Acronyms, Initialisms &
Abbreviations Dictionary

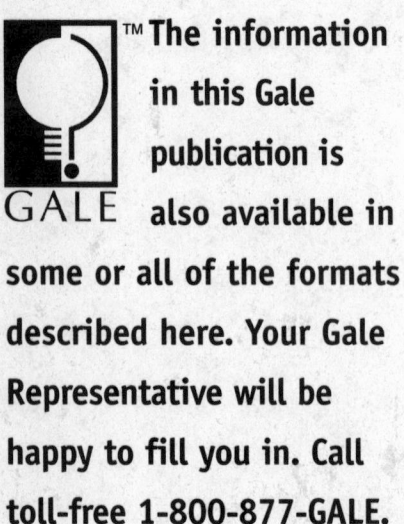

ISSN 0270-4404

Acronyms, Initialisms & Abbreviations Dictionary

A Guide to Acronyms, Abbreviations,
Contractions, Alphabetic Symbols, and Similar Condensed Appellations

Covering: Aerospace, Associations, Banking, Biochemistry, Business, Data Processing,
Domestic and International Affairs, Economics, Education, Electronics, Genetics,
Government, Information Technology, Investment, Labor, Law, Medicine, Military Affairs,
Pharmacy, Physiology, Politics, Religion, Science, Societies, Sports, Technical
Drawings and Specifications, Telecommunications, Trade, Transportation, and Other Fields

25th Edition

Volume 1

Part 2

G-O

Mary Rose Bonk,
Editor

Pamela Dear,
Associate Editor

GALE

DETROIT • LONDON

Editor: Mary Rose Bonk

Associate Editor: Pamela Dear

Contributing Editor: Mildred Hunt

Data Entry Manager: Eleanor M. Allison
Data Entry Coordinator: Kenneth Benson

Production Director: Mary Beth Trimper
Production Assistant: Carolyn Fischer

Graphic Services Manager: Barbara J. Yarrow
Graphic Artist: Gary Leach

Manager, Technical Support Services: Theresa A. Rocklin
Programmer: Charles Beaumont

Library of Congress Catalog Card Number 84-643188
ISBN 0-7876-2423-3 (Volume 1 Complete)
ISBN 0-7876-2424-1 (Part 1: A-F only)
ISBN 0-7876-2425-X (Part 2: G-O only)
ISBN 0-7876-2426-8 (Part 3: P-Z only)
ISSN 0270-4404

Printed in the United States of America

Contents

Volume 1

Part 1 A-F

Volume 1

Part 2 G-O

Volume 1

Part 3 P-Z

Gale's publications in the acronyms and abbreviations field include:

***Acronyms, Initialisms & Abbreviations Dictionary* series:**

Acronyms, Initialisms & Abbreviations Dictionary (Volume 1). A guide to acronyms, initialisms, abbreviations, and similar contractions, arranged alphabetically by abbreviation.

Acronyms, Initialisms & Abbreviations Dictionary Supplement (Volume 2). An interedition supplement in which terms are arranged alphabetically both by abbreviation and by meaning.

Reverse Acronyms, Initialisms & Abbreviations Dictionary (Volume 3). A companion to Volume 1 in which terms are arranged alphabetically by meaning of the acronym, initialism, or abbreviation.

***Acronyms, Initialisms & Abbreviations Dictionary* Subject Guide series:**

Computer & Telecommunications Acronyms (Volume 1). A guide to acronyms, initialisms, abbreviations, and similar contractions used in the field of computers and telecommunications in which terms are arranged alphabetically both by abbreviation and by meaning.

Business Acronyms (Volume 2). A guide to business-oriented acronyms, initialisms, abbreviations, and similar contractions in which terms are arranged alphabetically both by abbreviation and by meaning.

***International Acronyms, Initialisms & Abbreviations Dictionary* series:**

International Acronyms, Initialisms & Abbreviations Dictionary (Volume 1). A guide to foreign and international acronyms, initialisms, abbreviations, and similar contractions, arranged alphabetically by abbreviation.

Reverse International Acronyms, Initialisms & Abbreviations Dictionary (Volume 2). A companion to Volume 1, in which terms are arranged alphabetically by meaning of the acronym, initialism, or abbreviation.

***Periodical Title Abbreviations* series:**

Periodical Title Abbreviations: By Abbreviation (Volume 1). A guide to abbreviations commonly used for periodical titles, arranged alphabetically by abbreviation.

Periodical Title Abbreviations: By Title (Volume 2). A guide to abbreviations commonly used for periodical titles, arranged alphabetically by title.

New Periodical Title Abbreviations (Volume 3). An interedition supplement in which terms are arranged alphabetically both by abbreviation and by title.

User's Guide

The following examples illustrate possible elements of entries in *AIAD:*

①   ②   ③   ④   ⑤

FATAC... Force Aerienne Tactique [*Tactical Air Force*] [*French*] (NATG)

⑥   ⑦

MMT... Multiple-Mirror Telescope [*Mount Hopkins, AZ*] [*Jointly operated by Smithsonian Institution and the University of Arizona*] [*Astronomy*]

⑧

①   Acronym, Initialism, or Abbreviation

②   Meaning or Phrase

③   English Translation

④   Language (for non-English entries)

⑤   Source code (Allows you to verify entries or find additional information. Decoded in the List of Selected Sources)

⑥   Location or Country of origin (Provides geographic identifiers for airports, colleges and universities, libraries, military bases, political parties, radio and television stations, and others)

⑦   Sponsoring organization

⑧   Subject category (Clarifies entries by providing appropriate context)

The completeness of a listing is dependent upon both the nature of the term and the amount of information provided by the source. If additional information becomes available during future research, an entry is revised.

Arrangement of Entries

Acronyms, initialisms, and abbreviations are arranged alphabetically in letter-by-letter sequence. Spacing, punctuation, and capitalization are not considered. If the same term has more than one meaning, the various meanings are subarranged in word-by-word sequence.

Should you wish to eliminate the guesswork from acronym formation and usage, a companion volume could help. *Reverse Acronyms, Initialisms and Abbreviations Dictionary* contains essentially the same entries as *AIAD,* but arranges them alphabetically by meaning, rather than by acronym or initialism.

List of Selected Sources

Each of the sources included in the following list contributed at least 50 terms. It would be impossible to cite a source for every entry because the majority of terms are sent by outside contributors, are uncovered through independent research by the editorial staff, or surface as miscellaneous broadcast or print media references.

For sources used on an ongoing basis, only the latest edition is listed. For most of the remaining sources, the edition that was used is cited. The editors will provide further information about these sources upon request.

Unless further described in an annotation, the publications listed here contain no additional information about the acronym, initialism, or abbreviation cited.

(AABC)   *Catalog of Abbreviations and Brevity Codes.* Washington, DC: U.S. Department of the Army, 1981. [Use of source began in 1969]

(AAG)   *Aerospace Abbreviations Glossary.* Report Number AG60-0014. Prepared by General Dynamics/Astronautics. San Diego, CA: 1962.

(AAGC)   *Acronyms and Abbreviations in Government Contracting.* 2d ed. By Patricia A. Tobin and Joan Nelson Phillips. Washington, DC: George Washington University, 1997.

(AAMN)   *Abbreviations and Acronyms in Medicine and Nursing.* By Solomon Garb, Eleanor Krakauer, and Carson Justice. New York, NY: Springer Publishing Co., 1976.

(ABBR)   *Abbreviations: The Comprehensive Dictionary of Abbreviations and Letter Symbols.* Vol. 1 C. By Edward Wall. Ann Arbor, MI: The Pierian Press, 1984.

(AC)   *Associations Canada 1995/96.* Edited by Ward McBurney. Toronto, Canada: Canadian Almanac & Directory Publishing Co. Ltd., 1995.

(ACII)   *"Acronym and Initials Index."* 7 February 1996. <http://www.ioi.ie/~readout/cl.html> (7 November 1996).

(AD)   *Abbreviations Dictionary.* 8thed. By Ralph De Sola. Boca Raton, FL: CRC Press, 1992.

(ADA)   *The Australian Dictionary of Acronyms and Abbreviations.* 2nd ed. Compiled by David J. Jones. Leura, NSW, Australia: Second Back Row Press Pty. Ltd., 1981.

(ADDR)   *Army Dictionary and Desk Reference.* By Tim Zurick. Harrisburg, PA: Stackpole Books, 1992.

(AEBS)   *Acronyms in Education and the Behavioral Sciences.* By Toyo S. Kawakami. Chicago, IL: American Library Association, 1971.

(AEE)   *American Educators' Encyclopedia.* By Edward L. Dejnozka and David E. Kapel. Westport, CT: Greenwood Press, 1991.

(AF)   *Reference Aid: Abbreviations in the African Press.* Arlington, VA: Joint Publications Research Service, 1979.

(AFIT)   *Compendium of Authenticated Systems and Logistics.* Washington, DC: Air Force Institute of Technology, 1984.

(AFM)   *Air Force Manual of Abbreviations.* Washington, DC: U.S. Department of the Air Force, 1975. [Use of source began in 1969]

(AIA)   *Aviation Insurance Abbreviations, Organisations and Institutions.* By M.J. Spurway. London, England: Witherby & Co. Ltd., 1983.

(AIE)   *Acronyms and Initialisms in Education.* 6th ed. Compiled by John Hutchins. Norwich, England: Librarians of Institutes and Schools of Education, 1995.

(ANA)   *"Abbreviations" - U.S. Navy Dictionary.* 3rd revision. Washington DC: DCP, 1989.

(APTA)   *Australian Periodical Title Abbreviations.* Compiled by David J. Jones. Leura, NSW, Australia: Second Back Row Press Pty. Ltd., 1985.

(ARC)   *Agricultural Research Centres: A World Directory of Organizations and Programmes.* 2 vols. Edited by Nigel Harvey. Harlow, Essex, England: Longman Group, 1983.
               A world guide to official, educational, industrial, and independent research centers
               which support research in the fields of agriculture, veterinary medicine, horticulture,
               aquaculture, food science, forestry, zoology, and botany.

(ARCH)   *Dictionary of Architecture and Construction.* Edited by Cyril M. Harris. New York, NY: McGraw-Hill, Inc., 1975.

(ASF)   *Guide to Names and Acronyms of Organizations, Activities, and Projects.* By Food and Agriculture Organization of the United Nations. Fishery Information, Data, and Statistics Service and U.S. National Oceanic and Atmospheric Administration. Aquatic Sciences and Fisheries Information System Reference Series, Number 10, 1982. n.p.

(BABM)   *Bailliere's Abbreviations in Medicine.* 5th ed. By Edwin B. Steen. London, England: Bailliere Tindall, 1984.

(BARN)   *The Barnhart Abbreviations Dictionary.* Edited by Robert K. Barnhart. New York, NY: John Wiley & Sons, Inc., 1995.

(BI)   *British Initials and Abbreviations.* 3rd ed. By Ian H. Wilkes. London, England: Leonard Hill Books, 1971.

(BIB)   *Bibliotech.* Ottawa, Canada: National Library of Canada, 1988-89.

(BJA)   *Biblical and Judaic Acronyms.* By Lawrence Marwick. New York, NY: Ktav Publishing House, Inc., 1979.

(BRI)   *Book Review Index.* 1997 Cumulation. Edited by Beverly Baer. Detroit, MI: Gale Research, 1998.

(BROA)   *Broadcasting and Cable Yearbook 1997.* 2 vol. New Providence, NJ: R.R. Bowker, 1997.

(BTTJ)   *Breaking Through Technical Jargon: A Dictionary of Computer and Automation Acronyms.* By Mark S. Merkow. New York, NY: Van Nostrand Reinhold, 1990.

(BUR)   *Computer Acronyms and Abbreviations Handbook.* Tokyo, Japan: Burroughs Co. Ltd., 1978.

(BYTE)   *Byte: The Small Systems Journal.* Peterborough, NH: McGraw-Hill Information Systems, Inc., 1987-89.

(CAAL)   *CAAL COMOPTEVFOR Acronym and Abbreviation List.* Norfolk, VA: (CAAL-U) Operational Test and Evaluation Force, 1981.

(CB)   *Centres & Bureaux: A Directory of Concentrations of Effort, Information and Expertise.* Edited by Lindsay Sellar. Beckenham, Kent, England: CBD Research Ltd., 1987.
> A guide to British organizations which include the words "centre" or "bureau" in their names. Entries include name and address; telephone and telex numbers; chief official; and a description of the purposes, activities, and services of the organization.

(CDAI)   *Concise Dictionary of Acronyms and Initialisms.* By Stuart W. Miller. New York, NY: Facts on File Publications, 1988.

(CDE)   *The Computer Desktop Encyclopedia.* By Alan Freedman. New York, NY: AMACOM, 1996.

(CDI)   *The Cancer Dictionary.* By Roberta Altman and Michael Sarg, M.D. New York, NY: Facts on File, 1992.

(CED)   *Current European Directories.* 2nd ed. Edited by G.P. Henderson. Beckenham, Kent, England: CBD Research, 1981.

(CET)   *Communications-Electronics Terminology.* AFM 11-1. Vol. 3. U.S. Department of the Air Force, 1973.

(CINC)   *A CINCPAC Glossary of Commonly Used Abbreviations and Short Titles.* By Ltc. J.R. Johnson. Washington, DC: 1968.

(CMD)   *Complete Multilingual Dictionary of Computer Terminology.* Compiled by Georges Nania. Chicago, IL: National Textbook Co., 1984.
> Computer-related terms in Spanish, French, Italian, Portuguese, and English. Indexes in French, Italian, Spanish, and Portuguese are also provided.

(CNC)   *American National Standard Codes for the Representation of Names of Countries, Dependencies, and Areas of Special Sovereignty for Information Interchange.* U.S. National Bureau of Standards. Washington, DC: Government Printing Office, 1986. [Use of source began in 1977]
> These standard codes, approved by the International Organization for Standardization and the American National Standards Institute, are used in the international interchange of data in many fields.

(CPH)   *The Charles Press Handbook of Current Medical Abbreviations.* 3rd ed. Philadelphia, PA: The Charles Press Publishers, Inc., 1991.

(CRD)   *Computer-Readable Databases: A Directory and Data Sourcebook.* 6th ed. Edited by Kathleen Young Marcaccio. Detroit, MI: Gale Research, 1990.
> A guide to online databases, offline files available in various magnetic formats, and CD-ROM files. Entries include producer name, address, telephone number, description of coverage, vendors, and contact person.

(CROSS)   *Cross-Border Links: A Directory of Organizations in Canada, Mexico, and the United States.* Edited by Ricardo Hernandez and Edith Sanchez. Albuquerque, NM: Inter-Hemispheric Education Resource Center, 1992.

(CSR)   *Computer Science Resources: A Guide to Professional Literature.* Edited by Darlene Myers. White Plains, NY: Knowledge Industry Publications, Inc., 1981.

                 Covers several types of computer-related literature including journals, technical reports, directories, dictionaries, handbooks, and university computer center newsletters. Five appendices cover career and salary trends in the computer industry, user group acronyms, university computer libraries, and trade fairs and shows.

(CTT)   *Corporate TrendTrac.* Edited by A. Dale Timpe. Detroit, MI: Gale Research, 1988-89.

                 Covers mergers and acquisitions, stock exchange listings and suspensions, company name changes, bankruptcies, liquidations, and reorganizations.

(DA)   *Dictionary of Aviation.* By R. J. Hall and R. D. Campbell. Chicago, IL: St. James Press, 1991.

(DAS)   *Dictionary of Abbreviations and Symbols.* By Edward Frank Allen. London, England: Cassell and Co. Ltd., 1949.

(DAVI)   *The Davis Book of Medical Abbreviations: A Deciphering Guide.* By Sarah Lu Mitchell-Hatton. Philadelphia, PA: F. A. Davis Co., 1991.

(DBA)   *Directory of British Associations.* Edited by G. P. Henderson and S. P. A. Henderson. Beckenham, Kent, England: CBD Research, Ltd., 1990.

(DBQ)   *A Dictionary of British Qualifications.* London, England: Kogan Page Ltd., 1985.

(DCTA)   *Dictionary of Commercial Terms and Abbreviations.* By Alan E. Branch. London, England: Witherby & Co. Ltd., 1984.

(DD)   *The Financial Post Directory of Directors 1997.* Toronto, Canada: The Financial Post, 1996.

(DEN)   *Dictionary of Electronics and Nucleonics.* By L.E.C. Hughes, R. W. B. Stephens and L. D. Brown. New York, NY: Barnes & Noble, 1969.

(DFIT)   *Dictionary of Finance and Investment Terms.* 4th ed. Edited by John Downes and Jordan Elliot Goodman. Hauppauge, NY: Barron's Educational Series, 1995.

(DGA)   *Dictionary of Graphic Arts Abbreviations.* By L. W. Wallis. Rockport, MA: Rockport Publishers, Inc., 1986.

(DHSM)   *Dictionary of Health Services Management.* 2nd ed. By Thomas C. Timmreck. Owings Mills, MD: Rynd Communications, 1987.

(DI)   *The Dictionary of Initials-What They Mean.* Compiled and edited by Harriette Lewis. Kingswood, Surrey, England: Paper Fronts Elliot Right Way Books, 1983.

(DICI)   *The Dictionary of Initials.* By Betsy M. Parks. Secaucus, NJ: Citadel Press, 1981.

(DIT)   *Dictionary of Informatics Terms in Russian and English.* By G. S. Zhdanov, E. S. Kolobrodov, V. A. Polushkin, and A. I. Cherny. Moscow: Nauka, 1971.

(DLA)   *Bieber's Dictionary of Legal Abbreviations.* 3rd ed. By Mary Miles Prince. Buffalo, NY: William S. Hein & Co., 1988.

(DMA)   *Dictionary of Military Abbreviations: British, Empire, Commonwealth.* By B. K. C. Scott. Hastings, East Sussex, England: Tamarisk Books, 1982.

(DMAA)   *Dictionary of Medical Acronyms and Abbreviations.* 3rd ed. Edited by Stanley Jablonski. Philadelphia, PA: Hanley & Belfus, Inc., 1998.

(DMC)   *Webster's New World Dictionary of Media and Communications.* Revised ed. By Richard Weiner. New York, NY: Macmillan, 1996.

(DNAB)   *Dictionary of Naval Abbreviations.* 3rd ed. Compiled and edited by Bill Wedertz. Annapolis, MD: Naval Institute Press, 1984.

(DOAD)   *The Dictionary of Advertising.* Edited by Laurence Urdang. Lincolnwood, IL: NTC Business Books, 1986.

(DOG)   *A Dictionary of Genetics.* 5th ed. By Robert C. King and William D. Stansfield. New York, NY: Oxford University Press, 1997.

(DOGT)   *"List of Acronyms."* <http://www.em.doe.gov/rtc1994/loa.html> (5 March 1997).

(DOM)   *The Dictionary of Multimedia: Terms & Acronyms.* By Brad Hansen. Wilsonvillee, OR: Franklin, Beedle & Associates, 1997.

(DOMA)   *Dictionary of Military Abbreviations.* By Norman Polmar, Mark Warren, and Eric Wertheim. Annapolis, MD: Naval Institute Press, 1994.

(DS)   *Dictionary of Shipping International Trade Terms and Abbreviations.* 3rd ed. By Alan E. Branch. London, England: Witherby & Co. Ltd., 1986.

(DSA)   *Dictionary of Sigla and Abbreviations to and in Law Books before 1607.* By William Hamilton Bryson. Charlottesville, VA: University Press of Virginia, 1975.

(DSUE)   *A Dictionary of Slang and Unconventional English.* 8th ed. By Eric Partridge. New York, NY: Macmillan Publishing Co., 1984.

(DUND)   *Directory of United Nations Databases and Information Services.* 4th ed. Compiled by the Advisory Committee for the Coordination of Information Systems. New York, NY: United Nations, 1990.
           A guide to computerized databases and information systems/services. Entries include sponsoring organization, year established, type, scope, coverage, timespan, and contact information.

(DWSG)   *Defense Weapon Systems Glossary.* By David Trotz. Piscataway, NJ: Target Marketing, 1992.

(EA)   *Encyclopedia of Associations.* 29th ed. Vol. 1, National Organizations of the U.S. Edited by Carol A. Schwartz and Rebecca L. Turner. Detroit, MI: Gale Research, 1995 (and supplement 1995) [Use of source began in 1960]
           A guide to trade, professional, and other nonprofit associations that are national and international in scope and membership and that are headquartered in the United States. Entries include name and address; telephone and telex number; chief official; and a description of the purpose, activities, and structure of the organization.

(EAAP)   *Encyclopedia of Associations: Association Periodicals.* 3 vols. Edited by Denise M. Allard and Robert C. Thomas. Detroit, MI: Gale Research, 1987.
           A directory of publications issued by all types of national nonprofit organizations in the United States. Entries include title and organization name, address, telephone number; description of periodical, frequency of publication, and price.

(EAIO)   *Encyclopedia of Associations: International Organizations.* 29th ed. Edited by Linda Irvin. Detroit, MI: Gale Research, 1995. [Use of source began in 1985]
           A guide to trade, professional, and other nonprofit associations that are national or international in scope and membership and that are headquartered outside the United States. Entries include name and address; principal foreign language name; telephone and telex number; chief official; and a description of the purpose, activities, and structure of the organization.

(ECED)   *The European Communities Encyclopedia and Directory 1992.* London, England: Europa Publications Ltd., 1991; distributed in U.S. by Gale Research, Detroit, MI.
           A comprehensive guide to the European Communities. Entries explain widely-used acronyms and include address, telephone, telex, fax numbers and chief officers for EC-level organizations.

(ECII)   *Electronics, Computers and Industrial Instrumentation Abbreviations and Acronyms.* Edited by Sergio Sobredo. Miami, FL: Sergio Sobredo Technical Services, 1986.

(ECON)   *The Economist.* London, England: The Economist Newspaper Ltd., 1997. [Use of source began in 1988]

(EDAC)   *Dictionary of Educational Acronyms, Abbreviations, and Initialisms.* 2nd ed. Edited by James C. Palmer and Anita Y. Colby. Phoenix, AZ: Oryx Press, 1985.

(EE)   *Eastern Europe and the Commonwealth of Independent States 1992.* London, England: Europa Publications Ltd., 1992; distributed in U.S. by Gale Research, Detroit, MI.

(EECA)   *Dictionary of Electrical, Electronics, and Computer Abbreviations.* By Phil Brown. London, England: Buttersworth, 1985.

(EG)   *Environmental Glossary.* 4th ed. Edited by G. William Frick and Thomas F.P. Sullivan. Rockville, MD: Government Institutes, Inc., 1986.

(EGAO)   *Encyclopedia of Governmental Advisory Organizations.* 9th ed. Edited by Donna Batten. Detroit, MI: Gale Research, 1994-95 (and supplement, 1995). [Use of source began in 1975]
           A reference guide to permanent, continuing, and ad hoc U.S. presidential advisory committees, interagency committees, and other government-related boards, panels, task forces, commissions, conferences, and other similar bodies serving in a consultative, coordinating, advisory, research, or investigative capacity. Entries include name and address, telephone number, designated federal employee, history, recommendation and findings of the committee, staff size, publications, and subsidiaries. Also includes indexes to personnel, reports, federal agencies, presidential administration, and an alphabetical and keyword index.

(EMRF)   *The St. James Encyclopedia of Mortgage & Real Estate Finance.* By James Newell, Albert Santi, and Chip Mitchell. Chicago, IL: St. James Press, 1991.

(EPA)   *Glossary of EPA Acronyms.* Washington, DC: Environmental Protection Agency, 1987.

(ERG)   *Environmental Regulatory Glossary.* 5th ed. Edited by G. William Frick and Thomas F. P. Sullivan. Rockville, MD: Government Institutes, Inc., 1990.

(EY)   *The Europa World Year Book 1992.* London: Europa Publications Ltd., 1992. distributed in U.S. by Gale Research, Detroit, MI.
> An annual survey containing detailed information about the political, economic, statistical, and commercial situation of the regions and countries covered.

(FAAC)   *Contractions Handbook.* Changes. U.S. Department of Transportation. Federal Aviation Administration, 1993. [Use of source began in 1969]

(FAAL)   *Location Identifiers.* U.S. Department of Transportation. Federal Aviation Administration. Air Traffic Service, 1982.

(FEA)   *The Far East and Australasia 1987.* 18th ed. London, England: Europa Publications Ltd., 1986; distributed in U.S. by Gale Research, Detroit, MI.
> An annual survey containing detailed information about the political, economic, statistical, and commercial situation of the regions and countries covered.

(FFDE)   *The Facts on File Dictionary of Environmental Science.* By L. Harold Stevenson and Bruce Wyman. New York, NY: Facts on File, 1991.
> Defines terms from disciplines as diverse as biology, chemistry, geology, physics, engineering, meteorology, social science, medicine, and economics.

(GAAI)   *"Glossary of Abbreviations, Acronyms, and Initialisms."* 17 February 1998.
    <http://www.em.doe.gov/idb97/acropdf.html

(GAVI)   *"Glossary of Aviation Acronyms and Abbreviations."*
    <http://olias.arc.nasa.gov/AFO_Acronyms_.html> (5 March 1997).

(GEA)   *Government Economic Agencies of the World: An International Directory of Governmental Organisations Concerned with Economic Development and Planning.* A Keesing's Reference Publication. Edited by Alan J. Day. Harlow, Essex, England: Longman Group Ltd., 1985.
> Covers over 170 countries and territories. Two introductory sections for each area cover economic data and prevailing economic and political conditions. Individual entries provide title, address, and names of chief officials of each agency. Current activities and financial structure of each agency are also detailed. An index of agency officials is provided.

(GFGA)   *Guide to Federal Government Acronyms.* Edited by William R. Evinger. Phoenix, AZ: The Oryx Press, 1989.

(GNE)   *The Green Encyclopedia.* By Irene Franck and David Brownstone. New York, NY: Prentice Hall General Reference, 1992.

(GPO)   *Style Manual.* Washington, DC: Government Printing Office, 1984. Terms are included in Chapter 24, Foreign Languages.

(GRD)   *Government Research Directory.* 8th ed. Edited by Joseph M. Palmisano. Detroit, MI: Gale Research, 1994. (and supplement, 1994).
> A descriptive guide to U.S. government research and development centers, institutes, laboratories, bureaus, test facilities, experiment stations, data collection and analysis centers, and grants management and research coordinating offices in agriculture, business, education, energy, engineering, environment, the humanities, medicine, military science, and basic applied sciences.

(HCT)   *Health Care Terms*. 2nd ed. By Vergil N. and Debora A. Slee. St. Paul, MN: Tringa Press, 1991.

(HGAA)   *The Handy Guide to Abbreviations and Acronyms for the Automated Office*. By Mark W. Greenia. Seattle, WA: Self-Counsel Press Inc., 1986.

(IAA)   *Index of Acronyms and Abbreviations in Electrical and Electronic Engineering*. Compiled by Buro Scientia. New York, NY: VCH Publishers, 1989.

(IBMDP)   *IBM Data Processing Glossary*. 6th ed. White Plains, NY: IBM Corp., 1977.

(ICAO)   *Aircraft Type Designators*. 13th ed. International Civil Aviation Organization, August, 1981.

(ICDA)   *Designators for Aircraft Operating Agencies, Aeronautical Authorities and Services*. 49th ed. International Civil Aviation Organization, June, 1982.
            Document also includes telephony designators and postal and telegraphic
            addresses of government civil aviation authorities.

(ICLI)   *Location Indicators*. 51st ed. International Civil Aviation Organization, February, 1987.
            Document also contains addresses of flight information centers.

(IDOE)   *The Illustrated Dictionary of Electronics*. 6th ed. By Stan Gibilisco. New York, NY: TAB Books, 1994.

(IEEE)   *IEEE Standard Dictionary of Electrical and Electronics Terms*. Edited by Frank Jay. New York, NY: The Institute of Electrical and Electronics Engineers, Inc., 1977, 1984.
            Includes definitions for thousands of electrical and electronics terms. Each entry
            includes a numeric source code.

(IIA)   *Index of Initials and Acronyms*. Compiled by Richard Kleiner. New York, NY: Auerbach Publishers, 1971.

(IID)   *Information Industry Directory*. 15th ed. Edited by Annette Novallo. Detroit, MI: Gale Research, 1995. (and supplement, 1995).
            An international guide to computer-readable databases, database producers, and
            publishers, online vendors and time-sharing companies, telecommunications
            networks, and many other information systems and services. Entries include name
            and address, telephone number, chief official, and a detailed description of the
            purpose and function of the system or service.

(ILCA)   *Index to Legal Citations and Abbreviations*. By Donald Raistrick. Abingdon, Oxfordshire, England: Professional Books Ltd., 1981.

(IMH)   *International Marketing Handbook*. 2nd ed. Edited by Frank Bair. Detroit, MI: Gale Research, 1985.
            An in-depth guide to commercial and trade data on 142 countries of the world.
            Features include a list of European trade fairs and a report on growth markets in
            Western Europe.

(INF)   *Infantry*. Fort Benning, GA: U.S. Army Infantry Training School, 1996. [Use of source began in 1983]

(IRC)   *International Research Centers Directory 1992-93*. 6th ed. Edited by Annette Piccirelli. Detroit, MI: Gale Research, 1991.
            A world guide to government, university, independent, nonprofit, and commercial
            research and development centers, institutes, laboratories, bureaus, test facilities,

experiment stations, and data collection and analysis centers, as well as foundations, councils, and other organizations which support research.

(IRUK)   *Industrial Research in the United Kingdom*. 12th ed. Harlow, Essex, England: Longman Group UK Ltd., 1987.
>A guide to all groups conducting or funding research relevant to British industrial development. Entries include name, address, telephone and telex numbers; chief officials; and scope of activities.

(IT)   *Information Today: The Newspaper for Users and Producers of Electronic Information Services*. Medford, NJ: Learned Information Inc., 1988-89.

(ITD)   *International Tradeshow Directory*. 5th ed. Frankfurt, Germany: M + A Publishers for Fairs, Exhibitions and Conventions Ltd., 1989.
>A guide to trade fairs and exhibitions throughout the world. Entries include event name, dates, frequency, location, description of purpose, profile of exhibitors and attendees.

(IYR)   *The 1989-92 International Yacht Racing Rules*. London, England: International Yacht Racing Union, 1989.

(KSC)   *A Selective List of Acronyms and Abbreviations*. Compiled by the Documents Department, Kennedy Space Center Library, 1971, 1973.

(LAIN)   *Latest Intelligence: An International Directory of Codes Used by Government, Law Enforcement, Military, and Surveillance Agencies*. By James E. Tunnell. Blue Ridge Summit, PA: TAB BOOKS, 1990.

(LCCP)   *MARC Formats for Bibliographic Data*. Appendix II. Washington, DC: Library of Congress, 1982.

(LCLS)   *Symbols of American Libraries*. 14th ed. Edited by the Enhanced Cataloging Division. Washington, DC: Library of Congress, 1992. [Use of source began in 1980]

(LWAP)   *Legal Words and Phrases: Speed Abbreviations*. By Joel Larus. Boston, MA: Aurico Publishing, 1965.

(MAE)   *Medical Abbreviations and Eponyms*. By Sheila B. Sloane. Philadelphia, PA: W.B. Saunders Co., 1985.

(MAH)   *Medical Abbreviations Handbook*. 2nd ed. Oradell, NJ: Medical Economics Co., Inc., 1983.

(MCD)   *Acronyms, Abbreviations, and Initialisms*. Compiled by Carl Lauer. St. Louis, MO: McDonnell Douglas Corp., 1989. [Use of source began in 1969]

(MDG)   *Microcomputer Dictionary and Guide*. By Charles J. Sippl. Champaign, IL: Matrix Publishers, Inc., 1975.
>A listing of definitions for over 5,000 microelectronics terms. Seven appendices.

(MEDA)   *Medical Acronyms*. 2nd ed. By Marilyn Fuller Delong. Oradell, NJ: Medical Economic Books, 1989.

(MENA)   *The Middle East and North Africa 1987*. 33rd ed. London, England: Europa Publications Ltd., 1986; distributed in U.S. by Gale Research, Detroit, MI.
>An annual survey containing detailed information about the political, economic, statistical, and commercial situation of the regions and countries covered.

(MHDB)   *McGraw-Hill Dictionary of Business Acronyms, Initials, and Abbreviations*. By Jerry M. Rosenberg. New York, NY: McGraw-Hill, Inc., 1992.

(MHDI)   *McGraw-Hill Dictionary of Information Technology and Computer Acronyms, Initials, and Abbreviations*. By Jerry M. Rosenberg. New York, NY: McGraw-Hill, Inc., 1992.

(MHDW)   *McGraw-Hill Dictionary of Wall Street Acronyms, Initials, and Abbreviations*. By Jerry M. Rosenberg. New York, NY: McGraw-Hill, Inc., 1992.

(MSA)   *Military Standard Abbreviations for Use on Drawings, and in Specifications, Standards, and Technical Documents*. MIL-STD-12D. U.S. Department of Defense, 1981. [Use of source began in 1975]

(MSC)   *Annotated Acronyms and Abbreviations of Marine Science Related Activities*. 3rd ed. Revised by Charlotte M. Ashby and Alan R. Flesh. Washington, DC: U.S. Department of Commerce. National Oceanographic and Atmospheric Administration. Environmental Data Service. National Oceanographic Data Center, 1976, 1981.

(MUGU)   *The Mugu Book of Acronyms and Abbreviations*. Missile Range, California: Management Engineering Office, 1963, 1964.

(NADA)   *The New American Dictionary of Abbreviations*. By Mary A. De Vries. New York, NY: Signet, 1991.

(NASA)   *Space Transportation System and Associated Payloads: Glossary, Acronyms, and Abbreviations*. Washington, DC: U.S. National Aeronautics and Space Administration, 1985.

(NATG)   *Glossary of Abbreviations Used in NATO Documents*. AAP 15(B), n.p., 1979. [Use of source began in 1976]

(NCC)   *NCC The National Centre for Information Technology. Guide to Computer Aided Engineering, Manufacturing and Construction Software*. Manchester, England: NCC Publications. The National Computing Centre Ltd., 1985.
        Includes software classifications and descriptions, names and addresses of suppliers, processor manufacturers, and operating systems.

(NFD)   *The NSFRE Fund-Raising Dictionary*. Edited by Barbara R. Levy. New York, NY: John Wiley & Sons, Inc., 1996.

(NFPA)   *Standard for Fire Safety Symbols/NFPA170*. Quincy, MA: National Fire Protection Association, 1994.

(NG)   *NAVAIR Glossary of Unclassified Common-Use Abbreviated Titles and Phrases*. NAVAIRNOTE 5216 AIR-6031, n.p., July, 1969.

(NGC)   *Catalogue of the National Gallery of Canada*. Compiled by National Gallery of Canada. Ottawa, Canada: National Gallery of Canada, 1998.

(NHD)   *The New Hacker's Dictionary*. Edited by Eric Raymond. Cambridge, MA: MIT Press, 1991.

(NITA)   *Dictionary of New Information Technology Acronyms*. 2nd ed. By Michael Gordon, Alan Singleton, and Clarence Rickards. London, England: Kogan Page, Ltd., 1986.

(NLC)   *Symbols of Canadian Libraries*. 12th ed. National Library of Canada. Minister of Supply and Services Canada, 1987.

(NOAA)   *NOAA Directives Manual*. 66-13 Acronyms. 1977.

(NQ)   *NASDAQ Company Directory*. New York, NY: National Association of Securities Dealers, Inc., 1990. [Use of source began in 1983]
> Entries include company name, SIC code, contact person's name, title, address, and telephone number.

(NRCH)   *A Handbook of Acronyms and Initialisms*. Washington, DC: U.S. Nuclear Regulatory Commission. Division of Technical Information and Document Control, 1985.

(NTCM)   *NTC's Mass Media Dictionary*. R. Terry Ellmore. Lincolnwood, IL: National Textbook Co., 1991.

(NUCP)   *A Dictionary of Nuclear Power and Waste Management with Abbreviations and Acronyms*. Foo-Sun Lau. Letchworth, England: Research Studies Press, Ltd., 1987.

(NVT)   *Naval Terminology*. NWP3. Rev. B. U.S. Department of the Navy. Office of the Chief of Naval Operations, 1980. [Use of source began in 1974]
> Includes a section on definitions of naval terminology.

(OA)   *Ocran's Acronyms: A Dictionary of Abbreviations and Acronyms Used in Scientific and Technical Writing*. By Emanuel Benjamin Ocran. London, England: Routledge & Kegan Paul Ltd., 1978.

(OAG)   *Official Airline Guide Worldwide Edition*. Oak Brook, IL: Official Airlines Guide, Inc., 1984. [Use of source began in 1975]

(OCD)   *Oxford Classical Dictionary*. 2nd ed. Edited by N.G. Hammond and H.H. Scullard. London, England: Oxford University Press, 1970.

(OCLC)   *OCLC Participating Institutions Arranged by OCLC Symbol*. Dublin, OH: OCLC, 1981.

(ODBW)   *The Oxford Dictionary for the Business World*. New York, NY: Oxford University Press, Inc., 1993.

(OICC)   *Abbreviations and Acronyms*. Des Moines, IA: Iowa State Occupational Information Coordinating Committee, 1986.

(OLDSS)   *Online Database Search Services Directory*. 2nd ed. Edited by Doris Morris Maxfield. Detroit, MI: Gale Research, 1988.
> Provides detailed descriptions of the online information retrieval services offered by libraries, private information firms, and other organizations in the United States and Canada. Entries include name and address, telephone number, and key contact, as well as online systems accessed, frequently searched databases, and access hardware.

(OPSA)   "*Official Postal Service Abbreviations.*" <http://www.usps.gov/ncsc/lookups/abbr_suffix.txt> (17 December 1996).

(OSI)   *OSI Standards and Acronyms*. 3rd ed. Compiled by Adrian V. Stokes. United Kingdom: Stokes, 1991.

(PAZ)   *Parenting A to Z*. By Irene M. Franck and David M. Brownstone. New York, NY: HarperCollins Publishers, Inc., 1996.

(PCM)   *PC Magazine*. New York, NY: Ziff-Davis Publishing Co., 1997. [Use of source began in 1987]

(PD)   *Political Dissent: An International Guide to Dissident, Extra-Parliamentary, Guerrilla and Illegal Political Movements.* A Keesing's Reference Publication. Compiled by Henry W. Degenhardt. Edited by Alan J. Day. Harlow, Essex, England: Longman Group, 1983.
> Includes the history and aims of approximately 1,000 organizations, with details of their leaderships.

(PDAA)   *Pugh's Dictionary of Acronyms and Abbreviations: Abbreviations in Management, Technology and Information Science.* 5th ed. By Eric Pugh. Chicago, IL: American Library Association, 1987.

(PGP)   *Peterson's Graduate Programs in the Humanities, Arts & Social Sciences.* 31st ed. Princeton, NJ: Peterson's 1997.

(PPE)   *Political Parties of Europe.* 2 vols. Edited by Vincent E. McHale. The Greenwood Historical Encyclopedia of the World's Political Parties. Westport, CT: Greenwood Press, 1983.
> One of a series of reference guides to the world's significant political parties. Each guide provides concise histories of the political parties of a region and attempts to detail the evolution of ideology, changes in organization, membership, leadership, and each party's impact upon society.

(PPW)   *Political Parties of the World.* 2nd ed. A Keesing's Reference Publication. Compiled and edited by Alan J. Day and Henry W. Degenhardt. Harlow, Essex, England: Longman Group, 1980, 1984.
> Covers historical development, structure, leadership, membership, policy, publications, and international affiliations. For each country, an overview of the current political situation and constitutional structure is provided.

(PS)   *Popular Science.* New York, NY: Times-Mirror Magazines, Inc., 1995. [Use of source began in 1992]

(RCD)   *Research Centers Directory.* 19th ed. Edited by Thomas J. Cichonski. Detroit, MI: Gale Research, 1994. [Use of source began in 1986]
> A guide to university-related and other nonprofit research organizations carrying on research in agriculture, astronomy and space sciences, behavioral and social sciences, computers and mathematics, engineering and technology, physical and earth sciences and regional and area studies.

(RDA)   *Army RD and A Magazine.* Alexandria, VA: Development, Engineering, and Acquisition Directorate, Army Materiel Command, 1997. [Use of source began in 1979]

(ROG)   *Dictionary of Abbreviations.* By Walter T. Rogers. London, England: George Allen & Co. Ltd., 1913; reprinted by Gale Research, 1969.

(SAA)   *Space-Age Acronyms, Abbreviations and Designations.* 2nd ed. By Reta C. Moser. New York, NY: IFI/Plenum, 1969.

(SAG)   *Stock Abbreviation Guide.* New York, NY: Associated Press. [Database]

(SDI)   *Report to the Congress on the Strategic Defense Initiative.* U.S. Department of Defense. Strategic Defense Initiative Organization, April, 1987.

(SEIS)   *Seismograph Station Codes and Characteristics.* Geological Survey. Circular 791. By Barbara B. Poppe, Debbi A. Naab, and John S. Derr. Washington, DC: U.S. Department of the Interior, 1978.

(SLS)   *World Guide to Scientific Associations and Learned Societies/Internationales Verzeichnis Wissenschaftlicher Verbande und Gesellschaften.* 4th ed. Edited by Barbara Verrel. New York, NY: K.G. Saur, 1984.
    A directory of more than 22,000 societies and associations in all fields of science, culture, and technology. International, national, and regional organizations from 150 countries are also included.

(SPSG)   *Security Owner's Stock Guide.* New York, NY: Standard & Poor's Corp., 1994. [Use of source began in 1988]

(SRA)   *State and Regional Associations of the United States.* 9th ed. Edited by Tracey E. Chirico, Buck J. Downs and John J. Russell. Washington, DC: Columbia Books, Inc., 1997.

(SSD)   *Space Station Directory and Program Guide.* Edited and compiled by Melinda Gipson, Jane Glass, and Mary Linden. Arlington, VA: Pasha Publications Inc., 1988.

(TAG)   *Transportation Acronym Guide 1996.* U.S. Department of Transportation. Washington, DC: Bureau of Transportation Statistics, 1996.

(TDOB)   *The Dictionary of Banking.* By Charles J. Woelfel. Chicago, IL: Probus Publishing Company, 1994.

(TEL)   *Telephony's Dictionary.* 2nd ed. By Graham Langley. Chicago, IL: Telephony Publishing Corp., 1986.
    Includes definitions for U.S. and international telecommunications terms. Ten appendices.

(TNIG)   *Telecommunications, Networking and Internet Glossary.* By George S. Machovec. Chicago, IL: American Library Association, 1993.

(TOCD)   *The Official Catholic Directory 1997.* New Providence, NJ: P.J. Kenedy & Sons, 1997.

(TSPED) *Trade Shows and Professional Exhibits Directory.* 2nd ed. Edited by Robert J. Elster. Detroit, MI: Gale Research, 1987. [Use of source began in 1986]
    A guide to scheduled events providing commercial display facilities including conferences, conventions, meetings, fairs and festivals, etc. Entries include name of trade show; sponsor name, address, and telephone number; attendance figures; principal exhibits; special features; publications; and date and location of shows.

(TSSD)   *Telecommunications Systems and Services Directory.* 4th ed. (and supplement). Edited by John Krol. Detroit, MI: Gale Research, 1989. [Use of source began in 1985]
    An international descriptive guide to telecommunications organizations, systems, and services. Entries include name and address, telephone number, chief official, and a description of the purposes, technical structure, and background of the service or system.

(USDC)   *"Glossary of Acronyms".* U.S. Department of Commerce.
    <http://www.pmel.noaa.gov/pubs/acronym.html> (5 March 1997).

(USGC)   *"U.S. Government Commonly Used Abbreviations and Acronyms."*
    <http://www.fed.gov/hptext/infohwy/gov_acro.html> (5 March 1997).

(VNW)   *Words of the Vietnam War.* By Gregory R. Clark. Jefferson, NC: McFarland and Co., Inc., 1990.

(VRA)   *VRA Special Bulletin. No. 2, 1987: Standard Abbreviaitons for Image Descriptions for Use in Fine Arts Visual Resources Collections.* Compiled by Nancy S. Schuller. Austin, TX: Visual Resources Association, 1987.

(WDAA)   *Webster's New World Dictionary of Acronyms and Abbreviations.* By Auriel Douglas and Michael Strumpf. New York, NY: Webster's New World, 1989.

(WDMC)   *Webster's New World Dictionary of Media and Communications.* Revised and updated ed. By Richard Weiner. New York, NY: Webster's New World, 1996.

(WGA)   *Webster's Guide to Abbreviations.* Springfield, MA: Merriam-Webster Inc., 1985.

(WYGK)   *HR Words you Gotta Know!* By William R. Tracey. New York, NY: AMACOM, 1994.

Acronyms, Initialisms & Abbreviations Dictionary

G-O

G
By Acronym

G................ Acceleration Force (DMAA)
G................ Air Force Training Category [*12 training periods and zero days active duty training per year*]
G................ Application for Writ of Error Granted [*Legal term*] (DLA)
G................ Chicago [*Branch in the Federal Reserve regional banking system*] (BARN)
G................ Ciba-Geigy AG [*Switzerland*] [*Research code symbol*]
G................ Conductance [*Symbol*] [*IUPAC*]
G................ Dividends and Earnings in Canadian Dollars [*Investment term*] (DFIT)
G................ Federal Republic of Germany [*IYRU nationality code*] (IYR)
G................ Fire Control [*JETDS nomenclature*]
G................ Gage (IAA)
G................ Gain
G................ Gale [*Meteorology*]
G................ Gale's English Exchequer Reports [*A publication*] (DLA)
G................ Galliot [*Ship's rigging*] (ROG)
G................ Gallop [*Cardiology*] (DAVI)
G................ Gambia [*Country in West Africa*] (ROG)
G................ Game
G................ Games Played [*Sports statistics*]
G................ Gamma
G................ Gamut [*Music*] (ROG)
G................ Gandulphus [*Flourished, 1160-85*] [*Authority cited in pre-1607 legal work*] (DSA)
G................ Ganglion [*Medicine*]
G................ Ganz [*White Blot*] [*Rorschach*] [*Psychology*]
G................ Gaon (BJA)
G................ Gap in Cell Cycle [*Cytology*]
G................ Garage
(g)............... Gas [*Chemistry*]
G................ Gas Oil
G................ Gas Shutoff [*NFPA pre-fire planning symbol*] (NFPA)
g................ Gastralia [*Osteology*]
G................ Gastrin [*Biochemistry*]
G................ Gate [*Electronics*]
g................ Gate (IDOE)
g................ Gauche [*Chemical conformation*]
g................ Gauche [*Left*] [*French*]
G................ Gauge
g................ Gauge (WDMC)
G................ Gauss [*Unit of magnetic flux density*] [*Preferred unit is T, Telsa*]
G................ Gear (AAG)
G................ Ge'ez (BJA)
G................ Gelaendegaengig [*Having cross-country mobility*] [*German military - World War II*]
G................ Gelding [*Thoroughbred racing*]
g................ Gemeisamer Faktor [*General Factor*] [*Rorschach*] [*Psychology*]
G................ Gemini Airline [*British*]
G................ Gender
G................ General
G................ General Audiences [*All ages admitted*] [*Movie rating*]
G................ General Duties [*Ranking title*] [*British Women's Royal Naval Service*]
G................ General Factor (ADA)
G................ General Intelligence
G................ Generalist [*Ecology*]
G................ Generalized Feeder [*Ichthyology*]
G................ General List [*Navy British*]
G................ Generally Labeled [*Radioactive compounds*]
G................ General Procedures
G................ General-Purpose Freight Container (DCTA)
G................ General Staff Branch [*Army British*]
G................ Generating Item [*Military*]
g................ Generator (IDOE)
G................ Generators, Power [*JETDS nomenclature*] [*Military*] (CET)
G................ Genitive [*Case*] [*Grammar*]
g................ Genome [*Genetics*]
G................ Geography [*Secondary school course*] [*British*]
G................ Geometric Efficiency (DMAA)
G................ Geonic (BJA)
G................ George [*Phonetic alphabet*] [*Royal Navy World War I Pre-World War II*] [*World War II*] (DSUE)
G................ George [*King of England*] (DLA)
G................ Georgia State Library, Atlanta, GA [*Library symbol Library of Congress*] (LCLS)
G................ Georgics [*of Vergil*] [*Classical studies*] (OCD)
G................ Gericht [*Court*] [*German*] (ILCA)

G................ German [*or Germanic*]
G................ Germanischer Lloyd [*Shipping*] (ROG)
G................ Germany (WDAA)
G................ Gerontology [*American Occupational Therapy Association*]
G................ Geschichte [*History*] [*German*] (ILCA)
G................ Gesetz [*Law*] [*German*] (ILCA)
G................ Ghost
G................ Giant Slalom [*In Olympics event, Super-G*]
G................ Gibbs Energy [*Symbol*] [*IUPAC*]
G................ Gibbs Function [*Preferred term is Gibbs Energy*]
G................ Giemsa [*Method*] [*Chromosome stain*]
g................ GIF [*Graphics Interchange Format*] [*Computer science*] [*Telecommunications*]
G................ Gift Tax (DLA)
G................ Giga [*A prefix meaning multiplied by 10⁹*] [*SI symbol*]
G................ Gigabyte
G................ Gilbert [*A unit of magnetomotive force*]
G................ Gilbertus [*Flourished, 13th century*] [*Authority cited in pre-1607 legal work*] (DSA)
G................ Gillette Co. [*NYSE symbol*] (SAG)
G................ Gilt [*Bookbinding*]
G................ Gingiva (DMAA)
G................ Gingival [*Dentistry*]
G................ Girder [*Technical drawings*]
G................ Girls School [*British*]
G................ Givenchy [*Couturier*]
G................ Glabella [*Medicine*] (DMAA)
G................ Gladstonian [*Politics, 1868-1894*] [*British*] (ROG)
G................ Glasgow [*Postcode*] (ODBW)
(g)............... Glass (AAG)
G................ Glider
G................ Glimpse [*Optics*]
G................ Globular [*Referring to proteins*] [*Biochemistry*] (DAVI)
G................ Globulin
G................ Gloom
G................ Glucinium [*Also, Gl*] [*Old name for chemical element beryllium*]
G................ Glucose [*Also, Glc, GLUC*] [*A sugar*]
G................ Glycine [*One-letter symbol; see Gly*] [*An amino acid*]
G................ Glycogen [*Biochemistry*]
g................ Go [*to*] [*Computer science*] [*Telecommunications*]
G................ Goal [*A position in lacrosse, soccer, hockey, etc.*]
G................ Goalkeeper [*Sports*] (BARN)
G................ Goat [*Veterinary medicine*]
G................ Gofredus de Trano [*Deceased, 1245*] [*Authority cited in pre-1607 legal work*] (DSA)
G................ Gold
G................ Goldcorp Investments Ltd. [*Toronto Stock Exchange symbol*]
G................ Gold Inlay [*Dentistry*]
G................ Golf [*Phonetic alphabet*] [*International*] (DSUE)
G................ Gonidial [*With reference to colonies of bacteria*]
G................ Good (DAVI)
G................ Good [*Condition*] [*Antiquarian book trade, numismatics, etc.*]
g................ Good (WDMC)
G................ Good Skiing Conditions
G................ Gourde [*Monetary unit*] [*Haiti*]
G................ Government
G................ Government Expenditure [*Economics*]
G................ Government Purchases
G................ Grade (ADA)
G................ Grafenberg Spot [*Medicine*] (DMAA)
g................ Graft (Polymer) [*Organic chemistry*]
G................ Grain
g................ Gram
g................ Gram (WDMC)
G................ Grammar School [*British*]
g%............... Gram Percent [*Meaning grams per deciliter*] [*Measurement*] (DAVI)
G................ Grand [*Slang term for 1,000 dollars*]
G................ Grand-Orgue [*Great Organ*] [*Music*]
G................ Granite
G................ Granted [*Legal term*] (ILCA)
G................ Granular
G................ Graph (OA)
G................ Graphed [*Quilting*]
G................ Graphite
G................ Grass [*Botany*]
G................ Gravel

G................ Gravida [Obstetrics]
G................ Gravitational Constant [or Newtonian Constant] [Physics] (DAVI)
G................ Gravity [or the force or acceleration produced by it]
g................ Gravity (IDOE)
G................ Great
G................ Greek
G................ Green
G................ Greenhouse Plant [Botany]
G................ Greenwich Meridian [Upper branch]
g................ Greenwich Meridian [Lower branch]
G................ Greenwich Time
G................ Gregarious [Biology]
G................ Gregorowski's Reports of the High Court [A publication] (DLA)
G................ Grid [Electronics]
g................ Grid (IDOE)
G................ Grog [i.e., entitled to draw a daily rum ration and doing so] [See also, T, UA] [Obsolete] [Navy] [British]
G................ Grondwet [Constitution] [Netherlands] (ILCA)
G................ Gros [Large] [French]
G................ Groschen [Monetary unit] [Austria]
G................ Gross [Leukemia antigen] [Immunochemistry]
G................ Groszy [Monetary unit] [Poland]
G................ Ground
G................ Ground Control [Aviation] (DA)
G................ Grounded [Electronics]
G................ Ground Foraging [Ecology]
G................ Ground, General [JETDS nomenclature]
G................ Ground Swell
G................ Group
G................ Growth [Business term]
G................ Grumman American Aviation [ICAO aircraft manufacturer identifier] (ICAO)
G................ Gruppenfuehrer [Squad Leader] [German military - World War II]
G................ Guanidine [Biochemistry] (DAVI)
G................ Guanine [Also, Gua] [Biochemistry]
G................ Guanosine [One-letter symbol; see Guo]
G................ Guarani [Monetary unit] [Paraguay]
G................ Guard [Position in football, basketball, etc.]
G................ Guardian
G................ Guarnerius [Irnerius] [Flourished, 1113-18] [Authority cited in pre-1607 legal work] (DSA)
G................ Gucci [Designer]
G................ Guide
G................ Guided Tour [On a bus] [British]
G................ Guido de Baysio [Deceased, 1313] [Authority cited in pre-1607 legal work] (DSA)
G................ Guido de Suzaria [Deceased, 1293] [Authority cited in pre-1607 legal work] (DSA)
G................ Guilder [Modification of gulden] [Monetary unit] [Netherlands]
G................ Guillelmus de Tocco [Authority cited in pre-1607 legal work] (DSA)
G................ Guilty
G................ Guinea [Monetary unit] [Obsolete British]
G................ Guirsh [Monetary unit] [Saudi Arabia]
G................ Guitar [Music]
G................ Guizzardinus [Deceased, 1222] [Authority cited in pre-1607 legal work] (DSA)
G................ Gulden [Monetary unit] [Netherlands]
G................ Gules [Heraldry]
G................ Gulf [Maps and charts]
G................ Gun
g................ Gunnery [Navy British]
G................ Guttae [Drops of liquid] [Pharmacy] (CPH)
G................ Gutter Ball [Bowling]
G................ Gynoecium [Botany]
G................ Gyromagnetic Ratio
G................ Halls (Noncommercial) [Public-performance tariff class] [British]
G................ HMV [His Master's Voice], Gramophone Co. [Record label] [Great Britain, Europe, etc.]
G................ Longitude
G................ Obstetrics and Gynaecology [Medical Officer designation] [British]
G................ Permanently Grounded [Aircraft classification letter]
G................ Promoted to Glory [Salvation Army]
G................ Ranger [Army skill qualification identifier] (INF)
G................ Reports of the High Court of Griqualand [1882-1910] [South Africa] [A publication] (DLA)
G................ Shear Modulus [Symbol] [IUPAC]
g................ Statistical Weight [Symbol] [IUPAC]
G................ Surface Attack [Missile mission symbol]
G................ Telegraph [JETDS nomenclature]
G................ Teletype [JETDS nomenclature]
G................ Unit of Acceleration [Military]
G................ Unit of Gravitational Force (NASA)
G................ Weight [Symbol] [IUPAC]
G................ Workout from Starting Gate [Horse racing]
G1................ Government Current Expenditure [Economics]
G-1................ Personnel Section [of an Army or Marine Corps division general staff, or Marine brigade or aircraft wing general staff; also, the officer in charge of this section]
G^1 .... Staff Officer for Personnel [Army] [Marine Corps] (DOMA)
G1P................ Glucose-1-phosphate [Biochemistry]
G2................ Government Capital Expenditure [Economics]
G-2................ Military Intelligence Section [of an Army or Marine Corps division general staff, or Marine brigade or aircraft wing general staff; also, the officer in charge of this section]
G^2 .... Staff Officer for Intelligence [Army] [Marine Corps] (DOMA)

G2W................ Glaube in der 2. Welt [Faith in the Second World - FSW] [An association Switzerland] (EAIO)
G3................ Gadolinium, Gallium, Garnet
G3................ [The] Godfather Part III [Motion picture]
G-3................ Operations and Training Section [of an Army or Marine Corps division general staff or Marine brigade or aircraft wing general staff; also, the officer in charge of this section]
G^3 .... Staff Officer for Operations [Army] [Marine Corps] (DOMA)
G-3-P................ Glyceraldehyde-3-Phosphate [Biochemistry] (DAVI)
G-4................ Logistics Section [of an Army or Marine Corps division general staff, or Marine brigade or aircraft wing general staff; also, the officer in charge of this section]
G^4 .... Staff Officer for Supply/Logistics [Army] [Marine Corps] (DOMA)
G-5................ Civil Affairs Section [of an Army division or brigade general staff; the officer in charge of this section]
G5................ Group of Five [United States, Japan, West Germany, France, and Britain]
G^5 .... Staff Officer for Planning [Army] [Marine Corps] (DOMA)
G-6-Pase .... Glucose-6-Phosphatase [Organic chemistry] (DAVI)
G6PD .... Glucose-6-phosphate Dehydrogenase [Also, GPD, G6PDH] [An enzyme]
G6PDH .... Glucose-6-phosphate Dehydrogenase [Also, GPD, G6PD] [An enzyme]
G-6-PDHA .... Glucose-6-Phosphate Dehydrogenase Enzyme Variant A [Organic chemistry] (DAVI)
G-7................ Group of Seven [United States, Japan, West Germany, France, Britain, Italy, and Canada]
G7................ Grumpy Seven [Facetious translation for the Group of Seven: United States, Japan West Germany, France, Britain, Italy, and Canada] (ECON)
G-8................ Group of Eight [Nations] (EERA)
G-10................ Group of Ten [Nations] (EERA)
G10................ Group of Ten [United States, Japan, West Germany, France, Britain, Italy, Canada, Sweden, Holland, Belgium, and Switzerland] [There are actually eleven member countries]
G18 IYRA .... Geary 18 International Yacht Racing Association (EA)
G24................ Group of 24 [A clearinghouse for monetary aid to Eastern Europe] (ECON)
G30................ Group of Thirty [Financial think-tank] (ECON)
G-77................ Group of 77 [Coalition of environmentalists representing developing countries]
Ga................ Airway Conductance [Medicine] (DAVI)
GA................ Atlanta Public Library, Atlanta, GA [Library symbol Library of Congress] (LCLS)
GA................ Decisions of General Appraisers [United States] [A publication] (DLA)
GA................ Gabon [ANSI two-letter standard code] (CNC)
GA................ Gage
GA................ Gain of Antenna (IEEE)
GA................ Galatians [New Testament book]
GA................ Galatians [New Testament book]
Ga................ Galileo Number
GA................ Gallic
Ga................ Gallium [Chemical element]
GA................ Galvanizers Association [British] (EAIO)
GA................ Gamblers Anonymous (EA)
GA................ Games Abroad [Baseball]
GA................ Games Ahead [Baseball]
Ga................ Gandulphus [Flourished, 1160-85] [Authority cited in pre-1607 legal work] (DSA)
GA................ Gardens for All [Later, National Association for Gardening] (EA)
GA................ Garin Arava (EA)
GA................ Garrison Adjutant [Military British]
GA................ Garrison Artillery [British military] (DMA)
GA................ Garuda Indonesia [Airline flight code] (ODBW)
GA................ Garuda Indonesian Airways [ICAO designator] (AD)
GA................ Gas Amplification
GA................ Gas Analysis (NRCH)
GA................ Gasoline Stowage and Fuel System Man [Navy]
GA................ Gas or Air [Transportation]
GA................ Gastric Analysis
GA................ Gastric Antrum [Medicine] (DMAA)
GA................ Gate
GA................ Gated Attenuation [Computer science]
GA................ Gauge (AAG)
ga................ Gauge [of needles] [Measurement] (DAVI)
GA................ Gauge Man [Navy]
GA................ Gear Assembly
GA................ Gelbray Association [Later, GI] (EA)
GA................ Gemini Agena [NASA] (KSC)
GA................ Gemmological Association [British] (DBA)
GA................ General Accident [British insurance organization]
GA................ General Accounting (AAG)
GA................ General Activities (ADA)
GA................ General Agent [Insurance]
GA................ General Aircraft Ltd.
GA................ General Alert (NATG)
GA................ General American [A type of spoken American English] (BARN)
GA................ General Anesthesia [Medicine]
GA................ General Appearance [On physical examination] [Medicine] (DAVI)
GA................ General Appraisers' Decisions [A publication] (DLA)
GA................ General Arrangement (MCD)
GA................ General Assembly
GA................ General Assignment (ADA)
GA................ General Assistance [A form of public charity]

GA .... General Atomics [Division of General Dynamics Corp.]
GA .... General Atomics Corporation
GA .... General Attention [Medicine]
GA .... General Automation, Inc. [AMEX symbol]
GA .... General Average [Insurance]
GA .... General Avia SpA [Italy ICAO aircraft manufacturer identifier] (ICAO)
GA .... General Aviation
GA .... General of the Army (AABC)
GA .... Genetic Algorithm [Computer science]
GA .... Genl Automation [NYSE symbol] (TTSB)
GA .... Gentisic Acid [Analgesic drug]
GA .... [The] Geographical Association [British]
GA .... Geographical Association [British] (DBA)
GA .... Geological Abstracts
GA .... Geologists' Association [British]
GA .... Geometrical Acoustics
GA .... Georgia [Postal code] (AFM)
Ga .... Georgia (ODBW)
GA .... Georgia Railroad Co. [AAR code]
GA .... Georgia Supreme Court Reports [A publication] (DLA)
GA .... Geriatric Authority (DICI)
GA .... German Army (NATG)
GA .... Germanium Alloy (IAA)
GA .... Gesammelte Abhandlungen [A publication] (BJA)
GA .... Gesellschaft fuer Arzneipflanzenforschung [Society for Medicinal Plant Research] (EA)
GA .... Gestational Age [Medicine]
GA .... Getting Along [Psychological testing]
GA .... Giant Axon [Neurology]
GA .... Gibberellic Acid [Also, GA$_3$] [Plant growth hormone]
GA .... Gimbal Angle (KSC)
GA .... Gimbal Assembly
ga .... Ginger Ale
GA .... Gingivoaxial [Dentistry]
GA .... Gland Anlage
GA .... Glide Angle [Aviation]
GA .... Global Address
GA .... Global Assessment [Psychiatric evaluation test]
GA .... Global Auto [Computer science]
G/A .... Globulin/Albumin [Ratio] [Medicine] (DMAA)
GA .... Glucoamylase [An enzyme]
GA .... Glucose/Acetone [Biochemistry] (DAVI)
GA .... Glucuronic Acid [Also, GlcUA] [Biochemistry]
GA .... Glutamic Acid [See also Glu] [An amino acid]
GA .... Glutaraldehyde [Biochemistry]
GA .... Glyoxylic Acid [Biochemistry] (OA)
GA .... Gnomes Anonymous [New Malden, Surrey, England] (EA)
GA .... Go Ahead [or resume sending] [Communications]
GA .... Goal Attack [Netball]
GA .... Goals Against [Hockey]
GA .... Go Around (MCD)
GA .... Golgi Apparatus [Medicine] (DMAA)
GA .... Government Actuary [Australia]
GaAIAs .... Government Agency (AAG)
GA .... Governmental Affairs (DLA)
GA .... Government Architect (ADA)
GA .... Grade Age [Education]
GA .... Graduate Assistant
GA .... Graduate in Agriculture
G/A .... Grains per Anther [Botany]
Ga .... Gramicidin A [Antibiotic]
GA .... Grand Admiral [Freemasonry] (ROG)
GA .... Grand Almoner [Freemasonry]
GA .... Grand Architect [Freemasonry]
GA .... Grand Award [Record label]
GA .... Grands Arrets de la Jurisprudence Civile [A publication] (ILCA)
GA .... Grant Aid [Military] (AFM)
GA .... Grant Application [Job Training and Partnership Act] (OICC)
GA .... Grant Award [Job Training and Partnership Act] (OICC)
GA .... Granulocyte Agglutination [Hematology]
GA .... Granulomatous Angiitis [Medicine]
GA .... Graphic Ammeter (MSA)
GA .... Graphic Artists Guild (EA)
GA .... Graphics and Administration [Military] (GFGA)
GA .... Grapple Adapter [Nuclear energy] (NRCH)
GA .... Great Artists [A publication]
GA .... Great Attractor [Galactic science]
GA .... Green Alliance Senate - New South Wales [Political party Australia]
GA .... Greenhouse Annual [Horticulture] (ROG)
GA .... Greening Australia (EERA)
GA .... Gross Asset [Business term]
GA .... Ground Attack [Military]
GA .... Ground Attacker Aircraft
G-A .... Ground-to-Air [Communications, weapons] (MSA)
GA .... Group Atmosphere (PDAA)
GA .... Guanosine Triphosphatase Activating [Biochemistry]
GA .... Guardian Angels (EA)
GA .... Guardian Association (EA)
GA .... Guessed Average
GA .... Guidance Amplifier (IAA)
GA .... Gunlayer Armourer [British military] (DMA)
GA .... Gut-Associated [Medicine]
GA .... Gypsum Association (EA)
GA .... Gyrate Atrophy [Medicine]
GA .... Gyro Assembly (NASA)

GA .... L-Glutamic [acid] and L-Alanine [Copolymer]
GA .... Tabun [Nerve gas] [Army symbol]
GA$_3$ .... Gibberellin A$_3$ [Also, GA] [Plant growth hormone]
GAA .... Atlanta College of Art Library, Atlanta, GA [OCLC symbol] (OCLC)
GAA .... Atlanta School of Art, Atlanta, GA [Library symbol Library of Congress] (LCLS)
GAA .... Business Express [ICAO designator] (FAAC)
GAA .... Gaelic Athletic Association
GAA .... Gaelic Athletic Association of Australia
GAA .... Gain Adjuster Adapter
GAA .... Gale Auto Annual [A publication]
GaA .... Gallium Arsenide [Semiconductor]
GAA .... Gay AA (EA)
GAA .... Gay Activists' Alliance [Defunct]
GAA .... General Account of Advances
GAA .... General Agency Agreement [Navy] (AABC)
GAA .... General Aviation Authority [FAA] (TAG)
GAA .... Georgia Apartment Association (SRA)
GaA .... Georgia Appeals Reports [A publication] (DLA)
GAA .... Gift Association of America (EA)
GAA .... Girls Athletic Association [Local school affiliates of National Girls Athletic Association] [Defunct]
GAA .... Glacial Acrylic Acid [Organic chemistry]
GAA .... Gospel and the Age Series [A publication]
GAA .... Gossypol Acetic Acid (DMAA)
GAA .... Government Administrators Association (SRA)
GAA .... Government Advertising Agency [New South Wales, Australia]
GAA .... Grand National Resources, Inc. [Vancouver Stock Exchange symbol]
GAA .... Grandparents Association of America (EA)
GAA .... Grants for Aboriginal Advancement [Australia]
GAA .... Graphic Arts Association (SRA)
GAA .... Gravure Association of America (EA)
GAA .... Grease, Artillery/Automotive [Military] (INF)
GAA .... Greenhouse Action Australia (EERA)
GAA .... Greening Australia Action
GAA .... Grenfell Association of America (EA)
GAA .... Gross Average Audience [Nielsen rating] [Television] (WDMC)
GAA .... Ground-Aided Acquisition
GAA .... Ground Area Attainable
GAA .... GTO [Gran Torismo Omologato] Association of America (EA)
GAAA .... General Aviation Activity and Avionics [FAA] (TAG)
GAAA .... General Aviation Association Australia
GAAB .... Alston & Bird, Law Library, Atlanta, GA [Library symbol] [Library of Congress] (LCLS)
GAAC .... Graphic Arts Advertisers Council [Later, GAAEC]
GA Admin Comp... Official Compilation of the Rules and Regulations of the State of Georgia [A publication] (DLA)
GAAE .... Graphic Arts Association Executives [Defunct] (EA)
GAAEC .... Graphic Arts Advertisers and Exhibitors Council [Defunct] (EA)
GAAEF .... Grupo de Abogados Argentinos en el Exilio en Francia
GAAG .... Guerrilla Art Action Group
GAAI .... Atlanta Art Institute, Atlanta, GA [Library symbol] [Library of Congress] (LCLS)
GaAlAs .... Gallium Aluminum Arsenide (SSD)
GAAM .... Guided Antiaircraft Missile [Military] (IAA)
GA & CS .... Ground Acquisition and Command Station (MCD)
GAAO .... Ansongo [Mali] [ICAO location identifier] (ICLI)
GAAP .... Gateway Army Ammunition Plant
GAAP .... Generally Accepted Accounting Principles [or Procedures]
GA App .... Georgia Appeals Reports [A publication] (DLA)
Ga App .... Georgia Court of Appeals Reports [A publication] (AAGC)
GA App (NS)... Georgia Appeals Reports [A publication] (DLA)
GAARD .... General Automation Automatic Recovery Device (IAA)
GAARS .... Global Atmospheric and Aerosol Radiation Study
GAART .... Government Astronomy Administration Round Table
GaAs .... Gallium Arsenide [Semiconductor] (IEEE)
GAAS .... Generally Accepted Auditing Standards
GAAS .... German Association for American Studies (EAIO)
GAAS .... Goldberg Anorectic Attitude Scale [Medicine] (DMAA)
GAASD .... Gallium Arsenide [Phosphide Semiconductor]
GaAs FET .... Gallium Arsenide Field-Effect Transistor [Electronics] (LAIN)
GaAsP .... Gallium Arsenide Phosphide [Semiconductor] (IEEE)
GAASS .... Government Agency Arbitrage and Swap System (MHDW)
GAAT .... Gunner-Assisted Autotracking
GAATS .... Gander Automated Air Traffic System
GAATV .... Gemini Atlas/Agena Target Vehicle [NASA] (MCD)
GAB .... Gabbs [Nevada] [Seismograph station code, US Geological Survey Closed] (SEIS)
GAB .... Gabbs, NV [Location identifier FAA] (FAAL)
GAB .... Gabbs Resources Ltd. [Vancouver Stock Exchange symbol]
GAB .... Gabelli Equity Trust, Inc. [NYSE symbol] (SPSG)
GAB .... Gable
GAB .... Gabon [ANSI three-letter standard code] (CNC)
GAB .... Gendall Air Ltd. [Canada ICAO designator] (FAAC)
GAB .... General Adjustment Bureau [Insurance]
GAB .... General Arrangements to Borrow [United Nations] (EY)
GAB .... Georgia Association of Broadcasters (SRA)
GAB .... Gospel Association for the Blind (EA)
GAB .... Government Affairs Branch [European Theater of Operations] [World War II]
GAB .... Graphic Adapter Board
GAB .... Great Artesian Basin [Australia]
GAB .... Great Australian Bight [Region] (EERA)
GAB .... Great Australian Bight Trawl Fishery (EERA)
GAB .... Group Announcement Bulletin [Defense Documentation Center]

GAB .... Guardianship and Administration Board [*Victoria, Australia*]
GABA .... Gambling and Betting Addiction
GABA .... Gamma-Aminobutyric Acid [*Biochemistry*]
GA Back...... Great American Backrub Store, Inc. [*Associated Press*] (SAG)
GABA-T....... Gamma-Aminobutyric Acid Transaminase [*Pharmacology*] (DMAA)
Gabb Cr Law... Gabbett's Criminal Law [*A publication*] (DLA)
Gabb Stat L.. Gabbett. Abridgment of Statute Law [*1812-18*] [*A publication*] (ILCA)
GABC .... GAB Bancorp [*NASDAQ symbol*] (SAG)
GABC .... German Amer Bancorp [*NASDAQ symbol*] (TTSB)
GABC .... German American Bancorp [*NASDAQ symbol*] (SAG)
GABCC .... Great Australian Bight Consultative Committee
GA Bcp ...... Great American Bancorp, Inc. [*Associated Press*] (SAG)
GabCv .... Gabelli Convertible Securities Fund [*Associated Press*] (SAG)
GABD .... Bandiagara [*Mali*] [*ICAO location identifier*] (ICLI)
GABD .... Gauge Board
Gabeli .... Gabelli Equity Trust [*Associated Press*] (SAG)
Gabelli .... Gabelli Equity Trust, Inc. [*Associated Press*] (SAG)
GABF .... Bafoulabe [*Mali*] [*ICAO location identifier*] (ICLI)
GABG .... Bougouni [*Mali*] [*ICAO location identifier*] (ICLI)
GabGloM ..... Gabelli Global Multimedia Trust, Inc. [*Associated Press*] (SAG)
GabGM .... Gabelli Global Multimedia Trust, Inc. [*Associated Press*] (SAG)
GABH .... Georgia Baptist Hospital, Medical Library, Atlanta, GA [*Library symbol Library of Congress*] (LCLS)
GABH-N ...... Georgia Baptist Hospital, School of Nursing, Atlanta, GA [*Library symbol Library of Congress*] (LCLS)
GABHS .... Group A Beta-Hemolytic Streptococcus [*Pathology*]
GABIA .... Great Australian Bight Industry Association (EERA)
GablRsd...... Gables Residential Trust [*Associated Press*] (SAG)
GABN .... Ground-to-Air Broadcast Network
GaBnd........ Georgia Bonded Fibers, Inc. [*Associated Press*] (SAG)
GABOA .... Gamma-Amino-Beta-Hydroxybutyric Acid (DMAA)
GABOB....... Gamma-Amino-beta-hydroxybutyric Acid [*Pharmacology*]
GABR .... Bourem [*Mali*] [*ICAO location identifier*] (ICLI)
GABRA .... Gamma-Aminobutyric Acid Alpha Receptor (DMAA)
GABS .... Bamako/Senou [*Mali*] [*ICAO location identifier*] (ICLI)
GA Bus Law... Georgia Business Lawyer (DLA)
GABV .... Bamako [*Mali*] [*ICAO location identifier*] (ICLI)
GAC .... Armstrong State College, Savannah, GA [*OCLC symbol*] (OCLC)
GAC .... Clark College, Atlanta, GA [*Library symbol Library of Congress*] (LCLS)
GAC .... Galvanized Aircraft
GAC .... Geac Computer Corp. Ltd. [*Toronto Stock Exchange symbol*]
GAC .... General Acceptance Corp. (MHDW)
GAC .... General Access Copy (MHDI)
GAC .... General Advisory Committee [*to the AEC, later, the Energy Research and Development Administration*]
GAC .... General Agency Check [*Army*]
GAC .... General Air Cargo [*Venezuela*] [*ICAO designator*] (FAAC)
GAC .... General Areas of Competence [*Education*] (AIE)
GAC .... General Average Certificate [*Business term*] (DS)
GAC .... Ghost in Addition to Crew [*Sailing*]
GAC .... Gimbal Angle Change
GAC .... Gimbal Angle Controller
GAC .... Gippsland Agriculture Centre [*Australia*]
GAC .... Global Area Coverage [*Meteorology*]
GAC .... Goodyear Aerospace Corp.
GAC .... Government Advisory Committee on International Book and Library Programs [*Terminated, 1977*] (EGAO)
GAC .... Grand Assistant Conductor [*Freemasonry*] (ROG)
GAC .... Granular Activated Carbon
GAC .... Granular Activated Carbon Absorption
GAC .... Graphic Art Club, Toronto [*c.1903, SGA from 1912, CSGA from 1923*] [*Canada*] (NGC)
GAC .... Grilled American Cheese Sandwich
GAC .... Gross Available Capacity [*Electronics*] (IEEE)
GAC .... Ground Attitude Control (MCD)
GAC .... Groundwater Activated Carbon (EPA)
GAC .... Group Access Capabilities [*Library automation*]
GAC .... Grumman Aerospace Corp. [*of Grumman Corp.*]
GAC .... Guidance and Control [*Military*] (IAA)
G Ac .... Guillelmus de Accursio [*Deceased, 1314*] [*Authority cited in pre-1607 legal work*] (DSA)
GAC .... Gustavus Adolphus College [*St. Peter, MN*]
GACA .... American College of Applied Arts, Atlanta, GA [*Library symbol*] [*Library of Congress*] (LCLS)
GACC .... Atlanta Chamber of Commerce, Atlanta, GA [*Library symbol Library of Congress*] (LCLS)
GACC .... General Acceptance Corp. [*NASDAQ symbol*] (SAG)
GACC .... Genl Acceptance [*NASDAQ symbol*] (TTSB)
GACC .... Guidance Alignment and Checkout Console (IAA)
GACC .... Guidance and Control Coupler (IAA)
GACCC .... Coca-Cola Co., Technical Information Services, Atlanta, GA [*Library symbol Library of Congress*] (LCLS)
GACCLC ...... Cooperative College Library Center, Inc., Atlanta, GA [*Library symbol Library of Congress*] (LCLS)
GACCP........ Georgia Agricultural Commodity Commission for Peanuts (SRA)
GACDC........ Center for Disease Control, Main Library, Atlanta, GA [*Library symbol Library of Congress*] (LCLS)
GACDC-FP ... Center for Disease Control, Family Planning Evaluation Division, Atlanta, GA [*Library symbol Library of Congress*] (LCLS)
GACDL .... Georgia Association of Criminal Defense Lawyers (SRA)
GACEP .... Guidance and Control Equipment Performance (IAA)
GACHA........ Georgia Automated Clearing House Association
GACI .... Geographic Area Code Index [*Bureau of Census*]
GACIA .... Guidance and Control Information [*DoD*] (MCD)

GACIAC........ Guidance and Control Information Analysis Center [*Chicago, IL DoD Also, an information service or system*]
GACIC .... German Australian Chamber of Industry and Commerce [*Australia*]
GACL .... Crawford W. Long Memorial Hospital, Atlanta, GA [*Library symbol Library of Congress*] (LCLS)
GACNA........ Graphic Arts Council of North America (EA)
GACo .... Coca-Cola Co., Marketing Information Center, Atlanta, GA [*Library symbol Library of Congress*] (LCLS)
GA Code ...... Code of Georgia [*A publication*] (DLA)
GA Code Ann... Georgia Code, Annotated [*A publication*] (DLA)
G/A COMM... Ground-to-Air Communications (MCD)
G/A Con ...... General Average Contribution [*Marine insurance*] (DS)
GA Const .... Georgia Constitution [*A publication*] (DLA)
GACP .... Gunner's Accuracy Control Panel (MCD)
GACS .... Georgia Association of Christian Schools (SRA)
GACS .... Georgia Association of Convenience Stores (SRA)
GACS .... Gun Alignment and Control System (MCD)
GACSC .... Contel Service Corp., Atlanta, GA [*Library symbol*] [*Library of Congress*] (LCLS)
GACSU .... Singapore Government Administrative and Clerical Services' Union
GACT .... Generally Available Control Technology [*Environmental chemistry*]
GACT .... Graphic Analysis and Correlation Terminal (MCD)
GACT .... Greenwich Apparent Civil Time [*Astronomy*] (IAA)
GACTAI .... General Arbitration Council of the Textile and Apparel Industries (EA)
GACTFOSIF... Graphic Analysis and Correlation Terminal Fleet Ocean Surveillance Information Facility (DNAB)
GACTI .... General Arbitration Council of the Textile Industry [*Later, GACTAI*] (EA)
GACU .... Ground Air Conditioning Unit (MCD)
GACU .... Ground Avionics Cooling Unit
GAD .... Gadabout (DSUE)
GAD .... Gadsden [*Alabama*] [*Airport symbol*] (OAG)
GAD .... Gallium Arsenide Diode
GAD .... Galvanized and Dipped Metal (IAA)
GAD .... General Anthropology Division (EA)
GAD .... General Assembly Data
GAD .... Generalized Anxiety Disorder [*Medicine*] (DMAA)
GAD .... Germanium Alloy Diffused (IAA)
GAD .... Germersheim Army Depot (MCD)
GAD .... Gladstone Resources [*Vancouver Stock Exchange symbol*]
GAD .... Glutamate Acid Decarboxylase [*An enzyme*]
GAD .... Glutamate Decarboxylase [*An enzyme*]
GAD .... Government Actuary's Department
GAD .... Government Archives Division [*National Archives of Canada*] [*Information service or system*] (IID)
GAD .... Graduate Assistantship Directory [*A publication*]
GAD .... Grand Alliance for Democracy [*Philippines*] [*Political party*]
GAD .... Grants Administration Division [*Environmental Protection Agency*]
GAD .... Graphic Active Device [*Computer science*] (MHDI)
GAD .... Great American Dream
GAD .... Guards' Armoured Division [*Military unit*] [*British*]
GAD .... Guards Artillery Division [*British*]
GAD .... Guide to American Directories [*A publication*]
GADA .... Dioila [*Mali*] [*ICAO location identifier*] (ICLI)
GADAR .... Guild of Antique Dealers and Restorers [*British*] (DBA)
GADC .... General Audio and Data Communications Ltd. (NITA)
GA Dec .... Georgia Decisions [*A publication*] (DLA)
GA Dec (Dudley)... Dudley's Georgia Reports [*A publication*] (DLA)
GADEF .... Groupement des Associations Dentaires Francophones [*Group of Francophone Dentists' Associations*] [*Paris, France*] (EAIO)
G/A Dep...... General Average Deposit [*Marine insurance*] (DS)
GADES .... Gun Air Defense Effectiveness Study (MCD)
GADH.......... Gastric Alcohol Dehydrogenase [*An enzyme*]
GADL .... Ground-to-Air Data Link
GADNA........ Gduei Noar [*Youth Battalions*] [*Israel*]
GADNPH ...... Glycolic Aldehyde Dinitrophenylhydrazone [*Organic chemistry*]
GADO .... General Aviation District Office [*FAA*]
GADPET .... Graphic Data Presentation and Edit (PDAA)
GADPS .... Graphic Automatic Data Processing System (MCD)
GADR .... Guided Air Defense Rocket
GADS .... Gate-Assignment and Display System [*United Air Lines, Inc.*]
GADS .... Geographic and Alphanumeric Display System (MCD)
GADS .... Gonococcal Arthritis/Dermatitis Syndrome [*Medicine*]
GADS .... Goose Air Defense Sector
GADSCO ...... Gages Documentation Scheduling Committee
GADT .... Graded Assessment in Design and Technology (AIE)
GADT .... Ground/Air Defense Threat (MCD)
GADZ .... Douentza [*Mali*] [*ICAO location identifier*] (ICLI)
GADZ .... Gadzooks, Inc. [*NASDAQ symbol*] (SAG)
Gadzks........ Gadzooks, Inc. [*Associated Press*] (SAG)
gae .... Gaelic (Scots) [*MARC language code Library of Congress*] (LCCP)
GAE .... Gale Environmental Almanac [*A publication*]
GAE .... Gallic Acid Equivalent [*Wine analysis*]
GAE .... GAO [*General Accounting Office*] Denver Regional Office, Denver, CO [*OCLC symbol*] (OCLC)
GAE .... Gaslite Petroleum [*Vancouver Stock Exchange symbol*]
GAE .... General Administrative Expense [*A budget appropriation title*]
GAE .... General Air Express
GAE .... General American English
GAE .... General Analytical Evaluation
GAE .... General Classification Test/Arithmetic Test/Electronics Technician Selection Test [*Military*] (DNAB)
GAE .... Gibbs Adsorption Equation [*Physical chemistry*]
GAE .... Graphic Arts Employers of America (EA)

GAE............. Grupos Armados Espanoles [*Armed Spanish Groups*] [*Political party*] (PD)
GAE............. Gummed All Edges [*Envelopes*] (DGA)
GAE............. Gunner Aiming Error (MCD)
GAE-BPH...... Georgia State Department of Education, Division of Public Library, Library for the Blind and Physically Handicapped, Atlanta, GA [*Library symbol Library of Congress*] (LCLS)
GAEC .... Goodyear Aircraft and Engineering Corp.
GAEC .... Greek Atomic Energy Commission
GAEC .... Grumman Aircraft Engineering Corp. [*Later, Grumman Corp.*]
GAEI............ Equifax, Inc., Atlanta, GA [*Library symbol Library of Congress*] (LCLS)
GAEL........... Gaelic [*Language, etc.*]
GAEL........... Georgia Association of Educational Leaders (SRA)
GAELIC .... Grumman Aerospace Engineering Language for Instructional Checkout
GAEO .... Galileo Electro-Optics [*NASDAQ symbol*] (TTSB)
GAEO .... Galileo Electro-Optics Corp. [*NASDAQ symbol*] (NQ)
GAE-P .... Georgia State Department of Education, Division of Public Library Services, Atlanta, GA [*Library symbol Library of Congress*] (LCLS)
GAERF .... Graphic Arts Education and Research Foundation (DGA)
GAES .... Gas Appliance Engineers Society [*Later, ASGE*] (EA)
GAESDA....... Graphic Arts Equipment and Supply Dealers Association [*Defunct*] (EA)
GAESRE .... Genealogical Association of English-Speaking Researchers in Europe (EAIO)
GAF............. GA Financial [*AMEX symbol*] (TTSB)
GAF............. GA Financial, Inc. [*AMEX symbol*] (SAG)
GAF............. Gamma-Activated Factor [*Biochemistry*]
GAF............. GAO [*General Accounting Office*] Boston Regional Office, Boston, MA [*OCLC symbol*] (OCLC)
GAF............. German Air Force [*German Luftwaffe*]
GAF............. German Air Force [*ICAO designator*] (FAAC)
GAF............. Government Affairs Foundation [*Defunct*] (EA)
GAF............. Government Aircraft Facilities
GAF............. Grafton, ND [*Location identifier FAA*] (FAAL)
GAF............. Growth of the American Family [*A study*]
GAFA .... German-American Football Association [*Later, CSL*]
GAFADS........ German Air Force Air Defense School (MCD)
GAFB .... George Air Force Base [*California*] (MCD)
GAFB .... Goodfellow Air Force Base [*Texas*]
GAFB .... Griffiss Air Force Base [*New York*]
GAFC .... Fulton County Court House, Atlanta, GA [*Library symbol Library of Congress*] (LCLS)
GAFCOR....... Gas and Fuel Corp. [*Victoria, Australia*] [*Commercial firm*]
GAFD .... Faladie [*Mali*] [*ICAO location identifier*] (ICLI)
GAFD .... Guild of American Funeral Directors [*Defunct*]
GAFD .... United States Food and Drug Administration, Atlanta, GA [*Library symbol Library of Congress*] (LCLS)
GAFET......... Gallium Arsenide Field-Effect Transistor (MCD)
GAFG .... General Aviation Flight Guide [*British*] (AIA)
GAFG .... Goal Attainment Follow-Up Guide (DMAA)
GAFIA .... German Armed Forces Intelligence Agency (MCD)
GAFL........... Fulton County Law Library, Atlanta, GA [*Library symbol Library of Congress*] (LCLS)
GAFM.......... Fulton County Medical Society, Atlanta, GA [*Library symbol Library of Congress*] (LCLS)
GA Fncl........ GA Financial, Inc. [*Associated Press*] (SAG)
GAFPG .... General Aviation Facilities Planning Group
GAFR .... Federal Reserve Bank of Atlanta, Research Library, Atlanta, GA [*Library symbol Library of Congress*] (LCLS)
GAFS .... Gentile Air Force Station [*Ohio*]
GAFS .... United States Forest Service, Atlanta, GA [*Library symbol Library of Congress*] (LCLS)
GAFSC .... Fernbank Science Center, Atlanta, GA [*Library symbol Library of Congress*] (LCLS)
GAFSC .... German Air Force Southern Command (MCD)
GAFTA .... Grain and Food Trade Association [*British*]
GAFTAC....... German Air Force Tactical Air Command (MCD)
GAFTO .... Germany Air Force Technical Order (MCD)
GAFW .... United States Fish and Wildlife Service, Atlanta, GA [*Library symbol Library of Congress*] (LCLS)
GAG .... Cologne Air Transport [*Germany*] [*FAA designator*] (FAAC)
GAG .... Gage, OK [*Location identifier FAA*] (FAAL)
GAG .... Gallant Gold Mines Ltd. [*Vancouver Stock Exchange symbol*]
GAG .... GAO [*General Accounting Office*] Philadelphia Regional Office, Philadelphia, PA [*OCLC symbol*] (OCLC)
GAG .... Glycosaminoglycan [*Biochemistry*]
GAG .... Glyoxal Bis(guanylhydrazone) [*Organic chemistry*]
GAG .... Grand Aleph Godol (BJA)
GAG .... Graphic Artists Guild (EA)
GAG .... Gross Available Generation [*Electronics*] (IEEE)
GAG .... Gross Gradability [*Truck specification*]
GAG .... Ground-to-Air-to-Ground [*Aviation*]
GAG .... Group-Specific Antigen Gene (DMAA)
GAGAS........ Generally Accepted Government Auditing Standards [*A publication*] (AAGC)
GAGB .... Gemmological Association of Great Britain (BI)
GAGB .... General Association of General Baptists (EA)
GAGDT........ Ground-to-Air-to-Ground Data Terminal [*Air Force*] (MCD)
GAGE .... Global Atmospheric Gases Experiment (EERA)
GAGE .... Global Atmospheric Gases Experiment [*Environmental science*]
GAGF .... Graphic Artists Guild Foundation (EA)

GAGI .... Goethe Institute, German Culture Institute, Atlanta, GA [*Library symbol Library of Congress*] (LCLS)
GAGK .... Graphic Arts Guidance Kit
GAGL .... Aguelhoc [*Mali*] [*ICAO location identifier*] (ICLI)
GAGM .... Georgia Mental Health Institute, Atlanta, GA [*Library symbol Library of Congress*] (LCLS)
GAGM .... Goundam [*Mali*] [*ICAO location identifier*] (ICLI)
GAGO .... Gao [*Mali*] [*ICAO location identifier*] (ICLI)
GAGP .... Georgia Power Co., Atlanta, GA [*Library symbol Library of Congress*] (LCLS)
GAGR .... Courma-Rharous [*Mali*] [*ICAO location identifier*] (ICLI)
GAGR .... Georgia Retardation Center, Atlanta, GA [*Library symbol Library of Congress*] (LCLS)
GAGTh .... Gammon Theological Seminary, Atlanta, GA [*Library symbol Library of Congress*] (LCLS)
GaGulf .... Georgia Gulf Corp. [*Associated Press*] (SAG)
GAH .... Games at Home [*Baseball*]
GAH .... Gayndah [*Australia Airport symbol*] (OAG)
GAH .... Grand American Handicap [*Shooting competition*]
GAH .... Wren's Nest [*Joel Chandler Harris Home*], Atlanta, GA [*Library symbol Library of Congress*] (LCLS)
GAHB .... Hombori [*Mali*] [*ICAO location identifier*] (ICLI)
GAHF .... Grapple Adapter Handling Fixture [*Nuclear energy*] (NRCH)
GAHH .... Good American Helping Hands (EA)
GAHi .... Atlanta Historical Society, Atlanta, GA [*Library symbol Library of Congress*] (LCLS)
GAHM .... High Museum of Art, Atlanta, GA [*Library symbol Library of Congress*] (LCLS)
GAHoM .... Home Mission Board of the Southern Baptist Convention, Atlanta, GA [*Library symbol*] [*Library of Congress*] (LCLS)
GAHR .... Georgia Department of Human Resources, Atlanta, GA [*Library symbol Library of Congress*] (LCLS)
GAHSC........ Georgia Association of Homes and Services for Children (SRA)
GAHu .... Hurt, Richardson, Garner, Law Library, Atlanta, GA [*Library symbol Library of Congress*] (LCLS)
GAI............. Gaithersburg, MD [*Location identifier FAA*] (FAAL)
GAI............. Gate Alarm Indicator [*RADAR*]
GAI............. Gay American Indians (EA)
GAI............. General Accounting Instructions
GAI............. Generalized Area of Intersection (OA)
GAI............. Geophysical Associates International
GAI............. Gibbs Adsorption Isotherm [*Physical chemistry*]
GAI............. Gilbert Associates, Inc.
GAI............. [*A*] Glossary of the Aramaic Inscriptions [*A publication*] (BJA)
GAI............. Governmental Affairs Institute [*Later, VPS*] (EA)
GAI............. Guaranteed Annual Income
GAI............. Guild of Architectural Ironmongers [*British*] (BI)
GAIA .... Graphic Arts Industries Association
GAIC .... Gallium Arsenide Integrated Circuit [*Computer chip*]
GAIF .... General Assembly of International Sports Federations [*Later, GAISF*] (EA)
GAIF .... Gimbal Angle Information Failure
GAIFC .... Gene Autry International Fan Club (EA)
Gaii .... Gaii Institutionum Commentarii [*Gaius' Institutes*] [*A publication*] (DLA)
Gai Inst........ Gaius, Institutiones [*Second century AD*] [*Classical studies*] (OCD)
GAIL .... Gas Authority of India Ltd. (ECON)
GAIL .... Gate Array Interface Language (NITA)
GAIL .... General Atomic In-Pool Loop (SAA)
GAIL .... Glide Angle Indicator Light [*Aviation*] (DNAB)
GAILL .... Groupement des Allergologistes et Immunologistes de Langues Latines [*Latin Languages Speaking Allergists - LLSA*] (EAIO)
GAIM .... Global Analyses, Interpretation, and Modeling [*Task Force*] [*Marine science*] (OSRA)
GAIM .... Global Analysis, Interpretation and Modelling [*Climate*] (EERA)
GAIN .... Federal and State Governments Assistance Programs [*Database*] [*Australia*]
GAIN .... Gas Appliance Improvement Network
GAIN .... Gifted Advocacy Information Network [*Defunct*] (EA)
GAIN .... Global Automation Information Network [*An association*]
GAIN .... Graphic Aids for Investigating Networks [*NASA*] (NASA)
GAINS.......... Gimballess Analytic Inertial Navigation System
GAINS.......... Global Airborne Integrated Navigation System [*Military*] (IAA)
GAINS.......... Graphic Administrative Information System (DNAB)
GAINS.......... Growth and Income Security [*Finance*]
GAINS.......... Guaranteed Annual Income System
Gainsco .... Gainsco, Inc. [*Associated Press*] (SAG)
GAInv.......... General American Investors Co., Inc. [*Associated Press*] (SAG)
GAIS .... Gallium Arsenide Illuminator System
GAIS .... General Aviation Inspection Aids Summary [*FAA*]
GAISF .... General Association of International Sports Federations [*Formerly, GAIF*] (EA)
GAISO .... Gam-Anon International Service Office (EA)
GAISSAR...... Gilbert Associates, Incorporated, Standard Safety Analysis Report [*Nuclear energy*] (NRCH)
GAIT .... Government and Industry Team
G/AIT .... Ground/Airborne Integrated Terminal [*Air Force*] (DOMA)
GAIT........... Langer Biomechanics Group [*NASDAQ symbol*] (SAG)
GAIT........... Langer Biomechanics Grp [*NASDAQ symbol*] (TTSB)
GAITh.......... Interdenominational Theological Center, Atlanta, GA [*Library symbol Library of Congress*] (LCLS)
GAIU .... Graphic Arts International Union [*Later, GCIU*]
Gaius .... Gaius' Institutes [*A publication*] (DLA)
Gaius Inst .... Gaius' Institutes [*A publication*] (DLA)

GAJ.............. Atlanta Junior College, Atlanta, GA [Library symbol Library of Congress] (LCLS)
GAJ.............. Gaseous Axisymmetric Jet
GAJ.............. Guild of Agricultural Journalists
GAJ.............. Yamagata [Japan] [Airport symbol] (OAG)
GAJC........... Jimmy Carter Library, Atlanta, GA [Library symbol Library of Congress] (LCLS)
GAK .... Gakona, AK [Location identifier FAA] (FAAL)
GAK .... Galactokinase [Also, GALK] [An enzyme]
GAKA.......... Kenieba [Mali] [ICAO location identifier] (ICLI)
GAKL.......... Kidal [Mali] [ICAO location identifier] (ICLI)
GAKM......... Ke-Macina [Mali] [ICAO location identifier] (ICLI)
GAKN......... Kolokani [Mali] [ICAO location identifier] (ICLI)
GAKO......... Koutiala [Mali] [ICAO location identifier] (ICLI)
GAKT......... Kita [Mali] [ICAO location identifier] (ICLI)
GAKY......... Kayes [Mali] [ICAO location identifier] (ICLI)
GAI.............. Albany Public Library, Albany, GA [Library symbol Library of Congress] (LCLS)
GAL.............. Anti-Terrorist Liberation Group [Undercover anti-Basque terrorist interior-ministry network] [Acronym is based on foreign phrase Spain] (ECON)
GAL............ Galactic (KSC)
Gal............. Galactose [A sugar]
GAL............ Galactosyl [Biochemistry] (DAVI)
Gal............. Galatians [New Testament book]
Gal............. Galen [Second century AD] [Classical studies] (OCD)
GAL............ Galena [Alaska] [Airport symbol] (OAG)
GAL............ Galerazamba [Colombia] [Seismograph station code, US Geological Survey] (SEIS)
gal............. Galileo [Unit of acceleration]
gal .... Galla [MARC language code Library of Congress] (LCCP)
GAL............ Gallery
Gal............. Gallison's United States Circuit Court Reports [A publication] (DLA)
GAL............ Gallium Arsenide LASER
GAL............ Gallon (AAG)
gal............. Gallon (ODBW)
gal............. Gallon
GAL............ Gallons of Fuel ["Energy equivalent" abbreviation - biomass agriculture and conversion] [Fuel chemistry]
GAL............ Gallop [Music] (ROG)
GALIC......... Gallup Public Library, Gallup, NM [OCLC symbol] (OCLC)
GAL............ Gallus-adeno-like [Avian virus]
GAL............ Galoob (Lewis) Toys [NYSE symbol] (TTSB)
GAL............ Galoob [Lewis] Toys, Inc. [NYSE symbol] (SPSG)
gal............. Galvanized Iron (ADA)
GAL............ Galveston-Houston [Diocesan abbreviation] [Texas] (TOCD)
GAL............ Galveston Resources Ltd. [Toronto Stock Exchange symbol Vancouver Stock Exchange symbol]
GAL............ Galway [County in Ireland] (ROG)
GAL............ Gas-Analysis Laboratory [NASA]
GAL............ Gemini Airlines Ltd. [Ghana] [ICAO designator] (FAAC)
GAL............ General Administration Letter (OICC)
GAL............ General George A. Lincoln [World War II]
GAL............ Generalized Assembly Language [Computer science] (MHDB)
GAL............ Generic Array Logic [Computer science]
GA L......... Georgia Lawyer [A publication] (DLA)
GA L......... Georgia Sessions Laws [A publication] (DLA)
GAL............ German Atlantic Line [Steamship] (MHDB)
GAL............ Get a Life
GAL............ Gimbal Angle Loss
GAL............ Graphics Application Language (BYTE)
GAL............ Greening Australia Limited (EERA)
GAL............ Grupos Armados Libertarios [Armed Libertarian Groups] [Spain Political party] (PD)
Gal............. Gualcosius [Flourished, 11th-12th century] [Authority cited in pre-1607 legal work] (DSA)
GAL............ Guaranteed Access Level [Foreign Trade]
GAL............ Guardian Ad Litem [Social services] (PAZ)
GAL............ Guggenheim Aeronautical Laboratory [California Institute of Technology]
GAL............ Guild of American Luthiers (EA)
GAL............ Guinea Airways Ltd.
gal-1-P....... Galactose-1-Phosphate [Organic chemistry] (DAVI)
GALA .... Gay and Lesbian Atheists [Defunct] (EA)
GALA .... Graduated Audio Level Adjustment
GALA .... Graphic Arts Literature Abstracts [A publication]
GALA .... Grupo de Artistas Latino Americanos [An association]
GALA .... Guidance and Learner Autonomy [Project] (AIE)
GALAC........ Gay and Lesbian Association of Choruses (EA)
GalaGen...... GalaGen, Inc. [Associated Press] (SAG)
Gal & Dav ... Gale and Davison's English Queen's Bench Reports [1841-43] [A publication] (DLA)
GA Law Reporter... Georgia Law Reporter [A publication] (DLA)
GALAXY ...... General Automatic Luminosity and X-Y [Engine technology] (PDAA)
GALB .... Galbanum [Agum] [Pharmacology] (ROG)
Galb........... Galbraith's Reports [9-11 Florida] [A publication] (DLA)
G-ALB........ Globulin-Albumin [Biochemistry] (DAVI)
Galb & M..... Galbraith and Meek's Reports [9-12 Florida] [A publication] (DLA)
Galb & M (Fla)... Galbraith and Meek's Reports [9-12 Florida] [A publication] (DLA)
Galbraith ..... Galbraith's Reports [9-12 Florida] [A publication] (DLA)
GalC.......... Galactocerebroside [Biochemistry]
GALC .... Galactosylceramidase [An enzyme]
GALC .... Groupement des Associations de Libraries de la CEE [Group of Booksellers Associations in the EEC] (ECED)

GAL CAP...... Gallon Capacity (WDAA)
GALCIT .... Graduate Aeronautical Laboratories - California Institute of Technology [Research center] (RCD)
GALCIT .... Guggenheim Aeronautical Laboratory, California Institute of Technology (MCD)
GAID .... Dougherty County Court House, Albany, GA [Library symbol Library of Congress] (LCLS)
GALD .... Greatest Axial Linear Dimension
GAIDC.......... Darton College, Albany, GA [Library symbol] [Library of Congress] (LCLS)
Gale............ Gale on Easements [A publication] (DLA)
GALE........... Galerias de Arte y Salas de Exposiciones [Ministerio de Cultura] [Spain Information service or system] (CRD)
Gale............ Gale's English Exchequer Reports [A publication] (DLA)
Gale............ Gale's New Forest Decisions [England] [A publication] (DLA)
GALE........... Gaseous and Liquid Effluent [Nuclear energy] (NRCH)
GALE........... Genesis of Atlantic Lows Experiment (USDC)
GALE........... Genesis of Atlantic Tropical Lows Experiment [National Oceanic and Atmospheric Administration]
Gale & D .... Gale and Davison's English Queen's Bench Reports [1841-43] [A publication] (DLA)
Gale & Dav... Gale and Davison's English Queen's Bench Reports [1841-43] [A publication] (DLA)
Gale & D (Eng)... Gale and Davison's English Queen's Bench Reports [1841-43] [A publication] (DLA)
Gale & Whatley Easem... Gale and Whatley [later, Gale] on Easements [A publication] (DLA)
Gale & Wh Eas... Gale and Whatley [later, Gale] on Easements [A publication] (ILCA)
Gale Eas..... Gale on Easements [A publication] (ILCA)
Gale's St .... Gale's Statutes [A publication] (DLA)
Gale Stat .... Gale's Statutes [A publication] (DLA)
GaleyL........ Galey & Lord, Inc. [Associated Press] (SAG)
GALF .... Groupement des Acousticiens de Langue Francaise [Group of French-Speaking Acousticians] (EA)
GAL/(FT² D)... Gallons per Square-Foot per Day
GAL/(FT D)... Gallons per Foot per Day
GAL/H .... Gallons per Hour (MCD)
GALH .... General Association of Ladies Hairdressers [British] (BI)
GAL/(HP H).. Gallons per Horsepower-Hour
GALIC .... General American Life Insurance Co.
Galileo......... Galileo Electro-Optics Corp. [Associated Press] (SAG)
GA LJ.......... Georgia Law Journal [A publication] (DLA)
GAIJC.......... Albany Junior College, Albany, GA [Library symbol Library of Congress] (LCLS)
GALK .... Galactokinase [Also, GAK] [An enzyme]
GALL .... Gallae [Nut Galls] [Pharmacology] (ROG)
GALL .... Gallery (MSA)
gall .... Gallery (VRA)
Gall .... Gallison's United States Circuit Court Reports [A publication] (DLA)
GALL .... Gallon
gall .... Gallon (ODBW)
GALL .... Galloway [District in Scotland] (ROG)
Gallagr .... Gallagher [Arthur J.] & Co. [Associated Press] (SAG)
Gallaudet U... Gallaudet University (GAGS)
Gall CCR..... Gallison's United States Circuit Court Reports [A publication] (DLA)
Gall Cr Cas.. Gallick's Reports (French Criminal Cases) [A publication] (DLA)
GALLEX....... Gallium Experiment
GallHist ...... Gallery of History, Inc. [Associated Press] (SAG)
Gall Int L .... Gallaudet on International Law [A publication] (DLA)
Gallison...... Gallison's United States Circuit Court Reports [A publication] (DLA)
Gallison's Rep... Gallison's United States Circuit Court Reports [A publication] (DLA)
GALLSMIN... Gallons per Minute (IAA)
GALLY .... Gallery (ROG)
GAL/MIN ..... Gallons per Minute
GalN .... Galactosamine [Biochemistry]
GalNac........ N-Acetylgalactosamine
Galob......... Galoob [Lewis] Toys, Inc. [Associated Press] (SAG)
Galoob........ Galoob [Lewis] Toys, Inc. [Associated Press] (SAG)
GALOVAL..... Grappling and Lock-On Validation
GALP .... Good Automated Laboratory Practice [Environmental Protection Agency]
GALPAT....... Galloping Pattern Memory
GA L Rep.... Georgia Law Reporter [A publication] (DLA)
GAL/S .... Gallons per Second
GALS .... General Aerodynamic Lifting Surface (KSC)
GALS .... Generalized Assembly Line Simulator [General Motors Corp.]
GALS .... Geographic Adjustment by Least Squares (PDAA)
GAISC .... Albany State College, Albany, GA [Library symbol Library of Congress] (LCLS)
GALSFC ...... Ginger Alden "Lady Superstar" Fan Club (EA)
GALT.......... Galactotransferase [Cell strain deficient in galactose-1-phosphate uridyltransferase]
GALT.......... Gut-Associated Lymphoid Tissue [Medicine]
GALTS .... Generated Author Language Teaching System (EDAC)
GALV .... Galvanic [or Galvanized]
galv .... Galvanized (VRA)
GALV .... Galvanometer
GALV .... Galveston [Texas]
GALV .... Gibbon Ape Leukemia Virus
GALVI .... Galvanized Iron
GALVND...... Galvannealed
GALVNM...... Galvanometer

galvo .... Galvanometer [*An instrument for detecting and measuring an electric current*] (WDMC)
GALVS .... Galvanized Steel
GALV TND ... Galvanized or Tinned [*Freight*]
GALVWG...... Gemini Agena Launch Vehicle Working Group [*NASA*] (KSC)
GALW .... Galway [*County in Ireland*]
GALX .... Galaxy Foods [*NASDAQ symbol*] (TTSB)
GALX .... Galaxy Foods Co. [*NASDAQ symbol*] (SAG)
GalxCbl........ Galaxy Cablevision Ltd. [*Associated Press*] (SAG)
GALXY .... Galaxy
GALY .... Galley (MSA)
GALZ........... Gays and Lesbians of Zimbabwe [*An association*]
GAM .... Gambell [*Alaska*] [*Airport symbol*] (OAG)
GAM .... Gambia
GAM .... Gameness (DSUE)
GAM .... Gamin Resources, Inc. [*Vancouver Stock Exchange symbol*]
GAM .... Gamma (NASA)
Gam............ Gamma Biologicals, Inc.
GAM .... Gamut [*Music*] (ROG)
GAM .... General Accounting Material (DNAB)
GAM .... General Accounting Office, Los Angeles Region, Los Angeles, CA [*OCLC symbol*] (OCLC)
GAM .... General Aeronautical Material
GAM .... General American Investors Co., Inc. [*NYSE symbol*] (SPSG)
GAM .... General Audit Manual
GAM .... Genl Amer Investors [*NYSE symbol*] (TTSB)
GAM .... Georgia Motor Trucking Association [*STAC*]
GAM .... German Army [*ICAO designator*] (FAAC)
GAM .... Global Asset Management [*Commercial firm British*] (ECON)
GAM .... Globe and Mail [*Newspaper databank*] [*Canada*] (NITA)
GAM .... Globe and Mail Data Base [*Info Globe*] [*Information service or system*] (CRD)
GAM .... Golf Association of Michigan (SRA)
GAM .... Graduate Aerospace Mechanical Engineering
GAM .... Grants Administration Manual [*HEW*]
GAM .... Graphic Arts Monthly [*A publication*] (DGA)
GAM .... Graphics Access Method (BUR)
GAM .... Ground-to-Air Missile (AAG)
GAM .... Groupement des Associations Meunieres des Pays de la CEE [*Flour Milling Associations Group of the EEC Countries*] (EAIO)
GAM........... Grupo de Apoyo Mutuo [*Group for Mutual Support*] [*Mexico Political party*]
GAM .... Guaranteed Annual Minimum
GAM .... Guest Aerovias Mexico, SA
GAM .... Guided Aircraft Missile [*Obsolete*]
GAM .... Guided Air Missile (AAGC)
GAM .... Morehouse College, Atlanta, GA [*Library symbol Library of Congress*] (LCLS)
GAMA .... Game Manufacturers Association (EA)
GAMA .... Gas Appliance Manufacturers Association (EA)
GAMA .... General Agents & Managers Association [*Insurance*]
GAMA .... General Aviation Manufacturers Association (EA)
GAMA .... Graphic Arts Machinery Association (DGA)
GAMA .... Graphics-Assisted Management Application [*Computer science*] (BUR)
GAMA .... Groupe d'Analyse Macroeconomique Appliquee [*Group for Applied Macroeconomic Analysis*] [*University of Paris - Nanterre*] [*Information service or system*] (IID)
GAMA .... Guitar and Accessory Manufacturers Association [*Formerly, NAMMM*]
GAMA .... Markala [*Mali*] [*ICAO location identifier*] (ICLI)
GAMAA .... Graphic Arts Merchants' Association of Australia
GamaB......... Gamma Biologicals, Inc. [*Associated Press*] (SAG)
GAMARTA.... Metropolitan Atlanta Rapid Transit Authority, Atlanta, GA [*Library symbol Library of Congress*] (LCLS)
GAMAS .... Gamma Activation Materials Assay System [*Mobile laboratory*]
GAMAS .... General Atomic Material Assay System [*Nuclear energy*] (NRCH)
GAMAS .... Gulf Atomic Mobile Assay System
GAMAST ...... Girls and Mathematics and Science Teaching
GAMB .... Gambro [*A.B.*], Inc. [*NASDAQ symbol*] (NQ)
GAMB .... Mopti/Barbe [*Mali*] [*ICAO location identifier*] (ICLI)
GAMB .... Morris Brown College, Atlanta, GA [*Library symbol Library of Congress*] (LCLS)
Gamb & Barl... Gamble and Barlow's Digest [*Ireland*] [*A publication*] (DLA)
GAMBICA..... Group of Association of Manufacturers of British Instrumentation, Control and Automation (ECII)
GAMBICA..... Group of Association of Manufacturers of British, Instruments, Control and Automation (ACII)
GAMBIT ...... Gate-Modulated Bipolar Transistor (MCD)
Gamboa .... Gamboa's Introduction to Philippine Law [*A publication*] (DLA)
Gamboa Philippine Law... Gamboa's Introduction to Philippine Law [*A publication*] (DLA)
GAMBOG...... Gambogia [*Gamboge*] [*Pharmacology*] (ROG)
Gambro........ Gambro [*A. B.*], Inc. [*Associated Press*] (SAG)
GAMC .... General Agents and Managers Conference of NALU [*Washington, DC*] (EA)
GAMD .... Gallium Arsenide Microwave Diode
GAME .... Gametek, Inc. [*NASDAQ symbol*] (SAG)
GAME.......... GEWEX [*Global Energy and Water Cycle Experiment*] [*Marine science*] (OSRA)
GAMECOIN... Game Conservation International (EA)
GameFn........ Game Financial Corp. [*Associated Press*] (SAG)
GAMET........ Gyro Accelerometer Misalignment Erection Test
GAMETAG .... Global Atmospheric Measurements Experiment on Tropospheric Aerosols and Gases [*National Science Foundation*]
Gametek....... Gametek, Inc. [*Associated Press*] (SAG)

GAmG .... Georgia Southwestern College, Americus, GA [*Library symbol Library of Congress*] (LCLS)
GAMHTE ...... General Association of Municipal Health and Technical Experts (EA)
GAMI .... Great American Management & Investment, Inc. [*NASDAQ symbol*] (NQ)
GAMIC .... Gamma Incomplete [*Chemistry*] (IAA)
GAMIg .... Goat Anti-Mouse Immunoglobulin [*Immunology*]
GAMIN .... General Activity, Ascendence-Submission, Masculinity-Femininity, Inferiority Feelings, Nervousness [*Psychology*] (AEBS)
GamingW .... Gaming World International, Inc. [*Associated Press*] (SAG)
GAMIS .... General Analytical Methods Information Service [*Laboratory of the Government Chemist*] [*British*] (NITA)
GAMIS .... Graphic Arts Marketing Information Service (EA)
GAMK .... Martin Luther King, Jr., Memorial Center, Atlanta, GA [*Library symbol Library of Congress*] (LCLS)
GAMK .... Menaka [*Mali*] [*ICAO location identifier*] (ICLI)
GAMLOGS.... Gamma Ray Logs (IEEE)
GamLott....... Gaming Lottery Corp. [*Associated Press*] (SAG)
GAMM .... German Association for Applied Mathematics and Mechanics
GAMM .... Gimbal Angle Matching Monitor
GAM-M .... Morehouse College, School of Medicine, Atlanta, GA [*Library symbol Library of Congress*] (LCLS)
GAMMA ...... Generalized Automatic Method of Matrix Assembly [*Computer science*] (IAA)
GAMMA ...... Graphically-Aided Mathematical Machine
GAMMA ...... Guitar and Accesories Music Marketing Association (EA)
GAMMA ...... Guns and Magnetic Material Alarm [*Weapon-detecting device to prevent skyjacking*]
GAMNA .... Gambia News Agency (EY)
Gamng........ Gaming Corporation of America [*Associated Press*] (SAG)
GamngCp.... Gaming Corporation of America [*Associated Press*] (SAG)
GAMO .... German Army Material Office
GAMO .... Ground and Amphibious Military Operations [*Army*]
GAMP .... Global Atmospheric Measurements Program [*National Science Foundation*]
GAMP .... Guided Antiarmor Mortar Projectile (INF)
GAMPS .... Gander Automated Message Processing System [*ICAO*] (DA)
GAMRA .... Graphic Arts Manufacturers' Representative Association
GAMS .... Gas Analysis Modeling System [*Department of Energy*] (GFGA)
GAMS .... Groupement pour l'Avancement des Methodes Spectroscopiques et Physio-Chimiques d'Analyse [*Group for the Advancement of Spectroscopic Methods and Physicochemical Analysis*] [*Information service or system*] (IID)
GAMSA .... Glutamylaminomethylsulfonic Acid [*Biochemistry*]
GAMSA .... Management Science America, Inc., Atlanta, GA [*Library symbol Library of Congress*] (LCLS)
GAM/SP ...... Graphics Access Method/System Product [*IBM Corp.*]
GAMTA .... General Aviation Manufacturers' and Traders' Association [*British*] (DA)
GAMU .... Mercer University, Atlanta, GA [*Library symbol Library of Congress*] (LCLS)
GAMU-P...... Mercer University, Southern School of Pharmacy, Atlanta, GA [*Library symbol Library of Congress*] (LCLS)
GAMV .... Galinsoga Mosaic Virus [*Plant pathology*]
GamW .... Gaming World International, Inc. [*Associated Press*] (SAG)
GAN .... Gandalf Technologies, Inc. [*Toronto Stock Exchange symbol*]
GAN .... Gander Aviation Ltd. [*Canada ICAO designator*] (FAAC)
Gan .... Gandulphus [*Flourished, 1160-85*] [*Authority cited in pre-1607 legal work*] (DSA)
GAN .... GAO [*General Accounting Office*] Norfolk Regional Office, Virginia Beach, VA [*OCLC symbol*] (OCLC)
GAN .... Garan, Inc. [*AMEX symbol*] (SPSG)
GAN .... Gaseous Nitrogen (PDAA)
GAN .... Generalized Activity Network (IEEE)
GAN .... Generating and Analyzing Networks [*Computer science*]
GAN .... Generating and Assembly Networks (NITA)
GAN .... Giant Axon Neuropathy [*Medicine*] (DMAA)
GAN .... Global Area Network (IAA)
GAN .... Goldfields Air Navigation [*Australia*]
GAN .... Greenwich Apparent Noon (ROG)
GAN .... Ground Attack Night (MCD)
GAN .... Guidance and Navigation
GAN .... Gyro-Compass Automatic Navigation [*System*] (RDA)
GAN .... Net Gradability [*Truck specification*]
Ganatra........ Ganatra's Criminal Cases [*India*] [*A publication*] (DLA)
Gand........... Gandulphus [*Flourished, 1160-85*] [*Authority cited in pre-1607 legal work*] (DSA)
G and A .... Gas and Air [*Medicine*]
G & A .... General and Administrative
GANDALF.... General Alpha-Numeric Direct Access Library Facility [*Search system*]
G & B .... Gloucester and Bristol [*Diocese*] (ROG)
G & B .... Gordon & Breach [*Publisher*] [*British*]
G and B .... Grafton and Belington Railroad [*Initialism refers to a settlement of Indians who lived near this railroad*]
G&C .... Glass & Ceramic Division (ACII)
G & C .... Gonville and Caius College [*Cambridge University*] (ROG)
G & C .... Goodrich and Clincher (ROG)
G & C .... Guidance and Control [*Military*] (CAAL)
G & CC .... Guidance and Control Coupler (KSC)
G & CEP ...... Guidance and Control Equipment Performance (KSC)
G & CS .... Guidance and Control System
G & D .... Gale and Davison's English Queen's Bench Reports [*1841-43*] [*A publication*] (DLA)
G & D .... Grosset & Dunlap [*Publisher*]

G & D	Growth and Development [*Pediatrics*] (DAVI)
G and D	Guts and Determination (DSUE)
G & E	Ground and Environmental (KSC)
Gander	Gander Mountain, Inc. [*Associated Press*] (SAG)
GANDER	Guidance and Navigation Development and Evaluation Routine (PDAA)
GANDF	Gandalf Technologies [*NASDAQ symbol*] (TTSB)
GANDF	Gandalf Technologies, Inc. [*NASDAQ symbol*] (NQ)
G & F	Georgia & Florida R. R.
G & G	Gems & Gemology [*A publication*] (EAAP)
G & G	Goldsmith and Guthrie's Appeals Reports [*Missouri*] [*A publication*] (DLA)
G & G	Gyandoh and Griffiths. Sourcebook of the Constitutional Law of Ghana [*A publication*] (ILCA)
G & G (MO)	Goldsmith and Guthrie's Appeals Reports [*Missouri*] [*A publication*] (DLA)
G & H	Gavin and Hord's Indiana Statutes [*A publication*] (DLA)
G & H	Gibbs & Hill, Inc. (NRCH)
G & J	Gill and Johnson's Maryland Court of Appeals Reports [*1829-42*] [*A publication*] (DLA)
G & J	Glyn and Jameson's English Bankruptcy Reports [*1821-28*] [*A publication*] (DLA)
G & J	Gruner & Jahr AG & Co. [*Magazine publisher*] [*Germany*]
G & J (MD)	Gill and Johnson's Maryland Reports [*A publication*] (DLA)
G & Jo	Gill and Johnson's Maryland Reports [*A publication*] (DLA)
G & John	Gill and Johnson's Maryland Reports [*A publication*] (DLA)
G & K	G & K Services, Inc. [*Associated Press*] (SAG)
Gandlf	Gandalf Technologies, Inc. [*Associated Press*] (SAG)
G & L Rty	G & L Realty Corp. [*Associated Press*] (SAG)
G & M	General and Municipal
G & M	Geraghty & Miller, Inc.
G & M	Girth and Mirth (EA)
G & M	Gulf & Mississippi Railroad
G & N	Greenville & Northern Railway Co. (IIA)
G & N	Guidance and Navigation [*System*] [*Apollo*] [*NASA*]
G & O	Gas and Oxygen [*Medicine*]
G & OA	Glycerine and Oleochemicals Association (EA)
G & PA	Girls and Physical Activity National Newsletter [*A publication*]
G & P RR Laws	Gregg and Pond's Railroad Laws of the New England States [*A publication*] (DLA)
G & R	Geldert and Russell's Nova Scotia Reports [*A publication*] (DLA)
G & RS	Guidance and Reporting System [*Army*]
G & S	Gilbert and Sullivan
G & Sh RR	Godefroi and Shortt's Law of Railway Companies [*A publication*] (DLA)
G & SI	Gulf & Ship Island Railroad Co.
G & SS	Gilbert and Sullivan Society [*Australia*]
G & SW	Glasgow & South-Western [*Railway*] [*Scotland*]
G & SWR	Glasgow & South-Western Railway [*Scotland*]
G & T	Gin and Tonic
G&T	Goals and Timetables (AAGC)
G & T	Gould and Tucker's Notes on Revised Statutes of United States [*A publication*] (DLA)
G & T	Gowns and Towels [*Medicine*] (DMAA)
G & U	Grafe & Unzer [*Publisher*] [*German*]
G & W	Genesee & Western Railroad (IIA)
G & W	Gulf & Western Industries, Inc.
G & Wh Eas	Gale and Whatley [*later, Gale*] on Easements [*A publication*] (ILCA)
G & WI	Gulf & Western Industries, Inc.
G & W New Tr	Graham and Waterman on New Trials [*A publication*] (DLA)
Gane	Eastern District Court Reports [*South Africa*] [*A publication*] (DLA)
GANEFO	Games of the New Emerging Forces [*A counter-attraction to the Olympic Games*] [*Indonesia*]
GANF	Ganfield [*England*]
GANF	Niafunke [*Mali*] [*ICAO location identifier*] (ICLI)
GANG	Ganglion [*Medicine*]
gangl	Ganglion [*or Ganglionic*] [*Neurology*] (DAVI)
GANH	Northside Hospital, Atlanta, GA [*Library symbol Library of Congress*] (LCLS)
GANIP	Graphic Approach to Numerical Information Processing (IAA)
GANK	Nara/Keibane [*Mali*] [*ICAO location identifier*] (ICLI)
GANNET	General Administrative Network [*Computer linkup*] [*British*]
Gannett	Gannett Co., Inc. [*Associated Press*] (SAG)
Gannon U	Gannon University (GAGS)
GANO	[*The*] Georgia Northern Railway Co. [*AAR code*]
GANPAC	German American National Political Action Committee (EA)
GANR	Nioro [*Mali*] [*ICAO location identifier*] (ICLI)
GANS	Granulomatous Angiitis of the Nervous System [*Medicine*] (DMAA)
GANS	Guidance and Navigation System [*Apollo*] [*NASA*] (IAA)
GANSAT	Gannett Satellite Information Network
Gantos	Gantos, Inc. [*Associated Press*] (SAG)
Gantt Dig	Gantt's Digest of Arkansas Statutes [*A publication*] (DLA)
Gantts Dig	Gantt's Digest of Arkansas Statutes [*A publication*] (DLA)
ganz	Ganzlich [*Complete*] [*German*] (BARN)
GAO	GARP Activities Office [*Marine science*] (MSC)
GAO	General Accounting Office [*of the US government*]
GAO	General Accounting Office, Technical Information Sources and Service, Washington, DC [*OCLC symbol*] (OCLC)
GAO	General Administrative Order
GAO	General Agricultural Officer [*Ministry of Agriculture, Fisheries, and Food*] [*British*]
GAO D	General Alert Order (NATG)
GAO	German Army Office
GAO	Glycolic Acid Oxidase [*An enzyme*]
GAO	Golden Air Commuter AB [*Sweden ICAO designator*] (FAAC)

GAO	Government Accounting Office (MCD)
GAO	Guantanamo [*Cuba*] [*Airport symbol*] (OAG)
GAO	Gummed All Over [*Envelopes*] (DGA)
GAOC	Oglethorpe University, Atlanta, GA [*Library symbol Library of Congress*] (LCLS)
GAO/CED	General Accounting Office/Community and Economic Development Division
GAOF	Gummed All Over Flap [*Envelopes*]
GAO/FGMSD	General Accounting Office/Financial and General Management Studies Division
GAO/FPCD	General Accounting Office/Federal Personnel and Compensation Division
GAO/GGD	General Accounting Office General Government Division
GAOHP	General Alliance of Operative House Painters [*A union*] [*British*]
GAO/HRD	General Accounting Office Human Resources Division
GAO/LCD	General Accounting Office/Logistics and Communications Division
GAO Let Rep	General Accounting Office Letter Report [*A publication*] (DLA)
GAO/MASAD	General Accounting Office Mission Analysis and Systems Acquisition Division
GAO NOTE	General Accounting Office, Notice of Execution (DNAB)
GAO/NSIAD	General Accounting Office National Security and International Affairs Division
GAO/PAD	General Accounting Office Program Analysis Division
GAO/PEMD	General Accounting Office Program Evaluation and Methodology Division
GAO/PSAD	General Accounting Office/Procurement and Systems Acquisition Division
GAOR	General Accounting Office Review
GAOR	General Assembly Official Record [*United Nations*] [*A publication*] (DLA)
GAOTU	Grand Architect of the Universe [*Freemasonry*] (ROG)
GAOW	General Accounting Office, Washington
GAP	Atlanta Public Library, Atlanta, GA [*OCLC symbol*] (OCLC)
GAP	Atlanta Public Schools, Professional Library, Atlanta, GA [*Library symbol Library of Congress*] (LCLS)
GAP	Gadolinium Aluminium Perovskite [*Inorganic chemistry*]
Gap	Gap, Inc. [*Formerly, Gap Stores, Inc.*] [*Associated Press*] (SAG)
GAP	Garmisch-Partenkirchen [*Federal Republic of Germany*] [*Seismograph station code, US Geological Survey*] (SEIS)
GAP	Gastric and Peptic Ulcer [*A laboratory test kit*] [*Medicine*]
GAP	General Accounting Package (IAA)
GAP	General and Practical Energy Information Data Base (MCD)
GAP	General Antenna Package [*COMSAT*]
GAP	General Application Plan (AFIT)
GAP	General Assembly Program [*Computer science*]
GAP	Geographic Applications Program [*United States Geological Survey*] (IID)
GaP	Georgia Power [*Associated Press*] (SAG)
GAP	Ghetto Arts Program [*Later, Urban Arts Corps*] (EA)
GAP	Glyceraldehyde Phosphate [*Biochemistry*]
GAP	Glycidyl Azide Polymer [*Chemistry*]
GAP	GnRH [*Gonadotropin Releasing Hormone*] Associated Peptide [*Endocrinology*]
GAP	GOAL [*Ground Operations Aerospace Language*] Automatic Procedure [*NASA*] (NASA)
GAP	Good Agricultural Practice [*Toxicology*]
GAP	Goodyear Associative Processor [*Computer science*]
GAP	Government Accountability Project (EA)
GAP	Government Aircraft Plant
GAP	Government of Alberta Publications [*Alberta Public Affairs Bureau*] [*Canada Information service or system*] (CRD)
GAP	Grand Anatolia Project [*Dam system*] [*Turkey*] (ECON)
GAP	Grant Air Program [*DoD*] (MCD)
GAP	Graphical Automatic Programming [*Computer science*]
GAP	Graphics Adapter Processor [*Baytec*]
GAP	Graphics Application Program
GAP	Great Atl & Pac Tea [*NYSE symbol*] (TTSB)
GAP	Great Atlantic & Pacific Tea Co., Inc. [*NYSE symbol*] (SPSG)
GAP	Greater Access to Publishing [*British*]
GAP	Greenwood, Archer, and Pine [*Major streets in Tulsa, OK*] [*In musical group "The GAP Band"*]
GAP	Gross Agricultural Product (WDAA)
GAP	Group Attainment Program
GAP	Group for Aquatic Primary Productivity [*ICSU*]
GAP	Group for the Advancement of Psychiatry (EA)
GAP	Growth-Associated Protein [*Cytochemistry*]
GAP	Grupo de Auto-Defensa [*Self-Defense Group*] [*Uruguay*] [*Political party*] (PD)
GAP	Guanosine Triphosphatase Activating Protein [*Biochemistry*]
GAP	Guided Antitank Projectile (MCD)
GAP	Gusap [*Papua New Guinea*] [*Airport symbol Obsolete*] (OAG)
GAPA	Greek American Progressive Association (EA)
GAPA	Ground-to-Air Pilotless Aircraft [*Early US test missiles*]
GaPac	Georgia-Pacific Corp. [*Associated Press*] (SAG)
GAPAN	Guide to Air Pilots and Air Navigation [*A publication*]
GAPAN	Guild of Air Pilots and Air Navigators (MCD)
GAPB	General Aptitude Test Battery (DNAB)
GaPC	Georgia Power Capital Ltd. [*Associated Press*] (SAG)
GaPC	Georgia Power Capital Trust I [*Associated Press*] (SAG)
GAPCE	General Assembly of the Presbyterian Church of England (DAS)
GAP CON	Gap Conductance (GAAI)
Ga-PD	Gallium Arsenide Phosphide Photodiode
GAPD	Garrett Auxiliary Power Division [*Military contractor*] (RDA)
GAPD	Glyceraldehyde Phosphate Dehydrogenase [*Organic chemistry*] (MAH)

GAPD .... Government and Aeronautical Products Division [*Honeywell, Inc.*]
GAPDH .... Glyceraldehydephosphate Dehydrogenase [*Also, GPDH*] [*An enzyme*]
GAPE .... General Aviation Pilot Education [*Safety project*]
GAPE .... Geographical Association Package Exchange (AIE)
GAPE .... Graphic Acids to Packaging Equipment (PDAA)
GAPE .... Ground Anchor Placement Equipment
GAPEA .... Graphic Arts Platemakers Employers' Federation (DGA)
GAPh .... Southern School of Pharmacy, Mercer University, Atlanta, GA [*Library symbol Library of Congress*] (LCLS)
GAPHYOR .... Gaz-Physique-Orsay Database [*Universite de Paris-Sud*] [*Information service or system*]
GAPie .... Piedmont Hospital, Atlanta, GA [*Library symbol Library of Congress*] (LCLS)
GAPL .... Group Assembly Parts List (MCD)
GAPL .... Group Assembly Provisioning List (MCD)
GAPM .... Generalized Access Path Method [*Computer science*] (MHDB)
GAPO .... Growth Retardation, Alopecia, Pseudo-Anodontia, and Optic Atrophy Syndrome [*Medicine*] (DMAA)
GAPP .... Geometric Arithmetic Parallel Processor [*Computer science*]
GAPR .... Grant Application Request (WDAA)
GA Prac .... Stand's Georgia Practice [*A publication*] (DLA)
GAPS .... Geo-Assimilated Positioning System [*Navigation systems*]
GAPS .... Government Accountability Property System (MCD)
GAPSALS .... Give a Pint, Save a Life Society [*World War II organization which encouraged donating blood*]
GAPSAT ...... Gap-Filler Satellite [*RADAR*] (NVT)
GAPSATCOM... Gap-Filler Satellite Communication System (MCD)
GA PSC ...... Georgia Public Service Commission Reports [*A publication*] (DLA)
GAPSF .... Government Agricultural Policy and Services for Farmers [*British*]
GAPSFAS ..... Graduate and Professional School Financial Aid Service (GAGS)
GAPSS .... Graphical Analysis Procedures for System Simulation (PDAA)
GAPT .... Generalized Atomic Polar Tensor [*Physical chemistry*]
GAPT .... Graphical Automatically Programmed Tools [*Computer science*]
GaPw .... Georgia Power Co. [*Associated Press*] (SAG)
GAQ .... Gao [*Mali*] [*Airport symbol*]
GAQ .... Golfe Air Quebec Ltd. [*Canada ICAO designator*] (FAAC)
GAQ .... Good Average Quality (ADA)
GAQ .... Graphic Arts Quality (DGA)
GAQA .... Government Acquisition Quality Assurance (MCD)
GAR .... Commodore Aviation [*Australia ICAO designator*] (FAAC)
GAR .... GAO [*General Accounting Office*] San Francisco Regional Office, San Francisco, CA [*OCLC symbol*] (OCLC)
GAR .... Garage
GAR .... Garaina [*Papua New Guinea*] [*Airport symbol*] (OAG)
GAR .... Garamond [*Typography*] (DGA)
GAR .... Garden Lake Resources [*Vancouver Stock Exchange symbol*]
GAR .... Garm [*Former USSR Seismograph station code, US Geological Survey*] (SEIS)
GAR .... Garrison (MUGU)
GAR .... General Adverse Reaction [*Noise*]
GaR .... Georgia Reports [*A publication*] (DLA)
Ga R .... Georgia Review [*A publication*] (BRI)
G-Ar .... Georgia State Department of Archives and History, Atlanta, GA [*Library symbol Library of Congress*] (LCLS)
GAR .... German Army
GAR .... Gimbal Angle Rate
GAR .... Gimbal Angle Readout
GAR .... Glass Accumulation Rate [*Oceanography*]
GAR .... Global Atmospheric Research (NOAA)
GAR .... Go-Around (GAVI)
GAR .... Goat Anti-Rabbit [*Also, GARb*] [*Immunology*]
GAR .... Golden Age Records [*Record label*]
GAR .... Government Authorized Representative
GAR .... Grand Army of the Republic (GPO)
GAR .... Graphics Action Request (MCD)
GAR .... Ground Accident Report (MCD)
GAR .... Growth Analysis and Review (BUR)
GAR .... Gruppi Armati Radicali per il Comunismo [*Armed Radical Groups for Communism*] [*Italy*] (PD)
GAR .... Guided Aerial Rocket
GAR .... Guided Aircraft Rocket
GAR .... Guided Antiarmor Rocket
GAR .... Gummed All Round [*Envelopes*] (DGA)
GARA .... Garamond [*Typography*] (WDAA)
Garan .... Garan, Inc. [*Associated Press*] (SAG)
garb .... Garbage (BARN)
GARb .... Goat Anti-Rabbit [*Also, GAR*] [*Immunology*]
GARB .... Green, Amber, Red, Blue [*Priority of the airways*]
GARB .... Guided Antiradiation Bomb
Garbage ...... Garbage: The Independent Environmental Quarterly [*A publication*] (BRI)
GARBC .... General Association of Regular Baptist Churches (EA)
GARBD .... Garboard [*Naval architecture*]
GARC .... Graphic Arts Research Center [*Later, T & E Center*] [*Rochester Institute of Technology*]
GARC .... Great Atlantic Radio Conspiracy (EA)
GARC .... Retail Credit Co., Atlanta, GA [*Library symbol Library of Congress*] (LCLS)
GARCH .... Generalized Auto-Regressive Conditional Heteroskedacity [*Business term*] (ECON)
G Arch .... Graduate in Architecture
GARD .... Gamma Atomic Radiation Detector
gard .... Garden (VRA)
GARD .... Gardener (ROG)

Gard .... Gardens (BARN)
GARD .... General Address Reading Devices [*Computer science*]
GARD .... General Aviation Recovery Device
GARD .... Gimbal Angle Runaway Detector
GARD .... Graphic Analyzer of Resistance Defects
GARDAE .... Grumman-Alderson Research Dummy [*Aircraft ejection seats*]
GARDAE .... Gathers Alarms, Reports, Displays, and Evaluates
GardDen ...... Gardner Denver Machinery, Inc. [*Associated Press*] (SAG)
GARDE .... Gather, Alarm, Report, Display, and Evaluate (IAA)
GARDEN ...... Garden [*Commonly used*] (OPSA)
Gardenhire ... Gardenhire's Reports [*14, 15 Missouri*] [*A publication*] (DLA)
GARDENS ..... Gardens [*Commonly used*] (OPSA)
Gard Ev ...... Garde on Evidence [*1830*] [*A publication*] (DLA)
GARDN .... Garden [*Commonly used*] (OPSA)
GardnFr .... Garden Fresh Restaurant Corp. [*Associated Press*] (SAG)
Gardn PC .... Gardner's Peerage Case, Reported by Le Marchant [*A publication*] (DLA)
GardnR .... Garden Ridge Corp. [*Associated Press*] (SAG)
Gard NY Rep... Gardienier's New York Reporter [*A publication*] (DLA)
Gard NY Rept... Gardienier's New York Reporter [*A publication*] (DLA)
Gard NY Rptr... Gardienier's New York Reporter [*A publication*] (DLA)
Gard Pl .... Garde's First Principles of Pleading [*A publication*] (DLA)
GardStat ...... Garden State Bancshares [*Associated Press*] (SAG)
GARDTRAK... Gamma Absorption and Radiation Detection Tracking (IAA)
GARE .... Guidelines for Authority and Reference Entries [*Cataloguing*] [*Association for Library Collections and Technical Services*]
GA Rep .... Georgia Reports [*A publication*] (DLA)
GA Rep Ann... Georgia Reports, Annotated [*A publication*] (DLA)
GAREX .... Ground Aviation Radio Exchange System (MCD)
GARF .... Graphic Arts Research Foundation (EA)
GARF .... Ground Approach Radio Fuse (IAA)
GARF .... Guam Acoustic Range Facility [*Military*] (CAAL)
GARG .... Gargarisma [*Gargle*] [*Pharmacy*]
GarG .... Garment Graphics, Inc. [*Associated Press*] (SAG)
GARGAR ...... Gargarisma [*Gargle*] [*Pharmacy*] (ROG)
GARGD .... Garaged [*Automotive advertising*]
GARGG .... Goat Antiserum to Rabbit Gamma-Globulin [*Immunology*]
GARH .... Georgia Regional Hospital at Atlanta, Atlanta, GA [*Library symbol Library of Congress*] (LCLS)
GARI .... Goat Anti-Rabbit Immunoglobulin [*Immunochemistry*]
GARI .... Groupe d'Action Revolutionnaire Internationaliste [*International Revolutionary Action Group*] [*France Political party*] (PD)
GARI .... Grupo de Accion Revolucionaria Internacional [*International Revolutionary Action Group*] [*Spain Political party*]
GARIOA....... Government and Relief in Occupied Areas [*Post-World War II*]
Garkreba...... Garantie- und Kreditbank [*Guaranty and Credit Bank*] [*Germany*] (EG)
GARL .... Group Action Request Lists
GarmGph .... Garment Graphics, Inc. [*Associated Press*] (SAG)
GARMI .... General Aviation Radio Magnetic Indicator
GArmO........ Group Armaments Officer [*British military*] (DMA)
GARN.......... Garnet Resources [*NASDAQ symbol*] (TTSB)
GARN.......... Garnet Resources Corp. [*NASDAQ symbol*] (NQ)
GARN.......... Garnish [*Automotive engineering*]
GARN.......... Garnishee Order (DCTA)
GARNEE ...... Garnishee [*Legal shorthand*] (LWAP)
Garnet .... Garnet Resources Corp. [*Associated Press*] (SAG)
GARNOR ...... Garnishor [*Legal shorthand*] (LWAP)
GARP .... Global Atmospheric Research Program [*Terminated National Science Foundation*]
GARP .... Growth at the Right Price
GARS .... Generic Airborne RADAR System (DWSG)
GARS .... Geological Applications of Remote Sensing
GARS .... Glycine Amide Phosphoribosyl Synthetase (DMAA)
GARS .... Grand Assistant Recording Scribe [*Freemasonry*] (ROG)
GART .... Gartner Group'A' [*NASDAQ symbol*] (TTSB)
GART .... Gartner Group, Inc. [*NASDAQ symbol*] (NQ)
Gartner .... Gartner Group, Inc. [*Associated Press*] (SAG)
GAS .... Autonomous Anarchist Groups [*Spanish*] (PD)
GAS .... Gach Saran [*Iran*] [*Airport symbol*] (AD)
GAS .... Galactorrhea-Amenorrhea Syndrome [*Medicine*] (DMAA)
GAS .... Galena Air Services, Inc. [*ICAO designator*] (FAAC)
GAS .... Gallipolis, OH [*Location identifier FAA*] (FAAL)
GAS .... Gallium Arsenide [*Semiconductor*]
GAS .... Gamma-Activated Site [*Biochemistry*]
GAS .... Garissa [*Kenya*] [*Airport symbol*] (OAG)
GAS .... Gas Acquisition System
GAS .... Gas Anti-Solvent [*Chemical engineering*]
GAS .... Gas-Insulated Switchgear
GAS .... Gasoline (AFM)
GAS .... Gasoline
GAS .... Gastric Acid Secretion [*Medicine*] (DMAA)
GAS .... Gastroenterology [*Medicine*]
GAS .... Gauss [*Later, GTT*] [*Federal Republic of Germany*] [*Geomagnetic observatory code*]
GAS .... General Adaptation Syndrome [*Medicine*]
GAS .... General Air Staff (NATG)
GAS .... General Aptitude Series [*Test*]
GAS .... General Automotive Support
GAS .... General Aviation Simulator [*Computer science NASA*]
GAS .... Generalized Arteriosclerosis [*Medicine*]
GAS .... Generalized Audit Software [*Computer science*]
GAS .... Get Away Special (MCD)
GAS .... Giant Air Shower
GAS .... Giant Attribute Survey

GAS .... Glass Art Society (EA)
GAS .... Global Address Space (MHDI)
GAS .... Global Analysis Systems [*Information service or system*] (IID)
GAS .... Global Anxiety Score [*Medicine*] (DMAA)
GAS .... Global Assessment Scale [*Psychiatric evaluation test*]
GAS .... Goal Attainment Scale
GAS .... Goilala Air Services [*Australia*]
GAS .... Government Accounting Service [*British*]
GAS .... Government-Assisted Students
GAS .... Government of American Samoa (MUGU)
GAS .... Grand Annual Sojourner [*Freemasonry*] (ROG)
GAS .... Graphics Application Program [*Computer science*] (MHDI)
GAS .... Graphics Attachment Support (IAA)
GAS .... Gray Area Systems (MCD)
GAS .... Group A Streptococci [*Medicine*]
GAS .... Growth Arrest-Specific Gene [*Medicine*] (DMAA)
GAS .... Guild of All Saints [*British*] (ROG)
GAS .... Guild of All Souls [*British*]
GAS .... Gun Accessory System (MCD)
GAS .... Gun Aiming Sensor (MCD)
GAS .... Gunner's Auxiliary Sight (MCD)
GAS .... Gust Alleviation System [*Aviation*] (MCD)
GAS .... NICOR, Inc. [*Formerly, Northern Illinois Gas Co.*] [*NYSE symbol*] (SPSG)
GAS .... Southern Technical Institute, Marietta, GA [*OCLC symbol*] (OCLC)
GASA .... German Australian Society of Australia
GASA .... Graphic Arts Suppliers Association (EA)
GASA .... Growth-Adjusted Sonographic Age [*Obstetrics*] (DMAA)
GASANSW ... Graphic Arts Services Association of New South Wales [*Australia*]
GASAV .... Graphic Arts Services Association of Victoria [*Australia*]
GASB .... Governmental Accounting Standards Board [*Stamford, CT*] (EA)
GASBIINDO... Gabungan Serikat Buruh Islam Indonesia [*Federation of Indonesian Islamic Trade Unions*]
GASC .... Gas-Analysis Sample Container [*Apollo*] [*NASA*]
GASC .... Georgia, Ashburn, Sylvester & Camilla R. R. [*AAR code*]
GASC .... German-American Securities Corp. (BARN)
GASC .... Graphic Arts Show Co., Inc. (DGA)
GASC .... Gurkha Army Service Corps [*British military*] (DMA)
GAS Can ...... Get-Away-Special Cannister [*NASA*]
GASD .... Government Aerospace Systems Division [*Harris Corp.*]
GASDA .... Gasoline and Automotive Service Dealers Association (EA)
Gas de Cal... Gaspar de Calderinis [*Deceased, 1390*] [*Authority cited in pre-1607 legal work*] (DSA)
Gas de Cald... Gaspar de Calderinis [*Deceased, 1390*] [*Authority cited in pre-1607 legal work*] (DSA)
GASDSAS .... Gust Alleviation and Structural Dynamic Stability Augmentation [*Aviation*]
GASEQ .... Graziers' Association of South East Queensland [*Australia*]
GASER .... Gamma Ray LASER (NATG)
GASERBUN... Gabungan SB2 Non-Vakcentral [*Federation of Non-Affiliated Trade Unions*] [*Indonesia*]
GASES .... Gravity-Anchored Space Experiments Satellite (MCD)
GASF .... Graphic Arts Sales Foundation (EA)
GASFET .... Gallium Arsenide Field-Effect Transistor
GASG .... Segou [*Mali*] [*ICAO location identifier*] (ICLI)
GASGASGAS... Gild of Ancient Suppliers of Gas Appliances, Skills, Gins, Accessories, and Substances (EA)
GASH .... Guanidine Aluminum Sulfate Hexahydrate [*Insecticide*]
GASH .... Guanidine Aluminum Sulfate Hydrate [*Ferroelectrics*]
GASHA .... Golden American Saddlebred Horse Association (EA)
GASI .... Greenwich Air Services, Inc. [*NASDAQ symbol*] (SAG)
GASIA .... Greenwich Air Services 'A' [*NASDAQ symbol*] (TTSB)
GASIB .... Greenwich Air Svcs 'B' [*NASDAQ symbol*] (TTSB)
GASJ .... Saint Joseph's Infirmary, Atlanta, GA [*Library symbol Library of Congress*] (LCLS)
GASK .... Sikasso [*Mali*] [*ICAO location identifier*] (ICLI)
GASKET .... Graphic Surface Kinetics [*Computer program*] (KSC)
GASL .... General Activity Simulation Language [*Computer science*]
GASL .... General Applied Science Laboratory
GASL .... Southeastern Library Network [*SOLINET*], Atlanta, GA [*Library symbol*] [*Library of Congress*] (LCLS)
GASLAB ...... Global Atmospheric Sampling Laboratory (EERA)
GASM .... Graphic Arts Spray Manufacturers [*Defunct*] (EA)
GAS-MOP ... Gulf of Alaska Mesoscale Oceanographic Processes
GASN .... San [*Mali*] [*ICAO location identifier*] (ICLI)
GASO .... Gasoline
GASOHOL .... Gasoline/Ethanol [*Automotive fuel*]
Gasonics ..... Gasonics International Corp. [*Associated Press*] (SAG)
GASP .... Galloping Acronyms Save Paper
GASP .... Gas Annulus Sizing Program
GASP .... Gas Plasma Display (HGAA)
GASP .... Gas Properties [*NASA computer program*]
GASP .... General Activity Simulation Program [*Programming language*] [*1970*] [*Computer science*] (BUR)
GASP .... General All-Purpose Simulation Package [*McDonnell Douglas Automation Co.*] (MCD)
GASP .... General Analysis of System Performance (IAA)
GASP .... General Assembly to Stop the Powerline (EA)
GASP .... Generalized Academic Simulation Program [*Computer science*] (IEEE)
GASP .... Generalized Aerospace Program (KSC)
GASP .... Generalized Antisymmetric Potential
GASP .... Generalized Audit Software Package [*Computer science*] (MHDI)
GASP .... Gevic Arithmetic Simulation Program
GASP .... Global Assimilation and Prognosis System (EERA)

GASP .... Global Atmospheric Sampling Program [*NASA*]
GASP .... Goldfields Against Serious Pollution [*Australia*]
GASP .... Graded Assessment in Science Project (AIE)
GASP .... Grand Accelerated Space Platform
GASP .... Graphic Applications Subroutine Package [*Computer science*] (BUR)
GASP .... Gravity-Assisted Space Probe [*NASA*]
GASP .... Greater [*name of city*] Alliance to Stop Pollution
GASP .... Grip, Aim, Stance, and Posture [*Golf*]
GASP .... Ground Avoidance Simulation Program (MCD)
GASP .... Group Against Smokers' Pollution (EA)
GASP .... Groups Against Sewage Pollution [*Australia*]
Gaspar .... Gaspar's Small Cause Court Reports [*Bengal*] [*A publication*] (DLA)
Gasp de Cald... Gaspar de Calderinis [*Deceased, 1390*] [*Authority cited in pre-1607 legal work*] (DSA)
GASPE .... Gated Spin Echo [*Nuclear magnetic resonance*]
GASPI .... Guidance Attitude Space Position Indicator (MCD)
GASPT .... Generalized Axially-Symmetrical Potential Theory (PDAA)
GASR .... Guided Air-to-Surface Rocket (IAA)
GASS .... American Resources, Inc. [*NASDAQ symbol*] (SAG)
GASS .... Amer Resources Del [*NASDAQ symbol*] (TTSB)
GASS .... Generalized Assembly System [*Computer science*] (IEEE)
GASS .... Geomagnetic Airborne Survey System
GASS .... Gimbal Assembly Storage System
GASS .... Great American Shoe Store [*Advertising slogan of Kinney Shoe Corp.*]
GASS .... Great Analog Signal Saver
GASS .... Guidance Accuracy Study for SPRINT [*Missile*] [*Army*] (AABC)
GASSAR....... Gilbert Associates [*or General Atomic*] Standard Safety Analysis Report [*Nuclear energy*] (NRCH)
GASSER ...... Geographic Aerospace Search RADAR
GASSP .... Gas Source Seismic Section Profiler
GASSW .... Amer Res Del Wrrt [*NASDAQ symbol*] (TTSB)
GAST .... Gastric (WDAA)
GAST .... Gastronomia Espanola [*Ministerio de Cultura*] [*Spain Information service or system*] (CRD)
GAST .... Geraeteausgabestelle [*Equipment distributing point*] [*German military - World War II*]
GAST .... Globally Averaged Surface Temperature (EERA)
GAST .... Greenwich Apparent Sidereal Time (PDAA)
GASTA .... Gimbal Angle Sequencing Transformation Assembly (KSC)
GASTRN....... Gastrin [*Gastroenterology*] (DAVI)
GASTRNTRLGST... Gastroenterologist
GASTRNTRLY... Gastroenterology
Gastro .... Gastroenterology (DAVI)
Gastro .... Gastrointestinal [*Gastroenterology*] (DAVI)
GASTROC .... Gastrocnemius [*Muscle*] [*Anatomy*]
GASU .... Georgia State University, Atlanta, GA [*Library symbol Library of Congress*] (LCLS)
GASU-D ...... Georgia State University, Documents Library, Atlanta, GA [*Library symbol*] [*Library of Congress*] (LCLS)
GASU-I........ Georgia State University, Instructional Resource Center, Atlanta, GA [*Library symbol*] [*Library of Congress*] (LCLS)
GASU-L........ Georgia State University, Law Library, Atlanta, GA [*Library symbol Library of Congress*] (LCLS)
GA Sup .... Georgia Reports, Supplement [*A publication*] (DLA)
GA Supp ...... Georgia Reports, Supplement [*A publication*] (DLA)
GAS/W........ Gas Weld
GASWOA...... Great American Station Wagon Owner's Association [*Defunct*] (EA)
GAt............. Athens Regional Library, Athens, GA [*Library symbol Library of Congress*] (LCLS)
GAT............. Gate-Associated Transistor (MCD)
GAT............. Gelatin-Agglutination Test [*Clinical chemistry*]
GAT............. Gemini Agena Target [*NASA*]
GAT............. General Air Traffic [*Europe-Asia*]
GAT............. General Air Training
GAT............. General Analysis Technique
GAT............. General Aptitude Test [*Psychometrics*]
GAT............. General Aviation Trainer
GAT............. General Aviation Transponder
GAT............. Generalized Algebraic Translator [*Computer science*]
GAT............. Georgetown Automatic Translator [*Computer science*]
GAT............. Georgia Institute of Technology, Atlanta, GA [*Library symbol Library of Congress OCLC symbol*] (LCLS)
GAT............. Geriatric Assessment Team [*Medicine*] (DMAA)
GAT............. Gerontological Apperception Test [*Medicine*] (DMAA)
GAT............. Goodyear Atomic Corp. (KSC)
GAT............. Government Acceptance Test (MCD)
GAT............. Graphic Arts Terminal [*Phototypesetting*] (NITA)
GAT............. Great American Trials [*A publication*]
GAT............. Greenwich Apparent Time
GAT............. Ground Attack Tactics [*for air delivery of weapons against a ground target*]
GAT............. Ground-to-Air Transmitter
GAT............. Ground-to-Air Transmitter Gate (MCD)
GAT............. Group Adjustment Therapy [*Psychology*] (DAVI)
GAT............. Gulf Air, Inc. [*ICAO designator*] (FAAC)
GAT............. Guyane Air Transport [*Airline*] [*French Guiana*]
GAT$_{10}$ .... Glutamic Acid-Alanine-Tyrosine [*Biopolymer*]
GATA .... Glass and Allied Traders' Association [*British*] (DBA)
GATAC .... General Assessment Tridimensional Analog Computer (IEEE)
GATAE .... Graphic Arts Trade Association Executives [*Later, GAAE*]
GAtAR......... United States Department of Agriculture, Russell Agriculture Research Center, Athens, GA [*Library symbol Library of Congress*] (LCLS)
GATB .... General Aptitude Test Battery

GATB .... General Avionics Testbed [Military]
GATB .... Graphical Articulted Total Body
GATB .... Tombouctou [Mali] [ICAO location identifier] (ICLI)
GATBY .... General Aptitude Test Battery
GATCO .... Guild of Air Traffic Control Officers [British]
GATD .... Graphic Analysis of Three-Dimensional Data
GATE .... GARP [Global Atmospheric Research Program] Atlantic Tropical Experiment [National Oceanic and Atmospheric Administration]
GATE .... Gateway 2000 [NASDAQ symbol] (TTSB)
GATE .... Gateway 2000, Inc. [NASDAQ symbol] (SAG)
GATE .... General Access Transportation Extention [Telecommunications] (TSSD)
GATE .... Generalized Algebraic Translator Extended [Computer science]
GATE .... General-Purpose Automatic Test Equipment [Army] (RDA)
GATE .... Gifted and Taleted Education Program [California] (EDAC)
GATE .... Graduate Aid to Employment (OICC)
Gate2000 ..... Gateway 2000, Inc. [Associated Press] (SAG)
GATEOR ...... Gas-Assisted Thermal-Enhanced Oil Recovery
GATERS ...... Ground-Air Telerobotic Systems [Marine Corps] (DOMA)
GATEWAY .... Gateway [Commonly used] (OPSA)
GATEWY ...... Gateway [Commonly used] (OPSA)
GATF .... Graphic Arts Technical Foundation (EA)
GATH .... Gatha [Language, etc.] (ROG)
GAThS .... Theosophical Society, Atlanta, GA [Library symbol Library of Congress] (LCLS)
GAtL .... Athens Regional Library, Athens, GA [Library symbol] [Library of Congress] (LCLS)
GATN .... Taoudenni [Mali] [ICAO location identifier] (ICLI)
GATP .... Ground Acceptance [or Article] Test Procedure (MCD)
GATR .... Great American Truck Racing (EA)
GATR .... Gross Average Tax Rate
GATR .... Ground-to-Air Transmitting-Receiving [Station]
GATRI .... Gamma Technology Research Irradiator (ADA)
GATS .... General Acceptance Test Software
GATS .... General Agreement on Trade in Services
GATS .... GPS [Global Positioning System] Aided Targeting System [Army] (DOMA)
GATS .... Guidance Acceptance Test Set
GATS .... Tessalit [Mali] [ICAO location identifier] (ICLI)
GAtT .... Athens Are Technical Institute, Athens, GA [Library symbol] [Library of Congress] (LCLS)
GATT .... Gate Assisted Turnoff Thyristor [NASA] (NASA)
GATT .... General Agreement on Tariffs and Trade [Organization, and the concept it represents, concerned with adjustment of tariffs among 73 member nations] [See also AGTDC] [Switzerland] [Also, an information service or system]
GATT .... General Agreement on Tariffs and Trade (EERA)
GATT .... Ground-to-Air Transmitter Terminal
GATTC .... General Aviation Technical Training Conference
GATTIS .... Georgia Institute of Technology and Technical Information Science (HGAA)
GATTIS .... Georgia Institute of Technology Technical Information Service (NITA)
GATTS .... General Area Time-Based Train Simulator (PDAA)
GATU .... Geophysical Automatic Tracker Unit
GATV .... Gemini Agena Target Vehicle [NASA]
GATWAY ...... Gateway [Commonly used] (OPSA)
G AT WT .... Gram Atomic Weight (WDAA)
GATX .... GATX Corp. [Formerly, General American Transportation Corp.] [Associated Press] (SAG)
GAU .... Atlanta University, Atlanta, GA [Library symbol Library of Congress] (LCLS)
GAu .... Augusta-Richmond County Library, Augusta, GA [Library symbol Library of Congress] (LCLS)
GAU .... Gauhati [India] [Airport symbol] (OAG)
Gau .... Gauss [Unit of magnetic flux density]
GAU .... Gay Academic Union [Defunct] (EA)
gau .... Georgia [MARC country of publication code Library of Congress] (LCCP)
GAU .... Geriatric Assessment Unit [Australia]
GAU .... Glen Auden Resources Ltd. [Toronto Stock Exchange symbol]
GAU .... Glucoamylase Unit [Of hydrolytic enzyme activity]
GAU .... Grupos de Accion Unificadora [Groups for Unified Action] [Uruguay] (PD)
GAU .... Gun Automatic (MCD)
GAuA .... Augusta College, Augusta, GA [Library symbol Library of Congress] (LCLS)
GAuACH ...... Augusta Chronicle-Herald, Augusta, GA [Library symbol Library of Congress] (LCLS)
GAuAH .... Aquinas High School, Augusta, GA [Library symbol Library of Congress] (LCLS)
GAuAR .... Academy of Richmond County, Augusta, GA [Library symbol Library of Congress] (LCLS)
GAuBH .... Butler High School, Augusta, GA [Library symbol Library of Congress] (LCLS)
GAuCL .... Augusta-Richmond County Library, Augusta, GA [Library symbol] [Library of Congress] (LCLS)
GAUGE .... General Automation Users Group Exchange [Defunct] (EA)
GAuJ .... T. W. Josey High School, Augusta, GA [Library symbol Library of Congress] (LCLS)
GAUK .... Gamekeepers' Association of the United Kingdom (BI)
Gaul .... Gaulish [Language] (BARN)
GAuL .... Lucey C. Laney High School, Augusta, GA [Library symbol Library of Congress] (LCLS)
GAuM .... Medical College of Georgia, Augusta, GA [Library symbol Library of Congress] (LCLS)

GA (UN) ...... General Assembly of the United Nations
GAuP .... Paine College, Augusta, GA [Library symbol Library of Congress] (LCLS)
GAuRC .... Richmond County Law Library, Augusta, GA [Library symbol Library of Congress] (LCLS)
GAUSA .... Georgian Association in USA (EA)
GAUSS .... Gravity Association for Universal Scientific Study
GAuT .... Augusta Technical Institute, Augusta, GA [Library symbol] [Library of Congress] (LCLS)
GAuU .... University Hospital, Augusta, GA [Library symbol Library of Congress] (LCLS)
GAuV-F .... United States Veterans Administration Hospital, Forest Hills Division, Augusta, GA [Library symbol Library of Congress] (LCLS)
GAuV-L .... United States Veterans Administration Hospital, Lenwood Division, Augusta, GA [Library symbol Library of Congress] (LCLS)
G/AV .... General Average (WDAA)
GAV .... Geschichte des Alten Vorderasien [A publication] (BJA)
GAV .... Glen Avon [California] [Seismograph station code, US Geological Survey] (SEIS)
GAV .... Granada Aviacion [Spain ICAO designator] (FAAC)
GAV .... Gross Annual Value [Accounting] (ODBW)
GAV .... Gustavus, AK [Location identifier FAA] (FAAL)
GAVA .... Gavotto [Gavotte] [Music] (ROG)
GAvA .... Guild of Aviation Artists (DA)
GAvA .... Guild of Aviation Artists [British] (DBA)
GAVA .... United States Veterans Administration Hospital, Atlanta, GA [Library symbol Library of Congress] (LCLS)
Gav & H Rev St... Gavin and Hord's Revised Indiana Statutes [A publication] (DLA)
GAVRS .... Ground Attitude Vertical Reference System [Aviation]
GAW .... Airway Conductance [The reciprocal of airway resistance] [Medicine] (DAVI)
GAW .... Gambia Airways [ICAO designator] (FAAC)
GAW .... Gangaw [Myanmar] [Airport symbol] (OAG)
GAW .... Global Atmosphere Watch [Marine science] (OSRA)
GAW .... Global Atmospheric Watch (USDC)
GAW .... Global Atmospheric Watch (EERA)
GAW .... Gram Atomic Weight [Chemistry]
GAW .... Guaranteed Annual Wage
GAW .... Guided Atomic Warhead
GAWA .... Geographical Association of Western Australia
GAWAM .... Great American Wife and Mother [Slang]
GAWBS .... Guided Acoustic Wave Brillouin Scattering [Physics]
GAWF .... General Arab Women Federation (EA)
GAWR .... Gross Axle Weight Rating [Auto safety]
GAWRF .... Gross Axle Weight Rating Front [Auto safety]
GAWRR .... Gross Axle Weight Rating Rear [Auto safety]
GAWS .... German American World Society (EA)
GAWS .... Grandmothers of America in War Service [World War II]
GAWS .... Westminster School, Carlyle Fraser Library, Atlanta, GA [Library symbol] [Library of Congress] (LCLS)
GAWTS .... Genetic Amplification with Transverse Sequencing [Genetics]
GAWTS .... Genomic Amplification with Transcript Sequencing [Genetics]
GAWU .... General Agricultural Workers' Union [Kenya]
GAW/V$_1$ ...... Specific Conductance [Expressed per liter of lung volume at which G is measured] [Medicine] (DAVI)
GAWW .... Woodrow Wilson College of Law, Atlanta, GA [Library symbol Library of Congress] (LCLS)
GAX .... Gamba [Gabon] [Airport symbol] (OAG)
GAX .... GAO [General Accounting Office] Seattle Regional Office, Seattle, WA [OCLC symbol] (OCLC)
GAY .... Galvasay [Former USSR Seismograph station code, US Geological Survey Closed] (SEIS)
GAY .... Gaylord [Diocesan abbreviation] [Michigan] (TOCD)
GAY .... Government Accumulation Yard
Gayarre ...... Gayarre's Annual Reports [25-28 Louisiana] [A publication] (DLA)
GAYE .... Yelimane [Mali] [ICAO location identifier] (ICLI)
GAYIG .... Gallium Substituted Yttrium Iron Garnet
Gay (LA) ..... Gayarre's Annual Reports [25-28 Louisiana] [A publication] (DLA)
GaylC .... Gaylord Container Corp. [Associated Press] (SAG)
GaylCn .... Gaylord Container Corp. [Associated Press] (SAG)
GaylEnt .... Gaylord Entertainment [Associated Press] (SAG)
Gaylord .... Gaylord Companies, Inc. [Associated Press] (SAG)
Gaylrd .... Gaylord Companies, Inc. [Associated Press] (SAG)
GAZ .... GAO [General Accounting Office] Atlanta Regional Office, Atlanta, GA [OCLC symbol] (OCLC)
GAZ .... Gazette [or Gazetteer]
GAZ .... Gazette
GAZ .... General Allied Oil [Vancouver Stock Exchange symbol]
GAZ .... Gesamtverzeichnis Auslaendischer Zeitschriften [Cumulative List of Foreign Periodicals]
GAZ .... Globe, AZ [Location identifier FAA] (FAAL)
GAZ .... Gruene Aktion Zukunft [Green Action for the Future] [Germany] (PPW)
Gaz .... Weekly Law Gazette [Ohio] [A publication] (DLA)
Gaz & BC Rep... Gazette and Bankrupt Court Reporter [New York] [A publication] (DLA)
GAZ B .... Gazette of Bankruptcy [A publication] (ROG)
Gaz Bank .... Gazette of Bankruptcy [A publication] (DLA)
Gaz Bank Dig... Gazzam's Digest of Bankruptcy Decisions [A publication] (DLA)
Gaz Bankr .... Gazette of Bankruptcy [A publication] (DLA)
Gaz LR .... Gazette Law Reports [New Zealand] [A publication] (DLA)
Gaz LR (NZ)... New Zealand Gazette Law Reports [A publication] (DLA)
Gaz L Soc of Upper Can... Gazette. Law Society of Upper Canada [A publication] (DLA)

GAZS	Gesamtverzeichnis Auslaendischer Zeitschriften und Serien [*Cumulative List of Foreign Periodicals and Serials*]
Gaz Zan EA	Gazette for Zanzibar and East Africa [*A publication*] (ILCA)
GB	Air Inter Gabon [*ICAO designator*] (AD)
GB	Der Grosse Brockhaus [*A publication*]
GB	Gain Bandwidth (DEN)
GB	Galaxy Books [*Oxford University Press*]
GB	Gall Bladder [*or a patient with an affliction of this organ*] [*Medicine*]
GB	Games Behind [*Baseball*]
GB	G & B Automated Equipment Ltd. [*Toronto Stock Exchange symbol*]
GB	Ganzer Bogen [*Full Bow*] [*Music*]
GB	Garanti Bankasi [*Guarantee Bank*] [*Turkey*]
GB	Gardner's Books Ltd. [*British*]
GB	Gemeinde Berlin (BJA)
GB	Gemini B
GB	General Background
GB	General Board [*Military judicial or investigative body*]
GB	General Bronze Corp. (MCD)
GB	General Business (MHDI)
GB	Generation Breakdown
GB	Geschichtsbetrachtung und Geschichtliche Ueberlieferung bei den Vorexilischen Propheten [*A publication*] (BJA)
Gb	Gibbsite [*A mineral*]
Gb	GigaBIT [*Binary Digit*] [10^9 *BITs*]
Gb	Gigabyte [10^9 *bytes*]
Gb	Gigabyte [*Computer science*] (EERA)
Gb	Gilbert [*A unit of magnetomotive force*] (CET)
gb	Gilbert Islands [*gn (Gilbert and Ellice Islands) used in records cataloged before October 1978*] [*MARC country of publication code Library of Congress*] (LCCP)
GB	Ginzburg's Bible [*New Massoretico-Critical Text of the Hebrew Bible*] [*A publication*] (BJA)
GB	Girls Brigade [*British*] (BI)
GB	Glass Block (DAC)
GB	Glass Bowl
GB	Glial Bundle [*Medicine*] (DMAA)
GB	Glide Bomb [*Air Force*]
GB	Gold Black [*Ultrafine gold metal particles*]
GB	Gold Bond [*Bond payable in gold coin*]
GB	[*The*] Golden Bough [*A publication*] (OCD)
GB	Good-By [*Amateur radio*]
GB	Goofball [*Barbiturate pill*]
GB	Gould Belt [*Galactic science*]
GB	Governing Body
G/B	Government Boat
GB	Government Bunkers
GB	Grab Bar [*Technical drawings*]
GB	Grand Bounce [*Suspension or dismissal*] [*Slang*]
GB	Grassland Biome [*Ecological biogeographic study*]
GB	Great Barrier Airlines [*Airline code*] [*Australia*]
GB	Great Books
GB	Great Britain [*International automobile identification tag*]
GB	Green Bay [*Diocesan abbreviation*] [*Wisconsin*] (TOCD)
GB	Green Belt Act [*Town planning*] [*British*]
GB	Greenhouse Biennial [*Horticulture*] (ROG)
GB	Greenish Blue
GB	Grid Base [*Electronics*] (EECA)
GB	Grid Bearing [*Navigation*]
GB	Grid Bias (DEN)
GB	Griffiths & Bedell's [*System of stud tramways*] [*British*] (ROG)
GB	Ground Beacon [*Navigation*] (IAA)
GB	Grounded Base
GB	Grundbuch [*Land Register*] [*German*] (ILCA)
GB	Guaranteed Bond [*Business term*]
GB	Guard Book (DGA)
GB	Guardbridge Papers [*Manufacturer*] [*British*]
GB	Guardian Bancorp [*AMEX symbol*] (SPSG)
GB	Guardianship Board [*Tasmania, Australia*]
GB	Guidebook
GB	Guild of Bricklayers [*British*] (BI)
GB	Guillain-Barre [*Syndrome*] [*Medicine*]
GB	Gun Board [*British*]
GB	Gunboat [*Naval*]
GB	Gun Branch [*Electronics*] (OA)
GB	Gun-Bus [*Gun-carrying plane*] [*Air Force British*]
GB	Sarin [*Nerve gas*] [*Army symbol*]
GB	United Kingdom [*ANSI two-letter standard code*] (CNC)
GBA	Alderney [*International vehicle registration*] (ODBW)
GBA	Ganglionic-Blocking Agent [*Medicine*]
GBA	Gauribidanur Array [*India*] [*Seismograph station code, US Geological Survey*] (SEIS)
GBA	Georgian Bay Airways [*Canada ICAO designator*] (FAAC)
GBA	Gingivobuccoaxial [*Dentistry*]
GBA	Girls' Brigade Australia
GBA	Give Better Address [*Communications*]
GBA	Global Alert System [*Vancouver Stock Exchange symbol*]
GBA	Global Biodiversity Assessment [*Book*] (EERA)
GBA	Governing Bodies Association [*Organization of school officials*] [*British*]
GBA	Grammatik des Biblische-Aramaeischen [*A publication*] (BJA)
GBA	Gross Building Area (ADA)
GBA	Grundbuchamt [*Land Registry*] [*German*] (ILCA)
GBaB	Bainbridge Junior College, Bainbridge, GA [*Library symbol Library of Congress*] (LCLS)
GB & A	Grosvenor Barber and Associates (IID)
GB & I	Great Britain and Ireland
GB & W	Green Bay & Western Railroad Co.
GBAO	Graham Bond Appreciators Organization [*Defunct*] (EA)
GBAPS	Governing Bodies Association of Public Schools [*British*]
GBaS	Southwest Georgia Regional Library, Bainbridge, GA [*Library symbol Library of Congress*] (LCLS)
GBAT	Graduate Business Admission Test
GBB	General Banner Bearer [*Freemasonry*] (ROG)
GBB	Guild of British Butlers [*British*] (EAIO)
GBBA	Glass Bottle Blowers Association of the United States and Canada [*Later, GPPAW*]
GBBHS	Group B Beta-Hemolytic Streptococcus [*Bacteriology*] (DAVI)
GBBS	Group B Beta-Hemolytic Streptococcus [*Medicine*] (MEDA)
GBC	Berry College, Mount Berry, GA [*OCLC symbol*] (OCLC)
GBC	General Binding Corp.
GBC	Globe Air Cargo [*Antigua and Barbuda*] [*ICAO designator*] (FAAC)
GBC	Gold-Braid Chaser [*Refers to a woman who dates only officers*] [*Slang British*] (DSUE)
GBC	Greenland Base Command
GBC	Ground-Based Computer
GBC	Guantanamo Bay [*Cuba*] [*Seismograph station code, US Geological Survey Closed*] (SEIS)
GBCB	GBC Bancorp [*NASDAQ symbol*] (NQ)
GBC Bc	GBC Bancorp [*Associated Press*] (SAG)
GBCC	Great Britain Collectors Club (EA)
GBCI	Glacier Bancorp, Inc. [*NASDAQ symbol*] (SPSG)
GBCL	Glacier Bancorp [*NASDAQ symbol*] (TTSB)
GBCO	Greif Brothers Corp. [*NASDAQ symbol*] (SAG)
GBCOA	Grief Bros CI'A' [*NASDAQ symbol*] (TTSB)
GBCOB	Greif Bros 'B' [*NASDAQ symbol*] (TTSB)
GBCS	Global Casinos [*NASDAQ symbol*] (SAG)
GBCS	Ground-Based Common Sensor
GBCSCMC	General Board of Christian Social Concerns of the Methodist Church (EA)
GBCS-L/H	Ground Based Common Sensor-Light/Heavy [*Military*]
GBCT	GBC Technologies, Inc. [*NASDAQ symbol*] (SAG)
GBCT	Guild of British Camera Technicians (DBA)
GBC Tch	GBC Technologies, Inc. [*Associated Press*] (SAG)
GBCW	Governing Body of the Church in Wales (DAS)
GBD	Gale's Business Directory [*A publication*]
GBD	Gallbladder Disease [*Gastroenterology*] (DAVI)
GBD	Gamma Ray Burst Detector [*Instrumentation*]
GBD	General Board
GBD	Geometric Data Base (DOMA)
GBD	Global Burden of Disease
GBD	Grain Boundary Dislocation
GBD	Great Bear Development [*Vancouver Stock Exchange symbol*]
GBD	Great Bend [*Kansas*] [*Airport symbol*] (OAG)
GBDO	Guild of British Dispensing Opticians (BI)
GBDV	Gate Breakdown Voltage
GBE	Dame Grand Cross of the Order of the British Empire (ADA)
GBE	Gaborone [*Botswana*] [*Airport symbol*] (OAG)
GBE	Gilt Beveled Edges [*Bookbinding*]
GBE	Ginkgo Biloba Extract [*Biochemistry*]
GBE	Goal-Based Evaluation
GBE	Groupement Belge des Banques d'Epargne [*Banking association*] [*Belgium*] (EY)
GBE	Grubb & Ellis [*NYSE symbol*] (TTSB)
GBE	Grubb & Ellis Co. [*NYSE symbol*] (SPSG)
GBE	Knight Grand Cross of the [*Order of the*] British Empire
GBERL	Gulf Breeze Environmental Research Laboratory [*Environmental Protection Agency*] (MSC)
GBF	Gay Black Female [*Classified advertising*] (CDAI)
GBF	Geographic Base File [*Civil Defense*]
GBF	Grand Ballon [*France*] [*Seismograph station code, US Geological Survey Closed*] (SEIS)
GBF	Great Bear Foundation (EA)
GBF	Great Books Foundation (EA)
GBF	Ground-Based Field
GBFC	GB Foods [*NASDAQ symbol*] (TTSB)
GBFC	GB Foods Corp. [*NASDAQ symbol*] (SAG)
GBF/DIME	Geographic Base File/Dual Independent Map Encoding [*BTS*] (TAG)
GB Fds	GB Foods [*Associated Press*] (SAG)
GBFE	Golden Books Family Ent [*NASDAQ symbol*] (TTSB)
GBFE	Golden Books Family Entertainment, Inc. [*NASDAQ symbol*] (SAG)
GBFEL	Ground Based Free Electron LASER Proposal
GBG	Galesburg [*Illinois*] [*Airport symbol*] (OAG)
GBG	Garbage (MSA)
GBG	Glycine-Rich Beta-Globulin [*Immunology*]
GBG	Gonadal Steroid-Binding Globulin [*Medicine*] (DMAA)
GBG	Gordon Junior College, Barnesville, GA [*Library symbol*] [*Library of Congress*] (LCLS)
GBG	Governor's Bodyguard [*British military*] (DMA)
GBG	Greensboro [*Georgia*] [*Seismograph station code, US Geological Survey*] (SEIS)
GBG	Greensburg [*Diocesan abbreviation*] [*Pennsylvania*] (TOCD)
GBG	Guernsey [*International vehicle registration*] (ODBW)
GBGSA	Governing Body of Girls' Schools Association [*British*]
GBH	Galbraith Lake, AK [*Location identifier FAA*] (FAAL)
GBH	Gamma Benzene Hexachloride [*Also, BHC, HCH*] [*Insecticide*]
GBH	Garbell Holdings Ltd. [*Toronto Stock Exchange symbol*]
GB H	Gas Bath Heater [*Classified advertising*] (ADA)
GBH	Girth Breast Height (WGA)
GBH	Graphite-Benzalkonium-Heparin [*Medicine*] (MAE)
GBH	Great British Holiday [*Television movie*]

GBH .... Grievous Body Harm
GBH .... Group Busy Hour [Telecommunications] (TEL)
GBHA .... Glyoxal Bis(o-hydroxyanil) [An indicator] [Chemistry]
GBHP .... Gross Brake Horsepower (MCD)
GBHRG .... Ground-Based Hypervelocity Rail Gun [Military] (SDI)
GBHRS .... Granite Belt Horticultural Research Station [Australia]
GBI .... Blufete Industrial S.A. ADS [NYSE symbol] (TTSB)
GBI .... Bufete Industrial SA [NYSE symbol] (SPSG)
GBI .... Buffalo, NY [Location identifier FAA] (FAAL)
GBI .... Gabriel Resources, Inc. [Vancouver Stock Exchange symbol]
GBI .... Gained by Inventory (DNAB)
GBI .... Gesellschaft fuer Betriebswirtschaftliche Information mbH [Society for
             Business Information] [Germany Database producer]
GBI .... Global Brain Ischemia
GBI .... Globulin-Binding Insulin [Medicine] (DMAA)
GBI .... Governesses Benevolent Institute [British] (AIE)
GBI .... Grace Bible Institute [Nebraska]
GBI .... Grand Bahama Island (KSC)
GBI .... Gridlays Bank International Zambia Ltd.
GBI .... Ground Backup Instrument (MUGU)
GBI .... Ground-Based Interceptor [Army] (DOMA)
GBI .... Guanidinebenzimidazole [Biochemistry]
GBIA .... Guthrie Bacterial Inhibition Assay [Medicine] (MAE)
GBII .... Ground-Based Infrared Instrumentation
GBIIS .... Ground-Based Infrared Instrumentation System
GBiP .... German Books in Print [A publication]
GBIT .... Gigabit (MHDB)
GBIT .... Global Intellicom [NASDAQ symbol] (TTSB)
GBIT .... Global Intellicom, Inc. [NASDAQ symbol] (SAG)
GBIU .... Geoballistic Input Unit
GBI-X .... Ground-Based Interceptor-Experiment [US Army Strategic Defense
             Command] (RDA)
GBIZ .... Grow Biz International [NASDAQ symbol] (TTSB)
GBIZ .... Grow Biz International, Inc. [NASDAQ symbol] (SAG)
GBJ .... Glass Bell Jar
GBJ .... Jersey [Great Britain]
GBJ .... Marie Galante [French Antilles] [Airport symbol] (OAG)
GBK .... Gbangbatok [Sierra Leone] [Airport symbol] (OAG)
GBL .... Gable Mountain [Washington] [Seismograph station code, US
             Geological Survey] (SEIS)
GBL .... Games behind Leader [Baseball]
GBL .... Gamma Biologicals [AMEX symbol] (TTSB)
GBL .... Gamma Biologicals, Inc. [AMEX symbol] (SPSG)
GBL .... Gamma-Butyrolactone [Organic chemistry]
GBL .... GB Airways Ltd. [British ICAO designator] (FAAC)
GBL .... General Bearing Line [Navy] (NVT)
GBl .... Gesetzblatt [Gazette] [German] (DLA)
GBL .... Glomerular Basal Lamina [Medicine] (DAVI)
GBL .... Goldenbell Resources, Inc. [Toronto Stock Exchange symbol
             Vancouver Stock Exchange symbol]
GBL .... Goulburn Island [Australia Airport symbol Obsolete] (OAG)
GBL .... Government Bill of Lading
GBL .... Ground-Based LASER (MCD)
GBL .... Guide to Baseball Literature [A publication]
GBLADING ... Government Bill of Lading
GBLIC .... Gaussian Band Limited Channel (NITA)
GBLOC .... Government Bill of Lading Office Code (AFIT)
GBLV .... Grapevine Bulgarian Latent Virus [Plant pathology]
GBM .... Gain Band Merit
GBM .... Galilean Baptist Mission (EA)
GBM .... Gay Black Male [Classified advertising] (CDAI)
GBM .... Gesellschaft Fuer Biochemie Und Molekularbiologie [Germany]
GBM .... Gibraltar Mines Ltd. [Toronto Stock Exchange symbol Vancouver
             Stock Exchange symbol]
GBM .... Glass-Bonded Mica
GBM .... Glomerular Basement Membrane [Medicine]
GBM .... Glycerine Ball Memory
GBM .... Granite Butte [Montana] [Seismograph station code, US Geological
             Survey Closed] (SEIS)
GBM .... Grape Berry Moth
GBM .... Greater Britain Movement [British]
GBM .... Ground-Based Measurement (MCD)
GBM .... Isle Of Man (Great Britain)
GBMA .... Golf Ball Manufacturers Association (EA)
GBMA .... Great Britain Ministry of Aviation
GBMC .... Golf Ball Manufacturers' Conference [British] (BI)
GBMC .... Grain Bin Manufacturers Council [Later, GEMC] (EA)
GBMD .... Global Ballistic Missile Defense
GBMI .... Ground-Based Midcourse Interceptor [Military] (SDI)
GBMI .... Guilty-but-Mentally-Ill [Legal term]
GBMP .... General Benchmark Program (MHDB)
GBM-rAb .... Glomerular Basement Membrane-Reactive Antibodies [Immunology]
GBN .... Gila Bend, AZ [Location identifier FAA] (FAAL)
GBN .... Golden Band Resources [Vancouver Stock Exchange symbol]
GBND .... General Binding Corp. [NASDAQ symbol] (NQ)
GBND .... Genl Binding [NASDAQ symbol] (TTSB)
GBNE .... Guild of British Newspapers Editors (BI)
GBO .... Gissel Bargaining Order [Labor relations] (WYGK)
GBO .... Goods in Bad Order
GBO .... Ogooue Air Cargo [Gabon] [ICAO designator] (FAAC)
GBOA .... Gale Book of Averages [A publication]
GboSidek .... Grupo Sidek SA de CV [Associated Press] (SAG)
GBOT .... Garden Botanika [NASDAQ symbol] (TTSB)
GBowdC ..... Bowdon College, Bowdon, GA [Library symbol Library of Congress
             Obsolete] (LCLS)

GBP .... Gables Residential Trust [NYSE symbol] (SPSG)
GBP .... Gain-Bandwidth Product
GBP .... Galactose-Binding Protein [Biochemistry]
GBP .... Gas Bearing Part
GBP .... Gastric Bypass [Surgery]
GBP .... Gated Blood Pool [Hematology] (DMAA)
GBP .... Glutamate-Binding Protein [Biochemistry]
GBP .... Glycophorin Binding Protein [Biochemistry]
GBP .... Great Britain Pound [Banking]
GBP .... Great British Public
GBP .... Guanylate-Binding Protein [Biochemistry]
GBP .... Guinea-Bissau Peso [Monetary unit]
GBPA .... Gettysburg Battlefield Preservation Association [Defunct] (EA)
GBPC .... Gold Bondholders Protective Council (EA)
GBPR .... Grain-Burning Pattern Regulation (MCD)
GBPS .... Gemini B Procedures Simulator (MCD)
GBPS .... GigaBIT [Binary Digits] per Second [Transmission rate] [Computer
             science] (TSSD)
Gbps .... Gigabits per Second (EERA)
GBPW .... Great Bay Power [NASDAQ symbol] (TTSB)
GBPW .... Great Bay Power Corp. [NASDAQ symbol] (SAG)
GBq .... Gigabecquerel (NUCP)
GBR .... Gas-Cooled Breeder Reactor [Nuclear energy] (NRCH)
GBR .... Give Better Reference [Communications]
GBR .... Glass Bead Rating (MCD)
GBR .... Glutathione Bicarbonate Ringer [Solution mixture]
GBR .... Golden Bear Resources Ltd. [Vancouver Stock Exchange symbol]
GBR .... Grain Boundary Relaxation
GBR .... Great Barrier Reef (EERA)
GBR .... Great Barrington, MA [Location identifier FAA] (FAAL)
GBR .... Greenbriar Corp. [AMEX symbol] (SAG)
GBR .... Greenbriar Corp. [AMEX symbol] (TTSB)
GBR .... Ground-Based RADAR [Military]
GBR .... Ground-Based Radiometer
GBR .... Gun, Bomb, and Rocket
GBR .... Rader Aviation, Inc. [ICAO designator] (FAAC)
GBR .... United Kingdom [ANSI three-letter standard code] (CNC)
GBRCC .... Great Barrier Reef Consultative Committee [Australia]
GBRMP .... Great Barrier Reef Marine Park [Region] (EERA)
GBRMPA ..... Great Barrier Reef Marine Park Authority [Commonwealth] (EERA)
GBRP .... General Bending Response Program [Computer] [Navy]
GBR-P .... Ground-Based RADAR Prototype [Military]
GBR-PO ...... Ground-Based RADAR Project Office [Military] (RDA)
GBru .... Brunswick Regional Library, Brunswick, GA [Library symbol Library of
             Congress] (LCLS)
GBruJC .... Brunswick Junior College, Brunswick, GA [Library symbol Library of
             Congress] (LCLS)
GBruM .... MAP International, Brunswick, GA [Library symbol] [Library of
             Congress] (LCLS)
GBR-X .... Ground Based RADAR-Experimental [Army]
GBS .... Gall Bladder Series [Radiography]
GBS .... Gallbladder Stone [Medicine]
GBS .... Gas Bearing System (KSC)
GBS .... Gas Bioassay System [NASA]
GBS .... General Business System (MHDW)
GBS .... George Bernard Shaw [Irish-born playwright, 1856-1950]
GBS .... GigaBIT [Binary Digit] per Second [Computer science] (IAA)
GBS .... Glycine-Buffered Saline [Microbiology]
GBS .... Government Bureau of Standards
GBS .... Grain Boundary Segregation [Metallurgy]
GBS .... Granular Boundary Segregation [Petrology]
GBS .... Great Big Star [in the movies]
GBS .... Ground-Based Scanner
GBS .... Ground Based Sensor [Radar]
GBS .... Ground-Based Software (MCD)
GBS .... Ground Beacon System (MCD)
GBS .... Group B Streptococci [Medicine]
GBS .... Guillain-Barre Syndrome [Medicine]
GBSAS .... Ground-Based Scanning Antenna System (IAA)
GBSCA .... Greater Blouse and Skirt Contractors Association [Later, GBSUA]
             (EA)
GBSE .... Gibbs Construction [NASDAQ symbol] (TTSB)
GBSE .... Gibbs Construction, Inc. [NASDAQ symbol] (SAG)
GBSEW .... Gibbs Construction Wrrt [NASDAQ symbol] (TTSB)
GBSFI .... Guillain-Barre Syndrome Foundation International (EA)
GBSM .... Graduate of the Birmingham School of Music [British] (DBQ)
GBSM .... Guild of Better Shoe Manufacturers
GBSR .... Graphite-Moderated Boiling and Superheating Reactor
GBSS .... Gey's Balanced Salt Solution [Medium] [Cell culture]
GBSSG .... Guillain-Barre Syndrome Support Group [Later, GBSFI] (EA)
GBSSGI .... Guillain-Barre Syndrome Support Group International [Later,
             GBSFI] (EA)
GBST .... Grassi Block Substitution Test [Psychology]
GBSUA .... Greater Blouse, Skirt, and Undergarment Association (EA)
GBSVC .... General Broadcast Signaling Virtual Channel [Telecommunications]
             (ACRL)
GBT .... Der Babylonische Talmud [Goldschmidt] [A publication] (BJA)
GBT .... Generalized Burst Trapping
GBT .... Global Ballistic Transport [Military]
GBT .... Gold Belt Air Transport, Inc. [Canada ICAO designator] (FAAC)
GBT .... Graded Base Transistor
GBT .... Great Bustard Trust [An association] (EA)
GBT .... Ground-Based Telemetry
GBT .... Gunboat
GBTA .... Guild of Business Travel Agents [British] (DBA)

GBTBC .... Graham Brothers Truck and Bus Club (EA)
GBTC .... Generalized Burst Trapping Code (PDAA)
GBTI .... Gray-Body Temperature Index [for thermal ecology of lizards]
GBTS .... General Banking Terminal System (MHDW)
GBTS .... Gold Beaters' Trade Society [A union] [British]
GBTV .... Granite Broadcasting Corp. [NASDAQ symbol] (SPSG)
GBTVK .... Granite Broadcasting [NASDAQ symbol] (TTSB)
GBTVP .... Granite Brdcst $1.9375 Cv Pfd [NASDAQ symbol] (TTSB)
GBU .... Geschichtsbetrachtung und Geschichtliche Ueberlieferung bei den
                Vorexilischen Propheten [A publication] (BJA)
GBU .... Glide Bomb Unit [Air Force] (MCD)
GBU .... Ground Backup (DNAB)
GBU .... Groupes Bibliques Universitaires [University Biblical Groups]
                [Canada]
GBU .... Guided Bomb Unit (MCD)
GBU .... Khasm el Girba [Sudan] [Airport symbol] (AD)
GBU .... Transports Aeriens de la Guinee-Bissau [Guinea-Bissau] [ICAO
                designator] (FAAC)
GBV .... Gate Breakdown Voltage
GBV .... Gibb River [Australia Airport symbol Obsolete] (OAG)
GBV .... Globe Ball Valve
GBV .... Green Bank [West Virginia] [Seismograph station code, US
                Geological Survey] (SEIS)
GBviz .... Gall Bladder Visualization [Medicine]
GBW .... Gain Bandwidth
GBW .... Good Bears of the World (EA)
GBW .... Green Bay & Western Railroad Co. [AAR code]
GBW .... Guild of Book Workers (EA)
GBWA .... Georgia Beer Wholesalers Association (SRA)
GBX .... GBX Resources [Vancouver Stock Exchange symbol]
GBX .... Ginkgo Biloba Extract [Biochemistry]
GBX .... [The] Greenbrier Companies, Inc. [NYSE symbol] (SAG)
GBX .... Greenbrier Cos. [NYSE symbol] (TTSB)
GBX .... Ground Branch Exchange (DNAB)
GBY .... Giant Bay Resources Ltd. [Toronto Stock Exchange symbol]
G-B-Y .... God Bless You
GBY .... Greate Bay Casino [AMEX symbol] (SAG)
GBYD .... Banjul [Gambia] [ICAO location identifier] (ICLI)
G by Pos ..... Games by Position [Baseball]
GBZ .... Gibraltar
GBZ .... Glass-Bonded Zeolite
GBZ .... Great Barrier [New Zealand] [Seismograph station code, US
                Geological Survey] (SEIS)
GBZ .... Great Barrier Island [Australia Airport symbol] (OAG)
GBZ .... Tampa, FL [Location identifier FAA] (FAAL)
GC .... Gain Control
GC .... Galactic Center
GC .... Galactocerebroside [Biochemistry]
GC .... Galvanized Corrugated [Metal industry]
GC .... Game Conservancy [British]
GC .... Ganglion Cell [Medicine]
GC .... Garbage Collection [Slang Computer science]
GC .... Garrison Co. [British military] (DMA)
GC .... Gas Chromatograph [or Chromatography]
GC .... Gas Council [British]
G/C .... Gas-to-Cloth [Ratio] (FFDE)
GC .... Gastrocnemius [A muscle]
GC .... Gavel Clubs (EA)
GC .... Geiger-Mueller Counter [Nucleonics] (IAA)
GC .... Gel Chromatography
GC .... General Cable (IAA)
GC .... General Circular
GC .... General Code [A publication] (DLA)
GC .... General Condition [Medicine]
GC .... General Contractor [Technical drawings]
GC .... General Control
GC .... General Council (IAA)
GC .... General Counsel
GC .... General Cover [Insurance]
GC .... General Cueing
GC .... Generative Cell [Botany]
GC .... Generic Code (AFM)
GC .... Geneva Convention Relative to Protection of Civilian Persons in Time
                of War [Army] (AABC)
GC .... Gentleman Cadet [British]
GC .... Geopolitical Code [Military] (AFIT)
GC .... George Cross [British]
GC .... Geriatric Care
GC .... Geriatric Chair (DAVI)
GC .... Germinal Center [Immunochemistry]
Gc .... Gigacycle [Measurement]
GC .... Gimbal Case (KSC)
GC .... Gin Cocktail [Slang]
GC .... Girls' College (ADA)
GC .... Glass Capillary
GC .... Glassy Carbon
GC .... Gliding Club [British] (ADA)
GC .... Global Control (IAA)
GC .... Globular Cluster [Astrophysics]
GC .... Glucocorticoid [Endocrinology]
GC .... Gnome Club (EA)
GC .... Gold Coast [Later, Ghana] (ROG)
GC .... Gold Corp. [Western Australia] [Commercial firm]
GC .... Golden Companions [An association] (EA)
GC .... Goldsmith's College [London, England]

GC .... Golf Club
GC .... Gonococcal [Clinical chemistry]
GC .... Gonorrhea Case [Medical slang]
gc .... Good Condition [Doll collecting]
GC .... Good Conduct [Military decoration]
GC .... Governing Council (EERA)
GC .... Government Communications (TEL)
GC .... Government Contractor
GC .... Government Contribution
GC .... Governors' Conference
Gc .... Gradational, Calcareous [Soil]
GC .... Graham Center [An association] (EA)
GC .... Graham County Railroad Co. [AAR code]
GC .... Grain Count [Measurement of cell labeling]
GC .... Grain Cubic (DS)
G-C .... Gram-Negative Cocci [Clinical chemistry] (DAVI)
G+C .... Gram-Positive Cocci [Clinical chemistry] (DAVI)
GC .... GranCare, Inc. [NYSE symbol] (SPSG)
GC .... Grand Canyon [Arizona]
GC .... Grand Chancellor
GC .... Grand Chaplain
GC .... Grand Chapter
GC .... Grand Commander
GC .... Grand Conductor
GC .... Grand Council [Freemasonry] (ROG)
GC .... Grand Cross
GC .... Grantsmanship Center (EA)
GC .... Granular Cast [Medicine]
GC .... Granular Cyst [Medicine] (MAE)
GC .... Granulocyte Cytotoxic [Hematology]
GC .... Granulosa Cells [Cytology]
GC .... Graphics Conferencing (MCD)
GC .... Grazing Capacity [Agriculture]
GC .... Great Central Railway [British] (ROG)
GC .... Great Churchmen [A publication]
GC .... Great Circle
GC .... Greek Church (ROG)
GC .... Green Currency [EEC]
GC .... Greenhouse Corps [Australia]
GC .... Greenland Cruiser
GC .... Grid Course [Navigation]
GC .... Grolier Club (EA)
GC .... Ground Control (AFM)
GC .... Grounded Collector
GC .... Group Captain
GC .... Group Code [Dialog] [Searchable field] [Information service or
                system] (NITA)
GC .... Group Cohesiveness [Psychological testing]
GC .... Groupe de Chasse [French aircraft fighter unit] [World War II]
Gc .... Group-Specific Component [A serum group]
GC .... Guanine, Cytosine [Type] [Biochemistry]
GC .... Guidance Computer
GC .... Guidance Control [NASA] (NASA)
GC .... Gun Camera (MCD)
GC .... Gun Capital (DNAB)
GC .... Gun Captain
GC .... Gun Carriage
GC .... Gun Control
GC .... Gyro Compass
GC .... Gyro Control
GC .... Lina-Congo [ICAO designator] (AD)
GCA .... Gain Control Amplifier
GCA .... Garden Centers of America (EA)
GCA .... Garden Centres of Australia
GCA .... Garden Club of America (EA)
GCA .... Garden Club of Australia
GCA .... Gastric Cancer Area [Medicine] (DMAA)
GCA .... Gauge Control Analyzer
GCA .... Genealogy Club of America [Defunct] (EA)
GCA .... General Claim Agent
GCA .... General Combining Ability
G-C .... General Control Approach
GCA .... Geophysics Corp. of America
GCA .... Giant Cell Arteritis [Medicine]
GCA .... Girls Clubs of America [Later, GI] (EA)
GCA .... Glass Crafts of America [Defunct] (EA)
GCA .... Glen Canyon [Arizona] [Seismograph station code, US Geological
                Survey] (SEIS)
GCA .... Global Citizens Association [Quebec, PQ] (EAIO)
GCA .... Gold Clause Agreement [Shipping] (DS)
GCA .... Golf Course Association (EA)
GCA .... Government Contract Advisor [CD-ROM] [Published by Clark
                Boardman] (AAGC)
GCA .... Grains Council of Australia (EERA)
GCA .... Graphic Communications Association (EA)
GCA .... Great China Airlines [Taiwan] [ICAO designator] (FAAC)
GCA .... Green Coffee Association of New York City (EA)
GCA .... Greeting Card Association (EA)
GCA .... Greyhound Club of America (EA)
GCA .... Ground Communication Activity (IAA)
GCA .... Ground-Controlled Aircraft (AFM)
GCA .... Ground-Controlled Apparatus [RADAR]
GCA .... Ground-Controlled Approach [for lateral and vertical guidance of
                landing aircraft through use of ground RADAR and radio
                communications]

GCA .... Grounded Cathode Amplifier
GCA .... Group Capacity Analysis [or Assessment]
GCA .... Guacamayas [Colombia] [Airport symbol] (OAG)
GCA .... Guidance and Control Assembly (NG)
GCA .... Guidance Control and Adapter Section (MCD)
GCA .... Gun Control Act [1968]
GCA .... Gun Control Australia
GCA .... Gunite Contractors Association (EA)
GCA .... Gyro Control Assembly
GCAA .... Golf Coaches Association of America (EA)
GCAA .... Guidance, Control, and Airframe (IAA)
GCABY .... General Cable PLC [NASDAQ symbol] (SAG)
GCABY .... Genl Cable plc.ADS [NASDAQ symbol] (TTSB)
GCA-CTS ...... Ground-Controlled Approach - Controller Training System (MCD)
GCAD .... Granite City Army Depot (AABC)
GCai .... Roddenbery Memorial Library, Cairo, GA [Library symbol Library of Congress] (LCLS)
GCAL .... Gram Calorie
g-cal .... Gram-Calorie (IDOE)
GCAM .... Gaming Corp. of America [NASDAQ symbol] (SAG)
GCAM .... Groupement de la Caisse des Depots Automatisation pour le Management [Bank Group for Automation in Management] [Information service or system] (IID)
GC & A .... Guidance, Control, and Airframe
GC & O .... Guidance, Control, and Ordnance
GC & SF ...... Gulf, Colorado & Santa Fe Railway Co.
GCanS .... Sequoyah Regional Library, Canton, GA [Library symbol Library of Congress] (LCLS)
GCA of NO ... Green Coffee Association of New Orleans (EA)
GCAP .... Generalized Circuit Analysis Program (IEEE)
GCAP .... Germ-Cell Alkaline Phosphatase (DMAA)
GCAPEF ...... Grace Contrino Abrams Peace Education Foundation (EA)
G/Capt .... Group Captain [British military] (DMA)
GCarrS .... Southwire Co., Carrollton, GA [Library symbol Library of Congress] (LCLS)
GCarrWG ..... West Georgia College, Carrollton, GA [Library symbol Library of Congress] (LCLS)
GCAS .... Ground Collision Avoidance System [Army]
GCAT .... Guidance and Control Analysis Team [Space Flight Operations, NASA]
GCatO .... Group Catering Officer [British military] (DMA)
GCAU .... Grain-Consuming Animal Unit [Agricultural Statistics] (BARN)
GCAutrey ..... Grupo Casa Autrey [Associated Press] (SAG)
GCB .... Dame Grand Cross of the Order of the Bath [British] (ADA)
GCB .... General Circuit Breaker (MHDI)
GCB .... Generator Control Breaker
GCB .... German Convention Bureau (EA)
GCB .... Ghana Commercial Bank
GCB .... Ghanian Cocoa Butter
GCB .... Gonococcal Base [Broth] [Growth medium]
GCB .... Good Conduct Badge [British]
GCB .... Graphitized Carbon Black
GCB .... Gravity Cutback (NRCH)
GCB .... Great-Circle Bearing [Navigation] (IAA)
GCB .... Guthrie, C. B., Tariff Bureau Inc., Washington DC [STAC]
GCB .... Knight Grand Cross of the [Order of the] Bath [British]
GCB .... Lignes Nationales Aeriennes - Linacongo [Congo] [ICAO designator] (FAAC)
GCBA .... Golf Course Builders of America (EA)
GCBC .... Goucher College Babylonian Collection (BJA)
GCBK .... Great Country Bank [NASDAQ symbol] (NQ)
GCBM .... Gas Chromatography in Biology and Medicine [British]
GCBR .... Gas-Cooled Breeder Reactor [Nuclear energy]
GCBS .... General Council of British Shipping
GCBS .... Ground-Control Bombing System (NG)
GCBW .... Global Cooperation for a Better World [Australia]
GCC .... Coca-Cola Co., Business Information, Atlanta, GA [OCLC symbol] (OCLC)
GCC .... Garden Cat Club (EA)
GCC .... General Cinema Corp. [Chestnut Hill, MA]
GCC .... General Commission on Chaplains and Armed Forces Personnel [Later, NCMAF] (EA)
GCC .... Georgian Court College [Lakewood, NJ]
GCC .... Giannini Controls Corp. (AAG)
GCC .... Gillette [Wyoming] [Airport symbol] (OAG)
GCC .... Girton College [Cambridge University] (DAS)
GCC .... Global Climate Coalition [A US lobby group]
GCC .... Global Climatic Change (USDC)
GCC .... Global Climatic Change [Marine science] (OSRA)
GCC .... Global Competitiveness Council [Defunct] (EA)
GCC .... Glove Collector Club (EA)
GCC .... Goddard Communications Center [NASA]
GCC .... Goddard Computing Center [NASA]
GCC .... Goebel Collectors' Club [Later, MIHC] (EA)
GCC .... Gogebic Community College [Ironwood, MI]
GCC .... Golden Concord Mining [Vancouver Stock Exchange symbol]
GCC .... Gonville and Caius College [Cambridge University] (ROG)
GCC .... Good Counsel College [New York]
GCC .... Government Contract Committee [Later, OFCCP] [Department of Labor]
GCC .... Graduated Combat Capability [Military]
GCC .... Grand Canyon College [Phoenix, AZ]
GCC .... Granite Creek [California] [Seismograph station code, US Geological Survey] (SEIS)
GCC .... Graphic Control Center [Touch-activated CRT display]

GCC .... Greenfield Community College [Massachusetts]
GCC .... Grid Cooperating Centre (EERA)
GCC .... Ground Calcium Carbonate [Inorganic chemistry]
GCC .... Ground Communications Controller
GCC .... Ground Communications Coordinator [NASA] (NASA)
GCC .... Ground Computer Controller
GCC .... Ground-Control Center
GCC .... Group Change Control
GCC .... Group Control Center (MCD)
GCC .... Grove City College [Pennsylvania]
GCC .... Guidance and Control Computer
GCC .... Guidance Checkout Computer
GCC .... Gulf Cooperation Council [Consists of Saudi Arabia, Bahrain, Kuwait, Oman, Qatar, and the United Arab Emirates]
GCC .... Gulf Cooperative Council (EERA)
GCC .... Gun Control Console [Military] (CAAL)
GCCA .... Gambling Chip Collectors Association (EA)
GCCA .... G-Cat Class Association (EA)
GCCA .... Graphic Communications Computer Association [Printing Industries of America] [Later, GCA]
GCCA .... Greater Clothing Contractors Association (EA)
GCCA .... Greeting Card and Calendar Association [British]
GCCC .... Canarias [Canary Islands] [ICAO location identifier] (ICLI)
GCCC .... Ground-Control Computer Center (MCD)
GCCEA .... General Committee of the Comite Europeen des Assurances [France] (EAIO)
GCCF .... Governing Council of the Cat Fancy [British] (BI)
GCCG .... German Colonies Collectors Group (EA)
GCCNPIP ..... General Conference Committee of the National Poultry Improvement Plan [Department of Agriculture] (EGAO)
GCCO .... Granite Construction [NASDAQ symbol] (TTSB)
GCCO .... Granite Construction, Inc. [NASDAQ symbol] (SAG)
GCCO .... Ground-Control Checkout (MCD)
GC Cos .... GC Companies [Associated Press] (SAG)
GCCS .... Geneva Convention on the Continental Shelf (NOAA)
GCCS .... Global Command and Control System
GCCS .... Government Code and Cypher School [Later, GCHQ] [Sometimes facetiously translated as Golf, Chess, and Cheese Society] [British]
GCCW .... United Gas, Coke, and Chemical Workers of America [Later, OCAW]
GCD .... DeKalb Community College, Clarkston, GA [OCLC symbol] (OCLC)
GCD .... Gain Control Driver (CET)
GCD .... Gate-Controlled Diode (IAA)
GCD .... General and Complete Disarmament
GCD .... Gold Coupling Dendrite
GCD .... Golden Cadillac Resources Ltd. [Vancouver Stock Exchange symbol]
GCD .... Good Conduct Discharge
GCD .... Graft Coronary Disease [Cardiology] (DMAA)
GCD .... Graphic Codepoint Definition [Telecommunications]
GCD .... Great Circle Distance
GCD .... Greatest Common Denominator
GCD .... Greatest Common Divisor
GCD .... Gyro-Compass, Desired Cluster Orientation (MCD)
GCDC .... Gold Coast Divisional Court Reports [A publication] (DLA)
GCDC .... Grace Cancer Drug Center [Roswell Park Memorial Institute] [Research center] (RCD)
GCDC .... Ground Checkout Display and Control [NASA] (NASA)
GCDCS .... Ground Checkout Display and Control System (MCD)
GCDFP .... Gross Cystic Disease Fluid Protein (DAVI)
GCDI .... Galacticomm Custom Device Interface [Galacticomm, Inc.] [Telecommunications]
GCDIS .... Global Change Data and Information System [Marine science] (OSRA)
GCDIS .... Global Change Data and Information System (USDC)
GC Div C ..... Selected Judgments of the Divisional Courts [Ghana] [A publication] (DLA)
GC Div Ct .... Gold Coast Selected Judgments of the Divisional Courts [A publication] (DLA)
GCDP .... Global Change Database Project (EERA)
GCDP .... Gunner's Control and Display Panel [Military] (RDA)
GCDU .... Grupo de Convergencia Democratica en Uruguay [Group of Democratic Convergence in Uruguay] (EA)
GCE .... Commission for Geographical Education (EA)
GCE .... General Certificate of Education [British]
GCE .... General Consumers Electronics (NITA)
GCE .... Glassy Carbon Electrode
GCE .... Government Capital Expenditure [Finance]
GCE .... Government Computer Expo (HGAA)
GCE .... Great Canadian Cider [Vancouver Stock Exchange symbol]
GCE .... Greenwood Cotton Exchange (EA)
GCE .... Ground Checkout Equipment [Aerospace] (AAG)
GCE .... Ground Combat Element [Marine Corps] (DOMA)
GCE .... Ground Communications Equipment
GCE .... Ground-Control Equipment
GCE .... Gun Control Equipment (DNAB)
GCEBT .... Galveston Cotton Exchange and Board of Trade (EA)
GC-EC .... Gas Chromatography with Electron Capture
GCEC .... Gold Coast Environment Centre (EERA)
GC/ECD .... Gas Chromatograph with Electron Capture Detector [Chemical analysis]
GCECEE ...... Groupement des Caisses d'Epargne de la CEE [Savings Bank Group of the European Economic Community]
GCEG .... Grid-Controlled Electron Gun
GCEOS .... Group Contribution Equation of State
GCEP .... Gas Centrifuge Enrichment Plant [Department of Energy]

GCEP .... Governing Council for Environmental Programs [*United Nations*]
GCER .... Growth Environmental, Inc. [*NASDAQ symbol*] (SAG)
GCertClinInstr... Graduate Certificate in Clinical Instruction [*Australia*]
GCertEd .... Graduate Certificate in Education [*Australia*]
GCertEdStudies... Graduate Certificate in Educational Studies [*Australia*]
GCertMaths & MathEd... Graduate Certificate in Mathematics and Mathematics Education [*Australia*]
GCertMusMgmt... Graduate Certificate of Museum Management [*Australia*]
GCertSc & TechWriting... Graduate Certificate of Scientific and Technical Writing [*Australia*]
GCertSocAdmin... Graduate Certificate in Social Administration [*Australia*]
GCES .... Generalized Constant Elasticity of Substitution (PDAA)
GCES .... Glen Canyon Environmental Studies [*Department of the Interior*]
GCESq .... Geodetic Communications and Electronics Squadron [*Air Force*] (AFM)
G-CEU .... General Certified End User [*Department of Commerce export license*]
GCF .... Generation Control Function [*Telecommunications*] (TEL)
GCF .... Greatest Common Factor
GCF .... Greenhouse Crisis Foundation (EA)
GCF .... Gross Capacity Factor (IEEE)
GCF .... Ground Command Facility
GCF .... Ground Communications Facility [*NASA*]
GCF .... Growth-Rate-Controlling Factor [*Medicine*] (DMAA)
GCFA .... Gridded Crossed Field Amplifier (IAA)
GCFAP .... Guidance and Control Flight Analysis Program [*Aerospace*]
GCFBR .... Gas-Cooled Fast Breeder Reactor
GCFC .... Glen Campbell Fan Club (EA)
GCFC .... Gold Coast Full Court Selected Judgments [*A publication*] (DLA)
GCFC .... Gulf Coast Fisheries Center
GCF-CS .... Ground Communications Facility - Communications Switcher [*NASA*]
GCFI .... Gulf and Caribbean Fisheries Institute (EA)
GC-FID .... Gas Chromatography with Flame Ionization Detection
GCFLH .... Grand Cross of the French Legion of Honour
GCFR .... Gas-Cooled Fast Reactor
GCFRE .... Gas-Cooled Fast Reactor Experiment (IEEE)
GCFT .... Gonorrhea Complement Fixation Test [*Medicine*]
GC/FTIR ...... Gas Chromatography plus Fourier Transform Infrared Spectrometry
GCFU .... Germinal Center-Forming Unit (DNAB)
GCFV .... Puerto Del Rosario/Fuerteventura [*Canary Islands*] [*ICAO location identifier*] (ICLI)
GCG .... General Electric Capital Exchange [*AMEX symbol*] (SAG)
GCG .... Genl Chemical Group [*NYSE symbol*] (TTSB)
GCG .... Glucagon (DMAA)
GCG .... Gorham Collectors' Guild [*Defunct*] (EA)
GCG .... Grand Captain General [*Freemasonry*]
GCG .... Grand Captain of the Guard [*Freemasonry*]
GCG .... Gravity-Controlled Gyro
GCG .... Greenhouse Coordinating Group [*Australia*]
GCG .... Ground Command Guidance
GCG .... Guardian Capital Group Ltd. [*Toronto Stock Exchange symbol*]
GCG .... Guatemala City [*Guatemala*] [*Seismograph station code, US Geological Survey Closed*] (SEIS)
GCG .... Guidance Control Group [*Military*]
GCG .... Gyro Control Gunsight
GCGLD .... Grants, Contracts, and General Law Division [*Environmental Protection Agency*] (GFGA)
GCGR .... Glucagon Receptor (DMAA)
GCGR .... Glucocorticoid Receptor (DMAA)
GCGS .... Gravity-Controlled Gyro System
G CH .... [*The*] Gardeners' Chronicle [*A publication*] (ROG)
GCH .... Gas Collection Header (NRCH)
GCH .... Generalized Continuum Hypothesis [*Logic*]
GCH .... Germinal Center Hyperplasia [*Medicine*]
GCH .... Gigacharacters
GCH .... Global Community Health
GCH .... Glucocorticoid Hormone [*Endocrinology*]
GCH .... Golden Chance Resources, Inc. [*Vancouver Stock Exchange symbol*]
GCH .... Grand Captain of the Host [*Freemasonry*]
GCH .... Grand Chapter of Harodim [*Freemasonry*]
GCH .... [*The*] Greater China Fund [*NYSE symbol*] (SAG)
GCH .... Guidance Capsule Handling
GCH .... Knight Grand Cross of the Guelphic Order of Hanover [*British*]
GCHC .... Gulf Coast Hydroscience Center [*Department of the Interior*] [*National Space Technology Laboratories Station, MS*] (GRD)
GCHI .... Giant Cement Holding [*NASDAQ symbol*] (TTSB)
GCHI .... Giant Cement Holding, Inc. [*NASDAQ symbol*] (SAG)
GCHI .... Hierro [*Canary Islands*] [*ICAO location identifier*] (ICLI)
GCHQ .... Government Code Headquarters [*Formerly, GCCS*] [*British*] (INF)
GCHQ .... Government Communications Headquarters [*British*]
GCHR .... Guatemala Committee for Human Rights (EAIO)
GCHWR .... Gas-Cooled, Heavy-Water-Moderated Reactor [*Nuclear energy*] (NRCH)
GCHX .... Ground Cooling Heat Exchanger [*NASA*] (NASA)
GCI .... Gannett Co. [*NYSE symbol*] (TTSB)
GCI .... Gannett Co., Inc. [*NYSE symbol*] (SPSG)
GCI .... Gas Chromatograph Intoximeter [*Measure-of-intoxication test for drunk drivers*]
GCI .... General Capital Increase [*Banking*]
GCI .... General Cognitive Index [*Medicine*] (DMAA)
GCI .... General Communication, Inc. [*Anchorage, AK*] [*Telecommunications*] (TSSD)
GCI .... Generalized Communication Interface
GCI .... Genie Climatique International (EA)

GCI .... Getty Conservation Institute [*Database producer*] (IID)
GCI .... Gnostic Concepts, Inc. [*San Mateo, CA*] [*Database producer*] [*Information service or system*] [*Telecommunications*] (TSSD)
GCI .... Grand China Resources Ltd. [*Vancouver Stock Exchange symbol*]
GCI .... Graphic Communications, Inc. [*Computer science*]
GCI .... Graphic Converter Interface [*Computer science*] (DGA)
GCI .... Graphics Command Interpreter (IAA)
GCI .... Gray Cast Iron
GCI .... Ground Clearance Intercept [*System similar to US commercial RADAR for ground control of aircraft*] [*North Vietnam*]
GCI .... Ground-Controlled Interception [*RADAR*]
GCI .... Groupe des Communications Informatiques [*Computer Communications Group*] [*Canada*]
GCI .... Guernsey [*Channel Islands*] [*Airport symbol*] (OAG)
GCI .... Gulf Communications, Inc. [*Melbourne, FL*] [*Telecommunications service*] (TSSD)
GCIA .... Granite Cutters' International Association [*Later, Tile, Marble, Terrazzo, Finishers, Shopworkers, and Granite Cutters International Union*]
GCIAA .... Granite Cutters' International Association of America (DICI)
GCI/ADC ...... Ground-Controlled Intercept/Air Defense Center (DNAB)
GCIC .... Gifted Children's Information Centre [*British*] (CB)
GCIC .... Groupement Cinematographique International de Conciliation (EA)
GCICU .... German Chamber of Industry and Commerce in the United Kingdom (EAIO)
GCIE .... Knight Grand Commander of the [*Order of the*] Indian Empire [*British*]
GCIIG .... Glass and Ceramics Industry Instrumentation Group (ACII)
GCIIS .... Glucose Controlled Insulin Infusion System [*Medicine*] (DMAA)
GCIL .... Ground-Control Interface Logic (MCD)
GCILC .... Ground-Control Interface Logic Controller (MCD)
GCILU .... Ground-Control Interface Logic Unit (MCD)
GCIP .... GEWEX [*Global Energy and Water Cycle Experiment*] Continental-Scale International Project [*World Climate Research Program*] [*Geoscience*]
GCIP .... Guidance Correction Input Panel
GC/IR .... Gas Chromatography/Infrared
GCIRC .... Glass Container Industry Research Corp. [*An association*] (EA)
GCIRC .... Groupe Consultatif International de Recherche sur le Colza [*International Consultative Research Group on Rape Seed*] (EAIO)
GC-IRMS ..... Gas Chromatography - Isotope-Ratio Mass Spectrometry [*Chemistry*]
GCIS .... Grade Crossing Inventory System [*BTS*] (TAG)
GCIS .... Ground-Control Intercept Squadron
GCISD .... Guidance, Control, and Information Systems Division [*NASA*]
GCIT .... Ground Control Interception Team (IAA)
GCITING ...... Ground-Control Intercept Training [*Navy*] (ANA)
GCITNG .... Ground-Control Intercept Training (NVT)
GCIU .... Graphic Communications International Union (EA)
GCJB .... Guidance Checkout Junction Box
GCK .... Garden City [*Kansas*] [*Airport symbol*] (OAG)
GCK .... Glomerulocystic Kidney [*Nephrology*]
GCK .... Grid-Controlled Klystron
GCK .... Grocka [*Yugoslavia*] [*Geomagnetic observatory code*]
GCKP .... Grand Commander of the Knights of Saint Patrick
GCL .... Columbia Theological Seminary, Decatur, GA [*OCLC symbol*] (OCLC)
GCL .... Galactic Center Lobe
GCL .... Ganglion Cell Layer [*Neuroanatomy*]
GCL .... Gas-Cooled Loop [*Nuclear energy*] (NRCH)
GCL .... Generic Control Language [*Computer science*] (TEL)
GCL .... Globoid Cell Leukodystrophy [*Medicine*] (DMAA)
GCL .... Golden Circle Ltd. [*Australia Commercial firm*]
GCL .... Grand Cross (of the Order) of Leopold (ROG)
GCL .... Great Cameron Lake Resources, Inc. [*Vancouver Stock Exchange symbol*]
GCL .... Greenclose Aviation Services Ltd. [*British ICAO designator*] (FAAC)
GCL .... Ground-Control Landing
GCL .... Ground Coolant Loop (MCD)
GCL .... Guidance Control Laboratory (AAG)
GCL .... Guide to Computing Literature [*A publication*] (IT)
GCL .... Guild of Catholic Lawyers (EA)
GCL .... Guild of Cleaners and Launderers [*British*] (DBA)
GCL .... Gulf Canada Ltd. [*UTLAS symbol*]
GCLA .... Group Carry Look-Ahead (MHDI)
GCLA .... La Palma [*Canary Islands*] [*ICAO location identifier*] (ICLI)
GCLC .... Greater Cincinnati Library Consortium [*Library network*]
GCLC .... Guidance Control Launch Console (IAA)
GCLCS .... Groundcrew Liquid Cooling System
GCLH .... Knight Grand Cross of the Legion of Honour [*British*]
GC LISP ...... Golden Common LISP [*List Processor*] [*Artificial intelligence language*]
GCLJ .... Grand Cross, St. Lazarus of Jerusalem (DD)
GCLLM .... Groupement Canadien des Locataires des Logements Municipaux [*Canadian Organization of Public Housing Tenants*]
GCLP .... Gran Canaria [*Canary Islands*] [*ICAO location identifier*] (ICLI)
GC/LRMS ..... Gas Chromatography/Low Resolution Mass Spectrometry
GCLWD .... Gulf Coast Low Water Datum
GCM .... Gaussian Cosine Modulation (PDAA)
GCM .... Gay Christian Movement [*British*]
GCM .... General Circulation Model [*Meteorology*] [*Computer science*]
GCM .... General Counsel's Memorandum [*Internal Revenue Service*]
GCM .... General Court-Martial
GCM .... General George C. Marshall [*World War II*]
GCM .... Generator Coordinate Method [*Physics*]

GCM............ Geriatric-Care Manager
GCM............ Glazed Ceramic Mosaic (DICI)
GCM............ Global Circulation Model [National Center for Atmospheric Research]
GCM............ Global Circulation Models [Climate] (EERA)
GCM............ Global Climate Model
GCM............ Good Company Man [Theater term] (DSUE)
GCM............ Good Conduct Medal [Military decoration]
g-cm........... Gram-Centimeter (AAMN)
GCM............ Grand Cayman [West Indies] [Airport symbol] (OAG)
GCM............ Great Central Mines [Vancouver Stock Exchange symbol]
GCM............ Greatest Common Measure
GCM............ Greatest Common Multiple (ADA)
GCM............ Greenwich Street California Municipal Fund, Inc. [AMEX symbol] (SAG)
GCM............ Greenwich Street CA Muni Fd [AMEX symbol] (TTSB)
GCM............ Ground-Control Message
GCM............ Groupement Carte a Memoire [Group promoting use of 'smart' credit cards] [France] (NITA)
GCM............ Guild of Church Musicians [British] (DBA)
G/CM²........ Grams per Square Centimeter
G/CM³........ Grams per Cubic Centimeter
GCMA......... General Court-Martial Authority
GCMA......... Glazed Cement Manufacturers Association Ltd. [British] (BI)
GCMA......... Government Contract Management Association (AAGC)
GCMA......... Government Contract Management Association of America (EA)
GCMAPA..... Gay Caucus of Members of the American Psychiatric Association [Later, AGLP] (EA)
GCMC......... Good Conduct Medal Clasp
GCMCA....... General Court-Martial Convening Authority [DoD]
GCMD......... Global Change Master Director (EERA)
GCMDL....... Good Conduct Medal [Military decoration] (AABC)
GCMF......... George C. Marshall Foundation (EA)
GCMG........ Dame Grand Cross of the Order of Saint Michael and Saint George [British] (ADA)
GCMG........ Knight Grand Cross of St. Michael and St. George [Facetiously translated "God Calls Me God"] [British]
GCMI.......... Glass Container Manufacturers Institute [Later, GPI] (EA)
GCMJ.......... General Court-Martial Jurisdiction
GCMO......... General Court-Martial Order
GCMP......... General Court-Martial Prisoner
GCMP......... Greater Cleveland Mathematics Program [Education]
GCMPC....... General Chairman-Member Pickwick Club [From "The Pickwick Papers" by Charles Dickens]
GCMPS....... Gyro Compass
GCMR......... Ground-Control Message Request (MCD)
GCMRF....... George C. Marshall Research Foundation (EA)
GCMRGlc.... Global Cerebral Metabolic Rate for Glucose [Brain research]
GCMRJS..... Great Central Midland [or Metropolitan] Joint Stock [Railroad] [British] (ROG)
GCMS......... Gas Chromatography and Mass Spectroscopy
GC/MS....... Gas Chromatography/Mass Spectrometry
GCMSC....... George C. Marshall Space Flight Center [Also known as MSFC] [NASA]
GCMSFC..... George C. Marshall Space Flight Center [Also known as MSFC] [NASA]
GCMTW...... Guild of Canadian Musical Theatre Writers [Canada] (WWLA)
GCMU........ Glazed Concrete Masonry Units [Technical drawings]
GCMV........ Grapevine Chrome Mosaic Virus [Plant pathology]
GCN........... Gauge Code Number
GCN........... Geometric Constraint Network (DMAA)
GCN........... Giant Cerebral Neuron [Brain anatomy]
GCN........... Gold Canyon Mines, Inc. [Vancouver Stock Exchange symbol]
GCN........... Government Computer News
GCN........... Grand Canyon [Arizona] [Airport symbol] (OAG)
GCN........... Greenwich Civil Noon
GCN........... Ground Communications Network
GCN........... Ground-Control Network [NASA] (NASA)
GCN........... Gulf Central Airlines, Inc. [ICAO designator] (FAAC)
GCNA......... Guild of Carillonneurs in North America (EA)
GcNM......... GCN/Microfilm, Boston, MA [Library symbol Library of Congress] (LCLS)
GC-NPD..... Gas Chromatography-Nitrogen Phosphorus Detector
GCNPP....... Gay Community News Prisoner Project [An association] (EA)
GCNPP....... Greene County Nuclear Power Plant (NRCH)
GCNR......... Gas Core Nuclear Rocket
GCNSW...... Gas Council of New South Wales [Australia]
GCO........... Columbus College, Library, Columbus, GA [OCLC symbol] (OCLC)
GCO........... GC Optronics, Inc.
GCO........... GENESCO, Inc. [NYSE symbol] (SPSG)
GCO........... Georgetown College Observatory (MCD)
GCO........... Glenco International Corp. [Vancouver Stock Exchange symbol]
GCO........... Government Concept of Operations (RDA)
GCO........... Governor's Commissioned Officer [British military] (DMA)
GCO........... Ground Checkout [NASA] (NASA)
GCO........... Ground Cutout
GCO........... Guidance Control Officer (AAG)
GCO........... Gun Control Officer [Navy]
gCO2.......... Grams of Carbon Dioxide Equivalent (EERA)
GCOC......... General Conditions of Contract
GCOC......... Gun Control Officer Console [Military] (CAAL)
GCocM....... Middle Georgia College, Cochran, GA [Library symbol Library of Congress] (LCLS)
GCOE......... Ground-Control Operational Equipment (IAA)
GColu......... W. C. Bradley Memorial Library, Columbus, GA [Library symbol Library of Congress] (LCLS)

GColuC....... Columbus College, Columbus, GA [Library symbol Library of Congress] (LCLS)
GColuGS.... Church of Jesus Christ of Latter-Day Saints, Genealogical Society Library, MaconBranch, Columbus, GA [Library symbol Library of Congress] (LCLS)
GCom......... Grand Commander [or Commandery] [Freemasonry]
GCON........ Grand Cross, Order of the Niger [British]
GConT........ Monastery of the Holy Ghost, Conyers, GA [Library symbol Library of Congress] (LCLS)
GCOR......... Gencor Industries, Inc. [NASDAQ symbol] (NQ)
GCOS......... General Comprehensive Operating Supervisor [Computer science]
GCOS......... General Comprehensive Operating System (NITA)
GCOS......... General Computer Operational System [NASA]
GCOS......... Global Climate Observing System (USDC)
GCOS......... Global Climate Observing System [Marine science] (OSRA)
GCOS......... Great Canadian Oil Sands Ltd.
GCOS......... Ground Computer Operating System [NASA] (NASA)
GCP........... Gain Control Pulse (IAA)
GCP........... Gaining Command Program (MCD)
GCP........... Generalized Computer Program
GCP........... Generator Control Panel (DNAB)
GCP........... Gift Coupon Programme [Later, Co-Action] [UNESCO]
GCP........... Golden CommPass [Front-end computer processor] (PCM)
GCP........... Good Clinical Practice [Medicine]
GCP........... Government Contracts Program [George Washington University Law Center] (DLA)
GCP........... Grancamp Resources [Vancouver Stock Exchange symbol]
GCP........... Graphics Control Program [IBM Corp.] (PCM)
GCP........... Green Circle Program (EA)
GCP........... Gross Criminal Product
GCP........... Ground Control Point
GCP........... Guidance Checkout [or Control] Package (NG)
GCP........... Guild of Catholic Psychiatrists [Later, National Guild of Catholic Psychiatrists] (EA)
GCP........... Guild of Computer Practitioners [British] (DBA)
GCPA......... Grammatik des Christlich-Palaestinischen Aramaeisch [A publication] (BJA)
GCPD......... Grade Crossing Protection Device
GCPPD....... Global Committee of Parliamentarians on Population and Development (EA)
GCPPI........ Gifted Children's Pen Pals International (EA)
GCPR......... General Ceiling Price Regulation (DLA)
GCPS......... Gigacycles per Second (MUGU)
GCPS......... Global Climate Perspectives System [Marine science] (OSRA)
GCPS......... Global Climate Perspectives System (USDC)
GCPS......... Greig Cephalopolysyndactyly Syndrome [Medicine]
GCPS......... Ground Claims Processing System
GCPS......... Group Claims Processing System [McAuto]
GCQ........... Group Climate Questionnaire [Occupational therapy]
GCR........... Gain Control Range
GCR........... Galactic Cosmic Radiation [or Ray]
GCR........... Galvanocutaneous Reaction
GCR........... Gamma Cosmic Ray [Geophysics]
GCR........... Gas-Cooled Reactor
GCR........... Gaylord Container'A' [AMEX symbol] (TTSB)
GCR........... Gaylord Container Corp. Class A [AMEX symbol] (SPSG)
GCR........... General Cargo Rates [Business term]
GCR........... General Commodity Rate [Shipping] (DS)
GCR........... General Component Reference (IEEE)
GCR........... Generator Control Relay [Electronics] (OA)
GCR........... Geneva Consultants Registry [Alpha Systems Resource] [Database]
GCR........... Ghost Canceling Reference [Television technology]
GCR........... Glencair Resources, Inc. [Toronto Stock Exchange symbol]
GCR........... Glomerular Complement Receptor [Immunology]
GCR........... Glucocorticoid Receptor (DMAA)
GCR........... Glucose Consumption Rate
GCR........... Glucuronidase [An enzyme]
GCR........... Glycinecresol Red [An indicator] [Chemistry]
GCR........... Gold Coast Regiment [British military] (DMA)
GCR........... Government Contracts Reporter [A publication] (AAGC)
GCR........... Grand Central Rocket Co. (AAG)
GCR........... Grandparents'/Children's Rights (EA)
GCR........... Gray-Component Replacement [Color reproduction technology]
GCR........... Grayling Creek [Montana] [Seismograph station code, US Geological Survey] (SEIS)
GCR........... Great Central Railway [British]
GCR........... Great Circle Route (WDAA)
GCR........... Grignard's Chemical Reaction
GCR........... Ground-Controlled RADAR
GCR........... Group Coded Recording [Computer science] (BUR)
GCR........... Group Code Recording [Data storage method] (NITA)
GCR........... Group Conformity Rating (DMAA)
GCR........... Group Encoded Recording (NITA)
GCR........... Guerrilleros de Cristo Rey [Warriors of Christ and King] [Revolutionary Group Spain]
GCRA......... Gas-Cooled Reactor Associates (NRCH)
GCRA......... Giant Chinchilla Rabbit Association (EA)
GCRA......... Global Coral Reef Alliance (EA)
GCRC......... General Clinical Research Center [Stanford University] (RCD)
GCRC......... General Clinical Research Center [University of Virginia] (RCD)
GCRC......... General Clinical Research Center [University of Alabama in Birmingham] (RCD)
GCRC......... General Clinical Research Center [Scripps Clinic and Research Foundation]
GCRCH....... General Council and Register of Consultant Herbalists [British] (DBA)

GCRCPB....... General Clinical Research Center Program Branch [*National Institutes of Health*]
GCRE .... Gas-Cooled Reactor Experiment (NRCH)
GCREF .... GCR Hldgs Ltd [*NASDAQ symbol*] (TTSB)
GCRES .... Ground Combat-Readiness Evaluation Squadron
GCRF .... Greensboro Civil Rights Fund [*Defunct*] (EA)
GCRG .... Giant Cell Reparative Granuloma [*Oncology*]
GCRG .... Gun Carriage
GCRI .... Georgetown Clinical Research Institute [*FAA*]
GCRI .... German Carpet Research Institute [*See also TFI*] (EAIO)
GCRI .... Gillette Co. Research Institute
GCRL .... Glass House Crops Research Institute [*Agricultural Research Council*] (PDAA)
GCRL .... Gulf Coast Research Laboratory [*Ocean Springs, MS*]
GCRN .... General Council and Register of Naturopaths [*British*] (DBA)
GCRO .... General Council and Register of Osteopaths Ltd. [*British*]
GCRP .... Galactic Cosmic Ray Particle
GCRP .... Global Change Research Plan [*Program*] [*Marine science*] (OSRA)
GCRP .... Global Change Research Plan/Program (USDC)
GCRP .... Global Change Research Program (EERA)
GCRR .... Arrecife/Lanzarote [*Canary Islands*] [*ICAO location identifier*] (ICLI)
GCRV .... Ground Cruising Recreational Vehicle [*Owosso Motor Car Co.*] [*Owosso, MI*]
GCRWS .... Gaylord Container Wrrt [*AMEX symbol*] (TTSB)
GCS .... Gas Cleaning System [*Combustion technology*]
GCS .... Gas Cylinder System
GCS .... Gate-Controlled Switch
GCS .... General Clinical Service (MAE)
GCS .... General Communications System [*Sperry Univac*] (NITA)
GCS .... General Communication Subsystem [*Computer science*]
GCS .... General Computer Systems (NITA)
GCS .... General Computer Systems, Inc.
GCS .... Generator Control Switch (MCD)
GCS .... Geostationary Communications Satellite [*WARC*]
GCS .... Gifted Child Society (EA)
Gc/s .... Gigacycles per Second [*IEEE*]
GCS .... Glasgow Coma Score [*Medicine*]
GCS .... Golden Crown Resources Ltd. [*Vancouver Stock Exchange symbol*]
GCS .... Golf Collectors' Society (EA)
GCS .... Government Contractors Subcontractors
GCS .... Grand Commander (of the Order) of Spain (ROG)
GCS .... Graphic Compatibility System
GCS .... Graphic Compatibility System [*US Military Academy*] (NITA)
GCS .... Graphics Compatibility Standard [*For image processing*]
GCS .... Gray Communications Systems [*NYSE symbol*] (SAG)
GCS .... Ground Command System
GCS .... Ground Communications System
GCS .... Ground-Control Station (MCD)
GCS .... Guidance Cutoff Signal [*NASA*] (NASA)
GCS .... Gyroless Control System
GCS .... Portland, ME [*Location identifier FAA*] (FAAL)
GCSA .... Galloway Cattle Society of America (EA)
GCSA .... Gross Cell-Surface Antigen [*Immunology*]
GCSAA .... Golf Course Superintendents Association of America (EA)
GCSA/NJ ..... Golf Course Superintendents Association of New Jersey (SRA)
GCSC .... Guidance Control and Sequencing Computer
GCSE .... General Certificate of Secondary Education [*British*]
GCSE .... General Certificate of Secondary Education (BARN)
GCSE .... Generalized Convulsive Status Epilepticus [*Medicine*] (CPH)
Gc/sec .... Gigacycles per Second [*AIP*]
G-CSF .... Granulocyte-Colony Stimulating Factor [*Hematology*]
GCSF .... Gulf, Colorado & Santa Fe Railway Co. [*AAR code*]
GCSG .... Graphic Communications Societies Group [*British*] (NITA)
GCSG .... Knight Grand Cross of St. Gregory the Great [*British*]
GCSI .... Knight Grand Commander of the [*Order of the*] Star of India [*British*]
GC-SICM ..... Gas Chromatography - Single Ion Current Monitoring (PDAA)
GCSM .... Glandless Cottonseed Meal [*Animal feed*]
GCSM .... Ground Composite Signal Mixer
GCSP .... Guidance and Control Set Processor
GCSRW - UMC... General Commission on the Status and Role of Women - United Methodist Church (EA)
GCSS .... GEWEX [*Global Energy and Water Cycle Experiment*] Cloud System Study (EERA)
GCSS .... Global Communications Satellite System
GCSS .... Ground-Controlled Space System
GCSS .... Knight Grand Cross of St. Sylvester [*British*]
GCStJ.......... Bailiff Grand Cross of [*the Order of*] Saint John of Jerusalem [*British*] (ADA)
GCStJ.......... Dame Grand Cross of [*the Order of*] Saint John of Jerusalem [*British*] (ADA)
GCStJ.......... Knight Grand Cross of [*the Order of*] St. John of Jerusalem [*British*]
GCSU .... Government Clerical Services' Union [*Ceylon*]
GCSV .... Groundnut Chlorotic Spot Virus
GCSW .... Graduate Certificate of Social Work
GCT............. Coca-Cola Co., Technical Information Services, Atlanta, GA [*OCLC symbol*] (OCLC)
GCT............. Galactic Center Transient [*Astronomy*]
GCT............. General Classification Test [*Military*]
GCT............. Gesture Comprehension Test [*Occupational therapy*]
GCT............. Giant Cell Tumor [*Oncology*]
GCT............. Giro [*Money Order*] Credit Transfer (DI)
GCT............. Glasgow College of Technology (AIE)
GCT............. Glass Cloth Tape
GCT............. Government Competitive Testing
GCT............. Grand Cadence de Tir [*Self-propelled howitzer*] (RDA)

GCT............. Graphics Communications Terminal
GCT............. Great Circle Track
GCT............. Greenwich Central Time [*Astronomy*] (IAA)
GCT............. Greenwich Civil Time
GCT............. Greenwich Conservatory Time
GCT............. Ground Checkout and Test [*Aerospace*]
GCT............. Guidance Command Test
GCT............. Guidance Computer Test
GCT............. Gun Compatibility Test
GCT............. Gun Control Tower [*British military*] (DMA)
GCT............. Gyro-Compass Trial (IAA)
GCTA .... Ground Commanded [*or Controlled*] Television Assembly [*Apollo*] [*NASA*]
GCTC .... Giant Cell Tumor Cells [*A cell line*]
GCTE .... Global Change and Terrestrial Ecosystems [*Marine science*] (OSRA)
GCTE .... Global Change and Terrestrial Ecosystems (USDC)
GCTE .... Guidance Computer Test Equipment
GCTEV .... Garland Chrysanthemum Temperate Virus [*Plant pathology*]
GCTF .... Gold Coast Territorial Force [*British military*] (DMA)
GCTM.......... Global Chemical Transport Model [*Marine science*] (OSRA)
GCTOA .... Greek Cultural and Theatrical Organisation of Australia
GCtryB .... Great Country Bank [*Associated Press*] (SAG)
GCTS .... Gas Component Test Stand (MCD)
GCTS .... Ground Communications Tracking Systems
GCTS .... Tenerife-Reina Sofia [*Canary Islands*] [*ICAO location identifier*] (ICLI)
GCTW.......... Gross Combination Test Weight [*Automotive engineering*]
GCU .... Gas-Cooled Unit
GCU .... General Control Unit (MCD)
GCU .... Generator Control Unit [*Aviation*] (NASA)
GCU .... Generator/Converter Unit
GCU .... Gold Canyon Resources [*Vancouver Stock Exchange symbol*]
GCU .... Gonococcal Urethritis [*Medicine*] (DMAA)
GCU .... Ground Checkout Unit [*Aerospace*] (MCD)
GCU .... Ground-Control Unit (AAG)
GCU .... Ground Cooling Unit [*NASA*] (NASA)
GCU .... Guidance and Control Unit (NATG)
GCU .... Guidance Coupler Unit
GCU .... Gunner's Control Unit
GCU .... Gyro Coupling Unit (KSC)
GCuA .... Andrew College, Cuthbert, GA [*Library symbol Library of Congress*] (LCLS)
GCUGA........ Grounded Current Unity-Gain Amplifier
GCUUSA ...... Greek Catholic Union of the USA (EA)
GCV .... Chattahoochee Valley Regional Library, Columbus, GA [*OCLC symbol*] (OCLC)
GCV .... Gabelli Convertible Securities Fund [*NYSE symbol*] (SAG)
GCV .... Gabelli Conv Securities Fd [*NYSE symbol*] (TTSB)
GCV .... Gaseous Oxygen Control Valve (NASA)
GCV .... Great Cardiac Vein [*Medicine*] (DMAA)
GCV .... Gross Caloric Value
GCV .... Leakesville, MS [*Location identifier FAA*] (FAAL)
GCVF .... Great Cardiac Vein Flow [*Medicine*] (DMAA)
GCVO .... Dame Grand Cross of the Royal Victorian Order [*British*] (ADA)
GCVO .... Knight Grand Cross of the Royal Victorian Order [*British*]
GCVS .... General Catalog of Variable Stars [*Astronomy*] (OA)
GCVW.......... Gross Combination Vehicle Weight [*Automotive engineering*]
GCW .... Coca-Cola Co., Law Library, Atlanta, GA [*OCLC symbol*] (OCLC)
GCW .... [*The*] Garden City Western Railway Co. [*AAR code*]
GCW .... General Continuous Wave (IAA)
GCW .... Generative Cell Wall [*Botany*]
GCW .... Global Chart of the World [*Air Force*]
GCW .... Glomerular Capillary Wall [*Anatomy*]
GCW .... Grand Coulee [*Washington*] [*Seismograph station code, US Geological Survey Closed*] (SEIS)
GCW .... Gridiron Club of Washington, DC (EA)
GCW .... Gross Combination Weight [*for tractor and loaded trailer*]
GCWDA .... Gulf Coast Waste Disposal Authority [*Governmental industrial waste disposal system*]
GCWIU .... General Cigarette Workers' Industrial Union [*British*]
GCWM .... General Conference on Weights and Measures
GCWR .... Global Congress of the World's Religions (EA)
GCWR .... Gross Combination Weight Rating [*Environmental Protection Agency*]
GCX .... GC Companies [*NYSE symbol*] (SAG)
GCXO .... Tenerife [*Canary Islands*] [*ICAO location identifier*] (ICLI)
GCY .... Gastroscopy [*Medicine*] (DMAA)
GCY .... General Cybernetics Corp. [*Vancouver Stock Exchange symbol*]
GCY .... Glen Cove [*New York*] [*Seismograph station code, US Geological Survey*] (SEIS)
GCY .... Greeneville, TN [*Location identifier FAA*] (FAAL)
GCYF .... Grantmakers for Children, Youth, and Families (NFD)
GD .... Air Antilles [*Airline*] (MHDB)
GD .... Air North [*ICAO designator*] (AD)
GD .... DeKalb County Library System, Regional Service-Rockdale and Newton Counties, Decatur, GA [*Library symbol Library of Congress*] (LCLS)
GD .... Diganglioside [*Chemistry*]
Gd .... Gadolinium [*Chemical element*]
GD .... Gaol Delivery [*Legal*] [*British*] (ROG)
GD .... Gap Detector
GD .... Gas Dragster [*Class of racing cars*]
GD .... Gas Drainage
GD .... Gate Driver
GD .... Gave Delivery
GD .... Gear Down [*Aviation*]
GD .... Gel Destainer [*Analytical chemistry*]

GD .... Gel Dryer [Chromatography]
GD .... General Delivery
GD .... General Delivery (DD)
GD .... General Design (AAG)
GD .... General Development
GD .... General Diagram
GD .... General Discharge
GD .... General Dispensary [Military]
GD .... General Duty
GD .... General Dynamics Corp. [NYSE symbol] (SPSG)
GD .... Genl Dynamics [NYSE symbol] (TTSB)
GD .... Geographic Digest [A publication British]
GD .... Geographic Distribution
GD .... Gestational Day
GD .... Glass Door (ADA)
GD .... Global Data Systems [Vancouver Stock Exchange symbol]
GD .... Glow Discharge [Photovoltaic energy systems]
GD .... Glutamate Dehydrogenase [An enzyme]
GD .... Glutaraldehyde-Dichromate [Fixative]
GD .... Glyceryl Distearate [Organic chemistry]
GD .... Goal Defence [Netball]
GD .... God Damn
GD .... Golden Dawn [In occult society name, Hermetic Order of the Golden Dawn]
GD .... Gonadal Dysgenesis [Endocrinology]
GD .... Good
GD .... Good [Track condition] [Thoroughbred racing]
GD .... Good Delivery [Business term]
Gd .... Government Expenditure [Economics]
GD .... Grade [Technical drawings]
GD .... Graduate Diploma
GD .... Graduate in Divinity
GD .... Granddaughter
GD .... Grand Deacon [Freemasonry]
GD .... Grand Division
GD .... Grand Duchess [or Duke]
GD .... Grand Duchy
GD .... Grand Duke (WGA)
GD .... Grandes Decisions de la Jurisprudence Administrative [A publication]
GD .... Graphic Demand Meter
GD .... Graphic Display
GD .... Grave's Disease [Endocrinology]
GD .... Gravimetric Density
Gd .... Greenside Darter [Ichthyology]
GD .... Greenwich Date
GD .... Grenada [ANSI two-letter standard code] (CNC)
gd .... Grenada [MARC country of publication code Library of Congress] (LCCP)
GD .... Gross Debt [Business term]
GD .... Ground
GD .... Ground Detector (MSA)
GD .... Ground Directional (IAA)
GD .... Group Delay Distortion (LAIN)
GD .... Grouping Distance [Industrial engineering]
GD .... Grove Dictionary of Music and Musicians [A publication]
GD .... Grown Diffused
GD .... Guard (AABC)
GD .... Gudermannian Amplitude
GD .... Gundeck
GD .... Gunnery Division [British military] (DMA)
GD .... Guntersville Dam [TVA]
GD .... Nerve Gas [US Chemical Corps symbol]
GD .... Soman [Nerve gas] [Army symbol]
GDA .... Galvo-Drive Amplifier
GDA .... General Disposal Authority
GD/A .... General Dynamics/Astronautics
GDA .... General Dynamics Astronautics
GDA .... Germine Diacetate [Medicine] (DMAA)
GDA .... Gimbal Drive Actuator [or Assembly] (KSC)
GDA .... Global Data Administrator (MHDI)
GDA .... Global Data Area
GDA .... Global Directory Agent
GDA .... Glycidyldiisopropylidenearabitol [Organic chemistry]
GDA .... Goat Dairymen's Association [Australia]
GDA .... Goldera Resources, Inc. [Vancouver Stock Exchange symbol]
GDA .... Graduate Diploma in Administration
Gda .... Granddaughter
GDA .... Gun Damage Assessment (NVT)
GDA .... Gun-Defended Area
GDAA .... Gift and Decorative Accessories Association of America [Later, GAA] (EA)
GDahN .... North Georgia College, Dahlonega, GA [Library symbol Library of Congress] (LCLS)
GDAIS .... Atlanta Information Services, Decatur, GA [Library symbol Library of Congress] (LCLS)
GDal .... Dalton Regional Library, Dalton, GA [Library symbol Library of Congress] (LCLS)
GDalC .... Dalton College, Dalton, GA [Library symbol] [Library of Congress] (LCLS)
GDAM .... Graduate Division of Applied Mathematics
GD & R .... Grinning, Ducking, and Running (CDE)
GD & T .... Geometric Dimensioning and Tolerancing
GDanH .... Heritage Papers, Danielsville, GA [Library symbol Library of Congress] (LCLS)

GDAP .... GEOS [Geodetic Earth-Orbiting Satellite] Data Adjustment Program
GDAP .... Government Document Application Profile [Telecommunications] (OSI)
GDAS .... Geokinetic Data Acquisition System (PDAA)
GDAS .... Ground Data Acquisition System
GDAU .... General Data Acquisition Unit (MCD)
GDB .... Gas Density Balance [Medicine] (DMAA)
GDB .... Genome Data Base [Genetics]
GDB .... Geometric Database (MCD)
GDB .... Global Database
GDB .... Government Development Bank of Puerto Rico
GDB .... Guide Dogs for the Blind (EA)
GDBA .... Guide Dogs for the Blind Association [British] (EAIO)
GDBMS .... Generalized Data Base Management Systems [Air Force]
GDBS .... Generalized Database System (NASA)
GDBusAd .... Graduate Diploma in Business Administration
GDC .... Columbia Theological Seminary, Decatur, GA [Library symbol Library of Congress] (LCLS)
GDC .... Garage Door Council (EA)
GDC .... Gas Discharge Counter
GDC .... Gas Displacement Chromatography
GDC .... Gel Dryer with Clamps [Chromatography]
GDC .... Gel Drying Cart [Chromatography]
GDC .... General Data Comm (NITA)
GDC .... General DataComm Industries, Inc. [NYSE symbol] (SPSG)
GDC .... General Dental Council [British]
GDC .... General Design Criteria (NRCH)
GDC .... General Development Corp. (AAG)
GDC .... General [Purpose] Digital Computer
GD/C .... General Dynamics/Convair
GDC .... General Dynamics, Convair
GDC .... General Dynamics Corp.
GDC .... Genl DataComm Ind [NYSE symbol] (TTSB)
GDC .... Geocentric Dust Cloud
GDC .... Geodetic Data Center [Environmental Science Services Administration]
GDC .... Geological Data Center [University of California, San Diego] (IID)
GDC .... Geomagnetic Data Center [National Oceanic and Atmospheric Administration]
GDC .... Geophysical Data Center
GDC .... Gettysburg College, Gettysburg, PA [OCLC symbol] (OCLC)
GDC .... Giant Dopamine-Containing Cell [Medicine] (DMAA)
GDC .... Governmental Defence Council [British]
GDC .... Grand-Dad's Day Council [Defunct] (EA)
GDC .... Grand Deacon of Ceremonies [Freemasonry] (ROG)
GDC .... Granduc Mines Ltd. [Toronto Stock Exchange symbol Vancouver Stock Exchange symbol]
GDC .... Graphic Display Console (MCD)
GDC .... Gravity Die-Cast [Automotive engineering]
GDC .... Gross Dependable Capacity [Electronics] (IEEE)
GDC .... Ground Digit Control (IAA)
GDC .... Guidance Data Converter [Aerospace] (AAG)
GDC .... Guidance Display Computer (DNAB)
GDC .... Guild of Dyers and Cleaners [British] (BI)
GDC .... Gun Direction Computer
GDC .... Gyro Display Coupler (MCD)
GDC .... Society of Graphic Designers of Canada (EAIO)
GDCA .... Great Dane Club of America (EA)
GDCH .... Glycerol Dichlorohydrin [Organic chemistry]
GDCH .... Graduate Diploma in Community Health
GDCI .... Gypsum Drywall Contractors International [Later, AWCI]
GDCR .... Glacial Debris Conjugate Region [Oceanography]
GDCS .... Government Documents Catalog Service [Information service or system] (IID)
GDCS .... Ground Distributed Control System (SSD)
GD/CV .... General Dynamics/Convair Division (MCD)
GDD .... DeKalb Historical Society, Decatur, GA [Library symbol Library of Congress] (LCLS)
GDD .... Gas Discharge Display (IAA)
GDD .... Gay Disaster Disease [Also called AIDS] (DAVI)
GDD .... Geddes Resources Ltd. [Toronto Stock Exchange symbol]
GDD .... General Design Document [Computer science] (MHDI)
GD/D .... General Dynamics/Daingerfield (SAA)
GDD .... Global Developmental Delay
GDD .... Group Display Device (MCD)
GDD .... Growing Degree Day [Agriculture] (PDAA)
GDDL .... Graphical Data Definition Language
GDDM .... Graphical Data Display Manager [Computer science]
GDDQ .... Group Dimensions Descriptions Questionnaire [Psychology]
GDDS .... DeKalb County School System, Decatur, GA [Library symbol] [Library of Congress] (LCLS)
GDDS .... Gamma Dose Detector System
GD/DS .... Generalized Dictionary/Directory System [Computer science] (MHDB)
GDE .... Beaumont, TX [Location identifier FAA] (FAAL)
GD/E .... General Dynamics/Electronics (SAA)
GDE .... Generalized Data Entry (ADA)
GDE .... Gibbs-Duhem Equation [Physical chemistry]
GDE .... Gilt Deckled Edge [Bookbinding]
GDE .... Gode [Ethiopia] [Airport symbol] (OAG)
GDE .... Golden Dawn Explorations Ltd. [Vancouver Stock Exchange symbol]
GDE .... Gourde [Monetary unit] [Haiti]
GDE .... Graduate Diploma in Educational Studies
GDE .... Graduate Diploma in Extension (ADA)
GDE .... Gross Domestic Expenditure (WDAA)
GDE .... Ground Data Equipment [Electronics]

GDE	Guide [*or Guided*] (MSA)
GDE	Servicios Aereos Gadel SA de CV [*Mexico ICAO designator*] (FAAC)
GD/EB	General Dynamics/Electric Boat Division (KSC)
G de Bay	Guido de Baysio [*Deceased, 1313*] [*Authority cited in pre-1607 legal work*] (DSA)
G de Ca	Guillelmus de Cabriano [*Deceased, 1201*] [*Authority cited in pre-1607 legal work*] (DSA)
G de Cal	Gaspar de Calderinis [*Deceased, 1390*] [*Authority cited in pre-1607 legal work*] (DSA)
G de Cu	Guillelmus de Cuneo [*Deceased, 1335*] [*Authority cited in pre-1607 legal work*] (DSA)
G de Fr	Guillelmus de Ferreriis [*Deceased, 1295*] [*Authority cited in pre-1607 legal work*] (DSA)
G de Mon	Guillelmus de Monte Lauduno [*Deceased, 1343*] [*Authority cited in pre-1607 legal work*] (DSA)
G de Mon Lau	Guillelmus de Monte Lauduno [*Deceased, 1343*] [*Authority cited in pre-1607 legal work*] (DSA)
G de Mon Laud	Guillelmus de Monte Lauduno [*Deceased, 1343*] [*Authority cited in pre-1607 legal work*] (DSA)
GDemP	Piedmont College, Demorest, GA [*Library symbol Library of Congress*] (LCLS)
G-Dest	General Destination
G de Suz	Guido de Suzaria [*Deceased, 1293*] [*Authority cited in pre-1607 legal work*] (DSA)
GDEU	Guidance Digital Evaluation Unit
GDF	Gas Dynamic Facility [*Air Force*]
GDF	Geographic Data File [*LPC, Inc.*] [*Information service or system*] (IID)
GDF	Gibraltar Defence Force [*British military*] (DMA)
GDF	Global Partners Income Fd [*NYSE symbol*] (TTSB)
GDF	Global Partners Income Fund [*NYSE symbol*] (SPSG)
GDF	Goldfarb Corp. [*Toronto Stock Exchange symbol*]
GDF	Granular Diffusion Flame (MCD)
GDF	Ground Decommutation Facility
GDF	Ground Defense Forces
GDF	Ground Diverted Force [*Military*] (CINC)
GDF	Group Distributing Frames
GDF	Group Distribution Frame [*Telecommunications*] (NITA)
GDF	Growth Differentiation Factor [*Embryology*]
GDF	Guyanese Defense Force
GDFB	Guide Dog Foundation for the Blind [*Also known as Second Sight Guiding Eyes - Guide Dog Foundation*] (EA)
GDFCF	Gross Domestic Fixed Capital Formation (EERA)
GDFF	Geographic Distribution of Federal Funds Information System [*Comptroller General of the United States*]
GD/FW	General Dynamics/Fort Worth (KSC)
GDG	Gas Discharge Gauge
GD(G)	General Duties (Ground) [*British military*] (DMA)
GDG	Generation Data Group [*Computer science*] (BUR)
GDG	Golden Glory [*Vancouver Stock Exchange symbol*]
GDG	Group Display Generator
GDG	Guarding [*Bookbinding*] (DGA)
GDGA	Garment Dyers Guild of America (EA)
GD/GA	General Dynamics/General Atomic (KSC)
GDGIP	Gas-Driven Gyro Inertial Platform [*Aerospace*] (AAG)
GDGS	Guidance Digital Ground Station (IAA)
GDH	DeKalb General Hospital, Decatur, GA [*Library symbol Library of Congress*] (LCLS)
GDH	Glutamate Dehydrogenase [*An enzyme*]
GDH	Glycerophosphate Dehydrogenase (MAE)
GDH	Godhavn [*Greenland*] [*Seismograph station code, US Geological Survey*] (SEIS)
GDH	Goldsearch, Inc. [*Vancouver Stock Exchange symbol*]
GDH	Gonadotropic Hormone [*Endocrinology*]
GDH	Goods on Hand (DS)
GDH	Grand Ducal Highness (ROG)
GDH	Ground Data Handling
GDH	Growth and Differentiation Hormone [*Endocrinology*]
GDH	Sargodha [*Pakistan*] [*Airport symbol*] (AD)
GDHC	Ground Data Handling Centre [*Canada*]
GDHS	Ground Data Handling System (MCD)
GDHSE	Guardhouse (AABC)
GDHSWT	General Dynamics High-Speed Wind Tunnel
GDI	Gas-Driven Intensifier Pump (MCD)
GDI	Gasoline Direct Injection
GDI	Generalized Database Interface [*Computer science*] (MHDB)
GDI	God Damned Independent [*College slang for student not affiliated with a fraternity or sorority*]
GDI	Graphic Display Interface (MCD)
GDI	Graphics Device Interface
GDI	Ground Detector Indicator
GDI	New York, NY [*Location identifier FAA*] (FAAL)
GDI	Sammlung der Griechischen Dialektinschriften [*A publication*] (OCD)
GDIAN	Guardian (ROG)
GDIFS	Gray and Ductile Iron Founders' Society [*Later, Iron Castings Society - ICS*]
GdIG	Gadolinium Iron Garnet (IEEE)
GDIM	Graduate Diploma in Industrial Management [*Australia*]
GDIP	Gale Directory of International Publications [*A publication*]
GDIP	General Defense Intelligence Program [*DoD*]
GDip	Graduate Diploma (DD)
GDipA(Couns)	Graduate Diploma in Arts (Counselling)
GDipCD	Graduate Diploma in Child Development
GDipCh	Graduate Diploma in Chiropractic
GDipClinSc	Graduate Diploma in Clinical Science

GDipCompSt	Graduate Diploma in Computer Studies
GDipEc	Graduate Diploma in Economics
GDipErg	Graduate Diploma in Ergonomics
GDipExerSpSc	Graduate Diploma in Exercise and Sport Science
GDipHA	Graduate Diploma in Health Administration
GDipHC	Graduate Diploma in Health Counselling
GDipHSM	Graduate Diploma in Health Services Management
GDipHumNut	Graduate Diploma in Human Nutrition
GDipLS	Graduate Diploma in Legal Studies
GDipM	Graduate Diploma in Management
GDipMLS	Graduate Diploma in Medical Laboratory Science
GDIPP	General Defense Intelligence Proposed Program [*DoD*] (MCD)
GDipPEC	Graduate Diploma in Parent Education and Counselling
GDipPHC	Graduate Diploma in Primary Health
GDipPrfMgt	Graduate Diploma in Professional Management
GDipPubL	Graduate Diploma in Public Law
GDIS	Gier-Dunkle Integrating Sphere
Gdk	Gdansk [*Poland*] (BARN)
GDL	Gas Discharge Lamp
GDL	Gas Dynamic LASER
GDL	Gas Dynamics Laboratory
GDL	Gladstone-Dale Law
GDL	Glass Delay Line
GDL	Glass Development LASER
GDL	Global Data Link
GDL	Glow-Discharge Lamp [*Spectrometry*]
GDL	Glucono-delta-Lactone [*Organic chemistry*]
GDL	Graphic Display Library
GDL	Graphic Drawing Library [*Graphic Data Ltd.*] [*Software package*] (NCC)
GDL	Graphics Display List [*Graphic Data Ltd.*] [*Software package*] (NCC)
GDL	Guadalajara [*Mexico*] [*Airport symbol*] (OAG)
GDLB	Glendale Federal Bank FSB [*NASDAQ symbol*] (SAG)
GDLE	Graduate Diploma in Land Economy
GDLEW	Glendale Fed Bk FSB Wrrt [*NASDAQ symbol*] (TTSB)
GDLK	Grid Leak
GDLP	Grenada Democratic Labour Party [*Political party*] (EY)
GDLP	Ground Data Link Processor (GAVI)
GDLS	General Dynamics [*Corp.*] Land Systems Division
GDLS	General Dynamics Land Systems Inc. [*A publication*] (AAGC)
GDLS	Glow-Discharge Lamp Source [*Spectrometry*]
GDLS	Graduate Diploma in Library Science (ADA)
GDM	Gardner, MA [*Location identifier FAA*] (FAAL)
GDM	General Design Memorandum [*US Army Corps of Engineers*]
GDM	General Development Map [*or Model*]
GDM	Geodetic Distance Measurement
GDM	Gestational Diabetes Mellitus [*Medicine*]
GDM	Ghana Democratic Movement [*Political party*] (EY)
GDM	Gibraltar Democratic Movement [*Political party*] (PPE)
GDM	Global Data Manager
GDM	Gravitational Dipole Moment (PDAA)
GDM	Grenada Democratic Movement [*Political party*] (EAIO)
GDM	Grid-Dip Meter (IAA)
GDM	Grid-Dip Modulator
GDM	Guidance Design Manager (MCD)
GDMA	Glycol Dimethacrylate (MCD)
GDManTher	Graduate Diploma in Manipulative Therapy
GdmCl	Guanidinium Chloride [*Biochemistry*]
GDMCN	Ground Data Management and Communications Network (MCD)
GDME	Glycol Dimethyl Ether [*Organic chemistry*]
GDMI	Gardner Denver Machinery [*NASDAQ symbol*] (TTSB)
GDMI	Gardner Denver Machinery, Inc. [*NASDAQ symbol*] (SAG)
GDMK	GoodMark Foods [*NASDAQ symbol*] (TTSB)
GDMK	GoodMark Foods, Inc. [*NASDAQ symbol*] (NQ)
GDML	Gas Dynamic Mixing LASER [*Navy*]
GDMO	General Duties Medical Officer
GDMS	Generalized Data Management System [*Computer science*] (BUR)
GDMS	Geographic Data Management System [*Computer science*]
GDMS	Global Data Management System
GDMS	Glow-Discharge Mass Spectroscopy [*or Spectrometry*]
GDMS	Graphics Display Management System (MCD)
GDMT	Gemini Detailed Maneuver Table (IAA)
GDN	Garden
GDN	Garden
GDN	Gdansk [*Poland*] [*Airport symbol*] (OAG)
GDN	Giant Descending Neuron [*Neurology*]
GDN	Glycol Dinitrate [*Organic chemistry*]
GDN	Golden News Resources Corp. [*Vancouver Stock Exchange symbol*]
GDN	Government Data Network [*Telecommunications*] (OSI)
Gdn	Guanidine [*Biochemistry*]
GDN	Guardian
GDNC	Guidance (MSA)
GDNCE	Guidance (AFM)
GDNF	Glial-Derived Growth Factor [*Biochemistry*]
GDNS	Gardens (MCD)
Gdns	Gardens (DD)
GDNS	Gardens
GDO	Garage Door Opener (NG)
gdo	Gate-Dip Oscillator (IDOE)
GDO	General Development Order [*Town and country planning*] [*British*]
GDO	Grid-Dip Oscillator
gdo	Grid-Dip Oscillator (IDOE)
GDO	Gross Domestic Output [*Economics*]
GDO	Guasdualito [*Venezuela*] [*Airport symbol*] (OAG)
GDO	Guidance Officer (KSC)

GDO .... Gun Direction Officer (NATG)
GDO .... Gunn Diode Oscillator [Electronics] (PDAA)
GDOA .... Graphic Data Output Area (CMD)
GDO(A) .... Guild of Dispensing Opticians (Australia)
GDOC .... University of Guelph Document Holdings [Database] [No longer available online]
GDOccHlth ... Graduate Diploma in Occupational Health
GDOES .... Glow-Discharge Optical Emission Spectroscopy
GDOFA .... Guide Dog Owners and Friends' Association [Australia]
GDOP .... Geometric Degradation of Position [Aerospace]
GDOP .... Geometric Dilution of Precision
GDoS .... South Georgia College, Douglas, GA [Library symbol Library of Congress] (LCLS)
GDP .... Gaede Diffusion Pump
GDP .... Gale Directory of Publications [Later, GDPBM] [A publication]
GDP .... Gallium Photo Diode
GDP .... Gaseous Diffusion Plant [Nuclear energy] (NUCP)
GDP .... Gaseous Discharge Principle
GDP .... Gel Diffusion Precipitin [Biochemistry] (DAVI)
GDP .... General Defense Plan [Formerly, EDP] [NATO] (NATG)
GDP .... General Development Plan (MUGU)
GDP .... Generalized Data Base Processor [Computer science] (MHDI)
GDP .... Generalized Distributor Program [Computer science]
GDP .... Generalized Documentation Processor (NASA)
GDP .... Generalized Drawing Primitive
GDP .... Gesamtdeutsche Partei [All-German Party] [Political party] (PPE)
GDP .... Giant Depolarizing Potential [Neurophysiology]
GDP .... Giant Depolarizing Synaptic Potential [Neurochemistry]
GDP .... Goal-Directed Programming
GDP .... Golden Pond Resources [Vancouver Stock Exchange symbol]
GDP .... Goodrich Petroleum [NYSE symbol] (SAG)
GDP .... Government Data Publications [Information service or system] (IID)
GDP .... Government Development Platform [Marine science] (OSRA)
GDP .... Government Development Platform (USDC)
GDP .... Graphic Display Processor
GDP .... Grid Driving Power
GDP .... Gross Domestic Product [Economics]
GDP .... Grounded into Double Plays [Baseball]
GDP .... Groupe des Democrates Patriotes [Burkina Faso] [Political party] (EY)
GDP .... Guadalupe Pass, TX [Location identifier FAA] (FAAL)
GDP .... Guanosine Diphosphate [Biochemistry]
GDP .... Guanosine Dyphosphate [Biochemistry]
GDP .... Gun Defence Position [Navy British]
GDP .... Gun Director Pointer [Naval gunnery]
GDPA .... General Dental Practitioner's Association [British]
GDPA .... Graduate Diploma in Public Accountancy (DD)
GDPA .... Graduate Diploma in Public Accounting (DD)
GDPA .... Graduate Diploma in Public Administration (PGP)
GDP (A) .... Gross Domestic Product (Average) [Economics]
GDPAP .... Goodrich Petrol 8% Cv'A'Pfd [NASDAQ symbol] (TTSB)
GDPAP .... Goodrich Petroleum [NASDAQ symbol] (SAG)
GDPBM .... Gale Directory of Publications and Broadcast Media [Formerly, GDP] [A publication]
GDP(CL) ...... Gun Director Pointer (Cross Leveler) [Naval gunnery]
GD/PD .... General Dynamics, Pomona Division
GDP (E) .... Gross Domestic Product (Expenditure) [Economics]
GDPGM .... Ground Delay Program [Aviation] (FAAC)
GDP (I) .... Gross Domestic Product (Income) [Economics]
GDP(L) .... Gun Director Pointer (Leveler) [Naval gunnery]
GDPMan ...... Guanosine Diphosphomannose [Biochemistry]
GDP (P) .... Gross Domestic Product (Production) [Economics]
GDP(P) .... Gun Director Pointer (Pointer) [Naval gunnery]
GDPS .... General Disk Programming System [Computer science] (IAA)
GDPS .... Global Data Processing System [World Meteorological Organization]
GDPS .... Government Document Publishing Service
GDP(SS) ...... Gun Director Pointer (Sight Setter) [Naval gunnery]
GDP(T) .... Gun Director Pointer (Trainer) [Naval gunnery]
GDQ .... Golden Dragon Resources [Vancouver Stock Exchange symbol]
GDQ .... Gondar [Ethiopia] [Airport symbol] (OAG)
GDQ .... Lincoln, Nebraska Air National Guard [FAA designator] (FAAC)
GDQF .... Graphical Display and Query Facility [IBM Corp.]
GDR .... Gaol Delivery Roll (ROG)
GDR .... Gaucher's Disease Registry [National Gaucher Foundation - NGF] [Superseded by] (EA)
GDR .... Geodetic Data Reduction
GDR .... Geophysical Data Record
GDR .... German Democratic Republic [East Germany]
GDR .... Giant Dipole Resonance
GDR .... Graphic Depth Recorder
GDR .... Grid Dead Reckon [Military] (CAAL)
GDR .... Ground Delay Response [Telecommunications] (OA)
GDR .... Group Delay Response (IAA)
GDR .... Groupement des Democrates Revolutionnaires [Burkina Faso] [Political party] (EY)
GDR .... Guard Rail (AAG)
GDRC .... Gyro Drift Rate Compensation
GdrcCa .... Goodrich, BF Capital [Associated Press] (SAG)
GDRDA .... Genetically Directed Representational Difference Analysis
GDRE .... Graduate Diploma in Religious Education (PGP)
Gdrich .... [The] Goodrich [B.F.] Co. [Associated Press] (SAG)
GDS .... Agnes Scott College, Decatur, GA [Library symbol Library of Congress] (LCLS)
GDS .... Gas Deployed Skirt (MCD)
GDS .... Gas Dynamic System

GDS .... GDP [Guanosine Diphosphate] Dissociation Stimulator [Biochemistry]
GDS .... Gel Drying System [Chromatography]
GDS .... Gendis, Inc. [Toronto Stock Exchange symbol]
GDS .... General Data Stream [Computer science]
GDS .... General Declassification Schedule (MCD)
GDS .... General Drafting System [Applied Research of Cambridge Ltd.] [Software package] (NCC)
GDS .... Geodetic Data Site
GDS .... Geriatric Depression Scale [Medicine] (DMAA)
GDS .... Gesell Developmental Schedules [Education]
GDS .... Global Deterioration Scale [Medicine]
GDS .... Global Directory Service
GDS .... Global Distribution Systems
GDS .... Glow-Discharge Spectrometry
GDS .... GNC [Guidance and Navigation Computer] Dynamic Simulator [NASA] (NASA)
GDS .... Goldstone, CA [Spaceflight tracking and data network] [NASA] (NASA)
GDS .... Goods
GDS .... Gordon Diagnostic System (EDAC)
GDS .... Government Disclosure Service [A publication] (AAGC)
GDS .... Gradual Dosage Schedule [Medicine] (DMAA)
GDS .... Graphical Display System [Station control and data acquisition] (IEEE)
GDS .... Graphic Data System
GDS .... Graphic Design System
GDS .... Graphic Display Segment
GDS .... Great Dark Spot [Image on Neptune] [Astronomy]
GDS .... Great Dark Spot on Neptune [Astronomy]
GDS .... Ground Data System
GDS .... Ground Display System
Gds .... Guards [British military] (DMA)
GDS .... Gun Display System (MCD)
GDSA .... Goal-Directed Serial Alternation
GDSafH .... Graduate Diploma in Safety and Health
GDSafS .... Graduate Diploma in Safety Science
GDSBFC .... Good Day Sunshine Beatles Fan Club (EA)
GDSC .... Gateway Data Sciences [NASDAQ symbol] (TTSB)
GDSC .... Gateway Data Sciences Corp. [NASDAQ symbol] (SAG)
GDSC .... Geodesic
GDSC .... Graduate Diploma in Social Communication (ADA)
GDSCC .... Goldstone Deep Space Communications Complex [NASA]
GDSD .... Ground Data Systems Divsion [NASA] (NASA)
GDSDF .... Generalized Data Structure Definition Facility [Computer science] (MHDB)
GDSIB .... Global Digital Sea Ice Data Bank (USDC)
GDSIDB .... Global Digital Sea Ice Data Bank [Marine science] (OSRA)
GDSL .... Graduate Diploma in School Librarianship (ADA)
GDSM .... Ground Data Systems Manager (MCD)
GDSM .... Guardsman [Military]
GDSN .... Global Digital Seismic Network
GDSN .... Global Digital Seismograph Network [Earthquake study]
GDSO .... Ground Data Systems Officer (MCD)
GDSS .... Global Decision Support System (MCD)
GDSSc .... Graduate Diploma in Sport Science
GDSSR .... GDSD [Ground Data Systems Division] Staff Support Room [NASA] (NASA)
GDT .... Gas Decay Tank (NRCH)
GDT .... Gas Discharge Tube
GD/T .... General Dynamics/Telecommunications
GDT .... Generator Development Tools [Silicon Design Laboratories] (NITA)
GDT .... Geographic Data Technology, Inc. [Information service or system] (IID)
GDT .... Global Descriptor Table [Computer science]
GDT .... Golden Diamond Travel and Tourism Agency [Saudi Arabia]
GDT .... Graduate Diploma in Taxation (PGP)
GDT .... Graduate Diploma in Theology (PGP)
GDT .... Grand Turk [British West Indies] [Airport symbol] (OAG)
GDT .... Graphic Display Terminal
GDT .... Ground Data Terminal
GDT .... Ground Delay Time (IAA)
GDT .... Guidant Corp. [NYSE symbol] (SAG)
GDTE .... Graduate Diploma in Technological Entrepreneurship (PGP)
GDTL .... Graduate Diploma in Teacher Librarianship (ADA)
GDTR .... Global Descriptor Table Register [Computer science] (PCM)
GDTS .... Gliding Deceleration Technology System
GDU .... Garbage Disposal Unit (ADA)
GDU .... Gastroduodenal Ulcer [Medicine] (DMAA)
GDU .... Glendale Resources, Inc. [Vancouver Stock Exchange symbol]
GDU .... Graphic Display Unit
GDU .... Guide Dog Users (EA)
GDunGS .... Church of Jesus Christ of Latter-Day Saints, Genealogical Society Library, SandySprings Georgia Branch, Dunwoody, GA [Library symbol Library of Congress] (LCLS)
G Dur .... Guillelmus Durandi [Deceased, 1296] [Authority cited in pre-1607 legal work] (DSA)
G Duran .... Guillelmus Durandi [Deceased, 1296] [Authority cited in pre-1607 legal work] (DSA)
GDurng .... Grupo Industrial Durango SA de CV [Associated Press] (SAG)
GDuV .... United States Veterans Administration Center, Dublin, GA [Library symbol Library of Congress] (LCLS)
GDV .... Gastric Dilatation Volvulus
GDV .... Geomagnetic Daily Variations
GDV .... Glendive [Montana] [Airport symbol] (OAG)

GdVP .... Grossdeutsche Volkspartei [*Pan-German People's Party*] [*Austria Political party*] (PPE)
GDVS .... Greater Delaware Valley Savings Bank [*NASDAQ symbol*] (SAG)
GDVS .... Greater Del Valley Svgs [*NASDAQ symbol*] (TTSB)
GDW .... Gladwin, MI [*Location identifier FAA*] (FAAL)
GDW .... Glass-Distilled Water [*Medicine*] (DMAA)
GDW .... Golden West Financial Corp. [*NYSE symbol*] (SPSG)
GDW .... Golden West Finl [*NYSE symbol*] (TTSB)
GDW .... Goldwest Resources Ltd. [*Vancouver Stock Exchange symbol*]
GDWND .... Gradient Wind (NOAA)
GDX .... Gated-Diode Crosspoint [*Electronics*] (PDAA)
GDX .... Genovese Drug Stores, Inc. [*AMEX symbol*] (SPSG)
GDX .... Glycidydiisopropylidenexylitol [*Organic chemistry*]
GDX .... Goldstone, California [*Spaceflight Tracking and Data Network*] [*NASA*]
GDX .... Grandex Resources Ltd. [*Vancouver Stock Exchange symbol*]
GDX .... Gun Direction Exercise [*British military*] (DMA)
GDX .... Upperville, VA [*Location identifier FAA*] (FAAL)
GDXA .... Genovese Drug Str'A' [*AMEX symbol*] (TTSB)
GDY .... Grundy, VA [*Location identifier FAA*] (FAAL)
GdyFam ...... Goody's Family Clothing [*Associated Press*] (SAG)
GDYL .... Great Dictionary of the Yiddish Language [*Columbia University Department of Linguistics*] [*Information service or system*] (IID)
GDYN .... Geodynamics Corp. [*NASDAQ symbol*] (NQ)
GDYS .... Goody's Family Clothing [*NASDAQ symbol*] (SPSG)
GE .... Federal Republic of Germany [*NATO*]
GE .... Garrison Engineer [*British military*] (DMA)
GE .... Garrison Extracts [*Army*]
GE .... Gas Ejection [*Opening*] [*Technical drawings*]
GE .... Gas Examiner [*British*]
GE .... Gastroemotional [*Medicine*] (MAE)
GE .... Gastroenterology [*Medicine*]
GE .... Gastroenterostomy [*Medicine*]
GE .... Gastroesophageal [*Medicine*] (CPH)
GE .... Gateway Exchange [*Telecommunications*]
GE .... Gauge
GE .... Gaussian Elimination (IEEE)
Ge .... Gecelinus [*Zenzelinus de Cassanis*] [*Deceased, 1334*] [*Authority cited in pre-1607 legal work*] (DSA)
GE .... Gel Electrophoresis [*Analytical chemistry*]
GE .... General Election
GE .... General Electric (NITA)
GE .... General Electric Co. [*NYSE symbol*] (SPSG)
GE .... General Electric Vallecitos Nuclear Center (DOGT)
GE .... General Examination
GE .... General Expenses
GE .... Generator of Excitation [*Medicine*] (DMAA)
GE .... Gentamicin [*Antibacterial compound*] [*Generic form*]
GE .... Geoscience Electronics (MCD)
Ge .... Germanium [*Chemical element*]
GE .... Germany (NATG)
ge .... Germany, East [*MARC country of publication code Library of Congress*] (LCCP)
GE .... Gilbert Islands [*ANSI two-letter standard code Obsolete*] (CNC)
GE .... [*The*] Gilgamesh Epic and Old Testament Parallels [*A publication*] (BJA)
ge .... Gilt-Edge (WDMC)
GE .... Gilt Edges [*Bookbinding*]
GE .... Gimbal Electronics
GE .... Gnome Engine [*Hovercraft*]
GE .... Good Evening [*Amateur radio*]
GE .... Grand Earl [*Freemasonry*] (ROG)
GE .... Grand East [*Freemasonry*] (ROG)
GE .... Grand Encampment [*Freemasonry*]
GE .... Grand Expert [*Freemasonry*] (ROG)
GE .... Grand Ezra [*Freemasonry*] (ROG)
G/E .... Granulocyte-Erythroid (Ratio) [*Hematology*]
G/E .... Graphite Epoxy (NASA)
GE .... Gravissimam Educationis [*Declaration on Christian Education*] [*Vatican II document*]
G-E .... Gravity Eliminated (DAVI)
GE .... Great Educators [*A publication*]
GE .... Greater than or Equal To [*FORTRAN*]
GE .... Great Exuma [*Bahama Islands*]
GE .... Gripper Edge [*Bookbinding*] (DGA)
GE .... Gross Earnings [*Business term*]
GE .... Grounded Emitter
GE .... Ground Equipment
GE .... Group Engineer
GE .... Group of Experts (NATG)
GE .... Guernsey Airlines [*ICAO designator*] (AD)
GE .... Gyro Error
GEA .... Farbenfabriken Bayer [*Germany*] [*Research code symbol*]
GEA .... Gale Environmental Almanac [*A publication*]
GEA .... Gamma Energy Analysis [*Nuclear energy*] (NUCP)
GEA .... Garage Equipment Association (EAIO)
GEA .... Gas Evolution Analysis (DICI)
GEA .... Gastric Electrical Activity [*Medicine*] (DMAA)
GEA .... General Electric-ARSD, Sunnyvale, CA [*OCLC symbol*] (OCLC)
GEA .... Georgia Air [*Czechoslovakia*] [*ICAO designator*] (FAAC)
GEA .... German East Africa [*Obsolete*] (ROG)
GEA .... Gigabit Ethernet Alliance [*Telecommunications*] (ACRL)
GEA .... Global Education Associates (EA)
GEA .... Glossary of EPA [*Environmental Protection Agency*] Acronyms [*A publication*] (EPA)

GEA .... Gravure Engravers Association (EA)
GEA .... Greater East Asia [*Used by Japanese in such terms as War of Greater East Asia and Greater East Asia Co-Prosperity Sphere*] [*World War II*]
GEA .... Greater Ecosystem Alliance (EA)
GEA .... Gross External Area
GEA .... Grupo de Economistas y Asociados [*Provides economic analysis in Mexico and abroad*] (CROSS)
GEA .... Noumea [*New Caledonia*] Magenta Airport [*Airport symbol*] (OAG)
GEAAE .... Groupement Europeen des Artistes des Ardennes et de l'Eifel [*European Group of Artists of the Ardennes and the Eifel*] (EAIO)
GEAB .... Geophysical Abstracts [*A publication*]
GEADGE .... German Air Defense Ground Environment
GEAG .... General Electric Airborne Guidance (AAG)
GEAMR .... Groupement Europeen des Associations des Maisons de Reforme [*EC*] (ECED)
GE & JR ..... Great Eastern & Joint Railway [*British*] (ROG)
GE-ANPD ..... General Electric Aircraft Nuclear Propulsion Department (SAA)
GEANS .... Gimbaled Electrostatic-Gyro Aircraft Navigation System [*Air Force*]
GEaO .... Ocmulgee Regional Library System, Eastman, GA [*Library symbol*] [*Library of Congress*] (LCLS)
GEAP .... General Electric Atomic Power [*or Products*]
GEAP .... Groupe Europeen d'Administration Publique [*European Group of Public Administration - EGPA*] [*Brussels, Belgium*] (EAIO)
GEAPS .... Grain Elevator and Processing Society (EA)
GEAR .... Great Eastern Australian Rally [*Cycling*]
Gear Landl & T... Gear on Landlord and Tenant [*A publication*] (DLA)
GEASCOP .... General Asymptotic Composition Program [*Computer science*]
GE/ASD .... General Electric/Apollo Support Division (KSC)
GEAU .... Groupe d'Etudes et d'Actions Urbaines [*Canada*]
GEAV .... Guidance Error Analysis Vehicles [*Air Force*]
GEB .... Geboren [*Born*] [*German*]
GEB .... Gebrueder [*Brothers*] [*German*]
GEB .... Gebunden [*Bound*] [*Publishing*] [*German*]
GEB .... General Engine Bulletin
GEB .... Guiding Eyes for the Blind (EA)
GEBA .... Global Energy Balance Archive [*A publication*]
GEBA .... Global Energy Balance Archive
GEBA .... Government Excess Baggage Authorization
GEBCO .... General Bathymetric Chart of the Oceans [*International Hydrographic Bureau*]
GEC .... Galactose Elimination Capacity
GEC .... Gaseous Electronics Conference
GEC .... Geauga County Public Library, Chardon, OH [*OCLC symbol*] (OCLC)
GEC .... GEICO Corp. [*NYSE symbol*] (SPSG)
GEC .... General Electric Capital Exchange [*Associated Press*] (SAG)
GEC .... General Electric Co.
GEC .... General Electrodynamics Corp. (MCD)
GEC .... General Equipment Command [*Army*]
GEC .... Generalized Equivalent Cylinder (OA)
GEC .... Geneva Executives Club (EA)
GEC .... German Cargo Services [*ICAO designator*] (FAAC)
GEC .... Global Environmental Change [*Marine science*] (OSRA)
GEC .... Glomerular Epithelial Cell [*Medicine Medicine*] (DMAA)
GEC .... Government Employees Council [*Later, PED*] (EA)
GEC .... Graphic Export Center [*Netherlands*]
GEC .... Grolier Educational Corp. (AEBS)
GEC .... Ground Environment Complex (MCD)
GEC .... Lufthansa Cargo, AG [*Germany*] [*FAA designator*] (FAAC)
GECA .... Government Employees' Compensation Act [*1908*]
GECAL .... General Electric Caliber [*Gatling Gun*]
GECAL .... General Electric Credit Auto Lease, Inc.
GECC .... Gasoline Engine, Close-Coupled
GECC .... General Electric Capital Corp.
GECC .... Government Employees Clinic Center [*British*]
GECCMSEF.... Group to Establish Criteria for Certifying Munitions Systems to Electromagnetic Fields [*DoD*] (RDA)
GECCS .... General Electric Company Computer Services [*British*] (NITA)
GECE .... Groupement Europeen des Caisses d'Epargne [*European Savings Bank Group*] [*EC*] (ECED)
GECECS .... General Electric Chemical Engineering Calculation System
Gecel .... Gecelinus [*Zenzelinus de Cassanis*] [*Deceased, 1334*] [*Authority cited in pre-1607 legal work*] (DSA)
GECEP .... General Civil Engineering Package (IAA)
GECM .... GENICOM Corp. [*NASDAQ symbol*] (NQ)
GECO .... Guidance Engine Cutoff [*NASA*] (KSC)
GECOM .... General Compiler (NITA)
GECOM .... Generalized Compiler [*Computer science*]
GECOR .... General Communication Routine (IAA)
GECOS .... General Comprehensive Operating Supervisor [*Computer science*]
GECOS .... General Comprehensive Operating System
GECOS .... General Electric Comprehensive Operating System [*Computer science*] (NHD)
GECR .... Global Environment Change Report (EERA)
GECS .... Graphite-Epoxy Composite Structure (PDAA)
GECS .... Ground Environmental Control System (IAA)
GED .... Gasoline Engine Driven
GED .... Gas-Phase Electron Diffraction [*Physics*]
Ged .... Gedaagde [*Defendant*] [*Netherlands*] (ILCA)
GED .... Gedampft [*Muted*] [*Music*]
GED .... Gedeh [*Java*] [*Seismograph station code, US Geological Survey Closed*] (SEIS)
GED .... General Educational Development [*Test*]
GED .... General Equivalency Diploma [*For nongraduates*]
GED .... Geo-Data International [*Vancouver Stock Exchange symbol*]

GED .... Georgetown [Delaware] [Airport symbol] (AD)
GED .... Georgetown, DE [Location identifier FAA] (FAAL)
GED .... Global Engineering Documents [Santa Ana, CA] [Information service or system]
GED .... Government Electronics Division
GED .... Gross Earnings Deflator [Economics] (BARN)
GED .... Group on Electronic Devices
GED .... Gunn Effect Device
GEDA .... Goldfields Esperance Development Authority [Australia]
GEDA .... Goodyear Electronic Differential Analyzer (IAA)
GEDAC .... General Electric Detection and Automatic Correction (NASA)
GEDAN .... General Data Analyzer (IAA)
GEDI .... General Educational Development Institute (EA)
GEDI .... Groupe d'Etudes en Developpement International [International Development Studies Group] [Canada]
GEDIS .... Geological, Exploration and Development Information System [Australia]
GEDIS .... Groupement Europeen des Enterprises de Distribution Integrees [European Multiple Retailers Association] [Belgium EC] (ECED)
GEDIT .... General-Purpose Text Editor [Computer science] (MHDB)
GEdO .... Group Education Officer [British military] (DMA)
GEDP .... General Educational Development Program [Army] (AABC)
GEDPD .... Gallaudet Encyclopedia of Deaf People and Deafness [A publication]
GEDRT .... Group European d'Echange d'Experience sur la Direction de la Recherche Textil e [European Group for the Exchange of Information on Textile Research] (PDAA)
GEDS .... Gaseous Emissions Data System [Environmental Protection Agency] (GFGA)
GEDT .... General Educational Development Test
GEDU .... Gun Elevation Displacement Unit (DNAB)
GEE .... Geehi [Australia Seismograph station code, US Geological Survey Closed] (SEIS)
GEE .... Geeseair [Canada ICAO designator] (FAAC)
GEE .... General Estimating Equation [Mathematics]
GEE .... General Evaluation Equipment
GEE .... Generalized Estimating Equation (DMAA)
GEE .... Geneseo, NY [Location identifier FAA] (FAAL)
GEE .... Glycine Ethyl Ester (MAE)
GEE .... Gross Ecosystem Exchange [Biology]
GEE .... Group for Environmental Education
GEE .... Group of Economic Experts (EERA)
GEEB .... Geerlings & Wade [NASDAQ symbol] (TTSB)
GE economic forecasts... General Economic Forecasts [Databank] (NITA)
GEEIA .... Ground Electronics Engineering Installation Agency [Air Force]
GEEK .... Geomagnetic Electrokinetograph [Equipment for exploring ocean depths]
GEEL .... General Election Expenditure Limit [Federal Election Commission]
GE ENG ...... Geological Engineer (WDAA)
Ge Engr ...... Geological Engineer
GEEP .... General Electric Electronic Processor
GEEP .... Group of Experts on Environmental Pollutants (EERA)
GEER .... Geerlings & Wade, Inc. [NASDAQ symbol] (SAG)
GeerlWd ..... Geerlings & Wade, Inc. [Associated Press] (SAG)
GEESE .... General Electric Electronic System Evaluator
GEF .... Air GEFCO [France ICAO designator] (FAAC)
GEF .... Gauss Error Function [Mathematics]
GEF .... Gel Electrofocusing [Analytical chemistry]
GEF .... General Electric Co. and Fanuc Automation Corp.
GEF .... Global Environment Facility [Implemented jointly by the World Bank, the United Nations Environment Program, and the United Nations Development Program]
GEF .... Global Environment Fund [of the World Bank] (EERA)
GEF .... Gonadotropin Enhancing Factor [Endocrinology]
GEF .... Gradient Elution Fractionation
GEF .... Gravure Education Foundation (EA)
GEF .... Greenville, FL [Location identifier FAA] (FAAL)
GEF .... Ground Equipment Failure [Air Force]
GEF .... Guanine-Nucleotide-Exchange Factor [Biochemistry]
GEF .... Guanine-Nucleoxide Exchange Factor [Biochemistry]
GEFA .... Gulf-European Freight Association [Defunct]
GEFACS ...... Groupement des Fabricants d'Appareils Sanitaires en Ceramique de la CEE [Group of Manufacturers of Ceramic Sanitary Ware of the European Economic Community] (PDAA)
GEFAP .... Groupement Europeen des Associations Nationales des Fabricants de Pesticides [European Group of National Pesticide Manufacturer' Associations] [Common Market]
GEFDU .... Groupe Europeen des Femmes Diplomees des Universites [University Women of Europe - UWE] (EA)
GEFFEN .... Gay Extremists Fighting Fascistic Entertainment Normalcy [Focus group of Queer Nation]
GEFP .... Guild of Ethical Funeral Practice (EA)
GEFRC .... General File/Record Control [Honeywell, Inc.]
GEFS .... General Electric Financial Services [Australia Commercial firm]
GEFS .... General Electric Flame Site (MUGU)
GEFT .... Group Embedded Figure Test [Education]
GEG .... Gamma Eta Gamma [Fraternity]
GEG .... Gegechkori [Former USSR Seismograph station code, US Geological Survey Closed] (SEIS)
GEG .... Generalized Euclidian Geometry (OA)
GEG .... Grange Gold Corp. [Vancouver Stock Exchange symbol]
GEG .... Gravure Engraving [British] (DBA)
GEG .... Gun Evaluation Group [Military] (CAAL)
GEG .... Spokane [Washington] [Airport symbol] (OAG)
GEGAS .... General Electric Gas [Process]
GEGB .... General Electricity-Generating Board (OA)

GEGID .... Global Spill Mgmt [NASDAQ symbol] (TTSB)
GE-GLOSS ... Group of Experts on the Global Sea-Level Observing System [Marine science] (OSRA)
GEGP .... Golden Eagle Group [NASDAQ symbol] (TTSB)
GEGP .... Golden Eagle Group, Inc. [NASDAQ symbol] (SAG)
GEGPW .... Golden Eagle Group Wrrt [NASDAQ symbol] (TTSB)
GEGR .... General Grant National Memorial
GEGS .... General Electric Guidance System [Aerospace] (AAG)
Geh .... Gehalt [Contents] [German]
Geh .... Geheimrat [Privy Councillor] [German] (ILCA)
GEH .... George Eastman House [Rochester, NY]
GE-HAPO ..... General Electric Hanford Atomic Products Operation (SAA)
GEHL .... Gehl Co. [NASDAQ symbol] (NQ)
GEHME .... General Electric Heavy Military Electronics (IAA)
GEI .... Geisinger Medical Center, Medical Library, Danville, PA [OCLC symbol] (OCLC)
GEI .... Gender Equality Indicator [Australia]
GEI .... Geographic Enforcement Initiative [Environmental Protection Agency] (EPA)
GEI .... Graphics Engine Interface [Computer science]
GEI .... Graymoor Ecumenical Institute (EA)
GEI .... Grenlock Energy, Inc. [Vancouver Stock Exchange symbol]
GEI .... Gruppo Esponenti Italiani (EA)
GEICO .... GEICO Corp. [Associated Press] (SAG)
GEICO .... Government Employees Insurance Co.
GEIDC .... Greater Erie Industrial Development Corp. [Pennsylvania]
GEIL .... Greenfield Industries [NASDAQ symbol] (TTSB)
GEIMS .... General Electric Inventory Management System (IAA)
GEIP .... Greenhouse Education and Information Program (EERA)
GEIPS .... General Electric Industrial and Power Systems [Australia Commercial firm]
GEIR .... GPETE End Item Replacement (NVT)
GEIS .... GE [General Electric Co.] Information Services [Information service or system] (IID)
GEIS .... Generalized Environmental Impact Statement
GEIS .... Generic Environmental Impact Statement [or Study] [Nuclear energy] (NRCH)
GEISA .... Gestion et Etude des Informations Spectroscopiques Atmospheriques [Database] [Laboratoire de Meteorologie Dynamique du CNRS] [French] [Information service or system] (CRD)
GEISCO .... General Electric Information Services Co. [General Electric Co.] [Software manufacturer] [Information service or system Telecommunications] (IID)
GEISHA .... Geodetic Inertial Survey and Horizontal Alignment (IEEE)
GEISHA .... Gun Electron-Induced Semiconductor Hybrid Amplifier
GEJ .... Gaseous Ejection (KSC)
GEJ .... Gastroesophageal Junction [Anatomy] (DAVI)
GEK .... Ganes Creek, AK [Location identifier FAA] (FAAL)
GEK .... Geomagnetic Electrokinetograph [Equipment for exploring ocean depths]
GEL .... Gambcrest Enterprises Ltd. [Gambia] [ICAO designator] (FAAC)
GEL .... Gelatin
gel .... Gelatin [Theatrical lighting] (WDMC)
gel .... Gelatin (VRA)
GEL .... General Electric Laboratory
GEL .... General Electric Lighting [Australia Commercial firm]
GEL .... General Emulation Language
GEL .... Genesis Energy LP [NYSE symbol] (SAG)
GEL .... Gilbert Islands [ANSI three-letter standard code Obsolete] (CNC)
GEL .... Goldenlode Resources Ltd. [Vancouver Stock Exchange symbol]
GEL .... Groupement Europeen de Lymphologie [European Lymphology Group - ELG] [Brussels, Belgium] (EAIO)
GEL .... Guaranteed Employment Level
GEL .... Santo Angelo [Brazil] [Airport symbol] (OAG)
GELAC .... Georgia Division, Lockheed Aircraft Corp.
GELAP .... General Electric Computer Analysis Program
GELC .... Groupe des Editeurs de Livres de la CEE [Book Publishers Group of EEC] (EAIO)
Gelcap .... Gelatin-Coated Capsule [Pharmacy]
Geld & M.... Geldart and Maddock's English Chancery Reports [6 Maddock's Reports] [A publication] (DLA)
Geld & O .... Nova Scotia Decisions, by Geldert and Oxley [A publication] (DLA)
Geld & Ox .. Nova Scotia Decisions, by Geldert and Oxley [A publication] (DLA)
Geld & R .... Geldert and Russell's Nova Scotia Reports [A publication] (DLA)
Geldart .... Geldart and Maddock's English Chancery Reports [6 Maddock's Reports] [A publication] (DLA)
GElektr .... Grupo Elektra SA de CV [Associated Press] (SAG)
GELFAC .... Gel Frontal Analysis Chromatography
GELIS .... Ground Emitter Location and Identification System [Army]
GELIS-H ..... Ground Emitter Location and Identification System - High [Army]
GELME .... General Electric Light Military Electronics (IAA)
GelmSci ...... Gelman Sciences, Inc. [Associated Press] (SAG)
GELOAD ...... General Loader [Honeywell] (NITA)
GELOC .... Geolocation (DOMA)
GEL QUAV .. Gelatina Quavis [In Any Kind of Jelly] [Pharmacy] (ROG)
GelTex .... GelTex Pharmaceuticals, Inc. [Associated Press] (SAG)
GELTSPAP ... Group of Experts on Long-Term Scientific Policy and Planning [UNESCO]
GELX .... GelTex Pharmaceuticals [NASDAQ symbol] (TTSB)
GELX .... GelTex Pharmaceuticals, Inc. [NASDAQ symbol] (SAG)
GEM .... Bristol BAE [British ICAO designator] (FAAC)
GEM .... Gamma-Electron-Muon [Particle detector]
GEM .... Gas Energy Management
GEM .... Gas Engine Management [Alternative fuel conversion equipment]
GEM .... Gas Equipment Manufacturers' Group (IIA)

GEM............ Gas Exchange Module [Cell culture]
GEM............ Gateway to Educational Materials
GEM............ Gateway to Educational Materials
Gem............ Gemara (BJA)
Gem............ Geminatae (BJA)
gem............ Geminate [Chemistry]
Gem............ Gemini [Constellation]
GEM............ General Effectiveness Model (DNAB)
GEM............ General Electric Motors [Australia Commercial firm]
GEM............ General Enrollment Manual
GEM............ General Epitaxial Monolith (IEEE)
GEM............ Generic Electronic Module (SSD)
GEM............ Generic Experiment Module
GEM............ Genetically Engineered Microorganism
gem............ Germanic [MARC language code Library of Congress] (LCCP)
GEM............ GeV Electron Microtron [Atomic accelerator] [Proposed]
GEM............ Giant Earth Mover [Machine]
GEM............ Giotto Extended Mission [European Space Agency]
GEM............ Goddard Earth Model [NASA]
GEM............ Government-Education-Medical
GEM............ Government Electronics Market (IAA)
GEM............ Graduated [or Growing] Equity Mortgage
GEM............ Graff Electronic Machines Ltd. [British]
GEM............ Graphic Engine Monitor (DA)
GEM............ Graphics Environment Manager [Computer science]
GEM............ Graphite Electrode Contouring Machine (PDAA)
GEM............ Graphite Epoxy Motor (MCD)
GEM............ Ground Effect Machine (NG)
GEM............ Ground Electronics Maintenance
GEM............ Ground Elevation Meter (PDAA)
GEM............ Ground Exploitation Module
GEM............ Groupes Evangile et Mission [Institute of the Heart of Jesus - IHJ] [France] (EA)
GEM............ Growing Equity Mortgage
GEM............ Growth with Equity in Mindano [A USAID backed organization] [Philippines]
GEM............ Grupo Embotellador de Mexico [NYSE symbol] (SAG)
GEM............ Grupo Embotellador Mex GDS [NYSE symbol] (TTSB)
GEM............ Guidance Evaluation Missile
GEM............ Guild of Experienced Motorists [British] (DBA)
GEM............ Gulf Energy & Minerals Co.
GEM............ Gun Effectiveness Model
GEM............ Gunn Effect Material
GEM............ Gyro Energy & Minerals Corp. [Vancouver Stock Exchange symbol]
GEM............ Miami, FL [Location identifier FAA] (FAAL)
GEMl............ National Consortium for Graduate Degrees for Minorities in Engineering (EA)
GEMA........... Gale Encyclopedia of Multicultural America [A publication]
GEMA........... Grain Equipment Manufacturers Association (EA)
GEMA........... Gymnastic Equipment Manufacturers' Association [British] (BI)
GE/MAC...... General Electric Measurement and Control
GEMAGS...... General Electric Magnetically Anchored Gravity System
GEMAS........ Groupement Europeen des Maisons d'Alimentation et d'Approvisionnement a Succursales [European Group of Food and Provision Chain Stores] [Common Market Brussels, Belgium]
GEmbMx...... Grupo Embotellador de Mexico [Associated Press] (SAG)
GEMC.......... Geriatric & Medical Companies [NASDAQ symbol] (NQ)
GEMC.......... Geriatric & Medl Cos. [NASDAQ symbol] (TTSB)
GEMCO........ Global Electronic Markets Co. [Joint venture of Citicorp and McGraw-Hill, In c. to provide computerized buying, selling, shipping, and insuring services for commodities traders]
GEMCO........ Groote Eylandt Mining Co. [Australia Commercial firm]
GEMCOS...... Generalized Message Control System (BUR)
Gemi.......... Gemini [Constellation]
Gemi.......... Geminiano [Flourished, 1407-09] [Authority cited in pre-1607 legal work] (DSA)
GEMI.......... Global Environmental Management Initiative [Environmental science]
GemlI.......... Gemini II Fund, Inc. [Associated Press] (SAG)
GEMIM........ Group of Experts on Marine Information Management [Marine science] (OSRA)
GEML.......... Melilla [Spain ICAO location identifier] (ICLI)
GEMM......... Generalized Electronics Maintenance Model
GEMM......... Generic Missile Model (MCD)
GEMM......... Gilt-Edged Market Maker [London Stock Exchange] [England]
GEMM......... Granulocyte, Erythroid, Macrophage, Megakaryocyte [Hematology]
GEMMA....... Gilt-Edged Market Makers' Association [London Stock Exchange] [England]
GEMMS....... Geophysical Exploration Manned Mobile Submersible
GEMMSS..... Ground Emplaced Mine Scattering System [Military] (RDA)
GEMO.......... Ground Electronic Maintenance Officer [NASA] (NG)
GEMP.......... Government Energy Management Program [Australia]
GEMS......... Gender Equality in Mathematics and Science
GEMS......... General Education Management System [Computer science] (IEEE)
GEMS......... General Electrical and Mechanical Systems (IAA)
GEMS......... General Electric Manufacturing Simulator (IEEE)
GEMS......... General Electric Medical Systems [Australia Commercial firm]
GEMS......... General Energy and Materials Balance System [Chemical engineering] [Computer science]
GEMS......... General Engine Management System
GEMS......... General Equipment Maintenance System [Software] [Diagonal Data Corp.] [Automotive engineering]
GEMS......... Generalized Evaluation Model Simulator [NASA]
GEMS......... Geostationary European Meteorological Satellite
GEMS......... German Mass Spectrometer

GEMS......... Glass with Embedded Metal and Sulphide [In interplanetary dust particles]
GEMS......... Glenayre Technologies [NASDAQ symbol] (TTSB)
GEMS......... Glenayre Techs, Inc. [NASDAQ symbol] (SAG)
GEMS......... Global Environment Monitoring System [UNEP] [Database producer] (IID)
GEMS......... Good Emergency Mother Substitute [Pediatrics] (DAVI)
GEMS......... Government Expenditure Management System [Australia]
GEMS......... Graphical Exposure Modeling System [For estimating pollutants]
GEMS......... Graphics Engineering and Mapping System [Navy] (GFGA)
GEMS......... Ground Emplaced Mine Scattering System [Military] (AABC)
GEMS......... Ground Equipment Maintenance Squadron
GEMS......... Growth, Economy, Management, and Customer Satisfaction [Procedure for establishing management goals]
GEMSA........ Guanidinoethylmercaptosuccinic Acid [Biochemistry]
GeMSAEC..... General Medical Sciences and Atomic Energy Commission
GEMSAT ...... Girls' Education in Mathematics, Science, and Technology (AIE)
GEMSERVICE... Global Electronic Mail Service [Electronic Mail Corp. of America] [Old Greenwich, CT] [Telecommunications] (TSSD)
GEMSI .... Group of Experts on Methods, Standards, and Intercalibration [Oceanography] (MSC)
GEMSIP ...... Gemini Stability Improvement Program [NASA]
GEMSS .... Ground Emplaced Mine Scattering System [Military] (RDA)
Gemstr........ Gemstar International Group Ltd. [Associated Press] (SAG)
GEMSVD .... General Electric Missile and Space Vehicle Department [Military] (IAA)
GEMT........... Group of European Metallurgical Thermodynamicists [National Physical Laboratory] [Databank] (NITA)
GEMU .... German Economic and Monetary Union
GEN .... Business Operations Support Services [British] [FAA designator] (FAAC)
Gen............ Gecelinus [Zenzelinus de Cassanis] [Deceased, 1334] [Authority cited in pre-1607 legal work] (DSA)
GEN .... Genavco Air Ltd. [British ICAO designator] (FAAC)
GEN .... Gender
GEN .... Genealogy
GEN .... General (AABC)
Gen............ General (ODBW)
GEN .... General
gen............ General (VRA)
gen............ General (DMAA)
GEN .... General Electric Network [Computer science]
GEN .... Generate
gen............ Generate [News media] (WDMC)
GEN .... Generation (MSA)
GEN .... Generator [Computer science] (AAG)
gen............ Generator (IDOE)
GEN .... Generic
Gen............ Genesis [Old Testament book]
GEN .... Genetics
GEN .... Geneva [City in Switzerland]
GEN .... Genital
gen............ Genital [Medicine] (DMAA)
GEN .... Genitive [Case] [Grammar]
GEN .... Genoa [Italy] [Seismograph station code, US Geological Survey Closed] (SEIS)
GEN .... GenRad, Inc. [NYSE symbol] (SPSG)
GEN .... Genuine (ADA)
GEN .... Genus [Biology]
GEN .... Gerin, Inc. [Toronto Stock Exchange symbol]
GEN .... Gilgamesh, Enkidu, and the Netherworld (BJA)
GEN .... Greater Lenora Resources Corp. [Toronto Stock Exchange symbol Vancouver Stock Exchange symbol]
GEN .... Oslo [Norway] Ardermoen Airport [Airport symbol] (OAG)
GENA .... Ground Environment and Navigational Aid (PDAA)
Gen Abr Cas Eq... General Abridgment of Cases in Equity [Equity Cases Abridged] [1677-1744] [A publication] (DLA)
Gen AF .... General of the Air Force (WGA)
Gen An .... De Generatione Animalium [of Aristotle] [Classical studies] (OCD)
GEN AV....... General Average (WDAA)
GENB .... [The] Genesee Brewing Co., Inc. [NASDAQ symbol] (NQ)
GENB .... Genessee Brewing [NASDAQ symbol] (SAG)
GENBANK .... Genetic Sequences Databank [Intelligenetics, Inc.] [Information service or system] (IID)
GENBB........ Genesee Corp. 'B' [NASDAQ symbol] (TTSB)
GENC .... General Electric Nose Cone [Aerospace] (AAG)
GEN CAR ..... General Cargo [Shipping] (DS)
GENCHEM .... General Chemical Indicators [Database] [Probe Economics, Inc.] [Information service or system] (CRD)
Gen Con ..... General Counsel (AAGC)
GENCONV .... Geneva Conventions [Military] (NVT)
Gencor........ Gencor Industries, Inc. [Associated Press] (SAG)
Gen Corr...... De Generatione et Corruptione [of Aristotle] [Classical studies] (OCD)
GenCrp........ GenCorp, Inc. [Associated Press] (SAG)
GEND .... Generated Data File [Computer science]
GENDA .... General Data Analysis and Simulation (IAA)
GENDARME... Generalized Data Reduction, Manipulation, Evaluation
GEN DEL ...... General Delivery
GENDEP....... General Depot [Military]
GENDET....... General Detail [Coast Guard]
Gen Dig ...... General Digest [A publication] (DLA)
Gen Dig NS... General Digest, New Series [A publication] (DLA)
GENDIS........ General Distribution [Pentagon security classification code]
GENDISP...... General Dispensary [Military]

GENDYN ..... General Dynamics
GENE .... Genome Therapeutics [*NASDAQ symbol*] (TTSB)
GENE .... Genome Therapeutics Corp [*NASDAQ symbol*] (SAG)
GENEAL ..... Genealogy
GenEl .... General Electric Co. [*Associated Press*] (SAG)
GeneLTc ..... GeneLabs Technologies, Inc. [*Associated Press*] (SAG)
GeneMed .... GeneMedicine, Inc. [*Associated Press*] (SAG)
GENENG ..... Generalized Engine [*Computer science*]
Genentc ...... Genentech, Inc. [*Associated Press*] (SAG)
Generation... Generations [*A publication*] (BRI)
GENESCO .... General Shoe Corp. [*Acronym now official name of firm*]
GenesCp ..... [*The*] Genessee Brewing Company, Inc. [*Associated Press*] (SAG)
GENESIS ..... Generation Simulation System [*Power systems*]
Genesis ...... Genesis Health Ventures, Inc. [*Associated Press*] (SAG)
GenesisH.... Genesis Health Ventures, Inc. [*Associated Press*] (SAG)
GENESSIS .... Generic Scene Simulation Software (EERA)
GENESYS .... General Engineering System
GENESYS .... Generalized System [*Computer program*] (NITA)
GENESYS .... Graduate Engineering Education System
GENET .... Genetics
GenetI.......... Genetics Institute, Inc. [*Associated Press*] (SAG)
GenetInst.... Genetics Institute, Inc. [*Associated Press*] (SAG)
GENETOX..... Genetic Toxicity [*Database*] [*Environmental Protection Agency Information service or system*] (CRD)
gen et sp nov... Genus et Species Nova [*New Genus and Species*] [*Latin*] (DMAA)
GENFAP ...... General Nonlinear Frame Analysis Program [*Structures & Computers Ltd.*] [*Software package*] (NCC)
GENG .... Gasoline Engine
GENI .... Genetics Institute, Inc. [*NASDAQ symbol*] (NQ)
GENI .... Global Energy Network International
Genicm ...... GENICOM Corp. [*Associated Press*] (SAG)
GEnie .... General Electric Network for Information Exchange [*General Electric Co.*] [*Online information service*] (IID)
GENIE .... General Information Environment [*Data Dynamics, Inc.*] [*Portland, OR*] [*Telecommunications service*] (TSSD)
GENIE .... General Information Extractor
GENIP .... Geographic Education National Implementation Project [*National Geographic Society*]
GENIRAS..... General Information Retrieval and Application System (PDAA)
GENISYS..... General Inferencing System
GENIT .... Genitalia [*Medicine*]
GENIT .... Genitive [*Case*] [*Grammar*]
GENIZ .... Genetics Institute Dep Shrs [*NASDAQ symbol*] (TTSB)
GenKinet..... General Kinetics, Inc. [*Associated Press*] (SAG)
GENL .... General
GEN L .... General Licence [*British*] (ROG)
GENLED ...... General Ledger
genlock....... Generator Lock (CDE)
GenlRe .... General Re Corp. [*Associated Press*] (SAG)
GENLY .... Generally (ROG)
Genlyte....... Genlyte Group, Inc. [*Associated Press*] (SAG)
GenManCert... General Management Certificate
GEN MGR .... General Manager (WDAA)
GENMISH..... US Military Mission with the Iranian Gendarmerie
GENMO........ Generalissimo [*Commander-in-Chief*] [*Spanish*] (ROG)
GENMOD...... General Model (RDA)
Gen Mtge..... General Mortgage [*Bond*] (MHDW)
gen nov .... Genus Novum [*New Genus*] [*Latin*] (DAVI)
GenNutr...... General Nutrition Co. [*Associated Press*] (SAG)
Genome....... Genome Therapeutics Corp. [*Associated Press*] (SAG)
Gen Ord Ch... General Orders of the English High Court of Chancery [*A publication*] (DLA)
GENOS........ Generate Operating System [*Computer program*]
GENOT .... General Notice
GENP .... Gentamicin Peak [*Level*] [*Immunology*] (DAVI)
GEN PRAC ... General Practice (WDAA)
GENPRL ...... General Precision Laboratory
GEN PROC ... General Procedure (BABM)
GENPS .... Genital Neoplasm-Papilloma Syndrome [*Medicine*] (DMAA)
GENR .... Generate (AABC)
genr............ Generation (BARN)
GenR .... Genesis Rabbah (BJA)
GenRabb ..... Genesis Rabbah (BJA)
GENREP...... General Reports [*Military*]
GENS .... General Soviet [*Later, A Group*] [*Division of National Security Agency*]
GENSAL ...... Generic Structure Language
GenScan ..... General Scanning, Inc. [*Associated Press*] (SAG)
Gensco .... Genesco, Inc. [*Associated Press*] (SAG)
GENSER ...... General Service [*Military*] (MCD)
GENSER ...... General Services Intelligence [*Military*] (CAAL)
GENSESS ..... General Sessions (ADA)
GENSH........ Generate Shell [*Computer science*] (PCM)
Gensia........ Gensia Pharmaceuticals, Inc. [*Associated Press*] (SAG)
GenSignl..... General Signal Corp. [*Associated Press*] (SAG)
GensisE ...... Genesis Energy LP [*Associated Press*] (SAG)
GENSIT .... General Situation [*Military*] (NVT)
GENSPECS... General Specifications (DNAB)
GENSTAN..... Generalized Data Standardizer [*Bureau of the Census*] (GFGA)
GENSUP...... General Support [*Army*]
GENSURG .... General Surgery (AABC)
GenSurg ..... General Surgical Innovations, Inc. [*Associated Press*] (SAG)
GENSV .... General Service [*Military*]
GENSYM ..... Generated Symbol [*Computer science*] (NHD)
Gen T.......... General Term (DLA)

GENT .... Gentamicin [*Antibacterial compound*]
GENT E .... Gentamicin Trough [*Level*] [*Immunology*] (DAVI)
GENT .... Gentleman
Genta .... Genta, Inc. [*Associated Press*] (SAG)
GENTEL ...... General Telephone & Electronics Corp.
GENTEX ...... General Telegraph Exchange (IAA)
Gentex........ Gentex Corp. [*Associated Press*] (SAG)
GENTN .... Gentleman [*or Gentlemen*] (ROG)
Gentnr .... Gentner Communications Corp. [*Associated Press*] (SAG)
GENTRAS..... General Training System (MHDB)
GenuPrt ...... Genuine Parts Co. [*Associated Press*] (SAG)
Genus .... Genus, Inc. [*Associated Press*] (SAG)
GenvDr .... Genovese Drug Stores, Inc. [*Associated Press*] (SAG)
Gen View Cr L... Stephen's General View of the Criminal Law [*2nd ed.*] [*1890*] [*A publication*] (DLA)
GENVST ...... General Public Visiting [*Navy*] (NVT)
GenWyo ...... Genessee and Wyoming, Inc. [*Associated Press*] (SAG)
GENY .... Generally
GENZ .... Genzyme Corp. [*NASDAQ symbol*] (NQ)
GENZ .... Genzyme Corp.-Genl Div [*NASDAQ symbol*] (TTSB)
GENZL .... Genzyme Corp.-Tissue Repair [*NASDAQ symbol*] (TTSB)
Genzy.......... Genzyme Corp. [*Associated Press*] (SAG)
Genzym....... Genzyme Corp. [*Associated Press*] (SAG)
GenzyT........ Genzyme Corp. [*Associated Press*] (SAG)
GenzyTis..... Genzyme Corp. [*Associated Press*] (SAG)
GenzyTr...... Genzyme Transgenics Corp. [*Associated Press*] (SAG)
GENZZ .... Genzyme Corp. Wrrt [*NASDAQ symbol*] (TTSB)
GEO .... Air Georgia [*Former USSR*] [*FAA designator*] (FAAC)
GEO .... Genetically Engineered Organism
GEO .... Geographic
GEO .... Geographic Division [*Census*] (OICC)
GEO .... Geologist
GEO .... Geomaque Explorations [*TS, exchange symbol*] (TTSB)
GEO .... Geometry
GEO .... Geophysical Report [*Oil industry term*] (DSUE)
GEO .... Georgetown [*Guyana*] [*Airport symbol*] (OAG)
GEO .... Georgetown [*District of Columbia*] [*Seismograph station code, US Geological Survey*] (SEIS)
GEO .... Georgetown, OH [*Location identifier FAA*] (FAAL)
GEO .... Georgia [*Obsolete*] (ROG)
geo .... Georgian [*MARC language code Library of Congress*] (LCCP)
Geo .... Georgia Reports [*A publication*] (DLA)
GEO .... Geoscience Electronics (MCD)
GEO .... Geostationary Earth Orbit
GEO .... Geosynchronous [*Satellite orbit*] (CDE)
GEO .... Geosynchronous Earth Orbit
GEO .... Geotech Capital [*Vancouver Stock Exchange symbol*]
GEO .... Glosa Education Organisation (EAIO)
GEOARCHIVE... Geology Archive [*Database on earth science*] [*British*] (NITA)
GEOBASE..... Geographic Cross-Reference Data [*Claritas LP*] [*Information service or system*] (CRD)
GEOC .... GeoTel Communications Corp. [*NASDAQ symbol*] (SAG)
GEOCEIVER... Geodetic Receiver
GEOCHEM.... Geochemical
GEOD .... Geodesy [*Science of measuring the earth*] (ROG)
GEOD .... Geodetic
GEODAS...... Geophysical Data System (EERA)
Geod E........ Geodetic Engineer
Geo Dec ..... Georgia Decisions [*A publication*] (DLA)
GEODES...... Ground-based Electro-Optical Deep Space Surveillance (DICI)
GEODIAL...... Geoscience Data Index for Alberta [*Alberta Research Council*] [*Information service or system*] (IID)
Geo Dig ...... George's Mississippi Digest [*A publication*] (DLA)
GEODIS....... Geographic Design and Implementation System [*Australian Capital Territory*] (EERA)
GeoDIS .... Geographic Districting Information System for Maryland [*Maryland State Department of State Planning*] [*Baltimore*] [*Information service or system*] (IID)
GEODSS...... Ground-Based Electro-Optical Deep Space Surveillance [*Satellite-tracking network*]
Geodyn ...... Geodynamics Corp. [*Associated Press*] (SAG)
GEO-EAS...... Geostatistical Environmental Assessment Software [*US Environmental Protection Agency*]
GEOFILE ..... Geographic File [*DoD*]
GEOFIZ .... Geosciences Information Center [*Federal Institute for Geosciences and NaturalResources*] [*Information service or system*] (IID)
Geog .... Geographia [*of Ptolemy*] [*Classical studies*] (OCD)
Geog .... Geographical [*A publication*] (BRI)
GEOG .... Geography [*or Geographer*] (AFM)
Geog.......... Geography (DD)
GEOGNOS.... Geognosy [*A knowledge of the structure of the earth*] (ROG)
GEOGRAPHY... George Emerson's Old Grandmother Rode a Pig Home Yesterday [*Mnemonic guide for spelling "geography"*]
Geogr Ed ..... Geographical Education [*A publication*]
Geogrph...... Geographics, Inc. [*Associated Press*] (SAG)
GEOG T....... Geographical Teacher [*A publication*] (ROG)
GEOI .... Georesources, Inc. [*NASDAQ symbol*] (NQ)
GEOIS .... Geographic Information System [*Computer science*]
GEOL .... Geologist
GEOL .... Geology [*or Geologist*] (AFM)
Geol........... Geology (DD)
GEOL .... Georesources Inc. [*NASDAQ symbol*] (TTSB)
Geol E......... Geological Engineer
GEOLGCL..... Geological
GEOLGY....... Geology

Geo Lib........ George on Libel [1812] [A publication] (DLA)
GEOLOC.... Geographical Location [Military] (AABC)
GeolSci........ Geological Science (DD)
GEOM........ Geometry [or Geometric]
GEOMAG..... Geomagnetism
GEOMAN.... Global Energy Operations & Management Co.
Geo Mason U... George Mason University (GAGS)
GEOMOD...... Geometric Modeller [GE CAE International] [Software package] (NCC)
GEON.......... Gyro Erected Optical Navigation
GEONAMES... Geologic Names of the United States [US Geological Survey] [Information service or system] (IID)
GEONAV...... Geographic Navigation [Navy] (CAAL)
Geon Co ...... [The] Geon Co. [Associated Press] (SAG)
GEOP.......... General Emergency Operations Plan (CINC)
GEOPAUSE... Geodetic Satellite in Polar Geosynchronous Orbit [NASA] (NASA)
GE-OPC....... Group of Experts on Ocean Processes and Climate [Marine science] (OSRA)
Geo Peabody C... George Peabody College for Teachers of Vanderbilt University (GAGS)
Geoph........ Geophysics (DD)
GEOPHYS..... Geophysical
GEOPHYS ... Geophysical
geopol .... Geopolitics (BARN)
Geopp.......... Geopposserde [Defendant] [Netherlands Legal term] (DLA)
GEOPS.......... Geodetic Estimates from Orbital Perturbation of Satellites (IAA)
GEOPS .... Geodetic Estimates from Orbital Perturbations of Satellites
GEOREF....... Geographic Reference System [Civil Defense]
GEOREF....... Geological Reference File [American Geological Institute] [Bibliographic database] [Information service or system] (IID)
Geo Rep ...... Georgia Reports [A publication] (DLA)
GEOREQ....... Relocation Request [Code] [Military] (MCD)
Geores........ Georesources, Inc. [Associated Press] (SAG)
GEORG........ Georgics [Poetry] (ROG)
GEORGE....... General Organizational Environment [Computer science] (BUR)
George........ George's Reports [30-39 Mississippi] [A publication] (DLA)
George Partn... George on Partnership [A publication] (DLA)
GEORGETN... Georgetown (ROG)
Georgetown C... Georgetown College (Kentucky) (GAGS)
Georgetown U... Georgetown University (District of Columbia) (GAGS)
George Washington U... [The] George Washington University (GAGS)
Georgia........ Georgia Reports [A publication] (DLA)
Georgia C Milledgeville... Georgia College of Milledgeville (GAGS)
Georgia Inst Tech... Georgia Institute of Technology (GAGS)
Georgia Rep... Georgia Reports [A publication] (DLA)
Georgia So U... Georgia Southern University (GAGS)
Georgia St U... Georgia State University (GAGS)
Georg Nat.... Georgius Natta [Flourished, 1477-95] [Authority cited in pre-1607 legal work] (DSA)
GEOS .... Geodetic Earth-Orbiting Satellite
GEOS .... Geodetic Observation Satellite
GEOS .... Geodynamic Experimental Ocean Satellite
GEOS .... Geological (Research) Satellite
GEOS .... Geosynchronous Earth Observation System (IEEE)
GEOS .... Geosynchronous Earth Orbit Satellites (ACRL)
GEOS .... Graphic Environment Operating System [Commodore 64]
GEOSAR....... Geosynchronous Synthetic Aperture RADAR (IEEE)
GEOSAT....... Geodesy Satellite
Geosat........ Geodesy Satellite [Instrument] (EERA)
Geosat........ Geodetic Satellite
GEOSAT....... Geodynamic Experimental Ocean Satellite (MCD)
GEOSCAN .... Ground-Based Electronic Omnidirectional Satellite Communications Antenna
GEOSECS..... Geochemical Ocean Sections Study [Submarine ocean exploration by US for International Decade of Ocean Exploration]
GEOSECS..... Geochemical Sections Study (USDC)
GEOSEPS..... Geosynchronous Solar Electric Propulsion Stage [NASA] (NASA)
GEO/SIT ...... Geographical Situation (MCD)
GEOSS........ Geophysical Survey System [Naval Oceanographic Office]
GeoSSR........ Georgian Soviet Socialist Republic
GeoTk........ Geotek Communications, Inc. [Associated Press] (SAG)
GeoTICo....... GeoTel Communications Corp. [Associated Press] (SAG)
GEOU.......... Graphics Entity and Operation Unification [Computer science]
GEOW .... GeoWaste, Inc. [NASDAQ symbol] (SPSG)
Geo Williams C... George Williams College (GAGS)
Geoworks...... GeoWorks [Associated Press] (SAG)
GeoWste...... GeoWaste, Inc. [Associated Press] (SAG)
GEP........... Gastroenteropancreatic System [Medicine]
GEP........... General Electric Plastics [Australia Commercial firm]
GEP........... General Enrollment Plan [Insurance]
GEP........... General Entry Permit
GEP........... Geological Echo Profiler [Oceanography] (MSC)
GEP........... Goddard Experimental Package [NASA]
GEP........... Good Engineering Practice (EG)
GEP........... Grasslands Ecology Program (EERA)
GEP........... Great Pacific Resources [Vancouver Stock Exchange symbol]
GEP........... Grolier Electronic Publishing, Inc. [Information service or system] (IID)
GEP........... Gross Energy Product
GEP........... Ground Effects Phenomenon
GEP........... Ground Entry Point (NVT)
GEP........... Group Employment Plan (MCD)
GEP........... Gulf Environmental Measurements Program (MCD)
GEP........... Gustatory Evoked Potential [Medicine] (DMAA)
GEP........... Minneapolis, MN [Location identifier FAA] (FAAL)

GEPA .... General Education Provisions Act [1970]
GEPAC........ General Electric Process Automation Computer
GEPAC........ General Electric Programmable Automatic Comparator [or Computer]
GEPB .... Grievance and Employment Policy Board [Army]
GEPC.......... German External Property Control Commission [Minden] [Allied German Occupation Forces]
GEPDS........ General Electric Process Design System
GEPE.......... GATE [GARP Atlantic Tropical Experiment] Equatorial Profiling Experiment [Marine science] (MSC)
GEPE.......... Groupe d'Etudes Politiques Europeennes (EA)
GEPEXS ...... General Electric Parts Explosion System
GEpFAR ...... Federal Archives and Records Center, General Services Administration, Atlanta Region, East Point, GA [Library symbol Library of Congress] (LCLS)
GEPI.......... Gestioni e Partecipazioni Industriali [Industrial Management and Participation] [Italian government-sponsored agency to aid ailing companies]
GEPL.......... General Equipment and Packaging Laboratory [Army]
GEPLACEA ... Grupo de Paises Latinoamericanos y del Caribe Exportadores de Azucar [Group of Latin American and Caribbean Sugar Exporting Countries - GLACSEC] (EAIO)
GEPOL .... Generalized Processor for Command-Oriented Language (DNAB)
GEPURS ...... General Electric General Purpose
GEPVP .... Groupement Europeen des Producteurs de Verre Plat [European Group of Flat Glass Manufacturers] (EAIO)
GEQ .... Moline, IL [Location identifier FAA] (FAAL)
GEQUIV ...... Gram Equivalent [Chemistry] (IAA)
GER .... Gardiner Resources [Vancouver Stock Exchange symbol]
GER .... Gastroesophageal Reflux [See also GERD] [Medicine]
GER .... General Engineering Research
GER .... Geomagnetic Electrorinetograph
Ger.......... Gerard Pucelle [Deceased, 1184] [Authority cited in pre-1607 legal work] (DSA)
GER .... Geriatrics
Ger........... Gerim (BJA)
ger........... German [MARC language code Library of Congress] (LCCP)
GER .... German [Language, etc.]
GER .... Germany
Ger........... Germany (VRA)
GER .... Germany Fund [NYSE symbol] (TTSB)
GER .... Germany Fund, Inc. [NYSE symbol] (SPSG)
GER .... Gerontology [American Occupational Therapy Association]
GER .... Gerund
GER .... Goodyear Engineering Report (MCD)
GER .... Gran Enciclopedia Rialp [A publication]
GER .... Great Eastern Railway [British]
GER .... Guernsey Airlines Ltd. [British ICAO designator] (FAAC)
GER .... Guilde Europeenne du Raid [European Expedition Guild - EEG] (EAIO)
GER .... Nueva Gerona [Cuba] [Airport symbol] (OAG)
GERA .... Guard's Expense in Returning Absentee [Army]
GerABcp ...... German American Bancorp [Associated Press] (SAG)
GerAE .... German Antarctic Expedition [1901-03,1911-12,1938-39]
GERBIL .... Great Education Reform Bill [British]
GerbSc........ Gerber Scientific, Inc. [Associated Press] (SAG)
GERD .... Gastroesophageal Reflux Disease [Gastroenterology] (DAVI)
GERD .... Gross Expenditure on Research Development
GERDAT ...... Groupement d'Etudes et de Recherche pour le Developpement de l'Agronomie Tropicale [Group for the Study and Research of Tropical Agronomy] [International Cooperation Center of Agricultural Research for Development] [Information service or system] (IID)
GER DEM REP... German Democratic Republic (WDAA)
GERD/GDP ... Gross Expenditure on Research and Development/Gross Domestic Product [Ratio]
GEREP .... Generalized Equipment Reliability Evaluation Procedure
Gereq......... Gerequireerde [Defendant] [Netherlands] (ILCA)
GerFd......... Germany Fund, Inc. [Associated Press] (SAG)
GERG .... Groupe Europeen de Recherches Gazieres [European Gas Research Group] (EAIO)
GERI .... Geriatric
geri........... Geriatrics [Medicine] (DAVI)
GERIACT...... Great Education Reform Act [1988] (AIE)
GERIAT .... Geriatrics
GeriMed...... Geriatric & Medical Companies, Inc. [Associated Press] (SAG)
GERIS .... Graphic Expression Reading Improvement System
GERL .... Golgi-Associated Endoplasmic Reticulum Lysosomes
GERM .... Generalized Entity-Relationship Model (HGAA)
GERM .... German [Language, etc.] (ROG)
Germ .... Germania [of Tacitus] [Classical studies] (OCD)
GERM .... Ground Effect Research Machine
GERMA .... Groupe d'Etude des Ressources Maritimes [Universite du Quebec a Rimouski] [Canada Research center]
German........ Germanicus [15BC-19AD] [Classical studies] (OCD)
German Yb Int'l L... German Yearbook of International Law [A publication] (DLA)
GERMDF ...... German Ministry of Defense
GERME .... Groupe d'Etude en Regulation Metabolique [University of Quebec at Rimouski] [Research center] (RCD)
Germfask...... Grant, Edge, Robinson, Mead, French, Ackley, Shephard, and Knaggs [Founders of a town in Michigan's Upper Peninsula that derived its name from the initial letters of their surnames]
GermJud...... Germania Judaica [A publication] (BJA)
GERN .... Geron Corp. [NASDAQ symbol] (SAG)
GerNew........ Germany Fund New [Associated Press] (SAG)
GERNORSEA... German Naval Forces, North Sea Subarea [NATO] (NATG)

GERO......... George Rogers Clark National Historical Park
GERO......... GE [*General Electric Co.*] Robot
GERO......... Global Environmental Research Organization
GeronCp..... Geron Corp. [*Associated Press*] (SAG)
Gerontol ...... Gerontology [*or Gerontologist*] [*Geriatrics*] (DAVI)
GEROS .... General Routing Optimization System (IAA)
GERPAT ...... German Patent (IAA)
Ger Q .... German Quarterly [*A publication*] (BRI)
GERRI .... Geriatric Evaluation by Relative Rating Instrument [*Medicine*] (DMAA)
Gerrity .... Gerrity Oil & Gas [*Associated Press*] (SAG)
GERSAL ...... General Electric Symbolic Assembly Language (IAA)
GERSIS .... General Electric Range Safety Instrumentation System [*Aerospace*]
GERT .... Graphical Evaluation and Review Technique
GERTIE .... GEORGE [*General Organizational Environment*] Remote Terminal Interrogative Environment [*Computer science*] (IAA)
Ger Tit .... Gerard's Titles to Real Estate [*A publication*] (DLA)
GERTS .... General Electric Radio [*or Range*] Tracking System [*Aerospace*]
GERTS .... General Electric Remote Terminal Supervisor
GERTS .... General Electric Remote Terminal System (IEEE)
GERTS .... General Remote Terminal System (NITA)
GERV .... General Electric Reentry Vehicle [*Aerospace*] (AAG)
GES .... Gale Environmental Sourcebook [*A publication*]
GES .... Gamma European System (IAA)
GES .... General Edit System [*Computer science*] (IAA)
GES .... General Educational Services Corp.
GES .... General Electric Semiconductor
GES .... General Electric Silicones [*Australia Commercial firm*]
GES .... General Engineering Squadron
GES .... General Estimates System [*NHTSA*] (TAG)
GES .... General Santos [*Philippines*] [*Airport symbol*] (OAG)
GES .... Generic Environmental Statement [*Nuclear energy*] (NRCH)
GES .... Genesis Resource Corp. [*Vancouver Stock Exchange symbol*]
GES .... Gesellschaft [*Company*] [*German*]
Ges .... Gesellschaft [*Company*] [*German*] (ODBW)
ges............. Gesso (VRA)
GES .... Gestair Executive Jet [*Spain ICAO designator*] (FAAC)
GES .... Gilt-Edged Securities [*Business term*]
GES .... Glucose Electrolyte Solution [*Medicine*]
GES .... Goddard Experiment Support System [*NASA*] (MCD)
GES .... Gold Exchange Standard
GES .... Goliath Edison Screw
GES .... Gordon, E. S., Joplin MO [*STAC*]
GES .... Government Economic Service [*British*]
GES .... Government Evacuation Scheme [*British World War II*]
GES .... Green Extension System [*Traffic signal*] (DICI)
GES .... Grips Strong and Equal [*Medicine*] (MEDA)
GES .... Ground Earth Station [*Telecommunications*]
GES .... Ground Electronic System
GES .... Ground Entry Station (MCD)
GES .... Ground Equipment System
GES .... Groupe d'Etudes Sartriennes (EAIO)
GES .... Group Encounter Survey
GES .... Group Environment Scale [*Personality development test*] [*Psychology*]
GESAANP/NW... GE [*General Electric Co.*] Stockholders' Alliance Against Nuclear Power/Nuclear Weapons (EA)
Ges Abh...... Gesammelte Abhandlungen zur Roemischen Religions- und Stadtgeschichte [*A publication*] (OCD)
GESAC .... General Electric Self-Adaptive Control System
GESAL .... General Electric Symbolic Assembly Language (IAA)
GESAMP ...... Group of Experts on the Scientific Aspects of Marine Environmental Protection [*Marine science*] (OSRA)
GESAMP ...... Group of Experts on the Scientific Aspects of Marine Pollution [*ICSU*] (EAIO)
GESASA ...... Greek Ex-Servicemen's Association of South Australia
GESB .... General Export Services Branch [*Department of Trade*] [*British*]
GesB .... Hebraeisches und Aramaeisches Handwoerterbuch ueber das Alte Testament [*W. Gesenius and F. Buhl*] [*A publication*] (BJA)
GESBT .... Generic Expert System Building Tool
GESC .... Government EDP [*Electronic Data Processing*] Standards Committee [*Canada*]
Gesch .... Geschichte [*of Germanicus*] [*Classical studies*] (OCD)
GESCH .... Geschichte [*History*] [*German*]
GESCO........ General Electric Supply Corp.
GESCOM...... General Electric Scientific Color Matching (IAA)
GESEM........ Groupement Europeen des Sources d'Eaux Minerales Naturelles [*European Group ofNatural Mineral Water Sources*] (EAIO)
GESH .... Grain Effect Screenless Halftone [*Printing technique*]
GESHUA...... General Electric Six Hundred Users' Association [*Later, HLSUA*] [*Computer science*]
GESMAR ..... Geodetic Survey Marks Register [*of Western Australia*] [*State*] (EERA)
GESMO .... General Environmental Statement for Mixed Oxide Fuel
GESO .... Group Equipment Staff Officer [*British military*] (DMA)
GESOC........ General Electric Satellite Orbit Control [*Aerospace*]
GESP .... General Extrasensory Perception [*Parapsychology*]
GESPL .... General Edit System Programming Language (IAA)
GESPL .... Generalized Edit System Programming Language [*Computer science*] (PDAA)
GESS .... Generator Exhaust Signature Suppression (PDAA)
Ges Schr ..... Gesammelte Schriften [*A publication*]
GesStud...... Gesammelte Studien [*A publication*] (BJA)
GEST.......... Gas Explosive Simulation Technique [*Air Force*]
GEST.......... Gemini Slowscan Television [*NASA*]
GEST.......... General Systems Theory

GEST.......... Gestational [*Pediatrics*]
GEST.......... Gestorben [*Died*] [*German*]
gest .... Gesture [*Theater*] (WDMC)
GEST.......... Guest Supply [*NASDAQ symbol*] (TTSB)
GEST.......... Guest Supply, Inc. [*NASDAQ symbol*] (NQ)
GESTA........ Gesetzgebungsstand [*Database*] [*Deutscher Bundestag*] [*German*] [*Information service or system*] (CRD)
GESTAPO...... Geheime Staats Polizei [*Secret State Police*] [*Germany*]
GESTAPU...... Gerkang, September, Tigapuluh [*See also GESTOK*] [*Plot against the government of Indonesia beginning on September 30, 1965*]
GESTOK...... Gerkang Oktober [*See also GESTAPU*] [*Plot against the government of Indonesia which began on September 30, 1965 and continued into October*]
GET .... Gaming Entertainment Television [*Interactive-gambling TV station*] (ECON)
GET .... Gas, Electric, Telephones [*of GET, Inc., a consumer group*]
GET .... Gastric Emptying Time [*Medicine*]
GET .... Gaylord Entertainment [*NYSE symbol*] (SPSG)
GET .... Gaylord Entertainment 'A' [*NYSE symbol*] (TTSB)
GET .... Generator Environmental Tester
GET .... Geraldton [*Australia Airport symbol*] (OAG)
GET .... Germanium Transistor [*Electronics*] (IAA)
Get............. Geteilt [*Divided*] [*Music*]
GET .... Graded Treadmill Exercise Test [*Medicine*] (DMAA)
GET .... Graduate Employment and Training [*British*]
GET .... Graduate Employment and Training Survey (AIE)
GET .... Gross Error Test (PDAA)
GET .... Ground Elapsed Time [*Aerospace*]
GET .... Ground Entry Terminal (MCD)
GET$_{1/2}$.... Gastric Emptying Half-Time [*Gastroenterology*] (DAVI)
GETA.......... GeneralEndotracheal Anesthesia [*Medicine*] (DAVI)
GETA.......... General Equipment Test Activity [*Army*]
GETA.......... Government Employees Training Act [*1966*]
GETAB........ General Electric BWR [*Boiling Water Reactor*] Thermal Analysis Branch (NRCH)
GE/TAC .... General Electric Telemetering and Control (IEEE)
GETAC .... General Electric Telemetering and Control
GetchGld...... Getchell Gold Corp. [*Associated Press*] (SAG)
GETEL .... General Electric Test Engineering Language [*Computer science*] (IEEE)
GETF........... Global Environmental Trust Fund [*GEF-Core Fund*] (EERA)
GETh........... [*The*] Epic of Gilgamesh [*R. C. Thompson*] [*A publication*] (BJA)
GETI........... Ground Elapsed Time of Ignition [*Aerospace*] (KSC)
GETIL .... Ground Elapsed Time of Landing
GETIS .... Ground Environment Technical Installation System [*NATO*] (NATG)
GETL .... Ground Elapsed Time of Landing [*NASA*] (GFGA)
GETLO .... Obtain by Local Purchase [*Military*]
GETMA .... Obtain by Local Manufacture [*Military*]
GETO .... Ground Equipment Turn Off (KSC)
GETOL .... General Electric Training Operational Language (MCD)
GETOL .... General Electric Training Operational Logic [*Computer science*] (IEEE)
GETOL .... Ground Effect Takeoff and Landing
GETR .... General Electric Test Reactor
GETS .... General Electric Transportation Systems [*Australia Commercial firm*]
GETS .... Generalized Electronic Troubleshooting (IAA)
GETS .... General Track Simulation [*NASA*] (KSC)
GETS .... Ground Equipment Test Set
GETSC .... General Electric Technical Services Company
GETSCO ...... General Electric Technical Services Co. (NRCH)
GETSS .... General Electric Time Sharing System (IAA)
GETT .... German Tactical Truck (MCD)
GETT .... Gettysburg National Military Park
GETT .... Grants Equal to Taxes
GETTY .... Getty Communications [*NASDAQ symbol*] (SAG)
Getty .... Getty Petroleum Corp. [*Associated Press*] (SAG)
GettyCo....... Getty Communications [*Associated Press*] (SAG)
Getuig......... Getuigenis [*Roermond/Maaseik*] (BJA)
GETY .... Gettysburg Railroad Co. [*AAR code*]
Getz F .... Getz's Forms in Conveyancing [*A publication*] (DLA)
GEU .... Emory University, Atlanta, GA [*Library symbol Library of Congress*] (LCLS)
GEU .... Genetic Evaluation and Utilization (PDAA)
GEU .... Geothermal Energy Update [*A publication*]
GEU .... Geriatric Evaluation Unit [*Veterans Administration*] (GFGA)
GEU .... Grossesse Extra-Uterine [*Medicine*]
GEU .... Ground Electro-Optic Unit
GEU-B .... Emory University, School of Business Administration, Atlanta, GA [*Library symbol Library of Congress*] (LCLS)
GEU-D .... Emory University, School of Dentistry, Atlanta, GA [*Library symbol Library of Congress*] (LCLS)
GEU-L .... Emory University, Lamar School of Law, Atlanta, GA [*Library symbol Library of Congress*] (LCLS)
GEU-LS .... Emory University, Division of Librarianship, Atlanta, GA [*Library symbol Library of Congress*] (LCLS)
GEU-M .... Emory University, A. W. Calhoun Medical Library, Atlanta, GA [*Library symbol Library of Congress*] (LCLS)
GEU-S .... Emory University, Special Collections Department, Atlanta, GA [*Library symbol*] [*Library of Congress*] (LCLS)
GEU-T .... Emory University, Candler School of Theology, Atlanta, GA [*Library symbol Library of Congress*] (LCLS)
GEU-Y .... Emory University, Yerkes Primate Research Center, Atlanta, GA [*Library symbol Library of Congress*] (LCLS)
GEV............ Gallivare [*Sweden*] [*Airport symbol*] (OAG)
GeV............ Giga Electron Volt

GEV	Ground Effect Vehicle
GEV	Groundnut Eyespot Virus
GEVIC	General Electric Variable Increment Computer
GEVNC	General Electric Vallecitos Nuclear Center [*Vallecitos, CA*] (GAAI)
GEVST	Gordon Environmental Studies Laboratory [*University of Montana*] [*Research center*] (RCD)
GEW	Gas, Electricity, Water [*Department of Employment*] [*British*]
GEW	Gewoya [*Papua New Guinea*] [*Airport symbol*] (OAG)
GEW	Glazed Earthenware
GEW	Gram Equivalent Weight
GEW	Ground Effect Wing (PDAA)
GEWA	George Washington Birthplace National Monument
GEWEX	Global Energy and Water Cycle Experiment [*World Climate Research Program*] [*Geo science*]
GEWEX	Global Energy and Water Cycle Experiment [*Marine science*] (OSRA)
GEWP	George Washington Memorial Parkway [*National Park Service designation*]
GEX	Gas Exchange
GEX	Government Employees Exchange
GEX	Granges Exploration Ltd. [*Toronto Stock Exchange symbol*]
GEY	Getty Resources Ltd. [*Toronto Stock Exchange symbol*]
GEY	Geuserland Airways Ltd. [*New Zealand*] [*ICAO designator*] (FAAC)
GEY	Greybull, WY [*Location identifier FAA*] (FAAL)
GEZ	Garretson - Elmendorf - Zinov, Architects and Engineers [*San Francisco, CA*] [*Telecommunications service*] (TSSD)
GEZ	General Electric Canada, Inc. [*Toronto Stock Exchange symbol*]
GEZ	Gosudarstvennoe Knigoizdatelstvo [*State Publishing House*] [*Former USSR*]
GEZERD	Alfarbandishe Gezelshaft far Ainordenen Yidn af Erd in FSSR [*A publication*] (BJA)
GF	French Guiana [*ANSI two-letter standard code*] (CNC)
GF	Gain Factor [*Computer science*]
GF	Galois Field [*Mathematics*] (IAA)
GF	Galvanized Steel Fastenings
GF	Games Finished [*Baseball*]
GF	G and A Factor
GF	Gap Filler [*RADAR*]
GF	Garage Forecourts [*Public-performance tariff class*] [*British*]
GF	Gas Filled (MSA)
GF	Gas-Freeing System
GF	Gasoline-Fueled [*Automotive engineering*]
GF	Gastric Fistula [*Gastroenterology*] (DAVI)
GF	Gastric Fluid [*Medicine*] (MAE)
GF	Gaudeamus Foundation [*Netherlands*] (EAIO)
GF	Gauge Factor (MCD)
GF	Gelatinous Fiber [*Botany*]
GF	General Foods Corp. (CDAI)
G/F	General within Families (DICI)
GF	Generator Field
GF	Generic Failure
GF	Gentleman Friend
GF	Georgia & Florida R. R. [*AAR code*]
GF	Germfree [*Medicine*]
GF	Girl Friend [*Slang*]
GF	Girl Friends (EA)
GF	Glaciofluvial Soil [*Agronomy*]
GF	Glass Factor [*Tissue culture*]
GF	Glass Fiber
GF	Globular-Fibrous [*Biochemistry*]
GF	Glomerular Filtrate [*Medicine*]
GF	Gluten-Free [*Diet*]
GF	Goals For [*Hockey*]
GF	Gold Field
GF	Goldfinch [*Ornithology*]
GF	Goldflow (AFM)
GF	Gonococcus Filus [*A microorganism*]
GF	Good Faith [*Legal shorthand*] (LWAP)
GF	Gordon Fraser [*Publisher*] [*British*]
GF	Gorilla Foundation (EA)
GF	Government Form
GF	Government Funded (BABM)
GF	Gram Force (IAA)
gf	Gram-Force (DMAA)
gf	Grandfather
GF	Grand Fleet [*British military*] (DMA)
GF	Grand Format [*Graphic arts*] (DGA)
GF	Grayson Foundation [*Later, GJC*] (EA)
GF	Great Falls-Billings [*Diocesan abbreviation*] [*Montana*] (TOCD)
GF	Great Fire [*of London, 1666*]
GF	Greensward Foundation (EA)
GF	Grinding Fixture (MCD)
GF	Ground Face [*Technical drawings*]
G/F	Ground/Flight Test
GF	Ground Fog [*Meteorology*]
GF	Ground Foraging [*Ecology*]
GF	Ground Forces [*Military*]
GF	Group of Fourteen [*NATO countries minus France*] (NATG)
GF	Growth Factor [*Endocrinology*] (DAVI)
GF	Growth Fraction [*Endocrinology*]
GF	Guggenheim Foundation (BARN)
GF	Guinean Franc [*Monetary unit*] (ODBW)
GF	Gulf Air [*ICAO designator*] (AD)
GF	Gunnery Flight
GF	New Germany Fund [*NYSE symbol*] (SPSG)
GFA	Federal Aviation Administration, Southern Region, East Point, GA [*OCLC symbol*] (OCLC)
GFA	Gasket Fabricators Association (EA)
GFA	General Fitness Assessment
GFA	General Forestry Assistance
GFA	General Freight Agent
GFA	Giddens Family Associates (EA)
GFA	Gideon Family Association (EA)
GFA	Glial Fibrillary Acidic Protein [*Also, GFAP*] [*Biochemistry*]
GFA	Gloucester Fisheries Association (EA)
GFA	Gold Filled Association [*Defunct*] (EA)
GFA	Goodenow Family Association (EA)
GFA	Good Fair Average [*Insurance*]
GFA	Government-Furnished Ammunition (MCD)
GFA	Government-Furnished Articles (KSC)
GFA	Grain Futures Administration [*Superseded by Commodity Exchange Administration, 1936*]
GFA	Graves Family Association
GFA	Great Falls, MT [*Location identifier FAA*] (FAAL)
GFA	Gross Floor Area (ADA)
GFA	Group Feedback Analysis
GFA	Guitar Foundation of America (EA)
GFA	Gulf Air [*United Arab Emirates*] [*ICAO designator*] (FAAC)
GFA	Gunfire Area
GFA	Gust Front Algorithm (USDC)
GFAA	Game Fishing Association of Australia (EERA)
GFAA	Graphite-Furnace Atomic Absorption [*Spectroscopy*] [*Physics*]
GFAAS	Graphite Furnace Atomic Absorption Spectroscopy [*Physics*]
GFAC	Ground Forward Air Controller (MCD)
GFADS	Grand Forks Air Defense Sector [*North Dakota*] (SAA)
GFAE	Government-Furnished Accessory Equipment
GFAE	Government-Furnished Aeronautical Equipment (AFM)
GFAE	Government-Furnished Aerospace Equipment
GFAE	Government-Furnished Aircraft Equipment
GFAEL	Government-Furnished Aeronautical Equipment List (MCD)
GFAM	Graphics Flutter Analysis Methods [*Computer science*]
GF & A	Gulf Florida & Alabama Railway
GF & P	Gases, Fluids, and Propellants [*NASA*] (NASA)
GFAP	Glial Fibrillary Acidic Protein [*Also, GFA*] [*Biochemistry*]
GFB	Go for Broke [*Slang*]
GFB	Government Facilities Brochure
GFB	Government-Furnished Baseline
GFBA	Graduate Fellowships for Black Americans (EA)
GFBI	Grand Fleet Battle Instructions [*British military*] (DMA)
GFbIS	United States Army, Infantry School, Fort Benning, GA [*Library symbol Library of Congress*] (LCLS)
GFBN	Bonthe [*Sierra Leone*] [*ICAO location identifier*] (ICLI)
GFBO	Grand Fleet Battle Orders [*British military*] (DMA)
GfBV	Gesellschaft fuer Bedrohte Voelker [*Society for Threatened Peoples*] (EAIO)
GFC	Gas-Filled Counter
GFC	Gas Filter Correlation [*NASA*] (KSC)
GFC	Gas Frontal Chromatography
GFC	Gel Filtration Chromatography
GFC	General Failure Criteria
GFC	Generic Flow Control [*Telecommunications*] (ACRL)
GFC	Genstar Financial Corp. [*Toronto Stock Exchange symbol*]
GFC	George Fox College [*Oregon*]
GFC	Get Fresh Crew [*Rap recording group*]
GFC	Glass Filter Covers
GFC	Global Forcing Contribution [*Environmental science*]
GFC	Goldwing Flyers Club (EA)
GFC	Grand Falls Central Railway Co. Ltd. [*AAR code*]
GFC	Graphite Fiber Composite
GFC	Gun Feed Control (MCD)
GFC	Gunfire Control (DOMA)
GFCB	Ground Fault Circuit Breaker [*Electronics*]
GFCC	Gun Fire Control Computer [*Military*] (CAAL)
GFCE	Government-Furnished Capital Equipment (MCD)
GFCE	Gross Fixed Capital Expenditure
GFCES	Glider Flight Control Electronics Subsystem
GFCF	Gross Fixed Capital Formation
GFCG	Government Fluidic Coordinating Group
GFCI	Gay Fathers Coalition International [*Later, GLPCI*] (EA)
GFCI	Ground Fault Circuit Interrupter [*Electronics*]
GFCM	General Fisheries Council for the Mediterranean [*ICSU*]
GF/CM²	Gram Force per Square Centimeter
GFCO	Glenway Financial Corp. [*NASDAQ symbol*] (SAG)
GFCO	Glenway Fin'l [*NASDAQ symbol*] (TTSB)
GFCO	Good Faith Charitable Organization (EA)
GFCR	Gas Filter Correlation Radiometer [*NASA*]
GFCRP	Gap-Filler Control and Reporting Post [*RADAR*] (IAA)
GFCS	Gaseous Flowmeter Calibration Stand
GFCS	Gunfire Control System
GFCS-B	Gunfire Control System-Backup (DNAB)
GFCSMT	Generalized Fire-Control System Maintenance Trainer [*Spacecraft*] [*Navy*]
GFCSS	Gunfire Control Subsystem (DNAB)
GFCS SATSIM	Gun Fire Control System Satellite Simulation [*Military*] (CAAL)
GFCV	Gas and Fuel Corp. of Victoria [*Australia*]
GFD	Gallons per Square-Foot per Day
GFD	Gap-Filler Data [*RADAR*]
GFD	Gemini Food Corp. [*Toronto Stock Exchange symbol*]
GFD	General Freight Department
GFD	General Functional Description [*Military*] (AABC)

GFD .... Geophysical Fluid Dynamics Laboratory [*National Oceanic and Atmospheric Administration*]

GFD .... Gesellschaft fur Flugzieldarstellung GmbH [*Germany ICAO designator*] (FAAC)

GFD .... Gingival Fibromatosis-Progressive Deafness Syndrome [*Medicine*] (DMAA)

GFD .... Glucose-Free Dialysate [*Nephrology*]

GFD .... Gluten-Free Diet

GFD .... Gone for the Day

GFD .... Goodenough Figure Drawing [*Psychology*] (DAVI)

GFD .... Government-Furnished Data (NASA)

GFD .... Government-Furnished Documentation (KSC)

GFD .... Greenfield, IN [*Location identifier FAA*] (FAAL)

GFD .... Ground Forces Training Devices (Provisional) [*Army*] (RDA)

GFD .... Group Finance Department

GFD .... Guilford Mills [*NYSE symbol*] (SAG)

GFDA .... Gust Front Detection Algorithm (USDC)

GFDC .... Group Fire Distribution Center [*Army*] (AABC)

GFDD .... Gunfire Detection Device

GFDL .... Geophysical Fluid Dynamics Laboratory [*Princeton, NJ*] [*National Oceanic and Atmospheric Administration*]

GFDNA .... Grain and Feed Dealers National Association [*Later, NGFA*] (EA)

GFDP .... Geophysical Fluid Dynamics Program [*National Oceanic and Atmospheric Administration*] (GFGA)

GFE .... Gays for Equality

GFE .... Gibbs Free Energy [*Physical chemistry*]

GFE .... Goal-Free Evaluation [*Education*] (AEE)

GFE .... Government-Furnished Equipment

GFE .... Greater Fuel Economy

GFE .... Gross Feasibility Estimator (MCD)

GFEAM .... Government-Furnished Equipment and Material (IAA)

GFE & D ..... Government-Furnished Equipment and Data

GFE & M..... Government-Furnished Equipment and Material (NRCH)

GFEC .... Graphite-Fiber Epoxy-Composite

GFED .... Guaranty Federal Savings Bank [*NASDAQ symbol*] (SAG)

GFED .... Guaranty Fedl Svgs [*NASDAQ symbol*] (TTSB)

GFE/GFAE ... Government-Furnished Equipment / Government-Furnished Aircraft Equipment (SAA)

GFE/I .... Government-Furnished Equipment/Information (AAGC)

GFEL........... Government-Furnished Equipment List (MCD)

GFEM........... Graphics Finite Element Module [*McDonnell-Douglas Automation Corp.*]

GFER .... Government-Furnished Equipment Records

GFERC .... Grand Forks Energy Research Center [*Energy Research and Development Administration*]

GFERR .... Government-Furnished Equipment Requirements Request

GFETC .... Grand Forks Energy Technology Center [*Later, University of North Dakota Energy Research Center*] [*Department of Energy*] (GRD)

GFF .... Glass-Fiber Filter [*Separation technology*]

GFF .... Government-Furnished Facilities (MCD)

GFF .... Granolithic Finish Floor [*Technical drawings*]

GFF .... Graphic Firing Fan [*Weaponry*] (INF)

GFF .... Griffith [*Australia Airport symbol*] (OAG)

GFF .... Griffon Corp. [*NYSE symbol*] (SAG)

GFFAR .... Guided Folding-Fin Aircraft Rocket

GFFC .... Geophysical Fluid Flow Cell [*Instrumentation*]

GFFC .... Gibb Family Friendship Club (EA)

GFFD .... Gross Failed Fuel Detector [*Nuclear energy*] (NRCH)

GFFIL .... Groupement Francais des Fournisseurs d'Information en Ligne [*French Association of Online Information Providers*] [*Paris*] [*Information service or system*] (IID)

GFFPrl .... Griffon Corp. 2nd Cv Pfd [*NYSE symbol*] (TTSB)

GFFS .... Glycogen and Fat-Free Solid (DMAA)

GFG .... Geographical Field Group [*British*]

GFG .... Glare Free Gloss [*Paper*]

GFG .... [*The*] Good Food Guide [*A publication British*]

GFG .... Governor's Foot Guard

GFG .... Grafton Group Ltd. [*Toronto Stock Exchange symbol*]

GFG .... Leesburg, VA [*Location identifier FAA*] (FAAL)

GFGA .... Gippsland Fruit Growers' Association [*Australia*]

GFgC .... United States Army, Civil Affairs School, Fort Gordon, GA [*Library symbol Library of Congress*] (LCLS)

GFGCA .... Gympie Fruit Growers' Cooperative Association [*Australia*]

GFGF .... Group Fore Golf Foundation (EA)

GFGK .... Gbangbatok [*Sierra Leone*] [*ICAO location identifier*] (ICLI)

GFgML........ United States Army, Medical Library, Fort Gordon, GA [*Library symbol Library of Congress*] (LCLS)

GFgMP........ United States Army, Military Police School, Fort Gordon, GA [*Library symbol Library of Congress*] (LCLS)

GFgS........... United States Army, Special Services Library, Fort Gordon, GA [*Library symbol Library of Congress*] (LCLS)

GFgSS .... United States Army, Southeastern Signal School, Fort Gordon, GA [*Library symbol Library of Congress*] (LCLS)

GFH .... Glucose-Free Hanks [*Cell incubation medium*]

GFHA .... Gaelic Football and Hurling Association [*Australia*]

GFHA .... Hastings [*Sierra Leone*] [*ICAO location identifier*] (ICLI)

GFHR .... Gas-Filled Hydrophobic Region

GFI .... Gap-Filler Input [*RADAR*]

GFI .... Gas Flow Indicator [*NASA*]

GFI .... General Format Identifier [*Computer science*] (TNIG)

GFI .... Global Finance Information [*Information service or system*] (IID)

GFI .... Glucagon-Free Insulin [*Medicine*] (DMAA)

GFI .... Gmelin Formula Index [*Gmelin-Institut fuer Anorganische Chemie und Grenzgebiete*] [*Germany Information service or system*] (CRD)

GFI .... Government Final Inspection

GFI............. Government Free Issue (AABC)

GFI............. Government-Furnished Information

GFI............. Government-Furnished Items [*DoD*]

GFI............. Government-Owned Financial Institution (ADA)

GFI............. Graham-Field Health [*NYSE symbol*] (TTSB)

GFI............. Graham Field Health Products [*NYSE symbol*] (SAG)

GFI............. Greyvest Financial Services, Inc. [*Toronto Stock Exchange symbol*]

GFI............. Ground Fault Interrupter [*Electronics*]

gfi............. Ground-Fault Interrupter (IDOE)

GFI............. Group Fuel Injection [*Automotive engineering*]

GFI............. Guided Fault Isolation

GFII........... Greenfield Industries, Inc. [*NASDAQ symbol*] (SAG)

GFIN .... Game Financial Corp. [*NASDAQ symbol*] (SAG)

GFIN .... Gam Financial [*NASDAQ symbol*] (TTSB)

GFinSerf ..... Grupo Fnanciero Serfin SA [*Associated Press*] (SAG)

GFIP........... Gross Fault Indicator Panel (SAA)

GFIT........... Glass-Fiber Insulation Tubing

GFK........... Grand Forks [*North Dakota*] [*Airport symbol*] (OAG)

GFK........... Grand Forks Mines [*Vancouver Stock Exchange symbol*]

GFKB .... Kabala [*Sierra Leone*] [*ICAO location identifier*] (ICLI)

GFKE .... Kenema [*Sierra Leone*] [*ICAO location identifier*] (ICLI)

GFL........... Geoffrion, Leclerc, Inc. [*Toronto Stock Exchange symbol*]

GFL........... Giant Follicular Lymphoma [*Medicine*] (DMAA)

GFL........... Glens Falls [*New York*] [*Airport symbol*] (AD)

GFL........... Glens Falls, NY [*Location identifier FAA*] (FAAL)

GFL........... Glossary Function List

GFL........... Government-Furnished List

GFL........... Green Forest Lumber Ltd. [*Canada ICAO designator*] (FAAC)

GFL........... Ground Fire Locator

GFL........... Guide to Football Literature [*A publication*]

GFLAAL...... Gesellschaft zur Foerderung der Literatur aus Afrika, Asien, und Lateinamerika (EAIO)

GFLD .... Generator Field

GFLL........... Freetown/Lungi [*Sierra Leone*] [*ICAO location identifier*] (ICLI)

GFLOPS...... Giga Floating Operations per Second [*Computer science*]

GFLOPS...... One Billion Floating Point Operations per Second (ACRL)

GFLS .... Ground Fire Locating System

GFLU .... General Federation of Labor Unions [*Syria*]

GFLV .... Grapevine Fan Leaf Virus [*Plant pathology*]

GFM........... Glass-Fiber Material

GFM........... Goldfinch Mineral Ltd. [*Vancouver Stock Exchange symbol*]

GFM........... Government-Furnished Material

GFM........... Government-Furnished Missile

GFM........... Graphics Function Monitor [*Tektronix*] (NITA)

GFM........... Gravitational Field Measurements (SAA)

GFM........... Greyhound Food Management

GFMA .... Gold-Filled Manufacturers Association [*Later, GFA*] (EA)

GFmA.......... United States Army, Fort McPherson Post Library, Fort McPherson, GA [*Library symbol Library of Congress*] (LCLS)

GFMD .... Gold Film Mercury Detector [*Spectrometry*]

GFME .... Government-Furnished Missile Equipment (AAG)

GFMM .... Gaussian Fast Multipole Method [*Physics*]

GFMP.......... Marampa [*Sierra Leone*] [*ICAO location identifier*] (ICLI)

GFMS .... Gaseous Flow Measuring System

GFMS .... Generalized File Maintenance System (ADA)

GFMVT........ General Foods Moisture Vapor Transmission

GFN........... Global Futures Network [*India*] [*India*] (EAIO)

GFN........... Grafton [*Australia Airport symbol*] (OAG)

GFN........... Grafton [*New York*] [*Seismograph station code, US Geological Survey Closed*] (SEIS)

GFNL.......... Granite Financial, Inc. [*NASDAQ symbol*] (SAG)

GFO........... Bartica [*Guyana*] [*Airport symbol*] (OAG)

GFO........... Gap-Filler Output [*RADAR*]

GFO........... Gas-Fired Oven

GFO........... General Freight Office

GFO........... GEOSAT [*Geodesy Satellite*] Follow-On (USDC)

GFO........... GEOSAT [*Geodetic Satellite*] Follow On [*Marine science*] (OSRA)

GFO........... German Foreign Office [*British World War II*]

GFO........... Gulf, Mobile & Ohio [*Railroad*] (MHDB)

GFO........... Gulf, Mobile & Ohio Railroad [*Later, Illinois Central Gulf Railroad*] (IIA)

GFOA .... Government Finance Officers Association of United States and Canada (EA)

GFOAR .... Global Family of Operational [*Plan*] Assessment Report (DOMA)

GFoF........... Fort Valley State College, Fort Valley, GA [*Library symbol Library of Congress*] (LCLS)

GForsT .... Tift College, Forsyth, GA [*Library symbol Library of Congress*] (LCLS)

GFP........... Gas Flow Programmer [*Chromatography*]

GFP........... Geheime Feldpolizei [*Secret Police*] [*German*]

GFP........... General Forecasting Program (BUR)

GFP........... General Foreign Policy [*A publication*]

GFP........... Generalized File Processor

GFP........... Generations for Peace (EA)

GFP........... Glass-Fiber Pulling [*Materials processing*]

GFP........... Government-Funded Procurement

GFP........... Government-Funded Program

GFP........... Government-Furnished Parts (AFM)

GFP........... Government-Furnished Property

GFP........... Green Fluorescent Protein [*Biochemistry*]

GFP........... Ground Fault Protector (PDAA)

GFP........... Ground Fine Pitch (AIA)

GFP & S ..... Government-Furnished Property and Services (MSA)

GFPBBD....... Groupement Francais des Producteurs de Bases et Banques de Donnees [*French Federation of Data Base Producers*] [*Information service or system*] (IID)

GF-PET .... Glass-Fiber Polyethylene Terephthalate [*Plastics technology*]

GFPL............ Government-Furnished Property List (MCD)

GFPM........... Gas Fission Products Monitor

GFPM........... Gate Frequency Position Modulation (IAA)

GFP/M .... Government-Furnished Property and Material

GFPO .... Grand Forks Project Office [*Grand Forks, ND*] [*Terminated Department of Energy*] (GRD)

GFPO .... Port Loko [*Sierra Leone*] [*ICAO location identifier*] (ICLI)

GFQ .... Austin, TX [*Location identifier FAA*] (FAAL)

GFR .... Federal Reserve Bank of Atlanta, Atlanta, GA [*OCLC symbol*] (OCLC)

GFR .... Gap-Filler RADAR

GFR .... Gas-Filled Rectifier

GFR .... General Flight Rules [*CAB*] [*A publication*] (DLA)

GFR .... General Functional Requirements

GFR .... Generator Field Regulator (IAA)

GFR .... Geotechnical Fabrics Report [*A publication*] (EAAP)

GFR .... German Federal Republic [*West Germany*]

GFR .... Glass and Fiber Resin

GFR .... Glass-Fiber Reinforced

GFR .... Glomerular Filtration Rate [*Nephrology*]

GFR .... Government Facilities Request (AAG)

GFR .... Government Flight Representative

GFR .... Granville [*France*] [*Airport symbol*] (AD)

GFR .... Grim File Reaper [*Computer hacker terminology*] (NHD)

GFRC .... Gas Flow Radiation Counter [*Nucleonics*] (IAA)

GFRC .... General File/Record Control [*Honeywell, Inc.*] (IAA)

GFRC .... Glass Fiber Reinforced Concrete

GFRHS........ Germans-from-Russia Heritage Society (EA)

GF/RP .... Gap-Filler/Reporting Post [*RADAR*]

GFRP .... Gap Filler/Reporting Post

GFRP .... Glass-Fiber-Reinforced Plastic [*Also, GIFRP*]

GFRP .... Government Furnished Repair Parts

GFRP .... Graphite-Fiber-Reinforced Plastic [*Also, GrFRP*] (NASA)

GFRS .... Ground Forces Replacement Service [*World War II*]

GFRT .... Gas-Filled Rectifying Tube

GFRTP .... Glass-Fiber-Reinforced Thermoplastic (MCD)

GFS .... Fernbank Science Center, Atlanta, GA [*OCLC symbol*] (OCLC)

GFS .... Giant Foods [*AMEX symbol*] (SAG)

GFS .... Girls' Friendly Society of the USA (EA)

GFS .... Global Financial Studies

GFS .... Global Focal Sclerosis [*Medicine*] (DMAA)

GFS .... Goffs, CA [*Location identifier FAA*] (FAAL)

GFS .... Government Finance Statistics (NITA)

GFS .... Government-Furnished Services (KSC)

GFS .... Government-Furnished Software (NASA)

GFS .... Gower Federal Service [*Rocky Mountain Mineral Law Foundation*] [*Information service or system*] (CRD)

GFS .... Grandfather-Father-Son [*Computer science*] (PCM)

GFS .... Grand Financial Scribe [*Freemasonry*] (ROG)

GFS .... Group Final Selector (IAA)

GFS .... Guernsey Freight Services [*British*]

GFS .... Gulfstream Airlines, Inc. [*ICAO designator*] (FAAC)

GFS .... Gunfire Support (NVT)

GFSA .... Goldfish Society of America (EA)

GFSB .... GFS Bancorp [*NASDAQ symbol*] (SAG)

GFSB B .... GFSB Bancorp, Inc. [*Associated Press*] (SAG)

GFS Bcp ..... GFS Bancorp [*Associated Press*] (SAG)

GFSC .... Goddard Flight Space Center [*NASA*] (AAGC)

GFSE .... Government-Furnished Support Equipment (MCD)

GFsH.......... United States Army, Fort Stewart/Hunter AAF Library, Fort Stewart, GA [*Library symbol Library of Congress*] (LCLS)

GFSL.......... Gaffsail [*Ship's rigging*] (ROG)

GFSM.......... Government-Furnished Surplus Material (MCD)

GFSP .... Government-Furnished Support Property (KSC)

GFSR .... General Function System Requirement

GFSR .... Generalized Feedback Shift Register [*Mathematics*]

GFSS .... Gunfire Support Ship

GFST.......... Ground Fuel Start Tank (AAG)

GFSUSA...... Girls' Friendly Society of the USA (EA)

GFSY .... Government Finance Statistics [*International Monetary Fund*] [*Information service or system*] (CRD)

GFT............. Generalized Fast Transform (PDAA)

GFT............. Glass Fabric Tape

GFT............. Glass-Forming Tendency [*Materials science*]

GFT............. (Glucopyranosyl)fluorothymine [*Biochemistry*]

GFT............. Graphic Firing Table [*Weaponry*] (NATG)

GFT............. Green Forest Lumber Corp. [*Toronto Stock Exchange symbol*]

GFT............. Gruppo Finanziario Tessile [*Commercial firm*]

GFT............. Guided Flight Test (MCD)

GFT............. Gulfstream International Airlines, Inc. [*ICAO designator*] (FAAC)

G/FT² .... Grams per Square Foot

GFTA.......... Goldman-Fristoe Test of Articulation [*Education*]

GFTANSW.... Grain and Feed Trade Association of New South Wales [*Australia*]

GFTC-ER ..... General Freight Traffic Committee - Eastern Railroads

GFTO .... Tongo [*Sierra Leone*] [*ICAO location identifier*] (ICLI)

GFTU .... General Federation of Trade Unions [*Various countries*]

GFTU .... General Federation of Trade Unions [*British*] (DBA)

GFTWR........ Giftwear

GFU .... Glazed Facing Units [*Technical drawings*]

GFUT .... Ground Fuel Ullage Tank (AAG)

GFV............. Fort Valley State College, Fort Valley, GA [*OCLC symbol*] (OCLC)

GFV............. Goldfever Resources Ltd. [*Vancouver Stock Exchange symbol*]

GfV............. Gueterfernverkehr [*Carriage of Goods*] [*German Business term*] (ILCA)

GFV............. Guided Flight Vehicle

GFW .... General Flight Work

GFW .... Gesellschaft fuer Weltraumforschung [*Society for Space Research*] [*Germany*]

GFW .... GFW Aviation [*Australia*] [*FAA designator*] (FAAC)

GFW .... Glass Filament Wound (IAA)

G-F-W .... Goldman-Fristoe-Woodcock Test of Auditory Discrimination [*Education*]

GFW .... Gram Formula Weight [*Chemistry*]

GFW .... Great French Writers [*A publication*]

GFWC .... Ground-Fault Warning (IEEE)

GFWC .... General Federation of Women's Clubs (EA)

GFWO .... Gulfwest Oil Co. [*NASDAQ symbol*] (SAG)

GFX .... Ghuraf [*South Arabia*] [*Airport symbol*] (AD)

GFX .... Grandfield, OK [*Location identifier FAA*] (FAAL)

GFX .... PLM Equipment Growth Fund I Ltd. [*AMEX symbol*] (SPSG)

GFY .... Government Fiscal Year (MCD)

GFY .... Grootfontein [*South-West Africa*] [*Airport symbol*] (OAG)

GFY .... PLM Equipment Growth Fund II Ltd. [*AMEX symbol*] (SPSG)

GFYE .... Yengema [*Sierra Leone*] [*ICAO location identifier*] (ICLI)

GFZ .... Greenfield, IA [*Location identifier FAA*] (FAAL)

GFZ .... PLM Equipment Growth Fund III Ltd. [*AMEX symbol*] (SPSG)

GG .... Galloping Gourmet [*TV program*]

GG .... Gamma Globulin [*Medicine*]

GG .... Gas Generator (AAG)

GG .... Gatling Gun

GG .... Gem State Airlines [*ICAO designator*] (AD)

GG .... Gender Gap [*Refers to women's tendency to vote for Democratic over Republican candidates, a phenomenon noticed by pollsters beginning with the 1980 election*]

GG .... Generator Gas [*System*] [*Nuclear energy*] (NRCH)

GG .... Genito-Genital [*Medicine*]

GG .... Gewehrgranate [*Rifle Grenade*] [*German military - World War II*]

Gg .... Gigagram

GG .... Girl Guides (BARN)

GG .... Glass Glover [*Commercial firm British*]

Gg .... Glucagon [*Endocrinology*]

GG .... Glyceryl Guaiacolate [*Expectorant*] (AAMN)

GG .... Glycylglycine [*Organic chemistry*]

GG .... Goal Gradient [*Psychology*]

GG .... Goldcorp [*NYSE symbol*] (SAG)

GG .... Golden Gloves Association of America [*Later, GGA of A*]

GG .... Government Girl

GG .... Government Grade [*Followed by a number, 1-18; National Security Agency Employee Grade*]

GG .... Governor General

GG .... Grand Guardian [*Freemasonry*]

GG .... Grant Greater Than [*Dialog*] [*Searchable field*] [*Information service or system*] (NITA)

GG .... Gravity Gradient (KSC)

GG .... Great Gatsby [*Describes clothing style modeled after the type worn by characters in F. Scott Fitzgerald's novel, "The Great Gatsby"*]

GG .... Great Gross [*144 dozen*] [*Also, GGR*]

GG .... Grenadier Guards [*Military British*]

GG .... Groove Gauge

GG .... Grounded Grid [*Valve*] (DEN)

GG .... Ground Guidance [*Aerospace*] (AAG)

GG .... Ground Gunner [*Air Force British*]

G-G .... Ground-to-Ground [*Communications, weapons, etc.*] (MSA)

G/G .... Ground-to-Ground (IDOE)

GG .... Guaifenesin [*An expectorant*] [*Pharmacology*] (DAVI)

GG .... Guinea Gulf Line [*Steamship*] (MHDB)

GG .... Gutenberg Gesellschaft

GGA .... Gale Global Access [*Also, GGAEA*]

GGA .... General Gonadotropic Activity [*Endocrinology*] (MAE)

GGA .... Generalized Gradient Approximation [*Mathematics*]

GGA .... Girl Guides Association [*British*]

GGA .... Golden Glacier [*Vancouver Stock Exchange symbol*]

GGA .... Good Gardeners' Association [*British*]

GGA .... Grounded Grid Amplifier

GGA .... Group Gross Assets (ADA)

GGA .... Guernsey Growers Association [*British*] (DBA)

GGA .... Gulf General Atomic [*Commercial firm*]

GGA .... Girl Guides Association of Australia

GGAA .... Golden Gloves Association of America [*Later, GGA of A*] (EA)

GGaB .... Brenau College, Gainsville, GA [*Library symbol Library of Congress*] (LCLS)

GGAB .... Ghana Geographical Association. Bulletin [*A publication*]

GGaC .... Gainesville Junior College, Gainesville, GA [*Library symbol*] [*Library of Congress*] (LCLS)

GGaCL .... Chestatee Regional Library System, Gainsville, GA [*Library symbol*] [*Library of Congress*] (LCLS)

GGAEA .... Gale Global Access, Encyclopedia of Associations [*Also, GGA*]

GGA of A ..... Golden Gloves Association of America (EA)

GGAR .... Gas-Guided Aircraft Rocket

GGAWA .... Grape Growers' Association of Western Australia

GGBB .... Bambadinca [*Guinea-Bissau*] [*ICAO location identifier*] (ICLI)

GGBE .... Bedanda [*Guinea-Bissau*] [*ICAO location identifier*] (ICLI)

GGBF .... Bafata [*Guinea-Bissau*] [*ICAO location identifier*] (ICLI)

GGBG .... Governor-General's Bodyguard [*British military*] (DMA)

GGBI .... Bissora [*Guinea-Bissau*] [*ICAO location identifier*] (ICLI)

GGBO .... Bolama [*Guinea-Bissau*] [*ICAO location identifier*] (ICLI)

GGBU .... Bubaque [*Guinea-Bissau*] [*ICAO location identifier*] (ICLI)
GGC .... Gamma-Glutamyl Carboxylase (DMAA)
GGC .... General Grand Chapter [*Freemasonry*]
GGC .... Georgia College, Milledgeville, GA [*OCLC symbol*] (OCLC)
GGC .... Georgia Gulf Corp. [*NYSE symbol*] (SPSG)
GGC .... Golden Gate College [*California*]
GGC .... Grey Goose Corp. Ltd. [*Toronto Stock Exchange symbol*]
GGC .... Ground Guidance Computer [*Aerospace*]
GGC .... Gun Group Commander [*British military*] (DMA)
GGCC .... Cacine [*Guinea-Bissau*] [*ICAO location identifier*] (ICLI)
GGCC .... Grand Gaming Corp. [*NASDAQ symbol*] (SAG)
GGCCW .... Grand Gaming Wrrt [*NASDAQ symbol*] (TTSB)
GGCF .... Cufar [*Guinea-Bissau*] [*ICAO location identifier*] (ICLI)
GGCG .... Cantchungo [*Guinea-Bissau*] [*ICAO location identifier*] (ICLI)
GGCST .... Gleb-Goldstein Color Sorting Test [*Psychology*]
GGCT .... Catio [*Guinea-Bissau*] [*ICAO location identifier*] (ICLI)
GGCV .... Caravela [*Guinea-Bissau*] [*ICAO location identifier*] (ICLI)
GGD .... General Government Division [*GAO*] (AAGC)
GGD .... Gold Bridge Development [*Vancouver Stock Exchange symbol*]
GGD .... Great Granddaughter
GGD .... Gregory Downs [*Australia Airport symbol Obsolete*] (OAG)
GGDA .... Geocentric Datum of Australia [*Geographic*] (EERA)
GGDC .... G. G. Drayton Club (EA)
GGDF .... Gas Gathering Data File [*Phillips Petroleum*]
GGDPAC ..... Government Geoscience Database Policy Advisory Committee [*Commonwealth*] (EERA)
GGE .... Gauge
GGE .... Generalized Glandular Enlargement [*Medicine*]
GGE .... Georgetown, SC [*Location identifier FAA*] (FAAL)
GGE .... Golden Group Explorations, Inc. [*Vancouver Stock Exchange symbol*]
GGE .... Gospelrama Gospel Expo [*An association*] (EA)
GGE .... Gradient Gel Electrophoresis
GGE .... Griffin Gaming & Entertainment [*AMEX symbol*] (SAG)
GGE .... Ground Guidance Equipment [*Aerospace*]
GGEN .... GalaGen, Inc. [*NASDAQ symbol*] (SAG)
GGEN .... GalaGen Inc. [*NASDAQ symbol*] (TTSB)
GGEP .... Empada [*Guinea-Bissau*] [*ICAO location identifier*] (ICLI)
GGF .... Glass and Glazing Federation [*British*]
GGF .... Glial Growth Factor [*Biochemistry*]
GGF .... Global Government Plus Fund Ltd. [*Toronto Stock Exchange symbol*]
GGF .... Granges-Gontardes [*France*] [*Seismograph station code, US Geological Survey Closed*] (SEIS)
GGF .... Grant, NE [*Location identifier FAA*] (FAAL)
GGF .... Ground Gained Forward [*Aerial photography*]
GGFC .... Girl Groups Fan Club (EA)
GGFC .... Go Go's Fan Club [*Defunct*] (EA)
GGFO .... Formosa [*Guinea-Bissau*] [*ICAO location identifier*] (ICLI)
GGFR .... Farim [*Guinea-Bissau*] [*ICAO location identifier*] (ICLI)
G/G/FRIS ..... Gal/Guy Fridays [*Classified advertising*]
GGFRJ .... Gas Generator Fueled Ramjet (MCD)
GGFU .... Fulacunda [*Guinea-Bissau*] [*ICAO location identifier*] (ICLI)
GGG .... Gadolinium, Gallium, Garnet [*Also, G3*] [*Substrate for magnetic film*]
GGG .... Gladewater-Kilgore-Longview [*Texas*] [*Airport symbol*] (AD)
GGG .... Glycine-Rich Gamma-Glycoprotein [*Immunology*]
GGG .... Goat Gamma-Globulin [*Immunology*]
GGG .... Graco, Inc. [*NYSE symbol*] (SPSG)
GGG .... Gummi Guttae Gambiae [*Gamboge*] [*Pharmacology*] (ROG)
GGG .... Gunnar Gold, Inc. [*Toronto Stock Exchange symbol*]
GGG .... Longview [*Texas*] [*Airport symbol*] (OAG)
GGGA .... Galinhas [*Guinea-Bissau*] [*ICAO location identifier*] (ICLI)
GGGB .... Gabu [*Guinea-Bissau*] [*ICAO location identifier*] (ICLI)
GGHP .... General Grand High Priest [*Freemasonry*]
GGI .... Greenhouse Gas Index
GGIA .... Granite Grit Institute of America (EA)
GGIT .... Geographics Inc. [*NASDAQ symbol*] (TTSB)
GGIT .... Geographics, Inc. [*NASDAQ symbol*] (SAG)
GGK .... Goldstein Golub Kessler [*Commercial firm*]
GGL .... Gain Guided LASER (IAA)
GGL .... Gerle Gold Ltd. [*Vancouver Stock Exchange symbol*]
GGL .... Gissing, Glen L., Evansville WI [*STAC*]
GGL .... Gravity-Gradient Libration [*Damper*]
GGL .... Ground Glass
GGL .... Guild of Guide Lecturers [*British*]
GGL .... Titusville, FL [*Location identifier FAA*] (FAAL)
GGIF .... Federal Law Enforcement Training Center, Glynco, GA [*Library symbol Library of Congress*] (LCLS)
GGM .... Geographici Graeci Minores [*A publication*] (OCD)
GGM .... Glitter Gold Mines [*Vancouver Stock Exchange symbol*]
GGM .... Glucose/Galactose Malabsorption [*Medicine*]
GGM .... Gravity Gradiometer Mission [*NASA*]
GGM .... Ground-to-Ground Missile
GGMA .... Glassine and Greaseproof Manufacturers Association [*Later, API*] (EA)
GGMA .... Government Gold Mining Areas
GGMK .... Great, Grand Master Key [*Locks*] (ADA)
GGMMA .... Gabriel Garcia Moreno Memorial Association (EA)
GGMS .... Mansoa [*Guinea-Bissau*] [*ICAO location identifier*] (ICLI)
GGMWA .... Grace of God Movement for the Women of America [*Later, GGMWW*] (EA)
GGMWW ..... Grace of God Movement for the Women of the World (EA)
GGN .... Air Georgian [*Canada*] [*FAA designator*] (FAAC)
GGN .... Gagnoa [*Ivory Coast*] [*Airport symbol*] (OAG)
GGNG .... Gelatin Glass Negative (VRA)
GGNI .... Governor-General of Northern Ireland (DAS)

GGNRA .... Golden Gate National Recreation Area Advisory Commission [*National Park Service*] [*San Francisco, CA*] (EGAO)
GGNRACAC... Golden Gate National Recreation Area Advisory Commission [*National Park Service*] [*San Francisco, CA*] (EGAO)
GGNS .... Genus, Inc. [*NASDAQ symbol*] (CTT)
GGNS .... Grand Gulf Nuclear Station (NRCH)
GGO .... Getchell Gold Corp. [*AMEX symbol*] (SAG)
GGO .... Glavnaya Geofizicheskaya Observatory [*Main Geophysical Observatory*] [*Former USSR*]
GGO .... Governor-General's Order [*British military*] (DMA)
GGO .... Greater Greensboro [*North Carolina*] Open [*Golf tournament*]
GGO .... Guiglo [*Ivory Coast*] [*Airport symbol*] (OAG)
GG or S ...... Glands, Goiter, or Stiffness [*Medicine*]
GGOV .... Bissau/Oswaldo Vieira International [*Guinea-Bissau*] [*ICAO location identifier*] (ICLI)
GGP .... Gas-Gathering Pipeline
GGP .... Gateway-to-Gateway Protocol [*Computer science*] (TNIG)
GGP .... General Growth Properties [*NYSE symbol*] (SPSG)
GGP .... Genl Growth Properties [*NYSE symbol*] (TTSB)
GGP .... George Resources Co. [*Vancouver Stock Exchange symbol*]
GGP .... Golden Gate Productions [*San Francisco, CA*] [*Telecommunications*] (TSSD)
GGP .... Good Gay Poets [*EA*]
GGP .... GPS [*Global Positioning System*] Guidance Package
GGP .... Gross Global Product
GGP .... Logansport, IN [*Location identifier FAA*] (FAAL)
GGPA .... Graduate Grade-Point Average [*Higher education*]
GGPC .... Pecixe [*Guinea-Bissau*] [*ICAO location identifier*] (ICLI)
GGPF .... Glial Growth Promoting Factor [*Neurology*]
GGPL .... Glycine, Glycine Phenylalanine, Leucine [*A synthetic peptide*]
GGPP .... Giant Gaseous Protoplanet [*Planetary science*]
GGPR .... Pirada [*Guinea-Bissau*] [*ICAO location identifier*] (ICLI)
GGQ .... Gagnoa [*Ivory Coast*] [*Airport symbol*] (AD)
GGR .... Gallagher Explorations Ltd. [*Vancouver Stock Exchange symbol*]
GGR .... Geschichte der Griechischen Religion [*A publication*] (OCD)
GGR .... Great Gross [*144 dozen*] [*Also, GG*]
GGR .... Ground Gunnery Range
GGRA .... Gelatine and Glue Research Association [*British*] (BI)
G Gracch ..... Gaius Gracchus [*of Plutarch*] [*Classical studies*] (OCD)
GGraG .... Gracewood State School and Hospital, Gracewood, GA [*Library symbol Library of Congress*] (LCLS)
GGriEx .... University of Georgia, Experiment Station, Griffin, GA [*Library symbol Library of Congress*] (LCLS)
GGS .... Gates-Gaudin-Schuhmann [*Particle size distribution*]
GGS .... Girls' Grammar School (ADA)
GGS .... Global Geospace Science
GGS .... Global Geospace Study [*Proposed*] [*United States, Japan, and Europe*]
GGS .... Gobernador Gregores [*Argentina*] [*Airport symbol*] (OAG)
GGS .... Graphic Generator System
GGS .... Gravity-Gradient Satellite
GGS .... Gravity-Gradient Sensor
GGS .... Great Grandson
GGS .... Ground Gained Sideways [*Aerial photography*]
GGS .... Ground Guidance System [*Aerospace*] (AAG)
GGSA .... German Genealogical Society of America (EA)
GGSD .... Sao Domingos [*Guinea-Bissau*] [*ICAO location identifier*] (ICLI)
GGSE .... Gravity-Gradient Stabilization Experiment
GGSM .... Graduate Diploma of the Guildhall School of Music [*British*] (DBQ)
GGSP .... Giant-to-Giant Interneuron Synaptic Potential [*Neurochemistry*]
GGSPFWFH... Goose and Gander, Society for the Preservation of First Wives and First Husbands (EA)
GGT .... Gabelli Global Multimedia Tr [*NYSE symbol*] (TTSB)
GGT .... Gabelli Global Multimedia Trust, Inc. [*NYSE symbol*] (SAG)
GGT .... Gamma-Glutamyltransferase [*Also, GGTP, GT*] [*An enzyme*]
GGT .... Gamma-Glutamyl Transpeptidase [*Also, GGT, GT*] [*An enzyme*] (DAVI)
GGT .... George Town [*Bahamas*] [*Airport symbol*] (OAG)
GGT .... Georgetown, NY [*Location identifier FAA*] (FAAL)
GGT .... Gravity-Gradient Torque
GGT .... Greater Temagami [*Vancouver Stock Exchange symbol*]
GGTI .... GTI Corp. [*NASDAQ symbol*] (SAG)
GGTP .... Gamma-Glutamyl Transpeptidase [*Also, GGT, GT*] [*An enzyme*]
GGTS .... Gravity-Gradient Test Satellite [*NASA*]
GGTT .... Tite [*Guinea-Bissau*] [*ICAO location identifier*] (ICLI)
GGU .... Giant Gastric Ulcer [*Medicine*]
GGUALE .... Golden Gate University Advanced Legal Education Program (DLA)
GGUN .... Uno [*Guinea-Bissau*] [*ICAO location identifier*] (ICLI)
GGUY .... [*The*] Good Guys, Inc. [*NASDAQ symbol*] (NQ)
GGV .... Gabriel Gonzalez Videla [*Antarctica*] [*Seismograph station code, US Geological Survey Closed*] (SEIS)
GGV .... Gas Generator Valve (KSC)
GGV .... Kwigillingok, AK [*Location identifier FAA*] (FAAL)
GGVB .... Gelatin, Glucose, and Veronal Buffer [*Medicine*] (DMAA)
GGVR .... Varela [*Guinea-Bissau*] [*ICAO location identifier*] (ICLI)
GGW .... Glasgow [*Montana*] [*Airport symbol*] (OAG)
GGX .... Golden Gate Explorations [*Vancouver Stock Exchange symbol*]
GGY .... Clanton, AL [*Location identifier FAA*] (FAAL)
GGY .... Greentree Energy [*Vancouver Stock Exchange symbol*]
GGZ .... Akron, OH [*Location identifier FAA*] (FAAL)
GH .... Gaseous Hydrogen (KSC)
GH .... Gate House (NRCH)
GH .... Gemini Hatch [*NASA*]
GH .... General Headquarters [*Military*] (CDAI)
GH .... General Health (DMAA)

GH .... General Hospital [*Initialism also refers to a TV program*]
GH .... General Host Corp. [*NYSE symbol*] (SPSG)
GH .... Genetic Hypertension [*Medicine*] (DMAA)
GH .... Genl Host [*NYSE symbol*] (TTSB)
GH .... George Horne [*Refers to old news*] [*Slang*] (DSUE)
GH .... Ghana [*ANSI two-letter standard code*] (CNC)
gh .... Ghana [*MARC country of publication code Library of Congress*] (LCCP)
GH .... Ghana Airways [*ICAO designator*] (AD)
GH .... Gilt Head [*Bookbinding*] (ROG)
GH .... Glenohumeral [*Joint*] [*Anatomy*] (DAVI)
GH .... Glenohumeral Joint [*Anatomy*] (DAVI)
G-H .... Goodenough-Harris Drawing Test [*Education*]
GH .... Government House [*Canada*]
GH .... Gray Herbarium [*Harvard University*] [*Cambridge, MA*]
GH .... Grid Heading [*Navigation*]
GH .... Ground Handling [*Aerospace*]
GH .... Growth Hormone [*Somatotrophin*] [*Also, SH, STH Endocrinology*]
GH .... Guardhouse
GH .... Guest House
GH₂ .... Gaseous Hydrogen [*NASA*] (KSC)
GHA .... General Housekeeping Area [*NASA*] (NASA)
GHA .... Georgia Hospital Association [*Atlanta*] (TSSD)
GHA .... Georgia Southwestern College, Americus, GA [*OCLC symbol*] (OCLC)
GHA .... Gesneriad Hybridizers Association (EA)
GHA .... Ghana [*ANSI three-letter standard code*] (CNC)
GHA .... Ghana Airways Corp. [*ICAO designator*] (FAAC)
GHA .... Ghardaia [*Algeria*] [*Airport symbol*] (OAG)
GHA .... Glashutten [*Austria*] [*Seismograph station code, US Geological Survey*] (SEIS)
GHA .... Glucoheptanoic Acid [*Biochemistry*] (DAVI)
GHA .... Golden Hat Resources [*Vancouver Stock Exchange symbol*]
GHA .... Grassland Husbandry Adviser [*Ministry of Agriculture, Fisheries, and Food*] [*British*]
GHA .... Greenwich Hour Angle
GHA .... Ground Hazard Area (MUGU)
GHA .... Gyro Header Assembly
GHAA .... Group Health Association of America (EA)
GhAF .... Ghanaian Air Force
GHAF .... Grosvenor House Antiques Fair [*British*] (ITD)
GHAMS .... Greenwich Hour Angle of Mean Sun
GHANABATT... Ghana Battalion [*Military*]
GHAQ .... General High Altitude Questionnaire (PDAA)
GHARS .... Gyroscopic Heading and Altitude Reference System (SAA)
GHAT .... Ground Handling and Transportation [*Aerospace*] (KSC)
GHATS .... Greenwich Hour Angle of True Sun
GHB .... Gamma Hydroxy Butyrate [*Steroid*]
GHB .... Gamma-Hydroxybutyric Acid [*Organic chemistry*]
GHb .... Glycohemoglobin [*Biochemistry, medicine*]
GHB .... Glycosylated Hemoglobin [*Clinical chemistry*]
GHB .... Governor's Harbour [*Bahamas*] [*Airport symbol*] (OAG)
GHBA .... Galiceno Horse Breeders Association (EA)
GHBP .... Growth Hormone Binding Protein (DMAA)
GHC .... Gating Half-Cycle [*Computer science*]
GHC .... Generalized Hyperbolic Class
GHC .... Gold Hill [*California*] [*Seismograph station code, US Geological Survey*] (SEIS)
GHC .... Grays Harbor College [*Washington*]
GHC .... Great Harbour Cay [*Bahamas*] [*Airport symbol*] (OAG)
GHC .... Greyhound Computer of Canada Ltd. [*Toronto Stock Exchange symbol*]
GHC .... Ground Half Coupling (KSC)
GHC .... Group Health Cooperative (DMAA)
GHC .... Guidance Heater Control
GHC .... Halic Havacilik, AS [*Turkey*] [*FAA designator*] (FAAC)
GHCI .... Guanidine Hydrochloride [*Organic chemistry*]
GHCN .... Global Historical Climate Network (USDC)
GHCN .... Global Historical Climate Network [*Marine science*] (OSRA)
GHCP .... Georgia Hospital Computer Group
GHCR .... Gross Henle Chromoreaction [*Clinical chemistry*]
GHCS .... Good Housekeeping Check Sheet (AAG)
GHD .... Growth Hormone Deficiency [*Endocrinology*]
GHDT .... Goodenough-Harris Drawing Test [*Psychology*] (DAVI)
GHDV .... Gasoline-Engine Heavy-Duty Vehicle
GHE .... Gable House Estates Ltd. [*British*]
GHE .... Garachine [*Panama*] [*Airport symbol*] (OAG)
GHE .... Gaseous Helium (KSC)
GHE .... Gauss Hypergeometric Equation [*Mathematics*]
GHE .... Gibbs-Helmholtz Equation [*Physical chemistry*]
GHE .... Ginn, Herbert E., South Portland ME [*STAC*]
GHE .... Golden Hemlock [*Vancouver Stock Exchange symbol*]
GHE .... Ground Handling Equipment [*Aerospace*]
G Heb .... Gospel of the Hebrews [*Apocryphal work*]
GHEF .... Givat Haviva Educational Foundation (EA)
GHF .... Gauss Hypergeometric Function [*Mathematics*]
GHF .... Gradient Heating Facility
GHF .... Grassland Heritage Foundation (EA)
GHF .... Growth Hormone Transcription Factor [*Endocrinology*]
GHFC .... Gebhardt-Heriot Foundation for All Cats (EA)
GHFC .... Gunilla Hutton Fan Club (EA)
GHFF .... George Hamilton IV and Friends [*Defunct*] (EA)
GHG .... Galactic Hitchhiker's Guild (EA)
GHG .... [*The*] Good Hotel Guide [*A publication British*]
GHG .... Governor's Horse Guard

GHG .... Greenhouse Gas [*Climatology*]
GHG .... Greenhouse Gases (EERA)
GHG .... Grosshandelsgesellschaft [*Wholesale Business Establishment*] [*German*]
GHH .... Galveston, Houston & Henderson Railroad Co. [*AAR code*]
GHi .... Georgia Historical Society, Savannah, GA [*Library symbol Library of Congress*] (LCLS)
GHI .... German Historical Institute (EA)
GHI .... GHI Mortgage Investors [*Vancouver Stock Exchange symbol*]
GHI .... Gilbert Hill [*Idaho*] [*Seismograph station code, US Geological Survey Closed*] (SEIS)
GHI .... Global High Inc. Dollar Fd [*NYSE symbol*] (TTSB)
GHI .... Global High Income Dollar Fund [*NYSE symbol*] (SPSG)
GHI .... Group Health Insurance [*British*]
GHI .... Growth Hormone Insufficiency
GHIA .... Genealogical and Heraldic Institute of America (EA)
GHJ .... Gastonia, NC [*Location identifier FAA*] (FAAL)
GHK .... Greyhawk Resources Ltd. [*Vancouver Stock Exchange symbol*]
GHK .... Grosshandelskontor [*Wholesale Business Office*] [*German*]
GHK .... Handkommentar zum Alten Testament (Goettingen) [*A publication*] (BJA)
GHL .... Gatwick Handling Ltd. [*British ICAO designator*] (FAAC)
GHL .... George Henry Lewes [*Initials used as pseudonym*]
GHL .... [*A*] Grammar of the Hurrian Language [*A publication*] (BJA)
GHL .... Greyhound Lines of Canada Ltd. [*Toronto Stock Exchange symbol*]
GHL .... Guardhouse Lawyer [*Military slang*]
GH/LCD .... Guest-Host/Liquid Crystal Display [*Telecommunications*] (TEL)
GHLI .... Guilford-Holley L Inventory [*Psychology*]
GHM .... Aero Service Bolivia [*ICAO designator*] (FAAC)
GHM .... Centerville, TN [*Location identifier FAA*] (FAAL)
GHM .... Going-Home Money
GHM .... Graham Corp. [*AMEX symbol*] (SPSG)
GHM .... Guaranteed Hourly Minimum
GH-MATRIX... Generalized Hadamand Matrix
GHME .... Gott Hilf Mir Elenden [*God Help Miserable Me*] [*Motto of Eleonore, Electress of Brandenburg (1583-1607)*] [*German*]
GHMI .... Generalized Human-Machine Interface (MCD)
GHMS .... Home Mission Sisters of America (Glenmary) (TOCD)
GHN .... Generalized Hypertrophic Neuropathy
GHN .... Ghana Navy
GHN .... Goldhaven Resources Ltd. [*Vancouver Stock Exchange symbol*]
GHN .... Groupe Hygiene Naturelle [*European Natural Hygiene Society - ENHS*] (EAIO)
GHO .... Grahamstown [*South Africa*] [*Airport symbol*] (AD)
GHO .... Greater Hartford [*Connecticut*] Open [*Golf tournament*]
Ghose Mort... Ghose on Mortgages in India [*A publication*] (DLA)
GHOST .... Global Horizontal Sounding Technique [*Meteorology*]
GHOST .... Golf Head Optical Speed Trap [*Golf self-improvement program*]
GHP .... Gas High Pressure
GHP .... Grand High Priest [*Freemasonry*]
GHP .... Greater Hartford Process [*An association*] (EA)
GHP .... Great Hungarian Plain [*Geology*]
GHP .... Greenwich Hospital Pension [*British military*] (DMA)
GHP .... Gross Horsepower [*Engineering*]
GHP .... Guild of Hospital Pharmacists [*British*] (DBA)
GHPM .... General Health Policy Model
GHPP .... Genetically Handicapped Persons Program (MEDA)
GHPR .... Gliding Horse and Pony Registry (EA)
GHQ .... General Headquarters [*Military*]
GHQ .... General Health Questionnaire [*Personality development test*] [*Psychology*]
GHQAF .... General Headquarters Air Force
GHQC .... GH [*General Hospital*] Questionnaire Club [*Defunct*] (EA)
GHQF .... General Headquarters File [*Army*]
GHQS .... General Headquarters Exercise
GHR .... Golden Hope Resources, Inc. [*Vancouver Stock Exchange symbol*]
GHR .... Granulomatous Hypersensitivity [*Medicine*] (DMAA)
GHR .... Gross Heat Rate (DNAB)
GHR .... Growth Hormone Receptor [*Biochemistry*]
GH-RF .... Growth Hormone Releasing Factor [*Somatoliberin*] [*Also, GH-RH, GRF Endocrinology*]
GHRF .... Guardians of Hydrocephalus Research Foundation (EA)
GH-RH .... Growth Hormone Releasing Hormone [*Somatoliberin*] [*Also, GH-RF, GRF Endocrinology*]
GH-RIF .... Growth Hormone Release Inhibiting Factor [*Also, GH-RIH, GRIF, SRIF, SS*] [*Endocrinology*]
GH-RIH .... Growth Hormone Release Inhibiting Hormone [*Also, GH-RIF, GRIF, SRIF, SS*] [*Endocrinology*]
GHRP .... Growth Hormone Releasing Peptide [*Endocrinology*]
GHRS .... Goddard High-Resolution Spectrograph
GHRSP .... Guatemalan Health Rights Support Project (EA)
GHR/USA .... Guatemalan Human Rights Commission/USA (EA)
GHS .... Garden History Society [*British*]
GHS .... Gatari Hutama Air Services PT [*Indonesia*] [*ICAO designator*] (FAAC)
GHS .... General Household Survey [*Office of Population Census and Surveys*] [*British*]
GHS .... Getchell Resources, Inc. [*Vancouver Stock Exchange symbol*]
GHS .... Gilroy Hot Springs [*California*] [*Seismograph station code, US Geological Survey*] (SEIS)
GHS .... Global Health Sciences Fd [*NYSE symbol*] (TTSB)
GHS .... Global Health Sciences Fund [*NYSE symbol*] (SPSG)
GHS .... Ground Handling System [*Aerospace*] (AAG)
GHS .... Group Health Service (GHCT)
GHS .... Growth Hormone Secretagogue [*Biochemistry*]
GHS .... Grunberg Hydrofoil System

GHSE .... Ground Handling and Servicing Equipment [*Aerospace*] (IAA)
GHSG .... Guest Housing [*Army*] (AABC)
GHSI .... GHS, Inc. [*Formerly, Global Health Systems, Inc.*] [*NASDAQ symbol*] (NQ)
GHS Inc ...... GHS, Inc. [*Associated Press*] (SAG)
GHSV .... Gas Hour Space Velocity [*Chemical engineering*]
GHT .... Ghat [*Libya*] [*Airport symbol*] (OAG)
GHT .... Golden Hour Tango
GHT .... Goldhurst Resources [*Vancouver Stock Exchange symbol*]
GHT .... Ground Handling Test
GHU .... Gualeguaychu [*Argentina*] [*Airport symbol*] (OAG)
GHV .... Genesis Health Ventures [*NYSE symbol*] (SPSG)
GHV .... Genesis Hlth Ventures [*NYSE symbol*] (TTSB)
GHV .... Golden Hind Ventures Ltd. [*Vancouver Stock Exchange symbol*]
GHV .... Goose Hepatitis Virus [*Medicine*] (DMAA)
GHV .... Growth Hormone Variant [*Medicine*] (DMAA)
GHVL .... Groot Hertog von Luxemberg [*Grand Duke of Luxemburg*] [*Numismatics*] (ROG)
GHVM .... Global High-Visibility Mast
GHW .... Garrison Hill [*Washington*] [*Seismograph station code, US Geological Survey*] (SEIS)
GHW .... General Housewares Corp. [*NYSE symbol*] (SPSG)
GHW .... Genl Housewares [*NYSE symbol*] (TTSB)
GHW .... Guaranteed Hourly Wage
GHWP .... Greenhouse Warming Potential [*Environmental chemistry*]
GHWS .... Gas Hot Water Service [*Classified advertising*] (ADA)
GHX .... Graham, TX [*Location identifier FAA*] (FAAL)
GHX .... Ground Heat Exchanger
GHz .... Gigahertz [*1,000 megahertz*]
GHZ .... Golden Horizon [*Vancouver Stock Exchange symbol*]
GI .... Air Guinee [*ICAO designator*] (AD)
GI .... Galvanized Iron
GI .... Gastroenterology (DAVI)
GI .... Gastrointestinal [*Medicine*]
GI .... Gelatin Infusion [*Medium*] [*Biochemistry*] (DAVI)
GI .... Gelatin Infusion Medium [*Medicine*] (BABM)
GI .... Gelbray International (EA)
GI .... Gemeinschaft der Ikonenfreunde [*Society of Friends of Icons - SFI*] (EAIO)
GI .... Genealogical Institute (EA)
GI .... General Index
GI .... General Indulgence (ROG)
GI .... General Infantry [*Soldier*] [*Army*] (DAVI)
GI .... General Information (IAA)
GI .... General Input [*Computer science*] (IAA)
GI .... General Inspection [*Military*] (AABC)
GI .... General Instruments
GI .... General Issue
GI .... Generic Identifier [*Telecommunications*] (TEL)
GI .... Genesis Information (EA)
GI .... Genesis Institute [*An association*] (EA)
GI .... Genetics Institute, Inc.
GI .... Geodesic Isotensoid (IEEE)
GI .... Geographically Impossible (ADA)
GI .... Geometric Intelligence
GI .... Geophysical Institute [*University of Alaska, Fairbanks*] [*Research center*]
GI .... Gerson Institute (EA)
GI .... Giant Industries [*NYSE symbol*] (SPSG)
GI .... Giant Interneurons [*Neurology*]
GI .... Gibraltar [*ANSI two-letter standard code*] (CNC)
gi .... Gibraltar [*MARC country of publication code Library of Congress*] (LCCP)
GI .... Gideons International (EA)
GI .... Gilbert [*A unit of magnetomotive force*]
GI .... Gill
GI .... Gingival Index [*Dentistry*]
GI .... Girls, Inc. (EA)
GI .... Glazed Interior [*Title*] (DICI)
GI .... Globin Insulin
GI .... Glomerular Index [*Medicine*] (AAMN)
GI .... Glomus intraradices [*A fungus*]
GI .... Goethe Institute (EA)
GI .... Gold Institute [*Also known as L'Institut de l'Or*] (EA)
GI .... Government and Industrial (IEEE)
GI .... Government Initiated (IEEE)
GI .... Government Issue [*Army*]
GI .... Government of India
GI .... Graded Index [*Optics*]
GI .... Grand Island [*Diocesan abbreviation*] [*Nebraska*] (TOCD)
GI .... Granuloma Inguinale [*Endocrinology*] (DAVI)
GI .... Grassroots International (EA)
GI .... Gravida I [*Gynecology and obstetrics*] (DAVI)
GI .... Gray Iron (MSA)
GI .... Gray's Inn [*London*] [*One of the Inns of Court*]
GI .... Great Indulgence
GI .... Green Island [*Plant pathology*]
GI .... Greenpeace International (EA)
GI .... Grid Interval (IAA)
GI .... Gross Impression [*Television ratings*] (NTCM)
GI .... Gross Income
GI .... Gross Inventory (MHDB)
GI .... Gross Investment
GI .... Ground Interception (IAA)
GI .... Group Insurance

GI .... Growth and Income [*Business term*]
GI .... Growth Index
GI .... Growth Inhibiting
GI .... Guidance Inventory [*Psychology*]
GI .... Guided Imagery [*Psychology*]
GI .... Guido de Suzaria [*Deceased, 1293*] [*Authority cited in pre-1607 legal work*] (DSA)
GI .... Gunner Instructor [*Navy British*]
GI .... Gyro International (EA)
GI .... Royal Glasgow Institute of Fine Arts [*Scotland*]
GI .... Soldier [*Slang, probably from Government Issue*]
GIA .... Armed Islamic Group [*Anti-government faction*] [*Algeria*] [*Acronym is based on foreign phrase*] (ECON)
GIA .... Garden Industry of America [*Inactive*] (EA)
GIA .... Garuda Indonesian Airways Ltd.
GIA .... Garuda Indonesia PT [*ICAO designator*] (FAAC)
GIA .... Gastrointestinal Anastomosis [*Medicine*] (DAVI)
GIA .... Gemological Institute of America (EA)
GIA .... General Industry Applications (MCD)
GIA .... General International Agreement [*Legal term*] (DLA)
GIA .... Geographical Information Analysis (EERA)
GIA .... Geophysical Institute, University of Alaska [*Alaska*] [*Seismograph station code, US Geological Survey Closed*] (SEIS)
GIA .... Glacial Isostatic Adjustment [*Geophysics*]
GIA .... Glacial Isostatic Adjustment [*Geophysics*]
GIA .... Goodwill Industries of America (EA)
GIA .... Government Information and Advertising [*New South Wales, Australia*]
GIA .... GPC [*General Purpose Computer*] Interface Adapter (NASA)
GIA .... Grants-in-Aid
GIA .... Gross Internal Area
GIA .... Group Interaction Analysis
GIA .... Gummed Industries Association (EA)
GIABS .... Gastrointestinal Absorption Database [*Environmental Protection Agency Information service or system*] (CRD)
GIAC .... General Industry Advisory Committee
GIAM .... Global Impacts of Applied Microbiology [*International conferences*]
GIANT .... Genealogical [*or Geological*] Information and Name Tabulating System [*Computer science*] (IEEE)
GIANT .... General Information and Analysis Tool
GIANT .... General Instrument Advanced Nitride Technology (IAA)
GIANT .... General Integrated Analytical Triangulation Program [*National Oceanic and Atmospheric Administration*]
GIANT .... Geographic Intelligence and Topographic System
GIANT .... Giant Group Ltd. [*Associated Press*] (SAG)
GIANT .... Graphic Interactive Analytic Network Technique (MCD)
GiantCmt .... Giant Cement Holding, Inc. [*Associated Press*] (SAG)
GiantFd .... Giant Foods [*Associated Press*] (SAG)
GiantIn .... Giant Industries [*Associated Press*] (SAG)
GIANTS .... Greater Independent Association of National Travel Services (EA)
GIAO .... Gauge-Invariant Atomic Orbital [*NASA*]
GIAR .... Grants-in-Aid of Research
GIAS .... Global Integration and Synthesis [*Climate change*] (EERA)
Giauq El ..... Giauque's Election Laws [*A publication*] (DLA)
GIAWA .... Gas Industry Association of Western Australia
GIB .... Air Guinea [*Guinea*] [*ICAO designator*] (FAAC)
GIB .... Gastric Ileal Bypass [*Medicine*] (DAVI)
GIB .... Gastrointestinal Bleeding [*Medicine*] (DMAA)
GIB .... General Information Booklet [*Navy*]
GIB .... General Instruction Book
Gib .... Gibbon's Reports, New York Surrogate Court [*A publication*] (DLA)
GIB .... Gibilmanna [*Sicily*] [*Seismograph station code, US Geological Survey*] (SEIS)
GIB .... Gibraltar [*Airport symbol*] (OAG)
GIB .... Gibraltar [*ANSI three-letter standard code*] (CNC)
Gib .... Gibraltar (ODBW)
GIB .... Good in Bed (DSUE)
GIB .... GPS [*Global Positioning System*] Integrity Broadcast [*Navigation systems*]
GIB .... Gulf International Bank [*Bahrain*] (EY)
GIB .... Guy in the Back [*Copilot*] [*Air Force slang*]
Gib Aids ..... Gibson's Aids to the Examinations [*A publication*] (DLA)
GIBAIR .... Gibraltar Airways Ltd.
Gib & Na Eq Jur... Gibbons and Nathans' Equitable Jurisdiction of County Courts [*A publication*] (DLA)
GIBAPA .... Guild of International Butler Administrators and Personal Assistants [*British*] (EAIO)
Gibbon .... Gibbon on Nuisances [*A publication*] (DLA)
Gibbon Rom Emp... Gibbon's History of the Decline and Fall of the Roman Empire [*A publication*] (DLA)
Gibbons .... Gibbon's Reports, New York Surrogate Court [*A publication*] (DLA)
Gibbons (NY)... Gibbon's Reports, New York Surrogate Court [*A publication*] (DLA)
Gibb Rom Emp... Gibbon's History of the Decline and Fall of the Roman Empire [*A publication*] (DLA)
Gibbs .... Gibbs' Reports [*2-4 Michigan*] [*A publication*] (DLA)
GibbsC .... Gibbs Construction, Inc. [*Associated Press*] (SAG)
GibbsCn .... Gibbs Construction, Inc. [*Associated Press*] (SAG)
Gibbs F .... Gibbs' Practical Forms [*A publication*] (DLA)
Gibbs' Jud Chr... Gibbs' Judicial Chronicle [*A publication*] (DLA)
GIBBSSAR ... Gibbs & Hill, Inc., Standard Safety Analysis Report [*Nuclear energy*] (NRCH)
Gibb Sur ...... Gibbon's Reports, New York Surrogate Court [*A publication*] (DLA)
Gibb Surr..... Gibbon's Reports, New York Surrogate Court [*A publication*] (DLA)
Gib Civ L ..... Gibbons on the Civil Law [*A publication*] (DLA)
Gib Cod ...... Gibson's Codex Juris Ecclesiastia Anglicani [*A publication*] (DLA)

Gib Cont	Gibbons on Contracts [*A publication*] (DLA)
Gib Dec	Gibson's Scottish Decisions [*A publication*] (DLA)
Gib Dil	Gibbon's Dilapidations and Nuisances [*2nd ed.*] [*1849*] [*A publication*] (DLA)
GIBF	Gastrointestinal Bacterial Flora [*Medicine*] (MEDA)
Gib Fix	Gibbon's Law of Fixtures [*1836*] [*A publication*] (DLA)
GIBG	Gibson Greetings [*NASDAQ symbol*] (TTSB)
GIBG	Gibson Greetings, Inc. [*NASDAQ symbol*] (NQ)
GI (Bill)	Veterans Benefits Act, Public Law 345, 1944
GIBIS	Graphical IBIS [*Issue-Based Information System*] [*Computer science*] (BYTE)
Gib Lim	Gibbons' Lex Temporis, Limitations and Prescription [*A publication*] (DLA)
Gib LN	Gibson's Law Notice [*1882-84*] [*A publication*] (DLA)
Gib Lynd	Gibson's Memoir of Lord Lyndhurst [*A publication*] (DLA)
GIBMED	Gibraltar Mediterranean Command [*NATO*] (NATG)
Gib Nui	Gibbon's Dilapidations and Nuisances [*2nd ed.*] [*1849*] [*A publication*] (DLA)
GibPack	Gibraltar Packaging Group [*Associated Press*] (SAG)
Gibr	Gibraltar
GibrStl	Gibraltar Steel Corp. [*Associated Press*] (SAG)
GIBS	Guy in the Backseat [*Copilot*] [*Air Force slang*]
Gibs Camd	Gibson's Edition of Camden's Britannia [*A publication*] (DLA)
Gibs Code	Gibson's Codex [*A publication*] (DLA)
Gibs LN	Gibson's Law Notes [*1882-84*] [*A publication*] (DLA)
GibsnG	Gibson Greetings, Inc. [*Associated Press*] (SAG)
Gibson	(Gibson of) Durie's Decisions, Scotch Court of Session [*1621-42*] [*A publication*] (DLA)
GIC	Compagnie de Bauxites de Guinee [*Guinea*] [*ICAO designator*] (FAAC)
GIC	Galit Resource Corp. [*Vancouver Stock Exchange symbol*]
GIC	General Immunocompetence [*Immunology*] (DAVI)
GIC	General Improvement Contractors Association (EA)
GIC	General Input Channel (NITA)
GIC	General Input/Output Channel
GIC	General Instrument Corp. [*NYSE symbol*] (SPSG)
GIC	Generalized Immittance [*or Impedance*] Converter (IEEE)
GIC	Genl Instrument [*NYSE symbol*] (TTSB)
GIC	Geomagnetically Induced Current
GIC	German Information Center [*Information service or system*] (IID)
GIC	Glass-Ionomer Cement [*Dental material*]
GIC	Global Interdependence Center (EA)
GIC	Goods in Custody (ADA)
GIC	GPS [*Global Positioning Systems*] Integrity Channel [*Navigation systems*]
GIC	Graduate Induction Campaign [*Australia*]
GIC	Grains Industry Council [*Australia*]
GIC	Graphite Intercalation Compound [*Inorganic chemistry*]
GIC	Guaranteed Income Contract
GIC	Guaranteed Investment Contract
GIC	Gulf Intercoastal Conference
GICA	Gastrointestinal Cancer Antigen [*A tumor marker*] (CDI)
GICA	Goat Industry Council of Australia
GICC	Government-Industry Coordinating Committee
GICCW	Government-Industry Conference against Chemical Weapons (EERA)
GICL	Gila Cliff Dwellings National Monument
GICL	Graphics Language [*Computer science*] (HGAA)
GICLDC	GI Civil Liberties Defense Committee
GICLE	Institute of Continuing Legal Education in Georgia [*University of Georgia School of Law*] (DLA)
GICORP	Government-Industry Cooperative Oyster Research Program
GICR	Goodwin Institute for Cancer Research [*Nova University*] [*Research center*] (RCD)
GICS	Geographic Identification Code Scheme [*Bureau of the Census*] (GFGA)
GICS	Global Instrumentation Control System (IAA)
GICS	Grant Information and Control System [*Environmental Protection Agency*] (GFGA)
GICS	Ground Instrumentation and Communications System (IAA)
GICWG	Government Interface Control Working Group [*Military*]
GID	Channel Aviation Ltd. [*British ICAO designator*] (FAAC)
GID	Gastrointestinal Dialysis [*Medicine*]
GID	Gender Identity Disorder [*Medicine*] (DMAA)
GID	General Installation Dolly
GID	Gesellschaft fuer Information und Dokumentation mbH [*Society for Information and Documentation*] [*Information service or system*] (IID)
GID	Gitega [*Burundi*] [*Airport symbol*] (OAG)
GID	Grupo Indl Durango ADS [*NYSE symbol*] (TTSB)
GID	Grupo Industrial Durango SA de CV [*NYSE symbol*] (SAG)
GID	Guilde International du Disque [*Record label*] [*France*]
GID	Sud Air Transport SA [*Guinea*] [*ICAO designator*] (FAAC)
GIDAP	Guidance Inertial Data Analysis Program
GIDAS	Geoanomaly Interactive Data Analysis System (MCD)
GIDEON	Global Infectious Disease and Epidemiology Network
GIDEP	Government-Industry Data Exchange Program [*Formerly, IDEP*] [*Navy Information service or system*]
GID-IZ	Gesellschaft fuer Information und Dokumentation - Informationszentrum fuer Informationswissenschaft und -Praxis [*Information Center for Information Science and Information Work*] [*Society for Information and Documentation*] (IID)
GIDL	Giddings & Lewis [*NASDAQ symbol*] (TTSB)
GIDL	Giddings & Lewis, Inc. [*NASDAQ symbol*] (NQ)
GidLew	Giddings & Lewis, Inc. [*Associated Press*] (SAG)
GIDP	Gale International Directory of Publications [*A publication*]

GIDP	Grounded into Double Plays [*Baseball*]
GIE	Galapagos Islands [*Ecuador*] [*Seismograph station code, US Geological Survey*] (SEIS)
GIE	Glycerinisopropylidene Ether [*Organic chemistry*]
GIE	Ground Instrumentation Equipment
GIE	Grupo Interamericano de Editores [*Interamerican publishers group*] (NITA)
GIE	Guinee Inter Air [*Guinea*] [*ICAO designator*] (FAAC)
GIEA	German-American Information and Education Association (EA)
GIEE	Graduate of the Institute of Electrical Engineers [*British*] (DAS)
GIER	General Industrial Equipment Reserve
GIEUS	Guide to International Education in the US [*A publication*]
GIE VI	Groupe International Postal d'Echanges d'Information et d'Experience [*International Group for the Exchange of Information and Experience Among Postal Savings Institutions*] (EAIO)
GIEWS	Global Information and Early Warning System [*FAO*] [*United Nations*] (DUND)
GIF	General Image Format [*Marine science*] (OSRA)
GIF	General Image Format (USDC)
GIF	General Insurance Fund [*Federal Housing Administration*]
GIF	German-Israeli Foundation [*US and Israel*]
GIF	Gesellschaft fuer Informationsmarkt-Forschung [*Society for Information-Market Research*] [*Database producer*] (IID)
Gif	Giffard's English Vice-Chancellors' Reports [*65-66 English Reprint*] [*A publication*] (DLA)
GIF	Gifu [*Japan*] [*Seismograph station code, US Geological Survey*] (SEIS)
gif	Graphic Interchange Format [*Computer science*]
GIF	Graphics Interchange Format [*Computer technology*]
GIF	Gravito-Inertial Force
GIF	Growth Inhibiting Factor [*Endocrinology*] (MAE)
GIF	Guardian International Income Fund Units [*Toronto Stock Exchange symbol*]
GIF	Guinee Air Lines SA [*Guinea*] [*ICAO designator*] (FAAC)
GIF	Gulf It to FORTRAN [*Translator*] [*Computer science*]
GIF	Guy in the Front Seat [*Pilot*] [*Slang*] (DSUE)
GIF	Winter Haven, FL [*Location identifier FAA*] (FAAL)
GIFA	General Iron Fitters Association [*A union*] [*British*]
GIFA	Geneva Infant Feeding Association
GIFA	Governing International Fisheries Agreements
GIFA	Governing International Fishing Agreement (MSC)
GIFAP	Groupement International des Associations Nationales de Fabricants de Produits Agrochimiques [*International Group of National Associations of Manufacturers of Agrochemical Products*] (EAIO)
GIFC	Gilligan's Island Fan Club (EA)
Giff	Giffard's English Vice-Chancellors' Reports [*65-66 English Reprint*] [*A publication*] (DLA)
Giff & H	Giffard and Hemming's English Chancery Reports [*A publication*] (DLA)
Giff (Eng)	Giffard's English Vice-Chancellors' Reports [*65-66 English Reprint*] [*A publication*] (DLA)
GIFFI	Group Inventory for Finding Interests [*Educational test*]
GIFH	Golden Isles Financial Holdings, Inc. [*NASDAQ symbol*] (SAG)
GIFH	Golden Isles Finl Hldg [*NASDAQ symbol*] (TTSB)
GIFHU	Golden Isles Finl Hldg Unit [*NASDAQ symbol*] (TTSB)
GIFI	General Information File Interrogation (PDAA)
GI for SS	Goddard Institute for Space Studies [*NASA*]
GIFOV	Ground Instantaneous Field-of-View (MCD)
GIFS	Generalized Interrelated Flow Simulation (IEEE)
GIFS	Gospel-in-Film Service [*Australia*]
GIFS	Gray Iron Founders Society (EA)
GIFS	Guggenheim Institute of Flight Structures (MUGU)
GIFT	Gamete Intrafallopian Transfer [*Fertilization technique*]
GIFT	Gas-Insulated Flow Tube (NRCH)
GIFT	General Internal FORTRAN Translator [*Computer science*] (IEEE)
GIFT	Geometric Information for Targets (MCD)
GIFT	Glasgow International Freight Terminal [*Scotland*] (DS)
GIFT	Group Inventory for Finding Creative Talent [*Educational test*]
GIFTPOOL	Datenbank ueber Gifte und Vergiftungen [*Databank for Poisons and Poisoning*] [*German*]
GIFTS	Graphics-Oriented Interactive Finite Element Time-Sharing System (PDAA)
Gig	De Gigantibus [*Philo*] (BJA)
GIG	Genetics Interest Group [*British*]
GIG	Gesellschaft fuer Internationale Geldgeschichte (EAIO)
GIG	Gigi Resources Ltd. [*Vancouver Stock Exchange symbol*]
GIG	Gluten Intolerance Group [*Later, GIGNA*] (EA)
GIG	Glycidylisopropylideneglycerol [*Organic chemistry*]
GIG	Rio De Janeiro [*Brazil*] [*Airport symbol*] (OAG)
GIG	Scottsbluff, NE [*Location identifier FAA*] (FAAL)
GIGA	Giga-Tronics, Inc. [*NASDAQ symbol*] (NQ)
giga	One Billion (WDMC)
GigaInfo	Giga Information Group, Inc. [*Associated Press*] (SAG)
GigaTr	Giga-Tronics, Inc. [*Associated Press*] (SAG)
GIGI	Gamma Inspection of Grain Integrity
GIGI	General Imaging Generator and Interpreter (IAA)
GIGL	Gale Information Guide Library [*Publication series*]
GIGNA	Gluten Intolerance Group of North America (EA)
GIGO	Garbage In, Garbage Out [*Computer science*]
gigo	Garbage In Garbage Out [*Computer science*] (ODBW)
GIGS	Gemini Inertial Guidance System [*NASA*] (KSC)
GIGS	Gravity-Gradient Test Satellite
GIGX	Giga Information Group, Inc. [*NASDAQ symbol*] (SAG)
GIH	Gastrointestinal Hemorrhage [*Medicine*] (DMAA)
GIH	Gastrointestinal Hormone [*Endocrinology*]

GIH .... Groupe International Hachette [*France*]
GIH .... Growth Inhibiting Hormone [*Endocrinology*] (MAE)
GIH .... United States Geological Survey, Water Resources Division, Helena, MT [*OCLC symbol*] (OCLC)
GII .... Gastrointestinal Infection [*Medicine*]
GII .... Greiner Engineering, Inc. [*NYSE symbol*] (SPSG)
GII .... Guillevin International, Inc. [*Toronto Stock Exchange symbol*]
G-II .... Gulfstream II [*Shuttle training aircraft*] [*NASA*] (NASA)
GII .... Siguiri [*Guinea*] [*Airport symbol*] (AD)
GIID .... GENSER Integration Information Display (MCD)
GIIGNL .... Groupe Internationale des Importateur du Gaz Natural Liquefie
GIII .... G-III Apparel Group Ltd. [*NASDAQ symbol*] (NQ)
G-III .... GThree Apparel Group Ltd. [*Associated Press*] (SAG)
GIIP .... Groupement International de l'Industrie Pharmaceutique des Pays de la CEE [*International Pharmaceutical Industry Group for the EEC Countries*]
GIIR .... Government Idle Industrial Reserve (AAG)
GIIV .... Gated Image Intensifier Viewer
GIK .... Glucose, Insulin, and Potassium [*Solution*] [*Medicine*]
GIKA .... Gifts In Kind America (NFD)
GIL .... Gaseous Ion LASER
GIL .... General-Purpose Interactive Programming Language [*Computer science*] (MHDB)
Gil .... Gilbert [*A unit of magnetomotive force*]
Gil .... Gilbert's Cases in Law and Equity [*A publication*] (DLA)
Gil .... Gilbert's English Chancery Reports [*1705-27*] [*A publication*] (DLA)
Gil .... Gilfillan's Reports [*1-20 Minnesota*] [*A publication*] (DLA)
GIL .... Gilgit [*Pakistan*] [*Airport symbol*] (AD)
GIL .... Gill Aviation Ltd. [*British ICAO designator*] (FAAC)
Gil .... Gilman's Reports [*6-10 Illinois*] [*A publication*] (DLA)
Gil .... Gilmer's Virginia Reports [*21 Virginia*] [*A publication*] (DLA)
GIL .... Gilmore Creek [*Alaska*] [*Seismograph station code, US Geological Survey*] (SEIS)
GIL .... Grain Isolation Liner (MCD)
GIL .... Green Indicating Lamp
GIL .... Group Investment-Linked (ADA)
Gil .... Guillelmus Durandi [*Deceased, 1296*] [*Authority cited in pre-1607 legal work*] (DSA)
GIL .... United States Geological Survey, Metairie, LA [*OCLC symbol*] (OCLC)
Gil & Fal ..... Gilmour and Falconer's Cases, Scotch Court of Session [*A publication*] (DLA)
GilatSat .... Gilat Satellite Networks Ltd. [*Associated Press*] (SAG)
GILB .... Gilbert Associates, Inc. [*NASDAQ symbol*] (NQ)
Gilb .... Gilbert's Cases in Law and Equity [*A publication*] (DLA)
Gilb .... Gilbert's English Chancery Reports [*1705-27*] [*A publication*] (DLA)
GILBA .... Gilbert Assoc'A' [*NASDAQ symbol*] (TTSB)
Gilb Bank ..... Gilbert on Banking [*A publication*] (DLA)
Gilb Cas ..... Gilbert's Cases in Law and Equity [*A publication*] (DLA)
Gilb Cas L & Eq... Gilbert's Cases in Law and Equity [*A publication*] (DLA)
Gilb Cas L & Eq (Eng)... Gilbert's Common Pleas [*93 English Reprint*] [*A publication*] (DLA)
Gilb Ch .... Gilbert's English Chancery Reports [*1705-27*] [*A publication*] (DLA)
Gilb Com Pl... Gilbert's Common Pleas [*93 English Reprint*] [*A publication*] (DLA)
Gilb CP .... Gilbert's Common Pleas [*93 English Reprint*] [*A publication*] (DLA)
Gilb Debt ..... Gilbert on the Action of Debt [*A publication*] (DLA)
Gilb Dev ..... Gilbert's Law of Devises [*A publication*] (DLA)
Gilb Dis ..... Gilbert on Distress and Replevin [*A publication*] (DLA)
Gilb Ej .... Gilbert on Ejectments [*A publication*] (DLA)
Gilb Eq .... Gilbert's English Equity Reports [*25 English Reprint*] [*1705-27*] [*A publication*] (DLA)
Gilb Eq (Eng)... Gilbert's English Equity Reports [*25 English Reprint*] [*1705-27*] [*A publication*] (DLA)
Gilb Eq Rep... Gilbert's English Equity Reports [*1705-27*] [*A publication*] (DLA)
Gilbert Ev .... Gilbert's Law of Evidence [*A publication*] (DLA)
Gilbert Uses by Sugd... Gilbert's Uses and Trusts by Sugden [*A publication*] (DLA)
Gilb Ev .... Gilbert's Law of Evidence [*A publication*] (DLA)
Gilb Ex .... Gilbert's Executions [*A publication*] (DLA)
Gilb Exch ..... Gilbert's English Exchequer Reports [*A publication*] (DLA)
Gilb Exch Pr... Gilbert's History and Practice of the Exchequer [*A publication*] (DLA)
Gilb For Rom... Gilbert's Forum Romanum [*A publication*] (DLA)
Gilb Forum Rom... Gilbert's Forum Romanum [*A publication*] (DLA)
Gilb Hist CP... Gilbert's History of Common Pleas [*A publication*] (DLA)
Gilb KB .... Gilbert's Cases in Law and Equity [*A publication*] (DLA)
Gilb Lex Pr... Gilbert's Lex Praetoria [*A publication*] (DLA)
Gilb PC .... Gilbert's Common Pleas [*93 English Reprint*] [*A publication*] (DLA)
Gilb Rem ..... Gilbert's Remainders [*A publication*] (DLA)
Gilb Rents ... Gilbert's Treatise on Rents [*A publication*] (DLA)
Gilb Rep .... Gilbert's English Chancery Reports [*1705-27*] [*A publication*] (DLA)
Gilb Repl ..... Gilbert on Replevin [*A publication*] (DLA)
Gilb RR .... Gilbert's Railway Law of Illinois [*A publication*] (DLA)
GilbtA .... Gilbert Associates, Inc. [*Associated Press*] (SAG)
Gilb Ten .... Gilbert on Tenures [*A publication*] (DLA)
Gilb Uses ..... Gilbert on Uses and Trusts [*A publication*] (DLA)
Gilchr .... Gilchrist's Local Government Cases [*A publication*] (DLA)
Gild .... Gildersleeve's Reports [*New Mexico*] [*A publication*] (DLA)
GILD .... Gilead Sciences [*NASDAQ symbol*] (TTSB)
GILD .... Gilead Sciences, Inc. [*NASDAQ symbol*] (SPSG)
Gildersleeve... Gildersleeve's Reports [*New Mexico*] [*A publication*] (DLA)
Gildersleeve (N Mex)... Gildersleeve's Reports [*New Mexico*] [*A publication*] (DLA)
Gildr .... Gildersleeve's Reports [*New Mexico*] [*A publication*] (DLA)
Gil Dur .... Guillelmus Durandi [*Deceased, 1296*] [*Authority cited in pre-1607 legal work*] (DSA)
Gilead .... Gilead Sciences, Inc. [*Associated Press*] (SAG)
Gilfillan .... Gilfillan's Reports [*1-20 Minnesota*] [*A publication*] (DLA)
Gilg .... Gilgames (BJA)
GILL .... Gillingham [*Municipal borough in England*]
Gill .... Gill's Maryland Court of Appeals Reports [*1843-51*] [*A publication*] (DLA)
Gill & J .... Gill and Johnson's Maryland Reports [*A publication*] (DLA)
Gill and J (Maryland)... Gill and Johnson's Maryland Reports [*A publication*] (DLA)
Gill & J (MD)... Gill and Johnson's Maryland Reports [*A publication*] (DLA)
Gill & Johns... Gill and Johnson's Maryland Reports [*A publication*] (DLA)
Gillete .... Gillette Co. [*Associated Press*] (SAG)
Gillett Cr Law... Gillett's Treatise on Criminal Law and Procedure in Criminal Cases [*A publication*] (DLA)
Gill (MD) .... Gill's Maryland Reports [*A publication*] (DLA)
Gill Pol Rep... Gill's Police Court Reports [*Boston, MA*] [*A publication*] (DLA)
Gilm .... Gilman's Reports [*6-10 Illinois*] [*A publication*] (DLA)
Gilm .... Gilmer's Virginia Reports [*21 Virginia*] [*A publication*] (DLA)
Gilm .... Gilmour's Reports, Scotch Court of Session [*A publication*] (DLA)
Gilman .... Gilman's Reports [*6-10 Illinois*] [*A publication*] (DLA)
Gilm & F ..... Gilmour and Falconer's Decisions, Scotch Court of Session [*1961-66*] [*A publication*] (DLA)
Gilm & Fal... Gilmour and Falconer's Decisions, Scotch Court of Session [*1961-66*] [*A publication*] (DLA)
Gilm & Falc... Gilmour and Falconer's Reports, Scotch Court of Session [*A publication*] (DLA)
GilmC .... Gilman & Ciocia, Inc. [*Associated Press*] (SAG)
Gilm Dig ..... Gilman's Illinois and Indiana Digest [*A publication*] (DLA)
Gilmer .... Gilmer's Virginia Reports [*21 Virginia*] [*1820-21*] [*A publication*] (DLA)
GILMER .... Guardian of Impressive Letters and Master of Excellent Replies
Gilmer (VA)... Gilmer's Virginia Reports [*21 Virginia*] [*A publication*] (DLA)
Gilm (Ill) .... Gilman's Reports [*6-10 Illinois*] [*A publication*] (DLA)
Gil (Minn)... Gilfillan's Edition [*1-20 Minnesota*] [*A publication*] (DLA)
GilmnCio .... Gilman & Ciocia, Inc. [*Associated Press*] (SAG)
GILN .... Glosa International Language Network (EAIO)
Gilp .... Gilpin's United States District Court Reports [*A publication*] (DLA)
Gilp Opin ..... Gilpin's Opinions of the United States Attorneys-General [*A publication*] (DLA)
GILS .... Government Information Locator Service [*Internet*] (AAGC)
GILSP .... Good Industrial Large-Scale Practice
GILT .... General Internal Logic Test (PDAA)
GILT .... Gilat Satellite Networks Ltd. [*NASDAQ symbol*] (SAG)
GILTF .... Gilat Satellite Networks [*NASDAQ symbol*] (TTSB)
GIM .... Gaining Inventory Managers (AFM)
GIM .... Gas Injection Molding [*Plastic fabrications*]
GIM .... Geldermann Investment Management [*Finance British*]
GIM .... General Instrument Microelectronics [*British*] (NITA)
GIM .... Generalized Information Management [*Language*]
GIM .... Geneva Informal Meeting [*of International Non-Governmental Organizations*] [*British*]
GIM .... Glashow-Iliopoulos-Maiani [*Theory in particle physics*]
GIM .... Glass Insulation Material
GIM .... Gonadotropin-Inhibitory Material [*Endocrinology*] (MAE)
GIM .... Grace's Insect [*Growth*] Medium [*Microbiology*]
GIM .... Gruppe Internationale Marxisten [*International Marxist Group*] [*Germany Political party*] (PPW)
GIM .... Gulf International Minerals [*Vancouver Stock Exchange symbol*]
GIM .... Miele Mimbale [*Gabon*] [*Airport symbol*] (AD)
GIM .... Templeton Global Income [*NYSE symbol*] (SPSG)
GIMA .... Garden Industry Manufacturers Association [*British*] (DBA)
Gima .... Grupo Independente de Macau [*Independent Group of Macao*] [*Political party*] (PPW)
GIMADS .... Generic Integrated Maintenance and Diagnostic System (MCD)
GIMB .... Gimbal (KSC)
GI Mech E ... Graduate of the Institution of Mechanical Engineers [*British*]
GIMI .... Graduate of the Institute of the Motor Industry [*British*] (DBQ)
GIMIC .... Guard Ring Isolated Monolithic Integrated Circuit
GIMMIS .... G-I Manpower Management Information System
GIMMS .... Geographic Information Mapping and Management System (EERA)
GIMMS .... Global Inventory Modeling and Monitoring Study (EERA)
GIMP .... Gimbal Positioning
GIMPY .... Growing, Improving, Maturing - Puppy of the Year [*Canine award*]
GIMR .... Garvan Institute of Medical Research [*Australia*]
GIMRADA .... Geodesy, Intelligence, and Mapping Research and Development Agency [*Army*]
GIMS .... Geographic-Based Information Management System (PDAA)
GIMS .... Global Integrated Monitoring System (EERA)
GIMS .... Graduates of Italian Medical Schools (EA)
GIMS .... Ground Identification of Missions in Space
GIMT .... Gott Ist Mein Teil [*God Is My Portion*] [*Motto of Friedrich IV, Duke of Liegnitz (1552-96)*] [*German*]
GIMT .... Gott Ist Mein Trost [*God Is My Comfort*] [*Motto for a number of 16th and 17th century German and Bavarian rulers*]
GIMU .... Gimballess Inertial Measuring Unit
GIN .... Association de Recherche et d'Exploitation de Diamant et de l'Or [*Guinea*] [*ICAO designator*] (FAAC)
GIN .... Galilean Resources Corp. [*Vancouver Stock Exchange symbol*]
GIN .... Gimbaled Integral Nozzle
GIN .... Global Imaging Networks (DGA)
GIN .... Global Information Network (EA)
gin .... Glutamine [*Also, Q*] [*An amino acid*] (DOG)
GIN .... Greenland-Iceland-Norway [*Gap*] (DOMA)
GIN .... Guinea [*ANSI three-letter standard code*] (CNC)
GIN .... Stromboli-Ginostra [*Italy*] [*Seismograph station code, US Geological Survey*] (SEIS)
GINA .... Gas Industries Network Analyzer (PDAA)

GINA	Graphical Interactive NMR Analysis [Computer science]
GINETEX	Groupement International d'Etiquetage pour l'Entretien des Textiles [International Association for Textile Care Labelling] [Barcelona, Spain] (EA)
GING	Gingiva [Gum] [Latin]
GINI	Gazette International Networking Institute (EA)
GINLC	Grosse Ile Nature and Land Conservancy
G in N	Graduate in Nursing
GINNI	Generic Interactive Neural Network Interpreter
GINNIE MAE	Government National Mortgage Association [See also GNMA]
GINO	Graphical Input/Output
GINO-F	Graphical Input and Output in FORTRAN [GST Computer Systems Ltd.] [Software package] [Computer science] [British]
GInstM	Graduate of the Institute of Marketing [British] (DBQ)
GINTRAP	European Guide to Industrial Trading Regulations and Practice [EC] (ECED)
GIO	Gas Identification Officer
GIO	Generalist Intelligence Officer
GIO	Generic Interface for Operations [Telecommunications] (ACRL)
GIO	Giocossamente [Humorously] [Music] (ROG)
GIO	Golden Trio Minerals [Vancouver Stock Exchange symbol]
GIO	Government Information Organization [Later, NAGC]
GIO	Group Intelligence Officer [British military] (DMA)
GIO	Guaranteed Insurability Option
GIO	Guild of Insurance Officials [British] (BI)
GIO	Regionnair, Inc. [Canada ICAO designator] (FAAC)
GIOA	Gregorian Institute of America [Record label]
GIOC	Generalized Input/Output Controller [Computer science] (IEEE)
GIOP	General-Purpose Input/Output Processor [Computer science]
GIOR	GPETE Initial Outfitting Requirement [Military] (CAAL)
GIP	Galvanized Improved Plow [Steel]
GIP	Gastric Inhibitory Peptide [Gastroenterology] (DAVI)
GIP	Gastric [or Gastrin] Inhibitory Principle [or Polypeptide] [Medicine]
GIP	Gaussian Image Point [Optics]
GIP	General Implementation Plan
GIP	General Information Programme (NITA)
GIP	General Insertion Protein [Genetics]
GIP	General Internal Process [Computer science] (IAA)
GIP	Genetic Improvement Programs [Queensland] (EERA)
GIP	Giant Cell Interstitial Pneumonia [Medicine] (MAE)
GIP	Gileppe [Belgium] [Seismograph station code, US Geological Survey] (SEIS)
GIP	Glazed Imitation Parchment
GIP	Gonorrheal Invasive Peritonitis [Medicine] (DMAA)
GIP	Great Indian Peninsular R. R.
GIP	Great Irish Painter [Reference to Jack B. Yeats, ca. 1905]
GIP	Gross Internal Product
GIP	Ground Instructor Pilot (DNAB)
GIP	Gunnery Improvement Program [Military] (CAAL)
GIPD	B. F. Goodrich Institute for Personnel Development
GIPEC	Groupe d'Etudes International pour l'Utilization de Profils Creux dans la Construction [International Study Group on the Use of Hollow Sections in Construction] [Switzerland] (PDAA)
GIPEIE	Groupe International Postal d'Echanges d'Information et d'Experience [International Group for the Exchange of Information and Experience among Postal Savings Institutions - IGEIEPSI] (EAIO)
GIPGS	Greenhouse Information Program Grants Scheme (EERA)
GI/PI	General Inspection/Procurement Inspection (MCD)
GIPME	Global Investigation of Pollution in the Marine Environment [National Science Foundation]
GIPS	Geographical Information Processing System (EERA)
GIPS	Giga-Instructions per Second [Computer science] (NHD)
GIPS	Government Imprinted Penalty Stationery Society (EA)
GIPS	Ground Information Processing System
GIPSE	Gravity Independent Photosynthetic Gas Exchanger
GIPSY	Generalized Information Processing System
GIQ	Giant Imperial Quart [of beer]
GIR	Girder [Technical drawings]
GIR	Global Improvement Rating (DMAA)
GIR	Glucose Infusion Rate [Physiology]
GIR	Golden Lion Resources Ltd. [Vancouver Stock Exchange symbol]
GIR	Graduated Interest Rate [Finance] (BARN)
GIR	Greens in Regulation Golf (BARN)
GIR	Resource Appraisal Group Library, United States Geological Survey, Denver, CO [OCLC symbol] (OCLC)
GIRA	Gallups Island Radio Association (EA)
GIRA	Groupement Independant de Reflexion et d'Action [Independent Grouping of Reflection and Action] [Central Africa] (PD)
GIRA	Group Individual Retirement Account
GIRAFFE	Graphic Interface for Finite Elements [Graphics data processing]
GIRAS	Geographic Information Retrieval and Analysis System [Department of the Interior]
GIRAST	Groupe Interdisciplinaire de Recherche pour l'Amelioration des Situations de Travail [University of Quebec at Rimouski] [Canada Research center] (RCD)
GIRD	General Incentive for Research and Development [Canada]
GIRD	Good Industrial Relations Directors [Meetings sponsored by Master Printers of America]
GIRD	Grants for Industrial Research and Development (EERA)
GIRD	Ground Integration Requirements Document (MCD)
GIREP	International Group for the Advancement of Physics Teaching (AIE)
GIRGV	Groupe International des Ressources Genetiques Vegetales [International Board for Plant Genetic Resources - IBPGR] (EA)

GIRL	Generalized Information Retrieval Language [US Defense Nuclear Agency]
GIRL	Graph Information Retrieval Language [1970] [Computer science] (CSR)
GIRLS	General Indexing in Reciprocal Lattice Space (KSC)
GIRLS	Generalized Information Retrieval and Listing System
GIRLS	Global Interrogation Recording and Location System (MCD)
GIRM	Generalized Internal Reference Method [Statistical procedure]
GIRMS	Geographical Inter-University Resource Management Seminar
GIRO	General Instructions for Routing and Reporting Officers
GIROQ	Groupe Interuniversitaire des Recherches Oceanographiques du Quebec [Interuniversity Group for Oceanographic Research of Quebec] [Laval University] [Canada] [Research center] (RCD)
GIRPB	Groupe International de Recherches sur la Preservation du Bois [Sweden] (EAIO)
GIRS	Gallaudet Information Retrieval Service
GIRS	Gimballess Inertial Reference System
GIRSO	Groupement International pour la Recherche Scientifique en Stomatologie et Odontologie [International Group for Scientific Research on Stomato-Odontology] (EA)
GIRSS	General Information Retrieval System Simulation
GIRSTERM	Groupe Interdisciplinaire de Recherche Scientifique et Appliquee en Terminologie [INFOTERM]
Gir WC	Girard's Will Case Report [A publication] (DLA)
GIS	Gas in Stomach (MAE)
GIS	Gas-Scintillation Imaging Spectrometer
GIS	Gastrointestinal Series [Radiology]
GIS	Gastrointestinal System [Gastroenterology] (DAVI)
GIS	General Installation Subcontractor
GIS	Generalized Information System [IBM Corp.]
GIS	Generalized Inquiry System [Computer science]
GIS	General Mills, Inc. [NYSE symbol] (SPSG)
GIS	Genl Mills [NYSE symbol] (TTSB)
GIS	Geographic Information System (EERA)
GIS	Geographic Information Systems [Fish and Wildlife Service] (IID)
GIS	Geological Information Systems [University of Oklahoma] [Information service or system] (IID)
GIS	Geoscience Information Society (EA)
GIS	Gisborne [New Zealand] [Airport symbol] (OAG)
GIS	Gismondine [A zeolite]
GIS	Gissar [Former USSR Seismograph station code, US Geological Survey Closed] (SEIS)
GIS	Global Indexing System (GNE)
GIS	Global Information Services, Inc. [Flushing, NY] [Telecommunications] (TSSD)
GIS	Global Ionospheric Studies
GIS	Global Issues [Program] [Department of State]
GIS	Golden Iskut Resources [Vancouver Stock Exchange symbol]
GIS	Government Information Service (WDAA)
GIS	Government Information Services [Republic of Ireland]
GIS	Government Information Subcommittee [American Library Association]
GIS	Grain Inventory System [Department of Agriculture] (GFGA)
GIS	Grand Inside Sentinel [Freemasonry] (ROG)
GIS	Grant Information System [Oryx Press] (IID)
GIS	Graphic Information System [Computer databases]
GIS	Graphic Input System
GIS	Grazing-Incidence Spectrometer (PDAA)
GIS	Greatness Is Simplicity [See also SIG]
GIS	Greenland Ice Sheet
GIs	Gross Impressions [Advertising] (WDMC)
GIS	Ground Instrumentation System (IAA)
GIS	Guaranteed Income Stream [UAW program included in the union's 1982 contract with General Motors Corp.]
GIS	Guaranteed Income Supplement [Program] [Canada]
GIS	Guidance Information System [Houghton Mifflin Co.] [Information service or system] (IID)
GIS	Guidelines Implementation Staff [Environmental Protection Agency] (GFGA)
GIS	Guild for Infant Survival [Later, ICIS]
GIS	Guild of the Infant Saviour [Defunct] (EA)
GIS	Guinee Air Service [Guinea] [ICAO designator] (FAAC)
GIS	United States Department of the Interior, United States Geological Survey, Reston, VA [OCLC symbol] (OCLC)
GISA	Government in the Sunshine Act [1976]
GISAT	Ground Identification of Satellites (MCD)
GISC	Generic Intelligent Control System
GISC	Government Information Services Committee [Special Libraries Association]
GISC	Grail International Student Center [Defunct] (EA)
GISE	Generalized Integrated Square Error [Aeronautics]
GI Sec	General Inspectorate Section [European Theater of Operations] [World War II]
GISGE	Good Intent Society of Galvanizers and Enamellers [A union] [British]
GISH	Gish Biomedical [NASDAQ symbol] (TTSB)
GISH	Gish Biomedical, Inc. [NASDAQ symbol] (NQ)
GishBi	Gish Biomedical, Inc. [Associated Press] (SAG)
GISL	Graphic Imaging Specification Language [Printing technology]
GISMO	General Interpretative System for Matrix Operations [Data processing system used in engineering] [Navy]
GISOF	Gas Industry Salaried Officers' Federation [Australia]
GISP	General Information System for Planning (IAA)
GISP	Grain Income Stabilization Plan
GISP	Greenland Ice Sheet Project [National Science Foundation]

GISPA .... Guide to International Scientific Publications and Associations [*A publication*]
GISPRI .... Global Industrial and Social Progress Research Institute
GISS .... Goddard Institute for Space Studies [*NASA*]
GIST .... GARP International Sea Trial [*National Science Foundation*]
GIST .... Girls into Science and Technology [*British*] (DI)
GIST .... Global Information System Technology, Inc. (PCM)
GIST .... Gochnour Idiom Screening Test
GISTA .... Gruppo Italiano di Studio Tubercolosi e AIDS
GISTI .... Groupe d'Information et de Soutien des Travailleurs Immigres [*Information and Support Group for Immigrant Workers*] [*France*] (EAIO)
GISVS .... Generalized Information System Virtual Storage (IAA)
GIT .... Gastrointestinal Tract [*Medicine*]
GIT .... General Information Test
GIT .... Georgia Institute of Technology [*Atlanta*]
GIT .... Gilgit [*Pakistan*] [*Geomagnetic observatory code*]
Git .... Gittin (BJA)
GIT .... Glucose Infusion Test [*Diabetes detection*] (CPH)
GIT .... Glutathione-Insulin Transhydrogenase [*An enzyme*] (MAE)
GIT .... Graduate Institute of Technology [*University of Arkansas at Little Rock*] [*Research center*] (RCD)
GIT .... Graph Isomorphism Tester
GIT .... Grease Interceptor Trap
GIT .... [*The*] Great Ideas Today [*A publication*]
GIT .... Grit Resources, Inc. [*Vancouver Stock Exchange symbol*]
GIT .... Grooved for Iron Tongues
GIT .... Group Inclusive Tour [*Airline fare*]
GITC .... Government of Israel Trade Center (EA)
GITG .... Ground Interface Technical Group [*NASA*] (NASA)
GITI .... Global Information and Telecommunications Industries
GITI .... Government Issue Technical Inspection (INF)
GITIS .... Georgia Institute of Technology School of Information Science [*Report series code*] (NITA)
GITL .... Government/Industry Technical Liaison Committee [*Australia*]
GITP .... Ground Integration Test Program (KSC)
GITS .... Gastrointestinal Therapeutic System [*Medicine*]
GITSG .... Gastrointestinal Tumor Study Group [*Oncology*] (DAVI)
GITT .... Glucose Insulin Tolerance Test [*Medicine*]
GITU .... Gastrointestinal Transcription Unit [*Medicine*]
GIU .... Gateway Interface Unit (DGA)
GIU .... General Intelligence Unit [*US, London*]
GIU .... Geoballistic Input Unit
GIU .... Guidance Integration Unit (MCD)
GIU .... Union Guineene de Transports [*Guinea*] [*ICAO designator*] (FAAC)
GIUK .... Greenland-Iceland-United Kingdom [*NATO naval defense line*]
GIuscII .... Grupo Iusacell SA de CV [*Associated Press*] (SAG)
GIuscI IL ..... Grupo Iusacell SA de CV [*Associated Press*] (SAG)
GIV .... Given
GIV .... Grivco International Ltd. [*Romania*] [*FAA designator*] (FAAC)
GIVE .... Government's Involvement in Volunteer Efforts Programs
GIVN .... Given (DAVI)
GIVS .... Goodwill Industries Volunteer Services (EA)
GIW .... Glass-Insulated Wire
GIW .... Greenwood, SC [*Location identifier FAA*] (FAAL)
GIW .... Gulf Intracoastal Waterway
GIWG .... Ground Interface Working Group
GIWW .... Gulf Intracoastal Waterway
GIX .... Global Industrial Tech [*NYSE symbol*] (TTSB)
GIX .... Global Industrial Technologies [*NYSE symbol*] (SAG)
GIX .... Government Information Exchange [*Internet*] (AAGC)
GIXD .... Grazing-Incidence X-Ray Diffraction
GIXS .... Grazing-Incidence X-Ray Scattering [*Imaging technique*]
GIXU .... Grain Inspection X-Ray Unit (IAA)
GIY .... Glamorgan Imperial Yeomanry [*British military*] (DMA)
GIZ .... Gizan [*Saudi Arabia*] [*Airport symbol*] (OAG)
GIZ .... Gizo [*Solomon Islands*] [*Seismograph station code, US Geological Survey*] (SEIS)
GIZ .... Marshfield, WI [*Location identifier FAA*] (FAAL)
GIZH .... Gosudarstvennyi Institut Zhurnalistiki
GJ .... Ansett Airlines of South Australia [*ICAO designator*] (AD)
GJ .... British Guiana General Jurisdiction (Official Gazette) [*1899-*] [*A publication*] (ILCA)
GJ .... Gap Junction [*Cytology*]
GJ .... Gastric Juice [*Medicine*] (DMAA)
GJ .... Gastrojejunostomy [*Surgery*] (DAVI)
GJ .... General Journal [*Accounting*]
GJ .... Geographical Journal [*A publication*] (BRI)
GJ .... Germania Judaica (BJA)
GJ .... German Jewish (BJA)
GJ .... Gigajoule
GJ .... Gill and Johnson's Maryland Reports [*A publication*] (DLA)
GJ .... Goldreich-Julian [*PULSAR theory*]
GJ .... Graduate Jeweller
GJ .... Grand Jury
GJ .... Grapefruit Juice [*Restaurant slang*]
GJ .... Greenwich & Johnsonville Railway Co. [*AAR code*]
GJ .... Group Junction (MCD)
GJ .... Grown Junction (IEEE)
G+J .... Gruner + Jahr [*A publisher*] [*Hamburg, Germany*] (WDMC)
GJB .... Marie-Galante Island [*Guadeloupe*] [*Airport symbol*] (AD)
GJB .... Trans-Air Link Corp. [*ICAO designator*] (FAAC)
GJC .... Gainesville Junior College [*Later, Cooke County Junior College*] [*Texas*]
GJC .... Grayson-Jockey Club Research Foundation (EA)

GJCFC .... George Jones Country Fan Club (EA)
GJCO .... Gaylord Companies, Inc. [*NASDAQ symbol*] (SAG)
GJCO .... Gaylord Cos. [*NASDAQ symbol*] (TTSB)
GJCOW .... Gaylord Cos. Wrrt [*NASDAQ symbol*] (TTSB)
GJD .... Channel Aviation Ltd. [*British*] [*FAA designator*] (FAAC)
GJD .... Germanium Junction Diode (IDOE)
GJD .... Global Jewish Database [*Bar-Ilan University*] [*Information service or system*] (CRD)
GJD .... Grand Junior Deacon [*Freemasonry*]
GJE .... Gauss-Jordan Elimination (IEEE)
GJF .... Greensboro Justice Fund (EA)
GJFC .... George Jones Fan Club (EA)
GJG .... Augusta College, Augusta, GA [*OCLC symbol*] (OCLC)
GJI .... Ghetto Job Information [*US Employment Service*] [*Department of Labor*]
GJL .... Geographical Journal (London) [*A publication*]
GJL .... Jijel [*Algeria*] [*Airport symbol*] (OAG)
GJM .... Guajara Mirim [*Brazil*] [*Airport symbol*] (AD)
GJO .... Grand Junction Office [*Grand Junction, CO*] [*Department of Energy*]
GJO .... Greater Jacksonville [*Florida*] Open [*Golf tournament*]
GJOA .... G. J. Orphan & Associates [*Telecommunications service*] (TSSD)
GJP .... Galactic Jupiter Probe [*NASA*]
GJP .... Grand Jury Project (EA)
GJP .... Graphic Job Processor (MCD)
GJPA .... Grammatik des Juedisch-Palaestinischen Aramaeisch [*A publication*] (BJA)
GJPO .... Grand Juction Projects Office [*Department of Energy*] [*Grand Juction, CO*] (GAAI)
GJPO .... Grand Junction Project Office (DOGT)
GJPO .... Grand Junction Project Office [*Department of Energy*]
GJR .... Gjogur [*Iceland*] [*Airport symbol*] (OAG)
GJRAP .... Grand Junction Remedial Action Project [*Department of Energy*] [*Colorado*] (GAAI)
GJS .... Ghana Journal of Sociology [*A publication*]
GJT .... Grand Junction [*Colorado*] [*Airport symbol*] (OAG)
GJTA .... Goldsmiths' and Jewellers' Trade Association [*A union*] [*British*]
GJV .... Geschichte des Juedischen Volkes im Zeitalter Jesu Christi [*A publication*] (BJA)
GJW .... Grand Junior Warden [*Freemasonry*]
GJW .... Great Jurists of the World, by Sir John MacDonnel and Edward Manson [*1913*] [*A publication*] (DLA)
GK .... Geographenkalender (BJA)
GK .... Ginze Kedem (BJA)
GK .... Glycerol Kinase [*An enzyme*] (MAE)
GK .... Goalkeeper (WGA)
GK .... Goal Keeper [*Netball*]
GK .... Grand King [*Freemasonry*]
GK .... Granular Kidney [*Medicine*] (ROG)
GK .... Greek
GK .... Hebraeische Grammatik Voellig Umgearbeitet [*Gesenius and E. Kautzsch*] [*A publication*] (BJA)
GK .... Laker Airways [*ICAO designator*] (AD)
GK-101 .... N-Monochloroglycine [*Dental caries treatment named for patent holders, Goldman and Kronman*]
GKA .... Garter King of Arms
GKA .... Goroka [*Papua New Guinea*] [*Airport symbol*] (OAG)
GKA .... Goroka [*Papua New Guinea*] [*Seismograph station code, US Geological Survey Closed*] (SEIS)
GKA .... Grounded Kathode Amplifier
GKa .... Hebraeische Grammatik Voellig Umgearbeitet [*Gesenius and E. Kautzsch*] [*A publication*] (BJA)
GKA .... US Army Aeronautical Services [*ICAO designator*] (FAAC)
GKABL .... George Khoury Association of Baseball Leagues (EA)
GKB .... Garantie- und Kreditbank [*Guaranty and Credit Bank*] [*Germany*] (EG)
GKBZH .... Glowna Komisja Badania Zbrodni Hitlerowskich [*A publication*] (BJA)
GKC .... Gilbert Keith Chesterton [*British journalist and author*]
GKC .... Gold King Construction [*Vancouver Stock Exchange symbol*]
GKC .... Gold King River [*Alaska*] [*Seismograph station code, US Geological Survey*] (SEIS)
GKC .... Hebrew Grammar Gesenius, Kautzsch, Cowley [*A publication*] (BJA)
GKCS .... G. K. Chesterton Society (EA)
GKD .... Glycerol Kinase Deficiency [*Medicine*]
GKF .... Florence, SC [*Location identifier FAA*] (FAAL)
GKH .... G. K. Hall Co. [*Publisher*]
GKI .... General Kinetics, Inc. [*AMEX symbol*] (SPSG)
GKI .... Genl Kinetics [*AMEX symbol*] (TTSB)
GKI .... Glon Kristy Resources [*Vancouver Stock Exchange symbol*]
GKJ .... Kennesaw College, Marietta, GA [*OCLC symbol*] (OCLC)
GKJ .... Meadville, PA [*Location identifier FAA*] (FAAL)
GKL .... Great Keppel Island [*Australia Airport symbol*] (OAG)
GKLC .... Law Companies Group, Inc., Kennesaw, GA [*Library symbol*] [*Library of Congress*] (LCLS)
GKLL .... Garage Keeper's Legal Liability [*Insurance*]
GKMDT .... Graham-Kendall Memory for Designs Test [*Psychology*] (DAVI)
GKN .... Guest, Kean & Nettlefolds [*Steel-forging company*] [*British*]
GKN .... Gulkana [*Alaska*] [*Airport symbol*] (OAG)
GKN .... Gulkana, AK [*Location identifier FAA*] (FAAL)
GKNHS .... Golden Key National Honor Society (EA)
GKNT .... Gosudarstvennyy Komitet po Nauki i Teknologii [*State Committee for Science and Technology*] [*Former USSR*] (LAIN)
GKO .... Gosudarstvennyi Komitet Oborony [*State Defense Committee*] [*Former USSR World War II*]
GKO .... Kongo Boumba [*Gabon*] [*Airport symbol*] (AD)
GkOd .... Greek Odeon [*Record label*]

GKQ .... Newark, NJ [*Location identifier FAA*] (FAAL)

GKR .... Goddard Kay Rogers Ltd. [*British*]

GKR .... Golden Knight Resources, Inc. [*Toronto Stock Exchange symbol Vancouver Stock Exchange symbol*]

GKR .... Government of the Khmer Republic [*Anticommunist government of Cambodia during the early seventies*] (VNW)

GKRV .... Golden Knight Resources, Inc. [*NASDAQ symbol*] (NQ)

GKRVE .... Golden Knight Res [*NASDAQ symbol*] (TTSB)

GKS .... Gesamtverzeichnis der Kongressschriften [*Union List of Conference Proceedings*] [*Deutsches Bibliotheksinstitut*] [*Germany*] [*Information service or system*] (CRD)

GKS .... Grand Keeper of the Seals [*Freemasonry*]

GKS .... Graphical Kernel System [*International Standards Organization*] [*Computer science*]

GKSRA .... G & K Services CI'A' [*NASDAQ symbol*] (TTSB)

GKT .... Gasket [*Technical drawings*]

GKT .... General Knowledge Test

GKT .... Goldteck Mines Ltd. [*Toronto Stock Exchange symbol*]

GKTW .... Give Kids the World (EA)

GKW .... God Knows What

GKY .... Golden Key Resources Ltd. [*Vancouver Stock Exchange symbol*]

Gl .... Galatians [*New Testament book*] (BJA)

GL .... Galeries Lafayette [*Department store*] [*Paris, France*]

Gl .... Galleon [*Spanish vessel*] (DS)

Gl .... Gallon (MCD)

Gl .... Galvanized [*Metallurgy*]

GLA .... Gas LASER

GL .... Gate Leads (IEEE)

GL .... Gauge Length

glab .... Gear Lubricant [*Automotive engineering*]

GL .... General Laws [*A publication*] (DLA)

GL .... General Ledger (AABC)

GL .... General Letter

GL .... General Liability [*Insurance*]

GL .... General Linear [*Group theory, mathematics*]

GL .... General List [*Navy British*] (DMA)

GL .... Generator Lorry [*British*]

GL .... Genius Loci [*Genius of the Place*] [*Latin*] (ROG)

GL .... Geographic Location (NITA)

GL .... Germanischer Lloyd [*German ship classification society*] (DS)

gl .... Gill [*Oceanography*] (DAVI)

Gl .... Gill [*Unit of weight*]

GL .... Gilt Leaves [*Bookbinding*] (ROG)

GL .... Gilt Lines [*Bookbinding*] (ROG)

GL .... Gimbal Limit Prearming Inhibiting Signal

GL .... Giustizia e Liberta [*Italy*] [*Political party*]

GL .... Glabella [*Anatomy*] (ROG)

GL .... Glacier (ROG)

GL .... Gladstonian Liberal [*British*] (ROG)

gl .... Gland

GL .... Glass

GL .... Glaucolacustrine Soil [*Agronomy*]

GL .... Glaze

Gl .... Gleaver's Reports [*Jamaica*] [*A publication*] (ILCA)

GL .... Glebe [*Ecclesiastical*] (ROG)

GL .... Global Learning (EA)

Gl .... Globigerina [*Quality of the bottom*] [*Nautical charts*]

Gl .... Globus (BJA)

GL .... Gloria [*Glory*] [*Latin*]

Gl .... Gloss (DSA)

gl .... Gloss (WDMC)

GL .... Glossary (ROG)

gl .... Glossy (WDMC)

Gl .... Glucinium [*Also, G*] [*Old name for chemical element beryllium*]

GL .... Glycosphingolipid [*Biochemistry*]

GL .... Gold Lease (ADA)

GL .... Go Long [*Investment term*]

GL .... Good Luck (MHDB)

GL .... Gothic Letter

GL .... Government Laboratory (BARN)

GL .... Grade Line

GL .... Graduate in Law

G/L .... Grams per Liter

GL .... Grand Larceny

GL .... Grand Lodge [*Freemasonry*]

GL .... Grand Lot

GL .... Grant Less Than [*Dialog*] [*Searchable fields*] [*Information service or system*] (NITA)

GL .... Graphic Library

GL .... Greater London [*England*]

GL .... Greatest Length

GL .... Great Lakes [*Vessel load line mark*]

GL .... Great Lakes Forest Products Ltd. [*Toronto Stock Exchange symbol*]

gl .... Greenland [*MARC country of publication code Library of Congress*] (LCCP)

GL .... Greenland [*ANSI two-letter standard code*] (CNC)

GL .... Green Library [*See also BVM*] [*France*] (EAIO)

GL .... Green Light (MSA)

GL .... Grenade Launcher (AABC)

GL .... Grid Leak

GL .... Gronlandsfly [*ICAO designator*] (AD)

GL .... Gross Line [*Insurance*]

GL .... Ground Level

GL .... Guild Library [*Church of Scotland*] [*A publication*]

GL .... Gun Lay [*or Laying*] [*RADAR*]

GL .... Gun Licence [*British*] (DAS)

GL .... Gunnery Lieutenant [*British military*] (DMA)

GL .... Gustatory Lacrimation [*Medicine*] (DMAA)

GL .... Lanier Lake Regional and Gwinnett County Library, Lawrenceville, GA [*Library symbol Library of Congress*] (LCLS)

GL .... L-Glutamic [*acid*] and L-Lysine [*Copolymer*]

GLA .... Gamma-Linoleic Acid [*Organic chemistry*]

GLA .... Gamma-Linolenic Acid

GLA .... General Laboratory Associates

GLA .... General Learning Ability

GLA .... General Ledger Account (AFM)

GLA .... General Lighthouse Authority [*British*]

GLA .... Gingivolinguoaxial [*Dentistry*]

GLA .... Glamis [*California*] [*Seismograph station code, US Geological Survey*] (SEIS)

GLA .... Glasgow [*Scotland*] [*Airport symbol*] (OAG)

GLA .... Glass [*Automotive engineering*]

GLA .... Gold Star Resources, Inc. [*Vancouver Stock Exchange symbol*]

GLA .... Grain Legume Association [*Australia*]

GLA .... Great Lakes Aviation Ltd. [*ICAO designator*] (FAAC)

GLA .... Gross Leasable Area

GLA .... Groupe de Liberation Armee [*Armed Liberation Group*] [*Guadeloupe*] (PD)

GLA .... Group Life Assurance [*British*]

GLA .... Guadeloupe Liberation Army

GLA .... Gulkana, AK [*Location identifier FAA*] (FAAL)

GLA .... Gust Load Alleviation [*Aviation*]

GLAAD .... Gay and Lesbian Alliance Against Defamation (EA)

GLAADS ...... Gun Low-Altitude Air Defense System (NASA)

glab .... Glabrous [*Botany*] (BARN)

GLAC .... Gay and Lesbian Association of Choruses (EA)

GLAC .... General Ledger Account Code

glac .... Glacial [*Chemistry*] (DAVI)

GLAC .... Glacial

GLAC .... Glacier National Park

GLAC .... Grain Legume Advisory Committee [*Australia*]

GLACSEC .... Group of Latin American and Caribbean Sugar Exporting Countries [*See also GEPLACEA*] [*Mexico City, Mexico*] (EAIO)

GLAD .... Gay and Lesbian Advocates and Defenders (EA)

GLAD .... Gladiator Fighter Aircraft [*British*] (DSUE)

GLAD .... Gladiolus (DSUE)

GLAD .... Glancing Angle Deposition [*Coating technology*]

GLAD .... GLOTRAC [*Global Tracking*] Adjustment

GLAD .... Gold-labelled Antigen Detection [*Medicine*] (DMAA)

GLAD .... Government and Legal Affairs Division [*American Occupational Therapy Association*]

GLAD .... Grenade Launcher Attachment Development (MCD)

GLAD .... Group Learning about Drugs

GLADIS .... Ground-LASER Attack Designator/Identification System (MCD)

GLADS .... Great Falls Air Defense Sector [*Montana*] (SAA)

GLADS .... Gun Low-Altitude Air Defense System

GLAFLI .... Graded Levels of Achievement in Foreign Language Learning (AIE)

GLAG .... Ginzburg-Landau-Abrikosov-Gorkov [*Superconductivity theory*]

GLagC .... La Grange College, La Grange, GA [*Library symbol Library of Congress*] (LCLS)

GLagCM ...... Callaway Mills Co., Technical Library, LaGrange, GA [*Library symbol Library of Congress*] (LCLS)

GLagTAr ..... Troup County Archives, La Grange, GA [*Library symbol*] [*Library of Congress*] (LCLS)

GLAI .... Green Leaf Area Index (MCD)

GLAKES ...... Great Lakes (MUGU)

GLAM .... Glamorganshire [*County in Wales*]

GLAM .... Greying, Leisured, Affluent, and Married [*Lifestyle classification British*]

Glamis .... Glamis Gold Ltd. [*Associated Press*] (SAG)

GLAMIS .... Grant/Loan Accounting and Management Information System [*Department of Commerce*] (GFGA)

GLAMS .... Glamorganshire [*County in Wales*]

GLANCE ...... Global Lightweight Airborne Navigation Computer Equipment

gland .... Glandula [*Gland*] [*Endocrinology*] (DAVI)

Gl & J .... Glyn and Jameson's English Bankruptcy Reports [*1821-28*] [*A publication*] (DLA)

Glan El Cas... Glanville's English Election Cases [*A publication*] (DLA)

Glanv El Cas... Glanville's English Election Cases [*A publication*] (DLA)

GLAP .... Gay Legal Advice Project [*British*] (DI)

GLAPPAR .... General Ledger, Accounts Payable, and Accounts Receivable [*Accounting*]

GLAR .... Glas-Aire Indus Grp Ltd [*NASDAQ symbol*] (TTSB)

GLAR .... Glas-Aire Industries Group Ltd. [*NASDAQ symbol*] (SAG)

GLARE .... Glass Reinforced [*Organic chemistry*]

GLARE .... Ground-Level Attack, Reconnaissance, and Electronic Countermeasures (MCD)

GLARP .... Grupo Latinoamericano de Rehabilitacion Profesional [*Latin American Vocational Rehabilitation Group*] [*Bogata, Colombia*] (EAIO)

Glas .... Glascock's Reports in All the Courts of Ireland [*A publication*] (DLA)

GLAS .... Glasgal Communications [*NASDAQ symbol*] (TTSB)

GLAS .... Glasgal Communities [*NASDAQ symbol*] (SAG)

GLAS .... Glasgow [*Scotland*]

GLAS .... Goddard Laboratory for Atmospheric Sciences (MCD)

GLAS .... Goddard Laboratory of Atmospheric Sciences [*Marine science*] [*Army*] (OSRA)

GlasAire ...... Glas-Aire Industries Group Ltd. [*Associated Press*] (SAG)

GLAS & SW... Glasgow & South-Western [*Railway*] [*Scotland*] (ROG)

Glasc .... Glascock's Reports in All the Courts of Ireland [*A publication*] (DLA)

Glascock...... Glascock's Reports in All the Courts of Ireland [*A publication*] (DLA)

GLASG .... Glasgow [Scotland] (ROG)
Glasgal .... Glasgal Communities [Associated Press] (SAG)
GLASLA ...... Great Lakes - St. Lawrence Association
GLASOD ...... Global Assessment on Soil Degradation (EERA)
GLASS .... Geodetic LASER Survey System
GLASS .... Germanium-Lithium Argon Scanning System (NRCH)
GLASS .... Good Luck and Smooth Sailing [Slang Military] (DNAB)
Glassboro St C... Glassboro State College (GAGS)
GLASSEX ..... Glass Technology and Fabrication Exhibition (TSPED)
Glassf Ev ..... Glassford on Evidence [A publication] (DLA)
Glassmst ..... Glassmaster Co. [Associated Press] (SAG)
GLAST .... Gamma Large Array Space Telescope [A collaboration of physics groups]
GLAST .... Gamma-Ray Large Area Space [Proposed, 1996]
GLASU .... Glasgal Communications Unit [NASDAQ symbol] (TTSB)
GLASW .... Glasgal Communications Wrrt [NASDAQ symbol] (TTSB)
GLAT .... Government Lot Acceptance Test [Military] (CAAL)
Glatflt .... Glatfelter [P.H.] Co. [Associated Press] (SAG)
GLAU .... General Labourers' Amalgamated Union [British]
glau .... Glaucous [Botany] (BARN)
GLAVATOM... Chief Directorate to the Council of Ministries for the Utilisation of Atomic Energy [British] (NUCP)
GlaxcWeL ..... Glaxo Wellcome PLC [Associated Press] (SAG)
GLB .... Galactosidase Beta (DMAA)
GLB .... Gas [or Grease] Lubricated Bearing
GLB .... Gilbues [Brazil] [Airport symbol] (AD)
GLB .... Girls' Life Brigade [British]
GLB .... Glass Block (AAG)
GLB .... Glass in Barrels [Freight]
GLB .... Glenborough Realty Trust [NYSE symbol] (TTSB)
GLB .... Glenborough Realty Trust, Inc. [NYSE symbol] (SAG)
GLB .... Global Air [Bulgaria] [ICAO designator] (FAAC)
GLB .... Great Lakes Freight Bureau Inc., Cleveland OH [STAC]
GLBA .... Glacier Bay National Monument
GLBA .... Great Lakes Booksellers Association (EA)
GLBC .... Great Lakes Basin Commission [Terminated, 1981] (EGAO)
GlbCasn ...... Global Casinos [Associated Press] (SAG)
GlbDir .... Global Directmail Corp. [Associated Press] (SAG)
GLBE .... Globe Business Resources [NASDAQ symbol] (TTSB)
GLBE .... Globe Business Resources, Inc. [NASDAQ symbol] (SAG)
GlbeBus ...... Globe Business Resources, Inc. [Associated Press] (SAG)
GlbGvt .... Global Government Plus Fund, Inc. [Associated Press] (SAG)
GlbHlt .... Global Health Sciences Fund [Associated Press] (SAG)
GLBK .... Glendale Co-Operative Bank [NASDAQ symbol] (SAG)
GLBK .... Glendale Co. Operative Bk [NASDAQ symbol] (TTSB)
GLBL .... Global
GLBL .... Global Industries [NASDAQ symbol] (TTSB)
GLBL .... Global Industries Ltd. [NASDAQ symbol] (SAG)
GlblOcn .... Global Ocean Carriers Ltd. [Associated Press] (SAG)
GlblOne .... Global One Distribution & Merchandising, Inc. [Associated Press] (SAG)
GLBM .... Ground-Launched Ballistic Missile
GlbMktl .... Global Market Information, Inc. [Associated Press] (SAG)
GlbRsc .... Global Resources, Inc. [Associated Press] (SAG)
GLBS .... Globes [Freight]
GlbSpill .... Global Spill Management [Associated Press] (SAG)
GLBT .... Glastonbury Bank & Trust Co. [NASDAQ symbol] (SAG)
GlbTel .... Global Telecommunications Solutions, Inc. [Associated Press] (SAG)
GLBU .... Buchanan [Liberia] [ICAO location identifier] (ICLI)
GlbVilag ...... Global Village Communictions, Inc. [Associated Press] (SAG)
GLC .... Gas-Liquid Chromatography [Analytical chemistry]
GLC .... Gate Leakage Current
GLC .... Gay and Lesbian Caucus (EA)
GLC .... General Learning Corp. [of Time, Inc.]
GLC .... Generator Line Contractor (NASA)
GLC .... German Language Club (EA)
GLC .... Glace
GLC .... Glaucoma
GLC .... Global LORAN Navigation Chart [Air Force]
Glc .... Glucose [Also, G, GLUC] [A sugar]
GLC .... Greater London Council [Information service or system] (IID)
GLC .... Great Lakes Club (EA)
GLC .... Great Lakes Commission (EA)
GLC .... Great Little Car [Mazda Motors of America]
GLC .... Ground Level Concentration (EG)
GLC .... Philadelphia, PA [Location identifier FAA] (FAAL)
GLCA .... Gallery of Living Catholic Authors [Defunct] (EA)
GLCA .... Glen Canyon National Recreation Area
GlcA .... Gluconic Acid [Biochemistry]
GLCA .... Great Lakes Colleges Association (EA)
GLCCF .... Gaming Lottery [NASDAQ symbol] (TTSB)
GLCCF .... Gaming Lottery Corp. [NASDAQ symbol] (SAG)
GLCES .... Great Lakes Coastal Forecasting System [Marine science] (OSRA)
GLCFS .... Great Lakes Coastal Forecasting System (USDC)
GLCM .... Graduate Diploma of the London College of Music [British] (DBQ)
GLCM .... Ground-Launched Cruise Missile [Pronounced "glick-em"]
GLCM .... Robertsport/Cape Mount [Liberia] [ICAO location identifier] (ICLI)
GlcN .... Glucosamine [Biochemistry]
GLCNA .... German Lutheran Conference of North America (EA)
GlcNac .... N-Acetylglucosamine
GLCNSW ..... Gem and Lapidary Council of New South Wales [Australia]
GLCP .... Harper/Cape Palmas [Liberia] [ICAO location identifier] (ICLI)
GlcrBc .... Glacier Bancorp, Inc. [Associated Press] (SAG)
GLC/SBS ..... Great Little Computer/Small Business System [Business software] [Cumulus Computer Corp.] (PCM)

GLCSNSW.... Gay and Lesbian Counselling Service of New South Wales [Australia]
GLCSSA .... Gay and Lesbian Counselling Service of South Australia
GLCTS .... Global Land Cover Test Sites [Remote sensing] (EERA)
GlcUA .... Glucuronic Acid [Also, GA] [Biochemistry]
GlcWatr .... Glacier Water Services, Inc. [Associated Press] (SAG)
GLD .... Cases in the Griqualand West Local Division of the Supreme Court [1910-46] [South Africa] [A publication] (DLA)
GLD .... Gas Leak Detector
GLD .... General Learning Disability
GLD .... Glider
GLD .... Glide Slope [Aviation] (NASA)
GLD .... Glutamate Dehydrogenase (DMAA)
GLD .... Gold (MSA)
GLD .... Golden [Colorado School of Mines] [Colorado] [Seismograph station code, US Geological Survey] (SEIS)
GLD .... Golden Star Air Cargo Co. Ltd. [Sudan] [ICAO designator] (FAAC)
GLD .... Goodland [Kansas] [Airport symbol] (OAG)
GLD .... Gross Logical Design
GLD .... Ground-LASER Designators (RDA)
GLD .... Guild
GLD .... Guild
Gld .... Guilder [Modification of gulden] [Monetary unit] [Netherlands]
GLD .... Santa Fe Pacific Gold Corp. [NYSE symbol] (SAG)
GLD .... Sante Fe Pacific Gold [NYSE symbol] (TTSB)
GLDA .... Gay and Lesbian Democrats of America [Defunct] (EA)
GLDB .... Gold Banc Corp., Inc. [NASDAQ symbol] (SAG)
GldBear .... Golden Bear Golf, Inc. [Associated Press] (SAG)
GLDC .... Golden Enterprises [NASDAQ symbol] (TTSB)
GLDC .... Golden Enterprises, Inc. [NASDAQ symbol] (NQ)
GldEagl .... Golden Eagle Group, Inc. [Associated Press] (SAG)
GldEg .... Golden Eagle Group, Inc. [Associated Press] (SAG)
GLDF .... Gold Fields of South Africa Ltd. [NASDAQ symbol] (NQ)
GldFld .... Goldfield Corp. [Associated Press] (SAG)
GLDFY .... Gold Fields S. Africa ADR [NASDAQ symbol] (TTSB)
GLDH .... Glutamate Dehydrogenase [Organic chemistry]
GldKngt .... Golden Knight Resources, Inc. [Associated Press] (SAG)
GLDMS .... Groupe de Liaison de Docimologues en Milieu Scolaire [Canada]
gldn .... Golden [Philately]
GLDN .... Golden
GLDN .... Golden Systems, Inc. [NASDAQ symbol] (SAG)
GldnSyst ...... Golden Systems, Inc. [Associated Press] (SAG)
GLDP .... Ginn Language Development Program (EDAC)
GLD PLTD.... Gold Plated [Freight]
GldPoul .... Golden Poultry Co., Inc. [Associated Press] (SAG)
GldQual .... Golden Quail Resources Ltd. [Associated Press] (SAG)
GLDR .... Glider (FAAC)
GLDR .... Gold Reserve [NASDAQ symbol] (TTSB)
GLDR .... Gold Reserve Corp. [NASDAQ symbol] (NQ)
GLDR .... Groupe Liberal, Democratique, et Reformateur (EAIO)
GLDS .... Gemini Launch Data System [NASA] (MCD)
GLDS .... Ground LASER Designator Station (PDAA)
GldStarR ...... Golden Star Resources Ltd. [Associated Press] (SAG)
GldStd .... Gold Standard, Inc. [Associated Press] (SAG)
GLDT .... Gas LASER Discharge Tube
GLDTR .... Gladiator
GldWF .... Golden West Financial Corp. [Associated Press] (SAG)
GldwSam ..... Goldwyn [Samuel] Co. [Associated Press] (SAG)
GLE .... Gainesville, TX [Location identifier FAA] (FAAL)
GLE .... Gemini LASER Experiment [NASA] (IAA)
GLE .... Gleason Corp. [NYSE symbol] (SPSG)
GLE .... Glenmuick [New Zealand] [Seismograph station code, US Geological Survey Closed] (SEIS)
GLE .... GLE Resources Ltd. [Vancouver Stock Exchange symbol]
GLE .... Gloss Low Emission [Ink] (DGA)
GLE .... Government-Loaned Equipment (MSA)
GLE .... Grade Level Equivalent [Educational testing]
GLE .... Grand Larousse Encyclopedique [A publication]
GLE .... Ground-Level Event [Geophysics]
GLE .... Ground Liaison Element (MCD)
GLEAM .... Gummed Long Edge [Envelopes] (DGA)
GLEAM .... Graphic Layout and Engineering Aid Method
GleasC .... Gleason Corp. [Associated Press] (SAG)
GLEDIC .... Great Lakes Environmental Information Center [Ann Arbor, MI]
GLEEP .... Graphite Low-Energy Experimental Pile [Nuclear reactor] [British]
GLEF .... Geothermal Loop Experimental Facility [Department of Energy]
GLEIS .... Great Lakes Environmental Information Sharing
GLEMEDS ... Great Lakes Embryo Mortality, Edema, and Deformities Syndrome [Marine birds]
GLEN .... Glen [Commonly used] (OPSA)
Glenayr .... Glenayre Techs, Inc. [Associated Press] (SAG)
Gl Ency .... Globe Encyclopaedia [A publication] (ROG)
GLENDAL .... Glendalough [Valley in Ireland] (ROG)
GlendCo ...... Glendale Co-Operative Bank [Associated Press] (SAG)
GlenF .... Glendale Federal Bank Federal Savings Bank [Associated Press] (SAG)
GlenF .... Glendale Federal Bank FSB [Associated Press] (SAG)
GlenFed .... Glendale Federal Bank Federal Savings Bank [Associated Press] (SAG)
Glen High ... Glen's Highway Laws [A publication] (DLA)
Glenn .... Glenn's Annual Reports [16-18 Louisiana] [A publication] (DLA)
Glen Pub H.. Glen on the Public Health Laws [A publication] (DLA)
Glen Reg .... Glen on Registration of Births and Deaths [A publication] (DLA)
GlenRT .... Glenborough Realty Trust, Inc. [Associated Press] (SAG)
GLENS .... Glens [Commonly used] (OPSA)

Glenway	Glenway Financial Corp. [*Associated Press*] (SAG)
GLEP	Group for Lunar Exploration and Planning (MCD)
GLERL	Great Lakes Environmental Research Laboratory [*Ann Arbor, MI*] [*National Oceanic and Atmospheric Administration*] (GRD)
GLERR	Great Lakes Ecosystem Restoration and Rehabilitation [*Canada*] (ASF)
GLES	Great Lakes Forecasting System [*Marine science*] (OSRA)
GLET	Government Logistics Evaluation and Testing (MCD)
GLF	Gaussian Lens Formula [*Optics*]
GLF	Gay Liberation Front
GLF	Generalized Lambda Family [*Statistics*]
GLF	General Telephone Co. of Florida [*NYSE symbol*] (SPSG)
GLF	Glass Fiber [*Technical drawings*]
GLF	Golfito [*Costa Rica*] [*Airport symbol*] (OAG)
GLF	Great Lakes Fisheries Laboratory, Ann Arbor, MI [*OCLC symbol*] (OCLC)
GLF	GTE Florida, Inc. [*NYSE symbol*] (SAG)
GLF	Gulfstream Aerospace Corp. [*ICAO designator*] (FAAC)
GLF	McGill University, Law Library [*UTLAS symbol*]
GLFALSK	Gulf of Alaska (FAAC)
GLFC	Georganne LaPiere Fan Club (EA)
GLFC	Ginger Lynn Fan Club [*Defunct*] (EA)
GLFC	Gloria Loring Fan Club [*Defunct*] (EA)
GLFC	Great Lakes Fishery Commission [*Canada and United States*] (NOAA)
GLFC	Guiding Light Fan Club (EA)
GLFCAL	Gulf of California (FAAC)
GlfCda	Gulf Canada Resources Ltd. [*Associated Press*] (SAG)
GLFD	Guilford Pharmaceuticals [*NASDAQ symbol*] (TTSB)
GLFD	Guilford Pharmaceuticals, Inc. [*NASDAQ symbol*] (SAG)
GLFDCC	Great Lakes Fish Disease Control Committee [*Canada*] (ASF)
GLFE	Golf Enterprises [*NASDAQ symbol*] (TTSB)
GLFE	Golf Enterprises, Inc. [*NASDAQ symbol*] (SAG)
GL/FICS	General Ledger / Financial Information and Control System
GLFL	Great Lakes Fishery Laboratory [*Department of the Interior*] (GRD)
GLFMEX	Gulf of Mexico (FAAC)
Glfmrk	Gulfmark International [*Associated Press*] (SAG)
GLFPrA	GTE Fla $1.25 Pfd [*NYSE symbol*] (TTSB)
GLFPrB	GTE Fla $1.30cm B Pfd [*NYSE symbol*] (TTSB)
GLFPrC	GTE Fla 8.16% Pfd [*NYSE symbol*] (TTSB)
GLFRB	Great Lakes Fisheries Research Branch [*Canadian Department of Fisheries and Oceans*] [*Research center*] (RCD)
GLFRC	Great Lakes Forest Research Centre [*Environment Canada*] [*Research center*] (RCD)
GIFRP	Glass-Fiber-Reinforced Plastic [*Also, GFRP*]
GLFS	Great Lakes Forecasting System (USDC)
GLFSTLAWR	Gulf of St. Lawrence (FAAC)
GlfSU	Gulf States Utilities Co. [*Associated Press*] (SAG)
GLG	Glamis Gold Ltd. [*Toronto Stock Exchange symbol NYSE symbol*]
GLG	Glengyle [*Australia Airport symbol*] (OAG)
GLG	La Grange College, La Grange, GA [*OCLC symbol*] (OCLC)
GLGE	Greenville/Sinoe [*Liberia*] [*ICAO location identifier*] (ICLI)
GLGL	Gwinnett County Law Library, Lawrenceville, GA [*Library symbol*] [*Library of Congress*] (LCLS)
GLGS	Gwinnett County Public Schools, Lawrenceville, GA [*Library symbol*] [*Library of Congress*] (LCLS)
GLGT	Gwinnett Technical Institute, Lawrenceville, GA [*Library symbol*] [*Library of Congress*] (LCLS)
GLH	Gentleman's Left Handed [*Golf club*]
GLH	Giant Lymph Node Hyperplasia [*Medicine*] (DMAA)
GLH	Glue Line Heating
GLH	Go Like Hell [*In model name Omni GLH, proposed for Dodge car designed by Carroll Shelby*]
GLH	Greenville [*Mississippi*] [*Airport symbol*] (OAG)
GLHA	Great Lakes Harbor Association (EA)
GLH-S	Goes Like Hell - Some More [*In model "GLH-S," Dodge car designed by Carroll Shelby*] [*Facetious translation: "Goes Like Hell - Squared"*]
GLHS	Great Lakes Historical Society (EA)
GLHS	Ground-Launched HELLFIRE System (MCD)
GLHSC	Gay and Lesbian History on Stamps Club (EA)
GLI	Gale's Literary Index [*CD-ROM*]
GLI	Gallic Aviation [*France ICAO designator*] (FAAC)
GLI	Gamma LINAC Instrumentation
GLI	Glen Innes [*Australia Airport symbol*] (OAG)
GLI	Glicentin [*Biochemistry*]
GLI	Glider
GLI	Glucagon-Like Immunoreactivity [*or Immunoreactant*] [*Endocrinology*]
GLI	Grandma Lee's, Inc. [*Toronto Stock Exchange symbol*]
GLI	Gurkha Light Infantry [*British military*] (DMA)
GLIA	Gliatech, Inc. [*NASDAQ symbol*] (SAG)
GLIAC	Great Lakes Intercollegiate Athletic Conference
Gliatech	Gliatech, Inc. [*Associated Press*] (SAG)
GLIB	Gay and Lesbian Information Bureau (IID)
GliBad	Glider Badge [*Military decoration*]
GLIC	General Ledger Identification Code (AFM)
GLIFWC	Great Lakes Indian Fish and Wildlife Commission (EA)
GLIM	Generalised Linear Interactive Modelling System [*Software*] (EERA)
GLIM	General Light Inter-Reflection Model (PDAA)
GLIM	General Linear Modeling Program [*Computer science*]
GlimchRt	Glimcher Realty Trust [*Associated Press*] (SAG)
GLIMPCE	Great Lakes International Multidisciplinary Program on Crustal Evolution [*Geophysics*]
GLIMPSE	Global Limb Photometric Scanning Experiment (MCD)
GLIN	Georgia Library Information Network [*Library network*]
GLIN	Great Lakes Information Network
GLINN	Government Libraries Information Network in New South Wales [*Australia*]
GLINT	Global Intelligence (IEEE)
GLINT	Gospel Literature International (EA)
glio	Glioma [*Neurology*] (DAVI)
GLIP	Glide and Skip [*Bombing mission*]
GLIPAR	Guide Line Identification Program for Antimissile Research [*ARPA*]
GLIPAR	Guidelines for Investigation, Planning, and Research
GLIS	Gleaner Life Insurance Society [*Adrian, MI*] (EA)
GLIS	Glissando [*Gliding*] [*Music*] (ROG)
GLIS	Global Land Information System (EERA)
GLISA	Government Losses in Shipment Act [*1937*]
Gliss	Glissando [*Gliding*] [*Music*]
glit	Glitter (VRA)
GLITCH	Goblin Loose in the Computer Hut [*Computer science*]
GLJ	Global Getra Ltd. [*Bulgaria*] [*ICAO designator*] (FAAC)
GLK	Golden Lake Resources Ltd. [*Vancouver Stock Exchange symbol*]
GLK	Great Lakes Chemical [*NYSE symbol*] (TTSB)
GLK	Great Lakes Chemical Corp. [*NYSE symbol*] (SPSG)
GLL	Galileo [*NASA*]
GLL	Gay and Lesbian Literature
GLL	General Leaseholds Ltd. [*Toronto Stock Exchange symbol*]
GLL	Gilgames and the Land of the Living (BJA)
GLL	Gill, CO [*Location identifier FAA*] (FAAL)
GLL	Great Lakes Laboratory [*State University College at Buffalo*] [*Research center*] (RCD)
GLL	McGill University Library [*UTLAS symbol*]
GLLB	Buchanan [*Liberia*] [*ICAO location identifier*] (ICLI)
GLLD	Ground-LASER Locator Designator (MCD)
GLLD-E	Ground-LASER Locator Designator-Evaluator (MCD)
GLLD-TNS	Ground-LASER Locator Designator-Thermal Night Sight (MCD)
GLLD/VLLD	Ground-LASER Locator Designator/Vehicular LASER Locator Designator (MCD)
GLLKA	Great Lakes Lighthouse Keepers Association (EA)
GLLO	Great Lakes Licensed Officers' Organization
GLLRY	Gallery
GLM	Generalized Lagrangian Multiplier [*Military*] (AFIT)
GLM	Generalized Linear Model [*Statistics*]
GLM	Generalized Linear Models [*Computer science*] (EERA)
GLM	Gigabit Link Module [*Computer science*]
GLM	Gilmore [*Alaska*] [*Also, GLN*] [*Seismograph station code, US Geological Survey*] (SEIS)
GLM	Global Marine [*NYSE symbol*] (TTSB)
GLM	Global Marine, Inc. [*NYSE symbol*] (SPSG)
GLM	Gold Life-Saving Medal [*Military decoration*] (GFGA)
GLM	Government-Loaned Material
GLM	Graduated Length Method [*of learning to ski*] [*Later, Accelerated Length Method*]
GLM	Grand Livre du Mois [*Best-selling book of the month*] [*French*]
GLM	Graphics Lathe Module [*McDonnell-Douglas Automation Co.*]
GLM	Great Lakes Megalopolis [*Proposed name for possible "super-city" formed by growth and mergers of other cities*]
GLM	Growth-Limiting Medium [*For microorganisms*]
GLM	McGill University, Medical Library [*UTLAS symbol*]
GLMA	Glassmaster Co. [*NASDAQ symbol*] (SAG)
GLMA	Great Lakes Mink Association (EA)
GLMC	Gay and Lesbian Media Coalition
GLMC	Monrovia City [*Liberia*] [*ICAO location identifier*] (ICLI)
GLMI	Great Lakes Maritime Institute (EA)
GIMkt	Global Market Information, Inc. [*Associated Press*] (SAG)
GLMMM	Grand Lodge of Mark Master Masons [*Freemasonry*]
GLMMS	Groupement Latin et Mediterraneen de Medecine du Sport [*Latin and Mediterranean Group for Sport Medicine - LMGSM*] (EAIO)
GLMR	Monrovia/Spriggs Payne [*Liberia*] [*ICAO location identifier*] (ICLI)
GImRS	Glutaminyl-RNA Synthetase [*An enzyme*]
GLMWC	Great Lakes and Marine Waters Center [*University of Michigan*] [*Research center*] (RCD)
Glmy	[*The*] Glenmary Home Missioners (TOCD)
glmy	The Glenmary Home Missioners (TOCD)
GLN	Gilmore [*Alaska*] [*Also, GLM*] [*Seismograph station code, US Geological Survey*] (SEIS)
GLN	Glen
GLN	Glen
GLN	Glenayre Electronics Ltd. [*Toronto Stock Exchange symbol*]
GLN	Glendale Federal Bank [*NYSE symbol*] (SPSG)
Gln	Glucagon [*Medicine*] (DMAA)
Gln	Glutamine [*or Glu(NH$_2$)*] [*Also, Q An amino acid*]
GLN	Lennox Airways, Gambia Ltd. [*ICAO designator*] (FAAC)
GLNA	Nimba [*Liberia*] [*ICAO location identifier*] (ICLI)
GLNH	Giant Lymph Node Hyperplasia [*Medicine*] (DMAA)
GLNPO	Great Lakes National Program Office [*Environmental Protection Agency*]
GLNPrE	Glendale Fed Bk Cv'E'Prd [*NYSE symbol*] (TTSB)
GlnRS	Glutamine-Transfer Ribonucleic Acid Synthetase
GLNS	Glens
GLNS	Glens [*Postal Service standard*] (OPSA)
GLNSW	Gould League of New South Wales [*Australia*]
GLNTC	Great Lakes Naval Training Center
GLO	Cheltenham-Gloucester [*England*] [*Airport symbol*] (AD)
GLO	Clovis, NM [*Location identifier FAA*] (FAAL)
GLO	General Land Office [*Became part of Bureau of Land Management, 1946*]
GLO	Get the Lead Out [*Of GLO week, sponsored by American Oil Co.*]
Glo	Global

GLO .... Global Ocean Carriers [*AMEX symbol*] (TTSB)
GLO .... Global Ocean Carriers Ltd. [*AMEX symbol*] (CTT)
GLO .... Gloria [*Kyrgyzstan*] [*FAA designator*] (FAAC)
glo .... Gloss (VRA)
GLO .... Gloucester [*Massachusetts*] [*Seismograph station code, US Geological Survey*] (SEIS)
GLO .... Gloucester [*British depot code*]
GLO .... Glyoxalase [*An enzyme*]
GLO .... Goddard Launch Operations [*NASA*]
GLO .... Gospel literature Outreach [*Australia*]
G LO .... Grand Lodge [*Freemasonry*] (ROG)
GLO .... Greens in Lowe [*Political party Australia*]
GLO .... Ground Liaison Officer [*Military*]
GLO .... Ground Logistics Operations [*NASA*] (KSC)
GLO .... Guaiacol-Linoleic Acid Hydroperoxide Oxidoreductase [*An enzyme*]
GLO .... Gunnery Liaison Officer [*Navy*]
GLO .... GVN [*Government of Vietnam*] Liaison Officer
GLO .... L-Gulanolactone Oxidase [*An enzyme*]
GLO .... Ultra Glow Cosmetics [*Vancouver Stock Exchange symbol*]
Gloag & Henderson... Gloag and Henderson's Introduction to the Law of Scotland [*7th ed.*] [*1968*] [*A publication*] (DLA)
GLOAS .... German Liaison Office for the Armament Sector [*Military*]
GLOB .... Globular
GLOB .... Globulin
GlobalPh.... Global Pharmaceutical Corp. [*Associated Press*] (SAG)
Globalstr.... Globalstar Telecommunications Ltd. [*Associated Press*] (SAG)
GLOBE .... Gay, Lesbian, or Bisexual Employees [*An association*]
GLOBE .... Global Backscatter Experiment [*NASA/MSFC*]
GLOBE .... Global Backscatter Experiment (USDC)
GLOBE .... Global Backscatter Experiment [*Marine science*] (OSRA)
GLOBE .... Global Learning and Observations to Benefit the Environment [*NASA*]
GLOBE .... Global Legislators Organization for a Balanced Environment [*International coalition*]
GLOBE .... Global Lending and Overseas Banking Evaluator [*Chase Econometrics*] [*Database*]
GLOBE .... Global Observations to Benefit the Environment (EERA)
Globec......... Global Ocean Ecosystem Dynamics or Global Ocean-Ecosystem Coupling (USDC)
GLOBECOM... Global Communications System [*Air Force*]
GlobHi .... Global High Income Dollar Fund [*Associated Press*] (SAG)
GlobIndl....... Global Industrial Technologies [*Associated Press*] (SAG)
GLOBIXS.... Global Information Exchange System (DOMA)
GloblInd....... Global Industries Ltd. [*Associated Press*] (SAG)
Globlink....... Globalink, Inc. [*Associated Press*] (SAG)
GloblInt........ Global Intellicom, Inc. [*Associated Press*] (SAG)
Globlstr........ Globalstar Telecommunications Ltd. [*Associated Press*] (SAG)
GlobM.......... Global Marine, Inc. [*Associated Press*] (SAG)
GlobNR........ Global Natural Resources, Inc. [*Associated Press*] (SAG)
GlobOut ...... Global Outdoors, Inc. [*Associated Press*] (SAG)
GlobPart ..... Global Partners Income Fund [*Associated Press*] (SAG)
GlobSml ..... Global Small Cap Fund, Inc. [*Associated Press*] (SAG)
GlobTele...... Global Telecommunications Solutions, Inc. [*Associated Press*] (SAG)
GlobTR........ Global Total Return Fund [*Associated Press*] (SAG)
G-LOC......... Gravity-Induced Loss of Consciousness [*Aviation*]
GLOC .... Ground Line of Communications (AFM)
GLOCHANT... Global Change and the Antarctica (EERA)
GLOCK .... Glockenspiel [*Music*]
GLOCOM ..... Global Communications System [*Air Force*]
GLODIS........ General Language-Operated Decision Implementation System (PDAA)
GLOL .... Golay Logic Operating Language
GLOM .... Gross Lift-Off Mass [*NASA*] (KSC)
GLOMB .... Glide Bomb [*Air Force*]
GLOMEX ...... Global Oceanographic and Meteorological Experiment [*Marine science*] (MSC)
GLOMR........ Global Low-Orbiting Message Relay [*Satellite*]
GLONASS ... Global Navigation Satellite System [*Military*]
GLONASS ... Global Orbiting Navigational Satellite System [*FAA*] (TAG)
GLOP .... Gevic Logic Operation Program
GLOP .... Guidance and Launch Operation [*Aerospace*] (IAA)
GLOPAC....... Gyroscopic Low-Power Attitude Control
GLOPC .... Gyroscopic Lower Power Control (IAA)
Gl Ord .... Glossa Ordinaria [*A publication*] (DSA)
GLORIA........ Geological Long-Range Inclined ASDIC
GLOS .... Glossary
GLOS .... Gloucestershire [*County in England*]
Glos .... Gloucestershire [*County in England*] (ODBW)
GLOS .... Gun Line of Site [*Tank*] [*Army*]
GLOSS .... Global Ocean Surveillance System (IEEE)
GLOSS .... Global Sea Level Observing System
GLOSS .... Global Sea Level Observing System [*Marine science*] (OSRA)
GLOSS .... Glossary
Gloss Lat .... Glossaria Latina [*A publication*] (OCD)
GLOSTER ..... Gloucester [*City in England*] (ROG)
GLOTOS....... Graphical Representation of Language for Temporal Ordering Specification [*Telecommunications*] (OSI)
GLOTRAC..... Global Tracking [*RADAR*]
GLOUC........ Gloucester [*City in England*] (ROG)
GLOUC........ Gloucestershire [*County in England*] (ROG)
Gloucester .. Gloucestershire [*County in England*] (BARN)
GLOUC R .... Gloucestershire Regiment [*Military British*] (ROG)
GLOUCS....... Gloucestershire [*County in England*]
GLOV .... Gays and Lesbians Opposing Violence [*An association*]
Glov Mun Cor... Glover's Municipal Corporations [*A publication*] (DLA)

GLOW .... Giving and Learning Our Way [*An association*]
GLOW .... Global RADAR for Ocean Waves
GLOW .... Gross Lift-Off Weight [*NASA*]
GLOW .... Ground Lift-Off Weight [*NASA*] (NASA)
GLOWATS.... Global War Avoidance Telecommunications System (MCD)
GLP .... Gallup [*Diocesan abbreviation*] [*New Mexico*] (TOCD)
GLP .... Gelled Liquid Propellant
GLP .... Generalized Lattice-Point
GLP .... General Layout Plan (NATG)
GLP .... General Letter Package (PDAA)
GLP .... Glucagon-Like Peptide [*Biochemistry*]
GLP .... Glucose-L-Phosphate (DMAA)
GLP .... Glycolipoprotein (DMAA)
GLP .... GOAL [*Ground Operations Aerospace Language*] Language Processor
GLP .... Golden Princess [*Vancouver Stock Exchange symbol*]
GLP .... Golpazari [*Turkey*] [*Also, GPA*] [*Seismograph station code, US Geological Survey*] (SEIS)
GLP .... Good Laboratory Practice [*FDA*]
GLP .... Gospel Light Publications [*British*]
GLP .... Government-Lent Property (NG)
GLP .... Greek Literary Papyri [*A publication*] (OCD)
GLP .... Gross Lawyer Product [*Term for measurement of the income of attorneys*]
GLP .... Group-Living Program (DAVI)
GLP .... Guadeloupe [*ANSI three-letter standard code*] (CNC)
GLP .... Guide Line Paper [*of Washington Standardization Officers*] [*Military*]
GLP .... Guyana Labour Party [*Political party*] (EY)
GLPA .... Gay and Lesbian Press Association (EA)
GLPA .... Great Lakes Pilotage Administration [*Department of Transportation*]
GLP-AACR ... Gibraltar Labour Party - Association for the Advancement of Civil Rights [*Political party*] (PPW)
GLPC .... Gas-Liquid Partition Chromatography
GLPC .... Global Pharmaceutical Corp. [*NASDAQ symbol*] (SAG)
GLPCI .... Gay and Lesbian Parents Coalition International (EA)
GLPG .... Glow Plug
GLPIAC .... Great Lakes Physical Information Analysis Center
GLPP .... Glucose, Post Prandial [*Clinical chemistry*]
GLPR .... Goldstone Predict [*Orbit identification*] [*NASA*]
GL-PTC .... Gas Liquid Phase Transfer Catalysis [*Physical chemistry*]
GLQ .... Golden Adit Resources [*Vancouver Stock Exchange symbol*]
GLQ .... Greater-than-Lot Quantities
GLR .... Central Mountain Air Ltd. [*Canada ICAO designator*] (FAAC)
GLR .... G & L Realty Corp. [*NYSE symbol*] (SPSG)
GLR .... Gaylord, MI [*Location identifier FAA*] (FAAL)
GLR .... Gazette Law Reports [*New Zealand*] [*A publication*] (DLA)
GLR .... General Line Rate [*Advertising*]
GLR .... Gladiator Resources Ltd. [*Vancouver Stock Exchange symbol*]
GLR .... Glass LASER Rod
GLR .... Government Land Register [*of Western Australia*] [*State*] (EERA)
GLR .... Graphic Level Recorder
GLR .... Great Lakes Rules [*Boating*] (DICI)
GLR .... Groom Lake Road [*Nevada*] [*Seismograph station code, US Geological Survey*] (SEIS)
GLR .... McGill University Rare Books [*UTLAS symbol*]
GLRA .... Gun-Launched/Rocket-Assisted (MCD)
GL RADAR ... Gun Laying RADAR
GLR-AV........ Grapevine Leafroll-Associated Virus [*Plant pathology*]
GLRB .... Monrovia/Roberts International [*Liberia*] [*ICAO location identifier*] (ICLI)
GLRC .... Gas-Liquid Radiochromatography [*Analytical chemistry*]
GLRC .... Grain Legume Research Council (EERA)
GLRC .... Grain Legumes Research Council [*Australia*]
GLRE .... Geniki Laiki Rizospastiki Enosis [*General Union of Populists and Radicals*] [*Greek*] (PPE)
GLR (NZ) .... Gazette Law Reports [*New Zealand*] [*A publication*] (DLA)
GLRS .... Geodynamics LASER Ranging System [*NASA*]
GLRS .... Global Outdoors, Inc. [*NASDAQ symbol*] (SAG)
GLRS .... Global Res [*NASDAQ symbol*] (TTSB)
GLRS .... Global Resources, Inc. [*NASDAQ symbol*] (SAG)
GLRSHLD .... Glare Shield (MCD)
GLS............. Galveston [*Texas*] [*Airport symbol*] (OAG)
GLS............. Gaylord Circulation Control System [*Information service or system*] (IID)
GLS............. Generalized Least Squares [*Statistics*]
GLS............. Generalized Lymphadenopathy Syndrome [*Medicine*] (DMAA)
GLS............. General Ledger System [*Accounting*] (IAA)
GLS............. General Lighting Service
GLS............. General Lighting System [*Incadescent lighting*]
GLS............. General Line School
GLS............. Giles [*Australia Seismograph station code, US Geological Survey*] (SEIS)
GLS............. Glass
gls .... Glass (VRA)
GLS............. Glide Slope [*Aviation*] (MSA)
GLS............. Global International Ltd. [*Bulgaria*] [*ICAO designator*] (FAAC)
GLS............. Golden Shield Resources Ltd. [*Toronto Stock Exchange symbol Vancouver Stock Exchange symbol*]
GLS............. Government Launch Service (SSD)
GLS............. Graduate Library School
GLS............. Grand Lodge of Scotland [*Freemasonry*]
GLS............. Great Lakes Screw
GLS............. Green LASER System
GLS............. Ground Launch Sequence [*or Sequencer*] (NASA)
GLS............. Gypsy Lore Society, North American Chapter (EA)

GLS............. Schuller Corp. [NYSE symbol] (SAG)
GLS............. Schuller Corp. [NYSE symbol] (TTSB)
GLSA .... General Ledger Subsidiary Account (AFM)
GLSA .... General Livestock Agent
GLSA .... Government Large Structures Assembly (SSD)
GLSA .... Gray Line Sightseeing Association [Commercial firm] (EA)
GLSA .... Great Lakes Seaplane Association [Defunct] (EA)
GLSBG .... Great Lakes Sugar Beet Growers (EA)
GLS(C)........ Government Launch Service (Cryogenic) (SSD)
GLSE.......... Generalized Weighted Least Squares Estimates [Statistics]
GLSECT....... Ground Liaison Section [Military British]
GLSFC........ Great Lakes Sport Fishing Council (EA)
GLSGW .... Glasgow [Scotland]
GLSK .... Sanniquellie [Liberia] [ICAO location identifier] (ICLI)
GLSM.......... Gold Life Saving Medal [Military decoration]
glsn............. Glassine (VRA)
GLSOA .... Great Lakes Ship Owners Association (EA)
GLSP .... Good Large Scale Practice
GLSS .... Ground-Launch Support System (MCD)
GLST.......... Sasstown [Liberia] [ICAO location identifier] (ICLI)
GLSTM......... Graduate of the London School of Tropical Medicine (DAS)
Glstnbry....... Glastonbury Bank & Trust Co. [Associated Press] (SAG)
GLT............. Gas LASER Tube
GLT............. General Corporation for Light Air Transport & Technical Sevices [Libya] [ICAO designator] (FAAC)
GLT............. General Labor and Trades
glt............... Gilding (VRA)
glt............... Gilt (VRA)
GLT............. Gilt [Bookbinding] (ROG)
GLT............. Gladstone [Australia Airport symbol] (OAG)
GLT............. Glass Lined Tubing
GLT............. Glatfelter [P. H.] Co. [AMEX symbol] (SPSG)
GLT............. Gloss Low Tack [Ink] (DGA)
GLT............. Golden Lion Tamarin [South American monkey]
GLT............. Greeting Letter Telegram (ADA)
GLT............. Gridded Line of Thrust (MCD)
GLT............. Ground-LASER Tracking
GLT............. Guide Light (AAG)
GL(T)......... Gun-Laying (Turret) (DEN)
GLTB.......... Goleta National Bank [NASDAQ symbol] (SAG)
GLTB.......... Greater London Training Board [British] (AIE)
GLTMC........ Golden Lion Tamarin Management Committee (EA)
GlTN.......... Glomerulo-Tubulo-Nephritis [Medicine]
GLTN .... Guillotine (MSA)
GLTN .... Tchien [Liberia] [ICAO location identifier] (ICLI)
GLU .... Gambia Labour Union
GLU .... General Logic Unit [Computer chip]
GLU .... Global Land Use [NASA]
GLU .... Glucose [Organic chemistry] (DAVI)
glu .... Glutamate [An amino acid] (DOG)
glu .... Glutamic Acid [An amino acid] (DOG)
Glu .... Glutamic Acid [Also, E, GA] [An amino acid]
Glu .... Glutamine [An amino acid] (DAVI)
GLU .... Great Lakes United (EA)
GLU .... Green Lake Resources Ltd. [Vancouver Stock Exchange symbol]
GLU .... Gruene Liste Umweltschutz [Green List Ecology] [Germany] (PPE)
GLU-5 .... Five-Hour Glucose Tolerance Test [Medicine] (DMAA)
GLUC .... Glucose [Also, G, Glc] [A sugar]
GLUC .... Glucosidase (DMAA)
GLUCEPTATE... Glucoheptonate [USAN] [Organic chemistry]
GLUC-S ...... Urin Glucose Spot [Test] [Endocrinology] (DAVI)
Glucur........ Glucuronide [Biochemistry] (AAMN)
GLULAM ...... Glued Laminated Wood (PDAA)
GluN .... Glutamine [An amino acid] (BARN)
Glu(NH₂)..... Glutamine [or Gln] [Also, Q An amino acid]
glu ox .... Glucose Oxidase [Also, GO, GOD] [An enzyme] (AAMN)
GluR .... Glutamate Receptor [Biochemistry]
GLUT .... Glucose Transporter [Biochemistry]
GLUTAM ...... Glutamine [An amino acid] (DAVI)
GLUX .... Great Lakes Aviation [NASDAQ symbol] (TTSB)
GLUX .... Great Lakes Aviation Ltd. [NASDAQ symbol] (SAG)
GLV............ Gemini Launch Vehicle [NASA]
GLV............ Gibbon Ape Leukemia Virus (DMAA)
GLV............ Globe Valve (AAG)
GLV............ Glove
GLV............ Golden Vale Explorations Corp. [Vancouver Stock Exchange symbol]
GLV............ Golovin [Alaska] [Airport symbol] (OAG)
GLV............ Gould League of Victoria [Australia]
GLV............ Gross Leukemia Virus
GLVA .... Voinjama [Liberia] [ICAO location identifier] (ICLI)
GLVNZNG .... Galvanizing
GLW............ Corning Delaware LP [NYSE symbol] (SAG)
GLW............ Corning, Inc. [Wall Street slang name: "Glow Worm"] [NYSE symbol] (SPSG)
GLW............ Glasgow, KY [Location identifier FAA] (FAAL)
GLW............ Gunnery Lieutenant's Writer [British military] (DMA)
GLWB.......... Glazed Wallboard [Technical drawings]
GLWCAP...... Great Lakes Wetlands Conservation Action Plan [Canada]
GLWDA....... Great Lakes Waterways Development Association (EA)
GLWPrM....... Corning Del L.P. 6% 'MIPS' [NYSE symbol] (TTSB)
GLWQA....... Great Lakes Water Quality Agreement [Environmental Protection Agency]
GLWR .... Glassware
GLX............ Galela [Indonesia] [Airport symbol] (OAG)

GLX............ Glaxo Ltd. ADR [Formerly, Glaxo Holdilngs Ltd. ADR] [NYSE symbol] (SPSG)
GLX%......... Glaxo Wellcome plc ADR [NYSE symbol] (TTSB)
Glx............. Glutamic Acid [or Glutamine] [Also, Z An amino acid]
GLX............ Goldex Mines Ltd. [Toronto Stock Exchange symbol]
GLX............ McGill University RECON [UTLAS symbol]
GlxyFd........ Galaxy Foods Co. [Associated Press] (SAG)
GLY............ Clinton, MO [Location identifier FAA] (FAAL)
GLY............ Galaxy Minerals, Inc. [Toronto Stock Exchange symbol]
Gly............. Glycerol [Organic chemistry] (DAVI)
gly............. Glycinate [Organic chemistry]
Gly............. Glycine [Also, G] [An amino acid]
gly............. Glycine [An amino acid] (DOG)
GLY............ Glycol (KSC)
gly............. Glyph (VRA)
GLY............ Gully (ADA)
GLYC .... Glycerin
glyc............ Glyceritum [Glycerite] (MAE)
GLYCEROPH... Glycerophophas [Pharmacy] (ROG)
Glyc in W .... Glycerin in Water [Medicine] (DHSM)
GLYCN........ Glycerine
GLYCYRRH... Glycyrrhiza [Licorice] [Pharmacology] (ROG)
Gly-IPC....... Glycinergic Interplexiform Cell [Physiology]
GLYME........ Ethylene Glycol Dimethyl Ether [Also, DME, EGDE] [Organic chemistry]
Glyn & J...... Glyn and Jameson's English Bankruptcy Reports [1821-28] [A publication] (DLA)
Glyn & Jam... Glyn and Jameson's English Bankruptcy Reports [1821-28] [A publication] (DLA)
Glyn & J (Eng)... Glyn and Jameson's English Bankruptcy Reports [1821-28] [A publication] (DLA)
Glynn Wat Pow... Glynn on Water Powers [A publication] (DLA)
glypto .... Glypototheca (VRA)
GlyR .... Glycine Receptor [Organic chemistry]
GLYT........... Genlyte Group, Inc. [NASDAQ symbol] (NQ)
GLZ............. Glaze (MSA)
GLZ............. Glaze
glz............. Glaze (VRA)
glz............. Glazed (VRA)
GLZ............. Great Lakes Group, Inc. [Toronto Stock Exchange symbol]
GLZD........... Glazed
GM............ Air America [ICAO designator] (AD)
GM............ Gabexate Mesilate [A proteolytic enzyme inhibitor]
GM............ Gainesville Midland Railroad Co. [AAR code]
G/M........... Gallons per Minute
GM............ Gambia [ANSI two-letter standard code] (CNC)
gm............ Gambia [MARC country of publication code Library of Congress] (LCCP)
Gm............ Gamma [Subgroup of IgG] [Immunology]
GM............ Gamma [Third letter of the Greek alphabet] (DAVI)
GM............ Gaseous Mixture (MSA)
GM............ Gas Meter
GM............ Gastric Mucosa [Medicine]
GM............ Gated Memory (IAA)
GM............ Gay Male [Classified advertising]
G-M........... Geiger-Mueller [Radiation counter]
GM............ Generalized Myotonia [Medicine]
GM............ General Maintenance [Army]
GM............ General Maintenance Aptitude Area [Military] (AFIT)
GM............ General Manager
GM............ General Medical (MAE)
GM............ General Medicine
GM............ General Meetings [Quakers]
GM............ General Merchandise
GM............ General Merit [Military]
GM............ General MIDI [Musical Instrument Digital Interface] (CDE)
GM............ General Mortgage [Bond]
GM............ General Motors Corp. [NYSE symbol Toronto Stock Exchange symbol] (SPSG)
GM............ Genl Motors [NYSE symbol] (TTSB)
GM............ Gentamicin [Antibacterial compound]
GM............ Gentil Membre [Guest of Club Mediterranee, a vacation cooperative]
GM............ Geometric Mean
GM............ George Medal [British]
GM............ Giant Melanoma [Oncology]
gm............ Gigameter
GM............ Gill-Morrell [Valve oscillator] (DEN)
GM............ Glass Metal (IAA)
GM............ Global Directmail Corp. [NYSE symbol] (SAG)
GM............ Global Marketplace
GM............ Gluteus Medius [Anatomy]
GM............ Gold Medal
GM............ Gold Medallist (DAS)
GM............ Golf Course Operations and Management Programs [Association of Independent Colleges and Schools specialization code]
GM............ Good Mason [Freemasonry] (ROG)
GM............ Good Morning [Amateur radio]
GM............ Gradient Mixer [Chromatography]
GM............ Grail Movement (EA)
GM,........... Gram
gm............ Gram (IDOE)
g-m........... Gram-Meter (MAE)
GM............ Gramophone Motor (DEN)
Gm%......... Gram Percent [Grams per deciliter] [Measurement] (DAVI)
GM............ Grand Mal [Epilepsy]

GM............. Grand Marshal [Freemasonry] (ROG)
GM............. Grand Master [Freemasonry]
GM............. Grand Medal [Ghana]
GM............. Grand Minister [Freemasonry] (ROG)
GM............. Grandmother
GM............. Grand Multiparity [Obstetrics]
G/M............. Granulocyte/Macrophage [Ratio] [Hematology]
GM............. Gravitational Mass
GM............. Greater Manchester [County in England]
GM............. Great Musicians [A publication]
GM............. Greenwich Meridian
GM............. Grid Modulation
G-M............. Grid-to-Magnetic Angle [Navigation] (INF)
GM............. Grog Money [British military] (DMA)
GM............. Gross Motor
GM............. Ground Malfunction
GM............. Ground Mode
GM............. Group Mark [Computer science]
GM............. Group Mobile (CINC)
GM............. Group MODEM (MCD)
GM............. Group per Message (IAA)
GM............. Guam [IYRU nationality code] (IYR)
GM............. Guard Mail
GM............. Guessed Mean [Psychology] (BARN)
GM............. Guided Missile
GM............. Gun-Laying Mark I [RADAR]
GM............. Gunmetal
GM............. Gun Mount [Military] (CAAL)
GM............. Gunner's Mate [Navy rating]
GM............. Gypsy Moths [An association] (EA)
GM............. Metacentric Height [Naval architecture]
GM............. Monosialoganglioside [Chemistry]
Gm............. Mutual Conductance
GM............. Washington Memorial Library, Middle Georgia Regional Library, Macon, GA [Library symbol Library of Congress] (LCLS)
GM1............. Gunner's Mate, First Class [Navy rating]
GM^2............. Grams per Square Meter (WDAA)
GM2............. Gunner's Mate, Second Class [Navy rating]
GM3............. Gunner's Mate, Third Class [Navy rating]
GM100......... Groupement Mobile 100 [Elite French armed forces stationed in Vietnam] (VNW)
GMA............. Gama Aviation Ltd. [British ICAO designator] (FAAC)
GMA............. Game Manufacturers Association (EA)
GMA............. Garment Manufacturers' Association [Australia]
GMA............. Gas Metal Arc
GMA............. Gated Mode Acquisition [Telecommunications] (LAIN)
GMA............. Gemena [Zaire] [Airport symbol] (OAG)
GMA............. General Maintenance Aptitude [Military] (MCD)
GMA............. General Marketing Application
GMA............. General Mental Ability
GMA............. Geomechanics Abstracts [Rock Mechanics Information Service] [Bibliographic database] [British]
GMA............. Giant Molecular Association [Galactic science]
GMA............. Gilt Market Analysis [MMS International] [Information service or system] (CRD)
GMA............. Glyceryl Methacrylate [Organic chemistry] (DAVI)
GMA............. Glycidyl Methacrylate [Organic chemistry]
GMA............. Glycol Methacrylate [Organic chemistry]
GMA............. Good Morning America [Television program]
GMA............. Gospel Music Association (EA)
GMA............. Government Modification Authorization (AAG)
GMA............. Grail Movement of Australia
GMA............. Granite Mountain [Alaska] [Seismograph station code, US Geological Survey] (SEIS)
GMA............. Grocery Manufacturers of America (EA)
GMA............. Grocery Manufacturers of Australia (EERA)
GMA............. Gross Motor Activities (HGAA)
GM/A............. Ground Meat/Analyzer [USDA]
GMA............. Growth and Maturation Activity [Biochemistry]
GMA............. Growth Management Act
GMA............. Guided Missile Ammunition (AABC)
GMA............. Whitefield, NH [Location identifier FAA] (FAAL)
GMAA.......... Agadir/Inezgane [Morocco] [ICAO location identifier] (ICLI)
GMAA.......... Gold Mining Association of America
GMAA.......... Graduate Management Association of Australia
GMAB.......... Guided Missile Assembly Building (SAA)
GMAC.......... Gaining Motor Air Command (MCD)
GMAC.......... Gas Metal Arc Cutting [Welding]
GMAC.......... General Motors Acceptance Corp.
GMAC.......... Genetic Manipulation Advisory Committee (EERA)
GMAC.......... Graduate Management Admission Council [Los Angeles, CA] (EA)
GMAD.......... General Motors Allison Division
GMAD.......... General Motors Assembly Division
GMAG.......... Genetic Manipulation Advisory Group [British]
GMagic....... General Magic, Inc. [Associated Press] (SAG)
GMAI.......... Greg Manning Auctions [NASDAQ symbol] (TTSB)
GMAI.......... Greg Manning Auctions, Inc. [NASDAQ symbol] (SAG)
GMAI.......... Manning [Greg] Auctions, Inc. [NASDAQ symbol] (SAG)
GMAIC........ Guided Missile and Aerospace Intelligence Committee (AFM)
GMAIW........ Greg Manning Auctions Wrrt [NASDAQ symbol] (TTSB)
GMAJCOM.... Gaining Major Command [Military] (AFM)
GMAL.......... General Electric Macro Assembly Language (NASA)
GM & N...... Gulf Mobile & Northern Railroad
GM & O...... Gulf, Mobile & Ohio Railroad [Later, Illinois Central Gulf Railroad]
GM & S....... General Medicine and Surgery

GMann........ Greg Manning Auctions, Inc. [Associated Press] (SAG)
GMann........ Manning [Greg] Auctions, Inc. [Associated Press] (SAG)
GManning.... Greg Manning Auctions, Inc. [Associated Press] (SAG)
GManning.... Manning [Greg] Auctions, Inc. [Associated Press] (SAG)
GMAP........ Generalized Macroprocessor
GMAP........ General Macroassembly Program [Honeywell, Inc.]
GMarC........ Cobb County-Marietta Public Library, Marietta, GA [Library symbol Library of Congress] (LCLS)
GMarK........ Kennesaw College, Marietta, GA [Library symbol Library of Congress] (LCLS)
GMarLC...... Life College, Marietta, GA [Library symbol] [Library of Congress] (LCLS)
GMarLG...... Lockheed-Georgia Co., Scientific and Technical Information Department, Marietta,GA [Library symbol Library of Congress] (LCLS)
GMarRR...... Reid-Rowell, Marietta, GA [Library symbol] [Library of Congress] (LCLS)
GMarS........ Southern Technical Institute, Marietta, GA [Library symbol Library of Congress] (LCLS)
GMAS......... Glovers' Mutual Aid Society [A union] [British]
GMAS......... Ground Munitions Analysis Study (AABC)
GMasec...... Grupo Industrial Maseca SA de CV [Associated Press] (SAG)
GMaseca..... Grupo Industrial Maseca SA de CV [Associated Press] (SAG)
GMASI........ Graduate Member of the Ambulance Service Institute [British] (DBQ)
GMason...... George Mason Bankshares [Commercial firm Associated Press] (SAG)
GMAT......... General Mathematical Aptitude Test (BARN)
GMAT......... Graduate Management Admission Test
GMAT......... Greenwich Mean Astronomical Time
GMAT......... Tan-Tan/Plage Blanche [Morocco] [ICAO location identifier] (ICLI)
GMATS....... General Motors Air Transport System
GMAW........ Gas Metal Arc Welding
GMAWA...... Glass Merchants' Association of Western Australia
GMAW-P..... Gas Metal Arc Welding - Pulsed Arc
GMAW-S..... Gas Metal Arc Welding - Short Circuiting Arc
GMAX........ Graphics Multi-Axis Module [McDonnell-Douglas Automation Co.]
GMAZ........ Zagora [Morocco] [ICAO location identifier] (ICLI)
GMB.......... Gambela [Ethiopia] [Airport symbol] (OAG)
GMB.......... Gambia [ANSI three-letter standard code] (CNC)
GMB.......... General Mortgage Bond
GMB.......... Glass Microballoon (MCD)
GMB.......... Global Management Bureau
GMB.......... Good Merchantable Brand [Business term]
GMB.......... Good Morning Britain [Early morning television program] [ITV] [British]
GMB.......... Grand Master of the Bath [British]
GMB.......... Green Mountain Boy [Pseudonym used by Henry Stevens]
GMB.......... Guided Missile Brigade [Army]
GMBATU...... General Municipal Boilermakers' and Allied Trades Union [British]
GMBE......... Grand Master of the Order of the British Empire (EY)
GMBF......... Gastric Mucosal Blood Flow [Medicine]
GmbH........ Gesellschaft mit Beschraenkter Haftung [Limited Liability Company] [German]
GmbH & CoKG... Gesellschaft mit Beschraenkter Haftung und Kommanditgesellschaft [Combined Limited Partnership and Limited Liability Company] [German]
GmbHG....... Gesetz Betreffend der Gesellschaft mit Beschraenkter Haftung [Law Governing Limited Liability Company] [German] (ILCA)
GMBIM....... Genetics and Molecular Biology of Industrial Microorganisms [Conference]
GMBL......... Gimbal (AAG)
GMBS......... George Mason Bankshares [NASDAQ symbol] (SAG)
GMBS......... Glenn Miller Birthplace Society (EA)
GMC.......... Ganglion Mother Cell [Cytology]
GMC.......... General Medical Council [British]
GmC.......... General Microfilm Co., Cambridge, MA [Library symbol Library of Congress] (LCLS)
GMC.......... General Military Course (AFM)
GMC.......... General Monte Carlo Code [Computer science]
GMC.......... General Motors Corp. [ICAO designator] (FAAC)
GMC.......... Georgia Military College [Milledgeville]
GMC.......... Geostar Mining Corp. [Vancouver Stock Exchange symbol]
GMC.......... Germanic [Language, etc.]
GMC.......... Giant Molecular Cloud [Cosmology]
GMC.......... Gordon Military College [Georgia]
GMC.......... Great Midwestern Conference [College reports]
GMC.......... Grivet Monkey Cell Line
GMC.......... Gross Maximum Capacity [Electronics] (IEEE)
GMC.......... Ground Mobile Cenetheodolite
GMC.......... Ground Movement Controller
GMC.......... Groundwater Management Caucus (EA)
GMC.......... Guaranteed Mortgage Certificate [Federal Home Loan Mortgage Corp.]
GMC.......... Guard-Cell Mother Cell [Botany]
GMC.......... Guided Missile Committee [Army]
GMC.......... Guided Missile Control (AAG)
GMC.......... Guild of Memorial Craftsmen [British] (BI)
GMC.......... Gun Motor Carriage
GMC.......... Gunner's Mate, Chief [Navy rating]
GMC.......... Middle Georgia College, Cochran, GA [OCLC symbol] (OCLC)
gm-cal....... Gram Calorie (IDOE)
GMCB......... Gunner's Mate, Construction Battalion [Navy rating]
GMCBA....... Gunner's Mate, Construction Battalion, Armorer [Navy rating]
GMCBP....... Gunner's Mate, Construction Battalion, Powderman [Navy rating]
GMCC......... General Magnaplate Corp. [NASDAQ symbol] (NQ)

GMCC .... General NAS Maintenance Control Center [*FAA*] (TAG)
GMCC .... Genl Magnaplate [*NASDAQ symbol*] (TTSB)
GMCC .... Geophysical Monitoring for Climate Change (EERA)
GMCC .... Geophysical Monitoring for Climatic Change [*National Oceanic and Atmospheric Administration*]
GMCC .... Ground Mobile Command Center
GMCF .... Goddard Mission Control Facility [*NASA*] (KSC)
GMCF .... Guided Missile Control Facility (AAG)
GMCI .... Giftware Manufacturers' Credit Interchange (EA)
GMCL .... Ground Measurements Command List (MCD)
gm-cm .... Gram-Centimeter (IDOE)
GMCM .... Guided Missile Countermeasure [*NATO*]
GMCM .... Gunner's Mate, Master Chief [*Navy rating*]
GMCO .... Guided Missile Control Officer (AAG)
GMCP .... Guided Missile Control Party (IAA)
GMCR .... Globe Mackay Cable and Radio Corp. [*Philippines*] [*Telecommunications*]
GMCR .... Green Mountain Coffee [*Commercial firm NASDAQ symbol*] (SAG)
GMCS .... Gunner's Mate, Senior Chief [*Navy rating*]
GM-CSA .... Granulocyte-Macrophage Colony-Stimulating Activity [*Hematology*]
GM-CSF .... Granulocyte-Macrophage Colony-Stimulating Factor [*Biochemistry*]
GMCT .... Giftware Manufacturers Credit Interchange (EA)
GMCY .... Grant-Makers for Children and Youth (EA)
GMD .... General Management Directive
GMD .... General Marine Distress
GMD .... Geometric Mean Distance
GMD .... Geometrodynamics
GMD .... Gesellschaft fuer Mathematik und Datenverarbeitung [*Society for Mathematics and Data Processing*] [*Germany Information service or system*] (IID)
GMD .... Government Maintenance Depot (MCD)
GMD .... Ground Meteorological Detector [*or Device*]
GMD .... Groupo Mexicano Desarrollo [*NYSE symbol*] (SPSG)
GMD .... Grupo Mex de Desarrollo 'L'ADS [*NYSE symbol*] (TTSB)
GMD .... Grupo Mexicano Desarrollo [*NYSE symbol*] (SAG)
GMDA .... Golf Manufacturers and Distributors Association (EA)
GMDA .... Groundwater Management Districts Association (EA)
GMDA .... Group Method of Determining Arguments [*Equation*]
GMDC .... General Merchandise Distributors Council [*Colorado Springs, CO*] (EA)
GMDD .... Guided Missile Development Division [*NASA*] (KSC)
GMDEP .... Guided Missile Data Exchange Program [*Navy*]
GMDesB .... Grupo Mexicano Desarrollo [*Associated Press*] (SAG)
GMDH .... Group Method of Data Handling [*Mathematical technique*]
GMDIL .... General Motors Distribution Ireland Ltd. [*Dublin, Ireland*]
GMD-IZ .... GMD-Informationszentrum fuer Informationswissenschaft und -Praxis [*GMD Information Center for Information Science and Information Work*] [*Information service or system*] (IID)
GMDP .... Guaranteed Minimum Delivery Price (ADA)
GMDRL .... General Motors Defense Research Laboratory (MCD)
GMDS .... German Military Documents Section [*of AGO, Army*] [*World War II*]
GMDSS .... Global Maritime Distress and Safety System (DA)
GM Dud .... Dudley's Georgia Reports [*A publication*] (DLA)
GM Dudl ...... Dudley's Georgia Reports [*A publication*] (DLA)
GME .... Gelatine Manufacturers of Europe (EAIO)
GME .... General Microelectronics
GME .... General Motors Corp. [*NYSE symbol*] (SAG)
GME .... General Motors Europe
GME .... Generic Macro Expander [*Telecommunications*] (TEL)
GME .... Genl Motors CI'E' [*NYSE symbol*] (TTSB)
GME .... German Minimum Economy [*Allied German Occupation Forces*]
GME .... Gilt Marbled Edges [*Bookbinding*]
GME .... Gimbal Mounted Electronics (KSC)
GME .... Glimmer Resources, Inc. [*Vancouver Stock Exchange symbol*]
GME .... Globe Microphone Evaluation
GME .... Gmelinite [*A zeolite*]
GME .... Graduate Medical Education [*Program*] [*Army*]
GME .... Greater Middle East
GME .... Great Meteor East [*Nuclear energy*] (NUCP)
GME .... Green, M. E., Jefferson City MO [*STAC*]
GME .... Group Modulation Equipment (IAA)
GME .... Guided Missile Evaluator
GMED .... GeneMedicine, Inc. [*NASDAQ symbol*] (SAG)
GM/EDS .... General Motors Electronic Data Systems (NITA)
GMEFC .... Golden Memories of Elvis Fan Club (EA)
GMEI .... Gulf of Mexico Estuarine Inventory (PDAA)
GMEL .... Groupement des Mathematiciens d'Expression Latine [*Group of Mathematicians of Romance Languages - GMRL*] (EAIO)
GMEM .... GPC [*General Purpose Computer*] Memory (NASA)
G-MEM .... GPC [*General Purpose Computer*] Memory
GMENAC .... Graduate Medical Education National Advisory Committee [*Department of Health and Human Services*]
GME-PC .... General Motors Europe - Passenger Cars [*Switzerland*]
GMERD .... Government Minimum Essential Requirements Document
GMET .... Graphical Munitions Effects Tables (MCD)
GMET .... Gun Metal
GMetO .... Group Meteorological Officer [*British military*] (DMA)
GMEV .... General Motors Electric Vehicle [*General Motors Corp*]
GMEVALU ...... Guided Missile Evaluation Unit (MUGU)
GMexDes ..... Grupo Mexicano Desarrollo [*Associated Press*] (SAG)
GMF .... Galactic Magnetic Field
GMF .... Generalized Mainline Framework [*Computer science*]
GMF .... General Motors Corp. and Fanuc Ltd. [*In company name GMF Robotics Corp.*]
GMF .... Glass Manufacturers Federation

GMF .... Glass Microfilter
GMF .... Glial Maturation Factor [*Biochemistry*]
GMF .... Global Matching Figures Test [*Education*] (EDAC)
GMF .... Ground Mobile Forces [*Military*] (RDA)
GMF .... Ground Monitor Facility (MCD)
GMF .... Guided Missile Facilities (NG)
GMF .... Milwaukee, WI [*Location identifier FAA*] (FAAL)
GMFA .... Ouezzane [*Morocco*] [*ICAO location identifier*] (ICLI)
GMFC .... Gary Morris Fan Club (EA)
GMFC .... Guided Missile Fire Control
GMFCS .... Guided Missile Fire Control System (NG)
GMFF .... Fes/Saiss [*Morocco*] [*ICAO location identifier*] (ICLI)
GMFI .... Ifrane [*Morocco*] [*ICAO location identifier*] (ICLI)
GMFJ .... Ghana Movement of Freedom and Justice [*Political party*]
GMFK .... Er-Rachidia [*Morocco*] [*ICAO location identifier*] (ICLI)
GMFM .... Meknes/Bassatine [*Morocco*] [*ICAO location identifier*] (ICLI)
GMFMC .... Gulf of Mexico Fishery Management Council (MSC)
GMFN .... Nador/Taouima [*Morocco*] [*ICAO location identifier*] (ICLI)
GMFO .... Oujda/Angads [*Morocco*] [*ICAO location identifier*] (ICLI)
GMFP .... Guided Missile Firing Panel
GMFS .... Ground Mobile Forces/Tactical Satellite Communications Program
GMFSC .... Ground Mobile Forces Satellite Communications (MCD)
GMFT .... Touahar [*Morocco*] [*ICAO location identifier*] (ICLI)
GMF/TACSAT... Ground Mobile Forces/Tactical Satellite Communications (MCD)
GMFU .... Fes/Sefrou [*Morocco*] [*ICAO location identifier*] (ICLI)
GMFZ .... Taza [*Morocco*] [*ICAO location identifier*] (ICLI)
GMG .... Gott Mein Gut [*God Is My Good*] [*Motto of Karl, Margrave of Baden-Durlach (1529-77); Ernst Friedrich, (1560-1604)*] [*German*]
GMG .... Grand Metropolitan and Guinness [*Proposed company*]
GMG .... Grenade Machine Gun [*Military*]
GMG .... Gross Maximum Generation [*Electronics*] (IEEE)
GMG .... Gunner's Mate, Guns [*Navy rating*]
GMG1 .... Gunner's Mate, Guns, First Class [*Navy rating*] (DNAB)
GMG2 .... Gunner's Mate, Guns, Second Class [*Navy rating*] (DNAB)
GMG3 .... Gunner's Mate, Guns, Third Class [*Navy rating*] (DNAB)
GMGB .... Guards Machine Gun Battalion [*British military*] (DMA)
GMGC .... General Magic, Inc. [*NASDAQ symbol*] (SAG)
GMGC .... Gunner's Mate, Guns, Chief [*Navy rating*] (DNAB)
GMGR .... Guards Machine Gun Regiment [*British military*] (DMA)
GMGRU .... Guided Missile Group (MUGU)
GMGS .... Guided Missile General Support (MCD)
GMGSA .... Gunner's Mate, Guns, Seaman Apprentice [*Navy rating*] (DNAB)
GMGSN .... Gunner's Mate, Guns, Seaman [*Navy rating*] (DNAB)
GMH .... General Motors Corp. [*NYSE symbol*] (SAG)
GMH .... General Motors-Holden's Ltd. [*Australia*] (ADA)
GMH .... Georgia Mental Health Institute, Atlanta, GA [*OCLC symbol*] (OCLC)
gmh .... German, Middle High [*MARC language code Library of Congress*] (LCCP)
GMH .... Germinal Matrix Hemorrhage [*Medicine*] (DMAA)
GMH .... Greenville, KY [*Location identifier FAA*] (FAAL)
GMH .... Hughes Aircraft Co. (Aeronautical Operations) [*ICAO designator*] (FAAC)
GMHC .... Gay Men's Health Crisis (EA)
GMHC .... Grease Monkey Hldg [*NASDAQ symbol*] (TTSB)
GMHC .... Grease Monkey Holding Corp. [*NASDAQ symbol*] (NQ)
GMHE .... General Motors Hughes Electronics Corp.
GMI .... Galtaco, Inc. [*Toronto Stock Exchange symbol*]
GMI .... Garnes Mountain [*Idaho*] [*Seismograph station code, US Geological Survey*] (SEIS)
GMI .... Gasmata [*Papua New Guinea*] [*Airport symbol*] (OAG)
GMI .... Gelatin Manufacturers Institute of America (EA)
GMI .... Gemini Fund, Inc. [*NYSE symbol*] (SPSG)
GMI .... Gemini II [*NYSE symbol*] (TTSB)
GMI .... General Medical Intelligence (MCD)
GMI .... General Mills, Incorporated, Minneapolis, MN [*OCLC symbol*] (OCLC)
GMI .... General Motors Institute
GMI .... Genini II Fund [*NYSE symbol*] (SAG)
GMI .... Germania Fluggesellschaft Koln [*Germany ICAO designator*] (FAAC)
GMI .... Global Marine, Inc. (NOAA)
GMI .... Goddard Management Instruction [*NASA*]
g/mi .... Gram per Mile [*Automotive engineering*]
GMI .... Guaranteed Minimum Income (ADA)
GMI .... Guarantee Material Inspection (MCD)
GMIA .... Gelatin Manufacturers Institute of America (EA)
GMIC .... Graphic Memory Interface Controller [*Computer chip*]
GMIE .... Grand Master of the Order of the Indian Empire [*British*]
GMI-EMI ...... General Motors Institute - Engineering and Management Institute [*Flint, MI*]
GMIF .... Gandhi Memorial International Foundation (EA)
GMIFC .... George Michael International Fan Club (EA)
GMII .... Guaranteed Market Index Investment [*Canada*]
GMiM .... Georgia Military College, Milledgeville, GA [*Library symbol Library of Congress*] (LCLS)
GMI Mech E ... Graduate Member of the Institution of Mechanical Engineers [*British*]
GMIP .... General Motors Improvement Project [*Investigating team sponsored by consumer-advocate Ralph Nader*]
GMIPr .... Gemini II cm Income Shrs [*NYSE symbol*] (TTSB)
GMIS .... Generalized Management Information System
GMIS .... GMIS, Inc. [*NASDAQ symbol*] (SPSG)
GMIS .... Government Management Information Sciences (EA)
GMIS .... Grants Management Information System [*Department of Health and Human Services*] (GFGA)
GMISCA .... General Motors Information System and Communications Activity (HGAA)

GMiW .... Georgia College, Milledgeville, GA [*Library symbol Library of Congress*] (LCLS)
GMJ .... Macon Junior College, Macon, GA [*Library symbol Library of Congress*] (LCLS)
GMJC .... Green Mountain Junior College [*Vermont*]
GMJSU .... Gems, Minerals, and Jewelry Study Unit (EA)
GMK .... Gold Mark Minerals [*Vancouver Stock Exchange symbol*]
GMK .... Grand Master Key [*Locks*] (ADA)
GMK .... Green Monkey Kidney Cell
GMK .... Gyromagnetic Kompass
GMKP .... Grand Master of the Knights of St. Patrick
GMKT .... Global Market Information, Inc. [*NASDAQ symbol*] (SAG)
GML .... Galvanometer-Mirror Lightbeam
GML .... Gemial [*Slovakia*] [*ICAO designator*] (FAAC)
GML .... Generalized Markup Language [*Computer science*]
GML .... General Measurement Loop (MCD)
GML .... Generic Markup Language (NITA)
GML .... Global DirectMail [*NYSE symbol*] (TTSB)
GML .... Glycerol Monolaurate [*Food-grade lipid*] [*Pharmacology*]
GML .... Gold Maple Leaf [*Canadian coin*]
GML .... Gold-Medal Resources Ltd. [*Vancouver Stock Exchange symbol*]
GML .... Gorgas Memorial Laboratory [*Panama*] [*Research center*] (RCD)
gm/l .... Grams per Liter (MAE)
GML .... Grand Master's Lodge [*Freemasonry*] (ROG)
GML .... Graphic Machine Language
GML .... Guided Missile Launcher (NG)
GML .... Mercer University, Law Library, Macon, GA [*OCLC symbol*] (OCLC)
GMLDG .... Garnish Molding [*Mechanical engineering*]
GMLR .... Guided Missile and Large Rocket
GMLS .... Guided Missile Launching System
GMLSC .... Guided Missile Launching System Control (DWSG)
GMM .... Galvanomagnetic Method (IAA)
GMM .... Gamboma [*Congo*] [*Airport symbol*] (AD)
GMM .... General Matrix Manipulator (OA)
GMM .... General Methods of Moments [*Statistics*]
GMM .... Geometric Math Model (SSD)
GMM .... Goldsmith Minerals [*Vancouver Stock Exchange symbol*]
gm-m .... Gram Meter
GMM .... Graphical Multi-Meter
GMM .... Graphics Mill Module [*McDonnell-Douglas Corp.*]
GMM .... Gunner's Mate, Missile [*Navy rating*]
GMM .... Mercer University, Macon, GA [*Library symbol Library of Congress*] (LCLS)
GMM .... Mercer University, School of Medicine, Macon, GA [*OCLC symbol*] (OCLC)
GMM1 .... Gunner's Mate, Missile, First Class [*Navy rating*] (DNAB)
GMM2 .... Gunner's Mate, Missile, Second Class [*Navy rating*] (DNAB)
GMM3 .... Gunner's Mate, Missile, Third Class [*Navy rating*] (DNAB)
GMMA .... Gas Meter Makers' Association [*A union*] [*British*]
GMMA .... Gloucester Master Mariners Association (EA)
GMMA .... Golda Meir Memorial Association (EA)
GMMB .... Ben Slimane [*Morocco*] [*ICAO location identifier*] (ICLI)
GMMC .... Casablanca/ANFA [*Morocco*] [*ICAO location identifier*] (ICLI)
GMMC .... Gunner's Mate, Missile, Chief [*Navy rating*] (DNAB)
GMMD .... Beni-Mellal [*Morocco*] [*ICAO location identifier*] (ICLI)
GMME .... Rabat/Sale [*Morocco*] [*ICAO location identifier*] (ICLI)
GMMF .... Sidi Ifni [*Morocco*] [*ICAO location identifier*] (ICLI)
GMMG .... Grand Master of the Order of St. Michael and St. George [*British*]
GMMI .... Essaouira [*Morocco*] [*ICAO location identifier*] (ICLI)
GMMJ .... El Jadida [*Morocco*] [*ICAO location identifier*] (ICLI)
GMMK .... Khouribga [*Morocco*] [*ICAO location identifier*] (ICLI)
GMML .... Ground Master Measurements List
GMM-L .... Mercer University, School of Law, Macon, GA [*Library symbol Library of Congress*] (LCLS)
GMMM .... Casablanca [*Morocco*] [*ICAO location identifier*] (ICLI)
GMMN .... Casablanca/Mohamed V [*Morocco*] [*ICAO location identifier*] (ICLI)
GMMO .... Taroudant [*Morocco*] [*ICAO location identifier*] (ICLI)
GM MOL ..... Gram-Molecule (WDAA)
GMMR .... General Mobilization Material Readiness [*DoD*]
GMMRI .... Georgia Mining and Mineral Research Institute [*Georgia Institute of Technology*] [*Research center*] (RCD)
GMMS .... Safi [*Morocco*] [*ICAO location identifier*] (ICLI)
GMMSA .... Gunner's Mate, Missile, Seaman Apprentice [*Navy rating*] (DNAB)
GMMSN .... Gunner's Mate, Missile, Seaman [*Navy rating*] (DNAB)
GMMT .... Casablanca/Tit-Mellil [*Morocco*] [*ICAO location identifier*] (ICLI)
GMMX .... Marrakech/Menara [*Morocco*] [*ICAO location identifier*] (ICLI)
GMMY .... Kenitra/Tourisme [*Morocco*] [*ICAO location identifier*] (ICLI)
GMMZ .... Quarzazate [*Morocco*] [*ICAO location identifier*] (ICLI)
GMN .... Gorman [*TACAN station*] (MCD)
GMN .... Gorman, CA [*Location identifier FAA*] (FAAL)
GMN .... Greenman Brothers, Inc. [*AMEX symbol*] (SPSG)
GMN .... Greenwich Mean Noon (ROG)
GMNA .... Glutamyl(methoxy)naphthylamide [*Biochemistry*]
GmNE .... Graphic Microfilm of New England, Waltham, MA [*Library symbol Library of Congress*] (LCLS)
GmNY .... Graphic Microfilm Corp., Valley Stream, NY [*Library symbol Library of Congress*] (LCLS)
GMO .... Gadolinium Molybdate
GMO .... General Medical Officer [*Navy*] (DNAB)
GMO .... Genetically-Manipulated Organism [*Biochemistry*]
GMO .... Gill-Morrell Oscillator
GMO .... Glyceryl Monooleate [*Organic chemistry*]
GMO .... Groupe de Travail Charge de la Mise en Oeuvre de l'Information et de la Statistique Juridique [*Implementation Work Group on Justice Information and Statistics - IWG*] [*Canada*]

GMO .... Guided Missile Officer
GMO .... Gulf, Mobile & Ohio Railroad [*Later, Illinois Central Gulf Railroad*] [*AAR code*]
GMoC .... Colquitt-Thomas Regional Library, Moultrie, GA [*Library symbol Library of Congress*] (LCLS)
GMOCU .... Guided Missile Operation and Control Unit
GMODC .... General Motors Overseas Distribution Corp.
GMOL .... Gram Molecule [*or Molecular*] [*Chemistry*] (IAA)
GMOO .... Guided Missile Operations Officer (AAG)
GMorC .... Clayton Junior College, Morrow, GA [*Library symbol*] [*Library of Congress*] (LCLS)
GMorGE ...... Genealogical Enterprises, Morrow, GA [*Library symbol Library of Congress*] (LCLS)
GMOS .... Generic Message Orientation System (SSD)
GMOs .... Genetically Manipulated Organisms (EERA)
GMot .... General Motors Corp. [*Associated Press*] (SAG)
GMOV .... Glycine Mottle Virus [*Plant pathology*]
GMP .... Gap Media Project [*An association*] (EA)
GMP .... Garrison Military Police [*British*]
GMP .... Gay Men's Press [*GMP is now the name of the company*]
GMP .... Gemini Management Panel [*NASA*] (KSC)
GMP .... General Management Plan [*National Park Service*]
GMP .... General Matrix Program
GMP .... General Medical Practice (WDAA)
GMP .... General Medical Problem
GMP .... Geometric Modelling Project [*Software*] [*British*] (NITA)
GMP .... Georgia Milk Producers (SRA)
GMP .... Glycomacropeptide [*Biochemistry*]
G-MP .... G-Myeloma Protein [*Biochemistry*] (MAH)
G-MP .... G-Myeloma Proteins [*Biochemistry*] (DAVI)
GMP .... Good Management Practice
GMP .... Good Manufacturing Practice
GMP .... Grand Master of the Order of St. Patrick
GMP .... Granule Membrane Protein
GMP .... Grass-Model Polygraph
GMP .... Green Mountain Power Corp. [*NYSE symbol*] (SPSG)
GMP .... Green Mountain Pwr [*NYSE symbol*] (TTSB)
GMP .... Ground Map Pencil (DNAB)
GMP .... Ground Movement Planner [*Aviation*] (OA)
GMP .... Groundwater Modeling Program [*US Army Engineer Waterways Experiment Station*] (RDA)
GMP .... Guanosine Monophosphate [*Biochemistry*]
GMP .... Guaranteed Minimum Pension [*British*]
GMP .... Guaranteed Minimum Price
GMP .... Guild of Metal Perforators [*British*] (DBA)
GMP .... Gurkha Military Police [*British military*] (DMA)
GMPA .... Game Meat Processors of Australia
GMPA .... General Material and Petroleum Activity [*NCAD*] [*Army*] (MCD)
GMPC .... Green Mountain Power Corp. (NRCH)
GMPCS .... Global Mobile Personal Communications System [*International Telecommunications Union*] [*Geneva, Switzerland*] (ECON)
GMPG .... General Motors Proving Grounds [*Automotive engineering*]
GMPI .... Guilford-Martin Personnel Inventory [*Psychology*]
GMPMA ...... General Material and Petroleum Management Agency (MCD)
GMPPAW ..... Glass, Molders, Pottery, Plastics, and Allied Workers International Union (EA)
GMPR .... General Maximum Price Regulation [*World War II*]
GMPrD .... General Motors 7.92% Dep Pfd [*NYSE symbol*] (TTSB)
GMPrG .... General Motors 9.12% Dep Pfd [*NYSE symbol*] (TTSB)
GMPrQ .... General Motors 9.125% Dep Pfd [*NYSE symbol*] (TTSB)
GMPS .... Great Masters in Painting and Sculpture [*A publication*]
GMPT .... Gum Print [*Gum bichromates*] (VRA)
GMQ .... Geomaque Explorations Ltd. [*Toronto Stock Exchange symbol*]
GMQ .... Good Marketable Quality [*Business term*]
GMR .... Gambier Island [*French Polynesia*] [*Airport symbol*] (OAG)
GMR .... General Mobilization Reserves [*DoD*]
GMR .... General Modular Redundancy
GMR .... General Motors Research
GMR .... Geometric Mean Radii
GMR .... Giant Magnetoresistance [*Materials science*]
GMR .... Giant Magnetoresistive (CDE)
GMR .... Graduated Mobilization Response (DOMA)
GMR .... Grampian Helicopter Charter Ltd. [*British ICAO designator*] (FAAC)
GMR .... Graphics Metafile Resources [*Computer science*]
GMR .... Ground Mapping RADAR
GMR .... Ground Mobile RADAR
GMR .... Ground Movement RADAR [*Military*]
GMR .... Group Medical Report
GMR .... Grupo Marxista Revolucionario [*Marxist Revolutionary Group*] [*Portuguese Political party*] (PPE)
GMRAO .... General Mobilization Reserve Acquisition Objective [*DoD*]
GMRC .... Green Mountain Railroad Corp. [*AAR code*]
GMRD .... Guards Motorized Rifle Division (MCD)
GMRD .... Guided Missile Range Division [*NASA*] (KSC)
GMRE .... General Motors Rotary Engine [*Automotive engineering*]
GMRK .... Gulfmark International [*NASDAQ symbol*] (SPSG)
GMRL .... General Motors Corp. Research Laboratories [*Warren, MI*]
GMRL .... Grain Marketing Research Laboratory [*Manhattan, KS*] [*Department of Agriculture*] (GRD)
GMRL .... Group of Mathematicians of Romance Languages [*See also GMEL*] [*Coimbra, Portugal*] (EAIO)
GMRMLN ..... Greater Midwest Regional Medical Library Network [*Illinois, Kentucky, Michigan, Ohio, S. Dakota*] (NITA)
GMRMO ...... General Mobilization Reserve Materiel Objective [*DoD*]
GMRMR .... General Mobilization Reserve Materiel Requirement [*DoD*]

GMROI......... Gross Margin Return on Investment [*Air carrier designation symbol*]
GMRS .... General Mobile Radio Service [*Telecommunications*] (TSSD)
GMRS .... General Mobilization Reserve Stock [*DoD*]
GMRS .... Ground Marker Release System [*Army*] (INF)
GMRSO .... General Mobilization Reserve Stockage Objective [*DoD*]
GMRT .... Gates MacGinitie Reading Test [*Educational test*]
GMRT .... Giant Meterwave Radio Telescope [*India*]
GMRWG...... Guided Missile Relay Working Group [*Navy*]
GMS............ Gabriel Marcel Society (EA)
GMS............ Gas Measurement System
GMS............ Gelatin Matrix System
GMS............ Gemini Mission Simulator [*NASA*]
GMS............ General Maintenance System [*Computer science*] (BUR)
GMS............ General Material Services
GMS............ General Medical Services [*British*]
GMS............ General Micro Systems Ltd. (NITA)
GMS............ General Military Science
GMS............ General Milk Sales [*Inactive*] [*An association*] (EA)
GMS............ Generation Management Station
GMS............ Genomic Mismatch Scanning [*Genetic technique*]
GMS............ Geophysical Monitoring Satellite [*DoD, NOAA*]
GMS............ George MacDonald Society [*Lincoln, England*] (EAIO)
GMS............ Geostationary Meteorological Satellite [*Japan*]
GMS............ Geriatric Mental State [*Medicine*] (DMAA)
GMS............ Giant Motor Synapse [*Anatomy*]
GMS............ Gichner Mobile Shelters (MCD)
GMS............ Gilbert-Meulengracht Syndrome [*Medicine*] (DMAA)
GMS............ Gilbert M. Smith Herbarium [*Stanford University*] [*Pacific Grove, CA*]
GMS............ Glen Miller Society (EAIO)
GMS............ Glyceryl Monostearate [*Organic chemistry*]
GMS............ Gomori Methenamine Silver Stain [*Medicine*] (DMAA)
GMS............ Gomori's Methenamine Silver [*A biological stain*]
GMS............ Goniodysgenesis-Mental Retardation-Short Stature Syndrome [*Medicine*] (DMAA)
GMS............ Grant Maintained School (AIE)
GMS............ Grant-Maintained Status (ODBW)
G/MS.......... Graphics and/or Media Specialist
GMS............ Gravitational Mass Sensor
GMS............ Gravity Measuring System
GMS............ Greater Mekong Sub-Region [*East Asian development zone*]
GMS............ Ground Maintenance Support
GMS............ Ground Mapping [*or Marking*] System
GMS............ Groundwater Modeling System
GMS............ Group Membership Scores [*Psychometrics*]
GMS............ Guardian-Morton Shulman Precious Metals, Inc. [*Toronto Stock Exchange symbol Vancouver Stock Exchange symbol*]
GMS............ Guidance Monitor Set [*Aerospace*] (AAG)
GMS............ Guided Missile School [*Dam Neck, VA*]
GMS............ Guided Missile Simulator [*Military*] (CAAL)
GMS............ Guided Missile System
GMS............ Master Construction Specification [*Canada*]
GMS............ Morehouse College, School of Medicine, Atlanta, GA [*OCLC symbol*] (OCLC)
GMSA .... General Motors South African
GMSA .... German Minesweeping Administration [*Allied German Occupation Forces*]
GMSA .... Seaman Apprentice, Gunner's Mate, Striker [*Navy rating*]
GMSC .... General Medical Services Council [*British*] (BI)
GMSER .... Guided Missile Service Report (NG)
GMSFC .... George Marshall Space Flight Center [*Huntsville, AL*] (IEEE)
GMSFN .... Global Manned Space Flight Network (SAA)
GMSI .... Grand Master of the Order of the Star of India [*British*]
GMSIA .... Guided Missile System, Intercept-Aerial (MCD)
GMSK .... Gaussian Filtered Minimum Shift Keying (MCD)
GMSK .... Gaussian Mean Shift Keying
G/MSL .... Guided Missile
GMSL .... Sidi Slimane [*Morocco*] [*ICAO location identifier*] (ICLI)
GMSN .... Seaman, Gunner's Mate, Striker [*Navy rating*]
GMSO .... German Mine Supplies Organization [*Allied German Occupation Forces*]
GMSQUAD ... Guided Missile Squadron (MUGU)
GMSR .... Guided Missile Service Record
GMSR .... Guided Missile Service Report (MCD)
GMSR .... Gunner's Mate, Ship Repair [*Navy rating Obsolete*]
GMSRON .... Guided Missile Service Squadron (MUGU)
GMSRP .... Gunner's Mate, Ship Repair, Powderman [*Navy rating Obsolete*]
GMSS .... Graphical Modeling and Simulation System
GMST .... General Military Subjects Test
GMST .... Glossary of Merchant Ship Types (MCD)
GMST .... Greenwich Mean Sidereal Time (WGA)
GMSTE .... Gemstar Intl. [*NASDAQ symbol*] (TTSB)
GMSTF .... Gemstar International Group Ltd. [*NASDAQ symbol*] (SAG)
GMSTS .... Guided Missile System Test Set (NATG)
GMSU .... General Maritime Stevedores' Union [*Philippines*]
GMSU .... Guided Missile Service Unit [*Air Force*]
GMSW .... Gross Maximum Shipping Weight
GMT............ Garment
GMT............ Gas Missile Tube
GMT............ GATX Corp. [*Formerly, General American Transportation Corp.*] [*NYSE symbol*] (SPSG)
GMT............ Geiger-Mueller Tube
GMT............ Gemini Technology, Inc. [*Toronto Stock Exchange symbol Vancouver Stock Exchange symbol*]
GMT............ Generalized Multitasking
GMT............ General Machine Test [*Computer science*] (BUR)

GMT............ General Military Training (AFM)
GMT............ Generic Mapping Tools [*Marine science*] (OSRA)
GMT............ Generic Mapping Tools (USDC)
GMT............ Geomarine Technology
GMT............ Geometric Mean Titer [*Analytical chemistry*]
GMT............ Gingival Margin Trimmer [*Medicine*] (DMAA)
GMT............ Glass-Mat Reinforced Thermoplastic [*Automotive engineering*]
GMT............ Glass-Mat Thermoplastic
GMT............ Government Maturity Test (MCD)
GMT............ Governor Macquarie Tower [*Sydney, New South Wales, Australia*]
GMT............ Graphics Mouse Technology (DGA)
GMT............ Greenwich Mean [*or Meridian*] Time
GMT............ Grupoaereo Monterrey, SA de CV [*Mexico*] [*FAA designator*] (FAAC)
GMT............ Guided Missile Target (NG)
GMT............ Guided Missile Trainer
GMT............ Gunner's Mate, Technician [*Navy rating*]
GMT1.......... Gunner's Mate, Technician, First Class [*Navy rating*] (DNAB)
GMT2.......... Gunner's Mate, Technician, Second Class [*Navy rating*] (DNAB)
GMT3.......... Gunner's Mate, Technician, Third Class [*Navy rating*] (DNAB)
GMTA .... Al Hoceima/Cote Du Rif [*Morocco*] [*ICAO location identifier*] (ICLI)
GMTA .... Great Minds Think Alike [*Internet language*] (PCM)
GMtbC .... Berry College, Mount Berry, GA [*Library symbol Library of Congress*] (LCLS)
GMTC .... Chief Gunner's Mate, Technician [*Navy rating*]
GMTC .... Glutamate Manufacturers Technical Committee (EA)
GMTCM .... Master Chief Gunner's Mate, Technician [*Navy rating*]
GMTCS .... Senior Chief Gunner's Mate, Technician [*Navy rating*]
GMTF .... Gay Media Task Force (EA)
GMTF .... Geometric Modulation Transfer Function (MCD)
GMTI .... Greenman Technologies [*NASDAQ symbol*] (TTSB)
GMTI .... Greenman Technologies, Inc. [*NASDAQ symbol*] (SAG)
GMTI .... Ground Moving Target Indicator
GMTIW .... Greenman Technologies Wrrt [*NASDAQ symbol*] (TTSB)
GMTN .... Tetouan/Sania R'Mel [*Morocco*] [*ICAO location identifier*] (ICLI)
GMTO .... General Military Training Office
GMTOA .... Green Mountain Textile Overseers Association (EA)
GMTPr .... GATX Corp. $2.50 Cv Pfd [*NYSE symbol*] (TTSB)
GMTPrA ...... GATX Corp. $3.875 cm Cv Pfd [*NYSE symbol*] (TTSB)
GMTR .... Guided Missile Test Round [*Military*] (CAAL)
GMTRB .... General Military Training Review Board (AFM)
GMTRY .... Geometry (MSA)
GMTS .... Guided Missile Test Set (AFM)
GMTSA .... Gunner's Mate, Technician, Seaman Apprentice [*Navy rating*]
GMTSN .... Gunner's Mate, Technician, Seaman [*Navy rating*]
GMTT .... Tanger/Boukhalf [*Morocco*] [*ICAO location identifier*] (ICLI)
GMTTR .... Geometric Mean Time to Repair [*Military*] (CAAL)
GMTU .... Guided Missile Test Unit (IAA)
GMTU .... Guided Missile Training Unit [*Navy*]
GMtvB .... Brewton-Parker College, Mount Vernon, GA [*Library symbol Library of Congress*] (LCLS)
GMU .... Gadjah Mada University [*Indonesia*]
GMU .... George Mason University [*Virginia*]
GMU .... Goose Management Unit
GMU .... Gospel Missionary Union (EA)
GMU .... Granite Mountain [*Utah*] [*Seismograph station code, US Geological Survey*] (SEIS)
GMU .... Greenville, SC [*Location identifier FAA*] (FAAL)
GMU .... Guided Missile Unit
GMU .... Mercer University, Macon, GA [*OCLC symbol*] (OCLC)
GMUS .... Guildhall Museum [*London*]
GMusRNCM(Hons)... Graduate in Music of the Royal Northern College of Music [*British*] (DBQ)
GMUTS .... General Motors Uniform Test Standards [*Automotive engineering*]
GMV .... Galinsoga Mosaic Virus
GMV .... Generalized Minimum Variance [*Control technology*]
GMV .... Glycine Mosaic Virus [*Plant pathology*]
GMV .... Government Motor Vehicle (DNAB)
GMV .... Gram Molecular Volume [*Chemistry*]
GMV .... Grand Master of the Vails [*Freemasonry*]
GMV .... Guaranteed Minimum Value
GMVDC....... Gay Men's VD Clinic (EA)
GMVLS .... Guided Missile Vertical Launch System [*Canadian Navy*]
GMW .... General Microwave Corp. [*AMEX symbol*] (SPSG)
GMW .... Generic Maintenance Workstation (SSD)
GMW .... Genl Microwave [*AMEX symbol*] (TTSB)
GMW .... Gold Mountain [*Washington*] [*Seismograph station code, US Geological Survey*] (SEIS)
GMW .... Gram Molecular Weight [*Chemistry*]
GMW .... Guevara-McInteer-Wageman
GMW .... Wesleyan College, Macon, GA [*Library symbol Library of Congress*] (LCLS)
GMWA .... Gospel Music Workshop of America (EA)
GMWC........ Graphite Moderated, Water Cooled (PDAA)
GM/WM ...... Group Mark/Word Mark [*Computer science*] (OA)
GMWS .... Guided Missile Weapon System [*Military*] (CAAL)
GMWU........ General and Municipal Workers' Union [*British*]
GMX........... Gasket Material Expert [*Automotive engineering*]
GMZ........... Bowie, TX [*Location identifier FAA*] (FAAL)
GMZFO .... Gouvernement Militaire de la Zone Francaise d'Occupation [*Military Government of the French Zone of Occupation*] [*of Germany*]
GN .... Air Gabon [*ICAO designator*] (AD)
GN .... Gain (NASA)
GN .... Ganglion Nodosum [*Neurology*]
GN .... Gathering of Nations (EA)
GN .... Gaussian Noise (IAA)

GN .... Gaylactic Network [An association] (EA)
GN .... General (WGA)
GN .... General Note (MSA)
GN .... Generator (IAA)
Gn. .... Genesis [Old Testament book]
GN .... [The] Georgia Northern Railway Co. (IIA)
GN .... German
gn .... Gilbert and Ellice Islands [Tuvalu] [gb (Gilbert Islands) or tu (Tuvalu) used in records cataloged after October 1978] [MARC country of publication code] [Library of Congress] (LCCP)
GN .... Girls Nation (EA)
GN .... Glomerular Nephritis [Medicine]
G:N .... Glucose:Nitrogen [Ratio]
GN .... Gnotobiote [Medicine] (DMAA)
GN .... Godfrey-Nash [Forerunner of British HRG and Frazer-Nash automobiles]
GN .... Golden Nematode [A worm]
GN .... Golden Number [Number used to fix the date of Easter]
GN .... Golden Titan Resources [Vancouver Stock Exchange symbol]
GN .... Goldneck Summer Squash
Gn .... Gonadotropin [Endocrinology]
GCM .... Gonococcus [Medicine] (MEDA)
GN .... Good Night [Amateur radio]
Gn .... Gradational, Non-Calcareous [Soil]
GN .... Graduate Nurse
GN .... Grain (MCD)
GN .... Gram-Negative [Also, GRN] [Microbiology]
GN .... Grand National [Automobile racing]
GN .... Grand Nehemiah [Freemasonry] (ROG)
GN .... Grandnephew (ADA)
GN .... Grandniece (ADA)
GN .... Grant Number (NITA)
GN .... Great Northern Railway (MHDW)
GN .... Green [Maps and charts]
GN .... Grid North [Army] (ADDR)
GN .... Ground Nester [Ornithology]
GN .... Ground Network
GN .... Ground Network [Remote sensing] (EERA)
GN .... Groundnut Meal (PDAA)
GN .... Group Number [Dialog] [Searchable fields] [Information service or system] (NITA)
GN .... Guanine Nucleotide [Biochemistry]
GN .... Guide-Number [Photography]
GN .... Guinea [ANSI two-letter standard code] (CNC)
GN .... Gun [s] [Freight]
GN₂ .... Gaseous Nitrogen [NASA]
GNA .... Gainsco, Inc. [AMEX symbol] (SPSG)
GNA .... Gay Nurses' Alliance (EA)
GNA .... General Nursing Assistance (DMAA)
GNA .... Georgia Nurses Association (SRA)
GNA .... Ghana News Agency
GNA .... Global Network Academy [On-line education] [Information retrieval]
GNA .... Gnangara [Australia Geomagnetic observatory code]
GNA .... Granada Exploration Corp. [Vancouver Stock Exchange symbol]
GNA .... Grants Pass, OR [Location identifier FAA] (FAAL)
GNA .... Graphics Network Architecture
GNA .... Graysonia, Nashville & Ashdown Railroad Co. [AAR code]
GNA .... Servicios Aereos Gana SA de CV [Mexico] [FAA designator] (FAAC)
GNAACBJA... Greater North American Aviculturist and Color Bred Judges Association [Formerly, GNACBJA] (EA)
GNAB .... Guide to New Australian Books [A publication]
GNAC .... Guidance, Navigation and Control [Military] (IAA)
GNACBJA..... Greater North American Color-Bred Judge Association [Later, GNAACBJA] (EA)
GnAcpt......... General Acceptance Corp. [Associated Press] (SAG)
GNADS......... Gimbaled Night and Day Sight
GNAGS........ Ground Adjutant General Section [World War II]
GNAIW........ Glacial North Atlantic Intermediate Water
GNAL .... Georgia Nuclear Aircraft Laboratory (SAA)
GN & C .... Guidance, Navigation, and Control (MCD)
GNAS .... General NAS [FAA] (TAG)
GNAS .... Grand National Archery Society [British]
G Nas .... Guillelmus Naso [Flourished, 1220-34] [Authority cited in pre-1607 legal work] (DSA)
GNAT .... General Numerical Analysis of Transport [Computer program]
GNAT .... Global Network of Astronomical Telescopes [Proposed network]
GNATS .... General Noise and Tonal System (NVT)
GNATS .... General Nonlinear Analysis of Two-Dimensional Structures [Computer program]
GnAuto......... General Automation, Inc. [Associated Press] (SAG)
GNavO .... Group Navigation Officer [British military] (DMA)
GNB .... Global Air Link [Nigeria] [ICAO designator] (FAAC)
GNB .... Good News Bible [Today's English Version] [A publication] (BJA)
GNB .... Gram-Negative Bacillus [Microbiology]
GNB .... Granby, CO [Location identifier FAA] (FAAL)
GNB .... Granby Resources Ltd. [Vancouver Stock Exchange symbol]
GNB .... Grenoble [France] [Airport symbol] (OAG)
GNB .... Guinea-Bissau [ANSI three-letter standard code] (CNC)
GNBM .... Gram-Negative Bacillary Meningitis [Medicine]
GnBnd......... General Binding Corp. [Associated Press] (SAG)
GNC .... General Nautical Chart [Navy]
GNC .... General Nursing Care [Medicine]
GNC .... General Nursing Council
GNC .... Geologic Names Committee [US Geological Survey]
GNC .... Geriatric Nurse Clinician (DMAA)

GNC .... Global Navigation Chart [Military]
GNC .... Goddard Network Control [NASA] (MCD)
GNC .... Grand National Championship [Motorcycle racing]
GNC .... Graphic Numerical Control [Deltacam Systems Ltd.] [Software package] [British] (MCD)
GNC .... Grid North Correction
GNC .... Gross Neutron Counter (PDAA)
GNC .... Guaranty National [NYSE symbol] (TTSB)
GNC .... Guaranty National Corp. [NYSE symbol] (SPSG)
GNC .... Guidance and Navigation Computer [NASA] (KSC)
GNC .... Guidance, Navigation, and Control (NASA)
GNC .... Seminole, TX [Location identifier FAA] (FAAL)
GnCable ...... General Cable PLC [Associated Press] (SAG)
GNCAM .... Glia-Neuron Cell Adhesion Molecule [Cytology]
GNCCA .... Grand National Curling Club of America
GNCEW .... General Nursing Council for England and Wales
GNCFTS ...... GN & C [Guidance, Navigation, and Control] Flight Test Station (MCD)
GNCI .... General Nutrition Co. [NASDAQ symbol] (SAG)
GNCI .... Genl Nutrition [NASDAQ symbol] (TTSB)
GNCIS .... Guidance, Navigation, and Control Integration Simulator (NASA)
GNCM .... General Communication, Inc. [NASDAQ symbol] (NQ)
GNCMA .... Genl Communication'A' [NASDAQ symbol] (TTSB)
GNCN .... Goran Capital, Inc. [NASDAQ symbol] (SAG)
GNCNF........ Goran Capital [NASDAQ symbol] (TTSB)
GnCom......... General Communications, Inc. [Associated Press] (SAG)
GNCS .... Guidance, Navigation, and Control System (MCD)
GNCSA........ Good Neighbour Council of South Australia
GNCT .... Good Neighbour Council of Tasmania [Australia]
GNCTS........ GN & C [Guidance, Navigation, and Control] Test Station (MCD)
GND .... Gram-Negative Diplococci [Medicine] (MEDA)
GND .... Grand Airways, Inc. [FAA designator] (FAAC)
GND .... Grand Casinos [NYSE symbol] (TTSB)
GND .... Grand Casinos, Inc. [NYSE symbol] (SAG)
GND .... Grandview Resources, Inc. [Toronto Stock Exchange symbol Vancouver Stock Exchange symbol]
GND .... Grenada [Windward Islands] [Airport symbol] (OAG)
GND .... Ground (AAG)
gnd .... Ground (IDOE)
GND .... Ground-Detonated Flares [Military] (INF)
GND .... Grounded [Electricity] [Electronics]
GND .... North Georgia College, Stewart Library, Dahlonega, GA [OCLC symbol] (OCLC)
GnData .... General DataComm Industries, Inc. [Associated Press] (SAG)
GNDCG .... Ground Forces Commanding General [World War II]
GNDCK........ Ground Check [Aviation]
GND C/O ..... Ground Checkout [NASA] (NASA)
GNDCON ..... Ground Control
GNDCP .... Ground Command Post [Army]
GNDI .... Gross National Disposable Income [Economics]
GNDR.......... Gander Mountain [NASDAQ symbol] (TTSB)
GNDR.......... Gander Mountain, Inc. [NASDAQ symbol] (NQ)
GnDyn......... General Dynamics Corp. [Associated Press] (SAG)
GNE .... Gane Energy Corp. Ltd. [Toronto Stock Exchange symbol]
GNE .... Genentech, Inc. [NYSE symbol] (SPSG)
GNE .... Government Nomenclature Equipment (DNAB)
GNE .... Gross National Effluent
GNE .... Gross National Expenditure
GNE .... Guidance and Navigation Electronics (KSC)
GNE .... Guidance and Navigation Equipment
GNEC .... General Nuclear Engineering Corp. (MCD)
GNEM .... Global Network for Environmental Monitoring [Defunct] (EA)
GnEmp........ General Employment Enterprises, Inc. [Associated Press] (SAG)
GNESIT .... Greater New England Society of Inhalation Therapists
GNF .... Gannett Newspaper Foundation
GNFC .... Graceland News Fan Club [Defunct] (EA)
GNFMS .... Gaseous Nitrogen Flow Measuring System
GNG .... Gaussian Noise Generator [Electronics]
GNG .... Generation Gather Group [Computer science]
GNG .... Gooding, ID [Location identifier FAA] (FAAL)
GNG .... Granger Resources Corp. [Vancouver Stock Exchange symbol]
GNGCS........ Ground Forces Chief of Staff [World War II]
GNGDC........ Ground Forces Deputy Chief of Staff [World War II]
GNGPS........ Ground Forces Plans Section [World War II]
GNGRBRD.... Gingerbread
GnGrth........ General Growth Properties [Associated Press] (SAG)
GNGS .... Genoa Nuclear Generating Station (NRCH)
GNGSE........ Ground Forces Secretariat [World War II]
GNH .... Grand National Hunt [British]
GNH .... Gross Night Hour [Advertising] (WDMC)
GnHost........ General Host Corp. [Associated Press] (SAG)
GnHous....... General Housewares Corp. [Associated Press] (SAG)
GNI .... Genco Industry, Inc. [Vancouver Stock Exchange symbol]
GNI .... Generation of New Ideas (MHDB)
GNI .... [The] GNI Group, Inc. [Associated Press] (SAG)
GNI .... Grand Isle, LA [Location identifier FAA] (FAAL)
GNI .... Great Northern Iron Ore Properties [NYSE symbol] (SPSG)
GNI .... Grid Node Interface (PDAA)
GNI .... Gross National Income [Economics]
GNI .... Gross National Investment (EERA)
GNIB .... Guatemala News and Information Bureau (EA)
GNIC .... Gay News Information and Communication Network [Information service or system] (IID)
GNID........... Gram-Negative Intracellular Diplococci [Microbiology]
GNIron........ Great Northern Iron Ore Properties [Associated Press] (SAG)

GNIS .... Geographic Names Information System [*US Geological Survey*] [*Information service or system*]
GNIS .... Geographic Names Information System
GNIS .... Global Names Information System [*Computer science*]
GNJ .... Lexington, KY [*Location identifier FAA*] (FAAL)
GNK .... Globalink, Inc. [*AMEX symbol*] (SAG)
GNL .... Galey & Lord, Inc. [*NYSE symbol*] (SAG)
GNL .... General
GNL .... Georgia Nuclear Laboratory [*AEC*]
GNL .... Great National Land [*Vancouver Stock Exchange symbol*]
GNL .... Greenwood [*Mississippi*] [*Airport symbol*] (AD)
GNLB .... Genelabs Technologies [*NASDAQ symbol*] (SPSG)
GNLTD .... Granulated (MSA)
GNM .... Genetron Marine, Inc. [*Vancouver Stock Exchange symbol*]
GNM .... Golden [*New Mexico*] [*Seismograph station code, US Geological Survey*] (SEIS)
GNM .... Good News Mission (EA)
GNM .... Guanambi [*Brazil*] [*Airport symbol*] (OAG)
GNMA .... Government National Mortgage Administration (AAGC)
GNMA .... Government National Mortgage Association [*Nickname: Ginnie Mae*]
GnMag .... General Magnaplate Corp. [*Associated Press*] (SAG)
GnMicr .... General Microwave Corp. [*Associated Press*] (SAG)
GnMill .... General Mills, Inc. [*Associated Press*] (SAG)
GnMotr .... General Motors Corp. [*Associated Press*] (SAG)
GNMP .... Government Network Management Profile [*National Institute of Standards and Technology*]
GNMS .... Gaseous Nitrogen Measuring System
GNMS .... Ground Network Management System [*Aviation*] (DA)
GNN .... Ghinnir [*Ethiopia*] [*Airport symbol*] (AD)
GNN .... Giant North Resources Ltd. [*Vancouver Stock Exchange symbol*]
GNN .... Global Network Navigator [*An on-line publication and Internet reference guide*] (ECON)
GNN .... Gunnerudssatern [*Sweden*] [*Seismograph station code, US Geological Survey*] (SEIS)
GNO .... Golden North Resource Corp. [*Toronto Stock Exchange symbol Vancouver Stock Exchange symbol*]
GNOC .... Graphic Network Operator Console [*Hughes Network Systems, Inc.*]
GN of I .... Great Northern of Ireland [*Railway*] (ROG)
Gnom .... Gnomon [*Munich*] [*A publication*] (BJA)
GNOMAC ...... Greater New Orleans Microform Cooperative [*Library network*]
G-NORM .... Grounded - Not Operationally Ready Maintenance (MCD)
G-NORS .... Grounded - Not Operationally Ready Supply (MCD)
GNOS .... Goddard Network Operations Support [*NASA*] (KSC)
GNOZ .... Grease Nozzle
GNP .... Gas, Nonpersistent
GNP .... Geriatric Nurse Practitioner (DMAA)
GNP .... Gerontological Nurse Practitioner
GNP .... Good Neighbour Program [*Australia*]
GNP .... Graphics Nesting Processor (MCD)
GNP .... Graphics Nesting Program (MCD)
GNP .... Grenada National Party [*Political party*] (PPW)
GNP .... Gross National Product [*Economics*]
GNP .... Tulsa, OK [*Location identifier FAA*] (FAAL)
GNP & BR ... Great Northern Piccadilly & Brompton Railway [*British*] (ROG)
GnPara .... General Parametrics Corp. [*Associated Press*] (SAG)
GNPC .... Global Navigation and Planning Chart [*Military*]
GnPhys .... General Physics Corp. [*Associated Press*] (SAG)
GNpN .... Norman Junior College, Norman Park, GA [*Library symbol Library of Congress*] (LCLS)
GNPP .... Ginna Nuclear Power Plant (NRCH)
GNPP .... Great Nigeria People's Party [*Political party*] (PPW)
GnPrcl .... General Parcel Service, Inc. [*Associated Press*] (SAG)
GNPT .... GP Financial Corp. [*NASDAQ symbol*] (SAG)
GNQ .... Equatorial Guinea [*ANSI three-letter standard code*] (CNC)
GNR .... Gaseous Nuclear Rocket
GNR .... General Roca [*Argentina*] [*Airport symbol*] (OAG)
GNR .... Geographical Names Register [*New South Wales*] [*State*] (EERA)
GNR .... Global Natural Res [*NYSE symbol*] (TTSB)
GNR .... Global Natural Resources, Inc. [*NYSE symbol*] (SPSG)
G/N R .... Glucose to Nitrogen Ratio [*Medicine*] (AAMN)
GNR .... Gram-Negative Rods (DMAA)
GNR .... Great Northern Railway
GNR .... Guest Name Record (IAA)
GNR .... Gunner (AFM)
G n R .... Guns n' Roses [*Rock recording group*]
GNRA .... Gateway National Recreation Area [*New York*] [*Department of the Interior*]
GNRA .... Government National Railway Association [*Proposed*] [*Nickname: Ginnie Rae*]
GNRA .... Grand National Racing Association (EA)
GnRad .... GenRad, Inc. [*Associated Press*] (SAG)
GNRB .... Grid Navigational Reference Beacon [*Navy*] (CAAL)
GNRE .... Gross National Recreation Experience [*Refers to cost of recreation in relation to gross national product*]
GnRF .... Gonadotropin-Releasing Factor [*Also, GnRH, LH-RF, LH-RH, LH-RH/FSH-RH, LRF, LRH*] [*Endocrinology*]
GnRH .... Gonadotropin-Releasing Hormone [*Also, GnRF, LH-RF, LH-RH, LH-RH/FSH-RH, LRF, LRH*] [*Endocrinology*]
GnRHA .... Gonadotropin-Releasing Hormone Agonist [*Endocrinology*]
GNRP .... General Neighborhood Renewal Plan
GNRP .... Guanine Nucleotide Release Protein [*Biochemistry*]
GNRS .... Great Northern Railway Society [*British*] (DBA)
GNRTN .... Generation
GNRTNG ...... Generating
GNRTR .... Generator

GNRY .... Great Northern Railway
GNRY .... Gunnery (AFM)
GNS .... Eastern Executive Air Charter Ltd. [*British*] [*FAA designator*] (FAAC)
GNS .... Gannett News Service
GNS .... General Naval Staff [*NATO*] (NATG)
GN's .... Global Negotiations
G/NS .... Glucose in Normal Saline [*Medicine*]
GNS .... Glutamine Synthetase [*Also, GS*] [*An enzyme*]
GNS .... Goose NORAD [*North American Air Defense*] Sector (IAA)
GNS .... Grain Neutral Spirits [*Alcohol*]
GNS .... Gram-Negative Sensitivity [*to antibiotics*]
GNS .... Grand National Sportsman [*Car racing division*]
GNS .... Great North of Scotland Railway (ROG)
GNS .... Griffin's Nautical Series [*A publication*]
GNS .... Group of Negotiations on Services [*European Community*]
GNS .... Guidance and Navigation System
GNS .... Guineas [*Monetary unit*] [*Obsolete British*]
GNSA .... Gensia Inc. [*NASDAQ symbol*] (TTSB)
GNSA .... Gensia Pharmaceuticals, Inc. [*NASDAQ symbol*] (SAG)
GNSAW .... Gensia Pharmaceuticals Wrrt [*NASDAQ symbol*] (TTSB)
GNSH .... Grey Nuns of the Sacred Heart [*Roman Catholic religious order*]
GNSI .... Guild of Natural Science Illustrators (EA)
GNSM .... Gensym Corp. [*NASDAQ symbol*] (TTSB)
GNSM .... Graduate of the Northern School of Music [*Obsolete British*] (DBQ)
GNSMTH ...... Gunsmith
GNSO .... Goddard Network Support Operations [*King's College*] [*Wilkes-Barre, PA*] [*NASA*] (KSC)
GNSP .... Gross National Sports Product [*Economics*]
GNSR .... Great North of Scotland Railway
GNSS .... Genesis
GNSS .... Global Navigation Satellite System
GNSS .... Global Navigation Satellite System
GNSS .... Global Navigation Satellite System
GNsS .... Grammatik der Neusyrischen Sprache [*A publication*] (BJA)
GNST .... Glossary of Naval Ship Types (MCD)
GNSW .... Governor of New South Wales [*Australia*]
GNSWBR ...... Great New South Wales Bike Ride [*Australia*]
GNT .... Business Air Ltd. [*British ICAO designator*] (FAAC)
GNT .... General Naval Training [*British military*] (DMA)
GNT .... Giant
GNT .... Grant Exploration [*Vancouver Stock Exchange symbol*]
GNT .... Grants, NM [*Location identifier FAA*] (FAAL)
GNT .... Great Northern Telegraph Co. [*Denmark*] [*Telecommunications*] (TEL)
GNT .... Green Tree Financial, Inc. [*NYSE symbol*] (SPSG)
GNT .... Green Tree Finl [*NYSE symbol*] (TTSB)
GNT .... Ground Test [*NASA*] (KSC)
GNTA .... Genta, Inc. [*NASDAQ symbol*] (SPSG)
GNTC .... Girls' Naval Training Corps [*British*]
GnthrInt .... Gunther International Ltd. [*Associated Press*] (SAG)
GNTLMN ...... Gentlemen
GNTO .... Greek National Tourist Organization (EA)
GNTP .... Graduate Nurse Transition Program
GNTR .... Generator (FAAC)
GNTX .... Gentex Corp. [*NASDAQ symbol*] (NQ)
GNU .... Golden Rule Resources Ltd. [*Toronto Stock Exchange symbol*]
GNU .... Goodnews Bay [*Alaska*] [*Airport symbol*] (OAG)
GNUC .... [*The*] GNI Group, Inc. [*NASDAQ symbol*] (NQ)
GNV .... Gainesville [*Florida*] [*Airport symbol*]
GNV .... Geneva Steel Co. [*NYSE symbol*] (SPSG)
GNV .... Geneva Steel Co.'A' [*NYSE symbol*] (TTSB)
GNV .... Genoveva Resources, Inc. [*Vancouver Stock Exchange symbol*]
GNV .... Glycinenaphthol Violet [*An indicator*] [*Chemistry*]
GNV .... Grand Airways, Inc. [*ICAO designator*] (FAAC)
GNVN .... Government of North Vietnam
GNVQ .... General National Vocational Qualification [*British*] (ODBW)
GnvStl .... Geneva Steel [*Associated Press*] (SAG)
GNW .... Greenwell Resources Corp. [*Vancouver Stock Exchange symbol*]
GNWP .... Gross National Waste Product Forum [*Defunct*] (EA)
GNWR .... Genessee & Wyoming Railroad Co. [*AAR code*]
GNX .... Genex Resources [*Vancouver Stock Exchange symbol*]
GNY .... Fort Jay, NY [*Location identifier FAA*] (FAAL)
GNY .... German Navy [*ICAO designator*] (FAAC)
GNYADA .... Greater New York Automobile Dealers Association (SRA)
GNYCFS .... Greater New York Council for Foreign Students [*Later, English in Action*]
GNYO .... Guild of New York Opera [*Record label*]
GNZ .... Ghanzi [*Botswana*] [*Airport symbol*] (AD)
GNZ .... Gisborne [*New Zealand*] [*Seismograph station code, US Geological Survey*] (SEIS)
GNZ .... Government of New Zealand
GO .... Canada - Transport Canada [*Canada ICAO designator*] (ICDA)
go .... Gabon [*MARC country of publication code Library of Congress*] (LCCP)
GO .... Galactose Oxidase [*An enzyme*]
GO .... Gambia Air Shuttle [*ICAO designator*] (AD)
GO .... Garrison Orders [*British military*] (DMA)
GO .... Gasoffizier [*Gas Officer*] [*German military - World War II*]
GO .... Gas Oil [*Also, G*] [*Petroleum technology*]
GO .... Gas Operated (ADA)
GO .... Gaussian Orbitals [*Atomic physics*]
GO .... Generale Occidentale [*Commercial firm*]
GO .... Generalized Operations (MCD)
GO .... Generaloberst [*Full General*] [*German military - World War II*]
GO .... General Obligation [*Bond*] [*Business term*]

GO	General Office [*or Officer*] [*Military*]
GO	General Order
GO	General Organization [*Identification card used at Madison Square Garden*]
GO	Generated Output
GO	Genius Operator Advertising Data Bank [*Gert Richter*] [*Germany Information service or system*] (CRD)
GO	Gentil Organisateur [*Genial Host*] [*Employee of Club Mediterranee, a vacation cooperative*]
GO	Geometry-Optimized [*Calculations*]
GO	Global Options (EA)
GO	Global Outreach [*An association*] (EA)
GO	Glucose Oxidase [*Also, glu ox, GOD*] [*An enzyme*]
Go	Godecke AG [*Germany*] [*Research code symbol*]
Go	Goebel's Probate Court Cases [*Ohio*] [*A publication*] (DLA)
GO	Goethite [*A mineral*]
Go	Gofredus de Trano [*Deceased, 1245*] [*Authority cited in pre-1607 legal work*] (DSA)
go	Gold (VRA)
GO	Goniometer [*JETDS nomenclature*] [*Military*] (CET)
Go	Gonion (DMAA)
Go	Gothic [*Language, etc.*] (ROG)
GO	Government Obligation [*Economics*]
GO	Government Operations Committee [*US Senate*]
GO	Government Owned
GO	Graduate Opportunities [*British*]
GO	Grand Orator [*Freemasonry*]
GO	Grand Organist [*Freemasonry*] (ROG)
GO	Grand Orient [*Freemasonry*] (ROG)
GO	Grasp Objects [*Psychometric test*]
GO	Great Organ [*Music*]
GO	Ground Out [*Baseball*]
GO	Group Officer [*British military*] (DMA)
G-O	Grumman Olson [*Grumman Corp.*]
GO	Guest Option [*Hotel plan, Hilton hotels*]
GO	Gummed Only [*Envelopes*]
GO	Gunnery Officer [*Navy British*]
GO	Gunn Oscillator
GO	Gurkha Officer [*British military*] (DMA)
GO2	Gaseous Oxygen (MCD)
GO3OS	Global Ozone Observing System (USDC)
GOA	Alberta Government [*Canada ICAO designator*] (FAAC)
GOA	Generalized Osteoarthritis [*Medicine*]
GOA	General Operating Agency
GOA	Genoa [*Italy*] [*Airport symbol*] (OAG)
GOA	Georgia Oilmen's Association (SRA)
GOA	Georgia Optometric Association (SRA)
GOA	Glacier-Ocean-Atmosphere [*Global system used for modelling*]
GOA	Goa [*Panjim*] [*India*] [*Seismograph station code, US Geological Survey*] (SEIS)
GOA	Golden Seal Resources Ltd. [*Vancouver Stock Exchange symbol*]
GOA	Gone on Arrival [*Police terminology*] (IIA)
GOA	Government-Owned Aircraft
GOA	Group, Operations Analysis [*Air Force*] (MCD)
GOA	Gun Owners of America (EA)
GOA	Gyro Output Amplifier
GOAC	Geographic OPAREA [*Operating Area*] Coordinates (DNAB)
GOAC	Gun Owners Action Committee (EA)
GOAD	Group of Ancient Drama
GOAL	Ascent Entertainment Group, Inc. [*NASDAQ symbol*] (SAG)
GOAL	Ascent Entertainment Grp [*NASDAQ symbol*] (TTSB)
GOAL	Game Oriented Activities for Learning (AIE)
GOAL	General Organization Analysis Language (IAA)
GOAL	Generator for Optimized Application Language (IAA)
GOAL	Ground Operations Aerospace Language [*Computer science NASA*]
GOAL	Ground Operations Assembly Language [*Computer science*]
GOALI	Grant Opportunities for Academic Liaison with Industry [*National Science Foundation*]
GOALS	Generalized Officer Assignment On-Line System [*Navy*] (NVT)
GOALS	General Operations and Logistics Simulation [*Boeing*]
GOALS	General Optronics Line of Sight Atmospheric Lightwave Communication System [*General Optronics Corp.*] [*Edison, NJ*] [*Telecommunications service*] (TSSD)
GOALS	Geometrical Optical Analysis of Lens Systems (PDAA)
GOALS	Global Ocean-Atmosphere-Land-Surface Interactions (EERA)
GOALS	Global Ocean-Atmosphere-Land System [*Program*] [*Marine science*] (OSRA)
GOALS	Global OCean-Atmosphere-Land System [*Program*] (USDC)
GOALS	Goal-Oriented Approach to Life Cycle Software
GOALS	Greater Orlando Area Legal Services [*Florida*]
GOAM	Government-Owned and Maintained [*Telecommunications*] (TEL)
GOAR	Ground Observer Aircraft Recognition [*Army*]
GOAS	Guidance Optical Alignment Shelter (KSC)
GOASEX	Gulf of Alaska SEASAT Experiment [*National Oceanic and Atmospheric Administration*]
GOAT	Galveston Orientation and Amnesia Test [*Medicine*] (DMAA)
GOAT	Gerber Oscillogram Amplitude Translator
GOAT	Goes Over All Terrain [*Vehicle*]
GOAT	Goings On About Town [*The New Yorker magazine*] (WDMC)
GOAT	Grouped Optimal Aggregation Technique (MCD)
GOATS	Group Operational Access Tester System [*AT & T*]
GOB	General Obligation Bonds [*Finance*]
GOB	General Officers Branch [*Air Force*]
GOB	General Order of Battle

GOB	Glass Oceanographic Buoy
GOB	Goba [*Ehtiopia*] [*Airport symbol*] (AD)
GOB	Gobble (DSUE)
GOB	Goldbrae Development Ltd. [*Vancouver Stock Exchange symbol*]
GOB	Good Ordinary Brand [*Business term*]
gob	Good Ordinary Brand [*Business term*] (ODBW)
GOB	Government of Bangladesh
GOB	Government Of Bangladesh
GOB	Government of Burma (CINC)
GOB	Grants Operations Balance [*Environmental Protection Agency*] (ERG)
GOB	Ground Order of Battle (AFM)
GOBAB	Gamma-Hydroxy-beta-aminobutyric Acid [*Pharmacology*]
GOBAC	Gold-Plating Bath Analyzer and Controller (PDAA)
GOBEP	Generalized One-Boson Exchange Potential
GOBI	Growth Monitoring, Oral Rehydration, Breastfeeding, and Immunization [*Program*] [*UNICEF plan to reduce child mortality in Third World countries*]
GOBILS	Government Bill of Lading System
GOBR	Group of Officials on Biotechnology Regulation (EERA)
GOC	Gas-Oil Contact
GOC	Gas-Operated Core
GOC	General Officer Commanding [*Navy*]
GOC	General Operating Committee
GOC	General Optical Council [*British*]
GOC	Glas Owners Club (EA)
GOC	Glycidoxycoumarin [*Biochemistry*]
GOC	Gora [*Papua New Guinea*] [*Airport symbol*] (OAG)
GOC	Government Operations Committee
GOC	Graphic Option Controller (NITA)
GOC	Greatest Overall Coefficient (TEL)
GOC	Greek Orthodox Church (BARN)
GOC	Griffith Observatory [*California*] [*Seismograph station code, US Geological Survey*] (SEIS)
GOC	Ground Observer Corps
GOC	Ground Operations Coordinator [*NASA*] (NASA)
GOC	Group Operations Center (NATG)
GOC	Guaranteed One Coat [*Brand of house paint*]
GOC	Gunnery Officer's Console [*Army*] (AABC)
GOCA	Graphics Object Content Architecture (CDE)
GOCA	Ground Operations Control Area [*NASA*] (NASA)
GOCAP	Graphic Output Circuit Analysis Program
GOCC	GARP Operational Control Center [*Marine science*] (MSC)
GOCC	GATE [*GARP Atlantic Tropical Experiment*] Operational Control Centre [*Marine science*] (MSC)
GOCC	General Order of the Commander-in-Chief [*British military*] (DMA)
GOCC	Geodetic Operations Control Center [*NASA*]
GOCESS	Government-Operated Civil Engineering Supply Store
GOCHEM	Gulf Oil Chemicals Co.
GOCI	General Operator-Computer Interaction (IEEE)
GOCI	Graham Owners Club International (EA)
GOC-in-C	General Officer Commanding-in-Chief [*British*]
GOCMV	Greek Orthodox Community of Melbourne and Victoria [*Australia*]
GOCO	Golden Oil Co. [*NASDAQ symbol*] (NQ)
GOCO	Government-Owned/Commercial-Operated [*Facility*] (AFIT)
GO/CO	Government-Owned/Contractor-Operated [*Facility*] (NG)
GOCOM	General Officer Command [*US Army Reserve*] (AABC)
GOCR	Gated-Off Controlled Rectifier
GOCRM	General Officer Commanding Royal Marines [*British*]
GOD	Generation of Diversity [*Immunology*]
GOD	Glucose Oxidase [*Also, glu ox, GO*] [*An enzyme*]
God	Gofredus de Trano [*Deceased, 1245*] [*Authority cited in pre-1607 legal work*] (DSA)
GOD	Golden Sceptre Resources [*Toronto Stock Exchange symbol Vancouver Stock Exchange symbol*]
GOD	Government-Owned Depot
GOD	Grasped Objects Discrimination [*Psychometric test*]
GOD	Guaranteed Overnight Delivery
GOD	Guidance and Orbit Determination [*NASA*] (PDAA)
GODA	Guild of Drama Adjudicators [*British*] (BI)
GODAS	Graphically Oriented Design and Analysis System [*Computer science*]
Godb (Eng)	Godbolt's English King's Bench Reports [*78 English Reprint*] [*A publication*] (DLA)
Goddard	Goddard on Easements [*A publication*] (DLA)
Goddard C	Goddard College (GAGS)
Godd Ease	Goddard on Easements [*A publication*] (DLA)
Godd Easem	Goddard on Easements [*A publication*] (DLA)
GODE	Gulf Organization for Development in Egypt
Godef & Sh RC	Godefroi and Shortt on Railway Companies [*A publication*] (DLA)
Godefroi	Godefroi's Law of Trusts and Trustees [*A publication*] (DLA)
Godef Trust	Godefroi's Law of Trusts and Trustees [*A publication*] (DLA)
Godo	Godolphin on Admiralty Jurisdiction [*A publication*] (DLA)
Godo	Godolphin's Abridgment of Ecclesiastical Law [*A publication*] (DLA)
Godo	Godolphin's Orphan's Legacy [*A publication*] (DLA)
Godo	Godolphin's Repertorium Canonicum [*A publication*] (DLA)
Godol	Godolphin's Orphan's Legacy [*A publication*] (DLA)
Godolph Adm Jur	Godolphin on Admiralty Jurisdiction [*2nd ed.*] [*1685*] [*A publication*] (DLA)
Godolph Ecc Law	Godolphin's Ecclesiastical Law [*A publication*] (DLA)
Godolph Leg	Godolphin's Orphan's Legacy [*A publication*] (DLA)
Godolph Orph Leg	Godolphin's Orphan's Legacy [*A publication*] (DLA)
Godolph Rep Can	Godolphin's Repertorium Canonicum [*A publication*] (DLA)
GODORT	Government Documents Round Table [*American Library Association*]
GODORT ETF	GODORT [*Government Documents Round Table*] Education Task Force

GODORT FDTF... GODORT [*Government Documents Round Table*] Federal Documents Task Force
GODORT IDTF... GODORT [*Government Documents Round Table*] International Documents Task Force
GODORT MRGITF... GODORT [*Government Documents Round Table*] Machine-Readable Government Information Task Force
GODORT SLDTF... GODORT [*Government Documents Round Table*] State and Local Documents Task Force
GOD-POD..... Glucose Oxidase-Peroxidase [*Also, PGO*] [*Enzyme mixture*]
GODS.......... Geniuses of Distinction Society [*Later, SGD*] (EA)
GODSEP....... Guidance and Orbit Determination for Solar Electric Propulsion [*NASA*]
Godson......... Godson's Mining Commissioner's Cases [*Ontario*] [*A publication*] (DLA)
Gods Pat..... Godson on Patents [*2nd ed.*] [*1840*] [*A publication*] (DLA)
GOE........... Gas, Oxygen, Ether [*Anesthesiology*]
GOE........... General Operating Expenses (MCD)
GOE........... General Ordination Examination
GOE........... Geodome Resources Ltd. [*Toronto Stock Exchange symbol Vancouver Stock Exchange symbol*]
GOE........... Gonalia [*Papua New Guinea*] [*Airport symbol*] (OAG)
GOE........... Gore [*New Zealand*] [*Airport symbol*] (AD)
GOE........... Government-Owned Equipment (MCD)
GOE........... Ground Operational Equipment [*NASA*]
Goeb.......... Goebel's Probate Court Cases [*Ohio*] [*A publication*] (DLA)
Goebel........ Goebel's Probate Reports [*Ohio*] [*A publication*] (DLA)
Goebel (Ohio).. Goebel's Probate Court Cases [*Ohio*] [*A publication*] (DLA)
Goebel's Rep... Goebel's Probate Reports [*Ohio*] [*A publication*] (DLA)
GOE for OAO... Ground Operational Equipment for the Orbiting Astronomical Observatory [*NASA*] (MUGU)
GOE/RPIE..... Ground Operational Equipment/Real Property Installed Equipment [*NASA*] (AFM)
GOES.......... Geostationary Operational Environmental Satellite [*National Oceanic and Atmospheric Administration*]
GOES.......... Geostationary Operational Environmental Satellite [*Instrument*] (EERA)
GOES.......... Geostationary Orbital Earth Satellite (MCD)
GOES.......... Geosynchronous Operational Environmental Satellite [*NASA*] (NASA)
GOES.......... Geosynchronous Orbiting Earth Satellite
GOES.......... Global Omnibus Environmental Survey (EERA)
GOES/DCP .. Geostationary Operational Environmental Satellite Data Collection Platform (MSC)
GOESECS..... Geochemical Ocean Section Study [*International Decade of Ocean Exploration*] (USDC)
GOESECS..... Geochemical Ocean Section Study [*Marine science*] (OSRA)
GOES-Next... Next-Generation GOES [*Geostationary Operational Environmental Satellite*] (USDC)
GOEZS........ Global Ocean Euphotic Zone Study [*Marine science*] (OSRA)
Gof............. Gofredus de Trano [*Deceased, 1245*] [*Authority cited in pre-1607 legal work*] (DSA)
GOF .... Goodness of Fit (MCD)
GOF .... Good Old Friday [*Slang*]
GOF .... Government-Owned Facility
GOF .... San Angelo, TX [*Location identifier FAA*] (FAAL)
GOFAR........ Global Ocean Floor Analysis and Research [*Navy*]
GOF E .... Goffered Edges [*Bookbinding*] (DGA)
GOFS .... Global Ocean Flux Study [*Federal government*]
GOG .... GEOSECS Operations Group [*Marine science*] (MSC)
GOG .... Gerrity Oil & Gas [*NYSE symbol*] (SPSG)
GOG .... Golden Tag Resources [*Vancouver Stock Exchange symbol*]
GOG .... Government of Ghana
GOG .... Gynecologic Oncology Group (EA)
GOGAT........ Glutamate Synthase (BARN)
GOGECA...... Comite Generale de la Cooperation Agricole de la CEE [*General Committee of Agricultural Cooperation of the European Economic Community*] (PDAA)
GOGG........ Ziguinchor [*Senegal*] [*ICAO location identifier*] (ICLI)
GOGK........ Kolda [*Senegal*] [*ICAO location identifier*] (ICLI)
GOGO......... Global One Distribution & Merchandising, Inc. [*NASDAQ symbol*] (SAG)
GO/GO .... Government-Owned/Government-Operated [*Facility*]
Gog Or........ Goguet's Origin of Laws [*A publication*] (DLA)
GOGPr........ Gerrity O&G Cv Dep Pfd [*NYSE symbol*] (TTSB)
GOGS .... Cap Skirring [*Senegal*] [*ICAO location identifier*] (ICLI)
GOH .... Garments on Hangers [*Shipping*]
goh .... German, Old High [*MARC language code Library of Congress*] (LCCP)
GOH .... German Order of Harugari
GOH .... Geroderma Osteodysplastica Hereditaria [*Medicine*] (DMAA)
GOH .... Godthaab [*Denmark*] [*Airport symbol*]
GOH .... Goliath Gold Mines Ltd. [*Toronto Stock Exchange symbol Vancouver Stock Exchange symbol*]
GOH .... Goods on Hand (DS)
GOH .... Government of Honduras
GOH .... Nuuk [*Greenland*] [*Airport symbol*] (OAG)
GOI .... Fort Knox, KY [*Location identifier FAA*] (FAAL)
GOI .... General Oriental Investments Ltd. [*Vancouver Stock Exchange symbol*]
GOI .... Goa [*India*] [*Airport symbol*] (OAG)
GOI .... Government of Indonesia
GOI .... Government of Iran
GOI .... Government of Israel (MCD)
GOI .... Government of Italy
GOI .... Government-Owned Installation
GOI .... Group Operations Instruction [*British military*] (DMA)

GOI .... Gun Owners, Inc. (EA)
GOIC .... Gulf Organization for Industrial Consulting [*Doha, Qatar*] (EAIO)
GOIE .... Government-Owned Industrial Equipment (SAA)
GOIFE .... Government of Israel Furnished Equipment (MCD)
Goir Fr Co ... Goirand's French Code of Commerce [*A publication*] (DLA)
GOIT .... Goyer Organization of Ideas Test (EDAC)
GOJ .... Blytheville, AR [*Location identifier FAA*] (FAAL)
GOJ .... Eurojet Aviation Ltd. [*British ICAO designator*] (FAAC)
GOJ .... Government of Japan (CINC)
GOK .... God Only Knows [*Facetious diagnosis for a puzzling medical case*]
GOK .... Government of Korea
GOK .... Guthrie, OK [*Location identifier FAA*] (FAAL)
GOL .... General Operating Language [*Computer science*] (IEEE)
GOL .... Goal-Oriented Language
GOL .... Gold Beach, OR [*Location identifier FAA*] (FAAL)
GOL .... Golden [*Bergen Park*] [*Colorado*] [*Seismograph station code, US Geological Survey*] (SEIS)
GOL .... Goldlund Mines Ltd. [*Toronto Stock Exchange symbol*]
GOL .... Guinness Overseas Ltd. [*British*]
GOLD .... Gate-Drain Overlapped Device (MCD)
GOLD .... Generalized Organization of Large Databases (PDAA)
GOLD .... Geometric On-Line Definition [*Computer science*] (PDAA)
Gold........... Goldesborough's [*or Gouldsborough's*] English King's Bench Reports [*A publication*]
GOLD .... Graphic Online Language [*Computer science*] (IEEE)
GOLD .... Guild of Lady Drivers [*British*] (BI)
Gold & G ..... Goldsmith and Guthrie's Appeals Reports [*Missouri*] [*A publication*]
GOLD BDE ... Gold Bevelled Deckle Edges [*Printing*] (DGA)
GOLD BE ... Gold Bevelled Edges [*Printing*] (DGA)
GOLDBERG... Generally Operational Linear Digit-Controlled Biphase Electrical Retardance Gate [*IBM Corp.*]
GoldBks ...... Golden Books Family Entertainment, Inc. [*Associated Press*] (SAG)
GoldBnc ...... Gold Banc Corp., Inc. [*Associated Press*] (SAG)
Gold Coast... Judgments of the Full Court, Privy Council, and Divisional Courts, Gold Coast [*A publication*] (DLA)
Goldcp .... Goldcorp, Inc. [*Associated Press*] (SAG)
GoldcpA ...... Goldcorp [*Associated Press*] (SAG)
GoldcpB ...... Goldcorp [*Associated Press*] (SAG)
GOLD E ...... Gold Edges [*Printing*] (DGA)
GoldEn .... Golden Enterprises, Inc. [*Associated Press*] (SAG)
Golden Gate U... Golden Gate University (GAGS)
Goldes .... Goldesborough's [*or Gouldsborough's*] English King's Bench Reports [*A publication*] (DLA)
GOLDF .... Silverado Mines [*NASDAQ symbol*] (TTSB)
GoldFd .... Gold Fields of South Africa Ltd. [*Associated Press*] (SAG)
GoldIsl .... Golden Isles Financial Holdings, Inc. [*Associated Press*] (SAG)
GoldnOil ...... Golden Oil Co. [*Associated Press*] (SAG)
GoldRs .... Gold Reserve Corp. [*Associated Press*] (SAG)
Golds Eq ..... Goldsmith's Doctrine and Practice of Equity [*6th ed.*] [*1871*] [*A publication*] (DLA)
GOLD STAR... Generalized Organization of Large Databases / Set-Theoretic Approach to Relations
GoldTri .... Golden Triangle Industries, Inc. [*Associated Press*] (SAG)
GoldTri .... Golden Triangle Royalty & Oil, Inc. [*Associated Press*] (SAG)
GoletaN .... Goleta National Bank [*Associated Press*] (SAG)
GOLF .... Global Oscillations at Low Frequency [*Aerospace*]
go lf .... Gold Leaf (VRA)
Golf............. Olfactory G Protein [*Physiology*]
GOLF .... S 2 Golf [*NASDAQ symbol*] (TTSB)
GOLF .... STwo Golf, Inc. [*NASDAQ symbol*] (SAG)
Golf Ent ...... Golf Enterprises, Inc. [*Associated Press*] (SAG)
GolfTech ...... Golf Technology Holding, Inc. [*Associated Press*] (SAG)
GolfTS .... Golf Training Systems, Inc. [*Associated Press*] (SAG)
GolfTSy .... Golf Training Systems, Inc. [*Associated Press*] (SAG)
GOLIATH...... Giant On-Line Instrument for the Acquisition and Total Handling of Data (MCD)
GOLKAR...... Sekber Golongan Karya [*Joint Secretariat of Functional Groups*] [*Indonesia*] [*Political party*] (PPW)
GOLPH........ Giannetti On-Line Psychosocial History [*Personality development test*] [*Psychology*]
GOLPS .... Greek Orthodox Ladies Philoptochos Society (EA)
GOLS .... General Online Stack System (IAA)
GOM .... God's Own Medicine [*Also, God's Medicine*] [*Morphine*] [*Slang*]
GOM .... Golden Eye Minerals [*Vancouver Stock Exchange symbol*]
GOM .... Goma [*Zaire*] [*Airport symbol*] (OAG)
GOM .... Government of Malaysia (CINC)
GOM .... Government-Owned Material
GOM .... Grand Old Man [*A venerated man, especially in a specific field*] [*Political slang See also HOM*]
GOM .... Ground Operations Manager
GOM .... Group Occupancy Meter [*Telecommunications*] (NITA)
GOM .... Gulf of Mexico [*Also, GLFMEX*]
GOM .... Macon Junior College, Macon, GA [*OCLC symbol*] (OCLC)
GOM .... or WSMR [*Hugh L. Dryden Flight Research Center*] [*White Sands Missile Range*] (NASA)
GOMA .... General Officer Money Allowance [*Military*] (AABC)
GOMA .... Good Outdoor Manners Association (EA)
GOMAC....... Government Microcircuit Applications Conference
GOMAC....... Groupement des Opticiens du Marche Commun [*Common Market Opticians' Group*] [*Paris, France*]
GOMALCO... Gobel O'Malley Co. [*Entertainer George Gobel's firm; O'Malley is business ma nager*]
GOME .... Global Ozone Monitoring Experiment [*Marine science*] (OSRA)

GOMER........ Get Out of My Emergency Room [*Used as a noun in reference to an elderly, chronically ill patient*]
GOMMS....... Ground Operations and Material Management System (MCD)
GOMOS........ Global Ozone Monitoring by Occultation of Stars [*Marine science*] (OSRA)
GOMR......... Global Ozone Monitoring Radiometer
GOMR & R... Government-Owned Material Repair and Reimbursement (MCD)
GOMS......... Geostationary Operational Meteorological Satellite [*Marine science*] (OSRA)
GOMS......... Ground Operations Management System [*NASA*] (NASA)
GON.......... Geon Co. [*NYSE symbol*] (SPSG)
gon .... Gondi [*MARC language code Library of Congress*] (LCCP)
GON.......... Gonni Air Services Ltd. [*Suriname*] [*ICAO designator*] (FAAC)
GON.......... Gonococcal Ophthalmia Neonatorum [*Medicine*]
GON.......... New London [*Connecticut*] [*Airport symbol*] (OAG)
GOND......... Glaucomatous Optic Nerve Damage [*Medicine*] (DMAA)
GOND......... Gondola
GONG......... Global Oscillations Network Group [*National Science Foundation*]
GONIO........ Goniometer [*RADAR instrument*] (DSUE)
GONT......... Government on Taiwan
Gonzaga U... Gonzaga University (GAGS)
Gonz Pub Lab L Rep... Gonzaga Special Report. Public Sector Labor Law [*A publication*] (DLA)
GOO.......... Gastric Outlet Obstruction [*Gastroenterology*] (DAVI)
GOO.......... Generalized Overhauser Orbitals [*Atomic physics*]
GOO.......... Get Oil Out (EA)
GOO.......... Goldsil Resources Ltd. [*Toronto Stock Exchange symbol Vancouver Stock Exchange symbol*]
GOO.......... Goondiwindi [*Australia Airport symbol*] (OAG)
GOO.......... Goosecreekite [*A zeolite*]
GOO.......... Ground Observer Organization (NATG)
GOO.......... Ground Operation Order (NATG)
GOO.......... Group Operations Order [*British military*] (DMA)
GOOD......... Diourbel [*Senegal*] [*ICAO location identifier*] (ICLI)
Good & Wood... Full Bench Rulings, Edited by Goodeve and Woodman [*Bengal*] [*A publication*] (DLA)
GOOD-B'YE... God Be with You (ROG)
GOOD EGGS... Geriatric Order of Old Dolls Who Encourage the Generation Gap Singlemindedly [*Tongue-in-cheek teachers' organization*]
Good Ev...... Goodeve's Law of Evidence [*India*] [*A publication*] (DLA)
Goodeve...... Goodeve on Real Property [*1883-1906*] [*A publication*] (DLA)
Good Govt... Good Government [*A publication*]
GoodGy....... [*The*] Good Guys, Inc. [*Associated Press*] (SAG)
Goodmrk..... Goodmark Foods, Inc. [*Associated Press*] (SAG)
Good Pat..... Goodeve's Abstract of Patent Cases [*1785-1883*] [*England*] [*A publication*] (DLA)
Good Pr...... Goodwin's Probate Practice [*A publication*] (DLA)
Goodrch...... Goodrich, BF, Co. [*Associated Press*] (SAG)
Goodrich-Amram... Goodrich-Amram Procedural Rules Service [*A publication*] (DLA)
GoodrP....... Goodrich Petroleum [*Associated Press*] (SAG)
GoodrPet..... Goodrich Petroleum [*Associated Press*] (SAG)
Good Ry C... Goodeve on Railway Companies and Passengers [*A publication*] (DLA)
GoodT........ Good Times Restaurants, Inc. [*Associated Press*] (SAG)
GoodTm...... Good Times Restaurants, Inc. [*Associated Press*] (SAG)
Goodyear..... [*The*] Goodyear Tire & Rubber Co. [*Associated Press*] (SAG)
GOOFC....... Grand Ole Opry Fan Club (EA)
GOOG......... Linguere [*Senegal*] [*ICAO location identifier*] (ICLI)
GOOK......... Kaolack [*Senegal*] [*ICAO location identifier*] (ICLI)
GOOMBY..... Get Out of My Backyard [*Slang*]
GOONQ....... Grand Officier de l'Ordre National du Quebec [*Canada*] (DD)
GOONS .... Guild of One Name Studies [*Organization to link people with a common surname for the study of family history*] [*British*]
GOOO......... Dakar [*Senegal*] [*ICAO location identifier*] (ICLI)
GOOS......... Global Ocean Observation System (ECON)
GOOS......... Global Ozone Observing System [*Marine science*] (OSRA)
GOOS......... Gunnery Officers Ordnance School
GOOSE....... Waysgoose [*Country fair*] (ROG)
GOOV......... Dakar [*Senegal*] [*ICAO location identifier*] (ICLI)
GOOY......... Dakar/Yoff [*Senegal*] [*ICAO location identifier*] (ICLI)
GOP.......... General Operational Plot
GOP.......... General Outpost [*Army*] (AABC)
GOP.......... Gold Point Resources [*Vancouver Stock Exchange symbol*]
GOP.......... Gorakhpur [*India*] [*Airport symbol*] (OAG)
GOP.......... Government of Pakistan (ECON)
GOP.......... Government of the Philippines (CINC)
GOP.......... Government-Owned Property
GOP.......... Grand Old Party [*The Republican Party*]
GOP.......... Grille Opening Panel [*Automotive engineering*]
GOP.......... Ground Observer Post
GOP.......... Ground Operations Panel [*NASA*] (NASA)
GOP.......... Group of Paths (SAA)
GOP.......... Group of Pictures [*Computer science*]
GOPAC....... GOP Action Committee
GOPAL....... GOP [*Grand Old Party*] Women's Political Action League (EA)
GOPARS..... Government-Operated Parts Store
GOPE........ Government-Owned Plant Equipment
GOPG........ Ground Operations Planning Group [*NASA*] (NASA)
GOPIRB...... General Officer Product Improvement Review Board
GOPITS...... Grand Offertory Procession in the Sky [*Corporate sobriquet used by novelist William X. Kienzle*]
GOPL .... General Outpost Line [*Army*]
GOPO........ Government-Owned/Privately-Operated (GFGA)
GOPR........ General Officers' Protocol Roster

GOPRINT ..... Government Printer [*Queensland, Australia*]
GOPS......... Giga Operations Per Second (NITA)
GOQ.......... Genuine Occupational Qualification (DI)
GOQ.......... Golmud [*China*] [*Airport symbol*] (OAG)
GOQS......... General On-Line Query System (MCD)
GOR.......... Gained Output Ratio (IEEE)
GOR.......... Gas-Oil Ratio (IEEE)
GOR.......... General Ocean Research [*Navy ship symbol*]
GOR.......... General Officer Review
GOR.......... General Operating Room
GOR.......... General Operational Requirement
GOR.......... General Overruling Regulation [*Office of Price Stabilization*] (DLA)
GOR.......... Golden Range Resources, Inc. [*Toronto Stock Exchange symbol*]
GOR.......... Goldstack Resources [*Vancouver Stock Exchange symbol*]
GOR.......... Gore [*Ethiopia*] [*Airport symbol*] (OAG)
GOR.......... Gori [*Former USSR Seismograph station code, US Geological Survey*] (SEIS)
GOR.......... Gradual-Onset-Rate [*Air Force*] (DOMA)
GOR.......... Grille Opening Reinforcement [*Automotive engineering*]
GOR.......... Ground Operations Review (MCD)
GOR.......... Gun Operations Room [*British military*] (DMA)
GOR.......... Gurkha Other Rank [*Military British*]
GoranC....... Goran Capital, Inc. [*Associated Press*] (SAG)
Gord Dec ... Gordon on the Law of Decedents in Pennsylvania [*A publication*] (DLA)
Gord Dig..... Gordon's Digest of United States Laws [*A publication*] (DLA)
GORD HIGHRS... Gordon Highlanders [*Military British*] (ROG)
Gordon....... Gordon's Reports [*24-26 Colorado and 10-13 Colorado Appeals*] [*A publication*] (DLA)
Gord Tr...... Gordon's Treason Trials [*A publication*] (DLA)
Gore-B Comp.... Gore-Brown on Companies [*43rd ed.*] [*1977*] [*A publication*] (DLA)
GOREDCO.... Gulf Oil Real Estate Development Co.
GORF......... Goddard Optical Research Facility [*Goddard Space Flight Center*] [*NASA*]
GORG........ General Officers Review Group [*Air Force*]
Gorg.......... Gorgias [*483-376BC*] [*Classical studies*] (OCD)
G Org........ Grand-Orgue [*Great Organ*] [*Music*]
G ORG........ Great Organ [*Music*]
GORID .... Ground Optical Recorder for Intercept Determination
GORJE....... Generic Ordnance Ramjet Engine (MCD)
GORK........ God Only Really Knows [*Facetious diagnosis for a puzzling medical case*]
GormRup..... Gorman-Rupp Co. [*Associated Press*] (SAG)
GORP........ Ground Operational [*or Operations*] Requirements Plan [*NASA*]
GORP........ Ground Operations Review Panel [*NASA*] (NASA)
GORS......... Grant of Resident Status
GORS......... Ground Observation Reporting System
GORS......... Ground Observer RF [*Radio frequency*] System [*NASA*] (NASA)
GORSP....... Government Officials Responsible for Standardization Policies [*Economic Commission for Europe*] [*United Nations*] (PDAA)
GORT........ Gilmore Oral Reading Test [*Psychology*] (DAVI)
GORT........ Gray Oral Reading Tests
GORT-R ..... Gray Oral Reading Tests - Revised [*Educational test*]
GORX......... Graphite Oxidation from Reactor Excursion [*Engineering computer code*]
GOS.......... Gate Operating System [*Aviation*] (DA)
GOS.......... General Operating Specification [*Air Materiel Command*] (AAG)
GOS.......... General Overhaul Specification
GOS.......... Geodetic Optical System
GOS.......... Glasgow Outcome Score [*Medicine*] (DMAA)
GOS.......... Global Observing System (EERA)
GOS.......... Global Observing Systems [*Weather*]
GOS.......... Global Operating System (IAA)
GOS.......... Golden State Resources [*Vancouver Stock Exchange symbol*]
GOS.......... Goldfields Air Services [*Australia ICAO designator*] (FAAC)
GOS.......... Gosford [*Australia Airport symbol Obsolete*] (OAG)
GOS.......... Gossip (DSUE)
GOS.......... Government of Singapore (CINC)
GOS.......... Government of Spain
GOS.......... Government of Sweden (MCD)
GOS.......... Grade of Service
GOS.......... Grand Outside Sentinel [*Freemasonry*] (ROG)
GOS.......... Graphical Output Scheme (PDAA)
GOS.......... Graphics Operating System [*Tektronix*]
GOS.......... Gross Operating Surplus [*Economics*]
GOS.......... Ground Operations System (MCD)
GOS.......... Group Operating Services (NRCH)
GOS.......... Lakeview, OR [*Location identifier FAA*] (FAAL)
GOSC........ General Officer Steering Committee [*Military*] (MCD)
GOSEAC...... Group of Specialists on Environmental Affairs and Conservation (EERA)
Gosf.......... Gosford's Manuscript Reports, Scotch Court of Session [*A publication*] (DLA)
GOSG........ General Officer Steering Group
GOSH........ Graphical Operating System Hack [*Computer science*]
GOSH........ Grown Offspring, Still Home [*Lifestyle classification*]
GOSH........ Oshkosh B Gosh, Inc. [*NASDAQ symbol*] (SAG)
GOSHA....... Oshkosh B'Gosh CI'A' [*NASDAQ symbol*] (TTSB)
GOSHB....... Oshkosh B'Gosh CI'B' [*NASDAQ symbol*] (TTSB)
GOSIP....... Government Open Systems Implementation Protocol [*Telecommunications*]
GOSIP....... Government Open Systems Interconnection Profile [*National Institute of Standards and Technology*] (GFGA)
GOSIP....... Government Open Systems Interconnection Profiles Computer science (EERA)

GOSM.......... Matam/Ouro Sogui [Senegal] [ICAO location identifier] (ICLI)
GOSP.......... Gas-Oil Separation Plant
GOSP.......... Golden Spike National Historic Site
GOSP.......... Gospel (ROG)
GOSP.......... Podor [Senegal] [ICAO location identifier] (ICLI)
GOSPLAN .... Gosudarstvennaja Planovaja Komissija [Central Planning Commission] [Former USSR]
GOSR.......... Richard-Toll [Senegal] [ICAO location identifier] (ICLI)
GOSS.......... Gossamer Hat [Tall hat] (ROG)
GOSS.......... Ground Operational [or Operations] Support System [NASA]
GOSS.......... Saint Louis [Senegal] [ICAO location identifier] (ICLI)
GOSSTCOMP... Global Sea Surface Temperature Computation
GOSSTRAKH... Gosudarstvennoe Strakhovanie [State insurance] [Former USSR]
GOST.......... Goddard Satellite Tracking [NASA] (MCD)
GOST.......... Gossudarstvenny Obstschessojusny Standart [All-Union State Standard] [Former USSR]
GOST.......... Guidance Optics and Sighting
GOT.......... Air Express in Norrkoping AB [Sweden ICAO designator] (FAAC)
GOT.......... Aspartate Aminotransferase [An enzyme] (DAVI)
GOT.......... Glucose Oxidase Test [Organic chemistry] (DAVI)
GOT.......... Glutamic-Oxaloacetic Transaminase [Also, AAT, ASAT, AST] [An enzyme]
GOT.......... Goldbelt Mines [Vancouver Stock Exchange symbol]
GOT.......... Goteborg [Sweden] [Seismograph station code, US Geological Survey Closed] (SEIS)
GOT.......... Gothenburg [Sweden] [Airport symbol] (OAG)
got.......... Gothic [MARC language code Library of Congress] (LCCP)
GOT.......... Gottschalks, Inc. [NYSE symbol] (SPSG)
GOT.......... Government of Tunisia
GOT.......... Government-Owned Terminal
GOTA.......... Green Olive Trade Association (EA)
GOTB.......... Bakel [Senegal] [ICAO location identifier] (ICLI)
G/OTBSR...... Gas/Oil Tax Block Summary Record [IRS]
Gotchk.......... Gottschalks, Inc. [Associated Press] (SAG)
GOTCO.......... Gulf Oil Trading Co.
GOTG.......... Government of the Gambia
Goth.......... De Bello Gothico [of Procopius] [Classical studies] (OCD)
GOTH.......... Gothic [Language, etc.]
Goth.......... Gothic (VRA)
GOTH.......... Gothic Energy [NASDAQ symbol] (TTSB)
GOTH.......... Gothic Energy Corp. [NASDAQ symbol] (SAG)
GotHA.......... Goteborgs Hogskolas Arsskrift [Gothenburg] [A publication] (BJA)
GothE.......... Gothic Energy Corp. [Associated Press] (SAG)
Gothic.......... Gothic Energy Corp. [Associated Press] (SAG)
GothicEn.......... Gothic Energy Corp. [Associated Press] (SAG)
GOTHW.......... Gothic Energy Wrrt [NASDAQ symbol] (TTSB)
GOTHZ.......... Gothic Energy Wrrt [NASDAQ symbol] (TTSB)
GOTK.......... Geotek Communications, Inc. [NASDAQ symbol] (NQ)
GOTK.......... Goetek Communications [NASDAQ symbol] (TTSB)
GOTK.......... Kedougou [Senegal] [ICAO location identifier] (ICLI)
GOTLF.......... Gotaas-Larsen Shipping Corp. (MHDW)
GOTN.......... Niokolo Koba [Senegal] [ICAO location identifier] (ICLI)
GOTOH.......... Go to Heaven [Name of missionary, "Professor Gotoh," for Worldwide Church of God]
G/OTPSR...... Gas/Oil Tax Program Summary Record [IRS]
GOTR.......... Greek Orthodox Theological Review [A publication] (BJA)
GOTRAN.......... Load and Go FORTRAN [Computer science]
GOTS.......... Government Off- The Shelf (DOMA)
GOTS.......... Graphic-Oriented Timesharing System [Computer science] (IAA)
GOTS.......... Gravity-Oriented Test Satellite [NASA]
GOTS.......... Simenti [Senegal] [ICAO location identifier] (ICLI)
GOTT.......... Tambacounda [Senegal] [ICAO location identifier] (ICLI)
Gott Anz.......... Goettingischer Gelehrte Anzeigen [A publication] (OCD)
GOTTEX.......... Gottlieb Textiles
Gott Nachr.......... Nachrichten von der Gesellschaft der Wissenschaften zu Goettingen [A publication] (OCD)
Gottschall .... Gottschall's Dayton Superior Court Reports [Ohio] [A publication] (DLA)
GOTU.......... Glider Operational Training Unit [British military] (DMA)
GOTV.......... Get Out the Vote (GNE)
GOU.......... Garoua [Cameroon] [Airport symbol] (OAG)
gou.......... Gouache (VRA)
GOU.......... Government of Uganda (ECON)
GOU.......... Grupo de Oficiales Unidos [Group of United Officers] [Argentina]
GOU.......... Gulf Canada Resources [NYSE symbol] (TTSB)
GOU.......... Gulf Canada Resources Ltd. [AMEX symbol Toronto Stock Exchange symbol]
GOU.......... Oglethorpe University, Atlanta, GA [OCLC symbol] (OCLC)
Goucher C .. Goucher College (GAGS)
Goud Pand... Goudsmit's Pandects [Roman law] [A publication] (DLA)
Gould.......... Gouldsborough's English King's Bench Reports [A publication] (DLA)
Gould & T.... Gould and Tucker's Notes on Revised Statutes of United States [A publication] (DLA)
GouldP.......... Goulds Pumps, Inc. [Associated Press] (SAG)
Gould Pl ...... Gould on the Principles of Pleading in Civil Actions [A publication] (DLA)
Gouldsb .... Gouldsborough's English King's Bench Reports [A publication] (DLA)
Gouldsb (Eng)... Gouldsborough's English King's Bench Reports [A publication] (DLA)
Gould's Dig... Gould's Arkansas Digest of Laws [A publication] (DLA)
Gould Sten Rep... Gould's Stenographic Reporter [Monographic Series] [Albany, NY] [A publication] (DLA)
Gould Wat ... Gould on Waters [A publication] (DLA)
GOUPrA .... Gulf Can ResAdjcm Ser 1 Pref [NYSE symbol] (TTSB)
Gour.......... Gourick's Patent Digest [1889-91] [A publication] (DLA)

Gourl Gen Av... Gourlie on General Average [A publication] (DLA)
GOV .... Generator Output Voltage
GOV .... Global Government Plus Fund, Inc. [NYSE symbol] (SPSG)
GOV .... Golden Dividend Resources [Vancouver Stock Exchange symbol]
GOV .... Govalkot [India] [Seismograph station code, US Geological Survey Closed] (SEIS)
GOV .... Gove [Australia Airport symbol] (OAG)
GOV .... Govern (ROG)
GOV .... Government
gov.......... Government (VRA)
GOV .... Government-Owned Vehicle [GSA] (TAG)
GOV .... Governor (AFM)
gov.......... Governor (DD)
GOV .... Governor
GOVAIR.......... Government Aircraft (DNAB)
GOVAIRAUTHOUT... Travel via Government Aircraft Authorized Outside CONUS [Military]
GOVAIRAUTHVATL... Travel via Government Aircraft Authorized Outside CONUS Where Available [Military]
GOVAIRDIR... Travel via Government Aircraft Is Directed Where Necessary [Military]
GOVAIRDIROUT... Travel via Government Aircraft Is Directed Outside CONUS [Military]
GOVAIRDIRVAIL... Travel via Government Aircraft Is Directed Outside CONUS Where Available [Military]
GOVAIRPRI... Travel via Government Aircraft Outside CONUS Class _____ Priority Certified [Military]
GOVCOMLAIRAUTH... Travel via Government and/or Commercial Aircraft Authorized Where Necessary to Expedite Completion of Duty [Military]
GOVD.......... Governed (ROG)
GoVd.......... Go-Video, Inc. [Associated Press] (SAG)
Govett.......... Govett & Co. Ltd. [Associated Press] (SAG)
GOVG.......... Governing (MSA)
GoVideo.......... Go-Video, Inc. [Associated Press] (SAG)
GOV IS.......... Governor's Island [Massachusetts] (WDAA)
GOVMAR.......... Governor, Marshall Islands
GOVMERAIR... Government or Commercial Aircraft (DNAB)
GOVN.......... Govern (ROG)
Gov Ops.......... Government Operations Committee [House and Senate] (AAGC)
Govr.......... Governor
GOVS.......... Governments Division [Census] (OICC)
GOV STD ..... Government Standards
Gov St U ..... Governors State University (GAGS)
GOVT.......... Government (AFM)
govt.......... Government (DD)
GOVT.......... Government
GOVT.......... Govett & Co. Ltd. [NASDAQ symbol] (SAG)
Gov't Cont Rep... Government Contracts Reporter [Commerce Clearing House] [A publication] (DLA)
GOVTEL ...... Government Telegram (IAA)
GOVTHO ...... Government House [Canada] (DNAB)
GOVTL ...... Governmental
GOVTLAIRNOREUR... Commander, Allied Air Forces, Northern Europe
GOVTRANSDIROUT... Travel via Government Transportation Directed Outside CONUS [Military]
GOVTRANSDIRVAIL... Travel via Government Transportation Directed Outside CONUS Where Available [Military]
GOW .... Gowganda Resources, Inc. [Toronto Stock Exchange symbol Vancouver Stock Exchange symbol]
Gow .... Gow's English Nisi Prius Cases [171 English Reprint] [A publication] (DLA)
GOW .... Grand Old Woman [England's Queen Victoria]
GOW .... Gunnery Officer's Writer [Navy British]
GOWEX .... Geometry of the Wake Experiment [Military] (MCD)
GOWG .... Ground Operations Working Group (MCD)
GOWMA ...... Gulf Oil Wholesale Marketers Association (EA)
Gow NP ...... Gow's English Nisi Prius Cases [171 English Reprint] [A publication] (DLA)
Gow NP (Eng)... Gow's English Nisi Prius Cases [171 English Reprint] [A publication] (DLA)
GOWON .... Gulf Offshore Weather Observing Network (USDC)
GOWON .... Gulf Offshore Weather Observing Network [Marine science] (OSRA)
Gow Part .... Gow on Partnerships [A publication] (DLA)
GOWR .... Grand Order of Water Rats [British] (BI)
GOX .... Gaseous Oxygen
GOX .... Greenville, SC [Location identifier FAA] (FAAL)
GOY .... Gal Oya [Ceylon] [Airport symbol] (AD)
GOY .... Gorny [Former USSR Seismograph station code, US Geological Survey Closed] (SEIS)
GOY .... GWE [Global Weather Experiment] Operational Year [Marine science] (MSC)
GOYA.......... Get Off Your After-End [Slang Bowdlerized version]
GOYA.......... Greek Organisation of Young Australians
GOYA.......... Greek Orthodox Youth of America [Later, GOYAL] (EA)
GOYAL.......... Greek Orthodox Young Adult League (EA)
GOZ .... Gorna Orjachovica [Bulgaria] [Airport symbol] (OAG)
GP .... Albania [License plate code assigned to foreign diplomats in the US]
GP .... Ciba-Geigy AG [Switzerland] [Research code symbol]
GP .... Du Pont [E. I.] De Nemours & Co., Inc. [Research code symbol]
GP .... Galactic Plane [Astronomy]
GP .... Galactic Probe
GP .... Gallbladder Patient
GP .... Galley Proof (ADA)
GP .... Gallup Poll

GP	Galvanized Pipe [*Technical drawings*]
GP	Galvanized Plain [*Metal industry*]
GP	Games Played [*Sports statistics*]
GP	Gang Punch [*Computer science*]
GP	Gas, Persistent
GP	Gas-Plasma [*Computer display panel*]
GP	Gas Pressure (MUGU)
GP	Gas Projectile (MCD)
GP	Gastric Pressure [*Physiology*]
GP	Gastroplasty [*Medicine*]
GP	Gauge Pressure (IAA)
GP	Generalized Programming [*Computer science*]
GP	General Paralysis [*or Paresis*] [*Medicine*]
GP	General Pause [*Music*]
GP	General Plant Telephone [*Nuclear energy*] (NRCH)
GP	General Practice [*Medical specialty*] (DAVI)
GP	General Practitioner [*of medicine*]
GP	General Preferred Tariff [*Canada*]
GP	General Principles [*FBI standardized term*]
GP	General Processor
GP	General Product (BUR)
GP	General Protection [*Computer science*] (BYTE)
GP	General Provision
GP	General Public [*Merchandising slang*]
GP	General Publication (KSC)
GP	General Purpose
GP	General with Parents' Consent [*Motion picture rating*] (BARN)
GP	Genesis Project (EA)
GP	Genetic Prediabetes [*Endocrinology*]
GP	Geographical Pole
GP	Geographical Position
GP	Geographic Point
GP	Geometric Phase [*Mathematics*]
GP	Geometric Progression
GP	Georgia-Pacific [*NYSE symbol*] (TTSB)
GP	Georgia-Pacific Corp. [*NYSE symbol*] (SPSG)
GP	German Patent (IAA)
GP	Germinable Propagule [*Botany*]
GP	Giant Pulse
GP	Gimbal Package
GP	Gimbal Platform (AAG)
GP	Gimbal Point
GP	Girard-Point [*Virus*]
GP	Girls' PROUT [*Progressive Utilization Theory*] (EA)
GP	Glia Precursor [*Biochemistry*]
GP	Glide Path [*Aviation*]
GP	Gliomatosis Peritonei [*Oncology*]
GP	Globus Pallidus [*Brain anatomy*]
GP	Gloria Patri [*Glory to the Father*] [*Latin*]
GP	Glucose Phosphate [*Biochemistry*]
GP	Glutathione Peroxidase [*An enzyme*] (MAE)
GP	Glycerophosphate [*Biochemistry*]
GP	Glycogen Phosphorylase [*An enzyme*]
GP	Glycolyl Phthalate [*Organic chemistry*]
GP	Glycoprotein
GP	Goal Post
GP	Goal Programming
GP	Going Public [*Investment term*]
GP	Gold Points [*Investment term*]
GP	Goodpasture [*Syndrome*] [*Medicine*] (DAVI)
GP	Good Practice
GP	Government Property
GP	Government Publications [*Northern Territory, Australia*]
GP	Gozo Party [*Malta*] [*Political party*] (PPE)
GP	Grace Period [*Business term*]
G-p-ab	Graded Program
GP	Graduate in Pharmacy [*British*] (ROG)
GP	Gram-Positive [*Also, GRP*] [*Microbiology*]
GP	Grandmothers for Peace (EA)
GP	Grand Passion
GP	Grand Patron [*Freemasonry*]
GP	Grand Prelate [*Freemasonry*]
GP	Grand Prix
GP	Grand Pursuivant [*Freemasonry*] (ROG)
GP	Graphics Package [*Computer science*] (MHDI)
GP	Graphics Processor
G/P	Graphite Polyester
GP	Grass Pollen [*Immunology*]
GP	Gratitude Patient [*A nonpaying patient*] [*Medical slang*]
G/P	Gravida Para [*Gynecology and obstetrics*] (DAVI)
GP	Gravitational Redshift Space Probe [*Also, GRAVR*]
GP	Gray Panthers (EA)
GP	Great Peoples [*A publication*]
GP	Great Portland Street [*London*] (DSUE)
GP	Great Primer
GP	Greenhouse Perennial [*Horticulture*] (ROG)
GP	Greenpeace
G/P	Green Phone [*NASA*] (KSC)
GP	Grid Pulse (IAA)
GP	Gross Premium [*Insurance*] (AIA)
GP	Gross Profit [*Business term*]
GP	Ground Pneumatic (AAG)
GP	Ground Post (IAA)
GP	Ground-Protective [*Relay*]
GP	Ground Rods [*JETDS nomenclature*] [*Military*] (CET)
GP	Group (AFM)
gp	Group (VRA)
GP	Groupe de Paris [*France*] (EAIO)
GP	Growth in Total Profit (MHDB)
GP	Guadeloupe [*ANSI two-letter standard code*] (CNC)
gp	Guadeloupe [*MARC country of publication code Library of Congress*] (LCCP)
GP	Guidance Package
GP	Guided Projectile [*Military*] (CAAL)
GP	Guinea Pig
GP	Gun Pointer [*Naval gunnery*]
GP	Gun Program [*Military*] (MCD)
GP	Gutta-Percha [*Dentistry*] (MAE)
GP	Gutter Pair [*Philately*]
GP	GWEN [*Ground Wave Emergency Network*] Project (EA)
GP	Gyro Package
GP	Hadag Air Seebaederflug [*ICAO designator*] (AD)
GP	Parental Guidance Suggested [*Later, PG*] [*Movie rating*]
GPA	Ciba-Geigy Corp. [*Research code symbol*]
GPA	Gas Pressure Activator (MCD)
GPA	Gas Processors Association (EA)
GPA	Gate Pulse Amplifier [*Computer science*] (IAA)
GPA	Gay Press Association [*Later, GLPA*] (EA)
GPA	General Passenger Agent
GPA	General Public Assistance [*A form of public charity*]
GPA	General Purchasing Agency [*Allied German Occupation Forces*]
GPA	General-Purpose Amphibian [*Military vehicle*]
GPA	General-Purpose Amplifier
GPA	General-Purpose Analysis (IEEE)
GPA	General-Purpose Array
GPA	Georgians for Preservation Action [*An association*]
GPA	Geschichte der Perser und Araber zur Zeit der Sasaniden [*A publication*] (BJA)
GPa	Gigapascal [*SI unit of pressure*]
GPA	Global Program on AIDS [*Acquired Immune Deficiency Syndrome*] [*WHO*]
GPA	Glycerine Producers Association (EA)
GPA	Glycophorin A [*Biochemistry*]
GPA	Goat Producers Association [*British*] (DBA)
GPA	Gold Producers' Association [*Australia*]
GPA	Golpazari [*Turkey*] [*Also, GLP*] [*Seismograph station code, US Geological Survey*] (SEIS)
GPA	Government Property Administration (MCD)
GPA	Grade-Point Average [*Education*]
GPA	Graduation Pledge Alliance [*An association*] (EA)
GPA	Grandparents Anonymous (EA)
GPA	Graphical PERT [*Program Evaluation and Review Technique*] Analog [*Computer science*] (IEEE)
GPA	Graphics Philately Association (EA)
GPA	Graphics Preparatory Association (EA)
GPA	Green Party of Australia [*Political party*]
GPA	Greenpeace Australia
GPA	Green Peach Aphid [*Entomology*]
GPA	Grounded Plate Amplifier
GPA	Ground Plane Antenna
GPA	Group Practice Association [*Medicine*]
GPA	Guidance Platform Assembly [*Military*] (AABC)
GPA	Guidance Positioning Assembly
GPA	Guinea Pig Albumin
GPA	Guinness Peat Aviation [*Commercial firm British*]
GPA	Gulfcoast Pulpwood Association (EA)
GPA	Kingman Aviation, Inc. [*ICAO designator*] (FAAC)
GPA	United States Government Printing Office - Serials, Alexandria, VA [*OCLC symbol*] (OCLC)
GPAA	Gold Prospectors Association of America (EA)
g-p-ab	Gravida, Para, and Abortus [*Gynecology and obstetrics*] (DAVI)
GPABP	Guinea Pig Anti-Bovine Protection (OA)
GPAC	General-Purpose Analog Computer (DEN)
GPAC	Graphics Package [*Computer science*] (MHDI)
GPAC	Great Plains Agricultural Council (EA)
GPACK	General Utility Package (MHDB)
GPAD	Gallons per Acre per Day [*Irrigation*]
GPAD	Graphics Program for Aircraft Design
GPADS	Guided Parafoil Aerial Delivery System
GPADS-L	Delivery System-Light [*Army*] (INF)
GPAIS	Guinea Pig Anti-Insulin Serum [*Immunochemistry*] (MAE)
GPALS	Global Protection against Limited Strike [*Military*]
GPAM	General-Purpose Armor Machine Gun
GPAM	Graduated-Payment Adjustable Mortgage
GPAP	General Purpose Associative Processor (PDAA)
GPAR	General Parametrics Corp. [*NASDAQ symbol*] (NQ)
GPARM	Graduated-Payment Adjustable-Rate Mortgage (WDAA)
GPAS	General Performance Appraisals System
GPAS	General Product Acceptance Standard [*Automotive engineering*]
GPAS	General-Purpose Airborne Simulator
GPAT	General-Purpose Automatic Test [*Air Force*]
GPATE	General-Purpose Automatic Test Equipment [*Army*] (MSA)
GPATS	General-Purpose Automatic Test Set [*Air Force*] (IAA)
GPATS	General-Purpose Automatic Test Station
GPATS	General-Purpose Automatic Test System [*Air Force*]
GPAVTS	Great Planes Area Vocational Technical School [*Oklahoma*]
GPAX	General Purpose Automation Executive [*IBM*] (NITA)
GPAY	General Payments System
GPB	General Purchasing Board
GPB	General Purpose Basic [*Programming language*] (NITA)

GPB .... General-Purpose Buffer
GPB .... Geon Process Butadiene
GPB .... Glossopharyngeal Breathing
GPB .... Glucose Phosphorylase B [*An enzyme*]
GPB .... Glycoprotein B [*Biochemistry*]
GPB .... Government Patents Board [*Functions transferred to Secretary of Commerce, 1961*]
GP-B .... Gravity Probe-B [*Experiment to test Einstein's Theory of General Relativity*]
GPB .... Ground Power Breaker [*Electronics*] (OA)
GPB .... Pittsburgh, PA [*Location identifier FAA*] (FAAL)
GPBIM .... General-Purpose Buffer Interface Module [*Computer science*] (MCD)
GPBP .... Guinea Pig Myelin Basic Protein [*Immunochemistry*]
GPBS .... Gas Pressure Bending System
GPBTO .... General-Purpose Barbed Tape Obstacle [*Army*] (RDA)
GPC .... Gallons per Capita
GPC .... Gandhi Peace Center (EA)
GPC .... Gastric Parietal Cell [*Cytology*] (AAMN)
GPC .... Gastrointestinal Pathology Club [*Later, GPS*] (EA)
GPC .... Gauge Pressure Control
GPC .... Gay People at Columbia [*Later, CGLA*] (EA)
GPC .... Gel Permeation Chromatography
GPC .... General People's Congress [*or Committee*] [*Libya*] [*Political party*] (PPW)
GPC .... General People's Congress [*Yemen*] [*Political party*] (EY)
GPC .... General Peripheral Controller
GPC .... General Physical Condition [*Medicine*]
GPC .... General Precision Connector (IAA)
GPC .... General-Purpose Carrier [*Military*]
GPC .... General-Purpose Computer
GPC .... General Purposes Committee [*British*] (DCTA)
GPC .... Genuine Parts [*NYSE symbol*] (TTSB)
GPC .... Genuine Parts Co. [*NYSE symbol*] (SPSG)
GPC .... Geocentric Pendulum Control
GPC .... Georgia Peanut Commission (EA)
gpc............. Germanium Point-Contact (IDOE)
GPC. .... Ghana Publishing Co.
GPC .... Giant Papillary Conjunctivitis [*Ophthalmology*]
GPC .... Giant Piston Core [*Geology*]
GPC .... Glass-Polymer Composite (PDAA)
GPC .... Global Plotting Chart [*Air Force*]
GPC .... Global Processing Center (EERA)
GPC .... Glycerylphosphorylcholine [*Biochemistry*]
GPC .... Golay Pneumatic Cell
GPC .... Government Publications Center (SAA)
GPC .... Government Purpose Classification
GPC .... Gram-Positive Cocci [*Immunology*] (DAVI)
GPC .... Grande Prairie Regional College Library [*UTLAS symbol*]
GPC .... Granular Progenitor Cell [*Medicine*] (DMAA)
GPC .... Graphical Picture Drawing Language [*Computer science*] (PDAA)
GPC .... Grass Pollen Count [*Immunology*]
GPC .... Great Plains Coliseum [*Lawton, OK*]
GPC .... Gross Profit Contribution
GPC .... Ground Power Contactor
GPC .... Guinea Pig Complement [*Immunochemistry*]
GPC. .... Gulf Publishing Co.
GPC .... Gypsum-Plaster Ceiling [*Technical drawings*]
GPCA .... General-Purpose Communications Adapter
GPCA .... Golf Products and Components Association [*Defunct*] (EA)
GPCA .... Great Pyrenees Club of America (EA)
Gp Capt .... Group Captain [*British military*] (DMA)
GPCB .... General-Purpose Communications Base (MHDB)
GPCB .... GOAL [*Ground Operations Aerospace Language*] Program Control Block (MCD)
GPCC .... Global Precipitation Climatology Center [*Marine science*] (OSRA)
GPCC .... Global Precipitation Climatology Centre (EERA)
GPCC .... Grand Prix Contact Club [*British*] (DBA)
GPCD .... Gallons per Capita per Day
GPCE .... Groupement Pharmaceutique de la CE [*Pharmaceutical Group of the EC*] (ECED)
GPC-ERR ..... General Passenger Committee - Eastern Railroads [*Defunct*] (EA)
GPCF .... General-Purpose Computing Facility (MHDB)
GPCI .... Geographic Practice Cost Index [*Medicare*]
GPCL .... General-Purpose Closed Loop [*Nuclear energy*] (NRCH)
GP CMDR ... Group Commander [*Military*] (WDAA)
GPCO .... Global Perspective Country Outlooks [*Global Perspective, Inc.*] [*Information service or system*] (CRD)
GPCOC .... General-Purpose Central Office Concentrator [*Telecommunications*]
GPCP .... Generalized Process Control Programming [*Computer science*] (IEEE)
GPCP .... General-Purpose Contouring Program
GPCP .... General-Purpose Controller Processor (IAA)
GPCP .... Global Precipitation Chemistry Project [*Study of rain properties*]
GPCP .... Global Precipitation Climatology Project [*Marine science*] (OSRA)
GPCP .... Great Plains Conservation Program
GPCR .... Gas-to-Particle Conversion Rate [*Physics*]
GPCR .... G-Protein-Coupled Receptor [*Biochemistry*]
GPCR .... Great Proletarian Cultural Revolution [*People's Republic of China*]
GPcRE .... Great Pacific Real Estate Investment Trust, Inc. [*Associated Press*] (SAG)
GPCS .... General-Purpose Control System (IAA)
GPCS .... Guinea Pig Control Serum (OA)
GPCT .... George Peabody College for Teachers [*Later, George Peabody College for Teachers of Vanderbilt University*] [*Tennessee*]
GPD .... Gallons per Day

GPD .... General Pair Decomposition (IAA)
GPD .... General Passenger Department
GPD .... General Police Duties [*British military*] (DMA)
GPD .... General Political Department [*China*] [*Military*]
GPD .... General Protocol Driver (NITA)
GPD .... General-Purpose Data
GPD .... General-Purpose Discipline [*IBM Corp.*]
GPD .... Generals for Peace and Disarmament [*Ittervoort, Netherlands*] (EAIO)
GPD .... Gimbal Position Display (KSC)
GPD .... Glass Plasma Display [*Electronics*] (BARN)
GPD .... Glucose-6-phosphate Dehydrogenase [*Also, G6PD, G6PDH*] [*An enzyme*]
GPD .... Glycerophosphate Dehydrogenase
GPD .... Graduate Performance Diploma (PGP)
GPD .... Grams per Denier
GPD .... Greenpond [*New Jersey*] [*Seismograph station code, US Geological Survey*] (SEIS)
GPDA .... Grand Prix Drivers' Association
GPDA .... Gypsum Plasterboard Development Association [*British*] (BI)
GPDA .... Gypsum Products Development Association [*British*] (DBA)
GPDC .... Generalized Pressure Drop Correlation [*Chemical engineering*]
GPDC .... General-Purpose Digital Computer
GPDH .... Glycerolphosphate Dehydrogenase [*An enzyme*]
GPDM .... Geopotential Decameter [*Telecommunications*] (TEL)
GPDS .... General-Purpose Discrete Simulator (MHDI)
GPDS .... General-Purpose Display System
GPDSC .... Girl's Public Day School Co. [*British*] (ROG)
GPDST .... Girls' Public Day School Trust [*British*]
GPDU .... Groupe de Planification des Derives Urbaines [*Canada*]
GPDW .... Glacial Pacific Deep Water
GPDW .... Gypsum Dry Wall [*Technical drawings*]
GPE .... Gas Power Exchange
GPE .... General Precision Equipment (IAA)
GPE .... General-Purpose English (ADA)
GPE .... General-Purpose Equipment
GPE .... General-Purpose Evaporator [*Nuclear energy*] (NRCH)
GPE .... Geometric Position Error (MCD)
Gp E .... Geophysical Engineer
GPE .... Georgia Power Capital LP [*NYSE symbol*] (SAG)
GPE .... Georgia Power Capital Trust I [*NYSE symbol*] (SAG)
GPE .... Georgia Power Co. [*NYSE symbol*] (SPSG)
GPE .... Global Perspectives in Education (EA)
GPE .... Glycerylphosphorylethanolamine [*Biochemistry*] (MAE)
GPE .... Golden Pheasant [*Vancouver Stock Exchange symbol*]
GPE .... Government Preliminary Evaluation (MCD)
GPE .... GP Express Airlines, Inc. [*ICAO designator*] (FAAC)
GPE .... Grammaire du Palmyrenien Epigraphique [*A publication*] (BJA)
GPE .... Granulocyte Colony-Stimulating Factor Promoter Element (DMAA)
GPE .... Gravitational Potential Energy [*Geophysics*]
GPE .... Guinea Pig Embryo [*Medicine*] (DMAA)
GPE .... Los Angeles, CA [*Location identifier FAA*] (FAAL)
Gp Engr .... Geophysical Engineer
GPEP .... General Professional Education of the Physician [*Panel report*] [*Association of American Medical Colleges*]
GPEPr .... Georgia Pwr $7.72Pfd [*NYSE symbol*] (TTSB)
GPEPrB .... Georgia Pwr $7.80 Pfd [*NYSE symbol*] (TTSB)
GPEPrP .... Georgia Pwr $1.90'A'Pfd [*NYSE symbol*] (TTSB)
GPEPrQ .... Georgia Pwr $1.9875 'A' Pfd [*NYSE symbol*] (TTSB)
GPEPrR .... Georgia Pwr $1.9375'A'Pfd [*NYSE symbol*] (TTSB)
GPEPrS .... Georgia Pwr $1.925'A'Pfd [*NYSE symbol*] (TTSB)
GPER .... Gas Projectile, Extended Range (MCD)
GPER .... General Plant Equipment Requirements
GPERF .... Ground Passive Electronic Reconnaissance Facility
GPES .... Ground Proximity Extraction System
G Pet .... Gospel of Peter [*Apocryphal work*]
GPET .... Graphic Plan Evaluation Tool (DMAA)
GPETE .... General-Purpose Electronic Test Equipment (NVT)
GPEXS .... General Parts Explosion System (IAA)
GPF .... Gallons per Flush [*Plumbing*]
GPF .... Gandhi Peace Foundation [*India*] (EAIO)
GPF .... Gas Proof (AABC)
GPF .... Generalized Production Function [*Industrial economics*]
GPF .... General Protection Fault [*Computer programming*] (BYTE)
GPF .... General-Purpose Forces
GPF .... Glomerular Plasma Flow [*Medicine*] (DMAA)
GPF .... Grains per Foot
GPF .... Grande Puissance Filloux [*World War II*]
GPF .... Granulocytosis-Promoting Factor [*Hematology*]
GPF .... Groove between Parallel Folds
GPF .... Guardian Pacific Rim Corp. [*Toronto Stock Exchange symbol*]
GPF .... Guinea Pig Fibrinogen
GPF............. GUI [*Graphical User Interface*] Programming Facility [*Computer science*]
GPFC .... Galaxy Patrol Fan Club (EA)
GPFC .... Gene Pitney Fan Club (EA)
GPFC .... General-Purpose Function Code (NVT)
GPFI .... Grand Premier Financial, Inc. [*NASDAQ symbol*] (SAG)
GPFL .... Group Flashing [*Navigation signal lights*]
GPFLL .... Group Flashing Light [*Navigation*] (IAA)
GPFS .... General-Purpose Financial Statement (WDAA)
GPFS .... Greater Pacific Financial Services [*Australia*]
GPFU .... Gas Particulate Filter Unit (MCD)
GPG .... Gate Pulse Generator (IAA)
GPG .... General Planning Group

GPG............ Grains per Gallon [Unit of measure for water hardness]
GPG............ Grams per Gallon (GNE)
GPG............ Grande Portage [Vancouver Stock Exchange symbol]
GPG............ Ground Power Generator (DWSG)
GPG............ Guinness Peat Group [British]
GPGA........... Georgia Pecan Growers Association (SRA)
GPGA........... Georgia Propane Gas Association (SRA)
GP (Gas)..... Persistent Chemical Agent Gas
GPGG........... Guinea Pig Gamma Globulin [Immunochemistry]
GPGL........... General-Purpose Graphic Language [Computer science] (IEEE)
GPGS........... Government Purchases of Goods and Services [BTS] (TAG)
GPGS........... Ground Power Generator System (DWSG)
GPH............ Gallons per Hour
GPH............ General Physics Corp. [NYSE symbol] (SPSG)
GPH............ Genl Physics [NYSE symbol] (TTSB)
G Ph.......... Graduate in Pharmacy
GPH............ Graphite (MSA)
GPH............ Green Party of Hungary [Political party] (EAIO)
GPH............ Grenzpolizeihelfer [Border Police Aide] [German]
GPHA........... Great Plains Historical Association [Later, IGP] (EA)
GPHF.......... General Pulaski Heritage Foundation (EA)
GPHLV......... Guinea Pig Herpes-Like Virus [Medicine] (DMAA)
GPHMG......... General-Purpose Heavy Machine Gun (MCD)
GPHMO......... Group Practice Health Maintenance Organization [Insurance] (WYGK)
GPHN........... Giant Pigmented Hairy Nevus (DMAA)
GPHP.......... Give Peace Holiday Project (EA)
GPHS........... General-Purpose Heat Source [Nuclear energy]
GPHSC........ Group Project for Holocaust Survivors and Their Children (EA)
GPHV.......... Guinea Pig Herpes Virus (DMAA)
GPHW.......... Gay Public Health Workers Caucus [Later, LGCPHW] (EA)
GPI............ General Paralysis of the Insane [Literal translation, but also medical slang for eccentricity]
GPI............ General Patents Index [A publication]
GPI............ General Periodicals Index [Information Access Co.] [Information service or system] (CRD)
GPI............ General Precision, Inc.
GPI............ General Price Index (WDAA)
GPI............ General Printing Ink (DGA)
GPI............ General-Purpose Interface
GPI............ General-Purpose Inverter (KSC)
GPI............ Gimbal Position Indicator (KSC)
GPI............ Gingival-Periodontal Index [Dentistry]
GPI............ Glass Packaging Institute (EA)
GPI............ Glide Path Indicator [Aviation] (NATG)
GPI............ Glucophosphate Isomerase [An enzyme]
GPI............ Glycoprotein I (DMAA)
GPI............ Glycosyl-Phosphatidylinositol [Biochemistry]
GPI............ GOES [Geostationary Operational Environmental Satellite] Precipitation Index [Marine science] (OSRA)
GPI............ Gordon Personal Inventory [Psychology]
GPI............ Government Preliminary Inspection (MCD)
GPI............ Grain Products Irradiator [Nuclear energy]
GPI............ Graphics Programming Interface [IBM Corp.] (PCM)
GPI............ Great Pacific Industries, Inc. [Toronto Stock Exchange symbol Vancouver Stock Exchange symbol]
GPI............ Greenpeace International [Netherlands] (EAIO)
GPI............ Grocery Prices Index [British]
GPI............ Ground Point of Impact
GPI............ Ground Point of Intercept (AFM)
GPI............ Ground Position Indicator [Dead-reckoning computer]
GPI............ Guapi [Colombia] [Airport symbol] (OAG)
GPI............ Guardsman Products, Inc. [NYSE symbol] (SPSG)
GPI............ Guinea Pig Ileum (DMAA)
GPIA........... General-Purpose Interface Adapter (IEEE)
GPIA........... General Purpose Interface Adaptor (NITA)
GPIA........... Generic Pharmaceutical Industry Association (EA)
GPIB........... General-Purpose Instrument Bus (IAA)
GPIB........... General-Purpose Interface Bus [Computer science]
GPIB........... General Purpose Interface Bus
GPIC........... General-Purpose Intelligent Cable (MHDB)
GPIC........... General-Purpose Intercomputer [Test] (NVT)
GPID........... Guidance Package Installation Dolly [Polaris missile]
GPIEM......... International Marine Environment Award [Marine science] (OSRA)
GPII........... Geist Picture Interest Inventory [Psychology] (AEBS)
GPIMH........ Guinea Pig Intestinal Mucosal Homogenate (MAE)
GPIO........... General-Purpose Input/Output [Computer science]
GPIP........... Glide Path Intercept Point [Aviation]
GPIPID....... Guinea Pig Intraperitoneal Infectious Dose [Clinical chemistry] (MAE)
GPIS........... Gemini Problem Investigation Status [NASA] (IEEE)
GPIS........... Groundwater Pumping Incentives Scheme [Victoria] (EERA)
GPJ............ Great Peace Journey [Sweden] (EAIO)
GPK............ Gentleman's Pocket Knife
GPK............ Goldpac Investments Ltd. [Vancouver Stock Exchange symbol]
GPK............ Guinea Pig Kidney Antigen [Immunochemistry] (MAE)
GPKA........... Guinea Pig Kidney Absorption (Test) [Clinical chemistry]
GPKD........... General-Purpose Keyboard and Display Control [Computer science] (MDG)
GPKT.......... Grand Priory of the Knights of the Temple [Freemasonry]
GPL............ Gallahad Petroleum [Vancouver Stock Exchange symbol]
GPL............ Generalized Programming Language [Computer science]
GPL............ General Precision Laboratory
GPL............ General Price Level (ADA)
GPL............ General Public License (NHD)
GPL............ General-Purpose Laboratory (KSC)

GPL............ General-Purpose Language [Computer science] (CSR)
GPL............ General Purpose Loader (NITA)
GPL............ General-Purpose Loop [Nuclear energy] (NRCH)
GPL............ Geographic Position Locator [Navigation]
GPL............ Giant Pulse LASER
GPL............ Gimbal Pickoff Loop
GPL............ GOAL [Ground Operations Aerospace Language] Processing Language (MCD)
GPL............ Gravatom Projects Ltd. [British] (IRUK)
GPL............ Group Processing Logic (TEL)
GPL............ Guapiles [Costa Rica] [Airport symbol] (OAG)
GPL............ Guymon Public Library, Guymon, OK [OCLC symbol] (OCLC)
GPL............ Gypsum Lathe [Technical drawings]
GPLA........... General Price Level Accounting (ADA)
GPLA........... General Price-Level Adjusted [Finance] (PDAA)
GPLAN......... Generalized Database Planning System
GPLB.......... Grand Prix Association of Long Beach [NASDAQ symbol] (SAG)
GPLC.......... Guild of Professional Launderers and Cleaners [British] (BI)
GPLD.......... Government Property Lost or Damaged [or Destroyed]
GPLE.......... Global Program Line Editor [Beagle Bros.]
GPLI........... Group-Page-Line-Inserts (MCD)
GPLP.......... General-Purpose Linear Programming [Computer science] (IEEE)
GPLR.......... Government-Purpose License Rights (AAGC)
GPLRG......... Gay Parents Legal and Research Group [Defunct] (EA)
GPLS........... Giant Pulse LASER System
GPLS........... Glide Path Landing System [Aviation] (IAA)
GPLY.......... Gingivoplasty [Dentistry]
GPM........... Gallons per Mile
GPM........... Gallons per Minute
GPM........... Gas-Permeable Membrane
GPM........... Gas Plasma Monitor
GPM........... General Preventive Medicine
GPM........... General-Purpose Macrogenerator [Computer science] (IEEE)
GPM........... General-Purpose Maneuver
GPM........... General-Purpose Missile
GPM........... General-Purpose Module (MHDB)
GPM........... Geopotential Meter
GPM........... Georgia Southern College, Statesboro, GA [OCLC symbol] (OCLC)
GPM........... Gepanzerte Pioniermaschine [Armored Engineer Vehicle] [General Electric Co.] [German] (MCD)
GPM........... Giant Pigmented Melanosome [Medicine] (DMAA)
GPM........... Goettinger Predigt-Meditationen [A publication] (BJA)
GPM........... Gradient Pump Module
GPM........... Graduated Payment Mortgage [Sometimes referred to as "Jeep"]
GPM........... Grams per Mile
GPM........... Grand Past Master [Freemasonry]
GPM........... Grand Prairie, TX [Location identifier FAA] (FAAL)
GPM........... Graphics Postprocessor Module [McDonnell-Douglas Corp.]
GPM........... Grey Power Movement [Australia]
GPM........... Gross Processing Margin (MHDB)
GPM........... Gross Profit Margin (WDAA)
GPM........... Ground Potential Model [Physics]
GPM........... Groups [of code transmitted] per Minute [or Message] [Telecommunications]
GPM........... Gunnery Prize Money [British military] (DMA)
GPMA.......... Gasoline Pump Manufacturers Association (EA)
GPMAL......... Gravida, Para, Multiple Births, Abortions, Live Births [Obstetrics]
GPMC.......... Grocery Products Manufacturers of Canada [See also FCPA]
GPMC.......... Group and Pension Marketing Conference [LIMRA]
GPME.......... Gas-Porous Membrane Electrode [Electrochemistry]
GPME.......... General-Purpose Mission Equipment (NASA)
GPMF.......... Gram Parsons Memorial Foundation (EA)
GPMFGND ... Great Peace March for Global Nuclear Disarmament [Defunct] (EA)
GPMG.......... General-Purpose Machine Gun [Military]
GPMH.......... Good Practices in Mental Health (PDAA)
GPMMA........ Grain Processing Machinery Manufacturers Association (EA)
GPMR.......... Gallons Per Mile Ratio [DOE] (TAG)
GPMS.......... Galileo Probe Mass Spectrometer
GPMS.......... General-Purpose Microprogram Simulator [Computer science] (IEEE)
GPMS.......... General-Purpose Multiplex System [Aviation]
GPMS.......... Gross Performance Measuring System [Air Force]
GPMU.......... Graphical, Paper and Media Union [British]
GPN........... Garden Point [Australia Airport symbol] (OAG)
GPN........... General Performance Number
GPN........... Glass Plate Negative
GPN........... Gold-Pan Resources, Inc. [Vancouver Stock Exchange symbol]
GPN........... Government Packet Network [Canada]
GPN........... Graduate Practical Nurse
GPN........... Grey Power News [Australia A publication]
GPNITL....... Great Plains National Instructional Television Library
GPO........... Gemini Program [or Project] Office [NASA] (KSC)
GPO........... General Periodicals Ondisc [Database]
GPO........... General Pico [Argentina] [Airport symbol] (OAG)
GPO........... General Post Office [British Defunct]
GPO........... General Practitioner Obstetrician
GPO........... General-Purpose Oscilloscope
GPO........... General-Purpose Outlet (ADA)
GPO........... General-Purpose Output [Space Flight Operations Facility, NASA]
GPO........... Genprobe Tech [Vancouver Stock Exchange symbol]
GPO........... GIANT Group [NYSE symbol] (TTSB)
GPO........... Giant Group Ltd. [NYSE symbol] (SPSG)
GPO........... Government Printing Office
GPO........... Granulopoietin [Hypothetical substance] [Hematology]
GPO........... Gross Product Originating [Department of Transportation]
GPO........... Guaranteed Purchase Option [Insurance]

GPO .... Gunner's Primary Optics (MCD)
GPO .... Gun Position Officer (NATG)
GPO .... Library of Congress, Government Printing Office [Source file] [UTLAS symbol]
GPO .... Portland, OR [Location identifier FAA] (FAAL)
GPO .... United States Government Printing Office, Alexandria, VA [OCLC symbol] (OCLC)
GPOA .... Guild of Prescription Opticians of America [Later, OAA] (EA)
GPOA .... Gun Position Officer's Assistant [British military] (DMA)
GPOB .... Government Printing Office Bookstore (OICC)
GPOCC .... Group Occulting Lights [Navigation signal]
Gp Offr .... Group Officer [British military] (DMA)
GpoImsa ...... Groupo Imsa Sa de CV [Associated Press] (SAG)
GpoRadio .... Grupo Radio Centro [Associated Press] (SAG)
GPOS .... General-Purpose Operating System
GPP .... Gambia People's Party [Political party] (EY)
GPP .... Generalized Post-Processor
GPP .... General Plant Project
GPP .... General Print and Punch (NITA)
GPP .... General Purchasing Power [Accounting]
GPP .... General Purpose Processor (MHDI)
GPP .... General-Purpose Programming [Computer science]
GPP .... Giant Pacific Petroleums, Inc. [Vancouver Stock Exchange symbol]
GPP .... Glycosylated Plasma Protein [Clinical chemistry]
GPP .... Goal Programming Problem
GPP .... Gordon Personal Profile [Psychology]
GPP .... Graphic Part Programmer (PDAA)
GPP .... Gross Primary Productivity
GPP .... Ground Power Panel
GPP .... Guarapuava [Brazil] [Airport symbol] (AD)
GPP .... Guild of Pastoral Psychology [British] (DBA)
GPP .... Guild of Public Pharmacists [British] (BI)
GPP .... Gyro Pitch Position
GPPA .... Georgia Peanut Producers Association (SRA)
GPPA .... Georgia Pork Producers Association (SRA)
GPPA .... Georgia Psychiatric Physicians Association (SRA)
GPPA .... Government Patent Policy Act [1981]
GPPAW .... Glass, Pottery, Plastics, and Allied Workers International Union (EA)
GPPB .... Gemini Program Planning Board [NASA] (KSC)
GPPB .... Government Procurement Practices Board [Proposed]
GPP-I .... Gordon Personal Profile and Inventory [Personality development test] [Psychology]
GPPIPCEE .... Groupement Professionel des Pharmaciens de l'Industrie Pharmaceutique de la CEE [Professional Grouping of Pharmacists of the Pharmaceuticals Industry of the EEC] (ECED)
GPPL .... Gypsum Plaster [Technical drawings]
gppm .... Graphics Pages per Minute [Printer technology] (PCM)
GPPQ .... General-Purpose Psychiatric Questionnaire
GPPS .... General Provisions Policy Statement (MCD)
GPPT .... Group Personality Projective Test [Psychology]
GPPV .... Graff Pay per View [NASDAQ symbol] (SAG)
GPQ .... Carrollton, GA [Location identifier FAA] (FAAL)
GPR .... General-Purpose RADAR (MCD)
GPR .... General-Purpose Radiometer
GPR .... General-Purpose Receiver
GPR .... General-Purpose Register [Computer science] (MDG)
GPR .... General-Purpose Relay
GPR .... General-Purpose Representative
GPR .... Genio Populi Romani [To the Genius of the Roman People] [Latin]
GPR .... Glider Pilot Regiment [Military unit] [British]
GPR .... Golden Pyramid Resources, Inc. [Vancouver Stock Exchange symbol]
GPR .... Government Plant Representative
GPR .... Government Property Register [of New South Wales] [State] (EERA)
GPR .... Government Purpose Rights (AAGC)
GPR .... Grain-Burning Pattern Regulation (MCD)
GPR .... Gran Premio Romeo [Alfa Romeo race car] [Italian]
GPR .... Great Pacific Real Estate Investment Trust, Inc. [AMEX symbol] (SAG)
GPR .... Ground-Penetrating RADAR
GPRA .... General Practice Reform Association [Medicine] (DAVI)
GPRA .... Gouvernement Provisoire de la Republique Algerienne [Provisional Government of the Algerian Republic]
GPRA .... Govenment Performance and Results Act [1993]
GPRA .... Government Performance and Results Act [1993] (RDA)
GPRA .... Government Public Relations Association [Defunct]
GPRC .... Geophysical and Polar Research Center [University of Wisconsin]
GPrcl .... General Parcel Service, Inc. [Associated Press] (SAG)
GPRF-G .... General-Purpose Rocket Furnace - Gradient
GPRF-I .... General-Purpose Rocket Furnace - Isothermal
GPRG .... Gadsden Purchase Refund Group [Formerly, PRI] [Defunct] (EA)
GPRL .... Giant Pulse Ruby LASER (IAA)
GPRL .... Gulf Puerto Rico Lines [Steamship] (MHDB)
GPRMC .... Groupement des Plastiques Renforces et Materiaux Composites [Organization of Reinforced Plastics and Composite Materials] (EAIO)
GPRN .... GOAL [Ground Operations Aerospace Language] Test Procedure Release Notice [NASA] (NASA)
GPRP .... Government Production and Research Property (SSD)
GPRR .... General-Purpose Radio Receiver
GPRS .... General Parent Ring System [Proposed chemical classification]
GPRS .... General Plumbing & Roofing Services [Commercial firm] [British]
GPRSS .... General-Purpose Remote Sensor System (PDAA)
GPRT .... General-Purpose Radio Transmitter
GPRT .... Guanine Phosphoribosyltransferase [An enzyme]

GPS .... Galapagos Islands [Ecuador] [Airport symbol] (OAG)
GPS .... Gallons per Second
GPS .... Gap, Inc. [Formerly, Gap Stores, Inc.] [NYSE symbol] (SPSG)
GPS .... Gastrointestinal Pathology Society (EA)
GPS .... Gauge Pressure Switch
GPS .... Generality and Problem Solving
GPS .... Generalized Preference Scheme [Tariff policy]
GPS .... General Pavement Studies [FHWA] (TAG)
GPS .... General Problem Solver [Computer science]
GPS .... General Processing Subsystem (MCD)
GPS .... General Process Simulator
GPS .... General-Purpose Shelter
GPS .... General-Purpose Simulation [Formerly, Systems Simulator] [IBM Corp.] [Computer science] (IAA)
GPS .... Generic Processing System [Computer science] (TEL)
GPS .... Germany Philatelic Society (EA)
GPS .... GigaBIT [Binary Digits] per Second [Transmission rate] [Computer science]
GPS .... Global Positioning Satellite
GPS .... Global Positioning System [Formerly, NAVSTAR] [Air Force]
GPS .... Global Position System [Instrument] (EERA)
GPS .... Global Precision System
GPS .... Goodpasture's Syndrome [Medicine] (DAVI)
GPS .... Government Paper Specification Standards
GPS .... Government Procurement Service
GPS .... Graduated Pension Scheme [British] (BARN)
GPS .... Grams per Second
GPS .... Grand Past Sojourner [Freemasonry] (ROG)
GPS .... Grand Principal Sojourner [Freemasonry]
GPS .... Graphic Programming Services [Computer science] (IBMDP)
GPS .... Gray Platelet Syndrome [Medicine] (DMAA)
GPS .... Ground Plane Simulator
GPS .... Ground Power Supply [NASA] (NASA)
GPS .... Ground Processing Simulation (MCD)
GPS .... Ground Processing System [Aviation]
GPS .... Ground Proximity Sensor
GPS .... Ground Water Protection Strategy [Environmental Protection Agency] (GFGA)
GPS .... Groups of Pulses per Second (DEN)
GPS .... Guidance Power Supply
GPS .... Guinea Pig Serum
GPS .... Guinea Pig Spleen
GPS .... Gunner's Primary Sight (MCD)
GPS .... Gyroscope Parameter Shift
GPSA .... Gas Processors Suppliers Association (EA)
GPSA .... Global Positioning System-Active
GPSC .... Gas Proportional Scintillation Counters [Spectroscopy]
GPSC .... Guinea Pig Spinal Cord
GPSCO .... Global Position System Consortium (EERA)
GPSCS .... General-Purpose Satellite Communication System (MCD)
GPSDIC .... General-Purpose Scientific Document Image Code [System] [National Institute of Standards and Technology]
GPSDW .... General-Purpose Scientific Document Writer [National Institute of Standards and Technology]
GPSE .... General-Purpose Simulation Environment [Computer science]
GPSE .... Gunner's Primary Sight Extension
GPSG .... Generalized Phrase Structure Grammar [Artificial intelligence]
GPSIM .... Global Position System Integrity Monitoring [System] (EERA)
GPS/INS ...... Global Positioning System/Inertial Navigation System [Air Force]
GPSL .... General-Purpose Simulation Language [Computer science] (IAA)
GPSN .... General-Purpose Packet Satellite Network (MHDI)
GPS NCC ..... Global Positioning System Network Control Center [Air Force] (MCD)
GPSP .... General-Purpose Signal Processor
GPSP .... General-Purpose Software Program [Computer science]
GPSP .... General-Purpose String Processor (IAA)
GPSP .... Global Positioning System-Passive
GPS PC .... Global Positioning System Program Contractor [Air Force] (MCD)
GPSS .... General [or Generic] Problem Statement Simulator
GPSS .... General Process Simulation Studies
GPSS .... General-Purpose Simulation System [formerly, Systems Simulator] [IBM Corp. 1961] [Computer science]
GPSS .... General Purpose System Simulator (NITA)
GPSS .... Global Positioning Satellite System
GPSSM .... General-Purpose Surface-to-Surface Missile [Army]
GPSU .... Ground Power Supply Unit [NASA] (AAG)
GPSX .... General Parcel Service, Inc. [NASDAQ symbol] (NQ)
GPSX .... Genl Parcel Service [NASDAQ symbol] (TTSB)
GPSXW .... General Parcel Svc Wrrt [NASDAQ symbol] (TTSB)
GPT .... Gallons per Ton
GPT .... Gas Phase Titration
GPT .... Gas Power Transfer
GPT .... Gas Power Transfer (IEEE)
GPT .... GEC Plessey Telecommunications [British] (ECON)
GPT .... Gemini Pad Test [NASA] (KSC)
GPT .... General Perturbation Theory [Nuclear science]
GPT .... General Plant Telephone [Nuclear energy] (GFGA)
GPT .... General Preferred Tariff [Canada]
GPT .... General-Purpose Terminal
GPT .... General-Purpose Thermoplastic [Insulation]
GPT .... General-Purpose Tool
GPT .... General-Purpose Transport [British military] (DMA)
GPT .... Geometric and Positional Tolerance [Drafting symbol]
GPT .... Glass Precision Tubing
GPT .... Glass Probe Thermistor
GPT .... Glutamic-Pyruvic Transaminase [Also, AAT, ALAT, ALT] [An enzyme]

GPT............ Goldpost Resources, Inc. [Toronto Stock Exchange symbol]
GPT............ Governor Phillip Tower [Sydney, New South Wales, Australia]
GPT............ Grayson Perceptualization Test [Psychology]
GPT............ Greenpoint Financial Corp. [NYSE symbol] (SAG)
GPT............ Greenpoint Finl [NYSE symbol] (TTSB)
GPT............ Grid Pool Tank
GPT............ Group Projective Test [Psychology] (BARN)
GPT............ Guidance Position Tracking [Aerospace] (AAG)
GPT............ Gulfport/Biloxi [Mississippi] [Airport symbol] (OAG)
GPT............ Gypsum Tile [Technical drawings]
GPTA........... Gupta Corp. [NASDAQ symbol] (SAG)
GPTAE......... Gupta Corp. [NASDAQ symbol] (TTSB)
GPT-C......... Glutamic-Pyruvic Transaminase-C [An enzyme] (OA)
GPTE........... General-Purpose Test Equipment (MCD)
GpTh........... Group Therapy
GPTI............ General-Purpose Terminal Interchanges [Airline communication system] [Raytheon Co.]
GPTR........... General-Purpose Tape Routine [Computer science] (PCM)
GPTR........... Guidance Power Temperature Regulator
GPTS........... Geomagnetic Polarity Timescale
GPTU........... Glass Painters' Trade Union [British]
GPU............ Gas Power Unit (MUGU)
GPU............ Gas Pump Unit
GPU............ General Postal Union [Later, UPU]
GPU............ General Processor Unit
GPU............ General Public Utilities Corp. [NYSE symbol] (SPSG)
GPU............ Generating Power Unit
GPU............ Genl Public Util [NYSE symbol] (TTSB)
GPU............ Geopotential Unit (IAA)
GPU............ Gosudarstvennoe Politicheskoe Upravlenie [Government Political Administration] [Soviet secret service organization, also known as OGPU Later, KGB]
GPU............ Graphics Processing Unit
GPU............ Ground Power Unit
GPU............ Guinea Pig Unit [Endocrinology]
GPUN.......... General Public Utilities Nuclear Corp. (NRCH)
GPUR.......... GOAL [Ground Operations Aerospace Language] Test Procedure Update Request (MCD)
GPUSA........ Greenpeace USA (EA)
GPUT.......... Galactose Phosphate Uridyl Transferase [An enzyme] (MAE)
GPV............ General Public Virus [Computer science] (NHD)
GPV............ General-Purpose Vehicle
GPV............ General-Purpose Vessel
GPV............ Gereformeerd Politiek Verbond [Reformed Political League] [Netherlands Political party] (PPE)
GPV............ Gyroscope Pickoff Voltage
GPVB.......... General-Purpose Video Buffer
GPVEH........ General-Purpose Vehicle
GPW........... Geneva Convention Relative to Treatment of Prisoners of War, 12 August 1949 [Army] (AABC)
GPW........... Global Point Warning [Military]
GPW........... Gold Power Resources Corp. [Vancouver Stock Exchange symbol]
GPW........... Great Plains Wheat, Inc. (EA)
GPW........... Green Pulse Width [Instrumentation]
GPW........... Gypsum-Plaster Wall [Technical drawings]
GPW 1929 ... Geneva Convention Relative to Treatment of Prisoners of War, 27 July 1929 [Army]
GPWA.......... Grain Pool of Western Australia
GPWC.......... Great Pines Water [NASDAQ symbol] (TTSB)
GPWC.......... Great Pines Water Co. [NASDAQ symbol] (SAG)
GPWD.......... General Political Warfare Department [Military]
GPWM......... Guild for the Promotion of Welsh Music (EAIO)
GPWS.......... General-Purpose Workstation (SSD)
GPWS.......... Ground Proximity Warning System [FAA]
GPWU.......... Granite Polishers' and Workers' Union [British]
GPX............ Generalized Programming Extended [Livermore Atomic Research Computer] [Sperry UNIVAC]
GPx............ Glutathione Peroxidase [An enzyme]
GPX............ Greyhound Package Express
GPY............ Government Property Yard
GPY............ Gypsy Resources Ltd. [Vancouver Stock Exchange symbol]
GPYS.......... General-Purpose Yard Simulator (PDAA)
GPZ............ Gazpromavia [Former USSR] [FAA designator] (FAAC)
GPZ............ Gebbies Pass [New Zealand] [Seismograph station code, US Geological Survey] (SEIS)
GPZ............ Grand Rapids [Minnesota] [Airport symbol] (OAG)
GPZOA........ GPz Owners of America [Defunct] (EA)
GQ .... Big Sky Airlines [ICAO designator] (AD)
GQ .... Equatorial Guinea [ANSI two-letter standard code] (CNC)
GQ .... General Quarters [General Alert] [Navy]
GQ .... Golden West Airlines (MHDW)
GQ .... Governor of Queensland [Australia]
GQ .... Great Quotations [A publication]
GQ .... North Korea [License plate code assigned to foreign diplomats in the US]
GQA............ Get Quick Answer [Communications]
GQA............ Give Quick Answer [Communications]
GQA............ Government Quality Assurance (NATG)
GQ & A........ General's Branch, Quarter Master's Branch, and Adjutant's Branch [Main divisions of Staff Duties] [Military British]
GQE............ Generalized Queue Entry [Computer science]
GQE............ Gilmore, AR [Location identifier FAA] (FAAL)
GQG............ Gallaudet College, Washington, DC [OCLC symbol] (OCLC)
GQG............ Grand Quartier-General [French GHQ]

GQK .... Gallaudet College, Kendall Demonstration School, Washington, DC [OCLC symbol] (OCLC)
GQM .... Gallaudet College, Montessori School, Washington, DC [OCLC symbol] (OCLC)
GQM .... Golden Queen Mining [Vancouver Stock Exchange symbol]
GQMS .... Garrison Quartermaster-Sergeant [British military] (DMA)
GQN .... U.S. Air Force Reserve (440th Airlift Wing) [FAA designator] (FAAC)
GQNA .... Aioun El Atrouss [Mauritania] [ICAO location identifier] (ICLI)
GQNB .... Boutilimit [Mauritania] [ICAO location identifier] (ICLI)
GQNC .... Tichitt [Mauritania] [ICAO location identifier] (ICLI)
GQND .... Tidjikja [Mauritania] [ICAO location identifier] (ICLI)
GQNE .... Bogue [Mauritania] [ICAO location identifier] (ICLI)
GQNF .... Kiffa [Mauritania] [ICAO location identifier] (ICLI)
GQNH .... Timbedra [Mauritania] [ICAO location identifier] (ICLI)
GQNI .... Nema [Mauritania] [ICAO location identifier] (ICLI)
GQNJ .... Akjoujt [Mauritania] [ICAO location identifier] (ICLI)
GQNK .... Kaedi [Mauritania] [ICAO location identifier] (ICLI)
GQNL .... Moudjeria/Letfotar [Mauritania] [ICAO location identifier] (ICLI)
GQNM .... Timbedra/Dahara [Mauritania] [ICAO location identifier] (ICLI)
GQNN .... Nouakchott [Mauritania] [ICAO location identifier] (ICLI)
GQNR .... Rosso [Mauritania] [ICAO location identifier] (ICLI)
GQNS .... Selibabi [Mauritania] [ICAO location identifier] (ICLI)
GQNT .... Tamchakett [Mauritania] [ICAO location identifier] (ICLI)
GQNU .... M'Bout [Mauritania] [ICAO location identifier] (ICLI)
GQNV .... Nouakchott [Mauritania] [ICAO location identifier] (ICLI)
GQP .... Gas Quenching Process
GQPA .... Atar [Mauritania] [ICAO location identifier] (ICLI)
GQPF .... F'Derick [Mauritania] [ICAO location identifier] (ICLI)
GQPP .... Nouadhibou [Mauritania] [ICAO location identifier] (ICLI)
GQPT .... Bir Moghrein [Mauritania] [ICAO location identifier] (ICLI)
GQPZ .... Zouerate [Mauritania] [ICAO location identifier] (ICLI)
GQQ .... Galion [Ohio] [Airport symbol] (OAG)
GQR .... Gauss Quadrature Rule
GQR .... Golden Quail Resources Ltd. [Vancouver Stock Exchange symbol]
GQRV .... Golden Quail Resources Ltd. [NASDAQ symbol] (NQ)
GQRVF .... Golden Quail Res Ltd [NASDAQ symbol] (TTSB)
GQW .... Denver, CO [Location identifier FAA] (FAAL)
GQX .... Goldquest Exploration, Inc. [Toronto Stock Exchange symbol]
GR .... Aurigny Air Services [ICAO designator] (AD)
GR .... Carnegie Library, Rome, GA [Library symbol Library of Congress] (LCLS)
GR .... Gambia Regiment [British military] (DMA)
GR .... Game Reserve [State] (EERA)
GR .... Gamma Ray [or Roentgen]
GR .... Gas Ratio
GR .... Gastric Resection [Medicine]
GR .... Gear (MSA)
GR .... Geared Radial [Aircraft engine]
GR .... Gear Ratio
GR .... General Purpose Register (NITA)
GR .... General Radio
GR .... General Reader
GR .... General Reconnaissance [Marine Corps]
GR .... General Register [Computer science]
GR .... General Relativity [Physics]
GR .... General Research
GR .... General Reserve
GR .... Generator Run (IAA)
GR .... Genesis Rabbah (BJA)
GR .... Gentleman Rider [Horsemanship]
GR .... Georgist Registry [An association] (EA)
GR .... Georgius Rex [King George]
GR .... Germanium Rectifier
GR .... German Reports (MCD)
GR .... German Roach [Immunology]
GR .... Germ Ring [Embryology]
GR .... Glass-Reinforced
GR .... Glaxo Laboratories Ltd. [Great Britain] [Research code symbol]
GR .... Gloucestershire Regiment [Military unit] [British]
GR .... Glucocorticoid Receptor [Endocrinology]
GR .... Glutathione Reductase [An enzyme]
G-R .... Gnome-Rhone [Aircraft engine]
G-R .... Goldbarg-Rutenberg [Enzyme unit]
GR .... Golden Rule [Freemasonry] (ROG)
GR .... Gold Reserve
GR .... [The] Goodrich [B. F.] Co. [NYSE symbol] (SPSG)
GR .... Gospel Recordings (EA)
GR .... Government Regulation (AAG)
GR .... Government Report (AAG)
GR .... Government Reserve [British] (ADA)
GR .... Government Responsibility (MCD)
gr .... Government Revenue (MENA)
GR .... Government Rubber [Synthetic rubber] (IIA)
GR .... Grab Rod (AAG)
GR .... Grade (KSC)
gr .... Grade (WDMC)
GR .... Gradual-Release [Pharmacy]
GR .... Graduate
GR .... Graduation Requirement (MCD)
GR .... Grain (KSC)
gr .... Grain (WDMC)
gr .... Grains (ODBW)
GR .... Gram (KSC)
GR .... Grammar
gr- .... Gram-Negative [Bacteria] (DAVI)

G-R .... Gram-Negative Rods [*Biochemistry*] (DAVI)
gr+ .... Gram-Positive [*Bacteria*] (DAVI)
G+R .... Gram-Positive Rods [*Biochemistry*] (DAVI)
GR .... Grand [*Title*]
GR .... Grand Rapids, Michigan
GR .... Grand Recorder [*Freemasonry*]
GR .... Grand Registrar [*Freemasonry*] (ROG)
GR .... Grange [*or Manor, a religious residence*]
GR .... Gran Rabinato (BJA)
GR .... Grant
GR .... Grant Recipient [*Job Training and Partnership Act*] (OICC)
Gr .... Grant's Jamaica Reports [*A publication*] (DLA)
Gr .... Grant's Pennsylvania Cases [*A publication*] (DLA)
Gr .... Grant's Upper Canada Chancery Reports [*A publication*] (DLA)
GR .... Granular Snow [*Skiing condition*]
GR .... Granum [*Grain*] [*Latin*]
GR .... Graphic Reproduction [*A publication*] (DGA)
Gr .... Graphite
Gr .... Grashof Number [*IUPAC*]
Gr .... Grasp
GR .... Grass (ROG)
GR .... Grasse River R. R. Corp. [*AAR code*]
GR .... Grass Extract [*Immunology*]
GR .... Grave Record [*Genealogy*]
GR .... Graves Registration [*Military*]
Gr .... Gravida [*Obstetrics*] (DAVI)
GR .... Gravity
GR .... Gray
gr .... Gray [*Unit*] [*Radiation therapy*] (DAVI)
GR .... Gray [*Thoroughbred racing*]
GR .... Great (MCD)
GR .... Great Roll [*of the Pipe*] [*British*]
GR .... Grecian (ROG)
GR .... Greece [*ANSI two-letter standard code*] (CNC)
gr .... Greece [*IYRU nationality code*] [*MARC country of publication code Library of Congress*] (LCCP)
GR .... Greek
Gr .... Greenleaf's Reports [*1-9 Maine*] [*A publication*] (DLA)
Gr .... Green's Reports [*A publication*] (DLA)
GR .... Grid Resistor
GR .... Grid Return
GR .... Grind (ADA)
GR .... Grooved Roofing [*Lumber*]
GR .... Gross
gr .... Gross (ODBW)
gr .... Gross (WDMC)
GR .... Gross Rate [*Insurance*] (AIA)
GR .... Gross Receipts [*Business term*]
GR .... Gross Requirement (AABC)
GR .... Gross Revenue [*Business term*]
Gr .... Ground
GR .... Ground Range
GR .... Ground Rent (ROG)
GR .... Ground Rule (MCD)
GR .... Group
gr .... Group (WDMC)
GR .... Group Report
GR .... Grove (ADA)
GR .... Growth (SSD)
GR .... Growth Rate [*Biology*]
GR .... Guardrail
GR .... Guard Ring (BARN)
GR .... Gulf Rijad Bank [*Bahrain*]
GR .... Gulielmus Rex [*King William*]
GR .... Gun Control RADAR [*Military*] (CAAL)
GR .... Gunner
GR .... Gunnery Range
GR .... Gurkha Rifles [*British military*] (DMA)
GR .... Gypsum Requirement (OA)
GR .... Hail [*ICAO*] (FAAC)
GRA .... Fayetteville, NC [*Location identifier FAA*] (FAAL)
GRA .... Gamma Ray Amplification
GRA .... Gated Radionuclide Angiography [*Medicine*] (DMAA)
GRA .... German Research Association (EA)
GRA .... Girls Rodeo Association [*Later, WPRA*] (EA)
GRA .... Glucocorticoid-Remediable Aldosteronism [*Medicine*]
Gra .... Glyceraldehyde [*Biochemistry*]
GRA .... Gombarts Reducing Agent [*Medicine*] (AAMN)
GRA .... Gonadotropin-Releasing Agent [*Endocrinology*] (MAE)
GRA .... Governmental Research Association (EA)
GRA .... Government Reports Announcements [*Department of Commerce*] [*Database producer*]
GRA .... Government Responsibility Action
GRA .... Government Responsibility Authorized (MCD)
GR-A .... Government Rubber-Acrylonitrile [*Synthetic rubber*]
GRA .... Grace [*W. R.*] & Co. [*NYSE symbol*] (SPSG)
GRA .... Grace (W.R.) [*NYSE symbol*] (TTSB)
GRA .... Graduate Research Assistant
Gra .... Graham's Reports [*98-107 Georgia*] [*A publiclation*] (DLA)
Gra .... Grant [*Legal term*] (DLA)
GRA .... Grant Aid [*Military*] (AABC)
GRA .... Graphic Recording Ammeter (IAA)
gra .... Graphics (VRA)
GRA .... Grass Roots Association (EA)

Gra .... Gratianus [*Flourished, 1151-59*] [*Authority cited in pre-1607 legal work*] (DSA)
GRA .... Gray (MSA)
GRA .... Graz [*Steiermark*] [*Austria*] [*Seismograph station code, US Geological Survey*] [*Closed*] (SEIS)
GRA .... Great American Airways [*ICAO designator*] (FAAC)
GRA .... Growth Rate Adjustment [*Business term*]
GRA .... Guild for Religious Architecture [*Later, IFRAA*]
GRA .... Gyro Reference Assembly
GRAAL .... Graph Algorithmic Language [*Computer science*]
Gra & Wat NT... Graham and Waterman on New Trials [*A publication*] (DLA)
GRAB .... Galactic Radiation and Background (MCD)
GRAB .... Galatic Radiation and Background
GRAB .... Group Room Availability Bank [*Sheraton Corp.*]
GRABS .... Giant Reusable Air Blast Simulator [*Air Force*]
GRAC .... Grand Royal Arch Captain [*Freemasonry*]
GRAC .... Grand Royal Arch Chapter [*Freemasonry*] (ROG)
GRAC .... Groupe de Recherche sur les Attitudes Envers la Criminalite [*Canada*]
Grace .... Grace [*W.R.*] & Co. [*Associated Press*] (SAG)
GRACE .... Graphic Arts Composing Equipment
GRACE .... Grass Roots Art and Community Effort [*Vermont*]
GRACE .... Group Routing and Charging Equipment [*British*]
GRACE .... Mrs. Gould's Residential Advisory Centre for the Elderly [*British*] (CB)
Graco .... Graco, Inc. [*Associated Press*] (SAG)
GRACO .... Gray Co., Inc.
GRAD .... Generalized Remote Access Database
GRAD .... General Recursive Algebra and Differentiation (IEEE)
GRAD .... Gradatim [*Gradually*] [*Pharmacy*]
GRAD .... Gradient (AFM)
GRAD .... Grading (WDAA)
GRAD .... Gradual
GRAD .... Graduate (AFM)
GRAD .... Graduate
GRAD .... Graduate Resume Accumulation and Distribution [*Computer science*]
GRADB .... Generalized Remote Access Database (IEEE)
GradBHI .... Graduate of the British Horological Institute (DBQ)
GradCert .... Graduate Certificate
GradCertBus .... Graduate Certificate in Business [*Australia*]
GradCertCommunic... Graduate Certificate in Communication [*Australia*]
GradCertFin... Graduate Certificate in Finance [*Australia*]
GradCertHelpSkills... Graduate Certificate in Helping Skills [*Australia*]
GradCertHRD... Graduate Certificate in Human Resource Development [*Australia*]
GradCertIndRels... Graduate Certificate in Industrial Relations [*Australia*]
GradCertLitEd... Graduate Certificate in Literacy Education [*Australia*]
GradCertMarkt... Graduate Certificate in Marketing [*Australia*]
GradCertMngt... Graduate Certificate in Management [*Australia*]
GradCertTESOL... Graduate Certificate in Teaching of English to Speakers of Other Languages [*Australia*]
Gradco .... Gradco Systems, Inc. [*Associated Press*] (SAG)
GradDIndDes... Graduate Diploma in Industrial Design [*Australia*]
GradDipA.... Graduate Diploma of Arts [*Australia*]
GradDipAbIsEd... Graduate Diploma in Aboriginal and Islander Education [*Australia*]
GradDipAcc... Graduate Diploma in Accounting [*Australia*]
GradDipAccom... Graduate Diploma in Accompaniment [*Australia*]
GradDipAcct... Graduate Diploma in Accounting
GradDipActng... Graduate Diploma in Accounting
GradDipAdmin... Graduate Diploma in Administration
GradDipAdultEd & Train... Graduate Diploma in Adult Education and Training [*Australia*]
GradDipAdvAcctg... Graduate Diploma in Advanced Accounting
GradDipAltDispRes... Graduate Diploma in Alternative Dispute Resolution [*Australia*]
GradDipAnalytChem... Graduate Diploma in Analytical Chemistry
GradDipAppCommunications... Graduate Diploma in Applied Communications
GradDipAppEc... Graduate Diploma in Applied Economics [*Australia*]
GradDipAppHist... Graduate Diploma in Applied History
GradDipAppLing... Graduate Diploma in Applied Linguistics
GradDipAppSc... Graduate Diploma in Applied Science [*Australia*]
GradDipAppScGenStud... Graduate Diploma in Applied Science, General Studies [*Australia*]
GradDipAppStats... Graduate Diploma in Applied Statistics
GradDipArts(ChLit)... Graduate Diploma in Arts (Children's Literature) [*Australia*]
GradDipArts(WelfAdmin)... Graduate Diploma in Arts (Welfare Administration) [*Australia*]
GradDipAsianLaw... Graduate Diploma in Asian Law [*Australia*]
GradDipAsianStudies... Graduate Diploma in Asian Studies
GradDipASOS... Graduate Diploma in Antarctic and Southern Ocean Studies [*Australia*]
GradDipAud... Graduate Diploma in Audiology [*Australia*]
GradDipAud... Graduate Diploma in Internal Auditing
GradDipBldgProjMgt... Graduate Diploma in Building Project Management
GradDipBus... Graduate Diploma in Business [*Australia*]
GradDipBusAdmin... Graduate Diploma in Business Administration
GradDipBusComp... Graduate Diploma in Business Computing
GradDipCCC... Graduate Diploma of Computer Control and Communications [*Australia*]
GradDipChildLit... Graduate Diploma in Children's Literature
GradDipClinBiochem... Graduate Diploma in Clinical Biochemistry
GradDipClinDent... Graduate Diploma in Clinical Dentistry [*Australia*]
GradDipCmlComptg... Graduate Diploma in Commercial Computing
GradDipComEd... Graduate Diploma in Commercial Education [*Australia*]
GradDipComLaw... Graduate Diploma of Commercial Law [*Australia*]

GradDipCommDataProc... Graduate Diploma in Commercial Data Processing
GradDipCommn... Graduate Diploma in Communication
GradDipCommunicationMgt... Graduate Diploma in Communication Management
GradDipComMus... Graduate Diploma of Community Music [*Australia*]
GradDipComMusMgmt... Graduate Diploma of Community Museum Management [*Australia*]
GradDipCompContSys... Graduate Diploma in Computer Controlled Systems
GradDipCompEd... Graduate Diploma in Computers in Education [*Australia*]
GradDipCompEng... Graduate Diploma in Digital Computer Engineering
GradDipCompSc... Graduate Diploma of Computer Science [*Australia*]
GradDipCompStud... Graduate Diploma in Computer Studies
GradDipComptgSc... Graduate Diploma in Computing Science
GradDipConfRes... Graduate Diploma in Conflict Resolution [*Australia*]
GradDipCouns... Graduate Diploma in Counselling
GradDipCPPhty... Graduate Diploma in Cardio Pulmonary Physiotherapy
GradDipCurric... Graduate Diploma in Curriculum [*Australia*]
GradDipDatAnal... Graduate Diploma in Data Analysis
GradDipDemog... Graduate Diploma in Demography
GradDipDesStud... Graduate Diploma in Design Studies
GradDipDiplSt... Graduate Diploma in Diplomatic Studies [*Australia*]
GradDipDP... Graduate Diploma in Data Processing
GradDipDramaEd... Graduate Diploma in Drama in Education [*Australia*]
GradDipE..... Graduate Diploma in Engineering [*Australia*]
GradDipEarlyChildSt... Graduate Diploma in Early Childhood Studies [*Australia*]
GradDipEc ... Graduate Diploma in Economics
GradDipEcDev... Graduate Diploma in Economics of Development
GradDipEcHist... Graduate Diploma in Economic History
GradDipEcmetrics... Graduate Diploma in Econometrics
GradDipEconDev... Graduate Diploma in Economic Development [*Australia*]
GradDipEconGeol... Graduate Diploma in Economic Geology [*Australia*]
GradDipEconHist... Graduate Diploma in Economic History [*Australia*]
GradDipEconom... Graduate Diploma in Econometrics [*Australia*]
GradDipEd... Graduate Diploma in Education
GradDipEdAdmin... Graduate Diploma in Educational Administration [*Australia*]
GradDipEdCouns... Graduate Diploma in Educational Counseling [*Australia*]
GradDipEdCouns... Graduate Diploma in Educational Counselling (ADA)
GradDipEd(IndArts)... Graduate Diploma in Education (Industrial Arts)
GradDipEdStSptTchg... Graduate Diploma in Educational Studies Support Teaching [*Australia*]
GradDipEdStudies... Graduate Diploma in Educational Studies
GradDipEd(TAFE)... Graduate Diploma in Education (Technical and Further Education)
GradDipEdTrain... Graduate Diploma in Education and Training [*Australia*]
GradDipEmpRels... Graduate Diploma in Employment Relations
GradDipEng... Graduate Diploma in Engineering [*Australia*]
GradDipEng-PlantMgnt... Graduate Diploma in Engineering - Plant Management
GradDipEnv & MunEng... Graduate Diploma in Environmental and Municipal Engineering
GradDipEnvSt... Graduate Diploma in Environmental Studies [*Australia*]
GradDipEpi... Graduate Diploma in Epidemiology [*Australia*]
GradDipExerSportSc... Graduate Diploma in Exercise and Sport Sciences
GradDipFA... Graduate Diploma of Fine Arts [*Australia*]
GradDipFamLaw... Graduate Diploma of Family Law [*Australia*]
GradDipFilm & Tele in Ed... Graduate Diploma in Film and Television in Education
GradDipFin... Graduate Diploma in Finance
GradDipFineArt... Graduate Diploma in Fine Art
GradDipForOdont... Graduate Diploma in Forensic Odontology [*Australia*]
GradDipGalSt... Graduate Diploma in Gallery Studies [*Australia*]
GradDipGeol... Graduate Diploma for Science Teachers (Geology)
GradDipGeront... Graduate Diploma in Gerontology
GradDipGraphCommEd... Graduate Diploma in Graphic Communication Education [*Australia*]
GradDipHealthServMgmt... Graduate Diploma in Health Services Management
GradDipHIM... Graduate Diploma in Health Information Management
GradDipHumanPhysiol & Pharmacol... Graduate Diploma in Human Physiology and Pharmacology [*Australia*]
GradDipImmunolMicrobiol... Graduate Diploma in Immunology and Microbiology [*Australia*]
GradDipIndDes... Graduate Diploma in Industrial Design
GradDipInfoMgt... Graduate Diploma in Information Management [*Australia*]
GradDipInfServ... Graduate Diploma in Information Services
GradDipInfStudies... Graduate Diploma in Information Studies
GradDipInfTech... Graduate Diploma in Information Technology [*Australia*]
GradDipIntComLaw... Graduate Diploma in International and Commercial Law [*Australia*]
GradDipIntLaw... Graduate Diploma in International Law
GradDipIntPropLaw... Graduate Diploma in Intellectual Property Law [*Australia*]
GradDipKnowlBasSys... Graduate Diploma in Knowledge Based Systems
GradDipLabRelLaw... Graduate Diploma in Labour Relations Law [*Australia*]
GradDipLandArch... Graduate Diploma in Landscape Architecture
GradDipLandDatMan... Graduate Diploma in Land Data Management
GradDipLangTchg... Graduate Diploma in Language Teaching [*Australia*]
GradDipLD... Graduate Diploma in Landscape Design
GradDipLegalPrac... Graduate Diploma in Legal Practice
GradDipLegSt... Graduate Diploma of Legal Studies [*Australia*]
GradDipLeisureStud... Graduate Diploma in Leisure Studies
GradDipLibInfStud... Graduate Diploma in Librarianship and Information Studies
GradDipLibSc... Graduate Diploma in Library Science (ADA)
GradDipLocalGovtEng... Graduate Diploma in Local Government Engineering
GradDipLoc & AppHist... Graduate Diploma in Local and Applied History
GradDipManipTh... Graduate Diploma in Manipulative Therapy
GradDipMatAnth... Graduate Diploma of Material Anthropology [*Australia*]
GradDipMatEng... Graduate Diploma in Materials Engineering [*Australia*]
GradDipMathMethods... Graduate Diploma in Mathematical Methods
GradDipMathSc... Graduate Diploma in Mathematics Science [*Australia*]

GradDipMathsEd... Graduate Diploma in Mathematics Education [*Australia*]
GradDipMediaComm & TechLaw... Graduate Diploma in Media Communications and Technology Law [*Australia*]
GradDipMelSt... Graduate Diploma of Melanesian Studies [*Australia*]
GradDipMentHlthSc... Graduate Diploma in Mental Health Science [*Australia*]
GradDipMgmt... Graduate Diploma in Management
GradDipMidwif... Graduate Diploma in Midwifery [*Australia*]
GradDipMinRes... Graduate Diploma in Mineral Resources
GradDipMktg... Graduate Diploma in Marketing
GradDipMolBiol... Graduate Diploma in Molecular Biology [*Australia*]
GradDipMovement & Dance... Graduate Diploma in Movement and Dance [*Australia*]
GradDipMultiStudies... Graduate Diploma in Multicultural Studies [*Australia*]
GradDipMunEng... Graduate Diploma in Municipal Engineering [*Australia*]
GradDipMus... Graduate Diploma in Music [*Australia*]
GradDipMusCur... Graduate Diploma of Museum Curatorship [*Australia*]
GradDipMusMgmt... Graduate Diploma in Museum Management [*Australia*]
GradDipMus(Op)... Graduate Diploma in Music (Opera) [*Australia*]
GradDipMus(Perf)... Graduate Diploma in Music (Performance) [*Australia*]
GradDipMus(Rep)... Graduate Diploma in Music (Repetiteur) [*Australia*]
GradDipNatResourcesLaw... Graduate Diploma in Natural Resources Law [*Australia*]
GradDipNurs... Graduate Diploma in Nursing
GradDipNursStudies... Graduate Diploma in Nursing Studies
GradDipNutr & Diet... Graduate Diploma in Nutrition and Dietetics
GradDipOffshEng... Graduate Diploma in Offshore Engineering [*Australia*]
GradDipOH & S... Graduate Diploma in Occupational Health and Safety
GradDipOR... Graduate Diploma in Operations Research
GradDipOrgDev... Graduate Diploma in Organisation Development
GradDipPaedPhty... Graduate Diploma in Paediatric Physiotherapy
GradDipPPT... Graduate Diploma in Pulp and Paper Technology [*Australia*]
GradDipProjMgt... Graduate Diploma in Project Management [*Australia*]
GradDipProp... Graduate Diploma in Property
GradDipPSM... Graduate Diploma in Public Sector Management
GradDipPsych... Graduate Diploma of Psychology [*Australia*]
GradDipPubEcPol... Graduate Diploma in Public Economic Policy
GradDipPubLaw... Graduate Diploma in Public Law
GradDipPubPol... Graduate Diploma in Public Policy
GradDipQlty... Graduate Diploma in Quality
GradDipQualTech... Graduate Diploma in Quality Technology
GradDipRc... Graduate Diploma in Rehabilitation Counselling
GradDipSc... Graduate Diploma in Science
GradDipScSoc... Graduate Diploma of Science and Society [*Australia*]
GradDipSEAsianStud... Graduate Diploma in Southeast Asian Studies
GradDipSecStud... Graduate Diploma in Secretarial Studies
GradDipSocAdmin... Graduate Diploma in Social Administration [*Australia*]
GradDipSocEcol... Graduate Diploma in Social Ecology [*Australia*]
GradDipSpecEd... Graduate Diploma in Special Education [*Australia*]
GradDipStats... Graduate Diploma in Statistics
GradDipStratSt... Graduate Diploma in Strategic Studies [*Australia*]
GradDipStrucEng... Graduate Diploma in Structural Engineering [*Australia*]
GradDipStudWel... Graduate Diploma in Student Welfare [*Australia*]
GradDipSurFin... Graduate Diploma in Metal Finishing and Surface Protection
GradDipSurvPrac... Graduate Diploma in Surveying Practice
GradDipT..... Graduate Diploma in Teaching (ADA)
GradDipTax... Graduate Diploma in Taxation
GradDipTchrLib... Graduate Diploma in Teacher Librarianship (ADA)
GradDipTeach... Graduate Diploma in Teaching [*Australia*]
GradDipTeachLib... Graduate Diploma in Teacher Librarianship
GradDipTourism... Graduate Diploma of Tourism [*Australia*]
GradDipTrans & Dist... Graduate Diploma in Transport and Distribution
GradDipUEM... Graduate Diploma in Urban Estate Management
GradDipUltr... Graduate Diploma in Ultrasonography
GradDipUrb & RegPlan... Graduate Diploma in Urban and Regional Planning
GradDipURP... Graduate Diploma in Urban and Regional Planning
GradDip(VisArts)... Graduate Diploma in Visual Arts
GradDipWaterEng... Graduate Diploma in Water Engineering [*Australia*]
GradDipWeldTech... Graduate Diploma in Welding Technology
GradDipWelfAdmin... Graduate Diploma in Welfare Administration [*Australia*]
GradDipWomen'sStudies... Graduate Diploma in Women's Studies [*Australia*]
GradDipWomHlth... Graduate Diploma in Women's Health [*Australia*]
GRADE........ Gestalt Recognition by Asymptotic Differential Equations
GRADE........ Graphical Airspace Design Environment [*FAA*] (TAG)
Gradell........ Gradell Industries, Inc. [*Associated Press*] (SAG)
GRADEX...... Graded Exercise (NVT)
Grad Fix ...... Grady on Fixtures [*A publication*] (DLA)
Grad Hind Inh... Grady's Hindoo Law of Inheritance [*A publication*] (DLA)
Grad Hind L... Grady's Manual of Hindoo Law [*A publication*] (DLA)
GradIAE....... Graduate of the Institution of Automobile Engineers [*British*]
GradIElecIE... Graduate of the Institution of Electrical and Electronics Incorporated Engineers [*British*] (DBQ)
Grad IERE.... Graduate of the Institution of Electronic and Radio Engineers [*British*]
GradIISec .... Graduate of the Institute of Industrial Security [*British*] (DBQ)
Grad IM ...... Graduate of the Institute of Metallurgists (BARN)
GradIMA...... Graduate Member of the Institute of Mathematics and Its Applications [*British*] (DBQ)
GradIManf .... Graduate Member of the Institute of Manufacturing [*British*] (DBQ)
Grad I Mech E... Graduate of the Institution of Mechanical Engineers [*British*]
GradIMF ...... Graduate of the Institute of Metal Finishing [*British*] (DBQ)
GradIMS ...... Graduate of the Institute of Management Specialists [*British*] (DBQ)
Grad Ind Co... Grady's Indian Codes [*A publication*] (DLA)
Grad Inst BE... Graduate Member of the Institute of British Engineers
GradInstBTM... Graduate of the Institute of Business and Technical Management [*British*] (DBQ)
GradInstNDT... Graduate of the British Institute of Non-Destructive Testing (DBQ)

Grad Inst P... Graduate Member of the Institute of Physics and the Physical Society [*British*]
GradInstPS... Graduate of the Institute of Purchasing and Supply [*British*] (DBQ)
GradIOP...... Graduate of the Institute of Printing [*British*] (DBQ)
GradIPM...... Graduate of the Institute of Personnel Management [*British*] (DBQ)
GradIS........ Graduate Member of the Institute of Statisticians [*British*] (DBQ)
GradISM...... Graduate of the Institute of Supervisory Management [*British*] (DBQ)
Grad MNDTS... Graduate Member of the Non-Destructive Testing Society of Great Britain
GradNIH...... Graduate of the National Institute of Hardware [*British*] (DBQ)
GradPRI...... Graduate of the Plastics and Rubber Institute [*British*] (DBQ)
Grad RIC...... Graduate Member of the Royal Institute of Chemistry [*British*]
GRADS........ Generalized Remote Access Database System (IEEE)
GRADS........ Ground RADAR Aerial Delivery System (MCD)
GRADSCOPE... Graduate Search by Computer after Personal Evaluation (AIE)
GradSCP...... Graduate of the Society of Certified Professionals [*British*] (DBQ)
GradSLAET... Graduate of the Society of Licensed Aircraft Engineers and Technologists [*British*] (DBQ)
GRADU........ Gradual
Graduate IElecIE... Graduate of the Institution of Electrical and Electronics Incorporated Engineers [*British*] (DBQ)
GradWeldI... Graduate of the Welding Institute [*British*] (DBQ)
GRAE.......... Generally Regarded [*or Recognized*] as Effective [*Medicine*]
GRAE.......... Gouvernement de la Republique de l'Angola en Exile [*Government of the Republic of Angola in Exile*]
GRAE.......... Governo Revolucionario de Angola no Exilio [*Revolutionary Angolan Government-in-Exile*] [*Portuguese*] (PD)
GR Aero S... Graduate of the Royal Aeronautical Society [*British*]
GRAF.......... Graffiti [*Slang*] [*British*]
GRAF.......... Graphic Addition to FORTRAN [*Computer science*]
GRAF.......... Ground Replay and Analysis Facility (GAVI)
GRAFCET..... Graphe de Commande Etape-Transition [*State transition command graph*] [*Computer language*] (CDE)
GRAFEM...... Graphic Finite Element Modeling [*Software*] [*Automotive engineering*]
GraffPay...... Graff Pay per View [*Associated Press*] (SAG)
GRAFMA...... Grand Rapids Area Furniture Manufacturers Association (EA)
GRAFTABL... Load Graphics Table [*Computer science*]
Grafton....... Smith's New Hampshire Reports [*A publication*] (DLA)
Graham....... Graham Corp. [*Associated Press*] (SAG)
Grah & W New Trials... Graham and Waterman on New Trials [*A publication*] (DLA)
GRAI.......... Government Reports Announcements and Index [*Department of Commerce A publication*]
GRAID......... Graphical Aid [*Computer science*]
GRAIL......... Graphic Input Language [*Computer science*] (PDAA)
GRAIN........ Genetic Resources Action International [*Spain*]
GRAIN........ Graphics-Oriented Relational Algebraic Interpreter
GRAINCORP... New South Wales Grain Corp. [*Australia Commercial firm*]
Graingr....... Grainger [*W.W.*], Inc. [*Associated Press*] (SAG)
GRAL......... General (ROG)
Gram........ De Grammaticis [*of Suetonius*] [*Classical studies*] (OCD)
GRAM......... Global Reference Atmosphere Model (SSD)
GRAM......... Grammar [*or Grammatical*]
gram.......... Grammar [*Copyediting*] (WDMC)
Gram......... Gramophone [*Division of Record Corp. of America*] [*Record label*]
GRAM......... Granulocyte Activating Mediator [*Immunochemistry*]
Gramm Lat... Grammatici Latini [*A publication*] (OCD)
Gramm Rom Frag... Grammaticae Romana Fragmenta [*A publication*] (OCD)
gram-neg..... Gram-Negative [*Biochemistry*] (DAVI)
Gramo........ Gramola [*Record label*] [*Belgium*]
GRAMP....... Generalized Reliability and Maintainability Program [*Military*]
GRAMPA...... General Analytical Model for Process Analysis (IEEE)
GRAMPA...... Ground Resonance Automatic Multi-Point Apparatus (PDAA)
GRAMPIES... Growing Retired Active Monied Person in Excellent State [*Lifestyle classification*]
gram-pos..... Gram-Positive [*Biochemistry*] (DAVI)
GRAMPS...... Graphics for the Multipicture System [*Computer graphics*]
GRAMS........ Generalized Reliability and Maintainability Simulator (MCD)
GRAMS........ Gramophone Records [*Music or sound effects*]
GRAN.......... Bank of Granite [*NASDAQ symbol*] (SAG)
GRAN.......... Bank of Granite [*NASDAQ symbol*] (TTSB)
GRAN......... Global Rescue Alarm Network [*Program*] [*Navy*]
GRAN......... Gombarts Reducing Agent - Negative [*Medicine*] (AAMN)
GRAN......... Grain
GRAN......... Grandmother (DSUE)
GRAN......... Granite (MSA)
gran.......... Granite (VRA)
GRAN......... Granodize
GRAN.......... Granular (WDAA)
GRAN......... Granulatus [*Granulated*] [*Pharmacy*]
GRANADA.... Grammatical Nonalgorithmic Data Description
GRANAS...... Global Radio Navigation System [*Aviation*] (DA)
GRANAT...... Great Annihilator [*Commonwealth - French satellite*] (ECON)
GranBd....... Granite Broadcasting Corp. [*Associated Press*] (SAG)
GranCr....... GranCare, Inc. [*Associated Press*] (SAG)
Grand......... Grand Gaming Corp. [*Associated Press*] (SAG)
GRAND AM... Grand Marnier and Amaretto
GRANDE...... Gamma Ray and Neutrino Detector Experiment [*Proposed*] [*University of California, Irvine*]
GrandG....... Grand Gaming Corp. [*Associated Press*] (SAG)
GRANDO...... Grandioso [*Majestic*] [*Music*]
GR & P....... Grand Rapids & Petoskey Railway
GR & R....... Gauge Repeatability and Reproducibility [*Materials testing*]
GrandTel..... GrandeTel Technologies, Inc. [*Associated Press*] (SAG)
Grang......... Granges, Inc. [*Associated Press*] (SAG)

Granger....... Granger's State Reports [*22-23 Ohio*] [*A publication*] (DLA)
GRANIS....... Graphical Natural Inference System
GRANITE...... Gamma Ray Astrophysics New Imaging Telescope
GranitFn ..... Granite Financial, Inc. [*Associated Press*] (SAG)
GRANL........ Granulated
GRANO........ Granolithic
Grant.......... Grant of Elchies' Scotch Session Cases [*A publication*] (DLA)
Grant.......... Grant's Chancery Chamber Reports [*1850-65*] [*Upper Canada*] [*A publication*] (DLA)
Grant.......... Grant's Jamaica Reports [*A publication*] (DLA)
Grant.......... Grant's Pennsylvania Cases [*A publication*] (DLA)
Grant.......... Grant's Upper Canada Chancery Reports [*A publication*] (DLA)
Grant Bank... Grant on Banking [*A publication*] (DLA)
Grant Cas .... Grant's Pennsylvania Cases [*A publication*] (DLA)
Grant Cas (PA)... Grant's Pennsylvania Cases [*A publication*] (DLA)
Grant Ch..... Grant's Upper Canada Chancery Reports [*A publication*] (DLA)
Grant Ch (Can)... Grant's Upper Canada Chancery Reports [*A publication*] (DLA)
Grant Corp... Grant on Corporations [*A publication*] (DLA)
Grant E & A... Grant's Error and Appeal Reports [*A publication*] (DLA)
Grant Err & App... Grant's Error and Appeal Reports [*A publication*] (DLA)
Grant Jamaica... Grant's Jamaica Reports [*A publication*] (DLA)
Grant PA..... Grant's Pennsylvania Cases [*A publication*] (DLA)
Gra N Tr..... Graham on New Trials [*A publication*] (DLA)
Grant's R..... Grant's Jamaica Reports [*A publication*] (DLA)
GrantSt....... Granite State Bankshares, Inc. [*Associated Press*] (SAG)
Grant UC..... Grant's Upper Canada Chancery Reports [*A publication*] (DLA)
granulo........ Granulocyte [*Hematology*] (DAVI)
GRAO.......... Gamma Ray Astronomy Observatory
GRAP......... Greatest Response Amplitude Probability
GRAPD........ Greatest Response Amplitude Probability Data
GRAPD........ Guard Ring Avalanche Photodiode (IAA)
GRAPDEN ... Graphic Data Entry Unit [*Computer science*]
GRAPE........ Gamma Ray Attenuation Porosity Evaluator
GRAPE........ Graphical Analysis of Program Execution [*Computer science*]
GRAPE-4..... GRAvity PipE no. 4 [*Computer science*]
GRAPH........ Graphic
GRAPH........ Graphical Repair Discard Analysis Procedure Handbook
GRAPH........ Graphology (WDAA)
GRAPHDEN... Graphical Data Entry [*Computer science*] (MUGU)
GraphxZn.... Graphix Zone, Inc. [*Associated Press*] (SAG)
Grap Just.... Grapel's Translation of the Institutes of Justinian [*A publication*] (DLA)
GRAPO......... Grupos de Resistencia Anti-Fascista Primero de Octubre [*October First Antifascist Resistance Groups*] [*Spain Political party*] (PPE)
Gra Pr......... Graham's Practice of the New York Supreme Court [*A publication*] (DLA)
Grap Rom Law... Grapel's Sources of the Roman Civil Law [*A publication*] (DLA)
GRAR.......... Government Report Authorization and Record (AAG)
GRAR.......... Grinding Arbor
GRARD........ Goddard Range and Range Data [*NASA*] (KSC)
GRARE......... Ground-Receiving and Analog Ranging Equipment [*AFSCF*] (MCD)
GRARR......... Goddard Range and Range Rate [*Tracking system*] [*NASA*]
GRAS.......... Generally Recognized [*or Regarded*] as Safe [*FDA term*]
GRAS.......... Ground Return Area Suppression (NATG)
GRASER....... Gamma Ray Amplification by Stimulated Emission of Radiation
GRASER....... Gamma Ray LASER (MCD)
GRASP........ Gamma Ray Astronomy with Spectroscopy and Positioning
GRASP........ GAO [*General Accounting Office*] Review and Approval of Accounting Systems Project (GFGA)
GRASP........ Generalized Read and Simulate Program
GRASP........ Generalized Reentry Application Simulation Program [*NASA*] (KSC)
GRASP........ Generalized Remote Acquisition and Sensor Processing
GRASP........ Generalized Retrieval and Storage Program [*Computer science*]
GRASP........ Generally Recognized as Safe Petition [*FDA*]
GRASP........ General Reduction and Analysis Support Package [*Military*] (CAAL)
GRASP........ General Resource Allocation and Selection Program [*NASA*] (KSC)
GRASP........ Generic RADAR Analysis and Synthesis Program
GRasp......... Graphic Animation System for Professionals [*Software package*] [*Paul Mace Software*] (PCM)
GRASP........ Graphics-Augmented Structural Post-Processing [*Module*]
GRASP........ Graphic Service Program (IEEE)
GRASP Lab... General Robotics and Active Sensory Processing Laboratory [*University of Pennsylvania*] [*Research center*] (RCD)
GRASR........ General Railroad and Airline Stabilization Regulations [*A publication*] (DLA)
GRASS........ Gamma Ray Ablation Sensing System (SAA)
GRASS........ Gas Release and Swelling Subroutine (PDAA)
GRASS........ Generalized Reactor Analysis Subsystem
GRASS........ General Random Audit Sample Selection Technique [*Military*] (AFIT)
GRASS........ Geographical Resources Analysis Support System [*Software*] [*Computer science*] (EERA)
GRASS........ Geographic Resources Analysis Support System [*Army*] (RDA)
GRASS........ Germinating Ray Acoustics Simulation System (MCD)
GRASS........ Grassland Research and Serengeti Systems [*Model for simulation*]
GRASS........ Great Revolutionary American Standard System [*Book title*]
GRASS........ Ground-to-Air Scanner Surveillance
Grass R ...... Grass Roots [*A publication*]
GRAT.......... Gratis [*Free*] [*Latin*] (ROG)
Grat .... Grattan's Virginia Reports [*A publication*] (DLA)
GRAT.......... Gratuity (AABC)
Grat Act...... Gratiarum Actio [*of Ausonius*] [*Classical studies*] (OCD)
GRATE......... Growth Rate [*Botany*]
GRATIS........ Generation, Reduction, and Training Input System (IEEE)
Gratt.......... Grattan's Virginia Supreme Court Reports [*1844-80*] [*A publication*] (DLA)

Gratt (VA).... Grattan's Virginia Reports [*A publication*] (DLA)
GRAUL........ Grand Rapids Area Union List of Serials [*Library network*]
GRAV......... Gravid [*Pregnant*] [*Medicine*]
GRAV......... Gravitational
grav........... Gravity (CPH)
Grav De Jur Nat Gent... Gravina's De Jure Naturale Gentium, Etc. [*A publication*] (DLA)
Graves........ Proceedings in English King's Council [*1392-93*] [*A publication*] (DLA)
GRAVR....... Gravitational Redshift Space Probe [*Also, GP*]
Gray........... Gray's Massachusetts Supreme Judicial Court Reports [*67-82 Massachusetts*] [*1854-60*] [*A publication*] (DLA)
Gray........... Gray's Reports [*112-22 North Carolina*] [*A publication*] (DLA)
Gray Att Pr... Gray's Country Attorney's Practice [*9th ed.*] [*1869*] [*A publication*] (DLA)
GrayC........ Gray Communications Systems [*Associated Press*] (SAG)
GrayCom..... Gray Communications Systems [*Associated Press*] (SAG)
Gray Forms... Graydon's Forms of Conveyance [*A publication*] (DLA)
Gray (Mass)... Gray's Massachusetts Reports [*A publication*] (DLA)
Gray Perpetuities... Gray's Rule Against Perpetuities [*A publication*] (DLA)
GRAZ......... Grazioso [*Gracefully*] [*Music*]
GRAZO........ Grazioso [*Gracefully*] [*Music*]
GRB........... Gamma Ray Burst
GRB........... Garbo Industries [*Vancouver Stock Exchange symbol*]
GRB........... Geophysics Research Board
GRB........... Gerber Scientific [*NYSE symbol*] (TTSB)
GRB........... Gerber Scientific, Inc. [*NYSE symbol*] (SPSG)
GRB........... Government Reservation Bureau
GRB........... Granatbuechse [*Antitank Grenade Rifle*] [*German*]
GRB........... Granolithic Base
GRB........... Green Bay [*Wisconsin*] [*Airport symbol*] (OAG)
GRBC......... Goose Red Blood Cell
GRBDS........ Gyroscopes-Rate Bomb-Direction System (AAG)
GRBF......... Generalized Radial Basis Function [*Mathematics*]
GRBL......... Garble (FAAC)
GRBM......... Global Range Ballistic Missile [*Air Force*]
GRBNKS...... Grand Banks (FAAC)
Gr Br.......... Great Britain (WGA)
Gr Brice...... Green's Edition of Brice's Ultra Vires [*A publication*] (DLA)
Gr Brit........ Great Britain
GRBX......... Gearbox
GRC........... Gale Research Co. [*Later, GRI*]
GRC........... Garchy [*France*] [*Seismograph station code, US Geological Survey*] (SEIS)
GRC........... Gearcase (MSA)
GRC........... Gendarmerie Royale du Canada [*Royal Canadian Mounted Police - RCMP*]
GRC........... General Railway Classification [*British*]
GRC........... General Research Corp. [*Information service or system*] (IID)
GRC........... Generation Review Committee [*Nuclear Regulatory Commission*] (NRCH)
GRC........... Geographic Resources Center [*University of Missouri - Columbia*] [*Research center*] (RCD)
GRC........... Geotechnical Research Centre [*McGill University*] [*Canada Research center*] (RCD)
GRC........... Geothermal Resources Council (EA)
GRC........... Gerontology Research Center [*Department of Health and Human Services*] [*Research center*]
GRC........... Glass-Fiber Reinforced Concrete
GRC........... Glass-Reinforced Composite
GRC........... Glenmary Research Center (EA)
GRC........... Global Reference Code [*Developed by Smithsonian Institution*]
GRC........... Gorman-Rupp [*AMEX symbol*] (TTSB)
GRC........... Gorman-Rupp Co. [*AMEX symbol*] (SPSG)
GRC........... Government of the Republic of China
GRC........... Government Research Centers Directory [*Later, GRD*] [*A publication*]
GRC........... Government Research Corp. [*Information service or system*] (IID)
GRC........... Grace
GRC........... Graduate Research Center of the Southwest [*Later, University of Texas at Dallas*]
GRC........... Grafted Rubber Concentrate [*Organic chemistry*]
GRC........... Grand Cess [*Liberia*] [*Airport symbol*] (OAG)
GRC........... Greece [*ANSI three-letter standard code*] (CNC)
grc........... Greek, Ancient [*MARC language code Library of Congress*] (LCCP)
GRC........... Greene County District Library, Xenia, OH [*OCLC symbol*] (OCLC)
GRC........... Greenlandair Charter AS [*Denmark ICAO designator*] (FAAC)
GRC........... Gross Replacement Cost (ADA)
GRC........... Guard Ring Capacitor
GRCA......... Glassfibre Reinforced Cement Association [*British*]
GRCA......... Golden Retriever Club of America (EA)
GRCA......... Grand Canyon National Park
Gr Ca......... Grant's Cases [*A publication*] (DLA)
GRCA......... Ground Reference Coverage Area (DOMA)
Gr Capt....... Group Captain [*British military*] (DMA)
GRCD......... German Rhine Coordination Directorate [*Allied German Occupation Forces*]
GRCDA....... Governmental Refuse Collection and Disposal Association (EA)
GR CHAP .... Grand Chapter [*Freemasonry*] (ROG)
GRCHRSCHR... Die Griechische Christliche Schriftsteller der Ersten Drei Jahrhunderten (BJA)
GR/CIDS...... Genetic Resources/Communication, Information and Documentation System [*Databank*] (NITA)
GRC Int....... GRC International [*Associated Press*] (SAG)
GRCM......... Graduate of the Royal College of Music [*British*]
GRCO......... Gradco Systems [*NASDAQ symbol*] (TTSB)

GRCO......... Gradco Systems, Inc. [*NASDAQ symbol*] (NQ)
GR/CP........ Group Registration for Contributions to Periodicals [*US Copyright Office form*]
GrCr.......... Grande Croix (EY)
GRCS......... Guard Rail Common Sensor [*Army*] (DOMA)
GR/CS........ Guardrail/Common Sensor System [*Military*]
GRCSCC...... Golden Ring Council of Senior Citizens Clubs [*Defunct*] (EA)
GRCSW....... Graduate Research Center of the Southwest [*Formerly, Southwest Center for AdvancedStudies; later, University of Texas at Dallas*]
GRCTS........ Ground Combat Training Squadron
GrCu......... University of Crete, Crete, Greece [*Library symbol*] [*Library of Congress*] (LCLS)
GRCV......... Ground Cover [*Ecology*]
GRCV......... Guard Receiver (MCD)
GRCWA...... Grain Research Committee of Western Australia
GRD........... Gastroesophageal Reflux Disease [*Gastroenterology*] (DAVI)
GRD........... General Radio Discriminator (IAA)
GRD........... Geophysics Research Directorate [*US*]
GRD........... Goldrich Resources, Inc. [*Vancouver Stock Exchange symbol*]
GRD........... Government Research Directory [*A publication*]
GRD........... Grading
GRD........... Gramicidin [*Antimicrobial compound*]
GR D.......... Grand Duchess [*or Duke*] (ROG)
GRD........... Greatest Response Data
GRD........... Greenwood [*South Carolina*] [*Airport symbol*] (OAG)
GRD........... Grenada [*ANSI three-letter standard code*] (CNC)
GRD........... Grind (MSA)
GRD........... Ground
grd........... Ground (VRA)
GRD........... Ground Detector
GRD........... Ground Resolved Distance [*Satellite camera*]
GRD........... Ground Rule Double [*Baseball*]
Grd........... Ground Shells [*Quality of the bottom*] [*Nautical charts*]
GRD........... Guaranteed
GRD........... Guard
GRD........... Guard
GRD........... National Grid Co. [*British ICAO designator*] (FAAC)
GRDA......... Gin Rectifiers and Distillers Association [*British*] (DBA)
GRDAU....... Granddaughter (ROG)
GRDB......... Geoscientific Resource Data Base [*Queensland*] [*State*] (EERA)
GRDC......... Grains Research and Development Corporation [*Commonwealth*] [*State*] (EERA)
GrdCasn...... Grand Casinos, Inc. [*Associated Press*] (SAG)
GRDCUS...... Gulf Range Drone Control Upgrade System
GRDE......... Grade
GrDelV........ Greater Delaware Valley Savings Bank [*Associated Press*] (SAG)
GRDEN....... Garden [*Commonly used*] (OPSA)
GRDF......... Gypsum Roof Deck Foundation [*Later, NRDCA*] (EA)
GRDG......... Garden Ridge [*NASDAQ symbol*] (TTSB)
GRDG......... Garden Ridge Corp. [*NASDAQ symbol*] (SAG)
GRDL......... Geodetic Research and Development Laboratory [*Rockville, MD*] [*Department of Commerce*] (MSC)
GRDL......... Gradell Industries, Inc. [*NASDAQ symbol*] (SAG)
GRDL......... Gradual [*NWS*] (FAAC)
GRDL......... Griddle (MSA)
GRDN......... Garden (ADA)
GRDN......... Garden State Bancshares [*NASDAQ symbol*] (SAG)
GRDN......... Guardian
GRDN......... Guardian Technologies International, Inc. [*NASDAQ symbol*] (SAG)
GrdnB........ Guardian Bancorp [*Associated Press*] (SAG)
GRDNR....... Gardener
GRDNS....... Gardens [*Commonly used*] (OPSA)
GRDNU....... Guardian Tech Intl Unit [*NASDAQ symbol*] (TTSB)
GR/D/O....... Granddaughter Of [*Genealogy*]
GRDP......... Graphic Data Processing (IAA)
GrdPrd........ Guardsman Products, Inc. [*Associated Press*] (SAG)
GRDPRO...... Grid Procedure (SAA)
GrdPrx........ Grand Prix Association of Long Beach [*Associated Press*] (SAG)
GRDQ......... Groupe de Recherche sur la Demographie Quebecoise [*Research Group on Quebec Demography*] [*Canada*] (IRC)
GrdRnd....... Ground Round Restaurants, Inc. [*Associated Press*] (SAG)
GRDSR....... Geographically Referenced Data Storage and Retrieval System [*Canada*]
GrdTch........ Guardian Technologies International, Inc. [*Associated Press*] (SAG)
GRDTN....... Graduation (MSA)
Grdwtr....... Groundwater Technology, Inc. [*Associated Press*] (SAG)
GRE........... Gamma Ray Experiment
GRE........... Gamma Ray Explorer (NASA)
GRE........... Generated Repeatable Exams [*Education*]
GRE........... Generic Routing Encapsulation [*Computer science*]
GRE........... Glucocorticoid Responsive Element [*Endocrinology*]
GRE........... Gradient-Recalled Echo [*Physics*]
GRE........... Graduate Record Exam (GAGS)
GRE........... Graduate Record Examination [*Higher education*]
GRE........... Graduate Record Examinations Board (EA)
GRE........... Graduate Reliability Engineering
GRE........... Grant-Related Expenditure [*British*]
GRE........... Graphite-Reinforced Epoxy
GRE........... Gravitational Redshift Experiment (SSD)
GRE........... Greece (WDAA)
Gre........... Greece (WDAA)
gre........... Greek, Modern [*MARC language code Library of Congress*] (LCCP)
GRE........... [*The*] Greens [*Australia Political party*]
GRE........... Greenstone Resources Ltd. [*Toronto Stock Exchange symbol*]
GRE........... Greenville, IL [*Location identifier FAA*] (FAAL)

GRE .... Grenada [*Seismograph station code, US Geological Survey*] (SEIS)
GRE .... Ground RADAR Equipment (IAA)
GRE .... Ground Reconnaissance Equipment
GRE .... Ground Reconstruction Electronics [*Used in photographing moon*] [*NASA*]
GRE .... Ground Reconstruction Equipment
GRE .... Ground Run-Up Enclosure [*Aviation*] (DA)
GRE .... Grove Real Estate Asset Trust [*AMEX symbol*] (SAG)
GRE .... Guardian Royal Exchange Assurance [*British*]
Gre .... National Library of Greenland [*Nunatta Atuagaategarfi*], Nuuk, Greenland [*Library symbol*] [*Library of Congress*] (LCLS)
GRE .... SEEA-Southeast European Airlines [*Greece*] [*ICAO designator*] (FAAC)
GREA .... Grant-Related Expenditure Assessments [*British*]
GRE & E Div... Graves Registration and Effects Division [*Military*]
GREAT .... Geriatric Education and Training Act [*1985*]
GREAT .... Gifted Resources Education Action Team Project (EDAC)
GREAT .... Gorda Ridge Eruption Assessment Team [*Marine science*] (OSRA)
GREAT .... Grampian Region Early Anistreplase Trial [*Cardiology study*]
Greav Cr L... Greaves. Criminal Consolidation [*2nd ed.*] [*1862*] [*A publication*] (DLA)
Greaves .... Judgments of the Windward Islands Court of Appeal [*1866-1904*] [*A publication*] (DLA)
Greav Russ... Greaves' Edition of Russell on Crimes [*A publication*] (DLA)
GREB .... Galactic Radiation Experiment Background Satellite [*Navy transit satellite*]
GREB .... General Reciprocating Engine Bulletin [*A publication*] (DNAB)
GREB .... Graduate Records Examination Board (WDAA)
GRECC .... Geriatric Research, Education, and Clinical Center [*Veterans Administration*]
GRED .... Generalized Random Extract Device [*Computer science*]
GREDI .... Groupe d'Etudes en Developpement International [*International Development Studies Group*] [*Canada*]
GREE .... General Requests for Ground-Based Electronics Equipment [*NASA*]
GREEMAIN... Agreement to Remain on Active Duty Until Date Specified (DNAB)
GREEN .... Green [*Commonly used*] (OPSA)
Green .... Green's Reports [*A publication*] (DLA)
GREEN .... Guild to Revive Exhausted Nurses
Green & H Conv... Greenwood and Horwood's Conveyancing [*A publication*] (DLA)
GreenAP ...... Green [*A. P.*] Industries, Inc. [*Associated Press*] (SAG)
Green Bag.... Green Bag; A Legal Journal [*Boston*] [*A publication*] (DLA)
Green BL ..... Green's Bankrupt Law [*A publication*] (DLA)
Greenbr .... [*The*] Greenbrier Companies, Inc. [*Associated Press*] (SAG)
Greenbri ...... Greenbriar Corp. [*Associated Press*] (SAG)
Green Bri ..... Green's Edition of Brice's Ultra Vires [*A publication*] (DLA)
Green Conv... Greenwood's Manual of Conveyancing [*9th ed.*] [*1897*] [*A publication*] (DLA)
Green Cr...... Green's Criminal Law [*England*] [*A publication*] (DLA)
Green Cr Cas... Green's Criminal Cases [*A publication*] (DLA)
Green Crim Reports... Criminal Law Reports, by Green [*United States*] [*A publication*] (DLA)
Green Cr Law R... Green's Criminal Law Reports [*A publication*] (DLA)
Green Cr L Rep... Green's Criminal Law Reports [*A publication*] (DLA)
Green Cr Rep... Criminal Law Reports, by Green [*United States*] [*A publication*] (DLA)
Green Cruise... Greenleaf's Edition of Cruise's Digest of Real Property [*A publication*] (DLA)
Green Cts .... Greenwood on Courts [*A publication*] (DLA)
Greene......... Greene's Reports [*7 New York Annotated Cases*] [*A publication*] (DLA)
Green Ev...... Greenleaf on Evidence [*A publication*] (DLA)
Green Forms... Greening's Forms of Declarations, Pleadings, Etc. [*A publication*] (DLA)
Greenh Pub Pol... Greenhood's Doctrine of Public Policy in the Law of Contracts [*A publication*] (DLA)
Greenh Sh ... Greenhow's Shipping Law Manual [*A publication*] (DLA)
Greenl .... Greenland (BARN)
Greenl .... Greenleaf's Reports [*1-9 Maine*] [*A publication*] (DLA)
Greenl Cr..... Greenleaf's Edition of Cruise's Digest of Real Property [*A publication*] (DLA)
Greenl Cruise... Greenleaf's Edition of Cruise's Digest of Real Property [*A publication*] (DLA)
Greenl Cruise Real Prop... Greenleaf's Edition of Cruise's Digest of Real Property [*A publication*] (DLA)
Greenl Ev..... Greenleaf on Evidence [*A publication*] (DLA)
Greenl Ov Cas... Greenleaf's Over-Ruled Cases [*A publication*] (DLA)
Greenl Test Ev... Greenleaf on the Testimony of the Evangelists [*A publication*] (DLA)
Greenman.... Greenman Technologies, Inc. [*Associated Press*] (SAG)
Green (NJ)... Green's New Jersey Law or Equity [*A publication*] (DLA)
Green Ov Cas... Greenleaf's Over-Ruled Cases [*A publication*] (DLA)
Green (RI) ... Green's Reports [*Rhode Island*] [*A publication*] (DLA)
Green Rom Law... Green's Outlines of Roman Law [*A publication*] (DLA)
GREENS....... Greens [*Commonly used*] (OPSA)
GreenS .... GreenStone Industries, Inc. [*Associated Press*] (SAG)
Green Sc Cr Cas... Green's Criminal Cases [*A publication*] (DLA)
Green Sc Tr... Green's Scottish Trials for Treason [*A publication*] (DLA)
Green Ship... Greenhow's Law of Shipowners [*A publication*] (DLA)
GreenSt .... Green Street Financial Corp. [*Associated Press*] (SAG)
GreenStn .... GreenStone Industries, Inc. [*Associated Press*] (SAG)
GreenTR ...... GreenTree Financial Corp. [*Associated Press*] (SAG)
Greenw & M Mag Pol... Greenwood and Martin's Magistrates' Police Guide [*A publication*] (DLA)
Greenw Conv... Greenwood's Manual of Conveyancing [*9th ed.*] [*1897*] [*A publication*] (DLA)

Greenw Cts... Greenwood on Courts [*A publication*] (DLA)
GreenwSt.... Greenwich Street Municipal Fund, Inc. [*Associated Press*] (SAG)
Greer .... Greer's Irish Land Acts, Leading Cases [*1872-1903*] [*A publication*] (DLA)
GREF .... General Reserve Engineer Force [*British military*] (DMA)
GREFICOR ... Groupe de Recherche sur l'Efficacite Organisationnelle [*University of Quebec at Hull*] [*Research center*] (RCD)
G/REG .... Generator-Regulator [*Automotive engineering*]
G REG .... Grand Registrar [*Freemasonry*] (ROG)
GREG .... Gregorian (ROG)
Greg........... Gregorowski's Reports of the High Court [*A publication*] (DLA)
GregLA .... Pontificiae Universitatis Gregorianae Liber Annuus [*Rome*] [*A publication*] (BJA)
GRegO .... Group Regiment Officer [*British military*] (DMA)
Gregorowski... High Court Reports, Orange Free State [*A publication*] (DLA)
GREI .... Groupe de Recherche en Enseignement Individualise [*Canada*]
GreifBrA...... Greif Brothers Corp. [*Associated Press*] (SAG)
GreifBrB...... Greif Brothers Corp. [*Associated Press*] (SAG)
Greiner .... Greiner Engineering, Inc. [*Associated Press*] (SAG)
Grein Pr...... Greiner's Louisiana Practice [*A publication*] (DLA)
GREM .... Geopotential Research Explorer Mission (MCD)
GREM .... Gremlin [*Refers to a person unskilled in skateboarding*] [*Slang British*] (DSUE)
GREMAS ..... Genealogische Recherche mit Magnetband-Speicherung [*Organic chemistry coding system*]
GREMAS ..... Generic Retrieval by Magnetic-Tape Storage [*Computer science*] (PDAA)
GREMEX ...... Goddard Research and Engineering Management Exercise [*NASA*]
GREMF .... Groupe de Recherche et d'Echange Multidisciplinaires Feministes [*Universite Laval, Quebec*] [*Canada*]
GREN .... Grenade (AABC)
Gren........... Grenier's Ceylon Reports [*A publication*] (DLA)
GRENAP...... Greenlease Kidnapping
GRENDR...... Grenadier (AABC)
Grenfld .... Greenfield Industries, Inc. [*Associated Press*] (SAG)
Grenier .... Grenier's Ceylon Reports [*A publication*] (DLA)
Grenm .... Greenman Brothers, Inc. [*Associated Press*] (SAG)
grep .... Global Regular Expression and Print [*Computer science*] (CDE)
GREP .... Global Regular-Expression Purser [*Computer science*]
GREPAT ...... Greenland Patrol [*Navy*]
GrEq........... Gresley's Equity Evidence [*A publication*] (DLA)
GRER .... Greenstone Resources Ltd. [*NASDAQ symbol*] (NQ)
GRERF .... Greenstone Res Ltd [*NASDAQ symbol*] (TTSB)
Gre Rom Law... Greene's Outlines of Roman Law [*A publication*] (DLA)
GRES .... Global Renewable Energy Services [*Swinden, England*] [*Commercial firm*]
GRES .... Greatest Amount of Resources
Gres EqEv... Gresley's Equity Evidence [*A publication*] (DLA)
GRESLET .... Groupe de Recherche en Semantique, Lexicologie, et Terminologie [*Universite de Montreal, Quebec*] [*Canada*]
GRETA .... Ground RADAR Emitter for Training Aviators [*Army*] (RDA)
GR et I....... Georgius Rex et Imperator [*George, King and Emperor*]
Gretton .... Oxford Quarter Sessions Records [*Oxford Record Society, No. 16*] [*A publication*] (DLA)
GrEv.......... Greenleaf on Evidence [*A publication*] (DLA)
GREY .... Grey Advertising [*NASDAQ symbol*] (TTSB)
GREY .... Grey Advertising [*NASDAQ symbol*] (SAG)
GreyAd........ Grey Advertising, inc. [*Associated Press*] (SAG)
Grey Deb ..... Grey's House of Commons Debates [*A publication*] (DLA)
GreyhndL..... Greyhound Lines [*Associated Press*] (SAG)
GreyLne...... Greyhound Lines, Inc. [*Associated Press*] (SAG)
GRF .... Garbell Research Foundation (MCD)
GRF .... Gelatin, Resorcinol, and Formaldehyde
GRF .... Genetically-Related Factor [*Immunology*]
GRF .... Geographic Reference File [*Bureau of the Census*] (GFGA)
GRF .... Gerald Rudolf Ford [*US president, 1913-*]
GRF .... Gesneriad Research Foundation (EA)
GRF .... Golden Rule Foundation (EA)
GRF .... Gonadotropin-Releasing Factor [*Also, GnRF, GnRH, LH-RF, LH-RH/FSH-RH, LRF, LRH*] [*Endocrinology*]
GRF .... Graefenberg Array [*Erlangen*] [*Federal Republic of Germany*] [*Seismograph station code, US Geological Survey*] (SEIS)
GRF .... Grain Research Foundation [*Australia*]
GRF .... Grandfather
GRF .... Graphic Reproduction Federation (DGA)
GRF .... Grassland Research Foundation (EA)
GRF .... Gravity Research Foundation (EA)
GRF .... Ground Reaction Force [*Army*] (INF)
GRF .... Group Repetition Frequency
GRF .... Growth Hormone Releasing Factor [*Somatoliberin*] [*Also, GH-RF, GH-RH Endocrinology*]
GRF .... Guaranty Reserve Fund
GRF .... Guild Resource File [*Guild Products, Inc.*] [*Computer science*] (PCM)
GRF .... Tacoma/Fort Lewis, WA [*Location identifier FAA*] (FAAL)
GRFC .... Growth Financial Corp. [*NASDAQ symbol*] (SAG)
GR-FeSV ..... Gardner-Rasheed Feline Sarcoma Virus
GRFF .... General Radio Frequency Fitting (IAA)
G/Rfg .... Grooved Roofing [*Lumber*] (DAC)
GRFL .... Gerald R. Ford Library
GRFM .... General Radio Frequency Meter (IAA)
GRFMA .... Grand Rapids Furniture Market Association [*Inactive*] (EA)
GRFO .... Gun Range-Finder Operator
GrFRP........ Graphite-Fiber-Reinforced Plastic [*Also, GFRP*]
GRFX .... Grinding Fixture
GRG .... Gastroenterology Research Group [*Defunct*] (EA)

GRG .... Gearing (MSA)
GRG .... Generalized Reduced Gradient
GRG .... General Recurrent Grant
GRG .... Georgetown [Guyana] [Airport symbol] (AD)
GRG .... Glass-Fiber Reinforced Gypsum [Substitute wood]
GRG .... Glycine-Rich Glycoprotein (DMAA)
GRG .... Gordetsky [G.R.] Telecommunications and General Management Consulting [San Diego, CA] [Telecommunications] (TSSD)
Grg .... Gorgias [of Plato] [Classical studies] (OCD)
GRG .... Grandparents Raising Grandchildren (EA)
GRG .... Graphical Rewriting Grammar
GRG .... Gross Reserve Generation [Electronics] (IEEE)
GRGDB .... Gryehound Racing Grounds Development Board [Victoria, Australia]
GRGE .... Garage [Classified Advertising] (ADA)
GRGE .... Garage
GRGE .... Gorge [Board on Geographic Names]
Gr Gesch ..... Griechische Geschichte [A publication] (OCD)
GRGI .... Greenery Rehabilitation Group, Inc. (MHDW)
GRGL .... Groundwater Residue Guidance Level [Environmental Protection Agency]
GRGS .... Ground Roll Guidance System (MCD)
GRH .... Garuahi [Papua New Guinea] [Airport symbol] (OAG)
GRH .... Gas Recycle Hydrogenation [Petroleum engineering]
GRH .... Gentlemen's Right Handed [Golf club]
GRH .... Grahamstown [South Africa] [Seismograph station code, US Geological Survey Closed] (SEIS)
GRH .... Gramm-Rudman-Hollings [Law]
GRH .... Gramm-Rudman-Hollings Budget Deficit Control Act (AAGC)
GRH .... GRC International [NYSE symbol] (SPSG)
GRH .... Growth Hormone Releasing Hormone [Somatoliberin] [Also, GH-RF, GRF Endocrinology] (MAE)
GrhmFL .... Graham-Field Health Products, Inc. [Associated Press] (SAG)
GRHQU .... Gruppen-Hauptquartier [Group Headquarters] [German military - World War II]
GRHS .... Germans-from-Russia Heritage Society (EA)
GRI .... Gabriel Richard Institute (EA)
GRI .... Gale Research, Inc.
GRI .... Gallaudet Research Institute [Gallaudet College] [Research center] (RCD)
GRI .... Gamma Ray Inspection
GRI .... Gas Research Institute (EA)
GRI .... Generic Run-Time [Computer science]
GRI .... Geophysical Research Institute [University of New England, Australia]
GRI .... Geoscience Research Institute
GRI .... Gidley Research Institute [Research center] (RCD)
GRI .... Ginseng Research Institute (EA)
GRI .... Glider Developments, Inc. [Vancouver Stock Exchange symbol]
GRI .... Global Readiness Index
Gri .... Glyceric Acid [Biochemistry]
GRI .... Gospel Recordings, Inc.
GRI .... Government of the Ryukyu Islands
GRI .... Government Reports Index [Formerly, USGRDR-I] [Department of Commerce]
GRI .... Government Research Index (MCD)
GR-I .... Government Rubber-Isobutylene [Synthetic rubber]
GRI .... Grand Island [Nebraska] [Airport symbol] (OAG)
GRI .... Grassland Research Institute [Research center British] (IRC)
GRI .... Grassroots International (EA)
GRI .... Gravure Research Institute [Later, GAA] (EA)
GRI .... Groupe de Recherche et d'Intervention en Ideologie [Universite du Quebec a Montreal] [Canada]
GRI .... Group Repetition Interval (IEEE)
GRI .... Guaranteed Retirement Income
GRIB .... Gridded Binary [Data Format] [Marine science] (OSRA)
GRIB .... Gridded Binary Form [Computer science]
GRIBAT .... Graphics Interface Basic Acceptance Test (MCD)
GRIC .... Global Reach Internet Connection [Computer science]
GRIC .... Global Roaming Internet Connection [Computer science]
GRIC .... Graduate Member of the Royal Institute of Chemistry [British] (DBQ)
GRID .... Gas Research Institute Digest [Acronym is used as title of publication] [A publication]
GRID .... Gay-Related Immunodeficiency [Also, AID, AIDS] [Medicine]
GRID .... GEC [General Electric Company] Rectangular Image Data Processor (NITA)
GRID .... Global Resource Information Database [NASA]
GRID .... Global Resource Information Data Base [UNEP] [Nairobi, Kenya] [Information service or system] (IID)
GRID .... Graphic Interactive Display (IEEE)
GRID .... Graphic Reproduction by Integrated Design
GRID .... Graphic Retrieval and Information Display (NASA)
grid .... Gridiron [Typography] [Theater] (WDMC)
GRIDEQ .... Groupe de Recherche en Developpement de l'Est du Quebec [Canada]
GRIDS .... Geophysical Range Input Detection System
GRIDS .... Guidelines for Review and Internal Development in Schools (AIE)
GRIF .... Government Research Institute of Formosa
GRIF .... Griffin Technology, Inc. [NASDAQ symbol] (NQ)
GRIF .... Growth Hormone Release Inhibiting Factor [Also, GH-RIF, GH-RIH, SRIF, SS] [Endocrinology]
Grif Cr .... Griffith on Arrangements with Creditors [A publication] (DLA)
Grif Ct Mar... Griffith on Military Law and Courts-Martial [A publication] (DLA)
Grif Eq .... Griffith's Institutes of Equity [A publication] (DLA)
GRIFF .... Groupe de Recherches Interdisciplinaires des Fertilisation des Forets [Joint federal-provincial project] [Canada]

Griffin Pat Cas... Griffin's Patent Cases [1866-87] [A publication] (DLA)
Griffin PC... Griffin's Abstract of Patent Cases [England] [A publication] (DLA)
Griffith .... Griffith's Reports [1-5 Indiana Appeals and 117-132 Indiana] [A publication] (DLA)
Griffon .... Griffon Corp. [Associated Press] (SAG)
Griff Pat Cas... Griffin's Patent Cases [1866-87] [A publication] (DLA)
GrifGam .... Griffin Gaming & Entertainment [Associated Press] (SAG)
Grif Inst .... Griffith's Institutes of Equity [A publication] (DLA)
Grif Jud Acts... Griffith on the Judicature Acts [A publication] (DLA)
Grif L Reg ... Griffith's Law Register [Burlington, NJ] [A publication] (DLA)
Grif Mar Wom... Griffith's Married Women's Property Act [A publication] (DLA)
Grif Mil Law... Griffith on Military Law and Courts-Martial [A publication] (DLA)
Grif Pat C ... Griffin's Patent Cases [1866-87] [A publication] (DLA)
Grif PC .... Griffin's Patent Cases [1866-87] [A publication] (DLA)
Grif PLC ...... Griffin's London Poor Law Cases [1821-31] [A publication] (DLA)
Grif PL Cas... Griffin's London Poor Law Cases [1821-31] [A publication] (DLA)
Grif Pr .... Griffith's Practice [A publication] (DLA)
Grif PRC ..... Griffith's Poor Rate Cases [A publication] (DLA)
Grif PR Cas... Griffith's English Poor Rate Cases [A publication] (DLA)
Grif St .... Griffith's Stamp Duties [A publication] (DLA)
GrifTch .... Griffin Technology, Inc. [Associated Press] (SAG)
GRIL .... Gale Research International Ltd.
GRIL .... Grill Concepts [NASDAQ symbol] (TTSB)
GRIL .... Grill Concepts, Inc. [NASDAQ symbol] (SAG)
GrillCon .... Grill Concepts, Inc. [Associated Press] (SAG)
Grim Bank .. Grimsey's Proceedings in Bankruptcy [A publication] (DLA)
Grimke Ex... Grimke on Executors and Administrators [A publication] (DLA)
Grimke Jus... Grimke's Justice [A publication] (DLA)
Grimke PL... Grimke's Public Laws of South Carolina [A publication] (DLA)
GRIN .... Germplasm Resources Information Network [Department of Agriculture] [Beltsville, MD]
GRIN .... Graded-Index Fiber (ACRL)
GRIN .... Graded Refractive-Index [Optics]
GRIN .... Gradient of Refractive Index [Optics]
GRIN .... Grands Toys Intl [NASDAQ symbol] (TTSB)
GRIN .... Grand Toys International [NASDAQ symbol] (SAG)
GRIN .... Graphical Input [Language] [Computer science]
GRIN .... Great Plains [AAR code]
GRIN-2......... Graphical Interaction [Language] [Computer science]
GRIND .... Grinding
GRIND .... Group Index (MCD)
GRINDER .... Graphical Interactive Network Designer
GRINS......... General Retrieval Inquiry Negotiation Structure
GRINS......... Graphical Input of SMILES [Simplified Molecular Line Editor System] Input
GRINW........ Grand Toys Intl Wrrt [NASDAQ symbol] (TTSB)
GRIP .... Gemini Reentry Integration Program [NASA]
GRIP .... General Retrieval of Information Program [Computer science]
GRIP .... General Retrieval of Information Program [Hoechst Pharmaceutical Research Laboratories] [Personal indexing system] [British] (NITA)
GRIP .... Glutamate Receptor Interacting Protein [Neurochemistry]
GRIP .... Grandmet Information Processing [British]
GRIP .... Graphics Interaction with Proteins [Computer graphics]
GRIP .... Graphics Interactive Program (NITA)
GRIP .... Graphics Interactive Programming
GRIP .... Graphics Interactive Programming Language [McDonnell-Douglas Corp.]
GRIP .... Greenland Icecore Project [Europe] [Marine science] (OSRA)
GRIP .... Greenland Icesheet Program [Europe] [Marine science] (OSRA)
GRIP .... Greenland Icesheet Program [Europe] (USDC)
GRIP .... Groupe de Recherche sur les Insectes Piqueurs [University of Quebec at Trois-Rivieres] [Canada Research center] (RCD)
GRIP .... Guaranteed Recovery of Investment Principal [Economics]
GRIP .... International Grouping of Pharmaceuticals Distributors in the EEC (ECED)
GRIP .... Royal Grip [NASDAQ symbol] (TTSB)
GRIP .... Royal Grip, Inc. [NASDAQ symbol] (SAG)
GRIPHOS .... General Retrieval and Information Processor for Humanities Oriented Studies
GRIPS......... Gaming, Random Interfacing, and Problem Structuring (PDAA)
GRIPS......... General Relation Based Information Processing System (IAA)
GRIPS......... Graphic Image Pagination System [Penta Systems International]
GRIPS......... Ground Reconnaissance Information Processing System (DNAB)
GRIR .... Groupe de Recherche et d'Intervention Regionales [Universite du Quebec a Chicoutimi] [Canada]
GRIS .... Gamma-Ray Imaging Spectrometer
GRIS .... Global Resources Information System
gris .... Grisaille (VRA)
GRIS .... Grisons [Canton in Switzerland] (ROG)
GRIS .... Groupe de Recherche Interdisciplinaire en Sante [Interdisciplinary Health Research Group - IHRG] [Universite de Montreal] [Canada] [Research center]
GRISAH........ Groupe de Recherche et d'Intervention sur les Systemes d'Activities Humaines [University of Quebec at Rimouski] [Research center] (RCD)
GRISS .... Golombok Rust Inventory of Sexual Satisfaction [Test] [Psychology]
GRIST .... Grazing-Incidence Solar Telescope
GristMil .... Grist Mill Co. [Associated Press] (SAG)
GRISUR .... Grupo de Informacion y Solidaridad Uruguay [Switzerland]
Grisw.......... Griswold's Reports [14-19 Ohio] [A publication] (DLA)
Griswold ..... Griswold's Reports [14-19 Ohio] [A publication] (DLA)
Grisw Und ... Griswold's Fire Underwriter's Text-Book [A publication] (DLA)
GRIT .... Graduated Reduction in Tensions [Cold War term]
GRIT .... Grantor-Retained Income Trust [Estate planning]

GRITS .... Gamma Ray Imaging Telescope System
GRITS .... Geothermal Resource Interactive Temporal Simulation (PDAA)
GRITS .... Goddard Range [*and Range Rate*] Instrumentation Tracking System [*NASA*] (AAG)
GRJ .... George [*South Africa*] [*Airport symbol*] (OAG)
GRJ .... Gorje [*Yugoslavia*] [*Seismograph station code, US Geological Survey Closed*] (SEIS)
GRJC .... Grand Rapids Junior College [*Michigan*]
GRK .... Gear Rack
GRK .... Golden Rock Resources Ltd. [*Vancouver Stock Exchange symbol*]
GRK .... Goroka [*Papua New Guinea*] [*Seismograph station code, US Geological Survey Closed*] (SEIS)
GRK .... Greek [*Language, etc.*]
GRK .... Killeen, TX [*Location identifier FAA*] (FAAL)
GRL .... General
GRL .... Geophysical Research Letters [*A publication*]
GRL .... Gerontology Research Center, Baltimore, MD [*OCLC symbol*] (OCLC)
GRL .... Goldenrod Resources & Technology, Inc. [*Vancouver Stock Exchange symbol*]
GRL .... Grain Research Laboratory [*Canadian Grain Commission*] [*Research center*] (RCD)
GRL .... Greenland [*ANSI three-letter standard code*] (CNC)
GRL .... Grill
GRL .... Grille
GRL .... Gronlandsfly Ltd. [*Denmark ICAO designator*] (FAAC)
GRL .... Gross Reference List (DNAB)
GRL .... Grundrichtungslinie [*Base line, a gunnery term*] [*German military - World War II*]
Grld .... Greenland (VRA)
GRLL .... Roadhouse Grill, Inc. [*NASDAQ symbol*] (SAG)
GRLP .... Ground Lamp (IAA)
GRLS .... Great River Library System [*Library network*]
GRM .... Generalized Reed-Muller [*Codes*] (IEEE)
GRM .... Generalized Report Module Program [*Computer science*]
GRM .... Geophysical Research Mission [*Marine science*] (OSRA)
GRM .... Geopotential Research Mission [*NASA*]
GRM .... Germ [*or Germination*] (WGA)
GRM .... Global Range Missile [*Air Force*]
GRM .... Grahamstown [*South Africa*] [*Seismograph station code, US Geological Survey*] (SEIS)
GRM .... Gram (ADA)
GRM .... Gramme [*Gram*] [*French*] (ROG)
GRM .... Grand Marais, MN [*Location identifier FAA*] (FAAL)
GRM .... Grand Metropolitan ADS [*NYSE symbol*] (SPSG)
GRM .... Grandmother
GRM .... Graziano, R. M., Washington DC [*STAC*]
GRM .... Great Renunciation Movement (EA)
GRM .... Gross Rent Multiplier [*Business term*] (EMRF)
GRM .... Gruppe Revolutionaerer Marxisten [*Group of Revolutionary Marxists*] [*Austria Political party*] (PPE)
GRM .... Guarded Relay Multiplexer
GRM .... Guidance Rate Measurement
GRMN .... Garment Graphics [*NASDAQ symbol*] (TTSB)
GRMN .... Garment Graphics, Inc. [*NASDAQ symbol*] (SAG)
GRMNW ...... Garment Graphics Wrrt'A' [*NASDAQ symbol*] (TTSB)
GRMNZ .... Garment Graphics Wrrt'B' [*NASDAQ symbol*] (TTSB)
GrMonk .... Grease Monkey Holding Corp. [*Associated Press*] (SAG)
GRMPrA ...... Grand Met Del L.P. 9.42% Pfd [*NYSE symbol*] (TTSB)
GRMRA .... Gift Retailers, Manufacturers, and Reps Association (EA)
GRMT .... Garment
grmt .... Garment (VRA)
GRMT .... Grommet [*Automotive engineering*]
GRN .... General Re Corp. [*NYSE symbol*] (SPSG)
Grn .... Glycerone [*Biochemistry*]
GRN .... Gordon, NE [*Location identifier FAA*] (FAAL)
Gr N .... Graduate Nurse
GRN .... Gram-Negative [*Also, GN*] [*Microbiology*]
GRN .... Granite [*Technical drawings*]
GRN .... Granule [*Medicine*]
GRN .... Granulin (DMAA)
grn .... Green (VRA)
GRN .... Green (KSC)
GRN .... Green
GRN .... Greenair Hava Tasimaciligi AS [*Turkey*] [*ICAO designator*] (FAAC)
GRN .... Greens [*Political party Australia*]
GRN .... Greenville & Northern Railway Co. [*AAR code*]
GRN .... Greenwich Library, Greenwich, CT [*OCLC symbol*] (OCLC)
GRN .... Grenoble [*France*] [*Seismograph station code, US Geological Survey*] (SEIS)
GRN .... Grenoble Energy [*Vancouver Stock Exchange symbol*]
gRNA .... Guide Ribonucleic Acid [*Genetics*]
GRNC .... Group Number No Count [*Military communication*]
GRNCM .... Graduate of the Royal Northern College of Music [*British*] (DBQ)
GRND .... Grand
GRND .... Grand
GRND .... Ground (ADA)
GrnDan .... Green [*Daniel*] Co. [*Associated Press*] (SAG)
GrndM .... Grand Metropolitan Delaware Ltd. [*Associated Press*] (SAG)
GRNDMA ..... Grandma
GrndMet ...... Grand Metropolitan Ltd. [*Associated Press*] (SAG)
GRNDPA ...... Grandpa
GrndPr .... Grand Premier Financial, Inc. [*Associated Press*] (SAG)
GRNDR .... Grinder
GRNDR .... Grinder [*s*] [*Freight*]

Grnds .... Grounds (DD)
GrndToy ...... Grand Toys International [*Associated Press*] (SAG)
GrndUn .... Grand Union Co. [*Associated Press*] (SAG)
GRNHS .... Greenhouse
GRNL .... Gay Rights National Lobby (EA)
grnln .... Granulation (VRA)
Grnmn .... Greenman Technologies, Inc. [*Associated Press*] (SAG)
GrnMtn .... Green Mountain Coffee [*Associated Press*] (SAG)
GRNP .... Grant Geophysical, Inc. [*NASDAQ symbol*] (SAG)
GrnPtFin ...... Greenpoint Financial Corp. [*Associated Press*] (SAG)
GRNR .... [*The*] Grand River Railway Co. [*AAR code*]
GRNS .... Greens
GRNS .... Greens [*Postal Service standard*] (OPSA)
grnsh .... Greenish [*Philately*]
GrnStCA ...... Greenwich Street California Municipal Fund, Inc. [*Associated Press*] (SAG)
GrnstR .... Greenstone Roberts Advertising, Inc. [*Associated Press*] (SAG)
GrnstRs .... Greenstone Resources Ltd. [*Associated Press*] (SAG)
GRNT .... Granite
GRNT .... Grant Geophysical [*NASDAQ symbol*] (TTSB)
GRNT .... Grant Geophysical, Inc. [*NASDAQ symbol*] (SPSG)
GRNTD .... Guaranteed
GrnteC .... Granite Construction, Inc. [*Associated Press*] (SAG)
GrntG .... Grant Geophysical, Inc. [*Associated Press*] (SAG)
GrntGeo ...... Grant Geophysical, Inc. [*Associated Press*] (SAG)
GRNTP .... Grant Geophysical $2.4375 Cv Pfd [*NASDAQ symbol*] (TTSB)
GrntrSft .... Greentree Software, Inc. [*Associated Press*] (SAG)
GrntT .... Grant Tensor Geophysical Corp. [*Associated Press*] (SAG)
GrnwAir .... Greenwich Air Services, Inc. [*Associated Press*] (SAG)
GRO .... Gamma Ray Observatory [*NASA*] (EGAO)
GRO .... Gasoline Range Organic [*Chemistry*]
GRO .... General Register Office [*British*]
GRO .... General Routine Order
GRO .... Gerona [*Spain*] [*Airport symbol*] (OAG)
Gro .... Glycerol [*Biochemistry*]
GRO .... Government Reform and Oversight Committee [*House of Representatives*] (AAGC)
GRO .... Grandparents Rights Organization (EA)
GRO .... Graves Registration Officer [*Military*]
GRO .... Greenwich Royal Observatory [*British*] (BARN)
GRO .... Gross (MSA)
Gro .... Gross' Select Cases Concerning the Law Merchant [*Selden Society*] [*A publication*] (DLA)
Gro .... Grotius' Rights of War and Peace [*Many eds.*] [*1625-1901*] [*A publication*] (DLA)
GRO .... Ground Risks Only [*Insurance*] (AIA)
GRO .... Group (WGA)
GRO .... Grove
GRO .... Growth Investment Corp. [*Toronto Stock Exchange symbol*]
GRO .... Growth-Related Protein (DMAA)
GRO .... Grozny [*Former USSR Seismograph station code, US Geological Survey*] (SEIS)
GRO .... Lineas Aereas Allegro SA de CV [*Mexico ICAO designator*] (FAAC)
GRO .... Rota Island, TT [*Location identifier FAA*] (FAAL)
GROBDM ..... General Register Office for Births, Deaths, and Marriages [*A publication*] (DLA)
GROC .... Grocery (WDAA)
GROC .... Grocery
GROCAP ...... Gross Capability Estimator [*Air Force*]
GROFIS .... Ground Forces Intelligence Study (MCD)
GROJ .... Get Rid of Junk [*Garage sale sign*]
GROM .... Graphic Read-Only Memory [*Computer science*] (IAA)
GROM .... Grommet (KSC)
Gron .... Gronningen. Siglum for Tablets [*Leiden*] [*A publication*] (BJA)
GROOM .... Grooming
GROOVE ..... Generated Real-Time Output Operations on Voltage-Controlled Equipment [*Computer science*]
GROPAC ..... Group Pacific
GROS .... Grossman's, Inc. [*NASDAQ symbol*] (NQ)
gros .... Grossus [*Coarse*] [*Latin*] (MAE)
Grosmn .... Grossman's, Inc. [*Associated Press*] (SAG)
Gross St ..... Gross' Illinois Compiled Statutes [*A publication*] (DLA)
gro t .... Gross Tons (ODBW)
GROT .... Grote [*or Grotius*] [*Literature*] (ROG)
GROT .... Grotesque (ADA)
GROT .... Grotto (ROG)
Grot De JB... Grotius. De Jure Belli et Pacis [*A publication*] (DLA)
Grot De JrB... Grotius. De Jure Belli et Pacis [*A publication*] (DLA)
Grotius .... Grotius. Latin Law [*A publication*] (DLA)
Grotius De Jure Belli... Grotius. De Jure Belli et Pacis [*A publication*] (DLA)
Grot Soc'y ... Transactions. Grotius Society [*England*] [*A publication*] (DLA)
Groupe .... Groupe AB SA [*Associated Press*] (SAG)
Group1 .... Group 1 Software, Inc. [*Associated Press*] (SAG)
Group Legal Rev... Group Legal Review [*A publication*] (DLA)
GROV .... Grove [*Commonly used*] (OPSA)
GROV .... Grove Bank for Savings [*NASDAQ symbol*] (NQ)
GROV .... Grove Bank (MA) [*NASDAQ symbol*] (TTSB)
GROVE .... Grove [*Commonly used*] (OPSA)
GroveB .... Grove Bank for Savings [*Associated Press*] (SAG)
GroveR .... Grove Real Estate Asset Trust [*Associated Press*] (SAG)
GROVES ...... Groves [*Commonly used*] (OPSA)
GROW .... Greater Opportunities through Work [*Proposed federal program*]
GROW .... Group Relations Ongoing Workshops
Grow .... Growth [*A publication*]
GROW .... US Global Investors, Inc. [*NASDAQ symbol*] (SAG)

GrowBiz...... Grow Biz International, Inc. [Associated Press] (SAG)
GROWBY ..... Green, Red, Orange, White, Blue, Yellow [Military system of indicating what day of the week food products were made through colored packaging]
GROWN ...... Get-Rid-of-Westmoreland-Now [Secret society whose members were junior Pentagon officers] (VNW)
GROWTH ..... Get Rid of Waste through Team Harmony
GRP .... Gamma Ray Projector
GRP .... Gastrin-Releasing Peptide [Endocrinology]
GRP .... Gaussian Random Process [Mathematics]
GRP .... Gelatin Rigidized Panel
GRP .... General Receptor for Phosphoinositide [Biochemistry]
GRP .... Geographical Reference Points (GAVI)
GRP .... Giant Reef Petroleums [Vancouver Stock Exchange symbol]
GRP .... Glass-Reinforced Plastic [or Polyester]
GRP .... Glucocorticoid Receptor Protein [Biochemistry]
GRP .... Glucose Regulated Protein [Biochemistry]
GRP .... Gram-Positive [Also, GP] [Microbiology]
GRP .... Granite Point, AK [Location identifier FAA] (FAAL)
GRP .... Grant-Related Poundage [British]
GRP .... Greatest Response Probability
GrP .... Greenwood Publishing Corp., Westport, CT [Library symbol Library of Congress] (LCLS)
GRP .... Gross Rating Point [Television]
GRP .... Gross Regional Product
GRP .... Ground Relay Panel [Aerospace] (AAG)
GRP .... Group (KSC)
grp .... Group (DD)
GRP .... Group
GRP .... Group Reference Pilot [Telecommunications] (TEL)
GRP .... Grundrichtungspunkt [Base point, a gunnery term] [German military - World War II]
GRP .... Guardia Republicana [Peru]
GRP .... Guyana Republican Party [Political party] (EA)
GrPAB .... Gravida, Para, and Abortus [Gynecology and obstetrics] (DAVI)
GRPC .... Gulf Regional Planning Commission
Grp Capt .... Group Captain [British military] (DMA)
GRPH .... Graphic (MSA)
GRPH .... Graphic Industries [NASDAQ symbol] (TTSB)
GRPH .... Graphic Industries, Inc. [NASDAQ symbol] (NQ)
grph .... Graphite (VRA)
GRPHC .... Graphic
GrphIn .... Graphic Industries, Inc. [Associated Press] (SAG)
GRPJ .... Glass-Reinforced Plastic Joint
GRPL .... Grand Rapids Public Library [Michigan]
GRPP .... Glass-Reinforced Polypropylene (PDAA)
GRPS .... Glucose-Ringer-Phosphate Solution
GrpTech ..... Group Technologies Corp. [Associated Press] (SAG)
GRQ .... Goldrite Mining [Vancouver Stock Exchange symbol]
GRQ .... Groningen [Netherlands] [Airport symbol] (OAG)
GRQU .... Gran Quivira National Monument
GRR .... Asia Tigers Fund [NYSE symbol] (SPSG)
GRR .... Gastric Reservoir Reduction [Morbid obesity surgical treatment]
GRR .... Gear Reduction Ratio [Military] (CAAL)
GRR .... Geneva Radio Regulations
GRR .... Genotypic Relative Risk [Genetics]
GRR .... Georgetown Railroad Co. [AAR code]
GRR .... Golden Rim Resources, Inc. [Vancouver Stock Exchange symbol]
GRR .... Gorron [France] [Seismograph station code, US Geological Survey] (SEIS)
GRR .... Government Research and Development Reports
GRR .... Grand Rapids [Michigan] [Airport symbol] (OAG)
GRR .... Greek Research Reactor
GRR .... Guidance Reference Release (KSC)
GRR .... Kent County International Airport [FAA] (TAG)
GRRA .... Gramophone Record Retailers Association [British] (BI)
GRRC .... Gurkha Rifles Regimental Centre [British military] (DMA)
GRREG .... Graves Registration [Military]
GRRI .... Greenstone Roberts Adv [NASDAQ symbol] (TTSB)
GRRI .... Greenstone Roberts Advertising, Inc. [NASDAQ symbol] (SAG)
GRRRS .... Goddard Range and Range Rate System [NASA] (IAA)
GRS .... Beta-Glucuronidase [Organic chemistry] (DAVI)
GRS .... Gamma Radiation Source
GRS .... Gamma Radiation Spectrometer
GRS .... Gamma Ray Spectrometer
GRS .... Gamma Ray Spectrum
GRS .... Gaseous RADWASTE System [Nuclear energy] (NRCH)
GRS .... Generalized Retrieval System [Computer science]
GRS .... General Radio Service [Canada]
GRS .... General Reconnaissance School [British military] (DMA)
GRS .... General Records Schedules [Military] (AABC)
GRS .... General Register Set/Stack [Computer science]
GRS .... General Reporting System
GRS .... General Revenue Sharing [Office of Revenue Sharing]
GRS .... German Dermatological Society (EAIO)
GRS .... German Research Satellite [NASA]
GRS .... Ghost Research Society (EA)
GRS .... Golabi-Rosen Syndrome [Medicine] (DMAA)
GRS .... Golden Rule Society (EA)
GRS .... Goris [Former USSR Seismograph station code, US Geological Survey] (SEIS)
GR-S .... Government Rubber-Styrene [Also, SBR] [Synthetic rubber]
GRS .... Graduate Rabbinical School (BJA)
GRS .... Grand Recording Scribe [Freemasonry] (ROG)
GRS .... Grandson (ROG)

GRS .... Grass [Maps and charts]
GRS .... Gratiam Resources [Vancouver Stock Exchange symbol]
GRS .... Graves Registration Service [Military]
GRS .... Gravity Reference Signal [or System]
GRS .... Grease (MSA)
GRS .... Great Red Spot [on planet Jupiter]
GRS .... Grid Reference Ship [Navy] (NVT)
GRS .... Grigori Rasputin Society (EA)
GRS .... Grosseto [Italy] [Airport symbol] (AD)
GRS .... Groupe Revolutionnaire Socialiste [Socialist Revolution Group] [France] [Political party]
GRS .... Groupe Revolutionnaire Socialiste [Socialist Revolution Group] [Martinique] [Political party] (PPW)
GRS .... Gyro Reference System (AAG)
GRS .... Shorter College, Rome, GA [Library symbol Library of Congress] (LCLS)
GRSA .... Germersheim Reserve Storage Activity (MCD)
GRSA .... Great Sand Dunes National Monument
GRS & MIC... Gross and Microscopic [Medicine] (MEDA)
GRSC .... Graduate of the Royal Society of Chemistry [British] (DBQ)
GRSE .... Gamma Ray Spectrometric Equipment
GRSE .... Guild of Radio Service Engineers (BARN)
GRSHFT ...... Gearshaft (MSA)
GrSimec ..... Grupo Simec [Commercial firm Associated Press] (SAG)
GRSL .... Guam Reference Standards Laboratory (DNAB)
GRSLND ..... Grassland (RDA)
GRSM .... Graduate of the Royal Schools of Music [British]
GRSM .... Great Smoky Mountains National Park [Also, GSMNP]
GR/S/O........ Grandson Of [Genealogy]
GRSP .... General Range Safety Plan [NASA]
GRSP .... Glass-Reinforced Structural Plastic
GRSS .... IEEE Geoscience and Remote Sensing Society (EA)
GRST .... Grist Mill [NASDAQ symbol] (TTSB)
GRST .... Grist Mill Co. [NASDAQ symbol] (NQ)
GR ST .... Groom of the Stole [British]
GRST .... Gross Tons
GrStCA........ Greenwich Street California Municipal Fund, Inc. [Associated Press] (SAG)
GRSU .... Geography Remote Sensing Unit [University of California, Santa Barbara]
GRT .... Gabon-Air-Transport [ICAO designator] (FAAC)
GRT .... Gamma Ray Telescope
GRT .... Gamma Ray Tube
GRT .... General Reactor Technology (NRCH)
GRT .... Geriatric Rehabilitation Team [Australia]
GRT .... Glimcher Realty Trust [NYSE symbol] (SPSG)
GRT .... Government Rate Tender
GRT .... Graduate Respiratory Therapist
Grt .... Grant's Pennsylvania Cases [A publication] (DLA)
grt............... Graphic Technician [MARC relator code] [Library of Congress] (LCCP)
GRT .... Gratio [Tennessee] [Seismograph station code, US Geological Survey] (SEIS)
GRT .... Great (ROG)
GRT .... Great
GRT .... Gross Registered Tonnes (EERA)
GRT .... Gross Registered Tons [Navigation]
GRT .... Ground-Received Times [Solar wind measurements]
GRT .... Ground Resistance Tester
GRT .... Group Rapid Transit [TRB] (TAG)
GRT .... GTC Transcontinental Group Ltd. [Toronto Stock Exchange symbol]
GRT .... Gujrat [Pakistan] [Airport symbol] (AD)
Gr(T)........... Gunner (Torpedo) [British military] (DMA)
GRT .... Tri-County Regional Library, Rome, GA [Library symbol Library of Congress] (LCLS)
GRTA .... Government Reports and Topical Announcements [Later, WGA] [National Technical Information Service]
GRTA .... Group Relations Training Association (AIE)
GrtBay .... Great Bay Power Corp. [Associated Press] (SAG)
GrtBayPw.... Great Bay Power Corp. [Associated Press] (SAG)
GRTC .... Green River Test Complex
GRTC .... Groupe de Recherches pour les Transports au Canada [Canadian Transportation Research Forum]
GrtCtrl........ Great Central Mines [Associated Press] (SAG)
GRTE .... Grand Teton National Park
GrteBayC .... Greate Bay Casino [Associated Press] (SAG)
GrtFncl....... Great Financial Corp. [Associated Press] (SAG)
GRTG .... Granting
GRTG .... Grating (MSA)
GRTG .... Greeting
GRTH .... Growth
GRTK .... Group Technologies [NASDAQ symbol] (TTSB)
GRTK .... Group Technologies Corp. [NASDAQ symbol] (SAG)
GRTLKS ...... Great Lakes (FAAC)
GRTLS .... Glide Return to Landing Site (NASA)
GRTLS .... Glide Return to Launch Site (MCD)
GRTM .... Geared Roller Test Machine
GRTM .... Gross Ton-Mile (ADA)
GRTN .... Grid Return (MSA)
GrToy .... Grand Toys International [Associated Press] (SAG)
GRTP .... Glass-Fiber Reinforced Thermoplastics (PDAA)
GRTP .... Glass Reinforced Thermoplastic
GrtPines ..... Great Pines Water Co. [Associated Press] (SAG)
GRTR .... Grater (MSA)
GRTR .... Greater [Freight]

GRTR .... Greater
GRTR .... [*The*] Greater New York Savings Bank [*NASDAQ symbol*]   (NQ)
GRTR .... Greater N.Y. Svgs Bk [*NASDAQ symbol*]   (TTSB)
GRTS .... General Electric Remote Terminal Supervisor [*Honeywell*]   (NITA)
GRTS .... General Remote Terminal Supervisor
GRTS .... Geomagnetic Reversal Time Scale
GRTS .... Goddard Real Time System [*NASA*]   (IAA)
GRTS .... Ground Tracking System   (MCD)
GRTSFC .... Ginger Rogers: The Star Fan Club   (EA)
GrtSoB .... Great Southern Bancorp, Inc. [*Associated Press*]   (SAG)
GrtSoBcp ..... Great Southern Bancorp, Inc. [*Associated Press*]   (SAG)
Grtv ADR ..... Grootvlei Proprietary Mines Ltd. [*Associated Press*]   (SAG)
GrtWall .... Great Wall Electronic Internationl Ltd. [*Associated Press*]   (SAG)
GRU .... Genetic Resources Unit   (GNE)
GRU .... Glavnoe Razvedivatelnoe Upravlenie [*Chief Administration for Intelligence*] [*Division of the General Staff of the Soviet Army*] [*Former USSR*]
GRU .... Gold Ridge Resources [*Vancouver Stock Exchange symbol*]
GRU .... Grajau [*Brazil*] [*Airport symbol*]   (AD)
GRU .... Grid Reference Unit [*Military*]   (CAAL)
GRU .... Group
Gru .... Grus [*Constellation*]
GRU .... Guidance Regulator Unit
GRU .... Gyroscope Reference Unit   (MCD)
GRUB .... Grocery Update and Billing
GrubbEL .... Grubb & Ellis Co. [*Associated Press*]   (SAG)
GRUCOM ...... Group Commander
Grudman ...... Gramm-Rudman-Hollings Bill [*Proposed deficit-reducing bill, 1985-1986*]
GrUff .... Grand Ufficiale [*Grand Officer*]   (EY)
GRUMB .... Grumbalds [*England*]
Grumpie ...... Grim Ruthless Upwardly Mobile Professional [*Lifestyle classification*]
Grumpie ...... Grown-Up Mature Person [*Lifestyle classification*]
GRUNCH ...... Gross Universal Cash Heist [*Techno-economic term coined by Buckminster Fuller*]
GRUR .... Gewerblicher Rechtsschutz und Urheberrecht [*A publication*]   (ILCA)
GRUR Int ...... Gewerblicher Rechtsschutz und Urheberrecht, Internationaler Teil [*A publication*]   (ILCA)
GRUSL .... Group Sail [*Navy*]   (NVT)
GRV .... Grantsville, MD [*Location identifier FAA*]   (FAAL)
GRV .... Granville Island Brewing Co. Ltd. [*Vancouver Stock Exchange symbol*]
GRV .... Graphic Recording Voltmeter   (IAA)
GRV .... Graphite Rod Vaporization
grv .... Gravure   (VRA)
GRV .... Greenville [*Lake Wappapelo*] [*Missouri*] [*Seismograph station code, US Geological Survey*] [*Closed*]   (SEIS)
GRV .... Groove   (KSC)
GRV .... Grosvenor Aviation Services [*British ICAO designator*]   (FAAC)
GRV .... Ground Reaction Vector   (DMAA)
GRV .... Grove
GRV .... Grove
GRVA .... Graphic Varmeter
GRVD .... Grooved
GRVG .... Grooving
GR VJ POND... Grana Sex Pondere [*Six Grains by Weight*] [*Pharmacy*]   (ROG)
GRVL .... Gravel
GRVL .... Gravel
GRVR .... Groover
GRVS .... Groves [*Postal Service standard*]   (OPSA)
GRW .... Galactic Radio Wave
GRW .... General Railway Warrants [*US Military Government, Germany*]
GRW .... Giant Ragweed Test [*Medicine*]   (DMAA)
GRW .... Goodyear-Reston-Winthrop [*Publishing group*]
GRW .... Graciosa Island [*Azores*] [*Airport symbol*]   (OAG)
GRW .... Graphic Recording Wattmeter   (IAA)
GRW .... Greenwich [*United Kingdom*] [*Later, HAD*] [*Geomagnetic observatory code*]
GRW .... Greenwich Resources Ltd. [*Toronto Stock Exchange symbol Vancouver Stock Exchange symbol*]
GRW .... Greenwood, MS [*Location identifier FAA*]   (FAAL)
GRWS .... Gimbaled Reaction Wheel Scanner
GRWT .... Gross Weight
GRX .... Granada [*Spain*] [*Airport symbol*]   (OAG)
GRXR .... Ground Round Rest [*NASDAQ symbol*]   (TTSB)
GRXR .... Ground Round Restaraunts, Inc. [*NASDAQ symbol*]   (SAG)
GRY .... Gary [*Diocesan abbreviation*] [*Indiana*]   (TOCD)
GRY .... Gray   (ADA)
GRY .... Greyhound Racing
GRY .... Greymouth [*New Zealand*] [*Seismograph station code, US Geological Survey Closed*]   (SEIS)
GRY .... Grey Power [*Political party Australia*]
GRY .... Greystoke Exploration [*Vancouver Stock Exchange symbol*]
GRY .... Grimsey [*Iceland*] [*Airport symbol*]   (OAG)
gry .... Gross Redemption Yield   (BARN)
GryCm .... Gray Communications Systems [*Associated Press*]   (SAG)
GRYP .... Gryphon Holdings [*NASDAQ symbol*]   (SAG)
Gryphon .... Gryphon Holdings [*Associated Press*]   (SAG)
grysh .... Grayish [*Philately*]
GRZ .... Galapagos Rift Zone [*Marine science*]   (MSC)
GRZ .... Granophyric Roof Zone [*Geology*]
GRZ .... Graz [*Austria*] [*Airport symbol*]   (OAG)
GS.............. BAS Airlines [*ICAO designator*]   (AD)
G-S .... Gallard-Schlesinger [*Chemical manufacturing corporation*]
G/S .... Gallons per Second

GS.............. Galpin Society   (EA)
GS.............. Galvanized Steel [*Telecommunications*]
GS.............. Games Started [*Baseball*]
GS.............. Gap Separation
GS.............. Gardner Syndrome [*Medicine*]
GS.............. Gasoline Supply
GS.............. Gas Servicer   (MCD)
GS.............. Gas Sulfide [*Process for obtaining heavy water*]
GS.............. Gastric Shield [*Medicine*]
GS.............. Gaudium et Spes [*Pastoral Constitution on the Church in the Modern World*] [*Vatican II document*]
GS.............. Gauss [*Unit of magnetic flux density*] [*Preferred unit is T, Telsa*]
GS.............. General Schedule [*Federal employee job classification GS-1 to GS-18*]
GS.............. General Search   (IAA)
GS.............. General Secretariat
GS.............. General Secretary
GS.............. General Semantics
GS.............. General Service [*Literal translation, but used in sense of "excessively keen," or "overly acute"*] [*Army British*]
GS.............. General Sessions
GS.............. General Solution   (OA)
GS.............. General Specials
GS.............. General Speed [*Military*]
GS.............. General Staff [*Military*]
GS.............. General Statistics
GS.............. General Storage   (IAA)
GS.............. General Strike
GS.............. General Subjects   (MCD)
GS.............. General Superintendent
GS.............. General Support [*Military*]
GS.............. General Surgery
GS.............. Geochemical Society   (EA)
GS.............. Geological Society [*British*]   (EAIO)
GS.............. Geological Survey [*Department of the Interior*]
GS.............. German Silver
GS.............. Gerontological Society [*Later, GSA*]   (EA)
GS.............. Gesetzsammlung [*Collection of Statutes, Gazette*] [*German*]   (ILCA)
GS.............. Giant Slalom
GS.............. Gilbert's Syndrome [*Medicine*]
GS.............. Girl Scouts of the USA   (EA)
GS.............. Girls' School   (ADA)
GS.............. Glamour Stock [*Investment term*]
GS.............. Gland Seal [*System*] [*Nuclear energy*]   (NRCH)
GS.............. Glazounov Society   (EA)
GS.............. Glide Slope [*Aviation*]
GS.............. Gliding School [*British military*]   (DMA)
GS.............. Glomerular Sclerosis [*Medicine*]
GS.............. Glucose and Saline [*Medicine*]
GS.............. Glutamine Synthetase [*Also, GNS*] [*An enzyme*]
GS.............. Glycolytic Substrate
GS.............. Goal Shooter [*Netball*]
GS.............. Goldenhar Syndrome [*Medicine*]   (DMAA)
GS.............. Golden Shamrock Resources Corp. [*Vancouver Stock Exchange symbol*]
GS.............. Gold Smoke [*Dispersion of ultrafine metal particles*]
GS.............. Gold Standards
GS.............. Goudy Society   (EA)
GS.............. Government Security [*Business term*]
GS.............. Government Service
GS.............. Government Staffs [*British*]
GS.............. Grab Sample [*Analytical technique*]
GS.............. Grade System   (AAG)
GS.............. Grain Size Metal   (IAA)
GS.............. Grammar School
GS.............. Grand Scribe [*Freemasonry*]
GS.............. Grand Secretary [*Freemasonry*]
GS.............. Grand Sentinel [*Freemasonry*]
GS.............. Grand Sentry [*Freemasonry*]
GS.............. Grandson
GS.............. Grand Speed   (BARN)
GS.............. Grand Steward [*Freemasonry*]
GS.............. Gran Sport [*Automobile model designation*]
GS.............. Graphics and Sound [*in Apple IIGS*] [*Apple Computer, Inc.*]
G/S .... Gravity per Second   (KSC)
GS.............. Great Seal [*British*]
GS.............. Greenhouse Shrub [*Horticulture*]   (ROG)
GS.............. Grip Strength
GS.............. Grocery Store
GS.............. Gross Sales [*Business term*]
GS.............. Gross Spread [*Business term*]
GS.............. Ground Sensor
GS.............. Ground Speed [*Aviation*]
GS.............. Ground Stabilized   (MUGU)
GS.............. Ground Station [*Aerospace*]   (AAG)
GS.............. Ground Surface   (IAA)
GS.............. Ground System   (MCD)
G/S .... Ground to Slant   (MCD)
GS.............. Group Selector [*Telecommunications*]   (TEL)
GS.............. Group Separator [*Computer science*]
gs.............. Group Specific [*Antigen*] [*Immunology*]
GS.............. Group Structured [*Counseling group*]
GS.............. Growth Stage
GS.............. Growth Stock [*Investment term*]
GS.............. Grupo Socialista [*Socialist Group*] [*Portugal Political party*]   (PPE)

GS .... Guardship
GS .... Guard Society (EA)
GS .... Guard Squadron
GS .... Guidance Simulator
GS .... Guidance Station [*Aerospace*] (AAG)
GS .... Guidance System [*Aerospace*] (AAG)
GS .... Guide Slope (MUGU)
GS .... Guild of Surveyors [*Middlesex, England*] (EAIO)
GS .... Gulf Shelf [*Marine science*] (OSRA)
GS .... Gulf Shelf (USDC)
GS .... Gum Skips [*Philately*]
GS .... Gungywamp Society (EA)
GS .... Gunnery and Searchlight [*Control*] [*British World War II*]
GS .... Gunnery School [*Air Force*]
GS .... Gunnery Sergeant
GS .... Gunnery Support
GS .... Gyroscope (IAA)
GS .... Gyrostabilizer
GS .... Pfizer Ltd. [*Great Britain*] [*Research code symbol*]
GS .... Savannah Public and Chatham-Effingham-Liberty Regional Library, Savannah, GA [*Library symbol Library of Congress*] (LCLS)
GS .... Snow Pellets [*ICAO*] (FAAC)
GSA .... Armstrong State College, Savannah, GA [*Library symbol Library of Congress*] (LCLS)
GSA .... Gardenia Society of America (EA)
GSA .... Garden Seed Association
GSA .... Garden State Airlines, Inc. [*ICAO designator*] (FAAC)
GSA .... Gastroenterological Society of Australia
GSA .... Geinsheim Staging Activity
GSA .... General Services Administration (AAGC)
GSA .... General Services Administration [*Washington, DC*]
GSA .... General Services Administration, Washington, DC [*OCLC symbol*] (OCLC)
GSA .... General Somatic Afferent [*Nerve*] [*Anatomy*]
GSA .... General Studies Association [*British*]
GSA .... General Support Announcement [*Public television*]
GSA .... General Syntax Analyzer [*Sperry UNIVAC*]
GSA .... Genetics Society of America (EA)
GSA .... Geographic Systems Analysis [*Information service or system*] (IID)
GSA .... Geological Society of America (EA)
GSA .... Geological Society of Australia (EERA)
GSA .... Germanistic Society of America (EA)
GSA .... Gerontological Society of America (EA)
GSA .... Girl Scouts of America
GSA .... Girls' Schools Association [*British*]
GSA .... Glasgow School of Art [*Scotland*]
GSA .... Glass-Steagal Act [*1933*]
GSA .... Glide Slope Antenna [*Aviation*]
GSA .... Glutamatesemialdehyde [*Organic chemistry*]
GSA .... Goldfish Society of America (EA)
GSA .... Gourd Society of America [*Superseded by AGS*] (EA)
GSA .... Governor of South Australia
GSA .... Great Salinity Anomaly [*Marine science*] (OSRA)
GSA .... Greenhouse Suppliers Association (EA)
GSA .... [*The*] Green Party South Australia [*Political party*]
GSA .... Gross Sarcoma Virus Antigen [*Immunology*] (MAE)
GSA .... Gross Soluble Antigen
GSA .... Ground-Based Surface-to-Air (MCD)
GSA .... Ground Safety Approval (MUGU)
GSA .... Groundstar Resources Ltd. [*Vancouver Stock Exchange symbol*]
GSA .... Group-Specific Antigen [*Immunology*]
GSA .... GS Financial Products [*NYSE symbol*] (SAG)
GSA .... Guanidinosuccinic Acid (MAE)
GSA .... Guidance System Analyst [*Aerospace*] (IAA)
GSA .... Guild of Saint Alban
GSA .... Gulf & South American Steamship Co. (MHDB)
GSA .... Gusau [*Nigeria*] [*Airport symbol*] (AD)
GSA/ADTS.... General Services Administration/Automated Data and Telecommunications Services (OICC)
GSA-AT .... Glutamate Semialdehyde Aminotransferase [*An enzyme*]
GSAB .... General Surveys and Analysis Branch [*Department of Education*] (GFGA)
GSA-BCA..... General Services Administration - Board of Contract Appeals
GSA-CPO ... General Services Administration - Civilian Personnel Office
GSA DPA ..... GSA Delegation of Procurement Authority (AAGC)
GSA/FPRS.... General Services Administration/Federal Property Resources Services (OICC)
GSA/FSS ..... General Services Administration/Federal Supply Services (OICC)
GSAGR........ General Short Arc Geodetic Reduction (PDAA)
GSAI .... El Aaiun [*Western Sahara*] [*ICAO location identifier*] (ICLI)
GSAL .... Grupo de Solidariedade com America Latina [*Portugal*]
GSAM .... Generalized Sequential Access Method [*Computer science*]
GSAM .... Generalized Standard Addition Method [*Mathematics*]
GSA/NARS.... General Services Administration/National Archives and Records Services [*Franklin D. Roosevelt Library*] [*Hyde Park, NY*] (OICC)
GS & F .... Georgia Southern & Florida Railway Co.
GSA/OFR..... General Services Administration/Office of the Federal Register (OICC)
GSA-OP....... General Services Administration - Office of Preparedness
GSAP .... General Supported Accommodation Program [*New South Wales, Australia*]
GSAP .... Gun Sight Aiming Point
GSA-PBS..... General Services Administration - Public Building Service
GSAR .... General Services Acquisition Regulation

GSAR .... General Services Administration Acquisition Regulations [*A publication*] (AAGC)
GSARRTS .... Generator, Starter, Alternator, Regulator, and Rectifier Test Stand (MCD)
GSAT .... General Satellite (NASA)
GSAT .... Gesammelte Studien zum Alten Testament [*A publication*] (BJA)
GSAT .... Global Satellite Data Acquisition Team [*Marine science*] (OSRA)
GSAT .... Global Satellite Data Acquisition Team (USDC)
GS/ATE .... General Support/Automatic Test Equipment (MCD)
GS/ATSS ..... General Support/Automatic Test Support System (MCD)
GSB .... Gastric Stress Bleeding [*Medicine*]
GSB .... General School Budget (AIE)
GSB .... General Services Building [*Nuclear energy*] (NRCH)
GSB .... General Stud Book [*Horses*]
GSB .... Goldsboro, NC [*Location identifier FAA*] (FAAL)
GSB .... Gold Surface Barrier
GSB .... Government Savings Bank [*Australia*]
GSB .... Graduate School of Business [*University of Chicago*] (ECON)
GSB .... Grand Standard Bearer [*Freemasonry*] (ROG)
GSB .... Grand Sword-Bearer [*Freemasonry*]
GSB .... Gypsum Sheathing Board [*Technical drawings*]
GSBC .... Great Southern Bancorp [*NASDAQ symbol*] (TTSB)
GSBC .... Great Southern Bancorp, Inc. [*NASDAQ symbol*] (NQ)
GSBCA .... General Services Board of Contract Appeals
GSBG .... Gonadal Steroid-Binding Globulin [*Medicine*]
GSBI .... Gabungan Serikat Buruh Indonesia [*Federation of Indonesian Trade Unions*]
GSBI .... Granite State Bancshares [*NASDAQ symbol*] (TTSB)
GSBI .... Granite State Bankshares, Inc. [*NASDAQ symbol*] (NQ)
GSBP .... Glycosylation Site Binding Protein [*Biochemistry*]
GSBPS .... Global Space-Based Positioning and Navigation System
GSBR .... Gravel-Surface Built-Up Roof [*Technical drawings*]
GSC .... Galapagos Spreading Center [*Oceanography*]
GSC .... Gascoyne Junction [*Australia Airport symbol Obsolete*] (OAG)
GSC .... Gas-Solid Chromatography
GSC .... Gelman Sciences [*AMEX symbol*] (TTSB)
GSC .... Gelman Sciences, Inc. [*AMEX symbol*] (SPSG)
GSC .... General Service Corps [*Military unit*] [*British*]
GSC .... General Staff Corps [*Military*]
GSC .... General Staff Council [*Military*] (AABC)
GSC .... General Support Company [*Army*] (VNW)
GSC .... Genetically Significant Concentration [*Mutagenesis*]
GSC .... Geodetic Spacecraft (AAG)
GSC .... Geological Survey of Canada [*Marine science*] (MSC)
GSC .... Giant Serotonin-Containing [*Neuron*]
GSC .... Girls' School Company Ltd. [*British*] (BI)
GSC .... Gland Seal Condenser [*Nuclear energy*] (NRCH)
GSC .... Gland Steam Condenser [*Nuclear energy*] (NRCH)
GSC .... Glasgow [*Coma*] Scale [*Neurology*] (DAVI)
GSC .... Glenville State College [*West Virginia*]
GSC .... Golden Star Resources Ltd. [*Toronto Stock Exchange symbol*]
GSC .... Goldstone [*California*] [*Seismograph station code, US Geological Survey*] (SEIS)
GSC .... Good Samaritan Coalition [*Defunct*] (EA)
GSC .... Gravity Settling Culture
GSC .... Great Southwest Corp.
GSC .... Grid Spot Converter (NVT)
GSC .... Ground Services Cart
GSC .... Ground-Speed Continuing [*Aviation*]
GSC .... Ground Station Control (SSD)
GSC .... Group Study Course
GSC .... Group Switching Center [*British Telecommunications*] (TEL)
GSC .... GSA [*General Services Administration*] Stock Catalog
GSC .... Guardianship for Senior Citizens
GSC .... Guiana Space Center (MCD)
GSC .... Guidance Shipping Container
GSC .... Guidance System Console [*Aerospace*] (AAG)
GSCA .... Giant Schnauzer Club of America (EA)
GSCA .... Gordon Setter Club of America (EA)
GSCARNGARP... General Staff Committees on Army National Guard and Army Reserve Policy (AABC)
GSCC .... General Steel Casting Corp.
GSCC .... Global Simulation Control Center
GSCC .... Greater Siamese Cat Club (EA)
GSCF .... Geriatric Sentence Completion Form [*Personality development test*] [*Psychology*]
GSCG .... Ground Systems Coordination Group
GSCI .... GeoScience Corp. [*NASDAQ symbol*] (TTSB)
GSCI .... Ground Sound Control, Inc.
GSCM .... Gas Turbine Systems Technician, Master Chief [*Navy rating*] (DNAB)
GSCN .... General Scannning, Inc. [*NASDAQ symbol*] (SAG)
GSCN .... Genl Scanning [*NASDAQ symbol*] (TTSB)
GSCN .... Giant Serotonin-Containing Neuron (BABM)
GSCNY .... German Society of the City of New York (EA)
GSCO .... Guidance Sustainer Cutoff [*Aerospace*] (AAG)
GSCS .... Gas Turbine Systems Technician, Senior Chief [*Navy rating*] (DNAB)
GSCT .... Goldstein-Scheerer Cube Test [*Psychology*]
GSCT .... Guild of Sorting Clerks and Telegraphists [*A union*] [*British*]
GSCU .... Ground Service [*or Support*] Cooling Unit (KSC)
GSCW .... General Society of Colonial Wars (EA)
GSCW .... Georgia State College for Women [*Later, Women's College of Georgia*] (AEBS)
GSCWPPC... Guam Stamp Club and Western Pacific Philatelic Collectors (EA)
GSD .... Gate Stealer Display (MCD)
GSD .... General Sewing Data

GSD .... General Supply Depot
GSD .... General Support Division [*Air Force*]
GSD .... General System Description [*Military*] (AABC)
GSD .... General System Development [*or Design*] (IAA)
GSD .... General Systems Division [*IBM Corp.*]
GSD .... Generating Significant Dose [*Nuclear energy*] (NRCH)
GSD .... Generator Starter Drive
GSD .... Generic Structure Diagram [*Telecommunications*] (TEL)
GSD .... Genetically Significant Dosage [*X-Ray*]
GSD .... Genetic Sex Determination [*Biology*]
GSD .... Genotypic Sex Determination [*Embryology*]
GSD .... Geographical Data of Sweden [*Sweden*] (EERA)
GSD .... Geometric Standard Deviation [*Statistics*]
GSD .... German Shepherd Dog (DI)
GSD .... Gesco Industries, Inc. [*Toronto Stock Exchange symbol*]
GSD .... Glycogen Storage Disease [*Medicine*]
GSD .... Government Support Date (MCD)
GSD .... Grand Senior Deacon [*Freemasonry*]
GSD .... Grid Sphere Drag [*DoD satellite*]
GSD .... Ground Station Data
GSDA .... Great Southern Development Authority [*Western Australia*]
GSDA .... Grounded Surface Distribution Apparatus (IAA)
GSDA .... Ground-Speed Drift Angle [*Aviation*] (NG)
GSDB .... Geophysics and Space Data Bulletin [*A publication Air Force*]
GSDC .... Get Set Day Care Program [*Later, CDCP*] (EA)
GSDCA .... German Shepherd Dog Club of America (EA)
GSDF .... Ground Self-Defense Force [*Japan*]
GSDFJ .... Ground Self-Defense Force Japan
GSDL .... Ground Software Development Laboratory [*NASA*] (NASA)
GSDN .... Garden Supply Dealers National (EA)
GSDO .... General [*Aviation*] Safety District Office
GSDS .... General Status Display System [*Graphics system*] (NITA)
GS/DS .... General Support/Direct Support
GSDS .... Goldstone Duplicate Standard [*Deep Space Instrumentation Facility*] [*NASA*]
GSDT .... Generalized Syntax-Directed Translation (PDAA)
GSE .... General Somatic Efferent [*Nerve*] [*Anatomy*]
GSE .... General Support Equipment [*Military*] (MUGU)
GSE .... Geocentric Solar Ecliptic [*System*] [*NASA*]
GSE .... Geometric Standard Error (PDAA)
GSE .... Glutagen Sensitive Enteropathy [*Medicine*]
GSE .... Gluten-Sensitive Enteropathy [*Medicine*]
GSE .... Government-Specified Equipment [*Military*] (DNAB)
GSE .... Government Sponsored Enterprise [*FNMA*] (EMRF)
GSE .... Graphics Screen Editor (NITA)
GSE .... Grip Strong and Equal [*Neurology*] (DAVI)
GSE .... Gross Subsidy Equivalent [*Tariffs*] [*Australia*]
GSE .... Ground Service Equipment [*Air Force*]
GSE .... Ground Support Equipment [*Aviation*]
GSE .... Group of Scientific Experts
GSE .... Group Support Equipment
GSE .... Guias y Scouts de Europa [*Spain*] (EAIO)
GSE1 .... Gas Turbine Systems Technician, Electrical, First Class [*Navy rating*] (DNAB)
GSE2 .... Gas Turbine Systems Technician, Electrical, Second Class [*Navy rating*] (DNAB)
GSE3 .... Gas Turbine Systems Technician, Electrical, Third Class [*Navy rating*] (DNAB)
GSE-BI .... Ground Support Equipment-Base Installation [*Aviation*] (SAA)
GSEC .... Gas Turbine Systems Technician, Electrical, Chief [*Navy rating*] (DNAB)
G SEC .... Grand Secretary [*Freemasonry*] (ROG)
GSECP .... Ground Support Engineering Change Proposal [*Aerospace*] (AAG)
GSED .... Ground Support Equipment Division [*Naval Air Engineering Center*]
GSEE .... Geniki Synomospondia Ergaton Hellados [*General Confederation of Greek Labor*]
GSEEI .... Ground Support Equipment End Item [*Military*]
GSEF .... Ground Subsystem Evaluation Facility [*Army*] (RDA)
GSEFA .... Gas Turbine Systems Technician, Electrical, Fireman Apprentice [*Navy rating*] (DNAB)
GSEFN .... Gas Turbine Systems Technician, Electrical, Fireman [*Navy rating*] (DNAB)
GSEI .... Ground Support Equipment Illustration [*Military*] (MCD)
GSEID .... Ground Support Equipment Illustration Data [*Military*] (MCD)
GSEL .... Government Specified Equipment List [*Military*] (CAAL)
GSEL .... Ground Support Equipment List [*NASA*] (NASA)
GSEL .... Guidance System Evaluation Laboratory [*Military*] (CAAL)
GSE-M .... Ground Support Equipment-Mechanical [*Aviation*] (SAA)
GSE-ME ...... Ground Support Equipment-Maintenance Equipment [*Aviation*] (SAA)
GSE-MF ...... Ground Support Equipment-Maintenance Facility [*Aviation*] (SAA)
GSERD .... Ground Support Equipment Recommendation Data [*Military*] (MCD)
GSES .... Government-Sponsored Enterprises [*Federal National Mortgage Association, Student Loan Marketing Association, etc.*]
GSE-S .... Ground Support Equipment-Structure [*Aviation*] (SAA)
GSES .... GSE Systems [*NASDAQ symbol*] (TTSB)
GSES .... GSE Systems, Inc. [*NASDAQ symbol*] (SAG)
GSESD .... Ground Support Equipment Statistical Display (DNAB)
GSE-SE .... Group Support Equipment-Support Equipment [*Aviation*] (SAA)
GSE-SS .... Ground Support Equipment-Strategic System [*Aviation*] (SAA)
GSE-SS .... Ground Support Equipment-System and Service [*Aviation*] (SAA)
GSE-SS .... Ground Support Equipment-Systems Specification (IAA)
GSE Sy .... GSE Systems, Inc. [*Associated Press*] (SAG)
GSE-T & H... Ground Support Equipment-Transportation and Handling [*Aviation*] (SAA)
GSETD .... General Systems Engineering and Technical Direction

GSE-TS .... Ground Support Equipment-Test Stand [*Aviation*] (SAA)
GSE-WSR .... Ground Support Equipment-Weapon System Requirement [*Aviation*] (SAA)
GSF .... ACM Government Securities [*NYSE symbol*] (SPSG)
GSF .... ACM Gvt Securities [*NYSE symbol*] (TTSB)
GSF .... Galactosemic Fibroblasts [*Medicine*]
GSF .... General Semantics Foundation (EA)
GSF .... General Supply Fund
GSF .... General Support Force [*Air Force*]
GSF .... Genital Skin Fibroblast [*Medicine*] (DMAA)
GSF .... Georgia Southern & Florida Railway Co. [*AAR code*]
GSF .... Global Strategy Fund [*British*]
GSF .... Grenade Safety Fuze
GSF .... Ground Support Facilities [*Later, MGE*] [*Aerospace*] (AAG)
GSF .... Ground Support Fighter (MCD)
GSF .... Group of Soviet Forces
GSF .... Group of Soviet Forces in Germany (MCD)
GSF .... Gulf Sea Frontier
GSFA .... Genealogical Society of Flemish Americans (EA)
GSFC .... George Strait Fan Club (EA)
GSFC .... Goddard Space Flight Center [*Greenbelt, MD*] [*NASA*]
GSFC .... Green Street Financial [*NASDAQ symbol*] (TTSB)
GSFC .... Green Street Financial Corp. [*NASDAQ symbol*] (SAG)
GSFG .... Group of Soviet Forces in Germany (NATG)
GS Fin .... GS Financial Products [*Associated Press*] (SAG)
GSFLT .... Graduate School Foreign Language Test
GSFR .... Granulocyte Colony-Stimulating Factor Receptor (DMAA)
GSFS .... General Specifications for Ships (DNAB)
GSFSR .... Ground Safety and Flight Safety Requirements (AAG)
GSFU .... Glazed Structural Facing Units [*Technical drawings*]
GSG .... Garment Salesmen's Guild of New York [*Later, AG*] (EA)
GSG .... General Support Group [*Army*] (AABC)
GSG .... Glasgow, MT [*Location identifier FAA*] (FAAL)
GSG .... Glass-Silicone-Glass [*Electronics*] (DEN)
GSG .... Global Small Cap Fund [*AMEX symbol*] (TTSB)
GSG .... Global Small Capital Fund [*AMEX symbol*] (SPSG)
GSG .... Grammar School for Girls (ADA)
GSG .... Grenzschutzgruppe [*Border Protection Group*] [*German*]
GSG .... Ground Studies Group [*Military*] (VNW)
GSG .... Ground Systems Group [*Hughes Aircraft Co.*]
GSGA .... Geode Specialty Growers Association (EA)
GSGB .... Golf Society [*British*] (DBA)
GSGG .... Gadolinium, Scandium, Gallium, Garnet (MCD)
GSGS .... Geographical Section General Staff [*British*]
GSGT .... Gunnery Sergeant (DNAB)
GSH .... Gambia Air Shuttle Ltd. [*ICAO designator*] (FAAC)
GSH .... Gas Space Heater
GSH .... Gas Surge Header [*Nuclear energy*] (NRCH)
GSH .... Global Schoolhouse [*Computer science Telecommunications*]
GSH .... Glomerular-Stimulating Hormone [*Endocrinology*] (MAE)
GSH .... Glutathione [*Biochemistry*]
GSH .... Glutathione-SH [*Reduced glutathione*] [*Biochemistry*]
GSH .... Goshen, IN [*Location identifier FAA*] (FAAL)
GSH .... Growth-Stimulating Hormone [*Endocrinology*] (DAVI)
GSH .... Guangshen Railway ADS [*NYSE symbol*] (TTSB)
GSH .... Reduced Gluthathione [*Biochemistry*] (DAVI)
GSHR .... Gandhi Society for Human Rights (EA)
GSHR .... Grand Slam Home Runs [*Baseball*]
GSHV .... Ground Squirrel Hepatitis Virus
GSI .... General Safety Inspector [*Aviation*]
GSI .... General Service Infantry [*Army*]
GSI .... Generic Safety Issue (NRCH)
GSI .... Genetic Stock Identification [*Pisciculture*]
GSI .... Genuine Stress Incontinence [*Urology*] (DAVI)
GSI .... Geographical Survey Institute (EERA)
GSI .... Geographic Systems, Inc. [*Information service or system*] (IID)
GSI .... Geophysical Service, Inc.
GSI .... Gesneriad Society International (EA)
GSI .... Giant Scale Integration (IAA)
GSI .... Gigascale Integration [*Electronics*]
GSI .... Glide Slope Indicator [*Aviation*]
GSI .... Glide Speed Indicator
GSI .... Global Severity Index [*Medicine*] (DMAA)
GSI .... Gonosomatic Indices
GSI .... Gordon Diagnostic System [*Attention deficit disorder test*]
GSI .... Government Source Inspection
GSI .... Grand Scale Integration (BUR)
GSI .... Graphic Structure Input
GSI .... Greenwich Street Municipal Fund, Inc. [*NYSE symbol*] (SAG)
GSI .... Greenwich Street Muni Fund [*NYSE symbol*] (TTSB)
GSI .... Ground-Speed Indicator [*Aviation*] (MCD)
GSI .... Guild of Saint Ives (EA)
GSICO .... Glaucoma Society of the International Congress of Ophthalmology (EA)
GSID .... Ground-Emplaced Seismic Intrusion Detector (NVT)
G/SIDBAD .... General Staff Identification Badge [*Military decoration*] (GFGA)
GSIDC .... Arab Gulf States Information Documentation Center [*Information service or system*] (IID)
GSidekB........ Grupo Sidek SA de CV [*Associated Press*] (SAG)
GSIdentBad... General Staff Identification Badge [*Military decoration*] (AABC)
GSIFC .... Gene Summers International Fan Club (EA)
GSIFC .... Georgia Satellites International Fan Club (EA)
GSigsO .... Group Signals Officer [*British military*] (DMA)
GSIHS .... Group for the Study of Irish Historic Settlement [*British*]
GSII .... General Surgical Innovations, Inc. [*NASDAQ symbol*] (SAG)

GSII .... Genl Surgical Innovations [*NASDAQ symbol*] (TTSB)
GSIL............. German Silver
GSIO .... General Staff Interpreter Officer [*Military British*]
GSIS .... Group for the Standardization of Information Services (NITA)
GSISEA .... Government Service Insurance System Employees' Association [*Philippines*]
GSIT............ Group Shorr Imagery Test [*Personality development test*] [*Psychology*]
GSIU .... Ground Standard Interface Unit (MCD)
GSJ............. Gold Spring Resources [*Vancouver Stock Exchange symbol*]
GSJBS .... Goldsmiths', Silversmiths', and Jewellers' Benevolent Society [*British*]
GSJV .... Green Street Joint Venture (EERA)
GSK .... General Storekeeper [*Navy*]
GSK .... George Simon Kaufman [*American playwright, 1889-1961*]
GSK .... Glycogen Synthase Kinase [*An enzyme*]
GSK .... Gold Seeker Resources Ltd. [*Vancouver Stock Exchange symbol*]
GSKT .... Gasket (KSC)
GSL............. Generalized Simulation Language [*Computer science*] (MDG)
GSL............. General Service Launch [*British military*] (DMA)
GSL............. Generation Strategy Language [*Computer science*] (IEEE)
GSL............. Geographic Air Surveys Ltd. [*Canada ICAO designator*] (FAAC)
GSL............. Geographic Sciences Laboratory [*Fort Belvoir, VA*] [*United States Army Engineer Topographic Laboratories*] (GRD)
GSL............. Geographic Systems Laboratory [*US Army Engineer Topographic Laboratories*]
GSL............. Geological Society of London (BARN)
GSL............. Geophysical Sciences Laboratory [*New York University*]
GSL............. Georgia Department of Education, Atlanta, GA [*OCLC symbol*] (OCLC)
GSL............. Girls' Service League [*Later, YCL*] (EA)
GSL............. Glycosphingolipid [*Biochemistry*]
GSL............. Gold Cup Resources [*Vancouver Stock Exchange symbol*]
GSL............. Gorilla Sign Language (BYTE)
GSL............. Graduate Student Loan
GSL............. Great Salt Lake [*Utah*]
GSL............. Great Somalia League
GSL............. Ground Systems Laboratory
GSL............. Guaranteed Student Loan [*later, Stafford Loan*] [*Department of Education*]
GSLABHF..... Greater St. Louis Amateur Baseball Hall of Fame (EA)
GSLB .... Gold Star Lapel Button [*Military decoration*] (AABC)
GSLC .... Guaranty Financial [*NASDAQ symbol*] (TTSB)
GSLC .... Guaranty Financial Corp. [*NASDAQ symbol*] (SAG)
GSLC .... Guaranty Savings & Loan FA [*NASDAQ symbol*] (SAG)
GSLD .... Group Selector Long Distance [*Telecommunications*] (IAA)
GSLG .... German Studies Library Group (EAIO)
GSLO .... Gland Seal Leak Off [*Nuclear energy*] (NRCH)
GSLP .... Gibraltar Socialist Labour Party [*Political party*] (PPW)
GSLP .... Guaranteed Student Loan Program
GSLTA .... Girls' Schools Lawn Tennis Association [*British*] (BI)
GSLV .... Geostationary Launch Vehicle [*Indian Space Research Organization*]
GSLV .... Geostationary Satellite Launch Vehicle
GSM............. City of Savannah, Municipal Research Library, Savannah, GA [*Library symbol*] [*Library of Congress*] (LCLS)
GSM............. Garrison Sergeant-Major [*British*]
GSM............. Generalized Sequential Machine [*Computer science*]
GSM............. Generalized Sort/Merge [*Computer science*]
GSM............. General Sales Manager
GSM............. General Service Manager [*Automotive retailing*]
GSM............. General Service Medal [*British*]
GSM............. General Situation Map [*Military*] (NATG)
GSM............. General Stores Material [*Navy*]
GSM............. General Support Maintenance (MCD)
GSM............. General Synod Measures (ILCA)
GSM............. General System Mobile [*Telephone*]
GSM............. General System Model [*Computer science*] (EERA)
GSM............. Geocentric Solar Magnetospheric [*System*] [*NASA*]
GSM............. Geological Society of Malaysia (EAIO)
GSM............. Geological Survey of Great Britain and Museum of Practical Geology (BI)
GSM............. Gibson Spiral Maze [*Psychology*]
GSM............. Global System for Mobile Communication [*Computer science*]
GSM............. Global System for Mobiles [*European mobile-phone network*] (ECON)
GSM............. Gold Star Mothers
GSM............. Goldstream Resources Ltd. [*Vancouver Stock Exchange symbol*]
GSM............. Good Sound Merchantable
GSM............. Gradient Solidification Method [*Optics*]
GSM............. Grams per Square Meter
GSM............. Graphics Schematics Module [*McDonnell-Douglas Corp.*]
GSM............. Graphics System Module
GSM............. Grass Mountain [*Washington*] [*Seismograph station code, US Geological Survey*] (SEIS)
GSM............. Ground Signal Mixer
GSM............. Ground Station Modules [*Communications*] [*Army*]
GSM............. Ground Support Maintenance (MCD)
GSM............. Groupe Speciale Mobile [*European digital cellular radio standard*]
GSM............. Group Scout Master [*Scouting*]
GSM............. Guildhall School of Music [*London*]
GSM............. Guild of Saint Matthew
GSM1............ Gas Turbine Systems Technician, Mechanical, First Class [*Navy rating*] (DNAB)
GSM2............ Gas Turbine Systems Technician, Mechanical, Second Class [*Navy rating*] (DNAB)
GSM3............ Gas Turbine Systems Technician, Mechanical, Third Class [*Navy rating*] (DNAB)

GSMA .... Goldstone-SFOF [*Space Flight Operations Facility*] Microwave Assembly [*NASA*]
GSMB .... Grain Sorghum Marketing Board [*New South Wales, Australia*]
GSMB .... Graphic Standards Management Board
GSMBE .... Gas-Source Molecular Beam Epitaxy [*Coating technology*]
GSMC .... Gas Turbine Systems Technician, Mechanical, Chief [*Navy rating*] (DNAB)
GSMD .... General Society of Mayflower Descendants (EA)
GSMD .... Guildhall School of Music and Drama [*London*] (DI)
GSME .... Ground Support Maintenance Equipment [*Aerospace*]
GSMFA .... Gas Turbine Systems Technician, Mechanical, Fireman Apprentice [*Navy rating*] (DNAB)
GSMFC .... Gulf States Marine Fisheries Commission
GSMFN .... Gas Turbine Systems Technician, Mechanical, Fireman [*Navy rating*] (DNAB)
GSMI .... Global Spill Management, Inc. [*NASDAQ symbol*] (SAG)
GSML .... Generalized Standard Markup Language [*Also, SGML*]
GSML .... General Stores Material List
GSMNP .... Great Smoky Mountains National Park [*Also, GRSM*]
GSMS .... Government Securities Management System [*The Bond Buyer, Inc.*] [*Information service or system*] (IID)
GSMS .... Growth of Strategic Materials in Space (MCD)
GSMS .... Gulf South Medical Supply [*NASDAQ symbol*] (SAG)
GSMS .... Gulf South Medical Supply [*NASDAQ symbol*] (TTSB)
GSMT .... General Society of Mechanics and Tradesmen (EA)
GSN .... Gesneriad Saintpaulia News [*A publication*]
GSN .... Giant Serotonin-Containing Neuron [*Medicine*] (DMAA)
GSN .... Greenwich Sidereal Noon (ROG)
GSN .... Mount Gunson [*Australia Airport symbol*] (OAG)
GSN .... Saipan International Airport [*FAA*] (TAG)
GSNA .... Goethe Society of North America (EA)
GSNC .... General Steam Navigation Co. [*British*]
GSNCO......... General Steam Navigation Co. [*Shipping*] [*British*]
GSNS .... Guidance Control and Navigation Subsystem
GSNSW........ Geographical Society of New South Wales [*Australia*]
GSNT .... Genealogical Society of the Northern Territory [*Australia*]
GSNX .... GaSonics International [*NASDAQ symbol*] (TTSB)
GSNX .... Gasonics International Corp. [*NASDAQ symbol*] (SAG)
GSO .... General Salary Order [*United States*] (DLA)
GSO .... General Services Officer
GSO .... General Spin Orbitals [*Atomic physics*]
GSO .... General Staff Officer [*Military*]
GSO .... General Stores Officer
GSO .... General Submarine Officer (DOMA)
GSO .... General Supply Office
GSO .... General Support Office
GSO .... Geo. S. Olive & Co. [*Telecommunications service*] (TSSD)
GSO .... Geostationary Orbit (MCD)
GSO .... Geosynchronous Orbit
GSO .... Government Services Organization (DOMA)
GSO .... Government Solicitor's Office [*Australian Capital Territory*]
GSO .... Government Statistician's Office [*Queensland, Australia*]
GSO .... Government Superannuation Office [*Queensland, Australia*]
GSO .... Graduate School of Oceanography [*University of Rhode Island*]
GSO .... Graduate Service Overseas of the National Union of Students [*British*] (AEBS)
GSO .... Greensboro/High Point/Winston Salem [*North Carolina*] [*Airport symbol*]
GSO .... Ground Safety Office [*or Officer*] [*Air Force*]
GSO .... Ground-Speed Oscillator [*Aviation*]
GSO .... Ground Support Office [*or Officer*] [*Military*] (AFIT)
GSO .... Ground Support Operations [*Aerospace*] (MCD)
GSO .... Ground Systems Operations (MCD)
GSO .... Growth Stock Outlook Trust, Inc. (MHDW)
GSO .... GSR Goldsearch Resources [*Vancouver Stock Exchange symbol*]
GSO .... Gun Safety Officer
GSO .... Gyro Storage Oven
GSO .... Olive [*Geo S.*] & Co. [*Indianapolis, IN*] (TSSD)
GSO .... Piedmont Triad International Airport [*FAA*] (TAG)
GSoA .... Gerontological Society of America (DAVI)
GSOC .... Gold Star Owners Club (EA)
GSOF .... Group 1 Software [*NASDAQ symbol*] (TTSB)
GSOF .... Group 1 Software, Inc. [*NASDAQ symbol*] (NQ)
GS of W....... Grand Superintendent of Works [*Freemasonry*]
GSOIA .... General Security of Information Agreement
GSOP .... General Stock Ownership Plan
GSOP .... Guidance Systems Operation Plan [*NASA*] (KSC)
GSOR .... General Staff Operational Requirements [*Army*] (AABC)
GSOST .... Goldstein-Scheerer Object Sorting Test [*Psychology*]
GSOWM........ Global Spectral Ocean Wave Model
GSP .... Galvanic Skin Potential [*Physiology*]
GSP .... Gel Supported Precipitation [*Method*] [*Chemistry*]
GSP .... Genealogical Society of Pennsylvania (EA)
GSP .... Generalised System of Preferences (ECON)
GSP .... Generalized System of Tariff Preferences [*US Customs Service*]
GSP .... General Sea Harvest [*Vancouver Stock Exchange symbol*]
GSP .... General Semantic Problem (AAG)
GSP .... General Simulation Program [*Programming language*] (IEEE)
GSP .... General Strike for Peace
GSP .... General Strike Plan (NATG)
GSP .... General Syntactic Processor
GSP .... Geodetic Satellite Program
GSP .... German Society of Pennsylvania (EA)
GSP .... Girl Scouts of the Philippines

GSP .... Gladstone Stream [*New Zealand*] [*Seismograph station code, US Geological Survey*] (SEIS)
GSP .... Glycosylated Serum Protein
GSP .... Good-Service Pension [*Navy British*]
GSP .... Government Selected Price
GSP .... Government Sponsored Promotion (ADA)
GSP .... Government Standard Parts
GSP .... Graphics System Processor [*Texas Instruments, Inc.*] [*Computer hardware*]
GSP .... Graphic Subroutine Package [*Computer science*]
GSP .... Greenville/Spartanburg [*South Carolina*] [*Airport symbol*]
GSP .... Greer, SC [*Location identifier FAA*] (FAAL)
GSP .... Gross Social Product [*Economics*]
GSP .... Gross State Product (OICC)
GSP .... Ground Safety Plan (MUGU)
GSP .... Group Select Panel (ECII)
GSP .... Growth Fund of Spain [*NYSE symbol*] (SPSG)
GSP .... Guidance Signal Processor (KSC)
GSP .... M & M Aviation, Inc. [*ICAO designator*] (FAAC)
GSP .... Royal Geographical Society. Proceedings [*A publication*]
GSPA .... Gold Star Parents for Amnesty [*Defunct*] (EA)
GSPA .... Grain Sorghum Producers Association (EA)
GSPC .... Gas Scintillation Proportional Counter [*Instrumentation*]
GSPC .... Graphic Standards Planning Committee (NITA)
GSPCA .... German Shorthaired Pointer Club of America (EA)
GSPE .... Georgia Society of Professional Engineers (SRA)
GSPE .... Groupe Socialiste du Parlement Europeen [*Socialist Group in the European Parliament - SGEP*] (EAIO)
GSPHCT ...... Group Simplified Perturbed Hard Chain Theory [*Equation of state*]
GSPL .... Gospel
GSPMR .... General Services Administration Property Management Regulation [*A publication*] (AAGC)
GSPN .... Greater Superficial Petrosal Neurectomy [*Neurosurgery*] (DAVI)
GSPO .... Gemini Spacecraft Project Office [*NASA*] (MCD)
G (Spot) ...... Graefenberg Spot [*Gynecology*]
GSPR .... General Session of Peace Roll [*British Legal term*] (ROG)
GSPR .... GSA [*General Services Administration*] Procurement Regulations
GSP-R .... Guidance Signal Processor-Repeater (KSC)
GSPRT .... Generalized Sequential Probability Ratio Test (PDAA)
GSPS .... Generating Station Protection System [*Nuclear energy*] (NRCH)
GSPS .... Guidance Spare Power Supply
GSPTEK ...... Graphics Support Processor/Tektronix
GSPWA .... Georgia Southern Peanut Warehousemen's Association (SRA)
GSQ .... Generalized Sinusoidal Quantity
GSQ .... Genus Equity Corp. [*Toronto Stock Exchange symbol*]
GSQ .... Geological Survey of Queensland [*Australia*]
GSQC .... Ground Surveillance Qualification Course [*Army*]
GSQT .... Gun Ship Qualification Trials (MCD)
GSR .... Galvanic Skin Resistance [*Physiology*] (DAVI)
GSR .... Galvanic Skin Response [*or Reflex*] [*Physiology*]
GSR .... Galvanic Stimulation Rate [*Physiology*]
GSR .... Gardo [*Somalia*] [*Airport symbol*] (OAG)
GSR .... Generalized Schartzman Reaction [*Medicine*]
GSR .... General Service Recruit [*Navy*]
GSR .... General Staff Requirement [*British*] (RDA)
GSR .... General Support Reinforcing [*Army*] (AABC)
GSR .... General Systems Research Ltd. [*Vancouver Stock Exchange symbol*]
GSR .... Geological Survey, Reston [*Virginia*] [*Seismograph station code, US Geological Survey*] (SEIS)
gsr .... Georgian Soviet Socialist Republic [*MARC country of publication code Library of Congress*] (LCCP)
GSR .... Germanium Stack Rectifier
GSR .... German Sanchez Ruiperez [*Founder and chairman of Anaya, a Spanish publishing enterprise*]
GSR .... Gland Steam Regulator [*Nuclear energy*] (NRCH)
GSR .... Glide Slope Receiver [*Aviation*]
GSR .... Global Shared Resources [*Computer science*] (IBMDP)
GSR .... Golden Star Resources [*AMEX symbol*] (TTSB)
GSR .... Golden Star Resources Ltd. [*AMEX symbol*] (SPSG)
GSR .... Gongwer's State Reports [*Ohio*] [*A publication*] (DLA)
GSR .... Government Spares Release (MCD)
GSR .... Graphic Service Routines [*Computer science*] (MCD)
GSR .... Grid Space Relay
GSR .... Ground Sensor Relay (IAA)
GSR .... Ground Service Relay (MCD)
GSR .... Ground-Speed Returning [*Aviation*]
GSR .... Ground Surveillance RADAR
GSR .... Group Sales Representative [*Health insurance*] (GHCT)
GSR .... Group Selective Register
GSR .... Gunshot Residue [*Forensics*]
GSR .... Gun Sound Ranging [*An acoustic device*]
GSRB .... Glide Slope Reference Bar [*Aviation*]
GSRI .... Global Solar Radiation Index (PDAA)
GSRI .... Great Swamp Research Institute (EA)
GSRI .... Gulf South Research Institute
GSRP .... Gambian Socialist Revolutionary Party [*Political party*] (PD)
GSRS .... General Support Rocket System
GSRS .... Ground Support Rocket System (DWSG)
GSRS .... Ground Surveillance RADAR System
GSRT .... Gesell School Rediness Test (EDAC)
GSRVC .... Good Sam Recreational Vehicle Club (EA)
GSS .... Chieftain International Fund [*AMEX symbol*] (SPSG)
GSS .... Galvanized Steel Sheet [*Technical drawings*]
GSS .... Galvanized Steel Strand [*Telecommunications*] (TEL)
GSS .... Gamete Shedding Substance [*Endocrinology*]

GSS .... Gamma Scintillation System (MSA)
GSS .... Gamma Sigma Sigma (EA)
GSS .... General Service School [*Army*]
GSS .... General Simulation System [*Army*]
GSS .... General Social Survey [*National Opinion Research Center*]
GSS .... General Staff Support (IAA)
GSS .... General Supply Schedule
GSS .... General Support System
GSS .... Genesis Airways Ltd. [*British*] [*FAA designator*] (FAAC)
GSS .... Geodetic Stationary Satellite
GSS .... George Sand Studies (EA)
GSS .... Geostationary Satellite (PDAA)
GSS .... Gerontology Special Interest Section [*American Occupational Therapy Association*]
GSS .... Gerstmann-Staussler Syndrome [*Medicine*]
GSS .... Gerstmann-Straussler-Sheinker [*Disease*]
GSS .... Ghost Story Society [*British*] (DBA)
GSS .... Gilbert and Sullivan Society (EA)
GSS .... Global Space Station [*Proposed by NASA and ESA*]
GSS .... Global Subsurface System (DWSG)
GSS .... Global Surveillance Station (IAA)
GSS .... Global Surveillance System [*Air Force*]
GSS .... Gonad-Stimulating Substance [*Endocrinology*]
GSS .... Good Shepherd Sisters [*Australia*]
GSS .... Gossan Resources [*Vancouver Stock Exchange symbol*]
GSS .... Government Statistical Service [*British*]
GSS .... Graphic Software Systems Inc. (NITA)
GSS .... Graphic Support Software
GSS .... Gravity Sensors System [*Navigation*]
GSS .... Gray-Scale Sonography [*Medicine*]
GSS .... Ground Support Software [*NASA*] (NASA)
GSS .... Ground Support System [*Aerospace*] (AAG)
GSS .... Group Switching Subsystem (ACRL)
GSS .... Growth Space Station (KSC)
GSS .... Guidance System Simulator
GSS .... Rome, NY [*Location identifier FAA*] (FAAL)
GSSA .... General Support Service Area (MCD)
GSSA .... General Support Supply Activity (MCD)
GSSA .... Grassland Society of Southern Africa [*See also WVSA*] (EAIO)
GSSA .... Ground Support Systems Activation [*NASA*] (NASA)
GSSAPI .... Generic Security Service Application Program Interface
GSSC .... Greater Super Six Club [*Defunct*] (EA)
GSSC .... Ground Support Simulation Computer [*Aerospace*] (KSC)
GSSC .... Ground Support Systems Contractor [*NASA*] (NASA)
GSSC .... Savannah State College, Savannah, GA [*Library symbol Library of Congress*] (LCLS)
GSSD .... Gerstmann-Straeussler-Scheinker Disease [*Medicine*] (DMAA)
GSSF .... General Supply Stock Fund [*Air Force*] (AFM)
GSSF .... Government Satellite Services Facility (SSD)
GSSF .... Ground Special Security Forces
GSSG .... Glutathione [*Oxidized*] [*Biochemistry*]
GSSG-R .... Glutathione Reductase [*An enzyme*] (DAVI)
GSSI .... Ground Support System Integration (MCD)
GSsiHi .... Coastal Georgia Historical Society, St. Simons Island, GA [*Library symbol*] [*Library of Congress*] (LCLS)
GSsiM .... The Methodist Museum, St. Simons Island, GA [*Library symbol*] [*Library of Congress*] (LCLS)
GSSL .... General Staff Support Large (IAA)
GSSL .... Genoa, Savona, Spezia, or Leghorn [*Italian ports*] (DS)
GSSLD .... Group Selector of Secondary Long Distance [*Telecommunications*] (IAA)
GSSLNCV .... Genoa, Savona, Spezia, Leghorn, Naples, or Civita Vecchia [*Italian ports*] (DS)
GSSM .... General Staff Support Medium (IAA)
GSSO .... General Stores Supply Office
GSSP .... Global Stratotype Section and Point [*Paleontology*]
GSSPr .... Chieftain Intl Fd $1.8125 Cv Pfd [*AMEX symbol*] (TTSB)
GSSPS .... Gravitationally Stabilized Solar Power System
GSSq .... Geodetic Survey Squadron [*Air Force*] (AFM)
GSSR .... Generalized Sanarelli-Shwartzman Reaction [*Medicine*] (MAE)
GSSR .... General Salary Stabilization Regulations [*United States*] (DLA)
GSSR .... Ground Support System Review [*Aerospace*] (AAG)
GSSS .... Ground Support System Specification [*Aerospace*] (AAG)
GSSSP .... Graduate Science Student Support Postdoctorals Survey [*National Science Foundation*] (GFGA)
GSST .... Gatherer, Stitcher, Side Sewer, and Trimmer [*Publishing*]
GSST .... Goldstein-Scheerer Stick Test [*Psychology*]
GSSTFR .... Gas-Solid-Solid Trickle Flow Reactor [*Chemical engineering*]
GSSW .... Gas-Shielded Stud Welding (PDAA)
GST .... Flying Boat [*Russian aircraft symbol*]
GST .... Garter Stitch [*Knitting*] (ADA)
GST .... Gas Surge Tank [*Nuclear energy*] (NRCH)
GST .... Gate Sensitive Thyristor (IAA)
GST .... Gemini System Trainer [*NASA*] (IAA)
GST .... Genealogical Society of Tasmania [*Australia*]
GST .... General Scholarship Test for High School Seniors [*Education*] (AEBS)
GST .... General Screening Test
GST .... General Service Test (NATG)
GST .... General Service Truck [*British*]
GST .... General Staff Target (NATG)
GST .... General Staff with Troops [*Army*]
GST .... General Systems Theory
GST .... Generation-Skipping Transfer Tax
GST .... Generic Scan Tool [*Automobile service*]

GST	Geographical Specialist Team [*Army*] (AABC)
GST	Gesammelte Studien zum Alten Testament [*A publication*] (BJA)
GST	Glazed Structural Tile [*Technical drawings*]
GST	Global Space Transport (IAA)
GST	Glutathione S-Transferase [*An enzyme*]
GST	Gold Salt Therapy [*Medicine*] (DMAA)
GST	Gold Sodium Thiomalate [*Organic chemistry*] (DAVI)
GST	Goods and Services Tax [*Canadian*] (ODBW)
GST	Goods and Services Tax [*Canada*]
GST	Government Securities Trading [*Computer*]
GST	Government Steam Train [*British*]
GST	Graphic Stress Telethermometry [*Medicine*]
GST	Greenwich Sidereal [*or Standard*] Time
GST	Ground Sensor Terminal (AABC)
GST	Ground Surface Temperature
GST	Ground System Test [*NASA*] (NASA)
GST	GST Telecommunications [*AMEX symbol*] (TTSB)
GST	GST Telecommunications, Inc. [*AMEX symbol*] (SAG)
GST	Gunner Skills Test [*Army*] (INF)
GST	Gustavus [*Alaska*] [*Airport symbol*] (OAG)
GSTA	Ground Surveillance and Target Acquisition [*Military*] (MCD)
GSTAMIDS	Ground Standoff Minefield Detection System [*Military*] (RDA)
GSTANSW	General Studies Teachers' Association of New South Wales [*Australia*]
G ST B	Grand Standard Bearer [*Freemasonry*] (ROG)
GSTC	Gorham State Teachers College [*Merged with University of Maine*]
GSTD	Gold Standard [*NASDAQ symbol*] (TTSB)
GSTD	Gold Standard, Inc. [*NASDAQ symbol*] (NQ)
G STD B	Grand Standard Bearer [*Freemasonry*]
GSTDN	Ground Spacecraft Tracking and Data Network [*Computer science*] (MHDI)
GSTE	Guidance System Test Equipment
GSTF	Ground Systems Test Flow [*NASA*] (NASA)
GStG	Georgia Southern College, Statesboro, GA [*Library symbol Library of Congress*] (LCLS)
GSTK	Good Stuff to Know
GSTM	Gold Sodium Thiomalate [*Organic chemistry*] (DAVI)
GSTN	General Switched Telephone Nertwork [*Telecommunications*] (OSI)
GSTP	Generalized System of Tariff Preferences [*US Customs Service*] (MHDW)
GSTP	Global System of Trade Preferences [*United Nations Conference on Trade and Development*] [*Proposed*]
GSTP	Ground System Test Procedure (IAA)
GSTRF	Globalstar Telecommunications Ltd. [*NASDAQ symbol*] (SAG)
GSTRF	Golbalstar Telecommunications [*NASDAQ symbol*] (TTSB)
GSTS	German Student Travel Service
GSTS	Ground-Based Surveillance and Tracking System (MCD)
GSTS	Guidance System Test Set
GSTS	Gusts [*NWS*] (FAAC)
GSTT	Generation-Skipping Transfer Tax
GST Tele	GST Telecommunications, Inc. [*Associated Press*] (SAG)
GSTU	Guidance System Test Unit
GSTV	Digestive
GSTY	Gusty [*NWS*] (FAAC)
GSU	Entergy Gulf States [*NYSE symbol*] (SAG)
GSU	Gas Servicer Unit (MCD)
GSU	Gedaref [*Sudan*] [*Airport symbol*] (AD)
GSU	General Service Unit [*Marine Corps*]
GSU	General Support Unit [*Army*] (AABC)
GSU	Generator Step-Up Transformer [*Nuclear energy*] (NRCH)
GSU	Geographically Separated Units [*Military*] (AFM)
GSU	Georgia State University, Atlanta, GA [*OCLC symbol*] (OCLC)
GSU	Glazed Structural Unit [*Technical drawings*]
GSU	Golden Seven Industry [*Vancouver Stock Exchange symbol*]
GSU	Governors State University [*Illinois*]
GSU	Grain Services Union
GSU	Guaranteed Supply Unit [*Telecommunications*] (OA)
GSU	Guidance Switching Unit [*Aviation*]
GSU	Gulf States Utilities Co. [*NYSE symbol*] (SPSG)
GSUB	Glazed Structural Unit Base [*Technical drawings*]
GSUC	Ground Stub-Up Connection [*Aerospace*] (AAG)
GSUEG	Governors State University Energy Group (EA)
GSUG	Gross Seasonal Unavailable Generation [*Electronics*] (IEEE)
G (Suit)	Antigravity Suit [*Air Force clothing for supersonic flight*]
GSUPr	Entergy Gulf States $1.75 Pref [*NYSE symbol*] (TTSB)
GSUPrB	Entergy Gulf States $4.40 Pfd [*NYSE symbol*] (TTSB)
GSUPrD	Entergy Gulf States Dep Adj B Pfd [*NYSE symbol*] (TTSB)
GSUPrE	Entergy Gulf States $5.08 Pfd [*NYSE symbol*] (TTSB)
GSUPrG	Entergy Gulf States $4.52 Pfd [*NYSE symbol*] (TTSB)
GSUPrK	Entergy Gulf States $8.80 Pfd [*NYSE symbol*] (TTSB)
G SUPT	Grand Superintendent [*Freemasonry*]
GSUSA	Gallipoli Society in the United States of America (EA)
GSUSA	General Staff, United States Army
GSUSA	Girl Scouts of the USA (EA)
GSV	Gas Sampling Valve
GSV	Genealogical Society of Victoria [*Australia*]
GSV	Globe Stop Valve
GSV	Golden Seville Resources Ltd. [*Vancouver Stock Exchange symbol*]
GSV	Governor Steam Valve (IEEE)
GSV	Ground-to-Surface Vessel [*RADAR*] (NATG)
GSV	Grumman Submersible Vehicle
GSV	Guided Space Vehicle [*Air Force*]
GSV	Savannah Area Vocational/Technical School, Savannah, GA [*Library symbol*] [*Library of Congress*] (LCLS)
GSVAD	General Service Volunteer Aid Detachment [*British military*] (DMA)
GSVC	Generalized Supervisor Calls [*Computer science*] (IBMDP)
GSVO	Villa Cisneros [*Western Sahara*] [*ICAO location identifier*] (ICLI)
GSVP	Ground Support Verification Plan [*NASA*] (NASA)
GSVT	Ground System Validation Test (MCD)
GSW	Galvanized Steel Wire (IAA)
GSW	General Service Wagon [*British military*] (DMA)
GSW	Gold Star Wives of America (EA)
GSW	Grand Senior Warden [*Freemasonry*] (ROG)
GSW	Greater Southwest [*Ft. Worth and Dallas, Texas*] [*Airport symbol*] (AD)
GSW	Great Southwest Railroad, Inc. [*AAR code*]
GSW	Ground Saucer Watch (EA)
GSW	GSW, Inc. [*Toronto Stock Exchange symbol*]
GSW	Gunshot Wound [*Medicine*]
GSW 1812	General Society of the War of 1812 (EA)
GSWA	Gold Star Wives of America [*Later, GSW*] (EA)
GSWA	Gunshot Wound to the Abdomen
GSWA	International PEN - Centre of German-Speaking Writers Abroad (EAIO)
G SWD B	Grand Sword Bearer [*Freemasonry*]
GSwE	Emanuel County Junior College, Swainsboro, GA [*Library symbol Library of Congress*] (LCLS)
GSWR	Galvanized Steel Wire Rope
GS-WRD	Geological Survey - Water Resources Division
GSWT	General Staff with Troops [*Army*]
GSX	General Signal Corp. [*NYSE symbol*] (SPSG)
GSX	Genl Signal [*NYSE symbol*] (TTSB)
GSY	Global Strategy Corp. [*Vancouver Stock Exchange symbol*]
GSY	Gulf Science Year [*1970*]
GSYB	[*The*] Girls' School Year Book [*A publication*] (ROG)
GSZ	Golden Sitka Resources [*Vancouver Stock Exchange symbol*]
GSZ	Guernsey, WY [*Location identifier FAA*] (FAAL)
GT	Gabbart [*Ship's rigging*] (ROG)
GT	Gait Training [*Orthopedics*] (DAVI)
GT	Galactosyltransferase [*An enzyme*]
GT	Game Theory
GT	Gamma-Glutamyltransferase [*Also, GGT, GGTP*] [*An enzyme*]
GT	Gamow-Teller [*Transition*] [*Nuclear physics*]
GT	Garbage Truck
GT	Gas Tight
GT	Gastrin [*Biochemistry*]
GT	Gastrostomy [*Gastroenterology*] (DAVI)
GT	Gastrostomy Tube [*Gastroenterology*] (DAVI)
GT	Gastrotomy Tube [*Gastroenterology*] (DAVI)
GT	Gas Tube (IAA)
GT	Gas Turbine
GT	Gate Tube (IAA)
GT	Gelling Temperature [*Analytical biochemistry*]
GT	Gel Tube [*Electrophoresis*]
GT	Gemini-Titan [*NASA*]
GT	General Tariff (ADA)
GT	General Technical Aptitude Area
GT	General/Technical Score [*Standardized test*] [*Military*] (INF)
GT	General Test
GT	General Tool
GT	General Transport [*Military*]
GT	Generation Time [*Microbiology*]
GT	Genetic Therapy
GT	Genomic Tested [*Genetics*]
GT	Gentleman Traveller
GT	German Title (NITA)
GT	German Translation (MCD)
GT	Gibraltar Airways Ltd. [*British ICAO designator*] (ICDA)
GT	Gifted and Talented [*Education*]
GT	Gift Tax (DLA)
GT	Gigaton
Gt	gigatonne [*One billion tonnes*] (EERA)
GT	Gilt
GT	Gilt Top [*Bookbinding*]
gt	Gilt Top [*Bookbinding*] (WDMC)
GT	Gingiva Treatment [*Dentistry*] (MAE)
GT	Glacial Till Soil [*Agronomy*]
GT	Glanzmann Thrombasthenia [*Medicine*] (DMAA)
GT	Glass Tube (DEN)
GT	Globe Thermometer
GT	Glow Tube (IAA)
GT	Glucose Therapy [*Medicine*] (DMAA)
GT	Glucose Tolerance [*Medicine*]
GT	Glucose Transporter [*Biochemistry*]
GT	Glucose Turnover [*Physiology*]
GT	Glucuronosyltransferase [*An enzyme*]
GT	Glumitocin [*Endocrinology*]
GT	Glutamyl Transferase [*Liver-function test*] (CPH)
GT	Glutamyl Transpeptidase [*An enzyme*]
GT	Glycotyrosine [*Biochemistry*]
GT	Gnomonic Tracking Chart [*Air Force*]
GT	Good Templar
GT	Good Tidings (EA)
GT	Goodyear Canada, Inc. [*Toronto Stock Exchange symbol*]
GT	Goodyear Tire & Rub [*NYSE symbol*] (TTSB)
GT	[*The*] Goodyear Tire & Rubber Co. [*NYSE symbol*] (SPSG)
GT	Gopher Tape Armor [*Telecommunications*] (TEL)
GT	Governor of Tasmania [*Australia*]
g/t	Grams per Ton
GT	Grand Theft

GT............... Grand Tiler [Freemasonry]
GT............... Grand Touring [Automobile model designation]
GT............... Grand Treasurer [Freemasonry]
GT............... Grant [Legal shorthand] (LWAP)
GT............... Gran Turismo [Grand Touring] [Automotive term]
G/T............. Granulation Time
G/T............. Granulation Tissue
GT............... Graphics Terminal
GT............... Grease Trap (AAG)
GT............... Great
GT............... Greater Than [FORTRAN]
GT............... Greater Trochanter [Anatomy]
Gt............... Great Organ [Music]
GT............... Great Thoughts [A publication] (ROG)
GT............... Great Toe [Medicine] (DMAA)
GT............... Green Thumb (EA)
GT............... Green Thumbs [National Weather Service and Department of Agriculture Extension Service telecommunication system]
GT............... Greenwich Time
GT............... Greetings Telegram (IAA)
GT............... Gross Ton [or Tonnage]
GT............... Ground Team (MCD)
GT............... Ground Test [NASA] (NASA)
GT............... Ground Track
GT............... Ground Transmit (AFM)
GT............... Ground-Tree Foraging [Ecology]
GT............... Group Technology
GT............... Group Tensions [Medicine] (DMAA)
GT............... Group Therapy
GT............... Group Transformation
GT............... Grout [Technical drawings]
GT............... Guard of Tent [Oddfellows] (ROG)
GT............... Guatemala [ANSI two-letter standard code] (CNC)
gt............... Guatemala [MARC country of publication code Library of Congress] (LCCP)
GT............... Guidance Transmitter (NVT)
GT............... Gun Target (NVT)
GT............... Gun Tractor [British]
GT............... Gun Turret
GT............... Gutta [Drop of Liquid] [Pharmacy]
GT............... Gyro Torque (MCD)
GT............... Triganglioside [Chemistry]
GT1............. Glycogenosis Type 1 [Medicine]
GTA............. Gas Toxicity Analysis
GTA............. Gas Tungsten Arc
GTA............. Gay Theatre Alliance [Defunct] (EA)
GTA............. Gear Train Analyzer
GTA............. Gemini-Titan-Agena [NASA] (KSC)
GTA............. General Terms Agreement (MCD)
GTA............. General Training Assistance (ADA)
GTA............. Genetic Toxicology Association (EA)
GTA............. Gene Transfer Agent [Genetics]
GTA............. Gentra Inc. [TS, exchange symbol] (TTSB)
GTA............. German Teachers' Association [British]
GTA............. Gimbaled Telescope Assembly (MCD)
GTA............. Gitanair [Italy ICAO designator] (FAAC)
GTA............. Glass Tempering Association (EA)
GTA............. Glycerol Triacetate [Known as Triacetin] [Organic chemistry]
GTA............. Gospel Truth Association (EA)
GTA............. Government Telecommunications Agency [Canada]
GTA............. Graduate Teachers' Association [A union] [British]
GTA............. Graduate Teaching Assistant
GTA............. Grain Transportation Agency [Winnipeg, MB]
GTA............. Grand Theft Auto (WGA)
GTA............. Gran Turisimo Americano [In automobile name Pontiac Firebird GTA]
GTA............. Gran Turismo Automatico [Automobile model designation]
GTA............. Graphic Training Aid
GTA............. Gravure Technical Association [Later, GAA] (EA)
GTA............. Ground Test Access (MCD)
GTA............. Ground Test Article [NASA] (NASA)
GTA............. Ground Torquing Assembly (MCD)
GTA............. Ground Training Aid [Aerospace] (AAG)
GTA............. Groupement Technique de Assureurs du Canada [Government Telecommunications Agency] [Canada]
GTA............. Group Training Association [British] (DCTA)
GTA............. GT Aviation [British] [FAA designator] (FAAC)
GTA............. Guide Tube Assembly (NRCH)
GTA............. Gun Trade Association Ltd. [British] (BI)
GTA............. Gutta [Drop of Liquid] [Pharmacy] (ROG)
GTAA.......... Groupe de Travail Inter Agences sur l'Afrique Australe [Inter-Agency Working Group on Southern Africa - IAWGSA] [Canadian Council for International Cooperation]
GTAC.......... Gas Tungsten Arc Cutting [Welding]
GTAC.......... General Technical Advisory Committee [for fossil energy] [Energy Research and Development Administration]
GTAC.......... Ground-to-Air Cycle
GTAM.......... Ground-to-Air Missile (RDA)
GtAMg......... Great American Management & Investment, Inc. [Associated Press] (SAG)
GT & A....... Ground Test and Acceptance [NASA] (NASA)
GT & C....... General Terms and Conditions
GT & E....... General Telephone & Electronics (NITA)
GT & E....... General Telephone & Electronics Corp.
GT & TM..... General Traffic and Transportation Manager
GTAO.......... Graphic Training Aids Officer [Army]

GTASA........ Geography Teachers' Association of South Australia
GTASFA....... Grand Traverse Area Sportfishing Association [Michigan]
GtAtPc........ Great Atlantic & Pacific Tea Co., Inc. [Associated Press] (SAG)
GTAV.......... General Transport Administrative Vehicle
GTAW......... Gas Tungsten Arc Weld [or Welding]
GTAW-P...... Gas Tungsten Arc Welding - Pulsed Arc
GTAX......... Gilman & Ciocia, Inc. [NASDAQ symbol] (SAG)
GTAXW...... Gilman & Ciocia Wrrt [NASDAQ symbol] (TTSB)
GTB........... Fort Drum, NY [Location identifier FAA] (FAAL)
GTB........... Gastrointestinal Tract Bleeding [Medicine] (DMAA)
GTB........... General Tariff Bureau Inc. Lansing MI [STAC]
GTB........... General Trade Books [Publishing]
GTB........... Glycinethymol Blue [An indicator] [Chemistry]
GTB........... Grand Traverse Bay, Michigan
GTᴮ........... Gran Turismo Berlinetta [Automobile model designation]
GTB........... Guild of Traditional Butlers
GTBA.......... Gasoline-Grade Tertiary-Butyl Alcohol [Organic chemistry]
GTBA.......... Grade Tertiary Butyl Alcohol
GTBC.......... Guild of Teachers of Backward Children [British] (BI)
GTBicyc...... GT Bicycles, Inc. [Associated Press] (SAG)
GT BR........ Great Britain (ROG)
Gt Brit........ Great Britain (WGA)
GTBWI........ Grand Traverse Bay Watershed Initiative
GTBX.......... GT Bicycles [NASDAQ symbol] (TTSB)
GTBX.......... GT Bicycles, Inc. [NASDAQ symbol] (SAG)
GTC........... Gain Time Constant (MCD)
GTC........... Gain Time Control
GTC........... Gas Turbine Compressor
GTC........... Gateway to Care
GTC........... General Teaching Council [British]
GTC........... General Tool Contract (MCD)
GTC........... General Transistor Corp. (AAG)
GTC........... Georgia Teachers College [Later, Georgia Southern College] (AEBS)
GTC........... Giant Cell Thyroiditis [Medicine] (DMAA)
GTC........... Girls' Training Corps [British] (DAS)
GTC........... Global Tomorrow Coalition (EA)
GTC........... Global Tomorrow Coalition (GNE)
GTC........... Glycol Trim Console (MCD)
GTC........... Golder, Thoma & Cressey [Chicago, IL] [Telecommunications service] (TSSD)
GTC........... Good Till Canceled [as in a brokerage order]
GTC........... Government Telegraph Code [British World War II]
GTC........... Government Training Centre [British]
GTC........... Grand Touring Coupe [In automobile name Lincoln Mark VII GTC]
GTC........... Gran Turismo Cabriolet [Automobile model designation]
GTC........... Greater Toy Center (EA)
GTC........... Ground Test Conductor (MCD)
GTC........... Group for Technical Coordination [Marine science] (MSC)
GTC........... Group Training Command [Air Force British]
GTC........... Group Training Company
GTC........... Guanidinium Thiocyanate [Biochemistry]
GTC........... Guidance Transfer Container
GTC........... Guild of Television Cameramen [British] (EA)
GTC........... Gulf Transport [AAR code]
GTC........... Man, WV [Location identifier FAA] (FAAL)
GTCC.......... Gas Turbine Combined Cycle [Energy technology]
GTCC.......... German Touring Car Championship
GTCC.......... Government's Total Contract Cost (AAGC)
GTCC.......... Greater-than-Class-C [Radioactive waste level definition]
GTCC.......... Group Technology Characterization Code (IAA)
GtChina....... [The] Greater China Fund [Associated Press] (SAG)
GTCL.......... Graduate of Trinity College of Music, London
GTCM......... Great Central Mines [NASDAQ symbol] (SAG)
GTCMY....... Great Central Mines NL ADS [NASDAQ symbol] (TTSB)
GTCP.......... Gas Turbine Compressor and Power Unit (NG)
GTCP.......... General Telephone Call Processing
GTCP.......... Global Tropospheric Chemistry Program [Federal government]
GTCR.......... Gate-Turnoff Controlled Rectifier [Electronics] (IAA)
GTCS.......... General Teaching Council for School [British]
GTCU.......... Ground Thermal Conditioning Unit [NASA] (NASA)
Gtᴰ............ Duarte Variant Allele [Genetics] (DAVI)
GTD........... Gear Test Data
GTD........... General Traffic Department
GTD........... Geometrical Theory of Diffraction
GTD........... Geometric and Technical Draughting [British Olivetti Ltd.] [Software package] (NCC)
GTD........... Georgetown [Delaware] [Seismograph station code, US Geological Survey] (SEIS)
GTD........... Gestational Trophoblastic Disease [Medicine] (MAE)
GTD........... Graphic Tablet Display [Computer science] (IEEE)
GTD........... Ground Target Detection
GTD........... GT Global Developing Market Fund [NYSE symbol] (SPSG)
GTD........... G.T. Global Dvlp Mkt Fund [NYSE symbol] (TTSB)
GTD........... Guaranteed
GTD........... Guards Tank Division (MCD)
GTDB.......... Generic Transformed Database
GTDHD....... Give the Devil His Due [Slang]
GTDPL........ Generalized Top-Down Parsing Language
GTDR.......... General Technical Data Restricted
GTDS.......... Goddard Trajectory Determination System [NASA]
GTDvMk...... GT Global Developing Market Facts [Associated Press] (SAG)
GTE........... Gas Turbine Engine
GTE........... General-Purpose Thermoplastic Elastomer [Insulation]
GTE........... General Telephone and Electronics [Information service or system] (IID)

GTE............. General Telephone and Electronics [*Telecommunications company*] [*Stamford, CT*] (WDMC)
GTE............. General Telephone Equipment (MCD)
GTE............. Geothermal Energy
GTE............. Gilt Top Edge [*Bookbinding*]
GTE............. Global Tropospheric Experiment [*National Oceanic and Atmospheric Administration*]
GTE............. Gothenburg, NE [*Location identifier FAA*] (FAAL)
GTE............. Gran Turismo Europa [*Automobile model designation*]
GTE............. Groote Island [*Australia Airport symbol*] (OAG)
GTE............. Ground Telecommunication Equipment
GTE............. Ground Test Equipment
GTE............. Ground Training Engine [*Military*] (AFIT)
GTE............. Ground Transport Equipment (KSC)
GTE............. Group Translating Equipment
GTE............. GTE Corp. [*Formerly, General Telephone & Electronics Corp.*] [*NYSE symbol*] (SPSG)
GTE............. GTE Delaware LP [*NYSE symbol*] (SAG)
GTE............. Guidance Test Equipment
GTE............. Gunner Tracking Evaluator (PDAA)
GTEA........... Group Test Equipment Assembly
GTEC........... GTE California, Inc. [*Associated Press*] (SAG)
Gtech........... GTECH Holdings Corp. [*Associated Press*] (SAG)
GTED........... Gas Turbine Engine-Driven [*Generator*] (RDA)
GTEDE......... GTE Delaware Ltd. [*Associated Press*] (SAG)
GTEE........... Grantee [*Legal shorthand*] (LWAP)
GTEE........... Guarantee
GTEF........... GTE Florida, Inc. [*Associated Press*] (SAG)
GTEL........... GTE California, Inc. [*NASDAQ symbol*] (NQ)
GTelevsa ..... Grupo Televisa [*Associated Press*] (SAG)
GTELN........ GTE Calif 5% cm Pfd [*NASDAQ symbol*] (TTSB)
GTELO......... GTE Calif 4.50% cm Pfd [*NASDAQ symbol*] (TTSB)
GTELP......... GTE Calif 4.50% cm Pfd [*NASDAQ symbol*] (TTSB)
GT-ENDOR ... General Triple-Electron Nuclear Double Resonance [*Spectroscopy*]
GTEP........... General Telephone and Electronics Practice [*Telecommunications*] (TEL)
GTETDS ...... Gas Turbine and Engine Type Designation System
GTE TMD ..... Guillotine Trimmed [*Bookbinding*] (DGA)
GT Euro ...... GT Greater Europe Fund [*Associated Press*] (SAG)
GtewayD...... Gateway Data Sciences Corp. [*Associated Press*] (SAG)
GTF............. Generalized Trace Facility [*Computer science*] (MCD)
GTF............. Generalized Transformation Function
GT/F........... General Telephone Company of Florida (NITA)
GTF............. General Transcription Factor [*Genetics*]
GTF............. German Territorial Forces (MCD)
GTF............. Glucose Tolerance Factor [*Medicine*]
GTF............. Glucose Tolerance Factor [*Medicine*] (DMAA)
GTF............. Glucosyltransferase (DMAA)
GTF............. Government Test Facility
GTF............. Greater Than Flag (MHDB)
GTF............. Great Falls [*Montana*] [*Airport symbol*] (OAG)
GTF............. G.T. Greater Europe Fd [*NYSE symbol*] (TTSB)
GTF............. GT Greater Europe Fund [*NYSE symbol*] (SPSG)
GTF............. Guidance Test Fixture
GTF............. Guilt Free Goodies [*Vancouver Stock Exchange symbol*]
GTFN........... Great Financial [*NASDAQ symbol*] (TTSB)
GTFN........... Great Financial Corp. [*NASDAQ symbol*] (SAG)
GTFT........... Generous Tit-for-Tat [*Animal behavior*]
GTFT........... Generous Tit for Tat [*Game strategy*]
GtG............. Galactosemic Allele [*Genetics*] (DAVI)
GTG............. Game-Tying Goals [*Hockey*]
GTG............. Gas Turbine Generator
GTG............. Golden Trend Energy [*Vancouver Stock Exchange symbol*]
GTG............. Gold Thioglucose
GTG............. Grantsburg, WI [*Location identifier FAA*] (FAAL)
GTG............. Ground Timing Generator (IAA)
GTG............. Ground-to-Ground [*Communications, weapons, etc.*]
GTGEEEPS ... Groupe de Travail sur la Gestion de l'Energie dans les Etablissements d'Enseignement Post-Secondaire [*Postsecondary Education Task Force on Energy Management PETFEM*] [*Canada*]
GTGL .... Give the Gift of Literacy Foundation [*Duxbury, MA*]
GTGS .... Gas Turbine Generator Set (AABC)
GTGT .... Gun Target (AABC)
GTH .... Gas Tight High Pressure (IEEE)
GTH .... Genomic Thymus [*Genetics*]
GTH .... Gonadotropic Hormone [*Endocrinology*]
GTH .... Groton Minerals Ltd. [*Vancouver Stock Exchange symbol*]
GTH .... Guthrie, TX [*Location identifier FAA*] (FAAL)
GthEnvr....... Growth Environmental, Inc. [*Associated Press*] (SAG)
GthFn.......... Growth Financial Corp. [*Associated Press*] (SAG)
G Thom....... Gospel of Thomas [*Apocryphal work*]
GTHRNG ...... Gathering
GTHS .... German-Texan Heritage Society (EA)
GthSpn........ Growth Fund of Spain [*Associated Press*] (SAG)
GT-HTGR .... Gas Turbine High-Temperature Gas-Cooled Reactor [*Nuclear energy*] (NRCH)
GTI............. Atlas Air, Inc. [*ICAO designator*] (FAAC)
GTi............. Coastal Plains Regional Library, Tifton, GA [*Library symbol Library of Congress*] (LCLS)
GTI............. General Transportation Importance
GTI............. Genital Tract Infection [*Medicine*] (CPH)
GTI............. Glass Technical Institute [*Commercial firm*] (EA)
GTI............. Glentech International Ltd. [*British*]
GTI............. Grand Turk Island

GTI............. Ground Test Instrumentation (MCD)
GTI............. GTI Corp. [*Associated Press*] (SAG)
GTiA........... Abraham Baldwin Agricultural College, Tifton, GA [*Library symbol Library of Congress*] (LCLS)
GTiE........... Coastal Plains Experiment Station, Tifton, GA [*Library symbol Library of Congress*] (LCLS)
GTIG .... Gamma Thermometer Interest Group [*Nuclear energy*] (NRCH)
GT II .... Galactosyltransferase Isoenzyme II [*An enzyme*] (DAVI)
GTII............ Golden Triangle Ind [*NASDAQ symbol*] (TTSB)
GTII............ Golden Triangle Industries, Inc. [*NASDAQ symbol*] (SAG)
GTIM .... Good Times Restaurants [*NASDAQ symbol*] (TTSB)
GTIM .... Good Times Restaurants, Inc. [*NASDAQ symbol*] (SAG)
GTIMW .... Good Times Restaurants Wrrt [*NASDAQ symbol*] (TTSB)
GTIMZ .... Good Times Restaurants Wrrt'B' [*NASDAQ symbol*] (TTSB)
GTIP........... Ground Tilt Isolation Platform
GTIS .... Gloucestershire Technical Information Service (NITA)
GTIS .... Ground-Based Traffic Information System [*Aviation*] (DA)
GTIS .... GT Interactive Software [*NASDAQ symbol*] (TTSB)
GTJ .... Gold Torch Resources [*Vancouver Stock Exchange symbol*]
GTJ .... Gran Turismo Junior [*Automobile model designation*]
GTK .... Grand Turk [*British West Indies*]
GTK .... Grosser Touren Kombiwagen [*Grand Touring Station Wagon*] [*German*]
GTK .... Gross Tonne Kilometre (EERA)
GTK .... GTECH Holdings [*NYSE symbol*] (TTSB)
GTK .... GTECH Holdings Corp. [*NYSE symbol*] (SPSG)
GTL .... Gaseous Tritium Light [*Device*] [*Nuclear energy*] (NRCH)
GTL .... Gas Transport LASER
GTL .... Gas Turbine Laboratory [*MIT*] (MCD)
GTL .... Geomagnetic Tail Laboratory (MCD)
GTL .... Geometric and Technical Language [*British Olivetti Ltd.*] [*Software package*] (NCC)
GTL .... Georgia Tech Language [*Computer science*] (CSR)
GTL .... Glass Training Ltd. (AIE)
GTL .... Global Title Translation
GTL .... Government Test Laboratory (MSA)
GTL .... Great Lakes Nickel Ltd. [*Toronto Stock Exchange symbol*]
GTL .... Gun/Target Line [*Navy*] (NVT)
GT/LD .... Gifted & Learning Disabled
GtLkCh........ Great Lakes Chemical Corp. [*Associated Press*] (SAG)
GtLkeAv ...... Great Lakes Aviation Ltd. [*Associated Press*] (SAG)
GTLS........... Gaseous Tritium Light Source [*Nuclear energy*] (MCD)
GTM .... Abraham Baldwin Agricultural College, Tifton, GA [*OCLC symbol*] (OCLC)
GTM .... Gas to Methanol [*Process developed by ICI*]
GTM .... General Traffic Manager
GTM .... Geometry Technology Module [*NASA*]
GTM .... Getting the Message [*A reading program*]
GTM .... Good This Month [*Business term*]
GTM .... Ground Team Manager (MCD)
GTM .... Ground Test Missile
GTM .... Ground Test Motor (MCD)
GTM .... Group Talk Microphone
GTM .... Guatemala [*ANSI three-letter standard code*] (CNC)
GTM .... Guild of Temple Musicians (EA)
GTMA .... Galvanised Tank Manufacturers' Association [*British*] (BI)
GTMA .... Gauge and Toolmakers Association [*British*] (DS)
GTMHR .... Gas Turbine Modular Helium Reactor [*Nuclear reactor*]
GTMIE .... Global Telemedia Intl [*NASDAQ symbol*] (TTSB)
GTMMM .... Det Gamle Testament [*S. Michelet, S.Mowinckel, og N. Mersel*] [*Oslo*] [*A publication*] (BJA)
GTMO .... Guantanamo Bay, Cuba
GTMS .... Graphic Text Management System [*Computer science*] (DGA)
GTMS .... Ground Target Marking System
GTMV .... Gasoline-Tolerant Methanol Vehicle [*Chrysler Corp.*] [*Automotive engineering*]
GTN .... Gestational Trophoblastic Neoplasia [*Medicine*]
GTN .... Global Transportation Network (DOMA)
GTN .... Global Trend Network (GNE)
GTN .... Global Trends Network [*USA*] (EERA)
GTN .... Glomerulo-Tubulo-Nephritis [*Medicine*]
GTN .... Glyceryl Trinitrate [*Also, NG, NTG*] [*Explosive, vasodilator*]
GTN .... Gotenba [*Japan*] [*Seismograph station code, US Geological Survey Closed*] (SEIS)
GTN .... Government Telecommunications Network [*British*] (EECA)
GTN .... Great Eastern Line [*Vancouver Stock Exchange symbol*]
GTN .... Washington, DC [*Location identifier FAA*] (FAAL)
GTNR .... Gentner Communications [*NASDAQ symbol*] (TTSB)
GTNR .... Gentner Communications Corp. [*NASDAQ symbol*] (NQ)
GTNRW .... Gentner Communications Wrrt [*NASDAQ symbol*] (TTSB)
GTNW .... General Telephone Co. of the Northwest
GtNYSv........ [*The*] Greater New York Savings Bank [*Associated Press*] (SAG)
GTO .... Gate Turn Off [*Computer science*]
GTO .... Gaussian-Type Orbitals [*Atomic physics*]
GTO .... General Telecommunications Organization [*Oman*] [*Telecommunications service*]
GTO .... Geostationary Transfer Orbit [*Space technology*]
GTO .... Gigaton
GTO .... Golgi Tendon Organ [*Anatomy*]
GTO .... Gorontalo [*Indonesia*] [*Airport symbol*] (OAG)
GTO .... Grand Touring Over 3.0 Liters [*Class of racing cars*]
GTO .... Gran Turismo Omologato [*Grand Touring, Homologated*] [*Automotive engineering*] [*Italian*]
GTO .... Graphics Text Organizer [*Computer science*]
GTO .... Grenada Tourist Office (EA)

GTO .... Guaranteed Time Observer [*For telescope viewing*]
GTOL .... Graphic Take-Off Language [*Computer science*] (PDAA)
GTOL .... Ground Takeoff and Landing (AAG)
GTOR .... Grantor [*Legal shorthand*] (LWAP)
GT ORM H... Great Ormond Street Hospital for Children [*British*] (ROG)
GTOS .... Gantos, Inc. [*NASDAQ symbol*] (SAG)
GTO's .... Girls Together Outrageously [*or Organically*] [*Rock music group*]
GTOS .... Global Terrestrial Observing System [*Marine science*] (OSRA)
GTOS .... Global Terrestrial Observing System (USDC)
GTOS .... Ground Terminal Operations Support (SSD)
GTOSCR...... Gate Turnoff Silicon-Controlled Rectifier [*Electronics*] (IAA)
GTOSS .... Generalized Tethered Object System Simulation (SSD)
GTOT .... Gate Turn Off Thyristor (NITA)
GTOW .... Gross Takeoff Weight [*of an aircraft*] [*Also, GTW*]
GTOWFC...... George Takei's Official Worldwide Fan Club [*British*] (EAIO)
GTP............. Gas Turbine Power Unit (NG)
GTP............. General Test Plan (AAG)
GTP............. General Training Program
GTP............. Generate Target Position [*Military*] (CAAL)
GTP............. Global Time and Position [*Navigation systems*]
GTP............. Glutamyl Transpeptidase [*An enzyme*]
GTP............. Golay Transform Processor (IAA)
GTP............. Government Technology Productivity
GTP............. Grand Touring Prototype [*Race car designation*]
GTP............. Grand Trunk Pacific Railway
GTP............. Graphic Transform Package (MHDI)
GTP............. Great Northern Petroleums [*Vancouver Stock Exchange symbol*]
GTP............. Great Trunk Pacific Railway [*British*] (ROG)
GTP............. Green Tea Polyphenol [*Biochemistry*]
GTP............. Ground Test Plan (MCD)
GTP............. Ground Track Plotter
GTP............. Group-Transfer Polymerization [*Du Pont process*] [1983]
GTP............. Guanosine Triphosphate [*Biochemistry*]
GTPase .... Guanosine Triphosphatase [*An enzyme*]
GTPI .... Grupo de Trabajo para los Pueblos Indigenas [*Indigenous Peoples Working Group*] [*Netherlands*] (EAIO)
GTPR .... Grand Trunk Pacific Railway
GTPS .... Gas Turbine Power System
GTPS .... Great American Bancorp [*NASDAQ symbol*] (TTSB)
GTPS .... Great American Bancorp, Inc. [*NASDAQ symbol*] (SAG)
GTPSS .... Ground Test Plan Summary Sheets (MCD)
GTPT........... Geometrical and True Positioning Tolerance
GTPU .... Gas Turbine Power Unit (MCD)
GTR .... Columbus [*Mississippi*] [*Airport symbol*] (OAG)
GTR .... Gantry Test Rack [*Aerospace*] (AAG)
GTR .... Garter (MSA)
GTR .... General Theory of Relativity
GTR .... Geoid-to-Topography Ratio [*Planetary science*]
GTR .... Golden Terrace Resource Corp. [*Toronto Stock Exchange symbol*]
GTR .... [*The*] Goodyear Tire & Rubber Co.
GTR .... Government Technical Report
GTR .... Government Technical Representative
GTR .... Government Transportation [*or Travel*] Request
GTR .... Government Travel Request (MCD)
GTR .... Grand Trunk Railway
GTR .... Grantex Aviation [*British*] [*FAA designator*] (FAAC)
GTR .... Granulocyte Turnover Rate [*Hematology*]
GTR .... Great Barrier Island [*New Zealand*] [*Airport symbol*] (AD)
Gtr .... Greater (BARN)
GTR .... Ground Test Reactor [*Air Force*]
GTR .... Grupo Tribasa S.A. ADS [*NYSE symbol*] (TTSB)
GTR .... Grupo Tribasa SA de CV [*NYSE symbol*] (SPSG)
GT/R .... Guard Transmit/Receive (MCD)
GTR .... Guitar [*Music*]
GTR .... Gurkha Transport Regiment [*Military unit*] [*British*]
GTRB .... Gas Turbine
GTRD .... Greatest Total Resource Demand
GTRE .... Global Tape Recording Exchange (EA)
G TREAS...... Grand Treasurer [*Freemasonry*] (ROG)
GTRI .... Georgia Tech Research Institute [*Georgia Institute of Technology*] [*Research center*] (RCD)
GTribasa...... Grupo Tribasa SA de Cv [*Associated Press*] (SAG)
GTRN .... Great Train Store [*NASDAQ symbol*] (TTSB)
GTRN .... Great Train Stores Co. [*NASDAQ symbol*] (SAG)
GTRNW .... Great Train Store Wrrt [*NASDAQ symbol*] (TTSB)
GTRO .... Glyceryl Triricinoleate [*Organic chemistry*]
GTRO .... Golden Triangle Royalty & Oil, Inc. [*NASDAQ symbol*] (NQ)
GTRP .... General Transpose [*Computer science*]
GTRR .... Georgia Institute of Technology Research Reactor
GTRR .... Grand Trunk Railroad [*British*] (ROG)
GTRY .... Grand Trunk Railway
GTS............. Gas Turbine Ship (IIA)
GTS............. Gas Turbine Starter (MCD)
GTS............. Gated Transport Spectroscopy
GTS............. Generalized Transition State [*Physical chemistry*]
GTS............. General Tabulation System
GTS............. General Technical Services, Inc. (MCD)
GTS............. General Technical Services, Inc.
GTS............. General Telephone System (IAA)
GTS............. General Test Support (MCD)
GTS............. General Theological Seminary [*New York, NY*]
GTS............. General Troubleshooting
GTS............. Geostationary Technology Satellite
GTS............. Gilles de la Tourette Syndrome [*Medicine*] (DMAA)
GTS............. Gimbal Trim System

GTS............. Girls' Technical School (ADA)
GTS............. Glider Training School [*British military*] (DMA)
GTS............. Global Telecommunication System [*World Meteorological Organization*] (IID)
GTS............. Global Tracking Systems
GTS............. Global Treasury Services [*Barclays Bank*] [*British*]
GT's .... Globetrotters' Club (EAIO)
GTS............. GN & C [*Guidance, Navigation and Control*] Test Station [*NASA*] (NASA)
GTS............. Golden Tech Resources Ltd. [*Vancouver Stock Exchange symbol*]
GTS............. Golden Treasury Series [*A publication*]
GTS............. Goldstone Tracking Station [*NASA*]
GTS............. Grand Touring Supreme [*Auto racing*]
GTS............. Gran Turismo Spider [*Automobile model designation*]
GTS............. Graphics Terminal Scheduler (MCD)
GTS............. Graphics Terminal Services
GTS............. Graphics Terminal System
GTS............. Green Tobacco Sickness [*Illness resulting from exposure to dissolved nicotine*]
GTS............. Greenwich Time Signal (DEN)
GTS............. Ground Telemetry Subsystem
GTS............. Ground Terminal System
GTS............. Ground Test Station
GTS............. Ground Tracking System (MCD)
GTS............. Ground Training System (MCD)
GTS............. Ground Transportation Services [*MTMC*] (TAG)
GTS............. Group Technology System (MCD)
GTS............. Group Teleconferencing System [*Telecommunications*]
GTS............. Guam Tracking Station [*NASA*] (MCD)
GTS............. Guidance Test Set (AAG)
GTS............. Guinean Trawling Survey [*United Nations*]
GTS............. Gunnery Training School [*British military*] (DMA)
gts .... Guttae [*Drops*] [*Pharmacy*] (DAVI)
GTS............. Gyro Tilt Signal
GTSC .... German Territorial Southern Command [*NATO*] (NATG)
GTS Drtk..... GTS Duratek [*Associated Press*] (SAG)
GTSF .... Gifted and Talented Screening Form [*Educational test*]
GTSF .... Guidance Test and Simulation Facility
GTSI........... Government Technology Services [*NASDAQ symbol*] (SPSG)
GTSI........... Government Technology Svcs [*NASDAQ symbol*] (TTSB)
GTSPP .... Global Temperature and Salinity Pilot Project (EERA)
GTSS .... Gas Turbine Starting System (NG)
GTSS .... General Time Sharing System [*Computer science*]
GTST .... Global Telecomm Solutions [*NASDAQ symbol*] (TTSB)
GTST .... Global Telecommunications Solutions, Inc. [*NASDAQ symbol*] (SAG)
GTST .... Greatest (ABBR)
GTSTD .... Grid Test of Schizophrenic Thought Disorder [*Psychology*]
GTSTW .... Global Tele Solutions Wrrt [*NASDAQ symbol*] (TTSB)
GTSW .... Greentree Software, Inc. [*NASDAQ symbol*] (NQ)
GTSWC........ Greentree Software [*NASDAQ symbol*] (TTSB)
GTSX .... Golf Training Systems [*NASDAQ symbol*] (TTSB)
GTSX .... Golf Training Systems, Inc. [*NASDAQ symbol*] (SAG)
GTSXU .... Golf Training Systems Unit [*NASDAQ symbol*] (TTSB)
GTSXW .... Golf Training Sys Wrrt [*NASDAQ symbol*] (TTSB)
GTT............. Gelatin-Tellurite-Taurocholate [*Agar*] [*Medicine*] (MEDA)
GTT............. Gelatin-Tellurite-Taurocholate Agar [*Biochemistry*] (DAVI)
GTT............. Generated Target Tracking
GTT............. Geographical and Topographical Texts of the Old Testament [*A publication*] (BJA)
GTT............. Georgetown [*Australia Airport symbol*] (OAG)
GTT............. Glucose Tolerance Test [*Medicine*]
GTT............. Goettingen [*Federal Republic of Germany*] [*Geomagnetic observatory code*]
GTT............. Gone to Texas [*Sign on doors of New Englanders who had gone West, nineteenth century*]
GTT............. Gottingen [*Federal Republic of Germany*] [*Seismograph station code, US Geological Survey*] (SEIS)
GTT............. Grand Teton Industries, Inc. [*Vancouver Stock Exchange symbol*]
GTT............. Group Timing Technique [*Industrial engineering*]
GTT............. Guttae [*Drops of Liquid*] [*Pharmacy*]
GTTC........... Goodfellow Technical Training Center [*Military*]
GTTC........... Gulf Transportation Terminal Command
GTTF........... Gas Turbine Test Facility
GTTIF.......... Grande Tel Technologies [*NASDAQ symbol*] (TTSB)
GTTIF.......... GrandeTel Technologies, Inc. [*NASDAQ symbol*] (SAG)
GTT QUIBUSD... Guttis Quibusdam [*With Some Drops*] [*Pharmacy*] (ROG)
GtTrain .... Great Train Stores Co. [*Associated Press*] (SAG)
GtTrn.......... Great Train Stores Co. [*Associated Press*] (SAG)
GTTS........... Gyro Transfer Table System
GTU............. Gamma Theta Upsilon (EA)
GTU............. Gatelink Transceiver Unit [*Aviation*]
GTU............. Georgetown University, Medical Center Library, Washington, DC [*OCLC symbol*] (OCLC)
GTU .... Glycol Trim Unit (MCD)
GTU............. Graduate Theological Union, University of Saskatchewan [*UTLAS symbol*]
GTU .... Grand Touring Under 3.0 Liters [*Class of racing cars*]
GTU............. Ground Test Unit
GTU............. Guidance Test Unit
GTUC........... Ghana Trades Union Congress
GTUSIdentBad... Guard, Tomb of the Unknown Soldier Identification Badge [*Military decoration*] (AABC)
GTV............. Empresa de Aviacion Aerogaviota, SA [*Cuba*] [*FAA designator*] (FAAC)
GTV............. Galaxy Cablevision L.P. [*AMEX symbol*] (TTSB)

GTV	Galaxy Cablevision Ltd. [*AMEX symbol*] (SPSG)
GTV	Gas Toggle Valve
GTV	Gate Valve (AAG)
GTV	Gran Turismo Veloce [*Automobile model designation*]
GTV	Ground Test Vehicle (KSC)
GTV	Ground Transport Vehicle
GTV	Growth Test Vehicle (MCD)
GTV	Guidance [*or Guided*] Test Vehicle
GTV	Guided Tactical Vehicle [*Army*]
GTW	Gateway Aviation [*Zambia*] [*FAA designator*] (FAAC)
GTW	Global Technology Watch [*Information service or system*] (IID)
GTW	Good This Week [*Business term*]
GTW	Gottwaldov [*Former Czechoslovakia*] [*Airport symbol*] (OAG)
GTW	Grand Trunk Western Railroad Co. [*AAR code*]
GTW	Gross Takeoff Weight [*of an aircraft*] [*Also, GTOW*]
GTW	Gross Train Weight (DCTA)
GTW	Guild of Travel Writers [*British*]
GTWAY	Gateway [*Commonly used*] (OPSA)
GtWF	Great Western Financial [*Associated Press*] (SAG)
GtWF	Great Western Financial Corp. [*Associated Press*] (SAG)
GtWFn	Great Western Financial Corp. [*Associated Press*] (SAG)
GTWR	Gross Train Weight Rating
GTWT	Gridded Traveling-Wave Tube (MCD)
GTWY	Gateway (MCD)
GTWY	Gateway
gtwy	Gateway (VRA)
GtwyKY	Gateway Bancorp, Inc. (Kentucky) [*Associated Press*] (SAG)
GTX	Alma, MI [*Location identifier FAA*] (FAAL)
GTX	General Tool Experimental (MCD)
GTX	Gold Texas Resources Ltd. [*Vancouver Stock Exchange symbol*]
GTX	Gran Turismo Experimental [*Grand Touring, Experimental*] [*Automotive term*]
GTX	Graphics within Texts (NITA)
GTX	Ground Transport Express [*Airport baggage computer*]
GTXT	Generate Character Text [*Computer science*] (IAA)
GTY	Getty Petroleum [*NYSE symbol*] (TTSB)
GTY	Getty Petroleum Corp. [*NYSE symbol*] (SPSG)
GTY	Greatly (ABBR)
gty	Gritty [*Quality of the bottom*] [*Nautical charts*]
Gty	Guaranty (DLA)
GTY	Guaranty Trustco Ltd. [*Toronto Stock Exchange symbol*]
GTY	National Aviation Co. [*Egypt*] [*ICAO designator*] (FAAC)
GtyNtl	Guaranty National Corp. [*Associated Press*] (SAG)
GTZ	Gran Turismo Zagato [*Automobile model designation*]
GU	Aviateca [*ICAO designator*] (AD)
GU	Gasschutzoffizier [*Gas Noncommissioned Officer*] [*German military - World War II*]
GU	Gastric Ulcer [*Medicine*]
GU	Gear Up [*Aviation*]
GU	Generations United (EA)
GU	Generic Unit (TEL)
GU	Genitourinary [*Medicine*]
GU	Geographically Undesirable [*Slang*]
GU	Georgetown University [*Washington, DC*]
GU	Glycogenic Unit [*Medicine*]
GU	Gonococcal Urethritis [*Medicine*]
GU	Grafton & Upton Railroad Co. [*AAR code*]
GU	Grand United Friendly Society [*Australia*]
GU	Gravitational Ulcer [*Medicine*]
GU	Greater Union Organisation [*Australia*]
gu	Guam [*MARC country of publication code Library of Congress*] (LCCP)
GU	Guam [*Postal code*] [*ANSI two-letter standard code*] (CNC)
GU	Guanase [*An enzyme*]
GU	Guarantee
GU	Guatemala [*IYRU nationality code*] (IYR)
GU	Guidance Unit
Gu	Guillelmus de Tocco [*Authority cited in pre-1607 legal work*] (DSA)
GU	Guinea
GU	Gules [*Heraldry*]
GU	Gunner (ADA)
GU	University of Georgia, Athens, GA [*Library symbol Library of Congress*] (LCLS)
GUA	Aerotaxis de Aguascalientes SA de CV [*Mexico ICAO designator*] (FAAC)
GUA	Group of Units of Analysis [*Medicine*] (DMAA)
GUA	Guam [*Mariana Islands*] [*Seismograph station code, US Geological Survey*]
Gua	Guanine [*Also, G*] [*Biochemistry*]
gua	Guarani [*MARC language code Library of Congress*] (LCCP)
GUA	Guatemala City [*Guatemala*] [*Airport symbol*] (OAG)
GUA	Guidance Unit Assembly
GUA	Guinea [*Monetary unit*] [*Obsolete British*] (ROG)
GUA	International Guards Union of America
GUA	University of Georgia, Athens, GA [*OCLC symbol*] (OCLC)
GuaAF	Nieves M. Flores Memorial Library, Agana, Guam [*Library symbol Library of Congress*] (LCLS)
GUAD	Guadeloupe (ROG)
Gual	Gualcosius [*Flourished, 11th-12th century*] [*Authority cited in pre-1607 legal work*] (DSA)
Gualc	Gualcosius [*Flourished, 11th-12th century*] [*Authority cited in pre-1607 legal work*] (DSA)
GUALO	General Union of Associations of Loom Overlookers [*British*] (DCTA)
Guam Admin R	Administrative Rules and Regulations of the Government of Guam [*A publication*] (DLA)

Guam Civ Code	Guam Civil Code [*A publication*] (DLA)
Guam Code Civ Pro	Guam Code of Civil Procedure [*A publication*] (DLA)
Guam Gov't Code	Guam Government Code [*A publication*] (DLA)
Guam Prob Code	Guam Probate Code [*A publication*] (DLA)
GUAR	Guarantee (MSA)
GUAR	Guarantee Life Companies, Inc. [*NASDAQ symbol*] (SAG)
GUAR	Guarantee Life Cos [*NASDAQ symbol*] (TTSB)
Guar	Guarnerius [*Irnerius*] [*Flourished, 1113-18*] [*Authority cited in pre-1607 legal work*] (DSA)
GUARD	Government Employees United Against Discrimination [*An association*]
GUARD	Guaranteed Assignment Retention Detailing [*Navy*] (NVT)
GUARD FIST	Guard Unit Armor Device Full-Crew Interaction Simulation Trainer
GUARDS	Generalized Unified Ammunition Reporting Data System (MCD)
GUARDSMAN	Guidelines and Rules for Data Systems Management (TEL)
GuardTc	Guardian Technologies International, Inc. [*Associated Press*] (SAG)
GUAREE	Guarantee (ROG)
GuarFin	Guaranty Financial Corp. [*Associated Press*] (SAG)
GuarFS	Guaranty Federal Savings Bank [*Associated Press*] (SAG)
GuarLife	Guarantee Life Companies, Inc. [*Associated Press*] (SAG)
GUAROR	Guarantor [*Legal term*] (ROG)
GuarSL	Guaranty Savings & Loan FA [*Associated Press*] (SAG)
GUART	Guaranty (ABBR)
GUARTE	Guarantee (ABBR)
GUARTED	Guaranteed (ABBR)
GUARTEG	Guaranteeing (ABBR)
GUARTR	Guarantor (ABBR)
GUASO	Guatemalan Solidarity Committee (EA)
GUAT	Guatemala
Guat	Guatemala (VRA)
GuaU	University of Guam, Agana, GU [*Library symbol Library of Congress*] (LCLS)
GUB	Generalized Upper Bounding [*Computer science*]
GUB	Government Union of Burma
GUB	Greatest Upper Bound [*Computer science*]
GUB	Guerrero Negro [*Mexico*] [*Airport symbol*]
GUB	Law School Library, University of Georgia, Athens, GA [*OCLC symbol*] (OCLC)
GUBA	Growing Up Born Again [*Pronounced "goobah"*] [*Book published by Fleming H. Revell Co.*]
GUBER	Gubernatorial (ABBR)
GUBGF	General Union of Bellhangers and Gas Fitters [*British*]
GUBI	Gemeinschaft Unabhangiger Beratender Ingenieurbueros [*Association of German Consulting Engineers*]
GUBL	Beyla [*Guinea*] [*ICAO location identifier*] (ICLI)
GUBR	Gentleman Usher of the Black Rod [*British*] (ROG)
GUBSMW	General Union of Braziers and Sheet Metal Workers [*British*]
GUBTW	General Union of Bedding Trade Workers [*British*]
GUBU	Grotesque, Unbelievable, Bizarre, Unprecedented [*Term coined by an Irish politician to describe certain incidents in Irish politics*]
GUC	Good-until-Canceled Order [*Business term*]
GUC	Groupe d'Union Camerounaise [*Group for Cameroonian Union*]
GUC	Gucci Group NV [*NYSE symbol*] (SAG)
GUC	Gunnison [*Colorado*] [*Airport symbol*] (OAG)
GUC	Union Catalog of the Atlanta-Athens Area, Atlanta, GA [*OCLC symbol*] (OCLC)
Gucci	Gucci Group NV [*Associated Press*] (SAG)
GUCCIAAC	General Union of Chamber of Commerce, Industry and Agriculture for Arab Countries [*Lebanon*] (EAIO)
GUCCO	Guidance Computer Control Subsystem
GUCJ	General Union of Carpenters and Joiners [*British*]
GUCL	General-Use Consumable List [*Military*]
GUCO	Grand Union [*NASDAQ symbol*] (TTSB)
GUCO	Grand Union Co. [*NASDAQ symbol*] (SAG)
GUCO	Guilford Courthouse National Military Park
GUCOTROIS	Great, Unopposable Commandant of the Realm of Inextinguishable Sagacity [*Rank in Junior Woodchucks organization mentioned in Donald Duck comic by Carl Barks*]
GUCOW	Grand Un Wrrt Ser 1 [*NASDAQ symbol*] (TTSB)
GUCOZ	Grand Un Wrrt Ser 2 [*NASDAQ symbol*] (TTSB)
GUCP	Ground Umbilical Carrier Plate (MCD)
GUCY	Conakry/Gbessia [*Guinea*] [*ICAO location identifier*] (ICLI)
GUD	Goundam [*Mali*] [*Airport symbol*] (OAG)
GUD	Guardian Resources Corp. [*Vancouver Stock Exchange symbol*]
GUD	Guide (ABBR)
GUDBK	Guidebook (ABBR)
GUDD	Didi [*Guinea*] [*ICAO location identifier*] (ICLI)
GUDD	Guided (ABBR)
GU-De	University of Georgia, DeRenne Georgia Library, Athens, GA [*Library symbol Library of Congress*] (LCLS)
Gude Pr	Gude. Practice of the Crown Side of the Court of King's Bench [*1828*] [*A publication*] (DLA)
GUDG	Guiding (ABBR)
GUDNC	Guidance (ABBR)
GUDPST	Guidepost (ABBR)
GUDSPA	General Union Democratic Students and Patriotic Afghan (EA)
GUE	Graphical User Environment [*Computer science*]
GUE	Group for the European Unitarian Left [*EC*] (ECED)
GUE	University of Guelph [*UTLAS symbol*]
GUER	Guerilla
GUERAP	General Unwanted Energy Rejection Analysis Program [*Air Force*]
GUERL	Guerilla (ABBR)
Guern Eq Jur	Guernsey's Key to Equity Jurisprudence [*A publication*] (DLA)
Guern Ins	Guernsey on Questions of Insanity [*A publication*] (DLA)

Guern Mech L... Guernsey's Mechanics' Lien Laws of New York [*A publication*] (DLA)
GUESS......... General Purpose Expert System Shell [*Virginia Polytechnic Institute*] [*General framework for expert systems*] (NITA)
GuestS........ Guest Supply, Inc. [*Associated Press*] (SAG)
GUF............ French Guiana [*ANSI three-letter standard code*] (CNC)
GUF............ General University Funds (EERA)
GUF............ Global University Funding
GUF............ Grand Unified Force
GUFA.......... Fria [*Guinea*] [*ICAO location identifier*] (ICLI)
GUFEX........ Gulf Underwater Flare Experiment [*Marine science*] (MSC)
GUFFAW...... Government Undertaking for Finding Another Way [*Parliamentary slang*] [*British*] (DI)
GUFH.......... Faranah/Badala [*Guinea*] [*ICAO location identifier*] (ICLI)
GUFMEX..... Gulf of Mexico [*Project*] [*Marine science*] (OSRA)
GUFMEX..... Gulf of Mexico [*Project*] (USDC)
GUFS.......... Grand United Friendly Society [*Australia*]
GUFSA........ Griffith University Faculty Staff Association [*Australia*]
GUG............ Empresa Guatemalteca de Aviacion [*Guatemala*] [*ICAO designator*] (FAAC)
GUG............ Guari [*Papua New Guinea*] [*Airport symbol*] (OAG)
GUG............ N'Guigmi [*Niger*] [*Airport symbol*] (AD)
GUGA.......... Grounded Unity Gain Amplifier (IAA)
GuGIC......... Instituto de Nutricion de Centro America y Panama, Guatemala City, Guatemala [*Library symbol Library of Congress*] (LCLS)
GuGIN......... Instituto Centroamericano de Investigacion y Tecnologia Industrial, Guatemala City, Guatemala [*Library symbol Library of Congress*]
GuGIN......... Instituto Centro Americano de Investigacion y Tecnologia Industrial, Guatemala City, Guatemala [*Library symbol*] [*Library of Congress*] (LCLS)
GUGL.......... Gaoual [*Guinea*] [*ICAO location identifier*] (ICLI)
GUGO.......... Banankoro/Gbenko [*Guinea*] [*ICAO location identifier*] (ICLI)
GUGR.......... Gentleman Usher of the Green Rod [*British*] (ROG)
GuGS.......... Universidad de San Carlos de Guatemala, Ciudad Universitaria, Guatemala City, Guatemala [*Library symbol Library of Congress*] (LCLS)
GUH............ Gunnedah [*Australia Airport symbol*] (OAG)
GUHA.......... General Unary Hypothesis Automation (IEEE)
GUI............ Gay Union International [*Paris, France*] (EAIO)
GUI............ Genitourinary Infection [*Medicine*] (PDAA)
GUI............ Golfing Union of Ireland (EAIO)
GUI............ Graphical User Interface [*Computer science*] (PCM)
GUI............ Graphical User Interface [*Computer science*] (EERA)
GUI............ Guiana (ROG)
Gui............ Guido de Cumis [*Flourished, 13th century*] [*Authority cited in pre-1607 legal work*] (DSA)
Gui............ Guido de Suzaria [*Deceased, 1293*] [*Authority cited in pre-1607 legal work*] (DSA)
Gui............ Guillelmus de Accursio [*Deceased, 1314*] [*Authority cited in pre-1607 legal work*] (DSA)
Gui............ Guillelmus de Tocco [*Authority cited in pre-1607 legal work*] (DSA)
GUI............ Guiria [*Venezuela*] [*Airport symbol*] (OAG)
GUI............ Guitar [*Music*]
GUIAC......... Guaiacum [*Lignum Vitae*] [*Pharmacy*] (ROG)
GUIB........... Graphical User Interface for Blind People
GUID........... Globally Unique Identifier (PCM)
GUID........... Globally Unique Identifiers [*Microsoft Corp.*] [*Computer science*] (PCM)
GUID........... Guidance (AAG)
GUID........... Guide
GUID........... Kindia [*Guinea*] [*ICAO location identifier*] (ICLI)
Guidant....... Guidant Corp. [*Associated Press*] (SAG)
GUIDAR....... Guided Intrusion Detection and Ranging (PDAA)
GUIDE......... General Usage Inventory Director (MCD)
GUIDE......... Guidance for Users of Integrated Data Processing Equipment
Gui de Cu.... Guillelmus de Cuneo [*Deceased, 1335*] [*Authority cited in pre-1607 legal work*] (DSA)
Gui de Su.... Guido de Suzaria [*Deceased, 1293*] [*Authority cited in pre-1607 legal work*] (DSA)
Gui de Suz... Guido de Suzaria [*Deceased, 1293*] [*Authority cited in pre-1607 legal work*] (DSA)
Gui de Suza... Guido de Suzaria [*Deceased, 1293*] [*Authority cited in pre-1607 legal work*] (DSA)
GUIDN......... Guidance (AABC)
GUIDNC....... Guidance
GUIDO......... Guidance and Navigation Officer [*NASA*]
Guid Pancir... Guido Pancirolus [*Deceased, 1599*] [*Authority cited in pre-1607 legal work*] (DSA)
Guid Pancirol... Guido Pancirolus [*Deceased, 1599*] [*Authority cited in pre-1607 legal work*] (DSA)
Guid Pap..... Guido Papa [*Deceased, 1487*] [*Authority cited in pre-1607 legal work*] (DSA)
GUIL........... Guilder (ABBR)
Guil Bene.... Guillelmus de Benedictis [*Flourished, 16th century*] [*Authority cited in pre-1607 legal work*] (DSA)
GUILD......... Government, University, Industry, Laboratory Development [*Microelectronics*]
GUILDF........ Guildford [*City in England*] (ROG)
GUILDHL...... Guildhall (ABBR)
Guild Law.... Guild Lawyer [*National Lawyers' Guild*] [*New York Chapter*] [*A publication*] (DLA)
Guild Q....... National Lawyers Guild Quarterly [*A publication*] (DLA)
GUILFL........ Guileful (ABBR)
Guilford....... Guilford Mills, Inc. [*Associated Press*] (SAG)
GuilfrdP....... Guilford Pharmaceuticals, Inc. [*Associated Press*] (SAG)

GUILFY........ Guilefully (ABBR)
Guill............ Guillelmus Durandi [*Deceased, 1296*] [*Authority cited in pre-1607 legal work*] (DSA)
Guill de Montelaud... Guillelmus de Monte Lauduno [*Deceased, 1343*] [*Authority cited in pre-1607 legal work*] (DSA)
Guillel Bened... Guillelmus de Benedictis [*Flourished, 16th century*] [*Authority cited in pre-1607 legal work*] (DSA)
Guil Na....... Guillelmus Naso [*Flourished, 1220-34*] [*Authority cited in pre-1607 legal work*] (DSA)
GUILS.......... Guileless (ABBR)
GUILSY........ Guilelessly (ABBR)
GUIMARC..... Guidelines Marketing Corp.
GUIN........... Guinea [*Monetary unit*] [*Obsolete British*] (ROG)
Guin............ Guinea (VRA)
GUIRR......... Government-University-Industry Research Roundtable [*Academy of Sciences*]
GUISE.......... Guidance System Evaluation [*Military*] (IAA)
Guit............ Guitar [*Music*]
Guiz............ Guizzardinus [*Deceased, 1222*] [*Authority cited in pre-1607 legal work*] (DSA)
Guizot Rep Govt... Guizot's History of Representative Government [*A publication*] (DLA)
GUJ............ Guaratingueta [*Brazil*] [*Airport symbol*] (OAG)
guj............ Gujarati [*MARC language code Library of Congress*] (LCCP)
Guj Ind....... Gujarat, India (ILCA)
Guj L Rep.... Gujarat Law Reporter [*A publication*] (ILCA)
GUK............ Guanylate Kinase [*An enzyme*]
GUKE.......... Kerouane [*Guinea*] [*ICAO location identifier*] (ICLI)
GUKR.......... Glavnoe Upravlenie Kontrrazvedkoi [*Chief Administration for Counter-intelligence*] [*of the Ministry of War*] [*Former USSR*] [*World War II*]
GUKR.......... Kamsar/Kawass [*Guinea*] [*ICAO location identifier*] (ICLI)
GUKU.......... Kissidougou [*Guinea*] [*ICAO location identifier*] (ICLI)
GUL............ Georgetown University, Law Library, Washington, DC [*OCLC symbol*] (OCLC)
GUL............ GSE [*Ground Support Equipment*] Utilization List [*NASA*] (NASA)
Gul............ Guillelmus de Cuneo [*Deceased, 1335*] [*Authority cited in pre-1607 legal work*] (DSA)
GUL............ Gull Air [*ICAO designator*] (FAAC)
GUL............ Gull Laboratories [*AMEX symbol*] (TTSB)
GUL............ Gull Laboratories, Inc. [*AMEX symbol*] (SPSG)
GUL............ Gully (ABBR)
GUL............ Gulmarg [*India*] [*Geomagnetic observatory code*]
GU-L.......... University of Georgia, Law Library, Athens, GA [*Library symbol Library of Congress*] (LCLS)
GULAG........ Glavnoe Upravlenie Ispravitel'no-Trudovykh Lagerei [*Main Administration of Corrective Labor Camps*] [*Former USSR*]
GULB.......... Gullible (ABBR)
GULB.......... Labe/Tata [*Guinea*] [*ICAO location identifier*] (ICLI)
GULBLY........ Gullibly (ABBR)
GULBT......... Gullibility (ABBR)
GULC.......... Georgetown University Law Center (AAGC)
GULC.......... Glasgow University Language Centre [*University of Glasgow*] [*British*] (CB)
GULD.......... Goulds Pumps [*NASDAQ symbol*] (TTSB)
GULD.......... Goulds Pumps, Inc. [*NASDAQ symbol*] (NQ)
GULF.......... Gulfwest Oil [*NASDAQ symbol*] (TTSB)
GULFCOBASESERVUNIT... Gulf Coast Base Service Unit
GULFCON..... Gulf Control
GULFNAVFACENGCOM... Gulf Division Naval Facilities Engineering Command
GULFSEAFRON... Gulf Sea Frontier
GulfSou....... Gulf South Medical Supply [*Associated Press*] (SAG)
GulfSou....... Sulf South Medical Supply [*Associated Press*] (SAG)
Gulfwest...... Gulfwest Oil Co. [*Associated Press*] (SAG)
GULHEMP..... General Physique, Upper Extremity, Lower Extremity, Hearing, Eyesight, Mentality, and Personality [*Medicine*] (DMAA)
GULL........... Guillotine [*Bookbinding*] (DGA)
GullLb......... Gull Laboratories, Inc. [*Associated Press*] (SAG)
GULP.......... General Upgrade LAN [*Limited Access Network*] Program [*Computer science*] (PCM)
GULP.......... General Utility Library Program [*Computer science*]
GULP.......... Grenada United Labour Party [*Political party*] (PPW)
GULP.......... Group Universal Life Policy [*Insurance*] (DFIT)
GULP.......... Group Universal Life Program
GULT........... Gullet (ABBR)
GULTN......... Guillotine (ABBR)
GULTND........ Guillotined (ABBR)
GULTNG........ Guillotining (ABBR)
GULYG......... Gullying (ABBR)
GUM............ General Utility Mechanic
GUM............ Glavnoe Upravleniye Militsii [*Main Administration of Militia*] [*Former USSR*] (LAIN)
GUM............ Glavny Universalny Magazin [*Department store in USSR*]
GUM............ Gosudarstvennyi Universal'nyi Magazin [*Government Department Store*] [*Moscow*]
GUM............ Grand Unified Monopoles [*Cosmology*]
GUM............ Guadalajara [*Mexico*] [*Seismograph station code, US Geological Survey*] (SEIS)
GUM............ Guam [*ANSI three-letter standard code*] (CNC)
GUM............ Guam [*Marianas*] [*Airport symbol*] (AD)
GUM............ Gulderand Mining [*Vancouver Stock Exchange symbol*]
GUMA.......... Macenta [*Guinea*] [*ICAO location identifier*] (ICLI)
GUMM......... GumTech International, Inc. [*NASDAQ symbol*] (SAG)
GUMM......... GumTech Intl [*NASDAQ symbol*] (TTSB)
GUMMW...... GumTech Intl Wrrt [*NASDAQ symbol*] (TTSB)

GUMNS...... Gumminess (ABBR)
GUMO......... Guam [Mariana Islands] [Seismograph station code, US Geological Survey] (SEIS)
GUMP......... Gas, Undercarriage, Mixture, and Prop [Checkout procedure]
GumT......... GumTech International, Inc. [Associated Press] (SAG)
GumTch..... GumTech International, Inc. [Associated Press] (SAG)
GUMZ......... Glavnoye Upravleniye Mestami Zaklyucheniya [Main Administration of Places of Detention] [Former USSR] (LAIN)
GUN.......... Guaranteed Underwriting Facilities (TDOB)
GUN.......... Guncotton (ABBR)
GUN.......... Guncrete (ABBR)
GUN.......... Gundle Environmental Systems, Inc. [AMEX symbol] (SPSG)
GUN.......... Gundle/SLT Environmental [AMEX symbol] (TTSB)
GUN.......... Gunnery (MSA)
GUN.......... Gunny (ABBR)
GUN.......... Gunpowder (ABBR)
GUN.......... Gunsteel Resources, Inc. [Vancouver Stock Exchange symbol]
GUN.......... Montgomery, AL [Location identifier FAA] (FAAL)
GUNBT...... Gunboat (ABBR)
Gunby......... Gunby's District Court Reports [1885] [Louisiana] [A publication] (DLA)
Gunby (LA)... Gunby's District Court Reports [1885] [Louisiana] [A publication] (DLA)
Gunby's Dec... Gunby's District Court Reports [1805] [Louisiana] [A publication] (DLA)
GUND.......... Gunned (ABBR)
Gundle...... Gundle-SLT Environmental Systems, Inc. [Associated Press] (SAG)
Gundry...... Gundry. Manuscripts in Lincoln's Inn Library [A publication] (DLA)
GUNEX...... Gunnery Exercise [Navy] (NVT)
GUNFIT...... Gunfight (ABBR)
GUNFITR..... Gunfighter (ABBR)
GUNFR....... Gunfire (ABBR)
GUNG.......... Gunning (ABBR)
GUNMA...... Gunman (ABBR)
GUN MOLL... Gonif's Molly [Thief's Girl] [Yiddish]
Gunn Tolls... Gunning on Tolls [A publication] (DLA)
GUNPWDR... Gunpowder (ABBR)
GUNR.......... Gunner (ABBR)
GUNRY....... Gunnery (ABBR)
GUNSGT..... Gunnery Sergeant
GUNSH...... Gunshot (ABBR)
GUNSM...... Gunsmith (ABBR)
GUNSS........ Gunnery Schoolship [Navy] (NVT)
GUNST....... Gunstock (ABBR)
GUNWHL..... Gunwhale (ABBR)
GUNYBG..... Gunnybag (ABBR)
GUNZ.......... N,Zerekore/Konia [Guinea] [ICAO location identifier] (ICLI)
GUO.......... Georgetown, TX [Location identifier FAA] (FAAL)
GUO.......... Government Use Only (WDAA)
Guo.......... Guanosine [Also, G] [A nucleoside]
GUOK........ Boke/Baralande [Guinea] [ICAO location identifier] (ICLI)
GUOO........ Grand United Order of Oddfellows [Australia]
GUOOF...... Grand United Order of Odd Fellows (EA)
GUP.......... Gallup [New Mexico] [Airport symbol] (OAG)
GUP.......... Gas Under Pressure
GUP.......... Glass-Fiber-Reinforced Unsaturated Polyester [Organic chemistry]
GU-P......... Grifora Umbellata Polysaccharide [Antineoplastic drug]
GUP.......... Guppy (ABBR)
GU-P......... University of Georgia, School of Pharmacy, Athens, GA [Library symbol Library of Congress] (LCLS)
GUPAC....... Gulf Permanent Assistance Committee [Persian Gulf]
GUPB......... GFS Bancorp [NASDAQ symbol] (TTSB)
GUPB......... GFSB Bancorp, Inc. [NASDAQ symbol] (SAG)
GUPH........ Group for the Use of Psychology in History (EA)
Guppie....... Gay Urban Professional [Lifestyle classification]
GUPPY....... Greater Underwater Propulsive Power [Type of submarine]
GUPS........ Grand Unified Problem Solver
Gupta....... Gupta Corp. [Associated Press] (SAG)
GUQ.......... Guanare [Venezuela] [Airport symbol] (OAG)
GUR.......... Alotau [Papua New Guinea] [Airport symbol] (OAG)
GUR.......... Ground under Repair
GUR.......... Gulfstream Resources Canada Ltd. [Toronto Stock Exchange symbol]
GUR.......... Gurgu (ABBR)
GURC........ Gulf Universities Research Consortium (EA)
GURC........ Gulf Universities Research Corp.
GURGLD..... Gurgled (ABBR)
GURGLG..... Gurgling (ABBR)
GURNT....... Guarantee (ABBR)
GURNTD..... Guaranteed (ABBR)
GURNTG..... Guarantying (ABBR)
GURNTR..... Guarantor (ABBR)
GURNTY..... Guaranty (ABBR)
GURR........ Gentleman Usher of the Red Rod [British] (ROG)
GURS........ Kouroussa [Guinea] [ICAO location identifier] (ICLI)
GURTG....... Guaranteeing (ABBR)
Gus.......... Conductance of Upstream Segment [Physics] (DAVI)
GUS.......... Generic Update System [Computer science]
GUS.......... Generic User System [Computer science]
GUS.......... Genitourinary System [Medicine]
GUS.......... Give Up Smoking [Health Education Council campaign] [British]
GUS.......... Glucuronidase [An enzyme]
GUS.......... Great Universal Stores [Mail-order firm] [British]
GUS.......... Group Unit Simulator (MCD)
GUS.......... Gunflint Resources Ltd. [Vancouver Stock Exchange symbol]

GUS.......... Gusset (MSA)
GUS.......... Peru, IN [Location identifier FAA] (FAAL)
GUSA........ Sangaredi [Guinea] [ICAO location identifier] (ICLI)
GUSB........ Guided Unified S-Band (MCD)
GUSB........ Sambailo [Guinea] [ICAO location identifier] (ICLI)
GUSER....... GCOS Security Module
GUSH........ Fountain Oil [NASDAQ symbol] (TTSB)
GUSH........ Fountain Oil, Inc. [NASDAQ symbol] (SAG)
GUSHG...... Gushing (ABBR)
GUSHNS..... Gushiness (ABBR)
GUSHR...... Gushier (ABBR)
GUSHST..... Gushiest (ABBR)
GUSI......... Siguiri [Guinea] [ICAO location identifier] (ICLI)
GUSS........ Guided Social Simulation
GUSSIES..... Great Universal Stores [Mail-order firm] [British]
GUST........ Gusset (ABBR)
GUSTNS..... Gustiness (ABBR)
GUSTO...... Global Utilization of Streptokinase and Tissue Plasminogen Activator for Occluded Coronary Arteries [Cardiology study]
GUSTO...... Global Utilization of Streptokinase and TPA [Tissue Plasminogen Activator]for Occluded Arteries [Comparative study]
GUSTO...... Guidance Using Stable Tuning Oscillations
GUSTR...... Gustier (ABBR)
GUSTST..... Gustiest (ABBR)
GUSTY....... Gustily (ABBR)
GUT.......... Grand Unified Theory [Cosmology]
GUT.......... Gulf Titanium Ltd. [Vancouver Stock Exchange symbol]
GUT.......... Gutter (MSA)
GUT.......... Pittsburgh, PA [Location identifier FAA] (FAAL)
Gut Brac..... Guterbock's Bracton [A publication] (DLA)
GUTD........ Gutted (ABBR)
GUTG........ Gutting (ABBR)
Guth L & T... Guthrie's Landlord and Tenant [A publication] (DLA)
Guth Pr...... Guthrie's Principles of the Laws of England [1843] [A publication] (DLA)
Guthrie...... Guthrie's Reports [33-83 Missouri Appeals] [A publication] (DLA)
Guthrie...... Guthrie's Sheriff Court Cases [1861-92] [Scotland] [A publication] (DLA)
Guth Sh Cas... Guthrie's Sheriff Court Cases [1861-92] [Scotland] [A publication] (DLA)
Guth Sher Cas... Guthrie's Sheriff Court Cases [1861-92] [Scotland] [A publication] (DLA)
Guth Tr Un... Guthrie on Trade Unions [A publication] (DLA)
GUTR........ Gutter (ABBR)
GUTRL....... Gutteral (ABBR)
GUTRY...... Gutterally (ABBR)
GUTS........ Game on Urban Transport System [Kins Developments Ltd.] [Software package] (NCC)
GUTS........ Georgians Unwilling to Surrender [Organization founded by former governor, Lester Maddox]
GUTS........ Gothenburg University Terminal System [IBM Corp.] (EECA)
GUTS........ Ground Up-to-Space (MCD)
GUTS........ Guerilla Urban Traffic System [Refers to driving in Boston]
gutt......... Goutte [Drop] [Pharmacy]
GUTT........ Grand Unified Theory of the Tire
GUTT........ Guttae [Drops of Liquid] [Pharmacy]
GUTT........ Gutturi [To the Throat] [Pharmacy]
GUTTAT...... Guttatim [Drop by Drop] [Pharmacy] (GPO)
GUTT QUIBUSD... Guttis Quibusdam [With a Few Drops] [Pharmacy]
GUU......... Grundarfjordur [Iceland] [Airport symbol] (OAG)
GUU......... Gulu [Uganda] [Airport symbol] (AD)
GUUG........ Gross Unit Unavailable Generation [Electronics] (IEEE)
GUV.......... Gerecht und Volkommen [Correct and Complete] [German]
GUV.......... Guri [Venezuela] [Seismograph station code, US Geological Survey] (SEIS)
GUXD........ Kankan/Diankana [Guinea] [ICAO location identifier] (ICLI)
GUY.......... Air Guyane [France ICAO designator] (FAAC)
GUY.......... French Guiana Space Center
GUY.......... Guyana [ANSI three-letter standard code] (CNC)
GUY.......... Guymon, OK [Location identifier FAA] (FAAL)
Guy For Med... Guy's Forensic Medicine [7th ed.] [1895] [A publication] (DLA)
Guy Med Jur... Guy's Medical Jurisprudence [A publication] (DLA)
Guyot Inst Feod... Guyot's Instituts Feodales [A publication] (DLA)
Guy Rep...... Guy's Repertoire de la Jurisprudence [A publication] (DLA)
GUZ.......... Guiratinga [Brazil] [Airport symbol] (AD)
GUZL........ Guzzle (ABBR)
GUZLD....... Guzzled (ABBR)
GUZLG....... Guzzling (ABBR)
GUZLR....... Guzzler (ABBR)
GV........... Galvanized [Technical drawings]
GV........... Gastric Volume [Medicine] (DMAA)
GV........... Gas Ventilation [Medicine] (DMAA)
GV........... Gate Valve (DAC)
GV........... Genital Vein
GV........... Gentian Violet [Also, MRC] [A dye]
GV........... Germinal Vesicle (PDAA)
GV........... Gigavolt
GV........... Girls Volunteers [Australia]
GV........... Give (ABBR)
GV........... Goerz-Visier [Bomb sight manufactured by Goerz Co.] [German military - World War II]
GV........... Goldfield Corp. [AMEX symbol] (SPSG)
GV........... Gomphrena Virus [Plant pathology]
GV........... Governor (DSUE)
GV........... Governor of Victoria [Australia]

GV .... Granulosis Virus
GV .... Gravimetric Volume
G-V .... Gravity-Velocity (MCD)
GV .... Great Value [*In automobile name Yugo GV*]
GV .... Green Valley [*Plant pathology*]
GV .... Grid Variation [*Navigation*]
GV .... Gross Virus [*Leukemogenesis*] [*Immunochemistry*]
GV .... Ground Visibility
GV .... Groundwater Vistas [*Computer science*]
GV .... Groundwater Vistas
GV .... Group Velocity [*Physics*] (IAA)
GV .... Growth Vessel
GV .... Grow Victoria [*Mental health organisation*] [*Australia*]
GV .... Guard Vessel [*Nuclear energy*] (NRCH)
gv .... Guinea [*MARC country of publication code Library of Congress*] (LCCP)
G V .... Gulfstream V
GV .... Gulp Valve [*Automotive engineering*]
GV .... Talair [*ICAO designator*] (AD)
GVA .... Gamewardens of Vietnam Association (EA)
GVA .... Gay Veterans Association (EA)
GVA .... General Visceral Afferent [*Neurology*]
GVA .... Geneva [*Switzerland*] [*Airport symbol*] (OAG)
GVA .... Geschichte Vorderasien bis zum Hellenismus [*A publication*] (BJA)
GVA .... Golden Nevada [*Vancouver Stock Exchange symbol*]
GVA .... Golden Nevada Resources, Inc. [*Toronto Stock Exchange symbol*]
GVA .... Goulburn Valley Airlines [*Australia*]
GVA .... GOX [*Gaseous Oxygen*] Vent Arm (NASA)
GVA .... Grapevine Virus A [*Plant pathology*]
GVA .... Graphic Kilovolt-Ampere [*Meter*] (MSA)
GVA .... Gyroscope Vibration Absorber
GVA .... Henderson, KY [*Location identifier FAA*] (FAAL)
GVAC .... Amilcar Cabral International/Sal Island [*Cape Verde*] [*ICAO location identifier*] (ICLI)
GVAC .... Graphic Video Attributes Controller [*Computer chip*]
GVAO .... Gross Value of Agricultural Output
GVaP .... GEWEX [*Global Energy and Water Cycle Experiment*] Water Vapor Project [*Marine science*] (OSRA)
GVaP .... GEWEX [*Global Energy and Water Cycle Experiment*] Water Vapor Project (USDC)
GVaS .... Valdosta State College, Valdosta, GA [*Library symbol Library of Congress*] (LCLS)
GVAWY .... Giveaway (ABBR)
GVB .... Gelatine Veronal Buffer (PDAA)
GVB .... Generalized Valence Bond [*Physics*]
GVB .... Grapevine Virus B [*Plant pathology*]
GVB .... Guaranteed Voltage Breakdown
GVBA .... Boavista, Boavista Island [*Cape Verde*] [*ICAO location identifier*] (ICLI)
GVBD .... Germinal Vesicle Breakdown [*Cytology*]
GVC .... General Videotex Corp.
GVC .... Girls' Venture Corps [*British*] (BI)
GVC .... Glazed Vitrified Clay
GVC .... Grand View College [*Iowa*]
GVC .... Graphics Vendor Control
GVC .... Guild Vector Colorimeter
GVCAC .... Girls' Venture Corps Air Cadets [*British*] (DBA)
GVCO .... Grants to Voluntary Conservation Organisations (EERA)
GVD .... Gravdal [*Norway*] [*Airport symbol*] (AD)
GVD .... Group View Display (MCD)
GVDSN .... Gott Verlaeszt die Seinen Nicht [*God Forsakes Not His Own*] [*Motto of Dorothee, Duchess of Braunschweig-Wolfenbuttel (1607-34)*] [*German*]
GVE .... General Visceral Efferent [*Neurology*]
GVE .... Gordonsville, VA [*Location identifier FAA*] (FAAL)
GVE .... Group Value Engineering
GVE .... Grove (ADA)
GVF .... Garnisonsverwendungsfaehig Feld [*Fit for Garrison Duty in the Field*] [*German military - World War II*]
GVF .... Good Visual Field [*Ophthalmology*] (DAVI)
GVF .... Grazhdanskii Vozdushnyi Flot [*Civil Air Fleet*] [*Former USSR*]
GVFM .... Francisco Mendes, Santiago Island [*Cape Verde*] [*ICAO location identifier*] (ICLI)
GVG .... Flygaktiebolaget Gota Vingar [*Sweden*] [*FAA designator*] (FAAC)
GVG .... Gamma-Vinyl-GABA [*Biochemistry*]
GVG .... Giving (FAAC)
GVG .... Grundriss der Vergleichenden Grammatik der Semitischen Sprachen [*A publication*] (BJA)
GVGI .... General Visual Slope Indicator [*FAA*] (TAG)
GVGSS .... Grundriss der Vergleichenden Grammatik der Semitischen Sprachen [*A publication*] (BJA)
GVH .... Garnisonsverwendungsfaehig Heimat [*Fit for Garrison Duty in Zone of Interior*] [*German military - World War II*]
GVH .... Government Vehicle (FAAC)
GVH .... Graft Versus Host [*Immunology*]
GVHBCIFC .... Gene Vincent and His Blue Caps International Fan Club (EAIO)
GVHD .... Graft-Versus-Host Disease [*Immunology*]
GvHD .... Graft-Versus Host Disease [*Immunology*]
GVHR .... Graft-Versus-Host Reaction [*Immunology*]
GVHRR .... Geosynchronous Very-High-Resolution Radiometer
GVI .... Gas Vent Institute [*Defunct*] (EA)
GVI .... Global Vegetation Index (MCD)
GVI .... Green River [*Papua New Guinea*] [*Airport symbol*] (OAG)
GVIAO .... Gross Value of Industrial and Agricultural Output

GVidO .... Ohoopee Regional Library, Vidalia, GA [*Library symbol Library of Congress*] (LCLS)
GVIL .... Global Village Commun [*NASDAQ symbol*] (TTSB)
GVIL .... Global Village Communications, Inc. [*NASDAQ symbol*] (SAG)
GVIO .... Gross Value of Industrial Output
GVL .... Gainesville [*Georgia*] [*Airport symbol*] (AD)
GVL .... Gainesville, GA [*Location identifier FAA*] (FAAL)
GVL .... Gold Vapor LASER [*Physics*]
GVL .... Gold Ventures Ltd. [*Vancouver Stock Exchange symbol*]
GvL .... Graft-Versus-Leukemia [*Medicine*]
GVL .... Gravel (KSC)
G/VLLD .... Ground/Vehicle Laser Locator Designation [*Homing device*] (NITA)
G/VLLD .... Ground/Vehicular LASER Locator Designator (RDA)
G/VLL-D .... Ground Vehicular LASER Locator Designator [*Military*]
GVM .... Generating Volt Meter (PDAA)
GVMA .... Maio, Maio Island [*Cape Verde*] [*ICAO location identifier*] (ICLI)
GVMDS .... Ground Vehicle Mine Dispensing System [*Military*]
GVMR .... Gross Vehicle Mass Rating [*Load that a vehicle can carry*]
GVMT .... Mosteiros, Fogo Island [*Cape Verde*] [*ICAO location identifier*] (ICLI)
GVN .... Given (ABBR)
GVN .... Goodyear Video Network [*Training and motivational program*]
GVN .... Government of Vietnam
GVO .... Gaviota, CA [*Location identifier FAA*] (FAAL)
GVO .... Graeber-Verwaltungsoffizier [*Graves Registration Officer*] [*German military - World War II*]
GVO .... Gross Value of Output (MHDW)
GVP .... Gasoline Vapor Pressure (GNE)
GVP .... General Vice President (WDAA)
GVP .... Gesamtdeutsche Volkspartei [*All-German People's Party*] [*Germany Political party*] (PPE)
GVP .... Government Vehicle Pool [*Victoria, Australia*]
GVP .... Gravis Computer Peripherals, Inc. [*Vancouver Stock Exchange symbol*]
GVP .... Greater Victoria Public Library [*UTLAS symbol*]
GVP .... Gross Value of Production
GVP .... Group Visionary Productions, Inc. [*Studio City, CA*] [*Telecommunications*] (TSSD)
GVPF .... Guinea Pig Vascular Permeability Factor [*Biochemistry*]
GVPM .... Grootvlei Proprietary Mines Ltd. [*NASDAQ symbol*] (SAG)
GVPN .... Global Virtual Private Network [*Computer science*] (CDE)
GVPR .... Praia/Praia, Santiago Island [*Cape Verde*] [*ICAO location identifier*] (ICLI)
GVQ .... Batavia, NY [*Location identifier FAA*] (FAAL)
GVR .... Glyn Valley Railway [*Formerly, E & GVR*] [*Wales*]
GVR .... Governador Valadares [*Brazil*] [*Airport symbol*] (OAG)
GVR .... Granville Resources, Inc. [*Vancouver Stock Exchange symbol*]
GVR .... Gray-Votaw-Rogers [*Psychology*] (AEBS)
GVR .... Green Valley Road [*California*] [*Seismograph station code, US Geological Survey*] (SEIS)
GVRNMTL .... Governmental
GVS .... Global Videophone Standard [*Telecommunications*] (CDE)
GVS .... Government Vehicle Service [*Postal Service*]
GVS .... Graniteville [*South Carolina*] [*Seismograph station code, US Geological Survey Closed*] (SEIS)
GVS .... Ground Vibration Survey [*Aerospace*]
GVSC .... Sal Oceanic Area Control Center [*Cape Verde*] [*ICAO location identifier*] (ICLI)
GVSF .... Sao Felipe, Fogo Island [*Cape Verde*] [*ICAO location identifier*] (ICLI)
GVSN .... Sao Nicolau, Sao Nicolau Island [*Cape Verde*] [*ICAO location identifier*] (ICLI)
GV-SOLAS .... Gesellschaft fuer Versuchstierkunde - Society of Labortory Animal Science [*Switzerland*] (EAIO)
G vs T .... Deceleration Units of Gravity versus Time (KSC)
GVSU .... Grand Valley State University [*Michigan*]
G vs V .... Deceleration Units of Gravity Versus Velocity (KSC)
GVSV .... Sao Vicente, Sao Vicente Island [*Cape Verde*] [*ICAO location identifier*] (ICLI)
GVT .... Dean Witter Government Income Trust SBI [*NYSE symbol*] (SPSG)
GVT .... Dean Witter Gvt Income SBI [*NYSE symbol*] (TTSB)
GVT .... Gated Video Tracker
GVT .... Glenvet Resources Ltd. [*Vancouver Stock Exchange symbol*]
GVT .... Government (WDAA)
GVT .... Gravity Vacuum Tube System [*High-speed ground transportation*]
GVT .... Greenville, TX [*Location identifier FAA*] (FAAL)
GVT .... Ground Vibration Test [*Aerospace*] (MCD)
GVTA .... Ground Vibration Test Article [*Aerospace*] (NASA)
GvtTch .... Government Technology Services [*Associated Press*] (SAG)
GVTW .... Gross Vehicle Test Weight [*Automotive engineering*]
GVTY .... Gingivectomy [*Dentistry*]
GVU .... Graphic, Visualization, and Usability Center [*Georgia Institute of Technology*]
GVUGA .... Grounded Voltage Unity-Gain Amplifier (PDAA)
GVV .... Grangeville, ID [*Location identifier FAA*] (FAAL)
GVVA .... Goulburn Valley Viticultural Association [*Australia*]
GVW .... Grandview, MO [*Location identifier FAA*] (FAAL)
GVW .... Gross Vehicle Weight (MCD)
GVWR .... Gross Vehicle Weight Rating
GVX .... Extra-Great Value [*In automobile name Yugo GVX*]
GVX .... Gavle [*Sweden*] [*Airport symbol*] (OAG)
GVX .... Geevax Ltd. [*British ICAO designator*] (FAAC)
GVX .... Grove Explorations Ltd. [*Vancouver Stock Exchange symbol*]
GVX .... Gruver, TX [*Location identifier FAA*] (FAAL)
GVY .... Green Valley Mine [*Vancouver Stock Exchange symbol*]
GW .... Air Force Guide for Writing

GW............. Cases in the Griqualand West Local Division of the Supreme Court [1910-46] [South Africa] [A publication] (DLA)
GW............. Game Winning [Baseball]
GW............. Gastric Wrap [Morbid obesity surgical treatment]
GW............. General Warning
GW............. General Will [Collectivist theory of government]
GW............. George Washington [US general and president, 1732-1799]
GW............. George Washington University [Washington, DC]
gw............. Germany, West [MARC country of publication code Library of Congress] (LCCP)
GW............. Germ Warfare
GW............. Gigawatt
GW............. Glauben und Wissen (BJA)
GW............. Glazed Weatherproof [Tile] (DICI)
GW............. Global Water (EA)
G/W........... Glucose in Water [Medicine]
GW............. Glycerine in Water [Medicine]
GW............. Golden West Airlines [ICAO designator] (AD)
GW............. Good Words [A publication] (ROG)
GW............. Gradual Withdrawal [Medicine] (DMAA)
GW............. Grand Warder [Freemasonry]
GW............. Great Writers [A publication]
GW............. Green Weight (WDAA)
GW............. Grenzwache [Frontier Guard] [German military - World War II]
GW............. Gross Weight (NG)
GW............. Groundwater (EPA)
GW............. Ground Waves (NATG)
GW............. Groundwork for a Just World (EA)
G/W........... Group Work (MAE)
GW............. Growth [Business term]
GW............. Guardian Weekly [A publication] (BRI)
GW............. Guerrilla Warfare (AABC)
GW............. Guided Weapon [Air Force]
GW............. Guided Wire [British military] (DMA)
GW............. Guinea-Bissau [ANSI two-letter standard code] (CNC)
GWA .... General Work Area [NASA] (NASA)
GWA .... Governor of Western Australia
GWA .... Grand Worthy Associate [Freemasonry] (ROG)
GWA .... Great Wall Airlines [China] [ICAO designator] (FAAC)
GWA .... Great Westrn Air, Inc. [FAA designator] (FAAC)
GWA .... [The] Greens (Western Australia) Inc.
GWA .... Gunshot Wound of the Abdomen [Emergency medicine] (DAVI)
GWA .... International PEN - Guatemalan Writers Abroad (EA)
GWAA .... Garden Writers Association of America (EA)
GWAA .... Golf Writers Association of America (EA)
GWAD .... Great Warbirds Air Display [British]
GWAH........ Global Women of African Heritage (EA)
GWAI .... German Workshop on Artificial Intelligence [A publication]
GWAL .... Great Wall Electronic International Ltd. [NASDAQ symbol] (SAG)
GWALY .... Great Wall Electr Int. ADS [NASDAQ symbol] (TTSB)
GW & MRJS... Great Western & Midland Railway Joint Stock [British] (ROG)
GWasB........ Bartram Trail Regional Library, Washington, GA [Library symbol Library of Congress] (LCLS)
GWAY .... Galway [County in Ireland] (ROG)
GWayC......... Waycross Junior College, Waycross, GA [Library symbol Library of Congress] (LCLS)
GWAZB .... Gott Wende Alles zum Besten [May God Turn Everything to the Best] [Motto of Amoene Amalie, Princess of Anhalt (d. 1626)] [German]
GWB .... General Well-Being [Medicine] (DMAA)
GWB .... Gesetz Gegen Wettbewerbsbeschrankungen [German Law Against Restraint of Competition] (DLA)
GWB .... Glycosylated Whole Blood [Clinical chemistry]
GWB .... Gypsum Wallboard [Technical drawings]
GWBC .... Gateway Bancorp, Inc. Kentucky [NASDAQ symbol] (SAG)
GWBC .... Gateway Bancorp(Ky) [NASDAQ symbol] (TTSB)
GWBC .... Governor William Bradford Compact [An association] (EA)
GWBOT .... Greater Washington Board of Trade (SRA)
GWC .... Gardner-Webb College [Boiling Springs, NC]
GWC .... George Williams College [Downer's Grove, IL]
GWC .... Gippsland Waters Coalition (EERA)
GWC .... Global Weather Central
GWC .... Grand Worthy Chief [Templars] [Freemasonry] (ROG)
GWC .... Great Whale River [Quebec] [Seismograph station code, US Geological Survey Closed] (SEIS)
GWC .... Gross Weight Category (DNAB)
GWC .... Ground Water Council [Defunct]
GWC .... Guard Well Capacitor
GWC .... Omaha, NE [Location identifier FAA] (FAAL)
GWC .... West Georgia College, Carrollton, GA [OCLC symbol] (OCLC)
GWCA .... George Washington Carver National Monument
GWCC .... Georgia World Congress Center
GWCG........ General Wiring Cables Group [British] (DBA)
GW CHAP ... Grand Worthy Chaplain [Templars] [Freemasonry] (ROG)
GWCI .... Giftware Manufacturers' Credit Interchange [Buffalo, NY] (EA)
GWCSA .... Greater World Christian Spiritualist Association (EA)
GWCSWBD... Gunnery Weapon Control Switchboard
GWCT .... Grand Worthy Chief [Templars] [Freemasonry] (ROG)
GWCT .... Grand Worthy Chief Templar [Templars] [Freemasonry] (ROG)
GWD .... Gaseous Waste Disposal [System] [Nuclear energy] (NRCH)
GWd .... Gigawatt-days
GWD .... Grinding Wheel Dresser
GWD .... Gwadar [Pakistan] [Airport symbol] (OAG)
GWD .... South African Law Reports, Griqualand West Local Division [A publication] (DLA)
GWDB......... Groundwater Database

GWDM .... Grand Worthy Deputy Marshal [Templars] [Freemasonry] (ROG)
GWDRS....... Ground Winds Data Reduction System [NASA]
GWDS........ Graphic Weather Display System [FAA] (TAG)
GWE........... Gigawatt-Electric [DOE] (TAG)
GWe........... Gigawatt Electrical
GWE........... Global Weather Experiment [Marine science] (MSC)
GWE........... Glycerin and Water Enema [Medicine]
GWE........... Gwelo [Zimbabwe] [Airport symbol] (OAG)
GWEF......... Guided Weapons Evaluation Facility (MCD)
GWEN .... Ground Wave Emergency Network
GWEN .... Ground Wave Emergency Network
GWeP......... West Point-Pepperell, Inc., West Point, GA [Library symbol Library of Congress] (LCLS)
GWF........... Galveston Wharves [AAR code]
GWF........... Gating Waveform
GWF........... Gay White Female [Classified advertising] (CDAI)
GWF........... Global-Warming Factor [Meteorology]
GWF........... Great Western Financial Corp. [NYSE symbol] (SPSG)
GWF........... Great Westn Finl [NYSE symbol] (TTSB)
GWF........... Lancaster, CA [Location identifier FAA] (FAAL)
GWFN .... Global Weather Facsimile Network (MCD)
GWFPr........ Great Westn Finl CvDep Pfd [NYSE symbol] (TTSB)
GWFPrA ..... Great Westn Finl 8.30% Dep Pfd [NYSE symbol] (TTSB)
GWFPrT ..... Great Westn Fin l 8.25% 'TOPrS' [NYSE symbol] (TTSB)
GWG .... Game-Winning Goals [Hockey]
GWG .... Gaussian Wave Group [Physics]
GWG .... Generalized Wegener Granulomatosis [Medicine] (DMAA)
GWG .... Gottes Wille Geschehe [God's Will Be Done] [Motto of Juliane Ursula, Margravine of Baden (d. 1614)] [German]
GWG .... Groundwater Working Group [Australia]
GWG .... Gullwing Group (EA)
GWGI .... Gullwing Group International (EA)
GWh .... Gigawatt-Hour
GWH .... Gigawatt Hour [DOE] (TAG)
GWH .... Great Water Holt (EA)
GWH .... Guided Warheads
GWHF .... George Williams Hooper Foundation [Research center] (RCD)
GWHIS........ Global-Wide Help and Information Systems [On-line help system for Mosaic developers]
GWI .... Galvanized Wrought Iron (ADA)
GWI .... General Wage Increase (MCD)
GWI .... Global-Warming Index [Meteorology]
GWI .... Government-Wide Index [Later, USGRDR]
GWI .... Greenhouse Warming Index [Marine science] (OSRA)
GWI .... Greenhouse Warming Index (USDC)
GWI .... Grinding Wheel Institute (EA)
GWI .... Ground Water Institute [Defunct] (EA)
GWIBIT .... Guild of Washington Incompetent Bureaucratic Idea Throatcutters [An organizati on rumored to have been active in World War II]
GWIC .... Geothermal World Info Center [Later, REIC] (EA)
GWIC .... Global Warming International Center [An association] (EA)
GWIG .... Grand Worthy Inside Guard [Templars] [Freemasonry] (ROG)
GWIGWO ... Good Will In, Good Will Out [Computer science]
Gwil .... Gwillim's Tithe Cases [England] [1224-1824] [A publication] (DLA)
Gwill........... Gwillim's Tithe Cases [England] [A publication] (DLA)
Gwill Bac Abr... Gwillim's Tithe Cases [England] [A publication] (DLA)
Gwill T Cas... Gwillim's Tithe Cases [England] [A publication] (DLA)
Gwill Ti Cas... Gwillim's Tithe Cases [England] [A publication] (DLA)
Gwil Ti Cas... Gwillim's Tithe Cases [England] [A publication] (DLA)
GWIN .... Goodwin Railroad, Inc. [AAR code]
GWIRD........ Government-Wide Index to Research and Development
GWJ........... Chicopee Falls, MA [Location identifier FAA] (FAAL)
GWJ........... Glue Weld Joint
GWJC .... Gardner-Webb Junior College [Later, Gardner-Webb College] [North Carolina]
GWL........... George Washington University, Law Library, Washington, DC [OCLC symbol] (OCLC)
GWL........... Great-West Life Assurance Co. [Toronto Stock Exchange symbol]
GWL........... Grosswetterlage [Meteorology]
GWL........... Groundwater Level [Hydrology] (IAA)
GWL........... Gwalior [India] [Airport symbol] (OAG)
GWL........... Reports of Cases Decided in the Supreme Court of South Africa (Griqualand West Local Division), by Kitchin [A publication] (DLA)
GWLD .... Gaming World International, Inc. [NASDAQ symbol] (SAG)
GWLD .... Gaming World Intl. [NASDAQ symbol] (TTSB)
GWLD .... South Africa Law Reports, Griqualand West Local Division [A publication] (DLA)
GWLDW ...... Gaming World Intl. Wrrt'A' [NASDAQ symbol] (TTSB)
GWM .... Gay White Male [Classified advertising]
GWM .... George Washington University, Medical Library, Washington, DC [OCLC symbol] (OCLC)
GWM .... Grand Worthy Marshal [Templars] [Freemasonry] (ROG)
GWM .... Ground Water Monitor [A publication]
GWM .... Ground Water Monitoring
GWM .... Guam Tracking Station [NASA] (KSC)
GWM .... Guaranteed Weekly Minimum
GWMC .... Galvanized Ware Manufacturers Council (EA)
GWMD .... Ground Water Management District
GWMR .... Ground Water Monitoring Review [A publication]
GWMS .... Gaseous Waste Management System [Nuclear energy] (NRCH)
GWMS .... Gas-Water Module Storage [Nuclear energy] (NRCH)
GWMU .... Government Workforce Management Unit [Victoria, Australia]
GWN .... Golden West Network [Australia]
GWN .... Goldwinn Resources Ltd. [Vancouver Stock Exchange symbol]
GWND .... Gowned (ABBR)

GWO	General Watch Officer [Army] (AABC)
GWO	Great-West Lifeco, Inc. [Toronto Stock Exchange symbol]
GWO	Greenwood [Mississippi] [Airport symbol] (OAG)
GWOA	Guerrilla Warfare Operational Area [Army]
GWO & HP	Gas Wall Oven and Hot Plate [Classified advertising] (ADA)
GWOG	Grand Worthy Outside Guard [Templars] [Freemasonry] (ROG)
GWOTH	Ground Wave Over-the-Horizon RADAR (DNAB)
GWP	Gesellschaft fuer Wirtschaftspublizistik GmbH [Society for Public Economics] [Germany] (IID)
GWP	Gift with Purchase
g-w-p	Gift With Purchase [Retail] (WDMC)
GWP	Global-Warming Potential [Meteorology]
GWP	Government White Paper
GWP	Grand Worthy Patriarch [Freemasonry] (ROG)
GWP	Great Western Petroleum Corp. [Vancouver Stock Exchange symbol]
GWP	Greenhouse Warming Potential (EERA)
GWP	Gross World Product
GWP	Guided Writing Procedure [Reading improvement method]
GWPAS	General Work Force Performance Appraisal System [Marine science] (OSRA)
GWPAS	General Work Force Performance Appraisal System (USDC)
GWPCA	German Wirehaired Pointer Club of America (EA)
GWPM	Gross Words per Minute [Computer science] (IAA)
GWPMS	Ground Water Policy and Management Staff [Environmental Protection Agency] (GFGA)
GWPS	Gaseous Waste Processing System [Nuclear energy] (NRCH)
GWPS	Ground Water Protection Standard [Environmental Protection Agency] (GFGA)
GWpSO	Group Weapons Staff Officer [British military] (DMA)
GWPU	General Workers Professional Unions [Bulgaria]
GWQ	GWR Resources [Vancouver Stock Exchange symbol]
GWQ	San Francisco, CA [Location identifier FAA] (FAAL)
GWQAP	Government-Wide Quality Assurance Program
GWQE	General Water-Quality Engineering [Survey] [Army] (RDA)
GWR	General War Reserves [Army] (AABC)
GWR	Gill Withdrawal Reflex
GWR	[The] Great Western Railway Co. [Prior to nationalization] [AAR code]
GWR	Great World Resources [Vancouver Stock Exchange symbol]
GWR	Griqualand High Court Reports [A publication] (DLA)
GWR	Gwinner, ND [Location identifier FAA] (FAAL)
GW-RBI	Game-Winning Run Batted In [Baseball]
GWRDC	Grape and Wine Research and Development Corporation (EERA)
GWRDC	Grape and Wine Research and Development Council [Australia]
GWRI	Ground Water Resources Institute [Later, Ground Water Council]
GWRRA	Gold Wing Road Riders Association (EA)
GWRX	GeoWorks [NASDAQ symbol] (SAG)
GWRX	Geoworks [NASDAQ symbol] (TTSB)
GWS	Gar Wood Society (EA)
GWS	Gaseous Waste System [Nuclear energy] (NRCH)
GWS	GEEIA [Ground Electronics Engineering Installation Agency] Workload Schedule (AFM)
GWS	General War Subsystem (MCD)
GWS	Geneva Convention for the Amelioration of the Condition of the Wounded and Sick in Armed Forces in the Field, 12 August 1949 [Army] (AABC)
GWS	German Wine Society [Canada] (EAIO)
GWS	Glashow-Weinberg-Salam Theories [Physics]
GWS	Glenwood Springs, CO [Location identifier FAA] (FAAL)
GWS	Grand Worthy Scribe [Templars] [Freemasonry] (ROG)
GWS	Great Western Society (EA)
GWS	Great West Steel Industries Ltd. [Toronto Stock Exchange symbol Vancouver Stock Exchange symbol]
GWS	Great White Spot [Planetary science]
GWS	Guided Weapon Station (IAA)
GWS	Gulf War Syndrome [Medicine]
GWS	Gun Weapon System [Military] (CAAL)
GWS	Gwil Industries, Inc. [Toronto Stock Exchange symbol Vancouver Stock Exchange symbol]
GWS 1929	Geneva Convention for the Amelioration of the Condition of the Wounded and Sick in Armed Forces in the Field, 27 July 1929 [Army]
GWS-A & L	Girl Watchers Society - Ankle and Leg Division
GWSAE	Greater Washington Society of Association Executives (SRA)
GWSC	Ghana Water and Sewerage Corp.
GWSC	Greater World Spiritual Centre [British] (EAIO)
GWSF	Georgia Warm Springs Foundation [Later, RWSF] (EA)
Gw Sh	Gwynne on Sheriffs [A publication] (DLA)
GWSIP	Gun Weapon System Improvement Program [Military] (CAAL)
GWSR	General Wage Stabilization Regulations [United States] (DLA)
GWSRP	Gun Weapon System Replacement Program (NVT)
GWSS	Groundwater Supply Survey (GNE)
GWS Sea	Geneva Convention for the Amelioration of the Condition of the Wounded, Sick, and Shipwrecked Members of the Armed Forces at Sea, 12 August 1949 [Army] (AABC)
GWSTN	Ground Wireless Station (IAA)
GWSTV	Golden West Subscription Television [Cable TV programming service]
GWT	Chicopee Falls, MA [Location identifier FAA] (FAAL)
GWt	Gigawatt Thermal
GWT	Glazed Wall Tile [Technical drawings]
GWT	Grand Worthy Templar [Templars] [Freemasonry] (ROG)
GWT	Gross Weight
GWT	Ground Winds Tower [NASA] (NASA)
GWT	Gunshot Wound of the Throat [Emergency medicine] (DAVI)

GWT	Westerland [Germany Airport symbol] (OAG)
GWTA	Gift Wrappings and Tyings Association [Defunct] (EA)
GWTB	Glazed Wall Tile Base [Technical drawings]
GWTI	Groundwater Technology, Inc. [NASDAQ symbol] (NQ)
GW TREAS	Grand Worthy Treasurer [Templars] [Freemasonry] (ROG)
GWTUF	Government Workers' Trade Union Federation [Ceylon]
GWTW	Gone with the Wind [A novel by Margaret Mitchell; also, a motion picture]
GWU	George Washington University [Washington, DC]
GWU	Granite Workers' Union [British]
GWU	International Glove Workers' Union of America [Later, ACTWU]
GWV	Glendale, WV [Location identifier FAA] (FAAL)
GWVA	Great War Veterans' Association [Canada]
GWVSS	Ground Wind Vortex Sensing System [Aviation] (DA)
GWVT	Grand Worthy Vice Templar [Templars] [Freemasonry] (ROG)
GWW	Goldsboro, NC [Location identifier FAA] (FAAL)
GWW	Grainger, [W. W.] Inc. [NYSE symbol] (SPSG)
GWW	Grainger (W.W.) [NYSE symbol] (TTSB)
GWW	Ground Water for Windows [Computer program]
GWW	Guaranteed Weekly Wage
GWWS	Gott Wirds Wohl Schaffen [God Will Arrange] [Motto of Dorothee Auguste, Duchess of Braunschweig (1577-1625)] [German]
GWY	Galway [Ireland] [Airport symbol]
GWY	Goldways Resources [Vancouver Stock Exchange symbol]
GWY	Gwynedd-Mercy College, Gwynedd, PA [OCLC symbol] (OCLC)
GWYN	Gwynedd [County in Wales] (WGA)
GX	Gencor Indus [AMEX symbol] (TTSB)
GX	Gencor Industries [AMEX symbol] (SAG)
GX	Glycinxylidide [Biochemistry]
Gx	Graded Exercise
GX	Great Lakes Airlines [ICAO designator] (AD)
GXA	CountryBaskets [NYSE symbol] (SAG)
GXA	Countrybkts Australia Index Fd [NYSE symbol] (TTSB)
GXA	Gunn-Diode X-Band Amplifier
GXD	General X-Ray Diagnosis [Medicine]
GXD	Graded [Medicine] (DAVI)
GXD EKG	Graded Exercixe Electrocardiogram [Cardiology] (DAVI)
GXF	CountryBaskets [NYSE symbol] (SAG)
GXF	Countrybkts France Index Fd [NYSE symbol] (TTSB)
GXG	CountryBaskets [NYSE symbol] (SAG)
GXG	Countrybkts Germany Index Fd [NYSE symbol] (TTSB)
GXG	Negage [Angola] [Airport symbol] (OAG)
GXH	CountryBaskets [NYSE symbol] (SAG)
GXH	Countrybkts Hong Kong Index Fd [NYSE symbol] (TTSB)
GXI	CountryBaskets [NYSE symbol] (SAG)
GXI	Countrybkts Italy Index Fd [NYSE symbol] (TTSB)
GXI	Glenex Industries, Inc. [Vancouver Stock Exchange symbol]
GXI	Global Exchange, Inc.
GXJ	CountryBaskets [NYSE symbol] (SAG)
GXJ	Countrybkts Japan Index Fd [NYSE symbol] (TTSB)
GXK	CountryBaskets [NYSE symbol] (SAG)
GXK	Countrybkts UK Index Fd [NYSE symbol] (TTSB)
GXL	General-Purpose Crosslinked Polyethylene [Insulation]
GXL	Granges, Inc. [AMEX symbol Toronto Stock Exchange symbol] (SPSG)
GXL	Grinnell, IA [Location identifier FAA] (FAAL)
GXM	Gordex Minerals Ltd. [Toronto Stock Exchange symbol]
GXM	Medical College of Georgia, Augusta, GA [OCLC symbol] (OCLC)
G/XMTR	Guidance Transmitter (AAG)
GXO	Butler, PA [Location identifier FAA] (FAAL)
GXQ	Coyhaique [Chile] [Airport symbol]
GXQ	Coyhaique [Chile] [Airport symbol] (AD)
GXR	CountryBaskets [NYSE symbol] (SAG)
GXR	Countrybkts S.Africa Index Fd [NYSE symbol] (TTSB)
GXS	Goldex Resources [Vancouver Stock Exchange symbol]
GXSP	Guierrezia Xylem Sap Potential [Botany]
GXT	Graded Exercise Testing
GXU	CountryBaskets [NYSE symbol] (SAG)
GXU	Countrybkts US Index Fd [NYSE symbol] (TTSB)
GXU	Wrightstown, NJ [Location identifier FAA] (FAAL)
GXV	Golden Exodus [Vancouver Stock Exchange symbol]
GXY	Galaxy Airways Ltd. [Nigeria] [ICAO designator] (FAAC)
GXY	Galaxy Industry Ltd. [Vancouver Stock Exchange symbol]
GXY	Greeley, CO [Location identifier FAA] (FAAL)
GY	Gaily (ABBR)
GY	Galley
GY	Galley-Yarn [Crooked] [Slang British] (DSUE)
GY	Gardan [France ICAO aircraft manufacturer identifier] (ICAO)
GY	GenCorp [NYSE symbol] (TTSB)
GY	GenCorp, Inc. [NYSE symbol] (SPSG)
GY	Germany
Gy	Gray [Symbol] [SI unit for absorbed dose acceleration]
GY	Gray
GY	Greenish Yellow
GY	Grey [Unit of inpingent energy]
GY	Guaranty Trust Co. of Canada [Toronto Stock Exchange symbol]
GY	Guidance Year [DoD]
GY	Gunnery (ABBR)
GY	Gunnery
gy	Guyana [MARC country of publication code Library of Congress] (LCCP)
GY	Guyana [ANSI two-letter standard code] (CNC)
GY	Guyana Airways [ICAO designator] (AD)
GY	Gyro (ABBR)
GY	Gyrocar (ABBR)

GY.............. Gyrocompass (ABBR)
GY.............. Gyrodyne (ABBR)
GY.............. Gyroscope
Gy.............. Gyrus [Brain anatomy]
GYA .... Got Ya Again [Initialism used as name of second successful phony event staged by Washington, DC, law enforcement agents posing as fences] [See PFF Inc]
GYA .... Guayaramerin [Bolivia] [Airport symbol] (OAG)
GYA .... Guyana Airways Corp. [ICAO designator] (FAAC)
GyAR .... Rhein-Westfalische Technische Hochschule, Aachen, Germany [Library symbol Library of Congress] (LCLS)
GyAR .... Rhein-Westfalische Technische Hochschule, Aachen, Germany [Library symbol] [Library of Congress] (LCLS)
GyAsH .... Hofbibliothek, Aschaffenburg, Germany [Library symbol] [Library of Congress] (LCLS)
GyAsH .... Hofbibliothek, Aschaffenburg, Germany [Library symbol Library of Congress] (LCLS)
GYB .... Giddings, TX [Location identifier FAA] (FAAL)
GyBaA .... Archiv des Kreises Asch, Fernleihe, Bayern, Federal Republic of Germany [Library symbol Library of Congress] (LCLS)
GyBFU .... Freie Universitaet (Berlin), Garystrasse, Berlin, Germany [Library symbol Library of Congress] (LCLS)
GyBFU-P ...... Freie Universitaet (Berlin), Fachbereich Politische Wissenschaft, Bibliothek, Berlin, Germany [Library symbol Library of Congress] (LCLS)
GyBIAI .... Ibero-Amerikanisches Institu Preussicher Kulturbesitz, Berlin, Germany [Library symbol] [Library of Congress] (LCLS)
GyBiU .... Universitat Bielfeld, Kurt Schumacher, Bielfeld, Germany [Library symbol Library of Congress] (LCLS)
GyBochU ...... Ruhr-Universitat Bochum, Bochum, Germany [Library symbol Library of Congress] (LCLS)
GyBoDB .... Deutscher Bundestag, Abteilung Wissenschaftliche Dokumentation, Bonn, Germany [Library symbol Library of Congress] (LCLS)
GyBoFE .... Friedrich-Ebert-Stiftung, Archiv der Sozialen Demokratie, Bonn, Germany [Library symbol Library of Congress] (LCLS)
GyBoFN .... Friedrich-Naumann-Stiftung, Bonn, Germany [Library symbol Library of Congress] (LCLS)
GyBoGI .... Gesamtdeutsches Institut, Bonn, Germany [Library symbol Library of Congress] (LCLS)
GyBraTU ...... Technische Universitat Carolo Wilhelmina zu Braunschweig, Braunschweig, Federal Republic of Germany [Library symbol Library of Congress] (LCLS)
GyBrSU .... Staatsbibliothek und Universitatsbibliothek, Breitenweg, Bremen, Germany [Library symbol Library of Congress] (LCLS)
GyBrU .... Universitaet Bremen, Bremen, Germany [Library symbol Library of Congress] (LCLS)
GyBTU .... Technische Universitat Berlin, Berlin, Germany [Library symbol Library of Congress] (LCLS)
GYC .... Glasgow Yeomanry Cavalry [British military] (DMA)
GYC .... Global Energy Ltd. [Vancouver Stock Exchange symbol]
GYC .... Greater Yellowstone Coalition (EA)
GYC .... Young Harris College, Young Harris, GA [Library symbol Library of Congress] (LCLS)
GyDaD .... Deutsches Kunstoff-Institut, Darmstadt, Germany [Library symbol Library of Congress] (LCLS)
GyDaH .... Hessische Landes- und Hochschulbibliothek, Darmstadt (Schloss), Germany [Library symbol Library of Congress] (LCLS)
GyDaM .... E. Merck AG, Darmstadt, Germany [Library symbol Library of Congress] (LCLS)
GyDIZ .... Institut fur Zeitungsforschung, Dortmund, Germany [Library symbol Library of Congress] (LCLS)
GyDMA .... Mikrofilmarchiv der Deutschsparchigen Presse e.V., Dortmund, Germany [Library symbol Library of Congress] (LCLS)
GyDuiH .... Gesamthochschulbibliothek Duisburg, Duisburg, Germany [Library symbol Library of Congress] (LCLS)
GyDuU .... Universitat Dusseldorf, Grabbeplatz, Dusseldorf, Germany [Library symbol Library of Congress] (LCLS)
GYE............. Glory Explorations [Vancouver Stock Exchange symbol]
GYE............. Guayaquil [Ecuador] [Airport symbol] (OAG)
GyEU........... Friedrich-Alexander-Universitat zu Erlangen-Nurnberg, Erlangen, Germany [Library symbol Library of Congress] (LCLS)
GyFM.......... General Yielding Fracture Mechanics (OA)
GyFmB........ Beilstein-Institut, Frankfurt/Main, Germany [Library symbol Library of Congress] (LCLS)
GyFmDB ..... Deutsche Bibliothek, Zeppelinallee, Frankfurt am Main, Germany [Library symbol Library of Congress] (LCLS)
GyFmSU ...... Stadt u Universitatsbibliothek, Senckenbergische Bibliothek Fernleihe, Frankfurt/Main, Federal Republic of Germany [Library symbol Library of Congress] (LCLS)
GYG .... Grayling, MI [Location identifier FAA] (FAAL)
GYG .... Valdosta State College, Valdosta, GA [OCLC symbol] (OCLC)
GyGiU .... Justus Liebig Universitatsbibliothek Giessen, Giessen/Lahn, Federal Republic of Germany [Library symbol Library of Congress] (LCLS)
GyGoN .... Niedersachsische Staats- und Universitatsbibliothek, Gottingen, Germany [Library symbol Library of Congress] (LCLS)
GYH .... Greenville, SC [Location identifier FAA] (FAAL)
GyHanM....... Medizinische Hochschule, Karl Wiechert, Hannover-Kleefeld, Germany [Library symbol Library of Congress] (LCLS)
GyHaS .... Staats- und Universitatsbibliothek Hamburg, Hamburg, Germany [Library symbol Library of Congress] (LCLS)
GyHeM........ Max-Planck-Institut fuer Medizinisch Forschung, Heidelberg, Germany [Library symbol Library of Congress] (LCLS)

GyHeU-SS.... Universitat Heidelberg Sinologisches Seminar de Universitat Heidelberg, Heidelberg, Germany [Library symbol] [Library of Congress] (LCLS)
GyHGU........ University of Gottingen, Hannover, Germany [Library symbol Library of Congress] (LCLS)
GyHoU .... Universitat Hohenheim (Landwirtschaftliche Hochschule), Stuttgart-Hohenheim, Germany [Library symbol Library of Congress] (LCLS)
GyHTIB .... Universitaetsbibliothek der Technischen Universitaet Hannover und Technische Informationsbibliothek, Hannover, Federal Republic of Germany [Library symbol Library of Congress] (LCLS)
GYIL .... German Yearbook of International Law [A publication] (DLA)
GyJuK .... Kernforschungsanlage Julich, Julich, Germany [Library symbol Library of Congress] (LCLS)
GyKaU .... Universitat Trier-Kaiserslautern, Kaiserslautern, Germany [Library symbol Library of Congress] (LCLS)
GyKG .... Gesellschaft fuer Kernforschung mbH, Karlsruhe, Germany [Library symbol Library of Congress] (LCLS)
GyKiU .... Christian-Albrechts-Universitat Kiel, Kiel, Germany [Library symbol Library of Congress] (LCLS)
GyKoB .... Bundesanzeiger Verlagsgesellschaft, mbH, Koln, Germany [Library symbol] [Library of Congress] (LCLS)
GYM .... General Yardmaster [Railroading]
GYM .... Guaymas [Mexico] [Seismograph station code, US Geological Survey] (SEIS)
GYM .... Guaymas [Mexico] [Airport symbol] (OAG)
GYM .... Guaymas, Mexico [Remote site] [NASA] (NASA)
GYM .... Gymnasium
gym .... Gymnasium (VRA)
GYM .... Gymnastic
GYM .... Gymnastics (ADA)
GYM .... Sport Supply Group [AMEX symbol] (SAG)
GYM.. .... Sport Supply Group [NYSE symbol] (SPSG)
GyMB .... Boehringer Mannheim GmbH, Mannheim, Germany [Library symbol Library of Congress] (LCLS)
GYMB .... [The] Gymboree Corp. [NASDAQ symbol] (SAG)
Gymbree ...... [The] Gymboree Corp. [Associated Press] (SAG)
GyMIZ.......... Institut fur Zeitgeschichte [Institute of Modern History], Munchen, Federal Republic of Germany [Library symbol Library of Congress] (LCLS)
GyMLM........ Ludwig Maxmilians Universitatsbibliothek Munchen, Munich, Federal Republic of Germany [Library symbol Library of Congress] (LCLS)
GYMM .... HealthTech Intl [NASDAQ symbol] (TTSB)
GYMMW ...... HealthTech Intl Wrrt'A' [NASDAQ symbol] (TTSB)
GYMN .... Gymnasium (ABBR)
GYMNST...... Gymnast (ABBR)
GYMST .... Gymnast (ABBR)
GYMSTC ..... Gymnastic (ABBR)
GYMSTCY .... Gymnastically (ABBR)
GYMSTIC ..... Gymnastic [Freight]
GyMuW .... Westfalische Wilhelms-Universitat Munster, Munster, Germany [Library symbol Library of Congress] (LCLS)
GYM.WS ..... Sport Supply Grp Wrrt [AMEX symbol] (TTSB)
GYN .... Goiania [Brazil] [Airport symbol] (OAG)
GYN .... Gynecologist
GYN .... Gynecology
GYNAE........ Gynaecology [British]
GYNAEC...... Gynaecologist [or Gynaecology] [British] (ADA)
GYNAECOL... Gynaecology [British]
GYNC .... Gynecologic (ABBR)
GYNCL .... Gynecological (ABBR)
GYNCLGY .... Gynecology
GYNCLGY .... Gynecology
GYNE .... Gynecare [NASDAQ symbol] (SAG)
GYNE .... Gynecare Inc. [NASDAQ symbol] (TTSB)
gyne............ Gynecology [Medicine] (DAVI)
GyNeA .... Augustana Hochschule Bibliothek, Neuendettelsau, Federal Republic of Germany [Library symbol Library of Congress] (LCLS)
Gynecol ...... Gynecology
Gynecre ...... Gynecare, Inc. [Associated Press] (SAG)
GYNST........ Gynecologist (ABBR)
GyNU .... Friedrich-Alexander-Universitat zu Erlangen-Nurnberg, Abteilung fur Wirtschafts-und Socialwissenschaften, Nurnberg, Germany [Library symbol Library of Congress] (LCLS)
GYP .... CGC, Inc. [Toronto Stock Exchange symbol]
GYP .... Eagle Aviation [British] [FAA designator] (FAAC)
GYP .... Guild of Young Printers (DGA)
GYP .... Gympie [Australia Airport symbol]
GYP .... Gypsum (KSC)
GYP .... Gypsy (ABBR)
GYP .... Gyro Yaw Position
GYPD .... Gypped (ABBR)
GYPG .... Gypping (ABBR)
GYPS .... Gypsum
GYPSIOL ..... Gypsiologic (ABBR)
GYPSY .... General Image Processing System
GYR .... Gigayear [A billion years]
GYR .... Goodyear, AZ [Location identifier FAA] (FAAL)
GYR .... Gyrafrance [France ICAO designator] (FAAC)
GYR .... Gyration (ABBR)
GYR .... Gyrus (ABBR)
GYRA .... Gyrate (ABBR)
GYRAD........ Gyrated (ABBR)
GYRAG........ Gyrating (ABBR)

GYRAN........ Gyration (ABBR)
GYRAR........ Gyrator (ABBR)
GYRARY ...... Gyratory (ABBR)
GYRCMPS.... Gyrocompass (ABBR)
GYRMTR...... Gyrometer (ABBR)
GYRO.......... Gyrocompass (ABBR)
GYRO.......... Gyrodyne [*NASDAQ symbol*] (SAG)
GYRO.......... Gyrodyne Co. Amer [*NASDAQ symbol*] (TTSB)
GYRO.......... Gyroplane (ABBR)
GYRO.......... Gyroscope (AAG)
GYROCOMP... Gyroscope Compassing
GYROCOP ... Gyrocopter (ABBR)
GYrody........ Gyrodyne Company of America, Inc. [*Associated Press*] (SAG)
GYRODYN... Gyrodynamic (ABBR)
GYRPLN...... Gyroplane (ABBR)
GYRSCP....... Gyroscope (ABBR)
GYRSTBR .... Gyrostabilizer (ABBR)
GYRTD........ Gyrated (ABBR)
GyRU .... Universitat Regensburg, Regensburg, Germany [*Library symbol Library of Congress*] (LCLS)
GySalS......... Stadtbucherei Salzgitter, Joachim Campe, Salzgitter, Germany [*Library symbol Library of Congress*] (LCLS)
GySaU .... Universitat des Saarlandes, Saarbrucken, Germany [*Library symbol Library of Congress*] (LCLS)
GYSCO........ Great Yarmouth Shipping Co. (MHDW)
GYSGT........ Gunnery Sergeant
GySIA.......... Institut fuer Auslandsbeziehungen, Stuttgart, Germany [*Library symbol Library of Congress*] (LCLS)
GYSR.......... Geyser (ABBR)
GySU .... Universitat Stuttgart, Stuttgart, Germany [*Library symbol Library of Congress*] (LCLS)
GySW.......... Wuerttembergische Landesbibliothek, Konrad Adenauer, Stuttgart, Germany [*Library symbol Library of Congress*] (LCLS)
GyTrU .... Universitat Trier-Kaiserslautern, Schneidershof, Trier, Germany [*Library symbol Library of Congress*] (LCLS)
GYW .... International Finance Corp. [*AMEX symbol*] (SAG)
GyWitS........ Stadtbucherei Witten, Witten, Germany [*Library symbol Library of Congress*] (LCLS)
GyWK........ Kalle Aktiengesellschaft, Litteraturabteilung, Wiesbaden-Biebrich, Germany [*Library symbol Library of Congress*] (LCLS)
GyWoS........ Niedersachsische Staatsarchiv, Wolfenbuttel, Germany [*Library symbol Library of Congress*] (LCLS)
GYY .... Gary, IN [*Location identifier FAA*] (FAAL)
GZ................ Air Rarotonga [*ICAO designator*] (AD)
GZ................ Ganzfeld [*Whole Field*] [*ESP test*] [*German*]
gz................ Gaza Strip [*MARC country of publication code Library of Congress*] (LCCP)
GZ................ Gigahertz [*1,000 megahertz*] [*Preferred form is GHz*] (MCD)
Gz................ Graetz Number [*Physics*]
GZ................ Ground Zero [*Atomic detonation*]
GZ................ Ground Zero [*An association*] (EA)
GZ................ Guilford-Zimmerman Personality Test [*Psychology*] (MAE)
Gz................ Guizzardinus [*Deceased, 1222*] [*Authority cited in pre-1607 legal work*] (DSA)
GZA.............. Alverno College, Milwaukee, WI [*OCLC symbol*] (OCLC)
GZA.............. GZA GeoEnvironmental Technologies, Inc. [*Associated Press*] (SAG)
GZAS .... Guilford-Zimmerman Aptitude Survey [*Test*]
GZAS:GR...... Guilford-Zimmerman Aptitude Survey: General Reasoning [*Test*]
GZAS:NO...... Guilford-Zimmerman Aptitude Survey: Numerical Operations [*Test*]
GZAS:PS...... Guilford-Zimmerman Aptitude Survey: Perceptual Speed [*Test*]
GZAS:SO...... Guilford-Zimmerman Aptitude Survey: Spatial Orientation [*Test*]
GZAS:SV...... Guilford-Zimmerman Aptitude Survey: Spatial Visualization [*Test*]
GZAS:VC...... Guilford-Zimmerman Aptitude Survey: Verbal Comprehension [*Test*]
GZB.............. Carroll College, Waukesha, WI [*OCLC symbol*] (OCLC)
GZC.............. Carthage College, Kenosha, WI [*OCLC symbol*] (OCLC)
GZD .... Glazed (DGA)
GZD .... Milwaukee Public Library, Milwaukee, WI [*OCLC symbol*] (OCLC)
GZE.............. University of Wisconsin-Eau Claire, Eau Claire, WI [*OCLC symbol*] (OCLC)

GZEA........... GZA GeoEnvironmental Tech [*NASDAQ symbol*] (TTSB)
GZEA........... GZA GeoEnvironmental Technologies [*NASDAQ symbol*] (SAG)
GZEA........... GZA GeoEnvironmental Technologies, Inc. (NQ)
GZF.............. Eau Claire Public Library, Eau Claire, WI [*OCLC symbol*] (OCLC)
GZG .... Blackford, VA [*Location identifier FAA*] (FAAL)
GZG .... Brown County Library, Green Bay, WI [*OCLC symbol*] (OCLC)
GZG .... Gonzales Gold Mines Ltd. [*Vancouver Stock Exchange symbol*]
GZH .... University of Wisconsin-Madison, Health Sciences, Madison, WI [*OCLC symbol*] (OCLC)
GZI............... University of Wisconsin-Madison, Instructional Materials Center, Madison, WI [*OCLC symbol*] (OCLC)
GZII.............. Guilford-Zimmerman Interest Inventory [*Vocational guidance test*]
GZJ.............. University of Wisconsin-Milwaukee, School of Library Science, Milwaukee, WI [*OCLC symbol*] (OCLC)
GZK .... Oshkosh Public Library, Oshkosh, WI [*OCLC symbol*] (OCLC)
GZL.............. Gazelle Resources Ltd. [*Vancouver Stock Exchange symbol*]
GZL.............. Guzzle (ABBR)
GZL.............. University of Wisconsin-Madison, Law Library, Madison, WI [*OCLC symbol*] (OCLC)
GZLD .... Guzzled (ABBR)
GZLG .... Guzzling (ABBR)
GZLR .... Guzzler (ABBR)
GZM .... Gaz Metropolitain, Inc. [*Toronto Stock Exchange symbol*]
GZM .... University of Wisconsin-Madison, Madison, WI [*OCLC symbol*] (OCLC)
GZMG .... Gradient Zone Melting (IAA)
GZN .... Ground Zero [*Nevada*] [*Seismograph station code, US Geological Survey Closed*] (SEIS)
GZN .... University of Wisconsin-Milwaukee, Milwaukee, WI [*OCLC symbol*] (OCLC)
GZO .... Gizo [*Solomon Islands*] [*Airport symbol*] (OAG)
GZO .... University of Wisconsin-Oshkosh, Oshkosh, WI [*OCLC symbol*] (OCLC)
GZOB .... Glowna Zydowska Organizacja Bojowa [*A publication*] (BJA)
GZON .... Graphix Zone [*NASDAQ symbol*] (TTSB)
GZON .... Graphix Zone, Inc. [*NASDAQ symbol*] (SAG)
GZP............. University of Wisconsin-Parkside, Kenosha, WI [*OCLC symbol*] (OCLC)
GZPP .... Ground Zero Pairing Project (EA)
GZQ .... Marquette University, Milwaukee, WI [*OCLC symbol*] (OCLC)
GZR .... Golden Zone Resources [*Vancouver Stock Exchange symbol*]
GZR .... Wisconsin Department of Public Instruction, Reference and Loan Library, Madison,WI [*OCLC symbol*] (OCLC)
GZRC .... Ground Zero Resource Center [*Defunct*] (EA)
GZS.............. Gesellschaft fuer Zahlungssysteme [*International banking*] [*Germany*]
GZS.............. Gozaisho [*Japan*] [*Seismograph station code, US Geological Survey Closed*] (SEIS)
GZS.............. Pulaski, TN [*Location identifier FAA*] (FAAL)
GZS.............. University of Wisconsin-Stout, Menomonie, WI [*OCLC symbol*] (OCLC)
GZT............. Gaziantep [*Turkey*] [*Airport symbol*] (OAG)
GZT............. Greenwich Zone Time
GZT............. University of Wisconsin-Whitewater, Whitewater, WI [*OCLC symbol*] (OCLC)
GZTC........... Genzyme Transgenics [*NASDAQ symbol*] (TTSB)
GZTC........... Genzyme Transgenics Corp. [*NASDAQ symbol*] (SAG)
GZTPRD....... Ground Zero Tape Read (IAA)
GZTS........... Guilford-Zimmerman Temperament Survey [*Psychology*]
GZU .... University of Wisconsin-La Crosse, La Crosse, WI [*OCLC symbol*] (OCLC)
GZV............. University of Wisconsin-Platteville, Platteville, WI [*OCLC symbol*] (OCLC)
GZW............ University of Wisconsin-Green Bay, Green Bay, WI [*OCLC symbol*] (OCLC)
GZX............. La Crosse Public Library, La Crosse, WI [*OCLC symbol*] (OCLC)
GZX............. Peoria, IL [*Location identifier FAA*] (FAAL)
GZY............. Wisconsin Interlibrary Loan Service, Madison, WI [*OCLC symbol*] (OCLC)

H

By Acronym

H................	Air Force Training Category
H................	Altitude
H................	Altitude Rate [Symbol] (NASA)
H................	Atmospheric Head (AAG)
H................	Boltzmann Function [Physics] (BARN)
H................	Bracco Industria Chimica [Italy] [Research code symbol]
h................	Coefficient of Heat Transfer [Symbol] [Thermodynamics]
H................	Declared or Paid after Stock Dividend or Split-Up [Investment term] (DFIT)
h................	Dihydro [As substituent on nucleoside] [Biochemistry]
H................	Enthalpy [Symbol] [IUPAC] (DEN)
H................	Exposure [Symbol] [IUPAC]
h-----..........	French Union [MARC geographic area code Library of Congress] (LCCP)
h................	Hacia [Around] [Spanish]
H................	Haemaphysalis [A genus of tick] [Entomology] (DAVI)
H................	Haftarah (BJA)
H................	Hagelkorn [Hailstone] [Bomb] [German military - World War II]
H................	Haggai [Freemasonry]
H................	Hail [Meteorology]
H................	Haler [Monetary unit] [Former Czechoslovakia]
H................	Half
H................	Half-Word Designator [Computer science]
H................	Hall
H................	HALON [Halogenated Hydrocarbon] (NFPA)
H................	Halothane [Also, HAL] [An anesthetic]
H................	Halt [Computer science] (MDG)
H................	Hamiltonian Function [Mathematics]
H................	Hamlet
H................	Hamlyn Publishing [British]
H................	Hand [Music]
H................	Handbook (SAA)
H................	Handily [Horse racing]
h................	Hand-Rearing [of experimental animals] (DMAA)
H................	Handy's Ohio Reports [12 Ohio Decisions] [A publication] (DLA)
H................	Harbor [Maps and charts]
H................	Harcourt General [NYSE symbol] (TTSB)
H................	Harcourt General, Inc. [Formerly, General Cinema Corp.] [NYSE symbol] (SPSG)
H................	Hard [or Hardness] [Pencil leads]
H................	Hardness [Of precious stones]
H................	Hardware [Computer science] (MDG)
H................	Hardy [Horticulture]
H................	Hare's English Chancery Reports [A publication] (DLA)
H................	Harmonic (IDOE)
H................	Harmonic Mean [Psychology]
h................	Harmonized [Apparent inconsistency explained and shown not to exist] [Used in Shepard's Citations] [Legal term] (DLA)
H................	Harrier (ROG)
H................	Harry [Phonetic alphabet] [Royal Navy World War I Pre-World War II] (DSUE)
H................	Has
H................	Hassle [Sweden] [Research code symbol]
H................	Hatch [Technical drawings]
H................	Hauch [Antigen] [Immunology]
H................	Haustus [A Drink] [Pharmacy]
H................	Have (ROG)
H................	Haven (ADA)
H................	Hawaii Reports [A publication] (DLA)
(H)................	Hazardous [Task classification] [NASA] (NASA)
H................	Hazardous Cargo [Shipping]
H................	Haze [Weather reports]
H................	Hazor (BJA)
H................	Hazy (ABBR)
H................	H-Beam [Architecture]
H................	Head [Anatomy] (DAVI)
H................	Head [Linguistics]
H................	Head [Horse racing]
H................	Header (NFPA)
H................	Head, Hand, and Chest Sets [JETDS nomenclature] [Military] (CET)
H................	Headlines (ABBR)
H................	Headquarters (ABBR)
H................	Healthy
H................	Hearing Power (ROG)
H................	Heart [Freemasonry] (ROG)
H................	Hearts (ADA)

H................	Heart Trouble [Classification system used by doctors on Ellis Island to detain, re-examine, and possibly deny entry to certain immigrants]
H................	Heartwood [Forestry]
H................	Heat [or Heater]
H................	Heater (ABBR)
H................	Heaton Mint [British]
H................	Heavy (AAG)
H................	Heavy [Chain] [Biochemistry, immunochemistry]
H................	Heavy Lift Cargo Airlines Ltd. [British]
H................	Heavy Sea [Navigation]
H................	Hebrew (BJA)
h................	Hecto [A prefix meaning multiplied by 10^2] [SI symbol]
H................	Heel [Music]
H................	Heelstick [Medicine] (DAVI)
H................	Heft [Part] [German]
h................	Height [Symbol] [IUPAC]
H................	Height
H................	Heir
H................	Helicopter [When the second letter or only letter] [Designation for all US military aircraft]
H................	Helicopteros do Brasil SA [Brazil ICAO aircraft manufacturer identifier] (ICAO)
H................	Helium [Chemical symbol is He] (AAG)
H................	Helix
H................	Hemagglutinating [Virology]
H................	Hematite [A mineral]
H................	Hemic Subgroup [Magnetite, chromite, hematite] [CIPW classification Geology]
H................	Hemin [Hematology]
H................	Hemisphere [Anatomy] (DAVI)
H................	Hemophilus [Microbiology] (MAE)
H................	Hence
H................	Henry [Symbol] [SI unit of inductance]
H................	Henry (King of England) (DLA)
H................	Henry's Law Constant
H................	Heparin [Pharmacology] (DAVI)
h................	Heplode [Electronics] (OA)
H................	Herb [Botany]
H................	Herbivore
H................	Heres [Heir] [Legal term Latin]
H................	Hermit
H................	Hernia [Gastroenterology] (DAVI)
H................	Heroin [Slang]
H................	Hertzog's High Court Reports [South Africa] [A publication] (DLA)
H................	Heterophyes [A genus of trematode worms] [Gastroenterology] (DAVI)
H................	Heterozygosity [Cytology]
H................	Hettangian [Geology]
H................	Hexadecimal (BUR)
H................	Hexapole (OA)
H................	Hexode [Electronics] (OA)
H................	Hic [Here] [Latin]
H................	Hieroglyphics [Freemasonry] (ROG)
H................	High
H................	High [Engineering]
H................	Highest [Price Quoted of a Stock] [Finance] (BARN)
H................	High Season [Airline fare code]
H................	High-Viscosity Fuel
H................	Hilary Term [England] [Legal term] (DLA)
H................	Hilkoth (BJA)
H................	Hill (ROG)
H................	Hill's New York Reports [A publication] (DLA)
H................	Hindu (ABBR)
H................	Hinged [Philately]
H................	Hippelates [A genus of insects] [Entomology] (DAVI)
H................	Hispanic
H................	Histamine [Anesthesiology]
H................	Histidine [One-letter symbol]
H................	Histoplasma [Biochemistry] (DAVI)
H................	Historiae [of Sallust] [Classical studies] (OCD)
H................	Historical Re-Issue [Record cataloging]
H................	History [Secondary school course] [British]
H................	Hits [Baseball]
H................	Hoffmann [Reflex] [Neurology]
H................	Holding [Electronics]

H	Holiness (BJA)
H	Holland [*IYRU nationality code*] (IYR)
H	Holy
H	Holzknecht [*Unit*]
H	Home
H	Homobonus de Cremona [*Deceased, 1272*] [*Authority cited in pre-1607 legal work*] (DSA)
H	Homosexual
H	Honor
H	Honorary [*Academic degree*]
H	Hooker
H	Hope [*Freemasonry*] (ROG)
H	Hopper-Tainer [*A form of container*] [*British*] (DCTA)
h	Hora [*Hour*] [*Latin*]
H	Horizon (ABBR)
H	Horizontal
h	Horizontal (WDMC)
H	Horizontal Force of the Earth's Magnetism [*Amplitude of a tide*]
H	Hormone [*Endocrinology*]
H	Horn
H	Horrific [*Film certificate*] [*British*]
H	Horse [*Thoroughbred racing*]
H	Hose (NFPA)
H	Hospital (DAVI)
H	Hospital [*Traffic sign*] [*British*]
H	Hospital Plane [*When suffixed to Navy plane designation*]
H	Host [*Freemasonry*] (ROG)
H	Hostiensis [*Deceased, 1271*] [*Authority cited in pre-1607 legal work*] (DSA)
H	Hostile [*Military*]
H	Hot
H	Hotel
H	Hounsfield Unit [*Medicine*] (MAE)
H	Hour [*Also, h*]
h	Hour (WDMC)
H	House
H	House Bill [*Legal term*] (DLA)
H	House of Representatives
H	How [*Phonetic alphabet*] [*World War II*] (DSUE)
H	Howard's United States Supreme Court Reports [*42-65 United States*] [*A publication*] (DLA)
H	Hoy [*Ship's rigging*] (ROG)
H	Hoyre [*Conservative Party*] [*Norway Political party*] (PPE)
h	HTML [*Hypertext Markup Language*] [*Computer science*] [*Telecommunications*]
H	Hugolinus de Presbyteris [*Flourished, 1197-1238*] [*Authority cited in pre-1607 legal work*] (DSA)
H	Huguccio [*Deceased, 1210*] [*Authority cited in pre-1607 legal work*] (DSA)
H	Hull (ADA)
H	Human
h	Human (DMAA)
H	Human Being [*Rorschach*] [*Psychology*]
H	[*The*] Humanitarian [*A publication*] (ROG)
H	Humidity
H	Hundred
h	Hundred (WDMC)
H	Hungary
H	Hun-Stoffe [*Mustard gas*] [*Formerly, HS Also, HD, HT, M*]
H	Husband
H	Hussars [*Military unit*] [*British*]
H	Hydrant
H	Hydraulics (ADA)
H	Hydrodynamic Head
H	Hydrogen [*Chemical element*]
H	Hydrogen [*Chemical*] (EERA)
H	Hydrographic Survey [*Navy British*]
H	Hydrolysis
H	Hydroxydaunomycin [*See also ADR, Adriamycin*] [*Antineoplastic drug*]
H	Hygiene [*Preventive and Industrial Medicine*] [*Medical Officer designation*] [*British*]
H	Hymenolepis [*A genus of tapeworm*] [*Gastroenterology*] (DAVI)
H	Hyoscine [*Organic chemistry*]
H	Hypermetropia [*Ophthalmology*]
H	Hyperopia [*Ophthalmology*] (ROG)
H	Hyperphoria [*Ophthalmology*] (DAVI)
H	Hyperplasia [*Medicine*]
H	Hypodermic
h	Hypodermic (DMAA)
H	Hypothesis
H	Instructor [*Army skill qualification identifier*] (INF)
H	Magnetizing Force [*Symbol*] (DEN)
H	Momentum [*Measurement*]
H	Mustard Gas [*Also, HD, HS, HT, M*] [*Poison Gas US Chemical Corps symbol*]
H	Nondirectional Radio Homing Beacon [*Navigation charts*]
H	Oersted [*Unit of magnetizing force*] [*Physics*] (DMAA)
h	Planck Constant [*Symbol*] [*IUPAC*]
H	Regarding [*JETDS nomenclature*]
H	Restaurants, Cafes, and Hotel Lounges [*Public-performance tariff class*] [*British*]
H	Search/Rescue [*When the first letter of a pair*] [*Designation for all US military aircraft*]
H	Silo Stored [*Missile launch environment symbol*]

H	St Louis [*Branch in the Federal Reserve regional banking system*] (BARN)
H	Total Energy (ROG)
H	Turkiye Halk Bankasi [*Bank*] [*Turkey*]
H	Vectorcardiogram Electrode [*Cardiology*] (DAVI)
H_0	Hubble's Constant [*Astronomy*]
H_1	Alternative Hypothesis (DAVI)
H1	Haploid Cell Line 1
H^1	Protium [*or Light hydrogen*] [*Chemical element*] (DAVI)
H^2	Deuterium [*Also, D*] [*Radioisotope of hydrogen*]
H2	Hawaii (Kauai) [*Spaceflight Tracking and Data Network*] [*NASA*]
H^2	Hot and Heavy [*In reference to a romance*]
H2	Hydrogen
H_2BT	Hydrogen Breath Test
H2O	Water [*Compound*] (RDA)
H_2O	Water (GNE)
H_2O_2	Hydrogen Peroxide [*Pharmacology*] (DAVI)
H_2S	Hydrogen Sulfide (GNE)
H_2SO_4	Sulfuric Acid (GNE)
H_2SO_4	Sulfuric Acid [*Chemistry*] (DAVI)
H_2Urd	Dihydrouridine [*Also, D, hU*] [*A nucleoside*]
H_3	Tritium [*Also, T*] [*Radioisotope of hydrogen*]
H_3BO_3	Boric Acid [*Pharmacology*] (DAVI)
H_4	Solomon Islands [*Aircraft nationality and registration mark*] (FAAC)
H_4	Tetrahydro [*Biochemistry*]
$H_4folate$	Tetrahydrofolate [*Biochemistry*]
H_4furan	Tetrahydrofuran [*Organic chemistry*]
H_4pyran	Tetrahydropyranyl [*Organic chemistry*]
H5	Henry V [*Shakespearean work*]
H8	Henry VIII [*Shakespearean work*]
H24	Twenty-Four Hour [*Continuous*] Operation [*Aviation*]
HA	Apogee Altitude (NASA)
HA	CASA [*Construcciones Aeronauticas Sociedad Anonima*] [*Spain ICAO aircraft manufacturer identifier*] (ICAO)
HA	Chem. Werke Albert [*Germany*] [*Research code symbol*]
HA	Habitual Abortion [*Medicine*]
Ha	Hahnium [*Proposed name for chemical element 105*]
HA	Haiti [*or Haitian*] (WDAA)
HA	Half Adder [*Circuitry*] (MSA)
Ha	Hallah (BJA)
HA	Hallux Abductus [*Orthopedics*] (DAVI)
HA	Hand Actuated (IAA)
H/A	Hand/Automatic [*Nuclear energy*] (NRCH)
HA	Hardness Assurance (MSA)
HA	Hardware [*Computer science*] (IAA)
HA	Hardy Annual [*Horticulture*] (ROG)
Ha	Hare's English Vice-Chancellors' Reports [*66-68 English Reprint*] [*1841-53*] [*A publication*] (DLA)
HA	Harmonie Associates (EA)
HA	Harness Assembly
Ha	Hartmann Number [*IUPAC*]
HA	Hatch Act [*1887*]
HA	Hatchway (DS)
HA	Hawaii [*or Hawaiian*] (WDAA)
HA	Hawaiian Airlines 'A' [*AMEX symbol*] (TTSB)
HA	Hawaiian Airlines, Inc. [*AMEX symbol*] (SAG)
HA	Hawaiian Airlines, Inc. [*ICAO designator*] (ICDA)
HA	Hazard Analysis (NASA)
HA	Hazardous Area
HA	Headache
H/A	Headache (DMAA)
HA	Headmasters [*or Headmistresses*] Association (EA)
HA	Headquarters Administration Division [*Coast Guard*]
H/A	Head to Abdomen (DMAA)
HA	Health Act (OICC)
HA	Health Advisory (GNE)
HA	Health Affairs [*Army*] (DOMA)
HA	Health Alliance [*Consumer representation*] (ECON)
HA	Healthy America [*An association Defunct*] (EA)
HA	Hearing Aid
HA	Heavy Artillery
HA	Heavy Atoms
HA	Hectare (AAG)
ha	Hectare
ha	Hectare (DMAA)
HA	Hectocotylized Arm
HA	Heeres-Atmer [*Service Oxygen Breathing Apparatus*] [*German military - World War II*]
HA	Hefte von Auschwitz (BJA)
HA	Height Age (MAE)
HA	Height of Apogee
HA	Heir Apparent
HA	Hellenic Army (MCD)
HA	Hemadsorption [*Hematology*]
HA	Hemagglutinating Activity [*Hematology*] (DAVI)
HA	Hemagglutinating Antibody [*Hematology*] (DAVI)
HA	Hemagglutinating Antigen [*Hematology*] (DAVI)
HA	Hemagglutination [*Hematology*]
HA	Hemolytic Anemia [*Hematology*]
HA	Henry Adams, Inc. [*Baltimore, MD*] (TSSD)
HA	Henson Associates [*Television production company*]
HA	Hepatic Artery [*Anatomy*] (MAE)
HA	Hepatitis Associated [*Virus*]
HA	Herpes Association [*British*] (DBA)
HA	Heterophile Antibody [*Immunochemistry*]

HA..............	Heyden Antibiotic [*Pharmacology*]
HA..............	High Altitude
HA..............	High Amplitude (IAA)
HA..............	High Angle
HA..............	High Anxiety (MAE)
HA..............	High Authority of the ECSC [*European Coal and Steel Community*] (ILCA)
HA..............	Higher Authority
HA..............	Highways Act [*British*] (ILCA)
HA..............	Hiram Abiff [*Freemasonry*] (ROG)
HA..............	Historia Animalium [*of Aristotle*] [*Classical studies*] (OCD)
HA..............	Historical Association [*British*] (EAIO)
HA..............	History Abstracts [*Database*] (NITA)
HA..............	Hoc Anno [*This Year*] [*Latin*]
HA..............	Hockey Association [*British*]
H/A..............	Holding Activity
HA..............	Holiness Army (ROG)
HA..............	Home Address
HA..............	Homesteaders Association [*Defunct*] (EA)
HA..............	Horse Artillery
HA..............	Horticultural Abstracts
HA..............	Hosanna Army (ROG)
HA..............	Hospice Association (EA)
HA..............	Hospital Academy (EA)
HA..............	Hospital Admission
HA..............	Hospital Apprentice [*Navy rating*]
HA..............	Hostile Aeroplane [*British military*] (DMA)
HA..............	Hot Air
HA..............	Hounsfield Unit [*On computerized tomography*] [*Radiology*] (DAVI)
HA..............	Hour Angle [*Navigation*]
HA..............	House Account [*Business term*]
HA..............	House Administration (DLA)
HA..............	Housewives Association [*Australia*]
HA..............	Housing Allowance [*Military*]
HA..............	Housing Assistance [*HUD*]
HA..............	Housing Authority
HA..............	Hoverclub of America (EA)
H-A..............	Howson-Algraphy (DGA)
HA..............	Huius Anni [*This Year's*] [*Latin*]
HA..............	Human Adaptability
HA..............	Human Argininosuccinate Lyase [*An enzyme*]
HA..............	Humanitarian Assistance [*Military*] (INF)
HA..............	Humic Acid [*Organic chemistry*]
HA..............	Humor Association (EA)
HA..............	Humorolics Anonymous (EA)
HA..............	Hungarian Association [*Australia*]
HA..............	Hyaluronic Acid [*Biochemistry*]
HA..............	Hydraulic Association of Great Britain (BI)
HA..............	Hydrophone Allowance [*British military*] (DMA)
HA..............	Hydroxyapatite [*Also, HAP*] [*A mineral*]
HA..............	Hydroxylapatite [*Inorganic chemistry*]
HA..............	Hyperalimentation [*Intravenous feeding*] (DAVI)
HA..............	Hypermetropia, Absolute [*Ophthalmology*]
HA..............	Hypoglycemic Association [*Australia*]
HA..............	Hypothalmic Amenorrhea [*Medicine*] (DAVI)
HA..............	Netherlands [*IYRU nationality code*] (IYR)
HA1.............	Hemadsorption [*Virus*], Type 1 [*Hematology*] (DAVI)
HAA............	Haflinger Association of America (EA)
HAA............	Haitian-American Association [*Defunct*]
HAA............	Haloacetic Acids [*Environmental chemistry*]
HAA............	Handbooks of Archaeology and Antiquities [*A publication*]
HAA............	Handicapped Artists of America (EA)
HAA............	Hands Across America [*Defunct*] (EA)
HAA............	Harrison Air [*Canada ICAO designator*] (FAAC)
HAA............	Hasvik [*Norway*] [*Airport symbol*] (OAG)
HAA............	Head Access Area [*Nuclear energy*] (NRCH)
HAA............	Hearing Aid Amplifier
HAA............	Heater Amplifier Assembly
HAA............	Heavy Antiaircraft Artillery
HAA............	Height above Airport (AFM)
HAA............	Helicopter Airline Association (EA)
HAA............	Helicopter Association of America [*Later, HAI*] (EA)
HAA............	Helicopter Association of Australia
HAA............	Hemolytic Anemia Antigen [*Immunochemistry*]
HAA............	Hepatitis Associated Antigen [*Clinical chemistry*]
HAA............	Heptaminol Adenosinemonophosphate Amidate [*Biochemistry*]
HAA............	High-Altitude Abort [*NASA*] (KSC)
HAA............	High-Altitude Application
HAA............	Hispanic American Almanac [*A publication*]
HAA............	Historic Aircraft Association [*British*]
HAA............	Home Automation Association (EA)
HAA............	Honduran-American Association (EA)
HAA............	Horticulture Awareness Association (EA)
HAA............	Hospital Activity Analysis [*British*]
HAA............	Hotel Accountants Association of New York City (EA)
HAA............	Houseboat Association of America (EA)
HAA............	Housing Assistance Administration [*HUD*]
HAA............	Human Asset Accounting (ADA)
HAAA..........	Addis Ababa [*Ethiopia*] [*ICAO location identifier*] (ICLI)
HAAB..........	Addis Ababa/Bole International [*Ethiopia*] [*ICAO location identifier*] (ICLI)
HAAC..........	Heavy Attack Aircraft Commander (DNAB)
HAAC..........	Housing Aid & Advice Centre [*England*]
HAAC..........	Hydraulic Actuator Assembly Container
HAACT........	Heavy Attack Aircraft Commander Training (DNAB)

HAAD..........	Adaba [*Ethiopia*] [*ICAO location identifier*] (ICLI)
HAAD..........	High-Altitude Aircraft Detection
HAADA........	Horatio Alger Association of Distinguished Americans (EA)
HAAFCE......	Headquarters, Allied Air Force, Central Europe [*NATO*]
HAAFE........	Hawaiian Army and Air Force Exchange [*Military*]
HAAG..........	Agordat [*Ethiopia*] [*ICAO location identifier*] (ICLI)
HAAg..........	Hepatitis A Antigen [*Immunology*] (DAVI)
HAAL..........	Addis Ababa/Liddetta [*Ethiopia*] [*ICAO location identifier*] (ICLI)
HAALS.........	High-Accuracy Airborne Location System (MCD)
HAAM..........	Arba Minch [*Ethiopia*] [*ICAO location identifier*] (ICLI)
Ha & Tw......	Hall and Twell's English Chancery Reports [*1849-50*] [*A publication*] (DLA)
HAAO..........	High-Altitude Airborne Observation
HAAP..........	Hawthorne Army Ammunition Plant (MCD)
HAAP..........	High Air Pollution Potential
HAAP..........	High-Altitude Air Pollution Program [*FAA*] (MCD)
HAAP..........	Holston Army Ammunition Plant
HAAP..........	Home-Based Advanced Assignment Program [*Military*]
Ha App........	Appendix to Volume 10 of Hare's Vice-Chancellor's Reports [*England*] [*A publication*] (DLA)
HAARP........	High-Altitude Auroral Research Project [*Jointly operated by the Department of Defense and the Geophysical Institute at the University of Alaska*]
HAARS........	High-Altitude Airdrop Resupply System
HAARS........	Hourly Attendance and Absence Reporting System [*Military*] (MCD)
HAART........	Highly Active Antiretroviral Therapy [*Medicine*]
HAAS..........	Asmara App [*Ethiopia*] [*ICAO location identifier*] (ICLI)
HAAS..........	Honeywell Automotive Accounting System (IAA)
HAAT..........	Height above Average Terrain
HAAT..........	Height of Antenna Above Average Terrain [*Broadcasting*] (WDMC)
HAATC........	High-Altitude Air Traffic Control
HAAW..........	Awash [*Ethiopia*] [*ICAO location identifier*] (ICLI)
HAAW..........	Heavy Antitank/Assault Weapon [*Army*]
HAAX..........	Axum [*Ethiopia*] [*ICAO location identifier*] (ICLI)
HAAY..........	Asmara/Yohannes IV [*Ethiopia*] [*ICAO location identifier*] (ICLI)
HAB............	Habacuc [*Old Testament book*] [*Douay version*]
Hab............	Habakkuk [*Old Testament book*]
HAB............	Habitat [*Dwelling*] (ROG)
HAB............	Habitation
HAB............	Habitual [*FBI standardized term*]
HAB............	Haboro [*Japan*] [*Seismograph station code, US Geological Survey Closed*] (SEIS)
HAB............	Hamilton, AL [*Location identifier FAA*] (FAAL)
HAB............	Hazards Analysis Board [*Air Force*]
HAB............	Hearing Aid Battery
HAb............	Heart Antibody [*Medicine*] (CPH)
HAB............	Heavy Assault Bridge
HAB............	Hepatitis B [*Virus*] [*Infectious diseases*] (DAVI)
HAB............	High-Altitude Bombing [*Military*]
HAB............	High-Alumina Basalt [*Geology*]
HAB............	Hiram Abiff [*Freemasonry*] (ROG)
HAB............	Historic American Buildings [*Survey*] [*Library of Congress*]
HAB............	Home Address Block
HAB............	Horizontal Assembly Building [*NASA*] (KSC)
HAB............	Horizontal Axis Bearing
HAB............	Hot Air Balloon
HAB............	Hybrid Antibody [*Immunology*]
HABA..........	Health and Beauty Aids [*Retailing*] (AABC)
haba..........	Health and Beauty Aids [*Advertising*] (WDMC)
HABA..........	(Hydroxyazobenzene)benzoic Acid [*Also, HBABA*] [*Organic chemistry*]
HaBaD........	Hokhmah, Bimah, Daat [*Germinal, Developmental, and Conclusive Knowledge*] [*Hebrew*]
HABB..........	Bunno Bedele [*Ethiopia*] [*ICAO location identifier*] (ICLI)
HABBA........	(Hydroxyazobenzene)benzoic Acid [*Organic chemistry*]
HABC..........	Baco [*Ethiopia*] [*ICAO location identifier*] (ICLI)
HABC..........	Habersham Bancorp [*NASDAQ symbol*] (SAG)
HAB CORP...	Habeas Corpus [*You Have the Body*] [*Legal*] [*Latin*] (ROG)
HABD..........	Bahar Dar [*Ethiopia*] [*ICAO location identifier*] (ICLI)
HABD..........	Hydrazobenzene Derivative [*Organic chemistry*]
HABE..........	Beica [*Ethiopia*] [*ICAO location identifier*] (ICLI)
Habersh.......	Habersham Bancorp [*Associated Press*] (SAG)
HABF..........	Hepatic Artery Blood Flow
HAB FAC POSS...	Habere Facias Possessionem [*A writ to put the plaintiff in possession*] [*Latin Legal term*] (ROG)
Hab Fa Poss...	Habere Facias Possessionem [*A writ to put the plaintiff in possession*] [*Legal term Latin*]
HAB FA SEIS...	Habere Facias Seisenam [*A writ to put the plaintiff in actual possession*] [*Latin Legal term*] (ROG)
HAB FA SEIS...	Habere Facias Seisinam [*That You Cause to Have Seisin*] [*Latin Legal term*] (DLA)
HABGT........	Hutt Adaptation of the Bender-Gestalt Test
habit..........	Habitat (BARN)
HABP..........	Hypersonic Arbitrary Body Program [*NASA*]
HABS..........	High-Altitude Bombsight (NATG)
HABS..........	Historic American Buildings Survey [*Library of Congress*]
HABT..........	Habeat [*Let Him Have*] [*Pharmacy*]
HABT..........	Habitability Technology (SSD)
HABTA........	Habituate (ABBR)
HABTAD......	Habituated (ABBR)
HABTAG......	Habituating (ABBR)
HABTAN......	Habitation (ABBR)
HABTAN......	Habituation (ABBR)
HABTB........	Habitable (ABBR)
HABTL........	Habitual (ABBR)

HABTLNS..... Habitualness (ABBR)
HABTU......... Habitue (ABBR)
HABTY......... Habitually (ABBR)
HABU.......... Bulchi [Ethiopia] [ICAO location identifier] (ICLI)
HABY......... Haberdashery (DSUE)
HAC........... Hachijojima Island [Japan] [Airport symbol] (OAG)
HAC........... Hachinohe [Japan] [Seismograph station code, US Geological Survey] (SEIS)
HAC........... Haitian Air Corps
HAC........... Handicapped Action Committee
HAC........... Heading Alignment Circle [NASA] (NASA)
HAC........... Heading Alignment Cone [NASA] (NASA)
HAC........... Heading Alignment Cylinder (MCD)
HAC........... Headquarters Area Command [Military]
HAC........... Health Advisory Council [New South Wales, Australia]
HAC........... Health Advisory Council [Generic term] (DHSM)
HAC........... Hearing Aid with Compression
HAC........... Heavy-Aggregate Concrete (DEN)
HAC........... Heavy Antitank Convoy
HAC........... Heavy Attack Aircraft Commander
HAC........... Helicopter Air Control [Military] (CAAL)
HAC........... Helicopter Aircraft Commander (NVT)
HAC........... Hellenic Advancement Council [Australia]
HAC........... Henebury Aviation Co. [Australia ICAO designator] (FAAC)
HAC........... Herbicide Assessment Commission
HAC........... Hexamethylmelamine [Altretamine], Adriamycin, Cyclophosphamide [Antineoplastic drug regimen]
HAC........... Hierarchical Abstract Computer (MHDI)
HAC........... High-Acceleration Cockpit [Air Force]
HAC........... High-Altitude Compensation [Automotive engineering]
HAC........... High-Aluminous Concrete
HAC........... Highway Action Coalition
HAC........... Hines Administrative Center [Veterans Administration]
HAC........... Historians of American Communism (EA)
HAC........... Historical Artillery Corps [British] [An association] (DBA)
HAC........... Historical Atlas of Canada [Project]
HAC........... Holland America Cruises [Formerly, Holland-America Line]
HAC........... Holland Australia Club [Australia]
HAC........... Honourable Artillery Co. [Military unit] [British]
HAC........... Horticultural Advisory Council for England and Wales (BI)
HAC........... Hospitals Accreditation Committee [Australia]
HAC........... Hot and Cold (IAA)
HAC........... House Appropriations Committee [US Congress] (AAG)
HAC........... Housing Advisory Council [South Australia]
HAC........... Housing Assistance Council (EA)
HAC........... Hover and Approach Coupler (MCD)
HAC........... Hughes Aircraft Co.
HAC........... Human Artificial Chromosome [Genetics]
HAC........... Humanities Association of Canada [See also ACH]
HAC........... Hydrogenated Amorphous Carbon [Inorganic chemistry]
HACC......... Help and Action Coordinating Committee [Defunct France] (EAIO)
HACCP....... Hazard Analysis Critical Control Point [Quality control]
HACCP....... Hazard Analysis Critical Control Points
HACE......... High-Altitude Cerebral Edema [Medicine]
HACEK....... Hemophilus, Actinobacillus, Cardiobacterium, Eikenella, and Kingella [Gram-negative bacilli]
HACH........ Hach Co. [NASDAQ symbol] (NQ)
HACHD....... Hatched (ABBR)
HACHG....... Hatching (ABBR)
HAChT........ High-Affinity Choline Transport
HACHWY.... Hatchway (ABBR)
HACHY....... Hatchery (ABBR)
HACI.......... Hughes Aircraft Co., International Division
HACK........ Hackney [Borough of London]
Hack Gen Aw.. Hackett on the Geneva Award Acts [A publication] (DLA)
HACL......... Harvard Air Cleaning Laboratory (NRCH)
HACL......... Hostility Adjective Check List [Psychology]
HACLA....... Housing Authority of the City of Los Angeles
HACLCS..... Harpoon Aircraft Command and Launch Control Set [Missiles] (NVT)
HACLS....... Harpoon Aircraft Command and Launch Subsystem [Missiles] (MCD)
HACN........ Hacienda (ABBR)
HAC NOCT... Hac Nocte [Tonight] [Pharmacy]
HACOM...... Headquarters Area Command [Military]
HACR........ Hereditary Adenomatosis of the Colon and Rectum [Medicine] (DMAA)
HACS........ Hazard Assessment Computer System [Coast Guard]
HACS........ High-Angle Control System [British military] (DMA)
HACS........ Homeostatic Adaptive Control System
HACS........ Hyperactive Child Syndrome
HACSG....... Hyper Active Children's Support Group [British]
HACT......... High-Affinity Choline Transport
HACTU....... Human Action Counselling and Training Unit [British] (DI)
HACU........ Hispanic Association of Colleges and Universities
HAD.......... Casper, WY [Location identifier FAA] (FAAL)
HAD.......... Hadassah (BJA)
Had........... Haddington's Manuscript Reports, Scotch Court of Session [A publication] (DLA)
Had........... Hadley's Reports [45-48 New Hampshire] [A publication] (DLA)
HAD.......... Half Amplitude Duration [Telecommunications] (TEL)
HAD.......... Halmstad [Sweden] [Airport symbol] (OAG)
HAD.......... Handicappers for Accountable Democracy (EA)
HAD.......... Hardness Assurance Document
HAD.......... Hartland [United Kingdom] [Geomagnetic observatory code]
HAD.......... Hassan Addakhil Dam [Morocco] [Seismograph station code, US Geological Survey] (SEIS)

HAD.......... Hawaii Air Defense
HAD.......... Head Acceleration Device (PDAA)
HAD.......... Health Assessment Document [Environmental Protection Agency] (GFGA)
HAD.......... Health Care Alternatives Development (HCT)
HAD.......... Hearing Aid Dispenser [Otorhinolaryngology] (DAVI)
HAD.......... Heat-Activated Device (NRCH)
HAD.......... Helicopter Approach/Departure [Military] (CAAL)
HAD.......... Helicopteros Andes [Chile] [ICAO designator] (FAAC)
HAD.......... Helium Abundance Detector [Instrumentation]
HAD.......... Hemadsorption [Hematology]
HAD.......... Herein After Described [Legal] [British] (MHDI)
HAD.......... Hexamethylmelamine, Adriamycin, Diamminedichloroplatinum [Cisplatin] [Antineoplastic drug regimen]
HAD.......... High-Accuracy Data [System] (MUGU)
HAD.......... High Alcohol Drinking [Rat strain]
HAD.......... High-Altitude Density [Sounding rocket]
HAD.......... High-Altitude Diagnostic [Unit] [Rocket launcher]
HAD.......... Hole-Accumulated Diode [Sony Corp.]
HAD.......... Horizontal Array of Dipoles
HAD.......... Hospital Administration [or Administrator]
HAD.......... Hypersonic Aerothermal Dynamics (SAA)
HADA........ Hawaiian Defense Area
HADAPS..... Hydrographic Automated Data Acquisitioning and Processing System (MCD)
HADAS...... Helmet Airborne Display and Sight (MCD)
HADB........ Dagabour [Ethiopia] [ICAO location identifier] (ICLI)
HADB........ Hazardous Substances Data Bank [National Library of Medicine] [Information service or system]
HADB........ High-Altitude Dive Bomb [Military]
HADC........ Dessie/Combolcha [Ethiopia] [ICAO location identifier] (ICLI)
HADC........ HIV [Human Immunodeficiency Virus] -Associated Dementia Complex [Medicine]
HADC........ Holloman Air Development Center [Air Force]
Had Chy Jur... Haddan's Administrative Jurisdiction of the Court of Chancery [A publication] (DLA)
Hadco........ Hadco Corp. [Associated Press] (SAG)
HADD........ Dembidollo [Ethiopia] [ICAO location identifier] (ICLI)
Hadd......... Haddington's Manuscript Reports, Scotch Court of Session [A publication] (DLA)
HADD........ Hawaiian Air Defense Division
HADD........ Hydroxyapatite Deposition Disease [Medicine] (DAVI)
Haddington... Haddington's Manuscript Reports, Scotch Court of Session [A publication] (DLA)
HA-DEC....... Hour Angle-Declination [Type of antenna mounting]
HADES....... Hypersonic Air Data Entry System
HADIOS...... Honeywell Analog-Digital Input-Output Subsystem (IAA)
HADIS....... Hadamard Imaging Spectrometer (PDAA)
HADIS....... Huddersfield and District Information Service [British] (NITA)
HADIZ....... Hawaiian Air Defense Identification Zone
HADL........ Dallol [Ethiopia] [ICAO location identifier] (ICLI)
Hadl.......... Hadley's Reports [45-48 New Hampshire] [A publication] (DLA)
Hadley....... Hadley's Reports [45-48 New Hampshire] [A publication] (DLA)
Hadl Rom Law... Hadley's Introduction to the Roman Law [A publication] (DLA)
HADM........ Debre Marcos [Ethiopia] [ICAO location identifier] (ICLI)
HADM........ Heavy Atomic Demolition Munition [Military] (AABC)
HADN........ Danguilla [Ethiopia] [ICAO location identifier] (ICLI)
HAD(N)....... Head of Aircraft Department (Naval) [British]
Hadng........ Hardinge, Inc. [Associated Press] (SAG)
HADO........ Dodola [Ethiopia] [ICAO location identifier] (ICLI)
HADOPAD... High-Altitude Delayed Opening Parachute Actuation Device (MCD)
HADOSS..... HWWA-Dossiers [Society for Business Information] [Information service or system] (IID)
HADR........ Dire Dawa/Aba Tenna Dejazmatch Yilma [Ethiopia] [ICAO location identifier] (ICLI)
Hadr.......... Hadrian [of Scriptores Historiae Augustae] [Classical studies] (OCD)
HADR........ Hughes Air Defense RADAR [Military]
HADS........ Hawaii Air Defense System
HADS........ Hospital Anxiety and Depression Scale [Medicine] (DMAA)
HADS........ Hypersonic Air Data Sensor (IEEE)
HADT........ Debre Tabor [Ethiopia] [ICAO location identifier] (ICLI)
HADTS....... High-Accuracy Data Transmission System (MUGU)
HAE.......... Haemonetics Corp. [NYSE symbol] (SPSG)
HAE.......... Hannibal, MO [Location identifier FAA] (FAAL)
HAE.......... Hatia [Bangladesh] [Airport symbol] (AD)
HAE.......... Havasupai [Arizona] [Airport symbol] (OAG)
HAE.......... Health Appraisal Examination (DMAA)
HAE.......... Hearing Aid Evaluation [Otorhinolayrngology] (DAVI)
HAE.......... Hepatic Artery Embolization [Medicine] (DAVI)
HAE.......... Hereditary Angioneurotic Edema [Medicine]
HAEC........ High Altitude Economic Carrier (PDAA)
HAEC........ Human Aortic Endothelial Cell
HAEE........ Harwell Atomic Energy Establishment
HAEH........ Horizontal Axis Electrical Hairspring
HAEM........ Haemolysis [British]
HAEMAT...... Haematocrit [British]
HAEMATOL... Haematology [British]
Haemon...... Haemonetics Corp. [Associated Press] (SAG)
HAEMORRH... Haemorrhage [British]
HAEMP....... High-Altitude Electromagnetic Pulse
HAER........ Historic American Engineering Record [Department of the Interior]
HAES........ Hawaii Agricultural Experiment Station [Honolulu]
HAES........ High-Altitude Effects Simulation [Defense Nuclear Agency]
HAF.......... Haifa [Israel] [Seismograph station code, US Geological Survey Closed] (SEIS)

HAF	Half Moon Bay, CA [*Location identifier FAA*] (FAAL)
HAF	Hallmark Financial Services [*AMEX symbol*] (SAG)
HAF	Headquarters, Air Force (AFM)
HAF	Headquarters, Allied Forces
HAF	Heavy Aircraft Fuel (MSA)
HAF	Hebrew Arts Foundation (EA)
HAF	Helicopter Assault Force (NVT)
HAF	Hellenic Air Force [*Greece*] [*ICAO designator*] (FAAC)
HAF	Hellenic Armed Forces (NATG)
HAF	Helms Athletic Foundation [*Later, Citizens Savings Athletic Foundation*] (EA)
HAF	High-Abrasion Furnace (IEEE)
HAF	High-Altitude Fluorescence (IEEE)
HAF	High-Altitude Fuze [*To activate weapons*]
HAF	Human Antitumor Factor [*Biochemistry*]
HAF	Hypersonic Aerothermaldynamic Factor
HAFB	Heavy Assault Floating Bridge [*British military*] (DMA)
HAFB	Hill Air Force Base (SAA)
HAFB	Holloman Air Force Base [*New Mexico*]
HAFBLCK	High-Abrasion Furnace Black (IAA)
HAFC	High-Altitude Forecast Center
HAFC	Hoyt Axton Fan Club (EA)
HAFE	Harpers Ferry National Historical Park
HAFID	Hydrogen Atmosphere Flame Ionization Detector
HAFMED	Headquarters, Allied Forces, Mediterranean
HAFN	Fincha [*Ethiopia*] [*ICAO location identifier*] (ICLI)
HAFO	Home Accounting and Finance Office
HAFOE	High Air Flow with Oxygen Enrichment (PDAA)
HAFP	Hawaii Academy of Family Physicians (SRA)
HAFRA	Hat and Allied Feltmakers' Research Association [*British*] (BI)
HAFS	Homosexuals Anonymous Fellowship Services (EA)
HAFSE	Headquarters, Allied Forces, Southern Europe (NATG)
HafsInd	Hafslund Nycomed AS [*Associated Press*] (SAG)
HafsInd	Hafslund Nycomed AS [*Associated Press*] (SAG)
HAFTB	Holloman Air Force Test Base [*New Mexico*] (AAG)
Hag	Hagan's Reports [*West Virginia*] [*A publication*] (DLA)
Hag	Hagan's Reports [*Utah*] [*A publication*] (DLA)
Hag	Haggai [*Old Testament book*]
Hag	Haggard's English Admiralty Reports [*A publication*] (DLA)
Hag	Hagigah (BJA)
HAG	[*The*] Hague [*Netherlands*] [*Airport symbol*] (AD)
HAG	Harvest Aviation Ltd. [*British ICAO designator*] (FAAC)
HAG	Heat-Aggregated Globulin (DMAA)
HAG	Helicopter Action Group (NVT)
HAG	High-Explosive Antiarmor Grenade [*Weaponry*] (MCD)
HAG	Hold for Arrival of Goods
HAG	Home Address Gap [*Computer science*] (MHDB)
HAG	Housing Association Grant [*British*]
HAG	Humanitarian Assistance Group [*Iraq*]
HAG	Hydrothermally-Altered Granite [*Geology*]
HAG	Hydroxyaminoguanidine [*Biochemistry*]
Hag Adm	Haggard's English Admiralty Reports [*A publication*] (DLA)
Hagan	Hagan's Reports [*Utah*] [*A publication*] (DLA)
HAGB	Goba [*Ethiopia*] [*ICAO location identifier*] (ICLI)
HAG COM	Haga Comitum [*The Hague*] [*Imprint*] (ROG)
Hag Con	Haggard's English Consistory Reports [*161 English Reprint*] [*A publication*] (DLA)
Hag Ecc	Haggard's English Ecclesiastical Reports [*162 English Reprint*] [*A publication*] (DLA)
HAGG	Heat-Aggregated Gamma Globulin [*Clinical chemistry*]
HAGG	Hyperimmune Antivariola Gamma Globulin
Hagg Adm	Haggard's English Admiralty Reports [*A publication*] (DLA)
Hagg Adm (Eng)	Haggard's English Admiralty Reports [*161 English Reprint*] [*A publication*] (DLA)
Haggar	Haggar Corp. [*Associated Press*] (SAG)
Hagg Con	Haggard's English Consistory Reports [*161 English Reprint*] [*A publication*] (DLA)
Hagg Cons	Haggard's English Consistory Reports [*161 English Reprint*] [*A publication*] (DLA)
Hagg Consist	Haggard's English Consistory Reports [*161 English Reprint*] [*A publication*] (DLA)
Hagg Consist (Eng)	Haggard's English Consistory Reports [*161 English Reprint*] [*A publication*] (DLA)
Hagg Ecc	Haggard's English Ecclesiastical Reports [*162 English Reprint*] [*A publication*] (DLA)
Hagg Eccl	Haggard's English Ecclesiastical Reports [*162 English Reprint*] [*1827-33*] [*A publication*] (DLA)
Hagg Eccl (Eng)	Haggard's English Ecclesiastical Reports [*162 English Reprint*] [*A publication*] (DLA)
HAGH	Ghinnir [*Ethiopia*] [*ICAO location identifier*] (ICLI)
HAGH	Hydroxyacyl-Glutathione Hydrolase (DMAA)
HAGIOL	Hagiology (ABBR)
HAGL	Galadi [*Ethiopia*] [*ICAO location identifier*] (ICLI)
HAGL	Haggle (ABBR)
HAGL	Handheld Grenade-Launcher
HAGLD	Haggled (ABBR)
HAGLG	Haggling (ABBR)
HAGLR	Haggler (ABBR)
HAGLST	Hagiologist (ABBR)
HAGM	Gambella [*Ethiopia*] [*ICAO location identifier*] (ICLI)
HAGN	Gondar [*Ethiopia*] [*ICAO location identifier*] (ICLI)
Hagn & M	Hagner and Miller's Reports [*2 Maryland Chancery*] [*A publication*] (DLA)
Hagn & Mill	Hagner and Miller's Reports [*2 Maryland Chancery*] [*A publication*] (DLA)

HAGO	Gode [*Ethiopia*] [*ICAO location identifier*] (ICLI)
HAGO	Heavy Atmospheric Gas Oil [*Petroleum product*]
HAGR	Gore [*Ethiopia*] [*ICAO location identifier*] (ICLI)
HAGR	Hamilton Grange National Memorial
HAGTNS	Haughtiness (ABBR)
HAGTR	Haughtier (ABBR)
HAGTST	Haughtiest (ABBR)
HAGTY	Haughtily (ABBR)
HAGU	Gura [*Ethiopia*] [*ICAO location identifier*] (ICLI)
Hague Ct Rep	Hague Court Reports [*A publication*] (DLA)
HAH	Healthcare Association of Hawaii (SRA)
HAH	Jacksonville, NC [*Location identifier FAA*] (FAAL)
HAH	Moroni [*Comoro Islands*] Hahaia Airport [*Airport symbol*] (OAG)
HAHI	Help At Home [*NASDAQ symbol*] (TTSB)
HAHI	Help At Home, Inc. [*NASDAQ symbol*] (SAG)
HAHIW	Help At Home Wrrt [*NASDAQ symbol*] (TTSB)
HAHM	Debre Zeit/Harar Meda [*Ethiopia*] [*ICAO location identifier*] (ICLI)
HAHN	Hahn Automotive Warehouse [*NASDAQ symbol*] (TTSB)
HAHN	Hahn Automotive Warehouse, Inc. [*NASDAQ symbol*] (SAG)
HahnAut	Hahn Automotive Warehouse, Inc. [*Associated Press*] (SAG)
Hahnemann U	Hahnemann University (GAGS)
HAHO	Harmony Holdings [*NASDAQ symbol*] (TTSB)
HAHO	Harmony Holdings, Inc. [*NASDAQ symbol*] (SAG)
HAHO	High Altitude/High Opening [*Army*] (ADDR)
HAHR	Hispanic American Historical Review [*A publication*] (BRI)
HAHS	Hooved Animal Humane Society (EA)
HA(HS)	Hospital Apprentice, High School
HAHS	Hossana [*Ethiopia*] [*ICAO location identifier*] (ICLI)
HAHST	High-Altitude High-Speed Target [*Formerly, HAST*] (MCD)
HAHT	Hypersonic Arc-Heated Tunnel [*Langley Research Center*] [*NASA*]
HAHTG	Horse Anti-Human Thymus Globulin [*Immunology*] (MAE)
HAHU	Humera [*Ethiopia*] [*ICAO location identifier*] (ICLI)
HAI	Century Aviation International Ltd. [*Canada*] [*FAA designator*] (FAAC)
hai	Haida [*MARC language code Library of Congress*] (LCCP)
HAI	Haiti (ABBR)
HAI	Haiwee [*California*] [*Seismograph station code, US Geological Survey Closed*] (SEIS)
HAI	Hampton Indus [*AMEX symbol*] (TTSB)
HAI	Hampton Industries, Inc. [*AMEX symbol*] (SPSG)
HAI	Handwriting Analysts, International (EA)
HAI	Health Action International (EA)
HAI	Helicopter Association International (EA)
HAI	Helicopter Attitude Indicator
HAI	Hellenic Aerospace Industry [*Greek*]
HAI	Hellenic Arms Industry [*Greek*]
HAI	Hemagglutination Inhibition [*Immunochemistry*]
HAI	Hepatic Artery Infusion [*Chemotherapy*]
HAI	Holland Automation International [*Software retailer*] (NITA)
HAI	Hospital-Acquired Infection [*Medicine*]
HAI	Hospital Audiences (EA)
HAI	Hot Air Intake [*Automotive engineering*]
HAI	Three Rivers, MI [*Location identifier FAA*] (FAAL)
HAIA	Hearing Aid Industry Association [*British*] (DBA)
HAIA	Honorary Member, American Institute of Architects (DAC)
HAIC	Hearing Aid Industry Conference [*Later, HIA*] (EA)
HAIC	Hetero-Atom-in-Context
HAID	Hand-Emplaced Acoustic Intrusion Detector (NVT)
HAID	Hispanic Americans Information Directory [*A publication*]
HAIDE	Hostile Aircraft Identification Equipment (DWSG)
HAIDEX	Hughes Artificial Intelligence Diagnostic Expert [*Hughes Aircraft Co.*] [*Army*]
HAIIS	Headquarters Administrative Issuance Index System [*Military*] (DNAB)
Hailes	Dalrymple (Lord Hailes). Decisions of the Scotch Court of Session [*1776-91*] [*A publication*] (DLA)
Hailes Ann	Hailes' Annals of Scotland [*A publication*] (DLA)
Hailes Dec	Hailes' Decisions, Scotch Court of Sessions [*A publication*] (DLA)
HainFood	Hain Food Group, Inc. [*Associated Press*] (SAG)
Hain JP	Haine's Illinois Justice of the Peace [*A publication*] (DLA)
HAIR	Help Alopecia International Research [*Defunct*] (EA)
HAIR	High-Accuracy Instrumentation RADAR (DNAB)
HAIR-AN	Hyperandrogenism, Insulin Resistance, and Acanthosis Nigricans Syndrome [*Medicine*] (DMAA)
HAIRCTTNG	Haircutting
HAIRDS	High-Altitude Infrared Detecting Set (MCD)
HAIRS	High-Altitude Test and Evaluation of Infrared Sources (MCD)
HAISAM	Hashed Index Sequential Access Method (PDAA)
HAISS	High-Altitude Infrared Sensor System
HAIT	Haiti
HAIT	Hash Algorithm Information Table
HAJ	Hajvairy Airlines [*Pakistan*] [*ICAO designator*] (FAAC)
HAJ	Hanover [*Germany Airport symbol*] (OAG)
HAJC	Hawaiian Area Joint Committee [*Military*] (CINC)
HAJJ	Jijiga [*Ethiopia*] [*ICAO location identifier*] (ICLI)
HAJM	Jimma [*Ethiopia*] [*ICAO location identifier*] (ICLI)
HAK	Adelanto, CA [*Location identifier FAA*] (FAAL)
HAK	Haikou [*China*] [*Airport symbol*] (OAG)
HAK	Hakodate [*Japan*] [*Seismograph station code, US Geological Survey*] (SEIS)
HAK	Harka Air Services [*Nigeria*] [*FAA designator*] (FAAC)
HAK	Hawkish (ABBR)
HAK	Horizontal Access Kit (NASA)
HAKASH	Hayl Kashish [*Elderly Army*] [*Israel*]
HAKD	Kabre Dare [*Ethiopia*] [*ICAO location identifier*] (ICLI)
HAKL	Kelafo [*Ethiopia*] [*ICAO location identifier*] (ICLI)

Hal.............. Halakha (BJA)
Hal.............. Halieuticon Liber [*of Ovid*] [*Classical studies*] (OCD)
HAL............. Halifax [*Nova Scotia*] [*Seismograph station code, US Geological Survey*] (SEIS)
Hal.............. Hallah (BJA)
HAL............. Halliburton Co. [*NYSE symbol Toronto Stock Exchange symbol*] (SPSG)
HAL............. Halogen (WDAA)
hal .... Halogen (IDOE)
HAL............. Haloperidol [*A tranquilizer*]
HAL............. Halothane [*Also, H*] [*An anesthetic*]
HAL............. Hamburg-Amerika Linie [*Hamburg-America Steamship Co.*]
HAL............. Handicapped Assistance Loan
HAL............. Hardware Abstraction Layer [*Computer science*] (PCM)
HAL............. Harwell Automated Loans [*Library circulation system*]
HAL............. Hash Algorithm Library
HAL............. Hawaiian Airlines, Inc. [*ICAO designator*] (FAAC)
HAL............. Hazards Assessment Laboratory [*Colorado State University*] [*Research center*] (RCD)
H-A-L.......... Head-Arm-Leg [*Medicine*]
HAL............. Heads-Up Audio-Vision Logistics [*NASA*]
HAL............. Height above Landing [*Area*]
HA(L).......... Helicopter Attack Squadron (Light) (CINC)
HAL............. Hemispheric Activation Level [*Computer science*] (BYTE)
HAL............. Hepatic Artery Ligation [*Medicine*]
HAL............. Heuristically-Programmed Algorithmic [*Name of computer in film, "2001: A Space Odyssey." Acronym is also considered to have been formed by combining the letters before IBM in the alphabet*]
HAL............. Highly Active Liquid [*Nuclear energy*] (NUCP)
HAL............. Highly Automated Logic [*Computer science*]
HAL............. High-Order Algorithmic Language (SSD)
HAL............. High-Order Articulated Language [*Computer science*] (MCD)
HAL............. High-Order Assembly Language [*Computer science*] (NASA)
HAL............. Hindustan Aeronautics Ltd.
HAL............. Hoechst Australia Ltd. [*Commercial firm*]
HAL............. Holding and Approach-to-Land [*Procedure*] [*Aviation*]
HAL............. Holland-America Line [*Later, Holland America Cruises*]
HAL............. Home Automated Living
HAL............. Houston Aerospace Language [*NASA*] (NASA)
HAL............. Human Access Language [*Computer science*]
HAL............. Hyperalimentation [*Intravenous feeding*] (DAVI)
HAL............. Hypogastric Artery Ligation [*Medicine*]
HALA .... Awash [*Ethiopia*] [*ICAO location identifier*] (ICLI)
Hal Anal ...... Hale's Analysis of the Law [*A publication*] (DLA)
Hal & Tw ..... Hall and Twell's English Chancery Reports [*47 English Reprint*] [*A publication*] (DLA)
HALAT .... Hebraeisches und Aramaeisches Lexikon zum Alten Testament [*Leiden*] (BJA)
HALB .... Halberton [*England*]
Halbtn.......... Halliburton Co. [*Associated Press*] (SAG)
Halc............ Halcomb's Mining Cases [*England*] [*A publication*] (DLA)
HALC .... High Affinity-Low Capacity (DMAA)
HALCA .... Highly Advanced Laboratory for Communications and Astronomy [*Japanese satellite*]
Hal Civ Law... Hallifax's Analysis of the Civil Law [*A publication*] (DLA)
Halc Min Cas... Halcomb's Mining Cases [*England*] [*A publication*] (DLA)
HALCON...... High-Altitude Long-Focus Convergent Mapping System
Hal Const Hist... Hallam's Constitutional History of England [*A publication*] (DLA)
HALDIS........ Halifax and District Information Service [*British*] (NITA)
HALE........... Haleakala National Park
Hale............ Hale's English Common Law [*A publication*] (DLA)
Hale............ Hale's Reports [*33-37 California*] [*A publication*] (DLA)
HALE........... High-Altitude, Long-Endurance [*Proposed unmanned reconnaissance drone*] [*Military*]
HALE........... Hilevel Assembly Language Environment [*Hilever Technology Inc.*] [*Operating systems assembler*] (NITA)
Hale Anal .... Hale's Analysis of the Law [*A publication*] (DLA)
Hale C L ...... Hale's History of the Common Law [*A publication*] (DLA)
Hale Com Law... Hale's History of the Common Law [*A publication*] (DLA)
Hale Cr Prec... Hale's Precedents in (Ecclesiastical) Criminal Cases [*1475-1640*] [*A publication*] (DLA)
Hale De Jure Mar... Hale's De Jure Maris, Appendix to Hall on the Sea Shore [*A publication*] (DLA)
Hale De Port Mar... Hale's De Portibus Maris [*A publication*] (DLA)
Hale Ecc...... Hale's English Ecclesiastical Reports [*1583-1736*] [*A publication*] (DLA)
Hale Hist Eng Law... Hale's History of the English Law [*A publication*] (DLA)
Hale Jur HL... Hale's Jurisdiction of the House of Lords [*1796*] [*A publication*] (DLA)
HalEP.......... Hallwood Energy Partners Ltd. [*Associated Press*] (SAG)
Hale Parl ..... Hale's History of Parliament [*2nd ed.*] [*1745*] [*A publication*] (DLA)
Hale PC ...... Hale's Pleas of the Crown [*England*] [*A publication*] (DLA)
Hale PC (Eng)... Hale's Pleas of the Crown [*England*] [*A publication*] (DLA)
Hale Prec .... Hale's Precedents in (Ecclesiastical) Criminal Cases [*1475-1640*] [*A publication*] (DLA)
Hale's.......... Hale's Precedents in (Ecclesiastical) Criminal Cases [*1475-1640*] [*A publication*] (DLA)
Hale Sug CM... Hale's Suggestion on Courts-Martial [*A publication*] (DLA)
Hale Sum ..... Hale's Summary of the Pleas of the Crown [*England*] [*A publication*] (DLA)
Hal Ev .... Halsted's Digest of the Law of Evidence [*A publication*] (DLA)
HALF........... Half-plate (VRA)
HALFSEE...... Headquarters, Allied Land Forces, Southeastern Europe
halftmb........ Half-timber (VRA)
Halh Gent L... Halhed's Code of Gentoo Laws [*A publication*] (DLA)

Halifax......... Halifax Corp. [*Associated Press*] (SAG)
Halifax Anal... Halifax' Analysis of the Roman Civil Law [*A publication*] (DLA)
Hal Int Law... Halleck's International Law [*A publication*] (DLA)
Halk............ Halkerston's Compendium of Scotch Faculty Decisions [*A publication*] (DLA)
Halk............ Halkerston's Digest of the Scotch Marriage Law [*A publication*] (DLA)
Halk............ Halkerston's Latin Maxims [*A publication*] (DLA)
Halk Comp... Halkerston's Compendium of Scotch Faculty Decisions [*A publication*] (DLA)
Halk Dig ..... Halkerston's Digest of the Scotch Marriage Law [*A publication*] (DLA)
Halk Lat Max... Halkerston's Latin Maxims [*A publication*] (DLA)
Halk Max..... Halkerston's Latin Maxims [*A publication*] (DLA)
Halk Tech Terms... Halkerston's Technical Terms of the Law [*A publication*] (DLA)
Hall............ Decisions of the Water Courts [*1913-36*] [*South Africa*] [*A publication*] (DLA)
Hall............ Hallett's Reports [*1, 2 Colorado*] [*A publication*] (DLA)
Hall............ Hallmark [*Record label*] [*Canada*]
HALL.......... Hallmark Capital [*NASDAQ symbol*] (TTSB)
HALL.......... Hallmark Capital Corp. [*NASDAQ symbol*] (SAG)
Hall............ Hall's New York Superior Court Reports [*A publication*] (DLA)
Hall............ Hall's Reports [*56, 57 New Hampshire*] [*A publication*] (DLA)
HALL.......... Lalibela [*Ethiopia*] [*ICAO location identifier*] (ICLI)
Hall Adm ..... Hall's Admiralty Practice and Jurisdiction [*A publication*] (DLA)
Hall ALJ ..... Hall's American Law Journal [*A publication*] (DLA)
Hallam......... Hallam's Constitutional History of England [*A publication*] (DLA)
Hall Am LJ... Hall's American Law Journal [*A publication*] (DLA)
Hall & T ..... Hall and Twell's English Chancery Reports [*47 English Reprint*] [*A publication*] (DLA)
Hall & Tw..... Hall and Twell's English Chancery Reports [*47 English Reprint*] [*A publication*] (DLA)
Hall & Tw (Eng)... Hall and Twell's English Chancery Reports [*47 English Reprint*] [*A publication*] (DLA)
Hal Law...... Halsted's New Jersey Law Reports [*6-12 New Jersey*] [*A publication*] (DLA)
Hall Ch Pr ... Halliday's Elementary View of Chancery Proceedings [*A publication*] (DLA)
Hall Civ Law... Hallifax's Analysis of the Civil Law [*A publication*] (DLA)
Hall (Col)..... Hallett's Reports [*1, 2 Colorado*] [*A publication*] (DLA)
Hall Const Hist... Hallam's Constitutional History of England [*A publication*] (DLA)
Hall Const L... Hall's Tracts on Constitutional Law [*A publication*] (DLA)
Halleck Int Law... Halleck's International Law [*A publication*] (DLA)
Hall Emerig Mar Loans... Hall's Essay on Maritime Loans from the French of Emerigon [*A publication*] (DLA)
Hallett .... Hallett's Reports [*1, 2 Colorado*] [*A publication*] (DLA)
Hall Hist ..... Hallam's Constitutional History of England [*A publication*] (DLA)
Hallifax Anal (of Civil Law)... Hallifax's Analysis of the Civil Law [*A publication*] (DLA)
Hallif CL...... Hallifax's Analysis of the Civil Law [*A publication*] (DLA)
Hall Int Law... Halleck's International Law [*A publication*] (DLA)
Hall Int Law... Hall on International Law [*A publication*] (DLA)
Hall Jour Jur... Journal of Jurisprudence (Hall's) [*A publication*] (DLA)
Hall Law of W... Halleck's Law of War [*A publication*] (DLA)
Hall LJ........ Hall's American Law Journal [*A publication*] (DLA)
Hall Marit Loans... Hall's Essay on Maritime Loans from the French of Emerigon [*A publication*] (DLA)
Hall Mex Law... Hall's Laws of Mexico Relating to Real Property, Etc. [*A publication*] (DLA)
HallmF........ Halmark Financial Services [*Associated Press*] (SAG)
HallmkCa..... Hallmark Capital Corp. [*Associated Press*] (SAG)
Hall Neut..... Hall's Rights and Duties of Neutrals [*1874*] [*A publication*] (DLA)
Hall NH...... Hall's Reports [*56, 57 New Hampshire*] [*A publication*] (DLA)
Hall (NY)..... Hall's New York Superior Court Reports [*A publication*] (DLA)
HALLO .... Hang Alle Laffe Landverraders Op [*Hang All Cowardly Traitors to Their Country*] [*Greeting for Dutch Nazis allegedly coined by the Netherlands people during World War II*]
HALLO .... Hang Alle Landverraders Op [*Hang all traitors*] [*Dutch*] [*WWII phrase*]
Hall Profits a Prendre... Hall's Treatise on the Law Relating to Profits a Prendre, Etc. [*A publication*] (DLA)
HallRlty ...... Hallwood Realty Partners [*Associated Press*] (SAG)
HallRty ...... Hallwood Realty Partners Ltd. [*Associated Press*] (SAG)
Hall's Am LJ... Hall's American Law Journal [*A publication*] (DLA)
Hall Shores... Hall's Rights in the Sea Shores [*A publication*] (DLA)
Hall's J Jur... Journal of Jurisprudence (Hall's) [*A publication*] (DLA)
HALLUC....... Hallucination
Hallwd........ Hallwood Group, Inc. [*Associated Press*] (SAG)
HallwdCon... Hallwood Consolidated Resources [*Associated Press*] (SAG)
Hal Min Law... Halleck's Mining Laws of Spain and Mexico [*A publication*] (DLA)
HALO .... HA-LO [*NASDAQ symbol*] (SAG)
HALO .... HA-LO Industries [*NASDAQ symbol*] (TTSB)
HA-LO......... HA-LO Industries, Inc. [*Associated Press*] (SAG)
HALO .... Handling of Alarms with Logic [*Nuclear reactors*]
HALO .... High-Altitude Large Optics [*Air Force*] (MCD)
HALO .... High Altitude Long Operation [*Airplane*]
HALO .... High-Altitude, Low-Opening Parachute Jump
HALO .... High Arcal Learning Objectives (AIE)
HALO .... Hughes Automated Lunar Observer [*NASA*]
HALOE........ Halogen Occulation Experiment (MCD)
HALON........ Halogenated Hydrocarbon
HALP .... HAWK [*Homing All the Way Killer*] Equipment Logistics Program [*Army*]
HALP .... Husbands of Airline Pilots
HAL-PC .... Houston Area League of PC [*Personal Computer*] Users
HALPRO....... Halverson Project [*World War II plan to bomb Japan from China*]

Hals............ Halsted's New Jersey Law Reports [*6-12 New Jersey*] [*A publication*] (DLA)
HAL/S......... High-Order Assembly Language for Shuttle Flight Computer (MCD)
HAL/S......... High-Order Assembly Language for Spacelab Usage [*NASA*] (NASA)
HALS .... Hindered Amine Light Stabilizers [*for plastics*]
HALS .... Houston Area Library System [*Library network*]
HALS .... Hydrographic Airborne LASER Sounder (PDAA)
Halsbury...... Halsbury's Statutes of England [*A publication*] (DLA)
Halsbury's S Is... Halsbury's Statutory Instruments [*A publication*] (DLA)
Halsbury's Statutes... Halsbury's Statutes of England [*A publication*] (DLA)
Hals Ch...... Halsted's New Jersey Equity Reports [*A publication*] (DLA)
Hals Eq...... Halsted's New Jersey Equity Reports [*A publication*] (DLA)
Halsey........ Halsey Drug Co. [*Associated Press*] (SAG)
HALSIM ...... Hardware Logic Simulator [*Computer science*] (IEEE)
HALSOL....... High-Altitude Solar Energy (PS)
HALST .... Halstead [*Urban district in England*]
Halst........... Halsted's New Jersey Equity Reports [*A publication*] (DLA)
Halst........... Halsted's New Jersey Law Reports [*6-12 New Jersey*] [*A publication*] (DLA)
Halst Ch ..... Halsted's New Jersey Chancery Reports [*A publication*] (DLA)
HalstdE........ Halstead Energy Corp. [*Associated Press*] (SAG)
HalstdEn ..... Halstead Energy Corp. [*Associated Press*] (SAG)
Halsted (NJ)... Halsted's New Jersey Chancery Reports [*A publication*] (DLA)
Halst Ev ..... Halsted's Digest of the Law of Evidence [*A publication*] (DLA)
HALT........... Help Abolish Legal Tyranny [*In organization name HALT-ALR*] (EA)
HALT........... High-Altitude LASER Transmittance (MCD)
HALT........... Holdup Alert - Local Transmission [*Bank robbery alarm system*]
HALT........... Hungry Angry Lonely Tired [*Slogan used by Alcoholics Anonymous members to determine whether their emotions are so out of control that they may be tempted to take a drink*]
HALT-ALR.... HALT - An Organization of Americans for Legal Reform (EA)
HalterM .... Halter Marine Group, Inc. [*Associated Press*] (SAG)
HaLV........... Hamster Leukemia Virus
HalwdCn...... Hallwood Consolidated Resources Corp. [*Associated Press*] (SAG)
HAM........... Hairy Anatomy Marine [*See also BAM*] [*Slang term for male marines*] [*Bowdlerized version*]
HAM........... Hamarfly, AS [*Norway*] [*FAA designator*] (FAAC)
HAM........... Hamburg [*Germany Airport symbol*] (OAG)
HAM........... Hamburg [*Germany*] [*Seismograph station code, US Geological Survey*] (SEIS)
Ham............ (Hamilton of) Haddington's Manuscript Cases, Scotch Court of Session [*A publication*] (DLA)
Ham............ Hamlet [*Shakespearean work*]
ham............ Hammered (VRA)
Ham............ Hammond's India and Burma Election Cases [*A publication*] (DLA)
Ham............ Hammond's Reports [*1-9 Ohio*] [*A publication*] (DLA)
HAM........... Hampshire College, Amherst, MA [*OCLC symbol*] (OCLC)
HAM........... Hardware Associative Memory [*Computer science*] (DIT)
HAM........... Harry Armenius Miller [*Automotive engineer*]
HAM........... Hearing Aide of Minnesota (SRA)
HAM........... Hearing Aid Microphone
HAM........... Heavy Atom Method
HAM........... Heavy Automotive Maintenance
HAM........... Height Adjustment Maneuver (MCD)
HAM........... Hexamethylmelamine, Adriamycin, L-Phenylalanine Mustard [*Antineoplastic drug regimen*] (DAVI)
HAM........... Hexamethylmelamine, Adriamycin, Melphalan [*Antineoplastic drug regimen*]
HAM........... Hexamethylmelamine, Adriamycin, Methotrexate [*Antineoplastic drug regimen*]
HAM........... Hierarchical Access Method
HAM........... High-Activity Mode (IAA)
HAM........... High-Altitude Missile (MCD)
HAM........... High-Availability Manager (IAA)
HAM........... High-Speed Automatic Monitor
HAM........... Histocompatibility Antigen Modifier [*Genetics*]
HAM........... Hold and Modify [*Computer display mode*]
HAM........... Home Access Mortgage
HAM........... Home Amateur [*Radio*]
HAM........... Honda of America Manufacturing
HAM........... HTLV-1-Associated Myelopathy [*Medicine*]
HAM........... Human Albumin Microsphere [*Clinical anesthesiology*]
HAM........... Human Alveolar Macrophage [*Immunology*]
HAm........... Human Amnion (DMAA)
HAM........... Human Associative Memory
HAM........... Hymns Ancient and Modern
HAM........... Hypoparathyroidism, Addison's Disease, and Musculocutaneous Candidiasis [*Medicine*]
HAMA .... Hamilton Anxiety Scale [*Psychiatry*] (DMAA)
HAMA .... Human Anti-Mouse Antibody [*Medicine*]
HAMA .... Human Anti-Murine Antibody [*Medicine*] (DMAA)
Ham A & O... Hamerton, Allen, and Otter's English Magistrates' Cases [*3 New Sessions Cases*] [*A publication*] (DLA)
Ham & J..... Hammond and Jackson's Reports [*45 Georgia*] [*A publication*] (DLA)
HAMB .... Hambledon [*England*]
HAMB .... Hamburg [*West Germany*] (ROG)
HAMB .... Hamburger Hamlet Restaurants [*NASDAQ symbol*] (SPSG)
HAMBGR...... Hamburger
HAMCHAM... Haitian-American Chamber of Commerce and Industry (EA)
HAMCHAM... Honduran-American Chamber of Commerce [*See also CCHA*] (EA)
HAMCO........ HAWK [*Homing All the Way Killer*] Assembly and Missile Checkout (AAG)
Ham Cont .... Hammon on Contracts [*A publication*] (DLA)
Ham Cust..... Hamel's Laws of the Customs [*A publication*] (DLA)
HAM-D......... Hamilton Psychiatric Rating Scale for Depression

HAMD .... Helicopter Ambulance Medical Detachment
HAME.......... Mieso [*Ethiopia*] [*ICAO location identifier*] (ICLI)
Hamel Cust... Hamel's Laws of the Customs [*A publication*] (DLA)
Ham Fed...... Hamilton's Federalist [*A publication*] (DLA)
Hamilton...... (Hamilton of) Haddington's Manuscript Cases, Scotch Court of Session [*A publication*] (DLA)
Hamilton...... Hamilton on Company Law [*3 eds.*] [*1891-1910*] [*A publication*] (DLA)
Hamilton...... Hamilton's American Negligence Cases [*A publication*] (DLA)
HAMIM .... Hizbul Muslimin [*Islamic Front*] [*Malaysia*] [*Political party*] (FEA)
Ham Ins...... Hammond on Fire Insurance [*A publication*] (DLA)
Ham Ins...... Hammond on Insanity [*A publication*] (DLA)
Ham Int ...... Hamel's International Law [*A publication*] (DLA)
HAMJ........... Maji [*Ethiopia*] [*ICAO location identifier*] (ICLI)
HAMK.......... Makale [*Ethiopia*] [*ICAO location identifier*] (ICLI)
Haml........... Hamlet [*Shakespearean work*] (BARN)
HAML.......... Masslo [*Ethiopia*] [*ICAO location identifier*] (ICLI)
HamlFn........ Hamilton Financial Services Corp. [*Associated Press*] (SAG)
Hamlin........ Hamlin's Reports [*81-93 Maine*] [*A publication*] (DLA)
Hamline U.... Hamline University (GAGS)
HAMM .... Metema [*Ethiopia*] [*ICAO location identifier*] (ICLI)
Ham Mar Laws... Hammick's Marriage Laws [*2nd ed.*] [*1887*] [*A publication*] (DLA)
HAMMARR... Hazardous Materials Management and Resource Recovery [*University of Alabama*] [*Research center*] (RCD)
Hammond.... Hammond's Reports [*36-45 Georgia*] [*A publication*] (DLA)
Hammond.... Hammond's Reports [*1-9 Ohio*] [*A publication*] (DLA)
Hammond & Jackson... Hammond and Jackson's Reports [*45 Georgia*] [*A publication*] (DLA)
HAMN .... Mendi [*Ethiopia*] [*ICAO location identifier*] (ICLI)
Ham NP....... Hammond's Nisi Prius [*A publication*] (DLA)
HAMO .... Motta [*Ethiopia*] [*ICAO location identifier*] (ICLI)
HAMOS .... High-Altitude Synoptic Meteorological Observation (SAA)
HAMOTS ..... High-Altitude Multiple Object Tracking System [*Air Force*]
HAMP .... Hampshire Group Ltd. [*NASDAQ symbol*] (SAG)
HAMP .... Hampshire Group Ltd [*NASDAQ symbol*] (TTSB)
HAMP .... Hampstead [*Region of London*]
HAMP .... Hampton National Historic Site
HAMP .... Hexamethylmelamine, Adriamycin, Methotrexate, Cisplatin [*Antineoplastic drug regimen*] (DAVI)
HAMP .... High-Altitude Measurement Probe
HAMP .... Hop and Stamp [*Dance terminology*]
Ham Part..... Hammond on Parties to Action [*A publication*] (DLA)
Ham Parties... Hammond on Parties to Action [*A publication*] (DLA)
HampGp ...... Hampshire Group Ltd. [*Associated Press*] (SAG)
Ham Pl .... Hammond's Principles of Pleading [*1819*] [*A publication*] (DLA)
HAMPS .... Hampshire [*County in England*]
HAMPS .... Heavy Airborne Multipurpose System (MCD)
Hamps Co Cas... Hampshire County Court Reports [*England*] [*A publication*] (DLA)
HAMPS R..... Hampshire Regiment [*Military unit*] [*British*] (ROG)
Hamptl........ Hampton Industries, Inc. [*Associated Press*] (SAG)
Hampton U... [*The*] Hampton University (GAGS)
Hamp Tr ..... Hampson. Trustees [*2nd ed.*] [*1830*] [*A publication*] (DLA)
HAMR .... Mui River [*Ethiopia*] [*ICAO location identifier*] (ICLI)
HAMRC .... Hammers Plastic Recycling [*NASDAQ symbol*] (TTSB)
HAMS .... Hardness Assurance Monitoring System (MCD)
HAMS .... Headquarters and Maintenance Squad
HAMS .... Hour Angle of the Mean Sun [*Navigation*]
HAMS .... Massawa [*Ethiopia*] [*ICAO location identifier*] (ICLI)
HAMS .... Smithfield Companies [*NASDAQ symbol*] (SAG)
HAMS .... Smithfield Cos. [*NASDAQ symbol*] (TTSB)
HAMSA .... Hearing Aid Manufacturers' and Suppliers' Association [*British*] (BI)
HAMSDET.... Headquarters and Maintenance Squadron Detachment [*Marine Corps*] (DNAB)
HaMSV .... Harvey Murine Sarcoma Virus [*Medicine*] (MEDA)
HAMT.......... Human-Aided Machine Translation
HAMT.......... Mizan Teferi [*Ethiopia*] [*ICAO location identifier*] (ICLI)
HAMTC .... Hanford [*Washington*] Atomic Metal Trades Council
HAMTF........ Hispanic American Ministries Task Force of JSAC [*Joint Strategy and Action Committee*] [*Defunct*] (EA)
HaMuSV ..... Harvey Murine Sarcoma Virus
HAN........... Chandler, AZ [*Location identifier FAA*] (FAAL)
HAN........... Hambro Resources, Inc. [*Vancouver Stock Exchange symbol*]
Han............ Handy's Ohio Reports [*12 Ohio Decisions*] [*A publication*] (DLA)
HAN............ Hanford [*Washington*] [*Seismograph station code, US Geological Survey*] (SEIS)
Han............ Hannay's New Brunswick Reports [*12, 13 New Brunswick*] [*A publication*] (DLA)
HAN........... Hanoi [*Vietnam*] [*Airport symbol*] (OAG)
HAN........... Hanover [*Former state in Germany*]
Han............ Hansard's Book of Entries [*1685*] [*A publication*] (DLA)
HAN........... Hanson Ltd. [*AMEX symbol*] (SAG)
HAN........... Hanson PLC [*Associated Press*] (SAG)
HAN........... Hanson plc ADR [*NYSE symbol*] (TTSB)
Han............ Hanson's Bankruptcy Reports [*1915-17*] [*A publication*] (DLA)
HAN........... Hanson Trust Ltd. [*NYSE symbol*] (SPSG)
HAN........... Hawaii Association of Nurserymen (SRA)
HAN........... Health Activation Network [*Later, WHAN*] (EA)
HAN........... Heroin-Associated Nephropathy [*Medicine*] (DAVI)
HAN........... Hex Aluminum Nut
HAN........... Hydroxylamine Nitrate [*Organic chemistry*] (NUCP)
HAN........... Hydroxylammonium Nitrate [*Component of liquid propellants*] [*Inorganic chemistry*]
HAN........... Hydroxyl Ammonium Nitrate (MCD)
HAN........... Hyperplastic Alveolar Nodules [*Precancerous lesions in mice*]
HANA .... Halibut Association of North America (EA)

HANA.......... Helvetia Association of North America [*Defunct*] (EA)
HANBA........ Hollow Anistropic Beam Analysis (PDAA)
Hanb Pat ..... Hanbury's Judicial Error in the Law of Patents [*A publication*] (DLA)
Hanb Us ...... Hanbury-Jones on Uses [*A publication*] (DLA)
HancBT........ Hancock [*John*] Bank & Thrift Opportunity Fund [*Associated Press*] (SAG)
Hanc Conv ... Hancock's System of Conveyancing [*Canada*] [*A publication*] (DLA)
HancFab...... Hancock Fabrics, Inc. [*Associated Press*] (SAG)
HancHd........ Hancock Holding Co. [*Associated Press*] (SAG)
HAND.......... Handex Corp. [*NASDAQ symbol*] (TTSB)
HAND.......... Handex Environmental Recovery, Inc. [*NASDAQ symbol*] (NQ)
Hand............ Hand's Reports [*40-45 New York*] [*A publication*] (DLA)
Hand............ Handy's Ohio Reports [*12 Ohio Decisions*] [*A publication*] (DLA)
HAND.......... Have a Nice Day
H & A .... Health and Accident [*Insurance*]
H&A............ Honours and Awards (ACII)
H & A Ins .... Health and Accident Insurance (DAVI)
HandAms..... Handes Amsorya [*Vienna*] (BJA)
H & ASHD .. Hypertension and Arteriosclerotic Heart Disease [*Medicine*]
HANDB........ Handbook
H & B .... Holland & Barrett [*Grocery and health food shop chain*] [*British*]
H & B .... Hudson and Brooke's Irish King's Bench Reports [*1827-31*] [*A publication*] (DLA)
Handb Gk Myth... Handbook of Greek Mythology [*A publication*] (OCD)
Handb Mag... Handbook for Magistrates [*1853-55*] [*A publication*] (DLA)
H & BR........ Hull & Barnsley Railway [*British*] (ROG)
H & BT........ Huntingdon & Broad Top Railroad
H & BTM ..... Huntingdon & Broad Top Mountain Railroad & Coal Co. (IIA)
H & BTM ..... Huntington & Broad Top Mountain Railroad & Coal Co. (MHDB)
H & C .... Head and Cover (MSA)
H and C .... Heroin and Cocaine (DSUE)
H & C .... Hoffmann & Campe [*Publisher*] [*Germany*]
H&C............ Hot and Cold (DMAA)
H & C .... Hurlstone and Coltman's English Exchequer Reports [*A publication*] (DLA)
Hand Ch P ... Hand's Chancery Practice [*A publication*] (DLA)
H & Cie .... Hentsch & Compagnie [*Bank*] [*Switzerland*]
H&CP.......... Hospital and Community Psychiatry (DMAA)
H & CR........ Handling and Checkout Requirements
Hand Cr Pr... Hand's Crown Practice [*A publication*] (DLA)
H & D .... Hardened and Dispersed (AFM)
H & D .... Hurter and Driffield [*Chemists for whom H & D Curve and H & D Speed System are named*] (DEN)
H & D .... Lalor's Supplement to Hill and Denio's New York Reports [*A publication*] (DLA)
H & D Pr ..... Holmes and Disbrow's Practice [*A publication*] (DLA)
H & E............ Hematoxylin and Eosin [*Biological stain*]
H & E............ Hemorrhage and Exudate [*Medicine*]
H & E............ Heredity and Environment
H & E............ History and Examination
HANDE........ Hydrofoil Analysis and Design [*Computer science*]
Han Deb ...... Hansard's Parliamentary Debates [*A publication*] (DLA)
Handex........ Handex Environmental Recovery, Inc. [*Associated Press*] (SAG)
Hand Fines... Hand on Fines and Recoveries [*A publication*] (DLA)
H & G .... Harden and Grind [*Technical drawings*]
H & G .... Harris and Gill's Maryland Court of Appeals Reports [*1826-29*] [*A publication*] (DLA)
H & G .... Headed and Gutted [*Fish processing*]
H & G .... Hicks & Greist [*Advertising agency*]
H & G .... Home and Garden Bulletins [*A publication*]
H & G .... Hurlstone and Gordon's English Exchequer Reports [*A publication*] (DLA)
HandH......... Handy & Harman [*Associated Press*] (SAG)
H & H .... Harrison and Hodgin's Upper Canada Municipal Reports [*1845-51*] [*A publication*] (DLA)
H & H .... Hemoglobin and Hematocrit [*Clinical chemistry*]
H & H .... Holland & Holland [*Custom gun maker*]
H & H .... Horn and Hurlstone's English Exchequer Reports [*1838-39*] [*A publication*] (DLA)
H & HQ....... Headquarters and Headquarters Company [*Army*]
H & HS....... Headquarters and Headquarters Squadron [*Marine Corps*]
H & I .... Harassing and Interdiction
H and I .... Harassment and Interdiction Fires [*Military*]
HANDICP.... Handicap
HANDITAL.... Association of Italian Families and Friends of Handicapped Children [*Australia*]
H & J .... Harris and Johnson's Maryland Court of Appeals Reports [*1800-26*] [*A publication*] (DLA)
H & J .... Hayes and Jones' Irish Exchequer Reports [*1832-34*] [*A publication*] (DLA)
H & J .... Hyphenation and Justification [*Typography*]
H & J .... Hyphenation and Justification (CDE)
H & J Forms... Hayes and Jarman's Concise Forms of Wills [*18th ed.*] [*1952*]
H & J Ir .... Hayes and Jones' Irish Exchequer Reports [*1832-34*] [*A publication*] (DLA)
H & John..... Harris and Johnson's Maryland Reports [*A publication*] (DLA)
H & K .... Hill & Knowlton, Inc. [*Public relations firm*]
H & K .... Holbrook & Kellogg [*Publisher*] (AAGC)
H & L .... Heart and Lungs [*Medicine*]
HandIm........ Handleman Co. [*Associated Press*] (SAG)
H & M .... Hay and Marriott's English Admiralty Reports [*A publication*] (DLA)
H & M .... Hemming and Miller's English Vice-Chancellors' Reports [*A publication*] (DLA)
H & M .... Hening and Munford's Reports [*11-14 Virginia*] [*A publication*] (DLA)

H & M .... Hit and Miss (WDAA)
H & McH ..... Harris and McHenry's Maryland Court of Appeals Reports [*1785-99*] [*A publication*] (DLA)
H & M Ch .... Hemming and Miller's English Vice-Chancellors' Reports [*A publication*] (DLA)
H & McHenry... Harris and McHenry's Maryland Reports [*A publication*] (DLA)
handmd ...... Handmade (VRA)
H & MS .... Headquarters and Maintenance Squadron [*Marine Corps*]
H & M (VA).. Hening and Munford's Reports [*11-14 Virginia*] [*A publication*] (DLA)
H & N .... Head and Neck [*Medicine*]
H & N .... Holmes and Narver, Inc. (NRCH)
H & N .... Hum and Noise (DEN)
H & N .... Hurlstone and Norman's English Exchequer Reports [*156, 158 English Reprint*] [*A publication*] (DLA)
H & NH........ Hartford & New Haven Railroad
H & P .... History and Physical [*Examination*] [*Medicine*]
H & P .... Hopwood and Philbrick's English Election Cases [*1863-67*] [*A publication*] (DLA)
Hand Pat ..... Hand on Patents [*A publication*] (DLA)
H & Q .... Hambrecht & Quist [*Investment banking firm*]
H & Q Hlt .... H & Q Healthcare Fund [*Associated Press*] (SAG)
H & Q Lfe .... H & Q Life Sciences Investors [*Associated Press*] (SAG)
H & R.......... Harper & Row Publishers, Inc.
H & R.......... Harrison and Rutherfurd's English Common Pleas Reports [*1865-66*] [*A publication*] (DLA)
H & R.......... Holding and Reconsignment [*Military*]
H & R.......... Hysterectomy and Radiation [*Medicine*]
H & R Bank.. Hazlitt and Roche's Bankruptcy Reports [*A publication*] (DLA)
H & RPO..... Holding and Reconsignment Point [*Military*]
H & S .... Harris and Simrall's Reports [*49-52 Mississippi*] [*A publication*] (DLA)
H & S .... Head and Shoulders [*Photography*]
H & S .... Headquarters and Service [*Battery*] [*Army*]
H & S .... Headquarters and Supply Company [*Marine Corps*] (VNW)
HANDS........ High-Altitude Nuclear Detection Studies [*National Institute of Standards and Technology*]
H & S .... Hysterotomy and Sterilization [*Medicine*]
handscr....... Handscroll (VRA)
H & SCTB .... Heavy & Specialized Carriers Tariff Bureau
H & STR..... Headquarters and Service Troop [*Army*]
H & T.......... Hall and Twell's English Chancery Reports [*1849-50*] [*A publication*] (DLA)
H & T.......... Handling and Transportation (KSC)
H & T.......... Hardened and Tempered [*Steel*]
H & T.......... Hospitalization and Treatment
H & T Self-Def... Harrigan and Thompson's Cases on the Law of Self-Defense [*A publication*] (DLA)
H & Tw........ Hall and Twell's English Chancery Reports [*1849-50*] [*A publication*] (DLA)
H and V .... Heating and Ventilation (NATG)
H & V .... Hemigastrectomy and Vagotomy [*Medicine*]
H&V............ Horizontal and Vertical (WDMC)
H & W .... Harrison and Wollaston's English King's Bench Reports [*A publication*] (DLA)
H & W .... Hazzard and Warburton's Prince Edward Island Reports [*A publication*] (DLA)
H & W .... Holm & Wonsild [*Steamship*] (MHDB)
H & W .... Hurlstone and Walmsley's English Exchequer Reports [*1840-41*] [*A publication*] (DLA)
Handy......... Handy's Ohio Reports [*12 Ohio Decisions*] [*A publication*] (DLA)
Handy (Ohio)... Handy's Ohio Reports [*12 Ohio Decisions*] [*A publication*] (DLA)
Handy R ...... Handy's Cincinnati Superior Court Reports [*Ohio*] [*A publication*] (DLA)
HANE.......... Hereditary Angioneurotic Edema [*Medicine*]
HANE.......... High-Altitude Nuclear Effects [*Study*]
HANE.......... High-Altitude Nuclear Explosion
Hane Cr Dig... Hanes' United States Digest of Criminal Cases [*A publication*] (DLA)
Han Ent........ Hansard's Book of Entries [*1685*] [*A publication*] (DLA)
Hanes .... Hanes' English Chancery [*A publication*] (DLA)
HANES .... Health and Nutrition Examination Survey [*Public Health Service*]
Hanf........... Hanford's Entries [*1685*] [*A publication*] (DLA)
HANFORD .... Hanford Site [*Department of Energy*] [*Richland, WA*] (GAAI)
Hanfrd .... Hannaford Brothers, Inc. [*Associated Press*] (SAG)
HANG.......... Hawaiian Air National Guard (FAAC)
HANG.......... Neghelle [*Ethiopia*] [*ICAO location identifier*] (ICLI)
HangOr .... Hanger Orthopedic Group, Inc. [*Associated Press*] (SAG)
Hanh Mar Wom... Hanhart on the Laws Relating to Married Women [*A publication*] (DLA)
Han Hor....... Hanover on the Law of Horses [*A publication*] (DLA)
HANJ .... Nejjo [*Ethiopia*] [*ICAO location identifier*] (ICLI)
HanJI .... Hancock, John, Investors Trust [*Associated Press*] (SAG)
HanJI .... John Hancock Investors Trust [*Associated Press*] (SAG)
HanJS......... Hancock, John, Income Securities Trust [*Associated Press*] (SAG)
HanJS......... John Hancock Income Securities Trust [*Associated Press*] (SAG)
HANK.......... Nekemte [*Ethiopia*] [*ICAO location identifier*] (ICLI)
HAN/LCD..... Hybrid Assigned Nematic/Liquid Crystal Display (TEL)
Hanm.......... Lord Kenyon's English King's Bench Reports, Notes, Edited by Hanmer [*A publication*] (ILCA)
Han Mar Wom... Hanhart on the Laws Relating to Married Women [*A publication*] (DLA)
Hanmer........ Lord Kenyon's English King's Bench Reports, Notes, Edited by Hanmer [*A publication*] (DLA)
Hann........... Hannay's New Brunswick Reports [*12, 13 New Brunswick*] [*A publication*] (DLA)
Hanna......... Hanna [*M. A.*] Co. [*Associated Press*] (SAG)

Han (NB) ..... Hannay's New Brunswick Reports [*12, 13 New Brunswick*] [*A publication*] (DLA)
HanovGld..... Hanover Gold Company, Inc. [*Associated Press*] (SAG)
hANP .... Human Atrial Natriuretic Peptide [*Biochemistry*]
Han Prob ..... Hanson on the Probate and Legacy Acts [*A publication*] (DLA)
HanPtDiv ..... Hancock [*John*] Patriot Premium Dividend Fund I [*Associated Press*] (SAG)
HanPtDv2 .... Hancock [*John*] Patriot Premium Dividend Fund II [*Associated Press*] (SAG)
HanPtGlb ..... Hancock [*John*] Patriot Global Dividend Fund [*Associated Press*] (SAG)
HanPtPfd ..... Hancock, John, Patriot Preferred Dividend Fund [*Associated Press*] (SAG)
HanPtPfd ..... Hancock [*John*] Patriot Prferred Dividend Fund [*Associated Press*] (SAG)
HanPtSel ..... Hancock [*John*] Patriot Select Dividend Trust [*Associated Press*] (SAG)
HANS .... Hansen Nat [*NASDAQ symbol*] (TTSB)
Hans .... Hansen Natural Corp. [*Associated Press*] (SAG)
HANS .... Hansen Natural Corp. [*NASDAQ symbol*] (SAG)
HANS .... High-Altitude Navigation System
Hans Al....... Hansard on Aliens [*A publication*] (DLA)
Hansb .... Hansbrough's Reports [*76-90 Virginia*] [*A publication*] (DLA)
Hans Deb..... Hansard's Parliamentary Debates [*A publication*] (DLA)
Hansen .... Hansen Natural Corp. [*Associated Press*] (SAG)
Hans Ent..... Hansard's Book of Entries [*1685*] [*A publication*] (DLA)
Hanson .... Hanson Trust Ltd. [*Associated Press*] (SAG)
Hans Parl Deb... Hansard's Parliamentary Debates [*A publication*] (DLA)
Hans Pr ...... Hanson on Probate Acts [*A publication*] (DLA)
HANTS .... Hampshire [*County in England*]
HanvDir .... Hanover Direct, Inc. [*Associated Press*] (SAG)
HANYS........ Healthcare Association of New York State (SRA)
HAO .... Hamilton, OH [*Location identifier FAA*] (FAAL)
HAO .... Hardware Action Officer [*Military*] (AABC)
HAO .... Hearing Aid Follow-Up and Orientation [*Otorhinolaryngology*] (DAVI)
HAO .... High-Altitude Observatory [*Boulder, CO*] [*National Center for Atmospheric Research*]
HAO .... Hospitals, Administration, and Organizations [*British*]
HAOA .... High Angle of Attack [*Combat aircraft*] [*Navy*]
HAOC .... Haynes-Apperson Owners Club (EA)
HAOC .... Hexaazaoctadecahydrocoronene [*Organic chemistry*]
HAOG .... Handbuch der Altorientalischen Geisteskultur [*A publication*] (BJA)
HA or D ...... Havre, Antwerp, or Dunkirk [*Business term*]
HAOS .... Houston Area Oxidant Study [*Environmental Protection Agency*] (GFGA)
HAOS .... Hydroxylamine-ortho-sulfonic Acid [*Organic chemistry*]
HAOSS........ High-Altitude Orbital Space Station (IEEE)
HAP .... Hafnium Column Product [*Nuclear energy*] (NRCH)
HAP .... Hampshire Aircraft Parks [*British military*] (DMA)
HAP .... Handicapped Aid Program (DAVI)
HAP .... Happy
HAP .... Happy Bay [*Australia Airport symbol*] (OAG)
HAP .... Hardware Allocation Panel
HAP .... Harwood Academic Publishers [*British*]
HAP .... Hazardous Air Pollutant
HAP .... Heading Axis Perturbation
HAP .... Health Alliance Plan
HAP .... Heat Shock Activator Protein [*Biochemistry*]
HAP .... Height Above Plate [*Roofing*]
HAP .... Heredopathia Atactica Polyneuritiformis [*Medicine*]
HAP .... High-Acid Column Product (NRCH)
HAP .... High-Altitude Platform
HAP .... High-Altitude Probe (AAG)
HAP .... Histamine Phosphate Acid [*Biochemistry*] (DAVI)
HAP .... Home Owners Assistance Program [*Military*] (AABC)
HAP .... Honeycomb Aluminum Panel
HAP .... Hook-Associated Protein [*Genetics*]
HAP .... Horizontal Axis Pivot
HAP .... Host-Associated Population [*Ecology*]
HAP .... Housing Assistance Program
HAP .... Humoral Antibody Production [*Medicine*] (DMAA)
HAP .... Huntingtin-Associated Protein [*Biochemistry*]
HAP .... Hutch Apparel Ltd. [*Vancouver Stock Exchange symbol*]
HAP .... Hydrated Antimony Pentaoxide [*Inorganic chemistry*]
HAP .... Hydrolyzed Animal Protein [*Food technology*]
HAP .... Hydroxyacetophenone [*Organic chemistry*]
HAP .... Hydroxyapatite [*Also, HA*] [*A mineral*]
HAP .... Hydroxylamine Perchlorate [*Organic chemistry*]
HAP .... Hyperboloid Approximation Procedure
HAP .... Hyperpolarizing Afterpotential [*Electrophysiology*]
HAP .... Whitsunday Resort (Long Island) [*Australia Airport symbol*]
HAPA .... Handicapped Adventure Playground Association [*British*] (DBA)
HAPA .... Hemagglutinating Anti-Penicillin Antibody [*Virology*] (MAE)
HAPAB .... Health Aspects of Pesticides Abstract Bulletin [*Environmental Protection Agency*]
HAPC .... Hospital-Acquired Penetration Contact [*Medicine*] (MAE)
HAPCWS..... Holt-Atherton Pacific Center for Western Studies [*University of the Pacific*] [*Research center*] (RCD)
HAPDAR ..... Hard Point Demonstration Array RADAR
HAPDEC....... Hard Point Decoys (MCD)
HAPE .... High-Altitude Pulmonary Edema
HAPEMS ...... Hazardous Air Pollutants Enforcement Management System [*Environmental Protection Agency*] (GFGA)
HAPEX .... Hydrological Atmospheric Pilot Experiment [*Marine science*] (OSRA)
HAPEX .... Hydrological Atmospheric Pilot Experiments (EERA)

HAPFF-EUR... HAWK [*Homing All the Way Killer*] Project Field Facility - Europe (MCD)
HAPI .... Harris API [*Application Programming Interface*] [*Computer science*]
HAPI .... Helicopter Approach Path Indicator (MCD)
HAPI .... Holding as Previously Instructed [*Aviation*] (FAAC)
HAPI .... Host Application Programming Interface
HAP-NICA .... Humanitarian Assistance Project for Independent Agricultural Development in Nicaragua [*Defunct*] (EA)
HAPO .... Hanford Atomic Products Operations [*General Electric Co.*]
HAPO .... High-Altitude Pulmonary Oedema [*Medicine*] (DMAA)
HAPORTH .... Halfpennyworth [*British*] (ROG)
H App .... Heir Apparent (DAS)
HAPP .... High Air Pollution Potential
HAPP .... High-Altitude Pollution Project [*FAA*]
HAPP .... High-Altitude Powered Platforms (MCD)
HAPPE .... High-Altitude Particle Program Experiment [*NASA*]
HAPPE .... Honeywell Associative Parallel Processing Ensemble
HAPPI .... Height and Plan Position Indicator (PDAA)
HAPPI .... Household and Personal Products Industry [*A publication*]
Happiness ... Happiness Express, Inc. [*Associated Press*] (SAG)
HAPPS .... Hazardous Air Pollutant Prioritization System [*Environmental Protection Agency*] (GFGA)
HAPS .... Hazardous Air Pollutants
HAPS .... Health Aspects of Pesticides
HAPS .... Hepatic Arterial Perfusion Scintigraphy [*Cardiology*] (DAVI)
HAPS .... Historic Aircraft Preservation Society Ltd. [*British*] (BI)
HAPS .... Houston Automatic Priority Spooling [*Computer science*] (NRCH)
HAPS .... Hydroxyalkylpropyl Sephadex [*Analytical biochemistry*]
HAPT .... Haptoglobin [*Hematology*] (DAVI)
HAPTONG .... Haptong Tongsin [*Press agency*] [*South Korea*]
HAPUB .... High-Speed Arithmetic Processing Unit Board
HAP-USA .... Handicapped Aid Program - USA [*Defunct*] (EA)
HAPY .... Happiness Express [*NASDAQ symbol*] (TTSB)
HAPY .... Happiness Express, Inc. [*NASDAQ symbol*] (SAG)
HAQ .... Headache Assessment Questionnaire [*Neurology*] (DAVI)
HAQ .... Health Assessment Questionnaire (DMAA)
HAQO .... Hydroxyaminoquinoline Oxide [*Organic chemistry*]
Har............. Harari (BJA)
HAR .... Harbor (AFM)
HAR .... Harbor Advisory RADAR
HAR .... Harbor Airlines, Inc. [*ICAO designator*] (FAAC)
HAR .... Hardness Assessment Report
HAR .... Hardware Affiliated Representatives [*Defunct*] (EA)
HAR .... Harford Community College, Bel Air, MD [*OCLC symbol*] (OCLC)
HAR .... Harman International [*NYSE symbol*] (TTSB)
HAR .... Harman International Industries, Inc. [*NYSE symbol*] (SPSG)
HAR .... Harmonic
Har............. Harradine Group [*Australia Political party*]
Har............. Harrington's Delaware Reports [*A publication*] (DLA)
Har............. Harrington's Michigan Chancery Reports [*A publication*] (DLA)
HAR .... Harrisburg-New Cumberland [*Pennsylvania*] [*Airport symbol*] (AD)
HAR .... Harrisburg, PA [*Location identifier FAA*] (FAAL)
Har............. Harrison's Condensed Louisiana Reports [*A publication*] (DLA)
Har............. Harrison's Michigan Chancery Reports [*A publication*] (DLA)
Har............. Harrison's Reports [*15-17, 23-29 Indiana*] [*A publication*] (DLA)
HAR .... Hartford [*Connecticut*] [*Seismograph station code, US Geological Survey Closed*] (SEIS)
HAR .... Harum [*Of These*] [*Pharmacy*] (ROG)
HAR .... Hazard Action Report (MCD)
HAR .... Heinemann, A. R., East Saint Louis IL [*STAC*]
HAR .... High-Altitude Recombination Energy (IAA)
HAR .... Highway Advisory Radio [*Vehicle communications*]
HAR .... Highway Advisory Radio [*Federal program*]
HAR .... Home Address Register
HAR .... Homogeneous Aqueous Reactor [*Nuclear energy*] (NUCP)
HAR .... Honorary Air Reserve [*Air Force*]
HAR .... Horse of the Americas Registry (EA)
HAR .... Hover Agility Rotor (RDA)
HAR .... Hyperacute Rejection [*Medicine*]
H-Ar .... Public Archives, Honolulu, HI [*Library symbol Library of Congress*] (LCLS)
HARA .... High-Altitude RADAR Altimeter [*NASA*]
HARA .... High-Assault Risk Area [*DoD*]
HARAC .... High-Altitude Resonance Absorption Calculation (IEEE)
Har & G....... Harris and Gill's Maryland Reports [*A publication*] (DLA)
Har & Gil.... Harris and Gill's Maryland Reports [*A publication*] (DLA)
Har & Gill.... Harris and Gill's Maryland Reports [*A publication*] (DLA)
Har & G Rep... Harris and Gill's Maryland Reports [*A publication*] (DLA)
Har & J........ Harris and Johnson's Maryland Reports [*A publication*] (DLA)
Har & J (MD)... Harris and Johnson's Maryland Reports [*A publication*] (DLA)
Har & John... Harris and Johnson's Maryland Court of Appeals Reports [*1800-26*] [*A publication*] (DLA)
Har & Johns MD Rep... Harris and Johnson's Maryland Reports [*A publication*] (DLA)
Har & McH.... Harris and McHenry's Maryland Reports [*A publication*] (DLA)
Har and M'Hen... Harris and McHenry's Maryland Reports [*A publication*] (DLA)
Har & Ruth... Harrison and Rutherford's English Common Pleas Reports [*1865-66*] [*A publication*] (DLA)
Har & W ..... Harrison and Wollaston's English King's Bench Reports [*A publication*] (DLA)
Har & Woll... Harrison and Wollaston's English King's Bench Reports [*A publication*] (DLA)
Har App .... Hare's English Chancery Reports, Appendix to Vol. X [*A publication*] (DLA)
HARAS......... Hughes Active RADAR Augmentation System

HARB	Harbor [*Maps and charts*] (ROG)
HARB	Harbor Federal Savings Bank [*NASDAQ symbol*] (SAG)
HARB	Harbor Federal Svgs Bk [*NASDAQ symbol*] (TTSB)
Harb & Nav C	Harbors and Navigation Code [*A publication*] (DLA)
HarbFed	Harbor Federal Bancorp [*Associated Press*] (SAG)
Harbngr	Harbinger Corp. [*Associated Press*] (SAG)
HARBOR	Harbor [*Commonly used*] (OPSA)
HarborH	Harborside Healthcare Corp. [*Associated Press*] (SAG)
HARBORS	Harbors [*Commonly used*] (OPSA)
HarbourF	Harbourton Financial Services LP [*Associated Press*] (SAG)
HARBR	Harbor [*Commonly used*] (OPSA)
HarbrFd	Harbor Federal Savings Bank [*Associated Press*] (SAG)
Harbrgr	Harbinger Corp. [*Associated Press*] (SAG)
Har Bus R	Harvard Business Review [*A publication*] (BRI)
Harc	Harcarse's Decisions, Scotch Court of Session [*1681-91*] [*A publication*] (DLA)
HARC	Harcor Energy [*NASDAQ symbol*] (TTSB)
HARC	HarCor Energy Co. [*NASDAQ symbol*] (NQ)
HARC	Helical Axial Rate Control (MCD)
HARC	Hester Adrian Research Centre [*University of Manchester*] [*British*] (CB)
HARC	High-Altitude RADAR Controller
HARC	Houston Advanced Research Center
HARCFT	Harbor Craft
HarcG	Harcourt General, Inc. [*Associated Press*] (SAG)
HarcGn	Harcourt General, Inc. [*Associated Press*] (SAG)
Har Ch	Harrington's Michigan Chancery Reports [*A publication*] (DLA)
Har Ch Pr	Harrison's Chancery Practice [*A publication*] (DLA)
Har Chy	Harrington's Michigan Chancery Reports [*A publication*] (DLA)
HARCO	Hyperbolic Area Control (IAA)
HARCO	Hyperbolic Area Coverage [*Navigation*]
Har Col Jur	Hargrave's Collectanea Juridica [*1791-92*] [*A publication*] (DLA)
Har Com	Harrison's Compilation of the Laws of New Jersey [*A publication*] (DLA)
Har Com Proc	Harrison's Common Law Procedure Act [*Canada A publication*] (DLA)
HarcorE	HarCor Energy Co. [*Associated Press*] (SAG)
Har Ct Mar	Harwood's Practice of United States Naval Courts-Martial [*A publication*] (DLA)
HARCVS	Honorary Associate of the Royal College of Veterinary Surgeons [*British*]
Hard	Hardin's Kentucky Reports [*A publication*] (DLA)
Hard	Hardres' English Exchequer Reports [*145 English Reprint*] [*A publication*] (DLA)
HARD	Hardware (WDAA)
HARD	Horizontal Acoustic Range Depiction (NVT)
hardbd	Hardboard (VRA)
Hard Eccl L	Harding on Ecclesiastical Law [*A publication*] (DLA)
Har Del	Harrington's Delaware Reports [*1-5 Delaware*] [*A publication*] (DLA)
Hard El Pet	Hardcastle on Election Petitions [*A publication*] (DLA)
Hardes	Hardesty's Delaware Term Reports [*A publication*] (DLA)
HARDEX	Harbor Defense Exercise [*Navy*] (NG)
Har Dig	Harris' Georgia Digest [*A publication*] (DLA)
Har Dig	Harrison's Digest of English Common Law Reports [*A publication*] (DLA)
Hardin	Hardin Bancorp, Inc. [*Associated Press*] (SAG)
Hardin	Hardin's Kentucky Reports [*A publication*] (DLA)
Harding U	Harding University (GAGS)
Hardin (KY)	Hardin's Kentucky Reports [*A publication*] (DLA)
Hardin-Simmons U	Hardin-Simmons University (GAGS)
HARDIS	Hotel and Restaurant Design and Interiors Exhibition [*British*] (ITD)
HARDMAN	Hardware-Manpower Program [*Navy*]
HARDMON	Hardware Monitor [*Computer science*] (MHDI)
Hardr	Hardres' English Exchequer Reports [*145 English Reprint*] [*1655-69*] [*A publication*] (DLA)
Hardr (Eng)	Hardres' English Exchequer Reports [*145 English Reprint*] [*A publication*] (DLA)
Hardres	Hardres' English Exchequer Reports [*145 English Reprint*] [*A publication*] (DLA)
HARDS	High-Altitude Radiation Detection System (MCD)
Hard St L	Hardcastle on Statutory Law [*A publication*] (DLA)
Hard Tr M	Hardingham on Trade Marks [*A publication*] (DLA)
HARDTS	High-Accuracy RADAR Data Transmission System (MUGU)
Hardw	Cases Tempore Hardwicke, by Lee [*England*] [*A publication*] (DLA)
Hardw	Cases Tempore Hardwicke, by Ridgeway [*England*] [*A publication*] (DLA)
Hardw Cas Temp	Cases Tempore Hardwicke, by Lee and Hardwicke [*A publication*] (DLA)
Hardw (Eng)	Cases Tempore Hardwicke, by Lee [*England*] [*A publication*] (DLA)
Hardw (Eng)	Cases Tempore Hardwicke, by Ridgeway [*England*] [*A publication*] (DLA)
Hardw NB	Hardwicke's Note Books [*A publication*] (DLA)
HARDWR	Hardware [*Computer science*]
Hare	Hare's English Vice-Chancellors' Reports [*66-68 English Reprint*] [*1841-53*] [*A publication*] (DLA)
HARE	High-Altitude Ramjet Engine
HARE	High-Altitude Recombination-Energy Propulsion (AAG)
HARE	Humans Against Rabbit Exploitation (EA)
HARE	Hydrazine Auxiliary Rocket Engine
Hare & W	Hare and Wallace's American Leading Cases [*A publication*] (DLA)
Hare & Wallace Amer Leading Cases	American Leading Cases, Edited by Hare and Wallace [*A publication*] (DLA)
Hare & Wallace Lead Cases (Am)	American Leading Cases, Edited by Hare and Wallace [*A publication*] (DLA)

Hare & Wal LC	American Leading Cases, Edited by Hare and Wallace [*A publication*] (DLA)
Hare App	Hare's English Chancery Reports, Appendix to Vol. X [*A publication*] (DLA)
Hare Const Law	Hare's American Constitutional Law [*A publication*] (DLA)
Hare Disc	Hare on Discovery of Evidence [*A publication*] (DLA)
Hare Elec	Hare on Elections [*A publication*] (DLA)
Hare (Eng)	Hare's English Vice-Chancellors' Reports [*66-68 English Reprint*] [*1841-53*] [*A publication*] (DLA)
Hare Ev	Hare on Discovery of Evidence [*A publication*] (DLA)
HAREM	Heparin Assay Rapid Easy Method [*Medicine*] (DMAA)
HARES	High Altitude Radiation Environment Study [*FAA*] (PDAA)
HARF	Holland Australia Retirement Foundation of Victoria [*Australia*]
Harg	Hargrave's State Trials [*A publication*] (DLA)
Harg	Hargrove's Reports [*68-75 North Carolina*] [*A publication*] (DLA)
HARG	Harper Group [*NASDAQ symbol*] (TTSB)
HARG	Harper Group, Inc. [*NASDAQ symbol*] (NQ)
HARG	High-Speed Autoradiography
Harg & B Co Litt	Hargrave and Butler's Edition on Coke upon Littleton [*A publication*] (DLA)
Harg Co Litt	Hargrave's Notes to Coke on Littleton [*A publication*] (DLA)
Harg Coll Jur	Hargrave's Collectanea Juridica [*1791-92*] [*A publication*] (DLA)
Harg Exer	Hargrave's Jurisconsult Exercitations [*A publication*] (DLA)
Harg Jur Arg	Hargrave's Juridical Arguments and Collections [*A publication*] (DLA)
Harg Law Tracts	Hargrave's Law Tracts [*A publication*] (DLA)
Harg LT	Hargrave's Law Tracts [*A publication*] (DLA)
Hargrave & Butlers Notes on Co Litt	Hargrave and Butler's Notes on Coke upon Littleton [*A publication*] (DLA)
Hargr Co Litt	Hargrave's Notes to Coke on Littleton [*A publication*] (DLA)
Hargrove	Hargrove's Reports [*68-75 North Carolina*] [*A publication*] (DLA)
Harg State Tr	Hargrave's State Trials [*A publication*] (DLA)
Harg St Tr	Hargrave's State Trials [*A publication*] (DLA)
Harg Th	Hargrave on the Thellusson Act [*A publication*] (DLA)
HARH	High-Altitude Retinal Hemorrhage [*Medicine*]
Hari Rao	Indian Income Tax Decisions [*A publication*] (DLA)
HARIS	High-Altitude Radiological Instrumentation System
HarisHa	Harris & Harris Group [*Associated Press*] (SAG)
HarisSvg	Harris Savings Bank [*Associated Press*] (SAG)
Haristn	Hariston Corp. [*Associated Press*] (SAG)
Har Just	Harris' Justinian [*A publication*] (DLA)
HARK	Hardened Reentry Kill [*Air Force*]
Harken	Harken Energy Corp. [*Associated Press*] (SAG)
HARL	Harleysville Savings Association [*NASDAQ symbol*] (NQ)
HARL	Harleysville Savings Bank [*NASDAQ symbol*] (TTSB)
Harland	Manchester Court Leet Records [*A publication*] (DLA)
HARL CBM	Harleian Collection, British Museum (DLA)
HarleyD	Harley Davidson, Inc. [*Associated Press*] (SAG)
Harleys	Harleysville Group, Inc. [*Associated Press*] (SAG)
HARL MISC	Harleian Miscellany [*British*] (ROG)
HARL MSS	Harleian Manuscripts [*British*] (ROG)
Harlnd	Harland [*John H.*] Co. [*Associated Press*] (SAG)
HARLOT	Height [*Depth*] of Burst, Altitude of Targets, Resources, Location, Objectives, and Time [*Nuclear war games*]
HARLS	Horse Antiserum to Rabbit Lymphocytes [*Immunology*]
Harlyn	Harlyn Products, Inc. [*Associated Press*] (SAG)
HarlyNat	Harleysville National Corp. [*Associated Press*] (SAG)
HarlySV	Harleysville Savings Association [*Associated Press*] (SAG)
HARM	Harmonic (WDAA)
Harm	Harmonica [*of Ptolemy*] [*Classical studies*] (OCD)
Harm	Harmon's Reports [*13-15 California*] [*A publication*] (DLA)
Harm	Harmon's Upper Canada Common Pleas Reports [*A publication*] (DLA)
HARM	Harmony
HARM	Hazardous Atmospheric Release Model [*Marine science*] (OSRA)
HARM	Hazardous Atmospheric Release Model (USDC)
HARM	Heparin Assay Rapid Method (DMAA)
HARM	High-Acceleration Rocket-Missile
HARM	High-Speed Anti-RADAR Missile
HARM	Hypervelocity Antiradiation Missile (MCD)
Harma	Harmannus [*Authority cited in pre-1607 legal work*] (DSA)
Harman	Harman International Industries, Inc. [*Associated Press*] (SAG)
HarmBrk	Harmony Brook, Inc. [*Associated Press*] (SAG)
HarmLgt	Harmonic Lightwaves, Inc. [*Associated Press*] (SAG)
HarmLt	Harmonic Lghtwaves, Inc. [*Associated Press*] (SAG)
Harmon	Harmon Industries, Inc. [*Associated Press*] (SAG)
Harmon	Harmon's Upper Canada Common Pleas Reports [*A publication*] (DLA)
HarmPd	Harmony Products, Inc. [*Associated Press*] (SAG)
Harm Pens	Harmon's Manual of United States Pension Laws [*A publication*] (DLA)
HARN	Harness (MSA)
HARN	Harness
HARN	High Accuracy Reference Network [*Mathematics*]
HARNET	[*The*] Hong Kong Academic and Research Network [*Computer science*] (TNIG)
HARNG	Hawaii Army National Guard (CINC)
Harnish	Harnischfeger Industries, Inc. [*Associated Press*] (SAG)
Harold	Harold's Stores, Inc. [*Associated Press*] (SAG)
HAROTS	High-Accuracy RADAR Data Transmission System
HARP	Halpern's AntiRADAR Point
Harp	Harper's South Carolina Equity Reports [*A publication*] (DLA)
Harp	Harper's South Carolina Law Reports [*1823-30*] [*A publication*] (DLA)
Harp	Harpocration [*Classical studies*] (OCD)
HARP	Harpoon (WDAA)

HARP .... Harpsichord (WDAA)
HARP .... Hazard Assessment of Rocket Propellants
HARP .... Heater above Reheat Point (DNAB)
HARP .... Heating, Air Conditioning, Refrigeration, Plumbing (ADA)
HARP .... Heimlich-Armstrong-Rieveschl-Patrick [*Heart pump for aerospace use*]
HARP .... High-Altitude Reconnaissance Platform
HARP .... High-Altitude Relay Point
HARP .... High-Altitude Research Probe (IAA)
HARP .... High-Altitude Research Program [*or Project*] [*Military*]
HARP .... High-Altitude Rocket Probe [*Army*]
HARP .... Hitachi Arithmetic Processor [*Computer science*] (IEEE)
HARP .... Holding and Reconsignment Point (IAA)
HARP .... Homeless and At-Risk Population (DMAA)
HARP .... Hybrid Automated Reliability Predictor
Harp Con Cas... Harper's Conspiracy Cases [*Maryland*] [*A publication*] (DLA)
Har Pen Man... Harmon's Manual of United States Pension Laws [*A publication*] (DLA)
Harp Eq ...... Harper's South Carolina Equity Reports [*A publication*] (DLA)
Harp Eq (SC)... Harper's South Carolina Equity Reports [*A publication*] (DLA)
Harper .... Harper's Conspiracy Cases [*Maryland*] [*A publication*] (DLA)
Harper .... Harper's South Carolina Equity Reports [*A publication*] (DLA)
Harper .... Harper's South Carolina Law Reports [*1823-30*] [*A publication*] (DLA)
HarpGp .... Harper Group, Inc. [*Associated Press*] (SAG)
HARPI .... Hardpoint Interceptor
Harp L .... Harper's South Carolina Law Reports [*1823-30*] [*A publication*] (DLA)
Harp L (SC).. Harper's South Carolina Law Reports [*1823-30*] [*A publication*] (DLA)
HARPPS....... Heat, Absence of Use, Redness, Pain, Pus, Swelling [*Medicine*] (MEDA)
Har Prob ...... Harrison on Probate and Divorce [*A publication*] (DLA)
HARPS......... Hybrid AUTODIN Red Patch System (MCD)
HARPY .... Hydrofoil Advanced Research Study Program [*Navy*]
Harr .... Harrington's Delaware Reports [*1-5 Delaware*] [*A publication*] (DLA)
Harr .... Harrington's Michigan Chancery Reports [*A publication*] (DLA)
Harr .... Harrison's Law Reports [*16-19 New Jersey*] [*A publication*] (DLA)
Harr .... Harrison's Reports [*15-17, 23-29 Indiana*] [*A publication*] (DLA)
Harr .... Harris' Reports [*A publication*] (DLA)
Harr Adv ...... Harris' Hints on Advocacy [*18th ed.*] [*1943*] [*A publication*] (DLA)
HarrahE .... Harrahs Entertainment, Inc. [*Associated Press*] (SAG)
Harr & Cl Conv... Harris and Clarkson on Conveyancing, Etc. [*A publication*] (DLA)
Harr & G ...... Harris and Gill's Maryland Reports [*A publication*] (DLA)
Harr & H....... Harrison and Hodgin's Upper Canada Municipal Reports [*1845-51*] [*A publication*] (DLA)
Harr & Hodg... Harrison and Hodgin's Upper Canada Municipal Reports [*1845-51*] [*A publication*] (DLA)
Harr & J ...... Harris and Johnson's Maryland Reports [*A publication*] (DLA)
Harr & J (MD)... Harris and Johnson's Maryland Reports [*A publication*] (DLA)
Harr & M ..... Harris and McHenry's Maryland Reports [*A publication*] (DLA)
Harr & McH.. Harris and McHenry's Maryland Reports [*A publication*] (DLA)
Harr & McHen... Harris and McHenry's Maryland Reports [*A publication*] (DLA)
Harr & McH (MD)... Harris and McHenry's Maryland Reports [*A publication*] (DLA)
Harr & M'H... Harris and McHenry's Maryland Reports [*A publication*] (DLA)
Harr & R...... Harrison and Rutherford's English Common Pleas Reports [*1865-66*] [*A publication*] (DLA)
Harr & Ruth... Harrison and Rutherford's English Common Pleas Reports [*1865-66*] [*A publication*] (DLA)
Harr & Sim... Harris and Simrall's Reports [*49-52 Mississippi*] [*A publication*] (DLA)
Harr & W..... Harrison and Wollaston's English King's Bench Reports [*A publication*] (DLA)
Harr & W (Eng).. Harrison and Wollaston's English King's Bench Reports [*A publication*] (DLA)
Harr & Woll... Harrison and Wollaston's English King's Bench Reports [*A publication*] (DLA)
Harr Ch........ Harrington's Michigan Chancery Reports [*A publication*] (DLA)
Harr Ch (Mich)... Harrington's Michigan Chancery Reports [*A publication*] (DLA)
Harr Ch R .... Harrington's Michigan Chancery Reports [*A publication*] (DLA)
Harr Con LA R... Harrison's Condensed Louisiana Reports [*A publication*] (DLA)
Harr Cr L ..... Harris' Principles of the Criminal Law [*22nd ed.*] [*1973*] [*A publication*] (DLA)
Harr (Del)... Harrington's Delaware Reports [*1-5 Delaware*] [*A publication*] (DLA)
Harr Dig ...... Harrison's Digest of English Common Law Reports [*A publication*] (DLA)
Har Resp ..... De Haruspicum Responso [*of Cicero*] [*Classical studies*] (OCD)
Harr (GA).... Harris' Georgia Digest [*A publication*] (DLA)
Harr Hints.... Harris' Hints on Advocacy [*18th ed.*] [*1943*] [*A publication*] (DLA)
Harring .... Harrington's Delaware Reports [*1-5 Delaware*] [*A publication*] (DLA)
Harring .... Harrington's Michigan Chancery Reports [*A publication*] (DLA)
Harring Ch (Mich)... Harrington's Michigan Chancery Reports [*A publication*] (DLA)
Harrington ... Harrington's Delaware Supreme Court Reports [*1832-55*] [*A publication*] (DLA)
Harrington ... Harrington's Michigan Chancery Reports [*A publication*] (DLA)
Harris .... Harris Corp. [*Associated Press*] (SAG)
Harris .... Harris' Reports [*A publication*] (DLA)
Harris & G... Harris and Gill's Maryland Reports [*A publication*] (DLA)
Harris & Gill's MD R... Harris and Gill's Maryland Reports [*A publication*] (DLA)
Harris & J .... Harris and Johnson's Maryland Reports [*A publication*] (DLA)
Harris & S ... Harris and Simrall's Reports [*49-52 Mississippi*] [*A publication*] (DLA)
Harris & Sim... Harris and Simrall's Reports [*49-52 Mississippi*] [*A publication*] (DLA)
Harris & Simrall... Harris and Simrall's Reports [*49-52 Mississippi*] [*A publication*] (DLA)
HarrisCS ...... Harris Computer Systems Corp. [*Associated Press*] (SAG)
Harris Dig.... Harris' Georgia Digest [*A publication*] (DLA)

Harrison ...... Harrison's Law Reports [*16-19 New Jersey*] [*A publication*] (DLA)
Harrison ..... Harrison's Reports [*15-17, 23-29 Indiana*] [*A publication*] (DLA)
Harrison Ch.. Harrison's Chancery Practice [*A publication*] (DLA)
Harrison Dig... Harrison's Digest of English Common Law Reports [*A publication*]
Harr Just ..... Harris' Translation of the Institute of Justinian [*A publication*]
Harr (Mich)... Harrington's Michigan Chancery Reports [*A publication*] (DLA)
Harr Min ..... Harris on Titles to Mines [*A publication*] (DLA)
Harr Mun Law... Harrison's Municipal Law of Ontario [*A publication*] (DLA)
Harr NJ....... Harrison's Law Reports [*16-19 New Jersey*] [*A publication*] (DLA)
Harrod .... Harrodsburg First Financial Bancorp, Inc. [*Associated Press*] (SAG)
Harr Prin ..... Harris' Principiae Primae Legum [*A publication*] (DLA)
Harr Proc..... Harrison's Common Law Procedure Act [*Canada*] [*A publication*] (DLA)
Harr Rom Law... Harris' Elements of Roman Law [*A publication*] (DLA)
HARRS......... High-Altitude Radio Relay System (DNAB)
HARS .... Harris Savings Bank [*NASDAQ symbol*] (SAG)
HARS .... Harris Savings Bank [*NASDAQ symbol*] (TTSB)
HARS .... Hazardous Area Reporting Service [*Aviation*] (FAAC)
HARS .... Heading Attitude Reference System (MCD)
HARS .... Heavy Assault Rocket System (MCD)
HARS .... Helicopter Attitude Reference System (MCD)
HARS .... High Altitude Route System [*FAA*] (TAG)
HARS .... Historic Aircraft Restoration Society [*Australia*]
HARSAP....... Harbor Survey Assistance Program [*Naval Oceanographic Office*]
Harsco .... Harsco Corp. [*Associated Press*] (SAG)
Hars Pr....... Harston's California Practice and Pleading [*A publication*] (DLA)
Har St Tr ..... Hargrave's State Trials [*A publication*] (DLA)
HART .... Halt All Racist Tours [*British*] (DI)
HART .... Hardened Amplifier for Radiation Transients
Hart .... Hartley's Digest of Texas Laws [*A publication*] (DLA)
Hart .... Hartley's Reports [*4-10 Texas*] [*A publication*] (DLA)
HART .... Hayden Analysis and Reporting Tool [*Computer science*]
HART .... Heartland Wireless Commun [*NASDAQ symbol*] (TTSB)
HART .... Heartland Wireless Communications, Inc. [*NASDAQ symbol*] (SAG)
HART .... Heparin-Aspirin Reinfarction Trial [*Medicine*] (DMAA)
HART .... Heparin-Aspirin Reperfusion Trial [*Cardiology*]
HART .... High-Acceleration Rocket, Tactical (DNAB)
HART .... Highway Aid by Radio Truck (IAA)
HART .... Hospital Access and Response Terminal [*Health insurance*] (GHCT)
HART .... Hypervelocity Aircraft Rocket, Tactical
Hart & H..... Hartley and Hartley's Reports [*11-21 Texas*] [*A publication*] (DLA)
Hart Bank .... Hart's Bankrupt Law and Practice [*A publication*] (DLA)
HartC .... Hartford Capital I [*Associated Press*] (SAG)
HartC .... Hartford Capital II [*Associated Press*] (SAG)
Hart Dig ...... Hartley's Digest of Texas Laws [*A publication*] (DLA)
Hart Hartm... Hartmannus Hartmanni [*Deceased, 1586*] [*Authority cited in pre-1607 legal work*] (DSA)
HartHnk .... Harte Hanks Communications [*Associated Press*] (SAG)
Hartley........ Hartley's Reports [*4-10 Texas*] [*A publication*] (DLA)
Hartley & Hartley... Hartley and Hartley's Reports [*11-21 Texas*] [*A publication*] (DLA)
Hartley & Hartley Rep... Hartley and Hartley's Reports [*11-21 Texas*] [*A publication*] (DLA)
Hartman Pist... Hartmannus Pistoris [*Deceased, 1601*] [*Authority cited in pre-1607 legal work*] (DSA)
Hartm Pistor... Hartmannus Pistoris [*Deceased, 1601*] [*Authority cited in pre-1607 legal work*] (DSA)
Hartmx......... Hartmarx Corp. [*Associated Press*] (SAG)
Hart Pist...... Hartmannus Pistoris [*Deceased, 1601*] [*Authority cited in pre-1607 legal work*] (DSA)
HARTRAN .... Hardwell FORTRAN [*Computer science*] (IEEE)
HARTS .... Hardening Technology Studies Program (MCD)
HARU......... Handbuch fuer Rundfunk und Fernsehen [*Handbook for Radio and Television*] [*NOMOS Datapool Database*]
HARV .... Harassment Vehicle (MCD)
HARV .... Harvard University [*Massachusetts*]
Harv........... Harvard Vocarium [*Record label*]
HARV .... Harvest
HARV .... Harvey Universal, Inc. [*NASDAQ symbol*] (SAG)
HARVAN ...... Harriman and Vance [*Code name for 1968 Paris peace talks on Vietnam, derived from the surnames of US negotiators W. Averell Harriman and Cyrus R. Vance*]
HARV and MARV... Harvey Ratner and Marvin Wolfenson [*Proprietors of Target Centre basketball arena*] (ECON)
Harvard U .... Harvard University (GAGS)
Harv Bus World... Harvard Business World (DLA)
HarvCas....... Harveys Casinos Resorts [*Associated Press*] (SAG)
Harv CR CL Law Rev... Harvard Civil Rights - Civil Liberties Law Review [*A publication*] (ILCA)
Harv Ed Rev... Harvard Educational Review [*A publication*] (DLA)
Harv Env L Rev... Harvard Environmental Law Review [*A publication*] (DLA)
HARVEST ..... Highly Active Residues Vitrification and Engineered Storage [*Nuclear energy British*] (NUCP)
HARVEST..... Highly Active Residues Vitrification Engineering Studies [*Nuclear energy British*] (NUCP)
HarvestH...... Harvest Home Financial Corp. [*Associated Press*] (SAG)
HarveyE....... Harvey Entertainment Co. [*Associated Press*] (SAG)
HarveyU....... Harvey Universal, Inc. [*Associated Press*] (SAG)
HarvI.......... Harvard Industries, Inc. [*Associated Press*] (SAG)
HarvInd........ Harvard Industries, Inc. [*Associated Press*] (SAG)
Harv Int'l L Club Bull... Harvard International Law Club. Bulletin [*A publication*] (DLA)
Harv Int'l L Club J... Harvard International Law Club. Journal [*A publication*] (DLA)

Harv L Lib Inf Bull... Harvard Law Library. Information Bulletin [*A publication*] (DLA)
Harv LS Rec... Harvard Law School. Record [*A publication*] (DLA)
HarvstFn Harvest Financial Corp. [*Associated Press*] (SAG)
Harv Stud .... Harvard Studies in Classical Philology [*A publication*] (OCD)
Harv Women's LJ... Harvard Women's Law Journal [*A publication*] (DLA)
Harv W Tax Ser... Harvard World Tax Series [*A publication*] (DLA)
HARVY Harvard Securities Group PLC (MHDW)
HARW Harwich [*Municipal borough in England*]
HARWAS Horizontal-Axis Rotating-Wing Aeronautical System (PDAA)
HARY Harry's Farmers Market [*NASDAQ symbol*] (TTSB)
HARY Harry's Farmers Markets [*NASDAQ symbol*] (SAG)
HaryFar Harry's Farmers Markets [*Associated Press*] (SAG)
HARYOU-ACT... Harlem Youth Opportunities Unlimited - Associated Community Teams [*A kind of Peace Corps for Harlem area of New York City*]
HAS Hail [*Saudi Arabia*] [*Airport symbol*] (OAG)
HAS Hamburg Airlines, GmbH [*Germany ICAO designator*] (FAAC)
HAS Harassment Vehicle [*Military*]
HAS Hardened Aircraft Shelter [*British military*] (DMA)
HAS Hasbro, Inc. [*AMEX symbol*] (SPSG)
HAS Hastings [*New Zealand*] [*Seismograph station code, US Geological Survey Closed*] (SEIS)
HAS Heading Altitude Sensor (IAA)
HAS Heading Altitude System
HAS Health Advocacy Services [*AARP*]
HAS Helical Antenna System
HAS Helicopter Anti-Submarine
HAS Helicopter Avionics System [*Air Force*]
HAS Hellenic Affiliation Scale [*Psychology*]
HAS High-Altitude Sampler
HAS High-Angle Strafe
HAS Highest Asymptomatic [*Dose*] [*Medicine*]
HAS Highest Average Salary
HAS Holddown Alignment Support (NASA)
HAS Holograph Assessment System
HAS Horatio Alger Society (EA)
HAS Hospital Adjustment Scale [*Psychology*]
HAS Hospital Administrative Services
HAS Hospital Advisory Service [*British*]
HAS Hover Augmentation System
HAS Human Albumin Solution [*Clinical chemistry*]
HAS Hydraulic Actuation System (MCD)
HAS Hydraulic Adjustable Speed
HAS Hydrogen Actuation System (NASA)
HAS Hydroxy-Aluminosilicate [*Inorganic chemistry*]
HAS Hydroxylamine Acid Sulfate [*Inorganic chemistry*]
HAS Hydroxylammonium Sulfate [*Inorganic chemistry*]
HAS Hyperalimentation Solution [*Pharmacology*] (DAVI)
HAS Hypertensive Arteriosclerotic [*Cardiology*]
HAS Hypoxanthine and Azaserine [*Medium*]
HASAWA Health and Safety at Work Act [*1974*] [*British*] (NUCP)
HASB Assab [*Ethiopia*] [*ICAO location identifier*] (ICLI)
Hasb Hasbrouck's Reports [*Idaho*] [*A publication*] (DLA)
Hasbro Hasbro, Inc. [*Associated Press*] (SAG)
HASC Headquarters, Air Service Command [*Air Force*]
HASC Historical Automobile Society of Canada
HASC Hospitality Association of South Carolina (SRA)
HASC House Armed Services Committee [*US Congress*] (AABC)
HASC Hyderabad Army Service Corps [*British military*] (DMA)
HASCI Human Applications Standard Computer Interface [*Keyboard*] (MCD)
HASCO Haitian-American Sugar Co.
HASCO HAWK [*Homing All the Way Killer*] Assembly System Checkout (SAA)
HASCVD Hypertensive Arteriosclerotic Cardiovascular Disease [*Cardiology*] (MAE)
HASD Sodo [*Ethiopia*] [*ICAO location identifier*] (ICLI)
HASE Head Angulation Sighting Equipment [*British military*] (DMA)
HASE Hydrophobic Alkali Soluble Emulsion [*Paint technology*]
haSH Human Achaete-Scute Homologue [*Genetics*]
HASH Sheik Hussein [*Ethiopia*] [*ICAO location identifier*] (ICLI)
HASINS High Accuracy Submersible Inertial Navigation System (PDAA)
HASIS House Armed Services Investigation Subcommittee [*US Congress*]
HASJPL H. Allen Smith Jet Propulsion Laboratory [*Former name, JPL, continues to be used as official name*] [*Name adopted in 1973 to honor retiring congressman*]
Hask Haskell's Reports for United States Courts in Maine (Fox's Decisions) [*A publication*] (DLA)
Haskel Haskel International, Inc. [*Associated Press*] (SAG)
HASL Health and Safety Laboratory [*ERDA*]
HASL Hertfordshire Association of Special Libraries [*British*] (NITA)
HASL Hot-Air Solder Leveling [*Materials science*]
Hasl Med Jur Haslam's Medical Jurisprudence [*A publication*] (DLA)
HASO Assosa [*Ethiopia*] [*ICAO location identifier*] (ICLI)
HAsP Health Aspects of Pesticides [*Medicine*] (DMAA)
HASP High Altitude Sampling Plane
HASP High-Altitude Sampling Program [*Air Force*]
HASP High-Altitude Sounding Program (IAA)
HASP High-Altitude Sounding Projectile
HASP High-Altitude Space Platform
HASP High-Altitude Space Probe (IAA)
HASP High-Level Automatic Scheduling Program (BUR)
HASP Hospital Admission and Surveillance Program (MEDA)
HASP Houston Automatic Spooling Priority System [*Computer science*]

HASP Houston Automatic Spooling Processor [*IBM equipment operating system*] (NITA)
HASPA High-Altitude Superpressure Powered Aerostat [*Navy*]
HASPID House Armed Services Permanent Investigations Subcommittee [*US Congress*] (AAG)
HASPS Hardened Array Solar Power System [*Military*]
HASQ Hardware-Assisted Software Queue
HASR High-Altitude Sounding Rocket
HASRD Health and Safety Research Division [*Oak Ridge National Laboratory*]
HASSS High-Accuracy Spacecraft Separation System (IAA)
Hast Hastings' Reports [*69, 70 Maine*] [*A publication*] (DLA)
HAST High-Altitude Selection Test [*British military*] (DMA)
HAST High-Altitude Supersonic Target [*Later, HAHST*] (MCD)
HASTAM Health and Safety Technology Management (AIE)
Hast Cen R... Hastings Center Report [*A publication*] (BRI)
HASTE Hazard Assessment System for Toxic Emissions [*Computer-based emergency management system*] [*Environmental Research & Technology*]
HASTE Helicopter Assault Survivability in a Threat Environment (MCD)
HASTI High-Altitude Strike Indicator
Hasting Hastings Manufacturing Co. [*Associated Press*] (SAG)
Hastings C Law... University of California Hastings College of Law (GAGS)
Hast Int & Comp L Rev... Hastings' International and Comparative Law Review [*A publication*] (DLA)
Hast Tr Trial of Warren Hastings [*A publication*] (DLA)
HASVR High-Altitude Space Velocity RADAR (AAG)
HASWA Health and Safety at Work Act [*British*]
HAT Handbuch zum Alten Testament [*A publication*] (BJA)
HAT Handover Transmitter (IAA)
HAT Harbour Acceptance Trials [*Missile*] [*British*]
HAT Hardened and Tempered (IAA)
HAT Hardness Assurance Test
HAT Harmonic Attenuation Table [*or Test*] (DAVI)
Hat Hatran (BJA)
HAT Hatteras Income Sec [*NYSE symbol*] (TTSB)
HAT Hatteras Income Securities, Inc. [*NYSE symbol*] (SPSG)
HAT Hatteras, NC [*Location identifier FAA*] (FAAL)
HAT Hawaiian Archives for Tsunamis
HAT Head, Arms, and Trunk [*Anatomy*] (DAVI)
HAT Heathlands [*Australia Airport symbol Obsolete*] (OAG)
HAT Heavy Artillery Tractor [*British military*] (DMA)
HAT Height above Runway Touchdown Zone Elevation [*Aviation*]
HAT Height above Terrain
HAT Height Above Touchdown (PDAA)
HAT Helicopter Acquisition Test (MCD)
HAT High-Altitude Target
HAT High Altitude Temperature (PDAA)
HAT High-Altitude Temperature Rocket
HAT High-Altitude Testing [*Sounding rocket*]
HAT High-Altitude Transmitter
HAT High-Angle Threat
HAT Highest Astronomical Tide
HAT Highly Aphid Transmissible [*Plant pathology*]
HAT Histone Acetyltransferase [*An enzyme*]
HAT History Advertising Trust [*British*] (DBA)
HAT Home Area Toll [*Telecommunications*] (TEL)
HAT Horizontal Alidade Tie
HAT Hospital Alliance of Tennessee (SRA)
HAT Housing Action Trust [*British*] (ECON)
HAT Hug-a-Tree and Survive (EA)
HAT Hypoxanthine-Aminopterin-Thymidine [*Medium*] [*Biochemistry*]
HATACS Helicopter Air-to-Air Combat Simulation (MCD)
HATCDS High-Altitude Terrain Contour Data Sensor (MSA)
Hatcher's Kan Dig... Hatcher's Kansas Digest [*A publication*] (DLA)
HATF Hydraulic Actuator Test Fixture
HATFPEV Hatfield Peverel [*England*]
HATG Horse Anti-Human Thymocyte Globulin [*Immunology*] (AAMN)
HATH Hathaway Corp. [*NASDAQ symbol*] (NQ)
HATH Heterosexual Attitudes toward Homosexuality [*Scale*]
Hathwy Hathaway Corp. [*Associated Press*] (SAG)
HAT/LANT Habitability Assistance Team/Atlantic (DNAB)
HATLS Hostile Artillery Positions (RDA)
HATO Handling Tool (AAG)
HATO Tendaho [*Ethiopia*] [*ICAO location identifier*] (ICLI)
HATOFF Highest Astronomical Tide of the Foreseeable Future (PDAA)
HATOL Horizontal Altitude Take-Off and Landing (PDAA)
HATOM Highest Astronomical Tide of the Month (PDAA)
HATOY Highest Astronomical Tide of the Year (PDAA)
HATP Tippi [*Ethiopia*] [*ICAO location identifier*] (ICLI)
HAT/PAC Habitability Assistance Team/Pacific (DNAB)
HATR Hazardous Air Traffic Report
HATR Horizontal Attenuated Total Reflection [*Spectroscopy*]
HATRA Hosiery and Allied Trades Research Association [*British*] (BI)
HATRAC Handover Transfer and Receiver Accept Change [*SAGE*]
HATREMS Hazardous and Trace Emissions System [*Environmental Protection Agency*]
HATRICS Hampshire Technical Research Industrial and Commercial Service [*British*] (NITA)
HATRON Heavy Attack Squadron (MUGU)
HATS Hardened Tactical Shelters
Hats Hatsell's Parliamentary Precedents [*1290-1818*] [*A publication*] (DLA)
HATS Head and Torso Simulator [*A dummy developed by British Telecommunications Ltd.*]
HATS Heading, Altitude, True Airspeed [*Aviation*] (CAAL)

HATS .... Helicopter Advanced Tactical System (MCD)
HATS .... Helicopter Attack System
HATS .... Helmut Attitude Tracking System (MCD)
HATS .... Heuristic Automated Transportation System (MCD)
HATS .... High-Accuracy Targeting Subsystem
HATS .... High-Altitude Terrain Contour Data Sensor
HATS .... High-Altitude Test Stand
HATS .... Holden's Air Transport Services [Australia]
HATS .... Hour Angle of the True Sun [Navigation]
HATS .... Huntsville Association of Technical Societies
Hats .... Tessenei [Ethiopia] [ICAO location identifier] (ICLI)
Hats Pr .... Hatsell's Parliamentary Precedents [1290-1818] [A publication] (DLA)
Hats Prec ..... Hatsell's Parliamentary Precedents [1290-1818] [A publication] (DLA)
Hatt .... Hattusilis (BJA)
HATT .... Heparin-Associated Thrombocytopenia and Thrombosis [Medicine]
               (DMAA)
HATTS .... Hemagglutination Treponemal Test for Syphilis [Medicine] (DMAA)
HattSe .... Hatteras Income Securities, Inc. [Associated Press] (SAG)
HATU .... Heavy Air Training Unit
HATU .... Heavy Attack Training Unit
HATV .... High-Altitude Test Vehicle
HATWING .... Heavy Attack Wing
HATWINGLANT... Heavy Attack Wing, Atlantic Fleet
HATWINGPAC... Heavy Attack Wing, Pacific Fleet
HAU .... Haudompre [France] [Seismograph station code, US Geological
               Survey] (SEIS)
HAU .... Haugesund [Norway] [Airport symbol] (OAG)
HAU .... Haultain Resources Ltd. [Vancouver Stock Exchange symbol]
hau .... Hausa [MARC language code Library of Congress] (LCCP)
HAU .... Hebrew Actors Union (EA)
HAU .... Helena, MT [Location identifier FAA] (FAAL)
HAU .... Hemagglutination Unit [Hematology]
HAU .... Horizontal Arithmetic Unit
HAU .... Hybrid Arithmetic Unit
HAUL .... Allied Holdings [NASDAQ symbol] (TTSB)
HAUL .... Allied Holdings, Inc. [NASDAQ symbol] (SAG)
HAUP .... Hauppauge Digital [NASDAQ symbol] (TTSB)
HAUP .... Hauppauge Digital, Inc. [NASDAQ symbol] (SAG)
HaupD .... Hauppauge Digital, Inc. [Associated Press] (SAG)
HaupgD .... Hauppauge Digital, Inc. [Associated Press] (SAG)
HAUPTW .... Hauptwerk [Masterpiece] [German]
HAUPW .... Hauppague Digital Wrrt'A' [NASDAQ symbol] (TTSB)
HAURIEND ...... Hauriendus [To Be Drunk] [Pharmacy] (ROG)
HAUS .... Hauser Chemical Research [NASDAQ symbol] (TTSB)
HAUS .... Hauser Chemical Research, Inc. [NASDAQ symbol] (SAG)
HAUSch .... Hauser, Inc. [NASDAQ symbol] (SAG)
HausCh .... Hauser Chemical Research, Inc. [Associated Press] (SAG)
Hauser .... Hauser, Inc. [Associated Press] (SAG)
HAUST .... Haustus [A Drink] [Pharmacy]
HAUST PURG... Haustus Purgans [Purging Draught] [Pharmacy] (ROG)
HAUT .... Hautboy [Oboe]
Haut .... Heautontimorumenos [of Terence] [Classical studies] (OCD)
HAV .... Hallux Abducto Valgus [Orthopedics] (DAVI)
HAV .... Havana [Cuba] [Airport symbol] (OAG)
HAV .... Havering [Borough in England]
HAV .... Haversine [Mathematics]
HAV .... Havilah [California] [Seismograph station code, US Geological
               Survey Closed] (SEIS)
Hav .... Haviland's Prince Edward Island Chancery Reports, by Peters
               [1850-72] [Canada] [A publication] (DLA)
Hav .... Havildar [British military] (DMA)
HAV .... Heavily Armed Vessels
HAV .... Hepatitis A Virus
HAV .... High-Accuracy Voltmeter
HAV .... Hilprecht Anniversary Volume. Studies in Assyriology and
               Archaeology Dedicated to Hermann V. Hilprecht [Leipzig]
               [A publication] (BJA)
HAV .... Hot Air Vulcanization
HAV .... Hypovirulence-Associated Virus
HAVA .... Harvard Industries [NASDAQ symbol] (TTSB)
HAVA .... Harvard Industries, Inc. [NASDAQ symbol] (NQ)
HAVAg .... Hepatitis A Virus Antigen [Immunochemistry]
HAVC .... Health Audiovisual On-Line Catalog [Northeastern Ohio Universities]
               [Information service or system Defunct]
Hav Ch Rep... Haviland's Prince Edward Island Chancery Reports [1850-72]
               [A publication] (DLA)
HAVCO .... Have Complied
HAVE .... Heating and Ventilation Estimating [Tipdata Ltd.] [Software
               package] (NCC)
HAVE .... Height Average (IAA)
HAVE .... Homemaking and Volunteer Experience (DICI)
HAVEN .... Haven [Commonly used] (OPSA)
HAVEN .... Help Addicts Voluntarily End Narcotics
HavenB .... Haven Bancorp [Associated Press] (SAG)
Haverty .... Haverty Furniture Companies, Inc. [Associated Press] (SAG)
Havil .... Haviland's Prince Edward Island Reports [A publication] (DLA)
Hav-Maj .... Havildar-Major [British military] (DMA)
HAVN .... Haven [Commonly used] (OPSA)
HAVN .... Haven Bancorp [NASDAQ symbol] (SAG)
HAVO .... Hawaii Volcanoes National Park
HAVOC .... Histogram Average Ogive Calculator
Hav PEI....... Haviland's Prince Edward Island Reports [A publication] (DLA)
HAVREP .... Abridged Arrival Report [Navy] (NVT)
HAVREP .... Have Report [Navy] (ANA)
Havrfld........ Haverfield Corp. [Associated Press] (SAG)

Havrty .... Haverty Furniture Companies, Inc. [Associated Press] (SAG)
HAVS .... Harpoon Asset Visibility System (MCD)
HAVT .... Hardness Assurance Verification Testing (MCD)
HAVT .... Haverty Furniture [NASDAQ symbol] (TTSB)
HAVT .... Haverty Furniture Companies, Inc. [NASDAQ symbol] (NQ)
HAVTA .... Haverty Furniture'A' [NASDAQ symbol] (TTSB)
HAW .... Fargo, ND [Location identifier FAA] (FAAL)
HAW .... Hafnium Column Waste [Nuclear energy] (NRCH)
HAW .... Hawaii (KSC)
haw .... Hawaiian [MARC language code Library of Congress] (LCCP)
Haw .... Hawaii Supreme Court Reports [A publication] (DLA)
Haw .... Hawarde's Star Chamber Cases [A publication] (DLA)
Haw .... Hawkins' Annual Reports [19-24 Louisiana] [A publication] (DLA)
Haw .... Hawkins' Pleas of the Crown [England] [A publication] (DLA)
HAW .... Hawksbill Resources, Inc. [Vancouver Stock Exchange symbol]
Haw .... Hawley's Reports [10-20 Nevada] [A publication] (DLA)
HAW .... Heavy Antiarmor Weapon
HAW .... Heavy Antitank Weapon (INF)
HAW .... Heavy Assault Weapon
HAW .... Helicopter Assault Wave
HAW .... High-Acid Waste [Nuclear energy] (NRCH)
HAW .... High Active Waste [Nuclear energy]
HAW .... Highly Active Waste
HAW .... Holidays and Anniversaries of the World [A publication]
HAW .... Home All the Way [Military] (CAAL)
HAW .... Hypersonic Aerodynamic Weapon (DOMA)
HAWA .... Hawaii
Hawaii .... Hawaii Reports [A publication] (DLA)
Hawaiian Rep... Hawaii Reports [A publication] (DLA)
Hawaii BN ..... Hawaii Bar News [A publication] (DLA)
Hawaii Dist... United States District Court, District of Hawaii (DLA)
Hawaii PUC Dec... Hawaii Public Utilities Commission Decisions [A publication]
               (DLA)
Hawaii Rep... Hawaii Reports [A publication] (DLA)
Hawaii Rev Stat... Hawaii Revised Statutes [A publication] (DLA)
Hawaii Rules & Reg... Hawaii Rules and Regulations [A publication] (DLA)
Hawaii Sess Laws... Session Laws of Hawaii [A publication] (DLA)
HawAir .... Hawaiian Airlines, Inc. [Associated Press] (SAG)
Hawarde .... Hawarde's Star Chamber Cases [A publication] (DLA)
Hawarde St Ch... Hawarde's Star Chamber Cases [A publication] (DLA)
Haw Ass .... Hawes on Assignments [A publication] (DLA)
HAWB .... House Air Waybill [Shipping] (DS)
HAWC .... Homing and Warning Computer (MCD)
HAWC .... Wacca [Ethiopia] [ICAO location identifier] (ICLI)
Haw Cr Rep... Hawley's American Criminal Reports [A publication] (DLA)
HAWDC .... Hotel Association of Washington, D.C. (SRA)
HAWE .... Hamburg-Wechsler Intelligence Test [Psychology]
HawEl .... Hawaiian Electric Industries, Inc. [Associated Press] (SAG)
Hawes Jur ..... Hawes on Jurisdiction of Courts [A publication] (DLA)
Haw Fed .... Hawaii Federal [Legal term] (DLA)
HAWHA .... Heart of America Walking Horse Association (EA)
HAWIK .... Hamburg-Wechsler-Intelligenztest fuer Kinder [Hamburg-Wechsler
               Intelligence Test for Children] [Psychology]
HAWK .... Have Alimony, Will Keep
HAWK .... Hawkesbury [England]
Hawk .... Hawkins' Pleas of the Crown [England] [A publication] (DLA)
HAWK .... Hawks Industries [NASDAQ symbol] (TTSB)
HAWK .... Hawks Industries, Inc. [NASDAQ symbol] (NQ)
HAWK .... Homing All the Way Killer [Small missile]
HAWK .... Hunting and Angling With Kids
Hawk Abr.... Hawkins' Abridgment of Coke upon Littleton [A publication] (DLA)
HawkB .... Hawkeye Bancorp [Associated Press] (SAG)
HawkC .... Hawkins Chemical, Inc. [Associated Press] (SAG)
Hawk Coke Abr... Hawkins' Abridgment of Coke upon Littleton [A publication]
               (DLA)
Hawk Co Litt... Hawkins' Coke upon Littleton [A publication] (DLA)
Hawkins .... Hawkins' Annual Reports [19-24 Louisiana] [A publication] (DLA)
Hawk PC...... Hawkins' Pleas of the Crown [England] [A publication] (DLA)
Hawk Pl Cr... Hawkins' Pleas of the Crown [England] [A publication] (DLA)
Hawks .... Hawks Industries, Inc. [Associated Press] (SAG)
Hawks .... Hawks' North Carolina Reports [A publication] (DLA)
Hawks (NC)... Hawks' North Carolina Reports [A publication] (DLA)
Hawk Wills... Hawkins' Construction of Wills [A publication] (DLA)
Hawl .... Hawley's Reports [10-20 Nevada] [A publication] (DLA)
Hawl Cr R.... Hawley's American Criminal Reports [A publication] (DLA)
Hawley .... Hawley's American Criminal Reports [A publication] (DLA)
Hawley .... Hawley's Reports [10-20 Nevada] [A publication] (DLA)
Hawley's Crim Rep... Hawley's American Criminal Reports [A publication] (DLA)
Hawn .... Hawaii Reports [A publication] (DLA)
HAWP .... Homing and Warning Programmer (MCD)
HAWR .... Helicopter Attack Warning RADAR (NVT)
Haw Rep...... Hawaii Reports [A publication] (DLA)
Haw Rev Stat... Hawaii Revised Statutes [A publication] (DLA)
Haw Rev Stat Ann... Hawaii Revised Statutes Annotated [A publication] (AAGC)
HAWSEAFRON... Hawaiian Sea Frontier
Haw Sess Laws... Session Laws of Hawaii [A publication] (DLA)
HAWT .... Horizontal Axis Wind Turbine [Generator] [Also, HAWTG] (MCD)
HAWTADS... Helicopter All-Weather Target Acquisition and Designation System
HAWTADS.... HELLFIRE [Heliborne LASER Fire and Forget] All-Weather Target
               Acquisition and Destruction System (MCD)
HawtFn .... Hawthorne Financial Corp. [Associated Press] (SAG)
HAWTG .... Horizontal Axis Wind Turbine Generator [Also, HAWT]
Haw WC ...... Hawes' Will Case [A publication] (DLA)
HAX .... Hafnium Column Extractant [Nuclear energy] (NRCH)
HAX .... Hangar 5 Air Services Norway [FAA designator] (FAAC)

HAX .... Helicopter Armored Experiment
HAX .... Muskogee, OK [*Location identifier FAA*] (FAAL)
HAY .... Haycock, AK [*Location identifier FAA*] (FAAL)
HAY .... Hayes-Dana, Inc. [*Toronto Stock Exchange symbol*]
Hay .... Hayes' Irish Exchequer Reports [*1830-32*] [*A publication*] (DLA)
Hay .... Hayes' Reports [*Calcutta*] [*A publication*] (DLA)
HAY .... Hayes Wheels International [*NYSE symbol*] (SPSG)
HAY .... Hayfield [*California*] [*Seismograph station code, US Geological Survey*] (SEIS)
Hay .... Hay's High Court Appeals Reports [*1862-63*] [*Bengal, India*] [*A publication*] (DLA)
Hay .... Hay's Poor Law Decisions [*1711-1859*] [*Scotland*] [*A publication*] (DLA)
Hay .... Hay's Scotch Decisions [*A publication*] (DLA)
Hay .... Haywood's North Carolina Reports [*A publication*] (DLA)
Hay .... Haywood's Tennessee Reports [*A publication*] (DLA)
Hay Acc ...... Hay's Decisions on Accidents and Negligence [*1860*] [*Scotland*] [*A publication*] (DLA)
Hay & H ...... Hayward and Hazelton's United States Circuit Court Reports [*District of Columbia*] [*A publication*] (DLA)
Hay & Haz... Hayward and Hazelton's United States Circuit Court Reports [*District of Columbia*] [*A publication*] (DLA)
Hay & J ...... Hayes and Jones' Irish Exchequer Reports [*A publication*] (DLA)
Hay & Jo ..... Hayes and Jones' Irish Exchequer Reports [*1832-34*] [*A publication*] (DLA)
Hay & M ...... Hay and Marriott's English Admiralty Reports [*A publication*] (DLA)
Hay & Mar... Hay and Marriott's English Admiralty Reports [*A publication*] (DLA)
Hay & Marr... Hay and Marriott's English Admiralty Reports [*A publication*] (DLA)
Hay & M (Eng)... Hay and Marriott's English Admiralty Reports [*A publication*] (DLA)
Hay (Calc) ... Hay's Reports [*Calcutta*] [*A publication*] (DLA)
Hay Dec....... Hay's Decisions on Accidents and Negligence [*1860*] [*Scotland*] [*A publication*] (DLA)
Hay Eq .... Haynes' Outlines of Equity [*5th ed.*] [*1880*] [*A publication*] (DLA)
Hayes .... Hayes' Irish Exchequer Reports [*1830-32*] [*A publication*] (DLA)
Hayes .... Hayes Wheels International [*Associated Press*] (SAG)
Hayes & J ... Hayes and Jones' Irish Exchequer Reports [*1832-34*] [*A publication*] (DLA)
Hayes & J (Ir)... Hayes and Jones' Irish Exchequer Reports [*1832-34*] [*A publication*] (DLA)
Hayes & Jo... Hayes and Jones' Irish Exchequer Reports [*1832-34*] [*A publication*] (DLA)
Hayes & Jon... Hayes and Jones' Irish Exchequer Reports [*1832-34*] [*A publication*] (DLA)
Hayes & J Wills... Hayes and Jarman's Concise Forms of Wills [*18th ed.*] [*1952*] [*A publication*] (DLA)
Hayes Con Conv... Hayes' Concise Conveyancer [*A publication*] (DLA)
Hayes Conv... Hayes on Conveyancing [*A publication*] (DLA)
Hayes Cr & P... Hayes on Crimes and Punishments [*A publication*] (DLA)
Hayes Exch... Hayes' Irish Exchequer Reports [*1830-32*] [*A publication*] (DLA)
Hayes Exch (Ir)... Hayes' Irish Exchequer Reports [*1830-32*] [*A publication*] (DLA)
Hayes Heirs... Hayes' Dispositions to Heirs in Tail, Etc. [*A publication*] (DLA)
Hayes Intr.... Hayes' Introduction to Conveyancing [*A publication*] (DLA)
Hayes Lim ... Hayes on Limitations as to Heirs of the Body, Etc. [*A publication*] (DLA)
Hayes R Est... Hayes' Real Estate [*A publication*] (DLA)
Hayes UD & T... Hayes' Law of Uses, Devises, and Trust [*A publication*] (DLA)
Hay Exch ..... Hayes' Irish Exchequer Reports [*1830-32*] [*A publication*] (DLA)
Hay Exp ...... Hay on Expatriation [*A publication*] (DLA)
Hayford....... Gold Coast Native Institutions [*A publication*] (DLA)
Hayn Ch Pr.. Haynes' Chancery Practice [*1879*] [*A publication*] (DLA)
Hayn Eq....... Haynes' Outlines of Equity [*5th ed.*] [*1880*] [*A publication*] (DLA)
Haynes Eq .... Haynes' Outlines of Equity [*5th ed.*] [*1880*] [*A publication*] (DLA)
Hayn Lead Cas... Haynes' Students' Leading Cases [*A publication*] (DLA)
Hay PL........ Hay's Poor Law Decisions [*1711-1859*] [*Scotland*] [*A publication*] (DLA)
HAYR .... Hayridge [*England*]
HAYSTAQ..... Have You Stored Answers to Questions [*Computer science*]
Hayw .... Haywood's North Carolina Reports [*A publication*] (DLA)
Hayw .... Haywood's Tennessee Reports [*A publication*] (DLA)
Hayw & H.... Hayward and Hazelton's United States Circuit Court Reports [*District of Columbia*] [*A publication*] (DLA)
Hayw & HDC... Hayward and Hazelton's United States Circuit Court Reports [*District of Columbia*] [*A publication*] (DLA)
HaywdB....... Haywood Bancshares, Inc. [*Associated Press*] (SAG)
Hayw LR...... Hayward's Law Register [*Boston*] [*A publication*] (DLA)
Hayw Man ... Haywood's Manual of the Statute Laws of North Carolina [*A publication*] (DLA)
Hayw NC...... Haywood's North Carolina Reports [*A publication*] (DLA)
Haywood Tenn Rep... Haywood's Tennessee Reports [*A publication*] (DLA)
Hayw Tenn... Haywood's Tennessee Reports [*A publication*] (DLA)
HAZ............. Hazard [*or Hazardous*] (KSC)
HAZ............. Heat-Affected Zone
HAZ............. Heat-Annealed Zone [*Metallurgy*]
HAZAL .... Hahameinu Zikhronam Livrakha [*Our Sages of Blessed Memory*] [*Hebrew*]
HAZAN........ Hazard Analysis
Haz & R M War... Hazlitt and Roche on Maritime Warfare [*A publication*] (DLA)
HAZCHEM.... Hazardous Chemical
HAZCOM...... Hazardous Communication Standards [*Occupational Safety and Health Administration*] (RDA)
HAZCON...... Hazardous Condition (NVT)
HAZEL......... Homogeneous Assembly Zero Energy Level [*AERE*]
HAZFILE...... Hazards File [*National Chemical Emergency Centre*] [*British*] (NITA)

HAZINF .... Hazardous Chemicals Information and Disposal [*University of Alberta*] [*Canada Information service or system*] (CRD)
HAZMACON... West Coast Hazardous Materials Management Conference (TSPED)
HAZMAT ...... Hazardous Material
HAZMAT ...... Hazardous Material Response and Assessment Division [*Marine science*] (OSRA)
HAZMAT ...... Hazardous Materials Response and Assessment Division [*National Oceanic and Atmospheric Administration*] (USDC)
HAZMIN .... Hazardous Waste Minimization
HAZOP........ Hazard and Operability [*Chemical engineering*]
Haz PA Reg... Hazard's Pennsylvania Register [*A publication*] (DLA)
Haz PA Reg (PA)... Hazard's Pennsylvania Register [*A publication*] (DLA)
Haz P Reg ... Hazard's Pennsylvania Register [*A publication*] (ILCA)
Haz Reg....... Hazard's Pennsylvania Register [*A publication*] (DLA)
Haz US Reg... Hazard's United States Register [*A publication*] (DLA)
HAZWOPER.... Hazardous Waste Operations and Emergency Response Regulation
HAZWRAP.... Hazardous Waste Remedial Action Program [*Oak Ridge National Laboratory*]
HB................ Air Melanesiae [*ICAO designator*] (AD)
HB................ Bell Helicopter Co., Brantly Helicopter Corp., Brditschka [*Heinrich Brditschka Flugzeugbau*] [*ICAO aircraft manufacturer identifier*] (ICAO)
HB................ Brinell Hardness Number [*Also, BH, BHN, BHNo*]
H$_B$............... Deuterium [*Radioisotope of hydrogen*] (DAVI)
HB................ Farbwerke Hoechst AG [*Germany*] [*Research code symbol*]
Hb................ Habakkuk [*Old Testament book*]
HB................ Halfback [*Football*]
HB................ Half Bound [*Bibliography*]
HB................ Half Bow [*Music*] (ROG)
HB................ Half Breadth (AAG)
HB................ Halk Bankasi [*Peoples Bank of Turkey*] [*See also THB*]
HB................ Hallelujah Band
HB................ Halogen Bulb
HB................ Hampton & Branchville Railroad Co. [*AAR code*]
HB................ Handbook (NASA)
HB................ Handlebar (ROG)
HB................ Hard Black [*Pencil leads*]
HB................ Hardboard (ADA)
HB................ Hard-Boiled [*Egg*]
HB................ Hardy Biennial [*Horticulture*] (ROG)
HB................ Hatchback [*Automotive advertising*]
HB................ Headband (IAA)
HB................ Health Benefit
HB................ Health Board [*Ireland*]
HB................ Heart Block [*Medicine*]
HB................ Heat to Boiling Point [*Calorimetry*]
HB................ Heavy Barrel [*Rifles*]
HB................ Heavy Bombardment [*or Bomber*]
Hb................ Hebrew (BJA)
HB................ Heel to Buttock (DMAA)
HB................ Held Back (DMAA)
HB................ Hemoglobin [*Medicine*] (DMAA)
Hb................ Hemoglobin [*Biochemistry, medicine*]
HB................ Henricus Boich [*Flourished, 1320-30*] [*Authority cited in pre-1607 legal work*] (DSA)
HB................ Hepatitis B [*Medicine*]
HB................ Herba [*Herb*] [*Pharmacology*] (ROG)
HB................ Herders Bibelkommentar [*A publication*] (BJA)
HB................ Herri Batazuna [*Union of the People*] [*Spain Political party*] (PPE)
H-B............... Hexadecimal-to-Binary [*Computer science*] (IEEE)
HB................ High Band (AAG)
HB................ High Bay (KSC)
HB................ High Boilers
HB................ Highways and Byways [*A publication*]
HB................ Hill-Burton [*Federal grant and loan program for construction and modernization of medical facilities*]
HB................ Hillenbrand Indus [*NYSE symbol*] (TTSB)
HB................ Hillenbrand Industries, Inc. [*NYSE symbol*] (SPSG)
HB................ Hinged Block [*British military*] (DMA)
HB................ His Beatitude [*or His Blessedness*]
HB................ His Bundle [*Cardiology*]
HB................ Historical Branch [*Army*]
HB................ Hit by Ball [*or Hit Batsman*] [*Baseball*]
HB................ Hold Breakfast [*Medicine*]
HB................ Holiness Band
HB................ Hollowback (DAC)
HB................ Homing Beacon [*Aviation*]
HB................ Honey Bee
HB................ Honeywell-Bull
HB................ Horizontal Baffle (NRCH)
HB................ Horizontal Bands [*Navigation markers*]
HB................ Horizontal Bomber
HB................ Horizontal-Branch [*Astronomy*]
HB................ Horizontal Bridgman [*Crystal growing technique*]
HB................ Hormone Binding [*Endocrinology*]
HB................ Horn Book Magazine [*A publication*] (BRI)
HB................ Hose Bib (AAG)
HB................ Hospital Bed (DAVI)
HB................ Hot Boning [*Meat processing*]
HB................ House Bill [*In state legislatures*]
HB................ Housebound (MAE)
HB................ Housebreaking
HB................ Household Battalion [*British military*] (DMA)
HB................ Household Goods/Baggage
HB................ Housing Benefit [*British*]

HB.............. Human Behavior [National Science Foundation project]
HB.............. Human Being [Slang]
HB.............. Huntington Beach [California]
HB.............. Hybridoma [Cytology]
HB.............. Hybridoma Bank (DMAA)
HB.............. Hyoid Body (DMAA)
HBA............. Bible Atlas [Hurblut] [A publication] (BJA)
HBA............. General Hotel, Boarding House, and Apartments [British]
HBA............. Halley Bay [Antarctica] [Seismograph station code, US Geological Survey Closed] (SEIS)
HBA............. Handbook Art
HBA............. Handicapped Boaters Association [Defunct] (EA)
HBA............. Harrison Bay, AK [Location identifier FAA] (FAAL)
HBA............. Health and Beauty Aid [Retailing]
HBA............. Health Benefit Advisor [CHAMPUS]
HbA............. Hemoglobin, Adult [Medicine]
HBA............. Herring Buyers Association [British] (DBA)
HBA............. Hispanic Bar Association [EA]
HBA............. Hobart [Tasmania] [Airport symbol] (OAG)
HBA............. Home Baking Association (EA)
HBA............. Home Base [Military] (NVT)
HBA............. Honest Ballot Association (EA)
HBA............. Honours Bachelor of Arts in Business Administration (DD)
HBA............. Horizontal Baffle Assembly [Nuclear energy] (NRCH)
HBA............. Host Bus Adapter [Computer science]
HBA............. Hydraulic and Boatyard Association [A union] [British]
HBA............. Hydrazinobenzoic Acid [Organic chemistry]
HBA............. Hydrobenzoate [Organic chemistry]
HBA............. Hydrogen-Bond Acceptor [Chemistry]
HBA............. Trail Lake Flying Service, Inc. [ICAO designator] (FAAC)
HBAb........... Hepatitis B Antibody [Immunology]
HBABA......... (Hydroxybenzeneazo)benzoic Acid [Also, HABA] [Organic chemistry]
HBAG.......... Handbag
HBAg.......... Hepatitis B Antigen [Immunology]
HBAH.......... Hydroxybenzoic Acid Hydrazide [Reagent]
HBAM.......... Historic Buildings and Ancient Monuments Act [Town planning] [British]
HBAM.......... Home Builders Association of Maryland (SRA)
HBAM.......... Home Builders Association of Massachusetts (SRA)
HBAN.......... Huntington Bancshares [NASDAQ symbol] (TTSB)
HBAN.......... Huntington Bancshares, Inc. [NASDAQ symbol] (NQ)
HB & T....... Houston Belt & Terminal Railway Co.
HBAR.......... Head Bar Address Register [Computer science] (MHDB)
H-BAR........ Heavy Barrel [Rifles]
HBARO......... Barometric Altitude (GAVI)
HbAS.......... Hemoglobin A and Hemoglobin S [Medicine] (MEDA)
HBAT.......... Having Been Assigned to This Organization [or Headquarters]
HBAVS........ Human Betterment Association for Voluntary Sterilization [Later, AVS] (EA)
HBB............. Historic Buildings Bureau [British]
HBB............. Hobbs, NM [Location identifier FAA] (FAAL)
HBB............. Hook-Basal Body [Genetics]
HBB............. Hospital Blood Bank
HBB............. Human Beta-Globin [Genetics]
HBB............. Hydroxybenzyl Benzimidazole [Clinical chemistry] (MAE)
HBBA.......... Bujumbura [Burundi] [ICAO location identifier] (ICLI)
HBBD.......... Hydroxybenzylbutanediol [Clinical chemistry]
HBBE.......... Gitega [Burundi] [ICAO location identifier] (ICLI)
HBBI........... Home Building Bancorp [NASDAQ symbol] (SAG)
HBBK.......... Kiofi-Mosso [Burundi] [ICAO location identifier] (ICLI)
HBBL.......... Hydroxybenzylbutyrolactone [Clinical chemistry]
HBBL.......... Nyanza-Lac [Burundi] [ICAO location identifier] (ICLI)
HBBM.......... Mugera [Burundi] [ICAO location identifier] (ICLI)
HBBN.......... Nyakagunda [Burundi] [ICAO location identifier] (ICLI)
HBBW.......... Hold Breakfast for Blood Work [Medicine]
HBC............. Haitian Aviation Line SA [ICAO designator] (FAAC)
HBC............. Hajji Baba Club (EA)
HBC............. Handbooks for Bible Classes [A publication]
HBC............. Handlebar Control [Early automobiles] (ROG)
HBC............. Health Benefit Card (ADA)
Hb C............ Hemoglobin C [An abnormal hemoglobin] [Hematology] (DAVI)
HBc............. Hepatitis B Core [Immunology] (MAE)
HBC............. Highamerica Balloon Club (EA)
HBC............. High Blood Cholesterol
HBC............. High Breaking Capacity (IAA)
HBC............. Historic Buildings Council [British]
HBC............. [The] History Book Club
HBC............. Homogeneous Boundary Condition
HBC............. Honeywell Business Computer [or Compiler]
HBC............. Hong Kong Bank of Canada (ECON)
HBC............. Horseshoe Bay [British Columbia] [Seismograph station code, US Geological Survey Closed] (SEIS)
HBC............. Hostage Bracelet Committee (EA)
HBC............. House Budget Committee
HBC............. Hudson's Bay Co. [TS, exchange symbol] (TTSB)
HBC............. Hudson's Bay Company [Facetious translations include "Here before Christ," "Here before Columbus," and "Hungry Belly Co.."]
HBC............. Human Biology Council (EA)
HBC............. Human Body Counter (IAA)
HBC............. Hydrogen Bubble Chamber
HBC............. Hyperbaric Chamber (SSD)
HBcAb.......... Hepatitis B Core Antibody [Immunology] (MAE)
HBCAg.......... Hepatitis B Core Antigen [Immunology]
HBCC.......... Hosted Bus Controller Chip [Electronics]
HBCC.......... Hosted Bus Controller Chip

HBCC .... Hosted Bus Controller Circuit [Electronics]
HBCCA........ Heftel Broadcasting 'A' [NASDAQ symbol] (TTSB)
HBCCA........ Heftel Broadcasting Corp. [NASDAQ symbol] (SAG)
HBCD.......... Hexabromocyclododecane [Flame retardant] [Organic chemistry]
HBCF.......... Hydrobromofluorocarbons [Organic chemistry]
HBCI.......... Heritage Bancorp [NASDAQ symbol] (TTSB)
HBCI.......... Heritage Bancorp, Inc. [NASDAQ symbol] (SAG)
HBCN.......... Hazard Beacon (MSA)
HbCO.......... Hemoglobin, Carboxy [Biochemistry, medicine]
HBCO.......... Hungarian Broadcasting [NASDAQ symbol] (TTSB)
HBCO.......... Hungarian Broadcasting Corp. [NASDAQ symbol] (SAG)
HBCOW........ Hungarian Broadcasting Wrrt [NASDAQ symbol] (TTSB)
Hb CS .... Hemoglobin Constant Spring [An abnormal hemoglobin] [Hematology] (DAVI)
HBCU.......... Historically Black Colleges and Universities
HBCU/MI..... Historically Black Colleges, Universities, and Minority Institutions (RDA)
HBD............. Hardboard [Technical drawings]
HBD............. Has Been Drinking [Medical notation]
Hb D .... Hemoglobin D [An abnormal hemoglobin] [Hematology] (DAVI)
HBD............. Hepatobiliary Dysfunction [Medicine]
HBD............. Hormone Binding Domain [Endocrinology]
HBD............. Hubbard, OH [Location identifier FAA] (FAAL)
HBD............. Hydrogen Bond Donor [Solvent]
HBD............. Hydroxybutyrate Dehydrogenase [Also, HBDH] [An enzyme]
HBDC.......... Home Base Development Committee [Navy]
HBDE.......... Huntington Beach Development Engineering [McDonnell Douglas Aircraft Corp.]
HBDH.......... Hydroxybutyrate Dehydrogenase [Also, HBD] [An enzyme]
HBDMA........ Hat Block and Die Makers Association
HBDMI........ Historical Biographical Dictionaries Master Index [A publication]
HBDR.......... Helicopter Battle Damage Repair (RDA)
HBDS.......... Hypergraph-Based Data Structures
HBDT.......... High BIT [Binary Digit] Density Tape [Skylab] [NASA]
HBDT.......... Human Basophil Degranulation Test [Medicine] (DMAA)
HBE............. Hamilton Board of Education Schools [UTLAS symbol]
HBe............. Hepatitis B Early [Antibody or antigen] [Immunology] (DAVI)
HBE............. His Bundle Electrogram [Cardiology]
HBEA.......... Hawaii Business Education Association (EDAC)
HBeAb......... Hepatitis B Early Antibody [Immunology] (DAVI)
HBeAg......... Hepatitis B, Early Antigen [or Antibody] [Immunology]
HBED.......... Bis(hydroxybenzyl)ethylenediaminediacetic Acid [Organic chemistry]
HBEF.......... Health and Beauty Employers Federation [British] (DBA)
HBEF.......... Hubbard Brook Experimental Forest
HBEI.......... Home Bancorp of Elgin, Inc. [NASDAQ symbol] (SAG)
HBEN.......... High Byte Enable
HBEN.......... Home Beneficial Corp. [NASDAQ symbol] (NQ)
HBENB........ Home Beneficial Cl 'B' [NASDAQ symbol] (TTSB)
HBES.......... Human Behavior and Evolution Society [An association]
HBF............. Hamilton Board of Education [UTLAS symbol]
HBF............. Hand Blood Flow [Cardiology] (DAVI)
HBF............. Harts Bluff [South Carolina] [Seismograph station code, US Geological Survey] (SEIS)
HBF............. Hauptbahnhof [Main Railroad Station] [German]
HBF............. Hemispheric Blood Flow [Medicine] (DMAA)
HbF............. Hemoglobin, Fetal [Also, HgF] [Medicine]
HBF............. Hemoglobinuric Bilious Fever [Medicine] (DMAA)
HBF............. Hepatic Blood Flow
HBF............. High Bleeding Frequency [Medicine]
HBF............. House-Builders Federation [British] (DBA)
HBF............. Hypothalamic Blood FLow [Medicine] (DMAA)
HBFW.......... Home Bancorp [NASDAQ symbol] (SAG)
HBG............. Harrisburg [Diocesan abbreviation] [Pennsylvania] (TOCD)
HBG............. Hattiesburg [Mississippi] [Airport symbol] (AD)
HBG............. Hattiesburg, MS [Location identifier FAA] (FAAL)
HBG............. Hope Brook Gold, Inc. [Toronto Stock Exchange symbol]
HBG............. Hydroxybenzoylglycine [Biochemistry]
HBG............. (Hydroxybutyl)guanine [Biochemistry]
HBGF.......... Heparin-Binding Growth Factor [Biochemistry]
HBGI.......... Holson Burnes Group, Inc. [NASDAQ symbol] (SAG)
HBGM.......... Home Blood Glucose Monitoring [Medicine]
HBGM.......... Hypersonic Boost-Glide Missile
HB Guide .... Horn Book Guide [A publication] (BRI)
Hb H .... Hemoglobin H [An abnormal hemoglobin] [Hematology] (DAVI)
HBH............. History Behind the Headlines [A publication]
HBH............. Hobart Bay [Alaska] [Airport symbol] (OAG)
HBH............. Hydraulic Brake Hose [Automotive engineering]
HBHC.......... Hancock Holding [NASDAQ symbol] (TTSB)
HBHC.......... Hancock Holding Co. [NASDAQ symbol] (SAG)
HBHC.......... Hospital-Based Home Care
HBI............. Hemibody Irradiation [Oncology]
HbI............. Hemoglobin I [Biochemistry, medicine]
HBI............. High Serum-Bound Iron [Biochemistry] (MAE)
HBI............. Hindustan Bible Institute (EA)
HBI............. Horizontal Blanking Interval (DOM)
HBI............. Hospital Bureau, Inc. [Formerly, HBSS] (EA)
HBI............. Hot Biquetted Iron
HBI............. House-Breaking Implements [British police term]
HBI............. Houston Biotechnology [AMEX symbol] (TTSB)
HBI............. Houston Biotechnology, Inc. [AMEX symbol] (SPSG)
HBIA.......... Hairdressing and Beauty Industry Association [Australia]
HBIG.......... Hepatitis B Immune Globulin [Immunology]
HBJ............. High-Band Jammer (MCD)
HBK............. Habekacin [Antibacterial]
HBK............. Handbook

HBK .... Hardback [Book cover] (NTCM)
HBK .... Hardwood Bleached Kraft [Pulp and paper technology]
HBK .... Hartebeesthoek [South Africa] [Geomagnetic observatory code]
HBk .... Herders Bibelkommentar [A publication] (BJA)
HBK .... Hinchinbrook, AK [Location identifier FAA] (FAAL)
HBK .... Hollow Back [Of lumber] (BARN)
HBL .... Harbor Belt Line Railroad
HBL .... Heeresbetriebsstofflager [Army Gasoline-Supply Depot] [German military - World War II]
HBL .... Hepatoblastoma (DMAA)
HBL .... Huntington Beach Public Library, Huntington Beach, CA [OCLC symbol] (OCLC)
HBLB .... Horserace Betting Levy Board [British]
HBLLSB ...... Heard Best at Left Lower Sternal Border [Cardiology] (DAVI)
HBLO .... Home Base, Ledger Office [British military] (DMA)
HBLR .... Hidden Broad-Line Region [Spectra]
HBLRR .... Harbor Belt Line Railroad (MHDB)
HBLUSB...... Heard Best at Left Upper Sternal Border [Cardiology] (DAVI)
HBLV .... Human B-Lymphotropic Virus
HBM........... Half Bridge Monorail [Mobot Corp.] [Gantry robot] (NITA)
HBM........... Health Belief Model (DMAA)
HBM........... Heavy Ballistic Missile
HBM........... Held by Manufacturer
HbM........... Hemoglobin M [Biochemistry] (MAH)
HBM........... High-Beta Model (MCD)
HBM........... His [or Her] Britannic Majesty
HBM........... Hobart Mills [California] [Seismograph station code, US Geological Survey] (SEIS)
HBM........... Horizontal Boring Mill
HBM........... Hudson Bay Mining & Smelting Co. Ltd. [Toronto Stock Exchange symbol]
HBM........... Hydraulic Bore-Hole Mining [Coal]
HBM........... Hypertonic Buffered Medium (DMAA)
HBM........... Mali-Tinbouctou Air Service [ICAO designator] (FAAC)
HBMA .... Home-Based Maintenance Allowance
HBMC .... Homebush Bay Ministerial Council [New South Wales, Australia]
HBMS .... His [or Her] Britannic Majesty's Service
HBMS .... His [or Her] Britannic Majesty's Ship (ROG)
HBN .... Hazard Beacon
HBN .... Health-Based Number [Environmental science]
HB(N) .... Heavy Bomber (Night) [British military] (DMA)
HBNK .... Highland Federal Bank [NASDAQ symbol] (SAG)
HBNR .... Hydrogen-Bond Network Rearrangement [Physical chemistry]
HBO .... HBO & Co. [Associated Press] (SAG)
HBO .... Health Benefits Organization [Insurance]
H Bo .... Henricus Boich [Flourished, 1320-30] [Authority cited in pre-1607 legal work] (DSA)
HBO .... Home Box Office [Cable-television system]
HBO .... Horizontal-Branch Oscillation [Astronomy]
HBO .... Humboldt, NE [Location identifier FAA] (FAAL)
HBO .... Hyperbaric Oxygen [Also, HPO, OHP] [Medicine]
HBO .... Hyperbaric Oxygenation (DMAA)
HbO₂ .... Hemoglobin, Oxy [Biochemistry, medicine]
HBOC .... HBO & Co. [NASDAQ symbol] (NQ)
HBOI .... Harbor Branch Oceanographic Institution [Fort Pierce, FL]
H (Bomb)..... Hydrogen Bomb
HbOr .... Handbuch der Orientalistik [Leiden] [A publication] (BJA)
HBOT .... Hyperbaric Oxygen Therapy [Medicine] (DAVI)
HBP .... Dauphin County Library System, Harrisburg, PA [OCLC symbol] (OCLC)
HBP .... Hamilton Board of Education, Education Centre Library [UTLAS symbol]
HBP .... Handbook Production
HBP .... Heartbeat Period [Medicine] (DMAA)
HBP .... Held for Blueprint (MCD)
HBP .... Hepatic Binding Protein [Biochemistry]
HBP .... High Blood Pressure [Medicine]
HBP .... Highway Bridge Parapet (PDAA)
HbP .... Hilfsbuch des Pehlevi [A publication] (BJA)
HBP .... Hit by Pitcher [Baseball]
HBP .... Hospital-Based Practice (DMAA)
HBP .... Hospital Benefits Payment
HBP .... Hydraulic Bench Press
HBP .... Hydrocortisone(butyrate)propionate [Endocrinology]
HbP........... Primitive [Fetal] Hemoglobin
HBPA .... Horsemen's Benevolent and Protective Association (EA)
HBPA .... Hydrogenated Bisphenol A [Organic chemistry]
HBPE .... Health Based Physical Education
H-BPH........ Hawaii Regional Library for the Blind and Physically Handicapped, Honolulu, HI [Library symbol Library of Congress] (LCLS)
HBPIC .... High Blood Pressure Information Center [Public Health Service] (IID)
HBPM .... Home Blood Pressure Monitoring [Medicine]
HBPP .... Humboldt Bay Power Plant (NRCH)
HBPSA .... Hydroxybutylidene-p-aminobenzenesulfonic [Organic chemistry]
HBR .... Haibara [Japan] [Seismograph station code, US Geological Survey] (SEIS)
HBR .... Ham Band Receiver (IAA)
HBR .... Hansell's Bankruptcy Reports [1915-17] [A publication] (DLA)
HBR .... Harbor [Maps and charts]
HBR .... Harbor
HBR .... Harborside Healthcare Corp. [NYSE symbol] (SAG)
HBR .... Has Been Reviewed (AAG)
HBR .... High BIT [Binary Digit] Rate (KSC)
HBR .... High Burst Rate (PDAA)
HBR .... Hobart, OK [Location identifier FAA] (FAAL)

HBr .... Hydrobromic Acid (MAE)
HBRACW ..... Has Been Reviewed and Concurred With (AAG)
HBRDC........ Honey Bee Research and Development Council [Australia]
HBRF .... Hercules-Baachus Resin Formulation
HBRI .... Hospital Bureau Research Institute [Defunct] (EA)
H/BRK .... Hand Brake [Automotive engineering]
HBRK .... Harmony Brook [NASDAQ symbol] (TTSB)
HBRK .... Harmony Brook, Inc. [NASDAQ symbol] (SAG)
Hbr Mr .... Harbor Master
HBR-online... Harvard Business Review-Online [John Wiley & Son] (NITA)
HBRRP........ Highway Bridge Replacement and Rehabilitation Program [Department of Transportation]
HBRS .... Harbors
HBRS .... Harbors [Postal Service standard] (OPSA)
HBS .... Half Bar Symbology
HBS .... Hanks Balanced Salt [Solution] [Cell incubation medium]
HBS .... Harbor Boat Service [Military]
HBS .... Harvard Business School
HBS .... Harvard Business School, Boston, MA [OCLC symbol] (OCLC)
HBS .... Havergal Brian Society (EAIO)
HBS .... Haywood Bancshares, Inc. [AMEX symbol] (SAG)
HBS .... Health Behavior Scale [Psychiatry] (DAVI)
HBS .... Heavy Bomber Support
HBS .... Helicopter Blade Slap
HbS .... Hemoglobin, Sickle [Medicine]
HBS .... Henry Bradshaw Society [British]
HBₛ .... Hepatitis B Surface [Antibody or antigen] [Immunology] (DAVI)
HBS .... Hermanas Contemplativas del Buen Pastor (TOCD)
HBS .... Herringbone Strutting [Construction]
HBS .... High-Beta Stellarator (PDAA)
HBS .... High Byte Strobe [Computer science] (MHDI)
HBS .... Hoboken Shore Railroad [AAR code]
HBS .... Hole-Burning Spectroscopy
HBS .... Honey Bee Spiroplasma [Bacteriology]
HBS .... Hot Blade Stripper
HBS .... Hyperkinetic Behavior Syndrome [Medicine]
HBSA .... Historical Breechloading Smallarms Association [British] (DBA)
HBSA .... Hungarian Boy Scout Association (EA)
HBSAB .... Hepatitis B Surface Antibody [Immunology] (PDAA)
HBₛAg........ Hepatitis B Surface Antigen [Immunology] (DAVI)
HBSANSW ... Health and Building Surveyors' Association of New South Wales [Australia]
HBSC .... Hematopoietic Blood Stem Cell [Medicine] (DMAA)
HbSC .... Hemoglobin C Sickle Cell Disease [Medicine]
HBSG .... Home Birth Support Group [Australia]
HBSMA .... Hack and Band Saw Manufacturers Association of America
HBSMAA ..... Hack and Band Saw Manufacturers Association of America (EA)
HBSS .... Hanks Balanced Salt Solution [Cell incubation medium]
HBSS .... Hospital Bureau of Standards and Supplies [Later, HBI]
HBT .... Habeat [Let Him Have] [Pharmacy] (ROG)
HBT .... Harbor Bay Telecommunications [Alameda, CA] (TSSD)
HBT .... Harbourton Financial Services LP [NYSE symbol] (SAG)
HBT .... Harbourton Finl Svcs L.P. [NYSE symbol] (TTSB)
HBT .... Heflex Bioengineering Test [NASA]
HBT .... Herringbone Twill
HBT .... Heterojunction Bipolar Transistor [Electronics]
HBT .... Hetrojunction Bipolar Mobility Transistor (NITA)
HBT .... Hobart Mills [California] [Seismograph station code, US Geological Survey] (SEIS)
HBT .... Houston Belt & Terminal Railway Co. [AAR code]
HBT .... Human Brain Thromboplastin [Clinical chemistry]
HBT .... Human Breast Tumor [Type of cell line]
HBT .... Hydroxybenzotriazole [Organic chemistry]
HBT .... Sand Point, AK [Location identifier FAA] (FAAL)
HBTA .... HB [Homeward Bound Ministries] Tract Association (EA)
HBTA .... Hutchinson Board of Trade Association (EA)
HBTX .... High Beta Toroidal Experiment (PDAA)
HBU .... Aurora, OR [Location identifier FAA] (FAAL)
HBU .... Hollandsche Bank-Unie [Netherlands]
HBU .... Houston Baptist University [Texas]
HBUA .... Hungarian Baptist Union of America (EA)
HBV .... Harrisonburg [Virginia] [Seismograph station code, US Geological Survey] (SEIS)
HBV .... Hebbronville, TX [Location identifier FAA] (FAAL)
HBV .... Hepatitis B Vaccine
HBV .... Hepatitis B Virus
HBV .... Honey Bee Venom [Immunology]
HBVP .... Hepatitis B Virus Polymerase [An enzyme]
HBVS .... Hepatitis B Virus Integration Site [Medicine] (DMAA)
HBW .... Half Bandwidth [Electronics]
HBW .... High Birth Weight [Medicine] (MAE)
HBW .... High-Speed Black and White [Photography]
HBW .... Hillsboro, WI [Location identifier FAA] (FAAL)
HBw .... Historische Burowelt [A publication]
HBW .... Hot Bridgewire (KSC)
HBW .... Wolf [Howard B.], Inc. [AMEX symbol] (SPSG)
HBWA .... High-Band Warning Antenna (MCD)
HBWMA ...... Home Brewing and Winemaking Manufacturers Association [British] (DBA)
HBWR .... Halden Boiling Water Reactor [Norway Nuclear energy]
HBWR .... High-Band Warning Receiver (MCD)
HBWTA .... Home Brewing and Winemaking Trade Association [British] (DBA)
HBY .... Hereby (ROG)
HBZ............ Heber Springs, AR [Location identifier FAA] (FAAL)
HC .... Command Chaplain [AFSC]

HC..............	Critical Height [*Aviation*] (DA)
HC..............	Cross of Honour [*British military*] (DMA)
HC..............	Crystal Holder [*JETDS nomenclature*] [*Military*] (CET)
HC..............	Ecuador [*International civil aircraft marking*] (ODBW)
HC..............	Habeas Corpus [*You Have the Body*] [*Legal term Latin*] (DLA)
HC..............	Habitual Criminal
HC..............	Hague Convention
HC..............	Hair Cell [*Otology*]
HC..............	Haiti Air International [*ICAO designator*] (AD)
HC..............	Half Calf
HC..............	Half-Caste (ADA)
HC..............	Half-Changes [*Statistics*]
HC..............	Half Chest
HC..............	Half Covered [*Marine insurance*] (ROG)
HC..............	Handbooks for the Clergy [*A publication*]
H/C..............	Hand Carry (KSC)
HC..............	Hand Carry
HC..............	Hand-Colored [*Photography*]
HC..............	Hand Control [*Technical drawings*]
HC..............	Hand Crank
HC..............	Hand Cut [*Envelopes*]
HC..............	Hand-Held Unit Chromatography
HC..............	Handicapped [*Medicine*]
HC..............	Handling Capacity (DEN)
HC..............	Hanging Ceiling (OA)
HC..............	Hannibal Connecting R. R. [*AAR code*]
HC..............	Hard Copy [*Computer science*]
HC..............	Hardcore
HC..............	Hardware Capability (NITA)
HC..............	Hastings Center (EA)
HC..............	Hatz Club (EA)
HC..............	Hauling Class
HC..............	Hauling Code
HC..............	Haute-Contre [*Alto*] [*Music*]
HC..............	Hazardous Constitutients (GNE)
HC..............	Head Circumference [*Medicine*]
HC..............	Head Compression (AAMN)
HC..............	Headcount
HC..............	Headmaster Commander [*Navy British*]
HC..............	Headquarters City [*Dialog*] [*Searchable field*] [*Information service or system*] (NITA)
HC..............	Headquarters Command [*Military*]
HC..............	Health Certificate [*British*] (ADA)
HC..............	Heal the Children (EA)
HC..............	Healthy Control [*Medicine*] (DMAA)
HC..............	Heart Cycle [*Cardiology*] (MAE)
HC..............	Heat Capacity [*Electronics*] (EECA)
HC..............	Heat Control (IAA)
HC..............	Heated Coil (NITA)
HC..............	Heater Cord
HC..............	Heating Cabinet (AAG)
HC..............	Heating Coil (AAG)
HC..............	Heat of Combustion (ROG)
HC..............	Heavy Chain [*Immunoglobulin*]
HC..............	Heavy Current [*Electronics*] (IAA)
HC..............	Held Covered [*Insurance*]
HC..............	Helene Curtis Industries, Inc. [*NYSE symbol*] (SPSG)
H/C..............	Helicopter (NATG)
HC..............	Helicopter Combat (NVT)
HC..............	Helicopter Combat Support Squadron [*Navy*] (DNAB)
HC..............	Helicopter Command (NVT)
HC..............	Helicopter Coordinator [*Military*] (CAAL)
HC..............	Helicopter Council
HC..............	Helium Circulation [*System*]
HC..............	Helminthosporium carbonum [*A toxin-producing fungus*]
HC..............	Helper Component [*Biology*]
HC..............	Hematopoietic Cell [*Hematology*]
HC..............	Hemoglobin Concentration [*Medicine*] (HGAA)
HC..............	Hepatic Catalase [*An enzyme*] (MAE)
HC..............	Hepatic Coma [*Medicine*]
HC..............	Heralds' College [*British*]
HC..............	Herding Certified [*Purebred canine award*]
HC..............	Heritage Committee [*Australian Capital Territory*]
HC..............	Herzberg Continuum [*Spectral region*]
HC..............	Heuristic Concepts (IEEE)
HC..............	Hexachloroethane [*Organic chemistry*]
HC..............	Hickman Catheter [*Medicine*] (DAVI)
HC..............	High Calorie (AAMN)
HC..............	High-Capacity
HC..............	High Carbon [*Steel*]
HC..............	High Church
HC..............	High Churchman [*British*] (ROG)
HC..............	High Color (CDE)
HC..............	High Commissioner
HC..............	High Compression
HC..............	High Conditioners [*Psychology*]
HC..............	High Conductivity [*Copper*]
HC..............	High Cost of Living
HC..............	High Court
HC..............	High Current
HC..............	Higher Certificate [*Academic degree*] (AIE)
HC..............	Highland Cyclists [*British military*] (DMA)
HC..............	Highway Code [*A publication*] (DLA)
HC..............	Hippocampal
HC..............	Hire Car (ADA)

HC..............	Histamine Club [*Later, HRSNA*] (EA)
HC..............	Historical Commission
HC..............	Historical Cost (ADA)
HC..............	Hockey Club
HC..............	Holding Coil (MSA)
HC..............	Holding Company [*Business term*]
HC..............	Holiday Camps [*Public-performance tariff class*] [*British*]
HC..............	Hollow Core [*Technical drawings*]
HC..............	Holy Communion
HC..............	Holy Cross
HC..............	Home Care
HC..............	Home Computer (IAA)
HC..............	Honor Contracts [*Insurance*]
HC..............	Honoris Causa [*For the Sake of Honor, Honorary*] [*Latin*]
HC..............	Horizontal Cell [*Eye anatomy*]
HC..............	Horizontal Check (IAA)
Hc..............	Hornyhead Chub [*Ichthyology*]
HC..............	Hors Concours [*Not Competing*] [*French*]
HC..............	Hose Cabinet [*or Connection*] [*NFPA pre-fire planning symbol*] (NFPA)
HC..............	Hose Cart [*Early fire engines*] (ROG)
HC..............	Hose Clamp (MSA)
HC..............	Hospital Corps [*or Corpsman*] [*Navy*]
HC..............	Hospital Course (DAVI)
HC..............	Host Cell [*Parasitology*]
HC..............	Host Computer
HC..............	Host Country (NATG)
HC..............	Hostel Care
HC..............	Hot and Cold
HC..............	Hour Circle
HC..............	House Cable [*Telecommunications*] (TEL)
HC..............	House Call [*Medicine*]
HC..............	Household Cavalry [*British*]
HC..............	House of Commons [*British*]
HC..............	House of Correction
HC..............	Housing Census
HC..............	Housing Commission [*Australia*]
HC..............	Housing Corp. [*British*] (BI)
HC..............	Hroswitha Club (EA)
HC..............	Hug Club (EA)
HC..............	Humid Crepidations [*Medicine*] (ROG)
HC..............	Humidity Control
HC..............	Hungarian Congress (EA)
HC..............	Huntington's Chorea [*Medicine*]
HC..............	Hupmobile Club (EA)
HC..............	Hyaline Casts [*Clinical chemistry*]
HC..............	Hybrid Circuit [*Electronics*] (IAA)
HC..............	Hybrid Computer [*for processing both analog and digital data*] (NASA)
HC..............	Hyderabad Contingent [*British military*] (DMA)
HC..............	Hydranencephaly [*Medicine*] (AAMN)
HC..............	Hydraulic Clean (MSA)
HC..............	Hydraulic Coupling (DCTA)
HC..............	Hydraulic Cylinder
HC..............	Hydrocarbon [*Organic chemistry*]
HC..............	Hydrocarbons [*Chemical*] (EERA)
HC..............	Hydrocodone [*Medicine*] (MEDA)
Hc..............	Hydrocolloid (DMAA)
HC..............	Hydrocortisone [*Endocrinology*]
HC..............	Hydrocracking
HC..............	Hydrogen Chloride (AABC)
H/C..............	Hydrogen to Carbon Atomic Ratio (EG)
HC..............	Hydrographic Center [*Defense Mapping Agency*]
HC..............	Hypatia Cluster [*Defunct*] (EA)
HC..............	Hysteresis Comparator
HC..............	Pechiney-Progil [*France*] [*Research code symbol*]
HC..............	Reports of the High Court of Griqualand West [*South Africa*] [*A publication*] (DLA)
HC..............	Screening Smoke [*Mixture*]
HC4..............	Helicopterborne Command and Control Communications Central
HCA	Absent by Reason of Being Held by Civil Authorities [*Military*]
HCA	Big Spring [*Texas*] [*Airport symbol*] (AD)
HCA	Habitat Conservation Area
HCA	Haitian Coalition on AIDS (EA)
HCA	Harness and Cable Assembly
HCA	Head of Contracting Activity [*Military*] (AABC)
HCA	Head of Contracting Agency (DOMA)
HCA	Headquarters Commitment Authorization [*Military*] (DNAB)
HCA	Health Care Administration
HCA	Health Care Aide (DAVI)
HCA	Health Care Assistant (MEDA)
HCA	Heart Cell Aggregate [*Cytology*]
HCA	Heisey Collectors of America (EA)
HCA	Held by Civil Authorities
HCA	Helicopter Club of America (EA)
HC(A)...........	Helicopter Coordinator (Airborne) (NVT)
HCA	Hepatocellular Adenoma [*Medicine*]
HCA	Heterocyclic Antidepressant [*Psychopharmaceutical*]
HCA	Hexachloroacetone [*Organic chemistry*]
HCA	High Courts of Admiralty [*British*]
HCA	Hispanic Computing Association (EA)
HCA	Historic Cost Accounts [*London Stock Exchange*]
HCA	Hobby Clubs of America (EA)
HCA	Hobie Class Association (EA)
HCA	Hollow Cylinder Apparatus [*Nuclear energy*] (NUCP)

HCA	Holy Childhood Association (EA)
HCA	Home Care Aide [Medicine] (DMAA)
HCA	Homocysteate [Biochemistry]
HCA	Horizon Crossing Ascending
HCA	Hospital Caterers Association [British]
HCA	Hot Cranking Amperes [Battery] [Automotive engineering]
HCA	Human Component Analysis
HCA	Humanitarian and Civic Assistance (DOMA)
HCA	Humanitarian Civic Action
HCA	Hunter Club of America (EA)
HCA	Hunting-Clan Air Transport Ltd.
HCA	Hyderabad Contingent Artillery [British military] (DMA)
HCA	Hydrocortisone Acetate [Pharmacology]
HCA	Lake Havasu Air Service [ICAO designator] (FAAC)
HCAA	Hebrew Christian Alliance of America [Later, MJAA]
HCAAO	Hawaii Council of Associations of Apartment Owners (SRA)
HCAC	Hazardous Chemicals Advisory Committee [New South Wales, Australia]
HCAM	Health Care Association of Michigan (SRA)
HC & C	Harvard Capital & Consulting [An investment fund] [Czechoslovakia] (ECON)
HCAP	Handicapped
H-CAP	Hexamethylmelamine, Cyclophosphamide, Adriamycin, Platinol [Cisplatin] [Antineoplastic drug regimen]
HCAR	Historic Commands of the American Revolution (EA)
HCAS	Highway Cost Allocation Study [Also, FHCAS]
HCAV	Hunt Clubs Association of Victoria [Australia]
HCAV	Hyperactive Children's Association of Victoria [Australia]
HCAW	Home Care Association of Washington (SRA)
HCB	Hard Convex Body [Equation of state]
HCB	Hard-Covered Book (WDAA)
HCB	Heaviside-Campbell Bridge [Electronics]
HCB	Hemisphere Cylinder Body
HCB	Hexachlorobenzene [Organic chemistry]
HCB	High Capability Buoy [Marine science] (MSC)
HCB	High-Capacity Bomb
HCB	Highland Cyclist Battalion [British military] (DMA)
HCB	Hollow Concrete Block
HCB	Hoopes Conductivity Bridge [Electronics]
HCB	House of Commons Bill [British]
HCB	Hungarian Credit Bank
HCB	Hydrocortisone Butyrate [Glucocorticoid]
HCBD	Hexachlorobutadiene [Organic chemistry]
HCBI	Health Conference for Business and Industry [Defunct]
HCBK	Hudson Chartered Bancorp [NASDAQ symbol] (TTSB)
HCBK	Hudson Chartered Bancorp, Inc. [NASDAQ symbol] (SAG)
HCBP	Hexachlorobiphenyl [Organic chemistry]
HCBP	Hexachlorobiphenyl [Marine science] (OSRA)
HCBS	Home and Community-Based Services [Department of Health and Human Services] (GFGA)
HCBS	Host Computer Basic Software (IAA)
HCBWAG	Home and Community-Based Waiver for Aged [Department of Health and Human Services] (GFGA)
HCBWAGD	Home and Community-Based Waiver for Aged and Physically and Developmentally Disabled [Department of Health and Human Services] (GFGA)
HCBWAGPD	Home and Community-Based Waiver for Aged and Physically Disabled [Department of Health and Human Services] (GFGA)
HCBWMI	Home and Community-Based Waiver for Mentally Ill [Department of Health and Human Services] (GFGA)
HCBWMRDD	Home and Community-Based Waiver for Mentally Retarded and Developmentally Disabled [Department of Health and Human Services] (GFGA)
HCBWPDS	Home and Community-Based Waiver for Physically Disabled [Department of Health and Human Services] (GFGA)
HCC	Hand Control Clutch (DNAB)
HCC	Hardware Capability Code [Dialog] [Searchable field] [Information service or system] (NITA)
HCC	Harlem Cultural Council (EA)
HCC	Hawaii Control Center [Missiles] (MUGU)
HCC	HCC Insurance Hldgs [NYSE symbol] (TTSB)
HCC	HCC Insurance Holdings [NYSE symbol] (SAG)
HCC	Health Care Card (ADA)
HCC	Health Care Corp. [Proposed] (DHSM)
HCC	Health Coordinating Council
HCC	Heliax Coaxial Cable
HCC	Helicopter Control Center (NVT)
HCC	Helicopter Coordination Center
HCC	Helicopter Crash Crane (DNAB)
HCC	Hepatitis Contagiosa Canis [Virus]
HCC	Hepatocellular Carcinoma [Oncology]
HCC	Hereditary Colon Cancer
HCC	Hermetic Chip Carrier
HCC	Hibbing Community College, Hibbing, MN [OCLC symbol] (OCLC)
HCC	History of Chief Complaint [Medicine]
HCC	Hobart Chamber of Commerce [Australia]
HCC	Hollow Copper Conductor
HCC	Hollywood Comedy Club (EA)
HCC	Holy Cross [California] [Seismograph station code, US Geological Survey] (SEIS)
HCC	Holyoke Community College [Massachusetts]
HCC	Home Care Coordinator [Medicine]
HCC	Honda Car Club [Defunct] (EA)
HCC	Honda Civic Club [Later, H-I] (EA)
HCC	Honeycomb Corrugated Construction

HCC	Hospital Conveyance Corps [British military] (DMA)
HCC	Host Country Contributions [Peace Corps]
HCC	Hubcap Collector's Club (EA)
HCC	Hull Construction Certificate
HCC	Hummel Collectors Club (EA)
HCC	Humor Correspondence Club (EA)
HCC	Hyderabad Contingent Cavalry [British military] (DMA)
HCC	Hydraulic Cement Concrete
HCC	Hydrocarbon Concentration [Automotive engineering]
HCC	Hydroxycholecalciferol [Biochemistry]
HCCA	Heavy Construction Contractors Association
HCCA	Hellenic Chamber of Commerce in Australia
HCCA	Horseless Carriage Club of America (EA)
HCCAACT	Health Care Consumers' Association of the Australian Capital Territory
HCCAPS	Helmet Compatible Communications/Aural Protection System
HCCBE	Hungarian Central Committee for Books and Education (EA)
HCCC	Computer Center [Haverford College] [Research center] (RCD)
HCCC	HealthCare COMPARE [NASDAQ symbol] (TTSB)
HCCC	HealthCare COMPARE Corp. [NASDAQ symbol] (NQ)
HCCC	Health Care Complaints Commission [Australia]
HCCC	Helix Countercurrent Chromatography
HCCG	Discharge [from Military Service] under Honorable Conditions, Convenience of Government
HCCH	Hexachlorocyclohexane [Organic chemistry]
HCC Ins	HCC Insurance Holdings [Associated Press] (SAG)
HCCM	Discharge [from Military Service] under Honorable Conditions, Convenience of Man
HCCM	Hadley Centre Climate Model
HCCM	High-Performance Common Channel Module [Telecommunications]
HCCO	Hector Communications [NASDAQ symbol] (TTSB)
HCCO	Hector Communications Corp. [NASDAQ symbol] (SAG)
HCCP	Hexachlorocyclopentadiene [Also, HCP, HEX] [Organic chemistry]
HCCP	Honorary Certified Claims Professional
HC/CPP	Historical Cost/Current Purchasing Power
HCD	College of the Holy Cross, Worcester, MA [OCLC symbol] (OCLC)
HCd	Hair Cadmium Level [Medicine]
HCD	Handcarried (AABC)
HCD	Hard-Copy Device [Computer science] (ECII)
HCD	Heavy Chain Disease [Protein]
HCD	High Carbohydrate Diet [Medicine] (DMAA)
HCD	High-Current Density
HCD	High-Current Diode
HCD	Highest Common Denominator
HCD	Hoffman Core Driver
HCD	Hollow Cathode Discharge [Spectrometry]
HCD	Homologous Canine Distemper [Antiserum]
HCD	Horizon Crossing Descending
HCD	Horizontal Correlation Distance
HCD	Hot-Carrier Diode (IEEE)
HCD	Hughes Communications Division (SAA)
HCD	Hutchinson, MN [Location identifier FAA] (FAAL)
HCD	Hydrocolloid Dressing [Dermatology]
HCD	Hyundai California Design [Concept car]
HCDA	Housing and Community Development Act (GFGA)
HCDA	Hydrodynamic Core Disruptive Accident [Nuclear energy] (NRCH)
HCDA	Hypothetical Core Disruptive Accident [Nuclear energy]
HCDB	Historical Cost Database
HCDD	Hexachlorodibenzodioxin [Organic chemistry]
HCDE	Homothetic-Constant Differences of Elasticities of Substitution [Statistics]
HCDP	Discharge [from Military Service] under Honorable Conditions, Dependency Existing Prior to Enlistment
HCDR	Hardware Critical Design Review (MCD)
HCDR	Hours and Cost Detail Report
HCDV	Hilcoast Development [NASDAQ symbol] (TTSB)
HCDV	Hilcoast Development Corp. [NASDAQ symbol] (SAG)
hce	Hard-Coal Equivalents (BARN)
HCE	Haveth Childer Everywhere [Key phrase in "Finnegan's Wake"]
HCE	Health Care Education
HCE	Here Comes Everybody [Key phrase in "Finnegan's Wake"]
HCE	Hic Conditus Est [Here Lies Buried] [Latin]
HCE	Highly Compensated Employee [Human resources] (WYGK)
HCE	Hollow-Cathode Effect (IEEE)
HCE	Human-Caused Error
HCE	Humphrey Chimpden Earwicker [Hero of "Finnegan's Wake"]
HCEA	Hairdressers and Cosmetologists Employers' Association [Australia]
HCEA	Health Care Exhibitors Association (EA)
HCEA	Holland Cheese Exporters Association [Later, DDB] (EA)
HCEBT	Houston Cotton Exchange and Board of Trade [Defunct] (EA)
HCEC	Hospital Care Evaluation Committee (MEDA)
HCED	Hand Controller Engage Driver (NASA)
HCEE	Discharge [from Military Service] under Honorable Conditions, Expiration of Enlistment
HCEEP	Handicapped Children's Early Education Programs
HCEI	Hydrocarbon Emission Index [Automotive engineering]
HCEX	High-Speed Color Exterior
HCF	Fluorocarbon without Chlorine (ECON)
HCF	Hagerstown CATI [Computer-Assisted Telephone Interviewing] Facility [Bureau of the Census] (GFGA)
HCF	Halt and Catch Fire [Computer hacker terminology] (NHD)
HCF	Hardened Compact Fiber
HCF	Health Care Finder
HCF	[The] Healthcare Forum (EA)
HCF	Heat Control Filter

HCF............ Hebrew Christian Fellowship (EA)
HCF............ Hebrew Culture Foundation (EA)
HCF............ Height Correction Factor
HCF............ Hereditary Capillary Fragility [Medicine] (DMAA)
HCF............ High Carbohydrate, High Fiber [Nutrition]
HCF............ High-Carbon Ferrochrome [Metallurgy]
HCF............ High Circle Fatigue
HCF............ High Coefficient of Friction [Engineering]
HCF............ High-Cycle Fatigue [Rocket engine]
HCF............ Highest Common Factor [Mathematics]
HCF............ HIM [Hardware Interface Module] Configuration File [NASA] (NASA)
HCF............ Honeycomb Foundation (IIA)
HCF............ Honorary Chaplain to the Forces [British]
HCF............ Hood College, Frederick, MD [OCLC symbol] (OCLC)
HCF............ Host Command Facility
HCF............ Hungarian Cultural Foundation (EA)
HCFA .... Health Care Financing Administration [HHS]
HCFA .... [United States] Health Care Financing Administration
HCFAR .... Health Care Financing Administration Rulings [A publication] (DLA)
HCFC .... Helen Cornelius Fan Club (EA)
HCFC .... Hydrochlorofluorocarbon [Organic chemistry]
HCFC .... Hydrochlorofluorocarbons (EERA)
HCFD .... Hydrochemical Form Die [Tool] (AAG)
HCFF........... High-Capacity Fog Foam [Navy] (NVT)
HCFF/AFFF... High-Capacity Fog Foam/Aqueous Film-Forming Foam (DNAB)
HCFMS .... Holy Cross Foreign Mission Society (EA)
HCFP .... HealthCare Financial Partners, Inc. [NASDAQ symbol] (SAG)
HCFR .... Health Care Financing Review [A publication] (DLA)
HCF Rev ..... Health Care Financing Review [A publication] (DLA)
HCFSG .... Health Care Financing Study Group (EA)
HCFTA .... Home and Contract Furnishing Textiles Association [British] (DBA)
hCFTR .... Human Cystic Fibrosis Transmembrane Conductance Regulator [Genetics]
hCFU .... Human Colony-Forming Unit [Genetics]
HCG .... Griqualand High Court Reports [A publication] (DLA)
HCG .... Hardware Character Generator
HCG .... Hermanas Catequistas Guadalupanas [Sister Catechists of Guadeloupe] [Roman Catholic women's religious order]
HCG .... Home Capital Group, Inc. [Toronto Stock Exchange symbol]
HCG .... Horizontal Location of Center of Gravity
HCG .... Human Chorionic Gonadotrophin [Endocrinology]
hCG .... Human Chorionic Gonadotropin [A hormone] (PAZ)
HCGB .... Hover Club [British] (DBA)
HCGF .... Haematopoietic Cell Growth Factor [Biochemistry]
HCGN .... Hypocomplementemic Glomerulonephritis [Nephrology] (DAVI)
HCGO .... Heavy Coker Gas Oil [Petroleum technology]
hCGRP .... Human Calcitonin Gene-Related Peptide [Biochemistry]
HCGS .... Hope Creek Generating Station (NRCH)
HCH .... Crossville, TN [Location identifier FAA] (FAAL)
H-CH .... Handy-Cap Horizons [Defunct] (EA)
HCH .... Health Care for the Homeless (DMAA)
HCH .... Health-Chem [AMEX symbol] (TTSB)
HCH .... Health-Chem Corp. [AMEX symbol] (SPSG)
HCH .... Herbert Clark Hoover [US president, 1874-1964]
HCH .... Herding Champion [Prefix]
HCH .... Hexachlorocyclohexane [Also, BHC, GBH] [Insecticide]
HCHBK .... Hatchback [Automotive advertising]
HCHC .... High Carbon, High Chrome
HChD .... Diploma in Higher Chiropodial Theory of the Institute of Chiropodists [British] (DBQ)
HCHF .... High Carbohydrate, High Fiber [Nutrition]
Hchg .... Hechinger Co. [Associated Press] (SAG)
HCHGC .... Hollingworth Center for Highly Gifted Children (EA)
HCHO .... Aldehydes [Organic chemistry]
HCHO .... Formaldehyde (GNE)
HCHO .... Formaldehyde [Organic chemistry] (DAVI)
HCHP .... Harvard Community Health Plan (DMAA)
HCHP .... Health Care for the Homeless Program [Defunct] (EA)
HCHP .... High-Capacity Heat Pipe (SSD)
HCHS .... Handicapped Children's Home Service [Later, Easter Seal Home Service] (EA)
HCHWA-D ... Hereditary Cerebral Hemorrhage with Amyloidosis of the Dutch Type [Medicine]
HCI............. Handgun Control, Inc. (EA)
HCI............. Hardness-Critical Item (MSA)
HCI............. Hawthorne Communications, Inc.
HCI............. HCI Holdings Ltd. [Toronto Stock Exchange symbol]
HCI............. Health Care International [British]
HCI............. Health Commons Institute
HCI............. Hierarchically Classified Index
HCI............. High-Current Inductor
HCI............. Home Center Institute (EA)
HCI............. Host Computer Interface
HCI............. Hotel and Catering Institute [British] (BI)
HCI............. Hughes Communications, Inc. [Hughes Aircraft Co.] [Los Angeles, CA]
HCI............. Human-Computer Interaction [Computer science]
HCI............. Human-Computer Interface (RDA)
HCI............. Hybrid Computer Interface (MHDB)
HCI............. Hyderabad Contingent Infantry [India] [Army]
HCI............. Hydrochloride (CPH)
HCIA .... HCIA, Inc. [NASDAQ symbol] (SAG)
HCIA .... Highlander Class International Association (EA)
HCIL........... Human-Computer Interaction Laboratory [University of Maryland] (PCM)

HCIm .... HealthCare Imaging Services, Inc. [Associated Press] (SAG)
HCIMA .... Hotel Catering and Institutional Management Association [British] (DI)
HCIMA .... Hotel, Catering, and Institutional Management Association [British] (DBA)
HcIMP .... Hydrocolloid Impression [Dentistry]
HCIS .... Health Care Information System (DMAA)
HCIS .... Hospital Communication and Information System [McDonnell Douglas Automation Co.]
HCIS .... House Committee on Internal Security [Formerly, HUAC] [Dissolved, 1975 US Congress]
HCITB .... Hotel and Catering Industry Training Board [British] (BI)
HCITE......... Horizontal Cargo Integration Test Equipment (MCD)
HCJ........... High Court of Justice
HCJB .... High Court Junior Beadle [Ancient Order of Foresters]
HCJC .... Henderson County Junior College [Texas]
HCJC .... Howard County Junior College [Texas]
HCJFC......... Harry Connick, Jr., Fan Club (EA)
HC Jour ..... House of Commons Journals [England] [A publication] (DLA)
HCJW......... High Court Junior Woodward [Ancient Order of Foresters]
HCK .... Hematopoietic Cell Kinase (DMAA)
HCK .... Human Cervical Keratinocyte [Cytology]
HCKRY .... Hickory
HCL .... Central Hispano Capital Ltd. [NYSE symbol] (SAG)
HCL .... Hairy Cell Leukemia [Medicine]
HCL .... Hamburg-Chicago Line [Steamship] (MHDB)
HCL .... Hard Contact Lens [Ophthalmology]
HCL .... Harold Cohen Library [University of Liverpool] [British] (NITA)
HCL .... Harpoon Check List [Missiles] (MCD)
HCL .... Helium Cadmium LASER
HCL .... High, Common, Low [Relay] (IEEE)
HCL .... High Cost of Living
HCL .... Hollow Cathode Lamp
HCL .... Horizontal Center Line
HCL .... Human Cultured Lymphoblastoid [Cells]
HCL .... Human Cultured Lymphoblasts [Medicine] (DMAA)
HCL .... Huron College [UTLAS symbol]
HCL .... Husson College, Bangor, ME [OCLC symbol] (OCLC)
HCL .... Hyderabad Contingent Lancers [British military] (DMA)
HCl .... Hydrochloric Acid
HCl .... Hydrogen Chloride [Inorganic chemistry]
HCL .... International Hod Carriers', Building and Common Laborers' Union of America [Later, Laborers' International Union of North America]
HCLA .... Hungarian Catholic League of America (EA)
HCLD .... Housing Construction and Land Development
HCLE .... Humanities Center for Liberal Education
HCLF.......... Health Care Libraries Forum [Association of Specialized and Cooperative Library Agencies]
HCLF.......... High Carbohydrate, Low Fiber [Nutrition]
HCLF.......... Horizontal Cask Lifting Fixture [Nuclear energy] (NRCH)
HCLIP .... Harvard Computer-Aided Legal Instruction Project (DLA)
HcllMed....... Housecall Medical Resources, Inc. [Associated Press] (SAG)
HCLM......... Health Care Labor Manual [A publication] (DLA)
HC-LN......... High Control/Low Nurturance [Psychology]
HCLP .... Home Conversion Loan Program [Canada]
HCLPr......... Centl Hispano Cap 10.50% Pref [NYSE symbol] (TTSB)
HCLPrB........ Central Hispano Cap 9.43% Pref [NYSE symbol] (TTSB)
HCM .... Haitian Campaign Medal
HCM .... Half-Cycle Magnetizer (IDOE)
HCM .... Halifax Conservatory of Music
HCM .... Harcum, VA [Location identifier FAA] (FAAL)
HCM .... Hard Copy Module (NASA)
HCM .... Hard Core Monitor [Computer science] (IAA)
HCM .... HARDMAN [Hardware-Manpower Program] Comparability Methodology [Army]
HCM .... Health Care Maintenance (DAVI)
HCM .... High Capacity Multiplexing [Telecommunications] (ACRL)
HCM .... Highway Capacity Manual [FHWA] (TAG)
HCM .... His [or Her] Catholic Majesty
HCM .... Hundred Club of Massachusetts (EA)
HCM .... Hydraulic Core Mock-Up [Nuclear energy] (NRCH)
HCM .... Hydrocarbon Mass [Automotive engineering]
HCM .... Hypercalcemia of Malignancy [Medicine]
HCM .... Hypertrophic Cardiomyopathy [Cardiology]
HCMA .... Alula [Somalia] [ICAO location identifier] (ICLI)
HCMA .... Hotel Credit Managers Association [Defunct] (EA)
HCMB .... Baidoa [Somalia] [ICAO location identifier] (ICLI)
HCMC .... Candala [Somalia] [ICAO location identifier] (ICLI)
HCMC .... Ho Chi Minh City [Vietnam]
HCMD .... Bardera [Somalia] [ICAO location identifier] (ICLI)
HCME .... Eil [Somalia] [ICAO location identifier] (ICLI)
HCMF .... Bosaso [Somalia] [ICAO location identifier] (ICLI)
HCMF .... Henry Clay Memorial Foundation (EA)
HCMG .... Gardo [Somalia] [ICAO location identifier] (ICLI)
HCMH .... Hargeisa [Somalia] [ICAO location identifier] (ICLI)
HCMI .... Berbera [Somalia] [ICAO location identifier] (ICLI)
HCMI .... Homeless Chronically Mentally Ill [Medicine]
HCMJ .... Lugh Ferrandi [Somalia] [ICAO location identifier] (ICLI)
HCMK .... Kisimayu [Somalia] [ICAO location identifier] (ICLI)
HCML .... El Bur [Somalia] [ICAO location identifier] (ICLI)
HCMM .... Heat Capacity Map Mission [NASA]
HCMM .... Heat Capacity Mapping Mission [Satellite] (EERA)
HCMM .... Heavy Capability Mapping Mission [Satellite]
HCMM .... Hereditary Cutaneous Malignant Melanoma [Medicine] (DMAA)
HCMM .... Mogadishu [Somalia] [ICAO location identifier] (ICLI)

HCMMS	Health Care Material Management Society (EA)
HCMN	Belet Uen [*Somalia*] [*ICAO location identifier*] (ICLI)
HCMO	Obbia [*Somalia*] [*ICAO location identifier*] (ICLI)
HCMOS	High-Speed Complementary Metal-Oxide Semiconductor (MCD)
HCMP	Las Anod [*Somalia*] [*ICAO location identifier*] (ICLI)
HCMPA	Home Counties Master Printers' Alliance [*British*] (DGA)
HCMR	Galcaio [*Somalia*] [*ICAO location identifier*] (ICLI)
HCMR	Heat Capacity Mapping Radiometer [*NASA*]
HCMS	Discharge [*from Military Service*] under Honorable Conditions, Medical Survey
HCMS	Scusciuban [*Somalia*] [*ICAO location identifier*] (ICLI)
HCMTS	High-Capacity Mobile Telecommunications System (TEL)
HCMU	Discharge [*from Military Service*] under Honorable Conditions, under Age of Authorized Enlistment
HCMU	Erigavo [*Somalia*] [*ICAO location identifier*] (ICLI)
HCMU	Hebrew Cabinet Makers' Union [*British*]
HCMV	Burao [*Somalia*] [*ICAO location identifier*] (ICLI)
HCMV	Human Cytomegalovirus
HCMW	Discharge [*from Military Service*] under Honorable Conditions, Minor Enlisted Without Consent, under Eighteen at Time of Discharge
HCMW	United Hatters, Cap, and Millinery Workers International Union (EA)
HCN	Health Care REIT [*NYSE symbol*] (SAG)
HCN	Health Communications Network [*Medical University of South Carolina*] [*Charleston*] [*Telecommunications*] (TSSD)
HCN	Hilton Communications Network [*Hilton Hotels Corp.*] [*Beverly Hills, CA*] [*Telecommunications service*] (TSSD)
HCN	Historical Climate Network
HCN	Home Counties Newspapers [*British*] (DGA)
HCN	Hydrocyanic Acid [*Inorganic chemistry*]
HCN	Hydrogen Cyanide [*Also, AC*] [*Inorganic chemistry*]
HCN	Hygienic Community Network (EA)
HCN	Nereditary Chronic Nephritis [*Medicine*] (DMAA)
HCNSW	Heritage Council of New South Wales [*Australia*]
HCO	Hangar Control Officer [*Navy*]
HCO	Harco Air Services [*Nigeria*] [*ICAO designator*] (FAAC)
HCO	Harvard College Observatory
HCO	Head of Contracting Office [*Marine science*] (OSRA)
HCO	Head of Contracting Office (USDC)
HCO	Headquarters Catalog Office
HCO	Health Care Organization (HCT)
HCO	Hearing Carry-Over [*Hearing-impaired technology*]
HCO	Heavy Cycle Oil [*Petroleum technology*]
HCO	Helicopter Control Officer [*British military*] (DMA)
HCO	Higher Clerical Officer [*Civil Service*] [*British*]
HCO	Highly-Chlorinated Oil (IAA)
HCO	Horizontal Control Operator [*Military*]
HCO	Huntco, Inc. [*NYSE symbol*] (SAG)
HCO	Huntco Inc'A' [*NYSE symbol*] (TTSB)
HCO	Hydrogenated Coconut Oil (PDAA)
HCO₃	Bicarbonate [*Pharmacology*] (DAVI)
HCO₃	Bicarbonate (GNE)
HCOC	Honorary Colonel of the Corps [*Army*]
H Conf Rept	House of Representatives Conference Report (BARN)
HCONN	Hose Connector
H Con Res	House of Representatives Concurrent Resolution (DLA)
HCOP	Health Care Opportunities Program [*Department of Health and Human Services*]
HCOR	HealthCor Holdings, Inc. [*NASDAQ symbol*] (SAG)
HCOR	Honorary Colonel of the Regiment
HCP	Habitat Conservation Plan [*Ecology*]
HCP	Hamiltonian Cycle Problem [*Computer science*]
HCP	Handicap
HCP	Handicap Race [*Horse racing*]
HCP	Hangar Control Position [*Navy*]
HCP	Harbor Control Post
HCP	Hard Copy Printer [*Computer science*]
HCP	Hardness-Critical Process (MSA)
HCP	Health Care Products, Inc. [*Toronto Stock Exchange symbol*]
HCP	Health Care Property Investors, Inc. [*NYSE symbol*] (SPSG)
HCp	Health Care Prop Inv [*NYSE symbol*] (TTSB)
HCp	Heat of Combustion (of an Element under Constant Pressure) (ROG)
HCP	Hemispherical Candlepower [*Optics*] (IAA)
HCP	Hepatocatalase Peroxidase [*An enzyme*] (MAE)
HCP	Hereditary Coproporphyria [*Medicine*] (MAE)
HCP	Hexachlorocyclopentadiene [*Also, HCCP, HEX*] [*Organic chemistry*]
HCP	Hexachlorophene [*Germicide*]
HCP	Hexagonal Close-Packed [*Crystallography*]
HCP	High-Calcium Pyroxene [*Mineralogy*]
HCP	Holiday Caravan Parks [*Public-performance tariff class*] [*British*]
HCP	Home Consumption Price
HCP	Horizontal Candlepower
HCP	Host Communications Processor
HCP	Hybrid Combustion Process (RDA)
HCP	Hydrazine Catalytic Plenum
HCP	Hydroxycalcium Phenoxide [*Organic chemistry*]
HCP	Hydroxycyclopentenone
HCP	Hydroxyproline-Containing Protein
HCP	Hypervelocity Countermeasures Program
HCP	Hypothermal Coal Process (GNE)
HCPAA	Hungarian Catholic Priests' Association in America (EA)
HCPC	Health Care Compliance Packaging Council (EA)
HCPCS	HCFA [*Health Care Financing Administration*] Common Procedures Coding System [*Department of Health and Human Services*] (GFGA)
HCPDG	Health Care Professionals Discussion Group [*American Occupational Therapy Association*]
HCPNY	Harbor Carriers of the Port of New York (EA)
HCPOTP	Health Care Practitioner Other Than Physician (MEDA)
HCPOTP	Health Care Professionals other than Physicians (HCT)
HCPP	Health Care Prepayment Plan
HCPS	Hemispherical Candlepower Second [*Optics*] (IAA)
HCPS	Horizontal Candlepower Seconds
HCPT	Historic Churches Preservation Trust [*British*] (BI)
HCPT	Hydroxycamptothecin [*Antineoplastic drug*]
HCPTR	Helicopter (CINC)
HCPV	Hydrocarbon Pore Volume [*Petroleum technology*]
H/CQ	Habitability/Crew Quarters (KSC)
HCQ	Halls Creek [*Australia Airport symbol Obsolete*] (OAG)
HCQ	Harbours Corp. of Queensland [*Australia*]
HCQ	Hot Carrier Quad
HCQ	Hydroxychloroquine [*Disease modifying antirheumatic drug*]
HCQIA	Health Care Quality Improvement Act [*1986*] (HCT)
HCR	Hard Copy Response (SAA)
HCR	Hardware Check Routine
HCR	Hardware Correction Report
HCR	Haut Commissariat des Nations Unies pour les Refugies [*United Nations High Commission for Refugees - UNHCR*] [*Switzerland*]
HCR	Health Care & Retirement [*NYSE symbol*] (TTSB)
HCR	Health Care & Retirement Corp. [*NYSE symbol*] (SPSG)
HCR	HealthCare and Retirement Corp. [*Associated Press*] (SAG)
HCR	Height Cross Range (MCD)
HCR	Hemin Controlled Repressor [*Biochemistry*]
HCR	High Charge Retention (PDAA)
HCR	High Chief Ranger [*Ancient Order of Foresters*]
HCR	High Court Reports, India [*A publication*] (DLA)
HCR	High Cross Range
HCR	Highway Contract Route
HCR	Holy Cross [*Alaska*] [*Airport symbol*] (OAG)
HCR	House Concurrent Resolution [*US Congress*]
HCR	Household Cavalry Regiment [*British military*] (DMA)
HCr	Houston's Delaware Criminal Cases [*A publication*] (DLA)
HCR	Human-Controlled Repressor [*Genetics*] (DAVI)
HCR	Hurricane Rescue Craft, Inc. [*Vancouver Stock Exchange symbol*]
HCR	Hydrochloric Acid [*Organic chemistry*] (DAVI)
HCR	Hysterical Conversion Reaction [*Psychiatry*] (DAVI)
HCRC	Hallwood Consolidated Res. [*NASDAQ symbol*] (TTSB)
HCRC	Hallwood Consolidated Resources Corp. [*NASDAQ symbol*] (SAG)
HCRC	Hillsdale County Railroad Co., Inc. [*AAR code*]
HCRC	Hotel and Catering Research Centre [*British*] (IRUK)
HCRD	Health Care Research Division [*Brooke Army Medical Center*]
HCRE	Homeopathic Council for Research and Education (EA)
HCREF	Health Care Research and Educational Foundation [*Later, AAMAREF*] (EA)
HC Res	House of Representatives Concurrent Resolution [*Legal term*] (DLA)
HCRF	Health Care Research Foundation [*Australia*]
HCRI	Health Care Research Institution [*Australia*]
HCRIS	Hospital Cost Report Information System (MEDA)
H'CRIT	Hematocrit [*Medicine*]
HCRM	Holocaust Curriculum Resources Material (BJA)
HCRNWF	High Court Reports, North West Frontier [*A publication*] (DLA)
HCRNWP	High Court Reports, Northwest Provinces [*India*] [*A publication*] (DLA)
HCRO	High Cross-Range Orbiter (KSC)
HCRON	Helicopter Combat Support Squadron [*Navy*] (DNAB)
HCRP	Hominid Corridor Research Project [*Palaeontology*]
HCRR	Home Counties Reserve Regiment [*British military*] (DMA)
HCRS	Heritage Conservation Recreation Service [*Abolished, 1981, functions transferred to National Park Service*] [*Department of the Interior*]
HCRST	Hardware Clipping, Rotation, Scaling, and Translation (MHDI)
HCRSV	Hibiscus Chlorotic Ringspot Virus [*Plant pathology*]
HCRW	Hot and Cold Running Water
HCS	Hajdu-Cheney Syndrome [*Medicine*] (DMAA)
HCS	Hammered Chainmakers' Society [*A union*] [*British*]
HCS	Handicapped Children's Services
HCS	Hard-Clad Silica [*Materials science*]
HCS	Hard Copy System [*Computer science*] (MHDI)
HCS	Harris Consultive Services, Inc. [*Information service or system*] (IID)
HCS	Harry C. Stutz [*Designer of early automobile*]
HCS	Harvey Cushing Society [*Later, AANS*] (EA)
HCS	Hazard Communication Standard [*OSHA*]
HCS	Hazardous Chemicals Secretariat [*Victoria, Australia*]
HCS	Header Check Sequence [*Computer science*]
HCS	Health Care Support [*System*] [*IBM Corp.*]
HCS	Health Computing Services [*Australia*]
HCS	Healthy Cities Secretariat [*Australia*]
HCS	Helicopter Control Ship [*Navy*] (NVT)
HCS	Helium Circulator Seal (IEEE)
HCS	High-Carbon Steel
HCS	High Clad Silica (PDAA)
HCS	High-Compression Swirl [*Automotive engineering*]
HCS	High Court Secretary [*Ancient Order of Foresters*]
HCS	Histochemical Society (EA)
HCS	Home Civil Servant [*British*]
HCS	Home Civil Service [*British*]
HCS	Home Run Control System [*Computer science*]
HCS	Homogeneous Computer System
HCS	Hospital Car Service
HCS	Host Composition System [*Infograph Ltd.*] (NITA)
HCS	Hourglass Contraction of Stomach [*Gastroenterology*] (DAVI)

HCS .... House Committee Substitute [*US Congress*]
HCS .... Hover Coupler System (DWSG)
HCS .... HUD [*Housing and Urban Development*] Clearinghouse Service
HCS .... Human Chorionic Somatomammotrophin [*Also, CGP, hcs, HPL*] [*Endocrinology*]
HCS .... Human Cord Serum
HCS .... Hummocky Cross-Stratification [*Sedimentology*]
HCS .... Hundred Call Seconds [*Telecommunications*]
HCS .... Hybrid Computation and Simulation (SSD)
HCS .... Hydrogen Control System (NRCH)
HCS .... Hydromechanical Control System (KSC)
HCS .... Hydroxycorticosteroids [*Pharmacology*] (DAVI)
HCS .... Membership Section for Health Care Systems [*An association*] (EA)
HCSA .... Halogenated Cleaning Solvent Association (EA)
HCSA .... Hate Crimes Statistics Act
HCSA .... Hexylcarbonate of Salicylic Acid [*Analgesic*]
HCSA .... Hospital Consultants' and Specialists' Association [*British*] (DCTA)
HCSA .... House Committee on Space and Astronautics [*US Congress*] (AAG)
HCSB .... High Court Senior Beadle [*Ancient Order of Foresters*]
HCSBC .... Historical Commission, Southern Baptist Convention (EA)
HCSCIA .... Health Care Studies and Clinical Investigation Activity [*Fort Sam Houston, TX*] [*Army*]
HCSD .... Health Care Studies Division [*Academy of Health Sciences*] [*Army*]
HCSDS .... High-Capacity Satellite Digital Service [*AT & T*] (TSSD)
HCSF .... Histamine-Producing Cell-Stimulating Factor [*Biochemistry*]
HCSG .... Health Care Services Group [*NASDAQ symbol*] (SAG)
HCSG .... Healthcare Services Group, Inc. [*NASDAQ symbol*] (NQ)
HCSG .... Healthcare Svcs Group [*NASDAQ symbol*] (TTSB)
HCSG .... Hyperactive Children's Support Group [*England*]
HCSHT .... High-Carbon Steel, Heat-Treated
HCSI .... Hughes Communications Services, Inc. (NASA)
HCSL .... Hybrid Computational Science Laboratory
HCSL .... Hybrid Computation and Simulation Laboratory
HCSLP .... Hungarian Committee of Socialist Labor Party [*Defunct*] (EA)
HCSM .... Human Chorionic Somatomammotropin [*Endocrinology*]
HCSM .... Mogadishu [*Somalia*] [*ICAO location identifier*] (ICLI)
HCSNSW ...... Home Care Service of New South Wales [*Australia*]
HCSP .... High-Capacity Signal Processor
HCSPR .... Hundred Call Seconds Per Hour [*Telecommunications*] (ACRL)
HCSR .... E. O. Hulbert Center for Space Research (MCD)
HCSRDG ...... Health and Community Services Research and Development Grants [*Australia*]
HCSS .... Head Compartment Support Structure [*Nuclear energy*] (NRCH)
HCSS .... High-Capacity Storage System [*Novell, Inc.*] [*Computer science*] (PCM)
HCSS .... Home and Colonial School Society [*British*]
HCSS .... Hospital Computer Sharing System (IEEE)
HCSTR .... Homogeneous Continuous Stirred Tank Reactor [*Chemical engineering*]
HCSW .... High Court Senior Woodward [*Ancient Order of Foresters*]
HCT............. Hardware Compatibility Test [*Microsoft Corp.*] (PCM)
HCT............. Hayes Center, NE [*Location identifier FAA*] (FAAL)
HCT............. Health Check Test (DMAA)
HCT............. Heart-Circulation-Training [*Physical fitness*]
HCT............. Heater Center Tap [*Electronics*] (ECII)
HCT............. Heater Center Top
HCT............. Hematocrit [*Medicine*]
HCT............. High Commission Territories Corps [*Military unit*] [*British*]
H Ct .... High Court
HCT............. High Court Treasurer [*Ancient Order of Foresters*]
HCT............. Histamine Challenge Test [*Biochemistry*] (DAVI)
HCT............. Historic Control Trial [*Medicine*] (DMAA)
HCT............. Hollow Cathode Tube
HCT............. Homocytotropic [*Medicine*] (MAE)
HCT............. Hot Cathode Tube
HCT............. Howitzer Crew Trainer [*Military*]
HCT............. Hull Collector Tank
hCt .... Human Calcitonin [*Endocrinology*]
HCT............. Human Chorionic Thyrotrophin [*Endocrinology*]
HCT............. Hydraulic Components Test
HCT............. Hydrochlorothiazide [*Drug*] [*Also, HCTZ, HCZ*] [*Organic chemistry*]
HCT............. Hydrocortisone [*Endocrinology*]
HCTB .... Hotel and Catering Training Board [*British*]
HCTBA .... Hotel and Catering Trades Benevolent Association [*British*] (BI)
HCTC .... Hotel and Catering Training Co. (AIE)
HCTDS .... High-Capacity Terrestrial Digital Service [*AT & T*] (TSSD)
HCTF .... Helium Component Test Facility [*Nuclear energy*] (NUCP)
HCTL .... Healthcare Technologies Ltd. [*NASDAQ symbol*] (NQ)
HCTLF .... Healthcare Technologies Ltd [*NASDAQ symbol*] (TTSB)
HCTLR .... High Commission Territories Reports [*Basutoland, Bechuanaland, and Swaziland*] [*A publication*] (DLA)
HCTS .... House Call Tax Service
HCTSS .... Health Care Technology Study Section [*HEW*] (EGAO)
HCTU .... Home Cervical Traction Unit [*Medicine*] (DAVI)
HCTZ........... Hydrochlorothiazide [*Drug*] [*Also, HCT, HCZ*] [*Organic chemistry*]
HCU .... Handheld Computer Unit
HCU .... Harbor Clearance Unit [*Navy*] (NVT)
HCU .... Harbor Control Unit
HCU .... Hard Copy Unit
HCU .... Health Care Unit [*DoD*] (GFGA)
HCU .... Heavy Conversion Unit [*British military*] (DMA)
HCU .... Helicopter Control Unit (NVT)
HCU .... Helium Charging Unit (AAG)
HCU .... Homing Comparator Unit (AAG)
HCU .... Homocystinuria [*Medicine*]

HCU .... Horse Canyon [*Utah*] [*Seismograph station code, US Geological Survey*] (SEIS)
HCU .... Hydraulic Charging Unit (NASA)
HCU .... Hydraulic Control Unit [*Nuclear energy*] (NRCH)
HCU .... Hydraulic Coupling Unit [*Automotive engineering*]
HCU .... Hydraulic Cycling Unit (AFM)
HCU .... Hyperplasia Cystica Uteri [*Medicine*] (DMAA)
HCUA .... Honeywell Computer Users Association (HGAA)
HCUDET....... Harbor Clearance Unit Detachment [*Navy*] (DNAB)
HCUND .... Hospitality Committee for United Nations Delegations (EA)
HCUP .... Hospital Cost and Utilization Project [*Department of Health and Human Services*] (GFGA)
HCUS .... Discharge [*from Military Service*] under Honorable Conditions, Unsuitable
HCUT .... Homfray Carpets Unit Trust [*Commercial firm*] [*British*]
HCV .... Hand Control Valve (NRCH)
HCv .... Heat of Combustion (of an Element under Constant Volume) (ROG)
HCV .... Hepatitis C Virus
HCV .... Hercules Ventures [*Vancouver Stock Exchange symbol*]
HCV .... High Calorific Value [*of a fuel*]
HCV .... High Capacity Voice (ACRL)
HCV .... Hog Cholera Virus (DMAA)
HCV .... Hull Check Valve
HCV .... Human Coronavirus
HCV .... Hutchinson Cablevision [*British*]
HCV .... Hydraulic Check Valve (GFGA)
HCV .... Hydraulic Control Valve
HCVC .... Historic Commercial Vehicle Club [*British*] (DCTA)
HCVCS .... Historic Commercial Vehicle Cooperative Society [*Australia*]
HCVD .... Hypertensive Cardiovascular Disease [*Medicine*]
HCVIS .... High Clouds Visible [*NWS*] (FAAC)
HCVRCS....... Hill Counselor Verbal Response Category System (EDAC)
HCW .... Home Computing Weekly [*British*] (NITA)
HCW .... Paine Webber Group [*AMEX symbol*] (SAG)
HCWI .... High-Chromium White Iron
HC Wkly Inf Bull... House of Commons Weekly Information Bulletin [*A publication*] (DLA)
HCY .... Cowley/Lovell/Byron, WY [*Location identifier FAA*] (FAAL)
Hcy .... Homocysteine [*An amino acid*]
HCZ............ Hydrochlorothiazide [*Drug*] [*Also, HCT, HCTZ*] [*Organic chemistry*]
HCZ............ Hydrogen Convection Zone
HD .... Air-Conditioning Apparatus [*JETDS nomenclature*] [*Military*] (CET)
HD .... Air-Cushion Vehicle built by Hovercraft Development [*England*] [*Usually used in combination with numerals*]
HD .... Hajna-Damon Broth [*Medicine*] (DMAA)
HD .... Half Duplex Transmission [*Data communication*] (CET)
HD .... Hand (ROG)
HD .... Hand-Drawn
HD .... Hansen's Disease [*Leprosy*] [*Medicine*]
HD .... Harbor Defense [*Military*]
HD .... Hard (MSA)
HD .... Hard Disk [*Computer science*]
HD .... Hard-Drawn [*Metallurgy*]
HD .... Hardware Design
H-D .... Harley-Davidson
HD .... Harmonic Distortion
HD .... Hawaiian Department [*Army World War II*]
HD .... Head (AAG)
hd .... Head (WDMC)
HD .... Head Diameter
HD .... Head Driver (IAA)
HD .... Heading
Hd .... Headland [*Maps and charts*]
HD .... Heard (ROG)
HD .... Hearing Distance [*Medicine*]
HD .... Heart Disease [*Medicine*]
HD .... Heat Detector [*NFPA pre-fire planning symbol*] (NFPA)
HD .... Heat Dissipation (DNAB)
HD .... Heavy Distillate [*Fuel technology*]
HD .... Heavy-Duty
HD .... Helicopter Delivered
HD .... Helicopter Direction (DNAB)
HD .... Helicopter Director [*Military*] (CAAL)
HD .... Heloma Durum [*A hard corn*] [*Orthopedics*] (DAVI)
HD .... Hemidesmosome [*Cytology*]
HD .... Hemodialysis [*Nephrology*]
HD .... Hemodilution
HD .... Hemolyzing Dose [*Medicine*]
HD .... Henry Draper Catalogue [*Astronomy*]
HD .... Hepatosis Diaetetica [*Veterinary science*] (OA)
HD .... Herniated Disc [*Medicine*]
HD .... Hexadecimal Code [*Computer science*] (IAA)
H-D .... Hexadecimal-to-Decimal [*Computer science*] (IEEE)
HD .... Hexagonal Domain Structure
HD .... Hexanedione [*Organic chemistry*]
HD .... Hierarchical Direct
HD .... High Density
HD .... High Detergent (WGA)
HD .... High Dose [*Medicine*]
HD .... High Drag [*Navy*] (NVT)
HD .... High Dust
HD .... High Dynamic
HD .... Highland Division [*British military*] (DMA)
HD .... Highly Desirable (KSC)

HD .... Hilda Doolittle [Initials used as pen name of American poet, 1886-1961]
HD .... Hip Disarticulation [Medicine]
HD .... Hirschsprung's Disease [Medicine] (DMAA)
HD .... Histone Deacetylase [An enzyme]
HD .... Historical Development
HD .... Historical Division [Air Force]
HD .... Historic Deerfield (EA)
HD .... Hodgkin's Disease [Medicine]
HD .... Hogshead
H/D .... Holddown (AAG)
HD .... Holddown
HD .... Home Defence [British World War II]
HD .... Home Depot [NYSE symbol] (TTSB)
HD .... [The] Home Depot, Inc. [NYSE symbol] (SPSG)
HD .... Homoeodomain [Genetics]
HD .... Homoserine Dehydrogenase [An enzyme]
HD .... Honorable Discharge [Military]
HD .... Honorary Degree [Freemasonry] (ROG)
HD .... Hora Decubitus [At Bedtime] [Pharmacy]
HD .... Horizontal Distance [Photography] (OA)
HD .... Horizontal Drain
HD .... Horizontal Drive
HD .... Horse-Drawn
HD .... Hospital Day (DAVI)
HD .... Hourly Difference [Navigation]
HD .... House Document
HD .... House Dust (DMAA)
HD .... Housing Debtline [Telephone service] [British]
HD .... Housing Density
HD .... Huddersfield [Postcode] (ODBW)
HD .... Human Development
HD .... Humanitarian Deferment [Military]
HD .... Humper Dears (EA)
HD .... Hundred
HD .... Hunter and Driffield [System to indicate film emulsion speed] (BARN)
HD .... Huntington's Disease [Medicine]
HD .... Hurel Dubois [Societe de Construction des Avions Hurel Dubois] [France ICAO aircraft manufacturer identifier] (ICAO)
HD .... Hurricane Deck
HD .... Hydatid Disease [Medicine] (MAE)
HD .... Hydralazine [Antihypertensive drug]
HD .... Hydrogen Drain (MCD)
H-D .... Hypothetico-Deductive
HD .... Hypotonic Duodenogram [Medicine]
HD .... Mustard Gas [Also, H, HS, HT, M] [Poison gas US Chemical Corps symbol]
HD .... New York Helicopter [ICAO designator] (AD)
HDA .... Hail Detection Algorithm [Marine science] (OSRA)
HDA .... Hail Detection Algorithm (USDC)
HDA .... Halopredone Diacetate [Endocrinology]
HdA .... Handwoerterbuch des Deutschen Aberglaubens [A publication] (BJA)
HDA .... Harding Lake [Alaska] [Seismograph station code, US Geological Survey] (SEIS)
HDA .... Hardwood Distributors Association (EA)
HDA .... Harris Daishowa Australia Ltd. [Commercial] (EERA)
HDA .... Head Disk Assembly
HDA .... Headquarters, Department of the Army
HDA .... Heaviest Duty Available [Motor vehicle specifications]
HDA .... Heavy-Duty Amplifier
HDA .... Held for Detail Available (MCD)
HDA .... Heteroduplex Analysis (DMAA)
HDA .... Hexadecenyl Acetate [Pheromone] [Organic chemistry]
HDA .... Hexanediamine [or Hexamethylenediamine] [Organic chemistry]
HDA .... High-Density Acid
HDA .... High-Density Amorph [Materials science]
HDA .... High Duty Alloys Ltd.
HDA .... Higher Duties Allowance (ADA)
HDA .... Hodgkin's Disease Association [British] (DBA)
HDA .... Holddown Arm (KSC)
HDA .... Holistic Dental Association (EA)
HDA .... Honda [Colombia] [Airport symbol] (AD)
HDA .... Hong Kong Dragon Airlines Ltd. [ICAO designator] (FAAC)
HDA .... Horizontal Danger Angle [Navigation]
HDA .... Horticultural Dealers Association (EA)
HDA .... Hospital Doctors Association [British] (DBA)
HDA .... Housekeeping Data Acquisition (MCD)
HDA .... Housing and Development Administration [New York City]
HDA .... Housing Developers Association Ltd. [British] (BI)
HDA .... Huldra Silver [Vancouver Stock Exchange symbol]
HDA .... Huntington's Disease Association [Australia]
HDA .... Hydrogen Diffusion Anode [Electrochemistry]
HDA .... Hydroxydopamine [Also, HDM, OHDA] [Biochemistry]
HDAC .... Dictionary of the Apostolic Church [James Hasting] [A publication] (BJA)
HDAC .... Headache (KSC)
HDAC .... Heavy-Duty Air Cylinder
HDAg .... Hepatitis Delta Antigen [Immunology]
HDAL .... Hexadecenal [Pheromone] [Organic chemistry]
HDAM .... Hierarchical Direct Access Method [Computer science] (MCD)
HDAP .... Heavy-Duty Automatic Press
HDARAC .... High Dose Cytarabine [Medicine] (DMAA)
HDAS .... Hardened Digital Data Acquisition System [US Army Waterways Experiment Station] (RDA)
HDAS .... Historical Dictionary of American Slang [Random House]

HDAS .... Home Deposit Assistance Scheme [Australia]
HDAS .... House Defense Appropriations Subcommittee [US Congress] (AAG)
HDAS .... Hybrid Data Acquisition System
HDAS .... Hydrographic Data Acquisition System
HDASHY .... Haberdashery
HDATA .... Hydrogene Data [National College of Chemistry of Paris] [France] [Information service or system] (IID)
HDATZ .... High-Density Air Traffic Zone
HdAW .... Handbuch der Altertumswissenschaft [A publication] (BJA)
HDB .... [A] Dictionary of the Bible [James Hasting] [A publication] (BJA)
HDB .... Hamper, Deritend, Birmingham [Pseudonym used by William Hamper]
HDB .... Health Database Plus [Information Access Co.] [Information service or system] (PCM)
HDB .... Herpes-Dissociated Buffer [Medicine]
HDB .... High-Density Binary (TEL)
HDB .... High Density Bipolar (NITA)
HDB .... High-Density Bipolar Code [Telecommunications] (TEL)
HDB .... Horizontal Dynamic Balancing
HDB .... Hunter Development Board [Australia]
HDB3 .... High-Density Binary Three Level Signal (TEL)
HDB-3 .... High-Density Bipolar-3 (IDOE)
HDBA .... Horizontal Dynamic Balancing Adjustment
HDBD .... Hydroxybutyric Dehydrogenase [An enzyme] (DAVI)
HDBF .... Heavy Duty Business Forum (EA)
HDBH .... Hydroxybutyric Dehydrogenase [Clinical chemistry] (CPH)
HDBK .... Handbook (AFM)
hdbk .... Handbook (WDMC)
HDBMS .... Hierarchical Database Management System
HDC .... Claremont Men's College, Claremont, CA [OCLC symbol] (OCLC)
HDC .... Half Double Crochet
HDC .... Harbor Defense Command [Army]
HDC .... Harry Diamond Center [Army]
HDC .... Hasselblad Data Camera (MCD)
HDC .... Hawaiian Defense Command
HDC .... Heavy-Duty Contractor (MCD)
HDC .... Helicopter Direction Center
HDC .... Hierarchical Distributed Control [Computer science]
HDC .... High Dirt Capacity [A type of filter] [Pall Trinity Micro Corp.]
HDC .... High Duty Cycle (IAA)
HDC .... Histidine Decarboxylase [An enzyme]
HDC .... Holder in Due Course [Owner or holder of a negotiable instrument at some future time]
HDC .... Holston Defense Corp. (MCD)
HDC .... Hospital Data Center [American Hospital Association] [Information service or system] (IID)
HDC .... Hough Development Corp. [Cleveland]
HDC .... Housing Development Corp. (EA)
HDC .... Human Diploid Cell [Cytology] (DAVI)
HDC .... Hungarian Data Center [Defunct] (EA)
HDC .... Hybrid Device Controller (NASA)
HDC .... Hydrodynamic Chromatography
HDC .... Hydrogen Depolarized Carbon Dioxide Concentrator (OA)
HDCCAMS .... High-Dose Cyclophosphamide and Adriamycin [Antineoplastic drug regimen] (DAVI)
HDCD .... High Definition Compatible Digital [Compact-disc technology] (PS)
HDCES .... Hot/Dry Clothing and Equipment System [Army] (INF)
HDCG .... Dictionary of Christ and the Gospels [James Hasting] [A publication] (BJA)
HDCG .... Honorable Discharge, Convenience of Government [Military]
HDCH .... Headache
HDCM .... Honorable Discharge, Convenience of Man [Military]
HDCO .... Hadco Corp. [NASDAQ symbol] (NQ)
HDCOL .... Hand Colored (VRA)
HDCR .... Hard Chromium
HDCR(R) or (T) ... Higher Award in Radiodiagnosis or Radiotherapy, College of Radiographers [British] (DBQ)
HDCS .... Human Diploid Cell Strains [Immunology]
HDCV .... Human Diploid Cell Vaccine [For rabies]
HDD .... Halogenated Dibenzodioxin [Organic chemistry]
HDD .... Hard Disk Drive [Computer science]
HDD .... Head-Down Display [Aviation]
HDD .... Headsdown Display
HDD .... Heating Degree Days [Agriculture]
HDD .... Heavy-Duty Detergent
HDD .... Heavy-Duty Diesel [Vehicle]
HDD .... Heavy Duty Distribution [A publication]
HDD .... High-Density Data (KSC)
HDD .... High-Dosage Depth [Medicine] (DMAA)
HDD .... Higher Dental Diploma [British]
HDD .... Homopolar Disk Dynamo
HDD .... Human Disorientation Device
HDD .... Hyderabad [Pakistan] [Airport symbol] (OAG)
HDD .... Hydrogen Donor Diluents [Petroleum chemistry]
HDDA .... Hexadecadienyl Acetate [Pheromone] [Organic chemistry]
HDDA .... Hexanediol Diacrylate [Also, HDODA] [Organic chemistry]
HDDE .... Heavy-Duty Diesel Engine [Motor vehicle specifications]
HDDE .... Heavy Duty Diesel Engine
HD-DI .... Heavy-Duty Direct Injection [Diesel engines]
HDDP .... Honorable Discharge, Dependency Existing Prior to Enlistment [Military]
HDDP .... Hospital Discharge Demonstration Project (EDAC)
HDDR .... High-Density Digital Recording
HDDS .... High-Density Data System [Computer science]
HDDS .... Honorable Discharge, Dependency Arising Since Enlistment [Military]

HDDT	High-Density Digital Tape
HDDV	Heavy-Duty Diesel Vehicle
HDE	Heavy Duty Engine [Automotive engineering]
HDE	Heavy Duty Engine
HDE	High-Dose Epinephrine [Medicine]
HDE	Holdrege, NE [Location identifier FAA] (FAAL)
HDE	Homogeneous Differential Equation
HDEC	Holocaust Documentation and Education Center (EA)
HDED	Heavy-Duty Enzyme Detergent
HDEE	Honorable Discharge, Expiration of Enlistment [Military]
HDEG	Union List of Higher Degree Theses in Australian Libraries [University of Tasmania Library] [Australia Information service or system] (CRD)
HDeH	Hawker De Havilland [Australia]
HDEP	High Definition Electronic Production (NTCM)
HDEP	High-Density Electronic Packaging
HDES	Hydrodynamic Equilibrium System [For chromatography]
HDEU	Heating and Domestic Engineers' Union [British]
HDF	Haitian Development Fund [Later, MH] (EA)
HDF	Halogenated Dibenzofuran [Organic chemistry]
HDF	Handle Door Fastener
HDF	Hartmann Dispersion Formula
HDF	Hereditary Disease Foundation (EA)
HDF	Hierarchical Data Format [Computer science]
HDF	High-Density Flexible
HDF	High-Frequency Direction Finding [Electronics]
HDF	Horizontal Distributing Frame
HDF	Host Defensive Factor [Immunology] (AAMN)
HDF	Hubble Deep Field [Astronomy]
HDF	Human Diploid Fibroblasts [Cytology]
H/DF	Human/Dolphin Foundation (EA)
HDF	Hungarian Democratic Forum [Political party] (EY)
HDFP	Hypertension Detection and Follow-Up Program [NHLBI]
HDFRZ	Hard Freeze [NWS] (FAAC)
HDG	Halsey Drug [AMEX symbol] (TTSB)
HDG	Halsey Drug Co. [AMEX symbol] (CTT)
HDG	Heading (AFM)
HDG	Heavy-Duty Gasoline [Vehicle]
HDG	High-Dose Group [Medicine] (DMAA)
HDG	Hot Dip Galvanization
HDGA	Hot Dip Galvanizers Association [British] (BI)
HDGAF	Hot Dip Galvanizing After Fabrication [Metallurgy]
HDGCP	Human Dimensions of Global Change Programme [Canada] (EAIO)
HDGEC	Human Dimensions of Global Environmental Change (EERA)
HDGECP	Human Dimensions of Global Environmental Change Program [Marine science] (OSRA)
HDGP	High-Drag General-Purpose [Navy] (DNAB)
HDGS	High Dollar Group Sort (TDOB)
HDG SEL	Heading Select (GAVI)
HDH	Hauptverband der Deutschen Holz und Kunststoffe Verarbeitenden Industrie und Verwandter Industriezweige eV [Germany] (EY)
HDH	Heart Disease History [Medicine] (MAE)
HDH	Hemihydrate-Dihydrate [Chemical technology]
HDH	Histidinol Dehydrogenase [An enzyme]
HDH	Howden [D. H.] & Co. Ltd. [Toronto Stock Exchange symbol]
HDH	Hydrocracking-Distillation-Hydrotreatment (ECON)
HDH	Hydrogen Dehydrogenase [An enzyme]
HDH	Mokuleia, HI [Location identifier FAA] (FAAL)
HDHD	Hilf Du Heilige Dreifaltigkeit [Help Thou Holy Trinity] [Motto of Johann Georg I, Prince of Anhalt-Dessau (1567-1618)] [German]
HD/HE	Hospital Design/Hospital Equipment [British]
HDHL	High-Density Helicopter Landing [Army]
HDHQ	Hostility and Direction of Hostility Questionnaire [Psychology]
HDHS	Haul Down and Handling System [Canadian Navy]
HD-HT	Hemodilution Combined with Hypotension
HDHVPS	High-Density/High-Voltage Power Supply (DNAB)
HDI	Cleveland, TN [Location identifier FAA] (FAAL)
HDI	Hard Drives International (PCM)
HDI	Harley-Davidson [NYSE symbol] (TTSB)
HDI	Harley-Davidson, Inc. [NYSE symbol] (SPSG)
HDI	Hawaiian Development Irradiator [AEC]
HDI	Head-Disc Interference [Head crash] (NITA)
HDI	Headquarters Operating Instruction
HDI	Heavy-Duty Industrial [Internal combustion engines]
HDI	Helicopter Direction Inbound [Military] (CAAL)
HDI	Hemorrhagic Disease of Infants [Medicine] (DMAA)
HDI	Hexamethylene Diisocyanate [Organic chemistry]
HDI	High Definition Imaging
HDI	High-Density Interconnect
HDI	Horizontal Display Indicator (NG)
HDI	Hoteles Dinamicos SA de CV [Mexico ICAO designator] (FAAC)
HDI	House Dress Institute (EA)
HDI	Household Disposable Income
HDI	Human Development Index [Human Development Report] [United Nations Development Program]
HDI	Human Development Index (EERA)
HDI	Human Development Institute
HDIE	Healthdyne Info Enterprises [NASDAQ symbol] (TTSB)
HDIF	Heavy-Duty Industrial Filter
HDIL	Health and Drug Information Library
HDIP	Hazardous Duty Incentive Pay [Air Force] (AFM)
HDIP	High-Dose Immunological Paralysis [Medicine]
H Dip E	Higher Diploma in Education [British]
HDipEd	Higher Diploma in Education [Academic degree] (AIE)
HDipT	Higher Diploma of Teaching

HDIR	Heavy-Duty Industrial Relay
H Dist Ct	United States District Court, District of Hawaii (DLA)
HDIT	Hereditament [Legal shorthand] (LWAP)
HDIT	Home Drug Infusion Therapy [Medicine]
HDIV	Hughes Dynamic Imagery Viewer
HDK	Hidaka [Japan] [Seismograph station code, US Geological Survey] (SEIS)
HDK	Husband Doesn't Know (IIA)
HDKF	Handkerchief
HDL	Handel Society [Record label]
HDL	Handle (KSC)
HDL	Handleman Co. [NYSE symbol] (SPSG)
HDL	Hardware Description Language [Computer science]
HDL	Harry Diamond Laboratories [Formerly, DOFL] [Adelphi, MD] [Army]
HDL	Headline (WGA)
HDL	Hidalgo County Library System, McAllen, TX [OCLC symbol] (OCLC)
HDL	High-Density Lipoprotein [Biochemistry]
HDL	Holdenville, OK [Location identifier FAA] (FAAL)
HDL	Hydrologic Data Laboratory [Agricultural Research Service] (PDAA)
HDLA	High-Level Data Link Control Adapter [Data communication] (MHDI)
HDL-C	High-Density Lipoprotein - Cell Surface Receptor [Biochemistry]
HDLC	High-Density Lipoprotein Cholesterol [Physiology]
HDL-C	High Density Lipoprotein Fraction [Biochemistry] (DAVI)
HDLC	High-Level Data Link Control [International Standards Organization] [Data communication]
HDLD	Heavy-Duty Liquid Detergent
HDLE	Hurdle
HDLG	Handling (AABC)
HDLM	High-Level Data Linkage Module [Data communication] (MHDB)
HDLNR	Headliner
HDLP	High-Density Lipoprotein [Biochemistry] (AAMN)
HDLP	Holdup [FBI standardized term]
HDLR	Handler (AABC)
HDLR	Hexadecimal Symbolic Loader [Computer science] (MHDI)
HDLS	Hardware Description Language System (IAA)
HDLS	Headless (KSC)
HDLW	Distance at Which a Watch Is Heard with Left Ear [Medicine]
HDM	Haddam [Connecticut] [Seismograph station code, US Geological Survey] (SEIS)
HDM	Hamadan [Iran] [Airport symbol] (AD)
HDM	Hand-Deboned Meat
HDM	Harmonic Distortion Meter (DEN)
HDM	Hierarchical Development Method [Computer science]
HDM	High-Density Microsome [Cytology]
HDM	Hizbia Dighill e Mirifle [Somali political party]
HDM	Hot Dark Matter [Astronomy]
HDM	House Dust Mite
HDM	Hudson & Manhattan [AAR code]
HDM	Humic Degradation Matter (DICI)
HDM	Hydrodemetalation [Petroleum refining]
HDM	Hydrodynamic Machining [Manufacturing term]
HDM	Hydrodynamic Modulation
HDM	Hydroxydopamine [Also, HDA, OHDA] [Biochemistry]
HDMA	Hardwood Dimension Manufacturers Association [Later, NDMA] (EA)
HDMA	Heavy Duty Manufacturers' Association
HDMC	Helicopter Depot Maintenance Center (MCD)
HDMCC	Howdy Doody Memorabilia Collectors Club (EA)
HDMI	High-Density Multichip Interconnect [Semiconductor packaging]
HDML	Handheld Device Mark-up Language
HDML	Handheld Device Markup Language [Computer science] (PCM)
HDML	Harbor Defense Motor Launch [NATO] (NATG)
HDMP	Horizon Definition Measurement Program (DNAB)
HDMR	High-Density Moderated Reactor (IEEE)
HDMR	High-Density Multitrack Recording (MCD)
HDMS	High-Density Memory System
HDMS	High-Density MODEM System [Microcom] [Norwood, MA] [Computer science]
HDMS	Hizb Dastur Mustaghil Somalia [Somali Independent Constitution Party]
HDMS	Honeywell Distributed Manufacturing System (NITA)
HDMS	Honorable Discharge, Medical Survey [Military]
HDMSW	High-Density Mach Shock Wave
HDMT	High-Density Multi-Track
HDMTX	High Dose Methotrexate [Antineoplastic drug regimen]
HDMTX-CF	High-Dose Methotrexate-Citrovorum Factor [Antineoplastic drug regimen]
HDMTX-LV	High-Dose Methotrexate, Leucovorin [Antineoplastic drug regimen]
HDMU	Honorable Discharge, under Age of Authorized Consent [Military]
HDMW	Honorable Discharge, Minors Enlisted without Consent, under Eighteen at Discharge [Military]
HDN	Harden (KSC)
HDN	Hayden, CO [Location identifier FAA] (FAAL)
HDN	Hemolytic Disease of the Newborn [Medicine]
Hdn	Herodianus [Greek scholar, c. 200AD] [Classical studies] (OCD)
HDN	High-Density Nebulizer [Medicine] (MAE)
HDN	Hildon Mining [Vancouver Stock Exchange symbol]
HDN	Hydrodenitrogenation [of chemical compounds]
HDN	Steamboat Springs [Colorado] [Airport symbol Obsolete] (OAG)
hDNA	Deoxyribonucleic Acid, heteroduplex [Biochemistry, genetics]
hDNA	Deoxyribonucleic Acid, Histone [Biochemistry, genetics]
HDNA	Habonim Dror North America (EA)
HDNA	Hinged Deoxyribonucleic Acid [Biochemistry, genetics]
HDNG	Hardinge, Inc. [NASDAQ symbol] (SAG)
HDNPRSGR	Headquarters Squadron Personnel Group
HDNS	Hardness (MSA)

HDNSW........ High-Density Nuclear Shock Wave
HDNT............ Headnote
HdO .... Handbuch der Orientalistik [*Leiden*] [*A publication*] (BJA)
HDO .... Helicopter Direction Outbound [*Military*] (CAAL)
HDO .... Hondo, TX [*Location identifier FAA*] (FAAL)
HDOC .... Handy Dandy Orbital Computer (IEEE)
HDOC .... House Document
HDOCP........ Heavy-Duty Oil Classification Panel [*Automotive engineering*]
HDODA........ Hexanediol Diacrylate [*Also, HDDA*] [*Organic chemistry*]
HDOL .... Hexadecenol [*Pheromone*] [*Organic chemistry*]
HDOP............ Horizontal Dilution of Precision
HDOS .... Hard Disk Operating System
HDOT .... Inertial Vertical Speed (GAVI)
HDOV .... Hardover
HDP .... Hankyore Democratic Party [*South Korea Political party*] (EY)
HDP .... Harpoon Data Processor [*Missiles*] (MCD)
HDP .... Hearing Dog Project [*Later, HDRC*] (EA)
HDP .... Hexose Diphosphate [*Biochemistry*]
HDP .... Hiburd Properties [*Vancouver Stock Exchange symbol*]
HDP .... High-Density Plasma (SAA)
HDP .... High Detonation Pressure
HDP .... High-Discharge Pressure (IEEE)
HDP .... Holddown Post (NASA)
HDP .... Horizontal Data Processing
HDP .... Housing Development Program
HDP .... Huer Demokrat Parti [*Free Democrat Party*] [*Turkish Cyprus*] [*Political party*] (EY)
HDP .... Human Dimension of Global Environmental Change Programme [*The International Social Science Council*] (ECON)
HDP .... Huntington's Disease Protein [*Biochemistry*]
HDP .... Hydroxydimethylpyrimidine [*Organic chemistry*]
HDPAA........ Heparin-Dependent Platelet-Associated Antibody [*Medicine*] (DMAA)
HDPC........... Health Data Policy Committee [*Department of Health and Human Services*] (GFGA)
HDPE .... High-Density Polyethylene [*Plastics*]
HDPPA........ Housing Development and Public Participation Administration [*Turkey*] (ECON)
HDPS .... High-Density Power Supply
HDQ .... Headquarters [*Colorado*] [*Seismograph station code, US Geological Survey Closed*] (SEIS)
HDQR .... Headquarters
HDQRS .... Headquarters
HDQTRS ..... Headquarters (NASA)
HDQTRS ..... Headquarters
HDR .... Hair's Daily Requirement [*Brand of shampoo*]
HDR .... Hand Rail
HDR .... Hardening Design Responses
HDR .... Header [*Computer science*]
HDR .... Header [*Automotive engineering*]
HDR .... [*File*] Header Label [*Computer science*] (ECII)
HDR .... Health Data Recorder [*Computer science*] (PDAA)
HDR .... High Data Rate
HDR .... High Data Register
HDR .... High Definition RADAR
HDR .... High-Density Recorder [*Deep Space Instrumentation Facility, NASA*]
HDR .... High Density Recording (NITA)
HDR .... High Dose Rate [*Medicine*] (DMAA)
HDR .... Holddown and Release (AAG)
HDR .... Home Dockyard Regulations [*Navy*] (MCD)
H-Dr............. Horse-Drawn [*Obsolete Army*]
HDR .... Hot Dry Rock [*Geothermal science*]
HDR .... Humanitarian Daily Ration [*Army*] (INF)
HDRA .... Heavy Duty Representatives Association (EA)
HDRA .... Henry Doubleday Research Association [*Coventry, England*] (EAIO)
HDRA .... High-Data-Rate Assembly (MCD)
HDRA .... High Desert Racing Association
HDRAA........ Henry Doubleday Research Association of Australia
HDRANCE .... Hindrance (ROG)
HDRC........... Hearing Dog Resource Center (EA)
HDRF........... Heart Disease Research Foundation (EA)
HDRI .... Hannah Dairy Research Institute [*British*] (BI)
HDRL .... High-Data-Rate LASER (MCD)
HDRM........... High-Data-Rate Multiplexer (MCD)
HDRO........... House Democratic Research Organization [*Defunct*] (EA)
HDRR........... High-Data Rate Recorder
HDRR........... Holloman Development Research Report [*Air Force*] (MCD)
HDRS........... Hamilton Depression Rate Scale [*Psychiatry*] (DAVI)
HDRS........... High-Data Rate Switch (MCD)
HDRSS........ High-Data-Rate Storage System [*or Subsystem*] [*NASA*] (MCD)
HDRV........... Human Diploid-Cell Rabies Vaccine
HDRW........... Distance at Which a Watch Is Heard with Right Ear [*Medicine*]
HDS .... Handicapped Driving Systems [*Burnsville, MN*]
HDS .... Hardware Description Sheet (NASA)
HDS .... HDS Network Systems, Inc. [*Associated Press*] (SAG)
HDS .... Head of Defence Sales [*British*] (RDA)
HDS .... Heads [*Automotive engineering*]
HDS .... Head Set [*Telecommunications*] (TEL)
HDS .... Health and Diet Survey [*Department of Health and Human Services*] (GFGA)
HDS .... Help Desk Services
HDS .... Herdis International Canada, Inc. [*Vancouver Stock Exchange symbol*]
HDS .... Hermes Data System [*Hermes Precisa International*] (NITA)
HDS .... Herniated Disc Syndrome [*Medicine*]
HDS .... Hills Department Stores, Inc. [*NYSE symbol*] (SPSG)

HDS .... Hills Stores [*NYSE symbol*] (TTSB)
HDS .... Hills Stores Co. [*NYSE symbol*] (SAG)
HDS .... Historical Data System [*Air Force*] (MCD)
HDS .... History of Dermatology Society (EA)
HDS .... Holographic Diffractive Structure [*Advanced Environmental Research Group*]
HDS .... Holy Days of Obligation [*Roman Catholicism*] (ROG)
HDS .... Hospital Discharge Survey [*Public Health Service*]
HDS .... Household Delivery Service [*British Post Office facility*] (DCTA)
HDS .... Hrvatski Demokratski Stranka [*Croatian Democratic Party*] [*Political party*] (EY)
HDS .... Humungous Development Syndrome (EERA)
HDS .... Hybrid Development System
HDS .... Hydrodesulfurization
HDS .... Hydrogen Detection System
HDS .... Office of Human Development Services [*Department of Health and Human Services*]
HDSA .... Huntington's Disease Society of America (EA)
HDSB .... Heavy Dry Support Bridge [*Army*] (RDA)
HDSC .... Harpoon Data System Cabinet [*Missiles*] (MCD)
HdSchm....... Head Schoolmaster [*Navy British*]
HDSCS......... Hospital Disaster Support Communications System
HD(S)E......... Home Defence Security Executive [*British World War II*]
HDSHK........ Handshake [*Computers*] (MSA)
HDSL .... High Bit Rate Digital Subscriber Line [*Computer science*] (CDE)
HDSL .... High-Data-Rate Digital Subscriber Line [*Telecommunications*] (DOM)
HDSL .... High Data Rate Digital Subscriber Line [*Computer science*]
HDSL .... High-Speed Digital Subscriber Loop [*Computer science*]
HDSN .... Hudson Technologies Inc. [*NASDAQ symbol*] (TTSB)
HDSN .... Hudson Technology, Inc. [*NASDAQ symbol*] (SAG)
HDS-NA ...... High Definition System for North America
HDS Nt .... HDS Network Systems, Inc. [*Associated Press*] (SAG)
HDSP........... Hardship (AABC)
HDSPr......... Hills Stores Sr'A' Cv Pfd [*NYSE symbol*] (TTSB)
HDSR........... Historical Data Storage and Retrieval
HDSS........... Holographic Data Storage System
HDST........... Headset (MCD)
HDST........... Headstart [*Education*] (OICC)
HDST........... High-Density Shock Tube (IEEE)
HDSVLY....... Hudson Valley (FAAC)
HDSW........... Handwoerterbuch der Sozialwissenschaft [*Dictionary of the Social Sciences*] [*A publication*]
HDSX........... HDS Network Systems [*NASDAQ symbol*] (TTSB)
HDSX........... HDS Network Systems, Inc. [*NASDAQ symbol*] (SAG)
HDSXW....... HDS Network Sys Wrrt [*NASDAQ symbol*] (TTSB)
HDT .... Half Duplex Teletype (KSC)
HDT .... Hard Disk ToolKIT [*Computer science*]
HDT .... Heat Deflection Temperature [*of plastics*]
HDT .... Heat Distortion Temperature
HDT .... Heavy-Duty Thermoplastic Insulation [*Automotive engineering*]
HDT .... Heavy Duty Truck [*Environmental Protection Agency*]
Hdt.............. Herodotus [*Greek historian, c. 484BC*] [*Classical studies*] (OCD)
HDT .... Hexadecanethiol [*Organic chemistry*]
HDT .... Hi-Pot Dwell Time
HDT .... Host Digital Terminal [*Telecommunications*] (ACRL)
HDT .... Humboldt, TN [*Location identifier FAA*] (FAAL)
HDT .... Hydrotreating [*or Hydrotreated*] [*Petroleum technology*]
HDTA .... High-Density Traffic Airport
HDTC .... Healthdyne Technologies [*NASDAQ symbol*] (SAG)
HDTC .... Heavy Duty Transient Cycle
HDTCS......... Hexadecyltrichlorosilane [*Organic chemistry*]
HDTM .... Half-Duplex Transmission Module [*Telecommunications*] (ACRL)
HDTMA .... Heavy-Duty Truck Manufacturers Association (EA)
HDTMA .... Hexadecyltrimethylammonium
HDTV .... High-Definition Television [*Offers wider-screen pictures with high resolution that improves their depth, clarity, and detail*]
HDU .... Hard Disc Unit (NITA)
HDU .... Heads-Up Display Unit [*Aviation*] (RDA)
HDU .... Hemodialysis Unit [*Medicine*]
HDU .... High Dependency Unit [*Medicine*] (DMAA)
HDU .... Home Defence Unit [*British military*] (DMA)
HDU .... Hose Down Unit (DOMA)
HDU .... Hyde Park [*Utah*] [*Seismograph station code, US Geological Survey*] (SEIS)
HDUE .... High Dynamic User Equipment
HDUR........... Hungarian Democratic Union of Romania [*Political party*] (EY)
HDV .... Halt Device (IAA)
HDV .... Heavy Duty Vehicle [*Environmental Protection Agency*]
HDV .... Hepatitis Delta Virus
HDV .... Hepatitis D Virus [*Medicine*] (DMAA)
HDV .... High-Definition Video
HDV .... High-Dollar Value
HDV .... Horse-Drawn Vehicle
HDV .... Hydrodevanadization [*Petroleum technology*]
HDV .... Hydrodynamic Voltammogram [*Electrochemistry*]
HDV .... Hydrodynamic Volume [*Physical chemistry*]
HD Vest ...... H. D. Vest, Inc. [*Associated Press*] (SAG)
HDVIP.......... Heavy-Duty Vehicle Inspection Program
HDVS........... H.D.Vest [*NASDAQ symbol*] (TTSB)
HDVS........... High Definition Video System
HDVS........... Vest [*H.D.*], Inc. [*NASDAQ symbol*] (SPSG)
HDW .... Hard-Drawn Wire [*Metallurgy*] (IAA)
HDW .... Hardware [*Computer science*] (KSC)
HDW .... Hearing Distance with Watch [*Medicine*]
HDW .... High-Pressure Demineralized Water (NRCH)

HDW	Hydrodynamic Welding
HDWA	Hardware [Computer science] (IAA)
HDWA	Health Department of Western Australia
HDWC	Hardware Cloth
HDWD	Hardwood
HDWE	Hardware
hdwe	Hardware (VRA)
HDWND	Headwind (FAAC)
HDWR	Hardware
HDWRE	Hardware (WGA)
HDWS	How Do We Stand
Hdwt	Hundredweight
HDWY	Headway Corporate Resources
HDWY	Headway Corporate Resources, Inc. [NASDAQ symbol] (SAG)
HDWY	Hideaway
HDX	Half Duplex [Telecommunications] (NITA)
HDX	Half Duplex Transmission [Data communication]
HDX	Hand-Held Dental X-Ray (RDA)
HDY	Haadyai [Thailand] [Airport symbol] (OAG)
HDY	Heavy-Duty
HDYN	Healthdyne, Inc. [NASDAQ symbol] (NQ)
HDZ	Hrvatska Demokratska Zajednica [Croatian Democratic Union] [Political party] (EY)
HDZNV	De Handschriften van de Dode Zee in Nederlandse Vertaling [Amsterdam] [A publication] (BJA)
HE	Altitude Error (GAVI)
HE	Green Bay Aviation [ICAO designator] (AD)
HE	Hall Effect [Electromagnetism] (OA)
HE	Handling Equipment
HE	Hard Exudate [Ophthalmology] (DAVI)
HE	Hardware Evaluator [NASA]
HE	Hardware Executive
HE	Hawaiian Elec Indus [NYSE symbol] (TTSB)
HE	Hawaiian Electric Industries, Inc. [NYSE symbol] (SPSG)
he	Head [Anatomy] (DAVI)
HE	Head End
HE	Header Extension [Telecommunications] (ACRL)
HE	Hearing Examiner [Also, ALJ]
HE	Hearsay Evidence [Legal shorthand] (LWAP)
He	Heart (DMAA)
HE	Heat Engine
HE	Heat Exchange [or Exchanger]
HE	Heavy Enamel (AAG)
HE	Heavy Equipment (AFM)
HE	[The] Hebrew [A publication] (BJA)
HE	Hebrews [Old Testament book]
He	Hedstrom Number [Chemistry] (DAVI)
HE	Height of Eye [Navigation]
HE	Heinkel [German aircraft type] [World War II]
HE	Hektoen Enteric Agar [Medicine] (DMAA)
HE	Helio Aircraft Co. [ICAO aircraft manufacturer identifier] (ICAO)
He	Helium [Chemical element]
HE	Hemagglutinating Encephalomyelitis [Neurology] (DAVI)
HE	Hematoxylin and Eosin [Biological stain]
HE	Hemicylindrical [Leaf characteristic] [Botany]
HE	Hemoglobin Electrophoresis [Medicine] (AAMN)
HE	Hepatic Encephalography [Medicine]
HE	Hepatic Encephalopathy [Medicine]
HE	Hepatic Extraction [Endocrinology]
HE	Hereditary Elliptocytosis [Medicine]
HE	Hexane-Extractable Compound
HE	Hic Est [Here Is, That is, or This is] [Latin]
HE	High Efficiency
HE	High Energy (MCD)
HE	High-Energy Astrophysics (NASA)
HE	Higher Education [Educational Resources Information Center (ERIC) Clearinghouse] [George Washington University] (PAZ)
HE	Higher Elongation (MCD)
HE	Highest Electroendosmosis [Analytical biochemistry]
HE	High Explosive (AAG)
HE	His Eminence
HE	His [or Her] Excellency
HE	Historia Ecclesiastica [of Eusebius] [Classical studies]
HE	Historical Period Ending Date [Dialog] [Searchable field] [Information service or system] (NITA)
HE	Hoc Est [That Is or This Is] [Latin]
HE	Hollis & Eastern Railroad Co. [AAR code]
HE	Hollow Enzyme [Medicine] (DMAA)
HE	Holy Empire [Freemasonry]
HE	Holy Eucharist
HE	Home Economics [Secondary school course] [British]
HE	Honda Engineering
HE	Horizontal Equivalent
HE	Horticultural Enterprise [A publication]
HE	House Error [Publishing] (WDMC)
HE	Housekeeping Element (TEL)
HE	Hub End (BARN)
HE	Human Engineering
HE	Human Enolase [An enzyme]
HE	Human Enteric [Virology]
HE	Human Events [A publication] (BRI)
HE	Human Exposure Dose [Medicine]
HE	Hydraulics Engineer
HE	Hydroelectric (IAA)
HE	Hydrogen Embrittlement

HE	Hydromagnetic Emission (IAA)
HE	Hydrophone Effect [Navy] (NVT)
HE	Hydroxyecdysone [Endocrinology]
HE	Hygienic Effect
HE	Hygienic Electrician [British] (ROG)
HE	Hypo Eliminator [Photography] (DGA)
HE	Hypogonadotrophic Eunuchoidism [Medicine]
HE	Hypophysectomy [Medicine] (DAVI)
HEA	Centre des Hautes Etudes Americaines [Paris]
HEA	Health Education Authority [British]
HEA	Heliavia-Transporte Aereo Lda. [Portugal ICAO designator] (FAAC)
HEA	Hemorrhagic Arteries [Veterinary medicine]
HEA	Herat [Afghanistan] [Airport symbol Obsolete] (OAG)
HEA	Hexone-Extracted Acetone [Chemistry] (DAVI)
HEA	High-Efficiency Antireflection [Optics]
HEA	Higher Education Act [1965]
HEA	Higher Education Authority (ACII)
HEA	Higher Education Authority [Ireland] (AIE)
HEA	Higher Education Awards (ACII)
HEA	Horticultural Education Association [British]
HEA	Horticulture Exhibitors Association [British] (DBA)
HEA	Hot Electron Amplifier
HEA	Human Erythrocyte Antigen [Hematology] (DAVI)
HEA	Hunter Education Association (EA)
HEA	Hydroxyethyl Acrylate [Organic chemistry]
HEAA	Higher Education Act Amendment [1992]
HEAA	High-Explosive, Antiaircraft [Weaponry]
HEAA	High-Explosive, Antiarmor [Weaponry] (MCD)
HEAC	Higher Education Accommodation Consortium [British] (DBA)
HEAD	Hand-Held Encryption and Authentication Device (RDA)
Head	Head's Tennessee Supreme Court Reports [1858-59] [A publication] (DLA)
HEAD	Helium-Atom Diffraction (PDAA)
HEADCOM	Headquarters Command [Military]
HEADE	High Erucic Acid Development Effort
HEADSS	Helicopter Escort, Air Defense Suppression System
Head (Tenn)...	Head's Tennessee Reports [38-40 Tennessee] [A publication] (DLA)
Headway	Headway Corporate Resources, Inc. [Associated Press] (SAG)
HEAE	Hyperacute Experimental Autoimmune Encephalomyelitis [Medicine] (PDAA)
HEAF	Heavy End Aviation Fuel
HEAF	Higher Education Assistance Foundation
HEAF	High Explosives Application Facility
HEAFS	High-Explosive Anti-Tank Fin-Stabilized [Military] (PDAA)
HEAL	Health Education Assistance Loan [Bureau of Health Professions]
HEAL	Healthwatch, Inc. [NASDAQ symbol] (NQ)
HEAL	Human Ecology Action League (EA)
HEAL	Human Exposure Assessment Location [Environmental Protection Agency] (GFGA)
HEALD	Healthwatch Inc. [NASDAQ symbol] (TTSB)
Heal JS Comp...	Healy on Joint Stock Companies [A publication] (DLA)
Heal Pews ...	Heale's Law of Church Pews [A publication] (DLA)
HEALS	Honeywell Error Analysis and Logging System
HealSB	Health Standards Board
HEALT	Helicopter Employment and Assault Landing Table (NVT)
HEALTH	Happiness, Energy, and Longevity through Health [Title of 1979 film directed by Robert Altman]
Health & SC...	Health and Safety Code [A publication] (DLA)
HEALTHLINE...	Health Planning and Administration [National Library of Medicine] [Database]
HEAMF	Hydroxyethylated Acid Modified Flour (OA)
HEANET	Higher Education Authority Network [Irish] [Computer science] (TNIG)
HEAO	High-Energy Astronomy Observatory [Pronounced "hee-oh"] [NASA]
HEAP	Helicopter Extended Area Platform
HEAP	High-Energy Aim Point [Weaponry] (MCD)
HEAP	High-Explosive, Antipersonnel [Weaponry]
HEAP	High-Explosive Armor-Piercing [Weaponry]
HEAPS	Hawaiian Environmental Analysis and Prediction System (MUGU)
HEAPS	High Energy Alpha-Proton Spectrometer (PDAA)
HEAR	El Arish/El Arish [Egypt] [ICAO location identifier] (ICLI)
HEAR	Health Associated Representatives [Later, HIRA] (EA)
HEAR	Hearing
HEAR	Hearing Education and Awareness for Rockers [An association]
HEAR	Hearing Education through Auditory Research [In association name, HEAR Center] (EA)
HEAR	Hereafter (ROG)
HEAR	High Erucic Acid Rapeseed [Agricultural chemistry]
HEAR	Hospital Emergency Ambulance Radio (LAIN)
HEAR	Human Error Action Report [NASA] (KSC)
Heard Civ Pl...	Heard's Civil Pleading [A publication] (DLA)
Heard Cr Pl...	Heard's Criminal Pleading [A publication] (DLA)
Heard Cur Rep...	Heard's Curiosities of the Law Reporters [A publication] (DLA)
Heard Eq Pl...	Heard's Equity Pleading [A publication] (DLA)
Heard Lib & Sl...	Heard on Libel and Slander [A publication] (DLA)
Heard's Shortt Extr Rem...	Heard's Edition of Shortt on Extraordinary Legal Remedies [A publication] (DLA)
Hear Exam...	Hearing Examiner [Legal term] (DLA)
HEAR-FOUND...	Hearing, Educational Aid and Research Foundation [Defunct] (EA)
Hearnshaw...	Southampton Court Leet Records [A publication] (DLA)
HEARS	Higher Education Administration Referral Service [Defunct] (EA)
HEART	Hardened Electronic and Radiation Technology
HEART	Hardened Electronics and Radiation Technology (MCD)
HEART	Health Equity and Access Reform Today [Plan]

HEART .... Health Evaluation and Risk Tabulation (MCD)
HEART .... Higher Education Action Research Team (AIE)
HEART .... Household Employment Association for Reevaluation and Training
          [*Later, Personnel Resources*]
HEART .... Hydrometer Erosion and Recession Test (MCD)
HEARTHFIRE... High-Energy Accelerator and Reactor for Thermonuclear Fusion
          with Ion Beams of Relativistic Energies
HeartInd ...... Heartland Partners Ltd. [*Associated Press*] (SAG)
Heartprt ...... Heartport, Inc. [*Associated Press*] (SAG)
Heartsong R... Heartsong Review [*A publication*] (BRI)
Heartst .... Heartstream, Inc. [*Associated Press*] (SAG)
HeartTc .... Heart Technology, Inc. [*Associated Press*] (SAG)
Hearx .... Hearx Ltd. [*Associated Press*] (SAG)
HEAS .... Home Energy Advisory Service [*Victoria, Australia*]
HEASDA...... Home Economics Association of Seventh-Day Adventists (EA)
HEAST .... Health Effects Assessment Summary Tables
HEAT............ Asyut [*Egypt*] [*ICAO location identifier*] (ICLI)
HEAT............ Helicopter External Air Transport (MCD)
HEAT............ Helpdesk Expert Automation Tool [*Bendata Management Systems,
          Inc.*]
HEAT............ High-Enthalpy Ablation Test
HEAT............ High Enthalpy Arc Tunnel [*NASA*]
HEAT............ High-Explosive, Antitank [*Weaponry*]
HEAT............ Human Erythrocyte Agglutination Test [*Hematology*]
HEAT............ Petroleum Heat & Pwr'A' [*NASDAQ symbol*] (TTSB)
Heath .... Heath's Reports [*36-40 Maine*] [*A publication*] (DLA)
HEATH .... Higher Education and the Handicapped [*An association*] (EA)
Heath Max... Heath's Maxims [*A publication*] (DLA)
HEAT-MP .... High-Explosive Antitank, Multipurpose [*Weaponry*] (MCD)
HEAT-MP-T... High-Explosive Antitank, Multipurpose, Tracer [*Weaponry*] (MCD)
HEAT-T....... High-Explosive Antitank-Tracer [*Weaponry*] (AABC)
HEAT-TP ..... High-Explosive Antitank, Training Projectile [*Weaponry*] (MCD)
HEAT-TP-T... High-Explosive Antitank, Target Practice, Tracer [*Weaponry*] (MCD)
Heaven B..... Heaven Bone
HEAVYPHOTORON... Heavy Photographic Squadron
HEAX .... Alexandria [*Egypt*] [*ICAO location identifier*] (ICLI)
HEB............. Hebraic [*Language, etc.*] (ROG)
HEB............. Hebrew
heb............. Hebrew [*MARC language code Library of Congress*] (LCCP)
Heb............. Hebrews [*New Testament book*]
HEB............. Heinemann Educational Books [*London, England*]
HEB............. Hematoencephalic Barrier [*or Blood brain barrier*] [*Medicine*] (DAVI)
HEB............. Hepar Embryonis Bovis [*Embryonic bovine liver cells used in tissue
          culture studies of viruses*] [*Medicine*]
HEB............. Hollow Electron Beam
HEBAH......... Heat Engine/Battery Hybrid (PDAA)
HEBBLE....... High-Energy Benthic Boundary Layer Experiment [*Oceanography*]
HEBC........... Heavy Enamel Bonded Cotton [*Wire insulation*]
HEBD........... Hebdomada [*A Week*] [*Pharmacy*] (ROG)
HEBDC......... Heavy Enamel Bonded Double Cotton [*Wire insulation*] (AAG)
HEBDOM...... Hebdomada [*A Week*] [*Pharmacy*]
HEBDP .... Heavy Enamel Bonded Double Paper [*Wire insulation*] (AAG)
HEBDS........ Heavy Enamel Bonded Double Silk [*Wire insulation*] (AAG)
HEBE........... Higher Education Business Enterprises Ltd. (AIE)
HEBL........... Abu Simbel [*Egypt*] [*ICAO location identifier*] (ICLI)
HEBP .... Heavy Enamel Bonded Paper [*Wire insulation*]
Hebr........... Hebraic (BJA)
HEBR .... Hebrew
Hebrew C.... Hebrew College (GAGS)
HEBS .... Heavy Enamel Bonded Silk [*Wire insulation*]
HEBS .... High-Energy Battery System
HEBT .... High-Energy Beam Transport [*For protons*]
HEC............. Ecole des Hautes Etudes Commerciales, Bibliotheque [*UTLAS
          symbol*]
HEC............. Hamster Embryonic Cell
HEC............. Hardened Electronic Component
HEC............. Harken Energy [*AMEX symbol*] (TTSB)
HEC............. Harken Energy Co. [*AMEX symbol*] (SPSG)
HEC............. Hasselblad Electric Camera
HEC............. Hastings Environment Council (EERA)
HEC............. Hautes Etudes Commerciales (DD)
HEC............. Hazeltine Electronics Corp. (MCD)
HEC............. Header Error Control [*Telecommunications*] (ACRL)
HEC............. Health Education Council [*British*] (DAVI)
HEC............. Health Evaluation Center (DAVI)
HEC............. Heavy Enamel Single Cellophane [*Wire insulation*] (IAA)
HEC............. Heavy Enamel Single Cotton [*Wire insulation*] (AAG)
Hec............. Hecate [*A publication*]
HEC............. Hector, CA [*Location identifier FAA*] (FAAL)
HEC............. Hector Resources, Inc. [*Vancouver Stock Exchange symbol*]
Hec............. Hecuba [*of Euripides*] [*Classical studies*] (OCD)
HEC............. Helicopter Element Coordinator [*Navy*] (ANA)
HEC............. Heliservicio Campeche SA de CV [*Mexico ICAO designator*] (FAAC)
HEC............. Hella Electronics Corp. [*Automotive industry supplier*]
HEC............. Hepatoma Cells [*Oncology*]
HEC............. High Emission Cathode
HEC............. High-Energy Chemistry
HEC............. Higher Education (ECON)
HEC............. Hodgin's Election Cases [*Ontario*] [*A publication*] (DLA)
HEC............. Hollerith Electronic Computer
HEC............. Home Equity Conversion
HEC............. Human Economy Center (EA)
HEC............. Human Endometrial Cancer [*Oncology*]
HEC............. Human Endothelial Cell [*Cytology*]
HEC............. Human Enteric Coronavirus

HEC............. Human Environment Center (EA)
HEC............. Human Epithelial Cell [*Cytology*]
HEC............. Hydro Electricity Commission [*of Tasmania*] [*State*] (EERA)
HEC............. Hydrogen Embrittlement Cracking (PDAA)
HEC............. Hydrologic Engineering Center [*Davis, CA*] [*Army*] (GRD)
HEC............. Hydroxyergocalciferol [*Organic chemistry*] (MAE)
HEC............. (Hydroxyethyl)cellulose [*Organic chemistry*]
HEC............. Hydroxyethylcysteine [*Organic chemistry*]
HEC............. United States Department of Health and Human Services, Health
          Care Financial Administration, Baltimore, MD [*OCLC symbol*]
          (OCLC)
HECA........... Cairo/International [*Egypt*] [*ICAO location identifier*] (ICLI)
HECA........... Harpoon Environmental Correction Aid [*Navy*] (ANA)
HECAD........ Human Engineering Computer-Aided Design [*Air Force*]
HECATE....... Heat Exchanger Computerized Aid for Technical Engineering (IAA)
HECC .... Cairo [*Egypt*] [*ICAO location identifier*] (ICLI)
HECC .... Higher Education Coordinating Council of Metropolitan St. Louis
          [*Library network*]
HECC .... Hooker Electro-Chemical Co.
HECC .... House Energy and Commerce Committee (GFGA)
HECD .... Hall Electrolytic Conductivity Detector [*Analytical instrumentation*]
HECD .... Helium Cadmium [*LASER*] (DGA)
HECH .... Hechinger Co. [*NASDAQ symbol*] (NQ)
HECHA........ Hechinger Co. Cl'A' [*NASDAQ symbol*] (TTSB)
HECHB'....... Hechinger Co. Cl'B' Cv [*NASDAQ symbol*] (TTSB)
HECI........... Hawkins Energy [*NASDAQ symbol*] (TTSB)
HECI........... Hawkins Energy Corp. [*NASDAQ symbol*] (SAG)
HECI........... Human-Interface Equipment Catalog Item (TEL)
Heck Cas .... Hecker's Cases on Warranty [*A publication*] (DLA)
HeclaM........ Hecla Mining Co. [*Associated Press*] (SAG)
HECLINET .... Health Care Literature Information Network [*Institut fuer
          Krankenhausbau*] [*Germany Information service or system*] (IID)
HecIM.......... Hecla Mining Co. [*Associated Press*] (SAG)
HE Cls B ..... Heating Coils in Bunkers [*on a ship*] (DS)
HE Cls C ..... Heating Coils in Cargo Tanks [*on a ship*] (DS)
HECMAR ...... Human Engineering Criteria for Maintenance and Repair [*GE, NASA*]
HECP .... Harbor Entrance Control Post [*Nautical charts*]
HECRE .... High-Energy Cosmic Ray Experiment [*Balloon flight*] [*NASA*]
HECSA .... Humphreys Engineering Center Support Activity (AAGC)
HECSAGON... Horowitz-Eastman-Crane Symbol Array Governed by Orthodox
          Notation (NITA)
HECSE .... Higher Education Consortium on Special Education (EDAC)
HECSU .... Higher Education Careers Service Unit (AIE)
HECT........... Hectare (WDAA)
HectCm........ Hector Communications Corp. [*Associated Press*] (SAG)
HECTO......... Hectograph
HECTOG...... Hectogram
HECTOL....... Hectoliter
HECTOM...... Hectometer [*100 meters*]
HECTOR....... Heated Experimental Carbon Thermal Oscillator Reactor [*British*]
HECUA........ Higher Education Consortium for Urban Affairs (EA)
HECV .... Heavy Enamel Cotton Varnish [*Wire insulation*]
HECV .... Helium Check Valve (MCD)
HECV .... Human Enteric Coronavirus
HECVES....... Harbor Entrance Control Vessel
HED .... Hall Effect Device
HED .... Haut-Einheits-Dosis [*Unit Skin Dose*] [*Radiation therapy*]
HED .... Haut-Erythem-Dosis [*Skin erythema dose*] [*Radiation therapy*] (DAVI)
HED .... Hazard Evaluation Division [*Environmental Protection Agency*]
HED .... Headline [*Advertising*] (DOAD)
hed .... Headline (WDMC)
HED .... Headquarters (CINC)
HED .... Hedley Pacific Mining [*Vancouver Stock Exchange symbol*]
HED .... Herendeen Bay, AK [*Location identifier FAA*] (FAAL)
HED .... Hidrotic Ectodermal Dysplasia [*Dermatology*]
HED .... High-Energy Detector [*NASA*]
HED .... High-Explosive Delay [*Weaponry*] (MCD)
HED .... Historical Earthquake Data (NRCH)
HED .... Historical English Dictionary [*A publication*]
HED .... Horizontal Electrical Dipole (IEEE)
HED .... Howardite, Eucrite, Diogenite [*Meteorite composition*]
HED .... Human Engineering Data
HED .... Human Engineering Discrepancy [*Nuclear energy*] (NRCH)
HED .... Hydraulically Extendable Dipperstick [*for tractors*]
HED .... Hydrotropic Electron-Donor [*Medicine*] (DMAA)
HED .... Hymnal-Epic Dialect (BJA)
HED .... Hypohidrotic Ectodermal Dysplasia [*Medicine*]
HEDC .... Hasselblad Electric Data Camera
HEDC .... Heavy Enamel Double Cotton [*Wire insulation*]
HEDCC .... Human Error Data Control Center [*NASA*] (KSC)
HEDCOM...... Headquarters Command [*Military*]
HEDCV .... Heavy Enamel Double Cotton Varnish [*Wire insulation*] (AAG)
HEDDS......... Hawaii Educational Dissemination Diffusion System [*Hawaii State
          Department of Education*] [*Honolulu*] [*Information service or
          system*] (IID)
HEDF .... High Energy Density Facility [*Proposed site for testing nuclear
          bombs*]
HEDF .... High-Speed Electro-Drive Fan [*Automotive engineering*]
HEDGE .... Human Factor Evaluation Data for General Equipment
HEDGE .... Human Factors Engineering Data Guide for Evaluation
Hedges .... Hedges' Reports [*2-6 Montana*] [*A publication*] (DLA)
HEDH .... Hypohidrotic Ectodermal Dysplasia-Hypothyroidism [*Syndrome*]
          [*Medicine*] (DMAA)
HEDI .... High Endoatmospheric Defense Interceptor [*Military*] (RDA)
HEDING........ Hedingham [*England*]

HEDIS .... Health Plan Employer Data and Information Set
HEDL .... Hanford Engineering and Development Laboratory [*Richland, WA*] [*Department of Energy*]
HEDP .... Hearing Ear Dog Program (EA)
HEDP .... High-Explosive Dual-Purpose [*Cartridge*] (RDA)
HEDP .... (Hydroxyethylidene)diphosphonic Acid [*Also, EHDP*] [*Organic chemistry*]
HEDR .... Hanford Environmental Dose Reconstruction [*Radiobiology*]
HEDRON ..... Headquarters Squadron [*Obsolete*]
HEDRONFAIRWING... Headquarters Squadron Fleet Air Wing
HEDS .... Heavy Enamel Double Silk [*Wire insulation*]
HEDS .... Herpetic Eye Disease Study
HEDS .... High Endoatmospheric Defense System
HEDS .... Higher Education Data Sharing (EDAC)
HEDS .... High-Explosive, Discarding Sabot [*Weaponry*] (AAG)
HEDS .... Hydraulic End Design System [*Computer-aided design*]
HEDSUPPACT... Headquarters Support Activity
HEDSV .... Heavy Enamel Double Silk Varnish [*Wire insulation*] (AAG)
HEDTA .... Hydroxyethylenediaminetriacetic Acid [*Organic chemistry*]
HEE .... Heerlen [*Netherlands*] [*Seismograph station code, US Geological Survey*] (SEIS)
HEE............ Helena/West Helena, AR [*Location identifier FAA*] (FAAL)
HEE............ Heli Europe [*Belgium ICAO designator*] (FAAC)
HEE............ Hemiconvulsion, Hemiplegia, and Epilepsy Syndrome [*Neurology*] (DAVI)
HEE............ Household Earnings and Expenditure
HEEA.......... Home Economics Education Association (EA)
HEEB.......... High-Energy Electrolyte Battery
HEED.......... High-Energy Electron Diffraction
HEEDTA ...... (Hydroxyethyl)ethylenediaminetetracetate [*or -tetracetic*] Acid [*Organic chemistry*]
HEEEL......... High-Energy Electronically Excited LASER
HEEI........... (Hydroxyethyl)ethyleneimine [*Organic chemistry*]
HEEM.......... Embaba [*Egypt*] [*ICAO location identifier*] (ICLI)
HEEM.......... Hardsite Engagement Effectiveness Model (PDAA)
HEENT .... Head, Ears, Eyes, Nose, Throat
HEEO .... High Electroendosmosis [*Analytical biochemistry*]
HEEP .... Health Effects of Environmental Pollutants [*A publication*]
HEEP .... Health Effects of Environmental Pollution [*Database*] (NITA)
HEEP .... Highway Engineering Exchange Program (EA)
HEERA .... Higher Education External Relations Association (AIE)
HEF .... Hamster Embryo Fibroblast [*Medicine*] (DMAA)
HEF .... Health Education Foundation (EA)
HEF .... Hearth Electric Furnace
HEF .... Heat-Curing Epoxy Film
HEF .... Heated Effluents [*Cornell University*] [*Database*] (NITA)
HEF .... Heavy Element Facility [*Nuclear energy*] (NUCP)
HEF .... High Energy Forming
HEF .... High-Energy Fuel [*Air Force*]
HEF .... High-Expansion Foam
HEF .... Hispanic Energy Forum [*Defunct*] (EA)
HEF .... Human Ecology Fund (EA)
HEF .... Human Embryo Fibroblast [*A cell line*]
HEF .... Hydroxyethylflurazepam [*Sedative*]
HEF .... Manassas, VA [*Location identifier FAA*] (FAAL)
HEFA.......... Higher Education Facilities Act of 1963
HEFA.......... Higher Education Funding Act [*Australia*]
HEFC.......... Higher Education Facilities Commission
HEFC.......... Higher Education Funding Council (AIE)
HEFCE......... Higher Education Funding Council for England
HEFG.......... Hall Effect Function Generator
HEFOE......... Hydraulic, Engine, Fuel, Oxygen, Electrical (DNAB)
HEFRAG ...... High-Explosive, Fragmentation [*Artillery*] (INF)
HEFT .... Heavy-Element Fission Tracer
Heftel......... Heftel Broadcasting Corp. [*Associated Press*] (SAG)
HEFTH .... Henceforth (ROG)
HEFU .... High-Energy Firing Unit [*Army*] (AABC)
HEG .... Haftentschaedigungsgesetz [*A publication*] (BJA)
HEG .... Hall Effect Generator
HEG .... Heavy Enamel Single Glass [*Wire insulation*] (AAG)
HEG .... Helium Gauge (MCD)
HEG. .... Hemgold Resources Ltd. [*Vancouver Stock Exchange symbol*]
HEG .... Hemorrhagic Erosive Gastritis [*Gastroenterology*] (DAVI)
HEG .... Hexaethylene Glycol [*Organic chemistry*]
HEG .... Histioeosinophilic Granuloma [*Medicine*]
HEG .... Homogeneous Exposure Group [*Concept for acessing cancer risk*]
HEG .... Jacksonville, FL [*Location identifier FAA*] (FAAL)
HEGF.......... High-Energy Gas Fracturing [*For freeing natural gas from rock*]
HEGF.......... Human Epidermal Growth Factor [*Biochemistry*]
HEGIS .... Higher Education General Information Survey [*Office of Education*]
HEGN.......... Hurghada [*Egypt*] [*ICAO location identifier*] (ICLI)
HEGO.......... Heated Exhaust Gas Oxygen [*Automotive engineering*]
HEGOG........ Heated Exhaust Gas Oxygen Ground [*Automotive engineering*]
HEGR.......... El-Gora [*Egypt*] [*ICAO location identifier*] (ICLI)
HEGR.......... High-Energy Gamma Ray
HEGS .... Helicopter External Gondola System
HEGV.......... Helium Gauge Valve (MCD)
HEH .... Heho [*Myanmar*] [*Airport symbol*] (OAG)
HEH .... His [*or Her*] Exalted Highness [*Term applied only to personages of British India*]
HEH .... (Hydroxyethyl)hydrazine [*Organic chemistry*]
HEH .... Newark, OH [*Location identifier FAA*] (FAAL)
HEHC .... Hydroxyethylhomocysteine [*Organic chemistry*]
HEHF.......... Hanford Environmental Health Foundation [*Nuclear energy*]
HEHO.......... Herbert Hoover National Historic Site

HEHP .... Heavy Equipment Handling Package
HEHR .... Highest Equivalent Heart Rate [*Cardiology*] (DAVI)
HEHS .... Health, Education, and Human Services Division [*GAO*] (AAGC)
HEI .... Hall-Effect Imaging [*Medical imaging*]
HEI .... Hangar Engineering Item
HEI .... Health and Energy Institute (EA)
HEI .... Health Effects Institute [*Research center*] (RCD)
HEI .... Heat Exchange Institute (EA)
HEI .... Heico Corp. [*AMEX symbol*] (SPSG)
HEI .... Heidelberg [*Konigstuhl*] [*Federal Republic of Germany*] [*Seismograph station code, US Geological Survey*] (SEIS)
HEI .... Heidelberg College, Tiffin, OH [*OCLC symbol*] (OCLC)
HEI .... Hettinger, ND [*Location identifier FAA*] (FAAL)
HEI .... High-Energy Ignition (KSC)
HEI .... High-Energy Intermediate [*Medicine*] (DAVI)
HEI .... Higher Education Institute [*Australia*]
HEI .... Higher Education Institution
HEI .... High-Explosive, Incendiary [*Weaponry*]
HEI .... Holographic Exposure Index (PDAA)
HEI .... Homogeneous Enzyme Immunoassy [*Biochemistry*] (DAVI)
HEI .... Hospice Education Institute (EA)
HEI .... Hourly Earnings Index (OICC)
HEI .... House Ear Institute (EA)
HEI .... Human Embryonic Intestine Cells [*Medicine*] (DMAA)
HEI .... Human Engineering Institute
HEI .... Humidity-Electronic Indicator
HEIAC .... Hydraulic Engineering Information Analysis Center [*Army Corps of Engineers*] (IID)
HEI-AR........ Health Effects Institute-Asbestos Research
HEIAS .... Human Engineering Information and Analysis Service [*Tufts University*]
HEIB........... Home Economists in Business (EA)
HEIC........... Honourable East India Co. [*British*]
HE-ICM .... High Explosive - Improved Conventional Ammunition
HEICN......... Honourable East India Co. Navy [*British military*] (DMA)
Heico .... Heico Corp. [*Associated Press*] (SAG)
HEICS .... Honourable East India Company's Service [*British*]
HEID .... Heidemij NV [*NASDAQ symbol*] (SAG)
HEIDA .... (Hydroxyethyl)iminodiacetic Acid [*Organic chemistry*]
HEIDELB ..... Heidelberg [*City in Germany*] (ROG)
Heidemj...... Heidemij NV [*Associated Press*] (SAG)
HEIDF......... Heidemij N.V. [*NASDAQ symbol*] (TTSB)
HEIDI .... Higher Education Data Base [*Information service or system*] (IID)
HEIE .... High-Energy Isotope Experiment (SSD)
HEIFER .... High Frequency Relay (NVT)
HEIGHT .... Heights [*Commonly used*] (OPSA)
HEIGHTS..... Heights [*Commonly used*] (OPSA)
HEII........... HEI, Inc. [*NASDAQ symbol*] (NQ)
Heilig......... Heilig-Meyers Co. [*Associated Press*] (SAG)
HEI Mn .... HEI, Inc. [*Associated Press*] (SAG)
Hein.......... William S. Hein and Co., Inc. [*Publisher*] (DLA)
HE inj .... Hyperextension Injury [*Orthopedics*] (DAVI)
HeinWr .... Hein-Werner Corp. [*Associated Press*] (SAG)
Heinz .... Heinz [*H.J.*] Co. [*Associated Press*] (SAG)
HEIP........... High-Explosive, Incendiary Plug [*Weaponry*] (NATG)
HEIR .... Health Effects of Ionizing Radiation [*Medicine*] (DAVI)
HEIR .... High-Energy Ionizing Radiation [*Radiation therapy*] (DAVI)
HEIS .... High-Energy Ion Scattering Spectroscopy
HEIS .... Higher Education Information Service (AIE)
HEISD .... High-Explosive, Incendiary Self-Destroying [*Weaponry*] (NATG)
Heisk .... Heiskell's Tennessee Supreme Court Reports [*1870-74*] [*A publication*] (DLA)
Heisk (Tenn).. Heiskell's Tennessee Reports [*48-59 Tennessee*] [*A publication*] (DLA)
HEIST.......... High-Energy Isotope Spectrometer Telescope (MCD)
HeistC........ Heist [*C. H.*] Corp. [*Associated Press*] (SAG)
HEIT........... High-Explosive, Incendiary [*Shell*] Traced [*i.e., fitted with tracer*] [*Weaponry*]
HEITDISD.... High-Explosive, Incendiary Tracer, Dark Ignition, Self-Destroying [*Weaponry*] (NATG)
HEITSD .... High-Explosive, Incendiary Tracer, Self-Destroying [*Weaponry*] (NATG)
HEITV......... Higher Education Instructional Television [*West Virginia*] (EDAC)
HEK........... Heavy Enamel Single Cellophane [*Wire insulation*] (AAG)
HEK........... Hemingway, SC [*Location identifier FAA*] (FAAL)
HEK........... Human Embryo Kinase [*Medicine*] (DMAA)
HEK........... Human Embryonic Kidney [*Type of cell line*]
HEKB.......... El Nakab/El Nakab [*Egypt*] [*ICAO location identifier*] (ICLI)
HEL........... Handbooks of English Literature [*A publication*]
HEL........... Hardware Emulation [*Computer science*]
HEL........... Hardware Emulation Layer [*Computer science*]
HEL........... Header Extension Length [*Telecommunications*] (ACRL)
HEL........... Helena [*Diocesan abbreviation*] [*Montana*] (TOCD)
HEL........... Helicol Helicopteros Nacionales de Colombia [*ICAO designator*] (FAAC)
HEL........... Helicopter (AABC)
Hel........... Heliodor [*Record label*] [*Great Britain*]
hel........... Heliotrope [*Philately*]
HEL........... Hellenic Resources [*Vancouver Stock Exchange symbol*]
Hel........... Hellenistic [*Period*]
HEL........... Helsingfors [*Helsinki*] [*Finland*] [*Seismograph station code, US Geological Survey*] (SEIS)
HEL........... Helsinki [*Finland*] [*Airport symbol*] (OAG)
HEL........... Helvetia [*Switzerland*] (ROG)
HEL........... Hen-Egg White Lysozyme [*Also, HEWL*] [*An enzyme*]

HEL............	High-Energy LASER
HEL............	History of English Law, Edited by W. Holdsworth [*A publication*] (DLA)
HEL............	Home Equity Loan
HEL............	Hugoniot Elastic Limit [*Thermodynamics*]
HEL............	Human Embryonic Lung [*Type of cell line*]
HEL............	Human Engineering Laboratory [*Aberdeen Proving Ground, MD*] [*Army*]
HEL............	Human Erythroleukemia [*Type of cell line*]
HEL............	Hunting Engineering Ltd.
HEL............	Hydraulic Engineering Laboratory [*University of California at Berkeley*]
HeLa.........	Helen Lake [*Tumour cells*] [*Medicine*] (BABM)
HeLa.........	Henrietta Lacks [*Pseudonym, Helen Lake*] [*Line of tumor cells*]
HELAB	High-Energy LASER Assessment Board (MCD)
HELAC	Helix Linear Accelerator (PDAA)
HELAIRDET..	Helicopter Air Detachment [*Canadian Navy*]
HELANTISUBRON...	Helicopter Antisubmarine Squadron [*Navy*]
HELANTISUBRONDET...	Helicopter Antisubmarine Squadron Detachment [*Navy*] (DNAB)
HELAPS	High Efficiency Linear Amplification by Parametic Synthesis (PDAA)
HELASRON...	Helicopter Antisubmarine Squadron [*Navy*]
HELAST.......	Human Engineering Laboratory Armor Systems Test [*Army*] (RDA)
HELATKRON...	Helicopter Attack Squadron [*Navy*] (DNAB)
HELB.........	High-Energy LASER Beam
HELB.........	High-Energy Line Break [*Nuclear energy*] (NRCH)
HELBAT.......	Human Engineering Laboratories Battalion Artillery Test [*Army*]
HELCAP	Human Engineering Laboratory Counterair Program [*Army*] (RDA)
HELCAR	Helicopter Collision Avoidance RADAR (NG)
HELCIS	Helicopter Command Instrumentation System (MCD)
HELCM......	High-Energy LASER Countermeasures (MCD)
HELCO	Hartford Electric Light Co.
HELCOM	Baltic Marine Environment Protection Commission - Helsinki Commission (EAIO)
HELCOMBSUPPRON...	Helicopter Combat Support Squadron [*Navy*] (DNAB)
HELCOS	High-Energy LASER Component Servicing (MCD)
HELDREF	Helen Dwight Reid Educational Foundation
HELE	Helen of Troy Corp. [*NASDAQ symbol*] (NQ)
HELE	Helen of Troy Ltd [*NASDAQ symbol*] (TTSB)
HELEN	Hydrogenous Exponential Liquid Experiment [*British*]
HeleneC.....	Helene Curtis Industries, Inc. [*Associated Press*] (SAG)
HelenTr.......	Helen of Troy Corp. [*Associated Press*] (SAG)
HELEX	Helium Extraction
HELF...........	Human Embryonic Lung Fibroblasts [*Biochemistry*]
HELFAST.....	Human Engineering Laboratory Forward Area Supply and Transfer [*Army*] (RDA)
HEL-FI	Human Engineering Laboratory Field Office [*Charlottesville, VA*] [*Military*]
HEL-FIO	Human Engineering Laboratory Field Office [*Charlottesville, VA*] [*Military*]
HELHAT	Human Engineering Laboratory Helicopter Armament Test [*Army*] (RDA)
HELI...........	Helicopter (AFM)
HELI...........	Heliport [*ICAO designator*] (FAAC)
HELI...........	Helisys Inc. [*NASDAQ symbol*] (TTSB)
HELI...........	Helisys, Inc. [*NASDAQ symbol*] (SAG)
Helian........	Helian Health Group, Inc. [*Associated Press*] (SAG)
HELILEX......	Helicopter Landing Exercise [*Amphibious*] [*Navy*] (NVT)
HELIOD	Heliodorus [*Greek writer, c. 200AD*] (ROG)
Heliogab......	Heliogabalus [*of Scriptores Historiae Augustae*] [*Classical studies*] (OCD)
Heliont........	Helionetics, Inc. [*Associated Press*] (SAG)
Helios........	Helios - Joies de la Musique [*Record label*] [*France*]
HELIOS	Heteropowered Earth-Launched Inter-Orbital Spacecraft (KSC)
HELIP........	HAWK [*Homing All the Way Killer*] European Limited Improvement Program [*NATO*]
HELIPATH	Helicopter Position and Terrain Height
HELIST........	Human Engineering Laboratory Infantry System Test [*Army*] (RDA)
Helisys	Helisys, Inc. [*Associated Press*] (SAG)
HELITEAM....	Helicopter Team
HELITECH	International Helicopter Technology and Operations Conference and Exhibition [*British*] (ITD)
HELIVALS	Helicopter In-flight Validation System (PDAA)
HELIX.........	Harwell Electrochemical Ion Exchange Process [*British*] (NUCP)
HelixTch	Helix Technologies [*Associated Press*] (SAG)
Hell	Hellenica [*of Xenophon*] [*Classical studies*] (OCD)
HELL..........	Higher Education Learning Laboratory (EA)
Hell Dicht	Hellenistische Dichtung in der Zeit des Kallimachos [*A publication*] (OCD)
Hellen.........	Hellenic [*Classical studies*] (BARN)
HELLFIRE	Heliborne LASER Fire and Forget [*Missile system*] [*Army*] (RDA)
HELLFIRE/GLD...	HELLFIRE [*Heliborne LASER Fire and Forget*]/Ground LASER Designator [*Army*] (RDA)
HelloD	Hello Direct, Inc. [*Associated Press*] (SAG)
HELLOG	Human Engineering Laboratory Logistics [*Systems concept study*] (MCD)
Hell Oxy	Hellenica Oxyrhynchia [*Classical studies*] (OCD)
HELLP........	Hemolysis, Elevated Liver Enzymes, and Low Platelet Count [*Clinical chemistry*]
HELM..........	Helmet Cells [*Cytology*] (DAVI)
Helm..........	Helm's Reports [*2-9 Nevada*] [*A publication*] (DLA)
HELMEPA	Hellenic Marine Environmental Protection Association (EERA)
HELMEPA	Hellenic Marine Environmental Protection Association
HelmP	Helmerich & Payne, Inc. [*Associated Press*] (SAG)
HelmRes......	Helm Resources, Inc. [*Associated Press*] (SAG)

HELMS........	Helicopter Lift Margin System (MCD)
HELMS........	Helicopter Multifunction System
Helmstr.......	Helmstar Group [*Associated Press*] (SAG)
HELNAVS....	Helicopter Navigation System (RDA)
HELO	Heavy Lift Operability (PDAA)
HELO	Helicopter (NG)
HELO	Hello Direct [*NASDAQ symbol*] (TTSB)
HELO	Hello Direct, Inc. [*NASDAQ symbol*] (SAG)
HELO	High-Energy Liquid Oxidizer
HELO	Hispanic Elected Local Officials (EA)
HELOC	Home Equity Line of Credit (TDOB)
HELOPS	Helicopter Operations (DNAB)
HELOPSUPPFAC...	Helicopter Operational Support Facility (DNAB)
HELOQUALS...	Helicopter Qualifications [*Navy*] (NVT)
HELORADE...	Helicopter Operations in Selected RADAR Environment (MCD)
HELOS........	Harwell Electro Osmosis Process [*British*] (NUCP)
HELOS........	Highly Eccentric Lunar Occultation Satellite
HELOSID......	Helicopter-Delivered Seismic Intrusion Detector (NVT)
HELOTNG.....	Helicopter Training (NVT)
HELP..........	Harlem Eastside Lifesaving Program [*Television program*]
HELP..........	Harris Enhanced Language for Programmable Logic (NITA)
HELP..........	Hawaii Early Learning Profile [*Child development test*] [*Psychology*]
HELP..........	HAWK [*Homing All-the-Way Killer*] Equipment Logistics Program [*Military*] (GFGA)
HELP..........	Health and Energy Learning Project (EA)
HELP..........	Health Education Library Program [*Library network*]
HELP..........	Health Emergency Loan Program [*Planned parenthood*] (DAVI)
HELP..........	Health Evaluation and Learning Program
HELP..........	Health Evaluation through Logical Processing [*Computer science*] (DAVI)
HELP..........	Heat Escape Lessening Posture [*First aid technique*]
HELP..........	Heavy Vehicle Electronic License Plate
HELP..........	Helicopter Electronic Landing Path [*Army*]
HELP..........	Helium Liquid Program [*NASA*]
HELP..........	Help Establish Lasting Peace
HELP..........	HELP, International [*Defunct*] (EA)
HELP..........	Helpmate Robotics [*NASDAQ symbol*] (TTSB)
HELP..........	Helpmate Robotics, Inc. [*NASDAQ symbol*] (SAG)
HELP..........	Heroin Emergency Life Project
HELP..........	Herpetics Engaged in Living Productively [*Later, Herpes Research Center*] (EA)
HELP..........	High-Energy Lightweight Propellant
HELP..........	Highly Extendable Language Processor [*Computer science*]
HELP..........	Highly Extendable Language Processor (NITA)
HELP..........	Highway Emergency Locating Plan
HELP..........	Home Education Livelihood Program [*New Mexico*]
HELP..........	Home Emergency Ladies' Pal [*Book title*]
HELP..........	Homophile Effort for Legal Protection [*An association Defunct*] (EA)
HELP..........	Honeywell Equipment Lease Plan
HELP..........	Hospital Equipment Loan Project
HELP..........	Housewives Elect Lower Prices [*New York women's lobby group*]
HELP..........	Howitzer Extended Life Program
HELP..........	Hughes Emergency Locator Pack
HELP..........	Hydrologic Evaluation of Landfill Performance [*Environmental Protection Agency*]
HELPIS	Higher Education Learning Programmes Information Service [*British Universities Film & Video Council*] [*Database*]
HELPIS	Higher Education Learning Programmes Information Service (AIE)
Helpmte......	Helpmate Robotics, Inc. [*Associated Press*] (SAG)
HELPR	Handbook of Electronic Parts Reliability
HELPS	Handicapped Education Learner's Planning System [*Battelle Memorial Institute*] [*Information service or system*] (IID)
HELPS	Health Environment Long-Range Planning Support [*A computer model*]
HELPS	Helmet-Position Sensing System
HELPS	Highway Emergency Locating Paging Service [*For motorist assistance*]
HELPU	Helpmate Robotics Unit [*NASDAQ symbol*] (TTSB)
HELPW	Helpmate Robotics Wrrt [*NASDAQ symbol*] (TTSB)
HELRAS	Helicopter Long-Range Acoustic Sensor [*Military*] (CAAL)
HELRATS	High-Energy LASER RADAR Acquisition and Tracking System (MCD)
HELREC	Health Record
HelrFn	Heller Financial [*Associated Press*] (SAG)
HELRG	High-Energy LASER Review Group [*Terminated, 1977*] [*DoD*]
HELS	High-Energy LASER System
HELST........	Helston [*Municipal borough in England*]
HELSTF.......	High-Energy LASER System Test Facility (MCD)
HELSTF.......	High-Energy LASER System Test Facility [*Army*] (DOMA)
HELSUPPRON...	Helicopter Combat Support Squadron [*Navy*]
HELSUPPRONDET...	Helicopter Combat Support Squadron Detachment [*Navy*] (DNAB)
HELT	Hedonism Limitation Talks [*British*] (DI)
HELTAD	Helicopter Tank Destroyer [*Military*]
HELTADS	High-Energy LASER Tactical Air Defense System
HELTAS.......	High-Energy LASER Technology Applications Study (MCD)
HELTRARON...	Helicopter Training Squadron [*Navy*]
Helv..........	Ad Helviam [*of Seneca the Younger*] [*Classical studies*] (OCD)
HELV..........	Helvetica [*Typography*] (WDAA)
HELWS	High-Energy LASER Weapon System (MCD)
HELX.........	Helix Technology [*NASDAQ symbol*] (TTSB)
HELX.........	Helix Technology Corp. [*NASDAQ symbol*] (NQ)
HELX.........	Luxor [*Egypt*] [*ICAO location identifier*] (ICLI)
HEM..........	Hall Effect Multiplier
HEM..........	Handbook on Emergency Measures (NATG)
HEM..........	Harmonisation of Environmental Measurement (EERA)

HEM...........	Hatchlike Experiment Module [*NASA*] (NASA)
HEM...........	Heat Exchanger Method (RDA)
HEM...........	Heavy Equipment Maintenance
HEM...........	Hematite [*A mineral*]
HEM...........	Hematology [*Medicine*] (DHSM)
hem...........	Hematuria [*Urology*] (DAVI)
HEM...........	Hemisphere
HEM...........	Hemlo Gold Mines [*AMEX symbol*] (TTSB)
HEM...........	Hemlo Gold Mines, Inc. [*Toronto Stock Exchange symbol AMEX symbol*]
HEM...........	Hemmeter Aviation, Inc. [*ICAO designator*] (FAAC)
HEM...........	Hemoglobin [*Medicine*] (WDAA)
HEM...........	Hemolysis [*Medicine*]
Hem...........	Hemolytic [*Hematology*] (DAVI)
HEM...........	Hemorrhage [*Medicine*] (WDAA)
hem...........	Hemorrhoid [*Gastroenterology*] (DAVI)
HEM...........	HEPES-Buffered EMEM
HEM...........	Hitchhike Experiment Module (MCD)
HEM...........	Homogeneous Equilibrium Model (NRCH)
HEM...........	Human Exposure Modeling (GFGA)
HEM...........	Hybrid Electromagnetic [*Wave*]
HEM...........	Hydroxyethylmorpholine [*Organic chemistry*]
HEM...........	Sparta, TN [*Location identifier FAA*] (FAAL)
HEMA........	Health Education Media Association [*Defunct*] (EA)
HEMA........	HemaCare Corp. [*NASDAQ symbol*] (NQ)
HEMA........	Hematology Profile [*Medicine*] (DAVI)
HEMA........	Hot Melt Equipment Manufacturers Association (EA)
HEMA........	Hydroxyethyl Methacrylate [*Organic chemistry*]
HemaC........	HemaCare Corp. [*Associated Press*] (SAG)
HEMAC......	Hybrid Electromagnetic Antenna Coupler
Hemagn......	Hemagen Diagnostics [*Associated Press*] (SAG)
Hem & M....	Hemming and Miller's English Vice-Chancellors' Reports [*A publication*] (DLA)
Hem & M (Eng)...	Hemming and Miller's English Vice-Chancellors' Reports [*A publication*] (DLA)
Hem & Mill...	Hemming and Miller's English Vice-Chancellors' Reports [*A publication*] (DLA)
HEMAR.......	Human Engineering Criteria for Maintenance and Repair [*GE, NASA*]
Hemasure....	Hemasure, Inc. [*Associated Press*] (SAG)
HEMAT.......	Heavy Expanded Mobility Ammunition Trailer [*Military*]
hemat........	Hematocrit [*Medicine*] (DAVI)
HEMAT.......	Hematology [*Medicine*]
hemat ab....	Hematologic Abnormality [*Medicine*]
hematem.....	Hematemesis [*Gastroenterology*] (DAVI)
HEMATL.....	Hematologist
HEMATLGY...	Hematology
Hematol......	Hematology [*or Hematologist*] [*Medicine*]
HEMDE......	Hemdale Communications [*NASDAQ symbol*] (TTSB)
HEME........	Hostile Electromagnetic Emission (MCD)
HEME........	Hydroxyethyl Methyl (Cellulose) [*Organic chemistry*]
HEMF........	Handling Equipment Maintenance Facility [*Charleston Naval Shipyard*]
HEMF........	Hydroxy (Ethyl) Methyl Furanone [*Organic chemistry*]
Hemgn........	Hemagen Diagnostics [*Associated Press*] (SAG)
HEMI.........	Hemiparalysis [*Medicine*]
HEMI.........	Hemiplegia [*Medicine*]
Hemi.........	Hemisphere [*Neurology*] (DAVI)
HEMI.........	Hemispherical [*Automotive engineering*]
HEMI.........	Hemispherical [*S-band antenna*]
Heming......	Hemingway's Mississippi Reports [*A publication*] (DLA)
Heming (Miss)...	Hemingway's Mississippi Reports [*A publication*] (DLA)
HEMIS........	Hemisphere (AFM)
Hemis........	Hemispherx BioPharma, Inc. [*Associated Press*] (SAG)
HEMISEARCH...	Hemispherical Search [*First frequency-scanning RADAR*] (MCD)
Hemispx......	Hemispherx BioPharma, Inc. [*Associated Press*] (SAG)
HEML.........	High-Energy Microwave Laboratory [*Kirtland AFB*] [*Air Force*] (DOMA)
HEMLAW.....	Helicopter Mounted LASER Weapon (MCD)
Hemlo........	Hemlo Gold Mines, Inc. [*Associated Press*] (SAG)
HEMLOC.....	Heliborne Emitter Location/Countermeasures
HEMM........	Mersa-Matruh [*Egypt*] [*ICAO location identifier*] (ICLI)
Hemmant.....	Hemmant's Select Cases in Exchequer Chamber [*Selden Society Publications, Vol. 51*] [*1377-1460*] [*A publication*] (DLA)
HEMMS.......	Hand-Emplaced Minefield Marking System (MCD)
hemo.........	Hemoglobin [*Medicine*] (DAVI)
HEMO........	Hemolysis [*or Hemolyze*] [*Medicine*] (DAVI)
hemo.........	Hemophilia [*Medicine*] (DAVI)
hemocyt......	Hemocytometer (MAE)
HEMOR......	Hemorrhage [*Medicine*]
hemorr.......	Hemorrhage [*Medicine*] (DAVI)
HEMP........	Help End Marijuana Prohibition [*An association*]
Hemp.........	Hempstead's Arkansas Reports [*A publication*] (DLA)
Hemp.........	Hempstead's United States Circuit Court Reports [*A publication*] (DLA)
HEMP........	High-Altitude Electromagnetic Pulse (MCD)
HEMPA.......	Hexamethylphosphoric Triamide [*Also, HMP, HMPA, HMPT, HPT*] [*Organic chemistry*] (MCD)
HEMPAS.....	Hereditary Erythroblastic Multinuclearity Associated with a Positive Acidified-Serum Test [*Hematology*]
HEMPAS.....	Hereditary Erythrocytic Multinuclearity with a Positive Acidified-Serum [*Test*] [*Hematology*] (DAVI)
HEMPE.......	Henry, Edward, Mary, Philip, Elizabeth [*Bacon's prophecy*]
Hempst.......	Hempstead's Arkansas Reports [*A publication*] (DLA)
Hempst.......	Hempstead's United States Circuit Court Reports [*A publication*] (DLA)

HEMRI........	Hereditary Multifocal Relapsing Inflammation [*Medicine*] (DMAA)
HEMSiD......	Hemosiderin [*Hematology*] (DAVI)
HEMT........	HF Bancorp [*NASDAQ symbol*] (TTSB)
HEMT........	HF Bancorp, Inc. [*NASDAQ symbol*] (SAG)
HEMT........	High Electron Mobility Transistor [*Computer science*]
HEMT........	Hydrodynamic Elastic Magnets Plastic
HEMT FET...	High Electron Mobility Transistor FET [*Field Effect Transistor*] [*Honeywell*] (NITA)
HEMTT.......	Heavy Expanded Mobility Tactical Truck
HEMTT.......	Heavy Expanded Mobility Tactical Truck [*Army*] (RDA)
HEMT/UMHE...	Higher Education Ministries Team/United Ministries in Higher Education (EA)
HEMV........	Helium Manual Valve (MCD)
HEMW........	Hybrid Electromagnetic Wave (MSA)
HEMX........	Hemispherx BioPharma, Inc. [*NASDAQ symbol*] (SAG)
HEMXU......	Hemispherx BioPharma Unit [*NASDAQ symbol*] (TTSB)
HEN.........	Cape Henry (GAAI)
HEN.........	Harris Electronic News [*Service suspended*] [*Information service or system*] (IID)
HEN.........	Heat-Exchanger Network [*Chemical engineering*]
HEN.........	Hemorrhages, Exudates, and/or Nicking [*Ophthalmology*] (DAVI)
HEN.........	Hengchun [*Republic of China*] [*Seismograph station code, US Geological Survey*] (SEIS)
HEN.........	Henley International, Inc. [*Later, MAXXIM Medical*] [*AMEX symbol*] (SPSG)
Hen.........	Henricus Boich [*Flourished, 1320-30*] [*Authority cited in pre-1607 legal work*] (DSA)
Hen.........	Henry (King of England) (DLA)
HEN.........	Holistic Education Network (EDAC)
HEN.........	Home Enteral Nutrition [*Medicine*] (DMAA)
HEN.........	Home Entertainment Network [*Cable-television system*]
HEN.........	Hotel, Echo, November [*Russian submarine*]
HENA........	Hemeroteca Nacional [*Database*] [*Ministerio de Cultura*] [*Spanish*] [*Information service or system*] (CRD)
Hen Am Pl...	Hening's American Pleader [*A publication*] (DLA)
Hen & M...	Hening and Munford's Virginia Supreme Court Reports [*1806-10*] [*A publication*] (DLA)
Hen & Mun...	Hening and Munford's Reports [*11-14 Virginia*] [*A publication*] (DLA)
Hen Bo.......	Henricus Boich [*Flourished, 1320-30*] [*Authority cited in pre-1607 legal work*] (DSA)
HENDEL.....	Helium Engineering Demonstration Loop [*Nuclear energy*] (NUCP)
Henderson St U...	Henderson State University (GAGS)
HENE.........	Helium Neon [*LASER*] (DGA)
He-Ne........	Helium-Neon (IDOE)
Hen For L...	Henry on Foreign Law [*A publication*] (DLA)
Hen Forms...	Hennell's Forms [*A publication*] (DLA)
HENILAS.....	Helicopter Night-Landing System
Hen JP.......	Hening's Virginia Justice of the Peace [*A publication*] (DLA)
Hen LA Dig...	Hennen's Louisiana Digest [*A publication*] (DLA)
Hen Law.....	Hennepin Lawyer [*A publication*] (DLA)
Hen Man Cas...	Henry's Manumission Cases [*A publication*] (DLA)
Hen Max.....	Hening's Maxims [*A publication*] (DLA)
HENNA.......	Home Executives National Networking Association
HENP........	High Energy and Nuclear Physics Program [*Department of Energy*]
HENRE.......	High-Energy Neutron Reactions Experiment [*Nuclear energy*]
Henric.......	Henricus Boich [*Flourished, 1320-30*] [*Authority cited in pre-1607 legal work*] (DSA)
HenryJk......	Henry [*Jack*] & Associates, Inc. [*Associated Press*] (SAG)
Henry Judg...	Henry's Judgment in Ordwin V. Forbes [*A publication*] (DLA)
Hen St.......	Hening's Statutes [*Virginia*] [*A publication*] (DLA)
HENT.........	Head, Eyes, Ears, Nose, and Throat [*Medicine*] (HGAA)
Hent Forms...	Hent's Forms and Use of Blanks in California [*A publication*] (DLA)
HENV........	New Valley [*Egypt*] [*ICAO location identifier*] (ICLI)
HEO.........	High Earth Orbit (IEEE)
HEO.........	High Elliptical Orbit Satellite
HEO.........	High-Energy Orbit [*NASA*] (NASA)
HEO.........	Higher Executive Officer [*Civil service*] [*British*]
HEO.........	Higher Executive Order
HEO(A).......	Higher Executive Officer (Administration) [*Civil service*] [*British*]
HEOB........	High-Energy Organic Battery
HEOC........	Higher Education Opportunities Committee (EA)
HEOD........	Harbor Explosive Ordnance Disposal Team [*Navy*] (VNW)
HEOD........	Hexachloroepoxyoctahydro-exo-endo-dimethanonaphthalene [*Dieldrin*] [*Insecticide*]
HEOEBS.....	High-Energy Organic Electrolyte Battery System
HEOP........	Higher Equal Opportunity Program [*Education*]
HEOS........	Highly Eccentric [*or Elliptical*] Orbit Satellite
HEOY........	Handicapped Employee of the Year [*Award given to federal employees*] (RDA)
HEP.........	Habitat Evaluation Procedure [*Fishery science*]
HEP.........	Halkin Emek Partisi [*People's Labor Party*] [*Turkey Political party*] (EY)
HEP.........	Hall Effect Probe
HEP.........	Hallwood Energy Partners Ltd. [*AMEX symbol*] (SPSG)
HEP.........	Hallwood Energy Ptnrs L.P. [*AMEX symbol*] (TTSB)
HEP.........	Hardsite Engagement Program
HEP.........	Hepatic [*Pertaining to the liver*] [*Pharmacy*] (ROG)
hep.........	Hepatitis [*Gastroenterology*] (DAVI)
HEP.........	Hepatoerythropoietic Porphyria [*Medicine*]
HEP.........	Hepatology [*Gastroenterology*] (DAVI)
HEP.........	Heterogeneous Element Processor [*Computer science*] (RDA)
HEP.........	High Egg Passage [*Rabies vaccine*]
HEP.........	High-Energy Particle
HEP.........	High-Energy Phosphate [*Biochemistry*]
HEP.........	High-Energy Physics

HEP .... High-Energy Pulse
HEP .... Higher Education Panel (EA)
HEP .... High-Explosive Plastic [*Weaponry*]
HEP .... High-Explosive Plugged [*Weaponry*]
HEP .... High School Equivalency Program
HEP .... Hi-Peg Resources Ltd. [*Vancouver Stock Exchange symbol*]
HEP .... Hispanic Employment Program [*DoD*] (MCD)
HEP .... Histamine Equivalent Prick Unit [*Immunology*]
HEP .... Hole-Electron Pair
HEP .... Homogenous Element Processor (NITA)
HEP .... Human Engineering Plan
HEp .... Human Epithelial [*Cells*]
HEP .... Human Error Probability (IEEE)
HEP .... Hydrazine Electrolysis Plenum
HEP .... Hydroelectric Plant
HEP .... Hydroelectric Power
HEP .... Hydrogen Embrittlement Proof
HEPA .... High-Efficiency Particle Accumulator (NASA)
HEPA .... High-Efficiency Particulate Air [*Filter*]
HEPA .... Hydroxyethyl Phosphonic Acid [*Organic chemistry*]
HEP-AC .... Hepatitis Battery-Acute [*Gastroenterology*] (DAVI)
HEPAD .... High-Energy Proton and Alpha Detector
HEPAF .... High-Efficiency Particle Air Filter
HEPALIS ...... Higher Education Policy and Administration Library and Information
        Service
HEPAP .... High-Energy Physics Advisory Panel [*Department of Energy*
        Washington, DC] (EGAO)
HEPAT .... High-Explosive Plastic Antitank [*Weaponry*] (NATG)
Hepb .... Hepburn's Reports [*California*] [*A publication*] (DLA)
Hepb .... Hepburn's Reports [*Pennsylvania*] [*A publication*] (DLA)
HEPB .... High-Energy Pipe Break [*Nuclear energy*] (NRCH)
HEP.C .... Hallwood Energy Ptnrs L.P.'C' [*AMEX symbol*] (TTSB)
HEPC .... Hydro-Electric Power Commission [*Canada*] (PDAA)
HEPCA .... House Employees Position Classification Act [*1964*]
HEPCAT .... Helicopter Pilot Control and Training
HE-PD .... High-Explosive - Point Detonating [*Weaponry*] (MCD)
HEPDEX .... High-Energy Proton Detection Experiment
HEPDNP .... High-Explosive, Point Detonating Nose Plug [*Weaponry*] (NATG)
HEPES .... Hydroxyethylpiperazineethanesulfonic Acid [*A buffer*]
HEPI .... HEP [*High Energy Physics*] Index (NITA)
HEPI .... Higher Education Price Index (EDAC)
HEPL .... High-Energy Physics Laboratory [*Stanford University*] (MCD)
HEPL .... High-Energy-Pulse LASER (PDAA)
HEPM .... Hispanic Employment Program Manager [*DoD*]
HEPM .... Human Embryonic Palatal Mesenchymal [*Type of cell line*]
HEPnet .... High Energy Physics Network [*Computer science*] (TNIG)
HEPOD .... Hereditary Expansile Polyostotic Dysplasia [*Medicine*] (DMAA)
HEPP .... High-Energy Particle Physics Group [*Florida State University*]
        [*Research center*] (RCD)
HEPP .... Hoffmann Evaluation Program and Procedure (IAA)
HEPP .... Human Engineering Program Plan
HEPP .... Northwest Association of Horticulturists, Entomologists, and Plant
        Pathologists [*Defunct*] (EA)
HEPPS .... Hydroxyethylpiperazinepropanesulfonic Acid [*A buffer*]
HEPS .... Helicopter Personnel Escape, Protection, and Survival (DNAB)
HEPS .... High-Energy Particle Spectrometer (MCD)
HEPS .... High Energy Prespark [*Analytical chemistry*]
HEPS .... High-Energy Propellant Safety (MCD)
HEPS .... Port Said [*Egypt*] [*ICAO location identifier*] (ICLI)
HEPSS .... Helicopter Escape and Personnel Survival System (MCD)
HEP-T .... High-Explosive Plastic Tracer [*Weaponry*] (AABC)
HEP-UP .... High School Education Program at University of Pennsylvania
HE-PX .... High-Explosive Proximity Fuse [*Weaponry*] (MCD)
HEQ .... Holyoke, CO [*Location identifier FAA*] (FAAL)
HER .... Harvard Educational Review [*A publication*] (BRI)
HER .... Health and Education Resources (EA)
HER .... Hearsay Evidence Rule [*Legal shorthand*] (LWAP)
HER .... Hemorrhagic Encephalopathy of Rats (DMAA)
HER .... Heraklion [*Greece*] [*Airport symbol*] (OAG)
Her .... Herald [*Record label*] [*Great Britain*]
Her .... Heraldry
her .... Heraldry (VRA)
Her .... Hercules [*Constellation*]
her .... Herero [*MARC language code Library of Congress*] (LCCP)
HER .... Heres [*Heir*] [*Legal term Latin*]
HER .... Heritage Petroleum [*Vancouver Stock Exchange symbol*]
Her .... Hermannus [*Authority cited in pre-1607 legal work*] (DSA)
HER .... Hermanus [*South Africa*] [*Seismograph station code, US Geological
        Survey*] (SEIS)
Her .... Herne's Law of Charitable Uses [*A publication*] (DLA)
Her .... Herodian [*Period*]
Her .... Heroides [*of Ovid*] [*Classical studies*] (OCD)
HER .... Hershey Foods Corp., Hershey, PA [*OCLC symbol*] (OCLC)
HER .... Hex'air [*France ICAO designator*] (FAAC)
HER .... High-Efficiency Radiator [*General Motors Corp.*] [*Automotive
        engineering*]
HER .... High-Energy Ray
HER .... High-Energy Rotor [*Helicopter*] [*Army*]
HER .... HIM [*Hardware Interface Module*] Equipment Rack [*NASA*] (NASA)
HER .... Horizontal Earth Rate
HER .... Human EGF [*Epidermal Growth Factor*] Receptor [*Biochemistry*]
HER .... Human Embryonic Retinoblast
HER .... Human Error Rate
HER .... Human Estrogen Receptor [*Endocrinology*]
HER .... Hydrogen Evolution Reaction [*Metallurgy*]

HER .... Hyperenvironmental RADAR
Her .... Quis Rerum Divinarum Heres [*Philo*] (BJA)
HERA .... Hadron-Elektron-Ring Anlage [*Hadron-Electron Ring Accelerator*]
        [*Germany*]
HERA .... Heritage Australia Information System [*Computer science*] (EERA)
HERA .... High-Explosive Rocket Assisted [*Weaponry*]
HERA .... Homemakers Equal Rights Association [*Defunct*] (EA)
HERAC .... Health and Environmental Research Advisory Committee
        [*Department of Energy*] [*Washington, DC*] (EGAO)
Heracl .... Heraclidae [*of Euripides*] [*Classical studies*] (OCD)
Heraclid Pont... Heraclides Ponticus [*Fourth century BC*] [*Classical studies*] (OCD)
Her Aconza... Henricus Acconzaioco [*Flourished, 1374-82*] [*Authority cited in pre-
        1607 legal work*] (DSA)
HERALD .... Harbor Echo Ranging and Listening Device
HERALD .... Highly Enriched Reactor, Aldermaston [*British*] (DEN)
HERAP .... Health and Environmental Risk Analysis Program [*Department of
        Energy*]
HERAP .... Human Error Research and Analysis Program (MCD)
HERATES ..... Hourly Earnings Rate
HERB .... Herbaceous (WDAA)
HERB .... Herbalife International, Inc. [*NASDAQ symbol*] (NQ)
HERB .... Herbalife Intl. [*NASDAQ symbol*] (TTSB)
HERB .... Herbalist (ROG)
HERB .... Herbarium (WDAA)
Herb Ant ..... Herbert's Antiquities of the Inns of Court, Etc. [*A publication*] (DLA)
HERBB .... Hanscom Electronic Request [*for Proposals*] Bulletin Board [*Air
        Force*]
HERBIC .... Herbicide
Herblfe .... Herbalife International, Inc. [*Associated Press*] (SAG)
HERB RECENT... Herbarium Recentium [*Of Fresh Herbs*] [*Pharmacy*]
HERBRECS... Queensland Herbarium Plant Specimen Data Base [*State*] [*Computer
        science*] (EERA)
HERC .... Health Economics Research Center [*University of Wisconsin -
        Madison*] [*Research center*] (RCD)
HERC .... HERC Products [*NASDAQ symbol*] (SAG)
HERC .... H.E.R.C. Products [*NASDAQ symbol*] (TTSB)
Herc .... Hercules [*Constellation*]
HERC .... Home Education Resource Center [*Defunct*] (EA)
Her Char U... Herne's Law of Charitable Uses [*A publication*] (DLA)
Her Chat ..... Herman on Chattel Mortgages [*A publication*] (DLA)
HERCULES... Helicopter Remote Classification and Localization System (PDAA)
HERCULES... High-Energy Radiation Camera Using Light-Emitting Showers
Herculs .... Hercules, Inc. [*Formerly, Hercules Power Co.*] [*Associated Press*]
        (SAG)
HERD .... Health and Environmental Review Division [*Environmental Protection
        Agency*] (GFGA)
HERD .... High-Explosives Research and Development (MCD)
HerdCor .... Herder Correspondence [*London/New York*] [*A publication*] (BJA)
HERDESNAVAV... Hereby Designated as a Student Naval Aviator (DNAB)
HERDET .... Hereby Detached from Duty Assigned [*Military*]
HerdKor .... Herder-Korrespondenz [*Freiburg Im Breisgau*] [*A publication*] (BJA)
HERDUFLY... Hereby Detailed to Duty Involving Flying (DNAB)
HERE .... Hastings' Encyclopaedia of Religion and Ethics [*A publication*] (BJA)
HERE .... Herefordshire [*County in England*]
HERE .... Home Economics Resources in Education [*British*] (DBA)
HERE .... Hotel Employees and Restaurant Employees International Union
        (EA)
hered .... Hereditary (DMAA)
HERED .... Heredity
HEREDET ..... Hereby Detached from Duty Assigned [*Military*] (DNAB)
HEREDITS.... Hereditaments (ROG)
HEREF .... Herefordshire [*County in England*]
Hereford ...... Herefordshire [*County in England*] (BARN)
HEREFORDS... Herefordshire [*County in England*]
HEREFS .... Herefordshire [*County in England*]
Heref/Worcs... Hereford and Worcester [*County in Wales*] (WGA)
Herenn Modest... Herennius Modestinus [*Flourished, 3rd century*] [*Authority cited
        in pre-1607 legal work*] (DSA)
Her Est .... Herman's Law of Estoppel [*A publication*] (DLA)
Her Ex .... Herman's Law of Executors [*A publication*] (DLA)
HERF .... Hazards of Electromagnetic Radiation to Fuel (TEL)
HERF .... High Energy Radiation to Fuel
HERF .... High-Energy Rate Forging [*Metalworking*]
HERF .... High-Energy Rate Forming
HERI .... Heavy Oil/Enhanced Recovery Index [*Alberta Oil Sands Technology
        and Research Authority*] [*Information service or system*]
HERI .... Higher Education Research Institute [*University of California, Los
        Angeles*] [*Research center*]
HERI .... Home Economics Research Institute [*Iowa State University*]
        [*Research center*] (RCD)
HeritPpn ...... Heritage Propane Partners LP [*Associated Press*] (SAG)
HeritUS........ Heritage US Government [*Associated Press*] (SAG)
HERJ .... High-Explosive Ramjet [*Weaponry*]
Her Jur .... Heron's Jurisprudence [*1860*] [*A publication*] (DLA)
HERL .... Health Effects Research Laboratory [*Research Triangle Park, NC*]
        [*Environmental Protection Agency*] (GRD)
Herley .... Herley Industries, Inc. [*Associated Press*] (SAG)
Herm .... Hermand's Consistorial Decisions [*Scotland*] [*A publication*] (DLA)
Herm .... Hermogenianus [*Flourished, 4th century*] [*Authority cited in pre-1607
        legal work*] (DSA)
HERMAN...... Hierarchical Environmental Retrieval for Management Access and
        Networking [*Biological Information Service*] [*Database on
        biology*] (NITA)
HERMAN...... Hierarchical Environmental Retrieval for Management and Networking
        [*Biological Information Service*] [*Riverside, CA*]

Hermand...... Hermand's Consistorial Decisions [*Scotland*] [*A publication*] (DLA)

Herm Chat Mortg... Herman on Chattel Mortgages [*A publication*] (DLA)

Her (Mel).... Herald (Melbourne) [*A publication*]

HERMES ...... Heavy Element and Radioactive Material Electromagnetic Separator [*British*]

Herm Estop... Herman's Law of Estoppel [*A publication*] (DLA)

Herm Ex'ns.. Herman's Law of Executions [*A publication*] (DLA)

HERMIES ..... Hostile Environment Robotic Machine Intelligence Experiment Series [*Oak Ridge National Laboratory*]

Hermo .... Hermogenianus [*Flourished, 4th century*] [*Authority cited in pre-1607 legal work*] (DSA)

Her Mort...... Herman on Mortgages of Real Estate [*A publication*] (DLA)

Hermot........ Hermotimus [*of Lucian*] [*Classical studies*]

Herm Schil... Hermannus Schildis [*Deceased, 1357*] [*Authority cited in pre-1607 legal work*] (DSA)

HERN .... Hernia [*or Herniated*] [*Medicine*]

HERN .... High Explosive, Rocket-Assisted

HERN .... Ras-Nasrani [*Egypt*] [*ICAO location identifier*] (ICLI)

HERO .... Hazards of Electromagnetic Radiation to Ordnance

HERO .... Health Education Resource Organization (EA)

HERO .... Heath Educational Robot [*Heath Co.*]

HERO .... Heritage Education and Review Organization [*Defunct*] (EA)

He-Ro .... He-Ro Group [*Associated Press*] (SAG)

HERO .... High-Energy Radiation to Ordnance [*Army*]

HERO .... Historical Evaluation and Research Organization (AEBS)

HERO .... Home Economics Related Occupations

HERO .... Hot Experimental Reaction of O Power [*Nuclear energy*]

HERO .... Hydrothermal Environment Research Observatory [*US-French Marine collaboration*]

Herod.......... Herodas [*Third century BC*] [*Classical studies*] (OCD)

HEROD........ Herodotus [*Greek historian, c. 484BC*] [*Classical studies*] (ROG)

HERODIAN... Herodianus [*Greek scholar, c. 200AD*] [*Classical studies*] (ROG)

HERP .... Hazards of Electromagnetic Radiation to Personnel (TEL)

HERP .... Herpetology [*or Herpetologist*]

HERP .... High-Energy Radiation to Personnel

HERP .... Human Exposure Dose/Rodent Potency Dose [*Toxicology*]

HERPES ...... High-Energy Recovery Pressure and Enthalpy Sensor (IAA)

HERPET ...... Herpetology (ADA)

Her Prec ..... Herne's Precedents [*A publication*] (DLA)

HERR .... Home Economics Research Reports

HERS .... Hardware Error Recovery System [*Sperry UNIVAC*]

HERS .... Health Education Research Service [*Department of Health and Human Services*]

HERS .... Health Evaluation and Referral Service

HERS .... Heart and Estrogen/Progestin Replacement Study [*Medicine*]

HERS .... Heritage Financial Services, Inc. [*NASDAQ symbol*] (NQ)

HERS .... Heritage Finl Svcs [*NASDAQ symbol*] (TTSB)

HERS .... Herself

HERS .... High-Energy-Range Spectrometer [*Instrumentation*]

HERS .... Higher Education Resource Services (EA)

HERS .... Highway Economic Requirements System [*FHWA*] (TAG)

HERS .... Home Economics Reading Service [*Recipe clipping service*]

HERS .... Home Emergency Response System

HERS .... Home Energy Rating System [*Thermal technology*] (PS)

HERS .... Hyperion Energy Recovery System (GNE)

HERS .... Hysterectomy Educational Resources and Services Foundation (EA)

HERS .... National Heart Education Research Society (EA)

HERSCP...... Hazardous Exposure Reduction and Safety Criteria Plan [*NASA*] (NASA)

HERTF........ Hertford [*City in England*] (ROG)

HERTF........ High-Energy Radiation Test Facility [*Military*]

HertgBc....... Heritage Bancorp, Inc. [*Associated Press*] (SAG)

HertgFS....... Heritage Financial Services [*Associated Press*] (SAG)

HERTIS .... Hertfordshire Technical Library and Information Service [*British*] (NITA)

HERTIS .... High-Energy Real-Time Inspections System (PDAA)

Hert M & Serv... Hertslet on Master and Servant [*A publication*] (DLA)

Hert Map Eur... Hertslet's Map of Europe [*A publication*] (DLA)

HERTS .... Hertfordshire [*County in England*] (EY)

Herts.......... Hertfordshire [*County in England*] (ODBW)

Hert Treat.... Hertslet's Treaties [*A publication*] (DLA)

Hertzog....... Hertzog's Reports of Transvaal High Court [*A publication*] (DLA)

HertzT........ Hrtz Technology Group [*Associated Press*] (SAG)

HertzTc....... Hertz Technology Group [*Associated Press*] (SAG)

HERU .... Health Economics Research Unit [*University of Aberdeen*] [*Scotland*] (IRC)

HERV .... Hostile Environment Recovery Vehicle

HERV .... Human Endogenous Retrovirus

HervTS........ Hervormde Teologiese Studies [*Pretoria, South Africa*] [*A publication*] (BJA)

HervTST....... Hervormde Teologiese Studies [*Pretoria, South Africa*] [*A publication*] (BJA)

HERZ .... Hertz Technology Group [*NASDAQ symbol*] (SAG)

HerzfldC....... Herzfeld Caribbean Basin Fund [*Associated Press*] (SAG)

HES............ Hamlet Evaluation Survey [*South Vietnam*]

HES............ Hanford Engineering Service [*Nuclear energy*] (NRCH)

HES............ Harvard Expedition to Samaria (BJA)

HES............ Head End Steering

HES............ Healthcare Evaluation System [*National Planning Data Corp.*] [*Information service or system*] (CRD)

HES............ Health Examination Survey [*NCHS*]

HES............ Heavy Enamel Single Silk [*Wire insulation*] (AAG)

HES............ Heli Services [*France ICAO designator*] (FAAC)

HES............ Helium Emergency Supply

HES............ Hesiod [*Greek poet, c. 800BC*] [*Classical studies*] (ROG)

HES............ Hetastarch [*Biochemistry*]

HES............ Hic Est Sepultus [*Here Is Buried*] [*Latin*] (ROG)

HES............ High Early Strength Cement [*Technical drawings*]

HES............ Higher Elementary School (ADA)

HES............ High-Explosive Spotting [*Weaponry*]

HES............ History of Economics Society (EA)

HES............ History of Education Society (EA)

HES............ Home Entertainment Service [*Cable-television system*] (IAA)

HES............ Home Entertainment System

HES............ Homeowners Emergency Services, Inc.

HES............ House Exchange System [*Telecommunications*] (NITA)

HES............ Hughes Earth Station [*Aerospace*]

HES............ Human Embryonic Skin [*or Spleen*] [*Medicine*] (DMAA)

HES............ Hydroxyethyl Starch [*Plasma volume expander*]

HES............ Hypereosinophilic Syndrome [*Medicine*]

HES............ Hypertext Editing System [*Computer science*]

HES............ Lonely, AK [*Location identifier FAA*] (FAAL)

HESB .... Hahnemann Elementary School Behavior Rating Scale [*Test*]

HESB .... Hessische Bibliographie [*Database*] [*Arbeitsgemeinschaft Hessische Bibliographie*] [*German*] [*Information service or system*] (CRD)

HESC .... St. Catherine/St. Catherine [*Egypt*] [*ICAO location identifier*] (ICLI)

HESCA .... Health Sciences Communications Association (EA)

HESD .... High-Explosive, Self-Destroying [*Weaponry*] (NATG)

HESD .... Hospital Equipment and Supplies Directory [*A publication*]

HESDC .... Higher Education Student Data Collection [*Australia*]

HESDEP...... Helicopter Sensor Development Program

HESE .... Helium Selenium [*LASER*] (DGA)

HESES .... Higher Education Students Early Statistics (AIE)

HESF .... High-Energy Symmetric Fission

HESH .... High-Explosive, Squash Head [*Weaponry*] (NATG)

HESN .... Aswan [*Egypt*] [*ICAO location identifier*] (ICLI)

HESO .... High-Energy Solid Oxidizer

HESO .... Hospital Educational Services Officer [*Navy*]

HESODAC .... Helicopter SONAR Data Collection

HESP .... Health and Environmental Studies Program [*Department of Energy*] (IID)

HESP .... High-Efficiency Solar Panel

HESRE .... Hamlet Evaluation System Monthly Report (MCD)

HESS .... High-Energy Squib Simulator [*NASA*] (NASA)

HESS .... History of Earth Sciences Society (EA)

HESS .... Human Engineering Systems Simulator [*Air Force*]

HESSAD...... Household Expenditure Survey - Small Area Data [*Australian Bureau of Statistics*]

HESSES ...... High-Energy Squib Simulators [*NASA*] (KSC)

HEST .... HEAF Emergency Service Tanks

HEST .... High Energy Shock Tunnel (IAA)

HEST .... High Explosives Simulation Technique

HESV .... Heavy Enamel Single Silk Varnish [*Wire insulation*] (AAG)

HET .... Hall Effect Thruster [*Electric thruster type*]

HET .... Hall Effect Transducer

HET .... Harrah's Entertainment [*NYSE symbol*] (TTSB)

HET .... Harrahs Entertainment, Inc. [*NYSE symbol*] (SAG)

HET .... Health Education Technologies [*New York, NY*] (TSSD)

HET .... Health-Education Telecommunications [*HEW*]

HET .... Heavy Equipment Transporter

HET .... Helium Equilibration Time (MAE)

HET .... Henryetta, OK [*Location identifier FAA*] (FAAL)

HET .... Heterodyne (DEN)

HET .... Heterozygosity [*Cytology*]

Het............ Hetley's English Common Pleas Reports [*124 English Reprint*] [*A publication*] (DLA)

HET .... High-Energy Telescope [*Geophysics*]

HET .... Higher Educational Test [*British military*] (DMA)

HET .... High-Explosive [*Shell*] Traced [*i.e., fitted with tracer*] [*Weaponry*]

HET .... HITIL [*Hardware in-the-Loop*] Encapsulation Methodology

HET .... Hobby Eberly Telescope [*Texas*]

HET .... Hobby Eberly Telescope

HET .... Hohhot [*China*] [*Airport symbol*] (OAG)

HET .... Horizontal Electrical Tunnel (NRCH)

HET .... Houston - ET [*Texas*] [*Seismograph station code, US Geological Survey Closed*] (SEIS)

HET .... Hydroxyethyl Terephthalate [*Organic chemistry*]

HET .... TAF Helicopters SA [*Spain ICAO designator*] (FAAC)

HETA .... Hazard Evaluation and Technical Assistance [*National Institute for Occupational Safety and Health*]

HETAC .... Heavy Transport Aircraft [*Military*]

HETB .... Heart of England Tourist Board (DCTA)

HET-BE ...... Heterophile Beef [*Immunology*] (DAVI)

HETC .... Heavy Equipment Test Chamber (MCD)

Het CP .... Hetley's English Common Pleas Reports [*124 English Reprint*] [*A publication*] (DLA)

HETDI .... High-Explosive, Tracer, Dark Ignition [*Weaponry*] (NATG)

HETE .... High Energy Transient Experiment [*NASA*]

HETE .... High Energy Transient Explorer

HETE .... Higher Education Teachers of English (AIE)

HETE .... Hydroxyeicosatetraenoic Acid [*Biochemistry*]

Het (Eng).... Hetley's English Common Pleas Reports [*124 English Reprint*] [*A publication*] (DLA)

HETERO ...... Heterosexual (DSUE)

HETEROG ... Heterogeneous (ROG)

HETF .... Hill Engineering Test Facility [*Air Force*]

HET-GP ...... Heterophile Guinea Pig [*Immunology*] (DAVI)

Hetl........... Hetley's English Common Pleas Reports [*124 English Reprint*] [*A publication*] (DLA)

HETM .... Hybrid Engineering Test Model (NASA)

HETMA	Heavy Edge Tool Manufacturers' Association [British] (BI)
HETMAC	(Hydroxyethyl)trimethylammonium Chloride [Organic chemistry]
HETOC	Hudson-Essex-Terraplane Owners Club (EA)
HETP	Head End Treatment Plant [Nuclear energy British]
HETP	Height Equivalent to a Theoretical Plate [Chemical engineering]
HETP	Hexaethyl Tetraphosphate [Organic chemistry]
HETP	Human Engineering Test Plan
HET-PR	Heterophile Presumptive [Immunology] (DAVI)
HETR	El-Tor [Egypt] [ICAO location identifier] (ICLI)
HETS	Heavy Equipment Transporter System [Army] (RDA)
HETS	Height Equivalent to a Theoretical Stage [Chemical engineering] (NRCH)
HETS	High-Efficiency Transfer Solution [CINNA/BIOTECX International, Inc.] [Analytical biochemistry]
HETS	High-Energy Telescope System [Geophysics]
HETS	High-Energy Transfer Stage
HETS	Hyperenvironmental Test Station [or System] [Air Force]
HETSD	High Explosive, Tracer, Self-Destroying [Weaponry] (SAA)
HEU	Heulandite [A zeolite]
HEU	High Estimate Unconstrained
HEU	Highly Enriched Uranium [Nuclear reactor technology]
HEU	Hull Electronics Unit [Military] (RDA)
HEU	Hydroelectric Unit
HEU	Schenectady, NY [Location identifier FAA] (FAAL)
HEU EIS	Disposition of Surplus Highly Enriched Uranium Environmental Impact Statement
HEUI	Hydraulic Electronic Unit Injector [Fuel system] [Automotive engineering]
HEUR	Hydrophobic Ethoxylated Urethane Resin [Paint technology]
HEUS	High-Energy Upper Stage [NASA]
HEV	Health and Environment (AABC)
HEV	Hemagglutinating Encephalomyelitis Virus [Medicine] (DMAA)
HEV	High Endothelial Venule [Cytology]
HEV	High-Walled Endothelial Venule [Anatomy]
HEV	Human Enteric Virus
HEV	Hybrid-Electric Vehicle
Hev	Nahal Hever Caves (BJA)
HEVA	Hydrolyzed Ethylene-Vinyl Acetate [Plastics technology]
HEVAC	Heating, Ventilating, and Air-Conditioning Association [Federation of Environmental Trade Associations] [British]
HEVAC	Heating, Ventilating, and Air Conditioning Manufacturers Association Ltd. [British] (BI)
HEVR	Heavier (WDAA)
HEVS	Helenium Virus S [Plant pathology]
HEW	Department of Health, Education, and Welfare [Sometimes facetiously translated "Halls of Eternal Warfare"] [Later, HHS]
HEW	Department of Health, Education, and Welfare, Washington, DC [OCLC symbol] (OCLC)
HEW	Hanford Engineering Works [Nuclear energy]
HEW	Health, Education and Welfare (USDC)
HEW	Health Education and Welfare [Marine science] (OSRA)
HEW	Houston, TX [Location identifier FAA] (FAAL)
HEWC	Highly Enriched Waste Concentrate (PDAA)
HEWGAR	Department of Health, Education and Welfare Grant Appeals Board (AAGC)
HEWH	High-Explosive Warhead [Weaponry]
HEWL	Hen Egg White Lysozyme [Also, HEL] [An enzyme]
HewlPk	Hewlett-Packard Co. [Associated Press] (SAG)
HEWPR	Department of Health, Education, and Welfare [Later, HHS] Procurement Regulations
HEX	Handicapped Education Exchange [Amateur Radio Research and Development Corp.] [Information service or system] (IID)
HEX	Hatfield Executive Aviation Ltd. [British ICAO designator] (FAAC)
HEX	Heat Exchanger (KSC)
HEX	Hemlo Explorations [Vancouver Stock Exchange symbol]
HEX	Hexachlorocyclopentadiene [Also, HCCP, HCP] [Organic chemistry]
HEX	Hexachord [Music] (ADA)
HEX	Hexadecimal [System]
HEX	Hexagon [or Hexagonal]
HEX	Hexamethylmelamine [Altretamine] [Also, HMM, HXM] [Antineoplastic drug]
HEX	Hexateuch (ROG)
HEX	High Explosive (DNAB)
HEX	Hydraulics, External (DNAB)
HEX	Santo Domingo [Dominican Republic] [Airport symbol] (OAG)
HEXA	Hexamethylene Tetramine [Organic chemistry] (WDAA)
HEX-A	Hexosaminidase-A
Hexa-CAF	Hexamethylmelamine, Cyclophosphamide, Amethopterin [Methotrexate], Fluorouracil [Antineoplastic drug regimen]
HEX-B	Hexosominidase-B
HEX-BCH	Hexachloronorbornadiene [Organic chemistry] (EPA)
HEXCALC	Hexadecimal Calculator [Computer science] (MHDI)
Hexcel	Hexcel Corp. [Associated Press] (SAG)
HEXE	High Energy X-Ray Experiment
HEXFET	Hexagonal Field Effect Transistor (NITA)
HEXHD	Hexagonal Head
HEXIT	Hexadecimal Digit [Computer science] (NHD)
HEXL	Methohexital [A barbiturate] [Pharmacology] (DAVI)
HEY	Ozark/Fort Rucker, AL [Location identifier FAA] (FAAL)
Heyl Imp D	Heyl's United States Import Duties [A publication] (DLA)
HEYM	Herrold's Egg Yolk Medium [For growing microorganisms]
Heyw Ca	Heywood's Table of Cases [Georgia] [A publication] (DLA)
Heyw Co Ct	Heywood's County Courts Practice [4th ed.] [1876] [A publication] (DLA)
Heyw Elec	Heywood on Elections [A publication] (DLA)
Heywood & Massey	Heywood and Massey's Court of Protection Practice [9th ed.] [1971] [A publication] (DLA)
HEZ	Natchez [Mississippi] [Airport symbol] (OAG)
HEZOBOLLAH	Hezb Allah [Party of God] [Arabic] [An Irananian terrorist organization]
Hez-PBAN	Heliothis Zea Pheromone Biosynthesis Activating Neuropeptide
HF	Dorsey Laboratories [Research code symbol]
HF	First Air [ICAO designator] (AD)
Hf	Hafnium [Chemical element]
Hf	Hafnium (IDOE)
HF	Hageman Factor [Factor XII] [Hematology]
HF	Hale Foundation (EA)
HF	Half (AAG)
hf	Half (WDMC)
HF	Half Forward (ADA)
HF	Hammer Form (MCD)
H/F	Handling Fee [Coupon redemption]
HF	Handling Fixture (MCD)
HF	Handwriting Foundation
HF	Hankes Foundation (EA)
HF	Hanuman Foundation (EA)
HF	Harassing Fire [Military] (AABC)
HF	Hard Failure
HF	Hard Filled [Capsules] [Pharmacy]
HF	Hard Firm [Pencil leads]
HF	Harry Franco [Pseudonym used by Charles F. Briggs]
HF	Hartree-Fock [Orbitals] [Atomic structure]
HF	Hay Fever [Medicine]
HF	Hazard Function
HF	Haze Filter [Photography]
HF	Hazelden Foundation (EA)
HF	Heart Failure [Medicine]
HF	Heat Flow [Physiology]
Hf	Heat of Combustion of Fuel [Aviation] (DA)
HF	Heavy Fuel [Engine technology]
HF	Heeresfahrzeug [Army Vehicle] [German military - World War II]
HF	Height Finder [or Finding] [RADAR]
H/F	HeLa [Helen Lake]/Fibroblast [Hybrid] [Cytology] (DAVI)
H/F	Held For (AAG)
H/F	Held For [Investment term] (DFIT)
HF	Helper Factor [Immunology]
HF	Hemorrhagic Factor [Medicine]
HF	Hemorrhagic Fever [Medicine] (DAVI)
HF	Hepatic Fat
HF	Hercules Furens [of Euripides] [Classical studies] (OCD)
HF	Heritage Foundation [Washington, DC] (EA)
HF	Hesperian Foundation (EA)
HF	High Fat [Type of diet]
HF	High Field (IAA)
HF	High Flow (MAE)
HF	High Flux (IAA)
HF	High Foliage Forager [Ecology]
HF	High Food Density [Ecology]
HF	High Frequency [Electronics]
hf	High Frequency (WDMC)
HF	High Frontier (EA)
HF	High Rate Forward
HF	Hippocampal Fissure [Neuroanatomy]
HF	Hold Fire [Military]
HF	Holding Fixture (MSA)
HF	Hollow Fiber
H-F	Holstein-Friesian [Cattle breed]
HF	Holyearth Foundation (EA)
HF	Holy Father (ROG)
HF	Home Fleet [Obsolete British]
HF	Home Forces [Military British]
HF	Home Front
HF	Homeopathic Foundation [Later, FHR] (EA)
HF	Horizontal Flight (NASA)
HF	Hot Finished [Drawing] (DAC)
HF	Hot Firing (MCD)
HF	House File (OICC)
HF	House Formula [An in-house formula found in a particular hospital or clinic] (DAVI)
HF	House of Fabrics, Inc. [NYSE symbol] (SPSG)
HF	Hull Filter
HF	Human Factors
HF	Human Fibroblast [Medicine] (DMAA)
HF	Human Foreskin [Anatomy]
HF	Huna Forschunggesellschaft [Huna Research Association - HRA] [Switzerland] (EAIO)
HF	Hundred Feet
HF	Hydrogen Fill (MCD)
HF	Hydrogen Fluoride [Inorganic chemistry] (AFM)
HF	Hyperfiltration (NASA)
HF	Messerschmitt-Boelkow-Blohm [Germany ICAO aircraft manufacturer identifier] (ICAO)
HF	Wander AG [Switzerland] [Research code symbol]
HFA	Haemophilia Foundation of Australia
HFA	Haifa [Israel] [Airport symbol] (OAG)
HFA	Hardened Flexible Array
HFA	Hard Fibres Association (EA)
HFA	Hardware Federation of Australia
HFA	Harmelink Family Association (EA)
HFA	[The] Harry Fox Agency

HFA	Hartshorn Family Association (EA)
HFA	Hawaii Flooring Association (SRA)
HFA	Headquarters Field Army (NATG)
HFA	Heat and Flame Resistant, Armored (IAA)
HFA	Heavy Field Artillery
HFA	Hexafluoroacetone [Organic chemistry]
HFA	Hexafluoroaceytlacetone [Organic chemistry]
HFA	High Flow Alarm (IEEE)
HFA	High Force Actuator [Engineering]
HFA	High-Frequency Accelerometer (NASA)
HFA	High-Frequency Amplifier [Electronics] (IAA)
HFA	High-Frequency Antenna (KSC)
HFA	High Functioning Autism
HFA	Hired Fishermen's Association [A union] [British]
HFA	Historical Farm Association (EA)
HFA	Hitchhikers for America (EA)
HFA	Homofolic Acid [Biochemistry]
HFA	Hospital Finance Authority (GHCT)
HFA	Humane Farming Association (EA)
HFA	Hydrofluoroalkane [Organic chemistry]
HFA	Hydrogen-Fueled Aircraft
HFAA	Hardanger Fiddle Association of America (EA)
HFAA	High-Frequency Airborne Antenna
HFAA	Holstein-Friesian Association of America (EA)
HFAB	House of Fabrics, Inc. [NASDAQ symbol] (SAG)
HFAC	Human Factors Association of Canada
HFAF	Hawaii Foundation for American Freedoms (EA)
HFAJ	High-Frequency Antijam (DWSG)
HFAK	Hollow Fiber Artificial Kidney [Medicine] (AAMN)
HFAM	Helicopter Familiarization (MCD)
HF & OR	Human Factors and Operations Research [Army] (MCD)
HFARA	Honorary Foreign Associate of Royal Academy [British]
HFAS	High-Frequency Antenna System (KSC)
HFAS	Honeywell File Access System
HFB	Hand Form Block (MSA)
HFB	Helium Filled Bubble [For study of air flow]
HFB	Heptafluorobutyrate [or Heptafluorobutyric] [Organic chemistry]
HFB	Horizontal Flow Barrier [Computer science]
HFBA	Hebrew Free Burial Association (EA)
HFBA	Heptafluorobutyric Acid [Organic chemistry]
HFBC	High Frequency Broadcasting Schedule [Databank] (NITA)
HFBcp	HF Bancorp, Inc. [Associated Press] (SAG)
HF BD	Half-Bound [or Binding] (WDAA)
Hf-Bd	High-Frequency Band [Electricity]
HFBI	Heptafluorobutyrylimidazole [Organic chemistry]
HFBR	High-Flux Beam Reactor (GAAI)
HFBR	High Flux Beam Research Reactor [Nuclear energy]
HFBR	Hollow-Fiber Bioreactor [Chemical engineering]
HFBUP	High-Frequency Backup Program [Military] (CAAL)
HFC	Hand-Filled Capsules [Pharmacy] (DAVI)
HFC	Hard-Filled Capsules [Pharmacy] (DAVI)
HFC	Harpers Ferry Center [National Park Service] (GRD)
HFC	Heart Fan Club (EA)
HFC	Heat Flow and Convection (NASA)
HFC	High-Energy LASER Fire Control
HFC	Higher Fire Control [British military] (DMA)
HFC	High-Frequency Choke
HFC	High-Frequency Correction
HFC	High-Frequency Current
HFC	Histamine-Forming Capacity (DMAA)
HFC	Holy Family College [California, Pennsylvania, Wisconsin]
HFC	Holy Family College, Philadelphia, PA [OCLC symbol] (OCLC)
HFC	Home Finance Contract
HFC	Hope Foundation Communicators [Australia]
HFC	Hospital Financial Control [McDonnell Douglas Automation Co.]
HFC	Household Financing Corp. (CDAI)
HFC	Household Food Consumption
HFC	Human Factors Checklists [Navy]
HFC	Hybrid Fiber and Coax [Cable technology] (PCM)
HFC	Hybrid Fiber/Coax (ACRL)
HFC	Hybrid Fiber-Coax [Telecommunications]
HFC	Hydraulic Flight Control (NASA)
HFC	Hydrofluorocarbon [Organic chemistry]
HFC	Hyperfine Coupling [Spectroscopy]
HFCA	Holy Family Christian Association [In 1983 movie "Zelig"]
HFCAA	Hatters' Fur Cutters Association of America [Formerly, HFCAUS] (EA)
HFCAUS	Hatters' Fur Cutters Association of the United States [Later, HFCAA]
HFCC	Henry Ford Community College [Dearborn, MI]
HFCD	Hino Fuel Economy Clean Air High-Durability [Hino diesel engines]
HFCE	HFIR [High-Flux Isotope Reactor] Critical Experiment [Nuclear energy] (NRCH)
HF-CF	Half-Calf [Bookbinding] (DGA)
HF-CL	Half-Cloth [Bookbinding] (DGA)
HF-COL	Half Column [Advertisement] (DGA)
HFCRSP	High-Frequency Communications Replacement System Program (LAIN)
HFCS	Harpoon Fire Control System [Missiles] (MCD)
HFCS	High-Fructose Corn Sweetener [or Syrup]
HFCS	Honeywell Financial and Corporate Planning System (HGAA)
HFCT	Hydraulic Flight Control Test (NASA)
HFCUR	High-Frequency Current
HFCV	Helium Flow Control Valve (KSC)
HFCVD	Hot Filament Chemical Vapor Deposition [Coating technology]
HFD	Halifax Developments Ltd. [Toronto Stock Exchange symbol]

HFD	Hartford, CT [Location identifier FAA] (FAAL)
HFD	Hatfield BAE [British ICAO designator] (FAAC)
HFD	Held for Detail
HFD	Helium Fill to Distribution Unit [Aerospace] (AAG)
HFD	Hemorrhagic Fever of Deer [Medicine] (DMAA)
HFD	Hereford [British depot code]
HFD	Herefordshire [County in England] (ROG)
HFD	High-Fiber Diet (DMAA)
HFD	High Forceps Delivery [Obstetrics] (DAVI)
HFD	Home Furnishings Daily [A publication] [Formerly HFD-Weekly Home Furnishings] (WDMC)
HFD	Horizon Flight Director [Aircraft]
HFD	Hospital Field Director [Red Cross]
HFD	Host Funding 'A' [AMEX symbol] (TTSB)
HFD	Host Funding, Inc. [AMEX symbol] (SAG)
HFD	Hot Form Die
HFD	Human Factor Division [Air Research and Development Command] [Air Force] (AAG)
HFD	Human Factors Design (DMAA)
HFD	Human Figures Drawing Test [Education] (EDAC)
HFD	Hydro-Form Die
HFDA	High Film Density Area (DMAA)
HFDA	Hospital Food Directors Association
HFdeSJ	Franciscan Sisters of St. Joseph (Mexico City) (TOCD)
HFDF	High-Frequency Direction Finding [Pronounced "huff duff"] [Electronics]
HFDF	High-Frequency Distribution Frame (IEEE)
HF/DF	Hydrogen Fluoride/Deuterium Fluoride (MCD)
HFDK	Human Fetal Diploid Kidney [Type of cell line]
HFDL	Host Forms Description Language [Xerox software] (NITA)
HFDL	Human Fetal Diploid Lung [Type of cell line]
HFDM	High-Frequency Digital MODEM (LAIN)
HFDS	Hydrogen Fluid Distribution System (MCD)
HFdSvF	Home Federal Financial Corp. [Associated Press] (SAG)
HFE	Heat-Flow Electronics
HFE	Heat-Flow Experiment
HFE	Hefei [China] [Airport symbol] (OAG)
HFE	Helmholtz Free Energy
HFE	Hexafluorodiethyl Ether [Convulsant]
HFE	High Frequency Executive (NASA)
HFE	Hillside Energy [Vancouver Stock Exchange symbol]
HFE	Human Factors Engineering (AABC)
HFE	Human Factors Evaluation (MCD)
HFE	Human Factors in Electronics (MCD)
HFE	Hydrofluorether
HFE	Pittsburgh, PA [Location identifier FAA] (FAAL)
HFEA	Human Factors Engineering Analysis [or Assessment] [Army] (RDA)
HFEA	Human Fertilization and Embryology Authority [British]
HFEAA	Historic Fire Engine Association of Australia
HFEC	Human Foreskin Epithelial Cell [Medicine] (DMAA)
HFEF	High Flux Experimental Facility [Nuclear energy]
HFEF	Hot Fuel Examination Facility [Nuclear energy]
HFET	Hellmann-Feynmann Electrostatic Theorem [Physics]
HFET	Highway Fuel Economy Test [Environmental Protection Agency]
HFET	Human Factors Engineering Testing (MCD)
HFeU	Hepatic Iron (Ferrum) Uptake [Physiology]
HFF	Heavy Freight Flight [British military] (DMA)
HFF	High Flight Foundation (EA)
HFF	High-Frequency Furnace
HFF	Hoffman, NC [Location identifier FAA] (FAAL)
HFF	Horizontal Falling Film (PDAA)
hFF	Human Follicular Fluid [Physiology]
HFF	Human Foreskin Fibroblast [A cell line]
HFF	Hydraulic Fluid Filter
HFF	Hypervelocity Flow Field
HFFB	Harrodsburg First Financial Bancorp, Inc. [NASDAQ symbol] (SAG)
HFFB	Harrodsburg First Finl Bancorp [NASDAQ symbol] (TTSB)
HFFC	Hart Family Fan Club (EA)
HFFC	Helen Forrest Fan Club (EA)
HFFC	HF Financial [NASDAQ symbol] (TTSB)
HFFC	HF Financial Corp. [NASDAQ symbol] (SAG)
HFFF	Djibouti/Ambouli [Djibouti] [ICAO location identifier] (ICLI)
HFFF	Hungarian Freedom Fighters Federation USA (EA)
HFFF	Hypervelocity Free Flight Facility
HF Fnc	HF Financial Corp. [Associated Press] (SAG)
HFFS	HELLFIRE Fire and Forget Seeker [Missile]
HFG	Harmonic Frequency Generator
HFG	Heavy Free Gas (IEEE)
HFG	High Frequency Gas (WDAA)
HFG	Human Factors Group
HFGA	Hall of Fame for Great Americans (EA)
HFGI	Harrington Financial Group, Inc. [NASDAQ symbol] (SAG)
HFGI	Harrington Fin'l Grp [NASDAQ symbol] (TTSB)
HFH	Harnischfeger Industries [NYSE symbol]
HFHL	High-Frequency Hearing Loss [Otorhinolaryngology] (DAVI)
HFHT	Handling Fixture - Hoist Tool (MCD)
HFI	Health Facilities Information File [Australia]
HFI	Health First International (EA)
HFI	Helicopter Foundation International (EA)
HFI	Hereditary Fructose Intolerance [Medicine]
HFI	High Fidelity Institute
HFI	High-Frequency Input (IAA)
HFI	Hocker Federation International (EA)
HFI	Home for Incurables [Australia]
HFI	Hudson Foods Cl'A' [NYSE symbol] (TTSB)

HFI............. Hudson Foods, Inc., Class A [*NYSE symbol*] (SPSG)
HFI............. Human Fibroblast Interferon [*Medicine*] (DMAA)
HFI............. Hydraulic Fluid Index (PDAA)
HFI............. Hyperfine Interaction
HFIA......... Heat and Frost Insulators and Asbestos Workers (MHDB)
HFIA......... Home Furnishings International Association (EA)
HFIAW .... International Association of Heat and Frost Insulators and Asbestos Workers (EA)
HFIB......... Hexafluoroisobutylene [*Organic chemistry*]
HFIC......... Harpoon Firing Interlock Closed [*Missiles*] (MCD)
HFIC......... High-Frequency Intra-Task Force Communications (LAIN)
HFIC......... Home Furnishings Industry Committee [*Defunct*] (EA)
HFIC......... Human Factors Information Center (SAA)
HFID......... Heated Flame Ionization Detection [*Analytical chemistry*]
HFIF......... Human Fibroblast Interferon [*Cytology*]
HFIH......... High-Frequency Induction Heating (PDAA)
HFIM......... High-Frequency Instruments and Measurements (IEEE)
HFIP......... Hexafluoroisopropanol [*or Hexafluoroisopropyl*] [*Organic chemistry*]
HFIP......... High-Frequency Improvement Program (LAIN)
HFIR......... High Flux Isotope Reactor
HFITR .... High-Field Ignition Test Reactor [*Nuclear energy*] (MCD)
HFIW......... High-Frequency Induction Welding [*Manufacturing term*]
HFJ......... High-Frequency Jammer
HFJV......... High-Frequency Jet Ventilation [*Pulmonary ventilation*]
HFK......... Human Foreskin Keratinocyte [*Cytology*]
HFL............. Heliflyg AG [*Sweden ICAO designator*] (FAAC)
HFL............. Helium Fill Line
HFL............. Hesperia Fine Sandy Loam [*A soil type*]
HFL............. Human Factors Laboratory [*University of South Dakota*] [*National Institute of Standards and Technology Research center*]
HFL............. Human Fetal Lung
HFLA .... Handling Fixture - Line Accessory (MCD)
HFLD .... Handling Fixture - Line Dolly (MCD)
H flu .... Hemophilus Influenzae [*Bacteriology*] (DAVI)
HFM......... Hachette Filipacchi Magazines [*A publication*]
HFM......... Hachette Filipacchi Magazines
HFM......... Hand, Foot, and Mouth [*Disease*]
HFM......... Heavy Force Modernization [*Army*]
HFM......... Held for Manufacturing
HFM......... Held for Material
HFM......... Hemifacial Microsomia [*Medicine*] (DMAA)
HFM......... High-Field Magnetometer [*Instrumentation*]
HFM......... High-Frequency Mode (IAA)
HFM......... Hold for Money [*Business term*]
HFM......... Hollow Fiber Membrane (NASA)
HFM......... Horizonatal Flexible Mandrel (PDAA)
HFMA......... Healthcare Financial Management Association (EA)
HFMA......... Health Food Manufacturers Association [*British*] (DBA)
HFMA......... Hospital Financial Management Association [*Later, Healthcare Financial Management Association*] (EA)
HFMD .... Hand-Foot-and-Mouth Disease (PDAA)
HFMD .... Home Federal Corp. [*NASDAQ symbol*] (NQ)
HFMD .... Home Federal (MD) [*NASDAQ symbol*] (TTSB)
HFMF......... Hone-Finish Monolithic Floor [*Technical drawings*]
HFMI......... Highly Filled Materials Institute [*Stevens Institute of Technology*]
HF-MOR....... Half-Morocco [*Bookbinding*] (DGA)
HFMR......... HF [*High Frequency*] Modem Replacement (DOMA)
HFMRA .... Honorary Foreign Member of the Royal Academy
HFMS......... Highway Fleet Management System (MCD)
HFMS......... Human Factors Measurement System
HFMSS .... Heavy Force Modernization Survivability System
HFMSSP ...... Heavy Force Modernization System Safety Plan [*Army*]
HFMU......... High-Fidelity Mock-Up [*NASA*] (NASA)
HFN......... Hofn [*Iceland*] [*Airport symbol*] (OAG)
HFN......... Human Fibronectin [*Cytochemistry*]
HFNC......... HFNC Financial [*NASDAQ symbol*] (TTSB)
HFNC......... HFNC Financial Corp. [*NASDAQ symbol*] (SAG)
HFNCFn ...... HFNC Financial Corp. [*Associated Press*] (SAG)
HFO......... Heavy Fuel Oil
HFO......... Heavy Fuel Oils [*Database*] [*Department of Energy*]
HFO......... Height Finder Operator (MUGU)
HFO......... High-Frequency Oscillator
HFO......... Honolulu, HI [*Location identifier FAA*] (FAAL)
HFORL......... Human Factors Operation Research Laboratory [*Air Force*]
HFOSL .... Human Factors and Organizational Systems Laboratory [*Navy Personnel Research and Development Center*] [*San Diego, CA*]
HFOV .... High-Frequency Oscillatory Ventilation [*Medicine*] (DAVI)
HFP............. Hamdard Foundation Pakistan (EAIO)
HFP............. Held for Planning (MCD)
HFP............. Helical Flight Path
HFP............. Helium Fuel-Tank Pressurization (AAG)
HFP............. Hexafluoropropylene [*Organic chemistry*]
HFP............. Highfield Property Investments Ltd. [*Toronto Stock Exchange symbol*]
HFP............. Hostile Fire Pay [*Special pay for hazardous duty*] [*Military*] (AABC)
HFP............. Hot Full Power [*Nuclear energy*] (NRCH)
HFP............. Huron Forest Products Joint Venture [*Commercial*] (EERA)
HFP............. Hybrid Fabrication Procedure (MCD)
HFP............. Hypofibrinogenic Plasma
HFPA .... Hollywood Foreign Press Association (EA)
HFPA .... Home Fashions Products Association (EA)
HFPAC .... High Frequency Powder Air Conveyor (PDAA)
HFPCS .... Health Facilities Planning and Construction Service
HFPO .... Hexafluoropropylene Oxide [*Organic chemistry*]
HFPPV .... High-Frequency Positive Pressure Ventilation [*Medicine*]
HFPR .... Handling Fixture - Production (MCD)

HFPR .... Human Factors and Personnel Resources (DNAB)
HFPS .... Hay Fever Prevention Society
HFPS .... High-Frequency Phase Shifter [*Telecommunications*]
HFPS .... Home Fallout Protection Survey [*Formerly, EFPH*] [*Civil Defense*]
HFPSI .... Human Factors Personnel Selection Inventory [*Interpersonal skills and attitudes test*]
HFPT......... Health Fitness Physical Therapy [*NASDAQ symbol*] (SAG)
HFPT......... Held for Perishable Tools
HFPT......... Hlth Fitness Physl Therapy [*NASDAQ symbol*] (TTSB)
HFR......... Height Finder RADAR (CET)
HFR......... Heli France [*ICAO designator*] (FAAC)
HFR......... High Fill Rate [*Valve*] [*Automotive engineering*]
HFR......... High Flux Reactor [*Netherlands*] [*Nuclear energy*]
HFR......... High Frequency of Recombination [*Medicine*]
HFR......... High-Frequency Resistor
HFR......... Hold for Release [*Advertising*] (BARN)
HFR......... Human Factors Research
HFRA......... High-Frequency Recovery Antenna (KSC)
HFRA......... Honorary Fellow of the Royal Academy [*British*]
HFRDF......... High-Frequency Radio Direction Finding (IAA)
HFRDF......... High-Frequency Repeater Distribution Frame (DEN)
HFRE......... Hydraulic Fluid Replenishment Equipment
HFRG......... High-Frequency Radio Group [*Military*] (CAAL)
HFRO......... Hill Farming Research Organisation [*British*]
HFRS......... Hemorrhagic Fever with Renal Syndrome [*Medicine*]
HFRT .... High-Frequency Radio Transmitter
HFRW......... High-Frequency Resistance Welding [*Manufacturing term*]
HFRZ......... Halbfranzband [*Half-Calf Binding*] [*Publishing*] [*German*]
HFS............. French Frigate Shoals, HI [*Location identifier FAA*] (FAAL)
HFS............. Hagfors [*Sweden*] [*Seismograph station code, US Geological Survey*] (SEIS)
HFS............. Harrison Fisher Society (EA)
HFS............. Heat Flux Sensor
HFS............. Heavy Flushing Spray
HFS............. Hemifacial Spasm [*Medicine*]
HFS............. HFS, Inc. [*Associated Press*] (SAG)
HFS............. Hierarchical File Storage (ACRL)
HFS............. Hierarchical File System [*Computer science*]
HFS............. High-Frequency Stimulation [*Physiology*]
HFS............. Holstein Friesian Society of Great Britain and Ireland (DBA)
HFS............. Holy Family Seminary [*Connecticut*]
HFS............. Horizontal Flight Simulator (MCD)
HFS............. Hospital Financial Support (DMAA)
HFS............. Hospitality Franchise Systems [*NYSE symbol*] (SPSG)
HFS............. Hostile Fire Simulator [*Military*] (MCD)
HFS............. Household Financial Services [*Australia*]
HFS............. Human Factors Society (EA)
HFS............. Human Factors Study
HFS............. Hyperfine Structure
HFS............. Hypothetical Future Samples [*Statistics*]
HFSA......... Hardin Bancorp [*NASDAQ symbol*] (TTSB)
HFSA......... Hardin Bancorp, Inc. [*NASDAQ symbol*] (SAG)
HFSA......... Hydrofluorsilicic Acid [*Inorganic chemistry*]
HFSC......... Hamilton Financial Services Corp. [*NASDAQ symbol*] (SAG)
HFSC......... Human Fetal Spinal Cord
HFSC......... Hyperfine Splitting Constant [*Spectroscopy*]
HFSE......... High-Field-Strength Elements [*Geochemistry*]
HFSE......... Human Factors and Safety Engineering (DNAB)
HFSF......... Home Federal Financial Corp. [*NASDAQ symbol*] (SAG)
HFSG......... Healthcare Financing Study Group (EA)
HFSH......... Human Follicle Stimulating Hormone [*Endocrinology*]
HFSIW......... Hospitality Franchise Sys Wrrt [*NASDAQ symbol*] (TTSB)
HFSP......... Hanukah Factor Serine Protease (DMAA)
HFSP......... Human Frontier Science Program [*An international effort, proposed by Japan in 1987*]
HFSS .... High-Frequency Sounder System (SSD)
HFSSB .... High-Frequency Single Sideband [*Telecommunications*]
HFSSC .... High-Frequency Swept Spectrum Communications
HFST......... Hearing-for-Speech Test
HFST......... High-Flux Scram Trip [*Nuclear energy*] (IEEE)
HFSU......... Heat Flux Sensing Unit
HFSV......... High Flow Shutoff Valve
HFT......... Hachette-Filipacchi Telematique [*Information service or system*] (IID)
HFT......... Hammerfest [*Norway*] [*Airport symbol*] (OAG)
HFT......... Heavy Fire Team [*Military*]
HFT......... Heft (ROG)
HFT......... Heiney Family Tree (EA)
HFT......... Held for Tooling
HFT......... Hidden Frames Test [*Education*] (EDAC)
HFT......... High-Flux Telescope
HFT......... High-Frequency of Transduction [*Virology*]
HFT......... High-Frequency Transfer (DMAA)
HFT......... Hollyfordair Travel Ltd. [*New Zealand*] [*ICAO designator*] (FAAC)
HFT......... Horizontal Flight Testing [*NASA*] (KSC)
HFT......... Hot Functional Testing [*Nuclear energy*] (NRCH)
HFTA......... Hexafluorothioacetone [*Organic chemistry*]
HFTB......... Handling Fixture - Tow Bar (MCD)
HFTE......... Human Factors Test and Evaluation [*Military*] (MCD)
HFTF......... Horizontal Flight Test Facility [*NASA*] (NASA)
HFTL......... Held for Tool Liaison
HFTS......... Horizontal Flight Test Simulator [*NASA*] (NASA)
HFTS......... Human Factors Trade Studies [*Navy*]
HFU......... Hand-Foot-Uterus Syndrome [*Medicine*] (DMAA)
HFU......... Heat-Flow [*or Flux*] Unit [*Nuclear energy*]

HFU	Heeres-Funkstelle [Army Radio Station] [German military - World War II]
HFUPR	Hourly Fetal Urine Production Rate [Medicine] (AAMN)
HFUS	Historic Festivals of the United States [A publication]
HFV	High-Frequency Ventilation [Medicine]
HFV	Horizontal Flight Vector
HFV	Human Foamy Virus
HF-VEL	Half-Vellum [Bookbinding] (DGA)
HFW	Haverfordwest [Wales] [Airport symbol] (AD)
HFW	Hole Full of Water [Drilling] (DICI)
HFWA	High-Frequency Wave Analyzer
HFWB	High Freqency Wire Broadcasting (PDAA)
HFWE	Having Fun with Elvis [Fan club] (EA)
HFWF	Hired Farm Working Force
HFX	Halifax City Regional Library [UTLAS symbol]
HFX	High-Frequency Transceiver [or Transducer]
HG	Centreline Air Services Ltd. [British ICAO designator] (ICDA)
HG	Die Hethitischen Gesetze. Documenta et Monumenta Orientis Antiqui 7 [Leiden] [A publication] (BJA)
Hg	Haggai [Old Testament book]
HG	Half Gross (DNAB)
HG	Hammurabi's Gesetz (BJA)
HG	Hand Generator
HG	Hand Grip (DMAA)
HG	Harbor Airlines [ICAO designator] (AD)
HG	Hard Gelatin [Pharmacy]
HG	Harmonic Generator
HG	Harrogate [Postcode] (ODBW)
HG	Having (ROG)
HG	Head Gasket [Automotive engineering]
HG	Headgear [Mining engineering] (IAA)
HG	Hectogram
HG	Heliogram
HG	Hemoglobin [Biochemistry, medicine]
HG	Heptadecapeptide Gastrin [Endocrinology]
HG	Herpes Genitalis [Infectious disease] (DAVI)
HG	Herpes Gestationis [Medicine]
HG	Heschl's Gyrus [Brain anatomy]
Hg	Heterodera glycenes [A nematode]
HG	Hexylene Glycol [Organic chemistry]
HG	Higher Grade
HG	High German [Language, etc.]
HG	High Glucose [Clinical chemistry]
HG	High Grain (NASA)
HG	His [or Her] Grace
HG	Holy Ghost
HG	Home Guard [British]
HG	Homing Guidance (AAG)
HG	Horizon Grow [Astronomy] (OA)
HG	Horse Guards [British]
HG	Hotchkiss Gunner [British military] (DMA)
HG	Housing Guaranty
HG	Hull Gauge
HG	Human Gonadotrophin [Endocrinology]
HG	Human Growth [Factor] [Endocrinology] (DAVI)
Hg	Hydrargyrum [Mercury] [Chemical element]
HG	Hydrogen Gas [System] [Nuclear energy] (NRCH)
HG	Hydrogen Generator
HG	Hydrophilic Group [Surfactant technology]
HG	Hyperglycemic-Glycogenolytic [Factor] [Endocrinology]
HG	Hypertensive Group [Cardiology]
HG	Hypobranchial Gland
HG	Hypoglycemia [Medicine] (DMAA)
Hg	Mercury [Chemical] (EERA)
Hg	Mercury [Chemical element] (DOG)
HG	Workout Handily from Gate [Horse racing]
HGA	Hammel Green and Abrahamson, Inc. [A national leader in innovative design]
HGA	Handweavers Guild of America (EA)
HGA	Hang Glider Association (EA)
HGA	Hardware Graphics Accelerator [Computer science]
HGA	Hargeisa [Somalia] [Airport symbol] (OAG)
HGA	Harvey Gray & Associates
HGA	Heat Generator Assembly (KSC)
HGA	Heptagonal Games Association (EA)
HGA	Hercules Graphics Adapter (PCM)
HGA	Hereditary Grand Almoner [Freemasonry]
HGA	Heritage U.S. Government Income Fund [NYSE symbol] (SPSG)
HGA	Heritage U.S. Govt Income Fd [NYSE symbol] (TTSB)
HGA	High Gain Antenna
HGA	Hobby Greenhouse Association (EA)
HGA	Hobby Greenhouse Owners Association of America [Defunct] (EA)
HGA	Hobby Guild of America (EA)
HGA	Hogan Air [ICAO designator] (FAAC)
HGA	Homogentisate [Biochemistry]
HGA	Homogentisic Acid [Biochemistry] (MAE)
HGA	Hop Growers of America (EA)
HGA	Hotel Greeters of America [Later, HMGI]
HGAA	Hydride Generation Atomic Absorption [Analytical chemistry]
HGAC	High Gain Antenna Controller
H G & L Rev	Harvard Gay & Lesbian Review [A publication] (BRI)
HGAS	High Gain Antenna System (IEEE)
HGB	Handelsgesetzbuch [Commercial Code] [German Legal term] (DLA)
HGB	Hanford Gable Butte [Washington] [Seismograph station code, US Geological Survey] (SEIS)
HGB	Hemoglobin [Biochemistry, medicine]
HGB	Hot Gas Bonder
HGB	Household Goods Carriers' Bureau Agent, Arlington VA [STAC]
Hgb & Hct	Hemoglobin and Hematocrit [Hematology] (DAVI)
HGB EL	Hemoglobin Electrophoresis [Hematology] (DAVI)
HGB Elect	Hemoglobin Electrophoresis [Hematology] (DAVI)
Hgb F	Hemoglobin Fetal [Also, HbF, HgF] [Medicine] (DAVI)
HGBN	Herringbone [Electronics, engineering]
HGB-PL	Hemoglobin Plasma [Hematology] (DAVI)
HGBS	Methemoglobin-Sulfhemoglobin [Hematology] (DAVI)
HGC	Hercules Graphics [Computer science] (CDE)
HGC	Hudson General [AMEX symbol] (TTSB)
HGC	Hudson General Corp. [AMEX symbol] (SPSG)
HGC	Hypergolic Clean
HGCA	Home Grown Cereals Authority (PDAA)
HGCB	Household Goods Carriers' Bureau (EA)
HG-CSF	Human Granulocyte, Colony Stimulation Factor [Hematology]
HGCU	Heavy Glider Conversion Unit [British military] (DMA)
HGD	Hangard Aviation Ltd. [Mongolia] [ICAO designator] (FAAC)
HGD	Hawthorne Gold [Vancouver Stock Exchange symbol]
HGD	High Grade Dysplasia [Medicine]
HGD	Hogshead
HGD	Hourglass Device [Military decoration] (AFM)
HGD	Hughenden [Australia Airport symbol] (OAG)
hg den	Hearing Denied [Legal term] (HGAA)
HGDFS	High Gain Direction Finding System (PDAA)
HGDH	His [or Her] Grand Ducal Highness
HGDP	Human Genome Diversity Project [Genetics]
HGDS	Hazardous Gas Detection Systems (KSC)
HGE	Handling Ground Equipment
HGE	Hemorrhage [Medicine] (ROG)
HGE	Het Gilgamesj-Epos [A publication] (BJA)
HGE	Hinge [Automotive engineering]
HGE	Human Granulocytic Ehrlichiosis [Medicine]
HGE	Human Granulocytic Ehrlichiosis [Medicine]
HGE	Human Granulocytic Ehrlichiosis
HGE	Human Granulocytic Ehrlichiosis
HGE	Hybrid Geotempered Envelope [Architecture]
HGE	Hydraulic Grade Elevations (NRCH)
HGED	High-Gain Emissive Display [Technology]
HGF	Helmholtz-Gemeinschaft Deutscher Forschungs-zentren [Helmholtz association of German research centres]
HGF	Hematopoietic Growth Factor [Biochemistry Medicine]
HgF	Hemoglobin, Fetal [Also, HbF] [Medicine]
HGF	Hemopoietic Growth Factor [Hematology]
HGF	Hepatocyte Growth Factor [Biochemistry]
HGF	Household Goods Forwarders Tariff Bureau, Washington DC [STAC]
HGF	Human Growth Foundation (EA)
HGF	Hyperglycemic-Glycogenolytic Factor [Later, Glucagon] [Endocrinology]
HGFA	Henry George Foundation of America (EA)
HGFA	Household Goods Forwarders Association of America [Washington, DC]
HGG	Hot Gas Generator
HGG	Human Gamma-Globulin [Endocrinology]
HGGR	Haggar Corp. [NASDAQ symbol] (SAG)
HGH	Hangchow [China] [Airport symbol] (AD)
HGH	Hangzhou [China] [Airport symbol] (OAG)
HGH	Historische Grammatik der Hebraeischen Sprache [H. Bauer and P. Leander] [A publication] (BJA)
HGH	Human Growth Hormone [Also, hGH] [Endocrinology]
hGH	Human Growth Hormone (DOG)
HGHGHG	Hilf Gott, Hilf Gott, Hilf Gott [God Help, God Help, God Help] [Motto of Sophie Elisabeth, Countess of Schwarzenburg (1565-1621)]
Hghland	Highland Federal Bank [Associated Press] (SAG)
Hghlds	Highlands (DD)
HGHR	Higher
hGHR	Human Growth Hormone Receptor [Genetics] (DOG)
HghwyH	Highway Holdings Ltd. [Associated Press] (SAG)
HGI	Henry George Institute (EA)
HGI	HGI Realty [NYSE symbol] (TTSB)
HGI	Horizon Group, Inc. [NYSE symbol] (SAG)
HGI	Horizon Outlet Centers [NYSE symbol] (SPSG)
HGIC	Harleysville Group [NASDAQ symbol] (TTSB)
HGIC	Harleysville Group, Inc. [NASDAQ symbol] (NQ)
HGI Rlty	HGI Realty, Inc. [Associated Press] (SAG)
HGJ	Hongo [Japan] [Seismograph station code, US Geological Survey] (SEIS)
HGL	Hamilton Group Ltd. [Toronto Stock Exchange symbol]
HGL	Helgoland [Germany Airport symbol] (OAG)
HGL	Heregulin (DMAA)
HGL	High Gain Link
HGL	High Go Low Test
HGL	Homach Gap Lathe
HGL	Hyperbolic Type Gas Lens (IAA)
HGLDS	Highlands (MCD)
HGLF	High-Grain/Low-Fiber [Cereal] (OA)
HGLND	Highland
HGM	Hectogram (ROG)
HGM	Hereditary Grand Master [Freemasonry] (ROG)
HGM	Hot Gas Manifold (NASA)
HGM	Human Gene-Mapping
HGMAA	Hang Glider Manufacturers Association of America [Defunct] (EA)
HGMC	Harmony Gold Mining Co. Ltd. [NASDAQ symbol] (SAG)
HGMCR	Human Genetic Mutant Cell Repository

HGMF .... High-Gradient Magnetic Filtration
HGMGR........ Household Goods Military and Government Rate Tariff
HGML .... Human Gene-Mapping Library [Database]
HGMM .... Hereditary Grand Master Mason [Freemasonry]
HGMN .... Herb Growing and Marketing Network [EA]
HGMS .... Helicopter Gravity-Measuring System [Naval Oceanographic Office]
HGMS .... High-Gradient Magnetic Separator (NRCH)
HGMU .... Heavy Glider Maintenance Unit [British military] (DMA)
HGMUS........ Horizontal Generator Mock-Up System [NASA]
HGN .... Horizontal Gaze Nystagmus Test
HGN .... Hypogastric Nerve [Anatomy]
HGN .... Mae Hong Son [Thailand] [Airport symbol] (OAG)
HG/NG .... Hydrogen Gas/Nitrogen Gas (NRCH)
HGO .... Halsgerichtsordnung [German]
HGO .... Heavy Gas Oils [Petroleum product]
HGO .... Hepatic Glucose Output [Physiology]
HGO .... Hermes Global Orbiter [NASA, proposed]
HGO .... Hugo, CO [Location identifier FAA] (FAAL)
HGO .... Human Glucose Output [Hematology] (DMAA)
HGO .... Korhogo [Ivory Coast] [Airport symbol] (OAG)
HGP .... Hard Gas-Permeable [Contact lenses]
HGP .... Hepatic Glucose Production [Hematology] (DMAA)
HGP .... Horizontal Ground Plane [Automotive engineering]
HGP .... Hormonal Growth Promotant
HGP .... Human Genome Program [Genetics]
HGP .... Hyperglobulinemic Purpura [Medicine] (DMAA)
HGP-OIMLA... Hindustani Ghadar Party-Organization of Indian Marxist-Leninists Abroad
HGPRT........ Hypoxanthine-Guanine Phosphoribosyltransferase [AO HPRT] [An enzyme]
HG-PRTase... Hypoxanthine-Guanine Phosphoribosyltransferase [Also, HGPRT, HPRT] [An enzyme] (DAVI)
HGPS .... High-Grade Plow Steel
HGPS .... Hutchinson-Gilford Progeria Syndrome [Medicine] (DMAA)
HGR .... Hagerstown [Maryland] [Airport symbol] (OAG)
HGR .... Hangar (KSC)
HGR .... Hanger
HGR .... Hanger Orthopedic Group, Inc. [AMEX symbol] (SPSG)
HGR .... Hanger Orthopedic Grp [NASDAQ symbol] (TTSB)
HGR .... Haubitzgranate [Howitzer Shell] [German military - World War II]
HGR .... Headgear Receiver [Mining engineering] (IAA)
HGR .... High Group Receiving
HGR .... High River Resources Ltd. [Vancouver Stock Exchange symbol]
HGR .... Histoire Generale des Religions [A publication] (BJA)
HGR .... Hot Gas Reinjection (PDAA)
HGR .... Human Glucocorticoid Receptor [Endocrinology]
HGR & SPTFAC... Hangar and Support Facility [NASA] (NASA)
HGRF .... Hot Gas Radiating Facility
HGRF .... Human Growth-Hormone Releasing Factor [Biochemistry]
HGRM .... Hemogram [Hematology] (DAVI)
HGS .... Congregation de Hermanas Guadalupanas de la Salle (TOCD)
HGS .... Freetown [Sierra Leone] Hastings Airport [Airport symbol] (OAG)
HGS .... Hagensborg Resources Ltd. [Vancouver Stock Exchange symbol]
HGS .... Head-Up Guidance System [Aviation]
HGS .... Hot Gas System
HGS .... Human Genome Sciences
HGS .... Human Genome Sciences [Commercial firm]
H-GS .... Hurdy-Gurdy Society [British] (DBA)
HGS .... Hydrogen Gas Saver (MCD)
HGS .... Hyperbolic Grid System
HGSC .... Hoare Govett Small Companies Index [British]
HGSD .... Heavy Gauge Solid Drawn [Conduit]
HGSE .... Harvard Graduate School of Education
HGSE .... Hot Gas Soldering Equipment
HGSEI .... Home and Garden Show Executives International [Defunct] (EA)
HGSHS........ Harvard Group Scale of Hypnotic Susceptibility [Psychology]
HGSI .... Human Genome Sciences [NASDAQ symbol] (TTSB)
HGSI .... Human Genome Sciences, Inc. [NASDAQ symbol] (SAG)
HGSITVC...... Hot Gas Secondary Injection Thrust Vector Control (PDAA)
HGSW .... Heavy Gauge Screwed Welded [Conduit]
HGSW .... Horn Gap Switch
HGT .... Fort Hunter-Liggett (Jolon), CA [Location identifier FAA] (FAAL)
HGT .... Height (KSC)
HGT .... High Gelling Temperature [Analytical biochemistry]
HGT .... High Group Transmitting
HGT .... Household Goods Transportation Association, Washington DC [STAC]
HGT .... Hydrostatic-Gauging Technology [Engineering]
HGT .... Hypergeometric Group Testing [Computer science] (OA)
HGTA .... Honours Graduate Teachers' Association [British]
HGTMC........ Home Grown Timber Marketing Corp. Ltd. [British] (BI)
HGTS .... Heights [Commonly used] (OPSA)
HGTV .... Home & Garden Television
HGTV .... Home and Garden Television Network
HGTVC........ Hot Gas Thrust Vector Control
HGU .... Horizon Gyroscope Unit [Aviation] (AIA)
HGU .... Mount Hagen [Papua New Guinea] [Airport symbol] (OAG)
HGUC .... Helsinki Guarantees for Ukraine Committee [Defunct] (EA)
HGV .... Heavy Goods Vehicles
HGV .... Hepatitis G Virus
HGV .... Highgrade Ventures [Vancouver Stock Exchange symbol]
HGV .... Hydrogen Gas Valve (MCD)
HGVT .... Horizontal Ground Vibration Test [NASA] (NASA)
HGW .... Heat-Generative Radioactive Wastes [Nuclear energy]
HGW .... Hyper-Quenched Glassy Water [Material science]

HGWP .... Halocarbon Global-Warming Potential [Meteorology]
HGWS .... H. G. Wells Society (EA)
HGWY .... Highway (WGA)
HgwyH .... Highway Holdings Ltd. [Associated Press] (SAG)
HGX .... Lawrence, MA [Location identifier FAA] (FAAL)
HGZG .... Hilf Gott zu Glueck [May God Help Us to Fortune] [Motto of Magdalene, Princess of Anhalt (1585-1657)] [German]
HH .... Double Hard [Pencil leads]
HH .... Extra Hard [Pencil leads]
HH .... Fairchild/Republic [ICAO aircraft manufacturer identifier] (ICAO)
HH .... Habitat for Humanity (EA)
HH .... Half Hard [Metallurgy]
HH .... Half Hardy [Horticulture]
H/H .... Half Height [of an International Standards Organization container] (DCTA)
HH .... Halothane Hepatitis [Medicine] (DMAA)
HH .... Halothane Hypoxia [Medicine]
HH .... Hamish Hamilton [Publisher] [British]
HH .... Hamizrah Hehadash [Jerusalem] [A publication] (BJA)
HH .... Hampshire Hunt [British]
HH .... Handhole (AAG)
HH .... Hands [Units of measure, especially for the height of horses]
HH .... Hanging Handset [Telecommunications] (TEL)
HH .... Happy Humpers (EA)
HH .... Hard of Hearing
HH .... Harvest Help [An association British] (EAIO)
HH .... Hashomer Hatzair (EA)
HH .... Haunt Hunters (EA)
H/H .... Havre to Hamburg [Shipping]
HH .... Hawaii State Library System, Honolulu, HI [Library symbol Library of Congress] (LCLS)
HH .... Hayward and Hazelton's United States Circuit Court Reports [District of Columbia] [A publication] (DLA)
HH .... Head, Head [Coin-tossing possibility]
HH .... Headlamp Housing [Automotive engineering]
HH .... Head-to-Head [Polymer structure]
HH .... Healthy Hemophiliac [Medicine] (DMAA)
HH .... Heavy Helicopter [Military] (VNW)
HH .... Heavy Hinged [Philately]
HH .... Heavy Hydrogen
HH .... Heil Hitler [Political organization] [British]
HH .... Helen Hunt Jackson [American novelist, 1830-1885] [Initials used as pseudonym]
H-H .... Heli-Home [Recreational vehicle]
HH .... Hemmets Haerold [Record label] [Sweden]
HH .... Henderson and Haggard [Inhaler] [Medicine] (DAVI)
HH .... Herbig-Haro [Astronomy]
HH .... Hereditary Haemochromatosis [Medicine]
HH .... Here's Health [Exhibition] [British]
HH .... Herfindahl-Hirschman [Economic indicator]
HH .... Herman Hospital [Houston, TX]
HH .... Hertfordshire Hunt [British] (ROG)
HH .... Hetch Hetchy [Railroad] (MHDW)
HH .... Hetch Hetchy Railroad (IIA)
HH .... Hiatal Hernia [Medicine]
HH .... High-Powered, Nondirectional Radio Homing Beacon [Navigation]
HH .... His [or Her] Highness
HH .... His Holiness
HH .... His Honour [British] (ADA)
HH .... Historical Handbook
HH .... Hodgson's Horse [British military] (DMA)
HH .... Hogarth [H.] and Sons [Steamship line] (MHDW)
HH .... Hogshead (DNAB)
HH .... Hold Harmless (OICC)
HH .... Holidays for Humanity [An association] (EA)
HH .... Holistic Health [Medicine] (DAVI)
HH .... Home Health [Medicine] (DAVI)
HH .... Home Help [Medicine]
HH .... Hommel AG [Switzerland] [Research code symbol]
HH .... Homonymous Hemianopsia [Ophthalmology]
HH .... Hooper Holmes [AMEX symbol] (TTSB)
HH .... Hooper Holmes, Inc. [AMEX symbol] (SPSG)
HH .... Hour Hand [Clocks] (ROG)
HH .... Household
H/H .... House to House (ADA)
HH .... Hughes Helicopters (MCD)
HH .... Human Hair [Doll collecting]
HH .... Humbert Humbert [Character in Vladimir Nabokov's "Lolita"]
HH .... Hydroxyhexamide [Organic chemistry] (MAE)
HH .... Hydroxyhexenal [Organic chemistry]
HH .... Hyperactive Help [Australia]
HH .... Hypogonadism [Endocrinology] (DAVI)
HH .... Hypogonadotrophic [Endocrinology] (DAVI)
HH .... Hyporeninemic Hypoaldosteronism [Endocrinology]
HH .... Les Hieroglyphes Hittites [A publication] (BJA)
HH .... Rotary-Wing Air-Sea-Rescue Aircraft [Navy symbol] (MUGU)
HH .... Somali Airlines [ICAO designator] (AD)
HHA .... Anderson [H. H.] Line [Steamship] (MHDB)
HHA .... Half-Hardy Annual [Horticulture] (ROG)
H(Ha) .... Hare Tempore Wigram, Etc. [1841-53] [A publication] (DLA)
HHA .... Hatton Heritage Association (EA)
HHA .... Health Hazard Assessment [Army]
HHA .... Hereditary Hemolytic Anemia [Medicine]
HHA .... Hickory Handle Association (EA)
HHA .... High High Alarm (ECII)

HHA .... Historic House Association [British]
HHA .... Home Health Agency
HHA .... Home Health Aid (DAVI)
HHA .... Hungarian Horse Association (EA)
HHA .... Hydro Home Appliances Ltd. [Formerly, Hemgold Resources Ltd.] [Vancouver Stock Exchange symbol]
HHA .... Hypothalamo-Hypophyseal-Adrenal [Endocrinology]
HHAA .... Historic House Association of America (EA)
HHAG .... Human Health Assessment Group [Environmental Protection Agency]
HHALSA .... Heritage Hills Area Library Services Authority [Library network]
HHANES ...... Hispanic Health and Nutrition Examination Survey [Department of Health and Human Services] (GFGA)
HHAR .... Health Hazard Assessment Report [Army]
HHB .... Bernice Pauahi Bishop Museum, Honolulu, HI [Library symbol Library of Congress] (LCLS)
HHB .... Half-Hardy Biennial [Horticulture] (ROG)
HHB .... Happy Hours Brotherhood (EA)
HHB .... Hattiesburg, MS [Location identifier FAA] (FAAL)
HHB .... Headquarters and Headquarters Battery [Army]
HHb .... Hemoglobin, Reduced [Biochemistry, medicine]
HHb .... Hemoglobin Un-Ionized [Hematology] (DAVI)
HHBC .... Honourable Hudson's Bay Co. [Canada]
HHBLG .... Hobby Horse Brigade of the Legion of Guardsmen (EA)
HHC .... Chatham College, Pittsburgh, PA [OCLC symbol] (OCLC)
HHC .... Hammer Head Crane (NASA)
HHC .... Handheld Computer
HHC .... Harley Hummer Club (EA)
HHC .... Headquarters and Headquarters Company [Army]
HHC .... Heavy Helicopter Company [Military] (VNW)
HHC .... Higher Harmonic Control (MCD)
HHC .... Highland Crow Resources Ltd. [Toronto Stock Exchange symbol Vancouver Stock Exchange symbol]
HHC .... Home Health Care [Medicine] (DAVI)
HHC .... Honolulu Community College, Honolulu, HI [Library symbol Library of Congress] (LCLS)
HHC .... Hoover Historical Center (EA)
HHC .... Horizon/CMS Healthcare [NYSE symbol] (TTSB)
HHC .... Horizon CMS Healthcare Corp. [NYSE symbol] (SAG)
HHC .... Horizon Healthcare Corp. [NYSE symbol] (SPSG)
HHC .... Houdini Historical Center (EA)
HHC .... Hovercraft-Helicopter Carrier
HHC .... Hughes Helicopter Co.
HHC .... New York City Health and Hospitals Corp. (EA)
HHCA .... Home Health Corp. of Amer [NASDAQ symbol] (TTSB)
HHCA .... Home Health Corp. of America, Inc. [NASDAQ symbol] (SAG)
HHCC .... Higher Harmonic Circulation Control [Rotor] [Navy]
hHCF .... Human Humoral Hypercalcemic Factor [Oncology]
HHCL .... Hale's History of the Common Law [A publication] (DLA)
HHCL .... H-Hour Coordinating Line [Army] (AABC)
HHCL .... Howell Henry Chaldecott Lury [Advertising agency] [British]
HHD .... Doctor of Honorary Humanities
HHD .... Doctor of Humanities
HHD .... Headquarters and Headquarters Detachment [Army] (AABC)
HHD .... High Heparin Dose [Medicine] (DMAA)
HHD .... High Holy Days (BJA)
HHD .... Hogshead
HHD .... Home Dialysis [Medicine] (DMAA)
HHD .... Hypertensive Heart Disease [Medicine]
HHDDE .... Heavy Heavy-Duty Diesel Engine [Motor vehicle specifications]
HHDN .... Hexachlorohexahydrodimethanonaphthalene [Insecticide, commonly called Aldrin]
HHDW .... Heavy Handy Deadweight [Scrap] [Shipping]
HHDWS .... Heavy Handy Deadweight Scrap Iron [Shipping] (DS)
HHE .... Hand-Held Equipment (DWSG)
HHE .... Heli-Holland BV [Netherlands ICAO designator] (FAAC)
HHE .... Helium to Heat Exchanger (AAG)
HHE .... Hemiconvulsions, Hemiplegia, Epilepsy [Medicine]
HHE .... Herringer-Hulster Effect
HHE .... Household Economics Research Division [of ARS, Department of Agriculture]
HHE .... Household Effects [Insurance]
HHE .... Human Health and the Environment (GNE)
HHEC .... Hispanic Higher Education Coalition [Defunct] (EA)
HHEFG .... Hughes Hall Effect Function Generator
HHEG .... Hughes Hall Effect Generator
HHE-P .... East-West Center, Population Institute, Honolulu, HI [Library symbol Library of Congress] (LCLS)
HHES .... Hex Head Electrical Squib
HHES .... Housing and Household Economic Statistics [US Census Bureau]
HHESD .... Population Division and Housing and Household Economics Statistics Division [Bureau of the Census] [Also, an information service or system] (IID)
HHF .... Canadian, TX [Location identifier FAA] (FAAL)
HHF .... Friends of the Library of Hawaii, Honolulu, HI [Library symbol Library of Congress] (LCLS)
HHF .... Health for Haiti Foundation (EA)
HHF .... Household Furniture [Insurance]
HHF .... Hyper-High-Frequency (DEN)
HHFA .... Housing and Home Finance Agency [Terminated 1965, functions taken over by HUD]
HHFC .... Harvest Home Financial Corp. [NASDAQ symbol] (SAG)
HHFC .... Harvest Home Finl [NASDAQ symbol] (TTSB)
HHFC .... H. H. Franklin Club (EA)
HHFM .... High-Humidity Face Mask [Medicine] (MEDA)
HHFS .... Hilar High-Frequency Stimulation [Neurophysiology]

HHFT .... Heavy Helicopter Fire Team (DNAB)
HHFT .... Heavy Helo Fire Team [Military] (VNW)
HHFTH .... National Foundation for Happy Horsemanship for the Handicapped (EA)
HH-G .... Hitchhiker (Goddard Space Flight Center) [NASA]
HHG .... Household Goods [Insurance]
HHG .... Hypertrophic Hypersecretory Gastropathy [Medicine] (DMAA)
HHG .... Hypogonadotropic Hypogonadism [Medicine]
HHGCB .... Household Goods Carriers Bureau
HHGFAA ...... Household Goods Forwarders Association of America (EA)
HHGP .... Harris & Harris Group [NASDAQ symbol] (TTSB)
HHGP .... Harris & Harris Group, Inc. [NASDAQ symbol] (NQ)
HHGR .... Helian Health Group, Inc. [NASDAQ symbol] (NQ)
HHH .... Devine, TX [Location identifier FAA] (FAAL)
HHH .... Harrison Horncastle Holdings [Investment firm] [British]
HHH .... Hawaii Medical Library, Inc., Honolulu, HI [Library symbol Library of Congress] (LCLS)
HHH .... Helicsa [Spain] [FAA designator] (FAAC)
HHH .... Helm Resources [AMEX symbol] (TTSB)
HHH .... Helm Resources, Inc [AMEX symbol] (SAG)
HHH .... Hilton Head Island [South Carolina] [Airport symbol] (OAG)
HHH .... Hincherton Hayfever Helmet [Clear plastic head-enclosing device that allegedly relieves hayfever symptoms]
HHH .... Holistic Health Havens (EA)
HHH .... Hubert Horatio Humphrey [American politician, 1911-1978]
HHH .... Hyperornithinemia, Hyperammonemia, Homocitrillinuria Syndrome [Medicine] (DMAA)
HHH .... Triple Hard [Pencil leads]
HHHA .... Homemaker Home Health Aide (OICC)
HHH-CRC ..... Hubert H. Humphrey Cancer Research Center [Boston University] [Research center] (RCD)
HHHH .... FourHealth, Inc. [NASDAQ symbol] (SAG)
HHHH .... Head, Heart, Hands, and Health [As in 4H organizations]
HHHHH .... Hilf, Himmlischer Herr, Hoechster Hort [Help, Heavenly Father, Highest Treasure] [Motto of Elisabeth, Duchess of Saxony-Coburg (1540-94)] [German]
HHHMU .... Hydrazine Hand-Held Maneuvering Unit (MCD)
HHHO .... Hypotonia-Hypomentia-Hypogonadism-Obesity [Medicine]
HHI .... Ha-Hevra ha-Historit ha-Israelit [Historical Society of Israel] (EAIO)
HHI .... Harmony Heights [Idaho] [Seismograph station code, US Geological Survey Closed] (SEIS)
HHI .... Harness Horsemen International (EA)
HHi .... Hawaiian Historical Society, Honolulu, HI [Library symbol Library of Congress] (LCLS)
HHI .... Hawaii County Library, Hilo, HI [Library symbol Library of Congress] (LCLS)
HHI .... Head-of-Household Income (WDMC)
HHI .... Histologic HCM [Hypertrophic Cardiomyopathy] Index
HHI .... Home Holdings [NYSE symbol] (SPSG)
HHI .... Homer Hoyt Institute
HHI .... Horton Hydrocarbons, Inc. [Vancouver Stock Exchange symbol]
HHI .... Hughes Helicopter, Inc.
HHI .... Wahiawa, HI [Location identifier FAA] (FAAL)
HHIC .... Hilo College, Hilo, HI [Library symbol Library of Congress] (LCLS)
HHIP .... Hand-Held Information Processor
HHIRF .... Holifield Heavy Ion Research Facility [Department of Energy]
HHJ .... Hunt, Frank, Jr., Bala-Cynwyd PA [STAC]
HHK .... Kapiolani Community College, Honolulu, HI [Library symbol Library of Congress] (LCLS)
HHL .... Court of Session Cases, House of Lords [Scotland] [A publication] (DLA)
HHL .... Haddon Hall Library [A publication]
HHL .... Helicopter Hire Ltd. [British ICAO designator] (FAAC)
HHL .... Hollywood Hotline [Information service or system] (IID)
HHLD .... Household [Marketing]
HHLGCS ...... [Department of] Health, Housing, Local Government and Community Services (EERA)
HHLH .... Heaviest Heavy Lift Helicopter (MCD)
HHLR .... Hand-Held LASER Range-Finder [Military] (RDA)
HHLR .... Horace Hardy Lestor Reactor
HHLRF .... Hand-Held LASER Range-Finder [Military British] (INF)
HHIU-W .... University of Hawaii at Hilo, West Hawaii Library, Kealakekua, HI [Library symbol] [Library of Congress] (LCLS)
H + Hm .... Compound Hypermetropic Astigmatism [Ophthalmology]
HHM .... Hawkes Hospital of Mount Carmel, Mount Carmel Medical Center Library, Columbus, OH [OCLC symbol] (OCLC)
HHM .... Health and Healing Ministries (EA)
HH-M .... Hitchhiker (Marshall Space Flight Center) [NASA]
HHM .... Humoral Hypercalcemia of Malignancy [Medicine]
HHM .... Hungry Horse [Montana] [Seismograph station code, US Geological Survey] (SEIS)
HHM .... Kotzebue, AK [Location identifier FAA] (FAAL)
HHM .... Sisters of the Holy Humility of Mary [Roman Catholic religious order]
HHMC .... Hawaiian Mission Children's Society, Honolulu, HI [Library symbol Library of Congress] (LCLS)
HHMHDB ..... Hispanic Health and Mental Health Data Base [National Institute of Mental Health] [Information service or system] (CRD)
HHMI .... Howard Hughes Medical Institute
hh/mm .... Hours/Minutes (HGAA)
HHMS .... His Hellenic Majesty's Ship
HHMU .... Handheld Maneuvering Unit [NASA]
HHN .... Hahnemann Medical College and Hospital, Philadelphia, PA [OCLC symbol] (OCLC)
HHN .... Hand-Held Nebulizer [Pharmacology] (DAVI)
HHN .... Hot Hydrogen Nozzle

HHNC	His Highness the Nizam's Cavalry [*British military*] (DMA)
HHNC	Hyperglycemic Hyperosmolar Nonketotic Coma [*Endocrinology*] (CPH)
HHNK	Hyperosmolar Hyperglycemic Nonketotic (Coma) [*Also, NKHHC*] [*Medicine*]
HHO	Houston Helicopters, Inc. [*ICAO designator*] (FAAC)
HHOC	Holistic Health Organizing Committee (EA)
HHOCC	Holiday Happenings Ornament Collectors Club (EA)
HHOJ	Ha Ha Only Joking [*Computer hacker terminology*] (NHD)
HHOK	Ha Ha Only Kidding
HHOS	Ha Ha Only Serious
HHP	Half-Hardy Perennial [*Horticulture*] (ROG)
HHP	Handheld Processor
HHP	Head of Household Program [*IRS*]
HHP	Hospital Health Plan
HHP	Household Pet (WGA)
HHP	Hydraulic Hand Pump
HHP	Hydraulic Horse Power
HHP	Pineapple Research Institute, Honolulu, HI [*Library symbol Library of Congress*] (LCLS)
HHPA	Hexahydrophthalic Anhydride [*Organic chemistry*]
HHPC	Hale's History of the Pleas of the Crown [*A publication*] (DLA)
HHPC	Hand-Held Programmable Calculator (MCD)
HHPC	High Harmonic Pitch Control (PDAA)
HHPLA	Herbert Hoover Presidential Library Association (EA)
HHPP	Hydro-Hydrogen Pilot Project
HHPRT	Human Hypoxanthine Phosphoribosyltransferase [*An enzyme*]
HHPS	Hot High Pressure Separator [*Chemical engineering*]
HHR	Handheld RADAR (AABC)
HHR	Hawthorne, CA [*Location identifier FAA*] (FAAL)
HHR	High Reserve Resources [*Vancouver Stock Exchange symbol*]
HHR	Hydralazine, Hydrochlorothiazide, and Reserpine (DMAA)
HHRD	Horsehead Resource Dvlp [*NASDAQ symbol*] (TTSB)
HHREA	Health and Human Relations Education Association [*Australia*]
HHRH	Hereditary Hypophosphatemic Rickets with Hypercalciuria [*Medicine*] (DMAA)
HHRSD	Helicopter Hauldown and Rapid Securing Device [*Military*] (CAAL)
HHS	Department of Health and Human Services [*Formerly, HEW*]
HHS	Harte-Hanks Communications [*NYSE symbol*] (TTSB)
HHS	Harte-Hanks Communications, Inc. [*NYSE symbol*] (SPSG)
HHS	Hawaiian Sugar Planters' Association, Experiment Station, Honolulu, HI [*Library symbol Library of Congress*] (LCLS)
HHS	Health and Human Services (DICI)
HHS	[*Department of*] Health and Human Services
HHS	Hex Head Squib
HHS	Hex Head Steel (IAA)
HHS	Horse Hemolyzate Supernatant
HHS	Huguenot Historical Society (EA)
HHS	Hungarian Historical Society [*Australia*]
HHS	Hypothenar Hammer Syndrome [*Medicine*]
HHS	Society of Helpers (TOCD)
HHS	Society of Helpers of the Holy Souls [*Roman Catholic women's religious order*]
HHS	US Department of Health and Human Services (GNE)
HHSA	Home Health Services Association [*Later, HHSSA*] (EA)
HHSA	Honolulu Star-Bulletin and Advertiser, Honolulu, HI [*Library symbol Library of Congress*] (LCLS)
HHSAR	Department of Health and Human Services Acquisition Regulations (GFGA)
HHSAR	Health and Human Services Acquisition Regulation (AAGC)
HHSB	Hahnemann High School Behavior Rating Scale [*Psychology*]
HHSD	Holographic Horizontal Situation Display
HHSF	Habitat and Human Settlements Foundation [*United Nations*] (EY)
HHSG	Herpes Help Support Group [*Australia*]
HHSGAB	Department of Health and Human Services Grant Appeals Board (AAGC)
HHSI	High-Head Safety Injection [*Nuclear energy*] (NRCH)
HHSMU	Hand-Held Self-Maneuvering Unit (SAA)
HHSPR	Health and Human Services Procurement Regulations (AAGC)
HHSSA	Home Health Services and Staffing Association (EA)
HHSZYM	Hashomer Hatzair Socialist Zionist Youth Movement (EA)
HHT	Headquarters and Headquarters Troop [*Army*] (AABC)
HHT	Hereditary Hemorrhagic Telangiectasia [*Medicine*]
HHT	High-Temperature Helium Turbine (PDAA)
HHT	Holland Historical Trust (EA)
HHT	Homoharringtonine [*Antineoplastic drug*]
HHT	Horn-Hellersberg Test [*Psychology*]
HHT	Hurricane Hollow [*Tennessee*] [*Seismograph station code, US Geological Survey Closed*] (SEIS)
HHT	Hush House Tiedown
HHT	Hydroxyheptadecatrienoic Acid [*Organic chemistry*]
HHTG	House Heating [*Freight*]
HHTI	Hand-Held Thermal Imager [*Navy British*]
HHTM	United States Army, Tripler Army Medical Center, Honolulu, HI [*Library symbol Library of Congress*] (LCLS)
HHTNSW	Historic Houses Trust of New South Wales [*Australia*]
HHTR	Hand-Held Tactical RADAR (DNAB)
HHTT	Hexahexylthiotriphenylene [*Organic chemistry*]
HHTTFS	Huddersfield Healders and Twisters Trade and Friendly Society [*A union*] [*British*] (DCTA)
HHTV	Handheld Thermal Viewer (RDA)
HHV	Handheld Viewer
HHV	Heavy-High-mobility [*Multipurpose Wheeled*] Vehicle [*See also HMMWV*] (DOMA)
HHV	Help Hospitalized Veterans (EA)
HHV	High Heat [*or Heating*] Value
HHV	Human Herpes Virus
HHW	Higher High Water [*Tides and currents*]
HHW	High-Heat Waste (NRCH)
HHW	Household Hazardous Waste
HHWI	Higher High-Water Interval
HHWP	Household Hazardous Waste Project (EA)
HHX	Heavy-Lift Helicopter, Experimental (SAA)
HHY	Savannah, TN [*Location identifier FAA*] (FAAL)
HHYF	Harness Horse Youth Foundation (EA)
HI	Habitability Improvement [*Navy*] (NVT)
HI	Handicap Introductions (EA)
HI	Handling Instructions (MCD)
HI	Harcost Industries
HI	Hardware Interrupt
HI	Harold Institute [*Defunct*] (EA)
HI	Harvest Index [*Agronomy*]
HI	Hat Institute (EA)
HI	Hawaii [*Postal code*]
HI	Hawaiian Islands
HI	Hawaii Reports [*A publication*] (DLA)
HI	Hazard Index (GNE)
HI	Head Injury [*Neurology*] (DAVI)
HI	Health Inspector [*British military*] (DMA)
HI	Health Insurance
HI	Heard Island [*Region*] (EERA)
HI	Hearing Impaired (OICC)
HI	Heartland Institute [*Research center*] (RCD)
HI	Heat Index
HI	Heavily Included [*Colored gemstone grade*]
HI	Height Indicator (NVT)
HI	Hemagglutination Inhibition [*Immunochemistry*]
HI	Hepatobiliary Imaging [*Medicine*] (BABM)
HI	Hiburnium [*Supposed chemical element, discovered 1922*]
HI	Hic Iacet [*Here Lies*] [*Latin*]
HI	Hideaways International [*Commercial firm*] (EA)
HI	High [*Computer science*] (AAG)
HI	High Impact
HI	High Impulsiveness (MAE)
HI	High Intensity
HI	Hindi (WDAA)
HI	Hirth KG [*Germany ICAO aircraft manufacturer identifier*] (ICAO)
HI	Hispanic Institute (EA)
HI	Histadruth Ivrith of America
HI	Histidine [*An amino acid*] (MAE)
HI	Holton Inter-Urban Railway Co. [*AAR code*]
HI	Homicidal Ideation [*Psychiatry*] (DAVI)
H-I	Hondacar International (EA)
HI	Honeywell, Inc. (NASA)
HI	Horizontal Interval
HI	Hospital Insurance
HI	Hot Issue [*Investment term*]
HI	Household Capital Trust [*NYSE symbol*] (SAG)
HI	Household Capital Trust II [*NYSE symbol*] (SAG)
HI	Household International, Inc. [*NYSE symbol*] (SPSG)
HI	Household Intl [*NYSE symbol*] (TTSB)
HI	Housing Improvement
HI	Hudson Institute (EA)
HI	Human Interaction
HI	Human Interest
HI	Human Interface [*Computer science*] (EERA)
HI	Humidity Index
HI	Hybrid Index [*Botany*]
HI	Hydraulic Institute (EA)
HI	Hydriodic Acid [*Inorganic chemistry*]
HI	Hydrodynamic Interaction [*Chemistry*]
HI	Hydrogen Iodide [*Inorganic chemistry*]
HI	Hydronics Institute (EA)
HI	Hydroxyindole [*Biochemistry*] (DAVI)
HI	Hypomelanosis of Ito [*Medicine*] (DMAA)
HI	Methemoglobin [*Symbol*] [*Medicine*]
HI	Papillon Airways [*ICAO designator*] (AD)
HI-12	High Twelve International (EA)
HIA	Canadian Eagle Aviation Ltd. [*ICAO designator*] (FAAC)
HIA	Handkerchief Industry Association [*Defunct*] (EA)
HIA	Harrisburg International Airport (MCD)
HIA	Headwear Institute of America (EA)
HIA	Health Industries Association [*Later, HIMA*]
HIA	Hearing Industries Association (EA)
HIA	Heart Infusion Agar [*Medicine*]
HIA	Heat Infusion Agar [*Microbiology*] (DAVI)
HIA	Held [*or Hold*] in Abeyance [*Military*] (AFM)
HIA	Hemagglutination Inhibition Antibody [*Immunochemistry*]
HIA	Histadruth Ivrith of America (EA)
HIA	Hobby Industry Association of America
HIA	Hold in Abeyance [*Military*]
HIA	Homopolar Inductor Alternator (PDAA)
HIA	Horological Institute of America [*Later, AWI*]
HIA	Housing Industry Association
HIA	Whitehall, MT [*Location identifier FAA*] (FAAL)
HIAA	Health Insurance Association of America [*Washington, DC*] (EA)
HIAA	Hobby Industry Association of America (EA)
HIAA	Hydroxyindoleacetic Acid [*Organic chemistry*]
HIAC	Health Industry Advisory Committee [*Terminated, 1974*] (EGAO)
HIAC	Health Insurance Advisory Committee [*Australia*]

HIAC .... High Accuracy [*RADAR*]
HIAD .... Handbook of Instructions for Aircraft Designers
HIADS .... Hawaiian Integrated Air Defense System
HIAFSB .... Handbook of Instructions for Air Force Subsystem Designers
HIAG .... Healthcare International Audit Group (EA)
HIAGSE .... Handbook of Instructions for Aircraft Ground Support Equipment Designers
HIAGSED ...... Handbook of Instructions for Aircraft Ground Support Equipment Designers
HIAK .... Harpoon Interface Adapter Kit (DWSG)
HIALS .... High-Intensity Approach Lighting System [*Airport runways*]
HIALT .... High Altitude (MCD)
HI/AMBBA ..... Hair International/Associated Master Barbers and Beauticians of America (EA)
HI and RH ... His [*or Her*] Imperial and Royal Highness
HIAP .... Human Intracisternal A-Type Particle [*Cytology*]
HIAPSD .... Handbook of Instructions for Aerospace Personnel Subsystem Designers
HIARA .... Hail Insurance Adjustment and Research Association [*Later, NCIA*] (EA)
HIAS .... Hebrew Immigrant Aid Society
HIAS .... High Incidence Auto-Stabilizer (PDAA)
HIASD .... Handbook of Instructions for Aerospace Systems Design
HIAVED .... Handbook of Instructions for Aerospace Vehicle Equipment Design
HIB .... Haemophilus Influenzae, Type B
Hib .... Haemophilus Influenzae Type B (PAZ)
HIB .... Hawaiian Freight Tariff Bureau Inc., Maywood CA [*STAC*]
HIB .... Heart Infusion Broth [*Medicine*] (DMAA)
HIB .... Hemophilus Influenzae Type B [*Medicine*]
HIB .... Herring Industries Board [*British*]
HIB .... Hibbing [*Minnesota*] [*Airport symbol*] (OAG)
HIB .... Hibernia [*Ancient name for Ireland*] (ROG)
HIB .... Hibernia Corp. Cl'A' [*NYSE symbol*] (TTSB)
HIB .... Hibernia Corp. Class A [*NYSE symbol*] (SPSG)
HIB .... Hibiscus Air Services Ltd. [*New Zealand*] [*ICAO designator*] (FAAC)
HIB .... High-Impedance Bridge
HIB .... High Iron Briquetting (DICI)
HIB .... Hoop-Iron Bond [*Construction*]
HIBA .... Hawaiian International Billfish Association (EA)
HIBA .... Hydroxyisobutyric Acid [*Organic chemistry*]
HIBAC .... Health Insurance Benefits Advisory Council [*Department of Health and Human Services Inactive*]
HIBAL .... High-Altitude Balloon
Hibb .... Hibbard's Reports [*New Hampshire*] [*A publication*] (DLA)
Hibb .... Hibbard's Reports [*Opinions Attorneys-General*] [*A publication*] (DLA)
HIBB .... Hibbett Sporting Goods, Inc. [*NASDAQ symbol*] (SAG)
Hibbett .... Hibbett Sporting Goods, Inc. [*Associated Press*] (SAG)
HIBC .... Hydrogen-Induced Blister Cracking [*Metallurgy*]
HIBCC .... Health Industry Business Communications Council (EA)
Hibern .... Hibernia Corp. [*Associated Press*] (SAG)
Hibern .... Hibernia Corp, Class A [*Associated Press*] (SAG)
HiberSv .... Hibernia Savings Bank [*Associated Press*] (SAG)
HIBEX .... High-Impulse Booster Experiments [*DARPA/Army*]
HIBEX/HAPDAR... High Impulse Booster Experiment / Hardpoint Demonstration Array RADAR (SAA)
HiBiCMOS.... Hitachi Bipolar CMOS [*Complementary Metal Oxide Semiconductor*] (NITA)
HIBN .... Hibernia Foods Ltd. [*NASDAQ symbol*] (SAG)
HIBNY .... Hibernia Foods plc ADS [*NASDAQ symbol*] (TTSB)
HIBOR .... Hong Kong Interbank Offered Rate (DFIT)
HIBR .... Huxley Institute for Biosocial Research (EA)
HIBREL .... High-Brightness Relay [*Military*] (SDI)
HibrnFd .... Hibernia Foods Ltd. [*Associated Press*] (SAG)
HIBT .... High-Interest Books for Teens [*A publication*]
HIBT .... Howard Ink Blot Test [*Psychology*]
HIBU .... Hydrological Institute and Belgrade University [*Marine science*] [*Yugoslavia*] (OSRA)
HIBU .... Hydrological Institute and Belgrade University (USDC)
HIBUF .... Hibernia Foods PLC [*NASDAQ symbol*] (SAG)
HIBUF .... Hibernia Foods Unit [*NASDAQ symbol*] (TTSB)
HIBW .... Hibernia Foods PLC [*NASDAQ symbol*] (SAG)
HIBWF .... Hibernia Foods Wrrt'C' [*NASDAQ symbol*] (TTSB)
HIBZ .... Hibernia Foods PLC [*NASDAQ symbol*] (SAG)
HIBZF .... Hibernia Foods Wrrt'D' [*NASDAQ symbol*] (TTSB)
HIC .... Habitat International Council [*The Hague, Netherlands*] (EAIO)
HIC .... Hand Indicator Controller (NRCH)
HIC .... Happy Irish Celebration
HIC .... Hardware Indenture Code (KSC)
HIC .... Hayes International Corp.
HIC .... Head Injury Criteria [*Medicine*]
HIC .... Health Information Council [*An association*] (EA)
HIC .... Health Insurance Claim Number [*Medicare*] (DHSM)
HIC .... Health Insurance Council [*Later, Consumer and Professional Relations Division of HIAA*] (EA)
HIC .... Heart Information Center
HIC .... Heavy Ion Cloud [*Astrophysics*]
HIC .... Hemispheric Insurance Conference
HIC .... Hickam Air Force Base, Hawaii [*NASA*] (NASA)
HI-C .... High-Conversion Critical Experiment (IEEE)
HIC .... High Dielectric Constant (IAA)
HIC .... High-Integrity Containers (GAAI)
HIC .... High-Intensity Conflict [*Military*]
HIC .... Highlands Insurance Group [*NYSE symbol*] (TTSB)
HIC .... Highly Indebted Country
HIC .... Highly Ionized Cloud [*Galactic science*]

HIC .... Historical Intelligence Collection [*CIA*]
HIC .... Hole-in-Corner [*Paper*] (DSUE)
HIC .... Homosexual Information Center (EA)
HIC .... Honduras Information Center (EA)
HIC .... Hot Idle Compensation [*Automotive engineering*]
HIC .... Hot Isostatic Compaction
HIC .... Household and Industrial Chemical
HIC .... Humidity Indicator Controller [*Aerospace*]
HIC .... Hybrid Integrated Circuit
HIC .... Hydrogen-Induced Cracking [*Metallurgy*]
HIC .... Hydrographic Information Committee [*NATO*] (NATG)
HIC .... Hydrologist in Charge (NOAA)
HIC .... Hydrophobic Interaction Chromatography
HIC .... White Cloud, MI [*Location identifier FAA*] (FAAL)
HICA .... Honey Industry Council of America [*Defunct*] (EA)
HICA .... Hydroxyisocaproic Acid (DMAA)
hi-cal .... High Calorie [*or Caloric*] [*Type of diet*] (DAVI)
HICA/MYDP... Hazard Identification Capability Assessment and Multi-Year Development Plan [*Federal Emergency Management Agency*] (GFGA)
HICAP .... High-Capacity (IAA)
Hicap .... High-Capacity Digital Transport Service [*Pacific Bell*]
HICAP .... High-Capacity Projectile (NVT)
HICAP .... High [*Altitude*] Combat Air Patrol (NVT)
HICAPCOM... High-Capacity Communication System
HICAS .... High-Capacity Active Control Suspension [*Automotive engineering*]
HICAT .... High-Altitude Clear Air Turbulence [*Aviation*]
HI-CC .... High-Conversion Critical Experiment [*Nuclear energy*] (GFGA)
HICCUP .... Hearing Impaired Consultants Creating Unique Partnerships [*An association*]
H-ICDA .... International Classification of Diseases - Adopted Code for Hospitals
HICF .... Health Insurance Claim Form
HICHS .... Helicopter Internal Cargo Handling System
HICK .... Hickok Electrical Instrument Co. [*NASDAQ symbol*] (SAG)
HICK .... Hickok, Inc. [*NASDAQ symbol*] (SAG)
hick .... Hickory (VRA)
HICKA .... Hickok Inc. 'A' [*NASDAQ symbol*] (TTSB)
Hick Ct Mar... Hickman on Naval Courts-Martial [*A publication*] (DLA)
Hickok .... Hickok, Inc. [*Associated Press*] (SAG)
Hickory .... Hickory Tech Corp. [*Associated Press*] (SAG)
Hicks Ethics... Hicks' Organization and Ethics of Bench and Bar [*A publication*] (DLA)
Hicks Leg Research... Hicks on Materials and Methods of Legal Research [*A publication*] (DLA)
Hicks Men & Books... Hicks on Men and Books Famous in the Law [*A publication*] (DLA)
HICLASS ...... Hierarchical Classification [*Indexing*]
HI CLASS ..... Hughes Integrated Classification System [*Hughes Aircraft Co.*] (NITA)
HiCN .... Cyanmethemoglobin [*Immunology*] (DAVI)
HICOA .... Head Injury Council of Australia
HICOG .... High Commissioner for Germany
HICOM .... Heavy Industries Corp. of Malaysia (ECON)
HICOM .... High Command
HICOM .... High Commission [*or Commissioner*]
HICOMRY ...... High Commissioner of Ryukyu Islands
HICOMSEVONET... High Command Secure Voice Network [*Navy*] (NVT)
HICOMTERPACIS... High Commissioner Trust Territory, Pacific Islands
hi-con .... High Contrast [*Cinematography*]
HICRV .... Human Intracisternal Retrovirus [*Medicine*]
HICS .... Hardened Intersite Cable System (CET)
HICS .... Hierarchical Information Control System [*Japanese*]
HICS .... Holt International Children's Services (EA)
HID .... Hamer Butte [*Idaho*] [*Seismograph station code, US Geological Survey*] (SEIS)
HID .... Hardware Installation Data (CAAL)
HID .... Hardware Interface Device (NASA)
HID .... Headache, Insomnia, Depression [*Syndrome*]
HID .... Helium Ionization Detector [*Instrumentation*]
HID .... Herniated Intervertebral Disc [*Medicine*] (DMAA)
HID .... Hierarchical Identification
HID .... High Density (IAA)
HID .... High-Impact Design (NRCH)
HID .... High-Intensity Discharge [*Vapor lamp*]
HID .... High-Intensity Discharge
HID .... High-Iron Diamine
HID .... HIM [*Hardware Interface Module*] Interface Distributor (NASA)
HID .... Housing Industry Dynamics [*Originator and databank*] (NITA)
HID .... Human Immune Deficiency [*Immunology*]
HID .... Human Infectious Dose [*Medicine*] (DMAA)
HID .... Hyperkinetic Impulse Disorder [*Medicine*]
HIDA .... Health Industry Distributors Association (EA)
HIDA .... Hepatoiminodiacetic Acid [*Scan*] [*Radiology*] (DAVI)
HIDA .... Home Improvement Dealers Association of America (EA)
HID-AB .... High-Iron Diamine-Alcian Blue [*A biological stain*]
HIDACZ .... High-Density Airspace Control Zone (MCD)
HIDAD .... Helicopter Insecticide Dispersal Apparatus, Dry (NG)
HIDAF .... Helicopter Insecticide Dispersal Apparatus, Fog (NG)
HIDAL .... Helicopter Insecticide Dispersal Apparatus, Liquid (NG)
HIDAM .... Hierarchical Indexed Direct Access Method [*Computer science*] (BUR)
HIDAN .... High-Density Air Navigation
HIDB .... Highlands and Islands Development Board [*Scotland*] (ECON)
HIDC .... Housing Industry Development Council [*Australia*]
HIDE .... Helicopter Integrated Direction Equipment
HIDE .... High-Absorption Integrated Defense Electromagnetic Warfare System

HIDE	Human Insulin-Degrading Enzyme [An enzyme]
HIDEC	Highly Integrated Digital Engine Control (MCD)
HIDF	Horizontal Side of an Intermediate Distribution Frame [Telecommunications] (TEL)
HIDI	Health-Care Instruments and Devices Institute [State University of New York at Buffalo] [Research center] (RCD)
HiD/LoD	High-Density/Low-Density Tariff
HIDM	High Information Delta Modulation [Computer science] (BUR)
HIDTA	High Intensity Drug Trafficking Area
HIDTC	Hangar and Industrial Door Technical Council [Defunct] (MSA)
HIE	Heat Input Equivalent (PDAA)
HIE	Height Integration Equipment
HIE	Help in Emergency (ADA)
HIE	Hibernation Information Exchange [Later, IHS]
HIE	Homelessness Information Exchange (EA)
HIE	Human Intestinal Epithelium [Medicine] (DMAA)
HIE	Hypoxi-Ischemic Encephalopathy [Neurology] (DAVI)
HIE	Whitefield, NH [Location identifier FAA] (FAAL)
HIEAT	Highest Temperature Equaled for All Time [NWS] (FAAC)
HIEFM	Highest Temperature Equaled for the Month [NWS] (FAAC)
HIEFSS	Hospital, Institution, and Educational Food Service Society [Later, Dietary Managers Association - DMA] (EA)
HIER	Hieroglyphics (WDAA)
Hier	Hieronymus [Jerome] [348-420AD] (BJA)
HIER	Hierusolymo [Jerusalem] (ROG)
Hier Gabr	Hieronymus Gabrielius [Deceased, 1587] [Authority cited in pre-1607 legal work] (DSA)
hiergl	Hieroglyph (VRA)
Hiero	Hieroglyphics
Hiero Cag	Hieronymus Cagnolus [Deceased, 1551] [Authority cited in pre-1607 legal work] (DSA)
Hiero Cagno	Hieronymus Cagnolus [Deceased, 1551] [Authority cited in pre-1607 legal work] (DSA)
Hieron	Hieronymus [Jerome] [348-420AD] (OCD)
Hieron Cagno	Hieronymus Cagnolus [Deceased, 1551] [Authority cited in pre-1607 legal work] (DSA)
Hieron Gabriel	Hieronymus Gabrielius [Deceased, 1587] [Authority cited in pre-1607 legal work] (DSA)
Hieron Grat	Hieronymus Gratus [Deceased, 1544] [Authority cited in pre-1607 legal work] (DSA)
Hier Schurf	Hieronymus Schurff [Deceased, 1554] [Authority cited in pre-1607 legal work] (DSA)
Hier Torniel	Hieronymus Torniellus [Deceased, 1575] [Authority cited in pre-1607 legal work] (DSA)
HIES	Hadassah Israel Education Services [Jerusalem]
HIES	Health Insurance/Employer Survey [Department of Health and Human Services] (GFGA)
HIESE	Highest Temperature Equaled so Early [NWS] (FAAC)
HIESL	Highest Temperature Equaled so Late [NWS] (FAAC)
HIF	Health Information Foundation
HIF	Heavy Ion Fusion (PDAA)
HIAF	Higher Integrative Functions [Neurology]
HIF	High-Impedance Follower
HIF	Hocker International Federation (EA)
HIF	Horizontal Integral Float [Automotive engineering]
HIF	Housing Insurance Fund [New Deal]
HIF	Human-Initiated Failure
HIF	Hypoxia-Inducible Factor [Physiology]
HIF	International Helsinki Federation for Human Rights [Austria] (EAIO)
HIF	Ogden, UT [Location identifier FAA] (FAAL)
HIF	Salomon Bros High Income Fd [NYSE symbol] (TTSB)
HIF	Salomon Brothers High Income Fund [NYSE symbol] (SPSG)
HIFAM	High-Fidelity Amplitude Modulation (DEN)
HIFAR	High-Frequency Fixed Array RADAR
HIFBS	Heat-Inactivated Fetal Bovine Serum [Immunology]
HIFC	Hog Intrinsic Factor Concentrate
HIFI	Cambridge SoundWorks [NASDAQ symbol] (TTSB)
HIFI	Cambridge Soundworks, Inc. [NASDAQ symbol] (SAG)
HIFI	Hawaii Imaging Fabry-Perot Interferometer
HIFI	HFIR [High-Flux Isotope Reactor] Irradiation Facility Improvement [Nuclear energy]
HIFI	High Fibre Biscuits [British]
HI-FI	High-Fidelity [Usually, in reference to home sound-reproducing equipment]
hi-fi	High-Fidelity [Printing] (WDMC)
HIFI	High Fidelity Records [Record label]
HIFI	High-Intensity Food Irradiator
HIFO	Highest In, First Out [Accounting]
HIFO	High Input, First Output [Computer science] (ECII)
HIFOR	High-Level Forecast [Meteorology]
HIFPA	Hispanic Institute for the Performing Arts [Defunct] (EA)
HIFR	Helicopter In-Flight Refueling (NVT)
HIFRAG	High Fragmentation (MCD)
HIFRENSA	Sociedad Hispano-Francesa de Energia Nuclear SA [Nuclear energy Spanish] (NRCH)
HIFS	Hingham Institution for Savings [NASDAQ symbol] (CTT)
HIFT	Hardware Implemented Fault Tolerance
HIFT	Heard Island Feasibility Test [Marine science] (OSRA)
HIFT	Heard Island Feasibility Test (USDC)
HIFTO	How I Feel Toward Others [Psychology] (EDAC)
HIG	Hartford Capital I [NYSE symbol] (SAG)
HIG	Hartford Capital II [NYSE symbol] (SAG)
HIG	Hawaii Institute of Geophysics [Marine science] (OSRA)
HIG	Hawaii Institute of Geophysics [University of Hawaii] [Seismograph station code, US Geological Survey Research center] (SEIS)

HIG	Heli-Inter Guyane [France ICAO designator] (FAAC)
HIG	Hermetically Sealed, Integrating Gyroscope
HIG	Higginsville, MO [Location identifier FAA] (FAAL)
HIG	High Input Grant [Real estate] [Canada]
HIG	High-Integrating Gyroscope (KSC)
HIG	Honeywell Integrating Gyro
HIg	Human Immunoglobulin [Biochemistry] (MAE)
HIG	Hypervelocity Intercept Guidance
HIG	ITT Hartford Group [NYSE symbol] (TTSB)
HIGAD	High-Impulse Gun Airborne Demonstrator (MCD)
HIGE	Hovering in Ground Effect [Army]
HIGED	Handbook of Instructions for Ground Equipment Designers (MCD)
HIGFET	Heterostructure Insulated Gate Field Effect Transistor (NITA)
Higgins	Higgins' Tennessee Court of Civil Appeals Reports [A publication] (DLA)
HIGH	Highland Railway [British] (ROG)
HIGHB	Highbury College of Divinity [British] (ROG)
High Bail	Highmore on Bail [A publication] (DLA)
High Ct	High Court Reports, Northwest Provinces [India] [A publication] (DLA)
High Ex Rem	High on Extraordinary Legal Remedies [A publication] (DLA)
High Extr Leg Rem	High on Extraordinary Legal Remedies [A publication] (DLA)
HIGH GASSER	High Geographic Aerospace Search RADAR
High Inj	High on Injunctions [A publication] (DLA)
HighIdInc	Highlander Income Fund, Inc. [Associated Press] (SAG)
HIGH LI	Highland Light Infantry [Military British] (ROG)
High Lun	Highmore on Lunacy [A publication] (DLA)
High Mort	Highmore on Mortmain [A publication] (DLA)
High Rec	High on the Law of Receivers [A publication] (DLA)
HIGHRS	Highlanders [British]
Hight	Hight's Reports [57-58 Iowa] [A publication] (DLA)
Highvld	Highveld Steel & Vanadium Corporation Ltd. [Associated Press] (SAG)
HIGHWAY	Highway [Commonly used] (OPSA)
Highwd	Highwood Resources Ltd. [Associated Press] (SAG)
Highwd	Highwoods Properties, Inc. [Associated Press] (SAG)
HIGHWY	Highway [Commonly used] (OPSA)
Highwy	HighwayMaster Communications, Inc. [Associated Press] (SAG)
Highwym	HighwayMaster Communications, Inc. [Associated Press] (SAG)
Hig Pat Dig	Higgins' Digest of Patent Cases [1890] [A publication] (DLA)
HIGPrQ	Hartford Cap I 7.70% 'QUIPS' [NYSE symbol] (TTSB)
HIGS	Hypervelocity Interceptor Guidance Simulation
HIGSED	Handbook of Instructions for Aircraft Ground Support Equipment Designers
HIGSS	Hypervelocity Intercept Guidance Simulator Study
Hig Waterc	Higgins' Pollution and Obstruction of Watercourses [1877] [A publication] (DLA)
HIH	Greensboro, NC [Location identifier FAA] (FAAL)
HIH	His [or Her] Imperial Highness
HIH	Hypertensive Intracerebral Hemorrhage [Medicine] (DMAA)
HIHA	High Impulsiveness, High Anxiety [Psychology] (DAVI)
HIHAT	High-Resolution Hemispherical Reflector Antenna Technique
HIHE	Hunter Institute of Higher Education [Australia]
HI-HICAT	High High-Altitude Clear Air Turbulence [Aviation]
HIHO	Highway Holdings Ltd. [NASDAQ symbol] (SAG)
HIHOE	Hydrogen, Ions, Helium, Oxygen in the Exosphere (MUGU)
HIHRC	Humanitas International Human Rights Committee (EA)
HIHW	Highway Holdings Ltd. [NASDAQ symbol] (SAG)
HII	Health Images [NYSE symbol] (TTSB)
HII	Health Images, Inc. [NYSE symbol] (SPSG)
HII	Health Industries Institute (EA)
HII	Health Insurance Institute (EA)
HII	Heard Island [Seismograph station code, US Geological Survey Closed] (SEIS)
HII	Hemagglutination-Inhibition Immunoassay [Immunochemistry] (DAVI)
HII	Heritage Interpretation International
HII	High Input Impedance
HIID	Harvard Institute for International Development [Harvard University] [Research center] (RCD)
HIID	Heavy Ion-Induced Desorption [Analytical chemistry]
HiInco	High Income Advantage Trust [Associated Press] (SAG)
HiIncoOp	High Income Opportunity Fund [Associated Press] (SAG)
HiInIII	High Income Advantage Trust III [Associated Press] (SAG)
HIIP	High Impact Incarceration Program [60-day paramilitary regimen for prisoners]
HIIPS	HUD [Department of Housing and Urban Development] Integrated Information Processing Service (GFGA)
HIIS	Honeywell Institute for Information Science (IEEE)
HIiS	Schistocytes [Hematology] (DAVI)
HIJ	Hiroshima [Japan] [Airport symbol] (OAG)
HIJ	Sisters of the Holy Infant Jesus [Roman Catholic religious order]
HIJMS	His Imperial Japanese Majesty's Ship
HIK	High Permittivity (DEN)
HIK	Hikone [Japan] [Seismograph station code, US Geological Survey] (SEIS)
HIK	Honolulu, HI [Location identifier FAA] (FAAL)
HIL	Great Bend, KS [Location identifier FAA] (FAAL)
HIL	Hardware-in-the-Loop
HIL	Hees International Bancorp, Inc. [Toronto Stock Exchange symbol]
HIL	Helium Impurities Loop [Nuclear energy] (NRCH)
HIL	High-Intensity Light
Hil	Hilary Term [England] [Legal term] (DLA)
HIL	Hilo [Hawaii] [Seismograph station code, US Geological Survey] (SEIS)
HIL	Hypoxic-Ischemic Lesion [Medicine] (DAVI)

HILA............ High Impulsiveness, Low Anxiety (MAE)
HILAB.......... Heavy Ion Laboratory (PDAA)
Hil Abr......... Hilliard's American Law [*A publication*] (DLA)
HILAC.......... Heavy-Ion Linear Accelerator [*Nuclear energy*]
HILAP.......... High Latitude Particle (PDAA)
HILASD........ Hard Link Arm Safe Device (MCD)
HILAST........ High-Altitude Large Area Surveillance Tactic [*Military*] (CAAL)
HILAT.......... High-Latitude Research Satellite [*Defense Nuclear Agency*]
HilbRog........ Hilb, Rogal & Hamilton Co. [*Associated Press*] (SAG)
HILC............ Hampshire Inter-Library Center [*Library network*]
HILC............ High-Intermediate Level Cell [*Nuclear energy*] (NRCH)
HilcstDv....... Hilcoast Development Corp. [*Associated Press*] (SAG)
HILDCAA...... High-Intensity, Long-Duration, Continuous Aurora Event, Activity [*Astrophysics*]
Hild Ins....... Hildyard on Insurance [*A publication*] (DLA)
Hild Mar Ins... Hildyard's Marine Insurance [*A publication*] (DLA)
Hil Elem Law... Hilliard's Elements of Law [*A publication*] (DLA)
HILI............ Heavy Ion, Light Ion
HILI............ Higher Layers and Internetworking [*Computer science*] (ACRL)
HILI............ Hilite Industries [*NASDAQ symbol*] (TTSB)
HILI............ Hilite Industries, Inc. [*NASDAQ symbol*] (SAG)
HILIS.......... High Light Intensity System (PDAA)
Hilite.......... Hilite Industries, Inc. [*Associated Press*] (SAG)
HILL........... Hill [*Commonly used*] (OPSA)
Hill............ Hill's New York Supreme Court Reports [*1841-44*] [*A publication*] (DLA)
Hill............ Hill's South Carolina Law Reports [*A publication*] (DLA)
Hill Abr....... Hilliard's Abridgment of Real Property Law [*A publication*] (DLA)
Hill Am Jur... Hilliard's American Jurisprudence [*A publication*] (DLA)
Hill Am Law... Hilliard's American Law [*A publication*] (DLA)
Hill & D....... Lalor's Supplement to Hill and Denio's New York Reports [*A publication*] (DLA)
Hill & Den.... Lalor's Supplement to Hill and Denio's New York Reports [*A publication*] (DLA)
Hill & Den Supp... Lalor's Supplement to Hill and Denio's New York Reports [*A publication*] (DLA)
Hill & D Supp... Hill and Denio's Lalor's Supplement [*New York*] [*A publication*] (DLA)
Hill & Redman... Hill and Redman's Law of Landlord and Tenant [*16th ed.*] [*1976*] [*A publication*] (DLA)
Hill B & I.... Hilliard on Bankruptcy and Insolvency [*A publication*] (DLA)
Hill Bank..... Hilliard on Bankruptcy and Insolvency [*A publication*] (DLA)
HillBd......... Hillside Bedding Corp. [*Associated Press*] (SAG)
Hill Ch....... Hill's Equity South Carolina Reports [*1833-37*] [*A publication*] (DLA)
Hill Ch Pr.... Hill's Chancery Practice [*A publication*] (DLA)
Hill Cont...... Hilliard on Contracts [*A publication*] (DLA)
Hill Elem Law... Hilliard's Elements of Law [*A publication*] (DLA)
Hillenbd...... Hillenbrand Industries, Inc. [*Associated Press*] (SAG)
Hill Eq....... Hill's Equity South Carolina Reports [*1833-37*] [*A publication*] (DLA)
Hill Eq (SC)... Hill's Equity South Carolina Reports [*1833-37*] [*A publication*] (DLA)
Hill Fixt..... Hill's Law of Fixtures [*A publication*] (DLA)
Hilliard RP... Hilliard on Real Property [*A publication*] (DLA)
Hill Ill Chy... Hill's Illinois Chancery Practice [*A publication*] (DLA)
Hill Ill Com Law... Hill's Illinois Common Law Jurisdiction and Practice [*A publication*] (DLA)
Hill Inj...... Hilliard on the Law of Injunctions [*A publication*] (DLA)
Hill Lib & Law... Hill's Liberty and Law [*A publication*] (DLA)
Hill Mor...... Hilliard's Law of Mortgages [*A publication*] (DLA)
Hill Mortg.... Hilliard's Law of Mortgages [*A publication*] (DLA)
Hill New Trials... Hilliard on New Trials [*A publication*] (DLA)
Hill N Tr..... Hilliard on New Trials [*A publication*] (DLA)
Hill NY....... Hill's New York Reports [*A publication*] (DLA)
Hill NYR..... Hill's New York Reports [*A publication*] (DLA)
Hill Prob..... Hill's Illinois Probate Jurisdiction and Practice [*A publication*] (DLA)
Hill Real Prop... Hilliard on Real Property [*A publication*] (DLA)
Hill Rem..... Hilliard on Remedies for Torts [*A publication*] (DLA)
HILLS......... Hills [*Commonly used*] (OPSA)
Hill Sales.... Hilliard on Sales of Personal Property [*A publication*] (DLA)
Hill's Ann Codes & Laws... Hill's Annotated Codes and General Laws [*Oregon*] [*A publication*] (DLA)
Hill's Ann St & Codes... Hill's Annotated General Statutes and Codes [*Washington*] [*A publication*] (DLA)
HillsBd....... Hillside Bedding Corp. [*Associated Press*] (SAG)
Hill SC....... Hill's Equity South Carolina Reports [*1833-37*] [*A publication*] (DLA)
Hill SC....... Hill's South Carolina Law Reports [*A publication*] (DLA)
Hill's Code... Hill's Annotated Codes and General Laws [*Oregon*] [*A publication*] (DLA)
Hill's Code... Hill's Annotated General Statutes and Codes [*Washington*] [*A publication*] (DLA)
HillsStrs..... Hills Stores Co. [*Associated Press*] (SAG)
HillStr....... Hills Stores Co. [*Associated Press*] (SAG)
Hill Tax...... Hilliard on the Law of Taxation [*A publication*] (DLA)
Hill Torts.... Hilliard on the Law of Torts [*A publication*] (DLA)
Hill Tr....... Hill on Trustees [*A publication*] (DLA)
Hill Vend.... Hilliard on the Law of Vendors [*A publication*] (DLA)
Hillyer....... Hillyer's Reports [*20-22 California*] [*A publication*] (DLA)
HILNNEP..... Health Information Library Network of Northeastern Pennsylvania [*Library network*]
HiLo.......... Hi-Lo Automotive, Inc. [*Associated Press*] (SAG)
HILOW........ Health Information Libraries of Westchester [*Library network*]
HILP.......... Health Information Library Program [*Library network*]
HILS.......... Halogen Interchangeable Light Source
HILS.......... High-Intensity Learning Systems
HILS.......... High Intensity Lightweight Searchlight (PDAA)
HILT.......... High Impetus, Low Flame Temperature (MCD)

HILT.......... High-Intensity Language Training (AEBS)
Hil T......... Hilary Term [*England*] [*Legal term*] (DLA)
Hilt.......... Hilton's New York Common Pleas Reports [*A publication*] (DLA)
Hil Term 4 Will IV... Hilary Term 4, William IV [*A publication*] (DLA)
Hilt (NY).... Hilton's New York Common Pleas Reports [*A publication*] (DLA)
Hilton........ Hilton Hotels Corp. [*Associated Press*] (SAG)
Hil Torts..... Hilliard on the Law of Torts [*A publication*] (DLA)
HIL VAC...... Hilary Vacation [*British Legal term*] (DLA)
HILY SITTGS... Hilary Sittings [*British Legal term*] (ROG)
HIM........... Hardware Interface Module [*NASA*] (NASA)
HIM........... Hardware Interface Module Hierarchy of Interpretive Modules (MHDI)
HIM........... Health Insurance Manual
HIM........... Heavy Interdiction Missile
HIM........... Helps International Ministries (EA)
HIM........... Herald International Mailings Ltd. [*British*]
HIM........... High Impact
HIM........... High-Intensity Microphone
HIM........... Hill Interaction Matrix [*Psychology*]
him........... Himachali [*MARC language code Library of Congress*] (LCCP)
HIM........... Himac Resources Ltd. [*Vancouver Stock Exchange symbol*]
HIM........... Himeji [*Japan*] [*Seismograph station code, US Geological Survey*] (SEIS)
HIM........... His [*or Her*] Imperial Majesty
HIM........... Horizontal Impulse
HIM........... Host Interface Manager (NITA)
HIM........... Hotel Institute Montreux [*Switzerland*] (ECON)
HIM........... Hot Ionized Medium [*Astrophysics*]
HIM........... Human Individual Metamorphosis [*Flying saucer cult*]
HIM........... Human Integrated Manufacturing
HIM........... Hyperimmunoglobulin M Syndrome [*Medicine*]
HIM........... Hyper Immunoglobulin Syndrome [*Medicine*]
HIMA......... Health Industry Manufacturers Association (EA)
HIM-A........ Hill Interaction Matrix-A [*Personality development test*] [*Psychology*]
HIMAC....... Heavy-Ion Medical Accelerator in Chiba [*Japan*]
HIMAD....... High-to-Medium-Altitude Air Defense (AABC)
HIMAG....... High-Mobility-Agility [*Test for combat vehicles*] (RDA)
HIMARS...... High-Mobility Artillery Rocket System [*Military*]
HIMARS...... High Mobility Artillery Rocket System [*Army*] (DOMA)
HIMAT....... Highly Maneuverable Aircraft Technology Testbed [*Rockwell International Corp.*] (MCD)
HIMB......... Hawaii Institute of Marine Biology [*University of Hawaii*] [*Research center*] (RCD)
HIMC......... Hepatic Intramitochondrial Crystalloid [*Medicine*] (DMAA)
HIMD......... Handbook of Instructions for Missile Designers
HI MI........ High Mileage (WDAA)
HIMIC....... Highly-Indebted Middle-Income Country
HIMO........ High Mobility [*Vehicle analysis*] (MCD)
HIMOWC..... High-Mobility Weapons Carrier [*Army*] (MCD)
HIMP........ High-Dose Intravenous Methylprednisolone [*Medicine*] (DMAA)
HIMP........ High Impact
Him Pra...... All India Reporter, Himachal Pradesh [*A publication*] (DLA)
HIMR........ Handbook of Inspection Maintenance Requirements [*Navy*] (MCD)
HIMR........ Hearing-Impaired Mentally Retarded
HIMS........ Heavy Interdiction Missile System (MCD)
HIMS........ Helicopter In-Flight Monitoring System [*Army*] (RDA)
HIMS........ Himself
HIMS........ HMMWV [*High-Mobility Multipurpose Wheeled Vehicle*] Interchange Mount System [*Military*] (INF)
HIMS........ Housing Information Management System
HIMS........ HUMINT [*Human Intelligence*] Information Management System
HIMSEUR..... HAWK [*Homing All the Way Killer*] Intensified Management System Europe Program [*Military*]
HIMSS....... Healthcare Information and Management Systems Society (EA)
HIMT......... Hemagglutination Inhibition Morphine Test [*Immunochemistry*] (DMAA)
HIMV........ Hippeastrum Mosaic Virus [*Plant pathology*]
HIN........... Chadron, NE [*Location identifier FAA*] (FAAL)
HIN........... Health Identification Number
HIN........... Heli Inter [*France ICAO designator*] (FAAC)
HIN........... Heterotrophic Intestinal Nitrification [*Metabolism*]
HIN........... Hidden Lake Gold Mines [*Vancouver Stock Exchange symbol*]
HIN........... High Intensity
HIN........... High-Intensity Noise
HIN........... Hinchinbrook Island [*Alaska*] [*Seismograph station code, US Geological Survey*] (SEIS)
hin........... Hindi [*MARC language code Library of Congress*] (LCCP)
HIN........... Holocaust Information Network (EA)
HIN........... Hull Identification Number [*USCG*] (TAG)
HIN........... Hybrid Integrated Network [*Bell System*] [*Telecommunications*]
HIN........... Hydrocarbon-Induced Nephropathy [*Medicine*]
HINAS........ Historic Naval Ships Association of North America (EA)
HINASW...... Historic Naval Ships of the World [*Later, HINAS*] (EA)
HIncII........ High Income Advantage Trust II [*Associated Press*] (SAG)
Hincmar Epist... Hincmari Epistolae [*A publication*] (DLA)
HIND......... Health Care Item Name Directory [*A publication*]
HIND......... Hindi (WDAA)
HIND......... Hindu (WDAA)
Hind......... Hindustan
HIND......... Hindustani [*Language, etc.*]
H in DC...... Holder in Due Course [*Owner or holder of a negotiable instrument at some future time*]
Hinde Ch Pr... Hinde's Modern Practice of the High Court of Chancery [*A publication*] (DLA)
HINDEX...... HANES [*Health and Nutrition Examination Survey*] Data Index [*Department of Health and Human Services*] (GFGA)

Hind LJ..........	Hindu Law Journal [*A publication*] (DLA)
Hind LQ..........	Hindu Law Quarterly [*A publication*] (DLA)
Hind Pat......	Hindmarch on Patents [*A publication*] (DLA)
Hind Pr........	Hind's Practice [*A publication*] (DLA)
Hine & N Ass...	Hine and Nicholas on Assignment of Life Policies [*A publication*] (DLA)
Hine & N Dig...	Hine and Nicholas. Insurance Digest [*A publication*] (DLA)
HINEKF........	Hinekford [*England*]
Hines..........	Hines' Reports [*83-96 Kentucky*] [*A publication*] (DLA)
HINF..........	Hypodermoclysis Infusion [*Medicine*]
HING..........	High-Intensity Noise Generator
HingmS........	Hingham Institution for Savings [*Associated Press*] (SAG)
HINIL..........	High-Noise-Immunity Logic (MCD)
HINS..........	Health Information Network Services [*Database search service*] (OLDSS)
HINS..........	Helicopter Integrated Navigation System [*Canadian Navy*]
Hinsdle........	Hinsdale Financial Corp. [*Associated Press*] (SAG)
HINT..........	Happy Idiot News Team [*Also, Happy Idiot News Talk*] [*Broadcasting*] (WDMC)
HINT..........	High Intensity
HINT..........	Hinton [*Test*] [*Medicine*]
HINT..........	Housewares Industry News and Topics [*A publication*] (EAAP)
HIO..........	Health Insuring Organization (DMAA)
HIO..........	High Income Opp Fd [*NYSE symbol*] (TTSB)
HIO..........	High Income Opportunity Fund [*NYSE symbol*] (SAG)
HIO..........	Hillsboro, OR [*Location identifier FAA*] (FAAL)
HIO..........	Hypoiodism [*Medicine*]
HIO..........	Smith Barney High Income Opportunity Fund [*NYSE symbol*] (SPSG)
HIOMT........	Hydroxyindole O-Methyltransferase [*Also, HOMT*] [*An enzyme*]
HIOS..........	Headquarters Integrated Office System [*Military*] (GFGA)
HIOS..........	High Index of Suspicion [*Medicine*] (DMAA)
HIP..........	Habitability Improvement Plan [*Navy*]
HIP..........	Hanford Isotopes Plant [*Nuclear energy*]
HIP..........	Hardware Interface Program (NASA)
HIP..........	Harpoon Indicator Panel [*Missiles*] (MCD)
HIP..........	HAWK [*Homing All the Way Killer*] Improvement Program
HIP..........	Hazard Input Program (SAA)
HIP..........	Health Illness Profile (DMAA)
HIP..........	Health Insurance Plan
HIP..........	Hearing Impaired Peer
HIP..........	Help for Incontinent People (EA)
HIP..........	Hierachical Information Processor (PDAA)
HIP..........	High-Impact Pressure
HIP..........	High-Intent Priority [*In the record business, a heavily promoted disk*]
HIP..........	High Internal Phase [*Emulsion chemistry*]
HIP..........	Highly Ionized Plasma
HIPA..........	High-Potential Iron Protein
HIP..........	Homograft Incus Prosthesis [*Medicine*] (DMAA)
HIP..........	Hoover Institution Press (DGA)
HIP..........	Horizontal Injection Press
HIP..........	Hospital Improvement Project
HIP..........	Hospital Insurance Program
HIP..........	Host Information Processor (NITA)
HIP..........	Host Interface Port [*Computer science*]
HIP..........	Host Interface Processor [*Computer science*] (PDAA)
HIP..........	Hot Isostatically Pressed [*Materials processing*]
HIP..........	Housing Improvement Program [*Federal government*]
HIP..........	Howitzer Improvement Program
HIP..........	Hydrostatic Indifference Point
HIP..........	Hyperbolic Integer Programming [*Computer science*] (PDAA)
HIP..........	Hypnotic Induction Profile
HIPA..........	Health Insurance Persistency Award [*Later, HIQA*] [*LIMRA*]
HIPA..........	Heparin-Induced Platelet Activation [*Medicine*] (DMAA)
HIPA..........	Home Improvement Products Association [*Defunct*] (EA)
HIPAAS........	High-Performance Advanced Attack Systems (MCD)
HIPAAS........	High-Performance Attack Aircraft System (MCD)
HIPAC........	Heavy-Ion Plasma Accelerator (IAA)
HIPAC........	High-Performance Aircraft Cannon (MCD)
HIPAC........	Hitachi Parametron Automatic Computer
HIPAR........	High-Performance Precision Approach Control RADAR (MCD)
HIPAR........	High-Power Acquisition RADAR (AAG)
HIP/ATBM.....	HAWK [*Homing All the Way Killer*] Improvement Program / Anti-Tactical Ballistic Missile (SAA)
HIPC..........	Health Information Policy Council [*Department of Health and Human Services*] (GFGA)
HIPC..........	Health Insurance Purchasing Collective (DMAA)
HIPC..........	Health Insurance Purchasing Cooperative (ECON)
HIPC..........	Heavily Indebted Poor Country
HIPC..........	High Plains Corp. [*NASDAQ symbol*] (NQ)
HIPC..........	High Pressure Chamber
HIPE..........	Hospital In-Patient Enquiry [*British*]
HIPEG........	High-Performance External Gun
HIPEHT........	High-Performance Electrothermal Hydrazine Thruster (MCD)
HIPERARC.....	High-Performance Archiheater (MCD)
HI-PERF.......	High Performance [*Automotive engineering*]
HIPERFLIR....	High-Performance Forward-Looking Infrared (PDAA)
HIPERNAS.....	High-Performance Navigation System
HIPERTHINO...	High-Performance Throttleable Injector (KSC)
HIPEX........	Harmonic Identification Pitch Extraction (PDAA)
HIPG..........	Human Information Processing Group [*Princeton University*]
HI-PI..........	High-Performance Intercept
HIPIC..........	High-Pressure Impregnation Carbonization (MCD)
HIPIP..........	High Potential Iron Protein [*Biochemistry*]
HIPIR..........	High-Power Illuminator RADAR [*Army*] (AABC)
HiPlains.......	High Plains Corp. [*Associated Press*] (SAG)

HIPO..........	Hemihypertrophy, Intestinal Web, Preauricular Skin Tag, and Congenital Corneal Opacity Syndrome [*Medicine*] (DMAA)
HIPO..........	Hierarchical Input Process Output [*Diagram used in software assessment*] (NITA)
HIPO..........	Hierarchy plus Input-Process-Output [*Computer science*]
Hipo..........	High-Potential Employee
HIPO..........	Highway Post Office [*Bus or truck equipped with mail distribution facilities*]
HIPO..........	Hilfspolizei [*Auxiliary Police*] [*German*]
Hipo..........	Hippolytus Marsilius [*Deceased, 1529*] [*Authority cited in pre-1607 legal work*] (DSA)
HIPO..........	Hospital Indicator for Physicians' Orders
HIPOT........	High Potential (KSC)
hipot..........	High Potential (IDOE)
HIPOTT........	High-Potential Test (IEEE)
HIPOW........	Hot Isostatic Pressing of Waste [*Nuclear energy*] (NUCP)
HIPP..........	High-Energy Impulse Pumpable Propellant (MCD)
HIPP..........	Hippocrates [*Greek physician, 460 -377 BC*]
Hipp..........	Hippolytus [*of Euripides*] [*Classical studies*] (OCD)
Hipparch......	Hipparchus [*of Plato*] [*Classical studies*] (OCD)
Hipparcos....	High-Precision Parallax Collecting Satellite [*European Space Agency*]
Hipp Bonacoss...	Hippolytus Bonacossa [*Deceased, 1591*] [*Authority cited in pre-1607 legal work*] (DSA)
HIPPI..........	High Performance Parallel Interface [*Computer science*]
HIPPO........	High Internal Pressure Producing Orifice (MCD)
HIPPO........	Hippodrome [*London*] (DSUE)
HIPPO........	Hippopotamus (DSUE)
Hippoc........	Hippocrates [*Greek physician, 460 -377 BC*] [*Classical studies*] (OCD)
HIPPY........	Home Instruction Program for Preschool Youngsters [*Israel*]
HIPR..........	High Internal Phase Ratio
HIPR..........	High Pressure (KSC)
HIPRES........	High Pressure
HIPRI..........	High Priority (NG)
Hip Riminal...	Hippolytus Riminaldus [*Deceased, 1589*] [*Authority cited in pre-1607 legal work*] (DSA)
HIPrJ..........	Houshld 7.35% cm Dep Pfd [*NYSE symbol*] (TTSB)
HiPro..........	High-Protein (MEDA)
HIPrT..........	Househld Cap Tr 8.25% 'TOPrS' [*NYSE symbol*] (TTSB)
HIPrX..........	Househld 9.50%'91 cm Dep Pfd [*NYSE symbol*] (TTSB)
HIPrZ..........	Household 8.25% cm Dep Pfd [*NYSE symbol*] (TTSB)
HIPS..........	Health Insurance Plans Survey [*Department of Health and Human Services*] (GFGA)
HIPS..........	Helmet Initiated Pointing System (MCD)
HIPS..........	High-Impact Polystyrene [*Plastics technology*]
HIPS..........	Hyperintense Proximal Scanning
HIPSA..........	Hallicrafters Incremental Power Spectrum Analyzer
HIPSF..........	High-Performance Space Feed
HIQ..........	High Quality [*Home video system*] (IAA)
HIQ..........	Housing Intelligence Quotient
HIQ..........	New York, NY [*Location identifier FAA*] (FAAL)
HIQA..........	Health Insurance Quality Award [*Formerly, HIPA*] [*LIMRA*]
HIR..........	Hammersley Iron Proprietary Ltd. Railway [*Australia*] (DCTA)
HIR..........	Handbook of Inspection Requirements [*Navy*] (MCD)
HIR..........	Harvard International Review [*A publication*]
HIR..........	Hazardous Incident Report (MCD)
HIR..........	Head Injury Routine [*Medicine*] (DMAA)
HIR..........	Health Insurance Regulation
HIR..........	Helicopter Instrument Rules
HIR..........	HELWS-Integrated RADAR
HIR..........	Hierarchy [*Computer science*]
HIR..........	Hilton Resource Corp. [*Vancouver Stock Exchange symbol*]
HIR..........	Hiram College, Hiram, OH [*OCLC symbol*] (OCLC)
HIR..........	Hiring (ROG)
HIR..........	Hiroshima [*Japan*] [*Seismograph station code, US Geological Survey*] (SEIS)
HIR..........	Honiara [*Guadalcanal*] [*Airport symbol*] (OAG)
HIR..........	Horizontal Impulse Reaction (MSA)
HIR..........	Household Issuance Record [*Food Stamp Program*] (GFGA)
HIR..........	Human Insulin Receptor [*Biochemistry*]
HIR..........	Hydrospace Information Report (MCD)
HIR..........	Hydrostatic Impact Rocket (NATG)
HIRA..........	Handheld Infrared Alarm (PDAA)
HIRA..........	Health Industry Representatives Association (EA)
HIRAC........	High Random Access
HIRAN........	High-Precision SHORAN (AAG)
HIRAP........	High-Resolution Accelerometer Package (MCD)
HIRC..........	Head Injuries Rehabilitation Centre [*British*] (CB)
HIRC..........	Holy Innocents Reparation Committee (EA)
HIRCIS........	High-Resolution Capacitive Imaging Sensor [*Instrumentation*]
HIRD..........	High-Intensity Radiation Device
HIRDL........	High-Intensity Radiation Development Laboratory [*Brookhaven National Laboratory*] [*Department of Energy*]
HIRE..........	Help through Industry Retraining and Employment [*Program*] [*Department of Labor*]
HIREL........	High Reliability (IAA)
HirelHld........	Hirel Holdings, Inc. [*Associated Press*] (SAG)
HI Rep........	Hawaiian Islands Reports [*A publication*] (DLA)
HI-RES........	High Resolution [*Computer science*]
HIRES........	High-Resolution Echelle Spectrograph
HIRES........	Hypersonic In-Flight Refueling System
HIREWIMP......	High-Resolution Wind Measurement Program (MUGU)
HIRF..........	High-Intensity Radiated Field [*Aviation*]
HIRF..........	High-Intensity Reciprocity Failure
HIRI..........	Hi-Rise Recycling Sys [*NASDAQ symbol*] (TTSB)

HIRI .... Hi Rise Recycling Systems [*NASDAQ symbol*] (SAG)
HIRI .... Home Improvement Research Institute (EA)
HIRIS .... High-Resolution Imaging Spectrometer
HiRise .... Hi Rise Recycling Systems [*Associated Press*] (SAG)
HIRIV .... How Will Arrival Report Be Filed Concerning [*Aviation*] (FAAC)
HIRL .... High-Intensity Runway Lights [*Aviation*]
HIRL .... Hirel Holdings, Inc. [*NASDAQ symbol*] (SAG)
HIRM .... High-Incidence Research Model (MCD)
HIRO .... Health Insurance Regional Office
HIROP .... Hand-Held Infrared Controller Overpopulation [*Computer science*]
HIRS .... Harker's Information Retrieval Systems [*Harker's Specialist Book
                 Importers*] [*Information service or system*] (IID)
HIRS .... High-Impulse Retrorocket System
HIRS .... High-Resolution Infared Sounder [*Marine science*] (OSRA)
HIRS .... High-Resolution Infrared Radiation Sounder
Hirsch .... Hirsch International Corp. [*Associated Press*] (SAG)
HIRSO .... High-Resolution Solar Optical Telescope
HIRSS .... Hover Infrared Suppressor Subsystem
HIRT .... High Reynolds Number Tunnel
HIRTA .... High Intensity Radio Transmission Area [*Army*] (DOMA)
HIRUD .... Hirudo [*A Leech*] [*Pharmacy*] (ROG)
HIS .... CIGNA High Income Shares [*NYSE symbol*] (SPSG)
HIS .... CIGNA High Income Shs [*NYSE symbol*] (TTSB)
HIS .... Haptic Intelligence Scale [*Psychology*] (AEBS)
HIS .... Hardware Information System (MCD)
HIS .... Hardware Interrupt System (IAA)
HIS .... Hayman Island [*Australia Airport symbol*] (OAG)
HIS .... Health Information Series [*Federal government*]
HIS .... Health Information Services [*Australia*]
HIS .... Health Information Services [*Department of Health and Human
                 Services*]
HIS .... Health Information System (DMAA)
HIS .... Health Interview Survey [*National Institutes of Health*]
HIS .... Heavy-Ion Source
HIS .... Heiss Island [*Former USSR Geomagnetic observatory code*]
HIS .... Heliborne Illumination System (CINC)
HIS .... Hic Iacet Sepultus [*Here Lies Buried*] [*Latin*]
HIS .... Hierarchical Intensive Search [*of the literature*]
HIS .... High Integrity Systems [*Computer company*] [*British*] (NITA)
HIS .... High-Intensity Spectrometer
HIS .... High-Interest Shipping (MCD)
HIS .... High-Resolution Interferometer Spectrometer
HIS .... Hispaniola Airways [*Dominican Republic*] [*ICAO designator*] (FAAC)
HIS .... Histatin (DMAA)
His .... Histidine [*An amino acid*]
his .... Histidine [*An amino acid*] (DOG)
HIS .... Histogram Scanning
HIS .... Historian [*or History*] (EY)
HIS .... Hit Indicator System
HIS .... Homogeneous Information Sets
HIS .... Honeywell Information Systems, Inc. (IEEE)
HIS .... Hood Inflation System (DNAB)
HIS .... Horwitz Information Services [*Information service or system*] (IID)
HIS .... Hospital Infection Society [*British*] (DBA)
HIS .... Hospital Information System [*Computer science*]
HIS .... Hospitality and Information Service (EA)
HIS .... House Information Systems [*House of Representatives*] [*Washington,
                 DC*]
HIS .... Hunters' Improvement Society [*British*] (BI)
HIS .... Hybrid Infrared Source
HIS .... Hyperimmune Serum [*Medicine*] (DMAA)
HISA .... Hawaii International Services Agency
HISA .... Headquarters and Installation Support Activity [*Army*] (AABC)
HISAC .... High-Speed Airdrop Container [*Military*] (RDA)
HISAM .... Hardware Initiated Standalone Memory (NASA)
HISAM .... Hierarchical Indexed Sequential Access Method [*Computer
                 science*] (BUR)
HISAR .... Hughes Integrated Synthetic Aperture Radar [*Hughes Electronics*]
HISARS .... Hydrologic Information Storage and Retrieval System [*North Carolina
                 State University*] [*Raleigh, NC*]
HISB .... Health Insurance Standards Board
HISC .... House Internal Security Committee
HI-SCALE .... Heliospheric Instrument for Spectra, Composition, and Anisotropy at
                 Low Energies [*Astronomy*]
HISDAM .... Hierarchical Indexed Sequential Direct Access Method [*Computer
                 science*]
HISE .... High Interference Signaling Environment
HISEACOTS... High Sea State Container Transfer System [*Army*] (RDA)
HISG .... Human Immune Serum Globulin [*Immunochemistry*]
HiShear .... Hi-Shear Industries, Inc. [*Associated Press*] (SAG)
HiShearT ...... Hi Shear Technology Corp. [*Associated Press*] (SAG)
HiShearTc .... Hi Shear Technology Corp. [*Associated Press*] (SAG)
HISI .... Honeywell Information Systems, Inc.
HISKEW .... Health Insurance Skeleton Eligibility Write-off File [*Department of
                 Health and Human Services*] (GFGA)
HISM .... How I See Myself Scale [*Psychology*] (EDAC)
HISP .... Heat-Inactivated Serum Pool [*Clinical chemistry*]
Hisp .... Hispania [*A publication*] (BRI)
Hispa .... Hispavox [*Record label*] [*Spain*]
HISPA .... International Association for the History of Physical Education and
                 Sport [*Belgium*]
HISPID .... Herbarium Information Standards and Protocols for Interchange of
                 Data [*Australia*]
HISPOT .... High-Altitude Surveillance Platform for Over-the-Horizon Targeting
                 (MCD)

HISRAN .... High-Precision SHORAN [*Short-Range Navigation*]
HISS .... Healthcare Imaging Services [*NASDAQ symbol*] (TTSB)
HISS .... HealthCare Imaging Services, Inc. [*NASDAQ symbol*] (SAG)
HISS .... Helicopter Icing Spray System (RDA)
HISS .... Helicopter Inflight Spray System (MCD)
HISS .... Herpetological Information Search Systems
HISS .... High-Intensity Sound Simulator
HISS .... High-Intensity Sound System
HISS .... Holographic Ice Surveying System (PDAA)
HISSG .... Healthcare Information Systems Sharing Group (EA)
HiSSS .... High Speed Strike System [*Military*]
HISSZ .... Healthcare Imaging Sv Wrrt'B' [*NASDAQ symbol*] (TTSB)
HIST .... Gallery of History [*NASDAQ symbol*] (TTSB)
HIST .... Gallery of History, Inc. [*NASDAQ symbol*] (SAG)
HIST .... High Input Shock Test
Hist .... Histidinemia [*Medicine*] (AAMN)
HIST .... Histoire [*History*] [*French*] (ROG)
HIST .... Histology (ADA)
Hist .... Historia [*A publication*] (OCD)
Hist .... Historiae [*of Tacitus*] [*Classical studies*] (OCD)
HIST .... Historian [*or History*] (AFM)
HIST .... Historical [*Linguistics*]
hist .... History (VRA)
HIST .... Hospital In-Service Training
HIST .... Hyderabad Imperial Service Troops [*British military*] (DMA)
Hist An .... Historia Animalium [*of Aristotle*] [*Classical studies*] (OCD)
Hist Anc Geog... [*A*] History of Ancient Geography [*A publication*] (OCD)
Hist&PolSc... History & Political Science (DD)
Hist & T ...... History and Theory [*A publication*] (BRI)
Hist Athen Const... [*A*] History of the Athenian Constitution [*A publication*] (OCD)
Hist Aug ..... Historia Augusta [*A publication*] (OCD)
Hist Conscr... Quomodo Historia Conscribenda Sit [*of Lucian*] [*Classical studies*]
                 (OCD)
Hist Eccl ..... Historia Ecclesiastica [*of Eusebius*] [*Classical studies*] (OCD)
Hist Ed R .... History of Education Review [*A publication*]
HISTEP .... High-Speed Integrated Space Transportation Evaluation Program
                 (IAA)
Hist G .... History of Greece [*A publication*] (OCD)
Hist Gk Phil... History of Greek Philosophy [*A publication*] (OCD)
HISTL .... Historical
HISTLINE ..... History of Medicine On-Line [*National Library of Medicine*]
                 [*Bibliographic database*] (IID)
HISTN .... Historian (AABC)
Hist Num .... Historia Numorum [*A publication*] (OCD)
histo .... Histology [*Medicine*] (DAVI)
histo .... Histoplasma [*Medicine*] (DAVI)
histo .... Histoplasmin [*Skin test*] [*Medicine*] (DAVI)
histo .... Histoplasmosis [*Medicine*] (DAVI)
Hist of Greek Maths... History of Greek Mathematics [*A publication*] (OCD)
HISTOL .... Histology
Hist Pl .... Historia Plantarum [*of Theophrastus*] [*Classical studies*] (OCD)
HISTRAP ...... Heavy Ion Storage Ring for Atomic Physics
HISTRCL ...... Historical
Hist Rom Rel... Roemische Religions-Geschichte [*A publication*] (OCD)
HISTRU .... Hydraulic System Test and Repair Unit [*Army*] (MCD)
HISWA .... Herd Improvement Service of Western Australia [*Animal husbandry*]
HISXE .... Heavy Ion-Induced Satellite X-Ray Emission [*Analytical chemistry*]
HIT .... Hawthorn Institute of Technology [*Australia*]
HIT .... Hazard Information Transmission [*Chemical Manufacturers
                 Association*] (FFDE)
HIT .... Headline International Talent [*Commercial firm*]
HIT .... Health Indication Test [*Engine system*]
HIT .... Health Insurance Tax [*Social Security Administration*] (GFGA)
HIT .... HELWS-Integrated Tracker
HIT .... Hemagglutination Inhibition Test [*for pregnancy*] [*Medicine*]
HIT .... Heparin Induced Thrombocytopenia [*Hematology*] (DAVI)
HIT .... Heuristic Ideation Technique [*A procedure for generating ideas or
                 solutions to a problem by analyzing a series of generalizations*]
                 (WDMC)
HIT .... Hibernation Induction Trigger [*Biochemistry*]
HIT .... High Incidence Target [*Crime computer*]
HIT .... High Intensity Tutoring (EDAC)
HIT .... High-Interest Tracker (MCD)
HIT .... High Interest Tracks
HIT .... High-Isolation Transformer (IEEE)
HIT .... High Italian Technology [*Automotive engineering*]
HIT .... High-Level Interprocessor Transfer (DGA)
HIT .... High Torque [*Engineering*] (IAA)
HIT .... Histamine Inhalation Test [*Immunology*]
HIT .... Hitachi Ltd. [*NYSE symbol*] (SPSG)
HIT .... Hitachi,Ltd ADR [*NYSE symbol*] (TTSB)
Hit. .... Hittite (BJA)
HIT .... Holtzman Inkblot Test [*Psychology*]
HIT .... Homing Interceptor Technology [*Navigation*] (IEEE)
HIT .... Housing Investment Trust [*AFL-CIO*]
HIT .... Houston International Teleport [*Houston, TX*] [*Telecommunications*]
                 (TSSD)
HIT .... Hughes Improved Terminal [*Aviation*] (MCD)
HIT .... Hughes, Induced Turbulence
HIT .... Hunter Institute of Technology [*Australia*]
HIT .... Hypersonic Interference Technique
HIT .... Hypertrophic Infiltrative Tendinitis [*Medicine*] (MAE)
HIT .... Hypervelocity Impulse Tunnel (MCD)
HITA .... Hamper Industry Trade Association [*British*] (DBA)
HITAB .... High-Altitude Target and Background [*Program*] (MUGU)

HITAC .... Hitachi Computer (DIT)
HITAC .... Hitachi Computer Services (NITA)
Hitachi.......... Hitachi Ltd. [*Associated Press*] (SAG)
HITADS .... Helmet Integrated Tracking and Display System (MCD)
HITAHR .... Hawaii Institute of Tropical Agriculture and Human Resources [*University of Hawaii*] [*Research center*] (RCD)
HIT and MISS... Hitler and Mussolini [*Slang*] (DSUE)
HI/TC .... Half Inch Tape Cartridge [*Pressure group*] (NITA)
Hitch Pr & Proc... Hitch's Practice and Procedure in the Probate Court of Massachusetts [*A publication*] (DLA)
HiTcPhr....... Hi Tech Pharmacal Co. [*Associated Press*] (SAG)
HITEC.......... Health Information Technologies and Education Center [*University of Texas Health Science Center*] [*Houston, TX*] [*Computer science*]
HITEC.......... Highway Innovation Technology
HITECC .... Higher Introductory Technology and Engineering Conversion Courses [*Education*] [*British*]
HI TECH ...... High Technology (WDAA)
HI-TEMP ...... High Temperature (WDAA)
Hi Ten .... High Tensile
HITF .... Health Insurance Trust Fund
HitFd........... Hibernia Foods PLC [*Associated Press*] (SAG)
HITI .... High Integrity Trip Initiator (PDAA)
HITK........... Hi-Tech Pharmacal [*NASDAQ symbol*] (TTSB)
HITK........... Hi Tech Pharmacal Co. [*NASDAQ symbol*] (SAG)
HITL .... Hardware-in-the-Loop
HITLS.......... Hardware in the Loop Simulation [*Computer science*] (MCD)
HITMORE..... Helicopter Installed Television Monitor and Recorder (MCD)
HITMP .... Highest Temperature [*NWS*] (FAAC)
Hitox........... Hitox Corporation of America [*Associated Press*] (SAG)
HITP........... High-Ignition-Temperature Propellant
HITPRO........ Hit Probability [*Military*] (MCD)
HITP-SEAP... High-Ignition-Temperature Propellants Self-Extinguishing at Atmospheric Pressure [*Cartridge*] (RDA)
HITS .... Handbook of Information Technology Standards [*A publication*]
HITS .... HAWK [*Homing All the Way Killer*] Institutional Training System [*Military*] (RDA)
HITS .... Hercules Integrated Telecommunications System [*Telecommunications*]
HITS .... High Income Trust Securities [*Drexel Burnham Lambert, Inc.*]
HITS .... High-Rate Multiplexer Input/Output Test System (NASA)
HITS .... High-Speed Integrated Test System
HITS .... Hobbyist's Interchange Tape Standard [*Data recording*]
HITS .... Holloman Infrared Target Simulator (OA)
HITS .... Home Information Technology Study [*Department of Education*] (GFGA)
HITT............ Hittite
Hitt Cod .... Hittell's California Codes [*A publication*] (DLA)
Hittell's Laws... Hittell's California General Laws [*A publication*] (DLA)
HITTS........... Heparin-Induced Thrombosis-Thrombocytopenia Syndrome [*Medicine*] (DMAA)
HITWG .... Hole In The Wall Gang [*A sleep-away camp for kids with life-threatening illnesses*] (PCM)
hiu .... Hawaii [*MARC country of publication code Library of Congress*] (LCCP)
HIU .... Headseat Interface Unit (MCD)
HIU .... High Interest Unit [*Navy*] (ANA)
Hi-U .... High-Usage [*Telecommunications*]
HIU .... Higuerote [*Venezuela*] [*Airport symbol*] (AD)
HIU .... Homing Instrumentation Unit (MCD)
HIU .... Host Interface Unit
HIU .... Hyperplasia Interstitialis Uteri [*Medicine*] (DMAA)
HIUS .... Hispanic Institute in the United States [*Later, HI*] (EA)
HIV............. Helium Isolation Valve [*NASA*] (NASA)
HIV............. History Institute Victoria [*Australia*]
HIV............. Human Immunodeficiency Virus
HIV-1 PR ...... Human Immunodeficiency Virus-1 Protease [*An enzyme*]
HIVAC .... High-Value Accounting Control
HIVAC .... High-Value Asset Control
HIVAC .... Human Immunodeficiency Virus Vaccine [*Medicine*]
HI-VALU....... High-Priority Air Force Contract [*Generally in missile field*] (AAGC)
HIVAN .... Human Immunodeficiency Virus-Associated Nephropathy [*Medicine*] (DMAA)
HIVAP .... High Velocity Armor-Piercing Projectile (SAA)
HIVD .... Herniated Intervertebral Disc [*Medicine*] (DAVI)
HIVE........... High Integrity Voting Equipment (PDAA)
HIVES .... High-Volume Electrostatic Sampler (MCD)
HIVIES .... Human Immunodeficiency Virus Information Exchange and Support Group (EA)
HIVIG .... Human Immunodeficiency Virus Immunoglobulin [*Medicine*]
HiVit .... High Vitamin [*Pharmacology*] (DAVI)
hi-vol .... High-Volume Air Sampler [*Environmental science*] (FFDE)
HIVOS......... High-Vacuum Orbital Simulator
HIVOS......... Humanistisch Institut voor Ontwikkelings Samenwerking [*Humanistic Institute for Co-Operation with Developing Countries*] [*Hague, Netherlands*] (EAIO)
HIV-SF .... HIV-Suppressive Factors [*Medicine*]
HIW............ Highwoods Properties [*NYSE symbol*] (TTSB)
HIW............ Highwoods Properties, Inc. [*NYSE symbol*] (SAG)
HIWAS......... Hazardous Inflight Weather Advisory Service [*Aviation*] (FAAC)
HIWAY .... Highway [*Commonly used*] (OPSA)
HIWD.......... Highwood Resources Ltd. [*NASDAQ symbol*] (NQ)
HIWDF .... Highwood Res Ltd [*NASDAQ symbol*] (TTSB)
HIWRP .... Hoover Institution on War, Revolution, and Peace (EA)
HIWSC........ Health Industry Wage and Salary Committee [*Terminated, 1974*] (EGAO)

HIWSD........ Handbook of Instructions for Weapon Systems Designers
HIWY .... Highway [*Commonly used*] (OPSA)
HIX............ Heat-Inactivated Muscle Extract
HIX............ Helix Systems Ltd. [*Vancouver Stock Exchange symbol*]
HIX............ Hopkinsville, KY [*Location identifier FAA*] (FAAL)
HIXAT .... Highest Temperature Exceeded for All Time [*NWS*] (FAAC)
HIXFM .... Highest Temperature Exceeded for the Month [*NWS*] (FAAC)
HIXSE .... Highest Temperature Exceeded so Early [*NWS*] (FAAC)
HIXSL .... Highest Temperature Exceeded so Late [*NWS*] (FAAC)
HIY............ Hampshire Imperial Yeomanry [*British military*] (DMA)
HIY............ Hertfordshire Imperial Yeomanry [*British military*] (DMA)
HIY............ Holiday Inn of Yonkers (EA)
HiYdPl .... High Yield Plus Fund [*Associated Press*] (SAG)
HiYld .... High Yield Income Fund [*Associated Press*] (SAG)
HIZA........... Informationsdienst-AUSTAUSCH [*Information Service-EXCHANGE*] [*NOMOS Datapool Database*] (IID)
HJ .... Air-Cushion Vehicle built by Hoverjak [*England*] [*Usually used in combination with numerals*]
HJ .... Air-Cushion Vehicle built by Hoverjet [*Usually used in combination with n umerals*] [*Canada*]
HJ .... Halt and Jump [*Computer science*] (BUR)
HJ .... Heilige Johannes [*Saint John*] [*Freemasonry*] [*German*]
HJ .... Hepatojugular [*Reflex*] [*Medicine*]
HJ .... Hermanas Josefinas (TOCD)
HJ .... Heterojunction [*Electronics*]
HJ .... Hic Jacet [*Here Lies*] [*Latin*]
HJ .... High Jump
HJ .... Hinge Jaw (MSA)
HJ .... Holt-Jackson [*Commercial firm British*]
HJ .... Honest John [*A type of short range, unguided Army rocket*]
HJ .... Hose Jacket (KSC)
HJ .... Howell-Jolly [*Bodies*] [*Hematology*]
HJ .... Station Open from Sunrise to Sunset [*ITU designation*] (CET)
HJ .... Sunrise to Sunset [*ICAO*] (FAAC)
HJA .... Air Haiti [*ICAO designator*] (FAAC)
HJAS .... Harry James Appreciation Society (EAIO)
HJAS .... Harvard Journal of Asiatic Studies [*A publication*] (BRI)
HJB .... Howell-Jolly Bodies [*Hematology*] (DAVI)
HJB .... Hydrodynamic Journal Bearing
HJBT .... Heterojunction Bipolar Transistor (MCD)
HJC .... Hagerstown Junior College [*Maryland*]
HJC .... Hansoms of John Clayton [*An association*] (EA)
HJC .... Harcum Junior College [*Pennsylvania*]
HJC .... Heathrow Jet Charter Ltd. [*British ICAO designator*] (FAAC)
HJC .... Hibbing Junior College [*Later, Hibbing Community College*] [*Minnesota*]
HJC .... Highland Junior College [*Kansas*]
HJC .... Hinds Junior College [*Raymond, MS*]
HJC .... Holmes Junior College [*Goodman, MS*]
HJC .... Holyoke Junior College [*Later, Holyoke Community College*] [*Massachusetts*]
HJC .... Hutchinson Junior College [*Kansas*]
HJCC .... Honolulu Japanese Chamber of Commerce (EA)
HJD .... Heliocentric Julian Day [*Astronomy*]
HJD .... Heterojunction Device
HJD .... Las Hermanas de Juan Diego (TOCD)
HJD .... Los Hermanos de Juan Diego (TOCD)
HJE .... Hot Jet Exhaust
HJH .... Hebron, NE [*Location identifier FAA*] (FAAL)
HJI .... Hachtmann, J. I., Newark NJ [*STAC*]
HJJ .... Hachijojima [*Japan*] [*Seismograph station code, US Geological Survey*] (SEIS)
HJL .... Hamlin Jet Ltd. [*British ICAO designator*] (FAAC)
HJL .... Honest John Launcher [*See also HJ*] [*Army*]
HJM .... Akron-Canton, OH [*Location identifier FAA*] (FAAL)
HJM .... H. J. Mulliner [*British coachbuilder*]
HJM .... Hot Jet Model
H Joint Res... House Joint Resolution (AAGC)
HJP .... Hand Jewel Pusher
HJP .... Heat Jacketed Pump
HJPP.......... Heat Jacketed Proportioning Pump
HJR .... Hepatojugular Reflex [*Medicine*]
HJR .... Honest John Rocket [*See also HJ*] [*Army*]
HJR .... House Joint Resolution
HJR .... Khajuraho [*India*] [*Airport symbol*] (OAG)
HJ Res........ House Joint Resolution
HJS .... Hebrew Jewellers' Society [*A union*] [*British*]
HJS .... Helijet [*Spain ICAO designator*] (FAAC)
HJS .... Helsingen Juutalainen Seurakunta [*Finland*] [*A publication*] (BJA)
HJS .... Hic Jacet Sepultus [*Here Lies Buried*] [*Latin*]
HJSC.......... Hospital Junior Staff Committee [*British*] (DI)
HJT .... Head Joint [*Technical drawings*]
HK .... Handelskammer [*Chamber of Commerce*] [*German*]
HK .... Handkommentar zum Alten Testament [*Goettingen*] [*A publication*] (BJA)
H-K .... Hands to Knee [*Medicine*]
HK .... Hank [*Cotton*] (ROG)
HK .... Hauptwerk [*Masterpiece*] [*German*]
HK .... Hawker De Havilland Australia Pty. Ltd., Kaman Aircraft Corp. [*ICAO aircraft manufacturer identifier*] (ICAO)
HK .... Heater Kit
HK .... Heat Killed [*Medicine*] (MAE)
HK .... Heckler and Koch [*Machine gun*] (MCD)
H-K .... Heel to Knee
HK .... Heel-to-Knee (DMAA)

HK............ Hevra Kaddisha (BJA)
HK............ Hexokinase [*An enzyme*]
HK............ High-Priority Key [*IRS*]
HK............ Hoeheres Kommando [*Higher Command*] [*German military - World War II*]
HK............ Homoserine Kinase [*An enzyme*]
hk .... Hong Kong [*MARC country of publication code Library of Congress*] (LCCP)
HK............ Hong Kong [*ANSI two-letter standard code*] (CNC)
HK............ Hook
HK............ Hotkey [*Computer science*] (PCM)
HK............ Housekeeping
HK............ House of Keys [*Isle Of Man*]
Hk .... Hulk [*Nautical charts*]
HK............ Human Kidney
H-K .... Hunter-Killer [*Missile*] (MUGU)
H-K .... Hypoascorbemia-Kwashiorkor [*Orthomolecular medicine*]
H-K .... Knoop Hardness Number
HK............ People's Liberation [*Revolutionary group*] [*Turkey*]
HK............ South Pacific Island Airways [*ICAO designator*] (AD)
HKA .... Blytheville, AR [*Location identifier FAA*] (FAAL)
HKA .... Hand Knitting Association (EA)
HKA .... Hong Kong Airways Ltd.
HKA .... Superior Aviation, Inc. [*ICAO designator*] (FAAC)
HKAB .... Hong Kong Association of Banks (ECON)
HKAFO ...... Hip-Knee-Ankle-Foot Orthosis [*Medicine*]
HKAM .... Amboseli [*Kenya*] [*ICAO location identifier*] (ICLI)
HKamCF ...... Canada-France-Hawaii Telescope Corp. Kamuela, HI [*Library symbol*] [*Library of Congress*] (LCLS)
HKAO .... Hip-Knee-Ankle Orthosis [*Medicine*]
HkAT .... Handkommentar zum Alten Testament [*Goettingen*] [*A publication*] (BJA)
HKB .... Hard Kernel Bunch (IAA)
HKB .... Hepatitis Knowledge Base (NITA)
HKBA .... Busia [*Kenya*] [*ICAO location identifier*] (ICLI)
HKBA .... Hong Kong Bank Australia
HKBC .... Hong Kong Bank of Canada
HKBR .... Bura [*Kenya*] [*ICAO location identifier*] (ICLI)
HKBU .... Bungoma [*Kenya*] [*ICAO location identifier*] (ICLI)
HKC .... Henkel Corp., Minneapolis, MN [*OCLC symbol*] (OCLC)
HKC .... Hong Kong [*Seismograph station code, US Geological Survey*] (SEIS)
HKC .... Human Kidney Cell [*Medicine*] (DMAA)
HKC .... Shirley, NY [*Location identifier FAA*] (FAAL)
HKCC .... Hong Kong Cable Communications
HKCE .... Hong Kong Commodities Exchange
HKCS .... Hong Kong Chemical Society
HKD .... Hakodate [*Japan*] [*Airport symbol*] (OAG)
HKDS .... Croatian Christian Democratic Party [*Political party*]
HKEL .... Eldoret [*Kenya*] [*ICAO location identifier*] (ICLI)
HKEM .... Embu [*Kenya*] [*ICAO location identifier*] (ICLI)
HKES .... Eliye Springs [*Kenya*] [*ICAO location identifier*] (ICLI)
HKF .... Halbkettenfahrzeug [*Half-Track Vehicle*] [*German military - World War II*]
HKF .... Hancock Fabrics [*NYSE symbol*] (TTSB)
HKF .... Hancock Fabrics, Inc. [*NYSE symbol*] (SPSG)
HKF .... Handkerchief
HKF .... Middletown, OH [*Location identifier FAA*] (FAAL)
HKFE .... Hong Kong Futures Exchange
HKFG .... Kalokol [*Kenya*] [*ICAO location identifier*] (ICLI)
HKG .... Hong Kong [*Airport symbol*] (OAG)
HKG .... Hong Kong [*ANSI three-letter standard code*] (CNC)
HKG .... Hong Kong [*British Crown Colony*] [*Airport symbol*] (AD)
HKG .... Housekeeping (SSD)
HKGA .... Garissa [*Kenya*] [*ICAO location identifier*] (ICLI)
HKGS .... Church of Jesus Christ of Latter-Day Saints, Genealogical Society Library, Kaneohe Stake Branch, Kaneohe, HI [*Library symbol Library of Congress*] (LCLS)
HKGT .... Garba Tula [*Kenya*] [*ICAO location identifier*] (ICLI)
HKH .... Chicago, IL [*Location identifier FAA*] (FAAL)
HKHB .... Homa Bay [*Kenya*] [*ICAO location identifier*] (ICLI)
HKHO .... Hola [*Kenya*] [*ICAO location identifier*] (ICLI)
HKI .... Helen Keller International (EA)
HKI .... Husiki [*Japan*] [*Seismograph station code, US Geological Survey*] (SEIS)
HKIBOR ...... Hong Kong Inter-Bank Offered Rate (MHDW)
HKIS .... Isiolo [*Kenya*] [*ICAO location identifier*] (ICLI)
HKJ .... Hashemite Kingdom of Jordan (BARN)
HKK .... Hokitika [*New Zealand*] [*Airport symbol*] (OAG)
HKKA .... Kabarak [*Kenya*] [*ICAO location identifier*] (ICLI)
HKKE .... Keekorok [*Kenya*] [*ICAO location identifier*] (ICLI)
HKKG .... Kakamega [*Kenya*] [*ICAO location identifier*] (ICLI)
HKKI .... Kisumu [*Kenya*] [*ICAO location identifier*] (ICLI)
HKKK .... Helsingin Kauppakorkeakoulun Kirjasto [*Helsinki School of Economics Library*] [*Finland*] [*Information service or system*] (IID)
HKKL .... Kilaguni [*Kenya*] [*ICAO location identifier*] (ICLI)
HKKR .... Kericho [*Kenya*] [*ICAO location identifier*] (ICLI)
HKKS .... Kisii [*Kenya*] [*ICAO location identifier*] (ICLI)
HKKT .... Kitale [*Kenya*] [*ICAO location identifier*] (ICLI)
HKL .... Haleakala [*Hawaii*] [*Seismograph station code, US Geological Survey*] (SEIS)
HKL .... Hoyrekvinners Landsforbund [*Women's Organization of the Conservative Party*] [*Norway Political party*] (EAIO)
HKLG .... Lokitaung [*Kenya*] [*ICAO location identifier*] (ICLI)

HKLJ .... Hong Kong Law Journal [*A publication*] (DLA)
HKLK .... Lokichoggio [*Kenya*] [*ICAO location identifier*] (ICLI)
HKLM .... Heat-Killed Listeria Monocytogene [*Medicine*] (MAE)
HKLO .... Lodwar [*Kenya*] [*ICAO location identifier*] (ICLI)
HKLR .... Hong Kong Law Reports [*A publication*] (DLA)
HKLT .... Loitokitok [*Kenya*] [*ICAO location identifier*] (ICLI)
HKLU .... Lamu [*Kenya*] [*ICAO location identifier*] (ICLI)
HKLY .... Loyengalani [*Kenya*] [*ICAO location identifier*] (ICLI)
HKM .... Hypermetropic Keratomileusis [*Ophthalmology*]
HKM .... Hypervelocity Kill Mechanism [*Air Force*]
HKM .... Morgan Stanley Group, Inc. [*AMEX symbol*] (SAG)
HKMA .... Hawick Knitwear Manufacturers Association [*British*] (DBA)
HKMA .... Hong Kong Monetary Authority [*Banking*]
HKMB .... Mandera [*Kenya*] [*ICAO location identifier*] (ICLI)
HKMB .... Marsabit [*Kenya*] [*ICAO location identifier*] (ICLI)
HKMG .... Magadi [*Kenya*] [*ICAO location identifier*] (ICLI)
HKMI .... Maralal [*Kenya*] [*ICAO location identifier*] (ICLI)
HKMK .... Mulika [*Kenya*] [*ICAO location identifier*] (ICLI)
HKML .... Malindi [*Kenya*] [*ICAO location identifier*] (ICLI)
HKMO .... Mombasa/Moi International [*Kenya*] [*ICAO location identifier*] (ICLI)
HKMR .... Mackinnon Road [*Kenya*] [*ICAO location identifier*] (ICLI)
HKMSC ...... Hong Kong Military Service Corps [*British military*] (DMA)
HKMU .... Makindu [*Kenya*] [*ICAO location identifier*] (ICLI)
HKMY .... Moyale [*Kenya*] [*ICAO location identifier*] (ICLI)
HKN .... Harken Technologies, Inc. [*Vancouver Stock Exchange symbol*]
HKN .... Hoskins [*Papua New Guinea*] [*Airport symbol*] (OAG)
HKN .... Jim Hankins Air Service, Inc. [*FAA designator*] (FAAC)
HKNC .... Nairobi/Jomo Kenyatta International [*Kenya*] [*ICAO location identifier*] (ICLI)
HKNC .... Nairobi [*Kenya*] [*ICAO location identifier*] (ICLI)
HKNCDBYA.... Helen Keller National Center for Deaf-Blind Youths and Adults (EA)
HKNI .... Nyeri [*Kenya*] [*ICAO location identifier*] (ICLI)
HKNK .... Nakuru [*Kenya*] [*ICAO location identifier*] (ICLI)
HKNO .... Narok [*Kenya*] [*ICAO location identifier*] (ICLI)
HKNT .... Handkommentar zum Neuen Testament [*A publication*] (BJA)
HKNV .... Naivasha [*Kenya*] [*ICAO location identifier*] (ICLI)
HKNW .... Nairobi/Wilson [*Kenya*] [*ICAO location identifier*] (ICLI)
HKNY .... Nanyuki [*Kenya*] [*ICAO location identifier*] (ICLI)
HKO .... Hip-Knee Orthosis [*Medicine*]
HKP .... Hidden Lake [*Pennsylvania*] [*Seismograph station code, US Geological Survey Closed*] (SEIS)
HKP .... Hookup (MSA)
HKP .... Kaanapali [*Hawaii*] [*Airport symbol*] (OAG)
HKR .... Hallmark Resources [*Vancouver Stock Exchange symbol*]
HKR .... Hong Kong Regiment [*British military*] (DMA)
HKR .... Hooker [*Ship's rigging*] (ROG)
HKR .... Hydrolytic Kinetic Resolution
HKRE .... Nairobi/Eastleigh [*Kenya*] [*ICAO location identifier*] (ICLI)
HKS .... Heel-Knee-Shin [*Test*] [*Neurology*] (DAVI)
HKS .... Helikopter Service AS [*Norway ICAO designator*] (FAAC)
HKS .... Hyperkinesis Syndrome [*Medicine*] (DMAA)
HKS .... Jackson, MS [*Location identifier FAA*] (FAAL)
HKSA .... East African School of Aviation [*Kenya*] [*ICAO location identifier*] (ICLI)
HKSB .... Samburu [*Kenya*] [*ICAO location identifier*] (ICLI)
HKSC .... Hong Kong Study Circle (EA)
HKSRA ...... Hong Kong and Singapore Royal Artillery [*British military*] (DMA)
HKSRGA ...... Hong Kong and Singapore Royal Garrison Artillery [*British military*] (DMA)
HKSU .... Hong Kong Seamen's Union
HKT .... Hiram, King of Tyre [*Freemasonry*]
HKT .... Hockley [*Texas*] [*Seismograph station code, US Geological Survey*] (SEIS)
HKT .... Hollow Kathode Tube
HKT .... Hong Kong Telecom ADR [*NYSE symbol*] (TTSB)
HKT .... Hong Kong Telecommunications Ltd. [*NYSE symbol*] (CTT)
HKT .... Hot Kathode Tube
HKT .... Phuket [*Thailand*] [*Airport symbol*] (OAG)
HKTAG ...... Hong Kong Trade Advisory Group [*British Overseas Trade Board*] (DS)
HK Tel ...... Hong Kong Telecommunications Ltd. [*Associated Press*] (SAG)
HKU .... Hong Kong University
HkU .... University of Hong Kong, Hong Kong, Hong Kong [*UK*] [*Library symbol Library of Congress*] (LCLS)
HKUST ...... Hong Kong University of Science and Technology (ECON)
HKVC .... Hong Kong Volunteer Corps [*British military*] (DMA)
HKVO .... Voi [*Kenya*] [*ICAO location identifier*] (ICLI)
HKWJ .... Wajir [*Kenya*] [*ICAO location identifier*] (ICLI)
HKX .... Ellington Air Force Base, TX [*Location identifier FAA*] (FAAL)
HKY .... Canstar Sports, Inc. [*Toronto Stock Exchange symbol*]
HKY .... Hickory [*North Carolina*] [*Airport symbol*] (OAG)
HKYNA ...... Hydroxykynurenic Acid [*Organic chemistry*]
HKZ .... Minneapolis, MN [*Location identifier FAA*] (FAAL)
HL............ Das Heilige Land (BJA)
HL............ Hairline (DAVI)
HL............ Half Length [*Photography*] (DGA)
HL............ Half-Life [*of radioactive elements*]
HL............ Half Line [*Illustration*] (DGA)
hl .... Halite [*CIPW classification*] [*Geology*]
HL............ Hallux Limitus [*Podiatry*] (DAVI)
HL............ HALON [*Halogenated Hydrocarbon*] System [*NFPA pre-fire planning symbol*] (NFPA)
HL............ Haloperidol (DAVI)
HL............ Hand Lantern (AAG)
HL............ Hard Labor

HL............... Hardline (MCD)
HL............... Harelip
HL............... Hariana Lancers [*British military*] (DMA)
HL............... Haul (MSA)
HL............... Hawser Laid
HL............... Header Label [*Computer science*] (IAA)
HL............... Headlamp [*Automotive engineering*]
HL............... Head Linesman [*Football*]
HL............... Headmaster-Lieutenant [*Navy British*]
HL............... Hearing Level
HL............... Hearing Loss
HL............... Heavy Lift
HL............... Heavy Loading (IAA)
HL............... Hebrew Leader (BJA)
HL............... Hebrew Letters (BJA)
HL............... Hebrew Literature (BJA)
HL............... Hecla Mining [*NYSE symbol*] (TTSB)
HL............... Hecla Mining Co. [*NYSE symbol*] (SPSG)
HL............... Hectoliter (GPO)
HL............... Heel Line (MSA)
HL............... Height-Length
HL............... Height Loss [*Aviation*] (DA)
HL............... Heilig [*Holy, Saint*] [*German*]
HL............... Heir-at-Law
HL............... Helium Level
HL............... Heparin Lock [*Pharmacology*] (DAVI)
HL............... Herpetologists' League (EA)
HL............... Hickman Line [*Cardiology*] (DAVI)
HL............... High Level
H/L............... Highlight (DGA)
HL............... Highline (MSA)
H/L............... High or Low
HL............... Hill
HL............... Hill
HL............... Hinge Line [*Technical drawings*]
HL............... Histiocytic Lymphoma [*Oncology*]
HL............... Histocompatibility Locus [*Immunology*]
HL............... Hittite Laws (BJA)
HL............... Hoc Loco [*In This Place*] [*Latin*]
HL............... Hodges-Lehmann Estimator [*Statistics*]
HL............... Hodgkin's Lymphoma [*Medicine*]
HL............... Holiday Airlines (MHDW)
HL............... Home Lines [*Steamship*] (MHDW)
HL............... Honors List (ADA)
HL............... Horizontal Landing (KSC)
HL............... Horizontal Line
HL............... Host Language
HL............... Hot Line [*Alert system*] (AAG)
HL............... House of Lords [*British*]
HL............... House of Lords Cases (Clark) [*England*] [*A publication*] (DLA)
HL............... Howard League [*An association*] (EAIO)
HL............... Huius Loci [*Of This Place*] [*Latin*]
HL............... Human Lymphoid [*Immunology*]
HL............... Hyborean Legion (EA)
HL............... Hydrodynamics Laboratory [*MIT*] (MCD)
HL............... Hydrogen Line (MCD)
HL............... Hydrology Laboratory [*Department of Agriculture*] [*Information service or system*] (IID)
H/L............... Hydrophile/Lipophile [*Followed by a number*]
HL............... Hygienic Laboratory [*US*]
HL............... Hypermetropia, Latent [*Ophthalmology*]
HI............... Hypermetropia, Latent [*Medicine*] (DMAA)
HL............... Hyperopia Latent [*Ophthalmology*] (DAVI)
HL............... Hypertrichosis Lanuginosa [*Medicine*]
HL............... Law Reports, House of Lords, English and Irish Appeals [*1866-75*] [*A publication*] (DLA)
HL............... Mustard/Lewisite Mix [*Poisonous gas*] [*Army*]
HL............... VEB Deutsche Hydrierwerk, Rodleben [*East Germany*] [*Research code symbol*]
HLA............... Hall's Lagoon [*Australia Seismograph station code, US Geological Survey Closed*] (SEIS)
HLA............... Hat Leather Association (EA)
HLA............... Heavy-Lift Airship (MCD)
HLA............... Heavylift Cargo Airlines Ltd. [*British ICAO designator*] (FAAC)
HLA............... Helicopter Loggers Association (EA)
HLA............... Highlander Income Fund [*AMEX symbol*] (TTSB)
HLA............... Highlander Income Fund, Inc. [*AMEX symbol*] (SAG)
HLA............... High-Level Analog (MCD)
HLA............... High Level Architecture [*Department of Defense*]
HLA............... High Low Alarm [*Electronics*] (ECII)
HLA............... High-Speed Line Adapter (MHDI)
HLA............... Histocompatibility Locus Antigens [*System*] [*Immunology*]
HLA............... Historical Labor Applications [*Military*] (AFIT)
HLA............... Homologous Leucocytic Antibodies
HLA............... Horizontal Line Array (MCD)
HLA............... Human Leucocyte Antigen [*Immunology*]
HL-A............... Human Leukocyte- [*or Lymphocyte-*] Antigen [*System for recognizing foreign tissue*] [*Immunology*]
HLA............... Human Life Amendment
HLA............... Hydraulic Lash Adjuster [*Automotive engine design*]
HLA............... Hypoplastic Left Atrium [*Cardiology*] (DAVI)
HLaB............... Brigham Young University, Hawaii Campus, Laie, HI [*Library symbol Library of Congress*] (LCLS)
HLAC............... Host Link Adapter Card [*Ideacomm Gateway*]
HLAD............... Hearing-Lookout Assist Device [*Navigation*] (OA)

HLAD............... High-Level Air Defence [*Military British*]
HLAD............... Horse-Liver Alcohol Dehydrogenase [*Also, HLADH, HLALD*] [*An enzyme*]
HLADH............... Horse-Liver Alcohol Dehydrogenase [*Also, HLAD, HLALD*] [*An enzyme*]
HLA/DZ............... Helicopter Landing Area/Drop Zone [*Military*] (MCD)
HLA/DZS............... Helicopter Landing Area/Drop Zone Study [*Military*] (MCD)
HLAF............... High-Level Arithmetic Function
HLaGS............... Church of Jesus Christ of Latter-Day Saints, Genealogical Society Library, Laie Branch, Laie, HI [*Library symbol Library of Congress*] (LCLS)
HLAHWG............... High Level Ad Hoc Working Group [*NATO*] (NATG)
HLAIS............... High-Level Analog Input Subsystem [*Computer science*] (MHDI)
HLAIS............... High Level Analog Input System (NITA)
HLAL............... High-Level Assembly Language (MCD)
HLALD............... Horse-Liver Alcohol Dehydrogenase [*Also, HLAD, HLADH*] [*An enzyme*]
HL-A LD............... Human Lymphocyte-Antigen Lymphocyte Defined [*Immunology*]
H-LAND............... Headland (ADA)
HL & T............... Hunter's Landlord and Tenant [*Scotland*] [*A publication*] (DLA)
HLAS............... Handbook of Latin American Studies
HLAS............... Hot Line Alert System
HLASD............... Hand-Link Arm Safe Device
HL-A SD............... Human Lymphocyte-Antigen Serologically Defined [*Immunology*]
HLAV............... Horseradish Latent Virus [*Plant pathology*]
HLB............... Batesville, IN [*Location identifier FAA*] (FAAL)
HLB............... Federal Home Loan Bank Board, Accounts Payable, Washington, DC [*OCLC symbol*] (OCLC)
HLB............... High-Line Airways, Inc. [*Canada ICAO designator*] (FAAC)
HLB............... Hydrophile-Lipophile Balance [*Surfactant technology*]
HLB............... Hypotonic Lysis Buffer [*Analytical biochemistry*]
HLBB............... Home Loan Bank Board [*Federal agency*] (GPO)
HLBI............... Human Lymphoblastoid Interferon [*Antineoplastic drug*]
HLBR............... Heel Breaster
HLBRD............... Halberd
HLC............... HAWK [*Homing All the Way Killer*] Logistics Complex (MCD)
HLC............... Headmaster Lieutenant-Commander [*Navy British*]
HLC............... Heat Loss Center (DMAA)
HLC............... Heavy/Light Corps (MCD)
HLC............... Helicap [*France ICAO designator*] (FAAC)
HLC............... High-Level Cell [*Nuclear energy*] (NRCH)
HLC............... High-Level Center (IAA)
HLC............... High-Level Compiler (IAA)
HLC............... Hill City, KS [*Location identifier FAA*] (FAAL)
HLC............... Hispanic Literature Criticism [*A publication*]
HLC............... Homeowner's Land Corp. [*Federal agency formed in 1932*] [*Investment term*]
HLC............... Homogenized Leaf Curing [*Tobacco industry*]
HLC............... House of Lords Cases (Clark) [*England*] [*A publication*] (DLA)
HLC............... Human Lactation Center (EA)
HLC............... Human Life Center (EA)
HLCADS............... High-Level Container Airdrop System [*Army*] (RDA)
HL Cas............... House of Lords Cases (Clark) [*England*] [*A publication*] (DLA)
HL Cas (Eng)... House of Lords Cases [*A publication*] (DLA)
HLC-ATC............... Heavy-Lift Helicopter Advanced Technology Component [*Program*] [*Army*] (RDA)
HLCC............... Home-Laundering Care Code [*British*] (DI)
HLCC............... Home-Laundering Consultative Council [*British*] (DI)
HLCF............... Hardened Launch Control Facility (MUGU)
HLCF............... Heat-Labile Citrororum Factor [*Biochemistry*]
HLCF............... Holy Land Conservation Fund (EA)
HLCL............... Helical
HLCM............... Holy Land Christian Mission (EA)
HLCMI............... Holy Land Christian Mission International [*Later, HLCM*] (EA)
HLCPS............... Helical Compression
HLCPTR............... Helicopter (MSA)
HLCPTR............... Helicopter
HLCS............... Heat Limiter Control Switch
HLCS............... High-Level Compaction Station [*Nuclear energy*] (NRCH)
HLCS............... High-Level Control Station [*Hazardous materials control*]
HLCV............... Hot Leg Check Valve [*Nuclear energy*] (NRCH)
HLD............... Doctor of Humane Letters
HLD............... Hailar [*China*] [*Airport symbol*] (OAG)
HL-D............... Haloperidol Decanoate [*Pharmacology*] (DAVI)
HLD............... Harold's Stores [*AMEX symbol*] (TTSB)
HLD............... Harold's Stores, Inc. [*AMEX symbol*] (SPSG)
HLD............... Helium Leak Detector
HLD............... Herniated Lumbar Disc [*Medicine*]
hld............... Hold (WDMC)
HLD............... Hold
HLD............... Holdings [*Online database field identifier*]
HLD............... Holiday Airlines Havacilik Ve Turizm Sanayi Ve Ticaret, AG [*Turkey*] [*FAA designator*] (FAAC)
HLD............... Hollywood Investments [*Vancouver Stock Exchange symbol*]
HLD............... Home Laundry Detergent
HLD............... Hypersensitivity Lung Disease [*Medicine*]
HLDA............... Hold Acknowledge [*Computer science*]
HLDC............... High-Level Data Link Control (MCD)
HLDDN............... Holddown
HLDG............... Holding (MSA)
HLDH............... Heat-Stable Lactic Dehydrogenase [*Clinical chemistry*]
HLDI............... Highway Loss Data Institute (EA)
HLDLC............... High-Level Data Link Control [*Computer science*] (DOM)
HLDN............... Holddown (MSA)
HLDNG............... Holding

HLDR .... Holder
HLDS .... Hydrogen Leak Detection System (NASA)
HLDS .... Vermont-New Hampshire-New York Hospital Libraries [Library network]
HLDTL .... High Level Data Transistor Logic (NITA)
HLDTL .... High-Level Diode Transistor Logic [Computer science] (MHDI)
HLDY .... Holiday
HldyRV .... Holiday RV Superstores, Inc. [Associated Press] (SAG)
HLE .... First Air [British ICAO designator] (FAAC)
HLE .... Hailey, ID [Location identifier FAA] (FAAL)
HLE .... Hale Resources Ltd. [Toronto Stock Exchange symbol]
HLE .... Halle [German Democratic Republic] [Seismograph station code, US Geological Survey] (SEIS)
HLE .... Hazleton Laboratories Europe Ltd. [British] (IRUK)
HLE .... High-Low-Junction Emitter (PDAA)
HLE .... Human Leucocyte Elastase [An enzyme]
HLE .... Hydrogen Line Emission
HLEG .... Hydrolysate Lactalbumin Earle's Glucose [Medicine] (DMAA)
HLEXT .... Helical Extension
HLF .... Hall's Legal Forms [A publication] (DLA)
HLF .... Hapag Lloyd Fluggesellschaft GmbH [Germany ICAO designator] (FAAC)
HLF .... Heart and Lung Foundation [Defunct] (EA)
HLF .... Heat-Labile Factor
HLF .... Heller Financial [NYSE symbol] (SPSG)
HLF .... Hepatic Leukaemia Factor [Medicine]
HLF .... Hidden Lake Formation [Geology]
HLF .... High Loss Ferrite
HLF .... Holistic Life Foundation [Later, Feathered Pipe Foundation] (EA)
HLF .... Horizontal Line Frequency
HLF .... House Leadership Fund (EA)
HLF .... Hultsfred [Sweden] [Airport symbol] (OAG)
HLF .... Human Lactoferrin [Biochemistry]
HLF .... Human Life Foundation (EA)
HLF .... Human Lung Fluid [Medicine]
HLF .... Hyperbolic LOFAR Fix [Military] (CAAL)
HLFL .... Buattifel [Libya] [ICAO location identifier] (ICLI)
HLFM .... Half-Moon
HLFM .... High-Level Flux Monitor
HLFPrA .... Heller Finl 8.125% Sr'A' Pfd [NYSE symbol] (TTSB)
HLFT .... Holographic Lensless Fourier Transform (PDAA)
HLFTN .... Halftone (VRA)
HLG .... Dr. John W. Tintera Memorial Hypoglycemia Lay Group (EA)
HLG .... Hauling
HLG .... HAWK [Homing All the Way Killer] Logistics Group (AABC)
HLG .... Heligoland [Federal Republic of Germany] [Seismograph station code, US Geological Survey] (SEIS)
HLG .... High-Level Group [NATO]
HLG .... Historic Landscapes Group [British] (DBA)
HLG .... Hollinger, Inc. [Toronto Stock Exchange symbol Vancouver Stock Exchange symbol]
HLG .... Homing Level Gauge
HLG .... Hot Leg [Nuclear energy]
HLG .... Housing and Local Government [A publication] (DLA)
HLG .... Hybrid Lens Guide (PDAA)
HLG .... Wheeling [West Virginia] [Airport symbol] (AD)
HLGC .... Wheeling, WV [Location identifier FAA] (FAAL)
HLGC .... Hannibal-La Grange College [Missouri]
HLGL .... Giallo/Warehouse 59 E [Libya] [ICAO location identifier] (ICLI)
HLGRF .... Hollinger Inc. [NASDAQ symbol] (TTSB)
HLGS .... Hot Line Gunsight System
HLGT .... Ghat [Libya] [ICAO location identifier] (ICLI)
HLH .... Heavy-Lift Helicopter
HLH .... Helix-Loop-Helix [Genetics]
HLH .... Hertfordshire Light Horse [British military] (DMA)
HLH .... High-Level Heating [Nuclear science] (OA)
HLH .... Human Luteinizing Hormone [Endocrinology]
HLH .... Hypoplastic Left Heart [Cardiology]
HLH .... Ulanhot [China] [Airport symbol] (OAG)
HLHS .... Heavy-Lift Helicopter System
HLHS .... Hypoplastic Left-Heart Syndrome [Medicine]
HLI .... Hemolysis Inhibition [Medicine] (AAMN)
HLI .... Highland Light Infantry [Military unit] [British]
HLI .... Holly Springs, MS [Location identifier FAA] (FAAL)
HLI .... Holmium LASER Illuminator
HLI .... Host Language Interface
HLI .... Human Leukocyte Interferon [Medicine] (DMAA)
HLI .... Human Life International (EA)
HLIA .... Historic Landmarks of Irish America [A publication]
HLIC .... Highland Light Infantry of Canada [Military unit]
H/LIN .... Head Lining [Automotive engineering]
HLIT .... Harmonic Lightwaves [NASDAQ symbol] (TTSB)
HLIT .... Harmonic Lightwaves, Inc. [NASDAQ symbol] (SAG)
HLIV .... High-Level Input Voltage
HLIV .... Hot Leg Isolation Valve [Nuclear energy] (NRCH)
HLJ .... Hindu Law Journal [A publication] (DLA)
HL Jour .... House of Lords Journals [England] [A publication] (DLA)
HLK .... Haleakala [Hawaii] [Seismograph station code, US Geological Survey] (SEIS)
HLK .... Heart, Liver, Kidney [Medicine] (MAE)
HLK .... Heli-Link [Switzerland ICAO designator] (FAAC)
HLK .... Kauai Public Library Association, Linhue, HI [Library symbol Library of Congress] (LCLS)
HLK .... Salomon, Inc. [AMEX symbol] (SAG)
HLK .... Salomon Inc. 5.25% HP'ELKS' [AMEX symbol] (TTSB)

HLKF .... Kufra [Libya] [ICAO location identifier] (ICLI)
HLL .... Hallett [Antarctica] [Seismograph station code, US Geological Survey Closed] (SEIS)
HLL .... Halley Resources Ltd. [Vancouver Stock Exchange symbol]
HLL .... Hard Lunar Landing [Aerospace engineering] (IAA)
HLL .... Havelet Leasing Ltd. [British ICAO designator] (FAAC)
HLL .... Hebrew Language and Literature (BJA)
HLL .... High-Level Language [Computer science]
HLL .... High-Level Logic (IAA)
HLL .... High Liquid Level [Engineering]
HLL .... Hill [Board on Geographic Names]
HLL .... Hypoplastic Left Lung [Medicine] (DMAA)
HLLAPI .... High-Level Application Program Interface [Computer science] (PCM)
HLLAPI .... High Level Language Application Program Interface (NITA)
HLLB .... Benghazi/Benina [Libya] [ICAO location identifier] (ICLI)
HLLL .... Tripoli [Libya] [ICAO location identifier] (ICLI)
HLLMRK .... Hallmark
HLLO .... Metega [Libya] [ICAO location identifier] (ICLI)
HLLQ .... El Beida/Labraq [Libya] [ICAO location identifier] (ICLI)
HLLS .... Sebha [Libya] [ICAO location identifier] (ICLI)
HLLT .... Tripoli/International [Libya] [ICAO location identifier] (ICLI)
HLLV .... Heavy-Lift Launch Vehicle [Rocketry] (MCD)
HLLW .... High-Level Liquid Waste [Nuclear energy]
HLLW .... Hollow [Commonly used] (OPSA)
HLLWT .... High-Level Liquid Waste Tank [Nuclear energy] (NRCH)
HllywP .... Hollywood Productions, Inc. [Associated Press] (SAG)
HLM .... Hampshire Local Militia [British military] (DMA)
HLM .... Harpoon Logic Module [Missiles] (MCD)
HLM .... Helmstar Group [AMEX symbol] (SPSG)
HLM .... Helmville [Montana] [Seismograph station code, US Geological Survey Closed] (SEIS)
HLM .... Henry Louis Mencken [American author/critic]
HLM .... Heterogeneous LAN [Local Area Network] Manager (ACRL)
HLM .... High-Latitude Mode
HLM .... High-Level Meeting (DCTA)
HLM .... High-Level Mixer
HLM .... Holland, MI [Location identifier FAA] (FAAL)
HLMB .... Marsa Brega [Libya] [ICAO location identifier] (ICLI)
HLMI .... High-Load Melt Index [Plastics] [Automotive engineering]
HLML .... High-Level Microprogramming Language
HLMR .... Hunter-Leggitt Military Reservation (AABC)
HLMS .... High Latitude Monitoring Station [Marine science] (OSRA)
HLMS .... High Latitude Monitoring Station (USDC)
HLMS .... Holmes Protection Group [NASDAQ symbol] (TTSB)
HLMS .... Holmes Protection Group, Inc. [NASDAQ symbol] (SAG)
HLMT .... Helmet (NASA)
HLN .... Halton Reinsurance Co. Ltd. [Toronto Stock Exchange symbol]
HLN .... Helena [Montana] [Airport symbol] (OAG)
HLN .... Hellenic Air SA [Greece] [ICAO designator] (FAAC)
HLN .... Hualilan [Argentina] [Seismograph station code, US Geological Survey] (SEIS)
HLN .... Hyperplastic Liver Nodules [Medicine]
HLNCC .... High-Level Neutron Coincidence Counter [Nuclear energy] (NRCH)
HLND .... Highlands [Board on Geographic Names]
HLND .... Homeland Bankshares [NASDAQ symbol] (TTSB)
HLND .... Homeland Bankshares Corp. [NASDAQ symbol] (SAG)
HLNE .... Hillsboro & North Eastern Railway Co. [AAR code]
HLNF .... Ras Lanouf V 40 [Libya] [ICAO location identifier] (ICLI)
HLNFPF .... Human Life and Natural Family Planning Foundation [Defunct] (EA)
HLNG .... Headlining
HLNL .... Hydroxylysinonorleucine [Biochemistry]
HLNR .... Health Lawyers News Report [A publication] (DLA)
HLNSS .... Holiness
HLNW .... High-Level Nuclear Waste (BARN)
HLO .... High-Latitude Operation
HLO .... High-Level Override [Nuclear energy] (NRCH)
HLO .... Hi-Lo Automotive [NYSE symbol] (SPSG)
HLO .... Horizontal Lockout
HLO .... Samaritan Air Service Ltd. [Canada ICAO designator] (FAAC)
HLOA .... Heart Labs of America, Inc. [NASDAQ symbol] (SAG)
HLOAE .... Heart Labs Amer [NASDAQ symbol] (TTSB)
HLON .... Hon [Libya] [ICAO location identifier] (ICLI)
HLOV .... High-Level Output Voltage
HLOWE .... Heart Labs Amer Wrrt [NASDAQ symbol] (TTSB)
H/LP .... Headlamp [Automotive engineering]
HLP .... Heavy-Lift Pontoon
HLP .... Heavy-Lift Preposition [Ship] (DOMA)
HLP .... Hel [Poland] [Geomagnetic observatory code]
HLP .... Helper
HLP .... Help File [Computer science]
HLP .... Hilina Pali [Hawaii] [Seismograph station code, US Geological Survey] (SEIS)
HLP .... Home and Law Publishers [British]
HLP .... Hyperlipoproteinemia [Medicine]
HLP .... Hypersonic Local Pressure
HLP .... Jakarta [Indonesia] [Airport symbol] (OAG)
HLPH .... Holophane Corp. [NASDAQ symbol] (SAG)
HlpHm .... Help At Home, Inc. [Associated Press] (SAG)
HlpHme .... Help At Home, Inc. [Associated Press] (SAG)
HLPI .... Higher Layer Protocol Identifier [Telecommunications] (ACRL)
HLPI .... High-Level Programming Interface
HLPL .... Howard League for Penal Reform [An association British] (EAIO)
Hlpmte .... Helpmate Robotics, Inc. [Associated Press] (SAG)
Hlpr .... Helper (BARN)
HLPR .... Helper

HLPrB	Hecla Mining Sr'B'Cv Pfd [NYSE symbol] (TTSB)
HLPS	Heavy Lift Prepositioning Ship [Navy]
HLPS	Human Life Protection Society [Australia]
HLPSA	Hazardous Liquid Pipeline Safety Act (GFGA)
HLQ	High-Level Question (DMAA)
HLQ	Highly Luminous QUASAR [Astronomy]
HLQC	Hora Locoque Consuetis [At the Usual Time and Place] [Latin]
HLQL	High-Level Query Language
HLQN	Harlequin (WGA)
HLQS	Hora Locoque Solitis [At the Usual Time and Place] [Latin]
HLR	Hand-Held LASER Range-Finder
HLR	Harvard Law Review [A publication] (BRI)
HLR	Heart-Lung Resuscitation [or Resuscitator] [Medicine]
HLR	Heli Air Services [Bulgaria] [ICAO designator] (FAAC)
HLR	Helicopter LASER Range-Finder
HLR	Highland Ranch [Colorado] [Seismograph station code, US Geological Survey Closed] (SEIS)
HLR	High-Level Representation
HLR	High Level Resources Ltd. [Vancouver Stock Exchange symbol]
HLR	Holder (KSC)
HLR	Hollinger International, Inc. [NYSE symbol] (SAG)
HLR	Home Location Register (ACRL)
HLR	Home Location Register
HLR	Houston Law Review [A publication] (ILCA)
HLR	Killeen, TX [Location identifier FAA] (FAAL)
HLRA	Dahra/Warehouse 32 [Libya] [ICAO location identifier] (ICLI)
HLRA	Health Labour Relations Association [Canada]
HLRC	High Latitude Rocket Campaign [A cooperative study by 7 laboratories in the UK] (PDAA)
HL Rep	English House of Lords Reports [A publication] (DLA)
HLRF	Jaref/Sirte [ICAO location identifier] (ICLI)
HLRM	High-Level Radio Modulator
HLRO	House of Lords Record Office [British] (DLA)
HLRS	Homosexual Law Reform Society [British] (BI)
HLRSC	Holland Lop Rabbit Specialty Club (EA)
HLRT	HealthRite, Inc. [NASDAQ symbol] (SAG)
HLRV	Heavy Lift Research Vehicle [Military]
HLRV	Hibiscus Latent Ringspot Virus [Plant pathology]
HLRW	High-Level Radioactive Waste (GNE)
HLS	Haiti Air Freight [ICAO designator] (FAAC)
HLS	Harmonic Light Scattering [Physics]
HLS	Harvard Law School [Massachusetts]
HLS	Harvard University, Cambridge, MA [OCLC symbol] (OCLC)
HLS	Health Learning Systems
HLS	Heavy-Lift System
HLS	Heavy Logistics System
HLS	Helicopter Landing Site [Military] (INF)
HLS	High Level Scheduler [NITA]
HLS	High-Level Service [Computer science]
HLS	Hills (MCD)
HLS	Hills
HLS	Hippel-Lindau Syndrome [Medicine] (DMAA)
HLS	Hoc Loco Situs [Laid in This Place] [Latin]
HLS	Holes (ADA)
HLS	Holograph Letter Signed
HLS	Horizontal Liquid Spring
HLS	Hue, Lightness, and Saturation [Color model] (BYTE)
HLS	St. Helens [Tasmania] [Airport symbol] (AD)
HLSC	Helicopter Logistic Support Center (NVT)
HL Sc App Cas	English Law Reports, House of Lords, Scotch and Divorce Appeal Cases [1866-75] [A publication] (DLA)
HLSD	Essider [Libya] [ICAO location identifier] (ICLI)
HLSD	Heel Sanding
HLSE	High-Level, Single-Ended
HLSI	Hybrid Large Scale Integrated (PDAA)
HLSP	Heitler-London-Slater-Pauling [Method] [Physics]
HLSTO	Hailstones [NWS] (FAAC)
HLSUA	Honeywell Large Systems Users Association (EA)
HLSV	Helium Latching Solenoid Valve
HLSW	High-Level Solidified Waste [Nuclear energy] (NRCH)
HLT	Halt [Computer science] (MDG)
HLT	Hamilton [Australia Airport symbol] (OAG)
HLT	Heart-Lung Transplantation [Medicine] (DMAA)
HLT	Heli Transport [France ICAO designator] (FAAC)
HLT	Heterodyne Look-Thru [Telecommunications] (TEL)
HLT	Hierarchial Lapped Transform [Telecommunications]
HLT	High-Level Tactical
HLT	High-Level Terminal (CAAL)
HLT	Highly Leveraged Transaction [Banking]
HLT	Hilton Hotels [NYSE symbol] (TTSB)
HLT	Hilton Hotels Corp. [NYSE symbol] (SPSG)
HLT	Human Lipotropin [Medicine] (DMAA)
hLT	Human Lymphocyte Transformation [Immunology] (MAE)
HLTA	Halt Acknowledge [Computer science]
HltCmp	HealthCare COMPARE Corp. [Associated Press] (SAG)
HltcrIm	HealthCare Imaging Services, Inc. [Associated Press] (SAG)
HltcrRty	Healthcare Realty Trust [Associated Press] (SAG)
HltcrTc	Healthcare Technologies Ltd. [Associated Press] (SAG)
HLTD	Ghadames [Libya] [ICAO location identifier] (ICLI)
HLTF	High-Level Task Force (DOMA)
HLTH	Health
HLTH	Health
HlthCFP	HealthCare Financial Partners, Inc. [Associated Press] (SAG)
HlthCh	Health-Chem Corp. [Associated Press] (SAG)
HlthCor	HealthCor Holdings, Inc. [Associated Press] (SAG)

HlthCP	Health Care Property Investors, Inc. [Associated Press] (SAG)
HlthCr	Health Care REIT [Associated Press] (SAG)
HlthCSv	Health Care Services Group [Associated Press] (SAG)
Hlthdyn	Healthdyne, Inc. [Associated Press] (SAG)
HlthdynT	Healthdyne Technologies [Associated Press] (SAG)
HlthdyT	Healthdyne Technologies [Associated Press] (SAG)
HlthFit	Health Fitness Physical Therapy [Associated Press] (SAG)
HlthMSys	Health Management Systems, Inc. [Associated Press] (SAG)
Hlthpln	Healthplan Services Corp. [Associated Press] (SAG)
HlthplnSv	Healthplan Services Corp. [Associated Press] (SAG)
HlthPro	Health Professionals [Associated Press] (SAG)
HlthPwr	Health Power [Associated Press] (SAG)
HlthRite	HealthRite, Inc. [Associated Press] (SAG)
HlthRsk	Health Risk Management, Inc. [Associated Press] (SAG)
Hlthsrc	Healthsource, Inc. [Associated Press] (SAG)
Hlthsrce	Healthsource, Inc. [Associated Press] (SAG)
Hlthsth	Healthsouth Corp. [Associated Press] (SAG)
HlthSys	Health Systems Design Corp. [Associated Press] (SAG)
HlthSys	Health Systems International [Associated Press] (SAG)
HlthTc	HealthTech International, Inc. [Associated Press] (SAG)
HlthTch	HealthTech International, Inc. [Associated Press] (SAG)
HlthTech	HealthTech International, Inc. [Associated Press] (SAG)
Hlthwtch	Healthwatch, Inc. [Associated Press] (SAG)
Hltlmg	Health Images, Inc. [Associated Press] (SAG)
HLTL	High-Level Test Language
HLTL	High-Level Transistor Logic
HltMetr	Health O Meter Products [Associated Press] (SAG)
HltMgt	Health Management Associates, Inc. [Associated Press] (SAG)
HltMInc	Health Management, Inc. [Associated Press] (SAG)
HltMSys	Health Management Systems, Inc. [Associated Press] (SAG)
HLTP	Hilltop
HLTP	Hilltop [NWS] (FAAC)
HltPlanet	Healthy Planet Products, Inc. [Associated Press] (SAG)
Hltplx	Healthplex, Inc. [Associated Press] (SAG)
HltRet	Health & Retirement Property Trust [Associated Press] (SAG)
HLTRF	Hospitality Lodging and Travel Research Foundation [Also known as Research Foundation] (EA)
HLTTL	High-Level Transistor Translator Logic
HltwAm	Healthwise of America, Inc. [Associated Press] (SAG)
HLU	Heli Union Heli Prestations [France ICAO designator] (FAAC)
HLU	Houailou [New Caledonia] [Airport symbol] (OAG)
HLU	House Logic Unit
HLV	Hallsville, MO [Location identifier FAA] (FAAL)
HLV	Heavy-Lift Vehicle
HLV	Heliserv SA de CV [Mexico ICAO designator] (FAAC)
HLV	Heracleum Latent Virus [Plant pathology]
HLV	Herpes-Like Virus
HLV	Hypoplastic Left Ventricle [Cardiology] (DAVI)
HLVG	Das Heilige Land in Vergangenheit und Gegenwart [A publication] (BJA)
HLW	Halbleinwand [Half-Bound Cloth] [Bookbinding, publishing] [German]
HLW	Handbuch der Literaturwissenschaft [Potsdam] [A publication] (BJA)
HLW	Hattiesburg, Camp Shelby, MS [Location identifier FAA] (FAAL)
HLW	Helwan [Egypt] [Seismograph station code, US Geological Survey] (SEIS)
HLW	Higher Low Water
HLW	High-Level Waste [Nuclear energy]
HLWC	High-Level Waste Calcination [Nuclear energy] (NRCH)
HLWC	High-Level Waste Concentrate [Nuclear energy] (NRCH)
HLWD	High-Level Waste Concentrate Distillate [Nuclear energy] (NRCH)
HlwdE	Hallwood Energy Corp. [Associated Press] (SAG)
HlwdP	Hollywood Park, Inc. [Associated Press] (SAG)
HlwdPk	Hollywood Park, Inc. [Associated Press] (SAG)
HLWF	High-Level Waste Concentrator Feed [Nuclear energy] (NRCH)
HLWI	Higher Low-Water Interval
HLWIP	High Level Waste Immobilisation Program [Nuclear energy] (NUCP)
HL Wkly Inf Bull	House of Lords Weekly Information Bulletin [A publication] (DLA)
HLWN	Highest Low-Water Neap Tide (WDAA)
HLW/OC	Hard Labor without Confinement
HLWOG	High-Level Liquid Waste Off-Gas [Nuclear energy] (NRCH)
HLWS	High-Level Waste Surge [Nuclear energy] (NRCH)
HLX	Galax/Hillsville, VA [Location identifier FAA] (FAAL)
HLX	Halter Marine Group, Inc. [AMEX symbol] (SAG)
HLX	Helix
HLX	Helix Circuits, Inc. [Toronto Stock Exchange symbol]
HLXA	Helix Angle
HLY	Haley Industries Ltd. [Toronto Stock Exchange symbol]
HLY	Halley Bay [United Kingdom] [Geomagnetic observatory code]
HLY	Valparaiso, FL [Location identifier FAA] (FAAL)
HlyPd	Holly Products [Associated Press] (SAG)
HLYW	Hollywood Entertainment [NASDAQ symbol] (TTSB)
HLYW	Hollywood Entertainment Corp. [NASDAQ symbol] (SAG)
HlywdCa	Hollywood Casino Corp. [Associated Press] (SAG)
HlywdE	Hollywood Entertainment Corp. [Associated Press] (SAG)
HLZ	Hamilton [New Zealand] [Airport symbol] (OAG)
HLZ	Helicopter Landing Zone
HLZA	Zella 74 [Libya] [ICAO location identifier] (ICLI)
HLZBL	Holzblaeser [Woodwind Instrument] [Music]
HLZL	Helicopter Landing Zone Locator
HM	Air-Cushion Vehicle Built by Hovermarine [Usually used in combination with numerals]
HM	Air Mahe [ICAO designator] (AD)
HM	Habitation Module (SSD)
HM	Half Morocco

HM.............	Hallmark
HM.............	Hamarein Air [United Arab Emirates] [ICAO designator] (ICDA)
HM.............	Handmade
HM.............	Hand Motion [Vision] [Neurology] (DAVI)
HM.............	Hand Movement
HM.............	Hands of Mercy [An association] (EA)
HM.............	Harbor Master
HM.............	Hardness Maintenance (MSA)
HM.............	Hardware Multiple
HM.............	Harmonic Mean [Music]
HM.............	Harper's Magazine [A publication] (BRI)
HM.............	Hazardous Material (DNAB)
HM.............	Headmaster [or Headmistress]
HM.............	Head Motion [Gravity]
HM.............	Healthy Male (ROG)
HM.............	Heard and McDonald Islands [ANSI two-letter standard code] (CNC)
hm.............	Heard and McDonald Islands [MARC country of publication code Library of Congress] (LCCP)
HM.............	Heart Murmur [Cardiology] (MAE)
HM.............	Heater Middle (IAA)
HM.............	Heavy Maintenance [Ordnance]
HM.............	Heavy Metal [Inorganic chemistry]
HM.............	Heavy Metal [Rock music type]
HM.............	Heavy Mobile
HM.............	Hectometer [100 meters]
hm.............	Hematite [CIPW classification] [Geology]
H/m.............	Henry per Meter
HM.............	Hepatic Microcirculation [Physiology]
HM.............	Heritage Manor (BJA)
HM.............	Hermeter Master [Freemasonry] (ROG)
hM.............	Herrschende Meinung [Prevailing Opinion] [German] (ILCA)
HM.............	High-Meaningfulness [Psychology]
HM.............	High Melting (OA)
HM.............	High Molecular [Weight] [Also, HMW] [Organic chemistry]
HM.............	Hinge Mount (MCD)
HM.............	His [or Her] Majesty
HM.............	Hoc Mense [In This Month] [Latin]
HM.............	Hollow Metal [Technical drawings]
HM.............	Holter Monitoring [Medicine] (DMAA)
HM.............	Home (ROG)
HM.............	Home Mission
HM.............	Homestake Mining [NYSE symbol] (TTSB)
HM.............	Homestake Mining Co. [NYSE symbol] (SPSG)
HM.............	Homogenization Medium
HM.............	Honorary Member [Freemasonry] (ROG)
HM.............	Horizontal Marriage
HM.............	Horizontal Meridian [Optics, eye anatomy]
HM.............	Horniman Museum [London]
HM.............	Hoshen Mishpat, Shulhan 'Arukh (BJA)
HM.............	Hospital Corpsman [Navy rating]
HM.............	Houghton Mifflin Co. [Publisher]
HM.............	Hours, Minutes (ROG)
HM.............	House Magazine [Australia A publication]
HM.............	Housing Management [HUD]
HM.............	Huius Mensis [This Month's] [Latin]
HM.............	Human Milk [Biochemistry] (MAE)
HM.............	Huntingdon Militia [British military] (DMA)
HM.............	Hydatidiform Mole [Gynecology]
HM.............	Hydra Medium [Culture medium]
HM.............	Hydrogen MASER
HM.............	Hydrometeorological
hm.............	Hydroxymethyl [As substituent on nucleoside] [Biochemistry]
HM.............	Hyperimmune Mice
Hm.............	Hyperopia Manifest [Ophthalmology] (DAVI)
HM.............	Hypothetical Machine (MHDB)
HM.............	Hysteresis Motor [Electronics] (IAA)
Hm.............	Manifest Hypermetropia [Medicine]
HM.............	Marine Helicopter Squadron
HM.............	Master of Humanities
HM.............	Sandoz [Italy] [Research code symbol]
HM.............	Sisters of the Humility of Mary [Roman Catholic religious order]
HM1.............	Hospital Corpsman, First Class [Navy rating]
HM2.............	Hospital Corpsman, Second Class [Navy rating]
HM².............	Square Hectometer
HM³.............	Cubic Hectometer (WDAA)
HM3.............	Hospital Corpsman, Third Class [Navy rating]
HMA.............	Hardware Manufacturers' Association [British] (BI)
HMA.............	Hardwood Manufacturers Association (EA)
Hma.............	Harmona [Record label] [Austria]
HMA.............	Head Masters' Association (AIE)
HMA.............	Health Management Associates, Inc. [NYSE symbol] (SPSG)
HMA.............	Health Mgt Associates'A' [NYSE symbol] (TTSB)
HMA.............	Heteroduplex Mobility Analysis [Genetics]
HMA.............	High Memory Area [Computer science] (PCM)
HMA.............	His [or Her] Majesty's Airship
HMA.............	Hoist Manufacturers Association [Later, HMI] (EA)
HMA.............	Home Manufacturers Association [Later, HMC] (EA)
HMA.............	Home Medical Advisor [Schueler Corp.]
HMA.............	Home Mission Association [Episcopalian]
HMA.............	Hondo, TX [Location identifier FAA] (FAAL)
HMA.............	Hop Merchants Association [British] (BI)
HMA.............	Hot Melt Adhesive
HMA.............	Hot Melt Applicator
HMA.............	Hydroxymethyladenine [Biochemistry]
HMA.............	Hypergol Maintenance Area (MCD)
HMA.............	Hyundai Motor America, Inc.
HMA.............	Marine Attack Helicopter Squadron (VNW)
HMA.............	Marine Helicopter Squadron Attack (NVT)
HMAA.............	Haitian Medical Association Abroad [Later, AMHE] (EA)
HMAC.............	Hazardous Materials Advisory Council (EA)
HMAC.............	Health Manpower Advisory Council
HMAC.............	His [or Her] Majesty's Aircraft Carrier
HMAC.............	Horticultural Market Access Committee [Australia]
HMACI.............	His [or Her] Majesty's Alkali and Clean Air Inspectorate [British] (DCTA)
HMAF.............	His [or Her] Majesty's Armed Forces
H MAJ:T.............	Hans Majestaet [His Majesty] [Swedish]
HMANA.............	Hawk Migration Association of North America (EA)
HM & LP.............	Hand Motion and Light Perception [Medicine] (DAVI)
HM & M.............	Home Maintenance and Modification Program [Australia]
HM & SG.............	Hirshhorn Museum and Sculpture Garden [Smithsonian Institution]
HMAR.............	Hvide Marine Inc. [NASDAQ symbol] (SAG)
HMAS.............	Her Majesty's Australian Ship (DOMA)
HMAS.............	Hyperimmune Mouse Ascite [Medicine] (DMAA)
HmaScn.............	HumaScan, Inc. [Associated Press]
HMAV.............	His [or Her] Majesty's Army Vessel [British military] (DMA)
HMB.............	Garden City, KS [Location identifier FAA] (FAAL)
HMB.............	Haemophilus Maintenance Broth [Microbiology]
HMB.............	Hamburg [New York] [Seismograph station code, US Geological Survey Closed] (SEIS)
HMB.............	Hazara Mountain Battery [British military] (DMA)
HMB.............	Hexamethylbenzene [Organic chemistry]
HMB.............	Holderbank Management und Beratung AG [Switzerland]
HMB.............	Homatropine Methylbromide [Anticholinergic]
HMB.............	Hops Marketing Board
HMB.............	Hughes Mining Barge [Support vessel for Glomar Explorer]
HMB.............	Hydroxy(methoxy)benzaldehyde [Organic chemistry]
HMB.............	Hydroxymethoxybenzophenone [Organic chemistry]
HMBA.............	Hebrew Master Bakers Association [Defunct] (EA)
HMBA.............	Hexamethylene Bis(Acetamide) [Organic chemistry]
HMBA.............	Hotel and Motel Brokers of America (EA)
HMBA.............	Hydroxymethyl(methyl)benzanthracene [Organic chemistry]
HmBBc.............	Home Building Bancorp [Associated Press] (SAG)
HMBC.............	Heteronuclear Multiple-Bond Correlation [Physics]
HMBCEE.............	Horace Mann Bond Center for Equal Education [Defunct] (EA)
HMBDV.............	His [or Her] Majesty's Boom Defence Vessel
HmBElg.............	Home Bancorp of Elgin, Inc. [Associated Press] (SAG)
HmbHm.............	Hamburger Hamlet Restaurants, Inc. [Associated Press] (SAG)
H-MBP-H.............	Human-Mannose Binding Protein-H
HMBS.............	His [or Her] Majesty's British Ship
HMBT.............	Hydrazino(methyl)Benzothiazole [Organic chemistry]
HMC.............	Halley Multicolor Camera [Instrumentation]
HMC.............	Hammerson Canada, Inc. [Toronto Stock Exchange symbol]
HMC.............	Hand-Mirror Cell [Oncology]
HMC.............	Heading Marker Correction (SAA)
HMC.............	Head Masters' Conference [British]
HMC.............	Healing Ministry Centre [Australia]
HMC.............	Health Ministers Council (EERA)
HMC.............	Her Majesty's Customs and Excise [British] (BI)
HMC.............	Hermits of Mount Carmel (TOCD)
HMC.............	Heroin, Morphine, and Cocaine [Mixture] [Slang]
HMC.............	High Moisture Shelled Corn (OA)
HMC.............	High-Strength Sheet Molding Compound
HMC.............	His [or Her] Majesty's Council (ROG)
HMC.............	His [or Her] Majesty's Customs
HmC.............	Historian's Microfilm Co., Cazenovia, NY [Library symbol Library of Congress] (LCLS)
HMC.............	Historical Manuscripts Commission [British]
HMC.............	Holland Mills [Quebec] [Seismograph station code, US Geological Survey Closed] (SEIS)
HMC.............	Home Manufacturers Councils of NAHB [National Association of Home Builders of the US] (EA)
HMC.............	Honda Motor ADR [NYSE symbol] (TTSB)
HMC.............	Honda Motor Co. Ltd. [NYSE symbol] (SPSG)
HMC.............	Horizontal Motion Carriage [Engineering] (OA)
HMC.............	Horticultural Marketing Council [British] (BI)
HMC.............	Hospital Corpsman, Chief [Navy rating]
HMC.............	Houghton Mifflin Co., Boston, MA [OCLC symbol] (OCLC)
HMC.............	Household Mortgage Corp. (ODBW)
HMC.............	Howard Mold Count [Food quality measure]
HMC.............	Howitzer Motor Carriage
HMC.............	Hundred Million Club (EA)
HMC.............	Hybrid Microcircuit (NASA)
HMC.............	(Hydroxymethyl)carboline [Biochemistry]
HMC.............	Hydroxymethylcystosine [Organic chemistry]
HMC.............	Hydroxymethyl Cytosine [Biochemistry] (DAVI)
HMC.............	Hydroxypropyl(methyl)cellulose [Synthetic food gum] [Organic chemistry]
HMC.............	Hyoscine, Morphine, and Cactine [Tablets] [Medicine]
HMC.............	Hypergolic Maintenance and Checkout (NASA)
HMCA.............	Hospital and Medial Care Association [British] (DBA)
HMC & E.............	His [or Her] Majesty's Customs and Excise [British] (DCTA)
HMCC.............	Hazardous Materials Control Committee [General Motors Corp.]
HMCC.............	Housewife/Mother Career Concept (EDAC)
HMCC.............	Houston Mission Control Center [NASA] (KSC)
HMCC.............	Hypergolic Maintenance and Checkout Cell (NASA)
HMCCMP.............	Human Mammary Carcinoma Cell Membrane Proteinase [Medicine] (DMAA)
HMCF.............	Hypergolic Maintenance and Checkout Facility [NASA] (NASA)
HMCI.............	Homecorp, Inc. [NASDAQ symbol] (SAG)

HMCII .... Higher Military Command, Interior and Islands (MCD)
HMCL .... Hand-Mirror Cell Leukemia [*Oncology*]
HMCM .... Hospital Corpsman, Master Chief [*Navy rating*]
HMCN .... His [*or Her*] Majesty's Canadian Navy
HMCRI .... Hazardous Materials Control Research Institute (EA)
HMCS .... His [*or Her*] Majesty's Canadian Ship
HMCS .... His [*or Her*] Majesty's Civil Service
HMCS .... His [*or Her*] Majesty's Colonial Steamer [*In use in 19th century*]
HMCS .... Hoffman Modulation Contrast System
HMCS .... Hospital Corpsman, Senior Chief [*Navy rating*]
HMCV .... Human Cytomegalovirus
HMD .... Charlie Hammonds Flying Service, Inc. [*FAA designator*] (FAAC)
HMD .... Hamada [*Japan*] [*Seismograph station code, US Geological Survey*] (SEIS)
HMD .... Head-Mounted Display [*Virtual reality technology*] (PS)
HMD .... Heard Island and McDonald Islands [*ANSI three-letter standard code*] (CNC)
HMD .... Helmet-Mounted Display
HMD .... Heterodyne Matrix Detector
HMD .... His [*or Her*] Majesty's Destroyer [*British military*] (DMA)
HMD .... His [*or Her*] Majesty's Dockyard [*Navy British*]
HMD .... His [*or Her*] Majesty's Drifter
HMD .... Hollow-Metal Door (DAC)
HMD .... Homeopathic Medical Doctor [*Medicine*]
HMD .... Hot Metal Detector [*Electronics*] (IAA)
HMD .... Humid (MSA)
HMD .... Hyaline Membrane Disease [*Later, RDS*] [*Medicine*]
HMD .... Hydraulic Mean Depth
HMD .... HydrazinomethylDOPA [*Biochemistry*]
HMD .... Hydrostatic Motor-Driven
HMD .... Hydrostatic Motor-Driven
HMDA .... Hexamethylenediamine [*Organic chemistry*]
HMDA .... Home Mortgage Disclosure Act
HMDAA .... Hydroxymethyl Diacetone Acrylamide [*Organic chemistry*]
HMDBA .... Hollow Metal Door and Buck Association (EA)
HMDD .... Helmet-Mounted Display Device [*Military*]
HMDE .... Hanging Mercury Drop Electrode [*Electrochemistry*]
HMDF .... Hollow Metal Door and Frame [*Technical drawings*]
HMDF .... Horizontal Side of Main Distribution Frame (TEL)
hMDH .... Halophilic Malate Dehydrogenase [*An enzyme*]
HMDI .... Hexamethylene Diisocyanate [*Organic chemistry*]
HMDP .... Hydroxymethylenediphosphonate [*Organic chemistry*]
HMDS .... Hexamethyldisilazane [*Organic chemistry*]
HMDS .... Hexamethyldisiloxane [*Organic chemistry*]
HMDS .... Hospital Morbidity Data System
HMDSO .... Hexamethyldisiloxane [*Organic chemistry*]
HMDZ .... Hexamethyldisilazane [*Organic chemistry*]
HME .... Hassi Messaoud [*Algeria*] [*Airport symbol*] (OAG)
HME .... Health Media Education (EA)
HME .... Heat and Moisture Exchanger (MAE)
HME .... Heat, Massage, Exercise [*Medicine*]
HME .... High Vinyl-Modified Epoxy (MCD)
HME .... Home Medical Equipment
HME .... Home Properties of New York [*NYSE symbol*] (SAG)
HME .... Hull, Mechanical, Electrical [*Ship equipment*] [*Navy*]
HMEA .... Hatters Machinery and Equipment Association [*Defunct*] (EA)
HmeBc .... Home Bancorp [*Associated Press*] (SAG)
HMEC .... Human Mammary Epithelial Cell [*Cytology*]
Hmecrp .... Homecorp, Inc. [*Associated Press*] (SAG)
HMED .... Heavy Military Electronics Department (SAA)
HmeDep .... [*The*] Home Depot, Inc. [*Associated Press*] (SAG)
HMEED .... Heavy Military Electronic Equipment Division [*General Electric Co.*] (AAG)
HmeHlth .... Home Health Corporation of America, Inc. [*Associated Press*] (SAG)
HMEIA .... Health Manpower Education Initiative Award
HmeOil .... Home Oil Co. Ltd. [*Associated Press*] (SAG)
Hmeplx .... Homeplex Mortgage Investments [*Associated Press*] (SAG)
HmePrp .... Home Properties of New York [*Associated Press*] (SAG)
HMES .... Heavy Military Electronic System [*General Electric Co.*] (IAA)
HmeStat .... Home State Holdings, Inc. [*Associated Press*] (SAG)
HMF .... Handbook of Military Forces (MCD)
HMF .... Harbor Maintenance Fee [*Import/Export fee*]
HMF .... Hastings Manufacturing Co. [*AMEX symbol*] (SPSG)
HMF .... Hastings Mfg [*AMEX symbol*] (TTSB)
HMF .... Health Maintenance Facility (MCD)
HMF .... Heliospheric Magnetic Field [*Solar physics*]
HMF .... High Mach Flow
HMF .... High Magnetic Field
HMF .... His [*or Her*] Majesty's Forces
HMF .... Horizontal Mating Facility [*NASA*] (KSC)
HMF .... Hum Modulation Factor (DEN)
HMF .... Hydroxymethylfuraldehyde [*Organic chemistry*]
HMF .... Hydroxymethylfurfural [*Organic chemistry*] (DAVI)
HMF .... Hypergol Maintenance Facility [*NASA*] (NASA)
HmFedIN .... Home Federal Bancorp [*Associated Press*] (SAG)
HMFF .... Hoc Monumentum Fieri Fecit [*Caused This Monument to Be Made*] [*Latin*]
HMFG .... Heavy Metal Fluoride Glass
HMFI .... His [*or Her*] Majesty's Factory Inspectorate [*Department of Employment*] [*British*]
HMFIC .... Head Military Figure in Charge
HMFIHQ .... His [*or Her*] Majesty's Factory Inspectorate Headquarters [*Department of Employment*] [*British*]
HmFnFL .... Home Financial Corp. Florida [*Associated Press*] (SAG)
HMfW .... Help Model for Windows

HMG .... Hardware Message Generator [*Telecommunications*] (TEL)
HMG .... Harvard University, Gutman Library, Cambridge, MA [*OCLC symbol*] (OCLC)
HMG .... Heavy Machine Gun
HMG .... High-Mobility Group [*Genetics*]
HMG .... High Mobility Group [*of nonhistone proteins*] [*Biochemistry*]
HMG .... High Modulus Graphite [*Epoxy composite*] (MCD)
HMG .... His [*or Her*] Majesty's Government
HMG .... HMG/Courtland Prop [*AMEX symbol*] (TTSB)
HMG .... HMG Property Investors, Inc. [*Formerly, Hospital Mortgage Group*] [*AMEX symbol*] (SPSG)
HMG .... Human Menopausal Gonadotrophin [*Endocrinology*]
hMG .... Human Menopausal Gonadotropin [*Medicine*] (DMAA)
HMG .... Hydroxymethylglutaryl [*Biochemistry*]
HMGB .... His [*or Her*] Majesty's Gunboat
HMGC .... HMG Worldwide [*NASDAQ symbol*] (TTSB)
HMGC .... HMG Worldwide Corp. [*NASDAQ symbol*] (SAG)
HMGCC .... Her Majesty's Government Communications Centre [*British*] (PDAA)
HMGCO .... Hydroxymethylglutarylcoenzyme [*Organic chemistry*]
HMG CoA .... Hepatic Hydroxymethylglutaryl Coenzyme A [*Organic chemistry*] (DAVI)
HMG-CoA .... Hydroxy-Methylglutaryl-Coenzyme A Reductase [*Medicine*] (MEDA)
HMGF .... High Modulus Glass Fiber
HMGI .... Hotel-Motel Greeters International (EA)
HMGN .... Hemagen Diagnostics [*NASDAQ symbol*] (SAG)
HMGT .... Homegate Hospitality, Inc. [*NASDAQ symbol*] (SAG)
HMG Wd .... HMG Worldwide Corp. [*Associated Press*] (SAG)
HMH .... Heintz, M. H., Chicago IL [*STAC*]
HMH .... His [*or Her*] Majesty's Household
HMH .... Hispanic Marketing Handbook [*A publication*]
HMH .... Home Hill [*Australia Airport symbol*]
HMH .... Horizon Mental Health Management [*AMEX symbol*] (SAG)
HMH .... Marine Helicopter Squadron Heavy
HMHB .... Healthy Mothers, Healthy Babies (EA)
HMHB .... Healthy Mothers, Healthy Babies National Coalition (PAZ)
HMHCY .... Hexamethyl Hexacyclen [*Organic chemistry*]
HMHD .... High Molecular Weight, High Density
HMHEC .... Hydrophobically-Modified Hydroxyethylcellulose [*Organic chemistry*]
HMHF .... Hydrophobic Microporous Hollow Fiber [*Membranes for chemical reactions*]
HMHM .... Horizon Mental Health Management [*NASDAQ symbol*] (SAG)
HMHM .... Horizon Mental Health Mgmt [*NASDAQ symbol*] (TTSB)
HMHP .... Hospital Management, Hospital Problems [*British*]
HMHS .... His [*or Her*] Majesty's Hospital Ship
HMI .... Handbook of Maintenance Instructions
HMI .... Hardware Monitor Interface
HMI .... Hazardous Material Incident [*Nuclear energy*]
HMI .... Healed Myocardial Infarction [*Cardiology*] (AAMN)
HMI .... Hexamethyleneimine [*Trademark*] [*Celanese Corp.*]
HMI .... His [*or Her*] Majesty's Inspector
HMI .... Hoist Manufacturers Institute (EA)
HMI .... Horizontal Motion Index [*Printer technology*]
HMI .... Horticultural Marketing Inspectorate [*Ministry of Agriculture, Fisheries, and Food*] [*British*]
HMI .... Host Micro Interface [*CompuServe, Inc.*] [*Computer science*] (PCM)
HMI .... House Magazine Institute [*Later, NY/IABC*]
HMI .... Hub Management Interface [*Novell, Inc.*] (PCM)
HMI .... Human Machine Interface
HMI .... Hydragyrum Mercury Medium Arc Length and Iodide [*An arc lamp*] (WDMC)
HMI .... Hypomelanosis of Ito [*Medicine*] (DMAA)
HMIC .... Heinkel-Messerschmitt-Isetta Club [*Defunct*] (EA)
HMIF .... His [*or Her*] Majesty's Inspector of Factories (ROG)
HMII .... Health Mor, Inc. [*NASDAQ symbol*] (SAG)
HMII .... HMI Industries [*NASDAQ symbol*] (SAG)
HMI Ind .... HMI Industries [*Associated Press*] (SAG)
HMIMF .... His [*or Her*] Majesty's Indian Military Forces
HMIN .... His [*or Her*] Majesty's Indian Navy
HMIO .... Haitian Migrant Interdiction Operation [*Haitian-US agreement, allowing US Coast Guard to board Haitian vessels on high seas*]
HMIP .... His [*or Her*] Majesty's Inspectorate of Pollution [*British*]
hMIP .... Human Macrophage Inflammatory Protein [*Immunochemistry*]
HMIPI .... His [*or Her*] Majesty's Industrial Pollution Inspectorate for Scotland (DCTA)
HMIS .... Hazardous Materials Identification System [*National Paint and Coating Association*]
HMIS .... Hazardous Materials Information System (MCD)
HMIS .... Health Management [*NASDAQ symbol*] (TTSB)
HMIS .... Health Management, Inc. [*NASDAQ symbol*] (SAG)
HMIS .... His [*or Her*] Majesty's Indian Ship [*British military*] (DMA)
HMIS .... His [*or Her*] Majesty's Inspector of Schools (ROG)
HMIS .... Hospital Management Information System
HMIS .... Hospital Medical Information System [*Medicine*] (DMAA)
Hmisph .... Hemispherx BioPharma, Inc. [*Associated Press*] (SAG)
HMIT .... Her [*or His*] Majesty's Inspector of Taxes [*British*] (ODBW)
HMJ .... Homer, IL [*Location identifier FAA*] (FAAL)
HMK .... Heart Muscle Kinase [*An enzyme*]
HMK .... Highmark Resources [*Vancouver Stock Exchange symbol*]
HML .... Hamilton [*Ontario*] [*Seismograph station code, US Geological Survey Closed*] (SEIS)
HML .... Hammond Metallurgical Laboratory [*Yale*] (MCD)
HML .... Harbor Motor Launch
HML .... Hard Mobile Launcher [*Boeing Aerospace-Loral Defense Systems*]
HML .... Hardware Modelling Library [*Mentor Graphics*] (NITA)
HML .... Hawaii Medical Library, Inc., Honolulu, HI [*OCLC symbol*] (OCLC)

HML............ Heeresmunitionslager [*Army Ammunition Depot*] [*German military - World War II*]
HML............ His [*or Her*] Majesty's Lieutenant
HML............ Horace Mann League of the USA (EA)
HML............ Houston Metals Corp. [*Vancouver Stock Exchange symbol*]
HML............ Human Milk Lysozyme [*An enzyme*]
HML............ Huntsman Marine Laboratory [*Canada*] (MSC)
HML............ Marine Helicopter Squadron Light
HMLC.......... High-Mobility Load Carrier [*British military*] (DMA)
HMLD.......... Handmade Loft-Dried Paper (DGA)
HMLI............ Horace Mann-Lincoln Institute of School Experimentation [*Columbia University*] (AEBS)
HmInBk....... Homeland Bankshares Corp. [*Associated Press*] (SAG)
HMLR.......... His [*or Her*] Majesty's Land Registry
HMLT.......... Hamlet
HMM........... Hamamatsu [*Japan*] [*Seismograph station code, US Geological Survey*] (SEIS)
HMM........... Hamilton, MT [*Location identifier FAA*] (FAAL)
HMM........... Hammond Manufacturing Co. Ltd. [*Toronto Stock Exchange symbol*]
HMM........... Hardware Multiply Module
HMM........... Heavy Meromyosin [*Biochemistry*]
HMM........... Hexamethoxy(methyl)melamine
HMM........... Hexamethylmelamine [*Altretamine*] [*Also, HEX, HXM*] [*Antineoplastic drug*]
HMM........... Hidden Markov Modeling [*Computer science*]
HMM........... Marine Helicopter Squadron Medium
HMMA .... Hydroxymethoxymandelic Acid [*Also, VMA*] [*Biochemistry*]
HMMFC........ House Merchant Marine and Fisheries Committee
HMMHE....... High-Mobility Materiel Handling Equipment [*Army*]
HMML......... Hill Monastic Manuscript Library [*Saint John's University, Collegeville, MN*]
HMML......... His [*or Her*] Majesty's Motor Launch
HMMMS....... His [*or Her*] Majesty's Motor Mine Sweeper
HMMP .... HyperMedia Management Protocol [*Computer science*]
HMMR .... High-Resolution Multifrequency Microwave Radiometer (MCD)
HMMS .... HELLFIRE Modular Missile System
HMMS .... Hino Micro Mixing System [*Diesel engines*]
HMMS .... Hyper-Media Management Schema [*Computer science*]
HMMWV ..... High-Mobility Multipurpose Wheeled Vehicle [*Nicknamed "hummer"*] [*Army*] (RDA)
HMMWV-L... High-Mobility Multipurpose Wheeled Vehicle - Lightweight
HMN .... Alamogordo, NM [*Location identifier FAA*] (FAAL)
HMN .... Hemmings Motor News [*A publication*]
HMN .... Heptamethylnonane [*Fuel*]
HMN .... Horace Mann Educators [*NYSE symbol*] (TTSB)
HMN .... Horace Mann Educators Corp. [*NYSE symbol*] (SPSG)
HMN .... Human
HMN .... Human
HMNAO....... Her Majesty's Nautical Almanac Office [*British*] (PDAA)
HMNC......... Harmonic (MSA)
HMNF........ HMN Financial [*NASDAQ symbol*] (TTSB)
HMNF........ HMN Financial, Inc. [*NASDAQ symbol*] (SAG)
HMN Fn...... HMN Financial, Inc. [*Associated Press*] (SAG)
HMNIP........ Hydrophobically-Modified Nonionic Polymers [*Organic chemistry*]
HMNZS....... His [*or Her*] Majesty's New Zealand Ship
HMO .... Habitability Module Outfitting (SSD)
HMO .... Hardware Microcode Optimizer
HMO .... Health Maintenance Organization
HMO .... Heart Minute Output [*Cardiology*]
HMO .... Hermosillo [*Mexico*] [*Airport symbol*] (OAG)
HMO .... H. Mason [*Oregon*] [*Seismograph station code, US Geological Survey*] (SEIS)
HMO .... Honolulu Magnetic Observatory (CINC)
HMO .... Hueckel Molecular Orbital [*Atomic physics*]
HMOA......... Health Maintenance Organization Acts of 1973 and 1988 (WYGK)
HMOCS....... His [*or Her*] Majesty's Overseas Civil Service
HMOM........ HyperMedia Object Manager [*Computer science*]
HMOS......... Habitability Module Outfitting System (SSD)
HMOS......... Health Maintenance Organization Service [*Public Health Service*]
HMOS......... High-Speed Metal-Oxide Semiconductor [*ROM*]
HMOS-E...... HMOS [*High Speed Metal Oxide Semiconductor*] Erasable (NITA)
HMOW........ His [*or Her*] Majesty's Office of Works (ROG)
HmowG...... Homeowners Group, Inc. [*Associated Press*] (SAG)
HMOX........ Heme Oxygenase (DMAA)
HMP........... Habitat Management Plan
HMP........... Handmade Paper
HMP........... Harper's Magazine Press
HMP........... Helmet-Mounted Pick-Offs (MCD)
HMP........... Her [*or His*] Majesty's Prison [*British*] (BARN)
HMP........... Hexamethylphosphoramide [*or Hexamethylphosphoric Triamide*] [*Also, HEMPA, HMPA, HMPT, HPT*] [*Organic chemistry*]
HMP........... Hexasodium Metaphosphate [*Inorganic chemistry*]
HMP........... Hexose Monophosphate [*Biochemistry*]
HMP........... Hexose Monophosphate Pathway [*Biochemistry*] (DAVI)
HMP........... High Melting Point
HMP........... High-Methoxy Pectin [*Food technology*]
HMP........... Hoc Monumentum Posuit [*He, or She, Erected This Monument*] [*Latin*]
HMP........... Honda-Mrkos-Pajdusakova [*Comet*]
HMP........... Hot Moist Packs [*Medicine*]
HMP........... Humidity Monitoring Panel
HMP........... Hydraulic Maintenance Panel (AAG)
HMP........... Hydroxymethyl Hydroperoxide [*Organic chemistry*]
HMP........... Hydroxymethyl(methyl)propanediol [*Organic chemistry*]
HMP........... Hydrozene Monopropellant (MCD)

HMP............ Papair Terminal SA [*Haiti*] [*ICAO designator*] (FAAC)
HMPA .... Hexamethylphosphoramide [*or Hexamethylphosphoric Triamide*] [*Also, HEMPA, HMP, HMPT, HPT*] [*Organic chemistry*]
HMPA .... Hydroxymethyl Phosphonic Acid [*Organic chemistry*]
HMPAA .... Hydrophobically-Modified Polyacrylamide [*Organic chemistry*]
HMPAO .... Hexamethylpropylenamine Oxime [*Organic chemistry*]
HMPD .... Hoffman Military Products Division
HMPG .... Hydroxy(methoxy)phenylglycol [*Biochemistry*] (AAMN)
HMPGTS ..... His [*or Her*] Majesty's Procurator General and Treasury Solicitor
HMPI .... His [*or Her*] Majesty's Pollution Inspectorate [*British*] (DCTA)
HMPIPI .... Her Majesty's Industrial Pollution Inspectorate (EERA)
HMPMA ...... Historical Motion Picture Milestones Association
HMPP .... Hexose Monophosphate Pathway [*Biochemistry*]
HmPrt .... Home Port Bancorp, Inc. [*Associated Press*] (SAG)
HMPS .... Hexose Monophosphate Shunt [*Biochemistry*]
HMPSA .... Hot Melt Pressure Sensitive Adhesive
HMPT .... Hexamethylphosphoric Triamide [*Also, HEMPA, HMP, HMPA, HPT*] [*Organic chemistry*]
HMPT .... Human Factors, Manpower, Personnel, and Training [*Military*] (RDA)
HmpU .... Hampton Utilities Trust [*Associated Press*] (SAG)
HMQ .... Homer, LA [*Location identifier FAA*] (FAAL)
HMQC .... Heteronuclear Multiple-Quantum Coherence [*Physics*]
HMR .... Hamilton Ranch [*California*] [*Seismograph station code, US Geological Survey*] (SEIS)
HMR .... Hammer (MSA)
HMR .... Hazardous Materials Regulation [*Department of Transportation*]
HMR .... Headquarters Modification Request [*Military*] (CAAL)
HMR .... Health Management Resources [*Diet program*]
HMR .... High Moisture Resistant
HMR .... Histocytic Medullary Reticulosis [*Oncology*]
HMR .... HMR World Enterprise [*Vancouver Stock Exchange symbol*]
HMR .... Hoboken Manufacturers [*AAR code*]
HMR .... Hoechst Marion Roussel
Hmr .... Homer (DA)
HMR .... Hotel, Motel, Resort Database [*American Database Corp.*] [*Santa Barbara, CA*] [*Information service or system*] (IID)
HMR .... Human Milk Ribonuclease [*An enzyme*]
hMR .... Human Mineralocorticoid Receptor [*Endocrinology*]
HMR .... Hungry Mind Review [*A publication*] (BRI)
HMR .... Hybrid Modular Redundancy
HMRA .... Hadassah Medical Relief Association (EA)
HMRB .... Hazardous Materials Regulation Board
HMRI .... Huntington Medical Research Institutes [*Huntington Memorial Hospital*] [*Research center*] (RCD)
HMRL .... His [*or Her*] Majesty's Royal Licence (ROG)
HMRN......... Hull Moulding Release Note
H-mRNA ..... Ribonucleic Acid, H-Chain Messenger [*Biochemistry, genetics*]
HMRP .... Hurricane Microseismic Research Problem [*Aerology*]
HMRR .... His [*or Her*] Majesty's Reserve Regiment [*British military*] (DMA)
HMRRP .... Hazardous Materials Release Response Policy [*Stanford University*]
HMRS .... Historical Model Railway Society [*British*] (BI)
HMRTE .... Human Milk Reverse Transcriptase Enzyme [*Medicine*] (DMAA)
HMS .... Hammer Makers' Society [*A union*] [*British*]
HMS .... Hanford Meteorology Surveys [*Nuclear energy*] (NRCH)
HMS .... Hardened Memory System
HMS .... Harmonic Multiplier Source
HMS .... Harvard University Medical School, Countway Library of Medicine, Boston, MA [*OCLC symbol*] (OCLC)
HMS .... Hazardous Materials Safety [*RSPA*] (TAG)
HMS .... Hazardous Materials Systems [*A publication*] (EAAP)
HMS .... Hazards Monitoring System [*NASA*] (KSC)
HMS .... Health Mobilization Series
HMS .... Heavy Materiel Supply Units [*Military*]
HMS .... Heavy-Media Separation [*Mining engineering*] (IAA)
HMS .... Helmet-Mounted Sight [*Aviation*]
HMS .... Hemin Storage
HMS .... Hemus Air [*Bulgaria*] [*ICAO designator*] (FAAC)
HMS .... Hexagonal Mesoporous Silica [*Inorganic chemistry*]
HMS .... Hexose Monophospate Shunt (PDAA)
HMS .... Hierarchical Memory Storage [*Computer science*]
HMS .... High Melt Strength [*Plastic moldings*]
HMS .... Highway Mobile Source [*Environmental Protection Agency*] (GFGA)
HMS .... His [*or Her*] Majesty's Service
HMS .... His [*or Her*] Majesty's Ship
HMS .... His [*or Her*] Majesty's Steamer
HMS .... Historical Metallurgy Society [*British*] (EAIO)
HMS .... History Memory System (MCD)
HMS .... Honeywell's Manufacturing System [*Honeywell Information Systems Ltd.*] [*Software package*] (NCC)
HMS .... Hospital Marketing Services, Inc. [*Commercial firm*] (DAVI)
HMS .... Host Marriott Services [*NYSE symbol*] (TTSB)
HMS .... Host Marriott Services Corp. [*NYSE symbol*] (SAG)
HMS .... Hours, Minutes, Seconds
HMS .... Hull Monitoring System (PDAA)
HMS .... Humility of Mary Service (EA)
HMSA .... Hardware Manufacturers Statistical Association [*Later, BHMA*]
HMSA .... Hawk Mountain Sanctuary Association (EA)
HMSA .... Health Manpower Shortage Area
HMSA .... Historic Motor Sports Association (EA)
HMSA .... Hydroxymethanesulfonate [*Organic chemistry*]
HMSAS .... His [*or Her*] Majesty's South African Ship
HMSAS .... Hypertrophic Muscular Subaortic Stenosis [*Cardiology*] (MAE)
HMS(BOE) ... Hazardous Materials Systems (Bureau of Explosives) (EA)
HMSC .... Hatfield Marine Science Center [*Marine science*] (OSRA)
HMSC .... Hatfield Marine Science Center (USDC)

HMSC .... HumaScan, Inc. [*NASDAQ symbol*] (SAG)
HMSM .... Heavy Mortar, Smart Munition
HMS/M .... His [*or Her*] Majesty's Submarine
HMSO .... His [*or Her*] Majesty's Stationery Office
HMSO .... Honolulu Magnetic and Seismological Observatory
HMSR .... Hemasure, Inc. [*NASDAQ symbol*] (SAG)
HMSR .... HemaSure Inc. [*NASDAQ symbol*] (TTSB)
HMSRR .... Harpoon Missile Select Relay Rack [*Missiles*] (MCD)
HMSS .... Helmet-Mounted Sight Set
HMSS .... Hospital Management Systems Society [*Later, HIMSS*] (EA)
HMSS .... Religious Sisters of the Apostolate of the Blessed Sacrament (TOCD)
HMSS .... Sisters of Mercy of the Blessed Sacrament (TOCD)
HMSTD .... Homestead (WDAA)
HMSTD .... Homestead
Hmstke .... Homestake Mining Co. [*Associated Press*] (SAG)
HMSY .... Health Management Systems [*NASDAQ symbol*] (TTSB)
HMSY .... Health Management Systems, Inc. [*NASDAQ symbol*] (SAG)
HMT .... Air Nova [*British ICAO designator*] (FAAC)
HMT .... Hand Microtelephone (IAA)
HmT .... Helminthosporium maydis race T [*A toxin-producing fungus*]
HMT .... Hemet, CA [*Location identifier FAA*] (FAAL)
HMT .... Hexamethoxytriphenylene [*Organic chemistry*]
HMT .... Hexamethylenetetramine [*Also, HMTA*] [*Organic chemistry*]
HMT .... High Mobility Trailer
HMT .... His [*or Her*] Majesty's Transport
HMT .... His [*or Her*] Majesty's Trawler
HMT .... His [*or Her*] Majesty's Troopship [*British military*] (DMA)
HMT .... His [*or Her*] Majesty's Tug [*British military*] (DMA)
HMT .... Histamine Methyltransferase [*An enzyme*]
HMT .... Host Marriot [*Formerly, Marriott Corp.*] [*NYSE symbol*] (SPSG)
HMT .... Human Metallothioneine [*Biochemistry*]
hMT .... Human Molar Thyrotropin (MAE)
HMT .... Hydrazine Monopropellant Thruster
hMT .... Hydroxymethyl Uracil [*Organic chemistry*] (DAVI)
HMTA .... Hazardous Materials Transportation Act [*1975*]
HMTA .... Hexamethylenetetramine [*Also, HMT*] [*Organic chemistry*]
HMTA .... Hexamethylenetriamine [*Organic chemistry*]
HMTC .... Hazardous Materials Technical Center [*Rockville, MD*] [*DoD*] (GRD)
HMTPSD ..... HAWK [*Homing All the Way Killer*] Missile Test Program System Device (DWSG)
HMTS .... Health Message Testing Services [*Department of Health and Human Services*] (GFGA)
HMTS .... His [*or Her*] Majesty's Telegraph Ship
HMTSF .... Hexamethylenetetraselenafulvalenium [*Organic chemistry*]
HMTT .... Hexamethyltrithiane [*Organic chemistry*]
HMTT .... High-Mobility Tactical Trucks (MCD)
HMTT .... HMT Technology [*NASDAQ symbol*] (TTSB)
HMTT .... HMT Technology Corp. [*NASDAQ symbol*] (SAG)
HMTTch .... HMT Technology Corp. [*Associated Press*] (SAG)
HMTUSA ..... Hazardous Materials Transportation and Uniform Safety Act
HmtwBc .... Hometown Bancorp, Inc. [*Associated Press*] (SAG)
HMU .... Hammond, LA [*Location identifier FAA*] (FAAL)
HMU .... Hardware Mockup (NASA)
HMU .... Hydraulic Management Unit
HMU .... Hydraulic Mock-Up
HMU .... Hydromechanical Unit
HMU .... Hydroxymethyluracil [*Organic chemistry*]
HMUX .... Hybrid Multiplexer [*Telecommunications*]
HMV .... Henbane Mosaic Virus [*Plant pathology*]
HMV .... High Magnification Viewer
HMV .... High Mass Vehicle
HMV .... His Master's Voice [*Phonograph records*]
HMV .... Holston Mountain, TN [*Location identifier FAA*] (FAAL)
HMV .... Hydrodynamically Modulated Voltammetry [*Analytical chemistry*]
HMV .... Hydrogen Manual Valve (MCD)
HMVEC .... Human Dermal Microvascular Endothelial Cell [*Biochemistry*]
HMW .... High Molecular Weight [*Also, HM*] [*Organic chemistry*]
HMW .... How to Market to Women [*A publication*]
HMWA .... Hairdressing Manufacturers' and Wholesalers' Association [*British*] (BI)
HMWC .... Health of Munition Workers Committee [*World War I*] [*British*]
HMWC .... High-Mobility Weapons Carrier [*Army*]
HMWC/CSV... High-Mobility Weapons Carrier/Combat Support Vehicle [*Army*] (MCD)
HMWGP .... High Molecular Weight Glycoprotein [*Medicine*] (DMAA)
HMWK .... Advanced Voice Technologies [*NASDAQ symbol*] (TTSB)
HMWK .... Advanced Voice Technologies, Inc. [*NASDAQ symbol*] (SAG)
HMWK .... High Molecular Weight Kininogen [*Biochemistry*]
HMWKa .... High Molecular Weight Kallikrein [*Biochemistry*]
HMWKU .... Advanced Voice Tehcnol's 'Unit' [*NASDAQ symbol*] (TTSB)
HMWKW ...... Advanced Voice Technol Wrrt [*NASDAQ symbol*] (TTSB)
HMWP .... High-Molecular-Weight Protein [*or Polypeptide*] [*Biochemistry*]
HMWPE .... High-Molecular-Weight Polyethylene (MCD)
HMWRK .... Homework
HMX .... Denver, CO [*Location identifier FAA*] (FAAL)
HMX .... Hartmarx Corp. [*NYSE symbol*] (SPSG)
HMX .... Heat, Massage, Exercise [*Medicine*]
HMX .... High-Melting Explosive [*Proprietary name for cyclotetramethylene tetramintriamine*]
HMX .... Marine Helicopter Experimental Squadron
HMX-1 .... Marine Helicopter Experimental Squadron One [*Organized in 1947 for the development and study of helicopter tactics*]
HMXB .... High-Mass X-Ray Binary [*Star system*]
HMY/M .... Heilig-Meyers [*NYSE symbol*] (TTSB)
HMY .... Heilig-Meyers Co. [*NYSE symbol*] (SPSG)

HMY .... High Modulus Yarn
HMY .... His [*or Her*] Majesty's Yacht [*Navy British*]
HMY .... Lexington, OK [*Location identifier FAA*] (FAAL)
HMZ .... Nigerian International Air Services Ltd. [*ICAO designator*] (FAAC)
HN .... Hafslund Nycomed ADS [*NYSE symbol*] (SPSG)
HN .... Hardware Capability Name (NITA)
Hn .... Haven [*Maps and charts*]
HN .... Head and Neck (DMAA)
HN .... Headline News [*Cable television channel*]
HN .... Head Nurse
HN .... Headquarters Name [*Dialog*] [*Searchable field*] [*Information service or system*] (NITA)
HN .... Hear Now [*An association*] (EA)
HN .... Helium Neon [*LASER*] (DGA)
HN .... Hemagglutinin-Neuraminidase [*An enzyme*]
HN .... Hematemesis Neonatorum [*Medicine*] (DMAA)
HN .... Hemorrhage of Newborn [*Medicine*] (DMAA)
hn .... Henna [*Philately*]
Hn .... Henricus de Baila [*Flourished, 1169-70*] [*Authority cited in pre-1607 legal work*] (DSA)
HN .... Hereditary Nephritis [*Medicine*] (MAE)
HN .... Heroes of the Nations [*A publication*]
HN .... Herpes Network [*Defunct*] (EA)
hn .... Heterogeneous Nuclear [*Biochemistry*]
HN .... Hexagonal Nut
HN .... High Foliage Nester [*Ecology*]
HN .... High Necrosis [*Medicine*] (DMAA)
HN .... High Nitrogen [*Clinical chemistry*]
HN .... High Nutrition
HN .... Hilar Node [*Medicine*] (MAE)
HN .... Hindustan-Aeronautics Ltd. [*India*] [*ICAO aircraft manufacturer identifier*] (ICAO)
HN .... Hoc Nocte [*Tonight*] [*Pharmacy*]
HN .... Home Nursing
HN .... Honduras [*ANSI two-letter standard code*] (CNC)
HN .... Horn
HN .... Hospitalman [*Nonrated enlisted man*] [*Navy*]
HN .... Host Nation (AABC)
HN .... Host to Network [*Computer science*]
HN .... House Nigger [*Derogatory nickname for an obsequious black person*]
HN .... Human Nutrition [*Dietetics*] (DAVI)
HN .... Human Nutrition Research Division [*of ARS, Department of Agriculture*]
HN .... [*The*] Hutchinson & Northern Railway Co. [*AAR code*]
HN .... Hypertrophic Neuropathy [*Medicine*] (DMAA)
HN .... Naturalis Historia [*of Pliny the Elder*] [*Classical studies*] (OCD)
HN .... Nitrogen Mustard [*Also, M, MBA, NM*] [*Antineoplastic drug, war-gas base Army symbol used with numerals, as HN1*]
HN .... NLM-Dutch Airlines [*ICAO designator*] (AD)
HN .... Sunset to Sunrise [*ICAO*] (FAAC)
HN_2 .... Mechlorethamine [*Nitrogen mustard*] (MEDA)
HN_2 .... Nitrogen Mustard [*Antineoplastic drug*] (DAVI)
HNA .... Chicago, IL [*Location identifier FAA*] (FAAL)
HNA .... Hanamaki [*Japan*] [*Airport symbol Obsolete*] (OAG)
HNA .... Harrison Narcotic Act
HNA .... Heparin Neutralizing Activity [*Medicine*]
HNA .... Hierarchical Network Architecture
HNA .... High Nickel Alloy
HNA .... Hitachi Network Architecture
HNA .... Hockey North America (EA)
HNA .... Hospice Nurses Association (EA)
HNAA .... Holistic Nurses Association of Australia
HNAB .... Hexanitroazobenzene [*Organic chemistry*]
HNADC .... Honorary Naval Aide-de-Camp [*British*]
HNARMENTD... Hereinafter Mentioned [*Legal*] [*British*] (ROG)
HNB .... Hrvatska Narodna Banka [*Croatian National Bank*]
HNB .... Huntingburg, IN [*Location identifier FAA*] (FAAL)
HNB .... Hydroxynitrobenzyl [*Organic chemistry*]
HNB .... Hydroxynitrobenzylbromide [*Organic chemistry*] (MAE)
HNB .... New Britain General Hospital, Health Sciences Library, New Britain, CT [*OCLC symbol*] (OCLC)
HNBA .... Hispanic National Bar Association (EA)
HNBC .... Harleysville National Corp. [*NASDAQ symbol*] (SAG)
HNBC .... Harleysville Natl [*NASDAQ symbol*] (TTSB)
HNBEFMENTD... Hereinbefore Mentioned [*Legal*] [*British*] (ROG)
HNBK .... Handbook (WDAA)
HNC .... Center for Disease Control, Atlanta, GA [*OCLC symbol*] (OCLC)
HNC .... Hand Numerical Control (IAA)
HNC .... Higher National Certificate [*British*]
HNC .... High National Council
HNC .... Human Nutrition Center [*Oklahoma State University*] [*Research center*] (RCD)
HNC .... Hypothalamo-Neurohypophyseal Complex [*Endocrinology*]
HNC/D .... Higher National Certificate/Diploma (ACII)
HNCMT .... Hawkesbury Nepean Catchment Management Trust [*Resource management*] [*Australia*]
HNCS .... HNC Software [*NASDAQ symbol*] (TTSB)
HNCS .... HNC Software, Inc. [*NASDAQ symbol*] (SAG)
HNC Sft....... HNC Software, Inc. [*Associated Press*] (SAG)
HND .... Hand (WGA)
HND .... Higher National Diploma [*British*]
HND .... Highways for National Defense [*MTMC*] (TAG)
HND .... Honduras [*ANSI three-letter standard code*] (CNC)
HND .... Huntsville Nuclear Division [*Army Corps of Engineers*] (RDA)

HND .... State Historical Society of North Dakota, Bismarck, ND [*OCLC symbol*] (OCLC)
HND .... Tokyo [*Japan*] Haneda Airport [*Airport symbol*] (OAG)
HNDBK ...... Handbook
HNDCPD .... Handicapped
HNDCRFT .... Handicraft
HNDLER. ..... Handler (NASA)
HNDLR........ Handler
HNDP .... Handicap
HNDPRNT.... Handprint
HNDR.......... Heteronuclear Double Resonance (IAA)
HNDRL .... Hand Rail
HNDST......... Handset
HNDT .... Holographic Nondestructive Testing
HNDWL .... Handwheel
HNDY .... Handy
HNDYMN ..... Handyman
HNE .... Harriman & Northeastern R. R. [*AAR code*]
HNE .... HN Engineering, Inc. [*Burnaby, BC*] [*Telecommunications*] (TSSD)
HNE .... Human Neutrophil Elastase [*An enzyme*]
HNE .... Hydronuclear Experiment
HNE .... Hydronuclear Experiments [*Nuclear physics*]
HNE .... Hydroxynonenal [*Biochemistry*]
HNE .... National Institute of Environmental Health Sciences, Research Triangle Park, NC [*OCLC symbol*] (OCLC)
HNE .... Tahneta Pass Lodge, AK [*Location identifier FAA*] (FAAL)
HNED .... Horizontal Null External Distance (OA)
HNEI .... Hawaii Natural Energy Institute [*University of Hawaii at Manoa*] [*Research center*] (RCD)
HNET .... Houston Network Controller [*NASA*] (KSC)
HNF .... Hepatocyte Nuclear Factor [*Biochemistry*]
HNF1 .... Hepatocyte Nuclear Factor 1 [*Genetics*]
HNFBR....... Horn Fiber
HNFC .... Hinsdale Financial [*NASDAQ symbol*] (TTSB)
HNFC .... Hinsdale Financial Corp. [*NASDAQ symbol*] (SAG)
HNG .... Hanging (MSA)
hng .... Hanging (VRA)
HNG .... Heavy Narrow Gap [*Nuclear energy*] (NUCP)
HNG .... Hienghene [*New Caledonia*] [*Airport symbol Obsolete*] (OAG)
HNG .... Hilfsfonds fuer die Opfer der Nuernberger Gesetze [*A publication*] (BJA)
HNG .... Hinge (MSA)
HNG .... Hongo [*Japan*] [*Seismograph station code, US Geological Survey Closed*] (SEIS)
HNGL.......... Helium Neon Gas LASER
HNGR........... Hangar (KSC)
HNGR........... Hangar
HNGRY .... Hungry
hngscr .... Hanging Scroll (VRA)
HNH .... Handy & Harman [*NYSE symbol*] (SPSG)
HNH .... Hanover [*New Hampshire*] [*Seismograph station code, US Geological Survey*] (SEIS)
HNH .... Hoonah [*Alaska*] [*Airport symbol*] (OAG)
HNHIC......... Hepatic Nonheme Iron Content [*Physiology*]
HNI .... Health News Institute [*Defunct*]
HNI .... Holmes & Narver, Inc. (MCD)
HNI .... National Institutes of Health, Bethesda, MD [*OCLC symbol*] (OCLC)
HNIC .... Head Nigger in Charge [*Slang*]
HNIC .... Hockey Night in Canada [*Television program*]
HNickJS....... Hicksville Junior High School, Hicksville, NY [*Library symbol*] [*Library of Congress*] (LCLS)
HNIG .... Human Normal Immunoglobulin [*Medicine*] (PDAA)
HNIL .... High-Noise-Immunity Logic
HNIS .... Human Nutrition Information Service [*Hyattsville, MD*] [*Department of Agriculture*]
HNIW .... Hexanitrohexazaisowurtzitane [*An explosive*]
HN(JC) .... Hospitalman (Junior College) [*Navy*] (DNAB)
HNK .... Hancock, NY [*Location identifier FAA*] (FAAL)
HNK .... Hinchinbrook Island [*Australia Airport symbol*]
HNL .... Helium Neon LASER
HNL .... Holifield National Laboratory [*Later, Oak Ridge National Laboratory*]
HNL .... Honolulu [*Hawaii*] [*Airport symbol*] (OAG)
HNL .... Honolulu [*Hawaii*] [*Seismograph station code, US Geological Survey Closed*] (SEIS)
HNLC .... Hourly Noise Level
HNLC .... High Nutrient, Low Chlorophyll [*Biological oceanography*]
HNLG .... Handling
HNLM .... High Noise-Level Margin
HNM .... Hana [*Hawaii*] [*Airport symbol*] (OAG)
HNM .... Helicopter Noise Model [*OST*] (TAG)
HNM .... Hertzberg-New Method [*Standard periodical binding*]
HNM .... Hexanitromannite [*Organic chemistry*]
HNML .... Hindu Meal [*Airline notation*]
HNMR .... High-Resolution Nuclear Magnetic Resonance
HNMS .... Her Netherlands Majesty's Ship
HNMS .... High NATO Military Structure (NATG)
HNN .... Henderson, WV [*Location identifier FAA*] (FAAL)
HNO .... Henderson, TX [*Location identifier FAA*] (FAAL)
HNO .... Hercegnovi [*Yugoslavia*] [*Airport symbol*] (AD)
HNO .... Honcho Gold Mines, Inc. [*Vancouver Stock Exchange symbol*]
HNO .... Hrvatski Narodni Odbor [*Croatian National Resistance*] [*Former Yugoslavia*] (PD)
HNO₃........... Nitric Acid [*Chemistry*] (DAVI)
HNP .... Haddam Neck Plant [*Nuclear energy*] (NRCH)
HNP .... Hartsville Nuclear Plant (NRCH)

HNP .... Harvard Negotiation Project
HNP .... Herniated Nucleus Pulposus [*Medicine*]
HNP .... Herstigte Nasionale Party [*Reconstituted National Party*] [*South Africa*] [*Political party*] (PPW)
HNP .... High Needle Position [*on dial*]
HNP .... Huaneng Power International, Inc. [*NYSE symbol*] (SAG)
HNP .... Huaneng Power Intl ADS [*NYSE symbol*] (TTSB)
HNP .... Minneapolis, MN [*Location identifier FAA*] (FAAL)
HNP .... Parklawn Health Library, Rockville, MD [*OCLC symbol*] (OCLC)
HNPA .... Home Numbering Plan Area [*AT & T*]
HNPCC .... Hereditary Nonpolyposis Colon Cancer [*Medicine*]
HNPF .... Hallam Nuclear Power Facility [*Decommissioned*] [*AEC*]
HNPL .... High-Level Network Processing Language [*Computer science*] (MHDI)
HNPP .... Hereditary Neuropathy with Liability to Pressure Palsies
HNQ .... Hydroxynaphthoquinone [*Organic chemistry*]
HNR .... Haiti National Airlines [*ICAO designator*] (FAAC)
HNR .... Handwritten Numeral Recognition (IAA)
HNR .... Harlan, IA [*Location identifier FAA*] (FAAL)
HNR .... Heaston Resources Ltd. [*Vancouver Stock Exchange symbol*]
HNR .... Honiara [*Solomon Islands*] [*Seismograph station code, US Geological Survey*] (SEIS)
hnr .... Honoree [*MARC relator code*] [*Library of Congress*] (LCCP)
HNRC.......... USDA [*United States Department of Agriculture*] Human Nutrition Research Center on Aging at Tufts [*Tufts University*] [*Research center*] (RCD)
HNRIM .... Human Nutrition Research and Information Management System [*National Institute of Health*]
hnRNA .... Ribonucleic Acid, Heterogeneous Nuclear [*Biochemistry, genetics*]
hnRNP .... Ribonucleoprotein, Heterogeneous [*Biochemistry*]
HNRS .... Honors (ADA)
HNS .... Haines [*Alaska*] [*Airport symbol*] (OAG)
HNS .... Hamilton Normal School
HNS .... Haveeru News Service [*Maldives*] (EY)
HNS .... Hazardous and Noxious Substance
HNS .... Head and Neck Surgery [*Medical specialty*] (DHSM)
HNS .... Head, Neck, and Shaft [*of a bone*] [*Osteology*]
HNS .... Hexanitrostilbene [*High explosive*]
HNS .... Holy Name Society [*Defunct*] (EA)
HNS .... Home Nursing Supervisor [*Red Cross*]
HNS .... Host Nation Support [*Military*]
HNS .... Hrvatska Narodna Stranka [*Croatian People's Party*] [*Political party*]
HNS .... Hughes Network Systems
HNSA .... Host Nation Support Agreement [*Navy*] (ANA)
HNSD .... Hansard (DCTA)
HNSF .... Hungarian National Sports Federation (EA)
HNSHA .... Hereditary Nonspherocytic Hemolytic Anemia [*Medicine*]
HNST .... Hexanitrostilbene [*High explosive*] (MCD)
HNSX .... Honeywell-NEC Supercomputers, Inc.
HNT .... Handbuch zum Neuen Testament [*A publication*] (BJA)
HNT .... Helicopteros Internacionales, SA de CV [*Mexico*] [*FAA designator*] (FAAC)
HNT .... Hostage Negotiating Team (LAIN)
HNT .... National Center for Toxicological Research, Jefferson, AR [*OCLC symbol*] (OCLC)
HNTB .... Halstead Neuropsychological Test Battery (EDAC)
HNTD .... Highest Non-Toxic Dose (OA)
HNTG .... Hunting (MSA)
HntgIn .... Huntingdon International Holdings Ltd. [*Associated Press*] (SAG)
H-NTLA .... Hiskey-Nebraska Test of Learning Aptitude (EDAC)
HNTR .... Hunter
HNV .... Hanover Direct [*Formerly, Horn & Hardart Co.*] [*AMEX symbol*] (SPSG)
HNV .... Has Not Voided [*Urology*]
HNVS .... Helicopter Night Vision System (PDAA)
HNVS .... Hughes Night Vision System [*Aviation*]
HNW .... Head, Nut, and Washer [*Construction*]
HNW .... Heeresnachrichtenwesen [*Army Communications System*] [*German military - World War II*]
HNW .... Hein-Werner [*AMEX symbol*] (TTSB)
HNW .... Hein-Werner Corp. [*AMEX symbol*] (SPSG)
HNW .... Placerville, CA [*Location identifier FAA*] (FAAL)
HNY .... Hamilton [*New York*] [*Seismograph station code, US Geological Survey*] (SEIS)
HNY .... Happy New Year
HNY .... Hennessy Resource Corp. [*Vancouver Stock Exchange symbol*]
HNY .... Honey (WGA)
HNYB .... Honeybee
HNYCMB ...... Honeycomb
HNZ .... Havelock North [*New Zealand*] [*Seismograph station code, US Geological Survey Closed*] (SEIS)
HNZ .... Heinz [*H. J.*] Co. [*NYSE symbol*] (SPSG)
HNZ .... Heinz [*H.J.*] [*NYSE symbol*] (TTSB)
HNZPr.......... Heinz $1.70 cm Cv Pfd [*NYSE symbol*] (TTSB)
HO .... Airways International [*ICAO designator*] (AD)
HO .... Charterair [*ICAO designator*] (AD)
HO .... Haem Oxygenase [*An enzyme*]
HO .... Hale Observatories [*Formerly, Mount Palomar and Mount Wilson Observatories*]
H-O .... Half of 'O' Gauge [*Model railroading*]
HO .... Halogenated Organic Carbons (GNE)
HO .... Hand Orthosis [*Medicine*]
HO .... Hand Over (MCD)
H/O .... Handover
H/O .... Hard Over (KSC)

HO	Harmonic Oscillator
HO	Hazardous Organics [*Environmental science*]
HO	Head Office
HO	Heel Off Ground [*Medicine*]
H/O	Hematology and Oncology (DAVI)
HO	Heterotopic Ossification [*Osteology*]
HO	High Oblique [*Aerospace*]
HO	High Order [*Computer science*] (OA)
HO	High Output [*Automotive engineering*]
HO	High Oxygen (MAE)
HO	Hip Orthosis [*Medicine*]
H/O	History Of [*Medicine*]
HO	History Office (MCD)
HO	Hoist
HO	Hold [*Shipping*] (DS)
HO	Holding Out [*Cashier fraud*]
HO	Holdover [*Theater*]
Ho	Holmium [*Chemical element*]
HO	Holy Day of Obligation [*Roman Catholicism*]
HO	Holy Orders (ROG) -
HO	Home Office [*British*]
HO	Home Only [*British military*] (DMA)
HO	Homeowners' [*Insurance*]
Ho	Homobonus de Cremona [*Deceased, 1272*] [*Authority cited in pre-1607 legal work*] (DSA)
ho	Honduras [*MARC country of publication code Library of Congress*] (LCCP)
HO	Horizontally Opposed [*Automotive engineering*]
HO	Horizontal Output (IAA)
Ho	Horse (DMAA)
Ho	Hosea [*Old Testament book*] (BJA)
Ho	Hostiensis [*Deceased, 1271*] [*Authority cited in pre-1607 legal work*] (DSA)
HO	Hostilities Only [*Applied to men who joined for duration of war only*] [*Navy British World War II*]
HO	Hotel (ROG)
HO	Hours of Operation
HO	House
HO	House Officer
HO	Human Operator (IAA)
HO	Hunting Oscillator (IAA)
HO	Hydraulic Operator (NRCH)
HO	Hydrogen-Oxygen [*NASA*] (NASA)
HO	Hydrographic Office [*Terminated, 1963; later, NOO*] [*Navy*]
ho	Hydroxy [*As substituent on nucleoside*] [*Also, oh*] [*Biochemistry*]
HO	Hyperbaric Oxygen [*Medicine*]
HO	Observation Helicopter
Ho	Observed Altitude
HO	Service Available to Meet Operational Requirements [*ICAO*] (FAAC)
HOA	Hands Off - Automatic (AAG)
HOA	Heavy Observation Aircraft
HOA	Hechalutz Organization of America [*Defunct*] (EA)
HOA	Hip Osteoarthritis [*Medicine*] (DMAA)
HOA	Home Owner Association
HOA	Homeowners Assistance Fund, Defense [*DoD*]
HOA	Homeowner's Association [*Computer science*]
HOA	House of Assembly [*South Australia*]
HOA	(Hydroxyethyl)oxamic Acid [*Organic chemistry*]
HOA	Hypertrophic Osteoarthropathy [*Medicine*] (DMAA)
HOAB	Heptyloxyazoxybenzene [*Organic chemistry*]
HOACGA	Heart of America Carnival Glass Association (EA)
HOAI	Human Outreach and Advancement Institute
HOAL	Homes on Aboriginal Land [*Australia*]
HOALM	Holographic Optic Addressed Light Modulation (IAA)
HOAM	Healthwise of America, Inc. [*NASDAQ symbol*] (SAG)
HO & RC	Humble Oil & Refining Co. (MHDW)
HOANSW	Hospital Officers' Association of New South Wales [*Australia*]
HOAP	Home Ownership Assistance Program [*Farmers Home Administration*]
HOAP	Housing Opportunity Assistance Program [*Federal Home Loan Bank Board*]
HOAP	Hydroxydaunomycin [*Adriamycin*], Cytosine Arabinoside, Vincristine, Prednisone [*Antineoplastic drug regimen*] (DAVI)
HOAP-BLEO	, ara-C , Prednisone, Bleomycin [*Vincristine*] [*Cytarabine*] [*Antineoplastic drug regimen*]
HoaRhLG	Horse Anti-Rhesus Lymphocyte Globulin [*Immunology*]
HOARS	Hands-On Annotated Recorded Search (NITA)
HOATS	Human Ovarian Antitumor Serum [*Antineoplastic compound*]
HoaTTG	Horse Anti-Tetanus Toxoid Globulin [*Immunology*]
HOB	Half-Octave Bandwidth
HOB	Head of Bed [*Medicine*]
HOB	Head of Bus (ACRL)
HOB	Height [*Depth*] of Burst
Hob	Hobart's English King's Bench Reports [*80 English Reprint*] [*A publication*] (DLA)
HOB	Hobbs [*New Mexico*] [*Airport symbol*] (OAG)
HOB	Hobbs Public Library, Hobbs, NM [*OCLC symbol*] (OCLC)
HOB	Hobby
HOB	Home-on-Burn
HOB	Homing on Offset Beacon
HOB	Horizontal Oscillating Barrel (PDAA)
HOB	Hot Ore Briquetting (DICI)
HOB	House Office Building [*US Congress*]
HOBA	[*A*] History of the Book in Australia [*Project*]

Hobart	Hobart's English King's Bench Reports [*80 English Reprint*] [*A publication*] (DLA)
Hobart (Eng)	Hobart's English King's Bench Reports [*80 English Reprint*] [*A publication*] (DLA)
HOBE	Horseshoe Bend National Military Park
HOBGI	Honorable Order of the Blue Goose, International [*West Bend, WI*] (EA)
HOBIS	Home Ownership Building Industry Scheme [*Australia*]
HOBIS	Hotel Billing Information System [*Telecommunications*] (TEL)
HOBITS	Haifa On-line Bibliographic Text System [*University of Haifa Library*] [*Information service or system*] (IID)
HOBN	Home Office Business Network [*Information service or system*] (IID)
HOBO	Homing Optical Bomb (MCD)
Hobonus	Homobonus de Cremona [*Deceased, 1272*] [*Authority cited in pre-1607 legal work*] (DSA)
HOBOS	Homing Bomb System [*Air Force*]
HOBP	Hydroxy(octylidene)bis(phosphonic Acid) [*Organic chemistry*]
Hob R	Hobart's English Common Pleas Reports [*80 English Reprint*] [*1613-25*] [*A publication*] (DLA)
Hob R	Hobart's English King's Bench Reports [*80 English Reprint*] [*A publication*] (DLA)
HOBS	High-Orbital Bombardment System (KSC)
HOBS	Home and Office Banking Service [*Bank of Scotland*] (ECON)
HOBS	Homing Bomb System [*Air Force*]
HOBT	Hydroxybenzotriazole
HOBUPSOB	Head of Bed Up for Shortness of Breath [*Medicine*] (DAVI)
HOBY	Hugh O'Brian Youth Foundation (EA)
HOBYAA	Hugh O'Brian Youth Foundation Alumni Association (EA)
HOC	Halogenated Organic Compound [*Organic chemistry*] (FFDE)
HOC	Halogenated Organic Compounds
HOC	Handover Coordinator (SAA)
HOC	Hands-On Component
HOC	Health Officer Certificate (DAVI)
HOC	Heat of Combustion
HOC	Heavy Oil Cracking [*Process*] [*Petroleum industry*]
HOC	Height Overlap Coverage [*RADAR*]
HOC	Heterodyne Optical Correlation (IAA)
HOC	High Output Current
HOC	Hillman Owners Club [*Lancing, Sussex, England*] (EAIO)
HOC	Hillsboro, OH [*Location identifier FAA*] (FAAL)
HOC	History of Coverage (MCD)
HOC	Holly Corp. [*AMEX symbol*] (SPSG)
HOC	Hollywood Overseas Committee (IIA)
HOC	House of Commons [*British*]
HoC	Hoven & Co., Bakersfield, CA [*Library symbol Library of Congress*] (LCLS)
HOC	Human Ovarian Cancer [*Cytology*]
HOC	Hurricane Operations Center (AFM)
HOC	Hydraulic Overspeed Control [*Mechanical power transmission*]
HOC	Hydrofoil Ocean Combatant
HOC	Hydrophobic Organic Chemical [*Physical chemistry*]
HOC	Hydrophobic Organic Compound (USDC)
HOC	Hydrophobic Organic Compound [*Marine science*] (OSRA)
HOC	Hydrophobic Organic Contaminant [*Environmental science*]
HOC	Hydroxycorticosteroid [*Endocrinology*]
HOCA	High Osmolar Contrast Agent [*Medicine*]
HOCA	Hurst/Olds Club of America (EA)
HOCarm	Hermits of Our Lady of Mt. Carmel (TOCD)
HOCCU	Heavy Oil Catalytic Cracking Unit [*Petroleum refining*]
HOCM	Hypertrophic Obstructive Cardiomyopathy [*Cardiology*]
HOCOLEA	Heads of Commonwealth Operational Law Enforcement Agencies [*Australia*]
HoCT	Household Capital Trust [*Associated Press*] (SAG)
HoCT	Household Capital Trust II [*Associated Press*] (SAG)
HOCUS	Hand or Computer Universal Simulation [*PE Computer Services Ltd.*] [*Software package*] [*British*]
HOC VESP	Hoc Vespere [*Tonight*] [*Pharmacy*]
HOD	Head of Department
HOD	Heat of Detonation
HOD	Hebrew Order of David
HOD	Hodeidah [*Yemen Arab Republic*] [*Airport symbol*] (OAG)
Hod	Hodges' English Common Pleas Reports [*1835-37*] [*A publication*] (DLA)
HoD	Hodgkin's Disease [*Oncology*] (DAVI)
HOD	Hoffer-Osmond Diagnostic Test [*Psychology*]
HOD	Home on Decoy [*Military*] (CAAL)
HOD	Hurt on Duty
HOD	Hyperbaric Oxygen Drenching
HODA	Hawkfarm One Design Association (EA)
HODAG	Housing Development Action Grant [*HUD*]
HODCRA	Hampton One-Design Class Racing Association (EA)
Hodg	Hodges' English Common Pleas Reports [*1835-37*] [*A publication*] (DLA)
Hodg	Hodgin's Election Cases [*Ontario*] [*A publication*] (DLA)
Hodg Can Elec Cas	Hodgin's Canada Election Cases [*A publication*] (DLA)
Hodg El	Hodgins' Upper Canada Election Cases [*A publication*] (DLA)
Hodg El Cas	Hodgin's Election Cases [*Ontario*] [*A publication*] (DLA)
Hodg El Cas (Ont)	Hodgin's Election Cases [*Ontario*] [*A publication*] (DLA)
Hodge Presb Law	Hodge on Presbyterian Law [*A publication*] (DLA)
Hodges	Hodges' English Common Pleas Reports [*1835-37*] [*A publication*] (DLA)
Hodges (Eng)	Hodges' English Common Pleas Reports [*1835-37*] [*A publication*] (DLA)
Hodg Ont Elect	Hodgin's Election Cases [*Ontario*] [*A publication*] (DLA)
Hodg Ry	Hodges' Law of Railways [*A publication*] (DLA)

HODI	Homozygous Diabetes Insipidus [*A genetic variety of rat*]
HODS	Hydrographic Oceanographic Data Sheets (NG)
HOE	Height of Eye [*Navigation*]
HOE	Hoechst-Roussel Pharmaceuticals, Inc. [*Research code symbol*]
HOE	Holographic Optical Element
HOE	Homerville, GA [*Location identifier FAA*] (FAAL)
HOE	Homing Overlay Equipment (MCD)
HOE	Homing Overlay Experiment [*Ballistic missile defense*] (RDA)
HOE	Human and Organizational Errors [*Engineering*]
HOE	Hydraulically Operated Equipment
HOEI	Hover-One-Engine-Inoperative (PDAA)
HOEN	Hoenig Group [*NASDAQ symbol*] (TTSB)
HOEN	Hoenig Group, Inc. [*NASDAQ symbol*] (SPSG)
Hoenig	Hoenig Group, Inc. [*Associated Press*] (SAG)
HOET	Heavy Oil Engine Tractor [*British*]
HOF	Hafuf [*Saudi Arabia*] [*Airport symbol*] (OAG)
HOF	Hall of Fame
HOF	Head of Faculty [*Education*] (AIE)
HOF	Head of Form (IAA)
HOF	Heat of Formation
HoF	Height of Fundus [*Obstetrics*]
HOF	Hepatic Outflow [*Medicine*] (DMAA)
HOF	Hof [*Federal Republic of Germany*] [*Seismograph station code, US Geological Survey*] (SEIS)
HOF	Home Office Facility
HOF	Homing Fixture (MCD)
HOF	House of Fraser [*Department store conglomerate*] [*British*]
HOF	St. Paul, MN [*Location identifier FAA*] (FAAL)
HOFC	Hall and Oates Fan Club (EA)
H of C	House of Commons [*British*]
HOFCO	Horizontal Function Checkout (KSC)
HOFD	Heterogeneous Opposed Flow Diffusion
H of F	Hall of Fame (WDAA)
H of F	Height of Fundus [*Obstetrics*]
HofF	Height of Fundus [*Obstetrics*] (DAVI)
HOFF	Hoffmann [*Reflex*] [*Medicine*]
Hoff	Hoffman's Land Cases, United States District Court [*A publication*] (DLA)
Hoff	Hoffman's New York Chancery Reports [*A publication*] (DLA)
Hoff Ch	Hoffman's New York Chancery Reports [*A publication*] (DLA)
Hoff CR	Hoffman's New York Chancery Reports [*A publication*] (DLA)
Hoff Dec	Hoffman's Decisions [*A publication*] (DLA)
Hoff Ecc L	Hoffman's Ecclesiastical Law [*A publication*] (DLA)
Hoff Land	Hoffman's Land Cases, United States District Court [*A publication*] (DLA)
Hoff Land Cas	Hoffman's Land Cases, United States District Court [*A publication*] (DLA)
Hoff LC	Hoffman's Land Cases, United States District Court [*A publication*] (DLA)
Hoff L Cas	Hoffman's Land Cases, United States District Court [*A publication*] (DLA)
Hoff Lead Cas	Hoffman's Leading Cases [*A publication*] (DLA)
Hoff Leg St	Hoffman's Course of Legal Study [*A publication*] (DLA)
HOFFM	Hereditary Order of the First Families of Massachusetts (EA)
Hoffm	Hoffman's Land Cases, United States District Court [*A publication*] (DLA)
Hoffm	Hoffman's New York Chancery Reports [*A publication*] (DLA)
Hoffman Ch R	Hoffman's New York Chancery Reports [*A publication*] (DLA)
Hoffman's Ch R	Hoffman's New York Chancery Reports [*A publication*] (DLA)
Hoff Mast	Hoffman's Master in Chancery [*A publication*] (DLA)
Hoff Mast Ch	Hoffman's Master in Chancery [*A publication*] (DLA)
Hoffm Ch	Hoffman's Land Cases, United States District Court [*A publication*] (DLA)
Hoffm Ch	Hoffman's New York Chancery Reports [*A publication*] (DLA)
Hoffm Ch (NY)	Hoffman's New York Chancery Reports [*A publication*] (DLA)
Hoffm Dec (F)	Hoffman's Decisions, United States District Court [*A publication*] (DLA)
Hoffm Land Cas (F)	Hoffman's Land Cases, United States District Court [*A publication*] (DLA)
Hoffm Ops (F)	Hoffman's Opinions, United States District Court [*A publication*] (DLA)
Hoffm Rep Land Cases	Hoffman's Land Cases, United States District Court [*A publication*] (DLA)
Hoff NY	Hoffman's New York Chancery Reports [*A publication*] (DLA)
Hoff Op	Hoffman's Opinions [*A publication*] (DLA)
Hoff Out	Hoffman's Legal Outlines [*A publication*] (DLA)
Hoff Pr Rem	Hoffman's Provisional Remainders [*A publication*] (DLA)
Hoff Pub P	Hoffman's Public Papers [*New York*] [*A publication*] (DLA)
Hoff Ref	Hoffman on Referees [*A publication*] (DLA)
H of H	Holy of Holies [*Freemasonry*] (ROG)
H of IF	House of Ill Fame
H of J	Hospitallers of Jerusalem [*Freemasonry*] (ROG)
HOFL	Home Financial [*NASDAQ symbol*] (TTSB)
HOFL	Home Financial Corporation of Florida [*NASDAQ symbol*] (SAG)
H of N	Hydrographer of the Navy [*British*]
HOFR	Home of Franklin D. Roosevelt and Vanderbilt Mansion National Historic Sites
H of S	House of Solomon [*Freemasonry*] (ROG)
HOFS	Hydrogen-Oxygen Fuel System [*NASA*]
HOFSL	Home Office Forensic Science Laboratory [*British*]
Hofstra Lab LF	Hofstra Labor Law Forum [*A publication*] (DLA)
Hofstra Lab LJ	Hofstra Labor Law Journal [*A publication*] (DLA)
Hofstra U	Hofstra University (GAGS)
HOFTU	Hunter Operational Fighter Training Unit [*India*] [*Air Force*]
HOG	Halothane, Oxygen, and Gas [*Nitrous oxide*] [*Anesthesiology*] (DAVI)
HOG	Harley Owners' Group (EA)
HOG	Head End Off-Gas [*Nuclear energy*] (NRCH)
HOG	Head of Government (ADA)
HOG	Heavy Ordnance Gunship (NVT)
HOG	High Old Genius [*Slang British*]
Hog	(Hogan of) Harcarse's Scotch Session Cases [*A publication*] (DLA)
Hog	Hogan's Irish Rolls Court Reports [*A publication*] (DLA)
HOG	Holguin [*Cuba*] [*Airport symbol*] (OAG)
HOG	Homing Optical Guidance
HOG	Hondo Oil & Gas [*AMEX symbol*] (TTSB)
HOG	Hondo Oil & Gas Co. [*AMEX symbol*] (SPSG)
HOGA	Hyperornithinemia with Gyrate Atrophy [*Medicine*] (DMAA)
Hogan	(Hogan of) Harcarse's Scotch Session Cases [*A publication*] (DLA)
Hogan	Hogan's Irish Rolls Court Reports [*A publication*] (DLA)
Hogan	Hogan Systems, Inc. [*Associated Press*] (SAG)
Hogan (Ir)	Hogan's Irish Rolls Court Reports [*A publication*] (DLA)
HOGC	Handbook of Occupational Groups and Series of Classes
HOGE	Hover out of Ground Effect
HOGE	Hover-Out-of-Ground Environment
HOGEN	Hold Off Generator (MSA)
HOGN	Hogan Systems, Inc. [*NASDAQ symbol*] (NQ)
HOGS	Homing Optical Guidance System
Hog St Tr	Hogan's Pennsylvania State Trials [*A publication*] (DLA)
Hogue	Hogue's Reports [*1-4 Florida*] [*A publication*] (DLA)
HOH	Hard of Hearing (MAE)
HOH	Head of Household [*IRS*]
HOH	Heard on the Hill [*US Congress*]
HOH	Help Our Headaches Group [*Australia*]
HOH	Hereford Otter Hounds
HOH	High-Degree Helioseismometer
HOH	Hohenheim [*Federal Republic of Germany*] [*Seismograph station code, US Geological Survey Closed*] (SEIS)
HOH	Hydrogen-Oxygen-Hydrogen [*Water*] (HGAA)
HOHI	Handbook of Overhaul Instructions [*Navy*]
HOH of J	Holy Order of the Hospital of Jerusalem [*Freemasonry*] (ROG)
HOHP	Holocaust Oral History Project [*An association*] (EA)
HOI	Handbook of Operating Instructions [*Navy*]
HOI	Handbook of Overhaul Instructions [*Navy*] (MCD)
HOI	Hao Island [*French Polynesia*] [*Airport symbol*] (OAG)
HOI	Headquarters Office Instruction
HOI	Headquarters Operating Instructions [*Air Force*] (AFM)
HOI	Health Optimizing Institute (EA)
HOI	Hear O Israel (EA)
HOI	Hospital Onset of Infection [*Medicine*] (DMAA)
HOI	House of Issue [*Banking*]
Holg	Horse Immunoglobulin [*Immunology*]
HoInt	Household International, Inc. [*Associated Press*] (SAG)
HOIS	Hostile Intelligence Service [*Military*] (MCD)
HOJ	Home on Jamming
HOJ	Hope [*Jamaica*] [*Seismograph station code, US Geological Survey*] (SEIS)
HOJO	Howard Johnson [*Restaurant chain*] [*Slang*]
HOK	Hellmuth, Obata & Kassabaum [*Architectural firm*]
HOK	Hohkeppel [*Federal Republic of Germany*] [*Seismograph station code, US Geological Survey*] (SEIS)
HOK	Hoko Exploration [*Vancouver Stock Exchange symbol*]
HOK	Hooker Creek [*Airport symbol*]
HOK	House of Keys [*Isle Of Man*]
HOKEYS	Home Owners' Loan Corporation Bonds (MHDB)
HOL	Higher Order Logic [*Computer science*]
HOL	High- [*or Higher-*] Order Language [*Computer science*]
HOL	Holco Mortgage Acceptance Corp. [*AMEX symbol*] (SPSG)
HOL	Holiday (AFM)
HOL	Holiday Airlines, Inc. [*ICAO designator*] (FAAC)
HOL	Holiday and Leave [*Military*] (NVT)
HOL	Hollinger Argus Ltd. [*Toronto Stock Exchange symbol*]
HOL	Hollow (MSA)
HOL	House of Lords [*British*]
HOL	Humanization of Labor (IID)
HOLA	Hispanic Organization of Latin Actors (EA)
HOLA	Home Owners' Loan Act of 1933
HOLC	High-Order Language Computer (NASA)
HOLC	Home Owners' Loan Corp. [*Terminated, 1942*]
Ho L Cas	Clark's House of Lords Cases [*1847-66*] [*England*] [*A publication*] (DLA)
Holc Debt & Cr	Holcombe's Law of Debtor and Creditor [*A publication*] (DLA)
Holc Eq Jur	Holcombe's Equity Jurisdiction [*A publication*] (DLA)
Holc L Cas	Holcombe's Leading Cases of Commercial Law [*A publication*] (DLA)
Holco	Holco Mortgage Acceptance Corp. [*Associated Press*] (SAG)
HOLD	American Holdings, Inc. [*NASDAQ symbol*] (SAG)
HOLD	Call Hold [*Telecommunications*] (DOM)
HOLD	Hemostatic Occlusive Leverage Device [*Cardiology*] (DAVI)
HOLDET	Higher Order Language Development and Evaluation Tool [*Computer science*] (MHDB)
HOLF	Helicopter Outlying Field
Holg	Horse Immunoglobulin [*Immunology*] (DAVI)
holgr	Hologram (VRA)
HOLI	Hollinger International, Inc. [*NASDAQ symbol*] (SAG)
Holinger	Hollinger, Inc. [*Associated Press*] (SAG)
HOLL	Holland
Holl	Holland (VRA)
Holl	Hollinshead's Reports [*1 Minnesota*] [*A publication*] (DLA)
HOLLAND	Here Our Love Lives and Never Dies [*Correspondence*] (DSUE)
Holl Comp Deeds	Holland on Composition Deeds [*A publication*] (DLA)
Holl El Jur	Holland's Elements of Jurisprudence [*A publication*] (DLA)

Hollinger ..... Hollinger International, Inc. [*Associated Press*] (SAG)
Hollins C ..... Hollins College (GAGS)
Hollinshead... Hollinshead's Reports [*1 Minnesota*] [*A publication*] (DLA)
Holl Jur ...... Holland's Elements of Jurisprudence [*A publication*] (DLA)
Holl Just...... Holland's Institutes of Justinian [*A publication*] (DLA)
Hollng.......... Hollinger International, Inc. [*Associated Press*] (SAG)
HOLLOW....... Hollow [*Commonly used*] (OPSA)
HOLLOWS..... Hollow [*Commonly used*] (OPSA)
HollyCp........ Holly Corp. [*Associated Press*] (SAG)
HollyH......... Holly Holdings, Inc. [*Associated Press*] (SAG)
HollyHld....... Holly Holdings, Inc. [*Associated Press*] (SAG)
HollyP......... Holly Holdings, Inc. [*Associated Press*] (SAG)
HollyPd....... Holly Products [*Associated Press*] (SAG)
HOLM .... Higher-Order Language Machine [*Computer science*] (KSC)
Holm........... Holmes' Reports [*15-17 Oregon*] [*A publication*] (DLA)
Holm........... Holmes' United States Circuit Court Reports [*A publication*] (DLA)
Holm Com Law... Holmes on the Common Law [*A publication*] (DLA)
Holmes........ Holmes' United States Circuit Court Reports [*A publication*] (DLA)
HOLMES ...... Home Office Large Major Enquiry System [*Computer system*]
                [*British*]
HolmPr........ Holmes Protection Group, Inc. [*Associated Press*] (SAG)
Holm Statesman... Holmes' Statesman [*A publication*] (DLA)
HOLO .... Holograph (WDAA)
HOLO .... HoloPak Technologies [*NASDAQ symbol*] (SPSG)
HOLO .... Holotype
Hologic........ Hologic, Inc. [*Associated Press*] (SAG)
HoLoPak...... HoloPak Technologies [*Associated Press*] (SAG)
Holophne..... Holophane Corp. [*Associated Press*] (SAG)
Ho Lords C... Clark's House of Lords Cases [*1847-66*] [*England*] [*A publication*]
                (DLA)
Ho Lords Cas... Clark's House of Lords Cases [*1847-66*] [*England*]
                [*A publication*] (DLA)
HOLS .... Home Opportunity Loans Scheme [*Australia*]
HOLSA........ Health-Oriented Libraries of San Antonio [*Library network*]
HolsnB........ Holson Burnes Group, Inc. [*Associated Press*] (SAG)
HOLSW....... Holsworthy [*England*]
Holt............. Holt's English Equity Reports [*1845*] [*A publication*] (DLA)
Holt............. Holt's English King's Bench Reports [*A publication*] (DLA)
Holt............. Holt's English Nisi Prius Reports [*A publication*] (DLA)
Holt Adm ..... Holt's English Admiralty Cases (Rule of the Road) [*1863-67*]
                [*A publication*] (DLA)
Holt Adm Ca... Holt's English Admiralty Cases (Rule of the Road) [*1863-67*]
                [*A publication*] (DLA)
Holt Adm Cas... Holt's English Admiralty Cases (Rule of the Road) [*1863-67*]
                [*A publication*] (DLA)
Holt Eq .... Holt's English Equity Reports [*1845*] [*A publication*] (DLA)
Holthouse ... Holthouse's Law Dictionary [*A publication*] (DLA)
Holt KB....... Holt's English King's Bench Reports [*A publication*] (DLA)
Holt L Dic ... Holthouse's Law Dictionary [*A publication*] (DLA)
Holt Lib ...... Holt on Libels [*A publication*] (DLA)
Holt Nav ..... Holt on Navigation [*A publication*] (DLA)
Holt NP....... Holt's English Nisi Prius Reports [*A publication*] (DLA)
Holt Reg ..... Holt on Registration of Title [*A publication*] (DLA)
Holt R of R... Holt's English Admiralty Cases (Rule of the Road) [*A publication*]
                (DLA)
Holt Sh .... Holt on Shipping [*A publication*] (DLA)
Holt Shipp ... Holt on Shipping [*A publication*] (DLA)
HOLUA........ Home Office Life Underwriters Association [*St. Louis, MO*] (EA)
HOLUG........ Houston On Line Users Group (NITA)
HOLUPK....... Holiday, Upkeep [*Military*] (NVT)
HOLV .... Hop Latent Virus [*Plant pathology*]
HOLW .... Hollow
HOLW .... Hollow
HOLWG........ High- [*or Higher-*] Order Language Working Group [*Computer
                science*] (RDA)
HOLWS........ Hollow [*Commonly used*] (OPSA)
HOLX .... Holiday Airlines, Inc. [*Air carrier designation symbol*]
HOLX .... Hologic, Inc. [*NASDAQ symbol*] (SAG)
HOLX .... Hologic Inc. [*NASDAQ symbol*] (TTSB)
Holy Names C... Holy Names College (GAGS)
HOLZ .... Higher Order Laue Zone [*Crystal diffraction lines*]
HOM .... Heartless Old Man [*Alternative sobriquet for William Gladstone, 1809-
                98, British statesman and prime minister, who was known to
                admirers as GOM, which see*]
HOM .... Hectometric Emissions [*Radio astronomy*]
HOM .... Hexamethylmelamine, Oncovin [*Vincristine*], Methotrexate
                [*Antineoplastic drug regimen*] (DAVI)
HOM .... High-Order Multiplier (IAA)
HOM .... Homer [*Alaska*] [*Seismograph station code, US Geological Survey*]
                (SEIS)
HOM .... Homer [*Greek poet, c. 800BC*] [*Classical studies*] (ROG)
HOM .... Homer [*Alaska*] [*Airport symbol*] (OAG)
HOM .... Homily (ROG)
HOM .... Homing
Hom............. Homobonus de Cremona [*Deceased, 1272*] [*Authority cited in pre-
                1607 legal work*] (DSA)
Hom............. Homoptera [*Entomology*]
HoM............. Howell Microfilms Co., College, MD [*Library symbol Library of
                Congress*] (LCLS)
HOMA.......... Heads of Marine Agencies [*Commonwealth*] [*State*] (EERA)
HOMAC........ Home Mortgage Access Corp. (EMRF)
HomBen....... Home Beneficial Corp. [*Associated Press*] (SAG)
HomBib....... Homiletica en Biblica [*The Hague*] [*A publication*] (BJA)
HOME .... Home Centers (DIY) Ltd. [*NASDAQ symbol*] (SAG)

HOME .... Home Observation for Measurement of the Environment [*Child
                development test*] [*Psychology*]
HOME .... Home Oncology Medical Extension [*A home treatment program*]
HOME .... Home Oriented Maternity Experience [*Defunct*] (EA)
HOME .... Home Ownership Made Easy Association [*Defunct*] (EA)
Home........... Home's Manuscript Decisions, Scotch Court of Session
                [*A publication*] (DLA)
HOME .... Homestead National Monument
HOME .... Homeworkers Organized for More Employment (EA)
Home (Cl)..... Clerk Home's Decisions, Scotch Court of Session [*1735-44*]
                [*A publication*] (DLA)
Home (Clk)... Home's Manuscript Decisions, Scotch Court of Session
                [*A publication*] (DLA)
HomeCnt...... Home Centers (DIY) Ltd. [*Associated Press*] (SAG)
Home Ct of Sess... Home's Manuscript Decisions, Scotch Court of Session
                [*A publication*] (DLA)
HOMEF .... Home Centers [*NASDAQ symbol*] (TTSB)
Homegte...... Homegate Hospitality, Inc. [*Associated Press*] (SAG)
Home H Dec... Home's Manuscript Decisions, Scotch Court of Session
                [*A publication*] (DLA)
HomeHld...... Home Holdings [*Associated Press*] (SAG)
HOMEO .... Homeopathy (ADA)
HOMEOP...... Homeopathy [*Medicine*]
HOMER .... High-Altitude Ozone Measuring and Educational Rocket [*NASA*]
HOMES .... Homeowner-Mortgage Eurosecurities [*Salomon Brothers*] [*Real
                estate*]
HOMES .... Housing Operations Management System [*DoD*]
HOMES .... Huron, Ontario, Michigan, Erie, Superior [*Great Lakes*]
HomeSh....... Home Shopping Network, Inc. [*Associated Press*] (SAG)
HOMESWEST... Western Australian State Housing Commission
HomeTB....... Hometown Buffet, Inc. [*Associated Press*] (SAG)
HomeV......... Homestead Village, Inc. [*Associated Press*] (SAG)
HomeVil....... Homestead Village, Inc. [*Associated Press*] (SAG)
HOMF .... Home Fed Bancorp [*NASDAQ symbol*] (TTSB)
HOMG .... Homeowners Group [*NASDAQ symbol*] (TTSB)
HOMG .... Homeowners Group, Inc. [*NASDAQ symbol*] (NQ)
HOMI .... Homicide (DLA)
HOMIC .... Homicide [*Legal shorthand*] (LWAP)
HOMO .... Highest Occupied Molecular Orbital [*Atomic physics*]
HOMO .... Homeopath [*or Homeopathic*] (WDAA)
HOMO .... Homogenous
HOMO .... Homosexual
Homob......... Homobonus de Cremona [*Deceased, 1272*] [*Authority cited in pre-
                1607 legal work*] (DSA)
HOMOCO ..... Homemakers & Mothers Cooperatives, Inc.
HomoD........ Homo Dei. Przeglad Ascetyczno-Duszpasterski [*Warsaw/Wroclaw*]
                [*A publication*] (BJA)
HOMOEO...... Homoeopathy [*Medicine*]
HOMOLAT.... Homolateral [*Medicine*]
HOMP .... Halifax Ocean Meeting Point
HOMS .... Harbor Operations and Maintenance Support [*Navy*] (VNW)
HOMS .... Hellfire Optimized Missile System [*Army*] (DOMA)
HOMS .... Home State Holdings [*NASDAQ symbol*] (TTSB)
HOMS .... Home State Holdings, Inc. [*NASDAQ symbol*] (SAG)
HOMS .... Hydrological Operational Multipurpose Subprogramme [*World
                Meteorological Organization*] [*Information service or system*] (IID)
hom sap ..... Homo Sapiens (BARN)
HOMSTD...... Homestead (DLA)
HOMT .... Hydroxyindole O-Methyltransferase [*Also, HIOMT*] [*An enzyme*]
HOMV .... Hop Mosaic Virus [*Plant pathology*]
HON .... Handbook of the Nations [*A publication*]
HON .... Hazardous Organic NESHAP [*National Emission Standards for
                Hazardous Air Polluta nts*] (GNE)
HON .... Hazardous Organic NESHAP (National Emission Standards for
                Hazardous Air Pollutants) [*Environmental Protection Agency*]
HON .... Hold Off Normal
HON .... Honduras
HON .... Honey (DSUE)
HON .... Honeywell Electro-Optics Center Library, Lexington, MA [*OCLC
                symbol*] (OCLC)
HON .... Honeywell, Inc. [*Formerly, MH, M-H*] [*NYSE symbol*] (SPSG)
HON .... Honington FTU [*British ICAO designator*] (FAAC)
HON .... Honiton [*Municipal borough in England*]
HON .... Honolulu [*Hawaii*] [*Seismograph station code, US Geological
                Survey*] (SEIS)
HON .... Honorable
HON .... Honorable (DD)
HON .... Honorable
HON .... Honorary (MSA)
Hon............. Honorius de Kent [*Flourished, 1185-1208*] [*Authority cited in pre-
                1607 legal work*] (DSA)
HON .... Huron [*South Dakota*] [*Airport symbol*] (OAG)
HON .... Hydroxyoxo-L-norvaline [*Antibiotic*]
HONA.......... Health of Naval Aviation (DOMA)
HON AF....... Honorary Admiral of the Fleet [*Navy British*] (ROG)
Hon ARAM... Honorary Associate of the Royal Academy of Music [*British*]
HonARCM.... Honorary Associate of the Royal College of Music [*British*] (DI)
HonASTA .... Honorary Associate of the Swimming Teachers' Association
                [*British*] (DBQ)
HONBLE...... Honorable
HONCAUS.... Honoris Causa [*For the Sake of Honor, Honorary*] [*Latin*] (ADA)
HOND.......... Honduras
Hond.......... Honduras (VRA)
HOND.......... Honoured (ROG)
Honda........ Honda Motors Co. Ltd. [*Associated Press*] (SAG)

HonDLitt......	Honorary Doctor of Letters
Hondo.........	Hondo Oil & Gas Co. [*Associated Press*] (SAG)
HonDrRCA ...	Honorary Doctorate of the Royal College of Art [*British*] (DBQ)
HonDSc.......	Honorary Doctor of Science
HONEST......	Helicopter Operations in a Night Environment Against a Simulated Target [*Military*] (MCD)
HonFBID	Honorary Fellow of the British Institute of Interior Design (DBQ)
Hon FEIS	Honorary Fellow of the Educational Institute of Scotland
HonFHCIMA..	Honorary Fellow of the Hotel, Catering, and Institutional Management Association [*British*] (DBQ)
HonFIGasE...	Honorary Fellow of the Institution of Gas Engineers [*British*] (DBQ)
HonFIIM.......	Honorary Fellow of the Institution of Industrial Managers [*British*] (DBQ)
HonFIMarE...	Honorary Fellow of the Institute of Marine Engineers [*British*] (DBQ)
HonFIMechE..	Honorary Fellow of the Institution of Mechanical Engineers [*British*] (DBQ)
HonFIMM.....	Honorary Fellow of the Institution of Mining and Metallurgy [*British*] (DBQ)
HonFInstE....	Honorary Fellow of the Institute of Energy [*British*] (DBQ)
HonFInstMC...	Honorary Fellow of the Institute of Measurement [*British*] (DBQ)
HonFInstNDT...	Honorary Fellow of the British Institute of Non-Destructive Testing (DBQ)
HonFIOP	Honorary Fellow of the Institute of Printing [*British*] (DI)
HonFIQA	Honorary Fellow of the Institute of Quality Assurance [*British*] (DBQ)
HonFIRSE	Honorary Fellow of the Institution of Railway Signal Engineers [*British*] (DBQ)
HonFITD	Honorary Fellow of the Institute of Training and Development [*British*] (DI)
HonFIWHTE...	Honorary Fellow of the Institution of Works and Highways Technician Engineers [*British*] (DBQ)
Hon FNDTS...	Honorary Fellow of the Non-Destructive Testing Society of Great Britain
HonFPRI	Honorary Life Member of the Plastics and Rubber Institute [*British*] (DBQ)
Hon FRAM ...	Honorary Fellow of the Royal Academy of Music [*British*]
Hon FRPS ...	Honorary Fellow of the Royal Photographic Society [*British*]
HonFSCP	Honorary Fellow of the Society of Certified Professionals [*British*] (DBQ)
HonFSE.......	Honorary Fellow of the Society of Engineers, Inc. [*British*] (DBQ)
HonFSGT	Honorary Fellow of the Society of Glass Technology [*British*] (DBQ)
HonFSLAET...	Honorary Fellow of the Society of Licensed Aircraft Engineers and Technologists [*British*] (DBQ)
HonFWeldI...	Honorary Fellow of the Welding Institute [*British*] (DBQ)
Hong Kong LJ...	Hong Kong Law Journal [*A publication*] (DLA)
Hong Kong LR...	Hong Kong Law Reports [*A publication*] (DLA)
Hong Kong UL Jo...	Hong Kong University. Law Journal [*A publication*] (DLA)
HonGSM	Honorary Member of the Guildhall School of Music and Drama [*British*] (DBQ)
HONI...........	HON Indus [*NASDAQ symbol*] (TTSB)
HONI...........	Hon Industries, Inc. [*NASDAQ symbol*] (NQ)
HonInd........	Hon Industries, Inc. [*Associated Press*] (SAG)
HON L........	Honorary Lieutenant [*Navy British*] (ROG)
HON M........	Honorary Member (ROG)
HonMInst NDT...	Honorary Member of the British Institute of Non-Destructive Testing (DBQ)
Hon MNDTS...	Honorary Member of the Non-Destructive Testing Society of Great Britain
HonMRIN.....	Honorary Member of the Royal Institute of Navigation [*British*] (DBQ)
HonMWES ...	Honorary Member of the Women's Engineering Society [*British*] (DBQ)
HONO.........	Honolulu [*Hawaii*] (CINC)
Hon RAM	Honorary Member of the Royal Academy of Music [*British*]
HonRCM	Honorary Member of the Royal College of Music [*British*] (DBQ)
HonRNCM....	Honorary Member of the Royal Northern College of Music [*British*] (DBQ)
Hon RSCM...	Honorary Member of the Royal School of Church Music [*British*]
honry	Honorary (DD)
Hons	Honors (DD)
HONS...........	Honors
HON SCH MOD LANG...	Honour School of Modern Languages [*British*] (ROG)
HON SEC	Honorary Secretary (ROG)
HON SURG LIEUT COL...	Honorary Surgeon Lieutenant-Colonel [*Military British*] (ROG)
HON VA	Honorary Vice-Admiral [*Navy British*] (ROG)
HONY..........	Honorary (WGA)
Honywel......	Honeywell, Inc. [*Associated Press*] (SAG)
HOO	Avila College, Kansas City, MO [*OCLC symbol*] (OCLC)
HOO	Glacier Water Services [*AMEX symbol*] (TTSB)
HOO	Glacier Water Services, Inc. [*AMEX symbol*] (SAG)
HOO	Hanford Operations Office [*Nuclear energy*] (MCD)
HOO	Hiroo [*Japan*] [*Seismograph station code, US Geological Survey*] (SEIS)
HOO	Quang Duc [*South Vietnam*] [*Airport symbol*] (AD)
HOOD.........	Hereditary Osteo-Onychodysplasia [*Medicine*]
HOOD.........	Hierarchical Object-Oriented Design [*Computer science*] (ODBW)
Hood	Neighborhood [*Slang*]
Hood C	Hood College (GAGS)
Hood Ex	Hood on Executors [*A publication*] (DLA)
HOOK..........	Handbook of Occupational Keywords [*For use in employment services*] [*Department of Labor*]
Hook	Hooker's Reports [*25-62 Connecticut*] [*A publication*] (DLA)
HOOK..........	Redhook Ale Brewery [*NASDAQ symbol*] (TTSB)
HOOK..........	Redhook Ale Brewery, Inc. [*NASDAQ symbol*] (SAG)
Hooker	Hooker's Reports [*25-62 Connecticut*] [*A publication*] (DLA)
Hoon	Hoonahan's Sind Reports [*India*] [*A publication*] (DLA)

Hoonahan....	Hoonahan's Sind Reports [*India*] [*A publication*] (DLA)
HOOP	Handbook of Operating Procedures
HOOP	Sure Shot International, Inc. [*NASDAQ symbol*] (SAG)
HOOP	Sure Shot Intl Inc. [*NASDAQ symbol*] (TTSB)
HoopHI.......	Hooper Holmes, Inc. [*Associated Press*] (SAG)
HOOPS........	Hierarchical Object-Oriented Picture System [*Computer science*]
HOOPW.......	Sure Shot Intl Wrrt [*NASDAQ symbol*] (TTSB)
HOP	Handoff Point [*Aviation*] (FAAC)
HOP	HEDL [*Hanford Engineering Development Laboratory*] Overpower [*Nuclear energy*] (NRCH)
HOP	Helicopter Operations (FAAC)
HOP	Helium Oxidizer-Tank Pressure (AAG)
HOP	Help Other People [*Scout motto*]
HOP	High-Order Position (AFIT)
HOP	High Oxygen Pressure
HOP	Holding Procedures (SAA)
HOP	Hope [*Jamaica*] [*Seismograph station code, US Geological Survey Closed*] (SEIS)
HOP	Hopkinsville, KY [*Location identifier FAA*] (FAAL)
HOP	House Operating Tape [*Telecommunications*] (TEL)
HOP	Hybrid Operating Program [*Computer science*] (IEEE)
HOP	Hydrographic Office Publications [*Obsolete Navy*]
HOP	Hydroxydaunomycin [*Adriamycin*], Oncovin , Prednisone [*Vincristine*] [*Antineoplastic drug regimen*]
HOPA	Hopantenate Calcium [*Cerebral activator*]
Hop & C	Hopwood and Coltman's English Registration Appeal Cases [*A publication*] (DLA)
Hop & Colt...	Hopwood and Coltman's English Registration Appeal Cases [*A publication*] (DLA)
Hop & Ph.....	Hopwood and Philbrick's English Registration Appeal Cases [*A publication*] (DLA)
Hop & Phil....	Hopwood and Philbrick's English Registration Appeal Cases [*A publication*] (DLA)
HOPD.........	Hospital Out-Patient Department (MEDA)
HOPE	Hackers on Planet Earth [*An association*]
HOPE	Halley Optical Probe Experiment
HOPE	Health Opportunity for People Everywhere [*Philanthropic project operating hospital ship*]
HOPE	Health Organization to Preserve the Environment
HOPE	Health-Oriented Physician Education
HOPE	Help Obese People Everywhere
HOPE	Highlights of Personal Experience in Agriculture Department
HOPE	Highly Instrumented Orbiting Primate Experiment
HOPE	Hispanic Organization of Professionals and Executives [*Silver Spring, MD*] (EA)
HOPE	Holistic Orthogonal Parameter Estimation [*Medicine*] (DMAA)
HOPE	Home Ownership and Opportunity for People Everywhere [*Program*] [*HUD*]
HOPE	Homes of Private Enterprise (EA)
Hope	Hope (of Kerse). Manuscript Decisions, Scotch Court of Session [*A publication*] (DLA)
HOPE	Hospital-Oriented Programmed Environment
HOPE	Housing Our People Economically
HOPE	Humanistic Organization for Personal Expansion
HOPE	Hydrogen-Oxygen Primary Extraterrestrial [*Fuel cell*] [*NASA*]
HOPEC........	Hand-Operated Positive Energy Control
HOPEC........	Hydrogen Organization for Progress, Education, and Cooperation [*Defunct*] (EA)
Hope Com Law...	Hope's Compendium of the Commercial Law of the Pacific [*A publication*] (DLA)
Hope Dec.....	Hope (of Kerse). Manuscript Decisions, Scotch Court of Session [*A publication*] (DLA)
Hope Maj Pr...	Hope's Major Practicks [*Scotland*] [*A publication*] (DLA)
Hope Min Pr...	Hope's Minor Practicks [*Scotland*] [*A publication*] (DLA)
HOPES........	High Oxygen-Pulping Enclosed System (PDAA)
HOPG.........	Highly Oriented Pyrolytic Graphite [*Engineering*]
HOPH.........	Home of Peace Hospitals [*Australia*]
HOPI..........	Handbook of Operating Instructions [*Navy*] (MCD)
HOPI..........	History of Present Illness [*Medicine*] (HGAA)
HOPING	Helping Other Parents in Normal Grieving (EA)
Hopk..........	Hopkins' New York Chancery Reports [*A publication*] (DLA)
Hopk Adm ...	Hopkinson's Pennsylvania Admiralty Judgments [*A publication*] (DLA)
Hopk Adm Dec...	Admiralty Decisions of Hopkinson in Gilpin's Reports [*A publication*] (DLA)
Hopk Av......	Hopkins' Average [*4th ed.*] [*1884*] [*A publication*] (DLA)
Hopk CC	Hopkins' New York Chancery Reports [*A publication*] (DLA)
Hopk Ch......	Hopkins' New York Chancery Reports [*A publication*] (DLA)
Hopk Chanc Rep...	Hopkins' New York Chancery Reports [*A publication*] (DLA)
Hopk Judg...	Hopkinson's Pennsylvania Admiralty Judgments [*A publication*] (DLA)
Hopk Mar Ins...	Hopkins on Marine Insurance [*A publication*] (DLA)
Hopk Rep.....	Hopkins' New York Chancery Reports [*A publication*] (DLA)
Hopk W.......	Hopkinson's Works [*Pennsylvania*] [*A publication*] (DLA)
Hopk Wks	Hopkinson's Works [*Pennsylvania*] [*A publication*] (DLA)
Hopk Works (PA)...	Hopkinson's Works [*Pennsylvania*] [*A publication*] (DLA)
HOPL..........	History of Programming Languages
HOPM.........	Hydraulic Oil Power Module (DNAB)
Hop Min......	Hope's Minor Practicks [*Scotland*] [*A publication*] (DLA)
HOPO.........	Holders of Public Office
HOPR	Holly Holdings, Inc. [*NASDAQ symbol*] (SAG)
HOPR	Holly Products [*NASDAQ symbol*] (TTSB)
HOPRD........	Holly Products 10% Cv'D'Pfd [*NASDAQ symbol*] (TTSB)
HOPRW.......	Holly Products Wrrt [*NASDAQ symbol*] (TTSB)
HOPS..........	Hart Brewing [*NASDAQ symbol*] (TTSB)
HOPS..........	Helmet-Mounted Optical Projection System

HOPS	Heterodyne Optical Optimization Communication System with Stops [*NASA*]
HOPS	Host Proximity Service [*Computer science*]
HOPS	HOst Proximity Service [*Computer science*]
HOPT	Hypoparathyroidism [*Endocrinology*]
Hopw & C	Hopwood and Coltman's English Registration Appeal Cases [*A publication*] (DLA)
Hopw & Colt	Hopwood and Coltman's English Registration Appeal Cases [*A publication*] (DLA)
Hopw & P	Hopwood and Philbrick's English Registration Appeal Cases [*A publication*] (DLA)
Hopw & Phil	Hopwood and Philbrick's English Registration Appeal Cases [*A publication*] (DLA)
HOQ	Hansard Oral Questions [*Database*] [*House of Commons*] [*Canada*] [*Information service or system*] (CRD)
HOQ	Hof [*Germany Airport symbol*] (OAG)
HOQ	Home Office Quote (NITA)
HOQ	Hysteroid-Obsessoid Questionnaire [*Psychology*]
HOQNO	Heptyl(hydroxy)quinoline N-Oxide [*Organic chemistry*]
HOR	Heliocentric Orbit Rendezvous (MCD)
HOR	Holder of Record [*Investment term*]
HOR	Home of Record
HOR	Hoover-Owens-Rentschler [*Engines*]
HOR	Horace [*Roman poet, 65-8BC*] [*Classical studies*] (ROG)
Hor	Horayoth (BJA)
HOR	Horizon (KSC)
HOR	Horizon Air-Taxi Ltd. [*Switzerland ICAO designator*] (FAAC)
HOR	Horizontal
hor	Horizontal (WDMC)
Hor	Horizontal Lights [*Navigation signal*]
HOR	Horn & Hardart Co. [*Later, Hanover Direct*] [*AMEX symbol*] (SPSG)
Hor	Horologium [*Constellation*]
HOR	Horology
HOR	Horta [*Azores*] [*Airport symbol*] (OAG)
HOR	Horta [*Azores*] [*Seismograph station code, US Geological Survey*] (SEIS)
HOR	Hot Resources Ltd. [*Vancouver Stock Exchange symbol*]
HOR	Hydrogen-Oxygen Reaction (SAA)
HOR	University of Minnesota, the Hormel Institute, Austin, MN [*OCLC symbol*] (OCLC)
HORA	High Out of Range Alarm [*Electronics*] (ECII)
HORAD	Horizontal RADAR Display
Hor & Th Cas	Horrigan and Thompson's Cases on Self-Defense [*A publication*] (DLA)
HORA SOM	Hora Somni [*At Bedtime*] [*Latin*] (WDAA)
HORATIO	Human Operator Response Analyser and Timer for Infrequent Occurrences (PDAA)
Horat Mand	Horatius Mandosius [*Deceased, 1594*] [*Authority cited in pre-1607 legal work*] (DSA)
HOR CL	Horizontal Clearance [*Nautical charts*]
HORD	Hordeum [*Barley*] [*Pharmacy*] (ROG)
HOR DECU	Hora Decubitus [*At Bedtime*] [*Pharmacy*]
HOR DECUB	Hora Decubitus [*At Bedtime*] [*Pharmacy*] (ROG)
HO-RE-CA	Federation Internationale des Organisations d'Hoteliers, Restaurateurs, et Cafetiers [*International Organization of Hotel and Restaurant Associations*] (EAIO)
HORECOM	International Exhibition for the Hotel and Restaurant Trades Communities
HOREN	Horizontal Enlarger [*Photography*]
HOREP	Hot Photographic Report
HOREP	Hot Report
HOR INTERM	Horis Intermediis [*In the Intermediate Hours*] [*Pharmacy*]
Horitz	Horizontal (NITA)
HORIZ	Horizon (MSA)
HORIZ	Horizontal (AABC)
horiz	Horizontal (IDOE)
HORIZ	Horizontal Polarization
HorizFS	Horizon Financial Services Corp. [*Associated Press*] (SAG)
HorizMH	Horizon Mental Health Management [*Associated Press*] (SAG)
HoriznGp	Horizon Group, Inc. [*Associated Press*] (SAG)
HORM	Hybrid Orbital Rehybridization Method [*Atomic physics*]
Hormel	Hormel [*George*] & Co. [*Associated Press*] (SAG)
HorMn	Horace Mann Educators Corp. [*Associated Press*] (SAG)
HORMV	Hordeum Mosaic Virus [*Plant pathology*]
Horn & H	Horn and Hurlstone's English Exchequer Reports [*1838-39*] [*A publication*] (DLA)
Hornbk	Hornbeck Offshore Services, Inc. [*Associated Press*] (SAG)
Horne Dip	Horne on Diplomacy [*A publication*] (DLA)
Horne Mir	Horne's Mirror of Justice [*A publication*] (DLA)
Horne MJ	Horne's Mirror of Justice [*A publication*] (DLA)
Horner	Horner's Reports [*11-23 South Dakota*] [*A publication*] (DLA)
Horner's Ann St	Horner's Annotated Revised Statutes [*Indiana*] [*A publication*] (DLA)
Horner's Rev St	Horner's Annotated Revised Statutes [*Indiana*] [*A publication*] (DLA)
HORN GN	Hornblende Gneisses [*Geology*]
Horo	Horologium [*Constellation*]
HOROL	Horology
Horr & B Mun Ord	Horr and Bemis' Treatise on Municipal Police Ordinances [*A publication*] (DLA)
Horr & T Cas Self-Def	Horrigan and Thompson's Cases on Self-Defense [*A publication*] (DLA)
Horr & Th	Horrigan and Thompson's Cases on Self-Defense [*A publication*] (DLA)

HORSCERA	House of Representatives Standing Committee on the Environment (EERA)
HORSE	Heavy Operational Repair Squadron Engineer [*Air Force*] (AFM)
HORSE	Hydrofoil-Operated Rocket Submarine (NATG)
HORSEC	House of Representatives Standing Committee on Environment and Conservation (EERA)
Horsh	Horsham Corp. [*Associated Press*] (SAG)
Horshd	Horsehead Resource Development Company, Inc. [*Associated Press*] (SAG)
HOR SOM	Hora Somni [*At Bedtime*] [*Pharmacy*]
hort	Hortensis [*Of a Garden*] [*Latin*]
HORT	Horticulture
HORT	Horticulture
Hort	Horticulture [*A publication*] (BRI)
HORTI	Horticulture [*Freight*]
HORTIC	Horticulture
HORTL	Horticultural
HOR UN SPAT	Horae Unius Spatio [*At the End of an Hour*] [*Pharmacy*]
HOR UN SPATIO	Horae Unius Spatio [*At the End of an Hour*] [*Pharmacy*] (ROG)
HORV	Hydraulic and Optical Repair Vehicle (PDAA)
Horw YB	Horwood's Year Books of Edward I [*A publication*] (DLA)
HorzBcTx	Horizon Bancorp, Inc. (TX) [*Associated Press*] (SAG)
HorznFin	Horizon Financial Corp. [*Associated Press*] (SAG)
HOS	Croatian Defense Association [*Political party*]
HOS	Hardwire Operating System (IAA)
HOS	Health Online Service [*Computer science*] [*Medicine*]
HOS	Heated Oxygen Sensor [*Automotive engineering*]
HOS	Heat of Solution
HOS	Heckscher-Ohlin-Samuelson [*Theorem*]
HOS	Higher Order Software, Inc.
HOS	High-Order Software [*Computer science*] (NASA)
HOS	Home Orchard Society (EA)
HOS	Horizontal Obstacle SONAR (IAA)
HoS	Horse Serum [*Immunology*]
HOS	Hosana [*Ethiopia*] [*Airport symbol*] (AD)
Hos	Hosea [*Old Testament book*]
HOS	Hosebe, SIC [*Ukraine*] [*FAA designator*] (FAAC)
Hos	Hostiensis [*Deceased, 1271*] [*Authority cited in pre-1607 legal work*] (DSA)
HOS	Human Operator Simulator (MCD)
HOS	Human Osteosarcoma [*Medicine*]
HOS	Hydrographic Office Scale [*Obsolete*]
HOSA	Health Occupations Students of America (EA)
HOSA	Hearing Office Systems Administrator [*Computer science*]
HOSC	Hardened Operational Site Concept (AAG)
HOSC	History of Science Cases
HOSC	Huntsville Operations Support Center [*NASA*] (KSC)
HOSCORP	New York City Health and Hospitals Corp. (EA)
Hosea	Hosea's Reports [*Ohio*] [*A publication*] (DLA)
Hosea's Rep	Cincinnati Superior Court Decisions [*Ohio*] [*A publication*] (DLA)
HOSI	Handbook of Service Instructions
HOSJ	Sovereign Hospitaller Order of Saint John (EA)
Hoskins	Hoskins' Reports [*2 North Dakota*] [*A publication*] (DLA)
HOSP	Hospital
HOSP	Hospital
hosp	Hospital (VRA)
HOSP	Hospital Aircraft [*ICAO designator*] (FAAC)
HOSP	Hosposable Products [*NASDAQ symbol*] (TTSB)
HOSP	Hosposable Products, Inc. [*NASDAQ symbol*] (NQ)
HOSP	Hot Springs National Park
HOSPACT	Hospital Patient Accounting (PDAA)
Hosp Admin	Hospital Administration [*A publication*]
HOSPCO	Hospital Co. [*Marine Corps*]
Hosp Hlth Care	Hospital and Health Care [*A publication*]
Hosp Ins	Hospital Insurance (DAVI)
Hosp J	Hospital Journal [*A publication*]
Hosp J Aust	Hospital Journal of Australia [*A publication*]
Hospos	Hosposable Products, Inc. [*Associated Press*] (SAG)
HospPT	Hospitality Properties Trust [*Associated Press*] (SAG)
HOSPRATS	Hospital Rations [*Navy*]
Hosp Sgt	Hospital Sergeant (GFGA)
HospSt	Hospital Staffing Services, Inc. [*Associated Press*] (SAG)
HOSPTY	Hospitality
HospWwde	Hospitality Worldwide Services, Inc. [*Associated Press*] (SAG)
HOSS	Halo Orbit Space Station [*NASA*]
HOSS	Hand Order Transmeter
HOSS	Homing Optical System Study
HOSS	Homing System Survey (MCD)
HOSS	Hornbeck Offshore Services, Inc. [*NASDAQ symbol*] (NQ)
HOSS	Hydrogen/Oxygen Second Stage (MCD)
HOS-STPL	Hospital Operating System - Structured Programming Language [*Computer science*] (CSR)
HOST	Amerihost Properties [*NASDAQ symbol*] (TTSB)
HOST	Amerihost Properties, Inc. [*NASDAQ symbol*] (NQ)
HOST	Harmonic Optimized Stabilization Technique (IAA)
HOST	Hawaii Ocean Science and Technology Park [*Research center*] (RCD)
Host	Hostiensis [*Deceased, 1271*] [*Authority cited in pre-1607 legal work*] (DSA)
HOST	Hostile
HOST	Hot Spot Tracking (DNAB)
HOST	Hypo-Osmotic Shock Treatment [*Analytical biochemistry*]
HOSTAC	Helicopter Operations from Ships other than Aircraft Carriers [*Supplement*] (DOMA)
HOSTEX	Home Study Exchange (EA)

HostFdg ...... Host Funding, Inc. [*Associated Press*] (SAG)
Hosti .... Hostiensis [*Deceased, 1271*] [*Authority cited in pre-1607 legal work*] (DSA)
HOSTID .... Host Identifier (ACRL)
HostM .... Host Marriott Corp. [*Associated Press*] (SAG)
HostMar ...... Host Marriott Corp. [*Associated Press*] (SAG)
HostMS .... Host Marriott Services Corp. [*Associated Press*] (SAG)
HOSTS .... Hostess (ROG)
HOSTWOY ... Home of Selection and Completion of Travel within One Year Is Authorized [*Military*]
HOT .... Baltic Airlines Ltd. [*ICAO designator*] (FAAC)
HOT .... Birmingham Aerocentre, Ltd. [*British*] [*FAA designator*] (FAAC)
HOT .... Hand Over Transmitter
HOT .... Hands-on-Training
HOT .... HAT [*Hypoxanthine-Aminopterin-Thymidine*] with Ouabain [*Growth medium*] [*Biochemistry*]
HOT .... Hawaiian Ocean Time Series (USDC)
HOT .... High-Subsonic Optically Teleguided [*Antitank system*] (INF)
HOT .... Holographic One-Tube [*Goggles*] (MCD)
HOT .... Holographic-One-Two (PDAA)
HOT .... Home on Target [*Military*] (CAAL)
HOT .... Horizontal Output Transformer
HOT .... Horizontal Output Tube
HOT .... Hot Springs [*Arkansas*] [*Airport symbol*] (OAG)
HOT .... Human Old Tuberculin
HOT .... Hyperbaric Oxygen Therapy [*Medicine*] (DAVI)
HOT .... Hypertension Optimal Treatment [*Antihypertensive medicine*]
HOT .... Starwood Lodging Tr [*NYSE symbol*] (TTSB)
HOT .... Starwood Lodging Trust [*NYSE symbol*] (SAG)
HOT .... Starwood Lodging Trust [*AMEX symbol*] (SAG)
HOTAC .... Helicopter Optical Tracking and Control
HOTAC .... Hotel Accommodation Service [*British*]
HOTAS .... Hands on Throttle and Stick [*Aviation*] (MCD)
HOTAS .... Hands-on-Throttle-and-Stick [*Navy*] (DOMA)
HOTBUN ...... Have Not Yet Begun to Fight [*Simulated war game*]
HOTCE .... Hot Critical Experiments [*Nuclear energy*]
HOTCOG ...... Heart of Texas Council of Governments
HOTEF .... Helicopter Operational Test and Evaluation Flight [*Canadian Navy*]
HOTLIPS ...... Honorary Order of Trumpeters Living in Possible Sin
HOTO .... Health of the Oceans [*Marine science*] (OSRA)
HOTOL .... Horizontal Takeoff and Landing [*Name of proposed aircraft under development by the British government*]
HOTPHOTOREP... Hot Photographic Report (MCD)
HOTRAN ...... Hover and Transition [*Simulator*]
HOTREC .... Confederation of the National Hotel and Restaurant Associations in the EC (ECED)
HOTS .... Hands-On Training Simulator [*Vehicle*]
HOTS .... Hearing Office Tracking System [*Computer science*]
HOTS .... Higher Order Thinking Skills [*Education*]
HOT-SHOT ... Hydrogen-Oxygen Turbine: Super-High Operating Temperatures [*Hydrogen utilization technology*]
HOTSIT .... Hot Situation (MCD)
HOTT .... Hands-on Turret Trainer [*Military*]
HOTT .... Hot Topic, Inc. [*NASDAQ symbol*] (SAG)
HotTopic ...... Hot Topic, Inc. [*Associated Press*] (SAG)
HOTX .... Hands-On Training Exercise [*Military*] (ADDR)
HOU .... [*William P.*] Hobby Airport [*FAA*] (TAG)
HOU .... Houston [*Texas*] [*Seismograph station code, US Geological Survey*] (SEIS)
HOU .... Houston [*Texas*] [*Airport symbol*]
HOU .... Houston Indus [*NYSE symbol*] (TTSB)
HOU .... Houston Industries, Inc. [*NYSE symbol*] (SPSG)
Hou .... Houston's Delaware Reports [*A publication*] (DLA)
HOU .... United States Department of Housing and Urban Development, Washington, DC [*OCLC symbol*] (OCLC)
Hou Ang Sax Law... Houard's Anglo-Saxon Laws, Etc. [*A publication*] (DLA)
Houard Ang Sax Laws... Houard's Anglo-Saxon Laws [*A publication*] (DLA)
HouB........... Houston Biotechnology, Inc. [*Associated Press*] (SAG)
Houck Mech Lien... Houck on Mechanics' Lien Law [*A publication*] (DLA)
Houck Riv..... Houck on the Law of Navigable Rivers [*A publication*] (DLA)
Hou Dict ...... Houard's Dictionary of the Customs of Normandy [*A publication*] (DLA)
Hough Am Cons... Hough's American Constitutions [*A publication*] (DLA)
Hough CM ... Hough's Military Law and Courts-Martial [*A publication*] (DLA)
Hough C-M Cas... Hough's Court-Martial Case Book [*1821*] [*London*] [*A publication*] (DLA)
Houghtn....... Houghton Pharmaceuticals, Inc. [*Associated Press*] (SAG)
Houghton..... Houghton's Reports [*97 Alabama*] [*A publication*] (DLA)
Hough V-Adm... Reports of Cases in Vice-Admiralty of Province of New York [*1715-88*] [*1925 Reprint*] [*A publication*] (DLA)
HougM........ Houghton Mifflin Co. [*Associated Press*] (SAG)
HouInd........ Houston Industries, Inc. [*Associated Press*] (SAG)
HOUS.......... Housing
HOUS.......... Housing Division [*Census*] (OICC)
Hous .... Houston's Delaware Reports [*A publication*] (DLA)
Hous & Dev Rep... Housing and Development Reporter [*Bureau of National Affairs*] [*A publication*] (DLA)
HousBio....... Houston Biotechnology, Inc. [*Associated Press*] (SAG)
HOUSE-INFO... Homeowners Using Savings and Energy Information to Negotiate Fair Offers [*Student legal action organization*] (EA)
House Mag.... House Magazine [*A publication*]
House of L... House of Lords Cases [*A publication*] (DLA)
HOUSG .... Housing
HOUSHD ...... Household [*Marketing*] (ROG)
HoushInt....... Household International, Inc. [*Associated Press*] (SAG)

Housing & Devel Rep... Housing and Development Reporter [*Bureau of National Affairs*] [*A publication*] (DLA)
Housing Aust... Housing Australia [*A publication*]
Housing Vic... Housing Victoria [*A publication*]
Housing W Aust... Housing Western Australia [*A publication*]
Hous Law .... Houston Lawyer [*A publication*] (DLA)
Hous Life Ass... Houseman's Life Assurance [*9th ed.*] [*1977*] [*A publication*] (DLA)
Hous Pr .... Housman's Precedents in Conveyancing [*1861*] [*A publication*] (DLA)
Houst .... Houston's Delaware Reports [*A publication*] (DLA)
Houst Cr ...... Houston's Delaware Criminal Cases [*A publication*] (DLA)
Houst Cr Cas... Houston's Delaware Criminal Cases [*A publication*] (DLA)
Houst Crim Cas... Delaware Criminal Cases [*A publication*] (DLA)
Houst Crim Cases... Delaware Criminal Cases [*A publication*] (DLA)
Houst Crim (Del)... Houston's Delaware Criminal Cases [*A publication*] (DLA)
Houst Crim Rep... Delaware Criminal Cases [*A publication*] (DLA)
Houst Cr Rep... Delaware Criminal Cases [*A publication*] (DLA)
HoustEx ...... Houston Exploration Co. (The) [*Associated Press*] (SAG)
HoustInd ...... Houston Industries, Inc. [*Associated Press*] (SAG)
Houston ...... Houston's Delaware Supreme Court Reports [*1855-93*] [*A publication*] (DLA)
Houston Law... Houston Lawyer [*A publication*] (DLA)
Houst St Tr... Houston's Law of Stoppage in Transitu [*A publication*] (DLA)
HOV .... Heat of Vaporization
HOV .... High Occupancy Vehicle [*Commuter routes*] [*Acronym usually followed by a number indicating the minimum number of people per vehicle*]
HOV .... Homogeneity of Variance [*Statistics*]
Hov .... Hovenden on Frauds [*A publication*] (DLA)
Hov .... Hovenden's Supplement to Vesey, Jr.'s, English Chancery Reports [*1789-1817*] [*A publication*] (DLA)
HOV .... Hovercraft [*Military British*]
HOV .... Hovnanian Enterpr CI'A' [*AMEX symbol*] (TTSB)
HOV .... Hovnanian Enterprises, Inc. [*AMEX symbol*] (SPSG)
HOV .... Orsta/Volda [*Norway*] [*Airport symbol*] (OAG)
HOV .... United States Department of Housing and Urban Development, Region I, Boston, MA [*OCLC symbol*] (OCLC)
HOV .... Wichita, KS [*Location identifier FAA*] (FAAL)
Hov Ann ...... Hoveden's Annals [*A publication*] (DLA)
HOVE .... Hovenweep National Monument
Hoved .... Hoveden's Chronica [*A publication*] (DLA)
Hov Fr .... Hovenden on Frauds [*A publication*] (DLA)
HOVI .... Handbook of Overhaul Instructions [*Navy*]
HOVI .... Hopewell Village National Historic Site
Hovis .... Hominis Vis [*The Strength of Man*] [*Latin*]
HovnEn .... Hovnanian Enterprises, Inc. [*Associated Press*] (SAG)
Hov Sup...... Hovenden's Supplement to Vesey, Jr.'s, English Chancery Reports [*1789-1817*] [*A publication*] (DLA)
Hov Supp..... Hovenden's Supplement to Vesey, Jr.'s, English Chancery Reports [*1789-1817*] [*A publication*] (DLA)
HOVVAC....... Hovering Vehicle Versatile Automatic Control
HOW .... Handicapped Organized Women [*In association name, HOW, Inc.*] (EA)
HOW .... Hand over Word
HOW .... Happiness of Womanhood [*Also known as LOH*] [*Defunct*]
HOW .... Healing Our World [*An association*]
HOW .... Help Our World
HOW .... Hercules on Water [*Aircraft*] (MCD)
HOW .... High-Order Word (SSD)
HOW .... Home Owners Warranty [*National Association of Home Builders*]
How .... Howard's New York Practice Reports [*A publication*] (DLA)
How .... Howard's Reports [*2-8 Mississippi*] [*A publication*] (DLA)
How .... Howard's United States Supreme Court Reports [*42-65 United States*] [*A publication*] (DLA)
HOW .... Howell Indus [*AMEX symbol*] (TTSB)
HOW .... Howell Industries, Inc. [*AMEX symbol*] (SPSG)
How .... Howell's Reports [*22-26 Nevada*] [*A publication*] (DLA)
HOW .... Howitzer (KSC)
HOW .... Howrah [*India*] [*Seismograph station code, US Geological Survey*] (SEIS)
HO-W .... Hydrographic Office-Washington, DC [*Terminated, 1963; later, NOO*] [*Navy*] (MCD)
How A Cas... Howard's New York Appeal Cases [*A publication*] (DLA)
How & Beat... Howell and Beatty's Reports [*22 Nevada*] [*A publication*] (DLA)
How & H St... Howard and Hutchinson's Mississippi Statutes [*A publication*] (DLA)
How & N...... Howell and Norcross' Reports [*23, 24 Nevada*] [*A publication*] (DLA)
How & Nor... Howell and Norcross' Reports [*23, 24 Nevada*] [*A publication*] (DLA)
How Ann St... Howell's Annotated Statutes [*Michigan*] [*A publication*] (DLA)
How App..... Howard's New York Appeal Cases [*A publication*] (DLA)
How App Cas... Howard's New York Court of Appeals Cases [*A publication*] (DLA)
How App Cases... Howard's New York Court of Appeals Cases [*A publication*] (DLA)
Howard........ Howard's Mississippi Supreme Court Reports [*1834-43*] [*A publication*] (DLA)
Howard Pr ... Howard's New York Practice Reports [*A publication*] (DLA)
Howard Pr Rep... Howard's New York Practice Reports [*A publication*] (DLA)
Howard Rep... Howard's United States Supreme Court Reports [*A publication*] (DLA)
Howard SC... United States Reports [*Vols. 42-65*] [*A publication*] (DLA)
Howard's Prac Reports... Howard's New York Practice Reports [*A publication*] (DLA)
Howard's Practice... Howard's New York Practice Reports [*A publication*] (DLA)
Howard's Spec Term Rep... Howard's New York Practice Reports [*A publication*] (DLA)
Howard U .... Howard University (GAGS)
HOWBTRY ... Howitzer Battery (DNAB)

How C.........	Howard's Irish Chancery Practice [*A publication*] (DLA)
How Cas.....	Howard's New York Court of Appeals Cases [*A publication*] (DLA)
How Cas.....	Howard's Property Cases [*A publication*] (DLA)
How Ch......	Howard's Irish Chancery Practice [*A publication*] (DLA)
How Ch P...	Howard's Irish Chancery Practice [*A publication*] (DLA)
How Ch Pr...	Howard's Irish Chancery Practice [*A publication*] (DLA)
How Cr Tr...	Howison's Virginia Criminal Trials [*A publication*] (DLA)
How Ct App Cas...	Howard's New York Court of Appeals Cases [*A publication*] (DLA)
How EE......	Howard's Irish Equity Exchequer Reports [*A publication*] (DLA)
Howell NP....	Howell's Nisi Prius Reports [*Michigan*] [*A publication*] (DLA)
Howell St Tr...	Howell's English State Trials [*1163-1820*] [*A publication*] (DLA)
Howe Pr......	Howe's Practice [*Massachusetts*] [*A publication*] (DLA)
How Eq Exch...	Howard's Irish Equity Exchequer Reports [*A publication*] (DLA)
How J.........	Howard Journal [*A publication*] (DLA)
HOWL.........	Hands Off Wildlife [*British*] (DI)
HOWL.........	Help Our Wolves Live
HowlC.........	Howell Corp. [*Associated Press*] (SAG)
HowlCp.......	Howell Corp. [*Associated Press*] (SAG)
Howl In......	Howell Industries, Inc. [*Associated Press*] (SAG)
How L Rev...	Howard Law Review [*A publication*] (DLA)
HOWLS.......	Hostile Weapons Locator Study [*DARPA/Army*] (MCD)
How NP (Mich)...	Howell's Nisi Prius Reports [*Michigan*] [*A publication*] (DLA)
How NS	Howard's New York Practice Reports, New Series [*A publication*] (DLA)
How (NY).....	Howard's New York Practice Reports [*A publication*] (DLA)
How Pat.....	Howson on Patents [*A publication*] (DLA)
How Po Ca...	Howard's Property Cases [*A publication*] (DLA)
How Po Cas...	Howard's Irish Property Cases [*1720-73*] [*A publication*] (DLA)
How Pr.......	Howard's New York Practice Reports [*A publication*] (DLA)
How Prac....	Howard's New York Practice Reports [*A publication*] (DLA)
How Prac NS...	Howard's New York Practice Reports, New Series [*A publication*] (DLA)
How Prac (NY)...	Howard's New York Practice Reports [*A publication*] (DLA)
How Prac Rep...	Howard's New York Practice Reports [*A publication*] (DLA)
How Pr NS...	Howard's New York Practice Reports, New Series [*A publication*] (DLA)
How Prob Pr...	Howell's Probate Practice [*Ontario, Canada*] [*A publication*] (DLA)
How Pr Rep...	Howard's New York Practice Reports [*A publication*] (DLA)
How Pr Sup C...	Howard's New York Practice Reports [*A publication*] (DLA)
HOWR.........	However
Howr.........	Howitzer [*British military*] (DMA)
How SC.......	Howard's United States Supreme Court Reports [*A publication*] (DLA)
Hows Pat.....	Howson on Patents [*A publication*] (DLA)
HOWSR.......	Howsoever (ROG)
Hows Reis Pat...	Howson on Reissued Patents [*A publication*] (DLA)
How St.......	Howell's Annotated Statutes [*Michigan*] [*A publication*] (DLA)
How State Tr...	Howell's English State Trials [*1163-1820*] [*A publication*] (DLA)
How St Tr....	Howell's English State Trials [*1163-1820*] [*A publication*] (DLA)
HOWT.........	Howard Terminal [*Later, HT*] [*AAR code*]
HOWT.........	Howtek Inc. [*NASDAQ symbol*] (TTSB)
HOWT.........	Howtek, Inc. [*NASDAQ symbol*] (SAG)
Howtek	Howtek, Inc. [*Associated Press*] (SAG)
HOW-TO	Housing Operation with Training Opportunity [*Office of Economic Opportunity*]
How US	Howard's United States Supreme Court Reports [*A publication*] (DLA)
HOX...........	Homeobox [*Genetics*]
HOX...........	New Orleans, LA [*Location identifier FAA*] (FAAL)
HOY	Hoy Island [*Scotland*] [*Airport symbol Obsolete*] (OAG)
Hoyt Comp L...	Hoyt's Compiled Laws of Arizona [*A publication*] (DLA)
HOZ...........	Horizontal
HP...........	Air Hawaii [*ICAO designator*] (AD)
HP...........	ALAS, SA [*Uruguay*] [*ICAO designator*] (ICDA)
HP...........	All India Reporter, Himachal Pradesh [*A publication*] (DLA)
HP...........	America West Airlines [*ICAO designator*] (AD)
HP...........	Half Pay
HP...........	Half Plate [*Photography*]
HP...........	Half Price (ROG)
HP...........	Handicapped Person
H-P...........	Handley-Page Ltd.
HP...........	Handling and Propulsion (AAG)
HP...........	Handling Procedure (MCD)
HP...........	Handmade Paper
HP...........	Handpainted (WGA)
Hp...........	Haptoglobin [*Hematology*]
HP...........	Hard Plastic [*Doll collecting*]
HP...........	Hard Point
HP...........	Hardy Perennial [*Horticulture*] (ROG)
HP...........	Harmonic Progression
Hp...........	Harp [*Music*]
HP...........	Hauptpunkte [*Crystallography*]
HP...........	Haustus Purgans [*Purging Draught*] [*Pharmacy*] (ROG)
HP...........	Haut Parleur [*Loudspeaker*] [*French*]
HP...........	Hawker Siddeley Aviation Ltd. [*British ICAO aircraft manufacturer identifier*] (ICAO)
HP...........	Hay-Pasturage [*Agriculture*]
HP...........	Hazard Prevention [*A publication*] (EAAP)
HP...........	Head Postmaster [*British*] (DCTA)
HP...........	Headquarters Pamphlet [*Military*] (MCD)
HP...........	Healthcare Product
HP...........	Health Physics [*Nuclear energy*] (NRCH)
HP...........	Heating Plant (NATG)
HP...........	Heenan Petroleum Ltd. [*Toronto Stock Exchange symbol*]

HP...........	Height of Perigee
HP...........	Heir Presumptive
HP...........	Helicopter (NATG)
HP...........	Heliodor [*Record label*] [*Great Britain*]
HP...........	Hellas Planitia [*A filamentary mark on Mars*]
HP...........	Helmerich & Payne [*NYSE symbol*] (TTSB)
HP...........	Helmerich & Payne, Inc. [*NYSE symbol*] (SPSG)
HP...........	Hemel Hempstead [*Postcode*] (ODBW)
H/P...........	Hemipelvectomy [*Medicine*]
Hp...........	Hemiplegia [*Medicine*]
HP...........	Henderson & Pollard Ltd. [*New Zealand*]
HP...........	Heptode [*Electronics*] (IAA)
Hp...........	Heptyl [*Biochemistry*]
HP...........	Hesperian Foundation (EA)
HP...........	Hewlett-Packard Co.
HP...........	Hexamethylmelamine and Cisplatin [*Cisplatinum*] [*Antineoplastic drug*] (DAVI)
HP...........	Hiding Power [*Paint technology*]
HP...........	Highest Possible (ROG)
HP...........	Highly Purified
HP...........	High Pass [*Electronics*]
HP...........	High Performance
H/P...........	High Position (MDG)
HP...........	High-Positive (MDG)
HP...........	High-Potency [*Pharmacy*]
HP...........	High Power
HP...........	High Pressure
h-p...........	High-Pressure (IDOE)
HP...........	High-Pressure Cylinder [*Especially, a locomotive cylinder*]
HP...........	High Priest
HP...........	High Priority
HP...........	High Protein [*Nutrition*]
H-P...........	High Purity
HP...........	Hippocampal Pyramidal Cell [*Neuroanatomy*]
HP...........	Hire Purchase
HP...........	Historical Period [*Dialog*] [*Searchable field*] [*Information service or system*] (NITA)
HP...........	Hit by Pitcher [*Baseball*]
HP...........	Holding Pattern [*Aviation*]
HP...........	Holding Pipette
HP...........	Holding Potential [*Neurophysiology*]
HP...........	Holiday Pay [*Army*] (AABC)
HP...........	Holiday Project (EA)
HP...........	Hollow Point Bullet
HP...........	Homeopathic Pharmacopoeia
HP...........	Horizontal Parallax [*Navigation*]
HP...........	Horizontal Polarization
HP...........	Horsepower
hp...........	Horsepower (IDOE)
HP...........	Hospital Participation [*Blood program*] [*Red Cross*]
HP...........	Host Processor
HP...........	Hot Pack [*or Pad*] [*Physical therapy*]
HP...........	Hot Pilot [*An egotistic flying cadet*] [*Slang Air Force*]
HP...........	Hot-Pressed [*Paper*]
HP...........	House Painter (ROG)
HP...........	House Physician
HP...........	Houses of Parliament [*British*]
HP...........	Humanist Party [*Australia Political party*]
HP...........	Human Pituitary [*Endocrinology*] (MAE)
HP...........	Human Plasma [*Hematology*]
HP...........	Humeral Plate [*Entomology*]
HP...........	Hundred Pounds
HP...........	Hunger Project (EA)
HP...........	Hydrocollator Pack [*Physical therapy*] (DAVI)
HP...........	Hydrogen Purge (MCD)
HP...........	Hydrophilic Petrolatum [*Pharmacology*] (DAVI)
HP...........	Hydrostatic Pressure
HP...........	Hydroxyproline [*An amino acid*]
HP...........	Hygroscopicity Potential (PDAA)
HP...........	Hyperparathyroidism [*or Hyperthyroidism*] [*Endocrinology*]
HP...........	Hyperphoria
HP...........	Hyperpolarization
HP...........	Hypersensitivity Pneumonitis [*Medicine*]
HP...........	Hypertension and Proteinuria [*Medicine*]
HP...........	Hypertransfused Polycythemic [*Medicine*]
HP...........	Hypophsrynx [*Qtorhinolaryngology*] (DAVI)
HP...........	Hysterical Personality
HP...........	Perigee Altitude (NASA)
HP...........	Smith & Nephew Pharmaceuticals Ltd. [*Great Britain*] [*Research code symbol*]
HPA	Handley Page Association [*British*] (DBA)
HPA	Head of a Procuring Activity [*Army*] (AABC)
HPA	Head Post Assembly
HPA	Head Postmen's Association [*A union*] [*British*]
HPA	Heads of Procuring Activities (MCD)
HPA	Health Policy Agenda for the American People (HCT)
HPA	Hectopascal [*ICAO designator*] (FAAC)
HPA	Hen Packers Association [*British*] (DBA)
HPA	Heteropoly Acid [*Inorganic chemistry*]
HPA	Heuristic Path Algorithm
HPA	High-Power Amplifier
HPA	High-Pressure Air
HPA	Historical Preservation of America [*Publisher*] (EA)
HPA	Holding and Positioning Aid (IEEE)
HPA	Horizontal Planar Array (CAAL)

HPA .... Hospital Physicians Association [*British*]
HPA .... Host Processor Adapter (IAA)
HPA .... House Plants Australia
HPA .... Human Papillomavirus [*or Parvovirus*] (MAE)
HPA .... Hurlingham Polo Association [*Midhurst, Sussex, England*] (EAIO)
HPA .... Hybridization Protection Assay [*Analytical biochemistry*]
HPA .... Hydraulic Pneumatic Area (AAG)
HPA .... Hydroxypropyl Acrylate [*Organic chemistry*]
HPA .... Hypothalamic-Pituitary-Adrenal [*Axis*] [*Endocrinology*] (DAVI)
HPA .... Hypothalamic-Pituitary-Adrenocortical [*Endocrinology*]
HPA .... Lifuka [*Tonga Islands*] [*Airport symbol*] (OAG)
HPA .... Pearl Airways Compagne Haitienne [*Haiti*] [*ICAO designator*] (FAAC)
HPAA .... High-Performance Antenna Assembly (MHDI)
HPAA .... High-Pressure Air Accumulator
HPAA .... Hispanic Public Affairs Association (EA)
HPAA .... Housing Pressure Altitude Advance [*Automotive engineering*]
HPAA .... Hydroxyphenylacetic Acid [*Biochemistry*] (MAE)
HPAAS .... High-Performance Aerial Attack System (MCD)
HPAC .... Health Policy Advisory Center (EA)
HPAC .... High-Performance Affinity Chromatography
HPAC .... High-Pressure Air Compressor (NVT)
HP/A/C .... Home Port/Area/City [*Code*] [*Navy*] (DNAB)
H-PAC .... Human-Piloted Alien Craft [*Flying saucer*]
HPAC .... Hydropress Accessory [*Tool*] (AAG)
HPAC .... Hypothalamo-Pituitary-Adreno-Cortical [*Medicine*] (DMAA)
HPAD .... Host Packet Assembler/Disassembler (ACRL)
HPAE .... High-pH Anion-Exchange [*Analytical chemistry*]
HPAEC .... High pH Anion Exchange Chromatography
HPAF .... Hydraulic Performance Analysis Facility (MCD)
HPAG .... High-Performance Air-to-Ground
HPAH .... Hydroxy Polycyclic Aromatic Hydrocarbon [*Environmental chemistry*]
HPAL .... High Plains Agriculture Laboratory [*University of Nebraska - Lincoln*] [*Research center*] (RCD)
HP & A .... Hull Propulsion and Auxiliaries [*Navy*] (DNAB)
HP&R .... Highway Planning and Research [*MTMC*] (TAG)
HPANH .... Hydroxy Polycyclic Aromatic Nitrogen Heterocycle [*Environmental chemistry*]
HPAP .... Human Placental Alkaline Phosphatase [*An enzyme*]
HPAR .... Air-Resistance Horsepower [*Automotive engineering*]
HPAS .... High-Performance Adhesive System
HPASH .... Hydroxy Polycyclic Aromatic Sulfur Heterocycle [*Environmental chemistry*]
HPB .... Handmaids of the Precious Blood [*Roman Catholic religious order*]
HPB .... Hand-Printed Books
HPB .... Harbor Patrol Boat
HPB .... Helena Petrovna Blavatsky [*Famous 19th-century occultist*]
HPB .... Hepatobiliary [*Medicine*] (DMAA)
HPB .... High-Probability Behavior
HPB .... Hinged Plotting Board
HPB .... Hooper Bay [*Alaska*] [*Airport symbol*] (OAG)
HPBC .... Home Port Bancorp [*NASDAQ symbol*] (TTSB)
HPBC .... Home Port Bancorp, Inc. [*NASDAQ symbol*] (CTT)
HPBC .... Hyperpolarizing Bipolar Cell [*In the retina*]
HPBF .... Hepatotrophic Portal Blood Factor [*Medicine*] (DMAA)
HPBL .... Human Peripheral Blood Leukocyte
HPBN .... Hot-Pressed Boron Nitride [*Materials science and technology*]
HPBVWA ...... High-Power Broadband Vehicular Whip Antenna [*Army*]
HPBW .... Half-Power Beamwidth [*or Bandwidth*] (IEEE)
HPC .... Hale's Pleas of the Crown [*England*] [*A publication*] (DLA)
HPC .... Handheld PC [*Personal Computer*]
HPC .... Hard Processing Channel (IAA)
HPC .... Hawkins' Pleas of the Crown [*England*] [*A publication*] (DLA)
HPC .... Health Physics Center [*Nuclear energy*] (NRCH)
HPC .... Health Policy Council [*Defunct*] (EA)
HPC .... Helicopter Performance Computer (NG)
HPC .... Helicopter Plane Commander
HPC .... Hematopoietic Progenitor Cell [*Hematology*]
HPC .... Hemipalmitoylcarnitinium [*Biochemistry*]
HPC .... Hemisphere Publishing Co.
HPC .... Hercules, Inc. [*Formerly, Hercules Powder Co.*] [*NYSE symbol*] (SPSG)
HPC .... High Performance Computing (EGAO)
HPC .... High Point College [*North Carolina*]
HPC .... High-Pressure Compressor (MCD)
HPC .... High-Pressure Constant (DNAB)
HPC .... Hippocampal Pyramidal Cell [*Neuroanatomy*]
HPC .... Hippocampus [*Brain anatomy*]
HPC .... Hobart Peace Centre [*Australia*]
HPC .... Home Policy Committee of War Cabinet [*British World War II*]
HPC .... Hope, AR [*Location identifier FAA*] (FAAL)
HPC .... Horticultural Policy Council (EERA)
HPC .... Hot Pipe Chase [*Nuclear energy*] (NRCH)
HPC .... Howard Payne College [*Texas*]
HPC .... Hydraulic Package Container
HPC .... Hydraulic Piston Corer
HPC .... Hydroxyphenylcinchoninic Acid [*Pharmacology*]
HPC .... Hydroxypropylcellulose [*Organic chemistry*]
HPCA .... High-Performance Communications Adapter
HPCA .... High Performance Computing Act (TNIG)
HPCA .... Hiroshima Peace Center Associates [*Defunct*] (EA)
HPCA .... Housing Pressure Cold Advance [*Automotive engineering*]
HPCBR .... High-Pressure Chamber
HPCC .... High Performance Computing and Communication [*Computer science*]

HPCC .... High-Performance Computing and Communications [*Computer science*] (EERA)
HPCC .... High-Performance Computing and Communications Program [*Department of Energy*]
HPCC .... High Performance Computing and Communications Program and Information Technology (USDC)
HPCC .... High-Performance Control Center [*Aerospace*] (AAG)
HPCE .... High-Performance Capillary Electrophoresis [*Analytical biochemistry*]
HPCF .... High-Performance Carbon Fiber [*Materials science*]
HPCHD .... Harpsichord [*Music*]
HPCI .... High-Pressure Coolant Injection [*Nuclear energy*] (NRCH)
HPCIS .... High-Pressure Coolant Injection System [*Nuclear energy*] (NRCH)
HPcL .... Leeward Community College, Pearl City, HI [*Library symbol Library of Congress*] (LCLS)
HPCM .... Human Placenta Conditioned Medium
HPCM .... Hybrid Pulse Code Modulation (PDAA)
HPCO .... High-Pressure Cut-Off [*Air conditioning systems*] [*Automotive engineering*]
HPCPC .... High-Performance Centrifugal Partition Chromatography
HPCRB .... Hydraulic Power Control Relay Box
HPCRC .... High-Performance Computer and Research Center [*Department of Energy*]
HPCS .... High-Pressure Core Spray [*Nuclear energy*] (NRCH)
HPCUS .... Homeopathic Pharmacopoeia Convention of the United States
HP CYL .... High-Pressure Cylinder (WDAA)
HPD .... Dialysate of Hydropenic Plasma [*Hematology*] (DAVI)
HPD .... Haloperidol [*Tranquilizer*]
HPD .... Hammerson Properties Investment & Development Corp. Ltd. [*Toronto Stock Exchange symbol*]
HPD .... Hand-Point Defense [*Military*] (IIA)
HPD .... Hard Point Defense
HPD .... Hearing Protection Device
HPD .... Hematoporphyrin Derivative [*Antineoplastic compound*]
HPD .... Highly Probably Drink [*Chemical depedency*] (DAVI)
HPD .... High-Performance Drone
HPD .... High-Power Density
HPD .... High-Pressure Drain (DNAB)
HPD .... High-Protein Diet
HPD .... Home Peritoneal Dialysis [*Nephrology*] (DAVI)
HPD .... Horizontal Polar Diagram
H-PD .... Hough-Powell Digitizer
HPD .... Hourly Precipitation Data [*A publication*]
HPD .... Hydraulic Pump Discharge (AAG)
HPD .... Hydraulic Pump Drive [*Mechanical engineering*]
HPDC .... High Pressure Data Center [*National Institute of Standards and Technology Information service or system*] (IID)
HPDF .... High-Performance Demonstration Facility
HPDF .... Horizontal Payloads Processing Facility
HPDGF .... Human Platelet-Derived Growth Factor [*Biochemistry*]
HP-DHA .... High-Purity Dual Hardness Armor (KSC)
HPDI .... Hard Point Defense Interceptor
HPDIM .... Hard Point Defense Intercept Missile (MCD)
HPDLRL .... High-Power Diffraction Limited Raman LASER
HPDM .... High-Performance Demonstration Motor (MCD)
HPDO .... High Performance Diesel Oil (PDAA)
HPDP .... Hispanic Policy Development Project (EA)
HPDPI .... Health Promotion and Disease Prevention Initiative [*Pronounced "hippy dippy"*] [*Department of Health and Human Services*]
HpD-PT .... Hepatoporphyrin Derivative-Phototherapy [*Medicine*]
HPDS .... Hard Point Defense System
HPE .... Harbor Patrol Element [*Navy*] (VNW)
HPE .... Heat-Producing Element
HPE .... Heptasaccharide Phytoalexin Elicitor [*Organic chemistry*]
HPE .... High-Performance Estate Wagon [*Automobile model designation*]
HPE .... High-Power Effects [*Radio interference*]
HPE .... History and Physical Examination [*Medicine*]
HPE .... Human Proenkephalin [*Biochemistry*]
HPE .... Hydrogenous Polyethylene
HPcL .... Inomeni Parataksis Ethnikofronon [*United Front of Nationalists*] [*Political party*] (PPE)
HPEC .... High-Productivity Energy Crop
HP EGS .... Hewlett Packard Engineering Graphics System (NITA)
HPEK .... Paul B. Elder Co. [*Research code symbol*]
HPEL .... Horn Point Environmental Laboratories [*University of Maryland*] (PDAA)
HPEO .... Protonous Poly(ethylene oxide) [*Organic chemistry*]
HPER .... Hastings and Prince Edward Regiment [*British military*] (DMA)
HPER .... Health, Physical Education, and Recreation
HPERD .... Health, Physical Education, Recreation, and Dance (AEE)
HPES .... Human Performance Enhancement System [*Engineering*]
HPETE .... Hydroxyperoxyeicosatetraenoic Acid [*Biochemistry*]
HPEW .... High-Powered Early Warning (NATG)
HPF .... Hammond, LA [*Location identifier FAA*] (FAAL)
HPF .... Harbor Patrol Fleet
HPF .... Hazardous Processing Facility (SSD)
HPF .... Heat Pipe Furnace
HPF .... Heparin-Precipitable Fraction (MAE)
HPF .... Hepatic Plasma Flow [*Medicine*] (DMAA)
HPF .... Highest Possible [*or Probable*] Frequency [*Electronics*]
hpf .... Highest Possible Frequency (WDMC)
HPF .... High Pass Filter
HPF .... High Performance FORTRAN [*Computer language*]
HPF .... High-Power Field [*Microscopy*]
HPF .... High-Protein Fraction [*Food technology*]
HPF .... Historic Preservation Fund [*National Trust for Historic Preservation*]

HPF .... Historic Pullman Foundation (EA)
HPF .... Horizontal Position Finder (IAA)
HPF .... Horizontal Processing Facility [*Operation and Checkout*] [*NASA*] (NASA)
HPF .... Host Preparation Facility (MHDI)
HPF .... Hot-Pressed Ferrite (IAA)
HPF .... Human Powered Flight (DICI)
HPFC .... High-Performance Fuel Cell
HPFF .... High Pressure Fluid-Filled
HPFH .... Hereditary Persistence of Fetal Hemoglobin [*Hematology*]
HPFL .... Highpass Filter (MSA)
HPFL .... High-Performance Fuels Laboratory
HPFL .... Holly Park Field Laboratory [*University of Nevada - Reno*] [*Research center*] (RCD)
HPFM .... Hydropress Form [*Tool*] (AAG)
HPFP .... High-Pressure Fire Protection (NRCH)
HPFP .... High-Pressure Fuel Pump (KSC)
HPFS .... High-Performance File System [*Computer science*]
hPFSH .... Human Pituitary Follicle-Stimulating Hormone [*Endocrinology*] (MAE)
HPFT .... High-Pressure Fuel Turbopump (MCD)
HPFTP .... High-Pressure Fuel Turbopump (NASA)
HPG .... Harvard Presentation Graphics [*Software Publishing Corp.*] [*Computer software*]
HPG .... Heritage Propane Partners LP [*NYSE symbol*] (SAG)
HPG .... High-Power Generator
HPG .... High-Power Ground (IAA)
HPG .... High-Power Group
HPG .... High-Pressure Gas (KSC)
HPG .... High-Pressure Gelatine (IAA)
HPG .... Homopolar Generator [*To power high-technology experiments*]
HPG .... Horticultural Postharvest Group [*Queensland, Australia*]
HPG .... Human Pituitary Gonadotrophin [*Endocrinology*]
HPG .... Hydroxypropyl Guar [*Organic chemistry*]
HPG .... Hyperpure Germanium [*Also, HpGe*] [*Chemistry*]
HPG .... Hypothalamic, Pituitary, Gonadal [*Endocrinology*]
HPGC .... Heading per Gyro Compass [*Navigation*]
HPGC .... Hypopressure Gas Chromatography
HpGe .... Hyperpure Germanium [*Also, HPG*] [*Chemistry*]
HPGF .... Hybridoma/Plasmacytome Growth Factor [*Biochemistry*]
HPGL .... Gross Load Horsepower [*Automotive engineering*]
HPGL .... Hewlett-Packard Graphics Language
HPGMI .... Hunter Postgraduate Medical Institute [*Australia*]
HPGPM .... Hits per Gun per Minute (NVT)
hpGRF .... Human Pancreas Growth Hormone-Releasing Factor [*Immunochemistry*]
HPGS .... High-Performance Graphics System [*Computer science*] (MHDB)
HPGS .... High-Pressure Gas System (NASA)
HPH .... Harnischfeger Indus [*NYSE symbol*] (TTSB)
HPH .... Harnischfeger Industries [*NYSE symbol*] (SAG)
HPH .... High-Performance Hoist (MCD)
HPH .... High-Pressure Hose
HPH .... Horsepower-Hour
HPHC .... Harvard Pilgrim Healthcare
HPHC .... Harvard Pilgrim Health Care
HPHD .... High-Pressure High-Density
HPHF .... Hereditary Persistence of Hemoglobin F [*Genetics*] (DOG)
HPHP .... Hydroxypivalyl Hydroxypivalate [*Organic chemistry*]
HP-HR .... Horsepower-Hour
HPHT .... High Pressure High Temperature [*Engineering*]
HPI .... Cleveland, OH [*Location identifier FAA*] (FAAL)
HPI .... Handicap Problems Inventory [*Psychology*]
HPI .... Hardwood Plywood Institute [*Later, HPMA*] (EA)
HPI .... Health Practices Inventory (EDAC)
HPI .... Health Professionals [*AMEX symbol*] (TTSB)
HPI .... Health Professionals, Inc. [*AMEX symbol*] (SPSG)
HPI .... Heavy Positive Ion
HPI .... Heifer Project International (EA)
HPI .... Height-Position Indicator (DEN)
HPI .... Helpful Programs, Inc. [*Computer science*]
HPI .... Hepatic Perfusion Index [*Medicine*] (DMAA)
HPI .... High-Performance Insulation (MCD)
HPI .... High-Power Illuminator (NATG)
HPI .... High-Pressure Injection [*Nuclear energy*] (NRCH)
HPI .... History of Present Illness
HPI .... Homing Position Indicator (NATG)
HPI .... Hours Post Inoculation
HPI .... Howe Peak [*Idaho*] [*Seismograph station code, US Geological Survey*] (SEIS)
HPI .... Hull Product Improvement [*Navy*] (CAAL)
HPI .... Human Productivity Institute (EA)
HPI .... Hydraulic Pressure Indicator
HPI .... Hydrocarbon Processing Industry
HPIA .... (Hydroxyphenylisopropyl)adenosine
HP-IB .... Hewlett-Packard Interface Bus [*Instrumentation*]
HPIC .... Hearing Performance Inventory for Children
HPIC .... High-Performance Immunoaffinity Chromatography
HPIEC .... High-Performance Ion Exchange Chromatography
HPIEC .... High-Pressure Ion Exchange Chromatography
HP IL .... Hewlett Packard Interface Loop (NITA)
HPI-MSRG ... Human Performance International, Motor Sport Research Group [*Research center*] (RCD)
HPIP .... High-Pressure Intensifier Pump
HPIP .... Houghton Pharmaceuticals [*NASDAQ symbol*] (TTSB)
HPIP .... Houghton Pharmaceuticals, Inc. [*NASDAQ symbol*] (SAG)
HPIR .... High-Power Illuminator RADAR [*Army*] (AABC)

HPIR .... High-Probability-of-Intercept Receiver [*Telecommunications*] (IEEE)
HPIS .... High-Performance Insulation System
HPIS .... High-Pressure Injection System [*Nuclear energy*] (NRCH)
HPISS .... High-Power Illuminator Signal Source (MCD)
HPIT .... High-Performance Infiltrating Technique [*Materials science*]
HPJ .... Help Project [*Computer science*] (PCM)
HPJ .... High-Power Jammer
HPJ .... High-Pressure Jet
HPJC .... Highland Park Junior College [*Later, Highland Park College*] [*Michigan*]
HPK .... High-Power Klystron
HPK .... Histidine Protein Kinase [*An enzyme*]
HPK .... Honorary Physician to the King [*British*]
HPKA .... High-Power Klystron Amplifier
HPKMB .... Hieratische Papyrus aus den Koeniglichen Museen zu Berlin [*A publication*] (BJA)
HPL .... Hamilton Public Library [*UTLAS symbol*]
HPL .... Hartford Public Library, Hartford, CT [*OCLC symbol*] (OCLC)
HPL .... Heliportugal-Trabalhos e Transporte Aereo, Representacoes, Importaza e Exportacao Lda. [*Portugal ICAO designator*] (FAAC)
HPL .... High Polar Latitude [*Geophysics*]
HPL .... High-Power LASER
HPL .... Hotel Properties Ltd. [*Singapore*] (ECON)
HPL .... Human Pancreatic Lipase [*An enzyme*]
HPL .... Human Parotid Lysozyme [*An enzyme*]
HPL .... Human Performance Laboratory [*Ball State University*] [*Research center*] (RCD)
HPL .... Human Peripheral Lymphocyte
HPL .... Human Placental Lactogen [*Also, CGP, HCS*] [*Endocrinology*]
HPL .... Hybrid Programming Language [*Computer science*]
HPL .... Nucla, CO [*Location identifier FAA*] (FAAL)
HPLA .... Hydroxyphenyllactic Acid [*Pharmacology*] (MAE)
HPLAC .... High-Performance Liquid Affinity Chromatography
HPLAC .... High-Pressure Liquid-Affinity Chromatography (DMAA)
HPLAP .... Human Placental Alkaline Phosphatase [*An enzyme*]
HPLC .... High-Performance [*or High-Pressure*] Liquid Chromatography
HPLC .... High-Performance Liquid Chromatography (USDC)
HPLF .... High-Pressure Low-Flow
HPLF .... Hydrolyzed Polar Lipid Fraction [*Biochemistry*]
HPLJ .... High-Pressure Liquid Jet
HPLL .... High Pressure Life Laboratory (PDAA)
HPLL .... Hybrid Phase-Locked Loop (PDAA)
HPLO .... High-Performance, Low-Observable
HP/LP .... High-Power/Low-Power
HPLPC .... High-Performance Low-Pressure Chromatography
HPLR .... Hinge Pillar [*Technical drawings*]
HPLRP .... Health Professionals Loan Repayment Program [*Military*]
HPLV .... High-Pressure Low-Volume [*Automotive painting*]
HPLX .... Healthplex, Inc. [*NASDAQ symbol*] (NQ)
HPM .... Harding-Passey Melanoma [*Oncology*] (AAMN)
HPM .... Head Positioning Mechanism
HPM .... Head Position Monitor
HPM .... Head Postmaster's Manual [*British*] (DCTA)
HPM .... Hemiplegic Migraine [*Neurology*] (DAVI)
HPM .... High-Performance Membrane [*Medicine*] (DMAA)
HPM .... High-Polymer Molecular [*Film*]
HPM .... High-Power Microwave
HPM .... High-Power Multiplier (DNAB)
HPM .... High-Priority Mail (TSSD)
HPM .... Honeycomb Propellant Matrix (SAA)
HPM .... Horizontal Panel Mount
HPM .... Hot Press Molding
HPM .... How Products are Made [*A publication*]
HPM .... Human Performance Model [*Human Engineering Laboratory*] [*Aberdeen Proving Ground, MD*] (RDA)
HPM .... Human Peritoneal Macrophage [*Immunology*]
HPM .... Human Potential Movement [*Psychotherapy*]
HPM .... Hydraulic Punching Machine
HPM .... Hyper-Page-Mode [*Computer science*] (PCM)
HPMA .... Hardwood Plywood Manufacturers Association [*Reston, VA*] (EA)
HPMA .... Heat Pump Manufacturers' Association [*British*]
HPMA .... High-Power Microwave Assembly (AAG)
HPMA .... Hydroxypropyl Methacrylate [*Organic chemistry*]
HPMAA .... Honey Packers and Marketers' Association of Australia
HPMC .... High-Performance Membrane Chromatography
HPMC .... Housing Production and Management Credit [*HUD*]
HPMC .... Hydroxypropyl(methyl)cellulose [*Synthetic food gum*] [*Organic chemistry*]
HPMCF .... High Purity Milled Carbon Fiber
Hp Mi .... Hippias Minor [*of Plato*] [*Classical studies*] (OCD)
HPMM .... Horizontal Planar Motion Mechanism (PDAA)
HPMNJ .... High-Power Microelectronic Noise Jammer
HPMS .... High-Performance Main Storage (IAA)
HPMS .... Highway Performance-Monitoring System [*Department of Transportation*] (GFGA)
HPMSK .... High-Priority Mission Support Kit [*Military*] (AFIT)
HPMV .... High-Pressure Mercury Vapor
HPN .... Central Hispano International, Inc. [*NYSE symbol*] (SAG)
HPN .... Harrison, Purchase, and North Castle [*Airport*]
HPN .... Haustus Purgans Noster [*Purging Draught from the Doctor's Own Prescription*] [*Pharmacy*] (ROG)
HPN .... Health Physics Network [*Nuclear energy*] (NRCH)
HPN .... Heavy Primary Nuclei
HPN .... Hepsin (DMAA)

HPN	High Pass Network
HPN	High Pass Notch (IAA)
HPN	Home Parenteral Nutrition
HPN	Horsepower Nominal
HPN	Hydrogenation of Pyrolysis Naphtha [*Petroleum refining*]
HPN	Hydroxypropyl Nitrate [*Organic chemistry*]
HPN	Hypertension [*Medicine*]
HPN	White Plains [*New York*] [*Airport symbol*] (OAG)
HPND	Human Pronatriodilatin [*Endocrinology*]
HPNJ	High-Power Noise Jammer
HPnP	Home Plug and Play [*Technology*]
HPNPr	Centl Hispano Intl9.875% 'MIPS' [*NYSE symbol*] (TTSB)
HPNS	High-Pressure Nervous Syndrome [*Deep-sea diving*]
HPNS	Hunters Point Naval Shipyard
HPO	Head Post Office
HPO	Health Care Purchasing Organization [*Insurance*] (WYGK)
HPO	High-Performance Option (MCD)
HPO	High-Pressure Oxygen [*Also, HBO, OHP*]
HPO	Highway Post Office [*Bus or truck equipped with mail distribution facilities*]
HPO	Hippo Valley [*Zimbabwe*] [*Airport symbol*] (AD)
HPO	Home Port [*Navy*] (NVT)
HPO	Hourly Postflight (MCD)
HPO	Hydrogenated Palm Oil
HPO	Hydroperoxide (DMAA)
HPO	Hydrophilic Ointment [*Pharmacy*] (DAVI)
HPO	Hydroxylamine Phosphate Oxime [*Organic chemistry*]
HPO	Hypertrophic Pulmonary Osteoarthropathy [*Medicine*] (DAVI)
HPOD	Hydroperoxyoctadecadienoic Acid [*Organic chemistry*]
HPOF	High-Pressure Oil-Filled [*Cable*]
HPOL	Health Manpower Shortage Area Placement Opportunity List [*Department of Health and Human Services*] (GFGA)
HPOP	High-Pressure Oxidizer Pump (NASA)
HPOT	Helipotentiometer
HPOT	High Potential (IAA)
HPOT	High-Pressure Oxidizer Turbopump (MCD)
HPOT	Hydroperoxyoctadecatrienoic Acid [*Organic chemistry*]
HPOTP	High-Pressure Oxidizer Turbopump
HPOX	High-Pressure Oxygen (AFM)
HPP	Half Page Printer
HPP	Half Power Point [*LASER technology*]
HPP	Hamiltonian Path Problem [*Mathematics*]
HPP	Harvard Project Physics
HPP	Health Physics Program (NRCH)
HPP	Health Promotion Pilot
HPP	Healthy Planet Prod [*AMEX symbol*] (TTSB)
HPP	Healthy Planet Products, Inc. [*AMEX symbol*] (SAG)
HPP	Hepp [*Alaska*] [*Seismograph station code, US Geological Survey*] (SEIS)
HPP	Hereditary Pyropoikilocytosis [*Medicine*]
HPP	Hernieuwde Progressieve Partij [*Renewed Progressive Party*] [*Surinam*] [*Political party*] (PPW)
HPP	High-Performance Plastic
HPP	Holding under Promise of Payment
HPP	Hot Processing Plant [*Nuclear energy*]
HPP	Human Pancreatic Polypeptide [*Endocrinology*]
HPP	Hydraulic Pneumatic Panel (AAG)
HPP	Hydroxyphenyl Pyruvate [*Organic chemistry*]
HPPA	Horses' and Ponies' Protection Association [*British*] (DI)
HPPA	Hydroxyphenylpyruvic Acid [*Organic chemistry*]
HPPC	Health Plan Purchasing Cooperatives
HPPC	High Performance Computing and Communications (TNIG)
HP PCIB	Hewlett Packard Personal Computer Instruments Bus (NITA)
HPPCL	Hewlett-Packard Printer Control Language
HPPD	Hours per Patient Day [*Medicine*] (DMAA)
HPPF	Horizontal Payloads Processing Facility (MCD)
HPPH	(Hydroxyphenyl)phenylhydantoin [*Biochemistry*] (AAMN)
HPPI	High-Performance Parallel Interface [*Computer science*]
HPPLC	High-Performance Preparative Liquid Chromatography
HPPM	High-Performance Propulsion Module (MCD)
HPPO	High Pressure Partial Oxidation (PDAA)
HPPP	High-Priority Production Program [*NATO*] (NATG)
HPPR	Hydroxypyrazolopyrimidine Ribonucleoside [*Biochemistry*]
HPPS	Hewlett-Packard Printer Submodule (IAA)
HPPS	Hughes Post Processor, Surveyor
HPPT	Hypertext Text Transfer Protocol [*Computer science*] (TNIG)
HPPTS	Hydraulic Package Pressure Test Set
HPQ	Highly Polarized Quasar [*Galactic science*]
HPQY	High Purity Quartz Yarn [*Materials science*]
HPR	Halden Reactor Project [*Norway*]
HPR	Halt and Proceed [*Computer science*] (SAA)
HPR	Hardware Problem Report (MCD)
HPR	Heart Profile Recorder [*Medicine*]
HPR	Heat Pipe Reactor
HPR	Hic Pace Requiescat [*May He Here Rest in Peace*] [*Latin*] (ROG)
HPR	Highly Protected Risk [*Insurance*]
HPR	High Penetration Resistant (PDAA)
HPR	High-Performance Routing [*Computer science*] (CDE)
HPR	High-Polymer Rheology
HPR	High-Powered RADAR (NATG)
HPR	Holding Period Return (PDAA)
HPR	Hopper [*Freight*]
HPR	Horsepower
HPR	Hosptial Peer Review (MEDA)
HPR	Host-Plant Resistance [*Entomology, phytochemistry*]

HPR	Hot Particle Rolling (PDAA)
HPR	Housing and Planning References [*A publication*]
HPR	Howard's New York Practice Reports [*A publication*] (DLA)
HPr	Howard's New York Practice Reports, New Series [*A publication*] (DLA)
HPR	HPR, Inc. [*Associated Press*] (SAG)
HPR	Hughes Photoelectric Reader
HPR	Human Performance Reliability
HPR	Human Progesterone Receptor [*Endocrinology*]
HPR	Human Prolactin [*Endocrinology*]
HPR	Hydrogen Pressure Regulator (MCD)
HPR	Hydroxyphenylretinamide [*Biochemistry*]
HPR	Hyperion Resources [*Vancouver Stock Exchange symbol*]
HPrA	Rick Lucus Helicopters Ltd. [*New Zealand*] [*FAA designator*] (FAAC)
HPR	Harcourt Genl'A'cm CvStk [*NYSE symbol*] (TTSB)
HPRCC	High Plains Regional Climate Center [*NCPO*]
HPRES	Pressure Altitude (GAVI)
HPRF	High Pulse Recurrence Frequency (MCD)
HPRF	Hypersonic Propulsion Research Facility
HPRI	HPR Inc. [*NASDAQ symbol*] (SAG)
HPRK	Hollywood Park [*NASDAQ symbol*] (TTSB)
HPRK	Hollywood Park, Inc. [*NASDAQ symbol*] (SAG)
HPRKZ	Hollywood Park $0.70 Dep Cv Pfd [*NASDAQ symbol*] (TTSB)
HPRL	Human Performance Research Laboratory [*University of Utah*] [*Research center*] (RCD)
HPRL	Human Prolactin [*Endocrinology*]
HPRP	High-Performance Reporting Post (NATG)
HPRP	High-Powered RADAR Post (NATG)
HPRP	Homes Per Rating Point [*Advertising*] (DOAD)
HPRP	Human Platelet-Rich Plasma [*Medicine*] (DMAA)
HPRP	Human Potential Research Project [*University of Surrey*] [*British*] (AIE)
HPRPC	High-Performance Reversed Phase Chromatography
HPRR	Health Physics Research Reactor [*Oak Ridge, TN*] [*Oak Ridge National Laboratory*] [*Department of Energy*]
HPRS	High-Pressure Recirculation System [*Nuclear energy*] (NRCH)
HPRS	Hopkins Psychiatric Rating Scale [*Personality development test*] [*Psychology*]
HPRS	Houghton Poultry Research Station [*British*] (ARC)
HPRT	Heartport, Inc. [*NASDAQ symbol*] (SAG)
HPRT	Heartport Inc. [*NASDAQ symbol*] (TTSB)
HPRT	Hypoxanthine-Guanine-Phosphoribosyl Transferase (DOG)
HPRT	Hypoxanthine Phosphoribosyltransferase [*Also, HGPRT*] [*An enzyme*]
HPRU	Handicapped Persons Research Unit (NITA)
HPRV	High-Pressure Relief Valve (KSC)
HPS	Antisubmarine Helicopter (NATG)
HPS	Haitian Philatelic Society (EA)
HPS	Hanford Plant Standard [*Formerly, HWS*] [*Nuclear energy*] (NRCH)
HPS	Hanna Pacific [*Vancouver Stock Exchange symbol*]
HPS	Hantavirus Pulmonary Syndrome [*Medicine*]
HPS	Hardened Power System
HPS	Hardy Plant Society (EAIO)
HPS	Harpsicord [*Music*] (WGA)
HPS	Hazardous Polluting Substances [*Shipping*] (DCTA)
HPS	Health Physics Society (EA)
HPS	Health Physics Station [*Nuclear energy*] (NRCH)
HPS	HealthPlan Services [*NYSE symbol*] (TTSB)
HPS	Healthplan Services Corp. [*NYSE symbol*] (SAG)
HPS	Heat Protection System
HPS	Helium Pressure Switch (MCD)
HPS	Hematoxylin-Phloxine-Saffron [*Biochemistry*] (MAE)
HPS	Hermansky-Pudlak Syndrome [*Medicine*]
HPS	Hermetic Pivoting Seal
HPS	Hidden Predictive Saccades [*Ophthalmology*]
HPS	Highest Points Scored (ROG)
HPS	High-Pressure Separator [*Chemical engineering*]
HPS	High-Pressure Sintering [*Ceramic technology*]
HPS	High-Pressure Sodium
HPS	High-Pressure Steam [*Technical drawings*]
HPS	High Primary Sequence (IAA)
HPS	High-Protein Supplement [*Nutrition*]
HPS	Hospitalization Proneness Scale [*Psychometrics*]
HPS	Hull Pressure Switch
HPS	Hybrid Propulsion System
HPS	Hydraulic Power Section [*Later, HPU*] (AAG)
HPS	Hydraulic Power Supply
HPS	Hydraulic Power System (KSC)
HPS	Hydroxypropyl Starch [*Organic chemistry*]
HPS	Hypertrophic Pyloric Stenosis [*Medicine*]
HPSA	Health Professional Shortage Area (DMAA)
HPSA	Hellenic Philatelic Society of America (EA)
HPSA	Honors Program Student Association of the American Sociological Association (EA)
HPSA	Hydraulic Package Servovalve Actuator
HPSC	Heading per Standard Compass [*Navigation*]
HPSC	Health Programs Systems Center
HPSC	HPSC, Inc. [*NASDAQ symbol*] (NQ)
HPSC	Hydraulic Package Storage Container
HPSCI	House Permanent Select Committee on Intelligence (MCD)
HPSD	High-Power Switching Device
HPSEC	High-Performance Size Exclusion Chromatography
HPSEC	High-Pressure Size Exclusion Chromatography
HPSF	High-Pressure Stopped Flow [*Spectrometry*]
HPSG	Head Driven Phrase Structure Grammar [*Artificial intelligence*]

HPSI	Harpsichord [*Music*]
HPSI	Health Professions Stress Inventory [*Medicine*]
HPSI	High-Pressure Safety Injection (NRCH)
HPSIP	High-Pressure Safety Injection Pump (NRCH)
HPSIS	High-Pressure Safety Injection System (IEEE)
HPSK	Hydraulic Power Supply Kit
HPSL	Health Professions Student Loans
HPSN	Hot-Pressed Silicon Nitride (RDA)
HPSOM	High-Performance Stand-Off Motor (MCD)
HPSP	Health Professions Scholarship Program [*Army*]
HPSS	Hrvatska Pucka Seljacka Stranka [*Croatian People's Peasant Party*] [*Former Yugoslavia*] [*Political party*] (PPE)
HPSSNJ	High-Power Self-Screening Noise Jammer [*Military*] (CAAL)
HPSTGC	Heading per Steering Compass [*Navigation*]
HPSV	High-Pressure Solenoid Valve
HPSW	High-Pressure Service Water [*Nuclear energy*] (NRCH)
HPSW	Horizontally Polarized Shear Wave [*Physics*]
HPSWS	High-Pressure Service Water System [*Nuclear energy*] (NRCH)
HPT	Hampton, IA [*Location identifier FAA*] (FAAL)
HPT	Head per Track (BUR)
HPT	Hexamethylphosphoric Triamide [*Also, HEMPA, HMP, HMPA, HMPT*] [*Organic chemistry*]
HPT	High-Payoff Target [*Military*] (INF)
HPT	High-Performance Train (ADA)
HPT	High Point
HPT	High-Potential Test [*or Tester*]
HPT	High-Power Transmitter Memory (DWSG)
HPT	High-Pressure Tap
HPT	High-Pressure Test
HPT	High-Pressure Turbine (NRCH)
HPT	High Profile Terminal (IAA)
HPT	Home Port [*Navy*] (NVT)
HPT	Homonuclear Polarization Transfer [*Physics*]
HPT	Horizontal Plot Table
HPT	Hormone Pregnancy Test
HPT	Horsepower Tonnage (DOMA)
HPT	Hospitality Properties Trust [*NYSE symbol*] (SAG)
HPT	Human Placenta Thyrotrophin [*Endocrinology*]
HPT	Hydrocylic Pressure Testing
HPT	Hydropneumatic Trailer (MCD)
HPT	Hygromycin Phosphotransferase
HPT	Hyperparathyroidism [*or Hyperthyroidism*] [*Endocrinology*]
HPTA	High Pressure Technology Association [*British*]
HPTA	Hinckley Pilot 35 Association (EA)
HPTA	Hire Purchase Trade Association [*British*] (BI)
HPTB	High-Pressure Turbine [*on a ship*] (DS)
HPTD	High Point, Thomasville & Denton Railroad Co. [*AAR code*]
HPTDC	Himachal Pradesh Tourist Development Corp. [*India*]
HPTE	Bis(hydroxyphenyl)trichloroethane [*Organic chemistry*]
HPTE	Heptachlor Epoxide
HPTE	High-Performance Turbine Engine [*Air Force*]
HPTF	Hydraulic Power Transmission Fluid (MCD)
HPTH	Hyperparathyroidism [*Medicine*] (MEDA)
HPTL	High-Payoff Target List [*Military*] (INF)
HPTLC	High-Performance Thin-Layer Chromatography
HPTP	Hydraulic Power Transfer Panel
HPTS	High-Performance Third Stage [*Rocket*] [*Army*] (AABC)
HPTS	High-Powered Transmit Set (DWSG)
HPTS	Hydroxypyrenetrisulfonic Acid [*Organic chemistry*]
HPTW	Hauptwerk [*Masterpiece*] [*German*]
HPU	Hale Pohaku [*Hawaii*] [*Seismograph station code, US Geological Survey*] (SEIS)
HPU	Hansard's Publishing Union (ROG)
HPU	Heater Probe Unit (DMAA)
HPU	High-Pressure Unit
HPU	Hydraulic Power Unit (MCD)
HPU	Hydraulic Pumping Unit (AABC)
HP(UK)	Hunter Personnel (United Kingdom) Ltd.
HPUS	Homeopathic Pharmacopoeia of the United States
HPV	Helium Pressure Vessel
HPV	Hemophilus Pertussis Vaccine [*Medicine*] (MAE)
HPV	High-Passage Virus
HPV	High-Powered Vehicle
HPV	High-Power Veractor
HPV	High-Pressure Valve
HPV	High-Priority Violator (GNE)
HPV	High Production Volume [*Manufacturing*]
HPV	Human Papillomavirus [*or Parvovirus*]
HPV	Human-Powered Vehicle
HPV	Hypoxic Pulmonary Vasoconstriction [*Medicine*]
HPV	Princeville [*Hawaii*] [*Airport symbol*] (OAG)
HPVD	Hypertensive Pulmonary Vascular Disease [*Medicine*]
HPV-DE	High-Passage Virus [*Grown in*] Duck Embryo [*Cells*]
HPV-DK	High-Passage Virus [*Grown in*] Dog Kidney [*Cells*]
HPVG	Hepatic Portal Venous Gas (MAE)
HPVR	Hypoxic Pulmonary Vascular Response [*Anesthesiology*]
HPVS	Hydropneumatic Vehicle Suspension [*Automotive engineering*]
HP VUE	Hewlett-Packard Visual User Environment [*Computer science*]
HP/W	Health Promotion/Wellness Program [*Medicine*] (DMAA)
HPW	High-Purity Water
HPW	Hopewell, VA [*Location identifier FAA*] (FAAL)
HPW	Hot Pressure Welding
HPW	Hours per Week
HPW	Paine Webber Group [*AMEX symbol*] (SAG)
HPWO	High Performance Work Organization

HPWR	Health Power [*NASDAQ symbol*] (SAG)
HPWSol	High-Protein Wash Solution [*Clinical chemistry*]
HPX	Homeplex Mortgage Investments [*NYSE symbol*] (SPSG)
HPX	Homeplex Mtge Invmts [*NYSE symbol*] (TTSB)
HPX	(Hydroxypropyl)xylan [*Organic chemistry*]
HPY	Baytown, TX [*Location identifier FAA*] (FAAL)
HPY	HPY Industry Ltd. [*Vancouver Stock Exchange symbol*]
HPZ	Helicopter Protected Zone [*Military*] (DA)
HPZ	High-Pressure Zone
HPZE	High-Performance Zone Electrophoresis
HQ	Business Express [*ICAO designator*] (AD)
H-Q	Hamstring-Quadriceps [*Anatomy*]
HQ	Hawker Siddeley Aviation Ltd. [*British ICAO designator*] (ICDA)
HQ	Hazard Quotient [*Toxicology*]
HQ	Headquarters
HQ	Headquarters Companies [*San Francisco, CA*] (TSSD)
HQ	Health Systems International [*NYSE symbol*] (SAG)
HQ	Health Systems Intl'A' [*NYSE symbol*] (TTSB)
HQ	Heussler Air Service [*ICAO designator*] (AD)
HQ	Highly Qualified (AFM)
HQ	High Quality [*Home video systems*]
HQ	Historical Quotes [*Information retrieval*]
HQ	Hoc Quaere [*Look For This or See This*] [*Latin*]
HQ	Home Quarters Warehouse, Inc.
HQ	Hong Qi [*Red Flag*] [*China*]
HQ	Hoop Quotient [*Basketball*]
HQ	HQ Minerals Ltd. [*Vancouver Stock Exchange symbol*]
HQ	Hydro-Quebec [*Institut de Recherche d'Hydro-Quebec*] [*Canada*]
HQ	Hydroquinone [*Organic chemistry*]
HQ	Hydroxyquinoline [*Organic chemistry*]
HQ	New York Helicopter [*ICAO designator*] (AD)
HQ(A)	Headquarters Administration Office [*British police*]
HQA	Middletown, PA [*Location identifier FAA*] (FAAL)
HQ & SERV ...	Headquarters and Service [*Marine Corps*]
HQASC	Headquarters, Air Support Command [*NATO*] (NATG)
HQB	Los Angeles, CA [*Location identifier FAA*] (FAAL)
HQBA	Headquarters Base Area
HQBC	Headquarters, Bomber Command [*Later, HQSTC*] [*British*] (NATG)
HQBN	Headquarters Battalion (DNAB)
HQBP	High Quality Bonus Point [*Advancement system*] [*Navy*] (NVT)
HQBTRY	Headquarters Battery [*Military*] (DNAB)
HQC	Handling Quality Criteria
HQC	Headquarters Command [*Air Force*]
HQC	High "Q" Circuit [*or Coil*]
HQC	Hydraulic Quick Coupler
HQC	Hydroquinone Cream [*Pharmacy*] (DAVI)
HQC	Hydroxyquinoline Citrate [*Antiseptic*]
HQC	Hyperquasicenter
HQ-CAP	Headquarters, Civil Air Patrol
HQCC	Headquarters, Coastal Command [*British*] (NATG)
HQCDO	Headquarters Case Development Officer [*Environmental Protection Agency*] (GFGA)
HQCMD	Headquarters Command [*Military*]
HQCO	Headquarters Company [*Military*] (DNAB)
HQCOM	Headquarters Command [*Military*] (KSC)
HQCOMD	Headquarters Command [*Air Force*]
HQCOMDT	Headquarters Commandant (NATG)
HQCOMDUSAF...	Headquarters Command, United States Air Force
HQCS	Heraldic Quality Control System (AABC)
HQDA	Headquarters, Department of the Army
HQDM	Headquarters Data Manager (KSC)
HQDP	Headquarters, Department of the Pacific [*Marine Corps*]
HQ DSA	Headquarters, Defense Supply Agency
HQDTMS	Headquarters, Defense Traffic Management Service
HQE	Hansard Questions Ecrites [*Hansard Written Question - HWQ*] [*Database House of Commons*] [*French*] [*Information service or system*] (CRD)
HQE	Hardware Quality Engineer (MCD)
HQEARC	Headquarters, Equipment Authorization Review Center [*Army*]
HQES	High-Quality Epitaxial Silicon
HQF	High Quality Facsimile (DGA)
HQFC	Headquarters, Fighter Command [*NATO*] (NATG)
HQG	Hugoton, KS [*Location identifier FAA*] (FAAL)
HQH	H&Q Healthcare Inv [*NYSE symbol*] (TTSB)
HQH	H & Q Healthcare Investors [*NYSE symbol*] (SPSG)
HQHRA	Half-Quarter Horse Registry of America (EA)
HQIADS	Headquarters, Integrated Air Defense System [*Air Force*]
HQJTF	Headquarters, Joint Task Force (MCD)
HQK	Gulf of Mexico, LA [*Location identifier FAA*] (FAAL)
HQL	Cullowhee, NC [*Location identifier FAA*] (FAAL)
HQL	H&Q Life Sciences Investors [*NYSE symbol*] (TTSB)
HQL	H & Q Life Sciences Investors [*NYSE symbol*] (SAG)
HQL	High-Quality Life
HQM	Highland Queen Mines Ltd. [*Vancouver Stock Exchange symbol*]
HQM	High-Quality Matrix [*Electronics*]
HQM	Hoquiam, WA [*Location identifier FAA*] (FAAL)
HQM	Hydro-Quebec, Bibliotheque [*UTLAS symbol*]
HQMC	Headquarters, Marine Corps
HQMD	Headquarters Management Directive [*NASA*]
HQMME	Hydroquinone Monomethyl Ether [*Organic chemistry*]
HQMTMTS ...	Headquarters, Military Traffic Management Terminal Service (DNAB)
HQN	Haplequin Lake [*Alaska*] [*Seismograph station code, US Geological Survey*] (SEIS)
HQNAVMARCORMARSTA...	Headquarters, Navy-Marine Corps Military Affiliate Radio System Station (DNAB)

HQNAVMATCOM...	Headquarters, Naval Material Command
HQNMC........	Headquarters, Naval Material Command (AFIT)
HQNO............	Heptyl(hydroxy)quinoline N-Oxide [Organic chemistry]
HQO	Hansard Questions Orale [Hansard Oral Questions - HOQ] [Database House of Commons] [French] [Information service or system] (CRD)
HQOC..........	Headquarters Operational Command [Australia]
HQR	Handling Qualities Rating [Cooper-Harper]
HQRS..........	Handling Qualities Rating Scale (MCD)
HQS	Headquarters
HQS	Headquarters Staff [British military] (DMA)
HQS	High-Quality Silicon
HQS	High-Quality Sound [Home video system] (IAA)
HQSA	Hydroxyquinolinesulfonic Acid [Organic chemistry]
HQSC..........	Headquarters, Signals Command [British] (NATG)
HQSQ..........	Headquarters Squadron
HQSQDN......	Headquarters, Support Squadron [Military] (DNAB)
HQSQN	Headquarters Squadron [Marine Corps]
HQSRN	Headquarters Staff of the Royal Navy [British]
HQSTC.........	Headquarters, Strike Command [Formerly, HQBC] [British] (NATG)
HQSVCBN ...	Headquarters, Service Battalion [Military] (DNAB)
HQSVCCO ...	Headquarters, Service Company [Military] (DNAB)
HQT	Coats, NC [Location identifier FAA] (FAAL)
HQT	Halogen Quenched Tube
HQTC..........	Headquarters, Transport Command [British] (NATG)
HQTC..........	High "Q" Tuned Circuit
HQTR	Headquarters (KSC)
HQTV	High-Quality Television [Home video system] (IAA)
HQUSACE ...	Headquarters, U.S. Army Corps of Engineers
HQ USAF ...	Headquarters, United States Air Force (AFM)
HR	Air Bremen [ICAO designator] (AD)
HR	Hague Resolutions
HR	Hail and Rain [Meteorology] (BARN)
hr	Hair (VRA)
hr	Hairless Mouse [Endocrinology] (DMAA)
hr..............	Hairspace [Printing] (WDMC)
HR	Hair Space between Letters [Proofreader's mark]
HR	Half-Reversal [Psychometrics]
HR	Half-Yearly Review
HR	Hallux Rigidus [Orthopedics] (DAVI)
HR	Hall Wardrobes [Classified advertising] (ADA)
HR	Halorhodopsin [Biochemistry]
HR	Halstead-Reitan [Neuropsychological battery] (DAVI)
HR	Halton Rifles [British military] (DMA)
HR	Handling Room
HR	Hand RADAR (IAA)
HR	Hand Reach [Automotive engineering]
HR	Hand Receipt (AABC)
HR	Hand Reset
HR	Hard Rolled
HR	Hardware Reliability (MCD)
HR	Harrington Rod [Orthopedics] (DAVI)
HR	Hazard Report (MCD)
HR	Healthcare Realty Tr [NYSE symbol] (TTSB)
HR	Healthcare Realty Trust [NYSE symbol] (SPSG)
HR	Heart Rate [Medicine]
HR	Heart Rhythm [Cardiology]
HR	Heater (IAA)
HR	Heat Reflector
HR	Heat Resisting [Technical drawings]
HR	Heavy-Duty Relay (IAA)
HR	Height Range [RADAR]
HR	Heir (ROG)
HR	Helicopter Request [Military] (NVT)
HR	Helium Rebottled [System]
HR	Helium, Refrigerated (AAG)
HR	Hellenic Register [Greek ship classification society] (DS)
HR	Hemophilia Research [An association Defunct] (EA)
HR	Hemorrhagic Retinopathy [Ophthalmology]
Hr	Henricus de Baila [Flourished, 1169-70] [Authority cited in pre-1607 legal work] (DSA)
HR	Henry Russell [Astronomy]
HR	Hermetic Rite [Freemasonry] (ROG)
HR	Heroes of the Reformation [A publication]
HR	Herr [Sir, Mr.] [German]
H-R	Hertzsprung-Russell [Diagram] [Astronomy]
HR	Hessischer Rundfunk [Hessian Radio Network] [Germany]
HR	Heterosexual Relations [Scale]
HR	Higher (ROG)
HR	Higher Rate
HR	Highhams Railway [Wales]
HR	Highland Railway [Scotland]
HR	Highland Regiment [British military] (DMA)
HR	High-Range [RADAR] (DEN)
HR	High-Rate Reverse [Ecology]
HR	High Reduction [Microforms] (NITA)
HR	High Reflector (IAA)
HR	High Resilience [Plastics]
HR	High Resistance
HR	High Resolution (MCD)
HR	High Risk
HR	High Run
HR	High-Speed Radial [Automotive tires]
hr..............	Hinge Remnant [Philately]
HR	Histamine Release [Immunology]

HR	Historical Record (NASA)
HR	History Report (MCD)
HR	Hit Rate (MUGU)
HR	Hit Ratio
HR	Hoechst-Roussel Pharmaceuticals, Inc. [Research code symbol]
HR	Hoerner [Horns] [Music]
HR	Hoge Raad [Dutch Supreme Court] (DLA)
HR	Hojesteret [Supreme Court] [Netherlands] (ILCA)
HR	Holding Register
HR	Holiday Route (CDAI)
HR	Homeostatic Regulators [British]
HR	Home Rule
HR	Home Run [Baseball]
HR	Homoreactant [Medicine]
HR	Hook Rail (MSA)
HR	Horizontal Resistance [Plant pathology]
HR	Horizontal Retort
HR	Hormonal Response [Medicine] (DMAA)
HR	Hormone Receptor Complex [Endocrinology]
HR	Horology Program [Association of Independent Colleges and Schools specialization code]
HR	Hose Rack (AAG)
HR	Hospitalman Recruit
HR	Hospital Record
HR	Hospital Recruit
HR	Hospital Report (MAE)
HR	Hot Rolled (MSA)
HR	Hour (AAG)
hr..............	Hour (ODBW)
hr..............	Hour
hr..............	Hour (WDMC)
HR	Hourly Report (DNAB)
HR	House of Representatives
HR	House of Representatives Bill [with Number]
HR	House of Ruth (EA)
HR	House Recedes
HR	House Report
HR	House Resolution
HR	House Roll [Legal term] (DLA)
HR	Hudson Review [A publication] (BRI)
HR	Humanitarian Reassignment [Military] (AFM)
HR	Human Reliability
HR	Human Resources
HR	Human Rights Convention [Council of Europe] (DLA)
HR	Humber Register [St. Albans, Hertfordshire, England] (EAIO)
HR	Humidity, Relative
Hr	Hussar [British military] (DMA)
HR	Hydraulics Research Ltd. [British] (IRUK)
HR	Hydrogen Recombiner (NRCH)
HR	Hydrogen Relief (NASA)
HR	Hypersensitive Response [Biology]
HR	Hypophosphatemic Rickets [Medicine] (DMAA)
HR	Robin Avions [Pierre Robin] [France ICAO aircraft manufacturer identifier] (ICAO)
HR	Shore
HR2D	High-Resolution, Two-Dimensional [Electrophoresis]
HRA	Hard Replacement Assembly (MCD)
HRA	Harness Release Actuator (DNAB)
HRA	Haura [South Arabia (Yemen)] [Airport symbol] (AD)
HRA	Health Resources Administration [Abolished, 1982, functions transferred to Health Resources and Services Administration] [HEW]
HRA	Health Risk Appraisal [or Assessment] [Medicine]
HRA	Heart Rate Acceleration
HRA	Heart Rate Audiometry
HRA	Heavy Replaceable [or Replacement] Assembly
HRA	Heli-Iberica [Spain ICAO designator] (FAAC)
HRA	Hemispherical Reflective Antenna
HRA	HF [High-Frequency] Recovery Antenna
HRA	High-Radiation Area (DNAB)
HRA	High Right Atrium [Anatomy]
HRA	High-Speed Research Aircraft (PDAA)
HRA	Histamine Releasing Activity [Medicine] (DAVI)
HRA	Honorary Royal Academician [British]
HRA	Hour of Revival Association [British]
HRA	Housing Revenue Account [British]
HRA	Human Reliability Analysis [Engineering]
HRA	Human Resource Accounting (ADA)
HRA	Human Rights Advocates (EA)
HRA	Huna Research Association [See also HF] [Switzerland] (EAIO)
HRA	Hydraulic Rotary Actuator
HRA	Hypersonic Research Airplane [NASA]
HRAA	High-Rate Acquisition Assembly (MCD)
HRAA	Hire and Rental Association of Australia
HRAD	Hunger Relief and Development [An association] (EA)
HRA EIS....	Hanford Remedial Action Environmental Impact Statement
HRAF	Human Relations Area Files (EA)
HRAG..........	International Human Rights Advisory Group [Switzerland]
HRAI	Heating, Refrigerating, and Air Conditioning Institute of Canada
HRAI	Human Rights Advocates International (EA)
HRAM	Hazard Ranking and Allocation Methodology (MCD)
HRAM	Hierarchical Random Access Memory [Computer science]
HR & IH	His [or Her] Royal and Imperial Highness (ROG)
HRANSW	Harness Racing Authority of New South Wales [Australia]

HRAP .... Housing Relocation Assistance Program [*US Army Corps of Engineers*]
HRAR .... Hereafter
HRART .... Hampton Roads Army Terminal
HRAS .... High-Rate Activated Sludge [*Waste treatment*]
HRAT .... Hampton Roads Army Terminal
HRAT .... Hereat [*Legal*] [*British*] (ROG)
HRAV .... Human Resources Availability (NVT)
HRB .... Block (H&R) [*NYSE symbol*] (TTSB)
HRB .... Block [*H. & R.*], Inc. [*NYSE symbol*] (SPSG)
HRB .... Croatian Revolutionary Brotherhood [*Former Yugoslavia*] (PD)
HRB .... Harbin [*Manchuria*] [*Airport symbol*] (OAG)
HRB .... Hardship Relief Board [*Victoria, Australia*]
HRB .... Hazard Review Board
HRB .... High Rate Bioreactor [*Chemical Engineering*]
HRB .... High-Resolution Bathymetry [*Instrumentation*]
HRB .... Highway Research Board [*Later, TRB*] (EA)
HRB .... Hinged Rotor Blade
HRB .... Hockey Rules Board [*Walton-On-Thames, Surrey, England*] (EAIO)
HRB .... House of Representatives Bill
HRB .... Hurbanovo [*Czechoslovakia*] [*Seismograph station code, US Geological Survey*] (SEIS)
HRBA .... Havana Rabbit Breeders Association (EA)
HRBA .... Hoist Rotation Beam Assembly [*Military*] (CAAL)
HRBC .... Harbinger Corp. [*NASDAQ symbol*] (SAG)
HRBC .... Horse Red Blood Cells [*Also, HRC*]
HRBF .... Harbor Federal Bancorp [*NASDAQ symbol*] (SAG)
HRBI .... Hotot Rabbit Breeders International (EA)
HRBOR .... Harbor [*Commonly used*] (OPSA)
HRC .... Hairdressers' Registration Council [*British*] (BI)
HRC .... Haitian Refugee Center (EA)
HRC .... Hardness Rockwell C [*Materials testing*]
HRC .... Hardwood Research Council (EA)
HRC .... Harris Ranch [*California*] [*Seismograph station code, US Geological Survey Closed*] (SEIS)
HRC .... Hasselblad Reflex Camera (MCD)
HRC .... HEALTHSOUTH Corp. [*NYSE symbol*] (TTSB)
HRC .... HEALTHSOUTH Rehabilitation Corp. [*NYSE symbol*] (SPSG)
HRC .... HEATH [*Higher Education and the Handicapped*] Resource Center (EA)
HRC .... Helium Research Center
HRC .... Herpes Resource Center (EA)
HRC .... Highland Regional Council [*Scotland*]
HRC .... High-Rupturing Capacity
HRC .... Holiday Rambler Corp.
HRC .... Hollycroft Resource Corp. [*Vancouver Stock Exchange symbol*]
HRC .... Holocaust Resource Center (EA)
HRC .... Holy Roman Church (WDAA)
HRC .... Honda Racing Corp.
HRC .... Honey Research Council [*Australia*]
HRC .... Horizontal Redundancy Check (IEEE)
HRC .... Horse Red Blood Cells [*Also, HRBC*]
HRC .... Horticultural Research Center [*University of Massachusetts*] (RCD)
HRC .... Horticultural Research Center [*Southern Illinois University at Carbondale*] (RCD)
HRC .... Howard Research Corp.
HRC .... Human Relations Committee [*Military*] (VNW)
HRC .... Human Resources Center (EA)
HRC .... Human Resources Committee
HRC .... Human Resources Council (GNE)
HRC .... Human Rights Commission
HRC .... Human Rights Committee
HRC .... Huntingdon Research Centre Ltd. [*British*] (IRUK)
HRC .... Hunting Retriever Club (EA)
HRC .... Hybrid Receiver Circuit
HRC .... Hybrid Ring Control [*Computer science*] (TNIG)
HRC .... Hydraulics-Resonance Changer (DNAB)
HRC .... Hypertension Research Center [*Indiana University*] [*Research center*] (RCD)
HRC .... Hypothetical Reference Circuit [*Telecommunications*] (TEL)
HRC .... Rockwell Hardness (C Scale)
HRCA .... Honorary Royal Cambrian Academician [*British*]
HRCC .... High-Ratio Compact Chamber [*Automotive engineering*]
HRCC .... Humanities Research Council of Canada [*See also CCRH*] [*Later, SSHRCC*]
HRC/CCPR ... Human Rights Committee (EA)
HRCF .... Human Rights Campaign Fund (EA)
HR Con Res... House of Representatives Concurrent Resolution [*Legal term*] (DLA)
HRD .... Hannaford Bros [*NYSE symbol*] (TTSB)
HRD .... Hannaford Brothers, Inc. [*NYSE symbol*] (SPSG)
hrd .... Hard [*Quality of the bottom*] [*Nautical charts*]
HRD .... Harding Carpets Ltd. [*Toronto Stock Exchange symbol*]
HRD .... Hard Top [*Automotive advertising*]
HRD .... Harstad [*Norway*] [*Airport symbol*] (AD)
HRD .... Heroin-Related Death [*Epidemiology*]
HRD .... Hertzsprung-Russell Diagram [*Astronomy*]
HRD .... High-Rate Demultiplexer (SSD)
HRD .... High-Rate Discharge (MCD)
HRD .... High-Rate Dosimeter (MCD)
HRD .... High-Resolution Display
HRD .... High Roughage Diet (PDAA)
HRD .... Holocaust Remembrance Day (BJA)
HRD .... Human Related Deaths
HRD .... Human Resource Development (EERA)
HRD .... Human Resources Data

HRD .... Human Resources Development
HRD .... Human Resources Division [*GAO*] (AAGC)
HRD .... Hurricane Research Division [*Miami, FL*] [*National Oceanic and Atmospheric Administration*] (GRD)
HRD .... Hydraulic Rate Damper
HRD .... Kountze/Silsbee, TX [*Location identifier FAA*] (FAAL)
HRDA .... High-Rate Data Assembly (MCD)
HRDB .... Human Resources Development Branch [*Environmental Protection Agency*] (EPA)
HRDC .... Honeybee Research and Development Committee [*Australia*]
HRDC .... Human Resources Development Command [*Military*] (DNAB)
HRDG .... Harding Lawson Assoc Grp [*NASDAQ symbol*] (TTSB)
HRDG .... Harding Lawson Associates Group, Inc. [*NASDAQ symbol*] (SAG)
HRDG .... Human Resources Development Group [*British*]
HrdgLaw ...... Harding Lawson Associates Group, Inc. [*Associated Press*] (SAG)
HRDI .... High-Rate Demultiplexer Instrument (SSD)
HRDI .... High-Resolution Doppler Imager (MCD)
HRDI .... High-Resolution Dynamic Imaging [*Electrophoresis*]
HRDI .... Human Resources Development Institute (EA)
HRDITS .... Hereditaments [*Legal*] [*British*] (ROG)
HRDL .... Hudson River Day Line [*AAR code*]
HRDM .... High-Rate Demultiplexer (MCD)
HR Doc .... House of Representatives Document (DLA)
HRDP .... Human Resources [*Research*] and Development Program
HRDP .... Hypothetical Reference Digital Path [*Meteorology*]
HRDPO .... Human Resources Development Project Office [*Military*] (DNAB)
HRDR .... High-Rate Digital Recorder (MCD)
HRDRSSR ... Hairdresser
HRDS .... High-Rate Data Section (NASA)
HRDS .... Human Resource Development Staff
HRDTY .... Heredity
HRDWRE ..... Hardware (WGA)
HRE .... Aerosucre SA [*Colombia*] [*ICAO designator*] (FAAC)
HRE .... Harare [*Zimbabwe*] [*Airport symbol*] (OAG)
HRE .... High-Resolution Electrocardiography
HRE .... High-Resolution Electrophoresis [*Analytical biochemistry*]
HRE .... Highridge Exploration Ltd. [*Toronto Stock Exchange symbol*]
HRE .... Holy Roman Emperor [*or Empire*]
HRE .... Homogeneous Reactor Experiments (NRCH)
HRE .... Hormone Receptor Enzyme [*Endocrinology*] (DMAA)
HRE .... Hormone Regulatory Element [*Endocrinology*]
HRE .... Hormone-Responsive Element [*Endocrinology*]
HRE .... Hovering Rocket Engine (MCD)
HRE .... HRE Properties [*Formerly, Hubbard Real Estate Investments*] [*Associated Press*] (SAG)
HRE .... HRE Properties [*Formerly, Hubbard Real Estate Investments*] [*NYSE symbol*] (SPSG)
HRE .... Human Relations Education (MCD)
HRE .... Human Research and Engineering Directorate [*Army*] (RDA)
HRE .... Human Response Element of DNA [*Endocrinology*]
HRE .... Hydrazine Rocket Engine
HRE .... Hydro Reconnaissance Experimental [*British military*] (DMA)
HRE .... Hypersonic Ramjet Engine
HRE .... Hypersonic Research Engine [*NASA*]
HRE .... Hypoxia-Responsive Element [*Molecular medicine*]
HREAA .... Health and Research Employees' Association of Australia
HREBIU .... Hotel and Restaurant Employees and Bartenders International Union [*Later, HERE*] (EA)
HREC .... Health Record
H Rec A Sc.. Historical Records of Australian Science [*A publication*]
HREELS .... High-Resolution Electron Energy Loss Spectroscopy
HREF .... Hypertext Reference [*Computer science*] (CDE)
HREH .... High-Renin Essential Hypertension [*Medicine*] (DMAA)
HRELES .... High-Resolution Energy-Loss Electron Spectroscopy
HRELS .... High-Resolution Energy-Loss Spectroscopy (MCD)
HREM .... High-Resolution Electron Microscopy
HREOC .... Human Rights and Equal Opportunity Commission (EERA)
H Rep .... House of Representatives Report (AAGC)
HRept .... House of Representatives Reports [*A publication*] (DLA)
HRES .... High-Resolution Electronic System
H Res .... House Resolution, United States House of Representatives
HRET .... Health Related Fitness Test (EDAC)
HRET .... Hospital Research and Educational Trust (EA)
HREU .... Hotel and Restaurant Employees and Bartenders International Union [*Later, HERE*]
HRF .... Height-Ranger Finder
HRF .... Hemochromatosis Research Foundation (EA)
HRF .... Herb Research Foundation (EA)
HRF .... High Rate of Fire (NATG)
HRF .... High-Resolution Facsimile [*Telecommunications*]
HRF .... Histamine Releasing Factor [*Immunology*]
HRF .... History Record Folder (MCD)
HRF .... Human Research Facility (SSD)
HRF .... Hypersonic Rarefied Flow
HRF .... Sisters of the Holy Rosary of Fatima (Mexico) (TOCD)
HRFA .... High-Resolution Frequency Analysis [*of periodic phenomena*]
HRFA .... Hungarian Reformed Federation of America (EA)
HRFA .... Huron River Fishing Association [*Michigan*]
HRFAX .... High-Resolution Facsimile [*Telecommunications*] (TEL)
HRFBS .... Hill Radnor Flock Book Society [*British*] (DBA)
HRG .... Halford-Robins-Godfrey [*British sports car maker*]
HRG .... Harrington Public Library, Harrington, DE [*OCLC symbol*] (OCLC)
HRG .... Health Research Group
HRG .... Hearing (ROG)
HRG .... Hemispherical Resonating Gyro (PDAA)

HRG	Heritage Roses Group (EA)
HRG	He-Ro Group [NYSE symbol] (SPSG)
HRG	High River Gold [Vancouver Stock Exchange symbol]
HRG	High River Gold Mines Ltd. [Toronto Stock Exchange symbol]
HRG	Histidine-Rich Glycoprotein [Biochemistry]
HRG	Human Rights Group [Edinburgh, Scotland] [Defunct] (EAIO)
HRGC	Hurghada [Egypt] [Airport symbol] (OAG)
HRGC	High-Resolution Gas Chromatography
HRGM	High-Resolution Ground Map
HRGM	Hogg Robinson & Gardner Mountain [Insurance broker] [British]
HRGP	Hydroxyproline-Rich Glycoprotein [Biochemistry]
HRH	Hand Receipt Holder (MCD)
HRH	High-Rate Heat
HRH	Hilb, Rogal & Hamilton [NYSE symbol] (TTSB)
HRH	His [or Her] Royal Highness
HRH	Howard Robard Hughes [1905-1976] [American businessman]
HRH	Hypoplastic Right Heart [Cardiology]
HRH	Royal Tongan Airlines [Tonga] [ICAO designator] (FAAC)
HRHA	Honorary Member of the Royal Hibernian Academy [British]
HRHA	Hydronic Radiant Heating Association (EA)
HRHR	High-Risk Hearing Register
HR(HS)	Hospital Recruit (High School) [Navy] (DNAB)
HRI	Hannah Research Institute [British] (ARC)
HRI	Hard Rock International [Restaurant chain]
HRI	Harrington Rod Instrumentation [Orthopedics] (DAVI)
HRI	Hayes Resources, Inc. [Toronto Stock Exchange symbol]
HRI	Health Research, Inc. [New York State Department of Health] [Research center] (RCD)
HRI	Heart Research Institute [Australia]
HRI	Height-Range Indicator [Electronics]
HRI	Hierarchical Richness Index [Biodiversity] (EERA)
HRI	High-Resolution Image [or Imager] [Astronomy]
HrI	Holbrook Research Institute, Oxford, MA [Library symbol] [Library of Congress] (LCLS)
HRI	Holcomb Research Institute [Butler University]
HRI	Honorary Member of the Royal Institute of Painters in Water Colours [British]
HRI	Horizon Reference Indicator [Aerospace] (AAG)
HRI	Horticultural Research Institute (EA)
HRI	Hotel, Restaurant, and Institutional [Business]
HRI	Human Relations Inventory [Psychology]
HRI	Human Resources Institute [State University of New York at Buffalo] [Research center] (RCD)
HRI	Human Rights International (EA)
HRI	Human Rights Internet (EA)
HRIF	Histamine-Release Inhibitory Factor [Antiinflammatory]
HRIG	Human Rabies Immune Globulin [Immunology]
HRIN	Herein [Legal] [British] (ROG)
HRIN	Human Resource Information Network [Executive Telecom System, Inc.] [Information service or system] (IID)
HRINAR	Hereinafter [Legal] [British] (ROG)
HRINBEFE	Hereinbefore [Legal] [British] (ROG)
HRINBFR	Hereinbefore [Legal] [British] (ROG)
HRIO	Height-Range Indicator Operator [Electronics]
HRIO	Horticultural Research Institute of Ontario [Canada Research center] (RCD)
HRIP	Hic Requiescit in Pace [Here Rests in Peace] [Latin]
HRIP	Highway Research in Progress [British]
HRIR	High-Resolution Infrared Radiometer
HRIR	High Resolution Infrared Receiver (IAA)
HRIRS	High-Resolution Infrared Radiation Sounder
HRIRS	High Resolution Infra-Red Spectroscopy
HRIS	High-Repetition Illuminator System
HRIS	High Resolution Imaging Spectrometer [Instrument] (EERA)
HRIS	Highway Research Information Service [National Academy of Sciences] [Washington, DC]
HRIS	House of Representatives Information System
HRIS	Human Resources Information System (WYGK)
HRJ	High-Range Juno [Survey meter for radiation]
HRJ Res	House of Representatives Joint Resolution [Legal term] (DLA)
HRK	Hardrock Extension, Inc. [Toronto Stock Exchange symbol]
HRK	Kharkov [Former USSR Airport symbol] (OAG)
HRK	Racine, WI [Location identifier FAA] (FAAL)
HR-KMAG	Historical Report - Korea Military Advisory Group
HRL	Hardware Requirements List
HRL	Harlingen [Texas] [Airport symbol] (OAG)
HRL	Harlin Resources [Vancouver Stock Exchange symbol]
HRL	Head Rotated Left [Medicine]
HRL	Heat Rejection Loop
HRL	High Refraction Layer
HRL	High-Repetition LASER
HRL	High-Resolution LOFAR [Military] (CAAL)
HRL	Historical Record Log (SAA)
HRL	Horizontal Reference Line [Technical drawings]
HRL	Hormel [Geo. A.] & Co. [NYSE symbol] (SPSG)
HRL	Hormel Foods [NYSE symbol] (TTSB)
HRL	Hughes Research Laboratories [Hughes Aircraft Co.]
HRL	Human Resources Laboratory [Air Force] (MCD)
HRL	Hydraulics Research Laboratory [British]
HRL	Hydrological Research Laboratory [Silver Spring, MD] [National Weather Service] (GRD)
HRLA	Human Reovirus-Like Agent [Medicine] (DMAA)
HRLC	High-Resolution Liquid Chromatography
HRLI	High-Repetition LASER Illuminator
HRLIS	High-Repetition LASER Illuminating System

HRLM	High-Resolution Light Microscopy
HRLS	High-Repetition LASER System
HRLSD	Health and Rehabilitative Library Services Division [Later, ASCLA] [American Library Association]
HRLY	Herley Industries [NASDAQ symbol] (TTSB)
HRLY	Herley Industries, Inc. [NASDAQ symbol] (NQ)
HRM	Hardware Read-In Mode
HRM	Hermes Ventures [Vancouver Stock Exchange symbol]
HRM	High-Rate Multiplexer (MCD)
HRM	High-Ratio Multiplier (NASA)
HRM	High-Reliability Module (IAA)
HRM	High-Resolution Monitor (MCD)
HRM	His [or Her] Royal Majesty [British]
HRM	Holistic Resource Management (ECON)
HRM	Human Resources Management
HRM	University of Hartford, West Hartford, CT [OCLC symbol] (OCLC)
HRMA	[British Columbia] Human Resources Management Association (AC)
Hrm ADR	Harmony Gold Mining Co. Ltd. [Associated Press] (SAG)
HR Mag	HR Magazine [A publication] (BRI)
HR Mag	HR Magazine [A publication]
HRMC	Harts Range Meta-igneous Complex [Geology]
HRMC	Human Resources Management Center [Navy]
HRMC/D	Human Resources Management Center/Detachment [Navy] (DNAB)
HRMD	Human Resources Management Detachment [Navy] (DNAB)
HRMDDHG	Herr, Regiere Mich durch Deinen Heiligen Geist [Lord, Rule Me through Thy Holy Spirit] [Motto for a number of 16th and 17th century German and Bavarian rulers]
HrmHld	Harmony Holdings, Inc. [Associated Press] (SAG)
HRMI	Health Risk Management [NASDAQ symbol] (TTSB)
HRMI	Health Risk Management, Inc. [NASDAQ symbol] (SAG)
HRMI	Human Resources Management Instructor [Navy] (DNAB)
HRMN	Harmon Indus [NASDAQ symbol] (TTSB)
HRMN	Harmon Industries, Inc. [NASDAQ symbol] (NQ)
HRMOB	Association of Human Resources Management and Organizational Behavior [Later, AM] (EA)
HRMP	Harvard Radio Meteor Project
HRMR	Human Read/Machine Read [Microfilm memory system]
HRMS	Health Risk Management Service [Australian Capital Territory]
HRMS	Height Root Mean Square (IAA)
HRMS	High-Resolution Mass Spectrometry
HRMS	High Resolution Microwave Survey [Astronomy]
HRMS	Human Resource Management Services, Inc. [Database producer] (IID)
HRMS	Human Resource Management System
HRMS	Human Resources Management School [Navy] (DNAB)
HRMS	Human Resources Management Specialist [Navy] (NVT)
HRMSS	Human Resources Management Support System [Navy] (NVT)
HRMST	Human Resources Management Support Team [Navy] (DNAB)
HRMTG	Hermitage
HR/MTI	High-Resolution/Moving Target Indicator (DNAB)
HRMY	Harmony Products, Inc. [NASDAQ symbol] (SAG)
HRN	Airwork Ltd. [British ICAO designator] (FAAC)
HRN	Harlyn Products [AMEX symbol] (TTSB)
HRN	Harlyn Products, Inc. [AMEX symbol] (SPSG)
HRN	Harness
HRN	Harwin Exploration & Development, Inc. [Vancouver Stock Exchange symbol]
HRN	Herrn [Sirs, Gentlemen] [German] (ROG)
HRN	Hoerner [Horns] [Music]
HRN	Human Research Need (RDA)
HRN	Human Resources Need (MCD)
HRN	Human Resources Network [Information service or system] (EA)
HRN	Human Rights Network [British]
HRNA	Haflinger Registry of North America (EA)
hRNA	Ribonucleic Acid, Heterogeneous [Biochemistry, genetics]
HRNAR	Hereinafter
HRNB	History: Reviews of New Books [A publication] (BRI)
HRNES	Host Remote Node Entry System
HRNG	Hearing
HRNTWT	High Reynolds Number Transonic Wind Tunnel
HRO	Harrison [Arkansas] [Airport symbol] (OAG)
HRO	Hermiston [Oregon] [Seismograph station code, US Geological Survey] (SEIS)
HRO	HERO Industries Ltd. [Toronto Stock Exchange symbol Vancouver Stock Exchange symbol]
HRO	Homes Registration Office
HRO	Housing Referral Office [Military]
HROI	Honorary Member of the Royal Institute of Oil Painters [British]
HRON	Hereon [Legal] [British] (ROG)
HRP	Haitian Refugee Project [Defunct] (EA)
HRP	Health & Retirement Properties Trust [Formerly, Health/Rehabilitation Property] [NYSE symbol] (SPSG)
HRP	Health & Retirement Prop Tr [NYSE symbol] (TTSB)
HRP	Heat-Resistant Phenolic
HRP	Heat-Resisting Plastic
HRP	High-Risk Patient [Medicine] (DMAA)
HRP	Highway Regulating Point (AABC)
HRP	Histidine-Rich Protein [Biochemistry, immunochemistry]
HRP	Historical Review Press [British]
HRP	Holding and Reconsignment Point [Military] (AABC)
HRP	Horizontal Radiation Pattern [Electronics] (DEN)
HRP	Horseradish Peroxidase [An enzyme]
HRP	Human Reliability Program (AFM)
HRP	Human Rights Party [Ann Arbor, MI]

HRP	Human Rights Program [*Harvard University*] [*Research center*] (RCD)
HRP	Hypergroup Reference Pilot [*Telecommunications*] (NITA)
HRPA	Hebrew Religious Protection Association of Greater New York (EA)
HRPAC	Human Rights Political Action Committee (EA)
HRPC	High-Range Pressure Control
HRPD	Hamburg Rating Scale for Psychiatric Disorders [*Medicine*] (DMAA)
HRPD	High-Resolution Powder Diffractometer [*Crystallographic instrument*]
HRPI	High-Resolution Pointable Imager
HRPM	High-Resolution Permanent Magnet (MHDI)
HRPO	Horseradish Peroxidase [*Also, HRP*] [*An enzyme*]
HRPO	Hot Rolled, Pickled, and Oiled (MSA)
hr pp	Hours Postprandial [*Usually preceded by a numeral*] [*Pharmacology*] (DAVI)
HRPP	Human Rights Protection Party [*Western Samoa*] [*Political party*] (PPW)
HRPRAS	High-Risk, People-Related Accident Syndrome (DICI)
HRPS	Hazard Reduction Precedence Sequence (NASA)
HRPS	Human Resource Planning Service [*New York, NY*] (EA)
HRPS	Hydrogen Recombination and Purge System [*Nuclear energy*] (NRCH)
HRPT	High-Resolution Picture Transmission [*Service*]
HRPT	Highway Regulating Point Team [*MTMC*] (TAG)
HRPT	Hyperparathyroidism [*Medicine*] (DMAA)
HRPVD	High-Rate Physical Vapor Deposition [*Metal*]
HRQ	Hold Request (IAA)
HRQL	Health-Related Quality-of-Life [*Medicine*]
HRQOL	Health Related Quality of Life
HRQOL	Health-Related Quality of Life
HRR	Hardy-Rand Rittler [*Test for color vision*]
HRR	Head Rotated Right [*Medicine*]
HRR	Healy, AK [*Location identifier FAA*] (FAAL)
HRR	Heart Rate Range [*Medicine*]
HRR	Heat Rejection Radiator
HRR	Heat Release Rate [*Engineering*]
HRR	Heat Release Rate [*Flammability testing*] [*Fire safety*]
HRR	Heiliges Roemisches Reich [*Holy Roman Empire*] [*German*] (ROG)
HRR	Heron Resources Ltd. [*Vancouver Stock Exchange symbol*]
HRR	High-Reliability Relay
HRR	High-Resolution RADAR
HRRC	Hearing Rehabilitation Research Center [*Walt Disney*] (BABM)
HRRC	Home Recording Rights Coalition (EA)
HRRC	Human Resources Research Center
HRRC	Human Rights Resource Center (EAIO)
HRRC	Walt Disney Hearing Rehabilitation Research Center [*Ear Research Institute*]
HRRD	Human Resources Research Development Program
HR Rel	Historicorum Romanorum Reliquiae [*A publication*] (OCD)
HR Rep	House of Representatives Reports [*A publication*] (DLA)
HR Rept	House of Representatives Reports [*A publication*] (DLA)
HRRI	Heart Rate Retardation Index [*Medicine*] (DMAA)
HRRI	Human Resources Research Institute
Hrringtn	Harrington Financial Group, Inc. [*Associated Press*] (SAG)
HRRL	Human Resources Research Laboratory [*Air Force*] (MCD)
HRRM	High Range-Resolution Monopulse (PDAA)
hrRNA	Ribonucleic Acid, Heavy Ribosomal [*Biochemistry, genetics*]
HRRO	Human Resources Research Office [*NASA*] (AAG)
HRRVC	Holiday Rambler Recreational Vehicle Club (EA)
HRRWC	Hudson River Region Wine Council (EA)
HRS	Hair Replacement System
HRS	Hal Roach Studios, Inc.
HRS	Hamilton Rating Scale (MAE)
HRS	Hard Red Spring [*Wheat*]
HRS	Harp Renaissance Society [*Defunct*] (EA)
HRS	Harris Corp. [*NYSE symbol*] (SPSG)
HRS	Harris, GA [*Location identifier FAA*] (FAAL)
HRS	Hawaii Revised Statutes [*A publication*]
HRS	Hazard Ranking System [*Environmental Protection Agency*]
HRS	Heading Reference System (AAG)
HRS	Heat Rejection System
HRS	Hepatorenal Syndrome [*Medicine*]
HRS	High-Rate Station
HRS	High-Resolution Spectrograph [*Hubble Space Telescope*] [*NASA*]
HRS	High Resolution Spectrometer [*Marine science*] (OSRA)
HRS	High-Resolution System
HRS	Historic Record Society [*Record label*]
HRS	Home Reunion Society [*British*]
HRS	Honorary Reserve Section
HRS	Horizon Reference Set (MCD)
HRS	Horizontal Recovery System
HRS	Hormone Receptor Site [*Endocrinology*]
HRS	Hospital Reading Society [*Defunct*] (EA)
HRS	Host Resident Software
HRS	Hot Rolled Steel
HRS	Hours (NATG)
hrs	Hours (ODBW)
HRS	Housing Referral Service [*Military*] (AABC)
HRS	Hovering Rocket System [*Army*]
HRS	Human Resources System (MHDB)
HRS	Hunza Research Society [*Defunct*] (EA)
HRS	Hurricane Research Service [*Information service or system*] (IID)
HRS	Hussars [*Military unit*] [*British*]
HRS	Hydrant Refuelling System (IAA)
HRS	Hydraulics Research Station [*Research center British*]
HRS	Hyper-Rayleigh Scattering [*Physics*]
HRS	Missionary Sisters of Our Lady of the Holy Rosary [*Roman Catholic religious order*]
HRSA	Health Resources and Services Administration [*Department of Health and Human Services*]
HRSA	Historical Radio Society of Australia
HRSA	Honorary Member of the Royal Scottish Academy
HRSA	Hotel & Restaurant Suppliers Association Inc. (AC)
HRSC	Hudson River Sloop Clearwater (EA)
HRSCMR	High-Resolution Surface-Composition Mapping Radiometer (PDAA)
HRS-D	Hamilton Rating Scale for Deafness
HRS-D	Hamilton Rating Scale for Depression [*Medicine*] (DMAA)
HRSD	Hard Rock Silo Development
HRSD	Hazardous Response Support Division [*Environmental Protection Agency*]
HRSEM	High-Resolution Scanning Electron Microscopy (OA)
HRSG	Heat Recovery Steam Generator [*Industrial engineering*]
hrsg	Herausgegeben [*Edited, Published*] [*German*]
HRSH	Hirsch International Corp. [*NASDAQ symbol*] (SAG)
HRSH	Hirsch Intl. Corp'A' [*NASDAQ symbol*] (TTSB)
Hrshey	Hershey Foods Corp. [*Associated Press*] (SAG)
HRSI	High-Temperature Reusable Surface Insulation [*Space shuttle*] [*NASA*]
HRSN	Hariston Corp. [*NASDAQ symbol*] (SAG)
HRSNA	Histamine Research Society of North America (EA)
HRSNF	Hariston Corp. [*NASDAQ symbol*] (TTSB)
HRSP	Association of Human Resource Systems Professionals (EA)
HRSR	Heat Recovery/Seed Recovery [*System*]
HRSR	High Resolution Scanning Radiometer [*Instrument*] (EERA)
HRSS	Host Resident Software System
HRSS	Hrvatska Republikanska Seljacka Stranka [*Croatian Republican Peasant Party*] [*Former Yugoslavia*] [*Political party*] (PPE)
HRSSCC	High-Resolution Spin Scan Cloud Camera (NOAA)
HRSTYLNG	Hairstyling
HRSTYLST	Hairstylist
HRSV	Hydrangea Ringspot Virus [*Plant pathology*]
HRSW	Honorary Member of the Royal Scottish Water Colour Society
HRT	Arrhythmia Research Tech [*AMEX symbol*] (TTSB)
HRT	Arrhythmia Research Technology [*AMEX symbol*] (SPSG)
HRT	Hartford [*Diocesan abbreviation*] [*Connecticut*] (TOCD)
HRT	Hartwell Railway Co. [*AAR code*]
HRT	Heart
HRT	Heart
HRT	Heart Rate [*Cardiology*] (DAVI)
HRT	Heat Rejection and Transport (SSD)
HRT	Heavy Rail Transit (PDAA)
HRT	Helmholtz Reciprocal Theorem [*Physics*]
Hrt	Hertfordshire [*County in England*] (WGA)
HRT	High-Rate Telemetry [*NASA*]
HRT	High-Resolution Tracker
HRT	Hillcrest Resources Ltd. [*Toronto Stock Exchange symbol*]
HRT	Hiring, Retention, and Tenure [*of college professors*]
HRT	Homogeneous Reactor Test
HRT	Hormone Replacement Therapy [*Medicine*]
HRT	Hospitals Remuneration Tribunal [*Australia*]
HRT	Hostage Rescue Team [*Pronounced "hurt"*] [*FBI standardized term*]
HRT	Human Resources Training
HRT	Hydraulic Retention Time
HRT	Mary Esther, FL [*Location identifier FAA*] (FAAL)
HRT	Transporte Aereo Rioplatense [*Argentina ICAO designator*] (FAAC)
HRTC	Historic Rehabilitation Tax Credit
HrtCC	Heart Cubic Content (DAC)
HRTD	High-Rising Terminal Declarative [*Linguistics*]
HRTEM	High-Resolution Transmission Electron Microscope [*or Microscopy*]
HRTF	High-Resolution Tangential Flow Filtration
HrtFa	Heart Facial Area (DAC)
HrtfdSt	Hartford Steam Boiler & Inspection [*Associated Press*] (SAG)
HrtG	Heart Girth (DAC)
HRTG	Heritage
HrtgMd	Heritage Media Corp. [*Associated Press*] (SAG)
HrtgMda	Heritage Media [*Associated Press*] (SAG)
HrtLabs	Heart Labs of America [*Associated Press*] (SAG)
HrtLb	Heart Labs of America [*Associated Press*] (SAG)
HrtIndE	Heartland Express, Inc. [*Associated Press*] (SAG)
HRTS	High-Rate Telemetry System [*NASA*]
HRTS	High-Resolution Telescope and Spectrograph
HRTS	High-Risk Test Site [*Later, Research Test Site*]
HRTS	Hollywood Radio and Television Society (EA)
HRTT	Heart Technology, Inc. [*NASDAQ symbol*] (SAG)
HRTWD	Heartwood [*Forestry*] (WGA)
HrtWire	Heartland Wireless Communications, Inc. [*Associated Press*] (SAG)
HRTWN	Hawaii Regional Tsunami Warning Network [*Marine science*] (OSRA)
HRU	Harrisburg-Dayton [*Vancouver Stock Exchange symbol*]
HRU	Heading Reference Unit
HRU	Herrington, KS [*Location identifier FAA*] (FAAL)
HRU	Hostage Rescue Unit (LAIN)
HRUP	High-Risk Urban Problem [*Environmental Protection Agency*] (GFGA)
HRV	Harvard - Oak Ridge [*Massachusetts*] [*Seismograph station code, US Geological Survey*] (SEIS)
HRV	Heat Rate Variability
HRV	Heat Recovery Ventilator
HRV	Heavy Recovery Vehicle [*Marine Corps*] (VNW)
HRV	High Resolution Visible [*Imager*]
HRV	Historical Records of Victoria [*A publication*]
HRV	Human Reovirus [*Medicine*] (DMAA)
HRV	Human Rhinovirus [*Medicine*]

HRV	Human Rotaviruses
HRV	Hydraulic Relief Valve
HRV	Hypersonic Research Vehicle
HRV	New Orleans, LA [*Location identifier FAA*] (FAAL)
HRVL	Human Resources, Veterans, and Labor [*Office of Management and Budget*]
HRVLA	Human Reovirus-Like Agent (CPH)
HRVY	Harvey Entertainment [*NASDAQ symbol*] (TTSB)
HRVY	Harvey Entertainment Co. [*NASDAQ symbol*] (SAG)
HRW	Hard Red Winter [*Wheat*]
HRW	Heated Rear Window [*Automotive accessory*]
HRW	Human Rights for Women (EA)
HRW	Human Rights Watch (EA)
HRWMC	House of Representatives Ways and Means Committee (WDAA)
HRWS	Helicopter Remote Wind Sensor
HRX	Hereford, TX [*Location identifier FAA*] (FAAL)
HRX	Hypothetical Reference Connection [*Meteorology*]
HRXRS	High-Resolution X-Ray Spectroscopy
HRY	Hallwood Realty Partners Ltd. [*AMEX symbol*] (SPSG)
HRY	Hallwood Rlty Ptnrs L.P. (New) [*AMEX symbol*] (TTSB)
HRY	Head Rice Yield
HRYG	Gisenyi [*Rwanda*] [*ICAO location identifier*] (ICLI)
HRYI	Butare [*Rwanda*] [*ICAO location identifier*] (ICLI)
HRYO	Gabiro [*Rwanda*] [*ICAO location identifier*] (ICLI)
HRYR	Kigali [*Rwanda*] [*ICAO location identifier*] (ICLI)
HRYU	Ruhengeri [*Rwanda*] [*ICAO location identifier*] (ICLI)
HRZ	High Rainfall Zone
HRZA	Kamembe [*Rwanda*] [*ICAO location identifier*] (ICLI)
HRZB	Horizon Bank [*NASDAQ symbol*] (NQ)
HRZB	Horizon Financial [*NASDAQ symbol*] (TTSB)
HRZB	Horizon Financial Corp. [*NASDAQ symbol*] (SAG)
HrzBcWV	Horizon Bancorp (West Virginia) [*Associated Press*] (SAG)
HrzBTX	Horizon Bancorp, Inc. (Texas) [*Associated Press*] (SAG)
HrzHlt	Horizon CMS Healthcare Corp. [*Associated Press*] (SAG)
HrzHlt	Horizon Healthcare Corp. [*Associated Press*] (SAG)
HrzMH	Horizon Mental Health Management [*Associated Press*] (SAG)
HRZN	Horizon (MSA)
HRZN	Horizon
HS	Aeronoleggi e Lavoro Aereo (AERAL) [*Italy ICAO designator*] (ICDA)
HS	Air-Cushion Vehicle built by Hoversport [*US*] [*Usually used in combination with numerals*]
HS	Die Heilige Schrift des Alten Testaments [*Bonn*] [*A publication*] (BJA)
HS	Habitability System [*NASA*] (KSC)
HS	Habituation Stimulus [*to light*]
HS	Hair Space [*Publishing*] (DGA)
HS	Hakluyt Society (EA)
HS	Halfsheet [*Publishing*] (DGA)
HS	Half Strength
HS	Half Subtractor [*Circuitry*]
H-S	Hamilton Standard (SAA)
HS	Handset
HS	Hand-Starter
HS	Hand Surgery [*Medical specialty*] (DHSM)
HS	Hand Switch [*Nuclear energy*] (NRCH)
HS	Hansard Society [*British*] (ILCA)
HS	Hardened Site
HS	Hardness Surveillance (MSA)
HS	Hard Sized Paper (DGA)
H/S	Hard/Soft [*Two tops for convertible automobile*]
HS	Hardstand
HS	Hard Stripping [*Agriculture*] (OA)
HS	Harmonised System [*Customs commodity coding and description*] [*British*]
HS	Harness or Saddlery
HS	Hartford & Slocomb Railroad Co. [*AAR code*]
HS	Hartman's Solution [*Dentistry*]
HS	Harvey Society (EA)
Hs	Hassium [*Proposed name and symbol for recently-discovered element*]
HS	Hauptsatz [*Leading Theme*] [*Music*]
HS	Hawker Siddeley Aviation Ltd. [*British ICAO aircraft manufacturer identifier*] (ICAO)
HS	Haydn Society [*Record label*]
HS	Headquarters State (NITA)
HS	Head Set [*Telecommunications*] (IAA)
HS	Head Sling
HS	Headspace [*Above liquids*]
HS	Headspace Sampler [*Instrumentation*]
HS	Head Suppression (AAG)
HS	Healthsource, Inc. [*NYSE symbol*] (SPSG)
HS	Heart Sounds [*Medicine*]
HS	Heather Society (EA)
HS	Heating Surface
HS	Heating System
HS	Heat Shield [*Aerospace*] (AAG)
HS	Heat Stable
HS	Heaviside [*Ionosphere*] (AAG)
HS	Heel Spur [*Orthopedics*] (DAVI)
HS	Heel Stick [*For blood samples*] [*Medicine*] (DAVI)
HS	Heel Strike [*Medicine*]
H-S	Heel-to-Shin [*Test*] [*Neurology*] (DAVI)
HS	Height above Spherical Earth
HS	Helicopter Squadron
HS	Helicopter Squadron, Antisubmarine (MCD)
HS	Helicopter System
HS	Helios Semiconductor (IAA)
HS	Helmet Shield
HS	Helminthosporium sacchari [*A toxin-producing fungus*]
H/S	Helper/Suppressor [*Cell ratio*]
HS	Heme Synthetase [*An enzyme*] (AAMN)
HS	Hemingway Society (EA)
HS	Hemlock Society (EA)
HS	Hemorrhagic Shock [*Medicine*]
HS	Hemstitched
HS	Henoch-Schoenlein Syndrome [*Medicine*]
HS	Heparin Sulfate [*Biochemistry*]
HS	Hepatic Scintigraphy [*Medicine*]
HS	Hepatosplenic Schistosomiasis [*Medicine*]
HS	Heraldisk Selskab [*Denmark*] [*An association*] (EAIO)
HS	Heraldry Society (EA)
HS	Hereditary Spherocytosis [*Medicine*]
HS	Hermetically Sealed (IAA)
HS	Herpes Simplex
HS	Hic Sepultus [*Here Is Buried*] [*Latin*]
HS	Hic Situs [*Here Lies*] [*Latin*] (GPO)
HS	Hidradenitis Suppurative [*Medicine*]
HS	Hierarchically Structured [*Indexing language*] (NITA)
HS	Highest Score (ADA)
HS	Highly Sensitive System (MCD)
HS	High School
HS	High Sensitivity
HS	High Shock Resistant (IAA)
HS	High-Similarity [*Psychology*]
HS	High Speed
HS	High-Speed Adapter (IAA)
HS	High-Speed Arithmetic (IAA)
HS	High Spontaneous Activity
HS	High Stage (MCD)
HS	High Strength [*Steel*] [*Automotive engineering*]
HS	Hindenberg Society (EA)
HS	Hinged Seat (AAG)
HS	Hinge Side
HS	Histamine Sensitive [*Immunology*]
HS	Historical Period Starting Date [*Dialog*] [*Searchable field*] [*Information service or system*] (NITA)
HS	Historical Survey
hs	History [*Medicine*] (DMAA)
HS	History Section [*Reference and Adult Services Division*] [*American Library Association*]
HS	Hoc Sensu [*In This Sense*] [*Latin*] (GPO)
HS	Hohenzollern Society (EA)
HS	Holographic Stereogram (OA)
HS	[*The*] Holy See
HS	Home Secretary [*British*]
HS	Home Station [*DoD*]
HS	Homestead (ADA)
HS	Home Surgeon [*Medicine British*]
HS	Homing Sequence (IAA)
HS	Homologous Serum
HS	Honorary Secretary
HS	Horae Soederblomianae (BJA)
HS	Hora Somni [*At Bedtime*] [*Pharmacy*]
HS	Horizon Scanner
HS	Horizon Sensor
HS	Horizontally Selective [*Medicine*] (DMAA)
HS	Horizontal Shear
HS	Horizontal Stripes [*On buoys, beacons*]
HS	Horizontal Synchronous [*Computer science*]
HS	Horizontal System [*Government arrangement*] (OICC)
HS	Horner Syndrome [*Medicine*] (DMAA)
HS	Horse Serum [*Immunology*]
HS	Hospital Ship
HS	Hospital Staff
HS	Hospital Surgeon [*British military*] (DMA)
HS	Hot Shop [*Nuclear energy*] (NRCH)
HS	Hot Soak [*Automotive engineering*]
HS	Hot Spraying
HS	Hot Stuff [*Slang Bowdlerized version*]
HS	Hours of Sleep [*Medicine*]
hs	House (VRA)
HS	House Supervisor
HS	House Surgeon
HS	Housing Scheme [*British*]
HS	Housing Statistics
HS	Housman Society (EA)
HS	Humane Society (ROG)
HS	Humanite Society (EA)
HS	Hume Society (EA)
HS	Humic Substances [*Biology*]
HS	Hundred Square Feet (DNAB)
HS	Hun-Stoffe [*US Chemical Corp. symbol for mustard gas*] [*Also, HD, HT, M Later, H*]
HS	Hurler's Syndrome [*Medicine*]
HS	Hybrid Switching [*Telecommunications*]
HS	Hydraulic Supply
HS	Hydraulic System
HS	Hydrazine Sulfate [*Toxic substance*] [*Inorganic chemistry*]
HS	Hydrofoil Ship
HS	Hydrogen Sulfide (GNE)
HS	Hydrogen Swelling [*Chemistry*]

HS .... Hypersonic
Hs .... Hypochondriasis [Psychology]
HS .... Hypothetical Syllogism [Rule of inference] [Logic]
HS .... Marshall's Air [ICAO designator]   (AD)
HS .... Sandoz Pharmaceuticals [Research code symbol]
HS .... Service Available During Scheduled Operations [ICAO]   (FAAC)
HS .... Siglum for Tablets in the Frau Professor Hilprecht Collection of
                  Babylonian Antiquities [Jena]   (BJA)
HS .... Thailand [International civil aircraft marking]   (ODBW)
HSA .... CHS Aviation Ltd. [Kenya] [ICAO designator]   (FAAC)
HSA .... Haiku Society of America   (EA)
HSA .... Handicapped SCUBA Association   (EA)
HSA .... Harvard Student Agencies [Inc.]
HSA .... Hawaii Surfing Association   (EA)
HSA .... Hawker Siddeley Aviation Ltd. [British]
HSA .... Hawley-Smoot Act [1930]
HSA .... Hazardous Substances Act   (DMAA)
HSA .... Headquarters Support Activity
HSA .... Health Service Action [Later, CNHS] [An association]   (EA)
HSA .... Health Service Agreement
HSA .... Health Service Area [Military]   (AABC)
HSA .... Health Services Administration [Abolished, 1982, functions
                  transferred to Health Resources and Services Administration]
HSA .... Health Systems Agency [New York, NY]
HSA .... Heat Shield Abort [Aerospace]   (IAA)
HSA .... Heat-Stable Antigen [Immunochemistry]
HSA .... Hegel Society of America   (EA)
HSA .... Hepatic Stimulating Activity [Physiology]
HSA .... Heraldry Society of Australia
HSA .... Herb Society of America   (EA)
HSA .... Hereditary Sideroblastic Anemia [Medicine]   (DMAA)
HSA .... High Specific Activity [Radioisotope]
HSA .... High-Strength Adhesive
HSA .... Highway Safety Act [1970]
HSA .... Hill Start Assist [Transmission and braking systems] [Automotive
                  engineering]
HSA .... Hispanic Society of America   (EA)
HSA .... Hispanic Surname American
HSA .... Hollandse Signaalapparaten [Dutch]
HSA .... Holly Society of America   (EA)
HSA .... Holocaust Survivors of Auschwitz   (EA)
HSA .... Homo Sapiens [Human species]
HSA .... Horizon Sensor Assembly
HSA .... Horsemanship Safety Association   (EA)
HSA .... Horse Serum Albumin [Immunology]
HSA .... Hospital Saving Association [British]   (BI)
HSA .... Hospital Savings Association   (DAVI)
HSA .... Humane Society of Australia
HSA .... Human Serum Albumin
HSA .... Hunt Saboteurs Association   (EAIO)
HSA .... Hydroponic Society of America   (EA)
HSA .... Hymn Society of America [Later, HSUSC]   (EA)
HSA .... Hypersomnia-Sleep Apnea Syndrome [Medicine]   (MAE)
HSA .... New Hampshire State Library, Processing Center, Concord, NH
                  [OCLC symbol]   (OCLC)
HSAA .... Health Sciences Advancement Award [National Institutes of Health]
HSAAP .... Holston Army Ammunition Plant   (AABC)
HSAB .... Hard and Soft Acids and Bases [Chemistry]
HSAB .... Hydroxy(succinimidyl)azidobenzoate [Organic chemistry]
HSAC .... Health Security Action Council   (EA)
HSAC .... Helicopter Safety Advisory Conference   (EA)
HSAC .... High-Speed Analog Computer   (DEN)
HSAC .... Historic Shipwrecks Advisory Committee [Victoria, Australia]
HSAC .... House Science and Astronautics Committee [US Congress]   (AAG)
HSAFOKF... Help Save America for Our Kids' Future   (EA)
HSAG .... HEPES-Saline-Albumin-Gelatin [Medium] [Microbiology]
HSAK .... Akobo [Sudan] [ICAO location identifier]   (ICLI)
HSALU .... High-Speed Arithmetic and Logic Unit   (IAA)
HSAM .... Helicopter Survivability Assessment Model   (MCD)
HSAM .... Hierarchical Sequential Access Method [Computer science]
HSAM .... High-Speed Accounting Machine   (IAA)
HS & O .... Heads of Services and Offices [Red Cross]
HS & SS ..... Headquarters and Service Squadron
HSANSW...... Health Services Association of New South Wales [Australia]
HSAP .... Heat-Stable Alkaline Phosphatase [An enzyme]
HSAP .... Honeycomb Sandwich Aluminum Panel
HSAPrA...... HSBC AmericasAdj Rt cm A Pfd [NYSE symbol]   (TTSB)
HSARG........ High-Speed Scintillation Autoradiography
HSAS .... Hard Stability Augmentation System
HSAS .... Headquarters Support Activity - Saigon [Obsolete Military]   (CINC)
HSAS .... Hypertrophic Subaortic Stenosis [Cardiology]
HSAT .... Atbara [Sudan] [ICAO location identifier]   (ICLI)
HSAT .... Die Heilige Schrift des Alten Testaments [Bonner Bibel]
                  [A publication]   (BJA)
H-SAT .... Heavy Satellite   (PDAA)
HSATes........ Die Heilige Schrift des Alten Testaments [Bonner Bibel]
                  [A publication]   (BJA)
HSA-UWC .... Holy Spirit Association for the Unification of World Christianity
HSAW .... Aweil [Sudan] [ICAO location identifier]   (ICLI)
HSB .... Harrisburg, IL [Location identifier FAA]   (FAAL)
HSB .... Hartford Steam Boiler Inspection & Insurance Co. [NYSE symbol]
                  (SPSG)
HSB .... Hartford Stm Boiler Ins [NYSE symbol]   (TTSB)
HSB .... Heat-Shield Boost [Aerospace]
HSB .... Helmet Stowage Bag [NASA]   (KSC)

HSB .... Hermetically Sealed Bushing
HSB .... High School and Beyond Survey [Department of Education]   (GFGA)
HSB .... High Speed Boat   (DOMA)
HSB .... High-Speed Buffer
HSB .... High-Speed Bus [Computer science]
HSB .... Hobbyists Sourcebook [A publication]
HSB .... Horizontal Sounding Balloon   (IAA)
HSB .... Hospitals Superannuation Board [Victoria, Australia]
HSB .... Hue/Saturation/Brightness [Color model] [Printer technology]   (PCM)
HSB .... Hunter-Schreger Bands [Tooth structure]
HSB .... Hutterian Brethren [Hutterian Society of Brothers] [Acronym is based
                  on former name,]   (EA)
HSBA .... Herdwick Sheep Breeders Association [British]   (DBA)
HSBA .... High Speed Bus Adaptor   (NITA)
HSBA .... Historic Statistics of Black America [A publication]
HSBA .... Horizontal Static Balancing Adjustment
HSBC .... Hongkong and Shanghai Banking Corp.
HSBG .... Heel Stick Blood Gas [Medicine]   (DAVI)
HSBI .... Hyde Stud Bloodstock Investments Ltd. [British]
HSBK .... Hibernia Savings Bank [NASDAQ symbol]   (NQ)
HSBK .... Hibernia Savings Bk [NASDAQ symbol]   (TTSB)
HSBP .... High-Speed Bench Press
HSBR .... Bor [Sudan] [ICAO location identifier]   (ICLI)
HSBR .... High-Speed Bombing RADAR
HSBT .... Bentu [Sudan] [ICAO location identifier]   (ICLI)
HS + C .... Half-Sample plus Complement [Statistics]
HS-C .... Hamilton Standard Carbon Dioxide Absorbent Material   (NASA)
HSC .... Hampden-Sydney College [Virginia]
HSC .... Hand-Schueller-Christian [Disease] [Medicine]
HSC .... Hardware-Software Configuration [Computer science]
HSC .... Hardware/Software Coordination   (NASA)
HSC .... Harmonized System Code [File indexing]
HSC .... Harsco Corp. [NYSE symbol]   (SPSG)
HSC .... Hawker Siddeley Canada, Inc. [Toronto Stock Exchange symbol
                  Vancouver Stock Exchange symbol
HSC .... Hawker Siddeley Cda [TS, exchange symbol]   (TTSB)
HSC .... Health and Safety Commission [Department of Employment] [British]
HSC .... Health Sciences Consortium   (EA)
HSC .... Health Services Centre [Institute of Organisation and Social Studies,
                  Brunel University] [British]   (CB)
HSC .... Health Services Command [Army]
HSC .... Heat-Shock Cognate [Biochemistry]
HSC .... Heat Sterilization Compound
HSC .... Heavy & Specialized Carriers Tariff Bureau, Washington DC [STAC]
HSC .... Hematopoietic Stem Cell [Hematology]
HSC .... Henderson State College [Later, Henderson State University]
                  [Arkansas]
HSC .... Heraldry Society of Canada   (EAIO)
HSC .... Hermetic-Sealed Container   (MSA)
HSC .... Hierarchical Storage Controller   (ACRL)
HSC .... Higher School Certificate [British]
HSC .... High School Completion   (OICC)
HSC .... High-Speed Carry
HSC .... High-Speed Channel [Computer science]
HSC .... High-Speed Concentrator
HSC .... High Sulphur Content   (PDAA)
HSC .... High-Swirl Combustion [Engine]
HSC .... Home Products Safety Council   (EA)
HSC .... Home Shopping Club [of the Home Shopping Network]
HSC .... Horizon Scanner   (MSA)
HSC .... Hospital for Sick Children [Toronto, ON] [Canada]
HSC .... Hot Stove Club   (EA)
HSC .... House Space Committee [US Congress]   (AAG)
HS/C .... House Spacecraft   (KSC)
HSC .... Human SERVE [Service Employees Registration and Voter
                  Education] Campaign   (EA)
HSC .... Human Skin Collagen
HSC .... Humboldt State College [Later, Humboldt State University]
                  [California]
HSC .... Humor Stamp Club   (EA)
HSC .... Hunting Surveys & Consultants [Commercial firm] [British]
HSC .... Huntington Society of Canada
HSC .... Hydrogen Stress Cracking   (PDAA)
HSCA .... Health Sciences Communications Association   (DAVI)
HSCA .... Horizontal Sweep Circuit Analyzer
HSCC .... Heavy Specialized Carriers Conference [Later, SC & RA]
HSCC .... Hollywood Studio Collectors Club   (EA)
HSCD .... Hand-Schueller-Christian Disease   (MEDA)
HSCD .... Hazardous Site Control Division [Environmental Protection Agency]
                  (GFGA)
HSCE .... Higher School Certificate Examination   (ADA)
HSCF .... Health Sciences Computing Facility [UCLA]
HSCG .... Erkowit/Carthago [Sudan] [ICAO location identifier]   (ICLI)
HSchein....... Henry Schein, Inc. [Associated Press]   (SAG)
H Sch M ...... High School Magazine [A publication]
H Sch M ...... High School Magazine [A publication]   (BRI)
HSCI .... High School Characteristics Index [Research test] [Psychology]
HSCL .... High-Speed Command Link
HSCL .... Housecall Medical Resources [NASDAQ symbol]   (TTSB)
HSCL .... Housecall Medical Resources, Inc. [NASDAQ symbol]   (SAG)
HSCLCS ...... Harpoon Shipboard Command and Launch Control Set [Missiles]
                  (NVT)
HSCLS .... Harpoon Shipboard Command and Launch Subsystem [Missiles]
                  (MCD)
HS-CoA .... Reduced Coenzyme A [Biochemistry]   (DAVI)

HSCOCS....... House Select Committee on the Outer Continental Shelf [*US Congress*] [*Marine science*] (MSC)
HSCOR .... House Staff Check on Rounds [*Medicine*]
HSCP .... Health Science Cluster Program [*University of Connecticut*] [*Research center*] (RCD)
HSCP .... Heat-Shock Cognate Protein [*Biochemistry*]
HSCP .... High-Speed Card Punch [*Computer science*] (AABC)
HSCP .... Historical Sources Collection Program
HSCR .... High-Speed Card Reader [*Computer science*] (AABC)
HSCR .... High-Strength Cold-Rolled (PDAA)
HSCR .... High Sub-Chief Ranger [*Ancient Order of Foresters*]
HSCRG .... Historic Stock Car Racing Group
HSCS .... Helicopter Subcontrol Ship [*Navy*] (NVT)
HSCT .... High-Speed Civil Transport [*Supersonic plane*]
HSCT .... High Speed Commercial Transport [*MTMC*] (TAG)
HSCT .... High-Speed Compound Terminal [*Computer science*] (MCD)
HSCT .... Hughes Satellite Communications Terminal
HSCT .... Hypersonic Commercial Transport [*Airplane*]
HSCTT .... High-Speed Card Teletypewriter Terminal [*Computer science*] (CET)
HSCU .... Helicopter Subcontrol Unit (NVT)
HSCU .... Hydraulic Supply and Checkout Unit (NASA)
HS/CV .... Home Shopper/Cable Value [*Cable television channel*]
HSCW .... Helicopter Sea Control Wing (NVT)
HSD .... Doctor of Health and Safety (PGP)
HSD .... Hamilton Standard Division (NASA)
HSD .... Hardsite Defense [*Army*] (AABC)
HSD .... Hard/Soft Display (NITA)
HSD .... Harnosand [*Sweden*] [*Airport symbol*] (AD)
HSD .... Hawker-Siddeley Dynamics
HSD .... Heat-Sensing Device (DNAB)
HSD .... Height Sensing Device
HSD .... Hemisphere Development Corp. [*Vancouver Stock Exchange symbol*]
HSD .... Hierarchical Structured Data Set (IAA)
HSD .... Higher Anti-Submarine Detector [*British military*] (DMA)
HSD .... High-Speed Data
HSD .... High-Speed Displacement (IEEE)
HSD .... High-Speed Draft [*Print quality*]
HSD .... High-Sulfur Diesel Fuel [*Petroleum marketing*]
HSD .... Hit Scoring Device
H(SD)........... Holtzman Sprague-Dawley Rat [*Medicine*] (DMAA)
HSD .... Homer Semana Dia (BJA)
HSD .... Home Satellite Dish (NTCM)
HSD .... Homestead Village, Inc. [*AMEX symbol*] (SAG)
HSD .... Honestly Significant Difference
HSD .... Horizontal Situation Display
HSD .... Hot Shutdown (IEEE)
HSD .... Hot Side
HSD .... Human Services Division [*Air Force*]
HSD .... Human Systems Division [*Brooks Air Force Base, TX*] [*United States Air Force Systems Command*] (GRD)
HSD .... Hydraulic Steering and Diving [*System*] (DNAB)
HSD .... Hydropneumatic Suspension Device
HSD .... Hydroxysteroid Dehydrogenase [*An enzyme*]
HSD .... Hypertonic Saline Dextran [*Medicine*]
HSDA .... Heat Strain Decision [*Army*] (RDA)
HSDA .... High-Speed Data Acquisition [*Computer science*]
HSDA .... High-Speed Data Assembly [*Ground Communications Facility, NASA*]
HS-DARS ..... High-Speed Data Acquisition and Reduction System
HSDB .... Debba [*Sudan*] [*ICAO location identifier*] (ICLI)
HSDB .... Hastings' Shorter Dictionary of the Bible [*A publication*] (BJA)
HSDB .... Hazardous Substances Data Bank [*National Library of Medicine*] [*Information service or system*] (IID)
HSDB .... High-Speed Data Buffer
HSDB .... High Speed Data Bus [*Computer science*] (DOMA)
HSDC .... Hawaii State Data Center [*Hawaii State Department of Planning and Economic Development*] [*Information service or system*] (IID)
HSDC .... Health Systems Design [*NASDAQ symbol*] (TTSB)
HSDC .... Health Systems Design Corp. [*NASDAQ symbol*] (SAG)
HSDC .... High-Speed Data Channel (IAA)
HSDE .... High School Driver Education [*Department of Transportation*]
HSDF .... High-Speed Digital Filter
HSDG .... Hamburg-Sudamerikanische Dampfschiffarts-Gesellschaft [*Hamburg-South American Steamship Co.*] [*Shipping*] (ROG)
HSDG .... High School Diploma Graduate [*Military*]
HSDI .... Health Self Determination Index (MEDA)
HSDI .... High-Speed Data Interface
HSDI .... High-Speed Direct Injection [*Diesel engines*]
HS Dir .... Director of Health and Safety (PGP)
HSDL .... Dilling [*Sudan*] [*ICAO location identifier*] (ICLI)
HSDL .... High-Speed Data Line [*or Link*]
HSDLA .... Home School Legal Defense Association (PAZ)
HSDM .... Dueim [*Sudan*] [*ICAO location identifier*] (ICLI)
HSDM .... High-Speed Die Mounter
HSDMS .... Highly Secure Database Management System [*Computer science*] (MHDI)
HSDN .... Dongola [*Sudan*] [*ICAO location identifier*] (ICLI)
HSDP .... Hardsite Data Processor [*Army*] (AABC)
HSDP .... Hungarian Social Democratic Party [*Political party*] (EY)
HSDS .... Horizontal Situation Display System
HSDT .... High-Speed Distributor Transmitter
HSDT .... Hopper Side Tanks [*on a ship*] (DS)
HSDZ .... Damazin [*Sudan*] [*ICAO location identifier*] (ICLI)
HSE .... Compania Helicopteros del Sureste SA [*Spain ICAO designator*] (FAAC)

HsE .... Hawker-Siddeley Electronics Ltd., Microform Division, Fairfield, V, Australia [*Library symbol Library of Congress*] (LCLS)
HSE .... Health and Safety Executive [*Department of Employment*] [*Sheffield, England*]
HSE .... Heat Shield Entry [*Aerospace*] (IAA)
HSE .... Heat-Shock Element [*Genetics*]
HSE .... Heat-Stable Esterase (PDAA)
HSE .... Helsinki Stock Exchange [*Finland*]
HSE .... Hemorrhagic Shock and Encephalopathy [*Medicine*] (DMAA)
HSE .... Herpes Simplex Encephalitis [*Medicine*]
HSE .... Hic Sepultus Est [*Here Lies Buried*] [*Latin*]
HSE .... Highly Siderophile Element [*Biology*]
HSE .... High School Equivalency (OICC)
HSE .... High-Speed Encoder (IAA)
HSE .... High-Speed Signal Control Equipment [*Data communication*] (MHDI)
HSE .... Historically Socialist Economy (ECON)
HSE .... Home Sports Entertainment [*Cable-television system*]
HSE .... Honolulu Stock Exchange [*Hawaii*]
HSE .... House
HSE .... House
HSE .... HS Resources [*NYSE symbol*] (TTSB)
HSE .... HS Resources, Inc. [*NYSE symbol*] (SAG)
HSEAD .... Historical Society of Early American Decoration [*Defunct*] (EA)
HSEC .... Historical Society of the Episcopal Church (EA)
HSEF .... High School Evangelism Fellowship (EA)
HseFbr .... House of Fabrics, Inc. [*Associated Press*] (SAG)
HseFbrc .... House of Fabrics, Inc. [*Associated Press*] (SAG)
HSEHLD .... Household
HSEHOLD .... Household
HSEKPR .... Housekeeper (ROG)
HSEL .... High-Speed Selector Channel
HSELINE ...... Health and Safety Executive Online [*Health and Safety Executive*] [*Bibliographic database*] [*British*]
HSEN .... Home Sports Entertainment Network [*Cable TV programming service*]
HSEP .... Heart Synchronized Evoked Potential [*Medicine*] (DMAA)
HSEP .... High-Speed Electrostatic Printer
HSEP .... Hospital Surgical Expansion Package [*Air Force*] (DOMA)
HSERC .... Historical Society of the Evangelical and Reformed Church [*Later, ERHS-UCC*] (EA)
H/serf .... High-Scope Educational Research Foundation (EA)
HSES .... Hemorrhagic Shock-Encephalopathy Syndrome [*Medicine*] (DMAA)
HSES .... Hughes Satellite Earth Station
HSES .... Hydrostatic Equilibrium System [*For chromatography*]
HSET .... Hino Super Flow Turbine [*Diesel engine*]
HSETC .... Health Sciences Education and Training Command [*Navy*] (DNAB)
HSEUBC .... Historical Society of the Evangelical United Brethren Church [*Later, General Commission on Archives and History of the United Methodist Church*] (EA)
HSF .... Hartford Seminary Foundation [*Connecticut*]
HSF .... Hawaiian Sea Frontier
HSF .... Heat-Shock Transcription Factor [*Genetics*]
HSF .... Heat-Stable Fraction
HSF .... Heat Stimulated Flow (PDAA)
HSF .... Hepatocyte Stimulating Factor [*Endocrinology*]
HSF .... High Seas Fleet [*British military*] (DMA)
HSF .... High-Starch Fraction [*Food technology*]
HSF .... Histamine-Induced Suppressor Factor [*Immunology*]
HSF .... Histamine-Sensitizing Factor [*Immunology*]
HSF .... Home Service Force [*British*] (BARN)
HSF .... Hotel Sundry Fund [*Air Force*]
HSF .... Human Services Forum [*Defunct*] (EA)
HSF .... Hyderabad State Force [*British military*] (DMA)
HSF .... Hypergol Servicing Facility [*NASA*] (NASA)
HSF .... Hypersonic Flow
HSF .... Hypothalamic Secretory Factor [*Endocrinology*]
HSF-ACTH .... Hypothalmic Secretory Factor for Adreno-Corticotropic Hormone (PDAA)
HSFAE .... High-Speed Fuel Air Explosive
HSFB .... High Speed Fleet Broadcast (DOMA)
HSFC .... Hank Snow Fan Club [*Defunct*] (EA)
HSFF .... High-Speed Force Feed
HSFG .... High Strength Friction Grip (PDAA)
HSFMCV ...... Huguenot Society of the Founders of Manakin in the Colony of Virginia (EA)
HSFO .... High Sulphur Fuel Oil
HSFPJ .... Holocaust Survivors and Friends in Pursuit of Justice (EA)
HSFS .... El Fasher [*Sudan*] [*ICAO location identifier*] (ICLI)
HSFS .... High-Speed Flight Station [*NASA*]
HSFV .... High Speed Freight Vehicle (PDAA)
HSG .... Harris Steel Group, Inc. [*Toronto Stock Exchange symbol*]
HSG .... Headquarters, Support Group [*Military*]
HSG .... Health and Safety Guide [*Toxicology*]
HSG .... Herpes Simplex Genitalis
HSG .... High School for Girls (ADA)
HSG .... High School Graduate [*Classified advertising*]
HSG .... High Sierra Group [*Nevada-based group proposing CD-ROM standards*]
HSG .... High Speed Generation [*Hybrid vehicles*] [*Automotive engineering*]
HSG .... High-Speed Grinding (PDAA)
HSG .... High Sustained G2 Acceleration [*NASA*] (NASA)
HSG .... Holy Shroud Guild (EA)
HSG .... Home-Station Gunnery [*Military*] (INF)
HSG .... Horizontal Sweep Generator [*Telecommunications*] (OA)
HSG .... Housing (AABC)

HSG .... Human Standard Globulin [*Medicine*]
HSG .... Hydroshift Gun
HSG .... Hysterectomy Support Group [*British*] (DBA)
HSG .... Hysterosalpingogram [*Gynecology*]
HSG .... Hysterosalpingography [*Medicine*] (DMAA)
HSGB .... Haflinger Society [*British*] (DBA)
HSGB .... Hysterosalpingography [*Gynecology*] (DAVI)
HSGBI .... Huguenot Society of Great Britain and Ireland (EAIO)
HS-GC .... Headspace Sampling-Gas Chromatography
HSGF .... Gedaref/Azaza [*Sudan*] [*ICAO location identifier*] (ICLI)
HSGF .... Human Skeletal Growth Factor
HSGG .... Dinder/Galegu [*Sudan*] [*ICAO location identifier*] (ICLI)
HSGM .... Honorary Sergeant Major of the Regiment
HSGMOC ..... Honorary Sergeant Major of the Corps [*Marine Corps*]
HSGMOR ..... Honorary Sergeant Major of the Regiment [*Army*]
HSGN .... Geneina [*Sudan*] [*ICAO location identifier*] (ICLI)
HSGO .... Gogerial [*Sudan*] [*ICAO location identifier*] (ICLI)
HSGP .... High School Geography Project [*Defunct*]
HSGPC .... High-Speed Gel Permeation Chromatography
HSGREFSVCSYS... Housing Referral Service Record System [*Military*] (DNAB)
HSGT .... High-Speed Ground Transportation
HSGTC .... High-Speed Ground Test Center [*Later, TTC*] [*Pueblo, CO*]
HSH .... Handmaids of the Sacred Heart of Pohang (TOCD)
HSH .... Hebrew School Headache (BJA)
HSH .... Heinemann's Scientific Handbooks [*A publication*]
HSH .... Helix-Span-Helix [*Protein structure*]
HSH .... His [*or Her*] Serene Highness [*Used for certain Continental European princes or princesses*]
HSH .... Horseshoe (ROG)
HSHH .... Hill Staffers for the Hungry and Homeless (EA)
H/SHLD .... Heat Shield [*Automotive engineering*]
HSHLD .... Household (MSA)
HSHP .... High School for Health Professions
HSHRSSS .... High-Speed/High-Resolution Side Scan Sonar System [*National Oceanic and Atmospheric Administration*]
HSI .... Handbook of Service Instructions (MCD)
HSI .... Hang Seng Index [*Hong Kong Futures Exchange Index*]
HSI .... Hardware/Software Interface (IAA)
HSI .... Harpoon Standard Initiator (MCD)
HSI .... Hastings [*Nebraska*] [*Airport symbol*] (OAG)
HSI .... Headquarters Staff Instruction
HSI .... Headquarters Staff Instructor (AAGC)
HSI .... Health Development Services, Inc. [*Toronto Stock Exchange symbol*]
HSI .... Heat Stress Index
HSI .... Heraldry Society of Ireland (EA)
HSI .... Herpes Simplex I [*Titer and virus*] [*Medicine*] (DAVI)
HSI .... HERTIS [*Hertfordshire Technical Library and Information Service*] Subj ect Index (NITA)
HSI .... High School Equivalency Index
HSI .... High Solar Intensity
HSI .... High Speed Impact (SAA)
HSI .... High-Speed Interferometer [*Measures chemical components of smog*] (KSC)
HSI .... High Strand Intensity
HSI .... Hi-Shear Indus [*NYSE symbol*] (TTSB)
HSI .... Hi-Shear Industries, Inc. [*NYSE symbol*] (SPSG)
HSI .... Hispanic Serving Institution
HSI .... Home and School Institute (EA)
HSI .... Horizontal Situation Indicator [*Aviation*]
HSI .... Hoya Society International (EA)
HSI .... Hsinkong [*Republic of China*] [*Also, SGK*] [*Seismograph station code, US Geological Survey*] (SEIS)
HSI .... Hue-Saturation-Intensity [*Video monitor*] (BYTE)
HSI .... Human Seminal Plasma Inhibitor [*Medicine*] (DMAA)
HSI .... Human Systems Integration
HSIA .... Halogenated Solvents Industry Alliance (EA)
HSIC .... Henry Schein, Inc. [*NASDAQ symbol*] (SAG)
HSIC .... Schein (Henry) [*NASDAQ symbol*] (TTSB)
HSIC .... Schein [*Henry*], Inc. [*NASDAQ symbol*] (SAG)
HSI/CDI .... Horizontal Situation Indicator / Course Deviation Indicator [*Aviation*] (PDAA)
HSICNI .... Honourable Society of the Inns of Court of Northern Ireland
HSIF .... Hardware/Software Integration Facility (SSD)
HSIIL .... High-Speed Integrated Injection Logic (IAA)
HSIL .... High-Grade Squamous Intraepithelial Lesions [*OCLC symbol*]
HSIM .... Hill Samuel Investment Management [*British*]
HSIMP .... High-Speed Interface Message Processor (IAA)
HSIP .... Hsinchu Science-Based Industrial Park [*Taiwan*] (ECON)
HSIQ .... High School Interest Questionnaire [*Vocational guidance test*]
H/SIR .... Hardware/Software Integration Review (MCD)
HSIRMC .... Hazardous Substance Incident Response Management Course [*Navy*]
HSIS .... Highway Safety Information Service [*National Highway Safety Administration*] (IID)
HSJ .... Heat Shield Jettison [*Aerospace*] (IAA)
HSJ .... Honeycombed Sandwich Joint
HSJ .... Hoshina [*Japan*] [*Seismograph station code, US Geological Survey*] (SEIS)
HSK .... Hackensack, MN [*Location identifier FAA*] (FAAL)
HSK .... Heat Sink Kit
HSK .... Herpes Simplex Keratitis [*Medicine*] (DMAA)
HSK .... Herpes Stromal Keratitis [*Medicine*]
HSK .... Honeysuckle Creek Tracking Station [*NASA*] (KSC)
HSK .... Honorary Surgeon of the King [*British*]
HSK .... Horizontal Sling Kit [*NASA*] (NASA)

HSK .... Hsinking [*Sirkyo, Chang Chun*] [*Republic of China*] [*Seismograph station code, US Geological Survey*] (SEIS)
HSK .... HSK Minerals Ltd. [*Toronto Stock Exchange symbol*]
HSKA .... Kassala [*Sudan*] [*ICAO location identifier*] (ICLI)
HSKG .... Khashm El Girba [*Sudan*] [*ICAO location identifier*] (ICLI)
HSKI .... Kosti/Rabak [*Sudan*] [*ICAO location identifier*] (ICLI)
HSKJ .... Kago Kaju [*Sudan*] [*ICAO location identifier*] (ICLI)
HSKL .... Haskel International, Inc. [*NASDAQ symbol*] (SAG)
HSKL .... Haskel Intl 'A' [*NASDAQ symbol*] (TTSB)
HSKP .... Kapoeta [*Sudan*] [*ICAO location identifier*] (ICLI)
HSKPG .... Housekeeping (AFM)
hskpr .... Housekeeper (BARN)
HSL .... Hardware Simulation Laboratory (NASA)
HSL .... Hazardous Substance List [*Code of Federal Regulations*] (FFDE)
HSL .... Health Service Laboratory [*Army*] (AABC)
HSL .... Heenan Senlac Resources Ltd. [*Toronto Stock Exchange symbol*]
HSL .... Helicopter Antisubmarine Squadron Light (NVT)
HSL .... Herpes Simplex Labialis
HSL .... High-Speed Launch [*Navy*]
HSL .... High-Speed Logic
HSL .... Highway Safety Literature [*Database*] (NITA)
HSL .... Highway Safety Literature Service [*National Academy of Science*] [*Washington, DC*]
HSL .... Hispania Lineas Aereas SL [*Spain ICAO designator*] (FAAC)
HSL .... Home-School Liaison (AIE)
Hsl .... Homoserine Lactone [*An amino acid*]
HSL .... Hormone-Sensitive Lipase [*An enzyme*]
HSL .... Hue, Saturation, Lightness [*Color model*] (PCM)
HSL .... Huslia [*Alaska*] [*Airport symbol*] (OAG)
HSL .... Hytran Simulation Language [*Computer science*] (PDAA)
HSLA .... High Speed Line Adaptor (NITA)
HSLA .... High-Strength Low-Alloy [*or Light-Alloy*] [*Steel*]
HSLAN .... High Speed Local Area Network [*Telecommunications*] (ACRL)
HSLC .... High-Speed Liquid Chromatography
HSLC .... High-Speed Single Line Controller (MHDB)
HSLCG .... Health Science Libraries of Central Georgia [*Library network*]
HSLDA .... Home School Legal Defense Association (EA)
HSLI .... Kadugli [*Sudan*] [*ICAO location identifier*] (ICLI)
HSLIC .... Health Science Libraries Information Cooperative [*Library network*]
HSLLADS ..... High-Speed, Low-Level Airdrop System [*Military*] (INF)
HSLLC .... High-Speed Liquid-Liquid Chromatography
HSLN .... High-Speed Local Network [*Telecommunications*] (OSI)
HSLP .... Haydn Society [*Record label*]
HSLR .... Lirangu [*Sudan*] [*ICAO location identifier*] (ICLI)
HSL'S .... Hlinkova Slovenska l'Udova Strana [*Hlinka's Slovak People's Party*] [*Also, SL'S*] [*Political party*] (PPE)
HSLWI .... Helical Spring Lock Washer Institute
HSM .... Hand and Shoe Monitor [*Radiation detection*]
HSM .... Hardened Silo Missile
HSM .... Hard Structure Module
HSM .... Hard Structure Munition
HSM .... Harmonic Subcarrier Method (MCD)
HSM .... Harvard Semitic Museum (BJA)
HSM .... Health Services and Mental Health Administration [*Later, ADAMHA*] [*Abolished, 1973*] [*HEW*]
HSM .... Hepatosplenomegaly [*Gastroenterology*] (DAVI)
HSM .... Hermit Sisters of Mary (TOCD)
HSM .... Hierarchical Storage Manager [*or Management*]
HSM .... High-Speed Machining (MCD)
HSM .... High-Speed Measurement (IAA)
HSM .... High-Speed Memory [*Computer science*]
HSM .... High-Speed Motor [*Electrical engineering*]
HSM .... His [*or Her*] Serene Majesty
HSM .... Holosystolic Murmur [*Cardiology*] (DAVI)
HSM .... Horsham [*Australia Airport symbol Obsolete*] (OAG)
HSM .... Horsham Corp. [*Toronto Stock Exchange symbol NYSE symbol*]
HSM .... Hospital - Surgical - Medical
HSM .... Humanitarian Service Medal (MCD)
HSM .... Hydraulic System Module (MCD)
HSMA .... Hotel Sales Management Association [*Later, HSMAI*] (EA)
HSMAI .... Hotel Sales and Marketing Association International (EA)
HSMAI-EO.... Hotel Sales and Marketing Association International - European Office [*Utrecht, Netherlands*] (EAIO)
HSMB .... Hybrid Superconducting Magnetic Bearing
HSMCDR...... High-Speed Multichannel Data Recorder [*Instrumentation*]
HSMD .... Maridi [*Sudan*] [*ICAO location identifier*] (ICLI)
HSMF .... Holocaust Survivors Memorial Foundation (EA)
HSMGC .... Heavy Section Machine Gun Corps [*British military*] (DMA)
HSMHA .... Health Services and Mental Health Administration [*Later, ADAMHA*] [*Abolished, 1973*] [*HEW*]
HSMIMP .... High-Speed Modular Interface Message Processor
HSMK .... Rumbek [*Sudan*] [*ICAO location identifier*] (ICLI)
HSMO .... High-Speed Membrane Osmometry (MCD)
HSMO .... Hospital Senior Medical Officer [*Australia*]
HSMO .... Hydraulic System Mineral Oil [*Mechanical engineering*]
HSMR .... Merowe [*Sudan*] [*ICAO location identifier*] (ICLI)
HSMS .... High-Speed Microwave Switch
HSMSR .... Hardsite Missile Site RADAR [*Army*] (AABC)
HSM-WA...... Hard Structure Munition Weaponization Analysis (MCD)
HSN .... Haglund Industry International [*Vancouver Stock Exchange symbol*]
HSN .... Hanson-Street Nail (MEDA)
HSN .... Hereditary Sensory Neuropathy [*Neurology*]
HSN .... Hermaphrodite-Specific Neuron [*Cytology*]
HSN .... High Speed Network
HSN .... Home Shopping Network [*Cable-television system*]

HSN .... Home Shopping Network, Inc. [*NYSE symbol*] (SPSG)
HSN .... Hospital Satellite Network [*Los Angeles, CA*] [*Cable-television system*]
HSN .... Hsinchu [*Republic of China*] [*Seismograph station code, US Geological Survey*] (SEIS)
HSN .... Hughes Sports Network [*Formerly, SNI*]
HSN .... Southern Air Ltd. [*British ICAO designator*] (FAAC)
HSNA .... Nasir [*Sudan*] [*ICAO location identifier*] (ICLI)
HSND .... Shendi [*Sudan*] [*ICAO location identifier*] (ICLI)
HSNG .... Housing
HSNG .... Housing
HSNH .... Nahud [*Sudan*] [*ICAO location identifier*] (ICLI)
H/SNK .... Heat Sink [*Automotive engineering*]
HSNL .... Nyala [*Sudan*] [*ICAO location identifier*] (ICLI)
HSNM .... Nimule/Nimule [*Sudan*] [*ICAO location identifier*] (ICLI)
HSNP .... Hawker-Siddeley Nuclear Power Co. Ltd. [*British*]
HSNP .... High-Speed Nonimpact Printer [*Acronym pronounced "hisnip"*] [*Computer science*]
HSNPP .... Hlinka Slovak National People's Party [*Political party*]
HSNR .... Halstead Energy [*NASDAQ symbol*] (TTSB)
HSNR .... Halstead Energy Corp. [*NASDAQ symbol*] (SAG)
HSNR .... Sennar [*Sudan*] [*ICAO location identifier*] (ICLI)
HSNS .... High School News Service [*Fleet Hometown News Center*] (DNAB)
HSNSW .... Haemophilia Society of New South Wales [*Australia*]
HSNT .... Historical Society of the Northern Territory [*Australia*]
HSNTA .... New Testament Apocrypha [*E. Henneke and W. Schneemelcher*] [*A publication*] (BJA)
HSNW .... New Halfa [*Sudan*] [*ICAO location identifier*] (ICLI)
HSNY .... Holland Society of New York (EA)
HSO .... Compania Helicopteros de Transporte SA [*Spain ICAO designator*] (FAAC)
HSO .... Habitation/Station Operations (SSD)
HSO .... Haifa Symphony Orchestra (BJA)
HSO .... Headquarters Signal Officer (NATG)
HSO .... Higher Scientific Officer [*British*]
HSO .... High Specific Output [*Automotive engineering*]
HSO .... High Speed Optimized [*General Tire Co.*] [*Automobile tires*]
HSO .... Hydrogen Seal Oil [*System*] (NRCH)
HSOB .... El Obeid [*Sudan*] [*ICAO location identifier*] (ICLI)
HSOD .... Human Superoxide Dismutase [*An enzyme*]
HSOM .... Habitation/Station Operations Module (SSD)
H SOM .... Hora Somni [*At Bedtime*] [*Pharmacy*]
HSORS .... High Seas Oil Recovery System
HSOT .... Howitzer Strap-On Trainer [*Military*] (RDA)
HSP .... Half-Shade Plate
HSP .... Hardwire Safing Panel
HSP .... Haute Societe Protestante [*Protestant High Society*] (IIA)
HSP .... Head Start Program [*Education*]
HSP .... Health Service Plan
HSP .... Health Stabilization Program [*NASA*] (NASA)
HSP .... Health Systems Plan [*HEW*]
HSP .... Heat Shock Protein [*Physiology*]
hsp .... Heat Shock Protein [*Gene*] (DMAA)
HSP .... Heavy, Stressed Platform
HSP .... Hemostatic Screening Profile [*Medicine*] (DMAA)
HSP .... Henoch-Schoenlein Purpura [*Medicine*] (AAMN)
HSP .... Heparin Sulfate Proteoglycan [*Biochemistry*]
HSP .... Hereditary Spastic Paraplegia [*Medicine*]
HSP .... High-Speed Printer [*Computer science*]
HSP .... High-Speed Pulse
HSP .... High-Speed Punch (IAA)
HSP .... Hollow Soft Point [*Bullet*] (DICI)
HSP .... Home Services Program [*Australia*]
HSP .... Hospital Service Plan [*British*]
HSP .... Hot Springs [*Virginia*] [*Airport symbol*] (AD)
HSP .... Hot Springs, VA [*Location identifier FAA*] (FAAL)
HSP .... Hot Stamping Press
HSP .... Hrvatska Stranka Prava [*Croatian Party of Rights*] [*Former Yugoslavia*] [*Political party*] (PPE)
HSP .... Human Sciences Project [*National Science Foundation*]
HSP .... Human Serum Prealbumin
HSP .... Hungarian Socialist Party [*Political party*] (EY)
HSP .... Hydrocarbon Solids Process [*Tosco Corp.*] [*Oil shale pyrolysis*]
HSPA .... Hawaiian Sugar Planters' Association (EA)
HSPA .... High-Speed Parallel Adder
HSPA .... Human Service Personnel Association [*Defunct*] (EA)
HSPA .... Pachalla [*Sudan*] [*ICAO location identifier*] (ICLI)
HSPC .... Heat Sterilizable Potting Compound
HSPC .... Hospice
HSPDP .... Hill State People's Democratic Party [*India*] [*Political party*] (PPW)
HSPE .... High Strength Polyethylene [*Organic chemistry*]
HSPF .... Heating Seasonal Performance Factor
HSPF .... Heating Seasonal Performance Factor
HSPF .... Hydrologic Simulation Program Fortran
HSPG .... Heparan Sulfate Proteoglycan [*Biochemistry*]
HSPI .... High-Speed Printer Interface (MCD)
HSPI .... Pibor [*Sudan*] [*ICAO location identifier*] (ICLI)
HSPLS .... Hawaii State Public Library System [*Hawaii State Department of Education*] [*Information service or system*] (IID)
HSPQ .... High School Personality Questionnaire [*Psychology*]
HSPR .... High School Percentile Rank
HSpS .... Daughters of the Holy Spirit Nazareth of the Good Shepherd (TOCD)
HSPS .... Heat Shock Protein Synthesis
HSPS .... Highway Safety Program Standard [*Department of Transportation*]
HSPS .... Hydrographic Survey Platform System (MCD)

HSPSD .... High-Speed Packet Switched Data [*Computer science*] (ACRL)
HSPT .... High School Placement Test
HSPTAL .... High-Speed Paper Tape Absolute Loader [*Computer science*] (MDG)
HSPTP .... High-Speed Paper Tape Punch [*Computer science*] (AABC)
HSPTR .... High-Speed Paper Tape Reader [*Computer science*] (CET)
HSPU .... Householders for Safe Pesticide Use [*Australia*]
HSQ .... Heat-Shield Qualification [*NASA*] (KSC)
HSQ .... Helping Smokers Quit [*American Cancer Society*] (EA)
HSQ .... Home Screening Questionnaire [*Test*] [*Psychology*]
HSQ .... Houston, TX [*Location identifier FAA*] (FAAL)
HSQB .... Health Standards and Quality Bureau [*HEW*]
HSQC .... Heteronuclear Single Quantum Coherence [*Spectrum*]
HSQC .... Heteronuclear Single Quantum Correlation [*Spectrum*]
HSQR .... High-Strength Quick Release (MCD)
HSR .... Hampshire Swine Registry (EA)
HSR .... Handbook of Structural Repair (MCD)
HSR .... Harbor Surveillance RADAR [*Navigation*] (IAA)
HSR .... Hardware Status Register (MCD)
HSR .... Harleco Synthetic Resin (MAE)
HSR .... Hart-Scott-Rodino Antitrust Improvements Act [*1976*]
HSR .... Health Service Region [*Army*] (AABC)
HSR .... Heated Serum Reagin [*Immunochemistry*] (DAVI)
HSR .... Heat Shield Recovery [*Aerospace*] (IAA)
HSR .... High School Percentile Rank
HSR .... High-Speed RADAR (MCD)
HSR .... High-Speed Rail
HSR .... High-Speed Reader [*Computer science*]
HSR .... High-Speed Relay
HSR .... High Stocking Rate [*Agriculture*] (OA)
HSR .... Hi-Shear Technology [*AMEX symbol*] (TTSB)
HSR .... Hi Shear Technology Corp. [*AMEX symbol*] (SAG)
HSR .... Homestead Resources, Inc. [*Vancouver Stock Exchange symbol*]
HSR .... Homogeneously Staining Region [*Cytology*]
HSR .... Horizontal Size Ratio [*Ophthalmology*]
HSR .... Hot Springs [*South Dakota*] [*Airport symbol*] (AD)
HSR .... Hot Springs, SD [*Location identifier FAA*] (FAAL)
HSR .... Human Science Research [*Concept car*] [*Automotive engineering*]
HSRA .... Half Saddlebred Registry of America (EA)
HSRA .... Harvard-Smithsonian Reference Atmosphere
HSRA .... Health Services and Resources Administration (DAVI)
HSRA .... High-Speed Data Regeneration Assembly [*Ground Communications Facility, NASA*]
HSRA .... High Speed Rail Association (EA)
HSRA .... Hollow Shaft Rotary Actuator
HSR & D .... Health Services Research and Development Service [*Washington, DC Veterans Administration*] (GRD)
HSRC .... Health Services Research Center [*Georgia Institute of Technology*] [*Research center*] (RCD)
HSRC .... High School Red Cross
HSRC .... Highway Safety Research Center [*University of North Carolina, Chapel Hill*] [*Research center*] (RCD)
HSRC .... Human Sciences Research Council [*South Africa*]
HSRC .... Human-Subjects Review Committee [*Medicine*] (BABM)
HSRD .... Health Services Research and Development [*Series*] [*A publication*]
HSRD .... Hypertension Secondary to Renal Disease [*Medicine*]
HSRFO .... High-Sulfur Residual Fuel Oil [*Petroleum technology*]
HSRI .... Health Systems Research Institute
HSRI .... Highly Sensitive Refractive Index
HSRI .... Highway Safety Research Institute [*University of Michigan*]
HSRIOP .... High Speed RAD [*Rapid Access Data Dram*] Input/Output Processor [*Xerox*] (NITA)
HSRJ .... Raga [*Sudan*] [*ICAO location identifier*] (ICLI)
HSR/MLA ...... High Speed Rail/Maglev Association
HSRN .... Heavy Straight Run Naphtha [*Petroleum chemistry*]
HSRN .... Renk [*Sudan*] [*ICAO location identifier*] (ICLI)
HSRO .... High-Speed Repetitive Operation
HSRP .... Headquarters Systems Replacement Program [*Military*] (GFGA)
HSRP .... High Speed Research Program [*NASA*] [*Marine science*] (OSRA)
HSRP .... High Speed Research Program [*National Aeronautics and Space Administration*] (USDC)
HSRP .... High-Speed Rotary Prism
HSRRB .... Human Subjects Research Review Board [*Army*] (RDA)
HSRS .... Health-Sickness Rating Scale (DMAA)
HSRS .... Hurricane Supersonic Research Site
HS Rsc .... HS Resources, Inc. [*Associated Press*] (SAG)
HSRTC .... Health and Safety Research and Test Center [*Bureau of Mines*]
HSRTM .... High-Speed Resin Transfer Molding [*Automotive engineering*]
HSRTP .... Health Services Research and Training Program [*Purdue University*] [*Research center*] (RCD)
HSRV .... Human Spumaretrovirus
HSS .... British Library Catalog: Humanities and Social Sciences [*Information service or system*] (CRD)
HSS .... Habitability Support System (MCD)
HSS .... Hallervorden-Spatz Syndrome [*Medicine*] (AAMN)
HSS .... Hardware Specification Sheet (IAA)
HSS .... Hars Systems, Inc. [*Vancouver Stock Exchange symbol*]
HSS .... Health Service Support [*Army*] (DOMA)
HSS .... Health Surveillance System [*Shell Oil Co.*]
HSS .... Heeres-Sauerstoffschutzgeraet [*Service Oxygen Breathing Apparatus*] [*German military - World War II*]
HSS .... Helmet Sight Subsystem (RDA)
HSS .... Hepatic Stimulator Substance
HSS .... Heraldry Society of Scotland [*Edinburgh*] (EAIO)
HSS .... Hermanas del Servico Social (TOCD)
HSS .... Hierarchy Service System [*Toshiba Corp.*]

HSS	High School Size
HSS	High-Speed Simultaneous [*Electric trip mechanism*]
HSS	High-Speed Storage [*Computer science*] (IEEE)
HSS	High-Speed Supernatant [*Medicine*] (DAVI)
HSS	High-Speed System [*Ground Communications Facility, NASA*]
HSS	High Spread Shears
HSS	High-Strength Stainless Steel (PDAA)
HSS	High-Strength, Steel
HSS	High-Stress Strain (MCD)
HSS	Hispano-Suiza Society (EA)
HSS	Historiae Societatis Socius [*Fellow of the Historical Society*] [*Latin*]
HSS	History of Science Society (EA)
HSS	Hokkaido University [*Japan*] [*Seismograph station code, US Geological Survey*] (SEIS)
HSS	Honeycomb-Supported Screen
HSS	Hospital and Specialist Services [*British*]
HSS	Hospital Staffing Services, Inc. [*NYSE symbol*] (SPSG)
HSS	Hospital Staffing Svcs [*NYSE symbol*] (TTSB)
HSS	Hot Springs, NC [*Location identifier FAA*] (FAAL)
HSS	Hrvatska Seljacka Stranka [*Croatian Peasant Party*] [*Former Yugoslavia*] [*Political party*] (PPE)
HSS	Hull Seal Section
HSS	Hybrid Simulation System
HSS	Hydraulic Subsystem Simulator (NASA)
HSS	Hydraulic System Simulator (MCD)
HSS	Hydrologic Sensing Satellite (DNAB)
HSS	Hydropneumatic Suspension System (MCD)
HSS	HyperSonic Sound
HSS	Hypertonic Saline Solution
HSS	Hypertrophic Subaortic Stenosis [*Cardiology*]
HSSA	Handbag Supply Salesmen's Association (EA)
HSSA	Health and Safety Science Abstracts [*Cambridge Scientific Abstracts*] [*Information service or system*] (CRD)
HSSA	High Speed Steel Association [*British*] (BI)
HSSALB	Health Service Support Air Land Battle
HSSC	Heavy SEAL [*Sea-Air-Land*] Support Craft (NVT)
HSSD	High-Speed Serial Data [*Automotive electronics*]
HSSD	Hospital Sterile Supply Department (DMAA)
HSSDB	High-Speed Serial Data Buffer (MCD)
HSSDS	High-Speed Switched Digital Service [*AT & T*] (TSSD)
HSSE	High Soap Suds Enema [*Gastroenterology*] (DAVI)
HSSG	Heeres-Sauerstoffschutzgeraet [*Service Oxygen Breathing Apparatus*] [*German military - World War II*]
HSSG	High-Speed Symbol Generator
HSSG	Holograph Stress Strain Gauge
HSSGT	High-Speed Guided Ground Transportation [*TXDOT*] (TAG)
HSSI	High-Speed Serial Interface [*Computer science*] (CDE)
HSSI	High-Speed Serial Interface [*Telecommunications*]
HSSI	High-Speed Synchronous Interface [*Computer science*]
HSSI	Highway Safety Statistical Indicator
HSSJ	Juba [*Sudan*] [*ICAO location identifier*] (ICLI)
HSSM	Malakal [*Sudan*] [*ICAO location identifier*] (ICLI)
HSSP	Port Sudan [*Sudan*] [*ICAO location identifier*] (ICLI)
HSSPF	Hoehere SS und Polizeifuehrer (BJA)
HSSR	Hermit Sisters of Romuald (TOCD)
HSSR	Hydrogeochemical and Stream Sediment Reconnaissance (PDAA)
HSSS	Khartoum [*Sudan*] [*ICAO location identifier*] (ICLI)
HSSSM	Highly Sensitive Ship Synthesis Model (DNAB)
HSSSR	High School Students for Social Responsibility (EA)
HSST	Heavy Section Steel Technology [*Nuclear Regulatory Commission*]
HSST	High-Speed Surface Transport (MCD)
HSSTD	Historical Sea Surface Temperature Data Project [*WMO*] (MSC)
HSSTD	Historical Sea Surface Temperature Dataset [*Marine science*] (OSRA)
HSSU	Hospital Sterile Supply Unit (DMAA)
HSSW	High Salinity Shelf Water [*Oceanography*]
HSSW	Wadi Halfa/Nuba Lake [*Sudan*] [*ICAO location identifier*] (ICLI)
HST	Harmonic and Spurious Totalizer
HST	Harry S Truman [*US president, 1884-1972*]
HST	Harvard Step Test [*Physical tolerance test*]
HST	Hawaiian-Aleutian Standard Time
HST	Hawaiian Standard Time
H ST	Head Steward [*Navy British*] (ROG)
HST	Health Screening Test (DAVI)
HST	Heat Shrinkable Tubing
HST	Heist [*C.H.*] Corp. [*AMEX symbol*] (SPSG)
HST	Helicopter Support Team [*Navy*] (NVT)
HST	Hexobarbital Sleeping Time [*In experimental animals*]
HST	High Speed Taxi-Way Turn Off [*Aviation*] (DA)
HST	High-Speed Technology [*Computer science*] (BYTE)
HST	High-Speed Telemetry
HST	High-Speed Train [*British*]
HST	High-Speed Tunnel [*NASA*]
HST	Hoist (MSA)
HST	Homestead [*Florida*] [*Airport symbol*] (OAG)
HST	Homestead, FL [*Location identifier FAA*] (FAAL)
HST	Homogenate Survival Time
HST	Horizontal Seismic Trigger (IEEE)
HST	Hot Shot Tunnel
HST	Housing Study Tours [*British*]
HST	Hubble Space Telescope [*Great Observatory Program*] [*NASA*]
HST	Hunter Stockton Thompson
HST	Hydrostatic Transmission [*Automotive engineering*]
HST	Hypersonic Transport [*Aircraft*]
HST	Hypervelocity Shock Tunnel (OA)

HSTA	Honda Sport Touring Association (EA)
HSTAMIDS	Handheld Standoff Minefield Detection System [*Military*] (RDA)
HSTAR	Helicopter Surveillance and Target Acquisition RADAR
HSTAT	Health Services/Technology Assessment Text [*National Library of Medicine*] [*Information service or system*]
HSTC	Henderson State Teachers College [*Later, HSC*] [*Arkansas*]
HSTCO	High-Stability Temperature-Compensated Crystal Oscillator [*Electronics*] (OA)
HSTCXO	High-Stability Temperature-Compensated Crystal Oscillator
H STEPH	Henricus Stephanus [*Imprint*] [*Latin*] (ROG)
HSTF	Heat-Shock Transcription Factor [*Genetics*]
HSTF	Human Serum Thymus Factor [*Immunochemistry*] (DAVI)
HSTH	Hose Thread
HSTK	Herpes Simplex Thymidine Kinase [*An enzyme*]
HSTL	Harry S Truman Library
HSTL	High-Speed Telemetry Link
HSTO	Tong [*Sudan*] [*ICAO location identifier*] (ICLI)
HSTP	Hard Stop (MCD)
HSTP	Heat Sterilization Test Program
HSTR	Amer Homestar [*NASDAQ symbol*] (TTSB)
HSTR	American Homestar Corp. [*NASDAQ symbol*] (SAG)
HSTR	Torit [*Sudan*] [*ICAO location identifier*] (ICLI)
HSTRA	High-Strength Thermal-Resistant Alloy
HSTRU	Hydraulic System Test and Repair Unit [*Army*] (RDA)
HSTS	High-Pressure Side Temperature Sensor [*Air conditioning systems*] [*Automotive engineering*]
HSTS	Horizontal Stabilizer Trim Setting
HSTS	Host Software Testing Section [*Social Security Administration*]
HSTS	Hydraulic Subsystems Test Station (MCD)
HSTSF	Harry S Truman Scholarship Foundation (EA)
HSTT	High-Speed Test Track
HSTTL	High-Speed Transistor-Transistor Logic
HSTU	Tumbura [*Sudan*] [*ICAO location identifier*] (ICLI)
HSTV	High-Survivability Test Vehicle (MCD)
HSTVL	High Survivability Test Vehicle, Lightweight [*Military*]
HSTW	Humane Society of Tinplate Workers [*A union*] [*British*]
HSU	Hardin-Simmons University [*Texas*]
HSU	Hartridge Smoke Unit [*Automotive engineering*]
HSU	Helium Service Unit (MCD)
HSU	Helium Speech Unscrambler [*Deep sea diving*]
HSU	Henderson State University [*Arkadelphia, AR*]
HSU	Hero of the Soviet Union [*Award*] (DOMA)
HSU	Highway Speed Uniformity [*Automotive tire testing*]
HSU	Humboldt State University [*Los Angeles, CA*]
HSU	Hydraulic Supply Unit
HSUA	Health Services Union of Australia
HSUG	Housing Statistics Users Group (EA)
HS/UMC	Historical Society of the United Methodist Church (EA)
HSUNA	Humanist Student Union of North America
HSUR	Half Symmetric Unstable Resonator (PDAA)
HSURIA	Half Symmetric Unstable Resonator with Intracavity Axicon (PDAA)
HSUS	Humane Society of the United States (EA)
HSUSA	Heraldry Society of the United States of America (EA)
HSUSC	Hymn Society in the United States and Canada (EA)
HSV	Haemophilia society of Victoria [*Australia*]
HSV	Head Small Veins [*Anatomy*]
HSV	Head Suppression Valve (AAG)
HSV	Heliservico-Sociedade Portuguesa de Exploracao de Meios Aeros Lda. [*Portugal ICAO designator*] (FAAC)
HSV	Herpes Simplex Virus
HSV	Highly Selective Vagotomy [*Medicine*]
HSV	High-Speed Video [*Instrumentation*]
HSV	High-Stage Valve (MCD)
HSV	Hop Stunt Viroid [*Medicine*] (DMAA)
HSV	Hue, Saturation, and Value [*Color model*] (BYTE)
HSV	Hull Solenoid Valve
HSV	Huntsville [*Alabama*] [*Airport symbol*]
HSV	Hydraulic Selector Valve
HSV	Hydrogen Saturated Vacancy [*Photovoltaic energy systems*]
HSV	Hydroxyinterlayered Smectite or Vermiculite
HSVA	Health Systems Vendors Association [*San Francisco, CA*] (EA)
HSVE	Herpes Simplex Virus Encephalitis [*Medicine*]
HSVgD	Herpes Simplex Virus Glycoprotein D [*Biochemistry*]
HSVL	Highveld Steel & Vanadium Corp. Ltd. [*NASDAQ symbol*] (NQ)
HSVLY	Highveld Steel & VanadiumADR [*NASDAQ symbol*] (TTSB)
HSVtk	Herpes Simplex Virus Thymidine Kinase [*Medicine*] (DMAA)
HSW	Aerocombi SA [*Spain ICAO designator*] (FAAC)
HSW	Heat Sink Welding [*Nuclear energy*] (NRCH)
HSW	Helena Southwestern Railroad Co. [*AAR code*]
HSW	Hot Spot [*Washington*] [*Seismograph station code, US Geological Survey Closed*] (SEIS)
HSWA	Hazardous and Solid Waste Amendments [*1984 amendments to RCRA*]
HSWDC	Historical Society of Washington, DC (EA)
HSWG	High-Speed Wire Guidance
HSWH	High-Solid Waste Header [*Nuclear energy*] (NRCH)
HSWP	Hungarian Socialist Workers' Party [*Political party*] (PPW)
HSWRS	Housewares
HSWW	Wau [*Sudan*] [*ICAO location identifier*] (ICLI)
HSX	Hollywood Stock Exchange
HSY	Hershey Foods Corp. [*NYSE symbol*] (SPSG)
HSY	Hosiery
HSYA	Yambio [*Sudan*] [*ICAO location identifier*] (ICLI)
HSYE	Yei [*Sudan*] [*ICAO location identifier*] (ICLI)
HSYL	Yirol [*Sudan*] [*ICAO location identifier*] (ICLI)

HSYNC........	Horizontal Synchronous [Computer science]
HSZA	Zalingei [Sudan] [ICAO location identifier] (ICLI)
HSZD	Hermetically Sealed Zener Diode
HT...............	Air Tchad [ICAO designator] (AD)
HT...............	Haavara-Transfer (BJA)
HT...............	Hadamard-Transform [Mathematics]
HT...............	Haiti [ANSI two-letter standard code] (CNC)
ht................	Haiti [MARC country of publication code Library of Congress] (LCCP)
HT...............	Half-Tilt Containers (DCTA)
HT...............	Half-Time [Survey] [Shipping]
HT...............	Half-Title [Publishing]
HT...............	Halftone [Photoengraving]
HT...............	Half Tone [Printing] (NITA)
ht................	Halftone [Photography] [Art] (WDMC)
HT...............	Half-Tracked [Vehicle] (NATG)
H-T.............	Half-Truck [British]
HT...............	Halt and Transfer
HT...............	Hammer Toe [Orthopedics] (DAVI)
HT...............	Hand-Held Terminal [Computer science] (MHDB)
HT...............	Handling Time
HT...............	Handmaids of the Most Holy Trinity (TOCD)
HT...............	Hand Test [Psychology]
HT...............	Hand Transceiver
HT...............	Hand Translation (MCD)
HT...............	Handy Talky [Radio]
HT...............	Hard Top [Automobile advertising]
HT...............	Hashimoto's Thyroiditis [Medicine] (DMAA)
HT...............	Haustus [A Drink] [Pharmacy]
HT...............	Hawaiian Territory [Prior to statehood]
HT...............	Hawaiian Theater [Military]
HT...............	Hawaiian Time
HT...............	Headed Type
H/T.............	Head per Track
HT...............	Head, Tail [Coin-tossing probability]
HT...............	Head-to-Tail [Polymer structure]
HT...............	Head Turn [Industrial engineering]
HT...............	Hearing Test (CPH)
HT...............	Heart
HT...............	Heart Tones [Medicine]
HT...............	Heart Transplantation
HT...............	Heat (AAG)
HT...............	Heat Transfer (NASA)
HT...............	Heat Treat
HT...............	Heavy Tank
HT...............	Heavy Terminal [AFSCF] (MCD)
HT...............	Heavy Thermoplastic (IAA)
HT...............	Hebrew Text (BJA)
HT...............	Height (AAG)
ht................	Height (VRA)
ht................	Height [Also, h] (WDMC)
HT...............	Height of Target
HT...............	Heights [Commonly used] (OPSA)
HT...............	Height Technician [Air Force]
HT...............	Height Telling [RADAR]
HT...............	Helen Thomas [British author]
HT...............	Helicopter Training Squadron [Navy symbol] (NVT)
HT...............	Hemagglutination Titer [Medicine] (MAE)
HT...............	Herd Test
Ht................	Heterozygote [Medicine] (DMAA)
HT...............	Hibernation Trigger (BARN)
HT...............	High Technology (MCD)
HT...............	High Temperature
HT...............	High Tension
HT...............	High Tide
HT...............	High Torque [Engineering] (IAA)
HT...............	High Transform [Computer science]
HT...............	High Treason
HT...............	Histologic Technician [or Technologist] (MAE)
HT...............	Histologic Transformation [Medicine]
HT...............	Historic Towns [A publication]
HT...............	History Today [A publication] (BRI)
HT...............	Hittite Texts in the Cuneiform Character from Tablets in the British Museum [London] (BJA)
HT...............	Hoc Tempore [At This Time] [Latin]
HT...............	Hoc Titulo [In, or Under, This Title] [Latin]
HT...............	Hoisting Tool (MCD)
HT...............	Holding Time [Telecommunications] (TEL)
HT...............	Hollow Tile [Technical drawings]
HT...............	Holy Trinity
HT...............	Home Treatment [Medicine]
HT...............	Homing Terrier [Missile]
HT...............	Homing Transponders
HT...............	Homing Type (NATG)
HT...............	Horizontal Tab [Computer science] (DOM)
HT...............	Horizontal Tabulate (NITA)
HT...............	Horizontal Tabulation [Computer science]
HT...............	Horological Times [A publication] (EAAP)
HT...............	Horsed Transport [Military]
HT...............	Horserace Totalisator [Set up in 1926 to provide alternative form of betting and to generate income from improvement of racing] [British]
HT...............	Hospital Train
HT...............	Hot Report (NATG)
HT...............	Hot Tin (MSA)
HT...............	Hot Transient Exhaust Emissions [Automotive engineering]
HT...............	Houma-Thibodaux [Diocesan abbreviation] [Louisiana] (TOCD)
HT...............	House Trailer (AFM)
HT...............	Howard Terminal [AAR code]
HT...............	Hubbard Tank [Medicine]
HT...............	Huhner Test [Gynecology]
HT...............	Hull Technician [Navy]
HT...............	Human Teratocarcinoma [A cell line]
HT...............	Human Thrombin [Cytochemistry]
HT...............	Human Tumor [Oncology]
HT...............	Hunter Transport [Commercial firm British]
HT...............	Hybrid Tea [Roses] (ROG)
HT...............	Hydrolyzable Tannin Level
HT...............	Hydrophobic Tail [Surfactant technology]
HT...............	Hydrotalcite [Mineralogy]
HT...............	Hydrotherapy [Medicine]
HT...............	Hydrotreating [Also, HDT] [Petroleum technology]
HT...............	Hydroxyl Terminated (MCD)
HT...............	Hydroxytryptamine [Biochemistry]
Ht................	Hypermetropia, Total [Ophthalmology]
Ht................	Hyperopia, Total [Ophthalmology] (AAMN)
HT...............	Hypertension [Cardiology] (DAVI)
HT...............	Hyperthyroidism [Endocrinology] (MAE)
HT...............	Hypertriglyceridemia [Medicine]
HT...............	Hypertropia [Medicine]
HT...............	Hypodermic Tablet [Medicine]
HT...............	Hypotension [Medicine]
HT...............	Hypothalamus [Neurology]
HT...............	Hypothermally Treated (GNE)
HT...............	Mustard Gas [Also, H, HD, HS, M] [Poison gas US Chemical Corps symbol]
HT1	Hull Maintenance Technician, First Class [Navy] (DNAB)
HT2	Hull Maintenance Technician, Second Class [Navy] (DNAB)
HT3	Hull Maintenance Technician, Third Class [Navy] (DNAB)
HTA	Handbooks of Theology [A publication]
HTA	Harness Tracks of America (EA)
HTA	Harris Tweed Association [British] (DBA)
HTA	Heavier than Air
HTA	Hedge-to-Arrive [Business term]
HTA	Help the Aged [AAIA] [Superseded by] (EA)
HTA	Herb Trade Association (EA)
HTA	Heteroduplex Tracking Analysis [Genetics]
HTA	Heterophil Transplantation Antigen [Medicine] (DMAA)
HTA	High-Temperature Adhesive
HTA	High-Temperature Alloy
HTA	High-Temperature Ashing [Analytical chemistry]
HTA	Highway Traffic Act
HTA	Hohenfels Training Area [NATO]
HTA	Horticultural Trades Association [British] (BI)
HTA	Household Textiles Association [British] (BI)
HTA	Humanist Teachers' Association [British]
HTA	Hydroxytryptamine [Biochemistry] (MAE)
HTA	Hyperion 1997 Term Trust [NYSE symbol] (SPSG)
HTA	Hypophysiotropic Area [of hypothalamus] [Endocrinology]
HTAB	Hexadecytrimethylammonium Bromide [Organic chemistry]
HTAC	Hexadecyltrimethylammonium Chloride [Organic chemistry]
HTAC	High-Tension Alternating Current (IAA)
HTACS	Human Thyroid Adenyl Cyclase Stimulator [Endocrinology]
HTAD	High Temperature Aerosol Decomposition [Chemistry]
ht aer..........	Heated Aerosol [Pharmacology] (DAVI)
HTAH	High-Temperature Air Heat [for magnetohydrodynamic power plants] (MCD)
HT & C	Heat Transfer and Cryogenics
HTANSW	History Teachers' Association of New South Wales [Australia]
HTAR	Arusha [Tanzania] [ICAO location identifier] (ICLI)
HTAS	Hug-a-Tree and Survive (EA)
HT(ASCP)	Histologic Technician (American Society of Clinical Pathologists) (DMAA)
HTAT	Human Tetanus Antitoxin [Medicine] (CPH)
HTB	Hairdressing Training Board (AIE)
HTB	Hair Tuning Bar
HTB	Heat Treat Block (MCD)
HTB	Hexadecimal-to-Binary [Computer science]
H-TB	High-Tension Battery
HTB	High-Tension Braided Sheath [Automotive engineering]
HTB	Highway Tariff Bureau [Later, AMCTB]
HTB	Hot Tub Bath [Medicine]
HTB	Howitzer Test Bed (RDA)
HTB	Human Tumor Bank [Medicine] (DMAA)
HTB	Hungarian Tourist Board (EAIO)
HTB	Hypergolic Test Building (KSC)
HTB	Hyperion 2002 Term Trust [NYSE symbol] (SPSG)
HTBA	Hood's Texas Brigade Association (EA)
HTBB	HomeTown Buffet [NASDAQ symbol] (TTSB)
HTBB	Hometown Buffet, Inc. [NASDAQ symbol] (SAG)
HTBDR	High-Temperature Burner-Duct Recuperator System
Htbk............	Hatchback (BARN)
HTBU	Bukoba [Tanzania] [ICAO location identifier] (ICLI)
HTC	Haiti Trans Air SA [ICAO designator] (FAAC)
HTC	Handicapped Travel Club (EA)
HTC	Hand Tool Carrier [NASA] (KSC)
HTC	Harris Teachers College [Missouri]
HTC	Harris Transducer Corp. (MCD)
HTC	Hartco Enterprises, Inc. [Toronto Stock Exchange symbol]
HTC	Head to Come [Publishing]
HTC	Health Care Telecommunications Corp. [Camp Hill, PA] (TSSD)

HTC.............	Heavy Teflon Coating
HTC.............	Heavy Terminal Complex (MCD)
HTC.............	Hebrew Teachers College [Massachusetts]
HTC.............	Hebrew Theological College [Skokie, IL] (BJA)
HTC.............	Height-to-Time Converter
HTC.............	Height Tracking Console (MCD)
HTC.............	Helicopter Transit Controller (MCD)
HTC.............	Hepatoma Cells [Cytology] (DAVI)
HTC.............	Hepatoma Tissue Culture [Medicine]
HTC.............	High-Tar Content [of cigarettes]
HTC.............	High-Temperature Carbonization
HTC.............	High-Temperature Catalyst
HTC.............	High-Temperature Coil
HTC.............	High-Temperature Conditioning
HTC.............	Highway Traffic Control
HTC.............	Homozygous Typing Cells [Immunochemistry]
HTC.............	Hughes Tool Co.
HTC.............	Hull Maintenance Technician, Chief [Navy] (DNAB)
HTC.............	Hungarian Tel & Cable [AMEX symbol] (TTSB)
HTC.............	Hungarian Telephone and Cable Corp. [AMEX symbol] (SAG)
HTC.............	Huston-Tillotson College [Austin, TX]
HTC.............	Huston-Tillotson College, Austin, TX [OCLC symbol] (OCLC)
HTC.............	Hybrid Technology Computer
HTC.............	Hydraulic Temperature Control (AAG)
HTC.............	Hydraulic Test Chamber (AAG)
HTC.............	Hydrofoil Test Craft
HTC.............	Hydrogen Transfer Catalysis [Chemistry]
HTC.............	Hypertensive Crisis [Cardiology] (DAVI)
HTCA...........	Human Tumor Clonogenic Assay [In-vitro testing system]
HTCC...........	Hungarian Telephone & Cable Corp. [NASDAQ symbol] (SAG)
HTCD...........	High-Temperature Catalytic Oxidation [Chemistry]
HTCH...........	Chunya [Tanzania] [ICAO location identifier] (ICLI)
HTCH...........	Hutchinson Technology [NASDAQ symbol] (TTSB)
HTCH...........	Hutchinson Technology, Inc. [NASDAQ symbol] (NQ)
HTCHNG......	Hitching
HTCHY........	Hatchery
HTCI...........	High-Tensile Cast Iron
HTCM...........	Master Chief Hull Maintenance Technician [Formerly, SFCM] [Navy rating]
HTCO...........	Hickory Tech [NASDAQ symbol] (TTSB)
HTCO...........	Hickory Tech Corp. [NASDAQ symbol] (SAG)
HTCO...........	High-Temperature Catalytic Oxidation [Chemistry]
HTCS...........	Senior Chief Hull Maintenance Technician [Formerly, SFCS] [Navy rating]
HTCV...........	Hop Trefoil Cryptic Virus [Plant pathology]
HTD.............	Hand Target Designator
HTD.............	Hand-Tool Dexterity [Motor performance test]
HTD.............	Heated (MSA)
HTD.............	Higher Telegraphist Detector [British military] (DMA)
HTD.............	High-Temperature Distillation
HTD.............	High-Torque Drive [Engineering]
HTD.............	Horizontal Tactical Display (NG)
HTD.............	Human Therapeutic Dose
HTD.............	Huntingdon International Holdings Ltd. [NYSE symbol] (CTT)
HTD.............	Huntingdon Intl ADR [NYSE symbol] (TTSB)
HTDA...........	Dar Es-Salaam/Dar Es-Salaam [Tanzania] [ICAO location identifier] (ICLI)
HTDC...........	Dar Es-Salaam [Tanzania] [ICAO location identifier] (ICLI)
HTDC...........	High-Tension Direct Current (IAA)
HTDE...........	High-Technology Demonstrator Engine (MCD)
HTDL...........	High-Temperature Detection Lens
HTDM...........	Helicopter Team Defense Missile
HTDO...........	Dodoma [Tanzania] [ICAO location identifier] (ICLI)
HTDQ...........	Dar Es-Salaam [Tanzania] [ICAO location identifier] (ICLI)
HTDS...........	Hydrofoil Tactical Data System
HTDT...........	Heavy Truck Driver Trainer [Army]
HTDU...........	Horizontal Tactical Display Unit
HTE.............	England AFB (Alexandria), LA [Location identifier FAA] (FAAL)
HTE.............	Heavy-Duty Thermoplastic Elastomer Insulation [Automotive engineering]
HTE.............	High-Temperature Electrolysis (MCD)
HTE.............	Hydraulic Test Equipment
HTE.............	Hypergroup Translating Equipment (NITA)
HTE.............	Hypertensive Encephalopathy [Medicine] (CPH)
HTEC...........	High Technology
HTEC...........	Hydrogen Technology Evaluation Center [Upton, NY] [Brookhaven National Laboratory] [Department of Energy] (GRD)
HTEC...........	Hydron Technologies [NASDAQ symbol] (TTSB)
HTEC...........	Hydron Technologies, Inc. [NASDAQ symbol] (SPSG)
HTEF...........	Heat Transfer Efficiency Factor [Engineering]
HTEL...........	Hungarian Teleconstruct [NASDAQ symbol] (SAG)
HTEM...........	Human Thymic Epithelial Medium [Endocrinology]
HTES...........	High-Technology Ejection Seat
HTES...........	High-Technology Escape System (MCD)
HTESP........	High-Temperature Electrostatic Precipitator [Anti-smoke pollution device]
HTEXCH......	Heat Exchanger (MCD)
HTF.............	Heat Transfer Fluid
HTF.............	Heat Treat Fixture (MCD)
HTF.............	Height Finding (MSA)
HTF.............	Heritage Trails Fund (EA)
HTF.............	Heterothyrotropic Factor [Medicine] (MAE)
HTF.............	Highway Trust Fund
HTF.............	House Tube Feeding [Medicine] (DMAA)
HTF.............	How-to-Fight [Manuals] [Military]

HTF.............	Hypersonic Tunnel Facility [NASA]
HTF.............	Societe Helitrans France [ICAO designator] (FAAC)
HTFA...........	Hull Maintenance Technician, Fireman Apprentice [Navy] (DNAB)
HTFC...........	High-Temperature Fuel Cell
HTFFR.........	High-Temperature Fast-Flow Reactor [See also HTFS]
HTFFS.........	Heat Transfer and Fluid Flow Service [British]
HTFFT.........	Heat Transfer Fluid Flow Thermodynamics (NRCH)
HTFI...........	Fort Ikoma [Tanzania] [ICAO location identifier] (ICLI)
HTFM...........	How to Fight Manual [Military] (MCD)
HTFMI.........	Heat Transfer and Fluid Mechanics Institute (MCD)
HTFN...........	Hull Maintenance Technician, Fireman [Navy] (DNAB)
HTFORE......	Heretofore (ROG)
HTFS...........	Heat Transfer and Fluid Flow Service [Also, HTFFS] [British]
HTF/S.........	How to Fight/How to Support [Military] (MCD)
HTFW...........	High-Temperature Fluid-Wall [Incineration process]
HTFX...........	Heat Treat Fixture
HTG.............	Handbuch Theologischer Grundbegriffe [Munich] [A publication] (BJA)
HTG	Heating (KSC)
HTG.............	Heating
HTG.............	Heritage Media'A' [AMEX symbol] (TTSB)
HTG.............	Heritage Media Corp. [AMEX symbol] (CTT)
HTG.............	High-Temperature Gas [Reactor]
HTG.............	Hobart Town Gazette [A publication]
HTG.............	Honest-to-God Cash Flow Yields [Finance] (EMRF)
HTG.............	Hypertriglyceridemia [Medicine]
HTGC...........	High-Temperature Gas-Cooled Reactor (BARN)
HTGCR........	High-Temperature Gas-Cooled Reactor
HTGF	Human Transforming Growth Factor [Biochemistry]
HTGL	Hepatic Triglyceride Lipase [An enzyme]
HTGL	High Temperature Gasdynamics Laboratory [Stanford University] [Research center] (RCD)
HTGPF	High-Temperature General-Purpose Furnace
HTGR...........	High-Temperature Gas-Cooled Reactor
HTGR...........	High Temperature Gas Reactor (EERA)
HTGR-CX	High-Temperature Gas-Cooled-Reactor Critical Experiment
HTGRE........	High-Temperature Gas-Cooled-Reactor Experiment
HTH	Hawthorne [Nevada] [Airport symbol Obsolete] (OAG)
HTH	Heart to Heart Foundation (EA)
HTH	Helix-Turn-Helix [Protein structure]
HTH	Hexagon Tungsten Honeycomb
HTH	High-Temperature Heater
HTH	High-Test Hypochlorite (WGA)
HTH	Homeostatic Thymus Hormone [Immunology]
HTH	Home Town Honey [Slang]
HTH	Hypothalamus [Medicine] (DMAA)
HTHA...........	Hearing and Tinnitus Help Association [Later, AEAR] (EA)
HtHaN.........	Northern Montana College, Havre, MT [Library symbol Library of Congress] (LCLS)
HTHD...........	Hypertensive Heart Disease [Medicine] (MAE)
HTHM...........	High Toxic Hazard Material
HTHR...........	Hawthorne Financial Corp. [NASDAQ symbol] (NQ)
HTHR...........	Hawthorne Finl [NASDAQ symbol] (TTSB)
HTHR...........	High-Tension/High-Resistance [Automotive engineering]
HT-HS.........	High-Temperature, High-Shear Viscometer
HTHSR........	High-Temperature, High-Shear-Rate [Viscosity measurement]
HTI.............	Haiti [ANSI three-letter standard code] (CNC)
HTI.............	Haiti International Air SA [ICAO designator] (FAAC)
HTI.............	Hamilton Island [Australia Airport symbol] (OAG)
HTI.............	Hamilton Technology, Inc.
HTI.............	Hand Tools Institute (EA)
HTI.............	Heat Transfer Instrument System [Nuclear energy] (NUCP)
HTI.............	Hemispheric Thrombotic Infarction [Medicine] (DMAA)
HTI.............	Hemorrhagic Toxin Inhibitor [Hematology]
HTI.............	High-Temperature Incinerator
HTI.............	High-Temperature Isotropic
HTI.............	Home Testing Institute, Inc. (NTCM)
HTI.............	Horizons Technology, Inc.
HTI.............	Horizontal Tactics Indicator
HTI.............	Horizontal Technology Insertion
HTI.............	Horizontal Technology Integration [Business term] (INF)
HTIG...........	Homologous Tetanus Immune Globulin [Medicine] (DMAA)
HTIR...........	Iringa [Tanzania] [ICAO location identifier] (ICLI)
HTIS...........	Heat Transfer Instrument System (NRCH)
HT/IT.........	Homing Terrier/Improved Tartar [Missile] (MCD)
HTJ.............	H-Plane Tee Junction
HTK.............	Hard-Target Kill [Military] (GFGA)
HTK.............	Head to Come [A notation on copy that the headline will be written and set later] (WDMC)
HTK.............	Head to Kum [Come] [Publishing]
HTK.............	Heel to Knee (DMAA)
HTKA...........	Kigoma [Tanzania] [ICAO location identifier] (ICLI)
HTKI...........	Kilwa Masoko [Tanzania] [ICAO location identifier] (ICLI)
HTKJ...........	Kilimanjaro [Tanzania] [ICAO location identifier] (ICLI)
HTKNT........	Herders Theologischer Kommentar zum Neuen Testament [Freiburg] [A publication] (BJA)
HTKO...........	Kongwa [Tanzania] [ICAO location identifier] (ICLI)
HTKP...........	Hard-Target Kill Potential [Military] (MCD)
HTKT...........	Kilimatinde [Tanzania] [ICAO location identifier] (ICLI)
HTL.............	Hearing Threshold Level
HTL.............	Heartland Partners L.P.'A' [AMEX symbol] (TTSB)
HTL.............	Heartland Partners Ltd. Class A [AMEX symbol] (SPSG)
HTL.............	Heat Transfer Laboratory [MIT] (MCD)
HTL.............	Heat Transfer Loop (NRCH)
HTL.............	Helicopter Transportable Launcher (MUGU)

HTL............ Helper T-Lymphocyte [*Immunology*]
HTL............ High-Temperature Lacquer
HTL............ High Threshold Logic
HTL............ High Turbulence Level
HTL............ Histologic Technologist [*Medicine*] (MEDA)
HTL............ Hotel (WDAA)
HTL............ Hotel
HTL............ Hotel Call, Time, and Charges Mandatory [*Telecommunications*] (TEL)
HTL............ Houghton Lake, MI [*Location identifier FAA*] (FAAL)
HTL............ Human Thymic Leukemia [*Medicine*]
HTLA.......... High-Titer, Low-Acidity [*Hematology*]
HTLA.......... Human T-Lymphocyte Antigen (DMAA)
HTL(ASCP)... Histotechnologist (American Society of Clinical Pathologists) (DMAA)
HTLB.......... High-Technology Light Brigade [*Army*] (INF)
HTLD.......... Heartland Express [*NASDAQ symbol*] (TTSB)
HTLD.......... Heartland Express, Inc. [*NASDAQ symbol*] (NQ)
HTLD.......... High-Technology Light Division [*DoD*]
HTLD.......... Houston Test for Language Development [*Education*]
HTLI........... Lindi [*Tanzania*] [*ICAO location identifier*] (ICLI)
HTLL.......... High Test Level Language (NASA)
HTLM.......... Lake Manyara [*Tanzania*] [*ICAO location identifier*] (ICLI)
HTLO.......... Lobo Wildlife Lodge [*Tanzania*] [*ICAO location identifier*] (ICLI)
HTLR.......... High-Tension/Low-Resistance [*Automotive engineering*]
HTLR.......... High Torque, Low Rev
HTLS.......... Higher Torque/Low-Speed (DNAB)
HTLT.......... HTL Telemanagement Ltd. [*Burtonsville, MD*] (TSSD)
HTLT.......... Hughes Transportable Link Terminal
HTLTR........ High-Temperature Lattice Test Reactor
HTLV.......... Human T-Cell Lymphotropic [*formerly, Leukemia*] Virus
HTLV-III...... Human T-Cell Lymphotrophic Virus-Type Three
HTLV-III/LAV... Human T-Cell Lymphotropic Virus Type Three/Lymphadenopathy-Associated Virus
HTLVR........ Human T-Cell Leukemia Virus Receptor [*Medicine*] (DMAA)
HTM........... Hard Tube Modulator [*Electronics*]
HTM........... Hard Tube Monitor [*Electronics*] (IAA)
HTM........... Harpoon Trainer Module [*Missiles*] (MCD)
HTM........... Heat Transfer Medium [*Engineering*]
HTM........... Heat Transfer Meter
HTM........... Heat Transfer Module [*Furnace*]
HTM........... High Temperature (IEEE)
HTM........... High-Temperature Materials
HTM........... High-Temperature Metallography
HTM........... High Throughput Mission (SSD)
HTM........... High-Trajectory Missiles (NRCH)
HTM........... Hypothesis Testing Model (IEEE)
HTM........... Whitman, MA [*Location identifier FAA*] (FAAL)
HTMA.......... Hydraulic Tool Manufacturers Association [*Milwaukee, WI*] (EA)
HTMA.......... Mafia [*Tanzania*] [*ICAO location identifier*] (ICLI)
HTMAEW..... Home Timber Merchants' Association of England and Wales (BI)
HTMB.......... Mbeya [*Tanzania*] [*ICAO location identifier*] (ICLI)
HTMD.......... High-Technology Motorized Division
HTMD.......... Hold Time Management Display [*NASA*]
HTMD.......... Mwadui [*Tanzania*] [*ICAO location identifier*] (ICLI)
HTM-DB....... High Temperature Materials Data Bank [*Commission of the European Communities*] [*Information service or system*] (IID)
HTMG.......... Morgororo [*Tanzania*] [*ICAO location identifier*] (ICLI)
HTMI........... Masasi [*Tanzania*] [*ICAO location identifier*] (ICLI)
HTMIAC...... High Temperature Materials Information Analysis Center Information Analysis Center [*Formerly, TEPIAC*] [*West Lafayette, IN*] [*DoD*] (GRD)
HTMK.......... Mikumi [*Tanzania*] [*ICAO location identifier*] (ICLI)
HTML.......... High Temperature Materials Laboratory [*Oak Ridge, TN*] [*Oak Ridge National Laboratory*] [*Department of Energy*] (GRD)
HTML.......... Hypertext Markup Language [*Computer science*]
html............ Hypertext Markup Language [*Computer science*]
HTML.......... Hypertext Markup Language [*Telecommunication*]
HTMMP....... Helo Transportable Mulit-Mission Platform [*Experimental military vehicle*]
HTMO.......... Mombo [*Tanzania*] [*ICAO location identifier*] (ICLI)
HTMP.......... High-Temperature Thermomechanical Processing [*Alloy heat resistance*]
HTMP.......... High-Temperature Thermomechanical Pulp [*Pulp and paper technology*]
HTMP.......... Hydroxy(tetramethyl)piperidineoxyl [*Organic chemistry*]
HTMP.......... Mpanda [*Tanzania*] [*ICAO location identifier*] (ICLI)
HTMR.......... High Temperature Metals Recovery [*For hazardous waste treatment*]
HTMR.......... High Threshold Mechanoreceptor [*Neurophysiology*]
HTMR.......... Msembe-Ruaha National Park [*Tanzania*] [*ICAO location identifier*] (ICLI)
HTMS.......... High-Temperature Mass Spectrometry
HTMS.......... Moshi [*Tanzania*] [*ICAO location identifier*] (ICLI)
HTMT.......... Mtwara [*Tanzania*] [*ICAO location identifier*] (ICLI)
HTMU.......... Musoma [*Tanzania*] [*ICAO location identifier*] (ICLI)
HTMW.......... Mwanza [*Tanzania*] [*ICAO location identifier*] (ICLI)
HTMX.......... Mpwapwa [*Tanzania*] [*ICAO location identifier*] (ICLI)
HTN............ Haiti North Airline [*ICAO designator*] (FAAC)
HTN............ Hantaan [*Virus*]
HTN............ HazTECH News [*A publication*]
HTN............ Heterodyne (FAAC)
HTN............ Hocking Technical College, Nelsonville, OH [*OCLC symbol*] (OCLC)
HTN............ Home Theatre Network [*In network name "HTN Plus"*] [*Cable-television system*]
HTN............ Hotan [*China*] [*Airport symbol*] (OAG)
HTN............ Houghton Mifflin [*NYSE symbol*] (TTSB)

HTN............ Houghton Mifflin Co. [*NYSE symbol*] (SPSG)
HTN............ HUD [*Department of Housing and Urban Development*] Teleprocessing Network
HTN............ Hughes Television Network [*New York, NY*] [*Cable-television system*]
HTN............ Hypertension [*Medicine*]
HTN............ Miles City, MT [*Location identifier FAA*] (FAAL)
HTNA.......... Nachingwea [*Tanzania*] [*ICAO location identifier*] (ICLI)
htnd........... Heightened (VRA)
HTNG.......... Ngerengere [*Tanzania*] [*ICAO location identifier*] (ICLI)
HTNJ.......... Njombe [*Tanzania*] [*ICAO location identifier*] (ICLI)
HTNR.......... High-Temperature Nitric Oxide Reduction [*Combustion technology*]
HTNSL......... High Tensile [*Mechanics*]
HTNT.......... High Technology National Training (AIE)
HTO............ East Hampton [*New York*] [*Airport symbol*] (OAG)
HTO............ Hereto (ROG)
HTO............ Heterotopic Ossification [*Orthopedics*] (DAVI)
HTO............ High-Temperature Oxidation (IEEE)
HTO............ High Throughput Screening [*Chemistry*]
HTO............ High Tibial Osteotomy [*Orthopedics*] (DAVI)
HTO............ Highway Transportation Officer [*Army*]
HTO............ Horizontal Takeoff
HTO............ Hospital Transfer Order
HTO............ Hydrous Titanium Oxide (PDAA)
HTO............ Hyperion 2005 Investment Grade Opportunity Term Trust [*NYSE symbol*] (SPSG)
HTO............ Hyperion 2005 Inv Grd Oppt Tr [*NYSE symbol*] (TTSB)
HTOFORE.... Heretofore
H to H......... Heel to Heel
HTOH.......... Hydroxytryptophol [*Laboratory*] (DAVI)
HTOHL........ Horizontal Takeoff, Horizontal Landing (KSC)
HTOL.......... Horizontal Takeoff and Landing [*Proposed aircraft under development by the British government*] (IAA)
HTOS.......... High Throughput Organic Synthesis [*Chemistry*]
HTOT.......... High-Temperature Operating Test (MCD)
HTOVL........ Horizontal Take-Off Vertical Landing [*Aviation*] (PDAA)
HTP............ Hardness Test Plan [*Army*] (AABC)
HTP............ Heat Transfer Printing [*Textile technology*]
HTP............ High Temperature and Pressure (GNE)
HTP............ High-Temperature Photochemistry [*Aerochem Research Laboratories, Inc.*] [*Analytical chemistry*]
HTP............ High-Temperature Photolysis [*Physics*]
HTP............ High-Test Hydrogen-Peroxide
HTP............ Highway Traffic Point [*MTMC*] (TAG)
H-T-P......... [*A*] House, a Tree, a Person [*Psychological drawing test*]
HTP............ Humidity Test Procedure
HTP............ Humor Test of Personality [*Psychology*]
HTP............ Hydroxytryptophan [*Biochemistry*]
HTPB.......... Hydroxyl-Terminated Polybutadiene [*Organic chemistry*]
HTPB.......... Hydroxyl-Terminated Polybutylene [*Organic chemistry*] (NASA)
HTPB.......... Hydroxy-Terminated Polybutadiene [*Organic chemistry*]
HTPE.......... Pemba [*Tanzania*] [*ICAO location identifier*] (ICLI)
HTPFP........ High Technology Professionals for Peace [*Defunct*] (EA)
HTPHA........ Huguenot-Thomas Paine Historical Association (EA)
HTPM.......... Harvard Total Project Manager [*Computer software*]
HTPN.......... Home Total Parenteral Nutrition [*Medicine*]
HTPO.......... Human Thyroid Peroxidase [*An enzyme*]
HTPP.......... Hardness Test Program Plan
HTPS.......... Hull-Turret Position Sensor [*Military*] (RDA)
HTPV.......... High-Temperature Power and Voltage (IAA)
HTR............ Halt and Transfer
HTR............ Hanford Test Reactor (NRCH)
HTR............ Hard Tissue Replacement [*Dentistry*]
HTR............ Hateruma [*Japan*] [*Airport symbol*] (OAG)
HTR............ Heated-Tube Reactor [*Chemical engineering*]
HTR............ Heater (AAG)
HTR............ Hemolytic Transfusion Reaction [*Medicine*]
HTR............ High-Temperature Reactor
HTR............ High-Temperature Resistor
HTR............ Highway Traffic Regulation (AABC)
HTR............ Hitachi Training Reactor [*Japan*]
HTR............ Holstenair Lubeck, Luftverkehrsservice GmbH [*Germany ICAO designator*] (FAAC)
HTR............ Homing Terrier Retrofit [*Missile*] (MCD)
HTR............ Homogeneous Thorium Reactor
HTR............ Hours to Run (ADA)
HTR............ Household Tracking Report [*Television ratings*] (NTCM)
HTR............ HTR Industries, Inc. [*Vancouver Stock Exchange symbol*]
HTR............ Human Transferrin Receptor [*Biochemistry*]
HTR............ Hyperion Total Return Fd [*NYSE symbol*] (TTSB)
HTR............ Hyperion Total Return Fund [*NYSE symbol*] (SPSG)
HTR............ Hypermetropia, Right [*Ophthalmology*] (DAVI)
HTRAC........ Half-Track [*A type of military vehicle*] (AABC)
HTRAP........ Height Reply Analysis Processor (SAA)
HTRB.......... High-Temperature Reverse Bias [*Electronics*] (IAA)
HTRD.......... Heat Transfer Rotating Disc [*Engineering*]
HTRDA........ High-Temperature Reactor Development Associates
HTRE.......... Heat Transfer Reactor Experiment
HTRE.......... High-Temperature Reactor Experiment [*Department of Energy*] (GAAI)
HTRF.......... Homogeneous Time Resolved Fluorescence [*Analytical Chemistry*]
HTRF.......... Human Telomeric Repeat-Binding Factor [*Genetics*]
HTRI.......... Heat Transfer Research Institute (NRCH)
HTRI.......... High Technology Recruitment Index [*A publication*]
HTRIN......... Holy Trinity
HTRK.......... Half-Track [*A type of military vehicle*]

HTROL.........	Help To Run Our-Lines [*Military*]
H TRON	Home TRON [*The Real-Time Operating System Nucleus*] (NITA)
HTRR..........	Harpoon Transfer Relay Rack [*Missiles*] (MCD)
HTRW..........	Hazardous, Toxic, and Radiological Waste [*US Army Corps of Engineers*]
HTS.............	Half-Time Survey [*Shipping*]
HTS.............	Hamden Testing Services, Inc.
HTS.............	Harness Tracks Security [*Defunct*] (EA)
HTS.............	Hawaiian Tracking Station
HTS.............	Head, Track, and Selector
HTS.............	Head Traumatic Syndrome [*Medicine*] (DMAA)
HTS.............	Heal-₁o-Shin [*Test*] [*Neurology*] (DAVI)
HTS.............	Heat Transfer Section
HTS.............	Heat Transfer System
HTS.............	Heat Transport Section [*Apollo*] [*NASA*]
HTS.............	Heat Transport System [*NASA*] (NASA)
HTS.............	Heat-Treated Steel
HTS.............	Heavy-Duty Thermoset Elastomer Insulation [*Automotive engineering*]
HTS.............	Heights (MCD)
Hts.............	Heights (DD)
HTS.............	Heights
HTS.............	Height-Telling Surveillance
HTS.............	HeLa Tumor Suppression [*Medicine*] (DMAA)
HTS.............	Helitrans Air Service, Inc. [*ICAO designator*] (FAAC)
HTS.............	Hemangioma-Thrombocytopenia Syndrome [*Medicine*] (MEDA)
HTS.............	High Technology Solution (DGA)
HTS.............	High-Temperature Steam
HTS.............	High-Temperature Superconductivity (ECON)
HTS.............	High-Temperature Superconductor [*Materials science*]
HTS.............	High-Tensile Steel
HTS.............	High Tensile Strength [*Mechanics*]
HTS.............	High-Tension Separation (IAA)
HTS.............	High-Tension Supply (IAA)
HTS.............	High-Tension Synthetic Insulation [*Automotive engineering*]
HTS.............	High Throughput Screening [*For drug screening*]
HTS.............	Home Team Sports [*Cable-television system*]
HTS.............	Host-to-Satellite
HTS.............	How to Support [*Manuals*] [*Military*] (MCD)
HTS.............	Human Thyroid Stimulator [*Endocrinology*]
HTS.............	Huntington [*West Virginia*] [*Airport symbol*] (OAG)
HTS.............	Hybrid Test Set
HTS.............	Hydraulic Test Set [*or Station*]
HTS.............	Hydrodynamic Test System
HTSA..........	History Trust of South Australia
HTSA..........	Host-Tenant Support Agreement [*Military*]
HTSC..........	High-Temperature Semiconductor [*Electronics*]
HTSC..........	High-Temperature Superconductivity [*Materials science*]
HTSC..........	High-Temperature Superconductor [*Materials science*]
HTSC..........	Highway Traffic Safety Center [*Michigan State University*]
HTSC..........	Hughes Technical Services Co.
HTSCA	Human Tumor Stem Cell Assay [*Oncology*]
HTSD..........	Singida [*Tanzania*] [*ICAO location identifier*] (ICLI)
HTSE..........	Same [*Tanzania*] [*ICAO location identifier*] (ICLI)
HTSEC	High-Temperature Size-Exclusion Chromatography
HTSF..........	High-Temperature Sodium Facility [*Nuclear energy*] (NRCH)
HTSF..........	Hydrated Textured Soy Flour
HTSH..........	Human Thyroid Stimulating Hormone [*Also, htsh*] [*Endocrinology*]
HTSH..........	Mafinga [*Tanzania*] [*ICAO location identifier*] (ICLI)
HTSHLD......	Heat Shield
HTSI...........	Human Thyroid-Stimulating Immunoglobulin (PDAA)
HTSIM........	Height Stimulator (IAA)
HTSK..........	Heat Sink (MSA)
HTSL..........	Heat Transfer Simulation Loop (IEEE)
HTSL..........	High Temperature Sodium Loop (PDAA)
HTSM..........	High-Temperature Skim Milk (OA)
HTSN..........	Seronera [*Tanzania*] [*ICAO location identifier*] (ICLI)
HTSO..........	Songea [*Tanzania*] [*ICAO location identifier*] (ICLI)
HTSR..........	High-Temperature Strain Gauge
HTSS..........	Honeywell Time-Sharing System [*Computer science*] (IEEE)
HTSSE	High-Temperature-Superconductivity Space Experiment [*Navy*]
HTST..........	Heartstream Inc. [*NASDAQ symbol*] (TTSB)
HTST..........	Heartstream, Inc. [*NASDAQ symbol*] (SAG)
HTSt............	Hervormde Teologiese Studies [*Pretoria, South Africa*] [*A publication*] (BJA)
HTST............	High-Temperature Short-Time [*Pasteurization*] [*Food processing*]
HTSU..........	Sumbawanga [*Tanzania*] [*ICAO location identifier*] (ICLI)
HTSUP........	Height Supervisor [*RADAR*]
HTSUS	Harmonized Tariff Schedule of the United States [*Formerly, TSUS*]
HTSY..........	Shinyanga [*Tanzania*] [*ICAO location identifier*] (ICLI)
HT/SZ..........	Height/Size (DNAB)
HTT.............	Air Tchad, Societe de Transport Aeriens [*Chad*] [*ICAO designator*] (FAAC)
HTT.............	Hallett [*Australia Seismograph station code, US Geological Survey*] (SEIS)
HTT.............	Heat-Treatment Temperature
HTT.............	Heavy Tactical Transport
HTT.............	High Technology Transfer Co. [*Czechoslovakia*] (ECON)
HTT.............	High-Temperature Tetragonal [*Physics*]
HTT.............	High-Temperature Thermomechanical Treatment [*Steel forging*]
HTT.............	High Temperature Treatment [*Materials science*]
HTT.............	High-Temperature Tunnel [*NASA*]
HTT.............	High-Tension Thermoplastic Insulation [*Automotive engineering*]
HTT.............	Hook Tongue Terminal
HTT.............	Hydraulics, Turbine Throttle (DNAB)
HTT.............	Hyperion 1999 Term Trust [*NYSE symbol*] (SPSG)
HTTA..........	Highway and Traffic Technicians Association [*British*] (EAIO)
HTTB..........	High-Technology Test Bed [*Army*]
HTTB..........	Tabora [*Tanzania*] [*ICAO location identifier*] (ICLI)
HTTG..........	Tanga [*Tanzania*] [*ICAO location identifier*] (ICLI)
HTTL..........	High-Power Transistor-Transistor Logic (IEEE)
HTTL..........	High-Speed Transistor-Transistor Logic (IAA)
HTTMT........	High-Temperature Thermomechanical Treatment [*Steel forging*]
HTTP..........	Hypertext Transfer Protocol [*Computer science*]
HTTP..........	Hypertext Transfer Protocol [*Telecommunication*]
HTTR..........	Heat Treat
HTTS..........	Hybrid Thermal Treatment System [*Incinerator*] [*IT Corp.*] (RDA)
HTTS..........	Hydroquench Thrust Termination System [*NASA*] (KSC)
HTTT..........	High-Temperature Turbine Technology [*Power generation*]
HTTU..........	Tunduru [*Tanzania*] [*ICAO location identifier*] (ICLI)
HTU.............	Handheld Terminal Unit
HTU.............	Handheld Thermal Unit
HTU.............	Heat Transfer Unit
HTU.............	Height of a Transfer Unit [*Distillation*]
HTU.............	Horizontal Trail Unit (MCD)
HTU.............	Hoyt Peak [*Utah*] [*Seismograph station code, US Geological Survey*] (SEIS)
HTUR..........	Urambo [*Tanzania*] [*ICAO location identifier*] (ICLI)
HTV.............	Half Thickness Value (NRCH)
HTV.............	Harlech Television [*Wales*]
HTV.............	Herpes-Type Virus
HTV.............	High-Altitude Test Vehicle (MUGU)
HTV.............	Hi Tech Ventures, Inc. [*Vancouver Stock Exchange symbol*]
HTV.............	Home Video Tutorial
HTV.............	Homing Test Vehicle (NG)
HTV.............	Hospital Patient Transport Vehicle
HTV.............	Hull Test Vehicle [*for submarines*] (MCD)
HTV.............	Hybrid Test Vehicle [*Gasoline and electric motor*]
HTV.............	Hydrothermal Vent [*Geology*]
HTV.............	Hypersonic Test Vehicle [*Air Force*]
HTVD..........	Hypertensive Vascular Disease [*Cardiology*] (DAVI)
HTW.............	Chesapeake, OH/Huntington, WV [*Location identifier FAA*] (FAAL)
HTW.............	Haystack [*Washington*] [*Seismograph station code, US Geological Survey*] (SEIS)
HTW.............	Hazardous and Toxic Waste
HTW.............	Helicopter Trap Weapon (SAA)
HTW.............	High-Temperature Water
HTW.............	High-Temperature Wire
HTW.............	Hoosac Tunnel & Wilmington R. R. [*AAR code*]
HTWH..........	Wazo Hill [*Tanzania*] [*ICAO location identifier*] (ICLI)
HTWK..........	Ngare Nairobi [*Tanzania*] [*ICAO location identifier*] (ICLI)
ht wkt	Hit Wicket [*Cricket*] (BARN)
HTWN..........	Hometown Bancorp [*NASDAQ symbol*] (TTSB)
HTWN..........	Hometown Bancorp, Inc. [*NASDAQ symbol*] (NQ)
HTWS	Hawaii Tsunami Warning System [*Marine science*] (OSRA)
HTXA..........	Hitox Corp. [*NASDAQ symbol*] (TTSB)
HTXA..........	Hitox Corp. of America [*NASDAQ symbol*] (CTT)
HTXGR........	Heat Exchanger (KSC)
HTXRD........	High-Temperature X-Ray Diffraction
HTY.............	Hatizyo [*Japan*] [*Geomagnetic observatory code*]
HTYP..........	Heliotype [*Modified collotype*] (VRA)
HTZ.............	Hato Corozal [*Colombia*] [*Airport symbol*] (OAG)
HTZA..........	Zanzibar [*Tanzania*] [*ICAO location identifier*] (ICLI)
HU.............	Central Airlines Ltd. [*Nigeria*] [*ICAO designator*] (ICDA)
hU.............	Dihydrouridine [*Two-letter symbol; see H₂Urd*]
HU.............	Haifa University (BJA)
HU.............	Hamburger University [*McDonald's Corp.*]
HU.............	Hangup [*Telecommunications*] (TEL)
HU.............	Harvard University [*Cambridge, MA*]
HU.............	Heat Unit (MAE)
H/U.............	Heatup [*Nuclear energy*] (NRCH)
HU.............	Hebrew University [*Jerusalem*] (BJA)
HU.............	Hemagglutinating Unit [*Immunochemistry*]
HU.............	Hemoglobin Unit [*Of hydrolytic enzyme activity*]
HU.............	Hemolytic Unit [*Hematology*]
HU.............	High-Usage [*Telecommunications*] (TEL)
HU.............	Horizontal Arithmetic Unit [*Computer science*] (MHDI)
HU.............	Hospital Unit (DOMA)
HU.............	Housing Unit [*Bureau of the Census*] (GFGA)
HU.............	Hubbert Unit [*Petroleum technology*]
Hu.............	Hughes' Kentucky Reports [*A publication*] (DLA)
HU.............	Hughes Tool Co. [*Aircraft Division*] [*ICAO aircraft manufacturer identifier*] (ICAO)
Hu.............	Hughes' United States Circuit Court Reports [*A publication*] (DLA)
Hu.............	Hugo de Alberico [*Flourished, 1168-71*] [*Authority cited in pre-1607 legal work*] (DSA)
Hu.............	Hugolinus de Presbyteris [*Flourished, 1197-1238*] [*Authority cited in pre-1607 legal work*] (DSA)
Hu.............	Huguccio [*Deceased, 1210*] [*Authority cited in pre-1607 legal work*] (DSA)
HU	Hull (DNAB)
HU	Human Urine [*Medicine*] (DMAA)
hu	Hungary [*MARC country of publication code Library of Congress*] (LCCP)
HU	Hungary [*ANSI two-letter standard code*] (CNC)
HU	Hydroxyurea [*Also, HYD, HYDREA*] [*Antineoplastic drug*]
HU	Hyperemia Unit
HU	Trinidad and Tobago Air Services [*ICAO designator*] (AD)
HU	University of Hawaii, Honolulu, HI [*Library symbol Library of Congress*] (LCLS)

HUA .... Hockey Umpires' Association [*British*]
HUA .... Huancayo [*Peru*] [*Seismograph station code, US Geological Survey*] (SEIS)
HUA .... Human Urinary Albumin [*Clinical chemistry*]
HUA .... Humber Aviation Ltd. [*British ICAO designator*] (FAAC)
HUA .... Huntsville, AL [*Location identifier FAA*] (FAAL)
HUAA .... Home Uterine Activity Assessment [*Medicine*] (DMAA)
HUAC .... House Un-American Activities Committee [*Later, HCIS*] [*US Congress*]
HUAM .... Home Uterine Activity Monitoring
HuanPw .... Huaneng Power International, Inc. [*Associated Press*] (SAG)
HUAR .... Arua [*Uganda*] [*ICAO location identifier*] (ICLI)
Hu-Ar .... Magyar Orszagos Leveltar, Budapest, Hungary [*Library symbol Library of Congress*] (LCLS)
HUB .... Handicapped United in Brotherhood
HUB .... Houston, TX [*Location identifier FAA*] (FAAL)
HUB .... Hub Airlines, Inc. [*FAA designator*] (FAAC)
HUB .... Hubbell [*Harvey*] [*NYSE symbol*] (SAG)
HUBA .... Hudson Bay [*AAR code*]
Hubb .... Hubbard's Reports [*45-51 Maine*] [*A publication*] (DLA)
Hubbard ...... Hubbard's Reports [*45-51 Maine*] [*A publication*] (DLA)
HubbelB .... Hubbell, Harvey [*Associated Press*] (SAG)
Hubb Succ ... Hubback's Evidence of Succession [*A publication*] (DLA)
HUBC .... HUBCO, Inc. [*NASDAQ symbol*] (SAG)
HUBCO .... HUBCO, Inc. [*Associated Press*] (SAG)
HubelA .... Hubbell [*Harvey*], Inc. [*Associated Press*] (SAG)
HubelB .... Hubbel [*Harvey*], Inc. [*Associated Press*] (SAG)
Hub Ev .... Hubback's Evidence of Succession [*A publication*] (DLA)
HUBF .... Human Upstream Binding Factor [*Genetics*]
HuBG .... Allamin Gorkij Konyvtar, Budapest, Hungary [*Library symbol Library of Congress*] (LCLS)
HUBG .... Hub Group 'A' [*NASDAQ symbol*] (TTSB)
HUBG .... Hub Group, Inc. [*NASDAQ symbol*] (SAG)
HubGrp .... Hub Group, Inc. [*Associated Press*] (SAG)
HuBKPV .... Human BK Polyomavirus
Hub Leg Direc... Hubbell's Legal Directory [*A publication*] (DLA)
HuBM .... Orszagos Muszaki Konyvtar es Dokumentacios Kozpont, Budapest, Hungary [*Library symbol Library of Congress*] (LCLS)
Hub Prael JC... Huber's Praelectiones Juris Civilis [*A publication*] (DLA)
Hub Suc .... Hubback's Evidence of Succession [*A publication*] (DLA)
HUBZone .... Historically Underutilized Business Zone (AAGC)
HUC .... Hebrew Union College [*Later, HUC-JIR*]
HUC .... Hebrew Union College, Jewish Institute of Religion, Cincinnati, OH [*OCLC symbol*] (OCLC)
HUC .... Hook Up and Commissioning Conference [*Offshore Conference and Exhibitions Ltd.*] [*British*]
HUC .... Humacao [*Puerto Rico*] [*Airport symbol*] (OAG)
HUC .... Hypouricemia [*Medicine*]
HUCI .... Haitian Unity Council, Inc. [*Defunct*] (EA)
HUC-JIR ...... Hebrew Union College - Jewish Institute of Religion [*Formerly, HUC*] [*Cincinnati, OH*]
HUCO .... Hughes NADGE [*NATO Air Defense Ground Environment*] Consortium
HUCR .... Harvard University Character Recognizer [*Computer science*]
HUCR .... Highest Useful Compression Ratio [*Aerospace*]
HUD .... Department of Housing and Urban Development
HUD .... Handicapped Users' Database [*CompuServe Information Service*] [*Information service or system*] (CRD)
HUD .... Headsup Display
HUD .... Head-Up Display
HUD .... Horizontal Unit Displacement [*Military*] (INF)
HUD .... Hudson Resources Ltd. [*Vancouver Stock Exchange symbol*]
HUDA .... Housing and Urban Development Act
HUDAC .... Housing and Urban Development Association of Canada
Hud & B ...... Hudson and Brooke's Irish King's Bench Reports [*1827-31*] [*A publication*] (DLA)
Hud & Br .... Hudson and Brooke's Irish King's Bench Reports [*1827-31*] [*A publication*] (DLA)
Hud & Bro ... Hudson and Brooke's Irish King's Bench Reports [*1827-31*] [*A publication*] (DLA)
HUDAR .... Housing and Urban Development Acquisition Regulations [*A publication*] (AAGC)
HUD BCA .... Department of Housing and Urban Development Board of Contract Appeals (AAGC)
HudCB .... Hudson Chartered Bancorp, Inc. [*Associated Press*] (SAG)
HUDD .... Housing and Urban Development Department [*More commonly, HUD*] (KSC)
HUDDLE ...... Hull Urban Design Development Laboratory Enterprises, Inc.
HUDE .... Head-Up Display Electronics (NASA)
HuDeAgE .... Debreceni Agrartudomanyi Egyetem, Debrecen, Hungary [*Library symbol Library of Congress*] (LCLS)
HU/DEAP .... Harvard University Division of Engineering and Applied Physics [*Cambridge, MA*]
HuDeK .... Debreceni Reformatus Kollegium Nagykonyvtara, Debrecen, Hungary [*Library symbol Library of Congress*] (LCLS)
HuDeOE ...... Debreceni Orvostudomanyi Egyetem, Debrecen, Hungary [*Library symbol Library of Congress*] (LCLS)
Hud Exec .... Hudson's Executor's Guide [*A publication*] (DLA)
HudGn .... Hudson General Corp. [*Associated Press*] (SAG)
HUDMAP ...... HUD [*Department of Housing and Urban Development*] Mortgage Accounting Project
HUDPR .... Housing and Urban Development [*Department*] Procurement Regulations
HUDS .... Hudson Hotels Corp. [*NASDAQ symbol*] (SAG)
HudsFd .... Hudson Foods, Inc. [*Associated Press*] (SAG)

HudsHotl ..... Hudson Hotels Corp. [*Associated Press*] (SAG)
HudsnCB ..... Hudson Chartered Bancorp, Inc. [*Associated Press*] (SAG)
Hudson .... Hudson on Building Contracts [*A publication*] (DLA)
HudsonTc.... Hudson Technology, Inc. [*Associated Press*] (SAG)
HUDU .... Heads-Up Display Unit [*Aviation*]
HUDWAC ...... Heads-Up Display Weapons Aiming Computer (IEEE)
HUDWAS ...... Heads-Up Display Weapons Aiming System [*Air Force*] (MCD)
Hud Wills .... Hudson on Wills [*A publication*] (DLA)
HUE .... Humera [*Ethiopia*] [*Airport symbol*] (OAG)
HUEC .... Entebbe Area Control Center [*Uganda*] [*ICAO location identifier*] (ICLI)
HUEN .... Entebbe/International [*Uganda*] [*ICAO location identifier*] (ICLI)
huEPO .... Human Erythropoietin [*Biochemistry*]
HUF .... Highway Users Federation for Safety and Mobility [*Later, ASF*] (EA)
HUF .... Huffy Corp. [*NYSE symbol*] (SPSG)
HUF .... Terre Haute [*Indiana*] [*Airport symbol*] (OAG)
Huffy .... Huffy Corp. [*Associated Press*] (SAG)
HUFP .... Fort Portal [*Uganda*] [*ICAO location identifier*] (ICLI)
HUFSAM ...... Highway Users Federation for Safety and Mobility [*FHWA*] (TAG)
HU-FSH .... Human Urinary Follicle-Stimulating Hormone [*Medicine*] (DMAA)
HUFSM .... Highway Users Federation for Safety and Mobility
HUG .... Hastech Users Group (EA)
HUG .... Head of Units Group [*American Library Association*]
HUG .... Hiram Ulysses Grant [*US general and president, 1822-1885*]
HUG .... Honeywell Users Group
HUG .... Hughes Supply [*NYSE symbol*] (TTSB)
HUG .... Hughes Supply, Inc. [*NYSE symbol*] (SPSG)
HUG .... Hug-Laf-Luv (EA)
Hug .... Hugo de Alberico [*Flourished, 12th century*] [*Authority cited in pre-1607 legal work*] (DSA)
Hug .... Hugolinus de Presbyteris [*Flourished, 1197-1238*] [*Authority cited in pre-1607 legal work*] (DSA)
Hug .... Huguccio [*Deceased, 1210*] [*Authority cited in pre-1607 legal work*] (DSA)
HUG .... Lonely, AK [*Location identifier FAA*] (FAAL)
HUGA .... Human Genome Analyzer [*System for analysis of DNA*] [*Institute of Physical and Chemical Research, Japan Genetics*]
HUGE .... High-Field, Ultrathin Gel Electrophoresis [*Analytical biochemistry*]
Hugh .... Hughes' Circuit Court Reports [*A publication*] (DLA)
Hugh .... Hughes' Kentucky Reports [*A publication*] (DLA)
Hugh Abr .... Hughes' Abridgment [*1663-65*] [*England*] [*A publication*] (DLA)
Hugh Con .... Hughes' Precedents in Conveyancing [*2nd ed.*] [*1855-57*] [*A publication*] (DLA)
Hugh Conv ... Hughes' Precedents in Conveyancing [*2nd ed.*] [*1855-57*] [*A publication*] (DLA)
Hugh Ent .... Hughes' Entries [*1659*] [*A publication*] (DLA)
Hugh Eq D ... Hughes' Edition of Van Heythuysen's Equity Draftsman [*A publication*] (DLA)
Hughes .... Hughes Air West [*ICAO designator*] (AD)
Hughes .... Hughes' Kentucky Supreme Court Reports [*1785-1801*] [*A publication*] (DLA)
Hughes .... Hughes Resources, Inc. [*Associated Press*] (SAG)
Hughes .... Hughes' United States Circuit Court Reports [*A publication*] (DLA)
Hughes Fed Prac... Hughes' Federal Practice [*A publication*] (DLA)
Hughes (US)... Hughes' Circuit Court Reports [*United States*] [*A publication*] (DLA)
Hugh Ins .... Hughes on Insurance [*A publication*] (DLA)
Hugh Prec ... Hughes' Precedents in Conveyancing [*2nd ed.*] [*1855-57*] [*A publication*] (DLA)
HughSp .... Hughes Supply, Inc. [*Associated Press*] (SAG)
Hugh Wills... Hughes on Wills [*A publication*] (DLA)
Hugh Wr .... Hughes on Writs [*A publication*] (DLA)
HUGO .... Highly Unusual Geophysical Operation [*A meteorological research vehicle*]
Hugo .... Hugolinus [*Authority cited in pre-1607 legal work*] (DSA)
HUGO .... Hugoton Energy [*NASDAQ symbol*] (TTSB)
HUGO .... Hugoton Energy Corp. [*NASDAQ symbol*] (SAG)
HUGO .... Human Genome Organization [*Genetics*]
Hugo Hist Dr Rom... Hugo's Histoire du Droit Romain [*A publication*] (DLA)
Hugo Hist du Droit Rom... Hugo's Histoire du Droit Romain [*A publication*] (DLA)
Hugol .... Hugolinus de Presbyteris [*Flourished, 1197-1238*] [*Authority cited in pre-1607 legal work*] (DSA)
HugotEn .... Hugoton Energy Corp. [*Associated Press*] (SAG)
HUG's .... Home User Groups [*Computer science*]
HUG-SMS .... Honeywell Users Group - Small and Medium Systems [*Later, NAHU*]
HUGU .... Gulu [*Uganda*] [*ICAO location identifier*] (ICLI)
Hugu .... Huguccio [*Deceased, 1210*] [*Authority cited in pre-1607 legal work*] (DSA)
HUH .... Huahine [*French Polynesia*] [*Airport symbol*] (OAG)
HUH .... Hualalai [*Hawaii*] [*Seismograph station code, US Geological Survey*] (SEIS)
HUH .... University of Hawaii, Hamilton Library, Honolulu, HI [*OCLC symbol*] (OCLC)
HUI .... Headache Unit Index [*Medicine*] (DMAA)
HUI .... Hue [*South Vietnam*] [*Airport symbol*] (AD)
HUIFM .... Human Leukocyte Interferon Milieu [*Biochemistry*] (DAVI)
HuIFN .... Human Interferon [*Biochemistry*]
HUIS .... High-Dose Urea in Invert Sugar (AAMN)
HUJ .... Hebrew University [*Jerusalem*] (BJA)
HuJCPV .... Human JC Polyomavirus
HUJI .... Jinja [*Uganda*] [*ICAO location identifier*] (ICLI)
HUK .... Human Urinary Kallikrein [*Medicine*] (DMAA)
HUK .... Hungarian-Ukranian Heavy Lift Ltd. [*Hungary ICAO designator*] (FAAC)
HUK .... Hunter-Killer [*Operations against submarines*] [*Navy*]
HUKASWEX... Hunter-Killer Antisubmarine Warfare Exercise [*Navy*] (NVT)

HUKB .... Hostile, Unknown, Faker, and Big Photo [*Used in Semi-Automatic Ground Environment to designate certain tracks and raids*] (SAA)

HUKB .... Kabale [*Uganda*] [*ICAO location identifier*] (ICLI)

HuKeAgE .... Agrartudomanyi Egyetem, Keszthely, Hungary [*Library symbol Library of Congress*] (LCLS)

HUKF .... Kabalega Falls [*Uganda*] [*ICAO location identifier*] (ICLI)

HUKFOR ...... Hunter-Killer Forces [*Navy*]

HUKFORLANT... Hunter-Killer Forces, Atlantic [*Navy*]

HUKFORPAC... Hunter-Killer Forces, Pacific [*Navy*]

HUKP .... Hostile, Unknown, Faker, and Pending [*Used in SAGE to designate certain tracks and raids*]

HUKP .... Hostile, Unknown, Faker, Pending Track Identities [*Used in Semi-Automatic Ground Environment to designate certain tracks and raids*] (SAA)

HUKS .... Hostile, Unknown, Faker, Special Track Identities [*Used in SAGE to designate certain tracks and raids*] (SAA)

HUKS .... Hukbong Mapagpalaya ng Bayan [*People's Liberation Army, Philippines*] (CINC)

HUKS .... Hunter-Killer Submarine [*Navy*]

HUKS .... Kasese [*Uganda*] [*ICAO location identifier*] (ICLI)

HUL .... Hardware Utilization List (NASA)

HUL .... Harvard University, Cambridge, MA [*OCLC symbol*] (OCLC)

HUL .... Home University Library [*A publication*]

HUL .... Houlton [*Maine*] [*Airport symbol*] (OAG)

HUL .... Houlton, ME [*Location identifier FAA*] (FAAL)

Hul .... Hullin (BJA)

HULA .... Lake George [*Uganda*] [*ICAO location identifier*] (ICLI)

HULI .... Lira [*Uganda*] [*ICAO location identifier*] (ICLI)

HULL .... High-Usage Load List (DNAB)

Hull Costs.... Hullock on Costs [*A publication*] (DLA)

Hult Conv.... Hulton's Convictions [*1835*] [*A publication*] (DLA)

HULTEC ...... Hull-to-Emitter Correlation [*Navy*] (CAAL)

HULTIS .... Hull Technical Interloan Scheme [*British*] (NITA)

HUM .... Health and Usage Monitoring (DA)

HUM .... Highly Unusual Methods (ECON)

HUM .... Houma [*Louisiana*] [*Airport symbol*] (OAG)

HUM .... Human (ROG)

HUM .... Humana, Inc. [*NYSE symbol*] (SPSG)

Hum .... Humanist [*A publication*] (BRI)

HUM .... Humanitarian (ROG)

HUM .... Humanities

HUM .... Humble (ROG)

HUM .... Humidity (NASA)

HUM .... Hummingbird Helicopters Maldives (Pvt) Ltd. [*ICAO designator*] (FAAC)

HUM .... Humorous (ADA)

Hum .... Humphrey's Tennessee Supreme Court Reports [*1839-51*] [*A publication*]

HU-M .... University of Hawaii, Leahi Hospital, Hastings H. Walker Medical Library, Honolulu, HI [*Library symbol Library of Congress*] (LCLS)

HUMA .... Mbarara/Obote [*Uganda*] [*ICAO location identifier*] (ICLI)

HUMAN .... Help Us Make a Nation (EA)

Humana .... Humana, Inc. [*Associated Press*] (SAG)

Human Rts J... Human Rights Journal [*A publication*] (DLA)

Human Rts Rev... Human Rights Review [*A publication*] (DLA)

HUMARIS .... Human Materials Resources Information System (DIT)

Humb .... Humble

Humber........ Humberside [*County in England*] (WGA)

Humber de Bou... Humbertus de Bouen [*Authority cited in pre-1607 legal work*] (DSA)

Humbird ...... Hummingbird Communication Industries [*Associated Press*] (SAG)

HUMCAT ...... Humanoid Catalog [*Mutual Unidentified Flying Object Network*]

HUMCF .... Hummingbird Communication Industries [*NASDAQ symbol*] (SAG)

HUMCF .... Hummingbird Communications [*NASDAQ symbol*] (TTSB)

Hume.......... Hume's Court of Session Decisions [*1781-1822*] [*Scotland*] [*A publication*] (DLA)

Hume Com... Hume's Commentaries on Crimes [*Scotland*] [*A publication*] (DLA)

Hume Hist Eng... Hume's History of England [*A publication*] (DLA)

HUMEVAC.... Humanitarian Emergency Evacuation [*Military*] (NVT)

HumGen ...... Human Genome Sciences, Inc. [*Associated Press*] (SAG)

HUMI .... Masindi [*Uganda*] [*ICAO location identifier*] (ICLI)

HUMID........ Hughes Unit Malfunction Isolation Detector

HUMINT....... Human Intelligence [*Spies, double agents, etc.*] [*CIA*] (AFM)

HUMO .... Moroto [*Uganda*] [*ICAO location identifier*] (ICLI)

HUMP .... Humphrey Hospitality Tr Inc. [*NASDAQ symbol*] (TTSB)

HUMP .... Humphrey Hospitality Trust, Inc. [*NASDAQ symbol*] (SAG)

Humph........ Humphrey's Tennessee Reports [*20-30 Tennessee*] [*A publication*] (DLA)

Humph Dist Reg... Humphreys. District Registry Practice and Procedure [*1977*] [*A publication*] (ILCA)

Humph Prec... Humphry's Common Precedents in Conveyancing [*2nd ed.*] [*1882*] [*A publication*] (DLA)

Humphry...... Humphrey Hospitality Trust, Inc. [*Associated Press*] (SAG)

HUMRESMANDET... Human Resources Management Detachment [*Navy*] (DNAB)

HUMRESMANSCOL... Human Resources Management School [*Navy*] (DNAB)

HUMRESMANSCOLDET... Human Resources Management School Detachment [*Navy*] (DNAB)

HumRRO ...... Human Resources Research Office [*George Washington University*]

HumRRO ...... Human Resources Research Organization (EA)

Hum Rts LJ... Human Rights Law Journal [*A publication*] (DLA)

Hum Rts Q.... Human Rights Quarterly [*A publication*] (DLA)

Hum Rts USSR... Human Rights in the Union of Soviet Socialist Republics [*A publication*] (DLA)

HUMS .... Humanitarian Reasons

HUN............ Hualien [*Taiwan*] [*Airport symbol*] (OAG)

HUN............ Hundersingen [*Federal Republic of Germany*] [*Seismograph station code, US Geological Survey*] (SEIS)

HUN............ Hundred (MUGU)

hun............ Hungarian [*MARC language code Library of Congress*] (LCCP)

HUN............ Hungary [*ANSI three-letter standard code*] (CNC)

Hun............ Hun's New York Appellate Division Supreme Court Reports [*A publication*] (DLA)

HUN............ Hunting Business Aviation [*British ICAO designator*] (FAAC)

HUN............ Huntington Resources, Inc. [*Vancouver Stock Exchange symbol*]

HUN............ Hunt Manufacturing Co. [*NYSE symbol*] (SPSG)

HUN............ Hunt Mfg. [*NYSE symbol*] (TTSB)

Hun............ New York Supreme Court Reports [*A publication*] (DLA)

HUNA.......... Namulonge Agrometeorology Station [*Uganda*] [*ICAO location identifier*] (ICLI)

HUND.......... Hundred

HUNDREDSB... Hundredsbarrow [*England*]

HUNG.......... Hungary

Hung.......... Hungary (VRA)

HungB......... Hungarian Broadcasting Corp. [*Associated Press*] (SAG)

HungBd........ Hungarian Broadcasting Corp. [*Associated Press*] (SAG)

HungBrd ...... Hungarian Broadcasting Corp. [*Associated Press*] (SAG)

HUNGF........ Hungerford [*England*]

HUNGN .... Hungarian

HungTel....... Hungarian Telephone and Cable Corp. [*Associated Press*] (SAG)

HungTelc ..... Hungarian Teleconstruction & Cable Corp. [*Associated Press*] (SAG)

Hunt........... Hunter's Torrens Cases [*Canada*] [*A publication*] (DLA)

Hunt........... Hunt's Annuity Cases [*England*] [*A publication*] (DLA)

Hunt Ann Cas... Hunt's Annuity Cases [*England*] [*A publication*] (DLA)

HuntBnk....... Huntington Bankshares [*Associated Press*] (SAG)

Hunt Bound... Hunt's Law of Boundaries and Fences [*A publication*] (DLA)

Hunt Cas...... Hunt's Annuity Cases [*England*] [*A publication*] (DLA)

Huntco........ Huntco, Inc. [*Associated Press*] (SAG)

Hunt Eq....... Hunt's Suit in Equity [*A publication*] (DLA)

Hunter C (CUNY)... Hunter College of The City University of New York (GAGS)

Hunter Rom Law... Hunter on Roman Law [*A publication*] (DLA)

Hunter Suit Eq... Hunter's Proceeding in a Suit in Equity [*A publication*] (DLA)

HUNTEST..... Hunting and Testing [*Apollo*] [*NASA*]

Hunt Fr Conv... Hunt's Fraudulent Conveyances [*2nd ed.*] [*1897*] [*A publication*] (DLA)

hunth .... Hundred Thousand (BARN)

HuntJB........ Hunt [*J.B.*] Transport Services, Inc. [*Associated Press*] (SAG)

Hunt L & T... Hunter's Landlord and Tenant [*Scotland*] [*A publication*] (DLA)

Hunt Mer Mag... Hunt's Merchants' Magazine [*A publication*] (DLA)

HuntMf........ Hunt Manufacturing Co. [*Associated Press*] (SAG)

Hunt Rom L... Hunter on Roman Law [*A publication*] (DLA)

HUNTS......... Huntingdonshire [*County in England*]

Hunt's AC ... Hunt's Annuity Cases [*England*] [*A publication*] (DLA)

Hunt Suit ..... Hunter's Proceeding in a Suit in Equity [*A publication*] (DLA)

Hunt Torrens... Hunter's Torrens Cases [*Canada A publication*] (DLA)

Hunt Tr .... Huntingdon's Trial [*A publication*] (DLA)

Huntwy .... Huntway Partners Ltd. [*Associated Press*] (SAG)

HUO .... Huguenot, NY [*Location identifier FAA*] (FAAL)

HuOSzK....... Orszagos Szechenyi Konyvtar [*National Szechenyi Library*], Budapest, Hungary [*Library symbol Library of Congress*] (LCLS)

HUP .... Hangup

HUP .... Harvard University Press (DGA)

HUP .... Helicopter Utility (Piasecki)

HUP .... Homogenous Uniparental Embryo [*Embryology*]

HUP .... Hospital of the University of Pennsylvania

HUP .... Hospital Utilization Project [*Western Pennsylvania*]

HUP .... Hudspeth, TX [*Location identifier FAA*] (FAAL)

hup .... Hupa [*MARC language code Library of Congress*] (LCCP)

HUP .... Hydrogen Uranyl Phosphate [*Inorganic chemistry*]

HuPaB .... Pannonhalmi Szent Benedek Rend Kozponti Konyvtara, Pannonhalma, Hungary [*Library symbol Library of Congress*] (LCLS)

HUPATS....... Heuristic Paper Trimming System (BUR)

HUPCM........ Hybrid Unidigit Pulse Code Modulation (IAA)

HuPE.......... Pecsi Tudomanyegyetem, Pecs, Hungary [*Library symbol Library of Congress*] (LCLS)

HUPPIE .... Hispanic Urban Professional [*Lifestyle classification*]

HUQ .... Houn [*Libya*] [*Airport symbol*] (OAG)

HUR .... Hardware Usage Report (MCD)

HUR .... Heat Up Rate (IEEE)

HUR .... Homes Using Radio [*Ratings*] (NTCM)

HUR .... Hurn [*England*] [*Airport symbol*] (AD)

HUR .... Hurricane [*Alaska*] [*Seismograph station code, US Geological Survey*] (SEIS)

HUR .... Hydroxyurea [*Antineoplastic drug*] (DAVI)

HUR .... Miami Air Charter [*ICAO designator*] (FAAC)

HURA.......... Health Underserved Rural Areas

HURC.......... Hurco Companies [*NASDAQ symbol*] (TTSB)

HURC.......... Hurco Companies, Inc. [*NASDAQ symbol*] (NQ)

HURCN........ Hurricane

Hurco.......... Hurco Companies, Inc. [*Associated Press*] (SAG)

Hurd F & B... Hurd on the Laws of Freedom and Bondage in the United States [*A publication*] (DLA)

Hurd Hab Cor... Hurd on the Writ of Habeas Corpus [*A publication*] (DLA)

Hurd Pers Lib... Hurd on Personal Liberty [*A publication*] (DLA)

Hurd's Rev St... Hurd's Illinois Revised Statutes [*A publication*] (DLA)

Hurd St........ Hurd's Illinois Statutes [*A publication*] (DLA)

HUREP .... Hurricane Report

HUREVAC .... Hurricane Evacuation (NVT)

HURI........... Harvard Ukrainian Research Institute

HURI........... Hughes Resources, Inc. [*NASDAQ symbol*] (SAG)

HURIDOCS... Human Rights Information and Documentation System (EA)
HURIDOCS... Human Rights International Documentation System (EA)
HURL.......... Hawaii Undersea Research Laboratory [University of Hawaii] [Research center] (RCD)
Hurl & C...... Hurlstone and Coltman's English Exchequer Reports [A publication] (DLA)
Hurl & Colt... Hurlstone and Coltman's English Exchequer Reports [A publication] (DLA)
Hurl & G...... Hurlstone and Gordon's English Exchequer Reports [A publication] (DLA)
Hurl & Gord... Hurlstone and Gordon's English Exchequer Reports [A publication] (DLA)
Hurl & N...... Hurlstone and Norman's English Exchequer Reports [156, 158 English Reprint] [A publication] (DLA)
Hurl & Nor... Hurlstone and Norman's English Exchequer Reports [156, 158 English Reprint] [A publication] (DLA)
Hurl & W..... Hurlstone and Walmsley's English Exchequer Reports [1840-41] [A publication] (DLA)
Hurl & Walm... Hurlstone and Walmsley's English Exchequer Reports [1840-41] [A publication] (DLA)
Hurl Bonds... Hurlstone on Bonds [A publication] (DLA)
Hurl Colt...... Hurlstone and Coltman's English Exchequer Reports [A publication] (DLA)
Hurls & W (Eng)... Hurlstone and Walmsley's English Exchequer Reports [1840-41] [A publication] (DLA)
Hurlst & C ... Hurlstone and Coltman's English Exchequer Reports [A publication] (DLA)
Hurlst & C (Eng)... Hurlstone and Coltman's English Exchequer Reports [A publication] (DLA)
Hurlst & G ... Hurlstone and Gordon's English Exchequer Reports [A publication] (DLA)
Hurlst & N (Eng)... Hurlstone and Norman's English Exchequer Reports [156, 158 English Reprint] [A publication] (DLA)
Hurlst & W ... Hurlstone and Walmsley's English Exchequer Reports [1840-41] [A publication] (DLA)
Hurr .... Hurrian (BJA)
HURRA .... Housing and Urban-Rural Recovery Act of 1983
HURRAH ...... Help Us Reach and Rehabilitate America's Handicapped [State-Federal rehabilitation program]
HURRAN....... Hurricane Analog
HURRAO....... Human Use Review and Regulatory Affairs Office [Army] (RDA)
HURR-EVAC... Hurricane Evacuation (DNAB)
HURT .... HealthRite, Inc. [NASDAQ symbol] (SAG)
HUS .... Helicopter Utility Squadron
HUS .... Hemolytic-Uremic Syndrome [Nephrology]
HUS .... Heussler Air Service Corp. [ICAO designator] (FAAC)
HUS .... Hughes [Alaska] [Airport symbol] (OAG)
HUS .... Husband [Legal shorthand] (LWAP)
HUS .... Hyaluronidase Unit for Semen (MAE)
HUSAFICPA... Headquarters, United States Army Forces, Central Pacific Area
HUSAFMIDPAC... Headquarters, United States Army Forces, Middle Pacific [World War II]
HUSAT .... Human Sciences Advanced Technology Unit [Longborough University] [British]
HUSAT .... Human Sciences and Advanced Technology Research Centre [University of Technology] [British] (CB)
husb............. Husband
HUSB .... Husbandry
HUSB & W... Husband and Wife (DLA)
HUSBD......... Husband (ROG)
Husb For Med... Husband's Forensic Medicine [A publication] (DLA)
Husb Mar Wom... Husband on Married Women [A publication] (DLA)
HUSBN......... Husbandman
HUSICON ..... Humanities, Science, and Conservation [Environment]
HUSO........... Soroti [Uganda] [ICAO location identifier] (ICLI)
HuSpK .... Sarospataki Reformatus Kollegium Nagykonyvtara, Sarospatak, Hungary [Library symbol Library of Congress] (LCLS)
HUSS........... Hussars [Military unit] [British] (ROG)
Hust .... Hustings Court [As in Virginia] [Legal term] (DLA)
HUSTLE ...... Helium Underwater Speech Translating Equipment
Hust L Tit ... Huston on Land Titles in Pennsylvania [A publication] (DLA)
HuSzOE....... Szegedi Orvostudomanyi Egyetem, Szeged, Hungary [Library symbol Library of Congress] (LCLS)
HUT .... Hard Upper Torso (MCD)
HUT .... HEDL [Hanford Engineering Development Laboratory] Up Transient [Nuclear energy] (NRCH)
HUT .... Held-Up Transient (IAA)
HUT .... Helsinki University of Technology
HUT .... High-Usage Intertoll Trunk [Data communication] (MHDI)
HUT .... Hold Up Tank (IEEE)
HUT .... Homes Using Television [Television ratings]
HUT .... Hopkins Ultraviolet Telescope
HUT .... Households Using Television [Television ratings]
HUT .... Humboldt Energy [Vancouver Stock Exchange symbol]
HUT .... Hutchinson [Kansas] [Airport symbol] (OAG)
Hut.............. Hutton's English Common Pleas Reports [1612-39] [A publication] (DLA)
HUTCH......... Humidity-Temperature Chart (PDAA)
Hutch .... Hutcheson's Reports [81-84 Alabama] [A publication] (DLA)
Hutch Car ... Hutchinson on Carriers [A publication] (DLA)
Hutch Carr... Hutchinson on Carriers [A publication] (DLA)
Hutch Code... Hutchinson's Code [Mississippi] [A publication] (DLA)
Hutch JP..... Hutcheson's Justice of the Peace [A publication] (DLA)
HutchT........ Hutchinson Technology, Inc. [Associated Press] (SAG)
Hut Ct Req... Hutton's Courts of Requests [A publication] (DLA)

HUTHAS...... Human Thymus Anti-Serum [Medicine] (MAE)
HUTO .... Tororo [Uganda] [ICAO location identifier] (ICLI)
HUTR .... Hubbell Trading Post National Historic Site
HUTRON ...... Helicopter Utility Squadron
HUTSAT ...... Helsinki University of Technology Satellite
Hutt............. Hutton's English Common Pleas Reports [1612-39] [A publication] (DLA)
Hutt Ct Req... Hutton's Courts of Requests [A publication] (DLA)
Hutton.......... Hutton's English Common Pleas Reports [1612-39] [A publication] (DLA)
Hutton (Eng)... Hutton's English Common Pleas Reports [1612-39] [A publication] (DLA)
HUU .... Detroit, MI [Location identifier FAA] (FAAL)
HUU .... Huanuco [Peru] [Airport symbol] (OAG)
HUV .... Hudiksvall [Sweden] [Airport symbol] (OAG)
HUV .... Human Umbilical Vein [Medicine] (DMAA)
HUVE .... Human Umbilical Vein Endothelial
HUVEC .... Human Umbilical Vein Endothelial Cell [Cytology]
HUX .... Harvard University [Cambridge, MA]
HUX .... Sacramento, CA [Location identifier FAA] (FAAL)
Hux Judg ..... Huxley's Second Book of Judgments [1675] [England] [A publication] (DLA)
HUY .... Hull [England] [Airport symbol] (AD)
HUY .... Humberside [England] [Airport symbol] (OAG)
HUZ .... Huaraz [Peru] [Seismograph station code, US Geological Survey] (SEIS)
HUZ .... Mesquite, TX [Location identifier FAA] (FAAL)
HUzT........... Hermeneutische Untersuchungen zur Theologie [Tuebingen] [A publication] (BJA)
HV............... Air Central [ICAO designator] (AD)
HV............... Air-Cushion Vehicle built by Hover Vehicles [New Zealand] [Usually used in combination with numerals]
HV............... Boeing-Vertol Division [The Boeing Co.] [ICAO aircraft manufacturer identifier] (ICAO)
HV............... Hallux Valgus [Orthopedics] (DAVI)
HV............... Hand Valve [Nuclear energy] (NRCH)
HV............... Hard Valve (DEN)
HV............... Hardware Virtualizer [Computer science] (IEEE)
HV............... Haricots Verts [Green Beans] [French]
HV............... Has Voided [Medicine] (DAVI)
HV............... Health Visitor
HV............... Heater Voltage
HV............... Heating and Ventilation (AAG)
HV............... Heat of Vaporization (ROG)
HV............... Heavy (AABC)
hv............... Heavy (VRA)
H-V............. Height-Velocity
HV............... Helminthosporium victoriae [A toxin-producing fungus]
HV............... Hepatic Vein [Anatomy]
HV............... Herpesvirus
HV............... Hic Verbis [In These Words] [Latin]
HV............... High in Volatiles [Commercial grading]
HV............... Highly Variegated Maize
HV............... High Vacuum (ADA)
HV............... High Velocity
HV............... High Visibility (DS)
HV............... High Voltage
HV............... High Volume
HV............... Hoc Verbum [This Word] [Latin]
HV............... HomeVideo [Videocassette tape] (NTCM)
HV............... Home Video [Television]
HV............... Horizontal-Vertical Intersection [Lighting] [Automotive engineering]
HV............... Hospital Visit (AAMN)
HV............... Hyaline-Vascular [Oncology]
HV............... Hydrogen Vent (MCD)
HV............... Hydroxyl Value [Analytical chemistry]
HV............... Hypervariable
HV............... Hypervelocity (AABC)
HV............... Hyperventilation
HV............... Vatican [International civil aircraft marking] (ODBW)
HV............... Vickers Hardness Number [Also, VH, VHN]
HV6............. Heracleum Virus 6 [Plant pathology]
HVA .... Analalava [Madagascar] [Airport symbol] (OAG)
HVA .... Health Visitors' Association [A union] [British] (DCTA)
HVA .... Heeresverwaltungsamt [Army Administration Office] [German military - World War II]
HVA .... Herpesvirus Ateles
HVA .... High-Velocity Anomaly [Seismology]
HVA .... High-Voltage-Activated [Neurochemistry]
HVA .... Homovanillic Acid [Biochemistry]
HVA .... Methoxy-Hydroxyphenylacetic Acid [Chemistry] (DAVI)
HVA .... Newair, Inc. [ICAO designator] (FAAC)
HVAA .... High-Value Airborne Assets (DOMA)
HVAC .... Heating, Ventilating, and Air Conditioning
HVAC .... Heating, Ventilation, Air Conditioning [Marine science] (OSRA)
HVAC .... High Vacuum (IEEE)
HVAC .... High-Voltage Actuator [Electronics] (IEEE)
HVAC .... High-Voltage Alternating Current
HVAC .... House Veterans' Affairs Committee [House of Representatives]
HVACC........ High-Voltage Apparatus Coordinating Committee [ANSI]
HVAF .... High-Velocity Air Filter (EG)
H vag.......... Hemophilus Vaginalis [Gynecology] (DAVI)
HV & C .... Heating, Ventilating, and Cooling (AAG)
HVAP.......... High-Velocity, Armor-Piercing [Projectile]
HVAPDS....... High-Velocity, Armor-Piercing, Discarding Sabot [Projectile]

HVAPDS....... Hypervelocity, Armor-Piercing, Discarding Sabot Projectile [Army] (SAA)

HVAPDSFS... High-Velocity, Armor-Piercing, Discarding Sabot, Fin Stabilized [Projectile] (MCD)

HVAPDSFS... Hypervelocity, Armor-Piercing, Discarding Sabot, Fin Stabilized Projectile [Army] (SAA)

HVAPFSDS... High-Velocity, Armor-Piercing, Fin Stabilized, Discarding Sabot [Projectile] (MCD)

HVAP-T........ Hypervelocity, Armor-Piercing - Tracer [Projectile] (AABC)

HVAR.......... High-Velocity Aircraft Rocket

HVAR(HE).... High-Velocity Aircraft Rocket (High Explosive) (DNAB)

HVAS.......... Hydraulic Valve Adjuster System [Automotive engineering]

HVAT.......... High-Velocity Antitank [Projectile]

HVATKRON... Heavy Attack Squadron (DNAB)

HVB .... Hauptverbandplatz [Clearing Station] [German military - World War II]

HVB .... Hervey Bay [Australia Airport symbol] (OAG)

HVB .... High-Voltage Bias

HVC .... Hardened Voice Channel [NASA] (KSC)

HVC .... Hardened Voice Circuit (CET)

HVC .... Haverford College, Haverford, PA [OCLC symbol] (OCLC)

HVC .... Hav-Info Computers, Inc. [Vancouver Stock Exchange symbol]

HVC .... Hayden's Viburnum Compound [Medicine]

HVC .... Health Visitor's Certificate [British]

HVC .... Hernandez Valley [California] [Seismograph station code, US Geological Survey] (SEIS)

HVC .... High-Velocity Cloud [Astronomy] (OA)

HVC .... High Vocal Center [Songbird anatomy]

HVC .... High-Voltage Connector

HVC .... High-Voltage Control

HVC .... Hopkinsville, KY [Location identifier FAA] (FAAL)

HVc .... Hyperstriatum Ventralis Pars Caudalis [Bird brain anatomy]

HVc .... Ventral Hyperstriatum Caudal Nucleus [Neuroanatomy]

HVCA .... Heating and Ventilating Contractors' Association [British]

HVCC .... Hairy Vetch as a Cover Crop [Agriculture]

HVCE .... High-Voltage Capillary Electrophoresis

HVCH .... Hardened Voice Channel (MSA)

HVCMOS...... High Voltage CMOS [Complementary Metal Oxide Semiconductor] (NITA)

HVCS .... High-Vacuum Calibration System (PDAA)

HVD .... Half-Value Depth (IAA)

HVD .... Heaters, Vents, and Drains [System] [Nuclear energy] (NRCH)

HVD .... Height-Velocity Diagram

HVD .... Hendrik Verwoerd Dam [South Africa] [Seismograph station code, US Geological Survey] (SEIS)

HVD .... High-Velocity Detonation

HVD .... High-Viscosity Dispenser [Packaging]

HVD .... Hydroviscous Drive (DNAB)

HVD .... Hypertensive Vascular Disease [Medicine]

HVDC .... High-Voltage Direct Current

HVDCT........ High-Voltage Direct-Current Transmission [Electronics]

HVDF .... High- and Very-High-Frequency Direction Finding

HVDP .... Heavy Drop [Military] (AABC)

HVDRR .... Hypocalcemic Vitamin D-Resistant Rickets [Medicine]

HVDS .... Hypergolic Vapor Detection System [NASA] (NASA)

HVE .... Hanksville, UT [Location identifier FAA] (FAAL)

HVE .... Hepatic Vascular Exclusion [Medicine] (MEDA)

HVE .... High-Vacuum Environment

HVE .... High-Vacuum Evaporator

HVE .... High-Voltage Electrophoresis (AAMN)

HVE .... Horizontal Vertex Error (OA)

HVEC .... High Voltage Engineering Corp.

HVEC .... Human Vascular Endothelial Cells

HVEF .... Harvest Financial Corp. [NASDAQ symbol] (SAG)

HVEL.......... Hypervelocity

HVEM.......... High-Voltage Electron Microscopy

HVES .... High-Vacuum Evaporation System

HVES .... High-Voltage Electrical Stimulation [Meat treatment]

HVF .... Harmonically Varying Field

HVF .... Haverford College, Haverford, PA [OCLC symbol] (OCLC)

HVF .... High-Viscosity Fuel Oil (DCTA)

HVFB .... High-Velocity Fluidized Bed [Chemical engineering]

HVFD .... Haverfield Corp. [NASDAQ symbol] (NQ)

HVFS .... High-Vacuum Flame Sterilization [Food technology]

HVG .... High-Voltage Generator

HVG .... High-Voltage Gradient

HVG .... Honningsvag [Norway] [Airport symbol] (OAG)

HVG .... Host Versus Graft [Medicine]

HVG .... Hypervelocity Gun [Military] (SDI)

HVGL .... High Velocity Grenade Launcher [Projectile] (PDAA)

HVGLS........ High-Velocity Grenade Launcher System [Projectile] (MCD)

HVGO.......... Hanover Gold [NASDAQ symbol] (TTSB)

HVGO.......... Hanover Gold Company, Inc. [NASDAQ symbol] (SAG)

HVGO.......... Heavy Vacuum Gas Oil [Petroleum product]

HVH .... Herpesvirus Hominis

HVH .... Hydrogen Vent Header [Nuclear energy] (NRCH)

HVHA .... High-Velocity Hot-Air [Oven]

HVHAI.......... High-Velocity Hot-Air Impingement [Organic chemistry]

HVHD .... High-Voltage-Hold-Down (PDAA)

HVHF .... High and Very-High Frequency (IAA)

HVHMA........ Herpesvirus Hominis Membrane Antigen [Medicine] (MEDA)

HVHMD........ Holographic Visor Helmet-Mounted Display [Air Force]

HVI............. Hartman Value Inventory [Psychology]

HVI............. Hepatic Volumetric Index

HVI............. High-Value Item (NATG)

HVI............. High Viscosity Index (IAA)

HVI............. High Viscosity Index [Lubricants]

HVI............. High-Volume Instrument [Agricultural research]

HVI............. Home Ventilating Institute [Later, HVIDAMCA] (EA)

HVI............. Horizon Village [Vancouver Stock Exchange symbol]

HVIC .... High-Voltage Integrated Circuit [Computer science]

HVIDAMCA... Home Ventilating Institute Division of the Air Movement Control Association (EA)

HVideM....... Hvide Marine, Inc. [Associated Press] (SAG)

HVIO .... High-Volume Industrial Organics [Environmental science] (GFGA)

HVIRS........ Hull Vibration Information Retrieval System (PDAA)

HVIT........... High-Volume Information Transfer

HVJ........... Hemagglutinating Virus of Japan [Medicine]

HVK........... Holmavik [Iceland] [Airport symbol] (OAG)

HVK........... Hovik Medical [Vancouver Stock Exchange symbol]

HVL........... Half-Value Layer [Radiology]

HVL........... Heeresverpflegungslager [Army Ration Depot] [German military - World War II]

HVL........... Highly Volatile Liquid (TAG)

HVL........... High Voltage Laboratory [MIT] (MCD)

HVL........... Hypervelocity Launcher [Military] (SDI)

HVLP .... High-Velocity, Low Penetration Paint

HVLP .... High-Volume Low-Pressure [Spray-painting process]

HVLS .... Huron Valley Library System [Library network]

HVM .... Heterodyne Vegetation Meter (IAA)

HVM .... High Velocity Metalworking (PDAA)

HVM .... High-Velocity Missile [Military] (DAVI)

HVM .... High-Voltage Mode

HVM .... Hydraulic Valve Motor

HVM .... Hypervelocity Missile

HVM .... Hypervelocity Munition

HVM .... Sisters, Home Visitors of Mary [Roman Catholic religious order]

HVMC .... High-Variation Medical Condition

HVMS .... Hypervelocity, Medium Support

HVMVI........ High-Voltage Mercury-Vapor Isolator

HVN .... Hang Khong Viet Nam [ICAO designator] (FAAC)

HVN .... Havana [Cuba] [Geomagnetic observatory code]

HVN .... Haven (MCD)

HVN .... Haven

HVN .... Home View Network [Cable-television system]

HVN .... New Haven [Connecticut] [Airport symbol] (OAG)

HVO .... Hawaiian Volcano Observatory [Kilauea] [Hawaii] [Seismograph station code, US Geological Survey] (SEIS)

HVO .... Health Volunteers Overseas (EA)

HVOC .... Halogenated Volatile Organic Compound

HVOF .... High-Velocity Oxygen/Fuel [Coating technology]

HVOSM........ Highway Vehicle Object Simulation Model [Computer-aided design] [Automotive engineering]

HVOT .... Hooper Visual Organization Test [Psychology]

HVP .... Half-Value Period

HVP .... Hardware Verification Program (CAAL)

HVP .... Hartman Value Profile [Personality development test] [Psychology]

HVP .... Hayes Verification Protocol [Computer science]

HVP .... Heart Valve Prostheses [Medicine]

HVP .... High-Vacuum Pump

HVP .... High-Value Product

HVP .... High Video Pass (NVT)

HVP .... High-Voltage Potential (IAA)

HVP .... High-Voltage Pump

HVP .... Host Vehicle Pallet

HVP .... Hydrolyzed Vegetable Protein [Food additive]

HVPE .... High-Voltage Paper Electrophoresis

HVPE .... Hydride Vapor Phase Epitaxy [Crystallography]

HVPF .... Human Vascular Permeability Factor [Biochemistry]

HVPG .... Hepatic Venous Pressure Gradient [Medicine]

HVPHOTORON... Heavy Photographic Squadron (DNAB)

HVPI .... High-Voltage Plasma Interaction (SSD)

HVPI .... Holland Vocational Preference Inventory [Psychology]

HVPR .... High-Voltage Phase Retard

HVPS .... High-Voltage Power Supply

HVPS .... High-Volume Printing System [Computer science]

HVPVE........ High-Voltage Photovoltaic Effect [Physics]

HVR .... Hardware Vector to Raster

HVR .... Havre [Montana] [Airport symbol] (OAG)

HVR .... Helicopter Visual Rules

HVR .... Highland Valley Resources Ltd. [Vancouver Stock Exchange symbol]

HVR .... Highly Variable Regions [Of chromosomes] [Genetics]

HVR .... High-Resolution Visible Range

HVR .... High-Vacuum Rectifier

HVR .... High-Voltage Rectifier

HVR .... High-Voltage Regulator (MSA)

HVR .... High-Voltage Relay

HVR .... High-Voltage Resistor

HVR .... Home Video Recorder (NTCM)

HVR .... Hover (MCD)

HVR .... Hyderabad Volunteer Rifles [British military] (DMA)

HVR .... Hypervariable Region [Genetics]

HVR .... Hypoxic Ventilatory Response [Medicine]

HVRA .... Heating and Ventilating Research Association [British]

HVRAP........ Hyper-Velocity Rocket-Assisted Projectile (PDAA)

HVRL .... High Voltage Research Laboratory [MIT] (MCD)

HVRNG........ Hovering

HVS .... Hartsville, SC [Location identifier FAA] (FAAL)

HVS .... Herpesvirus of Saimiri

HVS .... High-Voltage Switch

HVS .... Hue, Value, Saturation [*Graphic arts*] (WDMC)
HVS .... Human Vaginal Swab [*Medicine*]
HVS .... Human Visual System
HVS .... Hypersonic Vehicle Shield
HVSA .... High-Voltage Solar Array
HVSCR......... High-Voltage Selenium Cartridge Rectifier
HVSD .... Hydrogen-Detected Ventricular Septal Defect [*Medicine*] (MAE)
HVSE .... High-Voltage Solar Experiment
HVSF .... High Velocity Sheet Forming (PDAA)
HVSF .... Honeywell Verification Simulation Facility (NASA)
HVSL .... Holidays, Vacation, and Sick Leave (NASA)
hVSMC........ Human Vascular Smooth Muscle Cell [*Biology*]
HVSP .... High-Voltage Solar Panel
HVSS .... Horizontal Volute Spring Suspension [*Projectile*]
HVST .... High-Voltage Switching Transistor
HVSU .... Heating Ventilating Supply Unit (NRCH)
HVT............. Half-Value Thickness
HVT............. Hidden Variable Theory [*Physics*]
HVT............. High-Value Target (NVT)
HVT............. High-Voltage Termination
HVT............. High-Voltage Tester
HVT............. High-Voltage Threshold (IAA)
HVT............. High-Voltage Transformer
HVT............. Hydraulic Variable-Valve Train [*Automotive engine design*]
HVTB .... High-Voltage Thermal Battery (DNAB)
HVTP .... High-Velocity, Target-Practice [*Projectile*]
HVTP .... Hypervelocity, Target-Practice [*Projectile*]
HVTPDS...... High-Velocity, Target-Practice, Discarding Sabot [*Projectile*]
HVTP-T .... Hypervelocity, Target-Practice - Tracer [*Projectile*] (AABC)
HVTR .... Home Videotape Recorder (IAA)
HVTS .... High-Volume Time Sharing [*Computer science*]
HVU .... Altus, OK [*Location identifier FAA*] (FAAL)
HVU .... Hansel Valley [*Utah*] [*Seismograph station code, US Geological Survey*] (SEIS)
HVU .... Heating Ventilation Unit (MCD)
HVU .... High-Value Unit [*Torpedo defense system*] (MCD)
HVUCAP...... High-Value Unit Combat Air Patrol [*Navy*] (DOMA)
HVV .... Helium Vent Valve (MCD)
HVW .... High-Voltage Waveform
HVW .... High-Voltage Wire
HVWP......... Hospitalized Veterans Writing Project (EA)
HVWS .... Hebrew Veterans of the War with Spain (EA)
HVY .... Happy Valley, AK [*Location identifier FAA*] (FAAL)
HVY .... Harveys Casinos Resorts [*NYSE symbol*] (SAG)
HVY .... Heavy (AFM)
HVY .... Heavy
HW .... Hairy Woodpecker [*Ornithology*]
HW .... Half Wave
HW .... Half Word (CET)
HW .... Handset, Wall Model (TEL)
HW .... Handwritten (BJA)
HW .... Hardware [*Computer science*] (NASA)
H/W .... Hardware [*Computer science*] (EERA)
HW .... Hard Wired (NITA)
HW .... Hardwood
HW .... Hardy-Weinberg Equilibrium [*of genes*] [*Also, HWE*]
HW .... Hauptwachtmeister [*First Sergeant*] [*German military - World War II*]
HW .... Hauptwerk [*Masterpiece*] [*German*]
HW .... Havasu Airlines [*ICAO designator*] (AD)
HW .... Hazardous Waste (GFGA)
HW .... Headwaiter
HW .... Head Wardmaster [*Navy British*] (ROG)
HW .... Head Width
HW .... Head Wind [*Navigation*]
HW .... Healing Well (DMAA)
HW .... Heavy Wall
HW .... Heavy Water
HW .... Heavy Weapons [*British military*] (DMA)
HW .... Heparin Well [*Pharmacology*] (DAVI)
HW .... Herewith [*Enclosures*] [*Navy*]
HW .... Hethitisches Woerterbuch [*Heidelberg*] [*A publication*] (BJA)
HW .... High Water [*Tides and currents*]
H/W .... Highway
HW .... High Wing [*Aviation*] (AIA)
HW .... Hispanic Writers [*A publication*]
HW .... Hit Wicket
HW .... Homing Weapons (NVT)
HW .... Hot Water
HW .... Hotwell [*Nuclear energy*] (NRCH)
HW .... Hot Wire (KSC)
HW .... Housewife
HW .... How (WGA)
HW .... Howard Aero Manufacturing [*ICAO aircraft manufacturer identifier*] (ICAO)
HW .... Howler [*Communications; electronics*]
HW .... Hunter-Wheel
HW .... North-Wright Air Ltd. [*ICAO designator*] (AD)
HWA .... Hallman, W. A., St. Paul MN [*STAC*]
HWA .... Handwritten by Amanuensis (BJA)
HWA .... Hawa-Air [*Belgium ICAO designator*] (FAAC)
HWA .... Holloway White Allom [*Building contractor*] [*British*]
HWA .... Hops Warehousing Association [*British*] (BI)
HWA .... Horror Writers of America [*An association*]
HWA .... Hot Wire Anemometer

HWA .... Hwalien [*Karenko*] [*Republic of China*] [*Seismograph station code, US Geological Survey*] (SEIS)
HWAA.......... Heereswaffenamt [*Army Ordnance Office*] [*German military - World War II*]
HWAAP........ Hawthorne Army Ammunition Plant (AABC)
HWADM........ Hypersonic Wide-Area Defense Missile (MCD)
HWAI .... Horseback Writers and Artists, International (EA)
HWAIFC....... Hank Williams Appreciation International Fan Club (EA)
HWAL .... Holland West-Afrika Line [*Steamship*] (MHDB)
HWAY .... Highway [*Commonly used*] (OPSA)
HWB .... Handwoerterbuch [*Pocket Dictionary*] [*German*]
HWB .... Hot Water Boiler [*on a ship*] (DS)
hwb .... Hot Water Bottle
HWB .... Hot Weather Boot [*Military*] (INF)
HWBC .... Hartford Whalers Booster Club (EA)
HWBDU........ Hot Weather Battle Dress Uniform [*Army*] (INF)
HWBF .... High-Water-Based Fluid [*Hydraulic and cutting fluids*]
HWBI .... Handwoerterbuch des Islam [*Leiden*] [*A publication*] (BJA)
HWBR .... Half-Wave Bridge Rectifier
HWBTA .... Home Wine and Beer Trade Association (EA)
HWC .... Health and Welfare Canada
HWC .... Hot Water Circulating [*Technical drawings*]
HWC .... Hurricane Warning Center (USDC)
HWC .... Hurricane Warning Center [*Marine science*] (OSRA)
HWCA .... Housing of Working Classes Act [*British*] (ROG)
HWCC .... Harpoon Weapon Control Console [*Missiles*] (MCD)
HWCC .... Hollywood Casino 'A' [*NASDAQ symbol*] (TTSB)
HWCC .... Hollywood Casino Corp. [*NASDAQ symbol*] (SAG)
HWCF .... High-Water-Content Fluid [*Nonpetroleum lubricant*]
HWCF .... High Water Content Fluid [*Hydraulics*]
HWCI .... Hardware Configuration Item
HWCR .... Higher Worth Control Rod [*Nuclear energy*] (NUCP)
HWCS .... Helicopter Wire Cutter System (MCD)
HWCTR .... Heavy-Water Components Test Reactor [*Nuclear energy*]
HWCU .... Heated Window Control Unit
HWD .... Hardwood [*Technical drawings*]
HWD .... Hayward, CA [*Location identifier FAA*] (FAAL)
HWD .... Hazardous Waste Disposal
HWD .... Heartworm Disease (DMAA)
HWD .... Highwood Resources Ltd. [*Toronto Stock Exchange symbol*]
HWD .... Hill/Wendover/Dugway [*Ranges*] [*Military*] (MCD)
HWD .... Horizontal Weather Depiction
HWD .... Hot Wire Detector [*Analytical instrumentation*]
HWDMS........ Hazardous Waste Data [*or Disposal*] Management System [*Environmental Protection Agency*]
HWDYKY...... How Well Do You Know Yourself [*Psychological testing*]
HWE .... East West Center, Honolulu, HI [*OCLC symbol*] (OCLC)
HWE .... Hardy-Weinberg Equilibrium [*of genes*] [*Also, HW*]
HWE .... Hardy-Weinberg Expectation [*Genetics*]
HWE .... Healthy Worker Effect (DMAA)
HWE .... Hot Water Extract (DMAA)
HWEC .... Hallwood Energy Corp. [*NASDAQ symbol*] (NQ)
HWED .... Hazardous Waste Enforcement Division [*Environmental Protection Agency*] (EPA)
HWEP .... Hot Wire Emissive Probe
HWERL .... Hazardous Waste Engineering Research Laboratory [*Cincinnati, OH*] [*Environmental Protection Agency*] (GRD)
HWF .... Aberdeen/Amory, MS [*Location identifier FAA*] (FAAL)
HWF .... Hazardous Waste Federation (EA)
HWF & C ..... High-Water Full and Change [*Tides and currents*]
HWFET........ Highway Fuel Economy Test [*Environmental Protection Agency*]
HW-FW .... Half Wave - Full Wave (EPA)
HWG .... Hallwood Group [*NYSE symbol*] (TTSB)
HWG .... Hallwood Group, Inc. [*NYSE symbol*] (SPSG)
HWG .... House Wednesday Group (EA)
HWGCR .... Heavy-Water Moderated Gas-Cooled Reactor [*Nuclear energy*]
HWGTF .... Hazardous Waste Groundwater Task Force [*Environmental Protection Agency*] (GFGA)
HWGW........ Hiram Walker - Gooderham & Worts [*Canada*]
HWH............. Hot Water Heater (MSA)
HWHH.......... Half-Width at Half-Height (PDAA)
HWI .... Hardware Interpreter
HWI .... Hardware Wholesalers, Inc.
HWI .... Hawk Inlet, AK [*Location identifier FAA*] (FAAL)
HWI .... Hawkwatch International (EA)
HWI .... Head Width Index
HWI .... Helical Washer Institute [*Defunct*] (EA)
HWI .... High-Water Interval
HWIL .... Hardware-in-the-Loop
HWIM .... Hear What I Mean [*Speech recognition system*]
HWIN .... Hot Water-Insoluble Nitrogen [*Analytical chemistry*]
HWIR .... Hazardous Waste Indentification Rule [*Environmental Protection Agency*]
HWJFC........ Hank Williams Jr. Fan Club (EA)
HWK .... Hawker [*Australia Airport symbol*] (OAG)
HWK .... Hawk Resources, Inc. [*Vancouver Stock Exchange symbol*]
HWK .... Kaufman [*H. W.*] Financial Group, Inc. [*AMEX symbol*] (SPSG)
HWK .... Swazi Air Charter (Pty) Ltd. [*Swaziland*] [*ICAO designator*] (FAAC)
HWKB .... Hawkeye Bancorp [*NASDAQ symbol*] (NQ)
HwkEn......... Hawkins Energy Corp. [*Associated Press*] (SAG)
HWKN .... Hawkins Chemical [*NASDAQ symbol*] (TTSB)
HWKN .... Hawkins Chemical, Inc. [*NASDAQ symbol*] (NQ)
HWL .... Harvey Woods Ltd. [*Toronto Stock Exchange symbol*]
HWL .... Hauptwiderstandslinie [*Main line of resistance in a delaying action*] [*German military - World War II*]

HWL............ Henry Wadsworth Longfellow [*Initials used as pseudonym*]
HWL............ High-Water Line [*Technical drawings*]
HWL............ Historic World Leaders [*A publication*]
HWL............ Hot Water Line (AAG)
HWL............ Hotwell
HWL............ Howell Corp. [*NYSE symbol*] (SPSG)
HWLC......... Harold Washington Library Center [*Chicago Public Library*]
HWLC......... Hotwell Level Control [*System*] [*Nuclear energy*] (NRCH)
HWLI.......... High-Water Lunitidal Interval
HWLL.......... Howell Corp. [*NASDAQ symbol*] (SAG)
HWLLP .... Howell Corp.$3.50 Cv'A'Pfd [*NASDAQ symbol*] (TTSB)
HWLS.......... Hostile Weapons Locating System (MCD)
HWLT.......... Hazardous Waste Land Treatment (GNE)
HWLWR....... Heavy-Water-Moderated, Boiling Light-Water-Cooled Reactor [*Nuclear energy*] (NRCH)
HWM........... Hazardous Waste Management
HWM........... Hersham & Walton Motors [*British specialty car maker*]
HWM........... High Molecular Weight
HWM........... High-Water Mark [*Maps and charts*]
HWM........... High Wet Modulus [*Test for rayon*]
HWM........... Hot-Water-Cure Mortar (PDAA)
HWM........... Maui County Free Library, Wailuku, HI [*Library symbol Library of Congress*] (LCLS)
HWMA .... Hazardous Waste Management Association
HWMC........ House Ways and Means Committee
HWMD........ Hazardous Waste Management Division [*Environmental Protection Agency*] (GFGA)
HWMF .... Hazardous Waste Management Facility
HWMP .... Hazardous Waste Management Plan
HWMR .... Heavy Water Moderated Reactor [*Nuclear energy*] (NUCP)
HWN........... Haldwani [*India*] [*Airport symbol*] (AD)
HWN........... Hazard Warning Network
HWN........... High-Water Neaps
HWN........... Honolulu, HI [*Location identifier FAA*] (FAAL)
HWNA......... Hosiery Wholesalers National Association (EA)
HWO .... Hollywood, FL [*Location identifier FAA*] (FAAL)
HWO .... Homosexual World Organization
HWO .... Hot Water Oxidizer (PDAA)
HWO .... Hurricane Warning Office [*National Weather Service*]
HWOCR....... Heavy-Water Moderated Organic-Cooled Reactor [*Nuclear energy*]
HWOST........ High-Water Ordinary Spring Tides [*Maps and charts*]
HWP .... Half-Wave Plate
HWP .... Hardware Work Package (MCD)
HWP .... Harmonic Wire Projector (IAA)
HWP .... Heavy-Water Plant [*Nuclear energy*]
HWP .... Hewlett-Packard [*NYSE symbol*] (TTSB)
HWP .... Hewlett-Packard Co. [*NYSE symbol*] (SPSG)
HWP .... Hours Waiting Parts (MCD)
HWP .... Hungarian Workers' Party [*Political party*] (PPW)
HWPB .... Heavy Weather Patrol Boats (CINC)
HWPC......... Hollywood Women's Political Committee (EA)
HWQ .... Hansard Written Questions [*Database*] [*House of Commons*] [*Canada*] [*Information service or system*] (CRD)
HWQ .... Harlowton, MT [*Location identifier FAA*] (FAAL)
HWQ .... High-Water Quadrature
HWR .... Half-Wave Rectifier
HWR .... Heavy-Water Reactor [*Nuclear energy*]
HWR .... Hot Water Return
HWR .... Walker [*Hiram*] Resources Ltd. [*Toronto Stock Exchange symbol Vancouver Stock Exchange symbol*] (SPSG)
HWRC......... Hazardous Waste Research Center [*Louisiana State University*] [*Research center*] (RCD)
HWRC......... Hot-Water Recirculation (DAC)
HWRTF .... Hazardous Waste Restrictions Task Force (GNE)
HWS .... Hanford Works Standard [*or Specification*] [*Later, HPS*] [*Nuclear energy*] (NRCH)
HWS .... Harassment Weapon System (MCD)
HWS .... Harpoon Weapons System (NVT)
HWS .... Helicopter Weapons System
HWS .... High Water of Spring Tide
HWS .... Hot Water Soluble
HWS .... Hurricane Warning System (WDAA)
HWSA......... Hazardous Waste Services Association [*Defunct*] (EA)
HWSS .... Hazardous Waste and Superfund Staff [*Environmental Protection Agency*] (GFGA)
HWSSG........ Heavy Weapons Special Study Group [*Military*] (MCD)
HWSTD .... High Water Speed Technology Demonstrator [*Marine Corps*] (DOMA)
HW/SW....... Hardware/Software (MCD)
HWT............ Heavy-Weight Torpedo (DOMA)
HWT............ Hot Water Temperature
HWT............ Hypersonic Wind Tunnel
HWTC .... Hazardous Waste Treatment Council (EA)
HWTC .... Highway Traffic Control
HWTH .... Herewith (ROG)
HWTR .... Heavy Weapons Testing Range [*Military*] (MCD)
HWTS .... Humm-Wadsworth Temperament Scale [*Psychology*]
HWVE .... Hot-Wall Vacuum Evaporation [*Photovoltaic energy systems*]
HWVP .... Hanford Waste Vitrification Plant [*Department of Energy*] (GAAI)
HWVR .... However (FAAC)
HWW .... Horan, Wall & Walker [*Publisher*] (ADA)
HWW .... H. W. Wilson Co. [*Publisher*]
HWWB........ Hardwood Weather Board (ADA)
HWWS .... Hyperfiltration Wash Water Recovery System [*NASA*] (NASA)
HWY .... Highway
Hwy .... Highway (DD)

HWY .... Highway
HWY .... Hundred Woman Years [*of exposure*] [*Radiation*]
HWY .... Huntway Partners LP [*NYSE symbol*] (CTT)
HWYM......... HighwayMaster Communic [*NASDAQ symbol*] (TTSB)
HWYM......... HighwayMaster Communications, Inc. [*NASDAQ symbol*] (SAG)
HWYM......... HighwayMaster Communications, Inc. [*NASDAQ symbol*] (SAG)
HWZOA....... Hadassah, The Women's Zionist Organization of America (EA)
HX.............. Half Duplex (IAA)
HX.............. Halifax Corp. [*AMEX symbol*] (SPSG)
HX.............. Hamburg Airlines [*ICAO designator*] (AD)
HX.............. Heat Exchanger (MCD)
HX.............. Hereodox [*Commercial firm British*]
HX.............. Hexagonal [*Technical drawings*]
Hx.............. Hexode (DEN)
Hx.............. Hexyl [*Biochemistry*]
HX.............. Histiocytosis X [*or Histocytosis X*] [*Hematology*]
Hx.............. History [*Medicine*]
Hx.............. Hospitalization (DAVI)
HX.............. Hydrogen Exchange (PDAA)
Hx.............. Hypophysectomized [*Medicine*]
Hx.............. Hypoxanthine [*Also, Hyp, HYPX*] [*Biochemistry*]
HX.............. No Specific Working Hours [*ICAO*] (FAAC)
HXB .... Helix Biotech [*Vancouver Stock Exchange symbol*]
hXBP.......... Human X Box Binding Protein [*Genetics*]
HXBT .... Helicopter Expendable Bathythermograph [*Naval Oceanographic Office*]
HXC .... Bear Stearns Companies, Inc. [*AMEX symbol*] (SAG)
HxCDD........ Hexachlorodibenzo-para-dioxin [*Organic chemistry*]
HXCL.......... Hexcel
HXF............ Hartford, WI [*Location identifier FAA*] (FAAL)
HXIS .... Hard X-Ray Imaging Spectrometer
HXK .... Berlin, NH [*Location identifier FAA*] (FAAL)
HXL .... Hexcel Corp. [*NYSE symbol*] (SPSG)
HXM .... Hazleton, PA [*Location identifier FAA*] (FAAL)
HXM .... Helicopter Experimental, Medium (MCD)
HXM .... Hexamethylmelamine [*Altretamine*] [*Also, HEX, HMM*] [*Antineoplastic drug*]
HXO .... Oxford, NC [*Location identifier FAA*] (FAAL)
HXP .... Bear Stearns Companies, Inc. [*AMEX symbol*] (SAG)
HXQ .... Hard X-Ray Quanta
HXRBS .... Hard X-Ray Burst Spectrometer
HXT............ Hard X-Ray Telescope
HXV .... Herpes Simplex Virus [*Infectious disease*] (DAVI)
HXW .... Hopkinsville, KY [*Location identifier FAA*] (FAAL)
HXWXL....... Height by Width by Length (IEEE)
HXX .... Hay [*Australia Airport symbol*] (OAG)
Hy.............. All India Reporter, Hyderabad [*A publication*] (DLA)
HY.............. Heavy [*Track condition*] [*Thoroughbred racing*]
HY.............. Heavy (NATG)
HY.............. Hebrew Year [*Freemasonry*] (ROG)
HY.............. Henry
hy.............. Henry [*Variation of the preferred H*] (IDOE)
HY.............. Hertfordshire Yeomanry [*British military*] (DMA)
Hy.............. Highway
HY.............. High Yield [*Material Strength*] (DOMA)
H-Y............ Histocompatibility Y [*Immunology*]
Hy.............. History [*Medicine*]
HY.............. Hundred Yards
HY.............. Hydrant (ADA)
HY.............. Hydrocollator [*Hot*] Pack [*Medicine*]
HY.............. Hydrography
Hy.............. Hypermetropia [*Ophthalmology*]
Hy.............. Hyperopia [*Ophthalmology*] (MAE)
hy.............. Hypersthene [*CIPW classification*] [*Geology*]
HY.............. Hypobranchial [*Gland*]
Hy.............. Hypothenar [*Anatomy*]
hy.............. Hysteria [*Psychiatry*] (DAVI)
HY.............. Metro Airlines [*ICAO designator*] (AD)
HYA .... Hyack Air Ltd. [*Canada ICAO designator*] (FAAC)
HYA .... Hyannis [*Massachusetts*] [*Airport symbol*] (OAG)
Hya .... Hydrus [*Constellation*]
HYACS .... Hybrid Analog-Switching Attitude Control System for Space Vehicles
Hyacs......... Hydrofoil Air Cushlon Ship
HYAI .... Hear You Are, Inc. [*An association*] (PAZ)
HYAL .... Hyal Pharmaceutical Corp. [*NASDAQ symbol*] (SAG)
HYALF .... Hyal Pharmaceutical [*NASDAQ symbol*] (TTSB)
HyalPhr....... Hyal Pharmaceutical Corp. [*Associated Press*] (SAG)
HY & T .... Hooppole, Yorktown & Tampico Railroad (IIA)
HYAPP .... Hays Army Ammunition Plant
HYAS .... Hydrogasification [*Gas from coal fuel*]
HYB .... Hybrid (MSA)
HYB .... Hybrid Systems [*Telecommunications*] (NITA)
HYB .... Hyderabad [*India*] [*Seismograph station code, US Geological Survey*] (SEIS)
HYB .... Hyderabad [*India*] [*Geomagnetic observatory code*]
HYB .... New Amer Hi Income Fd [*NYSE symbol*] (TTSB)
HYB .... New American High Income Fund [*NYSE symbol*] (SPSG)
HYBALL .... Hybrid Analog Logic Language (MCD)
HYBD .... Hycor Biomedical [*NASDAQ symbol*] (TTSB)
HYBD .... Hycor Biomedical, Inc. [*NASDAQ symbol*] (NQ)
HYBDW .... Hycor Biomedical Wrrt [*NASDAQ symbol*] (TTSB)
HYBLOC ...... Hybrid Computer Block Oriented Compiler (IAA)
HYBMED ...... Hybrid Microelectronic Device (MSA)
HYBN .... Hybridon Inc. [*NASDAQ symbol*] (TTSB)
HYBN .... Hybridon, Inc. [*NASDAQ symbol*] (SAG)

Hybridon......	Hybridon, Inc. [Associated Press] (SAG)
HYC	Hampshire Yeomanry Cavalry [British military] (DMA)
HYC	Haney [British Columbia] [Seismograph station code, US Geological Survey] (SEIS)
HYC	Hertfordshire Yeomanry Cavalry [British military] (DMA)
HYC	Hydraulic Coupling [of a ship] (DS)
HYCATS	Hydrofoil Collision Avoidance and Tracking System [Developed by Sperry]
HYCOL	Hybrid Computer Link
HY-COM	Highway Communications
Hycor	Hycor Biomedical, Inc. [Associated Press] (SAG)
HYCOTRAN..	Hybrid Computer Translator
HYCOTRANS...	Hybrid Composit Structures for Crashworthy Body Shells and Safe Transportation Structures
HYCPP	High Yield Catalyst Polypropylene (PDAA)
Hyd	All India Reporter, Hyderabad [A publication] (DLA)
HYD	Coeur D'Alene, ID [Location identifier FAA] (FAAL)
HYD	Hyderabad [India] [Airport symbol] (OAG)
HYD	Hydrant (MSA)
HYD	Hydrargyrum [Mercury] [Pharmacy]
HYD	Hydrated
HYD	Hydraulic (AAG)
HYD	Hydroelectric Power [Type of water project]
HYD	Hydrogenation [Chemistry]
HYD	Hydrographic
HYD	Hydrostatics
HYD	Hydrous
HYD	Hydroxyurea [Also, HU, HYDREA] [Antineoplastic drug]
HYDAC	Hybrid Digital-Analog Computing [System] [Satellite]
HYDAP	Hybrid Digital-Analog Pulse Time (MCD)
HYDAPT	Hybrid Digital-Analog Pulse Time
HYDAS	Hydrographic Data Acquisition System (PDAA)
HYDAT	Hydrodynamic Analysis Tool (DNAB)
HYDATA	Hydrological Database & Analysis
HYDE	Hyde Athletic Industries, Inc. [NASDAQ symbol] (NQ)
Hyde	Hyde's Bengal Reports [India] [A publication] (DLA)
HYDEA	Hyde Athletic Indus'A' [NASDAQ symbol] (TTSB)
HydeAt	Hyde Athletic Industries, Inc. [Associated Press] (SAG)
HydeAth	Hyde Athletic Industries, Inc. [Associated Press] (SAG)
HYDEB	Hyde Athletic Indus'B' [NASDAQ symbol] (TTSB)
Hyderabad ...	Indian Law Reports, Hyderabad Series [A publication] (DLA)
Hydi	Hydrus [Constellation]
HYDICE	Hyper-spectral Digital Imagery Collection Experiment [National Oceanic and Atmospheric Administration]
HYDLAPS	Hydrographic Data Logging and Plotting System (EERA)
HYDM	Hydrometer
HYDO	Hydraulic Oil
HYD'PR........	Hydroxyproline [An amino acid] (DAVI)
HYD PRO UN...	Hydraulic Propulsion Units [on a ship] (DS)
HYDR	Hydragogue [Cathartic] [Pharmacy] (ROG)
HYDR	Hydraulic (MSA)
Hydr	Hydrographer [British military] (DMA)
HYDR	Hydrostatics (ROG)
HYDRA	Hydramatic [Automotive engineering]
HYDRA	Hydraulic [or Hydrologic] Analysis
HYDRA	Hydrographic Digital Positioning and Depth Recording [System] [NOO]
HYDRARG	Hydrargyrum [Mercury] [Pharmacy]
HYDRAT	Chloral Hydrate [Pharmacology] (DAVI)
HYDRAUL	Hydraulics (ROG)
HYDREA	Hydroxyurea [Also, HU, HYD] [Antineoplastic drug]
HYDRELC	Hydroelectric (MSA)
HYDRLC	Hydraulic
HYDRO	Hydrographic Office [Terminated, 1963; later, NOO] [Navy]
HYDRO	Hydrography
HYDRO	Hydropathic (ADA)
HYDRO	Hydrostatic (KSC)
HYDRO	Hydrotherapy [Medicine]
HYDRODYN...	Hydrodynamics
HYDROELEC...	Hydroelectric
Hydrog	Hydrogeography
Hydrog	Hydrographer of the Navy [British]
HYDROG	Hydrographic
HYDROL	Hydrologic
HYDROLANT...	Hydrographic Information for the Atlantic [Navy] (DNAB)
HYDROPAC...	Hydrographic Information for the Pacific [Navy] (DNAB)
HYDROPNEU...	Hydropneumatic [Freight]
hydros	Hydrostatics (BARN)
HYDROX	Hydrogen-Oxygen [Fuel system] (DNAB)
HYDRST	Hydrostatic (MSA)
HydrTch	Hydron Technologies, Inc. [Associated Press] (SAG)
HYDT	Hydrant (ADA)
HYDTD	Hydrated (MSA)
HYDX	Hydroxide (IAA)
HYE	Healthy Years Equivalent (DMAA)
HYE	Hyeres Aero Service [France ICAO designator] (FAAC)
HYF	Hayfields [Papua New Guinea] [Airport symbol] (OAG)
HYF	Humbligny [France] [Seismograph station code, US Geological Survey] (SEIS)
HyF	Hytone Film Lab, Inc., Des Moines, IA [Library symbol Library of Congress] (LCLS)
HYFAC	Hypersonic Research Facilities [NASA]
HYFES	Hypersonic Flight Environmental Simulator
HYFIX	Hyperbolic Fix
HYFT	High-Yield Fallout Trajectory (DNAB)

HYG	Hydaburg [Alaska] [Airport symbol] (OAG)
HYG	Hygiene
HYG	Hygroscopic
HYGAS	Hydrogen Gasification
HYGL	Hypergolic (KSC)
HYGN	Hygiene
HYGNST.......	Hygienist
HYGST	Hygienist (AABC)
HY/HS	High Yield/High Stereospecificity Technology [for polypropylene] [Himont Corp.]
HYI.............	High Yield Income Fd [NYSE symbol] (TTSB)
HYI.............	High Yield Income Fund [NYSE symbol] (SPSG)
HYL	Hollis, AK [Location identifier FAA] (FAAL)
HYL	Hoyle Resources Ltd. [Vancouver Stock Exchange symbol]
Hyl	Hydroxylysine [Also, Hylys] [An amino acid]
HYLA	Hybrid Language Assembler
HYLIFE	High-Yield Lithium Injection Fusion Energy (MCD)
HYLO	Hyaline [Cytology] (DAVI)
HYLO	Hybrid LORAN
Hylys	Hydroxylysine [or (OH)Lys] [Also, Hyl An amino acid]
HYM	Hyman, TX [Location identifier FAA] (FAAL)
Hym	Hymenoptera [Entomology]
HYMA	Hebrew Young Men's Association
HYMATIC	Hydraulic Multiplate Active Traction Intelligent Control [Automotive engineering]
Hymn Hom Ap...	Hymnus Homericus ad Apollinem [Classical studies] (OCD)
Hymn Hom Bacch...	Hymnus Homericus ad Bacchum [Classical studies] (OCD)
Hymn Hom Cer...	Hymnus Homericus ad Cererem [Classical studies] (OCD)
Hymn Hom Mart...	Hymnus Homericus ad Martem [Classical studies] (OCD)
Hymn Hom Merc...	Hymnus Homericus ad Mercurium [Classical studies] (OCD)
Hymn Hom Pan...	Hymnus Homericus ad Panem [Classical studies] (OCD)
Hymn Hom Ven...	Hymnus Homericus ad Venerem [Classical studies] (OCD)
HYMNS	Hydrogen MASER for Navigation Satellite (MCD)
HYMOSS.......	Hybrid Mosaic on Stacked Silicon [Materials science]
HYMV	Hypochoeris Mosaic Virus [Plant pathology]
HYN	Halcyon Resources Ltd. [Vancouver Stock Exchange symbol]
HYOSCYAM...	Hyoscyamus [Henbane] [Pharmacology] (ROG)
HYP	Harvard, Yale, and Princeton Universities
HYP	High Yield Plus Fund [NYSE symbol] (SPSG)
HYP	Hydroxybenzylpindolol [Neuropharmacology]
Hyp	Hydroxyproline [Also, Hypro] [An amino acid]
HYP	Hypergolic
HYP	Hyperresonance
HYP	Hypertrophy
HYP	Hyphen Character [Computer science]
HYP	Hypnosis
HYP	Hypodermic (ROG)
HYP	Hypotenuse [Mathematics]
HYP	Hypothalamus [Neuroanatomy]
HYP	Hypothesis
HYP	Hypothetical (WDAA)
Hyp	Hypoxanthine [Also, Hx, HYPX] [Biochemistry]
Hyp2005	Hyperion 2005 Investment Grade Opportunity Term Trust [Associated Press] (SAG)
HYPACE	Hybrid Programmable Attitude Control Electronics [NASA]
HYPAR.........	Hysterectomy Produced and Artificially Reared (PDAA)
HYPARS........	Hyperbolic Paraboloid Surface (MCD)
HYPER	Hydrographic Personnel [Navy]
HYPER	Hyperhydrated, Hyperventilating with Hyperpyrexia, Hyperexcitability, and Hyperrigidity [Characteristics of drowning]
hyperal	Hyperalimentation [Intravenous feeding] [Medicine] (DAVI)
HYPERB........	Hyperbola [Mathematics]
HYPERDOP....	Hyperbolic Doppler
HYPERIGN ...	Hypergolic Ignition (KSC)
hyperpara	Hyperparathyroidism [Endocrinology] (DAVI)
hyper T & A...	Hypertrophy of Tonsils and Adenoids [Medicine] (MAE)
hyper T & A...	Hypertropy of Tonsils and Adenoids [Otorhinolaryngology] (DAVI)
HYPH	Hydrophone
HypmdCm.....	Hypermedia Communications, Inc. [Associated Press] (SAG)
HYPN	Hypertension
hypn.	Hypertension (DMAA)
HYPNO.........	Hypnosis
HYPNOT.......	Hypnotism
HYPNS.........	Hypnosis
HYPO	High Power [Water boiler atomic reactor] [Dismantled]
HYPO	Hypochondria (DSUE)
hypo.	Hypochromasia [Hematology]
HYPO	Hypodermic
Hypo	Hypodermic (DMAA)
hypo.	Hyposulfate [Solium Thiosulphate] [A compound used in photography] (WDMC)
HYPO	Hyposulfite of Sodium [Photography] (ROG)
HYPOC.........	Hypochromasia [Hematology] (DAVI)
HYPOCON	Hypochondria (DSUE)
HYPOT.........	Hypotenuse [Mathematics] (ROG)
HYPOTH.......	Hypothesis (ADA)
HYPOTH.......	Hypothetical (MSA)
HYPOX	Hypophysectomy [Medicine]
HYPP	Hyperkalemic Periodic Paralysis [Medicine]
HYPP	Hypersegmented Neutrophil [Hematology] (DAVI)
HYPR	Hypermedia Communications [NASDAQ symbol] (SAG)
HYPR	HyperMedia Communications [NASDAQ symbol] (TTSB)
HYPREM	Hyperresponse Electric Motor
HyprnSft	Hyperion Software, Inc. [Associated Press] (SAG)
HyprnTR	Hyperion Total Return & Income Fund [Associated Press] (SAG)

Hypro .... Hydroxyproline [or (OH)Pro] [Also, Hyp An amino acid]
HyprSf .... Hyperion Software, Inc. [Associated Press] (SAG)
Hyps .... Hypsipyle [of Euripides] [Classical studies] (OCD)
HYPSES .... Hydrographic Precision Scanning Echo Sounder
hypst .... Hypostyle (VRA)
HypT02 .... Hyperion 2002 Term Trust [Associated Press] (SAG)
HypT97 .... Hyperion 1997 Term Trust [Associated Press] (SAG)
HypT99 .... Hyperion 1999 Term Trust [Associated Press] (SAG)
HYPUB .... Hypanthium Pubescence [Botany]
HYPX .... Hypoxanthine [Also, Hx, Hyp] [Biochemistry]
HYR .... Hayward [Wisconsin] [Airport symbol] (OAG)
HYR .... Hycroft Resources & Development Corp. [Vancouver Stock Exchange symbol]
HYRROM ..... Hydrological Rainfall Runoff Model
HYS .... Hays [Kansas] [Airport symbol] (OAG)
HYS .... Hysterectomy [Medicine] (AAMN)
HYS .... Hysteria
HYSAM .... Hypersonic Surface-to-Air Missile (MCD)
HYSAS .... Hydrofluidic Stability Augmentation System
HYSIM .... Highway Driving Simulator [MM] (TAG)
HY-SPLIT ..... Hybrid Single Particle Lagrangian Integrated Trajectories [Model] [Marine science] (OSRA)
HY-SPLIT ..... Hybrid Single Particle Lagrangian Integrated Trajectories [Model] (USDC)
hyst .... Hysterectomy [Medicine]
HYSTAD .... Hydrofoil Stabilization Device
HYSTCK .... Haystack
hyster .... Hysterectomy [Gynecology] (DAVI)
HYSTERO ...... Hysterosalpingogram [Gynecology] (DHSM)
HYSTRU .... Hydraulic System Test and Repair Unit [Army] (MCD)
HYSURCH .... Hydrographic Surveying and Charting [System] [NOO]
HYSW .... Hyperion Software [NASDAQ symbol] (TTSB)
HYSW .... Hyperion Software, Inc. [NASDAQ symbol] (SAG)
Hyswas .... Hydrofoil Small Waterplane Area Ship
HYT .... High Year of Tenure
HYT .... High-Yield Tax-Exempt [Finance] (BARN)
HYT .... Humaita [Brazil] [Airport symbol] (AD)
HYTAC .... Hydraulic Tachometer
HYTAM .... Hypersonic Tactical Missile (MCD)
HYTEC .... Hydrogen Thermal Electrochemical Converter
HYTIWYG ..... How You Test is What You Get [Education] (AIE)
HYTRAN .... Hybrid Translator (IAA)
HYTREC .... Hydrospace Target Recognition, Evaluation, and Control
HYTRESS ..... High-Test Recorder and Simulator System (IEEE)
HYTROSS .... High-Test Recorder and Simulator System
HYU .... Chesterfield, VA [Location identifier FAA] (FAAL)
HYU .... Lilly Contingent Payment Units [AMEX symbol] (SPSG)
HYU .... Lilly CtgntPymt Units [AMEX symbol] (TTSB)
HYV .... High Yielding Variety [Agriculture]
HYVE .... Hydrogen Ventilated Enclosure (PDAA)

HYVIA .... Hypervelocity Interceptor Armament
HYW .... Conway, SC [Location identifier FAA] (FAAL)
HYWAYS ...... Hybrid with Advanced Yield for Surveillance [Strategic Defense Initiative]
HYWN .... Hypersonic Wedge Nozzle (MCD)
HYWV .... High-Yielding Wheat Variety (GNE)
HYX .... Hydra Explorations Ltd. [Toronto Stock Exchange symbol]
HYZ .... Thief River Falls, MN [Location identifier FAA] (FAAL)
HZ .... Dust Haze [Aviation]
HZ .... Habitable Zone [Beyond the solar system]
HZ .... Haze (WDAA)
Hz .... Headquarters Zip Code [Dialog] [Searchable field] [Information service or system] (NITA)
HZ .... Henebery Aviation [ICAO designator] (AD)
HZ .... Herpes Zoster [Medicine]
Hz .... Hertz [Symbol] [SI unit of frequency] (AABC)
Hz .... Hertz (WDMC)
HZ .... Hydralazine [Antihypertensive agent]
HZ .... Saudi Arabia [International civil aircraft marking] (ODBW)
HZA .... Hauptzollamt [Chief Customs Office] [German] (DLA)
HZA .... Herut Zionists of America (EA)
HZBL .... Holzblaeser [Woodwind Instrument] [Music]
HZE .... High Z and E [Particles in outer space]
Hzea .... Heliothis Zea [Corn ear worm]
HZFO .... Hamster Zona-Free Ovum [Test] [Medicine] (MEDA)
HZFS .... Horizon Financial Services Corp. [NASDAQ symbol] (SAG)
HZFS .... Horizon Financial Svcs [NASDAQ symbol] (TTSB)
HZG .... Hanzhong [China] [Airport symbol] (OAG)
HZI .... Hy & Zel's, Inc. [Toronto Stock Exchange symbol]
HZK .... Atlanta, GA [Location identifier FAA] (FAAL)
HZK .... Husavik [Iceland] [Airport symbol] (OAG)
HZL .... Hazelton Airlines [Australia ICAO designator] (FAAC)
HZL .... Hazleton [Pennsylvania] [Airport symbol Obsolete] (OAG)
HZMP .... Horizontal Impulse (IEEE)
HZN .... Hazen, NV [Location identifier FAA] (FAAL)
HZN .... Horizon Airlines Ltd. [Nigeria] [FAA designator] (FAAC)
HzNPV .... Heliothis Zea Nuclear Polyhedrosis Virus
HZNT .... Handbuch zum Neuen Testament [Lietzmann] [A publication] (BJA)
HZO .... Herpes Zoster Ophthalmicus [Ophthalmology]
HZP .... Hot Zero Power [Nuclear energy] (NRCH)
HZP .... Hyperbolic Zone Plate (PDAA)
HZP .... Zionsville, IN [Location identifier FAA] (FAAL)
HZR .... New Roads, LA [Location identifier FAA] (FAAL)
HZRN .... Horizontal Reaction
HZV .... Herpes Zoster Virus
HZW .... Wichita, KS [Location identifier FAA] (FAAL)
HZWV .... Horizon Bancorp West Virginia [NASDAQ symbol] (SAG)
HZWV .... Horizon Bancorp (WV) [NASDAQ symbol] (SAG)
HZY .... Hazy (WGA)
HZYC .... Hadassah Zionist Youth Commission (EA)
HZYO .... Hashomer Hatzair Zionist Youth Organization [Later, HHSZYM] (EA)

I

By Acronym

I..................	Air Force Training Category [No training]
I..................	Angle of Incidence
I..................	Angle of Incidence (IDOE)
I..................	Carlo Erba [Italy] [Research code symbol]
I..................	Class Interval [Statistics]
I..................	Electric Current [Symbol] [IUPAC]
I..................	Fighter [Russian aircraft symbol]
I..................	First Interstate Bancorp. [NYSE symbol] (SPSG)
I..................	I-Beam [Structural metal shape]
I..................	Ibuprofen [A drug]
I..................	Iconoscope (IAA)
I..................	Id [That] [Latin] (GPO)
I..................	Idaho
I..................	Identification
I..................	Idus [The Ides] [Latin]
I..................	Ihr [Your] [German]
I..................	Illinois State Library, Springfield, IL [Library symbol Library of Congress] (LCLS)
I..................	Illite [A mineral]
I..................	Illuminated (WDMC)
I..................	Illumination (IAA)
I..................	Image [File] [Computer science] [Telecommunications]
I..................	Imaginary (IAA)
I..................	Imaginary Unit (WGA)
I..................	Immortalis [Immortal] [Latin] (GPO)
I..................	Imperator [or Imperatrix] [Emperor or Empress] [Latin]
I..................	Imperial
I..................	Imperial Paper (DGA)
I..................	Implicit
I..................	Impression (DAVI)
I..................	Improbatur [Latin]
I..................	Inactive [Chemistry]
I..................	Inboard (DS)
I..................	Incendiary [Bomb]
I..................	Incident Ray (IDOE)
I..................	Incisal [Dentistry] (DAVI)
I..................	Incisor (Deciduous) [Dentistry]
I..................	Incisor (Permanent) [Dentistry]
I..................	Inclination
I..................	Income
I..................	Incompatible
I..................	Incomplete
I..................	Incontinent [Medicine]
I..................	Incumbent (ROG)
I..................	Independent
I..................	Independent Pump [Liquid gas carriers]
I..................	Independent School [British]
I..................	Index
I..................	India [Phonetic alphabet] [International] (DSUE)
I..................	Indian (WGA)
I-----	Indian Ocean [MARC geographic area code Library of Congress] (LCCP)
I..................	Indicated [or Indicative]
I..................	Indicated Horsepower
I..................	Indicated Main Engine
I..................	Indicator
I..................	Induction
I..................	Industrial
I..................	Industrial Premises [Public-performance tariff] [British]
I..................	Industrial Training School [British] (ROG)
I..................	Inertia (AAG)
I..................	Infantry
I..................	Infield
I..................	Informal [FCC special temporary authorization] (NTCM)
I..................	Information [Computer science]
I..................	Infra (IAA)
I..................	Inhalation (DMAA)
I..................	Inhibitor (DMAA)
I..................	Inhibitory
I..................	Initial
I..................	Ink [Phonetic alphabet] [Royal Navy World War I Pre-World War II] (DSUE)
I..................	Ink (VRA)
I..................	Inlet [Rotary piston meter]
I..................	Inner
I..................	Inosine [One-letter symbol; see Ino]
I..................	Input
I..................	Inside
I..................	Inside Edge [Skating]
I..................	Insoluble
I..................	Inspector
I..................	Inspired [Medicine] (DAVI)
I..................	Instantaneous
I..................	Instantaneous Current (IDOE)
I..................	Instantaneous Value (IDOE)
I..................	Institute [or Institution]
I..................	Institutional (WDMC)
I..................	Instruction
I..................	Instructional Program (NTCM)
I..................	Instructor (WDAA)
I..................	Instrumental [or Instrumentation]
I..................	Instrument Correction
I..................	Insulated (DS)
I..................	Insulated Tank [Liquid gas carriers]
I..................	Intact (DAVI)
I..................	Intake (AAMN)
I..................	Integer (IAA)
I..................	Integral (IAA)
I..................	Intelligence
I..................	Intensity
I..................	Interbank [Credit cards]
I..................	Intercept-Aerial [Missile mission symbol]
I..................	Interceptor
I..................	Interchangeability (AAG)
I..................	Intercooled [Automotive engineering]
I..................	Interest [Economics]
I..................	Interference [Broadcasting]
I..................	Interim [FCC] (NTCM)
I..................	Interlocked Metallic Armor [Technical drawings]
I..................	Intermediate [Vessel load line mark]
I..................	Intermediate Slope [Skiing]
I..................	Intermittent (DMAA)
I..................	Intermittent Operation during the Time Indicated [Broadcasting]
I..................	Intern
I..................	Internal
I..................	Internal Medicine (AAMN)
I..................	International
I..................	Internist [Medicine]
I..................	Interphone (IAA)
I..................	Interpole (IAA)
I..................	Interpreter
I..................	Interrupt [Computer science Telecommunications]
I..................	Interstate [Highways]
I..................	Intestine
I..................	Intransitive
I..................	Intrapictures [Electronics] (ACRL)
I..................	Intrinsic Semiconductor (IDOE)
I..................	Intrinsic-Type, Semiconductor Material
I..................	Introduced [Ecology]
I..................	Invasive
I..................	Inventory
I..................	Inverted Sentence [Used in correcting manuscripts, etc.]
I..................	Inverter
I..................	Investment
I..................	Iodine [Chemical element]
I..................	Ionic Strength
I..................	Iota [Ninth letter of the Greek alphabet] (DAVI)
I..................	Iraqi
I..................	Ireland
I..................	Irnerius [Flourished, 1113-18] [Authority cited in pre-1607 legal work] (DSA)
I..................	Iron [Symbol is Fe] [Chemical element] (ROG)
I..................	Irradiated (NASA)
I..................	Irregular (ROG)
I..................	Irrigation [Medicine]
I..................	Island [Maps and charts]
I..................	Isle
i..................	Isochromosome (MAE)
I..................	Isoflurane [An anesthetic]
I..................	Isoleucine [One-letter symbol; see Ile] [An amino acid]
I..................	Isometric [Botany]
i..................	Isopentenyl [As substituent on nucleoside] [Biochemistry]

I.................	Isopin (WDAA)
I.................	Isoproterenol [An adrenergic]
I.................	Isotope (DMAA)
I.................	Israeli
I.................	Issue (ROG)
I.................	Italy [IYRU nationality code]
I.................	Item [Phonetic alphabet] [World War II] (DSUE)
I.................	Luminous Intensity [Symbol] [IUPAC]
I.................	Minneapolis [Branch in the Federal Reserve regional banking system] (BARN)
I.................	Moment of Inertia [Symbol] [IUPAC]
I.................	One [Roman numeral]
I.................	Paid This Year, Dividend Omitted, Deferred, or No Action Taken at Last Dividend Meeting [Investment term] (DFIT)
I.................	Radiant Intensity [Symbol] [IUPAC]
I.................	Registro Italiano [Shipping] (ROG)
I.................	Requires a Doctor [Search and rescue symbol that can be stamped in sand or snow]
i.................	Tourist Information [Traffic sign] [British]
I^0.................	Primary (DAVI)
I2.................	Image Intensification
I2.................	International Interchangeability
I$_2$.................	Iodine [Chemical element] (DAVI)
I^{2}C.................	Inter-Integrated Circuit [Philips] (NITA)
I^{2}L.................	Integrated Injection Logic (NITA)
I^{2}L.................	Integrated Injection Logic [Microprocessing]
I^{2L2}AS...........	Infantry Issues and Lessons Learned Analysis System [Software] (INF)
I^{2}R..............	Imaging Infrared [Pronounced "eye-squared ar"]
I2S.................	Integrated Information System [Marine Corps]
I2S2.................	Intelligence Information Subsystem [Military]
I2S(FIN)............	Integrated Information System (Financial) [Marine Corps]
I2S(LOG).....	Integrated Information System (Logistics) [Marine Corps]
I2S(MPR).....	Integrated Information System (Manpower) [Marine Corps]
I2S(MPR/MMS)...	Integrated Information System (Manpower and Functional Area Manpower Management System) [Marine Corps]
I2S(OPS).....	Integrated Information System (Operational) [Marine Corps]
I2T2.............	Intelligence Interactive Test Terminal
I^{3}L..............	Isoplanar Integrated Injection Logic
I5/W............	Invert Sugar [5%] in Water [Medicine]
I-10/S........	Invert Sugar [10%] in Saline [Medicine]
I14Y............	Interoperability [The 14 replaces the fourteen letters between I and Y] [Computer hacker terminology] (NHD)
I18N............	Internationalization [The 18 replaces the eighteen letters between I and N] [Computer hacker terminology] (NHD)
I-129........	Iodine-129
IA.................	Comando de Material - Fabrica Militar de Aviones [Argentina ICAO aircraft manufacturer identifier] (ICAO)
IA.................	IATA [International Air Transport Association] Containers [Shipping] (DCTA)
IA.................	Ibotenic Acid [Organic acid] (DMAA)
IA.................	Ice Age
IA.................	Ileostomy Association of Great Britain and Ireland
IA.................	Image Acquisition [Computer graphics]
IA.................	Image Amplification [Radiology] (DAVI)
IA.................	Imagery Analyst (MCD)
IA.................	Im Auftrage [By Order Of] [German]
IA.................	Imitation Art Paper (DGA)
IA.................	Immediate Access (IAA)
IA.................	Immediate Action [Military]
IA.................	Immediate Annuity
IA.................	Immediately Available
IA.................	Immune Adherence [Immunology]
Ia.................	Immune Region Associated Antigen [Immunology]
Ia.................	Immune Response Gene-Associated Antigen [Immunology] (DAVI)
IA.................	Immunobiologic Activity [Immunology] (AAMN)
IA.................	Impedance Angle
IA.................	Imperial Airways Ltd. [British] (ADA)
IA.................	Implementing Agency (KSC)
IA.................	Import Annual Data [Department of Commerce] (GFGA)
IA.................	Impotents Anonymous (EA)
IA.................	In Absentia [In Absence] [Latin]
IA.................	Inactive Account [Banking]
IA.................	Inactive Aerospace Vehicle [or Aircraft]
IA.................	Incentive Award [Military]
IA.................	Incidental Appendectomy [Medicine]
IA.................	Income Averaging (MHDB)
IA.................	Incorporated Accountant
IA.................	Incremental Analysis [Statistics]
IA.................	Incurred Accidentally [Medicine] (MEDA)
IA.................	Independent Action (EA)
IA.................	Independent Americans (EA)
IA.................	Index Array (IAA)
IA.................	India Alert [An association] (EA)
IA.................	Indiana [Obsolete] (ROG)
IA.................	Indian Affairs (DLA)
IA.................	Indian Airlines (PDAA)
IA.................	Indian Army
IA.................	Indian Artillery [British military] (DMA)
IA.................	Indicated Altitude [Navigation]
IA.................	Indicator of Authoritativeness [Library symbol]
IA.................	Indirect Address (NITA)
IA.................	Indirect Addressing
IA.................	Indo-Aryan [Linguistics]
IA.................	Indolaminergic-Accumulating [Cytology] (DAVI)
IA.................	Indulin Agar [Microbiology]
IA.................	Industrial Arts (OICC)
IA.................	Industry Application (IAA)
IA.................	Infected Area
IA.................	Inferior Angle [Anatomy]
IA.................	Information Agency
IA.................	Information America [Information service or system] (IID)
IA.................	Infra-Audible [Sound]
IA.................	Initial Appearance [RADAR]
IA.................	Initial Authorization
IA.................	Initiative America (EA)
I/A.................	Innovative/Alternative [Recycling technologies]
IA.................	Input Acknowledge (MCD)
IA.................	Input Axis (KSC)
IA.................	Insertion Approval (NRCH)
IA.................	Inspection Administration [Navy]
IA.................	Inspection Authorization (GAVI)
I/A.................	Installment Agreement
IA.................	Institut de l'Amiante [Asbestos Institute - AI] (EA)
IA.................	Institute of Actuaries [British]
IA.................	Institute of Architects [Australia]
IA.................	Instruction Address [Computer science]
IA.................	Instructional Allowance [British military] (DMA)
IA.................	Instrument Abstracts
IA.................	Instrument Air [System] [Nuclear energy] (NRCH)
IA.................	Instrumentation Amplifier (IEEE)
IA.................	Insulin Antibody [Immunology]
IA.................	Insurance Adjustment
I/A.................	Insurance Auditor
IA.................	Intangible Asset [i.e., Patented rights]
IA.................	Integrated Adapter
IA.................	Intelligence Analysis
IA.................	Intelligence Assessment (DOMA)
IA.................	Intelligent Actuatot (ACII)
IA.................	Intelligent Agent
IA.................	Intelligent Assistant [Computer science]
IA.................	Intelligenzalter [Mental Age] [Psychology]
IA.................	Intemperate to Alcohol [An alcoholic] [Slang]
IA.................	Inter-Action (MCD)
IA.................	Interagency Agreement (GNE)
IA.................	Inter Alia [Among Other Things] [Latin]
IA.................	Intercept Arm (MUGU)
IA.................	Intercessors for America (EA)
IA.................	Interchangeable Alternate
IA.................	Interchange Address (NITA)
IA.................	Interciencia Association [Caracas, Venezuela] (EAIO)
IA.................	Intercity Airways [Australia]
IA.................	Intercoiffure America (EA)
IA.................	Intercultural Awareness
I/A.................	Interface Adapter (NASA)
IA.................	Interface Amplifier
IA.................	Interflora Australia
IA.................	Intermediate Air [Combustion]
IA.................	Intermediate Amplifier
IA.................	Internal Audit
IA.................	Internal Auditory (Ear)
IA.................	International Affiliation of Independent Accounting Firms [Later, Independent Accountants International] (EA)
IA.................	International Alert (EA)
IA.................	International Alliance of Theatrical Stage Employees (NTCM)
IA.................	International Alliance of Theatrical Stage Employees and Moving Picture Machine Operators of the United States and Canada
IA.................	International Alphabet
IA.................	International Angstrom
IA.................	Interval Availability
IA.................	Intra-Amniotic [Medicine] (AAMN)
IA.................	Intra Aortic [Cardiology] (MAE)
IA.................	Intra-Arterial [Cardiology]
IA.................	Intra-Articular [Medicine]
IA.................	Intra-Atrial [Cardiology]
IA.................	Intra-Auricular [Cardiology] (DAVI)
IA.................	Inverter Assembly
IA.................	Iowa [Postal code]
IA.................	Iowa Reports [A publication] (DLA)
Ia.................	Iowa State Library Commission, Des Moines, IA [Library symbol Library of Congress] (LCLS)
IA.................	Iphigenia Aulidensis [of Euripides] [Classical studies] (OCD)
IA.................	Iraqi Airways [ICAO designator]
IA.................	Iron Age
IA.................	Irrigation Area (ADA)
IA.................	Irrigation Association (EA)
I/A.................	Isle Of Angelsey [Wales] (ROG)
IA.................	Isle Of Aran
IA.................	Isolation Amplifier
IA.................	Isophthalic Acid [Organic chemistry]
IA.................	Issuing Agency (AFM)
IA.................	Italian Army (NATG)
I/A.................	Item Accounting (MCD)
IA.................	Law Reports, Privy Council, Indian Appeals [India] [A publication] (DLA)
IA.................	Millenia, Inc. [AMEX symbol] (SAG)
IA.................	Telegraph and Public Address [JETDS nomenclature]
IA-1.................	Image Array Processor (NITA)
IA-2.................	International Alphabet-2 [Standard telegraphy code] (NITA)
IA-5.................	International Alphabet 5 (NITA)

IaA.............. Ames, Public Library, Ames IA [*Library symbol Library of Congress*] (LCLS)

IAA............. Chicago State University, Chicago, IL [*OCLC symbol*] (OCLC)

IAA............. Ibero-Armorican Arc [*A geological area of western Europe*]

IAA............. Illinois Agricultural Association (SRA)

IAA............. Imidazoleacetic Acid [*Also, I-AC, IMAA*] [*Biochemistry*]

IAA............. Immediate Action Authority (AAG)

IAA............. Inactive Aerospace Vehicle [*or Aircraft*] Authorization

IAA............. In Amguel [*Issek Toufreg*] [*Algeria*] [*Seismograph station code, US Geological Survey*] [*Closed*] (SEIS)

IAA............. Incorporated Accountants and Auditors [*British*] (DAS)

IAA............. Independent Administrators Association of California (SRA)

IAA............. Independent Airlines Association (EA)

IAA............. Indian Army Act [*British military*] (DMA)

IAA............. Indian Association of America (EA)

IAA............. Indoleacetic Acid [*Plant growth promoter*]

IAA............. Inex Adria Aviopromet [*Yugoslavia*] [*ICAO designator*] (FAAC)

IAA............. Inpatient Ambulatory Activity Questionnaire [*Medicine*]

IAA............. Institute for Alternative Agriculture (EA)

IAA............. Institute for Arthritis and Autoimmunity [*Nile Research Center*] [*West Haven, CT*]

IAA............. Institute of Administrative Accountants [*Sevenoaks, Kent, England*] (EAIO)

IAA............. Institute of Administrative Accounting and Data Processing Limited [*British*] (NITA)

IAA............. Institute of Arbitrators Australia

IAA............. Institute of Archeology and Anthropology [*University of South Carolina at Columbia*] [*Research center*] (RCD)

IAA............. Institute of Automobile Assessors [*British*] (BI)

IAA............. Instrumental Activation Analysis

IAA............. Insulin Autoantibody [*Immunology*]

IAA............. Insurance Accountants Association [*Later, SIA*]

IAA............. Intelligence Analysts Associates [*Air Force*]

IAA............. Interamerican Accounting Association [*Mexico City, Mexico*] (EA)

IAA............. Interim Access Authorization

IAA............. Interment Association of America [*Later, PIAA*] (EA)

IAA............. International Academy of Astronautics [*Paris, France*] (EA)

IAA............. International Acetylene Association [*Later, CGA*]

IAA............. International Advertising Association [*Later, AAF*] (EA)

IAA............. International Aerosol Association [*Zurich, Switzerland*] (EAIO)

IAA............. International Aerospace Abstracts [*American Institute of Aeronautics and Astronautics*] [*A publication*] (AEBS)

IAA............. International Antituberculosis Association (DAVI)

IAA............. International Apple Association [*Later, IAI*] (EA)

IAA............. International Arthroscopy Association (EA)

IAA............. International Association of Allergology [*Later, IAACI*]

IAA............. International Association of Art [*See also AIAP*] (EA)

IAA............. International Association of Astacology (EA)

IAA............. International Astrological Association

IAA............. International Aviation Affairs [*FAA*] (MCD)

IAA............. Interruption of the Aortic Arch [*Medicine*] (DMAA)

IAA............. Intimate Apparel Associates [*Defunct*] (EA)

IAA............. Inventors Association of America (EA)

IAA............. Investment Advisers Act [*1940*]

IAA............. Iodoacetamide [*Organic chemistry*]

IAA............. Iododacetic Acid [*Organic chemistry*]

IAA............. Iowa Auctioneers Association (SRA)

IAA............. Irish Astronomical Association (EAIO)

IAA............. Israel Antiquities Authority

IAAA........... Illinois Agricultural Aviation Association (SRA)

IAAA........... Inflammatory Abdominal Aortic Aneurysm [*Medicine*] (DMAA)

IAAA........... Institute of Afro-American Affairs [*New York University*] [*Research center*] (RCD)

IAAA........... Integrated Advance Avionics for Aircraft

IAAA........... Inter-American Accounting Association

IAAA........... Intermarket Association of Advertising Agencies [*Dayton, OH*] (EA)

IAAA........... International Academy of Aquatic Art (EA)

IAAA........... International Airforwarders and Agents Association (EA)

IAAAA......... Intercollegiate Association of Amateur Athletes of America (EA)

IAAABBP.... International Association of African and American Black Business People [*Detroit, MI*] (EA)

IAAAM........ International Association for Aquatic Animal Medicine (EA)

IaAAR......... United States Department of Agriculture, Agricultural Research Service, NationalAnimal Disease Laboratory, Ames, IA [*Library symbol Library of Congress*] (LCLS)

IAAATDC...... International Association for Advancement of Appropriate Technology for Developing Countries (EA)

IAAB........... Inter-American Association of Broadcasters [*Later, IAB-AIR*]

IAAB........... Interim Aviation Airframe Bulletin (DNAB)

IAABB......... International Association of Amateur Boat Builders (EA)

IAABO......... International Association of Approved Basketball Officials (EA)

IaAc........... Ackley Public Library, Ackley, IA [*Library symbol Library of Congress*] (LCLS)

IAAC........... Interagency Assessment Advisory Committee (GNE)

IAAC........... International Agricultural Aviation Centre [*Defunct*] (EA)

IAAC........... International Assets Holding Corp. [*NASDAQ symbol*] (SAG)

IAAC........... International Association of Art Critics [*Australia*]

IAAC........... Intl Asset Holding [*NASDAQ symbol*] (TTSB)

IAACC......... Ibero-American Association of Chambers of Commerce [*See also AICO*] [*Bogota, Colombia*] (EAIO)

IAACC......... Inter-Allied Aeronautical Commission of Control

IAACI......... International Association of Allergology and Clinical Immunology (EA)

IAACW....... International Assets Hldg Wrrt [*NASDAQ symbol*] (TTSB)

IaAcW......... World Journal, Ackley, IA [*Library symbol Library of Congress*] (LCLS)

IaAdeCoC..... Dallas County Courthouse, Adel, IA [*Library symbol Library of Congress*] (LCLS)

IaAdeN....... Dallas County News, Adel, IA [*Library symbol Library of Congress*] (LCLS)

IAADFS....... International Association of Airport Duty Free Stores (EA)

IaAdN......... Adair News, Adair, IA [*Library symbol Library of Congress*] (LCLS)

IAADS......... Integrated Antiairborne Defense System

IAAE.......... Institute of Automotive and Aeronautical Engineers (WDAA)

IAAE.......... International Association of Agricultural Economists (EA)

IAAEES....... International Association for the Advancement of Earth and Environmental Sciences (EA)

IAAEM....... International Association of Aquaculture Economics and Management

IAAER....... International Association for the Advancement of Educational Research

IAAF.......... International Agricultural Aviation Foundation (EA)

IAAF.......... International Amateur Athletic Federation [*See also FIAA*] [*British*] (EAIO)

IAAF.......... International Association of Art for the Future [*Indonesia*] (EAIO)

IAAFA......... Inter-American Air Force Academy [*Operated by US Air Force to provide training for Latin American countries*]

IAAFF......... Iona Appliances, Inc. [*NASDAQ symbol*] (SAG)

IaAfSE........ Afton Star-Enterprise, Afton, IA [*Library symbol Library of Congress*] (LCLS)

IAAG.......... Inter-American Association of Gastroenterology (EA)

IAAH.......... International Action Against Hunger (EAIO)

IAAHU....... International Association of Accident and Health Underwriters [*Later, NAHU*]

IAAI.......... Insurance Auto Auctions [*NASDAQ symbol*] (SPSG)

IAAI.......... International Association of Arson Investigators (EA)

IaAIBI........ IBIA News, Ames, IA [*Library symbol Library of Congress*] (LCLS)

IAAIP......... Inter-American Association of Industrial Property [*See also ASIPA*] [*Buenos Aires, Argentina*] (EAIO)

IaAIS.......... Iowa Starter, Iowa State University, Ames, IA [*Library symbol Library of Congress*] (LCLS)

IaAkRT....... Akron Register-Tribune, Akron, IA [*Library symbol Library of Congress*] (LCLS)

IAAL.......... International Association of Applied Linguistics (EA)

IaAlb.......... Albia Public Library, Albia, IA [*Library symbol Library of Congress*] (LCLS)

IaAlbMHi..... Monroe County Historical Society, Albia, IA [*Library symbol Library of Congress*] (LCLS)

IaAlbN....... Monroe County News, Albia, IA [*Library symbol Library of Congress*] (LCLS)

IaAlbUR...... Albia Union-Republican, Albia, IA [*Library symbol Library of Congress*] (LCLS)

IaAlcAM...... Appeal and Marathon Republic, Albert City, IA [*Library symbol Library of Congress*] (LCLS)

IaAld.......... Alden Public Library, Alden, IA [*Library symbol Library of Congress*] (LCLS)

IAALD......... International Association of Agricultural Librarians and Documentalists (EA)

IaAlg.......... Algona Public Library, Algona, IA [*Library symbol Library of Congress*] (LCLS)

IaAlgKA....... Kossuth County Advance, Algona, IA [*Library symbol Library of Congress*] (LCLS)

IaAlgUD...... Upper Des Moines, Algona, IA [*Library symbol Library of Congress*] (LCLS)

IaAll.......... Allerton Public Library, Allerton, IA [*Library symbol Library of Congress*] (LCLS)

IaAlnBCo..... Butler County Courthouse, Allison, IA [*Library symbol Library of Congress*] (LCLS)

IaAlnTJ....... Butler County Tribune-Journal, Allison, IA [*Library symbol Library of Congress*] (LCLS)

IaAlta......... Alta Public Library, Alta, IA [*Library symbol Library of Congress*] (LCLS)

IaAltaA....... Alta Advertiser, Alta, IA [*Library symbol Library of Congress*] (LCLS)

IaAltn......... Alton Public Library, Alton, IA [*Library symbol Library of Congress*] (LCLS)

IaAlto......... Altoona Public Library, Altoona, IA [*Library symbol Library of Congress*] (LCLS)

IaAltoH....... Herald-Mitchellville Index, Altoona, IA [*Library symbol Library of Congress*] (LCLS)

IAAM.......... Incorporated Association of Assistant Masters [*British*]

IAAM.......... Independent Accountants Association of Michigan (SRA)

IAAM.......... International Association of Auditorium Managers (EA)

IAAM.......... International Association of Automotive Modelers [*Defunct*] (EA)

IAAM.......... Irish Anti-Apartheid Movement (EAIO)

IAAMRH...... International Association of Agricultural Medicine and Rural Health (EA)

IaAna......... Anamosa Public Library, Anamosa, IA [*Library symbol Library of Congress*] (LCLS)

IaAnaE....... Anamosa Eureka, Anamosa, IA [*Library symbol Library of Congress*] (LCLS)

IaAnaJ....... Anamosa Journal, Anamosa, IA [*Library symbol Library of Congress*] (LCLS)

IA & T........ Integration, Assembly, and Test

IaAniF........ Fontanelle Observer, Anita, IA [*Library symbol Library of Congress*] (LCLS)

IaAniT....... Anita Tribune, Anita, IA [*Library symbol Library of Congress*] (LCLS)

IaAnk......... Kirkendall Public Library, Ankeny, IA [*Library symbol Library of Congress*] (LCLS)

IaAnkD....... Des Moines Area Community College, Ankeny, IA [*Library symbol Library of Congress*] (LCLS)

IaAnkFB...... Faith Baptist Bible College, Ankeny, IA [*Library symbol Library of Congress*] (LCLS)

IaAnkP .... Ankeny Press-Citizen, Ankeny, IA [*Library symbol Library of Congress*] (LCLS)

IaAnt .... Anthon Public Library, Anthon, IA [*Library symbol Library of Congress*] (LCLS)

IaAntH .... Anthon Herald, Anthon, IA [*Library symbol Library of Congress*] (LCLS)

IAAO .... International Association of Assessing Officers (EA)

IAAOC .... International Association of Addictions and Offender Counseling (EA)

IAAOPA .... International Association of Aircraft Owners and Pilots Association (BARN)

IaAp .... Aplington Legion Memorial Library, Aplington, IA [*Library symbol Library of Congress*] (LCLS)

IAAP .... International Association for Analytical Psychology (EA)

IAAP .... International Association of Amusement Parks [*Later, IAAPA*]

IAAP .... International Association of Applied Psychology [*Nijmegen, Netherlands*] (EA)

IAAP .... Iowa Army Ammunition Plant (AABC)

IAAPA .... International Association of Amusement Parks and Attractions (EA)

IAAPEA .... International Association Against Painful Experiments on Animals (EA)

IAAPF .... Iona Appliances [*NASDAQ symbol*] (TTSB)

IAAPO .... International Association of Amusement and Park Owners

IAAR .... Imidazoleacetic Acid Ribonucleotide (DMAA)

IAAR .... Independent Associaton of Accredited Registrars [*For quality control*]

IAAR .... United States Information Agency Acquisition Regulation [*A publication*] (AAGC)

IAARC .... International Administrative Aeronautical Radio Conference [*Also known as WARC*]

IaArl .... Arlington Public Library, Arlington, IA [*Library symbol Library of Congress*] (LCLS)

IaArmJ .... Armstrong Journal, Armstrong, IA [*Library symbol Library of Congress*] (LCLS)

IAAS .... Incorporated Association of Architects and Surveyors [*British*] (DBA)

IAAS .... Institute of Auctioneers and Appraisers in Scotland (EAIO)

IAAS .... International Association of Agricultural Students [*See also AIEA*] [*Uppsala, Sweden*] (EAIO)

IaAS .... Iowa State University of Science and Technology, Ames, IA [*Library symbol Library of Congress*] (LCLS)

IAASA .... Indian Australian Association of South Australia

IAASE .... Independent Appeals Authority for School Examinations (AIE)

IAASE .... Inter-American Association of Sanitary Engineering [*Later, Inter-American Association of Sanitary and Environmental Engineering*] (EA)

IAASEES ...... Inter-American Association of Sanitary Engineering and Environmental Sciences (EAIO)

IAASM .... International Academy of Aviation and Space Medicine (EAIO)

IAASP .... International Association of Airport and Seaport Police [*Canada*] (EAIO)

IAASS .... International Association of Applied Social Scientists [*Later, CCI*]

IaAS-V .... Iowa State University of Science and Technology, School of Veterinary Medicine, Ames, IA [*Library symbol Library of Congress*] (LCLS)

IaAT .... Ames Daily Tribune, Ames, IA [*Library symbol Library of Congress*] (LCLS)

IaAt .... Atlantic Public Library, Atlantic, IA [*Library symbol Library of Congress*] (LCLS)

IAAT .... International Association Against Torture (EAIO)

IAATI .... International Association Auto Theft Investigators (EA)

IaAtL .... Atlantic Public Library, Atlantic, IA [*Library symbol*] [*Library of Congress*] (LCLS)

IAATM .... International Association for Accident and Traffic Medicine (EA)

IaAtNT .... Atlantic News-Telegraph, Atlantic, IA [*Library symbol Library of Congress*] (LCLS)

IaAu .... Audubon Public Library, Audubon, IA [*Library symbol Library of Congress*] (LCLS)

IaAub .... Auburn Public Library, Auburn, IA [*Library symbol Library of Congress*] (LCLS)

IaAubE .... Auburn Enterprise, Auburn, IA [*Library symbol Library of Congress*] (LCLS)

IaAuCoC ...... Audubon County Courthouse, Audubon, IA [*Library symbol Library of Congress*] (LCLS)

IaAuNA .... Audubon News-Advocate, Audubon, IA [*Library symbol Library of Congress*] (LCLS)

IaAur .... Aurelia Public Library, Aurelia, IA [*Library symbol Library of Congress*] (LCLS)

IaAurS .... Aurelia Sentinel, Aurelia, IA [*Library symbol Library of Congress*] (LCLS)

IAAV .... Alliance of Atomic Veterans [*International Alliance of Atomic Vetrans*] [*Acronym is based on former name,*] (EA)

IaAv .... Avoca Public Library, Avoca, IA [*Library symbol Library of Congress*] (LCLS)

IAAV .... International Association of Airborne Veterans (EA)

IaAvJH .... Avoca Journal-Herald, Avoca, IA [*Library symbol Library of Congress*] (LCLS)

IaAWD .... Wildlife Disease Association, Ames, IA [*Library symbol Library of Congress*] (LCLS)

IAAWS .... Infantry Antiarmor Weapon Systems [*Military*] (INF)

IaB .... Burlington Free Public Library, Burlington, IA [*Library symbol Library of Congress*] (LCLS)

IAB .... Identa-Band (DAVI)

IAB .... Idle Air Bleed [*Fuel system*] [*Automotive engineering*]

IAB .... Immigration Appeal Board [*Canada*]

IAB .... Indirect Address Buffer

IAB .... Industrial Accident Board

IAB .... Industrial Advisers to the Blind Ltd. [*British*] (BI)

IAB .... Industrial Advisory Board [*World War II*]

IAB .... Industrial Arbitration Board [*British*]

IAB .... Institute of Animal Behavior [*Rutgers University*] [*Research center*] (RCD)

IAB .... Institute of Arctic Biology [*Research center*] (RCD)

IAB .... Institut fuer Arbeitsmarkt- und Berufsforschung [*Institute for Employment Research*] [*Federal Employment Institute*] [*Germany*] (IID)

IAB .... Instrumentation Analysis Branch (SAA)

IAB .... Interagency Board of Examiners [*Civil Service Commission*]

IAB .... Inter-America Bank (WDAA)

IAB .... Interim Airframe Bulletin (MCD)

IAB .... Interim Armament Bulletin (MCD)

IAB .... International Abstracting Board [*Also, ICSU AB*] [*International Council of Scientific Unions*]

IAB .... International Association of Bibliophiles [*See also AIB*] [*Paris, France*] (EAIO)

IAB .... International Association of Boards of Examiners in Optometry (EA)

IAB .... International Association of Bookkeepers [*British*] (EAIO)

IAB .... International Association of Broadcasting (NTCM)

IAB .... International Association of Business (EA)

IAB .... Internationale Akademie fuer Bader-, Sport-, und Freizeitheitbau [*International Board for Aquatic, Sports, and Recreation Facilities*] [*Bad Neustadt/Saale, Federal Republic of Germany*] (EAIO)

IAB .... Internet Architecture Board

IAB .... Interrupt Address to Bus [*Computer science*]

IAB .... Intra-Abdominal [*Artery*]

IAB .... Intra-Aortic Balloon [*Cardiology*]

IAB .... Iowa Administrative Bulletin [*A publication*] (AAGC)

IAB .... Irish Association for the Blind (BI)

IAB .... Island Arc Basalt [*Geology*]

IAB .... Italian American Business [*American Chamber of Commerce in Italy*] [*A publication*]

IAB .... IUS [*Interior Upper Stage*] Assembly Building [*NASA*] (MCD)

IAB .... John Crerar Library, Chicago, IL [*OCLC symbol*] (OCLC)

IAB .... Wichita, KS [*Location identifier FAA*] (FAAL)

IABA .... Inter-American Bar Association (EA)

IABA .... International Amateur Boxing Association

IABA .... International Association of Aircraft Brokers and Agents [*Norway*] (EAIO)

IABA .... Intra-Aortic Balloon Assist [*Cardiology*]

IABA .... Irish Amateur Boxing Association (BI)

IaBag .... Bagley Public Library, Bagley, IA [*Library symbol Library of Congress*] (LCLS)

IaBagG .... Bagley Gazette, Bagley, IA [*Library symbol Library of Congress*] (LCLS)

IAB-AIR .... International Association of Broadcasting - Asociacion Internacional de Radiodifusion [*Formerly, Inter-American Association of Broadcasters*] (EA)

IaBanR .... Bancroft Register, Bancroft, IA [*Library symbol Library of Congress*] (LCLS)

IA Bar Rev ... Iowa Bar Review [*A publication*] (DLA)

IaBatB .... Batavia Beacon, Batavia, IA [*Library symbol Library of Congress*] (LCLS)

IaBaxNE ...... Baxter New Era, Baxter, IA [*Library symbol Library of Congress*] (LCLS)

IaBaxWC ..... Baxter Women's Club, Baxter, IA [*Library symbol Library of Congress*] (LCLS)

IaBay .... Bayard Public Library, Bayard, IA [*Library symbol Library of Congress*] (LCLS)

IaBayN .... Bayard News, Bayard, IA [*Library symbol Library of Congress*] (LCLS)

IABB .... Inter-American Bank Bond (MHDW)

IABBE .... International Association for Better Basic Education (EA)

IABBE .... International Association of Black Business Educators [*Defunct*] (EA)

IABBS .... International Amateur Boat Building Society [*Defunct*]

IABC .... Idle Air Bypass Control [*Fuel system*] [*Automotive engineering*]

IABC .... International Association of Building Companions [*See also IBO*] [*Marche-En-Famenne, Belgium*] (EAIO)

IABC .... International Association of Business Communicators (EA)

IABC .... Intra-Aortic Balloon Catheter [*Cardiology*] (DAVI)

IABC .... Intra-Aortic Balloon Counterpulsation [*Cardiology*]

IaBclHi .... Ida County Historical Society, Battle Creek, IA [*Library symbol Library of Congress*] (LCLS)

IaBcT .... Battle Creek Times, Battle Creek, IA [*Library symbol Library of Congress*] (LCLS)

IaBDHi .... Des Moines County Historical Society, Burlington, IA [*Library symbol Library of Congress*] (LCLS)

IABE .... Ibero-American Bureau of Education [*See also OEI*] [*Madrid, Spain*] (EAIO)

IaBedTP .... Bedford Times-Press, Bedford, IA [*Library symbol Library of Congress*] (LCLS)

IaBelm .... Belmond Public Library, Belmond, IA [*Library symbol Library of Congress*] (LCLS)

IaBelmI .... Belmond Independent, Belmond, IA [*Library symbol Library of Congress*] (LCLS)

IaBepU .... Belle Plaine Union, Belle Plaine, IA [*Library symbol Library of Congress*] (LCLS)

IaBetN .... Bettendorf News, Bettendorf, IA [*Library symbol Library of Congress*] (LCLS)

IaBev .... Bellevue Public Library, Bellevue, IA [*Library symbol Library of Congress*] (LCLS)

IaBevHL ...... Bellevue Herald-Leader, Bellevue, IA [*Library symbol Library of Congress*] (LCLS)

IABF .... Inter-American Bar Foundation (EA)

IABF............	International Association of Business Forecasting (EA)
IABG	International Association of Botanic Gardens [*Australia*] (EA)
IABG	International Association of Buying Groups [*See also IVE*] (EAIO)
IABK............	International Association of Book-Keepers [*Sevenoaks, Kent, England*] (EA)
IaBI.............	Bloomfield Public Library, Bloomfield, IA [*Library symbol Library of Congress*] (LCLS)
IABL............	Independent Association of Builders' Labourers [*A union*] [*British*]
IABLA........	Inter-American Bank for Latin America (WDAA)
IaBlak.........	Blakesburg Public Library, Blakesburg, IA [*Library symbol Library of Congress*] (LCLS)
IaBlaSP.......	South Benton Star Press, Blairstown, IA [*Library symbol Library of Congress*] (LCLS)
IaBID	Bloomfield Democrat, Bloomfield, IA [*Library symbol Library of Congress*] (LCLS)
IaBIDR	Davis County Republican, Bloomfield, IA [*Library symbol Library of Congress*] (LCLS)
IaBIGen.......	Davis County Genealogical Society, Bloomfield, IA [*Library symbol Library of Congress*] (LCLS)
IABM...........	International Academy of Biological Medicine [*Defunct*] (EA)
IABM...........	International Association of Broadcasting Manufacturers [*Hayes, Middlesex, England*] (EAIO)
IABM...........	International Association of Broadcast Monitors (EA)
IaBo	Ericson Public Library, Boone, IA [*Library symbol Library of Congress*] (LCLS)
IABO	Internacia Asocio de Bibliistoj kaj Orientalistoj [*International Association of Biblicists and Orientalists - IABO*] (EA)
IABO	International Association for Biological Oceanography [*Aberdeen, Scotland*] (EAIO)
IaBoCoC......	Boone County Courthouse, Boone, IA [*Library symbol Library of Congress*] (LCLS)
IaBonR........	Bonaparte Record-Republican, Bonaparte, IA [*Library symbol Library of Congress*] (LCLS)
IaBoNR	Boone News-Republican, Boone, IA [*Library symbol Library of Congress*] (LCLS)
IaBonRR	Bonaparte Record-Republican, Bonaparte, IA [*Library symbol*] [*Library of Congress*] (LCLS)
IABP............	International Arctic Buoy Program [*Marine science*] (OSRA)
IABP............	International Association of Businessmen and Professionals (EA)
IABP............	Intra-Aortic Balloon Pump [*Cardiology*]
IABPA	Intra-Aortic Balloon Pumping Assistance [*Cardiology*] (AAMN)
IABPAI	International Association of Blue Print and Allied Industries [*Later, IRGBA, IRA*] (EA)
IABPBD.......	International Alliance of Bill Posters, Billers, and Distributors of US and Canada [*Defunct*]
IABPC	International Association of Book Publishing Consultants [*Inactive*] (EA)
IABPFF........	International Association of Black Professional Fire Fighters (EA)
IABR	Index to Australian Book Reviews [*A publication*]
IaBrBEN	Brighton Enterprise-News, Brighton, IA [*Library symbol*] [*Library of Congress*] (LCLS)
IaBreN	Breda News, Breda, IA [*Library symbol Library of Congress*] (LCLS)
IaBrEN	Brighton Enterprise-News, Brighton, IA [*Library symbol Library of Congress*] (LCLS)
IA B Rev	Iowa Bar Review [*A publication*] (DLA)
IaBriNT	Britt News-Tribune, Britt, IA [*Library symbol Library of Congress*] (LCLS)
IABRM	International Association for Bear Research and Management (EA)
IaBroC	Brooklyn Chronicle, Brooklyn, IA [*Library symbol Library of Congress*] (LCLS)
IABS...........	Installation Automated Budget System [*Army*]
IABS...........	International Absorbents [*NASDAQ symbol*] (SAG)
IABS...........	International Alban Berg Society (EA)
IABS...........	International Association for Byzantine Studies [*See also AIEB*] [*Thessaloniki, Greece*] (EAIO)
IABS...........	International Association of Biological Standardization [*See also AISB*] [*ICSU Geneva, Switzerland*] (EAIO)
IABS...........	International Association of Buddhist Studies (EA)
IABSE..........	International Association for Bridge and Structural Engineering [*ICSU*] [*Zurich, Switzerland*] [*Research center*] (EA)
IABSF.........	Intl Absorbents [*NASDAQ symbol*] (TTSB)
IABSIW	International Association of Bridge, Structural, and Ornamental Iron Workers (BARN)
IABSOIW......	International Association of Bridge, Structural, and Ornamental Iron Workers (EA)
IABT...........	Illinois Association of Biology Teachers (EDAC)
IABTI	International Association of Bomb Technicians and Investigators (EA)
IaBucCT	Buffalo Center Tribune, Buffalo Center, IA [*Library symbol Library of Congress*] (LCLS)
IABWMT	International Association of Black and White Men Together [*Later, NABWMT*] (EA)
IAC.............	Chicago, IL [*Location identifier FAA*] (FAAL)
IAC.............	De Paul University, Chicago, IL [*OCLC symbol*] (OCLC)
IAC.............	Iceberg Athletic Club (EA)
IAC.............	Identification Accuracy [*Rate*] (MCD)
IAC.............	Idle Air Control [*Automotive engineering*]
I-Ac............	Imidazoleacetic Acid [*Biochemistry*] (AAMN)
IAC.............	Immigration Appeal Cases [*Canada*] [*A publication*] (DLA)
IAC.............	Improved Anode Catalyst
IAC.............	Indiana Administrative Code [*A publication*] (AAGC)
IAC.............	Indian Airlines Corp. [*ICAO designator*] (FAAC)
IAC.............	Indian Army Circular [*British military*] (DMA)
IAC.............	Industrial Accident Commission Decisions [*A publication*] (DLA)
IAC.............	Industries Assistance Commission (EERA)
IAC.............	Industry Advisory Committee [*World War II*]

IAC.............	Industry Advisory Committee on Survey and Mapping [*Queensland*] [*State*] (EERA)
IAC.............	Industry Advisory Conference [*Underwriters Laboratories*] [*Telecommunications*]
IAC.............	Industry Advisory Council [*Formerly, DIAC*]
IAC.............	Ineffective Airway Clearance [*Medicine*] (DMAA)
IAC.............	Information Access Co. [*Information service or system*] (IID)
IAC.............	Information Analysis Center [*DoD*]
IAC.............	Information and Communication
IAC.............	Inheritance of Acquired Characteristics
IAC.............	Initial Approach Course [*Aviation*]
IAC.............	Inner Approach Channel
IAC.............	Installation and Checkout (IAA)
IAC.............	Instantaneous Airborne Count (MCD)
IAC.............	Institute for Advanced Concepts [*In 1980 film "Simon"*]
IAC.............	Institute for Antiquity and Christianity [*Claremont University*] [*Research center*] (RCD)
IAC.............	Institute of Amateur Cinematographers [*British*] (BI)
IAC.............	Institute of Applied Clicheology
IAC.............	Instrument Approach Chart (AAG)
IAC.............	Instrument Array Cable
IAC.............	Instrumentation and Control (IAA)
IAC.............	Insurance Advertising Conference [*Later, IMCA*] (EA)
IAC.............	Integrating Assembly Contractor
IAC.............	Integrating Associate Contractor
IAC.............	Integration, Assembly, and Checkout
IAC.............	Intelligence Advisory Committee
IAC.............	Intelligence Analysis Center [*Marine Corps*] (MCD)
IAC.............	Intelligent Asynchronous Controller [*Computer terminal connector*] (NITA)
IAC.............	Interactive Array Computer
IAC.............	Interagency Committee for Outdoor Recreation [*Department of the Interior*]
IAC.............	Interagency Conference (MCD)
IAC.............	Inter-American Council
IAC.............	Interapplication Communication [*Apple Computer, Inc.*]
IAC.............	InterApplication Communications [*Computer science*] (CDE)
IAC.............	Inter-Applications Communication [*Computer science*] (EERA)
IAC.............	Interarray Communications (NVT)
IAC.............	Interdepartmental Advisory Committee [*World War II*]
IAC.............	Interface Assurance Contractor
IAC.............	Intergrated Avionics Computer [*DA*]
IAC.............	Interim Acceptance Criteria (NRCH)
IAC.............	Interim Action Committee [*British*]
IAC.............	Intermediate Air Command [*Air Force*] (AFM)
IAC.............	Intermittent Abdominal Compression
IAC.............	Internal Auditory Canal [*Anatomy*]
IAC.............	International Academy of Ceramics [*See also AIC*] [*Geneva, Switzerland*] (EAIO)
IAC.............	International Academy of Cytology [*Quebec, PQ*] (EA)
IAC.............	International Activities Committee [*American Chemical Society*]
IAC.............	International Advisory Committee [*ANSI*]
IAC.............	International Advisory Council for Homosexual Men and Women in Alcoholics Anonymous (EA)
IAC.............	International Aerobatic Club (EA)
IAC.............	International Agricultural Club (EA)
IAC.............	International Air Convention
IAC.............	International Algebraic Compiler
IAC.............	International Analysis Code [*Meteorology*]
IAC.............	International Anti-Counterfeiting Coalition (EA)
IAC.............	International Artists' Cooperation (EAIO)
IAC.............	International Association for Cybernetics [*See also AIC*] [*Namur, Belgium*] (EAIO)
IAC.............	International Association of Charities [*See also AIC*] (EAIO)
IAC.............	International Astronautical Congress
IAC.............	Interposed Abdominal Counterpulsation [*Medicine*]
IAC.............	Interview-after-Combat
IAC.............	Intra-Arterial Chemotherapy [*Medicine*]
IAC.............	Inventory of Anger Communication [*Personality development test*] [*Psychology*]
IAC.............	Iowa Administrative Code [*A publication*] (AAGC)
IAC.............	Ipsilateral Associational-Commissural [*Anatomy*]
IAC.............	Irvine Apartment Communities [*NYSE symbol*] (SAG)
IAC.............	Isolated Adrenal Cell [*Endocrinology*] (DAVI)
IAC.............	Israel Aliyah Center (EA)
IAC.............	Italian Aircraft Corp.
IaCa............	Duncan Memorial Library, Casey, IA [*Library symbol Library of Congress*] (LCLS)
IACA...........	Independent Air Carriers Association [*Defunct*] (EA)
IACA...........	Indian Arts and Crafts Association (EA)
IACA...........	Inter-American College Association (EA)
IACA...........	Inter-American Cultural Association (EA)
IACA...........	International Air Carrier Association [*Zaventhem, Belgium*] (EAIO)
IACA...........	International Association for Classical Archaeology [*See also AIAC*] [*Rome, Italy*] (EAIO)
IACA...........	International Association of Consulting Actuaries (MHDB)
IACA...........	Intra-Application Communication Area [*Computer science*] (PCM)
IACA...........	Irish American Cultural Association (EA)
IACAAC	International Artists' Cooperation Audio Art Center [*Defunct*] (EA)
I-ACAC	Inter-American Commercial Arbitration Commission
IACAC	International Association of Civil Aviation Chaplains (EA)
IAC/ADP	Interagency Committee on Automatic Data Processing [*Office of Management and Budget*]
IACAPAP......	International Association for Child and Adolescent Psychiatry and Allied Professions [*Copenhagen, Denmark*] (EA)

IaCar............ Carroll Public Library, Carroll, IA [*Library symbol Library of Congress*] (LCLS)

IaCarCH....... Carroll County Historical Society Museum, Carroll, IA [*Library symbol Library of Congress*] (LCLS)

IaCarl........... Carlisle Public Library, Carlisle, IA [*Library symbol Library of Congress*] (LCLS)

IaCarlC........ Carlisle Citizen, Carlisle, IA [*Library symbol Library of Congress*] (LCLS)

IaCarsT........ Carson Times, Carson, IA [*Library symbol Library of Congress*] (LCLS)

IaCarTH....... Daily Times-Herald, Carroll, IA [*Library symbol Library of Congress*] (LCLS)

IaCasPA....... Cascade Pioneer-Advertiser, Cascade, IA [*Library symbol Library of Congress*] (LCLS)

IaCb............. Council Bluffs Free Public Library, Council Bluffs, IA [*Library symbol Library of Congress*] (LCLS)

IACB............ Indian Arts and Crafts Board [*Department of the Interior*]

IACB............ Inter-Agency Consultative Board (EY)

IACB............ International Advisory Committee on Bibliography [*UNESCO*] (WDAA)

IACB............ International Association of Convention Bureaus [*Later, IACVB*] (EA)

IACB............ Intra-Aortic Counterpulsation Balloon [*Cardiology*] (DAVI)

IACBD.......... International Academy for Child Brain Development (EA)

IACBDT........ International Advisory Committee on Bibliography, Documentation and Terminology (NITA)

IaCbN........... Nonpareil, Council Bluffs, IA [*Library symbol Library of Congress*] (LCLS)

IACC............ India-America Chamber of Commerce (EA)

IACC............ Indo-American Chamber of Commerce (PDAA)

IACC............ Industrial Analysis and Control Council

IACC............ Integrating Assembly and Checkout Contractor

IACC............ Inter-Agency Air Cartographic Committee

IACC............ Interamerican Confederation of Cattlemen (EA)

IACC............ Inter-American Cultural Council (EA)

IACC............ International Air Cargo Corp. [*Egypt*] [*ICAO designator*] (FAAC)

IACC............ International Alliance of Catholic Churches (EA)

IACC............ International Americas Cup Class [*Yachting*]

IACC............ International Anticounterfeiting Coalition (EA)

IACC............ International Art Cinemas Confederation (EAIO)

IACC............ International Association of Conference Centers (EA)

IACC............ Iran American Chamber of Commerce (EA)

IACC............ Island Arts and Crafts Club, Victoria [*1910, IACS from 1922*] (NGC)

IACC............ Israel-America Chamber of Commerce and Industry (EAIO)

IACC............ Italian-American Chamber of Commerce (EA)

IACc............ Italy-America Chamber of Commerce (EA)

IaCc .... John E. Clegg Library, Central City, IA [*Library symbol Library of Congress*] (LCLS)

IACCB .... Illinois Association of Community College Biologists (EDAC)

IACCE.......... Inter-American Confederation for Catholic Education [*Bogota, Colombia*] (EAIO)

IACCI .... International Association of Computer Crime Investigators [*Defunct*] (EA)

IACCI .... International Association of Credit Card Investigators (EA)

IaCcL .... Linn News-Letter, Central City, IA [*Library symbol Library of Congress*] (LCLS)

IACCN .... Inventory Accounting Cost Control Number System (MCD)

IACCP .... Inter-American Council of Commerce and Production

IACCP .... International Association for Cross-Cultural Psychology [*Canada*] (EA)

IAC-CPR...... Interposed Abdominal Compression - Cardiopulmonary Resuscitation

IACD .... International Association of Clothing Designers (EA)

IACD .... Irish Association for Curriculum Development (AIE)

IAC Dec ...... Decisions of the Industrial Accident Commission of California [*A publication*] (DLA)

IACDLA .... International Advisory Committee on Documentation, Libraries, and Archives [*UNESCO*] (DIT)

IACDT .... International Association of Certified Duncan Teachers (EA)

IACE............ Intergovernmental Advisory Council on Education (AEE)

IACE............ International Air Cadet Exchange

IACE............ International Association for Computing in Education [*Also, an information service or system*] (EA)

IACED .... Inter-African Advisory Committee on Epizootic Diseases

IACED .... Interagency Committee on Environment and Development (EERA)

IaCenv .... Drake Public Library, Centerville, IA [*Library symbol Library of Congress*] (LCLS)

IaCenvl .... Iowegian & Citizen, Centerville, IA [*Library symbol Library of Congress*] (LCLS)

IACESC .... Inter-American Council for Education, Science, and Culture

IACET.......... International Association for Continuing Education and Training (EA)

IaCf............. Cedar Falls Public Library, Cedar Falls, IA [*Library symbol Library of Congress*] (LCLS)

IACF............ Inter-American Cement Federation [*Colombia*] (EAIO)

IACF............ International Amateur Cycling Federation (EA)

IACF............ International Association for Cultural Freedom [*Defunct*] (EA)

IaCfE........... Eastern Area Library Cooperative, Cedar Falls, IA [*Library symbol Library of Congress*] (LCLS)

IACFHG....... Inter Action Council of Former Heads of Government (EA)

IaCfHi .... Cedar Falls Historical Society, Cedar Falls, IA [*Library symbol Library of Congress*] (LCLS)

IACFM.......... International Association of Concert and Festival Managers [*Later, ISPAA*] (EA)

IaCfNl .... Northern Iowan, Cedar Falls, IA [*Library symbol Library of Congress*] (LCLS)

IaCfR .... Cedar Falls Record, Cedar Falls, IA [*Library symbol Library of Congress*] (LCLS)

IaCfT .... University of Northern Iowa, Cedar Falls, IA [*Library symbol Library of Congress*] (LCLS)

IACG .... Institute for American Church Growth (EA)

IaCh .... Free Public Library, Chariton, IA [*Library symbol Library of Congress*] (LCLS)

IACH .... Inter-Association Committee on Health

IACHA.......... Iowa Automated Clearing House Association

IaChc .... Charles City Public Library, Charles City, IA [*Library symbol Library of Congress*] (LCLS)

IaChcP .... Charles City Press, Charles City, IA [*Library symbol Library of Congress*] (LCLS)

IaChe .... Cherokee Public Library, Cherokee, IA [*Library symbol Library of Congress*] (LCLS)

IACHE .... International Association of Cylindrical Hydraulic Engineers (EA)

IaCheCHi .... Cherokee County Historical Society, Cherokee, IA [*Library symbol Library of Congress*] (LCLS)

IaCheCoC.... Cherokee County Courthouse, Cherokee, IA [*Library symbol Library of Congress*] (LCLS)

IaChHP .... Chariton Herald-Patriot, Chariton, IA [*Library symbol Library of Congress*] (LCLS)

IaChL .... Chariton Leader, Chariton, IA [*Library symbol Library of Congress*] (LCLS)

IaChoT .... Charter Oak Times, Charter Oak, IA [*Library symbol Library of Congress*] (LCLS)

IACHR.......... Inter-American Commission on Human Rights (EA)

IaChu .... Churdan City Library, Churdan, IA [*Library symbol Library of Congress*] (LCLS)

IACI .... Idiopathic Arterial Calcification of Infancy [*Medicine*] (DMAA)

IACI .... Industrial Acoustics Co., Inc. [*NASDAQ symbol*] (NQ)

IACI .... Inter-American Children's Institute [*Uruguay*] [*Research center*] (IRC)

IACI .... Iran Aircraft Industries (MCD)

IACI .... Irish American Cultural Institute (EA)

IACIA .... Interagency Committee for International Athletics [*Defunct*]

IACID .... Inter-American Center for Integral Development [*OAS*]

IACITC .... International Advisory Committee of the International Teletraffic Congress (EAIO)

IACJ............ Inter-American Council of Jurists [*Organization of American States*] [*Washington, DC*]

IaCjGS .... Columbus Gazette & Columbus Safeguard, Columbus Junction, IA [*Library symbol Library of Congress*] (LCLS)

IACKL.......... Interrupt Acknowledgment Latency [*Computer science*]

IaCkvS .... Clarksville Star, Clarksville, IA [*Library symbol Library of Congress*] (LCLS)

IACL............ International Aeradio Caribbean Ltd.

IACL............ International Association of Constitutional Law [*See also AIDC*] [*Belgrade, Yugoslavia*] (EAIO)

IaCla .... Clarion Public Library, Clarion, IA [*Library symbol Library of Congress*] (LCLS)

IACLA.......... International Association of Clinical Laser Acupuncturists (EA)

IaClad .... Clarinda Public Library, Clarinda, IA [*Library symbol Library of Congress*] (LCLS)

IaCladHJ..... Clarinda Herald-Journal, Clarinda, IA [*Library symbol Library of Congress*] (LCLS)

IaClaM........ Wright County Monitor, Clarion, IA [*Library symbol Library of Congress*] (LCLS)

IaClar......... Edna Zybell Memorial Library, Clarence, IA [*Library symbol Library of Congress*] (LCLS)

IaClarCHi.... Cedar County Historical Society, Clarence, IA [*Library symbol Library of Congress*] (LCLS)

IACLE .... International Association of Contact Lens Educators

IACLEA........ International Association of Campus Law Enforcement Administrators (EA)

IaClfC.......... Clearfield Chronicle, Clearfield, IA [*Library symbol Library of Congress*] (LCLS)

IaCli .... Clinton Public Library, Clinton, IA [*Library symbol Library of Congress*] (LCLS)

IaCliC.......... Clinton Corn Processing Co., Clinton, IA [*Library symbol Library of Congress*] (LCLS)

IaCliCC .... Clinton Community College, Clinton, IA [*Library symbol Library of Congress*] (LCLS)

IaCliCHi....... Clinton County Historical Society, Clinton, IA [*Library symbol Library of Congress*] (LCLS)

IaCliH .... Clinton Herald, Clinton, IA [*Library symbol Library of Congress*] (LCLS)

IaCliM.......... Mount Saint Clare College, Clinton, IA [*Library symbol Library of Congress*] (LCLS)

IaCll .... Clear Lake Public Library, Clear Lake, IA [*Library symbol Library of Congress*] (LCLS)

IaClvS .... Clarksville Star, Clarksville, IA [*Library symbol Library of Congress*] (LCLS)

IACM............ International Association for Computational Mechanics [*International Council of Scientific Unions*]

IACM............ International Association of Circulation Managers

IACM............ International Association of Concert Managers [*Later, ISPAA*] (EA)

IACME.......... International Association of Coroners and Medical Examiners (EA)

IACME.......... International Association of Crafts and Small- and Medium-Sized Enterprises [*Switzerland*] (EY)

IACMHA....... Illinois Association of Community Mental Health Agencies (SRA)

IACNRE........ International Association for Conservation of Natural Resources and Energy

IACO .... Conservative Orthopedics International Association (EA)

IACO .... Illinois Association of County Officials (SRA)

IACO .... Integrated Assembly and Checkout (SSD)

IACO .... Inter-African Coffee Organization (EAIO)

IACO .... International Association of Correctional Officers (EA)

IACOA......... Independent Armored Car Operators Association (EA)

IACOCCA..... I Am Chairman of Chrysler Corp. of America [*Acronym formed from name of Chrysler chairman Lee Iacocca*]

IAC of Cal.... Decisions of the Industrial Accident Commission of California [*A publication*] (DLA)

IaCogM........ Coggan Monitor, Coggan, IA [*Library symbol Library of Congress*] (LCLS)

IaCol........... Colfax Free Public Library, Colfax, IA [*Library symbol Library of Congress*] (LCLS)

IaColJ.......... Jasper County Tribune, Colfax, IA [*Library symbol Library of Congress*] (LCLS)

IaColn.......... Collins Public Library, Collins, IA [*Library symbol Library of Congress*] (LCLS)

IACOMS........ International Advisory Committee on Marine Sciences [*UNESCO*] (ASF)

IaCon........... Conrad Public Library, Conrad, IA [*Library symbol*] [*Library of Congress*] (LCLS)

IaConR......... Conrad Record, Conrad, IA [*Library symbol Library of Congress*] (LCLS)

IaCoon......... Coon Rapids Enterprise, Coon Rapids, IA [*Library symbol Library of Congress*] (LCLS)

IACOP.......... International Armaments Cooperative Opportunities Plan

IaCorn.......... Corning Free Public Library, Corning, IA [*Library symbol Library of Congress*] (LCLS)

IaCornFP...... Adams County Free Press, Corning, IA [*Library symbol Library of Congress*] (LCLS)

IaCorrN........ Correctionville News, Correctionville, IA [*Library symbol Library of Congress*] (LCLS)

IaCorv.......... Coralville Public Library, Coralville, IA [*Library symbol Library of Congress*] (LCLS)

IaCorvC........ Coralville Courier, Coralville, IA [*Library symbol Library of Congress*] (LCLS)

IaCorwH....... Corwith Herald, Corwith, IA [*Library symbol Library of Congress*] (LCLS)

IaCoryTR...... Corydon Times-Republican, Corydon, IA [*Library symbol Library of Congress*] (LCLS)

IaCoryWC.... Wayne County Courthouse, Corydon, IA [*Library symbol*] [*Library of Congress*] (LCLS)

IaCoryWCoC.. Wayne County Courthouse, Corydon, IA [*Library symbol Library of Congress*] (LCLS)

IACP............. Industrial Arts Curriculum Project [*Education*] (AEE)

IACP............. Integrated Air Cancer Project [*Environmental Protection Agency*]

IACP............. International Association for Child Psychiatry and Allied Professions [*Later, IACAPAP*]

IACP............. International Association of Chiefs of Police (EA)

IACP............. International Association of Computer Programmers

IACP............. International Association of Cooking Professionals (EA)

IACP............. Intra-Aortic Counterpulsation [*Cardiology*] (DAVI)

IACPA.......... Inter-American Council of Psychiatric Associations (DAVI)

IACPAP........ International Association for Child Psychiatry and Allied Professions [*Later, IACAPAP*]

IACPP.......... International Association of Crime Prevention Practitioners (EA)

IACPR.......... Inter-American Committee of Presidential Representatives

IACPS.......... Inter-American Committee on Peaceful Settlement [*Defunct Defunct*] (EA)

IACPS.......... International Academy of Chest Physicians and Surgeons (EA)

IACPWR....... Inter-Allied Committee on Post-War Requirements [*World War II*]

IaCr.............. Cedar Rapids Public Library, Cedar Rapids, IA [*Library symbol Library of Congress*] (LCLS)

IACR .... Institue of Arable Crop Research [*British*]

IACR .... Inter-American Congress of Radiology

IACR .... International Agreement Competitive Restrictions (AAGC)

IACR .... International Association for Cryptologic Research (EA)

IACR .... International Association of Cancer Registries [*Lyon, France*] (EAIO)

IACRAO........ Illinois Association of Collegiate Registrars and Admissions Officers (SRA)

IaCrC .... Coe College, Cedar Rapids, IA [*Library symbol Library of Congress*] (LCLS)

IACRD.......... Inter-American Center for Regional Development (EAIO)

IACRDP........ International Association of Cross-Reference Directory Publishers (EA)

IACRDVT...... Inter-American Centre for Research and Documentation on Vocational Training [*See also CINTERFOR*] [*Montevideo, Uruguay*] (EAIO)

IaCre........... Cresco Public Library, Cresco, IA [*Library symbol*] [*Library of Congress*] (LCLS)

IACREE........ International Association of Corporate Real Estate Executives (EA)

IaCreHC....... Howard County Courthouse, Cresco, IA [*Library symbol*] [*Library of Congress*] (LCLS)

IACREOT...... International Association of Clerks, Recorders, Election Officials, and Treasurers (EA)

IaCres.......... Matilda J. Gibson Memorial Library, Creston, IA [*Library symbol Library of Congress*] (LCLS)

IaCresco ...... Cresco Public Library, Cresco, IA [*Library symbol Library of Congress*] (LCLS)

IaCrescoCoC.. Howard County Courthouse, Cresco, IA [*Library symbol Library of Congress*] (LCLS)

IaCrescoTP... Cresco Times-Plain Dealer, Cresco, IA [*Library symbol Library of Congress*] (LCLS)

IaCresNA ..... Creston News-Advertiser, Creston, IA [*Library symbol Library of Congress*] (LCLS)

IaCreTP........ Cresco Times-Plain Dealer, Cresco, IA [*Library symbol*] [*Library of Congress*] (LCLS)

IaCrG .... Cedar Rapids Gazette, Cedar Rapids, IA [*Library symbol Library of Congress*] (LCLS)

IaCrK .... Kirkwood Community College, Cedar Rapids, IA [*Library symbol Library of Congress*] (LCLS)

IACRL .... Italian-American Civil Rights League

IaCrL........... Linn County Heritage Society, Cedar Rapids, IA [*Library symbol Library of Congress*] (LCLS)

IACRLRD...... International Association for Comparative Research on Leukemia and Related Diseases (EA)

IaCrM........... Iowa Masonic Library, Cedar Rapids, IA [*Library symbol Library of Congress*] (LCLS)

IaCrMM......... Mount Mercy College, Cedar Rapids, IA [*Library symbol Library of Congress*] (LCLS)

IaCrMT......... Micro-Technology, Inc., Cedar Rapids, IA [*Library symbol Library of Congress*] (LCLS)

IaCroyHi....... Wayne County Historical Society, Croydon, IA [*Library symbol*] [*Library of Congress*] (LCLS)

IACRP .... International Association for the Child's Right to Play (EAIO)

IACRS .... International Association of Concrete Repair Specialists (EA)

IACS .... IAL Consultancy Services [*Southall, England*] [*Telecommunications*] (TSSD)

IACS .... Inertial Attitude Control System [*Aerospace*]

IACS .... Integrated Access and Crossconnect System (ACRL)

IACS .... Integrated Acoustic Communication System [*Military*] (NVT)

IACS .... Integrated Armament Control System (MCD)

IACS .... Integrated Avionics Control System (RDA)

IACS .... Interactive Computer System [*Information science*]

IACS .... Intermediate Altitude Communication Satellite (IAA)

IACS .... International Academy of Cosmetic Surgery [*Rome, Italy*] (EA)

IACS .... International Annealed Copper Standard

IACS .... International Arms-Control Symposium

IACS .... International Association of Classification Societies (EAIO)

IACS .... International Association of Cooking Schools (EA)

IACS .... International Association of Counseling Services (EA)

IACS .... Island Arts and Crafts Society, Victoria [*1922, founded 1910 as IACC*] (NGC)

IACS .... Italian-American Cultural Society (EA)

IACSE.......... Interagency Advisory Committee on Security Equipment

IACS-LDR .... Integrated Acoustic Communication System - Low Data Rate (MCD)

IACSM .... International Association of Computer Service Managers

IACSP .... International Association of Counterterrorism and Security Professionals

IACSS .... Inter-American Conference on Social Security [*See also CISS*] [*Mexico City, Mexico*] (EAIO)

IACSS .... International Association for Computer Systems Security (EA)

IACST........... Inter-American Committee for Science and Technology

IACST........... International Association for Commodity Science and Technology (EAIO)

IACSW .... Interstate Association of Commissions on the Status of Women

IACT............. Inter-Association Commission on Tsunami [*Brussels, Belgium*] (EAIO)

IACT............. International Association for Clear Thinking (EA)

IACT............. International Association of Counselors and Therapists (EA)

IACT............. International Association to Combat Terrorism [*Defunct*] (EA)

IACUC .... Institutional Animal Care and Use Committee [*Department of Agriculture*]

IACUG .... International Association of Computer Users Groups (EA)

IACV............. Idle Air Control Valve [*Fuel system*] [*Automotive engineering*]

IACVB .... International Association of Convention and Visitor Bureaus (EA)

IACVF........... International Association of Cancer Victors and Friends (EA)

I/ACVIA........ Interaction/American Council for Voluntary International Action (EA)

IACW .... Inter-American Commission of Women [*Organization of American States*] [*Washington, DC*]

IACW .... International Association of Crime Writers (EAIO)

IAD............... Eastern Illinois University, Charleston, IL [*OCLC symbol*] (OCLC)

IAD............... Immediate Action Directive

IAD............... Immediate Action Drill [*Military*] (LAIN)

IAD............... Inactivating Dose [*Medicine*] (DMAA)

IAD............... Index of Axis Deficiency [*Embryology*]

IAD............... Information and Documentation [*British Film Institute*]

IAD............... Initial Address Designator

IAD............... Initiation Area Discriminator [*RADAR*]

IAD............... Inland Steel Indus [*NYSE symbol*] (TTSB)

IAD............... Inland Steel Industries, Inc. [*NYSE symbol*] (SPSG)

IAD............... Installation, Assembly or Detail (AAG)

IAD............... Institute for American Democracy (EA)

IAD............... Instructional Advance Directive

IAD............... Integrated Access Device [*BBN Communications Corp.*]

IAD............... Integrated Airbase Defense

IAD............... Integrated Automatic Documentation [*System*]

IAD............... Interface Agreement Document (KSC)

IAD............... Interface Analysis Document (KSC)

IAD............... Internal Absorbed Dose

IAD............... Internal Audit Division [*Environmental Protection Agency*] (GFGA)

IAD............... International Association of Documentalists and Information Officers [*France*] (EY)

IAD............... International Astrophysical Decade

IAD............... Internationale Automotive Design

IAD............... Internationale Arbeitsgemeinschaft Donauforschung [*International Working Association for Danube Research*] (EAIO)

IAD............... Inventory Adjustment Document

IAD............... Inventory Available Date (TEL)

IAD............... Ion-Assisted Deposition [*Coating technology*]

IAD............... Ion Beam Activated Deposition [*Coating technology*]

IAD............... Washington [*District of Columbia*] Dulles Airport [*Airport symbol*]

IaDa............. Davenport Public Library, Davenport, IA [*Library symbol Library of Congress*] (LCLS)

IADA .... Idaho Automobile Dealers Association (SRA)
IADA .... Illinois Automobile Dealer Association (SRA)
IADA .... Independent Aeronautical Dealers Association [*Defunct*] (EA)
IADA .... Independent Automotive Damage Appraisers Association [*Milwaukee, WI*] (EA)
IADA .... Inland Auto Dismantlers Association (SRA)
IADA .... International Atomic-Development Authority [*Proposed by Bernard M. Baruch, 1946, but never created*]
IADA .... Internationale Arbeitsgemeinschaft der Archiv-, Bibliotheks-, und Graphikrestauratoren [*International Association for Conservation of Books, Paper, and Archival Material*] (EAIO)
IADA .... Interstate Agreement on Detainers Act [*1970*]
IADA .... Iowa Automobile Dealers Association (SRA)
IaDaCM .... Catholic Messenger, Davenport, IA [*Library symbol Library of Congress*] (LCLS)
IaDaCoC ...... Scott County Courthouse, Davenport, IA [*Library symbol Library of Congress*] (LCLS)
IaDaGL .... Grant Law Library, Davenport, IA [*Library symbol Library of Congress*] (LCLS)
IaDaM .... Davenport Public Museum, Davenport, IA [*Library symbol Library of Congress*] (LCLS)
IaDaMC .... Marycrest College, Davenport, IA [*Library symbol Library of Congress*] (LCLS)
IaDaP .... Palmer College of Chiropractic, Davenport, IA [*Library symbol Library of Congress*] (LCLS)
IaDaPM .... Putnam Museum, Davenport, IA [*Library symbol Library of Congress*] (LCLS)
IaDaQT .... Quad City Times, Davenport, IA [*Library symbol*] [*Library of Congress*] (LCLS)
IaDaSA .... Saint Ambrose College, Davenport, IA [*Library symbol Library of Congress*] (LCLS)
IADA-UT ...... Independent Auto Dealers Association - Utah (SRA)
IaDayR .... Dayton Review, Dayton, IA [*Library symbol Library of Congress*] (LCLS)
IADB .... Inter-American Defense Board (EA)
IADB .... Inter-American Development Bank [*Also, IDB*]
IADB-MED .... Inter-American Defense Board Medal [*Military decoration*]
IADBWA .... Inter-American Development Bank's Wives Association (EA)
IaDc .... Dallas Center Public Library, Dallas Center, IA [*Library symbol Library of Congress*] (LCLS)
IADC .... Inter-American Defense College [*Washington, DC*]
IADC .... Inter-American Development Commission
IADC .... Interdepartmental Advisory and Development Committee (EERA)
IADC .... International Alliance for Distribution by Cable [*Formerly, International Alliance for Distribution by Wire*] (EA)
IADC .... International Association of Defense Counsel (EA)
IADC .... International Association of Dentistry for Children [*British*] (EAIO)
IADC .... International Association of Dredging Companies [*The Hague, Netherlands*] (EA)
IADC .... International Association of Drilling Contractors
IaDCC .... College Chips, Luther College, Decorah, IA [*Library symbol Library of Congress*] (LCLS)
I/ADCSP .... Initial/Advanced Defense Communications Satellite Program (SAA)
I/ADCSP .... Interim/Advanced Defense Communications Satellite Program (DNAB)
IADE .... Integral of Absolute Delay Error (IAA)
IAdEM .... Internacia Asocio de Esperantistaj Matematikistoj [*International Association of Esperantist Mathematicians*] (EAIO)
IaDen .... Denison Carnegie Library, Denison, IA [*Library symbol Library of Congress*] (LCLS)
IaDenB .... Denison Bulletin, Denison, IA [*Library symbol Library of Congress*] (LCLS)
IaDenR .... Denison Review, Denison, IA [*Library symbol Library of Congress*] (LCLS)
IaDewO .... Observer, De Witt, IA [*Library symbol Library of Congress*] (LCLS)
IaDexM .... Dexter Museum, Dexter, IA [*Library symbol Library of Congress*] (LCLS)
IADF .... Icelandic Air Defense Force (MUGU)
IADF .... Inter-American Association for Democracy and Freedom (EA)
IADF .... Irish American Defense Fund [*Defunct*] (EA)
IADH .... Inappropriate Antidiuretic Hormone [*Endocrinology*] (MAE)
IADH .... International Association of Dentistry for the Handicapped [*Toronto, ON*] (EAIO)
IADHS .... Inappropriate Antidiuretic Hormone Syndrome [*Endocrinology*]
IaDiaR .... Diagonal Reporter, Diagonal, IA [*Library symbol Library of Congress*] (LCLS)
IADIC .... Integration Analog-to-Digital Converter (IEEE)
IADIS .... Irish Association for Documentation and Information Services (NITA)
IADIWU .... International Association for the Development of International and World Universities [*See also AIDUIM*] [*Aulnay-Sous-Bois, France*] (EAIO)
IaDJ .... Decorah Journal, Decorah, IA [*Library symbol Library of Congress*] (LCLS)
IADL .... Instrumental Activities of Daily Living Survey [*Department of Health and Human Services*] (GFGA)
IADL .... International Association of Democratic Lawyers [*Brussels, Belgium*] (EA)
IaDL .... Luther College, Decorah, IA [*Library symbol Library of Congress*] (LCLS)
IaDm .... Des Moines Public Library, Des Moines, IA [*Library symbol Library of Congress*] (LCLS)
IaDmB .... Iowa Commission for the Blind, Des Moines, IA [*Library symbol Library of Congress*] (LCLS)
IaDmBR .... Business Record, Des Moines, IA [*Library symbol*] [*Library of Congress*] (LCLS)

IaDmC .... Iowa State Commerce Commission, Records and Information Center, Des Moines, IA [*Library symbol Library of Congress*] (LCLS)
IaDmCI .... Central Iowa Regional Library System, Des Moines, IA [*Library symbol*] [*Library of Congress*] (LCLS)
IaDmD .... Drake University, Des Moines, IA [*Library symbol Library of Congress*] (LCLS)
IaDmDC .... Dowling College, Des Moines, IA [*Library symbol Library of Congress*] (LCLS)
IaDmD-L ...... Drake University, Law School, Des Moines, IA [*Library symbol Library of Congress*] (LCLS)
IaDmE .... Iowa State Education Association, Des Moines, IA [*Library symbol Library of Congress*] (LCLS)
IADMFR .... International Association of Dento-Maxillo-Facial Radiology (EAIO)
IaDmG .... Grand View College, Des Moines, IA [*Library symbol Library of Congress*] (LCLS)
IaDmHN .... Highland Park News, Des Moines, IA [*Library symbol Library of Congress*] (LCLS)
IaDmL .... Iowa Legionnaire, Des Moines, IA [*Library symbol Library of Congress*] (LCLS)
IaDmLN .... Lee Town News, Des Moines, IA [*Library symbol Library of Congress*] (LCLS)
IaDmMet ...... Des Moines Metropolitan Service Area Library Cooperative, Des Moines, IA [*Library symbol Library of Congress*] (LCLS)
IaDmOF .... Odd Fellows Temple, Des Moines, IA [*Library symbol Library of Congress*] (LCLS)
IaDmPH .... Pioneer Hi-Bred International, Inc., Des Moines, IA [*Library symbol Library of Congress*] (LCLS)
IaDmR .... Daily Record, Des Moines, IA [*Library symbol Library of Congress*] (LCLS)
IaDmRT .... Des Moines Register-Tribune, Des Moines, IA [*Library symbol Library of Congress*] (LCLS)
IaDmS .... College of Osteopathic Medicine and Surgery, Des Moines, IA [*Library symbol Library of Congress*] (LCLS)
IADMS .... International Association for Dance Medicine and Science
IaDmV .... United States Veterans Administration Hospital, Des Moines, IA [*Library symbol Library of Congress*] (LCLS)
IaDN .... Norwegian-American Historical Museum and Library, Decorah, IA [*Library symbol Library of Congress*] (LCLS)
IaDo .... Dows Community Library, Dows, IA [*Library symbol Library of Congress*] (LCLS)
IADO .... Instituto Argentine de Oceanografia [*Marine science*] (OSRA)
IaDon .... Donnellson Public Library, Donnellson, IA [*Library symbol Library of Congress*] (LCLS)
IaDonS .... Donnellson Star, Donnellson, IA [*Library symbol Library of Congress*] (LCLS)
IaDooP .... Press, Doon, IA [*Library symbol Library of Congress*] (LCLS)
IADP .... INTELSAT Assistance and Development Program
IADP .... Inter-American Driving Permit
IADP .... International Association of Dollbaby Parents [*Defunct*] (EA)
IADPC .... Interagency Data Processing Committee
IADPG .... Intelligence Automatic Data Processing Group (CINC)
IaDPO .... Decorah Public Opinion, Decorah, IA [*Library symbol Library of Congress*] (LCLS)
IaDQT .... Quad City Times, Davenport, IA [*Library symbol Library of Congress*] (LCLS)
IADR .... Institute for Animal Disease Research [*Research center British*] (IRC)
IADR .... International Association for Dental Research (EA)
IADRS .... International Association of Dive Rescue Specialists (EA)
IADS .... Integrated Air Defense System (MCD)
IADS .... International Agricultural Development Service [*Later, WIIAD*] [*Department of Agriculture*]
IADS .... International Association of Dental Students [*British*]
IADS .... International Association of Department Stores [*See also AIGM*] (EAIO)
IA DSA .... Intra-Arterial Digital Subtraction Arteriography [*Cardiology*] (DAVI)
IADSA .... Intraaterial Digital Subtraction Angiography [*Medicine*]
IADT .... Initial Active Duty for Training [*Military*] (AABC)
IADT .... Integrated Automatic Detection and Tracking [*Military*] (CAAL)
IaDu .... Carnegie-Stout Free Public Library, Dubuque, IA [*Library symbol Library of Congress*] (LCLS)
IaDuA .... Aquinas Institute, Dubuque, IA [*Library symbol Library of Congress*] (LCLS)
IaDuAn .... Antique Trade Weekly, Dubuque, IA [*Library symbol Library of Congress*] (LCLS)
IaDuCl .... Clarke College, Dubuque, IA [*Library symbol Library of Congress*] (LCLS)
IaDuCo .... Clarke Courier, Dubuque, IA [*Library symbol Library of Congress*] (LCLS)
IaDuL .... Loras College, Dubuque, IA [*Library symbol Library of Congress*] (LCLS)
IaDuLe .... Dubuque Leader, Dubuque, IA [*Library symbol Library of Congress*] (LCLS)
IaDuN .... New Melleray Abbey, Dubuque, IA [*Library symbol Library of Congress*] (LCLS)
IaDunR .... Dunlap Reporter, Dunlap, IA [*Library symbol Library of Congress*] (LCLS)
IaDuT .... Schools of Theology in Dubuque, Dubuque, IA [*Library symbol Library of Congress*] (LCLS)
IaDuU .... University of Dubuque, Dubuque, IA [*Library symbol Library of Congress*] (LCLS)
IaDuU-S ...... University of Dubuque, Theological Seminary, Dubuque, IA [*Library symbol Library of Congress*] (LCLS)
IaDuW .... Wartburg Theological Seminary, Dubuque, IA [*Library symbol Library of Congress*] (LCLS)

IaDuWi .... Dubuque Witness, Dubuque, IA [*Library symbol Library of Congress*] (LCLS)

IaDv .... Denver Public Library, Denver, IA [*Library symbol Library of Congress*] (LCLS)

IaDvF .... Forum, Denver, IA [*Library symbol Library of Congress*] (LCLS)

IADWS .... Interim Air Defense Weapon System [*Army*]

IaDy .... Matthias M. Hoffman Public Library, Dyersville, IA [*Library symbol Library of Congress*] (LCLS)

IaDyC .... Dyersville Commercial, Dyersville, IA [*Library symbol Library of Congress*] (LCLS)

IaDysR .... Dysart Reporter, Dysart, IA [*Library symbol Library of Congress*] (LCLS)

IaE .... Eagle Grove Public Library, Eagle Grove, IA [*Library symbol Library of Congress*] (LCLS)

IAE .... Felician College, Chicago, IL [*OCLC symbol*] (OCLC)

IAE .... In Any Event [*Internet language*] [*Computer science*]

IAE .... Information and Education (IAA)

IAE .... Infrared Auroral Emission

IAE .... Institut d'Administration des Entreprises [*Institute of Company Management*] [*Information service or system*] (IID)

IAE .... Institute for the Advancement of Engineering (EA)

IAE .... Institute of Atomic Energy [*Academy of Sciences, USSR*]

IAE .... Institute of Automobile Engineers

IAE .... Integral of Absolute Error

IAE .... Inter-Asia Equities [*Vancouver Stock Exchange symbol*]

IAE .... International Association of Ethicists (EA)

IAE .... Interstate Airlines Ltd. [*Nigeria*] [*ICAO designator*] (FAAC)

IAE .... Intra-Atrial Electrocardiogram [*Cardiology*] (MAE)

IAE .... Iscrizioni Antico-Ebraici Palestinesi (BJA)

IAE .... Iskra Associated Enterprise [*Yugoslavia*] [*Telecommunications*]

IAEA .... Institute of Automotive Engineer Assessors [*British*] (EAIO)

IAEA .... Inter-American Education Association (EA)

IAEA .... International Advertising Executives' Association (NTCM)

IAEA .... International Agricultural Exchange Association [*British*] (EA)

IAEA .... International Association for Educational Assessment (EA)

IAEA .... International Association of Empirical Aesthetics [*Paris, France*] (EAIO)

IAEA .... International Atomic Energy Accord (DOMA)

IAEA .... International Atomic Energy Agency [*Database originator and operator*] [*United Nations*] [*Austria*]

IAEAC .... International Association of Environmental Analytical Chemistry [*Therwil, Switzerland*] (EAIO)

IAEACPD ...... Inter-American Emergency Advisory Committee for Political Defense

IAEA-MEL .... International Atomic Energy Agency Marine Environmental Laboratory [*Marine science*] (OSRA)

IaEarE .... Earlham Echo, Earlham, IA [*Library symbol Library of Congress*] (LCLS)

IaEarv .... Ruth Suckhow Memorial Library, Earlville, IA [*Library symbol Library of Congress*] (LCLS)

IaEaryN .... Early News, Early, IA [*Library symbol Library of Congress*] (LCLS)

IAEC .... International Association of Electrical Contractors [*See also AIE*] (EAIO)

IAEC .... International Association of Environmental Coordinators [*Belgium*] (DCTA)

IAEC .... International Atomic Energy Committee

IAECOSOC ... Inter-American Economic and Social Council [*United Nations*]

IAED .... International Association of Exchange Dealers [*British*] (EA)

IaEdd .... Eddyville Public Library, Eddyville, IA [*Library symbol Library of Congress*] (LCLS)

IaEddT .... Eddyville Tribune, Eddyville, IA [*Library symbol Library of Congress*] (LCLS)

IaEdgR .... Edgewood Reminder, Edgewood, IA [*Library symbol Library of Congress*] (LCLS)

IAEDP .... International Association of Eating Disorders Professionals (EA)

IAEDT .... International Association of Equine Dental Technicians (EA)

IaEE .... Eagle, Eagle Grove, IA [*Library symbol Library of Congress*] (LCLS)

IAeE .... Institute of Aeronautical Engineers

IAEE .... International Association for Earthquake Engineering [*ICSU*] [*Tokyo, Japan*] (EAIO)

IAEE .... International Association for Energy Economics (EERA)

IAEE .... International Association of Energy Economists (EA)

IAEG .... International Association of Engineering Geology [*International Union of Geological Sciences*] [*ICSU Paris, France*] (EA)

IAEI .... International Association of Electrical Inspectors (EA)

IAEJ .... Interfaith Action for Economic Justice (EA)

IAEL .... Initial Allowance Equipage List [*Military*] (CAAL)

IAEL .... International Association for Esperanto in Libraries [*See also TEBA*] (EAIO)

IAEL .... International Association of Electrical Leagues [*Later, ILEA*] (EA)

IAEL .... International Association of Entertainment Lawyers [*Amsterdam, Netherlands*] (EAIO)

IaElbTHi .... Tama County Historical Society, Elberon, IA [*Library symbol Library of Congress*] (LCLS)

IaEld .... Eldon Carnegie Library, Eldon, IA [*Library symbol Library of Congress*] (LCLS)

IaEldF .... Eldon Forum, Eldon, IA [*Library symbol Library of Congress*] (LCLS)

IaEldoHHi .... Hardin County Historical Society, Eldora, IA [*Library symbol Library of Congress*] (LCLS)

IaEldoHi ...... Hardin County Historical Society, Eldora, IA [*Library symbol*] [*Library of Congress*] (LCLS)

IaEldoHL .... Herald-Ledger, Eldora, IA [*Library symbol Library of Congress*] (LCLS)

IaEldoI .... Hardin County Index, Eldora, IA [*Library symbol Library of Congress*] (LCLS)

IaEldr .... Scott County Library, Eldridge, IA [*Library symbol Library of Congress*] (LCLS)

IaEldrN .... North Scott Press, Eldridge, IA [*Library symbol Library of Congress*] (LCLS)

IaElgE .... Elgin Echo, Elgin, IA [*Library symbol Library of Congress*] (LCLS)

IaElk .... Elkader Public Library, Elkader, IA [*Library symbol Library of Congress*] (LCLS)

IaElkCR .... Clayton County Register, Elkader, IA [*Library symbol Library of Congress*] (LCLS)

IaElkHi .... Elkader Historical Society, Elkader, IA [*Library symbol Library of Congress*] (LCLS)

IaElkhR .... Elk Horn-Kimballton Review, Elk Horn, IA [*Library symbol Library of Congress*] (LCLS)

IaEll .... Elliott Public Library, Elliott, IA [*Library symbol Library of Congress*] (LCLS)

IaElmR .... Elma Reminder, Elma, IA [*Library symbol Library of Congress*] (LCLS)

IaEls .... Ellsworth Public Library, Ellsworth, IA [*Library symbol Library of Congress*] (LCLS)

IaEm .... Emmetsburg Public Library, Emmetsburg, IA [*Library symbol Library of Congress*] (LCLS)

IAEM .... International Atomic Energy Agency (USDC)

IaEmD .... Emmetsburg Democrat, Emmetsburg, IA [*Library symbol*] [*Library of Congress*] (LCLS)

IaEmR .... Emmetsburg Reporter, Emmetsburg, IA [*Library symbol*] [*Library of Congress*] (LCLS)

IAEMS .... International Association of Environmental Mutagen Societies [*Helsinki, Finland*] (EAIO)

IAEP .... International Academy of Eclectic Psychotherapists [*St. Ives, NSW, Australia*] (EAIO)

IaEpD .... Divine Word College, Epworth, IA [*Library symbol Library of Congress*] (LCLS)

IAEPO .... International Association of Educational Peace Officers (EA)

IAER .... Institute of Applied Economic Research [*Concordia University*] [*Canada Research center*] (RCD)

IaEs .... Estherville Public Library, Estherville, IA [*Library symbol Library of Congress*] (LCLS)

IAES .... Institute of Aerospace [*formerly, Aeronautical*] Sciences

IAES .... Interim Aquanaut Equipment System (PDAA)

IAES .... International Academy for Environmental Safety

IAES .... International Association of Electrotypers and Stereotypers [*Later, Printing Platemakers Association*]

IAESC .... Inter-American Economic and Social Council [*United Nations*]

IAESC .... International Association of Evening Student Councils [*Later, USAES*] (EA)

IaEsN .... Estherville Daily News, Estherville, IA [*Library symbol Library of Congress*] (LCLS)

IAESR .... Institute of Applied Economic and Social Research (EERA)

IAESTE .... International Association for the Exchange of Students for Technical Experience [*Lisbon, Portugal*] (EAIO)

IAESTE/US ... International Association for the Exchange of Students for Technical Experience - United States [*Later, AIPT*]

IaEsxFN .... First National Bank, Essex, IA [*Library symbol Library of Congress*] (LCLS)

IaEsxI .... Essex Independent, Essex, IA [*Library symbol Library of Congress*] (LCLS)

IAET .... In-Flight Aeromedical Evacuation Team

IAET .... International Association for Enterostomal Therapy (EA)

IAETF .... International Anti-Euthanasia Task Force

IAETL .... International Association of Environmental Testing Laboratories (EA)

IaEveN .... Everly News, Everly, IA [*Library symbol Library of Congress*] (LCLS)

IAEVG .... International Association for Educational and Vocational Guidance [*See also AIOSP*] [*Belfast, Northern Ireland*] (EAIO)

IAEVI .... International Association for Educational and Vocational Information [*See also AIISUP*] [*Paris, France*] (EAIO)

IaEvS .... Black Hawk County Sun, Evansdale, IA [*Library symbol Library of Congress*] (LCLS)

IAEWP .... International Association of Educators for World Peace (EA)

IaExJ .... Audubon County Journal, Exira, IA [*Library symbol Library of Congress*] (LCLS)

IAF .... EPAG - Group Air France [*ICAO designator*] (FAAC)

IAF .... First Australia Fund [*AMEX symbol*] (TTSB)

IAF .... First Australia Fund, Inc. [*AMEX symbol*] (SPSG)

IAF .... Governors State University, Park Forest South, IL [*OCLC symbol*] (OCLC)

IAF .... Idiopathic Alveolar Fibrosis [*Medicine*] (DMAA)

IAF .... Image Analysis Facility [*Computer science*] (PDAA)

IAF .... Immobilizing Accelerating Factor (PDAA)

IAF .... Independent Air Force [*British military*] (DMA)

IAF .... Indian Air Force

IAF .... Indian Army Form [*British military*] (DMA)

IAF .... Indian Auxiliary Force [*British*]

IAF .... Indium Arsenide Filter

IAF .... Indonesian Air Force

IAF .... Induced-Air Flotation [*Chemical engineering*]

IAF .... Industrial Air Filtration

IAF .... Industrial Areas Foundation (EA)

IAF .... Information and Forwarding (MUGU)

IAF .... Initial Approach Fix [*Aviation*] (AFM)

IAF .... Initiative America Foundation (EA)

IAF .... Institut Armand-Frappier [*University of Quebec*] [*Formerly, Institute of Microbiology and Hygiene of Montreal*] [*Research center*] (RCD)

IAF .... Institute for Alternative Futures [*Defunct*] (EA)

IAF .... Institute on American Freedoms [*Defunct*]

IAF .... Instrument Air Filter

IAF	Instrument Approach Fix
IAF	Interactive Facility [*Control Data Corp.*]
IAF	Interallied Force [*NATO*] (NATG)
IAF	Inter-American Foundation (MCD)
IAF	International Abolitionist Federation [*India*]
IAF	International Accreditation Forum [*For quality control*]
IAF	International Activities Fund [*Canadian Labour Congress*] [*See also FAI*]
IAF	International Aeronautical Federation
IAF	International Aikido Federation [*Tokyo, Japan*] (EAIO)
IAF	International Apparel Federation [*Berlin, Federal Republic of Germany*] (EAIO)
IAF	International Aquaculture Foundation (EA)
IAF	International Arab Federation
IAF	International Archery Federation (EA)
IAF	International Association for Falconry and Conservation of Birds of Prey (EAIO)
IAF	International Astronautical Federation [*ICSU*] [*Research center France*]
IAF	International Athletic Footwear and Apparel Manufacturers Association [*Zurich, Switzerland Defunct*] (EAIO)
IAF	International Autumn Fair [*British*] (ITD)
IAF	Intra-Alaska Facsimile [*National Weather Service*]
IAF	(Iodoacetamido)fluorescein [*Biochemical label*]
IAF	Islamic Action Front [*Political party*] [*Jordan*]
IAF	Israel Air Force (BJA)
IAF	Israeli Air-Force [*ICAO designator*] (FAAC)
IAF	Italian Air Force (NATG)
IAF	Italian American Forum [*Defunct*] (EA)
IAF	Office of Information for the Armed Forces (AABC)
IAFA	Inter-American Foundation for the Arts [*Defunct*]
IAFA	International Association for the Fantastic in the Arts (EA)
IAFA	International Aviation Facilities Act [*1948*]
IAFAE	Inter-American Federation for Adult Education
IaFair	Fairfield Public Library, Fairfield, IA [*Library symbol Library of Congress*] (LCLS)
IaFairL	Fairfield Daily Ledger, Fairfield, IA [*Library symbol Library of Congress*] (LCLS)
IaFairM	Maharishi International University, Fairfield, IA [*Library symbol Library of Congress*] (LCLS)
IaFarmL	Van Buren County Leader, Farmington, IA [*Library symbol Library of Congress*] (LCLS)
IAFAW	International Association of Friends of Angkor Wat (EAIO)
IaFay	Fayette Community Library, Fayette, IA [*Library symbol Library of Congress*] (LCLS)
IaFayHHi	Fayette County Helpers Club and Historical Society, Fayette, IA [*Library symbol Library of Congress*] (LCLS)
IaFayL	Fayette Leader, Fayette, IA [*Library symbol Library of Congress*] (LCLS)
IaFayU	Upper Iowa University, Fayette, IA [*Library symbol Library of Congress*] (LCLS)
IAFB	Interim Airframe Bulletin
IAFC	Instantaneous Automatic Frequency Control
IAFC	Inter-American Freight Conference - Section C (EA)
IAFC	Interim Airframe Change (NG)
IAFC	International Association of Financial Consultants (BARN)
IAFC	International Association of Fire Chiefs (EA)
IAFC	Irwin Allen Fan Club [*Defunct*] (EA)
IAFCF	International Association of Fire Chiefs Foundation (EA)
IAFCI	Inter-American Federation of the Construction Industry [*See also FIIC*] [*Mexico City, Mexico*] (EAIO)
IaFcS	Forest City Summit, Forest City, IA [*Library symbol Library of Congress*] (LCLS)
IAFCT	International Association of French-Speaking Congress Towns [*See also AIVFC*] [*France*] (EAIO)
IaFcW	Waldorf College, Forest City, IA [*Library symbol Library of Congress*] (LCLS)
IaFd	Fort Dodge Public Library, Fort Dodge, IA [*Library symbol Library of Congress*] (LCLS)
IAFD	International Association on Food Distribution
IaFdIC	Iowa Central Community College, Fort Dodge, IA [*Library symbol Library of Congress*] (LCLS)
IaFdM	Fort Dodge Messenger, Fort Dodge, IA [*Library symbol Library of Congress*] (LCLS)
IAFE	International Association of Fairs and Expositions (EA)
IAFE	International Association of Fish Ethologists [*Normal, IL*] (ASF)
IAFES	International Association for the Economics of Self-Management [*Belgrade, Yugoslavia*] (EAIO)
IAFF	International Air Freight Forwarder (AABC)
IAFF	International Association of Fire Fighters (EA)
IAFI	Infantile Amaurotic Family Idiocy [*Medicine*]
IAFIS	Integrated Automated Fingerprint Identification System [*FBI standardized term*]
IAFLUP	International Association of French-Language University Presses [*Defunct*] (EA)
IaFm	Cattermole Memorial Library, Fort Madison, IA [*Library symbol Library of Congress*] (LCLS)
IAFM	Integrated Air-Fuel Module
IaFmD	Fort Madison Democrat, Fort Madison, IA [*Library symbol Library of Congress*] (LCLS)
IaFmLHi	North Lee County Historical Society, Fort Madison, IA [*Library symbol Library of Congress*] (LCLS)
IAFMM	International Association of Fish Meal Manufacturers [*Potters Bar, Hertfordshire, England*] (EAIO)
IaFon	Fonda Public Library, Fonda, IA [*Library symbol Library of Congress*] (LCLS)
IaFonT	Fonda Times, Fonda, IA [*Library symbol Library of Congress*] (LCLS)
IaFontO	Fontanelle Observer, Fontanelle, IA [*Library symbol Library of Congress*] (LCLS)
IAFP	Intergovernmental Affairs Fellowship Program (RDA)
IAFP	International Alliance of Film Producers [*Later, IAIP*] (EA)
IAFP	International Association for Financial Planning (EA)
IAFP	International Association of Filipino Patriots (EA)
IAFPE	Indian American Forum for Political Education (EA)
IaFre	Upham Memorial Library, Fredericksburg, IA [*Library symbol Library of Congress*] (LCLS)
IaFremG	Fremont Gazette, Fremont, IA [*Library symbol Library of Congress*] (LCLS)
IaFreN	Fredericksburg News, Fredericksburg, IA [*Library symbol Library of Congress*] (LCLS)
IaFreR	Fredericksburg Review, Fredericksburg, IA [*Library symbol*] [*Library of Congress*] (LCLS)
IAFS	Integrated Air-Fuel System [*Automotive engineering*]
IAFS	Integrated Air/Fuel System [*Automotive engine design*]
IAFS	International Animated Film Society (EA)
IAFS	International Association for Food Self-Sufficiency (EA)
IAFS	International Association of Family Sociology (EA)
IAFS	International Association of Forensic Sciences [*Defunct*] (EA)
IAFSA	International Association of French-Speaking Aircrews (EAIO)
IAFSDEI	International Association of French-Speaking Directors of Educational Institutions (EAIO)
IAFTA	Integrated Avionics Fault Tree Analyzer (MCD)
IAFU	Improved Assault Fire Units [*Military*] (MCD)
IAFV	Infantry Armored Fighting Vehicle (NATG)
IAFVH	Indian Advanced Field Veterinary Hospital [*British military*] (DMA)
IAFWA	International Association of Fish and Wildlife Agencies (EA)
IAFWNO	Inter-American Federation of Working Newspapermen's Organizations
IAG	Epag-Group Air France [*FAA designator*] (FAAC)
IAG	Greenville College, Greenville, IL [*OCLC symbol*] (OCLC)
IAG	Industry Advisory Group [*Underwriters Laboratories*] [*Telecommunications*]
IAG	Institute for Australasian Geodynamics [*Flinders University*] [*Australia*]
IAG	Instruction Address Generation [*Computer science*]
IAG	Intelligence Analysis Group [*Military*]
IAG	Interactive Application Generator (HGAA)
IAG	Interagency Advisory Group [*Civil Service Commission*]
IAG	Interagency Agreement
IAG	Inter-Association Group
IAG	Intergovernmental Agreement on the Environment [*Commonwealth*] [*State*] (EERA)
IAG	International Academy of Gnathology - American Section (EA)
IAG	International Applications Group [*IFIP*]
IAG	International Art Guild (EA)
IAG	International Association of Geodesy [*ICSU*] [*Paris, France*] (EAIO)
IAG	International Association of Gerontology (EA)
IAG	International Auditing Guideline
IAG	Niagara Falls, NY [*Location identifier FAA*] (FAAL)
IaG	Stewart Public Library, Grinnell, IA [*Library symbol Library of Congress*] (LCLS)
IAGA	International Association of Geomagnetism and Aeronomy [*ICSU*] [*Scotland*] (ASF)
IAGA	International Association of Golf Administrators (EA)
IAGA	Irish Amateur Gymnastics Association (EAIO)
IAGAE	International Association for Gerda Alexander Eutony [*See also AIEGA*] [*Switzerland*] (EAIO)
IAGAL	Industry Advisory Group for Air Logistics
IaGar	Garner Public Library, Garner, IA [*Library symbol Library of Congress*] (LCLS)
IaGarL	Garner Leader and Signal and Herald, Garner, IA [*Library symbol Library of Congress*] (LCLS)
IaGavoHi	Garnavillo Historical Society, Garnavillo, IA [*Library symbol Library of Congress*] (LCLS)
IaGavoT	Granavillo Tribune, Granavillo, IA [*Library symbol Library of Congress*] (LCLS)
IaGc	Gilmore City Public Library, Gilmore City, IA [*Library symbol Library of Congress*] (LCLS)
IAGC	Instantaneous Automatic Gain Control [*or Circuit*] [*RADAR*]
IAGC	International Association of Geochemistry and Cosmochemistry [*Edmonton, AB*] (EA)
IAGC	International Association of Geophysical Contractors (EA)
IAGCW	International Association of Greeting Card Workers
IAGD	Iowa Academy of General Dentistry (SRA)
IaGen	Iowa State Genealogical Society, Genealogical Library, Des Moines, IA [*Library symbol Library of Congress*] (LCLS)
IaGeoN	Lyon County News, George, IA [*Library symbol Library of Congress*] (LCLS)
IaGeoR	Lyon county Register, George, IA [*Library symbol*] [*Library of Congress*] (LCLS)
IAGFA	International Association of Governmental Fair Agencies (EA)
IAGFCC	International Association of Game, Fish, and Conservation Commissioners [*Later, IAFWA*] (EA)
IaGG	Grinnell College, Grinnell, IA [*Library symbol Library of Congress*] (LCLS)
IaGHR	Herald-Register, Grinnell, IA [*Library symbol Library of Congress*] (LCLS)
IaGjG	Globe Free Press, Grand Junction, IA [*Library symbol Library of Congress*] (LCLS)

IAGL............ Interactive Applicon Graphics Language [*Automotive engineering*]

IaGle............ Glenwood Public Library, Glenwood, IA [*Library symbol*] [*Library of Congress*] (LCLS)

IaGleOT ...... Opinion-Tribune, Glenwood, IA [*Library symbol Library of Congress*] (LCLS)

IaGliG.......... Glidden Graphic, Glidden, IA [*Library symbol Library of Congress*] (LCLS)

IAGLL.......... International Association of Germanic Languages and Literatures [*See also IVG*] (EAIO)

IAGLO .... International Association of Governmental Labor Officials [*Later, NAGLO*] (EA)

IAGLP .... International Association of Great Lakes Ports (EA)

IAGLR .... International Association for Great Lakes Research (EA)

IAGM .... International Association of Garment Manufacturers [*Absorbed by NOSA*] (EA)

IAGMA .... Illuminating and Allied Glassware Manufacturers Association [*Defunct*] (EA)

IAGMA .... International Assembly of Grocery Manufacturers Associations (EAIO)

IAGOD.......... International Association of the Genesis of Ore Deposits [*ICSU*] [*Prague, Czechoslovakia*] (EAIO)

IaGow .... Gowrie News, Gowrie, IA [*Library symbol Library of Congress*] (LCLS)

IAGP .... Illinois Association of Groundwater Professionals (SRA)

IAGP .... International Antarctic Glaciological Project [*Defunct*] (EA)

IAGP .... International Association of Geographic Pathology (DAVI)

IAGP .... International Association of Group Psychotherapy (EA)

IaGra .... Graettinger Public Library, Graettinger, IA [*Library symbol Library of Congress*] (LCLS)

IaGraT .... Graettinger Times, Graettinger, IA [*Library symbol Library of Congress*] (LCLS)

IaGrc............ Grundy Center Public Library, Grundy Center, IA [*Library symbol Library of Congress*] (LCLS)

IaGrcI........... Iowa Farm Bureau Spokesman, Grundy Center, IA [*Library symbol Library of Congress*] (LCLS)

IaGrcR .... Grundy Center Register, Grundy Center, IA [*Library symbol Library of Congress*] (LCLS)

IaGre .... Greene Public Library, Greene, IA [*Library symbol Library of Congress*] (LCLS)

IAgrE.......... Institution of Agricultural Engineers (EAIO)

IAgrE.......... Institution of Agricultural Engineers [*British*] (DBA)

IaGrefFP ...... Adair County Free Press, Greenfield, IA [*Library symbol Library of Congress*] (LCLS)

IaGreR .... Greene Recorder, Greene, IA [*Library symbol Library of Congress*] (LCLS)

IaGrisA .... Griswold American, Griswold, IA [*Library symbol Library of Congress*] (LCLS)

IAgS............ Institute of Agricultural Secretaries (DBA)

IAGS .... Inter-American Geodetic Survey

IAGS .... International Association for Germanic Studies (EAIO)

IAGS .... Irish Assessment & Guidance Service (ACII)

IaGucG......... Guthrian, Guthrie Center, IA [*Library symbol Library of Congress*] (LCLS)

IaGucT .... Guthrie Center Times, Guthrie Center, IA [*Library symbol Library of Congress*] (LCLS)

IAGUS......... International Association of Genito-Urinary Surgeons (DAVI)

IaGut............ Guttenberg Public Library, Guttenberg, IA [*Library symbol Library of Congress*] (LCLS)

IaGutP .... Guttenberg Press, Guttenberg, IA [*Library symbol Library of Congress*] (LCLS)

IAH.............. Houston [*Texas*] Intercontinental [*Airport symbol*] (OAG)

IAH.............. Idiopathic Adrenal Hyperplasia [*Medicine*]

IAH.............. Illinois Institute of Technology, Chicago, IL [*OCLC symbol*] (OCLC)

IAH.............. Immune Adherence Haemagglutination [*Immunochemistry*] (PDAA)

IAH.............. Implantable Artificial Heart

IAH.............. Institute for Animal Health [*Agricultural and Food Research Council*] [*British*] (IRC)

IAH.............. Institute for the Advancement of Health [*Defunct*] (EA)

IAH.............. International Association of Hydrogeologists [*Arnhem, Netherlands*] (EA)

IAH.............. International Association of Hydrology

IAH.............. Internationales Arbeiter-Hilfswerk [*International Workers Aid*] [*Bonn, Federal Republic of Germany*] (EAIO)

IAHA .... Immune Adherence Hemagglutination [*Immunochemistry*]

IAHA .... Indiana Association of Homes for the Aging (SRA)

IAHA .... Institute for the Advancement of Hawaiian Affairs

IAHA .... Inter-American Hospital Association [*Defunct*]

IAHA .... Inter-American Hotel Association

IAHA .... International Arabian Horse Association (EA)

IAHA .... International Association of Historians of Asia [*Quezon City, Philippines*] (EA)

IAHA .... International Association of Hospitality Accountants [*Austin, TX*] (EA)

IAHA .... Iowa Association of Homes for the Aging (SRA)

Ia-HA .... Iowa State Department of History and Archives, Des Moines, IA [*Library symbol Library of Congress*] (LCLS)

IAHAIO........ International Association of Human-Animal Interaction Organizations (EA)

IaHamb........ Hamburg Public Library, Hamburg, IA [*Library symbol Library of Congress*] (LCLS)

IaHambR ...... Hamburg Reporter, Hamburg, IA [*Library symbol Library of Congress*] (LCLS)

IaHampC...... Hampton Chronicle, Hampton, IA [*Library symbol Library of Congress*] (LCLS)

IaHampCoC... Franklin County Courthouse, Hampton, IA [*Library symbol Library of Congress*] (LCLS)

IaHampFC.... Franklin County Courthouse, Hampton, IA [*Library symbol*] [*Library of Congress*] (LCLS)

IaHampFN ... US Farm News, Hampton, IA [*Library symbol Library of Congress*] (LCLS)

IaHampHi .... Franklin County Historical Society, Hampton, IA [*Library symbol Library of Congress*] (LCLS)

IaHampJ...... Dumont Journal, Hampton, IA [*Library symbol Library of Congress*] (LCLS)

IaHampT...... Hampton Times, Hampton, IA [*Library symbol Library of Congress*] (LCLS)

IaHar .... Harlan Public Library, Harlan, IA [*Library symbol Library of Congress*] (LCLS)

IaHarNA...... Harlan News-Advertiser, Harlan, IA [*Library symbol Library of Congress*] (LCLS)

IaHarS .... Shelby County Museum, Harlan, IA [*Library symbol Library of Congress*] (LCLS)

IaHarT .... Harlan Tribune, Harlan, IA [*Library symbol Library of Congress*] (LCLS)

IaHart .... Hartley Public Library, Hartley, IA [*Library symbol Library of Congress*] (LCLS)

IaHartP .... Hartley Public Library, Hartley, IA [*Library symbol*] [*Library of Congress*] (LCLS)

IaHartS .... Hartley Sentinel, Hartley, IA [*Library symbol Library of Congress*] (LCLS)

IaHaw .... Hawarden Public Library, Hawarden, IA [*Library symbol Library of Congress*] (LCLS)

IAHB .... Institute for the Advancement of Human Behavior (EA)

IAHB .... International Association of Human Biologists [*ICSU*] [*Newcastle-Upon-Tyne, England*] (EAIO)

IAHC .... International Ad Hoc Committee (PCM)

IAHC .... Internet Ad Hoc Coalition [*Computer science*]

IAHC .... Internet Ad Hoc Committee

IAHCP .... International Academy of Health Care Professionals (EA)

IAHCSM ...... International Association of Healthcare Central Service Materials Management (EA)

IAHD .... Idiopathic Acquired Hemolytic Disease [*Medicine*] (MAE)

IAHD .... International Association of Hillel Directors (EA)

IAHE .... International Association for Hydrogen Energy (EA)

IaHi.............. State Historical Society of Iowa, Iowa City, IA [*Library symbol Library of Congress*] (LCLS)

IAHIC .... International Association of Home Improvement Councils [*Defunct*] (EA)

IAHM .... Incorporated Association of Head Masters [*British*]

IAHM .... International Academy of the History of Medicine [*Defunct*] (EA)

IAHMS .... International Association of Hotel Management Schools (EA)

IaHoDHi....... Delaware County Historical Society, Hopkinton, IA [*Library symbol Library of Congress*] (LCLS)

IaHoDL .... Delaware County Leader, Hopkinton, IA [*Library symbol Library of Congress*] (LCLS)

IaHoL........... Lenox College, Hopkinton, IA [*Library symbol Library of Congress*] (LCLS)

IaHol............ Stubbs Public Library, Holstein, IA [*Library symbol Library of Congress*] (LCLS)

IaHolA .... Holstein Advance, Holstein, IA [*Library symbol Library of Congress*] (LCLS)

IAHP .... Institutes for the Achievement of Human Potential (EA)

IAHP .... International Association of Heart Patients [*Formerly, IAPP*] (EA)

IAHP .... International Association of Horticultural Producers

IAHR .... International Association for Hydraulic Research [*ICSU*] [*Delft, Netherlands*] (EA)

IAHR .... International Association for the History of Religions [*Marburg, Federal Republic of Germany*] (EAIO)

IAHRC .... Inter-American Human Rights Commission

IAHRONA ..... International Arabian Horse Registry of North America (EA)

IAHS .... International Academy of the History of Science [*Paris, France*] (EA)

IAHS .... International Association for Hospital Security [*Later, IAHSS*] (EA)

IAHS .... International Association for Housing Science (EA)

IAHS .... International Association of Hydrological Sciences

IAHS .... International Automotive Hall of Shame (EA)

IAHSS .... International Association for Healthcare Security and Safety (EA)

IAHSSP .... International Association of Home Safety and Security Professionals (EA)

IAHU .... International Association of Health Underwriters [*Later, NAHU*] (EA)

IaHubS......... South Hardin Signal-Review, Hubbard, IA [*Library symbol Library of Congress*] (LCLS)

IaHud .... Hudson Public Library, Hudson, IA [*Library symbol Library of Congress*] (LCLS)

IaHudH ...... Hudson Herald, Hudson, IA [*Library symbol Library of Congress*] (LCLS)

IaHul........... Sioux County Index, Hull, IA [*Library symbol Library of Congress*] (LCLS)

IaHulR .... Sioux County Index-Reporter, Hull, IA [*Library symbol Library of Congress*] (LCLS)

IaHum.......... Humbolt Public Library, Humbolt, IA [*Library symbol Library of Congress*] (LCLS)

IaHume........ Humeston Public Library, Humeston, IA [*Library symbol Library of Congress*] (LCLS)

IaHumeN....... Humeston New Era, Humeston, IA [*Library symbol Library of Congress*] (LCLS)

IaHumHi ...... Humbolt County Historical Association, Humbolt, IA [*Library symbol Library of Congress*] (LCLS)

IaHumI........ Humbolt Independent, Humbolt, IA [*Library symbol Library of Congress*] (LCLS)

IaHumR........ Humbolt Republican, Humbolt, IA [*Library symbol Library of Congress*] (LCLS)

IaHweye ...... Hawkeye Public Library, Hawkeye, IA [*Library symbol Library of Congress*] (LCLS)

IAI............ Hayner Public Library, Alton, IL [*Library symbol Library of Congress*] (LCLS)

IAI............ Illinois State University, Normal, IL [*OCLC symbol*] (OCLC)

IAI............ Inactive Aerospace Vehicle [*or Aircraft*] Inventory

IAI............ Independent Accountants International (EAIO)

IAI............ Indo-Africa, Inc. (ECON)

IAI............ Infertility Associates International [*Commercial firm*] (EA)

IAI............ Informational Acquisition and Interpretation

IAI............ Information Associates of Ithaca [*Information service or system*] (IID)

IAI............ Initial Address Information [*Telecommunications*] (TEL)

IAI............ Integrated Aircraft Instrumentation

IAI............ Inter-American Institute (USDC)

IAI............ Inter-American Institute for Global Change Research (USDC)

IAI............ Inter-American Institute for Global Change Research [*Marine science*] (OSRA)

IAI............ International African Institute [*British*]

IAI............ International Apple Institute (EA)

IAI............ International Association for Identification (EA)

IAI............ International Association of Incubators (EA)

IAI............ Intra-Abdominal Infection [*Gastroenterology*] (DAVI)

IAI............ Ion Acoustic Instability Enterprises (PDAA)

IAI............ Ion Atom Interaction

IAI............ Isethionyl Acetimidate [*Biochemistry*]

IAI............ Israel Aircraft Industries Ltd. [*ICAO designator*] (FAAC)

IAI............ Istituto Affari Internazionali [*Institute for International Affairs*] [*Italy*]

IAIA.......... Institute of American Indian and Alaska Native Culture and Arts Development (EA)

IAIA.......... International Association for Impact Assessment (EA)

Iala........... Iowa City Public Library, Iowa City, IA [*Library symbol Library of Congress*] (LCLS)

IAIAA .... International Association for Iranian Art and Archaeology (EA)

IAIABC .... International Association of Industrial Accident Boards and Commissions (EA)

IAIAD .... International Acronyms, Initialisms, and Abbreviations Dictionary [*A publication*]

IAIAF.......... International Affiliation of Independent Accounting Firms (EA)

IaIaI........... Daily Iowan, Iowa City, IA [*Library symbol Library of Congress*] (LCLS)

IAIALAR ...... Ibero-American Institute of Agrarian Law and Agrarian Reform [*See also IIDARA*] [*Mexida, Venezuela*] (EAIO)

IaIaP........... Iowa City Press-Citizen, Iowa City, IA [*Library symbol Library of Congress*] (LCLS)

IAIAS .... Inter-American Institute of Agricultural Sciences [*Later, IICA*] [*OAS*]

IaIaS........... Seven Rivers Library Cooperative, Iowa City, IA [*Library symbol Library of Congress*] (LCLS)

IAIB .... International Association of Islamic Banks

IAIC........... International Academy of Indian Culture (EAIO)

IAIC........... International Association of Insurance Counsel [*Later, IADC*] (EA)

IAICM......... International Association of Ice Cream Manufacturers [*Later, IICA*] (EA)

IAICU .... International Association of Independent Colleges and Universities (EA)

IAID .... Indium Arsenide Infrared Detector

IaIdgIHi....... Ida County Historical Society, Ida Grove, IA [*Library symbol Library of Congress*] (LCLS)

IaIdgPR....... Ida County Pioneer-Record, Ida Grove, IA [*Library symbol Library of Congress*] (LCLS)

IAIDPA........ International Association for Information and Documentation in Public Administration (EAIO)

IAIE........... Integral of Absolute Ideal Error (IAA)

IAIE........... Inter-American Institute of Ecology [*Ecological Society of America*]

IAIE........... International Association for Integrative Education [*Versoix, Switzerland*] (EAIO)

IAIES.......... Institute for Advanced Interdisciplinary Engineering Studies [*Purdue University*] (MCD)

IAIES.......... International Association of Intermodal Equipment Surveyors [*Defunct*] (EA)

IaIf........... Carnegie Ellsworth Public Library, Iowa Falls, IA [*Library symbol Library of Congress*] (LCLS)

IaIfC.......... Iowa Falls Citizen, Iowa Falls, Iowa [*Library symbol Library of Congress*] (LCLS)

IaIfE.......... Ellsworth Commumity College, Iowa Falls, IA [*Library symbol Library of Congress*] (LCLS)

IaIfT.......... Hardin County Times, Iowa Falls, IA [*Library symbol Library of Congress*] (LCLS)

IAIG .... Industrial Analytical Instrumentation Group (ACII)

IAII........... Inter-American Indian Institute [*OAS*] [*Mexico City, Mexico*] (EA)

IAIMS.......... Integrated Academic Information Management System [*Georgetown University Medical Center*]

IAIN .... International Association of Institutes of Navigation [*British*] (EAIO)

IaInd.......... Indianola Public Library, Indianola, IA [*Library symbol*] [*Library of Congress*] (LCLS)

IaIndianR..... Record-Herald and Tribune, Indianola, IA [*Library symbol Library of Congress*] (LCLS)

IaIndianS..... Simpson College, Indianola, IA [*Library symbol Library of Congress*] (LCLS)

IaIndpB .... Independence Bulletin-Journal, Independence, IA [*Library symbol*] [*Library of Congress*] (LCLS)

IaIndpBC..... Buchanan County Courthouse, Independence, IA [*Library symbol Library of Congress*] (LCLS)

IaIndpC....... Independence Conservative, Independence, IA [*Library symbol Library of Congress*] (LCLS)

IaIndpCoC... Buchanan County Courthouse, Independence, IA [*Library symbol Library of Congress*] (LCLS)

IaIndR......... Record-Herald and Tribune, Indianola, IA [*Library symbol*] [*Library of Congress*] (LCLS)

IaIndS......... Simpson College, Indianola, IA [*Library symbol*] [*Library of Congress*] (LCLS)

IaInwH .... West Lyon Herald, Inwood, IA [*Library symbol Library of Congress*] (LCLS)

IaIonCHi ...... Chickasaw County Historical Society, Ionia, IA [*Library symbol Library of Congress*] (LCLS)

IAIP .... Inorganic Ablative Insulative Plastic

IAIP .... International Association of Independent Producers (EA)

IAIP .... International Association of Individual Psychology (EA)

IAIPS .... Integrated Automated Intelligence Processing System (MCD)

IAIR .... International Association of Industrial Radiation [*France*] (PDAA)

IAIRI .... International Association of Insurance and Reinsurance Intermediaries [*See also BIPAR*] [*Paris, France*] (EAIO)

IAIRS .... Installation Aircraft Inventory Reporting System [*Army*]

IAIS .... Industrial Aerodynamics Information Service [*British*] (IID)

IAIS .... Insulin Autoimmune Syndrome [*Medicine*] (DMAA)

IAIS .... International Association of Independent Scholars (EA)

IAITO .... International Association of Independent Tanker Owners

IAIU .... Insurance Agents International Union

IAJ .... Idle Air Jet [*Fuel system*] [*Automotive engineering*]

IAJ .... Institute for Administrative Justice [*University of the Pacific*] [*Research center*] (RCD)

IAJ .... International Association of Judges [*Rome, Italy*] (EAIO)

IaJ .... Jefferson Public Library, Jefferson, IA [*Library symbol Library of Congress*] (LCLS)

IAJA .... International Association of Jazz Appreciation (EA)

IAJAM......... Industrial Association of Juvenile Apparel Manufacturers (EA)

IAJAP......... International Association of Jai Alai Players (EA)

IaJB .... Jefferson Bee, Jefferson, IA [*Library symbol Library of Congress*] (LCLS)

IAJBBSC ...... International Association of Jim Beam Bottle and Specialties Clubs (EA)

IAJC .... Inter-American Juridical Committee

IAJE .... Internacia Socio de Juristoj-Esperantistoj [*International Association of Esperantist Lawyers*]

IAJE .... International Association of Jazz Educators (EA)

IaJesC .... Jesup Citizen Herald, Jesup, IA [*Library symbol Library of Congress*] (LCLS)

IaJew.......... Montgomery Memorial Library, Jewell, IA [*Library symbol Library of Congress*] (LCLS)

IaJewR......... South Hamilton Record-News, Jewell, IA [*Library symbol Library of Congress*] (LCLS)

IAJFCM........ International Association of Juvenile and Family Court Magistrates [*Paris, France*] (EA)

IaJGCoC....... Greene County Courthouse, Jefferson IA [*Library symbol Library of Congress*] (LCLS)

IaJH .... Jefferson Herald, Jefferson, IA [*Library symbol Library of Congress*] (LCLS)

IaJoN .... Northern Polk County News, Johnston, IA [*Library symbol Library of Congress*] (LCLS)

IAJRC......... International Association of Jazz Record Collectors (EA)

IAJS .... International Al Jolson Society (EA)

IAJV .... International Association of Justice Volunteerism (EA)

IAK........... International Air Cargo Corp. [*Egypt*] [*ICAO designator*] (FAAC)

IAK........... Internationales Auschwitz-Komitee [*International Auschwitz Committee*] [*Warsaw, Poland*] (EAIO)

IaK .... Keokuk Public Library, Keokuk, IA [*Library symbol Library of Congress*] (LCLS)

IAK........... Lake Forest College, Lake Forest, IL [*OCLC symbol*] (OCLC)

IaKalN .... Kalona News, Kalona, IA [*Library symbol Library of Congress*] (LCLS)

IaKan .... Kanawha Public Library, Kanawha, IA [*Library symbol Library of Congress*] (LCLS)

IaKanR........ Kanawha Reporter, Kanawha, IA [*Library symbol Library of Congress*] (LCLS)

IaKanRL....... Rural Life, Kanawha, IA [*Library symbol Library of Congress*] (LCLS)

IAKE.......... International Association of Knowledge Engineers (EA)

IaKe .... Keosauqua Public Library, Keosauqua, IA [*Library symbol Library of Congress*] (LCLS)

IaKen .... Kensett Public Library, Kensett, IA [*Library symbol Library of Congress*] (LCLS)

IaKeoE .... Keota Eagle, Keota, IA [*Library symbol Library of Congress*] (LCLS)

IaKeVR .... Van Buren County Register, Keosauqua, IA [*Library symbol Library of Congress*] (LCLS)

IaKey .... Keystone Public Library, Keystone, IA [*Library symbol Library of Congress*] (LCLS)

IAKF.......... International Amateur Karate Federation (EA)

IaKG.......... Keokuk Gate City, Keokuk, IA [*Library symbol Library of Congress*] (LCLS)

IaKiN .... Kingsley News-Tribune, Kingsley, IA [*Library symbol Library of Congress*] (LCLS)

IaKK............ Keosippi Library Cooperative, Keokuk, IA [*Library symbol Library of Congress*] (LCLS)
IaKn............. Knoxville Public Library, Knoxville, IA [*Library symbol Library of Congress*] (LCLS)
IaKnE........... Knoxville Express, Knoxville, IA [*Library symbol Library of Congress*] (LCLS)
IaKnJ........... Knoxville Journal, Knoxville, IA [*Library symbol Library of Congress*] (LCLS)
IaKnV........... United States Veterans Administration Hospital, Knoxville, IA [*Library symbol Library of Congress*] (LCLS)
IAKS............ Internationaler Arbeitskreis Sport- und Freizeiteninrichtungen [*International Working Group for the Construction of Sports and Leisure Facilities*] (EAIO)
IaKS............ Keokuk Savings Bank and Trust Co., Keokuk, IA [*Library symbol*] [*Library of Congress*] (LCLS)
IAL............. Immediate Action Letter (NASA)
IAL............. Imperial Airways Ltd. [*British*]
IAL............. Imperial Art League [*British*] (BI)
IAL............. Indian Airlines (PDAA)
IAL............. Infrared Aiming Light [*Military*] (INF)
IAL............. Inland Airlines
IAL............. Installation and Logistics (IAA)
IAL............. Instrument Approach and Landing Chart [*Aviation*]
IAL............. Interlaminar Adhesive Layer
IAL............. International Aeradio Ltd. [*British*]
IAL............. International Aeradio PLC [*British ICAO designator*] (FAAC)
IAL............. International Affairs (London) [*A publication*]
IAL............. International Algebraic Language [*Programming language*] [*Replaced by ALGOL*]
IAL............. International Algorithmic Language [*Computer science*] (BUR)
IAL............. International Aluminum Corp. [*NYSE symbol*] (SPSG)
IAL............. International Association of Laryngectomees (EA)
IAL............. International Association of Limnology (PDAA)
IAL............. International Association of Linguistics (DIT)
IAL............. International Association of Theoretical and Applied Limnology [*ICSU*] (EA)
IAL............. Intl Aluminum [*NYSE symbol*] (TTSB)
IAL............. Investment Analysis Language [*Computer science*] (BUR)
Ia-L............ Iowa State Law Library, Des Moines, IA [*Library symbol Library of Congress*] (LCLS)
IAL............. Irish Academy of Letters (BI)
IaL............. Lamoni Public Library, Lamoni, IA [*Library symbol Library of Congress*] (LCLS)
IAL............. Loyola University, Chicago, IL [*OCLC symbol*] (OCLC)
IALA........... International African Law Association
IALA........... International Association of Lighthouse Authorities [*Paris, France*] (EA)
IALA........... International Auxiliary Language Association [*Later, UMI*]
IALA........... Islamic Alliance for the Liberation of Afghanistan (PD)
IALACS........ International Association of Latin American and Caribbean Studies (EAIO)
IaLamtL....... Lamont Leader, Lamont, IA [*Library symbol Library of Congress*] (LCLS)
IaLanJ......... Allamakee Journal, Lansing, IA [*Library symbol Library of Congress*] (LCLS)
IaLau.......... Laurens Public Library, Laurens, IA [*Library symbol Library of Congress*] (LCLS)
IaLauS........ Laurens Sun, Laurens, IA [*Library symbol Library of Congress*] (LCLS)
IAlb............ Albion Public Library, Albion, IL [*Library symbol Library of Congress*] (LCLS)
IA L Bull...... Iowa Law Bulletin [*A publication*] (DLA)
IALC........... Instantaneous Automatic Level Control (IDOE)
IALC........... Institute of Allegheny Life and Culture (EA)
IALC........... Instrument Approach and Landing Chart [*Aviation*]
IALC........... International Arid Lands Consortium (EERA)
IALC........... International Association of Lions Clubs
IALC........... International Association of Lyceum Clubs
IALC........... Irish-American Labor Coalition [*Later, ALCHRNI*] (EA)
IALC........... Italian American Librarians Caucus (EA)
IaLC........... Lamoni Chronicle, Lamoni, IA [*Library symbol Library of Congress*] (LCLS)
IaLcG.......... Lake City Graphic, Lake City, IA [*Library symbol Library of Congress*] (LCLS)
IALCO.......... International Aircraft Leasing Co.
IAICU.......... Alton Community Unit 11, Alton, IL [*Library symbol Library of Congress*] (LCLS)
IALD........... International Association of Lighting Designers (EA)
IAIE............ East Alton Elementary 13, Alton, IL [*Library symbol Library of Congress*] (LCLS)
IALE........... Instrumented Architectural Level Emulation
IALE........... Integral of Absolute Linear Error (IAA)
IALEFI......... International Association of Law Enforcement Firearms Instructors (EA)
IALEIA......... International Association of Law Enforcement Intelligence Analysts (EA)
IaLeIS.......... Daily Sentinel, Lellars, IA [*Library symbol*] [*Library of Congress*] (LCLS)
IaLem......... Le Mars Public Library, Le Mars, IA [*Library symbol Library of Congress*] (LCLS)
IaLemS........ Daily Sentinel, Le Mars, IA [*Library symbol Library of Congress*] (LCLS)
IaLemW........ Westmar College, Le Mars, IA [*Library symbol Library of Congress*] (LCLS)

IaLeo.......... Leon Public Library, Leon, IA [*Library symbol Library of Congress*] (LCLS)
IaLeoJR........ Leon Journal-Reporter, Leon, IA [*Library symbol Library of Congress*] (LCLS)
IaLew.......... Lewis Public Library, Lewis, IA [*Library symbol Library of Congress*] (LCLS)
IALF........... Inter-American Literacy Foundation (EA)
IALF........... International Association of Law Firms [*Defunct*] (EA)
IaLG........... Graceland College, Lamoni, IA [*Library symbol Library of Congress*] (LCLS)
IAIH........... Alton Memorial Hospital, Alton, IL [*Library symbol Library of Congress*] (LCLS)
IALHI.......... International Association of Labour History Institutions [*Zurich, Switzerland*] (EAIO)
IALL........... International Association for Learning Laboratories (EA)
IALL........... International Association of Law Libraries (EAIO)
IaLL............ Lamoni Public Library, Lamoni, IA [*Library symbol*] [*Library of Congress*] (LCLS)
IALL Bull..... Bulletin. International Association of Law Libraries [*A publication*] (DLA)
IALM........... Integrated Anchor Leg Mooring [*Naval engineering*]
IALMC.......... International Association of Lighting Maintenance Contractors [*Later, NALMCO*] (EA)
IaLmG.......... Lake Mills Graphic, Lake Mills, IA [*Library symbol Library of Congress*] (LCLS)
IAIMH.......... Alton Mental Health Center, Development and Training Center, Staff Library, Alton, IL [*Library symbol Library of Congress*] (LCLS)
IALMH......... International Academy of Law & Mental Health (AC)
IaLnP.......... Lost Nation Press, Lost Nation, IA [*Library symbol Library of Congress*] (LCLS)
IaLoH.......... Logan Herald-Observer, Logan, IA [*Library symbol Library of Congress*] (LCLS)
IaLoHi......... Harrison County Historical Society, Logan, IA [*Library symbol Library of Congress*] (LCLS)
IaLohr......... J. J. Hands Library, Lohrville, IA [*Library symbol Library of Congress*] (LCLS)
IaLowS....... Sun News, Lowden, IA [*Library symbol Library of Congress*] (LCLS)
IALP........... International Association of Logopedics and Phoniatrics [*Dublin, Republic of Ireland*] (EA)
IaLpcPR....... La Porte City Progress-Review, La Porte City, IA [*Library symbol Library of Congress*] (LCLS)
IaLpN.......... Lake Park News, Lake Park, IA [*Library symbol Library of Congress*] (LCLS)
IALRW......... International Association of Liberal Religious Women (EA)
IALS........... Institute of Applied Language Studies [*Edith Cowan University*] [*Australia*]
IALS........... International Association of Legal Science [*See also AISJ*] [*Paris, France*] (EAIO)
IAIsA.......... Alsip-Merrionette Park Library District, Alsip, IL [*Library symbol Library of Congress*] (LCLS)
IaLsH.......... Lime Springs Herald, Lime Springs, IA [*Library symbol Library of Congress*] (LCLS)
IALSSA........ International Air Line Stewards and Stewardesses Association
IAIStA......... Saint Anthony's Hospital, Medical Library, Alton, IL [*Library symbol Library of Congress*] (LCLS)
IAIStJ.......... Saint Joseph's Hospital, Medical Information Services, Alton, IL [*Library symbol Library of Congress*] (LCLS)
IAlta........... Altamont Public Library, Altamont, IL [*Library symbol Library of Congress*] (LCLS)
IaLtR.......... Lone Tree Reporter, Lone Tree, IA [*Library symbol Library of Congress*] (LCLS)
IaLuHi......... Lucas County Historical Society, Lucas, IA [*Library symbol Library of Congress*] (LCLS)
IaLv............ Lake View Public Library, Lake View, IA [*Library symbol Library of Congress*] (LCLS)
IaLvR.......... Lake View Resort, Lake View, IA [*Library symbol Library of Congress*] (LCLS)
IAM............ Altos Hornos de Mexico SA de CV [*NYSE symbol*] (SAG)
IAM............ Anderson Public Library, Anderson, IN [*OCLC symbol*] (OCLC)
IAM............ Ignition Ackowledge Module [*Diesel engine controls*] [*Automotive engineering*]
IAM............ ILA [*Instruction Look Ahead*] Associative Memory [*Computer science*]
IAM............ Image Analyzing Microscope (PDAA)
IAM............ Imagery Analysis Memorandum (MCD)
IAM............ Immobilized Artificial Membranes [*Chemistry*]
IAM............ Impulse Amplitude Modulation (IAA)
IAM............ In Amenas [*Algeria*] [*Airport symbol*] (OAG)
IAM............ Incidental Amplitude Modulation
IAM............ Indefinite Admittance Matrix [*Network analysis*] (IEEE)
IAM............ Information Asset Management (SSD)
IAM............ Initial Address Message (TEL)
IAM............ Innovation Access Method [*Computer science*] (MHDI)
IAM............ Inscriptions Antiques du Maroc (BJA)
IAM............ Institute of Administrative Management [*British*] (DCTA)
IAM............ Institute of Advanced Motorists [*British*]
IAM............ Institute of Appliance Manufacturers [*Later, GAMA*] (EA)
IAM............ Institute of Applied Mathematics [*University of British Columbia*] [*Canada Research center*] (RCD)
IAM............ Institute of Aviation Medicine [*Royal Canadian Air Force*]
IAM............ Institute of the American Musical (EA)
IAM............ Intelligent Actuation & Measurement (ACII)
IAM............ Interactive Algebraic Manipulation [*Computer science*]
IAM............ Interaural Amplitude Modulation [*Audiology*]
IAM............ Intermediate Access Memory (NITA)

IAM.............	Internal Acoustic Meatus [*Medicine*] (MAE)
IAM.............	Internal Auditory Meatus [*Anatomy*]
IAM.............	International Academy of Management [*Knoxville, TN*] (EA)
IAM.............	International Academy of Metabology (EA)
IAM.............	International Academy of Myodontics (EA)
IAM.............	International Academy of Myodontics, Oceanic Chapter [*Sydney, NSW, Australia*] (EAIO)
IAM.............	International Afro-American Museum [*Later, AAM*] (EA)
IAM.............	International Amco Corp. [*Toronto Stock Exchange symbol*]
IAM.............	International Association of Machinists and Aerospace Workers (EA)
IAM.............	International Association of Metaphysicians
Ia-M.............	Iowa State Medical Library, Des Moines, IA [*Library symbol Library of Congress*] (LCLS)
IAMA.............	Incorporated Advertising Managers' Association [*British*] (BI)
IAMA.............	Independent Agricultural Merchants' Association [*Australia*]
IAMA.............	Informed Americans Monitor (EA)
IAMA.............	International Abstaining Motorists' Association [*Hagersten, Sweden*] (EAIO)
IAMA.............	International Academy of Myodontics, Asian Chapter [*Tokyo, Japan*] (EAIO)
IAMA.............	International Arts Medicine Association [*Philadelphia, PA*]
IAMA.............	Intimate Apparel Manufacturers Association (EA)
IaMa.............	Marshalltown Public Library, Marshalltown, IA [*Library symbol Library of Congress*] (LCLS)
IAMACS	International Association for Mathematics and Computers in Simulation
IaMall.........	Mallard Public Library, Mallard, IA [*Library symbol Library of Congress*] (LCLS)
IaMalv	Malvern Public Library, Malvern, IA [*Library symbol Library of Congress*] (LCLS)
IaMalvL	Malvern Leader, Malvern, IA [*Library symbol Library of Congress*] (LCLS)
IAMAM.........	International Association of Museums of Arms and Military History [*Ingolstadt, Federal Republic of Germany*] (EA)
IaMancP	Manchester Press, Manchester, IA [*Library symbol Library of Congress*] (LCLS)
IAMANEH....	International Association for Maternal and Neonatal Health [*Zurich, Switzerland*] (EAIO)
IaMannM	Manning Monitor, Manning, IA [*Library symbol Library of Congress*] (LCLS)
IaManS........	Marion Sentinel, Marion, IA [*Library symbol Library of Congress*] (LCLS)
IaMansJ.......	Manson Journal, Manson, IA [*Library symbol Library of Congress*] (LCLS)
IaManT	Manilla Times, Manilla, IA [*Library symbol Library of Congress*] (LCLS)
IaManyS	Manly Signal, Manly, IA [*Library symbol Library of Congress*] (LCLS)
IAMAP	International Association of Meteorology and Atmospheric Physics (EA)
IaMap	Mapleton Public Library, Mapleton, IA [*Library symbol Library of Congress*] (LCLS)
IaMapP........	Mapleton Press, Mapleton, IA [*Library symbol Library of Congress*] (LCLS)
IaMaq	Maquoketa Free Public Library, Maquoketa, IA [*Library symbol Library of Congress*] (LCLS)
IaMaqHi......	Jackson County Historical Society, Maquoketa, IA [*Library symbol Library of Congress*] (LCLS)
IaMaqP........	Maquoketa Community Press, Maquoketa, IA [*Library symbol Library of Congress*] (LCLS)
IaMaqS	Jackson Sentinel, Maquoketa, IA [*Library symbol Library of Congress*] (LCLS)
IaMara.........	Marathon Public Library, Marathon, IA [*Library symbol Library of Congress*] (LCLS)
IaMarc	Marcus Public Library, Marcus, IA [*Library symbol Library of Congress*] (LCLS)
IaMare	Marengo Public Library, Marengo, IA [*Library symbol Library of Congress*] (LCLS)
IaMarePR	Marengo Pioneer-Republican, Marengo, IA [*Library symbol Library of Congress*] (LCLS)
IaMari..........	Marion Carnegie Library, Marion, IA [*Library symbol Library of Congress*] (LCLS)
IAMAS	International Association of Meteorology and Atmospheric Sciences (EERA)
IAMAT.........	International Association for Medical Assistance to Travellers (EA)
IaMaTR........	Marshalltown Times-Republican, Marshalltown, IA [*Library symbol Library of Congress*] (LCLS)
IAMAW	International Association of Machinists and Aerospace Workers (MCD)
IaMaxHi.......	Community Historical Society, Maxwell, IA [*Library symbol Library of Congress*] (LCLS)
IaMay	Maynard Community Library, Maynard, IA [*Library symbol Library of Congress*] (LCLS)
IaMayr.........	Mount Ayr Public Library, Mount Ayr, IA [*Library symbol Library of Congress*] (LCLS)
IaMayrHi......	Ringgold County Historical Society, Mount Ayr, IA [*Library symbol Library of Congress*] (LCLS)
IaMayrR.......	Record-News, Mount Ayr, IA [*Library symbol Library of Congress*] (LCLS)
IAMB...........	International Association for the Protection of Monuments and Restoration of Buildings (EAIO)
IAMB...........	Irish Association of Master Bakers (BI)
IAMBE.........	International Association of Medicine and Biology of Environment [*See also AIMBE*] [*Paris, France*] (EAIO)
IAMBI..........	Iambic Verse (DSUE)

IaMbr..........	Marble Rock Public Library, Marble Rock, IA [*Library symbol Library of Congress*] (LCLS)
IAMC...........	Indian Army Medical Corps
IAMC...........	Institute for Advancement of Medical Communication [*Defunct*] (EA)
IAMC...........	Institute of Association Management Companies (EA)
IAMC...........	Inter-American Markets Corp. [*Latin America*]
IAMC...........	Inter-American Music Council (EAIO)
IAMC...........	International Association for Mobilization of Creativity
IaMc	Mason City Public Library, Mason City, IA [*Library symbol Library of Congress*] (LCLS)
IAMCA	International Association of Milk Control Agencies (EA)
IaMcG	Mason City Globe-Gazette, Mason City, IA [*Library symbol Library of Congress*] (LCLS)
IaMcg	McGregor Public Library, McGregor, IA [*Library symbol Library of Congress*] (LCLS)
IaMcGG........	Mason City Globe-Gazette, Mason City, IA [*Library symbol*] [*Library of Congress*] (LCLS)
IaMcgHi.......	McGregor Historical Society, McGregor, IA [*Library symbol Library of Congress*] (LCLS)
IaMcgN.......	North Iowa Times, McGregor, IA [*Library symbol Library of Congress*] (LCLS)
IaMcN........	North Iowa Cooperative Library Extension, Mason City, IA [*Library symbol Library of Congress*] (LCLS)
IaMcNC.......	North Iowa Area Community College, Mason City, IA [*Library symbol Library of Congress*] (LCLS)
IAMCR	International Association for Mass Communication Research [*British*]
IAMCS	International Alliance of Messianic Congregations and Synagogues (EA)
IAME...........	International Association for Modular Exhibitry (EA)
IAME...........	International Association of Medical Esperantists (EA)
IaMedi	Mediapolis Public Library, Mediapolis, IA [*Library symbol Library of Congress*] (LCLS)
IaMediN......	New Era, Mediapolis, IA [*Library symbol Library of Congress*] (LCLS)
IaMel	Melvin Public Library, Melvin, IA [*Library symbol Library of Congress*] (LCLS)
IaMelbR.......	Melbourne Record, Melbourne, IA [*Library symbol Library of Congress*] (LCLS)
IaMer..........	Merrill Public Library, Merrill, IA [*Library symbol Library of Congress*] (LCLS)
IAMFC.........	International Association for Marriage and Family Counselors (EA)
IAMFE.........	International Association on Mechanization of Field Experiments [*Aas, Norway*] (EA)
IAMFES........	International Association of Milk, Food, and Environmental Sanitarians (EA)
IAMFPA.......	International Association of Mouth and Foot Painting Artists (EA)
IAMFS.........	International Association for Maxillo-Facial Surgery (EA)
IAMG	International Association for Mathematical Geology (EA)
IAMHIST	International Association of Audio-Visual Media in Historical Research and Education [*Bologna, Italy*] (EAIO)
IAMIC.........	International Association of Mutual Insurance Companies [*See also AISAM*] (EAIO)
IaMidaHA	Amana Heritage Society, Middle Amana, IA [*Library symbol*] [*Library of Congress*] (LCLS)
IaMil...........	Milo Public Library, Milo, IA [*Library symbol Library of Congress*] (LCLS)
IaMilf.........	Milford Memorial Library, Milford, IA [*Library symbol Library of Congress*] (LCLS)
IaMilfM.......	Milford Mail, Milford, IA [*Library symbol Library of Congress*] (LCLS)
IaMilfN	Milford News, Milford, IA [*Library symbol Library of Congress*] (LCLS)
IaMisv.........	Missouri Valley Public Library, Missouri Valley, IA [*Library symbol Library of Congress*] (LCLS)
IaMisvTN......	Missouri Valley Times-News, Missouri Valley, IA [*Library symbol Library of Congress*] (LCLS)
IAML...........	International Association of Music Libraries (NITA)
IAML...........	International Association of Music Libraries, Archives, and Documentation Centers (EA)
IAMLADP	Inter-Agency Meeting on Language Arrangements, Documentation, and Publications [*United Nations*]
IAMLO	International African Migratory Locust Organization [*See also OICMA*] (EA)
IAMLT.........	International Association of Medical Laboratory Technologists [*Bootle, Merseyside, England*] (EA)
IAMM..........	International Association of Medical Museums [*Later, IAP*]
IAMMA........	Institute of Agricultural Market Management & Administration [*India*]
IAMM & D ...	Institute for Advanced Materials, Mechanics, and Design [*Army Materiel Command*]
IAMMW	International Association of Margaret Morris Method [*Glasgow, Scotland*] (EAIO)
IAMN..........	Istanbul Asariatica Muzeleri Nesriyati (BJA)
i amniot......	Intra-Amniotic [*Medicine*] (AAMN)
IaMonM	Monroe Mirror, Monroe, IA [*Library symbol Library of Congress*] (LCLS)
IaMono	Murphy Memorial Library, Monona, IA [*Library symbol Library of Congress*] (LCLS)
IaMonoB	Monona Billboard, Monona, IA [*Library symbol Library of Congress*] (LCLS)
IaMonoHi.....	Monona Historical Society, Monona, IA [*Library symbol Library of Congress*] (LCLS)
IaMont........	Monticello Public Library, Monticello, IA [*Library symbol Library of Congress*] (LCLS)
IaMontE	Monticello Express, Monticello, IA [*Library symbol Library of Congress*] (LCLS)
IaMonteR....	Montezuma Republican, Montezuma, IA [*Library symbol Library of Congress*] (LCLS)

IaMontHi...... Jones County Historical Society, Monticello, IA [*Library symbol*] [*Library of Congress*] (LCLS)
IaMontJHi.... Jones County Historical Society, Monticello, IA [*Library symbol Library of Congress*] (LCLS)
IaMoraU...... Moravia Union, Moravia, IA [*Library symbol Library of Congress*] (LCLS)
IaMorn........ Mellinger Memorial Library, Morning Sun, IA [*Library symbol Library of Congress*] (LCLS)
IaMornN...... Morning Sun News-Herald, Morning Sun, IA [*Library symbol Library of Congress*] (LCLS)
IaMou........ Garrett Memorial Library, Moulton, IA [*Library symbol Library of Congress*] (LCLS)
IaMouT....... Moulton Weekly Tribune, Moulton, IA [*Library symbol Library of Congress*] (LCLS)
IAMP...... Imagery Acquisition and Management Plan
IAMP......... Inter-Agency Motor Pool (WDAA)
IAMP......... International Academy of Medicine and Psychology [*Australia*] (EA)
IAMP......... International Association of Mathematical Physics (EA)
IAMP......... International Association of Meat Processors (EA)
IAMP......... International Association of Mercury Producers [*Spain, Italy, Turkey, Yugoslavia, Peru, Algeria*]
IaMp .... Mount Pleasant Public Library, Mount Pleasant, IA [*Library symbol Library of Congress*] (LCLS)
IaMpl......... Iowa Wesleyan College, Mount Pleasant, IA [*Library symbol Library of Congress*] (LCLS)
IaMpN......... Mount Pleasant News, Mount Pleasant, IA [*Library symbol Library of Congress*] (LCLS)
IAMPTH ...... International Association of Master Penmen and Teachers of Handwriting (EA)
IAMR .... Institute of Arctic Mineral Resources [*University of Alaska*]
IAMR .... International Association for Medical Research and Cultural Exchange
IAMRC .... International Antarctic Meteorological Research Center (PDAA)
IAMRC .... International Antarctic Meteorological Research Centre (PDAA)
IAMS......... Individual Aerial Mobility System [*Military*] (MCD)
IAMS......... Initial Attack Management System [*Weather system*]
IAMS......... Instantaneous Audience Measurement System
IAMS......... Institute for Archaeo-Metallurgical Studies [*British*] (IRUK)
IAMS......... Institute of Advanced Manufacturing Sciences [*University of Cincinnati*]
IAMS......... Institute of Advanced Marketing Studies - American Marketing Association (EA)
IAMS......... Institute of Applied Mathematics and Statistics [*University of British Columbia*] [*Research center*] (RCD)
IAMS......... International Advanced Microlithography Society [*Defunct*] (EA)
IAMS......... International Association for Mission Studies [*Hamburg, Federal Republic of Germany*] (EAIO)
IAMS......... International Association of Microbiological Societies [*ICSU*] [*Later, IUMS*]
IAMS......... International Association of Municipal Statisticians [*Later, IARUS*]
IAMSLIC ...... International Association of Aquatic and Marine Science Libraries & Information Centers [*Marine science*] (OSRA)
IAMSLIC ...... International Association of Marine Science Libraries and Information Centers (EA)
IAMSO .... Inter-African and Malagasy States Organization (NATG)
IAMT......... International Association for Machine Translation
IAMTACT..... Institute of Advanced Machine Tool and Control Technology [*British*]
IAMTCT...... Institute of Advanced Machine Tool and Control Technology (MCD)
IAM/TMD .... Institute of Administrative Management / Telecommunications Managers Division (HGAA)
IAMTS........ International Association of Model and Talent Scouts (EAIO)
IaMu .... P. M. Musser Public Library, Muscatine, IA [*Library symbol Library of Congress*] (LCLS)
IaMuJ .... Muscatine Journal, Muscatine, IA [*Library symbol Library of Congress*] (LCLS)
IAMUS ...... Installation Automated Manpower Utilization System [*Army*]
IaMvC .... Cornell College, Mount Vernon, IA [*Library symbol Library of Congress*] (LCLS)
IaMvCor...... Cornellian, Mount Vernon, IA [*Library symbol Library of Congress*] (LCLS)
IaMvH......... Hawkeye and Libson Herald, Mount Vernon, IA [*Library symbol Library of Congress*] (LCLS)
IaMvS......... Sun Hawkeye Record, Mount Vernon, IA [*Library symbol Library of Congress*] (LCLS)
IAMW......... Improved Antimateriel Warhead
IAMWH......... Improved Antimateriel Warhead
IAMWMW .... International Association of Ministers' Wives and Ministers' Widows (EAIO)
IAN............ Compania Internadia de Aviacion [*Colombia*] [*ICAO designator*] (FAAC)
IAN............ Idiopathic Aseptic Necrosis [*Medicine*] (DMAA)
IAN............ Illustrated Australian News [*A publication*]
IAN............ Imagery Analysis Notice
IAN............ Informatsionnoye Agentstvo Novosti [*Novosti Press Agency*] [*Russian Federation*]
IAN............ Interim Admission Note [*Medical records*] (DAVI)
IAN............ Intern Admission Note [*Medical records*] (DAVI)
IAN............ International Artist Network (EA)
IAN............ Internationale des Amis de la Nature [*International Federation of Friends of Nature*]
IAN............ Kennedy-King College of the City College of Chicago, Chicago, IL [*OCLC symbol*] (OCLC)
IAN............ Kiana [*Alaska*] [*Airport symbol*] (OAG)
IANA .... Intermodal Association of North America
IANA .... International Alliance of Nutrimedical Associations (EA)

IANA .... Internet Address Naming Authority [*Computer science*] (ACRL)
IANA .... Internet Assigned Numbers Authority
IANA .... Internet Assigned Numbers Authority (PCM)
IANAD.......... I Am Not a Doctor [*Internet*]
IANAL.......... I Am Not a Lawyer [*Internet*]
IANAP .... Interagency Noise Abatement Program
IaNas.......... Nashua Public Library, Nashua, IA [*Library symbol Library of Congress*] (LCLS)
IaNasCHi ..... Chickasaw County Historical Society, Nashua, IA [*Library symbol*] [*Library of Congress*] (LCLS)
IaNasPN ...... Plainfield News, Nashua, IA [*Library symbol Library of Congress*] (LCLS)
IaNasR .... Nashua Reporter, Nashua, IA [*Library symbol Library of Congress*] (LCLS)
IANC .... International Academy of Nutritional Consultants [*AANC*] [*Absorbed by*] (EA)
IANC .... International Airline Navigators Council [*Defunct*]
IANC .... International Air Navigation Convention
IANC .... International Anatomical Nomenclature Committee [*British*] (EAIO)
IANC .... Invest-in-America National Council [*Later, RA*] (EA)
IANCA .... Interamerican Naval Coordinating Authority (CINC)
IAND .... International Association of Nitrox Divers
I & A .... Indexing and Abstracting (NITA)
I & A .... Information and Action (MUGU)
I & A .... Inspection and Acceptance
I & A .... Irrigation and Aspiration [*Ophthalmology*] (DAVI)
I & B .... Improvement and Betterments [*Real estate*]
I & C .... Impact and Capabilities [*Study*] [*DoD*]
I & C .... Incision and Curettage [*Medicine*] (CPH)
I & C .... Information and Coordination (ADA)
I & C .... Inspected and Condemned [*Military*] (AAG)
I & C .... Installation and Calibration (SAA)
I & C .... Installation and Checkout [*Military*] (AFM)
I & C .... Installation and Construction [*Military*]
I & C .... Instrument and Controls
I and C .... Instrumentation and Communication
I & C .... Instrumentation and Communications [*Cable system*] (KSC)
I & C .... Instrumentation and Control [*Aerospace*] (AAG)
I & C .... Integration and Checkout (KSC)
I & C .... Issues and Criteria
I & C in Scot... Instrumentation and Control in Scotland [*A publication*]
I & C/O .... Installation and Checkout (NASA)
I & CRB .... Investigation and Censure Review Branch [*BUPERS*]
I & C(S) .... Instrumentation and Communication (System)
I & D .... Incision and Drainage [*Medicine*]
I and D .... Information and Documentation (NITA)
I & D .... Initiation and Development
I & D .... Install and Dismantle [*Expositions and exhibitions*]
I & D .... Integrate and Dump Detection [*Telecommunications*] (TEL)
I & D .... Irrigation and Debridement [*Surgery*] (DAVI)
I & D .... Irrigation and Drainage [*Surgery*] (DAVI)
i&e............ Identification and Exposition [*Also, ident-and-expo*] (WDMC)
I & E .... Industrial and Entertainment Funds [*Correctional institutions*]
I & E .... Information and Editorial [*Career program*]
I & E .... Information and Education [*Military*]
I & E .... Innovation and Entrepreneurship
I & E .... Intake and Exhaust [*Automotive engineering*]
I & E .... Internally and Externally (NRCH)
I & H .... Information and Historical [*Military*]
I&I............ Illness and Injuries (DMAA)
I & I .... Industrial and Institutional [*Business term*]
I & I .... Infiltration and Inflow [*Environmental science*] (FFDE)
I & I .... Inspector and Instructor [*For reserve units*] [*Marine Corps*] (DOMA)
I & I .... Intelligence and Interdiction [*Military*] (VNW)
I & I .... Intoxication and Intercourse
I & IA .... Interior and Insular Affairs
I & KP .... Initial and Key Personnel
I & L .... Installations and Logistics
I & M .... Improvement and Modernization (AABC)
I & M .... Inspection and Maintenance
I & M .... Installation and Maintenance
I & MA .... Inventory and Management Analysis (AFM)
I & N .... Immigration and Nationality Laws Administrative Decisions [*Department of Justice*] [*A publication*] (DLA)
I & N .... Immigration and Naturalization [*Service*] [*Department of Justice*]
I & N Dec ...... Immigration and Nationality Laws Administrative Decisions [*A publication*] (DLA)
I & O .... In and Out (MAE)
I & O .... Inlet and Outlet (MSA)
I & O .... Intake and Output [*Medicine*]
I & O .... Issues & Observations [*A publication*] (EAAP)
I & OH .... Inlet and Outlet Head (MSA)
I & OM .... Intermediate and Organizational Maintenance (MCD)
I & OP .... In and Out Processing [*Computer science*] (AFM)
I & P .... Indexed and Paged
I & P .... Inerting and Preheating [*Nuclear energy*] (NRCH)
I & R .... Information and Referral [*Services*] [*Used to assist the handicapped*]
I & R .... Initiative and Referendum
I & R .... Instruction and Research [*Individually-guided education*] (AEE)
I & R .... Integrity and Reliability [*Military*] (AFIT)
I & R .... Intelligence and Reconnaissance
I & R .... Interchangeability and Replaceability [*or Replacement*] (AAG)
I & RS .... Instrumentation and Range Safety [*NASA*] (KSC)
I&S............ Industries & Science Department (ACII)
I & S .... Inspection and Security

I & S............ Installation and Services
I & S............ Interchangeability and Substitutability (AFM)
IANDS.......... International Association for Near-Death Studies [See also AEEPM] (EA)
I & S............ Investigation and Suspension
I & S............ Iron and Steel
I & SE.......... Installation and Service Engineering (IEEE)
I & SM.......... Iron & Steelmaker [A publication] (EAAP)
I & SSFR...... Investigation and Security Service Field Representative [Veterans Administration]
I & T............ Inspection and Test (NRCH)
I & T............ Installation and Test [Army] (AABC)
I & T............ Integration and Test
I&T............... Internal Thoracic Artery [Medicine] (DMAA)
I&T............... Intolerance and Toxicity [Medicine] (DMAA)
I & T(P)........ Inspection and Test (Planning) (MCD)
I & TT.......... Ike and Tina Turner [Singers]
IANEC.......... Inter-American Nuclear Energy Commission [Organization of American States] (NRCH)
IaNeoG........ Gazette Reporter and Minden-Shelby News, Neloa, IA [Library symbol Library of Congress] (LCLS)
IANET.......... Integrated Access Network [Computer science] (MHDB)
IaNev.......... Nevada Public Library, Nevada, IA [Library symbol Library of Congress] (LCLS)
IaNevJ........ Nevada Evening Journal, Nevada, IA [Library symbol Library of Congress] (LCLS)
IaNewM....... Newell Mirror, Newell, IA [Library symbol Library of Congress] (LCLS)
IaNewt........ Newton Public Library, Newton, IA [Library symbol Library of Congress] (LCLS)
IaNewtCoC... Jasper County Courthouse, Newton, IA [Library symbol Library of Congress] (LCLS)
IaNewtHi...... Newton Historical Society, Newton, IA [Library symbol Library of Congress] (LCLS)
IaNewtJC ..... Jasper County Courthouse, Newton, IA [Library symbol] [Library of Congress] (LCLS)
IaNewtN....... Newton Daily News, Newton, IA [Library symbol Library of Congress] (LCLS)
IANF............ Individual Account Number File [IRS]
IANF............ Inter-Allied Nuclear Force (AABC)
IaNhE.......... New Hampton Economist, New Hampton, IA [Library symbol Library of Congress] (LCLS)
IaNhT.......... New Hampton Tribune, New Hampton, IA [Library symbol] [Library of Congress] (LCLS)
IaNl............. H. J. Nugen Public Library, New London, IA [Library symbol Library of Congress] (LCLS)
IaNIJ........... New London Journal, New London, IA [Library symbol Library of Congress] (LCLS)
IA/NLP......... International Association for Neuro-Linguistic Programming (EAIO)
IANLS .... International Association for Neo-Latin Studies [St. Andrews, Scotland] (EAIO)
IaNm........... New Market Public Library, New Market, IA [Library symbol Library of Congress] (LCLS)
IaNmM........ New Market Monitor, New Market, IA [Library symbol Library of Congress] (LCLS)
IaNoengR .... North English Record, North English, IA [Library symbol Library of Congress] (LCLS)
IaNosA........ Nora Springs Advertiser, Nora Springs, IA [Library symbol Library of Congress] (LCLS)
IaNowdA...... Northwood Anchor, Northwood, IA [Library symbol Library of Congress] (LCLS)
IaNowdCoC... Worth County Courthouse, Northwood, IA [Library symbol Library of Congress] (LCLS)
IaNowdWC... Worth County Courthouse, Northwood, IA [Library symbol] [Library of Congress] (LCLS)
IaNowkN...... North Warren Town and County News, Norwalk, IA [Library symbol Library of Congress] (LCLS)
IANPE .... Institute for the Advancement of Notary Public Education (EA)
IANPM......... International Academy of Nutrition and Preventive Medicine (EA)
IANRP.......... International Association of Natural Resource Pilots (EA)
IANS .... Institute of Applied Natural Science (EA)
IaNsS........... New Sharon Star, New Sharon, IA [Library symbol] [Library of Congress] (LCLS)
IANSW .... Ileostomy Association of New South Wales [Australia]
IANTD .... International Association of Nitrox and Technical Divers
IANTN .... Inter-American Naval Telecommunications Network (MCD)
IANU .... Italo American National Union
IaNv............ New Virginia Public Library, New Virginia, IA [Library symbol Library of Congress] (LCLS)
IaNvN.......... New Virginian, New Virginia, IA [Library symbol Library of Congress] (LCLS)
IANVS .... International Association for Non-Violent Sport [See also AICVS] [Monte Carlo, Monaco] (EAIO)
IAO............. Immediately after Onset [Medicine]
IAO............. In and Out of Clouds [ICAO] (FAAC)
IAO............. Incorporated Association of Organists [British]
IAO............. Independent Aviation Operators
IAO............. Information Activities Office [or Officer]
IAO............. Institute of Ambulance Officers [Australia]
IAO............. Institute of Apostolic Oblates (EA)
IAO............. Insurers' Advisory Organization of Canada
IAO............. Intermittent Aortic Occlusion [Cardiology]
IAO............. Internal Automation Operation
IAO............. International Association of Orthodontics (EA)
IAO............. Northeastern Illinois University, Chicago, IL [OCLC symbol] (OCLC)
IAOA .... Indicated Angle-of-Attack (GAVI)

IAOAD .... International Association of Original Art Diffusors (EAIO)
IaOak.......... Eckels Memorial Library, Oakland, IA [Library symbol Library of Congress] (LCLS)
IaOakA........ Oakland Acorn, Oakland, IA [Library symbol Library of Congress] (LCLS)
IAOC .... Indian Army Ordnance Control [British]
IAOC .... Irish Amateur Open Championship [Golf] (ROG)
IaOcD.......... Democrat, Orange City, IA [Library symbol Library of Congress] (LCLS)
IaOch.......... Ocheyedan Public Library, Ocheyedan, IA [Library symbol Library of Congress] (LCLS)
IaOchMH...... Melvin News, Ocheyedan, IA [Library symbol Library of Congress] (LCLS)
IaOchMN..... Melvin News, Ocheyedan, IA [Library symbol] [Library of Congress] (LCLS)
IaOchP......... Ocheyedan Press, Ocheyedan, IA [Library symbol Library of Congress] (LCLS)
IaOcM......... Mid-America Reformed Seminary, Orange City, IA [Library symbol] [Library of Congress] (LCLS)
IaOcN......... Northwestern College, Orange City, IA [Library symbol Library of Congress] (LCLS)
IaOcSC........ Sioux County Capital, Orange City, IA [Library symbol Library of Congress] (LCLS)
IAOD .... In Addition to Other Duties [Military]
IAOD .... International Academy of Optimum Dentistry [Defunct] (EA)
IAOD .... International Association of Opera Directors (EAIO)
IaOdC.......... Odebolt Chronicle, Odebolt, IA [Library symbol Library of Congress] (LCLS)
IAOE .... International Association of Optometric Executives (EA)
IaOe .... Oelwein Public Library, Oelwein, IA [Library symbol Library of Congress] (LCLS)
IaOeR .... Daily Register, Oelwein, IA [Library symbol Library of Congress] (LCLS)
IaOgd .... Ogden Public Library, Ogden, IA [Library symbol Library of Congress] (LCLS)
IaOgdR .... Ogden Reporter, Ogden, IA [Library symbol Library of Congress] (LCLS)
IAOH .... In Appreciation of the Hollies (EA)
IAOHRA........ International Association of Official Human Rights Agencies (EA)
IAOL............ International Association of Orientalist Librarians (EA)
IAOM .... International Association of Oral Myology (DMAA)
IAOMO .... International Association of Olympic Medical Officers [Rugby, Warwickshire, England] (EAIO)
IAOMS .... International Association of Oral and Maxillofacial Surgeons (EA)
IAOMT .... International Academy of Oral Medicine and Toxicology
IaOn .... Onawa Public Library, Onawa, IA [Library symbol Library of Congress] (LCLS)
IaOnCoC ..... Monona County Courthouse, Onawa, IA [Library symbol Library of Congress] (LCLS)
IaOnD .... Onawa Democrat, Onawa, IA [Library symbol Library of Congress] (LCLS)
IaOnS.......... Onawa Sentinel, Onawa IA [Library symbol Library of Congress] (LCLS)
IAOO .... Irish Agricultural Officers Organisation (BI)
IAOP .... International Association of Oral Pathologists (EA)
IAOPA .... International Council of Aircraft Owner and Pilot Associations (EA)
IAOPS .... Indiana Association of Osteopathic Physicians and Surgeons (SRA)
IaOrM .... Mid-American Reformed Seminary, Orange City, IA [Library symbol Library of Congress] (LCLS)
IAOS .... International Association for Official Statistics [International Statistical Institute] [Voorburg, Netherlands] (EAIO)
IAOS .... International Association of Ocular Surgeons (EA)
IAOS .... International Association of Oral Surgeons (EAIO)
IAOS .... Irish Agricultural Organisation Society Ltd. (BI)
IaOsa .... Sage Library, Osage, IA [Library symbol Library of Congress] (LCLS)
IaOsaCoC.... Mitchell County Courthouse, Osage, IA [Library symbol Library of Congress] (LCLS)
IaOsaP......... Mitchell County Press-News, Osage, IA [Library symbol Library of Congress] (LCLS)
IaOsc .... Osceola Public Library, Osceola, IA [Library symbol Library of Congress] (LCLS)
IaOscCoC..... Clarke County Courthouse, Osceola, IA [Library symbol] [Library of Congress] (LCLS)
IaOscS......... Osceola Sentinel, Osceola, IA [Library symbol Library of Congress] (LCLS)
IaOsk .... Oskaloosa Public Library, Oskaloosa, IA [Library symbol Library of Congress] (LCLS)
IaOskH......... Oskaloosa Daily Herald, Oskaloosa, IA [Library symbol Library of Congress] (LCLS)
IaOskMHi..... Mahaska County Historical Society, Oskaloosa, IA [Library symbol Library of Congress] (LCLS)
IaOskW........ William Penn College, Oskaloosa, IA [Library symbol Library of Congress] (LCLS)
IaOss .... Ossian Public Library, Ossian, IA [Library symbol Library of Congress] (LCLS)
IaOssB......... Ossian Bee, Ossian, IA [Library symbol Library of Congress] (LCLS)
IAOT .... International Association for Oxygen Therapy
IAOT .... International Association of Organ Teachers USA [Later, KTA] (EA)
IaOt............. Ottumwa Public Library, Ottumwa, IA [Library symbol Library of Congress] (LCLS)
IaOtC .... Ottumwa Heights College, Ottumwa, IA [Library symbol Library of Congress] (LCLS)
IaOtCo .... Ottumwa Courier, Ottumwa, IA [Library symbol Library of Congress] (LCLS)

IaOtS .... Southern Iowa Library Cooperative, Ottumwa, IA [*Library symbol Library of Congress*] (LCLS)

IaOxj .... Wreigie Memorial Library, Oxford Junction, IA [*Library symbol Library of Congress*] (LCLS)

IAP .... Image Array Processor

IAP .... Imitation Art Paper (DGA)

IAP .... Immunosuppressive Acidic Protein [*Immunochemistry*] (DMAA)

IAP .... Improved Accuracy Program (MCD)

IAP .... Incentive Awards Program [*of the federal government, administered by CSC*]

IAP .... Indoor Air Pollution

IAP .... Industry Applications Programs [*Computer science*] (IBMDP)

IAP .... Inerting and Preheating (IAA)

IAP .... Inhibitor of Apoptosis Protein [*Cytology*]

IAP .... Initial Aiming Point [*Gunnery*]

IAP .... Initial Approach [*Aviation*]

IAP .... Initial Approved Program

IAP .... Inlet Absolute Pressure

IAP .... Inorganic Ablative Plastic

IAP .... Institute of Animal Physiology [*British*]

IAP .... Institute of Arthropodology and Parasitology [*Georgia Southern University*] [*Research center*] (RCD)

IAP .... Institute of Atmospheric Physics [*University of Arizona*] [*Research center*]

IAP .... Institution of Analysis and Programmers (WDAA)

IAP .... Instrument Approach Procedure [*Aviation*] (AFM)

IAP .... Insurance Accounting Principles

IAP .... Integrated Action Plan

IAP .... Integrated Aeronautic Program [*Military*] (AFIT)

IAP .... Interactive Programming [*Computer science*]

IAP .... Interarray Processor (NVT)

IAP .... Interceptor Aim Points

IAP .... Intermittent Acute Porphyria [*Medicine*]

IAP .... Internal Air Portability

IAP .... Internal Array Processor [*Data General Corp.*]

IAP .... International Academy of Pathology (EA)

IAP .... International Academy of Proctology [*Defunct*] (EA)

IAP .... International Activities Program [*US Army Western Command*]

IAP .... International Aero Press

IAP .... International Airport

IAP .... International Association of Parapsychologists (EA)

IAP .... International Association of Photoplatemakers (EA)

IAP .... International Association of Planetology [*Brussels, Belgium*] (EA)

IAP .... International Association of Pteridologists (EERA)

IAP .... Intra-Abdominal Pressure

IAP .... Intra-Arterial Pressure

IAP .... Intracisternal A-Particle [*Biochemistry*]

IAP .... Iodoantipyrine [*Biochemistry*]

IAP .... Iona Appliances, Inc. [*Toronto Stock Exchange symbol*]

IAP .... Iranian Aircraft Program [*Military*] (MCD)

IAP .... Islet-Activating Protein [*Biochemistry*]

IAP .... Isopropylantipyrine [*Biochemistry*]

IAP .... Oakton Community College, Morton Grove, IL [*OCLC symbol*] (OCLC)

IAP .... Portland, OR [*Location identifier FAA*] (FAAL)

IAPA .... Idaho Association of Public Accountants (SRA)

IAPA .... Illinois Academy of Physician Assistants (SRA)

IAPA .... Illinois Asphalt Pavement Association (SRA)

IAPA .... Industrial Accident Prevention Association [*Canada*] (HGAA)

IAPA .... Instrument Approach Procedures Automation [*FAA*] (TAG)

IAPA .... Inter-American Police Academy (AABC)

IAPA .... Inter-American Press Association (EA)

IAPA .... International Airline Passengers Association (EA)

IAPA .... International Association of Physicians in Audiology (EAIO)

IAPAC .... Injection Assistee par Air Comprise [*Pneumatic Direct Fuel Injection*] [*French*]

IaPal .... Palmer Public Library, Palmer, IA [*Library symbol Library of Congress*] (LCLS)

IaPanV .... Guthrie County Vedette, Panora, IA [*Library symbol Library of Congress*] (LCLS)

IaParE .... Eclipse-News-Review, Parkersburg, IA [*Library symbol Library of Congress*] (LCLS)

IaParnHi .... Iowa County Historical Society, Parnell, IA [*Library symbol Library of Congress*] (LCLS)

IaPau .... Paullina Free Public Library, Paullina, IA [*Library symbol Library of Congress*] (LCLS)

IaPauT .... Paullina Times, Paullina, IA [*Library symbol Library of Congress*] (LCLS)

IAPB .... Inter-Allied Personnel Board [*World War II*]

IAPB .... International Agency for the Prevention of Blindness (EA)

IAPB .... International Association for the Prevention of Blindness [*Later, International Agency for the Prevention of Blindness*] (EA)

IAPBPPV .... International Association of Plant Breeders for the Protection of Plant Varieties (EAIO)

IAPBT .... International Association of Piano Builders and Technicians (EA)

IAPC .... Institute for the Advancement of Philosophy for Children (EA)

IAPC .... Instrument Approach Procedure Chart [*Aviation*] (NOAA)

IAPC .... Inter-American Peace Committee [*Later, Inter-American Committee on Peaceful Settlement*] [*OAS*]

IAPC .... International Association for Pollution Control [*Defunct*] (EA)

IAPC .... International Association of Pet Cemeteries (EA)

IAPC .... International Association of Political Consultants (EA)

IAPC .... International Auditing Practices Committee

IaPcN .... Prairie City News, Prairie City, IA [*Library symbol Library of Congress*] (LCLS)

IAPCO .... International Association of Professional Congress Organizers [*Brussels, Belgium*] (EAIO)

IAPD .... International Association of Paediatric Dentistry [*British*] (EAIO)

IAPD .... International Association of Parents of the Deaf [*Later, ASDC*] (EA)

IAPE .... Independent Association of Publishers' Employees (EA)

IaPe .... Pella Public Library, Pella, IA [*Library symbol Library of Congress*] (LCLS)

IaPeC .... Central College, Pella, IA [*Library symbol Library of Congress*] (LCLS)

IaPeCh .... Pella Chronicle, Pella, IA [*Library symbol Library of Congress*] (LCLS)

IaPeCR .... Central Ray, Pella, IA [*Library symbol Library of Congress*] (LCLS)

IaPerC .... Chief, Perry, IA [*Library symbol Library of Congress*] (LCLS)

IaPersHi .... Harrison County Historical Society, Persia, IA [*Library symbol Library of Congress*] (LCLS)

IAPES .... International Association of Personnel in Employment Security (EA)

IAPESGW .... International Association of Physical Education and Sport for Girls and Women (EA)

IaPet .... Kirchner-French Memorial Library, Peterson, IA [*Library symbol Library of Congress*] (LCLS)

IaPetP .... Peterson Patriot, Peterson, IA [*Library symbol Library of Congress*] (LCLS)

IAPF .... Inter-American Peacekeeping Force

IAPG .... Iberian Atlantic Planning Guidance (NATG)

IAPG .... Interagency Advanced Power Group

IAPG .... Interagency Arctic Policy Group (USDC)

IAPG .... Interagency Arctic Policy Group [*Marine science*] (OSRA)

IAPG .... International Association of Physical Geography (BARN)

IAPG .... International Association of Psychoanalytic Gerontology [*Paris, France*] (EAIO)

IAPG .... Item Analysis Program, General (PDAA)

IAPGPD .... Inter-American Parliamentary Group on Population and Development (EA)

IAPGR .... Institute of Animal Physiology and Genetics Research [*Research center British*] (IRC)

IAPH .... International Association of Paper Historians (DGA)

IAPH .... International Association of Ports and Harbors [*Japan*]

IAPHC .... International Association of Printing House Craftsmen (EA)

IAPI .... Industrial Air Pollution Inspectorate (PDAA)

IAPI .... Institute of Advertising Practitioners in Ireland (BI)

IAPI .... Institute of American Poultry Industries [*Later, PEIA*] (EA)

IaPierP .... Pierson Press, Pierson, IA [*Library symbol Library of Congress*] (LCLS)

IAPIP .... International Association for the Protection of Industrial Property

IAPL .... Initial Allowance Parts List [*Military*] (CAAL)

IAPL .... International Association for Philosophy and Literature (EA)

IAPL .... International Association of Penal Law [*Freiburg, Federal Republic of Germany*] (EAIO)

IaPlaBHi .... Bremer County Historical Society, Plainsfield, IA [*Library symbol Library of Congress*] (LCLS)

IaPleN .... Marion County News, Pleasantville, IA [*Library symbol Library of Congress*] (LCLS)

IAPLLT .... Interamerican Program for Linguistics and Language Teaching (EA)

IAPLSP .... International Association for Philosophy of Law and Social Philosophy [*See also AIPDPS*]

IAPM .... Institute of Applied Physiology and Medicine [*Formerly, Institute of Environmenta l Medicine and Physiology*] [*Research center*] (RCD)

IAPM .... International Academy of Preventive Medicine (EA)

IAPM .... International Association of Photoplate Makers (DGA)

IAPMA .... International Association of Hand Papermakers and Paper Artists (EAIO)

IAPMO .... International Association of Plumbing and Mechanical Officials (EA)

IAPN .... International Association of Professional Numismatists [*See also AINP*] [*Zurich, Switzerland*] (EAIO)

IAPNH .... International Association of Professional Natural Hygienists (EA)

IAPO .... Industrial Accountable Property Officer [*Air Force*]

IAPO .... Interchangeable at Attachment Point Only (AAG)

IAPO .... International Association of Physical Oceanography [*Later, IAPSO*]

IAPO .... International Association of Printers' Overseers (DGA)

IaPocR .... Pocahontas Record Democrat, Pocahontas, IA [*Library symbol Library of Congress*] (LCLS)

IaPolc .... Polk City Community Library, Polk City, IA [*Library symbol Library of Congress*] (LCLS)

IaPolcN .... Big Creek News, Polk City, IA [*Library symbol Library of Congress*] (LCLS)

IaPom .... Pomeroy Public Library, Pomeroy, IA [*Library symbol Library of Congress*] (LCLS)

IaPomH .... Pomeroy Herald, Pomeroy, IA [*Library symbol Library of Congress*] (LCLS)

IaPos .... Postville Public Library, Postville, IA [*Library symbol Library of Congress*] (LCLS)

IaPosH .... Postville Herald, Postville, IA [*Library symbol Library of Congress*] (LCLS)

IAPP .... International Association for Plant Physiology [*Australia*] (EAIO)

IAPP .... International Association for Preventive Pediatrics

IAPP .... International Association of Pacemaker Patients [*Later, IAHP*] (EA)

IAPP .... International Association of Police Professors [*Later, ACJS*]

IAPP .... Ion Acoustic Plasma Pulse

IAPP .... Islet Amyloid Polypeptide [*Biochemistry*]

IAPPHAP .... International Association for Past and Present History of the Art of Printing (EA)

IAPPI .... International Association of Public Pawnbroking Institutions [*Milan, Italy*] (EA)

IAPPP .... International Amateur-Professional Photoelectric Photometry [*An association*]
IAPPW .... International Association of Pupil Personnel Workers (EA)
IAPR .... Institute of Advanced Philosophic Research (EA)
IAPR .... International Association for Pattern Recognition [*British*] (EA)
IAPR .... International Association for Psychotronic Research [*Prague, Czechoslovakia*] (EA)
IaPrcWHi ...... Wayne County Historical Society, Promise City, IA [*Library symbol*] [*Library of Congress*] (LCLS)
IaPreT .... Preston Times, Preston, IA [*Library symbol Library of Congress*] (LCLS)
IaPreWHi ..... Wayne County Historical Society, Promise City, IA [*Library symbol Library of Congress*] (LCLS)
IAPRI .... International Association of Packaging Research Institutes [*British*] (EAIO)
IaPri .... Primghar Public Library, Primghar, IA [*Library symbol Library of Congress*] (LCLS)
IaPriB .... O'Brien County Bell, Primghar, IA [*Library symbol Library of Congress*] (LCLS)
IAPS .... Incorporated Association of Preparatory Schools [*British*] (DCTA)
IAPS .... Independent Association of Preparatory Schools
IAPS .... Inductosyn Angle Position Simulator
IAPS .... Institute for Advanced Pastoral Studies (EA)
IAPS .... Interim Antenna Pointing Subsystem [*Deep Space Instrumentation Facility, NASA*]
IAPS .... International Association for the Properties of Steam [*Later, IAPWS*] (EA)
IAPS .... Ion Auxiliary Propulsion System [*for satellites*]
IAPSAC .... International Association of Parents and Professionals for Safe Alternatives in Childbirth (EA)
IAPSC .... Inter-African Phytosanitary Commission
IAPSC .... International Association of Pipe Smokers Clubs (EA)
IAPSC .... International Association of Professional Security Consultants (EA)
IAPSO .... International Association for the Physical Sciences of the Ocean (EA)
IAPSP .... Inter-American Program for Social Progress [*AID*]
IAPSRS .... International Association of Psycho-Social Rehabilitation Services (EA)
IAPT .... International Association for Plant Taxonomy [*Utrecht, Netherlands*] (EA)
IAPT .... International Association of Plant Taxonomists (EERA)
IA/PT .... Item Acquisition/Production Trade-Off Model
IAPTA .... International Allied Printing Trades Association (EA)
IAPTE .... International Academy of Pediatric Transdisciplinary Education [*British*] (EAIO)
IAPUP .... International Association on the Political Use of Psychiatry [*Amsterdam, Netherlands*] (EAIO)
IAPV .... Institute Against Prejudice and Violence (EA)
IAPV .... Intermittent Abdominal Pressure Ventilation [*Medicine*] (DMAA)
IAPW .... International Association for Personnel Women (EA)
IaPwdC .... Packwood Clarion, Packwood, IA [*Library symbol Library of Congress*] (LCLS)
IAPWS .... International Association for the Properties of Water and Steam (EA)
IAQ .... Independent Activities Questionnaire [*Psychology*]
IAQ .... Indoor Air Quality
IAQ .... International Academy for Quality [*Grobenzell, Federal Republic of Germany*] (EAIO)
IAQ .... Parkland College, Champaign, IL [*OCLC symbol*] (OCLC)
IAQA/C .... Interstate Air Quality Agencies /Commissions [*Environmental Protection Agency*]
IAQC .... International Association of Quality Circles (EA)
IAQDE .... Independent Association of Questioned Document Examiners (EA)
IAR .... Iliamna Air Taxi, Inc. [*ICAO designator*] (FAAC)
I-Ar .... Illinois State Library, Archives Division, Springfield, IL [*Library symbol Library of Congress*] (LCLS)
IAR .... Imagery Analysis Report (MCD)
IAR .... Inactive Air Reserve
IAR .... Indirect Address Register
IAR .... Individual Action Report
IAR .... Information Analysis and Retrieval [*Computer science*] (ECII)
IAR .... Initial Address Register [*Computer science*] (HGAA)
IAR .... Inspection Acceptance Record (SAA)
IAR .... Institute for Aerobics Research (EA)
IAR .... Institute for Air Research (WDAA)
IAR .... Institute of American Relations [*Defunct*] (EA)
IAR .... Institute of Andean Research (EA)
IAR .... Institute of Asian Research [*Canada*] (IRC)
IAR .... Instruction Address Register [*Computer science*] (MDG)
IAR .... Instrument Air Receiver (AAG)
IAR .... Integrated Alternator Regulator [*Automotive engineering*]
IAR .... Integrity and Reliability [*Military*] (AFIT)
IAR .... Intelligence and Reconnaissance (IAA)
IAR .... Interagency Rate (AFM)
IAR .... Interavia Aerospace Review [*Interavia Publications*] [*Information service or system*] (CRD)
IAR .... Interment Is Authorized for the Remains Of [*Military*]
IAR .... International Art Register
IAR .... International Association of Radiopharmacology (EA)
IAR .... Interrupt Address Register
IAR .... Intersection of Air Routes [*Aviation*]
IAR .... Inventory Adjustment Rate
IAR .... Inventory Adjustment Report [*Military*]
IARP .... Isobaric Analog Resonance [*Nuclear structure*]
IAR .... Roosevelt University, Chicago, IL [*OCLC symbol*] (OCLC)
IARA .... Industrial Arbitration Registrars' Association [*Australia*]
IARA .... Inter-Allied Reparations Agency [*Brussels*]

IARA .... International Animal Rights Alliance [*Defunct*] (EA)
IARA .... International Association of Rebekah Assemblies, IOOF [*Independent Order of Odd Fellows*] (EA)
IaRa .... Rake Public Library, Rake, IA [*Library symbol Library of Congress*] (LCLS)
IARASM .... Institute for Advanced Research in Asian Science and Medicine (EA)
IARB .... Inspection Analysis Review Board (MCD)
IArb .... Institute of Arbitrators [*British*] (DI)
IArc .... Arcola Public Library, Arcola, IL [*Library symbol Library of Congress*] (LCLS)
IARC .... Independent Assessment and Research Centre [*British*] (CB)
IARC .... International Action for the Rights of the Child [*See also AIDE*] [*Paris, France*] (EAIO)
IARC .... International Agency for Research on Cancer [*World Health Organization*] [*Lyon, France*] [*Research center*] (EAIO)
IARC .... International Agency for Research on Cancer (EERA)
IARC .... International Agricultural Research Center
IARC .... International Agricultural Research Centre (EERA)
IAR/C .... Interviewing, Assessment, and Referral or Counseling (ADA)
IARCA .... International Association Residential and Community Alternatives (EAIO)
IaRcA .... Rockwell City Advocate, Rockwell City, IA [*Library symbol Library of Congress*] (LCLS)
IARCC .... Interagency Arctic Research Coordinating Committee [*Terminated, 1978*] [*National Science Foundation*]
IaRcCHi ...... Calhoun County Historical Society, Rockwell City, IA [*Library symbol Library of Congress*] (LCLS)
IaRcfR .... Rockford Register, Rockford, IA [*Library symbol Library of Congress*] (LCLS)
IArcSD .... Arcola Community Unit School District, Arcola, IL [*Library symbol*] [*Library of Congress*] (LCLS)
IARD .... Information Analysis and Retrieval Division [*American Institute of Physics*] (PDAA)
IARD .... International Association for Rural Development (AIE)
IARE .... Improved Amphibious Reconnaissance Equipment [*Military*] (MCD)
IARE .... Institute of Animal Resource Ecology [*University of British Columbia*] [*Research center*] (RCD)
IARE .... International Association of Railway Employees (EA)
IAREC .... Irrigated Agriculture Research and Extension Center [*Washington State University*] [*Research center*] (RCD)
IaRedf .... Redfield Public Library, Redfield, IA [*Library symbol Library of Congress*] (LCLS)
IaRedfRS ..... Dexfield Review Sentinel, Redfield, IA [*Library symbol Library of Congress*] (LCLS)
IaRedo .... Red Oak Public Library, Red Oak, IA [*Library symbol Library of Congress*] (LCLS)
IaRedoE ...... Red Oak Express, Red Oak, IA [*Library symbol Library of Congress*] (LCLS)
IaReiC .... Reinbeck Courier, Reinbeck, IA [*Library symbol Library of Congress*] (LCLS)
IaRemBE ..... Remsen Bell-Enterprise, Remsen, IA [*Library symbol Library of Congress*] (LCLS)
IaRen .... Renwick Public Library, Renwick, IA [*Library symbol Library of Congress*] (LCLS)
IARF .... International Amateur Racquetball Federation (EA)
IARF .... International Association for Religious Freedom [*Germany*] (EY)
IARFA .... Independent Aluminum Residential Fabricators Association (EA)
IARFP .... International Association of Registered Financial Planners (EA)
IArg .... Argonne National Laboratory, Argonne, IL [*Library symbol Library of Congress*] (LCLS)
IArgoC .... CPC International, Inc., Argo, IL [*Library symbol Library of Congress*] (LCLS)
IARI .... Indian Agricultural Research Institute
IARI .... Industrial Advertising Research Institute [*Later, CMC*] (EA)
IaRicP .... Richland Plainsman, Richland, IA [*Library symbol Library of Congress*] (LCLS)
IARIGAI .... International Association of Research Institutes for the Graphic Arts Industry [*St. Gallen, Switzerland*]
IARIL .... International Association of Rural and Isolated Libraries [*Australia*]
IaRinD .... Ringsted Dispatch, Ringsted, IA [*Library symbol Library of Congress*] (LCLS)
IaRiR .... Riceville Record, Riceville, IA [*Library symbol Library of Congress*] (LCLS)
IARIW .... International Association for Research in Income and Wealth (EA)
IARIW .... International Association for Research on Income and Wealth (EERA)
IARLD .... International Association for Research in Learning Disabilities
IArlh .... Arlington Heights Public Library, Arlington Heights, IL [*Library symbol Library of Congress*] (LCLS)
IARM .... Inspectorate of Armaments (PDAA)
IARM .... Interim Antiradiation Missile (MCD)
IARMCLRS.... International Agreement Regarding the Maintenance of Certain Lights in the Red Sea (EA)
IARMI .... International Association of Rattan Manufacturers and Importers [*Defunct*] (EA)
IARN .... International Amateur Radio Network
IARO .... Indian Army Reserve of Officers
IaRol .... Rolfe Public Library, Rolfe, IA [*Library symbol Library of Congress*] (LCLS)
IaRolA .... Rolfe Arrow, Rolfe, IA [*Library symbol Library of Congress*] (LCLS)
IAROO .... International Association of Railway Operating Officers (EA)
IARP .... International Association for Religion and Parapsychology [*Tokyo, Japan*] (EA)
IARP .... International Association of Retired Persons [*Superseded by IFA*] (EA)

IARQ	Intellectual Achievement Responsibility Questionnaire [*Psychology*] (EDAC)
IARR	International Association for Radiation Research [*Rijswijk, Netherlands*] (EAIO)
IaRrLCoC	Lyon County Courthouse, Rock Rapids, IA [*Library symbol Library of Congress*] (LCLS)
IaRrLR	Lyon County Reporter, Rock Rapids, IA [*Library symbol Library of Congress*] (LCLS)
IARS	Improved Aerial Refueling System Program
IARS	Independent Air Revitalization System (NASA)
IARS	Institute for Advanced Russian Studies [*Smithsonian Institution*]
IARS	International Anesthesia Research Society (EA)
IARSA	Idiopathic Acquired Refractory Sideroblastic Anemia [*Medicine*] (DMAA)
IARSB	International Association of Rolling Stock Builders [*See also AICMR*] (EAIO)
IARSC	International Association of Religious Science Churches [*Later, RSI*] (EA)
IARSL	Institute of Agriculture Remote Sensing Laboratory [*University of Minnesota*]
IArt	Arthur Public Library, Arthur, IL [*Library symbol Library of Congress*] (LCLS)
IART	Integra Life Sciences [*NASDAQ symbol*] (TTSB)
IART	Integra LifeSciences Corp. [*NASDAQ symbol*] (SAG)
i arter	Intra-Arterial [*Cardiology*] (AAMN)
IArtSD	Arthur Community School District, Arthur, IL [*Library symbol*] [*Library of Congress*] (LCLS)
IARU	International Amateur Radio Union (EA)
IARU	Irish Amateur Rowing Union [*British*] (EAIO)
IaRu	Ruthven Public Library, Ruthven, IA [*Library symbol Library of Congress*] (LCLS)
IARUS	International Association for Regional and Urban Statistics [*Voorburg, Netherlands*] (EA)
IaRuZ	Ruthven Zipcode, Ruthven, IA [*Library symbol Library of Congress*] (LCLS)
IaRvB	Rock Valley Bee, Rock Valley, IA [*Library symbol Library of Congress*] (LCLS)
IARW	International Association of Refrigerated Warehouses (EA)
IAS	Iasi [*Romania*] [*Airport symbol*] (OAG)
IAS	Iasi [*Romania*] [*Seismograph station code, US Geological Survey*] (SEIS)
IAS	Ideal Adsorbed Solution [*Physical chemistry*]
IAS	IEEE Industry Applications Society (EA)
IAS	Illness Adaptation Scale (EDAC)
IAS	Immediate Access Storage (AFM)
IAS	Impact Assessment Sheet (NASA)
IAS	Impact Assessment Study
IAS	India-America Society
IAS	Indian Administrative Service [*British*]
IAS	Indian Astronautical Society
IAS	Indicated Air Speed
IAS	Inelastic Atom Scattering (PDAA)
IAS	Information Acquisition System (MCD)
IAS	Inspector of Army Schools [*British military*] (DMA)
IAS	Institute for Advanced Studies [*Army*]
IAS	Institute for American Strategy [*Later, ASCF*]
IAS	Institute for Atmospheric Sciences [*South Dakota School of Mines*] [*Research center Environmental Science Services Administration*]
IAS	Institute for the Advancement of Sailing [*Commercial firm*] (EA)
IAS	Institute of Advanced Studies [*Australian National University*]
IAS	Institute of Aerospace [*formerly, Aeronautical*] Sciences [*Later, AIAA*]
IAS	Institute of Alcohol Studies [*British*] (DBA)
IAS	Institute of Andean Studies (EA)
IAS	Institute of Animal Sciences (ASF)
IAS	Institute of Asian Studies (EA)
IAS	Institute of Aviation Studies [*University of Newcastle*] [*Australia*]
IAS	Instructor Aid System (MCD)
IAS	Instrument Air System [*Nuclear energy*] (NRCH)
IAS	Instrument Approach System
IAS	Integrated Analytical System (IAA)
IAS	Integrated AUTODIN [*Automatic Digital Information Network*] System [*DoD*]
IAS	Integrated Automation Systems
IAS	Integrated Avionics System (MCD)
IAS	Intelligence Analysis Squadron
IAS	Intelligent Array Subsystem Core
IAS	Intelligent Authoring Systems (EDAC)
IAS	Intellisoft Accounting Series [*Computer science*] (PCM)
IAS	Interactive Analysis System [*Computer science*] (PCM)
IAS	Interactive Applications Supervisor
IAS	Interactive Application System (IAA)
IAS	Inter-American System
IAS	Interatrial Septum [*Cardiology*] (MAE)
IAS	Interatrial Shunting [*Medicine*] (DMAA)
IAS	Interest Assessment Scales
IAS	Internal Alignment Sensor (MCD)
IAS	International Academy of Sciences (EAIO)
IAS	International Accountants Society
IAS	International Accounting Standards
IAS	International AIDS Society (EAIO)
IAS	International Air Service Co. [*ICAO designator*] (FAAC)
IAS	International Applied Systems (NITA)
IAS	International Army Staff (MCD)
IAS	International Aroid Society (EA)
IAS	International Association of Sedimentologists [*Liege, Belgium*] (EA)
IAS	International Association of Siderographers (EA)
IAS	International Atherosclerosis Society (EA)
IAS	International Audiovisual Society (EA)
IAS	International Aviation Service [*FAA*]
IAS	International Aviation Services [*Belgium*]
IAS	Intra-Amniotic Saline [*Infusion*] [*Medicine*]
IAS	Intra-Articular Steroid [*Physiology*]
IAS	Intrusion Alarm System
IAS	Invariant-Azimuth States (PDAA)
IAS	Inventory of American Sculpture
IAS	Isobaric Analog State
IAS	Israeli Air Services (MCD)
IAS	Los Angeles, CA [*Location identifier FAA*] (FAAL)
IAS	Sangamon State University, Springfield, IL [*OCLC symbol*] (OCLC)
IASA	Idaho Association of School Administrators (SRA)
IASA	Ileostomy Association of South Australia
IASA	Illinois Association of School Administrators (SRA)
IASA	Importers' Association of South Australia
IASA	Independent Automotive Service Association (EA)
IASA	Indo-American Sports Association [*Later, FIA-USC*]
IASA	INSCOM [*Intelligence and Security Command*] Automated Systems Support Activity [*Army*] (MCD)
IASA	Institute for Atomic Sciences in Agriculture
IASA	Institute of Agricultural Secretaries of Australasia
IASA	Insurance Accounting and Statistical Association [*Later, Insurance Accounting and Systems Association*] (EA)
IASA	Insurance Accounting and Systems Association [*Durham, NC*] (EA)
IASA	Integrated Assessment of Security Assistance [*Military*]
IASA	Integrated AUTODIN [*Automatic Digital Information Network*] System Architecture (MCD)
IASA	Interatrial Septal Aneurysm [*Medicine*] (DMAA)
IASA	International Air Safety Association (EA)
IASA	International Alliance for Sustainable Agriculture (EA)
IASA	International Alliance for Sustainable Agriculture (GNE)
IASA	International Association of Schools in Advertising
IASA	International Association of Sound Archives [*Milton, Keynes, England*] (EAIO)
IASA	Irish Amateur Swimming Association (EAIO)
IASAA	International Agricultural Students Association of the Americas (EA)
IaSab	Sabula Public Library, Sabula, IA [*Library symbol Library of Congress*] (LCLS)
IASAC	International Association of Silver Art Collectors (EA)
IaSacLS	Lytton Star, Sac City, IA [*Library symbol Library of Congress*] (LCLS)
IaSacS	Sac Sun, Sac City, IA [*Library symbol Library of Congress*] (LCLS)
IASAIL	International Association for the Study of Anglo-Irish Literature [*Maynooth, Republic of Ireland*] (EAIO)
IASAJ	International Association of Supreme Administration Jurisdictions GG2 [*See also AIHJA*] (EAIO)
IaSal	Crew Public Library, Salem, IA [*Library symbol Library of Congress*] (LCLS)
IaSan	Sanborn Public Library, Sanborn, IA [*Library symbol Library of Congress*] (LCLS)
IaSanP	Sanborn Pioneer, Sanborn, IA [*Library symbol Library of Congress*] (LCLS)
IASAP	Intercollegiate Association for Study of the Alcohol Problem (EA)
IASAP	International Arctic Seas Assessment Project [*Marine science*] (OSRA)
IASB	Illinois Association of School Boards (EDAC)
IASB	Installation Aviation Standardization Board (MCD)
IASB	International Academy at Santa Barbara (EA)
IASB	Iowa Association of School Boards (SRA)
IASBFLC	Institute for the Advanced Study of Black Family Life and Culture (EA)
IASC	Indexing and Abstracting Society of Canada [*Toronto, ON*]
IASC	Indian Army Service Corps [*British military*] (DMA)
IASC	Inter-American Safety Council (EA)
IASC	Inter-American Scout Committee [*See also CIE*] [*San Jose, Costa Rica*] (EAIO)
IASC	Inter-American Statistical Teaching Center
IASC	International Accounting Standards Committee [*of the International Federation of Accountants*] [*British*] (EAIO)
IASC	International Afroid Science Conference (MCD)
IASC	International Aloe Science Council (EA)
IASC	International Arctic Science Committee
IASC	International Association for Statistical Computing (EA)
IASC	International Association of Seed Crushers [*British*] (EAIO)
IASC	International Association of Skal Clubs [*Spain*] (EAIO)
IASC	Intimate Apparel Square Club (EA)
IASc	Italian American Stamp Club (EA)
IaSc	Sioux City Public Library, Sioux City, IA [*Library symbol Library of Congress*] (LCLS)
IASCA	International Auto Sound Challenge Association (EA)
IaScB	Briar Cliff College, Sioux City, IA [*Library symbol Library of Congress*] (LCLS)
IASCB	Ibero-American Society for Cell Biology [*See also SIABC*] (EAIO)
IASCB	International Association of Sand Castle Builders (EA)
IASCD	Idaho Association of Soil Conservation Districts (SRA)
IASCD	Illinois Association for Supervision and Curriculum Development (SRA)
IASCE	International Association for the Study of Cooperation in Education (EA)
IaSce	Sioux Center Public Library, Sioux Center, IA [*Library symbol Library of Congress*] (LCLS)
IaSceD	Dordt College, Sioux Center, IA [*Library symbol Library of Congress*] (LCLS)

IaSchH......... Schaller Herald, Schaller, IA [*Library symbol Library of Congress*] (LCLS)

IaSchIL......... Schleswig Leader, Schleswig, IA [*Library symbol Library of Congress*] (LCLS)

IaScM......... Morningside College, Sioux City, IA [*Library symbol Library of Congress*] (LCLS)

IaScNR....... Northwest Regional Library System, Sioux City, IA [*Library symbol Library of Congress*] (LCLS)

IASCO.......... International Association of Service Companies [*NACSA*] [*Absorbed by*] (EA)

IASCP......... Institute for Advanced Study of the Communication Processes [*University of Florida*] [*Research center*] (RCD)

IASCP......... International Association for the Study of Common Property (EA)

IASCS......... International Association for Shopping Center Security (EA)

IaScS.......... Siouxland Libraries Cooperative, Sioux City, IA [*Library symbol Library of Congress*] (LCLS)

IaScT.......... Trinity College, Sioux City, IA [*Library symbol Library of Congress Obsolete*] (LCLS)

IaScWI........ West Iowa Technical Community College, Sioux City, IA [*Library symbol Library of Congress*] (LCLS)

IASD............ Interatrial Septal Defect [*Cardiology*]

IASDI........... Inter-American Social Development Institute [*Later, IAF*]

IASEES........ International Association of South-East European Studies [*See also AIESEE*] [*Bucharest, Romania*] (EAIO)

IaSeyH......... Seymour Herald, Seymour, IA [*Library symbol Library of Congress*] (LCLS)

IASF............ Instrumentation in Aerospace Simulation Facilities

IASF............ International Amateur Surfing Federation (EA)

IASF............ International Amateur Swimming Federation (EA)

IASF............ International Atlantic Salmon Foundation [*Canada*] (EA)

IASF............ Irish American Sports Foundation (EA)

IASG........... Inflation Accounting Steering Group (MHDB)

IASH............ International Association of Scientific Hydrology [*Later, International Association of Hydrological Sciences*] [*of International Union of Geodesy and Geophysics*]

IASH............ Isolated Asymmetric Septal Hypertrophy [*Medicine*] (DMAA)

IASH............ Israeli Academy of Sciences and Humanities

IaSh............ Shenandoah Public Library, Shenandoah, IA [*Library symbol Library of Congress*] (LCLS)

IaShe........... Sheldon Public Library, Sheldon, IA [*Library symbol Library of Congress*] (LCLS)

IaShefP........ Sheffield Press, Sheffield, IA [*Library symbol Library of Congress*] (LCLS)

IaSheHi........ Sheldon County Historical Society, Sheldon, IA [*Library symbol Library of Congress*] (LCLS)

IaSheM........ Sheldon Mail, Sheldon, IA [*Library symbol Library of Congress*] (LCLS)

IaSheS......... Sheldon Sun, Sheldon, IA [*Library symbol Library of Congress*] (LCLS)

IaShr........... Shell Rock Public Library, Shell Rock, IA [*Library symbol Library of Congress*] (LCLS)

IaShrN......... Shell Rock News, Shell Rock, IA [*Library symbol*] [*Library of Congress*] (LCLS)

IASHS.......... Institute for Advanced Study in Human Sexuality (DAVI)

IASI............. Inter-American Statistical Institute (EA)

IASI............. Inter-American Statistical Institute

IASI............. International Alliance Services, Inc. [*NASDAQ symbol*] (SAG)

IASI............. International Association for Sports Information [*The Hague, Netherlands*] (EA)

IaSibCoC..... Osceola County Courthouse, Sibley, IA [*Library symbol*] [*Library of Congress*] (LCLS)

IaSibG......... Sibley Gazette and Tribune, Sibley, IA [*Library symbol*] [*Library of Congress*] (LCLS)

IaSidAH....... Sidney Argus-Herald, Sidney, IA [*Library symbol*] [*Library of Congress*] (LCLS)

IaSidCoC..... Fremont County Courthouse, Sidney, IA [*Library symbol*] [*Library of Congress*] (LCLS)

IaSigCoC...... Keokuk County Courthouse, Sigourney, IA [*Library symbol*] [*Library of Congress*] (LCLS)

IaSigNR....... Sigourney News-Review, Sigourney, IA [*Library symbol*] [*Library of Congress*] (LCLS)

IASILL.......... International Association for the Study of the Italian Language and Literature [*See also AISLLI*] [*Padua, Italy*] (EAIO)

IASL............ International Association for the Study of the Liver [*Gottingen, Federal Republic of Germany*] (EAIO)

IASL............ International Association of School Librarianship (PDAA)

IaSl............. Storm Lake Public Library, Storm Lake, IA [*Library symbol Library of Congress*] (LCLS)

IaSla........... Slater Public Library, Slater, IA [*Library symbol Library of Congress*] (LCLS)

IaSlaT.......... Tri County Times, Slater, IA [*Library symbol*] [*Library of Congress*] (LCLS)

IaSIB........... Buena Vista College, Storm Lake, IA [*Library symbol Library of Congress*] (LCLS)

IASLC.......... International Association for the Study of Lung Cancer (EA)

IASLIC......... Indian Association for Special Libraries and Information Centres (NITA)

IaSIPT.......... Storm Lake Pilot-Tribune, Storm Lake, IA [*Library symbol*] [*Library of Congress*] (LCLS)

IASM........... Independent Association of Stocking Manufacturers [*Defunct*]

IASM........... Institute of Aerospace Safety and Management [*University of Southern California*]

IASM........... International Association for Seminar Management (EA)

IASM........... International Association of Structural Movers (EA)

IASM........... Istituto per l'Assistenza allo Sviluppo del Mezzogiorno [*Italy*] (EY)

IASMHF....... International Association of Sports Museums and Halls of Fame (EA)

IASMIRT...... International Association for Structural Mechanics in Reactor Technology (EAIO)

IASMW........ International Association of Sheet Metal Workers (BARN)

IAS/NAB....... International Arthurian Society/North American Branch [*Canada*] (EAIO)

IASnet......... [*The*] Institute for Automated Systems Network (TNIG)

IASOC......... International Association for the Study of Organized Crime (EA)

IaSolE.......... Solon Economist, Solon, IA [*Library symbol*] [*Library of Congress*] (LCLS)

IASOR.......... Ice and Snow on Runway [*Aviation*]

IASOS.......... Institute of Antarctic and Southern Ocean Studies (EERA)

IASP............ Integrated Attack Sensor Package

IASP............ International Arts and Sciences Press

IASP............ International Association for Social Progress

IASP............ International Association for Suicide Prevention (EA)

IASP............ International Association for the Study of Pain (EA)

IASP............ International Association of Scholarly Publishers [*Norway*]

IASP............ International Association of Space Philatelists (EA)

IASP............ International Association of Sports Physicians [*Defunct*] (EA)

IASP............ International Association of Sublimation Printers (EA)

IASPA.......... International Auto Show Producers Association (EA)

IASPC.......... International Association of Strategic Planning Consultants [*Defunct*] (EA)

IaSpeHi........ Parker Historical Society of Clay County, Spencer, IA [*Library symbol*] [*Library of Congress*] (LCLS)

IASPEI......... International Association of Seismology and Physics of the Earth's Interior [*ICSU*] [*Newbury, Berkshire, England*] (EAIO)

IASPHA........ International American Saddlebred Pleasure Horse Association (EA)

IaSplB.......... Spirit Lake Beacon, Spirit Lake, IA [*Library symbol*] [*Library of Congress*] (LCLS)

IaSplCoC..... Dickinson County Courthouse, Spirit Lake, IA [*Library symbol*] [*Library of Congress*] (LCLS)

IASPM.......... International Association for the Study of Popular Music [*Berlin, German Democratic Republic*] (EAIO)

IASPPV........ International Association of Former Soviet Political Prisoners and Victims of Communist Regime

IaSpr........... Springville Public Library, Springville, IA [*Library symbol Library of Congress*] (LCLS)

IASPS.......... International Association for Statistics in Physical Sciences

IASR............ Intermediate Altitude Sounding Rocket (MUGU)

IASR............ Interruption Address Storage Register (NITA)

IASRA.......... International Arthur Schnitzler Research Association (EA)

IaSrBP.......... Bulletin-Press, Sioux Rapids, IA [*Library symbol*] [*Library of Congress*] (LCLS)

IASRR.......... Institute of African Studies. Research Review [*A publication*]

IASS............ Insurance Accounting and Statistical Society

IASS............ International Air Safety Seminar

IASS............ International Association for Scandinavian Studies [*Norwich, England*] (EAIO)

IASS............ International Association for Shell and Spatial Structures [*Madrid, Spain*] (EA)

IASS............ International Association of Sanskrit Studies (EA)

IASS............ International Association of Security Service (EA)

IASS............ International Association of Semiotic Studies [*Palermo, Italy*] (EA)

IASS............ International Association of Soil Science

IASS............ International Association of Survey Statisticians [*See also AISE*] [*France*] (EA)

IASS............ Inverter/ATCS [*Active Thermal Control Subsystem*] Support Structure (MCD)

IASSD.......... International Association of School Security Directors [*Later, NASSD*] (EA)

IASSIST....... International Association for Social Science Information Service and Technology (EA)

IASSIST....... International Association for Social Science Information Services and Technology (NITA)

IASSMD....... International Association for the Scientific Study of Mental Deficiency [*Dublin, Republic of Ireland*] (EA)

IASSRF........ International Amateur Snowshoe Racing Federation (EA)

IASSW......... International Association of Schools of Social Work [*Austria*]

IAST............ Instrument for the Analysis of Science Teaching (EDAC)

IAST............ Integrated Avionic System Trainer [*Military*] (CAAL)

IAST............ International Association of Scuba Technicians

IASTA.......... Institute for Advanced Studies in the Theatre Arts (EA)

IaStacM........ Monitor-Review, Stacyville, IA [*Library symbol*] [*Library of Congress*] (LCLS)

IaStaE.......... Saint Ansgar Enterprise, St. Ansgar, IA [*Library symbol Library of Congress*] (LCLS)

IaStan.......... Stanton Community Library, Stanton, IA [*Library symbol Library of Congress*] (LCLS)

IaStanV........ Stanton Viking, Stanton, IA [*Library symbol*] [*Library of Congress*] (LCLS)

IaStaw.......... Stanwood Public Library, Stanwood, IA [*Library symbol*] [*Library of Congress*] (LCLS)

IaStc........... Gutenkunst Public Library, State Center, IA [*Library symbol Library of Congress*] (LCLS)

IaStcE.......... State Center Enterprise, State Center, IA [*Library symbol*] [*Library of Congress*] (LCLS)

IASTED........ International Association of Science and Technology for Development [*Calgary, AB*] (EAIO)

IaStoc.......... Story City Public Library, Story City, IA [*Library symbol Library of Congress*] (LCLS)

IaStocH........ Story City Herald, Story City, IA [*Library symbol*] [*Library of Congress*] (LCLS)

IaStrp.......... Strawberry Point Public Library, Strawberry Point, IA [*Library symbol Library of Congress*] (LCLS)

IaStrpP .... Strawberry Point Press-Journal, Strawberry Point, IA [*Library symbol Library of Congress*] (LCLS)

IaStuH........ Stuart Herald, Stuart, IA [*Library symbol*] [*Library of Congress*] (LCLS)

IASTWL....... International Association for Social Tourism and Workers' Leisure (EAIO)

IaSu .... General N. B. Baker Library, Sutherland, IA [*Library symbol Library of Congress*] (LCLS)

IASU .... International Association of Satellite Users [*Later, IASUS*] (EA)

IA Sup Vol ... English Law Reports, Indian Appeals, Supplementary Volume [*A publication*] (DLA)

IASUS .... International Association of Satellite Users and Suppliers (EA)

IASV .... Internationale Arbeitsgemeinschaft von Sortimentsbuchhaendler Vereinigungen [*International Community of Booksellers' Associations*]

IaSwc.......... Swea City Public Library, Swea City, IA [*Library symbol Library of Congress*] (LCLS)

IASWR .... Institute for Advanced Studies of World Religions (EA)

IAsy .... Ashley Public Library, Ashley, IL [*Library symbol Library of Congress*] (LCLS)

IASY........... International Active Sun Years

IAsyCD........ Ashley Community Consolidated District 15, Ashley, IL [*Library symbol Library of Congress*] (LCLS)

IAT.............. Image Auto Tracker

IAT.............. Immunoaugmentative Therapy [*Oncology*]

IAT.............. Indexible Address Tag (SAA)

IAT.............. Indicated Air Temperature (AFM)

IAT.............. Indirect Antiglobulin Test [*Clinical chemistry*]

IAT.............. Individual Acceptance Tests

IAT.............. Individual Aircraft Tracking Program (MCD)

IAT.............. Information Assessment Team (NRCH)

IAT.............. Inside Air Temperature

IAT.............. Inspection Apply Template (MCD)

IAT.............. Institute for Academic Technology

IAT.............. Institute for Advanced Technology [*Control Data Corp.*] [*Bloomington, MN*] [*Telecommunications*]

IAT.............. Institute for Applied Technology [*Superseded by NEL*] [*National Institute of Standards and Technology*]

IAT.............. Institute of Animal Technology [*London*]

IAT.............. Institute of Asphalt Technology [*British*]

IAT.............. Intake Air Temperature [*Automotive engineering*]

IAT.............. Integrated Avionics Test (MCD)

IAT.............. Integration Acceptance Test [*Military*] (CAAL)

IAT.............. Intelligent Actuators & Transmitters (ACII)

IAT.............. Interactive Audio Teletraining System [*Valencia Community College*] [*Orlando, FL*] (TSSD)

IAT.............. Interionic Attraction Theory

IAT.............. Internal Air Transportability (MCD)

IAT.............. International Air Transport Association [*ICAO designator*] (FAAC)

IAT.............. International Association of Trichologists (EA)

IAT.............. International Atomic Time

IAT.............. International Automatic Time

IAT.............. Intraoperative Autologous Transfusion [*Medicine*]

IAT.............. Invasive Activity Test [*Oncology*]

IAT.............. Inventory of Affective Tolerance [*Psychology*]

IAT.............. Iodine Azide Test [*Medicine*]

IAT.............. Iowa Achievement Test [*Psychology*] (DAVI)

IAT.............. Iowa Terminal Railroad Co. [*AAR code*]

IAT.............. Southern Illinois University, Edwardsville Campus, Edwardsville, IL [*OCLC symbol*] (OCLC)

IATA............ International Air Transport [*formerly, Traffic*] Association [*Canada*]

IATA............ International Amateur Theatre Association [*Denmark*]

IATA............ International Appropriate Technology Association [*Defunct*] (EA)

IATA............ Is Amended to Add

IATACS........ Improved Army Tactical Communications System (DOMA)

IATADS........ Initial Airborne Target Acquisition Designation System (MCD)

IATAE......... International Accounting and Traffic Analysis Equipment [*Telecommunications*] (NITA)

IATAL.......... International Association of Theoretical and Applied Limnology [*See also SILTA*] (EA)

IATB............ International Aviation Theft Bureau [*ACPI*] [*Superseded by*] (EA)

IATC............ India America Trade Council

IATC............ Inter-American Telecommunications Commission

IATC............ Inter-American Travel Congresses

IATC............ International Air Traffic Communications

IATC............ International Association of Tool Craftsmen (EA)

IATC............ International Association of Torch Clubs (EA)

IATC............ Italian Association of Triathlon Clubs (EA)

IATCA.......... International Air Transportation Competition Act of 1979

IATCB.......... Interdepartmental Air Traffic Control Board

IATCL.......... International Association for Textile Care Labelling (EA)

IATCR.......... International Air Traffic Communications Receiver Station

IATCS.......... International Air Traffic Communications Station

IATCS.......... International Air Traffic Communications System (MCD)

IATCT.......... International Air Traffic Communications Transmitter Station

IATD............ Is Amended to Delete

IATDB .... Interim Air Toxics Data Base (GNE)

IATDP......... International Association of Textile Dyers and Printers [*See also AITIT*] (EAIO)

IATE............ Intermediate Automatic Test Equipment

IATE............ Intermediate-Level Automatic Test Equipment (PDAA)

IATE............ International Accounting and Traffic Analysis Equipment [*Telecommunications*] (TEL)

IATE............ International Association for Television Editors

IATE............ International Association for Temperance Education [*Later, IVES*] (EA)

IATE............ International Association of Trade Exchanges [*Later, IRTA*] (EA)

IATE............ International Association of Travel Exhibitors (EA)

IATEFL........ International Association of Teachers of English as a Foreign Language [*Whitstable, Kent, England*] (EAIO)

IATF............ Interagency Task Force [*for Indochina*] [*South Vietnam refugee relief*]

IATFAI........ Inter-Association Task Force on Alcohol Issues (EA)

IATG............ International Association of Teachers of German [*See also IDV*] [*Copenhagen, Denmark*] (EAIO)

IATI............. Inter-Alpha-Trypsin Inhibitor (DMAA)

IATI............. International Association of Teachers of Italian [*Belgium*] (EAIO)

IaTip............ Tipron Public Library, Tipron, IA [*Library symbol Library of Congress*] (LCLS)

IaTipCoC...... Cedar County Courthouse, Tipton, IA [*Library symbol*] [*Library of Congress*] (LCLS)

IaTit............ Titonka Public Library, Titonka, IA [*Library symbol Library of Congress*] (LCLS)

IATJ............ International Association of Travel Journalists (EA)

IATL............ International Academy of Trial Lawyers

IATL............ International Association of Theological Libraries

IATM............ International Association for Testing Materials (IEEE)

IATM............ International Association of Tour Managers (DI)

IATM............ International Association of Transport Museums [*See also AIMT*] [*Berne, Switzerland*] (EAIO)

IATM-NAR.... International Association of Tour Managers - North American Region (EA)

IATN............ International Association of Telecomputer Networks (EA)

IaTo............. Toledo Public Library, Toledo, IA [*Library symbol Library of Congress*] (LCLS)

IaToC........... Toledo Chronicle, Toledo, IA [*Library symbol*] [*Library of Congress*] (LCLS)

IATOD.......... In Addition to Other Duties [*Military*]

IATP............. Individual Aircraft Tracking Program (MCD)

IATP............. International Airlines Technical Pool (PDAA)

IATP............. International Association of Tungsten Producers

IATR............. Is Amended to Read

IATRA.......... International Academy of Toxicological Risk Assessment (EA)

IaTraS......... Traer Star-Clipper, Traer, IA [*Library symbol*] [*Library of Congress*] (LCLS)

IaTriL.......... Tripoli Leader, Tripoli, IA [*Library symbol*] [*Library of Congress*] (LCLS)

IATROS........ Organisation Mondiale des Medicins Independants [*International Organization of Private and Independent Doctors*] (EAIO)

IatrosHlt....... Iatros Health Network, Inc. [*Associated Press*] (SAG)

IATS............. Individual Accession and Training System (MCD)

IATS............. Institute for Advanced Talmudic Studies [*Beth Medrash Govoha*] [*Canada*] (IRC)

IATS............. Intake Air Temperature Sensor [*Automotive engineering*]

IATSC........... International Aeronautical Telecommunications Switching Center

IATSE........... International Alliance of Theatrical Stage Employees and Moving Picture Machine Operators of the US and Canada (EA)

IATSE........... International Alliance of Theatrical Stage Employes [*An AFL-CIO union*] [*New York, NY*] (WDMC)

IATSIS .... Institute of Aboriginal and Torres Strait Islander Studies [*Australia*]

IATSS .... International Association of Traffic and Safety Sciences [*Tokyo, Japan*] (EAIO)

IATT............. International Academy of Twirling Teachers (EA)

IATTC.......... Inter-American Tropical Tuna Commission (EA)

IATU............ Inter-American Telecommunications Union [*US*]

IATUL.......... International Association of Technological University Libraries [*Goteborg, Sweden*]

IATV............. ACTV, Inc. [*NASDAQ symbol*] (SAG)

IATV............. Income Approach to Value (MHDB)

IATV............. Interactive Alphanumeric Television

IAU.............. Austin College, Sherman, TX [*OCLC symbol*] (OCLC)

IAU.............. Infrastructure Account Unit (NATG)

IAU.............. Initial Alignment Unit

IAU.............. Institute for American Universities (EA)

IAU.............. Interface Adapter Unit [*Computer science*] (MCD)

IAU.............. International Academic Union (EA)

IAU.............. International Association of Universities [*France*]

IAU.............. International Astronomical Union [*ICSU*] [*Paris, France*] [*Research center*] (IRC)

IAU.............. Internationale Armbrustschutzen Union [*International Crossbow Shooting Union*] (EAIO)

iau .... Iowa [*MARC country of publication code Library of Congress*] (LCCP)

IAU.............. Italian Actors Union (EA)

IaU.............. University of Iowa, Iowa City, IA [*Library symbol Library of Congress*] (LCLS)

IAub .... Auburn Public Library, Auburn, IL [*Library symbol Library of Congress*] (LCLS)

IaU-B .... University of Iowa, Botany-Chemistry Library, Iowa City, IA [*Library symbol Library of Congress*] (LCLS)

IAUC............ Irish American Unity Conference (EA)

IAUD............ International Association for a Union of Democracies [*Defunct*] (EA)

IAUF............ Interamerican Underwater Festival

IAug............ Tri-County Public Library District, Augusta, IL [*Library symbol Library of Congress*] (LCLS)

IaU-L .... University of Iowa, College of Law, Iowa City, IA [*Library symbol Library of Congress*] (LCLS)

IaU-M .... University of Iowa, Health Sciences Library, Iowa City, IA [*Library symbol Library of Congress*] (LCLS)

IAUMS .... Installation, Administrative Use, and Command Design Motor Vehicle Management System [*Army*]

IAUP .... International Association of University Presidents

IAUPE .... International Association of University Professors of English [*British*]

IAUPL .... International Association of University Professors and Lecturers (EAIO)

IaUpV .... Vennard College, University Park, IA [*Library symbol Library of Congress*] (LCLS)

IAur .... Aurora Public Library, Aurora, IL [*Library symbol Library of Congress*] (LCLS)

IAur .... Aurora Public Library, Aurora, IL [*Library symbol*] [*Library of Congress*] (LCLS)

IAUR .... Institute for Art and Urban Resources (EA)

IaUr .... Urbandale Public Library, Urbandale, IA [*Library symbol Library of Congress*] (LCLS)

IAurC .... Aurora College, Aurora, IL [*Library symbol Library of Congress*] (LCLS)

IAurC .... Aurora College, Aurora, IL [*Library symbol*] [*Library of Congress*] (LCLS)

IAURIF .... Institut d'Amenagement et d'Urbanisme de la Region de l'Ile de France (NITA)

IaUrN .... Urbandale News, Urbandale, IA [*Library symbol*] [*Library of Congress*] (LCLS)

IaUrP .... Urbandale Public Library, Urbandale, IA [*Library symbol*] [*Library of Congress*] (LCLS)

IaUte .... Ute Public Library, Ute, IA [*Library symbol Library of Congress*] (LCLS)

IAV .... Airavia [*France ICAO designator*] (FAAC)

IAV .... Identified Aerial Vehicle

IA(V) .... Ileostomy Association (Victoria) [*Australia*]

IAV .... Index of Adjustment and Values (AEBS)

IAV .... Indium Antimode Varactor

IAV .... Innotech Aviation Enterprises Ltd. [*Toronto Stock Exchange symbol*]

IAV .... Institute for American Values (EA)

IAV .... Intermittent Assisted Ventilation [*Medicine*] (MEDA)

IAV .... Intra-Arterial Vasopressin [*Cardiology*]

IAV .... Intransit Asset Visibility (MCD)

IAV .... Inventory Adjustment Voucher [*Military*] (AFM)

IAV .... Island-Arc Volcanic [*Geology*]

IAV .... Issue Authority Voucher

IAV .... Southern Illinois University, School of Medicine, Springfield, IL [*OCLC symbol*] (OCLC)

IAV .... VIDION/International Association of Video (EA)

IAVA .... Industrial Audio-Visual Association [*Later, AVMA*] (EA)

IaVaO .... Vail Observer, Vail, IA [*Library symbol*] [*Library of Congress*] (LCLS)

IAVC .... Indian Army Veterinary Corps [*British military*] (DMA)

IAVC .... Instantaneous Automatic Video Control (IEEE)

IAVC .... Instantaneous Automatic Volume Control [*Electronics*]

IAVCEI .... International Association of Volcanology and Chemistry of the Earth's Interior [*Germany*]

IAVCM .... International Association of Visual Communications Management [*Formerly, SRE*]

IAVD .... Interactive Videodisc [*Army*] (INF)

IAVE .... Industrial Arts and Vocational Education (AEBS)

IAVE .... International Association for Volunteer Education (EA)

IAVE .... International Association of Volunteer Effort (EA)

IAVFH .... International Association of Veterinary Food Hygienists

IAVG .... International Association for Vocational Guidance

IAVI .... International AIDS Vaccine Initiative

IAVI .... International Association of Voice Identification [*Later, IAI*] (EA)

IaViiR .... Villisca Review, Villisca, IA [*Library symbol*] [*Library of Congress*] (LCLS)

IaVin .... Vinton Public Library, Vinton, IA [*Library symbol Library of Congress*] (LCLS)

IaVinT .... Cedar Valley Times, Vinton, IA [*Library symbol*] [*Library of Congress*] (LCLS)

IaVol .... Volga Public Library, Volga, IA [*Library symbol Library of Congress*] (LCLS)

IAVRT .... Independent Association of Victorian Registered Teachers [*Australia*]

IAVS .... International Association for Vegetation Science [*See also IVV*] [*Gottingen, Federal Republic of Germany*] (EAIO)

IAVSD .... International Association for Vehicle Systems Dynamics [*ICSU*] [*Delft, Netherlands*] (EAIO)

IAVTC .... International Audio-Visual Technical Centre [*Netherlands*]

IAW .... Improved Antimateriel Warhead

IAW .... In Accordance With

IAW .... Institute of the American West [*Later, INAW*] (EA)

IAW .... International Alliance of Women [*See also AIF*] [*Valetta, Malta*] (EAIO)

IAWP .... International Association of Wholesalers [*Defunct*]

IAW .... Iraqi Airways [*ICAO designator*] (FAAC)

IAW .... Isotopic Atomic Weight

IAW .... Triton College, River Grove, IL [*OCLC symbol*] (OCLC)

IaW .... Waterloo Public Library, Waterloo, IA [*Library symbol Library of Congress*] (LCLS)

IAWA .... Independent American Whiskey Association [*Later, ABAA*] (EA)

IAWA .... International Association of Wood Anatomists [*Utrecht, Netherlands*] (EA)

IAWA .... Irish Amateur Weightlifting Association (EAIO)

IAWA .... Irish Amateur Wrestling Association (EAIO)

IaWa .... Washington Public Library, Washington, IA [*Library symbol Library of Congress*] (LCLS)

IaWaJ .... Washington Evening Journal, Washington, IA [*Library symbol Library of Congress*] (LCLS)

IaWal .... Walnut Public Library, Walnut, IA [*Library symbol Library of Congress*] (LCLS)

IaWall .... Wall Lake Public Library, Wall Lake, IA [*Library symbol Library of Congress*] (LCLS)

IaWap .... Wapello Public Library (Keck Memorial Library), Wapello, IA [*Library symbol Library of Congress*] (LCLS)

IaWapCoC .... Louisa County Courthouse, Wapello, IA [*Library symbol*] [*Library of Congress*] (LCLS)

IaWapR .... Wapello Republican, Wapello, IA [*Library symbol*] [*Library of Congress*] (LCLS)

IaWas .... Washta Library, Washta, IA [*Library symbol Library of Congress*] (LCLS)

IaWauE .... Jerico Community Echo, Waucoma, IA [*Library symbol Library of Congress*] (LCLS)

IaWaukAC .... Allamakee County Courthouse, Waukon, IA [*Library symbol*] [*Library of Congress*] (LCLS)

IaWaukCoC ... Allamakee County Courthouse, Waukon, IA [*Library symbol Library of Congress*] (LCLS)

IaWaukD .... Waukon Democrat, Waukon, IA [*Library symbol Library of Congress*] (LCLS)

IaWauke ...... Waukee Public Library, Waukee, IA [*Library symbol Library of Congress*] (LCLS)

IaWaukR .... Waukon Republican-Standard, Waukon, IA [*Library symbol Library of Congress*] (LCLS)

IaWavBHi ..... Bremer County Historical Society, Waverly, IA [*Library symbol Library of Congress*] (LCLS)

IaWavCoC ..... Bremer County Courthouse, Waverly, IA [*Library symbol Library of Congress*] (LCLS)

IaWavD .... Waverly Democrat, Waverly, IA [*Library symbol Library of Congress*] (LCLS)

IaWavH .... Waverly House, Waverly, IA [*Library symbol Library of Congress*] (LCLS)

IaWavI .... Bremer County Independent, Waverly, IA [*Library symbol Library of Congress*] (LCLS)

IaWavW .... Wartburg College, Waverly, IA [*Library symbol Library of Congress*] (LCLS)

IaWayN .... Wayland News, Wayland, IA [*Library symbol Library of Congress*] (LCLS)

IaWb .... Enlow Public Library, West Branch, IA [*Library symbol Library of Congress*] (LCLS)

IaWbe .... West Bend Public Library, West Bend, IA [*Library symbol Library of Congress*] (LCLS)

IaWbeJ .... West Bend Journal, West Bend, IA [*Library symbol Library of Congress*] (LCLS)

IaWbH .... Herbert Hoover Presidential Library, West Branch, IA [*Library symbol Library of Congress*] (LCLS)

IaWbT .... West Branch Times, West Branch, IA [*Library symbol Library of Congress*] (LCLS)

IaWbuN .... Des Moines County News, West Burlington, IA [*Library symbol Library of Congress*] (LCLS)

IaWC .... Daily Courier, Waterloo, IA [*Library symbol Library of Congress*] (LCLS)

IAWC .... In Accordance with Contract

IAWCC .... International Association of Wall and Ceiling Contractors [*Later, AWCI*] (EA)

IAWCC/GD ... International Association of Wall and Ceiling Contractors - Gypsum Drywall Contractors International [*Later, AWCI*] (EA)

IAWCM .... International Association of Wiping Cloth Manufacturers (EA)

IaWdmB .... New Iowa Bystander, West Des Moines, IA [*Library symbol Library of Congress*] (LCLS)

IaWdmGS .... Church of Jesus Christ of Latter-Day Saints, Genealogical Society Library, Des Moines Branch, West Des Moines, IA [*Library symbol Library of Congress*] (LCLS)

IaWdmNB ..... New Iowa Bystander, West Des Moines, IA [*Library symbol Library of Congress*] (LCLS)

IAWE .... International Association for Wind Engineering [*Aachen, Federal Republic of Germany*] (EAIO)

IaWec .... Kendall Young Library, Webster City, IA [*Library symbol Library of Congress*] (LCLS)

IaWecAJ .... Aberdeen-Angus Journal, Webster City, IA [*Library symbol Library of Congress*] (LCLS)

IaWecF .... Freeman-Journal, Webster City, IA [*Library symbol Library of Congress*] (LCLS)

IaWelmA .... Wellman Advance, Wellman, IA [*Library symbol Library of Congress*] (LCLS)

IaWels .... Wellsburg Public Library, Wellsburg, IA [*Library symbol Library of Congress*] (LCLS)

IaWG .... Henry W. Grout Museum of History and Science, Waterlook, IA [*Library symbol Library of Congress*] (LCLS)

IAWG .... Interagency Working Group (MCD)

IAWG .... Inter-American War Game (MCD)

IAWGSA ...... Inter-Agency Working Group on Southern Africa [*Canadian Council for International Cooperation*]

IaWH .... Hawkeye Institute of Technology, Area VII, Waterloo, IA [*Library symbol Library of Congress*] (LCLS)

IAWH .... Improved Antimateriel Warhead

IaWhaP .... What Cheer Patriot-Chronicle, What Cheer, IA [*Library symbol Library of Congress*] (LCLS)

IaWhHi .... Loess Hills Historical Society of Monona County, Whiting, IA [*Library symbol*] [*Library of Congress*] (LCLS)

IaWhitC .... Whittmore Champion, Whittmore, IA [*Library symbol Library of Congress*] (LCLS)

IAWHPJ .... International Association of Women and Home Page Journalists (EA)

IaWij .... Wilton Public Library, Wilton Junction, IA [*Library symbol Library of Congress*] (LCLS)

IaWijS .... S-R Advocate News, Wilton Junction, IA [*Library symbol Library of Congress*] (LCLS)

IaWinfB .... Beacon and Wayland News, Winfield, IA [*Library symbol Library of Congress*] (LCLS)

IaWinN .... Winthrop News, Winthrop, IA [*Library symbol Library of Congress*] (LCLS)

IaWint .... Winterset Public Library, Winterset, IA [*Library symbol Library of Congress*] (LCLS)

IaWintM ...... Winterset Madisonian, Winterset, IA [*Library symbol Library of Congress*] (LCLS)

IAWISP .... International Accidental War Information Sharing Project [*Nuclear Age Peace Foundation*] (EA)

IaWl .... Free Public Library, West Liberty, IA [*Library symbol Library of Congress*] (LCLS)

IAWL .... International Association for Water Law [*See also AIDA*] [*Rome, Italy*] (EAIO)

IaWll .... West Liberty Index, West Liberty, IA [*Library symbol Library of Congress*] (LCLS)

IAWM .... International Association of Women Ministers (EA)

IaWmbgl ..... Iowa County Farmer, Williamsburg, IA [*Library symbol Library of Congress*] (LCLS)

IaWmbgJT ... Williamsburg Jounal-Tribune, Williamsburg, IA [*Library symbol Library of Congress*] (LCLS)

IAWMC .... International Association of Workers for Troubled Children and Youth [*See also AIEJI*] (EAIO)

IaWob .... Woodbine Public Library, Woodbine, IA [*Library symbol Library of Congress*] (LCLS)

IaWobT .... Woodbine Twiner, Woodbine, IA [*Library symbol Library of Congress*] (LCLS)

IaWow .... Woodward Public Library, Woodward, IA [*Library symbol Library of Congress*] (LCLS)

IaWowN ...... Northeast Dallas County Record, Woodward, IA [*Library symbol Library of Congress*] (LCLS)

IAWP .... Inter-National Association for Widowed People (EA)

IAWP .... International Association of Women Philosophers [*Zurich, Switzerland*] (EAIO)

IAWP .... International Association of Women Police (EA)

IaWp .... West Point Public Library, West Point, IA [*Library symbol Library of Congress*] (LCLS)

IaWpB .... West Point Bee, West Point, IA [*Library symbol Library of Congress*] (LCLS)

IAWPR .... International Association of Water Polo Referees (EA)

IAWPR .... International Association on Water Pollution Research [*Later, IAWPRC*]

IAWPRC ...... International Association on Water Pollution Research and Control [*British*] (EA)

IAWR .... Institute of Air Weapons Research [*Air Force*]

IAWR .... Internationale Arbeitsgemeinschaft der Wasserwerke im Rheineinzugsgebiet [*International Association of Waterworks in the Rhine Basin Area - IAWRBA*] (EAIO)

IAWRBA ...... International Association of Waterworks in the Rhine Basin Area (EAIO)

IAWRT .... International Association of Women in Radio and Television (NTCM)

IAWS .... Intercollegiate Association of Women Students (AEBS)

IAWS .... Irish Agricultural Wholesale Society Ltd. (BI)

IAWTC .... Integrated Air Warfare Training Complex [*Military*] (CAAL)

IaWu .... Heiseman Memorial Library, West Union, IA [*Library symbol Library of Congress*] (LCLS)

IaWuCoC ..... Fayette County Courthouse, West Union, IA [*Library symbol Library of Congress*] (LCLS)

IaWuU .... Fayette County Union, West Union, IA [*Library symbol Library of Congress*] (LCLS)

IAWWE .... International Association of Workshop Way Educators (EA)

IaWyo .... Roche Memorial Library, Wyoming, IA [*Library symbol Library of Congress*] (LCLS)

IAX .... University of Illinois at the Medical Center, Chicago, IL [*OCLC symbol*] (OCLC)

IAY .... Island Canyon Mines, Inc. [*Vancouver Stock Exchange symbol*]

IAY .... University of Illinois at Chicago Circle, Chicago, IL [*OCLC symbol*] (OCLC)

IAYB .... Interim Accessory Bulletin (DNAB)

IAYC .... Interim Accessory Change (MCD)

IAYM .... International Association of Youth Magistrates [*Later, IAJFCM*]

IAYMC .... International Association of Y's Men's Clubs [*Geneva, Switzerland*] (EA)

IAZ .... Industrie Air Charter [*France ICAO designator*] (FAAC)

IAZ .... Inner Artillery Zone

IAZ .... Western Illinois University, Macomb, IL [*OCLC symbol*] (OCLC)

IaZN .... Tri-County News, Zearing, IA [*Library symbol Library of Congress*] (LCLS)

IB .... I-Beam [*Lumber*] (DAC)

IB .... Iberia Air Lines of Spain [*ICAO designator*] (AD)

IB .... Ibidem [*In the Same Place*] [*Latin*]

ib .... Ibidem [*Latin*] [*In the same place*] (WDMC)

Ib .... Ibis [*of Ovid*] [*Classical studies*] (OCD)

IB .... Identification Beacon [*Aviation*] (IAA)

IB .... Identifier Block

IB .... Imbibition Printing [*Cinematography*] (WDMC)

IB .... Immune Body

IB .... Impact Bag (SAA)

IB .... Inboard (NASA)

IB .... In Bond [*Wines and Spirits*]

IB .... Inbound

IB .... In Bulk (IAA)

IB .... Incendiary Bomb

IB .... Incentive-Based Policy [*for environmental improvement*]

IB .... Inclusion Body [*Cytology*]

ib .... Indent Both (WDMC)

IB .... Index of Body Build [*Anatomy*]

IB .... India-Burma [*World War II*]

IB .... Individual Bias

IB .... Induction Balance (ADA)

IB .... Induction Brazing

IB .... Industrial Business [*Insurance term*] [*British*]

IB .... Industrialized Building (PDAA)

IB .... Inert Building [*NASA*] (KSC)

IB .... Infantry Battalion [*Army*]

IB .... Infantry Brigade [*British military*] (DMA)

IB .... Infectious Bronchitis [*Medicine*]

IB .... Information Bulletin

IB .... Information Bureau [*Telecommunications*] (TEL)

IB .... Information Bus (IAA)

IB .... Inner Bottom [*Technical drawings*]

IB .... Input Buffer [*Telecommunications*] (TEL)

IB .... Input Bus [*Computer science*]

IB .... Inspection Bulletin

IB .... Institute of Bankers [*Later, CIB*] [*British*] (DI)

IB .... Institute of Biology [*British*]

IB .... Institute of Brewing [*Also, IOB*] [*British*]

IB .... Institute of Building [*British*]

IB .... Instruction Bank [*Computer science*]

IB .... Instruction Book

IB .... Instruction Bus [*Computer science*]

IB .... Intelligence Branch

IB .... Interface Bus [*Computer science*]

IB .... Internal Bond [*Pulp and paper technology*]

IB .... Internal Browning [*of Fruits and Vegetables*] (BARN)

IB .... Internal Bus [*Computer science*]

IB .... International Baccalaureate

IB .... International Bank for Reconstruction and Development [*Also known as World Bank*]

IB .... International Broadcasting

IB .... International Butec Industry [*Vancouver Stock Exchange symbol*]

IB .... Interpreter's Bible

IB .... Introducing Broker (MHDB)

IB .... Investigation Branch [*British Australia*] (DCTA)

IB .... Invoice Book [*Business term*]

IB .... Irish Baron (ROG)

IB .... Iron Bolts

IB .... Ironing Board (MSA)

IB .... Is Between (MHDB)

IB .... Isolation Bed [*Infectious disease*] (DAVI)

IB .... Issue Book [*DoD*]

IB .... Issue Book (DOMA)

IB .... Lineas Aereas du Espanalos [*Iberia*] [*Spain ICAO designator*]

IB .... RAB [*Radio Advertising Bureau*] Instant Background [*A publication*]

IBa .... Barrington Area Library District, Barrington, IL [*Library symbol Library of Congress*] (LCLS)

IBA .... Bradley University, Peoria, IL [*OCLC symbol*] (OCLC)

IBA .... Ibadan [*Nigeria*] [*Airport symbol*] (OAG)

IBA .... Igniter Booster Assembly [*Aerospace*]

IBA .... Ignorant Bloody Aircrafthand [*British Royal Air Force slang*]

IBA .... Independent Bakers Association (EA)

IBA .... Independent Bar Association (EA)

IBA .... Independent Board Authority [*Board granting franchises to new companies*] [*British*]

IBA .... Independent Broadcasting Authority [*Formerly, ITA*] [*British*]

IBA .... Indian Banks Association (PDAA)

IBA .... Indolebutyric Acid [*Plant growth regulator*]

IBA .... Indonesian-British Association (DS)

IBA .... Industrial Bankers' Association [*British*] (BI)

IBA .... Industrial Biotechnology Association (EA)

IBA .... Inflatable Boat Association (EA)

IBA .... Inhomogeneously Broadened Absorber [*Optics*]

IBA .... Inner Blanket Assembly [*Nuclear energy*] (NRCH)

IBA .... Inspection by Attribute

IBA .... Institute for Bioenergetic Analysis [*Later, IIBA*] (EA)

IBA .... Institute for Briquetting and Agglomeration (EA)

IBA .... Institute of British Architects

IBA .... Institute of Business Appraisers (EA)

IBA .... Institution of Business Agents [*British*]

IBA .... International Backgammon Association (EA)

IBA .... International Backpackers Association [*Later, AHS*] (EA)

IBA .... International Balloon Association (EA)

IBA .... International Banana Association (EA)

IBA .... International Banker Association (EA)

IBA .... International Banking Act [*1978*]

IBA .... International Bar Association [*British*] (EA)

IBA .... International Bartenders Association [*Paris, France*] (EAIO)

IBA .... International Baseball Association (EA)

IBA .... International Basketball Association [*Defunct*] (EA)

IBA .... International Bauxite Association [*Kingston, Jamaica*]

IBA .... International Biliary Association [*Later, IHBPA*] (EAIO)

IBA .... International Biometric Association (EA)

IBA .... International Board of Auditors (NATG)

IBA .... International Bocce Association (EA)

IBA .... International Bodyguard Association (EA)

IBA .... International Border Area

IBA .... International Braford Association (EA)

IBA .... International Bridge Academy [*The Hague, Netherlands*] (EA)

IBA............ International Bryozoology Association [*See also AIB*] [*Paris, France*] (EAIO)
IBA............ Investing Builders Association
IBA............ Investment Bankers Association of America [*Later, SIA*] (EA)
IBA............ Iodosobenzoic Acid [*Organic chemistry*] (RDA)
IBA............ Ion-Backscattering Analysis (IAA)
IBA............ Ion Beam Analysis
IBA............ Isobutylamine [*Organic chemistry*]
IBA............ Lineas Aereas Iberoamericanas [*Chile*] [*FAA designator*] (FAAC)
IBAA.......... Independent Bankers Association of America (EA)
IBAA.......... International Business Aircraft Association (DA)
IBAA.......... Italian Baptist Association of America [*Later, AEIM*] (EA)
IBAC.......... Caligula [*the Poisoner*] [*the Hun the Emperor Initials that form the name of the villain in "Captain Marvel" comic strip and indicate the sources of his power*]
IBAC.......... Information Bulletin of Australian Criminology [*A publication*]
IBAC.......... Instantaneous Broadcast Audience Counting (IAA)
IBAC.......... International Business Aviation Council (EA)
IBACOS....... Integrated Building and Construction Solutions
IBAD.......... Ion-Beam-Assisted Deposition [*Organic chemistry*]
IBAF.......... Interim Brigade Afloat Force [*Prepositioning force*] [*Army*] (DOMA)
IBAG.......... Ich Bau auf Gott [*I Build on God*] [*Motto of Heinrich Posthumus, Count Reuss (1572-1635)*] [*German*]
IBAH.......... IBAH, Inc. [*NASDAQ symbol*] (SAG)
IBAHP........ Inter-African Bureau for Animal Health and Protection
IBAHRS....... Inflatable Body and Head Restraint System [*Aviation*] (RDA)
IBAHRS....... Inflatable Body and Head Restraint System (DOMA)
IBALS........ Interactive Balancing through Simulation (PDAA)
IBAN.......... Imperial Bancorp [*NASDAQ symbol*] (NQ)
I (Bank)...... Instruction Bank [*Computer science*]
IBAP.......... Intervention Board for Agricultural Products [*Government body*] [*British*]
I Bar.......... I Baruch [*Apocrypha*] (BJA)
IBAR.......... Inter-African Bureau of Animal Resources [*Kenya*]
IBarA......... American Can Co., Barrington, IL [*Library symbol Library of Congress*] (LCLS)
IBarAS....... Allstate Insurance Co., Barrington, IL [*Library symbol*] [*Library of Congress*] (LCLS)
IBarQ......... Quaker Oats Co., Research Library, Barrington, IL [*Library symbol Library of Congress*] (LCLS)
IBart......... Alpha Park Public Library, Bartonville, IL [*Library symbol Library of Congress*] (LCLS)
IBartL........ Limestone Community High School, Bartonville, IL [*Library symbol Library of Congress*] (LCLS)
IBAS.......... Improved Bradley Acquisition Subsystem [*Army*] (RDA)
IBAS.......... Improved Bradley Acquisition System [*Army*] (INF)
IBAS.......... Informationssystem Beliebiger Andwendungssystem [*Germany*] (NITA)
IBAS.......... Instructional-Based Appraisal System [*Education*]
IBAS.......... Intelligent Body Assembly System [*Robotics*] [*Nissan Motor Co. Ltd.*]
IBASF......... Intervals Between Aircraft in Stream Type Formation [*Aviation*] (FAAC)
IBAT.......... Improved Brilliant Anti-Armor [*Army*] (RDA)
IBAT.......... Independent Bankers Association of Texas (SRA)
IBAT.......... Intravascular Bronchoalveolar Tumor [*Medicine*] (DMAA)
IBatF......... FERMILAB, Batavia, IL [*Library symbol Library of Congress*] (LCLS)
IBB........... Binter Canarais [*Spain ICAO designator*] (FAAC)
IBB........... Chicago Transit Authority, Chicago, IL [*OCLC symbol*] (OCLC)
IBB........... Institute of British Bakers (BI)
IBB........... Intentional Bases on Balls [*Baseball*]
IBB........... International Bank Bond (MHDB)
IBB........... International Book Bank (EA)
IBB........... International Bowling Board (EA)
IBB........... International Brotherhood of Bookbinders [*Later, Graphic Arts International Union*]
IBB........... Intestinal Brush Border [*Medicine*] (MAE)
IBB........... Invest in Britain Bureau
IBB........... Isobutylbenzene [*Organic chemistry*]
IBBA.......... Inland Bird Banding Association (EA)
IBBA.......... International Brangus Breeders Association (EA)
IBBA.......... International Business Brokers Association [*Defunct*] (EA)
IBBA.......... Irish Basketball Association (DBA)
IBBBA........ International Bundle Branch Block Association (EA)
IBBC.......... International Business Communications Council [*Japan*] (ECON)
IBBCA........ International Bathymetric Chart of the Caribbean Sea and Gulf of Mexico [*Marine science*] (OSRA)
IBBFIC....... International B & B [*Bed and Breakfast*] Fly-Inn Club (EA)
IBBH.......... Internationaler Bund der Bau-Haolzarbeiter [*International Federation of Building and Woodworkers*]
IBBIT......... Internal Bean Bacterial Infusion Test [*Plant pathology*]
IBBL.......... Islamic Bank of Bangladesh [*Commercial bank*] (EY)
IBBM.......... Ion-Binding/Ion-Bouncing Model [*Physical chemistry*]
IBBM.......... Iron Body Bronze-Mounted
IBBN.......... Inhomogeneous Big Bang Nucleosynthesis [*Cosmology*]
IBBR.......... International Beefalo Breeders' Registry (EA)
IBBRIS....... International Biodeterioration Bulletin. Reference Index [*A publication*]
IBBTPS...... Ivory and Bone Brushmakers' Trade Protection Society [*A union*] [*British*]
IBBY.......... International Board on Books for Young People [*Basel, Switzerland*] (EA)
IBC........... De Paul University, Law Library, Chicago, IL [*OCLC symbol*] (OCLC)
IBC........... Iceland Base Command [*Army World War II*]
IBC........... Idaho Bean Commission (SRA)
IBC........... Imperial Bushmen Contingent [*British military*] (DMA)
IBC........... Independent Bakers' Cooperative [*W. E. Long Co.*] (EA)

IBC........... Informatica Bulgarien Corp. [*Bulgaria*] [*ICAO designator*] (FAAC)
IBC........... Information-Based Complexity [*Mathematics*]
IBC........... Input Bias Current
IBC........... Insect Biotech Canada [*Queen's University*] [*Research center*] (RCD)
IBC........... Inside Back Cover
IBC........... Institute for Biomedical Communication [*South African Medical Research Council*] [*Information service or system*] (IID)
IBC........... Institute of Building Control [*British*] (DBA)
IBC........... Institutional Biosafety Committee [*National Institutes of Health*]
IBC........... Instrument Bus Computer
IBC........... Insurance Bureau of Canada
IBC........... Integrated Block Channel (MHDB)
IBC........... Integrated Block Controller (NITA)
IBC........... Integrated Broadband Communications (MHDB)
IBC........... Integrated Business Communications [*British*] (NITA)
IBC........... Integrated Business Computers [*Manufacturer*] (NITA)
IBC........... Intelligent Broadband Controller (NITA)
IBC........... Intelligent Buildings Corp. [*Broomfield, CO*] [*Telecommunications service*] (TSSD)
IBC........... Interboard Committee for Christian Work in Japan [*Later, JNAC*] (EA)
IBC........... Interconnect Backplane Capability
IBC........... Intermediate Bulk Containers [*Shipping*]
IBC........... International Ballet Competition
IBC........... International Ballet Council
IBC........... International Banana Club (EA)
IBC........... International Banking Centre [*British*]
IBC........... International Bathymetric Chart [*Marine science*] (OSRA)
IBC........... International Betta Congress (EA)
IBC........... International Biographical Centre [*British*] (CB)
IBC........... International Biophysical Center
IBC........... International Biotoxicological Center [*World Life Research Institute*] [*US*] (ASF)
IBC........... International Board of Cytopathology [*International Academy of Cytology*] [*Quebec, PQ*] (EAIO)
IBC........... International Borzoi Council (EA)
IBC........... International BRCA [*Breast Cancer*] Consortium
IBC........... International Brightness Coefficient
IBC........... International Broadcasting Convention [*Legal term*] (DLA)
IBC........... International Broadcasting Corp. [*Vancouver Stock Exchange symbol*]
IBC........... International Bulk Chemical
IBC........... International Bus Collectors Club (EA)
IBC........... International Business Communications [*Commercial firm British*]
IBC........... International Business Consultants [*Commercial firm*]
IBC........... International Business Contacts
IBC........... International Business Corp.
IBC........... International Business Council (EA)
IBC........... International Federation of the Blue Cross [*Formerly, International Federation of the Temperance Blue Cross Societies*] (EA)
IBC........... Internet Business Center [*Information service or system*] (IID)
IBC........... Interstate Bakeries [*NYSE symbol*] (TTSB)
IBC........... Interstate Bakeries Corp. [*NYSE symbol*] (SPSG)
IBC........... Inverted Bowl Centrifuge
IBC........... Iodine Binding Capacity [*of starch*]
IBC........... Iowa Business Council (SRA)
IBC........... Iron-Binding Capacity [*Clinical chemistry*]
IBC........... Isobaric Cooling [*Geology*]
IBC........... World Institute of Buddhist Culture
IBCA.......... Department of the Interior Board of Contract Appeals
IBCA.......... Idaho Building Contractors Association (SRA)
IBCA.......... Illinois Bulk Carriers Association (SRA)
IBCA.......... Indiana Beef Cattle Association (SRA)
IBCA.......... Industry Bar Code Alliance (EA)
IBCA.......... Institute of Burial and Cremation Administration [*British*]
IBCA.......... Interior Board of Contract Appeals (in United States Interior Decisions) [*A publication*] (DLA)
IBCA.......... International Braille Chess Association [*Abcoude, Netherlands*] (EA)
IBCA.......... International Brick Collectors' Association (EA)
IBCA.......... Isobutyl Cyanoacrylate [*Organic chemistry*]
IBCAM........ Institute of British Carriage and Automobile Manufacturers (BI)
IBCASA....... International Banking Campaign Against South Africa [*Later, ICABA*] (EAIO)
IBCC.......... International Building Classification Committee [*Netherlands*]
IBCC.......... International Business Communications Council (ECON)
IBCC.......... International Business Contact Club
IBCC.......... Intra-Bureau Change Committee
IBCE.......... Indo-British Cultural Exchange
IBCE.......... International Binding Center at Elat [*Israel*]
IBCEA........ International Bathymetric Chart of the Central Eastern Atlantic [*Marine science*] (OSRA)
IBCFA........ Injected Beam Cross Field Amplifier (IAA)
IBCFP........ International Board of Standards and Practices for Certified Financial Planners (EA)
IBCL.......... Instrument Bus Control Language [*National Instruments Corp.*] [*Austin, TX*]
IBCL.......... Interface Bus Control Language [*Computer science*]
IBCM.......... Integrated Battlefield Casualty Manikin [*Medical training*] [*Navy*]
IBCM.......... International Business Council Midamerica (EA)
IBCN.......... Integrated Broadband Communication Network [*Telecommunications*]
IBCP.......... Imperial British Conservative Party [*Political party*] (ADA)
IBCP.......... Independent Bank [*NASDAQ symbol*] (TTSB)
IBCP.......... Independent Bank Corp. [*NASDAQ symbol*] (NQ)
IBCRSGA..... International Bathymetric Chart of the Red Sea and Gulf of Aden [*Proposed*] [*Marine science*] (OSRA)

IBCS............ Inflight Blood Collection System [*On space flights*]
IBCS............ Integrated Battlefield Control System [*Army*]
IBCS............ Interlink Business and Communications Services [*British telecommunications service company*] (NITA)
IBCS/TRICAP... Integrated Battlefield Communications Systems / Triple Capability-Armoured, Infantry and Air Cavalry [*Military*] (PDAA)
IBCSVP........ International Breeding Consortium for St. Vincent Parrot (EAIO)
IBCWIO........ International Bathymetric Chart of the Western Indian Ocean [*Marine science*] (OSRA)
IBCWP......... International Bathymetric Chart of the Western Pacific [*Marine science*] (OSRA)
IBD.............. Baylor College of Dentistry, Dallas, TX [*OCLC symbol*] (OCLC)
IBD.............. Ibadan [*Nigeria*] [*Geomagnetic observatory code*]
IBD.............. Identical-By-Descent [*Genetics*]
IBD.............. Incomplete Block Design (MCD)
IBD.............. Incorporated Institute of British Decorators and Interior Designers (BI)
IBD.............. Infectious Bursal Disease [*Avian pathology*]
IBD.............. Inflammatory Bowel Disease [*Medicine*]
IBD.............. Inhabited Building Distance [*Army*] (AABC)
IBD.............. Institute of Business Designers (EA)
IBD.............. Interest Bearing Deposit [*Banking*] (ADA)
IBD.............. Interior Ballistic Division [*Ballistic Research Laboratory*] [*Army*] (RDA)
IBD.............. Intermediate Block Diagram (IAA)
IBD.............. International Business Database [*Information service or system*] (IID)
IBD.............. International Business Development Program [*Northwestern University*] [*Research center*] (RCD)
IBD.............. Internationale Bildungs- und Informations- Datenbank [*International Education and Information Data Bank*] [*Thiede & Thiede Mittelstandische Systemberatung GmbH*] [*Information service or system*] (IID)
IBD.............. Investor's Business Daily [*A publication*]
IBD.............. Ion Beam Deposition [*Coating technology*]
IBD.............. Irritable Bowel Disease [*Medicine*] (DMAA)
IBD.............. Ischemic Bowel Disease [*Medicine*] (DAVI)
IBD.............. Sandoz Pharmaceuticals [*Research code symbol*]
IBDA............ Indirect Bomb-Damage Assessment
IBDA............ International Balance Disorder Association [*Defunct*] (EA)
IBD-APM...... Identity-By-Descent Affected-Pedigree-Member [*Genetics*]
IBDB............ Internationaal Belasting Documentatie Bureau [*International Bureau of Fiscal Documentation*] (EAIO)
IBDB............ International Battery Data Base [*Robert Morey Associates*] [*Information service or system*] (IID)
IBDCC.......... International Barbie Doll Collectors Club (EA)
IBDI............ International Bureau of Documentation and Information on Sport (NITA)
IBDM........... Interim Bomber Defense Missile
IBDN........... Insulated Building Distribution Network [*Northern Telecom*]
IBDPW......... International Brotherhood of Du Pont Workers (EA)
IBDS............ Improved Biological Detection System [*Military*] (MCD)
IBDT............ Insulation Breakdown Tester
IBDU............ Isobutylidenediurea [*Organic chemistry*]
IBDV............ Infectious Bursal Disease Virus
IBDVS.......... Indian Base Depot Veterinary Stores [*British military*] (DMA)
IBE.............. Ibague [*Colombia*] [*Airport symbol*] (OAG)
IBE.............. Iberia-Lineas Aereas de Espana SA [*Spain ICAO designator*] (FAAC)
IBE.............. Inert-Ion Beam Etching
IBE.............. Inner Back End (MSA)
IBE.............. Institute of British Engineers (DAS)
IBE.............. Institute of Broadcast Engineers [*Later, SBE*] (NTCM)
IBE.............. Institute of Building Estimators Ltd. [*British*] (BI)
IBE.............. Institution of Body Engineers [*British*] (BI)
IBE.............. International Beverage Co. [*Vancouver Stock Exchange symbol*]
IBE.............. International Bureau for Epilepsy [*Alderley Edge, Cheshire, England*] (EAIO)
IBE.............. International Bureau of Education [*See also BIE*] [*UNESCO*] (EAIO)
IBE.............. Interval Between Eruptions [*of Geyser*]
IBE.............. Inventory by Exception (MHDB)
IBE.............. Rosary College, River Forest, IL [*OCLC symbol*] (OCLC)
IBea............ Beardstown Public Library, Beardstown, IL [*Library symbol Library of Congress*] (LCLS)
IBEA............ Industrial Base Engineering Activity (RDA)
IBE(A).......... Institution of Biomedical Engineering (Australia)
IBEAR.......... International Business Education and Research Program [*University of Southern California*] [*Research center*] (RCD)
IBEC............ International Bank for Economic Cooperation [*Moscow, USSR*] (EY)
IBEC............ International Basic Economic Cooperation [*Investment term*] (DS)
IBECO.......... Inboard Booster Engine Cutoff (MCD)
IBED............ Inter-African Bureau for Epizootic Diseases [*Later, IBAR*]
IBEDOC........ International Bureau of Education Documentation and Information System (NITA)
IBEE............ International Builders Exchange Executives (EA)
IBEF............ International Bio-Environmental Foundation (EA)
IBEG............ International Book Export Group
IBel............. Belleville Public Library, Belleville, IL [*Library symbol Library of Congress*] (LCLS)
IBEL............ Interest-Bearing Eligible Liabilities
IBelC........... Belleville Area College, Belleville, IL [*Library symbol Library of Congress*] (LCLS)
IBelHS......... Altoff High School, Belleville, IL [*Library symbol Library of Congress*] (LCLS)
IBelHSD....... Harmony-Emge-Ellis School District 175, Belleville, IL [*Library symbol Library of Congress*] (LCLS)
IBelS........... Saint Henry's Seminary, Belleville, IL [*Library symbol Library of Congress*] (LCLS)
IBelSCM...... Saint Clair County Mental Health Board, Belleville, IL [*Library symbol Library of Congress*] (LCLS)
IBelSD........ Belleville Public Schools District 118, Belleville, IL [*Library symbol Library of Congress*] (LCLS)
IBelSH........ Saint Elizabeth's Hospital, Belleville, IL [*Library symbol Library of Congress*] (LCLS)
IBelTSD...... Belleville Township High School District 201, Belleville, IL [*Library symbol Library of Congress*] (LCLS)
IBelv........... Ida Public Library, Belvidere, IL [*Library symbol Library of Congress*] (LCLS)
IBelVS........ Belle Valley School, Belleville, IL [*Library symbol Library of Congress*] (LCLS)
IBelw.......... Bellwood Public Library, Bellwood, IL [*Library symbol Library of Congress*] (LCLS)
IBem........... Bement Township Library, Bement, IL [*Library symbol Library of Congress*] (LCLS)
IBEM........... International Board of Environmental Medicine (EA)
IBemSD....... Bement Community Unit School District, Bement, IL [*Library symbol*] [*Library of Congress*] (LCLS)
IBEN........... Incendiary Bomb with Explosive Nose
IB-EP.......... Immunoreactive Beta-Endomorphin [*Immunochemistry*] (DMAA)
IBEP........... Integrated Border Environment Plan [*Mexico/US border policy*] (CROSS)
IBer............ Berwyn Public Library, Berwyn, IL [*Library symbol Library of Congress*] (LCLS)
IBER........... Institute for Biomedical Engineering Research [*University of Akron*] [*Research center*] (RCD)
IBerk.......... Berkeley Public Library, Berkeley, IL [*Library symbol Library of Congress*] (LCLS)
IBERLANT.... Iberian Atlantic Area [*NATO*] (NATG)
IBerMH....... MacNeal Memorial Hospital, Berwyn, IL [*Library symbol Library of Congress*] (LCLS)
IBerO.......... Olympic Savings & Loan Association, Berwyn, IL [*Library symbol Library of Congress*] (LCLS)
IBES........... Institutional Brokers Estimate System [*Lynch, Jones & Ryan*] [*Database*] [*New York, NY Information service or system*] (IID)
IBES........... Integration Building and Equipment Scheduling (PDAA)
IBES........... International Bronchoesophagological Society (EA)
IBES........... International Business Earth Stations [*Communications Satellite Corp.*]
IBET........... Trans World Gaming [*NASDAQ symbol*] (TTSB)
IBET........... Trans World Gaming Corp. [*NASDAQ symbol*] (SAG)
IBETA......... Irish Business Equipment Trade Association (DBA)
IBETA......... Irish Business Equipment Trade Association (ACII)
IBeth.......... Bethalto Public Library, Bethalto, IL [*Library symbol Library of Congress*] (LCLS)
IBethCU...... Bethalto Community Unit 8, Bethalto, IL [*Library symbol Library of Congress*] (LCLS)
IBETW........ Trans World Gaming Wrrt [*NASDAQ symbol*] (TTSB)
IBEU........... Independent Bakery Employees Union (EA)
IBEW.......... International Brotherhood of Electrical Workers (EA)
IBEX........... International Building Exposition
IBF............. Chicago Municipal Reference Library, Chicago, IL [*OCLC symbol*] (OCLC)
IBF............. First Iberian Fund [*AMEX symbol*] (TTSB)
IBF............. First Iberian Fund, Inc. [*AMEX symbol*] (SPSG)
IBF............. Imaginary Basketball Federation (EA)
IBF............. Immature Brown-Fat [*Cells*]
IBF............. Immunoglobulin-Binding Factor [*Immunology*] (MAE)
IBF............. Input Buffer Full [*Computer science*] (MHDB)
IBF............. Institute of British Foundrymen (EAIO)
IBF............. Internally Blown Flap [*Aviation*]
IBF............. International Badminton Federation [*Cheltenham, Gloustershire, England*] (EAIO)
IBF............. International Balint Federation [*Brussels, Belgium*] (EAIO)
IBF............. International Balut Federation [*Bangkok, Thailand*] (EAIO)
IBF............. International Bandy Federation [*Lulea, Sweden*] (EAIO)
IBF............. International Banking Facility
IBF............. International Banking Facility (TDOB)
IBF............. International Bar Fly [*Sign in Harry's New York Bar, Paris*]
IBF............. International Bicycle Fund (EA)
IBF............. International Bobsled Federation
IBF............. International Booksellers Federation [*Formerly, ICBA*] [*Austria*] (EA)
IBF............. International Boxing Federation (EA)
IBF............. Internationales Begegnungszentrum Friedenshaus [*Germany*] (EAIO)
IBFAN........ International Baby Food Action Network (EA)
IBFC.......... Iron Butterfly Fan Club [*Later, IBIN*] (EA)
IBFCC........ International Border Fancy Canary Club (EA)
IBFD.......... International Bureau of Fiscal Documentation (EAIO)
IBFEG........ Internationaler Bund Freier Evangelischer Gemeinden [*International Federation of Free Evangelical Churches - IFFEC*] (EA)
IBFF........... Impulse Base Flow Facility [*NASA*]
IBFG.......... Internationaler Bund Freier Gewerkschaften [*International Confederation of Free Trade Unions*]
IBFI........... International Business Forms Industries (EA)
IBFM.......... Institute of Broadcasting Financial Management [*Later, BCFMA*]
IBFMP........ International Bureau of the Federations of Master Printers
IBFN.......... Integrated Broadband Fiber Optic Network [*Telecommunications*]
IBFO.......... International Brotherhood of Firemen and Oilers (EA)
IBFRBTWB... International Book Fair of Radical Black and Third World Books
IBFS.......... Interim Billing and Follow-Up System [*Social Security Administration*] (GFGA)
IBFS.......... International Benjamin Franklin Society [*Defunct*] (EA)
IBG............ CNA Financial Corp., Library, Chicago, IL [*Inactive*] [*OCLC symbol*] (OCLC)

IBG............ Incorporated Brewers' Guild [*British*] (EAIO)
IBG............ Insoluble Bone Gelatin [*Cardiology*] (DMAA)
IBG............ Institute for Behavioral Genetics [*University of Colorado - Boulder*] [*Research center*] (RCD)
IBG............ Institute of British Geographers (BI)
IBG............ Institute of British Geographers (DBA)
IBG............ Inter Block Gap
IBG............ Intermediate BTU [*British Thermal Unit*] Gas
IBG............ International Boxing Guild
IBG............ Internationale Begegnung in Gemeinschaftsdiensten [*Germany*] (EAIO)
IBG............ Internationale Brecht Gesellschaft [*International Brecht Society*] (EAIO)
IBG............ Internationale Bruckner Gesellschaft [*Vienna, Austria*] (EAIO)
IBG............ Internationales Buro fuer Gebirgsmechanik [*International Bureau of Strato-Mechanics - IBSM*] (EAIO)
IBH............ Initial Beachhead [*Military*]
IBHA.......... Insulation, Building, and Hard Board Association [*British*] (BI)
IBHA.......... International Buckskin Horse Association (EA)
IBHD.......... Initial Beachhead [*Military*]
IBHF.......... International Boxing Hall of Fame (EA)
IBHR.......... International Bibliography of the History of Religions [*A publication*] (BJA)
IBi............ Blue Island Public Library, Blue Island, IL [*Library symbol Library of Congress*] (LCLS)
i-bi--.......... British Indian Ocean Territory [*MARC geographic area code Library of Congress*] (LCCP)
IBI............ College of Du Page, Glen Ellyn, IL [*OCLC symbol*] (OCLC)
IBI............ Independent Black Institution
IBI............ Independent Broadcast Institute [*British*]
IBI............ Individualized Bilingual Instruction (EDAC)
IBI............ Information Builders, Inc. [*New York*] [*Commercial firm*] (CDE)
IBI............ Insulation Board Institute [*Later, ABPA*] (EA)
IBI............ Intelligent Buildings Institute (EA)
IBI............ Interburst Interval [*Electrophysiology*]
IBI............ Intergovernmental Bureau for Informatics [*Telecommunications*] (EA)
IBI............ Interim Ballistic Instrumentation
IBI............ Intermittent Bladder Irrigation [*Medicine*]
IBI............ International Bankers, Inc.
IBI............ International Biomass Institute (EA)
IBI............ International Biotechnologies, Inc.
IBI............ International Brace Resources [*Vancouver Stock Exchange symbol*]
IBI............ International Broadcast Institute [*Later, IIC*]
IBI............ International Bureau for Informatics (CSR)
iBi............ International Business Intelligence [*A publication*]
IBI............ Internationales Burgen-Institut [*International Castles Institute*] [*Rozendaal, Netherlands*] (EA)
IBI............ Interpersonal Behavior Inventory [*Veterans Administration*]
IBI............ Interview-Oriented Background Investigation (MCD)
IBI............ Intimate Brands 'A' [*NYSE symbol*] (TTSB)
IBI............ Intimate Brands, Inc. [*NYSE symbol*] (SAG)
IBI............ Invoice Book Inward [*Business term*]
IBI............ Ischemic Brain Infarction [*Medicine*] (DMAA)
IBI............ Islamic Bank International
IBIA.......... Institute of British Industrial Art
IBIA.......... Interior Board of Indian Affairs (in United States Interior Decisions) [*A publication*] (DLA)
IB (I and II)... Information Bank (I and II) (NITA)
IBIB.......... Isobutyl Isobutyrate [*Organic chemistry*]
IBIC.......... Interface Bus Interactive Control [*Computer science*]
IBICC.......... Incorporated British Institute of Certified Carpenters (BI)
IBICT.......... Instituto Brasileiro de Informacao em Ciencia e Tecnologia [*Brazilian Institute for Information in Science and Technology*] [*National Council of Scientific and Technological Development*] [*Information service or system*] (IID)
IBID.......... Ibidem [*In the Same Place*] [*Latin*]
IBID.......... International Bibliographical Description
IBI-ICC........ IBI [*Intergovernmental Bureau for Informatics*] International Computation Centre (NITA)
IBI-ICC........ Intergovernmental Bureau for Informatics - International Computation Center (CSR)
IBIN.......... Integrated Brands [*NASDAQ symbol*] (SAG)
IBIN.......... Integrated Brands 'A' [*NASDAQ symbol*] (TTSB)
IBIN.......... Iron Butterfly Information Network (EA)
IBiol.......... Institute of Biology [*British*] (DI)
IBIP.......... International Books in Print [*A publication*]
IBIS.......... Ibis Technology [*NASDAQ symbol*] (TTSB)
IBIS.......... Ibis Technology Corp. [*NASDAQ symbol*] (SAG)
IBIS.......... ICAO [*International Civil Aviation Organization*] Bird Strike Information System [*Information service or system*] (IID)
IBIS.......... Industrialk Base Information System (AAGC)
IBIS.......... Infrared Background Imaging Seeker (MCD)
IBiS.......... Initiative in Biomolecular Structures [*University of New South Wales*] [*Australia*]
IBIS.......... Inspectors Based in Schools [*British*] (AIE)
IBIS.......... Integrated Botanical Information System [*Computer database*]
IBIS.......... Integrated Building Industry System (PDAA)
IBIS.......... Intelligent Business Information System (NITA)
IBIS.......... Intense Bunched Ion Source (IEEE)
IBIS.......... Intensive Biometric Intertidal Survey [*Botany*]
IBIS.......... International Bank Information System
IBIS.......... International Book Information Service
IBIS.......... Intranet Business Information System (PDAA)
IBIS.......... Inventaire Bibliographique des Isiaca (BJA)
IBIS.......... Issue-Based Information System [*Computer science*]
IBiS.......... Saint Francis Hospital, Blue Island, IL [*Library symbol Library of Congress*] (LCLS)
IBisSD........ Bismarck-Henning Community Unit School District, Bismarck, IL [*Library symbol*] [*Library of Congress*] (LCLS)
IbisTc.......... Ibis Technology Corp. [*Associated Press*] (SAG)
IbisTech...... Ibis Technology Corp. [*Associated Press*] (SAG)
IBISW.......... Ibis Technology Wrrt [*NASDAQ symbol*] (TTSB)
IBIT............ ICBM [*Intercontinental Ballistic Missile*] Blast Interference Test (MCD)
IBIT............ Initiated BIT (MCD)
IBIT............ Issue by Issue Tally
IBJ............ Industrial Bank of Japan
IBJ............ Instrument Bearing Jewel
IBJ............ Loop College, Chicago, IL [*OCLC symbol*] (OCLC)
IBJCA.......... International Blue Jay Class Association (EA)
IBJ Data...... Industrial Bank of Japan Database [*Originator and databank on trade and economics*] [*Japan*] (NITA)
IBJI............ Industrial Bank of Japan International Ltd. (ECON)
IBJM.......... International Board of Jewish Missions (EA)
IBK............ Independent Bankshares [*AMEX symbol*] (TTSB)
IBK............ Independent Bankshares, Inc. [*AMEX symbol*] (SAG)
IBK............ [*The*] Industrial Bank of Kuwait
IBK............ Infectious Bovine Keratoconjunctivitis [*Veterinary medicine*]
IBK............ Innsbruck [*Austria*] [*Seismograph station code, US Geological Survey*] (SEIS)
IBK............ Institute of Bookkeepers [*British*] (DAS)
IBK............ Knox College, Galesburg, IL [*OCLC symbol*] (OCLC)
IBKA.......... Ikatan Buruh Kereta Api [*Railroad Workers' Union*] [*Indonesia*]
IBKB.......... Ikatan Buruh Kendaaran Bermotor [*Motor Transport Workers' Union*] [*Indonesia*]
IBKC.......... Infectious Bovine Keratoconjunctivitis (PDAA)
I BKR.......... Ice Breaker [*Freight*]
IBL............ Boehringer Mannheim Corp., Indianapolis, IN [*OCLC symbol*] (OCLC)
IBL............ Immunoblastic Lymphadenopathy [*Medicine*] (CPH)
IBL............ Inside of the Battery Limits [*Engineering Economics*]
IBL............ Interest-Bearing Liability
IBL............ Interior Ballistics Laboratory [*Aberdeen, MD*] [*Army*]
IBL............ Intermediate Behavioral Language (SAA)
IBL............ International Brotherhood of Longshoremen
IBLA.......... Inter-American Bibliographical and Library Association (EA)
IBLA.......... Interior Board of Land Appeals [*Department of the Interior*]
IBLC.......... International B-24 Liberator Club (EA)
IBLE.......... International Brotherhood of Locomotive Engineers (EA)
IBLM.......... International Bureau of Legal Metrology
IBlo............ Withers Public Library, Bloomington, IL [*Library symbol Library of Congress*] (LCLS)
IBloA.......... Illinois Agricultural Association, Bloomington, IL [*Library symbol Library of Congress*] (LCLS)
IBloC.......... Corn Belt Library System, Bloomington, IL [*Library symbol Library of Congress*] (LCLS)
IBloHi.......... McLean County Historical Society, Bloomington, IL [*Library symbol Library of Congress*] (LCLS)
IBloMH........ Mennonite Hospital Association, Medical-Nursing Library, Bloomington, IL [*Library symbol Library of Congress*] (LCLS)
IBloSF.......... State Farm Insurance Co., Bloomington, IL [*Library symbol*] [*Library of Congress*] (LCLS)
IBloStJ........ Saint Joseph's Hospital, Bloomington, IL [*Library symbol Library of Congress*] (LCLS)
IBloW.......... Illinois Wesleyan University, Bloomington, IL [*Library symbol Library of Congress*] (LCLS)
IBLS.......... International Brotherhood of Live Steamers (EA)
IBM............ Ice-Binding Motif [*Biochemistry*]
IBM............ Inclusion Body Myositis
IBM............ Individual-Based Model [*Marine science*] (OSRA)
IBM............ Individual-Based Model (USDC)
IBM............ Instant Big Mouth [*Martini*] [*Slang*]
IBM............ Institute of Baths Management [*British*] (BI)
IBM............ Institute of Builders Merchants [*British*] (DBA)
IBM............ Instituto de Biologia Marina, San Antonia [*Argentina*] [*Marine science*] (OSRA)
IBM............ Interacting Boson Model [*Of nuclear structure*]
IBM............ Intercontinental Ballistic Missile
IBM............ International Brotherhood of Magicians (EA)
IBM............ International Business Machines [*Associated Press*] (SAG)
IBM............ International Business Machines Corp. [*Facetious translations: I Buil t a Macintosh; I Buy Money; Inferior But Marketable; Insidious Black Magic; It'sBeen Malfunctioning; Incontinent Bowel Movement*] [*NYSE symbol Toronto Stock Exchange symbol*] (SPSG)
IBM............ Intl Bus. Machines [*NYSE symbol*] (TTSB)
IBM............ Kimball, NE [*Location identifier FAA*] (FAAL)
IBM............ Kirkland & Ellis, Chicago, IL [*OCLC symbol*] (OCLC)
IBMA.......... Independent Battery Manufacturers Association (EA)
IBMA.......... Interior Board of Mine Operations Appeals (in United States Interior Decisions) [*A publication*] (DLA)
IBMA.......... International Bluegrass Music Association (EA)
IBMA.......... Isobutoxymethyl Acrylamide [*Organic chemistry*]
IBMC.......... International Brotherhood of Motorcycle Campers (EA)
IBMC.......... International Buddhist Meditation Center (EA)
IBMCUA........ IBM Computer Users' Association (NITA)
IBME.......... Institute of Biomedical Engineering [*University of Toronto*] [*Research center*] (RCD)
IBMK.......... Isobutyl Methyl Ketone [*Organic chemistry*]
IBMM.......... Integrated Book Manufacturing Machine
IBMNSW...... Independent Bread Manufacturers of New South Wales [*Australia*]
IBMOC........ Intercontinental Ballistic Missile Operational Capability (AAG)

IBMP .... International Board of Medicine and Psychology [*Later, IAMP*] (EA)
IBMP .... Isobutyl(methoxy)pyrazine [*Organic chemistry*]
IBMPrA .... Intl Bus. Mach 7 1/2% Dep Pfd [*NYSE symbol*] (TTSB)
IBMS .... Ion Beam Mass Spectrometer
IBMTR .... International Bone Marrow Transplant Registry
IBM TSS .... International Business Machine's Timesharing System (TEL)
IBM WU .... IBM Workers United (NITA)
IBMX .... Isobutylmethylxanthine [*Also, MIX*] [*Biochemistry*]
IBN .... Blackburn College, Carlinville, IL [*OCLC symbol*] (OCLC)
IBN .... Identification Beacon
IBN .... Indexed by Name (IAA)
IBN .... Institut Belge de Normalisation [*Belgian Institute for Standardization*] [*Information service or system*] (IID)
IBN .... International Biosciences Network
IBNJ .... Independence Bancorp, Inc. [*NASDAQ symbol*] (SAG)
IBNJ .... Independence Bancorp NJ [*NASDAQ symbol*] (TTSB)
IBNJP .... Independence Banc 9% Cv Pfd [*NASDAQ symbol*] (TTSB)
IBNR .... Incurred but Not Reported [*Insurance*]
IBNS .... Inter-Borough Nomination Scheme [*British*] (DI)
IBNS .... International Bank Note Society (EA)
IBO .... Ibotenic Acid [*Organic acid*]
IBO .... Idabel, OK [*Location identifier FAA*] (FAAL)
IBO .... Instruction by Objective
IBO .... International Baccalaureate Office [*See also OBI*] [*Later, International Baccalaureate Organization Grand-Saconnex, Switzerland*] (EAIO)
IBO .... International Bowhunting Organization
IBO .... International Broadcasting Organization
IBO .... Internationale Bouworde [*International Association of Building Companions - IABC*] [*Marche-En-Famenne, Belgium*] (EAIO)
IBO .... Invoice Book Outbound [*Business term*]
IBO .... Lutheran General Hospital, Park Ridge, IL [*OCLC symbol*] (OCLC)
IBOA .... Irish Bank Officials' Association [*Northern Ireland*]
IBOB .... International Brotherhood of Old Bastards (EA)
IBOC .... Iso and Bizzarrini Owners Club (EA)
IBOC .... Isobutoxycarbonylation [*Organic chemistry*]
IB of TCWHA... International Brotherhood of Teamsters, Chauffeurs, Warehousemen, and Helpers of America
IBOL .... Interactive Business-Oriented Language
IBOLS .... Integrated Business-Oriented Language Support (IAA)
IBOND .... IGOSS [*Integrated Global Ocean Station System*] Basic Observation Network Design [*Marine science*] (MSC)
IBOP .... Institute of British Oil Paintings
IBOP .... International Balance of Payments (AAGC)
IBOP .... International Balance of Payments Reporting System
IBOP .... International Brotherhood of Operative Potters [*Later, IBPAW*] (EA)
IBOS .... International Business Opportunities Service [*World Bank*] [*United Nations*] (DUND)
IBOT .... In-Branch Operator Training [*British*] (DCTA)
IBOT .... Introduction to the Books of the Old Testament [*A publication*] (BJA)
IBoT .... Istanbul Arkeoloji Muzelerinde Bulunan Bogazkoy Tableteri I and II [*Istanbul*] [*A publication*] (BJA)
IBP .... IBP, Inc. [*NYSE symbol*] (SPSG)
IBP .... Indicated Boiling Point [*Physics*]
IBP .... Industrial Base Program
IBP .... Informed Birth and Parenting [*Later, IH/IBP*] (EA)
IBP .... Initial Boiling Point (MCD)
IBP .... Inner [*Edge of*] Basal Piece
IBP .... Institute for Better Packaging [*Later, PPC*] (EA)
IBP .... Institute for Business Planning
IBP .... Institute of British Photographers (DGA)
IBP .... Insulated Binding Post
IBP .... Integrated Basic Research [*of ASRA*] [*National Science Foundation*]
IBP .... International Balance of Payments (AFM)
IBP .... International Biological Program [*Concluded, 1974*] [*National Academy of Sciences*]
IBP .... International Book Project (EA)
IBP .... Intra-Aortic Ballon Pumping [*Cardiology*] (DMAA)
IBP .... Intraspecific Brood Parasitism [*Biology*]
IBP .... Ion Beam Projector
IBP .... Iron-Binding Protein
IBP .... Principia College, Elsah, IL [*OCLC symbol*] (OCLC)
IBPA .... Illinois State Bowling Proprietors Association (SRA)
IBPA .... Iminobispropylamine [*Organic chemistry*]
IBPA .... Indiana Bowling Proprietors Association (SRA)
IBPA .... International Book Printers Association [*Later, NABM*] (EA)
IBPA .... International Bridge Press Association (EA)
IBPA .... International Business Press Associates (PDAA)
IBPAT .... International Brotherhood of Painters and Allied Trades (EA)
IBPAW .... International Brotherhood of Pottery and Allied Workers [*Formerly, IBOP*] (EA)
IBpB .... Bedford Park Public Library District, Bedford Park, IL [*Library symbol Library of Congress*] (LCLS)
IBPCA .... International Bureau of the Permanent Court of Arbitration (EAIO)
IBP/CT .... Internationale Biological Programme/Conservation of Terrestrial Biological Communities [*London, England*]
IBPCT .... International Customs Tariffs Bureau [*International Bureau for the Publi cation of Customs Tariffs*] [*Acronym is based on former name,*] (EA)
IBPDMS .... Improved Point Defense Missile System [*Sea Sparrow*] (DOMA)
IBPDSMS .... Improved Basic Point Defense Surface Missile System (DNAB)
IBPF .... International Black Peoples' Foundation [*Defunct*] (EA)
IBPFM .... Independent Board for Presbyterian Foreign Missions (EA)
IBPG .... Icon-Based Program Generators [*Software*] [*Computer science*]
IBPGR .... International Board for Plant Genetic Resources [*FAO*] [*Italy*]

IBPM .... International Brotherhood of Papermakers [*Later, United Paperworkers International Union*]
IBPMS .... Indirect Blood Pressure Measuring System
IBPO .... International Brotherhood of Police Officers (EA)
IBPOEW .... Improved Benevolent Protective Order of Elks of the World (EA)
IBQ .... Institutional Bond Quote Service [*Database*] [*Chase Econometrics Interactive Data*] [*Information service or system*] (CRD)
IBQ .... International Baron Resources [*Vancouver Stock Exchange symbol*]
IBQ .... Quincy College, Quincy, IL [*OCLC symbol*] (OCLC)
IBQA .... Institute of Building Quality Australia
IBR .... Iberia Air Lines of Spain (MCD)
IBR .... Infectious Bovine Rhinotracheitis [*Also, IBRV*] [*Virus*]
IBR .... Information Bearing Radiation
IBR .... Infrablack Region
IBR .... Institute for Basic Research [*National Institute of Standards and Technology*]
IBR .... Institute for Behavioral Research [*York University*] [*Canada Research center*] (IID)
IBR .... Institute for Biblical Research (EA)
IBR .... Institute for Biotechnology Research [*University of Waterloo*] [*Research center*] (RCD)
IBR .... Institute of Boiler and Radiator Manufacturers [*Later, Hydronics Institute*] (EA)
IBR .... Institutes for Behavior Resources (EA)
IBR .... Integral Boiling Reactor
IBR .... Integrated Bridge Rectifier (IEEE)
IBR .... International Business Reply [*Post Office*] [*British*]
IBR .... Irish Broadcasting Revenue
IBR .... Issues in Bank Regulation [*Bank Administration Institute*] [*A publication*]
IBR .... Rockford College, Rockford, IL [*OCLC symbol*] (OCLC)
IBra .... Bradford Public Library, Bradford, IL [*Library symbol Library of Congress*] (LCLS)
IBRA .... International Bee Research Association [*Cardiff, Wales*] (EA)
IBRA .... International Bible Reading Association [*Redhill, Surrey, England*] (EAIO)
IBRAPE .... Industria Brasileira de Produtos Eletronicos e Electricos, SA
IBRC .... Indiana Business Research Center [*Indiana University*] [*Bloomington, IN*] [*Information service or system*] (IID)
IBRD .... International Bank for Reconstruction and Development [*Also known as World Bank*]
IBre .... Breese Public Library, Breese, IL [*Library symbol Library of Congress*] (LCLS)
IBreD .... Breese Elementary District 12, Breese, IL [*Library symbol Library of Congress*] (LCLS)
IBreMHS ..... Mater Dei High School, Breese, IL [*Library symbol Library of Congress*] (LCLS)
IBreSJH ...... Saint Joseph's Hospital, Breese, IL [*Library symbol Library of Congress*] (LCLS)
IBRG .... International Biodeterioration Research Group (EA)
IBri .... Brighton Memorial Library, Brighton, IL [*Library symbol Library of Congress*] (LCLS)
IBRI .... Interdisciplinary Biblical Research Institute (EA)
IBRIC .... Institute for Behavioral Research in Creativity [*Research center*] (RCD)
IBritishE ...... Institute of British Engineers
IBRL .... Initial Bomb Release Line
IBRM .... Institute of Baths and Recreation Management [*British*]
IBRM .... Institute of Boiler and Radiator Manufacturers [*Later, Hydronics Institute*]
IBRM .... International Basic Res [*NASDAQ symbol*] (TTSB)
IBRM .... International Basic Resources, Inc. [*NASDAQ symbol*] (NQ)
IBRMA .... Institute for Biophysical Research and Macromolecular Assemblies [*Johns Hopkins University*]
IBRMR .... Institute for Basic Research on Mental Retardation
IBro .... Brookfield Free Public Library, Brookfield, IL [*Library symbol Library of Congress*] (LCLS)
IBRO .... International Brain Research Organization [*Paris, France*] (EA)
IBrov .... Broadview Public Library, Broadview, IL [*Library symbol Library of Congress*] (LCLS)
IBrowSD ...... Brownstown Community School District No. 201, Brownstown, IL [*Library symbol Library of Congress*] (LCLS)
IBRRC .... International Bird Rescue Research Center (EA)
IBRS .... Index to Book Reviews in the Sciences [*A publication*]
IBrS .... Suburban Library System, Burr Ridge, IL [*Library symbol Library of Congress*] (LCLS)
IBrus .... South County Public Library District of Calhoun County, Brussels, IL [*Library symbol Library of Congress*] (LCLS)
IBrusRSD .... Brussels-Richwood Community Consolidated School District 41, Brussels, IL [*Library symbol Library of Congress*] (LCLS)
IBrusSD ...... Brussels Community High School District 37, Brussels, IL [*Library symbol Library of Congress*] (LCLS)
IBrv .... Bridgeview Public Library, Bridgeview, IL [*Library symbol Library of Congress*] (LCLS)
IBRV .... Infectious Bovine Rhinotracheitis Virus [*Also, IBR*]
IBS .... Ball State University, Muncie, IN [*OCLC symbol*] (OCLC)
IBS .... Ibis [*Belgium ICAO designator*] (FAAC)
IBS .... Ichthyosis Bullosa of Siemens [*Medicine*]
IBS .... Identical by State [*Genetics*]
IBS .... Imidazole Buffered Saline [*Clinical chemistry*]
IBS .... Immediate Business Systems [*Commercial firm British*]
IBS .... Immunoblastic Sarcoma [*Medicine*] (DMAA)
IBS .... Impulse Balance System
IBS .... Incentive Bonus Scheme [*British*]

IBS............. Incorporated Bronte Society [*Keighley, West Yorkshire, England*] (EAIO)
IBS............. Inflatable Boat, Small (NVT)
IBS............. Institute for Basic Standards [*Later, NSL*] [*National Institute of Standards and Technology*]
IBS............. Institute for Biotechnological Studies [*University of Kent*] [*British*] (IRUK)
IBS............. Institute of Behavioral Science [*University of Colorado - Boulder*] [*Research center*] (RCD)
IBS............. Institute of Behavioural Studies [*University of Newcastle*] [*Australia*]
IBS............. Institute of Black Studies [*Defunct*] (EA)
IBS............. Integrated Booking System [*Army*] (RDA)
IBS............. Integrated Bridge System (MCD)
IBS............. Integrated Business Systems [*Trifid Software*] (NITA)
IBS............. INTELSAT Business Service [*MCI Communications Corp.*]
IBS............. Interbed-Storage Package [*Geological program*]
IBS............. Interbomb Spacing (DNAB)
IBS............. Inter-Byte Separation [*Automotive engineering Electronics*]
IBS............. Inter-Byte Spacing [*Computer science*]
IBS............. Intercollegiate Broadcasting System (EA)
IBS............. Interference Blanker Set
IBS............. International Bach Society [*Defunct*] (EA)
IBS............. International Bank for Settlements (MHDW)
IBS............. International Benchrest Shooters (EA)
IBS............. International Benevolent Society (EA)
IBS............. International Bentham Society (EAIO)
IBS............. International Bible Society (EA)
IBS............. International Bibliography of the Social Sciences, Economics, and Sociology [*International Committee for Social Science Information and Documentation*] [*Information service or system*] (CRD)
IBS............. International Bookbinders Secretariat (DGA)
IBS............. International Book Service, Inc.
IBSM............. International Boundary Study [*A publication*]
IBS............. International Brancusi Society (EA)
IBS............. International Brecht Society [*See also IBG*] (EA)
IBS............. International Bronchoesophagological Society (EA)
IBS............. International Bulb Society (EAIO)
IBS............. International Business Services [*Switzerland*] (ECON)
IBS............. International Business Services [*Telecommunications*] (TSSD)
IBS............. Interpersonal Behavior Survey [*Psychology*]
IBS............. Intron Binding Site [*Genetics*]
IBS............. Ion Beam Scanning
IBS............. Ion Beam Sputtering
IBS............. Ionospheric Beacon Satellite (PDAA)
IBS............. Iota Beta Sigma [*An association*] (WDMC)
IBS............. Irritable Bowel Syndrome [*Medicine*]
IBS............. Island Base Section [*Navy*]
IBS............. Isobaric Solution (DMAA)
IBSA............. Immunoreactive Bovine Serum Albumin [*Immunochemistry*]
IBSA............. International Barber Schools Association (EA)
IBSA............. International Bible Students Association (EA)
IBSA............. International Blind Sports Association [*See also AISA*] [*Farsta, Sweden*] (EAIO)
IBSA............. Iodinated Bovine Serum Albumin (DMAA)
IBSAC............. Industrialized Building Systems and Components (IEEE)
IBSAT............. Indexing by Statistical Analysis Techniques (PDAA)
IBSC............. Independent Banks of South Carolina (SRA)
IBSCA............. Ion Beam Spectrochemical Analysis (PDAA)
IB(Scot)............. Institute of Bankers in Scotland (ODBW)
IBSD............. Information-Based School Development
IBSDF............. International Business Schools [*NASDAQ symbol*] (SAG)
IBSDF............. Intl Business Schs [*NASDAQ symbol*] (TTSB)
IBSEDEX............. International Building Services Index [*Database*] [*BSRIA*] [*Information service or system*] (CRD)
IBSF............. IBS Financial [*NASDAQ symbol*] (TTSB)
IBSF............. IBS Financial Corp. [*NASDAQ symbol*] (SAG)
ibsf............. Little Brothers of Saint Francis (TOCD)
IBSFC............. International Baltic Sea Fishery Commission [*Warsaw, Poland*] (ASF)
IBS Fncl............. IBS Financial Corp. [*Associated Press*] (SAG)
IBSH............. Institute of the Brothers of the Sacred Heart [*See also IFSC*] [*Rome, Italy*] (EAIO)
IBSHR............. Integral Boiling and Superheat Reactor
IBSM............. Institute of Building Site Management [*British*] (BI)
IBSM............. International Bureau of Strata Mechanics [*See also IBG*] (EAIO)
IBSMA............. Interior Board of Surface Mine Appeals (in United States Interior Decisions) [*A publication*] (DLA)
IBSN............. Infantile Bilateral Striatal Necrosis [*Ophthalmology*]
IBSP............. Integrin-Binding Sialoprotein (DMAA)
IBSR............. Individual Battle Shooting Range (PDAA)
IBSR............. Interactive Bibliographic Search and Retrieval (NITA)
IBSR............. Inverse Boresight Ranging (MCD)
IBSRAM............. International Board for Soil Research and Management [*Thailand*]
IBSS............. Infrared Background Signature Survey [*Military*] (SDI)
IBSS............. Insect Balanced Salt Solution [*Cytology*]
IBS/SPS............. Inflatable Boat, Small/Silent Propulsion System (MCD)
IBSSU............. Internal Bearing Stabilized Sighting Unit (MCD)
IBST............. Institute of British Surgical Technicians (BI)
IBST............. International Bureau of Social Tourism [*See also BITS*] [*Brussels, Belgium*] (EAIO)
IBST............. International Bureau of Software Test
IBSTP............. International Bureau for the Suppression of Traffic in Persons (DI)
IBSWU............. International Boot and Shoe Workers' Union
IBSYS............. International Business Machines System
IBT............. Field Museum of Natural History, Chicago, IL [*OCLC symbol*] (OCLC)
IBT............. IBS Technologies Ltd. [*Vancouver Stock Exchange symbol*]

IBT............. Immunobead Binding Test [*Biochemistry*]
IBT............. Immunoblastic T-Cell [*Lymphadenopathy*]
IBT............. Implantable Beacon Transmitter [*Oceanography*]
IBT............. Inclined Bottom Tank [*Fermenter*]
IBT............. Income Before Taxes (AAGC)
IBT............. Incompatible Blood Transfusion (PDAA)
I-BT............. India-Burma Theater [*World War II*]
IBT............. Indianapolis Ballet Theatre
IBT............. Industrial Bio-Test Laboratories, Inc.
IBT............. Initial Boiling-Point Temperature
IBT............. Initial Brake Temperature [*Automotive engineering*]
IBT............. Ink Blot Test [*Rorschach test*] [*Psychology*] (DAVI)
IBT............. Instrumented Bend Test
IBT............. Insulation Breakdown Tester
IBT............. Integrated Business Terminal [*Computer science*] (PDAA)
IBT............. [*The*] International Bridge & Terminal Co. [*AAR code*]
IBT............. International Broadcasting Trust [*British*]
IBT............. International Brotherhood of Teamsters [*Union*]
IBT............. International Brotherhood of Teamsters, Chauffeurs, Warehousemen, and Helpers ofAmerica (EA)
IBT............. Ion Beam Technology
IBT............. Ion-Implanted Base Transistor
IBT............. Irrational Beliefs Test [*Psychology*]
IBT............. Isatin-beta-thiosemicarbazone [*Organic chemistry*]
IBTA............. Interest-Bearing Transaction Account (DICI)
IBTA............. International Baton Twirling Association of America and Abroad [*Defunct*] (EA)
IBTC............. International Brands and Their Companies [*Formerly, ITND*] [*A publication*]
IBTF............. Investment Bank for Trade and Finance [*United Arab Emirates*]
IBTMA............. International Black Toy Manufacturers Association (EA)
IBTO............. International Broadcasting and Television Organization (NTCM)
IBTOM............. Iranian B'nei Torah Movement (EA)
IBTS............. Insert Bit String [*Computer science*] (PCM)
IBTS............. International Beer Tasting Society (EA)
IBTS............. International Bicycle Touring Society (EA)
IBTTA............. International Bridge, Tunnel, and Turnpike Association (EA)
IBTU............. Instructors Basic Training Unit
IBU............. Eureka College, Eureka, IL [*OCLC symbol*] (OCLC)
IBU............. Ibukiyama [*Ibukisan*] [*Japan*] [*Seismograph station code, US Geological Survey*] [*Closed*] (SEIS)
IBU............. Ikatan Buruh Umum [*General Workers' Union*] [*Indonesia*]
IBU............. Imperial Bushel (WDAA)
IBU............. Independent Business Unit
IBU............. Instruction Buffer Unit [*Computer science*] (IAA)
IBU............. Interference Blanking Unit
IBU............. International Benzoate Unit [*Pharmacology*]
IBU............. International Broadcasting Union [*Defunct*] (NTCM)
IBU............. International Burgers Now Ltd. [*Vancouver Stock Exchange symbol*]
IBU............. International Business Unit [*British Information service or system*] (IID)
IBU............. Itambacuri [*Brazil*] [*Airport symbol*] (AD)
IBucSD............. Buckley-Loda Community Unit School District, Buckley, IL [*Library symbol*] [*Library of Congress*] (LCLS)
IBud............. Mason Memorial Public Library, Buda, IL [*Library symbol Library of Congress*] (LCLS)
IBun............. Bunker Hill Public Library, Bunker Hill, IL [*Library symbol Library of Congress*] (LCLS)
IBunMCD............. Macoupin Community District 8, Bunker Hill, IL [*Library symbol Library of Congress*] (LCLS)
ibuprofen............. Isobutylphenylpropionic Acid (BARN)
IBur............. South Stickney District Library, Burbank, IL [*Library symbol Library of Congress*] (LCLS)
IBure............. Leepertown Township Library, Bureau, IL [*Library symbol Library of Congress*] (LCLS)
IBureLSD............. Leepertown Consolidated Community School District 175, Bureau, IL [*Library symbol Library of Congress*] (LCLS)
IBV............. Infectious Bronchitis Vaccine [*Pharmacology*] (DAVI)
IBV............. Infectious Bronchitis Virus [*Avian*]
IBV............. Inspection by Variables
IBV............. International Bellevue Ventures Ltd. [*Vancouver Stock Exchange symbol*]
IBV............. Internationale Buchhandler-Vereinigung [*International Booksellers Federation - IBF*] (EAIO)
IBV............. Newberry Library, Chicago, IL [*OCLC symbol*] (OCLC)
IBVA............. Interactive Brain Wave Analyzer [*IBVA Technology*] [*Computer science*] (PCM)
IBVE............. Isobutyl Vinyl Ether [*Organic chemistry*]
IBVM............. Institute of the Blessed Virgin Mary [*Sisters of Loretto*] [*Roman Catholic religious order*]
IBW............. Borg-Warner Corp., Des Plaines, IL [*OCLC symbol*] (OCLC)
IBW............. Ideal Body Weight [*Medicine*]
IBW............. Impulse Bandwidth (MCD)
IBW............. In Black and White [*A publication*]
IBW............. Institute of the Black World [*Defunct*] (EA)
IBW............. Intelligence Bandwidth
IBW............. Internal Bore Weld [*Nuclear energy*] (NUCP)
IBW............. International Black Writers (EA)
IBW............. International Business Week
IBW............. Ion Beam Weapon
IBW............. Irrotationally Bound Water [*Biophysics*]
IBW............. Israel Book World [*A publication*]
IBWA............. International Bank for West Africa Ltd.
IBWA............. International Black Writers and Artists (EA)
IBWA............. International Bottled Water Association (EA)

IBWA	International Boxing Writers Association (EA)
IBWC	International Black Women's Congress (EA)
IBWC	International Black Writers Conference [Later, IBW] (EA)
IBWC	International Boundary and Water Commission
IBWCA	International Barbed Wire Collectors Association (EA)
IBWDA	Idaho Beer and Wine Distributors Association (SRA)
IBWM	International Bureau of Weights and Measures
IBWN	International Bureau of Weights and Measures (ECII)
IBX	Iberiotoxin [Biochemistry]
IBX	Integrated Business Exchange (MCD)
IBX	Schiff, Hardin & Waite, Chicago, IL [OCLC symbol] (OCLC)
IBY	International Bank of Yemen
IBY	International Biological Year
IBY	International Book Year [1972] [UNESCO]
IBY	International Business Aircraft, Inc. [FAA designator] (FAAC)
Ibyc	Ibycus [Sixth century BC] [Classical studies] (OCD)
IBYC	Institute in Basic Youth Conflicts (EA)
IBZ	Columbia College, Chicago, IL [Inactive] [OCLC symbol] (OCLC)
IBZ	Ibiza [Spain] [Airport symbol] (OAG)
IBZ	Inner Border Zone
IBZ	International Business Air [Sweden ICAO designator] (FAAC)
IC	Chicago Public Library, Chicago, IL [Library symbol Library of Congress] (LCLS)
IC	Ice Chest
IC	Ice Crystals
ic	Iceland [MARC country of publication code Library of Congress] (LCCP)
IC	Iceland [NATO]
IC	Icing [Aviation] (FAAC)
IC	Icon [Plate engraving]
IC	Icteric [Medicine] (DAVI)
IC	Identification Code
IC	Identity Card (BARN)
IC	Iesus Christus [Jesus Christ] [Latin]
IC	Ileocecal [Gastroenterology] (DAVI)
IC	Iliac Chamber [Anatomy] (IAA)
IC	Iliococcygeal [Muscle] [Anatomy] (DAVI)
IC	Iliocostal [Muscle] [Anatomy] (DAVI)
IC	Illinois Central [Illinois Central Gulf Railroad Co.] [AAR code]
IC	Illinois Central Corp. [NYSE symbol] (SPSG)
IC	Image Chamber (IAA)
IC	Image Check (IAA)
IC	Image Communications [Computer graphics]
IC	Immediate Constituent
IC	Immune Complex [Immunology]
IC	Immune Cytotoxicity [Immunochemistry] (DAVI)
IC	Immunocytochemistry [Immunochemstry] (DAVI)
IC	Implementation and Conversion (MCD)
IC	Implementation of Change
IC	Imported Content
IC	Impoverished Conditions
IC	Impression Cylinder [Typography] (DGA)
IC	Improved Capability [for aircraft] (MCD)
IC	Impulse Conductor (MSA)
IC	Incarnational Consecration (TOCD)
ic	In Casu [In This Case] [Latin]
IC	Incense Cedar [Botany]
IC	Incentive Compensation (MCD)
IC	In Charge Of
I/C	Incoming [Telecommunications] (TEL)
IC	In Command (ADA)
IC	In-Commission (MCD)
IC	Incomplete (DAVI)
IC	In Compliance [FDA]
IC	Increase (IAA)
IC	Incremental Cost (KSC)
IC	Incue [News broadcasting] (NTCM)
IC	Incurved Cactus [Horticulture]
IC	Independent Contractor
IC	Independent Telephone Co. [Telecommunications]
IC	Index Catalogue
IC	Index Chemicus [See also ICRS]
I/C	Index Concordance [International Serials Catalogue] [A publication]
IC	Index Correction [on a sextant] [Navigation]
IC	Index Correlation (WDAA)
IC	Index of Coincidence (MHDB)
IC	Indian Airlines [ICAO designator] (AD)
IC	Indian Cases [India] [A publication] (DLA)
IC	Indicating Controller (NRCH)
IC	Indication Cycle (IAA)
IC	Indicator and Control
IC	Indifference Curve [Economics]
IC	Indirect Calorimetry [Physiology] (DAVI)
IC	Individual/Collective (MCD)
IC	Individual Counsel (DNAB)
IC	Individual Counseling [Psychology] (DAVI)
IC	Indochina
IC	Inductance-Capacitance
IC	Inductive Coupling
I/C	Industrial/Commercial
IC	Industrial Concentration (MHDB)
IC	Industrial Court (DLA)
IC	Industry Competitive (AFIT)
IC	Inertial Component
IC	Infection Control (HCT)

IC	Inferior Colliculus [Also, ICC] [Brain anatomy]
IC	Infinite Capitalism [Book title]
IC	Informal Communication
IC	Information Center
IC	Information Circular
IC	Information Codes (NITA)
IC	Information Content (DEN)
IC	Infrastructure Committee of the North Atlantic Council [NATO]
IC	Ingenieur Constructeur [Academic degree]
IC	Inhibition Concentration [Biochemistry]
IC	Inhibitory Concentration [Toxicology]
IC	Iniciativia per Catalunya [Spain Political party] (EY)
IC	Initial Calibration
IC	Initial Conditions
IC	Initial Course [Navigation]
IC	Initiation of Contraction
IC	Inland Container [Shipping] (DCTA)
IC	Inlet Contact
IC	Inner Cabin
IC	Inner Canthal Distance [Medicine] (DMAA)
IC	Inner Circle [Numismatics]
IC	Inner Circle [An association] (EA)
IC	Inner Core [Geology]
IC	Innocent Civilian [Military]
IC	Inorganic Carbon
IC	Input Circuit
IC	Input Code (IAA)
I/C	Input Controller (MCD)
IC	Input Current
IC	Inscribed Circle (IAA)
IC	Inside Cloud Lightning [Meteorology]
IC	Inspected and Condemned [Military]
IC	Inspecting Commander [Military British] (ROG)
IC	Inspection Card
IC	Inspection Chamber
IC	Inspection Committee
IC	Inspiratory Capacity [Physiology]
IC	Inspiratory Center [Physiology]
IC	Installed Capacity [Electronics] (IEEE)
IC	Institute for Congress
IC	Institute of Ceramics [Stoke-On-Trent, Staffordshire, England] (EAIO)
IC	Institute of Charity [Rosminians] [Roman Catholic religious order]
ic	Institute of Charity (TOCD)
IC	Institute of Chemistry [British]
IC	Institutional Care [British]
IC	Institutional Characteristics [of the Integrated Postsecondary Education Data System] [Department of Education] (GFGA)
IC	Instruction Card (MSA)
IC	Instruction Cell
IC	Instruction Code (AAG)
IC	Instruction Counter [Computer science]
IC	Instruction Cycle [Computer science] (IAA)
IC	Instructor in Cookery [Navy British] (ROG)
IC	Instrumentation Controller (KSC)
IC	Instrument Correction
IC	Instrument Correlation (WDAA)
IC	Insulated Conductors (MCD)
IC	Insulating Compound (IAA)
IC	Intake Closes [Valve position]
IC	Integrated Chromatography
IC	Integrated Circuit [Electronics]
IC	Integrated Communications (MCD)
IC	Integrating Center
IC	Integrating Contractor (AAG)
IC	Integration Control (MCD)
IC	Integrator Card (IAA)
IC	Intelligence Center (CAAL)
IC	Intelligence Collator [British police term]
IC	Intelligence Collection [Military] (MCD)
IC	Intelligence Committee [NATO] (NATG)
IC	Intelligence Community [Military] (MCD)
IC	Intelligence Corps [Military unit] [British]
IC	Intelligence Cycle (LAIN)
IC	Intelligent Copier [Electrophotography] (DGA)
IC	Intensive Care [Medicine]
IC	Intercept Controller
IC	Interceptor Command
IC	Interceptor Computer (IAA)
I/C	Interchange
IC	Interchange Center
IC	Inter Cibos [Between Meals] [Pharmacy]
I/C	Intercom (KSC)
IC	Intercommunications
I/C	Intercommunicator
IC	Intercomputer (MCD)
IC	Intercomputer Channel (KSC)
IC	Interconnect Carrier [Telecommunications]
IC	Interconnection (IAA)
IC	Intercostal [Between the ribs] [Medicine]
IC	Intercrystalline Corrosion [Metallurgy]
IC	Interexchange Carrier [Telecommunications]
IC	Interface Control [or Controller]
IC	Interface Coordinator (MCD)
IC	Interfacial Communications (MCD)
IC	Interference Control (IAA)

IC	Interim Change (AFM)
IC	Interim Commission
IC	Interim Committee
IC	Interior Communication
IC	Interior Communications Electrician [*Navy rating*]
IC	Intermediate Care [*Medicine*]
IC	Intermediate Chain [*Biochemistry*]
IC	Intermediate Circuit (IAA)
IC	Intermediate Command
IC	Intermittent Catheterization [*Urology*] (DAVI)
IC	Intermittent Claudication [*Medicine*] (MAE)
IC	Internal Capsule [*Neuroanatomy*]
IC	Internal Carotid [*Artery*] [*Cardiology*] (DAVI)
IC	Internal Cerebral [*Neurology*] (DAVI)
IC	Internal Cholecystectomy [*Gastroenterology*] (DAVI)
IC	Internal Combustion
IC	Internal Communications (CAAL)
IC	Internal Conjugate [*Diameter*] [*Gynecology*] (DAVI)
IC	Internal Connection [*Electronics*]
IC	Internal Conversion [*Nuclear science*] (OA)
IC	International Classification (DAVI)
IC	International Conference
IC	International Control
IC	International Cooperation
IC	International Corp. [*Generic term*]
IC	International Curator Resources [*Vancouver Stock Exchange symbol*]
IC	Internment Camp
IC	Internuclear Company
IC	Interpretation Canada [*Federal agency*]
IC	Interrupting Capacity (IAA)
IC	Interruption Code (IAA)
IC	Interspecies Communication [*An association*] (EA)
IC	Interstate Club (EA)
IC	Interstate Commerce Reports [*A publication*] (DLA)
IC	Interstitial Cells [*Histology*]
IC	Interstitial Cyst [*Pulmonary medicine*]
IC	Interstitial Cystitis [*Nephrology*]
IC	Intervalve Coupling (DEN)
IC	Intracapsular (CPH)
IC	Intracardiac [*Medicine*]
IC	Intracarotid [*Medicine*] (MAE)
IC	Intracavitary [*Medicine*]
IC	Intracellular
IC	Intracerebral [*Medicine*]
ic	Intracerebroventricular [*Also, ICTV, ICV*] [*Brain anatomy*]
IC	Intracisternal [*Neruology*] (DAVI)
IC	Intracloud [*Climatology*]
IC	Intracoronary [*Cardiology*]
IC	Intracranial
IC	Intracutaneous [*Medicine*]
IC	Intraductal Carcinoma [*Medicine*] (MEDA)
IC	Intrapleural Catheter [*Medicine*] (DAVI)
IC	Inverse Check
IC	Investment Company
IC	Investment Counselor (MHDB)
IC	Investment Tax Credit
IC	Invited Contractor
IC	Ion Chamber [*Nucleonics*]
IC	Ion Chromatography
IC	Ionization Chamber
IC	Irish Constitution (ADA)
IC	Iron City [*Pittsburgh, PA*]
IC	Irregular Cavalry [*British military*] (DMA)
IC	Irritable Colon [*Medicine*]
IC	Ischemic Cardiomyopathy [*Cardiology*]
IC	Ischemic Contracture [*Hematology*]
IC	Islamic Congress
IC	Island of Calleja [*Neuroanatomy*]
IC	Islet Cells [*of the pancreas*] [*Endocrinology*]
IC	Isolation Condenser (NRCH)
IC	Isovolumic Contraction [*Medicine*] (DMAA)
IC	Izquierda Cristiana [*Christian Left*] [*Chile*] [*Political party*] (EY)
IC	Jesus [*First and third letters of His name in Greek*]
IC	Vietnamese Sisters Incarnational Consecration (TOCD)
IC1	Interior Communications Electrician, First Class [*Navy rating*]
IC2	Interior Communications Electrician, Second Class [*Navy rating*]
IC3	Interior Communications Electrician, Third Class [*Navy rating*]
IC4A	Intercollegiate Association of Amateur Athletes of America [*Also, IAAAA, ICAAAA*]
IC50	Inhibition of Protein Content, 50% [*Biochemistry*]
ICA	Art Institute of Chicago, Chicago, IL [*Library symbol Library of Congress*] (LCLS)
ICA	Aurora College, Aurora, IL [*OCLC symbol*] (OCLC)
ICa	Cairo Public Library, Cairo, IL [*Library symbol Library of Congress*] (LCLS)
ICA	Empresas ICA Socledad ADS [*NYSE symbol*] (SPSG)
ICA	Ica [*Peru*] [*Seismograph station code, US Geological Survey*] (SEIS)
ICA	Icabaru [*Venezuela*] [*Airport symbol*] (OAG)
ICA	Icabaru [*Venezuela*] [*Airport symbol*] (AD)
ICA	Icaro [*Italy*] [*FAA designator*] (FAAC)
ICA	Ice Cream Alliance Ltd. [*British*] (BI)
ICA	Idaho Cattle Association (SRA)
ICA	Ignition Control Additive (IAA)
ICA	Illinois Coal Association (SRA)
ICA	Illinois Cosmetology Association (SRA)

ICA	Immediate Constituent Analyzer [*Computer science*] (DIT)
ICA	Immunocytochemical Analysis
ICA	Immunological Chromatographic Analysis
ICA	Independent Cattlemen's Association of Texas (SRA)
ICA	Independent Colleges of Arkansas (SRA)
ICA	Independent Cost Analysis (AAGC)
ICA	Independent Cost Assessment (MCD)
ICA	Index of Competitive Ability (PDAA)
ICA	Indian Community Action
ICA	Indigenous Communications Association (EA)
ICA	Individual Combat Actions [*Army*]
ICA	Industrial Catering Association [*British*]
ICA	Industrial Communications Association (HGAA)
ICA	Industrial Cooperative Association (EA)
ICA	Industry and Commerce Association of South Dakota (SRA)
ICA	Initial Cruise Altitude
ICA	Inner Circle of Advocates [*Tucson, AZ*] (EA)
ICA	Institut Canadien d'Acupuncture [*Canadian Acupuncture Institute*]
ICA	Institut Canadien des Actuaires [*Canadian Institute of Actuaries*]
ICA	Institut Culturel Africain [*African Cultural Institute*] (EAIO)
ICA	Institute for Cell Analysis [*University of Miami*] [*Research center*] (RCD)
ICA	Institute of Chartered Accountants in England and Wales (BI)
ICA	Institute of Clinical Analysis
ICA	Institute of Company Accountants [*British*] (DAS)
ICA	Institute of Consumer Advisers [*British*] (DBA)
ICA	Institute of Contemporary Arts [*British*]
ICA	Institute of Cost Analysis [*Later, SCEA*] (EA)
ICA	Institute of Cultural Affairs (EA)
ICA	Instrumentation Control and Automation [*Water industry*] [*British*]
ICA	Instrument Compressed Air (AAG)
ICA	Instrument Control and Automation
ICA	Integrated Circuit Array
ICA	Integrated Communications Adapter (MCD)
ICA	Integrated Communications Architecture [*Navy*] (DOMA)
ICA	Integrated Conformal Array
ICA	Integrated Cost Accounting
ICA	Integration Change Allowance (MCD)
ICA	Intelligence Collection Area [*Military*] (NATG)
ICA	Intelligent Communications Adapter [*Computer hardware*] (PCM)
ICA	Intelligent Console Architecture (PCM)
ICA	Interapplication Communication Architecture [*Computer science*] (BTTJ)
ICA	Interbank Card Association [*Mastercard International*] (EA)
ICA	Inter City Airlines [*British*]
ICA	Intercompany Agreement (IAA)
ICA	Intercomputer Adapter
ICA	Interface Control Agreement
ICA	Intergovernmental Council for ADP [*Automatic Data Processing*]
ICA	Interlochen Center for the Arts (EA)
ICA	Intermountain College Association (AEBS)
ICA	Intermuseum Conservation Association (EA)
ICA	Internal Carotid Artery [*Anatomy*]
ICA	International Cartographic Association [*Australia*] (EA)
ICA	International Carwash Association (EA)
ICA	International Caterers Association [*Defunct*] (EA)
ICA	International Catholic Auxiliaries (EA)
ICA	International Center for Aquaculture [*Auburn University*] [*Research center*] (RCD)
ICA	International Ceramic Association (EA)
ICA	International Chefs' Association (EA)
ICA	International Chianina Association (EAIO)
ICA	International Chiropractors Association (EA)
ICA	International Claim Association [*Rock Island, IL*] (EA)
ICA	International Coffee Agreement [*Signed September, 1962*]
ICA	International College of Angiology (EA)
ICA	International Commercial Arbitration (BARN)
ICA	International Commission on Acoustics [*Aachen, Federal Republic of Germany*] (EAIO)
ICA	International Commodity Agreement
ICA	International Communication Agency [*Also, USICA*] [*Formerly called BECA and USIA, it later became known again as USIA*]
ICA	International Communication Association (EA)
ICA	International Communications Association (EA)
ICA	International Computer Association
ICA	International Confederation of Accordionists [*Vienna, Austria*] (EA)
ICA	International Conference of Administrators of Residential Centers for Youth [*Defunct*] (EA)
ICA	International Congress of Acarology
ICA	International Congress of Accountants
ICA	International Congress of Africanists [*Lagos, Nigeria*] (EAIO)
ICA	International Congress of African Studies (EAIO)
ICA	International Congress of Americanists [*Manchester, England*] (EA)
ICA	International Cooperation Administration [*Later, Agency for International Development*]
ICA	International Co-Operative Alliance [*Grand-Saconnex, Switzerland*] (EA)
ICA	International Copper Association [*British*] (IRC)
ICA	International Council on Archives [*UNESCO*] (EA)
ICA	International Credit Association [*St. Louis, MO*] (EA)
ICA	Interstate Commerce Act [*1887*]
ICA	Interstitial Cystitis Association (EA)
ICA	Intracranial Aneurysm [*Medicine*]
ICA	Invalid Care Allowance [*British*]
ICA	Inventors Clubs of America (EA)

ICA............. Investigative and Corrective Action (KSC)
ICA............. Investment Canada Act
ICA............. Investment Company Act [1940]
ICA............. Ionized Calcium Analyzer
ICA............. Iowa Cattlemen's Association (SRA)
ICA............. Iowa Code, Annotated [A publication] (DLA)
ICA............. Irish Countrywomen's Association (BI)
ICA............. Iron Caulkers' Association [A union] [British]
ICA............. Islet Cell Antibody [Immunology]
ICA............. Italian Charities of America (EA)
ICA............. Item Change Analysis (KSC)
ICA............. Item Control Area (NRCH)
ICAA........... Indian Church Aid [British] (BI)
ICAA........... Institut Canadien des Affaires Africaines [Canadian Institute of African Affairs]
ICAA........... Insulation Contractors Association of America (EA)
ICAA........... Integrated Cost Accounting Application
ICAA........... International Christian Accrediting Association (EA)
ICAA........... International Civil Airports Association [Orly, France] (EAIO)
ICAA........... International Civil Aviation Authority [Database originator] [Canada] (NITA)
ICAA........... International Committee on Arctic Arboviruses
ICAA........... International Council of Accrediting Agencies [Australia] (EAIO)
ICAA........... International Council on Alcohol and Addictions [Switzerland]
ICAA........... Invalid Children's Aid Association [London]
ICAA........... Investment Counsel Association of America (EA)
ICAAAA .... Intercollegiate Association of Amateur Athletes of America [Also, IAAAA, IC4A] (EA)
ICAAC .... Interscience Conference on Antimicrobial Agents and Chemotherapy
ICAAS .... Integrated Control and Avionics for Air Superiority (MCD)
ICAB........... International Cargo Advisory Bureau
ICAB........... International Council Against Bullfighting (EA)
ICABA .... International Campaign Against Banking on Apartheid (EAIO)
ICABF........ American Bar Foundation, Chicago, IL [Library symbol Library of Congress] (LCLS)
ICAC........... American College of Surgeons, Chicago, IL [Library symbol Library of Congress] (LCLS)
ICAC........... Independent College Assistance Center (EA)
ICAC........... Instrumentation Calibration and Checkout (IAA)
ICAC........... International Committee for Accounting Co-Operation
ICAC........... International Cotton Advisory Committee (EA)
ICACCP .... International Commission Against Concentration Camp Practices [Brussels, Belgium] [Defunct] (EAIO)
ICACGP....... International Commission on Atmospheric Chemistry and Global Pollution (USDC)
ICACGP....... International Commission on Atmospheric Chemistry Global Pollution [Marine science] (OSRA)
ICACM .... Associated Colleges of the Midwest, Periodical Bank, Chicago, IL [Library symbol Library of Congress] (LCLS)
ICACMu....... American Conservatory of Music, Chicago, IL [Library symbol Library of Congress] (LCLS)
ICAD .... Integrated Control and Display
ICAD .... Intelligent Computer-Aided Design
ICAD .... International Committee for Automobile Documentation
ICADA .... American Dental Association, Chicago, IL [Library symbol Library of Congress] (LCLS)
ICADE .... Interactive Computer-Aided Design Evaluation
ICADI .... Inter-American Center for Agricultural Documentation and Information (NITA)
ICADIS .... Instituto Centroamericano de Documentacion y Investigacion Social (EA)
ICADS .... Integrated Correlation and Display System [Air Force] (DOMA)
ICADS .... Integrated Cover and Deception Systems [Military] (MCD)
ICADTS .... International Committee on Alcohol, Drugs, and Traffic Safety [Linkoping, Sweden] (EA)
ICAE........... Integrated Communications Adapter Extended (BUR)
ICAE........... International Centre for Art Education (EAIO)
ICAE........... International Commission of Agricultural Engineering
ICAE........... International Commission on Atmospheric Electricity (EA)
ICAE........... International Conference of Agricultural Economists [Later, IAAE]
ICAE........... International Council for Adult Education [Toronto, ON] (EAIO)
ICAE........... United States Army, Corps of Engineers, Chicago, IL [Library symbol Library of Congress] (LCLS)
ICAEC......... International Confederation of Associations of Experts and Consultants [Paris, France] (EA)
ICAEO .... International Center for Athletic and Educational Opportunities (EA)
ICAEW .... Institute of Chartered Accountants in England and Wales
ICAF............ [The] Industrial College of the Armed Forces [Later, UND]
ICAF............ Industrial College of the Armed Forces (DOMA)
ICAF............ International Committee on Aeronautical Fatigue [Delft University of Technology] [Netherlands] (EAIO)
ICAF............ International Contemporary Art Fair [London, England]
ICAFFH .... International Committee for the Anthropology of Food and Food Habits [Defunct] (EA)
ICAG .... Althemer & Gray, Chicago, IL [Library symbol] [Library of Congress] (LCLS)
ICAH .... American Hospital Association, Chicago, IL [Library symbol Library of Congress] (LCLS)
ICah............ Cahokia Public Library, Cahokia, IL [Library symbol Library of Congress] (LCLS)
ICAhP......... Parks College of Saint Louis University, Cahokia, IL [Library symbol] [Library of Congress] (LCLS)
ICAhSD .... Cahokia Community Unit School District 187, Cahokia, IL [Library symbol Library of Congress] (LCLS)

ICAI............ American Institute of Baking, Chicago, IL [Library symbol Library of Congress] (LCLS)
ICAI............ Institut Canadien des Affaires Internationales [Canadian Institute of International Affairs]
ICAI............ Institute of Chartered Accountants in Ireland (EAIO)
ICAI............ Institute of Cultural Affairs International (EA)
ICAI............ Intelligent Computer-Assisted Instruction
ICAI............ International Commission for Agricultural Industries
ICAIE........... International Committee Against Involuntary Exile (EA)
ICAIF.......... International Computer-Assisted Instruction Facility (AEBS)
ICAITI........ Instituto Centroamericano de Investigacion y Tecnologia Industrial [Central American Institute of Research and Industrial Technology] [Guatemala] [Research center] (IRC)
ICAJ........... Institut Canadien d'Administration de la Justice (AC)
ICAK........... International College of Applied Kinesiology (EA)
ICaL........... Cairo Public Library, Cairo, IL [Library symbol] [Library of Congress] (LCLS)
ICAL........... Initiative on Communication Arts for Children (AIE)
ICALA......... American Library Association, Chicago, IL [Library symbol Library of Congress] (LCLS)
ICALEO .... International Congress on Applications of Lasers and Electro-Optics [Laser Institute of America]
ICALU .... International Confederation of Arab Labour Unions
ICAM........... American Medical Association, Chicago, IL [Library symbol Library of Congress] (LCLS)
ICAM........... Improved Cobra Agility and Maneuverability [Military] (MCD)
ICAM........... Institute of Corn and Agricultural Merchants Ltd. [British] (BI)
ICAM........... Integrated Communications Access Method [Computer science]
ICAM........... Integrated Computer-Aided Manufacturing (IEEE)
ICAM........... Intercellular Adhesion Molecule [Biochemistry]
ICAM........... International Confederation of Architectural Museums [Montreal, PQ] (EAIO)
ICAMAS ...... International Center for Advanced Mediterranean Agronomic Studies [FAO]
ICAMC .... International Conference on Automatic Control of Mines and Collieries
ICAME .... International Center for the Advancement of Management Education [Stanford University]
ICAME .... International Conference on the Applications of the Mossbauer Effect
ICAMI.......... International Committee Against Mental Illness (EA)
ICAMP .... Integrated Conventional Ammunition Maintenance Plan [DoD] (RDA)
ICAMQ .... International Committee of Automation of Mines and Quarries [Budapest, Hungary] (EAIO)
ICAMR .... Interagency [or Interdepartmental] Committee for Applied Meteorological Research
ICAMR .... Interdepartmental Committee for Applied Meteorological Research (USDC)
ICAMRS .... International Civil Aviation Message Routing System
ICAMS .... Industrial Central Atmosphere Monitoring System [Perkin Elmer Corp.] [Computer controlled chemical detection system] (NITA)
ICAMT......... International Centre of Ancient and Modern Tapestry
ICAN........... Individual Circuit Analysis [Telecommunications] (TEL)
ICAN........... Iniciativa Canaria [Spain Political party] (EY)
ICAN........... Integrated Circuit Analysis [Computer science]
ICAN........... Interlibrary Cooperation & Networking [Association of Specialized and Cooperative Library Agencies] [American Library Association]
ICAN........... International Cesarean Awareness Network [Formerly Cesarean Prevention Movement (CPM)] (PAZ)
ICAN........... International College of Applied Nutrition (EA)
ICAN........... International Commission for Air Navigation
ICAN........... Invalid Children's Aid Nationwide [British] (EAIO)
ICAN........... Iowa Computer-Assisted Network [Iowa State Library] [Des Moines] [Information service or system] (IID)
ICan........... Parlin-Ingersoll Public Library, Canton, IL [Library symbol Library of Congress] (LCLS)
ICA/NCC...... International Carwash Association/National Carwash Council [Later, ICA] (EA)
IC & C .... Installation Calibration and Checkout (KSC)
IC & C .... Instrumentation Calibration and Checkout (SAA)
IC & C .... Invoice Cost and Charges [Business term]
IC & CY .... Inns of Court and City Yeomanry [Military unit] [British]
IC & FCD ..... Interior Communication and Fire Control Distribution (MSA)
IC & RFS ..... Indoor Citrus and Rare Fruit Society [Defunct] (EA)
IC & RR ...... Inventory Control and Requirements Review Board [CNO]
ICanS.......... Spoon River College, Canton, IL [Library symbol Library of Congress] (LCLS)
ICAO .... American Osteopathic Association, Chicago, IL [Library symbol Library of Congress] (LCLS)
ICAO .... Internal Carotid Artery Occlusion [Medicine] (MAE)
ICAO .... International Civil Aviation Organization [Montreal, PQ] [United Nations]
ICAOPA........ International Council of Aircraft Owner and Pilot Associations (DI)
ICAP........... Improved Capability [for aircraft] (MCD)
ICAP........... Improved Cobra Armament Program [Military] (MCD)
ICAP........... Independent Cinema Artists and Producers (EA)
ICAP........... Indian Community Action Program (OICC)
ICAP........... Inductively Coupled Argon Plasma [Spectrometry]
ICAP........... Institute of Certified Ambulance Personnel [British] (BI)
ICAP........... Instituto Centroamericano de Administracion Publica [Central American Institute of Public Administration] [Costa Rica]
ICAP........... Integrated Correction Action Plan [Military] (MCD)
ICAP........... Integrated Criminal Apprehension Program
ICAP........... Inter-American Committee for the Alliance for Progress [Superseded by Permanent Executive Committee of the Inter-American Economic and Social Council]

ICAP............ Intermediate Communication Associative Processor [*Computer science*]

ICAP............ International Centre for the Application of Pesticides [*British*] (IRUK)

ICAP............ International Code of Advertising Practice (DI)

ICAP............ International College Art Program [*Red Cross Youth*]

ICAP............ International Committee of Architectural Photogrammetry

ICAP............ International Congress of Applied Psychology (PDAA)

ICAPP........... Integrated Conventional Ammunition Procurement Plan

ICAPR......... Interdepartmental Committee on Air Pollution Research [*British*]

ICAPR......... International Communications Agency Procurement Regulation [*A publication*]

ICAPS .... Integral Carrier ASW [*Antisubmarine Warfare*] Prediction System [*Marine science*] (MSC)

ICAPS .... Integrated Carrier Acoustic Prediction System [*Navy*] (NVT)

ICAPS .... Integrated Command ASW [*Antisubmarine Warfare*] Prediction System [*Navy*] (CAAL)

ICAPS .... Intelligence Civic Actions Program [*Army*] (VNW)

ICAPS .... Internal Control Audit Planning Summary (AAGC)

ICAQUO....... Inventory of Contaminants in Aquatic Organisms [*Databank*] (NITA)

ICAR .... ICAR [*Interstate Cinderellans and Revenuers*] Educational Club (EA)

ICAR .... Indian Council for Agricultural Research

ICAR .... Inner Circle of American Revenuers (EA)

ICAR .... Institute for Conflict Analysis and Resolution [*George Mason University*] [*Research center*] (RCD)

ICAR .... Integrated Command Accounting and Reporting

ICAR .... Intercargo Corp. [*NASDAQ symbol*] (NQ)

ICAR .... Interface Control Action Request (NRCH)

I-CAR .... Inter-Industry Conference on Auto Collision Repair (EA)

ICAR .... International Cannabis Alliance Reform (DI)

ICAR .... Inventory of Canadian Agri-Food Research [*Canandian Agricultural Research Council*] [*Information service or system*]

ICAR .... Investigation and Corrective Action Report (KSC)

ICARA .... International Child Abduction Remedies Act [*1988*]

ICARA .... International Conference on Assistance for Refugees in Africa [*See also CIARA*] [*United Nations Geneva, Switzerland*] (EAIO)

IC Arb Q ...... Indian Council of Arbitration. Quarterly [*A publication*] (DLA)

ICarbS .... Southern Illinois University, Carbondale, IL [*Library symbol Library of Congress*] (LCLS)

ICARDA....... International Center for Agricultural Research in Dry Areas [*Syria*]

ICARDS....... Integrated Carrier [*or Command*] ASW Prediction System

ICARE .... International Christian Aid Relief Enterprises [*Australia*]

ICARES .... Institut International Catholique de Recherches Socio-Ecclesiales [*International Catholic Institute for Socio-Religious Research*] [*Later, FERES*]

ICarl............. Carlinville Public Library, Carlinville, IL [*Library symbol Library of Congress*] (LCLS)

ICarlB .... Blackburn College, Carlinville, IL [*Library symbol Library of Congress*] (LCLS)

ICarlMCD..... Macoupin Community District 1, Carlinville, IL [*Library symbol Library of Congress*] (LCLS)

ICarly.......... Case-Halstead Library, Carlyle, IL [*Library symbol Library of Congress*] (LCLS)

ICarlyS........ Carlyle School, Carlyle, IL [*Library symbol Library of Congress*] (LCLS)

ICARMO....... International Council of the Architects of Historical Monuments

ICArmour ..... Armour & Co., Chicago, IL [*Library symbol Library of Congress Obsolete*] (LCLS)

ICarr .... Carrollton Public Library, Carrollton, IL [*Library symbol Library of Congress*] (LCLS)

ICarrCD........ Carrollton Community Unit, District 1, Carrollton, IL [*Library symbol Library of Congress*] (LCLS)

ICarSD .... Charleston Community Unit School District, Charleston, IL [*Library symbol*] [*Library of Congress*] (LCLS)

ICart............ Carthage Public Library, Carthage, IL [*Library symbol Library of Congress*] (LCLS)

ICARUS........ Index of Conservation and Analytical Records: Unified System [*Computer science*]

ICARUS........ Inter-Continental Aerospacecraft-Range Unlimited System

ICARVS .... Interplanetary Craft for Advanced Research in Vicinity of Sun

ICAS........... Acme Steel Co., Chicago, IL [*Library symbol Library of Congress*] (LCLS)

ICas .... Casey Township Library, Casey, IL [*Library symbol Library of Congress*] (LCLS)

ICAS........... Improved Cobra Armament System [*Military*] (MCD)

ICAS........... Independent Collision Avoidance System

ICAS........... Instant Computer Arbitration Search [*Database*] [*Labor Relations Press*] [*Information service or system*] (CRD)

ICAS........... Institute of Chartered Accountants of Scotland (AIE)

ICAS........... Institute of Combined Arms and Support [*Fort Leavenworth, KS*] [*Army*]

ICAS........... Institute of Contemporary Asian Studies [*Monash University*] [*Australia*]

ICAS........... Intel Communications Amplifications Specification [*Interface*]

ICAS........... Interdepartmental Committee for Atmospheric Sciences [*Terminated, 1976*]

ICAS........... Interdepartment Council on Radio Propagation and Standards (NTCM)

ICAS........... Interface Control Action Sheet (DNAB)

ICAS........... Intermittent Commercial and Amateur Service [*Radio*]

ICAS........... International Council of Air Shows (EA)

ICAS........... International Council of Associations of Surfing (EA)

ICAS........... International Council of the Aeronautical Sciences

ICAS........... Isolated Children's Assistance Scheme

ICA-S .... School of the Art Institute of Chicago, Chicago, IL [*Library symbol Library of Congress*] (LCLS)

ICASALS ...... International Center for Arid and Semi-Arid Land Studies [*Texas Technological University*]

ICASC .... Acme Steel Co., Chicago, IL [*Library symbol*] [*Library of Congress*] (LCLS)

ICASC .... International Contraception, Abortion, and Sterilization Campaign [*Later, WGNRR*] (EAIO)

ICASE........... Injection-Coupled Acoustic Stability Evaluation (MCD)

ICASE........... Institute for Computer Applications in Science and Engineering [*Universities Space Research Association*] [*Research center*] (RCD)

I-CASE......... Integrated Computer-Aided Software Engineering

ICASE........... International Council of Associations for Science Education [*See also FIAPS*] (EAIO)

ICASIS .... International Conference of African States on Insurance Supervision [*See also CICA*] [*Gabon*] (EAIO)

ICASO .... International Committee of Acquired Immunodeficiency Syndrome Service Organisations (DMAA)

ICasSD .... Casey Community Unit School District, Casey, IL [*Library symbol*] [*Library of Congress*] (LCLS)

ICASSP .... International Conference on Acoustics, Speech, and Signal Processing (MCD)

ICasv .... Caseyville Public Library, Caseyville, IL [*Library symbol Library of Congress*] (LCLS)

ICat............. Catlin Public Library, Catlin, IL [*Library symbol Library of Congress*] (LCLS)

ICAT........... In Commission, Active [*Vessel status*] [*Navy*] (DNAB)

I-CAT.......... Intelligent Computer-Aided Troubleshooting

ICAT........... International Committee for the Coordination of Clinical Application and Teaching of Autogenic Therapy [*North Vancouver, BC*] (EAIO)

ICATL.......... International Council of Associations of Theological Libraries (EA)

ICATS.......... Intermediate Capacity Automated Telecommunications System [*Air Force*] (CET)

ICATU.......... International Confederation of Arab Trade Unions

ICATVT........ International Centre for Advanced Technical and Vocational Training [*British*]

ICAV........... American Veterinary Medical Association, Chicago, IL [*Library symbol Library of Congress*] (LCLS)

ICAV........... Intracavity [*or Intracavitary*] [*Medicine*]

ICAVE.......... International Coalition Against Violent Entertainment (EA)

ICAVS .... United States Army, Medical Department, Veterinary School, Chicago, IL [*Library symbol Library of Congress*] (LCLS)

ICAWA .... Indo-Chinese Australian Women's Association [*Australia*]

ICB............ Barat College of the Sacred Heart, Lake Forest, IL [*OCLC symbol*] (OCLC)

ICB............ Icebird Airline Ltd. [*Iceland*] [*ICAO designator*] (FAAC)

ICB............ Image Capture Board [*Video monitor*] [*AT & T*] (BYTE)

ICB............ Incoming Call Barred [*Telecommunications*] (TEL)

ICB............ Individual Case Basis (TEL)

ICB............ Industrial and Commercial Bank [*China*]

ICB............ Inertia Compensated Balance

ICB............ Information Collection Budget [*Office of Management and Budget*] (GFGA)

ICB............ Inner-Core Boundary [*Geology*]

ICB............ Institute of Collective Bargaining and Group Relations (EA)

ICB............ Institute of Comparative Biology (BARN)

ICB............ Integrated Circuit Breadboard [*Electronics*] (IAA)

ICB............ Integration Change Board [*NASA*]

ICB............ InterCapital Income Securities, Inc. [*NYSE symbol*] (SPSG)

ICB............ InterCapital Inc. Sec [*NYSE symbol*] (TTSB)

ICB............ Interface Control Board (NRCH)

ICB............ Interim Change Bulletin (NASA)

ICB............ Interior Control Board

ICB............ Internal Common Bus [*Computer science*]

ICB............ International Christian Broadcasters [*Defunct*] (EA)

ICB............ International Competitive Bid (NATG)

ICB............ International Computer Bibliography [*A publication of National Computing Center*]

ICB............ International Container Bureau [*Paris*]

ICB............ International Co-operative Bulletin [*A publication*]

ICB............ Interrupt Control Block (NASA)

ICB............ Ivory Coast Basin [*Geology*]

ICBA........... International Community of Booksellers' Associations [*Later, IBF*]

ICBAH .... Booz, Allen & Hamilton, Inc., Chicago, IL [*Library symbol Library of Congress*] (LCLS)

ICBAM .... Interpersonal Communication Behavior Analysis Method (PDAA)

ICBB........... Ind Coope Burton Brewery [*British*]

ICBB........... International Commission for Bee Botany [*Later, ICPBR*] (EA)

ICBBA .... International Cornish Bantam Breeders' Association (EA)

ICBC........... Blue Cross Association, Chicago, IL [*Library symbol Library of Congress*] (LCLS)

ICBC........... Inclined Cleated Belt Conveyor

ICBC........... Institute of Certified Business Counselors (EA)

ICBC........... Interagency Committee on Back Contamination [*Aerospace*]

ICBC........... International Center for Biological Control [*University of California, Berkeley and Riverside*]

ICBC........... International Commercial Bank of China [*Taiwan*]

ICBCG......... Boston Consulting Group, Chicago, IL [*Library symbol Library of Congress*] (LCLS)

ICBCL......... Brook College, Chicago, IL [*Library symbol*] [*Library of Congress*] (LCLS)

ICBD .... International Children's Book Day [*Australia*]

ICBD .... International Council of Ballroom Dancing [*British*] (EAIO)

ICBD .... Ionized Cluster Beam Deposition [*Coating technology*]

ICBF............ Beatrice Foods Co., Chicago, IL [*Library symbol Library of Congress*] (LCLS)
ICBF............ Inner Cortical Blood Flow [*Medicine*] (DMAA)
ICBG............ Idiopathic Calcification of Basal Ganglia [*Medicine*] (DMAA)
ICBIF........... Inner City Business Improvement Forum
ICBK............ Intercontinental Bank [*NASDAQ symbol*] (SAG)
ICBK............ International Centrum voor Beurzen en Kongressen [*Belgium*] (EAIO)
ICBLB........... International Committee for Breaking the Language Barrier
ICBM............ Bank Marketing Association, Chicago, IL [*Library symbol Library of Congress*] (LCLS)
ICBM............ Intercontinental Ballistic Missile
ICBMS........... Intercontinental Ballistic Missile System
ICBMTMS .... Intercontinental Ballistic Missile Test Maintenance Squadron
ICBN............ International Code of Botanical Nomenclature
ICBN............ International Commission on the Biological Effects of Noise (GNE)
ICBo............ Bozzel & Jacobs Corp., Information Center, Chicago, IL [*Library symbol*] [*Library of Congress*] (LCLS)
ICBO .... International Conference of Building Officials (EA)
ICBO .... Interracial Council for Business Opportunity [*New York, NY*] (EA)
ICBOSS........ Interactive Computer-Based Office Support System [*Military*] (MCD)
ICBP............ International Council for Bird Preservation [*Cambridge, England*] (EAIO)
ICBP............ International Council for Bird Preservation (GNE)
ICBP............ Intracellular-Binding Proteins [*Medicine*]
ICBPA.......... Insurance Company and Bank Purchasing Agents Association
ICBP(AS)...... International Council for Bird Protection (Australian Section)
IC-BPH........ Illinois Regional Library for the Blind and Physically Handicapped, Chicago Public Library, Chicago, IL [*Library symbol Library of Congress*] (LCLS)
ICBR .... Ice-Cuber
ICBR .... Increased Chromosomal Breakage Rate [*Medicine*] (DMAA)
ICBR .... Input Channel Buffer Register [*Computer science*] (IAA)
ICBR .... Institute for Child Behavior Research (IID)
ICBRSD........ International Council for Building Research, Studies, and Documentation (DIT)
ICBS............ Impulsive Classroom Behavior Scale (EDAC)
ICBS............ Incorporated Church Building Society [*British*]
ICBS............ Interconnected Business System
ICBS............ International Cigar Band Society [*Defunct*] (EA)
ICBS............ National Association of Blue Shield Plans [*Later, BSA*], Chicago, IL [*Library symbol Library of Congress*] (LCLS)
ICBT............ Intercontinental Ballistic Transport
ICBT............ Intercostobronchial Trunk [*Medicine*] (DAVI)
ICBWR .... Improved-Cycle Boiling-Water Reactor [*Nuclear energy*]
ICC............. Article 19 - International Centre on Censorship (EAIO)
ICC............. Association Internationale de Chimie Cerealiere [*International Association for Cereal Chemistry*] [*Also, AICC*]
ICc .... Calumet City Public Library, Calumet City, IL [*Library symbol Library of Congress*] (LCLS)
ICC............. Calumet College, Whiting, IN [*OCLC symbol*] (OCLC)
ICC............. Cook County Clerk's Office, Chicago, IL [*Library symbol*] [*Library of Congress*] (LCLS)
ICC............. Ice Crystal Cloud
ICC............. Illinois Cancer Council Comprehensive Cancer Center [*Research center*] (RCD)
ICC............. Image Converter Camera
ICC............. Immunocompetent Cell [*Medicine*] (MAE)
ICC............. Immunocytochemistry [*Immunology*]
ICC............. Imperial Camel Corps [*British military*] (DMA)
ICC............. Imperial Communications [*World War II*]
ICC............. Inadequate Core Cooling [*Nuclear energy*] (NRCH)
ICC............. Income Capital Certificate
ICC............. Independent Community Consultants (EA)
ICC............. Index of Cranial Capacity [*Cladistics*]
ICC............. Indian Childhood Cirrhosis [*Medicine*] (MAE)
ICC............. Indian Claims Commission [*Terminated, 1976*]
ICC............. Indian Cultural Center [*Defunct*] (EA)
ICC............. Individual Concealment Cover
ICC............. Industrial and Commercial Company
ICC............. Industrial Capacity Committee of the Production Council [*British World War II*]
ICC............. Industrial Communication Council
ICC............. Industrial Control Center (NITA)
ICC............. Inferior Colliculus [*Also, IC*] [*Brain anatomy*]
ICC............. Infinity Color-Corrected System [*Optics*]
ICC............. Information and Coordination Central
ICC............. Information Center Complex [*ORNL*] (GRD)
ICC............. Information Control Center [*Military*] (IAA)
ICC............. Information Control Console (DNAB)
ICC............. Information Coordination Control [*Computer*] (MCD)
ICC............. Initial Communications Connectivity [*DoD*]
ICC............. Initial Contingency Capability (MCD)
ICC............. Injury Control Center [*An association*] (EA)
ICC............. Installation Calibration and Checkout (KSC)
ICC............. Institut Canadien de Conservation [*Canadian Conservation Institute - CCI*]
ICC............. Institute Circumpolaire Canadien [*Canadian Circumpolar Institute, University of Alberta*] (IRC)
ICC............. Institute of Chinese Culture (EA)
ICC............. [*Myasnikov*] Institute of Clinical Cardiology [*Russian*]
ICC............. Instituto Cartografico de Cataluna [*Spain ICAO designator*] (FAAC)
ICC............. Instrumentation Checkout Complex (MCD)
ICC............. Instrumentation Control Center (AAG)
ICC............. Instrument Control Center (KSC)
ICC............. Instrument Control Computer

ICC............. Integrated Chip Circuit
ICC............. Integrated Cluster Controller
ICC............. Integrated Communications Center (MCD)
ICC............. Integrated Communications Control (MCD)
ICC............. Intelligent Cruise Control [*Automotive engineering*]
ICC............. Intensive Care Certificate [*Medicine*]
ICC............. Intensive Coronary Care [*Medicine*]
ICC............. Inter-American Cultural Council
ICC............. Interchangeable Cycle Check (MCD)
ICC............. Interchannel Communicator (MCD)
ICC............. Inter-Company Correspondence
ICC............. Intercomputer Channel (NASA)
ICC............. Intercomputer Communication (MCD)
ICC............. Intercomputer Coupler (IAA)
ICC............. Interface Control Chart (NASA)
ICC............. Interior Communications Electrician, Chief [*Navy rating*]
ICC............. Intermediate Cryptanalysis Course [*Military*] (DNAB)
ICC............. Internal Conversion Coefficient [*Radiology*]
ICC............. International Association for Cereal Science and Technology [*Formerly, International Association of Cereal Chemists*] [*Acronym represents association's former name*] [*Austria*]
ICC............. International Cablecasting Technologies [*Vancouver Stock Exchange symbol*]
ICC............. International Camaro Club (EA)
ICC............. International Cello Centre [*Duns, Scotland*] (EAIO)
ICC............. International Chamber of Commerce [*See also CCI*] [*Paris, France*] (EAIO)
ICC............. International Chessology Club (EA)
ICC............. International Children's Centre [*Paris, France*]
ICC............. International Clergy Council (EA)
ICC............. International College in Copenhagen [*Denmark*]
ICC............. International College of Chiropractors (EA)
ICC............. International Color Consortium
ICC............. International Committee of ICOM [*International Council of Museums*] for Conservation [*Later, ICOM-CC*] (EAIO)
ICC............. International Communications Corp. [*Miami, FL*] (CSR)
ICC............. International Computaprint Corp. [*Fort Washington, PA*]
ICC............. International Computation Center [*Sponsored by UNESCO*] [*Rome, Italy*]
ICC............. International Computer Casting [*Information service or system*] (IID)
ICC............. International Computer Center (HGAA)
ICC............. International Computing Centre [*United Nations*] (ECON)
ICC............. International Conference on Communications [*IEEE*]
ICC............. International Congregational Council
ICC............. International Control Centre [*Telecommunications*] (NITA)
ICC............. International Control Commission [*Representatives of Canada, India, and Poland charged with supervising thecease-fire in Laos established at Geneva Conference of 1962*]
ICC............. International Controls Corp.
ICC............. International Convention Center [*British*] (ECON)
ICC............. International Cooperation Council [*Later, UDC*]
ICC............. International Coordinating Committee for the Presentation of Science and the Development of Out-of-School Scientific Activities [*See also CIC*] (EAIO)
ICC............. International Corrosion Council [*Orsay, France*] (EAIO)
ICC............. International Counseling Center (EA)
ICC............. International Cricket Conference (EA)
ICC............. [*The*] International Critical Commentary on the Holy Scriptures of the Old and New Testament [*Edinburgh*] [*A publication*] (BJA)
ICC............. Internet Content Coalition [*Computer science*]
ICC............. Interprocessor Communication and Control Routine (MCD)
ICC............. Interstate Carriers Conference (EA)
ICC............. Interstate Commerce Commission [*Independent government agency*]
ICC............. Interventional Cardiac Catheterization [*Medicine*]
ICC............. Intra-Class Correlation Coefficient
ICC............. Intracompany Correspondence (AAG)
ICC............. Inuit Circumpolar Conference [*Godthaab, Greenland, Denmark*] (EAIO)
ICC............. Invasive Cancer of the Cervix [*Oncology*]
ICC............. Inventory Control Center [*of Field Army Support Command*]
ICC............. Inventory Control Company
ICC............. Invitational Computer Conference
ICC............. Irish Council of Churches
ICC............. Issue Category Code (NITA)
ICC............. Italian Chamber of Commerce (EA)
ICC............. Italian Culture Council (EA)
ICC............. Item Category Code
ICC............. Item Characteristic Curve [*Statistics*]
ICCA........... Independent Computer Consultants Association (EA)
ICCA........... Infants' and Children's Coat Association [*Later, ICGSCA*] (EA)
ICCA........... Initial Cash Clothing Allowance [*Military*]
ICCA........... Institut Canadien de la Construction en Acier [*Canadian Institute of Steel Construction*]
ICCA........... Institut Canadien des Comptables Agrees [*Canadian Institute of Chartered Accountants*]
ICCA........... Interagency Coordinating Committee for Astronomy [*Federal Council for Science and Technology*] [*Terminated, 1976*]
ICCA........... InterAmericas Communications Corp. [*NASDAQ symbol*] (SAG)
ICCA........... International Commission on Commercial Activities (EAIO)
ICCA........... International Computer Chess Association
ICCA........... International Conference on Computer Applications [*in developing countries*] [*1977*]
ICCA........... International Congress and Convention Association [*Amsterdam, Netherlands*] (EA)
ICCA........... International Consumer Credit Association [*Later, ICA*] (EA)

ICCA............ International Conventions and Congresses Association [*Australia*]
ICCA............ International Correspondence of Corkscrew Addicts (EA)
ICCA............ International Corrugated Case Association [*Paris, France*] (EAIO)
ICCA............ International Council for Commercial Arbitration [*Vienna, Austria*] (EAIO)
ICCA............ International Council of Chemical Associations
ICCaC......... Carnow, Coninleas & Associates, Ltd., Chicago, IL [*Library symbol*] [*Library of Congress*] (LCLS)
ICCAC......... Interagency Clean Car Advisory Committee [*HEW Terminated*] (EGAO)
ICCAD......... International Center for Computer-Aided Design (MHDB)
ICCAD......... International Centre for Computer Aided Design (PDAA)
ICCAIA....... International Coordinating Council of Aerospace Industries Associations (EA)
ICCAM....... International Committee of Children's and Adolescents' Movements
ICCAP....... International Coordination Committee for the Accounting Profession
ICCARD....... International Commission for Central American Recovery and Development
ICCAS......... Chicago Academy of Sciences, Matthew Laflin Memorial Library, Chicago, IL [*Library symbol Library of Congress*] (LCLS)
ICCAS......... International Center for Communication Arts and Sciences
ICCAT.......... International Commission for the Conservation of Atlantic Tunas [*Spain*]
ICCATCI....... International Committee to Coordinate Activities of Technical Groups in CoatingsIndustry [*Paris, France*] (EAIO)
ICCB.......... Insulated Case Circuit Breaker (DWSG)
ICCB.......... Integrated Change Control Board [*NASA*] (NASA)
ICCB.......... Intermediate Change Control Board
ICCB.......... Intermediate Configuration Control Board [*Western Electric*] (AABC)
ICCB.......... International Catholic Child Bureau [*Geneva, Switzerland*]
ICCB.......... International Center for Cooperation in BioInformatics [*UNESCO*]
ICCB.......... Internet Control and Configuration Board [*Computer science*] (ACRL)
IC-CBPH...... Chicago Library Services for the Blind and Physically Handicapped (Subregional),Chicago Public Library, Chicago, IL [*Library symbol Library of Congress*] (LCLS)
ICCC.......... Columbia College, Chicago, IL [*Library symbol Library of Congress*] (LCLS)
ICCC.......... Ice Cream Connoisseurs Club [*Defunct*] (EA)
ICCC.......... ImmuCell Corp. [*NASDAQ symbol*] (NQ)
ICCC.......... Imperial College Computing Center (PDAA)
ICCC.......... Information Center on Children's Cultures [*Defunct*] (EA)
ICCC.......... International Center for Comparative Criminology (EA)
ICCC.......... International Color Computer Club (EA)
ICCC.......... International Concentration Camp Committee [*Vienna, Austria*] (EAIO)
ICCC.......... International Concerns Committee for Children (EA)
ICCC.......... International Conference of Catholic Charities
ICCC.......... International Conference of Coordination Chemistry
ICCC.......... International Conference on Circuits and Computers (MCD)
ICCC.......... International Council for Computer Communication (EA)
ICCC.......... International Council of Christian Churches (EA)
ICCC.......... International Council of Community Churches (EA)
ICCCA......... International C Class Catamaran Association of America (EA)
ICCCS......... Integrated Continuous Controlled Color System (DGA)
ICCD.......... Improved Computer-Controlled Dwell [*Automotive engineering*]
ICCD.......... Information Center on Crime and Delinquency [*National Council on Crime and Delinquency*] (IID)
ICCD.......... Institute of Chocolate and Confectionery Distributors [*British*] (BI)
ICCD.......... Intensified Charge-Coupled Device [*Electronics*]
ICCD.......... Intergovernmental Commission for Chagas Disease (ECON)
ICCD.......... Internal Coordination Control Drawing
ICCDP......... Integrated Circuit Communications Data Processor (MHDI)
ICCE.......... Iceland Communications and Control Enhancement
ICCE.......... International Congress on Combustion Engines
ICCE.......... International Council for Computers in Education (EA)
ICCE.......... International Council for Correspondence Education [*Later, ICDE*]
ICCE.......... International Council of Commerce Employers
ICCE.......... Intracapsular Cataract Extraction [*Ophthalmology*]
ICCEA.......... International Committee for the Study and Conservation of Earthen Architecture (EAIO)
ICCEC.......... India Chemists and Chemical Engineers Club (EA)
ICCEcPI........ Intracapsular Cataract Extraction with Peripheral Iridectomy [*Ophthalmology*]
ICCERSP...... Interagency Coordinating Committee for Earth Resource Survey Programs [*National Aeronautics and Space Council*]
ICCET.......... Imperial College of Science and Technology Centre for Environmental Technology [*British*] (IRUK)
ICCF.......... Interaction Computing and Control Facility (NITA)
ICCF.......... Interactive Computing and Control Facility [*IBM Corp. program product*]
ICCF.......... Interexchange Carrier and Carrier Forum [*Exchange Carriers Standards Association*] [*Telecommunications*]
ICCF.......... International Correspondence Chess Federation
ICCFM.......... International Confederation of Christian Family Movements (EAIO)
ICCFS.......... Imperial College of Science and Technology Centre for Fusion Studies [*British*] (IRUK)
ICCFTI.......... International Center for Companies of the Food Trade and Industry (EA)
ICCG .... Intercommunication-Communication Control Group [*Navy*] (NVT)
ICCG .... International Catholic Conference of Guiding (EAIO)
ICCG .... International Conference on Crystal Growth (PDAA)
ICCGB .... Indian Chamber of Commerce in Great Britain (DS)
ICCGB .... Italian Chamber of Commerce in Great Britain (DS)
ICCGR .... Intergranular Cyclic Crack Growth Rate [*Nuclear energy*] (NUCP)

ICCH .... Cook County Hospital, Dr. Frederick Tice Memorial Library, Chicago, IL [*Library symbol Library of Congress*] (LCLS)
ICch .... Country Club Hills Public Library District, Country Club Hills, IL [*Library symbol Library of Congress*] (LCLS)
ICCH .... International Catholic Confederation of Hospitals [*Later, IHF*] (EA)
ICCH .... International Commodities Clearing House [*British Business term*]
ICCH .... International Conference on Computers and the Humanities
ICCChC......... Chapman & Cutter, Law Library, Chicago, IL [*Library symbol*] [*Library of Congress*] (LCLS)
ICChH .... Children's Memorial Hospital, Joseph Brennemann Medical Library, Chicago, IL [*Library symbol Library of Congress*] (LCLS)
ICchP .... Country Club Hills Public Library District, Country Club Hills, IL [*Library symbol*] [*Library of Congress*] (LCLS)
ICCHRLA...... Inter-Church Committee on Human Rights in Latin America [*Canada*] (EAIO)
ICCHS .... Intercampus Committee for Handicapped Students (EA)
ICCIA .... Italian Chamber of Commerce and Industry in Australia
ICCICA .... Interim Co-ordinating Committee for International Commodity Arrangements
ICCICE .... Islamic Chamber of Commerce, Industry and Commodity Exchange [*See also CICIEM*] [*Karachi, Pakistan*] (EAIO)
ICCILMB ...... Interim Committee for Coordination of Investigations of the Lower Mekong Basin (EA)
ICCIR .... International Coordination Committee for Immunology of Reproduction [*Bulg aria*] [*Research center*] (IRC)
ICCJ .... International Committee for the Cooperation of Journalists (NATG)
ICCJ .... International Council of Christians and Jews [*Heppenheim, Federal Republic of Germany*] (EAIO)
ICCK.......... Chadwell, Kayser, Ruggles, McGee & Hasting, Chicago, IL [*Library symbol Library of Congress*] (LCLS)
ICCL.......... Cook County Law Library, Chicago, IL [*Library symbol Library of Congress*] (LCLS)
ICCL.......... Interface Control Configuration List
ICCL.......... International Committee for the Centennial of Light
ICCL.......... Irish Council for Civil Liberties (EAIO)
ICCLA.......... International Center for Coordination of Legal Assistance [*Switzerland*] (PDAA)
ICCLY.......... International Council to Combat Lethal Yellowing
ICCM.......... Idiopathic Congestive Cardiomyopathy [*Medicine*]
ICCM.......... Inadequate Core Cooling Monitor [*Nuclear energy*] (NUCP)
ICCM.......... Institute of Critical Care Medicine [*University of Southern California*] [*Research center*] (RCD)
ICCM.......... Intercontinental Cruise Missile (IAA)
ICCM.......... International Christian Classic Motorcyclists (EA)
ICCM.......... International Committee for the Conservation of Mosaics [*Hungerford, Berkshire, England*] (EAIO)
ICCM.......... International Council of Catholic Men [*See also FIHC*] [*Vatican City, Vatican City State*] (EAIO)
ICCM.......... Interstitial Cell-Conditioned Medium [*Clinical chemistry*]
ICCM.......... Master Chief Interior Communications Electrician [*Navy rating*]
ICCM.......... University of Health Sciences - Chicago Medical School, Chicago, IL [*Library symbol Library of Congress*] (LCLS)
ICCMB.......... International Committee for the Conservation of Mud-Brick (EAIO)
ICCMG.......... Clausen, Miller, Gorman, Caffrey & Witous, Chicago, IL [*Library symbol Library of Congress*] (LCLS)
ICCMHC....... Idiana Council of Community Mental Health Centers (SRA)
ICCN.......... Cook County School of Nursing, Chicago, IL [*Library symbol Library of Congress*] (LCLS)
ICCN.......... International Committee of Catholic Nurses [*See also CICIAMS*] [*Vatican City, Vatican City State*] (EAIO)
ICCNA.......... CNA Financial Corp., Chicago, IL [*Library symbol Library of Congress*] (LCLS)
ICCNA.......... International Center for Control of Nutritional Anemia [*University of Kansas*] [*Research center*] (RCD)
ICCO .... Chicago College of Osteopathic Medicine, Chicago, IL [*Library symbol Library of Congress*] (LCLS)
ICCO .... International Carpet Classification Organization [*Brussels, Belgium*] (EAIO)
ICCO .... International Cocoa Organization [*London, England*] (EAIO)
ICCO .... International Council of Containership Operators [*British*] (DCTA)
ICC of H & HH... International Club for Collectors of Hatpins and Hatpin Holders (EA)
ICComE........ Commonwealth Edison Co., Chicago, IL [*Library symbol Library of Congress*] (LCLS)
ICCon.......... Continental Group Co., Inc., Chicago, IL [*Library symbol Library of Congress*] (LCLS)
ICConB.......... Continental Illinois National Bank and Trust Co., Research and Information Services, Chicago, IL [*Library symbol*] [*Library of Congress*] (LCLS)
ICcP .... Calument City Public Library, Calumet City, IL [*Library symbol*] [*Library of Congress*] (LCLS)
ICCP.......... Impressed Current Corrosion Protection
ICCP.......... Information, Computer and Communications Policy (MHDI)
ICCP.......... Institute for Certification of Computer Professionals (EA)
ICCP.......... Integrated Communication Control Panel (MCD)
ICCP.......... Intelligence Civilian Career Program [*Army*] (AABC)
ICCP.......... Interface Coordination and Control Procedure (NASA)
ICCP.......... International Camp Counselor Program (EA)
ICCP.......... International Committee for Coal Petrology [*Liege, Belgium*] (EAIO)
ICCP.......... International Conference on Cataloging Principles
ICCP.......... International Council for Children's Play [*Groningen, Netherlands*] (EAIO)
ICCPBS .... International Chemical Congress of Pacific Basin Societies (EA)
ICCPC .... International Computing Center's Preparatory Committee
ICCR .... Interactive Cash and Credit Register [*Datacap Systems, Inc.*]

ICCR .... Interfaith Center on Corporate Responsibility (EA)
ICCR .... International Committee for Coal Research [*Brussels, Belgium*] (EAIO)
ICCR .... International Committee for Contraceptive Research
ICCR .... Interstate Commerce Commission Reports [*A publication*] (DLA)
ICCra .... Crane Co., Chicago, IL [*Library symbol Library of Congress*] (LCLS)
ICC Rep ...... Interstate Commerce Commission Reports [*A publication*] (DLA)
ICCROM .... International Centre for the Study of the Preservation and the Restoration of Cultural Property [*Rome, Italy*] (EAIO)
ICCS .... Integrated Carrier Catapult Station (MCD)
ICCS .... Integrated Carrier Catapult System (DNAB)
ICCS .... Integrated Catapult Control Station (MCD)
ICCS .... Integrated Chassis Control System [*Automotive*]
ICCS .... Integrated Communications Collection System [*Military*] (MCD)
ICCS .... Intercomputer Communication System
ICCS .... Interdisciplinary Center for Creative Studies [*State University College at Buffalo*] [*Research center*] (RCD)
ICCS .... Interface Configuration Control System (DNAB)
ICCS .... Interim Command and Control System (MCD)
ICCS .... International Center for Criminological Studies (BARN)
ICCS .... International Centre for Chemical Studies [*See also CIEC*] (EAIO)
ICCS .... International Classification of Clinical Services (HCT)
ICCS .... International Commission of Control and Supervision [*Composed of representatives of Canada, Hungary, Indonesia, and Poland, and charged with supervising the ceasefire in Vietnam, 1973*]
ICCS .... International Commission on Civil Status [*See also CIEC*] [*Strasbourg, France*] (EAIO)
ICCS .... International Committee of Creole Studies [*Aix-En-Provence, France*] (EAIO)
ICCS .... International Committee on Clinical Sociology [*See also CISC*] [*Later, International Group on Clinical Sociology*] (EAIO)
ICCS .... International Conference on Composite Structures [*Paisley, Scotland*] (EAIO)
ICCS .... International Convention on the Continental Shelf (NOAA)
ICCS .... International Cork Cutters' Society [*A union*]
ICCS .... International Council for Canadian Studies [*See also CIEC*]
ICCS .... International Group on Clinical Sociology [*Formerly, International Committee on Clinical Sociology*] (EA)
ICCS .... Senior Chief Interior Communications Electrician [*Navy rating*]
ICCSASW ..... International Commission for the Co-ordination of Solidarity among Sugar Workers [*Canada*]
ICCSHE .... Interagency Committee for Computer Support of Handicapped Employees [*General Services Administration*] (EGAO)
ICCSP .... Chicago School of Professional Psychology, Chicago, IL [*Library symbol Library of Congress*] (LCLS)
ICCSR .... Interagency Committee on Climate Services and Research
ICCSSSAR.... International Coordinating Committee on Solid State Sensors and Actuators Research (EA)
ICCSTR .... International Coordinating Committee on Solid State Transducers Research (EA)
ICCT .... Consoer, Townsend & Associates, Chicago, IL [*Library symbol Library of Congress*] (LCLS)
ICCT .... Initial Contact Control Time [*Aerospace*] (AAG)
ICCT .... Iowa Community College Telenetwork [*Marshalltown*] (TSSD)
ICCTA .... International Consultative Council of Travel Agents
ICC Tch .... ICC Technologies, Inc. [*Associated Press*] (SAG)
ICC-TM .... Interstate Commerce Commission Transport Mobilization [*Federal emergency order*]
ICCTR .... Intelligence Case Control and Time Reporting System [*IRS*]
ICCU .... Intensive Coronary Care Unit [*of a hospital*]
ICCU .... Inter-Channel Comparison Unit [*Nuclear energy*] (NRCH)
ICCU .... Intercomputer Communication Unit (IAA)
ICCU .... Intercomputer Compatibility Unit [*Computer science*]
ICCU .... Intermediate Coronary Care Unit [*Medicine*]
ICCU .... International Cross-Country Union (EA)
ICCUS .... International Claims Commission of the United States [*Abolished, 1954*] [*Department of State*]
ICCUSA .... Interagency Coordinating Committee on US-Soviet Affairs [*Department of State*]
ICCUSA .... International Child Care (USA) (EA)
ICC Valuation Rep... Interstate Commerce Commission Valuation Reports [*A publication*] (DLA)
ICCVAM .... Interagency Coordinating Committee on the Validation of Alternative Methods [*To amend for biological testing*]
ICCW .... In-Containment Chilled Water [*Nuclear energy*] (NRCH)
ICCY .... International Cultural Centers for Youth (EA)
ICCYM .... Central YMCA Community College, Chicago, IL [*Library symbol Library of Congress*] (LCLS)
ICD .... College of Saint Francis, Joliet, IL [*OCLC symbol*] (OCLC)
ICD .... De Paul University, Chicago, IL [*Library symbol Library of Congress*] (LCLS)
ICD .... Idiopathic Cerebral Dysfunction [*Medicine*] (CPH)
ICD .... Iesu Christo Duce [*With Jesus Christ as Leader*] [*Latin*]
ICD .... Imitative Communication Deception [*Military*]
ICD .... Immune Complex Disease
ICD .... Implantable Cardioverter-Defibrillator [*Medical device for heart patients*]
ICD .... Induced Circular Dichroism [*Physics*]
ICD .... Industrial Cooperation Division [*Navy*]
ICD .... Informal Clearance Document [*Customs*]
ICD .... Initial Case Design (MCD)
ICD .... Initiative Communications Deception (PDAA)
ICD .... Inland Clearance Depot [*Shipping*]
ICD .... Installation Completion Date (CET)
ICD .... Installation Control Drawing [*DoD*]
ICD .... Instantaneous Cardiac Death [*Cardiology*] (DAVI)
ICD .... Institute for Crippled and Disabled (DAVI)
ICD .... Institute of Civil Defence [*British*] (EAIO)
ICD .... Institute of Community Development [*British*] (DBA)
ICD .... Institute of Cooperative Directors (ODBW)
ICD .... Instrumentation Control Document (KSC)
ICD .... Inter Canadian Development [*Vancouver Stock Exchange symbol*]
ICD .... Intercanthal Distance [*Anatomy*]
ICD .... Interface Connecting Device [*Air Force*] (DOMA)
ICD .... Interface Control Diagram (NRCH)
ICD .... Interface Control Dimension (IAA)
ICD .... Interface Control Document [*Apollo*] [*NASA*]
ICD .... Interface Control Document
ICD .... Interface Control Drawings (NRCH)
ICD .... Interim Checkout Device
ICD .... International Candle
ICD .... International Center for the Disabled (EA)
ICD .... International Circulation Distributors, Inc.
ICD .... International Classification of Diseases [*A publication*]
ICD .... International Climatic Decades
ICD .... International Code Designator [*Telecommunications*] (OSI)
ICD .... International College of Dentists (EA)
ICD .... International Congress for Data Processing
ICD .... International Cooperation for Development [*Commercial firm British*] (ECON)
ICD .... Intracommunity Directive [*Meat-shipping plants*] [*European Community*]
ICD .... Intrauterine Contraceptive Device [*Medicine*]
ICD .... Investment Company Data, Inc. [*Database producer*] (IID)
ICD .... Ion-Controlled Diode [*Electronics*] (IAA)
ICD .... Ischemic Coronary Disease [*Medicine*]
ICD .... Isocitrate Dehydrogenase [*Also, ICDH, IDH*] [*An enzyme*]
ICD-9 .... International Classification of Diseases. 9th Revision [*A publication*] (DHSM)
ICD-9-CM..... International Classification of Diseases. 9th Revision. Clinical Modification [*A publication*] (DHSM)
ICDA .... Industrial Civil Defence Association [*British*] (BI)
ICDA .... Industrial Compressor Distributors Association (EA)
ICDA .... Infantry Combat Developments Agency [*Pronounced "ick-da"*] [*Army*]
ICDA .... Institute for Community Design Analysis (EA)
ICDA .... International Catholic Deaf Association (EA)
ICDA .... International Cheese and Deli Association [*Later, IDDA*] (EA)
ICDA .... International Classification of Diseases, Adopted for Use in the United States
ICDA .... International Coalition for Development Action [*See also CIAD*] (EAIO)
ICDA .... International Congress of Dealers Associations (EA)
ICDA .... International Cooperative Development Association [*Later, ACDI*]
ICDA-8 .... International Classification of Diseases, Adopted for Use in the United States. 8th Revision [*A publication*] (DHSM)
ICDB .... Integrated Corporate Database
ICDBL .... International Committee for the Defense of the Breton Language [*See also CISLB*] [*Brussels, Belgium*] (EAIO)
ICDC .... Industrial and Commercial Development Corp. [*Kenya*]
ICDC .... National Dairy Council, Chicago, IL [*Library symbol Library of Congress*] (LCLS)
ICDCP .... Interface Control Drawings Change Proposal (IAA)
ICDD .... International Center for Dynamics of Development (EA)
ICDDB .... DDB Needham Worldwide, Inc. Information Center, Chicago, IL [*Library symbol*] [*Library of Congress*] (LCLS)
ICDDB .... Internal Control Description Database
ICDDR .... International Center for Diarrhoeal Diseases Research (PDAA)
ICDDR .... International Centre for Diarrhoeal Disease Research [*Bangladesh*]
ICDDRB .... International Centre for Diarrhoeal Disease Research, Bangladesh (ECON)
ICDDS .... Institute of Civil Defence and Disaster Studies [*British*] (EAIO)
ICDE .... International Council for Distance Education [*Australia*] (EAIO)
ICDF .... International Christian Dance Fellowship (EAIO)
ICDFS .... Increased Capacity Drum Feed System (MCD)
ICDH .... Isocitrate Dehydrogenase [*Also, ICD, IDH*] [*An enzyme*]
ICDI .... Imperial Court, Daughters of Isis (EA)
ICD-L .... De Paul University, Law Library, Chicago, IL [*Library symbol Library of Congress*] (LCLS)
ICDL .... Integrated Circuit Description Language
ICDL .... Inter-Center Data Link (MCD)
ICDL .... Interface Control Documentation Log (KSC)
ICDL .... Internal Control Description Language
ICDL .... International Centre for Distance Learning [*United Nations University*] (DUND)
ICDLA .... Internal Control Description Language Analyzer [*Computer science*] (MHDI)
ICDM .... Industrial Civil Defense Management
ICDM .... Institut Canadien pour la Deficience Mentale [*Canadian Institute on Mental Retardation*] [*Canada*]
ICDMA .... Independent Carbon-Dioxide Manufacturers Association (EA)
ICDNA .... Imidazole (Carbonic Acid) Dinitroanilide [*Organic chemistry*]
ICDO .... International Civil Defence Organization [*Switzerland*]
ICDP .... Integrated Circuits Demonstration Plant [*Taiwan*] (NITA)
ICDP .... Intelligence Career Development Program (AFM)
ICDP .... International Center for Development Policy (EA)
ICDP .... International Confederation for Disarmament and Peace [*British*]
ICDP .... International Continental Scientific Drilling Program [*Originated by the US, China, and Germany*]
ICDR .... Incremental Critical Design Review (NASA)
ICDR .... International Council for Dispute Resolution (EA)

ICDR	Inward Call Detail Recording [*Telecommunications*] (TEL)
ICDR	Ion Cyclotron Double Resonance
IC DRUM	Intercommunication Drum (MSA)
ICDS	Improved Conventional Dive System (DOMA)
ICDS	Integrated Child Development Scheme (DMAA)
ICDS	Integrated Control and Display System (MCD)
ICDS	Interim Contractor Depot Support [*DoD*]
ICDS	International Cardiac Doppler Society (DMAA)
ICDSP	Interim Contractor Depot Support Plan [*DoD*]
ICDSRHP	International Committee for the Defense of Salman Rushdie and His Publishers (EAIO)
ICDT	Chicago Daily Tribune, Chicago, IL [*Library symbol Library of Congress*] (LCLS)
ICDT	Incident · (AABC)
ICDT	Inverse Discrete Cosine Transform [*Mathematics*]
ICDT	Islamic Centre for Development of Trade [*See also CIDC*] [*Casablanca, Morocco*] (EAIO)
ICDU	Inertial Coupling Data Unit (NASA)
ICDU	Inertial Coupling Display Unit (KSC)
ICDV	Import Certificate Delivery Verification [*Military*]
ICE	Concordia Teachers College, River Forest, IL [*OCLC symbol*] (OCLC)
ICE	Economist Newspapers, Chicago, IL [*Library symbol Library of Congress*] (LCLS)
ICE	Ice, Compression, Elevation (CPH)
ICE	Iceland
ICE	Icelandair [*ICAO designator*] (FAAC)
ice	Icelandic [*MARC language code Library of Congress*] (LCCP)
ICE	Ice Station Resources [*Vancouver Stock Exchange symbol*]
ICE	Illness-Correctional Environments
ICE	Immediate Cable Equalizer (IAA)
ICE	Implicit Continuous-Fluid Eulerian
ICE	Improved Cost Estimate (RDA)
ICE	Improving Career Education (OICC)
ICE	In-Car Entertainment [*Automotive audio system*]
ICE	Incidental Campaign Expense [*Ticket scalping*]
ICE	In-Circuit Emulator [*A trademark*]
ICE	Increased Combat Effectiveness (AFM)
ICE	Independent Cost Estimate
ICE	Index of Combat Effectiveness (CINC)
ICE	Indiana Computer Educators (EDAC)
ICE	Individual Career Exploration [*Vocational guidance test*]
ICE	Individual Commitment to Excellence [*DoD*]
ICE	Individual Compass Error (IAA)
ICE	Induction Certificate Examination [*British Institute of Innkeeping*]
ICE	Industrial Combustion Emissions Model [*Environmental Protection Agency*] (GFGA)
ICE	Industrial Computer Enclosure (IAA)
ICE	Industrial Cost Exclusion [*Amendment to Federal Clean Water Act which limits use of federal money*]
ICE	Information Center on Education [*New York State Education Department*] [*Albany*] [*Information service or system*] (IID)
ICE	Information Centre Exchange [*Canada*] (EAIO)
ICE	Information Collection and Exchange [*Peace Corps*]
ICE	Infrared Countermeasures Equipment [*Military Electronics*] (CAAL)
ICE	Initial Combat Employment [*of new munitions*]
ICE	Initial Cooling Experiment [*Nuclear physics research*]
ICE	Inner City Enterprises [*British*]
ICE	Input-Checking Equipment
ICE	Input Control Element (MCD)
ICE	Institute for Chemical Education (EA)
ICE	Institute for Christian Education [*Australia*]
ICE	Institute for Community Economics (EA)
ICE	Institute for Consumer Ergonomics [*British*] (IRUK)
ICE	Institute for Continuing Education (AIE)
ICE	Institute of Ceramic Engineers (NUCP)
ICE	Institution of Chemical Engineers [*British*] (EAIO)
ICE	Institution of Civil Engineers [*British*]
ICE	Instrumentation Communication Equipment (NASA)
ICE	Instrument Checkout Equipment [*NASA*] (KSC)
ICE	Instrument Communication
ICE	Integrated Circuits Engineering Corp.
ICE	Integrated Clinical Encounters
ICE	Integrated Coil Electronic [*Automotive engineering*]
ICE	Integrated Communications Environment [*Computer architecture*] (NITA)
ICE	Integrated Conceptual Environment [*Computer science*]
ICE	Integrated Cooling for Electronics
ICE	Integrated Curriculum Environment [*Army*]
ICE	Integration with Controlled Error (MCD)
ICE	Intelligence and Counterespionage [*Fictitious organization in the Matt Helm series of books and movies*]
ICE	Intelligent Concept Extraction [*Technology*] [*Computer science*]
ICE	Interactive Concurrent Engineering [*Software*]
ICE	Inter City Express [*Electric train*] [*Germany*]
ICE	Intercomputer Electronics (IAA)
ICE	Interface Cancellation Equipment [*Telecommunications*] (EECA)
ICE	Interfaith Coalition on Energy (EA)
ICE	Interference Cancellation Equipment [*Telecommunications*]
ICE	Interleukin-Converting Enzyme [*Biochemistry*]
ICE	Intermediate Cable Equalizers (IEEE)
ICE	Internal Combustion Engine
ICE DRUM	International Center for the Environment
ICE	International Centre for Economics [*British*]

ICE	International Cirrus Experiment [*Funded by West Germany, Britain, France, Sweden, and the European Communities Commission*] [*Climatology*]
ICE	International Cometary Explorer [*Formerly, International Sun-Ea rth Explorer*] [*NASA*]
ICE	International Commercial Exchange [*Defunct*] (EA)
ICE	International Computer Component Exchange
ICE	International Congress of Entomology [*Later, CICE*] (EA)
ICE	International Construction Equipment Exhibition (ITD)
ICE	International Council on Electrocardiology [*Glasgow, Scotland*] (EAIO)
ICE	International Cultural Exchange [*An association*] (EA)
ICE	Internet Commerce Exchange
ICE	Internet Connections for Engineering
ICE	Interstate Cost Estimate [*Federal Highway Administration*]
ICE	Inventory Control Effectiveness
ICE	Ion Chromatography Exclusion
ICE	Ion Convection Electrodynamics (MCD)
ICE	Irridescent Color Exchange [*Heat-sensitive clothing*]
ICE	Islamic Council of Europe
ICE	Isothermal Controlled Electrophoresis
ICE	Italian Cultural Exchange in the United States (EA)
ICE	It's Close Enough
ICEA	Institut Canadien d'Education des Adultes [*Canadian Institute of Adult Education*]
ICEA	Institution of Chemical Engineers in Australia
ICEA	Instrument Contracting and Engineering Association (EA)
ICEA	Insulated Cable Engineers Association (EA)
ICEA	International Childbirth Education Association (EA)
ICEA	International Christian Education Association (EA)
ICEA	International Christian Esperanto Association (EA)
ICEA	International Commission for Environmental Assessment (GNE)
ICEA	International Consulting Economists Association [*British*] (DBA)
ICEAM	Institute of Computer Aided Engineering and Management [*University of Dundee*] [*British*] (IRUK)
ICEAM	International Committee on Economic and Applied Microbiology [*ICSU*] (EAIO)
ICEATT	Index of Continuing Education Attitudes
ICEB	Indonesian Commodity Exchange Board [*Badan Pelaksana Bursa Komoditi*] [*Indonesia*] (FEA)
ICEBAC	International Council of Employers of Bricklayers and Allied Craftsmen (EA)
ICEC	Interagency Career Education Committee (OICC)
ICEC	International Committee of Enamelling Creators (EAIO)
ICEC	International Conference on Education in Chemistry
ICEC	International Cost Engineering Council (EA)
ICEC	International Council for Exceptional Children [*Later, CEC*]
ICEC	International Cryogenic Engineering Committee (EAIO)
ICEC	Interuniversity Consortium for Educational Computing [*Database*]
ICECA	Indochina Ethnic Chinese Association of Victoria [*Australia*]
ICECAN	Iceland-Canada Cable (NITA)
ICECAN	Iceland-Canada Submarine Cable System [*Telecommunications*] (TEL)
ICECAP	Infrared Chemistry Experiments Coordinated Auroral Program [*Defense Nuclear Agency*] (PDAA)
ICECON	Control of Sea Ice Information (NATG)
ICECS	Integrated Closed-Loop Environmental Control System (PDAA)
ICED	Industrial and Construction Equipment Division (EA)
ICED	Institute for Community Education Development [*Ball State University*] [*Research center*] (RCD)
ICED	Interface Control Envelope Drawings (KSC)
ICED	Interface Control Environment Drawing (IAA)
ICED	International Coalition on Energy for Development
ICED	International Congress on the Education of the Deaf
ICED	International Council for Educational Development (EA)
ICED	Interprofessional Council on Environmental Design (EA)
ICEDEFOR	Iceland Defense Force
ICEdit	EDITEC, Chicago, IL [*Library symbol Library of Congress*] (LCLS)
ICEDS	Insurance Company Education Directors Society (EA)
ICEEC	International Congress of Electrical and Electronic Communications
ICEED	International Center for Energy and Economic Development
ICEED	International Research Center for Energy and Economic Development [*University of Colorado*] [*Research center*]
ICEF	Institute for the Community as Extended Family (EA)
ICEF	Interactive Composition and Editing Facility [*IBM Corp.*]
ICEF	International Children's Emergency Fund [*United Nations*] (DLA)
ICEF	International Committee for Research and Study on Environmental Factors
ICEF	International Council for Educational Films [*Later, ICEM*]
ICEI	Independent Cold Extruders Institute
ICEI	Institution of Civil Engineers of Ireland (BI)
ICEI	Internal Combustion Engine Institute [*Later, EMA*] (EA)
Icel	Iceland (VRA)
ICEL	Icelandic
ICEL	Intercel, Inc. [*NASDAQ symbol*] (SAG)
ICEL	International Committee for Ethnic Liberty [*See also IKEL*] (EAIO)
ICEL	International Committee on English in the Liturgy
ICEL	International Council of Environmental Law [*Bonn, Federal Republic of Germany*] (EA)
ICEM	Incremental Cost Effectiveness Model
ICEM	Independent Cluster Emission Model [*Atomic physics*]
ICEM	Induced Contamination Experimental Monitor (MCD)
ICEM	Intergovernmental Committee for European Migration [*Later, ICM*]
ICEM	International Confederation for Electroacoustic Music (EA)
ICEM	International Council for Educational Media [*Formerly, ICEF*]

ICEM............ Inverted Coaxial Magnetron (MCD)
ICEM............ Irish Council European Movement
ICen............ Centralia Public Library, Centralia, IL [*Library symbol Library of Congress*] (LCLS)
ICEN............ [*The*] Israel Commercial Economic Newsletter [*A publication Also, an information service or system*] (IID)
ICEnB............ Encyclopaedia Britannica, Inc., Chicago, IL [*Library symbol*] [*Library of Congress*] (LCLS)
ICenC............ Centralia Correctional Center, Centralia, IL [*Library symbol Library of Congress*] (LCLS)
ICenHS........ Centralia District High School, District 200, Centralia, IL [*Library symbol Library of Congress*] (LCLS)
ICEOB............ Sea Ice Observation Code [*Marine science*] (MSC)
ICEP............ Iberoamerican Cultural Exchange Program [*An association*] (EA)
ICEP............ Institut Canadien d'Enseignement Personnalise Inc. (AC)
ICEP............ Institute for Cultural Exchange thru Photography (EA)
ICEP............ Instituto do Comercio Externo (Lisbon, Portugal) [*Institute of Commercial Exports*] (EY)
ICEPART...... Index of Continuing Education Participation
ICEPAT........ Iceland Patrol [*Navy*]
ICEPF............ International Commission for the Eriksson Prize Fund (EAIO)
ICEPM............ Internal Combustion Engine Powered Material (MCD)
ICEQ............ Individualized Classroom Environment Questionnaire (EDAC)
ICER............ Information Centre of the European Railways
ICER............ Infrared Cell, Electronically Refrigerated
ICER............ Institute for Central European Research (EA)
ICER............ Interdepartmental Committee of External Relations [*Canada*]
ICERA-VIC... Indo-Chinese Elderly Refugee Association of Victoria [*Australia*]
ICEROCC.... Iceland Regional Operational Control Center [*Aircraft surveillance*]
ICERP............ Internal Combustion Engine Repair Shop
ICERR............ Interstate Congress for Equal Rights and Responsibilities (EA)
ICES............ Ice, Compression, Elevation, Support [*Medicine*] (MEDA)
ICES............ Import Cargo Electronic System
ICES............ Information Collection and Evaluation System (DMAA)
ICES............ Institution of Civil Engineering Surveyors [*British*] (DBA)
ICES............ Institution of Surveyors in Civil Engineering [*British*]
ICES............ Instructor and Course Evaluation System (EDAC)
ICES............ Integrated Civil Engineering System [*Programming language*] [*Computer science*]
IC/ES............ Intercommunications/Emergency Station (MCD)
ICES............ International Centre for Ethnic Studies (EA)
ICES............ International Commission on Erosion Sedimentation (NUCP)
ICES............ International Council for the Exploration of the Sea [*Denmark*]
ICES............ International Cultural Exchange Service
ICES............ Interuniversity Centre for European Studies [*Canada*] (IRC)
ICES............ National Easter Seal Society for Crippled Children and Adults, Chicago, IL [*Library symbol Library of Congress*] (LCLS)
ICESA............ International Conference on Environmental Sensing and Assessment
ICESA............ Interstate Conference of Employment Security Agencies (EA)
ICESC............ Industry Crew Escape Systems Committee
ICESC............ International Committee for European Security and Co-Operation [*See also CISCE*] (EAIO)
ICESSP........ International Council for Elementary and Secondary School Philosophy (EA)
ICET............ Forty-Eight Item Counseling Evaluation Test [*Psychology*]
ICET............ Institute for Comparative and Environmental Toxicology [*Cornell University*] [*Research center*] (RCD)
ICET............ Institute for the Certification of Engineering Technicians [*Later, National Institute for Certification in Engineering Technologies*]
ICET............ Interagency Committee on Excavation Technology [*Federal Council for Science and Technology*] [*Terminated, 1976*]
ICET............ International Centre for Earth Tides [*See also CIMT*] [*Belgium*] (EAIO)
ICET............ International Council on Education for Teaching (EA)
ICETK............ International Committee of Electrochemical Thermodynamics and Kinetics (IEEE)
ICETT............ Industrial Council for Educational Training Technology [*British*] (DS)
ICEUM............ International Conference on Energy Use Management
ICEV............ Initial Condition Evaluation [*Orbit identification*]
ICEV............ Internal Combustion Engine Vehicle
ICEVH........ International Council for Education of the Visually Handicapped [*Bensheim, Federal Republic of Germany*] (EAIO)
ICEX............ Integrated Civil Engineering Executive (MHDI)
ICEX............ Intelligence Coordination and Exploitation [*Joint CIA-MACV program*]
ICF............ Field Museum of Natural History, Chicago, IL [*Library symbol Library of Congress*] (LCLS)
ICF............ George Williams College, Downers Grove, IL [*OCLC symbol*] (OCLC)
ICF............ Ice Cream Federation Ltd. [*British*] (BI)
ICF............ ICF Kaiser International [*NYSE symbol*] (SPSG)
ICF............ Indirect Centrifugal Flotation
ICF............ Industrial Christian Fellowship [*British*] (DBA)
ICF............ Inertial Confinement Fusion [*Nuclear physics*]
ICF............ Inspection Check Fixture (MSA)
ICF............ Installation Confinement Facility [*Army*] (AABC)
ICF............ Institut Canadien du Film [*Canadian Film Institute - CFI*]
ICF............ Institute for Canadian Futures
ICF............ Institute of Chart Foresters [*British*] (DBA)
ICF............ Integrated Catalog Facility (HGAA)
ICF............ Integrated Control Facility [*Sperry UNIVAC*]
ICF............ Integrated Crystal Filter (IAA)
ICF............ Intelligence Contingency Funds (CINC)
ICF............ Intensive Care Facility [*Medicine*]
ICF............ Interacting Correlated Fragment [*Physical chemistry*]
ICF............ Interactive Communications Feature [*IBM Corp.*]
ICF............ Interactive Computer Facility (NITA)

ICF............ Inter-Bureau Citation of Funds [*Navy*]
ICF............ Intercommunication Flip-Flop [*Computer science*]
ICF............ Interconnect Facility
ICF............ Interface Control Function (MCD)
ICF............ Intermediate Care Facility [*Medicine*]
ICF............ International Canoe Federation [*See also FIC*] [*Florence, Italy*] (EAIO)
ICF............ International Cardiology Foundation (EA)
ICF............ International Carpet Fair
ICF............ International Casting Federation (EAIO)
ICF............ International Cheerleading Foundation (EA)
ICF............ International Congregational Fellowship (EA)
ICF............ International Congress on Fracture [*ICSU*] [*Sendai, Japan*] (EAIO)
ICF............ International Consultants Foundation (EA)
ICF............ International Crane Foundation (EA)
ICF............ International Craniofacial Foundations (EA)
ICF............ International Cremation Federation (EAIO)
ICF............ International Curling Federation (EAIO)
ICF............ International Federation of Chemical and General Workers Union
ICF............ Intracellular Fluid [*Physiology*]
ICF............ Intravascular Coagulation and Fibrinolysis Syndrome [*Medicine*]
ICF............ Intrinsic Coercive Force
ICF............ Iota-Cam Fiberscope [*Also, ICFS*]
ICF............ Italian Catholic Federation Central Council (EA)
ICF-A........ Field Museum of Natural History, Edward E. Ayer Ornithological Library, Chicago,IL [*Library symbol Library of Congress*] (LCLS)
ICFA............ Fireman Apprentice, Interior Communications Electrician, Striker [*Navy rating*]
ICFA............ Independent College Funds of America [*Later, FIHE*] (EA)
ICFA............ Inland Commercial Fisheries Association (EA)
ICFA............ Institute of Chartered Financial Analysts [*Later, AIMR*] (EA)
ICFA............ International Committee on Future Accelerators [*International Union of Pure and Applied Physics*]
ICFA............ International Computer Facsimile Association (PS)
ICFAC............ Inertial Confinement Fusion Advisory Committee [*Department of Energy*]
ICFAD........ International Council of Fine Arts Deans (EA)
ICFAR........ Federal Archives and Records Center, General Services Administration, Chicago, IL [*Library symbol Library of Congress*] (LCLS)
ICFAR.......... Indianapolis Center for Advanced Research [*Indiana University - Purdue University at Indianapolis*] [*Research center*] (RCD)
ICFATCM...... Individual Cleared for Access to Classified Material (AAG)
ICFATCMUTAI... Individual Cleared for Access to Classified Material Up to and Including
ICFAX............ Integrated Circuit Failure Analysis Expert System
ICFC............ Felician College, Chicago, IL [*Library symbol Library of Congress*] (LCLS)
ICFC............ Industrial and Commercial Finance Corp. [*British*]
ICFC............ International Centre of Films for Children
ICFC............ International Council of Fan Clubs [*Defunct*] (EA)
ICFCB............ Foote, Cone & Belding Advertising, Inc., Corporate Inforamtion Center, Chicago, IL [*Library symbol*] [*Library of Congress*] (LCLS)
ICFCM............ International Convention of Faith, Churches, and Ministers (EA)
ICFCYP............ International Centre of Films for Children and Young People [*France*] (EY)
ICFE............ Independent Colleges of Further Education [*British*]
ICFE............ Institute for Consumer Financial Education (EA)
ICFE............ International Contract Flooring Exhibition [*British*] (ITD)
ICFE............ Intra-Collisional Field Effect (IAA)
ICFET............ Inhomogeneous Channel Field-Effect Transistor (PDAA)
ICFF............ International Contemporary Furniture Fair (ITD)
ICFFO............ International Council of Folklore Festival Organizations and Folk Art (EA)
ICFG............ International Commission on Fungal Genetics [*International Council of Scientific Unions*]
ICFI............ International Cooperative Fracture Institute
ICFI............ Iota-Cam Fiberscope Instrument
ICF Int.......... ICF Kaiser International [*Associated Press*] (SAG)
ICFK............ Friedman and Koven, Library, Chicago, IL [*Library symbol Library of Congress*] (LCLS)
ICFL............ International Council of the French Language [*See also CILF*] [*Paris, France*] (EAIO)
ICFLC............ International Curling Federation - Ladies Committee [*Defunct*] (EA)
ICFLPRMFS... Items Not Available through Cannibalization, Fabrication, or Local Procurement or Replacement from Maintenance Float Stock
ICFM............ In-Core Fuel Management (PDAA)
ICFM............ Inlet Cubic Feet per Minute (PDAA)
ICFM............ Institute of Charity Fundraising Managers [*British*] (DBA)
ICFM............ International Company for Finance and Investment [*Russian bank*]
ICFM............ International Convention of Faith Ministries (EA)
ICFMA............ International Cystic Fibrosis Mucoviscidosis Association (EA)
ICFMC............ FMC Corp., Chicago, IL [*Library symbol Library of Congress*] (LCLS)
ICFMH............ International Committee on Food Microbiology and Hygiene [*ICSU*] [*Frederiksberg, Denmark*] (EAIO)
ICFMR............ Intermediate Care Facility for the Mentally Retarded
ICF-MR/DD... Intermediate Care Facility for the Mentally Retarded/Developmentally Disabled
ICFN............ Fireman, Interior Communications Electrician, Striker [*Navy rating*]
ICFNB............ First National Bank of Chicago, Chicago, IL [*Library symbol Library of Congress*] (LCLS)
ICFP............ Institute of Certified Financial Planners (EA)
ICFPW............ International Confederation of Former Prisoners of War
ICFR............ Intercollegiate Conference of Faculty Representatives (EA)

ICFRB .... Federal Reserve Bank of Chicago, Chicago, IL [*Library symbol Library of Congress*] (LCLS)

ICFRU .... Idaho Cooperative Fishery Research Unit [*University of Idaho*] [*Research center*] (RCD)

ICFS .... Industry Coalition for Fire Safety [*Defunct*] (EA)

ICFS .... Installation CONUS FORSTAT System [*Military*]

ICFS .... Iota-Cam Fiberscope [*Also, ICF*]

ICFSHG .... International Committee of French-Speaking Historians and Geographers (EAIO)

ICFSRT .... International Council of French-Speaking Radio and Television (EAIO)

ICFTU .... International Confederation of Free Trade Unions [*Belgium*]

ICFTU-ARO... International Confederation of Free Trade Unions-Asian Regional Organisation [*India*]

ICFTUE .... International Center of Free Trade Unionists in Exile [*France Defunct*]

ICFU .... International Council on the Future of the University [*Defunct*]

ICG .... Icelandic Coast Guard [*ICAO designator*] (FAAC)

ICG .... ICG Communications, Inc. [*AMEX symbol*] (SAG)

ICG .... Icing [*Meteorology*] (BARN)

ICG .... Illinois Benedictine College, Lisle, IL [*OCLC symbol*] (OCLC)

ICG .... Illinois Central Gulf Railroad Co. [*AAR code*]

ICG .... Illinois Council for the Gifted (EDAC)

ICG .... Impedance Cardiogram [*Medicine*] (DMAA)

ICG .... Indochina Curriculum Group [*Defunct*] (EA)

ICG .... Indocyanine Green [*Liver function test*] [*Medicine*]

ICG .... In-Flight Coverall Garment [*Apollo*] [*NASA*]

ICG .... Integrated Combat Group [*Air Force*]

ICG .... Interactive Computer Graphics

ICG .... International Commission on Glass [*See also CIV*] [*Prague, Czechoslovakia*] (EAIO)

ICG .... International Conference Group [*Commercial firm*] (EA)

ICG .... International Congress of Genetics

ICG .... International Coordination Group (USDC)

ICG .... Interviewer's Classification Guide

ICG .... IntlCom Group [*AMEX symbol*] (TTSB)

ICG .... Isotope Cisternography (DMAA)

ICGA .... Directory of International and Corporate Giving in America and Abroad [*A publication*]

ICGA .... Illinois Corn Growers Association (SRA)

ICGA .... International Carnival Glass Association (EA)

ICGA .... International Conference on Genetic Algorithms

ICGA .... Iowa Corn Growers Association (SRA)

ICGB .... International Cargo Gear Bureau (EA)

ICGCD .... Gardner, Carton, and Douglas, Chicago, IL [*Library symbol Library of Congress*] (LCLS)

ICG Com ...... ICG Communications, Inc. [*Associated Press*] (SAG)

ICGE .... International Center of Genetic Epistemology [*Geneva, Switzerland*]

ICGEB .... International Centre for Genetic Engineering and Biotechnology [*United Nations Development Organization*] (EAIO)

ICGEBNET .... International Centre for Genetic Engineering and Biotechnology Network [*United Nations Development Organization*] (DUND)

ICGEC .... Interagency Collaborative Group on Environmental Carcinogenesis [*Bethesda , MD*] [*National Institutes of Health*] (EGAO)

ICGGI .... Internationale Coronelli-Gesellschaft fuer Globen- und Instrumentkunde [*International Coronelli Society - ICS*] (EAIO)

ICGH .... Greeley & Hansen Engineering Library, Chicago, IL [*Library symbol Library of Congress*] (LCLS)

ICGH .... International Confederation of Genealogy and Heraldry [*See also CIGH*] [*Paris, France*] (EAIO)

ICGI .... International Council of Goodwill Industries (EA)

ICGIC .... Icing in Clouds [*NWS*] (FAAC)

ICGICIP .... Icing in Clouds and Precipitation [*NWS*] (FAAC)

ICGIP .... Icing in Precipitation [*NWS*] (FAAC)

ICG-ITSU ...... International Coordination Group for the Tsunami Warning System in the Pacific [*Marine science*] (OSRA)

ICG/ITSU ...... Intrnational Coordination Group for the Tsunami Warning System in the Pacific (USDC)

ICGM .... Intercontinental Glide [*or Guided*] Missile (KSC)

ICGM .... International Colloquium about Gas Marketing (EA)

ICGN .... ICC Technologies [*NASDAQ symbol*] (TTSB)

ICGN .... ICC Technologies, Inc. [*NASDAQ symbol*] (SAG)

ICGR .... Gas Research Institute, Chicago, IL [*Library symbol*] [*Library of Congress*] (LCLS)

ICGR .... Ivory Coast - Ghana Ridge [*Geology*]

ICGRC .... International Connoisseurs of Green and Red Chile (EA)

ICGS .... Interactive Careers Guidance System (AIE)

ICGS .... International Catholic Girls' Society

ICGS .... Interreligious Committee of General Secretaries (EA)

ICGSCA .... Infants', Children's, and Girls' Sportswear and Coat Association (EA)

ICh .... Chicago Heights Free Public Library, Chicago Heights, IL [*Library symbol Library of Congress*] (LCLS)

ICH .... ICH Corp. [*Later, Southwestern Life*] [*AMEX symbol*] (SPSG)

ICH .... Ichthyology

ICH .... Idiopathic Cortical Hyperostosis [*Medicine*] (DMAA)

ICH .... Illinois College, Jacksonville, IL [*OCLC symbol*] (OCLC)

ICH .... Incumbent Come Home [*Political humor*] [*Pronounced "itch"*]

ICH .... Induction-Conduction Heating

ICH .... Infectious Canine Hepatitis [*Veterinary medicine*]

ICH .... Information Clearing House, Inc.

ICH .... Inhalation Cycle Histogram [*Biometrics*]

ICH .... Instituto Cubao de Higrafia [*Cuba*] [*Marine science*] (OSRA)

ICH .... Instructor Contact Hours (MCD)

ICH .... Interchange

ICH .... Interchanger (NASA)

ICH .... Intermediate Chain Home (IAA)

ICH .... International Conference Harmonization

ICH .... Intracerebral Hemorrhage [*Medicine*]

ICH .... Intracranial Hemorrhage [*Medicine*]

ICH .... Israel Chemical Ltd. [*NYSE symbol*] (SAG)

IChaAF .... United States Air Force, Chanute Air Force Base Library, Chanute Air Force Base, IL [*Library symbol*] [*Library of Congress*] (LCLS)

ICham .... Champaign Public Library, Champaign, IL [*Library symbol Library of Congress*] (LCLS)

IChamBH ..... Burnham City Hospital, Champaign, IL [*Library symbol Library of Congress*] (LCLS)

IChamCE ..... United States Army Construction Engineering Research Laboratory, Champaign, IL [*Library symbol Library of Congress*] (LCLS)

IChamGS ..... Church of Jesus Christ of Latter-Day Saints, Genealogical Society Library, Champaign Stake Branch, Champaign, IL [*Library symbol Library of Congress*] (LCLS)

IChamIG ...... Illinois State Geological Survey, Champaign,IL [*Library symbol*] [*Library of Congress*] (LCLS)

IChamL .... Lincoln Trail Libraries, Champaign, IL [*Library symbol Library of Congress*] (LCLS)

IChamMH .... Illinois Department of Mental Health and Developmental Disabilities, Herman M. Adler Center Library, Champaign, IL [*Library symbol Library of Congress*] (LCLS)

IChamNG ..... News-Gazette, Champaign, IL [*Library symbol*] [*Library of Congress*] (LCLS)

IChamP .... Parkland College, Champaign, IL [*Library symbol Library of Congress*] (LCLS)

ICHAP .... Improved Chaparral [*Military*] (MCD)

IChar .... Charleston Carnegie Public Library, Charleston, IL [*Library symbol Library of Congress*] (LCLS)

ICharE .... Eastern Illinois University, Charleston, IL [*Library symbol Library of Congress*] (LCLS)

ICharF .... Charleston Area Cooperative Film Library, Charleston, IL [*Library symbol*] [*Library of Congress*] (LCLS)

ICharH .... Charleston Community Memorial Hospital, Charleston, IL [*Library symbol Library of Congress*] (LCLS)

ICharSD .... Charleston Community Unit School District, Charleston, IL [*Library symbol*] [*Library of Congress*] (LCLS)

ICHC .... International Committee for Horticultural Congresses

ICHC .... International Congress of Heterocyclic Chemistry

ICHCA .... International Cargo Handling Coordination Association [*London, England*] (EA)

ICHD .... Inter-Society Commission for Heart Disease Resources (EA)

ICHDA .... International Cooperative Housing Development Association

ICHDR .... Intersociety Commission for Heart Disease Resources [*American Heart Assoc iation - AHA*] [*Absorbed by*]

I Ch E .... Institution of Chemical Engineers [*British*]

ICHE .... International Commission on Human Ecology (EA)

ICHE .... International Councils on Higher Education [*Defunct*]

I Chem E ..... Institution of Chemical Engineers [*British*]

ICHEO .... Interuniversity Council for Higher Education Overseas [*British*] (DI)

ICherSD .... Cherry School District 92, Cherry, IL [*Library symbol Library of Congress*] (LCLS)

IChevE .... Cherry Valley Elementary School, Cherry Valley, IL [*Library symbol*] [*Library of Congress*] (LCLS)

ICHF .... International Child Health Foundation (EA)

ICHFC .... Household Finance Corp., Chicago, IL [*Library symbol Library of Congress*] (LCLS)

ICHFST .... International Council of Health Fitness and Sports Therapists [*British*]

ICHG .... International Conference on the Holocaust and Genocide (EAIO)

IChGS .... Church of Jesus Christ of Latter-Day Saints, Genealogical Society Library, Chicago Heights Branch, Chicago Heights, IL [*Library symbol Library of Congress*] (LCLS)

ICHi .... Chicago Historical Society, Chicago, IL [*Library symbol Library of Congress*] (LCLS)

ICHID .... Harrington Institute of Interior Design, Chicago, IL [*Library symbol Library of Congress*] (LCLS)

IChil .... Chillicothe Township Free Public Library, Chillicothe, IL [*Library symbol Library of Congress*] (LCLS)

IChL .... Chicago Heights Free Public Library, Chicgo Heights, IL [*Library symbol*] [*Library of Congress*] (LCLS)

ICHLM .... International Conference of Historians of the Labour Movement [*Vienna, Austria*] (EAIO)

ICHM .... Institute of Care-Home Managers [*British*] (DBA)

ICHM .... International College of Hotel Management

ICHMH .... Interstate Clearing House on Mental Health [*Defunct*]

ICHMT .... International Centre for Heat and Mass Transfer (EAIO)

IChO .... International Chemistry Olympiad [*For high school students*]

ICHOHYP .... International Committee of Hard of Hearing Young People [*Frederiksberg, Denmark*] (EAIO)

ICHOR .... ICHOR Corp. [*Associated Press*] (SAG)

ICHP .... Illinois Council on Health System Pharmacists (SRA)

ICHP .... International Commission of Health Professionals for Health and Human Rights (EA)

ICHP .... Investors Chronicle/Hillier Parker [*British A publication*]

IChP .... Prairie State College, Learning Center, Chicago Heights, IL [*Library symbol Library of Congress*] (LCLS)

ICHPER .... International Council for Health, Physical Education, and Recreation (EA)

IChr .... Chrisman Public Library, Chrisman, IL [*Library symbol Library of Congress*] (LCLS)

ICHR .... ICHOR Corp. [*NASDAQ symbol*] (SAG)

ICHR .... Indian Council of Historical Research

ICHR .... Inter-American Commission on Human Rights [*OAS*] (PD)

ICHR .... Interfaith Council for Human Rights (EA)

I Ch R .... Irish Chancery Reports [*A publication*] (DLA)
ICHRI .... Islamic Committee for Human Rights in Iraq [*Later, IODHRI*] (EA)
ICHRPI .... International Commission for the History of Representative and Parliamentary Institutions [*Rome, Italy*] (EAIO)
ICHRT .... International Committee for Human Rights in Taiwan (EA)
ICHS .... Inter-African Committee for Hydraulic Studies [*See also CIEH*] [*Ouagadougou, Burkina Faso*] (EAIO)
ICHS .... International Center for Holocaust Studies (EA)
ICHS .... International Committee for Historical Sciences [*Paris, France*] (EA)
ICHS .... International Council of Homehelp Services [*See also CISAF*] [*Driebergen-Rijsenburg, Netherlands*] (EAIO)
ICHSMSS ..... International Commission for the History of Social Movements and Social Structures [*Paris, France*] (EAIO)
ICHSPP .... International Congress on High-Speed Photography and Photonics (EA)
ICHSWW ...... International Committee for the History of the Second World War (EAIO)
ICHT .... Harris Trust and Savings Bank, Chicago, IL [*Library symbol Library of Congress*] (LCLS)
ICHT .... International Council of Holistic Therapists [*British*]
ICHTH .... Ichthyology
ichthyol ...... Ichthyology (BARN)
ICHTHYS ...... Jesous Christos, Theou Uios Soter [*Jesus Christ, Son of God, Savior*]
ICHTSP .... International Conference on the Hydraulic Transport of Solids in Pipes (PDAA)
ICHY .... International Council of Hindoo Youth (EAIO)
ICI .... Cicia [*Fiji*] [*Airport symbol*] (OAG)
ICI .... Ice Condenser Instrumentation [*Nuclear energy*] (NRCH)
ICI .... ICI Pharmaceuticals [*Great Britain*] [*Research code symbol*]
ICI .... Illinois Institute of Technology, Chicago, IL [*Library symbol Library of Congress*] (LCLS)
ICI .... Imperial Chemical Industries Ltd. [*NYSE symbol*] (SPSG)
ICI .... Imprial Chem Ind ADR [*NYSE symbol*] (TTSB)
ICI .... Incoming Call Identification [*Telecommunications*]
ICI .... Independent Commercial Importer [*Automotive retailing*]
ICI .... Independent Curators, Inc. (EA)
ICI .... Individual/Collective Integration
ICI .... Information & Communications, Inc.
ICI .... Information Centre International [*Telecommunications service*] (TSSD)
ICI .... Information Concepts, Inc.
ICI .... Information Consultants, Inc. [*Information service or system*] (IID)
ICI .... Initial Capabilities Inspection [*Military*] (AFM)
ICI .... Institut Canadien des Ingenieurs [*Engineering Institute of Canada*]
ICI .... Institute of Chemistry of Ireland (BI)
ICI .... Intelligent Communications Interface (IEEE)
ICI .... Interagency Committee on Intelligence
ICI .... Interagency Cooperative Issuances (OICC)
ICI .... Inter-American Children's Institute [*OAS*]
ICI .... Inter-American Cooperative Institute
ICI .... Intercarrier Interface (ACRL)
ICI .... Interclick Interval [*Entomology*]
ICI .... Interexchange Carrier Interface [*Telecommunications*] (ACRL)
ICI .... Interim Cargo Integrator (MCD)
ICI .... Internal Change Identifier (MCD)
ICI .... International Castles Institute (EA)
ICI .... International Commission on Illumination [*Since 1951, has been known exclusively as CIE, which see*]
ICI .... Interpersonal Communication Inventory [*Interpersonal skills and attitudes test*]
ICI .... Intracardiac Infection [*Medicine*] (DMAA)
ICi .... Intracisternal (DMAA)
ICI .... Inuit Cultural Institute [*Canada*]
ICI .... Investment Casting Institute (EA)
ICI .... Investment Company Institute (EA)
ICI .... Ion Composition Instrument [*Cometary physics*]
ICI .... Istituto Chemioterapico Italiano [*Italy*] [*Research code symbol*]
ICI .... Italian Cultural Institute (EA)
ICI .... MacMurray College, Jacksonville, IL [*OCLC symbol*] (OCLC)
ICI-A .... Illinois Institute of Technology, Armour Research Foundation, Chicago, IL [*Library symbol Library of Congress*] (LCLS)
ICIA .... Industrial, Commercial, and Institutional Accountant (DD)
ICIA .... Institute of Cultural Affairs International [*Information service or system*] (IID)
ICIA .... International Center of Information on Antibiotics (EAIO)
ICIA .... International Communications Industries Association (EA)
ICIA .... International Conference Industry Association [*Defunct*] (EA)
ICIA .... International Credit Insurance Association [*Zurich, Switzerland*] (EAIO)
ICIA .... International Crop Improvement Association [*Later, AOSCA*] (EA)
ICIAO .... International Association of Assessing Officers, Chicago, IL [*Library symbol*] [*Library of Congress*] (LCLS)
ICIAP .... Interagency Committee on International Aviation Policy [*Department of State*] (AFM)
ICIASF .... International Congress on Instrumentation in Aerospace Simulation Facilities
ICic .... Cicero Public Library, Cicero, IL [*Library symbol Library of Congress*] (LCLS)
ICIC .... Interagency Committee on Intermodal Cargo
ICIC .... Interdisciplinary Committee on Institutes and Conferences
ICIC .... International Cancer Information Center [*Public Health Service*] [*Information service or system*] (IID)
ICIC .... International Copyright Information Centre [*UNESCO*] (PDAA)
ICIC .... International Copyrights Information Center (WDAA)

ICICI .... Industrial Credit & Investment Corp. of India Ltd.
ICICLE .... Integrated Cryogenic Isotope Cooling Equipment
ICicM .... Morton College, Cicero, IL [*Library symbol Library of Congress*] (LCLS)
ICICO .... Illinois College of Optometry, Chicago, IL [*Library symbol Library of Congress*] (LCLS)
ICICS .... International College of Surgeons, Chicago, IL [*Library symbol Library of Congress*] (LCLS)
ICI-D .... Illinois Institute of Technology, Institute of Design, Chicago, IL [*Library symbol Library of Congress*] (LCLS)
ICID .... Information Center for Individuals with Disabilities (EA)
ICID .... Intensified Charge Injection Device [*For television camera used in astronomy*]
ICID .... International Commission on Irrigation and Drainage [*See also CIID*] [*ICSU New Delhi, India*] (EAIO)
ICIDH .... International Classification of Impairments, Disabilities, and Handicaps [*Occupational therapy*]
ICIDI .... Independent Commission on International Development Issues [*Also known as the Brandt Commission*] [*Studies problems arising from the inequity between more developed Northern nations and less developed Southern countries*]
ICIDR .... International Collaboration in Infectious Diseases Research [*Tulane University*] [*Research center*] (RCD)
ICIDS .... Integrated Commercial Intrusion Detection System [*Army*]
ICIE .... Infogrow Communications Information Exchange [*Database directory*] (NITA)
ICIE .... Information Center for Internal Exposure [*Department of Energy*] [*Defunct*] (IID)
ICIE .... International Center for Industry and the Environment (DCTA)
ICIE .... International Council of Industrial Editors [*Later, IABC*]
ICIE .... International Council of Industrial Engineers
ICIEQ .... Illinois Institute for Environmental Quality, Chicago, IL [*Library symbol Library of Congress*] (LCLS)
ICIF .... Independent Colleges of Indiana Foundation (SRA)
ICIF .... International Cooperative Insurance Federation [*Manchester, England*] (EAIO)
ICIFI .... International Council of Infant Food Industries
ICI-G .... Illinois Institute of Technology, Institute of Gas Technology, Chicago, IL [*Library symbol Library of Congress*] (LCLS)
ICIg .... Intracytoplasmic Immunoglobulin
ICII .... Imperial Credit [*NASDAQ symbol*] (TTSB)
ICII .... Imperial Credit Industries, Inc. [*NASDAQ symbol*] (SAG)
ICII .... International Culture Institute [*Japan*] (EAIO)
ICIJ .... Institute for Juvenile Research, Chicago, IL [*Library symbol Library of Congress*] (LCLS)
ICI-K .... Illinois Institute of Technology, Chicago-Kent College of Law, Chicago, IL [*Library symbol Library of Congress*] (LCLS)
ICIL .... IFIP [*International Federation for Information Processing*] Committee for International Liaison
ICILB .... Isham-Lincoln-Beale, Chicago, IL [*Library symbol*] [*Library of Congress*] (LCLS)
ICIM .... Institute for Computer Integrated Manufacturing [*Strathclyde University*] [*British*]
ICIMOD .... International Centre for Integrated Mountain Development [*Kathmandu*] (ECON)
ICINR .... Institute of Natural Resources, Chicago, IL [*Library symbol Library of Congress*] (LCLS)
ICIntR .... Library of International Relations, Chicago, IL [*Library symbol Library of Congress*] (LCLS)
ICIO .... Interim Cargo Integration Operations (MCD)
ICIP .... Indirect Component Improvement Program
ICIP .... Institute for Psychoanalysis, Chicago, IL [*Library symbol Library of Congress*] (LCLS)
ICIP .... International Conference on Information Processing [*Paris, 1959*]
ICIP .... Vespasian Warner Public Library, Clinton, IL [*Library symbol*] [*Library of Congress*] (LCLS)
ICIPE .... International Centre of Insect Physiology and Ecology [*ICSU*] [*Nairobi, Kenya*] (EAIO)
ICipSD .... Cissna Park Community Unit School District, Cissna Park, IL [*Library symbol*] [*Library of Congress*] (LCLS)
ICIR .... In Commission, In Reserve [*Vessel status*] [*Navy*]
ICIREPAT ..... International Cooperation in Information Retrieval among Examining Patent Offices
ICIRO .... Interim Commission of the International Refugee Organization
ICIS .... ICIS Management Group, Inc. [*NASDAQ symbol*] (SAG)
ICIS .... ICIS Mgmt Group [*NASDAQ symbol*] (TTSB)
ICIS .... Independent Chemical Information Services Ltd. [*Information service or system*] (IID)
ICIS .... Integrated Chemical Information System [*Information Consultants, Inc.*] [*Information service or system*] (IID)
ICIS .... Intelligent Configuration Identification System [*NASA*]
ICIS .... Interactive Construction Industry System [*NCR Ltd.*] [*Software package*] (NCC)
ICIS .... Interdepartmental Committee on Internal Security [*Washington, DC*]
ICIS .... International Centre for Industrial Studies [*United Nations*]
ICIS .... International Council for Infant Survival [*Later, NCGIS*] (EA)
ICIS .... IUD Claims Information Source (EA)
ICis .... Willow Branch Library, Cisco, IL [*Library symbol Library of Congress*] (LCLS)
ICISI .... International Center for Interdisciplinary Studies of Immunology at Georgetown [*Georgetown University*] [*Research center*] (RCD)
ICIS Mgt ...... ICIS Management Group, Inc. [*Associated Press*] (SAG)
ICISS .... Impact-Collision Ion Scattering Spectroscopy

ICIST .... Institut Canadien de l'Information Scientifique et Technique [*Canadian Institute for Scientific and Technical Information - CISTI*]

ICIT .... Information Center on Instructional Technology

ICIT .... Intensified Conventional Insulin Therapy [*Medicine*]

ICITA .... International Chain of Industrial and Technical Advertising Agencies (EA)

ICITA .... International Cooperative Investigations of the Tropical Atlantic [*Navy*]

ICITAP .... International Criminal Investigative Training Assistance Program [*Department of Justice*]

ICITO .... Interim Commission for the International Trade Organization

ICIU .... University of Illinois at Chicago Circle, Chicago, IL [*Library symbol Library of Congress*] (LCLS)

ICIU-PM .... University of Illinois at Chicago Circle, Peoria School of Medicine, Peoria, IL [*Library symbol Library of Congress*] (LCLS)

ICIU-RM .... University of Illinois at Chicago Circle, Rockford School of Medicine, Rockford, IL [*Library symbol Library of Congress*] (LCLS)

ICIU-S .... University of Illinois at Chicago Circle, Science Library, Chicago, IL [*Library symbol Library of Congress*] (LCLS)

ICIWWW ...... International Congress of Industrial Waste Water and Wastes

ICIX .... Intermedia Communications [*NASDAQ symbol*] (TTSB)

ICIX .... Intermedia Communications, Inc. [*NASDAQ symbol*] (SAG)

ICJ .... Ileocecal Junction [*Anatomy*] (DAVI)

ICJ .... Ileocolonic Junction [*Anatomy*]

ICJ .... Incoming Junction [*Telecommunications*] (TEL)

ICJ .... International Commission of Jurists [*Switzerland*]

ICJ .... International Court of Justice [*United Nations*]

ICJ .... John Crerar Library, Chicago, IL [*Library symbol Library of Congress*] (LCLS)

ICJ .... McKendree College, Lebanon, IL [*OCLC symbol*] (OCLC)

ICJA .... Intelligence and Criminal Justice Academy [*Defunct*] (EA)

ICJA .... International Criminal Justice Association (EA)

ICJAS .... International Commission of Jurists Australian Section

ICJB .... Jenner and Block, Chicago, IL [*Library symbol Library of Congress*] (LCLS)

ICJC .... Immaculate Conception Junior College [*New Jersey*]

ICJC .... International Council of Jews from Czechoslovakia [*British Defunct*] (EAIO)

ICJC .... International Criminal Justice Clearinghouse [*Law Enforcement Assistance Administration*] [*Information service or system*]

ICJCM .... John T. and Catherine McArthur Foundation, Chicago, IL [*Library symbol*] [*Library of Congress*] (LCLS)

ICJCS .... International Conference of Jewish Communal Service [*Later, WCJCS*] (EA)

ICJKM .... Jesuit-Krauss-McCormick Library, Chicago, IL [*Library symbol Library of Congress*] (LCLS)

ICJL .... Institute for Computers in Jewish Life (EA)

ICJM .... John Marshall Law School, Chicago, IL [*Library symbol Library of Congress*] (LCLS)

ICJP .... Irish Commission for Justice and Peace [*An association*] (EAIO)

ICJR .... Institute for Criminal Justice, University of Richmond (DLA)

ICJS .... Independent Carpenters' and Joiners' Society [*A union*] [*British*]

ICJS .... Spertus College of Judaica, Chicago, IL [*Library symbol Library of Congress*] (LCLS)

ICJSh .... John G. Shedd Aquarium, Chicago, IL [*Library symbol Library of Congress*] (LCLS)

ICJST .... Jesuit School of Theology in Chicago, Chicago, IL [*Library symbol Library of Congress*] (LCLS)

ICJUB .... Intercontinental Jet Unmanned Bomber

ICJV .... Jewish Vocational Service Library, Chicago, IL [*Library symbol Library of Congress*] (LCLS)

ICJW .... International Council of Jewish Women (EA)

ICK .... Inscriptions Cuneiformes du Kultepe (BJA)

ICK .... Interdepartmental Committee on Nuclear Energy [*Netherlands*] (EY)

ICK .... International Cherokee [*Vancouver Stock Exchange symbol*]

ICK .... Metlakatla, AK [*Location identifier FAA*] (FAAL)

ICK .... Millikin University, Decatur, IL [*OCLC symbol*] (OCLC)

ICK .... Nieuw Nickerie [*Surinam*] [*Airport symbol*] (OAG)

ICKCMX ...... Integrated Circuit Keyset Central Multiplexer (CAAL)

ICKE .... Kirkland & Ellis, Chicago, IL [*Library symbol Library of Congress*] (LCLS)

ICKK .... Kennedy-King College of the City College of Chicago, Chicago, IL [*Library symbol Library of Congress*] (LCLS)

ICKL .... International Council of Kinetography Laban (EA)

ICKMC .... Keck, Mahin, and Cate, Chicago, IL [*Library symbol Library of Congress*] (LCLS)

ICKMZ .... Katten, Munchin & Zavis, Pearl, Greenburger & Galler, Chicago, IL [*Library symbol*] [*Library of Congress*] (LCLS)

ICL .... Cavei Avir Lemitanim [*Israel*] [*ICAO designator*] (FAAC)

ICL .... Clarinda, IA [*Location identifier FAA*] (FAAL)

ICL .... Income Contingent Loan

ICL .... Incoming Correspondence Log (AAG)

ICL .... Incoming Line

ICL .... Indal Ltd. [*Toronto Stock Exchange symbol*]

ICL .... Inflight Calibration Lamp [*Instrumentation*]

ICL .... Inserted Connection Loss [*Telecommunications*]

ICL .... Instructional Center Library

ICL .... Instrumentation Configuration Log (IAA)

ICL .... Instrument Calibration Laboratory

ICL .... Instrument Control Language [*Computer science*]

ICL .... Instrument-Controlled Landing [*Aviation*] (IAA)

ICL .... Integrated Circuit Logic

ICL .... Integrated Configuration List (NG)

ICL .... Intellicall, Inc. [*NYSE symbol*] (SPSG)

ICL .... Interactive Computer Learning

ICL .... Interagency Checklist [*United States Employment Service*] (OICC)

ICL .... Intercommunication Logic

ICL .... Intercomputer Communication Logic (NITA)

ICL .... Interdepartmental Committee on Land [*Canada*]

ICL .... Interest Checklist [*US Employment Service*] [*Department of Labor*]

ICL .... Internal Control Loop [*Chemical engineering*]

ICL .... International Cancer League [*Defunct*] (EA)

ICL .... International Catholic Library [*A publication*]

ICL .... International Christian Leadership (EA)

ICL .... International Clinical Laboratories, Inc.

ICL .... International Communications Ltd. [*Fayville, MA*] [*Telecommunications service*] (TSSD)

ICL .... International Computers Ltd. [*Great Britain*] [*Computer manufacturer*]

ICL .... International Cooperative Logistics (AFIT)

ICL .... International Council for Christian Leadership (EA)

ICL .... Interpersonal Check List [*Psychology*]

ICL .... Interpretive Coding Language

ICL .... Inter-Union Commission on the Lithosphere [*NASA*]

ICL .... Iris-Clip Lens (DMAA)

ICL .... Irish Central Library for Students (BI)

ICL .... Isocitrate Lyase [*An enzyme*]

ICL .... Isocitrate Lyase (DMAA)

ICL .... Loyola University, Chicago, IL [*Library symbol Library of Congress*] (LCLS)

ICL .... Monmouth College, Monmouth, IL [*OCLC symbol*] (OCLC)

ICl .... Vespasian Warner Public Library, Clinton, IL [*Library symbol Library of Congress*] (LCLS)

ICLA .... International Committee on Laboratory Animals

ICLA .... International Comparative Literature Association (EA)

ICLAE .... International Council of Library Association Executives (EA)

ICLAM .... International Committee for Life Assurance Medicine [*Zurich, Switzerland*] (EAIO)

ICLARM ...... International Center for Living Aquatic Resources Management [*Makati, Metro Manila, Philippines*] (EAIO)

ICLARM ...... International Center for Living Aquatic Resources Management

ICLAS .... Intracavity LASER Absorption Spectroscopy

ICLaw .... Chicago Law Institute, Chicago, IL [*Library symbol Library of Congress*] (LCLS)

ICL-B .... Loyola University, Julia Deal Lewis Library, Chicago, IL [*Library symbol Library of Congress*] (LCLS)

IcLc .... Identity Correct, Location Correct [*Psychology*]

ICLC .... International Centre for Local Credit [*The Hague, Netherlands*] (EAIO)

ICLC .... International Congress on Lightweight Concrete (PDAA)

ICLC .... International Criminal Law Commission (EA)

ICLCP .... International Conference on Large Chemical Plants [*Antwerp, Belgium*] (EAIO)

ICLD .... International Center for Law in Development (EA)

ICL-D .... Loyola University, Dental School, Chicago, IL [*Library symbol Library of Congress*] (LCLS)

ICLE .... Institute of Continuing Legal Education [*Research center*] (RCD)

ICLE .... Intacapsular Lens Extraction [*Ophthalmology*] (DAVI)

ICLEI .... International Council for Local Environmental Initiatives [*Marine science*] (OSRA)

ICLEI .... International Council for Local Environmental Initiatives (USDC)

ICLEP .... Individualized Computer Literacy Education Plan (EDAC)

ICLES .... International Common Law Exchange Society (EA)

ICLES .... International Conference on Large Electrical Systems

IClh .... Clarendon Hills Public Library, Clarendon Hills, IL [*Library symbol Library of Congress*] (LCLS)

ICLH .... Imperial College - London Hospital [*British*] (DI)

IClH .... John Warner Hospital, Clinton, IL [*Library symbol Library of Congress*] (LCLS)

IClhP .... Clarendon Hills Public Library, Clarendon Hills, IL [*Library symbol*] [*Library of Congress*] (LCLS)

IcLi .... Identity Correct, Location Incorrect [*Psychology*]

ICLID .... Incoming Caller Identification [*Telecommunications*]

ICL-L .... Loyola University, Law Library, Chicago, IL [*Library symbol*] [*Library of Congress*] (LCLS)

ICLM .... Induced Course Load Matrix (PDAA)

ICLM .... Inter-California Line in Mexico R. R. [*AAR code*]

ICLM .... International Christian Leprosy Mission (EA)

ICL-M .... Loyola University, School of Medicine, Maywood, IL [*Library symbol Library of Congress*] (LCLS)

ICLMC .... Intersociety Council on Laboratory Medicine of Canada

ICLoop .... Loop College, Chicago, IL [*Library symbol Library of Congress*] (LCLS)

ICLP .... Internal Connectionless Protocol [*Telecommunications*]

ICLR .... Interdepartmental Committee on Labour Requirements [*British World War II*]

ICLR .... International Committee for Lift Regulations [*See also CIRA*] [*Saint-Yvelines, France*] (EAIO)

ICLR .... Irish Common Law Reports [*A publication*] (DLA)

ICLR Can .... Index to Current Legal Research in Canada [*A publication*] (DLA)

ICLREW ...... Incorporated Council of Law Reporting for England and Wales [*Established in 1866*]

ICLRN .... Interagency Council on Library Resources for Nursing (EA)

ICLRSQ ...... Incorporated Council of Law Reporting for the State of Queensland [*Australia*]

ICLS .... Inequality Constrained Least-Squares [*Statistics*]

ICLS .... Instrument Carrier Landing System [*Navy*] (DOMA)

ICLS .... Integrated Carrier Landing System [*Military*] (MCD)

ICLS .... International Courtly Literature Society (EA)

ICLSA.......... United States League of Savings Associations, Chicago, IL [*Library symbol Library of Congress*] (LCLS)
ICLT............ International Committee of Lawyers for Tibet
ICLT............ Lutheran School of Theology, Chicago, IL [*Library symbol Library of Congress*] (LCLS)
ICLTC.......... Illinois Council on Long Term Care (SRA)
ICLW........... Latham & Watkins, Chicago, IL [*Library symbol*] [*Library of Congress*] (LCLS)
ICM............. Improved Capability Minuteman (SAA)
ICM............. Improved Capability Missile [*Air Force*]
ICM............. Improved Conventional Munitions
ICM............. In-Can Melter [*Nuclear energy*] (NUCP)
ICM............. Incoming Message [*Telecommunications*]
ICM............. Independent Citizens' Movement [*US Virgin Islands*] (PPW)
ICM............. Independent Color Matching [*Computer science*]
ICM............. Indian Campaign Medal
ICM............. Individual Case Management (WYGK)
ICM............. Individual Clutch Modulation [*Automotive engineering*]
ICM............. Infracostal Margin [*Anatomy*] (DAVI)
ICM............. Initiator Command Module
ICM............. Inner Cell Mass [*Embryology*]
ICM............. Installable Compression, Manager [*Computer science*]
ICM............. Instantaneous Center of Motion
ICM............. Institut Canadien de la Mediterranee [*Canadian Mediterranean Institute*]
ICM............. Institut Canadien des Mines et de la Metallurgie [*Canadian Institute of Mining and Metallurgy*] (EAIO)
ICM............. Institute for Complementary Medicine [*An association*] (EAIO)
ICM............. Institute for Composite Materials [*Defunct*] (EA)
ICM............. Institute for Court Management of the National Center for State Courts (EA)
ICM............. Institute of Caster Manufacturers (EA)
ICM............. Institute of Construction Management [*British*]
ICM............. Institute of Credit Management [*British*]
ICM............. Instituto de Ciencias del Mar [*Barcelona, Spain*] [*Marine science*] (OSRA)
ICM............. Instruction Control Memory
ICM............. Instrumentation and Communications Monitor
ICM............. Integral Charge-Control Model [*Electronics*] (OA)
ICM............. Integrated Catchment Management [*Water resources*]
ICM............. Integrated Circuit Mask
ICM............. Integrated Compact Mill [*Steel manufacture*]
ICM............. Integrated Controller Module [*Automotive engineering*]
ICM............. Integrated Crop Management [*Agriculture*]
ICM............. Interchangeable Control Media (MCD)
ICM............. Intercommunication (MSA)
ICM............. Intercontinental Missile (IAA)
ICM............. Intercostal Margin [*Anatomy*]
ICM............. Interface Coordination Memorandum (MCD)
ICM............. Interference Control Monitor (AAG)
ICM............. Interim Catalog Module [*MEDLARS*]
ICM............. Internacional De Ceramica ADS [*NYSE symbol*] (TTSB)
ICM............. Internacional de Ceramica SA de CV [*NYSE symbol*] (SAG)
ICM............. International Chaplain's Ministry (EA)
ICM............. International Colour Management [*Commercial firm British*]
ICM............. International Confederation of Midwives [*British*] (EAIO)
ICM............. International Congress of Mathematicians
ICM............. International Congress on Mechanical Behaviour of Materials (EAIO)
ICM............. International Control Mechanism
ICM............. International Creative Management [*Commercial firm*]
ICM............. Interoperability Configuration Manager
ICM............. Intracluster Medium [*Galactic science*]
ICM............. Intracompany Memorandum
ICM............. Inventory Control Manager (MCD)
ICM............. Investment Casting Mold (MCD)
ICM............. Ion Chromatography Module
ICM............. Ion Conductance Modulator [*Cytochemistry*]
ICM............. Irish Church Missions
ICM............. Ischemic Cardiomyopathy [*Also, IC*] [*Cardiology*]
ICM............. Isolation, Control, and Monitoring [*Pollution control*]
ICM............. Missionary Sisters of the Immaculate Heart of Mary (TOCD)
ICM............. Mundelein College, Chicago, IL [*OCLC symbol*] (OCLC)
ICM............. Soeurs Missionnaires du Coeur Immacule de Marie [*Missionary Sisters of the Immaculate Heart of Mary*] [*Italy*] (EAIO)
ICMA........... Imino(cyanomorpholinyl)deaminoadriamycin [*Antineoplastic drug*]
ICMA........... Independent Cabinet Makers' Association [*A union*] [*British*]
ICMA........... Independent Cable Makers' Association [*British*] (BI)
ICMA........... Initial Clothing Monetary Allowance [*Military*]
ICMA........... Institute for Computational Mathematics and Applications [*University of Pittsburgh*] [*Research center*] (RCD)
ICMA........... Institute of Certified Management Accountants [*Montvale, NJ*] (EA)
ICMA........... Institute of Cost and Management Accountants [*British*]
ICMA........... International Center of Medieval Art (EA)
ICMA........... International Christian Maritime Association [*Felixstone, Suffolk, England*] (EAIO)
ICMA........... International Cigarette Makers' Association [*A union*]
ICMA........... International Circulation Managers Association (EA)
ICMA........... International City Management Association [*Later, ICMA-The Professional Local Government Management Association*] (EA)
ICMAD......... Independent Cosmetic Manufacturers and Distributors (EA)
ICMARD....... International Center for Marine Resources Development (ASF)
ICMAREP..... Interagency Committee on Marine Environmental Prediction [*Marine science*] (OSRA)
ICMAREP..... Interagency Committee on Marine Environmental Prediction (USDC)

ICMASA....... Intersociety Committee on Methods for Air Sampling and Analysis (EA)
ICMay.......... Mayfair College, Chicago, IL [*Library symbol Library of Congress*] (LCLS)
ICMB........... International Center for Monetary and Banking Studies [*Switzerland*] (ECON)
ICMB........... Moody Bible Institute, Chicago, IL [*Library symbol Library of Congress*] (LCLS)
ICMBP........ Mayer, Brown & Platt Law Library, Chicago, IL [*Library symbol Library of Congress*] (LCLS)
ICMC.......... International Catholic Migration Commission [*See also CICM*] [*Geneva, Switzerland*] (EAIO)
ICMC.......... International Christian Media Commission (EA)
ICMC.......... International Cryogenic Materials Conference (EA)
ICMCA........ Museum of Contemporary Art, Chicago, IL [*Library symbol*] [*Library of Congress*] (LCLS)
ICMcC........ McCormick Theological Seminary, Chicago, IL [*Library symbol Library of Congress*] (LCLS)
ICMcDW...... McDermott, Will & Emory, Chicago, IL [*Library symbol*] [*Library of Congress*] (LCLS)
ICME.......... International Clearinghouse on the Military and the Environment (EA)
ICME.......... International Code of Medical Ethics
ICME.......... International Conference on Medical Electronics
ICME.......... International Conference on Medical Electronics (ECII)
ICME.......... International Congress on Mathematical Education (AIE)
ICME.......... International Congress on Mathematical Education [*International Council of Scientific Unions*]
ICME.......... International Contemporary Music Exchange (EA)
ICME.......... International Council on Metals and the Environment
ICMe.......... Meadville Theological School, Chicago, IL [*Library symbol Library of Congress*] (LCLS)
ICMEDC....... International Council of Masonry Engineering for Developing Countries [*Formerly, International Symposium on Reinforced and Prestressed Masonry*] (EA)
ICMen......... Chicago Mercantile Exchange, Chicago, IL [*Library symbol Library of Congress*] (LCLS)
ICMer.......... Charles E. Merriam Center for Public Administration, Merriam Center Library, Chicago, IL [*Library symbol Library of Congress*] (LCLS)
ICMG .... International Commission for Microbial Genetics [*International Council of Scientific Unions*]
ICMH .... Institut Canadien de Microreproductions Historiques [*Canadian Institute for Historical Microreproductions - CIHM*]
ICMH .... International Commission of Military History
ICMH .... Mercy Hospital and Medical Center, Chicago, IL [*Library symbol Library of Congress*] (LCLS)
ICMI........... Index of Childhood Memory and Imagination
ICMI........... Indonesian Muslim Intellectuals Association [*Political party*] (EY)
ICMI........... International Commission on Mathematical Instruction [*British*]
ICMICA....... Pax Romana, International Catholic Movement for Intellectual and Cultural Affairs [*See also MIIC*] [*Geneva, Switzerland*] (EAIO)
ICMID .... International Committee for Microbiological and Immunological Documentation [*International Council of Scientific Unions*]
ICMIS......... Integrated Computerized Management Information System (PDAA)
ICMJE......... International Committee of Medical Journal Editors [*An association*]
ICML.......... International Center for Medicine and Law (EA)
ICMLT........ International Congress of Medical Laboratory Technologists
ICMM......... Illinois Masonic Medical Center, Chicago, IL [*Library symbol Library of Congress*] (LCLS)
ICMM......... Incomplete Correlation Matrix Memory (PDAA)
ICMM......... International Committee of Military Medicine [*Belgium*] (EAIO)
ICMM......... International Congress of Maritime Museums (EA)
ICMMA....... Industrial Cleaning Machine Manufacturers Association [*British*] (DBA)
ICMMB....... International Conference on Mechanics in Medicine and Biology (EA)
ICM/MIRV.... Intercontinental Missile / Multiple Independently-Fuided Reentry Vehicle (PDAA)
ICMMP........ Integrated CONUS [*Continental United States*] Medical Mobilization Plan (DOMA)
ICMMP........ International Committee of Military Medicine and Pharmacy [*Belgium*]
ICMO.......... Indirect Cost Monitoring Office (AAGC)
ICMO.......... Integrated Configuration Management Office [*NASA*] (NASA)
ICMP.......... Interchannel Master Pulse
ICMP.......... International Confederation of Music Publishers [*British*] (EAIO)
ICMP.......... International Conference on Marine Pollution (ILCA)
ICMP.......... Internet Control and Message Protocol [*Telecommunications*]
ICMPD .... International Centre for Migration Policy Development [*Austria*] (ECON)
ICMPH .... International Center of Medical and Psychological Hypnosis [*Milan, Italy*] (EA)
ICMPS........ Induction Compass
ICMR .... Chicago Municipal Reference Library, Chicago, IL [*Library symbol Library of Congress*] (LCLS)
ICMR .... Indian Council of Medical Research
ICMR .... Instrument Calibration and Maintenance Record (MCD)
ICMR .... Interagency Committee on Medical Records (AAGC)
ICMRD .... International Center for Marine Resources Development [*University of Rhode Island*]
ICMREF....... Interagency Committee on Marine Science, Research, Engineering, and Facilities
ICMS........... Indirect Cost Management System (NASA)
ICMS........... Information Center Management System [*Cullinet*] (NITA)
ICMS........... Institute of Club Managers and Secretaries [*Australia*]
ICMS........... Instrument Calibration and Maintenance Schedule
ICMS........... Integrated Circuit and Message Switch

ICMS........... Interdepartmental Committee for Meteorological Services [*National Weather Service*]

ICMS........... International Centre for Mathematical Sciences [*Heriot-Watt University*] (ECON)

ICMS........... International Commission on Mushroom Science [*Later, ISMS*] (EA)

ICMS........... Intracortical Microstimulation [*For study of brain function*]

ICMSA........ Institute of Corporate Managers, Secretaries and Administrators [*Australia*]

ICMSA........ Irish Creamery Milk Suppliers' Association (BI)

ICMSE......... Interagency Committee on Marine Science and Engineering [*Federal Council for Science and Technology*]

ICMSF......... International Commission on Microbiological Specifications for Foods (EA)

ICMST......... International Conference on Machine Searching and Translation

ICMT........... Intercontract Material Transfer

ICMT........... International Commission on Mycotoxicology [*International Council of Scientific Unions*]

ICMTO........ Independent Carrier Military Traffic Office [*MTMC*] (TAG)

ICMU.......... Isolation Configuration and Monitor Unit (MCD)

ICMUA........ International Commission on the Meteorology of the Upper Atmosphere

ICMund....... Mundelein College, Chicago, IL [*Library symbol Library of Congress*] (LCLS)

ICMUP........ Instruction Control Memory Update Processor (MHDB)

ICMW.......... Inherent Corrective Maintenance Workload

ICMX.......... Malcolm X College of the City College of Chicago, Chicago, IL [*Library symbol Library of Congress*] (LCLS)

ICN............. ICN Pharmaceuticals [*NYSE symbol*] (TTSB)

ICN............. ICN Pharmaceuticals, Inc. [*Formerly, SPI Pharmaceuticals*] [*NYSE symbol*] (SPSG)

icn .... Icon (VRA)

ICN............. Idle Channel Noise (IAA)

ICN............. In Christi Nomine [*In the Name of Christ*] [*Latin*]

ICN............. Inclusion Conjunctivitis Neonate [*Ophthalmology*]

ICN............. Index of Community Noise

ICN............. Indicator Coupling Network (IAA)

ICN............. Inocan Technologies Ltd. [*Vancouver Stock Exchange symbol*]

ICN............. Instrumentation and Calibration Network (AAG)

ICN............. Integrated Computer Network

ICN............. Intensive Care Nursery [*Medicine*]

ICN............. Inter-Canadian [*ICAO designator*] (FAAC)

ICN............. Interface Change Notice (MCD)

ICN............. Interim Change Notice (AFM)

ICN............. International Communes Network (EAIO)

ICN............. International Conference on Nutrition [*United Nations*]

ICN............. International Council of Nurses [*Switzerland*] (EY)

ICN............. Intromogenous Computer Network

ICN............. Newberry Library, Chicago, IL [*Library symbol Library of Congress*] (LCLS)

ICN............. North Central College, Naperville, IL [*OCLC symbol*] (OCLC)

ICNA........... Infants' and Children's Novelties Association (EA)

ICNAF......... International Commission for the Northwest Atlantic Fisheries [*Superseded by NAFO*]

ICNAF......... International Council of North American Federation

ICNAF......... International Convention of the Northwest Atlantic Fisheries (USDC)

IC/NATAS.... International Council - National Academy of Television Arts and Sciences (EA)

IC/NATVAS... International Council of the National Academy of Television Arts and Sciences (EA)

ICNCP......... International Commission for the Nomenclature of Cultivated Plants [*Wageningen, Netherlands*] (EA)

ICND .... Irish Campaign for Nuclear Disarmament (EAIO)

ICNDT......... International Committee on NDT [*Nondestructive Testing*] [*Brazil*] (EAIO)

ICNDT......... International Conference on Non-Destuctive Testing (PDAA)

ICNE........... Northeastern Illinois University, Chicago, IL [*Library symbol Library of Congress*] (LCLS)

ICNEM........ Internacia Centro de la Neutrala Esperanto-Movado [*International Center of the Neutral Esperanto Movement*] [*Defunct*] (EAIO)

ICNEP......... Initiative Committee for National Economic Planning

ICNF .... Irredundant Conjunctive Normal Formula

ICNI .... Integrated Communication, Navigation, Identification [*System*]

ICNI .... Integrated Communications Network, Inc. [*NASDAQ symbol*] (SAG)

ICNI .... Integrated Commun Ntwk [*NASDAQ symbol*] (TTSB)

ICNIA......... Integrated Communication, Navigation, and Identification Avionics [*Air Force*]

ICNICP........ Integrated Communication/Navigation/Identification Control Panel (MCD)

ICNICS .... Integrated Communication/Navigation/Identification Control Set (MCD)

ICNND......... Interdepartmental Committee on Nutrition for National Defense

ICNP .... International Classification of Nursing Practice (DMAA)

ICNP .... International Commission on National Parks [*Later, CNPAA*] (EA)

ICN Ph........ ICN Pharmaceuticals, Inc. [*Formerly, International Chemical & Nuclear Corp.*] [*Associated Press*] (SAG)

ICNPT......... North Park College and Theological Seminary, Chicago, IL [*Library symbol Library of Congress*] (LCLS)

ICNS .... Information Center on Nuclear Standards [*American Nuclear Society*] [*Information service or system*]

ICNS .... Integrated Communications and Navigation System

ICNS .... National Safety Council, Chicago, IL [*Library symbol Library of Congress*] (LCLS)

ICNT........... INCOMNET, Inc. [*Formerly, Intelligent Commercial Net*] [*NASDAQ symbol*] (NQ)

ICNT........... Informal Composite Negotiating Text [*United Nations Conference on the Law of the Sea*]

ICNT........... Northern Trust Co., Chicago, IL [*Library symbol Library of Congress*]

ICNTG .... Intracoronary Nitroglycerine [*Pharmacology*]

ICNU .... National College of Education, Urban Campus, Chicago, IL [*Library symbol Library of Congress*] (LCLS)

ICNV .... International Committee on Nomenclature of Viruses [*Later, ICTV*]

ICNY .... International Center in New York (EA)

ICNY .... Islamic Center of New York (EA)

ICO............. ICO, Inc. [*Associated Press*] (SAG)

ICO............. Identified Camouflaged Objects [*Hunting*]

ICO............. Idiopathic Cyclic Oedema [*Medicine*] (DMAA)

ICO............. Illinois College of Optometry [*Chicago*]

ICO............. Illinois Wesleyan University, Bloomington, IL [*OCLC symbol*] (OCLC)

ICO............. Immediate Commanding Officer

ICO............. Impedance Cardiac Output [*Medicine*] (DMAA)

ICO............. In Case Of

ICO............. Independent Conducting Officer

ICO............. Indian Commissioned Officer [*British military*] (DMA)

ICO............. Information for the Contracting Officer (MCD)

ICO............. Input Current Offset [*Computer science*]

ICO............. Inspecting Chief Officer [*Military British*] (ROG)

ICO............. Institut Canadien des Oceans [*Oceans Institute of Canada*] (IRC)

ICO............. Institute of Careers Officers [*British*]

ICO............. Institute of Chemists-Opticians [*British*] (DAS)

ICO............. Instrumentation Control Officer (AAG)

ICO............. Integrated Checkout (NASA)

ICO............. Integrator Cutoff

ICO............. Interagency Committee on Oceanography [*Later, ICMSE*]

ICO............. Intercristo [*An association*] (EA)

ICO............. Intergovernmental Commission on Oceanography (NUCP)

ICO............. Interim Conservation Order

ICO............. International Carbohydrate Organization [*Aberdeen, Scotland*] (EAIO)

ICO............. International Cardero Resources [*Vancouver Stock Exchange symbol*]

ICO............. International Catholic Organizations

ICO............. International Civil Aviation Organization [*ICAO designator*] (FAAC)

ICO............. International Coffee Organization (EAIO)

ICO............. International College of Officers [*Salvation Army*]

ICO............. International Commission for Optics [*See also CIO*] [*ICSU Delft, Netherlands*] (EAIO)

ICO............. International Computer Orphanage (EA)

ICO............. International Council of Ophthalmology (EA)

ICO............. Internet Connectivity Option [*Galacticomm, Inc.*] [*Telecommunications*]

ICO............. Inventory Control Officer

ICO............. Le Iscrizioni Fenicie e Puniche delle Colonie in Occidente (BJA)

ICOA .... International Castor Oil Association (EA)

ICOA .... International CBX Owners Association (EA)

ICOBA......... International Confederation of Book Actors (EA)

ICOC .... ICO, Inc. [*NASDAQ symbol*] (NQ)

ICOC .... Instructions for Commodores of Convoys [*Navy Obsolete*]

ICOC .... International Commission for Orders of Chivalry (EA)

ICOCS......... Interim Circuit Order Control System [*Bell System*]

ICOCZ......... ICO Inc. 6.75% Cv Dep Pfd [*NASDAQ symbol*] (TTSB)

ICOD .... Intelligence Cutoff Date [*Military*] (MCD)

ICOD .... International Centre for Ocean Development [*See also CIEO*] [*Canada*]

ICOD .... International Council on Disability (EA)

ICODS......... Interagency Committee on Dam Safety [*Federal Emergency Management Agency*] [*Washington, DC*] (EGAO)

ICOE .... International Center for Orthopaedic Education

ICOEES .... Interagency Committee on Ocean Exploration and Environmental Services [*Terminated, 1971*] (NOAA)

ICOEES .... International Committee on Ocean Exploration and Environmental Services [*Defunct*] (USDC)

ICOEI .... Integral Components of End Items (MCD)

ICOF .... Industrial Common Ownership Finance [*An association British*]

I-COFT .... Institutional Conduct of Fire Trainer [*Army*]

ICOGRADA... International Council of Graphic Design Associations [*British*] (EA)

ICOH .... International Commission of Occupational Health (EA)

ICOH .... Olive-Harvey College Library, City Colleges of Chicago, Chicago, IL [*Library symbol*] [*Library of Congress*] (LCLS)

ICOHEPANS... International Conference on High Energy Physics and Nuclear Structure

ICOHH......... International Concatenated Order of Hoo-Hoo [*Later, International Order of Hoo-Hoo*] (EA)

ICOHTEC ...... International Committee for the History of Technology (EA)

ICOI .... International Congress of Oral Implantologists (EA)

ICO Inc .... ICO, Inc. [*Associated Press*] (SAG)

ICol............ Collinsville Public Library, Collinsville, IL [*Library symbol Library of Congress*] (LCLS)

IColCU .... Collinsville Community Unit 10, Collinsville, IL [*Library symbol Library of Congress*] (LCLS)

ICOLD .... International Commission on Large Dams [*See also CIGB*] [*ICSU Paris, France*] (EAIO)

ICOLP .... Industry Cooperative for Ozone Layer Protection

IColu .... Columbia Public Library, Columbia, IL [*Library symbol Library of Congress*] (LCLS)

IColuD .... Columbia Unit District 4, Columbia, IL [*Library symbol Library of Congress*] (LCLS)

ICOM .... Challenger International [*NASDAQ symbol*] (SAG)

ICOM .... Improved Conventional Mine System [*Military*] (MCD)

ICOM .... Industrial Common Ownership Movement [*British*]

ICOM .... Institute of Computational Mechanics [*University of Cincinnati*] [*Research center*] (RCD)
ICOM .... Intelect Communications Systems Ltd. [*NASDAQ symbol*] (SAG)
ICOM .... Intercommunications (NASA)
ICOM .... International Church of Metaphysics (EA)
ICOM .... International Council of Museums [*France*]
IComA .... Institute of Company Accountants [*British*] (EAIO)
ICOMC .... International Conference on Organometallic Chemistry
ICOM-CC ...... ICOM [*International Council of Museums*] Committee for Conservation (EAIO)
ICOME .... International Committee on Microbial Ecology [*ICSU*] (EAIO)
ICOMF .... Intelect Communications [*NASDAQ symbol*] (TTSB)
ICOMIA .... International Council of Marine Industry Associations [*Weybridge, Surrey, England*] (EA)
ICOMOS ...... International Council of Monuments and Sites [*France*] (EA)
ICOMP .... Iceland Ocean Meeting Point [*Navy*]
iCOMP .... Intel Comparative Microprocessor Performance Index (PCM)
ICOMP .... International Council on Management of Population Programmes [*Kuala Lumpur, Malaysia*] (EAIO)
ICON .... Iconoclasm (ADA)
ICON .... Iconography
ICON .... Imagery Communications and Operations Node (DOMA)
ICON .... Indexed Currency Option Note [*Student Loan Marketing Association*]
ICON .... Indexed Currency Option Notes (TDOB)
ICON .... Integrated COMSEC [*Communications Security*] [*Army*] (DOMA)
ICON .... Integrated Control
ICON .... Inter-Institutional Committee on Nutrition
ICON .... International Communication of Orthodox Nations
ICONCLASS... Iconography Classification [*Netherlands*] (NITA)
ICONDA .... International Construction Database [*Information Centre for Regional Planning and Building Construction of the Fraunhofer-Society*] [*Database*]
ICONMIG...... International Conference on Numerical Methods in Geomechanics
ICONS .... Information Center on Nuclear Standards [*American Nuclear Society*] [*La Grange Park, IL*] [*Information service or system*]
ICONS .... Inner Continental Shelf Sediments and Structure Program [*Army Corps of Engineers*] (GFGA)
ICONS .... International Communication and Negotiation Simulation
ICONS .... Isotopes of Carbon, Oxygen, Nitrogen, and Sulfur [*AEC project*]
iconst.......... Iconostasis (VRA)
ICOP .... Imported Crude Oil Processing
ICOP .... Intelligence Collect Program
ICOP .... Interagency Contingency Options Plan [*Military*]
ICOP .... Inventory Control Point
ICOPAMP ..... Integrated Circuit Operational Amplifier [*Electronics*] (IAA)
ICOPS .... Institute for the Comparative Study of Political Systems
ICOR .... In Charge of Room [*Military*] (DNAB)
ICOR .... Incremental Capital Output Ratio
ICOR .... Intergovernmental Conference on Oceanic Research
ICORRST...... Institution of Corrosion Science and Technology (PDAA)
ICORRT........ Institution of Corrosion Technology (PDAA)
ICORS .... International Conference of Raman Spectroscopy
ICOS .... ICOS Corp. [*NASDAQ symbol*] (SPSG)
ICOS .... Improved Crew Optical Sight (NASA)
ICOS .... Integrated Checkout System (KSC)
ICOS .... Integrated Cost Operation System (IAA)
ICOS .... Interactive COBOL Operating System
ICOS .... International Committee of Onomastic Sciences [*Belgium*]
ICOS .... Interpretation Canada. Ontario Section [*A publication*]
ICOS .... Irish Council for Overseas Students
ICOSA .... International Council of Seamen's Agencies (EA)
ICOSI .... International Committee on Smoking Issues [*Brussels, Belgium*] (EAIO)
ICOSO .... International Committee for Outer Space Onomastics
ICOSS .... Inertial-Command Off-Set System (MCD)
ICOT .... ICOT Corp. [*NASDAQ symbol*] (NQ)
Icot............ ICOT Corp. [*Associated Press*] (SAG)
ICOT .... Institute of Coastal Oceanography and Tides [*British*]
ICOT .... Institute of New Generation Computer Technology [*Japan*]
ICOTAS .... International Committee on the Organisation of Traffic at Sea [*British*] (DS)
ICOTS .... Interagency Committee on Transportation Security [*Department of Transportation*]
ICOTS .... International Conference on Teaching Statistics
ICOTT......... Industry Coalition on Technology Transfer (EA)
ICOTY .... Import Car of the Year [*Automotive promotion*]
ICOU .... International Consommateurs Organization des Unions [*International Organization of Consumers Unions*]
ICP............ ICS [*Interpretive Computer Simulator*] Control Program [*Army*]
ICP............ Ignition Control Programmer (MCD)
ICP............ Impact Copolymer Polypropylene [*Plastics*] [*Automotive engineering*]
ICP............ Incentive Compensation Plan (MCD)
ICP............ INCOLSA [*Indiana Cooperative Library Services Authority*] Processing Center, Indianapolis, IN [*OCLC symbol*] (OCLC)
ICP............ Incoming [*Message*] Process [*Telecommunications*] (TEL)
ICP............ Indian Communications Project
ICP............ Indicator Control Panel
ICP............ Indo-Chinese Communist Party [*Vietnam*] [*Political party*] (VNW)
ICP............ Inductively Coupled Plasma [*Spectrometry*]
ICP............ Inductively Coupled Plasma [*Chemical analysis*]
ICP............ Industrial Control Products (MCD)
ICP............ Industrial Coupling Program [*Refers to university-industry interaction*]
ICP............ Industry Cooperative Program [*United Nations*]
ICP............ Infection-Control Practitioner [*Medicine*]
ICP............ Infectious Cell Protein [*Genetics*]

ICP............ Initial Connection Protocol [*Computer science Telecommunications*]
ICP............ Inner City Partnership [*EEC and British program to regenerate blighted areas*]
ICP............ Insecticidal Crystal Protein [*Agrochemistry*]
ICP............ Installation Input Change Package (MCD)
ICP............ Instant Control Point [*British police*]
ICP............ Institute for Circadian Physiology [*Boston, MA*]
ICP............ Institute for Comprehensive Planning [*Defunct*] (EA)
ICP............ Institutional Conservation Program (GNE)
ICP............ Instructor Control Panel
ICP............ Instrument Calibration Procedure
ICP............ Insurance Conference Planners (EA)
ICP............ Integral Circuit Package
ICP............ Integrated Chemists of the Philippines
ICP............ Intelligence Collection Plan [*Military*] (AFM)
ICP............ Intelligent Communications Processor
IC-P........... Intelligent Copier-Printer [*Electrophotography*]
ICP............ Interdisciplinary Care Plan [*Information service or system*] (HCT)
ICP............ Interdisciplinary Communications Program
ICP............ Interface Change Proposal
ICP............ Interface Control Panel (MCD)
ICP............ Internal Combustion Powered (ADA)
ICP............ Internal Connection Protocol [*Telecommunications*]
ICP............ International Center of Photography (EA)
ICP............ International Classification of Patents [*Council of Europe*] (PDAA)
ICP............ International Comfort Products
ICP............ International Computer Programs, Inc. [*Indianapolis, IN*] [*Information service or system*]
ICP............ International Congress of Publishers (DIT)
ICP............ International Control Plan (MCD)
ICP............ International Council of Psychologists (EA)
ICP............ International Institute of Cellular and Molecular Pathology [*Belgium*] (IRC)
ICP............ Internet Content Provider [*Computer science*]
ICP............ Internet Control Protocol [*Telecommunications*] (PCM)
ICP............ Interoceanic Canal Project [*National Oceanic and Atmospheric Administration*] (NOAA)
ICP............ Inter-University Case Program
ICP............ Inter-University Cooperation Program [*EC*] (ECED)
ICP............ Intracarcass Pressure [*Tire technology*]
ICP............ Intracranial Pressure [*Medicine*]
ICP............ Intracuff Pressure [*In mechanical ventilation*] [*Medicine*]
ICP............ Intrinsically Conductive Plastic [*Organic chemistry*]
ICP............ Inventory Control Point
ICP............ Ion Coupled Plasma [*Oil analysis*]
ICP............ Iraqi Communist Party [*Political party*] (PPW)
ICP............ Irish Company Profiles [*Institute of Industrial Research and Standards - IIRS*] [*Dublin, Ireland*] [*Information service or system*] (IID)
ICP............ Ischemic Cardiac Pain [*Cardiology*]
ICP............ Islands of Cartilage Pattern [*Anatomy*]
ICP............ Italian Communist Party
ICP............ Item Control Point (AFM)
ICPA........... Information Centre for Polish Affairs (EAIO)
ICPA........... International Commission for the Prevention of Alcoholism [*Later, InternationalCommission for the Prevention of Alcoholism and Drug Dependency*]
ICPA........... International Conference of Police Associations [*Defunct*]
ICPA........... International Cooperative Petroleum Association (EA)
ICPA........... International Cruise Passengers Association (EA)
ICPA........... Public Administration Service, Joint Reference Library, Chicago, IL [*Library symbol Library of Congress*] (LCLS)
ICPAC .... Instantaneous Compressor Performance Analysis Computer
ICPADD....... International Commission for the Prevention of Alcoholism and Drug Dependency (EA)
ICP-AES ...... Inductively Coupled Plasma - Atomic Emission Spectrometry [*See also ICPES*]
ICPAM .... International Centre for Pure and Applied Mathematics [*United Nations*] (EA)
ICPAN .... Interfaith Council for the Protection of Animals and Nature (EA)
ICPAS .... Illinois Certified Public Accountants Society (SRA)
ICPAS .... Indiana Certified Public Accountants Society (SRA)
ICPas .... Passionist Academic Institute, Chicago, IL [*Library symbol Library of Congress*] (LCLS)
ICPB........... Inert Components Parts Building
ICPBC .... Institute of Certified Professional Business Consultants [*Chicago, IL*] (EA)
ICPBR .... International Commission for Plant-Bee Relationships (EAIO)
ICPC .... International Cable Protection Committee [*British*] (EAIO)
ICPC .... International Commission of Catholic Prison Chaplains (EA)
ICPC .... International Confederation of Popular Credit [*See also CICP*] [*Paris, France*] (EAIO)
ICPC .... International Conference of Police Chaplains (EA)
ICPC .... International Criminal Police Commission [*Later, INTERPOL*]
ICPC .... Interrange Communications Planning Committee
ICPC .... Intracranial Pressure Catheter [*Neurology*] (DAVI)
ICPCC .... International Council for Pastoral Care and Counselling (EAIO)
ICPCI .... International Conference on the Performance of Computer Installations (PDAA)
ICPDATA ...... Commodity Production Statistics [*United Nations Statistical Office*] [*Information service or system*] (CRD)
ICPDATA ...... International Commodity Production Data [*United Nations Statistical Office*] (NITA)
ICPDES .... International Cancer Patient Data Exchange System
ICPDS .... Interactive Continuous Process Dynamic Simulation (PDAA)

ICPE............ Internal Combustion Piston Engine (PDAA)
ICPE............. International Center for Public Enterprises in Developing Countries [Ljubljana, Yugoslavia] (EAIO)
ICPE............. International Commission on Physics Education [See also CIEP] (EA)
ICPE............. International Conference on Public Education [International Bureau of Education] [Switzerland]
ICPE............. Inventory Control Point Europe
ICPEAC .... International Conference on the Physics of Electronic and Atomic Collisions
ICPEM.......... Independent Computer Peripheral Equipment Manufacturers
ICPEMC........ International Commission for Protection Against Environmental Mutagens and Carcinogens [Rijswljk, Netherlands] (EAIO)
ICPERS .... Instant Computer Public Employment Relations Search [Database] [Labor Relations Press] [Information service or system] (CRD)
ICPES........... Inductively Coupled Plasma Emission Spectrometry [See also ICP-AES]
ICPES........... Intergovernmental Committee for Physical Education and Sport [United Nations France] (EY)
ICPFF........... Incentive Cost plus Fixed Fee [Contracts]
ICPFR .... International Council for Physical Fitness Research [Research center Canada] (IRC)
ICPG .... People Gas Light Co., Chicago, IL [Library symbol Library of Congress] (LCLS)
ICPHS .... International Council for Philosophy and Humanistic Studies [Paris, France]
ICPI............. Insurance Crime Prevention Institute [Westport, CT] (EA)
ICPI............. Interagency Committee on Product Information (EA)
ICPI............. Interlocking Concrete Pavement Institute
ICPI............. Intersociety Committee on Pathology Information (EA)
ICPIC .... International Cleaner Production Information Clearinghouse (GNE)
ICPIC .... International Conference on Phenomena in Ionised Gases (PDAA)
ICPIC .... International Council for Philosophical Inquiry with Children [Iceland] (EAIO)
ICPICH .... International Commission for the Preservation of Islamic Cultural Heritage (EA)
ICPIG .... International Conference on Phenomena in Ionised Gases (PDAA)
ICPIGP .... Internationale Chretienne Professionelle pour les Industries Graphiques et Papetieres [International Federation of Christian Trade Unions of Graphical and Paper Industries]
ICPIWC .... International Council for Philosophical Inquiry with Children (EA)
ICpKSD .... J. F. Kennedy Consolidated Community School District 129, Cedar Point, IL [Library symbol Library of Congress] (LCLS)
ICPL............ Initial Control Program Load [Computer science] (IAA)
ICPL............ International Committee of Passenger Lines (PDAA)
ICPL............ Iowa City Public Library [Iowa]
ICPLS .... International College of Podiatric Laser Surgery (EA)
ICPM........... Illinois College of Podiatric Medicine, Chicago, IL [Library symbol Library of Congress] (LCLS)
ICPM........... Institute of Certified Professional Managers [Harrisonburg, VA] (EA)
ICPM........... International Congress of Physical Medicine (PDAA)
ICPME......... International Center for Peace in the Middle East (EA)
ICPMM........ Incisors, Canines, Premolars, Molars [Dentistry]
ICPMM........ Peat, Marwick, and Mitchell, Chicago, IL [Library symbol Library of Congress] (LCLS)
ICPMP .... International Commission for the Protection of the Moselle Against Pollution (EA)
ICP-MS .... Inductively Coupled Plasma - Mass Spectrometry
ICPMS .... International Council of Prison Medical Services [Vancouver, BC] (EAIO)
ICPN .... International Committee of Plant Nutrition (EA)
ICPO .... Institute for Certified Park Operators (EA)
ICPO .... International CLIVAR [Climate Variability and Prediction] Project Office [Marine science] (OSRA)
ICPO .... International Criminal Police Organization [France]
ICPO .... Investment Co-Operative Programme Office [UNIDO]
ICPOA......... Intelligence Center, Pacific Ocean Areas [Obsolete]
ICP-OES ...... Inductively Coupled Plasma - Optical Emission Spectrometry
ICPP............ Idaho Chemical Processing Plant [AEC]
ICPP............ Institutional Child Protection Project [Ohio State University] (EDAC)
ICPP............ Interactive Computer Presentation Panel [To display computer-generated information for military use]
ICPP............ International Comparative Political Parties Project [Northwestern University] [Inactive] (IID)
ICPP............ Intubated Continuous Positive Pressure [Medicine] (DAVI)
ICPP............ Isochromic Color Perception Plates [Ophthalmology] (DAVI)
ICPR............ Incoming Capital Property Record
ICPR............ Industrial Cost and Performance Report (NG)
ICPR............ Integrated Circuit Parameter Retrieval [Information Handling Services] [Database]
ICPR............ Inter-University Consortium for Political Research [Later, ICPSR] (EA)
ICPRAP........ International Commission for the Protection of the Rhine Against Pollution [See also ICPRP, IKSR] [Germany] (EAIO)
ICPRB .... Interstate Commission on the Potomac River Basin
ICPRCPCO ... Intergovernmental Committee for Promoting the Return of Cultural Property to ItsCountries of Origin or Its Restitution in Case of Illicit Appropriation (EA)
ICPRCU....... Polish Roman Catholic Union of America, Chicago, IL [Library symbol Library of Congress] (LCLS)
ICPrM .... Provident Medical Center, Chicago, IL [Library symbol] [Library of Congress] (LCLS)
ICPRS .... Petersen, Ross, Schloerb & Seidel, Library, Chicago, IL [Library symbol Library of Congress] (LCLS)

ICPS............. ICBM [Intercontinental Ballistic Missile] Code Processing System (DWSG)
ICPS............. Industrial and Commercial Power Systems (MCD)
ICPS............. Institute for Cultural Policy Studies [Griffith University] [Australia]
ICPS............. Interamerican College of Physicians and Surgeons (EA)
ICPS............. International Carnivorous Plant Society (EA)
ICPS............. International Cerebral Palsy Society [British] (EAIO)
ICPS............. International Conference on the Properties of Steam
ICPS............. International Congress of Photographic Science
ICPS............. International Council of Perfusion Societies [Defunct] (EA)
ICPS............. Interpersonal Cognitive Problem-Solving Program (EDAC)
ICPSR .... Inter-University Consortium for Political and Social Research (EA)
ICPTO .... International China Painting Teachers Organization [Later, International Porcelain Artist Teachers]
ICPTUR .... International Conference for Promoting Technical Uniformity on Railways [Berne, Switzerland] (EAIO)
ICPU .... International Catholic Press Union [Later, UCIP]
ICPUAE .... International Conference on the Peaceful Uses of Atomic Energy
ICPV........... International Committee on Polar Viruses
ICPVT .... International Council for Pressure Vessel Technology (EA)
ICPYY .... Institute of Clinical Pharmacology PLC (MHDW)
i-cq-- .... Comoro Islands [MARC geographic area code Library of Congress] (LCCP)
ICQ............. Internal Control Questionnaire (ADA)
ICQ............. International Capri Resources [Vancouver Stock Exchange symbol]
ICQA .... International Columbian Quincentenary Alliance (EA)
ICQC .... International Conference on Quality Control (PDAA)
ICr.............. Chicago Ridge Public Library, Chicago Ridge, IL [Library symbol Library of Congress] (LCLS)
ICR............. Eagle Aero, Inc. [ICAO designator] (FAAC)
ICR............. Identification and Compliance Record (MCD)
ICR............. Iliac Crest [Anatomy]
ICR............. Illinois Central Railroad
ICR............. Illustration Change Request
ICR............. Immunodeficiency Cancer Registry
ICR............. In-Commission Rate
ICR............. Independent Component Release [Computer science] (IBMDP)
ICR............. Indirect Control Register [Computer science]
ICR............. Individual Census Report (GFGA)
ICR............. Individually Carried Records [Military]
ICR............. Inductance-Capacitance-Resistance
ICR............. Industrial Cases Reports [Law reports] [British] (DCTA)
ICR............. Industrial Cost Recovery [Environmental Protection Agency]
ICR............. Industrial Court Reports [England] [A publication] (DLA)
ICR............. Inertial Confinement Fusion Reactor [Nuclear energy] (MCD)
ICR............. Information Collection Request [Paperwork Reduction Act] (GFGA)
ICR............. Information Collection Rule [Environmental Protection Agency]
ICR............. Information Collection Rule [Environmental Protection Agency]
ICR............. Information Collection Rule (ACII)
ICR............. Input and Compare Register
ICR............. Input Control Register [Computer science]
ICR............. Instantaneous Center of Rotation
ICR............. Institute for Cancer Research (EA)
ICR............. Institute for Communications Research [Texas Tech University] [Research center] (RCD)
ICR............. Institute for Computer Research [University of Waterloo] [Canada Research center] (RCD)
ICR............. Institute for Constitutional Research (EA)
ICR............. Institute for Cooperative Research
ICR............. Institute for Creation Research (EA)
ICR............. Institute for Cultural Research [Research center British] (IRC)
ICR............. Institute of Coal Research [University of Newcastle] [Australia]
ICR............. Instruction Change Request (NASA)
ICR............. Instrumentation Control Racks (AAG)
ICR............. Insulated Core Reactor
ICR............. Integral Cesium Reservoir
ICR............. Integrated Color Removal [Printing technology]
ICR............. Integration of Cellular Responses [Research initiative] [bbswrc - Biotechnology and Biological Sciences Research Council] [British]
ICR............. Intelligence Collection Requirement [Army] (RDA)
ICR............. Intelligent Character Recognition [Computer science]
ICR............. Intensive Care Room [Medicine] (DAVI)
ICR............. Interactive Conflict Resolution (PDAA)
ICR............. Intercity Relay [Broadcasting] (NTCM)
ICR............. Intercolonial Railway [1858-1923] [Canada]
ICR............. Intercooled Recuperative [Engine] (DOMA)
ICR............. Intercultural Relations (DNAB)
ICR............. Interest Coverage Ratio
ICR............. Interface Compatibility Record (NASA)
ICR............. Interface Control Register (IAA)
ICR............. Intermediate Circulating Reflux [Chemical engineering]
ICR............. Intermittent Catheter Routine [Medicine] (DMAA)
ICR............. Internal Control Region [Genetics]
ICR............. Internal Control Review [DoD]
ICR............. International Committee on Refugees [World War II]
ICR............. International Computer Resources, Inc. [Information service or system] (IID)
ICR............. International Congress of Radiology
ICR............. International Consumer Reports [Consumers' Association] [British Information service or system] (IID)
ICR............. International Corona Resources Ltd. [Vancouver Stock Exchange symbol]
ICR............. International Council for Reprography
IC/R............. International Cruiser/Race Class [Yachting]

ICR.............. Interrupt Control Register [*Computer science*]
ICR.............. Intracardiac Catheter Recording [*Medicine*] (DMAA)
ICR.............. Intracranial Reinforcement
ICR.............. Inventory Change Report
ICR.............. Ion Cyclotron Radiation
ICR.............. Ion Cyclotron Resonance [*Spectrometry*]
ICR.............. Irish Chancery Reports [*A publication*] (DLA)
ICR.............. Irish Circuit Reports [*1841-43*] [*A publication*] (DLA)
ICR.............. Iron-Core Reactor (MSA)
ICR.............. Item Change Request (AFIT)
ICR.............. Nicaro [*Cuba*] [*Airport symbol Obsolete*] (OAG)
ICRA.......... Indian Civil Rights Act [*1968*]
ICRA.......... Industrial Chemical Research Association (EA)
ICRA.......... Industrial Copyright Reform Association [*British*] (DBA)
ICRA.......... Interagency Committee on Radiological Assistance
ICRA.......... International Cartridge Recycling Association (EA)
ICRA.......... International Catholic Rural Association
ICRA.......... International Centre for Research in Accounting [*University of Lancaster*] [*British*] (CB)
ICRA.......... Iowa Court Reporters Association (SRA)
ICRA.......... Islamic Correctional Reunion Association (EA)
ICRAEE........ International Commission on Rules for the Approval of Electrical Equipment [*Later, CEE*]
ICRAF.......... Institut Canadien de Recherches pour l'Avancement de la Femme [*Canadian Research Institute for the Advancement of Women*]
ICRAF.......... International Council for Research in Agroforestry [*See also ICRAF*] [*Kenya*] (EAIO)
ICRaH.......... Ravenswood Hospital Medical Center, Chicago, IL [*Library symbol Library of Congress*] (LCLS)
ICRand.......... Rand McNally & Co., Chicago, IL [*Library symbol Library of Congress*] (LCLS)
ICRAR.......... Interfaith Center to Reverse the Arms Race (EA)
ICRAS.......... International Committee for the Release of Anatoly Scharansky [*Defunct*] (EA)
ICRA(V)........ Indo-Chinese Refugee Association (Victoria) [*Australia*]
ICRB.......... International Center for Research on Bilingualism [*Universite Laval*] [*Canada*]
ICRB.......... International Co-Operative Reinsurance Bureau [*Manchester, England*] (EAIO)
ICRC.......... Imperial College Reactor Centre [*Imperial College of Science and Technology*] [*British*] (WND)
ICRC.......... Infant Care Review Committee [*Medicine*] (DMAA)
ICRC.......... Interagency Classification Review Committee [*Abolished, 1978*] [*DoD*]
ICRC.......... International Committee to the Red Cross [*Geneva, Switzerland*] (EAIO)
ICRC.......... Roosevelt University, Chicago, IL [*Library symbol Library of Congress*] (LCLS)
ICRC-N........ Roosevelt University, North Campus, Arlington Heights, IL [*Library symbol Library of Congress*] (LCLS)
ICRD.......... Index of Codes for Research Drugs [*A publication*]
ICRD.......... Input Collection Reports Data [*IRS*]
ICRD.......... Interior Committee on Research and Development
ICRD.......... Richard J. Daley College, Chicago, IL [*Library symbol*] [*Library of Congress*] (LCLS)
ICRDA.......... Independent Cash Register Dealers Association (EA)
ICRDB.......... International Cancer Research Data Bank [*National Cancer Institute*] [*Database producer*] (IID)
ICRDD.......... Institute for Community Resource Development [*Australia*]
ICre.............. Crete Public Library, Crete, IL [*Library symbol Library of Congress*] (LCLS)
ICRE.......... Ignitability Corrosivity, Reactivity, Extraction (GNE)
ICRE.......... International Commission on Radiological Education (DMAA)
ICREB.......... International Champlain-Richelieu Engineering Board [*Canada*]
ICREF.......... Institut Canadien de Recherches sur les Femmes (AC)
IC Rep.......... Interstate Commerce Commission Reports [*A publication*] (DLA)
ICRETT........ International Cancer Research Technology Transfer [*Program*]
ICREW.......... International Cancer Research Workshop
ICRF.......... Imperial Cancer Research Fund [*British*]
ICRF.......... Ion Cyclotron Radio Frequency
ICRF.......... Ion Cyclotron Resonance Frequency [*Nuclear energy*]
ICRF 159...... Imperial Cancer Research Fund 159 [*Razoxane*] [*Antineoplastic drug*]
ICRFSDD...... Independent Citizens Research Foundation for the Study of Degenerative Diseases (EA)
ICRGR.......... International Consultative Research Group on Rape [*See also GCIRC*] (EAIO)
ICRH.......... Information Center - Recreation for the Handicapped
ICRH.......... Institute for Computer Research in the Humanities [*New York University*]
ICRH.......... Ion Cyclotron Resonance Heating (MCD)
ICRH.......... Michael Reese Hospital and Medical Center, Lillian W. Florsheim Memorial Library, Chicago, IL [*Library symbol Library of Congress*] (LCLS)
ICRHO.......... Ross, Hardies, O'Keefe, Babcock, and Parsons, Chicago, IL [*Library symbol Library of Congress*] (LCLS)
ICRHS.......... Illinois Central Railroad Historical Society (EA)
ICRI.......... International Child Resource Institute (EA)
ICRI.......... International Coma Recovery Institute (EA)
ICRI.......... Iron Casting Research Institute (EA)
ICRI.......... Rehabilitation Institute of Chicago, Chicago, IL [*Library symbol*] [*Library of Congress*] (LCLS)
ICRICE.......... International Centre of Research and Information on Collective Economy

ICRIP.......... International Circle for Research in Philosophy [*Research center*] (RCD)
ICRISAT...... International Crops Research Institute for the Semi-Arid Tropics [*India*]
ICRL.......... Center for Research Libraries, Chicago, IL [*Library symbol Library of Congress*] (LCLS)
ICRL.......... Individual Component Repair List [*DoD*]
ICRL.......... Injury Control Research Laboratory [*HEW*]
ICRL(ARL).... Foreign Newspaper Microfilm Project, Association of Research Libraries, Center for Research Libraries, Chicago, IL [*Library symbol Library of Congress*] (LCLS)
ICRL(CAMP)... Cooperative Africana Microform Project, Archives-Libraries Committee, African Studies Association, Center for Research Libraries, Chicago, IL [*Library symbol Library of Congress*] (LCLS)
ICRlF.......... Follett Library Book Co., Crystal Lake, IL [*Library symbol*] [*Library of Congress*] (LCLS)
ICRL-LA...... Latin America Microform Project, Center for Research Libraries, Chicago, IL [*Library symbol*] [*Library of Congress*] (LCLS)
ICRLP.......... International Center for Research on Language Planning [*Laval University*] (IRC)
ICRL-RR...... Injury Control Research Laboratory Research Report [*HEW*]
ICRL(SAMP)... South Asian Microform Project, South Asian Microform and Library Committee, Association for Asian Studies, Center for Research Libraries, Chicago, IL [*Library symbol Library of Congress*] (LCLS)
ICRL-SEA..... South East Asia Microform Project, Center for Research Libraries, Chicago, IL [*Library symbol*] [*Library of Congress*] (LCLS)
I CRM.......... Ice Cream [*Freight*]
ICRM.......... Institute of Certified Records Managers (EA)
ICRM.......... Intercontinental Reconnaissance Missile (DNAB)
ICRM.......... International Carpet and Rug Market (ITD)
ICRM.......... International Cliff Richard Movement (EAIO)
ICRM.......... Rush Medical College, Chicago, IL [*Library symbol Library of Congress*] (LCLS)
ICRMS.......... Integrated Computer-Reactor Monitoring System (PDAA)
ICRO.......... Interallied Confederation of Reserve Officers [*See also CIOR*] (EAIO)
ICRO.......... International Cell Research Organization [*ICSU*] [*Paris, France*] (EAIO)
ICROSS........ International Community for the Relief of Starvation and Suffering (EA)
ICRP.......... Internal Control Review Program [*Air Force*] (DOMA)
ICRP.......... International Climatic Research Program
ICRP.......... International Commission on Radiological Protection [*International Society of Radiology*] [*British*]
ICRPDS........ Ion Cyclotron Resonance Photodissociation [*Spectrometry*]
ICRPG.......... Interagency Chemical Rocket Propulsion Group
ICRPMA...... International Committee for Recording the Productivity of Milk Animals [*See also CICPLB*] [*Rome, Italy*] (EAIO)
ICRS.......... Imagery Collection Requirements Subcommittee [*Military*]
ICRS.......... Index Chemicals Registry System [*Databank*] (NITA)
ICRS.......... Index Chemicus Registry System [*Information service or system A publication*]
ICRS.......... Institute of Contemporary Russian Studies [*Fordham University*]
ICRS.......... Instrument Calibration and Recall System [*Nuclear energy*] (NRCH)
ICRS.......... Integrated Chemical Retrieval System [*Pergamon InfoLine*] [*Computer science*]
ICRS.......... Intelligence Collection Reporting System [*Military*] (MCD)
ICRSC.......... International Council for Research in the Sociology of Co-operation
ICRSDT...... International Committee on Remote Sensing and Data Transmission [*Marine science*] (OSRA)
ICRT.......... Individual Criterion-Referenced Test [*Education*]
iCRT.......... Intelligent Content Recognition Technology [*Computer science*]
ICRU.......... International Commission on Radiation Units and Measurements (EA)
IcRU.......... University of Icelands (Haskoli Islands), Reykjavik, Iceland [*Library symbol Library of Congress*] (LCLS)
ICRUM.......... International Commission on Radiation Units and Measurements
ICRV.......... Inns of Court Rifle Volunteers [*Military British*] (ROG)
ICRW.......... International Center for Research on Women (EA)
ICRW.......... International Convention for the Regulation of Whaling (ASF)
ICRW.......... Rednik & Wolfe, Chicago, IL [*Library symbol*] [*Library of Congress*] (LCLS)
ICS.......... Identifying Criteria for Success [*Software package*] [*Development Dimensions Inc.*]
ICS.......... Ileocecal Sphincter [*Medicine*] (DMAA)
ICS.......... Illinois Chiropractic Society (SRA)
ICS.......... Immotile Cilia Syndrome [*Medicine*] (DMAA)
ICS.......... Immunochemistry System [*Medicine*]
ICS.......... Imperial College of Science [*British*]
ICS.......... Impulse Conducting System [*Physiology*]
ICS.......... In-Can System [*Device that improves quality of beer and ale*] [*British*]
ICS.......... Incident Command System [*Regional emergency response system*] (DHSM)
ICS.......... Indian Civil Service [*British*]
ICS.......... Induction Communications System
ICS.......... Industrial Control System
ICS.......... Infinity Color-Corrected System [*Optics*]
ICS.......... Information Calling Services [*Telecommunications*]
ICS.......... Information Centers Service [*United States Information Agency*] (IID)
ICS.......... Information Collection System (MHDI)
ICS.......... Information Computer System (IAA)
ICS.......... Information Control System [*Military*]
ICS.......... Infrared Calibration System

ICS.............. Infrared Camera System
ICS.............. Infrared Communications System
ICS.............. Infrared Countermeasures System [Military Electronics]
ICS.............. Injection Compression System
ICS.............. Inland Computer Service (IEEE)
ICS.............. Innes Clan Society (EA)
ICS.............. Input Contactor Switch
ICS.............. Input Control Subsystem
ICS.............. Insert Card Section
ICS.............. Institute for Chemical Studies (GNE)
ICS.............. Institute for Christian Studies
ICS.............. Institute for Cognitive Science [University of California, San Diego] [Research center] (RCD)
ICS.............. Institute for Computer Sciences (HGAA)
ICS.............. Institute for Contemporary Studies (EA)
ICS.............. Institute for Cultural Studies [Defunct] (EA)
ICS.............. Institute for the Comparative Study of History, Philosophy, and the Sciences Ltd. [British] (BI)
ICS.............. Institute of Chartered Shipbrokers [British]
ICS.............. Institute of Child Study [University of Toronto] [Research center] (RCD)
ICS.............. Institute of Cognitive Science [University of Colorado, Boulder] [Research center] (RCD)
ICS.............. Institute of Commonwealth Studies [British]
ICS.............. Institute of Complementary Sciences [Defunct] (EA)
ICS.............. Institute of Cornish Studies [British]
ICS.............. Institution of Computer Sciences [British] (DIT)
ICS.............. Instructional Communications Systems [University of Wisconsin] [Telecommunications service] (TSSD)
ICS.............. Instrumentation and Communication Subsystem [NASA] (KSC)
ICS.............. Instrumentation and Control Subsystem
ICS.............. Instrumentation Checkout Station (AAG)
ICS.............. Insurance Communication Service [IBM Information Network] [Tampa, FL] [Telecommunications] (TSSD)
ICS.............. Integrated Case Study [Medicine] (DMAA)
ICS.............. Integrated Checkout System (KSC)
ICS.............. Integrated Circuit System (IMH)
ICS.............. Integrated Collection System [IRS]
ICS.............. Integrated Combat Ship
ICS.............. Integrated Combat System
ICS.............. Integrated Command System
ICS.............. Integrated Communication Systems, Inc. [Roswell, GA] [Telecommunications] (IEEE)
ICS.............. Integrated Composite Spinning (PDAA)
ICS.............. Integrated Computer Solutions
ICS.............. Integrated Computer Systems [Culver City, CA] [Telecommunications service] (TSSD)
ICS.............. Integrated Configuration Summary (AAG)
ICS.............. Integrated Conning System (PDAA)
ICS.............. Integrated Control Storage [Computer science]
ICS.............. Integrated Control System (NRCH)
ICS.............. Intelligence Center and School [Army] (RDA)
ICS.............. Intelligence Community Staff [Military] (MCD)
ICS.............. Intensive Care Society [British] (EAIO)
ICS.............. Intensive Care, Surgical [Medicine]
ICS.............. Interactive Communications Software
ICS.............. Interactive Compatibility Software [Gateway Communications, Inc.] [Computer science] (PCM)
ICS.............. Interactive Counting System (IAA)
ICS.............. Interagency Communications System [Military]
ICS.............. InterCapital Ins Cal Muni Sec [NYSE symbol] (TTSB)
ICS.............. InterCapital Insured California Municipal Securities [NYSE symbol] (SAG)
ICS.............. Intercarrier Sound (IAA)
ICS.............. Intercellular Space (DMAA)
ICS.............. Inter-Celtic Society (EAIO)
ICS.............. Intercistronic Spacer [Genetics]
ICS.............. Intercockpit Communications System [Navy] (DOMA)
ICS.............. Intercommunication Control Station (KSC)
ICS.............. Intercommunications System
ICS.............. Intercontinental Church Society [British] (EAIO)
ICS.............. Intercostal Space [Medicine]
ICS.............. Interface Control Specification (MCD)
ICS.............. Interference Check Sample [Spectroscopy]
ICS.............. Interim Contractor Support (MCD)
ICS.............. Interior Contractor Support
ICS.............. Interlinked Computerized Storage and Processing System of Food and Agricultural Data [Databank] [United Nations Information service or system] (IID)
ICS.............. Intermittent Control Strategy [Environmental Protection Agency] (GFGA)
ICS.............. Intermittent Control System [Environmental Protection Agency]
ICS.............. Internal Chemical Shift
ICS.............. Internal Communication System [Space Flight Operations Facility, NASA]
ICS.............. Internal Countermeasures Set (MCD)
ICS.............. International Camellia Society [Worcester, England] (EAIO)
ICS.............. International Cardiovascular Society
ICS.............. International Catacomb Society (EA)
ICS.............. International Chamber of Shipping [British] (EAIO)
ICS.............. International Chemical Society [Proposed]
ICS.............. International Chemometrics Society [Brussels, Belgium] (EAIO)
ICS.............. International Chili Society (EA)
ICS.............. International Churchill Society (EA)
ICS.............. International Clarinet Society [Later, ICS/CI] (EA)

ICS.............. International Code of Signals (IAA)
ICS.............. International Cogeneration Society (EA)
ICS.............. International Cold Storage
ICS.............. International College of Scientists [See also ISK] [International Academy of Sciences] [Paderborn, Federal Republic of Germany] (EAIO)
ICS.............. International College of Surgeons (EA)
ICS.............. International Committee of Slavists [Sofia, Bulgaria] (EAIO)
ICS.............. International Committee on Sarcoidosis [British] (EAIO)
ICS.............. International Communications Sciences
ICS.............. International Communications System
ICS.............. International Computer System (IAA)
ICS.............. International Connecting Set (IAA)
ICS.............. International Conrad Society (EA)
ICS.............. International Controlled Industry [Vancouver Stock Exchange symbol]
ICS.............. International Coronelli Society [See also ICGGI] (EAIO)
ICS.............. International Correspondence School
ICS.............. International Craniopathic Society [SORSI] [Absorbed by] (EA)
ICS.............. International Crocodilian Society [Defunct] (EA)
ICS.............. Interphone Control Station
ICS.............. Interphone Control System
ICS.............. Interpretive Computer Simulator
ICS.............. Interpretive Computer System
ICS.............. Interviewer Card Scheme [Business term]
ICS.............. Intracapillary Space [In bioreactor]
ICS.............. Intracellular-Like Solution [Cardioplegic solution] [Pharmacology] (DAVI)
ICS.............. Intracommunication System
ICS.............. Intracranial Self-Stimulation [Also, ICSS] [Neurophysiology]
ICS.............. Intracranial Stimulation [Neurophysiology]
ICS.............. Inventory Control System [Computer science]
ICS.............. Inverse Conical Scan (DNAB)
ICS.............. Ion-Channel Switch [Biochemistry]
ICS.............. Ionization Current Source (PDAA)
ICS.............. Iowa Chiropractic Society (SRA)
ICS.............. Irish Computer Society
ICS.............. Iron Castings Society (EA)
ICS.............. Irritable Colon Syndrome [Medicine] (DMAA)
ICS.............. Isolation Containment Spray [Nuclear energy] (IEEE)
ICS.............. Issued Capital Stock
ICS.............. Saint Xavier College, Chicago, IL [OCLC symbol] (OCLC)
ICS.............. Society of Inter-Celtic Arts and Culture (EA)
ICS2............. Intelligent Communication Subsystem Two Board [Controls input from computer terminals to mainframe] [Prime Computer, Inc.]
ICSA......... In-Core Shim Assembly [Nuclear energy] (NRCH)
ICSA......... Indian Council of South America [See also CISA] [Lima, Peru] (EAIO)
ICSA......... Information and Computing Services Association (ACII)
ICSA......... Institute of Chartered Secretaries and Administrators (AIE)
ICSA......... International Cemetery Supply Association (EA)
ICSA......... International Chain Salon Association (EA)
ICSA......... International Christian Studies Association (EA)
ICSA......... International Claims Settlement Act of 1949
ICSA......... International Committee Against Apartheid, Racism, and Colonialism in Southern Africa [British Defunct] (EAIO)
ICSA......... International Computer Security Association
ICSA......... International Correspondence Society of Allergists (EA)
ICSA......... International Customer Service Association [Chicago, IL] (EA)
ICSA......... Intracranial Self-Administration [Neurophysiology]
ICSA......... Islet Cell Surface Antibody [Immunology]
ICSA......... Sidley and Austin Library, Chicago, IL [Library symbol Library of Congress] (LCLS)
ICSAB .... International Civil Service Advisory Board
ICSAC .... International Confederation of Societies of Authors and Composers
ICSac .... Sachnoff Weaver & Rubenstein, Chicago, II [Library symbol] [Library of Congress] (LCLS)
ICSAF .... International Commission for the Southeast Atlantic Fisheries [See also CIPASE] (EAIO)
ICSAL .... Integrated Communications System, Alaska [Air Force, FAA]
ICSAPI .... Internet Connection Services [Computer science] (PCM)
ICSB........... Interim Command Switchboard [Navy] (NVT)
ICSB........... International Committee on Systematic Bacteriology [London, ON] (EA)
ICSB........... International Council for Small Business (EA)
ICSBC .... Interstate Council of State Boards of Cosmetology [Later, NIC]
ICSBS .... International Chinese Snuff Bottle Society (EA)
ICSC........... Institute for Cardiovascular Studies [University of Houston] [Research center] (RCD)
ICSC........... Integrated Command Support Center [Military] (MCD)
ICSC........... Interim Commission on Satellite Communication (NITA)
ICSC........... Interim Communications Satellite Committee
ICSC........... Interior Communication Switching Center (DNAB)
ICSC........... International Civil Service Commission (EA)
ICSC........... International Commission for Supervision and Control [Composed of delegates from Canada, India and Poland established by the 1954 Geneva Accords] (VNW)
ICSC........... International Communications Satellite Consortium (MCD)
ICSC........... International Communications Systems Consultants [British] (NITA)
ICSC........... International Council of Shopping Centers (EA)
ICSC........... International Council of Shopping Centres [Australia]
ICSC........... Inter-Ocean Canal Study Commission (PDAA)
ICSC........... Irish Christian Study Centre [New University of Ulster] [British] (CB)
ICSC........... Irvine Computer Sciences Corporation (NITA)
ICSC........... Italy and Colonies Study Circle (EA)

ICSC............ Swift & Company, Research Laboratory Library, Chicago, IL [*Library symbol Library of Congress*] (LCLS)

ICSCA .... Institute for Computing Science and Computer Applications [*University of Texas at Austin*] [*Research center*] (RCD)

ICSch .... Schiff, Harden & Waite, Chicago, IL [*Library symbol*] [*Library of Congress*] (LCLS)

ICS/CI .... International Clarinet Society/Clarinetwork International (EA)

ICSCN .... Sonnenschein, Carlin, Nath & Rosenthal, Chicago, IL [*Library symbol*] [*Library of Congress*] (LCLS)

ICSD .... Inorganic Crystal Structure Database [*University of Bonn*] [*Germany*]

ICSD .... Ionization Chamber Smoke Detector [*Nuclear energy*] (NRCH)

ICSD .... Metropolitan Sanitary District of Greater Chicago, Chicago, IL [*Library symbol Library of Congress*] (LCLS)

ICS/DMC ...... Institute for Continuing Studies in Design, Management and Communication [*University of Cincinnati*] [*Research center*] (RCD)

ICSDV .... Ice-Cutter Semi-Submersible Drilling Vessel (PDAA)

ICSDW .... International Council of Social Democratic Women [*Later, SIW*] (EA)

ICSE .... Interdepartmental Committee on Software Engineering [*British*]

ICSE .... Intermediate Current Stability Experiment (DEN)

ICSEAF......... International Commission for the Southeast Atlantic Fisheries

ICSears........ Sears, Roebuck & Co., Chicago, IL [*Library symbol Library of Congress*] (LCLS)

ICSEES .... International Committee for Soviet and East European Studies (EAIO)

ICSEM.......... International Center of Studies on Early Music

ICSEM.......... International Commission for the Scientific Exploration of the Mediterranean Sea (EAIO)

ICSEMS........ International Commission for the Scientific Exploration of the Mediterranean Sea (NOAA)

ICSEP.......... International Center for the Solution of Environmental Problems (EA)

ICSEP.......... International Council of Sex Education and Parenthood (EA)

ICSey .... Seyfarth, Shaw, Fairweather & Geraldson, Chicago, IL [*Library symbol Library of Congress*] (LCLS)

ICSF .... International Collegiate Sports Foundation (EA)

ICSG .... International Center for Social Gerontology [*Later, TCSG*] [*Defunct*] (EA)

ICSH .... International Committee for Standardization in Haematology [*Louvain, Belgium*] [*Research center*] (EAIO)

ICSH .... Interstitial Cell Stimulating Hormone [*Also, LH, LSH*] [*Endocrinology*]

ICSHB .... International Committee for Standardization in Human Biology

ICSI............ Institut Canadien de la Sante Infantile [*Canadian Institute of Child Health*]

ICSI............ Institute for Clinical Systems Integration (DMAA)

ICSI............ International Commission on Snow and Ice

ICSI............ International Conference on Scientific Information

ICSI............ Intracytoplasmic Sperm Injection [*In vitro fertilization*]

ICSI............ Intracytoplasmic Sperm Injection

ICSID .... International Centre for Settlement of Investment Disputes (EA)

ICSID .... International Council of Societies of Industrial Design [*Helsinki, Finland*] (EA)

ICSISP .... International Center for Science Information Services in Phytovirology

ICSK........... International Cultural Society of Korea [*Seoul, Republic of Korea*] (EAIO)

ICSK........... Intracoronary Streptokinase [*An enzyme*]

ICSL............ Inner-City Simulation Laboratory [*Teacher training game*]

ICSL............ Inns of Court School of Law [*British*] (DI)

ICSL............ Interactive Computer Systems Ltd. (NITA)

ICSL............ Interactive Continuous Simulation Language [*Computer science*] (PDAA)

ICSL............ Presbyterian Saint Luke's Hospital, Chicago, IL [*Library symbol Library of Congress*] (LCLS)

ICSLS.......... International Convention for Safety of Life at Sea (BARN)

ICSM........... Instant Corn-Soya-Milk

ICSM........... International Confederation of Societies of Music (EA)

ICSMM .... International Conference on Superlattices, Microstructures, and Microdevices

ICSMP .... Integrated Command System Management Plan [*Military*] (DNAB)

ICSMP .... Interactive Continuous Systems Modeling Program

ICSMS .... Integrated Conventional Stores Management System [*DoD*] (DWSG)

ICSN .... Chicago Sun-Times and Chicago Daily News, Chicago, IL [*Library symbol Library of Congress*] (LCLS)

ICSOBA......... International Congress on Bauxite-Alumina-Aluminium (PDAA)

ICSOG .... International Correspondence Society of Obstetricians and Gynecologists (EA)

ICSOM .... International Conference of Symphony and Opera Musicians (EA)

ICSon.......... Sonicraft, Inc., Chicago, IL [*Library symbol Library of Congress*] (LCLS)

ICSP............ Illinois State Psychiatric Institute, Chicago, IL [*Library symbol Library of Congress*] (LCLS)

ICSP............ In Commission, Special [*Vessel status*] [*Navy*] (DNAB)

ICSP............ Interim Contractor Support Plan

ICSP............ International Council of Societies of Pathology (EA)

ICSPE.......... International Council of Sport and Physical Education

ICSPFT......... International Committee on the Standardization of Physical Fitness Tests

ICSPM .... Dr. William M. Scholl College of Podiatric Medicine, Chicago, IL [*Library symbol*] [*Library of Congress*] (LCLS)

ICSPRDC...... International Committee on Social Psychological Research in Developing Countries (EA)

ICSPRO........ Inter-Secretariat Committee on Scientific Problems Relating to Oceanography [*United Nations*]

ICS/R .... Individual Soldier's Computer/Radio [*Military*]

ICSR .... Interuniversity Centre for the Study of Religion [*Canada*]

ICSR .... Scottish Rite of Freemasonry Library, Chicago, IL [*Library symbol Library of Congress*] (LCLS)

ICSRE .... International Centre for Studies in Religious Education [*Brussels, Belgium*] (EAIO)

ICSRI .... Intelligent Computer Systems Research Institute [*University of Miami*] [*Research center*] (RCD)

ICSRI .... Interfaith Committee on Social Responsibility in Investments [*Later, ICCR*] (EA)

ICSS .... International Commission on Signs and Symbols

ICSS .... International Committee for the Sociology of Sport

ICSS .... International Conference on Solid Surfaces

ICSS .... International Council for the Social Studies (DIT)

ICSS .... Inter-University Committee on the Superior Student [*Defunct*] (EA)

ICSS .... Intracranial Self-Stimulation [*Also, ICS*] [*Neurophysiology*]

ICSSD .... International Committee for Social Science Information and Documentation [*Information service or system*] (IID)

ICSSD .... International Committee for Social Sciences Documentation and Information (NITA)

ICSSEA .... Integrated Communications System South-East Asia [*Australia*]

ICSSID .... International Committee for Social Science Information and Documentation [*Paris, France Information service or system*] (IID)

ICSSPE .... International Council of Sport Science and Physical Education (EA)

ICSST.......... Institute of Child Study Security Test [*Psychology*]

ICSST.......... International Conference on Solid State Transducers (EA)

ICSSVM .... International Commission for Small Scale Vegetation Maps [*Pondicherry, India*] (EAIO)

ICST............ Imperial College of Science and Technology (PDAA)

ICST............ Institute for Chemical Science and Technology [*Canada*]

ICST............ Institute [*formerly, Center*] for Computer Sciences and Technology [*Gaithersburg, MD*] (NIST)

ICST............ Institution of Corrosion Science and Technology (PDAA)

ICST............ Integrated Circuit Sys [*NASDAQ symbol*] (TTSB)

ICST............ Integrated Circuit Systems [*NASDAQ symbol*] (SPSG)

ICST............ Integrated Combined System Test

ICST............ International Concept Study Team [*for bridges*] [*US, Great Britain, Germany*] (RDA)

ICSTF.......... Integrated Combat Systems Test Facility (NVT)

ICSTI .... International Center for Scientific and Technical Information [*Moscow, USSR*] (EAIO)

ICSTI .... International Council for Scientific and Technical Information [*Information service or system*] (IID)

ICStJ........... St. Joseph Hospital, Chicago, IL [*Library symbol*] [*Library of Congress*] (LCLS)

ICSTK.......... Intracoronary Streptokinase [*An enzyme*]

ICSTND........ Information Center of Science and Technology for National Defense [*Chinese library*]

ICSTO.......... International Civil Service Training Organization

ICSU .... Chicago State University, Chicago, IL [*Library symbol Library of Congress*] (LCLS)

ICSU .... Independent Canadian Steelworkers' Union

ICSU .... International Council of Scientific Unions [*Research center France*]

ICSU AB....... International Council of Scientific Unions Abstracting Board [*Also, IAB*] [*Later, ICSTI*] (EA)

ICSU-CTS.... Committee on the Teaching of Science of the International Council of Scientific Unions [*York, England*] (EA)

ICSW .... Interdepartmental Committee on the Status of Women [*Terminated, 1978*]

ICSW .... International Committee on Seafarer's Welfare Office (EAIO)

ICSW .... International Conference of Social Work

ICSW .... International Council on Social Welfare (EA)

ICSW .... Sherwin Williams Chemicals, Chicago, IL [*Library symbol Library of Congress*] (LCLS)

ICSWBD....... Interior Communications Switchboard

ICSWSA....... International Chain Saw Wood Sculptors Association (EA)

ICSX........... Saint Xavier College, Chicago, IL [*Library symbol Library of Congress*] (LCLS)

ICT.............. Chicago Theological Seminary, Chicago, IL [*Library symbol Library of Congress*] (LCLS)

ICT.............. Icterus [*Jaundice*] [*Medicine*]

ICT.............. Iesu Christo Tutore [*With Jesus Christ as Protector*] [*Latin*]

ICT.............. Igniter Circuit Test (IAA)

ICT.............. Image Converter Tube

ICT.............. Image Creation Terminal (NITA)

ICT.............. Immunoreactive Calcitonin [*Endocrinology*]

ICT.............. In Circuit Test [*Electronics*] (EECA)

ICT.............. Incoming Trunk [*Telecommunications*] (BUR)

ICT.............. Indirect Coombs' Test [*Immunochemistry*]

ICT.............. Indirect Coulometric Titration [*Analytical chemistry*]

ICT.............. Individual Collective Training [*Army*]

ICT.............. Inflammation of Connective Tissue [*Medicine*]

ICT.............. Influence Coefficient Tests (MCD)

ICT.............. Information and Communication Technology

ICT.............. Insect Carrier Toxicant

ICT.............. Inspection Check Template (MSA)

ICT.............. Inspection Control Test (SAA)

ICT.............. Institut Canadien des Textiles [*Canadian Textiles Institute*] (EAIO)

ICT.............. Institute of Circuit Technology [*Oxford, England*] [*Defunct*] (EAIO)

ICT.............. Institute of Circuit Technology Ltd. (NITA)

ICT.............. Institute of Clay Technology [*British*]

ICT.............. Institute of Computer Technology

ICT.............. Institute of Concrete Technology [*British*]

ICT.............. Institution of Corrosion Technology (PDAA)

ICT.............. Insulated [*or Insulating*] Core Transformer

ICT.............. Insulin Coma Therapy [*Medicine*]

ICT............. Insulin Convulsive Therapy [*Medicine*] (MAH)
ICT............. Integrated Circuit Tester
ICT............. Integrated Computer Telemetry
ICT............. Integrated Concept Team [*Army*] (INF)
ICT............. Intelligence Cycle Time (MCD)
ICT............. Intensive Conventional Therapy [*Medicine*] (DAVI)
ICT............. Interaction Control Table [*Computer science*] (OA)
ICT............. Interactive Command Test [*Computer science*]
ICT............. Inter Cable Communications, Inc. [*Toronto Stock Exchange symbol*]
ICT............. Interchangeability Control Tool (MCD)
ICT............. Interchangeability Test (MCD)
ICT............. Intercontinental de Aviacion Ltd. [*Colombia*] [*ICAO designator*] (FAAC)
ICT............. Interface Control Tooling (NASA)
ICT............. Interference Compliance Test (SAA)
ICT............. Intermittent Cervical Traction [*Orthopedics*] (DAVI)
ICT............. Internal COMPOOL [*Communications Pool*] Table (SAA)
ICT............. International Call for Tenders (NATG)
ICT............. International Campaign for Tibet (EA)
ICT............. International Circuit Technology [*Electronics*] (IAA)
ICT............. International CMOS Technology [*Computer science*]
ICT............. International Commission on Trichinellosis (EA)
ICT............. International Computers and Tabulators Ltd. [*Later, ICL*]
ICT............. International Council of Tanners [*See also CIT*] [*Lewes, East Sussex, England*] (EAIO)
ICT............. International Critical Tables
ICT............. Intradermal Cancer Test [*Oncology*]
ICT............. Intramolecular Charge Transfer [*Physical chemistry*]
ICT............. Irrigated, Conventionally Tilled [*Agriculture*]
ICT............. Isometric Contraction Time [*Medicine*] (DAVI)
ICT............. Isovolumic Contraction Time [*Cardiology*]
ICT............. Trinity College, Deerfield, IL [*OCLC symbol*] (OCLC)
ICT............. Wichita [*Kansas*] [*Airport symbol*] (OAG)
ICTA........... Chicago Transit Authority, Chicago, IL [*Library symbol Library of Congress*] (LCLS)
ICTA........... Industry Council for Tangible Assets [*Washington, DC*] (EA)
ICTA........... Institute of Certified Travel Agents (EA)
ICTA........... International Center for the Typographic Arts
ICTA........... International Computer Training Association (PCM)
ICTA........... International Confederation for Thermal Analysis [*Jerusalem, Israel*] (EA)
ICTAA........ Imperial College of Tropical Agriculture Association [*British*] (BI)
ICTAB........ Institut Canadien de Tole d'Acier en Batiment [*Canadian Sheet Steel Building Institute*]
ICTAM....... International Congress of Theoretical and Applied Mechanics (PDAA)
ICTASD...... International Convention on Transistors and Semiconductor Devices
ICTB.......... International Companies and Their Brands [*A publication*]
ICTB.......... International Customs Tariffs Bureau (DLA)
ICTBA........ Infants', Children's, and Teens' Wear Buyers Association (EA)
ICTC.......... Inertial Components Temperature Controller (KSC)
ICTC.......... International Cooperative Training Center
ICTCD........ Insecticide (MSA)
ICTD.......... Individual and Collective Training Development (MCD)
ICTD.......... Inter-Channel Time Displacement
ICTE.......... Inertial Component Test Equipment
ICTED........ International Cooperation in the Field of Transport Economics Documentation [*European Conference of Ministers of Transport*] [*Information service or system*] (IID)
ICTF.......... Interagency Crisis Task Force
ICTF.......... International Cocoa Trades Federation [*British*]
ICTF.......... International Commission on the Taxonomy of Fungi
ICTF.......... International Conference on Thin Films (PDAA)
ICTG.......... ICT Group, Inc. [*NASDAQ symbol*] (SAG)
ICT Grp..... ICT Group, Inc. [*Associated Press*] (SAG)
ICTH.......... International Commission for the Teaching of History [*Brussels, Belgium*] (EA)
ICTH.......... International Committee on Thrombosis and Hemostasis
ICTI.......... International Committee of Toy Industries (EA)
ict ind....... Icterus Index [*Liver function test*] [*Medicine*] (AAMN)
ICTL.......... Image Control Table (MCD)
ICTL.......... Industrial Control (IAA)
ICTL.......... International Cabletel, Inc. [*NASDAQ symbol*] (SAG)
ICTL.......... Intl Cabletel [*NASDAQ symbol*] (TTSB)
ICTM......... International Coal Trade Model [*Department of Energy*] (GFGA)
ICTM......... International Council for Traditional Music (EA)
ICTME....... International Conference on Tribo-Terotechnology and Maintenance Engineering (PDAA)
ICTMM...... International Congresses on Tropical Medicine and Malaria
ICTN.......... Industry Center for Trade Negotiations [*Defunct*]
ICTOC........ Independent Corps Tactical Operations Center
ICTP.......... Individual/Collective Training Plan [*Army*]
ICTP.......... Institute for Certification of Tax Professionals (EA)
ICTP.......... Intensified Combat Training Program
ICTP.......... International Center for Theoretical Physics [*Trieste, Italy*] (EA)
ICTPDC...... Imperial College Thermophysical Properties Data Centre [*British*] (CB)
ICTR.......... Institut Canadien de Recherches en Telecommunications (AC)
ICTR.......... Institute of Commercial and Technical Representatives Ltd. [*British*] (BI)
ICTR.......... International Center of Theatre Research (EA)
ICTr........... Truman College, Chicago, IL [*Library symbol Library of Congress*] (LCLS)
ICTRM....... Interagency Committee on the Transportation of Radioactive Materials
ICTS.......... Idiopathic Carpal Tunnel Syndrome [*Medicine*] (DMAA)

ICTS.......... In-Car Temperature Sensor [*Automotive engineering*]
ICTS.......... Integrated Circuit Test Set
ICTS.......... Integrated Computerized Test Set
ICTS.......... Intermediate Capacity Transit System
ICTS.......... International Catholic Truth Society (EA)
ICTS.......... International Congress of the Transplantation Society
ICTSI......... International Container Terminal Services, Inc. [*Philippines*] [*Commercial firm*]
ICTT.......... Intensified Confirmatory Troop Test (AABC)
ICTU......... Catholic Theological Union, Chicago, IL [*Library symbol Library of Congress*] (LCLS)
ICTU......... Independent Canadian Transit Union
ICTU......... Iraqi Confederation of Trade Unions
ICTU......... Irish Congress of Trade Unions
ICTV......... Interactive Cable Television
ICTV......... International Committee on Taxonomy of Viruses [*ICSU*] [*Rennes, France*] (EAIO)
ICTV......... Intracerebroventricular [*Also, ic, ICV*] [*Brain anatomy*]
ICtvS........ Shawnee Library System, Carterville, IL [*Library symbol Library of Congress*] (LCLS)
ICTX......... Intermittent Cervical Traction [*Medicine*] (DMAA)
ICTZ......... I Corps Tactical Zone [*Vietnamese designation for both a military zone and a political region*]
ICU.......... ICG Utility Investments Ltd. [*Toronto Stock Exchange symbol*]
ICU.......... Immunologic Contact Urticaria [*Medicine*] (DMAA)
ICU.......... Indicator Control Unit
ICU.......... Industrial Control Unit (IAA)
ICU.......... Industry Capacity Utilization [*Engineering economics*]
ICU.......... Infant Care Unit [*Medicine*] (DMAA)
ICU.......... InfoColor Conversion Unit (DGA)
ICU.......... Informatie en Communicatie Unie [*Information and Communication United*] [*Dutch publishing house*]
ICU.......... Infrared Command Unit
ICU.......... Institut d'Urbanisme du Canada [*Town Planning Institute of Canada*]
ICU.......... Instruction Cache Unit [*Computer science*]
ICU.......... Instruction Control Unit
ICU.......... Integrated Control Unit
ICU.......... Integrated Control Unit (NITA)
ICU.......... Intelligent Connector Unit [*Telecommunications*] (TSSD)
ICU.......... Intensive-Care Unit [*of a hospital*]
ICU.......... Intensive Caring Unlimited [*An association*] (EA)
ICU.......... Interactive Chart Utility [*IBM Corp.*]
ICU.......... Interconnection Unit [*Computer science*]
ICU.......... Interface Control Unit [*Army*]
ICU.......... Interface Control Unit (NITA)
ICU.......... Intermediate Care Unit [*of a hospital*]
ICU.......... International Christian University [*Tokyo*]
ICU.......... International Christian University Library [*UTLAS symbol*]
ICU.......... International Code Use (BARN)
ICU.......... International [*or Internal*] Communication Unit [*Telecommunications*] (TEL)
ICU.......... International Cycling Union (EA)
ICU.......... Interrupt Control Unit [*Computer science*] (IAA)
ICU.......... Texas Christian University, Fort Worth, TX [*OCLC symbol*] (OCLC)
ICU.......... University of Chicago, Chicago, IL [*Library symbol Library of Congress*] (LCLS)
ICUA........ Institute for College and University Administrators [*Later, CPAA*] (EA)
ICUA........ Interdenominational Church Ushers Association
ICUAE....... International Congress of University Adult Education [*Fredericton, NB*] (EAIO)
ICUAER...... International Committee on Urgent Anthropological and Ethnological Research [*Vienna, Austria*] (EAIO)
ICUC........ Union Carbide Corp., Film-Packaging Division, Chicago, IL [*Library symbol Library of Congress*] (LCLS)
ICUD......... Index to Current Urban Documents [*Information service or system*] (IID)
ICU-D........ University of Chicago, Divinity School, Chicago, IL [*Library symbol Library of Congress*] (LCLS)
ICUE........ International Committee on the University Emergency (EA)
ICUEPR...... International Conference on University Education for Public Relations
ICU-FE...... University of Chicago, Far Eastern Library, Chicago, IL [*Library symbol Library of Congress*] (LCLS)
ICUFON...... Intercontinental UFO Galactic Spacecraft Research and Analytic Network (EA)
ICUFR....... International Council on United Fund Raising (EA)
ICUG......... United States Gypsum Co., Chicago, IL [*Library symbol*] [*Library of Congress*] (LCLS)
ICUGA....... International Computer Users Groups Association [*Defunct*] (EA)
ICU-H....... University of Chicago, Center for Health Administration Studies, Chicago, IL [*Library symbol Library of Congress*] (LCLS)
ICUI......... ICU Medical [*NASDAQ symbol*] (TTSB)
ICUI......... ICU Medical, Inc. [*NASDAQ symbol*] (SAG)
ICUIS....... Institute on the Church in Urban-Industrial Society [*Defunct*]
ICU-L....... University of Chicago, Law Library, Chicago, IL [*Library symbol Library of Congress*] (LCLS)
ICU-LS...... University of Chicago, Graduate Library School, Chicago, IL [*Library symbol Library of Congress*] (LCLS)
ICU-M........ University of Chicago, Bio-Medical Libraries, Chicago, IL [*Library symbol Library of Congress*] (LCLS)
ICU Med..... ICU Medical, Inc. [*Associated Press*] (SAG)
ICUMSA....... International Commission for Uniform Methods of Sugar Analysis [*Mackay, QLD, Australia*] (EAIO)
ICUnC........ University Club of Chicago, Chicago, IL [*Library symbol Library of Congress*] (LCLS)

ICUnW .... United Way of Metropolitan Chicago, Chicago, IL [*Library symbol Library of Congress*] (LCLS)
ICUP .... Individual Circuit Usage and Peg Count [*Telecommunications*] (TEL)
ICUP .... International Catholic Union of the Press (EA)
ICUPLANT.... Instructor's Computer Utility Programming Language for Interactive Teaching (IAA)
ICURR.......... Intergovernmental Committee on Urban and Regional Research [*Canada*]
ICUS .... Inside Continental United States [*Military*]
ICUS .... International Committee on Urgent Surgery [*Milan, Italy*] (EAIO)
ICUS .... International Conference on the Unity of the Sciences
ICUSA .... International Christians for Unity in Social Action (EA)
ICUSQ .... United States Quartermaster Corps, Food and Container Institute [*for the Armed Forces*], Chicago, IL [*Library symbol Library of Congress*] (LCLS)
ICUT .... Independent Colleges and Universities of Texas (SRA)
ICUT .... Initial COHORT [*Cohesion, Operational Readiness Training*] Unit Training [*Military*] (GFGA)
ICUT .... International Cutlery Ltd. [*NASDAQ symbol*] (SAG)
ICUT .... Intl Cutlery [*NASDAQ symbol*] (TTSB)
ICUTW .... Intl Cutlery Wrrt'A' [*NASDAQ symbol*] (TTSB)
ICUTZ .... Intl Cutlery Wrrt'B' [*NASDAQ symbol*] (TTSB)
ICU-Y .... University of Chicago, Yerkes Observatory, Williams Bay, WI [*Library symbol Library of Congress*] (LCLS)
ICUZ .... Integrated Compatible Use Zone [*Army*] (RDA)
ICV............ Elmhurst College, Elmhurst, IL [*OCLC symbol*] (OCLC)
ICV............ Ice-Cream Van [*Slang British*]
ICV............ Improved Capital Value [*Business term*] (ADA)
ICV............ Individual Cell Voltmeter (DNAB)
ICV............ Individually Controlled Ventilation
ICV............ Indoor Cricket Victoria [*Australia An association*]
ICV............ Infantry Combat Vehicle (MCD)
ICV............ Initial Calibration Verification
ICV............ Initial Chaining Value [*Computer science*]
ICV............ Inter-Center Vector (MCD)
ICV............ Interdecadal Climate Variability [*Marine science*] (OSRA)
ICV............ Internal Correction Voltage
ICV............ Interphase Chromosome Volume
ICV............ Intracellular Virus [*Medicine*] (PDAA)
ICV............ Intracerebroventricular [*Also, ic, ICTV*] [*Brain anatomy*]
ICV............ United States Veterans Administration, West Side Hospital, Chicago, IL [*Library symbol Library of Congress*] (LCLS)
ICVA........... International Council of Voluntary Agencies (GNE)
ICVAN .... International Committee on Veterinary Anatomical Nomenclature [*See also CINAV*] [*Zurich, Switzerland*] (EAIO)
ICVC........... VanderCook College of Music, Chicago, IL [*Library symbol Library of Congress*] (LCLS)
ICVD .... Inns of Court Volunteer Decoration [*Military British*] (ROG)
ICVD .... Isotopic Chemical Vapor Deposition (PDAA)
ICVF........... Inner-City Ventures Fund [*National Trust for Historical Preservation*]
ICVGAN........ International Committee on Veterinary Gross Anatomical Nomenclature [*Cornell University*] [*Ithaca, NY*] (EY)
ICVH .... Ischemic Cerebrovascular Headache [*Medicine*] (DAVI)
ICVI .... Isothermal Chemical Vapor Infiltration [*Materials science*]
ICVNA .... Visiting Nurses Association, Chicago, IL [*Library symbol Library of Congress*] (LCLS)
ICvR .... River Bend Library System, Coal Valley, IL [*Library symbol Library of Congress*] (LCLS)
ICVS........... International Cardiovascular Society (EA)
ICVS........... International Society for Cardiovascular Surgery (EA)
ICw .... Crestwood Library District, Crestwood, IL [*Library symbol Library of Congress*] (LCLS)
ICW............ In Compliance With (MUGU)
ICW............ In Conjunction With (AAGC)
ICW............ In Connection With
ICW............ India-China Wing [*World War II*]
ICW............ Initial Condition Word [*Computer science*]
ICW............ Input Command Word
ICW............ Input Control Word [*Computer science*] (MCD)
ICW............ Institute of Clay Workers [*British*] (BI)
ICW............ Institute of Clerks of Work (PDAA)
ICW............ Intake Cooling Water (IEEE)
ICW............ Interactive Courseware [*Air Force*]
ICW............ Inter-American Commission of Women [*OAS*]
ICW............ Interblock Communication Word (IAA)
ICW............ Intercoastal Waterway
ICW............ Interface Control Word [*Computer science*]
ICW............ International Chemical Workers Union
ICW............ International Council of Women [*France*]
ICW............ Internet Connection Wizard [*Computer science*]
ICW............ Interrupted Continuous Wave [*Electronics*]
ICW............ Intracellular Water [*Physiology*]
ICW............ Western Society of Engineers, Chicago, IL [*Library symbol Library of Congress*] (LCLS)
ICW............ Wheaton College, Wheaton, IL [*OCLC symbol*] (OCLC)
ICWA .... Indian Child Welfare Act [*1978*]
ICWA .... Institute of Cost and Works Accountants [*British*] (BI)
ICWA .... Institute of Current World Affairs (EA)
ICWA .... International Carwash Association
ICWA .... International Coil Winding Association (EA)
ICWAR .... Improved Continuous-Wave Acquisition RADAR [*Army*] (AABC)
ICWB .... Intermediate Cold-Wet Boot [*Military*] (INF)
ICWB .... World Book-Childcraft International, Inc., Chicago, IL [*Library symbol Library of Congress*] (LCLS)

ICWC .... Wilbur Wright Community College, Chicago, IL [*Library symbol Library of Congress*] (LCLS)
ICWD .... Interface Control/Weapon Delivery
ICWDP .... International Committee for World Day of Prayer (EA)
ICWeH .... Louis A. Weiss Memorial Hospital, Chicago, IL [*Library symbol Library of Congress*] (LCLS)
ICWES .... International Conference of Women Engineers and Scientists
ICWF .... Interactive Computer Worded Forecast [*Marine science*] (OSRA)
ICWF .... Interactive Computer Worded Forecast (USDC)
ICWG .... Interface Control Working Group [*NASA*] (KSC)
ICWG .... International Clubroot Working Group (EAIO)
ICWG .... International Co-operative Women's Guild
ICWG .... International Coordination Working Group (USDC)
ICWG .... International Coordination Working Group [*Marine science*] (OSRA)
ICWGA .... Interface Control Working Group Action [*NASA*] (KSC)
ICWHA .... Wildman, Harrold, Allen & Dixon, Chicago, IL [*Library symbol*] [*Library of Congress*] (LCLS)
ICWI........... International Car Wash Institute (EA)
ICwL .... Crestwood Library District, Crestwood, IL [*Library symbol*] [*Library of Congress*] (LCLS)
ICWL .... International Creative Writers League (EA)
ICWM .... Institute for Chemical Waste Management (GNE)
ICWM .... Interdepartmental Committee on Weather Modification [*Military*]
ICWM .... International Committee on Weights and Measures
ICWM .... International Congress on Women in Music [*Defunct*] (EA)
ICWMA .... International Country and Western Music Association (EA)
ICWO .... Indications Center Watch Officer [*Military*] (MCD)
ICWO .... Intercomponent Work Order
ICWORR .... International Conference on Waste Oil Recovery and Reuse
ICWP .... International Council of Women Psychologists [*Later, ICP*]
ICWP .... Interstate Conference on Water Policy (EA)
ICWR .... Interagency Committee on Water Resources
ICWS .... Improved Commander's Weapon Station
ICWS .... Institute of Civil War Studies (EA)
ICWS .... Winston & Strawn, Chicago, IL [*Library symbol Library of Congress*] (LCLS)
ICWSG .... Infants' and Children's Wear Salesmen's Guild (EA)
ICWT........... Inter-Component Work Transmitted (MCD)
ICWT........... Interrupted Continuous Wave Telegraphy (IAA)
ICWU .... International Chemical Workers Union (EA)
ICWWP .... Interagency Committee for World Weather Programs [*Department of Commerce*] (NOAA)
ICX............ Inferior Colliculus
ICX............ International Charter Xpress Limited Liability Co. [*ICAO designator*] (FAAC)
ICX............ International Computer Exchange (IAA)
ICX............ International Cultural Exchange
ICX............ Lewis University, Lockport, IL [*OCLC symbol*] (OCLC)
ICY............ Augustana College, Rock Island, IL [*OCLC symbol*] (OCLC)
ICY............ Instruction Cycle [*Computer science*] (IAA)
ICY............ International Christian Youth (EA)
ICY............ International Commission on Yeasts and Yeast-Like Microorganisms [*ICSU*] [*France*] (EAIO)
ICY............ International Cooperation Year [*1965*] [*20th anniversary of UN*]
I-cycle .... Instruction Cycle (NITA)
ICYE........... International Christian Youth Exchange (EA)
ICYF .... Institute for Children, Youth, and Families [*Michigan State University*] [*Research center*] (RCD)
ICYF .... International Catholic Youth Federation [*Later, WFCY*]
ICYO .... International Committee of Youth Organizations (EAIO)
ICYP .... Iodocyanopindolol [*Biochemistry*]
ICYRA .... Inter-Collegiate Yacht Racing Association [*of North America*] [*Later, ICYRA/NA*]
ICYRA/NA .... Inter-Collegiate Yacht Racing Association of North America (EA)
ICYT .... Instituto de Informacion y Documentacion en Ciencia y Tecnologia [*Institute for Information and Documentation in Science and Technology*] [*Database originator and host*] [*Information service or system*] [*Spain*] (IID)
ICZ............ International Climate Zone
ICZ............ Intertropical Convergence Zone [*Trade winds*] [*Meteorology*]
ICZ............ Isthmian Canal Zone
ICZ............ North Park College and Theological Seminary, Chicago, IL [*OCLC symbol*] (OCLC)
ICZM .... Integrated Coastal Zone Management [*Marine science*] (OSRA)
ICZN .... International Commission on Zoological Nomenclature [*British*] (EAIO)
ID................ Apollo Airlines [*ICAO designator*] (AD)
ID................ [*Official Decisions of the*] Department of Interior (AAGC)
ID................ Idaho [*Postal code*]
ID................ Idaho Operations Office [*Energy Research and Development Administration*]
ID................ Idaho Reports [*A publication*] (DLA)
Id................ Idaho State Library, Boise, ID [*Library symbol Library of Congress*] (LCLS)
ID................ Iddin-Dagan (BJA)
ID................ Idea [*Slang*]
ID................ Idem [*The Same*] [*Latin*]
ID................ Identification [*Computer science*]
ID................ Identification Data
ID................ Identification Date
ID................ Identification Dissector (MCD)
ID................ Identifier [*Online database field identifier*]
ID................ Identifier [*Dialog*] [*Searchable field*] (NITA)
ID................ Identify [*or Identification*] (DAVI)
ID................ Identity

ID................ [*The*] Ides
ID................ Iditol Dehydrogenase (MAE)
Id................ Idylls [*of Theocritus*] [*Classical studies*] (OCD)
ID................ Ifostamide, Doxorubicin [*Antineoplastic drug*] (CDI)
ID................ Image Digitizer [*Computer science*]
ID................ Image Dissector (KSC)
ID................ Immediate Delivery [*Shipping*]
ID................ Immunodeficiency [*Immunology*]
ID................ Immunodiffusion [*Immunology*]
ID................ Immunoglobulin Deficiency [*Immunology*] (AAMN)
ID................ Immunological Distance [*in primate phylogeny*]
ID................ Import Duty [*Customs*] (DS)
ID................ Inanna's Descent (BJA)
ID................ Inaugural Dissertation (BJA)
ID................ Inclusion Disease [*Medicine*]
ID................ Inclusive Depth [*Typography*] (DGA)
ID................ Income Debenture [*Type of bond*] [*Investment term*]
ID................ Increased Deployability [*Posture*] (DOMA)
ID................ Indefinite Delivery [*Shipping*]
ID................ Independence Dogs [*An association*] (EA)
ID................ Independent Dealer [*Automobile sales*]
ID................ Independent Distributor
ID................ Index of Discrimination
ID................ Index of Dissimilarity
ID................ Indicating Device
ID................ Indicator Driver (MSA)
ID................ Indirect Damage [*Insurance*]
ID................ Indirect Departmental (DGA)
I/D................ Indirect Labor (AAG)
ID................ Individual Development
ID$_{50}$........ Individual Dose [*Radioactivity calculations*]
ID................ Indonesia [*ANSI two-letter standard code*] (CNC)
ID................ Induced Draft
ID................ Inductance [*Electromagnetism*] (IAA)
ID................ Industrial Democracy
ID................ Industrial Design (WGA)
ID................ Industrial Development
ID................ Industrial Dynamics [*Management analysis*]
ID................ Inelastic Demand (MHDB)
ID................ Infant Death (MAE)
ID................ Infantry Division
ID................ Infectious Disease [*Medicine*]
ID................ Infective Dose
ID................ Inferior Division [*Medicine*] (DAVI)
ID................ Informal Decorative [*Horticulture*]
ID................ Information and Documentation [*Royal Tropical Institute*] [*Information service or system*] (IID)
ID................ Information Distributor
ID................ Inhibitory Dose [*Medicine*]
ID................ Initial Denial Authority (AAGC)
ID................ Initial Diagnosis [*Medicine*] (CPH)
ID................ Initial Distribution
ID................ Initial Dose [*Medicine*] (CPH)
ID................ Initial dyskinesia [*Medicine*] (DMAA)
ID................ Injected Dose
ID................ Inner Diameter
ID................ Inniskilling Dragoons [*Military British*]
ID................ Innovator's Digest [*The Infoteam, Inc.*] [*Information service or system*] (IID)
ID................ Inoculum Density
ID................ Input Display [*Computer science*] (IAA)
ID................ Insertion Device [*Series of magnets*] [*Physics*]
ID................ Inside Diameter
ID................ Inside Dimensions
ID................ Installation Data
ID................ Institute of Distribution [*Defunct*] (EA)
ID................ Instructional Developer (MCD)
I/D................ Instruction/Data (IEEE)
ID................ Instrumentation Directorate [*White Sands Missile Range*] [*Army*]
ID................ Insulation Displacement
ID................ Integral Derivative (IAA)
ID................ Integrated Diagnostics (AAGC)
ID................ Intellectual Digest [*A publication*]
ID................ Intelligence Department [*Army*] (MCD)
ID................ Intelligence Division [*NATO*] (NATG)
ID................ Intelligence Duties
ID................ Intelligent Digitizer
ID................ Intelligent Documentation [*Computer science*]
I-D................ Intensity Duration (Curve)
ID................ Interactive Debugging (IEEE)
ID................ Intercept Direction (SAA)
ID................ Intercommunication Devices (MCD)
ID................ Interconnection Device (MCD)
ID................ Interconnection Diagram (IAA)
ID................ Interdigital [*Telecommunications*] (IEEE)
ID................ Interdisciplinary
ID................ Interest Deductible [*Banking*] (ADA)
ID................ Interface Device (MCD)
ID................ Interface Document (NASA)
ID................ Interferometer and Doppler
ID................ Interim Dividend [*Investment term*]
ID................ Interior Department
ID................ Interior Department Decisions [*United States*] [*A publication*] (DLA)
ID................ Interlocking Directorate [*Business term*]
ID................ Intermediate Description (IEEE)

ID................ Intermittent Duty (IAA)
ID................ Intermodulation Distortion
ID................ Internal Diameter (MSA)
ID................ International Daleco Technology [*Vancouver Stock Exchange symbol*]
ID................ International Division [*Army Service Forces*] [*World War II*]
ID................ Interrectal Spike Discharge [*Neurophysiology*]
ID................ Intestinal Distress
ID................ Intradermal [*Medicine*]
ID................ Intraductal [*Anatomy*]
ID................ Intraduodenal [*Medicine*] (MAE)
ID................ Intrinsicoid Deflection [*Cardiology*]
ID................ Introduction (WDMC)
ID................ Inventory Difference [*Formerly, MUF*] [*NRC/ERDA*]
ID................ Invoice Distribution
ID................ Iraqi Dinar [*Monetary unit*] (BJA)
ID................ Iris Diaphragm [*Photography*]
ID................ Irish Duke (ROG)
ID................ Islamic Dinar [*Monetary unit*] (EY)
ID................ Island (ADA)
ID................ Isotope Dilution
ID................ Issue Date
ID................ Item Description
ID................ Item Documentation (IEEE)
ID................ Izquierda Democratica [*Democratic Left*] [*Ecuador*] [*Political party*] (PPW)
ID................ Noncathode Ray Tube Indicators [*JETDS nomenclature*] [*Military*] (CET)
ID................ Sumitomo Chemical Co. [*Japan*] [*Research code symbol*]
ID$_{50}$........ Infective Dose, Median
ID-86........ Infantry Division - 1986
ID................ Dallas Baptist College, Dallas, TX [*OCLC symbol*] (OCLC)
IDA................ Idaho
IDA................ Idaho Array [*Idaho*] [*Seismograph station code, US Geological Survey Closed*] (SEIS)
IDA................ Idaho Falls [*Idaho*] [*Airport symbol*] (OAG)
IDA................ Idaho Power [*NYSE symbol*] (TTSB)
IDA................ Idaho Power Co. [*NYSE symbol*] (SPSG)
Ida................ Idaho Reports [*A publication*] (DLA)
IDA................ Identification Data Accessory (NTCM)
IDA................ Image Display and Analysis (MAE)
IDA................ Iminodiacetic Acid [*Organic chemistry*]
IDA................ Immediate Damage Assessment
IDA................ Immortalis Dei Auspicio [*With the Help of God*] [*Latin*]
IDA................ Import Duty Act [*British*] (DS)
IDA................ In Defense of Animals (EA)
IDA................ Indicator Digest Average [*Stock exchange term*] (SPSG)
IDA................ Indonesia Air Transport PT [*ICAO designator*] (FAAC)
IDA................ Industrial Design Award
IDA................ Industrial Development Abstracts [*Database*] [*UNIDO*] (CRD)
IDA................ Industrial Development Authority [*Ireland*]
IDA................ Industrial Diamond Association of America (EA)
IDA................ Industry Development Arrangement
IDA................ Information, Decision, Action
IDA................ Infrared Detection Array
IDA................ Initial Denial Authority (AABC)
IDA................ Inpatient Data Administration (PDAA)
IDA................ Input Data Assembler
IDA................ Inspekteur der Artillerie [*Inspector of Artillery*] [*German military - World War II*]
IDA................ Institute for Defense Analyses (EA)
IDA................ Institute for Development Anthropology (EA)
IDA................ Integrated Data Access (NITA)
IDA................ Integrated Debugging Aid (IAA)
IDA................ Integrated Digital Access [*Telecommunications*]
IDA................ Integrated Digital Avionics (MCD)
IDA................ Integrated Disbursing and Accounting (MCD)
IDA................ Integrated Disk Adapter [*Sperry UNIVAC*]
IDA................ Integro-Differential Analyzer
IDA................ Intelligent Data Access
IDA................ Intelligent Database Assistant
IDA................ Intelligent Drive Array [*COMPAQ Computer Corp.*] [*Computer science*]
IDA................ Interactive Data on Accidents [*Engineering*]
IDA................ Interactive Debugging Aid
IDA................ Interactive Differential Analyzer
IDA................ Intercept Distance Aid (SAA)
IDA................ Intercollegiate Dramatic Association [*Defunct*] (EA)
IDA................ Interconnect Device Arrangement (HGAA)
IDA................ Interdigitated Array [*Electronics*]
IDA................ Inter-Divisional Agreement
IDA................ Interface Display Assembly [*NASA*] (NASA)
IDA................ International Dance Alliance (EA)
IDA................ International Data and Analysis [*Bureau of Mines*]
IDA................ International Database Association [*Defunct*] (EA)
IDA................ International Defenders of Animals (EA)
IDA................ International Deployment of Accelerometers [*Project*] [*Seismography*]
IDA................ International Desalination Association (EA)
IDA................ International Development Agency [*United Nations*] (NUCP)
IDA................ International Development Association (EA)
IDA................ International Discotheque Association [*Defunct*] (EA)
IDA................ International Dispensary Association [*Acronym is used as association name*] (EAIO)
IDA................ International Documentary Association (EA)
IDA................ International Doll Association [*Defunct*] (EA)

IDA............ International Downtown Association (EA)
IDA............ International Drapery Association (EA)
IDA............ International Dredging Association
IDA............ Intrusion Detection Alarm (CINC)
IDA............ Investment Dealers Association of Canada
IDA............ Ionospheric Dispersion Analysis [Air Force]
IDA............ Irish Dental Association (BI)
IDA............ Irish Drug Association (BI)
IDA............ Iron Deficiency Anemia [Medicine]
IDA............ Islamic Democratic Alliance [Pakistan] [Political party]
IDA............ Isotope Dilution Analysis
IDA............ Isotopic Dilution Analysis
IDA............ Iterative Differential Analyzer (IAA)
IDAA.......... Industrial Diamond Association of America
IDAA.......... International Diabetic Athletes Association (EA)
IDAA.......... International Dictionary of Architects and Architecture [A publication]
IDAA.......... International Doctors in Alcoholics Anonymous (EA)
IDAAS .... International Directory of Astronomical Associations and Societies [A publication]
IdAb............ Aberdeen Public Library, Aberdeen, ID [Library symbol] [Library of Congress] (LCLS)
IDAB .... Industrial Development Advisory Board [British]
IDABEE .... Institute of Defense Analysis Compiler (SAA)
ID AC.......... Idem Ac [The Same As] [Latin]
IDAC .... Industrial Data Acquisition Control (IAA)
IDAC .... Instant Data Access Control [National Design Center, Inc.] [Information service or system] (IID)
IDAC .... Integrated Data Acquisition and Control [Jet Propulsion Laboratory, NASA]
IDAC .... Integrated Digital-Analog Converter (MCD)
IDAC .... Interconnecting Digital-Analog Converter (NG)
IDAC .... Interim Digital-Analog Converter
IDAC .... International Decorative Accessories Center (EA)
IDAC .... International Disaster Advisory Committee
IDACE .... Association des Industries des Aliments Dietetiques de la CEE [Association of Dietetic Foods Industries of the European Economic Community]
ID-ACK........ Identification-Acknowledge (MCD)
IDACON........ Iterative Differential Analyzer Control
IDA-CRD ...... Institute for Defense Analysis-Communications Research Division
IDACS .... Integrated Detection and Classification Station
IDAD .... Internal Defense and Development [Army] (AABC)
IDADS.......... Interactive Drafting and Digitizing System (MCD)
IDAF............ International Defence and Aid Fund for Southern Africa [British] (EAIO)
IDAF............ International Defense and Aid Fund for Southern Africa, US Committee [Defunct] (EA)
IDAFIPS .... Integrated Disbursing and Accounting Financial Information Processing System [DoD]
IDAFMS .... Integrated Disbursing and Accounting Financial Management System (DNAB)
IDAGAM....... Institute for Defense Analysis Gaming Model (MCD)
IDA-HEAL-NET... Idaho Health Libraries Network [Library network]
Idaho .... Idaho Supreme Court Reports [A publication] (DLA)
Idaho Adm Code... Idaho Administrative Code [A publication] (AAGC)
Idaho LJ ...... Idaho Law Journal [A publication] (DLA)
Idaho NS ..... Idaho Reports, New Series [A publication] (DLA)
IdahoP......... Idaho Power Co. [Associated Press] (SAG)
Idaho Sess Laws... Session Laws of Idaho [A publication] (DLA)
Idaho St U ... Idaho State University (GAGS)
Ida IAB ...... Idaho Industrial Accident Board Reports [A publication] (DLA)
IdAl............ Albion Community Library, Albion, ID [Library symbol] [Library of Congress] (LCLS)
IdAL........... Indirect Data Address List [Computer science] (ECII)
IdAIN .... Albion State Normal School, Albion, ID [Library symbol Library of Congress] (LCLS)
IdAIS .... Southern Idaho College of Education, Albion, ID [Library symbol Library of Congress Obsolete] (LCLS)
IdAm........... American Falls District Library, American Falls, ID [Library symbol] [Library of Congress] (LCLS)
IDAM .... Indexed Direct Access Method
IdAmHS .... American Falls High School, American Falls, ID [Library symbol] [Library of Congress] (LCLS)
IDAMIS .... Integrated Drug Abuse Management Information Systems
IDAMS .... Image Display and Manipulation System [NASA]
IDAMS .... Isotope Dilution Analysis Mass Spectrometry
IDAMST....... Integrated Digital Avionics for Medium STOL Transport (MCD)
IDAN........... Idan Software Industries ISI Ltd. [NASDAQ symbol] (NQ)
I/D & C .... Instrumentation/Displays and Controls [Subsystem] (MCD)
ID & CA....... Inverter Distribution and Control Assembly (MCD)
ID & PD....... Industrial Democracy and Personnel Development
IDANF......... Idan Software Ind ISI [NASDAQ symbol] (TTSB)
IdanSft........ Idan Software Industries ISI Ltd. [Associated Press] (SAG)
IDanvi......... Danville Public Library, Danville, IL [Library symbol Library of Congress] (LCLS)
IDanviC....... Danville Junior College, Danville, IL [Library symbol Library of Congress] (LCLS)
IDanviCS...... Central Vermillion County Schools Cooperative, Danville, IL [Library symbol] [Library of Congress] (LCLS)
IDanviHS ..... Schlarman High School, Danville, IL [Library symbol] [Library of Congress] (LCLS)
IDanviL........ Lake View Memorial Hospital, Doctor's Library, Danville, IL [Library symbol Library of Congress] (LCLS)
IDanviSD ..... Danville Community Unit School District, Danville, IL [Library symbol] [Library of Congress] (LCLS)

IDanviSE...... Saint Elizabeth Hospital, Danville, IL [Library symbol] [Library of Congress] (LCLS)
IDanviStE..... Saint Elizabeth Hospital, Danville, IL [Library symbol Library of Congress] (LCLS)
IDanviVA..... United States Veterans Administration Hospital, Danville, IL [Library symbol Library of Congress] (LCLS)
IDAP .... Industrial Design Assistance Program [National Design Council, Canada]
IDAP .... Integrated Defensive Avionics Program [Navy] (DOMA)
IDAP .... Internal Development and Assistance Program (AFM)
IDAP .... International Development and Assistance Program (KSC)
IDAP .... Isomorphously Doped Ammonium Perchlorate
IDAP .... Iterative Differential Analyzer Pinboard
IDAPA......... Idaho Administrative Code [A publication] (AAGC)
IDAPI.......... Independent Database Application Program Interface (PCM)
IDAPR......... Individual DSS [Direct Support System] Activity Performance Report
IDAPS......... Image Data Processing System
IdAr............ Lost River District Library, Arco, ID [Library symbol] [Library of Congress] (LCLS)
IDARP......... Integrated Drug Abuse Reporting Process [National Institutes of Health]
IDART .... Individual Drill Attendance and Retirement Transaction [Military] (DNAB)
IdAs........... Ashton Public Library, Ashton, ID [Library symbol] [Library of Congress] (LCLS)
IDAS .... Industrial Data Acquisition System (IAA)
IDAS .... Information Displays Automatic Drafting System (IEEE)
IDAS .... Instrument Data Acquisition System
IDAS .... Integrated Data Acquisition System (MCD)
IDAS .... Integrated Defense Avionics System [Air Force] (DOMA)
IDAS .... Integrated Design Automation System (MCD)
IDAS .... Intelligent Data Acquisition System
IDAS .... International Database Access Service [Bahrain Telecommunications Co.] [Information service or system] (IID)
IDAS .... Intrusion Detection Alarm System
IDAS .... Isotope Dilution Alpha Spectrometry
IDAS .... Iterative Differential Analyzer Slave
IDAST .... Interpolated Data and Speech Transmission [Computer science]
Ida Supp..... Idaho Supplement [A publication] (DLA)
IDAT........... Interfacility Data (FAAC)
IDATU......... Irish Distributive and Administrative Trade Union (EAIO)
IDA (USA).... Indian Dental Association (USA) (EA)
IDAV........... Immune Deficiency Associated Virus
IdB............. Boise Public Library, Boise, ID [Library symbol Library of Congress] (LCLS)
IDB............ Illicit Diamond Buyer [or Buying]
IDB............ Illinois Central College, East Peoria, IL [OCLC symbol] (OCLC)
IDB............ Incomplete Data Base [Statistics] (DAVI)
IDB............ Inductance Decade Box
IDB............ Industrial Data Bank Department [Gulf Organization for Industrial Consulting] [Qatar] [Information service or system] (IID)
IDB............ Industrial Development Bank [Jordan]
IDB............ Industrial Development Bank [Kenya] (IMH)
IDB............ Industrial Development Board [Northern Ireland] (GEA)
IDB............ Industrial Development Bond
IDB............ Inertial Data Box (KSC)
IDB............ Infared Diving Binoculors (MCD)
IDB............ INPADOC [International Patent Documentation Center] Data Base [Information service or system] (CRD)
IDB............ Input Data Buffer
IDB............ Inspection Data Bulletin
IDB............ In-Suit Drink Bag [Aerospace] (MCD)
IDB............ Insurance Development Bureau [Guelph, ON] (EAIO)
IDB............ Integrated Data Base [Computer science]
IDB............ Interaction Database
IDB............ Inter-American Defense Board (EA)
IDB............ Inter-American Development Bank [Also, IADB]
IDB............ Intercept During Boost [Aerospace]
IDB............ Inter-Dealer Broker [British]
IDB............ Inter-Dynamic Balance
IDB............ International Data Base [Bureau of Census] [Database]
IDB............ Interpreter's Dictionary of the Bible
IDB............ Interpretive Debugger [Computer science] (ECII)
IDB............ Inverni & Della Beffa [Italy] [Research code symbol]
IDB............ Islamic Development Bank [Saudi Arabia]
IDB............ Israel Discount Bank
IDBA........... International Deli-Bakery Association [Defunct] (EA)
IdBB........... Boise State College, Boise, ID [Library symbol Library of Congress] (LCLS)
IdBBC......... Boise Bible College, Boise, ID [Library symbol] [Library of Congress] (LCLS)
IdBBC......... Boise Cascade Corp. Library, Boise, ID [Library symbol] [Library of Congress] (LCLS)
IdBC........... Ada County District Library, Boise, ID [Library symbol] [Library of Congress] (LCLS)
IdBCH .... CH2M Hill Library, Boise, ID [Library symbol] [Library of Congress] (LCLS)
IdBDB .... Diocese of Boise, Resource Center, Boise, ID [Library symbol] [Library of Congress] (LCLS)
IdBe............ Bellevue Public Library, Bellevue, ID [Library symbol] [Library of Congress] (LCLS)
IDBE........... ID Biomedical Corp. [NASDAQ symbol] (SAG)
IDBEF.......... ID Biomedical [NASDAQ symbol] (TTSB)
IdBEH.......... Idaho Elks Rehabilitation Hospital, Medical Library, Boise, ID [Library symbol] [Library of Congress] (LCLS)

IdBf .... Blackfoot Public Library, Blackfoot, ID [*Library symbol*] [*Library of Congress*] (LCLS)

IdBfBH .... Bingham Memorial Hospital, Medical Library, Blackfoot, ID [*Library symbol*] [*Library of Congress*] (LCLS)

IdBFG .... Fish & Game Library, Boise, ID [*Library symbol*] [*Library of Congress*] (LCLS)

IdBfGS .... Church of Jesus Christ of Latter-Day Saints, Genealogical Society Library, Blackfoot West Branch, Stake Center, Blackfoot, ID [*Library symbol Library of Congress*] (LCLS)

IdBfH .... State Hospital South, Medical Library, Blackfoot, ID [*Library symbol*] [*Library of Congress*] (LCLS)

IdBfS .... Snake River School and Community Library, Blackfoot, ID [*Library symbol*] [*Library of Congress*] (LCLS)

IdBG .... Genealogical Library, Boise, ID [*Library symbol*] [*Library of Congress*] (LCLS)

IdBHP .... Hewett-Packard, Boise Site Library, Boise, ID [*Library symbol*] [*Library of Congress*] (LCLS)

IDBI .... Industrial Development Bank of India (ECON)

IDBI .... Industrial Development Bank of Israel (IMH)

IdBI .... Information and Referral Service, Boise, ID [*Library symbol*] [*Library of Congress*] (LCLS)

ID Bio .... ID Biomedical Corp. [*Associated Press*] (SAG)

ID Biom ...... ID Biomedical Corp. [*Associated Press*] (SAG)

IdBL .... Idaho Legislative Council, Legislative Library, Boise, ID [*Library symbol*] [*Library of Congress*] (LCLS)

IdBLM-B ...... Bureau of Land Management, Boise, ID [*Library symbol Library of Congress*] (LCLS)

IDBMA .... International Data Base Management Association (EA)

IdBMK .... Morrison-Krudsen Co., Inc., Records and Micrographics Center, Boise, ID [*Library symbol Library of Congress*] (LCLS)

IDBMS .... Integrated Database Management System

IDBN .... Integrated Digital Backbone Network [*Telecommunications*]

IdBnf .... Boundary County Library District, Bonners Ferry, ID [*Library symbol*] [*Library of Congress*] (LCLS)

IDBPF .... Interdigital Band-Pass Filter [*Electronics*] (IAA)

Id-BPH .... Idaho State Library, Blind and Physically Handicapped Services, Boise, ID [*Library symbol Library of Congress*] (LCLS)

IdBr .... Bruneau District Library, Bruneau, ID [*Library symbol*] [*Library of Congress*] (LCLS)

IDBR .... Indirect Bilirubin [*Biochemistry*] (DAVI)

IDBR .... Input Data Buffer Register [*Computer science*] (MHDB)

IDBRA .... International Drivers' Behaviour Research Association [*Paris, France*] (EAIO)

IdBRC .... Roman Catholic Diocese of Boise, Boise, ID [*Library symbol*] [*Library of Congress*] (LCLS)

IdBRE .... Real Estate Comm. Library, Boise, ID [*Library symbol*] [*Library of Congress*] (LCLS)

IdBS .... Idaho Statesman Library, Boise, ID [*Library symbol*] [*Library of Congress*] (LCLS)

IdBSA .... Saint Alphonsus Regional Medical Center, Medical Library, Boise, ID [*Library symbol*] [*Library of Congress*] (LCLS)

IdBSH .... Boise Senior High School, Boise, ID [*Library symbol*] [*Library of Congress*] (LCLS)

IdBSL .... Saint Luke's Regional Center Medical Library, Boise, ID [*Library symbol*] [*Library of Congress*] (LCLS)

IDBT .... Industrial Development Bank of Turkey (PDAA)

IdBTI .... Mountain State Tumor Institute Medical Library, Boise, ID [*Library symbol*] [*Library of Congress*] (LCLS)

IdBuh .... Buhl Public Library, Buhl, ID [*Library symbol*] [*Library of Congress*] (LCLS)

IdBur .... Burley Public Library, Burley, ID [*Library symbol*] [*Library of Congress*] (LCLS)

IdBurGS .... Church of Jesus Christ of Latter-Day Saints, Genealogical Society Library, Burley Branch, Burley, ID [*Library symbol Library of Congress*] (LCLS)

IdBV .... United States Veterans Administration Medical Center, Medical Library, Boise, ID [*Library symbol*] [*Library of Congress*] (LCLS)

IdC .... Coeur D'Alene Public Library, Coeur D'Alene, ID [*Library symbol Library of Congress*] (LCLS)

IDC .... Idiopathic Dilated Cardiomyopathy [*Cardiology*]

IDC .... Image Dissector Camera

IDC .... IMBLMS [*Integrated Medical Behavioral Measurement System*] Digital Computer (MCD)

IDC .... Imperial Defence College [*British*]

IDC .... Indirect Costs

IDC .... Individual Defense Counsel

IDC .... Industrial Design Certificate [*British*]

IDC .... Industrial Development Certificate [*Department of Industry*] [*British*]

IDC .... Industrial Development Corp.

IDC .... Industries Development Committee

IDC .... Information and Direction Center

IDC .... Information and Documentation Center [*Royal Institute of Technology Library*] [*Information service or system*] (IID)

IDC .... Information Design Change (NG)

IDC .... Information Dynamics Corp.

IDC .... Infrared Detector Cryostat

IDC .... Inner Dead-Center (DNAB)

IDC .... Input Display Console [*Computer science*]

IDC .... Inspection Data Card (MCD)

IDC .... Insulation Displacement Connector [*Electronics*]

IDC .... Intangible Drilling Costs [*Petroleum industry*]

IDC .... Integrated Device Controller

IDC .... Integrated Disk Control [*NCR Corp.*]

IdBH .... Integrated Displays and Controls (MCD)

IDC .... Interactive Data Class [*Telecommunications*]

IDC .... Interactive Data Corporation (NITA)

IDC .... Interagency Defector Committee

IDC .... Interceptor Distance Computer

IDC .... Interdepartmental Committee

IDC .... Interdepartmental Communication

IDC .... Interdigital Communications [*AMEX symbol*] (SPSG)

IDC .... Interdigitating Cell [*Medicine*] (DMAA)

IDC .... Inter Documentation Co. AG, Zug, Switzerland [*Library symbol Library of Congress*] (LCLS)

IDC .... Interest During Construction

IDC .... Interface Document Control (MCD)

IDC .... Interior Designers of Canada [*See also DIC*]

IDC .... Internal Data Channel

IDC .... Internal Document Control

IDC .... International Dairy Committee

IDC .... International Dance Council [*See also CIDD*] (EAIO)

IDC .... International Data Connector

IDC .... International Data Consultants [*Market research organization*] (NITA)

IDC .... International Data Corp. [*Information service or system*] (IID)

IDC .... International Development Conference (EA)

IDC .... International Development Corp. [*Proposed corporation to combine Alliance for Progress and Agency for International Development*]

IDC .... International Diamond Council [*Antwerp, Belgium*] (EAIO)

IDC .... International Diastema Club (EA)

IDC .... International Display Corp. [*Vancouver Stock Exchange symbol*]

IDC .... International Documentation Center

IDC .... International Documentation in Chemistry (DIT)

IDC .... International Drycleaners Congress (EA)

IDC .... Internationale Democrate Chretienne [*Christian Democrat International*] [*Belgium*] (EAIO)

IDC .... Internationale Dokumentationsgesellschaft fuer Chemie [*International Company for Documentation in Chemistry*] [*Frankfurt, West Germany*]

IDC .... Internet Database Connector [*Computer science*] (PCM)

IDC .... Intraductal Carcinoma [*Oncology*]

IDC .... Intransit Data Card (AFM)

IDC .... Inventor's Desktop Companion [*A publication*]

IDC .... Iodine Dextrin Color

IDC .... Iranian Democratic Committee (EA)

IDC .... Irrigated, Double Cropped [*Agriculture*]

IDC .... Item Design Change

IDC .... Item Detail Card [*Military*] (AABC)

IDC .... Iterated Deferred Correction (PDAA)

IDC .... Peoples Gas, Light & Coke Co., Chicago, IL [*OCLC symbol*] (OCLC)

IdCa .... Caldwell Public Library, Caldwell, ID [*Library symbol Library of Congress*] (LCLS)

ID(C)A .... Indecent Displays (Control) Act [*British*]

IDCA .... Indian Diamond and Colorstone Association (EA)

IDCA .... International Design Conference in Aspen (EA)

IDCA .... International Development Cooperation Act of 1979

IDCA .... [*United States*] International Development Cooperation Agency (USGC)

IDCA .... International Dolphin Conservation Act [*1993*]

IDCA .... International Dragon Class Association (EAIO)

IdCaC .... College of Idaho, Caldwell, ID [*Library symbol Library of Congress*] (LCLS)

IdCaH .... West Valley Medical Center, Medical Library, Caldwell, ID [*Library symbol*] [*Library of Congress*] (LCLS)

IdCar .... Little Wood River District Library, Carey, ID [*Library symbol*] [*Library of Congress*] (LCLS)

IDCAS .... Industrial Development Center for Arab States [*Later, AIDO*]

IdCC .... Consolidated Free Library District, Coeur d'Alene, ID [*Library symbol*] [*Library of Congress*] (LCLS)

IDCC .... Integrated Data Communications Controller

IDCC .... Integrated Dual-Use Commercial Companies

IDCC .... INTEK Diversified [*NASDAQ symbol*] (TTSB)

IDCC .... INTEK Diversified Corp. [*NASDAQ symbol*] (NQ)

IDCC .... Interactive Display and Control Component (MCD)

IDCC .... Inter-Departmental Consultative Committee

IdCC-A .... Consolidated Free Library District, Athol Branch, Athol, ID [*Library symbol*] [*Library of Congress*] (LCLS)

IDCCC .... Interim Data Communications Collection Center

IDCCC .... International Dredging Conference Coordinating Committee (EAIO)

IdCCIN .... Cooperative Information Network, Coeur d'Alene, ID [*Library symbol*] [*Library of Congress*] (LCLS)

IdCC-R .... Consolidated Free Library District, Rathrum Branch, Rathrum, ID [*Library symbol*] [*Library of Congress*] (LCLS)

IdCC-SC .... Consolidated Free Library District, Service Center, Couer d'Alene, ID [*Library symbol*] [*Library of Congress*] (LCLS)

IdCC-SL .... Consolidated Free Library District, Spirit Lake Branch, Spirit Lake, ID [*Library symbol*] [*Library of Congress*] (LCLS)

IDCDA .... Independent Dealer Committee Dedicated to Action (EA)

IDCF .... Immunodiffusion Complement Fix [*Immunochemistry*] (DAVI)

IDCF .... Indirect Command File [*Computer science*] (WDAA)

IDCFC .... International David Cassidy Fan Club (EAIO)

IDCH .... International Directory of Company Histories [*A publication*]

IdCH .... Kootenai Medical Center, Medical Library, Couer d'Alene, ID [*Library symbol*] [*Library of Congress*] (LCLS)

IdCha .... Challis Public Library, Challis, ID [*Library symbol*] [*Library of Congress*] (LCLS)

IdCHM .... Hecla Mining Co. Library, Couer d'Alene, ID [*Library symbol*] [*Library of Congress*] (LCLS)

IdChP .... Portneuf Library District, Chubbuck, ID [*Library symbol*] [*Library of Congress*] (LCLS)

IdCHS .... Couer d'Alene High School, Couer d'Alene, ID [*Library symbol*] [*Library of Congress*] (LCLS)
IDCI .... Intradiplochromatid Interchange (PDAA)
IdCl .... Clarkia District Library, Clarkia, ID [*Library symbol*] [*Library of Congress*] (LCLS)
IDCL .... Coeur d'Alene Public Library, Coeur d'Alene, ID [*Library symbol*] [*Library of Congress*] (LCLS)
IDCL............ Information Design Change List (MCD)
IdCm .... Cambridge District Library, Cambridge, ID [*Library symbol*] [*Library of Congress*] (LCLS)
IDCMA .... Independent Data Communications Manufacturers Association (EA)
IDCN .... Interchangeability Document Change Notice (KSC)
IdCN .... North Idaho College, Coeur d'Alene, ID [*Library symbol Library of Congress*] (LCLS)
IDCNA.......... Insulation Distributor Contractors National Association [*Later, NICA*] (EA)
IdCnL .... Council District Library, Council, ID [*Library symbol*] [*Library of Congress*] (LCLS)
IDCNY.......... International Design Center, New York
IDCOP .... Integral Driver Coil on Plug
IDCOR......... Industry Degraded Core Rulemaking Program [*Nuclear industry sponsored group*]
IdCoStG ...... College of Saint Gertrude, Library, Cottonwood, ID [*Library symbol*] [*Library of Congress*] (LCLS)
IDCP .... International Data Collecting Platform (TEL)
IDCR .... Interchangeability Document Change Request (MCD)
IDCR .... International Decade of Cetacean Research
IdCs .... Cascade Public Library, Cascade, ID [*Library symbol*] [*Library of Congress*] (LCLS)
IDCS .... Image Dissector Camera System
IDCS .... Initial Defense Communications Satellite (MCD)
IDCS .... Instrumentation/Data Collection System
IDCS .... Integrated Data Coding System (NG)
IDCS .... Interdepartment Courier Service
IDCS .... International Digital Channel Service [*Federal Trade Commission*]
IDCSP .... Initial Defense Communications Satellite Program [*or Project*]
IDCSP .... Interim Defense Communications Satellite Program [*DoD*]
IDCSP-A....... Initial Defense Communications Satellite Program-Augmented (CET)
IDCSP/ADCSP... Initial Defense Communications Satellite Program / Advanced Defense Communications Satellite Program (SAA)
IDCSS .... Initial Defense Communications Satellite System (NATG)
IDCSS .... Intermediate Defense Communications Satellite System (IAA)
IDCT........... Integrated Daily Cycle Test (MCD)
IDCT........... Inverse Discrete Cosine Transform [*Electronics*] (ACRL)
IDCTR .... Inductor (MSA)
IDD .... Detroit Diesel Allison Division, General Motors Corp., Indianapolis, IN [*OCLC symbol*] (OCLC)
IDD .... Illicit Diamond Dealing (ROG)
IDD .... Image Definition Device
IDD ...,....... Indirect by Direct (MCD)
IDD .... Industrial Development Division [*Vietnam*]
IDD .... Infant Development Distress Syndrome [*Medicine*] (ADA)
IDD .... Institute for Drafting and Design [*Australia*]
IDD .... Insulin-Dependent Diabetes
IDD .... Integrated Data Dictionary
IDD .... Intelligence Data Handling Division [*United States European Command*]
IDD .... Inter-Director Designation (NG)
IDD .... Interface Definition Document (MCD)
IDD .... Interface Designation Drawing
IDD .... Interface Design Document (DOMA)
IDD .... Interim Drydocking [*Navy*] (NVT)
IDD .... International Defense Directory [*A publication*]
IDD .... International Direct Dialing [*Telecommunications*]
IDD .... International Dorado Resources [*Vancouver Stock Exchange symbol*]
IDD .... Inventory to Diagnose Depression [*Psychology*]
IDD .... Iodine Deficiency Disorders [*Medicine*]
IdD.............. South Bannock District Library, Downey Branch, Downey, ID [*Library symbol*] [*Library of Congress*] (LCLS)
IDDA .... Interior Decorators and Designers Association [*British*] (EAIO)
IDDA .... International Dairy-Deli Association (EA)
IDDAS .... Intelligent Dummy Data Acquisition System [*Crash testing*] [*Automotive engineering*]
IDDC .... International Demographic Data Center [*Bureau of the Census*] [*Database*] [*Information service or system*] (IID)
IDDC .... International Development Data Center [*Georgia Institute of Technology*]
IDDD .... International Demographic Data Directory [*Agency for International Development*] (IID)
IDDD .... International Direct Distance Dialing [*AT & T*]
IDDE .... Integrated Development and Debugging Environment [*Symantec Corp.*] [*Computer science*] (PCM)
IDDE .... Interactive Development and Debugging Environment (PCM)
IDDF .... Intermediate Digital Distribution Frame [*Telecommunications*] (TEL)
Iddings DRB... Iddings' Dayton Term Reports [*Ohio*] [*A publication*] (DLA)
Iddings TRD... Iddings' Dayton Term Reports [*Ohio*] [*A publication*] (DLA)
IDDIS .... IDD Information Services, Inc. (IID)
IDDJ .... Interim Decisions of the Department of Justice
IDDL .... Interactive Database Design Laboratory [*Computer science*] (MHDB)
IdD-L .... South Bannock District Library, Lava Hot Springs Branch, Lava Hot Springs, ID [*Library symbol*] [*Library of Congress*] (LCLS)
IDDM .... Insulin-Dependent Diabetes Mellitus
IDDP .... Interface Design Definition Paper [*Military*] (CAAL)

IDDP .... International Dairy Development Programme [*FAO/DANIDA Dairy Development P rogramme and International Scheme for the Coordination of Dairy Development*] [*Formed by a merger of United Nations*] (EAIO)
IDDP .... Isodecyl Diphenyl Phosphate [*Organic chemistry*]
IDDRG .... International Deep Drawing Research Group [*British*]
IdDrGS........ Church of Jesus Christ of Latter-Day Saints, Genealogical Society Library, Driggs Branch, Driggs, ID [*Library symbol Library of Congress*] (LCLS)
IDDS .... Implantable Drug Delivery System [*Pharmacology*] (DAVI)
IDDS .... Improved Data Display System
IDDS .... Institute for Defense and Disarmament Studies (EA)
IDDS .... Instrumentation Data Distribution System (MUGU)
IDDS .... Integrated Data Display System
IDDS .... Integrated Display Development Station (MCD)
IDDS .... International Dairy Development Scheme
IDDS .... International Digital Data Service [*Western Union Corp.*] [*Data transmission service*]
IDD TR........ Iddings' Dayton Term Reports [*Ohio*] [*A publication*] (DLA)
IDE............. Embedded Drive Electronics [*Computer science*]
IDE............. Independent Development Environment [*Computer science*] (PCM)
IDE............. Industry-Developed Equipment (AAG)
IDE............. Infrared Decoy Evaluator
IDE............. Initial Design Evaluation (MCD)
IDE............. Institute for Democratic Education [*Absorbed by Anti-Defamation League of B'nai B'rith*] (EA)
IDE............. Institute of Developing Economics, Tokyo [*UTLAS symbol*]
IDE............. Insulin-Degrading Enzyme [*Biochemistry*]
IDE............. Integrated Development Environment
IDE............. Integrated Device Electronics
IDE............. Integrated Drive Electronics [*Hard disk interface*] [*Computer science*] (PCM)
IDE............. Intelligent Distributed Editor (HGAA)
IDE............. Intelligent Drive Electronics
IDE............. Interactive Data Entry
IDE............. Interchange Data Element [*Telecommunications*] (OSI)
IDE............. Interdisciplinary Enquiry [*Education*] (AIE)
IDE............. Interim Data Element [*Army*] (AABC)
IDE............. Intrusion Detection Equipment
IDE............. Investigational Device Exemption [*Food and Drug Administration*]
IDE............. Isla Desecheo [*Puerto Rico*] [*Seismograph station code, US Geological Survey*] (SEIS)
IdEa .... Eagle Public Library, Eagle, ID [*Library symbol*] [*Library of Congress*] (LCLS)
IDEA............ IDEAssociates, Inc. [*Telecommunications*] (TSSD)
IDEA............ Identification, Distribution, and Exchange for Action [*Project*]
IDEA............ Improved Data Effectiveness and Availability
IDEA............ Index for Design Engineering Applications [*Data retrieval service*] [*Product engineering*]
IDEA............ Individuals with Disabilities Education Act [*Formerly, The Education for All Handicapped Children Act*] (PAZ)
IDEA............ Inductive Data Exploration and Analysis [*Computer science*]
IDEA............ Industrial Design Excellence Award
IDEA............ Innovasive Devices, Inc. [*NASDAQ symbol*] (SAG)
I/D/E/A......... Institute for Development of Educational Activities (EA)
IDEA............ Integrated Data for Enforcement Analysis System [*Environmental science*]
IDEA............ Integrated Design Engineering Aid [*Computer science*] (RDA)
IDEA............ Integrated Digital Electric Aircraft (PDAA)
IDEA............ Integrated Digital Electronic Automatic (PDAA)
IDEA............ Integrated Dose Environment Analysis
IDEA............ Interactive Data Entry Access [*Data General Corp.*]
IDEA............ Interactive Digital Electronic Appliance [*Computer science*]
IDEA............ Interactive Digital Electronic Appliances
IDEA............ Interface and Display Electronics Assembly
IDEA............ International Dalkon Shield Victims Education Association (EA)
IDEA............ International Dance-Exercise Association (EA)
IDEA............ International Data Encryption Algorithm [*Telecommunications*]
IDEA............ International Desalination and Environmental Association [*Later, IDA*] (EA)
IDEA............ International Diving Educators Association
IDEA............ International Downtown Executives Association [*Later, IDA*] (EA)
IDEA............ Isolation of Dimensions and Elimination of Alternatives
Idea .... Patent, Trademark, and Copyright Journal of Research and Education [*A publication*] (DLA)
IDEAL.......... Integrated Design Engineering and Logistics (PDAA)
IDEALS .... Ideal Design of Effective and Logical Systems
IDEALS .... Institute for the Development of Emotional and Life Skills (EA)
IDEAS .... Innovations Deserving Exploratory Analysis Program [*FHWA*] (TAG)
IDEAS .... Inquiry Data Entry Access System (IAA)
IDEAS .... Institutional Development and Economic Affairs Service [*Defunct*] (EA)
IDEAS .... Integrated Design Analysis System [*Space shuttle*] [*NASA*]
IDEAS .... Integrated Design and Engineering Automated System (IEEE)
IDEAS .... Intelligence Data Element Authorization Standards [*Military*] (MCD)
IDEAS .... Interest Determination and Assessment System [*Vocational guidance test*]
IDEAS .... International Data Exchange for Aviation Safety [*ICAO*] (DA)
IDEAS .... International Decade of Exploration and Assessment of the Seas [*Defunct*] (USDC)
IDEAS .... International Decade of Exploration and Assessment of the Seas [*Inactive*] [*Marine science*] (OSRA)
IDEAS .... International Development - Economics Awareness System
IDEB............ Intermittent Dual-Fluid Exhaust Burner

IDec .... Decatur Public Library, Decatur, IL [*Library symbol Library of Congress*] (LCLS)
IDEC .... IDEC Pharmaceuticals Corp. [*Associated Press*] (SAG)
IDEC .... Interior Design Educators Council (EA)
IDEC .... International Drug Enforcement Conference
IDECC .... Interstate Distributive Education Curriculum Consortium (EDAC)
IDecH .... Decatur Memorial Hospital, Medical Staff and Nursing School Library, Decatur, IL [*Library symbol Library of Congress*] (LCLS)
IDecJ .... James Millikin University, Decatur, IL [*Library symbol Library of Congress*] (LCLS)
IdEcL .... Elk City School/Community Library, Elk City, ID [*Library symbol*] [*Library of Congress*] (LCLS)
IDecM .... Adolph Meyer Mental Health Center, Decatur, IL [*Library symbol Library of Congress*] (LCLS)
IDecR .... Rolling Prairie Libraries, Decatur, IL [*Library symbol Library of Congress*] (LCLS)
IDecS .... A.E. Staley Manufacturing Co., Decatur, IL [*Library symbol*] [*Library of Congress*] (LCLS)
IDECS .... Image Discrimination, Enhancement, and Combination System [*Electronic optical system*]
IDecStM ...... Saint Mary's Hospital, Medical Staff and Nursing Library, Decatur, IL [*Library symbol Library of Congress*] (LCLS)
ID/ED .... Internal Diameter to External Diameter [*Ratio for cardiac valve replacement*] [*Cardiology*] (DAVI)
IDEDS .... International Development Education Documentation Service [*University of Pittsburgh*] (IID)
IdEdS .... Silver & Gold Senior Citizens Library, Eden, ID [*Library symbol*] [*Library of Congress*] (LCLS)
IDEE .... Institute for Democracy in Eastern Europe (EA)
IDEEA .... Information and Data Exchange Experimental Activities
IDEEA .... Instantaneous Drilling Evaluation Log (PDAA)
IDEEA .... International Defense Equipment Exhibitors Association (EA)
IDEF .... ICAM Definition (MCD)
IDEF .... Institut International de Droit d'Expression Francaise [*International Institute of Law of the French Speaking Countries - IILFSC*] [*Paris, France*] (EAIO)
IDEF .... Integrated System Definition Language [*Computer science*] (IEEE)
IDeKN .... Northern Illinois University, De Kalb, IL [*Library symbol Library of Congress*] (LCLS)
IDeKN-L ...... Northern Illinois University, College of Law, De Kalb, IL [*Library symbol*] [*Library of Congress*] (LCLS)
IDeKN-LS .... Northern Illinois University, Department of Library Sciences, De Kalb, IL [*Library symbol Library of Congress*] (LCLS)
IDelan .... Goose Creek Township Carnegie Library, De Land, IL [*Library symbol Library of Congress*] (LCLS)
IDelanSD ..... Bond County Community Unit, School District 2, De Land, IL [*Library symbol Library of Congress*] (LCLS)
IDelav .... Ayer Public Library, Delavan, IL [*Library symbol Library of Congress*] (LCLS)
IdEm .... Emmett Public Library, Emmett, ID [*Library symbol*] [*Library of Congress*] (LCLS)
iDEN .... Integrated Digital Enhanced Network [*Telecommunications*]
IDEN .... Interactive Data Entry Network [*Computer science*] (MHDB)
IDENT .... Identical (MSA)
IDENT .... Identification (AFM)
IDENT .... Identify (ECII)
IDENTIFD ..... Identified (ROG)
Identix .... Identix, Inc. [*Associated Press*] (SAG)
Ideo .... Ideological
Ideon .... Ideon Group, Inc. [*Associated Press*] (SAG)
IDep .... DePue Public Library, DePue, IL [*Library symbol Library of Congress*] (LCLS)
IDEP .... Industry Data Exchange Program
IDEP .... Institut Africain de Developpement Economique et de Planification [*African Institute for Economic Development and Planning*] [*Dakar, Senegal*] (AF)
IDEP .... Interagency Data Exchange Program [*Later, GIDEP*] (RDA)
IDEP .... Inter-Department Data Exchange Program [*Air Force*] (AFM)
IDEP .... International Data Exchange Program (NITA)
IDEP .... Interservice Data Exchange Program (AFIT)
IDEP .... Ion Density Electronics Package
IDepSD .... DePue Unit, School District 103, DePue, IL [*Library symbol Library of Congress*] (LCLS)
IdEr .... Elk River School/Community Library, Elk River, ID [*Library symbol*] [*Library of Congress*] (LCLS)
IDERA .... International Development Education Resources Association
i derm .... Intradermal [*Medicine*] (AAMN)
IDES .... Image Dissector Echelle Spectrograph [*Instrumentation*]
IDES .... Incoterm Data Entry Software [*Incoterm*] (NITA)
IDES .... Information and Data Exchange System (IAA)
IDES .... Institute for Demographic and Economic Studies [*Research center*] (RCD)
IDES .... Integrated Defense System
IDES .... Interactive Data Entry System [*Computer science*] (MHDI)
IDES .... Interactive Drawing Editing Station (MCD)
IDesA .... American Foundrymen's Society, Des Plaines, IL [*Library symbol Library of Congress*] (LCLS)
IDesB .... Borg-Warner Corp., Ingersoll Research Center, Des Plaines, IL [*Library symbol Library of Congress*] (LCLS)
IDesD .... De Soto, Inc., Des Plaines, IL [*Library symbol Library of Congress*] (LCLS)
IDesN .... National Association of Independent Insurers, Des Plaines, IL [*Library symbol Library of Congress*] (LCLS)
IDesS .... Signal Research Center, Inc., Des Plaines, IL [*Library symbol*] [*Library of Congress*] (LCLS)

IDesSC .... Sandoz Crop Protection Corp., Des Plaines, IL [*Library symbol*] [*Library of Congress*] (LCLS)
IDesU .... Universal Oil Products Co., Des Plaines, IL [*Library symbol Library of Congress*] (LCLS)
Idex .... IDEX Corp. [*Associated Press*] (SAG)
IDEX .... Initial Defense Experiment (IEEE)
IdexxLb .... IDEXX Laboratories, Inc. [*Associated Press*] (SAG)
IDF .... Belleville Area College, Belleville, IL [*OCLC symbol*] (OCLC)
IDf .... Deerfield Public Library, Deerfield, IL [*Library symbol Library of Congress*] (LCLS)
IDF .... Identifier (IAA)
IDF .... Image Description File
IDF .... Immune Deficiency Foundation (EA)
IDF .... Indicating Direction Finder (IAA)
IDF .... Indigenous Defense Fighter [*Military*]
IDF .... Industrial Diesel Fuel
IDF .... In-Flight Diverted Force (CINC)
IDF .... Innovative Design Fund, Inc. (EA)
IDF .... Instantaneous Direction Finding (MCD)
IDF .... Instructional Dialogue Facility (IAA)
IDF .... Integrated Data File
IDF .... Interactive Dialogue Facility [*Programming language*] (CSR)
IDF .... Interceptor Day Fighter (NATG)
IDF .... Intermediate Distributing Frame [*Telecommunications*]
IDF .... Intermediate Distribution Frame (ACRL)
IDF .... Internal Delay Factor [*Computer science*]
IDF .... Internal Distribution Frame [*Television*] (IAA)
IDF .... International Dairy Federation [*See also FIL*] [*Brussels, Belgium*] (EAIO)
IDF .... International Democratic Fellowship
IDF .... International Dental Federation [*British*]
IDF .... International Development Foundation (EA)
IDF .... International Diabetes Federation [*See also FID*] (EAIO)
IDF .... International Distress Frequency (MUGU)
IDF .... International Domesticated Furs Ltd. [*Vancouver Stock Exchange symbol*]
IDF .... International Drilling Federation (EA)
IDF .... International Drilling Fluids [*Singapore*]
IDF .... Inverse Document Frequency (NITA)
IDF .... Iron Dragon-Fly Ltd. [*Russian Federation*] [*ICAO designator*] (FAAC)
IDF .... Isotropic Distribution Function
IDF .... Israeli Defense Forces
IDF .... Item Data File (MCD)
IdFa .... Camas County District Library, Fairfield, ID [*Library symbol*] [*Library of Congress*] (LCLS)
IDFA .... Infant and Dietetic Foods Association [*British*] (DBA)
IDFA .... International Dairy Foods Association (EA)
IDFB .... Internationales Daunen- und Federn-Bureau [*International Down and Feather Bure au*] (EAIO)
IDFc .... Immature Dead Female Child [*Neonatology*] (DAVI)
IdFe .... Tri-Community Library, Fernwood, ID [*Library symbol*] [*Library of Congress*] (LCLS)
IDFF .... Internationale Demokratische Frauenfoederation [*Women's International Democratic Federation*]
IdFh .... Shoshone-Bannock Library, Fort Hall, ID [*Library symbol*] [*Library of Congress*] (LCLS)
IdFi .... Filer Public Library, Filer, ID [*Library symbol*] [*Library of Congress*] (LCLS)
IDFM .... Induced Directional FM
IDFN .... In Domino Fiducia Nostra [*In the Lord Is Our Trust*] [*Motto of August, Prince of Anhalt-Plotzkau (1575-1653)*] [*Latin*]
IDFOR .... Idle Waiting Convoy Forward [*Vessel status*] [*Navy*]
IdFr .... Franklin County District Library, Franklin, ID [*Library symbol*] [*Library of Congress*] (LCLS)
IDFR .... Identified Friendly [*Military*]
IDFS .... Interferometer Direction Finding System [*Military*] (CAAL)
IDFSS .... Infantry Direct-Fire Simulation System (MCD)
IDFT .... Inverse Discrete Fourier Transform [*Electronics*] (IEEE)
IDfT .... Trinity Evangelical Divinity School, Deerfield, IL [*Library symbol Library of Congress*] (LCLS)
IDFTA .... International Dwarf Fruit Trees Association (EA)
IDfTD .... Trinity Evangelical Divinity School, Deerfield, IL [*Library symbol Library of Congress*] (LCLS)
IDFUN .... International Dull Folks Unlimited [*Defunct*] (EA)
IDFV .... In Deo Faciemus Virtutem [*Through God We Shall Do Valiantly*] [*(Ps., IX. 12) Motto of August, Prince of Anhalt-Plotzkau (1575-1653)*] [*Latin*]
IDFW .... Institute for a Drug-Free Workplace (EA)
IDG .... Chicago Theological Seminary, Chicago, IL [*OCLC symbol*] (OCLC)
IDG .... Ida Grove, IA [*Location identifier FAA*] (FAAL)
IDG .... Immunodiffusion in Gel (PDAA)
IDG .... Indigo Technologies, Inc. [*Vancouver Stock Exchange symbol*]
IDG .... Individual Drop Glider
IDG .... Industrial Development Group (MCD)
IDG .... Inniskilling Dragoon Guards [*British military*] (DMA)
IDG .... Inspector of Degaussing [*Navy*]
IDG .... Integrated Drive Generator (MCD)
IDG .... Internal Drive Generator
IDG .... International Data Group [*Publisher of computer magazines*] [*Framingham, MA*]
IdGa .... Garden Valley District Library, Garden Valley, ID [*Library symbol*] [*Library of Congress*] (LCLS)
IdGc .... Garden City Public Library, Garden City, ID [*Library symbol*] [*Library of Congress*] (LCLS)
IDG/CMG ...... IDG Conference Management Group [*Framingham, MA*] (TSSD)

IdGf.............. Glenns Ferry Public Library, Glenns Ferry, ID [*Library symbol*] [*Library of Congress*] (LCLS)

IdGg.............. Grangeville Public Library, Grangeville, ID [*Library symbol*] [*Library of Congress*] (LCLS)

IdGi............... Gibbonsville Community Library, Gibbonsville, ID [*Library symbol*] [*Library of Congress*] (LCLS)

IDGIT .... Integrated Data Generation Implementation Technique

IdGo.............. Gooding Public Library, Gooding, ID [*Library symbol*] [*Library of Congress*] (LCLS)

IdGoPS ...... Gooding Public School District, Gooding, ID [*Library symbol*] [*Library of Congress*] (LCLS)

IdGoS........... Idaho State School for the Deaf and Blind, Gooding, ID [*Library symbol*] [*Library of Congress*] (LCLS)

IdGr .... Grace District Library, Grace, ID [*Library symbol*] [*Library of Congress*] (LCLS)

IdGv............. Eastern Owyhee County District Library, Grand View, ID [*Library symbol*] [*Library of Congress*] (LCLS)

IDH .... Isocitrate Dehydrogenase [*Also, ICD, ICDH*] [*An enzyme*]

IDH .... Meadville Theological School, Chicago, IL [*OCLC symbol*] (OCLC)

IDHA............ International District Heating Association [*Later, IDHCA*] (EA)

IdHamSD ..... Hamer Elementary School, Hamer, ID [*Library symbol*] [*Library of Congress*] (LCLS)

IdHb.............. Horseshoe Bend District Library, Horseshoe Bend, ID [*Library symbol*] [*Library of Congress*] (LCLS)

IDHCA.......... International District Heating and Cooling Association (EA)

IDHEC .... Institut des Hautes Etudes Cinematographiques [*French institute for the study of the motion picture*]

IDHF .... International Dental Health Foundation (EA)

IdHg............. Hagerman Public Library, Hagerman, ID [*Library symbol*] [*Library of Congress*] (LCLS)

IDHHB.......... Institute for the Development of the Harmonious Human Being (EA)

IdHi.............. Idaho State Historical Society, Boise, ID [*Library symbol Library of Congress*] (LCLS)

IDHIDH .... In dem Herrn Ist das Heil [*In the Lord Is Salvation*] [*Motto of Dorothee, Princess of Anhalt (1580-1618)*] [*German*]

IdHi-G........... Idaho Genealogical Society, Boise, ID [*Library symbol Library of Congress*] (LCLS)

IdHl.............. Hailey Public Library, Hailey, ID [*Library symbol*] [*Library of Congress*] (LCLS)

IdHIH .... Blaine County Medical Center, Medical Library, Hailey, ID [*Library symbol*] [*Library of Congress*] (LCLS)

IdHm............ Homedale Public Library, Homedale, ID [*Library symbol*] [*Library of Congress*] (LCLS)

IdHn............. Hansen Public Library, Hansen, ID [*Library symbol*] [*Library of Congress*] (LCLS)

IdHr .... Harrison Public Library, Harrison, ID [*Library symbol*] [*Library of Congress*] (LCLS)

IDHS .... Information Data Handling System

IDHS .... Integrated Data Handling System

IDHS .... Intelligence Data Handling System (AFM)

IDHSC.......... Intelligence Data Handling System Communications (MCD)

IdHyl............ Hayden Lake Library, Hayden Lake, ID [*Library symbol*] [*Library of Congress*] (LCLS)

IDI................ Bethany and Northern Baptist Theological Seminaries Library, Oak Brook, IL [*OCLC symbol*] (OCLC)

IDI................ Immunologically Detectable Insulin [*Medicine*] (DMAA)

IDI................ Improved Data Interchange

IDI................ Indiana, PA [*Location identifier FAA*] (FAAL)

IDI................ Indirect Injection Engine [*Engineering*]

IDI................ Induction-Delivery Interval [*Medicine*]

IDI................ Industrial Designers' Institute [*Later, IDSA*] (EA)

IDI................ Industrial Development Institute [*France*]

IDI................ Information Dimensions, Inc. [*Information service or system*] (IID)

IDI................ Initial Domain Identifier [*Computer science*] (TNIG)

IDI................ Initial Domain Part [*Telecommunications*] (OSI)

IDI................ Inspection Departmental Instruction (AAG)

IDI................ Instant Drug Index [*A publication*] (DAVI)

IDI................ Institut de Droit International [*Institute of International Law*]

IDI................ Instructional Dynamics, Inc. (AEBS)

IDI................ Instrumentation Data Items (NASA)

IDI................ Integrated Design Inspection (NRCH)

IDI................ Integrated Direct Ignition [*Automotive engineering*]

IDI................ Intelligent Dual Interface

IDI................ Intercomp Design, Inc. [*Neshanic Station, NJ*] [*Telecommunications*] (TSSD)

IDI................ Inter-Dentale Inferius [*Medicine*] (DMAA)

IDI................ Interdivision Invoice (AAG)

IDI................ International Development Institute [*Agency for International Development program*]

IDI................ International Diabetes Institute [*Australia*] (IRC)

IDI................ International Dialect Institute

IDI................ International Disaster Institute [*British*]

IDI................ Intractable Diarrhea of Infancy [*Pediatrics*]

IDI................ Ion Dipole Interaction

IDIA .... Industrial Disputes Investigation Act [*Canada*]

IDIA .... Internal Defense Identification Area (SAA)

IDIB .... Industrial Diamond Information Bureau [*British*] (BI)

IdIc............... Boise Basin District Library, Idaho City, ID [*Library symbol*] [*Library of Congress*] (LCLS)

IDIC .... Institut de Developpement International et de Cooperation [*Institute for International Development and Cooperation IIDC*] [*University of Ottawa*] [*Canada*]

IDIC .... Intelligence Division Indications Center [*Military*] (MCD)

IDIC .... Internal Dose Information Center [*ORNL*]

IDIC .... International Drought Information Center

IDID .... Comparator Sys [*NASDAQ symbol*] (TTSB)

IDID .... Comparator Systems Corp. [*NASDAQ symbol*] (SAG)

IDID .... Industrial Documentation and Information Department [*Industrial Development Center for Arab States*] [*Information service or system*] (IID)

IDIDAS........ Interactive Digital Image Display and Analysis System [*Marine science*] (OSRA)

IDIDAS........ Interactive Digital Image Display and Analysis System (USDC)

IdIf.............. Idaho Falls Public Library, Idaho Falls, ID [*Library symbol Library of Congress*] (LCLS)

IdIfA............ Aerojet Nuclear Co., Idaho Falls, ID [*Library symbol Library of Congress*] (LCLS)

IdIfAL.......... Argonne National Laboratory, Argonne-West Technical Library, Idaho Falls, ID [*Library symbol*] [*Library of Congress*] (LCLS)

IdIfC............ Bonneville County District Library, Idaho Falls, ID [*Library symbol*] [*Library of Congress*] (LCLS)

IdIfE............ Energy Incorp., Idaho Falls, ID [*Library symbol*] [*Library of Congress*] (LCLS)

IdIfEG......... EG & G Idaho, Inc., INEL Technical Library, Idaho Falls, ID [*Library symbol*] [*Library of Congress*] (LCLS)

IdIfGS .... Church of Jesus Christ of Latter-Day Saints, Genealogical Society Library, IdahoFalls Branch, Idaho Falls, ID [*Library symbol Library of Congress*] (LCLS)

IdIfH............ Eastern Idaho Regional Medical Center, Medical Library, Idaho Falls, ID [*Library symbol*] [*Library of Congress*] (LCLS)

IDIIOM........ Information Displays, Incorporated, Input-Output Machine

IDIM............ Integrated Departmental Instructions Manual

IDIMS .... Interactive Digital Image Manipulation System [*Minicomputer*]

Idings TRD... Iddings' Dayton Term Reports [*Ohio*] [*A publication*] (DLA)

IDIOT........... Instrumentation Digital On-Line Transcriber [*Computer science*]

IDIP .... Intelligence Data Input Package (MCD)

IDIP .... Intensified Drug Inspection Program [*FDA*]

IDIP .... International Directories in Print [*A publication*]

IDIQ .... Indefinite Delivery, Indefinite Quantity [*Type of contract*] (AAGC)

IDIQ .... Indefinite Delivery/Indefinite Quantity [*Military*] (RDA)

IDIS .... Idaho Drug Information Service [*Information service or system*] (IID)

IDIS .... Institut fuer Dokumentation, Information, und Statistik [*Institute for Documentation, Information, and Statistics*] [*Information service or system*] (IID)

IDIS .... Institut fuer Dokumentation und Information ueber Sozialmedizin und Oeffentliches Gesundheitswesen [*Institute for Documentation and Information in Social Medicine and Public Health*] [*Information retrieval Germany*]

IDIS .... Intrusion Detection and Identification System (PDAA)

IDIS .... Iowa Drug Information Service [*University of Iowa*] [*Information service or system*] (IID)

IDIU .... Interdivisional Information Unit [*Department of Justice intelligence unit*]

IDJ............... Catholic Theological Union, Chicago, IL [*OCLC symbol*] (OCLC)

IDJ............... I Dance Jazz [*Jazz music group*] (ECON)

IDJ............... Information Design Journal [*A publication*] (DGA)

IdJ............... Jerome Public Library, Jerome, ID [*Library symbol*] [*Library of Congress*] (LCLS)

IDJC............ India Docks Joint Committee (ROG)

IdJH............ Saint Benedict's Family Medical Center, Medical Library, Jerome, ID [*Library symbol*] [*Library of Congress*] (LCLS)

IdK.............. Community Library Association, Inc., Ketchem, ID [*Library symbol*] [*Library of Congress*] (LCLS)

IDK.............. Internal Derangement of Knee [*Medicine*] (DMAA)

IDK.............. Internal Derangement of Knee Joint

IDK.............. Jesuit-Krauss-McCormick Library, Chicago, IL [*OCLC symbol*] (OCLC)

IdKe............ Kellogg Public Library, Kellogg, ID [*Library symbol*] [*Library of Congress*] (LCLS)

IdKi............. Kimberly Public Library, Kimberly, ID [*Library symbol*] [*Library of Congress*] (LCLS)

IdKo............ Kooskia Public Library, Kooskia, ID [*Library symbol*] [*Library of Congress*] (LCLS)

IdKu............ Kuna School/Comm Library, Kuna, ID [*Library symbol*] [*Library of Congress*] (LCLS)

Id-L.............. Idaho Supreme Court, Idaho State Law Library, Boise, ID [*Library symbol Library of Congress*] (LCLS)

IDL.............. Ideal

IDL.............. Ideal Group of Companies, Inc. [*Toronto Stock Exchange symbol*]

IDL.............. Idler

IDL.............. Indentured Drawing List

IDL.............. Indianola, MS [*Location identifier FAA*] (FAAL)

ID(L).......... Infantry Division (Light) [*Army*] (INF)

IDL.............. Information Description Language

IDL.............. Insertion-Deletion Loop-Type [*Genetics*]

IDL.............. Instructional Development Laboratory [*University of Minnesota of Minneapolis Saint Paul*] [*Research center*] (RCD)

IDL.............. Instruction Definition Language

IDL.............. Instrument Detection Level [*Analytical chemistry*]

IDL.............. Instrument Development Laboratories

IDL.............. Interactive Data Language (USDC)

IDL.............. Interactive Data Language [*Marine science*] (OSRA)

IDL.............. Interdisciplinary Materials Laboratory [*Various universities*]

IDL.............. Interface Definition Language [*Computer science*]

IDL.............. Interfacility Data Link [*FAA*] (TAG)

IDL.............. Intermediate Density Lipoprotein [*Biochemistry*]

IDL.............. International Date Line (MCD)

IDL.............. Isotope Development Ltd.

IdL.............. Lewiston City Library, Lewiston, ID [*Library symbol*] [*Library of Congress*] (LCLS)

IDL .... Rush University, Chicago, IL [*OCLC symbol*] (OCLC)
IDL & RS ..... International Data Library and Reference Service
IDLC .... Integrated Digital Logic Circuit
IDLC .... Integrated Digital Loop Carrier [*Telecommunications*] (ACRL)
IdLe .... Leadore Community Library, Leadore, ID [*Library symbol*] [*Library of Congress*] (LCLS)
IdLES .... Lewiston Elementary Schools, Lewiston, ID [*Library symbol*] [*Library of Congress*] (LCLS)
IdLES-CM .... Lewiston Elementary Schools, Camelot Elementary School, Lewiston, ID [*Library symbol*] [*Library of Congress*] (LCLS)
IdLES-CN .... Lewiston Elementary Schools, Centennial Elementary School, Lewiston, ID [*Library symbol*] [*Library of Congress*] (LCLS)
IdLES-MG .... Lewiston Elementary Schools, McGhee Elementary School, Lewiston, ID [*Library symbol*] [*Library of Congress*] (LCLS)
IdLES-MS .... Lewiston Elementary Schools, McSorley Elementary School, Lewiston, ID [*Library symbol*] [*Library of Congress*] (LCLS)
IdLES-OR .... Lewiston Elementary Schools, Orchards Elementary School, Lewiston, ID [*Library symbol*] [*Library of Congress*] (LCLS)
IdLES-WB .... Lewiston Elementary Schools, Webster Elementary School, Lewiston, ID [*Library symbol*] [*Library of Congress*] (LCLS)
IdLES-WH .... Lewiston Elementary Schools, Whitman Elementary School, Lewiston, ID [*Library symbol*] [*Library of Congress*] (LCLS)
IdLGS .... Church of Jesus Christ of Latter-Day Saints, Genealogical Society Library, Lewiston Branch, Stake Center, Lewiston, ID [*Library symbol Library of Congress*] (LCLS)
IDLH .... Immediately Dangerous to Life and Health
IDLHC .... Immediately Dangerous to Life or Health Concentration [*Toxicology*]
IdLHS .... Lewiston High School, Lewiston, ID [*Library symbol*] [*Library of Congress*] (LCLS)
IdLI .... Independent School District No. 1, Lewiston, ID [*Library symbol*] [*Library of Congress*] (LCLS)
IdLI-C .... Independent School District No. 1, Curriculum Resource Center, Lewiston, ID [*Library symbol*] [*Library of Congress*] (LCLS)
IDLIS .... International Desert Locust Information Service
ID LJ .... Idaho Law Journal [*A publication*] (DLA)
IdLN .... Lewis-Clark State College, Lewiston, ID [*Library symbol Library of Congress*] (LCLS)
IdLNP .... Nez Perce County Free Library District, Lewiston, ID [*Library symbol Library of Congress*] (LCLS)
IdLNP-Cu .... Nez Perce County District Library, Culdesac Branch, Culdesac, ID [*Library symbol*] [*Library of Congress*] (LCLS)
IdLNP-L .... Nez Perce County District Library, Lapwai Branch, Lapwai, ID [*Library symbol*] [*Library of Congress*] (LCLS)
IdLNP-N ...... Nez Perce County District Library, Nez Perce Branch, Nez Perce, ID [*Library symbol*] [*Library of Congress*] (LCLS)
IdLNP-P ...... Nez Perce County District Library, Peck Branch, Peck, ID [*Library symbol*] [*Library of Congress*] (LCLS)
IdLNP-W ..... Nez Perce County District Library, Winchester Branch, Winchester, ID [*Library symbol*] [*Library of Congress*] (LCLS)
IDLOD .... Idle Waiting to Load [*Shipping*]
IDLR .... Instrumentation Development Laboratory Report (MCD)
IDLS .... Integrated Decoy Launching System [*Navy*] (CAAL)
IdLSJH .... Saint Joseph's Hospital, Medical Library, Lewiston, ID [*Library symbol*] [*Library of Congress*] (LCLS)
IDLT .... Identification Light
IDLT .... Increment-Decrement Life Table [*Statistics*]
IDM .... Idiopathic Disease of the Myocardium [*Cardiology*] (MAE)
IDM .... IDM Environmental Corp. [*Associated Press*] (SAG)
IDM .... Ignition Diagnostic Monitor [*Automotive engineering*]
IDM .... Illinois Valley Library System, Pekin, IL [*OCLC symbol*] (OCLC)
IDM .... Immune Defense Mechanism [*Medicine*] (DMAA)
IDM .... Improved Data Modem
IDM .... Improved Data Modem [*Air Force*] (DOMA)
IDM .... Indirect Method
IDM .... Induced Dipole Moment
IDM .... Infant of Diabetic Mother [*Medicine*]
IDM .... Information and Data Management (SSD)
IDM .... Information Document Matching Program [*IRS*]
IDM .... Instant Dimmer Memory (IAA)
IDM .... Integral and Differential Monitoring [*Telecommunications*] (OA)
IDM .... Integrated Delta Modulation (IAA)
IDM .... Integrated Design Methodology [*Electrical engineering*]
IDM .... Integrative Decision Making (MCD)
IDM .... Intelligent Database Machine [*Computer science*]
IDM .... Intelligent Document Management [*Computer science*]
IDM .... Interactive Data Machines [*British*] (NITA)
IDM .... Interdiction Mission [*Air Force*]
IDM .... Intermediate-Dose Methotrexate [*Medicine*] (DMAA)
IDM .... International Direct Mail [*British*]
IDM .... Interpolating Delta Modulator
IDM .... Ion Drift Meter [*Instrumentation*]
IDM .... Issue Definition Memorandum [*Jimmy Carter Administration*]
IDMA .... International Dancing Masters Association (BARN)
IDMA .... International Destination Management Association (EAIO)
IDMA .... International Doll Makers Association (EA)
IdMa .... Oneida County District Library, Malad City, ID [*Library symbol*] [*Library of Congress*] (LCLS)
IdMac .... Mackay District Library, Mackay, ID [*Library symbol*] [*Library of Congress*] (LCLS)
IdMaGS .... Church of Jesus Christ of Latter-Day Saints, Genealogical Society Library, MaladStake Branch, Malad City, ID [*Library symbol Library of Congress*] (LCLS)
IdMar .... Lizard Butte District Library, Marsing, ID [*Library symbol*] [*Library of Congress*] (LCLS)
IDMAS .... Interactive Database Manipulator and Summarizer

IDMB .... International Dictionary of Medicine and Biology [*A publication*]
IDMC .... IDM Environmental [*NASDAQ symbol*] (TTSB)
IDMC .... IDM Environmental Corp. [*NASDAQ symbol*] (SAG)
IDMC .... Immature Dead Male Child [*Neonatology*] (DAVI)
IDMC .... Interdigestive Motility Complex [*Gastroenterology*]
IDMC .... International Dull Men's Club (EA)
IdMC .... Moscow-Latah County Library System, Moscow, ID [*Library symbol*] [*Library of Congress*] (LCLS)
IdMC-D .... Moscow-Latah County District Library, Deary Branch, Deary, ID [*Library symbol*] [*Library of Congress*] (LCLS)
IdMC-G .... Moscow-Latah County District Library, Genesee Branch, Genesee, ID [*Library symbol*] [*Library of Congress*] (LCLS)
IdMC-J .... Moscow-Latah County District Library, Juliaetta Branch, Juliaetta, ID [*Library symbol*] [*Library of Congress*] (LCLS)
IdMcP .... McCall Public Library, McCall, ID [*Library symbol*] [*Library of Congress*] (LCLS)
IdMC-P .... Moscow-Latah County District Library, Potlatch Branch, Potlatch, ID [*Library symbol*] [*Library of Congress*] (LCLS)
IdMC-T .... Moscow-Latah County District Library, Troy Branch, Troy, ID [*Library symbol*] [*Library of Congress*] (LCLS)
IDMCW .... IDM Environmental Wrrt'A' [*NASDAQ symbol*] (TTSB)
IdMe .... Meridian Library District, Meridian, ID [*Library symbol*] [*Library of Congress*] (LCLS)
IdMen .... Jefferson County District Library, Menan Branch, Menan, ID [*Library symbol*] [*Library of Congress*] (LCLS)
IdMen-H ...... Jefferson County District Library, Hamer Branch, Hamer, ID [*Library symbol*] [*Library of Congress*] (LCLS)
IdMen-HV .... Jefferson County District Library, Heart of the Valley Branch, Terreton, ID [*Library symbol*] [*Library of Congress*] (LCLS)
IdMenSD ..... School District No. 251, Menan, ID [*Library symbol*] [*Library of Congress*] (LCLS)
IDM Env ...... IDM Environmental Corp. [*Associated Press*] (SAG)
IdMGH .... Gritman Memorial Hospital, Medical Library, Moscow, ID [*Library symbol*] [*Library of Congress*] (LCLS)
IDMH .... Input Destination Message Handler
IdMh .... Mountain Home Public Library, Mountain Home, ID [*Library symbol*] [*Library of Congress*] (LCLS)
IdMhAF .... United States Air Force, Mountain Home Air Force Base Library, Mountain Home, ID [*Library symbol*] [*Library of Congress*] (LCLS)
IdMhH .... Elmore Memorial Hospital, Medical Library, Mountain Home, ID [*Library symbol*] [*Library of Congress*] (LCLS)
IdMhP .... Prairie District Library, Mountain Home, ID [*Library symbol*] [*Library of Congress*] (LCLS)
IdMHS .... Moscow High School, Moscow, ID [*Library symbol*] [*Library of Congress*] (LCLS)
IDMI .... Interface Document Master Index (DNAB)
IDMI .... International Dun's Market Identifiers [*Dun & Bradstreet International*] [*Information service or system*] (IID)
IdMi .... Middleton Public Library, Middleton, ID [*Library symbol*] [*Library of Congress*] (LCLS)
IdMid .... Midvale District Library, Midvale, ID [*Library symbol*] [*Library of Congress*] (LCLS)
IdMin .... Minidoka-Acequia District Library, Minidoka, ID [*Library symbol*] [*Library of Congress*] (LCLS)
IdMJH .... Moscow Junior High School, Moscow, ID [*Library symbol*] [*Library of Congress*] (LCLS)
IDML .... Internal Data Manipulation Language [*Computer science*] (PDAA)
IDMM .... Intermediate and Depot Maintenance Manual (NASA)
IdMoGS .... Church of Jesus Christ of Latter-Day Saints, Genealogical Society Library, MooreBranch, Lost River Stake Center, Moore, ID [*Library symbol Library of Congress*] (LCLS)
IdMonB .... Bear Lake County District Library, Montpelier, ID [*Library symbol*] [*Library of Congress*] (LCLS)
IdMonB-P .... Bear Lake County District Paris Branch, Paris, ID [*Library symbol*] [*Library of Congress*] (LCLS)
IdMonGS ..... Church of Jesus Christ of Latter-Day Saints, Genealogical Society Library, Bear Lake Branch, Montpelier, ID [*Library symbol Library of Congress*] (LCLS)
IDMP .... Intraductal Mammary Pressure
IDMS .... Image and Document Management System [*Aquidneck Data Corp.*] (NITA)
IDMS .... Improved Deep Moored Sweep [*Military*] (MCD)
IDMS .... Information and Data Management System (SSD)
IDMS .... Information for Decision-Makers System (MCD)
IDMS .... Integrated Database Management System
IDMS .... Integrated Disposal Management System [*DoD*]
IDMS .... International Directory of Marine Scientists [*Marine science*] (OSRA)
IDMS .... Isotope Dilution Mass Spectrometry
IdMu .... Mullan Public Library, Mullan, ID [*Library symbol*] [*Library of Congress*] (LCLS)
I-DMV .... Internet Department of Motor Vehicles
IDN .... Chicago, IL [*Location identifier FAA*] (FAAL)
IDN .... Inanna's Descent to the Netherworld (BJA)
IDN .... Indagen [*Papua New Guinea*] [*Airport symbol*] (OAG)
IDN .... In Dei Nomine [*In God's Name*] [*Latin*]
IDN .... Indonesia [*ANSI three-letter standard code*] (CNC)
IDN .... Inspection Due Notice [*Military*]
IDN .... Integrated Digital Network [*Telecommunications*]
IDN .... Integrated Healthcare Network [*Health care provider*]
IDN .... Intelligent Data Network
IDN .... International Destron Technologies, Inc. [*Vancouver Stock Exchange symbol*]
IDN .... International Directory Network (USDC)

IdN.............. Nampa Public Library, Nampa, ID [*Library symbol*] [*Library of Congress*] (LCLS)

IDN .... United Way of Metropolitan Chicago, Chicago, IL [*OCLC symbol*] (OCLC)

IDNB .... Association of Registered Interior Designers of New Brunswick [*Association des Designers d'Interieur Immatricules du Nouveau-Brunswick*] (AC)

IDNC .... Integrated Direct Numerical Control [*Burroughs Machines Ltd.*] [*Software package*] (NCC)

IDNDR .... International Decade for Natural Disaster Reduction [*1990's*] [*United Nations*]

IDNE .... Indictione [*In the Indiction*] [*Latin*] (ROG)

IDNE .... Inertial Doppler Navigation Equipment (DNAB)

IDNF .... Irredundant Disjunctive Normal Formula

IdNI .... Idaho State School & Hospital, Medical Library, Nampa, ID [*Library symbol*] [*Library of Congress*] (LCLS)

IDNIYRA ...... International DN [*Detroit News*] Ice Yacht Racing Association (EA)

IdNm........... Meadows Valley Community Library, New Meadows, ID [*Library symbol*] [*Library of Congress*] (LCLS)

IdNMH .... Mercy Medical Center, Medical Library, Nampa, ID [*Library symbol*] [*Library of Congress*] (LCLS)

IdNN .... Northwest Nazarene College, Nampa, ID [*Library symbol Library of Congress*] (LCLS)

ID NO.......... Identification Number (DNAB)

IdNo............ Notus Public Library, Notus, ID [*Library symbol*] [*Library of Congress*] (LCLS)

IdNP........... Lewis County Free District Library, Nez Perce, ID [*Library symbol*] [*Library of Congress*] (LCLS)

IdNp-K .... Lewis County District Library, Kamiah Branch, Kamiah, ID [*Library symbol*] [*Library of Congress*] (LCLS)

IdNpm......... Armoral Tutle Public Library, New Plymouth, ID [*Library symbol*] [*Library of Congress*] (LCLS)

IDNS .... Illinois Department of Nuclear Safety (DOGT)

IDNS .... Illinois Department of Nuclear Safety

IDNSS......... International Directory of Non-Official Statistical Sources [*A publication*]

IdNTS.......... National Reactor Testing Station, Technical Library, Phillips Petroleum Co., Idaho Falls, ID [*Library symbol Library of Congress*] (LCLS)

IDNX .... Integrated Digital Network Exchange [*Telecommunications*] (ACRL)

IDO .... Idaho Operations Office [*Energy Research and Development Administration*] (MCD)

IDO .... Identification Officer [*Military*]

IDO .... Industrial Development Organization [*United Nations*]

IDO .... Industrial Diesel Oil (ADA)

IDO .... Infrared Drying Oven

IDO .... Inspekteur der Ordnungspolizei [*Inspector of Uniformed Police*] [*German military - World War II*]

IDO .... Intelligence Duty Officer

IDO .... Interdivisional Operations [*NASA*] (NASA)

IDO .... Interdivisional Order

IDO .... Interface Definition Object [*Computer science*]

IDO .... Interim Development Order (ADA)

IDO .... Internal Distribution Only (SAA)

IDO .... International Disarmament Organization

IDO .... International District Office

IdO .... Osburn Public Library, Osburn, ID [*Library symbol Library of Congress*] (LCLS)

IDO .... Santa Isabel Do Morro [*Brazil*] [*Airport symbol*] (OAG)

IdOa............ Oakley District Library, Oakley, ID [*Library symbol*] [*Library of Congress*] (LCLS)

IDOC .... Inside Diameter of Outer Conductor

IDOC .... International Documentation and Communication Center [*Formerly, Council for Development of Religious Information and Documentation - IDOC International*] [*Rome, Italy*] (SLS)

IDOC .... International Documentation on the Contemporary Church [*Later, International Documentation and Communication Center*] (EA)

IDOCS.......... Intrusion Detection Optical Communications System [*Computer system security*]

ID/OD .... Inside Diameter/Outside Diameter

IDOD .... International Directory of Directories [*A publication*]

IDOE .... International Decade of Ocean Exploration [*1970's*]

IDOFOR........ Improving the Definition of the Objective Force [*Military*]

IDol............. Dolton Public Library District, Dolton, IL [*Library symbol Library of Congress*] (LCLS)

IdOl............. Ola District Library, Ola, ID [*Library symbol*] [*Library of Congress*] (LCLS)

IDON .... Idongus [*Proper*] [*Pharmacy*] (ROG)

IDON VEHIC... Idoneo-Vehiculo [*In a Suitable Vehicle*] [*Pharmacy*]

IdOr .... Clearwater Memorial Public Library, Orofino, ID [*Library symbol*] [*Library of Congress*] (LCLS)

IdOrHS........ Orofino High School Library, Orofino, ID [*Library symbol*] [*Library of Congress*] (LCLS)

IDOS .... Interactive Disk Operating System [*Computer Associates, Inc.*]

IDOS .... Interrupt Disk Operating System

IDOT .... Instrumentation Online Transcriber (IDOE)

IDoV............ United States Veterans Administration Hospital, Downey, IL [*Library symbol Library of Congress*]

IDow .... Downers Grove Public Library, Downers Grove, IL [*Library symbol Library of Congress*] (LCLS)

IDowG.......... George Williams College, Downers Grove, IL [*Library symbol Library of Congress*] (LCLS)

IDP.............. Image Data Processor

IDP.............. Immunodiffusion Procedure [*Immunochemistry*]

IDP.............. Improvement Data Plan (MCD)

IDP.............. Incremental Dividend Preferred [*Share*] [*Investment term*]

IDP.............. Indenture Part List (KSC)

IDP.............. Independence [*Kansas*] [*Airport symbol*] (AD)

IDP.............. Independence, KS [*Location identifier FAA*] (FAAL)

IDP.............. Independence Petroleums [*Vancouver Stock Exchange symbol*]

IDP.............. Independent Democratic Party [*Gibraltar*] [*Political party*]

IDP.............. Independent Democratic Party [*Liberia*] [*Political party*] (EY)

IDP.............. Individual Development Plan (RDA)

IDP.............. Individual Development Program [*Civil Service Commission*]

IDP.............. Industrial Data Processing

IDP.............. Information and Data Base Publishing Report [*A publication*]

IDP.............. Information Data Processing

IDP.............. Initial Delay Position [*Military*] (AABC)

IDP.............. Initial Domain Part [*Telecommunications*] (OSI)

IDP.............. Initial Dose Period [*Medicine*] (MAE)

IDP.............. Inosine Diphosphate [*Biochemistry*]

IDP.............. Input Data Processor (CET)

IDP.............. Instantaneous Diastolic Pressure (MAE)

IDP.............. Institute of Data Processing [*Later, IDPM*]

IDP.............. Instructor Display Panel

IDP.............. Instrumentation Development Plan (MCD)

IDP.............. Integrated Data Presentation (MCD)

IDP.............. Integrated Data Processing

IDP.............. Intelligence Data Processing (MCD)

IDP.............. Interactive Database Processor [*Xerox Corp.*] (MCD)

IDP.............. Interactive Display Panel (MCD)

IDP.............. Intercept Deployment Plan [*National Security Agency*]

IDP.............. Interdigit Pause [*Telecommunications*] (TEL)

IDP.............. Interface Design Plan [*Air Force*]

IDP.............. Intermodulation Distortion Percentage

IDP.............. Internal Data Processing (IAA)

IDP.............. Internal Defense Plans (CINC)

IDP.............. Internal Design Pressure (PDAA)

IDP.............. Internal Development and Production Program

IDP.............. Internal Distribution Publication [*Navy*] (MCD)

IDP.............. Intern-Architect Development Program (DICI)

IDP.............. International Driving Permit

IDP.............. Internet Datagram Protocol [*Computer science*] (ACRL)

IDP.............. Interpersonal Diagnosis of Personality [*Psychology*]

IDP.............. Interplanetary Dust Particle

IDP.............. Investment Dollar Premium (ADA)

IDP.............. Isotope Development Program [*AEC*] (MCD)

IdP.............. Pocatello Public Library, Pocatello, ID [*Library symbol*] [*Library of Congress*] (LCLS)

IDPA .... Inland Daily Press Association

IDPAI .... International Directory of Professional Astronomical Institutions [*A publication*]

IDPAR .... Institute of Donations and Public Affairs Research [*Canada*]

IDPAR.......... Institute of Donations and Public Affairs Research [*Former name of Canadian Centre for Business in the Community*] (NFD)

IdPar........... Parma Public Library, Parma, ID [*Library symbol*] [*Library of Congress*] (LCLS)

IdPay .... Payette Public Library, Payette, ID [*Library symbol*] [*Library of Congress*] (LCLS)

IdPBH .... Bannock Regional Medical Center, Medical Library [*Library symbol*] [*Library of Congress*] (LCLS)

IDPC .... Integrated Data Processing Center

IDPF............ Integrated Digital Photogrammetric Facility [*National Oceanic and Atmospheric Administration*]

IdPf............. Post Falls Public Library, Post Falls, ID [*Library symbol Library of Congress*] (LCLS)

IDPG .... Impact Data Pulse Generator (IAA)

IdPGS .... Church of Jesus Christ of Latter-Day Saints, Genealogical Society Library, Pocatello Branch, Pocatello, ID [*Library symbol Library of Congress*] (LCLS)

IDPH .... IDEC Pharmaceuticals [*NASDAQ symbol*] (TTSB)

IDPH .... IDEC Pharmaceuticals Corp. [*NASDAQ symbol*] (SPSG)

IDPH .... Idiopathic Pulmonary Hemosiderosis [*Medicine*]

IdPH............ Pocatello Regional Medical Center, Medical Library, Pocatello, ID [*Library symbol*] [*Library of Congress*] (LCLS)

IdPI............. Idaho State University, Pocatello, ID [*Library symbol Library of Congress*] (LCLS)

IDPI .... International Data Processing Institute (MCD)

IdPi............. Pierce District Library, Pierce, ID [*Library symbol*] [*Library of Congress*] (LCLS)

IdPiES.......... Pierce Elementary School, Pierce, ID [*Library symbol*] [*Library of Congress*] (LCLS)

IdPin........... Pinehurst-Kingston Library, Pinehurst, ID [*Library symbol*] [*Library of Congress*] (LCLS)

IdPlu........... Plummer Public Library, Plummer, ID [*Library symbol*] [*Library of Congress*] (LCLS)

IDPM .... Industry Direct Purchase Manufacturer (AFIT)

IDPM .... Initial Draft Presidential Memorandum

IDPM .... Institute for Development Policy and Management [*University of Manchester*] [*British*] (ECON)

IDPM .... Institute of Data Processing Management [*DPMA and Institute of Data Proce ssing - IDP*] [*Formed by a merger of*] (EAIO)

IdPM .... Pocatello Regional Medical Center, Pocatello, ID [*Library symbol*] [*Library of Congress*] (LCLS)

IDPN .... Iminodipropionitrile [*Biochemistry*]

IdPr............. Priest River Library, Priest River, ID [*Library symbol*] [*Library of Congress*] (LCLS)

IdPre........... Preston Carnegie Library, Preston, ID [*Library symbol*] [*Library of Congress*] (LCLS)

IdPrP .... Priest Lake Community Library, Priest River, ID [*Library symbol*] [*Library of Congress*] (LCLS)
IDPS .... Improvement Data Plan Sheet (MCD)
IDPS .... Incremental Differential Pressure System (AAG)
IDPS .... Instrument Data Processing System
IDPS .... Integrated Data Processing System
IDPS .... Interactive Direct Processing System [*NCR Corp.*]
IDPS .... Interface Digital Processor (MCD)
IDPS/LF ...... IDPS/Large File (NITA)
IDPSS .... IGOSS [*Integrated Global Ocean Station System*] Data Processing and Services System (MSC)
IDPT .... Image Dissector Photomultiplier Tube
IDPT .... International Donkey Protection Trust (EAIO)
IDPTF .... Indirect Productive Time Factors (MCD)
IDQ .... Individualized Dementia Questionnaire [*Medicine*] (DMAA)
IDQ .... Industrial Development Quotient
IDQ .... International Delta Resources [*Vancouver Stock Exchange symbol*]
IDQ .... Quincy Public Library, Quincy, IL [*OCLC symbol*] (OCLC)
IDQA .... Individual Documented Quality Assurance
IDR .... Greeley & Hansen, Chicago, IL [*OCLC symbol*] (OCLC)
IDR .... Identification Record [*Computer science*] (MCD)
IDR .... Im Deutschen Reich. Zeitschrift des Central-Vereins Deutscher Staatsbuerger Juedischen Glaubens [*Berlin*] [*A publication*] (BJA)
IDR .... Iminodaunorubicin [*Antineoplastic drug*]
IDR .... Implementation Delay Report [*Social Security Administration*]
IDR .... Incremental Digital Recorder
IDR .... Independent Design Review (NRCH)
IDR .... Indian Defense Rules
IDR .... Indicator Co. [*Hungary*] [*FAA designator*] (FAAC)
IDR .... Individual Data Record
IDR .... Indore [*India*] [*Airport symbol*] (OAG)
IDR .... Indore [*India*] [*Airport symbol*] (AD)
IDR .... Industrial Damage Reports [*Formerly, ITR*] [*British World War II*]
IDR .... Industrial Data Reduction (MUGU)
IDR .... Industrial Development Revenue Bond [*Investment term*]
IDR .... Infantry Drill Regulations
IDR .... Infinite-Duration Impulse (IAA)
IDR .... Information Descriptor Record (MHDB)
IDR .... Information Dissemination and Retrieval [*System*] [*Reuters Ltd.*]
IDR .... Initial Design Review
IDR .... Input Data Request
IDR .... Inspection Discrepancy Report (MCD)
IDR .... Installation Data Record
IDR .... Institute for Delphinid Research (EA)
IDR .... Instrumentation Development Request (MCD)
IDR .... Integral Dryway Route [*Nuclear energy*] (NUCP)
IDR .... Integrated Dry Route (PDAA)
IDR .... Intelligent Disaster Recovery [*Computer science*]
IDR .... Intercept During Reentry [*Aerospace*] (IAA)
IDR .... Interface Data Report (NRCH)
IDR .... Interim Depot Repair
IDR .... Interim Design Review (MCD)
IDR .... Interim Development Report
IDR .... Interim Discrepancy Report
IDR .... Intermediate Design Review (NASA)
IDR .... Intermittent-Duty Rating
IDR .... Internal Development Report
IDR .... International Damascus Resources [*Vancouver Stock Exchange symbol*]
IDR .... International Defense Review [*Interavia Publications*] [*Information service or system A publication*] (CRD)
IDR .... International Depositary Receipt [*Investment term*]
IDR .... International Drawing Rights
IDR .... Internet Domain Registrars
IDR .... Intradermal Reaction [*Medicine*] (MAE)
IDR .... Invoice Discrepancy Report [*Business term*]
IdR .... Madison County Library District, Rexburg, ID [*Library symbol*] [*Library of Congress*] (LCLS)
IDR .... Winder, GA [*Location identifier FAA*] (FAAL)
IDRA .... Insanity Defense Reform Act of 1984
IDRA .... Intercultural Development Research Association (EA)
IDRA .... International Desert Racing Association [*Automobile racing*]
IDRA .... International Disaster Recovery Association (EA)
IDRA .... Irish Dinghy Racing Association (BI)
IDR & DS .... International Directory of Research and Development Scientists [*A publication*]
IDRB .... Industrial-Development Revenue Bond [*Issued by a state or local government to finance construction by a private company, which then becomes responsible for repaying the debt*] [*Investment term*]
IDRC .... Industrial Development Research Council (EA)
IDRC .... International Development Research Centre [*ICSU*] [*Research center Canada*]
IDRD .... Information Definition Requirements Document (NASA)
IDRD .... Internal Data Requirement Description (MCD)
IDREA .... Idle Other Reasons [*Vessel status*] [*Navy*]
IDRF .... International Development and Refugee Foundation
IdRg .... Salmon River Public Library, Riggins, ID [*Library symbol*] [*Library of Congress*] (LCLS)
IDRH .... Madison Memorial Hospital, Medical Library, Rexburg, ID [*Library symbol*] [*Library of Congress*] (LCLS)
IdRi .... Richfield District Library, Richfield, ID [*Library symbol*] [*Library of Congress*] (LCLS)
IdRig .... Rigby Public Library, Rigby, ID [*Library symbol*] [*Library of Congress*] (LCLS)

IdRir .... Ririe Public Library, Ririe, ID [*Library symbol*] [*Library of Congress*] (LCLS)
IDRL .... Intercompany Data Requirements List (MCD)
IdRMH .... Madison Memorial Hospital, Rexburg, ID [*Library symbol*] [*Library of Congress*] (LCLS)
IdRo .... Roberts Public Library, Roberts, ID [*Library symbol*] [*Library of Congress*] (LCLS)
IdRoc .... Rockland School/Community Library, Rockland, ID [*Library symbol*] [*Library of Congress*] (LCLS)
IDRP .... Intellectual Disability Review Panel
IDRP .... Interdomain Routing Protocol [*Computer science*] (TNIG)
IdRR .... Ricks College, Rexburg, ID [*Library symbol Library of Congress*] (LCLS)
IDRS .... Integrated Data Retrieval System [*Department of the Treasury*]
IDRS .... Intellectual Disability Rights Service
IDRS .... International Double Reed Society (EA)
IDRTY .... Indirectly
IdRu .... DeMary Memorial Public Library, Rupert, ID [*Library symbol*] [*Library of Congress*] (LCLS)
IdRuH .... Minidoka Memorial Hospital, Medical Library, Rupert, ID [*Library symbol*] [*Library of Congress*] (LCLS)
IDRV .... Ionic Drive
IDS .... Identification Section
IDS .... Identification Supervisor [*Military*]
IDS .... IDS Aircraft Lt. [*British*] [*FAA designator*] (FAAC)
IDS .... Iduronate Sulfatase [*An enzyme*]
IDS .... Image Display System
IDS .... Image Dissector Scanner [*Instrumentation*]
IDS .... Immune Deficiency State
IDS .... Improvement Data System (MCD)
IDS .... Impulse Duplexer Study
IDS .... Inadvertent Destruct [*Aerospace*] (AAG)
IDS .... Inclined Drive Shaft (DA)
IDS .... Income Data Service [*Research firm*] [*British*]
IDS .... Income Distribution Survey
IDS .... Incremented Dynamic Scanning (DAVI)
IDS .... India Development Service (EA)
IDS .... Indicator Drive Screw
IDS .... Industries Development Strategy
IDS .... Industry Data Sources [*Information Access Co.*] [*Information service or system*] (CRD)
IDS .... Inertial Data System
IDS .... Inertial Doppler System
IDS .... Infectious Disease Service (DAVI)
IDS .... Information Data Search, Inc. [*Information service or system*] (IID)
IDS .... Information Delivery Service [*Telecommunications*]
IDS .... Information Display System
IDS .... Information Dissemination System (OICC)
IDS .... Infrared Detection Set
IDS .... Infrared Discrimination System
IDS .... Inhibitor of DNA Synthesis [*Immunochemistry*]
IDS .... Input Data Strobe
IDS .... Institute for Democratic Socialism (EA)
IDS .... Institute of Development Studies [*University of Sussex*] [*British*]
IDS .... Institut fuer Deutsche Sprache [*Institute for German Language*] [*Information service or system*] (IID)
IDS .... Instruction Set Process (ECII)
IDS .... Instrument Data System
IDS .... Instrument Development Section
IDS .... Instrument Development Set
IDS .... Integral Direct Station Selection (PDAA)
IDS .... Integrated Data Storage (NITA)
IDS .... Integrated Data Store [*or System*] [*Honeywell, Inc.*] [*Computer science*]
IDS .... Integrated Defensive System
IDS .... Integrated Display Set
IDS .... Integrated Display Situation
IDS .... Intellectual Disability Services [*Australian Capital Territory, Queensland*]
IDS .... Intelligence Data System
IDS .... Intelligent Disk Subsystem [*Northgate Computer Systems*] [*Computer science*] (PCM)
IDS .... Intelligent Display System [*Computer science*]
IDS .... Interactive Data System [*Computer science*]
IDS .... Interactive Design Software (NITA)
IDS .... Interactive Display System
IDS .... Interagency Dialing System [*Telephones*]
IDS .... Interdepartmental Dial Service [*or System*] [*Telephones*]
IDS .... Interdictor Strike
IDS .... Inter-Disciplinary Studies [*Education*] (AIE)
IDS .... Interface Data Sheet (NASA)
IDS .... Interface Design Specification (CAAL)
IDS .... Interim Decay Storage [*Nuclear energy*] (NRCH)
IDS .... Interior Design Society (EA)
IDS .... Interlibrary Delivery Service of Pennsylvania [*Library network*]
IDS .... Intermediate Decay Storage [*Nuclear energy*] (NRCH)
IDS .... Intermediate Direct Support [*DoD*]
IDS .... Intermediate Drum Storage (CET)
IDS .... Internal Distribution System [*Television*]
IDS .... International Data Services Corp. [*Vancouver Stock Exchange symbol*]
IDS .... International Development Services
IDS .... International Development Strategy [*United Nations*]
IDS .... International Doctor's Society (EA)
IDS .... International Documents Service [*Defunct*] (EA)

IDS	International Dostoevsky Society (EA)
IDS	International Dove Society [Defunct] (EA)
IDS	Intrusion Detection System (MCD)
IDS	Investigative Dermatological Society (DAVI)
IDS	Investors Diversified Services, Inc. [Mutual funds]
IDS	Ion Dip Spectroscopy
IDS	Ion Drift Semiconductor
IDS	Isotope Detection System [Nuclear energy] (NRCH)
IDS	Item Description Sheet (NASA)
Id-S	Office of the Secretary of State, Boise, ID [Library symbol Library of Congress] (LCLS)
IdS	Shelley Public Library, Shelley, ID [Library symbol] [Library of Congress] (LCLS)
IDS	Spoon River College, Canton, IL [OCLC symbol] (OCLC)
IDSA	Industrial Designers' Society of America (EA)
IDSA	Industrial Services of America, Inc. [NASDAQ symbol] (SAG)
IDSA	Infectious Diseases Society of America (EA)
IDSA	International Dark-Sky Association (EA)
IDSA	International Diving Schools Association (EA)
IdSa	St. Anthony Public Library, St. Anthony, ID [Library symbol] [Library of Congress] (LCLS)
IdSaF	Fremont County District Library, St. Anthony, ID [Library symbol] [Library of Congress] (LCLS)
IdSal	Salmon Public Library, Salmon, ID [Library symbol] [Library of Congress] (LCLS)
IdSalH	Steel Memorial Hospital, Salmon, ID [Library symbol] [Library of Congress] (LCLS)
IdSan	East Bonner County Free Public Library District, Sandpoint, ID [Library symbol] [Library of Congress] (LCLS)
IdSan-C	East Bonner County District Library, Clark Fork Branch, Clark Fork, ID [Library symbol] [Library of Congress] (LCLS)
IdSanH	Bonner General Hospital, Medical Library, Sandpoint, ID [Library symbol] [Library of Congress] (LCLS)
IDSB	Independent Double Sideband
IDSC	International Die Sinkers' Conference (EA)
IdSc	Sugar Salem School/Community Library, Sugar City, ID [Library symbol] [Library of Congress] (LCLS)
IDSCM	Initial Defense Satellite Communication (KSC)
IDSCP	Initial Defense Satellite Communications Project [Telecommunications] (TEL)
IDSCS	Initial Defense Satellite Communication System (KSC)
IDSD	Institutional Data System Division [Johnson Space Center] [NASA] (NASA)
IDSEG	International Development Studies Group
IDSF	Intelligence Defector Source File [Military] (MCD)
IDSF	Inter-Agency Data Systems Facility [General Services Administration] (MCD)
IDSF	Interim Data Switching Facility (ADA)
IdSh	Shoshone Public Library, Shoshone, ID [Library symbol] [Library of Congress] (LCLS)
IDSI	Interactive Data Services, Inc. [Database producer] [Information service or system]
IDSIA	Immune Deficiency Syndrome "Innocently" Acquired (ADA)
IDS/IGS	Intermediate Direct Support/Intermediate General Support [Army]
IDSL	Intrusion Detection and Sensor Laboratory [Army] (RDA)
IDSM	Indian Distinguished Service Medal [British]
IDSM	Inertial Dampened Servomotor
IDSM	Integrated Direct Support Maintenance (MCD)
IDSm	Intermediate Direct Support Maintenance (MCD)
IdSm	St. Maries Public Library, St. Maries, ID [Library symbol] [Library of Congress] (LCLS)
IdSmB	Benewah County Library District, St. Maries, ID [Library symbol] [Library of Congress] (LCLS)
IDSO	Interdivisional Sales Order [NASA] (NASA)
IDSO	International Diamond Security Organization (BARN)
IDSOT	Interim Daily System Operational Test [Navy] (NG)
IDSRS	Ionization-Detected Stimulated Raman Spectroscopy
IDSS	ICAM [Integrated Computer-Aided Manufacturing] Decision Support System (IEEE)
IDSS	Image Data System Simulation [NASA]
IDSS	Information Decision Support System (MCD)
IDSS	International Development Support Services Pty. Ltd. [Australia] (ECON)
IdSs	Soda Springs Public Library, Soda Springs, ID [Library symbol] [Library of Congress] (LCLS)
IDST	Information and Documentation on Science and Technology (NITA)
IdSt	Stanley City Library, Stanley, ID [Library symbol] [Library of Congress] (LCLS)
IDSTO	Idle Used for Storage [Shipping]
IdSulGS	Church of Jesus Christ of Latter-Day Saints, Genealogical Society Library, Salmon Branch, Salmon River Stake Center, Salmon, ID [Library symbol Library of Congress] (LCLS)
IdSvH	Moritz Community Hospital, Medical Library, Sun Valley, ID [Library symbol] [Library of Congress] (LCLS)
IDT	I-Load Data Tape (NASA)
IDT	Image Dissector Tube
IDT	Immune Diffusion Test [Medicine] (DMAA)
IDT	Implantation Doping Technique
IDT	Improved Definition Television (NTCM)
IDT	Inactive Duty Training [Military] (AABC)
IDT	Industrial Data Terminal
IDT	Industrial Data Terminals Corporation (NITA)
IDT	Industrial Disputers Tribunal [British]
IDT	Inspection Discrepancy Tag (KSC)
IDT	Instillation Delivery Time [Medicine] (DMAA)

IDT	Instrument Definition Team
IDT	Integrated Device Technology, Inc. (PS)
IDT	Integrated Dynamic Tester
IDT	Intelligent Data Terminal
IDT	Interactive Display Terminal (MCD)
IDT	Interdigital Transducer [Physics]
IDT	Interdisciplinary Team [Education]
IDT	Interdivision Time [Cytology]
IDT	Interdivision Transfer (AAG)
IDT	International Diagnostic Technology [Medicine]
IDT	International Discount Telecommunications (ECON)
IDT	Interrupt-Descriptor Table [Computer science]
IDT	Intradermal Typhoid [Medicine] (DMAA)
IDT	Ion Doping Technique
IDT	Isodensitracer
IDT	Peoria Heights Public Library, Peoria Heights, IL [OCLC symbol] (OCLC)
IDTA	Institute of Drug Technology Australia
IDTA	Interdivisional Technical Agreement [NASA] (NASA)
IDTA	International Differential Treatment Association
IDTC	IDT Corp. [NASDAQ symbol] (TTSB)
IDTC	IDT Corp. [NASDAQ symbol] (SAG)
IDTC	Indefinite Delivery Type Contract [DoD]
IDTCorp	IDT Corp. [Associated Press] (SAG)
IDTE	ID Table Entry [Galaxy] [Computer science]
ID TER	Idaho Territory
IdTerSD	West Jefferson School District No. 253, Terreton, ID [Library symbol] [Library of Congress] (LCLS)
IDTF	International Documents Task Force [Government Documents Round Table] [American Library Association]
IdTf	Twin Falls Public Library, Twin Falls, ID [Library symbol Library of Congress] (LCLS)
IdTfGS	Church of Jesus Christ of Latter-Day Saints, Genealogical Society Library, Twin Falls Branch, Twin Falls, ID [Library symbol Library of Congress] (LCLS)
IdTfH	Magic Valley Regional Medical Center, Medical Library, Twin Falls, ID [Library symbol] [Library of Congress] (LCLS)
IdTfSI	College of Southern Idaho, Twin Falls, ID [Library symbol] [Library of Congress] (LCLS)
IDTI	Integrated Device Tech [NASDAQ symbol] (TTSB)
IDTI	Integrated Device Technology [NASDAQ symbol] (SAG)
IDTI	Integrated Device Technology, Inc. (NQ)
IDTIMS	Isotope Dilution Thermal Ionization Mass Spectrometry
IDTM	Integrated Development Test Matrix [Army]
IDTOC	Independent Division Tactical Operations Center [Army] (AABC)
IDTP	Integrated Data Transmittal Package
IDTR	Interdivisional Transfer Register
IDTS	Improved Doppler Tracking System
IDTS	Instrumentation Data Test Station
IDTS	Instrumentation Data Transmission System
IDTS	Integrated Development Test Schedule
IDTS	Iron Dressers Trade Society [A union] [British]
IDTSC	Instrumentation Data Transmission System Controller
IDTU	Intoxicated Driver Testing Unit [Criminology] (LAIN)
IDTV	Improved Definition Television
IDTW	International Union of Doll and Toy Workers of the US and Canada [Later, IUANPW] (EA)
IDTY	Intermittent Duty (MSA)
IDU	De Pauw University, Greencastle, IN [OCLC symbol] (OCLC)
idu	Idaho [MARC country of publication code Library of Congress] (LCCP)
IDU	Idle Signal Unit [Electronics] (EECA)
IDU	Idoxuridine [or Iododeoxyuridine] [Also, IDUR, IdUrd, IUDR] [Pharmacology]
IDU	Immunological Distance Unit [Genetics]
IDU	Indicator Drive Unit (IAA)
IDU	Industrial Development Unit (IEEE)
IDU	Industry, TX [Location identifier FAA] (FAAL)
IDU	Infrared Detection Unit
IDU	Injecting Drug User
IDU	Interface Demonstration Unit (NASA)
IDU	Intermittent Drive Unit
IDU	International Democrat Union (EA)
IDU	International Dendrology Union
IDU	Iododeoxyuridine (DMAA)
IdU	University of Idaho, Moscow, ID [Library symbol Library of Congress] (LCLS)
IdUA	Iduronic Acid
IDUD	Independent Deployable Unit Detachment (MCD)
IDUF	Interactive Display and Update Facility (SSD)
IdU-L	University of Idaho, Law Library, Moscow, ID [Library symbol Library of Congress] (LCLS)
IDun	Dunlap Public Library District, Dunlap, IL [Library symbol Library of Congress] (LCLS)
IDup	A. C. Dougherty Memorial Township Library, Dupo, IL [Library symbol Library of Congress] (LCLS)
IDupHS	Dupo Junior-Senior High School, Dupo, IL [Library symbol Library of Congress] (LCLS)
IDUR	Idoxuridine [or Iododeoxyuridine] [Also, IDU, IdUrd, IUDR]
IDUR	Intercept During Unpowered Rise [Aerospace] (IAA)
IdUrd	Iododeoxyuridine [Also, IDU, IDUR, IUDR] [Pharmacology]
IDV	Dunlap Public Library District, Dunlap, IL [OCLC symbol] (OCLC)
idv	Individuals
IDV	Initial Development Ltd. [Vancouver Stock Exchange symbol]
IDV	Integrating Digital Voltmeter

IDV............. Intermittent Demand Ventilation [*Medicine*]
IDV............. International Distillers & Vintners [*British*]
IDV............. Internationaler Deutschlehrerverband [*International Association of Teachers of German - IATG*] [*Copenhagen, Denmark*] (EAIO)
IdV............. Valley of Tetons District Library, Victor, ID [*Library symbol*] [*Library of Congress*] (LCLS)
IDVC .... Indwelling Venous Catheter [*Medicine*]
IDVID .... Immersed Deflection Vidicon Device (IAA)
IDVM .... Integrating Digital Voltmeter
IDVP .... Independent Design Verification Program (NRCH)
IDW .... Input Data Word
IDW .... Institut fuer Dokumentationswesen [*Germany*]
IdW............. Wallace Public Library, Wallace, ID [*Library symbol*] [*Library of Congress*] (LCLS)
IDW .... Washington Township Library, Washington, IL [*OCLC symbol*] (OCLC)
IDWA .... Interdivisional Work Authorization
IDWD .... Input Data Word (MCD)
IdWe........... Weippe Public Library, Weippe, ID [*Library symbol*] [*Library of Congress*] (LCLS)
IdWeES....... Weippe Elementary School, Weippe, ID [*Library symbol*] [*Library of Congress*] (LCLS)
IdWei.......... Weiser Public Library, Weiser, ID [*Library symbol*] [*Library of Congress*] (LCLS)
IdWen......... Wendell Public Library, Wendell, ID [*Library symbol*] [*Library of Congress*] (LCLS)
IdWenSD ..... Wendell School District, Wendell, ID [*Library symbol*] [*Library of Congress*] (LCLS)
IDWF .... Individual Drinking Water Flavors [*Developed by Natick Research and Development Center to encourage soldiers to drink more fluids to prevent dehydration*] (INF)
IDWI .... Imperial Direct West India Mail Service Co. (ROG)
IdWi............ Wilder District Library, Wilder, ID [*Library symbol*] [*Library of Congress*] (LCLS)
IDWO .... Inter-Division Work Order
IDWR .... Interim Design and Workmanship Rules (PDAA)
IDX............. Caterpillar Tractor Co., Peoria, IL [*OCLC symbol*] (OCLC)
IDX............. Identix, Inc. [*AMEX symbol*] (SPSG)
IDX............. Index (MSA)
IDX............. Individual Index File [*Computer science*] (PCM)
IDX............. Intelligent Digital Exchange (NITA)
IDXC .... IDX Systems Corp. [*NASDAQ symbol*] (SAG)
IDXC .... IDX Systmes [*NASDAQ symbol*] (TTSB)
IDXSys........ IDX Systems Corp. [*Associated Press*] (SAG)
IDXX .... IDEXX Laboratories [*NASDAQ symbol*] (SPSG)
IDY............. Fondulac Public Library District, East Peoria, IL [*OCLC symbol*] (OCLC)
IDYN .... Innerdyne, Inc. [*NASDAQ symbol*] (SAG)
IDZ............. Bank Marketing Association, Chicago, IL [*OCLC symbol*] (OCLC)
IDZ............. Inner Defense Zone
IE .... Evanston Public Library, Evanston, IL [*Library symbol Library of Congress*] (LCLS)
IE .... Idees pour l'Europe [*Paris, France*] (EAIO)
IE .... Id Est [*That Is*] [*Latin*]
IE .... Imbedded Error [*Factor analysis*]
IE .... Immediate-Early [*Genetics*]
IE .... Immobilized Enzyme [*Physiology*]
IE .... Immunitaetseinheit [*Immunizing Unit*] [*Medicine*]
IE .... Immunoelectrophoresis [*Analytical biochemistry*]
IE .... Import Executive [*British*]
IE .... Independent Estimate [*Army*]
IE .... Independent Evaluation (MCD)
IE .... Independent Expenditure [*Campaign-finance law provision*]
IE .... Index Error [*Navigation*]
IE .... Index of Enrichment
IE .... Indicator Equipment (IAA)
IE .... Indo-European
IE .... Industrial Electronics (MCD)
IE .... Industrial Engineer [*or Engineering*]
IE .... In Excess
IE .... Infection Efficiency [*Pathology*]
IE .... Infective Endocarditis [*Cardiology*]
IE .... Information and Education (AAGC)
IE .... Information Element (ACRL)
IE .... Information Engineering (CDE)
IE .... Information Enterprises [*Chesterfield, MO*] [*Telecommunications service*] (TSSD)
IE .... Information Environment
IE .... Infrared Emission
I/E .... Ingress/Egress
IE .... Initial Equipment [*Navy aircraft*]
IE .... Initial Establishment [*British military*] (DMA)
IE .... Initiating Event (NRCH)
IE .... Insert Exon [*Genetics*]
IE .... Insert Extract (IAA)
IE .... Inside Edge
IE .... Inspection and Enforcement (NRCH)
IE .... Inspection Equipment
IE .... Inspection Error (KSC)
I/E .... Inspiratory-Expiratory (Ratio) [*Physiology*]
IE .... Installation Equipment [*Army*] (AABC)
IE .... Institute of Energy [*An association*] (EAIO)
IE .... Institute of Engineers and Technicians [*British*]
IE .... Institute of Expertology (EA)
IE .... Institute of Export [*British*]

IE .... Instruction Execution (IAA)
IE .... Instrument Engineering
IE .... Intake (of a Unit of Food) Energy [*Nutrition*]
IE .... Interconnection Equipment
IE .... Intermediate Early [*Genetics*]
IE .... Intermediate Erection
IE .... Internal Elastica [*Artery anatomy*]
IE .... Internal Environment
IE .... International Exhibition (IMH)
IE .... Internet Explorer [*Microsoft Corp.*]
IE .... Interrogation Entry Register (IAA)
IE .... Interrupt Enable [*Computer science*]
I/E .... Introversion/Extroversion [*Psychology*] (AEE)
IE .... Ion Exchange (WDAA)
IE .... Ionization Energy [*Chemistry*]
IE .... Ionospheric Explorer [*NASA/National Bureau of Standards*]
ie .... Ireland [*MARC country of publication code Library of Congress*] (LCCP)
IE .... Ireland [*ANSI two-letter standard code*] (CNC)
IE .... Irish Earl (ROG)
IE .... Irradiation Effects (NRCH)
IE .... Isoetharine [*Medicine*]
IE .... Solomon Islands Airways [*ICAO designator*] (AD)
ie .... That Is [*Id est*] [*Latin*] (WDMC)
IEA .... American Hospital Supply Corp., Evanston, IL [*Library symbol Library of Congress*] (LCLS)
IEa .... East Alton Public Library, East Alton, IL [*Library symbol Library of Congress*] (LCLS)
IEA .... East Texas State University, Commerce, TX [*OCLC symbol*] (OCLC)
IEA .... Idaho Education Association (SRA)
IEA .... Illinois Education Association (SRA)
IEA .... Immuno-Electroadsorption [*Medicine*] (DMAA)
IEA .... Immunoenzyme Assay [*Biochemistry*] (DAVI)
IEA .... Import Entitlement Agreement [*United Arab Republic*]
IEA .... Index of Economic Activity (ADA)
IEA .... Indian-Eskimo Association of Canada [*Later, CASNP*] (EA)
IEA .... Indian Evidence Act (ROG)
IEA .... Indoleethanol [*Organic chemistry*]
IEA .... Industrial Editors Association
IEA .... Industrial Engineering Activity [*Army*] (AAGC)
IEA .... Infectious Equine Anemia [*Veterinary medicine*] (DMAA)
IEA .... Institute for Economic Analysis (EA)
IEA .... Institute for Educational Affairs (EA)
IEA .... Institute for Environmental Awareness (EA)
IEA .... Institute for Expressive Analysis (EA)
IEA .... Institute of Applied Economics [*University of Montreal*] [*Canada*] (IRC)
IEA .... Institute of Economic Affairs [*British*]
IEA .... Institute of Environmental Action (EA)
IEA .... Instruments, Electronics, and Automation [*Exhibit*]
IEA .... Integral Error Squared (PDAA)
IEA .... Integrated Electronic Assembly [*NASA*]
IEA .... Intereuropean Airways Ltd. [*British ICAO designator*] (FAAC)
IEA .... Interface Electronics Assembly
IEA .... Interment Exchange of America
IEA .... Intermountain Electrical Association (SRA)
IEA .... International Association for the Evaluation of Educational Achievement [*See also AIERS*] [*University of Stockholm*] [*Sweden*] (EAIO)
IEA .... International Economic Association [*See also AISE*] [*Paris, France*] (EAIO)
IEA .... International Education Act
IEA .... International Education Assembly [*World War II*]
IEA .... International Education Association
IEA .... International Emergency Action [*See also AUI*] [*Paris, France*] (EAIO)
IEA .... International Energy Agency [*OECD*] [*Research center France*] (IRC)
IEA .... International Entrepreneurs Association [*Later, AEA*] (EA)
IEA .... International Epidemiological Association (EA)
IEA .... International Ergonomics Association (EA)
IEA .... International Exchange Association (EA)
IEA .... International Executives Association (EA)
IEA .... International Exhibitors Association (EA)
IEA .... Intravascular Erythrocyte Aggregation [*Hematology*]
IEA .... Irish Exporters Association (EAIO)
IEAB .... Internacia Esperanto-Asocio de Bibliotekistoj [*International Association of Esperanto-Speaking Librarians*] [*Later, IAEL*] (EA)
IEAC .... IEEE [*Institute of Electrical and Electronics Engineers*] Automatic Control (IAA)
IEACS.......... Institut European des Armes de Chasse et de Sport [*European Institute of Hunting and Sporting Weapons - EIHSW*] (EAIO)
IEAF .... Imperial Ethiopian Air Force
IEAH .... American Hospital Supply Corp., Evanston, IL [*Library symbol*] [*Library of Congress*] (LCLS)
IEAHC .... Institute of Early American History and Culture (EA)
IEAJ .... Internacia Esperanto - Asocio de Juristoj [*International Esperanto - Association of Jurists*] [*Graz, Austria*] (EAIO)
IE & ID .... Interiors Engineering and Industrial Design (MCD)
IEAP........... Institut Europeen d'Administration Publique [*European Institute of Public Administration - EIPA*] (EAIO)
IEar .... Earl Township Public Library, Earlville, IL [*Library symbol Library of Congress*] (LCLS)
IEAR .... Internacia Esperanto-Amikaro de Rotarianoj [*International Esperanto Fellowship of Rotarians*] [*British*] (EAIO)

IEarFSD .... Freedom Community Unit, School District 245, Earlville, IL [*Library symbol Library of Congress*] (LCLS)

IEARN .... International Education and Resource Network [*Information service or system*] (IID)

IEarSD .... Earlville Community Unit, School District 9, Earlville, IL [*Library symbol Library of Congress*] (LCLS)

IEAS .... Institute of East Asian Studies [*University of California, Berkeley*] [*Research center*] (RCD)

IEAS .... International Economic Appraisal Service [*The Economist Publications Ltd.*] [*British Information service or system*]

IEATP .... Information Engineering Advanced Technology Programme [*British*]

IEB .... Elkhart Public Library, Elkhart, IN [*OCLC symbol*] (OCLC)

IEB .... Industrial Evaluation Board [*BDSA*]

IEB .... Infanterie-Ersatzbataillon [*Infantry Replacement Training Battalion*] [*German military - World War II*]

IEB .... Institute of Economic Botany [*New York Botanical Garden*]

IEB .... Interdiction Executive Board (MCD)

IEB .... International Energy Bank Ltd. [*British*]

IEB .... International Environmental Bureau for the Non-Ferrous Metals Industry

IEB .... International Executive Board [*UAW*]

IEB .... International Exhibitions Bureau

IEB .... Irish Evangelistic Band

IEB .... Irish Export Board

IEB .... Office of Inspection and Enforcement. Bulletin [*A publication*] (NRCH)

IEBL .... Inter-Entity Boundary Line [*Military*] (INF)

IEBM .... Institute of Epidemiology and Behavioral Medicine [*Medical Research Institute of San Francisco*] [*Research center*] (RCD)

IEBR .... Institute for Economic and Business Research [*University of Kansas*] [*Research center*] (RCD)

IEC .... Earlham College, Richmond, IN [*OCLC symbol*] (OCLC)

IEC .... Experimental Cardiology [*Russian*]

IEC .... Illinois Environmental Council (SRA)

IEC .... Imaginative Educational Cooperation Project (EDAC)

IEC .... Independent Electrical Contractors (EA)

IEC .... Industrial Electrification Council [*Later, TEC*] (EA)

IEC .... Industrial Energy Conservation (ODBW)

IEC .... Inflatable Exit Cone (MCD)

IEC .... Information Exchange Center

IEC .... Infused Emitter Coupling

IEC .... Inherent Explosion Clause [*Insurance*]

IEC .... Injection Electrode Catheter

IEC .... Inpatient Exercise Center [*Rehabilitation*] (DAVI)

IEC .... Institut d'Etudes Congolaises [*Congolese Institute of Studies*]

IEC .... Institute of Early Childhood [*Macquarie University*] [*Australia*]

IEC .... Institute of Educational Cinematography [*British*]

IEC .... Institute of Employment Consultants Ltd. [*British*]

IEC .... Institute of Engineers of Chile

IEC .... Institut Europeen de la Communication [*European Institute for the Media - EIM*] (EAIO)

IEC .... Integrated Electronic Components (BUR)

IEC .... Integrated Electronic Control

IEC .... Integrated Engine Control

IEC .... Integrated Environmental Control (AAG)

IEC .... Integrated Equipment Component

IEC .... Intelligence Evaluation Committee [*Department of Justice*]

IEC .... Interexchange Carrier [*Telecommunications*]

IEC .... Interface Efficiency Council [*Computer science*]

IEC .... Intermittent Electrical Contact (IAA)

IEC .... International Edsel Club (EA)

IEC .... International Educational and Cultural Exchange

IEC .... International Egg Commission [*British*] (EAIO)

IEC .... International Electronics Corp. (MUGU)

IEC .... International Electrotechnical Commission [*See also CEI*] [*Standards body Geneva, Switzerland*] (EAIO)

IEC .... International Electrotechnical Commission [*Geneva*]

IEC .... Interstate Electronics Corp. (MCD)

IEC .... Intraepithelial Carcinoma [*Medicine*]

IEC .... Intrinsic Electron Conduction (IAA)

IEC .... Inverse Electrode Current

IEC .... Ion Exchange Chromatography

IEC .... Iowa Egg Council (SRA)

IEC .... Iris Epithelium Cell [*Cytology*]

IEC .... Iso-Echo Contour

IEC .... Israel Economic Conference

IEC .... Item Entry Control (AFM)

IEC .... Office of Inspection and Enforcement. Circular [*A publication*] (NRCH)

IEC .... PEC Israel Economic [*NYSE symbol*] (TTSB)

IEC .... PEC Israel Economic Corp. Ltd. [*NYSE symbol*] (SAG)

IECA .... Independent Educational Consultants Association (EA)

IECA .... Independent Election Corp. of America (WDMC)

IECA .... Industry, Education Councils of America (OICC)

IECA .... International Erosion Control Association (EA)

IECC .... International Economic Conversion Campaign [*Defunct*] (EA)

IECD .... Ignition Energetics Characterization Device (MCD)

IECE .... IEC Electronics [*NASDAQ symbol*] (TTSB)

IECE .... IEC Electronics Corp. [*NASDAQ symbol*] (NQ)

IECE .... Institute on East Central Europe [*Columbia University*] [*Research center*] (RCD)

IECEC .... Intersociety Energy Conversion Engineering Conference

IECEE .... International Electrotechnical Commission System for Conformity Testing to Standards for Safety of Electrical Equipment [*Switzerland*] (EA)

IECEJ .... Institute of Electronic Communications Engineers of Japan

IECEJ .... Interreligious Emergency Campaign for Economic Justice (EA)

IEC Elc .... IEC Electronics Corp. [*Associated Press*] (SAG)

IECG .... Independent Energy Consultants Group [*British*]

IECG .... Interagency Emergency Coordinating Group [*Federal disaster planning*]

IECI .... Industrial Electronics and Control Instrumentation (MCD)

IECI .... Institute for Esperanto in Commerce and Industry (EA)

IECIC .... International Engineering and Construction Industries Council (PDAA)

IECL .... Instrumentation Equipment Configuration Log (SAA)

IECL .... International Esperanto Chess League [*See also ESLI*] (EAIO)

IECM .... Induced Environmental Contamination Monitor (MCD)

IECM .... Internal Electronic Countermeasure

IECMS .... Inflight Engine Condition Monitoring System [*Military*] (CAAL)

IECO .... Inboard Engine Cutoff

IECOK .... International Economic Consultative Organization for Korea [*Ten-nation consortium*]

IECP .... Injected Electric Current Perturbation

IECP .... Interface Engineering Change Procedure

IECPS .... International Electronic Packaging Symposium (MCD)

IECQU .... International Electrotechnical Commission Quality Assessment (PDAA)

IECS .... Igloo Environment Control Subsystem (MCD)

IECS .... Intelligence Evaluation Center [*Saigon*] [*Obsolete*] (CINC)

IECT .... IEEE [*Institute of Electrical and Electronics Engineers*] Circuit Theory (IAA)

IECT .... Impulsive Ergodic Collision Theory [*Mathematics*]

IEd .... Edwardsville Free Public Library, Edwardsville, IL [*Library symbol Library of Congress*] (LCLS)

IED .... Impact Energy Density

IED .... Improved Explosive Device

IED .... Improvised Explosive Device

IED .... Improvised Explosive Device Disposal (PDAA)

IED .... Incident Energy Density

IED .... Income Eligibility Determination [*Food and Nutrition Service*] [*Department of Agriculture*] (GFGA)

IED .... Income Equalization Deposit (ADA)

IED .... Independent Exploratory Development [*Navy*] (NG)

IED .... Individual Effective Dose (IEEE)

IED .... Inherited Epidermal Dysplasia [*Medicine*] (DMAA)

IED .... Initial Effective Data (IAA)

IED .... Initial Engine Development [*Air Force*]

IED .... Initiative Electronic Deception (ADDR)

IED .... Insertion/Extraction Device [*Aviation*]

IED .... Inspection Equipment Drawing

IED .... Institute for Educational Development [*Defunct*]

IED .... Institution of Engineering Designers [*British*] (BI)

IED .... Instrumental Engineering Division [*National Weather Service*]

IED .... Integrated Electric Drive [*Navy*] (DOMA)

IED .... Integrated Engineering Design Service (PDAA)

IED .... Integrated Environmental Design (PDAA)

IED .... Interacting Equipment Documents (MCD)

IED .... Intermittent Explosive Disorder

IED .... International Electron Devices Meeting (PDAA)

IED .... International Electronic Devices [*Conference*] (MCD)

IED .... Ion Exchange Desalination

IED .... Ionospheric Electron Density

IED .... Suburban Library System, Burr Ridge, IL [*OCLC symbol*] (OCLC)

IeDL .... Lembaga Ilmu Pengetahuan Indonesia, Pusat Dokumentasi Ilmiah Nasional, Jakarta, Indonesia [*Library symbol Library of Congress*] (LCLS)

IEdL .... Lewis and Clark Library System, Edwardsville, IL [*Library symbol Library of Congress*] (LCLS)

IEdL-A.......... Lewis and Clark Library System, Alhambra, Alhambra, IL [*Library symbol Library of Congress*] (LCLS)

IEdL-C.......... Lewis and Clark Library System, Chesterfield, Chesterfield, IL [*Library symbol Library of Congress*] (LCLS)

IEdL-H .... Lewis and Clark Library System, Hamel, Hamel, IL [*Library symbol Library of Congress*] (LCLS)

IEdL-HP .... Lewis and Clark Library System, Hillsboro Prison, Edwardsville, IL [*Library symbol Library of Congress*] (LCLS)

IeDLIP .... Lembaga Ilmu Pengetahuan Indonesia, Pusat Dokumentasi Ilmiah Nasional, Jakarta, Indonesia [*Library symbol*] [*Library of Congress*] (LCLS)

IEdL-L.......... Lewis and Clark Library System, Livingston, Livingston, IL [*Library symbol Library of Congress*] (LCLS)

IEdL-M......... Lewis and Clark Library System, Marine, Marine, IL [*Library symbol Library of Congress*] (LCLS)

IEdL-Mg....... Lewis and Clark Library System, Mulberry Grove, Mulberry Grove, IL [*Library symbol Library of Congress*] (LCLS)

IEdL-P.......... Lewis and Clark Library System, Palmyra, Palmyra, IL [*Library symbol Library of Congress*] (LCLS)

IEdL-Sh........ Lewis and Clark Library System, Shipman, Shipman, IL [*Library symbol Library of Congress*] (LCLS)

IEdL-StJ....... Lewis and Clark Library System, St. Jacob, St. Jacob, IL [*Library symbol Library of Congress*] (LCLS)

IEdMC.......... Pere Marquette Youth Center, Edwardsville, IL [*Library symbol*] [*Library of Congress*] (LCLS)

IEDO .... Institution of Economic Development Officers [*British*] (DBA)

IeDP............. Perpustakaan Museum Pusat, Jakarta, Indonesia [*Library symbol Library of Congress*] (LCLS)

IEDS............ Income Equalization Deposits Scheme

IEDS............ International Environmental Data Service [*European Commodities Exchange*] [*United Nations*] (DUND)

IEDS............ international Environment and Development Service (GNE)

IEdS............ Southern Illinois University, Edwardsville Campus, Edwardsville, IL [*Library symbol Library of Congress*] (LCLS)

IEdSD........... Edwardsville Community Unit, School District 7, Edwardsville, IL [*Library symbol Library of Congress*] (LCLS)

IEdS-D .... Southern Illinois University, School of Dental Medicine, Biomedical Library, Edwardsville, IL [*Library symbol Library of Congress*] (LCLS)

IEDSS .... Institute of European Defence and Strategic Studies [*British*] (DBA)

IEE .... Induced Electrical Effect

IEE .... Induced Electron Emission

IEE .... Industrial Electronic Engineer (IAA)

IEE .... Information Expert Environment [*Software*] [*Market research organization*] (NITA)

IEE .... Inner Enamel Epithelium [*Dentistry*]

IEE .... Institute for Earth Education (EA)

IEE .... Institute for Environmental Education (EA)

IEE .... Institute of Electrical Engineering [*Hitchin, Herts., England*] (NATG)

IEE .... Institute of Electrology Educators (EA)

IEE .... Institute of Environmental Engineers [*Later, IES*]

IEE .... Institution of Electrical Engineers [*London, England*] [*Database producer*]

IEE .... Intelligent Electronics Europa (NITA)

IEE .... Interim Expendable Emitter (NVT)

IEE .... International Institute for Hydraulic and Environmental Engineering [*Netherlands*] (IRC)

IEE .... National College of Education, Evanston, IL [*Library symbol Library of Congress*] (LCLS)

IEE .... North Suburban Library System, Wheeling, IL [*OCLC symbol*] (OCLC)

IEEC .... IEEE [*Institute of Electrical and Electronics Engineers*] Electronic Computer (IAA)

IEEC .... Integrated Electronics Engineering Center [*State University of New York, Binghamton*] [*Research center*] (RCD)

IEEE .... Institute of Electrical and Electronics Engineering (NITA)

IEEE .... Institute of Electrical and Electronics Engineering (USDC)

IEEE .... Institute of Electrical and Electronics Engineers (EA)

IEEE-CS ...... Institute of Electrical and Electronics Engineers - Computer Society

IEEE Exp ...... IEEE Expert: Intelligent Systems and Their Applications [*A publication*] (BRI)

IEEE/PES...... Power Engineering Society of the Institute of Electrical and Electronic Engineers (ITD)

IEEF .... Ion Exchange Evaporation Filter (PDAA)

IEEI .... IEEE [*Institute of Electrical and Electronics Engineers*] Electrical Insulation (IAA)

IEEI .... International Electronics Engineering, Inc. (AAG)

IEEI .... University of Illinois Hospital Eye and Ear Infirmary [*University of Illnois at Chicago*] [*Research center*] (RCD)

IEEIE .... Institution of Electrical and Electronics Inc. Engineers (DS)

IEELG .... International Education Exchange Liaison Group (EA)

IEENSW .... Institution of Electrical Engineers New South Wales [*Australia*]

IEEP .... Incapacitated Emergency Egress Practice [*NASA*] (KSC)

IEEP .... Institute for European Environmental Policy [*Germany*] (EAIO)

IEEP .... Interagency Energy/Environment Program [*Environmental Protection Agency*]

IEEPA .... International Emergency Economic Powers Act [*1977*]

IEES .... International Education Exchange Service [*Department of State*]

IEETE .... Institution of Electrical and Electronics Technician Engineers (MCD)

IEEU .... Instituto de Estudios de Estados Unidos [*Studies Mexico/US relations, US domestic politics, US economy, and US foreign policy*] [*Mexico*] (CROSS)

IEEV .... Institution of Electrical Engineers Victoria [*Australia*]

IE-Ex .... Evanston Public Library, Extension (Bookmobile), Evanston, IL [*Library symbol Library of Congress*] (LCLS)

IEF .... Indian Expeditionary Force [*British military*] (DMA)

IEF .... Information Engineering Facility (CDE)

IEF .... Instruction Execution Function (NITA)

IEF .... INTACT [*Infants Need to Avoid Circumcision Trauma*] Educational Foundation [*Later, NO-CIRC*] (EA)

IEF .... Integral Equation Formulation (PDAA)

IEF .... International Equestrian Federation (EAIO)

IEF .... International Exhibitions Foundation (EA)

IEF .... International Eye Foundation (EA)

IEF .... Isoelectric Focusing [*Analytical chemistry*]

IEF .... Israel Education Fund

IEF .... Italian Expeditionary Force

IEF .... Starved Rock Library System, Ottawa, IL [*OCLC symbol*] (OCLC)

IEFC .... International Emergency Food Council [*Post-World War II*]

IEFP .... International Exposition for Food Processors (ITD)

IEFR .... International Esperanto Fellowship of Rotarians [*See also IEAR*] (EAIO)

IEFS .... Integrated Electronic Filing System [*Computer science*] (DGA)

IEFUA .... International Electronic Facsimile Users Association (EA)

IEG .... Garrett-Evangelical Theological Seminary, Evanston, IL [*Library symbol Library of Congress*] (LCLS)

IEG .... Harry S Truman College, Chicago, IL [*OCLC symbol*] (OCLC)

IEG .... Imagery Exploitation Group

IEG .... Immediately Early Gene [*Genetics*]

IEG .... Imperial Ethiopian Government (CINC)

IEG .... Independent Evaluation Group (SDI)

IEG .... Industrial Electronics Group [*of General Motors Corp.*]

IEG .... Information Exchange Group [*National Institutes of Health*]

IEG .... Internal Engine Generator (PDAA)

IEG .... Internet Entertainment Group, Inc.

IEG .... Zielona Gora [*Poland*] [*Airport symbol*] (OAG)

IEGE .... IEEE [*Institute of Electrical and Electronics Engineers*] Geoscience Electronics (IAA)

IEGP .... Interagency Economic Growth Project [*Department of Transportation*]

IEH .... American Library Association, Chicago, IL [*OCLC symbol*] (OCLC)

IEHA .... International Economic History Association [*Paris, France*] (EA)

IEHD .... Institute for the Editing of Historical Documents

IEHIURM....... Institute for Encyclopedia of Human Ideas on Ultimate Reality and Meaning (EA)

IEHO .... Institute of Environmental Health Officers [*British*]

IEHS........... Evanston Township High School, Evanston, IL [*Library symbol Library of Congress*] (LCLS)

IEI .... Immunocytochemistry, ELISA [*Enzyme-Linked Immunosorbent Assay*], and Immunoblotting

IEI .... Indeterminate Engineering Items

IEI .... Indiana Energy [*NYSE symbol*] (TTSB)

IEI .... Indiana Energy, Inc. [*NYSE symbol*] (SPSG)

IEI .... Industrial Education Institute

IEI .... Industrial Engineering Institute

IEI .... Institute for Educational Innovation [*Later, Education Development Center*]

IEI .... Institution of Engineering Inspection [*British*] (BI)

IEI .... Institution of Engineers of Ireland (ACII)

IEI .... International Educator's Institute

IEI .... International Enamellers Institute [*Derby, England*] (EAIO)

IEI .... International Epitek, Inc. [*Toronto Stock Exchange symbol*]

IEI .... International Evaluations, Inc.

IEI .... Investment Education Institute (EA)

IEI .... Iran Electronics Industries

IEI .... Isoelectric Interval (DMAA)

IEIA .... Installation Environmental Impact Assessment (PDAA)

IEIA .... Insurance Employers' Industrial Association [*Australia*]

IEIA .... Integrated Educational Information System (PDAA)

IEIAS .... Institut Europeen Interuniversitaire de l'Action Sociale [*Inter-University European Institute on Social Welfare - IEISW*] (EAIO)

IEIB .... International Electronics, Inc. [*NASDAQ symbol*] (NQ)

IEIC .... Institution of Engineers-in-Charge [*British*] (BI)

IEIDATA ...... International Economic Indicators Database [*Columbia Business School*] [*Information service or system*] (CRD)

IEIE .... International Electrs [*NASDAQ symbol*] (TTSB)

IEIM .... IEEE [*Institute of Electrical and Electronics Engineers*] Instrumentation and Measurement Society (IAA)

IEIP .... Institut Europeen des Industries de la Pectine [*European Institute of the Pectin Industries*]

IEIP .... International Education Information Program

IEIS .... Integrated Engine Instrument System (MCD)

IEISW.......... Inter-University European Institute on Social Welfare (EA)

IEIT .... IEEE [*Institute of Electrical and Electronics Engineers*] Information Theory Society (IAA)

IEJ .... Deere & Co., Moline, IL [*OCLC symbol*] (OCLC)

IEJ .... Infite Ltd. [*British ICAO designator*] (FAAC)

IEJ .... Institut Europeen du Jouet [*European Toy Institute - ETI*] (EAIO)

IEJE .... Institut d'Etudes Juridiques Europeennes [*Benelux*]

IEK .... Kendall College, Evanston, IL [*Library symbol*] [*Library of Congress*] (LCLS)

IEKA .... Internacia Esperanto Klubo Automobilista [*International Automobile Esperanto Club*] (EAIO)

IEKKK.......... Invisible Empire Knights of the Ku Klux Klan (EA)

IEKV........... Internationale Eisenbahn-Kongress-Vereinigung [*International Railway Congress Association*]

IEL .... IE Industries, Inc. (MHDW)

IEL .... Improved Efficiency of Learning [*Project*] (AIE)

IEL .... Improved Erector-Launcher (SAA)

IEL .... Information Exchange List [*Military*] (AABC)

IEL .... Institute for Educational Leadership (EA)

IEL .... Internal Elastic Lamina [*Medicine*] (DMAA)

IEL .... International Electrochemical Commission

IEL .... Intraepithelial Lymphocyte [*Hematology*]

IEL .... Iota Exploration Ltd. [*Vancouver Stock Exchange symbol*]

IEL .... Parlin Public Library, Canton, IL [*OCLC symbol*] (OCLC)

IELA .... International Exhibition Logistics Associates [*Geneva, Switzerland*] (EAIO)

IEIg .... Gail Borden Public Library, Elgin, IL [*Library symbol Library of Congress*] (LCLS)

IELG .... International Esperantist League for Go (EA)

IEIgB .... Brethren Historical Library and Archives, Elgin, IL [*Library symbol Library of Congress*] (LCLS)

IEIgC .... Elgin Community College, Elgin, IL [*Library symbol Library of Congress*] (LCLS)

IEIm .... Elmhurst Public Library, Elmhurst, IL [*Library symbol Library of Congress*] (LCLS)

IEImC .... Elmhurst College, Elmhurst, IL [*Library symbol Library of Congress*] (LCLS)

IELS .... Isotope Exciter Light Source

IEIsP .... Principia College, Elsah, IL [*Library symbol Library of Congress*] (LCLS)

IEIw .... Morrison and Mary Wiley Public Library, Elmwood, IL [*Library symbol Library of Congress*] (LCLS)

IEIwp .... Elmwood Park Public Library, Elmwood Park, IL [*Library symbol Library of Congress*] (LCLS)

IEM .... East Texas State University, Metroplex Center, Commerce, TX [*OCLC symbol*] (OCLC)

IEM .... Ideal Effort Multiplier

IEM .... Immune Electron Microscopy

IEM .... Inactive Equipment Maintenance (DNAB)

IEM .... Inborn Error of Metabolism [*Medicine*]

IEM .... Individual Engagement Model (MCD)

IEM .... Industrial Engineer for Management

IEM .... Infrared Projector Energy Monitor (MCD)

IEM	Installation Equipment Management System (MCD)
IEM	Institute of Experimental Meteorology [Former USSR]
IEM	Interim Examination and Maintenance [Nuclear energy] (NRCH)
IEM	Internal Environment Monitoring
IEM	Intromission and Ejaculatory Mechanism [Physiology]
IEM	Ion Exchange Membrane
IEMA	Immunoenzymometric Assay [Clinical chemistry]
IEMA	Independent Electrical Manufacturers Association (EA)
IEMAE	Institute of Evolutionary Morphology and Animal Ecology [Commonwealth of Independent States]
IEMATS	Improved Emergency Message Automatic Transmission System (MCD)
IEMBA	International Executive Masters of Business Administration (PGP)
IEMC	IEEE [Institute of Electrical and Electronics Engineers] Electromagnetic Compatibility Society (IAA)
IEMC	Independent Electronic Music Center [Defunct]
IEMC	Industrial Equipment Manufacturers Council [Later, ICED] (EA)
IEMC	International Electronics Manufacturing Co. (AAG)
IEMCAP	Intrasystem Electromagnetic Compatibility Analysis Program [Computer science Air Force]
IEMD	Integrated Environmental Management Division [Environmental Protection Agency] (EPA)
IEME	Corps of Indian Electrical and Mechanical Engineers [British military] (DMA)
IEME	Inspectorate of Electrical and Mechanical Engineering [Military] (IAA)
IEMG	Integrated Electromyogram [Medicine]
IEMIS	Integrated Emergency Management Information System [Federal Emergency Management Agency] (GFGA)
IEMO	Installation Equipment Management Office [Military] (AFIT)
IEMP	Induced Electromagnetic Pulse (RDA)
IEMP	Institute of Environmental Medicine and Physiology
IEMP	Integrated Environmental Management Project [Environmental Protection Agency] (GFGA)
IEMP	Interior Electromagnetic Pulse (MCD)
IEMP	Internal Electromagnetic Pulse
IEMP	International Executive Masters Programme [London Business School]
IEMS	Installation Equipment Management System
I/EMS	Intergraph Corp./Engineering Modeling System
IEMS	Interim Electronic Maintenance Support (AFIT)
IEMSA	Iowa Emergency Medical Services Association (SRA)
IEMT	Intermediate Emergency Medical Technician [Also, EMT-I] (DHSM)
IEMTF	Interim Examination and Maintenance Training Facility [Nuclear energy] (NRCH)
IEMU	Integrated Extravehicular Mobility Unit (SSD)
IEMVT	Institut d'Elevage et de Medecine Veterinaire des Pays Tropicaux [Institute of Stockraising and Veterinary Medicine in Tropical Countries] [France]
IEN	Die Israelitischen Eigennamen [A publication] (BJA)
IE-N	Evanston Public Library, North Branch, Evanston, IL [Library symbol Library of Congress] (LCLS)
IEN	Interpenetrating Elastomeric Networks [Organic chemistry]
IEN	Northwestern University, Evanston, IL [Library symbol Library of Congress] (LCLS)
IEN-C	Northwestern University, Joseph Schaffner Library of Commerce, Chicago, IL [Library symbol Library of Congress] (LCLS)
IEN-D	Northwestern University, Dental School, Chicago, IL [Library symbol Library of Congress] (LCLS)
IEng	Incorporate Engineer (ACII)
IEN-L	Northwestern University, Law Library, Chicago, IL [Library symbol Library of Congress] (LCLS)
IEN-M	Northwestern University, Medical School, Chicago, IL [Library symbol Library of Congress] (LCLS)
IEN-Mu	Northwestern University, Music Library, Evanston, IL [Library symbol] [Library of Congress] (LCLS)
IEN-T	Northwestern University, Technological Institute, Evanston, IL [Library symbol Library of Congress] (LCLS)
IEN-Tr	Northwestern University, Transportation Library, Evanston, IL [Library symbol Library of Congress] (LCLS)
IEnvSc	Institution of Environmental Sciences [British] (DBA)
IEO	Incoherent Electronic Oscillator
IEO	Industry and Environment Office (GNE)
IEO	Installation Engineers Office (SAA)
I/EO	Instructor/Equipment Operator
IEO	Integrated Electronic Office (NITA)
IEO	Interim Engineering Order (AAG)
IEO	Intermediate Earth Orbit (SSD)
IEO	International Education Office [World War II]
IEO	International Exchange Office (AFM)
IEOCS	Interim Equipment Order Control System [Bell System]
IEON	International Esperantist Organization of Naturists [See also INOE] [Frankfurt, Federal Republic of Germany] (EAIO)
IEOP	Immunoelectroosmophoresis [Analytical biochemistry]
IEOS	Integrated Electronic Office System (IAA)
IEOTSG	Integral Economizer Once-Through Steam Generator (NRCH)
IEP	Evansville Public Library and Vanderburgh County Public Library, Evansville, IN [OCLC symbol] (OCLC)
IEp	Fondulac District Library, East Peoria, IL [Library symbol Library of Congress] (LCLS)
IEP	Image Edge Profile [Photography] (OA)
IEP	Immunoelectrophoresis [Analytical biochemistry]
IEP	Independent Evaluation Plan
IEP	Independent Exchange Plan
IEP	Indicateur Electronique de Pilotage [Electronic Pilotage Indicator] [Aviation]
IEP	Individual Education Plan
IEP	Individual Evaluation Plan [Army]
IEP	Individualized Education Plan [Special education] (PAZ)
IEP	Individualized Education Program [For the education of a handicapped person]
IEP	Information Exchange Program [or Project] [Military]
IEP	Ingestion Exposure Pathway [Nuclear emergency planning]
IEP	Initial Enrollment Period [Insurance]
IEP	Instantaneous Effective Photo
IEP	Institute for Ecological Policies [Defunct] (EA)
IEP	Institute for Experimental Psychiatry
IEP	Institut Europeen pour la Promotion des Entreprises
IEP	Institut fuer Europaeische Politik [Institute of European Politics] (EAIO)
IEP	Instrument for Evaluation of Photographs
IEP	Integrated Engineering Program
IEP	Intelligence Estimate for Planning
IEP	Internal Economic Problems [British]
IEP	International Economic Policy
IEP	International Education Project [American Council on Education] (PDAA)
IEP	International Energy Program
IEP	International Potential [Vancouver Stock Exchange symbol]
IEP	Intext Educational Publishers
IEP	Inverted Energy Population
IEP	Isoelectric Point [Also, IP, PH_1, pl] [Chemistry]
IEPA	Illinois Environmental Protection Agency
IEPA	Illinois Environmental Protection Agency (DOGT)
IEPA	Independent Electron Pair Approximation [Physics]
IEPA	International Economic Policy Act of 1972
IEPA	International Economic Policy Association (EA)
IEPA	International Environment Protection Act of 1983
IEPA	Intra-European Payments Agreement
IEPALA	Instituto de Estudios Politicos para America Latina y Africa [Spain]
IEPB	Interagency Emergency Planning Board [Federal disaster planning]
IEPC	Instantaneous Effective Photocathodes (MCD)
IEPC	Interagency Emergency Planning Committee
IEPD	Industrial and Extractive Processes Division [Environmental Protection Agency] (EPA)
IEpE	East Peoria Elementary School District, East Peoria, IL [Library symbol Library of Congress] (LCLS)
IEPFCHK	International Elvis Presley Fan Club, Hong Kong (EAIO)
IEPG	Independent European Program Group [NATO]
IEPG	Internet Engineering Planning Group
IEpI	Illinois Central College, East Peoria, IL [Library symbol Library of Congress] (LCLS)
IEPP	Institute of Earth and Planetary Physics [University of Alberta] [Research center] (RCD)
IEPPL	Integrated Engineering Planning Parts List
IEPR	Integrated Engine Pressure Ratio (GAVI)
IEPRC	International Electronic Publishing Research Centre [British] (IRC)
IEPS	International Electronics Packaging Society (EA)
IEQ	Illinois Prairie District Public Library, Metamora, IL [OCLC symbol] (OCLC)
IEQ	Index of Environmental Quality (WDAA)
IEQE	IEEE [Institute of Electrical and Electronics Engineers] Quantum Electronics (IAA)
I Eq R	Irish Equity Reports [A publication] (DLA)
IER	Independent Evaluation Report
IER	Individual Education Record
IER	Individual Evaluation Report
IER	Industrial Equipment Reserve
IER	Infanterie-Ersatzregiment [Infantry Replacement Training Regiment] [German military - World War II]
IER	Inherent Equipment Reliability
IER	Initial Engagement Range (MCD)
IER	Installation Enhancement Release [Computer science]
IER	Institute for Econometric Research (EA)
IER	Institute for Education by Radio [Defunct] (NTCM)
IER	Institute for Environmental Research [Environmental Science Services Administration]
IER	Institute of Educational Research [Defunct] (EA)
IER	Institute of Engineering Research [Research center British] (IRC)
IER	Institute of Engineering Research [University of California] [Research center] (MCD)
IER	Institute of Exploratory Research [Army]
IER	Interface Evaluation Report (KSC)
IER	Interim Engineering Report
IER	Internal Economic Rate of Return
IER	Inventory Equipment Requirement
IER	Ion Exchange Resin
IER	Irish Equity Reports [A publication] (DLA)
IER	Mackinaw Township Library, Mackinaw, IL [OCLC symbol] (OCLC)
IER	Natchitoches, LA [Location identifier FAA] (FAAL)
IER	Organization for International Economic Relations [Vienna, Austria] (EAIO)
IERC	Industrial Equipment Reserve Committee (SAA)
IERC	International Electronic Research Corp. (MCD)
IERD	Industry Energy Research and Development Program [Canada]
IERE	Institute of Electronics and Radio Engineers [British]
IERESM	Institut Europeen de Recherches et d'Etudes Superieures en Management [European Institute for Advanced Studies in Management - EIASM] [Brussels, Belgium] (EA)
IERF	International Education Research Foundation (EA)
IERI	Illuminating Engineering Research Institute (EA)

IERL............ Industrial Environmental Research Laboratory [*Environmental Protection Agency*]
IERM........... Individual Employment Rights Manual [*A publication*]
IERO .... Institute for Engineering Research in the Oceans [*Marine science*] (MSC)
IERS............ International Earth Rotation Services
IERS............ International Educational Reporting Service [*International Bureau of Education*] [*United Nations*] (EY)
IERS............ Inventory Equipment Requirement Specification
IERT............ Institute for Education by Radio-Television (NTCM)
IERTM.......... Institute for Environmental Research Technical Memorandum
IERW .... Initial Entry Rotary Wing [*Student*] (MCD)
IEs .... East St. Louis Public Library, East St. Louis, IL [*Library symbol Library of Congress*] (LCLS)
IES.............. Eli Lilly & Co., Indianapolis, IN [*OCLC symbol*] (OCLC)
IE-S............ Evanston Public Library, South Branch, Evanston, IL [*Library symbol Library of Congress*] (LCLS)
IES.............. Id, Ego, Superego [*Test*] [*Psychology*]
IES.............. IEEE Industrial Electronics Society (EA)
IES.............. IES Industries [*NYSE symbol*] (SPSG)
IES.............. Illuminating Engineering Society
IES.............. Illustrative Evaluation Scenario (DOMA)
IES.............. Imagery Exploitation System (DOMA)
IES.............. Income and Expense Statement (MHDW)
IES.............. Incoming Echo Suppressor [*Telecommunications*] (TEL)
IES.............. Independent Educational Services (EA)
IES.............. Indian Educational Service [*British*]
IES.............. Inductive Energy Storage
IES.............. Industrial Electronic System
IES.............. Industrial Engineering Services
IES.............. Industrial Engineering Standard (MCD)
IES.............. Information Exchange Systems [*British*]
IES.............. Institute for Earth Sciences [*Environmental Science Services Administration*]
IES .... Institute for Environmental Studies [*University of Wisconsin, Madison*] [*Research center*] (RCD)
IES .... Institute for Environmental Studies [*University of Washington*] [*Research center*] (RCD)
IES .... Institute for Environmental Studies [*University of Toronto*] [*Research center*] (RCD)
IES.............. Institute of Ecosystem Studies
IES.............. Institute of English Studies (DBA)
IES.............. Institute of Environmental Sciences (EA)
IES.............. Institute of European Studies (EA)
IES.............. Institution of Engineers and Shipbuilders [*Scotland*] (DI)
IES.............. Institution of Environmental Sciences (EAIO)
IES.............. Integral Error Squared (IEEE)
IES.............. Integrated Electronic System
IES.............. Intelligence Evaluation Staff
IES.............. Intelligence Exploitation Squadron [*Air Force*]
IES.............. Intensive Employability Services [*Work Incentive Program*]
IES.............. Inter-Island Air Services Ltd. [*Grenada*] [*ICAO designator*] (FAAC)
IES.............. Internal Environment Simulator
IES.............. International Ecology Society (EA)
IES.............. International Education Exchange Service [*Department of State*]
IES.............. International Education Series [*A publication*]
IES.............. International Exchange Service [*For publications*] [*Smithsonian Institution*]
IES.............. International Explorers Society
IES.............. Intrinsic Electric Strength (IEEE)
IES.............. Invariant-Ellipticity States (PDAA)
IES.............. Inventory Equipment Sheet
IES.............. Inverness Petroleum Ltd. [*Toronto Stock Exchange symbol*]
IES-........... Inverted Echo Sounder
IES.............. Ion Energy Selector
IES.............. Ion Engine Simulator
IES.............. Ion Engine System
IES.............. Irish Emigrant Society (EA)
IES.............. Irradiation Effects Simulation (NRCH)
IESA............ Instituto de Estudios Superiores de Administracion [*Institute of Higher Studies of Administration*] [*Venezuela*]
IESA............ Insurance Economics Society of America [*Defunct*] (EA)
IEsAHS........ Assumption High School, East St. Louis, IL [*Library symbol Library of Congress*] (LCLS)
IESC............ International Executive Service Corps [*Stamford, CT*] (EA)
IEsCH.......... Christian Welfare Hospital, East St. Louis, IL [*Library symbol Library of Congress*] (LCLS)
IEsCTH........ Centreville Township Hospital, East St. Louis, IL [*Library symbol Library of Congress*] (LCLS)
IESD........... Instrumentation and Electronic Systems Division [*NASA*] (MCD)
IES-DC .... IES [*Information Exchange System*] Data Collections [*Commission of the European Communities*] [*Information service or system*] (CRD)
IESG........... Internet Engineering Steering Group [*Computer science*] (ACRL)
IESM........... Inductive Energy Storage Modulator
IESNA .... Illuminating Engineering Society of North America (EA)
IESP............ Integrated Electronic Signal Processor
IEsP .... Parks College of Aeronautical Technology, East St. Louis, IL [*Library symbol Library of Congress*] (LCLS)
IEsPC.......... Project Choice, East St. Louis, IL [*Library symbol Library of Congress*] (LCLS)
IESq............ Intelligence Exploitation Squadron [*Air Force*]
IESR............ International English Shepherd Registry (EA)
IESRA .... Interim Employment Services Regulatory Authority
IESS............ Intergroup Ewing Sarcoma Study [*Medicine*] (DMAA)

IESS............ International Encyclopedia of the Social Sciences [*A publication*]
IESS............ Ion Engine System Section
IESSC.......... Irish El Salvador Support Committee (EAIO)
IEsSC.......... State Community College of East St. Louis, Learning Resources Center, East St. Louis, IL [*Library symbol Library of Congress*] (LCLS)
IEsSD.......... East Saint Louis Public School District 189, East St. Louis, IL [*Library symbol Library of Congress*] (LCLS)
IEsSMH....... Saint Mary's Hospital, East St. Louis, IL [*Library symbol Library of Congress*] (LCLS)
IEST............ Impulses, Ego, and Superego Test [*Psychology*] (AEBS)
IESU............ IEEE [*Institute of Electrical and Electronics Engineers*] Sonics and Ultrasonics (IAA)
IES Ut25 ..... IES Utilities [*Associated Press*] (SAG)
IESV............ Institute for Epidemiologic Studies of Violence (EA)
IET .... East Texas State University, Texarkana, Texarkana, TX [*OCLC symbol*] (OCLC)
IET .... Impact Excited Transmitter
IET .... Implanted Electrode Technique
IET .... Independent Evaluation Teams [*Army Systems Acquisitions Review Council*] (MCD)
IET .... Initial Engine Test
IET .... Initial Entry Training
IET .... Institute of Educational Technology [*British*]
IET .... Institute of Engineers and Technicians [*British*] (EAIO)
IET .... Instrument and Electrical Technician (MCD)
IET .... Integrated Equipment Test [*Nuclear energy*]
IET .... Interest Equalization Tax
IET .... Intermolecular Energy Transfer [*Chemistry*]
IET .... Interval Embossed Tube
IETA .... International Electrical Testing Association (EAIO)
IETAS.......... Interim Escort Towed Array System (MCD)
IETC............ Initial Education and Training Committee (ACII)
IETC............ Interagency Emergency Transportation Committee
IETC............ International Environmental Technology Centre [*United Nations*] (ECON)
IETCA.......... International E-22 Class Association (EA)
IETE .... Institution of Electronics and Telecommunications Engineers [*Information service or system*] (TSSD)
IETEJ .... Institute of Electronics & Telecommunications Engineers of Japan (NITA)
IETF .... Initial Engine Test Facility
IETF .... Initial Engine Test Firing (IAA)
IETF .... Integrated Equipment Test Facility [*Department of Energy*]
IETF .... International Engineering Task Force [*Computer science*]
IETF .... Internet Engineering Task Force
IETM............ Interactive Electronic Technical Manual [*Military*] (RDA)
IETP............ Individualized Education and Training Plan (OICC)
IETS............ Inelastic Electron Tunneling Spectroscopy
I-ETS........... Interim European Telecommunication Standard (OSI)
IETS............ Intermediate Examiner Training School [*Federal Home Loan Bank Board*]
IETS............ International Embryo Transfer Society (EA)
IETTAB........ International Environmental Technology Transfer Advisory Board [*Environmental Protection Agency*] (EGAO)
IEU .... Forum International: International Ecosystems University (EA)
IEU .... IES Util 7.875%JrSubDebs [*NYSE symbol*] (TTSB)
IEU .... IES Utilities [*NYSE symbol*] (SAG)
IEU .... Independent Education Union [*Australia*]
IEU .... Input Expansion Unit
IEU .... Instruction Execution Unit [*Computer science*] (IAA)
IEU .... Integrated Electronics Unit (MCD)
IEU .... Interface Electronics Unit [*NASA*]
IEU .... Intermediate Education Unit
IEU .... Ion Exchange Unit
IEU .... Lewis and Clark Library System, Edwardsville, IL [*OCLC symbol*] (OCLC)
IEuC .... Eureka College, Eureka, IL [*Library symbol Library of Congress*] (LCLS)
IEUP........... Institut fuer Europaeische Umweltpolitik [*Institute for European Environmental Policy - IEEP*] (EAIO)
IEV .... International Electrotechnical Vocabulary (IEEE)
IEV .... Intracellular Enveloped Virus
IEV .... Kewanee Public Library, Kewanee, IL [*OCLC symbol*] (OCLC)
IEV .... Kiev [*Former USSR Airport symbol*] (OAG)
IEVD............ Integrated Electronic Vertical Display
IEvp .... Evergreen Park Public Library, Evergreen Park, IL [*Library symbol Library of Congress*] (LCLS)
IEVS............ Income Eligibility Verification Systems (BARN)
IE-W........... Evanston Public Library, West Branch, Evanston, IL [*Library symbol Library of Congress*] (LCLS)
IEW .... Information Engineering Workbench (CDE)
IEW .... Intelligence and Electronic Warfare [*System*] [*Military*] (RDA)
IEW .... Pekin Public Library, Pekin, IL [*OCLC symbol*] (OCLC)
IEW .... Winters, TX [*Location identifier FAA*] (FAAL)
IEWCS .... Intelligent Electronic Warfare Common Sensor (DWSG)
I/EW FOSS... Intelligence/Electronic Warfare Family of Systems Study [*Military*] (MCD)
IEWI............ Indirect Environmental Warming Impact
IEWNI.......... Washington National Insurance Co., Evanston, IL [*Library symbol Library of Congress*] (LCLS)
IEWS........... Integrated Electronic Warfare System
IEWSE......... Intelligence Electronic Warfare Support Element (ADDR)
IEWT........... National Woman's Christian Temperance Union, Evanston, IL [*Library symbol Library of Congress*] (LCLS)

IEW-UAV.....	Intelligence/Electronic Warfare Unmanned Aerial Vehicle [*Army*]
IEX	Harrington Institute of Interior Design, Design Library, Chicago, IL [*OCLC symbol*] (OCLC)
IEX	IDEX Corp. [*NYSE symbol*] (SPSG)
IEX	Instruction Execution [*Computer science*] (IAA)
IEX	Ion Exchanger
IEX	Issue Exception Code [*Air Force*] (AFIT)
IEXPE	Institute of Explosive Engineers (PDAA)
IEXS	Integrated Expert System [*Computer science*]
IEY	Barrow, AK [*Location identifier FAA*] (FAAL)
IEY	Chicago Board of Trade, Chicago, IL [*OCLC symbol*] (OCLC)
IEY	International Education Year [*UN designation*]
IEZ	Cumberland Trail Library System, Flora, IL [*OCLC symbol*] (OCLC)
IEZ	Institut Europeen du Zinc [*European Zinc Institute - EZI*] (EA)
IF	Ice Fog
IF	Ideational Fluency [*Research test*]
IF	Idiopathic Fibroplasia [*Medicine*] (DMAA)
IF	Idiopathic Flushing [*Medicine*] (DMAA)
IF	Idirect Fluorescence [*Medicine*] (DMAA)
IF	Image Frequency (IAA)
I/F	Image-to-Frame Ratio (MUGU)
IF	Immersion Fixation [*Microbiology*]
IF	Immersion Foot [*Medicine*] (DMAA)
IF	Immunofluorescence [*Immunochemistry*]
IF	Imperial Father [*of the Chapel*] [*Unions*] [*British*] (DGA)
IF	Importance Factor [*Statistics*]
IF	Imprest Fund (MCD)
IF	Independent Force [*British military*] (DMA)
IF	Independent Foundation
IF	Indian Financial Questions [*British*]
IF	Indirect Fluorescent
IF	Indonesia Fund [*NYSE symbol*] (SPSG)
IF	Industrial Appointment Full Time [*Chiropody*] [*British*]
IF	Industrial Fund (AFM)
IF	Infielder [*Position in baseball*]
IF	In-Flight (AAG)
IF	Information Collector (SAA)
IF	Information Feedback
IF	Infrared (MCD)
IF	Infrared Filter
IF	In Full
IF	Inhibiting Factor
IF	Initiation Factor [*Protein biosynthesis*]
IF	Inner Forme [*Imposition*] (DGA)
IF	Inside Face (DAC)
IF	Inside Frosted
IF	Installation Fixtures (MCD)
IF	Instantaneous Flow [*Medicine*] (DMAA)
IF	Institute of Fuel [*British*]
IF	Instructional Television, Fixed [*FCC*] (NTCM)
IF	Instruction Field
IF	Instruction Folder (MSA)
IF	Instrument Flight (IAA)
IF	Instrument Flying [*Aviation*]
IF	Insufficient Funds
IF	Insular Force
IF	Integration Facility (MCD)
IF	Intellectual Framework
IF	Intellectual Freedom
IF	Intelligence Fusion [*Army*] (RDA)
IF	Intensity Factor
I/F	Interface [*Computer science*] (KSC)
IF	Interference Filter
IF	Interferon [*Also, IFN*] [*Biochemistry*]
IF	Interferon Foundation [*Defunct*] (EA)
IF	Interflug [*ICAO designator*] (AD)
IF	Interfuture (EA)
IF	Interior Facet [*Medicine*] (DMAA)
IF	Intermediate Filament [*Anatomy*]
IF	Intermediate Fix [*FAA*] (TAG)
IF	Intermediate Forward [*Army*]
IF	Intermediate Frequency [*Electronics*]
IF	Internal Fixation [*Orthopedics*] (DAVI)
IF	Internal Function [*Electronics*] (ECII)
IF	Internally Flawless [*Diamond clarity grade*]
IF	International Federation of American Homing Pigeon Fanciers (EA)
IF	International Forum (EA)
IF	International Foundation (EAIO)
IF	Interrupt Flag [*Computer science*]
IF	Interstitial Fluid [*Physiology*]
IF	Interstitial-Free [*Metallurgical engineering*]
IF	Interventional Fluoroscopy [*Medicine*] (DMAA)
IF	Intrinsic Factor [*Biochemistry*]
IF	Inventrepreneurs' Forum (EA)
IF	Inverted File (NITA)
IF	Involved Field [*Medicine*]
IF	Ipse Fecit [*He Did It Himself*] [*Latin*]
IF	Ipso Facto [*By the Fact Itself*] [*Latin*]
IF	Ireland Fund (EA)
IF	Irish Fusiliers [*British military*] (DMA)
IF	Irregular Force [*Military*] (CINC)
IF	Isotta-Fraschini [*Italian luxury auto maker*]
IFA	Association Internationale de l'Industrie des Engrais [*International Fertilizer Industry Association - IFA*] (EAIO)
IFA	FAI Airservice, Nurnberg [*Germany*] [*FAA designator*] (FAAC)
IFA	Fort Worth Public Library, Fort Worth, TX [*OCLC symbol*] (OCLC)
IFA	Idiopathic Fibrosing Alveolitis [*Medicine*] (DMAA)
IFA	Igniter-Fuel Assembly
IFA	Imero Fiorentino Associates, Inc. [*New York, NY*] [*Telecommunications*] (TSSD)
IFA	Immunofluorescence [*or Immunofluorometric*] Assay [*Also, IFMA*] [*Analytical biochemistry*]
IFA	Immunofluorescent Antibody [*Immunochemistry*]
IFA	Incomplete Freund's Adjuvant
IFA	Independent Fee Appraiser, Member [*National Association of Independent Fe e Appraisers, Inc.*] [*Designation awarded by*]
IFA	Independent Financial Adviser [*British*] (ECON)
IFA	Independent Financial Analysis (ADA)
IFA	Indirect Fluorescent Antibody [*Immunochemistry*]
IFA	Individualized Functional Assessment [*Social Security Administration*]
IFA	Industrial Forestry Association [*Later, NFA*] (EA)
IFA	In-Flight Abort (MCD)
IFA	In-Flight Alignment (PDAA)
IFA	In-Flight Analysis
IFA	Information Flow Analysis (MHDB)
IFA	Inslee Family Association (EA)
IFA	Institute of Field Archaeologists [*British*] (DBA)
IFA	Institute of Financial Accountants (EAIO)
IFA	Instrumented Fuel Assembly (PDAA)
IFA	Insulation Fabricators Association [*Defunct*] (EA)
IFA	Integrated Feed Antenna
IFA	Integrated File Adapter [*Computer science*] (BUR)
IFA	Intensive Flux Array (USDC)
IFA	Intensive Flux Array [*Marine science*] (OSRA)
IFA	Intercessors for America (EA)
IFA	Intercollegiate Fencing Association (EA)
IFA	Interface Functional Analysis (NASA)
IFA	Inter-Financial Association (EA)
IFA	Interim Functional Alternate
IFA	Intermediate Frequency Amplifier [*or Attenuator*]
IFA	International Federation of Accountants (ADA)
IFA	International Federation of Actors
IFA	International Federation of Airworthiness [*Middlesex, England*] (EAIO)
IFA	International Federation on Ageing [*Formerly, IARP*] (EA)
IFA	International Ferret Association (EA)
IFA	International Fertility Association [*Defunct*]
IFA	International Fertilizer Industry Association [*Paris, France*] (EAIO)
IFA	International Festivals Association (EA)
IFA	International Fiction Association (EAIO)
IFA	International Fighter Aircraft
IFA	International Filariasis Association (EA)
IFA	International Finance Alert [*Financial Times Business Information*] [*British Information service or system*] (CRD)
IFA	International Finn Association [*Madrid, Spain*] (EAIO)
IFA	International Fiscal Association [*Rotterdam, Netherlands*] (EAIO)
IFA	International Florists Association [*Later, National Florists Association*] (EA)
IFA	International Footprint Association (EA)
IFA	International Footwear Association (EA)
IFA	International Franchise Association (EA)
IFA	International Freight Apron
IFA	International Frisbee Association [*Later, IFDA*] (EA)
IFA	Interracial Family Alliance (EA)
IFA	Ionization Front Accelerator [*Physics*]
IFA	Iowa Falls, IA [*Location identifier FAA*] (FAAL)
IFA	Irish Features Agency [*News agency*]
IFA	Irish Football Association (BI)
IFA	Israel Folktale Archive (BJA)
IFA	Istituto di Fisica dell'Atmosfera [*Institute of Atmospheric Physics*] [*Italy*]
IFA	Majma'a al-Fiqh al-Islami [*Islamic Jurisprudence Academy - IJA*] (EAIO)
IFAA	International Federation of Advertising Agencies [*Sarasota, FL*] (EA)
IFAA	International Federation of Associations of Anatomists (EA)
IFAA	International Flight Attendants Association (EA)
IFAA	International Flow Aids Association (EA)
IFAA	International Furniture and Accessory Association (EA)
IFAAB	International Fiscal Association, Australian Branch
IFAB	Integrated Fire Direction System for the Artillery Battery [*German*]
IFABC	International Federation of Audit Bureaux of Circulations (EAIO)
IFAC	Independent Fee Appraiser/Counselor [*National Association of Independent Fee Appraisers, Inc.*] [*Designation awarded by*]
IFAC	Interfirm Accounting Project (IAA)
IFAC	International Federation of Accountants [*New York, NY*] (EA)
IFAC	International Federation of Automatic Control [*Laxenburg, Austria*]
IFAC	International Food Additives Council (EA)
IFACE	Interface Element (NITA)
IFAD	Interactive Finite Element Analysis and Design [*Software*] [*Automotive engineering*]
IFAD	International Foundation for Agricultural Development [*Defunct*] (EA)
IFAD	International Fund for Agricultural Development [*United Nations*]
IF-ADD ICMA...	Insular Force - Additional Initial Clothing Monetary Allowance [*Military*] (DNAB)
IFAE	International Farmers Association for Education [*Defunct*] (EA)
IFaf	Fairfield Public Library, Fairfield, IL [*Library symbol Library of Congress*] (LCLS)
IFAFA	Italian Folk Art Federation of America (EA)
IFAHPF	International Federation of American Homing Pigeon Fanciers (EA)
IFAI	Industrial Fabrics Association International (EA)
IFAI	International Fire Administration Institute

IFai .... Vance Township Library, Fairmount, IL [*Library symbol*] [*Library of Congress*] (LCLS)
IFALPA......... International Federation of Air Line Pilots Associations [*Egham, England*] (EAIO)
IFAM........... Initial-Final Address Message [*Telecommunications*] (TEL)
IFAM........... Inverted File Access Method
IFAMP......... If Approach Missed Proceed [*Aviation*] (FAAC)
IFAMS......... Integrated Force Administration System [*Bell System*]
IFAN........... Institut Francais d'Afrique Noire [*French Institute of Black Africa*]
IFAN........... Internationale Foderation der Ausschusse Normenpraxis [*International Federation for the Application of Standards*] (EAIO)
IFANC .... International Free Academy of New Cosmology (EA)
IF & F .... Intermediate Flush and Fill (AAG)
IFAO Bibl d'Et... Institut Francais d'Archeologie Orientale du Caire. Bibliotheque d'Etude [*A publication*] (BJA)
IFAP........... International Federation of Agricultural Producers (BARN)
IFAP........... International Foundation for Airline Passengers (EAIO)
IFAPA......... International Foundation of Airline Passengers Associations (EAIO)
IFAPAO .... International Federation of Asian and Pacific Associations of Optometrists [*Australia*] (EAIO)
IFAPP......... International Federation of Associations of Pharmaceutical Physicians [*Italy*] (EAIO)
IFAPWE....... Institute of Ferro-Alloy Producers in Western Europe [*Defunct*] (EA)
IFAR........... Injector Face Acoustic Resonator (MCD)
IFAR........... International Forum for AIDS Research [*Institute of Medicine*]
IFAR........... International Foundation for Art Research (EA)
IFARD .... International Federation of Agricultural Research Systems for Development [*Netherlands*]
IFarE.......... Farmington East Unit District No. 324, Farmington, IL [*Library symbol Library of Congress*] (LCLS)
IFARS .... Individual Flight Activity Reporting System [*Navy*]
IFAS........... Independent Fee Appraiser, Senior [*National Association of Independent Fe e Appraisers, Inc.*] [*Designation awarded by*]
IFAS........... International Federation for the Application of Standards (PDAA)
IFAS........... International Federation of Aquarium Societies
IFASC......... Integrated Functions Assessment Steering Committee [*NASA*] (NASA)
IFaSD......... Farina-LaGrove Community Unit, School District 206, Farina, IL [*Library symbol Library of Congress*] (LCLS)
IFAST......... Integrated Facility for Avionics System Test [*Air Force*]
IFAT........... Indirect Fluorescent Antibody Test [*Immunology*]
IFAT........... Indirect Immunofluorescent Antibody Test [*Clinical chemistry*]
IFATCA....... International Federation of Air Traffic Controllers' Associations [*Dublin, Republic of Ireland*] (EAIO)
IFATE......... International Federation of Airworthiness Technology and Engineering [*Later, IFA*]
IFATSEA...... International Federation of Air Traffic Safety Electronic Associations [*British*] (EAIO)
IFAVWU .... International Federation of Audio-Visual Workers Unions [*See also FISTA*] (EAIO)
IFAW.......... International Fund for Animal Welfare (EA)
IFAWPCA ..... International Federation of Asian and Western Pacific Contractors' Associations [*Pasig, Metro Manila, Philippines*] (EAIO)
IFAX........... International Facsimile Service [*Telecommunications*] (TEL)
IFAXA......... International Facsimile Association (EA)
IFB............ Fort Wayne Bible College, Fort Wayne, IN [*OCLC symbol*] (OCLC)
IFB............ Incendiary Fragmentation Bomb
IFB............ Independent Forward Bloc [*Mauritian political party*]
IFB............ Initiation for Bid
IFB............ Institute of Foreign Bankers [*New York, NY*] (EA)
IFB............ Internationales Federn-Bureau [*International Feather Bureau - IFB*] (EAIO)
IFB............ International Federation of the Blind [*Later, WBU*]
IFB............ Interrupted Feedback [*Wireless earphone*] (NTCM)
IFB............ Interrupt Feedback Line [*Computer science*] (IAA)
IFB............ Investment Finance Bank Ltd. [*Malta*]
IFB............ Invitation for Bid
IFB............ Invitation for Bid (DOMA)
IFB............ Invitation for Bid [*Marine science*] (OSRA)
IFBA.......... International Fire Buff Associates (EA)
IFBB.......... International Federation of Bodybuilders [*Montreal, PQ*] (EA)
IFBC.......... International Federation of the Blue Cross (EA)
IFBDO........ International Federation of Blood Donor Organizations [*See also FIODS*] [*Dole, France*] (EAIO)
IFBH.......... Intermediate Force Beachhead [*Military*] (DNAB)
IFBM.......... Improved Fleet Ballistic Missile
IFBPW........ International Federation of Business and Professional Women (EA)
IFBS.......... International Fashion and Boutique Show (ITD)
IFBSO .... International Federation of Boat Show Organisers (EA)
IFBSS......... Individual Flexible Barrier Shelter Systems (MCD)
IFBWW........ International Federation of Building and Wood Workers [*Sweden*]
IFC........... Cefi Aviation SRL [*Italy ICAO designator*] (FAAC)
IFC........... Franklin College of Indiana, Franklin, IN [*OCLC symbol*] (OCLC)
IFC........... If Clause
IFC........... Imasco Financial Corp. [*Vancouver Stock Exchange symbol Toronto Stock Exchange symbol*]
IFC........... Improved Flotation Chamber
IFC........... Incremental Frequency Control
IFC........... Independent Film Channel
IFC........... Independent Fire Control [*Area*] (NATG)
IFC........... Indicated Final Cost (SAA)
IFC........... Industrial Frequency Changer
IFC........... Infant Formula Council (EA)
IFC........... In-Flight Calibration (KSC)
IFC........... Infrared Fire Control

IFC........... Initial Floristic Composition [*Theory of plant succession*]
IFC........... Inside Front Cover [*Publishing*] (NTCM)
IFC........... Installed First Cost (ACRL)
IFC........... Instantaneous Frequency Correlation
IFC........... Institut Forestier du Canada [*Formerly, Canadian Society of Forest Engineers*] (AC)
IFC........... Instrument Flight Center [*Air Force*]
IFC........... Insulated Food Container [*Military*] (INF)
IFC........... Integrated Fire Control [*RADAR*]
IFC........... Integrated Forcing Contribution [*Environmental science*]
IFC........... Intellectual Freedom Committee [*American Library Association*]
IFC........... Interface Clear (IAA)
IFC........... Inter-Faith Compassionists (EA)
IFC........... Interfirm Comparison (ADA)
IFC........... Interfruitlet Corking [*of pineapple*]
IFC........... International Facilitating Committee [*World Resources Institute*]
IFC........... International Federation of Master-Craftsmen [*See also IFH*] (EAIO)
IFC........... International Film Completion Corp.
IFC........... International Finance Corp. [*Affiliate of International Bank for Reconstruction and Development*]
IFC........... International Fisheries Commission [*Later, IPHC*] [*US and Canada*]
IFC........... Interracial Family Circle [*An association*]
IFC........... Interstate and Foreign Commerce (DLA)
IFC........... Intrinsic Factor Concentrate [*Biochemistry*]
IFC........... Istituto di Fisica Cosmica [*Italy*]
IFCA.......... Independent Fundamental Churches of America (EA)
IFCA.......... Instrumentation to Follow the Course of an Accident [*Nuclear energy*] (NRCH)
IFCA.......... International Fan Club Association [*Formerly, FCA*] (EA)
IFCA.......... International Federation of Catholic Alumnae (EA)
IFCAA......... International Fire Chiefs' Association of Asia (EAIO)
IFCAM......... Industrial Fuel Choice Analysis Model [*Environmental Protection Agency*] (GFGA)
IFCAS......... Indirect Fire Casualty Assessment/Suppression System [*Military*] (MCD)
IFCATI........ International Federation of Cotton and Allied Textile Industries [*Later, ITMF*]
IFCB.......... International Federation of Cell Biology [*Toronto, ON*] (EAIO)
IFCB.......... International Friendly Circle of the Blind (EA)
IFCbl......... Intrinsic Factor Cobalamin (Complex) [*Biochemistry*]
IFCC.......... Iconized Flowchart Compilers [*Software*] [*Computer science*]
IFCC.......... Initial Fleet Command Center [*Navy*] (CAAL)
IFCC.......... Interim Fleet Command Center [*Navy*] (MCD)
IFCC.......... International Federation of Camping and Caravanning
IFCC.......... International Federation of Children's Communities [*Later, FICE*]
IFCC.......... International Federation of Clinical Chemistry [*Vienna, Austria*] (EA)
IFCCA......... International Federation of Community Centre Associations
IFCCTE........ International Federation of Commercial, Clerical, and Technical Employees
IFCDG .... Injection of Fuel Containing Dissolved Gas [*Diesel engines*]
IFCE.......... Integral Fire Control Equipment (AAG)
IFCE.......... International Federation of Consulting Engineers (NUCP)
IFCF.......... Integrated Fuel Cycle Facilities [*Nuclear energy*] (NRCH)
IFCF.......... Intermediate Frequency Crystal Filter
IFCF.......... International Frederic Chopin Foundation [*Poland*] (EAIO)
IFCGWU....... International Federation of Chemical and General Workers Union
IFCI.......... International Fibercom, Inc. [*NASDAQ symbol*] (SAG)
IFCI.......... Intl Fibercom Inc. [*NASDAQ symbol*] (TTSB)
IFCIW......... International Fibercom Wrrt [*NASDAQ symbol*] (TTSB)
IFCJ.......... International Federation of Catholic Journalists
IFCM.......... International Federation for Choral Music (EA)
IFCM.......... International Federation of Christian Metalworkers Unions
IFCMI......... International Federation of Children of Mary Immaculate [*Paris, France*] (EAIO)
IFCMU .... International Federation of Christian Miners' Unions
IFCN.......... Interfacility Communication Network
IFCN.......... Inter-Facility Flow Control Network [*FAA*] (TAG)
IFCN.......... International Federation of Clinical Neurophysiology (EAIO)
IFCO.......... International Fan Club Organization (EA)
IFCO.......... International Fisheries Cooperative Organization (BARN)
IFCO.......... Interreligious Foundation for Community Organization (EA)
IFCP.......... Institute for Financial Crime Prevention [*Later, NACFE*] (EA)
IFCP.......... International Federation of Catholic Pharmacists
IFCP.......... International Federation of the Cinematographic Press [*See also FIPRESCI*] (EAIO)
IFCP.......... International Fund for Concerned Photography [*Later, ICP*]
IFCPC......... International Federation of Cervical Pathology and Colposcopy [*Dundee, Scotland*] (EAIO)
IFCR.......... Interface Control Register (IAA)
IFCR.......... International Foundation for Cancer Research (EA)
IFCRM......... International Federation of Catholic Rural Movements (EAIO)
IFCS.......... Improved Fire Control System [*Military*] (MCD)
IFCS.......... Inactivated Fetal Calf Serum [*Medicine*] (DMAA)
IFCS.......... In-Flight Checkout System (IEEE)
IFCS.......... Infrared Fire Control System
IFCS.......... Institute for Family and Child Study [*Michigan State University*] [*Research center*] (RCD)
IFCS.......... Integrated Flight Control System
IFCS.......... Intergovernmental Forum on Chemical Safety
IFCS.......... International Federation of Computer Sciences
IFCSS.......... Independent Federation of Chinese Students and Scholars (EA)
IFCTIO .... International Federation of Commercial Travelers Insurance Organizations [*Later, CTIF*] (EA)

IFCTU.......... International Federation of Christian Trade Unions [*Often uses initialism CISC, based on name in French, to avoid confusion with ICFTU*]

IFCTUBWW... International Federation of Christian Trade Unions of Building and Wood Workers

IFCTUGP...... International Federation of Christian Trade Unions of Graphical and Paper Industries

IFCU.......... Interface Control Unit [*Army*] (IAA)

IFCU.......... International Federation of Catholic Universities [*See also FIUC*] [*Paris, France*] (EAIO)

IFCUAW........ International Federation of Christian Unions of Agricultural Workers

IFCWU........ International Federation of Chemical Workers' Unions

IFD.......... Idealization to Frustration to Demoralization

IFD.......... Image File Directory [*Computer science*]

IFD.......... Incipient Fire Detection

IFD.......... Indentation Force Deflection [*Automotive seat testing*]

IFD.......... In Flagrante Delicto [*Caught in the Act*] [*Latin*]

IFD.......... In-Flight Deployment

IFD.......... Infrared Detector

IFD.......... Initial Fill Date [*Army*] (AABC)

IFD.......... In-Line Filter Degasser

IFD.......... Instantaneous Frequency Discriminator (IEEE)

IFD.......... Integrated Flight Director [*Aviation*]

IFD.......... Intelligent Field Device (ACII)

IFD.......... Interfiber Distance

IFD.......... Inter-Fighter Director

IFD.......... Internal Friction Damping (PDAA)

IFD.......... Internationale Foderation des Dachdeckerhandwerks [*International Federation of Roofing Contractors*] (EAIO)

IFD.......... International Federation for Documentation [*Also, FID*] [*Later, IFID*]

IFD.......... International Foundation Directory [*A publication*]

IFDA.......... Independent Film Distributors' Association [*British*]

IFDA.......... Institutional Food Distributors of America [*Later, NAWGA*] (EA)

IFDA.......... International Foodservice Distributors Association (EA)

IFDA.......... International Foundation for Development Alternatives [*See also FIPAD*] [*Nyon, Switzerland*] (EAIO)

IFDA.......... International Franchised Dealers Association [*Later, SFDA*] (EA)

IFDA.......... International Frisbee Disc Association [*Formerly, IFA*] (EA)

IFDA.......... International Furnishings and Design Association (EA)

IFDAPS....... Integrated Flight Data Processing System [*Air Force*]

IFDAS........ International Federation of Dental Anesthesiology Societies [*British*] (EAIO)

IFDC.......... Industrial Funding Corp. [*NASDAQ symbol*] (NQ)

IFDC.......... Integrated Facilities Design Criteria (SAA)

IFDC.......... International Fertilizer Development Center (EA)

IFDC.......... Intraductal and Infiltrating Duct Carcinoma [*Oncology*]

IFDCAUS..... International Flying Dutchman Class Association of the US (EA)

IFDCO........ International Flying Dutchmen Class Organization [*Berlin, Federal Republic of Germany*] (EAIO)

IFDFA......... International Freeze-Dry Floral Association (EA)

IFDI.......... Israel Folk Dance Institute (EA)

IFDM.......... International Foundation of Doll Makers (EA)

IFDO.......... International Federation of Dalit Organizations (EA)

IFDO.......... International Federation of Data Organizations for the Social Sciences [*Amsterdam, Netherlands*] (EAIO)

IFDP.......... Institute for Food and Development Policy (EA)

IFDR.......... Interface Data Register (IAA)

IFDS.......... Inertial Flight Data System (KSC)

IFDS.......... Integrated Flagship Data System [*Navy*] (NG)

IFDVS........ Indian Field Depot Veterinary Stores [*British military*] (DMA)

IFE.......... Image Feature Extraction [*Air Force*]

IFE.......... Immunofixation Electrophoresis [*Clinical chemistry*]

IFE.......... Incipient Failure Everywhere [*Hypothesis descending forces in a sand-pile*]

IFE.......... In-Flight Emergency (MCD)

IFE.......... In-Flight Entertainment

IFE.......... Inner Front End (MSA)

IFE.......... Institute for Fluitronics Education (EA)

IFE.......... Institute of Financial Education [*Chicago, IL*] (EA)

IFE.......... Institute of Fire Engineers

IFE.......... Institut Francais de l'Energie [*French Institute of Energy*] [*Paris*] [*Information service or system*] (IID)

IFE.......... Intelligent Front End (NITA)

IFE.......... Internal Field Emission

IFE.......... International Family Entertainment

IFE.......... International Fasteners Exposition (ITD)

IFE.......... International Food and Drink Exhibition [*British*] (ITD)

IFE.......... Intl Flavors/Fragr [*NYSE symbol*] (TTSB)

IFEA.......... In-Flight Emergency Assistance [*FAA*] (TAG)

IFEA.......... Institute of Fire Engineers in Australia

IFEAT......... International Federation of Essential Oils and Aroma Trades [*British*] (EAIO)

IFEBP........ International Foundation of Employee Benefit Plans (EA)

IFEBS........ Integrated Foreign Exchange and Banking System (PDAA)

IFEC.......... International Foodservice Editorial Council (EA)

IFED.......... Integrated Fuel/Engine Display (MCD)

IFEEX........ International Fishing Equipment Exposition [*Canada*] (ITD)

IFEF.......... Internacia Fervojista Esperanto Federacio [*International Federation of Esperantist Railwaymen*] (EAIO)

IFEH.......... International Federation of Europe Houses [*See also FIME*] (EAIO)

IFEI.......... Integrated Fuel/Engine Instrument (MCD)

IFEL.......... Inverse Free Electron LASER [*Plasma physics*]

IFEM.......... In-Flight Engine Monitor (MCD)

IFEM.......... Institute of Fireplace Equipment Manufacturers (EA)

IFEMA........ Industrial Finishing Equipment Manufacturers Association (EA)

IFEMS........ International Federation of Electron Microscope Societies

IFEN.......... Institut Francais de l'Environnement [*Marine science*] [*France*] (OSRA)

IFenE........ Institute of Fence Engineers [*British*] (DBA)

IFEP.......... Inflation from an Energy Perspective [*Economic theory*]

IFEP.......... In-Flight Experiments Panel

IFEP.......... Integrated Front End Processor (NITA)

IFEPFC....... International Federation of Elvis Presley Fan Clubs [*Defunct*] (EA)

IFEPT......... International Federation for Enteric Phage Typing [*International Council of Scientific Unions*]

IFER.......... Internationale Foederation der Eisenbahn-Reklame-Gesellschaften [*International Federation of Railway Advertising Companies*] [*British*] (EA)

IFER.......... International Federation of Engine Reconditioners [*See also FIRM*] [*Paris, France*] (EAIO)

IFER.......... International Foundation for Ethical Research (EA)

IFERS........ International Flat Earth Research Society (EA)

IFES.......... Image Feature Extraction System [*Air Force*]

IFES.......... International Fellowship of Evangelical Students (EA)

IFES.......... International Foundation for Electoral Systems (EA)

IFESLG........ International Fellowship of Evangelical Students Link Group (EA)

IFeT.......... Intestinal Iron (Ferrum) Transport [*Physiology*]

IFEW.......... Inter-American Federation of Entertainment Workers

IFf.......... Frankfort Public Library District, Frankfort, IL [*Library symbol Library of Congress*] (LCLS)

IFF.......... Identification, Friend or Foe [*Military*]

IFF.......... If and Only If (IEEE)

IFF.......... Iffley [*Australia Airport symbol Obsolete*] (OAG)

IFF.......... Individual Freedom Federation (EA)

IFF.......... Induced Fluid Flow

IFF.......... Industrial Funding Fee (AAGC)

IFF.......... Inert Fluid Fill (AAG)

IFF.......... Institute for the Future

IFF.......... Institute of Freight Forwarders [*British*]

IFF.......... Institute of Natural Resources, Springfield, IL [*OCLC symbol*] (OCLC)

IFF.......... Intensity Fluctuation Factor [*Telecommunications*] (TEL)

IFF.......... Interchange File Format [*Computer science*]

IFF.......... Interfreight Forwarding Ltd. [*Sudan*] [*ICAO designator*] (FAAC)

IFF.......... International Federal Film [*Fictitious organization of agents in TV series "Scarecrow and Mrs. King"*]

IFF.......... International Federation of Falerists (EA)

IFF.......... International Fencing Federation [*Paris, France*] (EA)

IFF.......... International Film Foundation

IFF.......... International Flavors & Fragrances, Inc. [*NYSE symbol*] (SPSG)

IFF.......... International Flying Farmers (EA)

IFF.......... International Forum Foundation

IFF.......... International Freedom Foundation (EA)

IFF.......... Ionized Flow Field

IFF.......... Iran Freedom Foundation (EA)

IFF.......... Isoelectric Focusing Facility

IFF.......... Item Intelligence File [*DoD*]

IFFA.......... Independent Federation of Flight Attendants (EA)

IFFA.......... Interactive Flash Flood Analyzer

IFFA.......... International Federation of Film Archives

IFFA.......... International Fly Fishing Association (EAIO)

IFFA.......... International Frozen Food Association (EA)

IFFAA......... Inland Fish Farming Association of Australia

IFF/ATCRBS... Identification Friend or Foe/Air-Traffic Control RADAR Beacon System [*Military*]

IFFC.......... Integrated Flight and Fire Control

IFFCS........ International Fancy Food and Confection Show (ITD)

IFFEC........ International Federation of Free Evangelical Churches (EA)

IFFEX........ International Frozen Food Exhibition and Congress

IFFF.......... Internationale Frauenliga fuer Frieden und Freiheit [*Women's International League for Peace and Freedom*]

IFFH.......... International Federation for Family Health [*Bandung, Indonesia*] (EA)

IFFIT.......... International Facility for Food Irradiation Technology [*Netherlands*] (WND)

IFFJ.......... International Federation of Free Journalists [*British*]

IFFJP......... International Federation of Fruit Juice Producers [*See also FIJU*] [*Paris, France*] (EAIO)

IFFLP......... International Federation for Family Life Promotion (EA)

IFFN.......... Identification, Friend or Foe or Neutral (MCD)

IFFPA........ International Federation of Film Producers' Associations

IFFS.......... Identification, Friend or Foe, Switching Circuit [*Military*] (MSA)

IFFS.......... Intermediate Future Forecasting System [*Department of Energy*] (GFGA)

IFFS.......... International Federation of Fertility Societies (EAIO)

IFFS.......... International Federation of Film Societies

IFFSA......... Inflight Food Service Association (EA)

IFFSH........ Instrument Formation Flight System for Helicopters

IFF/SIF....... Identification, Friend or Foe/Selective Identification Feature [*Military*]

IFFT.......... Inverse Fast Fourier Transform (IAA)

IFFTU......... International Federation of Free Teachers' Unions [*See also SPIE*] [*Amsterdam, Netherlands*] (EAIO)

IFFU.......... Identification, Friend or Foe Unit (MCD)

IFF-UK....... International Freedom Foundation - United Kingdom Branch (EAIO)

IFG.......... Inferior Frontal Gyrus [*Brain anatomy*]

IFG.......... Inland Fisher Guide [*General Motors Corp.*]

IFG.......... Institute for Research on Educational Finance and Governance [*Department of Education*] (GRD)

IFG.......... Instream Flow Service Group [*United States Fish and Wildlife Service*]

IFG.......... International Fashion Group [*Later, Fashion Group International*] (EA)

IFG.............. Inter-Regional Financial Group, Inc. [*NYSE symbol*] (SPSG)
IFG.............. Inter-Regional Fin. Gr. [*NYSE symbol*] (TTSB)
IFG.............. Kaskaskia Library System, Smithton, IL [*OCLC symbol*] (OCLC)
IFGA.......... International Fancy Guppy Association (EA)
IFGA.......... International Federation of Grocers' Associations [*See also IVLD*] [*Bern, Switzerland*] (EAIO)
IFGAE........ International Federation for Gerda Alexander Eutony [*Belgium*] (EAIO)
IFGB.......... Institute of Chartered Foresters [*British*]
IFGE.......... International Foundation for Gender Education (EA)
IFGL.......... Initial File Generation Language
IFGMA .... International Federation of Grocery Manufacturers Associations (EA)
IFGO.......... International Federation of Gynecology and Obstetrics
IFGS.......... International Fantasy Gaming Society (EA)
IFGVP .... International Federation of Gastronomical and Vinicultural Press
IFH.......... Industrial Facilities Handbook [*A publication*] (AAGC)
IFH.......... In-Flight Helium
IFH.......... Internationale Foderation des Handwerks [*International Federation of Master-Craftsmen - IFMC*] [*Vienna, Austria*] (EAIO)
IFH.......... International Foundation for Homeopathy (EA)
IFH.......... Judson College Library, Elgin, IL [*OCLC symbol*] (OCLC)
IFHBT.......... International Federation of Health and Beauty Therapists
IFHE.......... International Federation for Home Economics [*See also FIEF*] [*Paris, France*] (EAIO)
IFHE.......... International Federation of Hospital Engineering (PDAA)
IFHG.......... Institute of Family History and Genealogy (EA)
IFhGS.......... Grant-Illini School 110, Fairview Heights, IL [*Library symbol Library of Congress*] (LCLS)
IFhGSD .... Grant Community Consolidated School District 110, Fairview Heights, IL [*Library symbol Library of Congress*] (LCLS)
IFHOH.......... International Federation of the Hard of Hearing [*Kampen, Netherlands*] (EAIO)
IFHOL.......... If Holding [*Aviation*] (FAAC)
IFHP.......... International Federation for Housing and Planning [*Netherlands*]
IFHP.......... International Federation of Health Professionals (EA)
IFHPM.......... International Federation of Hydraulic Platform Manufacturers [*Later, IPAF*] (EAIO)
IFHPMSM .... International Foundation for Hygiene, Preventative Medicine, Social Medicine (BABM)
IFhPSD .... Pontiac-William Holliday School District 105, Fairview Heights, IL [*Library symbol Library of Congress*] (LCLS)
IFHPSM .... International Federation for Hygiene, Preventive, and Social Medicine [*France*] (EAIO)
IFHRO.......... International Federation of Health Records Organizations [*Munich, Federal Republic of Germany*] (EAIO)
IFHS.......... Irish Family History Society (EA)
IFHTM.......... International Federation for the Heat Treatment of Materials (PDAA)
IFHTP.......... International Federation for Housing and Town Planning
IFI.......... Immune Interferon (DMAA)
IFI.......... Imperial Forestry Institute [*British*] (BI)
IFI.......... Industrial Fasteners Institute (EA)
IFI.......... Infisy Systems, Inc. [*Vancouver Stock Exchange symbol*]
IFI.......... In-Flight Insertion (NG)
IFI.......... Information for Industry Inc. (NITA)
IFI.......... Inter-Freight International [*Steamship*] (MHDB)
IFI.......... International Fabricare Institute (EA)
IFI.......... International Federation of Interior Architects/Interior Designers [*Amsterdam, Netherlands*] (EAIO)
IFI.......... International Feedstuffs Institute [*Utah State University*] [*Research center Defunct*] (RCD)
IFI.......... International Film Institute
IFI.......... International Financial Institution
IFI.......... International Foundation for Independence (EA)
IFI.......... International Fund for Ireland [*United States, Canada, and New Zealand*]
IFI.......... Italian for Idiots [*Facetious travel terminology*]
IFI.......... Kingfisher, OK [*Location identifier FAA*] (FAAL)
IFI.......... Sidley & Austin, Chicago, IL [*OCLC symbol*] (OCLC)
IFIA.......... Intermountain Forest Industry Association (EA)
IFIA.......... International Federation of Inventors' Associations [*Stockholm, Sweden*] (EAIO)
IFIA.......... International Federation of Ironmongers and Iron Merchants Associations [*See also FIDAQ*] [*Zurich, Switzerland*] (EAIO)
IFIA.......... International Fence Industry Association (EA)
IFIA.......... International Financial Institutions Act [*1977*]
IFIAS.......... International Federation of Institutes for Advanced Study [*ICSU*] [*Toronto, ON*] (EAIO)
IFIAT.......... International Federation of Independent Air Transport
IFIC.......... International Ferrocement Information Center [*Asian Institute of Technology*] (IID)
IFIC.......... International Food Information Council (EA)
IFICB.......... International Finance Investment and Commerce Bank Ltd. [*Bangladesh*] (EY)
IFICO .... Industrial Finance and Investment Corp. [*British*]
IFICS.......... In-Flight Interceptor Communications System [*Military*]
IFID.......... International Federation for Information and Documentation [*See also FIID*] (EAIO)
IFIDA.......... Independent Film Importers and Distributors of America [*Defunct*] (EA)
IFIEC.......... International Federation of Industrial Energy Consumers [*Geneva, Switzerland*] (EA)
I (field).......... Information Field (NITA)
IFIF.......... International Federation for Internal Freedom [*Later, Castalia Foundation*] (EA)

IFIF.............. International Federation of Industrial Organizations and General Workers' Unions
IFIFR.......... International Federation of International Furniture Removers [*See also FIDI*] [*Brussels, Belgium*] (EAIO)
IFIJG.......... International Federation of Infantile and Juvenile Gynecology [*See also FIGIJ*] [*Sierre, Switzerland*] (EAIO)
IFILE.......... Interface File (NITA)
IFIM.......... International Flight Information Manual
IFIN.......... Investors Financial Services Corp. [*NASDAQ symbol*] (SAG)
IFIN.......... Investors Finl Svcs [*NASDAQ symbol*] (TTSB)
IFINS.......... If Instrument Conditions Encountered [*Aviation*] (FAAC)
IFIO.......... Information for Industry Office [*Air Force*] (MCD)
IFIP.......... International Federation for Information Processing [*Formerly, IFIPS*] (EA)
IFIP.......... International Food Irradiation Project [*Food and Agricultural Organization*] (PDAA)
IFIPS.......... International Federation of Information Processing Societies [*Later, IFIP*]
IFIRA.......... Information Facility for Indigenous Resources for Australia
IFIS.......... Industry File Index System [*Chemical Information Systems, Inc.*] [*Information service or system*] (CRD)
IFIS.......... Infrared Flight Inspection System (IAA)
IFIS.......... Instrument Flight Instructors School [*Navy*]
IFIS.......... Integrated Flight Instrument System
IFIS.......... International Financial Intelligence Service (NITA)
IFIS.......... International Food Information Service [*Database producer*] [*Germany*]
IFISRR.......... International Federation of Institutes for Socio-Religious Research [*Louvain, Belgium*] (EA)
IFIWA.......... International Federation of Importers and Wholesale Grocers Associations [*The Hague, Netherlands*] (EAIO)
IFJ.......... Franklin-Johnson County Public Library, Franklin, IN [*OCLC symbol*] (OCLC)
IFJ.......... International Federation of Journalists [*See also FIJ*] [*Brussels, Belgium*] (EAIO)
IFJ.......... Isafjordur [*Iceland*] [*Airport symbol*] (OAG)
IFJ.......... Winnfield, LA [*Location identifier FAA*] (FAAL)
IFK.......... Installations Fragenkommission [*Later, International Commission on Rules for the Approval of Electrical Equipment*] [*CEE*]
IFK.......... Interfunk & Co. [*Yugoslavia*] [*ICAO designator*] (FAAC)
IFK.......... River Bend Library System, Coal Valley, IL [*OCLC symbol*] (OCLC)
IFKC.......... International Federation of Kennel Clubs (EA)
IFKM.......... Internationale Foederation fuer Kurzschrift und Maschinenschreiben [*International Federation of Shorthand and Typewriting*]
IFKT.......... International Federation of Knitting Technologists [*See also FITB*] [*Frauenfeld, Switzerland*] (EAIO)
IFL.......... Flora Carnegie Library, Flora, IL [*Library symbol Library of Congress*] (LCLS)
IFL.......... Icelandic Federation of Labor
IFL.......... Imperial Fascist League [*British*]
IFL.......... Induction Field Locator (IAA)
IFL.......... Inflatable (MSA)
IFL.......... Initial Flight Level
IFL.......... Innisfail [*Australia Airport symbol*]
IFL.......... Integer Function Language [*Computer science*] (PDAA)
IFL.......... Integrated Fuse Logic (NITA)
IFL.......... Intelligent Fault Locator [*McDonnell Douglas Helicopter Co.*] [*Army*]
IFL.......... Intelligent Forms Language [*Delrina Corp.*] [*Computer science*] (PCM)
IFL.......... Interfacility Link (LAIN)
IFL.......... International Frequency List (NATG)
IFL.......... International Friendship League [*Defunct*] (EA)
IFLA.......... International Federation of Landscape Architects [*Versailles, France*] (EAIO)
IFLA.......... International Federation of Library Associations (NITA)
IFLA.......... International Federation of Library Associations and Institutions
IFLA.......... International Finance and Leasing Association (MHDB)
IFLASC.......... International Federation of Latin American Study Centers [*Mexico City, Mexico*] (EAIO)
IFLB.......... Islamic Front for the Liberation of Bahrain [*Political party*] (PD)
IFLBP.......... International Federation of the Little Brothers of the Poor [*See also FIPFP*] (EAIO)
IFLC.......... International Frequency List Committee
IFICL.......... Cumberland Trail Library System, Flora, IL [*Library symbol Library of Congress*] (LCLS)
IFL-DFL........ Inflating-Deflating
IFLG.......... International Federation of Leather Guilds (EA)
IFLIPS.......... Integrated Flight Prediction System [*Aviation*] (DA)
IFLN.......... Interstate Freeze Lobbying Network (EA)
IFlo.......... Flossmoor Public Library, Flossmoor, IL [*Library symbol Library of Congress*] (LCLS)
IFLO.......... IFlow Corp. [*NASDAQ symbol*] (SAG)
IFLO.......... I-Flow Corp. [*NASDAQ symbol*] (TTSB)
IFLO.......... Islamic Front for Liberation of Oromo [*Ethiopia*] [*Political party*] (EY)
IFLOT.......... Intermediate Focal Length Optical Tracker
I-Flow.......... IFlow Corp. [*Associated Press*] (SAG)
IFLOWS .... Integrated Flood Observing and Warning System [*National Oceanic and Atmospheric Administration*]
IFLrA.......... Recombinant Human Leukocyte Interferon A [*Pharmacology*] (DAVI)
IFL Rev.......... International Financial Law Review [*A publication*] (DLA)
IFLRY.......... International Federation of Liberal and Radical Youth (EAIO)
IFLS.......... International Federation of Law Students (DLA)
IFLS.......... International Federation of Little Singers (EAIO)
IFLTT.......... Intermediate Focal Length Tracking Telescope (MUGU)
IFLWU .... International Fur and Leather Workers Union (MHDB)

IFM............	Improved Frequency Modulation (MCD)
IFM............	In-Flight Maintenance
IFM............	Instantaneous Frequency Measurement
IFM............	Institute of Fisheries Management [British]
IFM............	Instrument Flag Motor
IFM............	Integrating Fluctuation Meter
IFM............	Interactive File Manager [Computer science]
IFM............	Interfacial-Force Microscope
IFM............	Intermediate Frame Memory [Computer science]
IFM............	Internal Fetal Monitor [Medicine] (DMAA)
IFM............	International Falcon Movement
IFM............	International Finance Managers Study [Database] [Research Services Ltd.] [Information service or system] (CRD)
IFM............	International Financial Markets Trading Ltd.
IFM............	International Fund for Monuments
IFM............	Intrafusal Muscle [Anatomy]
IFM............	Iowa Farm-to-Market Carriers Tariff Bureau, Ottumwa IA [STAC]
IFM............	Tifton, GA [Location identifier FAA] (FAAL)
IFMA..........	Immunofluorescence [or Immunofluorometric] Assay [Also, IFA] [Analytical biochemistry]
IFMA..........	Immunofluorometric Assay [Analytical biochemistry]
IFMA..........	Independent Furniture Manufacturers' Associaiton [British] (DBA)
IFMA..........	Interdenominational Foreign Mission Association of North America (EA)
IFMA..........	International Facility Management Association (EA)
IFMA..........	International Farm Management Association [Reading, Berkshire, England] (EAIO)
IFMA..........	International Federation of Margarine Associations [Brussels, Belgium] (EAIO)
IFMA..........	International Foodservice Manufacturers Association (EA)
IFMA..........	Irish Flour Millers Association (BI)
IFMBE........	International Federation for Medical and Biological Engineering [ICSU] [Ottawa, ON] (EA)
IFMC..........	International Federation of Master-Craftsmen (EA)
IFMC..........	International Federation of Motorhome Clubs [Belgium] (EAIO)
IFMC..........	International Folk Music Council [Later, ICTM]
IFME..........	International Federation for Medical Electronics
IFME..........	International Federation of Municipal Engineers [See also FIIM] [British] (EAIO)
IF/MF........	Intermediate Frequency/Medium Frequency (NATG)
IFMIS........	Implementation Field Microfilm/Micrographics Information System
IFMIS........	Industrial Facilities and Material Information System
IFMIS........	Integrated Facilities Management Information System
IFML..........	International Film Management Ltd. [Australia]
IFMM..........	International Federation of Manual Medicine (EA)
IFMO..........	Imperial and Foreign Money Orders
IFMOD........	Interactive Forecasting Model (GFGA)
IFMP..........	International Federation for Medical Psychotherapy [See also IGAP] [Oslo, Norway] (EAIO)
IFMP..........	International Federation of Maritime Philately [Livorno, Italy] (EAIO)
IFMP..........	International Federation of Married Priests
IFMPO........	Integrated Farm Management Program Option [Department of Agriculture]
IFMS..........	Impact Force Measuring System
IFMS..........	In-Flight Management System
IFMS..........	Integrated Farm Management System
IFMS..........	Integrated Financial Management System (AABC)
IFMS..........	Interagency Fleet Management System (AAGC)
IFMS..........	Interagency Fleet Management System [GSA] (TAG)
IFMS..........	International Federation of Magical Societies [See also FISM] (EAIO)
IFMSA........	International Federation of Medical Students Associations [See also FIAEM] [Vienna, Austria] (EA)
IFM-SEI......	International Falcon Movement - Socialist Educational International
IFMSS.........	International Federation of Multiple Sclerosis Societies [British] (EAIO)
IFMX..........	Informix Corp. [NASDAQ symbol] (NQ)
IFN............	India Fund [NYSE symbol] (TTSB)
IFN............	India Fund, Inc. [NYSE symbol] (SAG)
IFN............	Information [Computer science] (MDG)
IFN............	Interferon [Also, IF] [Biochemistry]
IFN............	Interferon (DOG)
IFN............	International Feminist Network
IFN............	International Friends of Nature [See also NFI] [Zurich, Switzerland] (EAIO)
IFN............	Isfahan [Iran] [Airport symbol] (OAG)
IFN............	Items for Negotiation
IFNA..........	International Federation of Netball Associations [Glasgow, Scotland] (EAIO)
IFNA..........	International FidoNet Association [Defunct] (EA)
IFNA..........	International Flying Nurses Association (EA)
IFNC..........	Integrated Flight Control/Navigation Computer (MCD)
IFNE..........	International Federation for Narcotic Education
IFNG..........	Interferon Gamma [Medicine] (DMAA)
IFNP..........	International Federation of Newspaper Publishers (NTCM)
IFNs..........	Interferons [Biology] (DOG)
IFNS..........	Irish Family Names Society (EA)
IFNY..........	Infinity, Inc. [NASDAQ symbol] (SAG)
IFO............	Identified Flying Object [Air Force]
IFO............	Improved Fiber Optics
IFO............	Information Systems Office [NASA] (NASA)
IFO............	Info-Stop Communications [Vancouver Stock Exchange symbol]
IFO............	In Front Of (WDAA)
IFO............	International Fortran Organization (NITA)
IFOA..........	Isotta Fraschini Owner's Association [Defunct] (EA)
IFOAD.........	International Federation of Original Art Diffusors [France] (EAIO)

IFOAM.........	International Federation of Organic Agriculture Movements [Witzenhausen, Federal Republic of Germany] (EA)
IFOB..........	Improved Fiber Optics Bundle
IFOBRL........	In-Flight Operable Bomb Rack Lock (MCD)
IFOC..........	Intermountain Field Operations Center [Bureau of Mines] [Denver, CO] (GRD)
IFOCUS........	Interprofessional Fostering of Ophthalmic Care for Underserved Sectors [An association] (EA)
IFOFSAG......	International Fellowship of Former Scouts and Guides [Brussels, Belgium]
IFOG..........	Interferometric Fiber Optic Gyroscope
IFOMA.........	Independent Fuel Oil Marketers of America [Defunct] (EA)
IFOMA.........	Instructions for Mailers [A publication]
IFop............	Forest Park Public Library, Forest Park, IL [Library symbol Library of Congress] (LCLS)
IFOP..........	Institut Francais d'Opinion Publique [French Institute of Public Opinion]
IFOPA.........	International Fibrodysplasia Ossificans Progressiva Association (EA)
IFOR..........	Intelligent Forces [Army] (RDA)
IFOR..........	Interactive FORTRAN [Formula Translating System] [Computer science] (IAA)
IFOR..........	Internal Format Object Report (MCD)
IFOR..........	International Federation of Operation Research Societies (BARN)
IFOR..........	International Fellowship of Reconciliation [Alkmaar, Netherlands] (EA)
IFORD.........	Institut de Formation et de Recherche Demographiques [Institute for Training and Demographic Research - ITDR] (EAIO)
IFORO.........	Interphone (Service F) Resumed Operation [Aviation] (FAAC)
IFORS........	International Federation of Operational Research Societies [ICSU] [Lyngby, Denmark] (EAIO)
IFORVU........	International Federation of Recreational Vehicle Users [Later, FOR] (EA)
IFOS..........	International Federation of Ophthalmological Societies [Nijmegen, Netherlands] (EA)
IFOS..........	International Federation of Oto-Rhino-Laryngological Societies [Berchem, Belgium] (EAIO)
IFOS..........	Ion Formation from Organic Solids [International conference]
IFOSS.........	Intelligence Family of Systems Study [Military] (MCD)
IFOT..........	In-Flight Operations and Training (MCD)
IFOTES........	International Federation of Telephonic Emergency Services [Jorn, Sweden] (EA)
IFOV..........	Individual Field of View
IFOV..........	Instantaneous Field of View
IFOV..........	Instrument Field of View
IFP............	Illinois Functional Programming Language [Computer science]
IFP............	Imperial and Foreign Post (IAA)
IFP............	Independent Feature Project (EA)
IFP............	Indexes of Firepower Potential
IFP............	Inflammatory Fibroid Polyp [Gastroenterology]
IFP............	In-Flight Performance
IFP............	In Forma Pauperis [As a Pauper] [Latin]
IFP............	Inkatha Freedom Party [Afrikaans Political party] (ECON)
IFP............	Institute of Fluid Power
IFP............	Institute of Physical Problems [Former USSR] (MCD)
IFP............	Institut Francais du Petroles [French Institute of Petroleum] [Paris]
IFP............	Instruction Fetch Pipeline [Computer science]
IFP............	Integrated File Processor
IFP............	Intermediate Filament Protein (DMAA)
IFP............	International Federation of Pedestrians (EA)
IFP............	International Federation of Purchasing
IFP............	International Fixed Public
IFP............	International Forest Products Ltd. [Toronto Stock Exchange symbol Vancouver Stock Exchange symbol]
IFP............	Interns for Peace (EA)
IFP............	Intrapatellar Fat Pad (DMAA)
IFP............	Invitation for Proposal (NOAA)
IFPA..........	Independent Film Producers of America (NTCM)
IFPA..........	Independent Fluorspar Producers Association (EA)
IFPA..........	Independent Free Papers of America (EA)
IFPA..........	Industrial Fire Protection Association of Great Britain
IFPA..........	Information Film Producers of America [Later, Association of Visual Communicators] (EA)
IFPA..........	Institute for Foreign Policy Analysis, Inc. [Tufts University] [Research center] (RCD)
IFPA..........	International Federation of Photographic Art
IFPA..........	International Federation of Psoriasis Associations [Stockholm, Sweden] (EAIO)
IFPA..........	International Fighter Pilots Academy [Slovak Air Force]
IFPA..........	International Fire Photographers Association (EA)
IFPA..........	Isoelectric Focusing in Polyacrylamide [Gel] [Analytical chemistry]
IFPAAW.......	International Federation of Plantation, Agricultural, and Allied Workers [Switzerland]
IFPC..........	Integrated Flight and Propulsion Control (MCD)
IFPCA.........	International Federation of Press Cutting Agencies (EA)
IFPCS.........	International Federation of Unions of Employees in Public and Civil Services
IFPCW........	International Federation of Petroleum and Chemical Workers (EA)
IFPD..........	International Federation of Postcard Dealers (EA)
IFPDA.........	International Fine Print Dealers Association
IFPE..........	Institute of Fiscal and Political Education [Defunct] (EA)
IFPE..........	International Federation for Parent Education [See also FIEP] [Sevres, France] (EAIO)
IFPEC.........	Independent Film Producers Export Corp. [Defunct]
IFPFP.........	Individual Flight Plans from This Point [Aviation] (FAAC)
IFPI..........	International Federation of the Phonographic Industry (EAIO)

IFPI	International Federation of the Photographic Industry
IFPL	In-Flight Power Loss (MCD)
IFPL/SD	In-Flight Power Loss/Shutdown (MCD)
IFPM	In-Flight Performance Monitor
IFPM	International Federation of Physical Medicine
IFPMA	International Federation of Pharmaceutical Manufacturers Associations [See also FIIM] [Geneva, Switzerland] (EAIO)
IFPMM	International Federation of Purchasing and Materials Management [Aarau, Switzerland] (EAIO)
IFPMO	International Federation of Psychological-Medical Organizations [See also FIOPM] [Lausanne, Switzerland] (EAIO)
IFPMR	International Federation of Physical Medicine and Rehabilitation (EA)
IFPNT	International Federation of Practitioners of Natural Therapeutics [British]
IFPO	Institute of Fire Prevention Officers [British] (DBA)
IFPO	International Foundation for Protection Officers (EA)
IFPO	International Freelance Photographers Organization
IFPP	Imperial and Foreign Parcel Post (IAA)
IFPP	Industrial Facilities Protection Program [DoD]
IFPP	Industrial Fugitive Process Particulate (GNE)
IFPP	Irradiated Fuel Processing Plant (DEN)
IFPRA	Interamerican Federation of Public Relations Associations
IFPRA	International Family Planning Research Association [Later, ISRM] (EA)
IFPRA	International Federation of Park and Recreation Administration [Reading, England] (EAIO)
IFPRI	International Fine Particle Research Institute
IFPRI	International Food Policy Research Institute (EA)
IFPS	In-Flight Performance Signal [Aviation] (IAA)
IFPS	Integrated Initial Flight Plan Processing System [Aviation] (DA)
IFPS	Interactive Financial Planning System [Harris Systems Ltd.] [Software package] (NCC)
IFPS	International Federation of Palynological Societies (EAIO)
IFPS	International Federation of Philosophical Societies [See also FISP] [Fribourg, Switzerland] (EAIO)
IFPS	International Federation of Popular Sports [See also IVV] (EAIO)
IFPS	International Federation of Psychoanalytic Societies (EA)
IFPSM	International Federation for Preventive and Social Medicine (EAIO)
IFPTE	International Federation of Professional and Technical Engineers (EA)
IFPTO	International Federation of Popular Travel Organisations [Paris, France] (EAIO)
IFPTS	Intertype Fototronic Photographic System (DIT)
IFPV	International Federation of Pelota Vasca (EA)
IFPVP	International Federation of Phonogram and Videogram Producers (EA)
IFPW	International Federation of Petroleum Workers
IFPWA	International Federation of Protestant Workers' Associations
IFPWA	International Federation of Public Warehousing Associations [Formerly, IFPWKA] (EAIO)
IFPWKA	International Federation of Public Warehouse Keepers Associations [Later, IFPWA] (EAIO)
IFQ	Invitation for Quote (MCD)
IFR	Ifrane [Morocco] [Seismograph station code, US Geological Survey] (SEIS)
IFR	IFR Systems, Inc. [Associated Press] (SAG)
IFR	Image-to-Frame Ratio
IFR	Immediate Free Recall (PDAA)
IFR	Imported Food Regulations [British]
IFR	Impulse Fast Reactor [Former USSR]
IFR	Increasing Failure Rate
IFR	Incremental Financial Rate of Return
IFR	Indian Foodgrain Requirements [British]
IFR	In-Flight Refueling
IFR	In-Frame Response [Automotive engineering Electronics]
IFR	Infrared
IFR	Infrared Filter Radiometer
IFR	Inspiratory Flow Rate [Physiology]
IFR	Instantaneous Frequency [Indicating] Receivers (IEEE)
IFR	Institute of Fisheries Research [University of North Carolina]
IFR	Institute of Food Research [British]
IFR	Institut Federatif de Recherche [Federal Research Institute] [France]
IFR	Instituts Federatifs de Recherche [France]
IFR	Instrument Flight Recovery [NASA]
IFR	Instrument Flight Rules [Aviation]
IFR	Insufficient Data For Reporting (WDMC)
IFR	Integral Fast Reactor [Nuclear energy]
IFR	Interface Register
IFR	Interim Final Rule [RSPA] (TAG)
IFR	Intermediate Frequency Range (MCD)
IFR	Internal Function Register
IFR	Internationaler Frauenrat [International Council of Women]
IFR	International Fighter RADAR
IFR	International Film Representatives [Division of International Film Completion Corp.]
IFR	International Financing Review [A publication]
IFR	International Flyer Resources Ltd. [Vancouver Stock Exchange symbol]
IFR	Interrupt Flag Register [Computer science] (IAA)
IFR	Isolated Flow Responder [Physiology]
IFRA	INCA [International Newspaper Color Association]-FIEJ Research Association [Federation Internationale des Editeurs de Journaux] [Research center Germany] (IRC)
IFRA/SD	Increasing Failure Rate Average [Statistics]
IFRA	Independent Fabric Retailers Association [Defunct] (EA)

IFRA	Independent Footwear Retailers Association [British] (DBA)
IFRA	Indirect Fluorescent Rabies Antibody Test [Immunology] (MAE)
IFRA	Infrasonics, Inc. [NASDAQ symbol] (NQ)
IFRA	International Family Recreation Association (EA)
IFRA	International Foundation for Research in the Field of Advertising
IFRA	International Fragrance Association [Geneva, Switzerland] (EAIO)
IFRA	International Fund-Raising Association (EA)
IFRAA	Interfaith Forum on Religion, Art, and Architecture (EA)
IFRAC	Imported Food Risks Advisory Committee [Australia]
IFRAC	International Federation of Railway Advertising Companies [British] (EA)
IFRB	International Frequency Registration Board [ITU] [United Nations]
IFRC	Inland Forest Resource Council (EA)
IFRC	Instantaneous Frequency Correlation (NG)
IFRC	International Federation of Roofing Contractors [See also IFD] (EAIO)
IFRC	International Ford Retractable Club (EA)
IFRC	International Futures Research Conference (PDAA)
IFRCC	International Fight'n Rooster Cutlery Club (EA)
IFRD	International Federation of Retail Distributors (EAIO)
IFRE	Institute for Family Research and Education [Defunct] (EA)
IFREMER	Institut Francais de Recherche pour l'Exploitation de la Mer [French Research Institute for Ocean Utilization] [Research center] (IID)
IFREQ	Industrial Forecast Requirements (DNAB)
IFRF	International Federation of Resistance Fighters (BJA)
IFrHS	Freeburg Community High School 77, Freeburg, IL [Library symbol Library of Congress] (LCLS)
IFRI	International Fund-Raising Institute [Later, IFRA]
IFRIP	Institut Francais de Recherche et de Technologie Polaires [Public interest group] [French Southern and Antarctic Territories] (EY)
IFRIS	Intelligence Finished Reports Information Subsystem [Computer science]
IFRM	International Federation of Resistance Movements [Vienna, Austria] (EA)
IFRM	International Federation of the Rights of Man (EA)
IFRO	Internal Feed Rate Override
IFRP	International Fertility Research Program [Later, FHI]
IFRRO	International Federation of Reproductive Rights Organisations (AIE)
IFRS	IFR Systems [NASDAQ symbol] (TTSB)
IFRS	IFR Systems, Inc. [NASDAQ symbol] (NQ)
IFRS	Individuals for a Rational Society [Defunct] (EA)
IFRT	Intellectual Freedom Round Table [American Library Association]
IFRT	Internal Floating Roof Tank [Engineering]
IFRT	Involved Field Radiotherapy [Medicine] (DMAA)
IFRTA	International Federation of Railwaymen's Travel Associations (EA)
IFRU	In-Flight Replaceable Unit (KSC)
IFRU	Interference Frequency Rejection Unit [Military]
i-fs--	French Southern and Antarctic Lands [MARC geographic area code Library of Congress] (LCCP)
IFS	Identification, Friend or Foe, Switching Circuit [Military]
IFS	Inactivated Fetal-Calf Serum [Immunology]
IFS	In-Band Framing System [Simulation Laboratories, Inc.]
IFS	Increased Forward Stocking [Military] (DNAB)
IFS	Independent Front Suspension [Automotive engineering]
IFS	Indian Forest Service [British]
IFS	In-Flight Safety
IFS	Inflight Survey [USTTA] (TAG)
IFS	Information Flow Standards (KSC)
IFS	Infrared Frequency Synthesis
IFS	Inshore Fire Support Ship [Later, LFR]
IFS	Insignia Financial Group [NYSE symbol] (SAG)
IFS	Insignia Financial Grp'A' [NYSE symbol] (TTSB)
IFS	Installable File System [Computer science]
IFS	Institute for Fiscal Studies [British]
IFS	Institute of Financial Services [Australia]
IFS	Institute of Flight Structures [Columbia University]
IFS	Instructions for Service
IFS	Instrument Flight Simulator (MCD)
IFS	Integrated Facilities System [Army]
IFS	Integrated Flight System
IFS	Intelligent File Store [British]
IFS	Interactive File Sharing
IFS	Interactive Flow Simulator (TEL)
IFS	Interchange File Separator [Computer science] (BUR)
IFS	Interface Specification
IFS	Intermediate Frequency Strip
IFS	Internal Focus Sensor (PDAA)
IFS	International Federation of Settlements and Neighbourhood Centers (EAIO)
IFS	International Federation of Surveyors [See also FIG] (EAIO)
IFS	International Film Seminars (EA)
IFS	International Flying Services SRL [Italy ICAO designator] (FAAC)
IFS	International Focus Resources, Inc. [Vancouver Stock Exchange symbol]
IFS	International Foundation for Science [See also FIS] [ICSU Stockholm, Sweden] (EAIO)
IFS	International Foundation for Stutterers (EA)
IFS	International Frankenstein Society (EA)
IFS	Internationella Forsuringssekretariatet [International Secretariat on Acid Rain] [Sweden] (EAIO)
IFS	Interrelated Flow Simulation
IFS	Interstitial Fluid Space [Medicine] (DMAA)
IFS	Investment Feasibility Studies (TEL)
IFS	Ionospheric Forward Scatter (TEL)
IFS	Irish Free State [Later, Republic of Ireland]

IFS.......... Iron Fortified Common Salt [*Nutrition*]
IFS.......... Iterated Function System [*Computer science*] (BYTE)
IFSA.......... Instock Footwear Suppliers Association [*British*] (DBA)
IFSA.......... International Federation of Scoliosis Associations (EA)
IFSA.......... International Federation of Sports Acrobatics [*Sofia, Bulgaria*] (EAIO)
IFSA.......... International Fuzzy Systems Association (EA)
IFSA.......... Intumescent Fire Seals Association [*British*] (DBA)
IFSAL.......... Integral Frequency Scan Approach and Landing
IFSAR.......... Interferometric Synthetic Aperture RADAR (RDA)
IFSAS.......... Interim Fire Support Automation System [*Army*] (DOMA)
IFSAT.......... International Financial Services and Technology Exhibition [*British*]
IFSB.......... Independence Federal Savings Bank [*NASDAQ symbol*] (NQ)
IFSB.......... Independence Fed Svgs Bk [*NASDAQ symbol*] (TTSB)
IFSB.......... International Flying Saucer Bureau [*Defunct*]
IFSBAC.......... Institute for Folklore Studies in Britain and Canada
IFSC.......... Interferon Sciences [*NASDAQ symbol*] (TTSB)
IFSC.......... Interferon Sciences, Inc. [*NASDAQ symbol*] (NQ)
IFSC.......... International Federation of Surgical Colleges [*Dublin, Republic of Ireland*] (EAIO)
IFSC.......... Introduction to the Federal Supply Catalog System
IFSCC.......... International Federation of Societies of Cosmetic Chemists [*Luton, England*] (EAIO)
IFSCS.......... International Federation of the Societies of Classical Studies (EA)
IFSD.......... Inflight Shutdown (MCD)
IFSDA.......... International Federation of Stamp Dealers' Associations (EA)
IFSDP.......... International Federation of the Socialist and Democratic Press [*Milan, Italy*] (EAIO)
IFSEA.......... International Federation of Scientific Editors' Associations (EA)
IFSEA.......... International Food Service Executive's Association (EA)
IFSEC.......... International Fire and Security Exhibition and Conference [*British*] (ITD)
IFSECN.......... International Federation of Societies for Electroencephalography and Clinical Neurophysiology [*Amsterdam, Netherlands*] (EA)
IFSED.......... Initial Full-Scale Engineering Development
IFSEM.......... International Federation of Societies for Electron Microscopy (EA)
IFSF.......... Investment Feasibility Study Facility [*United Nations Development Programme*] [*Ghana*]
IFSF.......... Irradiated Fuels Storage Facility [*National Reactor Testing Station*]
IFSH.......... International Federation of Sound Hunters (EA)
IFSHC.......... International Federation of Societies for Histochemistry and Cytochemistry (EAIO)
IFSHJ.......... International Federation for Secular Humanistic Judaism (EA)
IFSI.......... Interface, Inc. [*NASDAQ symbol*] (NQ)
IFSIA.......... Interface Inc.'A' [*NASDAQ symbol*] (TTSB)
IF-SICMA.......... Insular Force - Special Initial Clothing Monetary Allowance [*Military*] (DNAB)
IFSIS.......... Iterated Function System-Image Synthesizer [*Computer science*] (BYTE)
IFSIT.......... In-Flight Safety Inhibit Test
IFSL.......... Indiana Federal [*NASDAQ symbol*] (TTSB)
IFSL.......... Indiana Federal Corp. [*NASDAQ symbol*] (NQ)
IFSL.......... Industrial Fire Safety Library [*National Fire Protection Association*]
IFSM.......... International Federation of Sports Medicine (EA)
IFSMA.......... International Federation of Shipmasters Associations [*See also FIAPN*] (EAIO)
IFSMTF.......... International Fusion Superconducting Magnet Test Facility [*Oak Ridge National Laboratory*]
IFSNC.......... International Federation of Settlements and Neighbourhood Centres [*Defunct*]
IFSO.......... International Federation of Sanitarians Organizations [*Defunct*] (EA)
IFSOT.......... Irradiated Fused Silica Open Tubular [*Column for chromatography*]
IFSP.......... Individualized Family Service Plan [*Required under the Individuals with Disabilities Education Act (IDEA)*] (PAZ)
IFSP.......... International Federation of Societies of Philosophy
IFSPO.......... International Federation of Senior Police Officers (EA)
IFSPS.......... International Federation of Students in Political Sciences
IFSR.......... International Federation for Systems Research (EAIO)
IFSRC.......... Independent Family Schools Resource Center (EA)
IFSRC.......... International Financial Services Research Center [*Massachusetts Institute of Technology*] [*Research center*] (RCD)
IFSS.......... If Signal Source (MCD)
IFSS.......... Index of Federal Specifications and Standards
IFSS.......... Inertia Fuel Shutoff Switch [*Automotive engineering*]
IFSS.......... Instrument Flight Safety System (MUGU)
IFSS.......... International Federation of Sleddog Sports (EA)
IFSS.......... International Fertilizer Supply Scheme [*FAO*] [*United Nations*]
IFSS.......... International Flight Service Station [*FAA*]
IFSSEC.......... International Fire, Security and Safety Exhibition and Conference (PDAA)
IFSSH.......... International Federation of Societies for Surgery of the Hand (EA)
IFSSO.......... International Federation of Social Science Organizations [*See also FIOSS*] [*Copenhagen, Denmark*] (EAIO)
IFST.......... Institute of Food Science and Technology of the United Kingdom
IFST.......... International Federation of Shorthand and Typewriting
IFSTA.......... International Fire Service Training Association (EA)
IFSTAD.......... Islamic Foundation for Science, Technology, and Development (BARN)
IFSTD.......... Interim Fund for Science and Technology for Development [*International Council of Scientific Unions*]
IFSTD.......... Islamic Foundation for Science, Technology and Development [*Saudi Arabia*] (PDAA)
IFSTM.......... International Federation of Sewing Thread Manufacturers (EA)
IFSW.......... International Federation of Social Workers [*Switzerland*]
IFSWA.......... International Figure Skating Writers Association [*Defunct*]
IFT.......... Immunofluorescence Test [*Immunology*]
IFT.......... Income Opportunities Fd 2000 [*NYSE symbol*] (TTSB)
IFT.......... Income Opportunities Fund 2000 [*NYSE symbol*] (SPSG)
IFT.......... Indexed, Folioed, and Titled [*Publishing*] (DGA)
IFT.......... Industrial Field Trip (DOMA)
IFT.......... In-Flight Test [*Air Force*]
IFT.......... Inland Fisheries Trust, Inc. [*Republic of Ireland*] (BI)
IFT.......... Innovative Feasibility Test
IFT.......... Input Frequency Tolerance [*Computer science*]
IFT.......... Instantaneous Field Tube [*Astrophysics*]
IFT.......... Instantaneous Fourier Transform [*Computer science*]
IFT.......... Institute of Family Therapy [*British*] (DBA)
IFT.......... Institute of Food Technologists (EA)
IFT.......... Instructor-Flown Advisory Target
IFT.......... Instrument Flight Trainer (MCD)
IFT.......... Interface Tool (MCD)
IFT.......... Interfacial Tension [*Physical chemistry*]
IFT.......... Interfacial Test
IFT.......... Interflight [*British ICAO designator*] (FAAC)
IFT.......... Intermediate Frequency Transformer
IFT.......... International Federation of Translators [*See also FIT*] [*Ghent, Belgium*] (EAIO)
IFT.......... International Foundation for Telemetering (EA)
IFT.......... International Foundation for Timesharing (EA)
IFT.......... International Frequency Tables
IFT.......... Io Flux Tube [*Cosmology*]
IFT.......... Ion Focusing Technique
IFT.......... Isolation Functional Testing (PDAA)
IFTA.......... In-Flight Thrust Augmentation
IFTA.......... In-Flight Training Aid
IFTA.......... International Federation of Teachers' Associations [*Later, WCOTP*] (EAIO)
IFTA.......... International Federation of Television Archives [*See also FIAT*] [*Madrid, Spain*] (EAIO)
IFTA.......... International Federation of Thanatologists Associations [*Saint-Ouen, France*] (EA)
IFTA.......... International Free Trade Area
IFTA.......... International Fuel Tax Agreement [*FHWA*] (TAG)
IFTAC.......... Inter-American Federation of Touring and Automobile Clubs [*See also FITAC*] (EAIO)
IF TACCA.......... Intermediate Frequency Time Averaged Clutter Coherent Airborne [*RADAR*] (DNAB)
IF TACCAR.......... Intermediate Frequency Time Averaged Clutter Coherent Airborne RADAR (NG)
IFTAD.......... Initial and Final Terminal Arrival Date [*Army*] (AABC)
IFTBCS.......... International Federation of the Temperance Blue Cross Societies [*Later, IBC*] (EA)
IFTC.......... International Federation of Thermalism and Climatism [*Bad Ragaz, Switzerland*] (EA)
IFTC.......... International Film and Television Council [*Rome, Italy*]
IFTC.......... International Fox-Tango Club [*Defunct*] (EA)
IFTDO.......... International Federation of Training and Development Organizations (EA)
IFTE.......... Integrated Family of Test Equipment [*Army*] (RDA)
IFTE.......... Intermediate Forward Test Equipment
IFTEX.......... International Flower Trades Exhibition [*British*] (ITD)
IFTF.......... Institute for the Future [*Research center Telecommunications*] (RCD)
IFTF.......... Inter-Faith Task Force (EA)
IFTF.......... International Federation of Teachers of French [*See also FIPF*] [*Sevres, France*] (EAIO)
IFTF.......... International Fur Trade Federation [*British*] (EAIO)
IFTI.......... Ionic Fuel Technology [*NASDAQ symbol*] (TTSB)
IFTI.......... Ionic Fuel Technology, Inc. [*NASDAQ symbol*] (SAG)
IFTIW.......... Ionic Fuel Technology Wrrt'A' [*NASDAQ symbol*] (TTSB)
IFTIZ.......... Ionic Fuel Technology Wrrt'B' [*NASDAQ symbol*] (TTSB)
IFTL.......... Institute for Friendship through Learning (EA)
IFTM.......... In-Flight Test and Maintenance (KSC)
IFTM.......... Inverse Fourier Transform Module [*An enzyme*] (MCD)
IFTO.......... International Federation of Tour Operators [*Lewes, East Sussex, England*] (EAIO)
IFTOA.......... Independent Fuel Terminal Operators' Association
IFToMM.......... International Federation for the Theory of Machines and Mechanisms [*Warsaw, Poland*] (EAIO)
IFTPNDC.......... Institute on the Federal Theatre Project and New Deal Culture [*George Mason University*] [*Research center*] (RCD)
IFTPP.......... International Federation of the Technical and Periodical Press (DIT)
IFTR.......... International Federation for Theatre Research [*British*] (EAIO)
IFTR.......... International Federation of Teachers of Rhythmics (EA)
IFTR.......... International Foundation for Theatrical Research (EA)
IFTRS.......... Individual Flying Time Report System [*Military*] (DNAB)
IFTS.......... In-Flight Test System
IFTS.......... International Federation of Teratology Societies (EA)
IFTS.......... Irradiated Fuel Transfer System [*Nuclear energy*] (NRCH)
IFTSSS.......... In-Flight Test System Scan Select (IAA)
IFTU.......... International Federation of Teachers' Unions
IFTU.......... International Federation of Trade Unions
IFTU.......... Iraq Federation of Trade Unions
IFTUTW.......... International Federation of Trade Unions of Transport Workers [*See also FIOST*] [*Brussels, Belgium*] (EAIO)
IFTW.......... International Federation of Tobacco Workers
IFTWA.......... International Federation of Textile Workers' Associations
IFTwA.......... International Federation of Tiddlywinks Associations (EA)
IFU.......... Inflatable Ward Unit (SAA)
IFU.......... Infusion-Forming Units [*Medicine*]
IFU.......... Instruction Fetch Unit [*Computer science*]
IFU.......... Integrated Fluorescence Unit [*Image formation*]

IFU	Intelligence Field Unit [Navy]
I/FU	Interface Unit [Computer science] (NASA)
IFU	Interferon Unit [Medicine] (DMAA)
IFUN	If Unable [Aviation] (FAAC)
IF/USA	Interfurnishings USA (TSPED)
IFUW	International Federation of University Women (EA)
IFV	Igniter-Fuel Valve (KSC)
IFV	Infantry Fighting Vehicle
IFV	Instantaneous Field of View (DNAB)
IFV	Internationaler Faustball-Verband (EAIO)
IFV	Intracellular Fluid Volume [Physiology]
IFVA	Independent Film and Video Makers' Association [British]
IFVC	International Federation for Victory over Communism
IF-VCA	Immunofluorescence-Viral Capsid Antigen [Clinical chemistry]
IFVH	Indian Field Veterinary Hospital [British military] (DMA)
IFVHSF	Federation of Health Funds - International [International Federation of Voluntary Health Service Funds] [Later, FHF] [Acronym is based on former name,] (EAIO)
IFVLS	If Flight Visibility Becomes Less Than [Aviation] (FAAC)
IFVM	Intermediate Frequency Video Microwave (MCD)
IFVME	Inspectorate of Fighting Vehicles and Mechanical Equipment [Military]
IFVPA	Independent Film, Video, and Photographers Association [British] (DBA)
IFVR	If Visibility Remains [Aviation] (FAAC)
IFVTCC	Internationale Foederation der Vereine der Textilchemiker und Coloristen [International Federation of Associations of Textile Chemists and Colorists] (EAIO)
IFW	International Federation of Wargaming [Defunct] (EA)
IFWA	International Federation for Weeks of Art
IFWC	Integrated Flight/Weapons Controls (MCD)
IFWEA	International Federation of Workers' Educational Associations [See also IVB] [Tel Aviv, Israel] (EAIO)
IFWG	Interface Working Group [NASA] (SSD)
IFWHA	International Federation of Women's Hockey Associations
IFWJ	Indian Federation of Working Journalists
IFWL	International Federation of Women Lawyers (EA)
IFWRI	Institute of the Furniture Warehousing and Removing Industry (EAIO)
IFWS	International Federation of Wines and Spirits [See also FIVS] (EAIO)
IFWSTI	International Federation of Wines and Spirits, Trade, and Industry (EA)
IFWTO	International Federation of Women's Travel Organizations (EA)
IFWTWA	International Food, Wine, and Travel Writers Association (EAIO)
IFX	Immunofixation [Clinical chemistry]
IFY	Independent Fission Yield
IFYC	International Federation of Young Cooperators
IFYE	International Farm Youth Exchange
IFYGL	International Field Year for the Great Lakes
IG	Alisarda [ICAO designator] (AD)
IG	ALISARDA SpA [Italy ICAO designator] (ICDA)
IG	Galesburg Public Library, Galesburg, IL [Library symbol Library of Congress] (LCLS)
IG	IGI, Inc. [AMEX symbol] (SPSG)
IG	Igloo [Spacelab Pallet Missions]
IG	Ignitor [Electron device] (MSA)
IG	Illawarra Greens [Political party Australia]
IG	Illustrators Guild [Later, GA] (EA)
IG	Image Generator (MCD)
IG	Immature Granule (DMAA)
IG	Immune Globulin
Ig	Immunoglobulin [Immunology]
IG	Immunology [Medical specialty] (DHSM)
iG	Immunoreactive Gastrin [Medicine] (MEDA)
IG	Imperial Gallon
IG	Impulse Generator (IAA)
IG	Index of Gravity [Engineering]
IG	Indicator Group (MCD)
I/G	Individual/Group (ACRL)
IG	Indo-Germanic [Language, etc.]
IG	Industrial Grade
IG	Industriegewerkschaft [Industrial Trade Union] [Germany]
IG	Inertial Guidance
IG	Inertial Gyroscope
IG	Ingot (DNAB)
IG	In-Ground (ADA)
IG	Inner Gimbal
IG	Inner Guard [Freemasonry]
IG	Inscriptiones Graecae [Epigraphic notation]
IG	Inside Guardian [Freemasonry] (ROG)
IG	Inspection Gauge (MCD)
IG	Inspector General [Air Force, Army, Marine Corps]
IG	[Office of the] Inspector General
IG	Instantaneous Grid (IAA)
IG	Institute of Geophysics [Later, IGPP] [University of California] (MCD)
IG	Institute of Groundsmanship (EA)
IG	Institution of Geologists (EAIO)
IG	Instruction [or Instructor] Guide
IG	Instructor in Gunnery [Military British]
IG	Instrumentation Group
IG	Instrument Ground (NASA)
IG	Insulated Gate (DEN)
IG	Insulin and Glucose [Medicine] (DMAA)
IG	Integrated Genetics
IG	Intelligence Generator
IG	Intendant-General

IG	Interagency Group [Federal government]
IG	Interconnect Group (CAAL)
IG	Interdepartmental Group [DoD]
IG	Interest Group
IG	Inter-Gas System
IG	Intergranular [Metallurgy]
IG	Inter-Granular (MCD)
IG	Internal Guidance (NASA)
IG	Internationale Kunstgilde [International Art Guild - IAG] (EAIO)
IG	International General (EA)
IG	International Graphics [Formerly, IGI] (EA)
IG	International Guides' Club (EAIO)
IG	Intestinal Groove
IG	Intragastric
IG	Inverse Gain (NVT)
IG	Inverse Gaussian [Statistics]
IG	Investment Grant [British]
IG	Iris Guide (PDAA)
IG	Irish Guards [Military unit]
IG	Irritable Gut [Medicine] (DMAA)
IG	Irvine Group [An association] (EA)
IG	Izmenyaemaya Geometriya [Variable Geometry] [Suffix letters on Soviet combat aircraft]
IGA	Dallas Public Library, Dallas, TX [OCLC symbol] (OCLC)
IGA	Great Inagua Island [Bahamas] [Airport symbol] (AD)
IgA	Human Immunoglobulin A (DOG)
IgA	Immunoglobulin A [Immunology]
IGA	Inagua [Bahamas] [Airport symbol] (OAG)
IGA	Independent Grocers Alliance Distributing Co. [Facetious translation: "I Get Attention"] (EA)
IGA	Industry and General Applications (MCD)
IGA	Infantile Genetic Agranulocytosis [Medicine] (DMAA)
IGA	Inhaled Gas Analyzer
IGA	Inner Gimbal Angle (NASA)
IGA	Inner Gimbal Assembly
IGA	Inner Gimbal Axis
IGA	Inscriptiones Graecae Antiquissimae (BJA)
IGA	Integrated Grant Administration
IGA	Integrating Gyro Accelerometer
IGA	Intergranular Attack [Nuclear energy] (NRCH)
IGA	International Galdos Association (EA)
IGA	International Gamers Association (EA)
IGA	International Gay Association - International Association of Lesbians/Gay Women and Gay Men (EAIO)
IGA	International General Aviation
IGA	International Geneva Association (EA)
IGA	International Geographical Association [Esperantist]
IGA	International Glaucoma Association (EAIO)
IGA	International Golf Association (EA)
IGA	International Graduate Achievement [Defunct] (EA)
IGA	International Grains Arrangement
IGA	International Green Alliance (EA)
IGA	Interstate Gambling Activities
IGA	Ion Gun Assembly
IGA	Irish Gas Association (BI)
IGAA	Intermountain Graphic Arts Association (DGA)
IGAAS	Integrated Ground/Airborne Avionics System (MCD)
IGAB	International Group of Agents and Bureaus (EA)
IGAC	International Global Atmospheric Chemistry [Project] (USDC)
IGAC	International Global Atmospheric Chemistry Program [Marine science] (OSRA)
IGACS	Integrated Guidance and Control System [Aerospace]
IGaDC	Illinois State Department of Conservation, Division of Parks and Memorials, Galena, IL [Library symbol Library of Congress] (LCLS)
IGADD	Intergovernmental Authority on Drought and Development [Djibouti] (EY)
IGAE	Intergovernmental Agreement on the Environment [Australia]
IGAEA	International Graphic Arts Education Association (EA)
IGAeM	Internationale Gesellschaft fuer Aerosole in der Medizin [International Society for Aerosols in Medicine - ISAeM] (EAIO)
IGAF	Intergovernmental Affairs Fellowship Program [Military] (MCD)
IgAIC	Immunoglobulin A Immune Complex [Immunochemistry]
IGal	Galva Township Library, Galva, IL [Library symbol Library of Congress] (LCLS)
IGAM	Internationale Gesellschaft fuer Allgemeinmedizin [International Society of General Medicine]
IGAM	International Game Technology (MHDW)
IgAN	Immunoglobulin A Nephropathy [Nephrology]
IG & GA	International Grooving and Grinding Association (EA)
IGAP	Institute for Grassland and Animal Production [Research center British] (IRC)
IGAP	Internationale Gesellschaft fuer Arztliche Psychotherapie [International Federation for Medical Psychotherapy - IFMP] [Oslo, Norway] (EAIO)
IGARSS	International Geoscience and Remote Sensing Symposium (MCD)
IGAS	Inspection Generale des Affaires Sociales [France]
IGAS	Inspection Generale des Affaires Sociales [General Inspection of Social Aff airs] [France]
IGAS	Interactive General Accounting System (MHDB)
IGAS	International General Assembly of Spiritualists [Later, LDTF] (EA)
IGAS	International Graphic Arts Society (EA)
IGAS	International Graphoanalysis Society (EA)
IGAUP	Interceptor Generation and Umpiring Program (SAA)
IGAX	Inner Gimbal Axis (NASA)

IGB............ Columbus, MS [*Location identifier FAA*] (FAAL)
IGB............ Illicit Gold Buyer [*or Buying*]
IGB............ Inlet Gear Box (MCD)
IGB............ Intercontinental Glide Bomber [*Unmanned*]
IGB............ Interference Guard Bands
IGB............ Inter-German Border (MCD)
IGB............ Intermediate Gearbox (DA)
IGB............ Internationaler Genossenschaftsbund [*International Cooperative Alliance*]
IGB............ Internationales Gewerkschafts Buro [*International Trades Union Office*]
IGB............ International Gravimetric Bureau [*Toulouse, France*] (EAIO)
IGB............ Israelitisches Gemeindeblatt [*Muelheim/Koeln*] [*A publication*] (BJA)
IGB............ National College of Education, Evanston, IL [*OCLC symbol*] (OCLC)
IGBC.......... Interagency Grizzly Bear Committee [*Forest Service*] [*Missoula, MT*] (EGAO)
IGBD.......... Impotent Grain Boundary Dislocation
IGBE.......... International Gold Bullion Exchange [*Bankrupt investment firm*]
IGBP.......... International Geosphere-Biosphere Program [*ICSU*] [*Proposed for 1992*]
IGBP.......... International Geosphere-Biosphere Programme [*Australia*]
IGBP-DIS..... Data and Information System [*Marine science*] (OSRA)
IGBS.......... International Gas Bearings Symposium (PDAA)
IGBST........ Interagency Grizzly Bear Study Team [*Montana State University*] [*Bozeman, MT*] (EGAO)
IGBT.......... Isolated Gate Bipolar Transistor [*Electronics*]
IGC............ Goshen College, Goshen, IN [*OCLC symbol*] (OCLC)
IGC............ Inspector-General of Communications [*British military*] (DMA)
IGC............ Institute for Global Communications (EA)
IGC............ Institute for Global Communications [*Internet*]
IGC............ Institute for Graphic Communication [*Defunct*] (EA)
IGC............ Intellectually Gifted Children
IGC............ Intelligence Graphics Controller [*Computer science*]
IGC............ Intergovernmental Committee on Refugees [*Post-World War II*] (DLA)
IGC............ Inter-Governmental Conference [*European Union*] (ECON)
IGC............ Inter-Governmental Conference
IGC............ Inter-Governmental Conferences [*European Community*]
IGC............ Intergovernmental Copyright Committee [*See also CIDA*] [*Paris, France*] (EAIO)
IGC............ Intergranular Corrosion (PDAA)
IGC............ Intermagnetics General Corp.
IGC............ Internal Gain Control (IAA)
IGC............ International Garden Club (EA)
IGC............ International Geological Congress
IGC............ International Geophysical Committee [*Also, CIG*]
IGC............ International Geophysical Cooperation [*World Meteorological Organization*]
IGC............ International Glaucoma Congress (EA)
IGC............ International Grassland Congress
IGC............ International Guides' Club (EAIO)
IGC............ Interstate General Ltd. [*AMEX symbol*] (SPSG)
IGC............ Interstate Genl L.P. [*AMEX symbol*] (TTSB)
IGC............ Inter-Union Geodynamics Commission [*Also, ICG*] (MSC)
IGC............ Inverse Gas Chromatography
IGC............ Ion Gun Collector
IGC............ Irish Goods Council (ACII)
IGC............ Isothermal Gas Chromatography
IGCA.......... Innovative Gaming Corp. [*NASDAQ symbol*] (SAG)
IGCA.......... Innovative Gaming Corp. Amer [*NASDAQ symbol*] (TTSB)
IGCA.......... International Guild of Candle Artisans (EA)
IGCA.......... Italian Greyhound Club of America (EA)
IGCBT........ Interagency Group for Computer-Based Training [*Later, IGITT*] (EA)
IGCC.......... Institute on Global Conflict and Cooperation [*University of California, Berkeley*]
IGCC.......... Insulating Glass Certification Council (EA)
IGCC.......... Integrated Gasification-Combined Cycle [*Chemical engineering*]
IGCC.......... Interagency Geothermal Coordinating Council
IGCC.......... Intergovernmental Copyright Committee [*See also CIDA*]
IGCC.......... Intergovernmental Panel on Climate Change [*World Meteorological Organization*]
IGCE.......... Independent Government Cost Estimate [*Army*]
IGCG.......... Inertial Guidance and Calibration Group [*Air Force*]
IGCI.......... Industrial Gas Cleaning Institute (EA)
IGCJAP....... International Guild of Craft Journalists, Authors, and Photographers [*Inactive*] (EA)
IGCO.......... International Genealogy Consumer Organization (EA)
IGCP.......... Intelligence Guidance for COMINT [*Communications Intelligence*] Programming (MCD)
IGCP.......... International Geological Correlation Programme [*See also PICG*] [*ICSU Paris, France*] (EAIO)
IGCPK........ Industrie Gewerkschaft Chemie, Papier, und Keramik [*West German union*]
IGCR.......... Intergovernmental Committee on Refugees [*Post-World War II*]
IGCS.......... Imperial Glass Collectors Society (EA)
IGCS.......... Integrated Guidance and Control System [*Aerospace*] (AAG)
IGCSE........ International General Certificate of Secondary Education (AIE)
IG-CUFMG ... Instituto de Geociencias Universidade Federal de Minas Gerais
IGD............ Illicit Gold Dealer
IgD............ Immunoglobulin D [*Immunology*]
IGD............ Indian Gold Resources Ltd. [*Vancouver Stock Exchange symbol*]
IGD............ Inspector General Division [*Environmental Protection Agency*] (GFGA)
IGD............ Inspector General's Department
IGD............ Institute of Grocery Distribution Ltd. [*British*]
IGD............ Interaction Graphics Display

IGD .... Interactive Grafics Digitizer [*Computer science*]
IGD .... Irma Graphics for DOS [*Digital Operation System*] [*DCA, Inc.*]
IGDM .... Infant of Gestational Diabetic Mother [*Obstetrics*]
IGDMR .... Initial Gross Depot Maintenance Requirement [*Military*]
IGDO .... International Guild of Opticians [*International Guild of Dispensing Optic ians*] [*Acronym is based on former name,*] (EAIO)
IGDOD .... Inspector General, Department of Defense (USGC)
IGDR .... Interim Geophysical Data Record [*From spacecraft data*]
IGDS .... Integrated Graduate Development Scheme [*British*]
IGDS .... Interactive Graphics Design System (MCD)
IGDS .... Interactive Graphics Display Systems [*Computer monitor*] [*Military*]
IGDS .... Iodine Generating and Dispensing System (NASA)
IGE .... Iguela [*Gabon*] [*Airport symbol Obsolete*] (OAG)
IgE .... Immunoglobulin E [*Immunology*]
IGE .... Impaired Gas Exchange (DMAA)
IGE .... Independent Government Estimate (MCD)
IGE .... Individually Guided Education [*for upgrading students' skills*]
IGE .... In-Ground Effect [*Aviation*] (NG)
IGE .... Institution of Gas Engineers [*British*] (DAS)
IGE .... Instrumentation Ground Equipment (MCD)
IGE .... International Geographics [*Vancouver Stock Exchange symbol*]
IGE .... International Geophysical Extension
IGE .... International Guiding Eyes (EA)
IGEB .... Intergency Global Positioning System Executive Board
IGEIEPSI ..... International Group for the Exchange of Information and Experience Among Postal Savings Institutions [*Geneva, Switzerland*] (EAIO)
IGEMS .... Interactive Generalized Modeling System (PDAA)
IGEN .... Current Source (MSA)
IGEN .... IGEN, Inc. [*NASDAQ symbol*] (SAG)
IGenD .... DuPage Library System, Geneva, IL [*Library symbol Library of Congress*] (LCLS)
IGeo .... Georgetown Public Library, Georgetown, IL [*Library symbol Library of Congress*] (LCLS)
IGeoSD .... Georgetown Community Unit School District, Georgetown, IL [*Library symbol*] [*Library of Congress*] (LCLS)
IGER .... Institute of Grassland and Environmental Research [*British*]
IGERT .... Integrating Graduate Education and Research Training [*National Science Foundation*]
IGES .... Initial Graphics Exchange Specification [*or System*] [*National Standards Institute*]
IGES .... International Graphics Exchange Specification [*Computer science*]
IGES .... International Graphics Exchange Standard (NITA)
IGES/PDES ... Initial Graphics Exchange Specification/Product Definition Exchange Specification
IGESUCO..... International Ground Environment Subcommittee [*NATO*]
IGF............ Fondation Internationale pour la Sauvegarde du Gibier [*International Foundation for the Conservation of Game*] (EAIO)
IGF............ IGF Metals, Inc. [*Vancouver Stock Exchange symbol*]
IGF............ Image Generation Facility (MCD)
IGF............ India Growth Fund [*NYSE symbol*] (TTSB)
IGF............ India Growth Fund, Inc. [*NYSE symbol*] (CTT)
IGF............ Inspector-General of Fortifications [*British*]
IGF............ Insulin Gene Family
IGF............ Insulin-Like Growth Factor
IGF............ International Genetics Federation [*See also FIG*] [*England*] (EA)
IGF............ International Graphical Federation [*See also FGI*] [*Berne, Switzerland*] (EAIO)
IGF............ International Gymnastic Federation [*See also FIG*] (EAIO)
IGF............ Irish Genealogical Foundation (EA)
IGF............ Island Games Foundation [*Canada*] (EAIO)
IGF-1 .... Insulin-Like Growth Factor-1
IGFA.......... Inspector General, Foreign Assistance [*Department of State*]
IGFA.......... Interessen Gemeinschaft der Farbenindustrie Aktiengesellschaft [*A dye trust*] [*Germany*]
IGFA.......... International Game Fish Association (EA)
IGFA.......... Isaac Garrison Family Association (EA)
IGFBP........ Insulin-Like Growth Factor Binding Protein [*Biochemistry*]
IGFES........ Interactive Graphics Finite Element System (RDA)
IGFET........ Insulated-Gate Field-Effect Transistor [*Electronics*]
IGFET........ Isolated-Gate Field-Effect Transistor [*Electronics*]
IGFL.......... Integral Green Fluorescence (DMAA)
IGFM.......... Internal Gamma Flux Monitor
IGFM.......... Internationale Gesellschaft fuer Menschenrechte [*International Society for Human Rights - ISHR*] (EA)
IGFO .... Inspector General Field Office [*Military*]
IGFOV........ Instantaneous Geometric Field of View
IGFPIL........ International Grotius Foundation for the Propagation of International Law
IGFR .... Insulin-Like Growth Factor Receptor (DMAA)
IGFR .... International Genealogical Fellowship of Rotarians (EA)
IGFS .... International Gem Finders Society
IGFVP .... Interservice Group for Flight Vehicle Power [*Military*]
IGG............ Igiugig [*Alaska*] [*Airport symbol*] (OAG)
IgG............ Immunoglobulin G [*Immunology*]
IGG............ Inert Gas Generator
IGG............ Internationale Gesellschaft fuer Geschichtsdidaktik [*International Society for History Didactics*] (EAIO)
IG-GCI........ International Geological-Geophysical Cruise Inventory [*Marine science*] (OSRA)
IGGDA........ International G. G. Drayton Association (EA)
IGGI.......... Inter-Governmental Group for Indonesia [*Defunct*]
IgGIC........ Immunoglobulin G Immune Complex [*Immunochemistry*]
IGGT .... Institute for Guided Ground Transport [*Canada*] (PDAA)
IGH............ Icy Grain Halo [*Model of comet structure*]
IGH............ Idiopathic Growth Hormone [*Medicine*] (MAE)

IgH .... Immunoglobulin Heavy Chain [*Biochemistry*]
IGH .... Immunoreactive Growth Hormone [*Immunology*] (MAE)
IGH .... Ingham [*Australia Airport symbol*]
IGH .... International Guild of Hypnotists (EA)
IGHAT .... Integrated Gasification Humid Air Turbine [*Chemical engineering*]
IGHD .... Isolated Growth Hormone Deficiency [*Medicine*]
IGHIA .... International Garden Horticultural Industry Association (EA)
IGHMHS ...... Inventory of General Hospital Mental Health Services [*Department of Health and Human Services*] (GFGA)
IGI .... IGI, Inc. [*Associated Press*] (SAG)
IGI .... Industrial Graphics International [*Later, IG*] [*An association*] (EA)
IGI .... Industrial Guest Investigator [*NASA*]
IGI .... Information Gatekeepers, Inc. [*Telecommunications Information service or system*] (IID)
IGI .... Information General, Inc. [*Information service or system*] (IID)
IGI .... Inner Grid Injection
IGI .... Institutional Goals Inventory [*Test*]
IGI .... Interlocked Grain Index [*Botany*]
IGI .... International Gallery Invitational (ITD)
IGI .... International Genealogical Index [*A publication Australia*]
IGI .... International Graphics, Inc. [*Defunct*] (EA)
IGI .... International Wallcovering Manufacturers Association [*Belgium*] (EAIO)
IGI .... Investigative Group International
IGI .... Investors Group, Inc. [*Toronto Stock Exchange symbol*]
IGIA .... Interagency Group on International Aviation
IGib .... Moyer Library, Gibson City, IL [*Library symbol Library of Congress*] (LCLS)
IGibH .... Gibson Community Hospital, Gibson City, IL [*Library symbol Library of Congress*] (LCLS)
IGibSD .... Gibson City Community Unit School District, Gibson City, IL [*Library symbol*] [*Library of Congress*] (LCLS)
IGIC .... International Gay Information Center [*Defunct*] (EA)
IGlcB .... Chicago Botanic Gardens, Glencoe, IL [*Library symbol*] [*Library of Congress*] (LCLS)
IGIER .... Innocenzo Gasparini Institute for Economic Research
IGIF .... Interferon Gamma-Inducing Factor [*Biochemistry*]
IGIF .... International Geographic Information Foundation
IGil .... Douglas Township Library, Gilman, IL [*Library symbol Library of Congress*] (LCLS)
IGill .... Gillespie Public Library, Gillespie, IL [*Library symbol Library of Congress*] (LCLS)
IGillMCD ...... Macoupin Community District 7, Gillespie, IL [*Library symbol Library of Congress*] (LCLS)
IGinseng ...... Imprial Ginseng Products Ltd. [*Associated Press*] (SAG)
IGIP .... Internationale Gesellschaft fuer Ingenieurpaedagogik [*International Society for Engineering Education*] (EAIO)
IGIPAS .... Interagency Group on International Programs in Atmospheric Science
IGir .... Girard Township Library, Girard, IL [*Library symbol Library of Congress*] (LCLS)
IGirMCD ...... Macoupin Community District 3, Girard, IL [*Library symbol Library of Congress*] (LCLS)
IGIS .... Intelligent Geographic System [*Computer science*]
IGITT .... Interagency Group for Interactive Training Technologies (EA)
IGIV .... Immune Globulin, Intravenous (CPH)
IGIW .... Indices of General Industrial Worth
IGK .... Infanteriegeschuetz - Kompanie [*Infantry Howitzer Co.*] [*German military - World War II*]
IGK .... Knox College, Galesburg, IL [*Library symbol Library of Congress*] (LCLS)
IGKB .... Internationale Gewasserschutz Kommission fur den Bodensee [*International Commission for the Protection of Lake Constance*] (EA)
IGKG .... Internationale Gesellschaft fuer Kiefer- und Gesichtschirurgie [*International Association for Maxillo-Facial Surgery*] (EAIO)
IGL .... Ideal Gas Law
IGL .... Igloolik [*Northwest Territories*] [*Seismograph station code, US Geological Survey*] (SEIS)
IGL .... IMC Global [*NYSE symbol*] (TTSB)
IGL .... IMC Global, Inc. [*Formerly, IMC Fertilizer Group*] [*NYSE symbol*] (SAG)
IGL .... Index Guided LASER (IAA)
IGL .... Information Grouping Logic [*Computer science*]
IGL .... Infrared Gunfire Locator
IGL .... Interactive Graphics Language
IGL .... Intergeniculate Leaflet [*Anatomy*]
IGL .... Internal Granule Layer [*Cytology*]
IGL .... Internationale Gesellschaft fuer Lymphologie [*International Society of Lymphology*] (EAIO)
IGL .... Ionized Gas LASER
IGL .... Izmir [*Turkey*] Cigli Airport [*Airport symbol*] (OAG)
IGlc .... Glencoe Public Library, Glencoe, IL [*Library symbol Library of Congress*] (LCLS)
IGlca .... Glen Carbon Library, Glen Carbon, IL [*Library symbol Library of Congress*] (LCLS)
IGLD .... International Great Lakes Datum
IGle .... Glen Ellyn Public Library, Glen Ellyn, IL [*Library symbol Library of Congress*] (LCLS)
IGleD .... College of Du Page, Glen Ellyn, IL [*Library symbol Library of Congress*] (LCLS)
IGleM .... Maryknoll Seminary, Glen Ellyn, IL [*Library symbol Library of Congress*] (LCLS)
IGLHRC ...... International Gay and Lesbian Human Rights Commission (EA)
IGLM .... Limnos [*Greece*] [*ICAO location identifier*] (ICLI)

IGIN .... United States Naval Training Center, Great Lakes, IL [*Library symbol Library of Congress*] (LCLS)
IGLOSS .... Integrated Global Ocean Station System [*Surrey, England*] [*See also IGOSS UNESCO*]
IGlvK .... Kraftco Corp., Research and Development Library, Glenview, IL [*Library symbol Library of Congress*] (LCLS)
IGlvK-L .... Kraft, Inc., Law Library, Glenview, IL [*Library symbol*] [*Library of Congress*] (LCLS)
IGlw .... Glenwood Public Library District, Glenwood, IL [*Library symbol Library of Congress*] (LCLS)
IGM .... I Got Mine [*Slang describing attitude of some nouveaux riches*]
IgM .... Immunoglobulin M [*Immunology*]
IgM .... Immunoglobulin Macro [*Also known as RF*] [*Immunology*]
IGM .... Inertial Guidance Mode
IGM .... Interactive Guidance Mode (NASA)
IGM .... Intergalactic Medium
IGM .... Internationale Gesellschaft fuer Menschenrechte [*International Society for Human Rights - ISHR*] (EAIO)
IGM .... International Grail Movement (EA)
IGM .... Interplanetary Global Model [*Marine science*] (OSRA)
IGM .... Interplanetary Global Model (USDC)
IGM .... Irma Graphics for Macintosh [*DCA, Inc.*]
IGM .... ISDN [*Integrated Services Digital Network*] Gateway Module [*Telecommunications*]
IGM .... Iterative Guidance Mode [*NASA*]
IGM .... Kingman [*Arizona*] [*Airport symbol*] (OAG)
IGMA .... International Guild of Miniature Artisans (EA)
IGMC .... Independent Gasoline Marketers Council [*Defunct*] (EA)
IGMCA .... Imperial German Military Collector's Association (EA)
IGMF .... Inertial Guidance Maintenance Facility (IAA)
IGMF .... Intergalactic Magnetic Fields
IGMG .... Institute of Geriatric Medicine and Gerontology [*British*]
IGMG .... Internationale Gustav Mahler Gesellschaft [*International Gustav Mahler Society*] (EA)
IgMIC .... Immunoglobulin M Immune Complex [*Immunochemistry*]
IGMP .... Internet Group Management Protocol [*Computer science*]
IGMP .... Internet Group Management Protocol [*Computer science*] (PCM)
IgM-RF .... Immunoglobulin M - Rheumatoid Factor [*Medicine*]
IGMT .... Impingement [*Engineering*]
IGN .... Ignition (KSC)
IGN .... Ignition
IGN .... Ignitron [*Electronics*]
IGN .... Ignorant
IGN .... Ignotus [*Unknown*] [*Latin*]
IGN .... Iligan [*Philippines*] [*Airport symbol*] (OAG)
IGN .... International-Great Northern [*AAR code*]
IGN .... Kingston, NY [*Location identifier FAA*] (FAAL)
IGNC .... International Good Neighbor Council [*See also CIBV*] [*Monterrey, Mexico*] (EAIO)
IgND .... Immunoglobulin ND [*Immunology, provisional class*]
IGNDET .... Ignition Detector
IGNET .... Inspector General Network [*Military*] (GFGA)
IGNR .... Igniter
IGNS .... Interactive Graphics Network System (MCD)
IGNTR .... Igniter (MSA)
IGO .... Chigorodo [*Colombia*] [*Airport symbol*] (OAG)
IGO .... Inspector General's Office [*Air Force*]
IGO .... Intergovernmental Organization [*Generic term*]
IGO .... Investment Grant Office [*British*]
IGOA .... Independent Garage Owners of America [*Later, Automotive Service Councils*] (EA)
IGoL .... Lewis and Clark Community College, Godfrey, IL [*Library symbol Library of Congress*] (LCLS)
IGOM .... Integrated Global Ocean Monitoring [*Marine science*] (OSRA)
IGoM .... Monticello College, Godfrey, IL [*Library symbol Library of Congress*] (LCLS)
IGOR .... Instrument Ground Optical Recording
IGOR .... Interactive Guidance on Routes [*FHWA*] (TAG)
IGOR .... Intercept Ground Optical Recorder [*NASA*]
IGORTT .... Intercept Ground Optical Recorder Tracking Telescope [*NASA*]
IGOS .... Inward Grade of Service (DNAB)
IGOSS .... Industry/Government Open Systems Specification (ACRL)
IGOSS .... Integrated Global Ocean Services System [*Marine science*] (OSRA)
IGOSS .... Integrated Global Ocean Station System [*See also IGLOSS*] [*UNESCO*] [*British*]
IGOSS .... International Group on Soil Sampling
IGP .... Gary Public Library, Gary, IN [*OCLC symbol*] (OCLC)
IGP .... Igap [*Former USSR*] [*FAA designator*] (FAAC)
IGP .... Igneous & Geothermal Processes (USDC)
IGP .... Igneous & Geothermal Processes [*Marine science*] (OSRA)
IGP .... Imidazole Glycerol Phosphate [*Biochemistry*]
IGP .... Imitation Greaseproof Parchment (DGA)
IGP .... Inertial Guidance Package
IGP .... Inertial Guidance Platform
IGP .... Inspection Gauges Production (MCD)
IGP .... Institute of the Great Plains (EA)
IGP .... Instituto Geofisico del Peru [*Marine science*] (OSRA)
IGP .... Intelligent Gateway Processor [*Computer science*]
IGP .... Intelligent Graphics Processor [*Computer science*] (PCM)
IGP .... Interior Gateway Protocol [*Computer science*] (TNIG)
IGP .... International Garment Processors
IGP .... International Geodynamics Project
IGP .... International Green Party - Ecologism USA (EA)
IGP .... International Guild of Prestidigitators [*Defunct*] (EA)
IGP .... Intestinal Glycoprotein [*Biochemistry*] (MAE)

IGP............ Inverted Groundplane (PDAA)
IGP............ Investment Guaranty Program [AID]
IGP............ Ion-Getter-Pumping [Electron microscopy]
IGPA.......... Igor-Patrick Air Force Base (KSC)
IGPAC........ Intergovernmental Policy Advisory Committee on Trade
IGPC.......... Inter-Governmental Philatelic Corp. (EA)
IGPD.......... Imidazoleglycerol-phosphate Dehydratase [An enzyme]
IGPE.......... International Guild of Professional Electrologists (EA)
IGPF.......... Canadian Imperial Ginseng Products Ltd. [NASDAQ symbol] (SAG)
IGPF.......... Imperial Ginseng Products Ltd. [NASDAQ symbol] (SAG)
IGPFF........ Imperial Ginseng Prod [NASDAQ symbol] (TTSB)
IGPM.......... Imperial Gallons per Minute
IGPP.......... Institute of Geophysics and Planetary Physics [Livermore, CA]
                [Department of Energy] (MCD)
IGPP.......... Interactive Graphics Packaging Program [Computer science]
IGR............ Grace College, Winona Lake, IN [OCLC symbol] (OCLC)
IGR............ Igitur [Therefore] [Latin] (ADA)
IGR............ Iguazu [Argentina] [Airport symbol] (OAG)
IGR............ Improved Ground Rents (ROG)
IGR............ Increased Growth Response [Botany]
IGR............ Infanteriegranate [Infantry Howitzer Shell] [German military - World
                War II]
IGR............ Inscriptiones Graecae ad Res Romanas Pertinentes [A publication]
                (BJA)
IGR............ Insect Growth Regulator
IGR............ Institute of Geomantic Research (EAIO)
IGR............ Inter-Globe Resources Ltd. [Vancouver Stock Exchange symbol]
IGR............ Intergovernmental Review System (OICC)
IGR............ Intrauterine Growth Retardation [Neonatology] (DAVI)
IGRA.......... Indian Gaming Regulatory Act
IGrac......... Granite City Public Library, Granite City, IL [Library symbol Library of
                Congress] (LCLS)
IGracCU...... Granite City Community Unit 12, Granite City, IL [Library symbol
                Library of Congress] (LCLS)
IGRAF........ Inspector-General of the Royal Air Force [British]
IGrafPM...... Pere Marquette Residential Center, Grafton, IL [Library symbol
                Library of Congress] (LCLS)
IGralC........ College of Lake County, Grayslake, IL [Library symbol Library of
                Congress] (LCLS)
IGR & P...... Inert Gas Receiving and Processing (NRCH)
IGranHS...... Hopkins Elementary School, Granville, IL [Library symbol Library of
                Congress] (LCLS)
IGranPSD.... Putnam County Community Unit, School District 535, Granville, IL
                [Library symbol Library of Congress] (LCLS)
IGRAP........ Inert Gas Receiving and Processing (IAA)
IGRDC........ Institute for Genome Research for Developing Countries [Tunisia]
                [Proposed for 1996]
IGRE.......... Improved Ground Reconnaissance Equipment [Military] (MCD)
IGref......... Greenfield Public Library, Greenfield, IL [Library symbol Library of
                Congress] (LCLS)
IGrefCU...... Greenfield Community Unit, District 10, Greenfield, IL [Library symbol
                Library of Congress] (LCLS)
IGrevi........ Greenville Public Library, Greenville, IL [Library symbol Library of
                Congress] (LCLS)
IGreviC....... Greenville College, Greenville, IL [Library symbol Library of
                Congress] (LCLS)
IGRF.......... International Geomagnetic Reference Field
IG Rom....... Inscriptiones Graecae ad Res Romanas Pertinentes [A publication]
                (OCD)
IGRP.......... Indus Group [NASDAQ symbol] (TTSB)
IGRP.......... Indus Group, Inc. (The) [NASDAQ symbol] (SAG)
IGRP.......... Interior Gateway Routing Protocol [Cisco Systems, Inc.]
IGRP.......... International Genetic Resources Programme [Later, RAFI-USA] (EA)
IGRP.......... Isophthalic Glass Reinforced Plastic [Materials science]
IGRPS........ Inert Gas Receiving and Processing System (NRCH)
IGRS.......... Irish Genealogical Research Society (EAIO)
IGrSD......... Grand Ridge Consolidated Community School District 95, Grand
                Ridge, IL [Library symbol Library of Congress] (LCLS)
IGRV.......... Improved Guard Rail V [Army] (DOMA)
IGRV.......... Integrated GUARDRAIL V
IGS............ Carl Sandburg Birthplace Association, Galesburg, IL [Library symbol
                Library of Congress] (LCLS)
IGS............ Gary Community School Corp., Gary, IN [OCLC symbol] (OCLC)
IGS............ Image Guided Surgery
IGS............ Image Guided Surgery
IGS............ Immigrant Genealogical Society (EA)
IGS............ Immunogold Stain [Cytochemistry]
IGS............ Imperial General Staff
IGS............ Improved Gray Scale
IGS............ Inappropriate Gonadotrophin Secretion [Endocrinology]
IGS............ Indicator Group Speed
IGS............ Inert Gas Storage
IGS............ Inert Gas System [Engineering]
IGS............ Inertial Guidance System [NASA]
IGS............ Information Group Separator
IGS............ Inner Glide Slope [Aviation] (NASA)
IGS............ Inner Gulf Shelf (USDC)
IGS............ Inner Gulf Shelf [Marine science] (OSRA)
IGS............ Institute of General Semantics (EA)
IGS............ Institute of Geological Sciences [British]
IGS............ Institute of Geological Sciences [British] [Marine science] (OSRA)
IGS............ Institute of Government Studies [University of California at Berkeley]
IGS............ Instrumentation Ground System
IGS............ Instrument Guidance System [Aviation] (DA)
IGS............ Integrated Graphics System [Computer science] (BUR)

IGS............ Interactive Graphics System [Computer science]
IGS............ Intercapillary Glomerulosclerosis (PDAA)
IGS............ Interchange Group Separator [Computer science] (BUR)
IGS............ Interchromatin Granular Cluster [Cytology]
IGS............ Intergenic Spacer [Genetics]
IGS............ Intermediate General Support [Army]
IGS............ Internal Guide Sequence [Genetics]
IGS............ International Geranium Society (EA)
IGS............ International Glaciological Society [Cambridge, England]
IGS............ International Graphological Society (EA)
IGS............ Irish Genealogical Society (EA)
IGS............ Irish Georgian Society (EA)
IGS............ Irish Graphical Society (BI)
IGS............ Isla Grande Flying School [Puerto Rico] [ICAO designator] (FAAC)
IGS............ Morgan StanGp 6.50% IGT'PERQS' [AMEX symbol] (TTSB)
IGS............ Morgan Stanley Group, Inc. [AMEX symbol] (SAG)
IGSA.......... Indoor Gardening Society of America (EA)
IGSA.......... International Golf Sponsors' Association [Later, AGS]
IGSC.......... Carl Sandburg College, Galesburg, IL [Library symbol Library of
                Congress] (LCLS)
IGSC.......... Inspector General, Supply Corps
IGSCC........ Intergranular Stress-Corrosion Cracking [Plant engineering]
IGSE.......... In-Space Ground Support Equipment [NASA] (NASA)
IGSE.......... Instrument Ground Support Equipment (MCD)
IgSF.......... Immunoglobulin Superfamily [Immunology]
IGSHPA....... International Ground Source Heat Pump Association (EA)
IGSM.......... Indian General Service Medal [British]
IGSM.......... Interim Ground Station Module [Joint Surveillance/Target Attack
                RADAR Syste m] (DOMA)
IGSM.......... International Graduate School of Management
IGSMA........ Inertial Guidance System Maintenance Area [Aerospace] (AAG)
IGSN.......... International Gravity Standardization Net (PDAA)
IGSOBM...... International Guild of Symphony, Opera, and Ballet Musicians (EA)
IGSP.......... Institute for Gravitational Strain Pathology
IGSP.......... Internationale Gesellschaft der Schriftpsychologie [International
                Society for the Psychology of Writing]
IGSP.......... International Greenland Sea Project (USDC)
IGSP.......... Interntional Greenland Sea Project [Marine science] (OSRA)
IGSPS........ International Gold and Silver Plate Society (EA)
IGSS.......... Immunogold Silver Staining [Cytochemistry]
IGSS.......... Inertial Guidance System Simulator [NASA] (IAA)
IGST.......... Intergovernmental Committee on Science and Technology (BARN)
IGSU.......... Improved Gunner's Sight Unit [Military] (MCD)
IGT............ Impaired Glucose Tolerance [Physiology]
IGT............ Improved Gas Turbine (MCD)
IGT............ Ingot (MSA)
IGT............ Ingot Resources Ltd. [Vancouver Stock Exchange symbol]
IGT............ Inspector-General of Transportation [British military] (DMA)
IGT............ Inspector-General to the Forces for Training [British military]
IGT............ Institute of Gas Technology (EA)
IGT............ Instrument Guide Tube [Nuclear energy] (NRCH)
IGT............ Insulated-Gate Tetrode (IAA)
IGT............ Integrated Ground Test
IGT............ Intelligent Graphics Terminal [Tektronix] (NITA)
IGT............ Interactive Graphics Terminal [Computer science]
IGT............ International Game Technology [NYSE symbol] (SPSG)
IGT............ Intl Game Technology [NYSE symbol] (TTSB)
IGT............ Intragastric Titration [Gastroenterology]
IGT............ Ionization Gauge Tube
IGT............ Nightmute, AK [Location identifier FAA] (FAAL)
IGTA.......... International Gay Travel Association (EA)
IGTC.......... Inertial Guidance Test Center [Aerospace] (IAA)
IGTC.......... International Glutamate Technical Committee (EA)
IGTDS........ Interactive Graphic Transit Design System (PDAA)
IGTI.......... Image Guided Technologies, Inc. [NASDAQ symbol] (SAG)
IGTI.......... International Gas Turbine Institute [Later, ASMEIGTI] (EA)
IGTS.......... Interactive Graphic Transit Simulator (PDAA)
IGTT.......... Intravenous Glucose Tolerance Test [Clinical medicine]
IGTYF........ International Good Templar Youth Federation [Oslo, Norway] (EAIO)
IGU............ Iguassu Falls [Brazil] [Airport symbol] (OAG)
IGU............ Infantile Gastroenteritis Virus [Medicine] (PDAA)
IGU............ Internationale Gewerbeunion [International Association of Crafts and
                Small and Medium Sized Enterprises - IACME] [Berne,
                Switzerland] (EAIO)
IGU............ International Gas Union [See also UIIG] (EAIO)
IGU............ International Geographical Union [ICSU] [Edmonton, AB] (EA)
IGU............ International Geophysical Union
IGUA.......... International Guards Union of America (EA)
IGUC.......... Information Gained per Unit Cost [Computer science]
IGUCC........ International Geographical Union Commission on Climatology
                [Switzerland] (EAIO)
IGV............ Incremental Growth Vehicle (MCD)
IGV............ Inlet Guide Valve (MCD)
IGV............ Inlet Guide Vane
IGV............ International Gravis Computer Technology, Inc. [Formerly, Gravis
                Computer Peripherals, Inc.] [Vancouver Stock Exchange symbol]
IGV............ Intrathoracic Gas Volume [Medicine] (MAE)
IGVP.......... International Guild of Vatican Philatelists [Defunct] (EA)
IGW............ Image West Entertainment Corp. [Vancouver Stock Exchange
                symbol]
IGW............ Information Group West Corp., Calgary, Alberta [National Library of
                Canad a] [Library symbol] (IID)
IGW............ Internal Gravity Wave [in the atmosphere]
IGW............ Irma Graphics for Windows [DCA, Inc.]

IGWAP .... CPA [*Canadian Psychological Association*] Interest Group on Women and Psychology
IGWES .... Inert Gas Wire Enamel Stripper (PDAA)
IGWF .... International Garment Workers' Federation
IGWIS .... Integrated Ground Water Information System
IGWMC .... International Ground Water Modeling Center [*Butler University*]
IGWP .... International Group of Women Pilots (EA)
IGWT .... Internationale Gesellschaft fuer Warenkunde und Technologie [*International Association for Commodity Science and Technology*] (EA)
IGWU .... International Glove Workers' Union of America [*Later, ACTWU*]
IGWUA .... International Glove Workers Union of America (MHDB)
IGY .... International Geophysical Year [*1958-1959*] [*ICSU*]
IGYN .... Imagyn Medical [*NASDAQ symbol*] (TTSB)
IGYN .... Imagyn Medical, Inc. [*NASDAQ symbol*] (SAG)
IGY-WDC ..... International Geophysical Year, World Data Center
IGZ .... Iguatu [*Brazil*] [*Airport symbol*] (AD)
IH .... Channel Flying [*ICAO designator*] (AD)
IH .... Hinsdale Public Library, Hinsdale, IL [*Library symbol Library of Congress*] (LCLS)
IH .... Iacet Hic [*Here Lies*] [*Latin*]
IH .... Ice Haulage
IH .... Idiopathic Hemachromatosis [*Medicine*]
IH .... Idiopathic Hypercalciuria [*Medicine*]
IH .... Immediate Hypersensitivity [*Immunology*]
IH .... Immobilized Histamine [*Biochemistry*]
IH .... Impact on Hunger (EA)
IH .... Incipient Heavies [*Slang for rising young bureaucrats in the foreign policy field*]
IH .... Indent Hanging [*Graphic arts*] (DGA)
IH .... Index of Homogeneity [*Botany*]
IH .... Indirect Hemagglutination [*Hematology*] (DAVI)
IH .... Indirectly Heated (DEN)
IH .... Indo-Hittite (BJA)
I/H .... Industria del Hierro [*Part of a large Mexican industrial complex*]
IH .... Industrial House (ROG)
IH .... Industrial Hygienist [*Occupational Safety and Health Administration*]
IH .... Infectious Hepatitis [*Medicine*]
IH .... Informed Homebirth [*Later, IH/IBP*] (EA)
IH .... Inguinal Hernia [*Gastroenterology*] (DAVI)
IH .... Inhibit
IH .... Inhibiting Hormone
IH .... In Home [*Men's lacrosse position*]
IH .... In-House
IH .... Initial Heading
IH .... Innateness Hypothesis [*Linguistics*]
IH .... Inner Half (MAE)
IH .... Inpatient, Hospital
IH .... Inside Height
IH .... Inside Home [*Baseball*]
IH .... Inspector-General of Hospitals and Fleets [*Navy British*] (ROG)
IH .... Inspired Humidity [*Anesthesiology*]
IH .... Installation Handbook
IH .... Institute of Housing [*British*]
IH .... Institute of Hydrology [*Research center British*]
IH .... Instrument Head
IH .... Interaction Handler [*Computer science*] (OA)
IH .... Internationale Horngesellschaft [*International Horn Society*] (EAIO)
IH .... International Harvester Co.
IH .... Interrupt Handler [*Computer science*] (IAA)
IH .... Irish Horse [*British military*] (DMA)
IH .... Iron Hematoxylin [*A dye*]
IH .... Isme-Dagan Hymn (BJA)
IH .... Israel's Herald [*A publication*] (BJA)
IH .... Itavia [*ICAO designator*] (AD)
IH3PA .... International Home and Private Poker Players Association (EA)
IHa .... Harvey Public Library, Harvey, IL [*Library symbol Library of Congress*] (LCLS)
IHA .... Idaho Hospital Association (SRA)
IHA .... Idiopathic Hyperaldosteronism [*Medicine*] (DMAA)
IHA .... Idiopathic Hyperplastic Aldosteronism [*Endocrinology*]
IHA .... Illinois Hospital and Health Systems Association (SRA)
IHA .... Immune Hemolytic Anemia [*Medicine*]
IHA .... Independent Hospitals Association [*British*] (DBA)
IHA .... Indian Housing Authorities (USGC)
IHA .... Indian Housing Authority [*Department of Housing and Urban Development*] (GFGA)
IHA .... Indirect Hemagglutination [*Clinical chemistry*]
IHA .... Indirect Hemagglutination Antibody [*Medicine*] (DMAA)
IHA .... Individual Housing Account
IHA .... Infusion Hepatic Angiography [*Medicine*]
IHA .... Institute of Hospital Administrators [*British*] (BI)
IHA .... Interfaith Hunger Appeal (EA)
IHA .... Interim Housing Allowance [*Military*] (AFM)
IHA .... International Hahnemannian Association [*Defunct*]
IHA .... International Hopkins Association
IHA .... International Hotel Association [*Paris, France*] (EA)
IHA .... International House Association [*Defunct*]
IHA .... Iowa Hospitality Association (SRA)
IHA .... Issuing Houses Association [*British Defunct*] (DI)
IHA .... Reese Hospital and Medical Center, Chicago, IL [*OCLC symbol*] (OCLC)
IHAB .... International Horticultural Advisory Board
IHAC .... Industrial Health Advisory Council [*British*]
IHAD .... I Have a Dream Foundation (EA)

IHADSS .... Integrated Helmet and Display Sight System
IHAF .... Institut d'Histoire de l'Amerique Francaise [*Institute of French America History*] [*Canada*]
IHAH .... Illustrated Handbooks of Art History [*A publication*]
IHai .... Ingalls Memorial Hospital, Harvey, IL [*Library symbol Library of Congress*] (LCLS)
IHAI .... Institute of Heating and Air-Conditioning Industries
IH & HU ...... Industrial Health and Hazards Update [*Merton Allen Associates*] [*Information service or system*] (CRD)
IH & MEE .... International Hotel and Motel Educational Exposition [*Later, IHM & RS*] (EA)
IH-ANES ...... Inhalation Anesthesia
IHAP .... International Human Assistance Programs (EA)
IHar .... Mitchell Carnegie Public Library, Harrisburg, IL [*Library symbol*] [*Library of Congress*] (LCLS)
IHardCSD .... Calhoun Community Unit, School District 40, Hardin, IL [*Library symbol Library of Congress*] (LCLS)
IHardR .... Hardin Reading Center, Hardin, IL [*Library symbol Library of Congress*] (LCLS)
IHart .... Hartford Public Library, Hartford, IL [*Library symbol Library of Congress*] (LCLS)
IHAS .... Icelandic Horse Adventure Society (EA)
IHAS .... Idiopathic Hypertrophic Aortic Stenosis [*Cardiology*] (DAVI)
IHAS .... Illinois Hearing Aid Society (SRA)
IHAS .... Integrated Helicopter Avionics System [*Navy*] (NG)
IHAS .... Iowa Hearing Aid Society (SRA)
IHASFC .... International Hearts Air Supply Fan Club [*Defunct*] (EA)
IHAS/ILAAS ... Integrated Helicopter Avionics System / Integrated Light Attack Avionics System [*Navy*] (SAA)
IHATIS .... International Hide and Allied Trades Improvement Society
IHAWK .... Improved Homing All the Way Killer [*Missile*]
IHB .... Barnes, Hickam, Pantzer & Boyd, Indianapolis, IN [*OCLC symbol*] (OCLC)
IHB .... Incomplete Heart Block [*Cardiology*] (DAVI)
IH/B .... Indiana Harbor Belt Railroad Co. [*AAR code*]
IHB .... Inhibin [*Biochemistry*]
IHB .... Internationale Hoptrenbaubuero [*International Hop Growers Convention*]
IHB .... International Hydrographic Bureau [*Later, IHO*] [*Monaco*]
IHBC .... International Health and Beauty Council [*British*]
IHBCA .... International H Boat Class Association (EA)
IHBPA .... International Hepato-Biliary-Pancreatic Association (EA)
IHBS .... International Hajji Baba Society (EA)
IHBT .... Incompatible Hemolytic Blood Transfusion
IHBTD .... Incompatible Hemolytic Blood Transfusion Disease (MAE)
IHC .... Hanover College, Hanover, IN [*OCLC symbol*] (OCLC)
IHC .... Idiopathic Hemochromatosis [*Medicine*] (CPH)
IHC .... Idiopathic Hypercalcemia [*Medicine*]
IHC .... Immaculate Heart College [*California*]
IHC .... Immobilization Hypercalcemia [*Medicine*] (DAVI)
IHC .... Immunohistochemical
IHC .... Immunohistochemistry
IHC .... Indian Heritage Council (EA)
IHC .... Indian Hospital Corps [*British military*] (DMA)
IHC .... Indirectly Heated Cathode
IHC .... Infant Hypercalcemia [*Medicine*]
IHC .... Inner Hair Cells [*of cochlea*] [*Anatomy*]
IHC .... Institute of Hospital Catering [*Australia*]
IHC .... Intelligence Handling Committee [*Military*]
IHC .... International Harvester Co.
IHC .... International Health Center
IHC .... International Health Consultants (EA)
IHC .... International Health Council (EA)
IHC .... International Help for Children
IHC .... International Hug Center [*Defunct*] (EA)
IHC .... Ionic Heated Cathode
IHCA .... Individual Health Care Account (HCT)
IHCA .... In Hands of Civil Authorities [*Military*]
IHCA .... International Hebrew Christian Alliance [*Ramsgate, Kent, England*] (EA)
IHCA .... International Hobie Class Association (EA)
IHCA .... Isocapnic Hyperventilation with Cold Air [*Medicine*] (DMAA)
IHCC .... Illinois Home Care Council (SRA)
IHCC .... Intensiva HealthCare Corp. [*NASDAQ symbol*] (SAG)
IHCC .... International Harvester Credit Corp. (ADA)
IHCM .... Idiopathic Hypertrophic Cardiomyopathy [*Cardiology*]
IHCOS .... Isotope-Heated Catalytic Oxidizer System (KSC)
IHCP .... Institute on Hospital and Community Psychiatry (EA)
IHCPV .... Initial Hydrocarbon Pore Volume [*Petroleum technology*]
IHCSERS ..... International Health Centre of Socio-Economics Researches and Studies [*See also CIERSES*] [*Lailly En Val, France*] (EAIO)
IHD .... American Hospital Association Library, Chicago, IL [*OCLC symbol*] (OCLC)
IHD .... In-Center Hemodialysis [*Medicine*] (DMAA)
IHD .... Indian Head, PA [*Location identifier FAA*] (FAAL)
IHD .... Institute of Human Development [*University of California, Berkeley*] [*Research center*] (RCD)
IHD .... Institut Henry-Dunant [*Henry Dunant Institute*] [*Geneva, Switzerland*] (EAIO)
IHD .... International Hard Suits [*Vancouver Stock Exchange symbol*]
IHD .... International Hydrological Decade [*UNESCO*] [*Later, IHP*]
IHD .... Intrahepatic Duct [*or Ductule*] [*Gastroenterology*] (DAVI)
IHD .... Ischemic Heart Disease
IHDI .... International Hearing Dog, Inc. (EA)

IHDP .... Independent Hungarian Democratic Party [*Political party Hungary*] (EAIO)
IHDP .... Infant Health and Development Program
IHDRT .... Interim High-Data Rate Terminal (CAAL)
IHDS .... Institute for Higher Defense Studies [*National Defense University*]
IHDS .... Integrated Helmet Display System
IHE .... Evanston Public Library, Evanston, IL [*OCLC symbol*] (OCLC)
IHE .... Insensitive High Explosive (MCD)
IHE .... Institute for the Human Environment (EA)
IHE .... Institute of Health Education [*British*]
IHE .... Institute of Higher Education
IHE .... Institute of Highway Engineers [*British*]
IHE .... Institute of Home Economics [*of ARS, Department of Agriculture*]
IHE .... Institute of Hospital Engineering (EAIO)
IHE .... Intergranular Hydrogen Embrittlement [*Metallurgy*]
IHE .... Intermediate Heat Exchanger [*Nuclear energy*]
IHE .... International Historic Enterprises
IHE .... International Institute for Hydraulic and Environmental Engineering [*Netherlands Universities Foundation for International Cooperation*] [*Research center*]
IHE .... Interservice Home Exchange [*Commercial firm*] (EA)
IHEA .... Industrial Heating Equipment Association (EA)
IHEA .... International Health Evaluation Association (EA)
IHEc .... Institute of Home Economics [*British*] (DBA)
IHEMI .... International Health Economics and Management Institute (EA)
IHen .... Henry Public Library, Henry, IL [*Library symbol Library of Congress*] (LCLS)
IHenn .... Putnam County Library, Hennepin, IL [*Library symbol Library of Congress*] (LCLS)
IHennC .... Hennepin Attendance Center, Hennepin, IL [*Library symbol Library of Congress*] (LCLS)
IHenn-G ...... Putnam County Library, Granville Branch, Granville, IL [*Library symbol Library of Congress*] (LCLS)
IHenn-H ...... Putnam County Library, Hennepin Branch, Hennepin, IL [*Library symbol Library of Congress*] (LCLS)
IHenn-M ..... Putnam County Library, Magnolia Branch, Magnolia, IL [*Library symbol Library of Congress*] (LCLS)
IHenn-Mc .... Putnam County Library, McNabb Branch, McNabb, IL [*Library symbol Library of Congress*] (LCLS)
IHenn-P ...... Putnam County Library, Condit Branch, Putnam, IL [*Library symbol Library of Congress*] (LCLS)
IHenn-S ...... Putnam County Library, Standard Branch, Standard, IL [*Library symbol Library of Congress*] (LCLS)
IHEP .... Insensitive High Explosives and Propellants [*DoD/DOE program*] (RDA)
IHEP .... Institute for High-Energy Physics [*China*]
IHEP .... Institute of High Energy Physics [*Former USSR*]
IHERC .... Inter-Hemispheric Education Resource Center (EA)
IHERS .... Institute of Higher Education Research and Services [*University of Alabama*] [*Research center*] (RCD)
IHES .... Idiopathic Hypereosinophilic Syndrome [*Medicine*] (DMAA)
IHETS .... Indiana Higher Education Telecommunication System [*Indianapolis*] [*Telecommunications*] (TSSD)
IHEU .... International Humanist and Ethical Union [*Utrecht, Netherlands*] (EA)
IHF .... Independent High Frequency (IAA)
IHF .... Industrial Health Foundation (EA)
IHF .... Industrial Hygiene Foundation of America
IHF .... Inhibit Halt Flip-Flop [*Computer science*]
IHF .... Inspection Holding Fixture (MCD)
IHF .... Institute of Gas Technology, Chicago, IL [*OCLC symbol*] (OCLC)
IHF .... Institute of High Fidelity [*Formerly, IHFM*] [*Later, EIA*] (EA)
IHF .... Integrated Hazard Function
IHF .... Integration Host Factor [*Genetics*]
IHF .... Intermediate High Frequency (IIA)
IHF .... International Handball Federation [*Basel, Switzerland*] (EA)
IHF .... International Health Foundation [*Brussels, Belgium*] (EAIO)
IHF .... International Helicopter Foundation [*Later, HFI*] (EA)
IHF .... International Helsinki Federation for Human Rights (ECON)
IHF .... International Hockey Federation (BARN)
IHF .... International Hospital Federation (EA)
IHF .... International Lawn Hockey Federation
IHF .... Inverse Hyperbolic Function
IHF .... Irish Heritage Foundation (EA)
IHF .... Irish Hotels Federation (EAIO)
IHF .... Isothermal Heating Furnace
IHF .... Israel Histadrut Foundation (EA)
IHFAS .... Integrated High-Frequency Antenna System
IHFF .... Inhibit Halt Flip-Flop [*Computer science*] (MSA)
IHFHR .... International Helsinki Federation for Human Rights (EA)
IHFM .... Institute of High Fidelity Manufacturers [*Later, IHF*]
IHFMA .... International Home Furnishings Marketing Association (EA)
IHFR .... Improved High-Frequency Radio (INF)
IHFR .... Institute of Health Food Retailing [*British*] (DBA)
IHFRA .... International Home Furnishings Representatives Association (EA)
IHG .... Internationale Hegel Gesellschaft (EA)
IHG .... Skokie Public Library, Skokie, IL [*OCLC symbol*] (OCLC)
IHGC .... International Hop Growers Convention [*See also CICH*] [*Zalec, Yugoslavia*] (EAIO)
IHGD .... Isolateral Human Growth Deficiency [*Medicine*] (DMAA)
IHGMA .... International Herb Growers and Marketers Association [*Defunct*] (EA)
IHGS .... Institute of Heraldic and Genealogical Studies [*British*]
IHh .... Eisenhower Public Library District, Harwood Heights, IL [*Library symbol Library of Congress*] (LCLS)
IHH .... Huntington College, Huntington, IN [*OCLC symbol*] (OCLC)
IHH .... Idiopathic Hypogonadotropic Hypogonadism [*Endocrinology*]

IHH .... Infectious Human Hepatitis [*Medicine*] (DMAA)
IHHA .... Indiana Hospital and Health Association (SRA)
IHHA .... International Halfway House Association (EA)
IHHI .... In Home Health, Inc. [*NASDAQ symbol*] (NQ)
IHHNV .... Infectious Hypodermal and Hematopoietic Necrosis Virus [*Aquaculture*]
IHHO .... Institute of Home Help Organisers [*British*]
IHHS .... Idiopathic Hyperkinetic Heart Syndrome [*Medicine*] (DMAA)
IHi .... Illinois State Historical Library, Springfield, IL [*Library symbol Library of Congress*] (LCLS)
IHI .... Impact of Hypertension Information Study [*Department of Health and Human Services*] (GFGA)
IHI .... Improved Holographic Image
IHI .... Institute for Healthcare Improvement (DMAA)
IHI .... Integrated Hit Indicator
IHI .... Ishikawajima-Harima Heavy Industries [*Japan*] (ECON)
IHI .... Ishikawajima-Harima Heavy Industries Co. Ltd. [*Japan*]
IHI .... Lincoln Trail Libraries System, Champaign, IL [*OCLC symbol*] (OCLC)
IHIA .... Include This Headquarters Information Addressee [*Army*] (AABC)
IHIA .... International Health Industries Association (EA)
IH/IBP .... Informed Homebirth/Informed Birth and Parenting (EA)
IHIE .... Institute of Highway Incorporated Engineers [*British*] (EAIO)
IHig .... Louis Latzer Memorial Library, Highland, IL [*Library symbol Library of Congress*] (LCLS)
IHigp .... Highland Park Public Library, Highland Park, IL [*Library symbol Library of Congress*] (LCLS)
IHigSD .... Highland Community Unit, School District 5, Highland, IL [*Library symbol Library of Congress*] (LCLS)
IHII .... Independent Health Insurance Institute [*Inactive*] (EA)
IHII .... Industrial Holdings [*NASDAQ symbol*] (TTSB)
IHII .... Industrial Holdings, Inc. [*NASDAQ symbol*] (SAG)
IHIIW .... Industrial Holdgs Wrrt'A' [*NASDAQ symbol*] (TTSB)
IHIIZ .... Industrial Hldgs Wrrt'B' [*NASDAQ symbol*] (TTSB)
IHil .... Hillside Public Library, Hillside, IL [*Library symbol Library of Congress*] (LCLS)
IHilb .... Hillsboro Public Library, Hillsboro, IL [*Library symbol Library of Congress*] (LCLS)
IHilbGC .... John A. Graham Correctional Center, Hillsboro, IL [*Library symbol*] [*Library of Congress*] (LCLS)
IHilbSD .... Hillsboro Community Unit, School District 3, Hillsboro, IL [*Library symbol Library of Congress*] (LCLS)
IHineJ .... John J. Madden Mental Health Center, Training Staff Development Library, Hines, IL [*Library symbol Library of Congress*] (LCLS)
IHineV .... United States Veterans Administration Hospital, Hines, IL [*Library symbol Library of Congress*] (LCLS)
IHIPIR .... Improved High-Power Illuminator RADAR [*IHAWK Missile*] (MCD)
IHIS .... Integrated Hit Indicator System
IHIS .... Integrated Hospital Information System (DMAA)
IHJ .... International Heroines of Jericho [*Later, General Conference of Grand Courts Heroines of Jericho, Prince Hall Affiliation, USA*] (EA)
IHK .... Imperial Holly Corp. [*AMEX symbol*] (SPSG)
IHK .... International Homestock Resources Ltd. [*Vancouver Stock Exchange symbol*]
IHK .... Ionic Heated Kathode
IHL .... Illinois Health Libraries Consortium [*Library network*]
IHL .... Imperial Light Horse [*Military British*] (ROG)
IHL .... International Hockey League (EA)
IHL .... International Homeopathic League
IHL .... Internet Header Length [*Computer science*] (ACRL)
IHLCADS ...... Interim High-Level Container Airdrop System
IHLS .... International Herring Larvae Survey
IHLZY .... Ichud Habonim Labor Zionist Youth (EA)
ihm .... Brothers of the Immaculate Heart of Mary (TOCD)
IHM .... Brothers of the Immaculate Heart of Mary (TOCD)
IHM .... [*The*] California Institute of the Sisters of the Most Holy and Immaculate Heart of the Blessed Virgin Mary (TOCD)
IHM .... Daughters of the Immaculate Heart of Mary [*Roman Catholic religious order*]
i-hm-- .... Heard and McDonald Islands [*MARC geographic area code Library of Congress*] (LCCP)
IHM .... Imitation Handmade Paper (DGA)
IHM .... Institute of Housing Managers [*British*] (BI)
IHM .... Mansfield, MA [*Location identifier FAA*] (FAAL)
IHM .... Sisters of the Immaculate Heart of Mary [*California Institute of the Most Holy and Immaculate Heart of the BVM*] [*Roman Catholic religious order*]
IHM .... Sisters of the Most Holy and Immaculate Heart of Blessed Virgin Mary (Wichita Foundation) (TOCD)
IHM .... Sisters, Servants of the Immaculate Heart of Mary [*Roman Catholic religious order*]
IHMA .... Indiana Hotel and Motel Association (SRA)
IHMA .... Industrialized Housing Manufacturer's Association (EA)
IHM & RS .... International Hotel/Motel and Restaurant Show (EA)
IHMDE .... Imitation Handmade Deckle Edges Paper (DGA)
IHMI .... Institute for Housing Management Innovations (EA)
IHMSA .... International Handgun Metallic Silhouette Association (EA)
IHM-SBF ...... Insan Haklari Merkezi, Siyasal Bilgiler Fakueltesi [*Turkey*]
IHN .... Infectious Hematopoietic Necrosis [*Fish pathology*]
IHN .... In His Name
IHN .... Integrated Delivery Networks [*Health care provider*]
IHN .... International Handicappers' Net (EA)
IHN .... Iron Horse Resources, Inc. [*Vancouver Stock Exchange symbol*]
IHNI .... Iatros Health Network [*NASDAQ symbol*] (TTSB)

IHNI	Iatros Health Network, Inc. [*NASDAQ symbol*] (SAG)
IHNIW	Iatros Health Network Wrrt [*NASDAQ symbol*] (TTSB)
IHo	Hoopestown Public Library, Hoopestown, IL [*Library symbol Library of Congress*] (LCLS)
IHO	Idiopathic Hypertrophic Osteoarthropathy [*Medicine*]
IHO	Impartial Hearing Officer
IHO	Impeded Harmonic Operation
IHO	In Honor Of
IHO	Inorganic Halogen Oxidizer
IHO	Institute of Human Origins (EA)
IHO	International Hydrographic Organization [*See also BHI*] [*Monaco*]
IHod	Hodgkins Public Library District, Hodgkins, IL [*Library symbol Library of Congress*] (LCLS)
IHoF	Vermilion County Elementary Film Library, Hoopeston, IL [*Library symbol*] [*Library of Congress*] (LCLS)
IHoH	Hoopestown Community Memorial Hospital, Hoopestown, IL [*Library symbol Library of Congress*] (LCLS)
IHom	Homer Community Library, Homer, IL [*Library symbol Library of Congress*] (LCLS)
IHOP	IHOP Corp. [*NASDAQ symbol*] (SAG)
IHOP	International House of Pancakes [*Restaurant chain*] [*Pronounced "eye-hop"*]
IHOP	Isophosphamide, Hydroxydaunomycin [*Adriamycn*], Oncovin , Prednisone [*Vincristine*] [*Antineoplastic drug regimen*] (DAVI)
IHOPCp	IHOP Corp. [*Associated Press*] (SAG)
IHOSPE	Institute of Hospital Engineering (PDAA)
IHot	Hometown Public·Library, Hometown, IL [*Library symbol Library of Congress*] (LCLS)
IHOU	Institute of Home Office Underwriters [*Louisville, KY*] (EA)
IHow	Homewood Public Library, Homewood, IL [*Library symbol Library of Congress*] (LCLS)
IHP	Hammond Public Library, Hammond, IN [*OCLC symbol*] (OCLC)
IHP	Idiopathic Hypoparathyroidism [*Medicine*]
IHP	Idiopathic Hypopituitarism [*Medicine*] (AAMN)
IHP	Indicated Horsepower
IHP	Individualized Habilitation Plan
IHP	Information Handling Project (DIT)
IHP	Inner Helmholtz Plane (IAA)
IHP	Inositol Hexaphosphate [*Biochemistry*]
IHP	Institute for Human Progress [*Defunct*]
IHP	Instrumentation Habitability Power (MCD)
IHP	Intergovernmental Council for the International Hydrological Programme (EA)
IHP	International Hydrographic Program
IHP	International Hydrological Program [*UNESCO*] [*France*]
IHP	Inverted Hand Position [*Neuropsychology*]
IHP	Isostatic Hot Pressing (PDAA)
IHPA	International Hardwood Products Association (EA)
IHPC	International Hydrolyzed Protein Council (EA)
IHPC	Intrahepatic Cholestasis [*Medicine*] (DMAA)
IHPD	International Health Physics Data Base [*Creative Information Systems, Inc.*] [*Information service or system*] (CRD)
IHPH	Indicated Horsepower-Hour
IHPH	Intrahepatic Portal Hypertension [*Medicine*] (MAE)
IHP-HR	Indicated Horsepower-Hour
IHPI	IHS [*Information Handling Services*] Product/Subject Index [*Information service or system*] (CRD)
IHPI	Improved High-Power Illuminator (CAAL)
IHPMI	International Health Policy and Management Institute (EAIO)
IHPO	International Health Program Office [*Atlanta, GA*] [*Department of Health and Human Services*] (GRD)
IHPP	Intergovernmental Health Policy Project (EA)
IHPRPT	Integrated High Payoff Rocket Propulsion Technology
IHPRS	International Husserl and Phenomenological Research Society (EA)
IHPST	Institute for the History and Philosophy of Science and Technology [*University of Toronto*] [*Canada*] (IRC)
IHPTET	Integrated High-Performance Turbine Engine Technology Initiative [*NASA and DOD*]
IHPVA	International Human Powered Vehicle Association (EA)
IHQ	International Headquarters (DNAB)
IHQ	Rolling Prairie Libraries, Decatur, IL [*OCLC symbol*] (OCLC)
IH/QAS	Indian Head [*Maryland*] - Quality Assurance Department [*Naval ordnance station*]
IHR	Carl Sandburg College, LRC, Galesburg, IL [*OCLC symbol*] (OCLC)
IHR	Cocoa, FL [*Location identifier FAA*] (FAAL)
IHR	Increased Hazard Rate
IHR	Infrared Heterodyne Radiometer
IHR	Institute for Historical Review (EA)
IHR	Institute of Horticultural Research [*Research center British*] (IRC)
IHR	Intrahepatic Resistance [*Medicine*] (MAE)
IHR	Intrinsic Heart Rate [*Cardiology*]
IHR	Ishihara [*Japan*] [*Seismograph station code, US Geological Survey Closed*] (SEIS)
IHRA	Increasing Hazard Rate Average
IHRA	International Hot Rod Association (EA)
IHRB	Industrial Health Research Board [*British*]
IHRBLR	International Human Resources, Business, and Legal Research Association (EA)
IHRC	Immigration History Research Center [*University of Minnesota*] [*Research center*] (RCD)
IHRC	In-Home Respite Care
IH/RE	Indian Head Research and Development Department [*Naval Ordnance Station*] [*Maryland*]
IHRG	Interdisciplinary Health Research Group [*See also GRIS*] [*Universite de Montreal*] [*Canada*] [*Research center*]
IHRLG	International Human Rights Law Group (EA)
IHRMA	Irish Hotel and Restaurant Managers' Association (BI)
IHRR	Institute for Human Rights Research (EA)
IHS	Fort Carson, CO [*Location identifier FAA*] (FAAL)
IHS	Idiopathic Headache Score [*Neurology*] (DAVI)
IHS	Iesous Hemeteros Soter [*Jesus, Our Savior*] [*Greek*]
IHS	Iesus Heiland Seligmacher [*Jesus, Savior, Sanctifier*] [*German*]
IHS	Iesus Hominum Salvator [*Jesus, Savior of Mankind*] [*Latin*] (ADA)
IHS	Immigration History Society (EA)
IHS	Improved HAWK Simulator [*Military*]
IHS	Inactivated Horse Serum [*Immunology*]
IHS	Inclined Heterolithic Stratification [*Geology*]
IHS	Indescor Hydrodynamics, Inc. [*Vancouver Stock Exchange symbol*]
IHS	Indian Health Service
IHS	Information Handling Services [*Englewood, CO*]
IHS	Infrared Homing System (AAG)
IHS	Infrared Horizon Sensor
IHS	In Hoc Signo (Vinces) [*In This Sign (You Will Conquer)*] [*Latin*]
IHS	Institute for Housing Urban Development Studies [*Netherlands*]
IHS	Institute for Humane Studies, Inc. [*Research center*] (RCD)
IHS	Institute for Hydrogen Systems [*UTLAS symbol*]
IHS	Institute of Home Safety [*British*] (DBA)
IHS	Institute of Hypertension Studies - Institute of Hypertension School of Research[*Later, NIHS*] (EA)
IHS	Integrated Headgear Subsystem [*Army*] (RDA)
IHS	Integrated Health Services, Inc. [*NYSE symbol*] (SPSG)
IHS	Integrated Health Svcs [*NYSE symbol*] (TTSB)
IHS	Integrated Heat Sink (PDAA)
IHS	Interactive Home System (PDAA)
IHS	International Health Society (EA)
IHS	International Hearing Society (PAZ)
IHS	International Heritage Site [*UNESCO*]
IHS	International Hibernation Society (EA)
IHS	International Horn Society (EA)
IHS	International Hurling Society
IHS	International Hydrofoil Society (EAIO)
IHS	Intrahepatic Arteriovenous Shunt [*Medicine*]
IHs	Iris Hamartoma [*Oncology*] (DAVI)
IHS	Isotope Heat Source
IHS	Italian Historical Society of America (EA)
IHS	Suburban Library System, Hinsdale, IL [*Library symbol Library of Congress*] (LCLS)
IHS	University of Texas, Health Science Center at Dallas, Dallas, TX [*OCLC symbol*] (OCLC)
IHSA	Intercollegiate Horse Show Association (EA)
IHSA	International Headquarters of the Salvation Army (EA)
IHSA	Iodinated Human Serum Albumin
IHSB	In-Flight Helmet Stowage Bag (KSC)
IHSBR	Improved High-Speed Bombing RADAR
IHSC	InSight Health Services Corp. [*NASDAQ symbol*] (SAG)
IHSD	Inertial Height Sensing Device
IHSD	In-House Systems Developer [*Personal computer*] (PCM)
IHSDC	Irish Health Services Development Corp.
IHSG	Internationale Heinrich Schutz-Gesellschaft [*International Heinrich Schutz Society*] (EAIO)
IHSGB	Icelandic Horse Society [*British*] (DBA)
IHSI	Induction Heating Stress Improvement [*Nuclear energy*] (NUCP)
IHSM	Institute of Health Services Management (DBA)
IHSPCB	International Healthcare Safety Professional Certification Board (EA)
IHSR	Improved High Speed Rail (PDAA)
IHSR	Institute for Health Services Research [*Tulane University*] [*Research center*] (RCD)
IH/SR	Integration Hardware and Software Review (MCD)
IHSRC	International Heat Stress Research Center [*Sudan*] (IRC)
IHSS	Idiopathic Hypertrophic Subaortic Stenosis [*Medicine*]
IHSS	In-Home Support Services [*Medicine*] (MEDA)
IHSS	Institute of Human Science and Services [*University of Rhode Island*] [*Research center*] (RCD)
IHSS	Integrated Hydrographic Survey System (PDAA)
IHSS	International Heinrich Schutz Society [*See also IHSG*] [*Germany*] (EA)
IHSS	International Humic Substances Society
IHT	Icelandic Horse Trekkers (EA)
IHT	Impact Hand Tool
IHT	Inheritance Tax [*British*]
IHT	Inspection Hold Tag
IHT	Institute of Heat Technology
IHT	Institution of Highways and Transportation [*British*] (DBA)
IHT	Insulin Hypoglycemia Test [*Endocrinology*] (DAVI)
IHT	International Association of Health and Therapy Instruments [*Japan*] (EAIO)
IHT	Intravenous Histamine Test [*Clinical Medicine*] (MAE)
IHT	Trinity Evangelical Divinity School, Rolfing Memorial Library, Deerfield, IL [*OCLC symbol*] (OCLC)
IHTA	International Health and Temperance Association (EA)
IH-TAS	Improved HAWK-Tracking Adjunct System [*Military*] (MCD)
IHTD	Improved HAWK Training Detachment
IHTS	Integrated Hybrid Transistor Switch (PDAA)
IHTS	Intermediate Heat Transport System [*Nuclear energy*] (NRCH)
IHTTA	International High-Technology Training Association (EA)
IHTU	Interservice Hovercraft Trials Unit [*Military*]
IHTV	Interim Hypersonics Test Vehicle [*NASA*] (NASA)
IHU	Chicago Mercantile Exchange, Chicago, IL [*OCLC symbol*] (OCLC)
IHU	Ihu [*Papua New Guinea*] [*Airport symbol*] (OAG)
IHU	Instantaneous Unit Hydrograph (PDAA)

IHU	Interservice Hovercraft Unit [Military]
IHumSD	Shiloh Community Unit School District, Hume, IL [Library symbol] [Library of Congress] (LCLS)
IHuSD	Hutsonville Community Unit, School District 1, Hutsonville, IL [Library symbol Library of Congress] (LCLS)
IHV	Highland Park Public Library, Highland Park, IL [OCLC symbol] (OCLC)
IHV	Independent Hardware Vendor [Computer science] (CDE)
IHV	Institute of Human Values [See also IMH] [Canada]
IHV	Institute of Human Virology [University of Maryland]
IHV	Internationale Hegel-Vereinigung [Munich, Federal Republic of Germany] (EAIO)
IHVE	Institution of Heating and Ventilating Engineers [Later, CIBSE]
IHVS	Intelligent Vehicle Highway Systems
IHW	Inner Heel Wedge [Orthopedics] (DAVI)
IHW	International Halley Watch [Defunct] (EA)
IHW	John G. Shedd Aquarium, Chicago, IL [OCLC symbol] (OCLC)
IHWG	Internationale Hugo Wolf Gesellschaft [Vienna, Austria] (EAIO)
IHWU	Independent Hospital Workers Union (EA)
IHX	Interim Hypersonics Test Vehicle
IHX	Interloop Heat Exchanger [NASA] (NASA)
IHX	Intermediate Heat Exchanger [Nuclear energy]
IHX	Western Illinois Library System, Monmouth, IL [OCLC symbol] (OCLC)
IHXGV	Intermediate Heat Exchanger Guard Vessel [Nuclear energy] (NRCH)
IHY	Ela Area Public Library District, Lake Zurich, IL [OCLC symbol] (OCLC)
IHY	I Heard You (MHDI)
IHYP	Iodohydroxybenzylpindolol [Organic chemistry]
IHZ	Warren-Newport Public Library District, Gurnee, IL [OCLC symbol] (OCLC)
II	Aer Arann Teoranta [Ireland] [ICAO designator] (ICDA)
ii	Bid in Die [Twice a Day] [Symbol] [Pharmacology] (DAVI)
I/I	Current to Current [Converter] (NRCH)
II	Igniter Initiator
II	Ikebana International [Japan]
I-I	Illegal Immigrant
II	Illegal Immigrant
II	Illinium [or Promethium] [Cardiology] (DAVI)
II	Image Intensifier
II	Imagery Interpretation
II	Immigrant Inspector [Immigration and Naturalization Service]
II	Imperial Airlines [ICAO designator] (AD)
II	Imperial Institute [British] (DAS)
II	Implementation Instructions (MCD)
II	Incarcerated Innocent
II	Independent Inspector (AIE)
ii	India [MARC country of publication code Library of Congress] (LCCP)
II	Individualized Instruction
II	Indochina Institute (EA)
I/I	Indorsement Irregular [Banking]
I/I	Industrial and Institutional [Waste] (GAAI)
II	Information Index [LIMRA]
II	Information Indicator (ACRL)
II	Ingot Iron
II	Initial Issue
II	Innovators International [Defunct] (EA)
II	Input Impedance
II	Insol International (EA)
I-I	Inspector-Instructor [Marine Corps]
II	Installation Instruction
II	Institute of Inventors [British] (BI)
II	Institutional Investor [Business term]
II	Instituto Interamericano (EA)
II	Instruction and Inspection (IAA)
II	Interlingua Institute (EA)
II	Interrupt Inhibit
II	Intersystems, Inc. [Formerly, Bamberger Polymers, Inc.] [AMEX symbol] (SPSG)
II	Interval International (EA)
II	Intransit Inventory (AFM)
II	Inventions and Inventors [A publication]
II	Inventory and Inspection Report [Army]
II	Irish Institute
II	Item Identification (MSA)
II	London City Airways [ICAO designator] (AD)
II	Requires Medical Supplies [Search and rescue symbol that can be stamped in sand or snow]
IIA	Carnegie Public Library, Angola, IN [OCLC symbol] (OCLC)
IIA	If Incorrect Advise [Aviation]
IIA	ILA [Instruction Look Ahead] Interrupt Address [Computer science]
IIA	Image Intensifier Assembly
IIA	Impotence Institute of America (EA)
IIA	Incinerator Institute of America [Later, NSWMA] (EA)
IIA	Independent Innkeepers Association (EA)
IIA	Independent Inspection Agency [RSPA] (TAG)
IIA	Indirect Immunofluorescence Assay [AIDS confirmation test] (CPH)
IIA	Inertial Instrument Assembly
IIA	Information Industry Association (EA)
IIA	Institute of Inter-American Affairs [Washington, DC]
IIA	Institute of Internal Affairs
IIA	Institute of Internal Auditors [Altamonte Springs, FL] (EA)
IIA	Institute of International Affairs
IIA	Institut International d'Anthropologie [International Institute of Anthropology] (EAIO)

IIA	Insurance Institute of America (EA)
IIA	Intelligence Industries Association (EA)
IIA	Interamericana de Aviacion Ltda. [Colombia] [ICAO designator] (FAAC)
IIA	Internatioal Internet Association
IIA	International Illawarra Association [Defunct] (EA)
IIA	International Imagery Association (EA)
IIA	International Information Administration [Transferred to U SIS, 1953] [Department of State]
IIA	International Institute of Agriculture
IIA	International Institute of Andragogy [See also INSTIA] (EAIO)
IIA	International Inventor's Association [Defunct] (EA)
IIA	International Investors Association
IIA	Invention Industry Association of America
IIA	Invert Indicator from Accumulator
IIAA	Independent Insurance Agents of America [New York, NY] (EA)
IIAA	Institute of Inter-American Affairs [United Nations]
IIAANY	Independent Insurance Agents Association of New York (SRA)
IIAAR	International Institute for Arab-American Relations [Defunct] (EA)
IIAC	Impulse International Auto Club [Defunct] (EA)
IIAC	Independent Insurance Agents of Connecticut (SRA)
IIAC	Industrial Injuries Advisory Council [British] (DCTA)
IIAC	Infrared Information and Analysis Center [University of Michigan] (MCD)
IIAC	Inter-Image Amplifying Chemistry [Color film technology]
IIAC	International Insurance Advisory Council [Later, IIC] (EA)
IIAD	Independent Insurance Agents of Delaware (SRA)
IIAF	Imperial Iranian Air Force
IIAFC	International Irwin Allen Fan Club (EA)
IIAG	Interbureau Insurance Advisory Group
IIAI	International Institute of American Ideals (EA)
IIAILS	Interim Integrated Aircraft Instrumentation and Letdown System
IIAL	International Institute of African Languages and Culture (BARN)
IIAL	International Institute of Arts and Letters
IIALM	International Institute for Adult Literacy Methods [Tehran, Iran] (EAIO)
IIANC	Independent Insurance Agents of North Carolina (SRA)
II & W	Intelligence Interface and Warning [Military] (MCD)
IIANH	Independent Insurance Agents of New Hampshire (SRA)
IIANJ	Independent Insurance Agents of New Jersey (SRA)
IIANM	Independent Insurance Agents of New Mexico (SRA)
IIAO	Independent Insurance Agents of Oregon (SRA)
IIAP	Independent Insurance Agents of Pennsylvania (SRA)
IIAP	Institut International d'Aluminium Primaire [International Primary Aluminum Institute] (EAIO)
IIAP	Insurance Institute for Asia and the Pacific (DS)
IIAR	Incurably Ill for Animal Research (EA)
IIAR	International Institute of Ammonia Refrigeration (EA)
IIARI	Independent Insurance Agents of Rhode Island (SRA)
IIAS	Institute of Interamerican Studies [University of Miami] [Research center] (RCD)
IIAS	International Institute for Advanced Studies (EA)
IIASA	Institute of Islamic and Arabic Sciences in America (EA)
IIASA	International Institute for Applied Systems Analysis
IIASC	Independent Insurance Agents of South Carolina (SRA)
IIAU	Independent Insurance Agents of Utah (SRA)
IIAV	Independent Insurance Agents of Vermont (SRA)
IIB	Butler University, Indianapolis, IN [OCLC symbol] (OCLC)
IIB	Illinois Intrastate Motor Carrier Rate & Tariff Bureau, Springfield IL [STAC]
IIB	Independence, IA [Location identifier FAA] (FAAL)
IIB	Independent Infantry Battalion
IIB	Industrial Information Bulletin [A publication]
IIB	Information Industry Bulletin [Digital Information Group] [Information service or system] (IID)
IIB	Institut International de Bibliographie
IIB	Institut International des Brevets [International Patent Institute]
IIB	Intense Ion Beam
IIB	International Institute of Biotechnology [University of Kent at Canterbury] [British] (IRC)
IIB	International Investment Bank [Moscow, USSR]
IIB	Internordic Investment Bank [Scandinavia]
IIB	Irish Intercontinental Bank Ltd.
IIB	Italian International Bank
IIBA	International Institute for Bioenergetic Analysis (EA)
IIBA	International Intelligent Buildings Association [Washington, DC] (EA)
II Bar	II Baruch [Pseudepigrapha] (BJA)
IIBC	International Institute of Biological Control [CAB International] [British] (IRC)
IIBD	Incorporated Institute of British Decorators (DAS)
IIBDID	Incorporated Institute of British Decorators and Interior Designers (BI)
IIBH	International Institute of Biological Husbandry [Ipswich, Suffolk, England] [Defunct] (EAIO)
IIBS	Interactive International Banking System [NCR Corp.]
IIBTT	Ion-Implanted Base Transistor Technology (IAA)
IIC	AMIGOS [Access Method for Indexed Data Generalized for Operating System] Bibliographic Council, Dallas, TX [OCLC symbol] (OCLC)
IIC	Igniter Initiator Cartridge [or Container]
IIC	Image Interpretation Cell
IIC	Imagery Interpretation Center
IIC	Impact Isolation Class [Noise rating of insulation]
IIC	Independent Insurance Conference
IIC	Independent Investment Co. [British]

IIC............... Industrial Intelligence Centre [*British World War II*]
IIC............... Inflation-Indexed Charge [*Medicare*] (GFGA)
IIC............... Information Industries Committee [*Information service or system*] (IID)
IIC............... Innovation Information Center [*George Washington University*] (PDAA)
IIC............... Insearch Institute of Commerce [*University of Technology, Sydney, Australia*]
IIC............... Institute of Insurance Consultants [*British*] (DBA)
IIC............... Institut International des Communications [*International Institute of Communications*] (EA)
IIC............... Instructional Improvement Committee [*Individually-guided education*] (AEE)
IIC............... Insurance Institute of Canada
IIC............... Integrated Interface Circuit (IAA)
IIC............... Intelligence Information Center [*Military*] (MCD)
IIC............... InterCapital California Insurance Municipal Income Fund [*NYSE symbol*] (SPSG)
IIC............... InterCapital Cal Ins Muni Inc. [*NYSE symbol*] (TTSB)
IIC............... Interceptor Identification Capability
IIC............... Interdepartmental Intelligence Conference [*Interagency conference of the National Security Council*] (EGAO)
IIC............... International Ice Patrol [*Coast Guard*]
IIC............... International Institute for Conservation of Historic and Artistic Works [*British*] (EAIO)
IIC............... International Institute for Cotton [*Belgium*] (FEA)
IIC............... International Institute for the Conservation of Museum Objects
IIC............... International Institute of Communications [*Formerly, IBI*] (EA)
IIC............... International Institute of Communications
IIC............... International Insurance Council (EA)
IIC............... International Ionarc, Inc. [*Vancouver Stock Exchange symbol*]
IIC............... Ion-Ion Collision
IIC............... Iron Information Center [*Battelle Memorial Institute*] [*Information service or system*] (IID)
IIC............... Isotopes Information Center [*ORNL*]
IIC............... Item Identification Code
IIC............... Rita Coyotepec [*Mexico*] [*Seismograph station code, US Geological Survey*] (SEIS)
IICA............... Indians into Communications Association (EA)
IICA............... Instituto Internacional de Ciencias Administrativas [*International Institute of Administrative Sciences*]
IICA............... Interamerican Institute for Cooperation on Agriculture [*Formerly, IAIAS*] (EA)
IICA............... International Ice Cream Association (EA)
IICA............... Islamic Information Center of America (EA)
IICBM............ Intermediate Intercontinental Ballistic Missile
IICC............... Institut International d'Etude et de Documentation en Matiere de Concurrence Commerciale [*International Institute for Commercial Competition*] [*Belgium*] (EA)
IICC............... International Institute for Study and Research in the Field of Commercial Competition
IICE............... Institute for Internal Combustion Engines (MCD)
IICE............... Institut International des Caisses d'Epargne [*International Savings Banks Institute - ISBI*] [*Geneva, Switzerland*] (EAIO)
IICG .... ICSU [*International Council of Scientific Unions*] Inter-Union Commission for Geodynamics [*Marine science*] (MSC)
IICHAW........ International Institute for Conservation of Historic and Artistic Works
IIC Ind .... IIC Industries, Inc. [*Associated Press*] (SAG)
IICL............... Institute of International Container Lessors (EA)
IICLRR........ International Institute for Children's Literature and Reading Research [*Vienna, Austria*] (EA)
IICMFA........ Integrated Information Centre of the Ministry of Foreign Affairs [*Saudi Arabia*] (NITA)
IICMSD .... International Institute for Comparative Music Studies and Documentation [*Berlin, Federal Republic of Germany*] (EA)
IiCN .... National Library of India, Calcutta, India [*Library symbol Library of Congress*] (LCLS)
IICNTR........ International Institute of Children's Nature and Their Rights (EA)
IICP............... Increased Intracranial Pressure (CPH)
IICP............... International Intersociety Committee on Pathology
IICR .... IIC Industries [*NASDAQ symbol*] (TTSB)
IICR .... IIC Industries, Inc. [*NASDAQ symbol*] (SAG)
IICR .... Inspection Item Change Request (MCD)
IICS............... Intelligent Image Caching Software [*Courtland Group, Inc.*] (PCM)
IICS............... International Interactive Communications Society [*San Francisco, CA*] [*Telecommunications service*] (TSSD)
IICU .... Infant Intensive Care Unit [*of a hospital*]
IICU .... Intermediate Intensive Care Unit [*Medicine*]
IICUC.......... International Institute of Carpet and Upholstery Certification (EA)
IICY............... International Independent Christian Youth [*See also JICI*] [*Paris, France*] (EAIO)
IID............... Iida [*Japan*] [*Seismograph station code, US Geological Survey*] (SEIS)
IID............... Image Intensifier Device
IID............... Impact Ionization Diode
IID............... Independent Identically Distributed [*Statistics*] (IEEE)
IID............... Information Industry Directory [*A publication*]
IID............... Infrared Intrusion Detection (NVT)
IID............... Institute for Integral Development (EA)
IID............... Insulin-Dependent Diabetes [*Mellitus*] [*Endocrinology*] (DAVI)
IID............... Insulin-Independent Diabetes Mellitus (MAE)
IID............... Insurgent Incident Data
IID............... Integrated Information Display (MCD)
IID............... Integrated Instrument Development
IID............... Interaural Intensity Disparity [*Audiology*]

IID............... Intermittent-Integrated Doppler (OA)
IID............... Intrinsic Infrared Detector
IID............... Investment in Default [*Business term*]
IID............... Ion Implantation Doping
IID............... Ionospheric Ion Density
IIDA .... Indivisualized Instruction for Data Access [*Drexel University and Franklin Institute*] [*Education package*] (NITA)
IIDA .... Instituto Interamericano de Direito de Autor [*Interamerican Copyright Institute*] (EAIO)
IIDARA........ Instituto Iberoamericano de Derecho Agrario y Reforma Agraria [*Ibero-American Institute of Agrarian Law and Agrarian Reform - IAIALAR*] (EAIO)
IiDaU .... University of North Bengal, Darjeeling District, West Bengal, India [*Library symbol Library of Congress*] (LCLS)
IIDC .... Institute for International Development and Cooperation [*University of Ottawa*] [*See also IDIC*] [*Canada*]
IIDD .... Interface Identification Data Document (DNAB)
IIDET........... International Institute of Dental Ergonomics and Technology [*Germany*] (EAIO)
IIDH .... Institut International de Droit Humanitaire [*International Institute of Humanitarian Law - IIHL*] (EAIO)
IIDH .... Instituto Interamericano de Derechos Humanos [*Inter-American Institute of Human Rights - IIHR*] (EA)
IIDLC .... Institut International de Droit Linguistique Compare [*International Institute of Comparative Linguistic Law*] (EAIO)
IIDP .... Integrated Instrument Development Program
IIDP .... Integrated Intelligence Development Plan (MCD)
IIDS .... Integrated Information Display System (MCD)
IIDS .... Integrated Instrumentation Display System
IIDT .... Ion Implantation Doping Technique
IIE............... Idiopathic Ineffective Erythropoiesis [*Hematology*] (AAMN)
IIE............... Imperial Institute of Entomology [*British*]
IIE............... Initial Ion Event
IIE............... Installation Identification Element (MCD)
IIE............... Institute for Independent Education (EA)
IIE............... Institute for International Economics
IIE............... Institute of Industrial Economics [*University of Newcastle*] [*Australia*]
IIE............... Institute of Industrial Engineers (EA)
IIE............... Institute of International Education (EA)
IIE............... Institut International de l'Epargne
IIE............... Instituto Interamericano de Estadistica [*Inter-American Statistical Institute - IASI*] [*Washington, DC*]
IIE............... Inter-American Institute of Ecology [*Ecological Society of America*]
IIE............... International Institute of Embryology [*Later, ISDB*]
IIEA............... Immediate Identifiable Emergency Action [*Red Cross*]
IIEA............... International Institute for Environmental Affairs [*Later, IIED*]
IIEC............... Inter-Industry Emission Control [*Program*] (EA)
IIEC............... International Institute for Energy Conservation (EA)
IIED............... International Institute for Environment and Development [*Research center British*] (IRC)
iied .... International Institute for Environment and Development [*British*]
IIEE............... Institut International d'Etudes sur l'Education [*International Institute for Education Studies*]
IIEG............... Interest Inventory for Elementary Grades [*Psychology*]
IIEL............... Institut International d'Etudes Ligures [*International Institute for Ligurian Studies - IILS*] (EAIO)
IIEP............... Illionois Inventory of Educational Progress (EDAC)
IIEP............... International Institute for Educational Planning [*Paris, France*] [*United Nations*] (EA)
IIEQ............... Illinois Institute for Environmental Quality (PDAA)
IIER............... International Institute for Economic Research (EA)
IIES............... International Institute for Environmental Studies (ASF)
IIETF............ Information Industries Education and Training Foundation [*Australia*]
IIExE............ Institution of Incorporated Executive Engineers [*British*] (DBA)
IIF............... IBM [*International Business Machines Corp.*] IGES Format [*Initial Graphics Exchange Specification*]
IIF............... Immune Interferon [*Cell biology*]
IIF............... Imprint Immuno-Fixation [*Immunochemistry*]
IIF............... Independent Investors Forum [*Information service or system*] (IID)
IIF............... Indirect Immunofluorescence [*Immunochemistry*]
IIF............... Institute of International Finance [*Washington, DC*] (EA)
IIF............... Institut International du Froid [*International Institute of Refrigeration*]
IIF............... Intense Irregular Field
IIF............... Internals Indexing Fixture (NRCH)
IIF............... International Institute of Forecasters [*See also IIM*] (EA)
IIF............... Morgan Stanley India Investment Fund [*NYSE symbol*] (SAG)
IIF............... Morgan Stanley India Inv Fd [*NYSE symbol*] (TTSB)
IIFA............... International Institute of Films on Art
IIFAR .... Incurably Ill for Animal Research (EA)
IIFAS............ Integration of Intelligence from All Sources (MCD)
IIFET .... International Institute of Fisheries Economics and Trade (EA)
IIFFL............ International Institute of Foods and Family Living (EA)
IIFP............... Institut International de Finances Publiques [*International Institute of Public Finance*] (EAIO)
IIFS............... Integrated Individual Fighting System [*US Army Natick Research, Development, and Engineering Center*] (INF)
IIFSO............ International Islamic Federation of Student Organizations [*Salimiyan, Kuwait*] (EAIO)
IIFSP........... Integrated Individual Fighting System Program [*Army*] (INF)
IIFT............... Indirect Immunofluorescence Technique [*Immunochemistry*]
IIFV............... Interim Infantry Fighting Vehicle [*Military*] (MCD)
IIG............... Illuminated Internal Graticule
IIG............... Imagery Intelligence Group [*Military*] (MCD)
IIG............... Investors Ins Group [*AMEX symbol*] (TTSB)

IIG .... Investors Insurance Group [*Formerly, Gemco National, Inc.*] [*AMEX symbol*] (SPSG)
IIG .... Item Identification Guide
IIGA .... IEEE [*Institute of Electrical and Electronics Engineers*] Industry and General Applications (IAA)
IIGB .... International Institute of Genetics and Biophysics [*Italy*]
IIGF .... Imperial Iranian Ground Forces
IIGR .... Ipsilateral Instinctive Grasp Reaction [*Medicine*] (DMAA)
IIGS .... Initial Image Generating Subsystem [*ERTS*] (MCD)
IIH .... Isoimmune Hydrops [*Medicine*]
IIHA .... Intercollegiate Ice Hockey Association [*Later, ECHA*] (EA)
IIHD .... Institute for International Health and Development (EA)
IIHF .... International Ice Hockey Federation (EAIO)
IIHHT .... International Institute of Health and Holistic Therapies [*British*]
IIHL .... International Institute for Home Literature [*See also MIKK*] [*Belgrade, Yugoslavia*] (EAIO)
IIHL .... International Institute of Humanitarian Law [*See also IIDH*] [*San Remo, Italy*] (EAIO)
IIHR .... Inter-American Institute of Human Rights [*See also IIDS*] [*San Jose, Costa Rica*] (EAIO)
IIHR .... International Institute of Human Rights (EA)
IIHR .... Iowa Institute of Hydraulic Research [*University of Iowa*] [*Research center*] (MCD)
IIHS .... Insurance Institute for Highway Safety (EA)
IIHSC .... Inter-Industry Highway Safety Committee [*Later, DSMC*] (EA)
III .... Idealist International, Inc. (EA)
III .... Illinois, Indiana, Iowa (IIA)
III .... Illumination Industries, Inc.
III .... Indiana Central University, Indianapolis, IN [*OCLC symbol*] (OCLC)
III .... Information Intelligence, Inc. [*Information service or system*] (IID)
III .... Information International, Inc. [*Phoenix, AZ*] [*Information broker*] (MCD)
III .... Innovative Interfaces, Inc. [*Information service or system*] (IID)
III .... Insteel Industries [*NYSE symbol*] (SAG)
III .... Insteel Industries Inc. [*NYSE symbol*] (TTSB)
III .... Institute for Information Industry [*Information service or system*] (IID)
III .... Institute of the Ironworking Industry (EA)
III .... Insurance Information Institute [*New York, NY*] (EA)
III .... Inter-American Indian Institute [*OAS*]
III .... International Industrial Information Ltd. [*Information service or system*] (IID)
III .... International Institute of Interpreters [*United Nations*] (BARN)
III .... International Insurance Intelligence
III .... International Intertrade Index [*No longer available online*] [*Information service or system*] (IID)
III .... Interstate Identification Index [*NCIC*]
III .... Investors in Industry [*British*]
III .... Sturgeon Bay, WI [*Location identifier FAA*] (FAAL)
iii .... Ter in Die [*Three Times a Day*] [*Symbol*] [*Pharmacology*] (DAVI)
III Bar .... III Baruch [*Pseudepigrapha*] (BJA)
IIIC .... International Irrigation Information Center (IID)
IIIC (LN) ...... International Institute of Intellectual Cooperation of the League of Nations [*Obsolete*]
IIIHS .... International Institute of Integral Human Sciences [*See also IISHI*] (EAIO)
IIII .... Innotech Inc. [*NASDAQ symbol*] (TTSB)
IIII .... Innotech, Inc. [*NASDAQ symbol*] (SAG)
IIIL .... International Institute of Iberoamerican Literature (EA)
IIIL .... Isoplanar Integrated Injection Logic (MCD)
IIIMB .... International Institute of Investment and Merchant Banking [*Washington, DC*] (EA)
IIIP .... Institute for International Information Programs [*University of Maryland*] (NITA)
IIIR .... Integrated Instructional Information Resource [*Educational Products Information Exchange Institute*] [*Information service or system*] (CRD)
IIIS .... Interim International Information Service [*World War II*]
IIIT .... International Institute of Instructional Technology [*British*]
IIIT .... International Institute of Islamic Thought (EA)
IIIVC .... Infrahepatic Interruption of the Inferior Vena Cava [*Medicine*] (AAMN)
IIJM .... Institut International Jacques Maritain [*International Jacques Maritain Institute - IJMI*] (EAIO)
IIK .... Imagery Interpretation Key
IIK .... Kipnuk, AK [*Location identifier FAA*] (FAAL)
IIL .... India International Airways (P) Ltd. [*ICAO designator*] (FAAC)
IIL .... Indianapolis Law Catalog Consortium, Indiana University School of Law Library, Indianapolis, IN [*OCLC symbol*] (OCLC)
IIL .... Induction Ion LASER
IIL .... Institute of Industrial Launderers (EA)
IIL .... Institute of International Law [*Geneva, Switzerland*] (EA)
IIL .... Integrated Injection Logic [*Microprocessing*] (BUR)
IIL .... Invert Indicator of the Left Half (IAA)
IILA .... Institute for the Integration of Latin America
IILA .... Instituto Italo Latino Americano [*Italo-Latin American Institute*] (EAIO)
IILA .... Istituto Italo-Latino-Americano [*Italian-Latin American Institute*] [*Rome, Italy*]
IILc .... Identity Incorrect, Location Correct [*Psychology*]
IILE .... Ion-Induced Light Emission (MCD)
IILFSC .... International Institute of Law of the French Speaking Countries [*See also IDEF*] [*Paris, France*] (EAIO)
IiLi .... Identity Incorrect, Location Incorrect [*Psychology*]
IILi .... Instituto Internacional de Literatura Iberoamericana [*International Institute of Iberoamerican Literature*] (EA)
IILP .... Index to Indian Legal Periodicals [*A publication*] (DLA)
IILP .... Institute of International Licensing Practitioners (EAIO)

IILP .... International Institute for Lath and Plaster (EA)
IILR .... Institute of International Labor Research (EA)
IILS .... International Institute for Labor Studies [*Switzerland*]
IILS .... International Institute for Ligurian Studies (EA)
IIM .... Children's Museum of Indianapolis, Indianapolis, IN [*OCLC symbol*] (OCLC)
IIM .... Institute for Information Management (EA)
IIM .... Institut International des Meteorologists [*International Institute of Forecasters*] (EAIO)
IIM .... Institut International du Manganese [*International Insitute of Manganese*] [*France*] (EAIO)
IIM .... Institution of Industrial Managers [*British*]
IIM .... Interagency Intelligence Memorandum (MCD)
IIM .... InterCapital Ins Muni Income [*NYSE symbol*] (TTSB)
IIM .... InterCapital Insurance Municipal Income Fund [*NYSE symbol*] (SPSG)
IIM .... International Investment Monitor [*Global Analysis Systems*] [*Information service or system*] (CRD)
IIM .... Inventory in Motion
IIM .... Item Intelligence Maintenance [*DoD*]
IIMA .... Insurance Industry Meetings Association [*St. Louis, MO*] (EA)
IIMC .... International Industrial Marketing Club [*Formerly, MMEC*] [*Defunct*] (EA)
IIMC .... International Institute of Maritime Culture (EA)
IIMC .... International Institute of Municipal Clerks (EA)
IIME .... Institute of International Medical Education
IIMI .... International Irrigation Management Institute [*Sri Lanka*] [*Research center*] (IRC)
I-IMP .... I-Labeled Iodoamphetamine
IIMS .... Intensive Item Management System (AABC)
IIMS .... Ion Implantation Manufacturing System
IIMT .... International Institute for the Management of Technology [*Defunct*] (EA)
IIN .... IBM [*International Business Machines Corp.*] Information Network (HGAA)
IIN .... Instituto Interamericano del Nino [*Inter-American Children's Institute*] [*Uruguay*] (EA)
IIN .... INX Insearch Group of Companies Ltd. [*Vancouver Stock Exchange symbol*]
IIN .... Item Identification Number (AFM)
IIN .... ITT Industries [*NYSE symbol*] (TTSB)
IIN .... ITT Industries, Inc. Indiana [*NYSE symbol*] (SAG)
IINA .... International Islamic News Agency [*Jeddah, Saudi Arabia*] (EAIO)
IiNaU .... University of Nagpur, Nagpur, India [*Library symbol Library of Congress*] (LCLS)
IINC .... International Institute of Novel Computing [*Japan*]
I Inf Sc .... Institute of Information Scientists [*British*] (DLA)
IiNI .... Indian National Scientific Documentation Center, Hillside Road, New Delhi, India [*Library symbol*] [*Library of Congress*] (LCLS)
IiNI .... Indian National Scientific Documentation Centre, New Delhi, India [*Library symbol Library of Congress*]
IiNN .... Nehru Memorial Museum and Library, New Delhi, India [*Library symbol Library of Congress*] (LCLS)
IINREN .... Interagency Interim National Research and Education Network (TNIG)
IINS .... Image Intensifier Night Sight
I/Ins .... Inactive Insurance (DLA)
IINS .... Incoherent Inelastic Neutron Scattering [*Physics*]
IINS .... Inelastic Incoherent Neutron Scattering [*Spectrometry*]
IINS .... Integrated Inertial Navigation System (MCD)
IINSE .... International Institute of Nuclear Science and Engineering
IINT .... Information International, Inc. [*NASDAQ symbol*] (NQ)
IINTE .... Instytut Informacji Naukowej, Technicznej, i Ekonomicznej [*Institute of Scientific, Technical, and Economic Information*] [*Information service or system*] (IID)
IIO .... Image Intensifier Orthicon
IIO .... Information Item Only
IIO .... Institute for International Order [*Later, IWO*]
IIO .... Inter-Allied Insurance Organization [*NATO*] (NATG)
IIOC .... Intelligent Input Output Channel (NITA)
IIODRFES ..... International Information Office of the Democratic Revolutionary Front of El Salvador [*See also OIIFDRES*] [*San Jose, Costa Rica*] (EAIO)
IIOE .... International Indian Ocean Expedition [*Navy*]
IIOIC .... International Intra-Ocular Implant Club (EAIO)
IIOP .... Integrated Input/Output Processor
IIOP .... Intelligent Input/Output Processor [*Disk Controller*]
IIOP .... Internet Inter-ORG [*Object Request Broker*] Protocol [*Computer science*]
IIP .... El Pinto [*Mexico*] [*Seismograph station code, US Geological Survey*] (SEIS)
IIP .... Immediate Impact Point (SAA)
IIP .... Implantable Insulin Pump
IIP .... Implementation/Installation Plan [*Telecommunications*] (TEL)
IIP .... Inadvertent Ignition Panel
IIP .... Increasing Intracranial Pressure [*Medicine*]
IIP .... Index of Industrial Production
IIP .... Individual Implementation Plan [*For the education of a handicapped person*]
IIP .... Industrial Incentive Plan [*NAVFAC*] (DNAB)
IIP .... Initial Issue Provisioning [*Marine Corps*] (DOMA)
IIP .... Inorganic Insulative Plastic
IIP .... Instantaneous Impact Points (KSC)
IIP .... Instantaneous Impact Predictor
IIP .... Institute of Incorporated Photographers [*British*]

IIP	Institut International de la Potasse [*International Potash Institute*] (EAIO)
IIP	Institut International de la Presse [*International Press Institute*]
IIP	Institut International de Philosophie [*International Institute of Philosophy*] (EAIO)
IIP	Interceptor Improvement Program
IIP	Intergovernmental Informatics Programme [*UNESCO*]
IIP	Interim Impact Predictor (AAG)
IIP	International Ice Patrol [*Coast Guard*]
IIP	International Institute for Peace [*Vienna, Austria*] (EA)
IIP	International Institute of Philosophy (AEBS)
IIP	International Inter-Visitation Program in Educational Administration [*UniverstiyCouncil for Educational Administration*] (AEE)
IIP	Irish Independence Party [*Political party*] (PPW)
IIPA	Institute of Incorporated Practitioners in Advertising [*British*] (BI)
IIPA	International Icelandic Pony Association (EA)
IIPA	International Intellectual Property Association (EA)
IIPACS	Integrated Information Presentation and Control System [*Aviation*]
IIPC	Image Intensifier Plumbicon Camera
IIPE	Institut International de Planification de l'Education [*International Institute for Educational Planning*]
IIPEC	Institute for Interconnecting and Packaging Electronic Circuits (EA)
IIPER	International Institute for Production Engineering Research (EAIO)
IIPF	International Institute of Public Finance [*Saarbrucken, Federal Republic of Germany*] (EAIO)
IIPG	International Institute of Practical Geomancy [*Formerly, Society for Symbolic Studies*] (EA)
IIPL	Independent Investor Protective League (EA)
IIPM	Irish International Peace Movement (EAIO)
IIPO	Illinois Inventory of Parent Opinion
IIPP	International Institute for Promotion and Prestige [*Geneva, Switzerland*] (EAIO)
IIPR	Installation Inspection Procedure Report
IIPR	Istituto Internazionale di Psicologia della Reliosita' [*International Institute for the Psychology of Religion*] [*Italy*] (IRC)
IIPS	Instantaneous Impact Prediction System (DNAB)
IIPS	Interactive Instructional Presentation System [*IBM*] (NITA)
IIQ	Initial Issue Quantities [*Military*]
IIR	Image Interpreter Response
IIR	Imaging Infrared [*Air Force*] (MCD)
IIR	Infinite-Duration Impulse-Response (IEEE)
IIR	Infinite Impulse Response [*Electronics*]
IIR	Institute of Industrial Relations [*Loyola University of Chicago*] [*Research center*] (RCD)
IIR	Institute of Intermodal Repairers (EA)
IIR	Institut International du Froid [*International Institute of Refrigeration*] [*France*] (EA)
IIR	Integrated Instrumentation RADAR
IIR	Intelligence Information Report (NVT)
IIR	Intercom Information Resources, Inc. [*Information service or system*] (IID)
IIR	Intermediate Infrared
IIR	International Impala Resources [*Vancouver Stock Exchange symbol*]
IIR	International Institute for Robotics (EA)
IIR	International Institute of Rehabilitation [*Defunct*] (EA)
IIR	International Inventors Registry (NITA)
IIR	Inventory and Inspection Report [*Army*] (MUGU)
IIR	Invert Indicator of the Right Half (SAA)
IIR	Isobutene-Isoprene Rubber
IIRA	Integrated Inertial Reference Assembly (PDAA)
IIRA	International Ice Racing Association
IIRA	International Industrial Relations Association [*Geneva, Switzerland*] (EA)
IIRB	Institut International de Recherches Betteravieres [*International Institute for Sugar Beet Research*] [*Brussels, Belgium*] (EA)
IIRC	Inactive Item Review Card [*Military*] (AFIT)
IIRC	Incident Investigation Review Committee [*Nuclear Regulatory Commission*] (NRCH)
IIRC	Indiana Interstate Railroad Co., Inc. [*AAR code*]
IIRC	Interrogation and Information Reception Circuit [*Telecommunications*] (OA)
IIRD	International Interdependent Research and Development (AABC)
IIRE	International Institute for Resource Economics [*Defunct*] (EA)
IIRF	Intergalactic Infrared Radiation Field
IIRG	Institut International de Recherches Graphologiques
IIRM	Improved Infrared Missile
IIRM	Irish Immigration Reform Movement (EA)
IIRMS	Industrial Information's Record Management System [*Computer science*]
IIRP	Integrated Installation Requirement Plan (MCD)
IIRR	Institute of Industrial Race Relations
IIRR	International Institute of Rural Reconstruction (EA)
IIRS	Institute of Industrial Research and Standards [*Ireland*] [*Research center Database producer*] (IID)
IIRS	Instrumentation Inertial Reference Set [*Aviation*]
IIRV	Improved Inter-Range Vector (MCD)
IIS	IBM [*International Business Machines Corp.*] Information Services (HGAA)
IIS	IIS Intelligent Information Systems [*Associated Press*] (SAG)
IIS	Image Intensified System
IIS	Imagery Interpretation System (MCD)
IIS	Improved Infrared Source
IIS	INA Investment Sec [*NYSE symbol*] (TTSB)
IIS	INA Investment Securities, Inc. [*NYSE symbol*] (SPSG)
IIS	Indexation Information Statement [*Accounting*]

IIS	Index to International Statistics [*A publication*]
IIS	Indirect Identification System [*Military*] (MCD)
IIS	Industrial Information Services [*Southern Methodist University*] [*Dallas, TX*]
IIS	Inflationary Impact Statement [*Economics*]
IIS	Infrared Imaging System
IIS	Infrared Instrumentation System
IIS	Inmate Information System [*Bureau of Prisons*] (GFGA)
IIS	Inspection Instruction Sheet
IIS	Inspection Item Sheet (MCD)
IIS	Inspections and Investigations Staff [*Vietnam*]
IIS	Institute for Information Studies [*Inactive*] [*Research center*] (RCD)
IIS	Institute for Intercultural Studies (EA)
IIS	Institute of Information Scientists [*British*] (EAIO)
IIS	Institute of International Studies (EA)
IIS	Institut International de la Soudure [*International Institute of Welding - IIW*] (EAIO)
IIS	Institut International de Statistique [*International Statistical Institute*]
IIS	Integrated Information System
IIS	Integrated Instrument Sheet (MCD)
IIS	Integrated Instruments System
IIS	Integrated Insulation System
IIS	Intelligence Information System [*Military*] (DNAB)
IIS	Intensive Immunosuppression [*Medicine*] (DMAA)
IIS	Interactive Instructional System [*IBM Corp.*]
IIS	Internationales Institut der Sparkassen [*International Savings Banks Institute*]
IIS	International Information Service Ltd. [*Information service or system*] (IID)
IIS	International Institute of Seismology and Earthquake Engineering [*Japan*] [*Seismograph station code, US Geological Survey*] (SEIS)
IIS	International Institute of Sociology
IIS	International Institute of Stress (EA)
IIS	International Institutional Services (EA)
IIS	International Insurance Seminars [*University, AL*] (EA)
IIS	International Insurance Society (EAIO)
IIS	International Isotope Society (EA)
IIS	International Medical Imagery [*Vancouver Stock Exchange symbol*]
IIS	Internet Information Server (PCM)
IIS	Internet Information Server [*Computer science*] (PCM)
IIS	Invert Indicator From Storage (SAA)
IIS	Investment Income Surcharge [*Finance*] (MHDW)
IIS	Ion Implantation Study
IIS	Irish Institute of Secretaries Ltd. (BI)
IIS	Nissan Island [*Papua New Guinea*] [*Airport symbol*] (OAG)
IISA	Institut International des Sciences Administratives [*International Institute for Administrative Sciences*]
IISA	Integrated Inertial Sensor Assembly (MCD)
IISA	Interservice/Interagency Support Agreement (MCD)
IISBR	International Institute for Sugar Beet Research (EA)
IISD	If Incorrect Service Direct (FAAC)
IISD	International Institute for the Study of Death (EA)
IISDI	International Institute for the Study of Death and Immortality [*Later, IISD*] (EA)
IISE	International Institute of Social Economics [*Hull, England*] (EAIO)
IISG	Internationaal Instituut voor Sociale Geschiedenis [*International Institute for Social History*] (EA)
IISHI	Institut International des Sciences Humaines Integrales [*International Institute of Integral Human Sciences - IIIHS*] (EAIO)
IISI	International Iron and Steel Institute [*Brussels, Belgium*] [*Research center*] (EA)
IISJ	Institute for Independent Social Journalism (EA)
IISL	IIS [*Intelligent Information Systems*] Ltd. [*NASDAQ symbol*]
IISL	International Institute of Space Law [*Baarn, Netherlands*] (EAIO)
IISL	Istituto Internazionale di Studi Liguri [*International Institute for Ligurian Studies*]
IISLF	I.I.S. Intellig't Info [*NASDAQ symbol*] (TTSB)
IISP	Improved Industrial Standard Process (MCD)
IISP	Interim Interswitch Signaling Protocol [*Telecommunications*] (ACRL)
IISP	International Institute of Site Planning (EA)
IISPA	Interactive Instructional Systems-Presentation and Authoring Special Interest Group [*Association for the Development of Computer-Based Instructional Systems*] (EDAC)
IISRP	International Institute of Synthetic Rubber Producers (EA)
IISS	Integrated Information Support System [*Computer science*]
IISS	Intelligence Information Subsystem [*Military*] (MCD)
IISS	International Institute for Strategic Studies (EA)
IISS	International Institute for the Science of Sintering [*Belgrade, Yugoslavia*] (EAIO)
IISSM	Istituto Internazionale Suore di Santa Marcellina [*Milan, Italy*] (EAIO)
IIST	Institute for Information Storage Technology [*University of Santa Clara*] [*Research center*] (RCD)
IIST	Intense Islet Stimulation Test [*Endocrinology*]
IIST	International Institute for Safety in Transportation [*Formerly, IST*] (EA)
IIST	International Institute of Sports Therapy [*British*]
IISWM	Institute of Iron and Steel Wire Manufacturers (MHDB)
IIT	Illinois Institute of Technology (IID)
IIT	Image Intensifier Tube
IIT	Inclinable Indexing Table
IIT	Individual Inclusive Tour [*Air fare plan*]
IIT	Indonesian Satellite Corp. [*NYSE symbol*] (SAG)
IIT	Industrial Information Transfer (NITA)
IIT	Ineffective Iron Turnover (DMAA)

IIT	Institut des Ingenieurs des Transports [*Institute of Transportation Engineers*] [*Canada*]
IIT	Institut Interafricain du Travail
IIT	Institut Internationale du Theatre [*International Theatre Institute - ITI*] (EAIO)
IIT	Integrated Information Transport (ACRL)
IIT	International Investment Trust
IIT	Intra-Industry Trade
IIT	Islet-Infiltrating T
IIT	Israel Institute of Technology (KSC)
IIT	Perusahaan PT IndoSatADS [*NYSE symbol*] (TTSB)
IITA	Information Infrastructure Technology Applications [*Marine science*] (OSRA)
IITA	Information Infrastructure Technology Applications (USDC)
IITA	Inland International Trade Association [*Sacramento, CA*] (EA)
IITA	International Institute of Tropical Agriculture [*Ibadan, Nigeria*] [*Research center*] (EAIO)
IITC	IITC Holdings Ltd. [*NASDAQ symbol*] (SAG)
IITC	Insurance Industry Training Council (PDAA)
IITC	Intera Information Technologies Corp. [*NASDAQ symbol*] (SAG)
IITC	International Indian Treaty Council (EA)
IITCF	IITC Holdings [*NASDAQ symbol*] (TTSB)
IITCHld	IITC Holdings Ltd. [*Associated Press*] (SAG)
IITCS	Igloo Internal Thermal Control Section [*Aerospace*] (MCD)
IITD	Institute of International Trade and Development (EA)
IITE	Information Infrastructure Task Force [*Marine science*] (OSRA)
I/ITEC	Interservice/Industry Training Equipment Conference [*Military*]
IITF	In-Core Instrument Test Facility [*Nuclear energy*] (IAA)
IITF	Information Infrastructure Task Force (USDC)
IITM	International Institute for Traditional Music [*Germany*] (EAIO)
IITPW	Inertial Interchange True Polar Wander [*Geophysics*]
IIT RES IN	Illinois Institute of Technology Research Institute (MCD)
IITRI	Illinois Institute of Technology Research Institute [*Information service or system*] (IID)
IITS	Igniter Initiator Test Set
IITS	Intratheater Imagery Transmission System [*Air Force*]
I/ITSC	Interservice/Industry Training Systems Conference [*Military*]
IITT-IITW	Institut International du Travail Temporaire - International Institute for Temporary Work (EAIO)
IITV	Image-Intensified Television (MCD)
IITYWYBMAD	If I Tell You, Will You Buy Me a Drink [*Tavern sign*]
IIU	Input Interface Unit [*Computer science*]
IIU	Instruction Input Unit
IIV	Image Intensifier Viewer
IIV	International Institute of Valuers (EA)
IIVD	Image Intensifier Viewing Device
IIVI	II-VI, Inc. [*NASDAQ symbol*] (NQ)
IIVI 0-7	International Institute for Visually Impaired, Zero-7 (EA)
IIVS	Intransit Item Visibility System (MCD)
IIVT	Intensive Intravenous Treatment [*Medicine*]
IIVW	Internationales Institut fuer Verwaltungswissenschaften [*International Institute of Administrative Sciences*]
IIW	International Institute of Welding [*See also IIS*] [*British*] (EAIO)
IIWG	International Industry Working Group [*of the Air Transport Association of America*] (EAIO)
IIWI	Interior Insulating Window Institute [*Defunct*] (EA)
IIWPA	International Information/Word Processing Association [*Formerly, IWPA*] [*Later, IWP*] (EA)
IIWPL	International Institute for Women's Political Leadership [*Defunct*] (EA)
IIWS	Intersystems Inc. Wrrt [*AMEX symbol*] (TTSB)
IIYA	Institute for International Youth Affairs
IJ	Ilejejunal [*Gastroenterology*] (DAVI)
IJ	Im Jahre [*In the Year*] [*German*]
IJ	Indian Jurist, Old Series [*A publication*] (DLA)
IJ	Indirect to Job Costs (DGA)
IJ	Institute of Journalists [*British*] (NTCM)
IJ	Instructor's Journal [*Air Force*]
IJ	Internal Jugular [*Anatomy*]
IJ	Internal Junctor [*Electronics*] (IAA)
IJ	Jacksonville Public Library, Jacksonville, IL [*Library symbol Library of Congress*] (LCLS)
IJ	Sisters of the Holy Infant Jesus [*Roman Catholic religious order*]
IJ	Sisters of the Infant Jesus (TOCD)
IJ	Touraine Air Transport [*ICAO designator*] (AD)
IJA	Imperial Japanese Army [*World War II*]
IJA	Institute of Jewish Affairs (EA)
IJA	Institute of Judicial Administration (EA)
IJA	International Jugglers Association (EA)
IJA	Inventory of Job Attitudes [*LIMRA*]
IJA	Irving Independent School District, Irving, TX [*OCLC symbol*] (OCLC)
IJA	Islamic Jurisprudence Academy [*See also IFA*] (EAIO)
IJAB	Internationaler Jugendaustausch und Besucherdienst der Bundesrepublik Deutschland [*International Youth Exchange and Visitor Service of the Federal Republic of Germany*]
IJAHS	International Journal of African Historical Studies [*A publication*]
IJAJ	Intentional Jitter Antijam [*Military*]
IJB	Internationale Jugendbibliothek [*International Youth Library - IYL*] [*Munich, Federal Republic of Germany*] (EAIO)
IJB	Interstate Job Bank
IJBBA	International Junior Brangus Breeders Association (EA)
IJBF	International Jacques Brel Foundation (EA)
IJBS	Integrated Joint Broadband System [*Army*] (AABC)
IJC	Interjob Communications (MHDB)
IJC	International Joint Commission (EA)
IJC	Irvine's Justiciary Cases [*England*] [*A publication*] (DLA)
IJC	Irving Public Library System, Irving, TX [*OCLC symbol*] (OCLC)
IJC	Itasca Junior College [*Later, Itasca Community College*] [*Minnesota*]
IJC	Itawamba Junior College [*Fulton, MS*]
IJCAI	International Joint Conference on Artificial Intelligence
IJ Cas	Irvine's Justiciary Cases [*England*] [*A publication*] (DLA)
IJCIC	International Jewish Committee on Interreligious Consultations (EA)
IJCNN	International Joint Conference on Neural Networks
IJCR	Institute for Jewish-Christian Relations (EA)
IJCS	Integrated Joint Communication System [*Military*] (AABC)
IJCS-PAC	Integrated Joint Communication System - Pacific [*Military*]
IJD	Inflammatory Joint Disease [*Medicine*] (DMAA)
IJD	Institutum Judaicum Delitzschianum (BJA)
IJDA	International Joseph Diseases Association (EA)
IJDF	International Joseph Diseases Foundation (EA)
IJDW	Im Jahre der Welt [*In the Year of the World*] [*German*]
IJE	Avijet SA de CV [*Mexico ICAO designator*] (FAAC)
IJE	Institute of Jewish Education [*British*] (DBA)
IJE	Inverse Joule Effect
IJe	Jerseyville Free Library, Jerseyville, IL [*Library symbol Library of Congress*] (LCLS)
IJeH	Jersey Community Hospital, Jerseyville, IL [*Library symbol Library of Congress*] (LCLS)
IJeSD	Jersey Community Unit, School District 100, Jerseyville, IL [*Library symbol Library of Congress*] (LCLS)
IJF	Internationale Judo Foederation [*International Judo Federation*] [*Germany*] (EA)
IJF	International Jazz Federation (EA)
IJF	Robinson Crusoe Island [*Juan Fernandez Archipelago*] [*Seismograph station code, US Geological Survey*] (SEIS)
IJFRS	Irish Joint Fiction Reserve Scheme (AIE)
IJI	Illegal Jewish Immigrant [*British occupation of Palestine, 1945-48*] (DI)
IJI	Illinois College, Jacksonville, IL [*Library symbol Library of Congress*] (LCLS)
IJI	Internationaal Juridisch Instituut [*International Juridical Institute*] [*BENELUX*]
IJI	Islamic Jamhoori Ittedad [*Islamic Democratic Alliance*] [*Pakistan*] [*Political party*]
IJIN	International Jensen, Inc. [*NASDAQ symbol*] (SAG)
IJIN	IntlJensen [*NASDAQ symbol*] (TTSB)
IJIR	International Journal of Impotence Research [*A publication*]
IJJU	Intentional Jitter Jamming Unit [*Military*]
IJK	Internationale Juristen-Kommission [*International Commission of Jurists*]
IJL	Institute of Jewish Life Media Project [*Later, JMS*]
IJL	International Journal of Leprosy [*A publication*]
IJL	Interstate/Johnson Lane [*NYSE symbol*] (TTSB)
IJL	Interstate Johnson Lane, Inc. [*NYSE symbol*] (SAG)
IJLB	International Jewish Labor Bund (EA)
IJMA	Infant and Juvenile Manufacturers Association (EA)
IJMac	MacMurray College, Jacksonville, IL [*Library symbol Library of Congress*] (LCLS)
IJMI	International Jacques Maritain Institute [*See also IIJM*] (EAIO)
IJMS	Interim JTIDS [*Joint Tactical Information Distribution System*] Message Standard
IJMVT	International Journal of Micrographics and Video Technology [*A publication*]
IJN	Imperial Japanese Navy [*World War II*]
IJN	International Justice Network [*Defunct*] (EA)
IJO	Independent Jewelers Organization (EA)
IJO	Individual Job Order
IJO	International Journal of Osteoarchaeology [*A publication*]
IJO	International Juridical Organization [*Later, IJOED*] (EAIO)
IJO	Inventory of Job Openings [*State Employee Security Agency*] (OICC)
IJOA	International Juvenile Officers' Association (EA)
IJOED	International Juridical Organization for Environment and Development (EAIO)
IJol	Joliet Public Library, Joliet, IL [*Library symbol Library of Congress*] (LCLS)
IJolStF	College of Saint Francis, Joliet, IL [*Library symbol Library of Congress*] (LCLS)
IJP	Idiopathic Juvenile Periodontitis [*Dentistry*] (PDAA)
IJP	Inhibitory Junction Potential [*Neurophysiology*]
IJP	Ink Jet Printing
IJP	Internal Job Processing (IAA)
IJP	Internal Jugular Pressure [*Medicine*] (MAE)
IJP	International Juvenile Publications
IJP	Israel Jewish Press (BJA)
IJPA	International Jelly and Preserve Association (EA)
IJPPR	Institute for Jewish Policy Planning and Research [*Defunct*] (EA)
IJPSMHI	Industrial Jacks Product Section of the Material Handling Institute [*Defunct*] (EA)
IJR	Institute for Justice Research [*American University*] [*Research center*] (RCD)
IJR	Institute for Juvenile Research [*Illinois Department of Mental Health-University of Illinois at Chicago*] [*Research center*] (RCD)
IJRCS	International Joint Rules Committee on Softball [*Later, ASA*] (EA)
IJS	Institute of Jazz Studies [*Rutgers University, University of New Jersey*] [*Research center*] (EA)
IJS	Interactive Job Submission [*Computer science*]
IJS	Interrupt Jet Sensor
IJS	Rutgers-[*The*] State University, Institute of Jazz Studies, Newark, NJ [*OCLC symbol*] (OCLC)
IJS	Silvair, Inc. [*ICAO designator*] (FAAC)

IJSBA	International Jet Ski Boating Association (EA)
IJSHOF	International Jewish Sports Hall of Fame
IJSS	International John Steinbeck Society (EA)
IJT	Interflight (Learjet) Ltd. [British ICAO designator] (FAAC)
IJU	Ijui [Brazil] [Airport symbol] (OAG)
IJV	Internal Jugular Vein [Medicine] (DMAA)
IJV	Jeffersonville Township Public Library, Jeffersonville, IN [OCLC symbol] (OCLC)
IJWU	International Jewelry Workers Union [Later, Service Employees International Union] (EA)
IJX	Jacksonville, IL [Location identifier FAA] (FAAL)
IJZ	Summersville, WV [Location identifier FAA] (FAAL)
IK	Eureka Aero Industries [ICAO designator] (AD)
IK	Ihud ha-Kibbutsim (BJA)
IK	Imitation Kraft [Paper] (DGA)
IK	Immobilized Knee [Orthopedics]
IK	Immunekoerper [Immune Bodies] [Medicine]
IK	Immunoconglutinin (MAE)
IK	Indicator Kit
IK	Infanteriekolonne [Infantry Supply Column] [German military - World War II]
IK	Infusoria Killing [Unit] [Medicine]
IK	Inner Keel
I/K	Inspector/Killer
IK	Interbank (ADA)
IK	Intercollegiate Knights [An association] (EA)
IK	Interkinase Domain [Genetics]
IK	[The] Interlake Corp. [NYSE symbol] (SPSG)
IK	Interlake Corp. [NYSE symbol] (TTSB)
IK	Interstitial Keratitis [Ophthalmology]
IK	Inverse Kinematics [Computer science]
IKA	International Kitefliers Association [Defunct] (EA)
IKampR	Kampsville Reading Center, Kampsville, IL [Library symbol Library of Congress] (LCLS)
IKan	Kansas Community Memorial Library, Kansas, IL [Library symbol Library of Congress] (LCLS)
IKanSD	Kansas Community Unit School District, Kansas, IL [Library symbol] [Library of Congress] (LCLS)
IKAR	Internationale Kommission fuer Alpines Rettungswesen [International Commission for Alpine Rescue] [Birchwil, Switzerland] (EAIO)
IKAT	Interactive Keyboard and Terminal [Computer science] (MCD)
IKB	Internationale Kommunistenbond [International Communist League] [Netherlands] (PPW)
IKB	International Klein Blue [Color named after French painter Yves Klein]
IKB	Wilkesboro, NC [Location identifier FAA] (FAAL)
IKBD	Intelligent Keyboard Device
IKBM	Integrated Knowledge Based Modelling (NITA)
IKBS	Intelligent Knowledge-Based System [Artificial intelligence]
IKC	Interkernal Communication (NITA)
IKC	International Kennel Club of Chicago (EA)
IKC	Kankakee Community College, Kankakee, IL [Library symbol Library of Congress] (LCLS)
ike	Iconoscope [A television camera tube] (WDMC)
IKE	Ion Kinetic Energy
IKe	Kewanee Public Library, Kewanee, IL [Library symbol Library of Congress] (LCLS)
IKEA	Ingvar Kamprad, Elmtaryd, Agunnaryd [Initialism is company name derived from the names of its founder, the farm on which he grew up, and a Swedish village]
IKeB	Black Hawk College, East Campus, Kewanee, IL [Library symbol Library of Congress] (LCLS)
IKEC	InterAction Media Corp. [NASDAQ symbol] (SAG)
IKEL	Internacia Komitato por Etnaj Liberecoj [International Committee for Ethnic Liberty - ICEL] [Eschweiler, Federal Republic of Germany] (EAIO)
IKES	Ion Kinetic Energy Spectrometry
IKET	Individual Knowledge Evaluation Test (AFM)
IKF	International Kart Federation (EA)
IKF	International Korfball Federation (EA)
IKF	International Kraft Federation (EA)
IKFC	International Knife and Fork Clubs (EA)
IKFS	International Kids Fashion Show (ITD)
IKG	Champaign Public Library, Champaign, IL [OCLC symbol] (OCLC)
IKG	Internationale Kommission fuer Glas [International Commission on Glass]
IKG	Israelitische Kultusgemeinde [Vienna] [A publication] (BJA)
IKH	Ihre Koenigliche Hoheit [His (or Her) Royal Highness] [German]
IKHS	International Kodak Historical Society (EA)
IKI	Iki [Japan] [Airport symbol] (OAG)
IKI	Institute of Space Research [Former USSR Acronym is based on foreign phrase]
IKIF	Individual Name and Address Key Index File [IRS]
IKIM	Institute of Islamic Understanding [Think-tank] [Malaysia] (ECON)
IKJ	Ikusaka [Japan] [Seismograph station code, US Geological Survey] (SEIS)
IKJ	Internationales Kuratorium fuer das Jugendbuch [International Board on Books for Young People]
IKK	Kankakee, IL [Location identifier FAA] (FAAL)
IKL	Ikela [Zaire] [Airport symbol] (AD)
IKL	Isaenmaallinen Kansanliike [Patriotic People's Movement] [Finland Political party] (PPE)
IKM	In Kind Matching (OICC)
IKM	Institut Kimia Malaysia

IKM	Texas State Library and Historical Commission, Austin, TX [OCLC symbol] (OCLC)
IKMB	Internationale Katholische Mittelstandsbewegung [International Catholic Union of the Middle Class]
IKN	Delco Electronics Division, General Motors Corp., Technical Library, Kokomo, IN [OCLC symbol] (OCLC)
IKN	Internationale Kommission fuer Numismatik [International Numismatic Commission]
IKO	Nikolski [Alaska] [Airport symbol] (OAG)
IKON	Olivet Nazarene College, Kankakee, IL [Library symbol Library of Congress] (LCLS)
IKOR	Immediate Knowledge of Results
IKOS	IKOS Systems [NASDAQ symbol] (TTSB)
IKOS	Ikos Systems, Inc. [NASDAQ symbol] (SAG)
IKP	Indiai Kommunista Part [Communist Party of India] [Political party]
IKP	Indian Communist Party [Political party]
IKP	Indonesian Communist Party [Political party]
IKP	Inkopah [California] [Seismograph station code, US Geological Survey] (SEIS)
IKP	Instructor and Key Personnel
IKP	Irakskaia Kommunisticheskaia Partiia [Iraqi Communist Party] [Political party]
IKP	Iranian Communist Party [Political party]
IKP	Iraqi Communist Party [Political party]
IKP	Irish Communist Party [Political party]
IKP	Israeli Communist Party [Political party]
IKP	Italian Communist Party [Political party]
IKP	Kokomo Public Library, Kokomo, IN [OCLC symbol] (OCLC)
IKPO	Internationale Kriminalpolizeiliche Organisation [International Criminal Police Organization]
IKPT	Instructor and Key Personnel Training
IKR	Ikaros DK [Denmark ICAO designator] (FAAC)
IKRA	International Kirlian Research Association (EA)
IKRD	Inverse Kinetics Rod Drop [Nuclear energy] (NRCH)
IKRK	Internationales Komitee vom Roten Kreuz [International Committee of the Red Cross]
IKS	Imaging Kernel System [Computer science] (BTTJ)
IKS	Integrated Key Set [Computer science]
IKS	International Kodaly Society (EAIO)
IKS	International Kolping Society [See also IKW] [Cologne, Federal Republic of Germany] (EAIO)
IKS	Inverse Kinetics Simulator
IKSR	Internationale Kommission zum Schutze des Rheins Gegen Verunreinigung [International Commission for the Protection of the Rhine Against Pollution - ICPRAP] (EAIO)
IKT	Iakutaviatrans [Russian Federation] [ICAO designator] (FAAC)
IKT	Irkutsk [Former USSR Airport symbol] (OAG)
IKTS	International Klaus Tennstedt Society [Defunct] (EA)
IKU	Interface Keying Unit [Computer science] (KSC)
IKUE	Internacia Katolica Unuigo Esperantista [International Catholic Esperanto Association] (EA)
IKV	Internationaler Kranckenhausverbaund [International Hospital Federation]
IKVSA	Internationale Katholische Vereinigung fuer Soziale Arbeit [Catholic International Union for Social Service]
IKW	Indicated Kilowatts per Hour [Engine emissions testing]
IKW	Internationales Kolpingwerk [International Kolping Society - IKS] [Cologne, Federal Republic of Germany] (EAIO)
IKX	Windsor Locks, CT [Location identifier FAA] (FAAL)
IL	Bomber [Russian aircraft symbol]
IL	Iceland [IYRU nationality code]
IL	Identification List
IL	Idle (BUR)
Il	Iliad [of Homer] [Classical studies] (OCD)
Il	Illinium (MAE)
IL	Illinois [Postal code]
IL	Illinois Supreme Court Reports [A publication] (DLA)
IL	Illite [A mineral]
IL	Illium [Anatomy] (IAA)
il	Illustrated [or Illustrator]
IL	Illustration
il	Ilmenite [Also, ILM] [CIPW classification Geology]
IL	Ilyushin [Former USSR ICAO aircraft manufacturer identifier] (ICAO)
IL	I'm Leavin' Elvis Photos, Exclusive (EA)
IL	Imperial Life Assurance Co. of Canada [Toronto Stock Exchange symbol]
I/L	Import License
IL	Incisolingual [Dentistry]
IL	Inclined Ladder (AAG)
IL	Including Loading
IL	Incoming Letter
IL	Indent Left [Typography] (DGA)
il	Indent Left (WDMC)
IL	Independent Living [An association Defunct] (EA)
IL	Index Linked [Government bonds] [British]
IL	Index Lists [DoD]
IL	Indicating Light
IL	Individualized Learning (OICC)
IL	Individual Line (IAA)
IL	Inertial Laboratory [NASA] (KSC)
IL	Information Labeling
IL	Injection Long Wheelbase [Automotive engineering]
IL	In Ladestreifen [Loaded in Clips] [German military - World War II]
I-L	In-Law
IL	In-Lock

IL	Insensible Weight Loss (MEDA)
IL	Insertion Loss
IL	Inside Layer [*Technical drawings*]
IL	Inside Left [*Soccer position*]
IL	Inside Leg (ADA)
IL	Inside Length [*Technical drawings*]
IL	Institute of Linguists [*British*] (BI)
IL	Instruction Leaflet (MSA)
IL	Instruction List
IL	Instructor-Lieutenant [*Navy British*]
IL	Instrumentation Laboratory (MCD)
IL	Instrument Landing (IAA)
IL	Insulation Level (IAA)
IL	Insulators [*JETDS nomenclature*] [*Military*] (CET)
IL	Intelligence Liaison [*Program*] [*Department of State*]
IL	Intensity Level [*Physics*] (IAA)
IL	Intereact Ltd. [*British*]
IL	Interior Length
IL	Interleukin [*Biochemistry*]
IL	Interline
IL	Intermediary Letter
IL	Intermediate Land (DNAB)
IL	Intermediate Language [*Computer science*] (BUR)
IL	Intermediate Level (MCD)
IL	Intermediate Loop
IL	International League [*Baseball*]
IL	International Library [*A publication*]
IL	International List
IL	International Logistics (AABC)
IL	Interpolated Learning [*Psychology*]
IL	Interpretive Language (PDAA)
IL	Intralipid [*Pharmacology*] (DAVI)
IL	Intraocular Lens [*Ophthalmology*] (DAVI)
IL	Irish Land Reports (Fitzgibbon) [*A publication*] (DLA)
IL	Island Air [*ICAO designator*] (AD)
IL	Israel [*ANSI two-letter standard code*] (CNC)
IL	Israel Lira (BJA)
IL	Italian Lira [*Monetary unit*]
IL	Item List (AFIT)
IL	Ives Laboratories [*Research code symbol*]
IL	Ivy League (EA)
IL	L'Internationale Liberale
IL	Lisle Library District, Lisle, IL [*Library symbol Library of Congress*] (LCLS)
IL 2d	Illinois Supreme Court Reports, Second Series [*A publication*] (DLA)
ILA	Ilan [*Giran*] [*Republic of China*] [*Seismograph station code, US Geological Survey*] (SEIS)
ILA	Illaga [*Indonesia*] [*Airport symbol*] (OAG)
IL A	Illinois Appellate Court Reports [*A publication*] (DLA)
ILa	Incisolabial [*Dentistry*]
ILA	Independent Label Association (EA)
ILA	Indian Limitation Act [*British*] (ROG)
ILA	Informationsstelle Lateinamerika [*Germany*]
ILA	Injection Locked Amplifier (PDAA)
ILA	Institute of Landscape Architects [*British*]
ILA	Instruction Look-Ahead [*Unit*] [*Computer science*]
ILA	Instrument Landing Aid
ILA	Instrument Landing Approach
ILA	Instrument Low Approach [*Aircraft landing method*]
ILA	Insulin-Like Activity
ILA	Insurance Logistics Automated (PDAA)
ILA	Integrated Laboratory Automation
ILA	Intelligent Line Adapter
ILA	Intermediate Level Amplifier (MHDB)
ILA	International Language for Aviation
ILA	International Laundry Association
ILA	International Law Association [*British*] (EA)
ILA	International Leprosy Association [*India*]
ILA	International Listening Association (EA)
ILA	International Llama Association (EA)
ILA	International Longshoremen's Association (EA)
ILA	Iterative Logic Array (MCD)
ILA	Lafayette School Corp., Lafayette, IN [*OCLC symbol*] (OCLC)
ILa	Lansing Public Library, Lansing, IL [*Library symbol Library of Congress*] (LCLS)
ILA	Williams, CA [*Location identifier FAA*] (FAAL)
IL A 2d	Illinois Appellate Court Reports, Second Series [*A publication*] (DLA)
IL A 3d	Illinois Appellate Court Reports, Third Series [*A publication*] (DLA)
ILAA	Independent Literary Agents Association (EA)
ILAA	International Lawyers in Alcoholics Anonymous (EA)
ILAA	International Legal Aid Association [*Defunct*]
ILAADS	Interim Low-Altitude Air Defense System
ILAAS	Integrated Light Attack Aircraft [*or Attack Avionics*] System
ILAAT	Interlaboratory Air-to-Air Missile Technology (MCD)
ILAB	Bureau of International Labor Affairs [*Department of Labor*]
ILAB	Instrumental Laboratory SpA [*NASDAQ symbol*] (SAG)
ILAB	International League of Antiquarian Booksellers [*See also LILA*] [*Bonn, Federal Republic of Germany*] (EAIO)
ILAB	Irish Laboratory Accreditation Board [*Now the Irish National Accreditation Board*] (ACII)
ILABC	Inter-Laboratory Committee (SAA)
I-Lac	Imidazolelactic Acid [*Medicine*] (MEDA)
ILAC	International Laboratory Accreditation Conference [*Gaithersburg, MD*] [*National Institute of Standards and Technology*] (EGAO)
ILACD	Ibero Latin American College of Dermatology (EA)
ILACDE	Instituto Latinoamericano de Cooperacion y Desarrollo [*Latin American Institute for Cooperation and Development*] (EAIO)
ILACO	International Land Development Consultants Ltd.
ILACS	Integrated Library Administration and Cataloguing System (PDAA)
ILad	Ladd Public Library, Ladd, IL [*Library symbol Library of Congress*] (LCLS)
ILADES	Instituto Latinoamericano de Doctrina y Estudios Sociales [*Latin American Institute of Social Doctrine and Social Studies*] [*Chile*] (EAIO)
ILadSD	Ladd Consolidated Community School District 94, Ladd, IL [*Library symbol Library of Congress*] (LCLS)
ILADT	Instituto Latinoamericano de Derecho Tributario [*Latin American Tax Law Institute*] (EAIO)
ILAE	International League Against Epilepsy (EA)
ILAEDS	Illinois Association for Educational Data Systems (EDAC)
ILAF	Identical Location of Accelerometer and Force [*NASA*]
ILAFA	Instituto Latinoamericano del Fierro y el Acero [*Latin American Iron and Steel Institute*] (EAIO)
ILAG	INLOGOV [*Institute of Local Government*] Local Authority Game
ILag	La Grange Public Library, La Grange, IL [*Library symbol Library of Congress*] (LCLS)
ILagp	La Grange Park Library District, La Grange Park, IL [*Library symbol Library of Congress*] (LCLS)
ILagpS	Suburban Audio-Visual Service, La Grange Park, IL (LCLS)
ILAI	Italo-Latin American Institute (EA)
ILAIS	Institute for Latin American and Iberian Studies [*Columbia University*] [*Research center*] (RCD)
ILAM	Institute of Leisure and Amenity Management (EAIO)
ILam	LaMoille-Clarion District Library, LaMoille, IL [*Library symbol Library of Congress*] (LCLS)
ILAMA	International Life-Saving Appliance Manufacturers Association (PDAA)
ILAMS	Infrared LASER Atmospheric Monitoring System
ILamSD	LaMoille Community Unit, School District 303, LaMoille, IL [*Library symbol Library of Congress*] (LCLS)
ILAN	Industrial Local Area Network [*Telecommunications*] (OSI)
ILAN	Industrial Local Area Network (NITA)
ILAN	[*The*] Israeli Academic Network [*Computer science*] (TNIG)
IL & FM	Assistant Secretary of the Army for Installations, Logistics, and Financial Management (MCD)
IL&FM	Installation, Logistics and Financial Management (AAGC)
IL & M	Ichthyological Laboratory and Museum [*University of Miami*]
ILAP	Integrated Local Area Planning
ILAR	Institute of Laboratory Animal Resources (EA)
ILAR	International League Against Rheumatism (EA)
ILAR	International League for Animal Rights (EA)
ILARTS	Integrated Launch and Recovery Television System (MCD)
ILAS	Improved Limb Atmospheric Spectrometer [*Matsushita Electronics*]
ILAS	Institute of Latin American Studies [*China*] (IRC)
ILAS	Instrument Landing Approach System [*Aviation*] (IAA)
ILAS	Instrument Low-Approach System [*Aircraft landing method*]
ILAS	International Laser Acupuncture Society (EA)
ILAS	Interrelated Logic Accumulating Scanner
ILas	LaSalle Public Library, LaSalle, IL [*Library symbol Library of Congress*] (LCLS)
ILasC	Carus Chemical Co., Inc., LaSalle, IL [*Library symbol Library of Congress*] (LCLS)
ILASE	Internacia Ligo de Agrikulturaj Specialistoj-Esperantistoj [*International League of Agricultural Specialists-Esperantists - ILASE*] (EAIO)
ILasH	Hygiene Institute, Medical Library, LaSalle, IL [*Library symbol Library of Congress*] (LCLS)
ILasJ	Jefferson Elementary School, LaSalle, IL [*Library symbol Library of Congress*] (LCLS)
ILasL	Lincoln Junior High School, LaSalle, IL [*Library symbol Library of Congress*] (LCLS)
ILasN	Northwest Elementary School, LaSalle, IL [*Library symbol Library of Congress*] (LCLS)
ILASS	Integrated Light Attack Avionics System [*Navy*] (NVT)
ILASS	Intermediate Level Avionics Support System (MCD)
ILasSD	LaSalle-Peru Township High School, LaSalle, IL [*Library symbol Library of Congress*] (LCLS)
I-LAW	Improved Light Antiarmor [*or Antitank*] Weapon (RDA)
ILaw	Lawrence Township Library, Lawrenceville, IL [*Library symbol Library of Congress*] (LCLS)
ILB	Eli Lilly & Co., Business Library, Indianapolis, IN [*OCLC symbol*] (OCLC)
ILB	Independent Lateral Band (IAA)
ILB	Infant, Low Birth Weight [*Medicine*] (DMAA)
ILB	Initial Load Block
ILB	Initial Lung Burden [*Medicine*] (DMAA)
ILB	Inner Lead Bond [*Integrated circuit technology*]
ILB	Inshore Life Boat (PDAA)
ILB	Insurance Law Bulletin [*Australia A publication*]
ILB	Involvement Limited to Bone [*Oncology*]
ILBA	International League for Bolivarian Action (EA)
ILBB	Improved Life Blower Bearing
ILBC	International Livestock Brand Conference (EA)
ILBE	International League of Blind Esperantists [*See also LIBE*] [*Belgrade, Yugoslavia*] (EAIO)
ILBFRLP	International Lelio Basso Foundation for the Rights and Liberation of Peoples (EA)
ILBTC	International Livestock Brand and Theft Conference (EA)
ILBW	Infant, Low Birth Weight
ILC	Ichthyosis Linearis Circumflex [*Medicine*] (DMAA)
ILC	Idiopathic CD4-Lymphocytopenia [*Medicine*]

ILC .... Idle Load Compensator [*Automotive engineering*]
ILC .... Improved Line Charge (DOMA)
ILC .... Incipient Lethal Concentration
ILC .... Independent Labor Congress [*Nigeria*]
ILC .... Industrial Liaison Centre [*British*]
ILC .... Industry-Labor Council (EA)
ILC .... Infantry Leader Course [*Army*] (INF)
ILC .... Initial Launch Capability [*Aerospace*]
ILC .... Input Language Converter [*Computer science*] (IAA)
ILC .... Institute for Liberty and Community (EA)
ILC .... Institute of Land Combat [*Army*]
ILC .... Instruction Length Code [*Computer science*] (BUR)
ILC .... Instruction Length Counter [*Computer science*] (IAA)
ILC .... Instruction Location Counter
ILC .... Instructor Lieutenant-Commander [*Navy British*]
ILC .... Integrated Launch Complex (MCD)
ILC .... Integrated Logic Circuit
ILC .... Intermediate-Level Cell [*Nuclear energy*] (NRCH)
ILC .... Internal Locus of Control [*Psychology*]
ILC .... International Labelling Centre [*Defunct*] (EA)
ILC .... International Labor Conference [*A section of the International Labor Organization*] [*United Nations*]
ILC .... International Latex Corp.
ILC .... International Law Commission [*United Nations*]
ILC .... International Law Commission (USDC)
ILC .... International Leadership Center [*Defunct*] (EA)
ILC .... International Legal Center [*Formerly, SAILER*] [*Later, International Center for Law and Development*] (EA)
ILC .... International Licensed Carrier [*Telecommunications*]
ILC .... International Lines of Communication (MCD)
ILC .... International Logistics Center [*Army*]
ILC .... Irrevocable Letter of Credit [*Business term*]
ILC .... ISDN [*Integrated Services Digital Network*] Link Controller [*Telecommunications*]
ILC .... Lake County Public Library, Merrillville, IN [*OCLC symbol*] (OCLC)
ILC .... Wilson Creek, NV [*Location identifier FAA*] (FAAL)
ILCA .... Belgique Judiciaire [*A publication*] (ILCA)
ILCA .... Indian Land Consolidation Act [*1983*]
ILCA .... Insurance Loss Control Association [*Indianapolis, IN*] (EA)
ILCA .... International Labor Communications Association (EA)
ILCA .... International Lactation Consultant Association (EA)
ILCA .... International Lightning Class Association (EA)
ILCA .... International Livestock Centre for Africa [*Addis Ababa, Ethiopia*]
ILCA .... Inverter Light Control Assembly (MCD)
ILCC .... Initial Launch Capability Complex [*Aerospace*]
ILCC .... Integrated Launch Control and Checkout (KSC)
ILCC .... Integrated Living Communities, Inc. [*NASDAQ symbol*] (SAG)
ILCC .... Italian Language and Culture Center [*Australia*]
ILCCG .... International Laity and Christian Community Group [*See also LAEEC*] [*Sion, Switzerland*] [*Defunct*] (EAIO)
IIC CI .... Illinois Court of Claims Reports [*A publication*] (DLA)
ILCCS .... Integrated Launch Control and Checkout System
ILCCTC .... International Liaison Committee on Co-Operative Thrift and Credit [*Paris, France*] (EA)
ILCEP .... Inter-Laboratory Committee on Editing and Publishing [*Navy*] (MCD)
ILCF .... Inter-Laboratory Committee on Facilities [*Navy*] (MCD)
ILCK .... Inductosyn Linearity Checkout Kit
ILCM .... Individual Level Cost Method [*Insurance*]
ILC Newl .... International Legal Center. Newsletter [*A publication*] (DLA)
ILCO .... Infrastructural, Logistics, Council Operations [*NATO*]
ILCO .... Instantaneous Launch Control Officer [*Aerospace*] (AAG)
ILCO .... Intercontinental Life Corp. [*NASDAQ symbol*] (NQ)
ILCO .... Intercontl Life [*NASDAQ symbol*] (TTSB)
ILCO .... International Logistics Control Office (AAGC)
ILCO .... International Logistics Control Office
ILCOP .... International Liaison Committee of Organizations for Peace
ILCORK .... International Liaison Committee for Research on Korea
ILCOS .... Instantaneous Lead Computing Optical Sight [*Gunsight*] [*Navy*] (DOMA)
ILCRPK .... International Liaison Committee for Reunification and Peace in Korea (EAIO)
ILCS .... Induction Loop Communications System
ILCT .... ILC Technology [*NASDAQ symbol*] (TTSB)
ILCT .... ILC Technology, Inc. [*NASDAQ symbol*] (NQ)
ILCTA .... International League of Commercial Travelers and Agents (EA)
ILC Tc .... ILC Technology, Inc. [*Associated Press*] (SAG)
ILC (UN) ..... International Law Commission of the United Nations
ILCV .... Inscriptiones Latinae Christianae Veteres
ILD .... Eli Lilly & Co., Agricultural Library, Greenfield, IN [*OCLC symbol*] (OCLC)
ILD .... I Love Dance [*Competition in US and Canada*]
ILD .... Indent Load Deflection [*Measure of hardness*]
ILD .... Inductive Loop Detector
ILD .... Information Lead Distance
ILD .... Initial Lung Deposit (PDAA)
ILD .... Injection LASER Diode (TEL)
ILD .... Injection Luminescence Device
ILD .... Inland Recovery Group [*Vancouver Stock Exchange symbol*]
ILD .... In-Lock Detector
ILD .... Instructional Logic Diagram (IAA)
ILD .... Instrument Loop Diagram (ACII)
ILD .... Integrating Light Detector (PDAA)
ILD .... Intermediate-Level Diagram (IAA)
ILD .... Internal Load Deflection [*Automotive seating*]
ILD .... International Labor Defense [*An association*]

ILD .... Intersection Loop Detection (MHDI)
ILD .... Interstitial Lung Disease
ILD .... Intraoperative Localization Device [*Medicine*] (DMAA)
ILD .... Ischemic Leg Disease [*Medicine*]
ILD .... Ischemic Limb Disease [*Medicine*]
ILD .... Isolated Lactase Deficiency [*Medicine*] (DMAA)
ILDA .... Industrial Lands Development Authority [*Australia*]
ILDA .... Industrial Lighting Distributors of America (EA)
ILDA .... Inter Laboratory Data Acceptance (PDAA)
ILDA .... International LASER Display Association (EA)
ILDA .... International Lutheran Deaf Association (EA)
ILDC .... International Legal Defense Counsel
ILDC .... Israel Land & Development Co. [*NASDAQ symbol*] (SAG)
ILDCSI .... Individual Learning Disabilities Classroom Screening Instruments
ILDCY .... Israel Ld Dev Ltd [*NASDAQ symbol*] (TTSB)
I L de Gaule... Inscriptions Latines des Trois Gaules [*A publication*] (OCD)
ILDIS .... International Legume Database and Information Service
ILDM .... Institute of Logistics and Distribution Management [*British*] (DBA)
ILDP .... Interlook Dormant Period (NVT)
ILDR .... Index of Limited Distribution Reports [*A publication*]
ILDS .... Integrated Logistics Data System
ILDS .... International League of Dermatological Societies [*Vancouver, BC*] (EAIO)
ILDSC .... Industrial Land Development Subcommittee [*New South Wales, Australia*]
ILDT .... Item Logistics Data Transmittal
ILDTF .... Item Logistics Data Transmittal Form (NATG)
ILE .... Ileum [*Anatomy*]
ILE .... Indiana Law Encyclopedia [*A publication*] (DLA)
ILE .... Inel Resources Ltd. [*Vancouver Stock Exchange symbol*]
ILE .... Institute of Legal Executives [*Australia*]
ILE .... Institution of Lighting Engineers (EAIO)
ILE .... Integral Linear Error (IAA)
ILE .... Intelligent Life Elsewhere
ILE .... Interface Latching Element
Ile .... Isoleucine [*or iLeu, Ileu*] [*Also, I An amino acid*]
ile .... Isoleucine [*An amino acid*] (DOG)
ILE .... Killeen [*Texas*] [*Airport symbol*] (OAG)
ILE .... Killeen, TX [*Location identifier FAA*] (FAAL)
ILE .... Lincolnwood Public Library District, Lincolnwood, IL [*OCLC symbol*] (OCLC)
ILEA .... Inner London Education Authority [*British*]
ILEA .... International League of Electrical Associations (EA)
ILeb .... Lebanon Public Library, Lebanon, IL [*Library symbol Library of Congress*] (LCLS)
ILebHS .... Lebanon High School, Lebanon, IL [*Library symbol Library of Congress*] (LCLS)
ILebM .... McKendree College, Lebanon, IL [*Library symbol Library of Congress*] (LCLS)
ILeD .... De Andreis Seminary, Lemont, IL [*Library symbol Library of Congress*] (LCLS)
ILEED .... Inelastic Low-Energy Electron Diffraction (IAA)
ILEF .... Internacia Ligo de Esperantistaj Foto-Kino-Magnetofon-Amatoroj [*International League of Esperantist Amateur Photographers, Cinephotographers, and Tape-Recording*] (EAIO)
ILEI .... Internacia Ligo de Esperantistaj Instruistoj [*International League of Esperantist Teachers*] (EAIO)
ILeISD .... Leland Community Unit, School District 1, Leland, IL [*Library symbol Library of Congress*] (LCLS)
ILEM .... Inter-Library Electronic Mail (NITA)
ILEMP .... Immigration Law Enforcement Monitoring Project [*American Friends Service Committee*] (CROSS)
ILEOA .... International Law Enforcement Officers Association (EA)
ILEP .... Federation Internationale des Associations Contre la Lepre [*International Federation of Anti-Leprosy Associations - ILEP*] (EAIO)
ILERA .... International League of Esperantist Radio Amateurs (EA)
ILERT .... Independent Librarians Exchange Round Table [*American Library Association*]
ILESA .... International Law Enforcement Stress Association (EA)
i-lesion .... Intralesional [*Medicine*] (MEDA)
ILET .... Instituto Latinoamericano de Estudios Transnacionales [*Latin American Institute for Transnational Studies - LAITS*] (EAIO)
Ileu .... Isoleucine [*or iLeu, Ile*] [*Also, I An amino acid*]
ILEV .... Inherently Low-Emissions Vehicle
ILE(V) .... Institute of Legal Executives (Victoria) [*Australia*]
ILEX .... ILX, Inc. [*NASDAQ symbol*] (SAG)
ILEX .... Institute of Legal Executives [*British*] (DBA)
ILEx .... Institute of Legal Executives (AIE)
ILF .... Idaho Laboratory Facility [*Later, IRC*] [*Idaho Falls, ID*] [*Department of Energy*] (GRD)
ILF .... Immigrants in the Labour Force [*British*]
ILF .... Indian Local Forces [*Military British*]
ILF .... Inductive Loss Factor (IEEE)
ILF .... Industrial Leathers Federation [*British*] (BI)
ILF .... Infra Low-Frequency [*Telecommunications*] (TEL)
ILF .... Integral Lift Fan [*Aviation*]
ILF .... Integrity Loss Factor
ILF .... International Falcon Resources Ltd. [*Vancouver Stock Exchange symbol*]
ILF .... International Lacrosse Federation (EA)
ILF .... International Landworkers' Federation [*Later, IFPAAW*]
ILF .... International Liaison Forum of Peace Forces [*See also FILFP*] [*Moscow, USSR*] (EAIO)
ILF .... International Lifeboat Federation [*England*] (EAIO)

ILF	International Lotto Fund
ILF	International Luge Federation [*Austria*]
ILf	Lake Forest Library, Lake Forest, IL [*Library symbol Library of Congress*] (LCLS)
ILF	Milford Haven [*Wales*] [*Airport symbol*] (AD)
ILfB	Barat College of the Sacred Heart, Lake Forest, IL [*Library symbol Library of Congress*] (LCLS)
ILFC	Immature Living Female Child [*Neonatology*] (DAVI)
ILfC	Lake Forest College, Lake Forest, IL [*Library symbol Library of Congress*] (LCLS)
ILFCG	International Logistics Functional Coordinating Group (MCD)
ILFI	International Labour Film Institute [*Defunct*]
ILFO	International Logistics Field Office [*Army*] (AABC)
ILFP-IM	Forum International de Liaison des Forces de la Paix [*International Liaison Forum of Peace Forces - ILF*] (EA)
ILFZ	Ivanhoe Lake Fault Zone [*Geology*] [*Canada*]
ILG	Consolidated Inland Recovery [*Vancouver Stock Exchange symbol*]
ILG	Inge Lehmann [*Greenland*] [*Seismograph station code, US Geological Survey Closed*] (SEIS)
ILG	Instrument Landing Guidance
ILG	International Leisure Group [*Commercial firm British*]
ILG	Irish Linen Guild [*Defunct*] (EA)
ILG	University of Illinois, Graduate School of Library Science, Urbana, IL [*OCLC symbol*] (OCLC)
ILG	Wilmington [*Delaware*] [*Airport symbol*] (OAG)
ILGA	Immiscible Lattice-Gas Automata [*Fluid mechanics*]
ILGA	Institute of Local Government Administration [*British*]
ILGA	International Lesbian and Gay Association [*Formerly, International Gay Association*] (EA)
ILGB	International Laboratory of Genetics and Biophysics
ILGF	Insulin-Like Growth Factor
ILGPNWU	International Leather Goods, Plastic, and Novelty Workers' Union (EA)
ILGSA	Indoor Light Gardening Society of America (EA)
ILGWU	International Ladies' Garment Workers' Union (EA)
ILH	Del Rio, TX [*Location identifier FAA*] (FAAL)
ILH	Immunoreactive Luteinizing Hormone (DMAA)
ILH	Imperial Light Horse [*Military British*] (ROG)
ILH	Jus Liberorum Habens [*Possessing the Right of Children*] [*Latin*]
ILH	Northern Illinois University, Department of Library Science, De Kalb, IL [*OCLC symbol*] (OCLC)
ILHA	International Labor History Association
ILHL	International Leisure Hosts Ltd. [*NASDAQ symbol*] (NQ)
ILHL	Intl Leisure Hosts [*NASDAQ symbol*] (TTSB)
ILHR	International League for Human Rights (EA)
ILI	Ili [*Former USSR Seismograph station code, US Geological Survey Closed*] (SEIS)
ILI	Iliamna [*Alaska*] [*Airport symbol*] (OAG)
ILI	Iliamna, AK [*Location identifier FAA*] (FAAL)
ILI	Indiana Limestone Institute of America (EA)
ILI	Indiana University, School of Law Library, Indianapolis, IN [*OCLC symbol*] (OCLC)
ILI	Influenza-Like Illness [*Medicine*]
ILI	Injection LASER Illuminator
ILI	Instant Lunar Ionosphere
ILI	Institute for Land Information [*Research center Information service or system*] (RCD)
ILI	Institute of Life Insurance [*Later, ACLI*] (EA)
ILI	Inter-African Labour Institute
ILI	Interamerican Labour Institute
ILI	Intercan Leasing, Inc. [*Toronto Stock Exchange symbol*]
ILI	International Law Institute (EA)
ILI	International Lottery, Inc. [*AMEX symbol*] (SAG)
ILIA	Indiana Limestone Institute of America
ILIA	International Livestock Investigators Association (EA)
ILib	Cook Memorial Public Library District, Libertyville, IL [*Library symbol Library of Congress*] (LCLS)
ILIC	In-Line Integrated Circuit
ILIC	International Library Information Center (EA)
IL-IC-IM	It's Life, I Can't, I Must [*Element of psychotherapist Joseph Bird's self-help theory*]
I-LIDS	Indian Legal Information Development Service (EA)
ILIF	International Logistics Information File (MCD)
ILIMA	International Licensing Industry and Merchandisers' Association (EA)
ILINC	Interactive Learning International Corp.
i-line	Identification Line [*Photojournalism*] (WDMC)
ILinL	Lincoln Christian College, Lincoln, IL [*Library symbol Library of Congress*] (LCLS)
ILinw	Lincolnwood Public Library, Lincolnwood, IL [*Library symbol Library of Congress*] (LCLS)
ILIOS	In-Line Infinity Optical System
ILIP	In-Line Instrument Package [*Nuclear energy*] (NRCH)
ILIR	In-House Laboratories Independent Research Program [*Army*] (RDA)
ILIR	Institute of Labor and Industrial Relations [*University of Illinois*] [*Research center*] (RCD)
ILIR	Institute of Labor and Industrial Relations [*University of Michigan*] [*Research center*] (RCD)
ILit	Litchfield Carnegie Public Library, Litchfield, IL [*Library symbol Library of Congress*] (LCLS)
I-LITE	Iowa Library Information Teletype Exchange [*Des Moines, IA*] [*Telecommunications Library network*]
ILitSD	Litchfield Community Unit, School District 12, Litchfield, IL [*Library symbol Library of Congress*] (LCLS)
ILivSD	Livingston Community Consolidated School District, Livingston, IL [*Library symbol Library of Congress*] (LCLS)

ILJ	Springfield, MO [*Location identifier FAA*] (FAAL)
ILK	IIT Chicago-Kent College of Law, Chicago, IL [*OCLC symbol*] (OCLC)
ILK	Integrin-Linked Kinase [*An enzyme*]
ILK	Interlock [*Technical drawings*]
ILKE	Internacia Libro-Klubo Esperantista (EA)
ILL	Illinois (AFM)
Ill	Illinois Reports [*A publication*] (DLA)
Ill	Illinois Reports [*A publication*] (AAGC)
ill	Illuminated (WDMC)
ILL	Illuminated (NTCM)
ILL	Illuminating [*Ammunition*] (NATG)
ILL	Illusion
ill	Illustrated (BJA)
ILL	Illustration
ill	Illustration (WDMC)
ill	Illustrator [*MARC relator code*] [*Library of Congress*] (LCCP)
ILL	Illustrissimus [*Most Illustrious*] [*Latin*]
ILL	Impact Limit Lines (MUGU)
ILL	Individual Learning Laboratory (OICC)
ILL	Input Logic Level
ILL	Institute of Languages and Linguistics (DIT)
ILL	Institute of Lifetime Learning (EA)
ILL	Institut Laue-Langevin [*Grenoble, France*] (ECON)
ILL	Interlibrary Loan
ILL	Intermediate Lymphocytic Lymphoma [*Medicine*]
ILL	International Larder Minerals, Inc. [*Toronto Stock Exchange symbol*]
ILL	Interstate Loan Library [*Council of State Governments*] (IID)
ILL	Intl Lottery [*AMEX symbol*] (TTSB)
ILL	Irving Langmuir Laboratory [*New Mexico Institute of Mining and Technology*] [*Research center*] (RCD)
ILL	Ontario Library Service - Escarpment, Hamilton [*UTLAS symbol*]
ILL	Willmar, MN [*Location identifier FAA*] (FAAL)
Ill 2d	Illinois Reports, Second Series [*A publication*] (DLA)
Ill A	Illinois Appellate Court Reports [*A publication*] (DLA)
Ill Adm Code	Illinois Administrative Code [*A publication*] (AAGC)
Ill Admin Code	Illinois Administrative Code [*A publication*] (AAGC)
Ill Admin Reg	Illinois Register [*A publication*] (DLA)
Ill Ann Stat	Smith-Hurd Illinois Annotated Statutes [*A publication*] (AAGC)
Ill Ann Stat	Smith-Hurd's Illinois Annotated Statutes [*A publication*] (DLA)
Ill Ap	Illinois Appellate Court Reports [*A publication*] (DLA)
Ill App	Illinois Appellate Court Reports [*A publication*] (DLA)
Ill App 2d	Illinois Appellate Court Reports, Second Series [*A publication*] (DLA)
Ill App 3d	Illinois Appellate Court Reports, Third Series [*A publication*] (DLA)
Ill App Ct Rep	Illinois Appellate Court Reports [*A publication*] (DLA)
Ill App Illinois	Appellate Court Reports [*A publication*] (AAGC)
Ill Apps	Illinois Appellate Court Reports [*A publication*] (DLA)
ILLB	Insurance and Liability Law Bulletin [*A publication*]
Ill BA Bull	Illinois State Bar Association. Quarterly Bulletin [*A publication*] (DLA)
Ill CC	Illinois Commerce Commission Opinions and Orders [*A publication*] (DLA)
Ill CC	Matthew and Bangs' Illinois Circuit Court Reports [*A publication*] (DLA)
Ill Cir	Illinois Circuit Court (DLA)
Ill Cir Ct	Illinois Circuit Court Reports [*A publication*] (DLA)
Ill Cont L Ed	Illinois Continuing Legal Education [*A publication*] (DLA)
ILLCS	Intralaunch Facility and Launch Control Facility Cabling Subsystem (IAA)
Ill Ct Cl	Illinois Court of Claims (AAGC)
ILLD	Illustrated (ROG)
Ill Dec	Illinois Decisions [*A publication*] (DLA)
ILLEGIT	Illegitimate (WDAA)
IL LF	Illinois Law Forum (DLA)
ILLIAC	Illinois Algorithmic Decoder [*Southern Illinois University*] (SAA)
ILLIAC	Illinois Institute for Advanced Computing
ILLIAC	Illinois Integrator and Automatic Computer [*University of Illinois*] (BUR)
ILLIC LAG OBTURAT	Illico Lagena Obturatur [*Stopper the Bottle at Once*] [*Pharmacy*]
IlliCtr	Illinois Central Corp. [*Associated Press*] (SAG)
ILLIN	Illinantur [*Anoint*] [*Pharmacy*] (ROG)
ILLINEND	Illinendus [*To Be Smeared*] [*Pharmacy*]
ILLINET	Illinois Library and Information Network [*Library network*]
IlliniSup	Illinois Superconductor Corp. [*Associated Press*] (SAG)
Illinois Rep	Illinois Reports [*A publication*] (DLA)
Illinova	Illinova Corp Holding Co. [*Formerly, Illinois Power*] [*Associated Press*] (SAG)
Ill Inst Tech	Illinois Institute of Technology (GAGS)
ILLIT	Illiterate
ILLL	International Lutheran Laymen's League (EA)
Ill Laws	Laws of Illinois [*A publication*] (DLA)
Ill LB	Illinois Law Bulletin [*A publication*] (DLA)
Ill Legis Serv	Illinois Legislative Service (West) [*A publication*] (DLA)
Ill Leg N	Illustrated Legal News [*India*] [*A publication*] (DLA)
Ill LQ	Illinois Law Quarterly [*A publication*] (DLA)
Ill L Rec	Illinois Law Record [*A publication*] (DLA)
ILLLTV	Integrated Low-Light-Level Television
ILLMO	Illustrissimo [*Most Illustrious*] [*Latin*]
ILLODIE-AIF	Illinois University Logical Design by Implicit Enumeration Using the All-Interconnection Inequality Formulation (PDAA)
illog	Antilog [*Mathematics*] (BARN)
Ill Op Att'y Gen	Illinois Attorney General's Opinion [*A publication*]
IIIP	Illinois Power Co. [*Associated Press*] (SAG)
ILLPC	Illinois Power Capital Ltd. [*Associated Press*] (SAG)
IIIPF	Illinois Power Financing I [*Associated Press*] (SAG)

Ill PUC Ops...	Illinois Public Utilities Commission Opinions and Orders [*A publication*] (DLA)
Ill R............	Illinois Reports [*A publication*] (DLA)
Ill R & WC...	Illinois Railroad and Warehouse Commission Reports [*A publication*] (DLA)
Ill R & WCD...	Illinois Railroad and Warehouse Commission Decisions [*A publication*] (DLA)
ILL rate.......	Illiteracy Rate
Ill Reg	Illinois Register [*A publication*] (AAGC)
Ill Rep	Illinois Reports [*A publication*] (DLA)
Ill Rev Stat...	Illinois Revised Statutes [*A publication*] (DLA)
Ill Rev Stat...	Illinois Revised Statutes [*A publication*] (AAGC)
ILLRI...........	Industrial Lift and Loading Ramp Institute [*Defunct*] (EA)
ILLRP..........	Inscriptiones Latinae Liberae Rei Publicae [*A publication*] (OCD)
ILLS	Illinois (ROG)
Ills	Illinois Reports [*A publication*] (DLA)
Ills App.......	Illinois Appellate Court Reports [*A publication*] (DLA)
Ill SBA........	Illinois State Bar Association. Reports [*A publication*] (DLA)
Ill SBAQB	Illinois State Bar Association. Quarterly Bulletin [*A publication*] (DLA)
Ills R	Illinois Reports [*A publication*] (DLA)
Ills Rep.......	Illinois Reports [*A publication*] (DLA)
ILLSTN........	Illustration
Ill St U.......	Illinois State University (GAGS)
ILLT...........	Illinois Terminal Railroad Co.
ILLUM.........	Illuminate (KSC)
illum..........	Illuminated (VRA)
ILLUS.........	Illustrate [*or Illustration*] (AABC)
illus	Illustrated (WDMC)
illus	Illustration (WDMC)
illus	Illustration (VRA)
illus	Illustrator (WDMC)
illus mat.....	Illustrative Material (VRA)
ILLUSTN	Illustration
ILLUSTR	Illustrator (ROG)
Ill WCC	Illinois Workmen's Compensation Cases [*A publication*] (DLA)
ILM	Iliamna [*Alaska*] [*Seismograph station code, US Geological Survey*] (SEIS)
ILM	Ilmenite [*Also, il*] [*Geology*]
ILM	Immobilized-Liquid Membrane [*Chemical engineering*]
ILM	Independent Landing Monitor [*RADAR-TV landing guidance*] [*NASA*]
ILM	Independent Learning Modules (ACII)
ILM	Industrial Learning Modules (ACII)
ILM	Industrial Light Magic [*Electronics Commercial firm*]
ILM	Information Logic Machine (IEEE)
ILM	Institute of Labour Management
ILM	Insulin-Like Material
ILM	Integrated Logistic Management (DNAB)
ILM	Interceptor Launch Module [*Military*]
ILM	Intermediate Language Machine [*Computer science*]
ILM	Internal Limiting Membrane [*Medicine*] (DMAA)
ILM	Lincoln Library, Springfield, IL [*OCLC symbol*] (OCLC)
ILM	Wilmington [*North Carolina*] [*Airport symbol*] (OAG)
ILM	Wilmington, NC [*Location identifier FAA*] (FAAL)
ILMA..........	Immunochemiluminometric Assay [*Analytical biochemistry*]
ILMA..........	Incandescent Lamp Manufacturers Association [*Defunct*] (EA)
ILMA..........	Independent Lubricant Manufacturers Association (EA)
ILMA..........	International Licensing and Merchandisers' Association [*Later, ILIMA*] (EA)
ILMA..........	Intraocular Lens Manufacturers Association [*Defunct*] (EA)
ILMA..........	Morton Arboretum, Lisle, IL [*Library symbol Library of Congress*] (LCLS)
ILMC..........	Immature Living Male Child [*Neonatology*] (DAVI)
ILMD..........	Item Logistics Management Data [*DoD*]
ILMH..........	Institute for Labor and Mental Health (EA)
ILMI...........	Index-Linked Mortgage and Investment (DI)
ILMI...........	Inferolateral Myocardial Infarct [*or Infarction*] [*Cardiology*] (DAVI)
ILMN..........	Incomplete Lower Motor Neuron [*Lesion*] [*Neurology*] (DAVI)
ILMO..........	Illustrissimo [*Most Illustrious*] [*Latin*] (WGA)
ILMP..........	Integrated Logistic Management Program (NG)
ILMP..........	International Literary Market Place [*A publication*]
ILMS..........	Improved Launcher Mechanical System [*Military*]
ILMT..........	Integrated Logistics Management Team
ILMT..........	Intermediate-Level Maintenance Training
ILMWSC	International Lifesaving Museum and Water Safety Center [*Defunct*] (EA)
ILN............	East Peoria Elementary Schools, East Peoria, IL [*OCLC symbol*] (OCLC)
ILN............	Idle Line Network
ILN............	Illinois League for Nursing (SRA)
ILN............	Illinova Corp. [*NYSE symbol*] (TTSB)
ILN............	Illinova Corp. Holding Co. [*Formerly, Illinois Power*] [*NYSE symbol*] (SAG)
ILN............	Illustrated London News [*A publication*] (BRI)
ILN............	International Law News [*A publication*]
ILN............	International Logistics Negotiations [*Military export sales*]
ILN............	Island Lagoon [*Australia Seismograph station code, US Geological Survey Closed*] (SEIS)
ILN............	Wilmington, OH [*Location identifier FAA*] (FAAL)
ILNY..........	International League of New York
ILo	Helen M. Plum Memorial Library, Lombard, IL [*Library symbol Library of Congress*] (LCLS)
ilo	Ilocano [*MARC language code Library of Congress*] (LCCP)
ILO............	Iloilo [*Philippines*] [*Airport symbol*] (OAG)
ILO............	Iloilo [*Philippines*] [*Seismograph station code, US Geological Survey Closed*] (SEIS)
ILO............	Individual Load Operation
ILO............	Industrial Liaison Organization [*MIT*]
ILO............	Injection-Locked Oscillator (IEEE)
ILO............	In Lieu Of
ILO............	Internally Linked Operation
ILO............	International Labor Office [*A section of the International Labor Organization*] [*United Nations*]
ILO............	International Labour Organisation [*Geneva, Switzerland*] [*United Nations*] (EA)
ILO............	Interservice Liaison Office [*Military*] (CAAL)
ILo.............	Iodine Lotion [*Medicine*]
ILO............	Islamic Liberation Organization
ILO............	School of the Art Institute of Chicago Library, Chicago, IL [*OCLC symbol*] (OCLC)
ILOA..........	Industrial Life Offices Association [*British*] (BI)
ILOAD........	Initialization Load (MCD)
ILOC..........	Irrevocable Letter of Credit [*Business term*] (DS)
ILoc	Lockport Township Public Library, Lockport, IL [*Library symbol Library of Congress*] (LCLS)
ILoC	National College of Chiropractic, Lombard, IL [*Library symbol Library of Congress*] (LCLS)
ILoCC........	National College of Chiropractic, Lombard, IL [*Library symbol*] [*Library of Congress*] (LCLS)
ILocL	Lewis University, Lockport, IL [*Library symbol Library of Congress*] (LCLS)
ILocL-L	Lewis University, College of Law, Glen Ellyn, IL [*Library symbol Library of Congress*] (LCLS)
ILod	Loda Public Library, Loda, IL [*Library symbol Library of Congress*] (LCLS)
ILoE	National College of Education, Lombard, IL [*Library symbol Library of Congress*] (LCLS)
ILOGS........	Integrated Logistics System [*Army*] (RDA)
ILoM	MidCon Corp., Lombard, IL [*Library symbol*] [*Library of Congress*] (LCLS)
ILOP..........	Initial Light Off Procedure (MCD)
ILos	Lostant Community Library, Lostant, IL [*Library symbol Library of Congress*] (LCLS)
ILosHSD	Lostant Consolidated High School District 400, Lostant, IL [*Library symbol Library of Congress*] (LCLS)
ILOSS	Integrated LASER Optical Sight Set
ILosSD	Lostant Consolidated Community School District 25, Lostant, IL [*Library symbol Library of Congress*] (LCLS)
ILOST.........	International Liaison Center of Schools of Cinema and Television
ILOSU........	International Labor Organization Staff Union [*Geneva, Switzerland*] (EAIO)
ILOUE........	In Lieu of Until Exhausted [*Military*]
ILovjD........	Lovejoy Unit, District 188, Lovejoy, IL [*Library symbol Library of Congress*] (LCLS)
ILP............	Clausen, Miller, Gorman, Caffrey & Witous, Chicago, IL [*OCLC symbol*] (OCLC)
ILP............	Ile Des Pins [*New Caledonia*] [*Airport symbol*] (OAG)
ILP............	Illinois Law and Practice [*A publication*] (DLA)
ILP............	Ilpo Aruba Cargo NV [*ICAO designator*] (FAAC)
ILP............	Independent Labour Party [*British*]
ILP............	Independent Liberal Party [*Israel*] [*Political party*] (BJA)
ILP............	Individual Learning Package (OICC)
ILP............	Individual Learning Programme (AIE)
ILP............	Industrial Liaison Program [*Refers to university-industry interaction*]
ILP............	In-Line Printer
ILP............	Instruction-Level Parallelism [*Computer science*]
ILP............	Integer Linear Programming Model [*Statistics*]
ILP............	Integrated Logistics Panel (NASA)
ILP............	Intermediate Language Processor [*Computer science*] (BUR)
ILP............	Intermediate Language Program [*Computer science*]
ILP............	International Links Program [*Overseas aid*] [*Australia*]
ILP............	International Logistics Program
ILP............	Irish Labour Party [*Political party*] (ROG)
ILP............	Islamic Liberation Party [*Tunisia*] [*Political party*] (MENA)
ILP............	Isle des Pins [*New Caledonia*] [*Airport symbol*] (AD)
ILP............	Israel Labor Party [*Political party*]
ILPA..........	International Labor Press Association (EA)
ILPA..........	Iowa Limestone Producers Association (SRA)
ILpB	Barber Colman Co., Technical Library, Loves Park, IL [*Library symbol*] [*Library of Congress*] (LCLS)
ILPBC........	International League of Professional Baseball Clubs (EA)
ILPC..........	International Linen Promotion Commission (EA)
ILPES........	Instituto Latinoamericano de Planificacion Economica y Social [*Latin American Institute for Economic and Social Planning*] [*Santiago, Chile*] [*United Nations*]
ILPF..........	Ideal Low Pass Filter
ILPH..........	International League for the Protection of Horses (DI)
ILPL	Index to Legal Periodical Literature [*1887-1937*] [*A publication*] (DLA)
IlPow	Illinois Power Co. [*Associated Press*] (SAG)
ILPPSM.......	International Library of Philosophy, Psychology, and Scientific Method [*Book publishing*] [*British*]
ILPS..........	Industrial Location Planning System [*Department of Commerce*] (GFGA)
ILPS..........	International Lecithin and Phospholipid Society
ILQ............	Chadwell, Kayser, Ruggles, McGee & Hastings, Chicago, IL [*OCLC symbol*] (OCLC)
ILQ............	Indian Law Quarterly [*A publication*] (DLA)
ILQ............	International Law Quarterly [*A publication*] (AAGC)
ILQR	Indian Law Quarterly Review [*A publication*] (DLA)
ILR............	Air Iliria [*Yugoslovia*] [*ICAO designator*] (FAAC)
ILR............	Burns, OR [*Location identifier FAA*] (FAAL)

ILR.............. Ilorin [*Nigeria*] [*Airport symbol*] (OAG)
ILR.............. Incurred Loss Ratio [*Insurance*]
ILR.............. Independent Local Radio [*British*]
ILR.............. Indian Law Reports [*A publication*] (DLA)
ILR.............. Indicating Light Relay
ILR.............. Industrial and Labor Relations
ILR.............. Industrial Law Review [*A publication*] (ILCA)
ILR.............. Infanterie-Lehrregiment [*Infantry Demonstration Regiment*] [*German military - World War II*]
ILR.............. In-Line Reciprocator
ILR.............. Inner Lindblad Resonance [*Galactic science*]
ILR.............. Institute of Library Research [*University of California*] (DIT)
ILR.............. Institute of Logistics Research [*Army*] (RDA)
ILR.............. Instruction Location Register (NITA)
ILR.............. Insurance Law Reporter [*A publication*] (DLA)
ILR.............. Interleukin Receptor [*Medicine*] (DMAA)
ILR.............. International Labour Review [*A publication*] (BRI)
ILR.............. International Laco Resources [*Vancouver Stock Exchange symbol*]
ILR.............. International Law Reports [*A publication*]
ILR.............. International Luggage Registry [*Computer system for recovery of airline luggage*]
ILR.............. Irish Law Reports [*A publication*] (DLA)
ILR.............. Irreversible Loss Rate (DMAA)
ILRA............ Inbred Livestock Registry Association (EA)
ILRA............ International Log Rolling Association
ILRAD.......... International Laboratory for Research on Animal Diseases [*Nairobi, Kenya*]
ILR All......... Indian Law Reports, Allahabad Series [*A publication*] (DLA)
ILR And........ Indian Law Reports, Andhra Series [*A publication*] (DLA)
ILR Assam... Indian Law Reports, Assam Series [*A publication*] (DLA)
ILR Bom....... Indian Law Reports, Bombay Series [*A publication*] (DLA)
ILRC............ Indian Law Reports, Calcutta Series [*A publication*] (DLA)
ILRC............ Indian Law Resource Center (EA)
ILRC............ International LASER RADAR Conference (PDAA)
ILR Cal........ Indian Law Reports, Calcutta Series [*A publication*] (DLA)
ILR Calc...... Indian Law Reports, Calcutta Series [*A publication*] (DLA)
ILR Cut........ Indian Law Reports, Orissa Series [*A publication*] (DLA)
ILRERF........ International Labor Rights Education and Research Fund (EA)
ILR Hyderabad... Indian Law Reports, Hyderabad Series [*A publication*] (DLA)
ILRIS........... Intermediate Long-Range Interceptor System
ILR Kar........ Indian Law Reports, Karachi Series [*A publication*] (DLA)
ILR Ker........ Indian Law Reports, Kerala Series [*A publication*] (DLA)
ILR Lah........ Indian Law Reports, Lahore Series [*A publication*] (DLA)
ILRLP.......... International League for the Rights and Liberation of Peoples [*Rome, Italy*] (EAIO)
ILR Luck...... Indian Law Reports, Lucknow Series [*A publication*] (DLA)
ILRM............ International League for the Rights of Man [*Later, ILHR*]
ILR Mad....... Indian Law Reports, Madras Series [*A publication*] (DLA)
ILR Madhya Bharat... Indian Law Reports, Madhya Bharat Series [*A publication*] (DLA)
ILR Mysore... Indian Law Reports, Mysore Series [*A publication*] (DLA)
ILR Nag........ Indian Law Reports, Nagpur Series [*A publication*] (DLA)
ILRO............ Industrial Labor Relations Office [*DoD*]
ILR Or.......... Indian Law Reports, Orissa Series [*A publication*] (DLA)
ILRP............ Indian Law Reports, Patna Series [*A publication*] (DLA)
ILR Pat........ Indian Law Reports, Patna Series [*A publication*] (DLA)
ILR Patiala... Indian Law Reports, Patiala Series [*A publication*] (DLA)
ILR Pun........ Indian Law Reports, Punjab Series [*A publication*] (DLA)
ILRR............ Industrial and Labor Relations Review [*A publication*] (BRI)
ILR Rajasthan... Indian Law Reports, Rajasthan Series [*A publication*] (DLA)
ILR Ran........ Indian Law Reports, Rangoon Series [*A publication*] (DLA)
ILR Rev........ Industrial and Labor Relations Review [*A publication*] (DLA)
ILRRJ........... International League for the Repatriation of Russian Jews (EA)
ILRRP........... International Long-Range Reconnaissance Patrol
ILRS............ International League of Religious Socialists [*Aerdenhout, Netherlands*] (EAIO)
ILRT............ Integrated Leak Rate Test [*Nuclear energy*] (NRCH)
ILRT............ Intermediate Level Reactor Test (IEEE)
ILR Trav-Cochin... Indian Law Reports, Kerala Series [*A publication*] (DLA)
ILRU............ Independent Living Research Utilization Program (PAZ)
ILRV............ In-Line Relief Valve
ILRV............ Integral [*or Integrated*] Launch and Recovery Vehicle [*or Reentry*] [*NASA*]
ILRVS.......... Integral [*or Integrated*] Launch and Recovery Vehicle System [*or Reentry*] [*NASA*]
ILRWG......... International Labor Rights Working Group (EA)
ILS.............. Ideal Liquidus Structures (IEEE)
ILS.............. Identification List
ILS.............. Illinois Benedictine College, Lisle, IL [*Library symbol Library of Congress*] (LCLS)
ILS.............. Incorporated Law Society [*British*]
ILS.............. Increase in Life-Span
ILS.............. Independent Living Skills [*Needed by the handicapped*]
ILS.............. Indiana Union List of Serials, Indianapolis, IN [*OCLC symbol*] (OCLC)
ILS.............. Industrial Locomotive Society [*British*]
ILS.............. Information & Library Services [*Information service or system*] (IID)
ILS.............. Infrared Live Scanner [*Medicine*] (DMAA)
ILS.............. Inland Library System [*Library network*]
ILS.............. Inspection Lot Size
ILS.............. Institute of Life Sciences [*British*] (DBA)
ILS.............. Institute of Lithuanian Studies (EA)
ILS.............. Instrument Landing System [*Aviation*]
ILS.............. Integrated Laboratory Sequence [*A system of teaching chemistry devised by Mary L. Good at Louisiana State University in New Orleans*]
ILS.............. Integrated LASER System [*Salford Engineering*]
ILS.............. Integrated LASER Systems [*Software*] [*British*]
ILS.............. Integrated Learning System (AIE)
ILS.............. Integrated Library System [*National Library of Medicine*] [*Information service or system*] (IID)
ILS.............. Integrated Logistics Support [*DoD*]
ILS.............. Integrated Logistics Support (AAGC)
ILS.............. Integrated Logistics System
ILS.............. Interactive Laboratory System (NITA)
ILS.............. Interferometric LASER Source
ILS.............. Intergovernmental Liaison Staff [*Environmental Protection Agency*] (GFGA)
ILS.............. International Latitude Service
ILS.............. International Laughter Society [*Commercial firm*] (EA)
ILS.............. International Learning Systems
ILS.............. International Lilac Society (EA)
ILS.............. International Limnological Society [*See also SIL*] (ASF)
ILS.............. International Line Selector
ILS.............. International Lunar Society [*Spain*]
ILS.............. Interrupt Level Subroutine (CMD)
ILS.............. Interstate Land Sales [*HUD*]
ILS.............. Inventory Locator Service [*Database*] [*Inventory Locator Service, Inc.*] [*Information service or system*] (CRD)
ILS.............. Irish Literary Supplement [*A publication*] (BRI)
ILSA............ Industry Large Structures Assembly (SSD)
ILSA............ Insured Locksmiths and Safemen of America [*Defunct*] (EA)
ILSA............ Integrated Logistic Support Analysis Paper (MCD)
ILSA............ Inter-American Legal Services Association (EA)
ILSA............ International Law Students Association (EAIO)
ILSA............ International Lending Supervision Act of 1983
ILSAA.......... Improved Lighting System for Army Aircraft (RDA)
ILSAC.......... International Legal Services Advisory Committee
ILSAC.......... International Lubricant Standardization and Approval Committee [*Automotive engine oils*]
ILSAM.......... International Language for Servicing and Maintenance (PDAA)
ILSAP.......... Instrument Landing System Approach [*Aviation*]
ILS(C).......... Industry Launch Service (Cryogenic) (SSD)
ILSC............ Integrated Logistics Support Cadre (AFIT)
ILSCM.......... Integrated Logistics Support Control Manual (MCD)
ILSCM.......... Integrated Logistics Support Coordination Meeting (MCD)
ILSDF.......... Integrated Logistics Support Data File
ILSDP.......... International Logistics Supply Delivery Plan (MCD)
ILS-DS......... Integrated Logistic Support - Detail Specification
ILSE............ Interagency Life Sciences Supporting Space Research and Technology Exchange
ILSE............ Intermediate-Level Support Equipment (MCD)
ILSF............ Incandescent Liquid Spheroidal Formation [*Combustion technology*]
ILSF............ Intermediate Level Sample Flow (IEEE)
ILSF............ Iterative Least-Squares Fitting [*Mathematics*]
ILSG............ Integrated Logistics Subgroup [*Military*] (MCD)
ILSG............ Interim Logistics Support Guide (NVT)
ILSGB.......... International Language Society of Great Britain
ILSI............. International Life Sciences Institute [*Later, ILSI-NF*] (EA)
ILSI............. International Life Services, Inc. (EA)
ILSI-NF........ International Life Sciences Institute - Nutrition Foundation (EA)
ILS/IS/D...... Integrated Logistics Support/Information System/Dictionary
ILS/LAR....... Integrated Logistics System and Logistics Assessment Review (MCD)
ILSM............ Integrated Logistics Support Manager [*Military*] (MCD)
ILSM............ Integrated Logistics Support Model [*Military*] (MCD)
ILSMH.......... International League of Societies for Persons with Mental Handicap [*Brussels, Belgium*] (EA)
ILSMP.......... Integrated Logistic Support Maintenance [*or Management*] Plan (MCD)
ILSMRS........ Integrated Logistics Support Milestone Reporting System [*Military*] (MCD)
ILSMRT........ Integrated Logistic Support Management Review Team
ILSMT.......... Integrated Logistic Support Management Team
ILSNI........... Incorporated Land Society of Northern Ireland
ILSO............ Incremental Life Support Operations
ILSO............ Integrated Logistic Support Office [*DoD*]
ILSOM.......... Improved Light-Scattering Dust Monitor (PDAA)
ILSP............ Integrated Logistics Support Plan
ILSP............ Integrated Logistic Support Plan [*or Program*]
ILSP............ International Library of Sports and Pastimes [*A publication*]
ILSPER........ Integrated Logistics Support Performance Evaluation Report [*Military*] (MCD)
ILSPIP......... International Logistics Supply Performance Improvement Program (NG)
ILSR............ Institute for Local Self-Reliance (EA)
ILSR............ Integrated Logistics Support Review [*Military*] (MCD)
ILSRO.......... Interstate Land Sales Registration Office [*HUD*] (IAA)
ILSS............ Industry Launch Services - Storable (SSD)
ILSS............ Integrated Life Support System [*NASA*]
ILSS............ Integrated Logistics Support System (SSD)
ILSS............ Interlaminar Shear Strength (MCD)
ILSSE.......... Integrated Life Science Shuttle Experiments (MCD)
ILSTAC........ Instrument Landing System and TACAN
ILSUS.......... Integrated Library System Users Society [*Defunct*] (EA)
ILS/VOR....... Instrument Landing System / VHF [*Very-High-Frequency*] Omnidirectional Range [*Aviation*] (SAA)
ILSW............ Interrupt Level Status Word
ILSWG......... Integrated Logistics Support Working Group (SSD)
ILT.............. Albuquerque, NM [*Location identifier FAA*] (FAAL)
ILT.............. Iliotibial Tract [*Medicine*] (DMAA)
ILT.............. Infantry Liaison Team (INF)

ILT	Infectious Laryngo-Tracheitis [*Medicine*] (ADA)
ILT	Inferolateral Trunk [*Neuroanatomy*]
ILT	In Lieu Thereof [*Military*]
ILT	Installation Lead Time
ILT	Interferometric Landmark Tracker (PDAA)
ILT	Interlayer Tunneling [*Model for superconductivity*]
ILT	Intermediate Lay-Up Tool [*Plastics technology*]
ILT	International Logistics Training
ILT	Ion Laser Technology [*AMEX symbol*] (TTSB)
ILT	Ion Laser Technology, Inc. [*AMEX symbol*] (SAG)
ILT	Iultin [*Former USSR Seismograph station code, US Geological Survey*] (SEIS)
ILT	Keck, Mahin & Cate, Chicago, IL [*OCLC symbol*] (OCLC)
ILTA	Independent Liquid Terminals Association (EA)
ILTC	International Leadership Training Conference
ILTCP	Inventory of Long-Term Care Places [*Department of Health and Human Services*] (GFGA)
ILTEB	Inner London Tertiary Education Board [*British*] (AIE)
ILTF	International Lawn Tennis Federation [*Later, ITF*]
ILT Jo	Irish Law Times Journal [*A publication*] (DLA)
ILTMS	International Leased Telegraph Message Switching Service [*British Telecom*] [*Telecommunications*] (TEL)
ILTO	Industrial Liaison Technical Officer [*British*] (DI)
ILTR	Irish Law Times Reports [*A publication*] (DLA)
ILTS	Industrial Language Training Service [*British*]
ILTS	Integration Level Test Series [*Psychology*]
ILTS	Intermediate Level Test Station (MCD)
ILTTA	International Light Tackle Tournament Association (EA)
ilu	Illinois [*MARC country of publication code Library of Congress*] (LCCP)
ILU	Illinois University (IEEE)
ilu	Illuminator [*MARC relator code*] [*Library of Congress*] (LCCP)
ILU	Institute of London Underwriters (ECON)
ILU	Inventory of Land Use (BARN)
ILU	Texas Tech University, Lubbock, TX [*OCLC symbol*] (OCLC)
ILUMS	Innovations in Land Use Management Symposium
ILUVM	I Love You Very Much [*Correspondence*] (DSUE)
ILV	Impatiens Latent Virus [*Plant pathology*]
ILV	Industrial Launch Vehicle
ILV	International Laser Tech, Inc. [*Vancouver Stock Exchange symbol*]
ILv	Lake Villa District Library, Lake Villa, IL [*Library symbol Library of Congress*] (LCLS)
ILV	Sonnenschein, Carlin, Nath & Rosenthal, Chicago, IL [*OCLC symbol*] (OCLC)
ILVBIDT	In Liebe Vereint bis in dem Tod [*United in Love until Death*] [*German*]
ILVSI	Instant Lead Vertical Speed Indicator (MCD)
ILW	Institute of Land Warfare [*Military*]
ILW	Institute of Land Warfare [*Association of the US Army*] (DOMA)
ILW	Intermediate-Level Wastes (IEEE)
ILW	International Association of Assessing Officers, Chicago, IL [*OCLC symbol*] (OCLC)
ILW	International Low Water
ILW	Investment Laws of the World [*A publication*] (DLA)
ILWAS	Integrated Lake-Watershed Acidification Study
ILWC	Intermediate-Level Waste Concentrate [*Nuclear energy*] (NRCH)
ILWC	International League of Women Composers (EA)
ILWCHSG	International Labor and Working Class History Study Group (EA)
ILWD	Intermediate-Level Waste Distillate [*Nuclear energy*] (NRCH)
ILWF	Intermediate-Level Waste Feed [*Nuclear energy*] (NRCH)
ILWML	International Lutheran Women's Missionary League (EA)
ILWS	Intermediate-Level Waste Storage [*Nuclear energy*] (GFGA)
ILWU	International Longshoremen's and Warehousemen's Union (EA)
ILX	Visiting Nurse Association of Chicago, Chicago, IL [*OCLC symbol*] (OCLC)
ILX Inc	ILX, Inc. [*Associated Press*] (SAG)
ILY	International Literacy Year
ILY	Islay [*Scotland*] [*Airport symbol*] (OAG)
ILY	Italian Liberal Youth [*Political party*] (EAIO)
ILy	Lyons Public Library, Lyons, IL [*Library symbol Library of Congress*] (LCLS)
ILY	Northern Illinois University, Law Library, Glen Ellyn, IL [*OCLC symbol*] (OCLC)
ILYA	Inland Lake Yachting Association (EA)
I-LYA	Inter-Lake Yachting Association (EA)
ILz	Ela Area Public Library, Lake Zurich, IL [*Library symbol Library of Congress*] (LCLS)
ILZ	Isham, Lincoln & Beale, Chicago, IL [*OCLC symbol*] (OCLC)
ILZ	Newport, RI [*Location identifier FAA*] (FAAL)
ILZRO	International Lead Zinc Research Organization (EA)
ILZSG	International Lead and Zinc Study Group [*British*] (EA)
IM	Ideal Modulation (IAA)
IM	Idle Money [*Business term*] (MHDB)
Im	Imaginary [*Mathematics*]
IM	Immature
IM	Im Mittel [*On an Average*] [*German*]
IM	Immunoassay [*Marine science*] (OSRA)
IM	Immunoassay (USDC)
IM	Immuno-Suppression Method [*For increasing fertility*]
IM	Impact Memorandum (MCD)
IM	Imperial Measure
IM	Implementation Monitoring (HCT)
IM	Import Monthly Data [*Department of Commerce*] (GFGA)
IM	Impulse Modulation
IM	Income Maintenance (OICC)

IM	Index Marker (MHDB)
IM	Individual Medley [*Swimming*]
IM	Indomethacin [*An analgesic*]
IM	Induced Magnetization
IM	Industrial Manager
IM	Industrial Medicine (DAVI)
IM	Industry Motion Picture [*FCC*] (MCD)
IM	Infantile Myofibromatosus [*Medicine*]
IM	Infant Mortality (ROG)
IM	Infectious Mononucleosis [*Medicine*]
IM	Informal Memorandum (MCD)
IM	Information Management (AAGC)
IM	Information Manager [*A publication*]
IM	Information Market [*Commission of the European Communities*] [*Information service or system*] (IID)
IM	Information Memory (MCD)
IM	Ingot Metallurgy
IM	Ingram Micro, Inc. [*NYSE symbol*] (SAG)
IM	Initial Mass [*Agronomy*]
IM	Injection Mold (MCD)
IM	Inland Marine [*Insurance*]
IM	In Maintenance
im	In Margine [*On the Margin*] [*Latin*]
IM	Inner Marker [*Part of an instrument landing system*] [*Aviation*]
IM	Inoffizielle Mitarbeiter [*Unofficial Collaborators*] [*German*]
IM	Insensitive Munitions (MCD)
I/M	Inside of Metal (MSA)
I/M	Inspection and Maintenance (ERG)
IM	Inspection Manual (MCD)
IM	Inspection Memorandum
IM	Inspector of Machinery
IM	Installation Material (AAGC)
IM	Installment Mortgage (WDAA)
IM	Instant Messaging [*Computer science*]
IM	Institute of Marketing (EAIO)
IM	Institute of Medicine [*National Academy of Sciences*]
IM	Institution of Metallurgists [*British*]
IM	Instruction Manual
IM	Instruction Memory
IM	Instrumentation (MDG)
IM	Instrumentation (ECII)
IM	Instrumentation and Measurement (MCD)
IM	Instrumentation Manager [*NASA*] (KSC)
IM	Instrumentman [*Navy rating*]
IM	Instrument Myopia (PDAA)
IM	Integrated Master (NRCH)
IM	Integrated MODEM
IM	Integration Modified
IM	Intelligence Memorandum
IM	Intelligent Measurement [*Function*] (ACII)
IM	Intensity Measuring Devices [*JETDS nomenclature*] [*Military*] (CET)
IM	Intensity Modulation
IM	Interactive Mode (IAA)
IM	Interact Ministries [*An association*] (EA)
IM	Interceptor Missile
IM	Interdepartmental Memorandum (AAG)
IM	Interface Module (MCD)
IM	Interfaith Movement [*Defunct*] (EA)
IM	Interim Measures
IM	Interim Memorandum
IM	Intermediate Maintenance (MCD)
IM	Intermediate Missile (MSA)
IM	Intermediate Modeling (USDC)
IM	Intermediate Modeling [*Marine science*] (OSRA)
IM	Intermediate Modulation
IM	Intermediate Moisture (KSC)
IM	Intermetatarsal [*Anatomy*] (DAVI)
IM	Inter Mirifica [*Decree on the Instruments of Social Communication*] [*Vatican II document*]
IM	Intermodulation
IM	Intermodulation Distortion (NTCM)
IM	Intermuscular [*Anatomy*] (DAVI)
IM	Internal Medicine
IM	Internal Memorandum
IM	International Missions [*An association*] (EA)
IM	Interrupt Mask
IM	Intestinal Metaplasia [*Medicine*]
IM	Intramedullary [*Medicine*]
IM	Intramural
IM	Intramuscular [*Injection*] [*Medicine*]
IM	In-Use Maintenance Test
IM	Invasive Mole
I/M	Inventory Management [*Business term*]
IM	Inventory Manager [*Military*]
IM	Inverted Microscope [*Instrumentation*]
IM	Invisible Ministry (EA)
IM	Iowa Mountaineers (EA)
IM	Irish Marquis (ROG)
IM	Isle of Man [*England*]
IM	Istanbuler Mitteilungen [*A publication*] (BJA)
IM	Item Management
IM	Item Manager (AAGC)
IM	Item Mark (BUR)
IM	Jamaire [*ICAO designator*] (AD)
IM	Sisters of Charity of the Infant Mary (TOCD)

IM1 .... Instrumentman, First Class [*Navy rating*]
IM2 .... Instrumentman, Second Class [*Navy rating*]
IM2 .... Integrated Materiel Management [*Military*]
IM3 .... Instrumentman, Third Class [*Navy rating*]
IMA .... Iamalele [*Papua New Guinea*] [*Airport symbol*] (OAG)
IMA .... Idaho Medical Association (SRA)
IMA .... Idaho Mining Association (SRA)
IMA .... Illinois Manufacturers Association (SRA)
IMA .... Immobilized Metal Affinity [*Protein chromatography*]
IMA .... Impedance Matching Attenuator
IMA .... Independent Manufacturing Assessment (MCD)
IMA .... Independent Midwives Association [*British*] (DBA)
IMA .... Independent Music Association (EA)
IMA .... Indiana Manufacturers Association (SRA)
IMA .... Indian Military Academy
IMA .... Indian Mountain [*Alaska*] [*Seismograph station code, US Geological Survey*] (SEIS)
IMA .... Individual Mobilization Augmentation [*or Augmentees*] [*DoD*]
IMA .... Individual Mobilization Augmentee (AAGC)
IMA .... Industrial Marketing Associates
IMA .... Industrial Medical Association [*Later, AOMA*] (EA)
IMA .... Inferior Mesenteric Artery [*Anatomy*]
IMA .... Information Medicale Automatisee [*Automated Medical Information*] [*INSERM*] [*Information service or system*] (IID)
IMA .... Information Mission Area
IMA .... Inherent Mobile Availability [*Military*]
IMA .... Initial Military Assistance (CINC)
IMA .... Input Message Acknowledgment [*Computer science*]
IMA .... Installation Maintenance Activity (MCD)
IMA .... Institute for Mathematics and Its Applications [*University of Minnesota*] [*Research center*] (RCD)
IMA .... Institute for Media Analysis (EA)
IMA .... Institute for Mediterranean Affairs (EA)
IMA .... Institute for Military Assistance [*Army*]
IMA .... Institute of Management Accounting (EA)
IMA .... Institute of Mathematics and Its Applications [*South-End-On-Sea, England*] (CSR)
IMA .... Instituto Magdalena Aulina [*Magdalena Aulina Institute*] [*Barcelona, Spain*] (EAIO)
IMA .... Integrated Modular Avionics [*Honeywell, Inc.*]
IMA .... Interactive Multimedia Association [*Database producer*] (IID)
IMA .... Interbank Merchants Association [*Pigeon Forge, TN*] (EA)
IMA .... Interchurch Medical Assistance (EA)
IMA .... Interdisciplinary Master of Arts (PGP)
IMA .... Interface Management Agent (MCD)
IMA .... Intermediate Maintenance Activity
IMA .... Inter-Mountain Airways [*ICAO designator*] (FAAC)
IMA .... Internal Mammary Artery (Implant) [*Medicine*]
IMA .... International Magnesium Association (EA)
IMA .... International Maintenance Agency
IMA .... International Management Association [*Later, AMA/I*] (EA)
IMA .... International Medical Assistance [*Society*]
IMA .... International Message Centre [*Vancouver Stock Exchange symbol*]
IMA .... International Messaging Associates [*Commercial firm*]
IMA .... International Metaphysical Association [*Defunct*] (EA)
IMA .... International MIDI [*Musical Instrument Digital Interface*] Association (EA)
IMA2 .... International Military Archives (EA)
IMA .... International Milling Association [*See also AIM*] [*Brussels, Belgium*] (EAIO)
IMA .... International Mineralogical Association [*ICSU*] [*Marburg, Federal Republic of Germany*] (EA)
IMA .... International Minilab Association (EA)
IMA .... International Mobjack Association (EA)
IMA .... International Mohair Association (EAIO)
IMA .... International Music Association
IMA .... International Mycological Association [*See also AIM*] [*England*] (EAIO)
IMA .... International Mycophagist Association (EA)
IMA .... Invalid Memory Address [*Computer science*]
IMA .... Inventory Management Activity
IMA .... Ion Microprobe Analyzer
IMA .... Irish Medical Association
IMA .... Iron Mining Association of Minnesota (SRA)
IMA .... Islamic Medical Association (EA)
IMA .... Islamic Mission of America (EA)
IMA .... Issues Management Association (EA)
IMA .... Item Manager [*DoD*]
IMAA .... Imidazoleacetic Acid [*Biochemistry*]
IMAA .... Industrial Medical Administrators' Association [*Later, OMAA*] (EA)
IMAA .... Institute for Mediterranean Art and Archaeology [*Defunct*] (EA)
IMAA .... Intelligence Mission Area Analysis [*Military*] (MCD)
IMAA .... International Marketing Audit Association (EA)
IMAA .... Iodinated Macroaggregated Albumin [*Medicine*] (MAE)
IMAAWS ...... Infantry Manportable Antiarmor Weapon System
IMAB .... Internal Mammary Artery Bypass [*Medicine*] (DMAA)
IMAC .... Ifosfamide, Mesna, Adriamycin, Cisplatin [*Antineoplastic drug*] (CDI)
IMAC .... Illinois Microfilm Automated Cataloging [*Illinois State Library*] (NITA)
IMAC .... Illinois State Library Microfilm Automated Catalog (PDAA)
IMAC .... Immobilized Metal Affinity Chromatography
IMAC .... Information Management, Archiving, and Communication (DMAA)
IMAC .... Integrated Microwave Amplifier Converter
IMAC2 .... International Metals Acquisition Corp. [*NASDAQ symbol*] (SAG)
IMAC .... International Movement of Apostolate of Children [*Paris, France*] (EA)

IMAC 90 ...... Immigration Act of 1990 (WYGK)
IMACA .... International Mobile Air Conditioning Association (EA)
IMACE .... Association des Industries Margarinieres des Pays de la CEE [*Association of Margarine Industries of the EEC Countries*] [*Belgium*]
IMACHA ...... Intermountain Automated Clearing House Association (MHDW)
IMacoW ...... Western Illinois University, Macomb, IL [*Library symbol Library of Congress*] (LCLS)
IMACS .... International Association for Mathematics and Computers in Simulation (EA)
IMAD .... Integrated Multisensor Airborne Display
IMad .... Madison Public Library, Madison, IL [*Library symbol Library of Congress*] (LCLS)
IMadCU ...... Madison Community, Unit 12, Madison, IL [*Library symbol Library of Congress*] (LCLS)
IMADE .... International Military and Defense Encyclopedia [*A publication*]
IMAF .... International Martial Arts Federation (EAIO)
IMAG .... IEEE [*Institute of Electrical and Electronics Engineers*] Magnetics (IAA)
IMAG .... Image Industries [*NASDAQ symbol*] (SAG)
IMAG .... Imagine [*or Imaginary*] (MSA)
Imag .... Imagines [*of Philostratus*] [*Classical studies*] (OCD)
IMAG .... Instituut voor Mechanistie Arbeid en Gebouwen [*Netherlands*] (NITA)
IMAG .... Internal Mammary Artery Graft [*Cardiology*] (DAVI)
IMAGE .... Information Management by Application Generation (IAA)
IMAGE .... Institute for Molecular and Agricultural Genetic Engineering [*University of Idaho*] [*Research center*]
IMAGE .... Instruction in Motivation Achievement and General Education [*YMCA program*]
IMAGE .... International Monitor for Auroral Geomagnetic Effects
IMAGE .... International Multicenter Angina Exercise (DMAA)
IMAGE .... Intruder Monitoring and Guidance Equipment (MCD)
ImageInd ...... Image Industries [*Associated Press*] (SAG)
ImagEn .... Image Entertainment, Inc. [*Associated Press*] (SAG)
ImageS .... Image Sensing Systems, Inc. [*Associated Press*] (SAG)
IMAGES ...... Instructional Material Adequacy Guide and Evaluation Standard (RDA)
IMAGES ...... Instrumental Manual Adequacy Guide and Evaluation Standard
IMAGES ...... Interactive Modal Analysis and Gain Estimation for Eigensystem [*NASA digital computer program*]
IMAGES ...... International Marine Global Change Study [*Research programs*]
ImageSft ...... Image Software, Inc. [*Associated Press*] (SAG)
Imagyn .... Imagyn Medical, Inc. [*Associated Press*] (SAG)
IMah .... Mahomet Township Public Library, Mahomet, IL [*Library symbol Library of Congress*] (LCLS)
IMAI .... Imaging Management Associates [*NASDAQ symbol*] (SAG)
IMAI .... Imaging Mgmt Assoc [*NASDAQ symbol*] (TTSB)
IMAI .... Internal Mammary Artery Implant [*Medicine*] (DMAA)
IMAJ .... Initiative d'Un Mouvement d'Animation Jeunesse pour l'Annee Internationale de laJeunesse en 1985 [*Canada*]
IMAK .... International Imaging Materials, Inc. [*NASDAQ symbol*] (SAG)
IMAK .... Intl Imaging Materials [*NASDAQ symbol*] (TTSB)
IMA MOD..... Information Mission Area Modernization [*Army*] (RDA)
IMan .... Blue Ridge Township Public Library, Mansfield, IL [*Library symbol Library of Congress*] (LCLS)
IMAN .... International Mail Art Network (EA)
IMANCO ...... Image Analysing Computers, Inc.
IM & AWU ... International Molders' and Allied Workers' Union [*AFL-CIO*] (EA)
IM & D .... Image Mapping and Display (NOAA)
IM & TPR .... Information Management and Telecommunications Pentagon Renovation (RDA)
IMANF .... Institute of Manufacturing [*Royal Leamington Spa, Warwickshire, England*] (EAIO)
IMAO .... In My Arrogant Opinion [*Computer hacker terminology*] (NHD)
IMAO .... International Military Assistance Office
IMAP.......... Immediately After Passing [*Aviation*] (FAAC)
IMAP.......... Institute of Materials and Advanced Processes [*University of Idaho*] [*Research center*] (RCD)
IMAP.......... Interactive Manpower Alternatives Processor (DNAB)
IMAP.......... Internet Mail Access Protocol [*Computer science*]
IMAP4 .... Internet Message Access Protocol 4 [*Electronic mail*]
IMAPPA ...... International Martial Arts Pen Pal Association [*Defunct*] (EA)
IMAPS .... Intake Manifold Absolute Pressure Sensor [*Automotive engineering*]
IMar.......... Markham Public Library, Markham, IL [*Library symbol Library of Congress*] (LCLS)
IMarE.......... Institute of Marine Engineers [*British Database producer*]
Imari .... Marion Carnegie Library, Marion, IL [*Library symbol*] [*Library of Congress*] (LCLS)
IMARPE ...... Instituto del Mar de Peru [*Marine science*] (OSRA)
IMars .... Marshall Public Library, Marshall, IL [*Library symbol Library of Congress*] (LCLS)
IMarse .... Marseilles Public Library, Marseilles, IL [*Library symbol Library of Congress*] (LCLS)
IMarseHS .... Marseilles High School, Marseilles, IL [*Library symbol Library of Congress*] (LCLS)
IMarseMSD... Miller Township Consolidated Community, School District 210, Marseilles, IL [*Library symbol Library of Congress*] (LCLS)
IMART .... International Medical Association for Radio and Television [*Brussels, Belgium*] (EAIO)
IMart.......... Martinsville Township Library, Martinsville, IL [*Library symbol Library of Congress*] (LCLS)
IMartSD ...... Martinsville Community Unit Schools District, Martinsville, IL [*Library symbol*] [*Library of Congress*] (LCLS)
IMaryR........ Maryville Reading Center, Maryville, IL [*Library symbol Library of Congress*] (LCLS)

IMAS............ Impurity Monitoring and Analysis System [*Nuclear energy*] (NRCH)
IMAS............ Industrial Management Assistance Survey [*Air Force*]
IMAS............ International Marine and Shipping Conference (NOAA)
IMas .... Mascoutah Public Library, Mascoutah, IL [*Library symbol Library of Congress*] (LCLS)
IMasHS........ Mascoutah High School, Mascoutah, IL [*Library symbol Library of Congress*] (LCLS)
IMAT............ Imatron, Inc. [*NASDAQ symbol*] (NQ)
IMAT............ Integrated, Modification and Trial
IMAT............ Interim Maintenance Assistance Team (MCD)
IMAT............ Intermodal Automated Transfer (PDAA)
IMAT............ International Mechanism for Appropriate Technology
IMat............ Mattoon Public Library, Mattoon, IL [*Library symbol*] [*Library of Congress*] (LCLS)
IMATA......... Independent Military Air Transport Association [*Later, Independent Airlines Association*]
IMATCE....... Information Mission Area Training Center of Excellence [*Army*] (RDA)
IMATDFW .... International Movement ATD Fourth World [*France*] (EAIO)
Imatec .... Imatec Ltd. [*Associated Press*] (SAG)
IMatH.......... Memorial Hospital District Library, Mattoon, IL [*Library symbol Library of Congress*] (LCLS)
IMatL.......... Sara Bush Lincoln Health Center, Mattoon, IL [*Library symbol Library of Congress*] (LCLS)
ImatLC........ Lake Land College, Mattoon, IL [*Library symbol Library of Congress*] (LCLS)
Imatrn.......... Imatron, Inc. [*Associated Press*] (SAG)
IMatt............ Matteson Public Library, Matteson, IL [*Library symbol Library of Congress*] (LCLS)
IMAU .... International Movement for Atlantic Union (EA)
IMAV........... Intermediate Maintenance Availability
IMAW.......... International Molders' and Allied Workers' Union [*AFL-CIO*]
IMAX........... Image-Maximum [*Photography*]
Imax Cp ...... Imax Corp. [*Associated Press*] (SAG)
IMAXF......... Imax Corp. [*NASDAQ symbol*] (SAG)
IMay .... Maywood Public Library, Maywood, IL [*Library symbol Library of Congress*] (LCLS)
IMB............. Imbaimadai [*Guyana*] [*Airport symbol*] (OAG)
IMB............. Independent Mixed Brigade [*Military*]
IMB............. Independent Mortar Battery [*British military*] (DMA)
IMB............. Indian Mountain Battery [*British military*] (DMA)
IMB............. Input Memory Buffer [*Computer science*]
IMB............. Institute for Marine Biochemistry [*British*]
IMB............. Institute of Microbiology
IMB............. Institute of Molecular Biophysics [*Florida State University*] [*Research center*] (RCD)
IMB............. Institute of Molecular Biotechnology [*Germany*]
IMB............. Instrument Material Bulletin (MCD)
IMB............. InterCapital Ins Muni Bd Fd [*NYSE symbol*] (TTSB)
IMB............. InterCapital Insurance Municipal Bond Fund [*NYSE symbol*] (SPSG)
IMB............. Intercontinental Medical Book Corp.
IMB............. Intermenstrual Bleeding [*Medicine*]
IMB............. Inter-Module Bus (NITA)
IMB............. Intermountain Tariff Bureau, Inc., Salt Lake City UT [*STAC*]
IMB............. Internationaler Metalarbeiterbund [*International Metalworkers' Federation*]
IMB............. International Maritime Bureau [*Research center British*] (IRC)
IMB............. International Mission Board (EA)
IMB............. Irvine/Michigan/Brookhaven [*Experiment on proton decay*]
IMB............. Kimberly, OR [*Location identifier FAA*] (FAAL)
IMBA......... Integrative Master of Business Administration (PGP)
IMBA......... International Master of Busness Administration [*University of South Carolina*]
IMBA......... International Media Buyers Association [*Defunct*] (EA)
IMBA......... International Morab Breeders Association (EA)
IMBA......... International Mountain Bicycling Association (EA)
IMBB......... Institute of Molecular Biology and Biochemistry [*Simon Fraser University*] [*Canada*]
IMBB......... Institute of Molecular Biology and Biotechnology [*Greece*]
IMBC.......... Indirect Maximum Breathing Capacity [*Medicine*]
IMBC.......... International Marine Biotechnology Conference
IMBE.......... Improved Multi-Band Encoding [*Telecommunications*] (ACRL)
IMBE.......... Institute for Minority Business Education [*Defunct*] (EA)
IMBEX........ International Men's and Boys' Wear Exhibition
IMBI.......... Institute of Medical and Biological Illustration [*British*]
IMBL.......... Independent Meat Buyers Ltd. [*British*] (BI)
IMBLM........ Integrated Medical and Behavioral Laboratory Management (DNAB)
IMBLMS....... Integrated Medical and Behavioral Laboratory Measurement System
IMBM......... Institute of Maintenance and Building Management [*British*] (DBA)
IMBM......... Institute of Municipal Building Management [*British*]
IMBO .... Indian and Metis Brotherhood Organization
IMBR .... Institute of Marine Biomedical Research [*University of North Carolina at Wilmington*] [*Research center*] (RCD)
IMBS.......... Individual Motor Behavior Survey [*Test*]
IMBT........... Iron Masters Board of Trade
IMC............. Chief Instrumentman [*Navy rating*]
IMC............. Consolata Missionaries (TOCD)
imc .... Consolata Missionaries (TOCD)
IMC............. Image Motion Compensation [*or Compensator*]
IMC............. Image Motion Configuration
IMC............. Imco Resources Ltd. [*Vancouver Stock Exchange symbol*]
IMC............. Improved Meteorological Conditions (MCD)
IMC............. Incident Management Center [*Nuclear Regulatory Commission*] (NRCH)
IMC............. Indigent Medical Care (HCT)

IMC............. Industrial Metal Containers Section of the Material Handling Institute (EA)
IMC............. Industrial Microcomputer
ImC............. Industrial Microfilm Co., Detroit, MI [*Library symbol Library of Congress*] (LCLS)
IMC............. Information Management Consultants [*Database producer*] (IID)
IMC............. Information-Memory-Concentration (DMAA)
IMC............. Initial Marks [*Held*] Constant [*Psychology*]
IMC............. Initial Moisture Content (IAA)
IMC............. In-Mold Coating [*Organic chemistry*]
IMC............. In-Mold Compounding
IMC............. Inspection Method Control
IMC............. Institute of Management Consultants [*New York, NY*] (EA)
IMC............. Institute of Measurement and Control [*British*]
IMC............. Institute of Motorcycling [*British*] (DBA)
IMC............. Instructional Materials Center
IMC............. Instrument [*Flight*] Meteorological Conditions [*Aviation*]
IMC............. Integrated Maintenance Chart [*or Concept*]
IMC............. Integrated Marketing Communications [*Advertising*] [*Public relations*] (WDMC)
IMC............. Integrated Microelectronic Circuitry (AAG)
IMC............. Integrated Microwave Circuit
IMC............. Integrated Monolithic Circuit
IMC............. Integrated Multiplexer Channel
IMC............. Intelligent Matrix Control [*T-Bar, Inc.*]
IMC............. Intensity Millicurie [*Nucleonics*] (IAA)
IMC............. Interactive Module Controller
IMC............. Interceptor Monitor and Controller
IMC............. Intercollegiate Men's Chorus, a National Association of Male Choruses (EA)
IMC............. Interdigestive Migrating Contractions [*Medicine*] (DMAA)
IMC............. Interdigestive Myoelectric Complex [*Gastroenterology*]
IMC............. Interim Message Change
IMC............. INTERMARC [*International Machine-Readable Cataloging*] [*French National Library Source file*] [*UTLAS symbol*]
IMC............. Intermediate Maintenance Costs (MCD)
IMC............. Intermediate Message Change (AAGC)
IMC............. Intermediate Metal Conduit
IMC............. Intermetallic Compound [*Materials science*]
IMC............. Intermetallic Matrix Composite [*Materials science*]
IMC............. Intermodal Marketing Company [*A third-party shipping broker*] (ECON)
IMC............. Intermodule Connector (SSD)
IMC............. Internal Mammary Chain [*Medicine*] (DAVI)
IMC............. Internal Management Control (DOMA)
IMC............. Internal Model Control [*Chemical engineering*] [*Computer science*]
IMC............. International Conference Management, Inc. [*Telecommunications service*] (TSSD)
IMC............. International Information Management Congress (EA)
IMC............. International Magazine Collection [*JA Micropublishing, Inc.*] [*Eastchester, NY*] [*Information service or system*] (IID)
IMC............. International Mailbag Club (EA)
IMC............. International Maintenance Control [*Telecommunications*]
IMC............. International Management Center [*Hungary*] (ECON)
IMC............. International Management Communications, Inc. [*Database producer*]
IMC............. International Management Council (EA)
IMC............. International Maritime Committee
IMC............. International Marketing Commission [*See also CIM*] [*Brixham, Devonshire, England*] (EAIO)
IMC............. International Materials Conference (DCTA)
IMC............. International Medical Centers
IMC............. International Medical Commission for Health and Human Rights [*Switzerland*]
IMC............. International Medical Corps (EA)
IMC............. International Meeting Center [*Germany*] (EAIO)
IMC............. International Meteorological Committee
IMC............. International Micrographic Congress (EA)
IMC............. International Minerals & Chemical Corp.
IMC............. International Missionary Council [*Later, CWME*]
IMC............. International Monetary Conference (ECON)
IMC............. International Morse Code (ADDR)
IMC............. International Multifoods Corp. [*NYSE symbol*] (SPSG)
IMC............. International Music Conference (AEBS)
IMC............. International Music Council [*Paris, France*] (EA)
IMC............. Internet Message Center
IMC............. Intestinal Mast Cells [*Anatomy*]
IMC............. Intl Multifoods [*NYSE symbol*] (TTSB)
IMC............. Inventory Management Center (MCD)
IMC............. Isochronous Maintenance Channel [*Electronics*]
IMC............. Item Management Coding [*Military*] (AABC)
IMC............. Item Management Concept
IMC............. Item Master Card [*Military*] (AABC)
IMC............. Marion College, Marion, IN [*OCLC symbol*] (OCLC)
IMC............. Preparatory Committee for the International Medical Commission for Health and Human Rights (EAIO)
IMCA......... Indian Major Crimes Act [*1909*]
IMCA......... Indian Motorcycle Club of America (EA)
IMCA......... Information Management and Consulting Association [*Information service or system*] (IID)
IMCA......... Insurance Marketing Communications Association (EA)
IMCA......... International Motor Contest Association (EA)
IMCA......... Investment Management Consultants Association (EA)
IMCAB .... Internal Mammary Coronary Artery Bypass [*Cardiology*]
IMCAR .... International Movement of Catholic Agricultural and Rural Youth G2 [*See also MIJARC*]

IMCARY ...... International Movement of Catholic Agricultural and Rural Youth [*See also MIJARC*] [*Louvain, Belgium*] (EAIO)
IMCAS .... Interactive Man/Computer Augmentation System
IMCAST ...... Instructor Model Characteristics for Automated Speech Technology (MCD)
IMCA-US ..... International Moth Class Association - US (EA)
IMCB .... Institute of Molecular & Cell Biology [*Singapore*]
IMCC .... Image Motion Compensation and Calibration
IMCC .... IMC Mortgage Co. [*NASDAQ symbol*] (SAG)
IMCC .... Integrated Mission Control Center [*NASA*]
IMCC .... Interstate Mining Compact Commission (EA)
IMCC .... Item Management Control Code (AABC)
IMcc .... McCook Public Library District, McCook, IL [*Library symbol Library of Congress*] (LCLS)
IMccA .... Armak Co., McCook, IL [*Library symbol Library of Congress*] (LCLS)
IMCCSRA ..... International MC Class Sailboat Racing Association (EA)
IMCD .... Information Management and Compliance Division [*Department of Education*] (GFGA)
IMCD .... Inner Medullary Collecting Ducts [*Kidney anatomy*]
IMCD .... Input Marginal Checking and Distribution
IMCE .... Institute for Molecular and Cellular Evolution [*University of Miami*] [*Research center*] (RCD)
IMCE .... International Meeting of Cataloging Experts
IMCEA .... International Military Club Executives Association (EA)
IMC Glob ..... IMC Global, Inc. [*Formerly, IMC Fertilizer Group*] [*Associated Press*] (SAG)
IMchF .... Follett Software Co., McHenry, IL [*Library symbol*] [*Library of Congress*] (LCLS)
IMCI .... Individual and Marriage Counseling Inventory [*Psychology*]
IMCI .... Infinite Machines [*NASDAQ symbol*] (TTSB)
IMCI .... Infinite Machines Corp. [*NASDAQ symbol*] (SAG)
IMC-IFR ...... Instrument [*Flight*] Meteorological Conditions - Instrument Flight Rules [*Aviation*] (DNAB)
IMCIW .... Infinite Machines Wrrt [*NASDAQ symbol*] (TTSB)
IMCJ .... International Movement of Catholic Jurists (EAIO)
IMCL .... ImClone Systems [*NASDAQ symbol*] (TTSB)
IMCL .... ImClone Systems, Inc. [*NASDAQ symbol*] (SPSG)
IMCL .... International Movement of Catholic Lawyers [*France*]
ImcIne .... ImClone Systems, Inc. [*Associated Press*] (SAG)
IMCM .... In Medio Currere Metuo [*I Fear to Go in the Middle*] [*Motto of Julius, Duke of Braunschweig-Wolfenbuttel (1529-89)*] [*Latin*]
IMCM .... Master Chief Instrumentman [*Navy rating*]
IMC Mt .... IMC Mortgage Co. [*Associated Press*] (SAG)
IMCO .... IMCO Recycling, Inc. [*Associated Press*] (SAG)
IMCO .... Improved Combustion
IMCO .... Intergovernmental Maritime Consultative Organization
IMCO .... International Maritime Consultive Organization
IMCO .... International Metered Communications
IMCOA .... Insulation Materials Corp. of America
IMCoS .... International Map Collectors' Society (EAIO)
IMCP .... Integrated Monitor and Control Panel (MCD)
IMCP .... Item Management Coding Program [*Military*] (AFM)
IMCPM .... Improved Capability Missile [*Air Force*] (IAA)
IMCR .... Institute for Mediation and Conflict Resolution (EA)
IMC/RMC .... Instructional Materials Centers/Regional Media Centers
IMCS .... Individual Microclimate Cooling System [*Army*] (INF)
IMCS .... Intelligent Motion Control System (PDAA)
IMCS .... Interactive Manufacturing Control System [*NCR Ltd.*] [*Software package*] (NCC)
IMCS .... International Meeting in Community Service [*Germany*] (EAIO)
IMCS .... International Movement of Catholic Students [*France*]
IMCS .... Pax Romana, International Movement of Catholic Students [*See also MIEC*] [*Fribourg, Switzerland Paris, France*] (EAIO)
IMCS .... Senior Chief Instrumentman [*Navy rating*]
IMCSAC .... International Movement of Catholic Students - African Secretariat [*An association*] (EAIO)
IMcSC .... John Swaney Attendance Center, McNabb, IL [*Library symbol Library of Congress*] (LCLS)
IMCSMHI ..... Industrial Metal Containers Section of the Material Handling Institute (EA)
IMCSRS .... Installation Materiel Condition Status Reporting System [*Army*]
IMCTS .... Intake Manifold Charge Temperature Sensor [*Automotive engineering*]
IMCU .... Intensity Millicurie [*Nucleonics*] (IAA)
IMCWR .... International Movement of Conscientious War Resisters [*Tel Aviv, Israel*] (EAIO)
IMCX .... ImageMatrix Corp. [*NASDAQ symbol*] (SAG)
IMD .... Immunologically Mediated Disease [*Medicine*]
IMD .... Imo Industries [*NYSE symbol*] (TTSB)
IMD .... Imo Industries, Inc. [*NYSE symbol*] (SPSG)
IMD .... Imonda [*Papua New Guinea*] [*Airport symbol*] (OAG)
IMD .... Incremental Multiple Development (PDAA)
IMD .... Independent Module Development (PDAA)
IMD .... Indianapolis-Marion County Public Library, Indianapolis, IN [*OCLC symbol*] (OCLC)
IMD .... Indian Medical Department [*British military*] (DMA)
IMD .... Inertia-Measuring Device [*Mechanical engineering*]
IMD .... Information Management Division [*Environmental Protection Agency*] (GFGA)
IMD .... Inhibit Momentum Dump
IMD .... Institute for Marine Dynamics [*Canada*] (PDAA)
IMD .... Institute for Muscle Disease [*Defunct*] (EA)
IMD .... Institut fur Maschinelle Dokumentation (NITA)
IMD .... Institutions for Mental Diseases [*Department of Health and Human Services*] (GFGA)

IMD .... Interactive Map Definition (IAA)
IMD .... Intercept Monitoring Display
IMD .... Intermediate (NASA)
IMD .... Intermittent Motion Driver
IMD .... Intermodulation Distortion (MSA)
IMD .... International Institute for Management Development
IMD .... International Market Development Program [*Department of Energy*]
IMD .... International MTM [*Methods-Time-Measurement*] Directorate (EA)
IMD .... Invasive Meningococcal Disease
IMD .... Ion Mobility Detector [*Instrumentation*]
IMD .... Isove's Modified Dulbrecco's Medium [*Oncology*]
IMDA .... Independent Medical Distributors Association (EA)
IMDA .... Indian Mineral Development Act of 1982
IMDA .... International Magic Dealers Association (EA)
IMDA .... International Mail Dealers Association (EA)
IMDA .... International Map Dealers Association (EA)
IMDB .... Integrated Maintenance Database (MCD)
IMDC .... Inamed Corp. [*NASDAQ symbol*] (NQ)
IMDC .... Instructional Media Distribution Center [*University of Wisconsin - Madison*] [*Research center*] (RCD)
IMDC .... Interceptor Missile Direction Center
IMDC .... Internal Message Distribution Center (NATG)
IMDC .... Intramedullary Metatarsal Decompression [*Medicine*] (DMAA)
IMDD .... Idiopathic Midline Destructive Disease [*Dentistry*]
IMDEG .... Insurance Management Decision Game
IMDES .... Item Management Data Element Standardization [*or System*] [*Military*]
IMDFNA ...... Inhibited Maximum Density Fuming Nitric Acid (MCD)
IMDG .... International Maritime Dangerous Goods
IMDGC .... International Maritime Dangerous Goods Code (MCD)
IMDI .... International Management and Development Institute
IMDL .... Inter-Laboratory Method Detection Limit [*Environmental Protection Agency*]
IM/DM .... Information Management / Data Management (HGAA)
IMDM .... Iscove's Modified Dulbecco's Medium [*For nematode culture*]
IMDO .... Installation and Materiel District Office [*FAA*]
IMDO .... Intelligence Material Development Office [*Military*] (MCD)
IMDP .... Integrated Management Development Program [*Australia*]
IMDQ .... Injected Minimum Detectable Quantity [*Analytical chemistry*]
IMDR .... Intelligent Mark Document Reader (MHDI)
IMDR .... Item Management Data Reply (MCD)
IMDS .... International Meat Development Scheme [*United Nations Defunct*] (EAIO)
IMDS .... International Microform Distribution Service (NITA)
IMDSO .... Intelligence Materiel Development and Support Office [*Army*] (RDA)
imdt .... Immediately (BARN)
IMDT .... International Institute for Music, Dance, and Theatre in the Audio-Visual Media [*Later, Mediacult International Institute for Audio-Visual Communication and Cultural Development*]
IMDTLY .... Immediately (WGA)
IMDur .... Inscriptiones Mithriacae Duranae (BJA)
IME .... Immobilized Enzyme
IME .... Incendiary Munitions Evaluation
IME .... Independent Medical Examination [*British*]
IME .... Independent Medical Examiner (HGAA)
IME .... Indiana & Michigan Power [*NYSE symbol*] (SAG)
IME .... Indirect Manufacturing Expense
IME .... Indirect Medical Education [*Department of Health and Human Services*] (GFGA)
IME .... Industria Machine Electroniche [*Computer manufacturer*] [*Italy*] (NITA)
IME .... Information Management & Engineering Ltd. [*Information service or system*] (IID)
IME .... Institute for Municipal Engineering
IME .... Institute of Makers of Explosives (EA)
IME .... Institute of Marine Engineers [*British*]
IME .... Institute of Mathematics Education [*La Trobe University*] [*Australia*]
IME .... Institute of Mechanical Engineers [*British*]
IME .... Institute of Mining Engineers [*British*]
IME .... Institute on the Military and the Economy (EA)
IME .... International Magnetospheric Explorer [*NASA/ESRO*]
IME .... International Materiel Evaluation Program [*Army*] (RDA)
IME .... International Medical Exchange [*Defunct*] (EA)
IME .... International Microcomputer Exhibition (NITA)
IME .... International Microcomputer Exposition
IME .... International Mirtone, Inc. [*Toronto Stock Exchange symbol*]
IME .... Interplanetary Meteoroid Experiment [*NASA*]
IME .... Mennonite Biblical Seminary Library, Elkhart, IN [*OCLC symbol*] (OCLC)
IMEA .... Indirect Medical Education Adjustment
IMEA .... International Middle East Association (EA)
IME(AB) .... Institution of Mechanical Engineers (Australian Branch)
IMEAC .... Northeast Interagency Motor Equipment Advisory Committee [*Terminated, 1981*] [*General Services Administration*] (EGAO)
IMEASY .... Integrated Management and Economic Analysis Model [*Federal Emergency Management Agency*] (GFGA)
IMEB .... International Movement of Esperantist Bicyclists [*See also BEMI*] [*The Hague, Netherlands*] (EAIO)
IMEC .... Imatec Ltd. [*NASDAQ symbol*] (SAG)
IMEC .... Institut Mondial d'Ecologie et de Cancerologie [*World Institute of Ecology and Cancer - WIEC*] (EAIO)
IMEC .... Interstate Migrant Education Council (EA)
IMEC .... Item Mission Essentially Code (MCD)
I Mech E ..... Institution of Mechanical Engineers [*British*]
IMECHIE ...... Institution of Mechanical Incorporated Engineers [*British*] (EAIO)

IMED .... Informedics, Inc. [*NASDAQ symbol*] (SAG)
IMEG .... Innovations in Medical Education Grant (DMAA)
IMEG .... International Management and Engineering Group [*British*]
IMEKO .... Internationale Messtechnische Konfoderation [*International Measurement Confederation*] [*ICSU Budapest, Hungary*] (EAIO)
IMEL .... IAEA [*International Atomic Energy Agency*] Marine Environment Laboratory [*Marine science*] (OSRA)
IMel .... Melvin Public Library, Melvin, IL [*Library symbol Library of Congress*] (LCLS)
IMelF .... Ford County Film Cooperative, Melvin, IL [*Library symbol*] [*Library of Congress*] (LCLS)
IMelp .... Melrose Park Public Library, Melrose Park, IL [*Library symbol Library of Congress*] (LCLS)
IMelpA .... Alberto-Culver Co., Melrose Park, IL [*Library symbol Library of Congress*] (LCLS)
IMelSD .... Melvin-Sibley Community Unit School District, Melvin, IL [*Library symbol*] [*Library of Congress*] (LCLS)
IMEM .... Improved Minimum Essential Medium [*Microbiology*]
IMEM .... International Mass Education Movement (EA)
IMEMME ...... Institution of Mining Electrical and Mining Mechanical Engineers (EAIO)
IMEMO .... Institute of World Economics and International Affairs [*Russian*] (BARN)
IMen .... Graves Public Library, Mendota, IL [*Library symbol Library of Congress*] (LCLS)
IMenHS .... Mendota High School, Mendota, IL [*Library symbol Library of Congress*] (LCLS)
IMenN .... Northbrook Elementary School, Mendota, IL [*Library symbol Library of Congress*] (LCLS)
IMEO .... Initial Mass in Earth Orbit [*NASA*]
IMEO .... Interim Maintenance Engineering Order (AAG)
IMEP .... Indicated Mean Effective Pressure [*Aerospace*]
IMEP .... International Materiel Evaluation Program [*Army*] (RDA)
IMER .... Immobilized-Enzyme Reactor
IMER .... Institute for Marine Environmental Research [*British*] (ARC)
IMerD .... Meredosia-Chambersburg River Valley Public Library District, Meredosia, IL [*Library symbol Library of Congress*] (LCLS)
IMES .... Integrated Missile Electronics Set
IMET .... International Military Education and Training [*Program of grant military training in the United States for foreign military and civilian personnel*]
I METH .... Independent Methodist (WDAA)
IMETP .... International Military Education and Training Program [*DoD*]
IMETS .... Integrated Meteorological System [*Army*] (RDA)
IMEX .... Imex Medical Systems [*NASDAQ symbol*] (TTSB)
IMEX .... Imex Medical Systems, Inc. [*NASDAQ symbol*] (NQ)
IMEX .... Integrated Manufacturing Exposition [*Penton/IPC*] (TSPED)
IMF .... Allen County Public Library, Fort Wayne, IN [*OCLC symbol*] (OCLC)
IMF .... Ifosfamide, Methotrexate, Fluorouracil (CDI)
IMF .... Image-Matched Filter (IAA)
IMF .... Immunofixation [*Analytical biochemistry*]
IMF .... Immunofluorescent [*Immunology*]
IMF .... Impact Mechanical Fuse (MCD)
IMF .... Imphal [*India*] [*Airport symbol*] (OAG)
IMF .... Impossible Mission Force [*Fictitious group of undercover agents in TV series, "Mission: Impossible"*]
IMF .... Individual Master File
IMF .... [*The*] Inefficient-Market Fund [*AMEX symbol*] (SPSG)
IMF .... Initial Mass Function [*Galactic science*]
IMF .... Installation Master File (MCD)
IMF .... Institut de Mecanique des Fluides [*Originator and database on fluid mechanics*] [*France*] (NITA)
IMF .... Institute for Metal Forming [*Lehigh University*] [*Research center*] (RCD)
IMF .... Institute for Monetary Freedom (EA)
IMF .... [*The*] Institute of Metal Finishing [*British*]
IMF .... Integrated Maintenance Facility
IMF .... Intense Magnetic Field
IMF .... Interactive Mainframe Facility (HGAA)
IMF .... Interim Minesweeping Force [*Military*]
IMF .... Intermaxillary Fixation (MAE)
IMF .... Intermediate Maintenance Facility
IMF .... Intermediate Moisture Food
IMF .... Internal Magnetic Focus
IMF .... International Marketing Federation [*Paris, France*] (EAIO)
IMF .... International Metalworkers Federation [*See also FIOM*] [*Geneva, Switzerland*] (EAIO)
IMF .... International Ministerial Federation [*Defunct*] (EA)
IMF .... International Monetary Fund [*United Nations*] (EA)
IMF .... International Myomassethics Federation (EA)
IMF .... Interplanetary Magnetic Field
IMF .... Inventory Master File (NASA)
IMF .... Israel Music Foundation (EA)
IMF .... Item Master File (MCD)
IMF .... Iuliu Maniu American Romanian Relief Foundation (EA)
i-mf-- .... Mauritius [*MARC geographic area code Library of Congress*] (LCCP)
IMFA .... Immigration Marriage Fraud Amendments Act of 1986
IMFC .... Immaculate Mary Fan Club (EA)
IMFC .... Iron Maiden Fan Club [*British*] (EAIO)
IMFET .... Internally Matched FETs [*Field Effect Transistor*] [*Avantek*] (NITA)
IMFHS .... Isle of Man Family History Society [*British*] (EAIO)
IMF/IBRD ..... International Monetary Fund and International Bank for Reconstruction and Development
IMFK .... Integrated Multifunction Keyboard (MCD)

IMFL .... Inventory of Marriage and Family Literature [*Sage Publications, Inc.*] (IID)
IM/FM .... Intensity Modulated / Frequency Modulated (WDAA)
IMFP .... Inelastic Mean Free [*or Face*] Path [*Surface analysis*]
IMFP .... Interaction Mean Free Path [*Astrophysics*]
IMFR .... Institute of Marriage and Family Relations (EA)
IMFRAD .... Integrated Multifrequency RADAR (MCD)
IMFSS .... Integrated Missile Flight Safety System
IMFU .... Imperial Military Foul-Up [*Bowdlerized version*] (DSUE)
IMFWUNA .... International Molders' and Foundry Workers' Union of North America [*Later, IM &AWU*]
IMG .... Image
IMG .... Image
IMG .... Immigration
ImG .... Immunogenetics
IMG .... Imperial Cargo Airlines Ltd. [*Ghana*] [*ICAO designator*] (FAAC)
IMG .... Inertial Measurement Group (KSC)
IMG .... Inferior Mesenteric Ganglia [*Anatomy*]
IMG .... Informational Media Guaranty
IMG .... Installation and Maintenance Guide
IMG .... Intermagnetics General Corp. [*AMEX symbol*] (SPSG)
IMG .... Internal Medicine Group [*Group practice*] (DAVI)
IMG .... International Mail Gram (MHDB)
IMG .... International Maintenance Group [*FAA*] (TAG)
IMG .... International Management Group
IMG .... International Marxist Group [*British*] (PPW)
IMG .... International Music Guide [*A publication*]
IMG .... Mead Johnson & Co., Research Library, Evansville, IN [*OCLC symbol*] (OCLC)
IMg .... Morton Grove Public Library, Morton Grove, IL [*Library symbol Library of Congress*] (LCLS)
IMGCN .... Integrated Missile Ground Control Network
IMGCSA .... Islamic Missionaries Guild of the Caribbean and South America (EAIO)
ImgeGud ...... Image Guided Technologies, Inc. [*Associated Press*] (SAG)
ImgeM .... ImageMatrix Corp. [*Associated Press*] (SAG)
ImgeMat ...... ImageMatrix Corp. [*Associated Press*] (SAG)
IMGG .... Institute of Marine Geology and Geophysics [*Russian Federation*] [*Marine science*] (OSRA)
IMGG .... Intramuscular Gammaglobulin [*Medicine*] (DMAA)
IMGI .... Improved Maintenance Guidance Information
ImgMgt .... Imaging Management Associates [*Associated Press*] (SAG)
IMGN .... Immuncogen, Inc. [*NASDAQ symbol*] (SAG)
IMGN .... ImmunoGen, Inc. [*NASDAQ symbol*] (NQ)
IMGNG .... Imaging
IMGNTN .... Imagination
IMgO .... Oakton Community College, Morton Grove, IL [*Library symbol Library of Congress*] (LCLS)
IMgO-Dp ..... Oakton Community Colleges, Learning Resources Center, Des Plaines, IL [*Library symbol Library of Congress*] (LCLS)
IMGT .... Interim Missile Guidance Test (MCD)
IMgT .... Travenol Laboratories, Morton Grove, IL [*Library symbol Library of Congress*] (LCLS)
IMGTechE ..... Institution of Mechanical General Technician Engineers [*British*]
IMGX .... Network Imaging Corp. [*NASDAQ symbol*] (SAG)
IMGXP .... Network Imaging $2.00 Cv Pfd [*NASDAQ symbol*] (TTSB)
IMGXW .... Network Imaging Wrrt [*NASDAQ symbol*] (TTSB)
IMH .... Idiopathic Myocardial Hypertrophy [*Cardiology*]
IMH .... Imperial Credit Mortgage Holdings, Inc. [*AMEX symbol*] (SAG)
IMH .... Imperial Credit Mtge Hldgs [*AMEX symbol*] (TTSB)
IMH .... Indirect Microhemagglutination Test [*Medicine*] (DMAA)
IMH .... Inlet Manhole [*Technical drawings*]
IMH .... Institut des Moeurs Humaines [*Institute of Human Values - IHV*] [*Canada*]
IMH .... Institute of Materials Handling [*British*] (BI)
IMH .... International Majestic Holdings Ltd. [*Formerly, Majestic Resources Corp.*] [*Vancouver Stock Exchange symbol*]
IMH .... International Marketing Handbook [*A publication*]
IMH .... Mennonite Historical Library, Goshen College, Goshen, IN [*OCLC symbol*] (OCLC)
IMHA .... Interamerican Medical and Health Association (EA)
IMHE .... Industrial Materials Handling Equipment
IMHE .... Institutional Management in Higher Education (AIE)
IMHEP .... Ideal Man Helicopter Engineering Project
IMHEPFC ..... Idol of My Heart Elvis Presley Fan Club (EA)
IMHI .... Infomed Holdings, Inc. [*NASDAQ symbol*] (SAG)
IMHI .... Institute for Mental Health Initiatives (EA)
IMHO .... In My Honest Opinion
IMHO .... In My Humble Opinion [*Internet language*] [*Computer science*]
IMHO .... Inventory of Mental Health Organizations [*Department of Health and Human Services*] (GFGA)
IMHOF .... International Motor Sports Hall of Fame [*Automotive racing history*]
IMHO/GHMHS... Inventory of Mental Health Organizations and General Hospital Mental Health Services [*Department of Health and Human Services*] (GFGA)
IMHP .... Iodomercuri-Hydroxypropane [*Chemistry*] (DAVI)
IMHP .... Isopropyl Methyl Pyrimidinone [*Organic chemistry*]
IMHQ .... International Military Headquarters (CINC)
IMHR .... International Miniature Horse Registry (EA)
IMHSSACE... Inventory of Mental Health Services in State Adult Correctional Facilites [*Department of Health and Human Services*] (GFGA)
IMHV .... Intermediate and Medial Part of the Hyperstriatum Ventrale [*Bird brain anatomy*]
IMI .... ICAN Minerals Ltd. [*Toronto Stock Exchange symbol*]
IMI .... Ignition Manufacturers Institute [*Later, TMI*] (EA)

ImI............ IMI of Philadelphia, Camp Hill, PA [*Library symbol Library of Congress*]　(LCLS)
IMI............ Imipramine [*Antidepressant*]
IMI............ Immunologically Measurable Insulin [*Medicine*]　(AAMN)
IMI............ Impact Message Inventory　(EDAC)
IMI............ Imperial Metal Industries Ltd. [*British*]
IMI............ Implantable Micro-Identification Device [*for laboratory animals*]
IMI............ Improved Manned Interceptor [*Proposed plane*] [*Air Force*]
IMI............ Improved Massed Intercept
IMI............ Incentives Management Index [*Test*]
IMI............ Ine [*Marshall Islands*] [*Airport symbol*]　(OAG)
IMI............ Inferior Myocardial Infarction [*Cardiology*]
IMI............ Information Marketing International [*Information service or system*]　(IID)
IMI............ Infrared Measurement Instrument
IMI............ Installation and Maintenance Instruction
IMI............ Institute for Marine Information [*Defunct*]　(EA)
IMI............ Institute of the Motor Industry, Inc. [*British*]　(BI)
IMI............ Institute on Money and Inflation　(EA)
IMI............ Institut Metapsychique International [*International Metaphysics Institute*] [*France*]　(EAIO)
IMI............ Integrally Molded Insulation
IMI............ Intensive Management Items　(MCD)
IMI............ Interim Manned Interceptor　(PDAA)
IMI............ Intermediate Machine Instruction
IMI............ Intermediate Manned Interceptor　(MUGU)
IMI............ International Maintenance Institute　(EA)
IMI............ International Management Institute [*Switzerland*]
IMI............ International Manganese Institute [*France*]　(EAIO)
IMI............ International Maple Institute
IMI............ International Marketing Institute　(EA)
IMI............ International Market Intelligence [*Databank originator*] [*Norway*]　(NITA)
IMI............ International Masonry Institute　(EA)
IMI............ International Meteorological Institute [*Marine science*]　(OSRA)
IMI............ International Ministries to Israel　(EA)
IMI............ International Missions　(EA)
IMI............ Intramuscular Injection [*Medicine*]　(MAE)
IMI............ Intraoperative Myocardial Ischemia [*Cardiology*]
IMI............ Invention Marketing, Inc. [*Information service or system*]　(IID)
IMI............ Invention Marketing Institute　(EA)
IMI............ Investment Management Institute [*Information service or system*]　(IID)
IMI............ Ion Microwelding Instrument
IMI............ Irish Management Institute　(EAIO)
IMI............ Istituto Mobiliare Italiano [*NYSE symbol*]　(SAG)
IMI............ Istituto Mobiliare Ital ADS [*NYSE symbol*]　(TTSB)
IMI............ Istituto Mobiliare Italiana [*Italian state-owned bank*]　(ECON)
IMI............ Marian College, Indianapolis, IN [*OCLC symbol*]　(OCLC)
IMIA............ Institute of Mathematics and Its Applications [*South-End-On-Sea, England*]
IMIA............ International Machinery Insurers Association [*Munich, Federal Republic of Germany*]　(EAIO)
IMIA............ International Medical Informatics Association [*IFIP special interest group*] [*Richmond Hill, ON*]　(EAIO)
IMIAT.......... International Masonry Institute Apprenticeship and Training　(EA)
IMIB............ Inland Marine Insurance Bureau [*Later, ISO*]　(EA)
IMIC............ Independent Medical Insurance Consultants Ltd. [*British*]
IMIC............ Industir-Matematik International Corp. [*NASDAQ symbol*]　(SAG)
IMIC............ Inhibitor of Mevalonate Incorporation to Cholesterol [*Food science*]
IMIC............ International Medical Information Center, Inc. [*Tokyo, Japan*]
IMIC............ International Music Industry Conference
IMIC............ Interval Modulation Information Coding　(PDAA)
IMID............ Inadvertent Missile Ignition Detection
IMID............ Infrared Miniaturized Intrusion Detector　(PDAA)
IMid............ Midlothian Public Library, Midlothian, IL [*Library symbol Library of Congress*]　(LCLS)
IMIDCA........ Interim Motorized Infantry Division Capability Analysis [*Military*]
IMIE............ Institution of Mining Engineers [*British*]
IMIF............ International Maritime Industries Forum [*British*]　(EAIO)
IMIG............ Intramuscular Immunoglobulin [*Immunology*]　(DAVI)
IMII............ Intelligent Medical Imaging, Inc. [*NASDAQ symbol*]　(SAG)
IMII............ Intelligent Med'l Imaging [*NASDAQ symbol*]　(TTSB)
IMil............ Milford Township Public Library, Milford, IL [*Library symbol Library of Congress*]　(LCLS)
IMilsSD........ Millstadt Community Consolidated School District 160, Millstadt, IL [*Library symbol Library of Congress*]　(LCLS)
IMiM.......... Inner Mitochondrial Membrane [*Cytology*]
IMIMI.......... Industrial Mineral Insulation Manufacturers Institute [*Later, TIMA*]
IMinE.......... Institution of Mining Engineers [*British*]
IMINICO....... Iranian Marine International Oil Co.
IMINT.......... Imaging Intelligence [*RADAR, photos, etc.*]
IMIP............ Industrial Management Improvement Program　(NG)
IMIP............ Industrial Modernization Improvement Plan [*DoD*]　(RDA)
IMIP............ Industrial Modernization Incentive Program [*DoD*]
IM/IPF........ Information Management / Information Processing Family　(HGAA)
IMIR............ Interceptor Missile Interrogation RADAR
IMIS............ Installation Management Information System [*Army*]
IMIS............ Instructional Materials Information System [*Database*]
IMIS............ Integrated Management Information System [*Air Force*]
IMIS............ Integrated Manufacturing Information System
IMIS............ Integrated Motorists' Information System [*Computerized guidance system to speed traffic and avoid tie-ups*]
IMIS............ Integrated Municipal Information System　(IAA)
IMIS............ Intelligence Management Information System [*Military*]　(MCD)

IMIS............ Interim Maneuver Identification System　(IAA)
IMIT............ Imitate [*or Imitative*]　(WDAA)
IMIT............ Imitation　(MSA)
IMIT............ Institute of Musical Instrument Technology [*British*]　(BI)
IM-IT.......... Insured Municipals-Income Trust [*Investment term*]
IMITAC........ Image Input to Automatic Computers
IMITS.......... Interim Mobile Independent Target System [*Military*]　(INF)
IMIX............ Imaging Workstation in X-Ray Microanalysis
IMJ............ Indiana & Michigan Power [*NYSE symbol*]　(SAG)
IMJ............ Indiana Mich Pwr 8%JrSubDebs [*NYSE symbol*]　(TTSB)
IMJ............ Infrared Miniaturized Jammer
IMJ............ RCA [*Radio Corp. of America*] Consumer Electronics Library, Indianapolis, IN [*OCLC symbol*]　(OCLC)
IMJHCA........ International Messianic Jewish Hebrew Christian Alliance [*British*]　(EAIO)
IMK............ Identification Mark　(IAA)
IMK............ Income Monitoring Kit
IMK............ Increased Maneuverability Kit
IMK............ Injection Molding Kit
IMK............ Instrument Marking Kit
IMK............ International Makaoo [*Vancouver Stock Exchange symbol*]
IMK............ Simikot [*Nepal*] [*Airport symbol*]　(OAG)
IMK............ Union Carbide Corp., Library, Indianapolis, IN [*OCLC symbol*]　(OCLC)
IMKE............ Inmark Enterprises, Inc. [*NASDAQ symbol*]　(SAG)
IMKR............ Inner Marker [*Part of an instrument landing system*] [*Aviation*]
IMKT............ Ingles Markets, Inc. [*NASDAQ symbol*]　(NQ)
IMKTA.......... Ingles Markets'A' [*NASDAQ symbol*]　(TTSB)
IML............ Imperial, NE [*Location identifier FAA*]　(FAAL)
IML............ Incoming Matching Loss [*Telecommunications*]　(TEL)
IML............ Indusmin Ltd. [*Toronto Stock Exchange symbol*]
IML............ Information Manipulation Language
IML............ Initial Machine Load [*Computer science*]　(IBMDP)
IML............ Initial Measurement List　(KSC)
IML............ Initial Microprogram Load [*Also, IMPL*] [*Computer science*]　(IBMDP)
IML............ Inside Mold Line [*Technical drawings*]
IML............ Institute of Modern Languages
IML............ Instructional Media Laboratory
IML............ Interactive Maintenance Language [*Denelcor*]　(NITA)
IML............ Intermediary Musical Language　(PDAA)
IML............ Intermediary Music Language　(NITA)
IML............ Intermediate Language [*Computer science*]　(TEL)
IML............ Intermediate Maintenance Level
IML............ Internal Medullary Lamina [*Neuroanatomy*]
IML............ International Microgravity Laboratory
ImL............ Irish Microforms Ltd., Dublin, Ireland [*Library symbol Library of Congress*]　(LCLS)
IML............ Irradiated Materials Laboratory
IML............ Island Air Ltd. [*Fiji*] [*ICAO designator*]　(FAAC)
IML............ Merrill Lynch & Co. [*NYSE symbol*]　(SAG)
IML............ Miles Laboratories, Inc., Library Resources and Services, Elkhart, IN [*OCLC symbol*]　(OCLC)
IMLA............ Intramural Left Anterior Artery [*Medicine*]　(DMAA)
IMLC............ Infantry Mortar Leader's Course [*Army*]　(INF)
IMLS............ Institute of Medical Laboratory Sciences [*British*]
IMLSG.......... Interim Mobile Logistic Support Group [*Military*]　(CAAL)
IMLSS.......... Integrated Maneuvering and Life Support System [*NASA*]
IMLT............ Institute of Medical Laboratory Technology [*British*]　(DI)
ImLy............ Immune Lysis [*Medicine*]　(DMAA)
IMM............ Immaculata College, Immaculata, PA [*OCLC symbol*]　(OCLC)
IMM............ Immediate
IMM............ Immersion　(ECII)
IMM............ Immokalee, FL [*Location identifier FAA*]　(FAAL)
IMM............ Immune [*or Immunization*]　(AFM)
IMM............ Impairing the Morals of a Minor [*Police terminology*]　(IIA)
IMM............ Independent Manned Manipulator [*NASA*]　(KSC)
IMM............ Inhibitor-Containing Minimal Medium [*Microbiology*]
IMM............ Inner Mitochondrial Membrane [*Cytology*]
IMM............ Institute for Manpower Management　(EA)
IMM............ Institute for Molecular Manufacturing
IMM............ Institute of Clinical Molecular Biology [*British*]　(DBA)
IMM............ Institute of Male Masseurs [*British*]　(DBA)
IMM............ Institute of Materials Management [*British*]　(DBA)
IMM............ Institution of Mining and Metallurgy [*London, England*]
IMM............ Integrated Magnetic Memory　(IAA)
IMM............ Integrated Maintenance Management
IMM............ Integrated Maintenance Manual
IMM............ Integrated Materiel Management [*or Manager*]
IMM............ Intelligent Memory Manager [*Computer science*]
IMM............ Intel Mobile Module
IMM............ Interactive Multimedia
IMM............ Intermediate Maintenance Manual [*Military*]　(CAAL)
IMM............ Internal Medial Malleolus [*Medicine*]　(DMAA)
IMM............ International Maggie Mines Ltd. [*Vancouver Stock Exchange symbol*]
IMM............ International Maritime Mobile [*Telecommunications*]
IMM............ International Monetary Market [*Chicago Mercantile Exchange*]
IMM............ International Money Management [*Business term*]
IMM............ Intersection Midblock Model [*Environmental Protection Agency*]　(GFGA)
IMMA............ Institute of Muslim Minority Affairs　(EAIO)
IMMA............ International Model Managers Association　(EA)
IMMA............ International Motorcycle Manufacturers Association　(EAIO)
IMMA............ Ion Microprobe Mass Analyzer
IMMAC.......... Immaculate
IMMAC.......... Inventory Management and Material Control　(IAA)

Imm AR .... Immigration Appeal Reports [*A publication*] (DLA)
IMMAT......... Immaterial (AABC)
IMMAT......... Immature
IMMC........... Interdigestive Migrating Motor Complex [*Medicine*] (DMAA)
IMMCLT....... Immaculate
IMMD........... Intensity-Maximizing Multidither (PDAA)
IMMDELREQ... Immediate Delivery Required (DNAB)
IMMDT......... Immediate
IMME.......... Institute of Municipal Maintenance Engineers [*British*] (BI)
IMME.......... Isobaric Multiplet Mass Equation
IMMED........ Immediate (AFM)
IMMEX........ Interactive Multi-Media Exercises [*A Windows-based program*]
IMMGRTN.... Immigration
IMMH.......... Indirect Maintenance Man-Hour
IMMI........... Inphynet Medical Management [*NASDAQ symbol*] (SAG)
IMMI........... International Irrigation Management Institute (GNE)
IMMI........... International Mass Media Institute (EA)
IMMIG .... Immigration
Immig & Naturalization Serv Mo Rev... United States Immigration and Naturalization Service, Monthly Review [*A publication*] (DLA)
Immig B Bull... Immigration Bar Bulletin [*A publication*] (DLA)
Immig Newsl... Immigration Newsletter [*A publication*] (DLA)
IMMIRS .... Integrated Maintenance Management Information Retrieval System [*DoD*]
IMMITTANCE... Impedance and Admittance (IAA)
IMMLEP....... Immunization Against Leprosy Program [*World Health Organization*]
IMMLS........ Interim Military Microwave Landing System (RDA)
IMMOB........ Immobilize [*Medicine*]
IMMOBIL..... Immobilize (BABM)
IMMP......... Information Management Master Plan [*DoD*]
IMMP......... Information Mission Management Plan
IMMP......... Integrated Maintenance Management Plan
IMMR......... Installation, Modification, Maintenance, and Repair (AAG)
IMMR......... Institute for Mining and Mineral Research [*University of Kentucky*] [*Research center*] (RCD)
IMMRL........ Individual Maintenance Material Readiness List (MCD)
IMMRRI...... Idaho Mining and Minerals Resources Research Institute [*University of Idaho*] [*Research center*] (RCD)
IMMS.......... Indore Mill Mazdoor Sangh [*Indore Textile Labour Association*] [*India*]
IMMS.......... Installation Maintenance Management System (MCD)
IMMS.......... Integrated Maintenance Management System [*Army*]
IMMS.......... Interactive Multimedia System (MCD)
IMMS.......... Interim Manpower Maintenance System
IMMS.......... International Material Management Society (EA)
IMMT......... Integrated Maintenance Management Team
IMMTS........ Indian Mercantile Marine Training Ship [*British*]
ImmU........ Immunizing Unit [*Medicine*] (MEDA)
IMMU......... Immunomedics, Inc. [*NASDAQ symbol*] (NQ)
IMMU......... Independent Munitions Maintenance Unit
IMMU........ InPhyNet Medical Mgmt [*NASDAQ symbol*] (TTSB)
ImmuCell...... ImmuCell Corp. [*Associated Press*] (SAG)
IMMUN .... Immunity
IMMUN .... Immunization (WDAA)
IMMUN .... Immunology (ADA)
IMMUNHMTLGY... Immunohematology
IMMUNO...... Immunoglobulin [*Immunology*] (DAVI)
IMMUNOL.... Immunology
Immut........ Quod Deus Sit Immutabilis [*Philo*] (BJA)
IMMV.......... Iris Mild Mosaic Virus
IMMY.......... Immediately
IMMY.......... Information Marketing Achievement Award [*Information Industry Association*]
IMN........... Idiopathic Membranous Nephropathy [*Nephrology*]
IMN........... Indicated Mach Number (AFM)
IMN........... Internal Mammary [*Lymph*] Node [*Medicine*] (DAVI)
IMN........... Internal-Mix Nozzle
IMN........... Manchester College, North Manchester, IN [*OCLC symbol*] (OCLC)
IMNB .... Isopropyl(methyl)nitrobenzene [*Organic chemistry*]
Imnet........... Imnet Systems, Inc. [*Associated Press*] (SAG)
IMNET......... International MarketNet [*System of broker work stations created by IBM Corp. and Merrill Lynch & Co.*] [*New York, NY*]
IMNH .... Idaho Museum of Natural History [*Idaho State University*] [*Research center*] (RCD)
IMNR .... Immune Response Corp. [*NASDAQ symbol*] (SAG)
IMNS .... Imperial Military Nursing Service [*British*]
IMNSHO...... In My Not-So-Humble Opinion [*Computer hacker terminology*] (NHD)
IMNT.......... IMNET Systems [*NASDAQ symbol*] (TTSB)
IMNT.......... Imnet Systems, Inc. [*NASDAQ symbol*] (SAG)
IMNX .... Immunex Corp. [*NASDAQ symbol*] (NQ)
IMO........... Asheville, NC [*Location identifier FAA*] (FAAL)
IMO........... Immobilized (NVT)
IMO........... Imperial Oil Ltd. [*AMEX symbol Toronto Stock Exchange symbol Vancouver Stock Exchange symbol*] (SPSG)
IMO............. Improper Order
IMO............. Indianapolis Museum of Art, Indianapolis, IN [*OCLC symbol*] (OCLC)
IMO............. In My Opinion [*Internet language*] [*Computer science*]
IMO............. Installation Maintenance Officer [*Military*] (AABC)
IMO............. Institute of Market Officers [*British*]
IMO............. Inter-American Municipal Organization
IMO............. Interband Magneto-Optic [*Effect*] (DEN)
IMO........... Interface Management Office
IMO........... International Maritime Organization [*See also OMI*] [*ICSU London, England*] (EAIO)
IMO........... International Materials Organization (NATG)

IMO........... International Mathematical Olympiad (RDA)
IMO........... International Messianic Outreach (EA)
IMO........... International Meteorological Organization [*Later, World Meteorological Organization*]
IMO........... International Money Order [*Business term*] (DS)
IMO........... Isla Mona [*Puerto Rico*] [*Seismograph station code, US Geological Survey*] (SEIS)
IMOA........... International Mercury Owners Association (EA)
IMOG .... Interagency Mechanical Operations Group [*Lawrence Livermore Laboratory*]
IMoH........... John and Mary Kirby Hospital, Monticello, IL [*Library symbol Library of Congress*] (LCLS)
ImoInd......... Imo Industries, Inc. [*Associated Press*] (SAG)
IMoI .... Moline Public Library, Moline, IL [*Library symbol Library of Congress*] (LCLS)
IMoIB.......... Black Hawk College, Moline, IL [*Library symbol Library of Congress*] (LCLS)
IMoID.......... Deere & Co., Moline, IL [*Library symbol Library of Congress*] (LCLS)
IMOM.......... Improved Many-on-Many [*Computer science*]
IMonC......... Monmouth College, Monmouth, IL [*Library symbol Library of Congress*] (LCLS)
IMont .... Allerton Public Library, Monticello, IL [*Library symbol Library of Congress*] (LCLS)
IMontF........ Piatt County Schools Film Library, Monticello, IL [*Library symbol*] [*Library of Congress*] (LCLS)
IMontSD ..... Monticello Community Unit School District, Monticello, IL [*Library symbol*] [*Library of Congress*] (LCLS)
IMonW........ Western Illinois Library System, Monmouth, IL [*Library symbol Library of Congress*] (LCLS)
IMOP.......... Infantry Mortar Program (MCD)
IMORL......... Infrared Mobile Optical Radiation Laboratory [*Navy*] (PDAA)
IMort.......... Morton Public Library, Morton, IL [*Library symbol Library of Congress*] (LCLS)
IMOS .... Inadvertent Modification of the Stratosphere [*Interagency government task force*]
IMOS .... Interactive Multiprogramming Operating System [*NCR Corp.*]
IMOS .... Ion-Implanted Metal-Oxide Semiconductor
IMOT.......... Installed Maximum Operating Time
IMOT.......... Interim Maximum Operating Time
IMOX-S....... Ion Implantation, Oxide Isolation with Scaling (NITA)
IMP............ Cargo Information Message Procedures [*IATA*] (DS)
IMP............ Idiopathic Myeloid Proliferation [*Medicine*] (DMAA)
IMP............ Illustrated Melbourne Post [*A publication*]
IMP............ Image Processing Program [*Computer program*]
IMP............ Immunoperoxidase [*An enzyme*]
IMP............ Impact (KSC)
IMP............ Impact
IMP............ Impaction [*or Impacted*] [*Medicine*] (DAVI)
imp............ Impaction [*Medicine*] (DMAA)
IMP............ Impact Predictor [*NASA*] (MUGU)
IMP............ Impaired
imp............ Impasse (DD)
IMP............ Impedance (KSC)
IMP............ Impeller
IMP............ Imperative
imp............ Imperative (WDMC)
IMP............ Imperator [*or Imperatrix*] [*Emperor or Empress*] [*Latin*]
IMP............ Imperatriz [*Brazil*] [*Airport symbol*] (OAG)
IMP............ Imperfect
imp............ Imperfect (WDMC)
IMP............ Imperial (AFM)
Imp............ Imperial [*Record label*]
IMP............ Imperial Air [*Peru*] [*ICAO designator*] (FAAC)
IMP............ Imperious [*Grammar*] (ROG)
IMP............ Imperium [*Empire*] [*Latin*]
IMP............ Impersonal
IMP............ Impersonating [*FBI standardized term*]
Imp............ Impetus [*A publication*]
IMP............ IMP, Inc. [*Associated Press*] (SAG)
IMP............ Implement (AFM)
IMP............ Implementation Language [*Edinburgh multiaccess system*] (CSR)
imp............ Import (WDMC)
imp............ Important (WDMC)
IMP............ Important
IMP............ Imported
IMP............ Importer (WDAA)
IMP............ Impracticable (FAAC)
IMP............ Impression
IMP............ Imprimatur [*Let It Be Printed*] [*Latin*]
imp............ Imprimatur [*Latin for let it be printed*] (WDMC)
Imp............ Imprime [*Printed*] [*French*] (ILCA)
Imp............ Imprimeur [*Printer*] [*French*] (ILCA)
IMP............ Imprimis [*In the First Place*] [*Latin*] (WGA)
IMP............ Imprint
IMP............ Impropriator (ROG)
IMP............ Improved
IMP............ Improved Maintenance Program [*Air Force*] (AFM)
IMP............ Improved Manufacturing Procedure [*Computer science*] (PDAA)
IMP............ Improved Mobility Package [*Wheelchair system*]
IMP............ Improvement [*Real estate*]
IMP............ Improvement Maintenance Program (MCD)
IMP............ Impulse (KSC)
IMP............ Impulse Generator
IMP............ Incomplete Male Pseudohermaphroditism [*Medicine*] (AAMN)
IMP-S......... Independent Motion Picture Co.

IMP	Indeterminate Mass Particle
IMP	Index to Maritime Publications [*A publication*]
IMP	Individual Merit Promotion
IMP	Industrial Management Program
IMP	Industrial Membrane Processing [*Chemical engineering*]
IMP	Industrial Mobilization Planning
IMP	Industrial Models and Patterns [*A publication*] (EAAP)
IMP	Industry Market Potential [*Business term*] (MHDW)
IMP	Infantry Mortar Plan (MCD)
IMP	Inflatable Micrometeoroid Paraglide
IMP	Information Management Plan [*DoD*]
IMP	Information Management Processor (NITA)
IMP	Information Management Program [*Army*]
IMP	Initial Memory Protection (MCD)
IMP	Initial Military Program (NATG)
IMP	Injection Microwave Plasma [*Oak Ridge National Laboratory*]
IMP	Inosine Monophosphate [*Biochemistry*]
IMP	Inosinic Acid [*Biochemistry*] (DAVI)
IMP	Inpatient Multidimensional Psychiatric Scale
IMP	Input Message Processor
IMP	Insoluble Metaphosphate [*Inorganic chemistry*]
IMP	Installation Master Planning [*Military*]
IMP	Institute of Modern Procedures [*Defunct*] (EA)
IMP	Institute of Molecular Pathology [*Austria*]
IMP	Instrumented Monkey Pod
IMP	Instrument Maintenance Procedure [*Nuclear energy*] (NRCH)
IMP	Integral Membrane Protein [*Cytology*]
IMP	Integrated Maintenance Plan [*or Procedure*]
IMP	Integrated Manufacturing Plan (IAA)
IMP	Integrated Master Plan [*Business term*] (RDA)
IMP	Integrated Mathematics Project (AIE)
IMP	Integrated Memory Processor
IMP	Integrated Message Processor (NITA)
IMP	Integrated Microprocessor [*National Semiconductor*]
IMP	Integrated Micro Products [*British*] (NITA)
IMP	Integrated Microwave Package (IAA)
IMP	Integrated Microwave Products (IEEE)
IMP	Integrated MIDI [*Musical Instrument Digital Interface*] Processor
IMP	Integrated Modular Personnel Software [*Percom*] (NITA)
IMP	Integrated Monitoring Panel
IMP	Integrating Motor Pneumotachograph
IMP	Intelligent Message Processor [*Delta Data Systems*] (NITA)
IMP	Intelligent Multiport Cards [*Computer hardware*] (PCM)
IMP	Interactive Mathematics Program [*High school curriculum*]
IMP	Interactive Microprogrammable Control (MCD)
IMP	Interagency Integrated Pest Management Coordinating Committee [*Terminated, 1980*] [*Council on Environmental Quality*] (EGAO)
IMP	Interface Management Plan [*Air Force*]
IMP	Interface Message Processor [*Computer science*]
IMP	Interim Monitoring Program
IMP	Inter-Industry Management Program (IAA)
IMP	Intermeccanica-Puch [*Italian-Austrian specialty car maker*]
IMP	Intermessage Processor (IAA)
IMP	Intermodulation Product
IMP	International Maple Leaf Resource Corp. [*Vancouver Stock Exchange symbol*]
IMP	International Match Point [*Game of bridge*]
IMP	International Microelectronic Products, Inc. [*Associated Press*] (SAG)
IMP	International Micro-Print Preservation, Inc.
IMP	International Mimes and Pantomimists [*Defunct*]
IMP	Interplanetary Magnetometer Probe
IMP	Interplanetary Measurement Probe
IMP	Interplanetary Monitoring Platform [*A spacecraft*]
IMP	Interplanetary Monitoring Probe [*A spacecraft*]
IMP	Intra-Industry Management Program [*Small Business Administration*]
IMP	Intramembranous Particle [*Cytology*]
IMP	Intramuscular Compartment Pressure [*Medicine*] (DMAA)
IMP	Intrinsic Multiprocessing (IEEE)
IMP	Inventory Management Plan [*Military*] (AFIT)
IMP	Ion Microprobe [*Surface analysis*]
IMP	Ion Moderated Partition [*Chromatography*]
IMP	Item Management Plan (AAGC)
IMP	Marathon, TX [*Location identifier FAA*] (FAAL)
IMP	Mishawaka Public Library, Mishawaka, IN [*OCLC symbol*] (OCLC)
IMPA	Incisal Mandibular Plane Angle [*Dentistry*]
IMPA	Independent Media Producers Association [*Later, IMPC*] (EA)
IMPA	Information Management and Processing Association [*Defunct*] (EA)
IMPA	Initialized Moore Probabilistic Automation (IAA)
IMPA	International Maritime Pilots Association (EAIO)
IMPA	International Master Printers Association [*Brussels, Belgium*]
IMPA	International Meat Processors Association (EA)
IMPA	International Motor Press Association (EA)
IMPA	International Museum Photographers Association (EA)
IMPA	International Myopia Prevention Association (EA)
IMPA	Ion Microprobe Analysis
IMPAC	Immediate Psychiatric Aid and Referral Center
IMPAC	Industrial Multilevel Process Analysis and Control (IAA)
IMPAC	Information for Management Planning Analysis and Coordination (PDAA)
IMPAC	Interagency Map and Publications Acquisitions Committee [*Department of State*] [*Washington, DC*]
IMPAC	International Merchant Purchases Authorization Care [*Visa*] (RDA)
IMPAC	International Microfiche Parts Access Catalogue [*Auto parts*] [*A publication*]

IMPACS	International Packet-Switching Service [*MCI International, Inc.*] [*Rye Brook, NY*] [*Telecommunications*] (TSSD)
IMPACT	Image Processing and Color Transmission [*Time, Inc. photograph transmission center*]
IMPACT	Implanted Advanced Composed Technology [*Texas Instruments, Inc.*]
IMPACT	Implementation Planning and Control Technique [*Computer science*]
IMPACT	Improved Management Procurement and Contracting Technique (AABC)
IMPACT	Improved Manpower Production and Controller Technique [*Navy*]
IMPACT	Improved Modern Pricing and Costing Techniques [*Air Force*] (MCD)
IMPACT	Integrated Management Planning and Control Technique [*British*]
IMPACT	Integrated Managerial Programming Analysis Control Technique [*Air Force*]
IMPACT	Integrated Materials Handling Production and Control Technology
IMPACT	Integrated Microform Parts Cataloging (PDAA)
IMPACT	Integrated Model of Plumes and Atmosphere in Complex Terrain [*Environmental Protection Agency*] (GFGA)
IMPACT	Intensive Matched Probation and After-Care Treatment (PDAA)
IMPACT	Interdisciplinary Model Programs in the Arts for Children and Teachers
IMPACT	International Marketing Program for Agricultural Commodities and Trade Center [*Washington State University*] [*Research center*] (RCD)
IMPACT	Intervention Moves Parents and Children Together [*Drug abuse treatment program sponsored by Phoenix House Foundation*]
IMPACT	Inventory Management Program and Control Technique [*IBM Corp.*] [*Computer science*]
Impacts Aust Econ	Impacts on the Australian Economy [*A publication*]
IMPALA	International Motion Picture and Lecturers Association (EA)
IMPAS-WG	Improved Military Parts Availability and Selection Working Group [*Army*] (RDA)
IMP-ATACMS	Improved Army Tactical Missile System (RDA)
Impath	Impath, Inc. [*Associated Press*] (SAG)
IMPATT	Impact Ionization Avalanche Transit Time [*Solid state diodes*] [*Transistor technology*]
IMPAV	Inter-Urban Microwave-Powered Air-Cushion Vehicle (PDAA)
IMPBA	International Model Power Boat Association (EA)
IMPC	Independent Media Producers Council (EA)
IMPC	Infantry Mortar Platoon Course (INF)
IMPC	Institutional and Municipal Parking Congress (EA)
IMPC	International Myopia Prevention Centre (DAVI)
IMPCA	International Methanol Producers and Consumers Association [*British*]
IMPCE	Importance
ImpCM	Imperial Credit Mortgage Holdings, Inc. [*Associated Press*] (SAG)
IMPCM	Improved Capability Missile [*Air Force*] (MCD)
ImpCMtg	Imperial Credit Mortgage Holdings, Inc. [*Associated Press*] (SAG)
IMPCON	Inventory Management and Production Control [*ISTEL*] [*Software package*] (NCC)
ImpCrd	Imperial Credit Industries, Inc. [*Associated Press*] (SAG)
ImpctSy	Impact Systems, Inc. [*Associated Press*] (SAG)
IMP CYL	Impression Cylinder [*Publishing*] (DGA)
IMPD	Impedance [*Electricity*]
IMPD	Improved [*Real estate*] (ROG)
IMPDAA	Independent Motion Picture Distributors Association of America
IMPDH	Inosine Monophosphate Dehydrogenase [*An enzyme*]
IMP DICT	Imperial Dictionary [*A publication*] (ROG)
IMPDMNT	Impediment
IMPE	Impregnate (IAA)
IMPEL	Insurance Management Performance Evaluation Life (MHDB)
IMPEND	Improved Effectiveness Nuclear Depth Bomb
IMPER	Imperative
IMPER	Imperfect
IMPER	Impersonal (ROG)
IMPERF	Imperfect
IMPERF	Imperforate [*Philately*]
IMPERS	Impersonal
IMPES	Implicit Pressure, Explicit Saturation [*Petroleum reservoir simulation*]
IMPF	Imperfect (MSA)
IMPFT	Imperfect (ADA)
IMPG	Imperial Group Ltd.
IMPG	Impregnate (KSC)
IMPGAC	Improved Guidance and Control (MCD)
IMPGEN	Impulse Generator (IAA)
IMPH	Impath, Inc. [*NASDAQ symbol*] (SAG)
IMPH	Impath Inc. [*NASDAQ symbol*] (TTSB)
ImpHly	Imperial Holly Corp. [*Associated Press*] (SAG)
IMPI	International Microwave Power Institute (EA)
IMPICS	Integrated Manufacturing Program Information and Control System (PDAA)
IMPIS	Indirect Material Purchasing Information Standards
IMPIS	Integrated Management Planning Information Systems [*Computer science*]
IMPL	Illustrated Maintenance Parts List
Impl	Imperial [*British military*] (DMA)
IMPL	Implement (AABC)
IMPL	Implement
IMPL	Implementation Language (NITA)
IMPL	Impulse (FAAC)
IMPL	Initial Microprogram Load [*Also, IML*] [*Computer science*]
IMPL	International Microwave Power Institute (PDAA)
IMPLNTN	Implementation
IMPLR	Impeller [*Mechanical engineering*]
IMPLS	Impulse (MSA)

Imp Man...... Impey's Law and Practice of Mandamus [*1826*] [*A publication*] (DLA)
IMPN......... Importation
IMPO......... Imposition (DSUE)
ImpOil........ Imperial Oil Ltd. [*Associated Press*] (SAG)
IMPOP....... Integrated Maintenance Program Operation (MCD)
IMPOS....... Interactive Multi-Programming Operating System (PDAA)
IMPOSN..... Imposition (ROG)
IMPOSS...... Impossible (ADA)
IMPOT........ Imposition (ROG)
IMPP......... Industrial Mobilization Production Planning [*DoD*]
IMPPA........ Independent Motion Picture Producers Association [*Defunct*] (EA)
Imp Pl........ Impey's Modern Pleader [*2nd ed.*] [*1814*] [*A publication*] (DLA)
Imp Pr CP... Impey's Practice, Common Pleas [*A publication*] (DLA)
Imp Pr KB... Impey's Practice, King's Bench [*A publication*] (DLA)
IMPR........ Impedor
IMPR........ Impractical (AABC)
IMPR........ Impression (ROG)
Impr........ Impressionism (VRA)
IMPR........ Imprint [*Online database field identifier*]
IMPR........ Imprint Records, Inc. [*NASDAQ symbol*] (SAG)
IMPR........ Improved
IMPRAC...... Impracticable (DSUE)
ImprAr....... Imperial Aramaic (BJA)
ImprBc....... Imperial Bancorp [*Associated Press*] (SAG)
IMPRD........ Impaired
IMPREG...... Impregnable (ADA)
IMPREG...... Impregnated (TEL)
IMPRESS..... Impression
IMPRESS..... Interdisciplinary Machine Processing for Research and Education in Social Sciences [*Dartmouth College, Hanover, NH*] [*Data processing system*]
IMPRG........ Impregnate (AABC)
IMPRIGA..... Imprimerie Centrale d'Afrique [*Publisher*] [*Gabon*] (EY)
IMPRINT..... Imbricated Program for Information Transfer [*Computer science*]
Imprint...... Imprint Records, Inc. [*Associated Press*] (SAG)
IMPRINT..... Improved Medical Programs and Readiness Immediately, Not Tomorrow [*TROA*]
ImprintR..... Imprint Records, Inc. [*Associated Press*] (SAG)
IMPRL........ Imperial (MSA)
IMPRL........ Imperial
imprm........ Imprimatura (VRA)
IMPROP...... Improper (ADA)
IMPROV...... Improvement (MSA)
IMPROVE.... Interagency Monitoring of Protected Visual Environments (USDC)
IMPROVE.... Interagency Monitoring of Protected Visual Environments [*Marine science*] (OSRA)
IMPROVE.... Inventory Management, Product Replenishment and Order Validity Evaluation (MHDB)
IMPRS........ Information Management Process Reporting System (HGAA)
IMPRSN...... Impression (MSA)
IMPRT........ Import
IMPRTD...... Imported
IMPRTNG..... Importing
IMPRTR...... Importer
IMPRV........ Improvement (AABC)
IMPRVMNT... Improvement
IMPRVMT.... Improvement
IMPS......... Imperial Tobacco Co. Shares [*Stock exchange term British*] (DSUE)
IMPS......... Impose (MSA)
IMPS......... Individual Multipurpose Shelter [*Army*] (INF)
IMPS......... Industry Media Publishing System [*Omni Industry Corp.*] [*Information service or system*] (IID)
IMPS......... Inpatient Multidimensional Psychiatric Scale
IMPS......... Institutional Meat Purchase Specification [*Department of Agriculture*]
IMPS......... Intact Months of Patient Survival [*Medicine*] (DMAA)
IMPS......... Integrated Mail Preparation System
IMPS......... Integrated Master Programming and Scheduling
IMPS......... Integrated Microcomputer Processing System [*Bureau of the Census*] (GFGA)
IMPS......... Integrated Modular Panel System
IMPS......... Interface Message Processors [*Computer science*] (NITA)
IMPS......... Intermediate Minimum Property Standards [*Department of Housing and Urban Development*] (GFGA)
IMPS......... International Microprogrammers' Society
IMPS......... International M [*formerly, Mensa*] Philatelists Society (EA)
Imp Sh........ Impey's Office of Sheriff [*6th ed.*] [*1835*] [*A publication*] (DLA)
impst......... Impasto (VRA)
impt......... Important (BARN)
Impt......... Imprisonment [*British military*] (DMA)
IMPT......... Improvement [*Real estate*] (ROG)
IMPT......... Integrated Micro Products [*NASDAQ symbol*] (SAG)
ImpThft....... Imperial Thrift & Loan Association [*Associated Press*] (SAG)
IMPTN........ Imputation
IMPTR........ Importer (ADA)
IMPTS........ Improved Programmer Test Station (IEEE)
IMPUTN...... Imputation
IMPV......... Imperative
IMPVD........ Improved [*Real estate*] (ROG)
IMPVE........ Improve [*Real estate*] (ROG)
Impx......... Impacted [*Medicine*] (DMAA)
IMPX......... Impaction [*Dentistry*]
IMPX......... Imperatrix [*Empress*] [*Latin*]
IMPX......... IMP, Inc. [*NASDAQ symbol*] (SAG)
IMQ......... Industrial Management Qualification
IMQ......... La Porte County Library, La Porte, IN [*OCLC symbol*] (OCLC)

IMR......... IMCO Recycling [*NYSE symbol*] (TTSB)
IMR......... IMCO Recycling, Inc. [*NYSE symbol*] (NQ)
IMR......... Impala Resources [*Vancouver Stock Exchange symbol*]
IMR......... Imperial Military Railways [*British military*] (DMA)
IMR......... Improved Military Rifle (PDAA)
IMR......... Impulse-Aero [*Russian Federation*] [*ICAO designator*] (FAAC)
IMR......... Independent Modification Review [*Military*] (AFIT)
IMR......... Individual Medical Record
IMR......... Infant Mortality Rate
IMR......... Infant Mortality Risk [*Medicine*] (DMAA)
IMR......... Infectious Mononucleosis Receptor [*Biochemistry*] (AAMN)
IMR......... Informal Memorandum Report
IMR......... Information Management Review [*A publication*] (NITA)
IMR......... Initial Missile Report (CINC)
IMR......... Initial Mortality Rate
IMR......... Inner Metropolitan Region (ADA)
IMR......... Institute for Materials Research [*Later, NSL*] [*National Institute of Standards and Technology*]
IMR......... Institute for Medical Research [*Camden, New Jersey*]
IMR......... Institute of Man and Resources
IMR......... Institute of Marine Resources [*University of California*] [*Research center*] (RCD)
IMR......... Institute of Masonry Research [*Defunct*] (EA)
IMR......... Institute of Metal Repair (EA)
IMR......... Institution for Mentally Retarded [*Generic term*] (DHSM)
IMR......... Integrated Multiport Repeater [*Computer science*] (PCM)
IMR......... Intelligent Machine Research (NITA)
IMR......... Internal Mold Release [*Plastics technology*]
IMR......... International Medical Research
IMR......... Interrupt-Mask Register [*Computer science*]
IMR......... Inventory Management Record [*Military*] (AFM)
IMR......... Inventory Management Review
IMR......... Inventory Modified Round
IMR......... Isla Mona [*Puerto Rico*] [*Seismograph station code, US Geological Survey Closed*] (SEIS)
IMR......... Isolation Mode Rejection (IAA)
IMR......... Monroe County Public Library, Bloomington, IN [*OCLC symbol*] (OCLC)
IMRA......... Incentive Manufacturers Representatives Association [*Naperville, IL*] (EA)
IMRA......... Independent Motorcycle Retailers of America [*Defunct*] (EA)
IMRA......... Industrial Marketing Research Association [*British*]
IMRA......... Infrared Monochromatic Radiation
IMRA......... Insurance Market Risk Assessment
IMRA......... International Manufacturers Representatives Association [*Tulsa, OK*] (EA)
IMRA......... International Military Recreation Association [*Defunct*] (EA)
IMRA......... International Mission Radio Association (EA)
IMRAD........ Introduction, Methodology, Results, and Discussion (WDMC)
IMRAD........ Introduction, Methods, Results, and Discussion [*Scientific writing*]
IMRADS...... Information Management, Retrieval, and Dissemination System (DIT)
IMRAN........ International Marine Radio Aids to Navigation
IMRB......... Improved Main Rotor Blade (RDA)
IMRC......... Indigenous Minorities Research Council [*British*]
IMRC......... Instructional Materials Reference Center [*American Printing House for the Blind - APH*] [*Absorbed by*] (EA)
IMRC......... Inventory [*or Item*] Management Responsibility Code
IMRE......... IMRE Corp. [*NASDAQ symbol*] (NQ)
IMRE......... Institute for Medical Record Economics (EA)
IMREC........ Interior Ministerial Real Estate Committee [*Vietnam*]
IMREP........ Immediately Report
IMRETES..... Immunization Readiness Training Exercises [*Army*]
IMRF......... Independent Manufacturers Representatives Forum (EA)
IMRF......... International Medical and Research Foundation [*Later, AMREF*] (EA)
IMRHS........ Inactive Materiel Request History and Status File [*Army*]
IMRI......... Integrated Medical Resources, Inc. [*NASDAQ symbol*] (SAG)
IMRI......... International Marian Research Institute [*University of Dayton*] [*Research center*] (RCD)
IMRL......... Immediate Material Requirement List
IMRL......... Individual Maintenance Readiness List
IMRL......... Individual Material Readiness List [*DoD*]
IMRL......... Integrated Materials Research Laboratory [*Sandia National Laboratories*]
IMRL......... Intermediate Maintenance Repair Level (MCD)
IMRL......... Intermediate Maintenance Requirements List
IMRO......... Internal Macedonian Revolutionary Organization [*Bulgaria*] [*Political party*] (PPE)
IMRO......... Interplant Material Requisition Order
IMRO......... Investment Managers Regulatory Organisation [*British*] (ECON)
IMRO-DPMNU... Internal Macedonian Revolutionary Organization - Democratic Party for Macedonian[*Bulgaria*] National Unity [*Political party*] (EY)
IMRP......... International Meeting on Radiation Processing (EA)
IMRR......... Isolation Mode Rejection Ratio (IAA)
IMRRS........ Installation Materiel Readiness Reporting System [*Army*]
IMRRS........ Institute of Market and Reward Regional Surveys [*British*]
IMRS......... Immersion (MSA)
IMRS......... Information Management Resources, Inc. [*NASDAQ symbol*] (SAG)
IM-RSI....... International Military Rationalization, Standardization, and Interoperability (RDA)
IMRT......... Infant Mortality Review Team [*Department of Health and Human Services*] (GFGA)
IMRU......... Institute of Microbiology, Rutgers University [*New Jersey*]
IMS......... Air Images [*British*] [*FAA designator*] (FAAC)
IMS......... Idle Matrix Search [*Computer science*]

IMS.............	IEEE Instrumentation and Measurement Society (EA)
IMS.............	Ignition Module Signal [*Automotive engineering*]
IMS.............	Image Management System [*Filenet*] (NITA)
IMS.............	Image Motion Simulator
IMS.	Imasco Ltd. [*Toronto Stock Exchange symbol Vancouver Stock Exchange symbol*]
ImS.............	Immune Serum [*Also, IS*]
IMS.............	Income Matching System
IMS.............	In-Core Monitoring System [*Nuclear energy*] (NRCH)
IMS.............	Incurred in Military Service [*Medicine*] (MAE)
IMS.............	Index Management System (PDAA)
IMS.............	Indianapolis Motor Speedway [*Auto racing venue*]
IMS.............	Indian Medical Service [*British*]
IMS.............	Indirect Measuring System
IMS.............	Individualized Mathematics System [*Education*]
IMS.............	Industrial Management Society (EA)
IMS.............	Industrial Mathematics Society (EA)
IMS.............	Industrial Measurement Systems/ Institute of Manpower Studies [*British*]
IMS.............	Industrial Methylated Spirit
IMS.............	Inertial Measuring Set [*or System*] (NVT)
IMS.............	In-Flight Management System
IMS.............	Information Management Specialists, Inc. [*Denver, CO*] [*Information service or system*] (IID)
IMS.............	Information Management Staff [*Environmental Protection Agency*] (GFGA)
IMS.............	Information Management System [*IBM Corp.*] [*Computer science*]
IMS.............	Infrared Measuring System
IMS.............	Initial Measurement System [*Nuclear missiles*]
IMS.............	In-Mold Surfacing [*Plastics technology*]
IMS.............	Inshore Minesweeper [*Navy British*]
IMS.............	Institute for Mesoamerican Studies [*State University of New York, Albany*] [*Research center*] (RCD)
IMS.............	[*The*] Institute of Management Sciences
IMS.............	Institute of Management Services [*British*]
IMS.............	Institute of Management Specialists [*Royal Leamington Spa, Warwickshire, England*] (EAIO)
IMS.............	Institute of Manpower Studies [*Department of Employment*] [*British*]
IMS.............	Institute of Marine Science [*University of Alaska*] [*Research center*]
IMS.............	Institute of Materials Science (KSC)
IMS.............	Institute of Mathematical Statistics (EA)
IMS.............	Institute of Mental Subnormality [*British*]
IMS.............	Institute of Museum Services [*National Foundation of the Arts and the Humanities*] (GRD)
IMS.............	Institute on Man and Science [*Formerly, Council on World Tensions*]
IMS.............	Instructional Management System (IEEE)
IMS.............	Instrumented Measuring System
IMS.............	Integrated Maintenance Schedule
IMS.............	Integrated Maintenance System
IMS.............	Integrated Manufacturing System (MHDI)
IMS.............	Integrated Mapping System
IMS.............	Integrated Master Schedule [*Business term*] (RDA)
IMS.............	Integrated Medical Services
IMS.............	Integrated Meteorological System [*Army*] (IEEE)
IMS.............	Integrated Microcomputer Systems, Inc.
IMS.............	Intelligent Manufacturing Systems [*Japan*] [*Agreement for conducting cooperative global research*]
IMS.............	Intensive Manpower Services (OICC)
IMS.............	Interactive Market Systems [*New York, NY Information service or system*] (IID)
IMS.............	Interactive Media Systems [*Information service or system*] (IID)
IMS.............	InterCapital Ins Muni Sec [*NYSE symbol*] (TTSB)
IMS.............	InterCapital Insured Municipal Securities [*NYSE symbol*] (SAG)
IMS.............	Interceptor Missile (IAA)
IMS.............	Interceptor Mission Sheet (SAA)
IMS.............	Interim Meteorological Satellite
IMS.............	Intermediate Maintenance Squadron (MCD)
IMS.............	Intermembrane Space [*Biochemistry*]
IMS.............	Inter-Message Separation [*Communications*]
IMS.............	Intermodal Management System [*VDOT*] (TAG)
IMS.............	Internal Management System [*Military*] (AFIT)
IMS.............	Internal Measurement System
IMS.............	International Magnetospheric Study [*1976-78*] [*National Science Foundation*]
IMS.............	International Maledicta Society (EA)
IMS.............	International Management Services, Inc. [*Framingham, MA*] [*Information service or system*] (IID)
IMS.............	International Marketing Services
IMS.............	International Measurement System [*Sailing*]
IMS.............	International Medication Systems [*Pharmacology*] (DAVI)
IMS.............	International Meditation Society
IMS.............	International Metallographic Society (EA)
IMS.............	International Metric System
IMS.............	International Military Services Ltd. [*Ministry of Defence*] [*British*]
IMS.............	International Military Staff [*NATO*]
IMS.............	International Monitoring System [*For nuclear tests*]
IMS.............	International Montessori Society
IMS.............	International Mountain Society (EA)
IMS.............	International Multihull Society [*Formerly, International Hydrofoil and Multihull Society*] [*Defunct*] (EA)
IMS	International Musicological Society [*Basel, Switzerland*] (EA)
IMS	Internet Multicasting Service [*Non-profit information service*]
IMS	Interplanetary Measurement Satellite (IAA)
IMS	Interplanetary Mission Support
IMS	Interplanetary Monitor Satellite (IAA)

IMS.............	Intrinsic Monomer Stress [*Physical chemistry*]
IMS.............	Inventory Management and Simulator
IMS.............	Inventory Management System (NASA)
IMS.............	Ionization and Momentum Sensor
IMS.............	Ion Mass Spectrometer
IMS.............	Ion Mobility Spectrometry
IMS.............	Irish Mathematics Society
IMS.............	Irradiance Measuring System
IMS.............	Island Missionary Society (EA)
IMS.............	Madison, IN [*Location identifier FAA*] (FAAL)
IMS.............	St. Mary-Of-The-Woods College, Library, St. Mary-Of-The-Woods, IN [*OCLC symbol*] (OCLC)
IMSA.............	Illinois Mathematics and Science Academy
IMSA.............	International Management Systems Association [*Later, Internet-International Management Systems Association*] (EA)
IMSA.............	International Metallic Silhouette Association (DICI)
IMSA.............	International Motor Sports Association (EA)
IMSA.............	International Municipal Signal Association (EA)
IMSA.............	Seaman Apprentice, Instrumentman, Striker [*Navy rating*]
IMSAM.............	Interceptor Missile, Surface-to-Air-Missile (MCD)
IMSAP	International Marine Sciences Affairs Panel [*Defunct*] (USDC)
IMSC.............	Industry Missile and Space Conference
IMSC.............	Integrated Measurement Sys [*NASDAQ symbol*] (TTSB)
IMSC.............	Integrated Measurement Systems [*NASDAQ symbol*] (SAG)
IMSC & D...	Inventory Manager Stock Control and Distribution [*Military*] (AFM)
IMSC & DS...	Inventory Manager Stock Control and Distribution System [*Military*]
IMSCO	Initial Maritime Satellite Consortium [*Six United States and two British oil companies and tanker operators*] (PDAA)
IMSCOM	International Military Staff Communication [*NATO*] (NATG)
IMSD	Information Management and Services Division [*Environmental Protection Agency*] (GFGA)
IMS-DB........	IMS-Database (NITA)
IMS-DC........	IMS-Data Communications (NITA)
IMSDP........	Innovator Multiple Source Drug Product
IMSE........	Integrated Mean Square Error [*Statistics*]
IMSE........	Interagency Materials Sciences Exchange
IMSE........	Intermediate Maintenance Support Equipment [*Army*]
IMSG........	Imperial Merchant Service Guild [*A union*] [*British*]
IMSI........	Information Management System Interface
IMSI........	International Maple Syrup Institute (EA)
IMSI........	International Microcomputer Software, Inc. [*NASDAQ symbol*] (SAG)
IMSI........	Intl Microcomputer Software [*NASDAQ symbol*] (TTSB)
IMSIM........	Information Management Simulation (KSC)
IMS INC.......	International Management Services, Inc. [*Franklyn, MA*] (TSSD)
IMS/INQ......	Information Management System Inquiry
IMSL........	International Mathematical and Statistical Libraries, Inc.
IMSL...........	International Mathematics and Statistics Library [*Marine science*] (OSRA)
IMSL........	International Mathematics and Statistics Library (USDC)
IMSM........	Institute of Marketing and Sales Management [*British*] (BI)
IMSM........	International Military Staff Memorandum [*NATO*] (NATG)
IMSN	Internal-Mix Spray Nozzle
IMSN	Seaman, Instrumentman, Striker [*Navy rating*]
IMSO	Initial Materiel Support Office [*Army*] (AABC)
IMSOC........	Interceptor Missile Squadron Operations Center [*Air Force*]
IMSP........	Integrated Mass Storage Processor
IMSR........	Interplanetary Mission Support Requirements
IMSS........	In-Flight Medical Support System [*Skylab*] [*NASA*]
IMSS........	Item Management Statistical Series
IMSSCE.......	Interceptor Missile Squadron and Supervisory Control Equipment
IMSSS	Institute for Mathematical Studies in the Social Sciences [*Stanford University*] [*Research center*] (RCD)
IMSSS	Interceptor Missile Squadron Supervisory Station
IMS/SSC	International Magnetospheric Study / Satellite Situation Committee [*NASA*] (PDAA)
IMST...........	Institute of Marine Sciences and Technology
IMST...........	International Mushroom Society for the Tropics (EAIO)
IMSTI...........	Institute of Marine Scientific and Technological Information [*China*] [*Marine science*] (OSRA)
IMSU...........	International Muslim Students Union (EA)
IMSUM........	International Military Staff Summary [*NATO*] (NATG)
IMS/VS	Information Management System/Virtual Storage (MCD)
IMSW...........	Institute of Medical Social Workers [*British*] (BI)
IMSWE........	Investigations of Marine Shallow Water Ecosystems (NOAA)
IMSWEP	Investigations of Marine Shallow-Water Ecosystems Program [*Smithsonian Institution*] (GFGA)
IMSWM........	International Military Staff Working Memorandum [*NATO*] (NATG)
IMT.............	Idaho Motor Tariff Bureau, Boise ID [*STAC*]
IMT.............	Immediate
IMT.............	Immediate Money Transfer (DCTA)
IMT.............	Impulse-Modulated Telemetry (IAA)
IMT.............	Independent Model Triangulation (PDAA)
IMT.............	Individual Movement Technique [*Military*] (INF)
IMT.............	Induced Muscular Tension [*Physiology*]
IMT.............	Industrial & Materials Technologies (ACII)
IMT.............	Information and Manufacturing Technologies Division [*British*]
IMT.............	Inspiratory Muscle Training [*Medicine*] (DMAA)
IMT.............	Institute of Municipal Transport [*British*] (DBA)
IMT.............	Integrated Microimage Terminal [*Kodak*] (NITA)
IMT.............	Intelligent Microimage Terminal [*Kodak*]
IMT.............	InterCapital Ins Muni Tr [*NYSE symbol*] (TTSB)
IMT.............	InterCapital Insured Municipal Trust [*NYSE symbol*] (SAG)
IMT.............	Intermachine Trunk [*Telecommunications*] (TEL)
IMT.............	Intermediate Maintenance Trainer [*Army*]
IMT.............	Intermediate Tape [*Telecommunications*] (TEL)

IMT	International Markatech [*Vancouver Stock Exchange symbol*]
IMT	International Military Tribunal [*Post-World War II*]
IMT	Intestinal Mutagenicity Test [*Clinical chemistry*]
IMT	Ion Microtomography [*High-resolution imaging technique*]
IMT	Iron Mountain [*Michigan*] [*Airport symbol*] (OAG)
IMT	Iron Mountain/Kingsford, MI [*Location identifier FAA*] (FAAL)
IMT	Morton Grove Public Library, Morton Grove, IL [*OCLC symbol*] (OCLC)
IMT-2000	International Mobile Telecommunications for the Year 2000
IMTA	Institut de la Medecine du Travail et des Ambiances [*Institute of Occupational and Environmental Health*] [*Canada*]
IMTA	Institute of Municipal Treasurers and Accountants [*Later, CIPFA*] [*British*]
IMTA	Intensive Military Training Area (DA)
IMTA	International Marine Transit Association (EA)
IMTA	International Mass Transit Association (EA)
IMTAC	Information Management Technology [*NASDAQ symbol*] (SAG)
IMTB	Isle Of Man Tourist Board (DCTA)
IMTC	Imtec, Inc. [*NASDAQ symbol*] (NQ)
IMTC	Infantry Moving Target Carrier [*Army*]
IMTC	International Multimedia Teleconferencing Consortium
IMtca	Mount Carmel Public Library, Mt. Carmel, IL [*Library symbol Library of Congress*] (LCLS)
IMtcaSD	Mount Carmel Community Unit School District No. 348, Mt. Carmel, IL [*Library symbol Library of Congress*] (LCLS)
IMTD	Institute of Master Tutors of Driving [*British*] (BI)
IMTE	Institut de la Medecine du Travail et de l'Environnement [*Institute of Occupational and Environmental Health*] [*Canada*]
IMTE	International Military Tribunal for Europe [*Post-World War II*]
Imtec	Imtec, Inc. [*Associated Press*] (SAG)
IMTEC	Institute of Marine and Terrestrial Ecology [*Research center*] (RCD)
IMTEC	International Marine Trades Exhibit and Convention [*National Marine Manufacturers Association*]
IMTEC	International Movements toward Educational Change [*Later, IMTEC-The International Learning Cooperative*] (EAIO)
IMTED	Information Management and Technology Division (AAGC)
IMTFC	International Movement for Therapeutic Free Choice [*France*] (EAIO)
IMTFJ	International Military Tribunal for Japan [*Post-World War II*]
IMTG	Internationale Moor und Torf-Gesellschaft [*International Peat Society - IPS*] (EAIO)
IMTK	Information Management Technology [*NASDAQ symbol*] (SAG)
IMTKA	Information Mgmt Tech'A' [*NASDAQ symbol*] (TTSB)
IMTKW	Information Mgmt Tech Wrrt'A' [*NASDAQ symbol*] (TTSB)
IMTLYM	Immature Lymphocytes [*Hematology*] (DAVI)
IMTN	Iron Mountain [*NASDAQ symbol*] (TTSB)
IMTN	Iron Mountain, Inc. [*NASDAQ symbol*] (SAG)
IMTNE	International Meteorological Teletype Network Europe (NATG)
IMto	Mount Olive Public Library, Mount Olive, IL [*Library symbol Library of Congress*] (LCLS)
IMtoMCD	Macoupin Community, District 5, Mount Olive, IL [*Library symbol Library of Congress*] (LCLS)
IMTP	Industrial Mobilization Training Program
IMTP	Injection-Molded Thermoplastic [*Materials science*]
IMTP	Integrated Maintenance Test Plan
IMTP	International Musa Testing Program [*United Nations*] (ECON)
IMTP	Itim Mizrah News Agency. Teleprinter Service (BJA)
IMTRAN	Implicit Transport (PDAA)
IMTRO	Integrated Maintenance Test Requirement Outline
IMTS	Improved Mobile Telephone Service [*Telecommunications*]
IMTS	Individualized Manpower Training System (OICC)
IMTS	International Machine Tool Show (ITD)
IMtv	Mount Vernon Public Library, Mt. Vernon, IL [*Library symbol Library of Congress*] (LCLS)
IMtvSD	Summersville School District 79, Mount Vernon, IL [*Library symbol Library of Congress*] (LCLS)
IMTWC	Information Management Technology [*NASDAQ symbol*] (SAG)
IMTX	Interactive Media Technologies, Inc. (NQ)
IMU	Immudyne, Inc. [*Vancouver Stock Exchange symbol*]
IMU	Impedance Matching Unit (MCD)
IMU	Income Maintenance Unit [*Work Incentive Program*] [*Department of Labor*]
IMU	Increment Memory Unit
IMU	Index of Medical Underservice (DMAA)
IMU	Inertial Measurement Unit
IMU	Information Management Unit (NITA)
IMU	Instruction Memory Unit
IMU	Interference Mockup (IAA)
IMU	Internal Measurement Unit (NASA)
IMU	Internationale Metall Union [*International Metal Union*] (EA)
IMU	International Mailers Union [*Later, International Typographical Union*] (EA)
IMU	International Mathematical Union [*See also UMI*] [*ICSU Helsinki, Finland*] (EAIO)
IMU	International Milliunit
IMU	Irish Missionary Union (EAIO)
IMU	Muncie Public Library, Muncie, IN [*OCLC symbol*] (OCLC)
IMUA	Inland Marine Underwriters Association [*New York, NY*] (EA)
IMUA	Interservice Materiel Utilization Agency [*Military*] (AABC)
Imucor	Immucor, Inc. [*Associated Press*] (SAG)
IMUDS	Illustration Makeup Data Sheet
IMUGSE	Inertial Measurement Unit Ground Support Equipment (SAA)
IMUL	ImmuLogic Pharmaceutical [*NASDAQ symbol*] (TTSB)
IMUL	ImmuLogic Pharmaceutical Corp. [*NASDAQ symbol*] (SPSG)
IMulgSD	Mulberry Grove Community Unit, School District 1, Mulberry Grove, IL [*Library symbol Library of Congress*] (LCLS)
ImuLog	ImmuLogic Pharmaceutical Corp. [*Associated Press*] (SAG)
IMunE	Institution of Municipal Engineers [*British*]
Imunex	Immunex Corp. [*Associated Press*] (SAG)
Imungn	Immuncogen, Inc. [*Associated Press*] (SAG)
Imunmd	Immunomedics, Inc. [*Associated Press*] (SAG)
ImunRsp	Immune Response Corp. [*Associated Press*] (SAG)
IMunS	Saint Mary of the Lake Seminary, Mundelein, IL [*Library symbol Library of Congress*] (LCLS)
IMUR	Interactive Multiple Regression System (MCD)
IMUS	Internal Measuring Unit System (MCD)
IMUS	Inventario Musical [*Database*] [*Ministerio de Cultura*] [*Spanish*] [*Information service or system*] (CRD)
IMUT	Imutec Corp. [*NASDAQ symbol*] (SAG)
Imutec	Imutec Corp. [*Associated Press*] (SAG)
IMUTF	IMUTEC Corp. [*NASDAQ symbol*] (TTSB)
IMUX	Intelligent Multiplexer [*Telecommunications*] (ACRL)
IMV	Cornell College, Mount Vernon, IA [*OCLC symbol*] (OCLC)
IMV	Industrija Motornih Vozil [*Yugoslav automaker*]
IMV	Inferior Mesenteric Vein [*Anatomy*]
IMV	Intermittent Mandatory Ventilation [*Respiratory therapy*] [*Medicine*]
IMV	Intermittent Mechanical Ventilation [*Respiratory therapy*] [*Medicine*] (DAVI)
IMV	Internal Motor Vehicle [*Type of tugboat*] (DS)
IMV	Internationaler Metzgermeisterverband [*International Federation of Meat Traders' Associations*] (EAIO)
IMV	Internationaler Milchwirtschaftverband [*International Dairy Federation*]
IMV	International Movie Group, Inc. [*Vancouver Stock Exchange symbol*]
IMV	Intracellular Mature Virus
IMV	Isophosphamide, Methotrexate, and Vincristine [*Medicine*] (DMAA)
IMVCi	Indole, Methyl-Red, Voges-Proskauer, Citrate Test [*Bacteriology*]
IM/VE	Information Management / Virtual Environment (HGAA)
IMVH	Indian Military Veterinary Hospital [*British military*] (DMA)
IMViC	Indole, Methyl Red, Voges-Proskauer, Citrate [*Reaction and test*] [*Biochemistry*] (DAVI)
IMViC	Indol, Methyl Red, Voges-Proskauer, Citrate Reactions [*Bacteriology*] [*Medicine*] (BABM)
IMVIC	International Motor Vehicle Inspection Committee [*Belgium*] (EAIO)
IMVP	Ifostamide, Methotrexate, VePesid (CDI)
IMVP	International Motor Vehicle Program [*MIT*]
IMVP-16	Isophosphamide, Methotrexate, Vesposide [*Antineoplastic drug regimen*] (DAVI)
IMVS	Indian Mobile Veterinary Stores [*British military*] (DMA)
IMVTS	Industrial Model Vocational Training Systems (EDAC)
IMW	Institute of Masters of Wine (BARN)
IMW	International Map of the World
IMW	Knox County Public Library, Vincennes, IN [*OCLC symbol*] (OCLC)
IMWA	International Mine Water Association [*Madrid, Spain*] (EAIO)
IMWA	International Ministers' and Widows' Association (EA)
IMWoodT	Institute of Machine Woodworking Technology [*British*] (BI)
IMX	Indiana Institute of Technology, McMillen Library, Fort Wayne, IN [*OCLC symbol*] (OCLC)
IMX	Inquiry Message Exchange
IMX	Island Mining [*Vancouver Stock Exchange symbol*]
IMX	Zimex Aviation Ltd. [*Switzerland ICAO designator*] (FAAC)
IMY	Groupo Imsa Sa de CV [*NYSE symbol*] (SAG)
IMY	Ida-May Resources Ltd. [*Vancouver Stock Exchange symbol*]
IMY	International Mahogany Corp. [*Toronto Stock Exchange symbol Vancouver Stock Exchange symbol*]
IMY	Michigan City Public Library, Michigan City, IN [*OCLC symbol*] (OCLC)
IMZ	Binghamton, NY [*Location identifier FAA*] (FAAL)
IMZ	Internationales Musikzentrum [*International Music Center*] [*Vienna, Austria*] (EAIO)
IM/ZEUS	Information Management / Zero Effort User System (HGAA)
IN	East Hampton Air [*ICAO designator*] (AD)
IN	Ice (Deposition) Nuclei [*Atmospheric science*]
IN	Icterus Neonatorum [*Medicine*]
IN	Idaho Nuclear (MCD)
IN	Ilioinguinal Nerve [*Anatomy*]
IN	Illinois Northern Railway [*AAR code*]
IN	Impetigo Neonatorum [*Medicine*] (DMAA)
in	Inch
in	Inch (IDOE)
IN	Inch (EY)
in	Inch (VRA)
in	Inches (VRA)
IN	Income
IN	India [*ANSI two-letter standard code*] (CNC)
IN	Indian (WDAA)
IN	Indiana [*Postal code*]
In	Indiana State Library, Indianapolis, IN [*Library symbol Library of Congress*] (LCLS)
IN	Indian Navy
In	Indian Reports [*A publication*] (DLA)
In	Indium [*Chemical element*]
IN	Inertial (MCD)
IN	Inertial Navigation (IAA)
IN	Infantry [*Army*]
IN	Information Systems Directorate [*Kennedy Space Center*] [*NASA*] (NASA)
IN	Ingress Node (ACRL)
IN	Initial Dose [*Medicine*]
IN	Inlet [*Maps and charts*]
IN	Input (MDG)
in	Input (IDOE)

IN.............. INS Insurance [*Vancouver Stock Exchange symbol*]
IN.............. Institute of Navigation [*US and British*]
IN.............. Institution [*Online database field identifier*]
In.............. Instructor [*Navy British*]
IN.............. Instructor Navigator (AFM)
IN.............. Instrumentation Notice (AAG)
IN.............. Instrument Note
IN.............. Insulated [*Shipping*] (DCTA)
IN.............. Insulin
In.............. Insurance
IN.............. Intake
IN.............. Integon Corp. [*NYSE symbol*] (SAG)
IN.............. Intelligence
IN.............. Intelligence Corps [*Army*] (RDA)
IN.............. Intelligent Network [*Telecommunications*]
IN.............. Intensity
IN.............. Interactive Network
IN.............. Interception [*Football*]
IN.............. Interconnecting Network (MHDI)
IN.............. Interest [*Finance, Law*] (ADA)
IN.............. Interference-to-Noise Ratio (IEEE)
IN.............. Intermittent Noise
IN.............. Internal Note
IN.............. International House - World Trade Center [*Later, WTC*] (EA)
IN.............. Internegative [*Photography*] (WDMC)
IN.............. Interneuron [*Neurology*] (DAVI)
IN.............. Interstitial Nephritis [*Medicine*] (DMAA)
IN.............. Intertechnique
IN.............. Intraductal [*Medicine*]
IN.............. Intranasal
In.............. Inulin [*Biochemistry*] (DAVI)
IN.............. Inventors [*Pergamon-Infoline*] (NITA)
IN.............. Inventory Nonrecurring (MCD)
IN.............. Investigator
IN.............. Investigator Name [*Dialog*] [*Searchable field*] (NITA)
IN.............. Irish Nationalist (ROG)
IN.............. Irritation of Nociceptors [*Medicine*] (DMAA)
IN.............. Italian Navy (NATG)
IN.............. Item Name [*Military*]
IN.............. Item Number (IAA)
I/N............. Item Number (WDAA)
IN.............. Neisler Laboratories, Inc. [*Research code symbol*]
IN.............. Office of Inspection and Enforcement Information Notice [*Nuclear energy*] (NRCH)
IN².............. Square Inch
IN³............. Cubic Inch
INA............. Anderson College, Anderson, IN [*OCLC symbol*] (OCLC)
INA............. Department of Indian and Northern Affairs Library [*UTLAS symbol*]
INA............. Icana [*Brazil*] [*Airport symbol*] (AD)
INA............. Iinan [*Japan*] [*Seismograph station code, US Geological Survey*] (SEIS)
INA............. Immigration and Nationality Act (GFGA)
INA............. Immunonephelometric Assay [*Clinical chemistry*]
INA............. Inactivator Accelerator [*Immunology*]
INA............. Independent Newsletter Association
InA............. Indiana Appellate Court Reports [*A publication*] (DLA)
INA............. Indian and Northern Affairs Department [*Canada*]
INA............. Indian National Airways
INA............. Indian National Army [*World War II*]
INA............. Individual Nonrecurrence Action (KSC)
INA............. Industrija Nafta [*State-owned company*] [*Yugoslavia*]
INA............. Infectious Nucleic Acid (DMAA)
INA............. Inferior Nasal Artery [*Medicine*] (DMAA)
INA............. Information Not Available (OICC)
INA............. Innopac, Inc. [*Toronto Stock Exchange symbol*]
INA............. Inspector of Naval Aircraft
INA............. Institute for Anthropology [*State University of New York at Albany*] [*Research center*] (RCD)
INA............. Institute for New Antibiotics [*Former USSR*]
INA............. Institute of Nautical Archaeology (EA)
INA............. Institution of Naval Architects [*British*]
INA............. Institut National de la Communication Audiovisuelle [*France*] (NITA)
INA............. Insurance Co. of North America
INA............. Integrated Network Architecture
INA............. Interair Aviation Ltd. [*British ICAO designator*] (FAAC)
INA............. International Nanny Association (EA)
INA............. International Naturopathic Association [*Later, IAHHP*] (EA)
INA............. International Neurological Association (DAVI)
INA............. International Neurotoxicology Association
INA............. International Newsreel and News Film Association [*Later, INANEWS*] (EAIO)
INA............. International Normal Atmosphere
INA............. International Nurses Anonymous (EA)
INA............. Iodonaphthyl Azide [*Organic chemistry*]
INA............. Iraqi News Agency
INA............. Irish Northern Aid
INA............. Iron Nickel Alloy
INA............. Isonicotinic Acid [*Organic chemistry*]
INA............. Israel News Agency
INA............. Jena Nomina Anatomic a [*Also, INA*] [*Anatomy*] (DAVI)
INAA........... Instrumental Neutron Activation Analysis
INAA........... Irish National Association of Australasia
INAAP......... Indiana Army Ammunition Plant (AABC)
INAB........... [*The*] Irish National Accreditation Board (ACII)

INABU......... Imprimerie Nationale du Burundi [*Government publishing house*] [*Burundi*] (EY)
INAC.......... Inacom Corp. [*NASDAQ symbol*] (SAG)
inac.......... Inactive
InAcdC-T...... Anderson College, Graduate School of Theology, Anderson, IN [*Library symbol Library of Congress*] (LCLS)
INACDUTRA... Inactive Duty Training [*Air Force*] (AFM)
Inacom........ Inacom Corp. [*Associated Press*] (SAG)
InAcous........ Industrial Acoustics Co., Inc. [*Associated Press*] (SAG)
INACS......... Interstate Airways Communications Station (IAA)
INACT......... Inactive (AABC)
INACTFLTLANT... Inactive Fleet, Atlantic Fleet (DNAB)
INACTFLTPAC... Inactive Fleet, Pacific Fleet
INACTLANT... Inactive Fleet, Atlantic Fleet
INACTPAC... Inactive Fleet, Pacific Fleet
INACTSERVCRAFAC... Inactive Service Craft Facility [*Military*] (DNAB)
INACTSHIPFAC... Inactive Ship Maintenance Facility [*Navy*]
INACTV........ Inactivate [*or Inactive*] (MSA) (MSA)
INAD........... Inadequate (AFM)
INAD........... Inadvertent
INAD........... Infantile Neuroaxonal Dystrophy [*Medicine*] (DMAA)
INAD........... Investigational New Animal Drug [*Food and Drug Administration*]
INADQT........ Inadequate (FAAC)
INAE........... International Newspaper Advertising Executives [*Later, INAME*] (EA)
INAETP........ Indian and Native American Employment and Training Program [*Department of Labor*]
InAF........... Indian Air Force
INAF........... Individual Name and Address File [*IRS*]
INAFBO........ International Association for Business Organizations [*Baltimore, MD*] (EA)
INAH.......... Interstitial Nuclei of the Anterior Hypothalamus [*Brain anatomy*]
INAH.......... Isonicotinic Acid Hydrazide [*See also INH, ISONIAZID*] [*Antituberculous agent*]
INAI........... IntelliCorp, Inc. [*NASDAQ symbol*] (NQ)
INAI........... Iowa Natural Areas Inventory [*Iowa State Conservation Commission*] [*Des Moines*] [*Information service or system*] (IID)
INA/IC........ Inactive - In Commission, In Reserve [*Vessel status*] [*Navy*]
INAIn.......... INA Investment Securities, Inc. [*Associated Press*] (SAG)
INA/IS........ Inactive - In Service, In Reserve [*Vessel status*] [*Navy*]
InAk.......... Akron Carnegie Public Library, Akron, IN [*Library symbol Library of Congress*] (LCLS)
IN AL......... Inter Alia [*Among Other Things*] [*Latin*] (WDAA)
InAlb.......... Noble County Public Library, Albion, IN [*Library symbol Library of Congress*] (LCLS)
InAle.......... Alexandria Public Library, Alexandria, IN [*Library symbol Library of Congress*] (LCLS)
InAleN........ Alexandria News, Alexandria, IN [*Library symbol Library of Congress*] (LCLS)
InAleTT........ Alexandria Times-Tribune, Alexandria, IN [*Library symbol Library of Congress*] (LCLS)
InAlGaP........ Indium Aluminum Gallium Phophide [*Organic chemistry*]
INAME........ International Newspaper Advertising and Marketing Executives (EA)
Inamed........ Inamed Corp. [*Associated Press*] (SAG)
InAnd.......... Anderson Carnegie Public Library, Anderson, IN [*Library symbol Library of Congress*] (LCLS)
InAndB........ Anderson Daily Bulletin, Anderson, IN [*Library symbol Library of Congress*] (LCLS)
InAndC........ Anderson College, Anderson, IN [*Library symbol Library of Congress*] (LCLS)
InAndC-T...... Anderson College, Graduate School of Theology, Anderson, IN [*Library symbol*] [*Library of Congress*] (LCLS)
IN & EA....... International Nuclear and Energy Association [*Defunct*] (EA)
InAndH........ Anderson Herald, Anderson, IN [*Library symbol Library of Congress*] (LCLS)
INANEWS... International Newsreel Association (EAIO)
InAng......... Carnegie Public Library, Angola, IN [*Library symbol Library of Congress*] (LCLS)
InAngT........ Tri-State University, Angola, IN [*Library symbol Library of Congress*] (LCLS)
InAnw.......... Andrews-Dallas Township Public Library, Andrews, IN [*Library symbol Library of Congress*] (LCLS)
INAO.......... Institut National des Appellations d'Origine [*Semigovernmental organization that fixes the appellations on all French wines*]
INA/OC........ Inactive - Out of Commission, In Reserve [*Vessel status*] [*Navy*]
INA/OS........ Inactive - Out of Service, In Reserve [*Vessel status*] [*Navy*]
INAP.......... Integrated Neutron Activation Prediction [*Code system*]
INap........... Nichols Library, Naperville, IL [*Library symbol Library of Congress*] (LCLS)
INapC......... College & Seminary Library, Inc., Naperville, IL [*Library symbol Library of Congress Obsolete*] (LCLS)
INAPEN....... International AIDS Prospective Epidemiology Network (EA)
INapGS........ Church of Jesus Christ of Latter-Day Saints, Genealogical Society Library, Naperville Branch, Naperville, IL [*Library symbol Library of Congress*] (LCLS)
INapN......... North Central College, Naperville, IL [*Library symbol Library of Congress*] (LCLS)
INapS......... Standard Oil Research Center, Naperville, IL [*Library symbol of Congress*] (LCLS)
InAr........... Argos Public Library, Argos, IN [*Library symbol Library of Congress*] (LCLS)
IN ARCH...... Inland Architect [*A publication*] (ROG)
InArcT.......... Tri Town Topics, Arcadia, IN [*Library symbol Library of Congress*] (LCLS)
InARP......... Inverse Address Resolution Protocol [*Telecommunications*] (ACRL)

InArT............ Argos Tribune, Argos, IN [*Library symbol Library of Congress*] (LCLS)
INAS .... Indexing and Abstracting Services
INAS .... Industrial Naval Air Stations (NG)
INAS .... Inertial Navigation and Attack System (MCD)
INAS .... Inpatient Non-Availability Statement [*DoD*]
INAS .... Interbank National Authorization System
INas .... Nashville Public Library, Nashville, IL [*Library symbol Library of Congress*] (LCLS)
INasHS .... Nashville High School, Nashville, IL [*Library symbol Library of Congress*] (LCLS)
INAsicrz ...... Istituto Nazionale Delle Assicoraziono SPA [*Associated Press*] (SAG)
INasSD .... Nashville Community High School District 99, Nashville, IL [*Library symbol Library of Congress*] (LCLS)
INat............. New Athens Public Library, New Athens, IL [*Library symbol Library of Congress*] (LCLS)
INATAPROBU... International Association of Professional Bureaucrats (EA)
INatCD .... New Athens Community Consolidated District 60, New Athens, IL [*Library symbol Library of Congress*] (LCLS)
INATS .... Interruption of Air Traffic Services (FAAC)
InAtt............ Attica Public Library, Attica, IN [*Library symbol Library of Congress*] (LCLS)
InAttCF........ Covington Friend, Attica, IN [*Library symbol Library of Congress*] (LCLS)
InAttFO........ Attica Friendly Oracle, Attica, IN [*Library symbol Library of Congress*] (LCLS)
InAttLT........ Attica Daily Ledger Tribune, Attica, IN [*Library symbol Library of Congress*] (LCLS)
InAub .... Eckhart Public Library, Auburn, IN [*Library symbol Library of Congress*] (LCLS)
InAubS........ Auburn Evening Star, Auburn, IN [*Library symbol Library of Congress*] (LCLS)
INAUG......... Inaugurated (ADA)
InAur........... Aurora Public Library, Aurora, IN [*Library symbol Library of Congress*] (LCLS)
IN AUR .... In Auri [*To the Ear*] [*Pharmacy*]
InAurHi .... Hillforest Historical Foundation, Inc., Aurora, IN [*Library symbol Library of Congress*] (LCLS)
InAusN........ Austin-Crothersville News, Austin, IN [*Library symbol Library of Congress*] (LCLS)
INAW .... Institute of the Northamerican West (EA)
INAZ............ Interference Accommodation Zone [*Geology*]
INB.............. Bartholomew County Library, Columbus, IN [*OCLC symbol*] (OCLC)
InB.............. Bedford Public Library, Bedford, IN [*Library symbol Library of Congress*] (LCLS)
IN B .... In Bonis [*In the Goods Of*] [*Latin*] (ADA)
INB.............. In Bono [*In Good Order*]
INB.............. Independence [*Belize*] [*Airport symbol*] (OAG)
INB.............. Indiana Motor Rate and Tariff Bureau Inc., Indianapolis IN [*STAC*]
INB.............. Instalbud [*Poland ICAO designator*] (FAAC)
INB.............. Interbev Packaging Corp. [*Vancouver Stock Exchange symbol*]
INB.............. Internuclear Bridging (DMAA)
INB.............. Intl Thunderbird Gaming [*Exchange symbol*] (TTSB)
INb.............. Northbrook Public Library, Northbrook, IL [*Library symbol Library of Congress*] (LCLS)
INB.............. Oakland, CA [*Location identifier FAA*] (FAAL)
INBA .... International Nubian Breeders Association (EA)
INBACS .... Infantry Battalion as a Combat System [*Study*] (MCD)
InBaHT........ Batesville Herald Tribune, Batesville, IN [*Library symbol Library of Congress*] (LCLS)
INbAS .... Allstate Insurance, Inc., Corporate Library, Northbrook, IL [*Library symbol*] [*Library of Congress*] (LCLS)
INBC .... InnoPet Brands Corp. [*NASDAQ symbol*] (SAG)
INBC .... Interlibrary Network of Baltimore County [*Library network*]
InBCR .... Lawrence County Recorder's Office, Bedford, IN [*Library symbol Library of Congress*] (LCLS)
INbD .... Dart & Kraft, Inc., Northbrook, IL [*Library symbol*] [*Library of Congress*] (LCLS)
INBD .... Inboard (KSC)
INBD .... Inbound
InBer........... Berne Public Library, Berne, IN [*Library symbol Library of Congress*] (LCLS)
INBH .... Brokaw Hospital Medical Center, Normal, IL [*Library symbol Library of Congress*] (LCLS)
INBI .... Industrial Bancorp [*NASDAQ symbol*] (TTSB)
INBI .... Industrial Bancorp, Inc. [*NASDAQ symbol*] (SAG)
InBiKN .... Knox County Daily News, Bicknell, IN [*Library symbol Library of Congress*] (LCLS)
INBio .... Biodiversity Institute [*Center established to inventory wildlife*] (PS)
INBIT .... Input BIT [*Binary Digit*] [*Computer science*] (NASA)
InBl............. Bloomfield Public Library, Bloomfield, IN [*Library symbol Library of Congress*] (LCLS)
InBlCR .... Greene County Recorder's Office, Bloomfield, IN [*Library symbol Library of Congress*] (LCLS)
InBLHi .... Lawrence County Historical Society, Bedford, IN [*Library symbol Library of Congress*] (LCLS)
InBlo .... Monroe County Public Library, Bloomington, IN [*Library symbol Library of Congress*] (LCLS)
InBloHT....... Bloomington Herald-Telephone, Bloomington, IN [*Library symbol Library of Congress*] (LCLS)
InBloKi........ Alfred C. Kinsey Institute for Sex Research, Bloomington, IN [*Library symbol Library of Congress*] (LCLS)
InBlu .... Bluffton-Wells County Public Library, Bluffton, IN [*Library symbol Library of Congress*] (LCLS)

InBlWN .... Bloomfield Evening World and News, Bloomfield, IN [*Library symbol Library of Congress*] (LCLS)
InBoM.......... Borden Museum, Borden, IN [*Library symbol Library of Congress Obsolete*] (LCLS)
InBoo.......... Boonville Warrick County Public Library, Boonville, IN [*Library symbol Library of Congress*] (LCLS)
InBooE........ Warrick Enquirer, Boonville, IN [*Library symbol Library of Congress*] (LCLS)
InBooS........ Boonville Standard, Boonville, IN [*Library symbol Library of Congress*] (LCLS)
InBosE .... Boswell Enterprise, Boswell, IN [*Library symbol Library of Congress*] (LCLS)
InBou.......... Bourbon Public Library, Bourbon, IN [*Library symbol Library of Congress*] (LCLS)
In-BPH .... Indiana State Library, Blind and Physically Handicapped Division, Indianapolis, IN [*Library symbol Library of Congress*] (LCLS)
INBR........... Inbrand Corp. [*NASDAQ symbol*] (SAG)
InBra........... Brazil Public Library, Brazil, IN [*Library symbol Library of Congress*] (LCLS)
InBraCHi ...... Clay County Historical Society, Brazil, IN [*Library symbol Library of Congress*] (LCLS)
Inbrand........ Inbrand Corp. [*Associated Press*] (SAG)
InBraT......... Brazil Times, Brazil, IN [*Library symbol Library of Congress*] (LCLS)
InBrb........... Brownsburg Public Library, Brownsburg, IN [*Library symbol Library of Congress*] (LCLS)
InBrbG .... Brownsburg Guide, Brownsburg, IN [*Library symbol Library of Congress*] (LCLS)
INBRD.......... Inboard (ADA)
InBre........... W. E. Walter Memorial Library (Bremen Public Library), Bremen, IN [*Library symbol Library of Congress*] (LCLS)
InBreE......... Bremen Enquirer, Bremen, IN [*Library symbol Library of Congress*] (LCLS)
InBri........... Bristol-Washington Township Public Library (Bristol Public Library), Bristol, IN [*Library symbol Library of Congress*] (LCLS)
InBriEHi....... Elkhart County Historical Society, Bristol, IN [*Library symbol Library of Congress*] (LCLS)
InBrkvA .... Brookville American, Brookville, IN [*Library symbol Library of Congress*] (LCLS)
InBrkvCR...... Franklin County Recorder's Office, Brookville, IN [*Library symbol Library of Congress*] (LCLS)
InBrkvD .... Brookville Democrat, Brookville, IN [*Library symbol Library of Congress*] (LCLS)
InBro........... Brook-Iroquois Public Library, Brook, IN [*Library symbol Library of Congress*] (LCLS)
InBroA .... George Ade Hazeldon Home, Brook, IN [*Library symbol Library of Congress*] (LCLS)
InBrt........... Brownstown Public Library, Brownstown, IN [*Library symbol Library of Congress*] (LCLS)
InBrtB .... Brownstown Banner, Brownstown, IN [*Library symbol Library of Congress*] (LCLS)
InBrtHi........ Jackson County Historical Society, Brownstown, IN [*Library symbol Library of Congress*] (LCLS)
INBSV .... Interim Narrow-Band Secure Voice (NVT)
InBTM.......... Bedford Times-Mail, Bedford, IN [*Library symbol Library of Congress*] (LCLS)
InBu .... Butler Carnegie Library, Butler, IN [*Library symbol Library of Congress*] (LCLS)
InBuB.......... Butler Bulletin, Butler, IN [*Library symbol Library of Congress*] (LCLS)
INbW........... Wiss, Janney, Elstner, & Associates, Northbrook, IL [*Library symbol Library of Congress*] (LCLS)
InC............. Crawfordsville District Public Library, Crawfordsville, IN [*Library symbol Library of Congress*] (LCLS)
INC............. Ice Navigation Center [*Marine science*] (MSC)
INC............. Idaho Nuclear Corp.
INC............. Iglesia Ni Cristo [*Religious organization*]
INC............. Igniter Nozzle Closure
INC............. Incendiary
INC............. Inchon [*Tyosen, Zinsen*] [*South Korea*] [*Seismograph station code, US Geological Survey*] [*Closed*] (SEIS)
INC............. Incidit [*Engraved*] [*Latin*] (ROG)
INC............. Incinerator
inc .... Incised (VRA)
inc .... Incision
INC............. Incisus [*Being Cut*] [*Pharmacy*] (ROG)
INC............. Inclosure
INC............. In Clouds [*ICAO*] (FAAC)
INC............. Including
INC............. Inclusive
INC............. Income (ROG)
inc .... Income (WDMC)
INC............. Incoming [*Telecommunications*] (KSC)
INC............. Incoming Trunk [*Telecommunications*] (TEL)
INC............. Incomplete
inc .... Incomplete (WDMC)
INC............. Inconclusive
INC............. Incontinent [*Medicine*]
INC............. Incorporated (EY)
INC............. Incorporated
inc .... Incorporated (WDMC)
inc .... Increase (WDMC)
INC............. Increase (AABC)
INC............. Increment
INC............. Incumbent (ROG)
inc .... Incurred

INC............... Indiana Cooperative Library Services Authority, Indianapolis, IN [*OCLC symbol*] (OCLC)
INC............... Indian National Congress
inc .... Indic [*MARC language code Library of Congress*] (LCCP)
INC............... Inertial Navigation Computer (MCD)
INC............... Information and Censorship [*Allied Forces*] [*World War II*]
INC............... In Nomine Christi [*In the Name of Christ*] [*Latin*]
INC............... Input Control System [*Military*]
INC............... Insectivorous Cyprinids [*Pisciculture*]
INC............... Insertable Nuclear Components (MCD)
INC............... Inside-the-Needle Catheter [*Cardiology*] (DAVI)
INC............... Installation Notice Card (KSC)
INC............... Installation Notification Certification (MCD)
INC............... Integrated Network Corp. (PCM)
INC............... Intelligence Coordination [*Program*] [*Department of State*]
INC............... International Negotiating Committee [*World Resources Institute*]
INC............... International Numismatic Commission
INC............... International Nut Council (EAIO)
INC............... Interstitial Nucleus of Cajal [*Brain anatomy*]
INC............... Invermay Resources [*Vancouver Stock Exchange symbol*]
INC............... Iraqi National Congress [*Political party*] (ECON)
INC............... Irish National Caucus (EA)
INC............... Ironfounders' National Confederation [*British*] (BI)
INC............... Item Name Code [*Military*] (AFM)
INC............... Jet Air Internacional Charters CA [*Venezuela*] [*ICAO designator*] (FAAC)
INC............... Yinchuan [*China*] [*Airport symbol*] (OAG)
INcA .... Abbott Laboratories, North Chicago, IL [*Library symbol Library of Congress*] (LCLS)
InCa .... Carlisle Public Library, Carlisle, IN [*Library symbol Library of Congress*] (LCLS)
INCA .... Idaho Nuclear Code Automation [*AEC*]
INCA .... Implementation of New Carrier Arrangements [*Telecommunications*]
INCA .... In-Core Analysis [*Nuclear energy*] (NRCH)
INCA .... Information Council of the Americas (EA)
INCA .... Innovation through Creative Analysis (PDAA)
INCA .... Institute for Numerical Computation and Analysis (MCD)
INCA .... Integrated Catalog Algorithm (MCD)
INCA .... Integrated Communications Agency [*Air Force*]
INCA .... Integrated Navigation and Communications, Automatic
INCA .... Integrated Network Communication Architecture (OSI)
INCA .... Integrated Nuclear and Chemical Analysis
INCA .... Integrated Nuclear Communications Assessment
INCA .... Integrated Numerical Control Approach
INCA .... Intelligence Communications Architecture
INCA .... International Narcotics Control Act
INCA .... International Newspaper and Colour Association [*Later, IFRA*] (EA)
INCA .... Inventory Control and Analysis (MHDB)
Inc Ab .... Incomplete Abortion [*Obstetrics*] (DAVI)
INCAD .... Incapacitated Passengers' Handling Advice [*British*]
INCAE .... Instituto Centroamericano de Administracion de Empresas [*Central American Institute of Business Administration*] [*Nicaragua*]
INCAIR .... Including Air
InCaL .... Carlisle Public Library, Carlisle, IN [*Library symbol*] [*Library of Congress*] (LCLS)
Incalz.......... Incalzando [*Music*]
InCam .... Camden-Jackson Township Public Library, Camden, IN [*Library symbol Library of Congress*] (LCLS)
INCAM .... Inducible Cell Adhesion Molecule [*Immunochemistry*]
InCan .... Cannelton Public Library, Cannelton, IN [*Library symbol Library of Congress*] (LCLS)
incan .... Incandescent (WDMC)
InCanCR ...... Perry County Recorder's Office, Cannelton, IN [*Library symbol Library of Congress*] (LCLS)
INCAND....... Incandescent (MSA)
INCAP .... Instituto de Nutricion de Centro America y Panama [*Institute of Nutrition of Central America and Panama*] [*Guatemala, Guatemala*] (EAIO)
InCar........... Carmel Public Library, Carmel, IN [*Library symbol Library of Congress*] (LCLS)
INCAR .... International Committee Against Racism (EA)
Incarnate Word C... Incarnate Word College (GAGS)
InCarNJ....... Carmel News Journal, Carmel, IN [*Library symbol Library of Congress*] (LCLS)
InCarS .... Carmel Clay Schools, Carmel IN [*Library symbol*] [*Library of Congress*] (LCLS)
INCAS .... Integrated Navigation and Collision Avoidance System (PDAA)
InCayHN ...... Cayuga Herald News, Cayuga, IN [*Library symbol Library of Congress*] (LCLS)
IncB .... Inclusion Body [*Cytology*]
INCB .... Indiana Cmnty Bk SB [*NASDAQ symbol*] (TTSB)
INCB .... Indiana Community Bank A Savings Bank [*NASDAQ symbol*] (SAG)
INCB .... International Narcotics Control Board (DMAA)
INCB .... International Nuclear Credit Bank (NRCH)
INCBE .... Israel National Committee on the Biosphere and Environment
INCBR .... Incubator (MSA)
InCc .... Cambridge City Public Library, Cambridge City, IN [*Library symbol Library of Congress*] (LCLS)
INCC .... Institut National du Cancer du Canada [*National Cancer Institute of Canada*] (EAIO)
INCC .... Interim National Coordinating Committee [*Ghana*] (PPW)
INCC .... International Network Controlling Center [*Telecommunications*] (TEL)
INCC .... International Newspaper Collector's Club (EA)
INCC .... International Nippon Collectors Club (EA)
INCC .... Internet Communications [*NASDAQ symbol*] (SAG)

InCcNR .... National Road Traveler, Cambridge City, IN [*Library symbol Library of Congress*] (LCLS)
INCD .... Incandescent
INCD .... Incendiary (AABC)
INCD .... Incorporated [*Legal term*] (EY)
INCD .... Infantile Nuclear Cerebral Degeneration [*Medicine*] (DMAA)
INCDT .... Incident (MSA)
InCe .... Centerville and Center Township Library, Centerville, IN [*Library symbol Library of Congress*] (LCLS)
INCE........... Institute of Noise Control Engineering (EA)
INCE........... Insurance
INCE........... International Network for Chemical Education [*Samoa*] (EAIO)
INCEP......... Interceptor
INCEPT .... Inception (ROG)
INCERFA...... Uncertainty Phase Code (Alerting Service) [*Aviation*] (FAAC)
IncFB .... Increase Feedback
INCFO .... Institute of Newspaper Controllers and Finance Officers [*Later, INFE*] (EA)
INCH .... Inchoative (WGA)
INCH .... Independent Channel Handler (IAA)
INCH .... Integrated Chopper
INCH .... Interim Charging [*Electric vehicle technology*]
INCH .... International Center for High Quality Scrap [*Scrap salvage*]
InCha .... Charlestown Township Public Library, Charlestown, IN [*Library symbol Library of Congress*] (LCLS)
InChe .... Westchester Public Library, Chesterton, IN [*Library symbol Library of Congress*] (LCLS)
InCheT .... Chesterton Tribune, Chesterton, IN [*Library symbol Library of Congress*] (LCLS)
INCHO........ Inchoate (ADA)
IN CH Q ...... Indian Church Quarterly Review [*A publication*] (ROG)
INCID......... Incide [*Cut*] [*Pharmacy*]
INCIDI........ Institut International des Civilisations Differentes [*International Institute of Differing Civilizations*]
INCIN......... Incinerator (MSA)
InCINC .... International Chemometrics Internet Conference
INCINC .... International Copyright Information Center (EA)
INCIRS .... International Communication Information Retrieval System [*University of Florida*] (PDAA)
INCIS .... Incisus [*Being Cut*] [*Pharmacy*] (ROG)
INCJHS .... International Network of Children of Jewish Holocaust Survivors (EA)
InCJR .... Crawfordsville Journal and Review, Crawfordsville, IN [*Library symbol Library of Congress*] (LCLS)
INCL .... Inclination [*Angular distance from equator in degrees*]
INCL .... Inclosure (AFM)
INCL .... Include [*or Including*] (EY)
incl .... Including (WDMC)
incl .... Inclusive (WDMC)
INCL .... Inclusive
INCL .... Incoming Line (IAA)
INCL .... Inconclusive
INCL .... In Control, Inc. [*NASDAQ symbol*] (SAG)
INCL .... Infantile Neuronal Ceroid Lipofuscinoses [*Medicine*]
InClcN........ Clay City News, Clay City, IN [*Library symbol Library of Congress*] (LCLS)
INCLD .... Including [*Freight*]
InCli .... Clinton Public Library, Clinton, IN [*Library symbol Library of Congress*] (LCLS)
InCliC .... Daily Clintonian, Clinton, IN [*Library symbol Library of Congress*] (LCLS)
INCLN .... Inclined (MSA)
INCLN .... Inclusion
INCLR .... Intercooler
INCLS .... Inclosure (MSA)
INCLU .... Inclusive (ROG)
INCLUDE..... Implementing New Concepts of the Library for Urban Disadvantaged Ethnics [*Cleveland Public Library*] (NITA)
INCLV .... Inclusive (FAAC)
InCLW......... General Lew Wallace Studio, Crawfordsville, IN [*Library symbol Library of Congress*] (LCLS)
INCM .... Income
INCM .... Incoming (MSA)
INCMG........ Incoming
INCND........ Incendiary (MSA)
INCNR .... Increment Number (DOMA)
InCo .... Connersville Public Library, Connersville, IN [*Library symbol Library of Congress*] (LCLS)
INCO .... INCO Ltd. [*Formerly, International Nickel Co. of Canada*] [*Associated Press*] (SAG)
INCO .... Installation and Checkout [*Military*] (CAAL)
INCO .... Instrumentation and Communications Officer [*NASA*]
INCO .... International Chamber of Commerce (IEEE)
INCO .... International Nickel Co.
InCoa .... Coatesville Public Library, Coatesville, IN [*Library symbol Library of Congress*] (LCLS)
InCODA........ International Congress of Dealers Associations (EA)
INCODEL..... Interstate Commission on the Delaware River Basin
incog .... Incognito [*Unknown*] [*Latin*]
INCOG........ Indian Nations Council of Governments
INCOH........ Incoherent (MSA)
IncoHm........ Inco Homes Corp. [*Associated Press*] (SAG)
InColc .... Peabody Library, Columbia City, IN [*Library symbol Library of Congress*] (LCLS)
InColcCR...... Whitley County Recorder's Office, Columbia City, IN [*Library symbol Library of Congress*] (LCLS)

InColf.......... Colfax Public Library, Colfax, IN [*Library symbol*] [*Library of Congress*] (LCLS)

InColo .... Bartholomew County Library, Columbus, IN [*Library symbol Library of Congress*] (LCLS)

INCOLR........ Intercooler

INCOLSA...... Indiana Cooperative Library Services Authority [*Indianapolis, IN*] [*Library network*]

InColu .... Bartholomew County Library, Columbus, IN [*Library symbol Library of Congress*] (LCLS)

InColuHi ...... Bartholomew County Historical Society, Columbus, IN [*Library symbol Library of Congress*] (LCLS)

InColuR........ Columbus Republic, Columbus, IN [*Library symbol*] [*Library of Congress*] (LCLS)

INCOM .... Incomplete (AABC)

INCOM .... Indicator Compiler (IAA)

INCOM .... Input Compiler (IAA)

INCOMEX ..... International Computer Exhibition

INCOMINDIOS... International Committee for the Indians of the Americas [*Kaiseraugst, Switzerland*] (EAIO)

Incomnt .... INCOMNET, Inc. [*Associated Press*] (SAG)

INCOMP....... Incomplete (MSA)

INCOMPAT... Incompatible [*Medicine*]

INCOMPL..... Incomplete

incompl .... Incomplete (WDMC)

InCon .... Converse Jackson Township Public Library, Converse, IN [*Library symbol Library of Congress*] (LCLS)

INCON......... Installation Console (MCD)

INCONCRYO-ISC... International Conference on Cryogenics - International Steering Committee (EAIO)

InCoNE........ Connersville News-Examiner, Connersville, IN [*Library symbol Library of Congress*] (LCLS)

incont .... Incontinent [*Medicine*] (DAVI)

InControl...... InControl, Inc. [*Associated Press*] (SAG)

InControl...... InControl, Inc. [*Associated Press*] (SAG)

IncOp2 .... Income Opportunities Fund II, Inc. [*Associated Press*] (SAG)

IncOp2000 ... Income Opportunities Fund 2000 [*Associated Press*] (SAG)

IncOpRT...... Income Opportunity Realty Trust [*Associated Press*] (SAG)

InCor........... Corydon Public Library, Corydon, IN [*Library symbol Library of Congress*] (LCLS)

INCOR......... Incorporated [*Legal term*]

INCOR......... Incorrect (MSA)

INCOR......... Intergovernmental Conference on Oceanographic Research (MCD)

InCorCP .... Harrison County Press, Corydon, IN [*Library symbol Library of Congress*] (LCLS)

InCorCR .... Harrison County Recorder's Office, Corydon, IN [*Library symbol Library of Congress*] (LCLS)

InCorD .... Corydon Democrat, Corydon, IN [*Library symbol Library of Congress*] (LCLS)

INCORE........ International Programme on Conflict Resolution and Ethnicity

INCORP........ Incorporated [*Legal term*] (EY)

INCORPN ..... Incorporation [*Legal term*] (ROG)

INCORR .... Incorrect (ADA)

INCOS......... Integrated Control System [*Navy*] (NVT)

INCOSAI...... International Congress of Supreme Audit Institutions (PDAA)

INCOT .... In-Core Test Facility [*Nuclear energy*] (NRCH)

INCOTEC ..... International Committee for Training and Education of Co-Operators (EAIO)

INCOTERM... International Commerce Term [*International Chamber of Commerce*]

INCOTERMS... International Contracting Terms (AAGC)

InCov .... Covington Public Library, Covington, IN [*Library symbol Library of Congress*] (LCLS)

InCovFS .... Fountain County Star, Covington, IN [*Library symbol Library of Congress*] (LCLS)

INCPD ACCT.. Incorporated Accountant [*British*] (ROG)

INCPEN .... Industry Committee for Packaging and the Environment [*British*] (DI)

INCPT .... Intercept

INCR .... Increase (AFM)

incr .... Increase (WDMC)

inc(r) .... Increase (Relative) (AAMN)

INCR .... Increment (AFM)

INCR .... Interrupt Control Register [*Computer science*] (MSA)

INCRA......... International Copper Research Association [*Research center British*] (IRC)

INCRAPLAN... Integrated Crew and Aircraft Planning (PDAA)

INCRE .... Increment

INCREM....... Incremental

INCREP........ Incident Report [*Military*] (CINC)

INCRNTN ..... Incarnation

InCrp........... Crown Point Center Public Library, Crown Point, IN [*Library symbol Library of Congress*] (LCLS)

InCrpCS .... Crown Point Community Schools, Crown Point, IN [*Library symbol Library of Congress*] (LCLS)

InCrpLS....... Lake County Star, Crown Point, IN [*Library symbol Library of Congress*] (LCLS)

INCS .... Incomplete Resolution, Scan to Follow [*Radiology*] (DAVI)

INCS .... Integrated Battlefield Control System (MCD)

INCS .... International Netsuke Collectors Society [*Commercial firm*] (EA)

INCSEA .... Incident at Sea [*Navy*] (NVT)

inc sed .... Incertae Sedis [*Uncertain Position*] [*Biology, taxonomy*]

INCSR......... International Narcotics Control Strategy Report [*Department of State*]

Incstar .... Incstar Corp. [*Associated Press*] (SAG)

INCT........... Incumbent (ROG)

Inc Tax Cas... Reports of Cases Relating to Income Tax [*A publication*] (DLA)

Inc Tax LJ ... Income Tax Law Journal [*India*] [*A publication*] (DLA)

Inc Tax R..... Income Tax Reports [*India*] [*A publication*] (DLA)

INCTN .... Incorporation

InCtPd......... Inter-City Products Corp. [*Associated Press*] (SAG)

INCTRL .... Installation Control [*Computer science*] (PCM)

InCu .... Culver Public Library, Culver, IN [*Library symbol Library of Congress*] (LCLS)

INCUMB....... Incumbent

INCUMBCE... Incumbrance (ROG)

INCUMBD .... Incumbered (ROG)

INCUN .... Incunabula (ADA)

INCUR......... Incurable [*Medicine*]

INCV .... Inclusive (MSA)

InCW .... Wabash College, Crawfordsville, IN [*Library symbol Library of Congress*] (LCLS)

INCWF .... Indian National Cement Workers' Federation

INCY .... Incendiary Bomb (DSUE)

INCY .... INCYTE Pharmaceuticals [*NASDAQ symbol*] (TTSB)

InCyA .... Cynthiana Argus, Cynthiana, IN [*Library symbol Library of Congress*] (LCLS)

Incyte.......... Incyte Pharmaceuticals, Inc. [*Associated Press*] (SAG)

Ind .... Adversus Indoctum [*of Lucian*] [*Classical studies*] (OCD)

IND .... American Industrial Properties [*Formerly, Trammell Crow Real Estate Investment*] [*NYSE symbol*] (SPSG)

IND .... Amer Industrial Prop [*NYSE symbol*] (TTSB)

IND .... Improvised Nuclear Device

IND .... Indecent [*FBI standardized term*]

IND .... Independent

ind .... Independent (WDMC)

Ind .... Independents [*Pakistan*] [*Political party*]

IND .... Index

ind .... Index (WDMC)

IND .... India [*IYRU nationality code*] [*ANSI three-letter standard code*] (CNC)

IND .... Indian (AABC)

IND .... Indiana

IND .... Indianapolis [*Indiana*] [*Airport symbol*] (OAG)

Ind .... Indiana Supreme Court Reports [*A publication*] (DLA)

IND .... Indicate [*or Indicator*] (KSC)

IND .... Indicative (ROG)

ind .... Indicator (IDOE)

IND .... Indies

IN D .... In Dies [*Daily*] [*Pharmacy*]

IND .... Indigo

ind .... Indigo (WDMC)

IND .... Indirect

IND .... Indomethacin [*An analgesic*]

ind .... Indonesian [*MARC language code Library of Congress*] (LCCP)

IND .... Indoors (ROG)

IND .... Indorse [*Legal term*] (AABC)

IND .... Induced Nuclear Disintegration

IND .... Inductance

ind .... Inductance (IDOE)

IND .... Induction (MSA)

ind .... Inductor (IDOE)

Ind .... Indus [*Constellation*]

IND .... Industrial

ind .... Industrial (DD)

IND .... Industrial

ind .... Industrial (WDMC)

IND .... Industrial Medicine (DMAA)

IND .... Industry (AFM)

IND .... Industry Division [*Census*] (OICC)

IND .... In Nomine Dei [*In the Name of God*] [*Latin*]

IND .... Intercept Director [*Military*]

IND .... Inter Mountain Development, Inc. [*Vancouver Stock Exchange symbol*]

IND .... International Number Dialing [*Telecommunications*] (TEL)

IND .... Investigational New Drug [*Application*] [*FDA*]

IND .... Investigational New Drug [*Medicine*] (DMAA)

IND(r) .... Iona National Airways Ltd. [*Republic of Ireland*] [*ICAO designator*] (FAAC)

IND .... University of Notre Dame, Notre Dame, IN [*OCLC symbol*] (OCLC)

INDA .... INDA, Association of the Nonwoven Fabrics Industry [*Formerly, International Nonwovens and Disposables Association*]

INDAC......... Industrial Data Acquisition and Control [*Computer science*] (MHDI)

Ind Acc Com... Decisions of the Industrial Accident Commission of California [*A publication*] (DLA)

Ind Acts....... Acts of Indiana [*A publication*] (DLA)

Ind A Dig..... United States Indian Affairs Office, Digest of Decisions [*A publication*] (DLA)

IndAdmin ..... Industrial Administration (DD)

Ind Admin R... Burns' Indiana Administrative Rules and Regulations [*A publication*] (DLA)

InDaDN....... Dale News, Dale, IN [*Library symbol*] [*Library of Congress*] (LCLS)

Ind Advocate... Indian Advocate [*A publication*] (DLA)

INDAIR........ Identification of Aircraft

InDair .... International Dairy Queen, Inc. [*Associated Press*] (SAG)

InDairA .... International Dairy Queen [*Associated Press*] (SAG)

InDairB........ International Dairy Queen [*Associated Press*] (SAG)

InDaN .... Dale News, Dale, IN [*Library symbol Library of Congress*] (LCLS)

InDan.......... Danville Public Library, Danville, IN [*Library symbol Library of Congress*] (LCLS)

InDanCR ...... Hendricks County Recorder's Office, Danville, IN [*Library symbol Library of Congress*] (LCLS)

Ind & Intell Prop Aust... Industrial and Intellectual Property in Australia [*A publication*] (DLA)

InDanN .... Central Normal College, Danville, IN [*Library symbol Library of Congress Obsolete*] (LCLS)
InDanR .... Danville Republican, Danville, IN [*Library symbol Library of Congress*] (LCLS)
Ind App .... Indiana Court of Appeals Reports [*A publication*] (DLA)
Ind App .... Law Reports, Indian Appeals [*A publication*] (DLA)
Ind App Ct ... Indiana Appellate Court Reports [*A publication*] (DLA)
Ind App Supp... Supplemental Indian Appeals, Law Reports [*A publication*] (DLA)
InDar .... Darlington Public Library, Darlington, IN [*Library symbol Library of Congress*] (LCLS)
INDASAT...... Indian Scientific Satellite
INDAT .... Incoming Data (MCD)
Ind Awards... Industrial Awards Recommendations [*New Zealand*] [*A publication*] (DLA)
INDB .... Independent Bank Corp. [*NASDAQ symbol*] (NQ)
INDB .... Independent Bank(MA) [*NASDAQ symbol*] (TTSB)
IndBc .... Independence Bancorp, Inc. [*Associated Press*] (SAG)
IndBkMA ...... Independent Bank Corp. Massachusetts [*Associated Press*] (SAG)
IndBkMI ...... Independent Bank Corp. Michigan [*Associated Press*] (SAG)
IndBnk .... Independent Bankshares, Inc. [*Associated Press*] (SAG)
INDC .... Indian National Democratic Congress (BARN)
INDC .... Indicate (FAAC)
INDC .... International Nuclear Data Committee [*of International Atomic Energy Agency*]
Ind Can L P Lit... Index to Canadian Legal Periodical Literature [*A publication*] (DLA)
Ind Cas........ Indian Cases [*India*] [*A publication*] (DLA)
Ind C Aw...... Industrial Court Awards [*England*] [*A publication*] (DLA)
Ind Code Ann... Burns' Indiana Statutes, Annotated Code Edition [*A publication*] (DLA)
Ind Com Law... Indermaur and Thwaites' Principles of the Common Law [*12th ed.*] [*1914*] [*A publication*] (DLA)
Ind Court Aw... Industrial Court Awards [*England*] [*A publication*] (DLA)
Ind Ct Awards... Industrial Court Awards [*England*] [*A publication*] (DLA)
Indctd .... Inducted [*Army*]
INDCTR........ Indicator
Ind Dec........ Indiana Decisions [*A publication*] (DLA)
Ind Dec........ Indiana Decisions and Law Reporter [*A publication*] (DLA)
Ind Dig .... All India Reporter, Indian Digest [*1946-52*] [*A publication*] (DLA)
Ind Div......... Inderwick's Divorce and Matrimonial Causes Acts [*1862*] [*A publication*] (DLA)
INDE .... IndeNet Inc. [*NASDAQ symbol*] (TTSB)
INDE .... IndeNet, Inc. [*NASDAQ symbol*] (SAG)
INDE .... Independence National Historical Park
INDE .... Independent TeleMedia Group [*NASDAQ symbol*] (SAG)
Ind E .... Industrial Engineer
INDE .... Integrated Nondestructive Evaluation (MCD)
Indebt .... Indebtedness [*Legal term*] (DLA)
InDec .... Decatur Public Library, Decatur, IN [*Library symbol Library of Congress*] (LCLS)
indec .... Indeclinable (BJA)
INDEC .... Independent Nuclear Disarmament Election Committee [*British*] (DI)
INDEC .... Interdepartmental Committee
InDecD........ Decatur Daily Democrat, Decatur, IN [*Library symbol*] [*Library of Congress*] (LCLS)
INDECL .... Indeclinable [*Grammar*]
INDECS .... Immigration and Nationality Department Electronic Computer System (BARN)
INDECS .... Interactive Design of Control Systems (DI)
INDEF .... Indefinite (AABC)
INDEFOPS... Indefinite Operations (NVT)
InDel........ Delphi Public Library, Delphi, IN [*Library symbol Library of Congress*] (LCLS)
INDEL .... Industry Education Liaison (AIE)
InDelCC ...... Carroll County Comet, Delphi, IN [*Library symbol Library of Congress*] (LCLS)
InDelCHi ...... Carroll County Historical Museum, Delphi, IN [*Library symbol Library of Congress*] (LCLS)
InDelCR ...... Carroll County Recorder's Office, Delphi, IN [*Library symbol Library of Congress*] (LCLS)
INDELISA..... Indirect Enzyme-Linked Immunosorbent Assay
INDELSEC... Industrial Electronic Security (AABC)
Indem .... Indemnity [*Legal term*] (DLA)
INDEMFY...... Indemnify [*Legal shorthand*] (LWAP)
INDEMTY...... Indemnity [*Legal shorthand*] (LWAP)
INDEMY ...... Indemnity (ROG)
INDEN........ IndeNet, Inc. [*Associated Press*] (SAG)
IndEng .... Industrial Engineering (DD)
Ind Eng 1922-1931 (NY)... Industrial Engineering 1922-1931 (New York) [*A publication*]
INDENT .... Indenture (ROG)
INDEP .... Independent (AFM)
IndepBc ...... Independence Bancorp, Inc. [*Associated Press*] (SAG)
INDEP CONTR... Independent Contractor
IndepHld ...... Independence Holding Co. [*Associated Press*] (SAG)
INDEP R ...... Independent Review [*London*] [*A publication*] (ROG)
INDEPTH...... International Deep Profiling of Tibet and the Himalaya [*Geology*] [*China*]
INDEPTY...... Independently (ROG)
INDESYS...... Information Delivery System Inc. [*Information service or system*] (NITA)
INDET .... Indeterminate (MSA)
indeterm........ Indeterminative (BJA)
Ind-Eur........ Indo-European
IN-DEV-IL ... Institute for the Development of Indian Law (EA)

INDEX .... Indiana Exchange, Inc.
INDEX .... Indian Ocean Experiment
INDEX .... Inter-NASA Data Exchange (IEEE)
IndFdg .... Industrial Funding Corp. [*Associated Press*] (SAG)
IndFdl .... Independence Federal Savings Bank [*Associated Press*] (SAG)
INDGF........ Indigo NV [*NASDAQ symbol*] (SAG)
INDH .... Independent Insurance Group, Inc. [*NASDAQ symbol*] (NQ)
INDH........ Indirect Hire [*Military*]
IndH .... Industrial Holdings, Inc. [*Associated Press*] (SAG)
IndHealth.... Industrial Health (DD)
ind i .... India Ink (VRA)
INDI .... Indiana
INDI .... Indicate
INDI .... Individual Investor Group [*NASDAQ symbol*] (SAG)
Indi .... Indus [*Constellation*]
INDI .... Irish Nutrition and Dietetics Institute (EAIO)
India AIR Manual... AIR [*All India Law Reporter*] Manual: Unrepealed Central Acts [*2nd ed.*] [*India*] [*A publication*] (DLA)
India Cen Acts... Central Acts, India [*A publication*] (DLA)
India Code Civ P... Code of Civil Procedure [*India*] [*A publication*] (DLA)
India Code Crim P... Code of Criminal Procedure [*India*] [*A publication*] (DLA)
India Crim LJR... Criminal Law Journal Reports [*India*] [*A publication*] (DLA)
IndiaFd .... India Fund, Inc. [*Associated Press*] (SAG)
IndiaG........ India Growth Fund, Inc. [*Associated Press*] (SAG)
India Gen R & O... General Rules and Orders, India [*A publication*] (DLA)
Indiana .... Indiana Reports [*A publication*] (DLA)
Indian App... Law Reports, Privy Council, Indian Appeals [*India*] [*A publication*] (DLA)
Indiana Sup Ct Rep... Indiana Reports [*A publication*] (DLA)
Indian Cas... Indiana Cases [*A publication*] (DLA)
Indian LJ ...... Indian Law Journal [*A publication*] (DLA)
Indian LR.... Indian Law Reports [*A publication*] (DLA)
Indian L R Calc... Indian Law Reports, Calcutta Series [*A publication*] (DLA)
Indian LR Mad... Indian Law Reports, Madras Series [*A publication*] (DLA)
Indian Rul ... Indian Rulings [*A publication*] (DLA)
Indian Terr... Indian Territory Reports [*A publication*] (DLA)
India Pen Code... Indian Penal Code [*A publication*] (DLA)
India S Ct... India Supreme Court Reports [*A publication*] (DLA)
India Subs Leg... Subsidiary Legislation [*India*] [*A publication*] (DLA)
INDIC .... Indicate (AABC)
INDIC .... Indication Report (MCD)
INDIC .... Indicative [*Grammar*]
INDIC .... Indicator (WDAA)
IndiCBk ...... Indiana Community Bank a Savings Bank [*Associated Press*] (SAG)
INDICN........ Indication
INDICOM...... Indications Communications (MCD)
indie .... Independent [*Filmmaking*] [*Slang*] (WDMC)
IndiEngy ...... Indiana Energy, Inc. [*Associated Press*] (SAG)
IndiFdl .... Indiana Federal Corp. [*Associated Press*] (SAG)
IndiFedl ...... Indiana Federal Corp. [*Associated Press*] (SAG)
INDIG........ Indigenous (AABC)
INDIGO .... Indian Ocean Geochemistry [*France*] [*Marine science*] (OSRA)
INDIGO .... Intelligence Division Gaming Operations
IndigoNV...... Indigo NV [*Associated Press*] (SAG)
IndiM........ Indiana & Michigan Power [*Associated Press*] (SAG)
IND IMP...... Indiae Imperator [*Emperor of India*] [*Latin*]
Ind Ind LP ... Index to Indian Legal Periodicals [*A publication*] (DLA)
IndInsr........ Independent Insurance Group, Inc. [*Associated Press*] (SAG)
INDIPEX...... India International Philatelic Exhibition
INDIR........ Indirect Coombs Test [*Hematology*] (DAVI)
INDIRS........ Indiana Information Retrieval System [*Library network*]
INDIS........ Industrial Information and Advisory Services [*UNIDO*] (IID)
INDIS .... Industrial Information System [*UN Industrial Development Organization*] (NITA)
INDIV........ Individual (AFM)
Individul ...... Individual, Inc. [*Associated Press*] (SAG)
INDIVL........ Individual [*Freight*]
Ind J Int'l L... Indiana Journal of International Law [*A publication*] (DLA)
Ind Jud Pr... Indermaur's Practice of the Supreme Court of Judicature [*12th ed.*] [*1919*] [*A publication*] (DLA)
Ind Jur........ Indian Jurist [*Calcutta or Madras*] [*A publication*] (DLA)
Ind Jur NS... Indian Jurist, New Series [*A publication*] (DLA)
Ind Jur OS... Indian Jurist, Old Series [*A publication*] (DLA)
Ind Jur Pr ... Indermaur's Practice of the Supreme Court of Judicature [*12th ed.*] [*1919*] [*A publication*] (DLA)
IND L .... Independent Liberal (WDAA)
INDL .... Industrial (MSA)
Ind LC Com Law... Indermaur's Leading Cases in Common Law [*10th ed.*] [*1921*] [*A publication*] (DLA)
Ind LC Eq.... Indermaur's Leading Cases in Conveyancing and Equity [*A publication*] (DLA)
Ind Led........ Individual Ledger [*Business term*] (MHDW)
Ind LH .... Indian Law Herald [*A publication*] (DLA)
Ind L Mag.... Indian Law Magazine [*A publication*] (DLA)
Ind LQ .... Indian Law Quarterly [*A publication*] (DLA)
Ind LQ Rev... Indian Law Quarterly Review [*A publication*] (DLA)
Ind LR .... Indiana Law Reporter [*1881*] [*A publication*] (DLA)
Ind LR .... Indiana Legal Register [*A publication*] (DLA)
Ind LR .... Indian Law Reports (East) [*A publication*] (DLA)
Ind LR .... Industrial Law Review [*A publication*] (ILCA)
Ind LR All... Indian Law Reports, Allahabad Series [*A publication*] (DLA)
Ind LR Alla... Indian Law Reports, Allahabad Series [*A publication*] (DLA)
Ind LR And... Indian Law Reports, Andhra Series [*A publication*] (DLA)
Ind LR Assam... Indian Law Reports, Assam Series [*A publication*] (DLA)
Ind LR Bomb... Indian Law Reports, Bombay Series [*A publication*] (DLA)

Ind LR Calc.... Indian Law Reports, Calcutta Series [*A publication*] (DLA)
Ind L Reg .... Indiana Legal Register [*A publication*] (DLA)
Ind L Rep .... Indiana Law Reporter [*1881*] [*A publication*] (DLA)
Ind L Rep .... Indian Law Reporter [*A publication*] (DLA)
Ind LR Hyderabad... Indian Law Reports, Hyderabad Series [*A publication*] (DLA)
Ind LR Kar... Indian Law Reports, Karachi Series [*A publication*] (DLA)
Ind LR Ker... Indian Law Reports, Kerala Series [*A publication*] (DLA)
Ind LR Lah... Indian Law Reports, Lahore Series [*A publication*] (DLA)
Ind LR Luck... Indian Law Reports, Lucknow Series [*A publication*] (DLA)
Ind LR Mad... Indian Law Reports, Madras Series [*A publication*] (DLA)
Ind LR Madhya Bharat... Indian Law Reports, Madhya Bharat Series
[*A publication*] (DLA)
Ind LR Mysore... Indian Law Reports, Mysore Series [*A publication*] (DLA)
Ind LR Nag... Indian Law Reports, Nagpur Series [*A publication*] (DLA)
Ind LR Or... Indian Law Reports, Orissa Series [*A publication*] (DLA)
Ind LR Pat... Indian Law Reports, Patna Series [*A publication*] (DLA)
Ind LR Patiala... Indian Law Reports, Patiala Series [*A publication*] (DLA)
Ind LR Pun... Indian Law Reports, Punjab Series [*A publication*] (DLA)
Ind LR Rajasthan... Indian Law Reports, Rajasthan Series [*A publication*] (DLA)
Ind LR Ran... Indian Law Reports, Rangoon Series [*A publication*] (DLA)
Ind LS......... Indiana Law Student [*A publication*] (DLA)
Ind L Stud ... Indiana Law Student [*A publication*] (DLA)
Ind LT......... Indian Law Times [*A publication*] (DLA)
INDM......... Indemnity [*Legal term*]
Ind M.......... Independent Monthly [*A publication*]
INDM......... Infant of Nondiabetic Mother [*Obstetrics*]
INDMAN..... Industrial Manager
IND METH... Independent Methodist (WDAA)
INDMGR ..... Industrial Manager
Ind Mining Stand... Industrial and Mining Standard [*A publication*]
INDMNTY..... Indemnity
INDN......... Indian
INDN......... Indication (WGA)
INDN......... Induction
IndNatuz..... Industrie Natuzzi SA [*Associated Press*] (SAG)
Ind News ..... Industry News [*A publication*]
IndO......... Indian Ocean
INDO......... Indomethacin [*An analgesic*]
INDO......... Indonesia
INDO......... Intermediate Neglect of Differential Overlap [*Quantum mechanics*]
INDOC......... Indochina [*or Indochinese*] (WDAA)
INDOC......... Indoctrinate (AABC)
INDOC......... Indonesian Documentation and Information Centre [*Leiden,
Netherlands*] (EAIO)
INDOC......... Information-Documentation and Communication (PDAA)
INDOCHEM... Indian Ocean GEOSECS Program (MSC)
INDOCNREGREPCEN... Indoctrination Naval Regional Reporting Center (DNAB)
INDO-EUR.... Indo-European (ROG)
INDO-GER.... Indo-Germanic [*Language, etc.*] (ROG)
Indo-Germ Forsch... Indogermanische Forschungen [*A publication*] (OCD)
Indon .... Indonesia (BARN)
Indones....... Indonesia Fund [*Associated Press*] (SAG)
INDOR .... Internuclear Double Resonance
IndoSatel..... Indonesian Satellite Corp. [*Associated Press*] (SAG)
IndoTel....... Indonesian Telekomunikas [*Associated Press*] (SAG)
Ind P......... Pharmacopoeia of India [*A publication*]
INDPDNC..... Independence
IND PENS ... Indian Pension [*Army British*] (ROG)
IND PH .... Indian Pharmacopoeia (ROG)
INDPNDNT... Independent
Ind Prog Dev... Industrial Progress and Development [*A publication*]
Ind Prop ..... Industrial Property [*Legal term*] (DLA)
Ind Prop Q... Industrial Property Quarterly [*A publication*] (DLA)
INDQ......... International Dairy Queen, Inc. [*NASDAQ symbol*] (NQ)
INDQA......... Intl Dairy Queen 'A' [*NASDAQ symbol*] (TTSB)
INDQB......... Intl Dairy Queen 'B' [*NASDAQ symbol*] (TTSB)
Ind R .... Indiana Reports [*A publication*] (DLA)
INDR .... Indicator (IAA)
INDRB .... Inactive Nondisability Retirement Branch [*BUPERS*]
INDRE .... Indenture
INDREG....... Inductance Regulator (IEEE)
Ind Rel J Econ & Soc... Industrial Relations: Journal of Economy and Society
[*A publication*] (DLA)
Ind Rep ..... Indiana Reports [*A publication*] (DLA)
INDS .... In-Core Nuclear Detection System [*Nuclear energy*] (IEEE)
Ind SBA ..... Indiana State Bar Association Reports [*A publication*] (DLA)
IndsBc .... Industrial Bancorp, Inc. [*Associated Press*] (SAG)
INDSCAL..... Individual Differences Scaling (PDAA)
IndSci......... Industrial Scientific Corp. [*Associated Press*] (SAG)
INDSL .... Industrial (WGA)
IndSqS....... Independence Square Income Securities [*Associated Press*] (SAG)
IndSqS....... Independence Square Income Securities, Inc. [*Associated Press*]
(SAG)
Ind St U....... Indiana State University (GAGS)
Ind Super..... Wilson's Indiana Superior Court Reports [*A publication*] (DLA)
INDT .... Indent (MSA)
IND T .... Indian Territory (ROG)
INDT .... Induction (DNAB)
INDT .... Institute for Non-Destructive Testing [*Milwaukee School of
Engineering*] (PDAA)
INDT .... Interceptor Director Technician (SAA)
Ind T Ann St... Indian Territory Annotated Statutes [*A publication*] (DLA)
IndTc .... Industrial Technologies, Inc. [*Associated Press*] (SAG)
IndTech....... Industrial Technologies, Inc. [*Associated Press*] (SAG)
INDTEL .... Industry and Teacher Education Liaison (AIE)

IND TER...... Indian Territory
Ind Ter......... Indian Territory Reports [*A publication*] (DLA)
Ind Terr ...... Indian Territory (DLA)
INDTNG....... Individual Training [*Navy*] (NVT)
INDTR......... Indicator-Transmitter
IndTrn......... Industrial Training Corp. [*Associated Press*] (SAG)
Indty .... Indemnity [*Legal term*] (DLA)
Ind U .... Indiana University (GAGS)
IndUAP .... Independent United Australia Party [*Political party*]
INDUC......... Induction (AABC)
Ind UCD...... Indiana Unemployment Compensation Division, Selected Appeal
Tribunal Decisions [*A publication*] (DLA)
Ind U Penn... Indiana University of Pennsylvania (GAGS)
IND U PR...... Indiana University Press (DGA)
Indus......... Industrialist
INDUS......... Industry
INDUS......... Interactive Duct Sizing [*Facet Ltd.*] [*Software package*] (NCC)
Indus & Lab Rel Rev... Industrial and Labor Relations Review [*A publication*]
(AAGC)
Indus Cas R... Industrial Cases Reports [*Law reports*] [*British*] (DLA)
IndusG .... Indus Group, Inc. (The) [*Associated Press*] (SAG)
IndusHld ..... Industrial Holdings, Inc. [*Associated Press*] (SAG)
Indus L Review... Industrial Law Review [*A publication*] (DLA)
INDUSMIN .. Industrial Mineral Service [*Midland, ON*]
IndusMt .... Industir-Matematik International Corp. [*Associated Press*] (SAG)
Indus Rel Guide... Industrial Relations Guide [*A publication*] (DLA)
INDUSSIM ... Total Industry Simulation [*Game*]
INDUST....... Industrial [*or Industry*]
INDUST....... Industry
Indust Acc Com... Decisions of the Industrial Accident Commission of California
[*A publication*] (DLA)
Indust Austn & Mining Std... Industrial Australian and Mining Standard
[*A publication*]
Indust Bull... Industrial Bulletin [*A publication*] (DLA)
Indust C Aw... Industrial Court Awards [*England*] [*A publication*] (DLA)
Indust Ct Aw... Industrial Court Awards [*England*] [*A publication*] (DLA)
INDUSTL...... Industrial
Indust Law Rev... Industrial Law Review [*A publication*] (DLA)
Indust L Rev... Industrial Law Review [*A publication*] (DLA)
Indust L Soc Bull... Bulletin. Industrial Law Society [*A publication*] (DLA)
Indust Prop... Industrial Property [*Legal term*] (DLA)
Indust Prop Q... Industrial Property Quarterly [*A publication*] (DLA)
Indust Prop'y Yb... Industrial Property Yearbook [*A publication*] (DLA)
INDUSTR .... Industrial (ROG)
Industr Prop'y Q... Industrial Property Quarterly [*A publication*] (DLA)
IndUtd .... Indiana United Bancorp [*Associated Press*] (SAG)
INDV .... Individual, Inc. [*NASDAQ symbol*] (SAG)
INDV .... Individual Inc. [*NASDAQ symbol*] (TTSB)
INDV .... Individually (MSA)
Indvl .... Individual Investor Group [*Associated Press*] (SAG)
IndvInv....... Individual Investor Group [*Associated Press*] (SAG)
Ind Wills ..... Inderwick on Wills [*1866*] [*A publication*] (DLA)
Ind YB Int'l Aff... Indian Yearbook of International Affairs [*A publication*] (DLA)
INE .... East Chicago Public Library, East Chicago, IN [*OCLC symbol*]
(OCLC)
InE .... Evansville Public Library and Vanderburgh County Public Library,
Evansville, IN [*Library symbol Library of Congress*] (LCLS)
INE .... Incorrect Negative Expectancy [*Psychometrics*]
ine .... Indo-European [*MARC language code Library of Congress*] (LCCP)
INE .... Inertial Navigation Equipment (MCD)
INE .... Infantile Necrotizing Encephalomyelopathy [*Medicine*] (MAE)
INE .... Initiatives for Not-for-Profit Entrepreneurship [*Research center*] (RCD)
INE .... Institution of Nuclear Engineers (PDAA)
INE .... International Kenergy Resource Corp. [*Vancouver Stock Exchange
symbol*]
INE .... Missoula, MT [*Location identifier FAA*] (FAAL)
INEA .... Internationaler Elektronik-Arbeitskreis [*International Electronics
Association*]
INEAC .... Institut National pour l'Etude Agronomique du Congo [*National
Institute for the Study of Agronomy in the Congo*]
InEaP .... Earl Park Public Library, Earl Park, IN [*Library symbol Library of
Congress*] (LCLS)
InEc .... East Chicago Public Library, East Chicago, IN [*Library symbol Library
of Congress*] (LCLS)
INEC......... Institut Europeen d'Ecologie et de Cancerologie [*European Institute
of Ecology and Cancer - EIEC*] (EA)
INEC......... Institut Europeen des Industries de la Gomme de Caroube [*European
Institute of Carob Gum Industries*] [*EC*] (ECED)
INECA .... Industrial Energy Conservation Abstracts [*UNIDO*] [*United Nations*]
(DUND)
InEcIP......... Indiana City Press, Indiana City, IN [*Library symbol Library of
Congress*] (LCLS)
InEd .... Edinburg Public Library, Edinburg, IN [*Library symbol*] [*Library of
Congress*] (LCLS)
INED .... Inedible
INED .... Inedites [*Unpublished*] [*French*] (ROG)
INED .... Ineditus [*Not Made Known*] [*Latin*]
INED .... Institute for New Enterprise Development (EA)
INED .... International Network for Educational Information (EAIO)
INEFFCY ..... Inefficiency
INEFFY....... Inefficiency (AABC)
InefMkt .... [*The*] Inefficient-Market Fund [*Associated Press*] (SAG)
INEGI......... Instituto Nacional de Estadistica, Geografia e Informatica [*Main
government clearinghouse for statistical information*] [*Mexico*]
(CROSS)

INEI............ Insituform East [*NASDAQ symbol*] (TTSB)
INEI............ Insituform East, Inc. [*NASDAQ symbol*] (NQ)
INEI............ International Exhibition of Industrial Electronics (MCD)
INEL........... Idaho National Engineering Laboratory [*Idaho Falls, ID*] [*Department of Energy*]
INEL........... Intelligent Electroncs [*NASDAQ symbol*] (TTSB)
INEL........... Intelligent Electronics, Inc. [*NASDAQ symbol*] (SAG)
INEL........... Intelligent Electronics, Inc. [*NASDAQ symbol*] (NQ)
InElk.......... Elkhart Public Library, Elkhart, IN [*Library symbol Library of Congress*] (LCLS)
InElkB....... Mennonite Biblical Seminary, Elkhart, IN [*Library symbol Library of Congress*] (LCLS)
InElkM...... Miles Laboratories, Inc., Elkhart, IN [*Library symbol Library of Congress*] (LCLS)
InElkT........ Elkhart Truth, Elkhart, IN [*Library symbol Library of Congress*] (LCLS)
InEllJ.......... Ellettsville Journal, Ellettsville, IN [*Library symbol Library of Congress*] (LCLS)
INELTEC...... Exhibition of Industrial Electronics, Electrical Engineering, and Technical Installation (TSPED)
InElw......... Elwood Public Library, Elwood, IN [*Library symbol Library of Congress*] (LCLS)
InElwCL...... Elwood Call-Leader, Elwood, IN [*Library symbol Library of Congress*] (LCLS)
InEM......... Mead Johnson Research Center, Evansville, IN [*Library symbol Library of Congress*] (LCLS)
InEng......... Crawford County Public Library, English, IN [*Library symbol Library of Congress*] (LCLS)
InEngD........ Crawford County Democrat, English, IN [*Library symbol Library of Congress*] (LCLS)
InENR........ Northside Reporter, Evansville, IN [*Library symbol Library of Congress*] (LCLS)
InEnt......... Inmark Enterprises, Inc. [*Associated Press*] (SAG)
INEOA........ International Narcotic Enforcement Officers Association (EA)
InEP.......... Evansville Press and Courier, Evansville, IN [*Library symbol Library of Congress*] (LCLS)
INEP.......... International Nurse Education Program
INep.......... Neponset Public Library, Neponset, IL [*Library symbol Library of Congress*] (LCLS)
INepL......... Neponset Public Library, Neponset, IL [*Library symbol*] [*Library of Congress*] (LCLS)
INEPT........ Insensitive Nuclei Enhanced by Polarization Transfer [*Spectroscopy*]
INER.......... Inertial (KSC)
INERT........ Index of National Enervation and Related Trends [*Department of Commerce*]
InES.......... Indiana State University, Evansville Campus, Evansville, IN [*Library symbol Library of Congress*] (LCLS)
INES.......... International Nuclear Event Scale
InESC......... Evansville-Vanderburgh School Corp., Library Services Center, Evansville, IN [*Library symbol Library of Congress*] (LCLS)
INET.......... Image Network (DMAA)
INET.......... Intelligent Network [*Telecom Canada*] [*Database*]
INET.......... Interbank Network for Electronic Transfer
INET.......... Intrenet, Inc. [*NASDAQ symbol*] (SAG)
InEU.......... University of Evansville, Evansville, IN [*Library symbol Library of Congress*] (LCLS)
In Evang Iohan... Tractatus in Evangelium Iohannis [*of Augustine*] [*Classical studies*] (OCD)
INew.......... Newman Township Library, Newman, IL [*Library symbol Library of Congress*] (LCLS)
InEW......... Willard Library, Evansville, IN [*Library symbol Library of Congress*] (LCLS)
INEWF........ Indian National Electricity Workers' Federation
INewm........ Newman Township Library, Newman, IL [*Library symbol*] [*Library of Congress*] (LCLS)
INEWS........ Integrated Electronic Warfare System
InEWS......... West Side Story, Evansville, IN [*Library symbol Library of Congress*] (LCLS)
INewt......... Newton Public Library, Newton, IL [*Library symbol Library of Congress*] (LCLS)
INEX.......... Inexperienced (DAVI)
IN EX.......... In Extenso [*At Full Length*] [*Latin*] (ROG)
INF............. Infamous [*FBI standardized term*]
INF............. Infant
INF............. Infantile (CPH)
inf.............. Infantile (DMAA)
INF............. Infantry (AFM)
inf.............. Infected (CPH)
INF............. Infection [*Medicine*]
INF............. Inferior
inf.............. Inferior (WDMC)
INF............. Infield (WGA)
IN F.......... In Fine [*Finally*] [*Latin*]
INF............. Infinite (MSA)
INF............. Infinite Resources, Inc. [*Vancouver Stock Exchange symbol*]
INF............. Infinitive
inf.............. Infinitive (WDMC)
INF............. Infinity
INF............. Infinity Broadcasting'A' [*NYSE symbol*] (TTSB)
INF............. Infinity Broadcasting Corp. [*NYSE symbol*] (SAG)
INF............. Infirmary
INF............. Influence (WDAA)
INF............. Influenza [*Medicine*]
INF............. In Folio (DGA)
INF............. Inform

INF............. Informaatiopalvelulaitos [*Information Service*] [*Technical Research Center of Finland Espoo*] [*Information service or system*] (IID)
INF............. Informal
INF............. Informant (WGA)
INF............. Information [*Computer science*]
inf.............. Information (WDMC)
INF............. Informationszentrum und Bibliotheken [*Information retrieval*]
INF............. Informed
Inf............. Infortiatum [*A publication*] (DSA)
INF............. Infra [*Beneath or Below*] [*Latin*]
INF............. Infunde [*Pour In*] [*Pharmacy*]
INF............. Infusion [*Medicine*]
INF............. Infusum [*Infusion*] [*Pharmacy*] (ROG)
INF............. Inland Navigation Facility
INF............. Interceptor Night Fighter (NATG)
INF............. Interface (KSC)
INF............. Interference (KSC)
INF............. Intermediate-Range Nuclear Forces
INF............. International Naturist Federation [*Antwerp, Belgium*] (EA)
INF............. International Nuclear Forces (NATG)
INF............. Iranian National Front (PPW)
INF............. Irredundant Normal Formula
INF............. ISDN [*Integrated Services Digital Network*] Numbering Forum (OSI)
INF............. Parke, Davis & Co. [*Great Britain*] [*Research code symbol*]
infa--........ Faroe Islands [*MARC geographic area code Library of Congress*] (LCCP)
INFA.......... International Federation of Aestheticians [*Brussels, Belgium*] (EAIO)
INFA.......... International Nuclear Fuel Authority
INFAC........ Instrumented Factory for Gears [*Illinois Institute of Technology Research Institute*] [*Research center*] (RCD)
INFACON...... International Ferro-Alloys Congress
INFACT........ Infant Formula Action Coalition (EA)
InFai.......... Fairmount Public Library, Fairmount, IN [*Library symbol Library of Congress*] (LCLS)
InFaiN....... Fairmount News, Fairmount, IN [*Library symbol Library of Congress*] (LCLS)
INFANT....... Interactive Networks Functioning on Adaptive Neural Topographies [*Robot*]
INFANT....... Iroquois Night Fighter and Night Tracker [*Military*] (MCD)
INFANTS...... Interested Future Attorneys Negotiating for Tot Safety [*Student legal action organization*]
InFarl......... Farmland Public Library, Farmland, IN [*Library symbol Library of Congress*] (LCLS)
InFb........... Fort Branch Public Library, Fort Branch, IN [*Library symbol Library of Congress*] (LCLS)
INFBAT....... Infantry Battalion [*Army*]
InFbT......... Fort Branch Times, Fort Branch, IN [*Library symbol Library of Congress*] (LCLS)
INF-C......... Influenza-C [*Medicine*]
INFCE........ Influence (ROG)
INFCE........ International Nuclear Fuel Cycle Evaluation
INFCO........ Information Committee [*International Organization for Standardization*] (IEEE)
INFCO........ Information Committee of the International Standards Organization (NITA)
INFCY........ Infancy (ROG)
INFD.......... Infodata Systems [*NASDAQ symbol*] (TTSB)
INFD.......... Infodata Systems, Inc. [*NASDAQ symbol*] (NQ)
INFD.......... Informed (ROG)
inf dis........ Infectious Disease (MEDA)
INFE.......... Instituto Nacional de Fomento de la Exportacion [*National Institute of Export Development*] [*Spain*] (EY)
INFE.......... International Newspaper Financial Executives (EA)
infec dis ...... Infectious Disease [*Medicine*] (CPH)
infect.......... Infection [*or Infectious*] (DAVI)
INFEDOP...... International Federation of Employees in Public Service [*Brussels, Belgium*] (EAIO)
InFerC......... Sisters of St. Benedict, Convent and Academy of the Immaculate Conception, Ferdinand, IN [*Library symbol*] [*Library of Congress*] (LCLS)
INFEREX...... Inference Execution Language
InFerN........ Ferdinand News, Ferdinand, IN [*Library symbol Library of Congress*] (LCLS)
Infernce...... Inference Corp. [*Associated Press*] (SAG)
InfFincl........ Infinity Financial Technology, Inc. [*Associated Press*] (SAG)
INFH.......... Ischemic Necrosis of Femoral Head [*Orthopedics*] (DAVI)
InfHA......... Influenza Virus Hemagglutinin [*Immunology*]
INFIC......... International Network of Feed Information Centers (EA)
infil............ Infiltrate [*or Infiltrated*] (DAVI)
INFIL/EXFIL... Infiltration and Exfiltration (DOMA)
INFIN......... Infinitive [*Grammar*]
InfinBr........ Infinity Broadcasting Corp. [*Associated Press*] (SAG)
InfinBrd........ Infinity Broadcasting Corp. [*Associated Press*] (SAG)
INFINET...... International Financial Networks
Infinity........ Infinity, Inc. [*Associated Press*] (SAG)
InFinSv........ Interchange Financial Services Corp. [*Associated Press*] (SAG)
INFINT........ Infinite
INFIRM........ Infirmary
INFIRS........ Invented-File-Search System (DICI)
INFIRS........ Inverted File Information Retrieval System [*UK Chemical Information Service*] (NITA)
INFIS.......... Indonesian Aquatic Sciences Fisheries Information System [*Marine science*] (OSRA)
InFl............. Flora-Monroe Public Library, Flora, IN [*Library symbol Library of Congress*] (LCLS)

INFL............ Inflammable
INFL............ Inflated (ADA)
infl............ Inflorescence [Botany]
INFL............ Influence
INFL............ Influx
In Flacc ...... In Flaccum [of Philo Judaeus] [Classical studies] (OCD)
INFLAM...... Inflammable
inflam.......... Inflammation [or Inflammatory] (DAVI)
INFLO.......... Integrated Flight Optimization (PDAA)
InFlt.......... Interactive Flight Technologies, Inc. Cl.A [Associated Press] (SAG)
INFM.......... Infectious Mononucleosis [Medicine] (DAVI)
INFM.......... Inform (ROG)
InfMach ...... Infinite Machines Corp. [Associated Press] (SAG)
InfMch ...... Infinite Machines Corp. [Associated Press] (SAG)
InfMgeR...... Information Management Resources, Inc. [Associated Press] (SAG)
InfMgt........ Information Management Technology [Associated Press] (SAG)
Inf MI.......... Inferior Myocardial Infarction [Cardiology]
inf mono...... Infectious Mononucleosis [Medicine] (MAE)
INFMRY ...... Infirmary
INFMTL...... Informational
INFN.......... Infinity Financial Technology, Inc. [NASDAQ symbol] (SAG)
INFN .... Information (ROG)
InFnDM...... International Finance Corp. [Associated Press] (SAG)
InFnDY...... International Finance Corp. [Associated Press] (SAG)
INFNET...... Istituto Nazionale Fisica Nucleare Network [National Institute for Nuclear Physics Network] [Italian] [Computer science] (TNIG)
INFNT .... Infant
INFNT .... Iroquois Night Fighter and Night Tracker [Military] (DNAB)
InFnYB........ International Finance Corp. [Associated Press] (SAG)
InFo .... Benton County Public Library, Fowler, IN [Library symbol Library of Congress] (LCLS)
INFO .... Infonautics, Inc. [NASDAQ symbol] (SAG)
INFO .... Infonautics Inc.'A' [NASDAQ symbol] (TTSB)
INFO .... Information (AFM)
info .... Information (DD)
INFO .... Information
INFO .... Information Network and File Organization [Computer science] (BUR)
INFO .... Information Network for Ontario [Canada]
INFO .... Information Network for Operations [Computer science]
INFO .... Integrated Fleet Operations
INFO .... Integrated Network Fiber Optics (MCD)
INFO .... International Fortean Organization (EA)
infobit........ Information Bit [Computer science] (BARN)
InfoCan...... Information Canada
INFOCEN...... Information Center (MCD)
INFOCLIMA... World Climate Data Information Referral Service [World Meteorological Organization] [Information service or system] (IID)
INFOCOMM... Information and Communications Technology Exposition (ITD)
InFoCR...... Benton County Recorder's Office, Fowler, IN [Library symbol Library of Congress] (LCLS)
InFocu .... In Focus System, Inc. [Associated Press] (SAG)
Infodat........ Infodata Systems, Inc. [Associated Press] (SAG)
INFODATA.... Database Information Science and Practice [Database]
INFO/DOC .... Information/Documentation [Information service or system] (IID)
INFOES .... In-Flight Operational Evaluation of a Space System
INFOEX........ Information Exchange, Inc. [Telecommunications service] (TSSD)
INFOHOST .. Database Guide to German Host Operators [Database]
INFOHOST .. Information on Hosts (NITA)
InfoIntl........ Information International, Inc. [Associated Press] (SAG)
INFOL........ Information Oriented Language [Information retrieval]
INFOLAC...... Information for Latin American Countries Project (NITA)
IN FOL ARG VOLVEND... In Folio Argenti Volvendae [To Be Silvered] [Pharmacy]
INFOMARK... Information Market News [Database] (ECED)
INFOMART... Information Market [Exhibition and conference centre] [Dallas] (NITA)
Infomed ...... Infomed Holdings, Inc. [Associated Press] (SAG)
INFONAC...... Instituto de Fomento Nacional [Industrial promotion agency] [Nicaragua]
Infonau...... Infonautics, Inc. [Associated Press] (SAG)
INFONET...... Information Network [British Telecommunications] (TEL)
INFOODS .. International Network of Food Data Systems [Massachusets Institute of Technology] [Cambridge] [Information service or system] (IID)
INFO PASS... Central Mississippi Library Council [Library network]
INFOR.......... Information (DSUE)
INFOR.......... Information Network and File Organization (MHDB)
INFOR.......... Interactive FORTRAN [Formula Translating System] [Computer science] (IAA)
INFORBW .... Information on Research in Baden-Wurttemberg [Fachinformationszentrum Karlsruhe GmbH] [Germany Information service or system] (CRD)
INFOREM..... Inventory Forecasting and Replenishment Modules [IBM Corp.]
INFOREP...... Information Report (CINC)
INFOREQ...... Information Requested [or Required]
InfoRes........ Information Resources, Inc. [Associated Press] (SAG)
INFORM...... Information
INFORM...... Information for Optimum Resource Management (MCD)
INFORM...... Information Network for Freight Overhead Billing, Rating, and Message Switching
INFORM....... International Reference Organization in Forensic Medicine and Sciences (EA)
INFORMAC... Immediate Information for Merchant and Customer (PDAA)
INFORMAL... Information for Avionics Laboratory
INFORMALUX... Information Luxembourg (NITA)
INFORMAP... Information Necessary for Optimum Resource Management and Protection (PDAA)
Informed...... Informedics, Inc. [Associated Press] (SAG)

INFORMN .... Information
INFORMS.... Information Organization Reporting and Management System (IAA)
Informx...... Informix Corp. [Associated Press] (SAG)
INFOS .... Information Network for Official Statistics [Department of Statistics] [Information service or system] (IID)
INFOS .... Informationszentrum fuer Schnittwerte [Cutting Data Information Center] [Germany Information service or system] (IID)
Infosafe ...... Infosafe Systems, Inc. [Associated Press] (SAG)
INFOSEC...... Information Systems Security (AAGC)
Infoseek ...... Infoseek Corp. [Associated Press] (SAG)
Infosf .... Infosafe Systems, Inc. [Associated Press] (SAG)
Infosfe .... Infosafe Systems, Inc. [Associated Press] (SAG)
INFOSOR .... Information Sources [Information service or system] (IID)
Infospecs .... Information Specialists Ltd. [Information service or system] (IID)
InfoStor...... Information Storage Devices, Inc. [Associated Press] (SAG)
INFOTERM ... International Information Centre for Terminology [UNESCO] (IID)
INFOTERRA... International Referral System for Sources of Environmental Information [Formerly, IRS] [United Nations Environment Program] (ASF)
INFOTEX .... Information via Telex [Telecommunications] (TEL)
INFP.......... Introverted, Intuitive, a Feeler, and Perceiver [Keirsey Temperament Test Result] [Psychology]
INFR .... Inference Corp. [NASDAQ symbol] (SAG)
INFR .... Inference Corp.'A' [NASDAQ symbol] (TTSB)
INFR .... Inferior (ROG)
INFRA .... Information Research Analysts [Database producer] (IID)
infra............ Infrared (VRA)
INFRA DIG .... Infra Dignitatem [Undignified] [Latin]
INFRAL........ Information Retrieval Automatic Language [Computer science]
INFRAPTUM... Infrascriptum [Written Below] [Latin] (ROG)
Infrasnc...... Infrasonics, Inc. [Associated Press] (SAG)
InFrem.......... Fremont Public Library, Fremont, IN [Library symbol Library of Congress] (LCLS)
InFren.......... Melton Public Library, French Lick, IN [Library symbol Library of Congress] (LCLS)
InFrenSH...... Springs Valley Herald, French Lick, IN [Library symbol Library of Congress] (LCLS)
InFrf.......... Frankfort Community Public Library, Frankfort, IL [Library symbol Library of Congress] (LCLS)
INF RHEI...... Infusum Rhei [Infusion of Rhubarb] [Pharmacy] (ROG)
INFRIC.......... Infricetur [Let It Be Rubbed In] [Pharmacy]
InFrl.......... Franklin Public Library, Franklin, IN [Library symbol Library of Congress] (LCLS)
InFrlC.......... Franklin College of Indiana, Franklin, IN [Library symbol Library of Congress] (LCLS)
InFrlCR .... Johnson County Recorder's Office, Franklin, IN [Library symbol Library of Congress] (LCLS)
InFrlJ.......... Franklin Daily Journal, Franklin, IN [Library symbol Library of Congress] (LCLS)
InFrlJM........ Johnson County Museum, Franklin, IN [Library symbol Library of Congress] (LCLS)
INFRM .... Infirm
INFRMRY.... Infirmary
INFRN.......... Inference (MSA)
INFROSS...... Information Requirements of the Social Sciences [British] (DIT)
INFROSS...... Investigation into Information Requirements of Social Sciences [1970s study] [British] (NITA)
InfRsc.......... Information Resource Engineering, Inc. [Associated Press] (SAG)
InFrv.......... Francesville-Salem Township Public Library, Francesville, IN [Library symbol Library of Congress] (LCLS)
InFrvT .... Francesville Tribune, Francesville, IN [Library symbol Library of Congress] (LCLS)
INFS.......... In Focus System, Inc. [NASDAQ symbol] (SAG)
INFS.......... In Focus Systems [NASDAQ symbol] (TTSB)
INFT............ Infant (ROG)
INFT............ Informal Training (NASA)
InFtbh.......... United States Army, Post Library, Fort Benjamin Harrison, IN [Library symbol] [Library of Congress] (LCLS)
InFtbhP........ United States Army, Post Library, Fort Benjamin Harrison, IN [Library symbol Library of Congress] (LCLS)
InFtv.......... Carnegie Public Library District, Fortville, IN [Library symbol Library of Congress] (LCLS)
InFtvT .... Fortville Tribune, Fortville, IN [Library symbol Library of Congress] (LCLS)
Infty............ Infantry [British military] (DMA)
INFU.......... Infu-Tech, Inc. [NASDAQ symbol] (SAG)
InFu............ Phyllis Meyer Library, Fulton, IN [Library symbol Library of Congress] (LCLS)
INFUND........ Infunde [Pour In] [Pharmacy]
INFUS.......... Infusum [Infusion] [Pharmacy] (ROG)
InfuTech...... Infu-Tech, Inc. [Associated Press] (SAG)
InFw.......... Public Library of Fort Wayne and Allen County, Fort Wayne, IN [Library symbol Library of Congress] (LCLS)
InFwAHi...... Allen County-Fort Wayne Historical Society Library, Fort Wayne, IN [Library symbol Library of Congress] (LCLS)
InFwB .... Fort Wayne Bible College, Fort Wayne, IN [Library symbol Library of Congress] (LCLS)
InFwC .... Concordia Senior College, Fort Wayne, IN [Library symbol Library of Congress] (LCLS)
InFwCS .... Fort Wayne Community Schools, Fort Wayne, IN [Library symbol] [Library of Congress] (LCLS)
InFwCT .... Concordia Theological Seminary, Fort Wayne, IN [Library symbol Library of Congress] (LCLS)

InFwGS........ Church of Jesus Christ of Latter-Day Saints, Genealogical Society Library, Fort Wayne Branch, Fort Wayne, IN [*Library symbol Library of Congress*] (LCLS)

InFwI .... Indiana Institute of Technology, Fort Wayne, IN [*Library symbol Library of Congress*] (LCLS)

InFwIP .... Indiana-Purdue University, Fort Wayne, IN [*Library symbol Library of Congress*] (LCLS)

InFwJG .... Fort Wayne Journal-Gazette, Fort Wayne, IN [*Library symbol Library of Congress*] (LCLS)

InFwL.......... Lincoln National Life Foundation, Fort Wayne, IN [*Library symbol Library of Congress*] (LCLS)

InFWl-F....... National Life Insurance Co., Lincoln National Life Foundation, Louis A. Warren Lincoln Library and Museum, Fort Wayne, IN [*Library symbol Library of Congress*] (LCLS)

InFwLW ...... Louis A. Warren Lincoln Library and Museum, Fort Wayne, IN [*Library symbol*] [*Library of Congress*] (LCLS)

InFwM .... Magnavox Co., Fort Wayne, IN [*Library symbol Library of Congress*] (LCLS)

InFwSF .... Saint Francis College, Fort Wayne, IN [*Library symbol Library of Congress*] (LCLS)

INFX........... Inspection Fixture

INFY............ Infancy [*Legal shorthand*] (LWAP)

Infy .... Infantry [*British military*] (DMA)

ING .... Ambler, PA [*Location identifier FAA*] (FAAL)

InG.............. Gary Public Library, Gary, IN [*Library symbol Library of Congress*] (LCLS)

ING .... Inactive National Guard

ING .... Inactive National Guard (DOMA)

ING .... Inertial Navigation and Guidance [*Aerospace*] (AAG)

ING .... Inertial Navigation Gyro

ING .... Ingenieur [*Engineer*] [*French*] (EY)

ing .... Ingenieur (DD)

ING .... Inglis Ltd. [*Toronto Stock Exchange symbol*]

ING .... Ingram Ranch [*California*] [*Seismograph station code, US Geological Survey*] (SEIS)

ING .... Inguinal [*Anatomy*]

ING .... Inside Nazi Germany [*A publication*]

ING .... Integrated News Gathering

ING .... Intense Neutron Generator

ING .... Internationale Nederlanden Groep [*Netherlands*] (ECON)

ING .... International Newspaper Group (EA)

ING .... Isotope Nephrogram (DMAA)

ING .... Lago Argentino [*Argentina*] [*Airport symbol*] (OAG)

INGA .... Indium Gallium Arsenide

INGA .... Inspection Gauge

INGA .... Interactive Graphics Analysis

INGAA......... Interstate Natural Gas Association of America (EA)

INGAALP..... Indium-Gallium-Aluminum Phosphide [*Light-emitting diode construction*]

InGaAs APD... Indium Gallium Arsenide Avalanche Photodiode

InGar .... Garrett Public Library, Garrett, IN [*Library symbol Library of Congress*] (LCLS)

InGarC .... Garrett Clipper, Garrett, IN [*Library symbol Library of Congress*] (LCLS)

INGAT .... Ingatestone [*Village in England*]

Ing B .... Ingenium Baccalaureus [*Bachelor of Engineering*]

InGc........... Gas City-Mill Township Public Library, Gas City, IN [*Library symbol Library of Congress*] (LCLS)

Ing Comp..... Ingram's Compensation for Interest in Lands [*2nd ed.*] [*1869*] [*A publication*] (DLA)

Ing D .... Ingenium Doctor [*Doctor of Engineering*]

Ing Dig .... Ingersoll's Digest of the Laws of the United States [*A publication*] (DLA)

InGe........... Geneva Public Library, Geneva, IN [*Library symbol Library of Congress*] (LCLS)

InGeL .... Limberlost State Memorial, Geneva, IN [*Library symbol Library of Congress*] (LCLS)

INGENINST... Office of the Inspector General Instructions [*Navy*]

INGER......... International Network on Genetic Evaluation in Rice (ECON)

IngerRd....... Ingersoll Rand [*Associated Press*] (SAG)

Ing Hab Corp... Ingersoll on Habeas Corpus [*A publication*] (DLA)

InGHi .... Gary Historical and Cultural Society, Gary, IN [*Library symbol Library of Congress*] (LCLS)

INGIFPI........ Irish National Group of International Federation of the Phonographic Industry (EAIO)

Ing Insolv .... Ingraham on Insolvency [*Pennsylvania*] [*A publication*] (DLA)

InglMkt .... Ingles Markets, Inc. [*Associated Press*] (SAG)

Ing M .... Ingenium Magister [*Master of Engineering*]

InGo............ Goshen College, Goshen, IN [*Library symbol Library of Congress*] (LCLS)

INGO .... International Non-Governmental Organization

InGoM.......... Mennonite Historical Library, Goshen College, Goshen, IN [*Library symbol Library of Congress*] (LCLS)

InGoN .... Goshen News, Goshen, IN [*Library symbol Library of Congress*] (LCLS)

InGoo.......... Goodland Public Library (Mitten Memorial Library), Goodland, IN [*Library symbol Library of Congress*] (LCLS)

InGoP.......... Goshen Public Library, Goshen, IN [*Library symbol Library of Congress*] (LCLS)

InGP........... Indol Glycerophosphate [*Biochemistry*]

InGPS .... Indoleglycerolphosphate Synthase [*Biochemistry*]

InGPT.......... Gary Post-Tribune, Gary, IN [*Library symbol Library of Congress*] (LCLS)

InGr .... Greencastle-Putnam County Library, Greencastle, IN [*Library symbol Library of Congress*] (LCLS)

INGR .... Intergraph Corp. [*NASDAQ symbol*] (NQ)

InGrBG .... Greencastle Banner-Graphic, Greencastle, IN [*Library symbol Library of Congress*] (LCLS)

InGrD .... De Pauw University, Greencastle, IN [*Library symbol Library of Congress*] (LCLS)

INGRD .... Ingredient

InGrD-Ar ...... De Pauw University, Archives, Greencastle, IN [*Library symbol Library of Congress*] (LCLS)

INGRDNT..... Ingredient

InGreb .... Greensburg Public Library, Greensburg, IN [*Library symbol Library of Congress*] (LCLS)

InGrebCR...... Decatur County Recorder's Office, Greensburg, IN [*Library symbol Library of Congress*] (LCLS)

InGrebDHi..... Decatur County Historical Society, Greensburg, IN [*Library symbol Library of Congress*] (LCLS)

InGrebHi....... Decatur County Historical Society, Greensburg, IN [*Library symbol Library of Congress*] (LCLS)

InGref .... Greenfield Public Library, Greenfield, IN [*Library symbol Library of Congress*] (LCLS)

InGrefL .... Eli Lilly & Co., Library Agricultural Services, Greenfield, IN [*Library symbol Library of Congress*] (LCLS)

InGrefR........ Greenfield Daily Reporter, Greenfield, IN [*Library symbol*] [*Library of Congress*] (LCLS)

INGRES........ Interactive Graphic and Retrieval System

InGretN .... Howard County News, Greentown, IN [*Library symbol Library of Congress*] (LCLS)

InGrew......... Greenwood Public Library, Greenwood, IN [*Library symbol Library of Congress*] (LCLS)

IngrmM......... Ingram Micro, Inc. [*Associated Press*] (SAG)

Ing Roc........ Ingersoll's Edition of Roccus' Maritime Law [*A publication*] (DLA)

InGS............ Gary School System, Gary, IN [*Library symbol Library of Congress*] (LCLS)

INGSOC....... English Socialism [*From George Orwell's novel, "1984"*]

Ing Ves........ Vesey, Junior's, English Chancery Reports, Edited by Ingraham [*A publication*] (ILCA)

INGYO.......... International Nongovernmental Youth Organization (PDAA)

INH .... Improved Nike Hercules [*Missile*]

IN/H .... Inches per Hour

INH .... Inhalation

INH .... Inhambane [*Mozambique*] [*Airport symbol*] (AD)

INH .... Inheritance [*Legal shorthand*] (LWAP)

INH .... Inhibit (NASA)

INH .... Isangel [*New Hebrides*] [*Seismograph station code, US Geological Survey*] (SEIS)

INH .... Isoniazid (DMAA)

INH .... Isonicotinic Acid Hydrazide [*or Isonicotinylhydrazine*] [*See also INAH, ISONIAZID*] [*Antituberculous agent*]

INHA .... Inhibin Alpha (DMAA)

INHAB........ Inhabitant

INHABD....... Inhabited (ROG)

InHag .... Hagerstown Public Library, Hagerstown, IN [*Library symbol Library of Congress*] (LCLS)

InHagE........ Hagerstown Exponent, Hagerstown, IN [*Library symbol Library of Congress*] (LCLS)

INHAL .... Inhalatio [*Inhalation*] [*Pharmacy*]

InhalTh .... Inhale Therapeutic Systems [*Associated Press*] (SAG)

InHam......... Hammond Public Library, Hammond, IN [*Library symbol Library of Congress*] (LCLS)

InHamP........ Purdue University, Calumet Campus, Hammond, IN [*Library symbol Library of Congress*] (LCLS)

InHamT........ Hammond Times, Hammond, IN [*Library symbol Library of Congress*] (LCLS)

InHan......... Hanover College, Hanover, IN [*Library symbol Library of Congress*] (LCLS)

InHar .... Hartford City Public Library, Hartford City, IN [*Library symbol Library of Congress*] (LCLS)

InHarBHi....... Blackford County Historical Society, Hartford City, IN [*Library symbol Library of Congress*] (LCLS)

InHazN......... White River News, Hazelton, IN [*Library symbol Library of Congress*] (LCLS)

INHB .... Inhibin Beta (DMAA)

INHB .... Inhibit (MSA)

INHBD .... Inhibited (DLA)

INHCE .... Inheritance [*Legal term*] (ROG)

InHeb .... Hebron Public Library, Hebron, IN [*Library symbol Library of Congress*] (LCLS)

InHebPH ...... Porter County Herald, Hebron, IN [*Library symbol Library of Congress*] (LCLS)

Inher........... Inheritance [*Legal term*] (DLA)

Inher Est & Gift Tax Rep (CCH)... Inheritance, Estate, and Gift Tax Reports (Commerce Clearing House) [*A publication*] (DLA)

InHhW .... Workingmen's Institute, New Harmony, IN [*Library symbol Library of Congress*] (LCLS)

InHi............ Indiana Historical Society, Indianapolis, IN [*Library symbol Library of Congress*] (LCLS)

INHIB.......... Inhibition

INHIGEO ...... International Commission on the History of the Geological Sciences [*ICSU*] [*Paris, France*] (EAIO)

INHL .... Inhale Therapeutic Sys [*NASDAQ symbol*] (TTSB)

INHL .... Inhale Therapeutic Systems [*NASDAQ symbol*] (SAG)

INHld.......... Industrial Holdings, Inc. [*Associated Press*] (SAG)

INHM .... Inco Homes [*NASDAQ symbol*] (TTSB)

INHM .... Inco Homes Corp. [*NASDAQ symbol*] (SAG)

INHO .... Independence Hldg [*NASDAQ symbol*] (TTSB)

INHO .... Independence Holding Co. [*NASDAQ symbol*] (NQ)

InHobG .... Hobart Gazette, Hobart, IN [*Library symbol*] [*Library of Congress*] (LCLS)

InHobHi .... Pleak Memorial Library/Hobart Historical Society, Hobart, IN [*Library symbol*] [*Library of Congress*] (LCLS)

InHoG .... Hobart Gazette, Hobart, IN [*Library symbol Library of Congress*] (LCLS)

InHoHi .... Pleak Memorial Library/Hobart Historical Society, Hobart, IN [*Library symbol Library of Congress*] (LCLS)

InHome........ In Home Health, inc. [*Associated Press*] (SAG)

INHS .... Illinois Natural History Survey [*Illinois Institute of Natural Resources*] [*Research center*] (RCD)

INHS .... Irish National Hunt Steeplechase (ROG)

InHu .... Huntington Public Library, Huntington, IN [*Library symbol Library of Congress*] (LCLS)

InHub........... Huntingburg Public Library, Huntingburg, IN [*Library symbol Library of Congress*] (LCLS)

InHuCR .... Huntington County Recorder's Office, Huntington, IN [*Library symbol*] [*Library of Congress*] (LCLS)

InHuH .... Huntington College, Huntington, IN [*Library symbol Library of Congress*] (LCLS)

InHuHi .... Huntington County Historical Society, Huntington, IN [*Library symbol Library of Congress*] (LCLS)

InHuHP .... Huntington Herald-Press, Huntington, IN [*Library symbol Library of Congress*] (LCLS)

INI............... Incipient Nonequilibrium Index

InI .... Indianapolis-Marion County Public Library, Indianapolis, IN [*Library symbol Library of Congress*] (LCLS)

INI............... Industrial Networking, Inc. [*Joint venture of Ungermann-Bass, Inc. and General Electric Corp.*]

INI............... Inner Integument [*Botany*]

INI............... In Nomine Iesu [*In the Name of Jesus*] [*Latin*]

INI............... Instituto Nacional de Industria [*National Institute for Industry*] [*Spain*]

INI............... Interface Noise Inverter

INI............... International Nonviolent Initiatives (EA)

INI............... Intervideo Network, Inc. [*Beverly Hills, CA*] [*Telecommunications*] (TSSD)

INI............... Intranuclear Inclusion

InIA .... Indiana Academy of Science, Indianapolis, IN [*Library symbol Library of Congress*] (LCLS)

InIAL........... American Legion, National Headquarters Library, Indianapolis, IN [*Library symbol Library of Congress*] (LCLS)

InIB .... Butler University, Indianapolis, IN [*Library symbol Library of Congress*] (LCLS)

INIBAP .... International Network for the Improvement of Banana and Plantain [*Affilia ted with the Consultative Group on International Agricultural Research*] [*France*]

InIBHM .... President Benjamin Harrison Memorial Home, Indianapolis, IN [*Library symbol Library of Congress*] (LCLS)

InIBHP .... Barnes, Hickam, Pantzer & Boyd, Law Library, Indianapolis, IN [*Library symbol Library of Congress*] (LCLS)

InIBio........... Bio-Dynamics, Inc., BMC Library, Indianapolis, IN [*Library symbol Library of Congress*] (LCLS)

InIB-P .... Butler University, College of Pharmacy, Indianapolis, IN [*Library symbol Library of Congress*] (LCLS)

InIBr............ Everett I. Brown Co., Indianapolis, IN [*Library symbol*] [*Library of Congress*] (LCLS)

INIC .... Ideal Current Negative Immittance Converter

InIC .... Indianapolis Commercial, Indianapolis, IN [*Library symbol Library of Congress*] (LCLS)

INIC .... Inverse Negative Impedance Converter (IAA)

InICC........... Indiana Central University, Indianapolis, IN [*Library symbol Library of Congress*] (LCLS)

INICE .... Inexpensive In-Circuit Emulator (NITA)

InICM........... Children's Museum of Indianapolis, Indianapolis, IN [*Library symbol Library of Congress*] (LCLS)

INICR .... Institute for Childhood Resources (EA)

InID............. General Motors Corp., Detroit Diesel Allison Division, Plant 8 Library, Indianapolis, IN [*Library symbol Library of Congress*] (LCLS)

INID .... Institutul National de Informare si Documentare [*National Institute for Information and Documentation*] [*National Council for Science and Technology*] [*Information service or system*] (IID)

INID/NOD ..... Immediate Network-In Dial/Network-Out Dial (DNAB)

InIDow .... DOWELANCO, Indianapolis, IN [*Library symbol*] [*Library of Congress*] (LCLS)

InIFHi........... Franklin Township Historical Society, Indianapolis, IN [*Library symbol Library of Congress*] (LCLS)

INIG .... International Nutritional Immunology Group (EA)

InIGS .... Church of Jesus Christ of Latter-Day Saints, Genealogical Society Library, Indianapolis Branch, Indianapolis, IN [*Library symbol Library of Congress*] (LCLS)

InIH .... Hudson Institute, Indiannapolis, IN [*Library symbol*] [*Library of Congress*] (LCLS)

InII .... Indiana Cooperative Library Service Authority (INCOLSA), Indianapolis, IN [*Library symbol Library of Congress*] (LCLS)

InIIY............ Indiana Youth Institute, Indianapolis, IN [*Library symbol*] [*Library of Congress*] (LCLS)

InIJ .... Herron School of Art, Indianapolis, IN [*Library symbol Library of Congress*] (LCLS)

InIL .... Eli Lilly & Co., Scientific Library, Indianapolis, IN [*Library symbol Library of Congress*] (LCLS)

InILB .... Eli Lilly & Co., Business Library, Indianapolis, IN [*Library symbol Library of Congress*] (LCLS)

InILL .... Eli Lilly & Co., Law Library, Indianapolis, IN [*Library symbol*] [*Library of Congress*] (LCLS)

InILS .... Indianapolis Law School, Indianapolis, IN [*Library symbol Library of Congress*] (LCLS)

InIM............ Marian College, Indianapolis, IN [*Library symbol Library of Congress*] (LCLS)

InIMa .... Indiana Masonic Library and Museum, Indianapolis, IN [*Library symbol*] [*Library of Congress*] (LCLS)

InIMu .... Indianapolis Museum of Art, Reference Library, Indianapolis, IN [*Library symbol Library of Congress*] (LCLS)

ININ............ InStent Inc. [*NASDAQ symbol*] (TTSB)

IN INIT......... In Initio [*In the Beginning*] [*Latin*]

INIP............ Institute of Non-Numerical Information Processing [*Switzerland*] [*Information service or system*] (IID)

InIPE........... Indiana University - Purdue University at Indianapolis, School of Physical Education, Indianapolis, IN [*Library symbol Library of Congress*] (LCLS)

InIR .... James Whitcomb Riley Home, Indianapolis, IN [*Library symbol Library of Congress*] (LCLS)

InIRCA .... RCA, Selectavision Video Disc Operations Library, Indianapolis, IN [*Library symbol Library of Congress*] (LCLS)

INIS .... International Nuclear Information System [*International Atomic Energy Agency*] (IID)

INIS .... Internation Nuclear Information Service [*International Atomic Energy Authority*] (NITA)

INIS ATOMINDEX... International Nuclear Information System [*International Atomic Energy Agency*] [*Vienna, Austria Bibliographic database*]

InISC........... Indiana Supreme Court Law Library, Indianapolis, IN [*Library symbol*] [*Library of Congress*] (LCLS)

InISIN .... Sigma Theta Tau International Nursing Library, Indianapolis, IN [*Library symbol*] [*Library of Congress*] (LCLS)

INIST .... Institute de l'Information Scientifique et Technique [*Institute of Scientific and Technical Information*] [*Information service or system*] (IID)

INISWF .... Indian National Iron and Steel Workers' Federation

InIT .... Christian Theological Seminary, Indianapolis, IN [*Library symbol Library of Congress*] (LCLS)

INIT............ Initial (AFM)

INIT............ Initial

INIT............ Initialization (KSC)

INIT............ Initial Training [*Aviation*] (FAAC)

INIT............ Initiate (NASA)

INIT............ Initiation (MSA)

INIT............ Initio [*In the Beginning*] [*Latin*] (ROG)

INIT & REF... Initiative and Referendum [*Legal term*] (DLA)

INITCCA ...... Initial Cash Clothing Allowance [*Military*] (DNAB)

INITCCCA ... Initial Civilian Cash Clothing Allowance [*Military*] (DNAB)

Initio........... Initio, Inc. [*Associated Press*] (SAG)

INITUNIFALW... Initial Uniform Allowance [*Military*]

InIU .... Indiana University - Purdue University at Indianapolis, Downtown Campus, Indianapolis, IN [*Library symbol Library of Congress*] (LCLS)

InIU-L .... Indiana University - Purdue University at Indianapolis, School of Law, Indianapolis, IN [*Library symbol Library of Congress*] (LCLS)

InIWis.......... Wishard Memorial Hospital, Indianapolis, IN [*Library symbol Library of Congress*] (LCLS)

InIZ .... Indianapolis, Zoological Society, Inc., Indianapolis, IN [*Library symbol*] [*Library of Congress*] (LCLS)

INJ.............. Inject

INJ.............. Injectio [*An Injection*] [*Pharmacy*]

INJ.............. Injector (KSC)

Inj............... Injunction [*Legal term*]

INJ.............. Injure (AABC)

INJ.............. Injury (CPH)

INJ.............. In Nomine Jesu [*In the Name of Jesus*] [*Latin*]

INJ.............. Interjet [*Greece*] [*FAA designator*] (FAAC)

INJ.............. International North American Resources, Inc. [*Vancouver Stock Exchange symbol*]

InJ .... Jasper Public Library, Jasper, IN [*Library symbol Library of Congress*] (LCLS)

InJa .... Jasonville Public Library, Jasonville, IN [*Library symbol*] [*Library of Congress*] (LCLS)

InJaL .... Jasonville Leader, Jasonville, IN [*Library symbol Library of Congress*] (LCLS)

InJamP .... Jamestown Press, Jamestown, IN [*Library symbol Library of Congress*] (LCLS)

INJCT.......... Injunction [*Legal term*]

INJCTN .... Injection

InJDHi .... Dubois County Historical Society, Jasper, IN [*Library symbol Library of Congress*] (LCLS)

InJe .... Jeffersonville Township Public Library, Jeffersonville, IN [*Library symbol Library of Congress*] (LCLS)

INJECT........ Injection [*Medicine*]

INJ ENEM .... Injiciatur Enema [*Let an Enema Be Injected*] [*Pharmacy*]

INJFACS ...... Injection Facilities (DNAB)

InJH .... Jasper Herald, Jasper, IN [*Library symbol Library of Congress*] (LCLS)

INJ HYP....... Injectio Hypodermica [*Hypodermic Injection*] [*Pharmacy*]

INJIC.......... Injiciatur [*Let It Be Given*] [*Pharmacy*] (ROG)

INJICIAT ...... Injiciatur [*Let It Be Given*] [*Pharmacy*] (ROG)

INJN........... Injunction [*Legal term*] (ROG)

InJo .... Jonesboro Public Library, Jonesboro, IN [*Library symbol Library of Congress*] (LCLS)

INJON .... Injunction [*Legal term*] (ROG)

INK............. International Coast Minerals Corp. [*Vancouver Stock Exchange symbol*]

INK............. Inuvik [*Northwest Territories*] [*Seismograph station code, US Geological Survey*] (SEIS)
INK............. Kentair (International) Ltd. [*British ICAO designator*] (FAAC)
INK............. Wink, TX [*Location identifier FAA*] (FAAL)
INKA........... Informationssystem Karlsruhe [*Karlsruhe Information System*] [*Information service or system Germany*]
INKA-CONF... Informationssystem Karlsruhe - Conference [*Database*]
INKA-CORP... Informationssystem Karlsruhe - Corporates in Energy [*Database*] [*Defunct*]
INKA-DATACOMP... Informationssystem Karlsruhe - Data Compilations in Energy and Physics [*Database*]
INKA-MATH... Informationssystem Karlsruhe - Mathematics [*Database*]
INKA-MATHDI... Informationssystem Karlsruhe - Mathematical Education [*Database*]
INKA-NUCLEAR... INKA Nuclear Science and Technology [*Database*] (NITA)
INKA-NUCLEAR PART INIS... Informationssystem Karlsruhe - Nuclear Database Part: International Nuclear Information System [*Database*]
INKA-NUCLEAR PART KKK... Informationssystem Karlsruhe - Nuclear Database Part: Conference Papers: NuclearResearch, Nuclear Technology [*Database*]
INKA-NUCLEAR PART NSA... Informationssystem Karlsruhe - Nuclear Database Part: Nuclear Science Abstracts [*Database*]
INKA-PHYS... Informationssystem Karlsruhe - Physics [*Database*]
InKend........ Kendallville Public Library, Kendallville, IN [*Library symbol Library of Congress*] (LCLS)
InKendNS... Kendallville News-Sun, Kendallville, IN [*Library symbol Library of Congress*] (LCLS)
InKent........ Kentland Public Library, Kentland, IN [*Library symbol Library of Congress*] (LCLS)
InKentCR..... Newton County Recorder's Office, Kentland, IN [*Library symbol Library of Congress*] (LCLS)
InKentE....... Newton County Enterprise, Kentland, IN [*Library symbol Library of Congress*] (LCLS)
InKew .... Kewanna Public Library, Kewanna, IN [*Library symbol Library of Congress*] (LCLS)
InKewO....... Kewanna Observer, Kewanna, IN [*Library symbol Library of Congress*] (LCLS)
InKir........... Kirklin Public Library, Kirklin, IN [*Library symbol Library of Congress*] (LCLS)
InKni.......... Knightstown Public Library, Knightstown, IN [*Library symbol Library of Congress*] (LCLS)
InKniB........ Knightstown Banner, Knightstown, IN [*Library symbol Library of Congress*] (LCLS)
InKno......... Henry F. Schricker Library, Knox, IN [*Library symbol Library of Congress*] (LCLS)
InKnoCHi.... Starke County Historical Museum, Knox, IN [*Library symbol Library of Congress*] (LCLS)
InKnoCR ..... Starke County Recorder's Office, Knox, IN [*Library symbol Library of Congress*] (LCLS)
InKo.......... Kokomo Public Library, Kokomo, IN [*Library symbol Library of Congress*] (LCLS)
InKoC......... Cabot Corp., Stellite Division, Kokomo, IN [*Library symbol Library of Congress*] (LCLS)
InKoT......... Kokomo Tribune, Kokomo, IN [*Library symbol Library of Congress*] (LCLS)
InKouT....... Kouts Times, Kouts, IN [*Library symbol Library of Congress*] (LCLS)
INL............. Inland Natural Gas Co. Ltd. [*Toronto Stock Exchange symbol Vancouver Stock Exchange symbol*]
inl............... Inlay (MAE)
inl............... Inlay (VRA)
INL............. Inlet (KSC)
INL............. Inner Nuclear Layer
INL............. Internal Noise Level (IEEE)
INL............. International Falls [*Minnesota*] [*Airport symbol*] (OAG)
INL............. International Falls, MN [*Location identifier FAA*] (FAAL)
INL............. Internodal Link (ACRL)
INL............. Morgan Intertrades Ltd. [*Nigeria*] [*FAA designator*] (FAAC)
InL............. tippecanoe County Public Library, Lafayette, IN [*Library symbol*] [*Library of Congress*] (LCLS)
InL............. Wells Memorial Library, Lafayette, IN [*Library symbol Library of Congress*] (LCLS)
INLA........... International Nuclear Law Association [*See also AIDN*] [*Brussels, Belgium*] (EAIO)
INLA........... Iowa Nursery and Landscape Association (SRA)
INLA........... Irish National Liberation Army
InLacN .... Lacrosse Regional News, La Crosse, IN [*Library symbol Library of Congress*] (LCLS)
InLad .... Ladoga-Clark Township Public Library, Ladoga, IN [*Library symbol Library of Congress*] (LCLS)
InLag .... LaGrange County Library, LaGrange, IN [*Library symbol Library of Congress*] (LCLS)
InLagHi....... LaGrange County Historical Society, LaGrange, IN [*Library symbol Library of Congress*] (LCLS)
InLagNS...... LaGrange News and Standard, LaGrange, IN [*Library symbol*] [*Library of Congress*] (LCLS)
INLAN .... Instant Language [*Trademark*] [*Computer science*]
InLap .... La Porte Public Library, La Porte, IN [*Library symbol Library of Congress*] (LCLS)
InLapHA...... LaPorte Herald-Argus, LaPorte, IN [*Library symbol Library of Congress*] (LCLS)
InLapHi....... LaPorte County Historical Society, LaPorte, IN [*Library symbol Library of Congress*] (LCLS)
InLaR......... Lapel Review, Lapel, IN [*Library symbol Library of Congress*] (LCLS)
InLasH........ Hygiene Institute, La Salle, IN [*Library symbol Library of Congress*] (LCLS)

INLAW .... Infantry LASER Weapon (MCD)
InLaw.......... Lawrenceburg Public Library, Lawrenceburg, IN [*Library symbol Library of Congress*] (LCLS)
InLawCR...... Dearborn County Recorder's Office, Lawrenceburg, IN [*Library symbol Library of Congress*] (LCLS)
IN/LB .... Inches per Pound
IN-LB .... Inch-Pound
In-LB........... Indiana Legislative Council, State House, Indianapolis, IN [*Library symbol Library of Congress*] (LCLS)
INLC........... Initial Launch Capability (IEEE)
InLcLM .... Lincoln Boyhood National Memorial, Lincoln City, IN [*Library symbol Library of Congress*] (LCLS)
INLD .... Inland Casino [*NASDAQ symbol*] (TTSB)
INLD .... Inland Casino Corp. [*NASDAQ symbol*] (SAG)
InldCas .... Inland Casino Corp. [*Associated Press*] (SAG)
InldRs .... Inland Resources [*Associated Press*] (SAG)
InldStI.......... Inland Steel Industries, Inc. [*Associated Press*] (SAG)
INLE .... Instituto Nacional del Libro Espanol
InLeb .... Lebanon Public Library, Lebanon, IN [*Library symbol Library of Congress*] (LCLS)
InLebCR...... Boone County Recorder's Office, Lebanon, IN [*Library symbol Library of Congress*] (LCLS)
InLebR........ Lebanon Reporter, Lebanon, IN [*Library symbol Library of Congress*] (LCLS)
INLET.......... Inlet [*Commonly used*] (OPSA)
InLib .... Union County Public Library, Liberty, IN [*Library symbol Library of Congress*] (LCLS)
InLibCN...... College Corner News, Liberty, IN [*Library symbol Library of Congress*] (LCLS)
InLibH........ Liberty Herald, Liberty, IN [*Library symbol Library of Congress*] (LCLS)
INLICA .... Indiana Land Improvement Contractors Association (SRA)
InLigAL....... Ligonier Advance-Leader, Ligonier, IN [*Library symbol Library of Congress*] (LCLS)
IN LIM .... In Limine [*At the Outset*] [*Latin*]
InLind .... Linden Public Library, Linden, IN [*Library symbol Library of Congress*] (LCLS)
INLINON ..... Interlineation (ROG)
InLint.......... Linton Public Library, Linton, IN [*Library symbol Library of Congress*] (LCLS)
InLintC........ Linton Daily Citizen, Linton, IN [*Library symbol Library of Congress*] (LCLS)
IN LITT .... In Litteris [*In Correspondence*] [*Latin*]
InLJC.......... Lafayette Journal and Courier, Lafayette, IN [*Library symbol Library of Congress*] (LCLS)
INLN .... Inland Resources [*NASDAQ symbol*] (SAG)
INLND......... Inland
INLO .... In Lieu Of
IN LOC........ In Loco [*In the Place Of*] [*Latin*]
IN LOC CIT.. In Loco Citato [*In the Place Mentioned*] [*Latin*] (ROG)
InLog .... Logansport-Cass County Public Library, Logansport, IN [*Library symbol Library of Congress*] (LCLS)
InLogCHi..... Cass County Historical Society Museum Library, Logansport, IN [*Library symbol Library of Congress*] (LCLS)
INLOGOV .... Institute of Local Government [*University of Birmingham*] [*British*] (AIE)
INLOGOV .... Institute of Local Government Studies [*British*]
InLogPT ...... Pharos-Tribune, Logansport, IN [*Library symbol Library of Congress*] (LCLS)
InLoo .... Frances L. Folks Memorial Library (Loogootee Public Library), Loogootee, IN [*Library symbol Library of Congress*] (LCLS)
InLooT .... Loogootee Tribune, Loogootee, IN [*Library symbol Library of Congress*] (LCLS)
InLow .... Lowell Public Library, Lowell, IN [*Library symbol Library of Congress*] (LCLS)
InLowT........ Lowell Tribune, Lowell, IN [*Library symbol Library of Congress*] (LCLS)
INLP.......... Integer Non-Linear Programming [*Computer science*] (PDAA)
InLP .... Purdue University, Lafayette, IN [*Library symbol Library of Congress*] (LCLS)
InLP-Ham .... Purdue University, Calumet Campus, Hammond, IN [*Library symbol Library of Congress Obsolete*] (LCLS)
INLQ .... INTERLING Software Corp. [*NASDAQ symbol*] (SAG)
INLQ .... Interlinq Software [*NASDAQ symbol*] (SAG)
INLQ .... INTERLINQ Software [*NASDAQ symbol*] (TTSB)
INLR .... Item No Longer Required
INLS.......... Individualized Learning System (DNAB)
InLS .... Lafayette Schools System, Lafayette, IN [*Library symbol Library of Congress*] (LCLS)
InLSEH....... St. Elizabeth Hospital Medical Center, Bannon Health Science Library, Lafayette, IN [*Library symbol*] [*Library of Congress*] (LCLS)
INLT.......... Inlet [*Board on Geographic Names*] (MCD)
INLT.......... Inlet
InLTHi......... Tippecanoe County Historical Association, Lafayette, IN [*Library symbol Library of Congress*] (LCLS)
InLv .... Lake Village Library, Lake Village, IN [*Library symbol Library of Congress*] (LCLS)
InLy .... Washington Township Public Library, Lynn, IN [*Library symbol Library of Congress*] (LCLS)
INM .... Imbokodvo National Movement [*Swaziland*] [*Political party*] (PPW)
INM .... Informed Notaries of Maine (SRA)
INM.......... Innamincka [*South Australia*] [*Airport symbol*] (AD)
INM.......... Inspector of Naval Machinery
INM.......... Inspector of Naval Material

INM............ Institute of Naval Medicine [*British*] (DMA)

INM............ Integrated Network Management [*for Companies*]

INM............ Interception Mission [*Air Force*]

INM............ International Narcotics Matters [*Department of State*]

INM............ International Nautical Mile

INM............ International Nuclear Model [*Department of Energy*] (GFGA)

INM............ Istel Network Monitoring System (NITA)

INMA.......... International Newspaper Marketing Association (EA)

Inmac......... Inmac Corp. [*Associated Press*] (SAG)

INMAC........ Instant Mini/Micro Computer Accessories and Cables [*Manufacturer/distributor*] [*British*] (NITA)

InMad......... Madison-Jefferson County Public Library, Madison, IN [*Library symbol Library of Congress*] (LCLS)

InMadC....... Madison Daily Courier, Madison, IN [*Library symbol Library of Congress*] (LCLS)

INMAP........ Independent Microelectronics Applications [*British*] (NITA)

InMar......... Marion Public Library, Marion, IN [*Library symbol Library of Congress*] (LCLS)

InMarC....... Marion College, Marion, IN [*Library symbol Library of Congress*] (LCLS)

InMarCT..... Marion Chronicle Tribune, Marion, IN [*Library symbol Library of Congress*] (LCLS)

InMarGHi.... Grant County Historical Society, Marion, IN [*Library symbol Library of Congress*] (LCLS)

INMARSAT.. International Maritime Satellite [*Satellite communications organization*] (NITA)

INMARSAT.. International Maritime Satellite Organization

InMart........ Morgan County Public Library, Martinsville, IN [*Library symbol Library of Congress*] (LCLS)

InMarV....... United States Veterans Administration Hospital, Marion, IN [*Library symbol Library of Congress*] (LCLS)

InMat......... Matthews Public Library, Matthews, IN [*Library symbol Library of Congress*] (LCLS)

INMC.......... Inmac Corp. [*NASDAQ symbol*] (NQ)

INMC.......... International Network Management Center [*Telecommunications*] (TEL)

INMD.......... IntegraMed America, Inc. [*NASDAQ symbol*] (SAG)

InMe.......... Bell Memorial Public Library, Mentone, IN [*Library symbol Library of Congress*] (LCLS)

INMED........ Indians into Medicine (EA)

InMelRP...... Richland Press, Mellott, IN [*Library symbol Library of Congress*] (LCLS)

IN MEM....... In Memoriam [*In Memory Of*] [*Latin*] (ROG)

INMEP........ Institute for a New Middle East Policy (EA)

InMerL....... Lake County Public Library, Merrillville, IN [*Library symbol Library of Congress*] (LCLS)

INMETRO.... Instituto Nacional de Metrologia, Normalizacao e Qualidade Industrial [*Government advisory body*] [*Brazil*] (EY)

INMHC........ International Network for Mutual Help Centers (EA)

INMHO........ In My Humble Opinion (BARN)

INMI.......... Institute of Microbiology (of the Academy of Sciences, USSR)

InMic......... Michigan City Public Library, Michigan City, IN [*Library symbol Library of Congress*] (LCLS)

InMicLM..... Old Lighthouse Museum, Michigan City, IN [*Library symbol Library of Congress*] (LCLS)

InMicND..... Michigan City News-Dispatch, Michigan City, IN [*Library symbol Library of Congress*] (LCLS)

InMid......... Middletown Public Library, Middletown, IN [*Library symbol*] [*Library of Congress*] (LCLS)

InMidb....... Middlebury Public Library, Middlebury, IN [*Library symbol Library of Congress*] (LCLS)

InMidbI...... Middlebury Independent, Middlebury, IN [*Library symbol Library of Congress*] (LCLS)

InMidN....... Middletown News, Middletown, IN [*Library symbol Library of Congress*] (LCLS)

InMil......... Milford Public Library, Milford, IN [*Library symbol Library of Congress*] (LCLS)

InMilMJ...... Milford Mail-Journal, Millford, IN [*Library symbol Library of Congress*] (LCLS)

InMis......... Mishawaka Public Library, Mishawaka, IN [*Library symbol Library of Congress*] (LCLS)

InMisB....... Bethel College, Mishawaka, IN [*Library symbol Library of Congress*] (LCLS)

InMisER..... Mishawaka Enterprise-Record, Mishawaka, IN [*Library symbol Library of Congress*] (LCLS)

InMit......... Mitchell Community Public Library, Mitchell, IN [*Library symbol Library of Congress*] (LCLS)

InmkEnt...... Inmark Enterprises, Inc. [*Associated Press*] (SAG)

INMM.......... Institute of Nuclear Materials Management (EA)

InMon........ Monon Town and Township Library, Monon, IN [*Library symbol Library of Congress*] (LCLS)

InMonN...... Monon News, Monon, IN [*Library symbol Library of Congress*] (LCLS)

InMont....... Monterrey-Tippecanoe Township Public Library Monterrey, IN [*Library symbol Library of Congress*] (LCLS)

InMoo........ Mooresville Public Library, Mooresville, IN [*Library symbol*] [*Library of Congress*] (LCLS)

InMop........ Montpelier Public Library, Montpelier, IN [*Library symbol Library of Congress*] (LCLS)

InMopH....... Montpelier Herald, Montpelier, IN [*Library symbol Library of Congress*] (LCLS)

InMotc....... Monticello Union Township Public Library, Monticello, IN [*Library symbol Library of Congress*] (LCLS)

InMotz........ Montezuma Public Library, Montezuma, IN [*Library symbol Library of Congress*] (LCLS)

INMR.......... Insider Network Market Report [*Information service or system*] (IID)

INMR.......... Instrumentarium Corp. [*NASDAQ symbol*] (NQ)

INMRY........ Instrumentarium 'B' ADR [*NASDAQ symbol*] (TTSB)

INMS.......... Integrated Network Management System [*Telecommunications*] (ACRL)

INMT.......... Intermet Corp. [*NASDAQ symbol*] (NQ)

InMtv......... Alexandrian Free Public Library, Mount Vernon, IN [*Library symbol Library of Congress*] (LCLS)

INMU.......... Inertial Navigation Measurement Unit (MCD)

InMu.......... Muncie Public Library, Muncie, IN [*Library symbol Library of Congress*] (LCLS)

InMuB........ Ball State University, Muncie, IN [*Library symbol Library of Congress*] (LCLS)

InMuMC...... Minnetrista Cultural Center, Muncie, IN [*Library symbol*] [*Library of Congress*] (LCLS)

InMuP........ Muncie Evening Press, Muncie, IN [*Library symbol Library of Congress*] (LCLS)

InMuSP...... Muncie Morning Star-Evening Press, Muncie, IN [*Library symbol Library of Congress*] (LCLS)

INMWF....... Indian National Mine Workers' Federation

INN............ ImagiNation Network [*Entertainment*]

INN............ Independent Network News [*Television*]

INN............ Inning (WGA)

INN............ Innsbruck [*Austria*] [*Airport symbol*] (OAG)

INN............ Innsbruck [*Austria*] [*Seismograph station code, US Geological Survey Closed*] (SEIS)

INN............ Intermediate Network Node (IAA)

INN............ International Nonproprietary Names [*World Health Organization*]

INN............ Minneapolis, MN [*Location identifier FAA*] (FAAL)

INN............ New Albany-Floyd County Public Library, New Albany, IN [*OCLC symbol*] (OCLC)

INNA.......... International Newsreel and News Film Association [*Belgium*] (EAIO)

InNap......... Nappanee Public Library, Nappanee, IN [*Library symbol Library of Congress*] (LCLS)

InNapAN..... Nappanee Advance News, Nappanee, IN [*Library symbol Library of Congress*] (LCLS)

InNas......... Brown County Public Library, Nashville, IN [*Library symbol Library of Congress*] (LCLS)

InNasBHi.... Brown County Historical Society, Nashville, IN [*Library symbol Library of Congress*] (LCLS)

InNasCR..... Brown County Recorder's Office, Nashville, IN [*Library symbol Library of Congress*] (LCLS)

InNasD........ Brown County Democrat, Nashville, IN [*Library symbol Library of Congress*] (LCLS)

InNcar........ New Carlisle and Olive Township Public Library, New Carlisle, IN [*Library symbol Library of Congress*] (LCLS)

InNcas........ New Castle - Henry County Public Library, New Castle, IN [*Library symbol Library of Congress*] (LCLS)

InNcasCT.... New Castle Courier Times, New Castle, IN [*Library symbol Library of Congress*] (LCLS)

InNcasHi..... Henry County Historical Society, Reference Room, New Castle, IN [*Library symbol Library of Congress*] (LCLS)

InNcasNR.... Henry County News-Republican, New Castle, IN [*Library symbol Library of Congress*] (LCLS)

INNCNT........ Innocent

InNd........... University of Notre Dame, Notre Dame, IN [*Library symbol Library of Congress*] (LCLS)

InNd-L........ University of Notre Dame, Law School, Notre Dame, IN [*Library symbol Library of Congress*] (LCLS)

InNd-LS...... University of Notre Dame, Life Sciences Research Library, Notre Dame, IN [*Library symbol Library of Congress*] (LCLS)

InNdS......... Saint Mary's College, Notre Dame, IN [*Library symbol Library of Congress*] (LCLS)

InNea......... New Albany-Floyd County Public Library, New Albany, IN [*Library symbol Library of Congress*] (LCLS)

Inn Eas...... Innes on Easements [*8th ed.*] [*1911*] [*A publication*] (DLA)

Inn Ease..... Innes on Easements [*8th ed.*] [*1911*] [*A publication*] (DLA)

InNeaTL...... New Albany Tribune and Ledger-Tribune, New Albany, IN [*Library symbol Library of Congress*] (LCLS)

InNeb......... Newburgh-Ohio Township Public Library, Newburgh, IN [*Library symbol Library of Congress*] (LCLS)

InNep......... Newport-Vermillion County Library, Newport, IN [*Library symbol Library of Congress*] (LCLS)

Innerdyn...... Innerdyne, Inc. [*Associated Press*] (SAG)

INNERTAP.... Information Network on New and Renewable Energy Resources and Technologies for Asia and the Pacific [*UNESCO*] (DUND)

INNERV....... Innervation [*Medicine*]

Innes......... Innes' Registration of Title [*A publication*] (ILCA)

INNF.......... Intermediate Naval Nuclear Forces (DOMA)

InNhvAT...... Allen County Times, New Haven, IN [*Library symbol Library of Congress*] (LCLS)

InNhW........ Workingmen's Institute, New Harmony, IN [*Library symbol*] [*Library of Congress*] (LCLS)

Innisfail Canegr... Innisfail Canegrower [*A publication*]

Innkeepr...... Innkeepers USA Trust [*Associated Press*] (SAG)

INNKPR........ Innkeeper

INNL.......... Improved Nonnuclear LANCE

INNO.......... Innocente [*Innocently*] [*Music*] (ROG)

Inno.......... Innovations [*Record label*]

INNO.......... Innovo Group [*NASDAQ symbol*] (TTSB)

INNO.......... Innovo Group, Inc. [*NASDAQ symbol*] (SAG)

InNob......... Noblesville Public Library, Noblesville, IN [*Library symbol Library of Congress*] (LCLS)

InNobL........ Noblesville Daily Ledger, Noblesville, IN [*Library symbol Library of Congress*] (LCLS)

Innodata ...... Innodata Corp. [*Associated Press*] (SAG)
InnoDev ...... Innovasive Devices, Inc. [*Associated Press*] (SAG)
InNoj .... North Judson-Wayne Township Public Library, North Judson, IN [*Library symbol Library of Congress*] (LCLS)
InnoM .... Innovative Medical Services [*Associated Press*] (SAG)
InNom .... North Manchester Public Library, North Manchester, IN [*Library symbol*] [*Library of Congress*] (LCLS)
InNoman ...... North Manchester Public Library, North Manchester, IN [*Library symbol Library of Congress*] (LCLS)
InNomanC .... Manchester College, North Manchester, IN [*Library symbol Library of Congress*] (LCLS)
InNomanNJ .. North Manchester News-Journal, North Manchester, IN [*Library symbol Library of Congress*] (LCLS)
InnoMed ...... Innovative Medical Services [*Associated Press*] (SAG)
InNomMC ..... Manchester College, North Manchester, IN [*Library symbol*] [*Library of Congress*] (LCLS)
InnoPet .... InnoPet Brands Corp. [*Associated Press*] (SAG)
InnoServe .... InnoServe Technologies, Inc. [*Associated Press*] (SAG)
Innotech ...... Innotech, Inc. [*Associated Press*] (SAG)
Innovex .... Innovex, Inc. [*Associated Press*] (SAG)
InnovirL .... Innovir Laboratories, Inc. [*Associated Press*] (SAG)
InNovJ .... Jennings County Public Library, North Vernon, IN [*Library symbol Library of Congress*] (LCLS)
Innovo .... Innovo Group, Inc. [*Associated Press*] (SAG)
InNovSP ...... North Vernon Sun-Plain Dealer, North Vernon, IN [*Library symbol*] [*Library of Congress*] (LCLS)
InnovT .... Innovative Tech Systems, Inc. [*Associated Press*] (SAG)
InnoVTch ..... Innovative Tech Systems, Inc. [*Associated Press*] (SAG)
Innovus .... Innovus Corp. [*Associated Press*] (SAG)
INNR .... Inner
INNS .... International Neural Network Society (EA)
Inn Sc Leg Ant ... Innes' Scotch Legal Antiquities [*A publication*] (DLA)
Innvr .... Innovir Laboratories, Inc. [*Associated Press*] (SAG)
INNVTN .... Innovation
INNVTV .... Innovative
INO .... Inongo [*Zaire*] [*Airport symbol*] (OAG)
Ino .... Inosine [*Also, I*] [*A nucleoside*]
INO .... Inosine (DMAA)
INO .... Inspector of Naval Ordnance [*British*]
INO .... Institute for Naval Oceanography [*Bay St. Louis, MS*] [*Navy*]
INO .... Internuclear Ophthalmoplegia
INO .... Inter-Oceanic Resources Ltd. [*Formerly, Inter-Oceanic Oil & Gas*] [*Vancouver Stock Exchange symbol*]
INO .... Intranuclear Ophthalmolplegia [*Ophthalmology*] (DAVI)
INO .... Irish Nurses Organisation (BI)
INO .... Issue Necessary Orders
INO .... Item Number
INO .... Iterative Natural Orbital [*Atomic physics*]
INO .... Northbrook Public Library, Northbrook, IL [*OCLC symbol*] (OCLC)
INOA .... International Norton Owners' Association (EA)
INOAVNOT ... If Not Available Notify This Office at Once
INOC .... Inoculation (AABC)
INOC .... Iraqi National Oil Co. [*Government company*]
INOC .... Isonicotinoyloxycarbonyl [*Medicine*] (DMAA)
InOcC .... Oakland City College, Oakland City, IN [*Library symbol Library of Congress*] (LCLS)
INOD .... Innodata Corp. [*NASDAQ symbol*] (SAG)
InOd .... Odon Winkelpeck Memorial Library, Odon, IN [*Library symbol Library of Congress*] (LCLS)
INODC .... Indian National Oceanographic Data Centre [*Information service or system*] (IID)
INODEP .... Institut Oecumenique pour le Developpement des Peuples [*Ecumenical Institute for the Development of Peoples*] [*Paris, France*] (EAIO)
InOdJ .... Odon Journal, Odon, IN [*Library symbol Library of Congress*] (LCLS)
Inodta .... Innodata Corp. [*Associated Press*] (SAG)
INODW .... Innodata Corp.Wrrt [*NASDAQ symbol*] (TTSB)
INOE .... Internacia Naturista Organizo Esperantista [*International Esperantist Organization of Naturists - IEON*] (EAIO)
IN OEDIB ..... In Oedibus [*In the House Of*] [*Latin*] (ROG)
INOF .... If Not Off (FAAC)
INok .... Nokomis Public Library, Nokomis, IL [*Library symbol Library of Congress*] (LCLS)
INokSD .... Nokomis Community Unit, School District 22, Nokomis, IL [*Library symbol Library of Congress*] (LCLS)
INol .... Northlake Public Library District, Northlake, IL [*Library symbol Library of Congress*] (LCLS)
INOP .... Inoperative
InOr .... Orleans Public Library, Orleans, IN [*Library symbol Library of Congress*] (LCLS)
INORG .... Inorganic
Inorg phos .. Inorganic Phosphorus [*Medicine*] (MEDA)
InOrPE .... Orleans Progress-Examiner, Orleans, IN [*Library symbol Library of Congress*] (LCLS)
inor phos .... Inorganic Phosphorus [*Biochemistry*] (DAVI)
INOS .... Isoform of Nitric Oxide Synthase [*An enzyme*]
INOSHAC .... Indian Ocean and Southern Hemisphere Analysis Center (BARN)
InOsJ .... Osgood Journal, Osgood, IN [*Library symbol Library of Congress*] (LCLS)
InOssJ .... Ossian Journal, Ossian, IN [*Library symbol Library of Congress*] (LCLS)
Inotek .... Inotek Technologies, Inc. [*Associated Press*] (SAG)
INOV .... Association Internationale du Nouvel Objet Visuel [*International Association for New Visual Objects*] [*Paris, France*] (EAIO)
InovGme ...... Innovative Gaming Corp. [*Associated Press*] (SAG)

InOw .... Owensville Public Library, Owensville, IN [*Library symbol Library of Congress*] (LCLS)
InOwSE .... Owensville Star-Echo, Owensville, IN [*Library symbol Library of Congress*] (LCLS)
InOx .... Oxford Public Library, Oxford, IN [*Library symbol Library of Congress*] (LCLS)
InOxG .... Oxford Gazette, Oxford, IN [*Library symbol Library of Congress*] (LCLS)
IN-OZ .... Inch-Ounce
INP .... FA Naval del Peru [*ICAO designator*] (FAAC)
INP .... If Not Possible (FAAC)
INP .... Indiana, PA [*Location identifier FAA*] (FAAL)
INP .... Indium Phosphide [*Inorganic chemistry*] (IAA)
INP .... Inert Nitrogen Protection (IEEE)
INP .... Information-Need-Product [*Sales technique*]
INP .... Initial Program Load [*Computer science*]
INP .... In Pace [*In Peace*] [*Latin*]
INP .... Input (MSA)
INP .... Insulator Nose Projection [*Automotive spark plugs*]
INP .... Integrated Network Processor
INP .... Intelligent Network Processor
INP .... International News Photo
INP .... Internet Nodal Processor [*Computer science*] (ACRL)
INP .... Inter-Net Predicts (MCD)
INPA .... International Newspaper Promotion Association (EA)
InPa .... Paoli Public Library, Paoli, IN [*Library symbol Library of Congress*] (LCLS)
INPADOC ..... INKA Patent Documentation (NITA)
INPADOC ..... International Patent Documentation Center [*Information service or system*] (IID)
InPaN .... Paoli News, Paoli, IN [*Library symbol Library of Congress*] (LCLS)
InPaR .... Paoli Republican, Paoli, IN [*Library symbol Library of Congress*] (LCLS)
INPB .... Irish National Pipe Band
INPBM .... Information Not Provided by Manufacturer
INPC .... Irish National Petroleum Corp.
INPC .... Irish National Productivity Committee (BI)
INPC .... Isopropyl Phenylcarbamate [*Also, IPC, IPPC*] [*Herbicide*]
InPen .... Pendleton and Fall Creek Township Public Library, Pendleton, IN [*Library symbol Library of Congress*] (LCLS)
InPenT .... Pendleton Times, Pendleton, IN [*Library symbol Library of Congress*] (LCLS)
InPer .... Peru and Miami County Public Library, Peru, IN [*Library symbol Library of Congress*] (LCLS)
InPerM .... Miami County Historical Museum, Peru, IN [*Library symbol Library of Congress*] (LCLS)
InPerT .... Peru Tribune, Peru, IN [*Library symbol Library of Congress*] (LCLS)
InPet .... Barrett Memorial Library, Petersburg, IN [*Library symbol Library of Congress*] (LCLS)
InPetPD .... Petersburg Press-Dispatch, Petersburg, IN [*Library symbol Library of Congress*] (LCLS)
INPEX .... International Postage Stamp Exhibition
INPFC .... International North Pacific Fisheries Commission (EA)
INPFC-US .... International North Pacific Fisheries Commission, United States Section
INPFL .... Independent National Patriotic Front of Liberia [*Political party*] (EY)
IN PH .... Indian Pharmacopoeia [*A publication*] (ROG)
INPH .... Interphase Corp. [*NASDAQ symbol*] (SAG)
INPH .... Interphone
INPH .... Iproniazid Phosphate [*Organic chemistry*]
InPHO .... Information Network for Public Health Officials [*CDC*]
InPHO .... International Photographic Historical Organization (EA)
Inphynet ...... Inphynet Medical Management [*Associated Press*] (SAG)
INPI .... Institut National de la Propriete Industrielle [*National Institute for Industrial Property*] [*France Information service or system*] (IID)
InPi .... Pierceton and Washington Township Library, Pierceton, IN [*Library symbol Library of Congress*] (LCLS)
INPI 1 .... INPI Database 1 [*Database on French patents*] (NITA)
INPI 2 .... INPI Database 2 [*Database on European patents*] (NITA)
InPla .... Plainfield Public Library, Plainfield, IN [*Library symbol Library of Congress*] (LCLS)
InPla-Hi .... Plainfield Public Library, Guilford Township and Hendricks County Historical Collection, Plainfield, IN [*Library symbol Library of Congress*] (LCLS)
InPly .... Plymouth Public Library, Plymouth, IN [*Library symbol Library of Congress*] (LCLS)
InPlyHi .... Marshall County Historical Society Library, Plymouth, IN [*Library symbol Library of Congress*] (LCLS)
INPM .... Integrated Network and Premise Management [*MUX Lab*]
INPO .... Institute for Nonprofit Organizations
INPO .... Institute of Nuclear Power Operations (EA)
INPOLSE ...... International Police Services
InPorP .... Portage Press, Portage, IN [*Library symbol Library of Congress*] (LCLS)
InPorS .... Portage Township Schools, Portage, IN [*Library symbol Library of Congress*] (LCLS)
InPosN .... Posey County News, Poseyville, IN [*Library symbol Library of Congress*] (LCLS)
INPOWER .... Independent Power Generation Conference and Exhibition [*British*] (ITD)
IN PR .... In Principio [*In the Beginning*] [*Latin*] (ROG)
INPR .... In Progress
INPR .... Institute for Natural Products Research [*University of Georgia*] [*Research center*] (RCD)
INPr .... Integon Cp $3.875 Cv Pfd [*NYSE symbol*] (TTSB)

InPr............	Princeton Public Library, Princeton, IN [*Library symbol Library of Congress*] (LCLS)
INPRA..........	International Public Relations Association
InPRC.........	Item Name Policy Review Committee [*DoD Washington, DC*] (EGAO)
InPrC	Princeton Daily Clarion, Princeton, IN [*Library symbol Library of Congress*] (LCLS)
INPRIS........	Investment Promotion Information System [*UNIDO*] [*United Nations*] (DUND)
INPRODE	Instituto Profesional para el Desarrollo [*Professional Development Institute*] [*Colombia*]
INPRONS	Information Processing in the Central Nervous System
INPS	Istituto Nazionale della Previdenza Sociale [*Italy*] (ECON)
IN-PT..........	Inpatient [*Medicine*] (DAVI)
INPT...........	In Port [*Navy*] (NVT)
InPtIC..........	Jay County Commercial Review, Portland, IN [*Library symbol Library of Congress*]
InPtICR........	Jay County Recorder's Office, Portland, IN [*Library symbol Library of Congress*] (LCLS)
IN PULM......	In Pulmento [*In Gruel*] [*Pharmacy*]
INPUT.........	Induced Pulse Transient (PDAA)
INPUT.........	International Public Television [*An association*] (NTCM)
InputOut......	Input Output, Inc. [*Associated Press*] (SAG)
INPV	Intermittent Negative-Pressure Ventilation [*Medicine*]
INQ	Index of Nutritional Quality
INQ	Inquire (ECII)
inq	Inquiry (WDMC)
INQ	Inquiry (AFM)
INQ	Intercontinental Venture [*Vancouver Stock Exchange symbol*]
INQ	Interior Nasal Quadrant [*Medicine*] (DMAA)
inq	Query (WDMC)
inq	Question (WDMC)
INQD..........	Inquired (ROG)
INQ PM.......	Inquisitio Post-Mortem [*Latin*] (ROG)
IN QRS	In Quires [*Publishing*] (DGA)
INQSTV.......	Inquisitive
INQT	Inquest (ROG)
INQUA.........	International Union for Quaternary Research [*Research center France*] (IRC)
INQY	Inquiry (ROG)
INR	Bureau of Intelligence and Research [*Department of State*]
INR	Image Navigation and Registration (GAVI)
INR	Impact Noise Rating [*of insulation*]
INR	Inertial Reference (MCD)
INR	Inner (MSA)
INR	Institute of Natural Resources [*University of Georgia*] [*Research center*] (RCD)
INR	Institute of Natural Resources [*Montana State University*] [*Research center*] (RCD)
INR	Institute of Nuclear Research [*Poland*]
INR	Institut National de Radiodiffusion [*Belgium*]
INR	Intelligence and Research (DNAB)
INR	Interaction Resources Ltd. [*Toronto Stock Exchange symbol*]
INR	Inter Air AB [*Sweden ICAO designator*] (FAAC)
INR	Interference-to-Noise Ratio
INR	International Normalized Ratio [*Hematology*]
INR	Morrisson-Reeves Public Library, Richmond, IN [*OCLC symbol*] (OCLC)
INRA	Individual Nonrecurrence Action (SAA)
INRA	Inland Navigational Rules Act of 1980
INRA	Institut National de la Recherche Agronomique (NITA)
INRA	International Network for Religion and Animals (EA)
INRAC.........	Immigration Nursing Relief Advisory Committee [*Department of Labor*] (EGAO)
INRAD.........	Interactive Real-Time Advanced Display
INRC	Indian Nation Restoration Committee
INRC	Innovative Naval Reserve Concept (DOMA)
InRCS	Richmond Community School, Richmond, IN [*Library symbol Library of Congress*] (LCLS)
INRCTN.......	Interaction
InRE...........	Earlham College, Richmond, IN [*Library symbol Library of Congress*] (LCLS)
IN RE..........	In Regard To
IN REF........	In Reference To
INREM.........	Internal REM [*Roentgen-Equivalent-Man*] [*Radiation dose*]
InRem..........	Remington Carpenter Township Public Library, Remington, IN [*Library symbol Library of Congress*] (LCLS)
InRen..........	Jasper County Public Library, Rensselaer, IN [*Library symbol Library of Congress*] (LCLS)
InRenS........	Saint Joseph's College, Rensselaer, IN [*Library symbol Library of Congress*] (LCLS)
INREP	Installation Damage Report [*Air Force*]
INREPL	Incoming Replacement [*Army*] (AABC)
INREQ.........	Information on Request (MCD)
INREQ.........	Information Requested
INREQS.......	Information Requests [*Army*] (AABC)
INRES	Independent Reservation System [*Hotels and motels*]
INRF	International Nutrition Research Foundation (EA)
INRH..........	Institut National de Recherches en Hydrologie [*National Hydrology Research Institute*] [*Canada*]
INRI	Iesus Nazarenus Rex Iudaeorum [*Jesus of Nazareth, King of the Jews*] [*Latin*]
INRI	Imperator Napoleon Rex Italiae [*Emperor Napoleon, King of Italy*] [*Latin*]

INRIA	Institut National de Recherche en Informatique et en Automatique [*National Institute for Research in Informatics and Automation*] [*Research center and database originator*] [*France Information service or system*] (IID)
InRid...........	Ridgeville Public Library, Ridgeville, IN [*Library symbol Library of Congress*] (LCLS)
InRis...........	Ohio County Public Library, Rising Sun, IN [*Library symbol Library of Congress*] (LCLS)
InRisCN	Ohio County News, Rising Sun, IN [*Library symbol Library of Congress*] (LCLS)
InRisCR	Ohio County Recorder's Office, Rising Sun, IN [*Library symbol Library of Congress*] (LCLS)
InRisHi	Ohio County Historical Society, Rising Sun, IN [*Library symbol Library of Congress*] (LCLS)
InRisR	Rising Sun Recorder, Rising Sun, IN [*Library symbol Library of Congress*] (LCLS)
InRM	Morrison-Reeves Public Library, Richmond, IN [*Library symbol Library of Congress*] (LCLS)
InRM	Wayne Township Library, Richmond, IN [*Library symbol*] [*Library of Congress*] (LCLS)
INRO	International Natural Rubber Organization [*Kuala Lumpur, Malaysia*] (EAIO)
INRO	International Naval Research Organization (EA)
InRo...........	Roachdale Public Library, Roachdale, IN [*Library symbol Library of Congress*] (LCLS)
InRoa..........	Roanoke Public Library, Roanoke, IN [*Library symbol Library of Congress*] (LCLS)
InRoc	Fulton County Public Library, Rochester, IN [*Library symbol Library of Congress*] (LCLS)
InRocCR	Fulton County Recorder's Office, Rochester, IN [*Library symbol Library of Congress*] (LCLS)
InRocFHi	Fulton County Historical Society, Rochester, IN [*Library symbol Library of Congress*] (LCLS)
InRocS........	Rochester Sentinel, Rochester, IN [*Library symbol Library of Congress*] (LCLS)
InRomS........	Gene Stratton-Porter Memorial, Rome City, IN [*Library symbol Library of Congress*] (LCLS)
InRoyR........	Royal Center Record, Royal Center, IN [*Library symbol Library of Congress*] (LCLS)
InRPI	Richmond Palladium-Item, Richmond, IN [*Library symbol Library of Congress*] (LCLS)
InRpt..........	Rockport-Ohio Township Public Library, Rockport, IN [*Library symbol Library of Congress*] (LCLS)
InRptD	Rockport Democrat, Rockport, IN [*Library symbol Library of Congress*] (LCLS)
InRptJ..........	Rockport Journal, Rockport, IN [*Library symbol Library of Congress*] (LCLS)
INRS	Institut National de la Recherche Scientifique [*National Institute for Scientific Research*] [*Canada Research center*]
INRS	Intranet Solutions, Inc. [*NASDAQ symbol*] (SAG)
INRT	Inertia (KSC)
INRTFLR	Inert Filler
INRTG.........	Inert Gas
INRTL	Inertial (MSA)
INRTLVEL	Inertial Velocity (MCD)
InRusCR	Rush County Recorder's Office, Rushville, IN [*Library symbol Library of Congress*] (LCLS)
InRusR........	Rushville Republican, Rushville, IN [*Library symbol Library of Congress*] (LCLS)
InRv	Rockville Public Library, Rockville, IN [*Library symbol Library of Congress*] (LCLS)
InRvCR	Parke County Recorder's Office, Rockville, IN [*Library symbol Library of Congress*] (LCLS)
INS	Idiopathic Nephrotic Syndrome
INS	Illinois State University, Normal, IL [*Library symbol Library of Congress*] (LCLS)
INS	Immigration and Naturalization Service [*Department of Justice*]
INS	Improved Navigational Satellite
INS	Improved Night Sight
INS	Inches (EY)
ins	Inches (ODBW)
IN/S	Inches per Second
INS	Independent News Service [*In TV series "The Night Stalker"*]
INS	Indian Springs, NV [*Location identifier FAA*] (FAAL)
INS	Indiopahtic Nephrotic Syndrome [*Nephrology*] (DAVI)
INS	Inelastic Neutron Scattering
INS	Inertial Navigation Sensor (IAA)
INS	Inertial Navigation System [*Aviation*]
INS	Information Network System [*Japan*]
INS	Information Systems (KSC)
INS	Initial Navigation System (AABC)
INS	Inlet Resources Ltd. [*Vancouver Stock Exchange symbol*]
Ins	Inositol [*Biochemistry*]
INS	Inrealistic Neutron Scattering [*Physics*]
INS	Insane (ROG)
INS	Inscribed
ins	Inscriber [*MARC relator code*] [*Library of Congress*] (LCCP)
INS	Inscription (ADA)
INS	Insect
INS.............	Insert (NVT)
INS	Insertion Burn [*Orbital Maneuvering Subsystem 1*] [*NASA*] (NASA)
INS	Insertion Mutation [*Genetics*]
INS	Insert Shot [*Film production*] (NTCM)
INS	Inside (MSA)
INS	In Situ [*In Place*] [*Latin*] (ADA)

Ins	Insolvency [Legal term] (DLA)
INS	Inspection Division [Coast Guard]
INS	Inspector
INS	Installation Squadron
ins	Instant (VRA)
INS	Institute for Naval Studies
INS	Institute for Nuclear Study [Japan]
INS	Institute of Neurological Science [University of Pennsylvania]
INS	Institute of Nuclear Studies [Oak Ridge, TN]
INS	Insular
INS	Insulate
Ins	Insulin [Endocrinology] (DAVI)
INS	Insurance (AFM)
ins	Insurance (ODBW)
INS	Insurance
INS	Insure
INS	Integrated Navigation System
INS	Integrated Network Systems, Inc.
INS	Integrated Nitrogen System (SSD)
INS	Intelligent Systems Corp. [AMEX symbol] (SPSG)
INS	Interceptor Simulator (SAA)
INS	Interchangeable-Substitute Items (AAG)
INS	Internal Navigation System
INS	International Navigation System
INS	International Network for Self-Reliance (EA)
INS	International News Service [Later, UPI]
INS	International Numismatic Society (EAIO)
INS	International Seaway Trading Corp. (MHDW)
I-NS	Inter-Nation Simulation [Simulation of international relations]
INS	Interstate Noise Suppression
INS	Intravenous Nurses Society (EA)
INS	Ion-Neutralization Spectroscopy
INS	Iron Nickel System
INS	Iron Soldering
INS	Isolated Neutron Star [Astrophysics]
INS	Israel Naval Ship (BJA)
INS	Israel News Service (BJA)
INS	Northern Illinois Library System, Rockford, IL [OCLC symbol] (OCLC)
InS	South Bend Public Library, South Bend, IN [Library symbol Library of Congress] (LCLS)
INSA	Institut National de Systematique Appliquee [Canada]
INSA	International Naples Sabot Association (EA)
INSA	International Shipowners' Association [See also MAS] [Gdynia, Poland] (EAIO)
InSa	Salem Public Library, Salem, IN [Library symbol Library of Congress] (LCLS)
INS AB	Insulin Antibody [Endocrinology] (DAVI)
INSAB	International Numismatic Society Authentication Bureau (EA)
INSAC	Interstate Airways Communications (IAA)
InSaCR	Washington County Recorder's Office, Salem, IN [Library symbol Library of Congress] (LCLS)
INSACS	Interstate Airways Communications Station
INSAG	International Nuclear Safety Advisory Group [United Nations] (EY)
INSAIR	Inspector of Naval Aircraft
InSaLD	Salem Leader/Democrat, Salem, IN [Library symbol Library of Congress] (LCLS)
INSAR	Instruction Address Register [Computer science]
INSAT	Indian Geostationary Satellite [Marine science] (OSRA)
INSAT	Indian National Satellite System [Bangalore, India] [Telecommunications]
INSAT	Indian Satellite (USDC)
INSAT	India Satellite [Telecommunications] (NITA)
INSATRAC ...	Interception with Satellite Tracking
InsAut	Insurance Auto Auctions [Associated Press] (SAG)
INSAV	Interim Shipboard Availability (MCD)
InSaWHi	Washington County Historical Society, Salem, IN [Library symbol Library of Congress] (LCLS)
INSB	Intelligence and Security Board [Army] (RDA)
In-SC	Indiana State Supreme Court, Law Library, Indianapolis, IN [Library symbol Library of Congress] (LCLS)
INSC	Inscribed [or Inscription] (MSA)
INSC	Insulating Concrete [Technical drawings]
Ins C	Insurance Code [A publication] (DLA)
INSC	Internal Shape Components (CINC)
InSc	Scott County Public Library, Scottsburg, IN [Library symbol Library of Congress] (LCLS)
INSCA	International Natural Sausage Casing Association (EA)
INSCAIRS ...	Instrumentation Calibration Incident Repair Service
INSCE	Insurance
Inschr	Inschrift (BJA)
INSCI	Information Science, Inc. [Information service or system] (IID)
Insci	Insci Corp. [Associated Press] (SAG)
INSCO	Intercontinental Shipping Corp. (MHDW)
INSCOM	Intelligence and Security Command [Army] (RDA)
INSCOPE	Information System for Coffee and Other Product Economics [International Coffee Organization] (NITA)
Ins Couns J ...	Insurance Counsel Journal [A publication] (DLA)
INSCR	Inscription
inscr	Inscription (VRA)
INSCTN	Insecure
INSCRPTN	Inscription
INSCRUIT ...	Inspector of Navy Recruiting and Naval Officer Procurement
INSD	Insured
INS Data Base...	United States International Air Travel Statistics Data Base [I. P. Sharp Associates] [Canada] (NITA)

INSDC	Indian National Scientific Documentation Centre [New Delhi]
INSDEN	Inspector of Dental Activities
INSDOC	Indian National Scientific Documentation Centre [Council of Scientific and Industrial Research]
Insd Val	Insured Value [Business term] (MHDB)
INSEA	International Society for Education through Art [Corsham, England]
INSEAD	Institut Europeen d'Administration des Affaires [European Business Management Institute] [France] (PDAA)
IN/SEC	Inches per Second (WDAA)
INSEC	Internal Security
INSECTI	Insecticide(s) [Freight]
INSEE	Institut National de la Statistique et des Etudes Economiques [National Institute of Statistics and Economic Research] [Paris, France]
InSelS	Sellersburg Star, Sellersburg, IN [Library symbol Library of Congress] (LCLS)
INSEM	Insemination
INSENG	Inspector of Naval Engineering
INSEP	Inseparable (MSA)
INSERM	Institut National de la Sante et de la Recherche Medicale [National Institute for Health and Medical Research] [France Information service or system] (IID)
INSERV	In Service [Military] (CAAL)
INSET	In-service Education for Teachers [Australia]
INSET	In-Service Training (PDAA)
InSey	Seymour Public Library, Seymour, IN [Library symbol Library of Congress] (LCLS)
InSeyT	Seymour Daily Tribune, Seymour, IN [Library symbol Library of Congress] (LCLS)
INSF	Insulating Fill [Technical drawings]
INSGCY	Insurgency (AABC)
INSGEN	Inspector General [Navy]
INSGENLANTFLT...	Inspector General, Atlantic Fleet [Navy]
INSGENPAC...	Inspector General, Pacific Fleet and Pacific Ocean Areas [Navy]
InsgFn	Insignia Financial Group [Associated Press] (SAG)
InSghtH	InSight Health Services Corp. [Associated Press] (SAG)
InsgSol	Insignia Solutions [Associated Press] (SAG)
InsgtEnt	Insight Entertainment Corp. [Associated Press] (SAG)
INSGY	Insignia Solutions [NASDAQ symbol] (SAG)
INSGY	Insignia Solutions ADS [NASDAQ symbol] (TTSB)
INSH	Inspection Shell
InShe	Shelbyville-Shelby County Public Library, Shelbyville, IN [Library symbol Library of Congress] (LCLS)
InSheCR	Shelby County Recorder's Office, Shelbyville, IN [Library symbol Library of Congress] (LCLS)
InSheN	Shelbyville News, Shelbyville, IN [Library symbol Library of Congress] (LCLS)
InSherN	Sheridan News, Sheridan, IN [Library symbol Library of Congress] (LCLS)
InSho	Shoals Public Library, Shoals, IN [Library symbol Library of Congress] (LCLS)
InShoD	Martin County Democrat, Shoals, IN [Library symbol Library of Congress] (LCLS)
InShoHi	Martin County Historical Society, Shoals, IN [Library symbol Library of Congress] (LCLS)
InShoN	Shoals News, Shoals, IN [Library symbol Library of Congress] (LCLS)
INSHOREPAT...	Inshore Patrol
INSHORUNSEAWARGRU...	Inshore Undersea Warfare Group [Navy]
INSI	INSCI Corp. [NASDAQ symbol] (TTSB)
Insight	Insight Enterprises, Inc. [Associated Press] (SAG)
INSIGHT	Interactive System for Investigation by Graphics of Hydrological Trends (PDAA)
Insignia	Insignia Systems, Inc. [Associated Press] (SAG)
Insilco	Insilco Corp. [Associated Press] (SAG)
INSILCO	International Silver Co. [Acronym now used as firm's name]
InSIN	Indianapolis Star and News, Indianapolis, IN [Library symbol] [Library of Congress] (LCLS)
INSINSTR	Inspector-Instructor, Naval Reserve
INSIS	Inter-Institutional Integrated Services Information System
INSITE	Information on Nuclear Site Data System [Nuclear Regulatory Commission] (GFGA)
InsitE	Insituform East, Inc. [Associated Press] (SAG)
INSITE	Institutional Space Inventory Technique [Computer science]
INSITE	Integrated Sensor Interpretation Techniques
InSiteVis	InSite Vision, Inc. [Associated Press] (SAG)
InsitTc	Insituform Technology [Associated Press] (SAG)
in situ	In Place (DOG)
INSIU	Insci Corp. [NASDAQ symbol] (SAG)
INSIW	INSCI Corp.Wrrt [NASDAQ symbol] (TTSB)
INSL	Insilco Crop. [NASDAQ symbol] (SAG)
INSL	Insulate
InSL	South Bend Public Library, South Bend, IN [Library symbol] [Library of Congress] (LCLS)
INSLAW	Institute for Law and Social Research (IID)
Ins Liability Rep...	Insurance Liability Reports [A publication] (DLA)
Ins LR	Insurance Law Reporter [A publication] (DLA)
Ins L Rep	Insurance Law Reporter [A publication] (DLA)
INSLTD	Insulated
INSLTN	Insulation
INSLUG	Insulating
INSM	Insituform Mid-America, Inc. [NASDAQ symbol] (NQ)
INSMACH	Inspector of Naval Machinery
INSMARSAT ...	International Maritime Satellite [Organization] (DOMA)
INSMAT	Inspector of Naval Material

INSMAT .... Material Inspection Service [*Navy*] (AAGC)
INSMAT PET... Inspector of Naval Material, Petroleum
INSMATS ..... Inspectors of Naval Material (AAGC)
Ins Mon .... Insurance Monitor [*A publication*] (DLA)
InsMuni .... Insured Municipal Income Fund [*Associated Press*] (SAG)
INSNA.......... International Network for Social Network Analysis [*University of Toronto*] [*Toronto, ON*] (EAIO)
INSNAVMAT... Inspector of Navigational Material
InSNHi .... Northern Indiana State Historical Society, South Bend, IN [*Library symbol Library of Congress*] (LCLS)
INSO .... InfoSoft International, Inc. [*NASDAQ symbol*] (SAG)
INSO .... INSO Corp. [*Associated Press*] (SAG)
INSO .... INSO Corp. [*NASDAQ symbol*] (SAG)
INSOL......... Insoluble (MSA)
INSOLT .... I've Never Seen One Like That [*Antiques market*]
Insolv......... Insolvency [*Legal term*] (DLA)
INSOLV .... Insolvent [*Legal term*] (ADA)
INSOLVT ...... Insolvent (ROG)
INSORD .... Inspector of Ordnance
INSORDINC... Inspector of Ordnance in Charge
InSow .... South Whitley Cleveland Township Public Library, South Whitley, IN [*Library symbol Library of Congress*] (LCLS)
InSowTN ...... South Whitley Tribune-News, South Whitley, IN [*Library symbol Library of Congress*] (LCLS)
INSP .... Inspect [*or Inspector*] (AFM)
INSP .... Inspiration
INSP .... Internet Name Server Protocol (TNIG)
InSp .... Speedway Public Library, Speedway, IN [*Library symbol Library of Congress*] (LCLS)
INSPAT .... Inshore Patrol
INSPCTN ...... Inspection
INSPCTR ...... Inspector
InSpe .... Spencer Public-Owen County Contractual Library, Spencer, IN [*Library symbol Library of Congress*] (LCLS)
INSPEC .... Information Service: Physics, Electrical and Electronics, and Computers and Con trol [*Information service*] [*British*] (NITA)
INSPEC .... Information Services in Physics, Electronics, and Computers [*Information service or system*]
INSPEC .... Initial Specialty [*Military*] (INF)
INSPEC .... Inspection
INSPEC .... International Information Services for the Physics and Engineering Communities
Inspector Gen Rep... Inspector General Reports (AAGC)
INSPEL .... International Newsletter of Special Libraries [*A publication*]
INSPETRES... Inspector of Petroleum Reserves
InSpeW .... Spencer Evening World, Spencer, IN [*Library symbol Library of Congress*] (LCLS)
INSPEX .... International Measurement and Inspection Technology Exposition
Insp Gen ..... Inspector General (WGA)
INSPINSTF... Inspector-Instructor Staff [*Military*] (DNAB)
INSP-INSTR... Inspector-Instruction [*Marine Corps*]
inspir.......... Inspiration [*or Inspiratory*] (CPH)
INSPIR .... Inspiretur [*Let It Be Inspired*] [*Pharmacy*]
INSPIRE....... Institute for Public Interest Representation [*Later, CCCIPR*] [*Georgetown University*]
INSP L .... Inspection Laws (DLA)
INSPON....... Inspection (ROG)
INSPR......... Inspector
INSPR......... Intelligence Systems Program Review [*Military*] (MCD)
INSP W & M... Inspector of Weights and Measures [*British*] (ROG)
INSR .... Insert (MSA)
INSR .... Insulin Receptor [*Medicine*] (DMAA)
INSRADMAT... Inspector of Radio Material
Ins Rep .... Insurance Reporter [*A publication*] (DLA)
INSRP......... Inter-Agency Network Safety Review Panel [*NASA*] (NASA)
INSRP......... Interagency Nuclear Safety Review Pane (USDC)
INSRP......... Interagency Nuclear Safety Review Panel
InSrvAm....... Industrial Services of America, Inc. [*Associated Press*] (SAG)
INSS .... International Network Services [*NASDAQ symbol*] (SAG)
INSS .... International Neuroblastoma Staging System [*Medicine*] (DMAA)
INSSCC .... Interim National Space Surveillance Control Center
Inst .... Coke's Institutes [*England*] [*A publication*] (DLA)
INST.......... Customs and Excise Institutions List [*Database*] (IID)
INST.......... In Nomine Sanctae Trinitatis [*In the Name of the Holy Trinity*] [*Latin*]
INST.......... Insert Screw Thread
INST.......... Installed
INST.......... Installment [*Business term*]
INST.......... Instans [*The Current Month*] [*Latin*]
INST.......... Instant
inst .... Instant (ODBW)
INST.......... Instantaneous (MSA)
INST.......... Institute [*or Institution*] (AFM)
INST.......... Institute
Inst .... Institutes of England, in Two Parts, or A Commentary upon Littleton by Sir Edward Coke [*A publication*] (DLA)
inst .... Institution (VRA)
Inst .... Institutio Oratoria [*of Quintilian*] [*Classical studies*] (OCD)
INST.......... Instruction [*or Instructor*] (AFM)
Inst .... Instructor [*A publication*] (BRI)
INST.......... Instrument (AAG)
INST.......... Instrumental Delivery [*Obstetrics*] (DAVI)
INST.......... International Numbering System for Tides (MSC)
INST.......... IPI, Inc. [*NASDAQ symbol*] (SAG)
INST.......... IPI, Inc. [*NASDAQ symbol*] (SAG)
Inst .... Justinian's Institutes [*A publication*] (DLA)

INST........... Revenue Canada - Customs and Excise Institutions List [*Revenue Canada - Customs and Excise*] [*Information service or system*] (CRD)
InST........... South Bend Tribune, South Bend, IN [*Library symbol Library of Congress*] (LCLS)
INSTA .... Instruments Authorized (FAAC)
INSTA .... Inter-Nordic Standardization
INSTA .... Interstate (FAAC)
INSTAAR ...... Institute of Arctic and Alpine Research [*University of Colorado*]
INSTAB .... Information Service on Toxicity and Biodegradability [*Water Pollution Research Laboratory*] [*British*] (IID)
InstAct .... Institute of Actuaries [*British*]
INSTAD .... Institute for Training and Development
Inst Ad Legal Stud Ann... Institute of Advanced Legal Studies. Annals [*A publication*] (DLA)
INSTAL .... Installation
INSTALLN .... Installation
INSTAR .... Inertialess Scanning, Tracking, and Ranging
INSTARS..... Information Storage and Retrieval System [*Computer science*]
in stat pup... In Statu Pupillari [*Subject to the Rule of the Institution*] [*Latin*] (BARN)
Inst BE........ Institution of British Engineers
INSTBY .... Instability (FAAC)
InstCES .... Institution of Civil Engineering Surveyors (DAC)
Inst Cler ...... Instructor Clericalis (DLA)
Inst Com Com... Interstate Commerce Commission Reports [*A publication*] (DLA)
INST/COMM... Instrumentation and Communication (MCD)
INSTCTL ...... Instrumentation and Control [*Aerospace*] (IAA)
INSTD......... Instead (ROG)
InstD.......... Institute of Directors [*British*]
InstDokAB... Institutionendokumentation zur Arbeitsmarkt- und Berufsforschung [*Database*] [*Institut fuer Arbeitsmarkt- und Berufsforschung der Bundesanstalt fuer Arbeit*] [*German*] [*Information service or system*] (CRD)
INSTEAD ...... Information Service on Technological Alternatives for Development [*ILO*] [*United Nations*] (DUND)
INSTEAD ...... International Student, Trade, Environment and Development Program (CROSS)
INSTEE........ Institution of Electrical Engineers (IAA)
Insteel .... Insteel Industries, Inc. [*Associated Press*] (SAG)
InStent........ Instent, Inc. [*Associated Press*] (SAG)
INSTEP .... Indian Steel Training and Education Program [*India*]
INSTEP .... In-Service Training and Education Panel (AIE)
Inst Epil...... Epilogue to (a Designated Part or Volume of) Coke's Institutes [*A publication*] (DLA)
InstF .... Institute of Fuel [*British*]
Inst Fed Tax... Institute on Federal Taxation (DLA)
INSTFLTNG... Instrument Flight Training (NVT)
INSTFURASPERS... Instruction and Further Assignment by Commander, Naval Military Personnel Command (DNAB)
Insti .... Institutes of Justinian [*Roman law*] [*A publication*] (DSA)
INSTIA .... Instituto Internacional de Andragogia [*International Institute of Andragogy - IIA*] (EAIO)
INSTILL....... Instillandus [*To Be Dropped In*] [*Pharmacy*]
INSTINET ..... Institutional Networks Corp.
Institutes .... Institutes of Justinian [*Roman law*] [*A publication*] (DLA)
Inst Iust...... Institutiones Iustiniani [*Classical studies*] (OCD)
InStjN .... Saint Joe News, Saint Joe, IN [*Library symbol Library of Congress*] (LCLS)
Inst Jur Angl... Institutiones Juris Anglicani, by Cowell [*A publication*] (DLA)
INSTL......... Installation (AFM)
instl .... Installation (VRA)
INSTL......... Installment
Inst Lab Rel Bull... Institute for Labor Relations. Bulletin [*A publication*] (DLA)
INSTL & C/O... Installation and Checkout (NASA)
INSTLLR ...... Installer
INSTLN .... Installation
INSTLR .... Installer
INSTLTN ...... Installation
INSTM .... Instrumentation (MSA)
InStmaS...... St. Mary-Of-The-Woods College, St. Mary-Of-The-Woods, IN [*Library symbol Library of Congress*] (LCLS)
INSTMC ...... Institute of Measurement and Control [*British*] (EAIO)
INST ME...... Institute of Mechanical Engineers [*British*] (WDAA)
Inst M E...... Institute of Media Executives [*British*]
InStme....... St. Meinrad College and Seminary, St. Meinrad, IN [*Library symbol Library of Congress*] (LCLS)
InstMet .... Institute of Metals [*British*]
Inst MM .... Institution of Mining and Metallurgy (BARN)
INSTMN ...... Instrumentation
INSTMNS..... Instrumentation Squadron [*Military*]
INSTMT .... Instrument (WGA)
INSTN .... Institution
INSTN .... Institution
INSTN .... Instruction [*Computer science*] (TEL)
INSTN .... Instrumentation (MUGU)
InSTN......... Tri-County News, South Bend, IN [*Library symbol Library of Congress*] (LCLS)
Inst NA .... Institution of Naval Architects (BARN)
INSTNL .... Institutional
INSTNL .... Institutional
INSTNS .... Institutions (ROG)
INSTNS .... Instructions
INSTNT .... Instant

Inst on Plan Zoning & Eminent Domain... Institute on Planning, Zoning, and Eminent Domain. Proceedings [*Southwestern Legal Foundation*] (DLA)

Inst on Priv Inv & Inv Abroad... Institute on Private Investments and Investors Abroad. Proceedings [*A publication*] (DLA)

INSTOP....... Instrument or on-Top-of-Clouds Authorized

INST P........ Institute of Physics [*British*] (WDAA)

Inst Plan & Zoning... Institute on Planning, Zoning, and Eminent Domain. Proceedings [*A publication*] (DLA)

Inst Plan Zoning & ED... Institute on Planning, Zoning, and Eminent Domain. Proceedings [*A publication*] (DLA)

INSTPN....... Instrument Panel

Inst Proem... Proeme [*Introduction to Coke's Institutes*] [*A publication*] (DLA)

InstPS....... Institute of Purchasing and Supply [*British*]

InstPubl...... [*The*] Instant Publishers, Inc. [*Associated Press*] (SAG)

INSTR....... Instruct [*or Instructor*] (AABC)

INSTR....... Instruction

INSTR....... Instrument

INSTR....... Instrument

instr........... Instrument (VRA)

instr........... Instrumental [*Grammar*]

INSTRAT...... Investment Strategy [*Game*]

INSTRAW..... International Research and Training Institute for the Advancement of Women [*Dominican Republic*] [*United Nations Research center*] (IRC)

Instr Cler... Instructor Clericalis (DLA)

INSTRCTR.... Instructor

INSTRD...... Instructed (ROG)

INSTRE...... Institute of Radio Engineers [*Later, IEEE*] (IAA)

INSTREF...... Instrument Reference (IAA)

INSTRL....... Instructional

InstrLab...... Instrumentation Laboratory SpA [*Associated Press*] (SAG)

INSTRM...... Instrumented

INSTRMNTN... Instrumentation

INSTRMT..... Instrument

INSTRN...... Instruction

INSTRNL..... Instructional

Instron........ Instron Corp. [*Associated Press*] (SAG)

INSTRONS.. Instructions (ROG)

INSTRPI...... Instrument Pilot Instructor [*Air Force*]

INSTRPIT..... Instructor Pilot [*Air Force*]

INSTRU....... Instrumentation

INSTRUC..... Instruction

InstruCp...... Instrumentarium Corp. [*Associated Press*] (SAG)

INSTRUCTA... Intelligent Naval Structures Assistant

INSTRUM..... Instrumentation Subsystem [*NASA*] (NASA)

Inst Sci & Indust Bull... Australia. Institute of Science and Industry. Bulletin [*A publication*]

Inst Sec Reg... Institute on Securities Regulation [*A publication*] (DLA)

Inst SMM... Institute of Sales and Marketing Management [*British*]

INSTSYS...... Instrumentation System (MCD)

InSU........... Indiana University at South Bend, South Bend, IN [*Library symbol Library of Congress*] (LCLS)

INSU.......... Insituform Technology [*NASDAQ symbol*] (SPSG)

INSU.......... Intensive Neurosurgery Unit (DAVI)

InSu........... Sullivan County Public Library, Sullivan, IN [*Library symbol Library of Congress*] (LCLS)

INSUA........ Insituform Technol'A' [*NASDAQ symbol*] (TTSB)

InSuC......... Sullivan County Public Library, Sullivan, IN [*Library symbol*] [*Library of Congress*] (LCLS)

InSuCR....... Sullivan County Recorder's Office, Sullivan, IN [*Library symbol Library of Congress*] (LCLS)

INSUF......... Insufficient (AABC)

INSUF......... Insufficient Scheduled Time Available [*Aviation*] (FAAC)

INSUFF....... Insufflatio [*An Insufflation*] [*Pharmacy*]

InSuHi........ Sullivan County Historical Society, Sullivan, IN [*Library symbol Library of Congress*] (LCLS)

INSUL........ Insulated [*or Insulation*]

INSULR....... Insulator

INSUPGENCRUIT... Inspect, Supervise, Generally Superintend Recruitment Methods

Insur.......... Insurance

INSURE....... Industry Network for Social, Urban, and Rural Efforts

Insur L Rep... Insurance Law Reporter [*A publication*] (DLA)

INSURR....... Insurrection (DLA)

Insur Rec Aust NZ... Insurance Record of Australia and New Zealand [*A publication*]

INSURV....... Board of Inspection and Survey [*Navy*]

INSURVINST... Board of Inspection and Survey, Instructions [*Navy*]

InSuT.......... Sullivan Daily Times, Sullivan, IN [*Library symbol Library of Congress*] (LCLS)

INSUWG..... Inshore Undersea Warfare Group [*Navy*]

INSV.......... InSite Vision [*NASDAQ symbol*] (TTSB)

INSV.......... InSite Vision, Inc. [*NASDAQ symbol*] (SAG)

InSw.......... Swayzee Public Library, Swayzee, IN [*Library symbol Library of Congress*] (LCLS)

InSy........... Syracuse Public Library, Syracuse, IN [*Library symbol Library of Congress*] (LCLS)

INSYD......... Instantaneous Systems Display [*Computer science*] (MHDB)

INT............ Ad Interim Specification [*Navy*]

Int............. De Interpretatione [*of Aristotle*] [*Classical studies*] (OCD)

INT............ Greensboro/High Point/West Salem [*North Carolina*] Reynolds [*Airport symbol*] (OAG)

INT............ Image 'N Transfer [*Developed by 3M Co.*] (WDMC)

INT............ Individual Needs Test (DNAB)

INT............ Induction Neutralizing Transformer [*Computer science*]

INT............ Infrared Nondestructive Testing [*Electrical technique*]

INT............ Initial (IAA)

INT............ Intair, Inc. [*Canada ICAO designator*] (FAAC)

INT............ Intake

INT............ Integer

INT............ Integral (MSA)

INT............ Integrase [*Biochemistry*]

INT............ Integrated (MCD)

INT............ Integrated Test (NASA)

INT............ Integrated Testing (NASA)

INT............ Intelligence

INT............ Intelligence and Law Enforcement Division [*Coast Guard*]

int............. Intense [*Philately*]

INT............ Intensifier [*Linguistics*]

INT............ Intensity

INT............ Intent [*FBI standardized term*]

INT............ Intercept [*or Interceptor*] (CINC)

INT............ Interchange

Int............. Interchange: Papers on Biblical and Current Questions [*A publication*] (APTA)

INT............ Interest [*Finance, Law*] (AFM)

int............. Interest (WDMC)

INT............ Interface

INT............ Interim (MSA)

INT............ Interior (KSC)

int............. Interior (WDMC)

int............. Interior (VRA)

INT............ Interjection

INT............ Interleaved (WGA)

int............. Interlingua [*MARC language code Library of Congress*] (LCCP)

INT............ INTERMARC [*International Machine-Readable Cataloging*] [*French National Library*] [*UTLAS symbol*]

INT............ Intermediate (MCD)

INT............ Intermetco Ltd. [*Toronto Stock Exchange symbol*]

INT............ Intermittent

INT............ Internal (AAG)

int............. Internal (WDMC)

int............. International (WDMC)

INT............ International (EY)

INT............ Interne [*Medicine British*]

INT............ Interned (AABC)

INT............ Internist [*Medicine*]

INT............ Internship (DAVI)

int............. Internus [*Internal*] [*Latin*]

INT............ Interphone (MDG)

INT............ Interpreter

INT............ Interrogate (MDG)

INT............ Interrogation [*British naval signaling*]

INT............ Interrupt

INT............ Interrupter (MSA)

INT............ Interstate [*Railroad*] (MHDW)

INT............ Interstate Railroad Co. [*AAR code*]

INT............ Interval

int............. Interval (WDMC)

INT............ Interview

int............. Interviewer

Int............. Intestinal (AAMN)

INT............ Intransitive

Int............. Introduction (DLA)

INT............ Introit

INT............ Iodonitrotetrazolium Violet

INT............ Irrigated, No Tillage [*Agriculture*]

INT............ Isaac Newton Optical Telescope

INT............ North Texas State University, Denton, TX [*OCLC symbol*] (OCLC)

INT............ Winston-Salem [*North Carolina*] [*Airport symbol*] (AD)

INT............ Winston-Salem, NC [*Location identifier FAA*] (FAAL)

INT............ World Fuel Services [*NYSE symbol*] (TTSB)

INT............ World Fuel Services Corp. [*NYSE symbol*] (SAG)

INTA.......... Intasys Corp. [*NASDAQ symbol*] (SAG)

INTA.......... International Association for the Development and Management of Existing and NewTowns (EAIO)

INTA.......... International New Thought Alliance (EA)

INTA.......... Interrupt Acknowledge [*Computer science*]

INTAAS....... Integrated Aircraft Armament System (MCD)

in-tab........ In-Tabulation [*Broadcasting*] (WDMC)

IntAbs........ International Absorbents [*Associated Press*] (SAG)

INTABS....... International Terminal Accounting and Banking Service [*Computer science*] (MHDB)

INTAC........ Intercept Tracking and Control Group

IntACom...... InterAmericas Communications Corp. [*Associated Press*] (SAG)

INTACS....... Integrated Tactical Communications Study [*or System*] [*Army*] (AABC)

INTAG........ Intaglio [*Engraving*] (ROG)

INTAG........ International Advisory Group on Technology Management [*Information broker and consultancy*] (NITA)

INTAGCY..... Interagency

INTAL........ Instituto para la Integracion de America Latina [*Institute for Latin American Integration*] (EAIO)

INT AL....... Inter Alia [*Among Other Things*] [*Latin*]

IntAlu......... International Aluminum Corp. [*Associated Press*] (SAG)

INTAMEL..... International Association of Metropolitan City Libraries [*The Hague, Netherlands*] (EA)

INTAMIC...... International Microcircuit Card Association [*Paris, France*] [*Defunct*] (EAIO)

INTAMP...... Intermediate Amplifier (IAA)
INTAP .... Interoperatbility Technology Association for Information Technology (OSI)
INTAPUC..... International Association of Public Cleansing [Later, ISWA]
INTAR .... International Arts Relations
Int Arb J ..... International Arbitration Journal [A publication] (DLA)
INTASAFCON... International Tanker Safety Conference (DS)
INTASAT...... Instituto Nacional de Tecnica Aeroespacial Satellite [Spain]
INTASGRO .. Interallied Tactical Study Group [NATO] (NATG)
Intasys........ Intasys Corp. [Associated Press] (SAG)
INTAV .... Interim Availability (DNAB)
INTAVA .... International Aviation Association
Int Bar J ..... International Bar Journal [A publication] (DLA)
IntBas......... International Basic Resources, Inc. [Associated Press] (SAG)
INTBUL .... Intelligence Bulletin (CINC)
Int Bull Indust Prop... International Bulletin of Industrial Property [A publication] (DLA)
Int Bus Lawy... International Business Lawyer [A publication] (DLA)
IntBusSch .... International Business Schools [Associated Press] (SAG)
INTC............. Intel Corp. [NASDAQ symbol] (NQ)
INTC............. Intelligence Corps [Army]
INTC............. Intercept (GAVI)
INTC............. International Nick Tate Club (EAIO)
InTc .... Tell City-Perry County Public Library, Tell City, IN [Library symbol Library of Congress] (LCLS)
IntCabl......... International Cablecasting Technologies, Inc. [Associated Press] (SAG)
IntcapIn .... Intercapital Insurance Municipal Bond Fund [Associated Press] (SAG)
IntcapIns..... InterCapital Insured Municipal Securities [Associated Press] (SAG)
IntCAQI....... Intercapital California Quality Municipal Security Trust [Associated Press] (SAG)
Intcardia...... Intercardia, Inc. [Associated Press] (SAG)
Int Cas........ Rowe's Interesting Cases [England and Ireland] [A publication] (DLA)
Int Case....... Rowe's Interesting Cases [England and Ireland] [A publication] (DLA)
IntCble......... International Cabletel, Inc. [Associated Press] (SAG)
INTCHG........ Interchangeable (MSA)
INTCHGR ..... Interchanger (NASA)
INT CIB .... Inter Cibos [Between Meals] [Pharmacy]
IntCm........... Interdigital Communications Corp. [Associated Press] (SAG)
InTcN........... Tell City News, Tell City, IN [Library symbol Library of Congress] (LCLS)
INTCNTL ..... Intercontinental
INTC/O......... Integrated Checkout (NASA)
INTCO .... International Code of Signals
INTCOL........ Intelligence Collection [Military] (NVT)
IntColng....... International Colin Energy [Associated Press] (SAG)
Int Com Com... Interstate Commerce Commission. Reports [A publication] (DLA)
Int Com Commn... Interstate Commerce Commission [Independent government agency] (DLA)
Int Com Rep... Interstate Commerce Commission Reports [A publication] (DLA)
INTCON .... Interconnection (MSA)
INTCP .... Intercept (AFM)
IntcpIM .... Intercapital Insured Municipal Income Trust [Associated Press] (SAG)
INTCP RNG... Intercept Range
IntCpt.......... Intersciences Computer Corp. [Associated Press] (SAG)
InTCS........... Commercial Solvents Corp., Terre Haute, IN [Library symbol Library of Congress Obsolete] (LCLS)
IntctlBk........ Intercontinental Bank [Associated Press] (SAG)
INTCW .... Intel Corp.Wrrt [NASDAQ symbol] (TTSB)
INTCYL .... Intercylinder
InTD............. Eugene V. Debs Foundation, Terre Haute, IN [Library symbol Library of Congress] (LCLS)
INTD .... Institut National des Techniques de la Documentation [National Institute for Information Science] [France Information service or system] (IID)
INTD .... InteliData Technologies Corp. [NASDAQ symbol] (SAG)
INTD .... Intend (FAAC)
INTDD......... Intended
INTDEPT ..... Interdepartmental
INTDISP....... Interdisciplinary
INTE............. Interactive Group [NASDAQ symbol] (TTSB)
INTE............. Interactive Group, Inc. [NASDAQ symbol] (SAG)
INTE............. Interrupt Enable [Computer science]
INTEC.......... Interface Technology [British] (NITA)
INTEC.......... Interference [Telecommunications] (MDG)
INTEC.......... International Technology Underwriters [Consortium, Washington] (NITA)
INTECH .... Instrument Technology-Journal of ISA (ACII)
INTECH .... Integrated Information Technology Conference and Exposition [National Trade Productions] (TSPED)
INTECOL...... International Association for Ecology [University of Georgia] [Athens, GA] (EAIO)
Integ............ Integ Inc. [Associated Press] (SAG)
INTEG .... Integrate [or Integrating] (MSA)
INTEG .... Integument [Dermatology] (DAVI)
IntegCirc...... Integrated Circuit Systems [Associated Press] (SAG)
IntegFn........ Integra Financial Corp. [Associated Press] (SAG)
IntegMed ..... IntegraMed America, Inc. [Associated Press] (SAG)
Integn.......... Integon Corp. [Associated Press] (SAG)
Integon........ Integon Corp. [Associated Press] (SAG)
INTEGR .... Integrate [or Integration] (NASA)
Integral........ Integral Systems, Inc. [Associated Press] (SAG)
Integrity....... Integrity, Inc. [Associated Press] (SAG)
IntegSrg....... Integrated Surgical Systems, Inc. [Associated Press] (SAG)

IntegTc........ Integrated Technology USA, Inc. [Associated Press] (SAG)
Intek .... INTEK Diversified Corp. [Associated Press] (SAG)
Intel .... Intel Corp. [Associated Press] (SAG)
INTEL.......... Intelligence (AABC)
Intelcal........ Intellicall, Inc. [Associated Press] (SAG)
INTELCAST... Intelligence Broadcast (DOMA)
INTELCEN .... Intelligence Center
INTELCENPAC... Intelligence Center, Pacific Ocean Areas [Obsolete]
Intelcm........ Intelcom Group [Associated Press] (SAG)
INTELCOM ... Worldwide Intelligence Communication (MCD)
Intelect........ Intelect Communications Systems Ltd. [Associated Press] (SAG)
IntelEl......... Intellignet Electronics, Inc. [Associated Press] (SAG)
INTELEVENT... International Televent (EA)
InteliDta....... InteliData Technologies Corp. [Associated Press] (SAG)
INTELL......... Intelligence (ROG)
Intellectual Property L Rev... Intellectual Property Law Review [A publication] (DLA)
Intellgrp....... Intelligroup, Inc. [Associated Press] (SAG)
Intelli.......... Intelli Corp., Inc. [Associated Press] (SAG)
INTELLIVISION... Intelligent Television [Home video game] [Mattel, Inc.]
INTELNET .... Intelligence Network (DOMA)
INTELO .... Intelligence Officer [Military]
INTELPOST... International Electronic Post [Postal Service]
INTELPOST... International Telecommunications Post [Facsimile transmission service] (NITA)
INTELSA ...... International Telecommunications Satellite Consortium [Later, International Telecommunications Satellite Organization] (IAA)
INTELSAT .... International Telecommunications Satellite Consortium (NITA)
Intelsat........ International Telecommunications Satellite Organization [Washington, D.C.] (WDMC)
INTELSAT .... International Telecommunications Satellite Organization (EA)
INTELTNG .... Intelligence Training [Military] (NVT)
INTEN .... Intensity (MSA)
Int Enc Comp Law... International Encyclopedia of Comparative Law [A publication] (DLA)
INTENS .... Intensive
Intensva....... Intensiva Healthcare Corp. [Associated Press] (SAG)
INTENT .... Initial Teacher Education and New Technology [Project] (AIE)
INTENTN...... Intention (ROG)
INTER .... Interception [Football]
INTER .... Interdenominational
Inter............ Interiors, Inc. [Associated Press] (SAG)
INTER .... Interleave (DGA)
INTER .... Intermediate (AAG)
INTER .... Intermediate
inter............ Intermediate (WDMC)
INTER .... Intermittent
INTER .... Internal (KSC)
INTER .... Interphone (MCD)
INTER .... Interrogation (ADA)
INTER .... Interrogative
INTER .... Interrupt
INTER .... Intertype (DGA)
Intera.......... Intera Information Technologies Corp. [Associated Press] (SAG)
INTERACT .... Integrated Research Aircraft Control Technology (MCD)
InterAct....... InterAction Media Corp. [Associated Press] (SAG)
Interact........ Interactive Group, Inc. [Associated Press] (SAG)
InteracT .... Interactive Technologies Corp., Inc. [Associated Press] (SAG)
INTERACT .... Interactive Television Network [Dartmouth-Hitchcock Medical Center] [Hanover, NH] [Telecommunications] (TSSD)
INTERALIS ... International Advanced Life Information System (BUR)
INTERALP .... Intercultural Action Learning Program
Inter American U... Inter American University (GAGS)
INTER ARTS... Intermediate of Arts [British] (ROG)
INTERASMA... International Association of Asthmology [Lisbon, Portugal] (EAIO)
INTERATOM... Internationale Atomreactorbau [German]
INTER BA .... Intermediate Bachelor of Arts [British] (ROG)
INTERBEV .... International Beverage Industry Exhibition and Congress [National Soft Drink Association]
INTERBOR ... Union Internationale des Techniciens Orthopedistes [International Association of Orthotists and Prosthetists] (EA)
INTERBRIGHT... International Literary and Information Centre in Science Extension (IID)
INTERCARGO... International Association of Dry Cargo Shipowners (EAIO)
INTERCEDE... International Coalition to End Domestics' Exploitation
Intercel........ Intercel, Inc. [Associated Press] (SAG)
INTERCENTRE... International Centre for the Terminology of the Social Sciences [Grand-Saconnex, Switzerland] (EA)
Interco .... Interco, Inc. [Formerly, International Shoe Co.] [Associated Press] (SAG)
INTERCO...... International Code of Signals (PDAA)
INTERCO...... International Council on Jewish Social and Welfare Services [Geneva, Switzerland] (EAIO)
INTERCODE... International CODEN Service [Chemical Abstracts Service] [Information service or system] (IID)
INTERCOL.... Intercolonial (ADA)
INTERCOM... Intercommunication System
INTERCOM... Intertribal Christian Communications
INTERCON ... Interconnection (KSC)
INTERCON ... Intercontinental
INTERCON ... Intermediate-Size Cargo Container
INTERCON ... International Convention
INTERCOOP... International Organization for Consumer Co-Operative Distributive Trade (EAIO)

INTERCOSMOS... Council on International Cooperation in the Study and Utilization of Outer Spac e

INTERDACO... Intercontinental Data Control Corp. Ltd. [Ottawa, ON] [Telecommunications] (TSSD)

INTERDEPT... Interdepartmental (KSC)

INTERDICT... Interference Detection and Interdiction Countermeasures Team [Electromagnetic compatibility programs]

InterDig...... Interdigital Communications Corp. [Associated Press] (SAG)

INTERDOC... Integrated Terminology Document Management System (IAA)

INTERDOK... International Documentation and Information Centre

INTEREG... Internationales Institut fuer Nationalitatenrecht und Regionalismus [International Institute for Ethnic Group Rights and Regionalism] (EA)

INTEREGEN... Internal Regenerative (KSC)

INTEREST.... Interactive Estimating [Camic Ltd.] [Software package] (NCC)

INTEREX..... International Exchangors Association (EA)

Interf.......... Interface Systems, Inc. [Associated Press] (SAG)

INTERF .... Interference (IAA)

INTERF .... Interferometer

INTERFAIS... International Food Aid Information System [World Food Program] [United Nations] (DUND)

Interfc.......... Interface Systems, Inc. [Associated Press] (SAG)

INTERFER .... Interference

INTERFILM... International Inter-Church Film Center [Hilversum, Netherlands] (EAIO)

INTERFOOD... International Exhibition of Foodstuffs, Fast Food, and Traditional and Mass Catering

INTERFRIGO... International Railway-Owned Company for Refrigerated Transport (EAIO)

INTERGALVA... International Galvanizing Conference (MCD)

INTERGOVT... Intergovernmental

INTERGU..... Internationale Gesellschaft fuer Urheberrecht [International Copyright Society] (EAIO)

INTERHYBRID... Association Intercontinentale du Mais Hybride

Interim.......... Interim Services, Inc. [Associated Press] (SAG)

Interior Dec... Decisions of the Department of the Interior [A publication] (DLA)

Interiors....... Interiors, Inc. [Associated Press] (SAG)

INTERJ.......... Interjection

interj............ Interjection (WDMC)

INTERLAINE... Comite des Industries Lainieres de la CEE [Committee of the Wool Textile Industry in the EEC] (EAIO)

Interlink...... Interlink Electronics, Inc. [Associated Press] (SAG)

Interlinq....... INTERLINQ Software Corp. [Associated Press] (SAG)

INTERMAC... International Association of Merger and Acquisition Consultants (EA)

INTERMAG... International Conference on Magnetics (MCD)

INTERMAMA... International Congress for Measurement and Automation (IEEE)

INTERMARC... International Machine Readable Catalogue

INTERMED... Intermediate (ADA)

INTERMET ... International Association for Metropolitan Research and Development

Intermex...... International Mexican Bank Ltd. [British] (EY)

INTERMILPOL... International Military Police [NATO]

INTERMORGEO... International Organization for Marine Geology [Council for Mutual Economic Assistance] [Riga, Union of Soviet Socialist Republics Defunct] (EAIO)

INTERMSTA... Intermediate Station

INTERMTRA... Intermediate Training [Naval Air]

INTERN....... Internal

INTERN....... International

Interna LN ... International Law Notes [London] [A publication] (DLA)

INTERNAT.... International

Internat Bar Assoc... International Bar Association (DLA)

Internat J of Leg Res... International Journal of Legal Research [A publication] (DLA)

INTERNATL... International

Internat LN.... International Law Notes [A publication] (DLA)

Interneur...... Interneuron Pharmaceuticals, Inc. [Associated Press] (SAG)

InterNIC...... Internet Network Information Center

InterNIC...... Internet Network Information Center [Computer science]

INTERNL...... Internal

INTER NOCT... Inter Noctem [During the Night] [Pharmacy]

INTERNST... Intenist

Internt.......... Internet Communications [Associated Press] (SAG)

INTEROBS... International Observations (DNAB)

INTEROG..... Interrogate (NASA)

INTEROP..... Interoperability

INTERP....... Interpreter

INTERPET... International Petroleum Co.

INTERPEX... International Philatelic Exhibition [American Stamp Dealers Association]

INTERPHES... International Pharmaceutical Cosmetics, Toiletry, and Allied Industries Exhibition [England]

INTERPHIL... International Standing Conference on Philanthropy [Yalding, Kent, England] (EAIO)

INTERPL...... Interplead [Legal shorthand] (LWAP)

INTERPLAN... International Group for Studies in National Planning

INTERPLAS... International Plastics and Rubber Exhibition [British Plastics Federation] (TSPED)

INTERPOL... International Criminal Police Organization

Interpol....... Interpool, Inc. [Associated Press] (SAG)

Interp Op..... Interpretative Opinion [Legal term] (DLA)

INTERPR..... Interpreter (WGA)

INTERPRO ... International Probation Organization (EA)

INTERPRON... Photointerpretation Squadron [Military]

interr.......... Interrogative (BJA)

INTERROG ... Interrogation

INTERROGS... Interrogatories (ROG)

INTERROGY... Interrogatory (ROG)

Inters Com Rep... Interstate Commerce Commission Reports [A publication] (DLA)

INTERSEARCH... International Productions and Safety Research [Auto accident reconstruction]

INTERSEC .... Intermediate Section

INTERSECT... International Security Technics [Organization in TV series "The Gemini Man"]

Interslv........ Intersolv, Inc. [Associated Press] (SAG)

INTERSPACE... Interactive System for Pattern Analysis, Classification, and Enhancement (PDAA)

INTERSPUTNIK... International Organization of Space Communications [Moscow, USSR] (EAIO)

INTERST ...... Interstate [Legal shorthand] (LWAP)

Interstate Com R... Interstate Commerce Reports [A publication] (DLA)

Interst Com R... Interstate Commerce Commission Reports [A publication] (DLA)

INTERSTENO... Federation Internationale de Stenographie et de Dactylographie [International Federation of Shorthand and Typewriting] [Bonn, Federal Republic of Germany] (EAIO)

INTERSTOL... Inter-City Short Takeoff and Landing [Aviation]

INTERTANKO... International Association of Independent Tanker Owners [Oslo, Norway] (EAIO)

INTERTEL... International Intelligence, Inc.

INTERTEL ... International Legion of Intelligence [Acronym is used as official name of association] (EA)

INTERTEST... Interactive Test Controller (MHDI)

INTERTEX ... International Textile and Fabrics Trade Fair

INTERV .... Interval

INTERV .... Interview

INTERV .... Interviewer

INTERVISION... International Television (IAA)

INTER/W..... Intersection With (WDAA)

INTERWOOLABS... International Association of Wool and Textile Laboratories (EAIO)

INTESCA...... Internacional de Ingenieria y Estudios Tecnicos SA [Spain] (PDAA)

INTEST......... Intestinal

Intevac......... Intevac, Inc. [Associated Press] (SAG)

INTEX......... Integer Extraction (PDAA)

INTEX......... International Fallout Warning Exercise (NATG)

INTEXT......... International Textbook Co.

INTF......... Interface (NASA)

INTF......... Interface Systems [NASDAQ symbol] (TTSB)

INTF......... Interface Systems, Inc. [NASDAQ symbol] (NQ)

IntF......... Internal Frosted (IAA)

IntF......... International Finance Corp. [Associated Press] (SAG)

IntFam......... International Family Entertainment [Associated Press] (SAG)

IntFast .... International Fast Food Corp. [Associated Press] (SAG)

INTFC......... Interface (MSA)

INTFC......... Interference (FAAC)

INTFER......... Interference (AABC)

Int FHR......... Internatl Fetal Heart Rate [Medicine] (MEDA)

IntFib......... International Fibercom, Inc. [Associated Press] (SAG)

IntFibcm .... International Fibercom, Inc. [Associated Press] (SAG)

IntFlav .... International Flavors & Fragrances, Inc. [Associated Press] (SAG)

INTFR......... Interference (KSC)

Intfrn......... Interferon Sciences, Inc. [Associated Press] (SAG)

INTFU......... Interface Unit [Computer science]

intg......... Intaglio (VRA)

INTG......... Integration (NASA)

INTG .... Intergroup Corp. [NASDAQ symbol] (TTSB)

INTG .... Interrogate (AABC)

IntGame......... International Game Technology [Associated Press] (SAG)

IntgDv......... Integrated Device Technology, Inc. [Associated Press] (SAG)

INTGEN......... Interpreter Generator

IntgHS......... Integrated Health Services, Inc. [Associated Press] (SAG)

INTGL......... Integral (KSC)

IntgMed......... Integrated Medical Resources, Inc. [Associated Press] (SAG)

IntgMic......... Integrated Micro Products [Associated Press] (SAG)

IntgMus .... Integrity Music, Inc. [Associated Press] (SAG)

Intgph......... Intergraph Corp. [Associated Press] (SAG)

INTGR......... Integrate (AABC)

IntgrBr......... Integrated Brands [Associated Press] (SAG)

INTGRD......... Integrated

Intgrp......... [The] Inner Group Corp. [Associated Press] (SAG)

INTGRTD......... Integrated

IntgSc......... Integrated Security Systems [Associated Press] (SAG)

IntgSec .... Integrated Security Systems [Associated Press] (SAG)

IntgSrg......... Integrated Surgical Systems, Inc. [Associated Press] (SAG)

IntgWst......... Integrated Waste Services, Inc. [Associated Press] (SAG)

INTH......... Intrathecal [Medicine]

InTho .... Thorntown Public Library, Thorntown, IN [Library symbol Library of Congress] (LCLS)

InThr......... International Thoroughbred Breeders, Inc. [Associated Press] (SAG)

InTI......... Indiana State University, Terre Haute, IN [Library symbol Library of Congress] (LCLS)

INTI......... Industrial Technologies [NASDAQ symbol] (TTSB)

INTI......... Industrial Technologies, Inc. [NASDAQ symbol] (SAG)

InTi......... Tipton County Public Library, Tipton, IN [Library symbol Library of Congress] (LCLS)

INTIB......... Industrial and Technological Information Bank [UNIDO] (IID)

INTIM......... Interrupt and Timing [Telecommunications] (TEL)

IntImag......... International Imaging Materials, Inc. [Associated Press] (SAG)

InTIMC......... IMC Chemical Group, Inc., Technical Library, Terre Haute, IN [Library symbol Library of Congress] (LCLS)

Intime......... Information on Technology in Manufacturing Engineering [*Society of Manufacturing Engineers*] [*Dearborn, MI*]
INTIME........ Interactive Textual Information Management Experiment (PDAA)
Intime......... Intime Systems International, Inc. [*Associated Press*] (SAG)
IntIMT........ Intercapital Insured Municipal Trust [*Associated Press*] (SAG)
Intimte........ Intimate Brands, Inc. [*Associated Press*] (SAG)
IntIns CA..... InterCapital Insured California Municipal Securities [*Associated Press*] (SAG)
INTIP .... Integrated Information Processing
InTip .... Tipton County Public Library, Tipton, IN [*Library symbol*] [*Library of Congress*] (LCLS)
INTIPS .... Integrated Information Processing System [*Air Development Center, Rome, NY*]
INTIW .... Industrial Technol Wrrt'A' [*NASDAQ symbol*] (TTSB)
INTIZ.......... Industrial Technol Wrrt'B' [*NASDAQ symbol*] (TTSB)
Int J Criminol... International Journal of Criminology and Penology [*A publication*] (DLA)
IntJen .... International Jensen, Inc. [*Associated Press*] (SAG)
IntJhn .... Interstate/Johnson Lane, Inc. [*Formerly, Interstate Securities, Inc.*] [*Associated Press*] (SAG)
Int J Pol ...... International Journal of Politics [*A publication*] (DLA)
Int Jurid Assn Bull... International Juridical Association. Bulletin [*A publication*] (DLA)
INTK.......... Inotek Technologies [*NASDAQ symbol*] (TTSB)
INTK.......... Inotek Technologies, Inc. [*NASDAQ symbol*] (SAG)
INTK.......... Intake (MSA)
INTK.......... Intertank (KSC)
INTL .... Internal
INTL .... International (AFM)
intl............. International (VRA)
intl............. International (WDMC)
INTL .... International Movement of Catholic Students [*France*]
INTL .... Inter-Tel, Inc. [*NASDAQ symbol*] (NQ)
INTL .... Inter-Tel Inc. [*NASDAQ symbol*] (TTSB)
IntlAffairs .... International Affairs (DD)
IntlAllSv...... International Alliance Services, Inc. [*Associated Press*] (SAG)
Int'l & Comp L Bull... International and Comparative Law Bulletin [*A publication*] (DLA)
Int'l Arb Awards... Reports of International Arbitral Awards [*A publication*] (DLA)
Int'l Arb J .... International Arbitration Journal [*A publication*] (DLA)
Int'l Assoc L Lib Bull... International Association of Law Libraries. Bulletin [*A publication*] (DLA)
IntlAsst .... International Assets Holding Corp. [*Associated Press*] (SAG)
IntlAst........ International Assets Holding Corp. [*Associated Press*] (SAG)
Int Law Tr.... International Law Tracts [*A publication*] (DLA)
Int'l BA Bull... International Bar Association. Bulletin [*A publication*] (DLA)
Int'l Bar J .... International Bar Journal [*A publication*] (DLA)
Int'l BJ........ International Bar Journal [*A publication*] (DLA)
Int L Bull .... International Law Bulletin [*A publication*] (DLA)
IntlBus........ International Business Schools, Inc. [*Associated Press*] (SAG)
Int'l Bus Lawyer... International Business Lawyer [*London, England*] [*A publication*] (DLA)
Int'l Bus Ser... International Business Series [*A publication*] (DLA)
IntlCable...... International Cabletel, Inc. [*Associated Press*] (SAG)
IntlCer .... Internacional de Ceramica SA de CV [*Associated Press*] (SAG)
INTL COMB... Internal Combustion [*Freight*]
Int'l Crim Pol Rev... International Criminal Police Review [*A publication*] (DLA)
IntlCt.......... International Cutlery Ltd. [*Associated Press*] (SAG)
IntlCut........ International Cutlery Ltd. [*Associated Press*] (SAG)
Int'l Dig Health Leg... International Digest of Health Legislation [*A publication*] (DLA)
Int Legal Materials... International Legal Materials [*A publication*] (DLA)
IntLeisr .... International Leisure Hosts Ltd. [*Associated Press*] (SAG)
IntlElec .... International Electronics, Inc. [*Associated Press*] (SAG)
Int'l Encycl Comp L... International Encyclopedia of Comparative Law [*A publication*] (DLA)
IntLfe .... Intercontinental Life Corp. [*Associated Press*] (SAG)
Int'l Fin L Rev... International Financial Law Review [*A publication*] (DLA)
IntlgC.......... Intelligent Controls, Inc. [*Associated Press*] (SAG)
IntlgSys .... Intelligent Systems Corp. [*Associated Press*] (SAG)
Int Lib .... Intrationum Liber [*A publication*] (DSA)
INTLINE .... International Online Data Base [*The WEFA Group*] [*Information service or system*]
IntLivC .... Integrated Living Communities, Inc. [*Associated Press*] (SAG)
Int'l J Crim & Pen... International Journal of Criminology and Penology [*A publication*] (DLA)
Int'l J Crimin & Penol... International Journal of Criminology and Penology [*A publication*] (DLA)
Int'l J Legal Res... International Journal of Legal Research [*A publication*] (DLA)
Int'l J Off Ther & Comp Crim... International Journal of Offender Therapy and Comparative Criminology [*A publication*] (DLA)
Int'l Jurid Ass'n Bull... International Juridical Association. Bulletin [*A publication*] (DLA)
INTLK.......... Interlock (MSA)
Int'l Lab Reports... International Labour Reports [*A publication*] (DLA)
Int'l L Ass'n.. Reports of the International Law Association [*A publication*] (DLA)
Int'l L Ass'n Bull... Bulletin. International Law Association [*1936-38*] [*A publication*] (DLA)
Int'l Law ...... International Law [*A publication*] (DLA)
IntlIcll........ Intellicell Corp. [*Associated Press*] (SAG)
Int'l L Comm'n... International Law Commission [*United Nations*] (DLA)
Int'l L Doc ... International Law Documents [*A publication*] (DLA)
Int'l Legal Ed Newsl... International Legal Education Newsletter [*A publication*] (DLA)
INTLLGNC.... Intelligence

Int'l LLL....... International Lutheran Laymen's League (EA)
Int'l L Persp.. International Law Perspective [*A publication*] (DLA)
Int'l LR .... International Law Reports [*A publication*]
Int'l L Rep ... International Law Reports [*A publication*] (DLA)
Int'l L Stud... International Law Studies [*Naval War College*] [*A publication*] (DLA)
Int LN .... International Law Notes [*A publication*]
Int L Notes... International Law Notes [*England*] [*A publication*] (DLA)
IntlNtwk....... International Network Services [*Associated Press*] (SAG)
IntlNurs........ International Nursing Services, Inc. [*Associated Press*] (SAG)
INTLOC........ Interdiction of Lines of Communication (PDAA)
IntLotry .... International Lottery, Inc. [*Associated Press*] (SAG)
IntLotTot...... International Lottery & Totalizator Systems [*Associated Press*] (SAG)
IntlPizza...... International Pizza Co. [*Associated Press*] (SAG)
IntlPlatin...... International Platinum Corp. [*Associated Press*] (SAG)
IntlPost....... International Post Ltd. [*Associated Press*] (SAG)
IntlPrec........ International Precious Metals [*Associated Press*] (SAG)
IntlPrecM..... International Precious Metals [*Associated Press*] (SAG)
Int'l Prop Inv J.. International Property Investment Journal [*A publication*] (DLA)
IntLR .... International Law Reports [*A publication*] (DI)
Int'l Rev Ad Sci... International Review of Administrative Sciences [*A publication*] (DLA)
Int'l Rev Crim Policy... International Review of Criminal Policy [*United Nations*] (DLA)
Int'l Soc'y of Barr Q... International Society of Barristers. Quarterly [*A publication*] (DLA)
IntlSpdw ..... International Speedway Corp. [*Associated Press*] (SAG)
IntlSpr .... International Sports Wagering, Inc. [*Associated Press*] (SAG)
IntlSrgL....... Intelligent Surgical LASERs, Inc. [*Associated Press*] (SAG)
Int'l Surv LDLL... International Survey of Legal Decisions on Labour Law [*1925-38*] [*A publication*] (DLA)
Int'l Sym Comp L... International Symposium on Comparative Law [*A publication*] (DLA)
Int'l Tax & Bus Law... International Tax and Business Lawyer [*A publication*] (DLA)
IntlTDS .... International Telecommunication Data Systems, Inc. [*Associated Press*] (SAG)
IntlVit......... International Vitamin Corp. [*Associated Press*] (SAG)
INTLVR .... Interleaver (MCD)
Int'l Woman Law... International Woman Lawyer [*A publication*] (DLA)
INTM.......... Interim Services [*NASDAQ symbol*] (TTSB)
INTM.......... Intermediate (KSC)
INTMA .... International Mail [*A publication*]
INTMD .... Intermediate (MSA)
INTMED .... Intermediate (AFM)
INTMED .... Internal Medicine (AABC)
IntMedI........ Intelligent Medical Imaging, Inc. [*Associated Press*] (SAG)
IntMet........ International Metals Acquisition Corp. [*Associated Press*] (SAG)
IntmetC........ Intermet Corp. [*Associated Press*] (SAG)
IntMicr........ International Microcomputer Software, Inc. [*Associated Press*] (SAG)
IntMJ.......... International Microfilm Journal of Legal Medicine, New York, NY [*Library symbol Library of Congress*] (LCLS)
IntMP.......... International Micro-Print Preservation, Inc., New York, NY [*Library symbol Library of Congress*] (LCLS)
INTMS .... Internal Messenger Service [*Hotels*]
INTMT.......... Intermittent (MSA)
IntMult........ International Multifoods Corp. [*Associated Press*] (SAG)
IntMur........ International Murex Technologies [*Associated Press*] (SAG)
INTN .... InStent, Inc. [*NASDAQ symbol*] (SAG)
INTN .... Intention
IntNDS........ Interstate National Dealer Services, Inc. [*Associated Press*] (SAG)
IntnetS......... Intranet Solutions, Inc. [*Associated Press*] (SAG)
IntnetSol...... Intranet Solutions, Inc. [*Associated Press*] (SAG)
INTNEW .... International News [*Database*] (IT)
INTN'L .... International
INT NOCT.... Inter Noctem [*During the Night*] [*Pharmacy*]
INTNS .... Intentions (FAAC)
INTNS .... In Transit
INTNTNL....... Intentional
IntNur.......... International Nursing Services, Inc. [*Associated Press*] (SAG)
IntNur.......... Interntional Nursing Services, Inc. [*Associated Press*] (SAG)
IntNYQ .... Intercapital New York Quality Municipal Security Trust [*Associated Press*] (SAG)
INTO .... Industrial Training Opportunities Exhibition (ITD)
INTO .... Inhibited Nitrogen Tetroxide
INTO .... Initio, Inc. [*NASDAQ symbol*] (SAG)
INTO .... Intelligence Officer [*Army*]
INTO .... Intuitive Network Total Office [*Benchmark Associates*] [*Computer science*]
INTO .... Iran National Tourist Organization
INTO .... Irish National Teachers' Organisation
int obst .... Intestinal Obstruction [*Medicine*] (MAE)
INTOP .... International Operations Simulation (IEEE)
INTOPS .... Interdiction Operations [*Navy*] (NVT)
INTOR .... International TOKAMAK Reactor [*Thermonuclear-fusion system*]
INTOR .... International Torus Design [*Nuclear energy*] (NUCP)
INTOSAI....... International Organization of Supreme Audit Institutions [*Vienna, Austria*] (EA)
InTour......... International Tourist Entertainment Corp. [*Associated Press*] (SAG)
INTOX......... Intoxication
INTOX L....... Intoxicating Liquor [*Legal term*] (DLA)
Int P........... International Pharmacopoeia [*A publication*]
INTP........... Interpoint [*NASDAQ symbol*] (SAG)
INTP........... Interpoint Corp. [*NASDAQ symbol*] (TTSB)
INTP........... Interport Trucking [*MTMC*] (TAG)
IntPack .... Integrated Packaging Assembly Corp. [*Associated Press*] (SAG)
IntPap......... International Paper Co. [*Associated Press*] (SAG)

IntpbGp........ [The] Interpublic Group of Companies, Inc. [Associated Press] (SAG)
INTPH......... Interphone
INTPHIBRFT... Interim Amphibious Refresher Training [Navy] (NVT)
Intphse........ Interphase Corp. [Associated Press] (SAG)
INTPHTR...... Interphase Transformer [Electronics]
INTPLDR...... Interpleader [Legal] [British] (ROG)
IntPly.......... Intertape Polymer Group [Associated Press] (SAG)
INTPN......... Interpretation (AFM)
Intpnt......... Interpoint Corp. [Associated Press] (SAG)
INTPO......... Interpole [Electromagnetics]
IntPoly........ Intertape Polymer Group [Associated Press] (SAG)
Intpore........ Interpore International [Associated Press] (SAG)
INTPR........ Interpret (AFM)
Intpr.......... Interpretation: A Journal of Bible and Theology [A publication] (BRI)
Int Private Law... Private International Law [A publication] (DLA)
IntPtr.......... International Petroleum Corp. [Associated Press] (SAG)
Int Qk........ Interrupted Quick [Flashing] Light [Navigation signal]
INTQKFL...... Interrupted Quick Flashing Light [Navigation signal]
IntQuest...... IntelliQuest Information Group, Inc. [Associated Press] (SAG)
intr............. Intarsia (VRA)
INTR.......... Interior (KSC)
INTR.......... Interior
INTR.......... Intermittent (AFM)
INTR.......... Internal (KSC)
INTR.......... Interrupt [Computer science Telecommunications]
INTR.......... Interscience Computer [NASDAQ symbol] (TTSB)
INTR.......... Intersciences Computer Corp. [NASDAQ symbol] (SAG)
INTR.......... Intransitive
INTR.......... Introduction
INTR.......... Intruder
InTR.......... Rose Polytechnic Institute, Terre Haute, IN [Library symbol Library of Congress] (LCLS)
INTRA........ International Travel (MCD)
Intra.......... Intramural (DLA)
INTRACONS... In-Transit Control System (PDAA)
IntrAct........ InterAction Media Corp. [Associated Press] (SAG)
INTRAFAX... Facsimile System [Western Union trade name]
INTRAFILM... International Travel-Adventure Film Guild [Defunct] (EA)
Intra L Rev (St LU)... Intramural Law Review (St. Louis University) [A publication] (DLA)
Intramural LJ... Intramural Law Journal [A publication] (DLA)
Intramural L Rev... Intramural Law Review [A publication] (DLA)
INTRAN...... Infrared Transmitting
INTRAN...... Input Translator [IBM Corp.] [Computer science]
INTRANS..... Intransitive (ROG)
IN TRANS... In Transitu [In Transit] [Latin] (ROG)
INTRANST... International Transportation Tracking System [Department of Transportation]
INTRAST..... Intrastate [Legal shorthand] (LWAP)
Intrav........ Intrav, Inc. [Associated Press] (SAG)
INTRC........ Intricate (MSA)
IntrCal........ Intercapital California Insured Municipal Income Trust [Associated Press] (SAG)
INTRCHNG... Interchange
IntrCm....... Intermedia Communications of Florida, Inc. [Associated Press] (SAG)
Intrcrgo....... Intercargo Corp. [Associated Press] (SAG)
INTRCTV..... Interactive
IntRect........ International Rectifier Corp. [Associated Press] (SAG)
INTREDIS..... International Tree Disease Register [US Forest Service] (NITA)
INTREDIS..... International Tree Disease Register System for Literature Retrieval in Forest Pathology [National Agricultural Library]
INTREP....... Intelligence Report (NATG)
INTREPT...... Intelligence Report
INT REV...... Internal Revenue (ROG)
Int Rev Bull... Internal Revenue Bulletin [A publication] (DLA)
Int Rev Crim Pol... International Review of Criminal Policy [United Nations] (DLA)
INTREX....... Information Transfer Exchange [Library science]
INTREX....... Information Transfer Experiment [Massachusetts Institute of Technology] (DIT)
INTRF........ Interference [Telecommunications] (MSA)
Intrfcln....... Interface, Inc. [Associated Press] (SAG)
IntrFlt......... Interactive Flight Technologies, Inc. [Associated Press] (SAG)
IntrFlt......... Interactive Flight Technologies, Inc. Cl.A [Associated Press] (SAG)
INTRFT....... Interim Refresher Training [Navy]
INTRFTH..... Interfaith
INTRG........ Integrate (AFIT)
INTRG........ Interrogate (MSA)
Intrirs........ Interiors, Inc. [Associated Press] (SAG)
INTRLCD..... Interlaced
Intrleaf....... Interleaf, Inc. [Associated Press] (SAG)
Intrlk......... Interlink Electronics, Inc. [Associated Press] (SAG)
INTRLKD..... Interlocked
Intrlke........ [The] Interlake Corp. [Associated Press] (SAG)
Intrlne........ Interline Resources Corp. [Associated Press] (SAG)
INTRLVR..... Interleaver (NASA)
Intrmagn..... Intermagnetics General Corp. [Associated Press] (SAG)
intr-md....... Inter-media (VRA)
INTRMT...... Interment (AABC)
INTRMTRGN... Inter-Mountain Region (FAAC)
Intrn.......... Interneuron Pharmaceuticals, Inc. [Associated Press] (SAG)
INTRN........ Intravenous [Medicine]
Intrnt......... Intranet, Inc. [Associated Press] (SAG)
INTRNTL...... International
Intrnu......... Interneuron Pharmaceuticals, Inc. [Associated Press] (SAG)
INTRO........ Introduction (MSA)

intro........... Introduction (WDMC)
intro........... Introductory (WDMC)
INTROD....... Introduction
INTROD....... Introduzione [Introductory Movement] [Music] (ROG)
INTROPTA.... Introscripta [Written Within] [Latin] (ROG)
int rot........ Internal Rotation [Orthopedics] (DAVI)
INTRP........ Interrupt
INTRPL....... Interpolation (MSA)
INTRPLRY.... Interpupillary
Intrpol........ Interpool, Inc. [Associated Press] (SAG)
INTRPT....... Interrupt (AFM)
INTRQ........ Interrupt Request [Computer science] (MHDI)
INTRST....... Interest
INTRSTG..... Interstage (KSC)
Intrsy........ Intersystems, Inc. [Associated Press] (SAG)
Intrsystm..... Intersystems, Inc. [Associated Press] (SAG)
Intrtan........ Intertan, Inc. [Associated Press] (SAG)
IntrTel........ Inter-Tel, Inc. [Associated Press] (SAG)
INTRW........ Interscience Computer Wrrt [NASDAQ symbol] (TTSB)
IntrWBcp..... InterWest Bancorp [Associated Press] (SAG)
INTS.......... Integrated Systems, Inc. [NASDAQ symbol] (SAG)
INTS.......... Intense
InTS.......... Terre Haute Spectator, Terre Haute, IN [Library symbol Library of Congress] (LCLS)
IntscCpt ...... Intersciences Computer Corp. [Associated Press] (SAG)
INTSCT....... Intersect (MSA)
INTSF........ Intensify
IntShip........ International Shipholding Corp. [Associated Press] (SAG)
INTSHP....... Intership
IntSilSy....... Integrated Silicon Systems [Associated Press] (SAG)
INTSORMIL... International Sorghum and Millet Research
INTSOY....... International Soybean Program
IntSpclty ..... International Specialty Products [Associated Press] (SAG)
IntSr.......... Intelligent Surgical Lasers, Inc. [Associated Press] (SAG)
INTST........ Intensity
INTST........ Interest [Finance, Law] (ROG)
IntStand...... International Standards Group Ltd. [Associated Press] (SAG)
IntstBak...... Interstate Bakeries Corp. [Formerly, Interstate Brands Corp.] [Associated Press] (SAG)
INTSTDTHD... International Standard Thread (MCD)
INTSTE....... Interstate
INTSTG....... Interstage
InstGC........ Interstate General Ltd. [Associated Press] (SAG)
InstNDS ..... Interstate National Dealer Services, Inc. [Associated Press] (SAG)
InstPw....... Interstate Power Co. [Associated Press] (SAG)
INTSTY....... Intestacy [Legal shorthand] (LWAP)
INTSUM....... Intelligence Summary
INTSV........ Intensive (WGA)
INTSY........ Intensify (DNAB)
IntSysC....... Integrated Systems Consulting Group, Inc. [Associated Press] (SAG)
INTT.......... Interest [Finance, Law] (ROG)
Int Tax Jour... International Tax Journal [A publication] (DLA)
IntTest........ International Testing Services Inc. [Associated Press] (SAG)
IntThr......... International Thoroughbred Breeders, Inc. [Associated Press] (SAG)
IntThrgh...... International Throughbred Breeders, Inc. [Associated Press] (SAG)
IntTourE...... International Tourist Entertainment Corp. [Associated Press] (SAG)
Int Trade LJ... International Trade Law Journal [A publication] (DLA)
InTTS.......... Terre Haute Tribune-Star, Terre Haute, IN [Library symbol Library of Congress] (LCLS)
INTU .... Intuit, Inc. [NASDAQ symbol] (SAG)
INTUC........ Indian National Trades Union Congress
INTUG......... International Telecommunications Users Group [Telecommunications Information service or system] (IID)
Intuit.......... Intuit, Inc. [Associated Press] (SAG)
INTURISMO... Instituto Nicaraguense de Turismo (EY)
INTV.......... Association of Independent Television Stations (EA)
INTV.......... Instrumentation Television (AFM)
INTV.......... Interview (CINC)
INTV.......... InterVoice [NASDAQ symbol] (TTSB)
INTV.......... InterVoice, Inc. [NASDAQ symbol] (NQ)
InTV.......... Vigo County Public Library, Terre Haute, IN [Library symbol Library of Congress] (LCLS)
IntVer......... International Verifact, Inc. [Associated Press] (SAG)
IntVerif........ International Verifact, Inc. [Associated Press] (SAG)
IntvisB........ Intervisual Books, Inc. [Associated Press] (SAG)
INTVL........ Interval (MSA)
INTVLM....... Intervalometer [Military ordnance]
Intvoice...... InterVoice, Inc. [Associated Press] (SAG)
InTVS.......... Vigo County School Corp., Instructional Materials Center, Terre Haute, IN [Library symbol Library of Congress] (LCLS)
INTVW........ Interview (AFM)
INTWF........ Indian National Textile Workers' Federation
InTWHi........ Wabash Valley Historical Society, Terre Haute, IN [Library symbol Library of Congress] (LCLS)
Int Woman L... International Woman Lawyer [A publication] (DLA)
INTWORLSA... International Third World Legal Studies Association (EA)
INTXA......... Interiors, Inc. [NASDAQ symbol] (SAG)
INTXA......... Interiors Inc.'A' [NASDAQ symbol] (TTSB)
INTXL......... Interiors Inc. Wrrt [NASDAQ symbol] (TTSB)
INTXP......... Interiors Inc.Cv'A'Pfd [NASDAQ symbol] (TTSB)
INTXW........ Interiors Inc. Wrrt'A' [NASDAQ symbol] (TTSB)
INTXZ......... Interiors Inc.Wrrt'B' [NASDAQ symbol] (TTSB)
INTY.......... Intestacy [Legal] (ROG)
IntYog........ International Yogurt Co. [Associated Press] (SAG)

inu .... Indiana [*MARC country of publication code Library of Congress*] (LCCP)

InU.............. Indiana University, Bloomington, IN [*Library symbol Library of Congress*] (LCLS)

INU .... Inertial Navigation Unit

INU .... Integration Unit

INU .... International Nutrition & Genetics Corp. [*Vancouver Stock Exchange symbol*]

INU .... Inuyama [*Japan*] [*Seismograph station code, US Geological Survey*] (SEIS)

INU .... Nauru [*Nauru*] [*Airport symbol*] (OAG)

InU-A .... Indiana University, Anatomy-Physiology Laboratory, Bloomington, IN [*Library symbol Library of Congress*] (LCLS)

InU-AT .... Indiana University, Archive of Traditional Music, Bloomington, IN [*Library symbol*] [*Library of Congress*] (LCLS)

InU-B .... Indiana University, Biology Library, Bloomington, IN [*Library symbol Library of Congress*] (LCLS)

InU-BA .... Indiana University, School of Business Administration, Bloomington, IN [*Library symbol Library of Congress*] (LCLS)

InUc .... Union City Public Library, Union City, IN [*Library symbol Library of Congress*] (LCLS)

INucE .... Institution of Nuclear Engineers [*British*]

InU-D .... Indiana University, School of Dentistry, Indianapolis, IN [*Library symbol Library of Congress*] (LCLS)

InU-Fw .... Indiana University, Fort Wayne Regional Campus, Fort Wayne, IN [*Library symbol Library of Congress*] (LCLS)

InU-I .... Indiana University, Indianapolis Regional Campus, Indianapolis, IN [*Library symbol Library of Congress*] (LCLS)

InU-ISR .... Indiana University, Institute for Sex Research, Bloomington, IN [*Library symbol Library of Congress*] (LCLS)

InU-K .... Indiana University, Kokomo Regional Campus, Kokomo, IN [*Library symbol Library of Congress*] (LCLS)

InU-L .... Indiana University, Law Library, Indianapolis, IN [*Library symbol Library of Congress*] (LCLS)

InU-Li .... Indiana University, Lilly Library, Bloomington, IN [*Library symbol Library of Congress*] (LCLS)

InU-M .... Indiana University, School of Medicine, Indianapolis, IN [*Library symbol Library of Congress*] (LCLS)

INUMRC...... Northwest Indiana Health Science Library Consortium [*Library network*]

InU-Mu .... Indiana University at Bloomington, Music Library, Bloomington, IN [*Library symbol*] [*Library of Congress*] (LCLS)

InU-N .... Indiana University, Northwest Regional Campus, Gary, IN [*Library symbol Library of Congress*] (LCLS)

InU-Nea .... Indiana University Southeast, New Albany, IN [*Library symbol Library of Congress*] (LCLS)

InU-O .... Indiana University, Optometry Library, Bloomington, IN [*Library symbol Library of Congress*] (LCLS)

InUpT.......... Taylor University, Upland, IN [*Library symbol Library of Congress*] (LCLS)

InU-R .... Indiana University at Bloomington, Lilly Rare Books, Bloomington, IN [*Library symbol Library of Congress*] (LCLS)

INUS .... Innovus Corp. [*NASDAQ symbol*] (TTSB)

INUS .... Innovus Corp. [*NASDAQ symbol*] (SAG)

INUS .... Inside the United States

InU-Sb .... Indiana University, South Bend Regional Campus, South Bend, IN [*Library symbol Library of Congress*] (LCLS)

InU-Se .... Indiana University, Southeastern Regional Campus, Jeffersonville, IN [*Library symbol Library of Congress*] (LCLS)

INUW .... Irish National Union of Woodworkers (BI)

INV.............. Inductive Null Voltage

INV.............. In-Line Needle Valve

INV.............. Invalid (IAA)

INV.............. Invasion

INV.............. Invective

INV.............. Invenit [*He, or She, Designed It*] [*Latin*]

INV.............. Invent (AABC)

INV.............. Inventory (AFM)

INV.............. Inveralochy [*Australia Seismograph station code, US Geological Survey*] (SEIS)

INV.............. Inverness [*Scotland*] [*Airport symbol*] (OAG)

INV.............. Inverse [*or Invert*]

inv .... Inverse (IDOE)

INV.............. Inversia [*Latvia*] [*ICAO designator*] (FAAC)

inv .... Inversion (DAVI)

INV.............. Inverter (KSC)

INV.............. Investigation

INV.............. Investment

INVS .... Invitation

INV.............. Invitational Race [*Harness racing*]

INV.............. Invoice [*Billing*] (AFM)

INV.............. Invoice

inv .... Invoice [*Billing*] (ODBW)

INV.............. Involuntary

INV.............. Iris Neovascularization [*Opthalmology*]

INVAC .... Investment Account [*Postal Service*] [*British*]

INVADJ .... Inventory Adjustment (MCD)

INVAL .... Invalid (IAA)

InVal .... Valparaiso-Porter County Public Library System, Valparaiso, IN [*Library symbol Library of Congress*] (LCLS)

InValCR .... Porter County Recorder's Office, Valparaiso, IN [*Library symbol Library of Congress*] (LCLS)

InValHi .... Historical Society of Porter County, Valparaiso, IN [*Library symbol Library of Congress*] (LCLS)

InValU .... Valparaiso University, Valparaiso, IN [*Library symbol Library of Congress*] (LCLS)

InValVM .... Valparaiso Vidette-Messenger, Valparaiso, IN [*Library symbol Library of Congress*] (LCLS)

INVAR.......... Invariant

InVb .... Van Buren Public Library, Van Buren, IN [*Library symbol Library of Congress*] (LCLS)

InvBank....... Investors Bank Corp. [*Associated Press*] (SAG)

Invcare .... Invacare Corp. [*Associated Press*] (SAG)

INVCE .... Invoice [*Billing*] (ROG)

INVCURR..... Inverse Current [*Electronics*] (IAA)

INVD .... Invalidate Data [*Cache*] [*Computer instruction*] (PCM)

INV DOC ATTACH... Invoice with Documents Attached [*Billing*] (ROG)

InVe .... Switzerland County Public Library, Vevay, IN [*Library symbol Library of Congress*] (LCLS)

InVeCR .... Switzerland County Recorder's Office, Vevay, IN [*Library symbol Library of Congress*] (LCLS)

INVECS .... Innovative Vehicle Electronic Control System [*Motor vehicles*]

INVECS .... Intelligent and Innovative Vehicle Electronic Control System

INVENT .... Institute for Ventures in New Technology

inver .... Inversion (DAVI)

InVeRE........ Vevay Reville-Enterprise, Vevay, IN [*Library symbol Library of Congress*] (LCLS)

INVERN........ Inverness [*County in Scotland*]

InVerR .... Versailles Republican, Versailles, IN [*Library symbol Library of Congress*] (LCLS)

InVerRHi...... Ripley County Historical Society, Versailles, IN [*Library symbol Library of Congress*] (LCLS)

INVERT .... Invertebrate (WGA)

INVERTEB .... Invertebrate

INVES .... Investigate [*or Investigation*] (AFM)

Invesco....... Invesco PLC [*Associated Press*] (SAG)

InvescoF...... Invesco Funding [*Associated Press*] (SAG)

InVeSD .... Switzerland Democrat, Vevay, IN [*Library symbol Library of Congress*] (LCLS)

INVEST .... Integrated Vehicle System Technology (MCD)

INVEST .... Investigation

INVEST .... Investment

invest.......... Investment (DD)

INVESTIG ..... Investigation

INVEX .... International Exhibition of Inventions and Novel Features (TSPED)

InvFnSv....... Investors Financial Services Corp. [*Associated Press*] (SAG)

InvGrMu....... Investment Grade Municipal Income Fund [*Associated Press*] (SAG)

INVI .... Invitro International [*Formerly, Ropak Laboratories*] [*NASDAQ symbol*] (SPSG)

InVi .... Vincennes and Knox County Public Libraries, Vincennes, IN [*Library symbol Library of Congress*] (LCLS)

InvIns.......... Investors Insurance Group [*Associated Press*] (SAG)

InViSC .... Vincennes Sun Commercial, Vincennes, IN [*Library symbol Library of Congress*] (LCLS)

InVision .... InVision Technologies, Inc. [*Associated Press*] (SAG)

INVIT .... Invitation (KSC)

Invitr........... Invitro International [*Associated Press*] (SAG)

InViU .... Vincennes University, Vincennes, IN [*Library symbol Library of Congress*] (LCLS)

InViU-Hi...... Vincennes University, Byron R. Lewis Historical Collections Library, Vincennes, IN [*Library symbol Library of Congress*] (LCLS)

Invivo.......... Invivo Corp. [*Associated Press*] (SAG)

INVLT.......... Involute

INV MGT...... Inventory Management (MCD)

INVN .... Inventory (MSA)

INVN .... InVision Technologies [*NASDAQ symbol*] (TTSB)

INVN .... InVision Technologies, Inc. [*NASDAQ symbol*] (SAG)

InVnCR........ Jennings County Recorder's Office, Vernon, IN [*Library symbol Library of Congress*] (LCLS)

INVOF .... In the Vicinity Of (FAAC)

INVOG......... Information Officers Working in Voluntary Organisations (AIE)

INVOL......... Involuntary

INVOLEX ..... Involuntary Extension

INVOLV .... Involve [*Coat*] [*Pharmacy*]

INVR .... Innovir Laboratories [*NASDAQ symbol*] (TTSB)

INVR .... Innovir Laboratories, Inc. [*NASDAQ symbol*] (SAG)

INVREC .... Inventory Record (MCD)

Inv Reg Cas... Notes of Decisions of Appeal Court of Registration at Inverness [*1835-53*] [*Scotland*] [*A publication*] (DLA)

Inv Rhet....... De Inventione Rhetorica [*of Cicero*] [*Classical studies*] (OCD)

INVRN......... Inversion [*NWS*] (FAAC)

INVRW........ Innovir Laboratories Wrrt'A' [*NASDAQ symbol*] (TTSB)

INVRZ......... Innovir Laboratories Wrrt'B' [*NASDAQ symbol*] (TTSB)

INVS .... Inverse (MSA)

INVST .... Invest

INVSTAR...... Investigate and Report (FAAC)

INVSTD .... Invested

INVSTGTN.... Investigation

INVSTGTV.... Investigative

INVSTMNT ... Investment

INVSTR........ Investigator

INVT .... Invenit [*He, or She, Designed It*] [*Latin*] (ROG)

INVT .... Inventory (AABC)

INVT .... Invert (MSA)

INVT .... Investext [*Business Research Corp.*]

InvTech........ Investment Technology Group [*Associated Press*] (SAG)

InvTitl......... Investors Title Insurance Co. [*Associated Press*] (SAG)

INVTNL........ Invitational

INVTR .... Inverter

INVTY	Inventory
INVV	Inverse Voltage [*Electronics*] (IAA)
INVX	Innovex, Inc. [*NASDAQ symbol*] (NQ)
INVY	Inventory (ROG)
INW	Internet World
INW	Winslow [*Arizona*] [*Airport symbol*] (OAG)
INW	Winslow, AZ [*Location identifier FAA*] (FAAL)
InWab	Wabash Carnegie Public Library, Wabash, IN [*Library symbol Library of Congress*] (LCLS)
InWabHi	Wabash County Historical Museum, Wabash, IN [*Library symbol Library of Congress*] (LCLS)
InWabPD	Wabash Plain Dealer, Wabash, IN [*Library symbol Library of Congress*] (LCLS)
InWak	Wakarusa Public Library, Wakarusa, IN [*Library symbol Library of Congress*] (LCLS)
InWal	Walkerton-Lincoln Township Public Library, Walkerton, IN [*Library symbol Library of Congress*] (LCLS)
InWalIN	Walkerton Independent-News, Walkerton, IN [*Library symbol Library of Congress*] (LCLS)
InWan	Wanatah Public Library, Wanatah, IN [*Library symbol Library of Congress*] (LCLS)
InWars	Warsaw Public Library, Warsaw, IN [*Library symbol Library of Congress*] (LCLS)
InWarsR	Kosciusko County Recorder's Office, Warsaw, IN [*Library symbol Library of Congress*] (LCLS)
InWarsTU	Warsaw Times-Union, Warsaw, IN [*Library symbol Library of Congress*] (LCLS)
InWas	Carnegie Public Library, Washington, IN [*Library symbol Library of Congress*] (LCLS)
INWAS	Inertial Navigation and Weapons Attack System (MCD)
InWasTH	Washington Times-Herald, Washington, IN [*Library symbol Library of Congress*] (LCLS)
InWat	Waterloo-Grant Township Public Library, Waterloo, IN [*Library symbol Library of Congress*] (LCLS)
INWATE	Integrating Waveguide Technology (PDAA)
INWATS	Inward Wide Area Telephone Service [*Bell System*]
InWav	Waveland Public Library, Waveland, IN [*Library symbol Library of Congress*] (LCLS)
INWD	Inward (MSA)
InWebaC	West Baden College, West Baden Springs, IN [*Library symbol Library of Congress*] (LCLS)
InWefG	GTE North, Inc., Westfield, IN [*Library symbol*] [*Library of Congress*] (LCLS)
InWele	West Lebanon Pike Township Public Library, West Lebanon, IN [*Library symbol Library of Congress*] (LCLS)
InWevP	Purdue University, North Central Campus, Westville, IN [*Library symbol Library of Congress*] (LCLS)
INWG	International Network Working Group [*International Federation for Information Processing*]
InWh	Whiting Public Library, Whiting, IN [*Library symbol Library of Congress*] (LCLS)
InWhC	Calumet College, Whiting, IN [*Library symbol Library of Congress*] (LCLS)
InWhHi	Whiting-Robertsdale Historical Society, Whiting, IN [*Library symbol Library of Congress*] (LCLS)
InWil	Williamsport-Washington Township Public Library, Williamsport, IN [*Library symbol Library of Congress*] (LCLS)
InWilCR	Warren County Recorder's Office, Williamsport, IN [*Library symbol Library of Congress*] (LCLS)
InWilR	Williamsport Review-Republican, Williamsport, IN [*Library symbol Library of Congress*] (LCLS)
InWina	Pulaski County Public Library, Winamac, IN [*Library symbol Library of Congress*] (LCLS)
InWincCR	Randolph County Recorder's Office, Winchester, IN [*Library symbol Library of Congress*] (LCLS)
InWinFM	Free Methodist Historical Center, Winona Lake, IN [*Library symbol Library of Congress*] (LCLS)
InWinG	Grace College, Winona Lake, IN [*Library symbol Library of Congress*] (LCLS)
INWL	International Network of Women Liberals (EAIO)
InWo	Worthington Jefferson Township Public Library, Worthington, IN [*Library symbol Library of Congress*] (LCLS)
InWol	Wolcott Public Library, Wolcott, IN [*Library symbol Library of Congress*] (LCLS)
InWolE	New Wolcott Enterprise, Wolcott, IN [*Library symbol Library of Congress*] (LCLS)
InWoT	Worthington Times, Worthington, IN [*Library symbol Library of Congress*] (LCLS)
INX	Inanwatan [*West Irian, Indonesia*] [*Airport symbol*] (AD)
INX	Index Character [*Computer science*]
INX	Inexco Oil Co. [*Toronto Stock Exchange symbol*]
INX	Ion Exchange (NRCH)
INXLTR	Input Translator [*IBM Corp.*] [*Computer science*] (MSA)
INY	Batesville, AR [*Location identifier FAA*] (FAAL)
INY	Ithaca [*New York*] [*Seismograph station code, US Geological Survey*] (SEIS)
INZ	In Salah [*Algeria*] [*Airport symbol*] (OAG)
INZ	Istituto Nazionale ADS [*NYSE symbol*] (TTSB)
INZ	Istituto Nazionale Delle Assicorazino SPA [*NYSE symbol*] (SAG)
InZSM	Sullivan Museum, Zionsville, IN [*Library symbol Library of Congress*] (LCLS)
IO	Air Paris [*ICAO designator*] (AD)
IO	British Indian Ocean Territory [*ANSI two-letter standard code*] (CNC)
IO	Image Orthicon
I/O	Inboard-Outboard [*Boating*]

IO	Incisal Opening [*Medicine*] (MAE)
IO	Incoming Orders
IO	Indian Ocean
IO	India Office [*British*]
io	Indonesia [*pt (Portuguese Timor) used in records cataloged before January 1978*] [*MARC country of publication code Library of Congress*] (LCCP)
IO	Industrial Operations (MCD)
I/O	Industry/Occupation (OICC)
IO	Infant Orphan [*British*] (ROG)
IO	Infantry Officer [*British military*] (DMA)
IO	Inferior Oblique [*Muscle*] [*Anatomy*]
IO	Inferior Olive [*Neuroanatomy*]
IO	Information Officer
IO	Information Operation [*Military*] (RDA)
IO	Information Overload
IO	Initial Only (AFM)
IO	Initial Opening [*Pressure*] [*Measurement*] (DAVI)
IO	Injector Orifice
IO	In Order
I/O	In-Port Operations [*USCG*] (TAG)
I/O	Input/Output [*Computer science*]
I/O	Input/Output [*Computer science*]
IO	Input Output, Inc. [*NYSE symbol*] (SAG)
IO	Input/Output Inc. [*NYSE symbol*] (TTSB)
IO	Inspection Opening (ADA)
IO	Inspection Order (NATG)
IO	Inspection Outline
IO	Institute for Oceanography [*Environmental Science Services Administration*]
I/O	Instructor/Operator
IO	Intake Opens [*Valve position*]
IO	Intelligence Office [*or Officer*]
IO	Intelligence Oversight (DOMA)
IO	Intercept Officer
IO	Interest Only [*Finance*]
IO	Interest Only Strip [*Mortgage security*]
IO	Intermediary Organization [*Physiology*]
IO	Internal Os [*or Orifice*] [*Medicine*] (DAVI)
IO	International Octal (IAA)
IO	International Organizations [*A publication*]
IO	Interpersonal Orientation (BARN)
IO	Interpreter Officer [*Military British*]
IO	Interpretive Operation
IO	Intestinal Obstruction [*Medicine*]
IO	Intraocular
IO	Inventory Objective
IO	Investigating Officer
io	Iodo [*As substituent on nucleoside*] [*Biochemistry*]
IO	Ion Engine (AAG)
Io	Ionium [*Th230, radioactive isotope of thorium*]
IO	Iowa
IO	Irish Office
IO	Issuing Office
IO	Iterative Operation
IOA	Illinois Optometric Association (SRA)
IOA	Imaging Optics Assembly (MCD)
IOA	Indiana Optometric Association (SRA)
IOA	Indian Ocean Area (MCD)
IOA	Indian Ocean Arts Association [*Australia*]
IOA	Indian Overseas Airways
IOA	Inflammatory Osteoarthritis [*Medicine*]
IOA	Initial Outfitting Allowance [*Navy*]
IOA	Input-Output Adapter [*Computer science*] (NASA)
IOA	Input-Output Address [*Computer science*] (KSC)
IOA	Input-Output Analysis [*Economics*]
IOA	Input-Output Assembly [*Computer science*] (MCD)
IOA	Institute of Acoustics [*British*] (DBA)
IoA	Institute of Administration [*University of New South Wales*] [*Australia*]
IOA	Institute of Outdoor Advertising [*New York, NY*] (EA)
IOA	Institute on Aging [*Portland State University*] [*Research center*] (RCD)
IOA	Institute on Aging [*University of Wisconsin - Madison*] [*Research center*] (RCD)
IOA	Instrumentation Operating Area
IOA	Instrument Operating Assembly
IOA	Interfaith Office on Accompaniment
IOA	International Office for Audiophonology (EA)
IOA	International Olympic Academy
IOA	International Omega Association (EA)
IOA	International Order of the Armadillo (EA)
IOA	International Orthoptic Association [*British*] (EAIO)
IOA	International Osteopathic Association (EA)
IOA	International Ozone Association (EA)
IOA	Interocular Asynchrony [*Ophthalmology*]
IOA	Intraoperative Autotransfusion [*Medicine*]
IOA	Ioannina [*Greece*] [*Airport symbol*] (OAG)
IOA	Iona Industries, Inc. [*Vancouver Stock Exchange symbol*]
IOA	Iowa Airways, Inc. [*ICAO designator*] (FAAC)
IOA	Irish Orienteering Association (EAIO)
IOa	Oak Park Public Library, Oak Park, IL [*Library symbol Library of Congress*] (LCLS)
IOAC	Infantry Officer Advanced Course [*Army*] (INF)
IOAC/RC	Infantry Officer Advanced Correspondence Course/Reserve Component (INF)

IOa-D .... Oak Park Public Library, Dole Branch, Oak Park, IL [*Library symbol Library of Congress*] (LCLS)

IOaHS .... Oak Park-River Forest High School, Oak Park, IL [*Library symbol Library of Congress*] (LCLS)

IOakSD .... Oakland Unit School District, Oakland, IL [*Library symbol*] [*Library of Congress*] (LCLS)

IOa-M .... Oak Park Public Library, Maze Branch, Oak Park, IL [*Library symbol Library of Congress*] (LCLS)

IOAN .... Inspect [*and Repair*] Only as Needed [*MTMC*] (TAG)

IOAT .... International Organization Against Trachoma [*Creteil, France*] (EA)

IOAU .... Input/Output Access Unit [*Computer science*]

IOAU .... Input/Output Arithmetic Unit [*Computer science*] (IAA)

IOaWH .... West Suburban Hospital, Oak Park, IL [*Library symbol Library of Congress*] (LCLS)

IOB .... Briar Cliff College, Sioux City, IA [*OCLC symbol*] (OCLC)

IOB .... Industrial Order of Battle (MCD)

IOB .... Information Officer, Basic [*DoD Information School*] (DNAB)

IOB .... Input/Output Block [*Computer science*] (CMD)

IOB .... Input-Output Box [*Computer science*] (MCD)

IOB .... Input-Output Buffer [*Computer science*]

I/OB .... Input/Output Bus [*Computer science*] (NASA)

IOB .... Installation Operation Budget (AABC)

IOB .... Institute of Bankers [*Later, CIB*] [*British*] (EAIO)

IOB .... Institute of Brewing [*Also, IB*] [*British*]

IOB .... Institute of Building [*or Builders*] [*British*]

IOB .... Insurance Ombudsman Bureau (PDAA)

IOB .... Intelligence Oversight Board [*Federal government*]

IOB .... Internal Operating Budget

IOB .... Inter-Organization Board for Information Systems [*United Nations*] (IID)

IOB .... Inter-Organization Board for Information Systems and Related Activities (NITA)

IOBB .... Independent Order of B'nai B'rith [*Later, BBI*]

IOBB .... International Organization of Biotechnology and Bioengineering [*Guatemala, Guatemala*]

IObC .... Chicago Bridge & Iron Co., Oak Brook, IL [*Library symbol Library of Congress*] (LCLS)

IOBC .... Indian Ocean Biological Center (BARN)

IOBC .... Infantry Officer Basic Course [*Army*]

IOBC .... International Organization for Biological Control of Noxious Animals and Plants [*See also OILB*] [*ICSU Montpellier, France*] [*Research center*] (EAIO)

IOBC-RC ...... Infantry Officer Basic Course-Reserve Component (INF)

IOBFR .... Input/Output Buffer

IOBPS .... Input-Output Box and Peripheral Simulator [*Computer science*] (MCD)

IOBS .... Input/Output Buffering System [*Computer science*]

IOBS .... Institute of Bankers in Scotland (DI)

IObSE .... Swift-Eckrich, Research and Development Information Center Library, Oak Brook, IL [*Library symbol*] [*Library of Congress*] (LCLS)

IObT .... Bethany and Northern Baptist Theological Seminaries Library, Oak Brook, IL [*Library symbol Library of Congress*] (LCLS)

IOC .... Clarke College, Dubuque, IA [*OCLC symbol*] (OCLC)

IOC .... Image Orthicon Camera

IOC .... Image Orthicon Control

IOC .... Immediate-or-Cancel Order [*Stock exchange term*]

IOC .... Imperial Owners Club, International (EA)

IOCTL .... Index of Cooperation

IOC .... Indian Ocean Commission [*Port Louis, Mauritius*] (EAIO)

IOC .... Indirect Operating Costs

IOC .... Initial Operating Capability

IOC .... Initial Operational Capability [*Military*]

IOC .... Initial Operational Capacity

IOC .... Initial Orbital Configuration (MCD)

IOC .... Initial Order Condition (MCD)

IOC .... Inorganic Chemical [*Environmental science*]

IOC .... In Our Culture

IOC .... In-Out Converter

IOC .... Input Offset Current

IOC .... Input-Output Channel [*Computer science*] (DIT)

IOC .... Input-Output Comparator [*Computer science*]

IOC .... Input/Output Connector (NITA)

I/OC .... Input/Output Console [*Computer science*] (CAAL)

IOC .... Input/Output Control (NITA)

I/OC .... Input/Output Controller (NITA)

IOC .... Input-Output Controller [*Computer science*]

IOC .... Input-Output Converter [*Computer science*]

IOC .... Installation and Operational Checkout

IOC .... Institute of Carpenters [*British*] (DBA)

IOC .... Institute of Chemistry [*British*] (DAS)

IOC .... Institute of Commerce [*British*] (DBA)

IOC .... Institutes for Oceanography [*Marine science*] (MSC)

IOC .... Integrated Optical Circuit [*or Component*]

IOC .... Integrated Optimization Control [*Engineering*]

IOC .... Integrated Optoelectronic Circuit

IOC .... Intelligence Operations Center [*Air Force*] (DOMA)

IOC .... INTELSAT Operations Center

IOC .... Intergovernmental Oceanographic Commission [*See also COI*] [*ICSU Paris, France*] (EAIO)

IOC .... Interim Operational Capability

IOC .... Internationaal Ontmoetings Centrum [*International Network for Self-Reliance - INS*] (EA)

IOC .... International Oceanographic Commission [*NASA*]

IOC .... International Olympic Committee

IOC .... International Ornithological Congress [*New Zealand*]

IOC .... International Ozone Commission [*IAMAP*] (NOAA)

IOC .... Intern on Call (HGAA)

IOC .... Inter-Office Channel [*Telecommunications*] (TSSD)

IOC .... Interoffice Correspondence

IOC .... Interstate Oil Compact

IOC .... Intraoperative Cholangiogram [*Radiology*] (DAVI)

IOC .... Iron Ore Co. of Canada Ltd.

IOC .... ISDN [*Integrated Services Digital Network*] Ordering Code (PCM)

IOC .... Iterative Orbit Calculator

IOC .... Kiowa, CO [*Location identifier FAA*] (FAAL)

IOCA .... Image Object Content Architecture (CDE)

IOCA .... Independent Oil Compounders Association [*Later, ILMA*] (EA)

IOCA .... Intercollegiate Outing Club Association (EA)

IOCARIBE ..... IOC [*Intergovernmental Oceanographic Commission*] Sub-commission for the Caribbean and Adjacent Region [*Marine science*] (OSRA)

IOC/B & CC... Intergovernmental Oceanographic Commission - Bureau and Consultative Council [*UNESCO*]

IOCC .... Infantry Officer Career Course [*Army*]

IOCC .... Input-Output Control Center [*or Command*] [*Computer science*]

I/OCC .... Input/Output Control Console [*Computer science*] (CAAL)

IOCC .... International Office of Cocoa and Chocolate [*Later, IOCCSC*] (EAIO)

IOCC .... Interstate Oil Compact Commission (EA)

IOCC Bull.... Interstate Oil Compact Commission. Bulletin [*A publication*] (DLA)

IOCCC .... International Office of Cocoa, Chocolate, and Sugar Confectionary [*Belgium*] (EAIO)

IOCCSC .... International Office of Cocoa, Chocolate, and Sugar Confectionary [*IOCC a nd International Sugar Confectionary Manufacturers Association*] [*Formed by a merger of*] (EAIO)

IOCD .... Initial Operation Capability Date [*Military*] (AABC)

IOCD .... Input Output under Count Control and Disconnect [*Computer science*] (SAA)

IOCD .... International Organization for Chemical Sciences in Development [*Brussels, Belgium*] (EA)

I/OCE .... Input/Output Control Element [*Computer science*] (MCD)

IOC/EC .... Intergovernmental Oceanographic Commission/Executive Council (MSC)

IOCF .... International Oil Compensation Fund

IOC-FDTE .... Initial Operational Capability - Force Development Testing and Experimentation

IOCG .... Industrial Oil Consumers Group (EA)

IOCG .... Intraoperative Cholecystogram [*Radiology*] (DAVI)

IOCHC .... International Organization for Cooperation in Health Care [*See also MMI*] [*Nijmegen, Netherlands*] (EAIO)

IOCHS .... International Organization for Cultivating Human Spirit [*Later, OISCA*]

IOCI .... Imperial Order of the Crown of India [*British*] (ROG)

IOCI .... Interstate Organized Crime Index [*Computer databank*]

IOCP .... Indian Overseas Communication Project

IOCP .... Input/Output Control Processor [*Computer science*]

IOCP .... Input/Output Control Program [*Computer science*]

IOCP .... Input/Output under Count Control and Proceed [*Computer science*] (IAA)

IOCR .... Input/Output Control Routine [*Computer science*] (IAA)

IOCS .... Input/Output Computer Service (IAA)

IOCS .... Input-Output Control System [*Computer science*]

IOCS .... Instant Ocean Culture System

IOCS .... Interoffice Comment Sheet (NATG)

IOCTL .... Indian Ocean Conventional Target List (MCD)

IOCTR .... Input/Output Controller (NITA)

IOCU .... Input-Output Control Unit [*Computer science*]

IOCU .... International Organization of Consumers Unions [*The Hague, Netherlands*] (EA)

IOCV .... International Organization of Citrus Virologists (EA)

IOC/VAP ...... Intergovernmental Oceanographic Commission/Voluntary Assistance Program (MSC)

IOC-VCP....... Intergovernmental Geographic Commission Voluntary Cooperation Program [*Marine science*] (OSRA)

IOD .... Drake University, Des Moines, IA [*OCLC symbol*] (OCLC)

IOD .... Identified Outward Dialing [*Telecommunications*] (TEL)

IOD .... Immediate Oxygen Demand [*Marine science*] (MSC)

IOD .... Imperial Order of the Dragon (EA)

IOD .... Information on Demand, Inc. [*Information service or system*] (IID)

IOD .... Injured on Duty

IOD .... Input/Output Device [*Telecommunications*] (TEL)

IOD .... Input/Output Dump Program [*Computer science*] (IAA)

IOD .... Institute of Directors [*British*] (DCTA)

IoD .... Institute of Directors [*British*] (ODBW)

IOD .... Institute of Diving (EA)

IOD .... Institute of Outdoor Drama (EA)

IOD .... Integrated Observation Device (MCD)

IOD .... Integrated Optical Density [*Instrumentation*]

IOD .... Interorbital Distance [*Ophthalmology*] (DAVI)

IOD .... Iron Overload Diseases Association (EA)

IOD .... Issue of Data

IODA .... Iron Overload Diseases Association (EA)

IODC .... Input-Output Data Channel [*Computer science*]

IODC .... Input-Output Delay Counter [*Computer science*]

IODD .... Ideal One-Dimensional Device (IAA)

IODD .... Input-Output Data Document [*Computer science*] (MCD)

IODE .... Imperial Order of Daughters of the Empire [*Canada*]

IODE .... International Oceanographic Data and Information Exchange [*Marine science*] (OSRA)

IODE .... International Oceanographic Data Exchange

IODHRI .... International Organization for the Defense of Human Rights in Iraq (EA)

IODM	Infant of Diabetic Mother [*Neonatology*] (DAVI)
IODMM	International Office of Documentation on Military Medicine (EA)
IODS	International Ocean Disposal Symposium (EA)
IODSTR	Input and Output Driven Selt-Timing Repeater (PDAA)
IOE	Buena Vista College, Storm Lake, IA [*OCLC symbol*] (OCLC)
IOE	Industrial and Operations Engineer (PGP)
IOE	Inlet Over Exhaust [*Automotive engineering*]
IOE	Input-Output Error Log Table [*Computer science*] (MCD)
IOE	Institute for the Officialization of Esperanto
IOE	Institute of Ecology [*Research center*] (RCD)
IOE	Institute of Offshore Engineering [*Heriot-Watt University*] [*Information service or system*] (IID)
IOE	Instrumentation Operations Engineer (MCD)
IOE	Intake Opposite Exhaust (IAA)
IOE	Intensity of Operational Employment [*Army*] (RDA)
IOE	International Office of Epizootics
IOE	International Organization of Employers [*Geneva, Switzerland*]
IOE	International Organization of Experts (EAIO)
IOE	Irregular Outer Edge [*Army*] (ADDR)
IOEBT	Intraoperative Electron Beam Therapy [*Medicine*] (DAVI)
IOEH	Institute of Occupational and Environmental Health [*See also IMTA, IMTE*]
IOEHI	International Organization for the Education of the Hearing Impaired (EA)
IOEMTFS	Independent Order of Engineers and Machinists Trade and Friendly Society [*A union*] [*British*]
IOf	Acorn Library District, Oak Forest, IL [*Library symbol Library of Congress*] (LCLS)
IOF	Graceland College, Lamoni, IA [*OCLC symbol*] (OCLC)
IOF	Income Opportunities Fd 1999 [*NYSE symbol*] (TTSB)
IOF	Income Opportunities Fund [*NYSE symbol*] (SPSG)
IOF	Independent Order of Foresters [*Buffalo, NY*] (EA)
IOF	Infrared Optical Film
IOF	Initial Operational Flight (MCD)
IOF	Input/Output Front End [*Computer science*]
IOF	Institute of Fuel [*British*] (BI)
IOF	Interactive Operations Facility [*Honeywell, Inc.*]
IOF	Internationale Orientierungslauf Foderation [*International Orienteering Federation*] (EA)
IOF	International Oceanographic Foundation (EA)
IOF	Intraocular Fluid [*Ophthalomology*] (DAVI)
I of A	Instructor of Artillery [*British*]
IOfa	O'Fallon Public Library, O'Fallon, IL [*Library symbol Library of Congress*] (LCLS)
IOfaCD	O'Fallon Community Consolidated District 90, O'Fallon, IL [*Library symbol Library of Congress*] (LCLS)
IOfaSD	O'Fallon Township High School District 203, O'Fallon, IL [*Library symbol Library of Congress*] (LCLS)
IOFB	Intraocular Foreign Body [*Ophthalmology*]
IOFC	Income Over Feed Cost [*Livestock*] (OA)
IOFC	Indian Ocean Fishery Commission [*FAO*] [*Italy United Nations*]
IofE	Institute of Electrolysis [*British*] (DBA)
IOfH	Oak Forest Hospital, Oak Forest, IL [*Library symbol Library of Congress*] (LCLS)
IOFI	International Organization of the Flavor Industry [*Geneva, Switzerland*] (EAIO)
I of M	Instructor of Musketry [*British*]
I of M	Isle of Man [*England*]
IOFOS	International Organization for Forensic Odonto-Stomatology [*Formerly, International Society of Forensic Odonto-Stomatology*] (EA)
IOFS	International Organ Festival Society (EA)
IOFSG	International Orienteering Federation, Scientific Group [*See also IOFWA*] (EAIO)
IOFSI	Independent Order of the Free Sons of Israel [*Freemasonry*] (ROG)
IOFT	Institution on Farm Training
I of W	Isle of Wight
IOFWA	Internationale Orientierungslauf Foderation, Wissenschaftliche Arbeitsgruppe [*International Orienteering Federation, Scientific Group - IOFSG*] (EAIO)
IOG	Grinnell College, Grinnell, IA [*OCLC symbol*] (OCLC)
IOG	Input-Output Gate [*Computer science*]
IOG	Institute of Groundsmanship [*British*] (ITD)
IOG	Intercollegiate Opera Group [*Defunct*] (EA)
IOg	Oglesby Public Library, Oglesby, IL [*Library symbol Library of Congress*] (LCLS)
IOGA	Industry-Organized Government-Approved
IOGAWV	Independent Oil and Gas Association of West Virginia (SRA)
IOgd	Rose Library, Ogden, IL [*Library symbol Library of Congress*] (LCLS)
IOGE	Integrated Operational Ground Equipment
IOGEN	Input-Output Generation [*Computer science*]
IOgIV	Illinois Valley Community College, Oglesby, IL [*Library symbol Library of Congress*] (LCLS)
IOGP	International Outboard Grand Prix
IOgPS	Oglesby Public Schools, Oglesby, IL [*Library symbol Library of Congress*] (LCLS)
IOGR	International Order of the Golden Rule [*Springfield, IL*] (EA)
IOGT	International Organization of Good Templars [*Oslo, Norway*] (EAIO)
IOH	Idiopathic Orthostatic Hypotension [*Medicine*]
IOH	Indication of Hostilities [*Military*]
IOH	Inside-Out Helmholtz
IOH	[*The*] Institute of Heraldry [*Military*]
IOH	Institute of Housing [*British*] (DBA)
IOH	Inventory on Hand
IOH	Item [*or Items*] on Hand

IOH	Luther College, Decorah, IA [*OCLC symbol*] (OCLC)
IOh	Ohio Township Library, Ohio, IL [*Library symbol Library of Congress*] (LCLS)
IOHE	Inter-American Organization for Higher Education [*See also OUI*]
IOHE	International Organization for Human Ecology (EAIO)
IOHFI	International Organization for Housing Finance Institutions (EA)
IOHH	International Order of Hoo-Hoo (EA)
IOHS	Integrated Operational Hydrological System [*Marine science*] (MSC)
IOI	Indication of Interest [*Business term*] (MHDW)
IOI	Interest on Investment (AFIT)
IOI	Interim Operating Instructions
IOI	Internal Operating Instruction
IOI	International Ocean Institute [*Valetta, Malta*] (EAIO)
IOI	International Ombudsman Institute [*University of Alberta*] [*Edmonton, AB*] [*Research center*] (EAIO)
IOI	International Orphans, Inc. (EA)
IOI	International Ozone Institute [*Later, IOA*] (EA)
IOI	Iori Enterprises, Inc. [*Vancouver Stock Exchange symbol*]
IOI	Iowa Wesleyan College, Mount Pleasant, IA [*OCLC symbol*] (OCLC)
IOIC	Integrated Operational Intelligence Center
IOICS	Integrated Operational Intelligence Center System [*Military*] (DNAB)
IOIH	Input/Output Interrupt Handler [*Computer science*]
IOIRS	International Online Information Retrieval Service [*Institute of Scientific and Technical Information of China*] [*Beijing*] [*Information service or system*] (IID)
IOIS	Integrated Operational Intelligence System (MCD)
IOITBAG	International Oil Industry TBA Group (EA)
IOJ	Institute of Journalists [*British*]
IOJ	International Organization of Journalists [*See also OIJ*] [*Prague, Czechoslovakia*] (EAIO)
IOJ	St. Ambrose College, Davenport, IA [*OCLC symbol*] (OCLC)
IOJD	International Order of Job's Daughters (EA)
IOJD	International Organization for Justice and Development (EAIO)
IOK	Industrial and Occupational Knowledge (AIE)
IOK	International Order of Kabbalists (EA)
IOK	Iokea [*Papua New Guinea*] [*Airport symbol*] (OAG)
IOK	Simpson College, Indianola, IA [*OCLC symbol*] (OCLC)
IOkCD	West Washington County Community District 10, Okawville, IL [*Library symbol Library of Congress*] (LCLS)
IOKDS	International Order of the King's Daughters and Sons (EA)
IOL	India Office Library and Records [*British*]
IOL	Induction of Labor [*Obstetrics*] (DMAA)
IOL	Initial Outfitting List [*for advanced naval bases*]
IOL	Instantaneous Overload
IOL	Intermediate Objective Lens
IOL	International Old Lacers (EA)
IOL	Intraocular Lens [*Ophthalmology*]
IOL	Loras College, Dubuque, IA [*OCLC symbol*] (OCLC)
IOl	Oak Lawn Public Library, Oak Lawn, IL [*Library symbol Library of Congress*] (LCLS)
IOLA	Input/Output Line Adaptor (NITA)
IOLA	Input/Output Link Adapter [*Computer science*]
IOlC	Christ Hospital, Oak Lawn, IL [*Library symbol Library of Congress*] (LCLS)
IOLC	Input/Output Link Control [*Computer science*]
IOLC	Input/Output Link Controller (NITA)
IOLC	Integrated Optical Logic Circuit
IOL/CR	Initial Outfitting List / Complete Repair, Parts, and Tools (SAA)
IOlE	Evangelical School of Nursing, Oak Lawn, IL [*Library symbol Library of Congress*] (LCLS)
IOLI	International Old Lacers, Inc. (EA)
IOLIM	International Online Information Meeting
IOLM	International Organization for Legal Metrology
IOln	Olney Carnegie Public Library, Olney, IL [*Library symbol Library of Congress*] (LCLS)
IOLS	Input/Output Label System [*Computer science*] (OA)
IOLS	Integrated Online Library Systems
IOLS	Iterated Ordinary Least Squares [*Statistics*]
IOLTA	Interest on Lawyers' Trust Accounts
IOLV	Independent Order Ladies of Vikings (EA)
IOM	Indian Order of Merit
IOM	Inert Operational Missile (NG)
IOM	Inferior Orbitomeatal Line [*Brain anatomy*]
IOM	Innovator of the Month
IOM	Input-Output Module [*Computer science*] (MCD)
I/OM	Input-Output Multiplexer [*Computer science*]
IOM	Insoluble Organic Material [*or Matter*] [*Analytical chemistry*]
IOM	Inspector of Ordnance Machinery [*British military*] (DMA)
IOM	Institute of Materials [*British*] (EAIO)
IOM	Institute of Meat [*British*] (DBA)
IOM	Institute of Medicine [*National Academy of Sciences*] (EA)
IoM	Institute of Medicine
IOM	Institute of Metals [*Institution of Metallurgists - IM and Metals Society - MS*] [*Formed by a merger of*] (EAIO)
IOM	Institute of Occupational Medicine [*British*] (IRUK)
IOM	Institute of Office Management [*British*] (BI)
IOM	International Options Market [*Australian Options Market, European Options Exchange in Amsterdam, Montreal Exchange, and Vancouver Stock Exchange*]
IOM	International Organization for Migration (EAIO)
IOM	International Organization for Mycoplasmology (EA)
IOM	Interoffice Memorandum
IOM	Island Aviation & Travel Ltd. [*British ICAO designator*] (FAAC)
IOM	Isle of Man [*England*] [*Airport symbol*] (OAG)
IOM	Morningside College, Sioux City, IA [*OCLC symbol*] (OCLC)

IOMA	Idaho Oil Marketers Association (SRA)
IOMA	Independent Oil Marketer's Association of New England (SRA)
IOMA	International Oxygen Manufacturers Association (EA)
IOMACI	Indian Ocean Marine Affairs Cooperation Conference
IOMC	International Organization for Medical Cooperation
IOME	Irgun Olej Merkas Europa (BJA)
Iomega	Iomega Corp. [*Associated Press*] (SAG)
IOMF	Inactive-Officer Master File (DNAB)
IOMG	Iomega Corp. [*NASDAQ symbol*] (NQ)
I/OMI	Integration/Operations and Maintenance Instruction [*NASA*] (NASA)
IOML	Infraorbitomeatal Line [*Anatomy*] (DAVI)
IOMMP	International Organization of Masters, Mates, and Pilots
IOMO	Invitation of Member Only
IOMP	Input/Output Message Processor [*Computer science*] (IAA)
IOMP	Input/Output Microprocessor (NITA)
IOMP	International Organization for Medical Physics (DAVI)
IOMR	Isle Of Man Railways [*British*] (ROG)
IOMS	Input-Output Management System [*Computer science*] (MHDI)
IOMS	Interim Operation Meteorological System
IOMS	International Organization for Masoretic Studies
IOMSPCo	Isle Of Man Steam Packet Co. [*British*] (ROG)
IOMT	Isomet Corp. [*NASDAQ symbol*] (NQ)
IOMTR	International Organization for Motor Trades and Repairs [*Rijswljk, Netherlands*] (EAIO)
IOMVM	International Organization of Motor Vehicle Manufacturers (EAIO)
ION	Bionaire, Inc. [*Toronto Stock Exchange symbol*]
ION	Biotech Electronics Ltd. [*Toronto Stock Exchange symbol*]
ION	Coe College, Cedar Rapids, IA [*OCLC symbol*] (OCLC)
ION	Impfondo [*Congo*] [*Airport symbol*] (OAG)
ION	Inferior Olivary Nucleus [*Neuroanatomy*]
ION	Institute for Optimum Nutrition [*British*]
ION	Institute of Navigation (EA)
ION	Institute of Navigation
ION	Institute of Neuroscience [*University of Oregon*] [*Research center*] (RCD)
ION	Institute of Neurotoxicology [*Yeshiva University*] [*Research center*] (RCD)
ION	International Organization of Nerds (EA)
ION	Ione, WA [*Location identifier FAA*] (FAAL)
ION	Ionic
ION	Ionics, Inc. [*NYSE symbol*] (SPSG)
ION	Ionosphere and Aural Phenomena Advisory Committee [*European Space Research Organization*] (IEEE)
ION	Ischemic Optic Neuropathy [*Medicine*]
ION	Isthmo-Optic Nucleus [*or Nuclei*] [*In midbrain of chick*]
Iona	De Iona [*Philo*] (BJA)
IOna	Onarga Public Library, Onarga, IL [*Library symbol Library of Congress*] (LCLS)
IonaApp	Iona Appliances, Inc. [*Associated Press*] (SAG)
Iona C	Iona College (GAGS)
IONDS	Initial Operational Nuclear Detection System
IONDS	Integrated Operational Nuclear Detonation Detection System
IONDT	Ischemic Optic Neuropathy Decompression Trial
Ionic	Ionic Fuel Technology, Inc. [*Associated Press*] (SAG)
IonicFuel	Ionic Fuel Technology, Inc. [*Associated Press*] (SAG)
Ionics	Ionics, Inc. [*Associated Press*] (SAG)
IonLaser	Ion Laser Technology [*Associated Press*] (SAG)
IonLsr	Ion Laser Technology, Inc. [*Associated Press*] (SAG)
ION-M	Integrated On-Line Non-Stop Manufacturing [*Safe Computing Ltd.*] [*Software package*] (NCC)
IONO	Ionosphere (MSA)
IONS	Institute of Noetic Sciences (EA)
IONS	Institute of Oceanography Nova Scotia [*Canada*] [*Marine science*] (OSRA)
IONS	Intraoperative Neurosonography [*Radiology*]
IOO	ICOR Oil & Gas Co. Ltd. [*Toronto Stock Exchange symbol*]
IOO	Idaho Operations Office [*Energy Research and Development Administration*]
IOO	Input/Output Operation (HGAA)
IOO	Inspecting Ordnance Officer
IOO	Northwestern College, Orange City, IA [*OCLC symbol*] (OCLC)
IOOC	Integrated Optics and Optical Fiber Communications (MCD)
IOOC	International Conference on Integrated Optics and Optical Fiber Communication (PDAA)
IOOC	International Olive Oil Council [*See also COI*] [*Madrid, Spain*] (EAIO)
IOOC	Iranian Oil Operating Companies
IOOF	Independent Order of Odd Fellows (EA)
IOOL	International Optometric and Optical League [*British*] (EAIO)
IOOP	Input/Output Operation [*Computer science*]
IOOSF	Integrated Orbital Operations Simulation Facility
IOOTS	International Organization of Old Testament Scholars
IOOW	In Our Own Way (EA)
IOP	Caliop [*France ICAO designator*] (FAAC)
IOP	Central College, Pella, IA [*OCLC symbol*] (OCLC)
IOP	Ibero-American Organization of Pilots [*See also OIP*] [*Mexico City, Mexico*] (EAIO)
I/OP	Inboard/Outboard Profile (NASA)
IOP	Initial Operating Production (MCD)
IOP	In-Orbit Plane (KSC)
IOP	Input-Output Package [*IBM Corp.*] [*Computer science*]
IOP	Input-Output Port (MCD)
IOP	Input-Output Processor [*Computer science*]
IOP	Input-Output Pulse [*Computer science*]
IOP	Inspection Operation Procedure (MCD)
IOP	Installation Operating Program (AABC)

IOP	Institute of Packaging [*British*] (BI)
IOP	Institute of Painters in Oil Colours [*British*]
IOP	Institute of Petroleum [*British*] (BI)
IOP	Institute of Physics [*British*] (EAIO)
IOP	Institute of Plumbing (EAIO)
IOP	Institute of Printing [*British*]
IOP	Institute of Pyramidology [*Harpenden, Hertfordshire, England*] (EA)
IOP	Integrated Obstacle Plan [*Military*]
IOP	Integrated Operation Plan [*NASA*] (NASA)
IOP	Integrated Ordnance Package (MCD)
IOP	Intensive Observation Period [*Marine science*] (OSRA)
IOP	Intensive Observing Period (USDC)
IOP	Interim Operating Procedure (NVT)
IOP	Internal Operating Procedure
IOP	International Organization of Palaeobotany [*British*]
IOP	International Organization of Psychophysiology [*See also IPO*] [*Montreal, PQ*] (EAIO)
IOP	International Potter Distilling Corp. [*Toronto Stock Exchange symbol Vancouver Stock Exchange symbol*]
IOP	Intraocular Pressure [*Ophthalmology*]
IOP	Ioma [*Papua New Guinea*] [*Airport symbol*] (OAG)
IOP	Iranian Oil Participants Ltd.
IOp	Orland Park Public Library, Orland Park, IL [*Library symbol Library of Congress*] (LCLS)
IOPA	International Organizations Procurement Act of 1947
IOPAB	International Organization for Pure and Applied Biophysics
IOPB	International Organization of Plant Biosystematists [*St. Anne De Bellevue, PQ*] (EA)
IOPC	Institute of Paper Conservation (EA)
IOPC	Interagency Oil Policy Committee
IOPC	International Oil Pollution Compensation [*In association name IOPC Fund*] [*See also FIPOL*]
IOPEC	International Oil Pollution Exhibition and Conference (PDAA)
IO/PG	Indian Ocean/Persian Gulf
IOPG	Input/Output Processor Group (NITA)
IOPI	International Organization for Plant Information
IOPKG	Input/Output Package [*IBM Corp.*] [*Computer science*]
IOPL	Instructional Objectives Preference List (AEBS)
IOPL	Integrated Open Problem List (NASA)
IOPL	Intermittent Operating Life (IAA)
IOPL	I/O [*Input/Output*] Privilege Level [*Computer science*]
IOPN	In Operation (IAA)
IOPO	Interest-Only/Principal-Only [*Stock exchange term*]
IoPP	Institute of Packaging Professionals (EA)
IOPP	International Oil Pollution Prevention
IOPS	Input-Output Programming System [*Computer science*]
IOQ	Input-Output Queue [*Computer science*] (IBMDP)
IOQ	Installational and Operational Qualifications [*Manufacturing*]
IOQ	Institute of Quarrying [*British*]
IOQ	Iowa State Historical Society, Iowa City, IA [*OCLC symbol*] (OCLC)
IOQE	Input-Output Queue Element [*Computer science*] (MCD)
IOR	Immediate Operational Requirement (MCD)
IOR	Independent Order of Rechabites
IOR	Index of Refraction (MCD)
IOR	Index of Response [*Medicine*] (DMAA)
IOR	Indian Ocean Region [*INTELSAT*]
IOR	Indian Other Rank [*British military*] (DMA)
IOR	Input-Output Register [*SAGE*]
IoR	Institute of Roofing [*British*] (DBA)
IOR	Instituto per le Opere di Religione [*Institute for Religious Works*] [*The Vatican bank*]
IOR	International Offshore Rule [*Yachting*]
IOR	International Order of Runeberg (EA)
IOR	Issue on Request [*or Requisition*]
IOR	Marycrest College, Davenport, IA [*OCLC symbol*] (OCLC)
IORB	Input/Output Record Block [*Computer science*]
IORC	Input-Output Read Control [*Computer science*] (MHDI)
IORD	International Organization for Rural Development
IOREG	Input/Output Register (IAA)
IOREQ	Input/Output Request [*Computer science*]
IORL	Input Output Requirements Language [*Teledyne Braun Engineering*] (NITA)
IORM	Improved Order of Red Men
IORS	Inflatable Occupant Restraint System
IORS	Input-Output Request Subroutine [*Computer science*] (MHDI)
IORT	Input Output of a Record and Transfer [*Computer science*] (SAA)
IORT	Input-Output Remote Terminal [*Computer science*] (MHDI)
IORT	Intraoperative Radiation Therapy [*Medicine*]
IORV	Inadvertent Opening of a Safety Relief Valve [*Nuclear energy*] (NRCH)
IOS	Davenport Public Library, Davenport, IA [*OCLC symbol*] (OCLC)
Ios	De Iosepho [*Philo*] (BJA)
IOS	IGOSS [*Integrated Global Ocean Station System*] Observing System [*Marine science*] (MSC)
IOS	Ilheus [*Brazil*] [*Airport symbol*] (OAG)
IOS	Image Optical Scanner
IOS	Image Orthicon System
IOS	Independent Order of Svithiod (EA)
IOS	Indian Ocean Ship
IOS	Indian Ocean Station (MCD)
IOS	Input-Output Selector [*Computer science*] (IEEE)
IOS	Input-Output Sense [*Computer science*] (KSC)
IOS	Input-Output Skip [*Computer science*]
IOS	Input/Output Subsystem (NITA)
IOS	Input-Output Supervision [*Computer science*] (NASA)

IOS.............. Input-Output Switch [Computer science]
IOS.............. Input/Output System [General Automation] [Computer science]
IOS.............. Inspection Operation Sheet (AAG)
IOS.............. Inspection Operation System (AAG)
IOS.............. Inspector of Schools [British] (DAS)
IOS.............. Institute for Objectivist Studies (EA)
IOS.............. Institute of Oceanographic Sciences [British Research center] (IRC)
IOS.............. Institute of Ocean Sciences [Canadian Department of Fisheries and Oceans] [Research center] (RCD)
IOS.............. Institute of Optimization and Systems Theory [Stockholm]
IOS.............. Institute of Statisticians [British] (DBA)
IOS.............. Instructor Operation Station [Army] (NASA)
IOS.............. Instrumentation Operation Station
IOS.............. Instrument Operating System
IOS.............. Integrated Observation System (MCD)
IOS.............. Integrated Office System [JSB Computer Systems/Olivetti] (NITA)
IOS.............. Integrated Operator System [Telecommunications]
IOS.............. Intelligence Operations Specialist [Military] (MCD)
IOS.............. Intelligence Oversight
IOS.............. Interactive Operating System [Computer science]
IOS.............. Interceptor Operator Simulator (IAA)
IOS.............. Interim Operational System
IOS.............. Internationale Organisation fuer Sukkulentenforschung [International Organization for Succulent Plant Study - IOS] (EAIO)
IOS.............. International Officer School [Military]
IOS.............. International Oleander Society (EA)
IOS.............. International Organization for Standardization [Official initialism is ISO]
IOS.............. International Orthokeratology Society (EA)
IOS.............. Intraoperative Sonography [Radiology] (DAVI)
IOS.............. Investors Overseas Services Ltd. [Firm which sells mutual funds in foreign countries]
IOS.............. Isle Of Skye [Scotland]
IOS.............. Isles of Scilly Skybus Ltd. [British ICAO designator] (FAAC)
IOs.............. Oswego Township Library, Oswego, IL [Library symbol Library of Congress] (LCLS)
IOSA............ Input/Output Systems Association [Defunct] (EA)
IOSA............ Integrated Optical Spectrum Analyzer (CAAL)
IOSA............ International Oil Scouts Association (EA)
IOSA............ Irish Offshore Services Association (EAIO)
IOSC............ Integrated Operations Support Center [NASA] (NASA)
IOSCS.......... International Organization for Septuagint and Cognate Studies (EA)
IOSD............ Information and Office Systems Division [Exxon Research and Engineering Co.] [Information service or system] (IID)
IOSD............ Initial Operational Support Date (MCD)
IOSDL.......... Institute of Oceanographic Sciences Deacon Laboratory [Natural Environment Research Council] [British] (IRC)
IOSEWR....... International Organization for the Study of the Endurance of Wire Ropes [Paris, France] (EAIO)
IOSGT.......... International Organization for the Study of Group Tensions (EA)
IOSH............ Independent Order Sons of Hermann
IOSH............ Institution of Occupational Safety and Health [British] (DBA)
IOSHD.......... International Organization for the Study of Human Development [Defunct] (EA)
IOSI............. International Oculoplastic Society, Inc. (EA)
IOSL............ Independent Order of St. Luke [Defunct] (EA)
IOSM........... Independent Order of Sons of Malta
IOSN........... Indian Ocean Standard Net
IOS/OSI....... International Organization for Standardization Open Systems Interconnection Model
IOSOT.......... International Organization for the Study of the Old Testament [British]
IOSP............ Input/Output under Signal and Proceed [Computer science] (IAA)
IOSS............ Indian Ocean Station Support
IOSS............ Input/Output Subsystem [NCR Corp.]
IOSS............ Integrated Ocean Surveillance System [Navy] (NG)
IOSS............ Integrated Operational Support Study (MCD)
IOSS............ Intelligence Organization Stationing Study [Army] (MCD)
IOSS............ Intraoperative Spinal Sonography [Radiology]
IOST............ Input/Output under Signal and Transfer [Computer science] (IAA)
IOSTA.......... Comission Internationale de l'Organisation Scientifique du Travail [International Committee of Work Study and Labour Management in Agriculture] (EAIO)
IOSTE.......... International Organisation for Science and Technology Education (AIE)
IOSV............ Interorbital Space Vehicle (MCD)
IOT.............. British Indian Ocean Territory [ANSI three-letter standard code] (CNC)
IOT.............. Dordt College, Sioux Center, IA [OCLC symbol] (OCLC)
IOT.............. Image Output Terminal [Computer science] (HGAA)
IOT.............. Income Opportunity Realty [AMEX symbol] (SPSG)
IOT.............. Income Opportunity Rlty [AMEX symbol] (TTSB)
IOT.............. Individual Operation Test
IOT.............. Induction Output Tube
IOT.............. Initial Operational Test [Army]
IOT.............. Initial Orbit Time [Aerospace]
IOT.............. Input/Output and Transfer (NITA)
IOT.............. Input/Output Termination [Computer science]
I/OT............ Input/Output Test [Computer science] (NASA)
IOT.............. Input/Output Transfer [Computer science]
IOT.............. Input-Output Trap [Computer science] (MHDI)
IOT.............. Input/Output Trunk (NITA)
IOT.............. Inspection Operation Tag
IOT.............. Institute of Operating Theatre Technicians [British]
IOT.............. International Optical Telecommunications, Inc. [Information service or system] (IID)

IOT.............. Interocular Transfer [Ophthalmology]
IOT.............. Interoffice Trunk (IAA)
IOT.............. Interorganizational Transfer (AAGC)
IOT.............. Intraocular Tension [Ophthalmology] (DAVI)
IOT.............. Intraocular Transfer [Ophthalmology] (DAVI)
IOT.............. Ipsilateral Optic Tectum [Medicine]
IOT.............. Iron Ore Transport [Steamship] (MHDW)
IOt.............. Reddick's Library, Ottawa, IL [Library symbol Library of Congress] (LCLS)
IOTA............ Inbound/Outbound Traffic Analysis [Military] (AABC)
IOTA............ Inbound Tourism Organisation of Australia
IOTA............ Information Overload Testing Aid [or Apparatus]
IOTA............ Information Overload Testing Apparatus (NITA)
IOTA............ Instant Oxide Thickness Analyzer (IAA)
IOTA............ Institute of Theoretical Astronomy [University of Cambridge]
IOTA............ Institute of Transport Administration [British] (DCTA)
IOTA............ Integrated On-Line Text Arrangement
IOTA............ Interest on Trust Accounts Program
IOTA............ International Occultation Timing Association (EA)
IOTAE.......... Initial Operating Test and Evaluation (IAA)
IOT & E....... Independent Operational Test and Evaluation [Military]
IOT & E....... Initial Operating Test and Evaluation (MCD)
IOT & E....... Initial Operational Test and Evaluation [Army] (DOMA)
IOtBD.......... LaSalle County Board for Developmentally Disabled, Ottawa, IL [Library symbol Library of Congress] (LCLS)
IOTC........... Infantry Officers Training Camp
IOTC........... International Originating Toll Center [Bell System]
IOtCE.......... LaSalle County Cooperative Extension, Ottawa, IL [Library symbol Library of Congress] (LCLS)
IOTCG......... International Organization for Technical Cooperation in Geology (EAIO)
IOtCH.......... Community Hospital of Ottawa, Ottawa, IL [Library symbol Library of Congress] (LCLS)
IOtDSD........ Deer Park Consolidated Community School District 82, Ottawa, IL [Library symbol Library of Congress] (LCLS)
IOTE........... Individual Operator Training Equipment (MCD)
IOTE........... Initial Outfitting Technical Evaluation (MCD)
IOTEP......... Initial Operating Test and Evaluation Period [Navy]
IOtES.......... LaSalle County Educational Service Region, Ottawa, IL [Library symbol Library of Congress] (LCLS)
IOtF........... Friendship Facilities, Ottawa, IL [Library symbol Library of Congress] (LCLS)
IOTG........... Input/Output Task Group [CODASYL]
IOTG........... Isooctyl Thioglycolate [Organic chemistry]
IOtGH.......... Ottawa General Hospital, Ottawa, IL [Library symbol Library of Congress] (LCLS)
IOtHS.......... Ottawa Township High School District 140, Ottawa, IL [Library symbol Library of Congress] (LCLS)
IOtM........... Marquette High School, Ottawa, IL [Library symbol Library of Congress] (LCLS)
IOTPD......... International Organization for the Transition of Professionals Dancers [Switzerland]
IOTR........... Intratrabecular Osteoclastic Tunneling Resorption [Medicine]
IOTR........... Item Operation Trouble Report (AAG)
IOtRP......... LaSalle County Regional Planning Commission, Ottawa, IL [Library symbol Library of Congress] (LCLS)
IOtRSD........ Rutland Consolidated Community School District 230, Ottawa, IL [Library symbol Library of Congress] (LCLS)
IOtS........... Starved Rock Library System, Ottawa, IL [Library symbol Library of Congress] (LCLS)
IOTT & E..... Improved Operational Test, Training, and Evaluation [Military]
IOTTSG........ International Oil Tanker Terminal Safety Group (PDAA)
IOtWSD........ Wallace Consolidated Community School District 195, Ottawa, IL [Library symbol Library of Congress] (LCLS)
IOU............. Immediate Operation Use
IOU............. Input-Output Unit [Computer chip]
IOU............. Input-Output Utility [Computer science]
IOU............. Intensive Care Observation Unit [Medicine] (DMAA)
IOU............. Intensive Therapy Observation Unit (MAE)
IOU............. Investor-Owned Utilities (BARN)
IOU............. I Owe You [Slang]
IOU............. Public Library of Des Moines, Des Moines, IA [OCLC symbol] (OCLC)
IOUBC.......... Institute of Oceanography, University of British Columbia
IOV............ Independent Order of Vikings [Des Plaines, IL] (EA)
IOV............ Initial Office Visit [Medicine] (DAVI)
IOV............ Input Offset Voltage
IOV............ Inside-Out Vesicle [Biochemistry]
IOV............ Institute of Virology [British] (ARC)
IOV............ University of Dubuque, Dubuque, IA [OCLC symbol] (OCLC)
IOVC........... In the Overcast [Aviation]
IOVST......... International Organization for Vacuum Science and Technology
IOW............ Inert Ordnance Warehouse
IOW............ In Other Words
IOW............ Input-Output Write [Computer science] (MHDI)
IOW............ Iowa City [Iowa] [Airport symbol] (AD)
IOW............ Iowa City, IA [Location identifier FAA] (FAAL)
Iow............ Iowa Reports [A publication] (DLA)
IOW............ Isle Of Wight
IOW............ Wartburg College, Waverly, IA [OCLC symbol] (OCLC)
IOWA.......... Interorganizational Work Authorization (KSC)
IOWA.......... Iowa Bancorporation, Inc. [NASDAQ symbol] (SAG)
Iowa.......... Iowa Supreme Court Reports [A publication] (DLA)
Iowa Acts..... Acts and Joint Resolutions of the State of Iowa [A publication] (DLA)
Iowa Admin Bull... Iowa Administrative Bulletin [A publication] (DLA)

Iowa Admin Code...   Iowa Administrative Code [*A publication*] (DLA)
Iowa Bar Rev...   Iowa Bar Review [*A publication*] (DLA)
IowaBcp.......   Iowa Bancorporation, Inc. [*Associated Press*] (SAG)
Iowa B Rev...   Iowa Bar Review [*A publication*] (DLA)
Iowa Code ...   Code of Iowa [*A publication*] (AAGC)
Iowa LB ......   Iowa Law Bulletin [*A publication*] (DLA)
Iowa L Bull..   Iowa Law Bulletin [*A publication*] (DLA)
Iowa Legis Serv...   Iowa Legislative Service (West) [*A publication*] (DLA)
Iowa RC......   Iowa Railroad Commissioners Reports [*A publication*] (DLA)
Iowa SBA....   Iowa State Bar Association. Proceedings [*A publication*] (DLA)
Iowa St BAQ...   Iowa State Bar Association. Quarterly [*A publication*] (DLA)
Iowa St U ....   Iowa State University of Science and Technology (GAGS)
Iowa Univ L Bull...   Iowa University. Law Bulletin [*A publication*] (DLA)
IOWE ....   International Office for Water Education [*Utah State University*]
IOWE ....   International Organization of Women Executives [*Defunct*] (EA)
IOWIT ....   International Organization of Women in Telecommunications [*Defunct*] (TSSD)
IOWMC ....   International Organization of Wooden Money Collectors (EA)
IOWQ ....   Input-Output Wait Queue [*Computer science*] (MHDI)
IOWT ....   International Organization of Women in Telecommunications [*Defunct*] (EA)
IOX..............   Input-Output Executive [*Computer science*] (MHDI)
IOX..............   William Penn College, Oskaloosa, IA [*OCLC symbol*] (OCLC)
IOY..............   Upper Iowa University, Fayette, IA [*OCLC symbol*] (OCLC)
IOZ..............   State Library Commission of Iowa, Des Moines, IA [*OCLC symbol*] (OCLC)
IOZP............   Indian Ocean Zone of Peace
IP................   Airlines of Tasmania [*ICAO designator*] (AD)
IP................   Cathode-Ray Tube Indicators [*JETDS nomenclature*] [*Military*] (CET)
I/P..............   Current/Pneumatic [*Nuclear energy*] (NRCH)
I/P..............   Current to Pressure [*Electropneumatic*] (ACII)
IP................   Empresa AVIAIMPORT [*Cuba ICAO designator*] (ICDA)
IP................   Ice Plow [*Coast Guard*] (DNAB)
IP................   Ice Point
IP................   Icterus Precox [*Medicine*]
IP................   Identification of Position
IP................   Identification Peculiarity
IP................   Identification Point
IP................   Identity Preserved [*Wheat*] [*Department of Agriculture*]
IP................   Igloo Pallet [*Spacelab*] [*NASA*] (NASA)
IP................   Ignition Point [*Chemistry*] (IAA)
IP................   Iliopsoas [*Muscle*] [*Anatomy*] (DAVI)
IP................   Image Previewer (DGA)
IP................   Image Process
IP................   Imaginary Part [*of a complex number*] (DEN)
IP................   Immediate Permanent Incapacitation [*Radiation casualty criterion*] [*Army*]
IP................   Immune Precipitate [*Immunology*]
IP................   Immunoperoxidase (Technique) [*Clinical chemistry*]
IP................   Impact Point (AFM)
IP................   Impact Predictor [*NASA*]
IP................   Impact Printer [*Computer science*]
IP................   Impact Prognosticator [*Aerospace*] (AAG)
IP................   Impedance Probe
IP................   Imperial Preference (ADA)
IP................   Impingement Point
IP................   Implementation of Plan (NG)
IP................   Implementation Period
IP................   Import Penetration
IP................   Impostor Phenomenon [*Subject of book "If I'm So Successful, Why Do I Feel Like a Fake - The Impostor Phenomenon" by Joan C. Harvey*] [*Psychology*]
IP................   Improvement Program (AFM)
IP................   Improvement Purchase (ADA)
iP ....   Impulse P Wave [*Earthquakes*] [*Exclamation point signifies a very sharp earthquake*]
IP................   Inca Pacific Resources [*VS, exchange symbol*] (TTSB)
IP................   Incentive Pay
IP................   Incisoproximal [*Dentistry*]
IP................   Incisopulpal [*Dentistry*]
IP................   Incubation Period [*Medicine*]
IP................   Index of Performance
IP................   Index of Preprogramming [*Computer science*] (PDAA)
IP................   Indian Pattern [*British military*] (DMA)
IP................   Indian Preference [*Civil Service*]
IP................   India Paper
IP................   Indicator Panel
IP................   Indirect Proof [*Method in logic*]
IP................   Indium Phosphide [*Materials science*]
IP................   Indochina Project [*An association*] (EA)
IP................   Induced Polarization [*Geophysical prospecting*]
IP................   Induced Protein [*Biochemistry*] (DAVI)
IP................   Induction Period [*Medicine*]
IP................   Industrial Participation [*Civil Defense*]
IP................   Industrial Planning
IP................   Industrial Police
IP................   Industrial Policy
IP................   Industrial Production
IP................   Industry Program [*Defense Systems Management College*] (DOMA)
IP................   Inertial Platform
IP................   Inertial Processing (MCD)
IP................   Infection Prevention
IP................   Information Packets [*or Packages*] (GNE)
IPaBcp........   Information Paper
IP................   Information Pool (IAA)

IP................   Information Processing (BUR)
IP................   Information Provider
IP................   Information Publication [*HUD*]
IP................   Information Publications [*Singapore, Hong Kong, Australia*]
IP................   Information Publishing
IP................   Infundibular Process [*Medicine*] (DMAA)
IP................   Infundibulopelvic [*Ligament*] [*Anatomy*] (DAVI)
IP................   Inhaled Particles [*or Particulates*] [*Environmental chemistry*]
IP................   Inhouse Publishing (IAA)
IP................   Initial Phase (IEEE)
IP................   Initial Point [*Military*]
IP................   Initial Position
IP................   Initial Post [*Military*]
IP................   Initial Pressure [*On lumbar puncture*] [*Neurosurgery*] (DAVI)
IP................   Initial Production
IP................   Initial Provisioning (MCD)
IP................   Inland Postage (IAA)
IP................   Innings Pitched [*Baseball*]
Ip................   Innings Played [*Baseball*]
IP................   Innovative Project
IP................   Inorganic Phosphorus (OA)
IP................   Inosine Phosphorylase [*An enzyme*] (MAE)
IP................   Inpatient [*Medicine*]
IP................   In-Phase [*Gynecology*]
IP................   In Place [*Dancing*]
IP................   In Plaster [*Medicine*] (DAVI)
IP................   In Process
I/P..............   In Progress (MCD)
I/P..............   Input [*Computer science*]
IP................   Input Power [*Computer science*]
IP................   Input Processor [*Computer science*]
IP................   Insolated Platform
IP................   Inspection Pit [*Motor garage*] (ROG)
IP................   Inspection Procedure [*Nuclear energy*] (NRCH)
IP................   Installation Procedure
IP................   Installment Paid [*Business term*]
IP................   Instantaneous Pressure [*Medicine*] (MAE)
IP................   Institute for Psychohistory (EA)
IP................   Institute of Petroleum [*British*]
IP................   Institute of Physics [*British*] (EAIO)
IP................   Institute of Printing [*British*]
IP................   Instructional Psychologist (MCD)
IP................   Instruction Pamphlet
IP................   Instruction Plate (MSA)
IP................   Instruction Pointer [*Computer science*]
IP................   Instruction Processor [*Computer science*]
IP................   Instruction Pulse (MSA)
IP................   Instructor-Patient [*Medicine*]
IP................   Instructor Pilot [*Air Force*] (AFM)
IP................   Instrumentation Papers [*Air Force*] (MCD)
IP................   Instrumentation Payload (NASA)
IP................   Instrumentation PCM [*Power Control Mission*] [*NASA*]
IP................   Instrumentation Plan (MUGU)
IP................   Instrumentation Power (MCD)
IP................   Instrument Panel [*Automotive engineering*]
IP................   Insulated Platform (MCD)
IP................   Insurance Patient [*Medicine*]
IP................   Integrated Processor [*Computer science*]
IP................   Intellectual Property (MCD)
IP................   Intelligence Publications (MCD)
IP................   Intelligent Peripheral [*Computer science*] (ACRL)
IP................   Interactive Processing (IAA)
IP................   Intercept Point [*Air Force*]
IP................   Interchangeable Solid and Screen Panels [*Technical drawings*]
IP................   Interdigital Pause [*Telecommunications*] (TEL)
IP................   Interelement Protection (IAA)
IP................   Interface Processor [*Computer science*]
IP................   Interface Program [*Computer science*] (IAA)
IP................   Interference Pattern (CAAL)
IP................   Intermediate Pallet (NASA)
IP................   Intermediate Pressure
IP................   Intermediate Processor (SSD)
IP................   Internal Phloem [*Botany*]
IP................   Internal Protocol (SSD)
IP................   International Paper Co. [*NYSE symbol*] (SPSG)
IP................   International Pharmacopoeia
IP................   International Programming (IAA)
IP................   Internet Protocol [*Computer science*] (PCM)
IP................   Interphalangeal [*Anatomy*]
IP................   Interplanetary
IP................   Interpositive [*Photography*] (WDMC)
IP................   Interscience Publishers
IP................   Intl Paper [*NYSE symbol*] (TTSB)
IP................   Intraperitoneal [*Medicine*]
IP................   Invalid Pension
IP................   Inverse Photoemission [*Spectroscopy*]
IP................   Ionization Potential
IP................   Ion-Pair [*Physical chemistry*]
IP................   Ipatropium [*Pharmacology*]
IP................   Irate Parent (ADA)
IP................   Irish Party (ROG)
IP................   Iron Pipe
I/P..............   Irregular Input Process [*Telecommunications*] (TEL)
IP................   Isidis Planitia [*A filamentary mark on Mars*]
IP................   Isoelectric Point [*Also, IEP, PH₁, pI*] [*Chemistry*]

IP	Isolation Pulse
IP	Isoproterenol [*An adrenergic*]
IP	Israeli Pound (BJA)
IP	Issue Paper
IP	Issue Price [*Business term*]
IP	Issuing Point
IP	Italian Patent (IAA)
IP	Item Processing
IP	Izquierda de los Pueblos [*Spain*] [*Political party*] (ECED)
IP	Office of International Programs [*Nuclear energy National Science Foundation*] (NRCH)
IP	Peer of Ireland (ROG)
IP	Peoria Public Library, Peoria, IL [*Library symbol Library of Congress*] (LCLS)
IP	Positive Identification (ECII)
IPA	Allied Agencies Center, Peoria, IL [*Library symbol Library of Congress*] (LCLS)
IPA	Image Power Amplifier (IAA)
IPA	Image Processing Applications [*Computer graphics*]
IPA	Immunoperoxidase Antibody Assay [*Clinical chemistry*]
IPA	Imperial Pale Ale
IPA	Including Particular Average [*Insurance*]
IPA	Incorporeal Personal Agency [*Parapsychology*]
IPA	Independent Physician Association (HCT)
IPA	Independent-Practice Association [*Medical insurance*]
IPA	Independent Product Assurance (SSD)
IPA	Independent Public Accountant
IPA	Independent Publishers' Association [*Canada*]
IPA	India Pale Ale
IPA	India Press Agency
IPA	Indicated Pressure Altitude
IPA	Individual Practice Association [*Medicine*]
IPA	Industrial Participation Association [*British*]
IPA	Industrial Perforators Association (EA)
IPA	Industrial Property Administration
IPA	Industrial Publicity Association (EA)
IPA	Information for Public Affairs, Inc. [*Information service or system*] (IID)
IPA	Information Process Analysis (BUR)
IPA	Information Processing Architecture (IAA)
IPA	Information Processing Association [*Israel*]
IPA	Information-technology Promotion Agency [*Japan*] (NITA)
IPA	In-Principle Agreement
IPA	Insolvency Practitioners Association [*British*] (EAIO)
IPA	Institute for Physics of the Atmosphere
IPA	Institute for Policy Analysis [*University of Toronto*] [*Canada*] (IRC)
IPA	Institute for Polyacrylate Absorbents (EA)
IPA	Institute of Practitioners in Advertising
IPA	Institute of Public Administration (EA)
IPA	Institute of Public Affairs [*Dalhousie University*] [*Canada Research center*]
IPA	Institutional Patent Agreements [*General Services Administration*]
IPA	Instrument Performance Assessment
IPA	Integrated Peripheral Adapter
IPA	Integrated Photodetection Assemblies (IEEE)
IPA	Integrated Plan of Action (MCD)
IPA	Integrated Printer Adapter
IPA	Intelligence Production Activity [*Military*] (MCD)
IPA	Interamerican Press Association
IPA	Intergovernmental Personnel Act [*1970*]
IPA	Interior Plantscape Association [*Later, ALCA/IPD*] (EA)
IPA	Intermediate Power Amplifier [*Electronics*]
IPA	International Association for the Child's Right to Play [*International PIayground Association*] [*Acronym is based on former name,*] (EA)
IPA	International Paddleball Association [*Later, AARA*] (EA)
IPA	International Palaeontological Association
IPA	International Patent Agreement
IPA	International Peace Academy (EA)
IPA	International Pediatric Association [*See also AIP*] [*Paris, France*] (EAIO)
IPA	International Petroleum Annual [*Department of Energy*] [*Database*]
IPA	International Phonetic Alphabet
IPA	International Phonetic Association [*University College*] [*Leeds, England*] (EA)
IPA	International Phototherapy Association (EA)
IPA	International Pietenpol Association (EA)
IPA	International Pinball Association (EA)
IPA	International Pipe Association [*Later, TPF*] (EA)
IPA	International Platform Association (EA)
IPA	International Police Academy [*Formerly, Inter-American Police Academy*]
IPA	International Police Association [*Maidstone, Kent, England*] (EAIO)
IPA	International Polka Association (EA)
IPA	International Porcelain Artist (EA)
IPA	International Prepress Association (EA)
IPA	International Press Association [*Defunct*] (EA)
IPA	International Psycho-Analytical Association [*British*] (EAIO)
IPA	International Psychogeriatric Association (EA)
IPA	International Psychohistorical Association (EA)
IPA	International Publishers Association [*See also UIE*] [*Geneva, Switzerland*] (EAIO)
IPA	International Pumpkin Association (EA)
IPA	Inter-Pacific Resource Corp. [*Vancouver Stock Exchange symbol*]
IPA	Invasive Pulmonary Aspergillosis [*Medicine*] (DAVI)
IPA	Investment Partnership Association (EA)
IPA	Ipec Aviation Pty Ltd. [*Australia ICAO designator*] (FAAC)
IPA	Ipota [*Vanuatu*] [*Airport symbol*] (OAG)
IPA	Isopentenyladenosine [*Biochemistry*]
IPA	Isophthalic Acid [*Organic chemistry*]
IPA	Isopropane [*Organic chemistry*]
IPA	Isopropyl Alcohol [*Organic chemistry*]
IPA	Issue-Position-Argument [*Computer science*] (BYTE)
IPAA	Independent Petroleum Association of America (EA)
IPAA	Industrial Photographers Association of America [*Later, Industrial Photographers of New Jersey*] (EA)
IPAA	Instrumental Photon Activation Analysis [*National Institute of Standards and Technology*]
IPAA	International Pesticide Applicators Association (EA)
IPAA	International Prisoners Aid Association (EA)
IPAA	Inventario del Patrimonio Arquitectonico [*Database*] [*Ministerio de Cultura*] [*Spanish*] [*Information service or system*] (CRD)
IPAB	International Program for Antarctic Buoys [*Marine science*] (OSRA)
IPAC	Independent Petroleum Association of Canada
IPAC	Information Processing and Control [*Systems Laboratory*] [*Northwestern University*]
IPAC	Institute of Public Administration of Canada
IPAC	Integrated Packaging Assembly [*NASDAQ symbol*] (TTSB)
IPAC	Integrated Packaging Assembly Corp. [*NASDAQ symbol*] (SAG)
IPAC	Intelligence Center, Pacific [*Military*] (MCD)
IPAC	Intelligence, Pacific Area Command (MCD)
IPACE	Interprovincial Advisory Council on Energy [*Canada*]
IPACK	International Packaging Material Suppliers (DGA)
IPACK	International Packaging Material Suppliers Association (PDAA)
IPACS	Integrated Power and Attitude-Control System [*NASA*]
IPACS	Interactive Pattern Analysis and Classification System (PDAA)
IPAD	Incoming Procurement Authorization Document [*Air Force*] (AFM)
IPAD	Integrated Program Aircraft Design
IPAD	Integrated Programs for Aerospace-Vehicle Design
IPAD	International Plastics Association Directors
IPADAE	Integrated Passive Action Detection Acquisition Equipment
IPADD	Intra-Governmental Professional Advisory Council on Drugs and Devices [*Inactive*] [*FDA*] (EGAO)
IPADE	Instituto Panamericano de Alta Direccion de Empresa [*Panamerican Institute for Business Management*] [*Mexico*] (PDAA)
IPADS	Interactive Processing and Display System (MCD)
IPAE	(Isopropylamino)ethanol [*Organic chemistry*]
IPAF	International Powered Access Federation (EAIO)
IPAFUG	International PAF User's Group (EA)
IPAHGEIS	Inter-Professional Ad Hoc Group for Environmental Information Sharing
IPAI	International Primary Aluminium Institute [*British*] (EAIO)
IPAL	Index to Periodical Articles Related to Law [*A publication*] (DLA)
IP/AL	Inland Printer / American Lithographer [*A publication*] (DGA)
IPal	Palatine Public Library District, Palatine, IL [*Library symbol Library of Congress*] (LCLS)
Ipalco	IPALCO Enterprises, Inc. [*Associated Press*] (SAG)
IPale	La Motte Township Library, Palestine, IL [*Library symbol Library of Congress*] (LCLS)
IPalH	William Rainey Harper College, Palatine, IL [*Library symbol of Congress*] (LCLS)
IPalmSD	Northwestern Community Unit, School District 2, Palmyra, IL [*Library symbol Library of Congress*] (LCLS)
IPALS	Integrated Pathology Audio-Visual Learning System (PDAA)
IPAMS	Independent Petroleum Association of Mountain States
IPANA	Indian People's Association in North America (EA)
IP & BE	Initial Program and Budget Estimate [*Army*]
IP & C	Instrumentation Program and Component (KSC)
IP & T	Intellectual Property and Technology
IPANY	Individual Psychology Association of New York
IPAP	Inspiratory Positive Airway Pressure [*Medicine*] (DMAA)
IPAP	Interagency Placement Assistance Program [*Office of Personnel Management*]
IPAP	Iodophenyl(piperidinoacetyl)piperazine [*Biochemistry*]
IPAR	Improved Pulse Acquisition RADAR (AABC)
IPAR	Innovative Photovoltaics Applications for Residences
IPAR	Institute of Personality Assessment and Research [*University of California*] [*Research center*]
IPAR	Institute of Policy Analysis and Research [*Nairobi, Kenya*] [*Research center*] (ECON)
IPAR	Intercepted Photosynthetically Active Radiation [*Photosynthesis*]
IPar	Paris Carnegie Public Library, Paris, IL [*Library symbol Library of Congress*] (LCLS)
IPAR	United States Department of Agriculture, Agricultural Research Service, NorthernResearch Center Library, Peoria, IL [*Library symbol Library of Congress*] (LCLS)
IPARA	International Publishers Advertising Representatives Association
I-Para	Primipara [*Obstetrics*] (DAVI)
IPARC	International Pesticide Application Research Centre [*Imperial College at Silwood Park*] [*British*] (CB)
IPARCOM	Interim Paris Commission [*British*]
IparF	Edgar County Film Library, Paris, IL [*Library symbol*] [*Library of Congress*] (LCLS)
IParH	Paris Community Hospital, Paris, IL [*Library symbol Library of Congress*] (LCLS)
Ipark	Park Ridge Public Library, Park Ridge, IL [*Library symbol*] [*Library of Congress*] (LCLS)
IParkA	American Society of Anesthesiologists, Park Ridge, IL [*Library symbol Library of Congress*] (LCLS)

IParkD .... Dames and Moore Chicago Branch Library, Park Ridge, IL [*Library symbol Library of Congress*] (LCLS)

IParkL .... Lutheran General Hospital, Park Ridge, IL [*Library symbol Library of Congress*] (LCLS)

IParP .... Paris Carnegie Public Library, Paris, IL [*Library symbol*] [*Library of Congress*] (LCLS)

IPARS .... International Passenger Airline Reservations System

IParSD .... Paris Union School District, Paris, IL [*Library symbol*] [*Library of Congress*] (LCLS)

IPAS .... Independants et Paysans d'Action Sociale [*Independents and Peasants of Social Action*] [*French*] (PPE)

IPAS .... Integrated Pneumatic Air System (MCD)

IPAS .... Interplatform Alignment System (MCD)

IPASS .... Interactive Policy Analysis Simulation System [*Department of Agriculture*]

IPAST .... IGOSS [*Integrated Global Ocean Services System*] Pilot Project on AlimetricSea-Surface Topography Data [*Marine science*] (OSRA)

IPAT .... Institute for Personality and Ability Testing [*Champaign, IL*]

IPAT .... International Porcelain Art Teachers [*Later, IPA*] (EA)

IPAT .... Inventario del Patrimonio Historico Artistico Espanol [*Ministerio de Cultura*] [*Spain Information service or system*] (CRD)

IPAT .... Iowa Pressure Articulation Test (DMAA)

IPat .... Patoka Public Library, Patoka, IL [*Library symbol Library of Congress*] (LCLS)

IPATA .... Independent Pet and Animal Transportation Association (EA)

IPAT CPQ ... Institute for Personality and Ability Testing, Children's Personality Questionnaire [*Psychology*] (AEBS)

IPAT NPFT ... Institute for Personality and Ability Testing, Neurotic Personality Factor Test [*Psychology*] (AEBS)

IPAVS .... International Project of the Association for Voluntary Sterilization

IPax .... Paxton Carnegie Library, Paxton, IL [*Library symbol Library of Congress*] (LCLS)

IPaxH .... Paxton Community Hospital, Paxton, IL [*Library symbol Library of Congress*] (LCLS)

IPB .... Bradley University, Peoria, IL [*Library symbol Library of Congress*] (LCLS)

IPB .... Ice-Penetrating Communications Buoy (DWSG)

IPB .... Illuminated Push Button (NASA)

IPB .... Illustrated Parts Book (IAA)

IPB .... Illustrated Parts Breakdown (AFIT)

IPB .... Inert Processing Building

IPB .... Information Parts Breakdown (MCD)

IPB .... Injury-Prone Behavior [*Medicine*] (DMAA)

IPB .... Installation Property Book [*Military*] (AABC)

IPB .... Institute of Professional Businesswomen (EA)

IPB .... Integrated Processor Board

IPB .... Intelligence Preparation of the Battlefield [*Army*] (RDA)

IPB .... Intelligence Preparatory Brief [*Army*] (DOMA)

IPB .... Intelligence Property Book [*Army*] (ADDR)

IPB .... Intercept Priorities Board [*Armed Forces Security Agency*]

IPB .... Interconnection and Program Bay (IAA)

IPB .... International Pathfinder, Inc. [*Toronto Stock Exchange symbol*]

IPB .... International Peace Bureau [*Geneva, Switzerland*] (EA)

IPB .... Interprocessor Buffer

IPB .... Irish Peat Board (EAIO)

IPB .... Jenner & Block, Chicago, IL [*OCLC symbol*] (OCLC)

IPBA .... India, Pakistan, and Bangladesh Association (PDAA)

IPBA .... Irish Paper Box Association (BI)

IPBC .... India, Pakistan, Bangladesh Conference (DS)

IPBC .... Iodopropynyl Butyl Carbamate [*Wood preservative*]

IPBM .... Integrated Program, Budget, Manpower [*System*] [*Defense Supply Agency*]

IPBM .... Interplanetary Ballistic Missile [*Air Force*]

IPBMM .... International Permanent Bureau of Motor Manufacturers (BARN)

IPBNet .... International Plant Biotech Network (EA)

IPBS .... Israel Plate Block Society (EA)

IPC .... Easter Island [*Chile*] [*Airport symbol*] (OAG)

IPC .... Idaho Potato Commission (EA)

IPC .... Illinois Power Co. [*NYSE symbol*] (SPSG)

IPC .... Illinois Power Financing I [*NYSE symbol*] (SAG)

IPC .... Illustrated Parts Catalog (AAG)

IPC .... Image Processing Center [*Drexel University*] [*Research center*] (RCD)

IPC .... Image Products Co.

IPC .... Imaging Proportional Counter [*Astronomy*]

IPC .... Impurity Photoconductivity (PDAA)

IPC .... Indirect Photometric Chromatography

IPC .... Indirect Pulp Capping [*Dentistry*]

IPC .... Individual Plan of Care

IPC .... Industrial Personal Computer (NITA)

IPC .... Industrial Planning Committee [*NATO*] (NATG)

IPC .... Industrial Policy Council [*Washington, DC*] (EA)

IPC .... Industrial Process Control [*by computers*]

IPC .... Industrial Programmable Controller (IAA)

IPC .... Industrial Property Committee [*US Military Government, Germany*]

IPC .... Industrial Publishing Co.

IPC .... Industry Planning Council (EA)

IPC .... Information Processing Center [*of General Motors Corp.*]

IPC .... Information Processing Code (DIT)

IPC .... Information Publishing Corp. [*Telecommunications service*] (TSSD)

IPCD .... Initial Planning Conference [*Military*] (INF)

IPC .... Institute for Interconnecting and Packaging Electronic Circuits [*Formerly, Institute of Printed Circuits*] (EA)

IPC .... Institute for Personal Computing (EA)

IPC .... Institute of Paper Chemistry [*Lawrence University*] [*Research center*] (EA)

IPC .... Institute of Paper Conservation [*Formerly, International Institute for Conservation of Historic and Artistic Works Paper Group*] (EA)

IPC .... Institute of Pastoral Care (EA)

IPC .... Institute of Printed Circuits (MCD)

IPC .... Institute of Production Control [*British*]

IPC .... Institute of Pure Chiropractic [*British*] (DBA)

IPC .... Institutional Population Component [*National Medical Expenditure Survey*] [*Department of Health and Human Services*] (GFGA)

IPC .... Instrumentation Package Container

IPC .... Instrument Panel Cluster [*Automotive engineering*]

IPC .... Integral Plate Chamber

IPC .... Integrated Peripheral Channel

IPC .... Integrated Peripheral Controller [*Computer chip*]

IPC .... Integrated Pest Control

IPC .... Integrated Pollution Control

IPC .... Integrated Procedures Control

IPC .... Integrated Process Control (IAA)

IPC .... Integrated Programme for Commodities [*UNCTAD*] (EY)

IPC .... Intelligence Priorities Committee [*British World War II*]

IPC .... Intelligent Peripheral Controller [*Computer science*]

IPC .... Inter-African Phytosanitary Commission

IPC .... Intercalated Polymer-Derived Carbon [*Chemistry*]

IPC .... Interconnections Packaging Circuitry (MCD)

IPC .... Intermediate Processing Centers

IPC .... Intermittent Positive Control [*Aviation*]

IPC .... Internal Positive Control [*Genetics*]

IPC .... International Pacific Cypress Minerals Ltd. [*Vancouver Stock Exchange symbol*]

IPC .... International Patent Classification

IPC .... International PBX [*Private Branch Exchange*]/Telecommunicators (EA)

IPC .... International Peace Campaign

IPC .... International Penpal Club (EAIO)

IPC .... International Pepper Community [*Indonesia*] [*Research center*] (IRC)

IPC .... International Petroleum Cartel

IPC .... International Photosynthesis Committee [*Stockholm, Sweden*] (EAIO)

IPC .... International Planning Corp.

IPC .... International Plasma Corp.

IPC .... International Poliomyelitis Congress

IPC .... International Poplar Commission [*FAO*] [*Rome, Italy*] [*United Nations*] (EA)

IPC .... International Procurement Committee [*ABA*] (AAGC)

IPC .... International Publishing Corp. [*England*]

IPC .... Interpenduncular Cistern [*Medicine*] (DAVI)

IPC .... Interplanetary Communications (AAG)

IPC .... Inter-Process Communication (NITA)

IPC .... Interprocess Controller

IPC .... Inter-Process Coupler (NITA)

IPC .... Interprocessor Channel (IAA)

IPC .... Interprocessor Communication (BUR)

IPC .... Interstate Processing Center [*Department of Labor*]

IPC .... Investment Promotion Centre [*Tanzania*]

IPC .... Investors Planning Corp.

IPC .... Ion-Pair Comonomers [*Organic chemistry*]

IPC .... Iraqi Petroleum Co.

IPC .... Irish Peace Council (EAIO)

IPC .... Irish Presbyterian Church (ROG)

IPC .... Irish Productivity Council (ACII)

IPC .... Iron Phosphate Coating

IPC .... Isolation-Physiological Characterization [*Microbiology*]

IPC .... Isopropyl Carbanilate [*Also, INPC, IPPC*] [*Herbicide*]

IPC .... Isopropyl Chlorophenyl [*Medicine*] (MAE)

IPC .... Item Processing Card

IPC .... Purdue University, Calumet Campus, Hammond, IN [*OCLC symbol*] (OCLC)

IPCA .... Independent Parametric Cost Analysis (MCD)

IPCA .... Independent Police Complaints Authority [*British*]

IPCA .... Industrial Pest Control Association [*British*] (BI)

IPCA .... International Plate Collectors Association (EA)

IPCA .... International Postcard Collectors Association (EA)

IPC-ASA ..... Intermittent Positive Control - Automatic Seperation [*Aviation*] (PDAA)

IPCC .... Infantry Precommand Course [*Army*] (INF)

IPCC .... Information Processing in Command and Control [*Air Force*]

IPCC .... Intergovernmental Panel on Climate Change [*World Meteorological Organization*]

IPCC .... International Pin Collectors Club (EA)

IPCCB .... Inter-Parliamentary Consultative Council of Benelux (EA)

IPCCC .... International Peace, Communication, and Coordination Center [*The Hague, Netherlands*] (EAIO)

IPCCIOS ...... Indo-Pacific Council of the International Committee of Scientific Management

IPCCS .... Information Processing in Command and Control Systems [*Air Force*]

IPCD .... Infantile Polycistic Disease (DAVI)

IPCDA .... International Penguin Class Dinghy Association (EA)

IPCE .... Independent Parametric Cost Estimate (AABC)

IPCEA .... Insulated Power Cable Engineers Association [*Later, ICEA*] (EA)

IPCF .... Interprocess Communication Facility [*Digital Equipment Corp.*]

IPCF .... Interprogram Communication Facility [*Prime Computer, Inc.*]

IPCG .... International Plate Collectors Guild

IPCHold .... IPC Holdings Ltd. [*Associated Press*] (SAG)

IPCI .... IPC Information Systems [*NASDAQ symbol*] (TTSB)

IPCI .... IPC Information Systems, Inc. [*NASDAQ symbol*] (SAG)

IPC Info ...... IPC Information Systems, Inc. [*Associated Press*] (SAG)

IPCIS .... Integrated Plant Control and Information System [*Nuclear energy*] (NUCP)
IPCL .... Central Illinois Light Co., Resource Center, Peoria, IL [*Library symbol Library of Congress*] (LCLS)
IPCL .... Instrumentation Program and Component List (NASA)
IPCL .... International Postal Collectors League [*Commercial firm*] (EA)
IPCO .... Idaho Power Co.
IPCO .... In-Place Cleanable Oilfilter
IPCO .... International Paper Co. (WDMC)
IPCOG .... Informal Policy Committee for Germany
IPCOG .... Interdepartmental Planning Committee on Germany [*US*]
IPCP .... Integrated Printing Collating Processing (DGA)
IPCP .... Interdisciplinary Patient Care Plan (HCT)
IPCPA .... Institute of Private Clinical Psychologists of Australia
IPCPP .... International Physicians Commission for the Protection of Prisoners (EA)
IPCPrA .... Illinois Pwr 4.08% Pfd [*NYSE symbol*] (TTSB)
IPCPrB .... Illinois Pwr 4.20% Pfd [*NYSE symbol*] (TTSB)
IPCPrC .... Illinois Pwr 4.26% Pfd [*NYSE symbol*] (TTSB)
IPCPrD .... Illinois Pwr 4.42% Pfd [*NYSE symbol*] (TTSB)
IPCPrE .... Illinois Pwr 4.70% Pfd [*NYSE symbol*] (TTSB)
IPCPrL .... Illinois Pwr Adj Rt A Pfd [*NYSE symbol*] (TTSB)
IPCPrM .... Illinois Pwr Cap 9.45%'MIPS' [*NYSE symbol*] (TTSB)
IPCPrT .... Illinois Pwr Fin I 8%'TOPrS' [*NYSE symbol*] (TTSB)
IPCR .... Inverse Polymerase Chain Reaction [*Genetics*]
IPCR .... IPC Holdings Ltd. [*NASDAQ symbol*] (SAG)
IPC Rept ..... International Procurement Committee Report [*ABA*] [*A publication*] (AAGC)
IPCRESS ...... Induction of Psychoneuroses by Conditioned Reflex under Stress [*In book and film "The Ipcress File"*]
IPCRF .... IPC Holdings [*NASDAQ symbol*] (TTSB)
IPCS .... Image Photon Counting System [*Instrumentation*]
IPCS .... Infrapatellar Contracture Syndrome [*Sports medicine*]
IPCS .... Institute of Professional Civil Servants [*British*]
IPCS .... Institution of Professional Civil Servants [*British*] (BI)
IPCS .... Integrated Powertrain Control System [*Automotive engineering*]
IPCS .... Integrated Propulsion Control System [*Air Force*]
IPCS .... Interactive Problem-Control System [*IBM Corp.*]
IPCS .... International Petula Clark Society (EAIO)
IPCS .... International Playing-Card Society (EA)
IPCS .... International Programme on Chemical Safety (EA)
IPCS .... International Program on Chemical Safety (GNE)
IPCS .... Interproject Control Station (IAA)
IPCS .... Intrauterine Progesterone Contraceptive System [*Gynecology*]
IPCT .... Caterpillar Tractor Co., Business Library, Peoria, IL [*Library symbol Library of Congress*] (LCLS)
IPCT-T .... Caterpillar Tractor Co., Technical Information Center, Peoria, IL [*Library symbol Library of Congress*] (LCLS)
IPCV .... Indian Peanut Clump Virus [*Plant pathology*]
IPD .... Idiopathic Parkinson's Disease [*Medicine*] (CPH)
IPD .... Illustrated Provisioning Document (MCD)
IPD .... Immediate Pigment Darkening [*Dermatology*]
IPD .... Impact Prediction Data (AFM)
IPD .... Implicit Price Deflator
IPD .... Improved Point Defense
IPD .... Individual Package Delivery [*Shipping*]
IPD .... Individual Protective Device [*Toxicology*]
IPD .... Inflammatory Pelvic Disease [*Medicine*] (MAE)
IPD .... Information Processing Division [*NASA*] (NASA)
IPD .... Initial Performance Data
IPD .... In Praesentia Dominorum [*In the Presence of the Lords of Session*] [*Latin*]
IPD .... Insertion Phase Delay
IPD .... Inspection Planning Document [*Military*] (MCD)
IPD .... Institute for Professional Development (EA)
IPD .... Institute of Professional Designers
IPD .... Instructional Program Development (NVT)
IPD .... Integrated Pin Diode
IPD .... Integrated Process Demonstration [*Nuclear energy*]
IPD .... Integrated Product Development [*Business term*] (RDA)
IPD .... Intelligence Planning Document [*Military*] (MCD)
IPD .... Intelligent Protection Device [*American Solenoid Co.*] [*Somerset, NJ*]
IPD .... Interaural Phase Disparity [*Audiology*]
IPD .... Intermediate Peritoneal Dialysis [*Medicine*] (BARN)
IPD .... Intermittent Peritoneal Dialysis [*Medicine*]
IPD .... International Police Dogs (EA)
IPD .... Inter-Provincial Diversified Holding Ltd. [*Toronto Stock Exchange symbol*]
IPD .... Interpupillary Distance
IPD .... Intra-Penile Device [*Contraceptive*] (DI)
IPD .... Inventory of Psychosocial Development
IPD .... Investment Property Databank [*London, England*]
IPD .... Isophorone Diamine [*Organic chemistry*]
IPD .... Isotope-Powered Device
IPD .... Issue Priority Designator
IPD .... Iterated Prisoner's Dilemma [*Psychology*]
IPDA .... International Periodical Distributors Association (EA)
IPDA .... Intrapulse Demodulation Analysis
IPD/AC .... Institut Panafricain pour le Developpement, Afrique Centrale [*Pan African Institute for Development, Central Africa*] [*Cameroun*] (PDAA)
IPDB .... Intelligence Production Database [*Military*] (MCD)
IPDC .... International Program for the Development of Communications [*UNESCO*]
IPDD .... Initial Project Design Description (NRCH)

IPDF .... Intensity Probability Density Function (PDAA)
IPDH .... In-Service Planned Derated Hours [*Electronics*] (IEEE)
IPDI .... Implicit Price Deflator Index [*Economics*]
IPDI .... Isophorone Diisocyanate [*Organic chemistry*]
IPDL .... Isotopes Process Development Laboratory [*AEC*]
IPDM .... Institute of Physical Distribution Management [*British*]
IPDMS .... Integrated Point Defense Missile System [*Military*] (CAAL)
IPDN .... International Paleoclimatic Data Network
IPDP .... Intervals of Pulsations of Diminishing Period
IPDP .... Isopropylphenyl(diphenyl)phosphate [*Fire-resistant hydraulic fluid*]
IPDR .... Incremental Preliminary Design Review (MCD)
IPDR .... Inter-Plan Data Reporting System [*Health insurance*] (GHCT)
IPDS .... IBM Personal Dication System [*Computer science*]
IPDS .... Imagery Processing and Dissemination System (DOMA)
IPDS .... Improved Point Defense Missile System [*Navy*] (DOMA)
IPDS .... Integrated Product Development System [*FAA*] (TAG)
IPDS .... Integrated Program Development Support System [*Allen Bradley*] (NITA)
IPDS .... Intelligent Printer Data Systems
IPDSMS .... Improved Point Defense Surface Missile System
IPDTAS .... Interim Point Defense Target Acquisition System [*Military*] (IAA)
IPDU .... Instantaneous Panoramic Display Unit
IPE .... Incentive PERT [*Program Evaluation and Review Technique*] Events
IPE .... Individual Protective Equipment
IPE .... Industrial Plant [*or Production*] Equipment
IPE .... Infectious Porcine Encephalomyelitis [*Medicine*] (DMAA)
IPE .... Information Processing Equipment
IPE .... Initial Portable Equipment
IPE .... Initial Psychiatric Evaluation (DAVI)
IPE .... Inscriptiones Orae Septentrionalis Ponti Euxini [*A publication*] (OCD)
IPE .... Institute for Program Evaluation (AAGC)
IPE .... Institute of Production Engineers [*British*]
IPE .... Institution of Plant Engineers [*British*]
IPE .... Intelligent Program Editor (PDAA)
IPE .... International Partners Facility
IPE .... International Petroleum Exchange [*British*]
IPE .... International Prism Exploration Ltd. [*Vancouver Stock Exchange symbol*]
IPE .... Interpret Parity Error
IPE .... Interstitial Pulmonary Emphysema [*Medicine*] (AAMN)
IPE .... Inverse Photoelectric Effect
IPE .... Isopropyl Ether [*Organic chemistry*]
IPe .... Peotone Township Library, Peotone, IL [*Library symbol Library of Congress*] (LCLS)
IPEA .... Independent Poster Exchanges of America (EA)
IPEC .... Integrated Process Equipment [*NASDAQ symbol*] (SAG)
IPEC .... International Patient Education Council (EAIO)
IPEC .... International Pharmaceutical Excipients Council (EA)
IPEC .... International Police Exhibition and Conference [*British*] (ITD)
IPEC .... International Power and Engineering Consultants
IPECAC .... Ipecacuanha [*Pharmacy*] (ROG)
IPECS .... Integrated Power and Environmental Control System (MCD)
IPEDS .... Integrated Postsecondary Education Data System [*National Center for Education Statistics*] (OICC)
IPEE .... Inclination of a Plane to the Plane of the Earth's Equator [*Aerospace*]
IPEE .... International Peace, Economy, and Ecology (EA)
IPEH .... Intravascular Papillary Endothelial Hyperplasia [*Medicine*]
IPek .... Pekin Public Library, Pekin, IL [*Library symbol Library of Congress*] (LCLS)
IPekC .... Pekin Community High School District No. 30, Pekin, IL [*Library symbol Library of Congress*] (LCLS)
IPekH .... Pekin Memorial Hospital, Pekin, IL [*Library symbol Library of Congress*] (LCLS)
IPEME .... International Program in Environmental Management Education
IPEN .... Pan American Institute of Naval Engineering (EAIO)
IPENEB .... International PEN [*Poets, Playwrights, Editors, Essayists, Novelists*]-Estonian Center (EAIO)
IPENHKE ..... International PEN - Hong Kong English (EAIO)
IPENI .... International PEN - Ireland (EAIO)
IPENS .... International PEN - Scotland (EAIO)
IPENUS .... International PEN - United States [*Later, PCUSAW*] (EA)
IPENWIE ...... International PEN [*Poets, Playwrights, Editors, Essayists, Novelists*]-Writers inExile [*British*] (EAIO)
IPENY .... International PEN - Yiddish (EA)
IPEP .... Integrated Performance Evaluation Program
IPER .... Industrial Production Equipment Reserve (NG)
IPer .... Peru Public Library, Peru, IL [*Library symbol Library of Congress*] (LCLS)
IPerIH .... Illinois Valley Community Hospital, Peru, IL [*Library symbol Library of Congress*] (LCLS)
i-periton ...... Intraperitoneal [*Medicine*] (MEDA)
IPERS .... Industrial Plant Equipment Reutilization System [*DoD*]
IPerSD .... Peru Consolidated Community School District 124, Peru, IL [*Library symbol Library of Congress*] (LCLS)
IPerStB .... Saint Bede Academy, Peru, IL [*Library symbol Library of Congress*] (LCLS)
IPES .... Inverse Photoemission Spectroscopy
IPE/T .... Improved Protective Entrance/Tent [*Army*]
IPET .... Independent Professional Electronic Technicians
IPetM .... Edgar Lee Masters Memorial Museum, Petersburg, IL [*Library symbol Library of Congress*] (LCLS)
IPEU .... International Photo-Engravers Union [*Later, GAIU*] (EA)
IPEX .... Instant Purchase Excursion Fares [*Aviation*]
IPEX .... International Printing Exhibition
IPF .... Idiopathic Pulmonary Fibrosis [*Medicine*]

IPF.............. Inches per Foot (IAA)
IPF.............. Indicative Planning Figure
IPF.............. Infection Potentiating Factor (AAMN)
IPF.............. Information Processing Facility (MHDI)
IPF.............. Initial Production Facilities (AABC)
IPF.............. Initial Protective Force
IPF.............. In-Process Factor
IPF.............. Institute of Public Finance [British] (ECON)
IPF.............. Insulin Promoter Factor [Biochemistry]
IPF.............. Intaken Piled Fathom [Shipping] (DS)
IPF.............. Integrated Processing Facility [DoD]
IPF.............. Intellectual Property Forum [A publication]
IPF.............. Interactive Productivity Facility (HGAA)
IPF.............. Intermediate Plot File
IPF.............. International Pain Foundation (EA)
IPF.............. International Pharmaceutical Federation [Netherlands] (EAIO)
IPF.............. International Pigeon Federation [See also FCI] (EAIO)
IPF.............. International Podrabinek Fund [Defunct] (EA)
IPF.............. International Poetry Forum (EA)
IPF.............. International Powerlifting Federation [Hagersten, Sweden] (EAIO)
IPF.............. International Prayer Fellowship (EA)
IPF.............. Interstitial Pulmonary Fibrosis [Medicine] (DMAA)
IPF.............. Iodine Protection Factor [Nuclear energy] (GFGA)
IPF.............. Irish Printing Federation (BI)
IPF.............. Isotope Production Facility
IPF.............. IUS Processing Facility [NASA] (NASA)
IPf.............. Park Forest Public Library, Park Forest, IL [Library symbol Library of Congress] (LCLS)
IPFA.............. Institute for Psychiatry and Foreign Affairs [Defunct] (EA)
IPFA.............. Insurance Premium Finance Association (EA)
IPFA.............. International Physical Fitness Association (EA)
IPFA.............. Member of the Chartered Institute of Public Finance and Accountancy [British]
IPFAA.............. International Police and Fire Athletic Association [Defunct] (EA)
iPFC.............. Indirect Plaque-Forming Cell [Immunology]
IPFC.............. Indo-Pacific Fisheries Commission [or Council] [FAO ICSU Bangkok, Thailand] [United Nations] (ASF)
IPFC.............. Indo-Pacific Fishery Commission (EAIO)
IPFD.............. Incident Power Flux Density (NITA)
IPFD.............. Intrapartum Fetal Distress [Obstetrics] (DAVI)
IPFEO.............. Institut des Producteurs de Ferro-Alliages d'Europe Occidentale [Institute of Ferro-Alloy Producers in Western Europe - IFAPWE] [Defunct] (EA)
IPFM.............. Integral Pulse Frequency Modulation (IEEE)
IPFP.............. Institut Professionnel de la Fonction Publique du Canada [Professional Institute of the Public Service of Canada - PIPS]
IPFP.............. Iterated Proportional Fitting Procedure [Statistics]
IPFR.............. Institute of Plasma and Fusion Research [University of California, Los Angeles] [Research center] (RCD)
IPFS.............. Integrated Polygenerator Fertilizer System
IPFS.............. International Pen Friend Service (EA)
IPfs.............. Park Forest South Public Library, Park Forest South, IL [Library symbol Library of Congress] (LCLS)
IPFSC.............. International Pacific Salmon Fisheries Commission [Marine science] (OSRA)
IPFSC.............. International Pacific Salmon Fisheries Commission (USDC)
IPfsG.............. Governors State University, Park Forest South, IL [Library symbol Library of Congress] (LCLS)
IPfsI.............. Inolex Pharmaceutical Co., Park Forest South, IL [Library symbol Library of Congress] (LCLS)
IPFW.............. Indiana University - Purdue University at Fort Wayne
IPG.............. Immediate Participation Guarantee Plan [Insurance]
IPG.............. Immobilized pH Gradients [Chemistry]
IPG.............. Impedance Plethysmography [Medicine]
IPG.............. In-Circuit Program Generator [Computer science] (PDAA)
IPG.............. Independent Publishers Group
IPG.............. Independent Publishers' Guild [British]
IPG.............. Individually Polymerized Grass [Organic chemistry] (DAVI)
IPG.............. Induction Plasma Gun
IPG.............. Industrial Painters Group [British] (BI)
IPG.............. Industrial Physics Group [University of Essex] [British] (IRUK)
IPG.............. Information Planning Group (SSD)
IPG.............. Information Policy Group (NITA)
IPG.............. Information Publishing Group [The Thomson Corp.]
IPG.............. Inositol-Phosphoglycan [Biochemistry]
IPG.............. INPADOC Patent Gazette (NITA)
IPG.............. Inspiration-Phase Gas (DMAA)
IPG.............. Institut de Physique du Globe [France]
IPG.............. Institute of Professional Goldsmiths [British] (DBA)
IPG.............. Interactive Presentation Graphics [IBM Corp.]
IPG.............. Internal Problem Generator (IAA)
IPG.............. International Pagurian Corp. Ltd. [Toronto Stock Exchange symbol Vancouver Stock Exchange symbol]
IPG.............. International Parliamentary Group for Human Rights in the Soviet Union (EA)
IPG.............. International Payments Group (NATG)
IPG.............. International Piano Guild (EA)
IPG.............. International Planning Group [Belgium, Germany, Netherlands] (AABC)
IPG.............. International Portrait Gallery
IPG.............. Interproject Group
IPG.............. [The] Interpublic Group of Companies, Inc. [NYSE symbol] (SPSG)
IPG.............. Interpublic Grp Cos. [NYSE symbol] (TTSB)
IPG.............. Isopropylidene Glycerol [Biochemistry]
IPG.............. Isopropylthiogalactoside [Also, IPTG] [Organic chemistry]

IPG.............. Isotope Power Generator
IPG.............. Issue Priority Group [Army]
IPG.............. Phoolbagh [India] [Airport symbol] (AD)
IPGA.............. Illinois Propane Gas Association (SRA)
IPGA.............. Indiana Propane Gas Association (SRA)
IPGA.............. Island Park Geothermal Area
IPGCU.............. International Printing and Graphic Communications Union
iPGE.............. Prostaglandin E, immunoreactive [Biochemistry]
IPGEN.............. Intersection Point Generator (PDAA)
IPGF.............. Immobilized pH Gradient Isoelectric Focusing [Analytical biochemistry]
IPGH.............. Instituto Panamericano de Geografia e Historia [Panamerican Institute of Geography and History] [Peru]
IPGI.............. Institute on Pluralism and Group Identity (EA)
IPGP.............. Illegal Possession of Government Property
IPGRI.............. International Plant Genetic Resources Institute [Italy]
IPGS.............. Intercollegiate Program of Graduate Studies
IPGS.............. Internationale Paracelsus-Gesellschaft zu Salzburg (EAIO)
IPGS.............. International Percy Grainger Society (EA)
IPH.............. Idiopathic Portal Hypertension [Medicine]
IPH.............. Idiopathic Pulmonary Hemosiderosis [Medicine]
IPH.............. Impressions per Hour [Printing]
IPH.............. Inches per Hour (TEL)
IPH.............. Industrial and Pastoral Holdings (ADA)
IPH.............. Industrial Process Heat
IPH.............. Inflammatory Papillary Hyperplasia [Dentistry]
IPH.............. Interdisciplinary Programs in Health [Harvard University]
IPH.............. International Association of Paper Historians (EA)
IPH.............. International Pharmadyne Ltd. [Vancouver Stock Exchange symbol]
IPH.............. Interphalangeal [Anatomy]
IPH.............. Intraparenchymal Hemorrhage [Medicine]
IPH.............. Ipoh [Malaysia] [Airport symbol] (OAG)
IPh.............. Peoria Heights Public Library, Peoria Heights, IL [Library symbol Library of Congress] (LCLS)
IphA.............. Illinois Pharmacists Association (SRA)
IPHA.............. Illinois Public Health Association (SRA)
IPHC.............. International Pacific Halibut Commission (EA)
IPHE.............. Individual Personal Hygiene Equipment (KSC)
IPHE.............. Institute of Public Health Engineers [British]
IPhe.............. Palos Heights Public Library, Palos Heights, IL [Library symbol Library of Congress] (LCLS)
IP/HHCL.............. Initial Point/H-Hour Control Line [Aviation]
IPhi.............. Green Hills Public Library District, Palos Hills, IL [Library symbol Library of Congress] (LCLS)
IPHi.............. Peoria Historical Society, Peoria, IL [Library symbol Library of Congress] (LCLS)
IPhil.............. Philo Township Public Library, Philo, IL [Library symbol Library of Congress] (LCLS)
IPhiM.............. Moraine Valley Community College, Palos Hills, IL [Library symbol Library of Congress] (LCLS)
IPhiP.............. Green Hills Public Library District, Palos Hills, IL [Library symbol Library of Congress] (LCLS)
IPHM.............. Individual Personal Hygiene Module (KSC)
IP-HPLC.............. Ion-Pair High-Performance Liquid Chromatography [Medicine]
IPHR.............. Inverted Polypoid Hamartoma of the Rectum [Medicine] (DMAA)
IPHRD.............. International Program for Human Resource Development [Defunct] (EA)
IPHT.............. Institute of Physical High Technology [Germany]
IPI.............. Identified Friendly Prior to Interception [Military]
IPI.............. Image Processing Interface [Computer science] (PCM)
IPI.............. Immigration Patrol Inspector [Immigration and Naturalization Service]
IPI.............. Implicit Price Index (MHDW)
IPI.............. Improved Processing Inspection [Food Safety and Inspection Service] [Department of Agriculture]
IPI.............. Income and Price Index (DICI)
IPI.............. INCYTE Pharmaceuticals, Inc. [AMEX symbol] (SPSG)
IPI.............. Index of Production Industries [Department of Employment] [British]
IPI.............. Individually Planned [or Prescribed] Instruction [Education]
IPI.............. Individually Presented Instruction (NITA)
IPI.............. Industrial Production Index (PDAA)
IPI.............. Infinite Position Indicator (PDAA)
IPI.............. Inflation Protected Income (DICI)
IPI.............. Information Professionals Institute (IID)
IPI.............. Information Publications International [Publisher] [British]
IPI.............. Initial Product Inspection
IPI.............. Initial Protocol Identifier [Computer science] (TNIG)
IPI.............. In Partibus Infidelium [In the Countries, Lands, or Regions of Unbelievers] [Latin]
IPI.............. Institute for Practical Idealism (EA)
IPI.............. Institute for Public Information
IPI.............. Institute of Patentees and Inventors [British] (ILCA)
IPI.............. Institute of Physical Medicine and Rehabilitation, Peoria, IL [Library symbol Library of Congress] (LCLS)
IPI.............. Institute of Poultry Industries
IPI.............. Institute of Professional Investigators (EA)
IPI.............. Insurance Periodicals Index [Nils Publishing Co.] [Chatsworth, CA] [Information service or system] (IID)
IPI.............. Integrated Position Indicator
IPI.............. Intelligence Publications Index [Published January, 1953, through February, 1968, by the Defense Intelligence Agency]
IPI.............. Intelligent Peripheral Interface [Computer science]
IPI.............. Intelligent Printer Interface
IPI.............. Intense Product Inspection
IPI.............. Interchemical Printing Inks
IPI.............. Internal Procedures Instruction

IPI	International Patent Institute [*Later, EPO*]
IPI	International Pesticide Institute
IPI	International Phototherapy Institute [*Defunct*] (EA)
IPI	International Population Institute [*Defunct*] (EA)
IPI	International Potash Institute [*See also IIP*] (EAIO)
IPI	International Press Institute [*British*]
IPI	International Press Institute [*Switzerland*] (PDAA)
IPI	International Press Institute, American Committee (EA)
IPI	International Psychosomatics Institute (EA)
IPI	Interpulse Interval
IPI	Intrapair Interval
IPI	Inventory, Print, and Index [*System*]
IPI	Iolani Place Irregulars (EA)
IPI	Ipiales [*Colombia*] [*Airport symbol*] (OAG)
IPIA	Independent Primary Inspection Agency [*Department of Housing and Urban Development*] (GFGA)
IPIA	Induced Psycho-Intellectual Activity (PDAA)
IPIACFA	International Private Investment Advisory Council on Foreign Aid [*Agency for International Development*] (EGAO)
IPiaMCD	Macoupin Community Unit, District 9, Piasa, IL [*Library symbol Library of Congress*] (LCLS)
IPiaSD	Southwestern Community Unit, School District 9, Piasa, IL [*Library symbol Library of Congress*] (LCLS)
IPIC	Institute of Personal Image Consultants (EA)
IPIC	Intelligent Power Integrated Circuit [*Electronics*]
IPIC	Interneuron Pharmaceuticals [*NASDAQ symbol*] (TTSB)
IPIC	Interneuron Pharmaceuticals, Inc. [*NASDAQ symbol*] (SAG)
IPICS	Initial Production and Information Control System [*Computer science*] (PDAA)
IPIE	Institute of Profit Improvement Executives [*British*] (DBA)
IPIECA	International Petroleum Industry Environmental Conservation Association [*British*] (EAIO)
IPIF	Institute of Pacific Islands Forestry [*Honolulu, HI*] [*Department of Agriculture*] (GRD)
IPI Inc	IPI, Inc. [*Associated Press*] (SAG)
IPI Inc	IPI, Inc. [*Associated Press*] (SAG)
IPI/MIS	Individually Planned Instruction/Management and Information System
IPI/MIS	International Press Institute/Management and Information System [*Switzerland*]
IPIN	Instituto Panamericano de Ingenieria Naval [*Pan American Institute of Naval Engineering*] (EAIO)
IPIN	Integrated Photogrammetric Instrument Network (PDAA)
IP/IN	Interpositive/Internegative [*Photography*] (WDMC)
IPIP	Implantable Programmable Infusion Pump [*Medicine*]
IPIP	Information Processing Improvement Program
IPip	Piper City Public Library, Piper City, IL [*Library symbol Library of Congress*] (LCLS)
IPIPS	Interactive Planetary Image Processing System
IPipSD	Ford Central Community Unit Shool District, Piper City, IL [*Library symbol*] [*Library of Congress*] (LCLS)
IPIR	Immediate Photograph Intelligence Report [*Military*] (AFM)
IPIR	Initial Photographic Interpretation Report [*Air Force*]
IPIR	Institute for Public Interest Representation [*Later, CCCIPR*] [*Georgetown University*]
IPIR	Integrated Personnel Information Report (AAG)
IPIS	Individually Prescribed Instructional Systems (OICC)
IPIS	Institute for Peace and International Security (EA)
IPIS	Instrument Pilot Instructor School [*Air Force*]
IPIS	International Peace Information Service [*Belgium*]
IPISD	Interservice Procedures for Instructional Systems Development
IPit	Pittsfield Public Library, Pittsfield, IL [*Library symbol Library of Congress*] (LCLS)
IPIV	Illinois Valley Library System, Peoria, IL [*Library symbol Library of Congress*] (LCLS)
IPJ	Institute for Peace and Justice (EA)
IPJ	Intellectual Property Journal [*A publication*]
IPJ	International Pursuit Corp. [*Toronto Stock Exchange symbol*]
IPJ	Interphalangeal Joint [*Anatomy*] (DAVI)
IPJP	Interpost Junction Panel
IPJT	Interplant Job Ticket
IPK	Interactive Press Kit [*Public relations*] (WDMC)
IPK	International Prototype Kilogram
IPK	Interphalangeal Keratosis [*Orthopedics*] (DAVI)
IPK	Intractable Plantar Keratosis [*Orthopedics*] (DAVI)
IPK	Painter Creek, AK [*Location identifier FAA*] (FAAL)
IPK	Peoria Kindergarten Primary Training School, Peoria, IL [*Library symbol Library of Congress*] (LCLS)
IPKC	International Pot and Kettle Clubs (EA)
IPKF	Indian Peace-Keeping Force [*Army*]
IPKO	International Information on Peace-Keeping Operations
IPL	Air Charter Services (Pty) Ltd. South Africa [*ICAO designator*] (FAAC)
IPL	El Centro/Imperial [*California*] [*Airport symbol*] (OAG)
IPL	Identified Parts List
IPL	Illustrated Parts List (NATG)
IPL	Illustrated Pocket Library [*A publication*]
IPL	Image Processing Laboratory [*University of Houston*] [*Research center*] (RCD)
IPL	Imperial, CA [*Location identifier FAA*] (FAAL)
IPL	Improved Position Locator (PDAA)
IPL	Indentured Parts List
IPL	Independent Publishers League [*Defunct*] (EA)
IPL	Individual Protection Laboratory [*Natick, MA*] [*Army*] (RDA)
IPL	Inferior Parietal Lobule [*Anatomy*]
IPL	Information Processing Language [*Computer science*]

IPL	Initial Program Load [*Computer science*]
IPL	Initial Provisioning List (MCD)
IPL	Inner Plexiform Layer [*Retina*]
IPL	Installation Parts List (AAG)
IPL	Institute of Professional Librarians [*Canada*]
IPL	Instrumentation Program List
IPL	Instrument Panel Lighting (MCD)
IPL	Instrument Pool Laboratory (IAA)
IPL	Integrated Payload [*NASA*]
IPL	Integrated Perceived Level [*Acoustics*]
IPL	Integrated Priority List [*DoD*]
IPL	Interconnected Porosity Level
IPL	Interested Parties List
IPL	Interim Parts List [*Navy*]
IPL	Interim Policy Letter [*Air Force*] (AAGC)
IPL	Interprovincial Pipe Line Ltd. [*Toronto Stock Exchange symbol*]
IPL	Interrupt Priority Level
IPL	Intrapleural
IPL	Iota Phi Lambda Sorority (AEBS)
IPL	IPALCO Enterprises [*NYSE symbol*] (TTSB)
IPL	IPALCO Enterprises, Inc. [*NYSE symbol*] (SPSG)
IPL	Purdue University, Lafayette, IN [*OCLC symbol*] (OCLC)
IPLA	Institute of Public Loss Assessors [*British*] (DBA)
IPLA	Instituto Pastoral Latinoamericano
IPLA	Interstate Producers Livestock Association (EA)
IPLAN	Joint IOC/WMO Planning Group for IGOSS [*Marine science*] (MSC)
IPlantE	Institution of Plant Engineers [*British*] (EAIO)
IPLC	International Private Leased Circuits [*British Telecom International*] (NITA)
IPLCA	International Pipe Line Contractors Association [*Later, IPOCA*] (EA)
IPLE	Institution of Public Lighting Engineers [*British*]
IPL En	IPL Energy, Inc. [*Associated Press*] (SAG)
IPLF	Isogrid Payload Fairing (MCD)
IPLGY	Institute for the Protection of Lesbian and Gay Youth (EA)
IPLOCA	International Pipe Line and Offshore Contractors Association [*Belgium*] (EAIO)
IPLS	IPL Systems CI'A' [*NASDAQ symbol*] (TTSB)
IPLS	IPL Systems, Inc. [*NASDAQ symbol*] (NQ)
IPL Sy	IPL Systems, Inc. [*Associated Press*] (SAG)
IPLV	Information Processing Language Five
IPLV	Intermediate Payload Launch Vehicle
IPlx	International Plant Index [*A publication*]
IPM	Illumination per Minute
IPM	Immediate Past Master [*Freemasonry*]
IPM	Imperial Metals Corp. [*Toronto Stock Exchange symbol Vancouver Stock Exchange symbol*]
IPM	Impulses per Minute [*Telecommunications*]
IPM	Inches Penetration per Month (IAA)
IPM	Inches per Minute
ipm	Inches per Minute (IDOE)
IPM	Incidental Phase [*or Pulse*] Modulation
IPM	Incident Power Monitor [*Military*] (CAAL)
IPM	Indomethacin-Treated Platelet Microsomes
IPM	Industrial Preparedness Measures
IPM	Infusible Platelet Membrane [*Substitute for blood tranfusion*]
IPM	Inhalable Particulate Matter (GNE)
IPM	Inner Peace Movement (EA)
IPM	Input Position Map [*Computer science*] (OA)
IPM	Insect Populations Management Research Unit [*Department of Agriculture*] (GRD)
IPM	Institute of Personnel Management [*British*] (DCTA)
IPM	Institute of Practical Mathematics [*Germany*]
IPM	Institute of Precious Metals [*China*]
IPM	Institute of Printing Management [*British*]
IPM	Instructional Programming Model [*Individually-guided education*] (AEE)
IPM	Integrated Pest Management [*Agronomy*]
IPM	Intelligent Power Management [*Laptop computers*] (BYTE)
IPM	Intelligent Processing of Materials [*Computer science*]
IPM	Intel Power Monitor (PCM)
IPM	Interaction Place Map (EDAC)
IPM	Interaural Phase Modulation [*Audiology*]
IPM	Interference Prediction Model
IPM	Internal Polarization Modulation (IEEE)
IPM	International Prison Ministry (EA)
IPM	International Prototype Meter
IPM	Internet Protection Module [*Computer science*]
IPM	Interpersonal Mail System [*Computer science*] (TNIG)
IPM	Interpersonal Messaging [*Telecommunications*] (OSI)
IPM	Interpersonal Messaging Service
IPM	Interpersonal Perception Method [*Psychology*]
IPM	Interphotoreceptor Matrix [*Ophthalmology*]
IPM	Interplanetary Medium
IPM	Inter-Processor/Multiplexer (MCD)
IPM	Interruptions per Minute
IPM	Inventory Policy Model (MHDI)
IPM	Isopropyl Myristate [*Pharmacology*]
IPM	Morrison and Mary Wiley Public Library, Elmwood, IL [*OCLC symbol*] (OCLC)
IPM	Peoria Masonic Temple, Peoria, IL [*Library symbol Library of Congress*] (LCLS)
IPMA	In-Plant Management Association (EA)
IPMA	In-Plant Printing Management Association
IPMA	Interlocking Paving Manufacturers Association [*Defunct*] (EA)
IPMA	International Personnel Management Association (EA)

IPMA............ International Planned Music Association (EA)
IPMA............ International Primary Market Association (EAIO)
IPMANA....... Interstate Postgraduate Medical Association of North America (EA)
IPMCF......... International Precious Metals [*NASDAQ symbol*] (SAG)
IPMH .... Methodist Hospital of Central Illinois, Peoria, IL [*Library symbol Library of Congress*] (LCLS)
IPMH-M .... Methodist Medical Center of Illinois, Medical Library, Peoria, IL [*Library symbol Library of Congress*] (LCLS)
IPMI............. Inferoposterior Myocardial Infarct [*or Infarction*] [*Cardiology*] (DAVI)
IPMI............. International Precious Metals Institute (EA)
IPMLF.......... Intl Precious Metals [*NASDAQ symbol*] (TTSB)
IPMP............ IEEE [*Institute of Electrical and Electronics Engineers*] Parts, Materials and Packaging (IAA)
IPMP............ Industrial Plant Modernization Program [*Air Force*]
IP/MP........... Inphase/Midphase (MHDI)
IPMP............ Isopropyl(methoxy)pyrazine [*Organic chemistry*]
IPMPCS .... Integrated Pest Management and Program Coordination Staff [*Environmental Protection Agency*] (GFGA)
IPMS........... Impact Predictor Monitor Set [*NASA*] (AAG)
IPMS........... Infinite Periodic Minimal Surface
IPMS........... Institute for Problems of Materials Science [*Ukraine*]
IPMS........... Institution of Professionals, Managers, and Specialists [*British*]
IPMS........... Integrated Program Management System [*Navy*]
IPMS........... International Plastic Modelers Society (EA)
IPMS........... International Polar Motion Service
IPMS........... International Primitive Money Society (EA)
IPM/S........... Interruptions per Minute/Second (DEN)
IPMS........... Investment Performance Monitoring Service [*British*]
IPMS/USA.... International Plastic Modelers Society/US Branch (EA)
IPN.............. Impulse Noise
IPN.............. Indigenous People's Network (EA)
IPN.............. Industri Pesawat Terbang Nusantara PT [*Indonesia*] [*ICAO designator*] (FAAC)
IPN.............. Infantile Periarteritis Nodosa [*Cardiology*] (DAVI)
IPN.............. Infectious Pancreatic Necrosis [*Medicine*]
IPN.............. Information Processing Network
IPN.............. Initial Priority Number [*Computer science*] (OA)
IPN.............. Initial Processing Number (NITA)
IPN.............. Inspection Progress Notification
IPN.............. Instant Private Network
IPN.............. Instrumentation Plan Number (MUGU)
IPN.............. Integrated Packet Network [*Hughes Network Systems, Inc.*]
IPN.............. Intellectual Property Network, Ltd. [*Information service or system*] (IID)
IPN.............. International Platinum Corp. [*Toronto Stock Exchange symbol*]
IPN.............. International Polio Network (EA)
IPN.............. International Publishing Newsletter (NITA)
IPN.............. Intern's Progress Note [*Medical records*] (DAVI)
IPN.............. Interpeduncular Nucleus [*Cytology*]
IPN.............. Interpenetrating Polymer Network [*Organic chemistry*]
IPN.............. Interplanetary Network [*Astronomy*]
IPN.............. Ipatinga [*Brazil*] [*Airport symbol*] (OAG)
IPN.............. Isophthalonitrile [*Organic chemistry*]
IPN.............. Purdue University, North Central Campus, Westville, IN [*OCLC symbol*] (OCLC)
IPNA .... International Pediatric Nephrology (EA)
IPNA .... Isopropylnoradrenaline
IPNC .... Independence Plan for Neighborhood Councils (EA)
IPNC .... International Council of Plant Nutrition [*Australia*] (EAIO)
IPNFC .... International Peter Noone Fan Club (EA)
IPng .... Internet Protocol Next Generation (CDE)
IPNJ............ Industrial Photographers of New Jersey (EA)
I/PNL .... Instrument Panel [*Automotive engineering*]
IPNL .... Integrated Perceived Noise Level [*Acoustics*]
IPNS .... Intense Pulsed Neutron Source
IPNS .... Interpenetrating Networks of Samples [*Statistics*]
IPNS .... Isopenicillin N Synthase [*An enzyme*]
IPNV .... Infectious Pancreatic Necrosis Virus
IPO.............. Crown Point Community Schools, Crown Point, IN [*OCLC symbol*] (OCLC)
IPO.............. Improved Pregnancy Outcome [*Medicine*] (DMAA)
IPO.............. Indophenol Oxidase [*An enzyme*]
IPO.............. Initial Planning Option [*Medicine*] (DAVI)
IPO.............. Initial Public Offering [*Business term*]
IPO.............. Initial Public Offering [*Stock exchange term*]
IPO.............. Input, Process, and Output (MHDB)
IPO.............. Inspection Planning Order
IPO.............. Installation Planning Order
IPO.............. Installation Production Order
IPO.............. Installation Productivity Option [*IBM Corp.*]
IPO.............. Instantaneous Power Output
IPO.............. Intellectual Property Owners (EA)
IPO.............. International Pact Organization
IPO.............. International Parents' Organization [*Later, PS*] (EA)
IPO.............. International Payment Order (DCTA)
IPO.............. International Progress Organization [*Vienna, Austria*] (EAIO)
IPO.............. Ipora [*Brazil*] [*Airport symbol*] (AD)
IPOC........... Iberian Peninsula Operating Committee [*World War II*]
IPOCA .... International Pipe Line and Offshore Contractors Association [*Belgium*] (EAIO)
IPOD .... International Program of Ocean Drilling [*Formerly, DSDP*] [*National Science Foundation*]
IPO/E .... Installation Productivity Option/Extended [*IBM Corp.*]
IPOEE.......... Institute of Post Office Electrical Engineers [*British*]
IPOFA .... Integrated Programmed Operational and Functional Appraisals

IPoH............ Saint James Hospital, Pontiac, IL [*Library symbol Library of Congress*] (LCLS)
IpOHA .... Isopropyl Oxalyl Hydroxamate [*Organic chemistry*]
IPOL............ Institute of Polarology [*British*]
IPOM .... Intelligent Plant Operating Manual [*Combustion Engineering Simcon, Inc.*]
IPOMS .... International Polar-Orbiting Meteorological Satellite
IP/OP........... Input/Output Interface Element [*Computer science*] (NITA)
IPOP........... Installer Point of Purchase
IPOR........... International Population Research Center [*University of California*] [*Defunct*]
IPOSA .... International Photo Optical Show Association [*Defunct*] (EA)
IPOSS .... Interim Pacific Oceanographic Support System (DNAB)
IPOT............ Inductive Potential Divider [*Electronics*] (ECII)
IPOT............ Inductive Potentiometer (MDG)
IPot............. Potomac Public Library, Potomac, IL [*Library symbol Library of Congress*] (LCLS)
IPOTMS .... Isopropenyloxytrimethylsilane [*Organic chemistry*]
IPP.............. British Institute of Practical Psychology
IPP.............. Imaging Polarimeter [*or Photopolarimetry*] [*NASA*]
IPP.............. Immediate Past President (ADA)
IPP.............. Imminent Peril to the Public (MHDB)
IPP.............. Impact Prediction Point [*NASA*]
IPP.............. Impaired Physician Program (EA)
IPP.............. Implementation Planning Program [*Environmental Protection Agency*] (GFGA)
IPP.............. Import Parity Pricing (ADA)
IPP.............. Inanities per Page [*Facetious criterion for determining insignificance of Supreme Court Justices*] [*Proposed by University of Chicago professor David P. Currie*]
IPP.............. Independent People's Party [*Political party Germany*] (EAIO)
IPP.............. Independent Power Producer
IPP.............. Independent Power Projects (AAGC)
IPP.............. Index of Prices Paid [*Economics*]
IPP.............. Indianapolis Public Schools, Indianapolis, IN [*OCLC symbol*] (OCLC)
IPP.............. Indian Print and Paper [*A publication*] (DGA)
IPP.............. India Paper Proofs
IPP.............. Individual Parameter Perturbation
IPP.............. Individual Program Plan
IPP.............. Industrial Partnering Program [*Department of Energy*]
IPP.............. Industrial Preparedness Planning [*DoD*]
IPP.............. Industrial Preparedness Program [*DOD*] (AAGC)
IPP.............. Inferior Point [*of the*] Pubic [*Bone*] [*Anatomy*] (DAVI)
IPP.............. Inflatable Penile Prosthesis [*Urology*] (DAVI)
IPP.............. Information Privacy Principle
IPP.............. Information Processing Professional
IPP.............. Infrared Pointer Package
IPP.............. Injury Prevention Program
IPP.............. In Propria Persona [*In Person*] [*Latin Legal term*] (DLA)
IPP.............. Input Processor Programs [*Computer science*]
IPP.............. Inspired Partial Pressure [*Physiology*]
IPP.............. Institute of Print Purchasing (DGA)
IPP.............. Integrated Plotting Package (NRCH)
IPP.............. Interface Program Plan (MCD)
IPP.............. Intermedia Priority Pollutant (GNE)
IPP.............. Intermittent Positive Pressure [*Medicine*]
IPP.............. Internal Packet Protocol [*Telecommunications*]
IPP.............. Internationally Protected Person (ADA)
IPP.............. International Partners in Prayer (EA)
IPP.............. International Phototelegraph Position [*Telecommunications*] (TEL)
IPP.............. International Price Program [*Bureau of Labor Statistics*] (GFGA)
IPP.............. International Priority Paid (ADA)
IPP.............. Interprocessor Process [*Telecommunications*] (TEL)
IPP.............. Intrapleural Pressure [*Biology*]
IPP.............. Inverse Polarity Protection
IPP.............. Investment Promotion Program
IPP.............. Ionospheric Propagation Path
IPP.............. Ipplepen [*England*]
IPP.............. Isopentenyl Pyrophosphate [*Organic chemistry*]
IPP.............. Isopropyl Percarbonate [*or Diisopropyl Peroxydicarbonate*] [*Organic chemistry*]
IPP.............. Isotactic Polypropylene [*Organic chemistry*]
IPP.............. Isothermal Pressure Profile
IPP.............. Itek Positive Plate [*Publishing*] (DGA)
IPp.............. Paw Paw Public Library, Paw Paw, IL [*Library symbol Library of Congress*] (LCLS)
IPPA............ Independent Programme Producers' Association [*British*]
IPPA............ Inspection, Palpation, Percussion, Auscultation [*Medicine*]
IPPA............ Instant Potato Products Association [*Defunct*] (EA)
IPPA............ Institute for Public Policy and Administration [*Later, CPPUI*] (EA)
IPPA............ Intensive Pig Producers of Australia
IPPA............ Intercontinental Press Publishing Association [*Defunct*] (EA)
IPPA............ International Paintball Players Association (EA)
IPPA............ International Pectin Producers Association [*Switzerland*] (EAIO)
IPPA............ International Pentecostal Press Association (EA)
IPPA............ International Printing Pressmen and Assistants' Union of North America [*Later, IPGCU*]
IPPA............ International Program for Population Analysis
IPPA............ Isopropylphenyl Acetate [*Organic chemistry*]
IPpa............ Palos Park Public Library, Palos Park, IL [*Library symbol Library of Congress*] (LCLS)
IPPAU.......... International Printing Pressmen and Assistants' Union of North America [*Later, IPGCU*] (EA)
IPPB............ Incremental Provisioning Parts Breakdown (SAA)
IPPB............ Intermittent Positive Pressure Breathing [*Medicine*]

IPPBA .... Intermittent Positive-Pressure Breathing Apparatus [*Medicine*] (MEDA)
IPPB/I .... Intermittent Positive Pressure Breathing/Inspiratory
IPPBS .... Integrated Personnel Planning and Budgeting System
IPPC............ Infrastructure Payments and Progress Committee [*NATO*] (NATG)
IPPC............ Integrated Pollution Prevention and Control [*Environmental science*]
IPPC............ International Penal and Penitentiary Commission [*Later, IPPF*]
IPPC............ International Philatelic Press Club (EA)
IPPC............ International Plant Protection Center [*Oregon State University*] [*Research center*] (RCD)
IPPC............ Isopropyl N-phenylcarbamate [*Also, INPC, IPC*] [*Herbicide*]
IPPCA .... Independent Professional Painting Contractors Association of America (EA)
IPPD .... Integrated Product and Process Development [*Business term*] (RDA)
IPPD .... Isopropyl(phenyl)para-phenylene Diamine [*Organic chemistry*]
IPPDSEU...... International Plate Printers, Die Stampers, and Engravers' Union of North America (EA)
IPPDT .... Integrated Product and Process Development Team [*Military*] (RDA)
IPPF............ Instruction Preprocessing Function
IPPF............ International Penal and Penitentiary Foundation [*See also FIPP*] [*Bonn, Federal Republic of Germany*] (EAIO)
IPPF............ International Planned Parenthood Federation (EA)
IPPF/WHR.... International Planned Parenthood Federation, Western Hemisphere Region (EA)
IPPH .... Proctor Community Hospital, Peoria, IL [*Library symbol Library of Congress*] (LCLS)
IPPHA .... International Peruvian Paso Horse Association (EA)
IPPI............ Instructional Procedures Preference Inventory
IPPI............ International Public Policy Institute
IPPI............ Interruption of Pregnancy for Psychiatric Indication
IPPIF.......... IPL Energy [*NASDAQ symbol*] (TTSB)
IPPIF.......... IPL Energy, Inc. [*NASDAQ symbol*] (SAG)
IPPJ............ Institute of Plasma Physics, Japan
IPPL............ Indentured Parts Price List (MCD)
IPPL............ Industrial Preparedness Planning List
IPPL............ Integrated Planning Parts List (MCD)
IPPL............ International Primate Protection League (EA)
IPPMA .... In-Plant Powder Metallurgy Association (EA)
IPPMA .... In-Plant Printing Management Association
IPPMHN....... International Post-Partum Mental Health Network (EA)
IPPNO .... International Philosophers for the Prevention of Nuclear Omnicide (EA)
IPPNW .... International Physicians for the Prevention of Nuclear War (EA)
IPPO .... Intermittent Positive Pressure with Oxygen [*Medicine*]
IPPP............ Industrial Preparedness Production Planning [*DOD*] (AAGC)
IPPP............ Industrial Property Policy Program [*Insurance*]
IPPP............ Institute for Philosophy and Public Policy (EA)
IPPP............ Institute of Private Practicing Psychologists [*Australia*]
IPPR............ Industrial Production Performance Reporting
IPPR............ Institute for Public Policy Research [*British*] (ECON)
IPPR............ Integrated Pancreatic Polypeptide Response [*Medicine*] (DMAA)
IPPR............ Intermittent Positive Pressure Respiration
IPPS............ Improved Processing System (MCD)
IPPS............ Infiniti Personalized Protection System
IPPS............ Institute of Physics and the Physical Society [*British*] (DI)
IPPS............ International Philippine Philatelic Society (EAIO)
IPPS............ International Plant Propagators Society, Eastern Region (EA)
IPpS............ Paw Paw School System, Paw Paw, IL [*Library symbol Library of Congress*] (LCLS)
IPPSA .... Israel-Palestine Philatelic Society of America [*Later, SIP*]
IPPSF.......... Isolated Perfused Porcine Skip Flap [*Clinical chemistry*]
IPPT............ Inter-Person Perception Test [*Personality development test*] [*Psychology*]
IPPUAD....... Immediate Postprandial Upper Abdominal Distress
IPPV............ Intermittent Positive Pressure Ventilation
IPQ.............. International Philosophical Quarterly [*A publication*] (BRI)
IPQ.............. International Praxis Resources [*Vancouver Stock Exchange symbol*]
IPQ.............. Intimacy Potential Quotient
IPQC............ In-Process Quality Control
IPQI............ Intermediate Personality Questionnaire for Indian Pupils [*Personality development test*] [*Psychology*]
IPR.............. Icar Airlines [*Ukraine*] [*FAA designator*] (FAAC)
IPR.............. Imposter Pass Rate (MHDI)
IPR.............. Inches per Revolution
IPR.............. Independent Professional Review [*Medicaid*] (DHSM)
IPR.............. Index of Prices Received [*Economics*]
IPR.............. Individual Pay Record [*Military*]
IPR.............. Indochina Postwar Reconstruction
IPR.............. Industry Planning Representative [*DoD*]
IPR.............. Inflation Pressure Retention [*Tire technology*]
IPR.............. Informal Progress Report
IPR.............. Initial Pressure Regulator [*Nuclear energy*] (NRCH)
IPR.............. In-Place Repair
IPR.............. In-Process Report
IPR.............. In-Process Review
IPR.............. In-Progress Review (DOMA)
IPR.............. In Pulse to Register [*Telecommunications*] (TEL)
IPR.............. Inspection Planning and Reliability (SAA)
IPR.............. Institute for Policy Research [*University of Wyoming*] [*Research center*] (RCD)
IPR.............. Institute for Policy Research [*University of Cincinnati*] [*Research center*] (RCD)
IPR.............. Institute for Public Research (AAGC)
IPR.............. Institute for Puerto Rican Policy, Inc. [*Research center*] (RCD)
IPR.............. Institute of Pacific Relations
IPR.............. Institute of Peace Research [*La Trobe University*] [*Australia*]
IPR.............. Institute of Population Registration [*British*]
IPR.............. Institute of Psychophysical Research [*British*]
IPR.............. Institute of Public Relations [*British*]
IPR.............. Insulin Production Rate [*Medicine*] (DMAA)
IPR.............. Intellectual Property Rights
IPR.............. Intelligence Production Requests
IPR.............. Intelligence Production Requirement (AFIT)
IPR.............. Interactive Photorealistic Rendering [*Computer-assisted design*]
IPR.............. Inter-City Products [*AMEX symbol*] (TTSB)
IPR.............. Inter-City Products Corp. [*AMEX symbol*] (SPSG)
IPR.............. Interdepartmental Procurement Request
IPR.............. Interdepartmental Purchase Request [*DoD*] (AFIT)
IPR.............. Interim Problem Report (NASA)
IPR.............. Interim Progress Report
IPR.............. Interior Procurement Regulations [*Department of the Interior*]
IPR.............. Internal Progress Report
IPR.............. International Public Relations (ADA)
IPR.............. Interpersonal Process Recall [*Psychology*]
IPR.............. Inward Processing Relief (DCTA)
IPR.............. Ion Production Rate
IPR.............. Isolated Pentagon Rule [*Physical chemistry*]
IPR.............. Isoproterenol [*An adrenergic*]
IPRA .... Illinois Park and Recreation Association (SRA)
IPRA .... In-Place Repairable Assembly (MCD)
IPRA .... Institute of Park and Recreation Administration [*British*] (BI)
IPRA .... International Paddle Racket Association [*Later, AARA*]
IPRA .... International Peace Research Association (EA)
IPRA .... International Professional Rodeo Association (EA)
IPRA .... International Public Relations Association [*London, England*] (WDMC)
IPRA .... International Public Relations Association, US Section (EA)
IPRA .... Iowa Park and Recreation Association (SRA)
IPra............. Vernon Area Library District, Prairie View, IL [*Library symbol*] [*Library of Congress*] (LCLS)
IPRB .... Installations Planning and Review Board [*DoD*]
IPRB .... Inter-Allied Postwar Requirements Bureau [*World War II*]
IPRC .... Information Privacy Research Center [*Purdue University*] (PDAA)
IPRE............ Incorporated Practitioners in Radio and Electronics Ltd. [*British*] (BI)
IPRE............ International Professional Association for Environmental Affairs (EA)
IPRI .... International Plant Research Institute (PDAA)
IPri............. Matson Public Library, Princeton, IL [*Library symbol Library of Congress*] (LCLS)
IPriBSD........ Bureau Township Consolidated School District 250, Princeton, IL [*Library symbol Library of Congress*] (LCLS)
I-PRIDE........ Interracial-Intercultural Pride (EA)
IPriDS.......... Douglas Elementary School, Princeton, IL [*Library symbol Library of Congress*] (LCLS)
IPriHi........... Bureau County Historical Society, Princeton, IL [*Library symbol Library of Congress*] (LCLS)
IPriJS........... Jefferson Elementary School, Princeton, IL [*Library symbol Library of Congress*] (LCLS)
IPriLH.......... Logan Junior High School, Princeton, IL [*Library symbol Library of Congress*] (LCLS)
IPriPH.......... Perry Memorial Hospital, Princeton, IL [*Library symbol Library of Congress*] (LCLS)
IPriv............ Lillie M. Evans Memorial Library, Princeville, IL [*Library symbol Library of Congress*] (LCLS)
IPriWS......... Washington Middle School, Princeton, IL [*Library symbol Library of Congress*] (LCLS)
IPRL............ Interceptor Pilot Research Laboratory (SAA)
I-PRO.......... Independent Professional Representatives Organization (EA)
I/Pro............ Interactive Profiles [*Computer science*]
IPRO............ International Pallet Recycling Organization (PDAA)
IPRO............ International Patent Research Office (IAA)
I/PRO.......... Internet Profiles Corp.
IProD .... Prospect Heights Public Library District, Prospect Heights, IL [*Library symbol Library of Congress*] (LCLS)
IProdE.......... Institute of Production Engineers [*British*] (DI)
I Prod E........ Institution of Production Engineers [*British*]
IPROP.......... Ionic Propulsion (IAA)
IPRP............ Institute for Puerto Rican Policy (EA)
IP-RPLC....... Ion-Pair-Reversed-Phase Liquid Chromatography
IPRR............ Integrated Personnel Requirement Report (AAG)
IPRS .... International Confederation for Plastic and Reconstructive Surgery [*Montreal, PQ*] (EAIO)
IPRT............ Industrial Platinum Resistance Thermometer (PDAA)
IPRT............ Interpersonal Reaction Test [*Medicine*] (MAE)
IPS.............. Ibero-American Philosophical Society [*Madrid, Spain*] (EAIO)
IPS.............. Idiopathic Pain Syndrome [*Medicine*] (DMAA)
IPS.............. Idiopathic Postprandial Syndrome [*Medicine*] (DMAA)
IPS.............. Ignition Pressure Switch [*Automotive engineering*]
IPS.............. Illinois Psychiatric Society (SRA)
IPS.............. Illustrative Planning Scenario [*DoD*]
IPS.............. Image Processing System (MCD)
IPS.............. Impact Predictor System [*NASA*]
IPS.............. Imperial Parliament Series [*A publication*]
IPS.............. Improved Plow Steel (PDAA)
IPS.............. Improved Processing System
IPS.............. Impulses per Second [*Telecommunications*] (TEL)
IPS.............. Inches per Second
ips .... Inches per Second (IDOE)
ips .... Inches per Second (DOM)
IPS.............. Incorporated Phonographic Society [*British*] (BI)
IPS.............. Incremental Purchasing System (SAA)

IPS............... Index Preparation System [*Foxon-Maddocks Associates*] [*Information service or system*] (IID)
IPS............... Indian Point Station [*Nuclear energy*] (NRCH)
IPS............... Indian Police Service [*British*]
IPS............... Indian Political Service [*British*]
IPS............... Industrial Planning Specification
IPS............... Inertial Positioning System (PDAA)
IPS............... Information Processing System
IPS............... Infundibular Pulmonic Stenosis [*Medicine*] (DAVI)
IPS............... Initial Prognostic Score [*Medicine*] (MAE)
IPS............... Initial Program Specification (SAA)
IPS............... Inlet Particle Separator (MCD)
IPS............... Inner Polar Site [*Cytology*]
IPS............... In-Pavement System
IPS............... In-Plant Support (MCD)
IPS............... In Pulse to Sender [*Telecommunications*] (TEL)
IPS............... Inside Pipe Size (DAC)
IPS............... Installation Performance Specification [*Computer science*] (IBMDP)
IPS............... Institute for Palestine Studies (EA)
IPS............... Institute for Policy Studies (EA)
IPS............... Institute of Plant Science [*Australia*]
IPS............... Institute of Polar Studies [*Ohio State University*] [*Later, BPRC*]
IPS............... Institute of Population Studies (BARN)
IPS............... Institute of Purchasing and Supply [*British*]
IPS............... Institutional Payment Summary [*Pell Grant Program*] [*Department of Education*] (GFGA)
IPS............... Instructions per Second [*Computer science*]
IPS............... Instrumentation Power Supply
IPS............... Instrumentation Power System [*or Subsystem*] [*NASA*] (NASA)
IPS............... Instrument Pointing System (MCD)
IPS............... Integrated Planning Summary (MCD)
IPS............... Integrated Power Semiconductors Ltd. [*British*] (NITA)
IPS............... Integrated Power System
IPS............... Integrated Procurement System [*Army*]
IPS............... Integrated Program Study (MCD)
IPS............... Integrated Program Summary [*Military*] (CAAL)
IPS............... Integrated Project Support (IAA)
IPS............... Integrated Propulsion System (MCD)
IPS............... Intelligent Power Management System [*Laptop computers*] (BYTE)
IPS............... Intelligent Power Switch [*Electronics*]
IPS............... Intelligent Printing System [*Dataroyal, Inc.*]
IPS............... Interactive Pictures Systems [*In IPS Dance, a computer program for choreographers*]
IPS............... Interceptor Pilot Simulator [*SSTM*]
IPS............... Interface Problem Sheet (NASA)
IPS............... Interim Policy Statement (NRCH)
IPS............... Interim POMSEE [*Performance, Operating, and Maintenance Standards for Electronic Equipment*] Sheet
IPS............... Interlink Press Service (EA)
IPS............... Intermolecular Pair Potential Surface [*Physical chemistry*]
IPS............... Intermolecular Potential (Energy) Surface [*Spectroscopy*]
IPS............... Internal Plate Screen (IAA)
IPS............... Internal Power Supply [*Computer science*]
IPS............... International Confederation for Plastic Surgery
IPS............... Internationale Paracelsus-Gesellschaft zu Salzburg [*International Paracelsus Society*] (EA)
IPS............... International Palm Society (EA)
IPS............... International Paracelsus Society [*Salzburg, Austria*] (EA)
IPS............... International Peat Society [*See also IMTG*] [*Helsinki, Finland*] (EAIO)
IPS............... International Perimetric Society (EA)
IPS............... International Phenomenological Society (EA)
IPS............... International Phycological Society (EA)
IPS............... International Pipe Standard
IPS............... International Planetarium Society (EA)
IPS............... International Plastics Selector, Inc. [*Information service or system*] (IID)
IPS............... International Polaris Energy Corp. [*Toronto Stock Exchange symbol*]
IPS............... International Preview Society (EA)
IPS............... International Primatological Society (EA)
IPS............... International Processes Simulation [*Game*]
IPS............... Internet Printing System [*Computer science*]
IPS............... Interplanetary Scintillation
IPS............... Inter/Press Service - Third World News Agency (EA)
IPS............... Interpretive Programming System
IPS............... Interruptions per Second
IPS............... Intractable Pain Society of Great Britain and Ireland
IPS............... Intrapartum Stillbirth [*Medicine*] (DMAA)
IPS............... Intraperitoneal Shock [*Psychology*]
IPS............... Introductory Physical Science [*Project*] [*Education*]
IPS............... Inventing and Patenting Sourcebook [*A publication*]
IPS............... Inventory of Perceptual Skills [*Visual and auditory test*]
IPS............... Inverse Photoemission Spectroscopy
IPS............... Inverter Power Supply (NASA)
IPS............... Investors Protection Scheme (DCTA)
IPS............... Ionospheric Prediction Service [*Telecommunications*] (TEL)
IPS............... Ion Plating Supply
IPS............... Iron Pipe Size (WGA)
IP's.............. Issue Priority Designators (AFIT)
IPS............... Item Processing System (BUR)
IPS............... Office of Information Programmes and Services [*UNESCO*] (IID)
IPSA............ Incremental Microwave Power Spectrum Analyzer [*Air Force*]
IPSA............ Independent Postal System of America [*Alternative to US Postal Service*]
IPSA............ Industrial Police and Security Association [*British*] (BI)

IPSA............ Institute for Psychological Study of the Arts [*University of Florida*] [*Research center*] (RCD)
IPSA............ International Passenger Ship Association [*Merger of Atlantic Passenger Steamship Conference, Trans-Atlantic Passenger Steamship Conference, Caribbean Cruise Association*] [*Defunct*]
IPSA............ International Political Science Association (EA)
IPSA............ International Professional Security Association [*Paignton, Devonshire, England*] (EAIO)
IPSA............ International Professional Surrogates Association (EA)
IPSAM........ International Presort Airmail [*US Postal Service*]
IPSANET...... Sharp [*I. P.*] Communications Network [*I.P. Sharp Associates Ltd.*] [*Toronto, ON*] (TSSD)
IPSAR......... Integrated Plant Safety Assessment Report [*Nuclear energy*] (NRCH)
IPSB............ Interprocessor Signal Bus
IPSC............ Information Processing Standards for Computers
IPSC............ Information Processing Supplies Council [*Defunct*] (EA)
IPSC............ Inhibitory Postsynaptic Current [*Neurophysiology*]
IPSC............ Interagency Primate Steering Committee [*National Institutes of Health*]
IPSC............ Ipsco, Inc. [*NASDAQ symbol*] (SAG)
IPSCF......... IPSCO Inc. [*NASDAQ symbol*] (TTSB)
Ipsco.......... Ipsco, Inc. [*Associated Press*] (SAG)
IPSD........... Interservice Procedures for Systems Development [*Military*]
IPSE............ Implementing Primary Science Education (AIE)
IPSE............ Integrated Programming Support Environment [*BIS Applied Systems*] [*British*]
IPSE............ Integrated Project Support Environment (NITA)
IPSEP......... International Project for Soft Energy Paths [*Defunct*] (EA)
IPSF............ Intermediate Postsurgical Fitting [*Medicine*]
IPSF............ International Pharmaceutical Students' Federation [*Jerusalem, Israel*] (EAIO)
IPSFC......... International Pacific Salmon Fisheries Commission [*Canada*] (EA)
IPSG........... International Programs Steering Group [*DoD*]
IPSICM....... International PSI Committee of Magicians [*See also CIEPP*] (EAIO)
IPSID.......... Immunoproliferative Small Intestinal Disease (MAE)
IPSJ............ Information Processing Society of Japan (NITA)
IPSL............ Interface Problem Status Log (NASA)
IPSLN......... Indo-Pacific Sea Level Network [*Marine science*] (OSRA)
IPSLN......... Indo-Pacific Sea Level Network (USDC)
IPSM.......... Improved Performance Space Motor (MCD)
IPSM.......... Institute of Physical Sciences in Medicine [*British*] (DBA)
IPSN........... Institute for Protection and Nuclear Safety (NUCP)
IPSO........... Initiating Production by Sales Order (PDAA)
IPSO........... Interface Peripheral Standard Olivetti (NITA)
IPSO........... International Programs and Studies Office [*Later, DIA*] (EA)
IPSOC......... Information Processing Society of Canada
IPSP........... Inhibitory Postsynaptic Potential [*Neurophysiology*]
IPSP........... Intelligence Priorities for Strategic Planning [*Military*]
IPSR........... Institute of Plant Science Research [*Research center British*] (IRC)
IPSRA......... International Professional Ski Racers Association (EA)
IPSS........... Information Processing System Simulator [*Computer science*] (MHDI)
IPSS........... Initial Pre-planned Supply Support (DOMA)
IPSS........... Institute of Planetary and Space Science (MCD)
IPSS........... Interactive Population Statistical System [*Computer science*]
IPSS........... Intermediate Plutonium Storage System [*Nuclear energy*] (NUCP)
IPSS........... International Packet Switched Service [*Telecommunications system*] (NITA)
IPSS........... International Packet Switching Service [*British Telecom International, Inc.*] [*Telecommunications service*] (TSSD)
IPSS........... International Packet Switch Stream [*Computer science*]
IPSS........... International Pilot Study of Schizophrenia [*WHO*]
IPSS........... Interprocessor Signaling System [*Telecommunications*] (TEL)
IPSSB......... Information Processing Systems Standards Board [*Later, Board of Standards Review of ANSI*] [*American Standards Association*]
IPSSG......... International Printers Supply Salesmen's Guild (EA)
IPST........... In-Process Self Test (MCD)
IPST........... Institute for Physical Science and Technology [*University of Maryland*] [*Research center*] (RCD)
IPST........... International Practical Scale of Temperature (PDAA)
IPST........... Israel Program for Scientific Translations [*An agency of the Government of Israel*]
IPStF.......... Saint Francis Hospital, Peoria, IL [*Library symbol Library of Congress*] (LCLS)
IPSW.......... Ipswich [*City in England*] (ROG)
IPSW.......... Ipswich Savings Bank [*NASDAQ symbol*] (SAG)
IPSW.......... Ipswich Svgs Bk Mass [*NASDAQ symbol*] (TTSB)
IpswchSv... Ipswich Savings Bank [*Associated Press*] (SAG)
IpswchSv... Ipswich Savings Bank [*Associated Press*] (SAG)
IPSY........... Interactive Planning System (MHDI)
IPT............. Icelandic Pony Trekkers [*Later, IHT*] (EA)
IPT............. Image Processing Technology [*Computer graphics*]
IPT............. Immunoprecipitation Technique [*Clinical chemistry*]
IPT............. Improved Programming Technologies (BUR)
IPT............. Inches per Tooth (IAA)
IPT............. Incremental Proof Testing
IPT............. Indexed, Paged, and Titled (ADA)
IPT............. Individual Perception Threshold (PDAA)
IPT............. Induction Plasma Torch
IPT............. Industrial and Performance Technology [*Human performance analysis*]
IPT............. Industrial Power Tube
IPT............. Information Presentation Technologies, Inc.
IPT............. Information Processing Technology
IPT............. Infrared Plume Target
IPT............. Initial Production Test [*Army*] (AABC)

IPT.............	In-Plant Test (KSC)
IPT.............	In-Plant Training
IPT.............	In-Plant Transporter (MCD)
IPT.............	In Port [*Navy*] (NVT)
IPT.............	In-Process Testing
IPT.............	Installation Preflight Test
IPT.............	Institute for Paralegal Training [*Later, Philadelphia Institute*] [*Commercial firm*] (EA)
IPT.............	Institute of Petroleum Technologists
IPT.............	Institute of Property Taxation (EA)
IPT.............	Instituto de Promocao Turistica [*Portugal*] (EY)
IPT.............	Integrated Process Team [*Business term*]
IPT.............	Integrated Product Team [*Business term*] (RDA)
IPT.............	Integrated Product Team
IPT.............	Intellectual Property Transfer
IPT.............	Intermediate Phase Training (DOMA)
IPT.............	Intermittent Pelvic Traction (DAVI)
IPT.............	Internal Pipe Thread
IPT.............	International Pipe Thread (NASA)
IPT.............	International Planning Team [*NATO*] (NATG)
IPT.............	International Production Technology (IAA)
IPT.............	Interpersonal Therapy [*Mental health treatment technique*]
IPT.............	Interphase Transformer [*Electronics*] (IAA)
IPT.............	Interplanetary Travel (AAG)
IPT.............	Interport Corp. [*ICAO designator*] (FAAC)
IPT.............	Io Plasma Torus [*Cosmology*]
IPT.............	IP Timberlands Cl'A' [*NYSE symbol*] (TTSB)
IPT.............	IP Timberlands Ltd. [*NYSE symbol*] (SAG)
IPT.............	IP Timberlands Ltd. [*NYSE symbol*] (SPSG)
IPT.............	Iron Pipe Thread (MSA)
IPT.............	Isopentenyl Transferase [*An enzyme*]
IPT.............	MAP International, Wheaton, IL [*OCLC symbol*] (OCLC)
IPT.............	Williamsport [*Pennsylvania*] [*Airport symbol*] (OAG)
IPT.............	Williamsport, PA [*Location identifier FAA*] (FAAL)
IPTA...........	International Patent and Trademark Association [*Later, IIPA*] (EA)
IPTA...........	International Piano Teachers Association [*Defunct*]
IPTAR.........	Institute for Psychoanalytic Training and Research
IPTC...........	International Polar Transportation Conference
IPTC...........	International Press Telecommunications Council [*See also CIPT*] [*Telecommunications An association Defunct*] (EA)
IPTCS.........	Igloo Passive Thermal Control Section [*Aerospace*] (MCD)
IPTEA.........	Internacia Postista kaj Telekomunikista Esperanto-Asocio [*International Esperanto Association of Post and Telecommunication Workers*] (EAIO)
IPTF...........	Indo-Pacific Theosophical Federation (EAIO)
IPTG..........	Isopropylthiogalactoside [*Also, IPG*] [*Organic chemistry*]
IPTH..........	Immunoreactive Parathyroid Hormone [*Endocrinology*]
IPTIC.........	International Pulse Trade and Industry Confederation [*FAO*]
IPTimb........	IP Timberlands Ltd. [*Associated Press*] (SAG)
IP Timb.......	IP Timberlands Ltd. [*Associated Press*] (SAG)
IPTM..........	Interval Pulse Time Modulation
IPTN...........	Independent Professional Typists Network (EA)
IPTO...........	International Pet Trade Organization [*Defunct*] (EAIO)
IPTP...........	In-Plant Test Program (IAA)
IPTPA........	International Professional Tennis Players Association (BARN)
IPTS..........	Integrated Powertrain Test System
IPTS..........	International Practical Temperature Scale [*National Institute of Standards and Technology*]
IPTS/PS......	Improved Programmer Test Station / Power Station (SAA)
IPTT..........	Internationale du Personnel des Postes, Telegraphes, et Telephones [*Postal, Telegraph, and Telephone International - PTTI*] [*Geneva, Switzerland*] (EAIO)
IPTV..........	Initial Propulsion Test Vehicle
IPTX..........	Intermittent Pelvic Traction [*Medicine*] (DMAA)
IPU............	Eastern New Mexico University, Portales, NM [*OCLC symbol*] (OCLC)
IPU............	Immediate Pick-Up (DNAB)
IPU............	Individual Patient Usage
IPU............	Information Processing Utility
IPU............	Initial Production Unit
IPU............	Inpatient Unit [*Medicine*]
IPU............	Input Preparation Unit [*Computer science*] (WDAA)
IPU............	Institute for Public Understanding (EA)
IPU............	Institute of Public Utilities (EA)
IPU............	Instruction Processing Unit (BUR)
IPU............	Integrated Physiological Unit
IPU............	Intelligent Processing Unit [*Canon, Inc.*] [*Computer science*] (PCM)
IPU............	Interface and Priority Unit
IPU............	International Paleontological Union
IPU............	International Peasant Union
IPU............	Inter-Parliamentary Union [*See also UI*] [*Switzerland*]
IPU............	Interphase Unit
IPU............	Interprocessor Unit
IPU............	Irish Postal Union
IPU............	Irish Print Union (DGA)
IPU............	Isotope Power Unit
IPV............	Imperative (WGA)
IPV............	Inaccessible Pore Volume [*Petroleum technology*]
IPV............	Inactivated Polio Vaccine [*Also, Salk vaccine*] (PAZ)
IPV............	Inactivated Poliovirus Vaccine
IPV............	Infectious Pustular Vaginitis [*Medicine*]
IPV............	Infectious Pustular Vulvovaginitis [*Veterinary medicine*]
IPV............	Injectable Polio Vaccine [*Medicine*]
IPV............	Inner Pilot Valve
IPV............	In-Plant Verification (AFIT)

IPV............	Internal Podalic Version [*Obstetrics*]
IPV............	International Prime Tech [*Vancouver Stock Exchange symbol*]
IPV............	Intrinsic Payload Value
IPV............	Isopycnic Potential Vorticity [*Oceanography*]
IPV............	Italian Polydor Variable Microgroove [*Record label*]
IPVG..........	Isopycnic Potential Vorticity Gradient [*Oceanography*]
IPVRA........	International Professional Vinyl Repair Association (EA)
IPVS..........	International Pig Veterinary Society [*Amer, Spain*] (EAIO)
IPVS..........	Ion Pump Vacuum System
IPW...........	International Peace Walk [*An association*] (EA)
IPW...........	International Powertech Systems, Inc. [*Vancouver Stock Exchange symbol*]
IPW...........	Interpole Winding [*Wiring*] (DNAB)
IPW...........	Interrogation Prisoner of War
IPW...........	Interstate Power [*NYSE symbol*] (TTSB)
IPW...........	Interstate Power Co. [*NYSE symbol*] (SPSG)
IPW...........	Ipswich [*England*] [*Airport symbol*] (AD)
IPWA..........	Invisible Panel Warming Association [*British*] (BI)
IPWF..........	International Public Works Federation (EA)
IPWI...........	Infrared Proximity Warning Indicator
IPWO..........	Interplant Work Order (MCD)
IPWR..........	Integrated Pressurized Water Reactor (PDAA)
IPWS.........	Iron Plate Workers' Society [*A union*] [*British*]
IPWSOM......	Institute of Practitioners in Work Study, Organisation, and Management (AIE)
IPX...........	International Phasor Telecom [*Vancouver Stock Exchange symbol*]
IPX...........	Internetwork Packet Exchange
IPX...........	Internetwork Protocol Exchange [*Novell, Inc.*] [*Computer science*] (PCM)
IPX...........	Interpool, Inc. [*NYSE symbol*] (SPSG)
IPXI...........	Intrinsic Peroxidase Inhibition Solution [*Clinical chemistry*]
IPXPrA........	Interpool Inc. 5.75% Cv Pfd [*NYSE symbol*] (TTSB)
IPX/SPX......	Internet Packet Exchange / Sequenced Packet [*Computer science*] (PCM)
IPY............	Inches per Year
IPY............	International Phoenix Energy [*Vancouver Stock Exchange symbol*]
IPY............	International Polar Year
IPY............	Ion Pair Yield
IPZ............	George A. Zeller Zone Center, Professional Library, Peoria, IL [*Library symbol Library of Congress*] (LCLS)
IPZ............	Insulin Protamine Zinc (DMAA)
IPZ............	Investment Promotion Zone
IPZ............	IPC International Prospector [*Vancouver Stock Exchange symbol*]
IPZ............	World Book - Childcraft International, Inc., Research Library, Chicago, IL [*OCLC symbol*] (OCLC)
IPZP..........	Iranian Peace Zebra Program [*Military*] (MCD)
IQ.............	Caribbean Airways [*ICAO designator*] (AD)
IQ.............	Ideal Quota [*Vitamin supplement*] [*British*]
IQ.............	Idem Quod [*The Same As*] [*Latin*]
IQ.............	Ideon Group, Inc. [*NYSE symbol*] (SAG)
IQ.............	Indefinite Quantity (AFM)
IQ.............	Inflation Quotient
IQ.............	Information Quick (PDAA)
I/Q............	In Phase/Quadrature (MCD)
IQ.............	Inquix Consulting Ltd. [*Information service or system*] (IID)
IQ.............	Installation Qualification (ACII)
IQ.............	Institute of Quarrying [*British*]
IQ.............	Instrument Quality (IAA)
IQ.............	Intelligence Quotient [*Psychological and educational testing*]
IQ.............	Intelligent Query
IQ.............	Intelligent Quisine [*Campbell Soup Co.*]
IQ.............	Internal Quality
IQ.............	International Quorum of Film and Video Producers (EA)
IQ.............	Interrupted Quick [*Flashing*] Light [*Navigation signal*]
IQ.............	Investment Quotient
IQ.............	Iowa Quality [*of pigs*]
IQ.............	I Quit [*Smoking*]
iq.............	Iraq [*MARC country of publication code Library of Congress*] (LCCP)
IQ.............	Iraq [*ANSI two-letter standard code*] (CNC)
IQ.............	Quincy Free Public Library, Quincy, IL [*Library symbol Library of Congress*] (LCLS)
IQA...........	Inertial Quality Attitude
IQA...........	Inspection Quality Assurance
IQA...........	Institute of Quality Assurance [*British*]
IQA...........	International Quality Award [*LIMRA*]
IQA...........	Irish Quality Association (ACII)
IqAF..........	Iraqi Air Force
IQ & S........	Iron, Quinine, and Strychnine [*Elixir*]
IQB...........	Individual Quick Blanching (DICI)
IQC...........	Indefinite-Quantity Contract (AAGC)
IQC...........	Industrial Quality Control
IQC...........	Institutional Quality Control [*Department of Education*] (GFGA)
IQC...........	Integrated Quality Control [*Department of Health and Human Services*] (GFGA)
IQC...........	InterCapital California Quality Municipal Securities [*NYSE symbol*] (SPSG)
IQC...........	InterCapital Cal Qual Muni Sec [*NYSE symbol*] (TTSB)
IQC...........	International Quality Centre
IQC...........	Quincy College, Quincy, IL [*Library symbol Library of Congress*] (LCLS)
IQCDPS.......	Integrated Quality Control Data Processing System [*Department of Health and Human Services*] (GFGA)
IQCODE.......	Informant Questionnaire on Cognitive Decline in the Elderly
IQCPP........	Institutional Quality Control Pilot Project [*Department of Education*] (GFGA)

IQE..............	Interruption Queue Element [*Computer science*] (MHDI)
IQED	Id Quod Erat Demonstrandum [*That Which Was to Be Proved*] [*Latin*]
IQF..............	Individually Quick-Frozen [*Food technology*]
IQF..............	Interactive Query Facility [*Computer science*]
IQF..............	International Quail Foundation [*Defunct*] (EA)
IQG	Great River Library System, Quincy, IL [*Library symbol Library of Congress*] (LCLS)
IQHE	Integer Quantum Hall Effect [*Solid state physics*]
IQHE	Integral Quantum Hall Effect [*Solid-state physics*]
IQI..............	Image Quality Indicator
IQI..............	Industrial Quality, Inc.
IQI..............	Instructional Quality Inventory
IQI..............	InterCapital Quality Municipal Income [*NYSE symbol*] (SPSG)
IQI..............	InterCapital Qual Muni Income [*NYSE symbol*] (TTSB)
IQIQ	Applied Intelligence Group, Inc. [*NASDAQ symbol*] (SAG)
IQISA	Interest Questionnaire for Indian South Africans [*Vocational guidance test*]
I Qk..............	Interrupted Quick [*Flashing*] Light [*Navigation signal*]
I Qk Fl	Interrupted Quick Flashing Light [*Navigation signal*]
IQL..............	Information Query Language (NITA)
IQL..............	Interactive Query Language [*Digital Equipment Corp.*] [*Computer science*]
IQL..............	Intermediate Query Language [*Computer science*]
IQM..............	Input Queue Manager (NITA)
IQM..............	InterCapital Quality Municipal Securities [*NYSE symbol*] (SPSG)
IQM..............	InterCapital Qual Muni Sec [*NYSE symbol*] (TTSB)
IQM..............	Qiemo [*China*] [*Airport symbol*] (OAG)
IQMF..........	Image Quality Merit Function [*Color image*]
IQMH	Input Queue Message Handler [*Computer science*]
IQMInc.........	Intercapital Quality Municipal Income Trust [*Associated Press*] (SAG)
IQMInv.........	Intercapital Quality Municipal Investment Trust [*Associated Press*] (SAG)
IQMS	Industrial Quality Management Science [*Quality control*]
IQMSec........	InterCapital Quality Municipal Securities [*Associated Press*] (SAG)
IQN	Inner Quantum Number
IQN	Intercapital New York Quality Municipal Securities [*NYSE symbol*] (SAG)
IQN	InterCapital N.Y.Qual Muni Sec [*NYSE symbol*] (TTSB)
IQN	Qingyang [*China*] [*Airport symbol*] (OAG)
IQO	Initial Quantity Order (NG)
IQPF..........	International Quick Printing Foundation [*Defunct*] (EA)
IQPP	Interactive Query Pre-Processor (NITA)
IQPS	Institute of Qualified Private Secretaries Ltd. [*British*] (BI)
IQQ	Caribbean Airways [*Barbados*] [*ICAO designator*] (FAAC)
IQQ	Iquique [*Chile*] [*Airport symbol*] (OAG)
IQQ	Iquique [*Chile*] [*Seismograph station code, US Geological Survey*] (SEIS)
IQR	Interquartile Range
IQRC	Institut Quebecois de la Recherche sur la Culture [*Database producer*]
IQRP	Interactive Query and Report Processor [*IBM Corp.*] [*Computer science*]
IQS..............	Initial Quality Survey
IQS..............	Institute of Quantity Surveyors [*Later, RICS*]
IQS..............	Interactive Query System [*Computer science*] (IAA)
IQS..............	International "Q" Signal
IQSoft	IQ Software Corp. [*Associated Press*] (SAG)
IQST..........	IntelliQuest Information Group, Inc. [*NASDAQ symbol*] (SAG)
IQST..........	ItelliQuest Info Group [*NASDAQ symbol*] (TTSB)
IQSU	International Quiet Sun Year [*1964-65*] [*Also, IQSY, IYQS*] (IAA)
IQSW	IQ Software [*NASDAQ symbol*] (TTSB)
IQSW	IQ Software Corp. [*NASDAQ symbol*] (SAG)
IQSY	International Quiet Sun Year [*1964-65*] [*Also, IYQS*]
IQT..............	Initial Qualification Training
IQT..............	Intercapital Quality Municipal Investment Trust [*NYSE symbol*] (SPSG)
IQT..............	InterCapital Qual Muni Inv [*NYSE symbol*] (TTSB)
IQT..............	Interquest Resources Corp. [*Toronto Stock Exchange symbol*]
IQT..............	Iquitos [*Peru*] [*Airport symbol*] (OAG)
IQU..............	University of New Mexico, Albuquerque, NM [*OCLC symbol*] (OCLC)
IQUE	In-Plant Quality Evaluation Program (AAGC)
IQV..............	Illinois Veterans Home, Quincy, IL [*Library symbol*] [*Library of Congress*] (LCLS)
IQV..............	Pekin Community High School, Pekin, IL [*OCLC symbol*] (OCLC)
IQW Fl	Individuelle Quantitative Wert [*Mean Total Ridge Count*] [*Anatomy*]
IQW	John Wood Community College, Quincy, IL [*Library symbol Library of Congress*] (LCLS)
IQW	Western New Mexico University, Silver City, NM [*OCLC symbol*] (OCLC)
IQX..............	Bradford Public Library, Bradford, IL [*OCLC symbol*] (OCLC)
IQY..............	Internet Query [*Computer science*]
IQY..............	Limestone High School, Bartonville, IL [*OCLC symbol*] (OCLC)
IQZ..............	Farmington East High School, Farmington, IL [*OCLC symbol*] (OCLC)
IR..............	Ice on Runway [*NWS*] (FAAC)
IR..............	Ice Rinks [*Public-performance tariff class*] [*British*]
IR..............	Illumination Rate (CAAL)
IR..............	Illuminator RADAR (NATG)
IR..............	Illustration Request
IR..............	Image Readout [*Computer graphics*]
IR..............	Image Rejection
IR..............	Imaging RADAR (MCD)
IR..............	Imitation Russia [*Bookbinding*] (DGA)
IR..............	Immediate Reserve [*Air Force British*]
IR..............	Immune Response [*Also, Ir*] [*Genetics*]

IR..............	Immunization Rate (AFM)
IR..............	Immunoreactive
IR..............	Improved Retrofit (CAAL)
IR..............	Impurity Removal Subsystem (MCD)
IR..............	Incidence Rate (WDAA)
IR..............	Incident Report
IR..............	Inclination of the Ascending Return [*Aviation*] (NASA)
IR..............	Indent Right [*Typography*] (DGA)
ir..............	Indent Right (WDMC)
IR..............	Independent Research (NG)
IR..............	Index of Response [*Medicine*] (MAE)
IR..............	Index Register (WDAA)
IR..............	Indiana Railroad System
IR..............	Indiana Register [*A publication*] (AAGC)
IR..............	Indian Rulings [*A publication*] (DLA)
IR..............	India-Rubber (DEN)
IR..............	Indicating Recorder [*Electronics*] (ECII)
IR..............	Indicator Reading (IAA)
IR..............	Indicator Register (IAA)
IR..............	Individual Recorder [*Sports*]
IR..............	Individual Referral (OICC)
IR..............	Industrial Registry [*New South Wales, Australia*]
IR..............	Industrial Relations
IR..............	Industrial Reports [*Australia A publication*]
I-R..............	Industrial Research
IR..............	Industry Remarketer (CDE)
IR..............	Inferior Rectus [*Muscle*] [*Anatomy*]
IR..............	Informal Report
IR..............	Information and Technology [*Educational Resources Information Center (ERIC) Clearinghouse*] [*Syracuse University*] (PAZ)
IR..............	Information Release (DLA)
IR..............	Information Report
IR..............	Information Request (AAG)
IR..............	Information Requirement [*Military intelligence*] (INF)
IR..............	Information Retrieval [*Computer science*]
IR..............	Infrared
IR..............	Infrared Radiation
IR..............	Infrared Radiometer
IR..............	Infrared Reconnaissance
IR..............	Infrared Reflectance (IAA)
Ir..............	Ingenieur [*Engineer*] [*French*]
IR..............	Ingersoll-Rand [*NYSE symbol*] (TTSB)
IR..............	Ingersoll-Rand Co. [*NYSE symbol*] (SPSG)
IR..............	Ingram-Rude Information Researchers [*Information service or system*] (IID)
IR..............	Ingreee Router (ACRL)
IR..............	Initial Reactive Results
IR..............	Initial Release (MCD)
IR..............	Initial Reserve
IR..............	Ink Receptivity
IR..............	Inland Revenue [*British*]
IR..............	Inner Roll Gimbal (NASA)
I/R..............	Inquiry/Response [*Automotive engineering Electronics*]
IR..............	Inside Radius [*Technical drawings*]
IR..............	Inside Right [*Soccer position*]
IR..............	Insoluble Residue
IR..............	Inspection Record (MCD)
IR..............	Inspection Rejection
IR..............	Inspection Release
IR..............	Inspection [*or Inspector's*] Report
IR..............	Inspection Request (IAA)
IR..............	Installation Report
IR..............	Installation Restoration (MCD)
IR..............	Instantaneous Relay
IR..............	Instantaneous Release (IAA)
IR..............	Instant Release [*Typography*] (DGA)
IR..............	Institute of Refrigeration [*British*]
IR..............	Instruction Register [*Computer science*]
IR..............	Instrumentation Report
IR..............	Instrumentation Requirements (MUGU)
I/R..............	Instrument Rating [*Aviation*] (AIA)
IR..............	Instrument Reading (AFM)
IR..............	Instrument Register (IAA)
IR..............	Instrument Restricted Controlled Airspace (DA)
IR..............	Insulation Resistance
IR..............	Intake Restriction [*Automotive engineering*]
IR..............	Intelligence Ratio
IR..............	Intelligence Report
IR..............	Intelligence Request (DOMA)
IR..............	Intelligence Requirement [*Military*] (INF)
IR..............	Intelligence Review
IR..............	Intensive Reading
IR..............	Interaction Resistance [*Plant pathology*]
IR..............	Interagency Report (PDAA)
IR..............	Intergovernmental Relations (OICC)
IR..............	Interim Report
IR..............	Intermediate Range (MCD)
IR..............	Intermediate Register [*Telecommunications*] (OA)
IR..............	Intermediate Review (NATG)
IR..............	Internal Register (IAA)
IR..............	Internal Reliability
IR..............	Internal Repeat [*Genetics*]
IR..............	Internal Report
IR..............	Internal Resistance
IR..............	Internal Revenue

IR.............. Internal Revenue Decisions [*Department of the Treasury*] [*A publication*] (DLA)
IR.............. Internal Review [*Army*] (AABC)
IR.............. Internal Rotation [*Myology*]
IR.............. Internationale de la Resistance [*Resistance International - RI*] (EAIO)
IR.............. International Randonneurs [*An association*] (EA)
IR.............. International Registration (BARN)
IR.............. International Rendezvous (MCD)
IR.............. International Rice (IIA)
IR.............. Interpretation Report
IR.............. InterRent [*Car rental group*]
IR.............. Interrogation Report
IR.............. Interrogator-Responder
IR.............. Interrupt Register (IAA)
IR.............. Interrupt Request [*Computer science*] (MHDB)
IR.............. Interval Rate [*Army*] (AABC)
IR.............. Invention Report
IR.............. Inversion Recovery [*NMR imaging*]
IR.............. Inverted Repeat [*Genetics*]
IR.............. Investigation Record
I-R.............. Investment Recurring (MCD)
IR.............. Investor Relations
ir.............. Iran [*MARC country of publication code Library of Congress*] (LCCP)
IR.............. Iran [*ANSI two-letter standard code*] (CNC)
IR.............. Iran Air [*ICAO designator*] (AD)
IR.............. Iran Air [*Airline flight code*] (ODBW)
IR.............. Iran National Airlines [*ICAO designator*] (AD)
Ir.............. Iredell's North Carolina Equity Reports [*A publication*] (DLA)
Ir.............. Iredell's North Carolina Law Reports [*A publication*] (DLA)
IR.............. Ireland [*IYRU nationality code*] (ROG)
Ir.............. Iridium [*Chemical element*]
IR.............. Irish
IR.............. Irish Law Reports [*A publication*] (DLA)
Ir.............. Irnerius [*Flourished, 1113-18*] [*Authority cited in pre-1607 legal work*] (DSA)
ir.............. Iron [*CIPW classification*] [*Geology*]
IR.............. Irradiance [*Electromagnetism*] (IAA)
IR.............. Irrelevancy [*Used in correcting manuscripts, etc.*]
IR.............. Isoprene Rubber
IR.............. Isotope Reactor [*Former USSR*]
IR.............. Item Record (AFIT)
I-R.............. Ito-Reenstierna [*Reaction*] [*Medicine*]
IR.............. Izquierda Republicana [*Republican Left*] [*Spain Political party*] (PPE)
IR.............. Rock Island Public Library, Rock Island, IL [*Library symbol Library of Congress*] (LCLS)
IR1.............. Iran Long-Period Array [*Iran*] [*Seismograph station code, US Geological Survey*] (SEIS)
IR2.............. Iran Long-Period Array [*Iran*] [*Seismograph station code, US Geological Survey*] (SEIS)
IR3.............. Iran Long-Period Array [*Iran*] [*Seismograph station code, US Geological Survey*] (SEIS)
IR4.............. Iran Long-Period Array [*Iran*] [*Seismograph station code, US Geological Survey*] (SEIS)
IR5.............. Iran Long-Period Array [*Iran*] [*Seismograph station code, US Geological Survey*] (SEIS)
IR6.............. Iran Long-Period Array [*Iran*] [*Seismograph station code, US Geological Survey*] (SEIS)
IR7.............. Iran Long-Period Array [*Iran*] [*Seismograph station code, US Geological Survey*] (SEIS)
IRA.............. Augustana College, Rock Island, IL [*Library symbol Library of Congress*] (LCLS)
IRA.............. Ileorectal Anastomosis [*Medicine*]
IRA.............. Immunoregulatory alpha-Globulin [*Immunology*]
IRA.............. Impact Ratio (AAGC)
IRA.............. Inactive Renin Activity [*Medicine*] (DMAA)
IRA.............. Independent Regulatory Agency [*US Government*]
IRA.............. Indian Registration Act [*British*] (ROG)
IRA.............. Indian Reorganization Act (OICC)
IRA.............. Indian Rights Association (EA)
IRA.............. Individual Retirement Account
IRA.............. Individual Retirement Annuity [*Insurance*]
IRA.............. Industrial Relations Act [*1971*] [*British*] (DCTA)
IRA.............. Information Resource Administration
IRA.............. Input Reference Axis (IEEE)
IRA.............. Inspector of the Royal Artillery [*British*]
IRA.............. Inspector's Report Addendum (AAG)
IRA.............. Institute of Registered Architects [*British*]
IRA.............. Instruction Register, Address Portion [*Computer science*] (MHDI)
IRA.............. Integrated RADOME [*RADAR Dome*] Antenna
IRA.............. Intelligence Related Activities [*Military*] (MCD)
IRA.............. Intercollegiate Rowing Association (EA)
IRA.............. Interim Response Actions [*Army*] (DOMA)
IRA.............. Internal Release Agent
IRA.............. Internal Revenue Act
IRA.............. International Racquetball Association [*Later, AARA*] (EA)
IRA.............. International Reading Association (EA)
IRA.............. International Recreation Association [*Later, WLRA*]
IRA.............. International Registration Authority [*Botany*] (PDAA)
IRA.............. International Reprographics Association
IRA.............. International Rodeo Association (EA)
IRA.............. International Roleo Association [*Later, International Log Rolling Association*] (EA)
IRA.............. International Rubber Association [*Kuala Lumpur, Malaysia*] (EAIO)
IRA.............. Investment Recovery Association (EA)
IRA.............. Investment-Return Assumption [*Finance*] (PDAA)

ira.............. Iranian [*MARC language code Library of Congress*] (LCCP)
IRA.............. Iranian Airways Co.
IRA.............. Iran National Airlines Corp. [*ICAO designator*] (FAAC)
IRA.............. Irish Republican Army
IRA.............. Ithaca Railroad Association [*Defunct*] (EA)
IRA.............. Kira Kira [*Solomon Islands*] [*Airport symbol*] (OAG)
IRA.............. Rutland, VT [*Location identifier FAA*] (FAAL)
IRAA.............. Independent Refiners Association of America [*Later, AIRA*] (EA)
IRAA & A.............. Increase and Replacement of Armor, Armament, and Ammunition [*Naval budget appropriation title*]
IRAAM.............. Improved Remote-Area Armor Mine (MCD)
IRAB.............. Index to Reviews of Australian Books [*A publication*]
IRAC.............. Indochina Resource Action Center (EA)
IRAC.............. Industrial Relations Advisory Council [*Australia*]
IRAC.............. Information Resources Administration Councils [*General Services Administration*] [*Washington, DC*] (EGAO)
IRAC.............. Infrared Advisory Center
IRAC.............. Infrared Array Camera
IRAC.............. Institut Royal d'Architecture du Canada [*Royal Architectural Institute of Canada*] (EAIO)
IRAC.............. Integrated Random Access Channel (PDAA)
IRAC.............. Intelligence Resources Advisory Committee [*To supervise US intelligence budget*]
IRAC.............. Interagency Research Animal Committee [*Department of Health and Human Services*] (GFGA)
IRAC.............. Interdepartment Radio Advisory Committee [*Department of Commerce*] (EGAO)
IRAC.............. Interfraternity Research and Advisory Council [*Defunct*] (EA)
IRAC.............. Interim Rapid Action Change (MCD)
IRAC.............. Issue, Rule, Application, Conclusions (AAGC)
IRACOR.............. Infrared Acquisition RADAR (MSA)
IRACQ.............. Infrared Acquisition RADAR
IRACQ.............. Instrumentation RADAR and Acquisition
IRACQ.............. Instrumented Range Acquisition (KSC)
IRACT.............. Incident Response Action Coordination Team [*Nuclear energy*] (NRCH)
IR-ACTH.............. Immunoreactive Adrenocorticotropic Hormone [*Medicine*] (DMAA)
IRAD.............. Independent Research and Development
IRAD.............. Infrared Ambush Device
IRAD.............. Institute for Research on Animal Diseases [*British*]
IRAD.............. Institutional Research and Development Office [*Kirksville College of Osteopathic Medicine*] [*Research center*] (RCD)
IRADDS.............. Infrared Air Defense Detection System
IRADS.............. Infrared Acquisition and Designation System (DOMA)
IRAF.............. Individual Retirement Account File [*IRS*]
IRAH.............. Infrared Active Homing (MCD)
IRAH.............. Infrared Alternate Head
IR All.............. Indian Rulings, Allahabad Series [*A publication*] (DLA)
IRAM.............. Improved Random Access Memory [*Computer science*]
IRAM.............. Improved Reliability and Maintainability
IRAM.............. Improved Repairables Asset Management (DNAB)
IRAM.............. Indexed Random Access Memory (NITA)
IRAM.............. Institut de Recherches et d'Applications des Methodes de Developpement [*Institute of Research and Application of Development Methods - IRAM*] (EAIO)
IRAM.............. Integrated Random-Access Memory [*Computer science*]
IRAMS.............. Infrared Automatic Mass Screening [*Electronics*]
IRAN.............. Inspect and Repair as Necessary [*Aviation*]
IRAN.............. Iranian [*Language, etc.*] (ROG)
IRanASD.............. Allen Township Consolidated Community School District 65, Ransom, IL [*Library symbol Library of Congress*] (LCLS)
IR & A.............. Information Research and Analysis [*Oak Ridge National Laboratory*] [*Oak Ridge, TN*] [*Department of Energy*] (GRD)
IR & AC.............. Internal Review and Audit Compliance [*Army*]
IR & D.............. Independent Research and Development
IR&D.............. Independent Research and Development (AAGC)
IR & D.............. Industrial Research and Development
IR & D.............. Internal Research and Development [*Army*]
IR & D/B & P.............. Independent Research and Development/Bid and Proposal
IRANDOC.............. Iranian Documentation Centre [*Ministry of Culture and Higher Education*] [*Tehran*]
IRANF.............. Immunoreactive Atrial Natriuretic Factor
IRANSAT.............. Iranian Government Communications Satellite [*NASA*] (NASA)
IRant.............. Rantoul Public Library, Rantoul, IL [*Library symbol Library of Congress*] (LCLS)
IRAP.............. Industrial Research Assistance Program [*Canada*]
IRAP.............. Interagency Radiological Assistance Program [*Nuclear Regulatory Commission*] (NRCH)
IRAP.............. Interleukin Receptor Antagonist Protein [*Biochemistry*]
IRAR.............. Impulse Response Area Ratio
IRAR.............. Individual Retirement Account Register [*IRS*]
IRAR.............. Infrared Airborne RADAR (PDAA)
IRAR.............. Infrared Augmentation Reliability (MCD)
IRAR.............. Integrator Register Address Register (PDAA)
IRAS.............. Information Retrieval Advisory Services Limited [*British*] (NITA)
IRAS.............. Infrared Astronomical Satellite [*NASA*] (MCD)
IRAS.............. Infrared Attack System
IRAS.............. Infrared Automatic System (DNAB)
IRAS.............. Infrared Reflection Absorption Spectroscopy [*Also, IRRAS, RAIR, RAIRS, RAIS*]
IRAS.............. Institute on Religion in an Age of Science (EA)
IRAS.............. Integrated RADOME [*RADAR Dome*] Antenna Structure
IRAS.............. Interdiction Reconnaissance Attack System (PDAA)
IRAS.............. Internet Routing and Access Service [*Computer science*] (ACRL)
IRASA.............. International Radio Air Safety Association

IRASER........ Infrared Amplification by Stimulated Emission of Radiation
IRASER........ Infrared MASER (CET)
IRASI........... Internal Review and System Improvement [*Army*]
IRAT........... Institut de Recherche Appliquee sur le Travail [*Canada*]
IRAT........... Institut de Recherches Agronomiques Tropicales et des Cultures
                Vivrieres [*Food and agricultural research foundation supported by
                France and several African states*]
IRATA .... Industrial Rope Access Trade Association [*British*] (DBA)
IRATA .... Irata, Inc. [*NASDAQ symbol*] (SAG)
IRATA .... Irata Inc.'A' [*NASDAQ symbol*] (TTSB)
IRATE........ Inertial Range Atmospheric Turbulence Entrainment (PDAA)
IRATE........ Intelligence Review and Assessment Task Element [*Study of the
                effectiveness of the air war in Southeast Asia*]
IRATE........ Interactive Retrieval and Text Editor [*Computer science*] (PDAA)
IRATW........ Interim Remote Area Terminal Equipment [*Air Force*]
IRATW........ Irata Inc.Wrrt [*NASDAQ symbol*] (TTSB)
IRAWS .... Infrared Attack Weapon System
IRayL........... Lincolnwood Community Reading Center, Raymond, IL [*Library
                symbol Library of Congress*] (LCLS)
IRaySD .... Panhandle Community Unit, School District 2, Raymond IL [*Library
                symbol Library of Congress*] (LCLS)
IRB............... Improved Ribbon-Type Bridge [*Military*] (RDA)
IRB............... Improved Rotor Blade [*Rotorcraft*]
IRB............... Impulse Resistance Bridge
IRB............... Individual Records Brief [*Military*] (AABC)
IRB............... Inducto-Ratio Bridge
IRB............... Industrial Readjustment Branch
IRB............... Industrial Relations Board [*Navy*]
IRB............... Industrial Relations Bulletin [*A publication*] (AAG)
IRB............... Industrial Revenue Bond
IRB............... Infinitely Rigid Beam [*Engineering*] (OA)
IRB............... Inflatable Rescue Boat
IRB............... Informationsverbundzentrum Raum und Bau [*Germany*] (NITA)
IRB............... Informationszentrum Raum und Bau [*Information Center for Regional
                Planning and Building Construction*] [*Germany Information
                service or system*] (IID)
IRB............... Infrared Binocular [*Military*] (VNW)
IRB............... Infrared Brazing
IRB............... Inner Radiation Belt
IRB............... Inside Reactor Building (NRCH)
IRB............... Inspection Review Board (KSC)
IRB............... Institutional Review Board
IRB............... Insurance Rating Board [*Later, ISO*]
IRB............... Internal Revenue Bulletin
IRB............... International Resources Bank
IRB............... International Rice Bran Industries Ltd. [*Vancouver Stock Exchange
                symbol*]
IRB............... International Rugby Board [*Australia*]
IRB............... Interrupt Request Block (CMD)
IRB............... Iranair Tours Co. [*Iran*] [*ICAO designator*] (FAAC)
IRB............... Irish Republican Brotherhood
IRB............... Iron Rotating Band
IRB............... Irregular Route Motor Carriers Bureau, Oklahoma City OK [*STAC*]
IRb............... Red Bud Public Library, Red Bud, IL [*Library symbol Library of
                Congress*] (LCLS)
IRBA........... International Rhythm and Blues Association (EA)
IRBAA .... Institute of Rural Business Administration of Australasia
IRBBB .... Incomplete Right Bundle Branch Block [*Cardiology*]
IRBEL........... Indexed References to Biomedical Engineering Literature
                [*A publication*] (IID)
IRBM........... Intermediate-Range Ballistic Missile
IRBO .... Infrared Homing Bomb (IEEE)
IR Bom .... Indian Rulings, Bombay Series [*A publication*] (DLA)
IRBP .... Interphotoreceptor Retinoid-Binding Protein [*Biochemistry*]
IRBP .... Interstitial Retinol-Binding Protein [*Biochemistry*]
IRbSCH........ Saint Clement Hospital, Red Bud, IL [*Library symbol Library of
                Congress*] (LCLS)
IRBT........... Infrared Brightness Temperature
IRBT........... Intelligent Remote Batch Terminal [*Computer science*] (IAA)
IRC............... Circle [*Alaska*] [*Airport symbol*] (OAG)
IRC............... Immediate Reaction Company [*Military*] (INF)
IRC............... Incident Response Center [*Nuclear Regulatory Commission*] (NRCH)
IRC............... Independent Record Charts (EA)
IRC............... Indicating Recording Controller [*Electronics*] (ECII)
IRC............... Indications Review Committee [*Military*] (CINC)
IRC............... Inductance, Resistance, Capacitance [*Electronics*] (BARN)
IRC............... Industrial Relations Center [*University of Minnesota*] [*Research
                center*] (RCD)
IRC............... Industrial Relations Council for the Plumbing and Pipe Fitting Industry
                [*Chicago, IL*] (EA)
IRC............... Industrial Relations Counselors [*New York, NY*] (EA)
IRC............... INEL [*Idaho National Engineering Laboratory*] Research Center
                [*Idaho Falls, ID*] [*Department of Energy*] (GRD)
IRC............... Infantry Reserve Corps (WDAA)
IRC............... Information Recovery Capsule
IRC............... Information Research Center (DIT)
IRC............... Information Resource Consultants [*Information service or system*]
                (IID)
IRC............... Information Resources Center [*of Mental Health Materials Center*]
IRC............... Information Retrieval Center [*BBDO International*] [*Information
                service or system*] (IID)
IRC............... Infrared Coagulator [*Hematology*] (DAVI)
IRC............... Infrared Countermeasures [*Military electronics*]
IRCI............. Initiative Resource Center [*Defunct*] (EA)
IRC............... Inland Revenue Commissioners [*British*]

IRC............... Inspection Record Card [*Navy*] (NG)
IRC............... Inspiratory Reserve Capacity [*Physiology*] (MAE)
IRC............... Institute for Research in Construction [*National Research Council of
                Canada*] [*Database producer*] (IID)
IRC............... Institutional Research Council [*Defunct*] (EA)
IRC............... Institutional Review Committee [*Generic term*]
IRC............... Insurance Research Council (EA)
IRC............... Integrated Radio Control (NVT)
IRC............... Integrator Register Counter (PDAA)
IRC............... Interchange Resource Center (EA)
IRC............... Interdisciplinary Research Centre [*British*]
IRC............... Intergovernmental Refugee Committee [*London*] [*World War II*]
IRC............... Interline Resources Corp. [*AMEX symbol*] (SAG)
IRC............... Internal Revenue Code
IRC............... International Radiation Commission [*of the International Association
                of Meteorology and Atmospheric Physics*] (EAIO)
IRC............... International Radio Carrier (NTCM)
IRC............... International Rainwear Council
IRC............... International Rating Class [*Yachting*]
IRC............... International Record Carrier [*Telecommunication companies providing
                international service*] (TSSD)
IRC............... International Red Cross and Red Crescent Movement (EAIO)
IRC............... International Reference Centre [*Community water supply and
                sanitation*] (NITA)
IRC............... International Relations Committee [*American Library Association*]
IRC............... International Relations Committee [*Library Association of Australia*]
IRC............... International Reply Coupon
IRC............... International Rescue Committee (EA)
IRC............... International Research Council [*Later, ICSU*]
IRC............... International Resistance Co. (AAG)
IRC............... International Resistor Center
IRC............... International Rice Commission [*See also CIR*] (EAIO)
IRC............... Internet Relay Chat [*Computer science*]
IRC............... Inter-Regional Capital Account [*Inter-American Development Bank*]
IRC............... Interservice Recruiting Committee [*Military*] (DNAB)
IRC............... Intrinsic Reaction Coordinate [*Physical chemistry*]
IRC............... Ionosphere Research Committee (MCD)
IRC............... Ion Recombination Chamber
IRC............... Iran Asseman Airline [*ICAO designator*] (FAAC)
IRC............... Iraqi Communist Party [*Also, ICP*] [*Political party*] (MENA)
IRC............... IRC International Water and Sanitation Centre [*International
                Reference Ce ntre for Community Water Supply and Sanitation*]
                [*Acronym is based on former name,*] (EAIO)
IRC............... Iron Canyon [*California*] [*Seismograph station code, US Geological
                Survey*] (SEIS)
IRC............... Ironclad
IRC............... Irregular Route Carrier
IRC............... Issue Restriction Code (MCD)
IRC............... Item Responsibility Code
IRCA........... [*The*] Immigration Reform and Control Act [*1986*] (ECON)
IRCA........... Immigration Reform and Control Act of 1986
IRCA........... International Radio Club of America (EA)
IRCA........... International Ragdoll Cat Association (EA)
IRCA........... International Railway Congress Association [*Belgium*]
IRCA........... International Remodeling Contractors Association (EA)
IRCA........... Intravascular Red Cell Aggregation [*Medicine*] (DMAA)
IR Cal......... Indian Rulings, Calcutta Series [*A publication*] (DLA)
IRC & M ..... Increase and Replacement of Construction and Machinery [*Naval
                budget appropriation title*]
IRCAR......... International Reference Center for Abortion Research (IID)
IRCAS......... Information Requirements Control Automated System [*Defense
                Supply Service/Pentagon*] (AABC)
IRCAT......... Infrared Radiometer Clear Air Turbulence [*Instrument*]
IRCC .... Instruction and Research Computer Center [*Ohio State University*]
                [*Research center*] (RCD)
IRCC .... International Radio Consultative Committee
IRCC .... International Record Collectors' Club [*Record label*]
IRCC .... International Red Cross Committee [*World War II*]
IRCCCOB...... Inter Research Council Coordinating Committee on Biotechnology
                (NITA)
IRCCD .... Infrared Charge-Coupled Device
IRCCM .... Infrared Counter-Countermeasures [*Military electronics*]
IRCCOPR ...... Inter-Research Council Committee on Pollution Research [*British*]
IRCCS .... Intrusion Resistant Communications Cable System (DNAB)
IRCD .... Information Retrieval Center on the Disadvantaged [*ERIC*]
IRCD .... International Research Centers Directory [*A publication*]
IRCDP .... International Research Career Development Program [*Public Health
                Service*]
IRC.EC......... Interline Resources [*Exchange symbol*] (TTSB)
IRCert .... Industrial Relations Certificate (ODBW)
Ir Ch .... Irish Chancery Reports [*A publication*] (DLA)
Ir Ch Rep ... Irish Chancery Reports [*A publication*] (DLA)
IRCICA .... Research Centre for Islamic History, Art, and Culture [*of the
                Organization of the Islamic Conference*] (EAIO)
IRCIHE .... International Referral Center for Information Handling Equipment
                [*Former Yugoslavia*] [*UNESCO*] (IID)
Ir Cir........... Irish Circuit Reports [*1841-43*] [*A publication*] (DLA)
Ir Cir Cas... Crawford and Dix's Irish Circuit Court Cases [*A publication*] (DLA)
Ir Circ Cas ... Irish Circuit Cases [*A publication*] (DLA)
Ir Circ Rep ... Irish Circuit Reports [*1841-43*] [*A publication*] (DLA)
Ir Cir Rep .... Reports of Irish Circuit Cases [*A publication*] (DLA)
IRCL........... International Research Centre on Lindane [*See also CIEL*] [*Brussels,
                Belgium*] (EAIO)
Ir CL........... Irish Common Law Reports [*A publication*] (DLA)
IRCL........... Irish Reports, Common Law Series [*A publication*] (DLA)

IRCM .... Infrared Countermeasures [*Military electronics*] (NVT)
IRCM .... Integrated Relay Controller Module [*Ford Motor Co.*] [*Automotive engineering*]
IRCM .... Intermediate Range Cruise Missile [*Military*] (CAAL)
IRCN .... Interagency Report Control Number
IRCND .... International Research Council of Neuromuscular Disorders (EA)
IRCNSW .... Industrial Relations Commission of New South Wales [*Australia*]
IRCO .... International Rubber Conference Organization (EAIO)
IRCOBI .... International Research Committee on the Biokinetics of Impacts [*Later, International Research Council on the Biokinetics of Impacts*] (EAIO)
IRCOL .... Institute for Information Retrieval and Computational Linguistics [*Bar Ilam University*] [*Israel*] (NITA)
Ir Com Law Rep ... Irish Common Law Reports [*A publication*] (DLA)
Ir Com L Rep ... Irish Common Law Reports [*A publication*] (DLA)
IR Comrs .... Inland Revenue Commissioners [*England*] (DLA)
IRCOPPS .... Interprofessional Research Commission on Pupil Personnel Services [*Defunct*]
IRCP .... Intermediate Range Construction Program [*Military*]
IRCPAL .... International Research Council on Pure and Applied Linguistics (EA)
IRCPPFI .... Industrial Relations Council for the Plumbing and Pipe Fitting Industry (EA)
IRCPUBS .... Publications of the Institute for Research in Construction [*National Research Council of Canada*] [*Information service or system*] (IID)
IRCQ .... Industrial Relations Commission of Queensland [*Australia*]
IRCR .... Integrator Register Control Register (PDAA)
IRCS .... Inertial Reference and Control System [*Aerospace*] (AAG)
IRCS .... Infrared Communications System
IRCS .... Interceptor Reaction Control System
IRCS .... Intercomplex Radio Communications System (IAA)
IRCS .... Interdisciplinary Research Center on Suicide [*Italy*] (EAIO)
IRCS .... International Radio Call Sign
IRCS .... International Research Communications System [*Electronic journal publisher*] [*British*]
IRCS .... Intersite Radio Communications System (MCD)
IRCS .... Italian Red Cross Society
IRCSA .... International Reference Collection of Soybean Arthropods [*INTSOY*]
IRCSI .... International Rabbinic Committee for the Safety of Israel (EA)
IRCT .... International Research on Communist Techniques
IRCV .... Industrial Relations Commission of Victoria [*Australia*]
IRD .... Ice-Rafted Debris [*Oceanography*]
IRD .... Immune Renal Disease [*Medicine*]
IRD .... Income in Respect of a Decedent [*Banking*]
IRD .... Information Requirements Description [*or Document*] (KSC)
IRD .... Infrared Detector
IRD .... Infrared Display
IRD .... Initiating Reference Document (MCD)
IRD .... Inland Rail Depot (DCTA)
IRD .... Institute on Religion and Democracy (EA)
I/RD .... Institutes and Research Divisions [*National Institutes of Health*]
IRD .... Integrated Receiver Decoder [*Telecommunications*]
IRD .... Interface Requirements Document
IRD .... Internal Revenue Department
IRD .... International Radiation Detectors [*Marine science*] (OSRA)
IRD .... International Radiation Detectors (USDC)
IRD .... International Research and Development
IRD .... International Research & Development Co. Ltd. [*Northern Engineering Industries*] [*British*] (IRUK)
IRD .... International Resource Development, Inc. [*Norwalk, CT*] [*Telecommunications Information service or system*] (IID)
IRD .... Iron Lady Resources [*Vancouver Stock Exchange symbol*]
IRD .... Ishurdi [*Bangladesh*] [*Airport symbol*] (OAG)
IRD .... Isotopes and Radiation Division [*American Nuclear Society*]
IRD .... Itinerant Recruiting Detail
IRDA .... Independent Reinol Distributors Association [*British*] (DBA)
IRDA .... Infraed Data Association (PS)
IrDA .... Infrared Data Association (PCM)
IRDA .... Infrared Detection Array
IRDA .... Infrared Developers Association (PCM)
IRDA .... Interactive Route Development and Analysis (CAAL)
IRDAC .... Industrial Research and Development Advisory Committee [*European Union*]
IRD & S .... International Research, Development, and Standardization [*Division*] [*Army*] (RDA)
IRDB .... Information Retrieval Databank (IEEE)
IRDC .... Improved RADAR Data Correlator (DWSG)
IRDC .... Industrial Research and Development Center [*University of Virginia*] (PDAA)
IRDC .... Intelligence Research and Development Council (MCD)
IRDC .... International Development Research Centre (GNE)
IRDC .... International Road Documentation Center
IRDC .... International Rubber Development Committee
IRDF .... Interactive Report Definition Facility (MCD)
IRDG .... Inter-Range Documentation Group [*White Sands Missile Range*]
IRDHS .... Imagery Related Data Handling System (MCD)
IRDIA .... Industrial Research and Development Investment Assistance [*Department of Industry*] [*Canada*] (PDAA)
IRDL .... Information Retrieval and Display Language [*Computer science*] (AABC)
IRDLO .... Infantry Research and Development Liaison Office [*Army*] (RDA)
IRDM .... Illuminated Runway Distance Marker (PDAA)
IRDM .... International Rendezvous and Docking Mission [*Aerospace*]
IRDN .... Illinois Resource and Dissemination Network [*Illinois State Board of Education*] [*No longer in operation*] [*Information service or system*] (IID)
IRDN .... Important Risk Data Notice [*Insurance*]
IRDO .... Infrared Drying Oven
IRDO .... Intermediate Retention of Differential Overlap [*Physics*]
IRDOE .... Institute for Research and Development in Occupational Education [*City University of New York*] [*Research center*] (RCD)
IRDP .... Icelandic Research Drilling Project
IRDP .... Industrial Regional Development Program [*Canada*]
IRDP .... Integrated Regional Development Planning (GNE)
IRDS .... Idiopathic Respiratory Distress Syndrome [*Pediatrics*]
IRDS .... Infant Respiratory Distress Syndrome [*Medicine*]
IRDS .... Information Resources Dictionary System (SSD)
IRDS .... Infrared Detecting Set [*or System*] (MCD)
IRDS .... Integrated Reliability Data System (AAG)
IRDS .... International Road Documentation Scheme (NITA)
IRDU .... Infrared Detection Unit
IRE .... Governor & Co. of the Bank of Ireland [*NYSE symbol*] (SAG)
IRE .... IFF Reply Evaluator
IRE .... Immediate Ready Element [*Military*] (AABC)
IRE .... Infrared Emission
IRE .... Institute for Responsive Education (EA)
IRE .... Institute of Radio Engineers [*Later, IEEE*]
IRE .... Institute of Refractories Engineers [*British*] (DBA)
IRE .... Instrument Rating Examiner [*Aviation*] (DA)
IRE .... Intelligence Resources [*Program*] [*Department of State*]
IRE .... Interferon Regulatory Element [*Biochemistry*]
IRE .... Internal Reflection Element [*Spectroscopy*]
IRE .... Internal Rotation in Extension [*Orthopedics*] (DAVI)
IRE .... International Association of Railway Employees
IRE .... International Relations Exercise (DNAB)
IRE .... International Research and Evaluation [*Research Center*] [*Also, an information service or system*] (IID)
IRE .... International Retail Systems, Inc. [*Toronto Stock Exchange symbol Vancouver Stock Exchange symbol*]
IRE .... International Royal Enterprises (EA)
IRE .... Investigative Reporters and Editors (EA)
IRE .... Ireland
Ire .... Ireland (VRA)
IRE .... Iron Replacement Element [*Biosynthesis*]
IRE .... Iron-Responsive Element [*Genetics*]
i-re-- .... Reunion [*MARC geographic area code Library of Congress*] (LCCP)
IREB .... Intense Relativistic Electron Beams [*Physics*]
IRE-BP .... Iron-Responsive Element - Binding Protein
IREC .... Increase and Replacement of Emergency Construction [*Ships*] [*Naval budget appropriation title*]
IREC .... International Registry of Early Corvettes (EA)
IREC .... International Rotary Engine Club [*Later, RX-7 Club of America*] (EA)
IRECA .... International Rescue and Emergency Care Association (EA)
Ir Eccl .... Irish Ecclesiastical Reports, by Milward [*1819-43*] [*A publication*] (DLA)
IRECUS .... Sherbrooke University Institut de Recherche et d'Enseignement pour les Cooperatives [*Canada Research center*] (RCD)
IRED .... Infrared-Emitting Diode (IEEE)
IRED .... Innovations et Reseaux pour le Developpement [*Development Innovations and Networks*] [*Geneva, Switzerland*] (EAIO)
IRED .... International Real Estate Directory [*Real estate computer site*]
Ired .... Iredell's North Carolina Equity Reports [*36-43 North Carolina*] [*A publication*] (DLA)
IREDA .... International Radio and Electrical Distributors Association (MHDB)
Ired Dig .... Iredell's North Carolina Digest [*A publication*] (DLA)
Ired Eq .... Iredell's North Carolina Equity Reports [*36-43 North Carolina*] [*A publication*] (DLA)
Ired Eq (NC) ... Iredell's North Carolina Equity Reports [*36-43 North Carolina*] [*A publication*] (DLA)
Ired L .... Iredell's North Carolina Equity Reports [*36-43 North Carolina*] [*A publication*] (DLA)
Ired L (NC) ... Iredell's North Carolina Law Reports [*A publication*] (DLA)
IreDNCA .... National College of Art and Design, Dublin, Ireland [*Library symbol*] [*Library of Congress*] (LCLS)
IreDNL .... National Library of Ireland, Dublin, Ireland [*Library symbol Library of Congress*] (LCLS)
IreDR .... Royal Dublin Society, Ballsbridge, Dublin, Ireland [*Library symbol Library of Congress*] (LCLS)
IreDT .... Trinity College, University of Dublin, Dublin, Ireland [*Library symbol Library of Congress*] (LCLS)
IREE .... Institut de Recherches et d'Etudes Europeennes [*Institute of European Research and Studies*] (EAIO)
IREF .... International Real Estate Federation
IREF .... Ischemia Research and Education Foundation
IREFAC .... International Real Estate Federation Australian Chapter
IREG .... Industriradets Industriregister [*Federation of Danish Industries' Register of Industries*] (EY)
IREG .... Information Res Engineering [*NASDAQ symbol*] (TTSB)
IREG .... Information Resource Engineering, Inc. [*NASDAQ symbol*] (SAG)
IREH .... Institute for Rural Environmental Health [*Colorado State University*] [*Research center*] (RCD)
IREHR .... Institute for Research and Education on Human Rights [*Defunct*] (EA)
IREI .... International Real Estate Institute (EA)
IRE-ITTD .... International Research and Evaluation - Information and Technology Transfer Database [*International Research and Evaluation*] [*Information service or system*] (CRD)
IREM .... Incorporation of Readiness into Effectivenss Modeling (MCD)

IREM............ Institut de Recherche en Exploration Minerale [*Mineral Exploration Research Institute*] [*Canada Research center*] (RCD)

IREM............ Institute of Real Estate Management [*Chicago, IL*] (EA)

IREM............ Integrated Regional Environmental Management Project (EA)

IREMAM ...... Institut de Recherches et d'Etudes sur le Monde Arabe et Musulman [*Institute for Research and Studies on the Arab and Muslim World*] [*France Information service or system*] (IID)

IREM-BASS... Improved Remotely Monitored Battlefield Sensor System

IRENE .... Industrial Restructuring and Education Network Europe

IREP............ Integrated Reliability Evaluation Program [*Nuclear energy*] (NRCH)

IREP............ Interdisciplinary Research Equipment Program

IREP............ Interim Reliability Evaluation Program [*Nuclear energy*]

IREP............ Internal Representation (MHDB)

IREPS .... Integrated Refractive Effects Prediction System [*Military*] (CAAL)

IREQ .... Institut de Recherche d'Hydro-Quebec [*Canada*]

IR Eq .... Irish Reports, Equity Series [*A publication*] (DLA)

Ir Eq Rep .... Irish Equity Reports [*A publication*] (DLA)

IRER .... Infrared Extra Rapid (ADA)

IRES............ Institute for Resource and Environmental Studies [*Dalhousie University*] [*Canada Research center*] (RCD)

IRES............ Internal Ribosomal Entry Site [*Genetics*]

IRES............ Internal Ribosome Entry Sequence [*To 21st site sequence*]

IRES............ IOC [*Intergovernmental Oceanographic Commission*] Group of Experts on Oceanographic Research as It Relates to IGOSS [*Marine science*] (MSC)

IRET............ Institute for Rational-Emotive Therapy (EA)

IRET............ Institute for Research on the Economics of Taxation [*Research center*] (RCD)

IRET............ Interrupt Return [*PC instruction*] (PCM)

IRETIJ......... Institut de Recherches et d'Etudes pour le Traitement de l'Information Juridique [*Institute of Research and Study for the Treatment of Legal Information*] [*University of Montpellier*] [*Information service or system*] (IID)

IRETP.......... Innovative Rural Education and Training Program

IRETS .... Infantry Remote Targeting System [*Army*] (RDA)

IREW .... Infrared Electronic Warfare

IREWS .... Infrared Early Warning System

IREX........... Ideas, Resources, Exchange [*Computer*] [*British*]

IREX........... International Research and Exchanges Board (EA)

IRF............. Idiopathic Retroperitoneal Fibrosis [*Medicine*] (DMAA)

IRF............. Immediate Reaction Force [*Military*] (AABC)

IRF............. Impedance-Reduction Factor (IAA)

IRF............. Induced Radiation Flux

IRF............. Inducing Resistance Factor [*Plant pathology*]

IRF............. Inherited Rights Filter [*Computer science*]

IRF............. Input Register Full

IRF............. Instrument Reliability Factor (PDAA)

IRF............. Instrument Response Function

IRF............. Interferon Regulatory Factor [*Biochemistry*]

IRF............. Intermittent Reinforcement [*Psychology*]

IRF............. Internal Rotation in Flexion [*Orthopedics*] (DAVI)

IRF............. International Racquetball Federation (EAIO)

IRF............. International Rectifier Corp. [*NYSE symbol*] (SPSG)

IRF............. International Reform Federation (EA)

IRF............. International Religious Fellowship (EA)

IRF............. International Research Fellowship Program [*Department of Health and Human Services*] (GFGA)

IRF............. International Road Federation (EA)

IRF............. International Rowing Federation

IRF............. Interrogation Repetition Frequency [*RADAR beacon*]

IRF............. Intl Rectifier [*NYSE symbol*] (TTSB)

IRF............. Intrinsic Rectifying Factor [*Biochemistry*]

IRF............. Islamic Research Foundation (EA)

IRF............. Island Resources Foundation (EA)

IRF............. Islands Research Foundation [*Inactive*] (EA)

IRFA........... Initial Regulatory Flexibility Analysis (AAGC)

IRFA........... Institut de Recherches sur les Fruits et Agrumes [*Institute of Research on Fruits and Citrus Fruits*] [*International Cooperation Center of Agricultural Research for Development Database producer*]

IRFAA .... International Rescue and First Aid Association [*Later, IRECA*] (EA)

IRFAP .... International Religious Fine Art Program (EA)

IRFB........... International Radio Frequency Board

IRFC........... Intermediate-Range Function Test (IAA)

IR Fed Ct .... Indian Rulings, Federal Court [*A publication*] (DLA)

IRFIS .... Inertial Referenced Flight Inspection System [*Aviation*] (PDAA)

IRFITS .... Infrared Fault Isolation Test System

IRFL........... Integral Red Fluorescence (DMAA)

IRFM........... Integral Reactor Flow Model [*Nuclear energy*] (NRCH)

IRFMS .... Interservice Radio Frequency Management School (DOMA)

IRFNA .... Inhibited Red Fuming Nitric Acid [*Rocket fuel*]

IRFN/UDMH... Inhibited Red Fuming Nitric Acid and Unsymmetrical Dimethylhydrazine [*Rocket fuel*]

IRFP........... International Relations and Foreign Policy [*Army British*]

IRFPA .... Infrared Focal Plane Array [*DoD*]

IRFRH......... Institut de Recherche et de Formation aux Relations Humaines [*Institute for Research and Training in Human Relations*] [*Research center France*] (IRC)

IRFT........... Interim Refresher Training [*Navy*] (NVT)

IRFU .... Irish Rugby Football Union (EAIO)

IRG............. Immunoreactive Gastrin [*Medicine*] (DMAA)

IRG............. Immunoreactive Glucagon [*Immunochemistry*]

IRG............. Industrial Reprocessing Group (SAA)

IRG............. Inertial Rate Gyro (KSC)

IRG............. Information Resource Group [*Information service or system*] (IID)

IRG .... Infrared Generator

IRG .... Initial Review Group [*National Institutes of Health*]

IRG .... Inner Roll Gimbal (MCD)

IRG .... Institut de Reescompte et de Garantie [*Development bank*] [*Belgium*] (EY)

IRG .... Interagency Regulatory Group

IRG .... Interagency Review Group [*Nuclear Regulatory Commission*] (NRCH)

IRG .... Interdepartmental Regional Group [*Army*] (AABC)

IRG .... Internationale des Resistants a la Guerre [*War Resisters International - WRI*] [*British*] (EA)

IRG .... International Register (IAA)

IRG .... International Research Group on Wear of Engineering Materials (PDAA)

IRG .... International Research Group on Wood Preservation [*Stockholm, Sweden*] (EAIO)

IRG .... Interrecord Gap (IAA)

IRG .... Inter-Record Gap [*Computer science Telecommunications*] (MCD)

IRG .... Interrelationship Graph (PDAA)

IRG .... Iron Range [*Queensland*] [*Airport symbol*] (AD)

IRG .... Lockhart Rivers [*Australia Airport symbol*] (OAG)

IRG .... Naft Air Lines [*Iran*] [*FAA designator*] (FAAC)

IRGA .... Infrared Gas Analyzer

IRgA........... International Reprographics Association (EA)

IRGAR......... Infrared Gas Radiation

IRGB........... Infrared Guided Bomb [*DoD*]

IRGBA......... International Repro Graphic Blueprint Association [*Later, IRA*] (EA)

IRGCVD....... International Research Group on Colour Vision Deficiencies [*Ghent, Belgium*] (EAIO)

IRGH .... Immunoreactive Growth Hormone [*Immunology*]

IR-GIP .... Immunoreactive Gastric Inhibitory Peptide [*Biochemistry*]

IRGI .... Immunoreactive Glucagon [*Immunochemistry*]

IRGL .... Indentation Residual Gauge Level [*Automotive engineering*]

IRGL .... Infrared Gunfire Locator

IRGMA........ Information Retrieval Group of the Museums Association [*British*] (NITA)

IRGP .... Infrared Guided Projectile (MCD)

IRGPG......... Inter-Range and Global Planning Group [*White Sands Missile Range*] (MUGU)

IRGRD......... International Research Group on Refuse Disposal [*Later, ISWA*]

IRGT .... Insulin-Regulatable Glucose Transporter [*Biochemistry*]

IRH .... Inductive Recording Head

IRH .... Infrared Heater

IRH .... Inspection Requirements Handbook [*Navy*] (NG)

IRH .... Institute for Reproductive Health (EA)

IRH .... Institute for Research in History

IRH .... Institute for Research in Hypnosis [*Later, IRHP*] (EA)

IRH .... Institutes of Religion and Health (EA)

IRH .... International Rhodes Resources [*Vancouver Stock Exchange symbol*]

IRHA .... Injured as Result of Hostile Action [*Military*] (NVT)

IRHA .... Interchurch Response for the Horn of Africa (EA)

IRHC .... Isolated Rat Hepatocyte Complex

IRHCS .... Immunoradioassayable Human Chorionic Somatomammotropin [*Medicine*] (MAE)

IRHD .... Internationaler Rat der Hauspflegedienste [*International Council of Home-Help Services*]

IRHD .... International Rubber Hardness Degree

IRHF .... Integral Radiative Heat Flux

IRHGH .... Immunoreactive Human Growth Hormone [*Immunology*] (AAMN)

IRHP .... Institute for Research in Hypnosis and Psychotherapy (EA)

IRHR .... Institute for Research in Human Relations (MCD)

IRHS .... Intact Reentry Heat Source (OA)

IRHS .... Intraoral Recurrent Herpes Simplex [*Medicine*]

IRI............. Image Resources, Inc. [*Winter Park, FL*] [*Telecommunications*] (TSSD)

IRI............. Immunobiology Research Institute [*Annandale, NJ*]

IRI............. Immunoreactive Insulin

IRI............. Inca Resources, Inc. [*Toronto Stock Exchange symbol Vancouver Stock Exchange symbol*]

IRI............. Industrial Research Institute [*Canada Research center*] (RCD)

IRI............. Industrial Risk Insurers (EA)

IRI............. Informal Reading Inventory [*Education*]

IRI............. Information Researchers, Inc. [*Information service or system*] (IID)

IRI............. Information Resources, Inc. [*Information service or system*] (IID)

IRI............. Information Retrieval, Inc.

IRI............. Infrared Imagery

IRI............. Infrared Instrumentation

IRI............. Innovative Resources, Inc.

IRI............. Institution of the Rubber Industry [*British*]

IRI............. Insulin Radioimmunoassay

IRI............. Insulin Resistance Index [*Medicine*] (DMAA)

IRI............. Integrated Range Instrumentation

IRI............. International Industrial Relations Institute

IRI............. International Reference Ionosphere

IRI............. International Relay, Inc. [*New York, NY*] [*Telecommunications*] (TSSD)

IRI............. International Remote Imaging Systems, Inc. [*AMEX symbol*] (SPSG)

IRI............. International Republican Institute (ECON)

IRI............. International Robotmotion Intelligence (NITA)

IRI............. International Roughness Index [*BTS*] [*FHWA*] (TAG)

IRI............. Intl Remote Imaging [*AMEX symbol*]

IRI............. Intravehicular Referenced Information [*NASA*]

IRI............. Inveresk Research International Ltd. [*British*] (IRUK)

IRI............. Iringa [*Tanzania*] [*Airport symbol*] (OAG)

iri............. Irish [*MARC language code Library of Congress*] (LCCP)

IRI.............. Istituto per la Ricostruzione Industriale [*Institute for Industrial Reconstruction*] [*Government holding company Italy*]
IRIA .... Infrared Information and Analysis Center [*University of Michigan*]
IRIA .... Institut de Recherche d'Informatique et d'Automatique [*French Research center*]
IRIAC .... Infrared Information and Analysis Center [*University of Michigan*]
IRIBS .... Inclination Removal Ionospheric Beacon Satellite (PDAA)
IRIC .... Information Resources [*NASDAQ symbol*] (TTSB)
IRIC .... Information Resources, Inc. [*NASDAQ symbol*] (NQ)
IRIC .... Infrared Image Converter
IRIC .... Inter-Regional Insurance Conference [*Later, ISO*]
IRICBM ...... Intermediate-Range Intercontinental Ballistic Missile
IRICON....... Infrared Vidicon Tube
IRICON....... International Information Service via a Computer-Oriented Network (TSSD)
IRICP .... International Research Institute for Climate Prediction [*Marine science*] (OSRA)
IRICP .... International Research Institute for Climate Prediction (USDC)
IRICU .... Intermountain Respiratory Intensive Care Unit [*Medicine*] (BABM)
IRicv .... Richview Township Public Library, Richview, IL [*Library symbol Library of Congress*] (LCLS)
IRid........... Elwood Township Carnegie Library, Ridge Farm, IL [*Library symbol Library of Congress*] (LCLS)
IRID .... Iridescent (WGA)
irid............ Irridescent (VRA)
Iridex......... Iridex Corp. [*Associated Press*] (SAG)
IRidSD........ Ridge Farm Community Unit School District, Ridge Farm, IL [*Library symbol*] [*Library of Congress*] (LCLS)
IRIE .... Infrared Information Exchange
IR/IED .... Independent Research/Independent Exploratory Development
IRIG .... Inertial Rate Integrating Gyro (NASA)
IRIG .... Inertial Reference Integrating Gyro [*NASA*] (NASA)
IRIg .... Insulin-Reactive Immunoglobulin [*Endocrinology*] (DAVI)
IRIG .... Inter-Range Instrumentation Group [*White Sands Missile Range*]
IRIG-B........ Inter-Range Instrumentation Group B [*NASA*] (GFGA)
IRIG-MWG... Inter-Range Instrumentation Group - Meteorological Working Group [*White Sands Missile Range*]
IR/IOD......... Independent Research/Independent Objectives Document [*Military*] (DNAB)
IRIRC .... International Refugee Integration Resource Centre [*Later, CDR*] (EAIO)
IRIS .... Center for Institutional Reform and the Informal Sector [*University of Maryland*] (ECON)
IRIS .... IBM [*International Business Machines Corp.*] Recruitment Information System
IRIS .... Incident Resource and Information System [*Police*] [*British*] (NITA)
IRIS .... Incorporated Research Institutions for Seismology
IRIS .... Increased Readiness Information System
IRIS .... Industrial Relations Information Service [*Labour Canada*]
IRIS .... Inertial Reactor with Internal Separation [*Coal furnace*] [*Tecogen, Inc.*]
IRIS .... Inertia Resonance Induction System [*Automotive engineering*]
IRIS .... Information Relayed Instantly from the Source [*Project*]
IRIS .... Information Resources Information System [*Library of Congress*]
IRIS .... Infrared Image Scanner
IRIS .... Infrared Imaging Seeker
IRIS .... Infrared Imaging System
IRIS .... Infrared Information System [*Sadtler Research Laboratories, Inc.*] [*Philadelphia, PA Database*]
IRIS .... Infrared Interferometer Spectrometer
IRIS .... Infrared Intruder System
IRIS .... Infrared Research Information Symposium (AAG)
IRIS .... Instant Response Information System (IEEE)
IRIS .... Institute for Regional and International Studies (EA)
IRIS .... Institute for Research in Information and Scholarship [*Brown University*] [*Research center*] (RCD)
IRIS .... Institute for Research on Interactive Systems [*Research center*] (TSSD)
IRIS .... Institute for Robotics and Intelligent Systems [*Research center*] (RCD)
IRIS .... Instructional Resources Information System [*Ohio State University*] [*Information service or system*]
IRIS .... Instruction and Research Information Systems [*Computer science*]
IRIS .... Insurance Regulatory Information System [*National Association of Insurance Commissioners*]
IRIS .... Integrated Radio and Intercommunications System [*Canada*]
IRIS .... Integrated Reconnaissance Intelligence System (IEEE)
IRIS .... Integrated Risk Information System [*Environmental Protection Agency*]
IRIS .... Intelligence Report Index Summary
IRIS .... Intelligence Reports Information Subsystem [*Computer science*]
IRIS .... Intelligent Remote Input Stand [*Computer science*]
IRIS .... Interactive Real-Time Information System [*Marine science*] (MSC)
IRIS .... Interactive Recorded Information Service [*British Telecommunications*] (TEL)
IRIS .... Interleukin Regulation of Immune System [*Medicine*] (DMAA)
IRIS .... International Radiation Investigation Satellite [*NASA*]
IRIS .... International Radio Interferometric Surveying [*International Association of Geodesy*]
IRIS .... International Recruitment Investigation in the Subarctic [*Marine science*] (OSRA)
IRIS .... International Recruitment Investigations in the Subarctic (USDC)
IRIS .... International Relations Information System [*Forschungsinstitut fuer Internationale Politik und Sicherheit*] [*Germany*] (IID)

IRIS .... International Remote Imaging Systems, Inc. [*Associated Press*] (SAG)
IRIS .... International Reporting and Information Services [*International Private Intelligence Service*] [*Terminated, 1983*]
IRIS .... International Reporting Information Systems
IRIS .... International Research Information Service [*American Foundation for the Blind*]
IRIS .... International Research on the Interior of the Sun
IRIS .... International REST [*Restricted Environmental Stimulation Techniques*] Investigators Society (EA)
IRIS .... International Rights Information Service
IRIS .... Internet Reach and Involvement Scale [*Advertising value of an Internet site*]
IRIS .... Interrogation Requirements Information System [*DoD*] (AFIT)
IRIS .... Italian Research Interim Stage (NASA)
IRISH .... Infrared Imaging Seeker Head (MCD)
IrishIn........ Irish Investment Fund [*Associated Press*] (SAG)
IRIS-M .... Infrared Interferometer Spectrometer - Michelson
IRISS .... Institute for Research in the Social Sciences [*University of York*] [*British*] (IRC)
IRIV .... Immunopotentiating Reconstituted Influenza Virosome [*Immunochemistry*]
IRIV .... Immunostimulating Reconstituted Influenza Virosome [*Immunochemistry*]
IRivd.......... Riverdale Library District, Riverdale, IL [*Library symbol Library of Congress*] (LCLS)
IRivf.......... River Forest Public Library, River Forest, IL [*Library symbol Library of Congress*] (LCLS)
IRivfR .... Rosary College, River Forest, IL [*Library symbol Library of Congress*] (LCLS)
IRivfT......... Concordia Teachers College, River Forest, IL [*Library symbol Library of Congress*] (LCLS)
IRivg.......... River Grove Public Library, River Grove, IL [*Library symbol Library of Congress*] (LCLS)
IRivgT........ Triton College, River Grove, IL [*Library symbol Library of Congress*] (LCLS)
IRivs.......... Riverside Public Library, Riverside, IL [*Library symbol Library of Congress*] (LCLS)
IRIX .... IRIDEX Corp. [*NASDAQ symbol*] (TTSB)
IRIX .... Iridex Corp. [*NASDAQ symbol*] (SAG)
IRJ............. Infrared Jammer
IRJ............. La Rioja [*Argentina*] [*Airport symbol*] (OAG)
IRJE.......... Infrared Jammer Equipment
IRJE.......... Interactive Remote Job Entry
IR Jour .... Indian Rulings, Journal Section [*A publication*] (DLA)
Ir Jur .... Irish Jurist Reports [*1849-66*] [*A publication*] (DLA)
Ir Jur Rep.... Irish Jurist Reports [*1849-66*] [*A publication*] (DLA)
IRK........... Infrared Kit
IRK........... Insulin Receptor Kinase [*An enzyme*]
IRK........... Interlake Development [*Vancouver Stock Exchange symbol*]
IRK........... Irkutsk [*Former USSR Seismograph station code, US Geological Survey*] (SEIS)
IRK........... Kirksville [*Missouri*] [*Airport symbol*] (OAG)
IRK........... Kirksville, MO [*Location identifier FAA*] (FAAL)
IRK........... Kish Air [*Iran*] [*ICAO designator*] (FAAC)
IRL........... Immigration Restriction League
IRL........... Indexed Repayment Loan
IRL........... Index Retrieval Language [*Computer science*] (PDAA)
IRL........... Industrial Reactor Laboratories [*New Jersey*]
IRL........... Industrial Research Laboratories [*A publication*]
IRL........... Indy Racing League [*Automobile racing*]
IRL........... Information Requirements List (KSC)
IRL........... Information Research Ltd. [*Information service or system*] (IID)
IRL........... Information Retrieval Language [*Computer science*]
IRL........... Information Retrieval Ltd. [*Database originator*] [*British Information service or system*]
IRL........... Infrared Lamp [*or Light*]
IRL........... Infrared Lens
IRL........... Initiating Reference Letter (MCD)
IRL........... Institute for Rational Living [*Absorbed by IRET*]
IRL........... Institute of Rural Life at Home and Overseas [*British*] (BI)
IRL........... Institute on Religious Life (EA)
IRL........... Interactive Reader Language [*Computer science*]
IRL........... Interactive Root Locus (PDAA)
IRL........... Interface Requirement List (NASA)
IRL........... Internationaler Ring fuer Landarbeit [*International Committee of Scientific Management in Agriculture*]
IRL........... International Meridian Resources [*Vancouver Stock Exchange symbol*]
IRL........... Interrogation and Locating
IRL........... Intersection of Range Legs
IRL........... Ionosphere Research Laboratory [*Pennsylvania State University*] (PDAA)
IRL........... Ireland [*ANSI three-letter standard code*] (CNC)
IRL........... Irish Air Corps [*ICAO designator*] (FAAC)
IRL........... Irish Investment Fund [*NYSE symbol*] (SAG)
IrL............. Irish Law Reports [*A publication*] (DLA)
IRLA.......... Independent Research Libraries Association (EA)
IRLA.......... Information Retrieval & Library Automation [*A publication*] (BRI)
IRLA.......... International Religious Liberty Association (EA)
IRLA.......... Item Repair Level Analysis [*DoD*]
IR Lah .... Indian Rulings, Lahore Series [*A publication*] (DLA)
IrL & Eq...... Irish Law and Equity Reports [*1838-50*] [*A publication*] (DLA)
IRLAS .... Infrared LASER

Ir Law & Ch... Irish Common Law and Chancery Reports, New Series [1850-53] [A publication] (DLA)
Ir Law & Eq... Irish Law and Equity Reports [1838-50] [A publication] (DLA)
Ir Law Rec... Irish Law Recorder [1827-38] [A publication] (DLA)
Ir Law Rec NS... Irish Law Recorder, New Series [1833-38] [A publication] (DLA)
Ir Law Rep... Irish Law Reports [A publication] (DLA)
Ir Law Rep NS... Irish Common Law Reports, New Series [A publication] (DLA)
IRLC............ Illinois Regional Library Council [Library network]
IRLCO-CSA... International Red Locust Control Organization for Central and Southern Africa (EAIO)
IRLCS .... International Red Locust Control Service
IRLD .... Institute for Research on Learning Disabilities [University of Minnesota] [Research center] (RCD)
IRLDA .... Independent Retail Lumber Dealers Association
IRLED .... Infrared Light Emitting Diode (PDAA)
IRLG .... Interagency Regulatory Liaison Group [Comprising several federal agencies] [Terminated, 1981]
Ir LJ .... Irish Law Journal [1895-1902] [A publication] (DLA)
Ir L NS....... Irish Common Law Reports, New Series [A publication] (DLA)
IRLR .... Industrial Relations Law Reports [British] (DCTA)
IRLR .... Infrared LASER Ranger (MCD)
Ir LR .... Irish Law Reports [A publication] (DLA)
Ir L Rec ...... Irish Law Recorder, First Series [1827-31] [A publication] (DLA)
Ir L Rec 1st Ser... Law Recorder, First Series [Ireland] [A publication] (DLA)
Ir L Rec NS... Law Recorder, New Series [Ireland] [A publication] (DLA)
IRLS............ Infrared LASER Spectrometer
IRLS............ Infrared Line Scanner (MCD)
IRLS............ Interrogation, Recording, and Locating System [Naval Oceanographic Office]
IRLSC .... Industrial Relations and Labor Studies Center [University of Maryland] [Research center] (RCD)
Ir LTJ .... Irish Law Times Journal [A publication] (DLA)
Ir LT Jour .... Irish Law Times Journal [A publication] (DLA)
Ir LTR .... Irish Law Times Reports [A publication] (DLA)
Ir LT Rep ...... Irish Law Times Reports [A publication] (DLA)
IRLWR .... Institute for Research on Land and Water Resources [Pennsylvania State University] (PDAA)
IRM............ Illinois Railway Museum (EA)
IRM............ Image Rejection Mixer [Electronics] (OA)
IRM............ Improved Risk Mutuals (EA)
IRM............ Induced Remanent Magnetization
IRM............ Information and Records Management
IRM............ Information Research Management (MCD)
IRM............ Information Resource Management [Computer science]
IRM............ Information Resources Management [Marine science] (OSRA)
IRM............ Information Resources Management (USDC)
IRM............ Infrared Mapper
IRM............ Infrared Measurement
IRM............ Inherited Releasing Mechanism [Psychiatry]
IRM............ Inherited Rights Mask (ACRL)
IRM............ Initial Release Memorandum
IRM............ Innate Release Mechanism [Endocrinology]
IRM............ Inspection Requirements Manual (AAG)
IRM............ Institute for Resource Management (EA)
IRM............ Institute of Rehabilitation Medicine (DAVI)
IRM............ Institute of Religion and Medicine [British] (DBA)
IRM............ Institute of Risk Management (EAIO)
IRM............ Integrated Range Missile (MCD)
IRM............ Integrated Range Mission [Military]
IRM............ Integrated Review Model
IRM............ Intelligent Remote Multiplexer [Computer science] (MHDI)
IRM............ Interactive Request Modification (IAA)
IRM............ Interference Reflection Microscopy
IRM............ Interim Remedial Measure (EPA)
IRM............ Interim Research Memo
IRM............ Intermediate Range Monitor (NRCH)
IRM............ Intermediate Remedial Measures (GNE)
IRM............ Intermediate Restorative Material [Dentistry]
IRM............ Internal Revenue (Service) Manual [A publication] (AAGC)
IRM............ International Royalon Minerals, Inc. [Vancouver Stock Exchange symbol]
IRM............ Iodine Radiation Monitor (IEEE)
IRM............ Ion Release Module [Spacecraft] [Germany]
IRM............ Isothermal Remanent Magnetization
IRMA .... Immunoradiometric Assay [Immunology]
IRMA .... Individual Retirement Mortgage Account
IRMA .... Individual Reverse Mortgage Account [American Homestead, Inc.]
IRMA .... Information Referral Manual
IRMA .... Information Revision and Manuscript Assembly
IRMA .... Infrared Milk Analyzer (PDAA)
IRMA .... Infrared Miss-Distance Approximator
IRMA .... Interactive Real-Time Music Assembler (PDAA)
IRMA .... International Rehabilitation Medicine Association (EA)
IRMA .... International Rock 'n' Roll Music Association (EA)
IRMA .... Intraretinal Microangiopathy [Ophthalmology]
IRMA .... Intraretinal Microvascular Abnormality [Ophthalmology]
IRMA .... Inverted Roof Membrane Assembly [Construction]
IRMAC .... Information Resource Management Association of Canada (EAIO)
IR Mad .... Indian Rulings, Madras Series [A publication] (DLA)
IRMAE .... Ius Romanum Medii Aevi [Latin]
IRMC .... Information Resource Management Council [DoD]
IRMC .... Information Resources Management College (USGC)
IRMC .... Institute of Risk Management Consultants [Later, SRMC] (EA)
IRMC .... Interagency Risk Management Council [Environmental Protection Agency] (EPA)

IRME......... Initiator Resistance Measuring Equipment (NASA)
IRMFSG ...... Inter-Range Missile Flight Safety Group [White Sands Missile Range]
IRMGSG .... Inter-Range Missile Ground Safety Group [White Sands Missile Range] (KSC)
IRMI............ Indirect Reading Measuring Instruments (DICI)
IRMI............ International Risk Management Institute [Dallas, TX] (EA)
IR Mim .... Internal Revenue Service Mimeographed Ruling (AAGC)
IR-MIM .... Published Internal Revenue Mimeograph [A publication] (DLA)
IRMJ .... Infrared Miniaturized Jammer
IRMMH .... Institute for Research into Mental and Multiple Handicap [British]
IRMO .... Information Resources Management Office [Army Corps of Engineers]
IRMP .... Industrial Readiness and Mobilization Production Planning [Military]
IRMP .... Infrared Measurement Program
IRMP .... Infrared Multiple-Photon [Physics]
IRMP .... Intermountain Regional Medical Program (BABM)
IRMP .... Interservice Radiation Measurement Program
IRMP .... Iron-Regulated Membrane Protein [Biochemistry]
IRMPC .... Industrial Raw Materials Planning Committee [NATO] (NATG)
IRMPD .... Infrared Multiple-Photon Dissociation [Physics]
IRMR .... Institute for Research into Mental Retardation
IRMRA .... Infrared Monochromatic Radiation (MSA)
IR/MRBM .... Intermediate-Range/Medium-Range Ballistic Missile (NG)
IRMS .... Information Resource Management Service [Veterans Administration Medical Center] [Information service or system] (IID)
IRMS .... Information Retrieval and Management System (IAA)
IRMS .... Infrared Mapping System
IRMS .... Integrated Radio Management System (MCD)
IRMS .... International Robert Musil Society [See also SIRM] [Saarbrucken, Federal Republic of Germany] (EAIO)
IRMS .... Isotope Ratio Mass Spectrometry
IRMT .... International Register of Manipulative Therapists
IRN .... Illinois Resource Network [University of Illinois] [Urbana] [Information service or system] (IID)
IRN .... Import Release Note (DS)
IRN .... Interface Revision Notice [NASA] (KSC)
IRN .... Interim Revision Notice (SAA)
IRN .... Internal Reference Number
IRN .... Internal Routing Network
IRN .... International Rivers Network (EA)
IRN .... Invoice Register Number [Business term] (MCD)
IRN .... Iran [ANSI three-letter standard code] (CNC)
IRN .... Iron [Chemical element] (DAVI)
IRN .... Iron or Steel [Freight]
IRN .... Iron River Resources [Vancouver Stock Exchange symbol]
IRN .... [The] Ironton Railroad Co. [Absorbed into Consolidated Rail Corp.] [AAR code]
IRN .... Item Removal Notice [Nuclear energy] (NRCH)
IRNA .... Iranian [or Islamic Republic] News Agency
I-RNA .... Ribonucleic Acid, Immune [Biochemistry, genetics]
IR Nag .... Indian Rulings, Nagpur Series [A publication] (DLA)
IRNDT .... Infrared Nondestructive Testing [Electrical technique]
IRNES .... Institut de Recherches et de Normalisation Economiques en Scientifiques [Canada]
IRNS .... Inertial Reference Navigational System
IRNU .... Institut de Recherche des Nations Unies pour le Developpement Social [United Nations Research Institute for Social Development]
IRNV .... Increase and Replacement of Naval Vessels [Naval budget appropriation title]
IRNWRK ...... Ironwork
IRO .... Birao [Central African Republic] [Airport symbol] (AD)
IRO .... CSA Air, Inc. [ICAO designator] (FAAC)
IRO .... Independent Retailer Organisation (EAIO)
IRO .... Industrial Relations Office [Army]
IRO .... Inflight Refueling Operator
IRO .... Infrared Oven
IRO .... Inland Revenue Office [or Officer] [British]
IRO .... Institute of Rent Officers [British] (DBA)
IRO .... Interim Range Operations (MUGU)
IRO .... Internal Revenue Office [or Officer]
IRO .... International Reception Operators [Defunct] (EA)
IRO .... International Refugee Organization [Later, UNHCR]
IRO .... International Relations Office [American Library Association]
IRO .... International Relief Organization [Post-World War II]
IRO .... Inventory Research Office [Army]
iro .... Iroquoian [MARC language code Library of Congress] (LCCP)
IRo .... Rockford Public Library, Rockford, IL [Library symbol Library of Congress] (LCLS)
IROA .... Independent Rabbinate of America
IRoAH .... Auburn High School, Rockford, IL [Library symbol] [Library of Congress] (LCLS)
IROAN .... Inspect and Repair Only as Necessary [or Needed] [Military]
IRob .... Robinson Public Library, Robinson, IL [Library symbol Library of Congress] (LCLS)
IRoBaE......... Barbour Elementary School, Rockford, IL [Library symbol] [Library of Congress] (LCLS)
IRobb .... Robbins Public Library District, Robbins, IL [Library symbol Library of Congress] (LCLS)
IRoBeE......... Beyer Elementary School, Rockford, IL [Library symbol] [Library of Congress] (LCLS)
IRoBIE......... Bloom Elementary School, Rockford, IL [Library symbol] [Library of Congress] (LCLS)
IRoBrE......... Brookview Elementary School, Rockford, IL [Library symbol] [Library of Congress] (LCLS)

RobSD	Robinson Community School District 2, Robinson, IL [*Library symbol Library of Congress*] (LCLS)
ROC	International Race of Champions [*Auto racing*]
ROC	International Rose O'Neill Club (EA)
RoC	Rockford College, Rockford, IL [*Library symbol Library of Congress*] (LCLS)
RoCaE	Carlson Elementary School, Rockford, IL [*Library symbol*] [*Library of Congress*] (LCLS)
RoChE	Church Elementary School, Rockford, IL [*Library symbol*] [*Library of Congress*] (LCLS)
Rockt	Talcott Free Public Library, Rockton, IL [*Library symbol Library of Congress*] (LCLS)
RocL	Flagg Township Library, Rochelle, IL [*Library symbol*] [*Library of Congress*] (LCLS)
RocN	Rochelle News, Rochelle, IL [*Library symbol*] [*Library of Congress*] (LCLS)
RoCoE	Conklin Elementary School, Rockford, IL [*Library symbol*] [*Library of Congress*] (LCLS)
ROD	Instantaneous Readout Detector [*Satellite instrument*]
RoDE	Dennis Elementary School, Rockford, IL [*Library symbol*] [*Library of Congress*] (LCLS)
RODP	International Registry of Organization Development Professionals (EA)
RODS	Inertial Rate of Descent Sensor (MCD)
RoEE	Ellis Elementary School, Rockford, IL [*Library symbol*] [*Library of Congress*] (LCLS)
RoEH	East High School, Rockford, IL [*Library symbol*] [*Library of Congress*] (LCLS)
RoEM	Einsehower Middle School, Rockford, IL [*Library symbol*] [*Library of Congress*] (LCLS)
ROF	Imagery Requirement Objectives File (MCD)
RoFE	Froberg Elementary School, Rockford, IL [*Library symbol*] [*Library of Congress*] (LCLS)
RO-FIET	Interamerican Regional Organization of the International Federation of Commercial, Clerical, Professional, and Technical Employees [*Willemstad, Netherlands Antilles*] (EAIO)
RoFM	B. W. Flinn Middle School, Rockford, IL [*Library symbol*] [*Library of Congress*] (LCLS)
RoFP	Fairview Preschool, Rockford, IL [*Library symbol*] [*Library of Congress*] (LCLS)
RoGaE	Garrison Elementary School, Rockford, IL [*Library symbol*] [*Library of Congress*] (LCLS)
RoGH	Guilford High School, Rockford, IL [*Library symbol*] [*Library of Congress*] (LCLS)
RoGrE	Gregory Elementary School, Rockford, IL [*Library symbol*] [*Library of Congress*] (LCLS)
RoHaE	Haskell Elementary School, Rockford, IL [*Library symbol*] [*Library of Congress*] (LCLS)
RoHgE	Haight Elementary School, Rockford, IL [*Library symbol*] [*Library of Congress*] (LCLS)
RoHiE	Hillman Elementary School, Rockford, IL [*Library symbol*] [*Library of Congress*] (LCLS)
RoHIE	Hallstrom Elementary School, Rockford, IL [*Library symbol*] [*Library of Congress*] (LCLS)
RoJaE	Jackson Elementary School, Rockford, IL [*Library symbol*] [*Library of Congress*] (LCLS)
RoJH	Jefferson High School, Rockford, IL [*Library symbol*] [*Library of Congress*] (LCLS)
RoJoE	Johnson Elementary School, Rockford, IL [*Library symbol*] [*Library of Congress*] (LCLS)
RoKE	King Elementary School, Rockford, IL [*Library symbol*] [*Library of Congress*] (LCLS)
RoKiE	Kishwaukee Elementary School, Rockford, IL [*Library symbol*] [*Library of Congress*] (LCLS)
RoKM	John F. Kennedy Middle School, Rockford, IL [*Library symbol*] [*Library of Congress*] (LCLS)
ROL	Imagery Requirements Objectives List (MCD)
RoLE	Lathrop Elementary School, Rockford, IL [*Library symbol*] [*Library of Congress*] (LCLS)
RoLM	Lincoln Middle School, Rockford, IL [*Library symbol*] [*Library of Congress*] (LCLS)
RoMcE	McIntosh Elementary School, Rockford, IL [*Library symbol*] [*Library of Congress*] (LCLS)
RoMH	Rockford Memorial Hospital, Rockford, IL [*Library symbol Library of Congress*] (LCLS)
RoMuE	Muhl Center Elementary School, Rockford, IL [*Library symbol*] [*Library of Congress*] (LCLS)
RON	Infrared Optical Noise (IAA)
Iron	Ironical (ROG)
RoN	Northern Illinois Library for Mental Health, Rockford, IL [*Library symbol Library of Congress*] (LCLS)
RoNaE	Nashold Elementary School, Rockford, IL [*Library symbol*] [*Library of Congress*] (LCLS)
RoNeE	Nelson Elementary School, Rockford, IL [*Library symbol*] [*Library of Congress*] (LCLS)
RoNL	Rockford Northern Illinois Library System, Rockford, IL [*Library symbol Library of Congress*] (LCLS)
RoNmE	New Milford Elementary School, Rockford, IL [*Library symbol*] [*Library of Congress*] (LCLS)
IronMnt........	Iron Mountain, Inc. [*Associated Press*] (SAG)
RONS	Iron and Total Iron Binding Capacity [*Hematology*] (DAVI)
Irons Pol Law...	Irons on Police Law [*A publication*] (DLA)
Irons Pub H...	Irons on Public Houses [*A publication*] (DLA)
Roo	Roodhouse Public Library, Roodhouse, IL [*Library symbol Library of Congress*] (LCLS)
IROP	Imagery Requirements Objectives Plan (MCD)
IROP	Infrared Optical Intelligence (MCD)
IROPG	Inter-Range Operations Planning Group [*White Sands Missile Range*]
IRoPpE	Page Park Center Elementary School, Rockford, IL [*Library symbol*] [*Library of Congress*] (LCLS)
IROQ	Iroquois Bancorp [*NASDAQ symbol*] (TTSB)
IROQ	Iroquois Bancorp, Inc. [*NASDAQ symbol*] (SAG)
Iroquoi	Iroquois Bancorp, Inc. [*Associated Press*] (SAG)
IroquoisB	Iroquios Bancorp [*Associated Press*] (SAG)
IROR	Improved Range-Only RADAR (MCD)
IROR	Inspection, Repair, Overhaul, and Rebuild
IROR	Interest Rate of Return [*Finance*]
IROR	Internal Rate of Return [*Telecommunications*] (TEL)
IRoR	Rockford Newspapers, Inc., Rockford, IL [*Library symbol Library of Congress*] (LCLS)
IRoRC	Teacher Resource Center, Rockford, IL [*Library symbol*] [*Library of Congress*] (LCLS)
IRoRgE	Rolling Green Elementary School, Rockford, IL [*Library symbol*] [*Library of Congress*] (LCLS)
IRoRrE	Rock River Elementary School, Rockford, IL [*Library symbol*] [*Library of Congress*] (LCLS)
IRoRvE	Riverdahl Elementary School, Rockford, IL [*Library symbol*] [*Library of Congress*] (LCLS)
IROS	Improved Reliability Operational System (MCD)
IROS	Increase Reliability of Operational Systems (AFM)
IROS	Infrared Operational Satellite (NOAA)
IROS	Instant Response Ordering System [*Teleordering system*] [*Information service or system*] (IID)
IROSA	Ipsilateral Routing of Signal
IRoSA	Sundstrand Aviation, Engineering Library, Rockford, IL [*Library symbol Library of Congress*] (LCLS)
IROSB	Inactive Reserve Officer Status Branch [*BUPERS*]
IRoScE	Spring Creek Elementary School, Rockford, IL [*Library symbol*] [*Library of Congress*] (LCLS)
IRoSH	Swedish-American Hospital, Rockford, IL [*Library symbol Library of Congress*] (LCLS)
IRoStA	Saint Anthony Hospital, Rockford, IL [*Library symbol Library of Congress*] (LCLS)
IRoStE	Stiles Elementary School, Rockford, II [*Library symbol*] [*Library of Congress*] (LCLS)
IRoStT	Saint Thomas High School, Rockford, IL [*Library symbol Library of Congress*] (LCLS)
IRoSuE	Summerdale Elementary School, Rockford, IL [*Library symbol*] [*Library of Congress*] (LCLS)
IRoSvE	Sky View Center Elementary School, Rockford, IL [*Library symbol*] [*Library of Congress*] (LCLS)
IROT	Infrared on Target
IRoTE	Thompson Elementary School, Rockford, IL [*Library symbol*] [*Library of Congress*] (LCLS)
IR Oudh	Indian Rulings, Oudh Series [*A publication*] (DLA)
IRoVC	Rockford Area Vocational Center, Rockford, IL [*Library symbol*] [*Library of Congress*] (LCLS)
IRoVE	Vandercook Elementary School, Rockford, IL [*Library symbol*] [*Library of Congress*] (LCLS)
IRoWaE	Walker Elementary School, Rockford, IL [*Library symbol*] [*Library of Congress*] (LCLS)
IRoWC	Washington Center, Rockford, IL [*Library symbol*] [*Library of Congress*] (LCLS)
IRoWeE	Welsh Elementary School, Rockford, IL [*Library symbol*] [*Library of Congress*] (LCLS)
IRoWH	West High School, Rockford, IL [*Library symbol*] [*Library of Congress*] (LCLS)
IRoWhE	Whitehead Elementary School, Rockford, IL [*Library symbol*] [*Library of Congress*] (LCLS)
IRoWM	Winnebago County Medical Society, Rockford, IL [*Library symbol Library of Congress*] (LCLS)
IRoWMS	Wilson Middle School, Rockford, IL [*Library symbol*] [*Library of Congress*] (LCLS)
IRoWsE	White Swan Elementary School, Rockford, IL [*Library symbol*] [*Library of Congress*] (LCLS)
IRoWvE........	West View Elementary School, Rockford, IL [*Library symbol*] [*Library of Congress*] (LCLS)
IRox	Roxana Public Library, Roxana, IL [*Library symbol Library of Congress*] (LCLS)
IRoxCU	Roxana Community Unit 1, Roxana, IL [*Library symbol Library of Congress*] (LCLS)
IRP	Ice on Runway - Patchy [*Aviation*]
IRP	Immunoglobulin Reference Preparation [*Clinical chemistry*]
IRP	Immunoreactive Peptides [*Biochemistry*]
IRP	Immunoreactive Plasma [*Immunochemistry*] (DMAA)
IRP	Immunoreactive Proinsulin [*Immunochemistry*]
IRP	Improved Replenishment-at-Sea Program (MCD)
IRP	Incus Replacement Prosthesis [*Medicine*] (DMAA)
IRP	Independent Routing Processor [*Telecommunications*] (ACRL)
IRP	Indianapolis Raceway Park [*Auto racing venue*]
IRP	Individualized Reading Program [*Education*]
IRP	Individual Responsibility Program [*Medicine*] (DHSM)
IRP	Industrial Readiness Planning [*Military*] (NG)
IRP	Industry Recognition Program (MCD)
IRP	Inertial Reference Package (MCD)
IRP	Information Reporting Program [*IRS*] (EGAO)
IRP	Information Resources Press [*Washington, DC*]
IRP	Information Return Program [*IRS*]
IRP	Information Returns Processing [*Computer science*]
IRP	Infrared Preamplifier

IRP..............	Infrared Projector (MCD)
IRP..............	Infrared Radiation Profile
IRP..............	Infrared Responsive Phosphor
IRP..............	Initial Receiving Point
IRP..............	Installation Restoration Program [Army] (RDA)
IRP..............	Institute for Research on Poverty [University of Wisconsin - Madison] [Research center] (RCD)
IRP..............	Institute for Retired Professionals (EA)
IRP..............	Institutional Revolutionary Party [Mexico Political party]
IRP..............	Instructional Resource Package (ACII)
IRP..............	Insulin-Releasing Polypeptide [Medicine] (DMAA)
IRP..............	Intelligence Report Plan (NATG)
IRP..............	Interference Reporting Point (NATG)
IRP..............	Intermediate Rated Power (MCD)
IRP..............	Intermediate Related Power
IRP..............	Intermediate Rotating Plug (NRCH)
IRP..............	Internal Reflection Plate
IRP..............	International Petroleum Corp. [Vancouver Stock Exchange symbol Toronto Stock Exchange symbol]
IRP..............	International Reference Preparation [World Health Organization]
IRP..............	International Rostrum of Young Performers [See also TIJE] (EAIO)
IRP..............	International Routing Plan [Telecommunications] (TEL)
IRP..............	Interrupt Processor (IAA)
IRP..............	Interstitial Radiation Pneumonitis [Medicine] (DMAA)
IRP..............	Inventory and Requirements Planning (MHDI)
IRP..............	Iron Regulatory Protein [Biochemistry]
IRP..............	Isiro [Zaire] [Airport symbol] (OAG)
IRP..............	Islahat Refah Partisi [Reformation and Welfare Party] [Turkish Cypriot] (PPE)
IRP..............	Islamic Renaissance Party [Commonwealth of Independent States] (ECON)
IRP..............	Islamic Republican Party [Iran] [Political party] (PPW)
IRP..............	Payam (Air Center Service) [Iran] [FAA designator] (FAAC)
IRp..............	Richton Park Library District, Richton Park, IL [Library symbol Library of Congress] (LCLS)
IRPA..........	Institut de Recherche sur le Profil d'Apprentissage [Canada]
IRPA..........	International Radiation Protection Association [Vienna, Austria] (EAIO)
IR Pat........	Indian Rulings, Patna Series [A publication] (DLA)
IRPC..........	Indian Rulings, Privy Council [1929-47] [A publication] (DLA)
IRPC..........	Indirect Reading Pocket Chamber
IRPC..........	Industrial Relations Policy Committee [General Council of British Shipping] (DS)
IRPD..........	Industrial Relations and Personnel Development [A publication]
IR-PERS-REC...	Industrial Relations Personnel Record [Military] (DNAB)
IR Pesh......	Indian Rulings, Peshawar Series [1933-47] [A publication] (DLA)
IR Peshawar...	Indian Rulings, Peshawar Series [1933-47] [A publication] (DLA)
Ir Pet SJ.....	Irish Petty Sessions Journal [A publication] (DLA)
IRPF..........	Independent Racing Pigeon Federation [Australia]
IRPFC........	International Ray Price Fan Club (EA)
IRPG..........	Iranian Research and Publication Group
IRPI..........	Individual Rod Position Indicator [Nuclear energy] (NRCH)
IRPIA........	Intelligence Information Report Photo Index [Military] (MCD)
IRPL..........	Index to Religious Periodical Literature [Database]
IRPL..........	Interim Repair Parts List
IRPL..........	Interservice Radio Propagation Laboratory (MCD)
IRPM..........	Individual Risk Premium Modification [Insurance]
IRPM..........	Infrared Physical Measurement
IRPMR........	Information Resources Procurement and Management Review (AAGC)
IRPOD........	Individual Repair Parts Ordering Data [Program] [DoD]
IRPOS........	Interdisciplinary Research Relevant to Problems of Our Society [Later, RANN] [National Science Foundation]
IRPP..........	Industrial Readiness Planning Program
IRPP..........	Infrared Pointer Package
IRPP..........	Institute for Research on Public Policy [Canada]
IRPP..........	International Petroleum Corp. [NASDAQ symbol] (SAG)
IRPPF........	Intl Petroleum [NASDAQ symbol] (TTSB)
IR Pr C......	Indian Rulings, Privy Council [1929-47] [A publication] (DLA)
IRPRI........	International Relations and Peace Research Institute [Guatemala] (EAIO)
IRPRL........	Initial Repair Parts Requirements List (MCD)
IRPS..........	Individual Resource Protection Sensor
IRPS..........	Institute for Research in Public Safety [Indiana University] [Research center] (RCD)
IRPS..........	Institute of Reconstructive Plastic Surgery [New York University] [Research center] (RCD)
IRPS..........	International Review of Publications in Sociology [Sociological Abstracts, Inc.] [Information service or system] (CRD)
IRPT..........	Inland Rivers Ports and Terminals (EA)
IRPTC........	International Register of Potentially Toxic Chemicals [United Nations Environment Program] [Geneva, Switzerland]
IRQ..........	Faraz Qeshm Airlines [Iran] [FAA designator] (FAAC)
IRQ..........	Interpersonal Relations Questionnaire [Personality development test] [Psychology]
IRQ..........	Interrupt Request [Computer science]
IRQ..........	Interrupt Request Line [Computer science]
IRQ..........	Intimate Relationship Questionnaire
IRQ..........	Iraq [ANSI three-letter standard code] (CNC)
IRQ..........	Rose-Hulman Institute of Technology Library, Terre Haute, IN [OCLC symbol] (OCLC)
IRQC..........	Infrared Quantum Counter
IRQR..........	Information Requirement [Military]
IRR..........	Immediate Ready Reserve [Army]
IRR..........	Improved Rearming Rates [Military] (NG)

IRR..........	Incidence Rate Ratio [Mathematics]
IRR..........	Indian Reservation Roads System [Bureau of Indian Affairs]
IRR..........	Indian River Resources, Inc. [Vancouver Stock Exchange symbol]
IRR..........	Individual Ready Reserve [Army]
IRR..........	Individual Retirement Record [Air Force] (AFM)
IRR..........	Industrial Retaining Ring Co.
IRR..........	Information Reduction Research [Information service or system] (IID)
IRR..........	Information Resource Repository
IRR..........	Infrared Radiometer
IRR..........	Infrared Receiver
IRR..........	Initial Rate of Return [Finance] (MCD)
IRR..........	Initial Reliability Review
IRR..........	Inspection Rejection Report [NASA] (KSC)
IRR..........	Installation and Removal Record [NASA] (KSC)
IRR..........	Institute for Reactor Research [Switzerland]
IRR..........	Institute for Rehabilitation and Research [Baylor College of Medicine] [Research center] (RCD)
IRR..........	Institute for Risk Research [University of Waterloo] [Canada Research center] (RCD)
IRR..........	Institute of Race Relations [British] (EAIO)
IRR..........	Institute of Resource Recovery (GNE)
IRR..........	Institute of Rubber Research (MCD)
IRR..........	Instrumentation Revision Record (IAA)
IRR..........	Integral Rocket Ramjet [Navy]
IRR..........	Integrated Radio Room (MCD)
IRR..........	Intelligence RADAR Reporting
IRR..........	Interface Requirements Review (SSD)
IRR..........	Interim Release Request (MCD)
IRR..........	Internal Rate of Return [Finance]
IRR..........	Internal Revenue Looseleaf Regulations System
IRR..........	International Rate of Return [Finance]
IRR..........	International Revenue Record [New York City] [A publication] (DLA)
IRR..........	Interrupt Return Register
IRR..........	Intrarenal Reflux [Medicine] (AAMN)
Ir R..........	Irish Law Reports [A publication] (DLA)
IRR..........	Irish Royal Rifles [Military British] (ROG)
IRR..........	Iron Range Research Center, Chisholm, MN [OCLC symbol] (OCLC)
irr..........	Irradiation
IRR..........	Irredeemable [Banking]
IRR..........	Irregular (WGA)
irr..........	Irrigate [or Irrigated] (DAVI)
IRR..........	Irrigation [Type of water project]
IRR..........	Irritant
IRR..........	Irritation (DAVI)
IRR..........	Israeli Research Reactor
IRR..........	Tara Air Line [Iran] [FAA designator] (FAAC)
IRRA..........	Industrial Relations Reform Act [Australia]
IRRA..........	Industrial Relations Research Association (EA)
IRRA..........	International Routing and Reporting Activity (DNAB)
IRRAD..........	Infrared Range and Detection
IRRADN.......	Irradiation
IR Ran.......	Indian Rulings, Rangoon Series [A publication] (DLA)
IRR & L.......	Irish Reports, Registry and Land Cases [A publication] (DLA)
IRRAPST.....	Individual Ready Reserve - Alternative Preassignment System Test (MCD)
IRRAS..........	Infrared Reflection Absorption Spectroscopy [Also, IRAS, RAIR, RAIRS, RAIS]
IRRB..........	International Rubber Research Board
IRRC..........	International Relief and Rescue Committee [Post-World War II]
IRRC..........	International Rubber Regulation Committee [World War II]
IRRC..........	Investor Responsibility Research Center (EA)
Ir R Ch......	Irish Chancery Reports [A publication] (DLA)
Ir R CL......	Irish Reports, Common Law Series [A publication] (DLA)
IRRCS..........	Institute for Regional, Rural, and Community Studies [Western Illinois University] [Research center] (RCD)
IRRD..........	Institute for Research of Rheumatic Diseases [Defunct] (EA)
IRRD..........	International Raod Research Documentation (NITA)
IRRDB..........	International Rubber Research and Development Board [Brickendonbury, Hertford, England] (EAIO)
IRRED..........	Irredeemable (ROG)
IRREG..........	Irregular (KSC)
irreg..........	Irregular (WDMC)
Irreg..........	Irregular Light [Navigation signal]
irreg..........	Irregularly (WDMC)
IR Rep.......	Reports of Inland Revenue Commissioners [A publication] (DLA)
Ir Rep Ch....	Irish Chancery Reports [A publication] (DLA)
Ir Rep CL....	Irish Reports, Common Law Series [A publication] (DLA)
Ir Rep Eq....	Irish Reports, Equity Series [A publication] (DLA)
Ir Rep NS....	Irish Common Law Reports, New Series [A publication] (DLA)
Ir Rep VR....	Irish Reports, Verbatim Reprint [A publication] (DLA)
Ir R Eq.......	Irish Reports, Equity Series [A publication] (DLA)
IRREV..........	Irrevocable
IRRF..........	Institut pour la Repression des Ravageurs Forestiers [Forest Pest Management Institute] [Canada]
IRRG..........	Irrigation
IRRGTN.......	Irrigation
IRRI..........	Industrial Relations Research Institute [University of Wisconsin - Madison] [Research center] (RCD)
IRRI..........	Interagency Rehabilitation Research Information System [National Institute on Disability and Rehabilitation Research] [Washington, DC Information service or system] (IID)
IRRI..........	International Rice Research Institute [Philippines]
IRRICAB.......	Current Annotated Bibliography of Irrigation [Bet Dagan, Israel] [A publication]
IRRIG..........	Irrigate

IRRIS	International Rehabilitation Research Information System [*National Institute of Handicapped Research*] [*Database*]
IRRL	Information Retrieval Research Laboratory [*University of Illinois*] [*Urbana*] [*Information service or system*] (IID)
IRRM	Information Requested in Above Referenced Message [*Army*] (AABC)
IRRMA	Institut Romand de Recherche Numerique en Physique des Materiaux
IRRMP	Infrared RADAR Measurement Program
IRRN	Illinois Research and Reference Center Libraries
Irr N	Tasmanian Irregular Notes [*A publication*]
IRR Newsl ...	Individual Rights and Responsibilities Newsletter [*A publication*] (DLA)
IRRP	Icefield Ranges Research Project
IRRP	Improved Rearming Rate Program [*Military*] (NVT)
IRRPOS........	Interdisciplinary Research Relevant to Problems of Our Society [*Later, RANN*] [*National Science Foundation*]
IRRR	Industrial Relations Review and Report [*A publication*]
IRRR	Interest Rate Reduction Refinancing [*Veterans Administration*]
Ir R Reg & L...	Irish Reports, Registry and Land Cases [*A publication*] (DLA)
Ir R Reg App...	Irish Reports, Registration Appeals [*1868-76*] [*A publication*] (DLA)
IRRS	Individual Ready Reserve System [*Military*]
IRRS	Infrared Reconnaissance Set
IRRS	Infrared Reconnaissance System (MCD)
IRRS	Infrared Reflection Spectroscopy
IRRS	Irish Railway Record Society
IRRSAM	Integral Rocket Ramjet Surface-to-Air Missile (MCD)
IRRSSM	Integral Rocket Ramjet Surface-to-Surface Missile (MCD)
IRRT	International Relations Round Table [*American Library Association*]
IRRTS	Infrared Resolution Target System (MCD)
IRRTTM	Integral Rocket Ramjet Torpedo Tube Missile (MCD)
IRRV	Institute of Revenues, Rating, and Valuation [*British*]
IRS	Identification and Reference Sheets (MCD)
IRS	Immunoreactive Secretin [*Endocrinology*]
IRS	Immunoreactive Somatostatin [*Endocrinology*]
IRS	Improved RADAR Simulation (DWSG)
IRS	Impurity Removal System
IRS	Inactive Reserve Section [*Military*]
IRS	Inboard Rotating Shield
IRS	Incident Reporting System [*IAEA*] (NUCP)
IRS	Incremental Range Summary
IRS	Independent Rear Suspension [*Automotive engineering*]
IRS	Independent Research Service [*Defunct*]
IRS	Indian Remote-Sensing Satellite
IRS	Indirect Representative Supplement [*British*]
IRS	Induction and Recruiting Station [*Marine Corps*]
IRS	Industrial Relations Section [*Princeton University*] [*Research center*] (RCD)
IRS	Industrial Relations Services [*Eclipse Group Ltd.*] [*British*] (ECON)
IRS	Ineligible Reserve Section
IRS	Inertial Reference Sensor
IRS	Inertial Reference System [*Aviation*]
IRS	Inertial Retical System
IRS	Infant Rating Scale [*Child development test*]
IRS	Infinitely Rigid System [*Engineering*] (OA)
IRS	Inflatable Restraint System [*Automotive engineering*]
IRS	Informal Routing Slip
IRS	Information Recovery [*or Retrieval*] System [*or Subsystem*]
IRS	Information Research Services [*Information service or system*] (IID)
IRS	Information Resources Specialists [*Information service or system*] (IID)
IRS	Information Retrieval Service [*Memphis State University Libraries*] (OLDSS)
IRS	Information Retrieval Service [*European Space Agency*] (IID)
IRS	Information Retrieval System (OICC)
IRS	Infrared RADAR Suppressor (MCD)
IRS	Infrared Reconnaissance Set (MCD)
IRS	Infrared Reflective Spectra
IRS	Infrared Soldering
IRS	Infrared Source
IRS	Infrared Spectrometer [*or Spectroscopy*]
IRS	Infrared Star (BARN)
IRS	Inorganic Resin System [*Fire-resistant cement*]
IRS	Input Read Submodule
IRS	Inquiry and Reporting System
IRS	Inspection Record Sheet
IRS	Inspector of Radio Services [*Military*] (IAA)
IRS	Installation Readiness System [*Army*]
IRS	Institute of Religious Studies [*Australia*]
IRS	Instructional Review System
IRS	Instrumentation RADAR Set
IRS	Instrument Retrieval System [*Containers*] [*Medicine*] (DAVI)
IRS	Insulin Receptor Species [*Medicine*] (DMAA)
IRS	Insulin Receptor Substrate [*Biochemistry*]
IRS	Intact Rock Strength [*Mining*]
IRS	Integrated Rate System
IRS	Integrated Record System (KSC)
IRS	Integrated Review Schedule [*Department of Health and Human Services*] (GFGA)
IRS	Integration Review Section [*Social Security Administration*]
IRS	Intelligence Research Specialist [*Military*] (MCD)
IRS	Interchange Record Separator [*Computer science*] (BUR)
IRS	Interface Requirements Document [*DoD*]
IRS	Interface Requirements Specification (MCD)
IRS	Interferon Response Sequence [*Genetics*]
IRS	Intergroup Rhabdomyosarcoma Study [*Oncology*]
IRS	Intermediate Reference Structure
IRS	Internal Reflection Spectroscopy
IRS	Internal Revenue Service [*Department of the Treasury*] [*Washington, DC*]
IRS	Internal Revenue Service Library, Washington, DC [*OCLC symbol*] (OCLC)
IRS	International Radio Silence
IRS	International Records Syndicate, Inc.
IRS	International Referral System [*United Nations Environment Programme*]
IRS	International Repeater Station [*Telecommunications*] (TEL)
IRS	International Rhinologic Society (EA)
IRS	International Rorschach Society [*Strasbourg, France*] (EA)
IRS	Internetwork Routing Service [*Telecommunications*] (OSI)
IRS	Interpersonal Relationship Scale [*EDAC*]
IRS	Interspersed Repetitive Sequence [*Genetics*]
IRS	Inverse Raman Scattering [*Spectroscopy*]
IRS	Iodine Removal System [*Nuclear energy*] (NRCH)
IRS	Ionospheric Radio Signal
IRS	Irish Standard (IAA)
IRS	IRSA Inversiones y Rep GDS [*NYSE symbol*] (TTSB)
IRS	IRSA Inversions y Representaciones SA [*NYSE symbol*] (SAG)
IRS	Isoleucyl-tRNA Synthetase [*An enzyme*]
IRS	Isotope Radiography System
IRS	Isotope Removal Service (IEEE)
IRS	Item Reduction Studies (MSA)
IRS	Sturgis, MI [*Location identifier FAA*] (FAAL)
IRS	Transavia Ltd. [*Romania*] [*FAA designator*] (FAAC)
IRSA	Idiopathic Refractory Sideroblastic Anemia [*Medicine*] (MAE)
IRSA	Improved Radiator Standards Association (EA)
IRSA	Independent Road Service Association (EA)
IRSA	International Racquet Sports Association [*Later, IRSAAQC*] (EA)
IRSA	International Rett Syndrome Association (EA)
IRSA	International Rural Sociology Association (EA)
IRSA	Iodinated Rat Serum Albumin (DMAA)
IRSA	Irish Research Scientists Association
IRSA	IRSA Inversiones y Representaciones SA [*Associated Press*] (SAG)
IRSAAQC....	IRSA [*International Racquet Sports Association*], the Association of Quality Clubs (EA)
IRSAC	Institut pour la Recherche Scientifique en Afrique Centrale [*Brussels*]
IRSB	Institute for Research in Social Behavior [*Research center*] (RCD)
IRSC	Institut de Recherches Scientifiques au Congo
IRSC	Internal Revenue Service Centers
IRSC	Inter-Regional Subject Coverage Scheme [*Libraries cooperative scheme*] [*British*] (NITA)
IRSCAN.......	Infrared Scanner
IRSCC	International Relief Service of Caritas Catholica [*Belgium*] (EAIO)
IRSCL	International Research Society for Children's Literature [*Cadaujac, France*] (EA)
IRSCOT.......	Infrared Structural Correlation Tables [*A publication*]
IRSD	Information and Regulatory Systems Division [*Environmental Protection Agency*] (GFGA)
IRSE	Infrared Systems Engineering
IRSE	Institution of Railway Signal Engineers [*British*]
IRSF	Inland Revenue Staff Federation [*A union*] [*British*] (DCTA)
IRSF	International Roller Skating Federation (EA)
IRSFC	International Rayon and Synthetic Fibres Committee [*See also CIRFS*] [*Paris, France*] (EAIO)
IRSG	Information Retrieval Specialist Group [*British Computer Society*] (NITA)
IRSG	Internationale Richard Strauss Gesellschaft [*An association*] (EAIO)
IRSG	International Rubber Study Group [*London, England*] (EAIO)
IRSG	Internet Research Steering Group [*Computer science*] (ACRL)
IRSGHL.......	Infrared Systems and Guidance Heads Laboratory
IRSH	Infrared Spectral Hygrometer (PDAA)
IRSI	Industrial Research and Service Institute
IRSI	International Remote Sensing Institute (MCD)
IR Sind	Indian Rulings, Sind Series [*A publication*] (DLA)
IRSIO	International Rationalization, Standardization, and Interoperability Office (MCD)
IRSLL	Image Recording System, Low Light
IRSM	Immunoreactive Somatomedin [*Endocrinology*]
IRSM	Infrared Systems Manufacturing
IRSN	Irvine Sensors [*NASDAQ symbol*] (TTSB)
IRSN	Irvine Sensors Corp. [*NASDAQ symbol*] (NQ)
IRSO	Infrared Solder Oven
IRSO	Institute of Road Safety Officers [*British*]
IRSO	International Rope Skipping Organization
IRSP	Infrared Spectrometer [*or Spectroscopy*]
IRSP	Irish Republican Socialist Party [*Pairti Poblachtach Soisialach na h-Eireann*] (PPW)
IRSPECT	Infrared Spectrometer [*or Spectroscopy*] (MCD)
IRSR	Immediate Replacement Support Requirement (MCD)
IRSS	Inertial Reference Stabilization System
IRSS	Infrared Search Set
IRSS	Infrared Search System [*Database*] [*Environmental Protection Agency Information service or system*] (CRD)
IRSS	Infrared Search System [*Institut za Nuklearne Nauke Boris Kidric*] [*Former Yugoslavia*] [*Information service or system*] (CRD)
IRSS	Infrared Sensor System
IRSS	Infrared Smoke Simulator (MCD)
IRSS	Infrared Surveillance Subsystem
IRSS	Institute for Religious and Social Studies (EA)

IRSS .... Institute for Research in Social Science [*University of North Carolina at Chapel Hill*] [*Research center*] (RCD)
IRSS .... Institute for Resource and Security Studies (EA)
IRSS .... Instrumentation and Range Safety System [*NASA*] (KSC)
IRSS .... Integrated Range Safety System (IAA)
IRSSO .... Infrared Search Set Operator
IRST .... Infrared Search and Track
Ir Stat .... Irish Statutes [*A publication*] (DLA)
IRSTDS .... Infrared Surveillance and Target Designation System (PDAA)
IRSTS .... Infrared Search and Track System
Ir St Tr .... Irish State Trials (Ridgeway's) [*A publication*] (DLA)
IRSU .... International Radio Scientific Union (DEN)
IRSU .... International Religious Studies Unit [*American Topical Association*] (EA)
IRSU .... ISDN [*Integrated Services Digital Network*] Remote Subscriber Unit [*Telecommunications*]
IRT .... Icing Research Tunnel [*Built at Lewis Research Center in 1944 by the National Advisory Committee for Aeronautics*]
IRT .... Image Rejection Technology [*RADAR detection*]
IRT .... Immunoreactive Trypsin
IRT .... Index Return Character [*Computer science*]
IRT .... Indicating Round Technique [*British*]
IRT .... Individual Reliability Test
IRT .... Industrial Reading Test
IRT .... Infinite-Resolution Trimmer
IRT .... Information Retrieval Technique (AAG)
IRT .... Infrared Radiation Thermometer (NOAA)
IRT .... Infrared Telescope
IRT .... Infrared Temperature
IRT .... Infrared Thermography
IRT .... Infrared Thermometer
IRT .... Infrared Tracker
IRT .... Infrared Tube
IRT .... Initialize Reset Tape
IRT .... Input Revision Typewriter
IRT .... In-Reactor Thimble (IEEE)
IRT .... In Reference To (NVT)
IRT .... In Regard To (MCD)
IRT .... In Reply To (NVT)
IRT .... In Response To (NVT)
IRT .... [*The*] Inscriptions of Roman Tripolitania (BJA)
IRT .... Institute for Radiological Technologists
IRT .... Institute for Rapid Transit [*Later, APTA*] (EA)
IRT .... Institute for Reality Therapy (EA)
IRT .... Institute for Research on Teaching [*East Lansing, MI*] [*Department of Education*] (GRD)
IRT .... Institute of Reprographic Technology
IRT .... Instrument Retrieval Containers [*Medicine*] (DAVI)
IRT .... Integrated Readiness Testing
IRT .... Intelcom Radiation Technology, Inc.
IRT .... Interboro Rapid Transit [*A New York City subway line*]
IRT .... Interim Remote Terminals (MCD)
IRT .... Intermediate-Range Technology
IRT .... Intermediate Rated Thrust [*Military*] (CAAL)
IRT .... Internal Reflection Technique
IRT .... International Research and Technology, Inc.
IRT .... Interot Air Service [*Germany ICAO designator*] (FAAC)
IRT .... Interresponse Time [*Psychometrics*]
IRT .... Interrogator-Responder-Transducer
IRT .... Interrupted Ring Tone [*Telecommunications*] (TEL)
IRT .... Interstitial Radiotherapy (DMAA)
IRT .... Inverse Reflex Tetrode [*Physics*]
IRT .... IRT Properities [*Formerly, Investors Realty Trust*] [*Associated Press*] (SAG)
IRT .... IRT Property [*NYSE symbol*] (TTSB)
IRT .... IRT Property Co. [*Formerly, Investors Realty Trust*] [*NYSE symbol*] (SPSG)
IRT .... Isometric Relaxation Time [*Medicine*] (DAVI)
IRT .... Isotope Ratio Tracer (PDAA)
IRT .... Isovolumic Relaxation Time [*Cardiology*]
IRT .... Item Response Theory (GFGA)
IRT .... Richmond Community Schools, Richmond, IN [*OCLC symbol*] (OCLC)
IRTA .... Independent Retail Tobacconists Association of America [*Defunct*] (EA)
IRTA .... International Reciprocal Trade Association (EA)
IRTA .... Intramural Research Training Award [*National Institutes of Health*]
IRTAC .... International Round Table for the Advancement of Counseling [*British*]
IRTAFS .... International Ready-to-Assemble Furniture Show (ITD)
IRTC .... Infantry Replacement Training Center
IRTCES .... International Research and Training Center on Erosion and Sedimentation [*China*] (EAIO)
IRTCG .... Installation Restoration Technology Coordinating Group [*Army*] (RDA)
IRTCM .... Integrated Real-Time Contamination Monitor [*Module*]
IRTD .... Infantry Reinforcement Training Depot [*British military*] (DMA)
IRTD .... Infrared Target Detector
IrTD .... Iranian Documentation Centre, Tehran, Iran [*Library symbol Library of Congress*] (LCLS)
IRTE .... Institut de Radio-Telediffusion pour Enfants [*Children's Broadcast Institute*] [*Canada*]
IRTE .... Institute of Road Transport Engineers (EAIO)
Ir Term Rep... Irish Term Reports, by Ridgeway, Lapp, and Schoales [*A publication*] (DLA)
IRTF .... Industry Restructuring Task Force

IRTF .... Infrared Telescope Facility
IRTF .... Intermediate-Range Task Force
IRTF .... International Radio and Television Foundation, Inc. [*International Radio and Television Society*] (NTCM)
IRTF .... Internet Research Task Force
IRTF .... Inter-Religious Task Force on Central America [*Defunct*] (EA)
IRTGSM .... Infrared Terminally-Guided Submunition
IRTIS .... Inter-Regional Training Information System [*International Labor Organization*] [*United Nations*] (DUND)
IRTM .... Infrared Thermal Mapper [*NASA*]
IRTP .... Initial Recruiting and Training Plan [*Military*]
IRTP .... Integrated Reliability Test Program
Ir TR .... Irish Term Reports, by Ridgeway, Lapp, and Schoales [*A publication*] (DLA)
IRTRAN .... Infrared Transmitting
IRTRN .... Infrared Transmission
IRTS .... Infrared Target Seeker (MSA)
IRTS .... Infrared Temperature Sounder (PDAA)
IRTS .... Interim Recovery Technical Specification (IEEE)
IRTS .... International Radio and Television Society (EA)
IRTTD .... Infrared Transmission through the Diffusion (PDAA)
IRTU .... Integrating Regulatory Transcription Units [*Genetics*]
IRTU .... Intelligent Remote Terminal Unit
IRTU .... International Railway Temperance Union
IRTV .... Information Retrieval Television [*Tele-education project*] (NITA)
IRTWG .... Interrange Telemetry Working Group
IRTWS .... Infrared Tail Warning Set (MCD)
IRU .... Immediate Response Unit [*Police*] [*British*] (DI)
IRU .... Indefeasible Right of User [*Telecommunications*] (TEL)
IRU .... Industrial Rehabilitation Units [*British*]
IRU .... Inertial Reference Unit
IRU .... Information Retrieval Unit (NITA)
IRU .... Interferon Reference Unit
IRU .... Intergenic Repeat Unit [*Genetics*]
IRU .... Internationale Raiffeisen-Union [*International Raiffeisen Union*] (EAIO)
IRU .... International Radium Unit
IRU .... International Raiffeisen Union (EA)
IRU .... International Relief Union
IRU .... International Road Transport Union [*Geneva, Switzerland*] (EAIO)
IRU .... International Romani Union (EA)
IRU .... Irvine Research Unit [*University of California, Irvine*]
IRU .... IVA [*Intravehicular Activity*] Replacement Unit (SSD)
IRU .... New Mexico State University, Las Cruces, NM [*OCLC symbol*] (OCLC)
IRUC .... Information and Research Utilization Center in Physical Education and Recreationfor the Handicapped [*American Association for Health, Physical Education, and Recreation*]
IRUC .... Intermediate Resource Usage Condition (MHDI)
IRUS .... Infantry Rifle Unit Study [*Army*]
IRut .... Rutland Community Library, Rutland, IL [*Library symbol Library of Congress*] (LCLS)
IR/UV-LS...... Infrared/Ultraviolet Line Scanner (PDAA)
IRV .... Improved Recovery Vehicle [*Army*] (RDA)
IRV .... Inglewood [*Forest*] Rifle Volunteers [*British military*] (DMA)
IRV .... Inspiratory Reserve Volume [*Physiology*]
IRV .... Internationale Rat fuer Vogelschutz [*International Council for Bird Preservation*]
IRV .... International Reference Version (OSI)
IRV .... International Rex Ventures, Inc. [*Vancouver Stock Exchange symbol*]
IRV .... Inter-Range Vector [*NASA*] (KSC)
IRV .... Interrupt Request Vector
IRV .... Inversed Ratio of Ventilation
Irv .... Irvine's Scotch Justiciary Reports [*1851-68*] [*A publication*] (DLA)
IRV .... Isotope Reentry Vehicle [*NASA*] (NASA)
IRV .... Item Rating Value (DNAB)
IRVAT .... Infrared Video Automatic Tracking (PDAA)
IRVAT .... Infrared Video-Auto Tracker (DWSG)
IRVB .... India-Rubber Vulcanized, Braided [*Wire insulation*] (IAA)
IRVC .... Indian Remount and Veterinary Corps [*British military*] (DMA)
Irv Civ Law... Irving's Civil Law [*A publication*] (DLA)
IRVH .... Integrated Reactor Vessel Head [*Nuclear energy*] (NRCH)
Irvine .... Irvine Sensors Corp. [*Associated Press*] (SAG)
IrvineApt..... Irvine Apartment Communities [*Associated Press*] (SAG)
Irvine Just Cas... Irvine's Justiciary Cases [*England*] [*A publication*] (DLA)
Irving Civ Law... Irving's Civil Law [*A publication*] (DLA)
Irv Just .... Irvine's Justiciary Cases [*England*] [*A publication*] (DLA)
IRVR .... Instrumented Runway Visual Range [*Aviation*] (DA)
IRVSS .... Infrared Vertical Sounding System [*Oceanography*] (MSC)
IRVW .... Integrated Research Volkswagen [*Automotive engineering*]
IRW .... Index of Relative Worth (MCD)
IRW .... Indirect Reference Word (BUR)
IRW .... Infrared Window
IRW .... Institute for Rural Water (EA)
IRW .... International Rehabilitation Week [*Trade show*]
IRW .... International Rocket Week
IRW .... Inverted Rib Waveguide (NITA)
IRWA .... International Right of Way Association (EA)
IRWA .... International Rodeo Writers Association [*Later, RMA*] (EA)
IRWC .... International Registry of World Citizens
Ir WCC .... Irish Workmen's Compensation Cases [*A publication*] (DLA)
IRWEP .... International Register for the White Eared Pheasant (EAIO)
IRWG .... Interface Requirements Working Group (SSD)
IrwinFin ...... Irwin Financial Corp. [*Associated Press*] (SAG)
Irwin's Code... Clark, Cobb, and Irwin's Code [*Georgia*] [*A publication*] (DLA)

r WLR	Irish Weekly Law Reports [*1895-1902*] [*A publication*] (DLA)
RWN	Irwin Financial Corp. [*NASDAQ symbol*] (SAG)
rwnFn	Irwin Financial Corp. [*Associated Press*] (SAG)
RWR	Infrared Warning Receiver [*Aviation*] (MCD)
RX	Interactive Resource Executive [*NCR Corp.*]
RY	Iron Bay Trust [*Toronto Stock Exchange symbol*]
RZ	Inner Radiation Zone
RZ	International Reference Zero [*Level for pure-tone audiometers*]
S	Eagle Air [*ICAO designator*] (AD)
S	Ibbi-Sin (BJA)
S	Iceland [*ANSI two-letter standard code*] (CNC)
S	Ice Screamers (EA)
S	Ideological Survey [*Psychology*]
S	IDS Aircraft Ltd. [*British ICAO designator*] (ICDA)
S	Ignition and Separation (IAA)
S	Image Stabilization [*Technology from Canon*]
S	Image Stabilizer [*Canon's technology for binoculars*]
S	Imaging Spectrometer (SSD)
S	Immortalist Society (EA)
S	Immune Serum [*Also, ImS*]
S	Immunological Similarity
S	Immunosuppressive [*Immunochemistry*]
S	Impact Switch (SAA)
S	Improved Suspension (MCD)
S	Incentive Spirometer [*or Spirometry*] [*Medicine*] (DMAA)
S	Including Sheeting
S	Incoherent Scatter
S	Income Statement [*Business term*]
S	Incomplete Sequence (MSA)
S	Independent School (BARN)
S	Independent Sector (EA)
S	Independent Shoemen of America [*Defunct*] (EA)
S	Independent Spherical Aluminum Tank [*on a ship*] (DS)
S	Indexed Sequential [*Computer science*]
S	Indexing in Source
S	Indian Standard (IAA)
S	Indicating Switch (NRCH)
S	Induced Sputum [*Otorhinolaryngology*] (DAVI)
S	Induction Soldering
S	Industrial School [*British*] (ROG)
S	Industrial Service [*Equipment specifications*]
S	Industrial Society (AIE)
S	Industrial Source (GNE)
S	Industrial Specialist
S	Industrial Systems (DS)
S	Inertial Systems (AFIT)
S	[*The*] Infantry School [*Army*] (MCD)
S	Infection Structure [*Plant pathology*]
S	Information Science (IEEE)
S	Information Seekers
S	Information Separation (NITA)
S	Information Separator [*Control character*] [*Computer science*]
S	Information Service
S	Information Services [*Portion of InterNIC General Atomics Corporation*]
S	Information System
S	Information Systems [*Ori, Inc.*] [*Information service or system*] (IID)
S	Infrared Spectrometer [*or Spectroscopy*] (IAA)
S	Infrasonic
S	Ingglish Speling 3soesiaesh3n [*An organization to reform spelling*] [*See also IS3*] (EA)
S	Initial Shortage (AFM)
S	Initiation Supervisor
S	Inner Sheath [*Botany*]
S	Input Secondary [*Electronics*]
S	Input Simulator
S	Insect Screen (AAG)
S	Insertion Sequence [*Genetics*]
S	In Service [*Telecommunications*] (TEL)
S	In Shop (MCD)
/S	Inside [*Automotive engineering*]
S	Inside Sentinel [*Freemasonry*]
S	In Situ [*In Place*] [*Latin*]
S	Inspection Services, Inc. (EA)
S	Installation of Systems (IAA)
S	Installation Start [*Telecommunications*] (TEL)
S	Installation Support (KSC)
S	Institute of Statisticians [*British*]
S	Instruction Section [*Association of College and Research Libraries*] [*American Library Association*]
S	Instruction Sheet
S	Instructions to Ship (AAG)
S	Instructor Squadron
S	Instrument (IAA)
S	Instrumentation Ships Project [*Navy*]
S	Instrumentation Summary (MUGU)
S	Instrumentation System (KSC)
S	Insufficiently Stamped [*Post office*] [*British*] (ROG)
S	Insulating Sleeve
S	Integrally Stiffened
S	Integrated Satellite [*Military spacecraft*]
S	Integrating Support
S	Intelligence in the Sky [*An extraterrestrial intelligence with whom Dr. Andrija Puharich and psychic Uri Geller claim to have communicated*]
IS	Intelligence Service (IAA)
IS	Intelligence Specialist [*Navy*]
IS	Intelligence Support [*Program*] [*Department of State*]
IS	Intelligence Systems [*Military*] (MCD)
IS	Interchangeability and Substitution
IS	Interconnecting Station (MCD)
IS	Intercostal Space [*Medicine*]
IS	Interference Suppressor (IEEE)
IS	Interim Standard (ACRL)
IS	Interim Status (GNE)
IS	Interior Surface
IS	Intermediate School
IS	Intermediate Suppression (MCD)
IS	Intermediate System [*Computer science*] (TNIG)
IS	Internal Security [*Military British*]
IS	Internal Shield [*Electronics*]
IS	Internal Standard [*Chemistry*]
IS	Internal Surface (AAG)
IS	Internationaler Suchdienst [*International Tracing Service*] (EAIO)
IS	Internationale Schutzenunion [*International Shooting Union*] (EAIO)
IS	International Services [*Red Cross*]
IS	International Socialists
IS	International Society of Sculptors, Painters, and Gravers
IS	International Staff (NATG)
IS	International Standard
IS	International Stock [*Business term*]
IS	Intersegmental
IS	Interservice
IS	Intership [*Freight forwarding company*] [*British*]
IS	Interspace
I/S	Interstage
IS	Interstate
IS	Interstate/Johnson Lane [*Formerly, Interstate Securities, Inc.*] [*NYSE symbol*] (SPSG)
IS	Interval Signal
IS	Intraspinal [*Injection*]
IS	Intraventricular Septum [*Cardiology*] (AAMN)
IS	Invalided from Service [*Medicine Navy*]
IS	Inventory Schedule
I/S	Inventory to Sales Ratio [*Business term*]
IS	Investment-Savings [*Economics*]
I-S	Investment-Savings Curve [*Economics*]
IS	Ion Source [*Spectroscopy*]
IS	Irish Society
IS	Irish Standard (IAA)
Is	Isaiah [*Old Testament book*]
Is	Isidore [*Authority cited in pre-1607 legal work*] (DSA)
Is	Islam (BJA)
IS	Island (DA)
IS	Island
Is	Islands [*Maps and charts*]
IS	Isle (EY)
I/S	Isle Of Skye [*Scotland*] (ROG)
IS	Isolated Step
IS	Isolation
IS	Isomeric Shift (OA)
IS	Isotopic Separation [*Subsystem*] (MCD)
is	Israel [*MARC country of publication code Library of Congress*] (LCCP)
Is	Israel [*IYRU nationality code*] (BJA)
IS	ISSN [*International Standard Serial Number*] [*Online database field identifier*]
IS	Issue Code [*Online database field identifier*]
IS	Issue Number [*Dialog*] [*Searchable field*] (NITA)
IS	Istituto Superiore di Sanita [*Italy*] [*Research code symbol*]
IS1	Intelligence Specialist, First Class [*Navy*] (DNAB)
IS2	Intelligence Specialist, Second Class [*Navy*] (DNAB)
IS3	Ingglish Speling 3soesiaesh3n [*English Spelling Association*] (EA)
IS3	Intelligence Specialist, Third Class [*Navy*] (DNAB)
ISA	Ibsen Society of America (EA)
ISA	Idle Speed Actuator [*Automotive engineering*]
ISA	Ignition and Separation Assembly
ISA	Illinois Sheriffs Association (SRA)
ISA	Illinois Sign Association (SRA)
ISA	Illinois Soybean Association (SRA)
ISA	Incest Survivors' Association [*Australia*]
ISA	Independent Scholars of Asia (EA)
ISA	Independent Schools Association [*British*] (AEBS)
ISA	Independent Shoemen of America [*Defunct*]
ISA	Independent Signcrafters of America (EA)
ISA	Independent Stores Association Ltd. [*British*] (BI)
ISA	Index of Spouse Abuse
ISA	Indiana Sheriffs' Association (SRA)
ISA	Individual Savings Account [*Proposed*]
ISA	Inductee Special Assignment
ISA	Industrial Security Acquisition (MCD)
ISA	Industry Standard Architecture [*Computer hardware*] (PCM)
ISA	Inertial Sensor Assembly [*Military*] (CAAL)
ISA	Infantry Sailing Association [*British*]
ISA	Information Systems Architecture [*AT & T*]
ISA	Information Systems Association (EA)
ISA	Innkeepers Society of America [*Defunct*] (EA)
ISA	Inorganic Sampling and Analysis
ISA	Insecta Research [*Vancouver Stock Exchange symbol*]
ISA	Installations and Services Agency [*Army Materiel Command*]

ISA............. Installation Supply Accounting
ISA............. Installation Supply Activity
ISA............. Institute for Scientific Analysis (EA)
ISA............. Institute for Sustainable Agriculture [*Australia*]
ISA............. Institute of Systems Analysis [*Army*]
ISA............. Institut Superieur des Affaires [*Chamber de Commerce et d'Industrie de Paris*] (ECON)
ISA............. Instructional Systems Association (EA)
ISA............. Instruction Set Architecture [*Computer science Army*] (RDA)
ISA............. Instrument Society of America (EA)
ISA............. Instruments, Systems, and Automation (ACII)
ISA............. Instrument Subassembly (IEEE)
ISA............. Insulating Siding Association [*Defunct*] (EA)
ISA............. Insurance Service Associates [*Later, Assurex International*]
ISA............. Integrated Support Area (NVT)
ISA............. Intelligence Support Activity [*Military*]
ISA............. Interactive Survey Analysis (IAA)
ISA............. Intercoastal Steamship Freight Association, New York NY [*STAC*]
ISA............. Interconexion Electrica, Sociedad Anonima
ISA............. Interface Switching Assembly
ISA............. Intergalactic SYSOP [*System Operator*] Alliance (EA)
ISA............. Interim Stowage Assembly
ISA............. Intermediate Specific Activity [*Radioisotope*]
ISA............. Intermediate Supply Activity [*Marine Corps*] (DOMA)
ISA............. Internal Storage Area [*Computer science*] (BYTE)
ISA............. International Safety Academy
ISA............. International Schools Association [*Geneva, Switzerland*] (EA)
ISA............. International Seabed Authority
ISA............. International Security Affairs [*DoD*]
ISA............. International Security Agency
ISA............. International Service Agencies
ISA............. International Shakespeare Association (EA)
ISA............. International Shipmasters' Association of the Great Lakes (EA)
ISA............. International Shuffleboard Association (EA)
ISA............. International Sign Association [*NESA*] [*Absorbed by*] (EA)
ISA............. International Silk Association - USA (EA)
ISA............. International Silo Association (EA)
ISA............. International Skateboard Association (EA)
ISA............. International Skeeter Association
ISA............. International Society of Appraisers [*Hoffman Estates, IL*] (EA)
ISA............. International Society of Arboriculture (EA)
ISA............. International Society of Women Airline Pilots (EA)
ISA............. International Sociological Association [*Research center Spain*] (IRC)
ISA............. International Soling Association [*Bordon, Hampshire, England*] (EAIO)
ISA............. International Songwriters' Association (EAIO)
ISA............. International Standard Atmosphere
ISA............. International Standard Atmosphere [*ICAO*] (FAAC)
ISA............. International Standards Association
ISA............. International Stiltwalkers Association (EA)
ISA............. International Strabismological Association (EAIO)
ISA............. International Studies Association (EA)
ISA............. International Sugar Agreement [*1958*]
ISA............. International Surfing Association [*Swansea, England*] (EAIO)
ISA............. International Swift Association (EA)
ISA............. International Symbol of Access [*Department of Transportation*] (EGAO)
ISA............. Interplant Shipping Authority
ISA............. Interrupt Storage Area
ISA............. Intersecting Storage Accelerator [*In name of atomic reactor, Isabelle*]
ISA............. Interservice Agreement [*DoD*]
ISA............. Interservice Support Agreement [*Military*]
ISA............. Intrinsic Sympathomimetic Activity [*Biochemistry*]
ISA............. Investment Savings Account (ADA)
ISA............. Iodinated Serum Albumin [*Medicine*]
ISA............. Ion Scattering Analysis
ISA............. Iowa Soybean Association (SRA)
ISA............. Irregular Serials and Annuals [*A publication*]
ISA............. Irregular Spiking Activity [*Electrophysiology*]
ISA............. Isabella [*California*] [*Seismograph station code, US Geological Survey*] (SEIS)
Isa .... Isaiah [*Old Testament book*]
ISA............. Isaias [*Old Testament book*] [*Douay version*]
ISA............. Island Airlines, Inc. [*ICAO designator*] (FAAC)
ISA............. Israel Space Agency [*Israel*]
ISA............. Mount Isa [*Australia Airport symbol*] (OAG)
ISA............. Santa Isabel ADS [*NYSE symbol*] (TTSB)
ISA............. Santa Isabel SA [*NYSE symbol*] (SAG)
ISA............. UNRWA [*United Nations Relief and Works Agency*] International Staff Association (EAIO)
ISA₅ .... Internal Surface Area of Lung at Volume of 5 Liters [*Medicine*] (MAE)
ISA + 21 ...... International Social Affiliation of Women Airline Pilots [*Later, ISWAP*] (EA)
ISAA............. Institute of Shops Acts Administration [*British*] (BI)
ISAA............. Insurance Service Association of America [*Later, Assurex International*] (EA)
ISAA............. Intercollegiate Soccer Association of America (EA)
ISAAA .... International Service for the Acquisition of Agri-Biotech Applications
ISAAC .... Information System for Advanced Academic Computing (IID)
ISAAC .... Integrated System for Automated Acquisition and Control
ISAAC .... International Society for Alternative and Augmentative Communication (EA)
ISAAI .... Illinois Society of Allergy, Asthma, and Immunology (SRA)
IS/A AMPE ... Inter-Service Agency Automated Message Processing Exchange

ISAARE .... Information System for Adaptive, Assistive, and Rehabilitation Equipment [*For the handicapped*]
ISAB .... Institute for the Study of Animal Behavior (BARN)
ISABC .... International Society Against Breast Cancer (EAIO)
ISABEL......... ISO [*International Organization for Standardization*] Status Accumulating Binaries Extraordinary Logic [*Using*]
ISABP .... International South Atlantic Buoy Program [*Marine science*] (OSRA)
ISABPS .... Integrated Submarine Automated Broadcasting Processing System (MCD)
ISABR .... International Society for Animal Blood Group Research [*Australia*] (EAIO)
ISABR .... International Society for Animal Genetics [*Australia*] (EAIO)
ISABS .... Integrated Submarine Automated Broadcast Processing System [*Navy*] (CAAL)
ISAC............. Industrial Safety Advisory Council [*British*]
ISAC............. Industrial Security Association of Canada
ISAC............. Industry Sector Advisory Committee [*Established by Trade Reform Act for industry-to-government advice*]
ISAC............. Information Systems Advisory Committee
ISAC............. In Service, Active [*Vessel status*] [*Navy*] (DNAB)
ISAC............. Institute for the Study of American Cultures (EA)
ISAC............. Instrumentation System Assessment Center (MCD)
ISAC............. International Security Affairs Committee
ISAC............. International Society for Analytical Cytology (EAIO)
ISAC............. International Society for Autistic Children [*Defunct*] (EA)
ISAC............. Interuniversity Southeast Asia Committee [*of the Association for Asia*]
ISACC .... Initial Satellite Command and Control Center (MCD)
ISACCC .... Initial Satellite Communications Control Center (MCD)
ISACMETU ... International Secretariat of Arts, Communications Media, and Entertainment TradeUnions (EAIO)
ISACS .... Independent Schools Association of the Central States (AEBS)
ISAD............. Information Science and Automation Division [*Later, LITA*] [*American Library Association*]
ISAD............. Integrate Sample and Dump [*Telecommunications*] (IAA)
ISADC......... Interim Standard Airborne Digital Computer (MCD)
ISADH......... Inappropriate Secretion of Antidiuretic Hormone [*Endocrinology*] (MAE)
ISADPM .... International Society for the Abolition of Data Processing Machines (EA)
ISADS .... Innovative Strategic Aircraft Design Studies (IEEE)
ISAE............. Internacia Scienca Asocio Esperantista [*International Association of Esperanto-Speaking Scientists*] [*Oslo, Norway*] (EA)
ISAE............. International Society for AIDS Education (EA)
Isae .... Isaeus [*Fourth century BC*] [*Classical studies*] (OCD)
ISAeM......... International Society for Aerosols in Medicine [*See also IGAeM*] (EAIO)
ISAF............. Intermediate Super-Abrasion Furnace
ISAF............. Isotopic Source Adjustable Fissometer [*Nuclear energy*] (NRCH)
IsAF............. Israeli Air Force
ISAG............. IGOSS [*Integrated Global Ocean Services System*] Scientific Advisory Group [*Marine science*] (OSRA)
ISAG............. Office of the Auditor General, Springfield, IL [*Library symbol Library of Congress*] (LCLS)
ISAGA .... International Simulation and Gaming Association (EA)
ISAGE .... International Symposium on Antarctic Glaciological Exploration
ISAGEX .... International Satellite Geodesy Experiment
ISAGL .... International Shipmasters Association of the Great Lakes
ISAGUG....... International Software AG Users Group (EA)
ISAI............. Independent Schools Association [*British*]
ISAI............. Independent Schools Association Inc. (AIE)
ISAI............. ISA [*Instruments, Systems and Automation*] International (ACII)
ISal............. Bryan-Bennett Public Library, Salem, IL [*Library symbol Library of Congress*] (LCLS)
ISAL............. Information System Access Lines [*Computer science*]
ISALC......... International Society of Animal License Collectors (EA)
ISalCD .... Selmaville Community Consolidated District 10, Salem, IL [*Library symbol Library of Congress*] (LCLS)
ISALPA .... Incorporated Society of Auctioneers and Landed Property Agents [*British*] (ILCA)
ISAM............. Indexed Sequential Access Method [*Pronounced "i-sam"*] [*Computer science*]
ISAM............. Index Sequential Access Method [*Telecommunications*] (ACRL)
ISAM............. Infant of Substance-Abusing Mother [*Pediatrics*]
ISAM............. Institute for Studies in American Music (EA)
ISAM............. Integrated Switching and Multiplexing [*IBM Corp.*]
ISAM............. International Society for Aerosols in Medicine (EAIO)
ISAM............. Intravenous Streptokinase in Acute Myocardial Infarction [*Cardiology study*]
ISAM............. Israeli Society for the Application of Mathematics (MCD)
ISAMS .... Improved Stratospheric and Mesospheric Sounder (MCD)
ISan............. Sandwich Township Public Library, Sandwich, IL [*Library symbol Library of Congress*] (LCLS)
ISanCH .... Sandwich Community Hospital, Sandwich, IL [*Library symbol Library of Congress*] (LCLS)
IS & CG ...... Information Systems and Communications Group (HGAA)
ISandSD .... Sandoval Community Unit School District 501, Sandoval, IL [*Library symbol Library of Congress*] (LCLS)
IS & T......... Industry, Science, and Technology
IS & T......... Innovative Science and Technology (DOMA)
ISanH......... Lynn G. Haskin School, Sandwich, IL [*Library symbol Library of Congress*] (LCLS)
ISanHS .... Sandwich Community High School, Sandwich, IL [*Library symbol Library of Congress*] (LCLS)
ISanJS .... Sandwich Junior High School, Sandwich, IL [*Library symbol Library of Congress*] (LCLS)

ISanP........... Prairie View School, Sandwich, IL [*Library symbol Library of Congress*] (LCLS)

I-SANTA...... Industrial Stapling and Nailing Technical Association (EA)

ISANTA ...... International Staple, Nail, and Tool Association (EA)

ISanW.......... W. W. Woodbury School, Sandwich, IL [*Library symbol Library of Congress*] (LCLS)

ISAO .... International Society for Artificial Organs (EA)

ISAP........... Individual System Automation Plans [*Military*]

ISAP........... Information Sort and Predict

ISAP........... Institute for the Study of Animal Problems [*Defunct*] (EA)

ISAP........... Instituto Sudamericano del Petroleo [*South American Petroleum Institute*]

ISAP........... Integrated Safety Assessment Program [*Nuclear energy*] (NRCH)

ISAP........... Interactive Survey Analysis Package (IAA)

ISAP........... International School Art Program [*Defunct*]

ISAP........... International Society of Art and Psychopathology [*Paris, France*] (EA)

ISAPA .... International Screen Advertising Producer's Association [*Defunct*] (EA)

ISAPC .... Incorporated Society of Authors, Playwrights, and Composers (BARN)

ISAPI .... Internet Server API [*All-Purpose Interface*] [*Microsoft and Process Software Corp.*] [*Computer science*]

ISAPI .... Internet Services API [*Computer science*]

ISAR .... Information Storage and Retrieval [*Computer science*] (DIT)

ISAR .... Institute for Soviet-American Relations (EA)

ISAR .... International Society for Animal Rights (EA)

ISAR .... International Society for Astrological Research (EA)

ISAR .... Inter-Seamount Acoustic Range

ISAR .... Inverse Synthetic Aperture RADAR [*Navy*] (ANA)

ISARC .... Installation Shipping and Receiving Capability [*Army*] (AABC)

ISAS........... Illinois State Academy of Science (PDAA)

ISAS........... Infrared Small Astronomical Spacecraft

ISAS........... Institute of Space and Aeronautical Science [*Japan*]

ISAS........... Integrated Smart Artillery Synthesis (RDA)

ISAS........... Integrated Spacecraft Avionics System (IAA)

ISAS........... International Society of African Scientists (EA)

ISAS........... Isotopic Source Assay System

ISAS........... Iterative Single Wavelength Anomalous Scattering [*Crystallography*]

ISASC .... International Society of Antique Scale Collectors (EA)

ISASI .... International Society of Air Safety Investigators (EA)

ISASNP .... International Symposium on Aerospace Nuclear Propulsion (MCD)

ISAST......... International Society for the Arts, Sciences, and Technology (EA)

ISAT .... Initial Surface Absorption Test

ISAT........... International Society of Analytical Trilogy [*See also SITA*] [*Sao Paulo, Brazil*] (EAIO)

ISAT........... Interrupt Storage Area Table [*Computer science*] (OA)

ISAT........... Invite, Show, and Test [*Military*] (SDI)

ISAUS .... Indonesian Students Association in the United States (EA)

ISAUS .... Iranian Students Association in the United States

ISAV........... Institute of Sound and Vibration (MCD)

ISAV........... Instituto de Sistemas Audio-Visuales [*Institute of Audio-Visual Media*] [*Colombia*]

ISAVVT .... International Symposium on the Aerodynamics and Ventilation of Vehicle Tunnels (PDAA)

ISAW .... International Society of Aviation Writers

ISAZ........... Isolation Accommodation Zone [*Geology*]

ISB............. Illinois Baptist Historical Library, Springfield, IL [*Library symbol Library of Congress*] (LCLS)

ISB............. Incentive Spirometry Breathing [*Medicine*] (DAVI)

ISB............. Independent Sideband

ISB............. Independent Society of Bricklayers [*A union*] [*British*]

ISB............. Industry Service Bureaus

ISB............. Information Services Branch [*Chalk River Nuclear Laboratories*] [*Atomic Energy of Canada Ltd.*] [*Information service or system*] (IID)

ISB............. Information Services Branch [*SHAPE Technical Center*] [*The Hague, Netherlands*]

ISB............. Information Systems Branch [*National Institutes of Health*] (IID)

ISB............. Initial Staging Base [*Army*] (DOMA)

ISB............. Institute of Scientific Business [*British*]

ISB............. Institute of Small Business [*British*]

ISB............. Intelligence and Security Board [*Military*] (MCD)

ISB............. Intelligence Systems Branch [*Military*] (IAA)

ISB............. Interchangeability Survey Board

ISB............. Interchange Financial Services Corp. [*Formerly, Interchange State Bank*] [*AMEX symbol*] (SPSG)

ISB............. Interchange Finl Svcs [*AMEX symbol*] (TTSB)

ISB............. Intermediate Sideband (NATG)

ISB............. Intermediate Staging Base

ISB............. Intermediate Support Base [*Military*] (NVT)

ISB............. Internationaler Studentenbund [*International Union of Students*]

ISB............. International Sinabarb [*Vancouver Stock Exchange symbol*]

ISB............. International Society of Bassists (EA)

ISB............. International Society of Biometeorology [*See also SIB*] [*Zurich, Switzerland*] (EAIO)

ISB............. International Society of Biorheology [*Germany*] (EAIO)

ISB............. International Symposium on Biomembranes

ISB............. Internet3D Space Builder

ISB............. Interstate Tariff Bureau, Inc., Lakewood OH [*STAC*]

ISB............. Investors Service Bureau [*Investment term*]

ISB............. Islamabad/Rawalpindi [*Pakistan*] [*Airport symbol*] (OAG)

ISB............. Nisab [*South Arabia*] [*Airport symbol*] (AD)

ISB............. Southern Methodist University, Bridwell Library, Dallas, TX [*OCLC symbol*] (OCLC)

ISBA........... Incorporated Society of British Advertisers [*British*]

ISBA........... Independent Safety Board Act of 1974

ISBA........... Independent Schools Bursars' Association [*British*]

ISBA........... International Sea-Bed Authority [*Marine science*] [*United Nations*] (OSRA)

ISBA........... International Ships-in-Bottles Association (EA)

ISBB........... International Society of Bioclimatology and Biometeorology (IEEE)

ISBC........... Infantry Squad Battle Course [*Army*]

ISBC........... Institute of Certified Business Counselors (EA)

ISBC........... Interdepartmental Savings Bond Committee [*Military*] (AABC)

ISBC........... International Society of Bible Collectors (EA)

ISBD........... International Soap Box Derby, Inc. (EA)

ISBD........... International Standard Bibliographic Description [*Library of Congress*]

ISBD(A)....... International Standard Bibliographic Description - Antiquarian

ISBD(CM) .... International Standard Bibliographic Description for Cartographic Materials [*Library of Congress*]

ISBD(CP) ..... International Standard Bibliographic Description (Component Parts)

ISBD(G) .... International Standard Bibliographic Description - General

ISBD(M)...... International Standard Bibliographic Description for Monographs [*Library of Congress*]

ISBD(NBM)... International Standard Bibliographic Description for Non-Book Materials

ISBD(PM) .... International Standard Bibliographic Description for Printed Music

ISBD(S)........ International Standard Bibliographic Description for Serials [*Library of Congress*]

ISBE........... Independent Small Business Employers of America (EA)

ISBE........... International Society for Boundary Elements (EAIO)

ISBE........... International Society for Business Education, US Chapter [*Reston, VA*] (EA)

ISBE........... International Standard Bible Encyclopaedia [*A publication*] (BJA)

ISBEA......... Independent Small Business Employers of America [*Later, ISBE*] (EA)

ISBF........... Interactive Search of Bibliographic Files

ISBF........... ISB Financial [*NASDAQ symbol*] (TTSB)

ISBF........... ISB Financial Corp. [*NASDAQ symbol*] (SAG)

ISB Fn .... ISB Financial Corp. [*Associated Press*] (SAG)

ISBGFH....... International Society for British Genealogy and Family History (EA)

ISBI........... International Savings Banks Institute [*See also IICE*] [*Geneva, Switzerland*] (EAIO)

ISBI........... International Society for Burn Injuries (EAIO)

ISBIC......... Interservice Balkan Intelligence Committee [*World War II*]

ISBL........... Information System Base Language

ISBL........... Inside Battery Limits [*Chemical engineering*]

ISBM......... Institute for the Study of Business Markets [*Pennsylvania State University*] [*Research center*] (RCD)

ISBM......... International Society of Biophysical Medicine [*British*] (IRUK)

ISBM......... Motorola Communications Sector Library, Schaumburg, IL [*Library symbol*] [*Library of Congress*] (LCLS)

ISBN........... International Standard Book Number [*Library of Congress*]

ISBO .... Islamic States Broadcasting Organization [*Jeddah, Saudi Arabia*] (EAIO)

ISBP........... International Society for Biochemical Pharmacology

ISBRA......... International Society Biomedical Research on Alcoholism (EAIO)

ISBS........... Integrated Small Business Software (NITA)

ISBS........... International Specialized Books Services [*Book distributor*]

ISBT........... International Society of Blood Transfusion (EA)

ISBX........... Integrated Services Branch Exchange [*Telecommunications*] (OSI)

ISC........... Concordia Theological Seminary, Springfield, IL [*Library symbol Library of Congress Obsolete*] (LCLS)

ISC........... Duneland School Corp., Chesterton, IN [*OCLC symbol*] (OCLC)

ISc........... Iconic Store, Central [*Psychophysiology*]

ISC........... Idaho State College [*Later, Idaho State University*] (AEBS)

ISC........... Idle Speed Control [*Automotive engineering*]

I-SC .... Illinois Supreme Court, Springfield, IL [*Library symbol Library of Congress*] (LCLS)

ISC........... Immune Spleen Cell

ISC........... Imperial Service College [*British*]

ISC........... Improved Submarine Communication (MCD)

ISC........... Incorporated Staff Sight-Singing College [*London*]

ISC........... Independent Search Consultants (EA)

ISC........... Index of Status Characteristics

ISC........... Indian Staff Corps [*British*] (ROG)

ISC........... Indirect Strike Control

ISC........... Individual Soldier's Computer [*Army*] (RDA)

ISC........... Indoor Sports Club (EA)

ISC........... Industrial Source Complex [*Environmental science*] (GFGA)

ISC........... Industrial Support Contractor (KSC)

ISC........... Inertial Start Command

ISC........... Infiltration Surveillance Center (CINC)

ISC........... Information Science Center (MCD)

ISC........... Information Science Corporation (NITA)

ISC........... Information Services Control Branch [*Control Commission for Germany*] [*World War II*]

ISC........... Information Services of Cranston [*Information service or system*] (IID)

ISC........... Information Society of Canada (MCD)

ISC........... Information Specialties Corp. (IID)

ISC........... Information Systems Command [*DoD*]

ISC........... Information Systems Committee [*Universities Funding Council*] (AIE)

ISC........... Infrared Sightline Control

ISC........... Infrastructure Special Committee [*NATO*] (NATG)

ISC........... Initial Slope Circuit [*Telecommunications*] (OA)

ISC........... Initial Software Configuration Map (MCD)

ISC........... Initial Student Characteristics

ISC........... In Situ Combustion [*Engineering*]

ISC.............. Insoluble Collagen [Biochemistry]
ISC.............. Inspection and Safety Center [Military]
ISC.............. Institute for the Study of Conflict [British]
ISC.............. Instruction Staticizing Control (IEEE)
ISC.............. Instrumentation System Corp. (MCD)
ISC.............. Instrumentation Systems Center [University of Wisconsin - Madison] [Research center] (RCD)
ISC.............. Insulated Signal Coupler (IAA)
ISC.............. Integrated Stage Concept (MCD)
ISC.............. Integrated Storage Control
ISC.............. Intelligence Subject Code
ISC.............. Intelligence Support Center
ISC.............. Intelligent Synchronous Controller [Computer science] (NITA)
ISC.............. Intelligent Systems Corp.
ISC.............. Interactive Sciences Corp. [Information service or system] (IID)
ISC.............. Interagency Staff Committee on Public Law 480 [Department of Agriculture] (EGAO)
ISC.............. Inter-American Society of Cardiology [Mexico City, Mexico] (EAIO)
ISC.............. Interceptor Subsystem Controller
ISC.............. Intercompany Services Coordination [Telecommunications] (TEL)
ISC.............. Intercomponent Subcontractor (MCD)
ISC.............. Interdisciplinary Scientific Commission [COSPAR]
ISC.............. Interface Signal Chart
ISC.............. International Cruiseships [Vancouver Stock Exchange symbol]
ISC.............. International Salmonella Center
ISC.............. International Salon of Cartoons (EA)
ISC.............. International Scientific Publications [Tel Aviv, Israel]
ISC.............. International Security Conference and Exposition (ITD)
ISC.............. International Security Council (EA)
ISC.............. International Seismological Centre [ICSU] [Newbury, Berkshire, England] (EAIO)
ISC.............. International Serials Catalogue [A publication]
ISC.............. International Sericultural Commission [See also CSI] [La Mulatiere, France] (EAIO)
ISC.............. International Signal and Control [Army]
ISC.............. International Society for Chronobiology (EA)
ISC.............. International Society of Cardiology [Later, ISFC]
ISC.............. International Society of Chemotherapy [Bad Heilbrunn, Federal Republic of Germany] (EAIO)
ISC.............. International Society of Citriculture (EA)
ISC.............. International Society of Copoclephologists [British] (EAIO)
ISC.............. International Society of Cryosurgery [Turin, Italy] (EAIO)
ISC.............. International Society of Cryptozoology (EA)
ISC.............. International Softball Congress (EA)
ISC.............. International Space Congress
ISC.............. International Space Corp.
ISC.............. International Statistical Classification
ISC.............. International Student Conference
ISC.............. International Sugar Council [London] [Later, ISO]
ISC.............. International Supply Committee [World War II]
ISC.............. International Supreme Council of World Masons (EA)
ISC.............. International Switching Center [Communications]
ISC.............. International Symposium on Chemiluminescence
ISC.............. Inter-Service Communication [British World War II]
ISC.............. Inter-Service Sports Council [Military]
ISC.............. Interservice Support Code [Military]
ISC.............. Inter-Shift Coordination [Medicine] (DMAA)
ISC.............. Intersociety Committee on Methods for Air Sampling and Analysis
ISC.............. Interstage Section Container
ISC.............. Interstate Commerce
ISC.............. Interstellar Communications (AAG)
ISC.............. Interstitial Cells [Histology]
ISC.............. Inter-System Communication (NITA)
ISC.............. Inter-System Crossing [Chemical Kinetics]
ISC.............. Intersystem Crossing [Physics]
ISC.............. Interval Selection Circuit
ISC.............. Interview Schedule for Children
ISC.............. Intrasite Cabling (CET)
ISC.............. Intuit Services Corp.
ISC.............. Invention Submission Corp. [Information service or system] (IID)
ISC.............. Iowa Safety Council (SRA)
ISC.............. Iowa State College of Agriculture and Mechanic Arts [Later, Iowa State University] (MCD)
ISC.............. Irreversibly Sickled Cell [Hematology]
ISC.............. Island Air Charters, Inc. [ICAO designator] (FAAC)
ISC.............. Isles Of Scilly [England] [Airport symbol] (OAG)
ISC.............. Italian Space Commission
ISC.............. Item Status Code (NATG)
ISCA.............. Idle Speed Control Actuator [Automotive engineering]
ISCA.............. Independent Safety Consultants Association (DBA)
ISCA.............. Industrial Specialty Chemical Association (EA)
ISCA.............. Interest Standby Credit Arrangement
ISCA.............. Interlake Sailing Class Association (EA)
ISCA.............. International Sailing Craft Association [Exeter, Devonshire, England] (EAIO)
ISCA.............. International Scientific Collectors Association (EA)
ISCA.............. International Senior Citizens Association (EA)
ISCA.............. International Shooting Coaches Association (EA)
ISCA.............. International Show Car Association (EA)
ISCA.............. International Society of Copier Artists (EA)
ISCA.............. International Speedway Corp. [NASDAQ symbol] (SAG)
ISCA.............. International Sunfish Class Association (EA)
ISCA.............. Irish Setter Club of America (EA)
IScAF.............. United States Air Force, Base Library, Scott AFB, IL [Library symbol Library of Congress] (LCLS)

IScAF-A........ United States Air Force, Airlift Operations School, Scott Air Force Base, IL [Library symbol Library of Congress] (LCLS)
IScAF-E........ United States Air Force, Environmental Technical Applications Center, Air Weather Service Technical Library, Scott Air Force Base, IL [Library symbol Library of Congress] (LCLS)
ISCAMPME... Iodosuccinyl CAMP Tyrosine Methyl Ester [Biochemistry]
ISCAMS .... Installation Standard Command Automated Data Processing Management System [Army]
ISCAN .... Inertialess Steerable Communications Antenna
ISCAN .... International Sanitary Convention for Air Navigation
ISCAS .... Integrated Submarine Communications Antenna System [Navy] (CAAL)
ISCAS .... International Symposium on Circuits and Systems [IEEE] (MCD)
ISCAY .... International Solidarity Committee with Algerian Youth
ISCB.............. Interallied Staff Communications Board [World War II]
ISCB.............. International Society for Cell Biology [Later, IFCB] (ASF)
ISCB.............. International Society for Classical Bibliography [Paris, France] (EAIO)
ISCB.............. International Society for Clinical Biostatistics (EAIO)
ISCBA .... Insulating Siding Core Board Association [Defunct] (EA)
ISCBMC .... International Single Comb Black Minorca Club (EA)
ISCC.............. International Service Coordination Center [Communications]
ISCC.............. International Somali Cat Club
ISCC.............. International Standard Commodity Classification of All Goods and Services
ISCC.............. Inter-Society Color Council (EA)
ISCC.............. Inter-Society Cytology Council [Later, American Society of Cytology - ASC]
ISCC.............. Interstate Solar Coordination Council (EA)
ISCC.............. Iranian Students Counseling Center (EA)
ISCCED .... Independent Sector Coordinating Committee on Environment and Development (GNE)
ISCCP .... International Satellite Cloud Climatology Project
ISCD.............. Interface Specification Control Document (KSC)
ISCD.............. International Society for Community Development (EA)
ISCDD .... International Scheme for the Coordination of Dairy Development (EAIO)
ISCDP .... International Standing Committee on Distribution Problems [International Water Supply Association]
ISCDS .... International Stop Continental Drift Society [Defunct] (EA)
ISCE.............. Institute for the Study of Conscious Evolution [Defunct] (EA)
ISCE.............. International Society for a Complete Earth (EA)
ISCE.............. International Society for Clinical Enzymology [Hanover, Federal Republic of Germany] (EAIO)
ISCE.............. International Society of Chemical Ecology (EA)
ISCE.............. International Society of Christian Endeavor (EA)
ISCE.............. Interstate Substitute Cost Estimate [Federal Highway Administration]
ISCEBS .... International Society of Certified Employee Benefit Specialists [Brookfield, WI] (EA)
ISCED .... International Society of Continuing Education in Dentistry [See also SIECD] [Brussels, Belgium] (EAIO)
ISCED .... International Standard Classification of Education (MCD)
ISCEH .... International Society for Clinical and Experimental Hypnosis [Charles University] (EA)
ISCERG .... International Society for Clinical Electroretinography
ISCET .... International Society of Certified Electronics Technicians (EA)
ISCF.............. Industrial Sentence Completion Form [Psychology]
ISCF.............. Inter-School Christian Fellowship [British] (BI)
ISCF.............. Interstitial Cell Fluid (DMAA)
ISCG.............. Institute of School and College Governors [British] (EAIO)
ISCG.............. Integrated Sys Consulting Gp [NASDAQ symbol] (TTSB)
ISCG.............. Integrated Systems Consulting Group, Inc. [NASDAQ symbol] (SAG)
ISCh.............. Incorporated Society of Chiropodists [British] (DI)
ISch.............. Steger-South Chicago Heights Library District, South Chicago Heights, IL [Library symbol Library of Congress] (LCLS)
ISCHDR........ Inter-Society Commission for Heart Disease Resources
ISCHE .... International Standing Conference for the History of Education (AIE)
ISCI.............. Information Systems Consultants, Inc. [Information service or system] (IID)
ISCII.............. International Standard Code for Information Interchange (NATG)
ISCJ.............. International Ski Club of Journalists (EAIO)
ISCL.............. Interim Status Compliance Letter [Environmental Protection Agency] (GFGA)
ISCLC.......... International Symposium on Column Liquid Chromatography [1986] [San Francisco, CA]
ISCLT.......... Industrial Source Complex Long-Term Model [Environmental Protection Agency] (GFGA)
ISCLT.......... International Society for Clinical Laboratory Technology (EA)
ISCM.......... International Society for Contemporary Music (EA)
ISCM.......... International Society of Cybernetic Medicine (EA)
ISCME .... International Society for Computational Methods in Engineering (EAIO)
ISCN.......... International System for Human Cytogenetic Nomenclature
ISCO.......... Illinois Superconductor [NASDAQ symbol] (TTSB)
ISCO.......... Illinois Superconductor Corp. [NASDAQ symbol] (SAG)
ISCO.......... Independent Schools Careers Organisation [British]
ISCO.......... Indicated Specific Carbon Monoxide
ISCO.......... Initial Systems Checkout
ISCO.......... Instrumentation Specialties Co.
ISCO.......... International Society of Corvette Owners
ISCO .... International Standard Classification of Occupations (WDAA)
Isco.......... Isco, Inc. [Associated Press]
ISCO .... Istituto Nazionale per lo Studio della Congiuntura [Data Resources, Inc.] [Database]
ISCOM .... Immunostimulatory Complex [Immunochemistry]
ISCOM .... Island Commander

ISCOMADEIRA... Island Commander Madeira (AABC)
ISCOMAZORES... Island Commander Azores
ISCOMBERMUDA... Island Commander Bermuda
ISCOMFAROES... Island Commander Faroes
ISCOMGREENLAND... Island Commander Greenland
ISCOMICELAND... Island Commander Iceland
ISCOR......... South African Iron & Steel Corp.
ISCORE........ Intelligence Score (MCD)
ISCOS....... Institute for Security and Cooperation in Outer Space (EA)
ISCOSS....... International Symposium on the Chemistry of the Organic Solid State
ISCP......... India Study Circle for Philately (EA)
ISCP......... Infection Surveillance and Control Program [*Medicine*] (DMAA)
ISCP......... Installation Spill Contingency Plan [*DoD*] (AFIT)
ISCP......... Integrated Subsystem Calibration Plan (SAA)
ISCP......... Intermediate Sodium Characterization Package [*Nuclear energy*] (NRCH)
ISCP......... International Society for Chinese Philosophy (EA)
ISCP......... International Society for Comparative Psychology (EA)
ISCP......... International Society of Clinical Pathology [*Later, WASP*]
ISCP......... International Society of Comparative Pathology (DMAA)
ISCP......... Inventory Stock Cataloging Program
ISCPET........ Illinois Statewide Curriculum Study Center in the Preparation of Secondary School English Teachers
ISCPP........ International Society of Crime Prevention Practitioners (EAIO)
ISCPVS........ Istituto Sindacale per la Cooperazione con i Paesi in Via di Sviluppo [*Trade Union Institute for Cooperation with Developing Countries*] [*Italy*] (EAIO)
ISC/R......... Individual Soldier's Computer/Radio [*Army*] (INF)
ISCRE...... International Symposium on Chemical Reaction Engineering
ISCRO....... Industrial Security Clearance Review Office [*DoD*]
ISCRP....... International Society of City and Regional Planners [*See also AIU*]
ISCS......... Information Service Computer System (DIT)
ISCS......... Integrated Submarine Communications System (MCD)
ISCS......... Interim Sea Control Ship (MCD)
ISCS......... Intermediate Science Curriculum Study
ISCS......... International Sand Collectors Society (EA)
ISCS......... International Society for Cardiovascular Surgery (DAVI)
ISCS......... International Society of Communications Specialists (EA)
ISCS......... International Stamp Collectors Society (EA)
ISCS......... International Symposium on Cooling Systems (PDAA)
ISCS......... Interservice/Cross Service [*Support*]
ISCSA....... Industrial Sports Clubs Secretaries' Association [*British*] (BI)
ISCSC....... International Society for the Comparative Study of Civilizations (EA)
ISCSH....... Independent Scientific Committee on Smoking and Health [*British*]
ISCST........ Industrial Source Complex Short-Term Model [*Environmental Protection Agency*] (GFGA)
ISCST2........ Industrial Source Complex Short-Term Model Version 2
ISCT......... Inner Seal Collar Tool [*Nuclear energy*] (NRCH)
ISCT......... Ito System Color Television [*Japan*]
ISCTF....... Interservice Committee on Technical Facilities [*Aerospace*] (AAG)
ISCTP....... International Study Commission for Traffic Police
ISC/USO....... Intercompany Services Coordination/Universal Service Order [*Telecommunications*] (TEL)
ISCV......... Idle Speed Control Valve [*Exhaust emissions*] [*Automotive engineering*]
ISCVS....... International Society of Cardiovascular Surgeons
ISCWFD...... Intergovernmental Steering Committee on World Food Day (EA)
ISCWQT...... International Standing Committee on Water Quality and Treatment [*International Water Supply Association*]
ISCX......... Industrial Scientific [*NASDAQ symbol*] (TTSB)
ISCX......... Industrial Scientific Corp. [*NASDAQ symbol*] (SAG)
ISCYRA....... International Star Class Yacht Racing Association (EA)
ISD......... Cabot Corp., Stellite Division, Kokomo, IN [*OCLC symbol*] (OCLC)
ISD......... IBM [*International Business Machines Corp.*] Standard Data (IAA)
ISD......... Immunosuppressive Drug [*Medicine*] (DMAA)
ISD......... Indian Stores Depot [*British military*] (DMA)
ISD......... Induction System Deposit
ISD......... Information Services Department [*Ohio State University Libraries*] [*Columbus*] [*Information service or system*] (IID)
ISD......... Information Services Division [*Mississippi State Research and Development Center*] [*Information service or system*] (IID)
ISD......... Information Services Division [*Scottish Health Service*] [*Research center*]
ISD......... Information Structure Design
ISD......... Information System Development [*Telecommunications*] (TEL)
ISD......... Information Systems Department [*Franklin Research Center, Inc.*] [*Information service or system*] (IID)
ISD......... Information Systems Division [*Ori, Inc.*] [*Bethesda, MD*]
ISD......... Infrared Suppression Device
ISD......... Inhibited Sexual Desire [*Sex therapy*]
ISD......... Initial Search Depth
ISD......... Initial Selection Done
ISD......... Initial Ship Design
ISD......... Innovative Software Design [*South Africa ICAO designator*] (FAAC)
ISD......... Insert Subcaliber Device [*Weaponry*] (INF)
ISD......... Installation Specification Drawing (MCD)
ISD......... Installation Start Date (CET)
ISD......... Installation Supply Division [*Military*] (AABC)
ISD......... Institute for Security Design (EA)
ISD......... Institute of Single Dynamics (EA)
ISD......... Institute of Surplus Dealers (EA)
ISD......... Instructional System Design Model
ISD......... Instructional Systems Design (DOM)
ISD......... Instructional Systems Development (AFM)
ISD......... Integrated Symbolic Debugger [*Computer science*] (IID)

ISD......... Integrated Systems Demonstrator (MCD)
ISD......... Intensity, Severity, and Discharge [*Medicine*] (DHSM)
ISD......... Interactive Screen Definition (IAA)
ISD......... Interim Simulation Display [*FAA*] (TAG)
ISD......... Interim Status Document [*Environmental Protection Agency*] (GFGA)
ISD......... Intermediate School District (AEE)
ISD......... Intermediate Storage Device
ISD......... Internal Security Division [*Abolished 1973; functions transferred to Criminal Division*] [*Department of Justice*]
ISD......... Internal Symbol Dictionary [*Computer science*] (OA)
ISD......... International Society of Dermatology: Tropical, Geographic, and Ecologic (EA)
ISD......... International Society of Differentiation (EA)
ISD......... International Society of Dramatists (EA)
ISD......... International Subscriber Dialing [*Later, IDD*] [*Telecommunications*]
ISD......... Intersystem Designation (CAAL)
ISD......... Invoice Shipping Documentation [*Business term*]
ISD......... Isosorbide Dinitrite [*Coronary vasodilator*]
ISD......... MENU - the International Software Database [*Menu the International Software Database Corp.*] [*Information service or system*] (CRD)
ISD......... Winner, SD [*Location identifier FAA*] (FAAL)
ISDA....... Indian Self-Determination Act [*1975*]
ISDA....... Institute for the Study of Drug Addiction [*Later, ISDM*] (EA)
ISDA....... International Sculpteurs et Designers Associes [*Paris, France*] (EAIO)
ISDA....... International Security and Detective Alliance (EA)
ISDA....... International Swap Dealers' Association
ISDA....... International Swaps and Derivatives Association (ECON)
ISDAIC....... International Staff Disaster Assistance Information Coordinator [*NATO*] (NATG)
ISDB....... Initial Subordinate Dominates Bystander [*Sociology*]
ISDB....... International Society of Development Biologists [*Formerly, IIE*] [*Nogent-Sur-Marne, France*]
ISDC....... Indiana State Data Center [*Indiana State Library*] [*Indianapolis*] [*Information service or system*] (IID)
ISDC....... Intense Sample Data Collection System (MCD)
ISDCC....... Illinois State Data Center Cooperative [*Illinois State Bureau of the Budget*] [*Springfield*] [*Information service or system*] (IID)
ISDCI....... International Society of Developmental and Comparative Immunology (EA)
ISDD....... Information Systems Development Division (SAA)
ISDD....... Institute for the Study of Drug Dependence [*London*]
ISDE....... Integral Square Delay Error (IAA)
ISDE....... International Seismic Data Exchange [*Geology*]
ISDE....... International Six Days Enduro [*Motorcycle racing*]
ISDE....... International Society for Diseases of the Esophagus [*Tokyo, Japan*] (EAIO)
ISDF....... Impact Short Delay Fuze (MCD)
ISDF....... Intermediate Sodium Disposal Facility [*Nuclear energy*] (NRCH)
ISDF....... International Shooter Development Fund [*National Rifle Association*]
ISDG....... Information Science Discussion Group [*British*] (NITA)
ISDI....... Information Storage Devices [*NASDAQ symbol*] (TTSB)
ISDI....... Information Storage Devices, Inc. [*NASDAQ symbol*] (SAG)
ISDI....... International Social Development Institute
ISDI....... International Society of Dietetic Including All Infant and Young Children Food Industries (EA)
ISDI....... International Special Dietary Foods Industries [*France*] (EAIO)
ISDIN....... Isosorbide Dinitrate [*Also, ISDN*] [*Coronary vasodilator*]
ISDM....... Indian Self-Determination Memorandum [*Indian Health Service*] [*Department of Health and Human Services*] (GFGA)
ISDM....... Institute for the Study of Drug Misuse [*Formerly, ISDA*] (EA)
ISDM....... International Society for Disaster Medicine (EA)
ISDN....... Information Service Data Network [*Telecommunications*]
ISDN....... Institute for the Study of Developing Nations (EA)
ISDN....... Integrated Services Digital Network [*Telecommunications*]
ISDN....... International Society for Developmental Neuroscience (EA)
ISDN....... International Standard Data Network (NITA)
ISDN....... Isosorbide Dinitrate [*Also, ISDIN*] [*Coronary vasodilator*]
ISDN....... It Still Does Nothing [*Facetious translation for ISDN - Integrated Services Digital Network*]
ISDNA....... Inverse Standard Deviation of Nucleolar Area [*Oncology*]
ISDO....... Institute for Systems Design and Optimization
ISDO....... International Staff Duty Officer [*NATO*] (NATG)
ISDOS....... Information Systems Design Optimization System
ISDP....... Income Survey Development Program [*Department of Health and Human Services*] (GFGA)
ISDP....... International Society for Developmental Psychobiology (EA)
ISDPG....... Independent Social Democratic Party of Germany [*Political party*] (EAIO)
ISDRA....... International Sled Dog Racing Association (EA)
ISDS....... Inadvertent Separation and Destruct System [*Aerospace*]
ISDS....... Institute for Social Dance Studies [*Defunct*] (EA)
ISDS....... Institute for the Study of Defects in Solids [*State University of New York at Albany*] [*Research center*] (RCD)
ISDS....... Instructional Systems Development Squadron
ISDS....... Instruction Set Design System (PDAA)
ISDS....... Integrated Ship Design System (IEEE)
ISDS....... Integrated Software Development System
ISDS....... Integrated Switched Data Service [*Telecommunications*] (TEL)
ISDS....... Intelligence Support Display System [*Military*] (MCD)
ISDS....... International Serials Data System [*Database*] (EA)
ISDS....... International Sheep Dog Society [*Bedford, England*] (EAIO)
ISDS....... International Society of Dermatologic Surgery (EA)
ISDSI....... Insulated Steel Door Systems Institute (EA)
ISDS/IC....... International Center of the International Serials Data System [*UNESCO*] (PDAA)

ISDT............ Instructional Systems Development Team [*Air Force*]
ISDT............ International Six Days Trial [*Motorcycling*]
ISDT............ International Symposium on Dredging Technology (PDAA)
ISDTS........ Iron and Steel Dressers Trade Society [*A union*] [*British*]
ISDU............ International Standard Density Unit (DGA)
ISDX............ Integrated Services Digital Exchange [*British*]
ISE............ Illogical Sequence Error (IAA)
ISE............ Independent Scheduled Exercises
ISE............ Independent Ship Exercise [*Navy*]
ISE............ Indiana State University, Evansville Campus, Evansville, IN [*OCLC symbol*] (OCLC)
ISE............ Indian Service of Engineers [*British*]
ISE............ Individual Ship Exercises [*Navy*]
ISE............ Individual Soldier Energy [*Military*] (RDA)
ISE............ Induced Surface Effect
ISE............ Information in Science Extension [*INTERBRIGHT database*] [*Budapest, Hungary*] [*Information service or system*] (IID)
ISE............ Information Services to Education [*American Society for Information Science*]
ISE............ Inhibited Sexual Excitement [*Medicine*] (DMAA)
ISE............ Initial Support Element (MCD)
ISE............ In-Service Education (ADA)
ISE............ In-Service Engineering [*Navy*]
ISE............ Installation Support and Evaluation (AAG)
ISE............ Institute for Software Engineering (EA)
ISE............ Institute of Sanitary Engineers [*British*] (DAS)
ISE............ Institute of Social Ethics (EA)
ISE............ Institution of Sales Engineers [*British*] (BI)
ISE............ Institution of Structural Engineers [*British*] (EAIO)
ISE............ Instrumentation Suitability Evaluation (MCD)
ISE............ In System Evaluator [*National Semiconductor Company*] (NITA)
ISE............ Integral Squared Error
ISE............ Integrated Safeguards Experiment
ISE............ Integrated Space Experiment (MCD)
ISE............ Integrated Storage Element [*Computer science*]
ISE............ Intelligence Support Element [*Military*] (MCD)
ISE............ Interactive Software Engineering
ISE............ Intercept System Environment [*Army*] (AABC)
ISE............ Intermountain Stock Exchange [*Salt Lake City, UT*]
ISE............ International Semi-Tech Microelectronics, Inc. [*Toronto Stock Exchange symbol*]
ISE............ International Society for Electrostimulation (EA)
ISE............ International Society of Electrochemistry [*Graz, Austria*] (EA)
ISE............ International Society of Endocrinology (EA)
ISE............ International Society of Endoscopy
ISE............ International Sports Exchange (EA)
ISE............ International Stock Exchange
ISE............ International Stock Exchange of the United Kingdom and the Republic of Ireland (DFIT)
ISE............ Interpret Sign Error
ISE............ Interrupt System Enable
ISE............ Inter System Emulator (NITA)
ISE............ Ion-Selective Electrode [*Instrumentation*]
ISE............ Ion-Sensitive Electrode [*Instrumentation*] (IAA)
ISE............ Irish School of Ecumenics
ISE............ Ise [*Japan*] [*Seismograph station code, US Geological Survey*] (SEIS)
i-se-- .... Seychelles [*MARC geographic area code Library of Congress*] (LCCP)
ISEA............ Industrial Safety Equipment Association [*Arlington, VA*] (EA)
ISEA............ Inland Seas Education Association
ISEA............ Inservice Engineering Agent [*Military*] (CAAL)
ISEA............ International Stamp Exchange Association
ISEANSW.... Institute of Senior Educational Administrators of New South Wales [*Australia*]
ISEAS.......... Institute of Southeast Asian Studies
ISEB............ Independent Schools Education Board [*Later, National Association of IndependentSchools*] (AEBS)
ISEB............ Interim Support Equipment Bulletin (MCD)
ISEC............ Information System Electronic Command [*Army*]
ISEC............ Information Systems Engineering Command (SSD)
ISEC............ Institute for Social Economic Change
ISEC............ International Solvent Extraction Conference [*Toronto, ON, 1977*] [*Canada*]
ISEC............ International Standard Electric Corp. (NATG)
ISEC............ International Statistical Education Centre [*India*]
ISECCo........ International Space Exploration and Colonization Company [*An association*] (EA)
ISECS.......... International Society for Eighteenth-Century Studies [*See also SIEDS*] [*Oxford, England*] (EAIO)
ISED............ Institute for Social Evaluation and Design
ISEE............ Incident-Shock Equilibrium Expansion
ISEE............ Initial System Evaluation Experiment [*Photovoltaic energy systems*]
ISEE............ International Society for Engineering Education [*Austria*] (EAIO)
ISEE............ International Sun-Earth Explorer [*NASA/ESRO satellite*]
ISEE............ International Sun-Earth Explorer [*Marine science*] (OSRA)
ISEE............ Sterling Vision [*NASDAQ symbol*] (TTSB)
ISEE............ Sterling Vision, Inc. [*NASDAQ symbol*] (SAG)
ISEEM.......... International Society for Economic Evaluation of Medicines
ISEEP.......... Infrared Sensitive Element Evaluation Program
ISEF............ International Science and Engineering Fair
ISEG............ Independent Safety Engineering Group [*Nuclear energy*] (NRCH)
ISEGR.......... Institute of Social, Economic, and Governmental Research [*Later, ISER*] [*University of Alaska*]
ISEI............ International Standard Engineering, Inc. (NATG)

ISEK............ International Society of Electromyographic Kinesiology (EA)
ISEK............ International Society of Electrophysiological Kinesiology [*Montreal, PQ*] (EA)
ISEL............ Institute of Shipping Economics and Logistics [*See also ISL*] [*Bremen, Federal Republic of Germany*] (EAIO)
ISELS.......... Institute of Society, Ethics, and Life Sciences [*Later, HC*] (EA)
ISEM.......... Immunosorbent Electron Microscopy
ISEM.......... Improved Standard Electronic Module (MHDB)
ISEM.......... Institute for the Study of Earth and Man [*Southern Methodist University*] [*Research center*] (RCD)
ISEM.......... Integrated Simulation Evaluation Model
ISEM.......... International Society for Ecological Modelling [*Vaerloese, Denmark*] (EAIO)
ISEMS.......... International Society of Emergency Medical Services (EA)
ISEN.......... Interactive Satellite Education Network [*IBM Corp.*] [*New York, NY*] (TSSD)
ISen............ Seneca Public Library, Seneca, IL [*Library symbol Library of Congress*] (LCLS)
ISenMS........ Miller Township Consolidated Community, School District 210, Seneca, IL [*Library symbol*] [*Library of Congress*] (LCLS)
ISEO............ Institute of Shortening and Edible Oils (EA)
ISEP............ Instructional Scientific Equipment Program [*National Science Foundation*]
ISEP............ International Society for Educational Planning (EA)
ISEP............ International Society for Evolutionary Protistology (EA)
ISEP............ International Society of Esperantist-Philologists [*See also IUEFI*] (EAIO)
ISEP............ International Standard Equipment Practice (MHDB)
ISEP............ International Student Exchange Program [*United States Information Agency*]
ISEP............ Interservice Experiments Program
ISEPS.......... International Sun-Earth Physics Satellite
ISER............ InnoServe Technologies, Inc. [*NASDAQ symbol*] (SAG)
ISER............ InnoServ Technologies [*NASDAQ symbol*] (TTSB)
ISER............ Institute of Sex Education and Research [*British*] (DBA)
ISER............ Institute of Social and Economic Research [*Formerly, ISEGR*] [*University of Alaska*]
ISER............ Institute of Social and Economic Research [*Memorial University of Newfoundland*] [*Research center Canada*] (RCD)
ISER............ Integral Systems Experimental Requirements (NRCH)
ISerSD .... Serena Consolidated High School District 390, Serena, IL [*Library symbol Library of Congress*] (LCLS)
ISES............ In Silentio et Spe [*In Silence and in Hope*] [*Motto of Bernhard, Prince of Anhalt (1572-96)*] [*Latin*]
ISES............ Institute for Socioeconomic Studies (EA)
ISES............ International Ship Electric Service Association [*British*] (EAIO)
ISES............ International Society of Explosives Specialists (EA)
ISES............ International Solar Energy Society [*Australia*] (EAIO)
ISES............ International Special Events Society (EA)
ISES............ Iron Safe Engineers' Society [*A union*] [*British*]
ISESCO .... Islamic Educational, Scientific, and Cultural Organization [*United Nations*]
ISETAP........ Intergovernmental Science, Engineering, and Technology Advisory Panel [*National Science Foundation*]
ISETC............ International Society for Environmental Toxicology and Cancer (EAIO)
ISETU.......... International Secretariat of Entertainment Trade Unions [*Geneva, Switzerland*]
ISEU.......... International Stereotypers and Electrotypers Union [*Later, IPGCU*]
ISEW.......... Index of Sustainable Economic Welfare (PS)
ISEW.......... Intelligence, Security, and Electronic Warfare [*DoD*]
ISF............ Alpha Park Public Library District, Pekin, IL [*OCLC symbol*] (OCLC)
ISF............ Imperial Smelting Furnace [*Zinc and lead*]
ISF............ Incremental Stretch Forming
ISF............ Indian States Force [*British military*] (DMA)
ISF............ Individual Store and Forward
ISF............ Industrial Space Facility [*Space Industries, Inc.*]
ISF............ Infant Soy Formula
ISF............ Information Systems Factory (NITA)
ISF............ Information Systems Flight [*Military*]
ISF............ Infrasonic Frequency
ISF............ Instrument Standards Foundation (ACII)
ISF............ Insurance, Surety, and Fidelity (MHDB)
ISF............ Integrated Subject File
ISF............ Integrated Support Facility (DWSG)
ISF............ Interdistrict Settlement Fund [*Banking*]
ISF............ Intermediate Scale Facility [*Department of Energy*]
ISF............ Internationale Schulsport Foderation [*International School Sport Federation*] (EAIO)
ISF............ International School Sport Federation (EAIO)
ISF............ International Science Foundation (EA)
ISF............ International Scleroderma Federation [*Later, SF*] (EA)
ISF............ International Shipping Federation [*British*] (EAIO)
ISF............ International Ski Federation
ISF............ International Snowshoe Federation (EA)
ISF............ International Society for Fat Research
ISF............ International Society of Financiers (EA)
ISF............ International Softball Federation (EA)
ISF............ International Spiritualist Federation [*British*]
ISF............ International Spring Fair [*British*] (ITD)
ISF............ Intersection of the Shift Fringes (PDAA)
ISF............ Interstitial Fluid [*Physiology*]
ISF............ Ionizer, Slab Fabrication
ISF............ Isfjord [*Norway*] [*Seismograph station code, US Geological Survey Closed*] (SEIS)

ISF............	Isotope Separation Factor (MCD)
ISFA.........	Intercoastal Steamship Freight Association (EA)
ISFA.........	International Scientific Film Association
ISFA.........	Isaac Garrison Family Association (EA)
ISFAA........	Intercollegiate Soccer-Football Association of America [*Later, ISAA*] (EA)
ISFAA........	International Society of Fine Arts Appraisers (EA)
IS-FACT	Irwin Stone Foundation for Ascorbate Capability and Therapy
ISFAHSIG....	International Society for the Advancement of Humanistic Studies in Gynecology (EA)
ISFC.........	Indicated Specific Fuel Consumption
ISFC.........	International Short Film Conference (EAIO)
ISFC.........	International Society and Federation of Cardiology [*International Cardiol ogy Federation and International Society of Cardiology - ISC*] [*Formed by a merger of*] (EAIO)
ISFC.........	International Symposium on Fluorine Chemistry
ISFD.........	Integrated Software Functional Design
ISFE.........	Incident-Shock Frozen Expansion
ISFE.........	Integrated Site Facilities and Equipment (MCD)
ISFE.........	International Society of Flying Engineers [*Defunct*] (EA)
ISFEA........	Infosafe Systems'A' [*NASDAQ symbol*] (TTSB)
ISFEA........	Infosafe Systems, Inc. [*NASDAQ symbol*] (SAG)
ISFET........	Ion-Selective Field Effect Transistor
ISFEU........	Infosafe Sys Units'99 [*NASDAQ symbol*] (TTSB)
ISFEW........	Infosafe Sys Wrrt'A' [*NASDAQ symbol*] (TTSB)
ISFEZ........	Infosafe Sys Wrrt'B [*NASDAQ symbol*] (TTSB)
ISFFSR	Institute for the Study of Fatigue Fracture and Structural Reliability [*George Washington University*]
ISFGW	International Society of Friendship and Good Will (EA)
ISFHC	International Society of Folk Harpers and Craftsmen (EA)
ISFIS	Selective Fisheries Information Service (IID)
ISFL.........	International Scientific Film Library
ISFL.........	International Society of Family Law [*Cambridge, England*] (EAIO)
ISFM.........	Indexed Sequential File Manager [*Computer science*]
ISFMP........	Interstate Fisheries Management Program (GNE)
ISFMS........	Indexed Sequential File Management System [*Computer science*] (BUR)
ISFNR........	International Society for Folk-Narrative Research [*Turku, Finland*] (EA)
ISFR.........	International Society for Fluoride Research
ISFSC........	International Society of Food Service Consultants [*Later, FCSI*] (EA)
ISFSC........	International Society of Free Space Colonizers [*Superseded by Political Action Caucus*] (EA)
ISFSF........	Independent Spent Fuel Storage Facility [*Department of Energy*] [*Nuclear energy*]
ISFSI........	Independent Spent Fuel Storage Installation [*Nuclear energy*] (NRCH)
ISFSI........	International Society of Fire Service Instructors (EA)
ISFSM........	Incompletely-Specified Finite State Machine (MHDB)
ISFV.........	Interstitial Fluid Volume [*Medicine*] (DMAA)
ISG..........	Ayer Public Library, Delavan, IL [*OCLC symbol*] (OCLC)
ISG..........	Idaho State Grange (SRA)
ISG..........	Immune Serum Globulin
ISG..........	Imperial Standard Gallon
ISG..........	Indiana State Grange (SRA)
ISG..........	Inland Shipping Group [*British*]
ISG..........	Institute for the Study of Genocide (EA)
ISG..........	Insurance Services Group
ISG..........	Integrated Survey Grid
ISG..........	Interchangeable and Substitute Group [*Military*] (AFIT)
ISG..........	Interconnected Systems Group
ISG..........	Interfacial Surface Generation [*Instrumentation*]
ISG..........	Internal Shutter Grid
ISG..........	International SYSOP [*System Operator*] Guild
ISG..........	Interservice Group [*Military*]
ISG..........	Intersubblock Gap
ISG..........	Ishigaki [*Japan*] [*Airport symbol*] (OAG)
ISG..........	ISS International Service Systems AS [*NYSE symbol*] (SAG)
ISG..........	ISS-Intl Service Sys ADS [*NYSE symbol*] (TTSB)
ISGA	Idaho Sugarbeet Growers Association (SRA)
ISGA	Illinois Specialty Growers' Association (SRA)
ISGA	Indiana Soybean Growers Association (SRA)
ISGA	International Stained Glass Association (EA)
ISGA	International Study Group for Aerogrammes
ISGC	International Society of Guatemala Collectors (EA)
ISGC	International Steel Guitar Convention (EA)
ISGD	International Study Group of Diabetes in Children and Adolescents [*Linkoping, Sweden*] (EAIO)
ISGE	International Society for Geothermal Engineering [*Defunct*] (EA)
ISGE	International Society of Gastroenterology
ISGF	Interferon-Stimulated Gene Factor [*Biochemistry*]
ISGI	International Sheep and Goat Institute [*Utah State University*] [*Research center*] (RCD)
ISGI	International Standards Group Ltd. [*NASDAQ symbol*] (SAG)
ISGI	Intl Standards Group Ltd [*NASDAQ symbol*] (TTSB)
ISG Intl	ISG International Software Group [*Associated Press*] (SAG)
ISGML	International Study Group for Mathematics Learning [*British*]
ISGN	Insignia (MSA)
ISGO	International Society of Geographic Ophthalmology [*Montreal, PQ*] (EAIO)
ISGOTT	International Safety Guide for Oil Tankers and Terminals (DS)
ISGP	International Society of General Practice [*Germany*] (PDAA)
ISGP	International Society of Geographical Pathology [*Australia*] (EY)
ISGRA	International Study Group on Risk Analysis

ISGS	Illinois State Geological Survey [*Champaign*] [*Information service or system*] (IID)
ISGS	International Society for General Semantics (EA)
ISGSH	International Study Group for Steroid Hormones [*Rome, Italy*] (EAIO)
ISGT........	ISG Technologies, Inc. [*NASDAQ symbol*] (SAG)
ISG Tech.....	ISG Technologies, Inc. [*Associated Press*] (SAG)
ISGTF........	I.S.G. Technologies [*NASDAQ symbol*] (TTSB)
ISgW.........	Waubonsee Community College, Sugar Grove, IL [*Library symbol Library of Congress*] (LCLS)
ISGWRCA	International Study Group for Waterworks in the Rhine Catchment Area [*See also IAWR*] (EAIO)
ISH..........	Caterpillar Tractor Co., Technical Information Center, Peoria, IL [*OCLC symbol*] (OCLC)
ISH..........	Icteric Serum Hepatitis [*Medicine*]
ISH..........	Information Superhighway [*Telecommunications*] (PCM)
ISH..........	Inner Self-Helper [*Mulitple personality*] [*Psychology*]
ISH..........	In Situ Hybridization [*Biology*]
ISH..........	Institute for Scientific Humanism [*Later, WISH*]
ISH..........	Interim Scout Helicopter (MCD)
ISH..........	Intermediate System Hello [*Computer science*] (TNIG)
ISH..........	International Shipholding Corp. [*NYSE symbol*] (NQ)
ISH..........	International Society of Hematology (DAVI)
ISH..........	International Society of Hypertension (EA)
ISH..........	International Sterling [*Vancouver Stock Exchange symbol*]
ISH..........	Intl Shipholding [*NYSE symbol*] (TTSB)
ISH..........	Ishtion [*Former USSR Seismograph station code, US Geological Survey*] (SEIS)
ISH..........	Isolated Systolic Hypertension [*Cardiology*] (DAVI)
ISHAE	International Society of Hotel Association Executives (EA)
ISHAM	International Society for Human and Animal Mycology [*London School of Hygiene and Tropical Medicine*] [*British*]
ISHC	Indicated Specific Hydrocarbon [*Automotive exhaust emission testing*]
ISHC	International Siberian Husky Club
ISHC	International Symposium on Homogeneous Catalysis
IShCoH	Shelby County Memorial Hospital, Shelbyville, IL [*Library symbol Library of Congress*] (LCLS)
ISHE	International Safety and Health Exhibition [*British*] (ITD)
ISHE	International Society for Human Ethology (EA)
ISHE	International Society of Healthcare Executives (EA)
IShe	Sheldon Township Public Library, Sheldon, IL [*Library symbol Library of Congress*] (LCLS)
ISherESD	Sheridan Elementary School District 272, Sheridan, IL [*Library symbol Library of Congress*] (LCLS)
ISHG	Indian Society of Human Genetics
ISHH	In Situ Hybridization Histochemistry
ISHI	Institute for the Study of Human Issues (EA)
ISHI	International Society for the History of Ideas (EA)
ISHK	Institute for the Study of Human Knowledge (EA)
ISHL	International Society for Historical Linguistics (EAIO)
ISHLT........	International Society for Heart and Lung Transplantation (EAIO)
ISHM	International Society for Hybrid Microelectronics (EA)
ISho	South Holland Public Library, South Holland, IL [*Library symbol Library of Congress*] (LCLS)
ISHOF	International Swimming Hall of Fame (EA)
IShoSHi	South Suburban Genealogical and Historical Society, South Holland, IL [*Library symbol Library of Congress*] (LCLS)
IShoT........	Thornton Community College, South Holland, IL [*Library symbol Library of Congress*] (LCLS)
ISHOW	Information System for Hazardous Organics in Water [*Database*] [*Environmental Protection Agency Information service or system*] (CRD)
(I)SHP........	(Intermediate) Shaft Horsepower
ISHPES	International Society for the History of Physical Education and Sport [*Belgium*] (EAIO)
ISHR	Intermediate Scale Homogeneous Reactor
ISHR	International Society for Heart Research [*Winnipeg, MB*] (EA)
ISHR	International Society for Human Rights [*See also IGM*] [*Frankfurt, Federal Republic of Germany*] (EAIO)
ISHR	International Society for the History of Rhetoric (EA)
ISHRA	Iron and Steel Holdings and Realisation Agency [*British*]
ISHS	Improved Spartan Homing Sensor [*Missiles*]
ISHS	International Society for Horticultural Science [*See also SISH*] [*ICSU Wageningen, Netherlands*] (EAIO)
ISHS	International Society for Humor Studies (EA)
ISHT	International Society for Heart Transplantation (EA)
ISHTAR	Inner Shelf Transfer and Recycling [*Marine science*] (OSRA)
ISHTCP	Inventory of Sources for History of Twentieth Century Physics [*University of California, Berkeley*] [*Information service or system*] (IID)
ISHTE	In-Situ Heat Transfer Experiment [*Nuclear energy*] (NUCP)
ISHVBS	International Society for Hildegard Von Bingen Studies (EA)
ISI............	Chillicothe Township Free Public Library, Chillicothe, IL [*OCLC symbol*] (OCLC)
ISI............	Indian Standards Institution
ISI............	Indian Statistical Institute
ISI............	Induced Spatial Incoherence [*Physics*]
ISI............	Industrial Security International
ISI............	Industrial Static Inverter
ISI............	Industry Standard Item (AAG)
ISI............	Infarct Size Index [*Cardiology*]
ISI............	Infodata Systems, Inc. [*Information service or system*] (IID)
ISI............	Informal Spelling Inventory [*Education*]
ISI............	Information Science, Inc.

ISI.............. Information Sciences Institute [*University of Southern California, Marina Del Rey*]
ISI.............. Information Service of India
ISI.............. Information Services, Inc. [*Information service or system*] (IID)
ISI.............. Information Services International [*Information service or system*] (IID)
ISI.............. Information Storage, Inc.
ISI.............. Inhibited Sporozoite Invasion [*Immunology*]
ISI.............. Initial Shipping Instructions (MCD)
ISI.............. Initial Support Increments [*Army*] (AABC)
ISI.............. Initial Support Item
ISI.............. Initial Systems Installation (NASA)
ISI.............. Injury Severity Index (MCD)
ISI.............. In-Service Inspection (NRCH)
ISI.............. In-Service Institute [*National Science Foundation*]
ISI.............. Institute for Scientific Information [*Philadelphia, PA*] [*Database producer*]
ISI.............. Institute for Social Inquiry [*University of Connecticut*] [*Storrs*] [*Information service or system*] (IID)
ISI.............. Instrumentation Support Instruction (KSC)
ISI.............. Integra Systems, Inc. [*Toronto Stock Exchange symbol Vancouver Stock Exchange symbol*]
ISI.............. Intelligent Serial Interface [*Computer science*]
ISI.............. Intercollegiate Studies Institute (EA)
ISI.............. Interim Support Item (MCD)
ISI.............. Internally Specified Index
ISI.............. International Safety Institute [*Defunct*] (EA)
ISI.............. International Satellite for Ionospheric Studies [*NASA-Canada*] (NOAA)
ISI.............. International Satellite, Inc. [*Telecommunications*]
ISI.............. International Sensitivity Index [*Hematology*]
ISI.............. International Statistical Institute [*ICSU*] [*Voorburg, Netherlands*] (EA)
ISI.............. International Students, Inc. (EA)
ISI.............. Interpersonal Style Inventory [*Personality development test*] [*Psychology*]
ISI.............. Inter-Sound Interval (EDAC)
ISI.............. Interspike Interval [*Neurophysiology*]
ISI.............. Interstimulus Interval
ISI.............. Intersymbol Interference
ISI.............. Ion Source Injector
ISI.............. Iron and Steel Institute (MCD)
ISI.............. Ishigakijima [*Ryukyu Islands*] [*Seismograph station code, US Geological Survey*] (SEIS)
ISI.............. Isisford [*Australia Airport symbol*] (OAG)
ISI.............. Italic Studies Institute (EA)
ISI.............. Item Station and Indenture (AAG)
ISIA.............. Ice Skating Institute of America (EA)
ISIA.............. International Ski Instructors' Association (ECON)
ISIA.............. International Snowmobile Industry Association (EA)
ISIA.............. Italo Svevo International Association [*Defunct*] (EA)
ISIAL.............. Incorporated Society of Irish/American Lawyers (EA)
ISIAME.............. International Symposium on the Industrial Applications of the Mossbauer Effect
ISIB.............. Institute for the Study of Intellectual Behavior [*University of Colorado*] (PDAA)
ISIB.............. Inter-Service Ionosphere Bureau [*Military*]
ISIC.............. Immediate Superior in Command [*Military*]
ISIC.............. Intelligence Support and Indications Center [*Military*] (MCD)
ISIC.............. International Standard Industrial Classification (EY)
ISIC.............. International Student Identity Card (BARN)
ISICCE.............. Intersymbol Interference Corrector
ISICCE.............. International Society of India Chemists and Chemical Engineers (EA)
ISICS.............. Indian Self-Identified Certified Staff (EDAC)
ISID.............. International Society of Interior Designers (EA)
ISid.............. Sidell District Library, Sidell, IL [*Library symbol Library of Congress*] (LCLS)
ISIDHI.............. International Society on Infectious Diseases and Human Infertility (EA)
ISidn.............. Sidney Community Library, Sidney, IL [*Library symbol Library of Congress*] (LCLS)
ISIDPP.............. Initial Shut-In Drill Pipe Pressure
ISidSD.............. Jamaica Community Unit School District, Sidell, IL [*Library symbol*] [*Library of Congress*] (LCLS)
ISIE.............. Integral Square Ideal Error (IAA)
ISIFM.............. International Society of Industrial Fabric Manufacturers (EA)
ISIG.............. Implementation Special Interest Group [*Association for the Development of Computer-Based Instructional Systems*] (EDAC)
ISIG.............. Insignia Sys [*NASDAQ symbol*] (TTSB)
ISIG.............. Insignia Systems, Inc. [*NASDAQ symbol*] (SAG)
ISIG.............. Irish Special Interest Group of American Mensa (EA)
ISIH.............. Interspike Interval Histogram [*Neurophysiology*]
ISII.............. International Society for Individualized Instruction (AIE)
ISI/IST.............. In-Service Inspections and In-Service Testing
ISI/ISTP & B... ISI/Index to Scientific and Technical Proceedings and Books [*Institute for Scientific Information*] [*Philadelphia, PA Bibliographic database*]
ISIJ.............. Iron and Steel Institute of Japan
ISIL.............. Interim Support Items List (NASA)
ISIL.............. International Society for Individual Liberty (EAIO)
ISILT.............. Information Science Index Language Text (NITA)
ISIM.............. Inhibit Simultaneity (IAA)
ISIM.............. [*The*] International School of Inforamtion Management, Inc. [*Denver, CO*] (ECON)
ISIM.............. [*The*] International School of Information Management, Inc. [*Denver, CO*] (ECON)

ISIM.............. International Society of Internal Medicine [*Langenthal, Switzerland*] (EA)
ISIM.............. Inventory Simulation (IAA)
ISIMC.............. International Study Institution of the Middle Classes [*Brussels, Belgium*] (EAIO)
ISIMEP.............. International Symposium on Identification and Measurement of Environmental Pollutants (PDAA)
ISIMM.............. International Society for the Interaction of Mechanics and Mathematics (EA)
ISINC.............. Immediate Superior in Command [*Military*]
ISIP.............. Indexed Security Investment Plan [*Canada*]
ISIP.............. Intelligence Support Interface Program
ISIP.............. Isis Pharmaceuticals [*NASDAQ symbol*] (SPSG)
ISIPP.............. Information System for Improved Plant Protection [*FAO*] [*United Nations*] (DUND)
ISIR.............. Initial Sample Inspection Report
ISIR.............. In Service, In Reserve [*Vessel status*] [*Navy*]
ISIR.............. Interactive Single Isomorphous Replacement [*Crystallographic procedure*]
ISIR.............. International Satellite for Ionospheric Research [*NASA Canada*] (IAA)
ISIR.............. International Society for the Immunology of Reproduction (EA)
ISIR.............. International Society of Invertebrate Reproduction (EA)
ISIR.............. International Symposium on Industrial Robots (PDAA)
ISIR.............. Iterative Single Isomorphous Replacement [*Crystallography*]
ISIRC.............. International Statistical Institute Research Center [*Research center Netherlands*] (IRC)
ISIRS.............. International Sorption Information Retrieval System [*Nuclear Energy Agency*] (EY)
ISIRTA.............. I'm Sorry, I'll Read That Again [*BBC radio comedy program*]
ISIS.............. Image-Selected in Vivo Spectroscopy
ISIS.............. Impact Shock Isolation System [*Tennis-racket technology*] [*Dunlop Slazenger Corp.*]
ISIS.............. Independence Square Income Securities [*NASDAQ symbol*] (SAG)
ISIS.............. Independence Square Income Securities, Inc. [*NASDAQ symbol*] (NQ)
ISIS.............. Independent Schools Information Service [*British*]
ISIS.............. Indian School of International Studies [*Delhi*]
ISIS.............. Individualized Science Instructional System [*National Science Foundation project*]
ISIS.............. Information System Indexing System [*Federal Judicial Center*] [*Database*]
ISIS.............. Instant Sales Indicator System (IAA)
ISIS.............. Institute for the Study of Inquiring Systems
ISIS.............. Institute of Scrap Iron and Steel [*Later, ISRI*] (EA)
ISIS.............. Institute of Strategic and International Studies [*Malaysia*] (ECON)
ISIS.............. Institutional Sector Investment Services [*Chase Manhattan Securities*] [*British*]
ISIS.............. Integral Service Information System (IAA)
ISIS.............. Integral Spar Inspection System
ISIS.............. Integrated Safeguard Information System (NRCH)
ISIS.............. Integrated Scientific Information System
ISIS.............. Integrated Set of Information Systems (IAA)
ISIS.............. Integrated Ship Instrumentation System (IAA)
ISIS.............. Integrated Side-Impact System [*Automotive safety*]
ISIS.............. Integrated Software Invocation System [*Computer science*] (MHDI)
ISIS.............. Integrated Statistical Information Service (WDAA)
ISIS.............. Integrated Strike and Interceptor System
ISIS.............. Integrated Surface Irradiance Study [*Marine science*] (OSRA)
ISIS.............. Integrated Surface Irradiance Study (USDC)
ISIS.............. Integrated System for Improved Separations [*Membrane filtration*]
ISIS.............. Integriertes Statistisches Informationssystem [*Integrated Statistical Information System*] [*Central Statistical Office Vienna, Austria*] [*Information service or system*] (IID)
ISIS.............. Interchangeability and Substitutability Item Subgroup (MCD)
ISIS.............. Intermarket Surveillance Information System (DFIT)
IS-IS.............. Intermediate System-to-Intermediate System [*Telecommunications*]
ISIS.............. Internally Switched Interface System [*Tymnet, Inc.*]
ISIS.............. Internationale de Services Industriels and Scientifiques
ISIS.............. Internationally Syndicated Information Services [*Information service or system Defunct*] (IID)
ISIS.............. International Satellite for Ionospheric Studies [*NASA-Canada*]
ISIS.............. International Science Information Services [*Earth sciences data center*] [*Dallas, TX*]
ISIS.............. International Shipping Information Service (DS)
ISIS.............. International Society of Introduction Services (EA)
ISIS.............. International Space Information System [*United Nations*] (DUND)
ISIS.............. International Species Information System (IID)
ISIS.............. International Species Inventory System [*Data processing for animal mating*] [*Minnesota Zoological Gardens Apple Valley, MN*]
ISIS.............. International Student Information Service
ISIS.............. International Study of Infarct Survival [*Medicine*]
ISIS.............. International Superconductivity Industry Summit [*Conference*]
ISIS.............. Interstate Settlement Information System [*AT & T*]
ISIS.............. Investigative Support Information System [*Federal Bureau of Investigation*]
Isis.............. Isis Pharmaceuticals, Inc. [*Associated Press*] (SAG)
ISIS.............. Item Standardization Information System [*DoD*]
ISIS.............. Women's International Information and Communication Service [*Italy and Switzerland*]
ISISA.............. Individual Scale for Indian South Africans [*Intelligence test*]
ISISC.............. Istituto Superiore Internazionale di Scienze Criminali [*Italy*]
ISISSAPORCI... International Section of ISSA [*International Social Security Association*] on the Prevention of Occupational Risks in the Construction Industry [*Boulogne-Billancourt, France*] (EAIO)

ISIS-WICCE...	ISIS [*Women's International Information Communication Service*] - Women's International Cross-Cultural Exchange (EAIO)
ISIS-X.........	International Satellites for Ionosphere Studies - Experimental [*NASA/Canada*] (SAA)
ISIT.............	Intensified Silicon Intensifier Target (MCD)
ISITB...........	Iron and Steel Industry Training Board [*British*] (BI)
ISIUP.........	Islamic Society for International Unity and Peace [*Pakistan*] (EAIO)
ISIYM.........	International Society of Industrial Yarn Manufacturers [*Later, ISIFM*] (EA)
ISJ.............	Institute for Social Justice (EA)
ISJ.............	Saint Joseph's College, Rensselaer, IN [*OCLC symbol*] (OCLC)
ISJAC..........	Independent Schools Joint Action Committee (AIE)
ISJC...........	Independent Schools Joint Council [*British*]
ISJCT..........	International Symposium on Jet Cutting Technology (PDAA)
IsJJNL.........	Jewish National and University Library, Hebrew University, Jerusalem, Israel [*Library symbol Library of Congress*] (LCLS)
ISJL............	International Society of Jewish Librarians (EA)
ISJP...........	International Society for Japanese Philately (EA)
ISJTA..........	Intensive Student Jet Training Area
ISK.............	Galva Township Public Library, Galva, IL [*OCLC symbol*] (OCLC)
ISK.............	Insert Storage Key (IEEE)
ISK.............	Instruction Space Key
ISK.............	Internacia Scienca Kolegio [*International College of Scientists - ICS*] [*Paderborn, Federal Republic of Germany*] (EAIO)
ISK.............	Internationale Seidenbau Kommission [*International Sericultural Commission*]
ISK.............	International Society of the Knee (EA)
ISK.............	Ion Source Kit
ISK.............	Iskenderon [*Turkey*] [*Airport symbol*] (AD)
ISK.............	Iskut Gold Corp. [*Vancouver Stock Exchange symbol*]
ISK.............	Istanbul-Kandilli [*Turkey*] [*Seismograph station code, US Geological Survey*] (SEIS)
ISK.............	Nasik [*India*] [*Airport symbol*] (OAG)
ISk.............	Skokie Public Library, Skokie, IL [*Library symbol Library of Congress*] (LCLS)
ISKA...........	International Saw and Knife Association (EA)
ISKCON........	International Society for Krishna Consciousness (EA)
ISKDC.........	International Study of Kidney Disease in Children
ISkH...........	Hebrew Theological College, Skokie, IL [*Library symbol Library of Congress*] (LCLS)
ISKI...........	International Secretariat of the Knitting Industries [*Paris, France*] (EAIO)
ISKO..........	International Society for Knowledge Organization [*Germany*] (EAIO)
ISKO..........	Isco, Inc. [*NASDAQ symbol*] (NQ)
ISkS...........	G. D. Searle & Co., Inc., Skokie, IL [*Library symbol Library of Congress*] (LCLS)
ISkT...........	Triodyne, Skokie, IL [*Library symbol Library of Congress*] (LCLS)
ISL.............	Eagle Air Ltd. [*Iceland*] [*ICAO designator*] (FAAC)
ISL.............	First Israel Fund [*NYSE symbol*] (TTSB)
ISL.............	Iceland [*ANSI three-letter standard code*] (CNC)
ISL.............	Immunodeficiency-Virus-Suppressing Lymphokine [*Virology*]
ISL.............	Inactive Status List (MUGU)
ISL.............	Indiana State Library, Indianapolis, IN [*OCLC symbol*] (OCLC)
ISL.............	Industrial Security Letter [*DoD*]
ISL.............	Inertial Systems Laboratory [*NASA*] (GFGA)
ISL.............	Informatics Services [*Oakville, ON*] [*Telecommunications service*] (TSSD)
ISL.............	Information Search Language
ISL.............	Information Services Ltd. [*Publisher*] [*British*]
ISL.............	Information System Language [*Computer science*] (IEEE)
ISL.............	Information Systems Laboratories, Inc.
ISL.............	Initial Spare Parts List (IAA)
ISL.............	Initial Stocks List
ISL.............	Initial System Loading
ISL.............	Injection Coupled Synchronous Logic (IAA)
ISL.............	Inner Scapular Line [*Medicine*] (DMAA)
ISL.............	In Situ Leaching (GAAI)
ISL.............	Institute of Space Law
ISL.............	Institut fuer Seeverkehrwirtschaft und Logistik [*Institute of Shipping Economics and Logistics - ISEL*] [*Bremen, Federal Republic of Germany*] (EAIO)
ISL.............	Instructional Systems Language [*Computer science*] (IEEE)
ISL.............	Instrument Standards Laboratory [*Space Flight Operations Facility, NASA*]
ISL.............	Integrated Schottky Logic (IEEE)
ISL.............	Integrated Stock Listing
ISL.............	Integrated Synthesis Logic [*Computer science*]
ISL.............	Interactive Simulation Language [*Computer science*] (IEEE)
ISL.............	Internally-Silvered Lamp [*Light bulb*] (DI)
ISL.............	Internal Standard Line
ISL.............	International Soccer League
ISL.............	International Society of Literature [*Ilkley, Yorkshire, England*] (EAIO)
ISL.............	International Society of Lymphology (EA)
ISL.............	International Subcommittee on Lactobacilli and Closely Related Organisms
ISL.............	Intersatellite Link
ISL.............	Interspinous Ligament [*Medicine*] (DMAA)
ISL.............	Intersystem Link
ISL.............	Island [*Board on Geographic Names*]
ISL.............	Isle
ISL.............	Islington (ROG)
ISL.............	Isolated Signal Line (IAA)
ISL.............	Item Selection List
ISL.............	Item Study Listings
ISL.............	Item Survey List (DNAB)
ISL.............	Lincoln Library, Springfield, IL [*Library symbol Library of Congress*] (LCLS)
ISLA...........	Information Services on Latin America (EA)
ISLA...........	International Survey Libraries Association [*University of Connecticut*] (NITA)
ISLA...........	International Survey Library Association (EA)
ISLADE........	Interactive Structural Layout and Design [*Module*]
ISLAN.........	Integrated Services Local Area Network [*Telecommunications*] (ACRL)
ISLAND.......	Island [*Commonly used*] (OPSA)
ISLANDS......	Islands [*Commonly used*] (OPSA)
ISLAR.........	International Symposium on Laboratory Automation and Robotics
ISLC...........	International Sporting and Leisure Club
ISLC...........	Lincoln Land Community College, Springfield, IL [*Library symbol Library of Congress*] (LCLS)
ISLCBS........	International Seal, Label, and Cigar Band Society (EA)
ISLD...........	Institute for the Study of Learning Difficulties [*Flinders University*] [*Australia*]
ISLD...........	International Special Librarians Day
ISLD...........	Inter-Services Liaison Department [*World War II*]
ISLE...........	Integral Square Linear Error (IAA)
ISLE...........	Integrated Simulation Language Environment [*Computer science*]
ISLE...........	Isle [*Postal Service standard*] (OPSA)
ISLEC.........	Institute for the Study of Labor and Economic Crisis (EA)
ISLER.........	Islander
ISLES.........	Isle [*Commonly used*] (OPSA)
ISLF...........	Improved Saturn Launch Facility
ISLFD.........	Incorporated Society of London Fashion Designers
ISLI...........	INTERSOLV [*NASDAQ symbol*] (TTSB)
ISLI...........	Intersolv, Inc. [*NASDAQ symbol*] (SAG)
ISLIC.........	Israel Society of Special Libraries and Information Centers
ISLL...........	International Survey of Legal Decisions on Labour Law [*1925-38*] [*A publication*] (DLA)
ISL/LAR.......	Integrated Logistics System and Logistics Assessment Review
ISLLSL........	International Society for Labor Law and Social Legislation [*Later, International Society for Labor Law and Social Security United States National Branch*] (EA)
ISLLSS........	International Society for Labor Law and Social Security [*International Congresses of Labour Law and International Society for Social Law*] [*Formed by a merger of*] (EAIO)
ISLM..........	Integration Shop/Laboratory Manager (MCD)
ISLM..........	Investment-Savings, Liquidity-Money [*Economics*] (ODBW)
ISLMA........	Illinois School Library Media Association (SRA)
ISLN..........	Isolation (MSA)
ISLND........	Island [*Commonly used*] (OPSA)
ISLNDS.......	Islands [*Commonly used*] (OPSA)
ISLP..........	IGOSS [*Integrated Global Ocean Services System*] Sea Level Project [*Marine science*] (OSRA)
ISLP-Pac.....	GOSS [*Integrated Global Ocean Station System*] Sea Level Project in the Pacific (USDC)
ISLP-Pac.....	IGOSS [*Integrated Global Ocean Services System*] Sea Level Project in the Pacific [*Marine science*] (OSRA)
ISLR..........	Initial Sample Laboratory Report
ISLR..........	Integrated Side-Lobe Ratio
ISLR..........	International Symposium on Laboratory Robotics
ISLR..........	Isolator (MSA)
ISLRS........	Inactive Status List Reserve Section
ISLS..........	Improved Side-Lobe Supression (PDAA)
ISLS..........	Intelligent Surgical Lasers, Inc. [*NASDAQ symbol*] (SAG)
ISLS..........	Interrogation Side-Lobe Suppression
ISLS..........	Islands [*Board on Geographic Names*]
ISLSCP........	International Satellite Land Surface Climatology Project [*Federal government*]
ISLT..........	International Snow Leopard Trust (EA)
ISLTS........	Incorporated Society of Licensed Trade Stocktakers [*British*] (DBA)
ISLW.........	Indian Spring Low Water [*Tides and currents*]
ISLWF........	International Shoe and Leather Workers' Federation
ISLWG........	Working Group on International Shipping Legislation [*UNCTAD*] (DS)
ISM..........	Iesus Salvator Mundi [*Jesus, Savior of the World*] [*Latin*]
ISM..........	Imperial Service Medal [*British*]
ISM..........	Improved Sensing Munitions (RDA)
ISM..........	Incorporated Society of Musicians [*British*]
ISM..........	Independent Subcarrier Method (PDAA)
ISM..........	Indian Supply Mission [*World War II*]
ISM..........	Industrial, Scientific, and Medical (IAA)
ISM..........	Industrial, Scientific and Medical Applications
ISM..........	Industrial Security Manual (MCD)
ISM..........	Information System Manager (NATG)
ISM..........	Information Systems for Management (IEEE)
ISM..........	Information Systems Marketing, Inc. [*Information service or system*] (IID)
ISM..........	Infrared Systems Manufacturing
ISM..........	Initial Segment Membrane
ISM..........	Inside of Metal
ISM..........	Institute for the Study of Man (EA)
ISM..........	Institute of Sanitation Management [*Later, EMA*] (EA)
ISM..........	Institute of Spiritualist Mediums [*British*] (DBA)
ISM..........	Institute of Sports Medicine [*British*]
ISM..........	Institute of Supervisory Management [*British*]
ISM..........	Instructional System in Mathematics Program (EDAC)
ISM..........	Insulation System Module [*Engineering*] (OA)
ISM..........	Integrated Sander Machine [*Disk controller*] [*Apple Computer, Inc.*] (BYTE)
ISM..........	Integrated Skills Method [*Education*]
ISM..........	Integrated Sustainment Maintenance

ISM............. Interactive Siting Method (PDAA)
ISM............. Interavia Space Markets [*Interavia Publications*] [*Information service or system*] (CRD)
ISM............. Interim Surface Missile (PDAA)
ISM............. International Camero Resources [*Vancouver Stock Exchange symbol*]
ISM............. International Society for Metaphysics (EA)
ISM............. International Society of Microbiologists (DAVI)
ISM............. International Software Marketing (HGAA)
ISM............. International Soil Museum
ISM............. International Standards Method (IAA)
ISM............. International Sweets Market [*Trade fair*] [*Cologne, West Germany 1982*]
ISM............. International Symposium on Microchemistry
ISM............. International Symposium on Microtechniques
ISM............. International Systems Meeting [*Computer science*]
ISM............. Interpretive Structural Modeling [*A computer-assisted learning process for structuring information*]
ISM............. Intersegmental Muscles [*Anatomy*] (DAVI)
ISM............. Interstellar Medium [*Planetary science*]
ISM............. Ion-Selective Material [*Chemistry*]
ISM............. Ion Selective Microelectrodes [*Instrumentation*]
ISM............. Irish School of Music (ROG)
ISM............. ISDN [*Integrated Services Digital Network*] Subscriber Module [*Telecommunications*]
ISM............. Istituto Internazionale Suore di Santa Marcellina [*Also, Instituto Marcelline*] [*Italy*] (EAIO)
ISM............. Kissimmee, FL [*Location identifier FAA*] (FAAL)
ISM............. Southern Methodist University, Central Library, Dallas, TX [*OCLC symbol*] (OCLC)
ISMA......... Indiana State Medical Association (SRA)
ISMA......... Industrial Silencer Manufacturers Association (EA)
ISMA......... Infantile Spinal Muscular Atrophy [*Medicine*] (DAVI)
ISMA......... Institute of Sisters of Mercy of Australia
ISMA......... International Security Management Association [*Boston, MA*] (EA)
ISMA......... International Shipmasters Association (EA)
ISMA......... International Superphosphate Manufacturers' Association [*Later, IFA*]
Is Mag...... Island Magazine [*A publication*]
ISMAP .... Indirect Source Model for Air Pollution [*Environmental Protection Agency*] (GFGA)
ISMAR .... International Society of Magnetic Resonance
ISMB......... Information System Management Board [*NATO*] (NATG)
ISMB......... International Society of Mathematical Biology [*See also SIBM*] [*Antony, France*] (EAIO)
ISMC......... Independent Schools Microelectronics Centre [*British*]
ISMC......... International Switching Maintenance Center [*Communications*]
ISMD......... Indian Subordinate Medical Department [*British military*] (DMA)
ISMDA .... Independent Sewing Machine Dealers Association (EA)
ISMDKTS .... Iron, Steel, Metal Dressers, and Kindred Trades Society [*A union*] [*British*]
ISME......... Institute of Sheet Metal Engineering [*British*]
ISME......... International Society for Music Education (EA)
ISME......... International Society of Marine Engineers
ISME......... International Society of Mechanical Engineers
ISME......... International Sympsosium on Marine Engineering (PDAA)
ISMEC......... Information Service in Mechanical Engineering [*Cambridge Scientific Abstracts*] [*British Information service or system*] (IID)
ISMED .... International Society on Metabolic Eye Disease (EA)
ISMES......... Experimental Institute for Models and Structures [*Italy*]
ISMET......... Inter-Service Metallurgical Research Council [*British*] (MCD)
ISMF......... Inactive Ship Maintenance Facility
ISMF......... International Sports Massage Federation (EA)
ISMG......... International Scientific Management Group [*GARP*] (NOAA)
ISMGF .... International Stoke Mandeville Games Federation [*Aylesbury, Buckinghamshire, England*] (EA)
ISMGR......... Island Manager (FAAC)
ISMH......... Input Source Message Handler
ISMH......... International Society of Medical Hydrology and Climatology
ISMHC .... International Society of Medical Hydrology and Climatology (EA)
ISMI......... Improved Space Manned Interceptor (IAA)
ISMIS......... Improved SAGE [*Semiautomatic Ground Environment*] Manned Intercept System (IAA)
ISMIS......... Interservice Depot Maintenance Interrogation Systems
ISMIT......... International Society for Mental Imagery Techniques [*France*] (EAIO)
ISmK......... Kaskaska Library System, Smithton, IL [*Library symbol Library of Congress*] (LCLS)
ISML......... Institute for the Study of Matrimonial Laws (EA)
ISML......... Intermediate System Mock-Up Loop (IEEE)
ISMLS......... Interim Standard Microwave Landing System [*Aviation*]
ISMM......... International Society for Music in Medicine (EAIO)
ISMM......... International Society of Mini- and Micro-Computers [*Calgary, AB*] (EAIO)
ISMMRRI .... Iowa State Mining and Mineral Resources Research Institute [*Iowa State University*] [*Research center*] (RCD)
ISMMS......... Integrated Stores Monitor and Management System [*Later, Armament Control Panel*] (MCD)
ISMN......... Isosorbide Mononitrate [*Coronary vasodilator*]
ISMO .... Ion-Sieve-Type Manganese Oxide [*Inorganic chemistry*]
ISMOD......... Index Sequential Module (IAA)
ISMPH......... International Society for Medical and Psychological Hypnosis (EA)
ISMR......... Independent Snowmobile Medical Research [*An association*] (EA)
ISMRC......... Inter-Services Metallurgical Research Council [*British*]
ISMS......... Illinois State Medical Society (SRA)
ISMS......... Image Store Management System

ISMS............. Improved SPRINT [*Solid-Propellant Rocket Intercept*] Missile Subsystem [*Army*]
ISMS............. Industrial Standards and Military Specifications [*Information Handling Services*] [*Information service or system*] (CRD)
ISMS............. Information Systems and Media Services [*Eastern Illinois University*] [*Information service or system*] (IID)
ISMS............. Infrared Spectral Measurement System (MCD)
ISMS............. Inherently Safe Mining Systems (PDAA)
ISMS............. Integrated Software Maintenance System
ISMS............. Interactive Solids Modeling System [*Gould Electronics Ltd. Computer Systems*] [*Software package*] (NCC)
ISMS............. International Society for Mushroom Science [*Braunschweig, Federal Republic of Germany*] (EA)
ISMS-D .... Improved SPRINT [*Solid-Propellant Rocket Intercept*] Missile Subsystem - Derated [*Army*]
ISMSD .... Istituto delle Suore Maestre di Santa Dorotea [*Rome, Italy*] (EAIO)
ISmSD .... Smithton Community Consolidated School District 130, Smithton, IL [*Library symbol Library of Congress*] (LCLS)
ISMT............. Indoor Simulated Marksmanship Trainer [*Military*]
ISMT............. Integrated System Maintenance Trainer (MCD)
ISMUN .... International Youth and Student Movement for the United Nations [*Geneva, Switzerland*] (EA)
ISMV............. Iris Severe Mosaic Virus
ISMX............. Integrated Subrate Data Multiplexer (TEL)
ISN .... Information Systems Network [*AT & T*] [*Telecommunications*]
ISN .... Initial Sequence Number (IAA)
ISN .... Instron Corp. [*AMEX symbol*] (SPSG)
ISN .... Internal Statement Number (IAA)
ISN .... International Society for Neurochemistry [*Kjeller, Norway*] (EA)
ISN .... International Society of Nephrology
ISN .... International Suneva Resources [*Vancouver Stock Exchange symbol*]
ISN .... Internment Serial Number
ISN .... Interplant Shipping Notice
ISN .... Ishinomaki [*Japan*] [*Seismograph station code, US Geological Survey*] (SEIS)
ISN .... Item Sequence Number (MCD)
ISN .... Saint Mary's College, Notre Dame, IN [*OCLC symbol*] (OCLC)
ISN .... Williston [*North Dakota*] [*Airport symbol*] (OAG)
ISN .... Williston, ND [*Location identifier FAA*] (FAAL)
ISNA .... International Society for New Atlantis (EA)
ISNA .... International Space: 1999 Alliance (EA)
ISNA .... International Symposium on Novel Aromatic Compounds
ISNAC............. Inactive Ships Navy Custody (NVT)
ISNAR............. International Service for National Agricultural Research [*The Hague, Netherlands*]
ISNE............. International Scale of Nuclear Events
ISNOX............. Indicated Specific Oxides of Nitrogen [*Automotive exhaust emission testing*]
ISNP............. Independent Scholarship National Program [*Defunct*] (EA)
ISNP............. International Society of Naturopathic Physicians
ISNR............. State of Illinois, Institute of Natural Resources, Energy Information Library, Springfield, IL [*Library symbol Library of Congress*] (LCLS)
ISNR-E........ State of Illinois, Institute of Natural Resources, Division of Environmental Management, Chicago, IL [*Library symbol Library of Congress*] (LCLS)
ISNS .... Image Sensing Systems [*NASDAQ symbol*] (TTSB)
ISNS .... Image Sensing Systems, Inc. [*NASDAQ symbol*] (SAG)
ISNS .... Institute for the Study of Natural Systems (EA)
ISNS .... International Society for Neoplatonic Studies (EA)
ISNSE .... International School for Nuclear Science and Engineering
ISNSL............. Incremental Stock Number Sequence List [*Military*] (CAAL)
ISNT............. Informal Single Negotiating Text [*Marine science*] (MSC)
ISNU............. Illinois State Normal University
ISNV............. Institute for the Study of Nonviolence [*Defunct*] (EA)
ISNY............. Insurance Society of New York [*New York, NY*] (EA)
ISO............. Illegal Support Officer [*CIA*] (LAIN)
ISO............. Imaging Spectrometric Observatory (MCD)
ISO............. Imperial Service Order [*British*]
ISO............. I'm So Optimistic [*Dance company*]
ISO............. Incentive Stock Option
ISO............. Independent Sales Organization (HGAA)
ISO............. Individual System Operation
ISO............. Industrial Safety Office
ISO............. Information Services Officer
ISO............. Information Systems Office [*Library of Congress*]
ISO............. Infrared Space Observatory
ISO............. In Search Of [*Classified advertising*]
ISO............. Inside-Out [*Biochemistry*]
ISO............. Installation Supply Officer [*Military*]
ISO............. Insurance Services Office [*An association*] (EA)
IS(O)............. Intelligence Section, Operations [*Control Commission for Germany*] [*World War II*]
ISO............. Intermediate Station Operation (IAA)
ISO............. Internal Standard Organization Code (CMD)
ISO............. Internal System Organization (ECII)
ISO............. International Organization for Standardization [*Geneva, Switzerland*] [*United Nations*]
ISO............. International Science Organization
ISO............. International Self-Service Organization
ISO............. International Shopfitting Organization [*Zurich, Switzerland*] (EAIO)
ISO............. International Sikh Organization (EA)
ISO............. International Socialist Organization (EA)
ISO............. International Society of Organbuilders [*Levallois-Perret, France*] (EAIO)

ISO............	International Standards Organization [*Communications*] (PCM)
ISO..............	International Sugar Organization [*See also OIA*] [*British*] (EAIO)
ISO..............	Interplant Shipping Order
ISO..............	Intraseasonal Atmospheric Oscillation (USDC)
ISO..............	ISG Technologies, Inc. [*Toronto Stock Exchange symbol*]
ISO..............	Isochromatic (ROG)
ISO..............	Isoflurane [*An anesthetic*]
ISO..............	Isola [*France*] [*Seismograph station code, US Geological Survey*] (SEIS)
iso	Isolated [*Slang*] (WDMC)
ISO..............	Isolated Camera (NTCM)
ISO..............	Isolation
ISO..............	Isolation
ISO..............	Isomedix, Inc. [*NYSE symbol*] (SAG)
ISO..............	Isomedix Inc. [*NYSE symbol*] (TTSB)
iso	Isometric (VRA)
ISO..............	Isometric (MSA)
Iso	Isophase
ISO..............	Isoproterenol [*An adrenergic*]
ISO..............	Isotope
ISO..............	Isotropic (KSC)
ISO..............	Isotype
ISO..............	Israel Students Organization
ISO..............	Kinston [*North Carolina*] [*Airport symbol*] (OAG)
ISO..............	Kinston, NC [*Location identifier FAA*] (FAAL)
ISO..............	South Bend Public Library, South Bend, IN [*OCLC symbol*] (OCLC)
ISOA	Improved State-of-the-Art (PDAA)
ISO-ALPHABET...	International Standards Organization-Authorized Alphabetic Characters (MCD)
ISOB	Incorporated Society of Organ Builders [*British*] (BI)
ISOB	International Society of Barristers (EA)
Isoc............	De Isocrate [*of Dionysius Halicarnassensis*] [*Classical studies*] (OCD)
ISOC	Individual System/Organization Cost (MHDB)
ISOC	Instituto de Informacion y Documentacion en Ciencias Sociales y Humanidades [*Institute for Information and Documentation in the Social Sciences and Humanities*] [*Higher Council for Scientific Research*] [*Information service or system*] (IID)
ISOC	Internet Society
ISOC	[*The*] Internet Society (TNIG)
Isoc............	Isocrates [*436-338BC*] [*Classical studies*] (OCD)
ISoCaRP	International Society of City and Regional Planners [*See also AIU*] [*The Hague, Netherlands*] (EAIO)
ISOCC	Input System for Operator Connected Calls (PDAA)
ISO-CMOS ...	Isolated Fully Recessed Complementary Metal-Oxide Semiconductor (TEL)
ISOD	International Society for Orbital Disorders (EAIO)
ISOD	International Sports Organization for the Disabled [*Farstn, Sweden*] (EA)
ISODARCO ...	International School of Disarmament and Research on Conflicts
ISODATA......	Iterative Self-Organizing Data Analysis Technique A [*Computer science*]
ISODIS	International Organization for Standardization Draft International Standard (IAA)
ISODOC........	International Information Centre for Standards in Information and Documentation (ADA)
ISOE	International Society for Optical Engineering (EA)
IsoENET.......	Isochronous Ethernet [*Computer science*] (CDE)
isoenz	Isoenzyme (AAMN)
ISOF	International Society for Ocular Fluorophotometry (EAIO)
IS of LANG...	Islets of Langerhans [*Anatomy*]
ISOHP	International Society for Organ History and Preservation (EA)
ISOL.............	IMAGE Software [*NASDAQ symbol*] (TTSB)
ISOL.............	Image Software, Inc. [*NASDAQ symbol*] (SAG)
isol	Isolate [*or Isolated*] (DAVI)
ISOL.............	Isolation (KSC)
ISOLDE	Isotopic Low-Weight Device (IAA)
ISOLN	Isolation
ISOLR	Isolationer
Isolyser.......	Isolyser Co., Inc. [*Associated Press*] (SAG)
ISOM	International Standard Orthopaedic Measurements [*Medicine*]
ISOM	Isometric (KSC)
ISom............	Somonauk Public Library, Somonauk, IL [*Library symbol Library of Congress*] (LCLS)
ISOMATA	Idyllwild School of Music and the Arts [*California*]
Isomdx........	Isomedix, Inc. [*Associated Press*] (SAG)
Isomet	Isomet, Corp. [*Associated Press*] (SAG)
ISOMITE	Isotope Miniature Thermionic Electric (IAA)
ISomSD	Somonauk Community Unit, School District 432, Somonauk, IL [*Library symbol Library of Congress*] (LCLS)
ISON	Isolation Network (PDAA)
ISONET	International Organization for Standardization Information Network [*United Nations*] [*Geneva, Switzerland*] (IID)
ISONIAZID ...	Isonicotinic Acid Hydrazide [*See also INAH, INH*] [*Antituberculous agent*]
ISOO	Information Security Oversight Office [*National Archives and Records Service*]
ISO/OSI........	International Standards Organization/Open System Interface [*Motorola, Inc.*]
ISOP	Integrated Spacecraft Operations Plan [*NASA*]
ISOP	Internal Standard Operating Procedure [*Military*] (MCD)
ISOPAR........	Improved Symbolic Optimizing Assembly Routine
ISOPE	International Society of Offshore and Polar Engineers
ISOPEDAC....	Integrated System of Pipework Estimating, Detailing, and Control (PDAA)
ISOPEP	Isometric Piping Efficiency Program

ISOPGU.......	International Security Officer's Police and Guard Union (EA)
IS(Ops)	Intelligence Section, Operations [*Joint Intelligence Subcommittee of Chiefs of Staff*] [*World War II*]
ISORID	International Information System on Research in Documentation [*International Federation for Documentation*] [*UNESCO*] (IID)
ISORT	Interdisciplinary Student-Originated Research Training [*National Science Foundation*]
ISOS	International Southern Ocean Study [*National Science Foundation*]
ISOS	Interplanetare Sonnensonde
ISOS	Isosceles [*Triangle*]
ISOSC	International Society for Soilless Culture [*Wageningen, Netherlands*] (EAIO)
ISOSJ..........	Institute of Social Order of the Society of Jesus [*Later, JCSS*] (EA)
ISOSS	Immobile Suspension Feeders on Soft Substrata [*Oceanography*]
ISOT	International Symposium on Olfaction and Taste
ISOTAP	Interservice Occupational Task Analysis Program [*Military*] (NVT)
ISOTEC	Isotope Thermoelectric Converter
ISOTH	Isothermal (KSC)
ISOU	International Society for Ophthalmic Ultrasound (EA)
ISOW	Iceland-Scotland Overflow Water [*Oceanography*]
ISP	Distance between Iliac Spines [*Anatomy*] (DAVI)
ISp	Henry Public Library, Henry, IL [*OCLC symbol*] (OCLC)
ISp	Iconic Store, Peripheral [*Psychophysiology*]
ISP	Image Stabilization Program [*Photography*]
ISP	Image Storage Panel [*Computer science*] (PDAA)
ISP	Image Store Processor [*Computer science*]
ISP	Image Synthesis Processor [*Computer science*]
ISP	Immunoreactive Substance P [*Immunology*]
ISP	Imperial Smelting Process
ISP	Implementation Support Package [*Army*]
ISP	Impulse, Specific (KSC)
ISP	Independent Service Provider [*Telecommunications*]
ISP	Independent Smallholders' Party [*Hungary Political party*] (EY)
ISP	Independent Studies Project [*Navy*]
ISP	Independent Study Program [*IBM Corp.*]
ISP	Indexed Sequential Processor
ISP	Index of Social Position [*Advertising*] (DOAD)
ISP	Individual Seal Packaging [*Food technology*]
ISP	Individual Service Plan
ISP	Industrial Security Plan [*Nuclear energy*] (NRCH)
ISP	Industrial Security Program [*Air Force, Army*]
ISP	Industry Service Package
ISP	Information Search and Processing [*Database search service*] (OLDSS)
ISP	Information System Plan (MCD)
ISP	Information Systems Plan [*USAID*] (ECON)
ISP	Information Systems Professional (DD)
ISP	Information Systems Program [*University of Oklahoma*] [*Norman, OK*]
ISP	Infrared Spectrophotometer
ISP	Initial Specific Impulse (MCD)
ISP	Initial Support Package (MCD)
ISP	Instantaneous Sound Pressure
ISP	Instant-Set Polymer (PDAA)
ISP	Institute for Studies in Pragmaticism [*Texas Tech University*] [*Research center*] (RCD)
ISP	Institute of Sales Promotion [*ICSU*] [*British*]
ISP	Institute of Store Planners (EA)
ISP	Instituto de Seguros de Portugal [*Insurance regulatory agency*] [*Portugal*] (EY)
ISP	Institut pour une Synthese Planetaire [*Institute for Planetary Synthesis - IPS*] [*Geneva, Switzerland*] (EAIO)
ISP	In-Store Promotions [*Marketing events for US goods held by retail establishments in foreign countries*] [*Department of Commerce*]
ISP	Instructional System Package (MCD)
ISP	Instruction Set Processor [*1971*] [*Computer science*]
ISP	Instruction Set Processor [*Computer science*] (ECII)
ISP	Instrumentation Support Plan (MCD)
ISP	Integrated Scientific Processor [*Sperry*] (NITA)
ISP	Integrated Shear Plate
ISP	Integrated Support Plan (MCD)
ISP	Integrated System Peripheral [*Computer science*]
ISP	Integrated Systems Planning, Inc. [*Baltimore, MD*] (TSSD)
ISP	Intensively Supervised Probation [*Legal term*] (BARN)
ISP	Interamerican Society of Psychology (EA)
ISP	Intergovernmental Science Programs
ISP	Interim Support Period
ISP	Interim Support Plan (MCD)
ISP	Internally Stored Program (AAG)
ISP	Internal Security Plan (CINC)
ISP	Internationale des Services Publics [*Public Service International - PSI*] [*Ferney Voltaire, France*] (EAIO)
ISP	International Shadow Project (EA)
ISP	International Society for Photogrammetry [*Later, ISPRS*]
ISP	International Society for Plastination (EA)
ISP	International Society of Postmasters [*Montreal, PQ*] (EAIO)
ISP	International Solar Polar [*Mission*] [*NASA*]
ISP	International Specialty Products [*NYSE symbol*] (SPSG)
ISP	International Streptomyces Project
ISP	International Student Pugwash [*Formerly, USSPC*] [*Later, Student Pugwash (USA)*]
ISP	International Study Program
ISP(s)	Internet Service Provider
ISP	Internet Service Providers [*Telecommunications*]
ISP	Interoperable Systems Project [*Computer science*]

ISP .... Interspace (MAE)
ISP .... Interspinal [Anatomy] (DAVI)
ISP .... Intl Specialty Products [NYSE symbol] (TTSB)
ISP .... Intraspinal
ISP .... Inverse Sampling Procedure
ISP .... Ipsco, Inc. [Toronto Stock Exchange symbol]
ISP .... Islip, NY [Location identifier FAA] (FAAL)
ISP .... Isolated Safflower Protein [Food technology]
ISP .... Isolated Soy Protein [Food technology]
ISP .... Isoproterenol (DMAA)
ISP .... Isotope Separation Power
ISP .... Italian Society of Physics
ISP .... Long Island [New York] MacArthur [Airport symbol] (OAG)
ISp .... Schiller Park Public Library, Schiller Park, IL [Library symbol Library of Congress] (LCLS)
ISP .... Specific Impulse (MCD)
ISPA .... International Screen Publicity Association
ISPA .... International Society for the Protection of Animals [Later, WSPA] [British] (EA)
ISPA .... International Society of Parametric Analysts (EA)
I/SPA .... International Spa and Fitness Association
ISPA .... International Sporting Press Association
ISPA .... International Squash Players Association [Cardiff, Wales] (EAIO)
ISPA .... Internet Service Provider Association
ISPA .... Inverted Socket Process Architecture [Computer science]
ISPAA .... International Society of Performing Arts Administrators (EA)
ISPAA .... International Society of Plastic and Audio-Visual Art
ISPBX .... Integrated Services PBX [Telecommunications] (NITA)
ISPC .... International Sound Programming Center [Telecommunications]
ISPC .... International Spotted Pony Club [Defunct] (EA)
ISPC .... International Statistical Programs Center [Department of Commerce] (IID)
ISPCA .... Irish Society for the Prevention of Cruelty to Animals (DBA)
ISPCAN .... International Society for Prevention of Child Abuse and Neglect (EA)
ISPCC .... Irish Society for the Prevention of Cruelty to Children (DI)
ISPD .... International Society for Peritoneal Dialysis (EA)
ISPE .... Improved SONAR Processing Equipment [Military] (CAAL)
ISPE .... Institute and Society of Practictioners in Electrolysis Ltd. [British] (BI)
ISPE .... Institute of Swimming Pool Engineers [British] (DBA)
ISPE .... International Society for Philosophical Enquiry (EA)
ISPE .... International Society of Pharmaceutical Engineers (EA)
ISPEC .... Independent Schools Physical Education Conference (AIE)
ISPEC .... Insulation Specification (MSA)
ISPER .... IPAC [Intelligence, Pacific Area Command] Special Report
ISPES .... Inner-Shell Photoelectron Spectroscopy
ISPF .... Integral Skinned Polyurethane Foam (PDAA)
ISPF .... Interactive System Productivity Facility [Computer science]
ISPF .... International Save the Pun Foundation (EA)
ISPF .... International Science Policy Foundation (EAIO)
ISPF/PDF .... Interactive System Productivity Facility/Program Development Facility [Computer science]
ISPG .... Institute of Sedimentary and Petroleum Geology [Geological Survey of Canada] [Research center] (RCD)
ISPG .... Institutional Support Planning Group [NASA] (NASA)
ISPH .... International Society for Professional Hypnosis (EA)
ISPH .... International Society for the Protection of Horses (DI)
ISPH .... International Society of Psychology of Handwriting [Milan, Italy] (EA)
ISPHS .... International Society for Phenomenology and Human Sciences (EA)
ISPhS .... International Society of Phonetic Sciences (EA)
ISPI .... Illinois State Psychiatric Institute
ISPI .... International Society for Prevention of Infertility (EAIO)
ISPICE .... Interactive Simulation Program with Integrated Circuit Emphasis [Computer science] (MHDI)
ISPK .... Insulin-Stimulated Protein Kinase [An enzyme]
ISPK .... Isolated Spontaneous Psychokinesis [Parapsychology]
ISPL .... Incremental System Programming Language [Computer science]
ISPL .... Initial Spare Parts List (IAA)
ISPL .... Instruction Set Processor Language [Computer science]
ISPL .... Interim Spare Parts List (AAG)
ISPL .... International Society for Phenomenology and Literature (EA)
ISPM .... International Society of Plant Morphologists [Delhi, India] (EAIO)
ISPM .... International Solar Polar Mission [NASA]
ISPM .... International Staff Planners Message [NATO] (NATG)
ISPM .... Interplanetary Shock Propagation Model [Marine science] (OSRA)
ISPM .... Interplanetary Shock Propagation Model (USDC)
ISPMB .... International Society for the Protection of Mustangs and Burros (EA)
ISPMB .... International Society of Plant Molecular Biology (EA)
ISPMEMO ... International Staff Planners Memo [NATO] (NATG)
ISPMM .... International Symposium on Purine Metabolism in Man
ISPN .... Integrated Surveys Processing Network [Bureau of the Census] (GFGA)
ISPN .... International Society for Pediatric Neurosurgery (EA)
ISPN .... International Standard Program Number [Numbering system for software]
ISPN .... International Students Peace Network (EA)
ISPO .... Industrial Staffing Plan Occupations (MCD)
ISPO .... Instrumentation Ships Project Office [Navy]
ISPO .... International Society for Preventive Oncology (EA)
ISPO .... International Society for Prosthetics and Orthotics - US National Member Organization (EA)
ISPO .... International Sports Equipment Fair [Germany]
ISPO .... International Statistical Programs Office [Department of Commerce] (IEEE)
ISPO .... Irradiation Special Purchase Order (SAA)

ISPOG .... International Society of Psychosomatic Obstetrics and Gynaecology (PDAA)
ISPOUSC ..... International Society for Prosthetics and Orthotics - US Committee [Later, ISPO] (EA)
ISPP .... Internationale Studiengemeinschaft fuer Pranatale Psychologie [International Society for the Study of Prenatal Psychology - ISPP] (EAIO)
ISPP .... International Society for Plant Pathology (EAIO)
ISPP .... International Society for Portuguese Philately (EA)
ISPP .... International Society for Retirement Planning [Later, ISRP] (EA)
ISPP .... International Society for the Study of Prenatal Psychology (EAIO)
ISPP .... International Society of Political Psychology (EA)
ISPP .... International Society of Prenatal and Perinatal Psychology and Medicine (EAIO)
ISPPP .... International Symposium on HLtd. of Proteins, Peptides, and Polynucleotides
ISPPS .... Item Support Plan Policies Statement (AFIT)
ISPR .... Infantry Systems Program Review [Army] (AABC)
ISPR .... Information Security Program Regulation (MCD)
ISPR .... Integrated Support Parts Requirement (KSC)
ISPR .... International Special Commission on Radio Interference (MCD)
ISPRS .... International Society for Photogrammetry and Remote Sensing [Royal Institute of Technology] [Research center Sweden] (IRC)
ISprv .... Spring Valley Public Library, Spring Valley, IL [Library symbol Library of Congress] (LCLS)
ISprvHSD .... Hall Township High School District 502, Spring Valley, IL [Library symbol Library of Congress] (LCLS)
ISprvSD ...... Spring Valley Consolidated Community School District 99, Spring Valley, IL [Library symbol Library of Congress] (LCLS)
ISPS .... Instruction Set Processor Specification [1977] [Computer science] (CSR)
ISPS .... Integrated Secondary Propulsion System (MCD)
ISPS .... International Society of Phonetic Sciences (EA)
ISPS .... International Standard Paper Sizes
ISPT .... Industry Superannuation Property Trust
ISPT .... Initial Satisfactory Performance Test (AAG)
ISPT .... Institute for Studies in Psychological Testing
ISPT .... Intergovernmental Science and Public Technology [of ASRA] [National Science Foundation]
ISPT .... Interspecies Ovum Penetration Test [Medicine] (BABM)
ISPW .... International Society for the Psychology of Writing (EA)
ISPWP .... International Society for the Prevention of Water Pollution [Alton, Hampshire, England] (EAIO)
ISPX .... Secular Institute of Pius X (EA)
ISQ .... In Status Quo
ISQ .... Lillie M. Evans Memorial Library, Princeville, IL [OCLC symbol] (OCLC)
ISQ .... Manistique, MI [Location identifier FAA] (FAAL)
ISQD .... Identification System for Questioned Documents [Book title]
ISQL .... Interactive SQL [Computer science]
ISR .... Ice Sounding RADAR
ISR .... Identification Safety Range [Military] (NVT)
ISR .... Image Storage Retrieval
ISR .... Impulse Sequencing Relay
ISR .... Incoherent Scatter RADAR [Instrumentation]
ISR .... Incstar Corp. [AMEX symbol] (SPSG)
ISR .... Indian State Railway (ROG)
ISR .... Indirect Source Review [Environmental Protection Agency] (FFDE)
ISR .... Individual Soldier Radio [Military] (INF)
ISR .... Individual Soldier's Report
ISR .... Industrial Security Regulations [DoD]
ISR .... Information Service Representative [Veterans Administration]
ISR .... Information Storage and Retrieval [Computer science]
ISR .... Infrared Scanning Radiometer (KSC)
ISR .... Initial Sample Report
ISR .... Initial System Release (MCD)
ISR .... Innovative Systems Research (NITA)
ISR .... Input Select and Reset (IAA)
ISR .... Input Shift Register
ISR .... In-Service Recruiter [Army]
ISR .... Institute for Sex Research, Inc. [National Institute of Mental Health] (IID)
ISR .... Institute for Social Research [University of Michigan] (EA)
ISR .... Institute for Social Research [York University] [Information service or system] (IID)
ISR .... Institute for Storm Research (MCD)
ISR .... Institute for Study of Regulation [Defunct] (EA)
ISR .... Institute of Seaweed Research [British]
ISR .... Institute of Semiconductor Research [Former USSR]
ISR .... Institute of Social Research [Indiana University] [Information service or system] (IID)
ISR .... Institute of Surgical Research [San Antonio, TX] [Army]
ISR .... Instructional System Review
ISR .... Instrumentation Status Report (MUGU)
ISR .... Insulin Secretion Rate [Medicine] (DMAA)
ISR .... Integral Superheat Reactor
ISR .... Integrated Secretory Response [Biochemistry] (DAVI)
ISR .... Integrated Support Requirements (AAG)
ISR .... Interagency Source Register [Intelligence] (MCD)
ISR .... Interim Scientific Report
ISR .... Interim System Review (SSD)
ISR .... Intermediate Session Routing (ACRL)
ISR .... Intermediate Sodium Removal [Nuclear energy] (NRCH)
ISR .... Internal Scientific Report

ISR.............	International Sacred Recordings, Christian Artists' Record Corp. [*Record label*]
ISR.............	International Sanitary Regulations [*World Health Organization*]
ISR.............	International Shasta Resources [*Vancouver Stock Exchange symbol*]
ISR.............	International Society of Radiology [*Berne, Switzerland*] (EA)
ISR.............	International Sourdough Reunion (EA)
ISR.............	International Star Registry
ISR.............	International Student Relief [*Later, WUS*]
ISR.............	International Survey Research [*London consultancy firm*]
ISR.............	International Synthetic Rubber Co. [*United Kingdom*]
ISR.............	Interrupt Service Routine (IEEE)
ISR.............	Interrupt Status Register (IAA)
ISR.............	Intersecting Storage Ring [*High-energy physics*]
ISR.............	Inventory Status Report
ISR.............	Israel [*ANSI three-letter standard code*] (CNC)
Isr.............	Israel (VRA)
ISR.............	Istra Air [*Slovakia*] [*ICAO designator*] (FAAC)
ISR.............	Methodist Medical Center of Illinois, Peoria, IL [*OCLC symbol*] (OCLC)
ISRA	Installment Sales Revision Act of 1980
ISRA	International Seabed Research Authority
ISRA	International Ski Racers Association [*Later, WPS-RA*]
ISRA	International Society for Research on Aggression (EA)
ISRA	Irish Squash Rackets Association (EAIO)
ISRAC	ITT [*International Telephone & Telegraph Corp.*] Secure Ranging and Communications System
ISRAD	Institute for Social Research and Development [*University of New Mexico*]
ISRAD	Integrated Software Research and Development Program (MCD)
Israel Ch......	Israel Chemical Ltd. [*Associated Press*] (SAG)
Israel Stud Criminol...	Israel Studies in Criminology [*Jerusalem, Israel*] [*A publication*] (DLA)
Isramc	Isramco, Inc. [*Associated Press*] (SAG)
ISRB	Inter-Service Research Bureau [*British*]
ISRC	International Service Robot Congress
ISRC	International Society of Radiology Congress
ISRC	International Survey Research Corp.
ISRCDVS.....	International Society for Research on Civilization Diseases and Vital Substances (PDAA)
ISRD	Information Storage Retrieval and Dissemination (NITA)
ISRD	International Society for Rehabilitation of the Disabled [*Later, RehabilitationInternational*]
ISRDS	Istituto di Studi sulla Ricerca e Documentazione Scientifica [*Institute for Study of Scientific Research and Documentation*] [*National Research Council*] [*Information service or system*] (IID)
ISRE	Interferon-Stimulated Response Element [*Medicine*]
ISRF..........	International Squash Rackets Federation [*Cardiff, Wales*] (EAIO)
ISRF..........	International Sugar Research Foundation [*Later, WSRO*] (EA)
ISRG	Independent Space Research Group (EA)
ISRGLU	Independent Ship, Riverside, and General Labourers' Union [*British*]
ISRHAI........	International Secretariat for Research on the History of Agricultural Implements [*Lyngby, Denmark*] (EAIO)
ISRIC	International Soil Reference and Information Centre [*Research center Netherlands*] (IRC)
ISRL..........	Isramco, Inc. [*NASDAQ symbol*] (NQ)
IsrlLd........	Israel Land & Development Co. [*Associated Press*] (SAG)
ISRLW........	Isramco Inc.Wrrt'A' [*NASDAQ symbol*] (TTSB)
ISRLZ........	Isramco Inc.Wrrt'B' [*NASDAQ symbol*] (TTSB)
ISRM	Index of Stability of Relative Magnitudes [*Statistics*]
ISRM	Information Systems Resource Manager
ISRM	International Society for Range Management (EA)
ISRM	International Society for Rock Mechanics [*Lisbon, Portugal*] (EA)
ISRM	International Society of Reproductive Medicine (EA)
ISRM	Inter-Service Radio Measurements [*British World War II*]
Isrm	Isramco, Inc. [*Associated Press*] (SAG)
ISRN	Incorporated Society of Registered Naturopaths [*British*]
ISRNI	Incest Survivors Resource Network, International (EA)
ISRO	Indian Space Research Organization
ISRO	International Securities Regulatory Organisation [*London, England*] [*Business term*]
ISRO	Isle Royale National Park
ISRP	Initial Spares and Repair Parts
ISRP	Internal Surface Reverse Phase [*Chromatography column*]
ISRP	International Society for Respiratory Protection (EA)
ISRP	International Society for Retirement Planning (EA)
ISRR	International Soundex Reunion Registry (EA)
ISRREC	Institute for Sex Research Library Records [*Database*] [*Kinsey Institute for Research in Sex, Gender, and Reproduction*] [*Information service or system*] (CRD)
ISRRT	International Society of Radiographers and Radiological Technicians [*Don Mills, ON*] (EA)
ISRS	Impulsive Stimulated Raman Scattering [*Physics*]
ISRS	Information Search and Recording System [*of UMREL*]
ISRS	Integrated Status Reporting System (MCD)
ISRSM	International Symposium on Rocket and Satellite Meteorology
ISRT	International Spinal Research Trust [*British*]
ISRT............	Iowa Silent Reading Tests [*Education*]
ISRT...........	Isotopes and Radiation Technology [*A publication*]
ISRU	Intergovernmental Science and Research Utilization [*National Science Foundation*]
ISRU	International Scientific Radio Union [*Also, URSI*]
IsRW...........	Weizmann Institute of Science, Rehovot, Israel [*Library symbol Library of Congress*] (LCLS)
ISS.............	Ideal Solidus Structures (IEEE)
ISS.............	Idiopathic Short Stature [*Medicine*] (DMAA)
ISS.............	Ignition Shielding System
ISS.............	Image Sensor System
ISS.............	Image Sharpness Scale [*Photography*] (OA)
ISS.............	Imaging Science Subsystem
ISS.............	Imperfect Single Stamp [*Philately*]
ISS.............	Imperial Service Sappers [*British military*] (DMA)
ISS.............	Independent Schools Section [*American Association of School Libraries*] [*American Library Association*]
ISS.............	Independent Sweep System
ISS.............	Index of Specifications and Standards (MCD)
ISS.............	Inductive Storage Switch
ISS.............	Industrial Security Section [*NATO*] (NATG)
ISS.............	Industry Sole Source (AFIT)
ISS.............	Industry Standard Specifications (AAG)
ISS.............	Inertial Sensor System (KSC)
ISS.............	Inertial Subsystem (MCD)
ISS.............	Information Sharing System (NITA)
ISS.............	Information Storage System (IEEE)
ISS.............	Information Support System [*Nondestructive Testing Information Analysis Center - NTIAC*] [*Southwest Research Institute*] [*Information service or system*] (CRD)
ISS.............	Information Systems Section [*Battelle Memorial Institute*] [*Information service or system*] (IID)
ISS.............	Information Systems Security
ISS.............	Information Systems Services [*Brigham Young University*] [*Research center*] (RCD)
ISS.............	Information Systems Specialists Office [*Library of Congress*] (NITA)
ISS.............	Information Systems Subdivision (MCD)
ISS.............	Infrared Sensor System
ISS.............	Infrared Surveillance Set
ISS.............	Inhibit/Override Summary Snapshot Display (NASA)
ISS.............	Initial Space Station (KSC)
ISS.............	Injury Severity Score [*Auto safety research*]
ISS.............	Input Subsystem
ISS.............	Inside Skin (MCD)
ISS.............	Inside Surface (MCD)
ISS.............	Installation Site Survey (MCD)
ISS.............	Installation Support School [*Army*]
ISS.............	Installation Support Services (NASA)
ISS.............	Institute for Socioeconomic Studies (EA)
ISS.............	Institute for Southern Studies (EA)
ISS.............	Institute for Space Studies [*NASA*]
ISS.............	Institute for Strategic Studies [*Later, IISS*] [*Obsolete*]
ISS.............	Institute of Salesian Studies
ISS.............	Institute of Social Studies [*Netherlands*]
ISS.............	Institute of Special Studies [*Army*]
ISS.............	Institute of Sports Sponsorship [*British*] (DBA)
ISS.............	Instruction Summary Sheet (NASA)
ISS.............	In-Structure Shock [*Army*] (RDA)
ISS.............	Instrumentation Support Service
ISS.............	Instrument Servo System
ISS.............	Integrated Satellite System
ISS.............	Integrated Sealift Study [*Army*] (AABC)
ISS.............	Integrated Separation Systems [*Electrophoresis*]
ISS.............	Integrated Sounding System [*Marine science*] (OSRA)
ISS.............	Integrated Sounding System (USDC)
ISS.............	Integrated Start System (AAG)
ISS.............	Integrated Storage System (NITA)
ISS.............	Integrated Structural Seat [*Automotive engineering*]
ISS.............	Integrated Switch Stick (IAA)
ISS.............	Integrated System Schematic (NASA)
ISS.............	Integration Support Service
ISS.............	Intelligence Support System
ISS.............	Intelligent Support System
ISS.............	INTERCO, Inc. [*Formerly, International Shoe Co.*] [*NYSE symbol*] (SPSG)
ISS.............	Intercommunication Service System Inc. [*Information service or system*] (IID)
ISS.............	Interface Signal Simulator (SAA)
ISS.............	Interface Simulation System (CAAL)
ISS.............	Interface Supply Support (SAA)
ISS.............	Interim Standard Set
ISS.............	Interim Status Standards (GNE)
ISS.............	Interim Stowage Shelf (KSC)
ISS.............	Intermediate Service School [*Military*] (AFM)
ISS.............	Internal Switching System
ISS.............	Internationale Gesellschaft fuer Stereologie [*International Society for Stereology*] (EAIO)
ISS.............	International Savant Society (EA)
ISS.............	International School of Sailing
ISS.............	International Schools Services (EA)
ISS.............	International Scientific Series [*A publication*]
ISS.............	International Scotist Society [*See also SIS*] [*Rome, Italy*] (EAIO)
ISS.............	International Seaweed Association (EAIO)
ISS.............	International Seaweed Symposium [*Trondheim, Norway*] (MSC)
ISS.............	International Self-Service Organization [*Cologne, Federal Republic of Germany*] (EAIO)
ISS.............	International Sinatra Society (EA)
ISS.............	International Skeletal Society (EA)
ISS.............	International Social Service [*See also SSI*] [*Geneva, Switzerland*] (EAIO)
ISS.............	International Society for Stereology (EA)
ISS.............	International Society of Shropshires (EA)
ISS.............	International Society of Surgery (DAVI)
ISS.............	International Softbill Society (EA)

ISS............ International Space Station
ISS............ International Steamboat Society (EA)
ISS............ International Students Society [Defunct] (EA)
ISS............ International Sunshine Society (EA)
ISS............ Interrupt Service Subroutine (CMD)
ISS............ Interservice Supply Support [Military] (AABC)
ISS............ Interstage Section Shell
ISS............ Interstellar Scattering [of radio waves in the galaxy]
ISS............ Interstellar [Phase] Scintillation [Galactic science]
ISS............ Intra-List Stimulus Similarity (PDAA)
ISS............ Inventory Service System (AFIT)
ISS............ Involuntary Servitude and Slavery
ISS............ Ionospheric Sounding Satellite [Japan]
ISS............ Ion-Scattering Spectrometer [or Spectrometry]
ISS............ Ion Silicon System (IAA)
ISS............ Ion Spectroscopy Scattering [Surface analysis]
ISS............ Iraqi Intelligence Service
ISS............ Iron and Steel Society - of AIME (EA)
ISS............ Islands
ISS............ Islands [Postal Service standard] (OPSA)
ISS............ Isotopic Separation Subsystem
ISS............ Issue (AABC)
ISS............ Issy-Les Moulineaux Airport [France]
ISS............ Meridiana SpA [Italy ICAO designator] (FAAC)
ISS............ Sangamon State University, Springfield, IL [Library symbol Library of Congress] (LCLS)
ISS............ St. Meinrad College, St. Meinrad, IN [OCLC symbol] (OCLC)
ISS............ Wiscasset, ME [Location identifier FAA] (FAAL)
ISS............ YMCA [Young Men's Christian Association] International Student Service (EA)
ISSA.......... Association Internationale des Ecoles de Voile [International Sailing Schools Association] [France] (EAIO)
ISSA.......... Information Systems Security Association (EA)
ISSA.......... Institute for the Study of Sexual Assault [Defunct] (EA)
ISSA.......... Institute of Social Services Alternatives [Defunct] (EA)
ISSA.......... Intelligence Specialist, Seaman Apprentice [Navy] (DNAB)
ISSA.......... International Sailing Schools Association (EA)
ISSA.......... International Sanitary Supply Association (EA)
ISSA.......... International Ship Suppliers Association [Wimbledon, England] (EA)
ISSA.......... International Slurry Seal Association (EA)
ISSA.......... International Slurry Surfacing Association (EAIO)
ISSA.......... International Social Security Association [Geneva, Switzerland] (EA)
ISSA.......... International Society of Stress Analysts (EA)
ISSA.......... International Strategic Studies Association (EA)
ISSA.......... Interservice Supply Support Agreements [Military]
ISSA.......... Irish Schools Swimming Association (EAIO)
ISSAA........ Information Systems Selection and Acquisition Agency (AAGC)
ISS/AB....... International Social Service, American Branch (EA)
ISSAB........ International Social Service, Australian Branch [An association]
ISSAC........ Integrated Surface Search and Attack Coordinate
ISSAS........ Interactive Structural Sizing and Analysis System [Computer science]
ISSB.......... Information Systems Standards Board [American National Standards Institute] [Telecommunications]
ISSB.......... Interservice Security Board [World War II]
ISSBB........ Inertial Sensor System Breadboard
ISSBD........ International Society for the Study of Behavioural Development [Nijmegen, Netherlands] (EAIO)
ISSC.......... Information Systems Software Center [Fort Belvoir, VA] [Army] (RDA)
ISSC.......... International Ship Structures Congress (NOAA)
ISSC.......... International Smart Shoppers Club (EA)
ISSC.......... International Snowshoe Council [Defunct] (EA)
ISSC.......... International Social Science Council [See also CISS] [Paris, France] [Research center] (EAIO)
ISSC.......... Interservice Sports Council [Later, ISC]
ISSC.......... Interservice Supply Support Committee [or Coordinator] [Military] (AABC)
ISSC.......... Interstate Shellfish Sanitation Conference
ISSCA........ International Swizzle Stick Collectors Association (EA)
ISSCAAP...... International Standard Statistical Classification of Aquatic Animals and Plants
ISSCB........ International Society for Sandwich Construction and Bonding
ISSCC........ International Solid State Circuits Conference (MCD)
ISSCM........ International Society for the Study of Church Monuments [Later, CMS] (EA)
ISSCO........ Integrated Software Systems Corp.
ISSCT........ International Society of Sugar Cane Technologists [Piracicaoa, Brazil] (EA)
ISSD.......... Information Systems and Services Division [Department of Commerce] (IID)
ISSD.......... International Society for Social Defence [See also SIDS] [Paris, France] (EAIO)
ISSDF......... International Society for the Study of Dendrobatid Frogs (EA)
ISSDN........ Integrated Services Satellite Digital Network (MCD)
ISSE.......... International Sight and Sound Exposition
ISSE.......... International Society for the Study of Expressionism [Formerly, ETMS] (EA)
ISSEC......... Internal Spectral Shifter and Energy Converter (MCD)
ISSE-ETMS... International Society for the Study of Expressionism - Ernst Toller Memorial Society (EA)
ISSEL......... University of Illinois Solid State Electronics Laboratory [Research center] (RCD)
ISSEM........ Information System Security Evaluation Method (IAA)
ISSEP......... Integrated System Safety Engineering Plan

ISSEP......... International Soros Science Education Program [Privately-funded program for former Soviet Republics]
ISSES......... International Stationary Steam Engine Society (EAIO)
ISSET......... International Symposium on Space Electronics (MCD)
ISSF.......... Industry Satellite Services Facility (SSD)
ISSG.......... Illustrated Shipboard Shopping Guide [Navy]
ISSG.......... Information Systems Support Group (AAGC)
ISSGA........ International Society for the Study of Ghosts and Apparitions
ISSHCAB..... International Society for the Study of the Human-Companion Animal Bond [Later, IAHAIO] (EA)
ISSI.......... Integrated Silicon Solution [NASDAQ symbol] (TTSB)
ISSI.......... Integrated Silicon Solution, Inc. [NASDAQ symbol] (SAG)
ISSI.......... International Social Science Institute [Later, International Academy at Santa Barbara] (EA)
ISSI.......... Interswitching System Interface [Telecommunications] (ACRL)
ISSID......... International Society for the Study of Individual Differences (EAIO)
ISS Int....... ISS International Service Systems AS [Associated Press] (SAG)
ISSIP......... Interswitching System Interface Protocol [Telecommunications] (ACRL)
ISSK.......... International Society for the Sociology of Knowledge [St. John's, NF] [Defunct] (EAIO)
ISSL.......... Initial Spares Support List (AFM)
ISSLS......... International Symposium on Subscribers' Loops and Services [Telecommunications] (TEL)
ISSM.......... Incompletely Specified Sequential Machine (PDAA)
ISSM.......... Independent Society of Stick Makers [A union] [British]
ISSM.......... Initialized Stochastic Sequential Machine (IAA)
ISSM.......... Institute of Sterile Services Management [British] (DBA)
ISSM.......... Interim Surface-to-Surface Missile [Military] (CAAL)
ISSM.......... Sangamon County Medical Society, Springfield, IL [Library symbol Library of Congress] (LCLS)
ISSM.......... Secular Institute of Schoenstatt Sisters of Mary (TOCD)
ISSMB........ Information Systems Standards Management Board
ISSMC........ Interim Surface-to-Surface Missile Capability [Military] (CAAL)
ISSMFE....... International Society for Soil Mechanics and Foundation Engineering [See also SIMSTF] (EA)
ISSMIS....... Integrated Support Services Management Information System (AABC)
ISSMPD...... International Society for the Study of Multiple Personality and Dissociation (EA)
ISSMS........ Interim Surface-to-Surface Missile System [Military] (NVT)
ISSN.......... Intelligence Specialist, Seaman [Navy] (DNAB)
ISSN.......... International Standard Serial Number [Library of Congress]
ISSO.......... Institute of Strategic and Stability Operations [Army]
ISSO.......... International Side-Saddle Organization (EA)
ISSOL......... International Society for the Study of the Origin of Life (EA)
ISSOP........ Intra-Fleet Supply Support Operations Program [Navy] (DNAB)
ISSOT........ Inactive Ship Supply Overhaul Team
ISSOT........ Intra-Fleet Supply Support Operations Team [Navy] (DNAB)
ISSP.......... Information Sciences and Systems Planning (SAA)
ISSP.......... International Society of Sports Psychology (EA)
ISSP.......... Interservice Supply Support Program [Military] (AABC)
ISSPA......... International Sport Show Producers Association (EA)
ISSPP......... Integrated System Safety Program Plan [DoD]
ISSR.......... Information Storage, Selection, and Retrieval [Computer science]
ISSR.......... Information System Service Request (DNAB)
ISSR.......... Institute for Social Science Research [Research center] (RCD)
ISSR.......... International Society for the Sociology of Religion [Italy] (EAIO)
ISSRO........ Interservice Supply Support Records Office [Military] (AABC)
ISSRT......... Illinois State Society of Radiologic Technologists (SRA)
ISSRU........ Information Science and Scientometrics Research Unit [Hungarian Academy of Sciences Library] [Budapest] [Information service or system] (IID)
ISSS.......... IBM Speech Server Series
ISSS.......... Inherent Secondary Shutdown System (PDAA)
ISSS.......... Installation Service Supply Support
ISSS.......... Institute for Space and Security Studies (EA)
ISSS.......... Institute for the Study of Sport and Society
ISSS.......... Integrated Silicon Systems [NASDAQ symbol] (SAG)
ISSS.......... Integrated Support System Sort [Computer science] (MHDB)
ISSS.......... International Seebeck Study Society (EA)
ISSS.......... International Seminars Support Scheme
ISSS.......... International Society for Socialist Studies
ISSS.......... International Society for the Study of Symbols
ISSS.......... International Society of Soil Science [See also AISS] [ICSU Wageningen, Netherlands] (EAIO)
ISSS.......... International Society of Sport Sponsors (EA)
ISSS.......... Schoenstatt Institute of Secular Priests (TOCD)
ISSSA......... International Society for Strategic Studies (Africa) [Formerly, Africa Society forStrategic Studies] (EA)
ISSSC......... Interservice Supply Support Subcommittee [Military] (CINC)
ISSSE......... International Society of Statistical Science in Economics (EA)
ISSSM........ Imaging Seeker Surface-to-Surface Missile (PDAA)
ISSSP........ International Sacerdotal Society Saint Pius X (EA)
ISSSS......... Integrated SONAR System for Surface Ships (SAA)
ISSST......... Integrated Submarine SONAR System Technician
ISST.......... Infrared Surveillance of Surface Targets [Military] (CAAL)
ISST.......... Institute for Space Science and Technology, Inc. [Research center] (RCD)
ISST.......... International Society for the Study of Time (EA)
ISST.......... Involuntary Second SEA [Southeast Asia] Tour [Air Force]
ISSTA......... Israel Student Tourist Association
ISSTDR....... International Society for STD [Sexually Transmitted Diseases] Research (EA)

ISStH .... Saint John's Hospital, Science Library, Springfield, IL [*Library symbol*] [*Library of Congress*] (LCLS)
ISSU .... Inter-Services Signals Unit [*British military*] (DMA)
ISSUE .... Information System Software Update Environment
ISSVD .... International Society for the Study of Vulvar Disease (DAVI)
ISSX .... International Society for the Study of Xenobiotics
IST .... Improved System Technology (NITA)
IST .... Incompatible Simultaneous Transfer (IAA)
IST .... Incredibly Small Transistor (IAA)
IST .... Incremental System Test
IST .... Indexing Slide Table
IST .... Indian Standard Time (IAA)
IST .... Individualized Study by Telecommunications [*Alaska*] (EDAC)
IST .... Individual Sales Transaction
IST .... Industrielle-Services Techniques Inc. [*Industrial Life-Technical Services Inc.*] [*Information service or system*] (IID)
IST .... Information Science and Technology (BUR)
IST .... Initial Service Test (AABC)
IST .... Initial Support Team [*Military*] (AFM)
IST .... Innovative Science and Technology [*DoD*]
IST .... Input Stack Tape (IAA)
IST .... Inside Trim (DAC)
IST .... Instantaneous Spatial Transference
IST .... Institute for Simulation and Training [*University of Central Florida*] [*Research center*] (RCD)
IST .... Institute of Science and Technology [*University of Michigan*] [*Research center*] (RCD)
IST .... Institutional Skill Training (OICC)
IST .... Instruction-Set Translator [*IBM Corp.*]
IST .... Instrumentation Support Team (KSC)
IST .... Instrumented Sensor Technologies
IST .... Insulin Sensitivity Test
IST .... Insulin Shock Therapy [*Psychiatry*]
IST .... Integral Simulation Test [*Nuclear energy*] (NRCH)
IST .... Integrated Switching and Transmission [*Telecommunications*] (TEL)
IST .... Integrated System (NITA)
IST .... Integrated Systems Technology (IAA)
IST .... Integrated Systems Test [*NASA*] (KSC)
IST .... Integrated System Trainer (MCD)
IST .... Integrated System Transformer (IEEE)
IST .... International Institute for Safety in Transportation [*Later, IIST*] (EA)
IST .... International Society on Toxicology (EA)
IST .... International Standard [*Vancouver Stock Exchange symbol*]
IST .... International Standard Thread (MSA)
IST .... Interstation Transmission (KSC)
IST .... Interstellar Travel (AAG)
IST .... Intraspecific Antigenic Typing (PDAA)
IST .... Iron, Steel and Heavy Transporters Association, Cleveland OH [*STAC*]
IST .... Isothermal Storage Test [*For hazardous chemicals*]
IST .... Istanbul [*Turkey*] [*Airport symbol*] (OAG)
IST .... Istanbul [*Turkey*] [*Seismograph station code, US Geological Survey*] (SEIS)
IST .... Istanbul Airlines [*Turkey*] [*ICAO designator*] (FAAC)
IST .... Morton Public Library, Morton, IL [*OCLC symbol*] (OCLC)
ISt .... Stickney-Forest View Library District, Stickney, IL [*Library symbol Library of Congress*] (LCLS)
ISTA .... Illinois School Transportation Association (SRA)
ISTA .... Illinois Seed Trade Association (SRA)
ISTA .... Independent Secretarial Training Association [*British*]
ISTA .... Indiana State Techers Association (SRA)
ISTA .... Intelligence, Surveillance, and Target Acquisition [*Military*]
ISTA .... International Seed Testing Association [*Switzerland*]
ISTA .... International Sightseeing and Tours Association [*Defunct*] (EA)
ISTA .... International Special Tooling Association [*Frankfurt, Federal Republic of Germany*] (EA)
ISTA .... Intertank Structural Test Assembly [*NASA*] (NASA)
ISTAC .... International Science and Technology Advisory Committee [*Australia*]
ISTAC .... International Skilled Trades Advisory Committee [*UAW*]
ISTAIA .... Institute for the Study of Traditional American Indian Arts (EA)
ISTAR .... Image Storage Translation and Reproduction
ISTAR .... Information Science Technology Assessment for Research [*Army*]
ISTAT .... International Society of Transport Aircraft Trading (EA)
I-STAT .... I-STAT Corp. [*Associated Press*] (SAG)
IStau .... Staunton Public Library, Staunton, IL [*Library symbol Library of Congress*] (LCLS)
IStauMCD .... Macoupin Community District 6, Staunton, IL [*Library symbol Library of Congress*] (LCLS)
ISTB .... Integrated Subsystem Test Bed (NASA)
ISTB .... Interstate Tariff Bureau, Inc.
ISTB .... Introductory Science Text-Books [*A publication*]
ISTC .... Incunable Short Title Catalogue [*British Library*] [*Information service or system*] (IID)
ISTC .... Industry, Science, and Technology Canada [*Government agency*]
ISTC .... Institute of Scientific and Technical Communicators [*British*]
ISTC .... Interdepartmental Screw Thread Committee [*Departments of Commerce and Defense*]
ISTC .... International Science & Technology Center
ISTC .... International Shade Tree Conference [*Later, ISA*] (EA)
ISTC .... International Society for Training and Culture
ISTC .... International Spa and Tub Council [*Defunct*] (EA)
ISTC .... International Stress and Tension Control Association (EA)
ISTC .... International Student Travel Confederation [*Switzerland*] (EAIO)
ISTC .... International Switching and Testing Center [*Communications*]
ISTC .... Iron and Steel Trades Confederation [*British*]
IStc .... Saint Charles Public Library District, Saint Charles, IL [*Library symbol Library of Congress*] (LCLS)
ISTD .... Imperial Society of Teachers of Dancing
ISTD .... Institute for the Study and Treatment of Delinquency [*British*]
ISTD .... International Society of Tropical Dermatology [*Later, International Society of Dermatology: Tropical, Geographic, and Ecologic - ISD*]
ISTD .... International Society of Tropical Dermatology (DAVI)
ISTD .... Inter-Service Topographical Department [*British*]
ISTDA .... Institutional and Service Textile Distributors Association (EA)
ISTDF .... Istec-Industries Technologies [*NASDAQ symbol*] (SAG)
ISTE .... International Society for Technology in Education (EAIO)
ISTE .... International Society for Tropical Ecology (EA)
ISte .... Saint Elmo Public Library, St. Elmo, IL [*Library symbol Library of Congress*] (LCLS)
ISTEA .... Initial Screening Training Effectiveness Analysis
ISTEA .... Intermodal Surface Transportation Efficiency Act [*1990*]
ISTEA .... Iron and Steel Trades Employers' Association [*British*] (BI)
ISTEC .... International Superconductivity Technology Center [*Japan*]
Istecln .... Istec-Industries Technologies [*Associated Press*] (SAG)
ISter .... Sterling Public Library, Sterling IL [*Library symbol*] [*Library of Congress*] (LCLS)
ISteSD .... Saint Elmo Community Unit, School District 202, Saint Elmo, IL [*Library symbol Library of Congress*] (LCLS)
ISTES TEMP ... Istesso Tempo [*Same Time*] [*Music*] (ROG)
ISTF .... Integrated Servicing and Test Facilities [*Canada*]
ISTF .... Integrated System Test Flow (NASA)
ISTF .... International Social Travel Federation [*See also FITS*] [*Brussels, Belgium*] (EAIO)
ISTF .... International Society of Tropical Foresters [*See also SIIFT*] (EA)
ISTFA .... International Society for Testing and Failure Analysis (MCD)
ISTFA .... International Symposium for Testing and Failure Analysis [*Annual electronics symposium*] (NITA)
ISTH .... International Society on Thrombosis and Hemostasis (EA)
ISTH .... Isthmus [*Board on Geographic Names*]
ISTHM .... Isthmian (ROG)
Isthm .... Isthmian Odes [*of Pindar*] [*Classical studies*] (OCD)
ISTI .... International Spa and Tub Institute (EA)
ISTIC .... Institute of Scientific and Technical Information of China [*INFOTERM*] [*Beijing*]
ISTIG .... Intercooled Steam-Injected Gas Turbine
ISTIM .... Interchange of Scientific and Technical Information in Machine Language [*Office of Science and Technology*]
ISTIP .... Information Systems Technical Integration Panel (SSD)
ISTIS .... International Scientific and Technical Information System (EAIO)
IStjo .... Saint Joseph Township Library (Swearingen Memorial Library), St. Joseph, IL [*Library symbol Library of Congress*] (LCLS)
IStJSD .... Tiraid Community Unit, School District 2, St. Jacob, IL [*Library symbol Library of Congress*] (LCLS)
ISTM .... Institute of Strata Title Management [*Australia*]
ISTM .... International Society for Testing Materials
ISTMC .... Instrumentation Section Test and Monitor Console (SAA)
ISTMH .... Indefinite Substitute Temporary Mail Handler [*US Postal Service employee classification*]
IstMobl .... Istituto Mobilaire Italiano [*Associated Press*] (SAG)
ISTN .... Integrated Switching and Transmission Network [*Telecommunications*] (TEL)
ISTN .... Interstate National Dealer Services, Inc. [*NASDAQ symbol*] (SAG)
ISTN .... Interstate Natl Dealer Svcs [*NASDAQ symbol*] (TTSB)
ISTNW .... Interstate Natl Dealer Wrrt [*NASDAQ symbol*] (TTSB)
ISTO .... Information Science and Technology Office [*Arlington, VA*] [*DoD*] (TSSD)
ISTP .... Information System Theory Project (IAA)
ISTP .... Interagency Solar Terrestrial Programme [*European Space Agency*]
ISTP .... International Society of Tropical Pediatrics [*Philippines*] (EAIO)
ISTP .... International Solar Terrestrial Physics [*Proposed NASA mission*]
ISTP .... Isotope
ISTP & B ..... Index to Scientific and Technical Proceedings and Books [*Institute for Scientific Information*] [*Database*]
ISTPW .... Impact Signature Training Practice Warhead [*Army*]
ISTR .... Incstar Corp. [*NASDAQ symbol*] (TTSB)
ISTR .... Indexed Sequential Table Retrieval
ISTR .... International Society for Third-Sector Research (NFD)
IStr .... Streator Public Library, Streator, IL [*Library symbol Library of Congress*] (LCLS)
ISTRA .... Interplanetary Space Travel Research Association
ISTRACON ... Interstation Supersonic Track Conferences (MCD)
IStrESD .... Eagle Elementary Consolidated School District 43, Streator, IL [*Library symbol Library of Congress*] (LCLS)
IStrHSD .... Streator Township High School District 40, Streator, IL [*Library symbol Library of Congress*] (LCLS)
ISTRO .... International Soil Tillage Research Organization [*Netherlands*] (EAIO)
IStrOSD .... Otter Creek Elementary School District 56, Streator, IL [*Library symbol Library of Congress*] (LCLS)
ISTRS .... Index of Submarine Technical Repair Standards [*Military*] (DNAB)
IStrSD .... Streator Elementary School District 45, Streator, IL [*Library symbol Library of Congress*] (LCLS)
IStrSMH .... Saint Mary's Hospital, Henegen Medical Library, Streator, IL [*Library symbol Library of Congress*] (LCLS)
ISTRUCTE .... Institution of Structural Engineers [*British*]
ISTS .... Institute for Space and Terrestrial Science [*Research center Canada*] (RCD)
ISTS .... International Simultaneous Translation Service
ISTS .... International Society for Twin Studies [*Rome, Italy*] (EA)
ISTS .... International Symposium on Space Technology and Science (MCD)

ISTS............ Intersite Transmission Subsystem [*Ground Communications Facility,* *NASA*]
ISTS............ Intradermal Skin Test Score [*Immunology*]
ISTSP.......... Independent Schools Talent Search Program [*Later, A Better Chance*] (EA)
ISTT............ In-Service Training of Teachers [*Scottish National Committee*]
ISTT............ International Society for Trenchless Technology (EAIO)
ISTT............ Intersegmental Travel Time [*Zoology*]
ISTU............ Isometric Strength Testing Unit [*Medicine*] (DMAA)
IsTU............ Tel Aviv University, Tel Aviv, Israel [*Library symbol Library of Congress*] (LCLS)
ISTV............ Insight Entertainment Corp. [*NASDAQ symbol*] (SAG)
ISTVS.......... International Society for Terrain-Vehicle Systems (EA)
IStw............ Popular Creek Public Library District, Streamwood, IL [*Library symbol*] [*Library of Congress*] (LCLS)
ISU............. In-Arm Suspension Unit [*Tank Technology*]
ISU............. Independent Signal Unit [*Telecommunications*] (TEL)
ISU............. Indiana State University [*Terre Haute*]
ISU............. Indiana State University, Terre Haute, IN [*OCLC symbol*] (OCLC)
ISU............. Inertial Sensing Unit
ISU............. Information Service Unit [*International Potato Center*] [*Information service or system*] (IID)
ISU............. Initial Signal Unit [*Telecommunications*] (TEL)
ISU............. Instruction Storage Unit
ISU............. Instruction Stream Unit (IAA)
ISU............. Integrated Sight Unit [*Weaponry*] (INF)
ISU............. Interface Sharing Unit
ISU............. Interface Surveillance Unit (SAA)
ISU............. Interface Switching Unit (BUR)
ISU............. Interference Suppression Unit (IAA)
ISU............. Internal Airlift/Helicopter Slingable Container Unit [*MTMC*] (TAG)
ISU............. International Salvage Union (PDAA)
ISU............. International Scientific Union
ISU............. International Seaman's Union
ISU............. International Shooting Union
ISU............. International Sigma Security, Inc. [*Vancouver Stock Exchange symbol*]
ISU............. International Skating Union [*See also UIP*] [*Davos-Platz, Switzerland*] (EAIO)
ISU............. International Society of Urology [*See also SIU*] [*Lille, France*] (EAIO)
ISU............. International Space University [*Strasbourg, France*]
ISU............. International Stereoscopic Union (PDAA)
ISU............. International System of Units
ISU............. Iowa Southern Utilities [*Southern Industrial Railroad, Inc.*] [*AAR code*]
ISU............. Iowa State University [*Ames*]
ISU............. Italian Service Unit [*Italian prisoners of war who became volunteers in the Allied war effort*]
ISu............. Summit-Argo Public Library, Summit, IL [*Library symbol Library of Congress*] (LCLS)
I-Sub........... Inhibitor Substance [*Medicine*] (DMAA)
ISU/CCL....... Iowa State University / Cyclone Computer Laboratory (PDAA)
ISUDO......... International Symposium on Ultrasonic Diagnostics in Ophthalmology [*Later, ISO U*] (EA)
ISUDS......... Iterative Scheme Using a Direct Solution
ISU-ERI....... Iowa State University - Engineering Research Institute (PDAA)
ISUH.......... Institute for the Study of Universal History through Arts and Artifacts [*Defunct*] (EA)
ISUM.......... Intelligence Summary
ISUM.......... Southern Illinois University, School of Medicine, Springfield, IL [*Library symbol Library of Congress*] (LCLS)
ISumSD....... Red Hill Community Unit, School District 10, Sumner, IL [*Library symbol Library of Congress*] (LCLS)
ISUP.......... Integrated Services User Part
ISUP.......... Iowa State University Press (DGA)
ISUP.......... ISDN [*Integrated Services Digital Network*] User Part [*Telecommunications*]
ISUPTTS...... International Sports Union of Post, Telephone, and Telecommunications Service (EA)
ISURSL........ Indiana State University Remote Sensing Laboratory [*Research center*] (RCD)
ISUS.......... International Society for Utilitarian Studies [*British*] (EAIO)
ISUSAIC...... Intelligence School, United States Army Intelligence Center
ISUSE......... International Secretariat for the University Study of Education (EA)
ISV............. Independent Software Vendor [*Computer science*]
ISV............. Input Signal Voltage
ISV............. In Situ Vitrification [*Radioactive waste cleanup*]
ISV............. Instantaneous Speed Variation [*Tape recorders*]
ISV............. International Scientific Vocabulary
ISV............. International Society for Vaccines [*Gaithersburg, MD*]
ISV............. International Society of Videographers (EA)
ISV............. Interorbital Space Vehicle
ISV............. Interval Service Value (BUR)
ISV............. Iron-Solution Value (PDAA)
ISV............. Irradiated Silicon Vidicon
ISV............. Islena de Inversiones SA [*Honduras*] [*ICAO designator*] (FAAC)
ISV............. Iso Ventures, Inc. [*Vancouver Stock Exchange symbol*]
ISV............. Neponset Public Library, Neponset, IL [*OCLC symbol*] (OCLC)
ISv............. Sauk Village Library District, Sauk Village, IL [*Library symbol Library of Congress*] (LCLS)
ISVA.......... Incorporated Society of Valuers and Auctioneers (EAIO)
ISVA.......... International Satellite Verification Agency
ISVA.......... International Society for Vibroacoustics (EAIO)
ISVBM........ International Society of Violin and Bow Makers [*Basel, Switzerland*] (EAIO)

ISVCS......... Improved Secure Voice Conferencing System [*Military*] (MCD)
ISVD.......... Information System for Vocational Decisions Program
ISVE.......... Istituto di Studi per lo Sviluppo Economico [*Institute for the Study of Economic Development*] [*Italy*]
ISVESTA...... Individual Survival Vest for Aircrew [*Army*] (RDA)
ISVL.......... Vachel Lindsay Association, Springfield, IL [*Library symbol Library of Congress*] (LCLS)
ISVP.......... International Society for Vehicle Preservation (EA)
ISVR.......... Institute of Sound and Vibration Research [*Southampton University, England*]
ISVR3......... Intel Smart Video Recorder III
ISVS.......... In Situ Vapro Stripping [*Environmental science*]
ISVS.......... Integrated Secure Voice System
ISVS.......... International Secretariat for Volunteer Service [*Defunct*]
ISVSK......... Internationaler Staendiger Verband fuer Schiffahrt-Kongresse [*Permanent International Association of Navigation Congresses*]
ISW............ Ice Shelf Water [*Oceanography*]
ISW............ Information Services of Warwick [*Rhode Island*] [*Information retrieval*] (IID)
ISW............ Initial Status Word (IAA)
ISW............ Institute for Solid Wastes
ISW............ Institute of Social Welfare [*British*] (BI)
ISW............ Integrated Sachs-Wolfe [*Effect in cosmic microwave background*]
ISW............ Integrated Software
ISW............ Intermediate Scale Warfare
ISW............ Internal Status Word (IAA)
ISW............ Interstitial Water [*Physiology*]
ISW............ Ion Switch (IAA)
ISW............ Serib Wings [*Italy ICAO designator*] (FAAC)
ISW............ Toulon Public Library, Toulon, IL [*OCLC symbol*] (OCLC)
ISW............ Wisconsin Rapids [*Wisconsin*] [*Airport symbol*] (OAG)
ISW............ Wisconsin Rapids, WI [*Location identifier FAA*] (FAAL)
ISWA.......... Association Internationale pour les Residus Solides et le Nettoiement des Vil les [*International Solid Wastes and Public Cleansing Association*] [*INTAPUC and IRGRD*] [*Formed by a merger of*] [*Denmark*] (EAIO)
ISWA.......... Insect Screening Weavers Association (EA)
ISWA.......... International Science Writers Association
ISWA.......... International Ski Writers Association [*Riehen, Switzerland*] (EA)
ISWAP........ International Society of Women Airline Pilots (EA)
ISWBBHA.... Iron, Steel, and Wood Barge Builders' and Helpers' Association [*A union*] [*British*]
ISWC.......... Industrial Social Welfare Center [*Columbia University*] [*Research center*] (RCD)
ISWC.......... International Society for the Welfare of Cripples [*Later, Rehabilitation International*]
ISWG.......... Imperial Standard Wire Gauge
ISWG.......... Independent Schools Working Group (AIE)
ISWG.......... Integrated Support Working Group (SDI)
ISWG.......... Item Selection Working Group [*NATO*] (NATG)
ISWI........... Incisional Surgical Wound Infection [*Medicine*] (DMAA)
ISWI........... International Sports Wagering, Inc. [*NASDAQ symbol*] (SAG)
ISWIM........ If You See What I Mean (PDAA)
ISWL.......... Isolated Single Wheel Load (AIA)
ISWM......... Institute of Solid Waste Management [*British*] (DCTA)
ISWM......... International Society of Weighing and Measurement (EA)
ISWNE........ International Society of Weekly Newspaper Editors (EA)
ISWRRI....... Iowa State Water Resources Research Institute [*Iowa State University*] [*Department of the Interior Research center*] (RCD)
ISWS.......... Illinois State Water Survey [*Illinois Department of Energy and Natural Resources*] [*Research center*] (RCD)
ISWSC........ International Society of Worldwide Stamp Collectors [*Formerly, Worldwide Collectors' Club - WCC*]
ISWT.......... International Society of Wine Tasters [*Defunct*] (EA)
ISWU.......... International Society of Wang Users (EA)
ISWU.......... Iron and Steel Workers' Union [*India*]
ISX............ Impurity Study Experiment [*Oak Ridge National Laboratory*]
ISX............ Information Switching Exchange (IAA)
ISX............ Wyoming Public Library, Wyoming, IL [*OCLC symbol*] (OCLC)
ISY............ Black Hawk College, East Campus, Gustav E. Lundberg Learning Center, Kewanee, I L [*OCLC symbol*] (OCLC)
ISY............ City Air Ltd. [*British ICAO designator*] (FAAC)
ISY............ Instrument Systems Corp. [*NYSE symbol*] (SAG)
ISY............ International Space Year [*1992*]
ISY............ Intrasynovial [*Medicine*]
ISy............ Sycamore Public Library, Sycamore, IL [*Library symbol Library of Congress*] (LCLS)
IsYAEC....... Israel Atomic Energy Commission, Soreq Nuclear Research Centre, Yavne, Israel [*Library symbol Library of Congress*] (LCLS)
ISYN.......... Inductosyn
ISYS.......... Integral Sys MD [*NASDAQ symbol*] (TTSB)
ISYS.......... Integral Systems, Inc. [*NASDAQ symbol*] (SAG)
ISYSCON..... Integrated System Control [*Military*]
ISYVC........ International Sivananda Yoga Vedanta Center (EAIO)
ISYVO........ International Sivananda Yoga Vedanta Organization [*Val Morin, PQ*] (EAIO)
ISZ............ Increment and Skip on Zero [*Computer science*]
ISZ............ Interplate Shear Zone [*Geology*]
ISZ............ Iskustvennyi Sputnik Zemil [*Former USSR*]
IT.............. Air Inter [*ICAO designator*] (AD)
IT.............. Air Inter, Societe [*France ICAO designator*] (ICDA)
It.............. Biblioteca Nazionale Centrale, Rome, Italy [*Library symbol Library of Congress*] (LCLS)
IT.............. Idaho Territory [*Obsolete*] (ROG)
IT.............. Identification and Traceability (IAA)

IT	Identification Transponder (MCD)
IT	Iliotibial [Anatomy] (DAVI)
IT	Illusion Theater (EA)
IT	Immediate Transient Incapacitation [Radiation casualty criterion] [Army]
IT	Immediate Transportation
IT	Immunity Test
IT	Immunoreactive Tag [Clinical chemistry]
IT	Immunotherapy [Medicine]
IT	Immunotoxin
IT	Immunoturbidimetry [Analytical biochemistry]
IT	Implantation Test [Medicine] (MAE)
IT	Implosive Therapy [Type of behavior therapy]
IT	Improved Tartar
IT	Improved Touring [Class of racing cars]
IT	Incentive Travel [Travel industry]
IT	Inclusive Tour (MCD)
IT	Income Tax
IT	Income Tax Unit Rulings [US Internal Revenue Service]
IT	Incomplete Translation [Telecommunications] (TEL)
IT	Indent Tab Character [Computer science]
IT	Independent Tank (DS)
IT	Index Term [Computer science]
IT	Index Translationum [UNESCO]
IT	Indian Territory [in United States]
IT	Individual Therapy
IT	Individual Training [Army]
IT	Individual Transportation [Urban planning]
IT	Industrial Technology
IT	Industrial Training
IT	Industrial Tribunal [British] (DCTA)
IT	Industry Telephone Maintenance [FCC] (IEEE)
IT	Industry Transistor [Electronics] (IAA)
IT	Infection Type [Pathology]
IT	Inferior Temporal [Anatomy]
IT	Inferior Turbinate [Otorhinolaryngology] (DAVI)
IT	Information Technology [Computer science] (ECON)
IT	Information Theory (MCD)
IT	Information Transform [Information service or system] (IID)
IT	Information Type (ACRL)
IT	Inhalation Test [Clinical medicine] (MAE)
IT	Inhalation Therapy [or Therapist] [Medicine]
I/T	Initial Track (MCD)
IT	Initiation Technician (SAA)
IT	Inner Temple
IT	Innovative Test
IT	Input Terminal
IT	Input Translator [IBM Corp.] [Computer science]
IT	Inspection and Test (IAA)
IT	Inspection Tag
IT	Inspiratory Time [Medicine] (DAVI)
IT	Installation Test (NASA)
IT	Instant Transaction (IAA)
IT	Institut du Textile [Textile Institute] (EAIO)
IT	Institute of Technology [Air Force]
IT	Institute of Trichologists (EAIO)
IT	Institutional Training (OICC)
IT	Instructional Technologist (EDAC)
IT	Instructional Technology
IT	Instruction Tag (MSA)
IT	Instructor Trainer [Red Cross]
IT	Instrumented Laboratory Training
IT	Instrument Technician
IT	Instrument Test [or Tree] [Nuclear energy] (NRCH)
IT	Instrument Transformer
IT	Insulated Tank Container [Shipping] (DCTA)
IT	Insulating Transformer (KSC)
IT	Intact (DAVI)
IT	Intelligent Terminal [Computer science]
IT	Intelligent Transaction Router [Telecommunications]
IT	Intelligent Transmitter (ACII)
IT	Intensity of Telephone Interference (IAA)
IT	Intensive Therapy [Medicine] (MAE)
IT	Interactive Television
IT	Interceptor Trap
IT	Interesting Transcript [genetics]
IT	Interfacial Tension [Physical chemistry] (IAA)
IT	Interfering Transmitter (IAA)
IT	Intermediate Technology [An association] (EA)
IT	Intermediate Treatment [Special provision of British law for juvenile offenders]
IT	Internal Thread
IT	Internal Translator [Carnegie Institute] [IBM Corp.]
IT	International Steam Table Calorie (IIA)
IT	International Technology Corp. [Associated Press] (SAG)
IT	International Tolerance
IT	International Traders Association (EA)
IT	International Travellers [YWCA]
IT	Interrogator-Transponder (KSC)
IT	Interstate Theft
I/T	Intertank (NASA)
IT	Intertoll [Trunk] [Telecommunications] (TEL)
IT	Intertuberous [Diameter] [Medicine]
IT	Interval Timer [Computer science]
IT	Interval Training [Physical fitness program]
IT	Intestinal Type [of epithelium]
IT	Intimal Thickening [Medicine] (MEDA)
IT	Intradermal Test [Medicine] (MAE)
IT	In Transitu [In Transit] [Latin]
IT	Intrathecal [Medicine]
IT	Intrathoracic [Medicine]
IT	Intratracheal [Medicine]
IT	Intratracheal Tube [Medicine]
IT	Intratumoral [Medicine] (MAE)
IT	Inventory Transfer
IT	Ion Trap [Instrumentation]
IT	Iphigenia Taurica [of Euripides] [Classical studies] (OCD)
IT	Irrelevant Talk [Slang]
IT	Ischial Tuberosity [Medicine]
IT	Island Telephone Co. Ltd. [Toronto Stock Exchange symbol]
It	Islet [Maps and charts]
IT	Isomeric Transition [Radioactivity]
IT	Isothermal Transformation [Metallurgy]
IT	Isotocin [Endocrinology]
IT	Italian
IT	Italic (IAA)
IT	Italy [ANSI two-letter standard code] (CNC)
it	Italy [MARC country of publication code Library of Congress] (LCCP)
It	Italy (VRA)
IT	Item (MCD)
IT	Item Transfer
IT	National Organization of Industrial Trade Unions
IT	Tour-Based Fare [Airline fare code]
it	Vetus Itala (BJA)
IT-95	Information Technology 1995 [Marine science] (OSRA)
IT-95	Information Technology 1995 (USDC)
ITA	Great River Library System, Quincy, IL [OCLC symbol] (OCLC)
ITA	Illinois Motor Truck Operators Association, Chicago IL [STAC]
IT-A	Immunotoxin with A-Chain
ITA	Income Tax Act Regulations [Commerce Clearing House Canadian Ltd.] [Information service or system] (CRD)
ITA	Independent Telecommunications Analysts [Boulder, CO] (TSSD)
ITA	Independent Television Association [British] (DBA)
ITA	Independent Television Authority [Later, IBA] [British]
ITA	Individual Task Authorization
ITA	Indoor Tennis Association [Later, NTA] (EA)
ITA	Industrial Technological Associates, Inc. [Information service or system]
ITA	Industrial Truck Association [Washington, DC] (EA)
ITA	Industry and Trade Administration [Later, International Trade Administration] [Department of Commerce]
ITA	Inferior Temporal Artery [Medicine] (DMAA)
ITA	Inferior Tympanic Artery [Anatomy]
i/t/a	Initial Teaching Alphabet [A 44-symbol alphabet planned to simplify beginning reading by representing sounds more precisely]
ITA	Inner Transport Area
ITA	Inside Wheel Turning Angle [Automotive engineering]
ITA	Inspection Test Assembly (MCD)
ITA	Institut du Transport Aerien [Institute of Air Transport] [Research center France] (IRC)
ITA	Institute for Telecommunications and Aeronomy [ESSA] (MCD)
ITA	Institute of the Arts [Australian National University]
ITA	Institute of Theoretical Astronomy [Leningrad, USSR]
ITA	Institute of Traffic Administration [British]
ITA	Institute of Transactional Analysis [British] (DBA)
ITA	Institute of Transport Administration [Later, IoTA] (EAIO)
ITA	Institute of Transport Aviation (KSC)
ITA	Institute of Travel Agents [British] (BI)
ITA	Instrumentation Technology Associates, Inc.
ITA	Instrument Time (Actual)
ITA	Integrated Test Area (MCD)
ITA	Integrated Thruster Assembly (KSC)
ITA	Interactive Television Association
ITA	Inter-Air, Inc. [ICAO designator] (FAAC)
ITA	Interface Test Adapters (MCD)
ITA	Intermediate Teachers Association
ITA	Intermediate Thrust Arc
ITA	Intermediate Training Assessment (DOMA)
ITA	Intermodal Transportation Association (EA)
ITA	International 210 Association (EA)
ITA	International Alphabet
ITA	International Tap Association (EA)
ITA	International Tape Association (NITA)
ITA	International Tape/Disc Association (EA)
ITA	International Taxicab Association (EA)
ITA	International Telegraph Alphabet (NATG)
ITA	International Temperance Association [Later, IHTA] (EA)
ITA	International Texcan Tech [Vancouver Stock Exchange symbol]
ITA	International Thermographers Association (EA)
ITA	International Tin Agreement
ITA	International Tire Association (EA)
ITA	International Tornado Association [Germany] (EAIO)
ITA	International Touring Alliance [Belgium] (EAIO)
ITA	International Track Association [Defunct]
ITA	International Trade Administration [Washington, DC Department of Commerce]
ITA	International Trade Association [BTS] (TAG)
ITA	International Trombone Association (EA)
ITA	International Tube Association [Leamington Spa, Warwickshire, England] (EAIO)

ITA............. International Tuberculosis Association (DAVI)
ITA............. International Tunnelling Association (EA)
ITA............. International Turquoise Association (EA)
ITA............. International Twins Association [*Defunct*] (EA)
ITA............. International Typographic Association (MCD)
ITA............. Interstate Towing Auxiliary (EA)
ITA............. Interstate Truckers Association
ITA............. Ionization Test Apparatus
ITA............. Itacoatiara [*Brazil*] [*Airport symbol*] (AD)
ITA............. Itaconic Acid [*Organic chemistry*]
ita............. Italian [*MARC language code Library of Congress*] (LCCP)
ITA............. Italy [*ANSI three-letter standard code*] (CNC)
ITA............. Italy Fund [*NYSE symbol*] (TTSB)
ITA............. Italy Fund, Inc. [*NYSE symbol*] (SPSG)
ITA............. Itapemirim Transportes Aereos SA [*Brazil*] [*ICAO designator*] (FAAC)
ITAA............. Independent Travel Agencies of America Association (EA)
ITAA............. Information Technology Association of America [*Arlington, VA*] (CDE)
ITAA............. International Theatrical Agencies Association (EA)
ITAA............. International Transactional Analysis Association (EA)
ITAADS .... Installation the Army Authorization Document System
ITAADS .... Interim Target Acquisition and Designation System
ITAAP........... Inspection Test and Analysis Plan (IAA)
ITAB............. Information Technology Advisory Board [*British*]
ITAB............. International Transportation Advisory Board [*BTS*] (TAG)
ITAC............. Information Technology Advisory Committee [*Office of Management and Budget*] (GFGA)
ITAC............. Integrated Tactical Aircraft Control [*Air Force*] (DOMA)
ITAC............. Intelligence and Threat Analysis Center [*Air Force*] (DOMA)
ITAC............. Intelligence and Threat Analysis Center
ITAC............. Intelligence Tracking Analysis and Correlation (MCD)
ITAC............. Interagency Textile Administrative Committee
ITAC............. International Target Audience Code [*International Federation of Library Associations*]
ITAC............. Intestinal Type Adenocarcinoma [*Oncology*]
ITACC........... Incremental Tactical Communications Capability Study [*Military*] (MCD)
ITACCS .... International Trauma Anesthesia and Critical Care Society (EA)
ITACO .... Integration Trade and Analysis-Cycle O (SSD)
ITACS........... Integrated Tactical Air Control System
ITAC-T......... International Telecommunication Advisory Committee-Telecommunications (ACRL)
ITAD........... Individual Training Analysis and Design (MCD)
ITAD........... Information, Training and Agricultural Development [*British consultancy and training service*] (ECON)
ITAD........... Intelligence Threat Analysis Detachment [*Army*] (RDA)
ITAE........... Integrated Time and Absolute Error
ITAffi2......... Internationality Alphabet ffi2 (MCD)
ITAG........... Intelligence Threat Analysis Group [*Military*] (DNAB)
ITAG........... Invalid Tricycle Action Group [*British*] (DI)
ITAK........... Illankai Tamil Arasu Kadchi [*Federal Party*] [*Sri Lanka*] [*Political party*] (PPW)
ITAL........... Information Technology and Libraries [*A publication*]
ITAL........... Information Technology for Libraries [*Formerly, JOLA*] [*A publication*] (NITA)
ITAL........... Initial Task Assignment List
ITAL........... Introductory Trials Allowance List [*Military*] (AFIT)
ITAL........... Inventory Trial Allowance List
ITAL........... Italian
ITAL........... Italian
ITAL........... Italic [*or Italics*]
ital........... Italic (WDMC)
ITALD........... Improved Tactical Air-Launched Decoy (DWSG)
Ital Dial....... Italic Dialects [*A publication*] (OCD)
Italian Yb of Int'l L... Italian Yearbook of International Law [*A publication*] (DLA)
Italy........... Italy Fund, Inc. [*Associated Press*] (SAG)
ITALY........... I Trust and Love You [*Correspondence*] (DSUE)
ITAM........... Immunoreceptor Tyrosine Activation Motif [*Biochemistry*]
ITAM........... Immunoreceptor Tyrosine-Based Activation Motif [*Immunology*]
ITAM........... Instituto Tecnologico Autonomo de Mexico [*Economic research*] [*Mexico*] (CROSS)
ITAM........... Integrated Training Area Management [*Military*] (INF)
ITAM........... Interactive Med Tech Ltd [*NASDAQ symbol*] (TTSB)
ITAM........... Interdata Telecommunications Access Method [*Computer science*] (MHDB)
ITAMA........... Information Technology Acquisition and Marketing Association [*Defunct*] (EA)
ITAM VETS... Italian American War Veterans of the United States [*Defunct*] (EA)
IT & AP... Inspection Test and Analysis Plan (NRCH)
IT & ME... Incentive Travel and Meeting Executives Show [*Trade show*]
IT and T...... International Telephone & Telegraph Corp. [*New York, NY*] [*Facetious translation: International Travel and Talk*]
IT & TS........ International Turtle and Tortoise Society (EA)
ITAP........... Information Technology Advisory Panel [*British*]
ITAP........... Integrated Technical Assessment Panel [*NASA*] (NASA)
ITAR........... International Trade and Arms Regulations
ITAR........... International Traffic in Arms Regulation [*US*]
ITAR........... Interstate Transportation in Aid of Racketeering
ITARS........... Integrated Terrain Access and Retrieval System [*Hughes Aircraft*] [*Digital mapping project*] (NITA)
ITARS .... Integrated Terrain Retrieval System (MCD)
ITAS .... Improved Tactical Attack System
ITAS........... Improved Target Acquisition System [*Army*]
ITAS........... Indicated True Air Speed [*Aviation*] (AFM)
ITAS........... Integrated Tactical Attack System (MCD)
ITAS........... Integrated Test and Alignment System

ITAS............. Inter-American Travel Agents Society (EA)
ITASS........... Interim Towed Array Surveillance System [*Military*] (NVT)
ITAV............. Individual Tactical Air Vehicle
ITAVS .... Integrated Testing, Analysis, and Verification System
ITAWDS .... Integrated Tactical Amphibious Warfare Data System [*Navy*] (NVT)
ITAX............. Intermountain Aviation, Inc. [*Air carrier designation symbol*]
ITAX............. Italics
ITB............. Abbott Laboratories, North Chicago, IL [*OCLC symbol*] (OCLC)
ITB............. Iliotibial Band [*Anatomy*]
ITB............. Individual Tour Basing [*Fares*]
ITB............. Industrial Training Board [*British*]
ITB............. Instantaneous Trip Block [*Computer science*] (IAA)
ITB............. Institut Technique du Batiment [*Technical Institute for Building*] [*France Information service or system*] (IID)
ITB............. Integral Terminal Block
ITB............. Integrated Test Block
ITB............. Integrated Training Brigade [*Navy*]
ITB............. Integrated Tug Barge (DS)
ITB............. Interbrasil Star, SA [*Brazil*] [*FAA designator*] (FAAC)
ITB............. Intermediate Text Block
ITB............. Intermediate Transmission Block [*Computer science*] (BUR)
ITB............. Intermountain Tariff Bureau, Inc.
ITB............. Internal Transfer Bus
ITB............. Internationaler Turnerbund [*International Gymnastic Federation*]
ITB............. International Thomson Books
ITB............. International Thoroughbred Breeders, Inc. [*AMEX symbol*] (SPSG)
ITB............. International Time Bureau
ITB............. International Training Branch [*Office of Education*]
ITB............. Internet Transaction Broker [*Computer science*]
ITB............. In the Business [*Refers to television and film industries*]
ITB............. Intl ThoroughBred [*AMEX symbol*] (TTSB)
ITB............. Invisible Trade Balance [*Business term*] (MHDW)
ITB............. Invitation to Bid
ITB............. Ion Thruster Beam
ITB............. Irish Tourist Board (EA)
ITB............. Island Tug & Barge [*AAR code*]
ItBa............. Biblioteca Comunale "Angelillo", Servizio Prestito, Bari, Italy [*Library symbol Library of Congress*] (LCLS)
ITBA............. Idaho Thoroughbred Breeders Association (SRA)
ITBA............. International Toy Buff's Association (EA)
ITBA............. Irish Ten Pin Bowling Association (EAIO)
ItBar............. Biblioteca Comunale di Barletta, Barletta, Italy [*Library symbol Library of Congress*] (LCLS)
ItBaU............. Universita degli Studi di Bari, Bari, Italy [*Library symbol Library of Congress*] (LCLS)
ITBC............. Instructional Television Funding Cooperative (NTCM)
ITBE............. Interchannel Time Base Error (IAA)
ITB-ID............. International Thomson Books - International Division
ITBL............. Incompressible Turbulent Boundary Layer
ITBOF............. Illinois Thoroughbred Breeders and Owners Foundation (SRA)
ITBP............. International Thomson Business Press, Inc. [*Publisher*]
ITBPrA............. Intl ThoroughBred A Pfd [*AMEX symbol*] (TTSB)
ITBS............. Iowa Tests of Basic Skills
ITBTP............. Institut Technique du Batiment et des Travaux Publics [*Technical Institute for Building and Public Works*] [*Information service or system*] (IID)
ITC............. Concordia Theological Seminary, Fort Wayne, IN [*OCLC symbol*] (OCLC)
ITC............. Igloo Thermal Control [*Aerospace*] (MCD)
ITC............. Illinois Terminal Railroad Co. [*AAR code*]
ITC............. Imidazolyl-Thioguanine Chemotherapy [*Medicine*] (MAE)
ITC............. Immediate Track Control [*Automotive engineering*]
ITC............. Imperial Tobacco Co. [*of Great Britain and Ireland*] Ltd.
ITC............. Inclusive Tour Charter
ITC............. Independent Tank Center [*of a ship*] (DS)
ITC............. Independent Television Commission [*British*] (ECON)
ITC............. Industrial Technology Centre [*Manitoba Research Council*] [*Canada Research center*] (RCD)
ITC............. Industrial Training Council
ITC............. Infantry Training Center [*Army*]
ITC............. Information Technology Ltd. [*British*] (NITA)
ITC............. Inland Transport Committee [*United Nations*]
ITC............. Institute of Tax Consultants (EA)
ITC............. Instructional Telecommunications Consortium (EA)
ITC............. Instructor Training Course
ITC............. Instrumentation Tracking Controller
ITC............. Integral Tube Component (IAA)
ITC............. Integrated Telemetry Complex
ITC............. Integrated Terminal Controller (NITA)
ITC............. Integrated Trajectory Computations
ITC............. Intelligent Controls, Inc. [*AMEX symbol*] (SAG)
ITC............. Intelligent Tape Controller (PDAA)
ITC............. Intelligent Telecommunication Controller (IAA)
ITC............. Intelligent Transaction Controller (MHDB)
ITC............. Intent to Change
ITC............. Interagency Testing Committee [*Toxicology*]
ITC............. Inter-American Travel Congresses
ITC............. Intercept [*Telecommunications*] (TEL)
ITC............. Interchurch Transportation Council [*Defunct*] (EA)
ITC............. Intercontinental Trailsea Corp.
ITC............. Interdata Transaction Controller [*Perkin-Elmer*]
ITC............. Intermediate Toll Center [*Telecommunications*] (TEL)
ITC............. Internationaal Instituut voor Lucht-en Ruimtekaartering an Aardkunde [*International Institute for Aerospace Survey and Earth Sciences*] [*Netherlands*] (EAIO)

ITC	International Air Carrier Association [ICAO designator] (FAAC)
ITC	International Chemalloy Corp. [Toronto Stock Exchange symbol]
ITc	International Table Calorie [Dietetics] (DAVI)
ITC	International Tar Conference [See also CIG] [Paris, France] (EAIO)
ITC	International Tea Committee (EAIO)
ITC	International Technology Council [Defunct] (EA)
ITC	International Telemetering Conference
ITC	International Telepresence Corp. (ECON)
ITC	International Teletraffic Congress [Telecommunications]
ITC	International Television Center [Communications]
ITC	International Tin Council [See also CIE] [Defunct] (EAIO)
ITC	International Toastmistress Clubs (EA)
ITC	International Trade Centre [Switzerland United Nations] (MCD)
ITC	International Trade Club of Chicago [Later, IBCM] (EA)
ITC	International Trade Commission [Databank originator]
ITC	International Trade Council (EA)
ITC	International Traders Club (EA)
ITC	International Trading Certificate (DS)
ITC	International Training College [Salvation Army]
ITC	International Training in Communication (EA)
ITC	International Trans Asia [Vancouver Stock Exchange symbol]
ITC	International Translations Centre [Formerly, ETC] (EA)
ITC	International Trypanotolerance Centre [Gambia]
ITC	International Tuberculosis Campaign
ITC	International Typeface Corp.
ITC	Intern Training Center [DARCOM]
ITC	Intertropical Convergence [Trade winds] [Meteorology]
ITC	Interval Time Control [Computer science] (OA)
ITC	In-Track Contiguous
ITC	Investment Tax Credit
ITC	Ionic Thermoconductivity [or Thermocurrent]
ITC	Isothermal Titration Calorimetry [Analytical chemistry]
ITC	Israel Trade Commission
ITC	Italian Tile Center (EA)
ITC	Italian Trade Commission (EA)
ITC	Spinivasan's Reports of Income Tax Cases [India] [A publication] (DLA)
ITC	Srinivasan's Reports of Income Tax Cases [India] [1886-] [A publication] (ILCA)
ITCA	Independent Television Companies Association [British]
ITCA	Indian Transcontinental Airways
ITCA	Inspector of Training Corps and Cadets [Military British]
ITCA	Instituto Tecnologico Centroamericano [El Salvador]
ITCA	Inter-American Technical Council on Archives (DIT)
ITCA	Intercollegiate Tennis Coaches Association (EA)
ITCA	International Technical Caramel Association (EA)
IT/CA	International Tele/Conferencing Association (EA)
ITCA	International Thunderbird Class Association (EA)
ITCA	International Typographic Composition Association [Later, TIA] (EA)
ITCA	Invest to Compete Alliance [Washington, DC] (EA)
ITCA	Irish Terrier Club of America (EA)
ITCABIC	Inter-Territorial Catholic Bishops' Conference (EAIO)
ITCAL	International Table Calorie
ITCAN	Inspect, Test, and Correct as Necessary (MCD)
ItCaU	Universita di Cagliari, Sardinia, Italy [Library symbol Library of Congress] (LCLS)
ITCC	Industrial Training [NASDAQ symbol] (TTSB)
ITCC	Industrial Training Corp. [NASDAQ symbol] (NQ)
ITCC	International Technical Communications Conference [Society for Technical Communication]
ITCC	Interstate Truckload Carriers Conference
ITCCU	Information Technology Centre Consultancy Unit [British] (AIE)
ITCG	Information Technology Co-Ordinating Group [International Electrotechnical Commission] [ISO] (DS)
ITCI	International Tree Crops Institute USA (EA)
ITCIS	Integrated Telephone Customer Information System [Telecommunications] (IAA)
ITCK	Issue Time Check [Aviation] (FAAC)
ITCM	Integrated Tactical Countermeasures [Army]
ITCOM	Information Technology and Communications Bureau [United Nations] (ECON)
IT Corp	International Technology Corp. [Associated Press] (SAG)
ITCP	Idiopathic Thrombocytopenic Purpura [Hematology] (DAVI)
ITCP	Integrated Test and Checkout Procedures (MCD)
ItcpSe	Intercapital Income Securities, Inc. [Associated Press] (SAG)
ItCr	Biblioteca Statale di Cremona, Cremona, Italy [Library symbol Library of Congress] (LCLS)
ITCS	Installation Training/Coordination Section [Social Security Administration]
ITCS	Institute for 21st Century Studies [Defunct] (EA)
ITCS	Integrated Target Central System [Military] (CAAL)
ITCS	Integrated Target Command [or Control] System (IAA)
ITCS	Integrated Target Control System (MCD)
ITCSA	Institute of Technical Communicators of Southern Africa (EAIO)
ITCTLA	ITC [International Trade Commission] Trial Lawyers Association (EA)
ITCU	Information Technology Consultancy Unit (NITA)
ITCUA	International Telephone Credit Union Association (EA)
ITCZ	Intertropical Convergence Zone [Trade winds] [Meteorology]
ITD	Idiopathic Torsion Dystonia [Medicine]
ITD	Idiopathic Torsion Dystonia [Medicine]
ITD	Idiopathic Torsion Dytonia [Medicine]
ITD	Inception-to-Date
ITD	Individual'naya Trudovaya Deyatel'nost' [Individual Labor Activity] [Government program designed to foster private enterprise] [Russian]
ITD	Industrial Technology Division [Environmental Protection Agency] (GFGA)
ITD	Information and Technology for the Disabled
ITD	Information Technology Development [Project] [DoD] (RDA)
ITD	Information Technology Directorate [British]
ITD	Information Technology Division [Naval Research Laboratory]
ITD	Information Trade Directory [Gale Research Co.] (NITA)
ITD	Infrared Target Detector
ITD	Inhalation Toxicology Division [Environmental Protection Agency] (GFGA)
ITD	Initial Temperature Difference (IAA)
ITD	Institute of Training and Development (EAIO)
ITD	Integral Trap Door [Technical drawings]
ITD	Integrated Technology Demonstration
ITD	Integrated Test Document (MCD)
ITD	Integration Test and Demonstration (SDI)
ITD	Intensely Transfused Dialysis [Medicine] (DMAA)
ITD	Interactive Terminal Display [Computer science] (DGA)
ITD	Interactive Typographic Display [Computer science] (DGA)
ITD	Interaural Time Difference [Andiology]
ITD	Interchannel Time Displacement [Magnetic recording]
ITD	Intercontinental Data [Vancouver Stock Exchange symbol]
ITD	Interface Timing Diagram
ITD	Interim Technical Directive (MCD)
ITD	Internal Test Directive (KSC)
ITD	Intertropical Discontinuity [Meteorology]
ITD	Ion Trap Detector [Spectroscopy]
ITD	University of Texas at Dallas, Richardson, TX [OCLC symbol] (OCLC)
ITDA	Independent Truckers and Drivers Association (EA)
ITDA	Indirect Target Damage Assessment (AAG)
ITDA	Integrated Tunnel Diode Amplifier
ITDAC	Interagency Trade Data Advisory Committee [Department of Commerce] (EGAO)
ITDD	Integrated Tunnel Diode Device (IAA)
ITDE	Interchannel Time Displacement Error [Magnetic recording]
ITDE	Intertrack Time Displacement Error (IAA)
ITDF	Interactive Transaction Dump Facility [Computer science] (MHDB)
ITDG	Intermediate Technology Development Group [Rugby, Warwickshire, England] (EAIO)
ITDG/NA	Intermediate Technology Development Group of North America (EA)
ITDM	Intelligent Time-Division Multiplexer
ITDN	Integrated Tactical-Strategic Data Network (DOMA)
ITDNS	Integrated Tour Operating Digital Network Service (MHDI)
ITDP	Institute for Transportation and Development Policy (EA)
ITDR	Institute for Training and Demographic Research (EA)
ITDS	Integrated Technical Data System (PDAA)
ITDS	International Telecommunication Data Systems, Inc. [NASDAQ symbol] (SAG)
ITDT	Integrated Technical Documentation and Training
ITDU	Infantry Trials and Development Unit [British military] (DMA)
ITDU	Infrared Tracking Display Unit
ITE	Indicated Terminal Efficiency (DNAB)
ITE	Indicated Thermal Efficiency [Automotive engineering]
ITE	Individual Training Evaluation (MCD)
ITE	Information Technology in Engineering [British]
ITE	Input Test Equipment
ITE	Institute of Telecommunications Engineers
ITE	Institute of Terrestrial Ecology [Research center British] (IRC)
ITE	Institute of Traffic Engineers (EA)
ITE	Institute of Transportation Engineers (EA)
ITE	Instrumentation Test Equipment (KSC)
ITE	Insufficient Therapeutic Effect [Medicine] (DAVI)
ITE	Integration Test Equipment (MCD)
ITE	Intercity Transportation Efficiency (OA)
ITE	Interestatal de Aviacion SA de CV [Mexico ICAO designator] (FAAC)
ITE	International Telephone Exchange [Telecommunications] (TEL)
ITE	Intersite Transportation Equipment [NASA] (NASA)
ITE	Interstrat Resources, Inc. [Vancouver Stock Exchange symbol]
ITE	In the Ear [Hearing aid]
ITE	Intrapulmonary Interstitial Emphysema [Medicine] (DMAA)
ITE	Inverse Time Element (MUGU)
ITEA	Infraestructura Teatral [Ministerio de Cultura] [Spain Information service or system] (CRD)
ITEA	International Technology Education Association (EA)
ITEA	International Test and Evaluation Association (EA)
ITEC	Information Technology Centre [Training centres] [British] (NITA)
ITEC	Information Technology Electronics and Computers [A publication]
ITEC	Integral Throat/Exit Cone (MCD)
ITEC	International Thoroughbred Exposition and Conference [Kentucky Thoroughbred Association, Inc.] (TSPED)
ITEC	International Tourist Entertainment Corp. [NASDAQ symbol] (SAG)
ITEC	International Transport Exhibition
ITECH	Joint IOC/WMO Group of Experts on IGOSS Technical Systems Design and Developmentand Service Requirements [Marine science] (MSC)
ITED	Integrated Trajectory Error Display [Aviation]
ITED	Iowa Tests of Educational Development
ITEF	Integrated Test Equipment Facility (MCD)
I-TEF	International Toxicity Equivalency Factor [Toxicology]
ITEF	International Trade Exhibitions in France (EA)
ITEG	Individual Training Evaluation Group (MCD)
ITEG	Isotope-Powered Thermoelectric Generator (PDAA)
ITEL	Joint WMO/IOC Group of Experts on Telecommunications (MSC)
ITEL	Wavetech Inc. [NASDAQ symbol] (TTSB)

ITELIS......... Irish Times Eurolex Legal Information Service [*Database*] (NITA)
ITEM............ Integrated Test and Maintenance (PDAA)
ITEM............ Integrated Theater Engagement Model
ITEM............ Intelligence Threat Evaluation Model [*Military*] (MCD)
ITEM............ Interference Technology Engineer's Master (IEEE)
ITEME......... Institution of Technician Engineers in Mechanical Engineering [*British*]
ITeMS......... Ideas in the Teaching of Mathematics and Science (AIE)
ITEMS......... INCOTERM [*International Commerce Term*] Transaction Entry Management System
ITEMS......... In-Service Inspection, Testing, Evaluation, and Monitoring Service
ITEP........... Individual Training and Evaluation Program [*Army*] (INF)
ITEP........... Integrated Test/Evaluation Program (AABC)
ITEP........... Interim Tactical ELINT [*Electronic Intelligence*] Processor
ITEP........... International Trade Enhancement Program
ITER........... International Thermonuclear Experimental Reactor
ITES........... Inelastic Tunnelling Electron Spectroscopy
ITESM......... Instituto Tecnologico de Estudios Superiores de Monterrey [*Research institute onMexico/US relations*] [*Mexico*] (CROSS)
ITEST......... Institute for Theological Encounter with Science and Technology (EA)
ITeuS......... Saint Joseph Seminary, Teutopolis, IL [*Library symbol Library of Congress*] (LCLS)
ITeuSD....... Teutopolis Community Unit, School District 50, Teutopolis, IL [*Library symbol Library of Congress*] (LCLS)
ITEWS......... Integrated Tactical Electronic Warfare System
ITEX........... Information Technology Exchange Exhibition [*British*] (ITD)
ITEX........... Internal Tide Experiment [*Marine science*] (MSC)
ITEX........... Itex Corp. [*NASDAQ symbol*] (SAG)
ItexCp........ Itex Corp. [*Associated Press*] (SAG)
ITF............. Air Inter, Societe [*France ICAO designator*] (FAAC)
ITF............. Impulse Transfer Function (KSC)
ITF............. Indian Territorial Force [*British military*] (DMA)
ITF............. Industrial and Trade Fairs Ltd. [*Solihull, West Midlands, England*] (TSSD)
ITF............. Industrial Technology Fund [*British*]
ITF............. Information Technology Fund (AAGC)
ITF............. Instant Transference
ITF............. Institute of Tropical Forestry [*Rio Piedras, PR*] [*Department of Agriculture*] [*Research center*]
ITF............. Institut Textile de France [*French Textile Institute*] [*Boulogne-Billancourt*] [*Information service or system*] (IID)
ITF............. Integrated Test Facility [*Computer science*]
ITF............. Integrated Thermal Flux (AAG)
ITF............. Intelligence Task Force (DOMA)
ITF............. Intelligence Terminal Family [*Military*] (MCD)
ITF............. Interactive Terminal Facility
ITF............. Interagency Task Force (AAGC)
ITF............. Interferon (DMAA)
ITF............. Interim [*Contact*] File (MCD)
ITF............. Intermediate Test Facility (MCD)
ITF............. International Tennis Federation [*Formerly, ILTF*] (EA)
ITF............. International Toll Free [*Telecommunications*]
ITF............. International Trade Fair [*New Zealand*]
ITF............. International Transport Workers' Federation [*London, England*] (EAIO)
ITF............. International Tremor Foundation (EA)
ITF............. Interstate Transportation of Fireworks
ITF............. Interstitial Transfer Facility [*Nuclear energy*] (NRCH)
ITF............. Intertropical Front [*Meteorology*] (BARN)
ITF............. Intestinal Trefoil Factor [*Biochemistry*]
ITF............. In Trust For [*Banking*]
ITF............. Inverse Trigonometric Function
ITF............. Italfarmaco [*Italy*] [*Research code symbol*]
ITFA........... Installation, Testing, and Firing Apparatus [*Military*] (INF)
ItFB............ Biblioteca Berenson, Florence, Italy [*Library symbol Library of Congress*] (LCLS)
ItFBM.......... Biblioteca Marucelliana di Firenze, Servizio Prestito, Florence, Italy [*Library symbol Library of Congress*] (LCLS)
ITFCA......... International Track and Field Coaches Association [*Athens, Greece*] (EAIO)
ITFCC......... Initial [*or Interim*] Tactical Flag Command Center (MCD)
ITFCS......... Institute for Twenty-First Century Studies (EA)
ITFF........... Intertrochanteric Femoral Fracture [*Medicine*] (MEDA)
ITFMC......... Indian Territorial Force Medical Corps [*British military*] (DMA)
ITFMSG....... Interscience Technological Forecasting Methodology Study Group
ITFO........... International Trade Fairs Office [*Department of Commerce*]
ITFS........... Incomplete Testicular Feminization Syndrome [*Medicine*] (AAMN)
ITFS........... Instructional Television Fixed Service [*Educational TV*]
ITFS........... International Tropical Fern Society [*Defunct*] (EA)
ITFTRIA....... Instrument Tree Flow and Temperature Removal Instrument Assembly [*Nuclear energy*] (NRCH)
ITFW.......... Industry Training Fund for Women [*Australia*]
ITG............. Australian Income Tax Guide [*A publication*]
ITG............. Industrial Tachometer Generator
ITG............. Industry Technology Group [*Air Force*] (MCD)
ITG............. Industry Test Group [*Air Force*]
ITG............. Information and Telecommunications Technologies Group [*Electronic Industries Association*] [*Washington, DC*] (TSSD)
ITG............. Innovationstechnik GmbH & Co. [*Database producer*] (IID)
ITG............. Institute Technical Group
ITG............. Integra Financial Corp. [*NYSE symbol*] (SPSG)
ITG............. Integrated Terminal Guidance
ITG............. Integrin (DMAA)
ITG............. Inter-Continental Energy [*Vancouver Stock Exchange symbol*]

ITG............. Interdiction Target Graphic (MCD)
ITG............. Interlace Airlines Ltd. [*Gambia*] [*FAA designator*] (FAAC)
ITG............. International Trumpet Guild (EA)
ITG............. Ion Temperature Gradient [*Physics*]
ITGA........... Integrin Alpha (DMAA)
ITGA........... Isothermogravimetric Analysis
ITGB.......... Institute of Transport of Great Britain
ITGB.......... Integrin Beta (DMAA)
ITGBL......... International through Government Bill of Lading
ItgCom........ Integrated Communications Network, Inc. [*Associated Press*] (SAG)
ITGD.......... Interstate Transportation of Gambling Devices
ITGI........... Investment Tech Group [*NASDAQ symbol*] (TTSB)
ITGI........... Investment Technology Group [*NASDAQ symbol*] (SAG)
ItgLfSci....... Integra LifeSciences Corp. [*Associated Press*] (SAG)
ITGLWF........ International Textile, Garment, and Leather Workers' Federation [*See also FITTHC*] [*Brussels, Belgium*] (EAIO)
ItgPrc......... Integrated Process Equipment [*Associated Press*] (SAG)
ITGR.......... Integrity, Inc. [*NASDAQ symbol*] (SAG)
ITGR.......... Integrity Music'A' [*NASDAQ symbol*] (TTSB)
ITGR.......... Integrity Music, Inc. [*NASDAQ symbol*] (SAG)
ItgSys........ Integrated Systems, Inc. [*Associated Press*] (SAG)
ITGWF........ International Textile and Garment Workers' Federation [*Later, ITGLWF*]
ITGWU........ Irish Transport and General Workers' Union (DCTA)
ITH............. Integrated Technology USA, Inc. [*AMEX symbol*] (SAG)
ITH............. Interstitial Hyperthermia [*Medicine*] (DMAA)
ITh............. Interthecal [*Anesthesiology*]
Ith............. Intrathecal [*Medicine*] (CPH)
ITH............. Intrathoracic [*Anatomy*]
ITH............. Island Technologies Corp. [*Vancouver Stock Exchange symbol*]
ITH............. Ithaca [*New York*] [*Airport symbol*] (OAG)
ITH............. Ithaca [*New York*] [*Seismograph station code, US Geological Survey Closed*] (SEIS)
ITH............. Ithaca, NY [*Location identifier FAA*] (FAAL)
ITh............. Thornton Public Library, Thornton, IL [*Library symbol Library of Congress*] (LCLS)
Ithaca C....... Ithaca College (GAGS)
ITHE.......... International Travel Host Exchange
i thec......... Intrathecal [*Medicine*] (AAMN)
ITHI........... International Thomson Holdings, Inc.
ITHI........... International Travelers Health Institute (EA)
ITHL.......... Internal Triangular Hinge Ligament [*of scallops*]
ITHOF........ International Tennis Hall of Fame (EA)
ITHP.......... Increased Take-Home Pay
ITI............. Iceberg Transport International Ltd. [*Saudi Arabia*] (PDAA)
ITI............. Immediate Transient Incapacitation [*Radiation casualty criterion*] [*Army*] (AABC)
ITI............. Indian Telephone Industries (NITA)
ITI............. Industrial Technology Institute [*Research center*] (RCD)
ITI............. Infaunal Trophic Index [*Marine pollution*]
ITI............. Information Transform, Inc. [*Information service or system*] (IID)
ITI............. Initial Task Index (AAG)
ITI............. Inspection and Test Instruction (NASA)
ITI............. Institute of Translation and Interpreting [*British*] (DBA)
ITI............. Institut TNO voor Toegepaste Informatica [*TNO Institute of Applied Computer Science*] [*Information service or system*] (IID)
ITI............. Insurance Testing Institute [*Malvern, PA*] (EA)
ITI............. Integrated Task Index (AAG)
ITI............. Intelligent Transportation Infrastructure
ITI............. Interactive Terminal Interface [*Computer science*] (IEEE)
ITI............. Interceptor Technology Integration
ITI............. Intermittent Trouble Indication [*Telecommunications*] (TEL)
ITI............. International Tax Institute (EA)
ITI............. International Technical Institute of Flight Engineers
ITI............. International Technology Institute (EA)
ITI............. International Telesis Industries Corp. [*Vancouver Stock Exchange symbol*]
ITI............. International Theatre Institute [*Paris, France*] (EAIO)
ITI............. International Thrift Institute
ITI............. International Training Institute
ITI............. Intertrial Interval [*Psychology*]
ITI............. Itapetinga [*Brazil*] [*Airport symbol*] (AD)
ITIA........... International Trade and Investment Act [*1984*]
ITIA........... International Tungsten Industry Association (EAIO)
ITIAL.......... Items Troop Installed or Authorized List (MCD)
ITIC........... Information Technology Industry Council (AAGC)
ITIC........... International Tsunami Information Center (EA)
ITIC........... Inter-Tribal Indian Ceremonial Association (EA)
ITIC........... Investors Title Co. [*NASDAQ symbol*] (TTSB)
ITIC........... Investors Title Insurance Co. [*NASDAQ symbol*] (SAG)
ITIES......... Interfaced between Two Immiscible Electrolyte Solutions [*Physical chemistry*]
ITIES......... Interservice Technical Information Exchange System [*Military*] (AFIT)
ITIF........... Individual Taxpayer Information File [*IRS*]
ITIG........... Intelligroup, Inc. [*NASDAQ symbol*] (SAG)
ITII........... Internal-to-Internal Interface (MCD)
ITII........... International Thomson Information, Inc. [*Later, ITLS*]
ITII........... ITI Technologies [*NASDAQ symbol*] (TTSB)
ITII........... ITI Technologies, Inc. [*NASDAQ symbol*] (SAG)
ITIM.......... Itonut Yisrael Meugedet [*ITIM News Agency of the Associated Israel Press Ltd.*]
ITIN........... Individual Taxpayer Identification Number
ITIN........... Itinerary (AFM)
ITIN........... Itinerating (ROG)
IT Info........ Income Tax Information Release (DLA)

ITIP	Improved Transtage Injector Program (MCD)
ITIP	International Technical Integration Panel
ITIP	International Thomson Industrial Press
ITIPAT	Institute for the Technology and Industrialization of Tropical Agricultural Products [Ivory Coast]
ITIPI	Interim Tactical Information Processing and Interpretation
ITIR	Intermediate Thermal Infrared Radiometer (SSD)
ITIRC	IBM Technical Information Retrieval Center [International Business Machines Corp.] [Armonk, NY]
ITIS	Industrial Technical Information Service [Singapore] (IID)
ITIS	Integrated Tank Insulation System
ITIS	Integrated Technical Information System [Department of Energy Information service or system] (IID)
ITIS	Interagency Taxonomy Information System [A database of all the flora and fauna in North America] [Created by the EPA and other agencies]
IT-IS	Intermediate Technology Industrial Services [ITDG] [British]
ITIS	Internal Translation Information Subsystem [Computer science]
ITIS	International Trade Information Service
ITIS	Italians in Service of the US [World War II]
ITis	Tiskilwa Township Library, Tiskilwa, IL [Library symbol Library of Congress] (LCLS)
ITISN	Information Technology Information Services Network [British] (NITA)
ITisP	Plow Creek Commune Library, Tiskilwa, IL [Library symbol Library of Congress] (LCLS)
ITISS	Integrated Tactical Intelligence Support System (MCD)
ITisSD	Tiskilwa Community Unit, School District 300, Tiskilwa, IL [Library symbol Library of Congress] (LCLS)
ITI Tech	ITI Technologies, Inc. [Associated Press] (SAG)
ITIU	Inventory Temporarily in Use [Army] (AABC)
ITI/US	International Theatre Institute of the United States (EA)
ITJ	Indian Tax Journal [A publication] (DLA)
ITJ	International Trojan Development Corp. [Vancouver Stock Exchange symbol]
ITJ	Itajai [Brazil] [Airport symbol] (AD)
ITJ	Societa' Italjet [Italy ICAO designator] (FAAC)
ITK	Itokama [Papua New Guinea] [Airport symbol] (OAG)
ITKF	International Traditional Karate Federation (EA)
ITL	Ignition Transmission Line
ITL	Incoming Transaction Listing (AFM)
ITL	Incomplete Task Log (AAG)
ITL	Industrial Test Laboratory [Philadelphia Navy Yard] [Navy]
ITL	Information Technology Laboratory [Army Corps of Engineers]
ITL	Information Technology Ltd. [British] (NITA)
ITL	Institute of Tape Learning [British] (DBA)
ITL	Instrumented Team Learning (ADA)
ITL	Integrate-Transfer-Launch [Complex] [NASA]
ITL	Intent to Launch (NG)
ITL	Interactive Technology Laboratory [New York Institute of Technology] [Research center] (RCD)
ITL	Interceptor/Transporter/Loader
ITL	Intermediate Text Language (NITA)
ITL	Intermediate Transfer Language
ITL	International Theological Library [A publication]
ITL	Inverse Taper Lens
ITL	Inverse Time Limit (MSA)
ITL	Isomeric Transition Level [Radioactivity]
ITL	Isothermal Luminescence (PDAA)
Itl	Italian (BARN)
ITL	ITL Industries Ltd. [Toronto Stock Exchange symbol]
ITL	Mikma Ltd. [Moldova] [FAA designator] (FAAC)
ITLA	Imperial Thrift & Loan [NASDAQ symbol] (TTSB)
ITLA	Imperial Thrift & Loan Association [NASDAQ symbol] (SAG)
ITLB	Instruction Translation Lookaside Buffer [Computer science] (PCM)
ITLB	International Trade Law Branch [United Nations] (DUND)
ITLBV	Individual Tactical Load Bearing Vest [Army] (INF)
ITLC	Instant Thin-Layer Chromatography
ITLC	Integrated Transfer Launch Complex (IAA)
ITLGSWF	Interamerican Textile, Leather, Garment, and Shoe Workers Federation (EA)
ITLJ	Income Tax Law Journal [India] [A publication] (DLA)
ITLMCF	Instrument Technicians Labor-Management Cooperation Fund (EA)
ItlOven	[The] Italian Oven, Inc. [Associated Press] (SAG)
ITLS	International Thomson Library Services
ITLSA	Integrated Torso Limb Suit Assembly [NASA] (KSC)
ITLT	Interstate Transportation of Lottery Tickets
ITM	Improved Thayer-Martin [Medium] (DMAA)
ITM	Inch Trim Moment [Nautical]
ITM	Index of Technical Manuals [Military] (DNAB)
ITM	Indirect Tag Memory
ITM	Induction Tube Modulation
ITM	Infantry Target Mechanism [Army]
ITM	Information Transfer Module [Telecommunications] (NITA)
ITM	Inspector of Torpedoes and Mines [Navy]
ITM	Institute of Thread Machiners [Defunct]
ITM	Integral Telemetry
ITM	Intelligent Tutoring Media [Artificial intelligence]
ITM	Interceptor Tactical Missile [Air Force]
ITM	Intercommunication Teleprocessing Monitor (IAA)
ITM	Interim Technical Memorandum
ITM	Internal Technical Memorandum
ITM	Internal Tympaniform Membrane [Zoology]
ITM	International Tourism Management [Australia]
ITM	Investment Trust Funds under Management

ITM	ISDN [Integrated Services Digital Network] Trunk Module [Telecommunications]
ITM	ITA [Itapemirim Transportes Aereos SA] [Brazil] [ICAO designator] (FAAC)
ITM	Item [Online database field identifier]
ITM	Ithomi [Greece] [Seismograph station code, US Geological Survey] (SEIS)
ITMA	Institute for Training in Municipal Administration (EA)
ITMA	Institute of Trade Mark Agents [British] (DI)
ITMA	International Tanning Manufacturers Association [Defunct] (EA)
ITMA	Investigation on Teaching Using Microcomputers as an Aid
ITMA	Irradiation Test Management Activity (NRCH)
ITMA	It's That Man Again [Long-running English radio comedy, 1939-1949]
ITMC	International Transmission Maintenance Center [Communications]
IT/ME	Incentive Travel and Meeting Executives Show [Trade show] (ITD)
ITMF	International Textile Manufacturers Federation [Zurich, Switzerland] (EA)
ITMG	Integrated Thermal Micrometeoroid Garment [Spacesuit]
ItMGM	Italian MGM [Record label]
ITMI	Industrial Technology and Machine Intelligence (NITA)
ITMID	Item Identification File
ITMIS	Integrated Transportation Management Information System [Army]
ITMJ	Incoming Trunk Message Junction [Telecommunications] (OA)
ITMRA	Information Technology Management Reform Act of 1996 (AAGC)
ITMRC	International Travel Market Research Council
ITMS	In-Core Temperature Monitoring System [Nuclear energy] (NRCH)
ITMS	Ingestible Thermal Monitoring System
ITMS	Integrated Training Management System [DoD]
ITMS	Interactive Tsunami Modeling System [Marine science] (OSRA)
ITMS	International Tax Management System [Price Waterhouse & Co.]
ITMS	Ion Trap Mass Spectrometer
ITMT	Intermediate Thermomechanical Treatment (MCD)
ITN	Independent Telecommunication Network (ACRL)
ITN	Independent Television News [British]
ITN	Industrias Titan SA [Spain ICAO designator] (FAAC)
ITN	Institute for TransPacific Networking [Oakland, CA] [Telecommunications service] (TSSD)
ITN	Integrated Teleprocessing Network
ITN	Interim Technical Note
ITN	International Television News [A publication] (EAAP)
ITN	International Turbine Tech [Vancouver Stock Exchange symbol]
ITN	Internegative [Photography] (NTCM)
ITN	InterTan, Inc. [NYSE symbol] (CTT)
ITN	In Touch Networks (EA)
ITN	Itabuna [Brazil] [Airport symbol] (OAG)
ITNA	Independent Television News Association [News service]
ITNC	In-Track Noncontiguous
ITND	International Trade Names Dictionary [Later, IBTC] [A publication]
ITNFSA	International Tanker Nominal Freight Scale Association
ITNL	Interactive Tech [NASDAQ symbol] (TTSB)
ITNL	Interactive Technologies Corp. [NASDAQ symbol] (SAG)
ITNL	Internal (ECII)
ITNOTGAOTU	In the Name of the Great Architect of the Universe [Freemasonry] (ROG)
ITNRNT	Itinerant (FAAC)
ITNS	Integrated Tactical Navigation System [Navy]
ITNS	International Transplant Nurses Society (EA)
ITNS/D-AHRS	Integrated Tactical Navigation System/Doppler - Altitude Heading Reference System
ItNU	Universita di Napoli, Naples, Italy [Library symbol Library of Congress] (LCLS)
ItNU-IC	Universita di Napoli, Istituto Chimico, Naples, Italy [Library symbol Library of Congress] (LCLS)
ITO	Hilo [Hawaii] [Airport symbol] (OAG)
ITO	Hilo, HI [Location identifier FAA] (FAAL)
ITO	Impulse Transfer Orbit
ITO	Income Tax Office (DAS)
ITO	Income Tax Order
ITO	Independent Television Organization (NTCM)
ITO	Indian Tribal Organization (GFGA)
ITO	Indium Tin Oxide
ITO	Individual Travel Order [Military] (CINC)
ITO	Industrial Therapy Organisation [British]
ITO	Inspecting Torpedo Officer [Navy]
ITO	Installation Transportation Office [or Officer] [Air Force] (AFM)
ITO	Institution of Training Officers [British]
ITO	Instrument Takeoff
ITO	Integration and Test Order (MCD)
ITO	Interim Technical Order (AFM)
ITO	Intermediate Training Objective [Army] (INF)
ITO	International Thomson Organisation [Later, The Thomson Corp.]
ITO	International Trade Organization
ITO	International Travel Orders
ITO	Invitational Travel Order [Army] (AABC)
ITO	Irish Tourist Office (BI)
ITO	Ito [Japan] [Seismograph station code, US Geological Survey Closed] (SEIS)
ITOA	Inbound Tourism Organisation of Australia
ITOA	Independent Tanker Owners Association (DS)
ITOA	Independent Terminal Operators Association (EA)
ITOF	Ion Time of Flight
ITOFCN	Interim Technical Order Field Change Notice [Air Force] (MCD)
ITOI	International Thomson Organisation, Inc.
ITOL	International Thomson Organisation Ltd. [Later, TTC]

ITol .... Toluca City Library, Toluca, IL [*Library symbol Library of Congress*] (LCLS)

ITolo .... Tolono Township Library, Tolono, IL [*Library symbol Library of Congress*] (LCLS)

ITolSD .... Toluca Community Unit, School District 2306, Toluca, IL [*Library symbol Library of Congress*] (LCLS)

ITOM .... Interstate Transportation of Obscene Matter

ITONA .... Iveco Trucks of North America, Inc.

ITonSD........ Tonica Consolidated Community School District 79 and Consolidated High School District 360, Tonica, IL [*Library symbol Library of Congress*] (LCLS)

I-TOO .... Independent Truck Owner/Operator Association (EA)

ITOO .... Independent Truck Owner-Operators Association

ITOP........... Integrated Test Operate Panel

ITOP........... International Test Operations Procedure [*DoD*]

ITOPF .... International Tanker Owners Pollution Federation

ITOPLC .... International Thomson Organisation Public Limited Co.

ITOR .... Intercept Target Optical Reader

ITOS........... Improved TIROS [*Television Infrared Observation Satellite*] Operational Satellite [*or System*] [*National Oceanic and Atmospheric Administration*]

ITOS........... Interactive Terminal Operating System (NITA)

ITOS........... Iterative Time Optimal System

ITOSS .... Integrated Toolkit for Operating System Security [*Computer security system*]

ITOU .... Intensive Therapy Observation Unit [*Medicine*] (DMAA)

ITou .... Toulon Public Library, Toulon, IL [*Library symbol Library of Congress*] (LCLS)

ITOW .... Improved Tube-Launched, Optically Tracked, Wire-Guided [*Weapon*] (RDA)

ITOY........... International Truck of the Year

ITOY........... International Truck of the Year

ItoYokd .... Ito-Yokado Co. Ltd. [*Associated Press*] (SAG)

ITP............. Idiopathic Thrombocytopenic Purpura [*Medicine*]

ITP............. Immune Thrombocytopenic Purpura [*Medicine*]

ITP............. Income Tax Professional (ADA)

ITP............. Independent Television Publications [*British*] (ECON)

ITP............. Index of Technical Publications [*Military*] (DNAB)

ITP............. Index to Proceedings [*Information service or system United Nations*] (DUND)

ITP............. Individual Training Plan [*Army*]

ITP............. Individual Training Program (MCD)

ITP............. Individual Treatment Plan [*For the medical care and the education of a handicapped person*]

ITP............. Inferior Thalamic Peduncle [*Anatomy*]

ITP............. Initial Trial Phase (NG)

ITP............. Innovative Training Project

ITP............. Inosine Triphosphate [*Biochemistry*]

ITP............. Input Translator Program [*Computer science*]

ITP............. Inspection Test Procedure

ITP............. Installation Test Program

ITP............. Instruction to Proceed (NATG)

ITP............. Integrated Test Package (CAAL)

ITP............. Integrated Test Plan (AAGC)

ITP............. Integrated Test Program

ITP............. Integrated Transaction Processor (MHDI)

ITP............. Intelligence Town Plan

ITP............. Intensive Training Program

ITP............. Interactive Terminal Protocol [*Computer science*]

ITP............. Interceptor Technology Program

ITP............. Intercon Petroleum, Inc. [*Vancouver Stock Exchange symbol*]

ITP............. Interim Test Procedure (MCD)

ITP............. Interim Training Program [*Army*] (INF)

ITP............. Intermin Treatment Plan [*Medicine*] (DAVI)

ITP............. International Test Pilot School [*British ICAO designator*] (FAAC)

ITP............. International Thomson Publishing [*Also, ITPI*]

ITP............. Interrupted Task Paradigm [*Psychometrics*]

ITP............. Intertape Polymer Group [*AMEX symbol*] (SAG)

ITP............. Intrathoracic Pressure [*Medicine*]

ITP............. Isotachophoresis [*Analytical biochemistry*]

ITP............. Italian Patent (IAA)

It P............. Italian Pharmacopoeia [*A publication*]

ITp............. Tinley Park Public Library, Tinley Park, IL [*Library symbol Library of Congress*] (LCLS)

ITPA........... Illinois Test of Psycholinguistic Abilities

ITPA........... Independent Telephone Pioneer Association (EA)

ITPA........... International Tea Promotion Association [*Defunct*] (EAIO)

ITPA........... International Trotting and Pacing Association (EA)

ITPA........... International Truck Parts Association (EA)

ITPA........... Irish Trade Protection Association (DBA)

ITPAC......... Imported Tobacco Products Advisory Council [*British*] (DBA)

ITPAIS .... Image Technology Patent Information System [*Printing technology*] [*Rochester Institute of Technology Rochester, NY*]

ItPavU........ Universita degli Studi, Pavia, Italy [*Library symbol Library of Congress*] (LCLS)

ITPB........... Integrated Test Program Board

ITPC........... International Television Program Center [*Telecommunications*] (TEL)

ITPFF .... Interstate Transportation of Prize Fight Films

ITPI........... International Thomson Publishing, Inc. [*Also, ITP*]

ITPI........... International Transfer Printing Institute (EA)

ITPIAL........ Infrared Target Pointer/Illuminator/Aiming Laser [*Military*] (INF)

ITP-ID .... International Thomson Publishing - International Division

ITpM .... Tinley Park Mental Health Center, Tinley Park, IL [*Library symbol Library of Congress*] (LCLS)

ITPMG .... Interstate Transportation of Prison-Made Goods

ITP-NSS ...... Innovative Training Projects - National Skills Shortage

ITPO........... International TOGA [*Tropical Ocean Global Atmosphere*] Project Office [*Geneva, Switzerland*] (EAIO)

ITPP........... Individual Training Plan Proposal [*Army*]

ITPP........... Institute of Technical Publicity and Publications [*British*] (BI)

ITPP........... International Thomson Professional Publishing

ITPR........... Infrared Temperature Profile Radiometer

ITPRL......... Individual Training and Performance Research Laboratory [*Army*] (RDA)

ITPS........... Income Tax Payers' Society [*British*] (BI)

ITPS........... Institute for Theological and Philosophical Studies (EA)

ITPS........... Integrated Technical Processing System (NITA)

ITPS........... Integrated Teleprocessing System (IEEE)

ITPS........... Interactive Teleprocessing System (NITA)

ITPS........... Interactive Test Preparation System [*Computer science*] (MHDI)

ITPS........... Interactive Text Processing System (NITA)

ITPS........... Internal Teleprocessing System (CMD)

ITPS........... International Thomson Publishing Services

ITQ............. Individual Transferable Quota

ITQ............. Infant Temperament Questionnaire

ITQ............. Inferior Temporal Quadrant [*Medicine*] (DMAA)

ITQ............. International Thesaurus of Quotations [*A publication*]

ITQ............. Invitation to Quote (MCD)

ITQ............. Itaqui [*Brazil*] [*Airport symbol*] (AD)

ITR............. Australian Income Tax Reports [*A publication*] (DLA)

ITR............. Ignition Test Reactor (MCD)

IT-R .... Immunotoxin with Ricin

ITR............. Improved Tartar Retrofit [*Missile*] (MCD)

ITR............. Income Tax Reports [*India*] [*A publication*] (DLA)

ITR............. In-Core Thermionic Reactor [*Nuclear energy*]

ITR............. Incremental Tape Recorder

ITR............. Indian Tax Reports [*A publication*] (ILCA)

ITR............. Individual Training Record [*Military*] (INF)

ITR............. Indoor Testing Range [*Golf*] (PS)

ITR............. Industrial Target Report [*Later, IDR*] [*British World War II*]

ITR............. Industrial Tribunal Reports (DCTA)

ITR............. Infantry Training Replacement

ITR............. Information Technology Research [*Waltham, MA*] [*Telecommunications*] (TSSD)

ITR............. Initial Training Requirement

ITR............. Initial Trouble Report (IAA)

ITR............. Inlet Temperature Rise

ITR............. Inspection Test Report

ITR............. Instrumentation Tape Recorder

ITR............. Instrumented Test Range [*Fort Huachuca, AZ*] [*United States Army Electronic Proving Ground*] (GRD)

ITR............. Instrument Test Rig [*Liquid Metal Engineering Center*] [*Energy Research and Development Administration*] (IEEE)

ITR............. Integrated Technology Rotor

ITR............. Integrated Telephone Recorder [*Telecommunications*] (TEL)

ITR............. Integrated Test Requirements

ITR............. Integrated Thyristor Rectifier (IAA)

ITR............. Integrated Tourism Resort

ITR............. Intelcom Group [*AMEX symbol*] (SPSG)

ITR............. Intense Thermal Radiation

ITR............. Interim Technical Report

ITR............. Interim Test Report

ITR............. Internal Technical Report

ITR............. Interstate Transport Region

ITR............. In-Transit Rendezvous

ITR............. Intraocular Tension Recorder

ITR............. Intratracheal [*Medicine*]

IT/R .... Inventory Transfer Receipt

ITR............. Inverse Time Relay (KSC)

ITR............. Inverted Terminal Repeat [*Genetics*]

ITR............. Invitation to Register (ADA)

ITR............. Irish Term Reports, by Ridgeway, Lapp, and Schoales [*A publication*] (DLA)

ITR............. Isolation Test Routine (IAA)

ITRA........... Integrated Test Requirements Analysis (CAAL)

ITRA........... International Truck Restorers Association (EA)

i trach .... Intratracheal [*Medicine*] (AAMN)

ITRAM .... International [*Passenger*] Traffic Management System [*MTMC*] (TAG)

ITRB........... Interservice Training Review Board (MCD)

ItRC .... Consiglio Nazionale delle Ricerche, Rome, Italy [*Library symbol Library of Congress*] (LCLS)

ITRC........... Intercardia, Inc. [*NASDAQ symbol*] (SAG)

ITRC........... Intercardia Inc. [*NASDAQ symbol*] (TTSB)

ITRC........... International Tin Research Council [*Middlesex, England*] (EAIO)

ITRC........... Interstate Transport Region Commission

ITRD .... Integrated Test Requirements Documents (MCD)

ITRDB .... International Tree-Ring Data Bank [*University of Arizona*] (IID)

ITRDS .... Integrated Test Requirements Documents (MCD)

ITRE .... Institute for Transportation Research and Education [*University of North Carolina*] [*Research center*] (RCD)

ITre .... Trenton Public Library, Trenton, IL [*Library symbol Library of Congress*] (LCLS)

ITreWHS ..... Weslin Junior-Senior High School, Trenton, IL [*Library symbol Library of Congress*] (LCLS)

ITRI........... Industrial Technology Research Institute [*Integrated Circuit Design Centre*] [*Taiwan*] (NITA)

ITRI........... Inhalation Toxicology Research Institute [*Albuquerque, NM*] [*Department of Energy*]

ItRI	Institute Centrale Catalogo Unico delle Bibliotheche Italiane e per le Informazioni Bibliografiche, Rome, Italy [*Library symbol*] [*Library of Congress*] (LCLS)
ITRI	International Tin Research Institute (EAIO)
ITRI	Invitation to Register Interest
ITRI	Itron, Inc. [*NASDAQ symbol*] (SAG)
ITRIA	Instrument Tree Removable Instrument Assembly [*Nuclear energy*] (NRCH)
ITRIS	Integrated Tsunami Research Information System [*Marine science*] (OSRA)
ITRIS	International Trade and Resource Information System [*University of Alaska at Anchorage*] [*Information service or system*] (CRD)
ITRL	Instrument Test Repair Laboratory (AAG)
ITRM	Inverse Thermoremanent Magnetization
ITRO	Installation Test Requirements Outline (MCD)
ITRO	Integrated Test Requirements Outline
ITRO	Interservice Training Review Organization [*Military*] (NVT)
ITro	Tri-Township Library, Troy, IL [*Library symbol Library of Congress*] (LCLS)
ITROD	Incendiary Torch Remote Opening Device (MCD)
ITRON	Industrial TRON (NITA)
Itron	Itron, Inc. [*Associated Press*] (SAG)
ITRP	Institute of Transportation and Regional Planning (EA)
ITRPF	International Tyre, Rubber, and Plastic Federation (EAIO)
ITRU	Industrial Training and Research Unit (ACII)
ItRU	Universita degli Studi, Biblioteca Alessandrina, Rome, Italy [*Library symbol Library of Congress*] (LCLS)
IT Rulings	Income Tax Rulings [*A publication*]
ItRUN	Centro di Documentazione Umberto Nobile, Museo Storico, Rome, Italy [*Library symbol*] [*Library of Congress*] (LCLS)
ITRY	Itinerary (FAAC)
ITS	Aeronautica Interespacial SA de CV [*Mexico ICAO designator*] (FAAC)
ITS	AmericaIntelligent Transportation Society of America [*Formerly, IVHS America*]
ITS	Idaho Test Station [*Nuclear energy*] (NRCH)
ITS	Idle Tracking Switch [*Automotive engineering*]
ITS	IEEE Information Theory Society (EA)
ITS	Ignition Test Simulator
ITS	Imaginary Transition Structure [*Organic chemistry*]
ITS	Import Tabulation System [*United Nations*] (PDAA)
ITS	Improved Third Stage [*of Minuteman rocket*]
ITS	Incident Tracking System
ITS	Inclusive Tour Service (ADA)
ITS	Incompatible Time-sharing System (NHD)
ITS	Independent Triggering System
ITS	Index to Speeches [*Information service or system United Nations*] (DUND)
ITS	Industrial Technology Securities [*Investment firm*] [*British*]
ITS	Industrial Television Society [*Later, ITVA*] (EA)
ITS	Industrial Training Service (AIE)
ITS	Industry Training Support
ITS	Indus Tsangpo Suture [*Paleogeography*]
ITS	Inertial Timing Switch (IAA)
ITS	Infective Toxic Shock [*Medicine*] (DMAA)
ITS	Infinite Time Span
ITS	Information Technology Services [*California State University, Long Beach*] [*Research center*] (RCD)
ITS	Information Technology Services [*National Library of Canada*] (TSSD)
ITS	Information Technology Services [*Stanford University*] [*Information service or system*] (IID)
ITS	Information Technology Systems
ITS	Information Transfer Satellite (KSC)
ITS	Information Transfer [*or Transmission*] System
ITS	Infrared Tracking System
ITS	Initial Training School [*British military*] (DMA)
ITS	Insertion Test Signal [*Telecommunications*] (TEL)
ITS	Institute for Telecommunication Sciences [*Formerly, ITSA*] [*Boulder, CO*] [*Department of Commerce*]
ITS	Institute for Transportation Studies [*University of Calgary*] [*Canada Research center*] (RCD)
ITS	Institute of Telecommunications Services (MSC)
ITS	Institute of Temporary Services [*Later, National Association of Temporary Services*] (EA)
ITS	Institute of Theoretical Science [*University of Oregon*] [*Research center*] (RCD)
ITS	Institute of Transportation Studies [*University of California*] [*Research center*] (RCD)
ITS	Institute of Turkish Studies (EA)
ITS	Instrumentation Telemetry Station [*NASA*] (NASA)
ITS	Instrumentation Telemetry System [*NASA*] (IAA)
ITS	Instrument Time (Simulated)
ITS	Insulation Test Specification (MSA)
ITS	In-Tank Solidification
ITS	Integrated Target System
ITS	Integrated Termination System (IAA)
ITS	Integrated Test Schedule [*Army*]
ITS	Integrated Test Software (CAAL)
ITS	Integrated Tracking System [*ARTRAC*] [*Obsolete*] (MCD)
ITS	Integrated Trajectory System
ITS	Intelligent Terminal System [*IBM Corp.*]
ITS	Intelligent Transportation Society [*formerly, IVHS, Intelligent Vehicle-Highway Society*]
ITS	Intelligent Transportation System [*FTA*] [*NHTSA*] (TAG)
ITS	Intelligent Transport System [*Traffic management*] (ECON)
ITS	Intelligent Tutoring System (RDA)
ITS	Interactive Terminal Service (NITA)
ITS	Interactive Terminal Support [*Computer science*]
ITS	Interim Table Simulation (SAA)
ITS	Interim Teleprinter System
ITS	Intermarket Trading System (IEEE)
ITS	Intermediate Tape Store (CET)
ITS	Intermediate-Term Standby [*Business term*] (EMRF)
ITS	Internal Time Sharing (IAA)
ITS	Internal Transcribed Spacer [*Genetics*]
ITS	International Technogeographical Society
ITS	International Technologies & Systems [*Computer science*]
ITS	International Telecommunications Society (EA)
ITS	International Telecom Systems, Inc. [*Madison, WI*] [*Telecommunications*] (TSSD)
ITS	International Teleproduction Society (EA)
ITS	International Television Service [*Turner Teleport, Inc.*] [*Atlanta, GA*] [*Telecommunications service*] (TSSD)
ITS	International Temperature Scale (MUGU)
ITS	International Tesla Society (EA)
ITS	International Thespian Society (EA)
ITS	International Time-Sharing Corporation [*Telecommunications*] (NITA)
ITS	International Tracing Service [*Arolsen, Germany*] (EAIO)
ITS	International Trade Secretariats [*ICFTU*]
ITS	International Training School
ITS	International Travel Show (ITD)
ITS	International Trucking Show (ITD)
ITS	International Turfgrass Society (EA)
ITS	International Twin Study [*University of Southern California*] [*Research center*] (RCD)
ITS	Intersectional Transportation Service
ITS	Interstate Energy [*Vancouver Stock Exchange symbol*]
ITS	Intertime Switch [*Connection or Call*] [*Telecommunications*] (TEL)
ITS	Invitation to Send [*Western Union*] [*Data communications*]
ITS	Ion Thrust System
ITS	Ion Trap System
ITS	Iowa Transfer System
ITS	Irish Texts Society (EAIO)
ITS	Islamic Texts Society [*British*] (DBA)
ITS	Tri-State University, Angola, IN [*OCLC symbol*] (OCLC)
ITSA	Information Technology Skills Agency (NITA)
ITSA	Information Technology Strategic Alliances Database (IID)
ITSA	Insider Trading Sanctions Act of 1984
ITSA	Installation and Test Support Associate Contractor [*Air Force*]
ITSA	Institute for Telecommunication Sciences and Aeronomy [*Later, ITS*] [*National Oceanic and Atmospheric Administration*]
ITSA	Institute of Trading Standards Administration [*British*]
ITSA	Interstate Transportation of Stolen Aircraft
ITSAADCOTFOIK	International Twelve-Star Admiral and Deputy Custodian of the Fountain of Inexhaustible Knowledge [*Rank in Junior Woodchucks organization mentioned in Donald Duck comic by Carl Barks*]
ITSAC	International Thermal Storage Advisory Council (EAIO)
ITSB	Interstate Transportation of Strikebreakers
ITSC	International Telecommunications Satellite Consortium [*Superseded by International Telecommunications Satellite Organization*]
ITSC	International Telephone Services Center [*Telecommunications*] (TEL)
ITSC	Interstate Transportation of Stolen Cattle
ITSC	It Scale for Children [*Psychology*]
ITSDC	Interagency Toxic Substances Data Committee [*Washington, DC*] [*Environmental Protection Agency*] (EGAO)
ITSE	Integral of Time Squared Error [*Statistics*] (PDAA)
ITSEC	Information Technology Standards Unit [*British*]
ITSI	International Lottery & Totalizator Systems [*NASDAQ symbol*] (SAG)
ITSI	International Totalizator Systems, Inc. [*NASDAQ symbol*] (NQ)
ITSI	Intl Lottery & Totalizator [*NASDAQ symbol*] (TTSB)
ITSL	Integrated Two-Step Liquefaction [*Chemical engineering*]
ITSL	International Translator (IAA)
ITSMV	Interstate Transportation of Stolen Motor Vehicle
ITSO	Instrument Technician Service Organization
IT/SP	Instrument Tree/Spool Piece [*Nuclear energy*] (NRCH)
ITSP	Integrated Training System Plan [*Army*]
ITSP	Interstate Transportation of Stolen Property
ITSS	Integrated Tactical Surveillance System
ITSS	Integrated Target Sensor Suite (MCD)
ITSS	Investment Trust Savings Scheme [*British*]
ITSTC	International Telecommunictaions Standards Technical Council (OSI)
ITSU	Information Technology Standards Unit (NITA)
ITSU	International Coordination Group for the Tsunami Warning System in the Pacific [*Marine science*] (OSRA)
ITSY	Innovative Tech Systems, Inc. [*NASDAQ symbol*] (SAG)
ITSYLF	Interactive Synthesizer of Letterforms
ITSYW	Innovative Tech Sys Wrrt'A' [*NASDAQ symbol*] (TTSB)
ITT	Federal Reserve Bank of Chicago Library, Chicago, IL [*OCLC symbol*] (OCLC)
ITT	Iliotibial Tract [*Orthopedics*] (DAVI)
ITT	Image Intensification Tube (MCD)
ITT	Impact Transition Temperature (MCD)
ITT	Incoming Teletype
ITT	Incoming Trunk Terminal [*Telecommunications*] (IAA)
ITT	Indicator Time Test [*Chemistry*]
ITT	Individual Technical Training [*Military*]
ITT	Initial Teacher Training (AIE)
ITT	Inside Trim Template (MSA)

ITT .... Institute of Textile Technology (EA)
ITT .... Institute of Travel and Tourism [*British*] (DBA)
ITT .... Insulin Tolerance Test [*Physiology*]
ITT .... Internal Tibial Torsion [*Orthopedics*] (DAVI)
ITT .... International Trade in Textiles [*Textile trade agreement*]
ITT .... Interpretative Trace and Trap Program (SAA)
ITT .... Interrogation-Translation Team [*Military*] (CINC)
ITT .... Inter-Theater Transfer [*Army*] (AABC)
ITT .... Intertoll Trunk [*Telecommunications*]
ITT .... Inter-Turbine Temperature (ADA)
ITT .... Intertype Training [*Navy*] (NVT)
ITT .... Inventaire des Tablettes de Tello. Mission Francaise en Chaldee [*Paris*] [*A publication*] (BJA)
ITT .... Invitation to Tender (SSD)
ITT .... ITT Canada Ltd. [*Toronto Stock Exchange symbol*]
ITT .... ITT Corp. [*Formerly, International Telephone & Telegraph Corp.*] [*Wall Street slang name: "It Girl," the sobriquet for early movie star Clara Bow*] [*NYSE symbol*] (SPSG)
ITT .... Wittenoom Gorge [*Western Australia*] [*Airport symbol*] (AD)
ITTA .... Independent Taxation with Transferable Allowance [*British*] (DI)
ITTA .... International Tropical Timber Agreement (ECON)
ITTA .... ITT [*Institute of Textile Technology*] Austria (NITA)
ITTAC .... Information Technology Training Accredition Council [*British*] (NITA)
ITTAC .... International Telegraph and Telephonic Advisory Committee (AABC)
ITTAP .... ITT [*Institute of Textile Technology*] Testability Analysis Program (NITA)
ITTC .... Inter-American Tropical Tuna Commission [*Scripps Institution of Oceanography*]
ITTC .... International Travel and Trailer Club (EA)
ITTC .... International Tropical Timber Council [*Australia*]
ITTCCS .... ITT Corporate Communications Services, Inc.
ITTCOINS ..... ITT [*Institute of Textile Technology*] Communications and Information Services Inc. (NITA)
ITTCOM .... International Telephone & Telegraph World Communications, Inc.
ITT Corp ...... ITT Corp. [*Associated Press*] (SAG)
ITT Cp .... ITT Corp. [*Formerly, International Telephone & Telegraph Corp.*] [*Wall Street slang name: "It Girl," the sobriquet for early movie star Clara Bow*] [*Associated Press*] (SAG)
ITTCS .... International Telephone and Telegraph Communication System
ITTD .... Information and Technology Transfer Database [*International Research and Evaluation*]
ITTE .... Institute for the Transfer of Technology to Education (EA)
ITTE .... Institute of Transportation and Traffic Engineering [*UCLA*]
ITTE .... Interim Terminal Test Environment [*FAA*]
ITT Ed .... ITT Educational Services, Inc. [*Associated Press*] (SAG)
ITTETS .... ITT Employment & Training Systems, Inc. [*Telecommunications service*] (TSSD)
ITTF .... International Table Tennis Federation [*British*]
ITTF .... International Telephone and Telegraph Federal Laboratories
ITTFA .... Iterative Target Transformation Factor Analysis [*Computer science*]
ITTFL .... International Telephone and Telegraph Federal Laboratories
ITTG .... Interdisciplinary Team Training in Geriatrics [*Veterans Administration*] (GFGA)
ITTGATC ...... ITT [*Institute of Textile Technology*] Gallium Arsenide Technology Cen ter (NITA)
ITT Inds ...... ITT Industries, Inc. Indiana [*Associated Press*] (SAG)
ITTL .... International Table Tennis League (EA)
ITTL .... International Telephone and Telegraph Laboratories (SAA)
ITTO .... International Tropical Timber Organization [*Yokohama, Japan*] [*United Nations*]
ITTP .... Instrument Technician Training Program (ACII)
ITT/PMD ...... Interpretative Trace and Trap Program Plus Modifications (SAA)
ITTS .... Instrumentation, Target, and Threat Simulator [*Army*] (RDA)
ITTT .... Individual Tactical Technical Training [*Military*] (MCD)
ITTT .... Institute of Transportation, Travel, and Tourism
ITTTA .... International Technical Tropical Timber Association
ItTU .... Biblioteca Nazional Universitaria di Torino, Servizio Prestito, Turin, Italy [*Library symbol Library of Congress*] (LCLS)
ITT-USTS ..... ITT United States Transmission Systems, Inc. [*Telecommunications service*] (TSSD)
ITU .... Income Tax Unit
ITU .... Input Terminal Unit (SSD)
ITU .... Instructional Technologist Unit
ITU .... Intensive Therapy Unit [*Medicine*] (MAE)
ITU .... Interface Transformation Unit (SAA)
ITU .... International Taurus Resources [*Vancouver Stock Exchange symbol*]
ITU .... International Telecommunications Union [*An association*] (PCM)
ITU .... International Telecommunication Union [*Formerly, International Telegraphic Union*] [*A specialized agency of the United Nations*] [*Switzerland Research center*]
ITU .... International Temperance Union
ITU .... International Triathlon Union (EAIO)
ITU .... International Typographical Union (EA)
ITU .... Inventory Temporarily in Use [*Army*] (AFIT)
ITU .... Investment Trust Unit [*British*]
ITU .... Taylor University, Upland, IN [*OCLC symbol*] (OCLC)
ITu .... Tuscola Public Library, Tuscola, IL [*Library symbol Library of Congress*] (LCLS)
ITUA .... Independent Trade Union Association [*Turkey*]
ITUC .... Irish Trade Union Congress
ITuCoH .... Douglas County Jarman Memorial Hospital, Tuscola, IL [*Library symbol Library of Congress*] (LCLS)
ITUCSTL ...... International Trade Unions Committee of Social Tourism and Leisure [*See also CSITSL*] [*Prague, Czechoslovakia*] (EAIO)

ITU-D .... International Telecommunication Union-Telecommunication Development Sector (ACRL)
ITUG .... Information Technology Users Group [*Exxon Corp.*]
ITUG .... International Tandem Users' Group (EA)
ITU-R .... International Telecommunication Union-Radio Communication Sector (ACRL)
ITUR .... Interstate Transportation of Unsafe Refrigerators
ITURM .... International Typographical Union Ruling Machine
ITUS .... Institute of Totally Useless Skills [*An association*] (EA)
ITUSA .... Information Technology Users' Standards Association [*British*]
ITUSAF .... Institute of Technology, United States Air Force [*Wright-Patterson Air Force Base, Dayton, OH*] (AAG)
ITUSFP .... Interreligious Taskforce on US Food Policy (EA)
ITU-T .... International Telecommunication Union-Telecommunication Standardization Sector (ACRL)
ITU-TSS .... International Telecommunications Union - Telecommunications Switching System (PCM)
ITV .... Improved TOW [*Tube-Launched, Optically Tracked, Wire-Guided (Weapon)*] Vehicle
ITV .... Independently Targeted Vehicle [*Military*] (DA)
ITV .... Independent Television
ITV .... Industrial Television
ITV .... Inferior Temporal Vein [*Medicine*] (DMAA)
ITV .... Instructional Television
ITV .... Instrumental Test Vehicle
ITV .... Integrated Technology Validation
ITV .... Interactive Television
ITV .... Intermediate Test Vessel (NRCH)
ITV .... Intervuelo SA [*Mexico ICAO designator*] (FAAC)
ITV .... Intranet Visability [*Army*]
ITV .... Israel Television (BJA)
ItV .... Italian RCA [*Victor*] [*Record label*]
ITVA .... International Industrial Television Association (NTCM)
ITVA .... International Television Association (EA)
ITVAC .... Industrial Transistor Value Automatic Computer
ITVAD .... Indwelling Transcutaneous Vascular Access Device [*Pharmacology*] (DAVI)
ITVB .... International Television Broadcasting
ITVETS .... Improved TOW [*Tube-Launched, Optically Tracked, Wire-Guided (Weapon)*] Vehicle Evasive Target Simulator [*Military*] (MCD)
ItVox .... Italian Vox [*Record label*]
ITVS .... Ignition Timing Vacuum Switch [*Automotive engineering*]
ITVS .... Independent Television Service
ITVSDA .... Independent Television Service Dealers' Association
ITVTP .... Internationale Tieraerztliche Vereinigung fuer Tierproduktion [*International Veterinary Association for Animal Production*]
ITW .... Illinois Tool Works [*NYSE symbol*] (TTSB)
ITW .... Illinois Tool Works, Inc. [*NYSE symbol*] (SPSG)
ITW .... Independent Tank Wing [*of a ship*] (DS)
ITW .... Independent True Whig Party [*Liberia*] [*Political party*]
ITW .... Inertia Test Weight [*Exhaust emissions*] [*Automotive engineering*]
ITW .... Initial Training Wing [*British military*] (DMA)
ITW .... Introducing the World [*An association Canada*]
ITWA .... International Tug-of-War Association (EA)
ITWC .... Inland Transport War Council [*World War II*]
ITWF .... International Transport Workers' Federation
ITWG .... Interface Technical Working Group
ITWI .... Interstate Transmission of Wagering Information
ITWO .... i2 Technologies [*NASDAQ symbol*] (TTSB)
ITWO .... Inspection Test Work Order (SAA)
ITWP .... Interstate Transportation of Wagering Paraphernalia
ITWS .... Integrated Terminal Weather System [*Marine science*] (OSRA)
ITWS .... Integrated Terminal Weather System (USDC)
ITX .... Iberiotoxin [*Biochemistry*]
ITX .... Inclusive Tour Excursion [*Airline fare*]
ITX .... Independent Tank Common [*of a ship*] (DS)
ITX .... Information Transfer Exchange (PDAA)
ITX .... Interactive Transaction
ITX .... International Technology Corp. [*NYSE symbol*] (SPSG)
ITX-T .... International Tillex Enterprises Ltd. [*Vancouver Stock Exchange symbol*]
ITX .... Intertriginous Xanthoma [*Medicine*] (AAMN)
ITX .... Intl Technology [*NYSE symbol*] (TTSB)
ITY .... Fort Riley, KS [*Location identifier FAA*] (FAAL)
ITY .... Information Technology Year [*1982*]
ITY .... Intensity Resources Ltd. [*Toronto Stock Exchange symbol*]
Ity .... Interchangeability
ITY .... International Tourist Year
ITZ .... Inter-Tropical Convergence Zone
IU .... Identification Unit (MSA)
IU .... Immunizing Unit [*Medicine*]
IU .... Impedance Unit (MCD)
IU .... Indianapolis Union [*AAR code*]
IU .... Indiana University
IU .... Industrial User (ERG)
IU .... Infectious Unit
IU .... Information Unit
IU .... Information Unlimited [*Information service or system*] (IID)
IU .... Input Unit
IU .... Instant Update [*Professional Farmers of America*] [*Information service or system*] (TSSD)
IU-D .... Instruction Unit [*Computer science*]
IU .... Instrument Unit [*NASA*]
IU .... Integer Unit [*Computer science*]
IU .... Interface Unit [*Computer science*] (MCD)

IU................ Interference Unit [Military]
IU................ Interlingue Union
IU................ International Unit
IU................ Internet University [Computer science]
IU................ Interval of Uncertainty [Psychology]
IU................ Intrauterine [Medicine]
IU................ In Utero [Gynecology]
iu................ Israel-Syria Demilitarized Zones [is (Israel) used in records cataloged after January 1978] [MARC country of publication code Library of Congress] (LCCP)
IU................ Izquierda Unida [United Left] [Peru] [Political party]
IU................ Izquierda Unida [United Left] [Spain] [Political party] (ECED)
IU................ Izquierda Unida [United Left] [Bolivia] [Political party] (EY)
IU................ Midstate Airlines [ICAO designator] (AD)
IU................ University of Illinois, Urbana, IL [Library symbol Library of Congress] (LCLS)
IUA............... Image Understanding Architecture [Computer science]
IUA............... Individual Unit Action Model
IUA............... Inertial Unit Assembly
IUA............... Inter-American University Association
IUA............... Interface Unit Adapter [Computer science] (MCD)
IUA............... Interlibrary Users Association [University of Maryland] [College Park, MD] [Library network]
IUA............... International Union of Academies (EA)
IUA............... International Union of Architects
IUA............... International University of America [San Francisco, CA] (ECON)
IUA............... Intrauterine Adhesion [Medicine] (DMAA)
IUA............... IOMEC Users Association [Formerly, DUA] [Defunct] (EA)
IUA............... University of Texas at Arlington, Arlington, TX [OCLC symbol] (OCLC)
IUAA............. International Union of Advertisers Associations [Later, WFA] (EAIO)
IUAA............. International Union of Alpine Associations
IUAC............ International Union Against Cancer [An association] (CDI)
IUACE.......... Indian University Association for Continuing Education
IUADM......... International Union of Associations of Doctor-Motorists
IUAES.......... International Union of Anthropological and Ethnological Sciences [See also UISAE] [ICSU Gwynedd, Wales] (EAIO)
IUAI............. International Union of Aviation Insurers [British] (EAIO)
IUAJ............ International Union of Agricultural Journalists
IUAM.......... Islamic Unity of Afghan Mujahadeen [Afghanistan] [Political party]
IUANPW...... International Union of Allied Novelty and Production Workers (EA)
IUAO........... Internationalen Union fuer Angewandte Ornithologie [International Union for Applied Ornithology] (EAIO)
IUAPPA....... International Union of Air Pollution Prevention Associations [See also UIAPPA] [England] (EAIO)
IUAR........... Institute for Urban Affairs and Research [Howard University] [Research center] (RCD)
IU-Ar........... University of Illinois, Archives, Urbana, IL [Library symbol Library of Congress] (LCLS)
IUAT........... International Union Against Tuberculosis [Later, IUATLD] (EAIO)
IUATLD....... International Union Against Tuberculosis and Lung Disease [See also UICTMR] (EAIO)
IUB............. Baltimore, MD [Location identifier FAA] (FAAL)
IUB............. Indiana University, School of Law Library, Bloomington, IN [OCLC symbol] (OCLC)
IUB............. Instruction Used BIT [Binary Digit] [Computer science] (MHDI)
IUB............. International Union of Biochemistry (EA)
IUB............. International Universities Bureau
IU-B........... University of Illinois, Biology Library, Urbana, IL [Library symbol Library of Congress] (LCLS)
IUBC.......... Indiana United Bancorp [NASDAQ symbol] (SAG)
IUBCTW...... International Union of Bakery, Confectionery, and Tobacco Workers (BARN)
IUBS.......... International Union of Biological Sciences [Paris, France]
IUBS-CBE.... IUBS Commission on Biological Education (AIE)
IUBSSA....... International Union of Building Societies and Savings Associations [Later, IOHFI] [Chicago, IL] (EA)
IUC............. Association for Higher Education, Dallas, TX [OCLC symbol] (OCLC)
IUC............. Idiopathic Ulcerative Colitis [Medicine]
IUC............. Immediate Unit Commander [Navy] (NVT)
IUC............. Incurred but Unreported Claims [Health insurance] (GHCT)
IUC............. Initial User Capability (SSD)
IUC............. Instructor Utilization Course (MCD)
IUC............. International Underwater Contractors, Inc.
IUC............. International Union of Crystallography
IUC............. International University Consortium for Telecommunications in Learning [Later, IUC] (EA)
IUC............. International University Contact for Management Education
IUC............. International University of Communication [Washington, DC]
IUC............. Inter-University Committee for Debate on Foreign Policy [Defunct]
IUC............. Inter-University Council
IUCAA......... Inter-University Center for Astronomy and Astrophysic [India]
IUCAB........ International Union of Commercial Agents and Brokers [EC] (ECED)
IUCADC....... Inter-Union Commission of Advice to Developing Countries [of the International Union of Geodesy and Geophysics] [Mississauga, ON] (EAIO)
IUCAF......... Inter-Union Commission on Frequency Allocations for Radio Astronomy and Space Science (EA)
IUCD........... Intrauterine Contraceptive Device [Medicine]
IUCED........ Inter-Union Commission of European Dehydrators [See also CIDE] [Paris, France] (EAIO)
IUCESD........ Inter-American University Council for Economic and Social Development (EA)
IUCF........... Indiana University Cyclotron Facility [Research center] (RCD)

IUCFA.......... Inter-Union Commission on Frequency Allocations for Radio Astronomy and Space Science (EA)
IUCI............ Inter-University Committee on Israel [Later, America-Israel Cultural Foundation] (EA)
IUCME......... International University Contact for Management Education
IUCN........... International Union for Conservation of Nature [World Conservation Union] (USDC)
IUCN........... International Union for Conservation of Nature and Natural Resources [Research Center] [ICSU] [Switzerland] (EA)
IUCN........... World Conservation Union
IUCNNR...... International Union for Conservation of Nature and Natural Resources [ICS U] [Research center Switzerland]
IUCNPSG..... International Union for the Conservation of Nature's Primate Specialist Group (EA)
IU Cr.......... International Union of Crystallography [See also UIC] (EA)
IUCRC......... Industry/University Cooperation Research Center [National Science Foundation]
IUCRCB....... Inter-University Committee for Research on Consumer Behavior (EA)
IUCRM........ Inter-Union Commission on Radio Meteorology [International Council of Scientific Unions] [Research center]
IUCS........... Instruction Update Command System
IUCS........... Instrumentation Unit Update Command System [NASA] (NASA)
IUCS........... Inter-Union Commission on Spectroscopy [International Council of Scientific Unions]
IUCSTP....... Inter-Union Commission on Solar-Terrestrial Physics (MCD)
IUCTG........ Inter-University Committee on Travel Grants
IUCW......... International Union for Child Welfare [Geneva, Switzerland] [Defunct]
IUD............ Indiana University, School of Dentistry, Indianapolis, IN [OCLC symbol] (OCLC)
IUD............ Industrial Union Department [of AFL-CIO] (EA)
IUD............ Institute for Urban Design (EA)
IUD............ Institute for Urban Development
IUD............ Internal Unstable Damper (MCD)
IUD............ Intrauterine Death [Medicine]
IUD............ Intrauterine Device [A contraceptive] [Medicine]
IUDH.......... In-Service Unplanned Derated Hours [Electronics] (IEEE)
IUdR.......... Iodouracildeoxyriboside [Biochemistry]
IUDWC....... Irish Union of Distributive Workers and Clerks (BI)
IUDZG........ International Union of Directors of Zoological Gardens [Canada] (EAIO)
IUE........... Interface Unit Error Count Table (MCD)
IUE........... International Thunderwood Explorations Ltd. [Vancouver Stock Exchange symbol Toronto Stock Exchange symbol]
IUE........... International Ultraviolet Explorer [NASA]
IUE........... International Union for Electroheat [Also, IUE-H]
IUE........... International Union of Electrical, Radio, and Machine Workers
IUE........... International Union of Electronic [Electrical, technical, salaried and machine workers] (NITA)
IUE........... International Union of Electronic, Electrical, Technical, Salaried, Machine, andFurniture Workers (EA)
IUE........... Niue Island [Niue] [Airport symbol] (OAG)
IUE........... University of Evansville, Evansville, IN [OCLC symbol] (OCLC)
IUEC.......... International Union of Elevator Constructors (EA)
IUEF.......... Internacia Unuigo de la Esperantistoj-Filologoj [International Union of Esperantist-Philologists - IUEP] [Sofia, Bulgaria] (EAIO)
IUEFI......... Internacia Unuigo de la Esperantistoj-Filologoj [International Union of Esperantist-Philologists - IUEP] [Sofia, Bulgaria] (EA)
IUEGS......... International Union of European Guides and Scouts [See also UIGSE] [Chateau Landon, France] (EAIO)
IUE-H......... International Union for Electroheat [Also, IUE]
IUEP.......... International Union of Esperantist-Philologists [Sofia, Bulgaria] (EAIO)
IUERMW..... International Union of Electrical, Radio, and Machine Workers (IAA)
IUEW......... International Union of Electrical Workers
IUF........... Interamerican Underwater Festival
IUF........... International Unicycling Federation (EA)
IUF........... International Union of Food and Allied Workers' Associations [See also IUL] [Petit-Lancy, Switzerland] (EAIO)
IUF........... International University Foundation (EA)
IUF........... Isolated Ultrafiltration [Organic chemistry] (DAVI)
IUF........... Southern Methodist University, Law Library, Dallas, TX [OCLC symbol] (OCLC)
IUFB.......... Intrauterine Foreign Body [Gynecology]
IUFD.......... Intrauterine Fetal Death [or Demise] [Obstetrics] (DAVI)
IUFDT........ International Union of Food, Drink, and Tobacco Workers' Associations
IUFGR........ Intrauterine Fetal Growth Retardation [Obstetrics] (DAVI)
IUFLJP........ International Union of French-Language Journalists and Press [See also UIJPLF] [Paris, France] (EAIO)
IUFO.......... International Union of Family Organizations [Paris, France]
IUFoST........ International Union of Food Science and Technology [ICSU] [Dublin, Republic of Ireland] (EAIO)
IUFRO........ International Union of Forestry Research Organizations [Vienna, Austria] [Research center] (EAIO)
Iug............ Bellum Iugurthinum [of Sallust] [Classical studies] (OCD)
IUG............ ICES [Integrated Civil Engineering System] Users Group [Defunct] (EA)
IUG............ Infusion Urogram [Medicine] (DMAA)
IUG............ Intelligence Users' Guide (MCD)
IUG............ Intercomm Users' Group (EA)
IUG............ Intrauterine Gestation [Obstetrics] (DAVI)
IUGB.......... International Union of Game Biologists [Canada] (EAIO)
IUGG......... International Union of Geodesy and Geophysics [Brussels, Belgium]
IUGGTC....... International Union of Geodesy and Geophysics Tsunami Commission [Marine science] (OSRA)
IUGG/TC..... IUGG Tsunami Commission (USDC)

IUGM .... International Union of Gospel Missions (EA)
IUGR .... Intrauterine Growth Rate [*Medicine*] (MAE)
IUGR .... Intrauterine Growth Retardation [*Medicine*]
IUGRI .... International Union of Graphic Reproduction Industries [*Later, IUI*] (EAIO)
IUGS .... International Union of Geological Sciences [*ICSU*] [*Trondheim, Norway*] (EA)
IU-GS .... University of Illinois, Illinois State Geological Survey, Urbana, IL [*Library symbol Library of Congress*] (LCLS)
IUH .... Indiana University, School of Medicine, Health Library Cooperative, Indianapolis, IN [*OCLC symbol*] (OCLC)
IUH .... Instantaneous Unit Hydrograph
IU-H .... University of Illinois, School of Basic Medical Sciences, Library of Public Health Sciences, Urbana, IL [*Library symbol Library of Congress*] (LCLS)
IUHE .... International Union of Health Education [*See also UIES*] [*Paris, France*] (EAIO)
IUHFI .... International Union of Housing Finance Institutions (EAIO)
IUHPS .... International Union of the History and Philosophy of Science [*ICSU*] [*Uppsala, Sweden*] (EAIO)
IUHR .... International Union of Hotel, Restaurant, and Bar Workers
IU-HS .... Illinois Historical Survey, University of Illinois, Urbana, IL [*Library symbol Library of Congress*] (LCLS)
IUI .... Interim Use Item (MCD)
IUI .... Intrauterine Insemination [*Medicine*] (DMAA)
IUI .... Shawnee Library System, Carterville, IL [*OCLC symbol*] (OCLC)
IUIEC .... Inter-University Institute of Engineering Control (PDAA)
IUIN .... International Union for Inland Navigation [*Strasbourg, France*] (EA)
IUIS .... International Union of Immunological Societies (EA)
IUJ .... International University of Japan (ECON)
IUJ .... John Marshall Law School, Chicago, IL [*OCLC symbol*] (OCLC)
IUJCD .... Internationale Union Junger Christlicher Demokraten [*International Union of Young Christian Democrats*]
IUJHUSC .... International Union of Journeymen Horseshoers of the United States and Canada (EA)
IUKADGE .... Improved United Kingdom Air Defense Ground Environment
Iul .... Divus Iulius [*of Suetonius*] [*Classical studies*] (OCD)
IUL .... Indiana University, Bloomington, IN [*OCLC symbol*] (OCLC)
IUL .... Indian Unattached List [*British military*] (DMA)
IUL .... Information Utilization Laboratory [*University of Pittsburgh*] (NITA)
IUL .... Institute of Urban Life (EA)
IUL .... Internationale Union der Lebens- und Genussmittelarbeiter-Gewerkschaften [*International Union of Food and Allied Workers Associations - IUF*] [*Petit-Lancy, Switzerland*] (EAIO)
IU/L .... International Units per Liter
IU-L .... University of Illinois, Lincoln Room, Urbana, IL [*Library symbol Library of Congress*] (LCLS)
IULA .... International Union of Local Authorities [*The Hague, Netherlands*] (EA)
IULC .... Committee on Instruction in the Use of Libraries [*Later, CUILL*] (EA)
IULC .... Independent United Labor Congress [*Nigeria*]
IULC-RAILS .... Interuniversity Library Council: Reference and Interlibrary Loan Service [*Library network*]
IULCS .... International Union of Leather Chemists Societies
IULCW .... International Union of Liberal Christian Women
IULD .... International Union of Lorry Drivers [*See also UICR*] [*Munich, Germany*] (EAIO)
IULEC .... Inter-University Labor Education Committee
IULIA .... International Union of Life Insurance Agents [*Milwaukee, WI*] (EA)
IULS .... Indiana Union List of Serials
IU-LS .... University of Illinois, Graduate School of Library Science, Urbana, IL [*Library symbol Library of Congress*] (LCLS)
IULVTFT .... International Union for Land Value Taxation and Free Trade [*British*] (EAIO)
IUM .... Honolulu, HI [*Location identifier FAA*] (FAAL)
IUM .... Indiana University, School of Medicine, Indianapolis, IN [*OCLC symbol*] (OCLC)
IUM .... Interim Use Material (MCD)
IUM .... Intrauterine Fetally Malnourished [*Medicine*] (MAE)
IU-M .... University of Illinois at the Medical Center, Chicago, IL [*Library symbol Library of Congress*] (LCLS)
IUMA .... Interim Use Material Authorization (MCD)
IUMA .... Internet Underground Music Archive
IU-MG .... University of Illinois, Map and Geography Library, Urbana, IL [*Library symbol*] [*Library of Congress*] (LCLS)
IUMI .... International Union of Marine Insurance [*Basel, Switzerland*]
IUMMSW .... International Union of Mine, Mill, and Smelter Workers [*Later, USWA*]
IUMP .... International Union of Master Painters [*See also UNIEP*] [*Brussels, Belgium*] (EAIO)
IUMP .... International Union of the Medical Press (DIT)
IUMS .... International Union for Moral and Social Action
IUMS .... International Union of Microbiological Societies [*University of Newcastle*] (EA)
IUMSBD .... International Union of Microbiological Societies Bacteriology Division [*B eckenham, Kent, England*] (EAIO)
IUMSWA .... Industrial Union of Marine and Shipbuilding Workers of America (EA)
IU-Mu .... University of Illinois, Music Library, Urbana, IL [*Library symbol Library of Congress*] (LCLS)
IUNA .... Irish United Nations Association (EAIO)
IUNDH .... In-Service Unit Derated Hours [*Electronics*] (IEEE)
IU-Ne .... University of Illinois at Urbana-Champaign, University of Illinois Newspaper Library, Urbana-Champaign, IL [*Library symbol Library of Congress*] (LCLS)
IU-NH .... University of Illinois, Illinois Natural History Survey, Urbana, IL [*Library symbol Library of Congress*] (LCLS)

IUNS .... International Union of Nutritional Sciences [*Wageningen, Netherlands*]
IUNT .... Interservice Undergraduate Navigator Training
IUO .... ICG Utilities (Ontario) Ltd. [*Toronto Stock Exchange symbol*]
IUOE .... International Union of Operating Engineers (EA)
IUOMWH .... Independent United Order of Mechanics - Western Hemisphere (EA)
IUOTO .... International Union of Official Travel Organisations [*Later, WTO*]
IUP .... Indiana University of Pennsylvania
IUP .... Indiana University Press
IUP .... Indiana University - Purdue University at Indianapolis, Indianapolis, IN [*OCLC symbol*] (OCLC)
IUP .... Industrial Union Party (EA)
IUP .... Installed User Program [*Computer science*]
IUP .... International Union of Phlebology [*Paris, France*] (EA)
IUP .... Intrauterine Pregnancy (CPH)
IUP .... Intrauterine Pressure [*Gynecology*]
IUP .... Irish University Press
IUP .... Israel Universities Press
IUPA .... International Union of Police Associations (EA)
IUPA .... International Union of Practitioners in Advertising
IUPAB .... International Union of Pure and Applied Biophysics [*ICSU*] [*Pecs, Hungary*] [*Research center*] (EA)
IUPAC .... International Union of Pure and Applied Chemistry [*Research center British*] (IRC)
IUPAP .... International Union of Pure and Applied Physics [*ICSU*] [*Goteborg, Sweden*] (EA)
IUPD .... Intrauterne Pregnancy, Delivered [*Obstetrics*] (DAVI)
IUPESM .... International Union for Physical and Engineering Sciences in Medicine [*ICSU*] [*Ottawa, ON*] (EAIO)
IUPHAR .... International Union of Pharmacology [*ICSU*] [*Buckingham, England*] (MSC)
IUPIW .... International Union of Petroleum and Industrial Workers (EA)
IUPLAW .... International Union for the Protection of Literary and Artistic Works
IUPM .... International Union for Protecting Public Morality [*Later, International Union for Moral and Social Action*]
IUPN .... International Union for the Protection of Nature [*Later, IUCN*]
IUPOV .... International Union for the Protection of New Varieties of Plants (GNE)
IUPPE .... Independent Union of Plant Protection Employees (EA)
IUPPR .... Institute for Urban and Public Policy Research [*University of Colorado - Denver*] [*Research center*] (RCD)
IUPPS .... International Union of Prehistoric and Protohistoric Sciences [*Ghent, Belgium*] (EAIO)
Iupp Trag .... Iuppiter Tragoedus [*of Lucian*] [*Classical studies*] (OCD)
IUPS .... International Union of Physiological Sciences [*ICSU*] [*Gif-sur-Yvette, France*] (ASF)
IUPS .... International Union of Psychological Science (EA)
IUPsyS .... International Union of Psychological Science (EA)
IUPT .... International Union of Public Transportation
IUPUI .... Indiana University - Purdue University at Indianapolis
IUPW .... International Union of Petroleum Workers [*Later, IUPIW*] (EA)
IUQ .... Interrupted Ultraquick [*Flashing*] Light [*Navigation signal*]
IUQ .... Quaker Oats Co., Research Library, Barrington, IL [*OCLC symbol*] (OCLC)
IUR .... Insured Unemployment Rate (OICC)
IUR .... International Union of Radioecologists (EA)
IUR .... International Union of Railways [*Paris*]
IUR .... International Union Resources, Inc. [*Vancouver Stock Exchange symbol*]
IUR .... Inter-User Reliability
IUR .... Inventory Update Rule [*Environmental Protection Agency*]
IU-R .... University of Illinois, Rare Book Room, Urbana, IL [*Library symbol Library of Congress*] (LCLS)
IUr .... Urbana Free Library, Urbana, IL [*Library symbol Library of Congress*] (LCLS)
IURAP .... International Users Resource Allocation Panel
IURC .... International Underwater Research Corp.
IURC .... International Union for Research of Communication [*Berne, Switzerland*] (EAIO)
IUrCD .... Clark Dietz Engineers, Urbana, IL [*Library symbol*] [*Library of Congress*] (LCLS)
IUrCH .... Carle Foundation Hospital, Urbana, IL [*Library symbol Library of Congress*] (LCLS)
IURD .... Institute of Urban and Regional Development [*University of California, Berkeley*] [*Research center*] (RCD)
IUrE-E .... Educational Resources Information Center, Elementary and Early Childhood Education (ERIC/ECE), Urbana, IL [*Library symbol Library of Congress*] (LCLS)
IUrE-NC .... Educational Resources Information Center, National Council of Teachers of English, Urbana, IL [*Library symbol Library of Congress*] (LCLS)
IUREP .... International Uranium Resources Evaluation Project
IURES .... International Union of Reticuloendothelial Societies (EA)
IUrG .... Illinois State Geological Survey, Urbana, IL [*Library symbol Library of Congress*] (LCLS)
IURGRQR .... Item Urgently Required [*Army*] (AFIT)
IUrH .... Mercy Hospital, Urbana, IL [*Library symbol Library of Congress*] (LCLS)
IURMS .... International Union of Railway Medical Services (EA)
IURP .... Integrated Unit Record Processor
IURP .... International Union of Roofing and Plumbing (EAIO)
IURS .... Institute of Urban and Regional Studies [*Washington University*] [*Research center*] (RCD)
IURS .... International Union of Radio Science (MSC)

IUrSD.......... Urbana Community Unit School District, Urbana, IL [*Library symbol*] [*Library of Congress*] (LCLS)
IUrW .... Illinois State Water Survey, Urbana, IL [*Library symbol Library of Congress*] (LCLS)
IUS .... Inertial [*formerly, Interim*] Upper Stage [*Air Force*]
IUS .... Information Unit Separator [*Computer science*]
IUS .... Initial Upper Stage [*NASA*]
IUS .... Initial Upper State (IEEE)
IUS .... Installed User System [*Computer science*] (IAA)
IUS .... Institute of Urban Studies, University of Winnipeg [*UTLAS symbol*]
IUS .... Interchange Unit Selector (NITA)
IUS .... Interchange Unit Separator [*Computer science*] (BUR)
IUS .... Interim Upper Stage [*Missile*]
IUS .... Interim Use Sheet (NASA)
IUS .... Interior Upper Stage (NASA)
IUS .... International Union of Speleology [*See also UIS*] [*Vienna, Austria*] (EAIO)
IUS .... International Union of Students [*See also UIE*] [*Prague, Czechoslovakia*] (EAIO)
IUS .... Inter-University Seminar on Armed Forces and Society (EA)
IUSA .... International Underwater Spearfishing Association (EA)
IUSA .... Interserve/USA [*An association*] (EA)
IUSAMH ...... International Union of Societies for the Aid of Mental Health [*Bordeaux, France*] (EAIO)
IUSB .... Indiana University at South Bend
IUSB .... International Universities' Sports Board [*Defunct*] (EA)
IUSC .... Inter-University Software Committee [*Inter-University Committee on Computing*] (AIE)
IUSDT .... International Union of Socialist Democratic Teachers (EAIO)
IUSF............ India-US Foundation (EA)
IUSF............ International Union for Surface Finishing (EAIO)
IUSF............ International Union of Societies of Foresters [*See also UISIF*] [*Ottawa, ON*] (EAIO)
IUSO .... Institute of University Safety Officers [*British*] (DBA)
IUSO .... International Union of Security Officers (EA)
IUSS .... Integrated Undersea-Surveillance System [*Oceanography*] (ECON)
IUSS .... Integrated Underwater Surveillance System [*Navy*] (USDC)
IUSS .... Integrated Underwater Surveillance System [*Navy*] [*Marine science*] (OSRA)
IUSSI .... International Union for the Study of Social Insects [*Utrecht, Netherlands*]
IUSSP .... International Union for the Scientific Study of Population [*Liege, Belgium*]
IUSTFI .... Institute on United States Taxation of Foreign Income [*Later, ITI*] (EA)
IUSTOC....... Independent US Tanker Owners Committee [*Defunct*] (EA)
IUSUHM...... International Union of School and University Health and Medicine [*See also UIHMSU*] [*Brussels, Belgium*] (EAIO)
IUSY .... International Union of Socialist Youth
IUT .... Implementation Under Test [*Telecommunications*] (OSI)
IUT............. Industrial Unit of Tribology [*University of Leeds*] [*An association Research center British*] (EA)
IUT............. Instructor Under Training [*Navy*] (NVT)
IUT............. International Union of Tenants [*Stockholm, Sweden*] (EAIO)
IUT............. Intrauterine Transfusion [*Gynecology*]
IUt............... Utica Public Library, Utica, IL [*Library symbol Library of Congress*] (LCLS)
IUTAM .... International Union of Theoretical and Applied Mechanics [*Germany*]
IUTAO .... International Union of Technical Associations and Organizations [*France*] (EAIO)
IUTCA .... International Union of Technical Cinematograph Associations [*See also UNIATEC*] [*Paris, France*] (EAIO)
IUTDM .... International Union of Tool, Die, and Mold Makers (EA)
IUTDMM ...... International Union of Tool, Die, and Mold Makers (EA)
IUTM .... International Union Against Tuberculosis (DAVI)
IUTOX .... International Union for Toxicology
IUTS .... Inter-University Transit System [*Interlibrary loan service*] [*Canada*] (NITA)
IUUCLGW .... International Union, United Cement, Lime and Gypsum Workers (MHDB)
IUUU............ Industrial Unit, University of Ulster [*British*] (IRUK)
IUUW .... International Union, United Welders [*Later, IUOE*]
IUV.............. IATA [*International Air Transport Association*] Unit of Value [*International airline currency*]
IU-V .... University of Illinois, Veterinary Medicine Library, Urbana, IL [*Library symbol Library of Congress*] (LCLS)
IUVDT .... International Union Against Venereal Diseases and Treponematoses (EAIO)
IUVSTA .... International Union for Vacuum Science, Technique, and Applications [*See also UISTAV*] (EAIO)
IUW .... Inshore Undersea Warfare [*Navy*]
IUWA .... International Union of Women Architects [*See also UIFA*] [*Paris, France*] (EAIO)
IUWC .... Inshore Undersea Warfare Craft [*Navy*]
IUWCC .... Inshore Undersea Warfare Control Center [*Navy*] (NVT)
IUWDS......... International URSI [*Union Radio Scientifique Internationale*]-gram and World Day Service
IUWG .... Inshore Undersea Warfare Group [*Navy*]
IU-WS .... University of Illinois, Illinois State Water Survey, Champaign, IL [*Library symbol Library of Congress*] (LCLS)
IUWSU .... Inshore Undersea Warfare Surveillance Unit [*Navy*] (DNAB)
IUWWML ...... International Union of Wood, Wire, and Metal Lathers (MHDB)
IUYCD .... International Union of Young Christian Democrats [*Rome, Italy*]
iv .... Air Gambia [*Airline flight code*] (ODBW)
IV................ British Island Airways [*ICAO designator*] (AD)

IV................ Evans Public Library, Vandalia, IL [*Library symbol Library of Congress*] (LCLS)
IV................ Iceland Veterans [*Defunct*] (EA)
IV................ Improved Value (ADA)
IV................ Increased Value
IV................ Independent Variable (IAA)
IV................ Induct Vent
IV................ Information Victoria [*Australia An association*]
IV................ Initial Value
IV................ Initial Velocity [*Ballistics*]
I/V............... Inlet Valve (MCD)
IV................ Input Voltage
I/V............... Instrument/Visual Controlled Airspace (DA)
IV................ Insurance Value (IAA)
IV................ Integrated Vehicle (MCD)
IV................ Intensifier Vidicon
IV................ Interactive Video (PDAA)
IV................ Interceptor Vehicle
IV................ Interface Volume (MCD)
IV................ Intermediate Voltage (MSA)
IV................ Internal Velocity
IV................ Interval (IAA)
IV................ Interventricular [*Medicine*]
IV................ Intervertebral [*or Intravertebral*] [*Medicine*]
IV................ Intravascular [*Medicine*]
IV................ Intravehicular (MCD)
IV................ Intravenous [*Medicine*]
IV................ Intraventricular [*Cardiology*]
IV................ Intravertebral [*Anatomy*] (DAVI)
IV................ In Vapour (ROG)
IV................ Invasive (MAE)
IV................ In Verbo [*Under the Word*] [*Latin*]
IV................ Inverted Vertical [*Aircraft engine*]
IV................ Inverter
IV................ Investigation [*Dialog*] [*Searchable field*] [*Information service or system*] (NITA)
IV................ In View
IV................ In Vitro [*Medicine*] (MAE)
IV................ In Vivo [*Medicine*] (MAE)
IV................ Invoice Value [*Business term*]
iv................. Invoice Value (ODBW)
IV................ Iodine Value [*Analytical biochemistry*]
IV................ Irish Viscount (ROG)
IV................ Irish Volunteers [*British military*] (DMA)
iv................. Ivory (VRA)
iv................. Ivory Coast [*MARC country of publication code Library of Congress*] (LCCP)
IV................ Mark IV Industries [*NYSE symbol*] (TTSB)
IV................ Mark IV Industries, Inc. [*NYSE symbol*] (SPSG)
IVA.............. Ambanja [*Madagascar*] [*Airport symbol*] (OAG)
IVA.............. Evansville-Vanderburgh School Corp., Evansville, IN [*OCLC symbol*] (OCLC)
IVA.............. Illinois Vocational Association (SRA)
IVA.............. Imposta sul Valore Aggiunto [*Value-Added Tax*] [*Italian*]
IVA.............. Independent Voters Association [*Political organization in North Dakota, 1918-1932*]
IVA.............. Indiana Veal Association (SRA)
IVA.............. Industrial Veterinarians' Association [*Later, AAIV*] (EA)
IVA.............. Inlet Vane Actuator
IVA.............. Innotech Aviation Ltd. [*Canada ICAO designator*] (FAAC)
IVA.............. Inspection Visual Aid (AAG)
IVA.............. Integrated Vulnerability Assessment [*Military*]
IVA.............. Interactive Video Association (EA)
IVA.............. Intermediate Volitility Agents (MCD)
IVA.............. Internationaler Verband fuer Arbeiterbildung [*International Federation of Workers' Educational Associations - IFWEA*] (EAIO)
IVA.............. Internationale Vereinigung der Anschlussgeleise-Benuetzer [*International Association of Users of Private Sidings*]
IVA.............. International Volleyball Association [*Defunct*] (EA)
IVA.............. International Voyage Alliance (EA)
IVA.............. Intraoperative Vascular Angiography [*Cardiology*]
IVA.............. Intravehicular Activity
IVA.............. Inventory Valuation Adjustment [*Business term*]
IVA.............. Isovaleric Acid (DMAA)
IVA.............. Ivac [*Intravenous monitor*] [*Medicine*] (DHSM)
IVA.............. Ivaco, Inc. [*Toronto Stock Exchange symbol*]
IVAAP .... International Veterinary Association for Animal Production [*See also AIVPA*] [*Brussels, Belgium*] [*Research center*] (EAIO)
IVAC............ International Video and Communications Exhibition [*British*] (ITD)
IVAC............ Intevac, Inc. [*NASDAQ symbol*] (SAG)
IVAC............ Intravenous Accurate Control [*Pharmacology*] (DAVI)
IVACG .... International Vitamin A Consultative Group (EA)
IVAG .... Institutionenverzeichnis Auslaendischer Gesellschaften [*NOMOS Database*] [*Information service or system*]
IVag .... Intravaginal [*Medicine*] (MAE)
IVAK............ Igloo Vertical Access Kit [*Aerospace*] (NASA)
IVALA .... Integrated Visual Approach and Landing Aid [*System*] [*RADAR*]
IValSD .... Valmeyer Community Unit School District 3, Valmeyer, IL [*Library symbol Library of Congress*] (LCLS)
IVAM .... Interorbital Vehicle Assembly Mode
IVAML .... Instrumental Variable-Approximate Maximum Likelihood (PDAA)
IV & T.......... Independent Verification and Test
IV & V .... Independent Validation and Verification (CAAL)
IV-ANES....... Intravenous Anesthetic [*Medicine*]

IVANS .... Insurance Value-Added Network Services [*Insurance Institute for Research*] (TSSD)
IVAP............ In Vivo Adhesive Platelet [*Medicine*] (MAE)
IVAR .... Insertion Velocity Adjust Routine [*NASA*]
IVAR .... Internal Variable (NASA)
IVAR .... International Voluntary Action and Voluntary Association Research Organization [*Defunct*] (EA)
IVAS............ International Veterinary Acupuncture Society (EA)
IVAS............ Internet Value-Added Service (PCM)
IvaxCp .... Ivaco Industries [*Associated Press*] (SAG)
IvB .... Innenstadt von Babylon [*A publication*] (BJA)
IVB .... Intermediate Vector Boson [*Physics*]
IVB .... Internationaler Verband fuer Arbeiterbildung [*International Federation of Workers' Educational Associations - IFWEA*] (EAIO)
IVB .... Intraventricular Block [*Medicine*] (DMAA)
IVB .... Mason Memorial Public Library, Buda, IL [*OCLC symbol*] (OCLC)
IVBA .... International Veteran Boxers Association (EA)
IVBA .... International Volleyball Association [*Defunct*]
IVBAT .... Intravascular Bronchoalveolar Tumor [*Oncology*]
IVBC .... Integrated Vehicle Baseline Configuration (MCD)
IVBC .... Intravascular Blood Coagulation [*Medicine*] (DMAA)
IVBF .... International Volleyball Federation (EA)
IVBH .... Internationale Vereinigung fuer Brueckenbau und Hochbau [*International Association for Bridge and Structural Engineering*]
IVBK............ Intervisual Books'A' [*NASDAQ symbol*] (TTSB)
IVBK............ Intervisual Books, Inc. [*NASDAQ symbol*] (SAG)
IVC .... Imperial Valley College [*California*]
IVC .... Independent Viewing Console
IVC .... Individual Viable Cells [*Metabolic studies*]
IVC .... Industrial View Camera
IVC .... Inferior Vena Cava [*Anatomy*]
IVC .... Inferior Venacavogram [*Cardiology*] (DAVI)
IVC .... Inspection Validation Center [*Nuclear energy*] (NUCP)
IVC .... Inspired Vital Capacity (AAMN)
IVC .... Installation Volunteer Coordinator
IVC .... Intake Valve Closing [*Automotive engineering*]
IVC .... Integrated Vacuum Circuit
IVC .... Interactive Videodisc Consortium [*Defunct*] (EA)
IVC .... Intermediate Velocity Cloud [*Astronomy*] (OA)
IVC .... Intervehicular Communication (KSC)
IVC .... Intravaginal Culture [*Alternative to traditional in-vitro fertilization (IVF)*] (PAZ)
IVCT .... Intravenous Cholangiography [*Medicine*]
IVC .... Intraventricular Cannula [*Medicine*]
IVC .... Intraventricular Catheter [*Cardiology*] (DAVI)
IVC .... Invercargill [*New Zealand*] [*Airport symbol*] (OAG)
IVC .... Invesco PLC [*NYSE symbol*] (SAG)
IVC .... INVESCO PLC ADS [*NYSE symbol*] (TTSB)
IVC .... Isovolumic Confraction [*Cardiology*]
IVC .... Permanent Committee for the International Veterinary Congresses
IVC .... Vandalia Correctional Center, Vandalia, IL [*Library symbol Library of Congress*] (LCLS)
IVC .... Vigo County Public Library, Terre Haute, IN [*OCLC symbol*] (OCLC)
IVCAP .... International Video Contest for Amateurs and Professionals [*British*]
IVCC .... Illinois Vocational Curriculum Center (EDAC)
IVCC .... Intravascular Consumption Coagulopathy [*Medicine*]
IVCD .... Indian Veterinary Convalescent Depot [*British military*] (DMA)
IVCD .... Intraventricular Conduction Defect [*Cardiology*]
IVCD .... Intraventricular Conduction Delay [*Cardiology*] (AAMN)
IVCD .... In-Vehicle Communications Device [*Highway safety research*]
IVCE .... International Video and Communications Exhibition (NITA)
IVCF............ Inter-Varsity Christian Fellowship of the United States of America (EA)
IVCh .... Intravenous Cholangiography [*or Cholangiogram*] [*Medicine*] (DAVI)
IVCH .... Intravenous Cholangiography [*Medicine*] (DMAA)
IVCI .... International Venture Capital Institute (EA)
IVCO .... International Vitamin Corp. [*NASDAQ symbol*] (SAG)
IVCO .... I V C Industries [*NASDAQ symbol*] (TTSB)
Iv Co .... Ivory Coast (VRA)
IVCOW .... I V C Industries Wrrt [*NASDAQ symbol*] (TTSB)
IVCP .... Inferior Vena Cava Pressure [*Medicine*]
IVCR .... Inferior Vena Cava Reconstruction [*Medicine*] (DMAA)
IVCR .... Invacare Corp. [*NASDAQ symbol*] (NQ)
IVCS .... Integrated Vehicular Communication System (MCD)
IVCS .... Integrated [*or Interior*] Voice Communications System (MCD)
Iv Cst .... Ivory Coast
IVCT .... Inferior Vena Cava Thrombosis [*Medicine*] (DMAA)
IVCT .... Intervalence Charge-Transfer [*Phyical chemistry*]
IVCU .... Isotope-Voiding Cystourethrogram [*Urology*] (DAVI)
IVCV .... Inferior Venacavography [*Medicine*]
IVCV .... Ivy Vein Clearing Virus [*Plant pathology*]
IVD .... Image Velocity Detector
IVD .... Indirect Video Display (MCD)
IVD .... Inductive Voltage Divider [*Electromagnetism*] (IAA)
IVD .... Information Viewing Device
IVD .... Intake Valve Detergent [*Automotive fuels*]
IVD .... Interactive Videodisc (INF)
IVD .... Internal Vapor Deposition (ACRL)
IVD .... International Vending Technologies Corp. [*Vancouver Stock Exchange symbol*]
IVD .... Interpolated Voice Data (IAA)
IVD .... Intervertebral Disc [*Medicine*]
IVD .... Intravenous Drip [*Pharmacology*] (DAVI)
IVD .... Invalid Decimal (IAA)
IVD .... In Vitro Diagnostics [*Clinical chemistry*]

IVD............. Ionized Vacuum Deposit (MCD)
IVD............. Ion Vapor Deposition [*Coating technology*]
IVD............. University of Dallas, Irving, TX [*OCLC symbol*] (OCLC)
IVDA .... Intravenous Drug Abuser
IVDA .... Investors Daily [*JA Micropublishing, Inc.*]
IVDBA .... Imperial Valley Dune Buggy Association
iv Dei .... Institut Voluntas Dei (EA)
IVDM .... Integrated Voice Data Multiplexer [*Telecommunications*] (ACRL)
IVDP .... Initial Vector Display Point (IAA)
IVDS .... Independent Variable Depth SONAR
IVDS .... Interactive Video and Data Service
IVDSA .... Intravenous Digital Subtraction Angiography
IVDT .... Integrated [*or Interactive*] Voice Data Terminal [*Telecommunications*]
IVDTS .... Integrated Voice and Data Telecommunications System (AAGC)
IVDU .... Intravenous Drug User
IVE .... Image of Vocational Education [*ERIC*]
IVE .... Institute of Vitreous Enamellers [*British*]
IVE .... Integrated Visualization Environment [*Computer science*] (BTTJ)
IVE .... Interactive Video Enterprises [*US West, Inc.*] (PCM)
IVE .... Interface Verification Equipment (NASA)
IVE .... Internationale Vereinigung der Eisenwaren- und Eisenhaendlerverbaende [*International Federation of Ironmongers and Iron Merchants Association*]
IVE .... Internationale Vereinigung von Einkaufsverbanden [*International Association of Buying Groups - IABG*] (EAIO)
IVE .... International Video Entertainment
IVE .... Investment Equipment (MCD)
IVE .... Isobutyl Vinyl Ether [*Organic chemistry*]
IVE .... University of Chicago, Graduate Library School, Chicago, IL [*OCLC symbol*] (OCLC)
IVEC .... In Vitro Expression Cloning [*Analytical biochemistry*]
IVen .... Venice Public Library, Venice, IL [*Library symbol Library of Congress*] (LCLS)
IVenCU .... Venice Community Unit 3, Venice, IL [*Library symbol Library of Congress*] (LCLS)
Iv Ersk .... Ivory. Notes on Erskine's Institutes [*A publication*] (ILCA)
IVES .... Internationaler Verband fuer Erziehung zu Suchtmittelfreiem Leben [*International Association for Education to a Life without Drugs*] (EAIO)
IVES............ International Teachers Temperance Association [*Denmark*] (EAIO)
Ives Mil Law... Ives on Military Law [*A publication*] (DLA)
IVESS........... Interactive Vehicle Scheduling System (MHDI)
IVET .... In Vivo Expression Technology [*Genetics*]
IVETA .... International Vocational Education and Training Association (EA)
IvexPkg .... Ivex Packaging Corp. [*Associated Press*] (SAG)
IVF .... Internationale Viola Forschunggesellschaft [*International Viola Society*] [*Germany*] (EAIO)
IVF .... Inter-Varsity Fellowship of Evangelical Unions [*British*] (BI)
IVF .... Interventricular Foramen [*Medicine*] (DMAA)
IVF .... Intravascular Fluid [*Medicine*]
IVF .... Intravenous Fluid [*Pharmacology*] (DAVI)
IVF .... In Vitro Fertilization [*Gynecology*]
IVF .... IVF America, Inc. [*Associated Press*] (SAG)
IVF .... Triodyne, Inc., Information Center, Skokie, IL [*OCLC symbol*] (OCLC)
IVFA .... IVF America [*NASDAQ symbol*] (TTSB)
IVFA .... IVF America, Inc. [*NASDAQ symbol*] (SAG)
IVF Am .... IVF America, Inc. [*Associated Press*] (SAG)
IVFE .... Intravenous Fat Emulsion [*Pharmacology*] (DAVI)
IVFET .... In Vitro Fertilization with Embryo Transfer [*Gynecology*]
IVFGR .... Internationale Vereinigung fuer Gewerblichen Rechtsschultz [*International Association for the Protection of Industrial Property*]
IVFZ .... International Veterinary Federation of Zootechnics [*Later, IVAAP*]
IVg .... Camargo Township Library, Villa Grove, IL [*Library symbol Library of Congress*] (LCLS)
IVG............. Internationale Vereinigung fuer Germanische Sprach - und Literaturwissenschaft [*International Association of Germanic Studies - IAGS*] [*Tokyo, Japan*] (EAIO)
IVG............. Interrupt Vector Generator
IVG............. Isotopic Ventriculogram [*Cardiology*] (DAVI)
IVGG .... Institute of Volcanic Geology and Geochemistry [*Commonwealth of Independent States*]
IVGGD......... Internationale Vereinigung fuer Geschichte und Gegenwart der Druckkunst [*International Association for Past and Present History of the Art of Printing*] (EAIO)
IVGMA .... International Violin and Guitar Makers Association (EA)
IVGTT .... Intravenous Glucose Tolerance Test [*Clinical medicine*]
IVGWP .... Internationaler Verband der Gastronomie- und Weinbau-Presse [*International Federation of Gastronomical and Vinicultural Press*]
IVH............. Independent Variable Hull [*Statistics*]
IVH............. Indian Veterinary Hospital [*British military*] (DMA)
IVH............. Intravenous Hyperalimentation [*Medicine*]
IVH............. Intraventricular Hemorrhage [*Cardiology*]
IVH............. Ivishak, AK [*Location identifier FAA*] (FAAL)
IVHESM .... International Voluntary Historical Enlightenment Society Memorial (EAIO)
IVHM .... In-Vessel Handling Machine [*Nuclear energy*] (NRCH)
IVHM-EM ..... In-Vessel Handling Machine-Engineering Model [*Nuclear energy*] (NRCH)
IVHP .... Intraventricular Hemorrhage Parents (EA)
IVHS .... Intelligent Vehicle/Highway System
IVHS .... Intelligent Vehicle Highway System (USGC)
IVHW .... Internationaler Verband fuer Hauswirtschaft [*International Federation for Home Economics*]
IVHX .... In-Vessel Heat Exchanger [*Nuclear energy*] (NRCH)

IVI .... American Conservatory of Music, Chicago, IL [*OCLC symbol*] (OCLC)
IVI .... Incremental Velocity Indicator [*NASA*]
IVI .... Indeo Video Interactive [*Computer science*]
IVI .... Initial Ventricular Impulse
IVI .... Initial Voluntary Indefinite [*Status*] [*Army*]   (INF)
IVI .... Instant Visual Index
IVI .... Internal Vibration Isolator
IVI .... International Vaccine Institute [*Korea*]
IVI .... International Verifact, Inc. [*Toronto Stock Exchange symbol*]
IVI .... Inventory Index   (MCD)
IVI .... Ivigtut [*Greenland*] [*Seismograph station code, US Geological Survey Closed*]   (SEIS)
IVI .... Tucson, AZ [*Location identifier FAA*]   (FAAL)
IVIA .... Interactive Video Industry Association   (EA)
IVIA .... International Videotex Industry Association
IVIAF .... International Verifact, Inc. [*NASDAQ symbol*]   (SAG)
IVIAF .... Intl Verifact [*NASDAQ symbol*]   (TTSB)
IVIAW .... International Verifact Wrrt [*NASDAQ symbol*]   (TTSB)
IVIE .... Independent Visually Impaired Enterprisers   (EA)
IVIE .... Interactive Video in Education [*National Interactive Video Centre*]   (AIE)
IVIG .... Intravenous Immunoglobulin [*Medicine*]   (CPH)
IVIM .... Intravoxel Incoherent Motion [*Imaging technique*]
IVING .... Ivinghoe [*England*]
IVIP .... Internationale Vereinigung fuer Individualpsychologie [*International Association of Individual Psychology*]
IVIP .... IVI Publishing [*NASDAQ symbol*]   (TTSB)
IVIP .... IVI Publishing, Inc. [*NASDAQ symbol*]   (SAG)
IVIPA .... International Videotex Information Providers' Association [*British Information service or system*]   (IID)
IVI Pub ...... IVI Publishing, Inc. [*Associated Press*]   (SAG)
IVird .... Virden Public Library, Virden, IL [*Library symbol Library of Congress*]   (LCLS)
IVirdMCD .... Macoupin Community District 4, Virden, IL [*Library symbol Library of Congress*]   (LCLS)
IVIS .... Integrated Vehicular Information System [*Army*]   (RDA)
IVIS .... International Visitors Information Service   (EA)
IVIS .... Intervehicular Information System [*Army*]   (RDA)
IViS .... Shawnee Correctional Center, Vienna, IL [*Library symbol*] [*Library of Congress*]   (LCLS)
IVIZ .... Institutionenverzeichnis fuer Internationale Zusammenarbeit [*Institutions for International Cooperation*] [*NOMOS Datapool Database*]   (IID)
IVJ .... Oak Lawn Public Library, Oak Lawn, IL [*OCLC symbol*]   (OCLC)
IVJC .... Intervertebral Joint Complex [*Medicine*]
IVJH .... Internationale Vereinigung fuer Jugendhilfe [*International Union for Child Welfare*]
IVJS .... International Jewish Vegetarian Society [*Formerly, Jewish Vegetarian Society*]   (EA)
IVKMH .... Internationale Vereinigung der Klein- und Mittelbetriebe des Handels [*International Federation of Small and Medium-Sized Commercial Enterprises*]
IVL .... Internationale Vereinigung der Lehrerverbaende [*International Federation of Teachers' Associations*]
IVL .... Internationale Vereinigung fuer Theoretische und Angewandte Limnologie [*International Association of Theoretical and Applied Limnology*]
IVL .... Intervalometer   (KSC)
IVL .... Invader Resources Ltd. [*Vancouver Stock Exchange symbol*]
IVL .... Inventory Validation Listing [*Computer science*]
IVL .... Involucrin   (DMAA)
IVL .... Ivalo [*Finland*] [*Airport symbol*]   (OAG)
IVLA .... International Visual Literacy Association   (EA)
IVLBW .... Infant of Very Low Birth Weight [*Neonatology*]   (DAVI)
IVLD .... Internationale Vereinigung der Organisationen von Lebensmittel-Detail-Listen [*International Federation of Grocers' Associations - IFGA*]   (EAIO)
IVLS .... Illinois Valley Library System [*Library network*]
IVM .... Improved Visible Marker
IVM .... Initial Virtual Memory
IVM .... Institute of Value Management [*British*]
IVM .... Integrated Vector Management [*Insect control*]
IVM .... Interface Virtual Machine [*Computer science*]
IVM .... Intravascular Mass   (MAE)
IVM .... Inventory Verification Manual
IVMA .... Idaho Veterinary Medical Association   (SRA)
IVMA .... Indiana Veterinary Medical Association   (SRA)
IVMA .... Industrial Vegetation Management Association [*Defunct*]   (EA)
IVMA .... Intermountain Veterinary Medical Association   (EA)
IVMA .... Iodovinylmethoprenol Analog [*Organic chemistry*]
IVMA .... Iowa Veterinary Medical Association   (SRA)
IVMB .... Internationale Vereinigung der Musikbibliotheken, Musikarchive, und Dokumentationszentren [*International Association of Music Libraries, Archives, and Documentation Centers*]
IVMF .... Inter-Varsity Missions Fellowship   (EA)
IVMP .... Intravenous Methylprednisolone [*Medicine*]
IVMS .... Instrumented Vibration Measuring System
IVMS .... Integrated Vehicle Management Subsystem   (MCD)
IVMS .... Integrated Voice Messaging System [*Commterm, Inc.*] [*Atlanta, GA*]   (TSSD)
IVMU .... Inertial Velocity Measurement Unit   (IEEE)
IVN .... Intercity Voice Network [*FTS*]   (DNAB)
IVN .... Internationale Vereniging voor Neerlandistiek [*International Association of Dutch Studies*]   (EAIO)

IVN .... Intravenous Nutrition [*Medicine*]
IVNAA .... In Vivo Neutron Activation Analysis [*Analytical chemistry*]
IVNTG .... Intravenous Nitroglycerin [*Medication order*]   (CPH)
IVO .... Improved Virtual Orbitals [*Atomic physics*]
IVO .... Inova Optics, Inc. [*Vancouver Stock Exchange symbol*]
IVO .... Input Voltage Offset
IVO .... Intake Valve Open [*Automotive engineering*]
IVOX .... Intravascular Oxygenator [*Artificial lung*] [*Medicine*]
IVP .... Imitation Vegetable Parchment [*Paper*]   (DGA)
IVP .... Implied Valve Position   (ACII)
IVP .... Initial Vapor Pressure
IVP .... Insecticidal Viral Product [*Agricultural chemistry*]
IVP .... Inspected Variety Purity [*Agriculture*]
IVP .... Installation Verification Procedure   (MCD)
IVP .... Interface Verification Procedure [*NASA*]   (IAA)
IVP .... Internationaler Verband der Pektinproduzenten [*International Pectin Producers Association*] [*Switzerland*]   (EAIO)
IVP .... Inter-Varsity Press [*British*]
IVP .... Intravenous Pitocin [*Pharmacology*]   (DAVI)
IVP .... Intravenous Push [*Medicine*]
IVP .... Intravenous Pyelogram [*Radiology*]
IVP .... Intraventricular Pressure [*Cardiology*]   (AAMN)
IVP .... Ion Vacuum Pump
IVPA .... Independent Video Programmers Association [*Defunct*]   (EA)
IVPB .... Intravenous Piggyback [*Method of drug administration*] [*Pharmacology*]
IVPC .... Internationaler Verband der Petroleum- und Chemiearbeiter [*International Federation of Petroleum and Chemical Workers*]
IV-PCA .... Intravenous-Patient-Controlled-Analgesia
IVPD .... In Vitro Protein Digestibility [*Nutrition*]
IVPF .... Isovolume Pressure Flow Curve [*Cardiology*]   (MAE)
IVPO .... Inside Vapor Phase Oxidation [*Glass technology*]
IVPP .... Institute of Vertebrate Palaeontology and Palaeoanthropology [*China*]
IVPT .... Inter-Vehicle Power Transfer   (MCD)
IVQ .... Individual Vessel Quota [*Fisheries management*]
IVQ .... Interrupted Very Quick [*Flashing*] Light [*Navigation signal*]
IVR .... Idioventricular Rhythm [*Cardiology*]   (DMAA)
IVR .... Inner Vertical Resonance [*Physics*]
IVR .... Instant Video Receiver [*Electronics*]
IVR .... Instrumented Visual Range   (IAA)
IVR .... Instrument Voltage Regulator [*Automotive engineering*]
IVR .... Integrated Voltage Regulator   (IEEE)
IVR .... Interactive Voice Response
IVR .... Internal Visual Reference [*Motion sickness*]
IVR .... International Association for the Rhine Vessels Register [*Netherlands*]   (EY)
IVR .... Internationale Vereinigung fuer Rechts- und Sozialphilosophie [*International Association for Philosophy of Law and Social Philosophy*]   (EAIO)
IVR .... Interventional Radiography [*Medicine*]
IVR .... Intramolecular Vibrational Redistribution [*Chemistry*]
IVR .... Intramolecular Vibrational Relaxation [*Organic chemistry*]
IVR .... Inverell [*Australia Airport symbol*]   (OAG)
IVR .... Irvco Resources [*Vancouver Stock Exchange symbol*]
IVR .... Isolated Volume Responders [*Physiology*]
IVR .... Isovolumic Relaxation [*Time*] [*Cardiology*]   (DAVI)
IVRD .... In Vitro Rumen Digestibility [*Nutrition*]
IVRET .... Intramolecular Vibration-Rotation Energy Transfer [*Chemistry*]
IVRG .... International Verticillium Research Group   (EAIO)
IVRG .... In-Vehicle Route Guidance System [*FHWA*]   (TAG)
IVRS .... Interactive Voice Response System [*Military*]   (INF)
IVRT .... Isovolumic Relaxation Time   (DMAA)
IVS .... Air Evasion [*France ICAO designator*]   (FAAC)
IVS .... Idle Validation Switch [*Automotive electronics*]
IVS .... Independent Vertical System
IVS .... Infrared Viewing Set
IVS .... Input Voltage Supply
IVS .... Insect Visual System
IVS .... Intact Ventricular System [*Cardiology*]
IVS .... Integrated Versaplot Software   (PDAA)
IVS .... Interactive Video Service   (LAIN)
IVS .... Interactive Voice System [*Electronics*]
IVS .... Interchange Units Separation   (ECII)
IVS .... International Vestor Resources [*Vancouver Stock Exchange symbol*]
IVS .... International Voluntary Services   (EA)
IVS .... Intervening Sequence [*Genetics*]
IVS .... Interventricular Septum [*Cardiology*]
IVS .... In-Vessel Storage [*Nuclear energy*]   (NRCH)
IVS .... Vigo County School Corp., Terre Haute, IN [*OCLC symbol*]   (OCLC)
IVSA .... International Veterinary Students Association [*Utrecht, Netherlands*]   (EAIO)
IVSAWS ...... In-Vehicle Safety Advisory and Warning System [*FHWA*]   (TAG)
IVSAWS ...... In-Vehicle Safety Advisory and Warning System
IVSD .... Interventricular Septal Defect [*Cardiology*]
IVSD .... Vandalia Community Unit, School District 203, Vandalia, IL [*Library symbol Library of Congress*]   (LCLS)
IVSET .... Interactive Videodisc for Special Education Technology   (EDAC)
IVSI .... Inertial Lead Vertical Speed Indicator   (IAA)
IVSI .... Instantaneous Vertical Speed Indicator [*NASA*]
IVSK .... Intravenous Streptokinase [*An enzyme*]
IVSM .... In-Vessel Storage Module [*Nuclear energy*]   (NRCH)
IVSN .... Initial Voice Switched Network [*NATO integrated communications system*]   (NATG)
IVSP .... In Vitro Synthesized Protein [*Biochemistry*]

IVSS............ Internationale Vereinigung fuer Soziale Sicherheit [*International Social Security Association*]

IVSS............ Intravenous Solu-Set [*Medicine*] (MEDA)

IVSU............ International Veterinary Students Union [*Later, IVSA*]

IVT............ Index of Vertical Transmission [*Cultural evolution*]

IVT............ Inferential Value Testing (KSC)

IVT............ Infinitely Variable Transmission [*Automotive engineering*] (PS)

IVT............ Input Value Table [*Computer science*] (ECII)

IVT............ Inspection Verification Tag

IVT............ Institute for Victims of Trauma (EA)

IVT............ Integrated Video Terminal

IVT............ Interactive Video Technology [*Database*] [*Heartland Communications*] [*Information service or system*] (CRD)

IVT............ Internationale Vereinigung der Textileinkaufsverbande [*International Association of Textile Purchasing Societies*]

IVT............ Intervalve Transformer (IAA)

IVT............ Intervehicular Transfer (KSC)

IVT............ Intravenous Transfusion [*Medicine*]

IVT............ Intraventricular [*Cardiology*]

IVT............ Iventronics Ltd. [*Toronto Stock Exchange symbol*]

IVTD............ Integrated Visual Testing Device

IVTM............ In-Vessel Transfer Machine [*Nuclear energy*] (NRCH)

IVTTT............ Intravenous Tolbutamide Tolerance Test [*Clinical medicine*] (MAE)

IVU............ International Vegetarian Union [*Stockport, Cheshire, England*]

IVU............ Intravehicular Umbilical [*NASA*] (KSC)

IVU............ Intravenous Urogram [*or Urography*] [*Medicine*]

IVU............ In-Vehicle Unit [*Electronic system for charging for road usage*] [*Singapore*] (ECON)

IVU............ Valparaiso University, Valparaiso, IN [*OCLC symbol*] (OCLC)

IVUS............ Intravascular Ultrasound [*Medicine*]

IVV............ Idle Vacuum Valve [*Exhaust emissions*] [*Automotive engineering*]

IVV............ Instantaneous Vertical Velocity

IVV............ Internationaler Volkssportverband [*International Federation of Popular Sports - IFPS*] (EAIO)

IVV............ Internationale Vereinigung fuer Vegetationskunde [*International Association for Vegetation Science - IAVS*] (EAIO)

IVV............ Intravenous Vasopressin [*Endocrinology*]

IVV............ Lebanon, NH [*Location identifier FAA*] (FAAL)

IVV............ Vincennes University, Vincennes, IN [*OCLC symbol*] (OCLC)

IVVI............ Instantaneous Vertical Velocity Indicator

IV vol............ Intravenous Volume [*Pharmacology*] (DAVI)

IVVS............ Instantaneous Vertical Velocity Sensor (NATG)

IVWO............ International Vine and Wine Office

IVWSR............ Internationaler Verband fuer Wohnungswesen, Staedtebau und Raumordnung [*International Federation for Housing and Planning*]

IVX............ Columbus, OH [*Location identifier FAA*] (FAAL)

IVX............ Imperial Valley College, Imperial, CA [*OCLC symbol*] (OCLC)

IVX............ IVAX Corp. [*AMEX symbol*] (SAG)

IVY............ Ivory Oil & Minerals [*Vancouver Stock Exchange symbol*]

IVYBR............ Ivybridge [*England*]

IVZ............ Valparaiso University, Law Library, Valparaiso, IN [*OCLC symbol*] (OCLC)

IW............ Impulse Weight (IAA)

IW............ Index Word [*Online database field identifier*]

IW............ Indications and Warning [*Subsystems*] [*Military*] (MCD)

IW............ Indirect Waste

IW............ Individual Weapon (MCD)

IW............ Induction Welding

IW............ Inertia Weight [*Exhaust emissions*] [*Automotive engineering*]

IW............ Information World [*A publication*]

IW............ Inland Waterways [*Organization that administered British canals during World War II*] [*Facetious translation: "Idle Women," due to high female workforce*]

IW............ Inner Wall [*Medicine*] (DMAA)

IW............ Inpatient Ward [*Medicine*] (DMAA)

IW............ Inside Width

IW............ Inside Wire [*Telecommunications*] (TEL)

IW............ Inspector of Works

IW............ Instruction Word [*Computer science*] (IAA)

I/W............ Interchangeable With (AAG)

IW............ Interior Width (IAA)

IW............ International Air Bahama [*ICAO designator*] (AD)

IW............ International Wattier [*Process*] [*A method of making transparencies for rotogravure plates*]

IW............ Iron-Wustite [*Geology*]

IW............ Isle of Wight

IW............ Isotopic Weight

iw............ Israel-Jordan Demilitarized Zones [*is (Israel) used in records cataloged after January 1978*] [*MARC country of publication code Library of Congress*] (LCCP)

IW............ Wheaton Public Library, Wheaton, IL [*Library symbol Library of Congress*] (LCLS)

IWA............ Independent Watchmen's Association (EA)

IWA............ Inland Waterways Association [*British*] (DCTA)

IWA............ Institute of World Affairs [*Later, UFSI-IWA*] (EA)

IWA............ Interdivisional Work Authorization (AAGC)

IWA............ International Waterproofing Association [*See also AIE*] [*Brussels, Belgium*] (EAIO)

IWA............ International Wheat Agreement [*London*]

IWA............ International Women's Auxiliary to the Veterinary Profession

IWA............ Internationale Woodworkers of America (EA)

IWA............ Iowa State University of Science and Technology, Ames, IA [*OCLC symbol*] (OCLC)

IWA............ Iwakuni [*Japan*] [*Airport symbol*] (AD)

IWAAC............ Inland Waterways Amenity Advisory Council [*British*] (DCTA)

I/WAC............ Interface/Weapon Aiming Computer (MCD)

IWAC............ International Women's Anthropology Conference (EA)

IWAHMA............ Industrial Warm Air Heater Manufacturers

IWAK............ Improved Water Analysis Kit

IWal............ Walnut Township Library, Walnut, IL [*Library symbol Library of Congress*] (LCLS)

IWalHSD............ Walnut Consolidated High School District 508, Walnut, IL [*Library symbol Library of Congress*] (LCLS)

IWalSD............ Walnut Consolidated Community School District 285, Walnut, IL [*Library symbol Library of Congress*] (LCLS)

IWaltSD............ Waltonville Community Unit, School District 1, Waltonville, IL [*Library symbol Library of Congress*] (LCLS)

IWARDS............ Iowa Water Resources Data System [*Iowa State Geological Survey*] [*Iowa City*] [*Information service or system*] (IID)

IWARS............ Installation Worldwide Ammunition Reporting System [*Army*]

IWas............ Washington Township Library, Washington, IL [*Library symbol Library of Congress*] (LCLS)

IWas-Su............ Washington Township Library, Sunnyland Branch, Sunnyland, IL [*Library symbol Library of Congress*] (LCLS)

IWat............ Watseka Public Library, Watseka, IL [*Library symbol Library of Congress*] (LCLS)

IWatF............ Iroquois County Film Library, Watseka, IL [*Library symbol*] [*Library of Congress*] (LCLS)

IWatH............ Iroquois Memorial Hospital, Watseka, IL [*Library symbol Library of Congress*] (LCLS)

IWatl............ Morrison-Talbott Library, Waterloo, IL [*Library symbol Library of Congress*] (LCLS)

IWatlGHS............ Gibault High School, Waterloo, IL [*Library symbol Library of Congress*] (LCLS)

IWatlSD............ Waterloo Community School District 3, Waterloo, IL [*Library symbol Library of Congress*] (LCLS)

IWau............ Waukegan Public Library, Waukegan, IL [*Library symbol Library of Congress*] (LCLS)

i-way............ Information Superhighway (CDE)

IWayc............ Wayne City Public Library, Wayne City, IL [*Library symbol Library of Congress*] (LCLS)

IWaycCD............ Wayne City Community Unit, District 100, Wayne City, IL [*Library symbol Library of Congress*] (LCLS)

IWB............ C. Berger & Co., Wheaton, IL [*Library symbol*] [*Library of Congress*] (LCLS)

IWB............ Council Bluffs Free Public Library, Council Bluffs, IA [*OCLC symbol*] (OCLC)

IWB............ Industry-Wide Bargaining (MHDB)

IWB............ Instruction Word Buffer (NITA)

IWB............ Intergalactic World Brain [*Underground press service*] (IIA)

IWBC............ Interim Wideband Communications (MCD)

IWBK............ InterWest Bancorp [*NASDAQ symbol*] (TTSB)

IWBK............ InterWest Savings Bank [*NASDAQ symbol*] (SAG)

IWBNI............ It Would Be Nice If [*Computer hacker terminology*] (NHD)

IWBP............ Integration with Britain Party [*Gibraltar*] (PPE)

IWBS............ Congregation of the Incarnate Word and the Blessed Sacrament [*Roman Catholic women's religious order*]

IWBS............ Indirect Work Breakdown Structure (NASA)

IWBS............ Integral Weight and Balance System [*Aviation*]

IWC............ Ice Water Content

IWC............ Imperial War Cabinet [*British military*] (DMA)

IWC............ Incarnate Word College [*Texas*]

IWC............ Individual Weapons Captured

IWC............ Inland Waterways Corp. [*Later, Federal Barge Lines, Inc.; liquidated, 1963*]

IWC............ Institute for Workers' Control

IWC............ In-Stream Waste Concentration [*Environmental science*] (GFGA)

IWC............ Interim Wilderness Committee [*Australia*]

IWC............ International Whaling Commission [*Cambridge, England*]

IWC............ International Wheat Council [*See also CIB*] [*British*] (EAIO)

IWC............ International Wildcat Resources [*Vancouver Stock Exchange symbol*]

IWC............ International Wildlife Coalition (EA)

IWC............ International Willow Collectors [*An association*] (EA)

IWC............ Iowa Wesleyan College

IWC............ IWC Resources Corp. [*Associated Press*] (SAG)

IWC............ Wabash College, Crawfordsville, IN [*OCLC symbol*] (OCLC)

IWCA............ Inside Wiring Cable [*Telecommunications*] (TEL)

IWCA............ International Windsurfer Class Association (EA)

IWCA............ International World Calendar Association (EA)

IWCA............ Irish Wolfhound Club of America (EA)

IWCB............ Internal Web Channel Bus (IAA)

IWCC............ International Women's Cricket Council [*Australia*] (EAIO)

IWCC............ International Wrought Copper Council [*British*] (EAIO)

IWCCA............ Inland Waterways Common Carriers Association [*Defunct*] (EA)

IWCI............ Industrial Water Conditioning Institute (EA)

IWCI............ Industrial Wire Cloth Institute [*Later, AWCI*] (EA)

IWCR............ IWC Resources Corp. [*NASDAQ symbol*] (NQ)

IWCS............ Integrated Weapons Control System

IWCS............ Integrated Wideband Communications System [*Military*]

IWCS............ Interceptor Weapon Control System

IWCS............ International Wood Collectors Society (EA)

IWCS/SEA............ Integrated Wideband Communications System/Southeast Asia (IEEE)

IWCT............ International War Crimes Tribunal

IWCTF............ Interdepartmental Workers' Compensation Task Force [*Department of Labor*] [*Terminated, 1976*] (EGAO)

IW/CW............ Infectious Waste / Chemotherapeutic Waste

IWD............ Drake University, Law Library, Des Moines, IA [*OCLC symbol*] (OCLC)

IWD............ Inland Waters Directorate [*Canada*]

IWD .... Integrated Weapons Display
IWD .... Intermediate Water Depth (MCD)
IWD .... International Women's Day
IWD .... International Women's Decade
IWD .... Iron or Wood [Freight]
IWD .... Ironwood [Michigan] [Airport symbol] (OAG)
IWD .... Ironwood, MI [Location identifier FAA] (FAAL)
IWDA .... Independent Wire Drawers Association [Later, AWPA]
IWDM .... Intermediate Water Depth Mine (MCD)
IWDS .... Interactive Wholesale Distribution System (MHDI)
IWDS .... International World Day Service
IWE .... Camden, AL [Location identifier FAA] (FAAL)
IWE .... Illustrated World Encyclopedia [A publication]
IWE .... Instantaneous Word Encoder (IAA)
IWE .... Institute for Wholistic Education [Later, SCIWE] (EA)
IWE .... Institute of Water Engineers [British]
IWE .... Institution of Water Engineers [British] (BI)
IWE .... Interpolated Water Elevation (PDAA)
IWe .... Westchester Public Library, Westchester, IL [Library symbol Library of Congress] (LCLS)
IWE .... Winnetka Public Library, Winnetka, IL [OCLC symbol] (OCLC)
IWedSD .... Wedron Consolidated Community School District 201, Wedron, IL [Library symbol Library of Congress] (LCLS)
IWEM .... Institution of Water and Environmental Management (EAIO)
IWem .... Westmont Public Library, Westmont, IL [Library symbol Library of Congress] (LCLS)
IWen .... Bond Public Library, Wenona, IL [Library symbol Library of Congress] (LCLS)
IWenSD .... Wenona Community Unit, School District 1, Wenona, IL [Library symbol Library of Congress] (LCLS)
IWERC .... Industrial Waste Elimination Research Center [Illinois Institute of Technology] [Research center] (RCD)
Iwerks .... Iwerks Entertainment, Inc. [Associated Press] (SAG)
IWERRI .... Idaho Water and Energy Resources Research Institute [University of Idaho] [Research center] (RCD)
IWES .... Inhibited White Fuming Nitric Acid (PDAA)
IWes .... West Salem Public Library, West Salem, IL [Library symbol Library of Congress] (LCLS)
IWesp .... Thomas Ford Memorial Library, Western Springs, IL [Library symbol Library of Congress] (LCLS)
IWev .... Westville Public Library, Westville, IL [Library symbol Library of Congress] (LCLS)
IWEWSULOTATDTO... I Wish Everyone Would Stop Using Letters of the Alphabet to Designate Their Organizations [Originated by Bea von Boeselager in "Line o' Type," Chicago Tribune]
IWEX .... Internal Wave Experiment (NOAA)
IWF .... International Weightlifting Federation [See also FHI] [Budapest, Hungary] (EAIO)
IWF .... International Woodworking Machinery and Furniture Supply Fair (ITD)
IWF .... Internetworking Function [Computer science] (ACRL)
IWFA .... Inhibited White Fuming Nitric Acid [Rocket fuel] (SAA)
IWFA .... Intercollegiate Women's Fencing Association [Later, NIWFA]
IWFA .... International Window Film Association (EA)
IWFA .... International Women's Fishing Association (EA)
IWFAI .... International Watch Fob Association, Inc. (EA)
IWFI .... Italian Wine and Food Institute (EA)
IWFNA .... Inhibited White Fuming Nitric Acid [Rocket fuel] (IAA)
IWFP .... International Women's Film Project (EA)
IWFS .... Industrial Waste Filter System (IEEE)
IWFS .... Integrated Waste Fluid System (SSD)
IWFS .... International Wine and Food Society [British] (EAIO)
IWG .... Grand View College, Des Moines, IA [OCLC symbol] (OCLC)
IWG .... Imperial Wire Gauge (ROG)
IWG .... Implementation Work Group [DoD]
IWG .... Implementation Work Group on Justice Information and Statistics [See also GMO] [Canada]
IWG .... Industry Working Group
IWG .... Intelligence Working Group [Military] (CINC)
IWG .... Interface Working Group [NASA] (NASA)
IWG .... Intergovernmental Working Group [United Nations]
IWG .... International Working Group [NATO] (NATG)
IWG .... International Writers Guild
IWG .... Investigator's Working Group [Spacelab mission]
IWG .... Iron Wire Gauge
IWGA .... International Wheat Gluten Association (EA)
IWGA .... International World Games Association (EA)
IWGC .... Imperial War Graves Commission [British]
IWGCS .... International Working Group in Clinical Sociology (EAIO)
IWGCSFIPERM... Inter-Service Working Group for Cooperation and Standardization of Foto Interpretation Procedures, Equipment, and Related Matters
IWGDE .... Interlaboratory Working Group for Data Exchange [Computer science] (MHDI)
IWGFR .... International Working Group on Fast Reactors (NRCH)
IWGGDM..... International Working Group on Graminaceous Downy Mildews [Defunct] (EAIO)
IWGIA .... International Work Group for Indigenous Affairs [Copenhagen, Denmark] (EAIO)
IWGM .... Intergovernmental Working Group on Monitoring or Surveillance [United Nations] (ASF)
IWGMP .... Intergovernmental Working Group on Marine Pollution [Inter-Governmental Maritime Consultative Organization]
IWGMS .... Intergovernmental Working Group on Monitoring or Surveillance [United Nations] (MSC)

IWH .... Wabash, IN [Location identifier FAA] (FAAL)
IWHC .... International Women's Health Coalition (EA)
IWhh .... White Hall Township Library, White Hall, IL [Library symbol Library of Congress] (LCLS)
IWhhB .... Beecham Laboratories, White Hall, IL [Library symbol Library of Congress] (LCLS)
IWhhSD ...... North Greene Community Unit, School District 3, White Hall, IL [Library symbol Library of Congress] (LCLS)
IWhl .... Indian Trails Public Library District, Wheeling, IL [Library symbol Library of Congress] (LCLS)
IWHM .... Institution of Works and Highways Management [British] (DBA)
IWHM .... Interwest Home Medical [NASDAQ symbol] (TTSB)
IWHM .... Interwest Home Medical, Inc. [NASDAQ symbol] (SAG)
IWhN .... North Suburban Library System, Wheeling, IL [Library symbol Library of Congress] (LCLS)
IWHS .... Institute of Works and Highways Superintendents [British]
IWHSD .... Irish War Hospital Supply Depot [British military] (DMA)
IWI .... International Werner Tech [Vancouver Stock Exchange symbol]
IWI .... Inventors' Workshop International [Later, IWIEF] (EA)
IWI .... Irreversible Warmup Indicator [To detect whether frozen foods have risen above an acceptable temperature level] [Pronounced "ee-wee"]
IWI .... Wishard Memorial Hospital, Indianapolis, IN [OCLC symbol] (OCLC)
IWi .... Witt Memorial Library, Witt, IL [Library symbol Library of Congress] (LCLS)
IWIEF .... Inventors Workshop International Education Foundation (EA)
IWI Hold ..... IWI Holding Ltd. [Associated Press] (SAG)
IWilB .... National Baha'i Museum, Wilmette, IL [Library symbol] [Library of Congress] (LCLS)
IWilGS .... Church of Jesus Christ of Latter-Day Saints, Genealogical Society Library, Wilmette Branch, Wilmette, IL [Library symbol Library of Congress] (LCLS)
IWin .... Winnetka Public Library, Winnetka, IL [Library symbol Library of Congress] (LCLS)
IWinfC .... Central DuPage Hospital, Medical Library, Winfield, IL [Library symbol] [Library of Congress] (LCLS)
IWin-N .... Winnetka Public Library District, Northfield Branch, Northfield, IL [Library symbol Library of Congress] (LCLS)
IWIPC .... Interim Wool Industry Policy Council [Australia]
IWIS .... Interceptor Weapons Instructor School [Air Force]
IWiSD .... Witt Community Unit, School District 66, Witt, IL [Library symbol Library of Congress] (LCLS)
IWISTK .... Issue While in Stock
IWIU .... Insurance Workers International Union
IWL .... Infant Water Loss [Medicine] (CPH)
IWL .... Insensible Water Loss [Medicine]
IWL .... Institute Warranty Limits [Shipping] (DS)
IWL .... International Walther League (EA)
IWL .... Italian Welfare League (EA)
IWL .... Willard Library, Evansville, IN [OCLC symbol] (OCLC)
IWLA .... Izaak Walton League of America (EA)
IWLAE .... Izaak Walton League of America Endowment (EA)
IWLE .... Individual Whole of Life and Endowment [Insurance] (ADA)
IWLF .... International Wilderness Leadership Foundation
IWLS .... Iterative Weighted Least Squares [Statistics]
IWM .... Bluffton-Wells County Public Library, Bluffton, IN [OCLC symbol] (OCLC)
IWM .... Imperial War Museum [England]
IWM .... Industrial Waste Management (MCD)
IWM .... Institute of Wastes Management [British]
IWM .... Institution of Works Managers [British]
IWM .... Integrated Woz Machine [Apple Computer, Inc.]
IWM .... Internal Waste Manifest [Stanford University]
IWM .... MAP International, Wheaton, IL [Library symbol Library of Congress] (LCLS)
IWMA .... Institute of Weights and Measures Administration [Wales]
IWMA .... International Wire and Machinery Association [Leamington Spa, Warwickshire, England] (EAIO)
IWMI .... Inferior Wall Myocardial Infarction [Cardiology]
IWMP .... International Women's Media Project [Defunct] (EA)
IWMS .... Integrated Weed Management System [Agriculture]
IWN .... Indigenous Women's Network (EA)
IWN .... North Iowa Area Community College, Mason City, IA [OCLC symbol] (OCLC)
IWO .... Institute for World Order (EA)
IWO .... Intelligence Watch Officer [Military] (MCD)
IWO .... Interdivisional Work Order (AAGC)
IWo .... Worth Public Library District, Worth, IL [Library symbol Library of Congress] (LCLS)
IWOC .... International Wizard of Oz Club (EA)
IWor .... Wood River Public Library, Wood River, IL [Library symbol Library of Congress] (LCLS)
IWordR .... Worden Reading Center, Worden, IL [Library symbol Library of Congress] (LCLS)
IWordSD ..... Worden Community Unit, School District 16, Worden, IL [Library symbol Library of Congress] (LCLS)
IWorH .... Wood River Township Hospital, Medical Library, Wood River, IL [Library symbol Library of Congress] (LCLS)
IWorHS .... East Alton-Wood River Community High School 14, Wood River, IL [Library symbol Library of Congress] (LCLS)
IWori .... Woodridge Public Library, Woodridge, IL [Library symbol Library of Congress] (LCLS)
IWOSC........ International Working-Group of Soilless Culture
IWP............. Idaho White Pine [Lumber]
IWP............. Illawarra Workers Party [Political party Australia]

IWP............ Indicative World Plan for Agricultural Development [*United Nations*]
IWP............ Indo-West Pacific [*Biogeographic region*]
IWP............ Internal Working Paper
IWP............ Internationale Weltfriedens Partei [*International World Peace Party*] [*Germany Political party*] (PPW)
IWP............ International Information/Word Processing Association [*Formerly, IWPA*] (EA)
IWP............ International Word Processing Association (NITA)
IWP............ International Working Party
IWP............ Inverse Wulff Plot (PDAA)
IWP............ Irish Workers' Party [*Political party*] (PPW)
IWP............ Sioux City Public Library, Sioux City, IA [*OCLC symbol*] (OCLC)
IWPA .... Independent Wire Producers Association [*Later, AWPA*] (EA)
IWPA .... International Word Processing Association [*Later, IIWPA, IWP*]
IWPA .... Irish Water Polo Association (EAIO)
IWPC .... Institute of Water Pollution Control [*Later, IWEM*] (EAIO)
IWPPA .... Independent Waste Paper Processors Association [*British*] (DBA)
IWR .... Cedar Rapids Public Library, Cedar Rapids, IA [*OCLC symbol*] (OCLC)
IWR .... Connecticut Institute of Water Resources [*Storrs, CT*] [*Department of the Interior*] (GRD)
IWR .... Improved Weather Reconnaissance
IWR .... Information World Review [*A publication Information service or system*] (IID)
IWR .... Infrared Warning Receiver [*Aviation*] (DNAB)
IWR .... Institute for Water Resources [*Fort Belvoir, VA*] [*Army*] (MSC)
IWR .... Institute for Wildlife Research [*Defunct*] (EA)
IWR .... Institute of Water Research [*Michigan State University*]
IWR .... Isle Of Wight Railway [*British*]
IWR .... Isle Of Wight Rifles [*British military*] (DMA)
IWR .... Isolated Word Recognition (MCD)
IWRA .... International Water Resources Association (EA)
IWRA .... International Wild Rice Association (EA)
IWRAW .... International Women's Rights Action Watch (EAIO)
IWRB .... International Waterfowl and Wetlands Research Bureau (EAIO)
IWRC .... Independent Wire Rope Center [*or Core*]
IWRC .... International Wildlife Rehabilitation Council (EA)
IWRC .... Iron Wire Rope Core [*Nuclear energy*] (NRCH)
IWRI .... Informal World Recognition Inventory [*Education*] (EDAC)
IWRK .... Iwerks Entertainment [*NASDAQ symbol*] (TTSB)
IWRK .... Iwerks Entertainment, Inc. [*NASDAQ symbol*] (SAG)
IWRM .... Integrated Warfare Requirements Methodology
IWRMA .... Independent Wire Rope Manufacturers Association (EA)
IWRMA .... Irish Wholesale Ryegrass Machiners Association (BI)
IWRO .... Interdepartmental Work Release Order
IWRP .... Individualized Written Rehabilitation Program [*Department of Education*]
IWRP .... Industrial Waste Reduction Program [*Environmental science*]
IWRRC .... International Wheelchair Road Racers Club (EA)
IWS .... Impact Warning System
IWS .... Industrial Water Society [*British*] (DBA)
IWS .... Industrial Water Supply
IWS .... Industrial Water System (KSC)
IWS .... Industrial Welfare Society [*British*] (ILCA)
IWS .... Information Warfare Squadron [*Air Force*]
IWS .... Inland Waterway Service
IWS .... Institute of Wood Science [*British*] (BI)
IWS .... Instruction Work Stack (MHDB)
IWS .... Integrated Water System (SSD)
IWS .... Integrated Weapon System
IWS .... Integrated Work Statement (MCD)
IWS .... Interactive Work Station (MHDB)
IWS .... International Wildrose Resources, Inc. [*Vancouver Stock Exchange symbol*]
IWS .... International Wine Society (EA)
IWS .... International Wool Secretariat [*British*]
IWS .... Ionizing Wet Scrubber [*Environmental science*] (GFGA)
IWS .... Western Iowa Technical Community College, Sioux City, IA [*OCLC symbol*] (OCLC)
IWSA .... International Water Supply Association [*British*] (EAIO)
IWSA .... International Workers Sport Association
IWSAW .... Institute for Women's Studies in the Arab World [*Beirut, Lebanon*] (EAIO)
IWSB .... Insect Wire Screening Bureau [*Later, Insect Screening Weavers Association*] (EA)
IWSc........... Institute of Wood Science Ltd. [*British*]
IWSC .... Internet & Web Services Corp.
IWSCA .... Irish Water Spaniel Club of America (EA)
IWSF .... Irish Waterski Federation (EAIO)
IWSG .... International Wool Study Group [*British Defunct*] (EAIO)
IWSI........... Integrated Waste Services, Inc. [*NASDAQ symbol*] (SAG)
IWSI........... Integrated Waste Svcs [*NASDAQ symbol*] (TTSB)
IWSI........... Irish Work Study Institute Ltd. (BI)
IWS/IT .... Integrated Work Sequence/Inspection Traveler (NRCH)
IWSM .... Integrated Weapon Support Management (AFM)
IWSO .... Instructor Weapons System Officer [*Military*]
IWSOE .... International Weddell Sea Oceanographic Expedition
IWSP .... Institute of Work Study Practitioners [*British*] (BI)
IWSP .... Integrated Weapon Secret Panel (MCD)
IWSR .... Integrated Weapon System Representative [*or Review*] (MCD)
IWSR .... International Wine and Spirit Record
IWSRA .... Irish Women's Squash Rackets Association (EAIO)
IWSS .... International Weed Science Society (EA)
IWSSA .... Interservice Warehousing Support Services Agreement
IWST........... Integrated Weapon System Training [*Air Force*]

IwstHM .... Interwest Home Medical, Inc. [*Associated Press*] (SAG)
IWT .... Industrial Waste Treatment Management (MCD)
IWT .... Inland Water Transport [*British*]
IWT .... Institute of Women Today (EA)
IWT .... Integrated Waste Water Treatment
IWT .... Internationaal Watertribunaal [*International Water Tribunal*] [*Netherlands*] (EAIO)
IWT .... International Working Team [*NATO*] (NATG)
IWT .... Irwin Toy Ltd. [*Toronto Stock Exchange symbol*]
IWT .... I Was There
IWT .... Schools of Theology in Dubuque, Dubuque, IA [*OCLC symbol*] (OCLC)
IWTC .... International Women's Tribune Centre (EA)
IWTF .... International Water Tribunal Foundation [*Netherlands*] (EAIO)
IWTO .... International Wool Testing Organisation [*Australia*]
IWTO .... International Wool Textile Organization [*See also FLI*] [*Brussels, Belgium*] (EAIO)
IWTS........... Indications and Warning Training System [*Military*] (MCD)
IWTS........... Individual Weapon Thermal Sight [*Army*] (INF)
IWTS........... Industrial Waste Treatment System (NRCH)
IWTS........... Integrated Wire Termination System (IAA)
IWTS........... Integrated Worldwide Topographic System (PDAA)
IWTT........... Industrial Wastewater Treatment Plant
IWU .... Illegal Wearing of Uniform
IWU .... Illinois Wesleyan University [*Bloomington*]
IWU .... Interworking Unit [*Computer science*] (TNIG)
IWU .... Isolation Working Unit [*Telecommunications*] (TEL)
IWU .... Texas Woman's University, Denton, TX [*OCLC symbol*] (OCLC)
IWUL .... Irrigators and Water Users' League [*Australia*]
IWV .... Internationale Warenhaus-Vereinigung [*International Association of Department Stores*]
IWV .... Waterloo Public Library, Waterloo, IA [*OCLC symbol*] (OCLC)
IWVA .... International War Veterans' Alliance (EA)
IWVMTS .... Interim Water Velocity Meter Test Set
IWW .... Industrial Workers of the World (EA)
IWW .... Inland Waterway (AABC)
IWW .... International Westward Development Corp. [*Vancouver Stock Exchange symbol*]
IWW .... International Who's Who [*A publication*]
IWW .... Intracoastal Waterway
IWW .... Kenai, AK [*Location identifier FAA*] (FAAL)
IWW .... Westmar College, Le Mars, IA [*OCLC symbol*] (OCLC)
IWW .... Wheaton College, Wheaton, IL [*Library symbol Library of Congress*] (LCLS)
IWWA .... International Wild Waterfowl Association (EA)
IWWCS .... International Who's Who in Community Service [*A publication*]
IWWG .... International Women's Writing Guild (EA)
IWW-G .... Wheaton College, Billy Graham Center, Wheaton, IL [*Library symbol Library of Congress*] (LCLS)
IWWM .... International Who's Who in Music and Musicians Directory [*A publication*]
IWWP .... International Who's Who in Poetry [*A publication*]
IWWRB .... International Waterfowl and Wetlands Research Bureau (EAIO)
IWY............. International Women's Year [*1975*]
IWY............. New York, NY [*Location identifier FAA*] (FAAL)
IWya .... Raymond A. Sapp Memorial Library, Wyanet, IL [*Library symbol Library of Congress*] (LCLS)
IWyaSD....... Wyanet Consolidated High School District 510, Wyanet, IL [*Library symbol Library of Congress*] (LCLS)
IWyo .... Wymoning Public Library, Wymoning, IL [*Library symbol Library of Congress*] (LCLS)
IX................ Flandre Air [*ICAO designator*] (AD)
IX................ Iesus Christus [*Jesus Christ*] [*Latin*]
IX................ In Christo [*In Christ*] [*Latin*]
IX................ Index [*Computer science*] (BUR)
IX................ Industry Manufacturers [*FCC*] (MCD)
IX................ Information Exchange [*Advanced photo system*]
ix................ Interactive Executive (HGAA)
IX................ Inter-Exchange [*Telecommunications*] (NITA)
IX................ Inverted Index (NITA)
IX................ Ion Exchanger (NRCH)
IX................ Unclassified Miscellaneous [*Navy ship symbol*]
IXA .... Agartala [*India*] [*Airport symbol*] (OAG)
i-xa-- .... Christmas Island [*Indian Ocean*] [*MARC geographic area code Library of Congress*] (LCCP)
IXA .... Ion-Excited X-Ray Analysis
IXA .... University of Texas at Austin, Austin, TX [*OCLC symbol*] (OCLC)
IXAE .... International X-Ray Astrophysics Explorer
IXB.............. Bagdogra [*India*] [*Airport symbol*] (OAG)
i-xb-- .... Cocos [*Keeling*] Islands [*MARC geographic area code Library of Congress*] (LCCP)
IXC.............. Chandigarh [*India*] [*Airport symbol*] (OAG)
IXC.............. Interexchange Carrier [*Telecommunications*] (PCM)
IXC.............. Interexchange Channel [*Telecommunications*]
IXC.............. Interexchange Circuit [*Telecommunications*] (TSSD)
IXC.............. Inter-Exchange Control (NITA)
IXC.............. Interexchange Mileage (CET)
IXC.............. Ixora Communications System [*Vancouver Stock Exchange symbol*]
i-xc--.......... Maldives [*MARC geographic area code Library of Congress*] (LCCP)
IXD.............. Allahabad [*India*] [*Airport symbol*] (OAG)
IXD.............. Olathe, KS [*Location identifier FAA*] (FAAL)
IXE.............. Mangalore [*India*] [*Airport symbol*] (OAG)
IXEE .... International X-Ray and Extreme Ultraviolet Explorer
IXES .... Information Exchange System [*or Subsystem*] [*Military*] (DNAB)
IXF.............. Industrial X-Ray Film

IXG.............	Belgaum [India] [Airport symbol] (OAG)
IXH.............	Kailashahar [India] [Airport symbol] (AD)
IXI.............	Lilabari [India] [Airport symbol] (OAG)
IXJ.............	Jammu [India] [Airport symbol] (OAG)
IXK.............	Keshod [India] [Airport symbol] (OAG)
IXL.............	Leh [India] [Airport symbol] (OAG)
IXM.............	Index Manager (MHDI)
IXM.............	Madurai [India] [Airport symbol] (OAG)
IXN.............	Khowai [India] [Airport symbol] (AD)
IXO.............	Inlet and Outlet
i-xo--	Socotra Island [MARC geographic area code Library of Congress] (LCCP)
IXOH	Inlet and Outlet Head
IXP.............	Information Exchange Protocol [Telecommunications] (NTCM)
IXP.............	Ivex Packaging Corp. [AMEX symbol] (SAG)
IXP.............	Pathankot [India] [Airport symbol] (AD)
IXQ.............	Kamalpur [India] [Airport symbol] (AD)
IXR.............	Integrated X-Ray Reflection
IXR.............	Intersection of Runways [Aviation]
IXR.............	Ranchi [India] [Airport symbol] (OAG)
IXRALM	Imaging Soft X-Ray LASER Microscope
IXS.............	Information Exchange System [or Subsystem] [Military] (CAAL)
IXS.............	Silchar [India] [Airport symbol] (OAG)
IXSD............	International Telex Subscriber Dialling (NITA)
IXSS............	Unclassified Miscellaneous Submarine [Navy symbol] (NVT)
IXT.............	Christian Theological Seminary, Indianapolis, IN [OCLC symbol] (OCLC)
IXT.............	Interaction Cross Talk [Telecommunications] (TEL)
IXT.............	Interexchange Channel [Computer science] (TNIG)
IXT.............	Ixtapalapa [Mexico] [Seismograph station code, US Geological Survey Closed] (SEIS)
IXT.............	Lineas Aereas de Ixtlan SA de CV [Mexico ICAO designator] (FAAC)
IXT.............	Pasighat [India] [Airport symbol] (AD)
IXTR............	Intelligible Crosstalk Ratio
IXU.............	Aurangabad [India] [Airport symbol] (OAG)
IXU.............	Index Translation Unit [Computer science] (MHDB)
IXV.............	Along [India] [Airport symbol] (AD)
IXW.............	Jamshedpur [India] [Airport symbol] (AD)
IXX.............	Dolphin Express Airlines, Inc. [FAA designator] (FAAC)
IXY.............	Kandla [India] [Airport symbol] (AD)
IXZ.............	Port Blair [Andaman Islands] [Airport symbol] (OAG)
IY.............	Imperial Yeomanry [British]
IY.............	Ionized Yeast
iy.............	Iraq-Saudi Arabia Neutral Zone [MARC country of publication code Library of Congress] (LCCP)
IY.............	Yemen Airlines [Airline flight code] (ODBW)
IY.............	Yemen Airways [ICAO designator] (AD)
IYA.............	Indian Youth of America (EA)
IYA.............	Irish Yachting Association (EAIO)
IYB.............	Imperial Yeomanry Bearer Corps [British military] (DMA)
IYC.............	Individual Yield Coverage Program [Department of Agriculture]
IYC.............	International Year of the Child [United Nations] (AEE)
IYC.............	International Youth Congress
IYC.............	International Youth Council (EA)
IYCM............	International Year of Canadian Music [1986]
IYCO	Ito-Yokado Co. Ltd. [NASDAQ symbol] (NQ)
IYCOY	Ito Yokado Ltd ADR [NASDAQ symbol] (TTSB)
IYCW	International Young Christian Workers [See also JOCI] (EAIO)
IYDP	International Year of the Disabled Person [1981]
IYDU	International Young Democratic Union [Defunct] (EAIO)
IYE.............	Yemenia, Yemen Airways [ICAO designator] (FAAC)
IYF.............	International Year of the Family
IYF.............	International Youth Federation for Environmental Studies and Conservation (EAIO)
IYFS............	International Young Fish Survey [Denmark, Great Britain, Norway, West Germany] [1987-88 Oceanography]
IYFS............	International Young Friends Society [Pakistan] (EAIO)
IYH.............	Imperial Yeomanry Hospitals [Military British] (ROG)
IY'H	Im Yirtseh Hashem (BJA)
IYHA............	Irish Youth Hostel Association (EAIO)
IYHF............	International Youth Hostel Federation [See also FAIJ] [Welwyn Garden City, Hertfordshire, England] (EAIO)
IYK.............	Inyokern [California] [Airport symbol] (OAG)
IYK.............	Inyokern, CA [Location identifier FAA] (FAAL)
IYL.............	International Youth Library [See also IJB] [Munich, Federal Republic of Germany] (EAIO)
IYP.............	Instant Yellow Pages [Information service or system]
IYPD............	International Year for the Preparation of Disarmament [Pugwash Conference]
IYQS	International Year of the Quiet Sun [1964-65] [Also, IQSY] (KSC)
IYRU	International Yacht Racing Union [British]
IYS.............	Inverted Y-Suspensor [Medicine]
IYSH............	International Year of Shelter for the Homeless [1987]
IYTA............	International Yoga Teachers Association (ADA)
IYU.............	Baylor University, Waco, TX [OCLC symbol] (OCLC)
IYWIP	International Year of the World's Indigenous People
IYY.............	International Youth Year [1985] (AIE)
IYYC............	International Youth Year Commission [Defunct] (EA)
IZ.............	Arkia-Israel Inland Airlines [ICAO designator] (AD)
IZ.............	Informationszentrum Sozialwissenschaften [Social Sciences Information Center] [Information service or system] (IID)
IZ.............	Inspection Zone
IZ.............	Interfacial Zone
IZ.............	Intermediate Zone
IZ.............	Isolation Zone [Nuclear energy] (NRCH)
IZ.............	Spofa Ltd. [Czechoslovakia] [Research code symbol]
IZ.............	Zion-Benton Public Library District, Zion, IL [Library symbol Library of Congress] (LCLS)
IZA.............	International Zen Association [Formerly, European Zen Association] (EA)
IZA.............	International Zeolite Association
IZAA............	Independent Zinc Alloyers Association (EA)
IZAA............	Isotope-Shift, Zeeman-Effect Atomic Absorption
IZBA............	International Zebu Breeders Association (EA)
IZBB............	Interagency Zero-Based Budgeting [Federal government]
IZC.............	International Zetcentrum [International Typesetting Center, The Netherlands]
IZCA............	International Zuma Class Association (EA)
IZD.............	Implanted Zener Diode (MCD)
IZD.............	Internationaler Zivildienst [International Voluntary Service]
IZE.............	Elizabeth City, NC [Location identifier FAA] (FAAL)
IZE.............	International Association of Zoo Educators (EA)
IZK.............	Iizuka [Japan] [Seismograph station code, US Geological Survey Closed] (SEIS)
IZK.............	Wilkes-Barre/Scranton, PA [Location identifier FAA] (FAAL)
IZL.............	Irgun Zeva'i Le'umi (BJA)
IZM.............	Izmir [Turkey] [Airport symbol] (OAG)
IZM.............	Izmir [Turkey] [Seismograph station code, US Geological Survey] (SEIS)
IZN.............	Izone International Ltd. [Vancouver Stock Exchange symbol]
IZO.............	Izumo [Japan] [Airport symbol] (OAG)
IZR.............	San Antonio, TX [Location identifier FAA] (FAAL)
IZS.............	Insulin Zinc Suspension
IZT.............	Ixtepec [Mexico] [Airport symbol] (AD)
IZTO............	Interzonal Trade Office [NATO] (NATG)
IZU.............	Izuhara [Japan] [Seismograph station code, US Geological Survey] (SEIS)
IZY.............	Intermediate Zone Yaw
IZY.............	International Zoo Yearbook [A publication]
IZZI............	Integrated Security Sys [NASDAQ symbol] (TTSB)
IZZI............	Integrated Security Systems [NASDAQ symbol] (SAG)
IZZIW	Integrated Sec Sys Wrrt [NASDAQ symbol] (TTSB)

J

By Acronym

J .... Action Variable [*Physics*] (BARN)
J .... Air Force Training Category [*Officer training program*]
J .... Angular Momentum [*Physics*] (BARN)
J .... Australian Journalist [*A publication*]
J .... Business Class [*Also, C*] [*Airline fare code*]
J .... Cable Jointing [*Section of the British Royal Navy*]
J .... Chain [*Symbol*] [*A part of the immunoglobulin molecular structure*] (DAVI)
J .... Clubs [*Public-performance tariff class*] [*British*]
j .... Dissenting Opinion Citation in Dissenting Opinion [*Used in Shepard's Citations*] [*Legal term*] (DLA)
J .... Electric Current Density [*Symbol*] [*IUPAC*] (DEN)
J .... Electromechanical [*JETDS nomenclature*]
J .... Flux [*Symbol*] [*IUPAC*]
J .... Institutes of Justinian [*Roman law*] [*A publication*] (DLA)
J .... Irradiation Correction
J .... Jack [*In card game*]
J .... Jack [*Technical drawings*]
J .... Jackpot Enterprises [*NYSE symbol*] (TTSB)
J .... Jackpot Enterprises, Inc. [*NYSE symbol*] (CTT)
J .... Jacobeian Determinant (ROG)
J .... Jacobus de Porta Ravennate [*Deceased, 1178*] [*Authority cited in pre-1607 legal work*] (DSA)
J .... January
J .... Japan [*IYRU nationality code*]
J .... Jargon [*Used in correcting manuscripts, etc.*]
j .... Jaundice [*Medicine*] (DMAA)
J .... Jerusalem Talmud (BJA)
J .... Jesus (ROG)
J .... Jet [*Aircraft*]
J .... Jet Fuel
J .... Jet Route [*Followed by identification*]
J .... Jewels Horology (BARN)
J .... Jewish
J .... Jewish Chaplain [*Territorial Force*] [*Military British*] (ROG)
J .... Jewish School [*British*]
J .... Jig [*Phonetic alphabet*] [*World War II*] (DSUE)
J .... Job (IEEE)
J .... Jobber [*Merchant middleman*]
J .... Johannes Galensis [*Flourished, 13th century*] [*Authority cited in pre-1607 legal work*] (DSA)
J .... Johnnie [*Phonetic alphabet*] [*Royal Navy World War I*] (DSUE)
J .... Johnny [*Phonetic alphabet*] [*Pre-World War II*] (DSUE)
J .... Johnson's New York Reports [*A publication*] (DLA)
J .... Join
J .... Joinable Containers [*Shipping*] (DCTA)
J .... Joiner [*Machinery*]
J .... Joining [*Also, JNG*] [*Genetics*]
J .... Joint
J .... Joint Matriculation Board [*British*]
J .... Joist [*Technical drawings*]
J .... Jonckheere Test [*Fisheries*]
J .... Joshua [*Old Testament book*] [*Freemasonry*]
J .... Joule [*Symbol*] [*SI unit of energy*] (GPO)
j .... Jour [*Day*] [*French*]
J .... Journal
J .... Journalism
J .... Judaeo-Persian
J .... Judean or Yahwistic [*Used in biblical criticism to designate Yahwistic material*]
J .... Judex [*Judge*] [*Latin*]
J .... Judge
J .... Judgment
J .... Juice
J .... Juliett [*Phonetic alphabet*] [*International*] (DSUE)
J .... July
J .... Junction
J .... Junction Devices [*JETDS nomenclature*] [*Military*] (CET)
J .... June
J .... Jungle
J .... Junior
J .... Jupiter
J .... Juris [*Of Law*] [*Latin*] (ADA)
J .... Jus [*Law*] [*Latin*]
J .... Justice [*i.e., a judge; plural is JJ*]
J .... Justiciary Cases [*Scotland*] [*A publication*] (DLA)

J .... Justification (WDMC)
J .... Juta's South African Reports [*A publication*] (DLA)
J .... Jute-Asphalted [*Nonmetallic armor*] (AAG)
J .... Juvenile
J .... Juvenile (Amaurotic Idiocy) [*Medicine*] (DAVI)
J .... Kansas City [*Branch in the Federal Reserve regional banking system*] (BARN)
J .... Lower Canada Jurist, Quebec [*1848-91*] [*A publication*] (DLA)
J .... Magnetic Poparization [*Physics*] (BARN)
J .... Massieu Function [*Symbol*] [*IUPAC*]
J .... Mechanical Equivalent of Heat [*Symbol*]
J .... Radiant Intensity [*Symbol*]
J .... Scottish Jurist [*1829-73*] [*A publication*] (DLA)
J .... Special Test, Temporary [*Aircraft classification letter*]
j .... Total Angular Momentum Quantum Number of a Single Particle [*Symbol*] [*Spectroscopy*]
J .... Total Angular Momentum Quantum Number of a System [*Symbol*] [*Spectroscopy*]
J .... VEB Fahlberg-List [*East Germany*] [*Research code symbol*]
J .... Yahwist Source [*Biblical scholarship*]
j .... Yellow [*Symbol*] (DAVI)
J-1 .... Jaeger Test Type One [*Ophthalmology*]
J-1 .... Personnel Section [*of a joint military staff; also, the officer in charge of this section*]
J2 .... Djibouti [*Aircraft nationality and registration mark*] (FAAC)
J-2 .... Intelligence Section [*of a joint military staff; also, the officer in charge of this section*]
J2 .... JTwo Communications [*Associated Press*] (SAG)
J2 Com .... JTwo Communications [*Associated Press*] (SAG)
J3 .... Grenada [*Aircraft nationality and registration mark*] (FAAC)
J-3 .... Operations and Training Section [*of a joint military staff; also, the officer in charge of this section*]
J-4 .... Logistics Section [*of a joint military staff; also, the officer in charge of this section*]
J-5 .... General Administration Section [*of a joint military staff; also the officer in charge of this section*]
J5 .... Guinea-Bissau [*International civil aircraft marking*] (ODBW)
J-6 .... Communications-Electronics Section [*of a joint military staff; also, the officer in charge of this section*]
J6 .... St. Lucia [*Aircraft nationality and registration mark*] (FAAC)
J7 .... Dominica [*Aircraft nationality and registration mark*] (FAAC)
J8 .... St. Vincent and the Grenadines [*Aircraft nationality and registration mark*] (FAAC)
J-14/CA .... Jet 14 Class Association (EA)
J31 .... British Aerospace Jetstream 31 [*Airplane code*]
JA .... Bankair [*ICAO designator*] (AD)
JA .... Jack Adapter
Ja .... Jacobus Balduini [*Deceased, 1235*] [*Authority cited in pre-1607 legal work*] (DSA)
Ja .... Jacobus de Albenga [*Flourished, 13th century*] [*Authority cited in pre-1607 legal work*] (DSA)
Ja .... Jacobus de Ravanis [*Deceased, 1296*] [*Authority cited in pre-1607 legal work*] (DSA)
ja .... Jade (VRA)
JA .... Jama'at Ahmadiyyah [*Ahmadiyya Muslim Association*] (EAIO)
JA .... Jamaica
JA .... January
ja .... Japan [*ry (Ryukyu Islands, Southern) used in records cataloged before January 1978*] [*MARC country of publication code Library of Congress*] (LCCP)
JA .... Jetevator Assembly
JA .... Jewelers of America (EA)
JA .... Jewish Art, An Illustrated History [*A publication*] (BJA)
JA .... Job Aid
JA .... Job Analysis
JA .... Jockey's Association [*Defunct*] (EA)
JA .... John Adams [*US president, 1735-1826*]
JA .... John Alden Financial [*NYSE symbol*] (SPSG)
JA .... Joint Account
JA .... Joint Agent
JA .... Journal Announcement [*Dialog*] [*Searchable field*] [*Information service or system*] (NITA)
JA .... Judge Advocate
JA .... Judge of Appeal
JA .... Judicature Act (ROG)
JA .... Judicial Authority [*British*]

JA .... Jump Address
JA .... Jump If Above [Computer science] (PCM)
JA .... Junior Achievement [Stamford, CT] (EA)
JA .... Junior Ambassadors [Defunct] (EA)
JA .... Justice of Appeal [Legal term] (DLA)
JA .... Juvenile Atrophy [Medicine] (DAVI)
JA .... Juxta-Articular [Orthopedics] (DAVI)
JAA .... American Dental Association, Chicago, IL [OCLC symbol] (OCLC)
JAA .... Jamiat Adduwal Alarabia [League of Arab States - LAS] (EAIO)
JAA .... Japan Asia Airways
JAA .... Japan Asia Airways Co. Ltd. [ICAO designator] (FAAC)
JAA .... Joint Airworthiness Authority [Aviation]
JAA .... Judge Advocates Association (EA)
JAAA .... Jabara Award for Airmanship [Military decoration]
JAAB .... Joint Airlift Allocations Board
JAAC .... Joint Airlift Allocations Committee
JAAC .... Journal of Aesthetics and Art Criticism [A publication] (BRI)
JAACS .... John A. Andrew Clinical Society (EA)
JA(ACT) ...... Jobless Action (Australian Capital Territory) [An association]
JAAF .... Japanese Army Air Force
JAAF .... Joint Action Armed Forces
JAAFAR ...... Joint Army-Air Force Adjustment Regulations
JAAFCTB .... Joint Army-Air Force Commercial Traffic Bulletin
JAAFPC ...... Joint Army-Air Force Procurement Circular
JAAFU .... Joint Anglo-American Foul Up [World War II slang] [Bowdlerized version]
JAAL .... Journal of Adolescent & Adult Literacy [A publication] (BRI)
JAAML .... Journal. American Academy of Matrimonial Lawyers [A publication] (DLA)
JAAMRS ..... Joint Air-to-Air Missile Requirement Study (MCD)
JAAOC .... Joint Antiaircraft Operation Center [NATO] (NATG)
JAAP .... Joint Airborne Advance Party [Military] (AFM)
JAAP .... Joliet Army Ammunition Plant (AABC)
JAAR .... Job Area Acceptance Range (AAGC)
JAAR .... Journal of the American Academy of Religion [A publication] (BRI)
Ja Are .... Jacobus de Arena [Deceased, 1297] [Authority cited in pre-1607 legal work] (DSA)
JAARS .... Jungle Aviation & Radio Service, Inc. [Mission plane service]
JAAS .... Jewish Academy of Arts and Sciences (EA)
JAAS .... Journal of Analytical Atomic Spectrometry [Formerly, ARAAS] [A publication]
JAAT .... Joint Air Attack Team [Military] (INF)
JAATT .... Joint Air Attack Team Tactics (MCD)
JA/ATT .... Joint Airborne/Air Transportability Training
JAAW .... Juvenile Arthritis Awareness Week [Arthritis Foundation]
JAB .... American Library Association, Booklist, Chicago, IL [OCLC symbol] (OCLC)
JAB .... January Assumption Budget [Budget based on economic forecasts available as of January]
JAB .... Jet Business Airlines [Belgium ICAO designator] (FAAC)
JAB .... Joint Activity Briefing [Military] (AFM)
JAB .... Joint Amphibious Board [Military]
JABES .... Just Another Break-Even Situation [Slang]
Jabil .... Jabil Circuit, Inc. [Associated Press] (SAG)
JABOWA ..... Janak-Botkin-Wallis [Data processing program regarding forest growth; named for three men involved in program]
JABPPC....... Joint Animal By Products Parliamentary and Advisory Committee [British] (DBA)
JABQC .... Job Assembly Breakdown and Quality Control Section [Social Security Administration]
JABRO .... James Broadwell [Custom-built racing car]
JABUP .... Joint Air Base Utilization Plan (MCD)
JAC .... CEGEP [College d'Enseignement General et Professionnel] John Abbott College Library [UTLAS symbol]
JAC .... Jackson [Wyoming] [Airport symbol] (OAG)
JAC .... Jacksonville [Florida] [Seismograph station code, US Geological Survey Closed] (SEIS)
JAC .... Jackson, WY [Location identifier FAA] (FAAL)
JAC .... Jacobean (WDAA)
Jac .... Jacob's English Chancery Reports [1821-22] [A publication] (DLA)
Jac .... Jacob's Law Dictionary [A publication] (DLA)
Jac .... Jacobus [James] [King of England] (DLA)
Jac .... Jacobus Balduini [Deceased, 1235] [Authority cited in pre-1607 legal work] (DSA)
JAC .... Japan Air Commuter Co. Ltd. [ICAO designator] (FAAC)
JAC .... Jet Age Conference
JAC .... Jet Aircraft Coating
JAC .... Jeunesse Anarchiste Communiste [French student group]
JAC .... Job Assistance Center (DOMA)
JAC .... Johnstown American Co. (MHDW)
JAC .... Joint Action Co. [Marine Corps]
JAC .... Joint Advisory Committee [Military]
JAC .... Joint Aircraft Committee [World War II]
JAC .... Joint Apprenticeship Committee
JAC .... Joint Arms Control
JAC .... Journal of Applied Chemistry [A publication]
JAC .... Junior American Citizens [An association] (EA)
JAC .... Junior Association of Commerce (BARN)
JACADS ...... Johnston Atoll Chemical Agents Disposal System
Jac & W ...... Jacob and Walker's English Chancery Reports [37 English Reprint] [A publication] (DLA)
Jac & Walk... Jacob and Walker's English Chancery Reports [37 English Reprint] [A publication] (DLA)

Jac & W (Eng)... Jacob and Walker's English Chancery Reports [37 English Reprint] [A publication] (DLA)
JACB-E........ Joint Acquisition Coordinating Board-Europe (AAGC)
Jacbn.......... Jacobean (VRA)
Jacbsn......... Jacobson Stores, Inc. [Associated Press] (SAG)
JACC.......... Jayhawk Acceptance [NASDAQ symbol] (TTSB)
JACC.......... Jayhawk Acceptance Corp. [NASDAQ symbol] (SAG)
JACC.......... Joint Airborne Communications Center (MCD)
JACC.......... Joint Air Command Center [Army] (DOMA)
JACC.......... Joint Alternate Command Center [Military] (CINC)
JACC.......... Joint Automatic Control Conference [IEEE]
JACC.......... Journalism Association of Community Colleges (EA)
JACCC........ Joint Air Control and Coordination Center [Air Force] (AFM)
JACC/CP ..... Joint Airborne Communications Center/Command Post (AFM)
JACCI......... Joint Allocation Committee Civil Intelligence [of US and Great Britain] [World War II]
J Account..... Journal of Accountancy [A publication] (BRI)
JACCP........ Joint Airborne Communication and Command Post (IAA)
J Acct .... Journal of Accountancy [A publication] (DLA)
Jac Dict ...... Jacob's Law Dictionary [A publication] (DLA)
JACE.......... Joint Allied Communications Element (AFM)
JACE.......... Joint Alternate Command Element
JACE.......... Just Another Confused Elephant
Jac Fish Dig... Jacob's American Edition of Fisher's English Digest [A publication] (DLA)
JACFU......... Joint American-Chinese Foul Up [World War II slang] [Bowdlerized version]
JACGUAR..... Johns and Call Girls United Against Repression (EA)
Jac Int .... Jacob's Introduction to the Common, Civil, and Canon Law [A publication] (DLA)
JACK.......... Golden Bear Golf, Inc. [NASDAQ symbol] (SAG)
JACK.......... Junior American Coin Klub (EA)
JACK.......... Junior Assistant Cook [British military] (DMA)
Jack & G Landl & Ten... Jackson and Gross' Treatise on the Law of Landlord and Tenant in Pennsylvania [A publication] (DLA)
Jack & L...... Jackson and Lumpkin's Reports [59-64 Georgia] [A publication] (DLA)
Jack Geo Ind... Jackson's Index to the Georgia Reports [A publication] (DLA)
JackHwt....... Jackson Hewitt [Associated Press] (SAG)
JACKPHY..... Japanese, Arabic, Chinese, Korean, Persian, Hebrew, Yiddish [Nonroman languages] [Library of Congress]
Jack Pl .... Jackson on Pleadings [1933] [A publication] (DLA)
Jackpot .... Jackpot Enterprises, Inc. [Associated Press] (SAG)
JACKPOT..... Joint Airborne Communications Center and Command Post
Jackpt......... Jackpot Enterprises [Associated Press] (SAG)
Jackson ...... Jackson's Reports [1-29 Texas Court of Appeals] [A publication] (DLA)
Jackson ...... Jackson's Reports [46-58 Georgia] [A publication] (DLA)
Jackson & Lumpkin... Jackson and Lumpkin's Reports [59-64 Georgia] [A publication] (DLA)
Jackson St U... Jackson State University (GAGS)
Jacksonville St U... Jacksonville State University (GAGS)
Jacksonville U... Jacksonville University (GAGS)
Jack Tex App... Jackson's Reports [A publication] (DLA)
JACL........... Japanese American Citizens League (EA)
Jac Law Dict... Jacob's Law Dictionary [A publication] (DLA)
Jac LD .... Jacob's Law Dictionary [A publication] (DLA)
Jac L Dict.... Jacob's Law Dictionary [A publication] (DLA)
Jac Lex Mer... Jacob's Lex Mercatoria [A publication] (DLA)
Jac LG .... Jacob's Law Grammar [A publication] (DLA)
Jaclyn......... Jaclyn, Inc. [Associated Press] (SAG)
JACNE......... Joint Advisory Committee on Nutrition Education [British]
JACO.......... Jaco Electronics [NASDAQ symbol] (TTSB)
JACO.......... Jaco Electronics, Inc. [NASDAQ symbol] (NQ)
JACO.......... Joint Actions Control Office (AABC)
Jacob .... Jacob's English Chancery Reports [1821-22] [A publication] (DLA)
Jacob .... Jacob's Law Dictionary [A publication] (DLA)
Jacob Ardiz... Jacobus de Ardizone [Flourished, 1213-50] [Authority cited in pre-1607 legal work] (DSA)
Jacobs .... Jacobs Engineering Group, Inc. [Associated Press] (SAG)
JacoEl......... Jaco Electronics, Inc. [Associated Press] (SAG)
JacoElec...... Jaco Electronics, Inc. [Associated Press] (SAG)
JACOPIS ..... Joint Advisory Committee on Pets in Society [British] (DI)
JacorC........ Jacor Communications, Inc. [Associated Press] (SAG)
JacorCm...... Jacor Communications, Inc. [Associated Press] (SAG)
JACP.......... Japanese American Curriculum Project (EA)
JacrCm....... Jacor Communications, Inc. [Associated Press] (SAG)
JACS.......... Japan-American Cultural Society (EAIO)
JACS.......... Jet Attitude Control System (KSC)
JACS.......... Jewish Alcoholics, Chemically Dependent Persons, and Significant Others
JACS........... Joint Action in Community Service (EA)
JACS........... JUMPS Army Coding System (MCD)
Jac Sea Laws... Jacobsen's Law of the Sea [A publication] (DLA)
JACSPAC ..... Joint Air Communications of the Pacific
JACT.......... [The] Joint Association of Classical Teachers [British]
JACTRU....... Joint Air Traffic Control RADAR Unit (IAA)
JACWA........ Joint Allied Command Western Approaches [NATO] (LAIN)
JAD .... Joint Application Design [Computer science]
JAD .... Joint Resource Assessment Database
JAD .... Wheaton Public Library, Wheaton, IL [OCLC symbol] (OCLC)
JADB .... Joint Air Defense Board
JADC .... Joint Administrative Committee [Military]
JADD .... Joint Air Defense Division (SAA)
JADE .... Japan Area Defense Environment

JADE...........	Japan Asian Dance Event
JADE...........	Japanese Air Defense Environment
JADE...........	Junior Administrator Development Examination (AFM)
JADF...........	Japan Air Defense Force
JADF...........	Joint Air Defense Force (AAG)
JADIS..........	Joint Air Defense Interoperability Study
JADITBHKNYC...	Just a Drop in the Basket Helps Keep New York Clean [*Antilitter campaign*]
JADO...........	Joint Air Defense Operations [*Marine Corps*] (DOMA)
JADOC	Joint Air Defense Operation Center
JADOR.........	Joint Advertising Directors of Recruiting [*Navy*] (NVT)
JADPU	Joint Automatic Data Processing Unit
JAD/RAD......	Joint Application Design/Rapid Application Design [*Computer science*]
JADREP	Joint Resource Assessment Data Base Report [*Military*] (AABC)
JADS...........	Journal Article Delivery Service [*Carnegie Mellon University*]
jadt............	Jadeite (VRA)
J Adv	Judge Advocate [*Legal term*] (DLA)
J Adv Ed	Journal of Advanced Education [*A publication*]
J ADV GEN...	Judge Advocate General [*Military*] (WDAA)
JADW..........	Joint Air Defense Wing (SAA)
JAE	Illinois Agricultural Association & Affiliated Co., Bloomington, IL [*OCLC symbol*] (OCLC)
JAE	Jacksonville [*Illinois*] [*Airport symbol*] (AD)
JAE	Japan Aviation Electronics Industry Ltd.
JAE	Joint Atomic Exercise [*NATO*] (NATG)
JAE	Journal of Advanced Education [*A publication*] (ADA)
JAE	Journal of Agricultural Economics [*A publication*]
JAE	Jump If Above or Equal [*Computer science*] (PCM)
JAEC..........	Japan Atomic Energy Commission
JAEC..........	Joint Atomic Energy Commission
JAEG..........	Jaegdtiger [*Tank-destroyer*] [*German military - World War II*]
Jaeger Labor Law...	Jaeger's Cases and Statutes on Labor Law [*A publication*] (DLA)
JAEH..........	Journal of Aquatic Ecosystem Health [*A publication*]
JAEIC	Joint Atomic Energy Intelligence Center [*Military*]
JAEIC	Joint Atomic Energy Intelligence Committee (KSC)
JAEIP	Japan Atomic Energy Insurance Pool
JAERI..........	Japan Atomic Energy Research Institute [*Tokyo*]
J Aes Ed	Journal of Aesthetic Education [*A publication*] (BRI)
JAEW.........	Japanese Airborne Early Warning
JAF	Corn Belt Library System, Normal, IL [*OCLC symbol*] (OCLC)
JAF	Jaffna [*Ceylon*] [*Airport symbol*] (AD)
JAF	James A. Fitzpatrick [*Nuclear power plant*] (NRCH)
JAF	Jamestown Area Furniture Haulers Association, Inc., Buffalo NY [*STAC*]
JAF	Japan-Australia Foundation
JAF	Japan Automobile Federation
JAF	Job Accounting Facility
JAF	John Augustus Foundation (EA)
JAF	Joint Attack Fighter [*Air Force*] [*Navy*] [*DoD*] (DOMA)
JAF	Jordanian Air Force
JAF	Journal of American Folklore [*A publication*] (BRI)
JAF	Judge Advocate of the Fleet
JAFC..........	James Allen Fan Club (EA)
JAFC..........	Jammie Ann Fan Club (EA)
JAFC..........	Japan Atomic Fuel Corp.
JAFC..........	John Anderson Fan Club [*Defunct*] (EA)
JAFC..........	Junior Acting Field Captain [*Military British*] (ROG)
JAFE..........	Joint Advanced Fighter Engine
JAFF..........	Electronic and Chaff Jamming (IEEE)
JAFHRO.......	Joint Armed Forces Housing Referral Office (MCD)
JAFNA........	Joint Air Force-NASA
JAFNC........	Joint Air Force-Navy Committee
JAFO	Junior Acting Field Officer [*Military British*] (ROG)
JAFP	Jewish Agency for Palestine
JAFPUB.......	Joint Armed Forces Publication
J African L...	Journal of African Law [*A publication*] (DLA)
JAG...........	Indian Trails Public Library District, Wheeling, IL [*OCLC symbol*] (OCLC)
JAG...........	Jaguar [*Automobile*]
JAG...........	James Abram Garfield [*US president, 1831-1881*]
JAG...........	Jetag AB [*Switzerland ICAO designator*] (FAAC)
JAG...........	Jobs for America's Graduates [*An association*] (EA)
JAG...........	Judge Advocate General [*Air Force, Army, Navy*]
JAGA.........	Military Affairs Division, Office of Judge Advocate General, United States Army (DLA)
JAGAR........	Judge Advocate General's Area Representatives
JAGB..........	Jockeys' Association [*British*] (DBA)
JAG Bull	Judge Advocate General Bulletin [*Air Force A publication*] (DLA)
JAGC.........	Judge Advocate General's Corps
JAG CMR (AF)...	Judge Advocate General Court-Martial Reports [*Air Force A publication*] (DLA)
JAG Comp CMO (Navy)...	Judge Advocate General Compilation of Court-Martial Orders [*Navy A publication*] (DLA)
JAGD	Judge Advocate General's Department [*Air Force, Army*]
JAG Dig Op...	Judge Advocate General Digest of Opinions [*A publication*] (DLA)
JAGDR........	Judge Advocate General's Department Reserve
Jagg Torts ...	Jaggard on Torts [*A publication*] (DLA)
JAGINST	Office of the Judge Advocate General Instructions [*Navy*]
JAGIT.........	Joint Air-Ground Instruction Team
JAG L Rev ...	United States. Air Force Judge Advocate General. Law Review [*A publication*] (DLA)
JAG Man......	Judge Advocate General Manual (Navy) [*A publication*] (DLA)
JAGN	Judge Advocate General of the Navy
JAGO	Judge Advocate General's Office
JAGOS	Joint Air-Ground Operations System [*Military*]
J Agric W Aust...	Journal of Agriculture of Western Australia [*A publication*]
J Agr Ind SA...	Journal of Agricultural Industry, South Australia [*A publication*]
J Agr Tax'n & L...	Journal of Agricultural Taxation and Law [*A publication*] (DLA)
JAGRY	Jaguar PLC (MHDW)
JAGS	Joint Army-Air Force Air-Ground Study
JAGS	Judge Advocate General's School (DLA)
JAGT.........	Procurement Division, Judge Advocate General, United States Army (DLA)
Ja Guara......	Jacobus Guaraguilia [*Authority cited in pre-1607 legal work*] (DSA)
JAGUAR-V ..	Jamming Guarded Radio - VHF [*Very High Frequency*] (PDAA)
JAH............	Glencoe Public Library, Glencoe, IL [*OCLC symbol*] (OCLC)
JAH............	Journal of African History [*A publication*]
JAH............	Journal of American History [*A publication*] (BRI)
JAHI..........	Jordan Amer Hldgs [*NASDAQ symbol*] (TTSB)
JAHI..........	Jordan American Holdings, Inc. [*NASDAQ symbol*] (SAG)
JAHIW	Jordan Amer Hldgs Wrrt [*NASDAQ symbol*] (TTSB)
Jahrb f Cl Phil Suppl...	Jahrbucher fuer Classische Philologie. Supplementband [*A publication*] (OCD)
Jahresb........	Jahresberichte ueber die Fortschritte der Altertumswissenschaft [1873-] [*A publication*] (OCD)
JAHWGS	Joint Ad Hoc Working Group on Shipping [*ASEAN*]
JAI	JAI Press [*Division of Johnson Associates, Inc.*]
JAI	Jaipur [*India*] [*Airport symbol*] (OAG)
JAI	Jaipur [*India*] [*Geomagnetic observatory code*]
JAI	Jami'at Al Islan [*Defunct*] (EA)
JAI	Japan-America Institute [*Defunct*] (EA)
JAI	Jewish Agency for Israel [*United Israel Appeal*] [*Absorbed by*] (EA)
JAI	Job Accounting Interface
JAI	Johnson Associates Inc. (GAAI)
Jai	Johnson Associates, Incorporated, Greenwich, CT [*Library symbol Library of Congress*] (LCLS)
JAI	Joint Administrative Instruction
JAI	Joint Staff Administrative Instruction [*Military*]
JAI	Juvenile Amaurotic Idiocy [*Medicine*]
JAI	Lake Forest Library, Lake Forest, IL [*OCLC symbol*] (OCLC)
JAI	M/S Jet Airways Ltd. [*India*] [*FAA designator*] (FAAC)
JAIA	Japan Automobile Importers Association
JAIA	Journal. Australian Indonesian Association [*A publication*]
JAIC	Joint Air Intelligence Center (DOMA)
JAICI.........	Japanese Association for International Chemical Information [*Tokyo*]
JAIEA	Joint Atomic Information Exchange Agency (SAA)
JAIEG.........	Joint Atomic Information Exchange Group [*DoD*]
JAIF	Japan Atomic Industrial Forum
JAII	Johnstown America Indus [*NASDAQ symbol*] (TTSB)
JAII	Johnstown America Industries, Inc. [*NASDAQ symbol*] (SAG)
JAIM	Job Analysis and Interest Measurement
JAIMS........	Japan-American Institute of Management Science
JAIO	Joint Assessment and Initiatives Office [*Military*]
Jaipur LJ	Jaipur Law Journal [*India*] [*A publication*] (DLA)
JAJ............	Waubonsee Community College, Sugar Grove, IL [*OCLC symbol*] (OCLC)
JAJC	Journalism Association of Junior Colleges [*Later, JACC*]
JAJO	January, April, July, and October [*Denotes quarterly payments of interest or dividends in these months*] [*Business term*]
Jakarta	Jakarta Growth Fund [*Associated Press*] (SAG)
JAKE	Jakes Pizza International [*NASDAQ symbol*] (SAG)
JAKE	Jakes Pizza Intl [*NASDAQ symbol*] (TTSB)
JakePza	Jakes Pizza International [*Associated Press*] (SAG)
JAKFORCE...	Jammu and Kashmir Force [*British military*] (DMA)
JAKIS........	Japanese Keyword Indexing Simulator
JAKK.........	JAKKS Pacific [*NASDAQ symbol*] (TTSB)
JAKK.........	Jakks Pacific, Inc. [*NASDAQ symbol*] (SAG)
JAL...........	Japan Air Lines
JAL...........	Japan Air Lines Ltd. [*ICAO designator*] (FAAC)
JAL...........	Jet Approach Landing Charts (FAAC)
JAL...........	Jewish Apocryphal Literature [*A publication*] (BJA)
JAL...........	Journal of Academic Librarianship [*A publication*] (BRI)
JAL...........	Judge Advocate Library, Department of the Navy, Alexandria, VA [*OCLC symbol*] (OCLC)
JALAP........	Jalapae [*Jalap*] [*Pharmacology*] (ROG)
Jalate	Jalate, Inc. [*Associated Press*] (SAG)
JALC	Jet Approach and Landing Chart (AFM)
JAlden	Alden [*John*] Financial Corp. [*Associated Press*] (SAG)
JALPG........	Joint Automatic Language Processing Group
JALT	Journal. Association of Law Teachers [*A publication*] (DLA)
JAM	Jail Accounting Microcomputer System
JAM	Jamaica [*ANSI three-letter standard code*] (CNC)
JAM	James [*New Testament Book*] (WDAA)
JaM	J A Micropublishing, Inc., Eastchester, NY [*Library symbol Library of Congress*] (LCLS)
JAM	Jamieson Scotch Dictionary [*A publication*] (ROG)
JAM	Jamming [*Military*] (NVT)
JAM	Jet Age Malfunction (IAA)
JAM	Job Analysis Memorandum
JAM	Job Assignment Memorandum
JAM	Joint Analysed Make-up [*Computer-controlled attachment*] (PDAA)
JAM	JUMPS [*Joint Uniform Military Pay System*] Action Memorandum (NVT)
JAM	Just a Minute [*Computer hacker terminology*] (NHD)
JAM	Moraine Valley Community College, Palos Hills, IL [*OCLC symbol*] (OCLC)
Jama	Jamaica (VRA)

JAMA............ Japan Automobile Manufacturers Association, Washington Office (EA)
JAMA............ Moslem People's Revolutionary Movement [*Iran*] [*Political party*] (PPW)
JAMAC......... Job Analysis Memorandum Activity Chart
JAMAC......... Joint Aeronautical Materials Activity [*Military*] (AABC)
JAMAG......... Joint American Military Advisory Group
JAMASS...... Japanese Medical Abstract Scanning System [*International Medical Information Center*] [*Japan*] (NITA)
JAMB............ Joint Air Movements Board [*Military*]
J Am Bankers' Assn... Journal. American Bankers Association [*A publication*] (DLA)
J Am Cult .... Journal of American Culture [*A publication*] (BRI)
James.......... James' Reports [*2 Nova Scotia*] [*A publication*] (DLA)
James & Mont... Jameson and Montagu's English Bankruptcy Reports [*Vol. 2 of Glyn and Jameson*] [*1821-28*] [*A publication*] (DLA)
James Bk L... James' Bankrupt Law PB (DLA)
James Const Con... Jameson's Constitutional Convention [*A publication*] (DLA)
James Ct Mar... James on Courts-Martial [*A publication*] (DLA)
James Fr Soc... James' Guide to Friendly Societies [*A publication*] (DLA)
James JS..... James' Law of Joint Stock Companies [*A publication*] (DLA)
James Madison U... James Madison University (GAGS)
JamesnIn..... Jameson Inns, Inc. [*Associated Press*] (SAG)
James (N Sc)... James' Reports [*2 Nova Scotia*] [*A publication*] (DLA)
James Op.... James' Opinions, Charges, Etc. [*A publication*] (DLA)
James Salv... James on Salvage [*1867*] [*A publication*] (DLA)
James Sel Cas... James' Select Cases [*1835-55*] [*Nova Scotia*] [*A publication*] (DLA)
James Sel Cases... James' Select Cases [*1835-55*] [*Nova Scotia*] [*A publication*] (DLA)
James Sh ... James' Merchant Shipping [*1866*] [*A publication*] (DLA)
JAMEX......... Jamming Exercise [*Military*] (NVT)
JAMG........... Jamming
JAMG........... Juvenile Autoimmune Myasthenia Gravis [*Medicine*] (DAVI)
JAMHEP....... Joint Aircraft Hurricane Plan
JAMIA.......... Journal of the American Medical Informatics Association [*A publication*] (DMAA)
JAMINTEL.... Jamaica International Telecommunications Ltd. [*Kingston*] [*Telecommunications service*]
JamKI-L....... Institute of Jamaica, National Library of Jamaica, Kingston, Jamaica [*Library symbol*] [*Library of Congress*] (LCLS)
JamKLS....... Jamaica Library Service, Kingston, Jamaica [*Library symbol Library of Congress*] (LCLS)
JamKU......... University of the West Indies, Mona, Kingston, Jamaica [*Library symbol Library of Congress*] (LCLS)
JAML............ Journal of Arts Management, Law & Society [*A publication*] (BRI)
Jam LJ .... Jamaica Law Journal [*A publication*] (DLA)
JAMMAT...... Joint American Military Mission for Aid to Turkey (MUGU)
JAMOT......... Julie/Jezebel [*Sonobuoy Systems*] Airborne Maintenance Operator Trainee [*Navy*] (MCD)
JAMP........... JINTACCS [*Joint Interoperability of Tactical Command and Control System*] Army Management Plan (MCD)
JAMPAC....... Jamming Package [*Air Force*]
JAMPACK .... Jamming Package [*Air Force*] (MCD)
JAMPO......... Joint Allied Military Petroleum Office [*NATO*]
JAMPS......... JINTACCS [*Joint Interoperability of Tactical Command and Control Systems*] Automated Message Preparation System (MCD)
JAMREP....... Jamming Report
JAMS............ Jameson Inns [*NASDAQ symbol*] (TTSB)
JAMS............ Jameson Inns, Inc. [*NASDAQ symbol*] (SAG)
JAMS............ Joint Agency for Municipal Securities Dealers
JAMS............ Journal. Academy of Marketing Science [*A publication*]
Jam St......... Jamaica Statutes [*A publication*] (DLA)
J Am St .... Journal of American Studies [*A publication*] (BRI)
JAMSTEC.... Japan Marine Science and Technology Center
JAMTO......... Joint Airlines Military Traffic Office
JAMTRAC .... Jammers Tracked by Azimuth Crossings [*RADAR*]
JAN............... Emerald Airways Ltd. [*British*] [*FAA designator*] (FAAC)
JAN............... Jackson [*Mississippi*] [*Airport symbol*] (OAG)
JAN............... Jackson, MS [*Location identifier FAA*] (FAAL)
JAN............... Janes Aviation 748 Ltd. [*British ICAO designator*] (FAAC)
JAN............... Janina [*Greece*] [*Seismograph station code, US Geological Survey*] (SEIS)
JAN............... Janitor
JAN............... Jantar Resources Corp. [*Vancouver Stock Exchange symbol*]
JAN............... January (EY)
Jan............... January (ODBW)
JAN............... Japanese Accepted Name (DMAA)
JAN............... Japanese Animation Network (EA)
JAN............... Jet Aircraft Noise
JAN............... Job Accommodation Network [*President's Committee on Employment of the Handicapped*] [*Information service or system*] (IID)
JAN............... Joint Army and Navy
JAN............... Judgment Analysis [*Psychology*]
JAN............... Justification for Authority to Negotiate [*Military*]
JAN............... Lincoln Christian College, Lincoln, IL [*OCLC symbol*] (OCLC)
JANA............ Jamahiriyah News Agency [*Libya*]
JANAC......... Joint Army-Navy Assessment Committee [*World War II*]
JANAF.......... Joint Army-Navy-Air Force
JANAFPAC.... Joint Army-Navy-Air Force, Pacific General Message [*Serially numbered*] (CINC)
JANAIA .... Joint Army-Navy Aircraft Instrument Action (MCD)
JANAIR .... Joint Army-Navy Aircraft Instrument Research
JANALP........ Joint Army-Navy-Air Force Logistics Policy
JANALP........ Joint Army-Navy-Air Force Logistics Publication

Jan Angl ...... Jani Anglorum Facies Nova [*1680*] [*A publication*] (DLA)
JANAP........... Joint Army-Navy-Air Force Procedure [*NATO*] (NATG)
JANAP........... Joint Army-Navy-Air Force Publication
JANARS......... Joint Army-Navy-Air Force Radiotelephone System (IAA)
JANAST......... Joint Army-Navy-Air Force Sea Transportation Message
JanBell.......... Jan Bell Marketing, Inc. [*Associated Press*] (SAG)
JANBMC........ Joint Army-Navy Ballistic Missile Committee
JANC............. Junior Army and Navy Club [*British*] (DSUE)
JANCOM........ Joint Army-Navy Communications
JANCWR....... Joint Army and Navy Committee on Welfare and Recreation
J & A............. Justification and Approval [*Army*]
J&A............... Justification and Approval (AAGC)
J & B............ Justerini and Brooks [*Scotch*]
J & C............ Jones and Cary's Irish Exchequer Reports [*1838-39*] [*A publication*] (DLA)
J & D............ June and December [*Denotes semiannual payments of interest or dividends in these months*] [*Business term*]
J & E............ Jehovistic and Elohistic [*Theology*]
J & F............ Job and Function [*Air Force*] (AAG)
J & H............ Johnson and Hemming's English Vice-Chancellors' Reports [*A publication*] (DLA)
J & H Hind L... Johnson and Houghton's Institutes of Hindoo Law [*A publication*] (DLA)
J & J............ January and July [*Denotes semiannual payments of interest or dividends in these months*] [*Business term*]
J & J............ Johnson and Johnson [*Commercial firm*] (DAVI)
J & J Sn........ J & J Snack Foods Corp. [*Associated Press*] (SAG)
J & K............ All India Reporter, Jammu and Kashmir [*A publication*] (DLA)
J & L............ Jones and La Touche's Irish Chancery Reports [*A publication*] (DLA)
J & La T....... Jones and La Touche's Irish Chancery Reports [*A publication*] (DLA)
J & L SpSt... J & L Specialty Steel [*Associated Press*] (SAG)
J & P............ Joannou & Paraskevaides [*Construction company*] [*British*]
J & P............ Joists and Planks [*Technical drawings*]
J & P............ Journal and Proceedings [*Australia A publication*]
J & P............ Justice and Peace [*An association Scotland*] (EAIO)
J & Proc Aust Chem Inst... Journal and Proceedings. Australian Chemical Institute. [*A publication*]
J & Proc Roy Soc WA... Journal and Proceedings. Royal Society of Western Australia [*A publication*]
J & S............ Jebb and Symes' Irish Queen's Bench Reports [*A publication*] (DLA)
J & S............ Jones and Spencer's Superior Court Reports [*33-61 New York*] [*A publication*] (DLA)
J & S............ Judah and Swan's Jamaica Reports [*1839*] [*A publication*] (DLA)
J & S Jam..... Judah and Swan's Jamaica Reports [*1839*] [*A publication*] (DLA)
J & V............ Jones and Varick's Laws of New York [*A publication*] (DLA)
J & W............ Jacob and Walker's English Chancery Reports [*A publication*] (DLA)
J & WO........ Jettison and Washing Overboard
JANE............. Joint Air Force-Navy Experiment (MUGU)
JANE............. Journalists Against Nuclear Extermination [*British*] (DI)
JANET........... Joint Academic Network [*Proposed supercomputer network*]
JANET........... Joint Army-Navy Experimental and Testing Board
JANET........... Just Another Network [*University of Waterloo*] [*Canada*]
Janex........... Janex International, Inc. [*Associated Press*] (SAG)
JANFU........... Joint Army-Navy Foul Up [*Military slang*] [*Bowdlerized version*]
JANGO.......... Junior Army-Navy Guild Organization [*Organization of teenage daughters of military officers, who helped out in war work*] [*World War II*]
JANGRID....... Joint Army-Navy Grid System [*NATO*]
JANIC............ Joint Army-Navy Information Center
JANIS............ Joint Army-Navy Intelligence Studies
JANMAT........ Joint Army-Navy Machine Tools Committee (AAG)
JANMAT........ Joint Army-Navy Material
JANMB.......... Joint Army and Navy Munitions Board [*Terminated, 1947*]
JANNAF .... Joint-Army-Navy-NASA-Air Force Interagency Propulsion Committee (MCD)
JANNF .... Jannock Ltd. [*NASDAQ symbol*] (SAG)
Jannock........ Jannock Ltd. [*Associated Press*] (SAG)
JANOT.......... Joint Army-Navy Ocean Terminal
JANP............. Joint Army-Navy Procedure
JANP............. Joint Army-Navy Publication
JANPPA......... Joint Army-Navy Petroleum Purchase Agency
JANS............. Jet Aircraft Noise Survey
JANS............. Joint Army-Navy Specification (IAA)
JANSPEC....... Joint Army-Navy Specification
JANSRP .... Jet Aircraft Noise Survey Research Program
JANSTD .... Joint Army-Navy Standard [*NATO*] (NATG)
JANTA........... Journal of the Australian Natural Therapists Association [*A publication*]
JANTAB......... Joint Army and Navy Technical Aeronautical Board
JANTRL......... Janitorial
JANTX........... Joint Army-Navy Tested Extra
JANUS........... Joint Analog Numeric Understanding System
JANV............. Janvier [*January*] [*French*]
JANWSA......... Joint Army-Navy War Shipping Administration
JANX............. Janex International, Inc. [*NASDAQ symbol*] (SAG)
JANX............. Janex Intl. [*NASDAQ symbol*] (TTSB)
JANXW.......... Janex Intl. Wrrt [*NASDAQ symbol*] (TTSB)
JANY............. January (ROG)
JAO............... Joint Area of Operations (DOMA)
JAO............... Prospect Heights Public Library District, Prospect Heights, IL [*OCLC symbol*] (OCLC)
JAOC............. Joint Air Operations Center [*Air Force*]
JAp .... Against Apion [*Josephus*] (BJA)
JAP............... G. D. Searle & Co., Inc., Skokie, IL [*OCLC symbol*] (OCLC)
JAP............... Japan (KSC)

Jap............... Japan (VRA)
JAP .... Japanese (ROG)
Jap............... Japanese (ODBW)
jap .... Japanned [*Finished with a hard, glossy varnish*] (BARN)
JAP .... Japan Photo [*Norway*] [*FAA designator*] (FAAC)
JAP .... J. A. Prestwick [*British auto and motorcycle engine maker*]
JAP .... Jerusalem Academic Press (BJA)
JAP .... Jewish Agency for Palestine
JAP .... Jewish-American Princess [*Slang*]
JAP .... Joint Acceptance Plan (AAG)
JAP .... Joint Apprenticeship Program [*Department of Labor*]
JAP .... Judicial Appointments Project (EA)
JAP .... Juntas de Accao Patriotica [*Patriotic Action Boards*] [*Portuguese Political party*] (PPE)
JAP .... Jupiter Atmospheric Probe
JAP .... Juventudes de Accion Popular [*Spanish*] (PPE)
JAPA .... Jane Addams Peace Association (EA)
JAPA .... Japan Area
JAPACS........ Japanese Pacific Climate Study [*Marine science*] (OSRA)
JAPACS........ Japanese Pacific Ocean Climate Studies (USDC)
Japan Ann L & Pol... Japan Annual of Law and Politics [*A publication*] (DLA)
JAPANMEC... Japan International Measuring and Control Industry Show
JapARE......... Japanese Antarctic Research Expedition [*1956-*]
JAPATIC....... Japan Patient Information Center [*Information service or system*] (IID)
JAPC............ Joint Air Photo Center [*NATO*] (NATG)
JAPCO .... Jamestown Paint & Varnish Co.
JAPCO .... Japan Atomic Power Co.
JAPIA.......... Japan Auto Parts Industries Association
JAPIC........... Japan Pharmaceutical Information Center [*Tokyo*] [*Information service or system*] (IID)
JAPIO.......... Japan Patent Information Organization [*Database producer*]
JAPIT.......... Japanese Association for the Promotion of International Trade (EY)
JAPN............ Japan Air Lines Co. Ltd. [*NASDAQ symbol*] (NQ)
JapnAr......... Japan Airlines [*Associated Press*] (SAG)
JapnAr......... Japan Airlines Co. Ltd. [*Associated Press*] (SAG)
JapnEq......... [*The*] Japan Equity Fund, Inc. [*Associated Press*] (SAG)
JAPNY .... Japan Airlines Co. Ltd ADR [*NASDAQ symbol*] (TTSB)
JAPO............ Joint Area Petroleum Office
JAPOS .... JAPOS Study Group [*Defunct*] (EA)
JAPOS .... Journalists, Authors and Poets on Stamps Study Unit (EA)
JAPP............ Japanese Patent (IAA)
Jap P .... [*The*] Pharmacopoeia of Japan [*A publication*]
JAPS............ Japanese American Philatelic Society [*Later, JASP*]
JAPS............ Joint Administrative Planning Section [*Joint Planning Staff*] [*World War II*]
JAPSS.......... Joint Automated Planning Support System [*of JOPS*] [*Military*]
JAQ.............. Jacquinot Bay [*Papua New Guinea*] [*Airport symbol*] (OAG)
JAQ.............. Job Activities Questionnaire
JAQ.............. Passionist Academic Institute, Chicago, IL [*OCLC symbol*] (OCLC)
JAR.............. Airlink Luftverkehrsgesellschaft GmbH [*Austria ICAO designator*] (FAAC)
JAR.............. Jamming Avoidance Response
JAR.............. Jargon (WDAA)
JAR.............. J. Arthur Rank [*Motion picture company in England*]
JAR.............. JavaSoft Java Archive [*Computer science*]
JAr.............. Jewish Aramaic (BJA)
JAR.............. Jewish Autonomous Region [*Eastern Siberia*]
JAR.............. Jews for Animal Rights (EA)
JAR.............. Job Appraisal Review (PDAA)
JAR.............. Joint Airworthiness Requirements (MCD)
JAR.............. Joint Aviation Requirement [*FAA*] (TAG)
JAR.............. Journal of Advertising Research [*Advertising Research Foundation*] [*A publication*]
JAR.............. Jump Address Register
JAR.............. Junior Admitting Resident [*Medicine*] (DAVI)
JAR.............. Justice Acquisition Regulation [*A publication*] (AAGC)
JAR.............. Zion-Benton Library District, Zion, IL [*OCLC symbol*] (OCLC)
Jar & By Conv... Jarman and Bythewood's Conveyancing [*A publication*] (DLA)
JARC............ Jewish Association for Retarded Citizens (EA)
JARC............ Joint Air Reconnaissance Center [*NATO*] (NATG)
JARCC.......... Joint Air Reconnaissance Coordination Center [*Military*] (MCD)
Jar Chy Pr ... Jarman's Chancery Practice [*A publication*] (DLA)
Jar Cr Tr...... Jardine's Criminal Trials [*A publication*] (DLA)
JARD .... Jardines
JardFICh...... Jardine Fleming China Region [*Associated Press*] (SAG)
Jard Ind...... Jardine's Index to Howell's State Trials [*A publication*] (DLA)
JARE........... Japanese Antarctic Research Expedition [*1956-*]
JARI........... Japan Automobile Research Institute
JARI........... Japan Automotive Research Institute
JARIB.......... Joint Air Reconnaissance Intelligence Board [*Australia*]
JARIC.......... Joint Aerial Reconnaissance Interpretation Center (MCD)
JARIC.......... Joint Air Reconnaissance Intelligence Centre [*British*]
Jar Pow Dev... Jarman's Edition of Powell on Devises [*A publication*] (DLA)
JARRP .... Japan Association for Radiation Research on Polymers
JARS........... Alltrista Corp. [*NASDAQ symbol*] (SAG)
JARS........... Job Accounting Report System (MHDI)
JARS........... Journalization and Recovery System (PDAA)
JARTRAN..... James A. Ryder Transportation [*Acronym is trade name of truck-rental firm*]
Jar Wills...... Jarman on Wills [*8 eds.*] [*1841-51*] [*A publication*] (DLA)
Jas.............. James [*New Testament book*]
JAS.............. Jamestown [*California*] [*Seismograph station code, US Geological Survey*] (SEIS)
JAS .... Jane Austen Society [*Basingstoke, Hampshire, England*] (EAIO)

JAS .... Japan Air System Co. Ltd. [*ICAO designator*] (FAAC)
JAS .... Jasper, TX [*Location identifier FAA*] (FAAL)
JAS .... Jazz Arts Society (EA)
JAS .... Jenkins Activity Survey [*Personality development test*] [*Psychology*]
JAS .... Jewish Agricultural Society (EA)
JAS .... Job Accounting System
JAS .... Job Activity Survey
JAS .... Job Analysis Schedule [*Department of Labor*]
JAS .... Job Analysis System [*Computer program*]
JAS .... Job Attitude Scale [*Employment test*]
JAS .... Johnny Alfalfa Sprout [*Defunct*] (EA)
JAS .... Joint Administration Services
JAS .... Joint Airmiss Section [*Aviation*] (DA)
JAS .... Joint Association Survey [*American Petroleum Institute, Independent Petroleum Association of America, and Mid-Continent Oil and Gas Association*]
JAS .... Journal Access Service [*Center for Research Libraries*]
JAS .... Journal of Asian Studies [*A publication*] (BRI)
JAS .... Journal of Atmospheric Sciences [*A publication*] (SSD)
JAS .... Journals Access Service [*Center for Research Libraries*]
J As .... Judicial Assessor [*Ghana*] [*A publication*] (DLA)
JAS .... Junior Astronomical Society (EAIO)
JAS .... Juvenile Ankylosing Spondylitis [*Medicine*] (DMAA)
JAS .... Lake Villa District Library, Lake Villa, IL [*OCLC symbol*] (OCLC)
JAS-1............ Japan Amateur Satellite-1
JASA .... Jewish Association for Services for the Aged (EA)
JASA .... Joint Antisubmarine Action
JASA .... Junior Assistant Stores Accountant [*British military*] (DMA)
JASAP .... Julie [*Sonobuoy System*] Automatic Search and Attack Plotter [*Navy*] (MCD)
JASAR .... Jittered and Swept Active RADAR
JASASA....... Joint Air-Surface Antisubmarine Action
JASB .... Joint Advisory Survey Board [*British*]
JASC .... Japan-America Student Conference (EA)
JASC .... Japan Asia Sea Cable
JASC .... JPL [*Jet Propulsion Laboratory*] Astronautical Star Catalog (KSC)
JASCO .... Joint Assault Signal Co. [*Small unit in Pacific amphibious warfare*] [*World War II*]
JASDA .... Julie [*Sonobuoy System*] Automatic Sonic Data Analyzer [*Navy*]
JASDF......... Japanese Air Self-Defense Force
JASG .... Joint Advanced Study Group
JASGP .... Joint Advanced Study Group
JASIN .... Joint Air Sea Interaction [*National Science Foundation/United Kingdom*]
JASIN.......... Joint Air-Sea Interaction Program [*Marine science*] (OSRA)
JASIN.......... Joint Air-Sea Interaction Program [*Global Atmospheric Research Program*] (USDC)
JASLS......... Japanese American Society for Legal Studies (EA)
JASMMM.... Joint Aviation Supply and Maintenance Material Management (DNAB)
JASMU........ Journal pour l'Avancement des Soins Medicaux d'Urgence [*A publication*]
JASN.......... Jason, Inc. [*NASDAQ symbol*] (NQ)
JASNA .... Jane Austen Society of North America (EA)
Jason.......... Jason, Inc. [*Associated Press*] (SAG)
JASORS ...... Joint Advanced Special Operations Radio System [*Military*] (RDA)
JASP .... Japanese American Society for Philately (EA)
JASPA......... Jesuit Association of Student Personnel Administrators (EA)
JASPER....... Joint Academic Services Providers to Education and Research (AIE)
JASPR .... Jasper [*Gem*] (ROG)
JASR.......... JTPA [*Job Training and Partnership Act*] Annual Status Report (OICC)
JASS........... Joint Antisatellite Study
JASS........... Joint Anti-Submarine School [*British military*] (DMA)
JASS........... JUMPS [*Joint Uniform Military Pay System*] Automated Support System [*or Supplemental*] [*Military*]
JASS-AC ...... JUMPS [*Joint Uniform Military Pay System*] Automated Supplemental System-Active Component [*Military*]
JASSC......... Japan-America Society of Southern California
JASSM......... Joint Acoustic Surveillance System Model [*Military*] (CAAL)
J Ass'n L Teachers... Journal. Association of Law Teachers [*A publication*] (DLA)
J Assoc L Teachers... Journal. Association of Law Teachers [*A publication*] (DLA)
JASS-RC ...... JUMPS [*Joint Uniform Military Pay System*] Automated Support System - Reserve Corps
JAST........... Jazz Action Society of Tasmania
JAST........... Joint Advanced Strike Technology [*DoD*]
JAST........... Joint Advanced Strike Technology [*Program*] [*Air Force*] [*Navy*] (DOMA)
JAST........... Joint Air Support Tactics [*Military*]
JASTD......... Junior Assistant Steward [*British military*] (DMA)
JASTOP....... Jet Assist Stop
JASU.......... Jet Aircraft Starting Unit (AFM)
JASW.......... Japan-America Society of Washington (EA)
JAT............ Jabat [*Marshall Islands*] [*Airport symbol*] (OAG)
JAT............ Jam Angle Tracking
JAT............ Job Accounting Table
JAT............ Joint Agency Training
JAT............ Jugoslovenski Aerotransport [*Yugoslav Air Transport*] [*ICAO designator*]
JAT............ Junior Aptitude Tests [*Educational test*]
JAT .... Mennonite Hospital, Health Sciences Library, Bloomington, IL [*OCLC symbol*] (OCLC)
JATAN.......... Japan Tropical Rainforest Action Network
JATC............ Joint Apprenticeship and Training Committee [*Bureau of Apprenticeship and Training*] [*Department of Labor*]
JATCC......... Joint Air Traffic Control Center [*Military*]

JATCCCP...... Joint Advanced Tactical Command, Control, and Communications Program [Military]
JATCCCS..... Joint Advanced Tactical Command, Control, and Communications System [Military] (MCD)
JATCCS....... Joint Advanced Tactical Command and Control System [Military] (SAA)
JATCO......... Japan Automatic Transmission Co.
JATE........... Joint Air Transport Establishment [Military British]
JATES......... Japan Techno-Economics Society (EA)
JATF........... Joint Amphibious Task Force (NVT)
JATLA......... Journal. American Trial Lawyers Association [A publication] (DLA)
JATM.......... Joint Antitactical Missile System (Provisional) [Army] (RDA)
JATMA........ Japan Automobile Tire Manufacturers Association
JATO.......... Jet-Assisted Takeoff
JATP........... Jazz at the Philharmonic
JATP........... Joint Air Training Plan
JATP........... Joint Air Transportation Plan (AABC)
JATS........... Joint Air Transportation Service
JAU........... American Hospital Supply Corp., Evanston, IL [OCLC symbol] (OCLC)
JAU........... Jacksboro, TN [Location identifier FAA] (FAAL)
JAUN.......... Jaundice [Medicine]
JAUND........ Jaundice [Medicine]
J Aust Stud... Journal of Australian Studies [A publication]
J Aus War M... Journal. Australian War Memorial [A publication]
JAV........... Chicago, IL [Location identifier FAA] (FAAL)
JAV........... Dr. William M. Scholl College of Podiatric Medicine, Chicago, IL [OCLC symbol] (OCLC)
JAV........... Janes Aviation Ltd. [British ICAO designator] (FAAC)
JAV........... Java
jav............ Javanese [MARC language code Library of Congress] (LCCP)
Jav........... Javolenus Priscus [Flourished, 60-120] [Authority cited in pre-1607 legal work] (DSA)
JAV........... Job Analysis Vocabulary (OICC)
JAVA.......... Jamaica Association of Villas and Apartments [Later, JRJ]
JAVA.......... Jamming Amplitude Versus Azimuth (NVT)
JAVA.......... Jandel Video Analysis System
JavaCt........ Java Centrale, Inc. [Associated Press] (SAG)
JavaCtrl...... Java Centrale, Inc. [Associated Press] (SAG)
JAVC.......... Java Centrale [NASDAQ symbol] (TTSB)
JAVC.......... Java Centrale, Inc. [NASDAQ symbol] (SAG)
JAVCF........ Japan Australia Venture Capital Fund
Javelin........ Javelin Systems, Inc. [Associated Press] (SAG)
Javole........ Javolenus Priscus [Flourished, 60-120] [Authority cited in pre-1607 legal work] (DSA)
JAVS.......... JOVIAL Automated Verification System (MCD)
JAW........... Jamahiriya Airways [Libya] [ICAO designator] (FAAC)
JAW........... Standard Oil Co. (Indiana), Central Research Library, Naperville, IL [OCLC symbol] (OCLC)
JAWF.......... Jet Augmented Wing Flap
JAWF.......... Joint Agriculture Weather Facility [Marine science] (OSRA)
JAWF.......... Joint Agriculture-Weather Facility (USDC)
JAWPB........ Joint Atomic Weapons Publications Board (AABC)
JAWPM....... Joint Atomic Weapons Planning Manual (AFM)
JAWPS........ Joint Atomic Weapons Publication System
JAWS......... Jamming and Warning System (MCD)
JAWS......... Japan Animal Welfare Society [London, England]
JAWS......... Jet Advance Warning System (PDAA)
JAWS......... Joint Airport Weather Studies [National Center for Atmospheric Research]
JAWS......... Joint Arctic Weather Stations [Canada-US]
JAWS......... Joint Attack Weapon System [Military] (MCD)
JAWS......... Josephson AttoWeber Switch [Data processor circuitry]
JAWS......... Junk Acronyms When Speaking [Program]
JAWS......... Just Another Work Station [Jargon] (NITA)
JAWTR........ Junior Assistant Writer [British military] (DMA)
JAWYS........ Join Airways (FAAC)
JAX........... Chicago School of Professional Psychology, Chicago, IL [OCLC symbol] (OCLC)
JAX........... Jacksonville [Florida] [Airport symbol] (OAG)
JAX........... JanAir, Inc. [ICAO designator] (FAAC)
JAX........... Mister Jax Fashions, Inc. [Toronto Stock Exchange symbol]
JAY........... J & J Air Charters Ltd. [British ICAO designator] (FAAC)
JAY........... Jayapura [Indonesia] [Seismograph station code, US Geological Survey] (SEIS)
JAY........... Travenol Laboratories, Morton Grove, IL [OCLC symbol] (OCLC)
JAYA......... Jayark Corp. [NASDAQ symbol] (NQ)
Jayark........ Jayark Corp. [Associated Press] (SAG)
Jayhwk....... Jayhawk Acceptance Corp. [Associated Press] (SAG)
JAYJ.......... Jay Jacobs [NASDAQ symbol] (TTSB)
JAYJ.......... Jay Jacobs, Inc. [NASDAQ symbol] (NQ)
JAYT.......... Jacobs [Jay], Inc. (MHDW)
JAZ........... Japan Air Charter Co. Ltd. [ICAO designator] (FAAC)
JB........... IML Air Services Ltd. [British ICAO designator] (ICDA)
Jb........... Jaarboek [Yearbook] [Netherlands] (BJA)
JB........... Jahrbuch [Yearbook] [German]
JB........... James Boswell [Initials used as pseudonym]
JB........... James Buchanan [US president, 1791-1868]
JB........... Jerusalem Bible
J-B........... Jet Barrier
JB........... Jet Black [Derogatory nickname for a black person]
JB........... Jet Bomb
JB........... Jiffy Bag
Jb........... Job [Old Testament book]
JB........... Job (MCD)

JB........... Job Bank (OICC)
JB........... Job Book
JB........... Joggle Blocks (MCD)
JB........... Johannes Baptista [John the Baptist] [Authority cited in pre-1607 legal work] (DSA)
JB........... John Bull [The typical Englishman]
JB........... Johore Bahru [Refers to Europeans named after Malaysian towns] (DSUE)
JB........... Joint Army-Navy Board
JB........... Joint Bond
JB........... Juggle Box
JB........... Jukeboxes [Public-performance tariff class] [British]
JB........... Jump If Below [Computer science] (PCM)
JB........... Junction Box [Technical drawings]
JB........... Junior Beadle [Ancient Order of Foresters]
JB........... Junior Birdman [Slang]
JB........... Junior Bookshelf [A publication] (BRI)
JB........... Juris Baccalaureus [Bachelor of Laws]
JB........... Lakeside Laboratories, Inc. [Research code symbol]
JB........... Pioneer Airways [ICAO designator] (AD)
JB........... Stetson Hat [After John Batterson Stetson, 19th-century American hat manufacturer] [Slang]
JBA........... Helijet Airways [Canada ICAO designator] (FAAC)
JBA........... Jewel Bearing Assembly
JBA........... John Burroughs Association (EA)
JBA........... Junction Box Assembly
JBA........... Junior Bluejackets of America (EA)
JBAFC........ Jan Berry and the Alohas Fan Club (EA)
JBAK......... Baker [J.], Inc. [NASDAQ symbol] (NQ)
JBAKC....... John Brown Anti-Klan Committee (EA)
JBANC....... Joint Baltic American National Committee (EA)
J-Bar......... Jet Runway Barrier [Aviation] (FAAC)
JBAS......... Jussi Bjorling Appreciation Society [British] (DBA)
JBBF......... Judo Black Belt Federation [Later, USJE]
JBBFC....... James Bond British Fan Club (EAIO)
JBBL......... Jamming of Beacons and Blind Landing [Aviation] (IAA)
JBC........... Jamaica Broadcasting Corp.
JBC........... [The] Jerome Biblical Commentary [Englewood Cliffs, NJ] [A publication] (BJA)
JBC........... Jesness Behavior Checklist [Psychology] (DAVI)
JBC........... Jewelers' Book Club (EA)
JBC........... Jewish Book Council [of the National Jewish Welfare Board] [Later, JWBJBC] (EA)
JBC........... Johnson Bible College [Tennessee]
JBC........... Joint Blood Council [Defunct] (EA)
JBC........... Joint Budget Committee (OICC)
JBC........... Journal. State Bar of California [A publication] (DLA)
JBCPS........ Journeyman Bakers' and Confectioners Pension Society [British] (BI)
JBCS......... James Branch Cabell Society (EA)
JBD........... Becton, Dickinson & Co., Paramus, NJ [OCLC symbol] (OCLC)
JBD........... James Brake [Aviation] (DA)
JBD........... Jet Blast Deflector
JBD........... Jewish Board of Deputies [Australia]
JBDAAFES ... Joint Board of Directors, Army-Air Force Exchange Service (AABC)
JBDFC....... James Bond 007 Fan Club [Defunct] (EA)
JBE........... Japanese B Encephalitis [Medicine]
JBE........... Jump If Below or Equal [Computer science] (PCM)
Jber.......... Jahresbericht [Journal, Annual Report] [German] (BJA)
JBES......... Jodrell Bank Experimental Station [British]
JBF........... James Beard Foundation (EA)
JBF........... James Buchanan Foundation (EA)
JBF........... Jeune Ballet de France
JBFC......... James Bond 007 Fan Club [British] (EAIO)
JBFC......... Jennifer Bassey Fan Club (EA)
JBFC......... Jennifer Burnett Fan Club (EA)
JBFC......... Johnny Bernard Fan Club (EA)
JBFCI........ Jon Beryl Fan Club International (EA)
JBFLP........ Journal of Banking and Finance Law and Practice [A publication]
JBFSAW..... Joint Board on Future Storage of Atomic Weapons
JBG........... Jewish Board of Guardians (EA)
JBHCPIUA.. Journeymen Barbers, Hairdressers, Cosmetologists and Proprietors' International Union of America (EA)
JBHT......... Hunt(JB)Transport [NASDAQ symbol] (TTSB)
JBHT......... Hunt [J. B.] Transport Services, Inc. [NASDAQ symbol] (NQ)
JBI........... Jacob Blaustein Institute for the Advancement of Human Rights (EA)
JBI........... Jewish Braille Institute of America (EA)
JBIA......... Jewish Braille Institute of America (EA)
JBIC......... Journal of Biological Inorganic Chemistry [A publication]
JBIL......... Jabil Circuit [NASDAQ symbol] (TTSB)
JBIL......... Jabil Circuit, Inc. [NASDAQ symbol] (SAG)
Jb Int R ...... Jahrbuch fuer Internationales und Auslaendisches Oeffentliches Recht [1948-] [A publication German] (ILCA)
JBJ........... Bellum Judaicum [Josephus] [Classical studies] (BJA)
JBJ........... James Bond Journalism [Term coined by leader Sinnathamby Bajaratman of Singapore and referring to Western journalism]
JBK........... Berkeley, CA [Location identifier FAA] (FAAL)
JBL........... James B. Lansing Sound, Inc.
JBL........... Jonesboro, LA [Location identifier FAA] (FAAL)
JBL........... Journal of Biblical Literature [A publication] (BRI)
JBL........... Jubilee
JBL........... Junior Bird League [British] (BI)
J/BLK........ Junction Block [Automotive engineering]
J Bl St .... Journal of Black Studies [A publication] (BRI)
JBM........... Jan Bell Marketing [AMEX symbol] (TTSB)
JBM........... Jan Bell Marketing, Inc. [AMEX symbol] (SPSG)

JBMA	John Burroughs Memorial Association (EA)
JBMI	Journalist Biographies Master Index [*A publication*]
JBMTO	Joint Bus Military Traffic Office (AABC)
JBNC	Jefferson Bancorp (FL) [*NASDAQ symbol*] (TTSB)
JBNC	Jefferson Bancorp, Inc. [*NASDAQ symbol*] (NQ)
JBNK	Jefferson Bankshares, Inc. [*NASDAQ symbol*] (NQ)
JBOH	Oxford [*J. B.*] Oxford Holdings [*NASDAQ symbol*] (SAG)
JBOR	Job Bank Operations Review [*Employment and Training Administration*] [*Department of Labor*]
JBOS	Job Banks Opening Summary [*Department of Labor*]
JB Oxfrd	JB Oxford Holdings [*Associated Press*] (SAG)
JBP	Jettison Booster Package [*NASA*]
JBP	John B. Pierce Foundation Laboratory [*New Haven, CT*]
JBP	Junior Bowhunter Program (EA)
JBPO	Joint Blood Program Office (DOMA)
JBR	Job Air Ltd. [*Czechoslovakia*] [*FAA designator*] (FAAC)
JBR	Jonesboro [*Arkansas*] [*Airport symbol*] (OAG)
JBR	Jonesboro, AR [*Location identifier FAA*] (FAAL)
J BRANNAM...	Just Brand Names [*Division of F. W. Woolworth Co.*]
J Broadcst	Journal of Broadcasting and Electronic Media [*A publication*] (BRI)
JBS	Jane Badler Society (EA)
JBS	Jewish Burial Society [*Australia*]
JBS	Job Search [*Job Training and Partnership Act*] (OICC)
JBS	John Birch Society (EA)
JBS	Joly Black Screen
JBS	Josephine Butler Society (EAIO)
JBSS	Sanfilippo [*John B.*] & Son [*NASDAQ symbol*] (SPSG)
JBT	Bethel, AK [*Location identifier FAA*] (FAAL)
JBT	Jewelers Board of Trade (EA)
JBU	John Brown University [*Siloam Springs, AR*]
JBUSDC	Joint Brazil-United States Defense Commission [*Terminated, 1977*]
JBUSMC	Joint Brazil-United States Military Commission
JBV	Jolt Beverage Co. Ltd. [*Vancouver Stock Exchange symbol*]
JC	Community Colleges [*Educational Resources Information Center (ERIC) Clearinghouse*] [*University of California at Los Angeles (UCLA)*] (PAZ)
JC	Jack Connection [*Electronics*] (IAA)
JC	Jack Cover
JC	Jakob-Creutzfeldt [*Disease or syndrome*] [*Neurology*] (DAVI)
JC	Janitor Closet (MSA)
JC	J. C. Smith Marketing Corp. [*Vancouver Stock Exchange symbol*]
JC	Jeanswear Communication (EA)
JC	Jefferson City [*Diocesan abbreviation*] [*Missouri*] (TOCD)
JC	Jenny Craig [*NYSE symbol*] (SPSG)
JC	Jersey Central Railroad
JC	Jesus Christ
JC	Jesus College [*Oxford or Cambridge*] [*England*] (DAS)
JC	Jewish Care [*British*] (EAIO)
JC	[*The*] Jewish Community: Its History and Structure to the American Revolution [*A publication*] (BJA)
JC	Jimmy Carter [*James Earl Carter, Jr.*] [*US president, 1924-*]
JC	Job Center
JC	Job Club
JC	Job Corps [*Department of Labor*]
JC	Jockey Club [*Later, TJC*] (EA)
JC	Johnson's New York Cases [*or Reports*] [*A publication*] (DLA)
JC	Joint Compound [*Plumbing*]
JC	Joule Cycle [*Physics*]
J/C	Joule per Coulomb [*Physics*] (DAVI)
JC	Journal Citation (NITA)
JC	Journal Code [*Online database field identifier*]
JC	Journal Coden [*Searchable fields*] (NITA)
JC	Journalists' Club [*Australia*]
JC	Journal of Chromatography [*A publication*]
JC	Journal of Communication [*A publication*] (BRI)
JC	JOVIAL Compiler [*Computer science*]
Jc	Juglans cinerea [*Butternut tree*]
jc	Juice
JC	Juice
JC	Julius Caesar [*Shakespearean work*]
JC	Jump on Condition [*Computer science*] (BUR)
JC	Jump-to-Contact [*Physics*]
JC	Junction (ADA)
JC	Junction Center [*Civil engineering*] (IAA)
JC	Junior Chamber of Commerce (WDAA)
JC	Junior Clinicians [*Medical students*] (DAVI)
JC	Junior College
JC	Jurisconsult
JC	Just Compensation [*Business term*] (MHDB)
JC	Justice Clerk
JC	Justiciary Cases [*Scotland*] [*A publication*] (DLA)
JC	Juvenile Court
JC	Rocky Mountain Airways [*ICAO designator*] (AD)
JCA	Jamming Control Authority (NATG)
JCA	Javelin Class Association (EA)
JCA	Jetcom SA [*Switzerland ICAO designator*] (FAAC)
JCA	Jewelry Crafts Association [*Later, JMA*]
JCA	Jewish Ceremonial Art [*A publication*] (BJA)
JCA	Jewish Colonization Association [*British*]
JCA	Joint Church Aid [*Biafra relief program in late 1960's*] [*Defunct*]
JCA	Joint Commission on Accreditation of Universities [*Military*]
JCA	Joint Communication Activity
JCA	Joint Communications Agency [*Military*]
JCA	Joint Construction Agency
JCA	Joint Cultural Appeal (EA)

JCA	Joint Custody Association (EA)
JCA	Junior Catering Accountant [*British military*] (DMA)
JCA	Juvenile Chronic Arthritis [*Medicine*] (DAVI)
JCAB	Japan Civil Aviation Bureau (MCD)
JCAC	Joint Civil Affairs Committee
JCACC	Joint Combat Airspace Command and Control Course (DOMA)
JCADIS	Joint Continental Aerospace Defense Integration Staff [*Military*] (AABC)
JCAE	Joint Committee on Atomic Energy [*of the US Congress*] [*Terminated*]
JCAEC	Joint Congressional Atomic Energy Commission (MUGU)
JCAH	Joint Commission on Accreditation of Hospitals [*Later, JCAHO*] (EA)
JCAHO	Joint Commission on Accreditation of Healthcare Organizations [*An association*]
JCAHPO	Joint Commission on Allied Health Personnel in Ophthalmology (EA)
JCAI	Joint Council of Allergy and Immunology (EA)
JCALM	Joint Committee on Aboriginal Lands and Mining [*Australia*]
JCALS	Joint Computer-Aided Acquisition and Logistic Support [*DoD*]
JCALS	Joint Computer-Aided Acquisition Logistics System [*Army*] (RDA)
JCAM	Joint Commission on Atomic Masses
J Can B	Juris Canna Baccalaureus [*Bachelor of Canon Law*]
J Cancer Res Comm	Journal. Cancer Research Committee. University of Sydney [*A publication*]
J Can D	Juris Canna Doctor [*Doctor of Canon Law*]
J Can M	Juris Canna Magister [*Master of Canon Law*]
JCAP	Joint Conventional Ammunition Program [*Army*]
JCAP	Joint Coordinated Ammunition Production (MCD)
JCAP-CG	Joint Conventional Ammunition Program Coordinating Group [*Army*]
JCAR	Joint Commission on Applied Radioactivity
J card	Jacket Card [*A printed card inside the box holding a cassette tape or compact disc*] (WDMC)
JCARD	Joint Committee on Agricultural Research and Development [*Agency for International Development*]
JCarlFut	Jack Carl/312 Futures, Inc. [*Associated Press*] (SAG)
J Car P & E	Journal of Career Planning and Employment [*A publication*] (BRI)
J-CATCH	Joint Countering Attack Helicopter Exercises (RDA)
JCA-USA	Joint Church Aid - United States of America [*See also JCA*] [*Defunct*] (EA)
JCB	Japan Convention Bureau (EA)
JCB	J. C. Bamford Excavators [*British*]
JCB	Joacaba [*Brazil*] [*Airport symbol*] (AD)
JCB	Job Control Block [*Computer science*] (BUR)
JCB	Joint Communications Board
JCB	Joint Computer Bureau [*Office of Population Census and Surveys*] [*British*]
JCB	Joint Consultative Board [*NATO*] (NATG)
JCB	Juris Canonici Baccalaureus [*Bachelor of Canon Law*]
JCB	Juris Civilis Baccalaureus [*Bachelor of Civil Law*]
JCBA	Jewish Conciliation Board of America (EA)
JCBC	Joint Committee on Building Codes [*Later, Model Code Standardization Council*] (EA)
JCBC	Jute Carpet Backing Council (EA)
JCBMI	Joint Committee for the British Memorial Industry (DBA)
JCBS	Jacobson Stores, Inc. [*NASDAQ symbol*] (NQ)
JCBSF	Joint Commission for Black Sea Fisheries
JCC	Jamestown Community College [*New York*]
JCC	Janney Cylinder Co.
JCC	Japanese Chamber of Commerce of New York [*Later, JCCINY*] (EA)
JCC	Jarvis Christian College [*Hawkins, TX*]
JCC	Jarvis Christian College, Hawkins, TX [*OCLC symbol*] (OCLC)
JCC	Jesus College, Cambridge [*England*] (ROG)
JCC	Jet Circulation Control
JCC	Jewish Chaplains Council (EA)
JCC	Jewish Community Center
JCC	Jharkhand Coordination Committee [*Jharkhand Samanvaya Samiti*] [*India*] [*Political party*]
JCC	Jilin Chemical Inc ADS [*NYSE symbol*] (TTSB)
JCC	Jilin Chemical Industrial Co. Ltd. [*NYSE symbol*] (SAG)
JCC	Job Control Card (MCD)
JCC	Job Corps Camp [*Department of Labor*]
JCC	Joint Committee on Contraception (DMAA)
JCC	Joint Communications Center (MCD)
JCC	Joint Computer Conference
JCC	Joint Consultative Committee [*of the National Joint Advisory Council*] [*British World War II*]
JCC	Joint Consultative Committee (NITA)
JCC	Joint Control Center (MCD)
JCC	Joint Coordination Center (NVT)
JCC	Jowett Car Club (EA)
JCC	Junior Chamber of Commerce
JCC	Junior Command Course [*British military*] (DMA)
JCC	San Francisco [*California*] China Bas [*Airport symbol*] (OAG)
JCCA	Japanese Canadian Citizens' Association
JCCA	Japanese Chin Club of America (EA)
JCCA	Joint CONEX [*Container Express*] Control Agency
JCCANA	Jewish Community Centers Association of North America (EA)
JCCB	Joint Configuration Control Board [*DoD*]
JCCC	Japanese Canadian Citizens' Council
JCCC	Joint Committee on Contemporary China (EA)
JCCC	Joint COMSEC Coordination Center (MCD)
JCCC	Joint Configuration Control Committee [*DoD*]
JCCD	Japanese Canadian Committee for Democracy
JCCDG	Joint Command and Control Development Group [*DoD*]
JCCEM	Joint Committee of Cultural and Education Ministers [*Australia*]
JCCEP	Joint Crisis Communications Exercise Program (MCD)

JCCFC.......... June Carter Cash Fan Club (EA)
JCCFE.......... Joint Coordination Center, Far East [Military] (CINC)
JCCFEP....... Joint Commission on Cooperation in the Field of Environmental Protection [US-USSR] [Marine science] (OSRA)
JCCFEP....... Joint Commission on Cooperation in the Field of Environmental Protection [US-USSR] (USDC)
JCC-FPM..... Joint Coordinating Committee on Fundamental Properties of Matter [US Department of Energy and USSR State Committee on Peaceful Uses of Atomic Energy]
JCCIS.......... Japan Chamber of Commerce and Industry, Sydney [Australia]
JCCIUK .... Japanese Chamber of Commerce and Industry in the United Kingdom (DS)
JCCL.......... Japanese Canadian Citizens' League
JCCLE.......... Joint Committee on Continuing Legal Education [Later, ALI-ABA Committee on Con tinuing Professional Education] (EA)
JCCO.......... Joint Container Control Office (MCD)
JCCOMNET... Joint Coordination Center Communications Network
JCCR.......... Joint Command and Control Requirements [Military] (GFGA)
JCCRG......... Joint Command and Control Requirements Group [Joint Chiefs of Staff] [DoD]
JCCS.......... Jewish Cultural Clubs and Societies (EA)
JCCSA.......... Joint Communications Contingency Station Activity (MCD)
JCCSC.......... Joint Command and Control Standards Committee (AFM)
JCCSMAS .... Joint Commission on Competitive Safeguards and the Medical Aspects of Sports [Later, JCSMS] (EA)
JCCSWO...... Joint Committee on Cooperation in Studies of the World Ocean [US-USSR] [Marine science] (OSRA)
JCCSWO...... Joint Committee on Cooperation on Studies of the World Ocean [US-USSR] (USDC)
JCCTC.......... Joint Customs Consultative Technical Committee [British] (DCTA)
JCD.......... John Chard Decoration [British military] (DMA)
JCD.......... Journal of Community Development [A publication]
JCD.......... Junior College District
JCD.......... Juris Canonici Doctor [Doctor of Canon Law] [Latin]
JCD.......... Juris Civilis Doctor [Doctor of Civil Law] [Latin]
JCDA.......... Junior Catholic Daughters of the Americas [Defunct] (EA)
JCDSG.......... Joint Civil Defense Support Group
JCDSIPS ..... Joint Continental Defense Systems Integration Planning Staff [Air Force]
JCDTA.......... Joint Commission on Dance and Theatre Accreditation (EA)
JCE.......... Joint Cadet Executive [British military] (DMA)
JCE.......... Journal of Chemical Education [A publication] (WDAA)
JCEA.......... Joint Committee for European Affairs [Defunct] (EA)
JCEADF....... Joint Central Air Defense Force (SAA)
JCEAG.......... Joint Civilian Employee Advisory Group [Military] (CINC)
JCEB.......... Joint Council on Educational Broadcasting [Later, JCET] (EA)
JCEC.......... Joint Chapters - Educational Council
JCEC.......... Joint Communications-Electronics Committee [Military]
JCECPAC..... Joint Communications-Electronics Committee, Pacific [Military] (CINC)
JCEE .... Joint Council on Economic Education (EA)
JCEG.......... Joint Communications-Electronics Group [Military]
JCEG.......... Joint Concepts and Evaluation Group [Military] (CINC)
JCEGP.......... Joint Communications-Electronics Group [Military]
JCEM.......... Joint Center for Energy Management [Research center] (RCD)
JCEM.......... Junior Control Electrical Mechanic [British military] (DMA)
JCENS.......... Joint Communications-Electronics Nomenclature System [Military]
JCEOI.......... Joint Communications-Electronics Operating Instructions [Military] (CET)
JCEPC.......... Joint United States/Canada Civil Emergency Planning Committee
JCET.......... Joint Council on Educational Telecommunications [Defunct] (EA)
JCEW.......... Joint Communications Electronic Warfare Simulation
JCEWG.......... Joint Communications and Electronics Working Group [NATO] (NATG)
JCEWS.......... Joint Command, Control, and Electronic Warfare School
J Ceylon Law... Journal of Ceylon Law [A publication] (ILCA)
JCF .... Jaycees Community Foundation [Australia]
JCF .... Jet Center Flight Training SA [Spain ICAO designator] (FAAC)
JCF .... Juvenile Calcaneal Fracture [Medicine] (DMAA)
JCFC.......... Jesse Couch Fan Club (EA)
JCFC.......... John Conlee Fan Club (EA)
JCFC.......... Judaica Captioned Film Center (EA)
JCFI.......... Job Control File Internal (IAA)
JCFR.......... Junior College of Flat River [Missouri]
JCFS.......... Job Control File Source (IAA)
JCFSBFC...... Jerry Campbell and Five Star Band Fan Club (EA)
JCFSO.......... Joint Council of Fire Service Organizations [Defunct] (EA)
JCG.......... Joint Conservation Group
JCG.......... Joint Coordinating Group [Military] (AFIT)
JCGRO......... Joint Central Graves Registration Office [Military] (CINC)
JCGRO......... Joint Central Graves Registration Office (DOMA)
JCGS.......... Joint Center for Graduate Study [Research center] (RCD)
J Ch.......... Johnson's New York Chancery Reports [A publication] (DLA)
JCHA.......... Joint Commission on Hospital Accreditation
J Chem Ed... Journal of Chemical Education [A publication] (BRI)
JCHST.......... Joint Committe on Higher Surgical Training [Royal College of Surgeons] (PDAA)
J Ch St .... Journal of Church and State [A publication] (BRI)
J Church S... Journal of Church and State [A publication] (DLA)
JCI.......... Jaycees International (EA)
JCI.......... Job Characteristics Inventory
JCI.......... Johnson Controls [NYSE symbol] (TTSB)
JCI.......... Johnson Controls, Inc. [NYSE symbol] (SPSG)
JCI.......... Joint Communications Instruction
JCI.......... Junior Chamber International (EAIO)

JCI .... Jute Corp. of India
JCI .... Olathe [Kansas] [Airport symbol] (OAG)
JCIC............. Jewish Community Information Center [Australia]
JCIC............. Joint Committee on Intersociety Coordination [Defunct] (EA)
JCIE/USA..... Japan Center for International Exchange (EA)
JCIFC............. Johnny Comfort International Fan Club [Defunct] (EA)
JCIHCA......... Joint Council to Improve Health Care of the Aged [Defunct] (EA)
JCIM............. Joint Council of Immunohistochemical Manufacturers
J Cin BA ...... Journal. Cincinnati Bar Association [A publication] (DLA)
JCIPP............. Jewish Committee for Israeli-Palestinian Peace (EA)
JCIWG............. Joint Cutover Integrated Working Group [Military] (RDA)
JCJC............. Jefferson City Junior College [Discontinued operation, 1958] [Missouri]
JCJC............. Jones County Junior College [Ellisville, MS]
JCJCCIFC..... Johnny Cash and June Carter Cash International Fan Club (EA)
JCK............. Jackson Air Services Ltd. [Canada ICAO designator] (FAAC)
JCK............. Joint Commission on Korea
JCK............. Julia Creek [Australia Airport symbol] (OAG)
JCL............. Jackson County Library System, Medford, OR [OCLC symbol] (OCLC)
JCL............. Jet Cargo-Liberia [ICAO designator] (FAAC)
JCL............. Job Command Language (NITA)
JCL............. Job Control Language [High-level programming language] [1979] [Computer science]
JCL............. John Crerar Library [National Translation Center]
JCL............. Johnny Come Lately [Slang]
JCL............. Journal of Contract Law [Australia A publication]
JCL............. Junior Classical League (EA)
JCL............. Juris Canonici Lector [Reader in Canon Law]
JCL............. Juris Canonici Licentiatus [Licentiate in Canon Law]
JCL............. Juris Civilis Licentiatus [Licentiate of Civil Law]
JCLA............. Joint Council of Language Associations [British]
JCLC............. Joint Committee [of Congress] on the Library of Congress
JCLE............. Joint Committee on Library Education
JCLGEN......... Job Control Language Generation [Computer science] (MHDB)
JCLIL............. Journal of Comparative Legislation and International Law [A publication]
J ClinPsyc .... Journal of Clinical Psychiatry [A publication] (BRI)
JCLL............. Joint Center for Lessons Learned (DOMA)
JCL-OMATIC... Job Control Language Automatic Generator [Computer science]
JCLOT............. Joint Closed Loop Operations Test (SAA)
JCLPREP...... Job Control Language Preprocessor [Computer science] (MHDB)
JCLS............. Junior College Libraries Section [Association of College and Research Libraries]
JCM............. Jacobina [Brazil] [Airport symbol] (OAG)
JCM............. Jettison Control Module
JCM............. Jeunesse Canada Monde (AC)
JCM............. Jeunesse Chretienne Malgache [Malagasy Christian Youth]
JCM............. Job Cylinder Map [Computer science] (IBMDP)
JCM............. Joint Conflict Model [Military]
JCM............. Joule Ceramic Melter (PDAA)
JCM............. Juris Civilis Magister [Master of Civil Law]
JCMA............. Junior Clergy Missionary Association [British]
JCMBS......... Journeymen Curriers' Mutual Benefit Society [A union] [British]
JCMC............. Joint Crisis Management Capability [DoD]
JCMC............. Junta Civico-Militar Cubana [An association] (EA)
JCMD............. Joint Committee on Mobility for the Disabled [British]
JCMHC......... Joint Commission on Mental Health of Children
JCMIH............. Joint Commission on Mental Illness and Health [Defunct] (EA)
JCML............. Juvenile Chronic Myelogenous [or Myelocytic] Leukemia [Medicine] (DMAA)
JCMPO......... Joint Cruise Missile Program [or Project] Office (MCD)
JCMST......... Journal of Computers in Math and Science Teaching (NITA)
JCMT............. James Clerk Maxwell Telescope [Mauna Kea, HI] [Operated by the Royal Observatory in Edinburgh, Scotland]
JCMT............. Joint Collection Management Tools [Army] (RDA)
JCN............. Job Change Notice [Form] (AAG)
JCN............. Job Control Number
JCN............. Joint Control Number
JCN............. Jump on Condition [Computer science]
JCN............. Junction (NITA)
JCNA............. Jaguar Clubs of North America (EA)
JCNFC............. Jimmy C. Newman Fan CLub (EA)
JCNMT......... Joint Committee of Nordic Marine Technology [See also NSTM] (EAIO)
JCNMT......... Joint Committee of Nordic Master Tailors (EA)
JCNNSRC..... Joint Committee of the Nordic Natural Science Research Councils (EA)
JCNSW......... Judicial Commission of New South Wales [Australia]
JCO............. Jesus College, Oxford [England] (ROG)
JCO............. Justification for Continued Operation [Nuclear energy] (NRCH)
JCOA............. Jazz Composers Orchestra Association (EA)
J-COARE...... Japanese COARE [Coupled Ocean-Atmosphere Response Experiment] (USDC)
JCOARE ...... Japanese Coupled Ocean-Atmosphere Response Experiment [Marine science] (OSRA)
JCOC............. Joint Civilian Orientation Conference [DoD]
JCOC............. Joint Combat Operations Center [Navy] (NVT)
JCOC............. Joint Command Operations Center [NATO] (NATG)
JCOCG......... Joint Cadre Operation Control Group [Military]
J-CODE......... Justification Code (LAIN)
JC of C .... Junior Chamber of Commerce
JCOMCEN..... Joint Communications Center
JCOME......... Jewish Committee on the Middle East (EA)
J Comm Mt Stud... Journal of Common Market Studies [A publication] (DLA)

J Comp Corp L... Journal of Comparative Corporate Law and Securities Regulation [*A publication*] (ILCA)
J Comp Leg... Journal. Society of Comparative Legislation [*A publication*] (DLA)
J Con A........ Journal of Consumer Affairs [*A publication*] (BRI)
J Conat Law... Journal of Conational Law [*A publication*] (DLA)
J Contemp RDL... Journal of Contemporary Roman-Dutch Law [*A publication*] (DLA)
J Copr Soc'y... Journal. Copyright Society of the USA [*A publication*] (DLA)
J Copyright Ent & Sports L... Journal of Copyright, Entertainment, and Sports Law [*A publication*] (DLA)
J Copyright Entertainment Sports L... Journal of Copyright, Entertainment, and Sports Law [*A publication*] (DLA)
JCOR .... Jacor Communications [*NASDAQ symbol*] (TTSB)
JCOR .... Jacor Communications, Inc. [*NASDAQ symbol*] (NQ)
J Corp Tax'n... Journal of Corporate Taxation [*A publication*] (DLA)
JCORW .... Jacor Communications Wrrt [*NASDAQ symbol*] (TTSB)
JCOS .... Job Corps Opportunity Specialist [*Department of Labor*]
JCOS .... Joint Chiefs of Staff [*Military*]
JCOT .... Joint Committee on College Teaching
JCP .... Janna Contact Personal [*Janna Systems*] [*Computer interface*] (PCM)
JCP .... Japan Communist Party [*Nikon Kyosanto*] [*Political party*] (PPW)
JCP .... Jetcopter [*Denmark ICAO designator*] (FAAC)
JCP .... Jettison Control Panel
JCP .... Jewish Communist Party [*Political party*] (BJA)
JCP .... Job Content Protection [*UAW*]
JCP .... Job Control Program (CMD)
JCP .... Job Creation Programme [*Manpower Services Commission*] (AIE)
JCP .... John Crowe Productions, Inc. [*Houston, TX*] [*Telecommunications*] (TSSD)
JCP .... Joint Chiefs of Staff Publications [*Military*]
JCP .... Joint [*Congressional*] Committee on Printing
JCP .... Joint Contact Point Division [*Desert Test Center*] [*Fort Douglas, UT*]
JCP .... Joint Power Conditions [*NASA*] (LAIN)
JCP .... Jordanian Communist Party [*Political party*] (PD)
JCP .... JOVIAL [*Joule's Own Version of the International Algorithmic Language*] Control Program [*Computer science*]
JCP .... Jungle Canopy Penetration
JCP .... Junior Collegiate Players [*Later, Associate Collegiate Players*] (EA)
JCP .... Justice of the Common Pleas [*Legal term*] (DLA)
JCP .... Penney [*J. C.*] Co., Inc. [*NYSE symbol*] (SPSG)
JCP .... Penney (J.C.) [*NYSE symbol*] (TTSB)
JCPC .... J. C. Penney Communications, Inc. [*J. C. Penney Co., Inc.*] [*Telecommunications service*] (TSSD)
JCPCap .... JCP & L Capital LP [*Associated Press*] (SAG)
JCPDS .... Joint Committee on Powder Diffraction Standards (MCD)
JCPES .... Joint Center for Political and Economic Studies (EA)
JCPOA .... Joint Council of Post Office Associations [*South Africa*]
JCPPRFNA.... Joint Commission on Political Prisoners and Refugees in French North Africa [*World War II*]
JCPS .... Joint Center for Political Studies [*Later, JCPES*] (EA)
JCPX .... Joint Command Post Exercise [*Military*] (AABC)
JCQ .... Jacqueline Gold [*Vancouver Stock Exchange symbol*]
JCQ .... Jefferson City, MO [*Location identifier FAA*] (FAAL)
JCQE .... Joint Council on Quantum Electronics (MCD)
JCR .... Jack Criswell Resources [*Vancouver Stock Exchange symbol*]
JCR .... Jesus Cares Refuge Incorporated [*Australia An association*]
JCR .... Johnson's New York Chancery Reports [*A publication*] (DLA)
JCR .... Joint Council for Repatriation (EA)
JCR .... Judicial Council Reports [*A publication*] (DLA)
JCR .... Junction Current Recovery [*in silicon devices*]
JCR .... Junior Common Room [*in British colleges and public schools*]
JCRA .... Jewish Committee for Relief Abroad
JCRC .... Jewish Community Relations Council (BARN)
JCRC .... Joint Casualty Resolution Center (MCD)
JCRC .... Joint Concept Review Committee (AAGC)
JCRe .... Judentum im Christlichen Religionsunterricht (BJA)
JC Rettie ..... Rettie, Crawford, and Melville's Session Cases, Fourth Series [*1873-98*] [*Scotland*] [*A publication*] (DLA)
JCRFC .... Jeannie C. Riley Fan Club (EA)
J Crim L & Crim... Journal of Criminal Law and Criminology [*A publication*] (DLA)
J Crim Sci ... Journal of Criminal Science [*A publication*] (DLA)
JCRPCC ...... Joint Council on Research in Pastoral Care and Counseling [*Later, COMISS*] (EA)
JCRR .... Joint Commission on Rural Reconstruction
JCRS .... Joint Casualty Resolution Center [*Established in 1973 to coordinate U.S. military activities regarding American MIA/POWs*] (VNW)
JCRWD .... Jersey Committee of Resistance Workers and Deportees (EAIO)
JCS .... Jaicos [*Brazil*] [*Airport symbol*] (AD)
JCS .... Japan Club of Sydney [*Australia*]
JCS .... Jazz Centre Society [*British*]
JCS .... Jersey Cattle Society [*British*] (DBA)
JCS .... Jewish Chautauqua Society (EA)
JCS .... Job Control Statement [*Computer science*]
JCS .... Job Control System (IAA)
JCS .... Job Cost Sheet (DGA)
JCS .... Job Creation Scheme [*Department of Employment*] [*British*]
JCS .... Joint Chiefs of Staff [*United States*] [*Military*]
JCS .... Journal of Chromatographic Science [*A publication*]
JCS .... Justices' Clerks' Society [*British*] (DBA)
JCSA .... Joseph Conrad Society of America (EA)
JCS-ACA ..... Joint Chiefs of Staff Automatic Conference Arranger [*Military*] (CET)
JCSAN .... Joint Chiefs of Staff Alerting Network [*Military*]
JCSAS .... Joint Chiefs of Staff Alerting System (MCD)

JC/SCAMEP... Joint Commonwealth/States Committee on the Adult Migration Education Program [*Australia*]
JCSCCF........ Joint Commission of the Socialist Countries on Cooperation in the Field of Fisheries (PDAA)
JCSE .... Joint Communications Support Element [*DoD*]
JCSE .... Joint Communications Systems Elements (MCD)
JCSI .... Joint Combat Systems Integrating
JCSIDBAD .... Joint Chiefs of Staff Identification Badge [*Military decoration*] (GFGA)
JCSIdentBad... Joint Chiefs of Staff Identification Badge [*Military decoration*] (AABC)
JCSIDTN ...... Joint Chiefs of Staff Interim Data Transmission Network [*Military*] (CET)
JCSIR .... Journal. Council for Scientific and Industrial Research (Australia) [*A publication*]
JCSLHG .... Joint Center for the Study of Law and Human Genetics
JCSM .... Joint Chiefs of Staff Memorandum [*Military*]
J/CSM.......... Junior Company Sergeant-Major [*British military*] (DMA)
JCSMS .... Joint Commission on Sports Medicine and Science (EA)
JCSNMCC .... Joint Chiefs of Staff National Military Command Center (DNAB)
JCSO .... Joint Chiefs of Staff Organization [*Military*] (MCD)
JCSOS .... Joint and Combined Staff Officer School
JCSP .... Joint Chiefs of Staff Plans
JCSPUB .... Joint Chiefs of Staff Publications [*Military*]
JCSRE .... Joint Chiefs of Staff Representative, Europe [*NATO*] (NATG)
JCSS .... Jesuit Center for Social Studies [*Defunct*] (EA)
JCSS .... Jesus Christ Superstar [*Rock opera*]
JCSS .... Joint Communications Support Squadron
JCSSAB........ Joint Committee of the States to Study Alcoholic Beverage Laws (EA)
JCS(SASM)... Joint Chiefs of Staff (Special Assistant for Strategic Mobility) (DNAB)
JCST .... Joint Combined System Test (KSC)
JCSTC .... Joint Council for Scientific and Technical Communication [*British*]
JCSTELECON... Joint Chiefs of Staff Teletypwriter Conference Network [*Military*] (MCD)
JCT .... Jacket (ROG)
JCT .... Jewett-Cameron [*Vancouver Stock Exchange symbol*]
JCT .... Jewish Cemetery Trust [*Australia*]
JCT .... Job Control Table (CMD)
JCT .... Johnstown/Consolidated Realty Trust (MHDW)
JCT .... Joint Committee on Taxation [*US Congress*]
JCT .... Jordan Cosmological Theory
JCT .... Journal Control Table (IAA)
JCT .... Junction [*Texas*] [*Seismograph station code, US Geological Survey*] (SEIS)
JCT .... Junction (AFM)
JCT .... Junction
JCT .... Junction, TX [*Location identifier FAA*] (FAAL)
JCT .... Jurisconsult (ROG)
JCT & M ..... Jordan, Case, Taylor & McGrath [*Advertising agency*]
JCTC .... Jewett-Cameron Trading Co. Ltd. [*NASDAQ symbol*] (SAG)
JCTCF .... Jewett-Cameron Trading [*NASDAQ symbol*] (TTSB)
JCTG .... Joint Contingency Task Group [*Military*] (VNW)
JCTI .... James Crowe Traders International [*Commercial firm British*]
JCTI .... Jurisconsulti [*Counselors at Law*] [*Latin*] (ROG)
JCTION .... Junction [*Commonly used*] (OPSA)
JCTN .... Junction [*Commonly used*] (OPSA)
JCTNS......... Junctions [*Commonly used*] (OPSA)
JCTPT .... Junction Point (IAA)
JCTS .... Junctions
JCTS .... Junctions [*Postal Service standard*] (OPSA)
JCTUS......... Jurisconsultus [*Counselor at Law*] [*Latin*] (ROG)
JCU .... John Carroll University [*University Heights, OH*]
JCU .... John Carroll University, Grasselli Library, University Heights, OH [*OCLC symbol*] (OCLC)
JCULS......... Joint Committee on the Union List of Serials
JCUS.......... Joint Center for Urban Studies of MIT [*Massachusetts Institute of Technology*] and Harvard University [*Research center*] (RCD)
JCV .... Jamestown Canyon Virus [*Medicine*] (DMAA)
JCV .... Jentech Ventures Corp. [*Vancouver Stock Exchange symbol*]
JCV .... Joule-Clausius Velocity [*Physics*]
JCVS........... JOVIAL Compiler Validation System [*Computer science*]
JCW .... Jim Creek [*Washington*] [*Seismograph station code, US Geological Survey*] (SEIS)
JCWG .... Joint Checklist Working Group [*Military*] (AFIT)
JCWI .... Joint Council for the Welfare of Immigrants [*British*] (DI)
JCWP .... Joint Conservation Working Party [*Australia Political party*]
JCY .... Johnson City, TX [*Location identifier FAA*] (FAAL)
JD .... Diploma in Journalism (ADA)
JD .... Doctor of Jurisprudence (DD)
JD .... Doctor of Jurisprudence (GAGS)
JD .... Jack Daniels [*A brand name of whiskey*]
JD .... J-Band Detector
JD .... Jejunal Diverticulitis [*Gastroenterology*] (DAVI)
JD .... Jet Driver (KSC)
JD .... Jewish Division [*New York Public Library*] (BJA)
JD .... Job Description [*Department of Labor*]
JD .... Job Development (OICC)
JD .... Joggle Die (MCD)
JD .... Joined (AABC)
JD .... Joint Determination (AFM)
JD .... Joint Dictionary [*Dictionary of US Military Terms for Joint Usage*] [*A publication*] (AFM)
JD .... Jordanian Dinar [*Monetary unit*] (BJA)
Jd .... Jude [*New Testament book*] (BJA)
JD .... Jugulodigastric [*Node*] [*Gastroenterology*] (DAVI)

JD .... Julian Date [or Day]
JD .... Junior Deacon [Freemasonry]
JD .... Junior Dean
JD .... Junior Division [British military] (DMA)
JD .... Junta Democratica [Democratic Junta] [Spain Political party] (PPE)
JD .... Jurisdiction [Legal shorthand] (LWAP)
JD .... Juris Doctor [Doctor of Jurisprudence] [Latin]
JD .... Jurum Doctor [Doctor of Laws] [Latin]
JD .... Jury Duty (WGA)
JD .... Justice Department
JD .... Juvenile Delinquency [or Delinquent]
JD .... Juvenile Diabetes [Medicine] (DAVI)
JD .... Toa Domestic Airlines [ICAO designator] (AD)
JDA .... Japan Domestic Airlines (PDAA)
JDA .... Japanese Defense Agency (MCD)
JDA .... Jefferson Davis Association (EA)
JDA .... Jewelery Distributors Association [British] (DBA)
JDA .... Joint Defense Appeal [Defunct] (EA)
JDA .... Joint Deployment Agency [DoD]
JDA .... Joint Development Agency [DoD]
JDA .... Joint Development Agreement [Business term] (PCM)
JDA .... Joint Duty Assignment (DOMA)
JDA .... Juvenile Delinquency Act
JDAL .... Joint Duty Assignment List (DOMA)
JDAL .... Jurisdictional [Legal shorthand] (LWAP)
JDAM .... Joint Direct Attack Munition (DOMA)
JDAM .... Joint Direct Attack Munitions [DoD]
JDAMIS .... Joint Duty Assignment Management Information System (DOMA)
JDAP .... Joint Direct Attack Program [Air Force] (DOMA)
JDAS .... JDA Software Group [NASDAQ symbol] (TTSB)
JDAS .... JDA Software Group, Inc. [NASDAQ symbol] (SAG)
JDASoft .... JDA Software Group, Inc. [Associated Press] (SAG)
JDB .... Japan Development Bank (PDAA)
JDBC .... Java Database Connect [Computer science]
JDC .... American Jewish Joint Distribution Committee (EA)
JDC .... Deere & Co. [ICAO designator] (FAAC)
JDC .... Japan Airlines Development Co.
JDC .... Japan Documentation Center [Columbia University]
JDC .... Jet Deflection Control (AAG)
JDC .... Jeunesse Democratique Camerounaise [Cameroonian Democratic Youth]
JDC .... Jewish Documentation Centre [See also BJVN] (EAIO)
JDC .... Job Description Card
JDC .... Joint Deployment Community [Military] (INF)
JDC .... Joint Development Community [DoD]
JDC .... Joslin Diabetes Center (EA)
JDC .... Junction Diode Circuit
JDC .... Just Discriminable Change (IAA)
JDCE .... Jeunes Democrates Chretiens Europeens [European Young Christian Democrats - EYCD] (EA)
JDCMC .... Joint Department of Defense Configuration Management Committee (MCD)
JDCS .... Joint Deputy Chiefs of Staff [Military]
JDDD .... Judicial Discipline and Disability Digest [American Judicature Society] [Information service or system] (CRD)
JDE .... Air Med Jetoperations [Austria ICAO designator] (FAAC)
JDEG .... Joules per Degree [Physics] (IAA)
JDENL .... Joined by Enlistment [Military]
J Denning LS... Journal. Denning Law Society [Tanzania] [A publication] (DLA)
J Denning L Soc'y... Journal. Denning Law Society [Tanzania] [A publication] (DLA)
JDEP .... Juvenile Delinquency Evaluation Project
JDES .... Joint Density of Electronic State [Semiconductor technology] (OA)
JDEWN .... John Denver Early Warning Network (EA)
JDF .... Jamaican Defense Forces
JDF .... Jamming Direction Finder [Military] (CAAL)
JDF .... Juiz De Fora [Brazil] [Airport symbol] (OAG)
JDF .... Juvenile Diabetes Foundation [Later, JDFI] (EA)
JDFC .... James Darren Fan Club [Defunct] (EA)
JDFC .... Jimmie Dale Fan Club (EA)
JDFC .... Joanie Dale Fan Club (EA)
JDFC .... Joint Danube Fishery Commission [See also ZKRVD] [Zilina, Czechoslovakia] (EAIO)
JDFI .... Joslin Diabetes Foundation, Inc. [Later, JDC] (EA)
JDFI .... Juvenile Diabetes Foundation International (EA)
JDFR .... Joined From [Military]
JdFR .... Juan de Fuca Ridge [Marine science] (OSRA)
JDFR .... Juan de Fuca Ridge (USDC)
JDG .... Judge
JDH .... Jodhpur [India] [Airport symbol] (OAG)
JDHE .... Joint Directory of Higher Education [A publication]
JDHHFC .... John Denver Heart to Heart Fan Club (EA)
JDHTC .... Jaguar-Daimler Heritage Trust Collection
JDI .... JDS Investments Ltd. [Toronto Stock Exchange symbol]
JDI .... Job Description Index
JDI .... Joint Declaration of Interest (DS)
JDIND .... Joined by Induction [Military]
JDipMA .... Joint Diploma in Management Accounting Services [British]
JDK .... Java Developer's Kit (PCM)
JDK .... Joodsch-Democratische Kiespartij [Political party] (BJA)
JDL .... Jewish Defense League (EA)
JDL .... Job Description Language [Computer science]
JDL .... Job Description Library
JDL .... Job Descriptor Language (NITA)
JDL .... Job Drawing List (MCD)

JDL .... Joint Directors of Laboratories [Military]
JDL .... Juneau, AK [Location identifier FAA] (FAAL)
JDL .... Lynn-01, AK [Location identifier FAA] (FAAL)
JDM .... Juvenile Diabetes Mellitus [Medicine]
JDMAG .... Joint Depot Maintenance Analysis Group [Military]
JDMC .... James Dean Memory Club (EA)
JDMS .... Juvenile Dermatomyositis [Medicine] (DAVI)
JDN .... JDN Realty [NYSE symbol] (TTSB)
JDN .... JDN Realty Corp. [NYSE symbol] (SAG)
JDN .... Jordan, MT [Location identifier FAA] (FAAL)
JDN .... Jordan Petroleum Ltd. [Toronto Stock Exchange symbol]
JDN .... Julian Day Number
JDO .... Jewish Defense Organization (EA)
JDO .... Job Delivery Orders (MCD)
JDO .... Junior Duty Officer (MCD)
JDOP .... Joint Development Objectives Plan (SAA)
JDOP .... Joint Doppler Operational Project [For tornado warning] [Meteorology]
JDOYM .... Jewish Defense Organization Youth Movement (EA)
JDP .... Covington/Cincinnati, OH [Location identifier FAA] (FAAL)
JDP .... Job Development Program
JDP .... Joint Declaration of Principles
JDP .... Joint Development Program
JDP .... Paris-Moulineaux [France] [Airport symbol] (OAG)
JDPA .... Japan Directory of Professional Associations [Japan Publications Guide Service] [Information service or system] (CRD)
JDPA .... Juvenile Justice Planning Agency (OICC)
JDPC .... Joint Defense Production Committee [Later, Joint War Production Committee] [World War II]
JDPC .... Junior Daughters of Peter Claver (EA)
JDR .... Juta's Daily Reporter, Cape Provincial Division [South Africa] [A publication] (DLA)
JDR3 .... John D. Rockefeller III [American philanthropist, 1906-1978]
JDREENL .... Joined by Reenlistment [Military]
JDRMA .... Japanese Digital Road Mapping Association
JDRP .... Joint Dissemination Review Panels
JDS .... Doctor of Juridical Science
JDS .... Jaguar Diagnostic System [Automotive engineering]
JDS .... JDS Capital Ltd. [Toronto Stock Exchange symbol]
JDS .... Job Data Sheet (IEEE)
JDS .... Job Diagnosis Survey (PDAA)
JDS .... John Dewey Society (EA)
JDS .... Joint Defense Staff [NATO] (NATG)
JDS .... Joint Deployment System
JDS .... Joint Disciplinary Scheme [British]
JDS .... Jugoslovenska Demokratska Stranka [Yugoslav Democratic Party] [Political party] (PPE)
JDS .... Julian Day of Spring
JDSCS .... Joint Defense Space Communications Station
JDSSC .... Joint Data Systems Support Center [Military]
JDT .... Joint Design Team [Military]
JDT .... Joint Development Team (MCD)
JDT .... Joint Development Testing
Jdt .... Judith [Old Testament book] [Roman Catholic canon]
JDT .... Judson Dance Theater
JDW .... Jacket Decladding Waste (PDAA)
JDWC .... Jazz Dance World Congress
JDY .... Downey, CA [Location identifier FAA] (FAAL)
JDYD .... Juvenile Delinquency and Youth Development Office [Federal government]
JDZ .... Jingdezhen [China] [Airport symbol] (OAG)
JE .... Jamin Effect [Electronics]
JE .... Jamming Equipment
JE .... Japanese Encephalitis [Medicine]
Je .... Jeremiah [Old Testament book] (BJA)
JE .... Jerseyville & Eastern [AAR code]
JE .... Jet Engine
JE .... Jet Exhaust
JE .... Jewish Encyclopaedia [A publication] (BJA)
JE .... Job Enlargement (MHDB)
JE .... Job Enrichment (MHDB)
JE .... Job Estimate (AAG)
JE .... Joint Engineers [Army] (RDA)
JE .... Joshi Effect [Physics]
JE .... Joule Effect [Physics]
JE .... Journal of Education [A publication] (BRI)
JE .... Jump If Equal [Computer science] (PCM)
JE .... Junctional Escape [Cardiology] (DAVI)
JE .... Junction Exchange [Telecommunications] (OA)
JE .... June
JE .... Manx Airlines [Airline flight code] (ODBW)
JE .... Yosemite Airlines [ICAO designator] (AD)
JEA .... Jersey European Airways [British ICAO designator] (FAAC)
JEA .... Jesuit Educational Association [Later split into AJCU and JSEA] (EA)
JEA .... Jewish Educators Assembly
JEA .... Joint Endeavor Agreement
JEA .... Joint Engineering Agency
JEA .... Joint Export Agent
JEA .... Joint Export Association [Department of Commerce]
JEA .... Journalism Education Association (EA)
JEAC .... Journal of Electroanalytical Chemistry [A publication]
JEADF .... Joint Eastern Air Defense Force (MUGU)
Jeaf .... Jeaffreson's Book about Lawyers [A publication] (DLA)
JEAH .... Jewish Endowment for the Arts and Humanities
JEAL .... Junction Emitting Avalanche Light

JEAN........... Jean Philippe Fragrances [*NASDAQ symbol*] (TTSB)
JEAN........... Jean Philippe Fragrances, Inc. [*NASDAQ symbol*] (NQ)
JEAN........... JOSS-Based Expression Analyser for the Nineteen Hundred (NITA)
JeanPhl....... Jean Philippe Fragrances, Inc. [*Associated Press*] (SAG)
JEARD......... Journal of Eastern African Research and Development [*A publication*]
JEASC.......... Journal. East African Swahili Committee [*A publication*]
JEAT........... Joint Emergency Airlift Traffic Management Plan [*DoD*]
JEB............. James Ewell Brown Stuart [*American Confederate general known as Jeb Stuart, 1833-1864*]
JEB............. Jewish Education Bureau [*British*] (CB)
JEB............. Joint Economy Board [*Abolished, 1947*] [*Army-Navy*]
JEB............. Joint Electronics Board
JEB............. Junctional Epidermolysis Bullosa [*Medicine*]
Jebb........... Jebb's Irish Crown Cases [*1822-40*] [*A publication*] (DLA)
Jebb & B..... Jebb and Bourke's Irish Queen's Bench Reports [*1841-42*] [*A publication*] (DLA)
Jebb & B (Ir)... Jebb and Bourke's Irish Queen's Bench Reports [*1841-42*] [*A publication*] (DLA)
Jebb & S.... Jebb and Symes' Irish Queen's Bench Reports [*A publication*] (DLA)
Jebb & S (Ir)... Jebb and Symes' Irish Queen's Bench Reports [*A publication*] (DLA)
Jebb & Sym... Jebb and Symes' Irish Queen's Bench Reports [*A publication*] (DLA)
Jebb CC....... Jebb's Irish Crown Cases [*1822-40*] [*A publication*] (DLA)
Jebb CC (Ir)... Jebb's Irish Crown Cases [*1822-40*] [*A publication*] (DLA)
Jebb Cr & Pr Cas... Jebb's Irish Crown and Presentment Cases [*A publication*] (DLA)
JEBC........... Jefferson Bancorp, Inc. (Los Angeles) [*NASDAQ symbol*] (SAG)
JEBC........... Jefferson Bancorp(LA) [*NASDAQ symbol*] (TTSB)
JEBM........... Jet Engine Base Maintenance
JEBM-RR..... Jet Engine Base Maintenance - Return Rate (PDAA)
JEC............. Jacobs Engineering Group, Inc. [*NYSE symbol*] (SPSG)
JEC............. Jacobs Engr Group [*NYSE symbol*] (TTSB)
JEC............. Japanese Electrotechnical Committee
JEC............. Jersey Electric Co. [*British*]
JEC............. Jeunesse Etudiante Catholique Internationale [*International Young Catholic Students*] (EAIO)
JEC............. Joint Economic Committee of Congress
JEC............. Joint Evaluation Committee [*NSF-UCAR*]
JEC............. Journal Editorial Committee (ACII)
JECA........... Jewel Cave National Monument
JECB........... Jet Engine Control Bearing
JECC........... Japan Electric Computer Corporation [*Japan*] (NITA)
JECC........... Japanese Electronic Computer Co.
JECC........... Joint Economic Committee of Congress (MCD)
JECC........... Joint Exercise Control Center (MCD)
JECFA......... Joint Expert Committee on Food Additives [*FDA/WHO*]
JECI............ Jeunesse Etudiante Catholique Internationale [*International Young Catholic Students*]
JECL............ Job Entry Control Language
JECMB......... Joint Executive Committee on Medicine and Biology
JECMOS...... Joint Electronic Countermeasures Operation Section [*NATO*] (NATG)
JECNS......... Joint Electronic Communications Nomenclature System [*Military*] (IAA)
JECS........... Job Entry Central Services (MCD)
JECSS......... Japan and East China Seas Study [*Marine science*] (OSRA)
JED............. Japan Economic Daily [*Database*] [*Kyodo News International, Inc.*] [*Information service or system*] (CRD)
JED............. Jeddah [*Saudi Arabia*] [*Airport symbol*] (OAG)
Jed.............. Jedediah (BJA)
JED............. Jet East, Inc. [*ICAO designator*] (FAAC)
JED............. Jet Engine Duct
JED............. Joint Educational Development (EA)
JED............. Julian Ephemeris Data (MCD)
JEDA........... Joint Environmental Data Analysis Center [*Army*] [*Marine science*] (OSRA)
JEDEC......... Joint Electron Device Engineering Council (EA)
JEDI............ Jobs for Employable Dependent Individuals Program [*Federal government*]
JEDI............ Joint Electronic Data Interchange [*International trade*]
JEDMICS...... Joint Engineering and Data Management Information and Control System [*Military*]
JEDPE.......... Joint Emergency Defense Plan Europe [*NATO*] (NATG)
JEDS........... Japanese Expeditions to the Deep Sea
JEDS........... Jedburgh Teams [*Allied intelligence-gathering units in Europe*] [*World War II*]
JEE............. Japanese Equine Encephalitis [*Medicine*]
JEE............. Jet Engine Exhaust
JEEC........... Kenneth E. Johnson Environmental and Energy Center [*University of Alabama in Huntsville*] [*Research center*] (RCD)
JEEP........... General-Purpose Quarter-Ton Military Utility Vehicle
Jeep............ Graduated Payment Mortgage (DFIT)
JEEP........... Joint Effort Evaluation Program [*Military*] (AFM)
JEEP........... Joint Emergency Evacuation Plan [*Military*] (AABC)
JEEP........... Joint Environmental Effects Program [*Military*] (AFM)
JEEP........... Joint Establishment Experimental Pile [*Nuclear reactor*] [*Norway*]
JEEP........... Joint Export Establishment Promotion [*Trade exhibition*] [*Department of Commerce*]
JEF............. Jacobi Elliptic Function [*Mathematics*]
JEF............. Jefferies Group [*NYSE symbol*] (TTSB)
JEF............. Jefferson City [*Missouri*] [*Airport symbol*] (OAG)
JEF............. Jefferson City, MO [*Location identifier FAA*] (FAAL)
JEF............. Jefferson Educational Foundation (EA)
JEF............. Jefjen Capital [*Vancouver Stock Exchange symbol*]
JEF............. Jet Engine Fuel
JEF............. Jetflite OY [*Finland ICAO designator*] (FAAC)
JEF............. Jeunesses Europeennes Federalistes
JefBsh......... Jefferson Bankshares, Inc. [*Associated Press*] (SAG)
JEFF........... JeffBanks, Inc. [*NASDAQ symbol*] (SAG)
JEFF........... Jefferson National Expansion Memorial National Historic Site
Jeff............ Jefferson's Virginia General Court Reports [*A publication*] (DLA)
JEFF........... Judiciously Efficient Fixed Frame [*Computer science*] (MCD)
JeffBanks..... JeffBanks, Inc. [*Associated Press*] (SAG)
JeffBcLA...... Jefferson Bancorp, Inc. [*Los Angles*] [*Associated Press*] (SAG)
JeffBcp........ Jefferson Bancorp, Inc. [*Associated Press*] (SAG)
Jeff Man...... Jefferson's Manual of Parliamentary Law [*A publication*] (DLA)
JeffPilot....... Jefferson-Pilot Corp. [*Associated Press*] (SAG)
JeffPlt......... Jefferson Pilot [*Associated Press*] (SAG)
JeffPOO....... Jefferson Pilot [*Associated Press*] (SAG)
JeffrGp........ Jefferies Group, Inc. [*Associated Press*] (SAG)
JeffSvg........ Jefferson Savings Bancorp [*Associated Press*] (SAG)
Jeff (VA)...... Jefferson's Virginia General Court Reports [*A publication*] (DLA)
JEFG........... Jefferies Group, Inc. [*NASDAQ symbol*] (NQ)
JEFM........... Jet Engine Field Maintenance
JefSmrf........ Jefferson Smurfit Corp. [*Associated Press*] (SAG)
JEG............. Joint Exploratory Group [*NATO*] (NATG)
JEGP........... Journal of English and Germanic Philology [*A publication*] (BRI)
JEH............. Journal of Economic History [*A publication*] (BRI)
JEHFC......... Jon-Erik Hexum Fan Club (EA)
JEHO........... Jehosaphat [*Biblical*] (ROG)
JEHU........... Joint Experimental Helicopter Unit [*British military*] (DMA)
JEI.............. Japan Economic Institute of America (EA)
JEIA........... Japanese Electronic Industries Association
JEIA........... Joint Electronics Information Agency
JEIA........... Joint Export-Import Agency [*Munich*] [*Allied German Occupation Forces*]
JEIDA.......... Japanese Electronic Industry Development Association (CDE)
JEIM........... Jet Engine Intermediate Maintenance
JEIPAC........ JICST [*Japan Information Center of Science and Technology*] Electronic Information Processing Automatic Computer (NITA)
JEIT............ Joint Equipment Identification Team [*Military*] (CINC)
JEJ............. Jejunum [*Medicine*]
JEJ............. Jets Ejecutivos SA [*Mexico ICAO designator*] (FAAC)
JEJUN......... Jejunectomy (ABBR)
JEJUN......... Jejunitis (ABBR)
JEL............. Aerojelk, SA de CV [*Mexico*] [*FAA designator*] (FAAC)
JEL............. Jackson Estuarine Laboratory [*University of New Hampshire*] [*Research center*] (RCD)
JEL............. Jeunesses Europeennes Liberales [*Liberal European Youth*]
JEL............. Journal of Economic Literature [*A publication*] (BRI)
JELC........... Joint Effort Against Lefthanded Complications
JELOS......... Jealous (ABBR)
JELOSY....... Jealousy (ABBR)
JEM............ Japanese Experiment Module
JEM............ Jerusalem and the East Mission
JEM............ Jet Engine Modulation (MCD)
JEM............ Joint Endeavor Manager
JEM............ Joint Exercise Manual (MCD)
JEM............ Journey's End Motel Corp. [*Toronto Stock Exchange symbol*]
JEM(A)........ Junior Electrical Mechanic (Air) [*British military*] (DMA)
JEM(AW)..... Junior Electrical Mechanic (Air Weapon) [*British military*] (DMA)
JEMC.......... Joint Engineering Management Conference
JEMIMA...... [*The*] Japan Electrical Measurements Manufacturers' Association (ACII)
JEMP.......... Joint Engineers Management Panel [*Army*] (RDA)
JEN............ Japan Economic Newswire [*Kyodo News International, Inc.*] [*Information service or system*] (CRD)
JEN............ Jena [*German Democratic Republic*] [*Seismograph station code, US Geological Survey Closed*] (SEIS)
JEN............ Jenair Ltd. [*Cyprus*] [*ICAO designator*] (FAAC)
JEN............ Junta de Energia Nuclear [*Spanish nuclear agency*]
JENAKAT..... Jeunesse Nationale Katangaise [*Katangan National Youth*]
Jenck Bills... Jencken's Bills of Exchange [*1880*] [*A publication*] (DLA)
Jenck Neg S... Jencken's Negotiable Securities [*1880*] [*A publication*] (DLA)
JenCrg........ Jenny Craig [*Associated Press*] (SAG)
JENER......... Joint Establishment for Nuclear Energy Research
J Energy & Devel... Journal of Energy and Development [*A publication*] (DLA)
JENEX......... Japanese El Nino Experiment [*Marine science*] (OSRA)
JenfCv......... Jennifer Convertibles, Inc. [*Associated Press*] (SAG)
Jenk............ Jenkins' Eight Centuries of Reports, English Exchequer [*145 English Reprint*] [*1220-1623*] [*A publication*] (DLA)
Jenk & Formoy... Jenkinson and Formoy's Select Cases in the Exchequer of Pleas [*Selden Society Publication, Vol. 48*] [*A publication*] (DLA)
Jenk Cent.... Jenkins' Eight Centuries of Reports, English Exchequer [*145 English Reprint*] [*1220-1623*] [*A publication*] (DLA)
Jenkins (Eng)... Jenkins' Eight Centuries of Reports, English Exchequer [*145 English Reprint*] [*1220-1623*] [*A publication*] (DLA)
Jenks.......... Jenks' Reports [*58 New Hampshire*] [*A publication*] (DLA)
Jenn........... Jennison's Reports [*14-18 Michigan*] [*A publication*] (DLA)
Jenn Sug A... Jennett's Sugden Acts [*A publication*] (DLA)
JENTAC....... Jentaculum [*Breakfast*] [*Pharmacy*]
JEOCN........ Joint European Operations Communications Network
JEOP.......... Jeopardy (ABBR)
JEOPZ......... Jeopardize (ABBR)
JEOPZD...... Jeopardized (ABBR)
JEOPZG...... Jeopardizing (ABBR)
Jep............ Jeopardy (BARN)
JEP............ Jet Engine Processor
JEP............ Jewish Elite Person

JEP .... Jupiter Entry Probe
JEPA .... Job Evaluation Policy Act of 1970
JEPAP .... Joint Emergency Personnel Augmentation Plan [*Military*] (CINC)
JEPG .... Joint Exercise Planning Group [*Military*]
JEPI .... Joint Electronic Payment Intitiative [*Proposed*] [*Computer science*]
JEPI .... Joint Electronic Payments Initiative
JEPI .... Junior Eysenck Personality Inventory [*Psychology*]
JEPIA .... Japan Electronic Parts Industry Association
JEPO .... Joint Engine Project Office (MCD)
JEPP .... Japan English Publications in Print [*Japan Publications Guide Service*] [*Japan Information service or system*] (CRD)
JEPP .... Japanese Earthquake Prediction Plan
JEPS .... Job Effectiveness Prediction System [*Test for insurance company employees*]
JEPS .... Job Entry Peripheral Services [*IBM Corp.*] (MCD)
JEPS .... Joint Exercise Planning Staff [*NATO*] (NATG)
JEQ .... Japan Equity Fund [*NYSE symbol*] (SPSG)
JEQ .... Jequie [*Brazil*] [*Airport symbol*] (OAG)
JER .... Japan Economic Review [*A publication*] (WDAA)
JER .... Japanese Erection Ring [*Medicine*] (BABM)
Jer .... Jeremiah [*Old Testament book*]
Jer .... Jeremias (BJA)
Jer .... Jericho (BJA)
JER .... Jersey [*Channel Islands*] [*Airport symbol*] (OAG)
JER .... Jerusalem [*Israel*] [*Seismograph station code, US Geological Survey*] (SEIS)
Jer .... Jerusalem Talmud (BJA)
Jer .... Jerushalmi (BJA)
JERA .... James E. Rush Associates, Inc. [*Also, an information service or system*] (IID)
JerC .... Jersey Central Power & Light [*Associated Press*] (SAG)
Jerc .... Junior Executive Research Consultant [*Fictitious position in Commerce Bank of Beverly Hills created for Jethro Bodine on the television show "The Beverly Hillbillies"*]
Jer Car ...... Jeremy on Carriers [*A publication*] (DLA)
Jer Dig .... Jeremy's Digest [*1817-49*] [*A publication*] (DLA)
Jeremy Eq ... Jeremy's Equity Jurisdiction [*A publication*] (DLA)
Jeremy Eq Jur... Jeremy's Equity Jurisdiction [*A publication*] (DLA)
Jer Eq Jur ... Jeremy's Equity Jurisdiction [*A publication*] (DLA)
JerM .... Jersey Microfilming, Clifton, NJ [*Library symbol Library of Congress*] (LCLS)
JEROB .... Jeroboam (WDAA)
JerPes .... Jerusalem Talmud. Pesahim (BJA)
Jerr Copyr ... Jerrold on Copyright [*A publication*] (DLA)
JERS .... Japan Earth Remote Sensing Satellite
JERS .... Joint Emergency Relocation Site
Jersey City St C... Jersey City State College (GAGS)
JERS-I .... Japan Earth Resources Satellite [*Marine science*] (OSRA)
JERU .... Joint Environmental Research Unit (MCD)
Jerus .... Jerusalem (BJA)
Jerv Cor ...... Jervis. Coroners [*9th ed.*] [*1957*] [*A publication*] (DLA)
Jerv NR ...... Jervis' New Rules [*A publication*] (DLA)
JerW .... Jerusalemer Warte (BJA)
JerYeb .... Jerusalem Talmud. Yebamoth (BJA)
Jes.............. Analysis and Digest of the Decisions of Sir George Jessel, by A. P Peter [*England*] [*A publication*] (DLA)
JES .... Japan Electronics Show
JES .... Japan Environmental Systems
JES .... Japanese Export Standard
JES .... Jes Air [*Bulgaria*] [*ICAO designator*] (FAAC)
JES .... Jesuit (DSUE)
JES .... Jesup, GA [*Location identifier FAA*] (FAAL)
JES .... Jesus
JES .... Jet Ejector System
JES .... Job Entry System [*or Subsystem*] [*IBM Corp.*] [*Computer science*]
JES .... John Ericsson Society (EA)
JES .... Joint Efficiency Study (AIE)
JESAP .... Jet Engine Smoke Abatement Program
JES COLL.... Jesus College [*Oxford or Cambridge*] [*England*] (ROG)
JESCOM....... Jesuits in Communication in the US (EA)
JESNA .... Jewish Education Service of North America (EA)
JESS .... Joint Exercise Simulation System [*DoD*]
JESS .... Joint Exercise Support System [*Military*]
JESSI .... Joint European Semiconductor Silicon Initiative
JESSI .... Joint European Submicron Silicon [*Project*]
JESSI .... Junior Engineers' and Scientists' Summer Institute
JEST .... Jungle Environmental Survival Training [*Military*]
JET.............. European Jet Ltd. [*British ICAO designator*] (FAAC)
JET.............. Frankfort, KY [*Location identifier FAA*] (FAAL)
JET.............. Jam Exceeds Threshold
JET.............. Jetronic Industries, Inc. [*AMEX symbol*] (SPSG)
JET.............. Jetsam (ABBR)
JET.............. Jettison
JET.............. Job Element Text (AFM)
JET.............. Job English Training
JET.............. Jobs Evaluation and Training
JET.............. Joint Economic Team
JET.............. Joint Effort for Talent [*Navy*] (NG)
JET.............. Joint European TOKAMAK [*Toroidal Kamera Magnetic*] [*or Torus Nuclear reactor*]
JET.............. Jointly Endorsed Training [*Union-management*]
JET.............. Journal Entries Transfer [*Computer science*] (MHDI)
JET.............. Judicial Education Teleseminar System [*Defunct*] (TSSD)
JET.............. Junior Enlisted Travel [*Entitlement*] (MCD)
JETAM .... Jet Engine Thrust Augmentation Mix (SAA)

JETAV .... Jet Aviation (SAA)
JETD .... Jetted (ABBR)
JETD .... Joint Electronics Type Designator [*Military*] (AABC)
JETDS .... Joint Electronics Type Designation System [*Military*] (AFM)
JETEC .... Joint Electron Tube Engineering Council [*Later, JEDEC*] (MCD)
JetForm .... Jet Form Corp. [*Associated Press*] (SAG)
JETG .... Jetting (ABBR)
J Eth L........ Journal of Ethiopian Law [*A publication*] (DLA)
JETLNR....... Jetliner (ABBR)
JETN .... Jettison
JETP .... Jet-Propelled
JETR .... Japan Engineering Test Reactor
JETR .... Jetevator
JETRO.......... Japan External Trade Organization [*New York, NY*] (EA)
Jetronic .... Jetronic Industries, Inc. [*Associated Press*] (SAG)
JETS .... Jet Express Ticketing System
JETS .... Job Executive and Transport Satellite [*NCR Corp.*]
JETS .... Joint Electronics Type [*Designation*] System [*Military*] (NASA)
JETS .... Joint Enroute Terminal System [*Canada*] (MCD)
JETS .... Junior Engineering Technical Society
JETT .... Jettison (KSC)
JEV .... Japanese Encephalitis Virus [*Medicine*]
Jev Cr Law... Jevons on Criminal Law [*A publication*] (DLA)
JEW .... Jewellery [*British*] (ROG)
JEW .... Jewish
JEWC .... Joint Electronic Warfare Center (MCD)
JEW COLL LOND... Jewish College, London [*England*] (ROG)
JEWEL .... Joint Endeavor for Welfare, Education, and Liberation [*Part of Grenadian political party, the New JEWEL Movement*]
JewettC .... Jewett-Cameron Trading Co. Ltd. [*Associated Press*] (SAG)
JEWLF .... IWI Holding Ltd. [*NASDAQ symbol*] (SAG)
JEWSOC .... Joint Electronic Warfare Staff Officer Course (DOMA)
JEWT .... Jungle Exercise without Trees [*British military*] (DMA)
Jew YB Int'l L... Jewish Yearbook of International Law [*A publication*] (DLA)
JEX .... Jenks, OK [*Location identifier FAA*] (FAAL)
JEX .... Jet Express, Inc. [*ICAO designator*] (FAAC)
JEX .... Joint Exercise (NVT)
JEZ .... Joint Engagement Zone [*Marine Corps*] (DOMA)
JEZEX .... Jezebel [*Sonobuoy*] Exercise [*Navy*] (NVT)
JF .... Jack Field
JF .... Jackstone Froster Ltd. [*Commercial firm British*]
JF .... Jamestown Foundation (EA)
JF .... Japan Foundation [*Also, Kokusai Koryu*] (EA)
JF .... Jefferson Foundation (EA)
JF .... Jet Flap
JF .... John Flanagan [*Designer's mark, when appearing on US coins*]
JF .... Joint Filler [*Technical drawings*]
JF .... Joint Fluid [*Orthopedics*] (DAVI)
JF .... Joint Force [*Military*]
JF .... Journal Folio (ROG)
JF .... Jugular Forainen [*Anatomy*] (DAVI)
JF .... Junctional Fold [*Anatomy*] (DAVI)
JF .... Junction Frequency [*Telecommunications*] (TEL)
JF .... Junctor Frame [*Telecommunications*] (TEL)
JF .... Jundt Growth Fund [*NYSE symbol*] (SPSG)
JF .... Justice Fellowship (EA)
JF .... LAB Flying Service [*ICAO designator*] (AD)
JF .... Trehaven Aviation Ltd. [*British ICAO designator*] (ICDA)
JFA .... Aviones Ejecutivos, JFA [*Mexico*] [*FAA designator*] (FAAC)
JFA .... Jaffa [*Israel*] [*Airport symbol*] (AD)
JFAAD .... Joint Forward-Area Air Defense (MCD)
JFAADS........ Joint Forward-Area Air Defense System
JFAC .... Joint Flight Acceptance Composite Test [*Gemini*] [*NASA*] (IAA)
JFACC .... Joint Force Air Component Commander (DOMA)
J-FACT.......... Joint Flight Acceptance Composite Test [*Gemini*] [*NASA*]
JFACTSU...... Joint Forward Air Controllers Training and Standards Unit [*British*]
JFAI .... Joint Formal Acceptance Inspection [*NATO*] (NATG)
JFAP .... Joint Frequency Allocation Panel
JFAST .... Joint Flow and Analysis System for Transportation [*Model USA*]
JFB .... Jet Flying Belt (PDAA)
JFC .... Jardine Fleming China Reg Fd [*NYSE symbol*] (TTSB)
JFC .... Jardine Fleming China Regular Fund [*NYSE symbol*] (SPSG)
JFC .... Jewish Folk Center [*Australia*]
JFC .... John Forsyth Co., Inc. [*Toronto Stock Exchange symbol*]
JFC .... Joint Force Commander [*DoD*]
JFC .... Jupiter-family Comets [*Astronomy*]
JFC .... LTV Jet Fleet Corp. [*ICAO designator*] (FAAC)
JFCB .... Job File Control Block [*Computer science*] (BUR)
JFCL .... Jump if Flag Set and Then Clear the Flag [*Computer science*] (NHD)
JFDA .... Jewish Funeral Directors of America (EA)
JFDP .... Joint Force Development Process [*or Program*] [*Army*]
JFE .... Joint Fighter Engine (DWSG)
JFEA .... Japan Federation of Employers Association
JFEA .... Joint Foreign Exchange Agency [*Berlin*] [*Post-World War II, Germany*]
JFED .... Junction Field-Effect Device
JFEO .... Japanese Federation of Economic Organizations
J Ferment Technol (1944-1976)... Journal of Fermentation Technology (1944-1976) [*Japan*] [*A publication*]
JFET.......... Junction Field-Effect Transistor
JFEW .... Jewish Foundation for Education of Women (EA)
JFF............. Aguadilla, PR [*Location identifier FAA*] (FAAL)
JFF............. Jobs for the Future [*An association*]
JFF............. Junior Fashion Fair International [*British*] (ITD)
JFFC .... Jewish Fighting Force Committee [*British*]

JFFC	John Fricke Fan Club [Defunct] (EA)
JFFC	Judy Fields Fan Club (EA)
JFG	Jumbogroup Frequency Generator [Bell System]
JFH	Jam Frequency Hopper
JFHQ	Joint Force Headquarters [Military]
JFI	James Franck Institute [University of Chicago] [Research center] (RCD)
JFI	Japanese Fermentation Institute
JFI	Jardine Fleming India Fund [NYSE symbol] (SAG)
JFI	Jet Flight Information (AFM)
JFI	John La Farge Institute (EA)
JFI	New Orleans, LA [Location identifier FAA] (FAAL)
JFIAP	Joint Foreign Intelligence Assistance Program (AFM)
JFIF	JPEG [Joint Photographic Experts Group] File Interchange Format [Computer science] (CDE)
J Film & Vid...	Journal of Film & Video [A publication] (BRI)
JFIndia	Jardine Fleming India Fund [Associated Press] (SAG)
JFIT	Joint Framework for Information Technology [British]
JFJ	Jewish Fund for Justice (EA)
JFJ	Jews for Jesus (EA)
JFK	John Fitzgerald Kennedy [US president, 1917-1963]
JFK	Kennedy International Airport [New York] [Airport symbol]
JFKC	John Fitzgerald Kennedy Center for the Performing Arts
JFKCTRMA...	John F. Kennedy Center for Military Assistance (MCD)
JFK FDC SU...	John F. Kennedy First Day Cover Study Unit (EA)
JFKL	John F. Kennedy Library
JFKLF	John F. Kennedy Library Foundation (EA)
JFKPS	John F. Kennedy Philatelic Society (EA)
JFKSC	John Fitzgerald Kennedy Spaceflight Center [Also known as KSC] [NASA]
JFL	Joint Frequency List
JFL	Judy Farquharson Ltd. [British]
JFLA	Jewish Free Loan Association (EA)
JFLC	Joint Forces Land Component (DOMA)
JFLCC	Joint Forces Land Component Commander (DOMA)
JFM	Jet Flap Model
JFM	Jews for Morality (EA)
JFM	Job Function Manual (AAG)
JFM	Joint Force Memorandum [Military]
JFM	Jupiter Flyby Mission [Aerospace]
JFMIP	Joint Financial Management Improvement Program
JFMO	Joint Frequency Management Office (MCD)
JFN	Jefferson, OH [Location identifier FAA] (FAAL)
JFN	Job File Number
JFNF	Jewish Family Name File [Association for the Study of Jewish Languages] [Information service or system] (CRD)
JFNP	Joseph M. Farley Nuclear Plant (NRCH)
JFNPP	James A. FitzPatrick Nuclear Power Plant (NRCH)
JFO	Just for Openers [An association] (EA)
J For Sci Soc...	Journal. Forensic Science Society [A publication] (DLA)
JFP	Jewish Family Purity (BJA)
JFP	Joint Frequency Panel
JFPH	JUMPS [Joint Uniform Military Pay System] Field Procedures Handbook (NVT)
JFR	Jamie Frontier Resources, Inc. [Toronto Stock Exchange symbol]
JFR	Jet Flap Rotor
JFR	Joint Fiction Reserve
JFRC	James Forrestal Research Center [Princeton University] (MCD)
JFS	Jamaica Freight and Shipping Co. Ltd. (EY)
JFS	Jet Fuel Starter
JFS	Jewish Family Service (EA)
JFS	Jewish Friends Society (EA)
JFS	Job Finder System
JFS	Johnston & Frye [Vancouver Stock Exchange symbol]
JFS	Joint Foundation Support (EA)
JFS	Juanda Flying School [Indonesia] [ICAO designator] (FAAC)
JFS	Jugular Foramen Syndrome [or Vernet's syndrome] [Medicine] (DAVI)
JFS	Jumbogroup Frequency Supply [Bell System]
JFSG	Joint Feasibility Study Group [Air Force] (MCD)
JFSNY	Jewish Folk Schools of New York (EA)
JFSP	Joint Forecast System Project (USDC)
JFSP	Joint Forecast System Project [Marine science] (OSRA)
JFSS	Joint Force Signals Staff [Military]
JFT	Jet Fret [France ICAO designator] (FAAC)
JFT	Job File Table (PCM)
JFT	Joint Field Trial (NATG)
JFTCG	Joint Flight Test Control Group (AAG)
JFTG	Joint Fuze Task Group [Army]
JFTOT	Jet Fuel Thermal Oxidation Test [or Tester] [Analytical chemistry] [Air Force]
JFTR	Joint Federal Travel Regulations (DOMA)
JFTS	Jet Fuel Thermal Stability
JFTU	Jordan Federation of Trade Unions
JFTX	Joint Field Training Exercise [Military]
JFU	Jersey Farmers' Union [British] (DBA)
JFUB	Joint Facilities Utilization Board [Military]
JFuU	Fukui University, Fukui-shi, Japan [Library symbol Library of Congress] (LCLS)
JFV	Jobs for Veterans National Committee [Defunct] (EA)
JFV	Jupiter Flyby Vehicle [Aerospace]
JFW	Justice for Women (EA)
JFY	Foster Yeoman Ltd. [British ICAO designator] (FAAC)
JFY	Japanese Fiscal Year (CINC)
JFY	Jiffy (ABBR)

JG	Jahrgang [Year of Publication/Volume] [German]
JG	Jerusalem und Seine Gelaende [A publication] (BJA)
JG	Jockeys' Guild (EA)
JG	Joules per Gram [Physics] (IAA)
Jg	Judges [Old Testament book] (BJA)
JG	Judgment [Legal shorthand] (LWAP)
JG	Juedisches Gemeindeblatt fuer die Britische Zone [A publication] (BJA)
JG	Junction Grammar [Computer science]
JG	Junction Grammar [Machine translation term] (NITA)
JG	June Grass [Test] [Medicine] (DAVI)
JG	Junior Girls [School department] [British] (DI)
JG	Junior Grade
JG	Juxtaglomerular [Histology]
JG	Swedair [ICAO designator] (AD)
JGA	Jamnagar [India] [Airport symbol] (OAG)
JGA	Jojoba Growers Association (EA)
JGA	Joseph Guzman & Associates, Inc. [Palatine, IL] [Telecommunications Defunct] (TSSD)
JGA	Juxtaglomerular Apparatus [Histology]
JGAB	Joint Government Agencies Board (SSD)
JG & C	Joint Guidance and Control (KSC)
JGB	Japanese Government Bond (ECON)
JGB	Jewish Guild for the Blind (EA)
JGC	Grand Canyon [Arizona] [Airport symbol] (OAG)
JGC	Jacob Gold Corp. [Vancouver Stock Exchange symbol]
JGC	JGC Corp. [Formerly, Japan Gasoline Co. Ltd.]
JGC	Juxtaglomerular Cells [Histology]
JGCC	Juxtaglomerular Cell Count [Endocrinology]
JGCT	Juxtaglomerular Cell Tumor [Histology] (DAVI)
JG/D	Judgement for the Defendant [Legal shorthand] (LWAP)
JGD	Junior Grand Deacon [Freemasonry]
J/Gdsmn	Junior Guardsman [British military] (DMA)
JGE	Jaguar Equity, Inc. [Vancouver Stock Exchange symbol]
JGE	Joint Group of Experts [Marine science] (MSC)
JGF	Jakarta Growth Fund [NYSE symbol] (SPSG)
JGF	Junctor Grouping Frame [Telecommunications] (TEL)
JGFC	Joe Gallison Fan Club (EA)
JGFC	John Gilbert Fan Club (EA)
JGFC	John Gill Fan Club (EA)
JGFET	Junction Gate Field-Effect Transistor [Electronics] (IAA)
JGH	Jig Grinder Head
JGI	Jejunogastric Intussusception [Gastroenterology] (DAVI)
JGI	Juxtaglomerular Granulation Index [Endocrinology]
JGI	Juxtaglomerular Index [Endocrinology]
JGIFC	John Gary International Fan Club (EA)
JGIN	JG Industries [NASDAQ symbol] (TTSB)
JGIN	JG Industries, Inc. [NASDAQ symbol] (NQ)
JG Ind	JG Industries, Inc. [Associated Press] (SAG)
JGLC	Joint Government Liaison Committee [Composed of Association of Brass and Bronze Ingot Manufacturers and Brass and Bronze Ingot Institute] (EA)
JGM	Jig Grinding Machine
JGM	Job Guide Manual (PDAA)
JGMC	Judy Garland Memorial Club (EA)
JGN	Junction Gate Number
JGOFS	Joint Global Ocean Flux Study [International experiment]
JGO-US	Job Guarantee Office of the United States (OICC)
J Gov Info...	Journal of Government Information [A publication] (BRI)
JGP	Houston [Texas] Greenway [Airport symbol] (OAG)
JGP	Jem Group Products [Vancouver Stock Exchange symbol]
JG/P	Judgement for the Plaintiff [Legal shorthand] (LWAP)
JGP	Juvenile General Paralysis [Medicine] (DAVI)
JGP	Juvenile General Paresis [Medicine] (DMAA)
JGPA	Jobbing Grinders' Provident Association [A union] [British]
JGQ	Houston [Texas] Guest Quarters [Airport symbol] (OAG)
JGR	Belize Trans Air [ICAO designator] (FAAC)
JGR	Journal of Geophysical Research
JGRIP	Japanese Government and Public Research in Progress [International database]
JGS	James Griffiths & Sons [AAR code]
JGS	Jewish Genealogical Society (EA)
JGS	Joint General Staff [Military] (NATG)
Jgs	Judges [Old Testament book]
JGSDF	Japanese Ground Self-Defense Forces (AABC)
JGSW	Jigsaw (ABBR)
JGT	Judgment [Legal term] (ROG)
JGT	Junction Growth Technique
JGTC	Junior Girls' Training Corps [British World War II]
JGTL	Job Grading System for Trades and Labor Occupations
JGTOI	[The] Judge GTO International
JGW	Junior Grand Warden [Freemasonry]
JGWTC	Jungle and Guerrilla Warfare Training Center [Army]
JH	Echovirus 28 [Virology] (DAVI)
JH	Harland [John H.] Co. [NYSE symbol] (SPSG)
JH	Harland (John H.) [NYSE symbol] (TTSB)
JH	Jacob's Horse [British military] (DMA)
JH	Journal of the House of Representatives [United States] [A publication] (DLA)
JH	Juvenile Hormone [Entomology]
JH	Nordeste-Lineas Aereas Regionais [ICAO designator] (AD)
JHA	Japan Hour Association [Later, JHB] (EA)
JHA	Job Hazard Analysis (PDAA)
JHA	John Howard Association (EA)
JHA	Juvenile Hormone Analog [Entomology]

JHB.............. Japan Hour Broadcasting (EA)
JHB.............. Johannesburg [South Africa] (ABBR)
JHB.............. Johore Bahru [Malaysia] [Airport symbol] (OAG)
JHBP............ Juvenile Hormone Binding Protein [Entomology]
JHC.............. Garden City [New York] [Airport symbol] (OAG)
JHC.............. Johnson Canyon [California] [Seismograph station code, US Geological Survey] (SEIS)
JHC.............. Joint High Command (DNAB)
JHCNHS....... John Henry Cardinal Newman Honorary Society [Defunct] (EA)
JHD.............. Jehuda [On Hebrew coins of the fourth century]
JHD.............. Joint Hypocenter Determination [Earthquake study]
JHDA............ Junior Hospital Doctors Association [British]
JHe.............. Jewish Heritage [A publication] (BJA)
JHE.............. Johns Hopkins University, Baltimore, MD [OCLC symbol] (OCLC)
JHE.............. Juvenile Hormone Esterase [An enzyme]
JHF.............. Jackson, MS [Location identifier FAA] (FAAL)
JHFC............ Jan Howard Friends Club (EA)
JHFC............ Jeff Healey Fan Club (EA)
JHG.............. Joule Heat Gradient (IEEE)
JHGA............ Jewish Historical General Archives [Jerusalem] (BJA)
JHGSOWA.... Joint Household Goods Shipping Office, Washington Area [Military] (AABC)
JHHGSO....... Joint Household Goods Shipping Office [Military]
JHI.............. Hancock, John, Investors Trust [NYSE symbol] (SAG)
JHI.............. John Hancock Investors Trust [NYSE symbol] (SPSG)
JHI.............. John Hancock Inv Tr [NYSE symbol] (TTSB)
JHI.............. Journal of the History of Ideas [A publication] (BRI)
J Hi E........ Journal of Higher Education [A publication] (BRI)
J Hist G...... Journal of Historical Geography [A publication] (BRI)
J Hist Soc SA... Journal. Historical Society of South Australia [A publication]
JHjelm......... Hjelms [Jim] Private Collection [Associated Press] (SAG)
JHjelm......... Jim Hjelms Private Collection [Associated Press] (SAG)
JHL.............. Jet Heritage Ltd. [British ICAO designator] (FAAC)
JHM.............. Juvenile Hormone Mimic [Entomology]
JHMCO .... J. H. Morgan Consultants [Morristown, NJ] [Information service or system Telecommunications] (TSSD)
JHMO.......... Junior Hospital Medical Officer
JHN.............. John Henry Newman [Initials used as pseudonym]
JHN.............. Johnson Air, Inc. [ICAO designator] (FAAC)
JHN.............. Johnson, KS [Location identifier FAA] (FAAL)
JHO.............. Junior House Officer [Military]
J Homosex... Journal of Homosexuality [A publication] (BRI)
JHP.............. Jacketed Hollow-Point [Ammunition]
JHP.............. Jackson Hole Preserve (EA)
JHP.............. Peabody Institute of Johns Hopkins University, Conservatory Library, Baltimore, MD [OCLC symbol] (OCLC)
JHPC............ Jim Hielms Private Coll'n [NASDAQ symbol] (TTSB)
JHPC............ Jim Hjelms Private Collection [NASDAQ symbol] (SPSG)
JHPS............ Judaica Historical Philatelic Society (EA)
JHQ.............. Joint Headquarters [British military] (DMA)
JHQ.............. Shute Harbour [Australia Airport symbol] (OAG)
JHR.............. Jarisch-Herxheimer Reaction [Immunology] (DAVI)
JHRP .... Joint Highway Research Project [Purdue University] [Research center] (RCD)
JHS.............. Hancock, John, Income Securities Trust [NYSE symbol] (SAG)
JHS.............. Jesus Hominum Salvator [Jesus, Savior of Men] (ROG)
JHS.............. Job Hunter's Sourcebook [A publication]
JHS.............. John Hancock Income Securities Trust [NYSE symbol] (SPSG)
JHS.............. John Hancock Inc. Sec [NYSE symbol] (TTSB)
JHS.............. Junior High School
JHS.............. School of Advanced International Studies, Johns Hopkins University, Washington, DC [OCLC symbol] (OCLC)
JHSE............ Jewish Historical Society of England
JHSN .... Journal. Historical Society of Nigeria [A publication]
JHTR............ Japan High Tech Review [Database] [Kyodo News International, Inc.] [Information service or system] (CRD)
JHU.............. Johns Hopkins University [Maryland]
JHU/APL ..... Johns Hopkins University Applied Physics Laboratory [Laurel, MD]
JHU-CRSC ... Johns Hopkins University - Center for Research in Scientific Communication (PDAA)
JHU-DDB ..... Johns Hopkins University - Dyslexia and Dysgraphia Batteries
JHVA.......... Jehovah (ROG)
JHVH.......... Jehovah (ABBR)
JHW.............. Jamestown [New York] [Airport symbol] (OAG)
JHW.............. Jamestown, NY [Location identifier FAA] (FAAL)
JHW.............. Johns Hopkins University, Welch Medical Library, Baltimore, MD [OCLC symbol] (OCLC)
JHWC............ Joint Hurricane Warning Center (CINC)
JI.............. Air Balear [ICAO designator] (ICDA)
JI.............. Gull Air [ICAO designator] (AD)
JI.............. Jamaat-i-Islami [Pakistan] [Political party] (FEA)
JI.............. Japan Institute [Defunct] (EA)
JI.............. Jazz Interactions (EA)
JI.............. Jazz International
JI.............. Jejunoileitis [Gastroenterology] (DAVI)
JI.............. Jejunoileostomy [Gastroenterology] (DAVI)
JI.............. Jersey Institute
JI.............. Jesness Inventory [Psychology]
JI.............. Jet Express [ICAO designator] (AD)
JI.............. Jet Interaction (RDA)
JI.............. Jigging Information
JI.............. Job Instruction
JI.............. Job Insurance [Job Service] (OICC)
ji.............. Johnston Atoll [MARC country of publication code Library of Congress] (LCCP)

JI.............. Joint Identification (DNAB)
JI.............. Josephson Interferometer [Optics] (IAA)
JI.............. Junction Isolation [Electronics]
JI.............. Jupiter Inlet [NASA] (KSC)
JIA.............. Jetstream International Airlines [ICAO designator] (FAAC)
JIA.............. Joint Interest Audiovisual Requirements (MCD)
JIA.............. Jordan International Airline
JIA.............. Jute Importers' Association [British] (DBA)
JIAA.............. Joint Institute for Aeronautics and Acoustics [Stanford University] (PDAA)
JIAD.............. Joint Integrated Avionics Directorate (DOMA)
JIAFS.......... Joint Institute for Acoustics and Flight Sciences (MCD)
JIAFS.......... Joint Institute for Advancement of Flight Science [Research center] (RCD)
JIAWG .... Joint Integrated Avionics Working Group [DoD]
JIB.............. Djibouti [Airport symbol] (OAG)
JIB.............. Jack-in-the-Box Dummy [CIA]
JIB.............. Jejunoileal Bypass [Gastroenterology] (DAVI)
JIB.............. Jewish Information Bureau [Defunct] (EA)
JIB.............. Job Information Block [Computer science] (BUR)
JIB.............. Jobs Impact Bulletin [National Committee for Full Employment] [A publication]
JIB.............. Joint Information Bureau [Military] (MCD)
JIB.............. Joint Intelligence Bureau [British] (MCD)
JIB.............. Jordan Information Bureau (EA)
JIB.............. Journal of International Business Studies [A publication] (BRI)
JIBEI.......... Joint Industry Board of the Electrical Industry (EA)
JIBG.......... Jibing (ABBR)
JIC.............. Jet-Induced Circulation [Combustor]
JIC.............. Jet Interaction Control (MCD)
JIC.............. Jewelry Industry Council (EA)
JIC.............. Job Information Centre [Canada]
JIC.............. Job Instruction and Communication (PDAA)
JIC.............. Joint Ice Center [Marine science] (MSC)
JIC.............. Joint Ice Center [US Navy] [Marine science] (OSRA)
JIC.............. Joint Implementation Committee [Military] (SAA)
JIC.............. Joint Industrial Council [Defunct] (EA)
JIC.............. Joint Industry Council (EAIO)
JIC.............. Joint Insurance Committee [under the Trading with the Enemy Act] [World War II]
JIC.............. Joint Intelligence Center
JIC.............. Joint Intelligence Committee
JIC.............. Joint Interrogation Center (MCD)
JIC.............. Junior International Club (EA)
JIC.............. Just in Case (WDMC)
JIC.............. Juventudes Inconformes de Colombia [Political party] (EY)
JIC.............. Morgan Stanley Group, Inc. [AMEX symbol] (SAG)
JICA.......... Japan International Cooperation Agency
JICA.......... Joint Intelligence Center, Africa
JICA.......... Joint Intelligence Collecting Agency
JICACBI........ Joint Intelligence Collecting Agency, China, Burma, India [World War II]
JICAME .... Joint Intelligence Collecting Agency, Middle East [World War II]
JICANA .... Joint Intelligence Collecting Agency, North Africa [World War II]
JICARC .... Joint Intelligence Collecting Agency, Reception Committee [Navy]
JICC.......... Job Item Cost Code (MCD)
JICCAR........ Joint Industry Committee for Cable Audience Research [Television] [British]
JICG.......... Joint International Coordination Group (MSC)
JICHS.......... Joint Industrial Conference on Hydraulic Standards
JICI.......... Jeunesse Independante Chretienne Internationale [International Independent Christian Youth - IICY] (EA)
JICJ.......... Journal. International Commission of Jurists [A publication] (DLA)
Jick Est.... Jickling. Legal and Equitable Estates [1829] [A publication] (DLA)
JICNARS...... Joint Industry Committee for National Readership Surveys [British]
JICOA.......... Japan Information and Communication Association [Information service or system] (IID)
JICPAC........ Joint Intelligence Center Pacific (DOMA)
JICPAS........ Joint Industry Committee for Poster Audience Surveys [British]
JICPOA........ Joint Intelligence Center, Pacific Ocean Areas
JICRAR........ Joint Industry Committee for Radio Audience Research [British]
JICS.......... Joint Intelligence Coordination Staff [Central Intelligence Agency] (AABC)
JICST.......... Japan Information Center for Science and Technology
JICST.......... Japan Information Center of Science and Technology [Tokyo] (IID)
JICST.......... Japan International Center of Science and Technology (USGC)
JICTAR........ Joint Industry Committee for Television Advertising Research [Database producer]
JICUF.......... Japan International Christian University Foundation (EA)
JID.......... Air Condal SA [Spain ICAO designator] (FAAC)
JIDA.......... Jewelry Industry Distributors Association (EA)
JIDS.......... Job Information Delivery System [US Employment Service] [Department of Labor]
JIE.......... Japan Information Exchange [Comtex Scientific Corp.] [Information service or system Defunct] (CRD)
JIE.......... Jobs in Energy (EA)
JIE.......... Junior Institute of Engineers
JIEE.......... Japanese Institute of Electrical Engineers
JIEO.......... Joint Interoperability and Engineering Organization [DoD]
JIEP.......... Joint Intelligence Estimate for Planning (AFM)
JIF.......... French Lick, IN [Location identifier FAA] (FAAL)
JIF.......... Janus Information Facility [Later, J2CP Information Services] (EA)
JIF.......... Jet Interaction Fuel
JIF.......... Joint Integrated Firepower [Task force] (MCD)
JIF.......... Joint Interrogation Facility (DOMA)

JIFC	Janis Ian Fan Club (EA)
JIFC	Julio Iglesias Fan Club [*Defunct*] (EA)
JIFDATS	Joint In-Flight Data Transmission System [*Army*] (MCD)
JIFE	Junta Internacional de Fiscalizacion de Estupefacientes [*International Narcotics Control Board*]
JIFSAN	Joint Institute of Food Safety and Applied Nutrition
JIFTS	Joint In-Flight Transmission System [*Army*] (IEEE)
JIG	Jinotega [*Nicaragua*] [*Seismograph station code, US Geological Survey*] (SEIS)
JIG	Joint Industry Group [*An association*] (EA)
JIG	Joint Intelligence Group [*Military*]
JIG	Joule Impulse Generator [*Physics*]
JIGFET	Junction and Insulated Gate Field Effect Transistor (MCD)
JIGG	Jet Interaction Gas Generator
JIGL	Jiggle (ABBR)
JIGLD	Jiggled (ABBR)
JIGLG	Jiggling (ABBR)
JIGLY	Jiggly (ABBR)
JIGR	Jigger (ABBR)
JIGS	Joule Impulse Generator System [*Physics*]
JIGTSC	Joint Industry-Government Tall Structures Committee
JIH	Joint Interval Histogram [*Histology*] (DAVI)
JIH	Journal of Interdisciplinary History [*A publication*] (BRI)
JII	John Innes Institute [*British*] (ARC)
JII	Johnston Industries [*NYSE symbol*] (TTSB)
JII	Johnston Industries, Inc. [*NYSE symbol*] (SPSG)
JIIB	Jewish Immigrants Information Bureau (BJA)
JIIG-CAL	Job Ideas and Information Generator - Computer Assisted Learning (AIE)
JIIKS	Joint Imagery Interpretation Key Structure (MCD)
JIIP	Joint Interface Implementation Program [*Army*] (MCD)
JIIST	Japan Institute for International Studies and Training
JIL	Jet-Induced Lift
JIL	Joy Industries Ltd. [*Vancouver Stock Exchange symbol*]
JILA	Joint Institute for Laboratory Astrophysics [*University of Colorado, National Bureau of Standards*] (EA)
JILA-IC	Joint Institute for Laboratory Astrophysics-Information Center [*University of Colorado*] (PDAA)
JILE	Joint Intelligence Liaison Element (MCD)
JilinCh	Jilin Chemical Industrial Co. Ltd. [*Associated Press*] (SAG)
JILL	Jobs Illustrated [*CD-ROM*]
JilEnt	Jillians Entertainment Corp. [*Associated Press*] (SAG)
JILO	Joint Information Liaison Office [*Military*]
JILTA	Journal. Indian Law Teachers Association [*A publication*] (DLA)
JIM	Jevreiski Istoriski Muzej (BJA)
JIM	Jimma [*Ethiopia*] [*Airport symbol*] (OAG)
JIM	Job Instruction Manual
JIM	Memphis, TN [*Location identifier FAA*] (FAAL)
JIM	Sark International Airways Ltd. [*British ICAO designator*] (FAAC)
JIMA	John Innes Manufacturers Association (DBA)
JIMAR	Joint Institute for Marine and Atmospheric Research [*Honolulu, HI*] [*National Oceanic and Atmospheric Administration*] (GRD)
JIMI	Jimi Hendrix Information Management Institute (EA)
JIMS	Joint Industrial Measurement Programme (ACII)
JIN	Jindabyne [*Australia Seismograph station code, US Geological Survey Closed*] (SEIS)
JIN	Jinja [*Uganda*] [*Airport symbol*] (AD)
JIN	Jump Indirectly [*Computer science*]
JIN	Justice Institute of British Columbia, Instructional Service [*UTLAS symbol*]
J Ind L Inst	Journal. Indian Law Institute [*A publication*] (DLA)
J Ind R	Journal of Industrial Relations [*A publication*]
J Indust Rel	Journal of Industrial Relations [*A publication*]
JINGLD	Jingled (ABBR)
JINGLG	Jingling (ABBR)
J INOR NUCL CHEM	Journal of Inorganic and Nuclear Chemistry [*A publication*] (WDAA)
JINR	Joint Institute of Nuclear Research [*Dubna, USSR*]
JINS	Juveniles in Need of Supervision [*Classification for delinquent children*]
JINSA	Jewish Institute for National Security Affairs (EA)
JINSTE	Junior Institution of Engineers [*British*]
J Inst Electr Eng (1949-63)	Journal. Institution of Electrical Engineers (1949-63) [*A publication*]
J Inst Electr Eng (1889-1940)	Journal. Institution of Electrical Engineers (1889-1940) [*A publication*]
J Instn Eng Aust	Journal. Institution of Engineers of Australia. [*A publication*]
JINTACCS	Joint Interoperability of Tactical Command and Control Systems (MCD)
JINTCCS	Joint Interoperability of Tactical Command and Control Systems (DOMA)
J Int'l & Comp L	Journal of International and Comparative Law [*A publication*] (DLA)
J Int'l Comm Jur	Journal. International Commission of Jurists [*A publication*] (DLA)
J Int'l L & Dipl	Journal of International Law and Diplomacy [*A publication*] (DLA)
J Int'l L & Pol	Journal of International Law and Politics [*A publication*] (DLA)
JIO	Joint Information Office [*Military*]
JIO	Joint Integration Office [*Department of Energy*] [*Albuquerque, NM*] (GAAI)
JIO	Ontario, CA [*Location identifier FAA*] (FAAL)
JIOA	Joint Intelligence Objectives Agency (MCD)
JIOC	Jensen Interceptor Owners Club (EA)
JIP	Jipijapa [*Ecuador*] [*Airport symbol*] (AD)
JIP	Job Improvement Plan
JIP	Job the Impatient (BJA)
JIP	Join in Progress [*Broadcasting*] (WDMC)
JIP	Joint Implementation Plan [*Military*]
JIP	Joint Input
JIP	Joint Input Processing (IEEE)
JIP	Joint Installation Plan (AAG)
JIP/AMD	JIP/Areal Marketing Database [*Toyo Keizai Shinposha Co. Ltd.*] [*Japan Information service or system*] (CRD)
JIPC	Joint Imagery Production Complex (DOMA)
JIPC	Jordan Is Palestine Committee (EA)
JIPDEC	Japan Information Processing Development Center (NITA)
JIPID	Japanese International Protein Information Database
JIPMER	Jawahrlal Institute of Postgraduate Medical Education and Research [*India*]
JIR	Jewish Institute of Religion
JIR	Jiri [*Nepal*] [*Airport symbol*] (OAG)
JIR	Job Improvement Request
JIRC	Journal of Information Research Communications [*British*] (NITA)
JIRCSM	Joint Industry Research Committee for Standardization of Miniature Precision Coaxial Connectors
JIRI	Johnson Informal Reading Inventory (EDAC)
JIRP	Juneau Icefield Research Project [*University of Idaho*] [*Research center*]
JIRS	Jewish Information and Referral Service Directory [*A publication*] (EAAP)
JIRS	Joint Information and Retrieval System [*DoD*] (MCD)
JIS	Japanese Industrial Standards
JIS	Japan Investment Service [*Reuters Holdings Ltd.*] [*British Information service or system*] (CRD)
JIS	Jet Inlet System
JIS	Jet Interaction Steering
JIS	Jewish Information Society of America (EA)
JIS	Job Information Service [*Department of Labor*]
JIS	Job Information Station [*Department of Labor*] (IAA)
JIS	Job Information System (NITA)
JIS	Job Input System (NITA)
JIS	Joint Integrated Simulation (NASA)
JIS	Joint Intelligence Staff
JIS	Joint Operations Interim Software (MCD)
JIS	Journal of Information Science [*A publication*] (NITA)
JIS	Juvenile Idiopathic Scoliosis [*Medicine*] (DMAA)
JISAO	Joint Institute for Study of the Atmosphere and Ocean [*Seattle, WA*] [*University of Washington, NOAA*] (GRD)
JISC	Japanese Industrial Standards Committee [*Agency of Industrial Science and Technology, Ministry of International Trade and Industry*]
JISETA	Joint Investigation of the Southeastern Tropical Atlantic [*Angola, US*] (MSC)
JI/SI	Jet Interaction / Secondary Injection
J Islam & Comp L	Journal of Islamic and Comparative Law [*Nigeria*] [*A publication*] (DLA)
JISO	Japanese International Satellite Organization [*Cable-television system*]
JISPB	Joint Intelligence Studies Publishing Board
JISR	Joint Information Search Unit Retrieval System (MCD)
JISS	Jet Impurity Survey Spectrometer [*Nuclear energy*] (NUCP)
JISTEC	Japan International Science and Technology Exchange Center
JIT	Jamiat-i-Talaba [*Pakistan*] [*Political party*] (PD)
JIT	Job Information Test [*Military*] (AFM)
JIT	Job Instruction Training
JIT	Joint Interest Test [*Navy*] (NG)
JIT	Just in Time
jit	Just-In-Time [*Industry*] (ODBW)
JIT	Just-in-Time Inventory (TDOB)
JITA	Japanese Industrial Technology Association
JITA	Jet Interaction Test Apparatus (MCD)
JITC	Jewelry Industry Tax Committee [*Defunct*] (EA)
JITF	Joint Interface Test Facility [*Army*] (RDA)
JITF	Joint Interface Test Force [*Military*] (RDA)
JITF	Joint Interservice Task Force (MCD)
JITR	Jitter (ABBR)
JITRBG	Jitterbug (ABBR)
JITRY	Jittery (ABBR)
JIU	Joint Inspection Unit [*United Nations*]
JIW	J. Inglis Wright [*Advertising agency*] [*New Zealand*]
JIW	Jiwani [*Pakistan*] [*Airport symbol*] (OAG)
JIWP	Joint Interim Working Party
JJ	Coddair Air East [*ICAO designator*] (AD)
JJ	Jaw Jerk [*Medicine*]
JJ	Jeep Junior [*Automobile model designation*]
JJ	Jejunojejunostomy [*Gastroenterology*] (DAVI)
JJ	Jennifer Jo [*In TV series "The Governor and JJ"*]
JJ	Jews for Jews [*Defunct*] (EA)
JJ	Josephson Junction [*Cryogenics*] (IAA)
JJ	Judges [*Old Testament book*]
JJ	Junior Judge [*Legal term*] (DLA)
JJ	Justices
JJA	Jack and Jill of America (EA)
JJA	Judges of Appeal [*Legal term*]
JJA	June-July-August [*Marine science*] (OSRA)
JJA	Justices of Appeal [*Legal term*] (DLA)
JJAF	Jack and Jill of America Foundation (EA)
JJAMD	Jaw Joints and Allied Musculo-Skeletal Disorders Foundation (EA)
JJC	Jackson Junior College [*Florida; Michigan*]
JJC	Jiffy Junction Connector

JJC	Joliet Junior College [*Illinois*]
JJDP	Juvenile Justice and Delinquency Prevention
JJDPA	Juvenile Justice and Delinquency Prevention Act
JJ FAD	Just Jammin' Fresh and Def [*Rap recording group*]
JJFC	Jana Jae Fan Club (EA)
JJFC	Jim and Jesse Fan Club (EA)
JJFC	Joan Jett Fan Club (EA)
JJFC	Johnny and Jack Fan Club (EA)
JJI	Juanjui [*Peru*] [*Airport symbol*] (OAG)
JJITC	Jayco Jafari International Travel Club (EA)
JJM	John Judkyn Memorial (EA)
JJ Marsh (KY)	Marshall's Reports [*Kentucky*] [*A publication*] (DLA)
JJMAS	Jack Jones Music Appreciation Society [*Defunct*] (EAIO)
JJN	Jinjiang [*China*] [*Airport symbol*] (OAG)
JJO	Mountain City, TN [*Location identifier FAA*] (FAAL)
JJP	Jatiya Janata Party [*National People's Party*] [*Bangladesh*] [*Political party*] (PPW)
JJS	James Joyce Society (EA)
JJSC	Jefferson Smurfit [*NASDAQ symbol*] (TTSB)
JJSC	Jefferson Smurfit Corp. [*NASDAQ symbol*] (SAG)
JJSC	Justices of the Supreme Court [*Legal term*] (DLA)
JJSF	J&J Snack Foods [*NASDAQ symbol*] (TTSB)
JJSF	J & J Snack Foods Corp. [*NASDAQ symbol*] (NQ)
J-J S-S	Jean-Jacques Servan-Schreiber [*French publisher*]
JJSWC	Jiffy Junction Single Wire Connector
JJT	Jumbo Jet Transport
JJU	Julienhaab [*Greenland*] [*Airport symbol*] (AD)
J Jur	Journal of Jurisprudence [*A publication*] (DLA)
J Jur Papyrol	Journal of Juristic Papyrology [*A publication*] (DLA)
JJW	Sternair, Inc. [*FAA designator*] (FAAC)
JJWC	Jiffy Junction Wire Connector
JJWFC	Jerry Jeff Walker Fan Club (EA)
JK	Flip-Flop Circuit [*Computer science*]
JK	Jack (MSA)
JK	Jishu Kanri [*Voluntary Management*] [*Japanese method for increasing productivity of industrial workers by involving them in planning*]
J/K	Joule per Kelvin [*Physics*]
JK	Junk [*Ship's rigging*] (ROG)
JK	Sun World [*ICAO designator*] (AD)
JK	Trabajos Aereos y Enlaces SA [*Spain ICAO designator*] (ICDA)
JKA	Jakarta [*Indonesia*] (ABBR)
Jk^a	Kidd A [*Blood group*] (DAVI)
JKAA	Japan Karate Association of Australia
J Kan B Ass'n	Journal. Kansas Bar Association [*A publication*] (DLA)
JK & A	John Krucek & Associates [*Telecommunications service*] (TSSD)
JKAS	Jackass (ABBR)
JKAS	Jack Knight Airmail Society (EA)
JKB	Justice of the King's Bench (ROG)
Jk^b	Kidd B [*Blood group*] (DAVI)
JKBIR	Justice of the King's Bench, Ireland (ROG)
JKBT	Jackboot (ABBR)
JKBX	Jukebox (ABBR)
JKC	Jidosha Kiki Co. Ltd.
JKC	Shreveport, LA [*Location identifier FAA*] (FAAL)
JKCL	Jockey Club, Inc. [*NASDAQ symbol*] (SAG)
JKD	Jacked (ABBR)
JKET	Jacket (ABBR)
JKETD	Jacketted (ABBR)
JKFC	Japan-Republic of Korea Joint Fisheries Commission [*Marine science*] (OSRA)
JKFCFC	Jimmy Kish "The Flying Cowboy" Fan Club (EA)
JKG	Jacking (ABBR)
JKG	Jonkoping [*Sweden*] [*Airport symbol*] (OAG)
J/kg	Joule per Kilogram [*Physics*]
J/(KG K)	Joules per Kilogram Kelvin
JKH	Chios [*Greece*] [*Airport symbol*] (OAG)
JKHY	Henry (Jack) & Assoc [*NASDAQ symbol*] (TTSB)
JKHY	Henry, Jack Associates [*NASDAQ symbol*] (SAG)
JKKB	Jeunesse du Kwilu-Kwango-Bateke [*Kwilu-Kwango-Bateke Youth*]
JkksPac	Jakks Pacific, Inc. [*Associated Press*]
JKL	Jackal (ABBR)
JKL	Jackson, KY [*Location identifier FAA*] (FAAL)
JKLF	Jammu and Kashmir Liberation Front [*India*] [*Political party*] (ECON)
JKMR	Jackhammer (ABBR)
JKMS	Jack Knight Air Mail Society (EA)
JKNC	Jammu and Kashmir National Conference [*India*] [*Political party*] (PPW)
JKNIF	Jackknife (ABBR)
JKP	James Knox Polk [*US president, 1795-1849*]
JKPC	Junior Knights of Peter Claver (EA)
JKPMA	James K. Polk Memorial Association (EA)
JKPT	Jackpot (ABBR)
JKPT	Jackpot Enterprises [*NASDAQ symbol*] (SAG)
JKPTW	Jackpot Enterprises Wrrt [*NASDAQ symbol*] (TTSB)
JKR	Janakpur [*Nepal*] [*Airport symbol*] (OAG)
JKS	Jacks (ABBR)
JKS	Jacks Creek, TN [*Location identifier FAA*] (FAAL)
JKS	Jackson [*Diocesan abbreviation*] [*Mississippi*] (TOCD)
JKSCR	Jackscrew [*Mechanical engineering*]
Jksnvll	Jacksonville Bancorp, Inc. [*Associated Press*] (SAG)
JksnvlSL	Jacksonville Savings & Loan Association [*Texas*] [*Associated Press*] (SAG)
JksnvSB	Jacksonville Savings Bank (Illinois) [*Associated Press*] (SAG)
JKST	Johnson-Kenney Screening Test [*Psychology*] (DAVI)
JKT	Djakarta [*Java, Indonesia*] [*Airport symbol*] (AD)
JKT	Jacket (KSC)
JKT	Jakarta [*Indonesia*] [*Airport symbol*] (OAG)
JKT	Job Knowledge Test [*Military*] (AFM)
JKTD	Jacketed (ABBR)
JKTG	Jacketing (ABBR)
JKU	Kyoto University, Kyoto, Japan [*Library symbol Library of Congress*] (LCLS)
JKW	Juvonen, K. W., Winnipeg, Manitoba CDA [*STAC*]
JL	Jadassohn-Lewandowsky [*Syndrome*] [*Thickening of the nails*] [*Medicine*] (DAVI)
JL	Jaffe-Lichtenstein [*Syndrome*] [*or Fibrous dysplasia Orthopedics*] (DAVI)
JL	JAG Listing [*Military*]
JL	J & L Specialty Steel [*NYSE symbol*] (SPSG)
JL	Japan Air Lines [*ICAO designator*] (OAG)
JL	Javan LASER
JL	Jazz-Lift [*Provides jazz records to persons in Iron Curtain countries*] [*Defunct*] (EA)
JL	Jefferson Lyons [*Commercial firm British*]
JI	Jejunoileal [*Medicine*] (MEDA)
JI	Joel [*Old Testament book*]
JL	Joule's Law [*Physics*]
JL	Journal (ROG)
JL	Journal [*Online database field identifier*]
JL	July
JL	Junior Leaders Regiment [*British military*] (DMA)
JL	Jurin Law [*Electronics*]
JL	JustLife [*Defunct*] (EA)
JL	Just Looking [*A browser*] [*Retail slang*]
JL	Lab. Jacques Logeais [*France*] [*Research code symbol*]
JLA	Cooper Landing, AK [*Location identifier FAA*] (FAAL)
JLA	Jack L. Ahr [*Designer's mark on US bicentennial quarter*]
JLA	Jalna Resources [*Vancouver Stock Exchange symbol*]
JLA	Jet Lift Aircraft
JLA	Jewish Librarians Association [*Later, AJL*] (EA)
JL & Com Soc	Journal. Law and Commerce Society [*Hong Kong*] [*A publication*] (DLA)
JL & Information Science	Journal of Law and Information Science [*A publication*]
JL & Pol	Journal of Law and Politics [*A publication*] (DLA)
JL & Religion	Journal of Law and Religion [*A publication*] (DLA)
JLAS	JUMPS [*Joint Uniform Military Pay System*] Leave Accounting System (DNAB)
J Law & Ed	Journal of Law and Education [*A publication*] (DLA)
J Law Reform	Journal of Law Reform [*A publication*] (DLA)
J Law Soc'y Scotland	Law Society of Scotland. Journal [*A publication*] (DLA)
JLB	Jewish Labor Bund (EA)
JLB	Jewish Lads' Brigade [*British*] (DI)
JLBD	Jailbird (ABBR)
JLBRK	Jailbreak (ABBR)
JLBTS	Japanese Land-Based Test Site (MCD)
JLC	Houston [*Texas*] Allen Center [*Airport symbol*] (OAG)
JLC	Japanese Linear Collider [*High energy physics*]
JLC	Jewish Labor Committee (EA)
JLC	Joint Logistics Commanders [*Military*]
JLC	Joint Logistics Committee [*Military*]
JLC	Junction Latching Circulator
JLC & E	Jonesboro, Lake City & Eastern Railroad
JLCAT	Joint Logistics Commanders' Action Team [*Military*]
JLCD	Joint Liaison Committee on Documents (DS)
J/L/Cpl	Junior Lance-Corporal [*British military*] (DMA)
J/Ldr	Junior Leader [*British military*] (DMA)
JLE	Jet Lift Engine
JLEM	Jerusalem (ABBR)
JLEN	Julienne (ABBR)
JLEP	Julep (ABBR)
JLF	Joint Landing Force
JLFB	Joint Landing Force Board
JLFC	Joan Lunden Fan Club [*Defunct*] (EA)
JLFC	Johnny Len Fan Club (EA)
JLG	Jewish Lawyers Guild (EA)
JLG	JLG Industries, Inc. [*Associated Press*] (SAG)
JLG	Joint Liaison Group (ECON)
JLGI	JLG Indus [*NASDAQ symbol*] (TTSB)
JLH	Arlington Heights, IL [*Location identifier FAA*] (FAAL)
JLHC	Just Like Home [*NASDAQ symbol*] (TTSB)
JLHC	Just Like Home, Inc. [*NASDAQ symbol*] (SAG)
JLI	Julian, CA [*Location identifier FAA*] (FAAL)
JLIOOF	Junior Lodge, Independent Order of Odd Fellows (EA)
JLM	Junior Legacy Melbourne [*Australia An association*]
JLMC	Joint Labor Management Committee of the Retail Food Industry (EA)
JLMIC	Japan Light Machinery Information Center (EA)
JLMSA	Jewish Liturgical Music Society of America (EA)
JLN	Jaclyn, Inc. [*AMEX symbol*] (SPSG)
JLN	Joplin [*Missouri*] [*Airport symbol*] (OAG)
JLN	Joplin, MO [*Location identifier FAA*] (FAAL)
JLO	Jesolo [*Italy*] [*Airport symbol*] (AD)
JLO	Junction Light Output
JLOIC	Joint Logistics, Operations, Intelligence Center [*NATO*] (NATG)
JLOTS	Joint Logistics Over-the-Shore [*Military*] (RDA)
JLP	Jamaica Labour Party [*Political party*] (PPW)
JLP	John Lewis Partnership [*British*] (ECON)
JLP	Juan-les-Pins [*France*] [*Airport symbol*] (AD)
JLP	Juvenile Laryngeal Papilloma [*Medicine*] (DAVI)

JLPB .... Joint Logistics Planning Board
JLPC .... Joint Logistics Plans Committee [*Military*]
JLPG .... Joint Logistics Plans Group [*Military*]
JLPPG .... Joint Logistics and Personnel Policy Guidance [*Military*] (AFM)
JLR .... Jabalpur [*India*] [*Airport symbol*] (OAG)
JLR .... Jailer (ABBR)
JLR .... Jailer
JLR .... Jamaica Law Reports [*1953-55*] [*A publication*] (DLA)
JLR .... Jeweler (ABBR)
JLR .... Johore Law Reports [*India*] [*A publication*] (DLA)
JLR .... Junior Leaders Regiment [*British military*] (DMA)
JLRB .... Joint Labor Relations Board
JLRB .... Joint Logistics Review Board [*Military*]
JLRC .... Jack London Research Center (EA)
JLREID ...... Joint Long-Range Estimative Intelligence Document [*Military*]
JLRPG .... Joint Long-Range Proving Ground (KSC)
JLRRT .... Jordan Left-Right Reversal Test [*Educational test*]
JLRSA .... Joint Long-Range Strategic Appraisal [*Military*]
JLRSE .... Joint Long-Range Strategic Estimates [*Military*]
JLRSS .... Joint Long-Range Strategic Study [*Military*] (AFM)
jlry .... Jewelry (VRA)
JLS .... Jet Alsace [*France ICAO designator*] (FAAC)
JLS .... Jet Lift System
JLS .... Jewels (ADA)
JLS .... Joint Least Squares [*Statistics*]
JLSC .... Joint Logistics System Command (DOMA)
J/L/Sgt ...... Junior Lance-Sergeant [*British military*] (DMA)
JL Soc .... Journal. Law Society of Scotland [*A publication*] (DLA)
JLSP .... Joint Logistics Support Plan
JLT .... Jalate, Inc. [*AMEX symbol*] (SAG)
JLT .... Jalate Ltd [*AMEX symbol*] (TTSB)
JLT .... Junior Lord of the Treasury
JLTF .... Jewish Librarians Task Force (EA)
JLTPB .... Joint Logistics Techniques and Procedures Board [*Military*]
JLTR .... Jilter (ABBR)
JLUAC .... Joint Land Use Advisory Committee
JLUS .... Jealous (ABBR)
JLUSLY ..... Jealously (ABBR)
JLUSNS ..... Jealousness (ABBR)
JLUSY .... Jealousy (ABBR)
JLW-155 .... Joint Lightweight 155mm Howitzer (RDA)
JLY .... Jelly (ABBR)
JLY .... Jena, LA [*Location identifier FAA*] (FAAL)
JLYBN .... Jellybean (ABBR)
JLYD .... Jellied (ABBR)
JLYFSH ..... Jellyfish (ABBR)
JLYLK .... Jellylike (ABBR)
JM .... Air Jamaica Ltd. [*ICAO designator*] (OAG)
JM .... Jactitation of Marriage [*Legal*] [*British*] (ROG)
JM .... Jamaica [*ANSI two-letter standard code*] (CNC)
jm .... Jamaica [*MARC country of publication code Library of Congress*] (LCCP)
Jm .... James [*New Testament book*] (BJA)
JM .... James Madison [*US president, 1751-1836*]
JM .... James Monroe [*US president, 1758-1831*]
J/M .... Jettison Motor (KSC)
JM .... Jewish Male [*Classified advertising*]
JM .... Jiyu-Minshuto [*Liberal-Democratic Party*] [*Japan Political party*]
JM .... John Mercanti [*Designer's mark, when appearing on US coins*]
JM .... Johns Manville Corp. (MCD)
JM .... Journal of Marketing [*A publication*] (BRI)
JM .... Journal of Micrographics (NITA)
JM .... Jugomaxillary [*Dentistry*] (DAVI)
JM .... Julia MacRae [*Publisher*] [*British*]
JM .... Julian Messner [*Publisher's imprint*]
JM .... Junction Module [*Deep Space Instrumentation Facility, NASA*]
JM .... Juris Magister [*Master of Laws*]
JM .... Justizminister [*Minister of Justice*] [*German*] (ILCA)
JM .... Justizministerium [*Ministry of Justice*] [*German*] (ILCA)
JM .... Juxtamembrane Domain
jM .... Mass Transfer Factor [*Physics*] (DAVI)
J/M² .... Joules per Square Meter
J/M³ .... Joules per Cubic Meter [*Physics*]
JMA .... Houston [*Texas*] Astrodome [*Airport symbol*] (OAG)
JMA .... James Martin Associates [*Database consulting group*] [*British*]
JMA .... Jamming Modulation Analysis
JMA .... Japanese Military Administration
JMA .... Japan Meteorological Agency
JMA .... Japan Microphotography Association
JMA .... Jewelry Manufacturers Association (EA)
JMA .... Jewish Music Alliance (EA)
JMA .... Joinery Managers' Association [*British*] (BI)
JMA .... Joint Mission Analysis
JMA .... Julia Morgan Association [*Defunct*] (EA)
JMA .... Junior Management Assistant
JMA .... Junior Medical Assistant [*British military*] (DMA)
JMA .... Junior Military Aviator
JMA .... Juvenile Missionary Association [*British*] (BI)
JMAAD ...... Joint Military Assistance Affairs Division (CINC)
JMAC .... Joint Munitions Allocation Committee
JMAHEP .... Joint Military Aircraft Hurricane Evacuation Plan (AFM)
J MAN GS .... Journal of the Manchester Geographical Society [*A publication*] (ROG)
JMAR .... JMAR Industries [*NASDAQ symbol*] (SPSG)
JMARW ...... JMAR Inds Wrrt [*NASDAQ symbol*] (TTSB)

J-Mass .... Joint-Modeling and Simulation System
JMB .... Jamb (ABBR)
JMB .... Jewelers Memorandum Bureau (EA)
JMB .... Johnson Matthey Bankers [*Commercial firm British*]
JMB .... Joint Matriculation Board [*British*] (DCTA)
JMB .... Joint Meteorological Board (AAG)
JMB .... Joint Movements Branch [*NATO*] (NATG)
JMBL .... Jumble (ABBR)
JMBLD .... Jumbled (ABBR)
JMBLG .... Jumbling (ABBR)
JMBRE .... Jamboree (ABBR)
JMC .... Joint Maritime Commission
JMC .... Joint Maritime Congress [*Washington, DC*] (EA)
JMC .... Joint Message Center
JMC .... Joint Meteorological Committee
JMC .... Joint Military Commission [*US, North Vietnam, South Vietnam, Viet Cong*]
JMC .... Justice Mining Corp. [*Vancouver Stock Exchange symbol*]
JMC .... Sausalito, CA [*Location identifier FAA*] (FAAL)
JMCA .... Jewish Ministers Cantors Association of America and Canada (EA)
JMCA .... Joint Movement Coordination Agency
JMCA .... Judges, Marshals, and Constables Association
JMCAA ...... Jewish Minister and Cantors Association of America [*Later, JMCA*] (EA)
JMCAAC .... Jewish Ministers Cantors Association of America and Canada (EA)
JMCC .... Joint Mobile Communications Center [*NATO*] (NATG)
JMCC .... Joint Movements Coordinating Committee [*British*]
JMCG .... JMC Group [*NASDAQ symbol*] (TTSB)
JMCG .... JMC Group, Inc. [*NASDAQ symbol*] (SAG)
JMC Gp. .... JMC Group, Inc. [*Associated Press*] (SAG)
JMCOL ...... JUMPS [*Joint Uniform Military Payment System*] Monthly Compute Output Listing [*Military*] (AABC)
JMCP .... Jefferson Medical College of Philadelphia
JMCQ .... Journalism & Mass Communication Quarterly [*A publication*] (BRI)
JMCY .... Joseph Malins Crusade of Youth [*British*] (BI)
JMD .... Joint Managing Director (DCTA)
JMD .... Joint Monitor Display
JMD .... Justice Management Division [*U.S. Department of Justice*] (BARN)
JMD .... Juvenile Macular Degeneration [*Medicine*] (MEDA)
JMDC .... Joint Manual Direction Center [*Air Force*]
JME .... James Industries [*Vancouver Stock Exchange symbol*]
JME .... Joint Maximum Effort
JME .... Juvenile Myoclonic Epilepsy [*Medicine*]
JMEA .... Jewish Music Educators Association [*Defunct*] (EA)
JMED .... Jones Medical Indus [*NASDAQ symbol*] (TTSB)
JMED .... Jones Medical Industries, Inc. [*NASDAQ symbol*] (NQ)
JMED .... Jungle Message Encoder-Decoder (MCD)
JMEM .... Job Memory [*Computer science*] (MHDB)
JMEM .... Joint Munitions Effectiveness Manual [*Military*] (AFM)
JMEM .... Junior Marine Engineering Mechanic [*British military*] (DMA)
JMEMS ...... Joint Munitions Effectiveness Manual [*Navy*] (DOMA)
JMEMT ...... John Morgan Evans of Merthyr Tydil [*An association*] (EA)
JMEMTF .... Joint Munitions Effectiveness Manual Task Force (MCD)
JMENS ...... Joint Mission Element Need Statement (MCD)
JMETL .... Joint Mission Essential Task List (DOMA)
JMF .... James Madison Foundation (EA)
JMF .... Java Media Framework [*Computer science*]
JMF .... Jet Mixing Flow
JMF .... Jewish Music Forum
JMF .... John Marshall Foundation (EA)
JMF .... Journal of Marriage and the Family [*A publication*] (BRI)
JMFC .... Jared Martin Fan Club [*Defunct*] (EA)
JMFC .... Jayne Mansfield Fan Club (EA)
JMFC .... Jimmy Murphy Fan Club (EA)
JMG .... Jewelry Manufacturers Guild (EA)
JMG .... Joint Meteorological Group [*DoD*]
JMH .... John Milton Hagen [*Antibody*] [*Immunology*] (DAVI)
JMH .... Journal of Modern History [*A publication*] (BRI)
JMI .... Jackson & Moreland, Inc. (MCD)
JMI .... Jan Mayen Island [*Seismograph station code, US Geological Survey*] (SEIS)
JMI .... John Muir Institute for Environmental Studies [*Defunct*] (EA)
Jml .... Jorm Microlab, Inc., Cedar Rapids, IA [*Library symbol*] [*Library of Congress*] (LCLS)
JMIE .... Joint Maritime Information Element [*Coast Guard*]
JMIE .... Joint Maritime Information Exchange
JMIFC .... Jeanette MacDonald International Fan Club (EA)
JMIFC .... Johnny Mathis International Fan Club (EA)
J Mil H .... Journal of Military History [*A publication*]
J Mil H .... Journal of Military History [*A publication*] (BRI)
JMJ .... James J. Johnston [*FAA designator*] (FAAC)
JMJ .... Jesus, Mary, and Joseph
JMK .... Mikonos [*Greece*] [*Airport symbol*] (OAG)
JML .... Job Method Learning (PDAA)
JML .... Taxi Aereo de Jimulco SA de CV [*Mexico ICAO designator*] (FAAC)
JMLS .... John Marshall Law School [*Chicago, IL*] (DLA)
JMLS .... John Menzies Library Services [*Information service or system*] (IID)
JMM .... Jacobi Matrix Method [*Mathematics*]
JMM .... Jamaica Merchant Marine (EY)
JMM .... Joint Man Machine (IAA)
JMM .... Journal of Molecular Medicine [*A publication*]
JMMF .... James Monroe Memorial Foundation (EA)
JMN .... Jeweled-Orifice Misting Nozzle
JMN .... Johan Mangku Negara [*Malaysian Honour*]
JMNA .... Joint Military Net Assessment [*A publication*] (RDA)

JMNCL	Jeunesse du Mouvement National Congolaise - Lumumba [*Youth of the Lumumba Wing of the Congolese National Movement*]
J/Mne	Junior Marine [*British military*] (DMA)
JMO	Jesuit Mission Office [*Australia*]
JMO	Jomsom [*Nepal*] [*Airport symbol*] (OAG)
JMO	Jugoslovenska Muslimanska Organizacija [*Yugoslav Moslem Organization*] [*Political party*] (PPE)
J/MOL	Joules per Mole [*Physics*]
J/(MOL K)	Joules per Mole Kelvin [*Physics*]
JMOS	Job Management Operations System (PDAA)
JMP	Jack Morton Productions, Inc. [*New York, NY*] [*Telecommunications*] (TSSD)
JMP	Jen Min Piao [*or Yuan*] [*Peoples money of China*] (BARN)
JMP	John M. Poindexter [*National Security Advisor during the Reagan Administration*]
JMP	Johnson Matthey Public Ltd. Co. [*Toronto Stock Exchange symbol*]
JMP	Joint Manpower Program [*Military*] (CINC)
JMP	Jump [*Computer science*]
JMPAB	Joint Materiel Priorities and Allocation Board [*Military*] (AABC)
JMPC	Joint Military Procurements Control [*World War II*]
JMPD	Jumped (ABBR)
JMPG	Jumping (ABBR)
JMPI	Jumpmaster Personnel Inspection [*Army*] (ADDR)
JMPNS	Jumpiness (ABBR)
JMPOF	Jumpoff (ABBR)
JMPP	Joint Munitions Production Panel (MCD)
JMPR	Jumper (MSA)
JMPT	Joint Military Potential Test (MCD)
JMPTC	Joint Military Packaging Training Center
JMR	Alexandair, Inc. [*Canada ICAO designator*] (FAAC)
JMR	Johannesburg Mounted Rifles [*British military*] (DMA)
JMRC	Joint Mobile Relay Center (MCD)
JMRO	Joint Medical Regulating Office (AABC)
JMRO	Joint Military Regulating Office
JMRP	Joint Meteorological Radio Propagation Committee [*British*] (MCD)
JMRT	Junior Members Round Table [*American Library Association*]
JMS	Jacob More Society (EA)
JMS	Jamestown [*North Dakota*] [*Airport symbol*] (OAG)
JMS	Jamestown, ND [*Location identifier FAA*] (FAAL)
JMS	Jewish Media Service [*Defunct*] (EA)
JMS	John Milton Society for the Blind [*Later, JMSB*] (EA)
JMS	Joint Movements Staff [*British*]
JMS	Jump to Subroutine Instruction [*Computer science*]
JMS	Junior Medical Student (DAVI)
JMS	Morgan Stanley Group, Inc. [*AMEX symbol*] (SAG)
JMSA	Japan Marine Safety Agency [*Marine science*] (OSRA)
JMSAC	Joint Meteorological Satellite Advisory Committee
JMSB	John Milton Society for the Blind (EA)
JmSC	Japan Microfilm Service Center Co. Ltd., Tokyo, Japan [*Library symbol Library of Congress*] (LCLS)
JMSDC	Joint Merchant Shipping Defence Committee [*General Council of British Shipping*] (DS)
JMSDF	Japanese Maritime Self-Defense Force
JMSEP	Joint Modeling and Simulation Executive Panel [*DoD*]
JMSLS	Joliet Three-Minute Speech and Language Screen [*Test*]
JMSNS	Justification of Major System New Start [*Military*]
JMSPO	Joint Meteorological Satellite Program Office
JMSW	Journal of Multicultural Social Work [*A publication*] (BRI)
JMSX	Job Memory Switch Matrix
JMT	Job Methods Training
JMT	Joint Management Team (MCD)
JMT	Judgment (DCTA)
JMTB	Joint Military Transportation Board
JMTC	Joint Military Transportation Committee
JMTG	Joint Military Task Group (MUGU)
JMTG	Joint Military Terminology Group (AFM)
JMTSS	Joint Multichannel Trunking and Switching System (MCD)
JMU	James Madison University [*Virginia*]
JMU	Jamshedpur Mazdoor Union [*India*]
JMU	John Moores University [*British*]
JMUA	Joint Meritorious Unit Award [*Military decoration*] (GFGA)
JMUSDC	Joint Mexican-United States Defense Commission
J/Musn	Junior Musician [*British military*] (DMA)
JMVB	Joint Merchant Vessels Board [*World War II*]
JMW	James McNeill Whistler [*Nineteenth-century American painter and etcher*]
JMX	Jumbogroup Multiplex [*Bell System*]
JMY	Jimmy (ABBR)
JMYG	Jimmying (ABBR)
jn	Jan Mayen [*MARC country of publication code Library of Congress*] (LCCP)
JN	Jannock Ltd. [*Toronto Stock Exchange symbol*]
J-N	Jet Navigation (AAG)
JN	Jet Navigation Chart
JN	Jim's Neighbors (EA)
JN	Job Number
Jn	John [*New Testament book*]
JN	Johnson Noise [*Thermal noise, that made by a resistor at a temperature above absolute zero*]
JN	Join (MSA)
JN	Journal Name [*Online database field identifier*]
Jn	Juglans nigra [*Eastern black walnut*]
JN	Junction
JN	June (ROG)
JN	Junior (ROG)
JN	Justice Now [*An association*]
Jn	King John [*Shakespearean work*]
JNA	Januaria [*Brazil*] [*Airport symbol*] (AD)
JNA	Jena Nomina Anatomica [*Also, INA*] [*Anatomy*]
JNA	Jewish News Agency (BJA)
JNA	John Nurminen, OY [*Finland*] [*FAA designator*] (FAAC)
JNA	Joint Navy (IAA)
JNA	Jordanian News Agency
JNA	Jump If Not Above [*Computer science*] (PCM)
JNA	Junior Naval Airman [*British military*] (DMA)
JNA	Northern Illinois University, De Kalb, IL [*OCLC symbol*] (OCLC)
JNA	Yugoslav People's Army
JNAC	Japan-North American Commission on Cooperative Mission (EA)
JNACC	Joint Nuclear Accident Coordinating Center
JNADPI	Japan National Assembly of Disabled Peoples' International (EAIO)
JNAE	Jump If Not Above or Equal [*Computer science*] (PCM)
JNAF	Japanese Navy Air Force
JNAF	Joint Navy-Air Force
JNAM	Junior Naval Air Mechanic [*British military*] (DMA)
JNA Referees Bank	Journal. National Association of Referees in Bankruptcy [*A publication*] (DLA)
JNB	Johannesburg [*South Africa*] [*Airport symbol*] (OAG)
JNB	Joinable (ABBR)
JNB	Jump If Not Below [*Computer science*] (PCM)
JNBE	Jump If Not Below or Equal [*Computer science*] (PCM)
JNC	Jet Navigation Chart
JNC	John Nuveen 'A' [*NYSE symbol*] (TTSB)
JNC	Joint National Council (AIE)
JNC	Joint Negotiating Council [*British*] (DCTA)
JNC	Jump If No Carry [*Computer science*] (PCM)
JNC	Junction (ADA)
JNC	Nuveen [*John*] & Co. [*NYSE symbol*] (SPSG)
JNCC	Junior Naval Command Course
JNCG	Japan Nuclear Codes Group
JNCIMC	Japanese National Committee of the International Music Council (EAIO)
JNCL	Joint National Committee for Languages (EA)
JNCN	Junction (ABBR)
JNCO	Junior Non-Commissioned Officer [*British military*] (DMA)
JNCP	Justification for Non-Competitive Procurement (GFGA)
JNC Referees Bank	Journal. National Conference of Referees in Bankruptcy [*A publication*] (DLA)
JNCUR	Juncture (ABBR)
JND	Air East Africa Ltd. [*Kenya*] [*FAA designator*] (FAAC)
JND	Joined (ABBR)
JND	Just Noticeable Difference [*Psychology*]
JNDR	Joinder (ABBR)
JNE	Ja Niin Edespain [*And So On*] [*Finnish*]
JNE	Journal of Negro Education [*A publication*] (BRI)
JNE	Jump Not Equal [*Computer science*] (OA)
JNE	June (ABBR)
JNF	Jewish National Fund (EA)
JNFA	Jewish National Fund of Australia
JNFC	Juice Newton Fan Club (EA)
JNG	[*The*] Jews in NAZI Germany; A Handbook of Facts Regarding Their Present Situation [*A publication*] (BJA)
JNG	Joining [*Also, J*]
JNGL	Jonquil (ABBR)
JNGL	Jungle (ABBR)
JNHAC	Jewish National Home for Asthmatic Children
JNI	Java Native Interface [*Computer science*]
JNJ	Johnson & Johnson [*NYSE symbol*] (SPSG)
JNKD	Junked (ABBR)
JNKG	Junking (ABBR)
JNKI	Junkie (ABBR)
JNKMA	Junkman (ABBR)
JNKT	Junket (ABBR)
JNKTD	Junketed (ABBR)
JNKTG	Junketing (ABBR)
JNKTR	Junketer (ABBR)
JNL	Atchison, KS [*Location identifier FAA*] (FAAL)
JNL	Japanese National Laboratory
JNL	Jenolan [*Australia Seismograph station code, US Geological Survey*] (SEIS)
JNL	Journal
JNLS	Journals (ADA)
JNLST	Journalist
JNMR	Joint National Media Research [*Database producer*]
JNND	Just Not Noticeable Difference (MSA)
JNOV	Judgment Not Withstanding Verdict (HGAA)
JNP	Jasper National Park [*Alberta*] [*Airport symbol*] (AD)
JNP	Joint Nuclear Plot (CINC)
JNP	Newport Beach, CA [*Location identifier FAA*] (FAAL)
JNPE	Joint Nuclear Planning Element (MCD)
JNPI	Jetevator Null Position Indicator
JNPR	Juniper (ABBR)
JNR	Japanesae National Railways (BARN)
JNR	Joiner (ABBR)
JNR	June Resources, Inc. [*Vancouver Stock Exchange symbol*]
JNR	Junior (EY)
JNR	Unalakleet, AK [*Location identifier FAA*] (FAAL)
JNRC	Joint Nuclear Research Center [*EURATOM*]
JNRI	Joint Nuclear Research Institute [*Former USSR*]
JNROTC	Junior Naval Reserve Officer Training Corps
JNS	Chic by HIS, Inc. [*NYSE symbol*] (SPSG)

JNS.............. International Graduate School, St. Louis, MO [*OCLC symbol*] (OCLC)
JNS.............. Jet Noise Survey
JNS.............. Jugoslovenska Nacionalna Stranka [*Yugoslav National Party*]
    [*Political party*] (PPE)
JNS.............. Just Noticeable Shift (PDAA)
JNS.............. Minneapolis, MN [*Location identifier FAA*] (FAAL)
JNSC.......... Joint Navigation Satellite Committee
JNT.............. Jaunt (ABBR)
JNT.............. Joint
JNT.............. Joint
JNT.............. Joint Network Scheme [*British*]
JNT.............. Joint Network Team [*British*] (NITA)
JNT.............. Jonathan [*Italy*] [*FAA designator*] (FAAC)
JNT.............. Junction (ABBR)
JNT.............. Juncture (ABBR)
JNT.............. New York, NY [*Location identifier FAA*] (FAAL)
JNTD.......... Jointed (ABBR)
JNTINS........ Jauntiness (ABBR)
JNTIR......... Jauntier (ABBR)
JNTLY......... Jauntily (ABBR)
JNTLY......... Jointly (ABBR)
JNTO.......... Japan National Tourist Organization (EA)
JNTR.......... Janitor (ABBR)
JNTR.......... Jointer (ABBR)
JNTST......... Jauntiest (ABBR)
JNT STK CO... Joint Stock Co. (DLA)
JNTUR........ Jointure (ABBR)
JNTURD...... Jointured (ABBR)
JNTURG...... Jointuring (ABBR)
JNT VEN ..... Joint Venture [*Legal term*] (DLA)
JNTY.......... Jaunty (ABBR)
JNTY.......... Jointly (ABBR)
JNU............ Juneau [*Alaska*] [*Airport symbol*] (OAG)
JNU............ Juneau, AK [*Location identifier FAA*] (FAAL)
JNU............ Universal Jet Navigation Charts [*Air Force*]
JNUL.......... Jewish National and University Library
JNuveen ...... Nuveen [*John*] Co. [*Associated Press*] (SAG)
JNVOA........ Jewish Nazi Victims Organization of America (EA)
JNW........... Joint Committee on New Weapons and Equipment
JNW........... Newport, OR [*Location identifier FAA*] (FAAL)
JNWOC....... Joint Warfare Operations Center
JNWP......... Joint Numerical Weather Prediction Unit (IAA)
JNWPS .... Joint Nuclear Weapons Publication Systems (MCD)
JNWPU....... Joint Numerical Weather Prediction Unit
JNX........... Jackson [*Michigan*] [*Airport symbol*] (AD)
JNY........... January (ABBR)
JNY........... Jenney Beechcraft, Inc. [*ICAO designator*] (FAAC)
JNY........... Jones Apparel Group [*NYSE symbol*] (SPSG)
JNZ........... Jennings, LA [*Location identifier FAA*] (FAAL)
JNZ........... Jump on Not Zero [*Computer science*] (PCM)
JO............. Holiday Airlines [*ICAO designator*] (AD)
JO............. Job Order
Jo............. Joel [*Old Testament book*] (BJA)
Jo............. Johannes Faventinus [*Deceased circa 1187*] [*Authority cited in pre-
    1607 legal work*] (DSA)
JO............. Joint Organization
JO............. Joint Ownership [*Business term*]
Jo............. Jones' Irish Exchequer Reports [*A publication*] (DLA)
jo............. Jordan [*MARC country of publication code Library of Congress*]
    (LCCP)
JO............. Jordan [*ANSI two-letter standard code*] (CNC)
Jo............. Joseph (BJA)
JO............. Journalist [*Navy rating*]
JO............. Journal Officiel des Communautes Europeennes [*Official Journal of
    the European Communities*] [*A publication*] (ILCA)
JO............. Judicial Officer [*Department of Agriculture*] (GFGA)
JO............. Junction Office [*Telecommunications*] (OA)
JO............. Junior Officer
JO............. Jupiter Orbiter [*NASA*]
JO............. Juvenile Offenders
JO1............ Journalist, First Class [*Navy rating*]
JO2............ Journalist, Second Class [*Navy rating*]
JO3............ Journalist, Third Class [*Navy rating*]
JOA........... Joint Objective Area (NVT)
JOA........... Joint Oceanographic Assembly [*Marine science*] (MSC)
JOA........... Joint Operating Agreement
Joa Bologne... Johannes Bolognetus [*Deceased, 1575*] [*Authority cited in pre-1607
    legal work*] (DSA)
JOAC.......... Joachim Bancorp [*NASDAQ symbol*] (TTSB)
JOAC.......... Joachim Bancorp, Inc. [*NASDAQ symbol*] (SAG)
Joachim....... Joachim Bancorp, Inc. [*Associated Press*] (SAG)
JOAD.......... Junior Olympic Archery Development
JOAG.......... Juvenile Open Angle Glaucoma [*Ophthalmology*]
JO AI.......... Jahreshefte des Oesterreichischen Archaeologischen Instituts in
    Wien [*A publication*] (OCD)
Joa Imo ...... Johannes de Imola [*Deceased, 1436*] [*Authority cited in pre-1607
    legal work*] (DSA)
Joan Andr.... Johannes Andreae [*Deceased, 1348*] [*Authority cited in pre-1607
    legal work*] (DSA)
Joan Bapt Villalob... Johannes Baptista Villalobos [*Authority cited in pre-1607 legal
    work*] (DSA)
Joan Bologne... Johannes Bolognetus [*Deceased, 1575*] [*Authority cited in pre-
    1607 legal work*] (DSA)
Joan Borcholt... Johannes Borcholten [*Deceased, 1593*] [*Authority cited in pre-
    1607 legal work*] (DSA)

Jo & Car...... Jones and Cary's Irish Exchequer Reports [*1838-39*] [*A publication*]
    (DLA)
Joan de Ces... Johannes de Cesena [*Flourished, 13th century*] [*Authority cited in
    pre-1607 legal work*] (DSA)
Joan de Lign... Johannes de Lignano [*Deceased, 1383*] [*Authority cited in pre-
    1607 legal work*] (DSA)
Jo & La T..... Jones and La Touche's Irish Chancery Reports [*A publication*] (DLA)
Joan Fan ..... Johannes Faventinus [*Deceased circa 1187*] [*Authority cited in pre-
    1607 legal work*] (DSA)
Joan Mon .... Johannes Monachus [*Deceased, 1313*] [*Authority cited in pre-1607
    legal work*] (DSA)
Joann.......... Johannes Teutonicus [*Deceased circa 1246*] [*Authority cited in pre-
    1607 legal work*] (DSA)
Joannes....... Johannes Franciscus Pavinus [*Flourished, 1448-82*] [*Authority cited
    in pre-1607 legal work*] (DSA)
Joan Teut... Johannes Teutonicus [*Deceased, 1246*] [*Authority cited in pre-1607
    legal work*] (DSA)
Joan Vaud ... Johannes Vaudus [*Flourished, 16th century*] [*Authority cited in pre-
    1607 legal work*] (DSA)
JOAP.......... Joint Oil Analysis Program [*Military*] (NVT)
JOAP-CG..... Joint Oil Analysis Program Coordinating Group (MCD)
JOAP-TSC ... Joint Oil Analysis Program Technical Support Center (MCD)
JOB........... Aerojobeni SA de CV [*Mexico ICAO designator*] (FAAC)
JOB........... General Employment Enterprises, Inc. [*AMEX symbol*] (SPSG)
JOB........... Genl Employ Enterpr [*AMEX symbol*] (TTSB)
JOB........... Jobber
Jo B........... Johannes Bassianus [*Flourished, 12th century*] [*Authority cited in
    pre-1607 legal work*] (DSA)
JOB........... Judicial Officers Bulletin [*A publication*]
JOB........... Just One Break (EA)
JOBAPT....... John the Baptist
JOBCAT....... Job Catalog (HGAA)
JOBD .... Jobbed (ABBR)
JOBG .... Jobbing (ABBR)
JOBHLDR.... Jobholder (ABBR)
JOBLIB........ Job Library [*Computer science*]
JOBR.......... Jobber (ABBR)
JOBS.......... Job Opportunities in the Business Sector (WDAA)
JOBS.......... Job Oriented Basic Skills [*Program*] [*Military*]
JOBTAP....... Job Training Assessment Program [*Vocational guidance test*]
JOC........... Cambria County Library System, Johnstown, PA [*OCLC symbol*]
    (OCLC)
JOC........... Chief Journalist [*Navy rating*]
JOC........... Jewett Owners Club (EA)
JOC........... Jewish Occupational Council [*Later, NAJVS*] (EA)
JOC........... Job Order Contracting
JOC........... Job Order Costing (MHDI)
JOC........... Jocose [*or Jocular*]
JOC........... Jocular (ABBR)
JOC........... John Coutts Library Services [*ACCORD*] [*UTLAS symbol*]
JOC........... Joint Operations Center
JOC........... Joint Organizing Committee [*Global Atmospheric Research Program*]
JOC........... Joint Organizing Committee [*Marine science*] (OSRA)
JOC........... Journal of Organic Chemistry [*A publication*]
JOC........... Junior Officer Council [*Army*]
JOC........... Junior Optimist Clubs (EA)
JOC........... New York, NY [*Location identifier FAA*] (FAAL)
JOCARG...... Joint Wideband Circuit Allocation and Requirement Group, Thailand
    [*Military*] (CINC)
JOCAS .... Job Order Cost Accounting System (MCD)
JOCC.......... Jeunesse Ouvriere Catholique Canadienne [*Young Canadian
    Catholic Workers*] [*Established 1930*]
JOCC.......... Joint Operations Control Center
J Occ Health Safety Aust... Journal of Occupational Health and Safety in Australia
    [*A publication*]
J Occup Health Safety... Journal of Occupational Health and Safety - Australia and
    New Zealand [*A publication*]
JOCG .... Joint Ordnance Commanders Group
Jo Ch.......... Johnson's New York Chancery Reports [*A publication*] (DLA)
JOCI........... Jeunesse Ouvriere Chretienne Internationale [*International Young
    Christian Workers - IYCW*] (EAIO)
JOCIT......... JOVIAL Compiler Implementation Tool [*Computer science*] (MCD)
JOCK.......... Jockey (ABBR)
JOCK.......... Jockstrap (ABBR)
JockeyC ...... Jockey Club, Inc. [*Associated Press*] (SAG)
JOCM.......... Master Chief Journalist [*Navy rating*]
JOCO.......... Jointly-Owned Contractor-Operated Facility (MCD)
Jo Comm Eur... Journal Officiel des Communautes Europeennes [*Official Journal
    of the European Communities*] [*A publication*] (ILCA)
JOCOTAS ..... Joint Committee on Tactical Shelters (MCD)
JOCR.......... Joint Observation for Cometary Research (MCD)
Jo Cre........ Johannes Bassianus de Cremona [*Flourished, 12th century*]
    [*Authority cited in pre-1607 legal work*] (DSA)
JOCS.......... Senior Chief Journalist [*Navy rating*]
JOCSG .... Joint Ordnance Commanders Supply Group [*DoD*]
J-OCT.......... Joint Operational Compatibility Tests
JOCT.......... Junior Officers Common Training
JOD........... Joint Occupancy Date (MCD)
JOD........... Juvenile Onset Diabetes [*Medicine*]
JODC.......... Japan Oceanographic Data Center [*Information service or system*]
    (IID)
JODC .... Juvenile Osteochondritis Dissecans [*Medicine*]
Jo de Ana.... Johannes de Anania [*Deceased, 1457*] [*Authority cited in pre-1607
    legal work*] (DSA)

Jo de Anna... Johannes de Anania [*Deceased, 1457*] [*Authority cited in pre-1607 legal work*] (DSA)

Jo de Bor..... Johannes de Borbonio [*Flourished, 1317-30*] [*Authority cited in pre-1607 legal work*] (DSA)

Jo de Cre..... Johannes Bassianus de Cremona [*Flourished, 12th century*] [*Authority cited in pre-1607 legal work*] (DSA)

Jo de F........ Johannes de Fintona [*Flourished, 13th century*] [*Authority cited in pre-1607 legal work*] (DSA)

Jo de Fi........ Johannes de Fintona [*Flourished, 13th century*] [*Authority cited in pre-1607 legal work*] (DSA)

Jo de Imol... Johannes de Imola [*Deceased, 1436*] [*Authority cited in pre-1607 legal work*] (DSA)

Jo de Mo..... Johannes de Monciaco [*Flourished, 1263-66*] [*Authority cited in pre-1607 legal work*] (DSA)

JODIN.......... Iodinium [*Iodine*] [*Symbol is I*] [*Chemical element Pharmacy*] (ROG)

JODIV .... John the Divine

JODM.......... Juvenile Onset Diabetes Mellitus [*Medicine*]

JOE.............. Joensuu [*Finland*] [*Airport symbol*] (OAG)

JOE.............. Joensuu [*Finland*] [*Seismograph station code, US Geological Survey Closed*] (SEIS)

JOE.............. Juvenile Opportunities Endeavor

JOEG............ Joint Operations Evaluation Group (AABC)

JOEG-V .... Joint Operations Evaluation Group, Vietnam [*Air Force*] (MCD)

JOEM.......... Junior Ordnance Electrical Mechanic [*British military*] (DMA)

JOERS .... Joint Opto-Electronics Research Scheme [*British*]

JOEVANG...... John the Evangelist

Jo Ex Ir .... Jones' Irish Exchequer Reports [*A publication*] (DLA)

Jo Ex Pro W... Jones' Exchequer Proceedings Concerning Wales [*1939*] [*A publication*] (DLA)

JOF.............. Japan OTC Equity Fund [*NYSE symbol*] (TTSB)

JOF.............. Japan OTC Equity Fund, Inc. [*NYSE symbol*] (SPSG)

Jo F .... Johannes de Fintona [*Flourished, 13th century*] [*Authority cited in pre-1607 legal work*] (DSA)

Jo Fa .... Johannes Faventinus [*Deceased circa 1187*] [*Authority cited in pre-1607 legal work*] (DSA)

Jo Fav .... Johannes Faventinus [*Deceased circa 1187*] [*Authority cited in pre-1607 legal work*] (DSA)

J of Ceylon L... Journal of Ceylon Law [*Colombo, Ceylon*] [*A publication*] (DLA)

J of E........... Journal of Education [*A publication*] (ROG)

J of EL........ Journal of Electric Lighting [*A publication*] (ROG)

J of Ethiop L... Journal of Ethiopian Law [*Addis Ababa, Ethiopia*] [*A publication*] (DLA)

J of Ins of Arbitrators... Journal. Institute of Arbitrators [*A publication*] (DLA)

JOFL............ Johnstown Flood National Memorial

JOFOC .... Justification for Other than Full and Open Competition (SSD)

JOG.............. Joggle [*Engineering*]

JOG.............. Jogyakarta [*Indonesia*] [*Airport symbol*] (OAG)

JOG.............. Joint Operating Group [*SLA/ASIS*]

JOG.............. Joint Operations Graphics [*Military*]

JOG.............. Joint Operations Group [*DoD*]

JOG.............. Junior Offshore Group [*Racing*] [*British*]

JOG-A .... Joint Operations Graphics - Air [*Military*] (PDAA)

JOGD .... Jogged (ABBR)

JOGG .... Jogging (ABBR)

JOG-G.......... Joint Operations Graphics - Ground (PDAA)

JOGL .... Joggle (ABBR)

JOGLD .... Joggled (ABBR)

JOGLG .... Joggling (ABBR)

JOGR .... Jogger (ABBR)

JOH.............. Johannesburg [*South Africa*] [*Seismograph station code, US Geological Survey Closed*] (SEIS)

Joh............... Johannine (BJA)

Joh............... John [*New Testament book*] (BJA)

JOH.............. Johnstone Point, AK [*Location identifier FAA*] (FAAL)

JOH.............. St. John's College [*Cambridge, England*] (DAS)

Joh Ch Rep... Johnson's New York Chancery Reports [*A publication*] (DLA)

John............. Chase's United States Circuit Court Decisions, Edited by Johnson [*A publication*] (DLA)

John............. Johnson's English Vice-Chancellors' Reports [*A publication*] (DLA)

John............. Johnson's Maryland Chancery Reports [*A publication*] (DLA)

John............. Johnson's New York Reports [*A publication*] (DLA)

John............. Johnson's New York Supreme Court Reports [*A publication*] (DLA)

John Am Not... John's American Notaries [*A publication*] (DLA)

John & H..... Johnson and Hemming's English Chancery Reports [*70 English Reprint*] [*A publication*] (DLA)

John Carroll U... John Carroll University (GAGS)

John Cas ..... Johnson's New York Cases [*A publication*] (DLA)

John Chan ... Johnson's New York Chancery Reports [*A publication*] (DLA)

John Ch Rep... Johnson's New York Chancery Reports [*A publication*] (DLA)

JohnCn........ Johnson Controls, Inc. [*Associated Press*] (SAG)

John Dict...... Johnson's English Dictionary [*A publication*] (DLA)

John Eng Ch... Johnson's English Vice-Chancellors' Reports [*A publication*] (DLA)

John Jay C (CUNY)... John Jay College of Criminal Justice of The City University of New York (GAGS)

JohnJn......... Johnson & Johnson [*Associated Press*] (SAG)

John Marshall Law Sch... John Marshall Law School (GAGS)

John Marshall LQ... John Marshall Law Quarterly [*A publication*] (DLA)

John Marsh LJ... John Marshall Law Journal [*A publication*] (DLA)

John Marsh LQ... John Marshall Law Quarterly [*A publication*] (DLA)

JOHNNIAC ... John's [*Von Neumann*] Integrator and Automatic Computer [*An early computer*]

John Oxley J... John Oxley Journal [*A publication*]

Johns........... Chase's United States Circuit Court Decisions, Edited by Johnson [*A publication*] (DLA)

Johns........... Johnson's English Vice-Chancellors' Reports [*A publication*] (DLA)

Johns........... Johnson's Maryland Chancery Reports [*A publication*] (DLA)

Johns........... Johnson's New York Supreme Court Reports [*A publication*] (DLA)

Johns & H..... Johnson and Hemming's English Chancery Reports [*70 English Reprint*] [*A publication*] (DLA)

Johns & Hem... Johnson and Hemming's English Chancery Reports [*70 English Reprint*] [*A publication*] (DLA)

Johns & H (Eng)... Johnson and Hemming's English Chancery Reports [*70 English Reprint*] [*A publication*] (DLA)

Johns Bills... Johnson's Bills of Exchange [*2nd ed.*] [*1839*] [*A publication*] (DLA)

Johns C ...... Johnson's New York Cases [*A publication*] (DLA)

Johns Cas..... Johnson's New York Cases [*A publication*] (DLA)

Johns Cases.. Johnson's New York Cases [*A publication*] (DLA)

Johns Cas (NY)... Johnson's New York Cases [*A publication*] (DLA)

Johns Ch .... Johnson's English Vice-Chancellors' Reports [*A publication*] (DLA)

Johns Ch .... Johnson's Maryland Chancery Decisions [*A publication*] (DLA)

Johns Ch .... Johnson's New York Chancery Reports [*A publication*] (DLA)

Johns Ch Cas... Johnson's New York Chancery Reports [*A publication*] (DLA)

Johns Ch (NY)... Johnson's New York Chancery Reports [*A publication*] (DLA)

Johns Civ L Sp... Johnson's Civil Law of Spain [*A publication*] (DLA)

Johns Ct Err... Johnson's New York Court of Errors Reports [*A publication*] (DLA)

Johns Dec ... Johnson's Maryland Chancery Decisions [*A publication*] (DLA)

Johns Eccl L... Johnson's Ecclesiastical Law [*A publication*] (DLA)

Johns Eng Ch... Johnson's English Chancery Reports [*A publication*] (DLA)

Johns Hopkins U... [*The*] Johns Hopkins University (GAGS)

Johns HRV... Johnson's English Chancery Reports [*A publication*] (DLA)

Johns Mar R... Johnson on Maritime Rights [*A publication*] (DLA)

Johns (NY)... Johnson's New York Reports [*A publication*] (DLA)

Johns NZ... Johnson's New Zealand Reports [*A publication*] (DLA)

Johnson...... Johnson's English Vice-Chancellors' Reports [*A publication*] (DLA)

Johnson...... Johnson's Maryland Chancery Decisions [*A publication*] (DLA)

Johnson...... Johnson's New York Reports [*A publication*] (DLA)

Johnson NYR... Johnson's New York Reports [*A publication*] (DLA)

Johnson R .... Johnson's New York Reports [*A publication*] (DLA)

Johnson's Quarto Dict... Johnson's Quarto Dictionary [*A publication*] (DLA)

Johnson's Rep... Johnson's New York Reports [*A publication*] (DLA)

Johns Pat Man... Johnson's Patent Manual [*A publication*] (DLA)

Johns R .... Johnson's New York Reports [*A publication*] (DLA)

Johns Rep ... Johnson's New York Supreme Court Reports [*A publication*] (DLA)

Johnst Inst... Johnston's Institutes of the Laws of Spain [*A publication*] (DLA)

JohnstnA...... Johnstown America Industries, Inc. [*Associated Press*] (SAG)

Johnst (NZ)... Johnston's New Zealand Reports [*A publication*] (DLA)

Johnston...... Johnston Industries, Inc. [*Associated Press*] (SAG)

Johns Tr ...... Johnson's Impeachment Trial [*A publication*] (DLA)

Johns US .... Johnson's Reports of Chase's United States Circuit Court Decisions [*A publication*] (DLA)

Johns VC .... Johnson's English Vice-Chancellors' Reports [*A publication*] (DLA)

Johns VC (Eng)... Johnson's English Vice-Chancellors' Reports [*A publication*] (DLA)

Johs............. Johannes Galensis [*Flourished, 13th century*] [*Authority cited in pre-1607 legal work*] (DSA)

Joh Teut ...... Johannes Teutonicus [*Deceased circa 1246*] [*Authority cited in pre-1607 legal work*] (DSA)

JOHX .... Johnson Flying Service [*Air carrier designation symbol*]

JOI............... Joint Oceanographic Institution (USDC)

JOI............... Joint Oceanographic Institutions, Inc. [*Research center*] (RCD)

JOI............... Joinville [*Brazil*] [*Airport symbol*] (OAG)

JOIDES .... JODC [*Japan Oceanographic Data Center*] On-Line Information and Data Exchange Service [*Marine science*] (OSRA)

JOIDES .... Joint Oceanographic Institutions for Deep Earth Sampling

JOIN............ Job Orientation in Neighborhoods (AEBS)

JOIN............ Jobs or Income Now [*Students for a Democratic Society*] [*Defunct*]

JOIN............ Joinery (ADA)

JOIN............ Joint Optical Information Network [*Army*]

JOIN............ Jones Intercable [*NASDAQ symbol*] (TTSB)

JOIN............ Jones Intercable, Inc. [*NASDAQ symbol*] (NQ)

JOINA.......... Jones Intercable Cl'A' [*NASDAQ symbol*] (TTSB)

JOINREP....... Joining Report (MCD)

JOIP............ Joint Operations Interface Procedure (NASA)

JOIS............ Japan Online Information System [*Database*]

JOJA .... July, October, January, and April [*Denotes quarterly payments of interest or dividends in these months*] [*Business term*]

Jo Jur .... Journal of Jurisprudence [*A publication*] (DLA)

JOK............. Airtaxi Bedarfsluftverkehrsges GmbH [*Austria ICAO designator*] (FAAC)

JOKG .... Joking (ABBR)

JOKGLY ...... Jokingly (ABBR)

JOKGY .... Jokingly (ABBR)

JOKI............ John Fitzgerald Kennedy National Historical Site

JOKING .... Joint Kinematics and Geometry (PDAA)

JOKP........... Junior Order, Knights of Pythias (EA)

JOKSTR .... Jokester (ABBR)

JOL............. Job Organization Language [*1979*] [*Computer science*] (CSR)

JOL............. Joilet in Illinois [*Diocesan abbreviation*] [*Illinois*] (TOCD)

JOL............. Jolo [*Philippines*] [*Airport symbol*] (OAG)

JOL............. Jolon [*California*] [*Seismograph station code, US Geological Survey*] (SEIS)

JOL............. Joule, Inc. [*AMEX symbol*] (SPSG)

JOLD........... Jollied (ABBR)

Jo Le .... Johannis Lectura [*A publication*] (DSA)

JOLT........... Juvenile Offenders Learn the Truth [*Program*]

JOLTGLY..... Joltingly (ABBR)

JOM............ Jeunesse Ouvriere Marocaine [*Moroccan Working Youth*]

JOM............ Job Operation Manual (AAG)

JOM............ Job-Oriented Manual (AAG)

JOM............ Johnson-O'Malley Act [*1934*]

JOM Njombe [*Tanzania*] [*Airport symbol*] (AD)
JOMAC Judgement, Orientation, Memory, Abstraction, and Calculation [*Medicine*] (DAVI)
JOMACI Judgment, Orientation, Memory, Abstraction, and Calculation Intact [*Medicine*] (DAVI)
JOMAR John and Margaret Seidel [*Children of US importer after whom British sports car was named*]
JOMN Jeweled-Orifice Misting Nozzle
JOMO Job Mix Optimization [*Computer science*] (MHDB)
Jo Mon Johannes Monachus [*Deceased, 1313*] [*Authority cited in pre-1607 legal work*] (DSA)
JOMU John Muir National Historic Site
JON Jeweled-Orifice Nozzle
JON Job Order Number (MCD)
JON Johnston Island [*Airport symbol*] (OAG)
Jon Jonah [*Old Testament book*]
JON Jonas [*Old Testament book*] [*Douay version*]
Jon Jones' Irish Exchequer Reports [*A publication*] (DLA)
JON Jonpol Explorations Ltd. [*Toronto Stock Exchange symbol*]
Jon & Car Jones and Cary's Irish Exchequer Reports [*1838-39*] [*A publication*] (DLA)
Jon & L Jones and La Touche's Irish Chancery Reports [*A publication*] (DLA)
Jon & La T Jones and La Touche's Irish Chancery Reports [*A publication*] (DLA)
Jonel Jones Intercable, Inc. [*Associated Press*] (SAG)
JoneInt Jones Intercable Investors Ltd. [*Associated Press*] (SAG)
Jones Jones' Irish Exchequer Reports [*A publication*] (DLA)
Jones Jones' North Carolina Equity Reports [*54-59*] [*1853-63*] [*A publication*] (DLA)
Jones Jones' North Carolina Law Reports [*A publication*] (DLA)
Jones Jones' Reports [*22-30 Missouri*] [*A publication*] (DLA)
Jones Jones' Reports [*11, 12 Pennsylvania*] [*A publication*] (DLA)
Jones Jones' Reports [*43-48, 52-57, 61, 62 Alabama*] [*A publication*] (DLA)
Jones Jones' Upper Canada Common Pleas Reports [*A publication*] (DLA)
Jones & C Jones and Cary's Irish Exchequer Reports [*1838-39*] [*A publication*] (DLA)
Jones & H Hind Law Jones and Haughton's Hindoo Law [*A publication*] (DLA)
Jones & L Jones and La Touche's Irish Chancery Reports [*A publication*] (DLA)
Jones & La T Jones and La Touche's Irish Chancery Reports [*A publication*] (DLA)
Jones & L (Ir) Jones and La Touche's Irish Chancery Reports [*A publication*] (DLA)
Jones & McM Jones and McMurtrie's Pennsylvania Supreme Court Reports [*A publication*] (DLA)
Jones & McM (PA) Jones and McMurtrie's Pennsylvania Supreme Court Reports [*A publication*] (DLA)
Jones & S Jones and Spencer's Superior Court Reports [*33-61 New York*] [*A publication*] (DLA)
Jones & Sp Jones and Spencer's Superior Court Reports [*33-61 New York*] [*A publication*] (DLA)
Jones & Spen Jones and Spencer's Superior Court Reports [*33-61 New York*] [*A publication*] (DLA)
Jones & V Laws Jones and Varick's Laws of New York [*A publication*] (DLA)
JonesAp Jones Apparel Group, Inc. [*Associated Press*] (SAG)
Jones B Jones' Law of Bailments [*A publication*] (DLA)
Jones Bailm Jones' Law of Bailments [*A publication*] (DLA)
Jones B & W (MO) Jones, Barclay, and Whittelsey's Reports [*31 Missouri*] [*A publication*] (DLA)
Jones Barclay & Whittelsey Jones, Barclay, and Whittelsey's Reports [*31 Missouri*] [*A publication*] (DLA)
Jones Ch Mort Jones on Chattel Mortgages [*A publication*] (DLA)
Jones Easem Jones' Treatise on Easements [*A publication*] (DLA)
Jones Eq Jones' North Carolina Equity Reports [*54-59*] [*1853-63*] [*A publication*] (DLA)
Jones Eq (NC) Jones' North Carolina Equity Reports [*54-59*] [*1853-63*] [*A publication*] (DLA)
Jones Exch Jones' Irish Exchequer Reports [*A publication*] (DLA)
Jones Fr Bar Jones' History of the French Bar [*A publication*] (DLA)
Jones French Bar Jones' History of the French Bar [*A publication*] (DLA)
Jones Inst Jones' Institutes of Hindoo Law [*A publication*] (DLA)
Jones Intr Jones' Introduction to Legal Science [*A publication*] (DLA)
Jones Ir Jones' Irish Exchequer Reports [*A publication*] (DLA)
Jones L Jones' Law Reports [*A publication*] (DLA)
Jones Law Jones' North Carolina Law Reports [*A publication*] (DLA)
Jones Lib Jones on Libel [*1812*] [*A publication*] (DLA)
Jones L Of T Jones on Land and Office Titles [*A publication*] (DLA)
JonesM Jones Medical Industries, Inc. [*Associated Press*] (SAG)
Jones Mort Jones on Mortgages [*A publication*] (DLA)
Jones NC Jones' North Carolina Law Reports [*A publication*] (DLA)
Jones PA Jones' Reports [*11, 12 Pennsylvania*] [*A publication*] (DLA)
JonesPl Jones Plumbing Systems, Inc. [*Associated Press*] (SAG)
Jones Pledges Jones on Pledges and Collateral Securities [*A publication*] (DLA)
Jones Ry Sec Jones on Railway Securities [*A publication*] (DLA)
Jones Salv Jones' Law of Salvage [*A publication*] (DLA)
Jones Securities Jones on Railroad Securities [*A publication*] (DLA)
JonesSp Jones Spacelink Ltd. [*Associated Press*] (SAG)
Jones UC Jones' Upper Canada Common Pleas Reports [*A publication*] (DLA)
Jones Uses Jones' Law of Uses [*A publication*] (DLA)
Jon Ex Jones' Irish Exchequer Reports [*A publication*] (DLA)
Jon Exch Jones' Irish Exchequer Reports [*A publication*] (DLA)
JonIcbl Jones Intercable, Inc. [*Associated Press*] (SAG)
Jon Ir Exch Jones' Irish Exchequer Reports [*A publication*] (DLA)
JONR Joiner (ABBR)
JONS Juntas de Ofensiva Nacional Sindicalista [*Syndicalist Juntas of the National Offensive*] [*Spain Political party*] (PPE)
JONSDAP Joint North Sea Data Acquisition Project [*An informal group of Belgian, Dutch, German, British, Dutch, and Swedish scientific institutes*] (PDAA)
JONSIS Joint North Sea Information Systems (PDAA)
JONSWAP Joint North Sea Wave Atmosphere Program [*Marine science*] (OSRA)
JONSWAP Joint North Sea Wave Atmosphere Program [*Global Atmospheric Research Program*] (USDC)
JONSWAP Joint North Sea Wave Project [*An informal group of Belgian, German, British, Dutch, and Swedish scientific institutes*] (PDAA)
JOO Jonesboro, GA [*Location identifier FAA*] (FAAL)
JOOD Junior Officer of the Day [*or Deck*] [*Navy*]
JOOMS Junior Observers of Meteorology [*Trainees for government service to replace Weather Bureau men who had gone to war*] [*World War II*]
JOOS Job-Oriented Organizational Structure (AAG)
JOOW Junior Officer of the Watch [*Navy*]
JOP Job Opportunity Program (OICC)
JOP Jobs Optional Program [*Combination job opportunities in the business sector and on the job training*] (OICC)
JOP Joint Observing Program [*NASA*]
JOP Joint Operating Plan
JOP Joint Operation Procedure (AAG)
JOP Joint Optoelectronics Project [*Japan*] [*Agreement for conducting cooperative global research*]
JOp Jupiter Orbiter Probe [*Later, Project Galileo*] [*NASA*]
JOPA Junior Officers and Professional Association
JOPA Juventud Organizada del Pueblo en Armas [*Armed People's Organized Youth*] [*Guatemala*] (PD)
JOPC Junior Olympic Pistol Championship [*National Rifle Association*]
JO/PCN Job Order/Program Control Number [*Army*]
JOPD Junior Officer Professional Development Program [*Army*] (RDA)
JOPES Joint Operation Planning and Execution System [*DoD*]
JOPES Joint Operations Planning and Execution System [*Military*]
JOPM Joint Occupancy Plan Memorandum (AAG)
JOPM Joint Operation Procedure Memorandum (AAG)
JOPP Joint Operational Policies and Procedures (MCD)
JOPR Joint Operation Procedure Report (AAG)
JOPREP Joint Operational Report [*Military*] (AFM)
JOPS Joint Operational Planning System [*Military*]
JOQ Job Order Quantity [*Military*] (AFIT)
JOR Jet Operations Requirements
JOR Job Operations Report
JOR Job Order Request (AAG)
JOR Joint Operations Requirements [*Military*] (AFM)
JOR Jordan [*ANSI three-letter standard code*] (CNC)
Jor Jordan (VRA)
JOR Yorkshire European Airways Ltd. [*British ICAO designator*] (FAAC)
Jo Radio Law Journal of Radio Law [*A publication*] (DLA)
JORC Junior Olympic Rifle Championship [*National Rifle Association*]
JORD Jordan (ABBR)
Jordan Jordan American Holdings, Inc. [*Associated Press*] (SAG)
Jord Jt St Comp Jordan on Joint Stock Companies [*A publication*] (DLA)
Jord PJ Jordan's Parliamentary Journal [*A publication*] (DLA)
JORG Joint Oceanographic Research Group
JORITDS Joint Optical Range Instrumentation Type Designation System
JOS Jeunesse Ouvriere du Senegal [*Senegalese Working Youth*]
JOS Job Order Supplement (MCD)
JOS Joint Operations Staff [*Military*]
JOS Jos [*Nigeria*] [*Airport symbol*] (OAG)
Jos Joseph (BJA)
Jos Joseph's Reports [*21 Nevada*] [*A publication*] (DLA)
Jos Josephus (BJA)
Jos Joshua [*Old Testament book*]
Jos Josiah (BJA)
JOS Joss Energy Ltd. [*Toronto Stock Exchange symbol*]
JOS Jostens, Inc. [*NYSE symbol*] (SPSG)
JOS Josvafo [*Hungary*] [*Seismograph station code, US Geological Survey*] (SEIS)
JOSA Seaman Apprentice, Journalist, Striker [*Navy rating*]
JOSAF Joint Operations Support Activity Frankfurt [*National Security Agency*]
Jos & Bev Joseph and Beven's Digest of Decisions [*Ceylon*] [*A publication*] (DLA)
JosAnt Jewish Antiquities [*Josephus*] (BJA)
JosApion Against Apion [*Josephus*] (BJA)
JOSB Bank [*Joseph A.*] Clothiers, Inc. [*NASDAQ symbol*] (SAG)
JOSB Jos.A. Bank Clothiers [*NASDAQ symbol*] (TTSB)
JOSB Joseph A Bank Clothiers [*NASDAQ symbol*] (SAG)
JosBank Bank [*Joseph A.*] Clothiers, Inc. [*Associated Press*] (SAG)
JosBank Joseph A. Bank Clothers [*Associated Press*] (SAG)
JOSCO Joint Overseas Shipping Control Office
Joseph Josephus [*First century AD*] [*Classical studies*] (OCD)
JOSH Job Safety and Health [*Bureau of National Affairs*] [*Information service or system*] (CRD)
Josh Joshua [*Old Testament book*]
JOSHUA Joint Sticking Hemoglobin Universal Assay [*Sickle cell anemia test*]
JO/SL Jupiter Orbiter Satellite Lander [*NASA*]
JosLife Life of Josephus (BJA)
JOSM Jesuit Office of Social Ministry [*Later, NOJSM*] (EA)
JOSN Seaman, Journalist, Striker [*Navy rating*]
JOSO Joint Organization for Solar Observations
JOSP Junior Olympic Shooting Program [*National Rifle Association*]
JOSPRO Joint Ocean [*or Overseas*] Shipping Procedure

JOSS............ JOHNNIAC [John's Integrator and Automatic Computer] Open Shop System [Time-sharing language] [Rand Corp. 1962] [Computer science]
JOSS............ Joint Ocean Surface Study
JOSS............ Joint Overseas Switching System [Military] (AABC)
Jostens........ Jostens, Inc. [Associated Press] (SAG)
JosWars...... Wars [Josephus] (BJA)
JOT.............. Jam on Target
Jo T............. John of Tynemouth [Deceased, 1221] [Authority cited in pre-1607 legal work] (DSA)
JOT.............. Joint Operational Test
JOT.............. Joliet, IL [Location identifier FAA] (FAAL)
JOTA............ Jamboree on the Air [Boy Scouts of America]
JOT & E...... Joint Operational Test and Evaluation (MCD)
JOTB............ Jungle Operations Training Battalion [Military]
JOTC........... Joint Oil Targets Committee [World War II]
JOTC........... Jungle Operations Training Center [Army] (INF)
JOTD........... Jotted (ABBR)
Jo Te........... Johannes Teutonicus [Deceased circa 1246] [Authority cited in pre-1607 legal work] (DSA)
JOTFOC...... Justification for Other than Full and Open Competition (AAGC)
JOTG........... Jotting (ABBR)
JOTR........... Joint Operational and Technical Reviews [Military] (AFIT)
JOTR........... Joshua Tree National Monument
JOTS........... Job-Oriented Training Standards (AFM)
JOTS........... Joint Operational Tactical System [Navy] (DOMA)
JOU............. Osaka University, Kita-ku, Osaka, Japan [Library symbol Library of Congress] (LCLS)
JOU............. Sioux Falls, SD [Location identifier FAA] (FAAL)
JOUAM........ Junior Order United American Mechanics
Joule........... Joules, Inc. [Associated Press] (SAG)
JOU-N......... Osaka University, Nakanishima Library, Osaka, Japan [Library symbol Library of Congress] (LCLS)
JOUR........... Journal (ABBR)
JOUR........... Journey (WGA)
JOUR........... Journeyman
Jour Comp Leg... Journal. Society of Comparative Legislation [A publication] (DLA)
Jour Conat Law... Journal of Conational Law [A publication] (DLA)
Jour Jur...... Journal of Jurisprudence [A publication] (DLA)
Jour Juris.... Hall's Journal of Jurisprudence [A publication] (DLA)
Jour Jur Sc... Journal of Jurisprudence and Scottish Law Magazine [A publication] (DLA)
Jour Law..... Journal of Law [A publication] (DLA)
JOURN......... Journal
Journ.......... Journalism (DD)
JOURN......... Journey (ABBR)
Journ Bib Lit... Journal of Biblical Literature [A publication] (OCD)
Journ Jur.... Journal of Jurisprudence [A publication] (DLA)
Journ Phil... Journal of Philology [A publication] (OCD)
Journ Sav.... Journal des Savants [A publication] (OCD)
Jour Ps Med... Journal of Psychological Medicine and Medical Jurisprudence [A publication] (DLA)
Jour Soc Civ... Journal des Societes Civiles et Commerciales [A publication] (DLA)
Jour Trib Com... Journal des Tribunaux de Commerce [A publication] (DLA)
Jov.............. Hymnus in Jovem [of Callimachus] [Classical studies] (OCD)
JOVE........... Jupiter Orbiting Vehicle for Exploration (MCD)
JOVIAL........ Joule's Own Version of the International Algebraic [or Algorithmic] Language [1958] [Computer science]
Jow Dict...... Jowitt's Dictionary of English Law [2nd ed.] [1977] [A publication] (DLA)
JOWIP......... Joint Ocean Wave Investigation Project [US and Canadian venture]
JOWOG........ Joint Working Group
JOY............. Job Opportunity for Youth [NASA employment program]
JOY............. Joy [Poland ICAO designator] (FAAC)
Joy Acc....... Joy's Evidence of Accomplices [1836] [A publication] (DLA)
Joyce Ins.... Joyce on Insurance [A publication] (DLA)
Joyce Lim.... Joyce on Limitations [A publication] (DLA)
Joyce Prac Inj... Joyce's Law and Practice of Injunctions [1872] [A publication] (DLA)
Joyce Prin Inj... Joyce's Doctrines and Principles of Injunctions [1877] [A publication] (DLA)
Joy Chal..... Joy's Peremptory Challenge of Jurors [1844] [A publication] (DLA)
Joy Conf..... Joy. Admissibility of Confessions [1842] [A publication] (DLA)
Joy Ev........ Joy's Evidence of Accomplices [1836] [A publication] (DLA)
Joy Leg Ed... Joy on Legal Education [A publication] (DLA)
Joyn Lim..... Joynes on Limitations [A publication] (DLA)
JOYS........... Journal of Youth Services in Libraries [American Library Association]
JOZ............. Jozini [South Africa] [Seismograph station code, US Geological Survey] (SEIS)
JP............... Adria Airways [Airline flight code] (ODBW)
JP............... Die Juedische Presse [The Jewish Press] [German] (BJA)
JP............... Fighter [Russian aircraft symbol]
JP............... Indo-Pacific International [ICAO designator] (AD)
JP............... Jack Panel
JP............... Jackson-Pratt [Drain] [Surgery] (DAVI)
JP............... Jacobi Polynomial [Mathematics]
JP............... James M. Peed [Designer's mark when appearing on US coins]
JP............... Janata Party [India] [Political party] (PPW)
JP............... Japan [ANSI two-letter standard code] (CNC)
JP............... Japan Paper
JP............... Jarrow Press, Inc.
JP............... Jatiya Party [Bangladesh] [Political party]
JP............... Jean Pierre Cosmetiques, Inc. [Vancouver Stock Exchange symbol]
JP............... Jefferson-Pilot [NYSE symbol] (TTSB)
JP............... Jefferson Pilot [NYSE symbol] (SAG)

JP............... Jefferson-Pilot Corp. [NYSE symbol] (SPSG)
JP............... Jet Penetration
JP............... Jet Petroleum (AFM)
JP............... Jet Pilot
JP............... Jet Pipe
JP............... Jet Power
JP............... Jet Propellant [or Propulsion]
JP............... Jet Propulsion Fuel
JP............... Jet Publications [DoD]
JP............... Jet Pump [Bioinstrumentation]
JP............... Jewish Press [Brooklyn, NY] [A publication] (BJA)
JP............... Jobbing Printer [A publication] (DGA)
JP............... Job Placement [Job Service] (OICC)
JP............... Job Processor
JP............... Jobst Pump [Medicine]
JP............... Job the Patient (BJA)
JP............... Joining Peptide [Medicine] (DMAA)
JP............... Joint Pacific [Military] (CINC)
JP............... Jones Party [Malta] [Political party] (PPE)
JP............... Jones Plug [Electricity] (IAA)
JP............... Joseph Pennell [Specification-made paper]
JP............... Journal of Parapsychology [A publication] (BRI)
JP............... Judge of Probate [British] (ROG)
JP............... Jumper (IAA)
JP............... Junction Panel [or Point] [Electronics]
JP............... Junge Pioniero
JP............... Jungle Penetrator [A helicopter rescue device] [Military] (VNW)
JP............... Junior Partner [i.e., a husband] [Slang]
JP............... Junior Principal [Freemasonry] (ROG)
JP............... Junior Probationer [British] (ROG)
JP............... Justice of the Peace
JP............... Justice of the Peace and Local Government Review [A publication] (DLA)
JP............... Justice of the Peace. Weekly Notes of Cases [England] [A publication] (DLA)
JP............... Justice Party [Turkey] [Political party]
JP............... Jute Protection [Telecommunications] (TEL)
JP............... Juvenile Periodontist [Dentistry] (DAVI)
JP............... Juventud Peronista [Peronist Youth] [Argentina]
JP............... Kim Jong Pil [South Korean politician]
JPA............. Jack Panel Assembly
JPA............. Japan Procurement Agency
JPA............. Jesuit Philosophical Association of the United States and Canada (EA)
JPA............. Jet Pioneers Association of the United States of America (EA)
JPA............. Jewish Palestinian Aramaic (BJA)
JPA............. Joao Pessoa [Brazil] [Airport symbol] (OAG)
JPA............. Job Pack Area [Computer science] (IBMDP)
JPA............. Job Performance Aid
JPA............. Joint Passover Association of the City of New York (EA)
JPA............. Joint Planning Activity [DoD]
JPA............. Junior Philatelists of America (EA)
JPA............. Justices of the Peace Association [Australia]
JPA............. Juvenile Pilocytic Astrocytoma [Medicine] (DMAA)
JPA............. La Porte, TX [Location identifier FAA] (FAAL)
J-PAAS........ Jubilation - Paul Anka Admiration Society [Defunct] (EA)
J Pac H....... Journal of Pacific History [A publication]
JPAM........... Joint Program Assessment Memorandum (MCD)
JPAO........... Joint Public Affairs Office (DOMA)
JPAP........... Jet Penetration Approach
JPAT........... Joint Process Action Team
JPATS......... Joint Primary Aircraft Training System
JPATS......... Joint Primary Aircraft Training System [Air Force] [Navy] (DOMA)
JPB............. Joint Planning Board
JPB............. Joint Procurement Board [Military] (AABC)
JPB............. Joint Production Board [US and Great Britain]
JPB............. Joint Purchasing Board
JPB............. Junctional Premature Beat [Cardiology]
JPBS........... Jettison Pushbutton Switch
JPC............. Jack Patch Cord
JpC............. Japanese Columbia [Record label]
JPC............. Jeunesse pour Christ [Youth for Christ International - YFCI] (EA)
JPC............. Jeunesse Progressiste Casamancaise [Casamance Progressive Youth] [Senegal]
JPC............. Joint Planning Center
JPC............. Joint Planning Committee
JPC............. Joint Power Conditioner
JPC............. Joint Production Committee [British] (DCTA)
JPC............. Journal of Popular Culture [A publication] (BRI)
JPC............. Judgement Purchase Court.
JPC............. Judge of the Prize Court (DLA)
JPC............. Judicial Planning Council (OICC)
JPC............. Junctional Premature Contraction [Cardiology]
JPC............. Justice of the Peace Clerk [British] (ROG)
JPC............. Just Prior Condition [Computer science]
JPC............. Polar Air Co. [Russian Federation] [ICAO designator] (FAAC)
JPCA........... Jewish Penicillin Connoisseurs Association (EA)
JPCC........... Joint Pacific Command Control Network (MCD)
JPCC........... Joint Petroleum Coordination Center/Committee [NATO] (NATG)
JPCD........... Just Perceptible Color Difference [Telecommunications] (TEL)
JPCG-CRM... Joint Policy Coordinating Group on Computer Resources Management (MCD)
JPCG/DIMM... Joint Policy Coordinating Group on Defense Integrated Materiel Management (AFIT)
JPCG-DMI... Joint Policy Coordinating Group on Depot Maintenance Interservicing

JP Ct............	Justice of the Peace's Court [*Legal term*] (DLA)
JPD..............	Japan Publishers Directory [*Japan Publications Guide Service*] [*Japan Information service or system*] (CRD)
JPD..............	Joint Potential Designator [*DoD*]
JPD..............	Juvenile Plantar Dermatosis [*Medicine*] (DAVI)
JPDC............	Japan Petroleum Development Co.
JPDR	Japan Power Demonstration Reactor
JPE..............	Job Performance Evaluation (PDAA)
JPE..............	Journal of Political Economy [*A publication*] (BRI)
JPE..............	JPE, Inc. [*Associated Press*] (SAG)
JPEC............	Joint Planning and Execution Community (DOMA)
JP ECON	Journal of Political Economy [*A publication*] (ROG)
J PED	Journal of Pedagogy [*New York*] [*A publication*] (ROG)
JPEG............	Joint Photographic Experts Group [*International video standard*] (PCM)
jpeg	Joint Photographic Experts Group [*Computer science*]
JPEG	Joint Photographic Experts Group [*Antineoplastic drug*]
JPEI	JPE, Inc. [*NASDAQ symbol*] (SAG)
JPESJ	Jewish Palestine Exploration Society. Journal [*A publication*] (BJA)
JPET............	Job Placement and Employment Training
JPF	Jewish Peace Fellowship (EA)
JPF	Jewish Philanthropic Fund of 1933 (EA)
JPF	Job Planning Form
JPF	Justice of the Peace Fiscal [*British*] (ROG)
JPFC............	Jane Powell Fan Club (EA)
JPFC............	Jeanne Pruett Fan Club (EA)
JPFC............	Judas Priest Fan Club (EA)
JPFO............	Jews for the Preservation of Firearms Ownership (EA)
JP Food	JP Foodservice, Inc. [*Associated Press*] (SAG)
JPFS............	JP Foodservice [*NASDAQ symbol*] (TTSB)
JPFS............	JP Foodservice, Inc. [*NASDAQ symbol*] (SAG)
JPFT............	Joiner Pilaster Fumetight [*Technical drawings*]
JPG..............	Jefferson Proving Ground [*Madison, IN*] [*Army*] (AABC)
JPG..............	Job Performance [*or Proficiency*] Guide (AFM)
JPG..............	Joint Planning Group [*NATO*] (NATG)
JPGC............	Joint Power Generation Conference
JPGS............	Japan Publications Guide Service [*Information service or system*] (IID)
JPH..............	Jones, Paul H., Romulus MI [*STAC*]
JPHA............	John Pelham Historical Association (EA)
J Phil	Journal of Philosophy [*A publication*] (BRI)
JPI	Jackson Personality Inventory [*Personality development test*] [*Psychology*]
JPI	Job Performance Illustrations (MCD)
JPI	Joint Packaging Instruction
JPI	Joint Precision Interdiction [*NATO*] (DOMA)
JPI	Jupiter National, Inc. (SPSG)
JPI	Sitka, AK [*Location identifier FAA*] (FAAL)
JPIC............	Joint Program Integration Committee [*NASA*] (NASA)
JPIM............	Journal of Product Innovation Management [*Product Development and Management Association*] [*A publication*]
JPJ..............	Justice of the Peace and Local Government Review [*A publication*] (DLA)
JPJ..............	Justice of the Peace Journal [*A publication*]
JPJ..............	Justice of the Peace. Weekly Notes of Cases [*England*] [*A publication*] (DLA)
JPJ..............	Paterson, NJ [*Location identifier FAA*] (FAAL)
JPJo...........	Justice of the Peace. Weekly Notes of Cases [*England*] [*A publication*] (DLA)
JPL	Jacksonville Public Library System, Jacksonville, FL [*OCLC symbol*] (OCLC)
JPL	Jet Propulsion Laboratory [*Renamed H. Allen Smith Jet Propulsion Laboratory, 1973, after a retiring congressman. However, JPL is used officially*] [*California Institute of Technology Pasadena, CA*] [*NASA*] [*Research center*]
JPL	Jewish Peace Lobby (EA)
JPL	Job Parts List (AAG)
JPLE............	Journal of Professional Legal Education [*Australia A publication*]
JPL/ETR.......	Jet Propulsion Laboratory Field Station, Air Force Eastern Test Range
JPL/PODS....	Jet Propulsion Laboratory/Pilot Ocean Data System (MCD)
JPL-STAR	Jet Propulsion Laboratory Self Testing and Repairing Computer [*California Institute of Technology*] (PDAA)
JPM............	Jet-Piercing Machine
JPM............	Job Performance Manual (MCD)
JPM............	Job Performance Measure
JPM............	Joint Project Manager
JPM............	Morgan [*J. P.*] & Co., Inc. [*NYSE symbol*] (SPSG)
JPM............	Morgan (J.P.) [*NYSE symbol*] (TTSB)
JPMA...........	Juvenile Products Manufacturers Association (EA)
JPMC...........	JPM Co. [*NASDAQ symbol*] (TTSB)
JPMCo.........	JPM Co. (The) [*Associated Press*] (SAG)
JPMO...........	Joint Program Management Office (MCD)
JPMPrA.......	Morgan(JP) Adj Rt A Pfd [*NYSE symbol*] (TTSB)
JPMPrH.......	Morgan(JP)6.625% Dep'H'Pfd [*NYSE symbol*] (TTSB)
JPMR..........	Joint Projected Manpower Requirements [*Military*] (AABC)
JPMS..........	J. P. Morgan Securities
JPMX...........	JPM Co. (The) [*NASDAQ symbol*] (SAG)
JPN.............	Japan [*ANSI three-letter standard code*] (CNC)
jpn	Japanese [*MARC language code Library of Congress*] (LCCP)
JPN.............	Memrykord Ltd. [*British ICAO designator*] (FAAC)
JPN.............	Washington, DC [*Location identifier FAA*] (FAAL)
JPNL............	Judged Perceived Noise Level (OA)
JPNT............	Joiner Pilaster Nontight [*Technical drawings*]
JPO.............	Joint Petroleum Office

JPO.............	Joint Program Office [*Military*] (SDI)
JPO.............	Joint Project Office [*or Officer*]
JPO.............	Junior Professional Officer [*United Nations*]
JPO.............	Juvenile Probation Officer (OICC)
JPO.............	Pomona [*California*] [*Airport symbol*] (AD)
JPOAA.........	Junior Panel Outdoor Advertising Association [*Later, ESOAA*]
JPO-BD.......	Joint Program Office for Biological Defense [*Army*] (RDA)
JPOC...........	JSC [*Johnson Space Center*] Payload Operations Center (MCD)
J Pol	Journal of Politics [*A publication*] (BRI)
J Pol Sci & Admin...	Journal of Police Science and Administration [*A publication*] (DLA)
J Pop F&TV...	Journal of Popular Film and Television [*A publication*] (BRI)
JpOTC.........	Japan OTC Equity Fund, Inc. [*Associated Press*] (SAG)
JPOTS..........	Joint Panel on Oceanographic Tables and Standards [*Marine science*] [*United Nations*] (OSRA)
JPO-TT........	Joint Program Offrice-Transition Team [*DoD*]
JPP.............	Jalkeen Puolenpaiuan [*Afternoon*] [*Finland*]
JPP.............	Japan Paper Proofs
JPP.............	Joint Planning Process [*Military*] (NVT)
JPP.............	Joint Program Plan (NASA)
JPPL............	Joint Personnel Priority List
JpPol...........	Japanese Polydor-Deutsche Grammophon [*Record label*]
JPPP............	Jewish People, Past and Present [*Jewish Encyclopedic Handbooks*] [*A publication*] (BJA)
JPPRI..........	Jewish Policy Planning and Research Institute [*Synagogue Council of America*]
JPPS...........	Jack Point Preservation Society (EA)
JPPSO	Joint Personal Property Shipping Office [*Military*] (DNAB)
JPPSOWA	Joint Personal Property Shipping Office, Washington, DC [*Military*] (AABC)
JPPSST........	Joseph Preschool and Primary Self-Concept Screening Test [*Child development test*] [*Psychology*]
JpPV...........	Japanese Polydor Variable Microgroove [*Record label*]
JPQ.............	Jung Personality Questionnaire [*Personality development test*] [*Psychology*]
JPR.............	Air International (Holdings) PLC [*British ICAO designator*] (FAAC)
JPR.............	Inversiones Ayacucho, SA, "Jet Privado" [*Peru*] [*FAA designator*] (FAAC)
JPR.............	Joint Procurement Regulations [*of Army and Air Force*]
JPR.............	Journal of Peace Research [*A publication*] (BRI)
JPR.............	Journal of Purchasing and Materials Management [*A publication*] (AAGC)
JPR.............	JP Realty [*NYSE symbol*] (SPSG)
jpr	Judaeo-Persian [*MARC language code Library of Congress*] (LCCP)
JPR.............	Justice of the Peace and Local Government Review Reports [*A publication*] (DLA)
JPR.............	Justice Procurement Regulation [*A publication*] (AAGC)
JPRA...........	Japanese Phonograph Record Association [*An association*] (NITA)
JPRC...........	Joint Personnel Recovery Center [*Military*]
J PR CT	Judge Prerogative Court, Canterbury [*British*] (ROG)
JPRDY	Jeopardy (ABBR)
JPRDZ	Jeopardize (ABBR)
JPRDZG	Jeopardizing (ABBR)
JP Rlty.........	JP Realty [*Associated Press*] (SAG)
JPRO...........	Joint Photographic Reconnaissance Organization [*World War II*]
JPROB.........	Judge of Probate [*British*] (ROG)
J Prod L	Journal of Products Law (DLA)
JPRS...........	Joint Publications Research Service [*Department of Commerce*]
JPRS-GUO ...	Joint Publications Research Service Translations - Government Use Only [*Department of Commerce*]
JPS	Japan Press Service
JPS	Jean Piaget Society [*Later, JPSSSKD*] (EA)
JPS	Jet Plume Simulation
JPS	Jeunesse Populaire Senegalaise [*Senegalese People's Youth*]
JPS	Jewish Publication Society (EA)
JPS	John Player Special [*Sponsor of British Lotus Formula I racing car*]
JPS	Joint Planning Staff [*US and Great Britain*] [*World War II*]
JPS	Joint Position Sense [*Medicine*]
JPS	Jones Plumbing Systems, Inc. [*AMEX symbol*] (SPSG)
JPS	Junior Philatelic Society [*British*] (BI)
JPSA...........	Jacob's Prevocational Skills Assessment
JPSA...........	Japanese Plating Supplier's Association [*Environmetal science*]
JPSA...........	Jewish Pharmaceutical Society of America (EA)
JPSA...........	Jewish Publication Society of America (DGA)
JPSA...........	Joint Program for the Study of Abortion
JPSA...........	Junior Philatelic Society of America [*Later, JPA*] (EA)
JPSC...........	Joint Production Survey Committee
JPSG...........	Joint Planning and Scheduling Group
JPSS...........	Just, Participatory, and Sustainable Society [*World Council of Churches*]
JPSSSKD	Jean Piaget Society: Society for the Study of Knowledge and Development (EA)
JPST...........	Journal of Parenteral Science and Technology [*A publication*] (EAAP)
JPSTH.........	Joint Peristimulus Time Histograms [*For study of physiology*]
J Psychological Medicine...	Journal of Psychological Medicine and Medical Jurisprudence [*A publication*] (DLA)
JPT.............	Houston [*Texas*] Park-Ten [*Airport symbol*] (OAG)
JPT.............	Japanese Proficiency Test [*Educational test*]
JPT.............	Jet Pipe Temperature
JPT.............	Job Progress Ticket
JPT.............	Jupitor Resources Ltd. [*Vancouver Stock Exchange symbol*]
JPTDS.........	Joint Photographic Type Designation System [*Military*]
JPTDS.........	Junior Participating Tactical Data System [*Also known as "Jeep"*] (MCD)
JPTF	Joint Parachute Test Facility [*DoD*]

JPTL .... Jet Pipe Temperature Limiter (MCD)
JPTO .... Jet-Propelled Takeoff
JPTS .... Jet Petroleum, Thermally Stable (DOMA)
JPU .... Job Processing Unit
JPU .... Just Publishable Unit
JpV .... Japanese Victor [Record label]
JPV .... Joint Pacific Voice [Military] (CINC)
JPW .... Job Processing Word
JPWC .... Joint Postwar Committee
JPWC .... Joint Psychological Warfare Committee (LAIN)
JQ .... Job Questionnaire
JQ .... Journalism Quarterly [A publication] (BRI)
JQ .... J-Q Resources, Inc. [Toronto Stock Exchange symbol]
JQ .... Trans-Jamaican Airlines [ICAO designator] (AD)
JQA .... John Quincy Adams [US president, 1767-1848]
JQA .... Trans Jamaican Airlines Ltd. [ICAO designator] (FAAC)
JQB .... Justice of the Queen's Bench [Legal term] (DLA)
JQC .... Dayton, OH [Location identifier FAA] (FAAL)
JQE .... Jaque [Panama] [Airport symbol] (OAG)
JQH .... Hammons [John Q.] Hotels, Inc. [NYSE symbol] (SAG)
JQHamm ...... Hammons [John Q.] Hotel, Inc. [Associated Press] (SAG)
JQR .... Hammons(John Q)Hotels'A' [NYSE symbol] (TTSB)
JR .... Jacobus Rex [King James]
JR .... James River Corp. [NYSE symbol] (TTSB)
JR .... James River Corp. of Virginia [NYSE symbol] (SPSG)
JR .... Jam Resistant
JR .... Jar (MCD)
Jr .... Jeremiah [Old Testament book] (BJA)
JR .... [The] Jewish Right (EA)
JR .... Jigger [Ship's rigging] (ROG)
JR .... Job Rotation [Computer science] (MHDB)
JR .... Job Routed [Military] (AFIT)
JR .... John Ross Ewing, Jr. [Character in TV series "Dallas"]
JR .... Johnson's New York Reports [A publication] (DLA)
JR .... Joint Resolution [Usually, of the US Senate and House of
　　　　　　　Representatives]
JR .... Joint Return (MHDB)
JR .... Joint Review
JR .... Jolly's Reaction [Neurology] (DAVI)
JR .... Jordan Register (EA)
JR .... Jour [Day] [French]
JR .... Journal (ADA)
JR .... Journal of Religion [A publication] (BRI)
JR .... Judges' Rules [A publication] (DLA)
Jr .... Juglans regia [Persian walnut]
JR .... Junctional Rhythm [Cardiology]
JR .... Junction Rack (KSC)
JR .... Junior
Jr .... Junior (DD)
JR .... Junior
Jr .... Junior (WDMC)
JR .... Jurist Reports [1873-78] [New Zealand] [A publication] (DLA)
JR .... Juror
JR .... Juvenile Rheumatoid Arthritis [Also, JRA] [Medicine] (DAVI)
JRA .... Jam-Resistant Antenna
JRA .... Japanese Racing Association
JRA .... Japan Racing Association (ECON)
JRA .... Jewish Royalty Association (EA)
JRA .... Job Release Analysis
JRA .... Juvenile Rheumatoid Arthritis [Medicine]
JRA .... New York, NY [Location identifier FAA] (FAAL)
JRAD .... Joint Resource Assessment Data
JRAD .... Judicial Recommendation against Deportation
J Radio L ..... Journal of Radio Law [A publication] (DLA)
JRAS .... Journal of the Royal Agricultural Society [A publication] (ROG)
JRATA .... Joint Research and Test Activity (MCD)
JRATA .... Joint Research and Test Agency [Terminated, 1966] [Military]
JRB .... Joint Radio Board
JRB .... Joint Reconnaissance Board [Military] (AABC)
JRB .... Joint Review Board (MCD)
jrb .... Judaeo-Arabic [MARC language code Library of Congress] (LCCP)
JRB .... New York, NY [Location identifier FAA] (FAAL)
JRBK .... James River Bankshares [NASDAQ symbol] (TTSB)
JRBK .... James River Bankshares, Inc. [NASDAQ symbol] (SAG)
JRC .... Jet Reaction Control
JRC .... Jewish Refugees Committee (EAIO)
JrC .... Johnson Reprint Corporation, New York, NY [Library symbol Library
　　　　　　　of Congress] (LCLS)
JRC .... Joint Railroad Conference
JRC .... Joint Reconnaissance Center [Military] (AFM)
JRC .... Joint Recovery Center (MCD)
JRC .... Joint Representation Committee [British] (DCTA)
JRC .... Joint Research Center [Commission of the European Communities]
JRC .... Junior Red Cross
JRCAT .... Joint Research Center for Atom Technology [Japan]
JRCC .... Joint Reconnaissance Control Center (MCD)
JRCC .... Joint Regional Continuing Committee [Later, RCEAC] [Civil Defense]
JRCC .... Joint Rescue Coordination Center [Military] (AFM)
JRC-CVT ...... Joint Review Committee on Education in Cardiovascular
　　　　　　　Technology (DAVI)
JRCDMS ...... Joint Review Committee on Education in Diagnostic Medical
　　　　　　　Sonography (EA)
JRC-EEG ..... Joint Review Committee on Education in Electroencephalographic
　　　　　　　[Technology] (DAVI)

JRCEMT-P ... Joint Review Committee on Educational Programs for the EMT
　　　　　　　[Emergency MedicalTechnician]-Paramedic (EA)
JRCEPEP .... Joint Review Committee on Educational Programs for the EMT
　　　　　　　[Emergency MedicalTechnician]-Paramedic (EA)
JRCEPPA .... Joint Review Committee on Educational Programs for Physician
　　　　　　　Assistants (EA)
JRCERT....... Joint Review Committee on Education in Radiologic Technology (EA)
JRCEST....... Joint Review Committee on Education for the Surgical Technologist
　　　　　　　(EA)
JRCI .... Jamming RADAR Coverage Indicator (MSA)
JRCI .... Journal of the Royal Colonial Institute (ROG)
JRC-NMT .... Joint Review Committee on Educational Programs in Nuclear
　　　　　　　Medicine Technology (DAVI)
JRCOMA ..... Joint Review Committee for the Ophthalmic Medical Assistant (EA)
JRCOMP ..... Joint Review Committee for Ophthalmic Medical Personnel (EA)
JRCP .... Joint Reinforced Concrete Pavement
JRC-PA .... Joint Review Committee on Educational Programs for Physician
　　　　　　　Assistants (EA)
JRCPE .... Joint Review Committee for Perfusion Education (DAVI)
JRCRTE....... Joint Review Committee for Respiratory Therapy Education (EA)
JRCS .... Jet Reaction Control System
JRCS .... John Reich Collectors Society (EA)
JRC-ST .... Joint Review Committee on Education for the Surgical Technologist
　　　　　　　(DAVI)
JRD .... Jarred (ABBR)
JRD .... Justification Review Document (AAGC)
JRD .... Riverside, CA [Location identifier FAA] (FAAL)
JRDA .... Jeunesse du Rassemblement Democratique Africain [Youth of the
　　　　　　　African Democratic Rally]
JRDACI .... Jeunesse du Rassemblement Democratique Africain de Cote d'Ivoire
　　　　　　　[Youth of the African Democratic Rally of the Ivory Coast]
JRDB .... Joint Research and Development Board [1946-1947]
JRDOD .... Joint Research and Development Objectives Document [Military]
　　　　　　　(AABC)
JRE .... JR Energy Ltd. [Vancouver Stock Exchange symbol]
JRE .... New York [New York] E. 60th Street [Airport symbol] (OAG)
JREA .... James Robison Evangelistic Association (EA)
J Rehab RD... Journal of Rehabilitation Research and Development
　　　　　　　[A publication] (BRI)
JREM .... Junior Radio Electrical Mechanic [British military] (DMA)
J Rep .... Johnson's Maryland Chancery Reports [A publication] (DLA)
J Rep .... Johnson's New York Reports [A publication] (DLA)
J Rep .... Johnson's Reports of Chase's United States Circuit Court Decisions
　　　　　　　[A publication] (DLA)
J Reprints Antitrust L & Econ... Journal of Reprints for Antitrust Law and
　　　　　　　Economics [A publication] (DLA)
JRF .... Jackie Robinson Foundation (EA)
JRF .... Jewish Reconstructionist Foundation (EA)
JRF .... John-Roger Foundation (EA)
JRF .... Judicial Research Foundation [Defunct]
JRFC .... Jerry Reed Fan Club [Defunct] (EA)
JRFC .... Johnny Rodriguez Fan Club (EA)
JRFL .... Jarful (ABBR)
JRFTNG ...... Jet Refresher Training [Navy] (NVT)
JRG .... Jarring (ABBR)
JRG .... Junction Register (IAA)
JRGN .... Jargon (ABBR)
JRH .... Jorhat [India] [Airport symbol] (OAG)
JR HS .... Junior High School (WDAA)
JRHSQ .... Journal. Royal Historical Society of Queensland [A publication]
JRI .... Jail Release Information
JRI .... Jewel Resources [Vancouver Stock Exchange symbol]
JRISDON ...... Jurisdiction (ROG)
JRivBsh .... James River Bankshares, Inc. [Associated Press] (SAG)
JRiver .... James River Corp. of Virginia [Associated Press] (SAG)
JRJ .... JAVA [Jamaica Association of Villas and Apartments] Reservations
　　　　　　　Jamaica (EA)
JRKD .... Jerked (ABBR)
JRKG .... Jerking (ABBR)
JRKIR .... Jerkier (ABBR)
JRKLY .... Jerkily (ABBR)
JRKN .... Jerkin (ABBR)
JRKNS .... Jerkiness (ABBR)
JRKR .... Jerker (ABBR)
JRKST .... Jerkiest (ABBR)
JRL .... Cincinnati G&E8.28%JrSubDebs [NYSE symbol] (TTSB)
JRL .... Cincinnati Gas & Electric [NYSE symbol] (SAG)
JRL .... Jarvis Resources [Vancouver Stock Exchange symbol]
JRL .... Jet Research Laboratory (MCD)
jrl .... Journal (DAVI)
Jr LS .... Junior Life Saving [Red Cross]
JRM .... Jettison Release Mechanism
JRM .... Joule-Rowland Method [Physics]
JRM .... McDermott [J. Ray] SA [NYSE symbol] (SAG)
JRMB .... Joint Requirements and Management Board [Later, JROC] [Military]
JRMB .... Joint Resources Management Board [Military]
JRMF .... Joseph R. McCarthy Foundation (EA)
JRMTO .... Joint Rail Military Traffic Office (AABC)
JRN .... Jet Rent SA [Mexico ICAO designator] (FAAC)
JRN .... Junior Resident Note [Medical records] (DAVI)
JrNAD .... Junior National Association for the Deaf [Defunct] (EA)
JRNDEX .... Journal Index
JRNIST .... Journalist
JRNL .... Journal
JRNL .... Journal

JRNLM.........	Journalism (ABBR)
JRNLSM......	Journalism (ABBR)
JRNLST.......	Journalist (ABBR)
JRNLST.......	Journalist
JRNLSTC......	Journalistic (ABBR)
JRNLT.........	Journalistic (ABBR)
JRNLTC.......	Journalistic (ABBR)
JRNLTCY......	Journalistically (ABBR)
JRNLZ.........	Journalize (ABBR)
JRNLZD	Journalized (ABBR)
JRNLZG	Journalizing (ABBR)
JRNLZR	Journalizer (ABBR)
JRNSCA	Jurist Reports, New Series, Court of Appeal [*New Zealand*] [*A publication*] (DLA)
JRNSML	Jurist Reports, New Series, Cases in Mining Law [*New Zealand*] [*A publication*] (DLA)
JRNSSC	Jurist Reports, New Series, Supreme Court [*New Zealand*] [*A publication*] (DLA)
JRNY	Journey (ABBR)
JRNY	Journey
JRNYD	Journeyed (ABBR)
JRNYG	Journeying (ABBR)
JRNYMAN	Journeyman (ABBR)
JRO............	Jicamarca Radar Observatory [*Peru*]
JRO............	Junior Radio Operator [*British military*] (DMA)
JRO............	Kilimanjaro [*Tanzania*] [*Airport symbol*]
JROC	Joint Requirements Oversight Council [*Military*]
JROFC	James "Rebel" O'Leary Fan Club (EA)
JROJATC......	James "Rebel" O'Leary and Jammie Ann Tape Club [*Defunct*] (EA)
JROTC	Junior Reserve Officers' Training Corps (AABC)
JRP	Job Readiness Posture (OICC)
JRP	Joint Requirements Planning (CDE)
JRPG	Joint RADAR Planning Group [*Military*] (CET)
JRPM	Joint Registered Publications Memorandum
JRPO	Joint Research Projects Office [*Army and NASA joint operation*] (RDA)
JRPrK	James River$3.375Cv Ex K Pfd [*NYSE symbol*] (TTSB)
JRPrL	James River Dep Cv Ex Pfd [*NYSE symbol*] (TTSB)
JRPrO	James River 8.25% Dep Pfd [*NYSE symbol*] (TTSB)
JRPrP	James River 9% 'DECS' [*NYSE symbol*] (TTSB)
JRR	Japanese Research Reactor
JRR	Juror (ABBR)
JRRC	Joint Regional Reconnaissance Center [*NATO*] (NATG)
JRRT	John Ronald Renel Tolkien [*British author, 1892-1973*]
JRS	Japanese Rocket Society
JRS	Jersey [*Channel Islands*] [*Seismograph station code, US Geological Survey Closed*] (SEIS)
JRS	Jerusalem [*Israel*] [*Airport symbol*] (OAG)
JRS	Jet Repair Service
JRS	Job Rehearsal Scheme (AIE)
JRS	Job Release Scheme (PDAA)
JRS	John R. Sinnock [*Designer's mark, when appearing on US coins*]
JRS	Joint Reporting Structure [*Military*] (AFM)
JRS	Journal. Roentgen Society [*A publication*] (ROG)
JRS	Junction Relay Set (IAA)
JRSC	Jam-Resistant Secure Communications
JRSC	Joint Resistant Secure Communications [*DoD*]
JRSDCNL	Jurisdictional (ABBR)
J/RSM.........	Junior Regimental Sergeant-Major [*British military*] (DMA)
JRSO	Jewish Restitution Successor Organization (EA)
JRSPDN	Jurisprudent (ABBR)
JRSPDNC	Jurisprudence (ABBR)
JRSPDTL	Jurisprudential (ABBR)
JRST	Jurist (ABBR)
JRS/USA......	Jesuit Refugee Service/USA (EA)
JRSVC	Jam-Resistant Secure Voice Communications (MCD)
JRSWG	Joint Reentry System Working Group
JRSY	Jersey (ABBR)
JRT	Jaguar-Rover-Triumph
JRT	Job Relations Training
JRT	Jugoslovenska Radiotelevizija [*Association of Yugoslav Radio and Television Organizations*] (EY)
JRT	Junctional Recovery Time [*Medicine*] (DMAA)
JRT	Tampa, FL [*Location identifier FAA*] (FAAL)
JRTC..........	Joint Readiness Training Center [*Fort Chaffee, AR*] (INF)
JRTCA........	Jack Russell Terrier Club of America (EA)
JRTC-IS	Joint Readiness Training Center Instrumentation System [*DoD*]
JRUSI	Journal of the Royal United Service Institution [*A publication*] (ROG)
JRV	Javelin Rocket Vehicle
JRvr	James River Corp. of Virginia [*Associated Press*] (SAG)
JRWG	Job Redesign Working Group
JRX	Joint Readiness Exercise (MCD)
JRY	Jury (ABBR)
JRYBLD	Jerrybuild (ABBR)
JRYBLDG	Jerrybuilding (ABBR)
JRYBLDR	Jerrybuilder (ABBR)
JRYBLT.......	Jerrybuilt (ABBR)
JryDeli........	Jerrys Famous Deli, Inc. [*Associated Press*] (SAG)
JRYMA........	Juryman (ABBR)
JRZ	Jugoslovenska Radikalna Zajednica [*Yugoslav Radical Union*] [*Political party*] (PPE)
JS	Jack Screw
JS	Jamestowne Society (EA)
J/S	Jamming to Signal
JS	Jam Strobe (IEEE)

J/S	Jam to Signal Ratio
JS	Japan Society (EA)
JS	Jargon Society (EA)
JCS	JCS [*Joint Chiefs of Staff*] Support (MCD)
JS	Jefferson Smurfit Group PLC [*NYSE symbol*] (SAG)
JS	Jefferson Smurfit Grp ADS [*NYSE symbol*] (TTSB)
JS	Jejunal Segment [*Gastroenterology*] (DAVI)
JS	Jetevator Sensor
JS	Jet Stabilization
JS	Jet Stream
JS	Jet Study (AAG)
JS	Jettison Signal
JS	Job Search [*Job Training and Partnership Act*] (OICC)
JS	Job Service (OICC)
JS	Job Specification [*Department of Labor*]
JS	Job Stream [*Computer science*]
JS	John R. Sinnock [*Designer's mark, when appearing on US coins*]
JS	Johnson Society (EA)
JS	Joint Services [*British military*] (DMA)
JS	Joint Spacing [*Mining technology*]
JS	Joint Staff [*Military*] (CINC)
JS	Joint Support [*Military*] (AFM)
JS	Jones and Spencer's Superior Court Reports [*33-61 New York*] [*A publication*] (DLA)
JS	Joshua [*Old Testament book*]
J/s	Joules per Second (IDOE)
JS	Jourdain Society [*British*]
JS	Judaisme Sepharadi (BJA)
JS	Judean Society (EA)
JS	Judgment Summons [*British*] (ROG)
JS	Judicial Separation [*British*] (ROG)
JS	Junctional Slowing [*Cardiology*] (DAVI)
JS	Junior Seaman [*British military*] (DMA)
JS	Junkman-Shoeller Unit (MAE)
JS	Jury Sittings (Faculty Cases) [*Scotland*] [*A publication*] (DLA)
J/S	Justified
JS	Justifying Space [*Typography*] (DGA)
JS	Just Scale
JS	Korean Airways [*ICAO designator*] (AD)
JS	Sea of Japan
JSA	Jammer System Analysis
JSA	Japanese Standards Association (NTCM)
JSA	Japan Silk Association (EA)
JSA	Jesuit Seismological Association (EA)
JSA	Jet Show Assembly
JSA	Jewelers Security Alliance of the US (EA)
JSA	Jewelers Shipping Association (EA)
JSA	Jewish Society of America
JSA	Job Safety Analysis
JSA	Job Search Allowance
JSA	Joint Security Area (MCD)
JSA	Joint Supportability Assessment [*Army*]
JSA	Journeymen Stone Cutters Association of North America [*Defunct*]
JSA	Junior Statesmen of America (EA)
Jsa	Sutter Antigen [*Of Kell system blood group*] [*Hematology*] (DAVI)
JSAAE	Japanese Society for Alternatives to Animal Experiments
JSAC	Jet Strategic Airlift Capability [*of Military Air Command*] (AAG)
JSAC	Joint Strategy and Action Committee [*Defunct*] (EA)
JSAG	Joint Service Advisory Group
JSAIS	Junior South African Individual Scales [*Intelligence test*]
J-SAK	Joint Attack of the Second Echelon (MCD)
JSAL	Journal of South African Law [*A publication*] (ILCA)
JSAM	Joint Security Assistance Memorandum [*Military*]
JSAM	Joint Service Achievement Medal [*Military decoration*]
JSAMSA.......	Joint Security Assistance Memorandum Supporting Analysis (MCD)
JSAP	Joint Statement of Agreed Principles [*US-USSR*]
JSAR	Joint Search and Rescue [*Military*] (DNAB)
JSAR	Joint Service Agreement Report [*Defense Supply Agency*]
JSARC	Joint Search and Rescue Center [*Military*] (AABC)
JSAS	Jammer System Analysis Simulator
JSAS	Journal Supplement Abstract Service [*American Psychological Association*]
JSAT	Japan Satellite Systems [*Commercial firm*]
JSAT	Joint System Acceptance Test (MCD)
JSAT	Junior Scholastic Aptitude Test [*Education*] (AEBS)
JSATG	Joint Services Actions Task Group (MCD)
JSATP	Joint Services Automatic Testing Panel (AAGC)
JSB	Bachelor of Judicial Science
JSB	Japanese Society in Brisbane [*Australia*]
JSB	Jaswant Singh and Bhattacharji [*Staining method for blood cells, named for its discoverers*] [*Medicine*]
JSB	Jewish Society for the Blind (EA)
JSB	Jewish Statistical Bureau (EA)
JSB	Joint-Stock Bank [*Banking*]
JSBA	Jefferson Savings Bancorp [*NASDAQ symbol*] (SAG)
JSBF	JSB Financial [*NASDAQ symbol*] (TTSB)
JSBF	JSB Financial, Inc. [*NASDAQ symbol*] (SPSG)
JSB Fn	JSB Financial, Inc. [*Associated Press*] (SAG)
JSBS	Joint Strategic Bomber Study
JSC	Jackson State College [*Later, Jackson State University*] [*Mississippi*]
JSC	Japanese Studies Center [*Monash University*] [*Australia*]
JSC	Jascan Resources, Inc. [*Toronto Stock Exchange symbol*]
JSC	Jenkinsville [*South Carolina*] [*Seismograph station code, US Geological Survey*] (SEIS)
JSC	Job-Site Component

JSC .... Johnson Space Center (USDC)
JSC .... Johnstown & Stony Creek Rail Road Co. [*AAR code*]
JSC .... Joint Scientific Committee [*WMO/ICSU*]
JSC .... Joint Security Control
JSC .... Joint Selection Committee
JSC .... Joint Service Committee [*Military*]
JSC .... Joint Setup Cost
JSC .... Joint Staff Council [*Japanese*] [*Military*] (CINC)
JSC .... Joint Standing Committee (ADA)
JSC .... Joint-Stock Company
JSC .... Joint Strategic Capabilities [*Military*]
JSC .... Joint Strategic Committee [*Military*]
JSC .... Joint Support Command [*Navy*]
JSC .... Joly Steam Calorimeter
JSC .... Judgments of the Supreme Court of Cyprus [*A publication*] (ILCA)
JSC .... Junior Staff Course [*British*]
JSC .... Justice of the Supreme Court
JSCA .... Japanese Spaniel Club of America [*Later, JCCA*] (EA)
JSCA .... Journeymen Stone Cutters Association of North America [*Defunct*] (EA)
JSCAACR .... Joint Steering Committee for Revision of AACR [*Anglo-American Cataloging Rules*]
JSCAEN ...... Joint Schools Committee for Academic Excellence Now (EA)
JSCAMPS .... Joint Service Common Airframe Multiple Purpose System [*Military*] (MCD)
JSCB .... Job Step Control Block [*Computer science*] (BUR)
JSCC .... Joint Service Coordination Committee [*DoD*]
JSCC .... Joint Service Coordination Committee [*Military*] (DOMA)
JSCC .... Joint Staff Consultative Committee [*British*] (DI)
JSCCB .... Joint Services Configuration Control Board [*Military*] (AFIT)
J Sc D .... Doctor of Juridical Science
JScE .... Eimac [*Division of Varian Associates*] Technical Library, San Carlos, CA [*Library symbol Library of Congress*] (LCLS)
JSCERDCG .. Joint Service Civil Engineering Research and Development Coordination Group [*Military*] (RDA)
J school .... Journalism School (WDMC)
J School Libr Ass Qd... Journal. School Library Association of Queensland [*A publication*]
JSCIC .... Joint Space Command Intelligence Center [*Air Force*]
JSCLC .... Joint Standing Committee on Library Cooperation [*British*] (NITA)
JSCM .... Joint Service Commendation Medal [*Military decoration*] (AFM)
JSCM .... JSC [*Johnson Space Center*] Manual [*NASA*] (NASA)
JSCMPO ...... Joint Service Cruise Missile Program Office (MCD)
JSCO .... Joint Staff Communications Office [*Military*] (AABC)
JSCO .... Journal Status Central Operations Table (SAA)
JSCOM .... Joint Services Commendation Medal (RDA)
JS Com Ind L... Journal. Society of Commercial and Industrial Law [*A publication*] (ILCA)
J Scott .... Reporter, English Common Bench Reports [*A publication*] (DLA)
JSCP .... Joint Strategic Capabilities Plan [*Military*]
JSCR .... Job Schedule Change Request
JSCS .... Job Shop Control System (MHDI)
JSCS .... Joint Strategic Connectivity Committee [*Joint Chiefs of Staff*]
JSCS .... Joint Strategic Connectivity Staff
JSCS .... Junior Slovak Catholic Sokol (EA)
JSCU .... Joint Supply Council for Union of South Africa [*World War II*]
JSD .... Doctor of Judicial [*or Juridical*] Science [*or Doctor of the Science of Law*]
JSD .... Doctor of Judicial Science (GAGS)
JSD .... Jackson System Development [*Systems development methodology*] (NITA)
JSD .... Jatiya Samajtantrik Dal [*National Socialist Party*] [*Bangladesh*] [*Political party*] (PPW)
JSD .... Jeunesse Social Democrate [*Social Democratic Youth*] [*Malagasy*]
JSD .... Jewish Society for the Deaf [*Later, New York Society for the Deaf*] (EA)
JSD .... JiJi Securities Data Service [*JiJi Press Ltd.*] [*Japan Information service or system*] (CRD)
JSD .... Justification Service Digit [*Telecommunications*] (TEL)
JSD .... Stratford, CT [*Location identifier FAA*] (FAAL)
JSDA .... Japanese Securities Dealers Association (ECON)
JSDA .... Japanese Self-Defense Agency
JSDF .... Japan Self-Defense Force (CINC)
JSDF .... Jin Shin Do Foundation for Bodymind Acupressure (EA)
JSDM .... June, September, December, and March [*Denotes quarterly payments of interest or dividends in these months*] [*Business term*]
JSDP .... Jewish Social Democratic Party [*Political party*] (BJA)
JSE .... Jam Strobe Extractor
JSEA .... Jesuit Secondary Education Association (EA)
JSEAC .... Joint Societies Employment Advisory Committee
J-SEAD .... Joint Suppression of Enemy Air Defenses [*Military*] (INF)
JSEI .... Joint Second Echelon Interdiction
JSEP .... Job Skills Education Program [*Military*]
JSEP .... Joint Services Electronics Program [*Military*]
JSESPO........ Joint [*Maritime Administration - Navy*] Surface-Effects Ship Program Office
JSeTU .... Tohoku University, Sendai, Japan [*Library symbol*] [*Library of Congress*] (LCLS)
JSEXP .... Joint Services Explosives Program (MCD)
JSEY .... Jersey [*One of the Channel Islands*] (ROG)
JSF .... Japan Scholarship Foundation (EA)
JSF .... Jesse Stuart Foundation (EA)
JSF .... Job Services File
JSF .... Joint Security Force [*Army*] (INF)

JSF .... Joint Stipulated Facts and Figures (AAGC)
JSF .... Joint Strike Fighter
JSF .... Junctor Switch Frame [*Telecommunications*] (TEL)
JSF .... Junior Statesmen Foundation (EA)
JSFC .... Jack Scalia Fan Club (EA)
JSFC .... Japanese-Soviet Fisheries Commission for the Northwest Pacific
JSFC .... Joe Stampley Fan Club [*Defunct*] (EA)
JSFP .... Joint Service Fuze Plan [*Army*]
JSG .... Jamaica (BWI) Study Group [*Defunct*] (EA)
JSG .... Job Seekers Guide to Private and Public Companies [*A publication*]
JSG .... Jugoslavia Study Group (EA)
JSGCC .... Joint Service Guidance and Control Committee
JSGOMRAM... Joint Study Group on Military Resources Allocation Methodology (MCD)
JSGRP .... Jewish Symbols in the Greco-Roman Period [*A publication*] (BJA)
JSH .... Jetstream Ltd. [*Hungary ICAO designator*] (FAAC)
JSH .... Journal of Southern History [*A publication*] (BRI)
JSHA .... Johannes Schwalm Historical Association (EA)
J Shaw .... John Shaw's Justiciary Reports [*1848-52*] [*Scotland*] [*A publication*] (DLA)
J Shaw Just... John Shaw's Justiciary Reports [*1848-52*] [*Scotland*] [*A publication*] (DLA)
JSHG .... Hokkai Gakuen University, Sapporo, Japan [*Library symbol Library of Congress*] (LCLS)
JSHS .... Jewish Society for Human Service [*British*]
JSHS .... Junior Science and Humanities Symposia [*Terminated, 1977*]
JSI .... Jansky Screening Index [*Psychology*] (DAVI)
JSI .... Job Satisfaction Inventory [*Guidance*]
JSI .... Job Schedule Items (MCD)
JSI .... Job Search Information
JSI .... Job Sensitivity Inventory [*Interpersonal skills and attitudes test*]
JSI .... Job Step Index [*Computer science*] (IAA)
JSI .... Joint Support Item (DNAB)
JSI .... Skiathos [*Greece*] [*Airport symbol*] (OAG)
JSIA .... Joint Service Induction Area
JSIA .... Justice System Improvement Act [*1979*]
JSIC .... Joint Space Intelligence Center
J-SIDS .... Joint Service Intrusion Detection System [*Military*] (INF)
JSIID .... Joint Service Interior Intrusion Detection Devices [*Military*] (MCD)
JSIIDS .... Joint Service Interior Intrusion Detection System [*Military*]
JSIM .... Joint Service Intelligence Manual
JSIMS .... Joint Simulation System [*DoD*]
JSIP .... Job Service Improvement Program [*Department of Labor*]
JSIPS .... Joint Services Imagery Processing System [*Military*]
JSIPS .... Joint Systems Integration Planning Staff [*Air Force*]
JSK .... St. Cloud, MN [*Location identifier FAA*] (FAAL)
JSL .... Jet Select Logic (MCD)
JSL .... Job Specification Language
JSL .... Johnson Society of London (EA)
JSL .... Joint Stock List [*Military*] (AFIT)
JSL .... Joint Support List [*Military*]
JSLB .... Joint Stock Land Banks [*New Deal*]
JSLGWCM.... Joint Services LASER-Guided Weapons Countermeasures (MCD)
JSLI .... Johnson-Sea-Link I [*A submersible for deep sea studies*]
JSLPC .... Joint Service Local Planning Committee
JSLRMDO .... Joint Service Large Rocket Motor Disposal Office [*Army*]
JSLS .... Japan Society of Library Science (NITA)
JSLS .... Joint Services Liaison Staff [*British*]
JSLWG........ Joint Spacelab Working Group [*NASA*] (NASA)
JSM .... Jesus Salvator Mundi [*Jesus the Savior of the World*] [*Latin*] (ROG)
JSM .... Job Stream Manager [*Computer science*] (IAA)
JSM .... Joint Staff Memorandum (MCD)
JSM .... Joint Staff Mission [*British World War II*]
JSM .... Jose de San Martin [*Argentina*] [*Airport symbol*] (OAG)
JSM .... Master of Judicial Science
JSMA .... Joint Sealer Manufacturers Association
JSMB .... Joint Sealift Movements Board [*Military*] (AFM)
JSME .... Japan Society of Mechanical Engineers
JSME .... Joint Soil Moisture Experiment
JSMIN .... Jasmine (ABBR)
JSMP .... JSIMS [*Joint Simulation (System)*] Master Plan [*DoD*]
JSmrfG .... Jefferson Smurfit Group PLC [*Associated Press*] (SAG)
JSMS .... Job Service Matching Systems [*US Employment Service*] [*Department of Labor*]
JSMSM........ Joint Service Meritorious Service Medal [*Military decoration*]
JSN .... Job Sequence Number
JSN .... Joint Space Narrowing [*Medicine*]
JSNA .... Jaspers Society of North America (EA)
JSNOOFC.... Judson Scott Is Number 1 Official Fan Club (EA)
JSNPE .... Joint Staff Nuclear Planning Element (MCD)
JSO .... Jacksonville, TX [*Location identifier FAA*] (FAAL)
JSO .... Joint Service Office
JSO .... Joint Specialty Officer (DOMA)
JSOA .... Joint Special Operations Area [*Military*] (INF)
JSOC .... Joint Ship Operations Center
JSOC .... Joint Ship Operations Committee
JSOC .... Joint Special Operations Center (MCD)
JSOC .... Joint Special Operations Command [*Military*]
JSOC .... Joint Strategic Operations Command (MCD)
J Soc H....... Journal of Social History [*A publication*] (BRI)
J Soc'y Comp Leg... Journal. Society of Comparative Legislation [*A publication*] (DLA)
JSOFI.......... Joint Special Operations Force Institute [*DoD*]
JSON .... Joint Services Operational Notice
JSONOM...... Joint Specialty Officer Nominee (DOMA)

JSOP...........	Dominican Oblates of Jesus (Spain) (TOCD)
JSOP...........	Joint Strategic Objectives Plan [*Military*]
JSOR...........	Joint Services Operational Requirement [*Military*]
JSOR...........	Joint Statements of Requirements (DOMA)
JSORD.........	Joint System Operational Requirements [*Document*] (DOMA)
JSORS.........	Joint Service Operational Requirement Statement (MCD)
JSOSE.........	Joint Special Operations Support Element [*DoD*]
JSOTF.........	Joint Special Operations Task Force [*DoD*]
JSOTF.........	Joint Special Operations Task Force (DOMA)
JSOW..........	Joint Standoff Weapons Program
JSP.............	Jacketed Soft-Point [*Ammunition*]
JSP.............	Jackson Structured Programming [*Program design tool*] (NITA)
JSP.............	Japan Socialist Party [*Nikon Shakaito*] [*Political party*] (PPW)
jsp.............	Jasper (VRA)
JSP.............	Job Support Program
JSP.............	Joint Services Development Program
JSP.............	Joint Services Publication
JSP.............	Joint Staff Planners [*Joint Chiefs of Staff*]
JSP.............	Judicial Selection Project (EA)
JSP.............	Jupiter, Saturn, and Pluto Mission (MCD)
JSP.............	Jurisdictional Separation Process
J Space L	Journal of Space Law (AAGC)
JSPB...........	Joint Staff Pension Board [*United Nations*]
JSPC...........	Japan Sports Prototype Championship [*Auto racing*]
JSPC...........	Joint Sobe Processing Center [*Okinawa*] [*Military*]
JSPC...........	Joint Strategic Plans Committee [*Military*]
JSPD...........	Joint Strategic Planning Document (MCD)
JSPD...........	Joint Subsidiary Plans Division [*Military*] (MUGU)
JSPDSA	Joint Strategic Planning Document Supporting Analysis [*Military*] (AABC)
JSPF...........	Joint Staff Pension Fund [*United Nations*]
JSPFL.........	Jointly Sponsored Program for Foreign Libraries [*Defunct*]
JSPG...........	Joint Strategic Plans Group [*Military*]
JSPMRC	Joint Service Program Management Review Committee [*Military*]
JSPOG........	Joint Strategic Plans and Operations Group
JSPP..........	Joint Service Program Plan [*Military*] (RDA)
JSPS..........	Japan Society for the Promotion of Science
JSPS..........	Jewish Student Press Service (EA)
JSPS..........	Joint Strategic Planning System [*Military*]
JSR.............	Jackson Resources Ltd. [*Vancouver Stock Exchange symbol*]
JSR.............	Jam to Signal Ratio (MCD)
JSR.............	Japan Science Review [*A publication*]
JSR.............	Japan Synthetic Rubber Co. Ltd.
JSR.............	Jessore [*Bangladesh*] [*Airport symbol*] (OAG)
JSR.............	Joint Staffing Review
JSR.............	Joint Strategic Review (DOMA)
JSR.............	Journal of Ship Research [*A publication*] (DNAB)
JSR.............	Journal of Spacecraft and Rockets [*A publication*] (AAGC)
JSR.............	Jump to Subroutine [*Computer science*] (BUR)
JSRA..........	Job Search and Relocation Assistance Projects (OICC)
JSRA..........	Joint Sponsored Research Agreement (GAVI)
JSRC..........	Junction Services Review Committee
JSRC..........	Joint Ship Repair Committee
JSRCC	Joint Search and Rescue Coordination Center (MCD)
JSRK..........	Jeunesse Socialiste Royale Khmere [*Royal Cambodian Socialist Youth*] [*Political party*]
JSRP..........	Joint Services Reading Panel [*Military British*]
JSRS..........	Jury System Reform Society [*British*]
JSRT..........	Joint Short-Range Technology (MCD)
JSRU..........	Joint Speech Research Unit [*British*] (NITA)
JSRWG	JSIMS [*Joint Simulation (System)*] Requirements Working Group [*Military*]
JSS	Jacob Sheep Society [*British*] (DBA)
JSS	Japanese Society of Sydney [*Australia*]
JSS	Jet Steering System
JSS	Jet Strip System (PDAA)
JSS	Jewish Social Studies [*A publication*] (BRI)
JSS	Jim Smith Society (EA)
JSS	Job Schedule Status (SAA)
JSS	Job Shop Simulator
JSS	Joint Surveillance System [*FAA Air Force*]
JSS	Junior Secondary School
JSSA..........	John Steinbeck Society of America (EA)
JSSA..........	Joint Stealth Strike Aircraft [*DoD*] (DOMA)
JSSAM........	Joint Service Small Arms Management Committee (MCD)
JSSAP........	Joint Service Small Arms Panel (MCD)
JSSAP........	Joint Service Small Arms Program (RDA)
JSSAP........	Joint Service Small Arms Program Office [*Dover, NJ*] [*Military*]
JSSC..........	Joint Services Staff College [*or Course*] [*Obsolete British*]
JSSC..........	Joint Shop Stewards Committee [*British*]
JSSC..........	Joint Strategic Survey Committee [*or Council*] [*DoD*]
JSSE..........	Japanese Software Support Environment
JSSIS.........	Joint Staff Support Information System [*Military*] (GFGA)
JSSM..........	Joint Services Staff Manual [*Military British*]
JSSPG........	Job Shop Simulation Program Generator (KSC)
JSST..........	Job Seeking Skills Training (OICC)
JSSUP........	Japanese Space Shuttle Utilization Program (MCD)
JSS/US.......	Japanese Sword Society of the United States (EA)
JST.............	Jamming Station (IAA)
JST.............	Japanese Standard Time
JST.............	Japan Universal System Transport Co. Ltd. [*ICAO designator*] (FAAC)
JST.............	Jet STOL [*Short Takeoff and Landing*] Transport [*Aircraft*]
JST.............	Job Skills Training
JST.............	Johnstown [*Pennsylvania*] [*Airport symbol*] (OAG)

JST	Johnstown, PA [*Location identifier FAA*] (FAAL)
JST	Joint Systems Test (KSC)
JSTA	Justice System Training Association [*Defunct*] (EA)
JSTARS........	Joint Surveillance and Target Attack RADAR System
JSTARS........	Joint Surveillance Target Attack Radar System
JSTARS-GSM...	Joint Surveillance/Target Attack RADAR System Ground Station Module (RDA)
J St Bar Calif...	Journal. State Bar of California [*A publication*] (DLA)
JSTC	Job Skills Training Course
JSTC	Justice
JSTE	Joint System Training Exercise [*Military*]
JstFeet........	Just For Feet, Inc. [*Associated Press*] (SAG)
JSTN	Justin Indus [*NASDAQ symbol*] (TTSB)
JSTN	Justin Industries, Inc. [*NASDAQ symbol*] (NQ)
JSTP	Job Search Training Program
JSTP	Joint System Test Plan [*Initial Defense Communications Satellite Program*] (DNAB)
JSTPA	Joint Strategic Target Planning Agency (NATG)
JSTPPC........	Joint Services Technical Publication Policy Committee [*Ministry of Defence*] (PDAA)
JSTPS.........	Joint Strategic Target Planning Staff [*DoD*]
JSTR...........	Joint Systematic Troop Review [*Military*]
J St Tax'n	Journal of State Taxation [*A publication*] (DLA)
JSTU	Tohoku University, Sendai, Japan [*Library symbol Library of Congress*] (LCLS)
JSTX	Joro Spider Toxin [*Biochemistry*]
JSU	Hokkaido University, Sapporo, Japan [*Library symbol Library of Congress*] (LCLS)
JSU	Jacksonville State University [*Jacksonville, AL*]
JSU	Junta Socialista Unida [*United Socialist Party*] [*Spain*]
JSU	Sukkertoppen [*Greenland*] [*Airport symbol*] (AD)
JSUN	Jupiter, Saturn, Uranus, and Neptune (PDAA)
JSV	Jerry-Slough Virus [*Medicine*] (DMAA)
JSVA	Jewish Socialist Verband of America [*Defunct*] (EA)
JSWAP........	Job Swapping Memory [*Computer science*] (MHDB)
JSWDL........	Joint Services Weapon Data Link (MCD)
JSWPB........	Joint Special Weapons Publications Board
JSYB..........	Jewish Socialist Youth Bund [*Later, MJSG*] (EA)
J Syd Univ Eng Soc...	Journal. Sydney University Engineering Society. [*A publication*]
JT	Iowa Airways [*ICAO designator*] (AD)
JT	James Taylor [*Singer*]
JT	Japan Times [*A publication*] (BARN)
JT	Jejunostomy Tube [*Medicine*] (DMAA)
JT	Jerusalem Talmud (BJA)
JT	Jig Template (MSA)
JT	Job Table [*Computer science*] (IAA)
JT	John Tyler [*US president, 1790-1862*]
JT	Joint
JT	Joint Tenancy (MHDW)
J-T	Joule-Thomson [*Physics*]
JT	Junction Transistor [*Electronics*] (IAA)
JT	Juridisk Tidsskrift [*A publication*] (ILCA)
JT	Juvenile Templar [*Freemasonry*]
JTA	Azia Keizai Kenkyujo [*Institute for Developing Economies*], Tokyo, Japan [*Library symbol Library of Congress*] (LCLS)
JTA	Japanese Technical Abstracts [*A publication*]
JTA	Japan Transocean Air Co. Ltd. [*ICAO designator*] (FAAC)
JTA	Jewish Telegraphic Agency (EA)
JTA	Job Task Analysis
JTA	Joint Table of Allowance
JTA	Joint Technical Architecture [*Office of the Secretary of Defense*]
JTA	Joint Tenancy Agreement [*Military*]
JTA-Army.....	Joint Technical Architecture-Army
JTAC...........	Joint Technical Advisory Committee [*Electronics*]
JTACC.........	Joint Tactical Air Control Center
JTACMIS-A...	Joint Tactical Missile System - Army
JTACMS.......	Joint Tactical Missile System
JTACMS-A ...	Joint Tactical Missile System - Army
JTACS.........	Joint Tactical Area Communications System [*Army*] (RDA)
JTAD..........	Joint Tactical Aids Detachment [*Military*]
JTAG..........	Japan Trade Advisory Group [*British Overseas Trade Board*] (DS)
JTAG..........	Joint Test Action Group [*European automotive industry*]
JTAGG	Joint Turbine Advanced Gas Generator [*DoD*]
JTAGS.........	Joint Tactical Ground Station [*Army*] (RDA)
JTAGS.........	Joint Target Acquistion Ground Station [*Military*]
JT AGT........	Joint Agent (WDAA)
JTA-M.........	Jewish Teachers Association - Morim (EA)
JT & E	Joint Test and Evaluation [*DoD*]
JT & SEV	Joint and Several [*Legal shorthand*] (LWAP)
JTARS.........	Joint Tactical Aerial Reconnaissance/Surveillance [*Military*] (DNAB)
JTARS MISREP...	Joint Tactical Aerial Reconnaissance/Surveillance Mission Report [*Military*] (DNAB)
JTASB.........	Joint Tactical Air Support Board
jt asp	Joint Aspiration [*Orthopedics*] (DAVI)
jt auth.........	Joint Author
JTAWG........	Joint Targeting and Weapon Guidance (MCD)
JTAX..........	Jackson Hewitt [*NASDAQ symbol*] (SAG)
JTB	Japanese Tourist Board
JTB	Joint Bar
JTB	Joint Transportation Board [*Military*]
JTBSMHS	Jacques Timothe Boucher Sieur de Montbrun Heritage Society (EA)
JTC	Houston [*Texas*] Town/Country [*Airport symbol*] (OAG)
JTC	Jets Corporativos SA de CV [*Mexico ICAO designator*] (FAAC)
JTC	Jewish Thought and Civilization (BJA)

JTC .... Joint Technical Committee (CDE)
JTC .... Joint Telecommunications Committee [*Military*] (AFM)
JTC .... Joint Transform Correlator [*Instrumentation*]
JTC .... Joke to Come (WDMC)
JTC .... Joule-Thomson Coefficient [*Physics*]
JTC .... Junior Training Corps [*British*]
JTC .... Jurong Town Corp. [*Singapore*]
JTC3A .... Joint Tactical Command, Control, and Communications Agency (USGC)
JTC³A .... Joint Tactical Command, Control, and Communications Agency [*Military*]
JTC³S .... Joint Tactical Command and Control and Communications System [*Military*] (RDA)
JTCC .... Joint Test Coordinating Committee (MCD)
JTCCCS ...... Joint Tactical Command, Control, and Communications System [*Military*] (MCD)
JTCCG .... Joint Technical Configuration Control Group [*Military*] (AABC)
JTCG .... Joint Technical Coordinating Group [*Military*] (MCD)
JTCG/ALNNO... Joint Technical Coordinating Group for Air Launched Non-Nuclear Ordnance [*Military*] (AFM)
JTCG/AS ...... Joint Technical Coordinating Group for Aircraft Survivability [*Military*]
JTCG-DLA .... Joint Technical Coordinating Group for Data Link Acquisitions (MCD)
JTCG-DMI .... Joint Technical Coordinating Group for Depot Maintenance Interservicing [*Military*] (AFIT)
JTCG-EER .... Joint Technical Coordinating Group for Electronic Equipment Reliability (MCD)
JTCG-ESR .... Joint Technical Coordinating Group for Electronics Systems Reliability (MCD)
JTCG/MD .... Joint Technical Coordinating Group for Munitions Development [*Military*]
JTCG/ME .... Joint Technical Coordinating Group for Munitions Effectiveness [*Military*] (AFM)
JTCG/MS ..... Joint Technical Coordinating Group on Munitions Survivability [*Military*] (RDA)
JTCGP .... Joint Technical Coordinating Group [*Military*]
JTCGP/ME.... Joint Technical Coordinating Group for Munitions Effectiveness [*Military*]
JTCGP-TACS... Joint Technical Coordinating Group for Tactical Air Control System [*Military*]
JTCG-STD .... Joint Technical Coordinating Group on Simulators and Training Devices (MCD)
JTCO .... Jacksonville Terminal Co. [*AAR code*]
JTCP .... JOVIAL [*Joule's Own Version of the International Algorithmic Language*] Test Control Program [*Computer science*] (SAA)
JTCTS .... Joint Tactical Combat Training System [*Military*]
JTCY-P........ Jig Transit Central Y-Plane
JTD .... Joint Table of Distribution [*Military*] (AFM)
JTD .... Joint Test Directorate [*Military*] (CAAL)
JTDA .... Joint Track Data Storage
JTDARMVAL... Joint Test Directorate Advanced Antiarmor Vehicle Evaluation [*Military*] (DNAB)
JTDE........... Joint Technology Demonstrator Engine [*Air Force*] (MCD)
JTDP........... Joint Technical Development Plan
JTDS........... Joint Track Data Storage
JTE............. Jamming Tactics Evaluation
JTE............. Joint Technical Evaluation (MCD)
JTE............. Joint Test Element
JTE............. Joule-Thomson Effect [*Physics*]
JTE............. Junction Tandem Exchange [*Electronics*] (IAA)
JTE............. Junction Termination Extension (PDAA)
J Teach Ed... Journal of Teacher Education [*A publication*] (BRI)
JTEC .... Japan Telecommunications Engineering and Consultancy
JTEC .... Jeep-Truck Engine Controller
JTEC .... Joint Training Enhancement Committee [*Military*]
JT ED.......... Joint Editor
J-TENS......... Joint Tactical Exploitation of National Systems [*Army*] (ADDR)
J Tert Ed Admin... Journal of Tertiary Educational Administration [*A publication*]
JTETF.......... Joint Test and Evaluation Task Force [*Air Force*]
JTEV .... Joint Tactical Electric Vehicle [*Military*]
JTF............. Japan Textile Federation
JTF............. Jet Tear-Down Facility (MCD)
JTF............. Joint Tactical Fusion [*Army*] (RDA)
JTF............. Joint Task Force [*Military*]
JTF............. Joint Test Force [*Military*]
JTF2........... Joule-Thomson Flow [*Physics*]
JTF2........... Joint Task Force Two [*Sandia Base, NM*]
JTFAK .... Joint Task Force Alaska [*Military*]
JTF/ASAS..... Joint Tactical Fusion/All Source Analysis System (AAGC)
JTF-FA......... Joint Task Force-Full Accounting [*DoD*]
JTFHQ......... Joint Task Force Headquarters [*Military*] (MCD)
JTFME .... Joint Task Force Middle East (DOMA)
JTFOA......... Joint Task Force Operating Area [*Military*] (NVT)
JTFP........... Joint Tactical Fusion Program [*Military*] (RDA)
JTFPMO....... Joint Tactical Fusion Program Management Office [*Army*] (RDA)
JTFREP........ Joint Task Force Report [*Military*]
JTFS .... Joint Tactical Fusion System [*Military*] (LAIN)
JTFS .... JTF [*Joint Task Force*] Simulation [*Model*] [*DoD*]
JTG .... Joint Task Group [*Military*]
JTG .... Joint Test Group [*Nuclear energy*] (NRCH)
JTG .... Joint Training Group [*NASA*] (NASA)
Jth .... Judith [*Old Testament book*] [*Roman Catholic canon*] (BJA)
JTHP .... Joule-Thomson High Pressure [*Physics*]
JTI .... Jatai [*Brazil*] [*Airport symbol*] (AD)
JTI .... Jydsk Teknologisk Institut [*Technological Institute of Jutland*] [*Denmark*]

JTIC .... Joint Transportation Intelligence Center [*MTMC*] (TAG)
JTIDS .... Joint Tactical Information Distribution System [*DoD*]
JTIDS .... Joint Tactical Information Distribution System
J-TIES .... Japan Technology Information and Evaluation Service (IID)
JTIG .... Joint Target Intelligence Group [*Military*] (CINC)
JTIS .... Japanese Technical Information Service [*University Microfilms International*] [*Information service or system*] (IID)
JTJ.............. Japan Information Center of Science and Technology, Tokyo, Japan [*Library symbol Library of Congress*] (LCLS)
JTKU........... Keio University, Tokyo, Japan [*Library symbol Library of Congress*] (LCLS)
JTL............. Jetall Holdings, Corp. [*Canada ICAO designator*] (FAAC)
JTL............. Josephson Transmission Line [*Physics*]
JTL............. Joutel Resources Ltd. [*Toronto Stock Exchange symbol*]
JTLAS .... Jet Transport Landing Approach Simulator
JTLS .... Joint Theater Level Simulation [*Model*] [*DoD*]
JTLY .... Jointly
JTM .... Job Transfer and Management (ACRL)
JTM .... Job Transfer and Manipulation [*Telecommunications*] (OSI)
JTMA .... Joint Traffic Management Agency (MCD)
JTM & H ...... Journal of Tropical Medicine and Hygiene [*A publication*] (WDAA)
JTMB .... Joint Transportation Movements Board [*Military*] (CINC)
JTMD .... Joint Theater Missile Defense [*DoD*]
JTML .... Junior Town Meeting League (EA)
JTMLS .... Joint Tactical Microwave Landing System (MCD)
JTMP .... Job Transfer and Manipulation Protocol (NITA)
JTMSS .... Joint Tactical Multichannel Switch System (MCD)
JTN .... Jewish Television Network
JTNDL .... Kokuritsu Kokkai Toshokan [*National Diet Library*], Tokyo, Japan [*Library symbol Library of Congress*] (LCLS)
JTNS........... Nihon Shinbun Kyokai [*Japanese Newspaper Association*], Tokyo, Japan [*Library symbol Library of Congress*] (LCLS)
JTO .... Jeunesse Travailleuse Oubanguienne [*Ubangi Working Youth*]
JTO .... Joint Technical Operations (AAG)
JTO .... Joint Test Organization [*Joint Tactical Communications Office*] [*Fort Huachuca, AZ*]
JTO .... JOPES [*Joint Operations, Planning, and Execution System*] Training Organization (DOMA)
JTO .... Jump Takeoff (WDAA)
JTO .... Junction Temperature, Operating
JTOC .... Joint Tactical Operations Center
JTOR........... Joint Terms of Reference (MCD)
JTP .... Job Training Package
JTP .... Job Training Program (OICC)
JTP .... Joint Technical Panel [*Aerospace*]
JTP .... Joint Training Package
JTP .... Journeyman Training Program
JTP .... Juventud Trabajadora Peronista [*Working Peronist Youth*] [*Argentina*]
JTPA .... Job Training Partnership Act [*Formerly, CETA*] [*1982*]
JTPA .... Job Training Partnership Administration
JTPS .... Job and Tape Planning System
JTPS .... Juvenile Tropical Pancreatitis Syndrome [*Medicine*] (DMAA)
JTPT .... Job Task Performance Test
JTQ .... Wrightstown, NJ [*Location identifier FAA*] (FAAL)
JTR .... Jet-Air Bedarfsflugunternehmen [*Austria ICAO designator*] (FAAC)
JTR .... Joint Tactical Radio [*Army*]
JTR .... Joint Termination Regulation
JTR .... Joint Travel Regulations
JTR .... Santorini [*Thira Islands*] [*Airport symbol*] (OAG)
JTR .... Thira [*Greece*] [*Airport symbol*] (AD)
JTRA .... Job Task Requirements Analysis (PDAA)
JTRAC......... JPL [*Jet Propulsion Laboratory*] Transient Radiation Analysis by Computer Program [*NASA*]
JTRB .... Joint Telecommunications Resource Board [*Office of Science and Technology Policy*] [*Washington, DC*] (EGAO)
JTRC .... Joint Theatre Reconnaissance Committee [*NATO*] (NATG)
JTRCP......... Joint Travel Regulations, Department of Defense Civilian Personnel
JTRE .... JIMAP [*Joint Institute for Marine and Atmospheric Research*] Tsunami Research Effort [*Marine science*] (OSRA)
JTRE .... JIMAR [*Joint Institute for Marine and Atmospheric Research*] Tsunami Research Effort (USDC)
JTRE .... Joint Tsunami Research Effort
JTRL .... Janitorial (ABBR)
JTRS .... Joint Tenant with Right of Survivorship [*Legal term*] (DLA)
JTRU .... Joint Tropical Research Unit [*Australia*]
JTRUS .... Joint Travel Regulations
JTS .... Arrendamiento de Aviones Jets, SA [*Mexico*] [*FAA designator*] (FAAC)
JTS .... Japan Troposcatter Systems
JTS .... Job Training Scheme [*Government initiative*] [*British*]
JTS .... Job Training Standard
JTS .... Joint Training Scheme (AIE)
JTS .... Joint Training Standards [*Military*] (KSC)
JTS .... JTS Corp. [*AMEX symbol*] (SAG)
JTS .... Justice Telecommunications Service [*Department of Justice*] (TSSD)
JTSA .... Jewish Theological Seminary of America
JTSA .... Joint Tactical Support Activity
JTSA .... Joint Technical Support Activity
JTSCC......... Joint Telecommunications Standards Coordinating Committee [*American National Standards Institute*] [*Telecommunications*]
JTS Corp..... JTS Corp. [*Associated Press*] (SAG)
JTSG .... Joint Trials Subgroup [*NATO*] (NATG)
JTSN .... Jettison (MSA)
JTST .... Jet Stream
JTSTR......... Jet Stream

JTT/CIBSM... Joint Tactical Terminal/Common Integrated Broadcast System Module [*Military*] (RDA)
JTTCW......... Jesus to the Communist World [*Later, CMCW*] (EA)
JTTP .... Joint Tactics, Techniques, and Procedures (DOMA)
JTTPRG........ Joint Tactics, Techniques, and Procedures Review Group
JTTU .... Jet Transitional Training Unit [*Navy*]
JTU .... Jackson Turbidity Unit [*Water pollution*]
JTU .... Jet Training Unit
JTUAC.......... Joint Trade Union Advisory Committee
JT-UAV .... Joint Tactical Unmanned Aerial Vehicle [*DoD*]
JTV .... Jet Test Vehicle
JTV .... Jones Intercable Inv CI'A' [*AMEX symbol*] (TTSB)
JTV .... Jones Intercable Investors Ltd. [*AMEX symbol*] (SPSG)
J-T-W .... Journey to Work [*FHWA*] (TAG)
JTWC........... Joint Typhoon Warning Center
JTWO .... J2 Communications [*NASDAQ symbol*] (TTSB)
JTWO .... JTwo Communications [*NASDAQ symbol*] (SAG)
JTWOW....... J2 Communications Wrrt'A' [*NASDAQ symbol*] (TTSB)
JTWROS ...... Joint Tenants with Right of Survivorship [*Legal term*]
JTWS .... Journal of Third World Studies [*A publication*]
JTX .... Jet Aspen Air Lines, Inc. [*FAA designator*] (FAAC)
JTX .... Joint Test Exercises
JTX .... Joint Training Exercise [*Military*]
JTZ .... Oklahoma City, OK [*Location identifier FAA*] (FAAL)
JU .... Jeunesse Universelle
JU .... Joint Use [*Military*] (AFIT)
JU .... Joint User [*Telecommunications*] (TEL)
JU .... Joygerms Unlimited (EA)
Ju .... Judges [*Old Testament book*] (BJA)
JU .... Julep (ROG)
JU .... Jump Unit
JU .... June
JU .... Junker [*German aircraft type*] [*World War II*]
JU .... Jure Uxoris [*In Right of His Wife*] [*Latin*] (ROG)
JU .... Yugoslav Airlines [*ICAO designator*] (AD)
JUA .... Joint Underwriting Association [*Generic term*] (DHSM)
JUB .... Job Unit Block [*Computer science*] (IAA)
JUB .... Juba [*Sudan*] [*Airport symbol*] (OAG)
JUB .... Jubilate
Jub .... Jubilees [*Pseudepigrapha*] (BJA)
JUB .... Justice of the Upper Bench [*Legal term*] (DLA)
JUBU .... Journalistutbildningsutredningen [*Sweden*]
JUCG .... Joint Utilization Coordination Group [*DoD*]
JUCO .... Junior College (OICC)
JUCUND...... Jucunde [*Pleasantly*] [*Latin*]
JUD .... Duluth, MN [*Location identifier FAA*] (FAAL)
JUD .... Jeunesse d'Union Dahomeene [*Dahomean Youth Union*]
JUD .... Judah (WDAA)
Jud .... Judaic (BJA)
JUD .... Judea (WDAA)
Jud .... Judean (BJA)
JUD .... Judge (WDAA)
JUD .... Judges [*Old Testament book*] (ROG)
JUD .... Judgment
JUD .... Judicial
Jud .... Judith [*Old Testament book*] [*Roman Catholic canon*]
JUD .... Juris Utrisque Doctor (DD)
JUD .... Juris Utriusque Doctor [*Doctor of Both Laws; i.e., Canon and Civil Law*]
JUD .... US Department of Justice [*ICAO designator*] (FAAC)
Jud & Sw..... Judah and Swan's Jamaica Reports [*1839*] [*A publication*] (DLA)
Jud Chr........ Judicial Chronicle [*A publication*] (DLA)
Jud Com PC... Judicial Committee of the Privy Council [*A publication*] (DLA)
Jud Conduct Rep... Judicial Conduct Reporter [*A publication*] (DLA)
Jud Coun (NY)... Judicial Council (New York). Annual Reports [*A publication*] (DLA)
Judd............ Judd's Reports [*4 Hawaii*] [*A publication*] (DLA)
JUDE............ Judicature (ROG)
JUDG .... Judge
Judg............ Judges [*Old Testament book*]
JUDG .... Judicate, Inc. [*NASDAQ symbol*] (NQ)
Jud GCC ...... Judgments, Gold Coast Colony [*A publication*] (DLA)
JUDGE .... Judged Utility Decision Generator
JUDGT......... Judgment
Judg UB....... Judgments of Upper Bench [*England*] [*A publication*] (DLA)
JUDIC .... Judicial
Judicate....... Judicate, Inc. [*Associated Press*] (SAG)
JUDL .... Judicial (ROG)
Jud Pan Mult Lit... Rulings of the Judicial Panel on Multidistrict Litigation [*A publication*] (DLA)
Jud QR .... Judicature Quarterly Review [*1896*] [*A publication*] (DLA)
JUDr............ Juris Utriusque Doctor [*Doctor of Both Laws; i.e., Canon and Civil Law*]
JUDRE .... Judicature
Jud Rep....... New York Judicial Repository [*A publication*] (DLA)
Jud Repos ... Judicial Repository [*New York*] [*A publication*] (DLA)
JUDY .... Just a Useful Device for You (PDAA)
JUE .... Julich [*Federal Republic of Germany*] [*Seismograph station code, US Geological Survey*] (SEIS)
JUG .... Joint Users Group [*Computer science*]
JUG .... Jugenheim [*Federal Republic of Germany*] [*Seismograph station code, US Geological Survey Closed*] (SEIS)
JUG .... Jugoslav (DSUE)
Jug............. Jugoton [*Former Yugoslavia*] [*Record label*]
jug .... Jugular [*Anatomy*] (DAVI)

JUG .... Jugulo [*To the Throat*] [*Pharmacy*]
JUG .... Junction Gate (IAA)
jug comp .... Jugular Compression [*Test*] [*Neurology*] (DAVI)
JUGFET....... Junction Gate Field-Effect Transistor (TEL)
Jughead....... Jonzy's Universal Gopher Hierachy Excavation and Display [*Internet*]
JUI .... Jamiatul Ulama-i-Islam [*Pakistan*] [*Political party*] (FEA)
JUI .... Juist [*Germany Airport symbol Obsolete*] (OAG)
Juilliard ...... [*The*] Juilliard School (GAGS)
JUJ .... Jujuy [*Argentina*] [*Seismograph station code, US Geological Survey*] (SEIS)
JUJ .... Jujuy [*Argentina*] [*Airport symbol*] (OAG)
JUJAMCYN... Jujamcyn Theaters [*Established by William McKnight, and named for his three grandchildren, Judy, James, and Cynthia*]
JUKE.......... Video Jukebox Network [*NASDAQ symbol*] (SAG)
JUKE.......... Video Jukebox Ntwk [*NASDAQ symbol*] (TTSB)
JUL .... Joint University Libraries
JUL .... Julepus [*Julep*] [*Pharmacy*] (ROG)
JUL .... Juliaca [*Peru*] [*Airport symbol*] (OAG)
JUL .... Julian [*Calendar*]
JUL .... Julianehab [*Denmark*] [*Later, NAQ*] [*Geomagnetic observatory code*]
JUL .... July (AFM)
Jul .... July (ODBW)
JUL .... Juris Utriusque Licentiatus [*Licentiate in Both Laws; i.e., Canon and Civil Law*]
Jul Caes ..... Julius Caesar [*Shakespearean work*] (BARN)
Jul Frontin... Julius Frontinus [*Roman soldier and author, 40-103*] (DLA)
Julian .... Julianus Imperator [*332-363AD*] [*Classical studies*] (OCD)
JULIE .... Joint Utility Locating Information for Excavators [*Telecommunications*] (TEL)
JULIEX........ Julie [*Sonobuoy System*] Exercise [*Navy*] (NVT)
JULLS .... Joint Universal Lessons Learned System (DOMA)
JUM .... Jumla [*Nepal*] [*Airport symbol*] (OAG)
JUMO........... Junkers-Motor [*Junkers aircraft engine*] [*German military - World War II*]
JUMP .... Joint UHF Modernization Project (MCD)
JUMPS........ Joint Uniform Military Pay Service [*or System*]
JUMPS/MMS... Joint Uniform Military Pay System/Manpower Management System (DNAB)
JUMPS-RC... Joint Uniform Military Pay System - Reserve Components (MCD)
JUN .... Jump Unconditionally [*Computer science*]
JUN .... Jundah [*Queensland*] [*Airport symbol*] (AD)
JUN .... June (AFM)
Jun .... June (ODBW)
JUN .... Juneau [*Diocesan abbreviation*] [*Alaska*] (TOCD)
JUN .... Junior
JUN .... Junius (ROG)
JUNAC .... Grupo Andino - Junta del Acuerdo de Cartagena [*Andean Group - Cartagena Agreement Board - ANCOM*] (EAIO)
JUNC .... Jeunesse d'Union Nationale Congolaise [*Congolese National Youth Union*]
JUNC .... Junction
JUNCT .... Junction
JUNCTION... Junction [*Commonly used*] (OPSA)
JUNCTIONS... Junctions [*Commonly used*] (OPSA)
JUNCTN ...... Junction [*Commonly used*] (OPSA)
JUNCTON.... Junction [*Commonly used*] (OPSA)
Jundt .... Jundt Growth Fund [*Associated Press*] (SAG)
JUNE........... Joint Utility Notification for Excavators (IEEE)
JUNET......... Japanese University Network (ACRL)
JUNET......... Japan UNIX Network [*Japan*] [*Computer science*] (TNIG)
JunF........... Juniper Features Ltd. [*Associated Press*] (SAG)
JUNI .... Juniper Features Ltd. [*NASDAQ symbol*] (SAG)
JUNIP .... Juniperus [*Juniper*] [*Pharmacy*] (ROG)
JuniprF .... Juniper Features Ltd. [*Associated Press*] (SAG)
JUNIW .... Juniper Features Wrr'A' [*NASDAQ symbol*] (TTSB)
JUNIZ .... Juniper Features Wrrt'B' [*NASDAQ symbol*] (TTSB)
JUNO .... Juno Lighting [*NASDAQ symbol*] (TTSB)
JUNO .... Juno Lighting, Inc. [*NASDAQ symbol*] (NQ)
JunoLt .... Juno Lighting, Inc. [*Associated Press*] (SAG)
JUNR .... Junior
JUNT .... Juntae (ROG)
Junta del Acuer... Grupo Andino - Junta del Acuerdo de Cartagena [*Andean Group - Cartagena Agreement Board - ANCOM*] (EA)
JUO .... Junior Under-Officer [*British military*] (DMA)
JUP .... Jamiatul Ulama-i-Pakistan [*Political party*] (FEA)
JUP .... Jupiter (KSC)
JUP .... Juventud Universitaria Peronista [*University Peronist Youth*] [*Argentina*]
JUP .... Juventud Uruguaya de Pie [*Upstanding Uruguayan Youth*] (PD)
JUP .... Upland, CA [*Location identifier FAA*] (FAAL)
JUPITER ...... Judicial Precedent Information Trace by Electronic Retrieval [*Database*] [*Toyo Information Systems Co.*] [*Information service or system*] (CRD)
JupNatl........ Jupiter National, Inc. [*Associated Press*] (SAG)
JUPPIE........ Japanese Urban Professional [*Lifestyle classification*]
JUR .... Julia Resources [*Vancouver Stock Exchange symbol*]
JUR .... Jurassic [*Period, era, or system*] [*Geology*]
JUR .... Juridical (ROG)
JUR .... Jurisprudence (ROG)
Jur .... [*The*] Jurist [*Washington, DC*] [*A publication*] (DLA)
Jur .... Jurist Reports [*18 vols.*] [*England*] [*A publication*] (DLA)
Jur .... London Jurist [*1854*] [*A publication*] (DLA)
J Urban H..... Journal of Urban History [*A publication*] (BRI)
JUR D.......... Juris Doctor [*Doctor of Law*] [*Latin*] (ADA)
JUR DIG ...... Jure Dignitatis [*By Right of Rank*] [*Latin*] (ROG)

JURE............ Junta Revolucionaria Cubana [Exile action group]
Jur Ex .... Hargrave's Francis-Jurisconsult Exercitations [A publication] (DLA)
JURG .... Joint Users Requirements Group (NASA)
Jurid Soc'y Pap... Juridical Society Papers [England] [A publication] (DLA)
JURIS .... Jurisdiction (AABC)
JURIS .... Jurisprudence (ADA)
JURIS .... Juristisches Informationssystem [Judicial Information System] [Federal Ministry of Justice Legal database] [Germany] (IID)
JURIS .... Justice Retrieval and Inquiry System [Department of Justice] [Legal databank] [Information service or system] (IID)
JURISD .... Jurisdiction
JURISDN ...... Jurisdiction (ROG)
JURISDON ... Jurisdiction (ROG)
JURISP .... Jurisprudence
Jurispr .... Jurisprudence (DLA)
Jur M .... Master of Jurisprudence
Jur Mar .... Molloy's De Jure Maritimo [A publication] (DLA)
Jur NY .... Jurist, or Law and Equity Reporter [New York] [A publication] (DLA)
Jur Ros........ Roscoe's Jurist [London] [A publication] (DLA)
Jur (Sc) .... [The] Scottish Jurist [Edinburgh] [A publication] (DLA)
Jur Sc D ...... Doctor of Judicial Science [or Doctor of the Science of Jurisprudence]
Jur Soc P.... Juridical Society Papers [1858-74] [Scotland] [A publication] (DLA)
Jur St .... Juridical Styles [Scotland] [A publication] (DLA)
JURUE .... Joint Unit for Research on the Urban Environment [British]
Jur Utr Dr ... Juris Utriusque Doctor [Doctor of Both Laws; i.e., Canon and Civil Law]
JUS............. Active Aero Charter [FAA designator] (FAAC)
JUS............. Department of Justice Library [UTLAS symbol]
Jus............. Jacobus de Porta Ravennate [Deceased, 1178] [Authority cited in pre-1607 legal work] (DSA)
JUS............. Justice
JUS............. Nenana, AK [Location identifier FAA] (FAAL)
JUS AVEN ... Jusculum Avenaceum [Gruel] [Pharmacy] (ROG)
JUSC.......... Jusculum [Broth] [Pharmacy] (ROG)
JUSCIMPC ... Joint United States/Canada Industrial Mobilization Planning Committee [NATO] (NATG)
Jus Code .... Code of Justinian [A publication] (DLA)
Jus Code .... Justices' Code [Oregon] [A publication] (DLA)
Juscul .... Jusculum [Broth] [Pharmacy]
JUSE.......... Japanese Union of Scientists and Engineers [Databank originator] (NITA)
JUSE.......... Japanese Union of Scientists and Engineers (ACII)
JUSE.......... Japan Union of Scientists and Engineers (BARN)
JUSE-AESOPP... JUSE [Japanese Union of Scientists and Engineers] an Estimator of Phy sical Properties (NITA)
Jus Inst....... Institutes of Justinian [Roman law] [A publication] (DLA)
JUSMAAG ... Joint United States Military Assistance Advisory Group
JUSMAG ...... Joint United States Military Advisory Group
JUSMAGG ... Joint United States Military Aid Group, Greece
JUSMAG-K... Joint United States Military Advisor Group-Korea (DOMA)
JUSMAGPHIL... Joint United States Military Advisory Group to the Republic of the Philippines [World War II]
JUSMAGTHAI... Joint United States Military Assistance Group, Thailand
JUSMAP ...... Joint United States Military Advisory and Planning Group
JUSMG .... Joint United States Military Group
JUSMGP ...... Joint United States Military Group
JUSMMAT.... Joint United States Military Mission for Aid to Turkey
Jus Nav Rhod... Jus Navale Rhodiorum [A publication] (DLA)
JUSO.......... Jungsozialist [Young Socialist] [Germany]
JUSPAO ...... Joint United States Public Affairs Office [Vietnam]
JUSS.......... Jussien (ROG)
JUSS.......... Jussive
JUSSC........ Joint United States Strategic Committee
JUSSIM....... Justice System Interactive Model (PDAA)
JUST.......... Justice (ROG)
Just............. Justices' Law Reporter [Pennsylvania] [A publication] (DLA)
Just............. Justiciary [Legal term] (DLA)
JUST .... Justification (AABC)
Just............. Justin (BJA)
JUST .... Justinian (ROG)
JUST .... Just Toys [NASDAQ symbol] (TTSB)
JUST .... Just Toys, Inc. [NASDAQ symbol] (SAG)
JUST ANGL ... Justiciarius Anglie [Chief Justiciary of England] [Latin] (ROG)
JUST CP ...... Justice of the Common Pleas (ROG)
Just Dig .... Digest of Justinian [A publication] (DLA)
JUSTICE...... Journeymen Under Specific Training in Construction Employment (PDAA)
Justices' LR (PA)... Justices' Law Reporter [Pennsylvania] [A publication] (DLA)
JUSTIFON ... Justification (ROG)
Justin.......... Justinian [483-565, Byzantine emperor] [Authority cited in pre-1607 legal work] (DSA)
Justin.......... Justin Industries, Inc. [Associated Press] (SAG)
Just Inst ...... Justinian's Institutes [A publication] (DLA)
JUSTIS .... Judicial State Information System (OICC)
JUST ITIN ... Justice Itinerant [Legal term] (DLA)
JUST KB ...... Justice of the King's Bench [British] (ROG)
JustLHo ...... Just Like Home, Inc. [Associated Press] (SAG)
Just LR .... Justices' Law Reporter [Pennsylvania] [A publication] (DLA)
Justn........... Justinian [Australia A publication]
Just P .... Justice of the Peace and Local Government Review [A publication] (DLA)
Just Peace... Justice of the Peace and Local Government Review [A publication] (DLA)
Just SL .... Justice's Sea Law [A publication] (DLA)

JustToys ...... Just Toys, Inc. [Associated Press] (SAG)
JUT............. Jet Utility Transport
JUT............. Jeunesse de l'Unite Togolaise [Togolese Unity Youth]
Juta .... Juta's Daily Reporter [South Africa] [A publication] (DLA)
Juta .... Juta's Prize Cases [South Africa] [A publication] (DLA)
Juta .... Juta's Supreme Court Reports [1880-1910] [Cape Of Good Hope, South Africa] [A publication] (DLA)
JUTCPS....... Joint Uniform Telephone Communications Precedence System (DNAB)
JUV............. Juvenal [Roman poet, 60-140AD] [Classical studies] (ROG)
JUV............. Juvenile
JUV............. Juvenis [Young] [Latin]
Juv & Dom Rel Ct... Juvenile and Domestic Relations Court [Legal term] (DLA)
Juv Ct J .... Juvenile Court Journal [A publication] (DLA)
JUVE........... Juvenile
juvenile SMA... Spinal Muscular Atrophy [Kugelberg-Welander disease] (PAZ)
JUV JUST ... Juvenile Justice [Legal term] (DLA)
JUVOS .... Joint Unemployment, Vacancy, and Operating Statistics [Department of Employment] [British]
JUWAT........ Joint Unconventional Warfare Assessment Team [Military]
JUWC......... Joint Unconventional Warfare Command (MCD)
JUWTF....... Joint Unconventional Warfare Task Force
JUWTFA...... Joint Unconventional Warfare Task Force, Atlantic
JUX............. Juxtaposition (WDAA)
JUXT........... Juxta [Near] [Pharmacy]
JUY............. Andalusia, AL [Location identifier FAA] (FAAL)
JV .... Air Charters [Senegal] [ICAO designator] (ICDA)
JV .... Bearskin Lake [ICAO designator] (AD)
JV .... Jagdverband [German aircraft fighter unit] [World War II]
JV .... Janesbury Valve [Aerospace] (KSC)
JV .... Japanese Vellum
JV .... Jersey European Airways [ICAO designator] (AD)
JV .... Jet Ventilation [Medicine]
JV .... Jewish Vegetarians of North America (EA)
JV .... Joint Venture [Legal term Business term]
JV .... Journal Voucher [Accounting]
JV .... Jugular Vein [Anatomy]
JV .... Jugular Venous [Pressure and pulse] [Cardiology] (DAVI)
JV .... Junin Virus [Medicine] (DMAA)
JV .... Junior Varsity
JVA............. Ankavandra [Madagascar] [Airport symbol] (OAG)
JVA............. Genavia SRL [Italy ICAO designator] (FAAC)
JVA............. Jet Vane Actuators
JVA............. Jewish Vacation Association [Superseded by Association of Jewish Sponsored Camps] (EA)
JVA............. Junior Victory Army [World War II]
JVAA........... Jewish Visual Artists Association [Defunct] (EA)
JVAS........... Jandel Video Analysis System
JVB............. James V. Brown Library of Williamsport and Lycoming County, Williamsport, PA [OCLC symbol] (OCLC)
JVB............. Joint Vulnerability Board
JVC............. Japan Victor Co.
JVC............. Jesuit Volunteer Corps: Northwest (EA)
JVC............. Jet Vane Control (MCD)
JVC............. Jewelers Vigilance Committee (EA)
JVC............. Jewelry Valuers' Council [Australia]
JVC............. Jugular Venous Catheter [Medicine] (DMAA)
JVC............. Jules Verne Circle (EA)
JVC............. Junior Vice Commander
JVD............. Jet Vapor Deposition [Coating technology]
JVD............. Jugular Venous Distention [Medicine]
JVD............. Juris Utriusque Doctor [Doctor of Both Laws; i.e., Canon and Civil Law]
JVDHS .... Jahresverzeichnis der Deutschen Hochschulschriften [A bibliographic publication] [Germany]
JVE............. Jeans Viscosity Equation [Physics]
JVER........... Journal of Vocational Education Research [A publication] (EAAP)
JVH............. Bangor, ME [Location identifier FAA] (FAAL)
JVIDS.......... Joint Visually Integrated Display System (DOMA)
JVIS............ Jackson Vocational Interest Survey [Vocational guidance test]
JVIS............ Joint Visual Information Services [DoD] (DOMA)
JVita........... Life of Josephus (BJA)
JVL............. Beloit/Janesville [Wisconsin] [Airport symbol] (OAG)
JVL............. Janesville, WI [Location identifier FAA] (FAAL)
JVLN........... Javelin Systems, Inc. [NASDAQ symbol] (SAG)
JVM............. Java Virtual Machine [Computer science]
JVM............. Java Virtual Machine [Computer science]
JVNC.......... John Von Neumann National Supercomputer Center [Princeton, NJ] (GRD)
JvNCnet ...... John Von Neumann Computer Center Network (ACRL)
JVNL........... Juvenile
J Voet Com ad Pand... Jan Voet's Commentarius ad Pandectas [A publication] (DLA)
JVP............. Janatha Vimukhti Peramuna [People's Liberation Front] [Sri Lanka] [Political party] (PPW)
JVP............. Japanese Vellum Proofs
JVP............. Joint Venture Partners
JVP............. Juedische Volkspartei (BJA)
JVP............. Jugular Vein [or Venous] Pulse [Medicine]
JVP............. Jugular Venous Pressure [Cardiology] (DAVI)
JVP............. Junior Vice-President [Freemasonry] (ROG)
JVPT........... Jugular Venous Pulse Tracing [Medicine]
JVR............. Jury Verdict Research, Inc. [Information service or system] (IID)
JVS............. Jewish Vegetarian Society - America [Later, JVSNA] (EA)
JVS............. Jewish Vocational Services

JVS .... Joint Venture Scheme
JVS .... Joint Vocational School
JVSNA .... Jewish Vegetarian Society-North America (EA)
JVSPLNMQNSC... Je Vous Salue par les Noms Maconniques que Nous Seul Connoissons [I Salute You by the Masonic Names, Which We Only Know] [Freemasonry] [French]
JVVVA .... Justice for Veteran Victims of the Veterans Administration (EA)
JVX .... Joint Service Vertical-Lift Aircraft, Experimental [Military] (RDA)
JVY .... Jeffersonville, IN [Location identifier FAA] (FAAL)
JW .... Jacket Water
JW .... Jehovah's Witnesses (ADA)
JW .... [The] Jewish War [A publication] (BJA)
JW .... John Wiley [& Sons] [Publisher]
JW .... Joint Warfare
JW .... Jordan Watch [Database] [Jordan & Sons Ltd.] [Information service or system] (CRD)
JW .... Jump Walker [Rehabilitation] (DAVI)
JW .... Junction Wide [Telecommunications] (OA)
JW .... Junior Warden [Freemasonry]
JW .... Junior Wolf [A young philanderer] [Slang]
JW .... Junior Woodward [Ancient Order of Foresters]
JW .... Polar Avia [ICAO designator] (AD)
JW .... Royal American [ICAO designator] (AD)
JW .... Wiley [John] & Sons [NYSE symbol] (SAG)
JWA .... Jetworld Airways Ltd. [Antigua and Barbuda] [ICAO designator] (FAAC)
JWA .... Johnson Worldwide Associates, Inc. [Associated Press] (SAG)
JWA .... Jwalamukhi [India] [Seismograph station code, US Geological Survey Closed] (SEIS)
JWADF .... Joint Western Air Defense Force (MUGU)
JWAI .... Johnson Worldwide Associates, Inc. [NASDAQ symbol] (NQ)
JWAIA .... Johnson Worldwide'A' [NASDAQ symbol] (TTSB)
JW & NW ... Jamestown, Westfield & Northwestern Railroad (IIA)
JWAR .... Jehovah's Witnesses for Animal Rights [An association] (EA)
JWB .... Joint Wages Board (DAS)
JWB .... National Jewish Welfare Board [Later, JCCANA] (EA)
JWBC .... Joint Whole Blood Center [Military]
JWBCA .... Joint Whole Blood Control Agency (MCD)
JWBJBC .... JWB [Jewish Welfare Board] Jewish Book Council (EA)
JWC .... Joint Warfare Center [DoD]
JWC .... Junction Wire Connector
JWC .... Jungle Warfare Course [Military] (MCD)
JWD .... Journal of Workforce Diversity [A publication]
JWE .... Joint Warfare Establishment [British]
JWEF .... Joinery and Woodwork Employers' Federation [British] (BI)
JWF .... Job Work Folder (AABC)
JWFC .... Jacky Ward Fan Club [Defunct] (EA)
JWFC .... Jimmy Wakely Fan Club [Defunct] (EA)
JWFC .... Joe Waters Fan Club (EA)
JWFC .... Joint Warfighting Center [DoD]
JWG .... Joint Working Group [Military]
JWG .... Jugendwohlfahrtsgesetz [Youth Welfare Law] [German] (ILCA)
JWGA .... Joint War Games Agency [JCS] [DoD]
JWGCG .... Joint War Games Control Group [Military] (CINC)
JWGM .... Joint Working Group Meeting [NASA] (KSC)
JWKB .... Jordan-Wentzel-Kramers-Brillouin [Physics]
JWLR .... Jeweler
JWLR .... Jeweller [British] (ADA)
JWLRY .... Jewelry (WDAA)
JWLRY .... Jewelry
JWNS .... Jewish News Service (BJA)
jwo .... Jettisoning and Washing Overboard [Inventor] (ODBW)
JWO .... Job Work Order
JWOD .... Javits-Wagner-O'Day Act
JWP .... Jamaican Workers' Party [Political party] (PPW)
JWP .... Joint Working Paper
JWP .... Joint Working Party (ADA)

JWPC .... Joint War Plans Committee
JWPC .... Joint War Production Committee
JWPNN .... Jobs with Peace National Network [Later, NJWPC] (EA)
JWPS .... Joint War Production Staff
JWPT .... Jersey Wildlife Preservation Trust (EAIO)
JWR .... Joint War Room [Military]
JWRA .... Joint War Room Annex [Military] (CINC)
JWRC .... Jewish Women's Resource Center (EA)
JWS .... Japanese Weekend School
JWS .... Jazz World Society (EA)
JWS .... Jewish Welfare Society [Australia]
JwS .... John Wiley & Sons, New York, NY [Library symbol Library of Congress] (LCLS)
JWS .... Joint Warfare Staff [British]
JWS .... Judson Welliver Society (EA)
JWSOL .... Joint Warfare Simulation Object Library [DoD]
JWSS .... James Willard Schultz Society (EA)
JWS/TD .... Jungle Warfare School Trial and Development Wing [Johore Bahru, Malaysia]
JWSTP .... Joint Warfighting Science and Technology Plan [Defense Technical Information Center]
JWTC .... Jungle Warfare Training Center [Army]
JWU .... International Jewelry Workers Union [Later, Service Employees International Union]
JWU .... Sumter, SC [Location identifier FAA] (FAAL)
JWV .... Jewish War Veterans of the USA (EA)
JWVA .... Jewish War Veterans of the USA - National Ladies Auxiliary (EA)
JWVUSANM... Jewish War Veterans USA National Memorial (EA)
JWY .... Jet Way, Inc. [ICAO designator] (FAAC)
JWYCC .... Jamestown-Williamsburg-Yorktown Celebration Committee
JX .... Bougair [ICAO designator] (AD)
JX .... Jesus Christus [Jesus Christ] [Latin] (ROG)
JX .... Jorex Ltd. [Toronto Stock Exchange symbol]
JXCG .... Joint Exercise Control Group [Military] (AABC)
JXG .... Juvenile Xanthogranuloma [Ophthalmology]
JXN .... Jackson [Michigan] [Airport symbol] (OAG)
JXSB .... Jacksonville Savings Bank (Illinois) [NASDAQ symbol] (SAG)
JXT .... Morristown, TN [Location identifier FAA] (FAAL)
JXVL .... Jacksonville Bancorp, Inc. [NASDAQ symbol] (SAG)
JXVL .... Jacksonville Savings & Loan Association [Texas] [NASDAQ symbol] (SAG)
J XXII .... Extravagantes Johannes XXII [A publication] (DSA)
Jy .... Jansky [A unit of electromagnetic flux density]
JY .... Japanese Yen [Monetary unit]
JY .... Jersey European [ICAO designator] (AD)
JY .... July
JY .... Jury [Ship's rigging] (ROG)
JYA .... Junior Year Abroad [Collegiate term]
JYC .... Jacques-Yves Cousteau [French marine explorer] [Initialism pronounced "Jheek" when used as nickname]
JYP .... JCP & L Capital LP [NYSE symbol] (SAG)
JYP .... Jersey Central Power & Light Co. [NYSE symbol] (SAG)
JYPPr .... Jersey Cent P&L 4%cmPfd [NYSE symbol] (TTSB)
JYPPrE .... Jersey Cent P&L7.88% Pfd [NYSE symbol] (TTSB)
JYPPrZ .... JCP&L Cap L.P.8.56%'MIPS' [NYSE symbol] (TTSB)
JYV .... Houston, TX [Location identifier FAA] (FAAL)
JYV .... Jyvaskyla [Finland] [Airport symbol] (OAG)
JZ .... Alamo Commuter Airlines [ICAO designator] (AD)
JZ .... Jazz [A radio station format] (WDMC)
JZ .... Juedische Zeremonialkunst [A publication] (BJA)
JZ .... Jump on Zero [Computer science] (PCM)
JZF .... Jannasch-Zafirion-Farrington [Marine sediment trap]
JZG .... Juedische Zeitschrift fuer Wissenschaft und Leben (A. Geiger) [A publication] (BJA)
JZI .... Charleston, SC [Location identifier FAA] (FAAL)
JZM .... Jazzman Resources, Inc. [Vancouver Stock Exchange symbol]
JZQ .... Norfolk, VA [Location identifier FAA] (FAAL)

K

By Acronym

K................. Absolute Zero [*Temperature*] (MAE)
K................. Amphibious [*JETDS*]
K................. Black (WDMC)
k................. Boltzmann Constant [*Symbol*] [*IUPAC*]
K................. Bulk Modulus of Elasticity [*Symbol*] (DEN)
K................. Calcium in the Solar Spectrum [*Astronomy*] (BARN)
K................. Calix [*Anatomy*] (MAE)
K................. Capacity (AAG)
K................. Capital [*Factor of production*]
K................. Capsular Antigen [*Immunology*] (MAE)
K................. Cara [*Dear One*] [*Latin*]
K................. Carat [*Unit of measure for precious stones or gold*]
K................. Care
K................. Carissimus [*Dearest*] [*Latin*]
K................. Carlo Erba [*Italy*] [*Research code symbol*]
K................. Carrying Capacity [*Genetics*] (DAVI)
K................. Carus
K................. Cathode [*Electron device*] (MSA)
K................. Cellophane (AAG)
K................. Certified Kosher [*Food labeling*]
K................. Chritiania Bank og Kreditkasse [*Bank*] [*Norway*]
K................. Circuses [*Public-performance tariff class*] [*British*]
K................. Coefficient of Alienation [*Psychology*]
K................. Coefficient of Scleral Rigidity [*Ophthalmology*] (DAVI)
K................. Cold Air Mass [*Meteorology*] (BARN)
K................. Computer [*JETDS nomenclature*]
K................. Consonantal [*Linguistics*]
K................. Constant
K................. Contract [*Legal shorthand*] (LWAP)
K................. Cretaceous [*Period, era, or system*] [*Geology*]
K................. Cumulus [*Cloud*] [*Meteorology*]
K................. Dallas [*Branch in the Federal Reserve regional banking system*] (BARN)
K................. Declared or Paid This Year on a Cumulative Issue with Dividends in Arrears [*Investment term*] (DFIT)
K................. Degrees Kelvin
K................. Dielectric Constant
K................. Electrostatic Capacity [*Symbol*] (AAMN)
K................. Equilibrium Constant [*Symbol*] [*Chemistry*]
K................. Ionization Constant [*Symbol*] [*Chemistry*]
K................. Kadenz [*Cadence*] [*Music*]
K................. Kaempferol [*Biochemistry*]
K................. Kainic Acid [*Biochemistry*]
K................. Kaiser [*In radio call signs west of the Mississippi River*] (ROG)
K................. Kaken Chemical Co. [*Japan*] [*Research code symbol*]
K................. Kalendas [*Calends*]
K................. Kalium [*Potassium*] [*Chemical element*]
K................. Kallikrein [*or Kininogenin*] Inhibiting Unit [*Hematology*]
K................. Kanamycin [*Antibacterial compound*]
K................. Kanone [*Gun*] [*German military - World War II*]
K................. Kansas State Library, Topeka, KS [*Library symbol Library of Congress*] (LCLS)
K................. Kappa [*Tenth letter of the Greek alaphabet*] (DAVI)
K................. Karat [*A twenty-fourth part; unit of value for gold*]
K................. Karolus de Tocco [*Flourished, 13th century*] [*Authority cited in pre-1607 legal work*] (DSA)
K................. Karyotype [*Clinical chemistry*]
K................. Kathode [*Cathode*]
K................. Kayak
K................. Kayser
K................. K Capture [*A type of radioactive decay*]
K................. Keel
K................. Keg
K................. Kell [*Blood group*]
K................. Kell Factor (DMAA)
K................. Kellogg Co. [*NYSE symbol*] (SPSG)
K................. Kelp [*Quality of the Bottom*] [*Nautical charts*]
K................. Kelvin [*Symbol*] [*SI unit of thermodynamic temperature*]
K................. Kennedy Space Center [*NASA*]
K................. Kensal Press [*Publisher*] [*British*]
K................. Kentish
K................. Kenyon's English King's Bench Reports [*A publication*] (DLA)
K................. Kerma (DMAA)
K................. Kern Wave [*Earthquakes*]
K................. Kerosene (AAG)
K................. Kerr Constant [*Optics*]

K................. Ketamine [*An anesthetic*]
K................. Ketch (ROG)
K................. Ketib (BJA)
K................. Ketotifen [*Pharmacology*]
K................. Key
K................. Keyes' New York Court of Appeals Reports [*A publication*] (DLA)
K................. KGB [*Komitet Gossudarstvennoi Bezopasnosti*] Agent
K................. Kicker [*Football*]
K................. Kidney [*Anatomy*] (MAE)
K................. Killed
K................. Killer [*Cells*] [*Cytology*] (DAVI)
K................. Kilo [*Phonetic alphabet*] [*International*] (DSUE)
k................. Kilo [*A prefix meaning multiplied by 10³*] [*SI symbol*]
K................. Kilo (WDMC)
K................. Kilobyte [*10³ bytes*] [*Computer science*]
K................. Kilocycle
K................. Kilogram [*Also, kg*] [*Symbol SI unit for mass*]
k................. Kilohm
K................. Kilometer (WDAA)
K................. Kilowatt (WDMC)
K................. Kindergarten
K................. Kinesthetic (AAG)
K................. Kinetic Energy [*Symbol*] [*IUPAC*]
K................. King [*Chess, card games*]
K................. King [*Phonetic alphabet*] [*Royal Navy*] (DSUE)
K................. King [*Monetary unit*] [*Papua, New Guinea*] (BARN)
K................. Kingdom (ROG)
K................. Kings [*Old Testament book*] (BJA)
K................. Kip [*1000 lbs.*]
K................. Kip [*Monetary unit*] [*Laos*]
K................. Kirk (ROG)
K................. Kirschner [*Wire*] [*Orthopedics*] (DAVI)
K................. Kitchen
K................. Klebsiella [*Genus of microorganisms*] (DAVI)
K................. Klinge [*Germany*] [*Research code symbol*]
K................. Klystron
K................. Knee [*Anatomy*] (DAVI)
K................. Knight [*Chess, card games*]
K................. Knighthood
K................. Knit
K................. Knock [*Cardiology*]
K................. Knots [*Also, KT*] [*Nautical speed unit*]
K................. Knudsen Number
K................. Koechel [*Catalogue of Mozart's works*] (ODBW)
K................. Kollaborateur [*Nickname given Alain Robbe-Grillet*] [*World War II*]
K................. Kontra [*Contra*] [*Music*]
K................. Kopeck [*Monetary unit*] [*Former USSR*]
K................. Koruna [*Monetary unit*] [*Former Czechoslovakia*]
K................. Kosher
K................. Kosmos [*Publisher*] [*Holland*]
K................. Kotze's Transvaal High Court Reports [*South Africa*] [*A publication*] (DLA)
K................. Kouyunjik [*or Kuyounjik*] [*Collection of cuneiform tablets from Kuyounjik in the British Museum, London*] (BJA)
K................. Kraft [*Paper*] (DGA)
K................. Kraftfahrwesen [*Motor transport*] [*German military - World War II*]
K................. Kraftrad [*Motorcycle*] [*German military - World War II*]
K................. Krazy Kat [*Cartoon character by George Herriman*]
K................. Krona [*Monetary unit*] [*Iceland, Sweden*]
K................. Krone [*Crown*] [*Monetary unit Denmark, Norway*]
K................. Kroon [*Monetary unit*] [*Estonia*]
K................. Krupp Gun
K................. Kurus [*Monetary unit*] [*Turkey*]
K................. Kwacha [*Monetary unit*] [*Malawi, Zambia*]
K................. Kyat [*Monetary unit*] [*Myanmar*]
K................. Luminous Efficiency [*Physics*] (BARN)
K................. Lysine [*One-letter symbol; see Lys*]
K................. Mass Transfer Coefficient [*Symbol*] [*IUPAC*]
K................. Motor Coordination [*Neurology and orthopedics*] (DAVI)
k................. Multiplication Factor [*or Constant*]
K................. NCO Logistics Program [*Army skill qualification identifier*] (INF)
K................. One Thousand (NASA)
K................. Phylloquinone [*Vitamin K*] [*Also, PMQ*] [*Biochemistry*]
K................. Potassium [*Chemical element*]
K................. Promotional Fare [*Also, L, Q, V*] [*Airline fare code*]

K .... Radius of Curvature of Flattest Meridian of Apical Cornea [*Ophthalmology*] (DAVI)
k .... Rate (DAVI)
k .... Rate Constant [*Symbol*] [*Chemistry*]
k .... Reaction Rate Constant [*Chemistry*] (DAVI)
K .... Red Star of Maximum Intensity of Metal [*Astronomy*] (BARN)
K .... Relay (CET)
K .... Required Rate of Return [*Finance*]
K .... Smoke [*Weather charts*]
K .... Solar Absorption Index (CET)
K .... Strikeout [*Baseball symbol*]
K .... Tanker [*Designation for all US military aircraft*]
K .... Telemetering [*JETDS*]
k .... Thermal Conductivity [*Symbol*] [*IUPAC*]
K .... Thousand (ADA)
k .... Torsion Constant [*Physics*] (BARN)
K .... United Kingdom [*IYRU nationality code*] (IYR)
k .... Velocity [*Physics*] (DAVI)
K .... Wetboek van Koophandel [*Commercial Code*] [*Dutch*] (ILCA)
K1 .... Kayak, Single Person (ADA)
K2 .... Kayak, Two Person (ADA)
K2 .... Mount Godwin-Austen [*Initialism denotes that mountain is second highest (to Everest) in the Karakoram range in the Himalayas*] [*Initialism also used as brand name of skiing equipment*]
K2Desgn .... K2 Design, Inc. [*Associated Press*] (SAG)
K2Dsgn .... K2 Design, Inc. [*Associated Press*] (SAG)
K-3 .... Krasnogorsk-3 [*A 16mm film camera*] (WDMC)
K-3 .... Kummer, Kneser, and Kodaira [*Surfaces*] [*Mathematics*]
K_3 .... Menadione [*Vitamin K_3*] (DAVI)
K4 .... Kayak, Four Person (ADA)
K_4 .... Menadiol Sodium Diphosphate [*Vitamin K_4*] (DAVI)
K9 .... Canine [*K9 Corps - Army Dogs*] [*World War II*]
K-12 .... Kindergarten through 12th Grade (WDAA)
K24H .... Potassium, Urine 24 Hour [*Biochemistry*] (DAVI)
K-25 .... Oak Ridge K-25 Site [*Department of Energy*] [*Oak Ridge, TN*] (GAAI)
K25 .... Oak Ridge Uranium Separation Plant [*Code designation*] (DEN)
K_a .... Acid Ionization Constant [*Physics*] (DAVI)
KA .... Alkair [*Denmark ICAO designator*] (ICDA)
KA .... Alkaline Phosphatase [*An enzyme*] (DAVI)
Ka .... Auroral Absorption Index (CET)
KA .... Australia [*IYRU nationality code*] (IYR)
Ka .... Cathode [*Electron device*] (AAMN)
KA .... Coastal Plains Commuter [*ICAO designator*] (AD)
KA .... Concrete Arch [*Bridges*]
KA .... Eha-Kibbuts ha-Artsi (BJA)
KA .... HMS King Alfred [*British military*] (DMA)
KA .... Kainic Acid [*Biochemistry*]
KA .... Kainic Acid (DMAA)
Ka .... Kallikrein (MEDA)
KA .... Kamov [*Former USSR ICAO aircraft manufacturer identifier*] (ICAO)
Ka .... Kaolinite [*A mineral*]
Ka .... Karolus de Tocco [*Flourished, 13th century*] [*Authority cited in pre-1607 legal work*] (DSA)
KA .... Kathode [*Cathode*] (AAG)
KA .... Keratoacanthoma [*Dermatology*] (DAVI)
KA .... Keren Ami (BJA)
KA .... Keto Acid (DMAA)
KA .... Ketoacidosis [*Medicine*]
K/A .... Ketogenic to Anti-Ketogenic [*Ratio*] [*In diets*]
KA .... Keyed Address (IAA)
KA .... Keyed Alike [*Locks*] (ADA)
ka .... Killed in Action
KA .... Kilmarnock [*Postcode*] (ODBW)
kA .... Kiloampere
KA .... King-Armstrong Unit [*Clinical chemistry*]
KA .... King of Arms
KA .... King Pin Angle [*Automotive engineering*]
KA .... Knight of St. Andrew [*Russia*] [*Obsolete*]
K/A .... Knights of the Altar (EA)
K-A .... Kuhlmann-Anderson Intelligence Tests [*Education*]
KA .... Kuwait Airways Corp.
KA .... Kynurenic Acid [*Biochemistry*] (OA)
KA .... Kypriakes Aerogrammes [*Cyprus Airlines*]
KA .... Thousands of Amperes
KAA .... Asia Aero Survey & Consulting Engineers, Inc. [*Korea*] [*ICAO designator*] (FAAC)
Ka A .... Kansas Appeals Reports [*A publication*] (DLA)
kaa .... Karakalpak [*MARC language code Library of Congress*] (LCCP)
KAA .... Karratha [*Australia Seismograph station code, US Geological Survey Closed*] (SEIS)
KAA .... Kasama [*Zambia*] [*Airport symbol*] (OAG)
KAA .... Keep-Alive Anode
KAAA .... Kingman, AZ [*AM radio station call letters*]
KAAB .... Batesville, AR [*AM radio station call letters*]
KAAD .... Kerosene, Alcohol, Acetic Acid, and Dioxane (DMAA)
KAAK .... Great Falls, MT [*FM radio station call letters*]
KAAL .... Austin, MN [*Television station call letters*]
KAAM .... Huntsville, MO [*FM radio station call letters*]
KAAM .... Plano, TX [*AM radio station call letters*] (RBYB)
KAAN .... Bethany, MO [*AM radio station call letters*]
KAAN-FM .... Bethany, MO [*FM radio station call letters*]
KAAO .... Kabul [*Afghanistan*] [*Seismograph station code, US Geological Survey*] (SEIS)
KAAP .... Kansas Army Ammunition Plant (AABC)
KAAQ .... Alliance, NE [*FM radio station call letters*]
KAAR .... Butte, MT [*FM radio station call letters*]
KAAS .... Keele Assessment of Auditory Style (DMAA)
KAAS .... Salina, KS [*Television station call letters*]
KAAT .... Oakhurst, CA [*FM radio station call letters*]
KAAX .... Avenal, CA [*FM radio station call letters*]
KAAY .... Little Rock, AR [*AM radio station call letters*]
KAb .... Abilene Free Public Library, Abilene, KS [*Library symbol Library of Congress*] (LCLS)
KAB .... Kabansk [*Former USSR Seismograph station code, US Geological Survey*] (SEIS)
KAB .... Kaneb Services [*NYSE symbol*] (TTSB)
KAB .... Kaneb Services, Inc. [*NYSE symbol*] (SPSG)
KAB .... Kariba Dam [*Zimbabwe*] [*Airport symbol*] (OAG)
KAB .... Katholieke Arbeidersbeweging [*Netherlands*]
KAB .... Keep America Beautiful (EA)
KAB .... Knowledge, Attitudes, and Behavior Survey [*Department of Health and Human Services*] (GFGA)
KABB .... San Antonio, TX [*Television station call letters*]
KABC .... Kaufman Assessment Battery for Children
K-ABC .... Kaufman Assessment Battery for Children [*Diagnostic assessment test*] (PAZ)
KABC .... Los Angeles, CA [*AM radio station call letters*]
KABCC .... Korea Australia Business Cooperation Council
KABC-TV .... Los Angeles, CA [*Television station call letters*]
KAbE .... Dwight D. Eisenhower Library, Abilene, KS [*Library symbol Library of Congress*] (LCLS)
KABF .... Little Rock, AR [*FM radio station call letters*]
KABH .... Shawnee, OK [*FM radio station call letters*]
KABI .... Abilene, KS [*AM radio station call letters*]
KABI .... Abilene/Municipal [*Texas*] [*ICAO location identifier*] (ICLI)
KABIR .... Kapitalist Birokrat [*Capitalist Bureaucrat*] [*Term for foreigner Indonesia*]
KABK .... Augusta, AR [*FM radio station call letters*]
KABL .... Oakland, CA [*AM radio station call letters*]
KABN .... Long Island, AK [*AM radio station call letters*]
KABPrA .... Kaneb Svc Adj Rt A Pfd [*NYSE symbol*] (TTSB)
KABQ .... Albuquerque/International [*New Mexico*] [*ICAO location identifier*] (ICLI)
KABQ .... Albuquerque, NM [*AM radio station call letters*]
KABR .... Alamo Community, NM [*AM radio station call letters*]
KABS .... Great Falls, MT [*FM radio station call letters*]
KABU-FM .... Fort Totten, ND [*FM radio station call letters*] (RBYB)
KABX .... Merced, CA [*FM radio station call letters*]
KABY .... Aberdeen, SD [*Television station call letters*]
kac .... Kachin [*MARC language code Library of Congress*] (LCCP)
KAC .... Kaman Aircraft Corp. (MCD)
KAC .... Kameshli [*Syria*] [*Airport symbol*] (OAG)
KAC .... Kamishli [*Syria*] [*Airport symbol*] (AD)
KAC .... Kinetics and Catalysis
KAC .... Komatsu America Corp.
KAC .... Korean American Coalition (EA)
KAC .... Kuwait Airways Corp. [*ICAO designator*] (FAAC)
KACB .... San Angelo, TX [*Television station call letters*]
KACC .... Alvin, TX [*FM radio station call letters*]
KACC .... Kaiser Aluminum & Chemical Corp. (MCD)
KACC .... Korean-American Chamber of Commerce [*Later, AAACC*]
KACD .... Kansas Association of Soil Conservation Districts (SRA)
KACD .... Santa Monica, CA [*FM radio station call letters*]
KACE .... Inglewood, CA [*FM radio station call letters*]
KACEE .... Kansas Advisory Council on Environmental Education (EDAC)
KACF .... Korean-American Cultural Foundation (EA)
KACH .... Preston, ID [*AM radio station call letters*]
KACHAPAG .... Karlsruhe Charged Particle Group (NITA)
KACI .... The Dalles, OR [*AM radio station call letters*]
KACIA .... Korea-American Commerce and Industry Association [*Later, KS*]
KACI-FM .... The Dalles, OR [*FM radio station call letters*]
KACK .... Nantucket [*Massachusetts*] [*ICAO location identifier*] (ICLI)
KACL-FM .... Bismarck, ND [*FM radio station call letters*] (RBYB)
KACO-FM .... Ardmore, OK [*FM radio station call letters*] (RBYB)
KACP .... Custer, SD [*FM radio station call letters*]
KACP .... Kansas Association of Chiefs of Police (SRA)
KACQ .... Lometa, TX [*FM radio station call letters*] (RBYB)
KACS .... Chehalis, WA [*FM radio station call letters*]
KACT .... Andrews, TX [*AM radio station call letters*]
KACT .... Waco/Waco Municipal [*Texas*] [*ICAO location identifier*] (ICLI)
KACT-FM .... Andrews, TX [*FM radio station call letters*]
KACU .... Abilene, TX [*FM radio station call letters*]
KACV .... Amarillo, TX [*FM radio station call letters*]
KACV-TV .... Amarillo, TX [*Television station call letters*]
KACW .... North Bend, OR [*FM radio station call letters*]
KACY .... Atlantic City/Atlantic City [*New Jersey*] [*ICAO location identifier*] (ICLI)
KACY .... Lafayette, LA [*AM radio station call letters*]
KAD .... Kadena Air Base, Ryuku Islands (NASA)
KAD .... Kadrey Energy [*Vancouver Stock Exchange symbol*]
KAD .... Kaduna [*Nigeria*] [*Airport symbol*] (OAG)
KAD .... Karad [*India*] [*Seismograph station code, US Geological Survey*] (SEIS)
KAD .... Keyboard and Display [*Computer science*]
KADA .... Ada, OK [*AM radio station call letters*]
KADA-FM .... Ada, OK [*FM radio station call letters*]
KADD .... Laughlin, NV [*FM radio station call letters*]
KADE .... San Luis Obispo, CA [*Television station call letters*]
KaDeWe .... Kaufhaus des Westens [*Department Store of the West*] [*Germany*]
KADF .... Kuwait Air Defense Force (MCD)

KADI	Republic, MO [*FM radio station call letters*]
KADM	Ardmore [*Oklahoma*] [*ICAO location identifier*] (ICLI)
KADM	Odessa, TX [*FM radio station call letters*]
KADN	Lafayette, LA [*Television station call letters*]
KADOS	Knowledge-Based Automated Design of Silencers [*Automotive engineering*]
KADP	Kaduna State Agricultural Development Project [*Nigeria*] (ECON)
KADQ	Rexburg, ID [*FM radio station call letters*]
KADR	Elkader, IA [*AM radio station call letters*]
KADS	Elk City, OK [*AM radio station call letters*]
KADS	Korea Air Defense System (CINC)
KADU	Hibbing, MN [*FM radio station call letters*]
KADU	Kenya African Democratic Union [*Political party*] (PPW)
KADV	Modesto, CA [*FM radio station call letters*]
KADW	Camp Springs/Andrews Air Force Base [*Maryland*] [*ICAO location identifier*] (ICLI)
KADX	Houston, AK [*FM radio station call letters*]
KADY	Oxnard, CA [*Television station call letters*]
KAE	Kaena [*Hawaii*] [*Seismograph station code, US Geological Survey*] (SEIS)
KAE	Kake [*Alaska*] [*Airport symbol*] (OAG)
KAE	Knitting Arts Expo (TSPED)
KAEC	Kentucky Association of Electric Cooperatives (SRA)
KAEDS	Keystone Association for Educational Data Systems (HGAA)
KAEF	Arcata, CA [*Television station call letters*]
KAEH	Beaumont, CA [*FM radio station call letters*]
KAEP	Spokane, WA [*FM radio station call letters*] (RBYB)
KAET	Phoenix, AZ [*Television station call letters*]
KAEX	Alexandria/England Air Force Base [*Louisiana*] [*ICAO location identifier*] (ICLI)
KAEZ	Amarillo, TX [*FM radio station call letters*]
KAF	Kafue International Air Services Ltd. [*Zambia*] [*ICAO designator*] (FAAC)
KAF	Kafue International Air Services Ltd. [*Zambia*] [*FAA designator*] (FAAC)
KAF	Karato [*Papua New Guinea*] [*Airport symbol*] (OAG)
KAF	Kenya Air Force
KAF	Khmer [*Cambodia*] Air Force (VNW)
KAF	Killer-Assistng Factor (DAVI)
KAF	Kinase-Activating Factor [*Organic chemistry*] (DAVI)
KAF	Kuwaiti Air Force (DOMA)
KAFB	Keesler Air Force Base [*Mississippi*]
KAFB	Kirtland Air Force Base [*New Mexico*]
KAFC	Kenny Antcliff Fan Club (EA)
KAFE	Bellingham, WA [*FM radio station call letters*]
KAFF	Flagstaff, AZ [*AM radio station call letters*]
KAFF-FM	Flagstaff, AZ [*FM radio station call letters*]
KAFFR	Kaffaria [*South Africa*] (ROG)
KAFH	Ku-Band Antenna Feed Horn
KAFO	Knee-Ankle-Foot Orthosis [*Medicine*]
KAFP	Kansas Academy of Family Physicians (SRA)
KAFP	Kentucky Academy of Family Physicians (SRA)
KAFR	Angel Fire, NM [*FM radio station call letters*]
KAFT	Fayetteville, AR [*Television station call letters*]
KAFU	Enid, OK [*Television station call letters*]
KAFW	Wilson, AR [*FM radio station call letters*] (RBYB)
KAFX-FM	Diboll, TX [*FM radio station call letters*]
KAFY	Bakersfield, CA [*AM radio station call letters*]
KAG	Cryptographic Aid, General Publication (CET)
KAG	Kagoshima [*Japan*] [*Seismograph station code, US Geological Survey*] (SEIS)
KAG	Kagoshima Space Center [*Japan*]
KAG	Kelvin Astatic Galvanometer [*Electronics*]
KAGA	Santa Ynez, CA [*FM radio station call letters*]
KAGC	Bryan, TX [*AM radio station call letters*]
KAGE	Winona, MN [*AM radio station call letters*]
KAGE-FM	Winona, MN [*FM radio station call letters*]
KAGG	Madisonville, TX [*FM radio station call letters*]
KAGH	Crossett, AR [*AM radio station call letters*]
KAGH-FM	Crossett, AR [*FM radio station call letters*]
KAGI	Grants Pass, OR [*AM radio station call letters*]
KAGI	Kesatuan Aksi Guru Indonesia [*Action Front of Indonesian Teachers*]
KAGJ	Ephraim, UT [*FM radio station call letters*]
KAGL	El Dorado, AR [*FM radio station call letters*] (RBYB)
KAGM	Strasburg, CO [*FM radio station call letters*]
KAGO	Klamath Falls, OR [*AM radio station call letters*]
KAGO-FM	Klamath Falls, OR [*FM radio station call letters*]
KAGP	Grants, NM [*FM radio station call letters*]
KAGR	Morro Bay, CA [*FM radio station call letters*] (RBYB)
KAGU	Spokane, WA [*FM radio station call letters*]
KAGY	Port Sulphur, LA [*AM radio station call letters*]
KAH	Keilschrifttexte aus Assur Historischen Inhalts [*A publication*] (BJA)
KAH	Kent Aviation Ltd. [*Canada ICAO designator*] (FAAC)
KAH	Kiloampere Hour (IAA)
KAHF-FM	Ortonville, MN [*FM radio station call letters*] (RBYB)
KAHI	Auburn, CA [*AM radio station call letters*]
KAHI	Keilschrifttexte aus Assur Historischen Inhalts [*A publication*] (BJA)
Kahler	Kahler Corp. [*Associated Press*] (SAG)
KAHM	Prescott, AZ [*FM radio station call letters*]
KAHO	Junction, TX [*FM radio station call letters*]
KAHP	Kentucky Allied Health Project (EDAC)
KAHR	Poplar Bluff, MO [*FM radio station call letters*]
KAHRP	Knob-Associated Histidine-Rich Protein [*Cytology*]
KAHS	Thousand Oaks, CA [*AM radio station call letters*] (RBYB)
KAHSLC	Knoxville Area Health Science Consortium [*Library network*]

KAHU	Hilo, HI [*AM radio station call letters*]
KAHX-FM	Ingleside, TX [*FM radio station call letters*] (RBYB)
KAHY	Myrtle Point, OR [*FM radio station call letters*]
KAHZ	Fort Worth, TX [*AM radio station call letters*]
KAI	Kaieteur [*Guyana*] [*Airport symbol*] (OAG)
KAI	Kaimata [*New Zealand*] [*Seismograph station code, US Geological Survey*] (SEIS)
KAI	Kanaanaeische und Aramaeische Inschriften [*A publication*] (BJA)
KAI	Kazan Aviation Institute
KAI	Keep America Independent [*Defunct*] (EA)
KAI	Korean Affairs Institute (EA)
KAI	Kurzweil Applied Intelligence [*Computer science*]
KAIC	Komatsu America Industries Corp.
KAID	Boise, ID [*Television station call letters*]
KAIG	Kearfott Acceleration Integrating Gyroscope
KAIH	Jacksboro, TX [*FM radio station call letters*] (RBYB)
KAII	Kiddie Academy International, Inc. [*NASDAQ symbol*] (SAG)
KAII	Kiddie Academy Intl [*NASDAQ symbol*] (TTSB)
KAII	Wailuku, HI [*Television station call letters*]
KAIIW	Kiddie Academy Intl Wrrt [*NASDAQ symbol*] (TTSB)
KAIL	Fresno, CA [*Television station call letters*]
KAIM	Honolulu, HI [*AM radio station call letters*]
KAIM-FM	Honolulu, HI [*FM radio station call letters*]
KAIN	Vidalia, LA [*AM radio station call letters*]
KAIR-AM	Atchison, KS [*AM radio station call letters*] (RBYB)
KAIR-FM	Horton, KS [*FM radio station call letters*] (RBYB)
KAIS	Korean Air Intelligence System (MCD)
KaisA	Kaiser Aluminum & Chemical Corp. [*Associated Press*] (SAG)
KaisAl	Kaiser Aluminum & Chemical Corp. [*Associated Press*] (SAG)
KAIST	Korea Advanced Institute of Science and Technology [*Seoul*] [*Information service or system*] (IID)
KaisVent	Kaiser Ventures, Inc. [*Associated Press*] (SAG)
KAIT	Jonesboro, AR [*Television station call letters*]
KAIT	Katzman Automatic Imaging Telescope [*University of California*]
KAJ	Kajaani [*Finland*] [*Airport symbol*] (OAG)
KAJ	Kashiwara [*Japan*] [*Seismograph station code, US Geological Survey*] (SEIS)
KAJ	Keilschrifttexte aus Assur Juridischen Inhalts [*A publication*] (BJA)
KAJA	San Antonio, TX [*FM radio station call letters*]
KAJI	Keilschrifttexte aus Assur Juridischen Inhalts [*A publication*] (BJA)
KAJI	Point Comfort, TX [*FM radio station call letters*] (RBYB)
KAJK	Fortuna, CA [*AM radio station call letters*]
KAJK-FM	Ferndale, CA [*FM radio station call letters*]
KAJL	Winters, TX [*FM radio station call letters*] (RBYB)
KAJN	Crowley, LA [*FM radio station call letters*]
KAJO	Grants Pass, OR [*AM radio station call letters*]
KAJP	Firebaugh, CA [*FM radio station call letters*] (RBYB)
KAJQ	Sibley, IA [*FM radio station call letters*] (RBYB)
KAJW	Tolleson, AZ [*Television station call letters*] (RBYB)
KAJX	Aspen, CO [*FM radio station call letters*]
KAJZ-FM	Killeen, TX [*FM radio station call letters*] (RBYB)
KAK	Kakioka [*Japan*] [*Seismograph station code, US Geological Survey*] (SEIS)
KAK	Key-Auto-Key [*Computer science*]
KAK	Kungliga Automobil Klubben
KAKC	Tulsa, OK [*AM radio station call letters*]
KAKD	Eureka, CA [*FM radio station call letters*] (RBYB)
KAKE	Wichita, KS [*Television station call letters*]
KAKJ	Marianna, AR [*FM radio station call letters*]
KAKM	Anchorage, AK [*Television station call letters*]
kakm	Kakemono (VRA)
KAKN	Naknek, AK [*FM radio station call letters*]
KAKO	Gooding, ID [*FM radio station call letters*] (RBYB)
KAKP	Bagdad, AZ [*FM radio station call letters*] (RBYB)
KAKQ	Fairbanks, AK [*FM radio station call letters*]
KAKQ-FM	Fairbanks, AK [*FM radio station call letters*]
KAKR	Akron [*Ohio*] [*ICAO location identifier*] (ICLI)
KAKR-FM	Sterling City, TX [*FM radio station call letters*] (RBYB)
KAKT-FM	Phoenix, OR [*FM radio station call letters*] (RBYB)
KAKU-FM	Springfield, MO [*FM radio station call letters*] (RBYB)
KAKV-FM	Lompoc, CA [*FM radio station call letters*] (RBYB)
KAKW	Kileen, TX [*TV station call letters*] (RBYB)
KAKX	Mendocino, CA [*FM radio station call letters*] (RBYB)
KAKZ	Juneau, AK [*AM radio station call letters*] (RBYB)
KAL	Caltech Data Ltd. [*Vancouver Stock Exchange symbol*]
KAL	Kalamazoo [*Diocesan abbreviation*] [*Michigan*] (TOCD)
KAL	Kalamein [*Trademark*]
KAL	Kalendae [*The Kalends*] [*First day of the ancient Roman month*]
KAL	Kalium [*Potassium*] [*Pharmacy*]
Kal	Kallah (BJA)
KAL	Kallmann [*Syndrome*] [*Medicine*] (DMAA)
KAL	Kalocsa [*Hungary*] [*Seismograph station code, US Geological Survey Closed*] (SEIS)
KAL	Kaltag [*Alaska*] [*Airport symbol*] (OAG)
KAL	Kappa Application Language [*Artificial intelligence system*] [*IntelliCorp*] (PCM)
KAL	Keywords and Learning (AIE)
KAL	Korean Air Lines Co. Ltd. [*ICAO designator*] (FAAC)
KAL	Korean Air Lines, Inc.
KALA	Davenport, IA [*FM radio station call letters*]
KALB	Albany/Albany [*New York*] [*ICAO location identifier*] (ICLI)
KALB-TV	Alexandria, LA [*Television station call letters*]
KALC	Denver, CO [*FM radio station call letters*]
KALC	Krypton Absorption in Liquid Carbon Dioxide [*Nuclear energy*] (NRCH)

KALD	Kalamein [Trademark] Door
KALDAS	Kidsgrove ALGOL [Algorithmic Language] Digital Analogue Simulation [Computer science British]
KALE	Richland, WA [AM radio station call letters]
KALF	Red Bluff, CA [FM radio station call letters]
KALG	Chadron, NE [FM radio station call letters] (RBYB)
KALI	Alice/International [Texas] [ICAO location identifier] (ICLI)
KALI	San Gabriel, CA [AM radio station call letters]
KALI-FM	Santa Ana, CA [FM radio station call letters] (RBYB)
KALK	Winfield, TX [FM radio station call letters]
KALL	Salt Lake City, UT [AM radio station call letters]
KALM	Thayer, MO [AM radio station call letters]
KALN	Iola, KS [AM radio station call letters]
KALO	Port Arthur, TX [AM radio station call letters]
KALP	Alpine, TX [FM radio station call letters]
KAL PPT	Kali Praeparatum [Prepared Kali] [Carbonate of potash] [Pharmacy] (ROG)
KALQ	Alamosa, CO [FM radio station call letters]
KALR	Hot Springs, AR [FM radio station call letters]
KalR	Kallah Rabbati (BJA)
KALS	Kalispell, MT [FM radio station call letters]
KALT	Atlanta, TX [AM radio station call letters]
KALU	Langston, OK [FM radio station call letters]
KALV	Alva, OK [AM radio station call letters]
KALW	San Francisco, CA [FM radio station call letters]
KALX	Berkeley, CA [FM radio station call letters]
KALY	Los Ranchos de Albuquerque, NM [AM radio station call letters]
KAM	Benedictine College, South Campus, Atchison, KS [Library symbol Library of Congress] (LCLS)
KAM	Kamaran Island [South Arabia (Yemen)] [Airport symbol] (AD)
kam	Kamba [MARC language code Library of Congress] (LCCP)
Kam	Kames' Dictionary of Decisions, Scotch Court of Session [A publication] (DLA)
Kam	Kames' Remarkable Decisions, Scotch Court of Session [2 vols.] [1716-52] [A publication] (DLA)
KAM	Kameyama [Japan] [Seismograph station code, US Geological Survey] (SEIS)
KAM	Keep-Alive Memory [Computer science]
KAM	Kehillath Anshe Mayriv (BJA)
KAM	Kenya African Movement
KAM	Kinematic Analysis Method
KAM	Knudsen Absolute Manometer [Physics]
KAM	Kolmogorov-Arnold-Moser [Statistical mechanics]
KAMA	Amarillo/Amarillo Air Terminal [Texas] [ICAO location identifier] (ICLI)
KAMA	El Paso, TX [AM radio station call letters]
Kaman	Kaman Corp. [Associated Press] (SAG)
KAMB	Merced, CA [FM radio station call letters]
KAMC	Komatsu America Manufacturing Corp. [Chattanooga, TN]
KAMC	Lubbock, TX [Television station call letters]
KAMD	Camden, AR [AM radio station call letters]
KAMD-FM	Camden, AR [FM radio station call letters] (RBYB)
KAME	Reno, NV [Television station call letters]
Kam Eluc	Kames' Elucidation of the Laws of Scotland [A publication] (DLA)
Kam Eq	Kames' Principles of Equity [A publication] (DLA)
Kames	Kames' Dictionary of Decisions, Scotch Court of Session [A publication] (DLA)
Kames	Kames' Remarkable Decisions, Scotch Court of Session [2 vols.] [1716-52] [A publication] (DLA)
Kames Dec	Kames' Dictionary of Decisions, Scotch Court of Session [A publication] (DLA)
Kames Dict Dec	Kames' Dictionary of Decisions, Scotch Court of Session [A publication] (DLA)
Kames Elucid	Kames' Elucidation of the Laws of Scotland [A publication] (DLA)
Kames Eq	Kames' Principles of Equity [A publication] (DLA)
Kames Rem	Kames' Remarkable Decisions, Scotch Court of Session [2 vols.] [1716-52] [A publication] (DLA)
Kames Rem Dec	Kames' Remarkable Decisions [Scotland] [A publication] (DLA)
Kames Sel Dec	Kames' Select Decisions [Scotland] [A publication] (DLA)
KAMFES	Kentucky Association of Milk, Food, and Environmental Sanitarians (SRA)
KAMFT	Kansas Association of Marriage and Family Therapy (SRA)
KAMFT	Kentucky Association for Marriage and Family Therapy (SRA)
KAMG	Victoria, TX [AM radio station call letters]
KAMI	Cozad, NE [AM radio station call letters]
KAMI	Kasatuan Aksi Mahasiswa Indonesia [Political party] (BARN)
KAMI-FM	Cozad, NE [FM radio station call letters]
KAMJ	Gosnell, AR [FM radio station call letters] (RBYB)
KAMK-FM	Forest City, IA [FM radio station call letters] (RBYB)
KAML	Gillette, WY [FM radio station call letters]
KAML	Kenedy-Karnes City, TX [AM radio station call letters]
Kam L Tr	Kames' Historical Law Tracts [Scotland] [A publication] (DLA)
KAMM	Madison, SD [FM radio station call letters] (RBYB)
KAMN	Kaman Corp. [NASDAQ symbol] (NQ)
KAMNA	Kaman Corp. Cl'A' [NASDAQ symbol] (TTSB)
KAMNZ	Kaman Cp $3.25 Ser 2 Cv Dep Pfd [NASDAQ symbol] (TTSB)
KAMO	Rogers, AR [AM radio station call letters]
KAMO-FM	Rogers, AR [FM radio station call letters]
KAMP	El Centro, CA [AM radio station call letters]
KAMQ	Carlsbad, NM [AM radio station call letters]
KAMR	Amarillo, TX [Television station call letters]
Kam Rem	Kames' Remarkable Decisions, Scotch Court of Session [2 vols.] [1716-52] [A publication] (DLA)
KAMS	Korea Ammunition Management System (MCD)
KAMS	Mammoth Spring, AR [FM radio station call letters]
Kam Sel	Kames' Select Decisions [Scotland] [A publication] (DLA)

Kam Sel Dec	Kames' Select Decisions [Scotland] [A publication] (DLA)
KAMT	Juneau, AK [FM radio station call letters] (RBYB)
KAMU	College Station, TX [FM radio station call letters]
KAMU-TV	College Station, TX [Television station call letters]
KAMX	Luling, TX [FM radio station call letters] (RBYB)
KAMY	Lubbock, TX [FM radio station call letters]
KAN	Kanazawa [Japan] [Seismograph station code, US Geological Survey] (SEIS)
kan	Kannada [MARC language code Library of Congress] (LCCP)
KAN	Kano [Nigeria] [Airport symbol] (OAG)
KAN	Kansas
Kan	Kansas (ODBW)
Kan	Kansas Supreme Court Reports [A publication] (DLA)
Kan	Kantorei [Record label] [Germany]
KAN	Kriegsausruestungsnachweisung [Table of Basic Allowances] [German military - World War II]
Kan Admin Regs	Kansas Administration Regulations [A publication] (DLA)
Kan Ann	Vernon's Kansas Statutes, Annotated [A publication] (DLA)
Kan App	Kansas Appeals Reports [A publication] (DLA)
Kanb	Kaneb Services, Inc. [Associated Press] (SAG)
Kan City L Rep	Kansas City Law Reporter [A publication] (DLA)
Kan City L Rev	Kansas City Law Review [A publication] (DLA)
Kan Civ Pro Stat Ann	Vernon's Kansas Statutes, Annotated, Code of Civil Procedure [A publication] (DLA)
Kan Civ Pro Stat Ann (Vernon)	Vernon's Kansas Statutes, Annotated, Code of Civil Procedure [A publication] (DLA)
Kan CL & IWC	Kansas Commission of Labor and Industry Workmen's Compensation Department Reports [A publication] (DLA)
Kan CL Rep	Kansas City Law Reporter [A publication] (DLA)
Kan Crim Code & Code of Crim Proc	Criminal Code and Code of Criminal Procedure [Kansas] [A publication] (DLA)
Kan Crim Code & Code of Crim Proc (Vernon)	Vernon's Kansas Statutes, Annotated, Criminal Code and Code of Criminal Procedure [A publication] (DLA)
Kan Ct App	Kansas Appellate Reports [A publication] (DLA)
KAND	Corsicana, TX [AM radio station call letters]
K & B	Kotze and Barber's Transvaal (High Court) Reports [1885-88] [A publication] (DLA)
K & B Dig	Kerford and Box's Victorian Digest [A publication] (DLA)
K & CL	Kensington and Chelsea Law Group [British]
K & D	Kitchen and Dining Room [Real estate terminology]
K & E Conv	Key and Elphinstone's Conveyancing [15th ed.] [1953-54] [A publication] (DLA)
K & F NSW	Knox and Fitzhardinge's New South Wales Reports [A publication] (DLA)
K & G	Keane and Grant's English Registration Appeal Cases [1854-62] [A publication] (DLA)
K & G	Kerbing and Guttering [British] (ADA)
K & Gr	Keane and Grant's English Registration Appeal Cases [1854-62] [A publication] (DLA)
K & GRC	Keane and Grant's English Registration Appeal Cases [1854-62] [A publication] (DLA)
KANDIDATS	Kansas Digital Data System
Kan Dig	Hatcher's Kansas Digest [A publication] (DLA)
K & J	Kay and Johnson's English Vice-Chancellors' Reports [69, 70 English Reprint] [A publication] (DLA)
K & J	Kenrick & Jefferson (DGA)
K & O	Knapp and Ombler's English Election Cases [A publication] (DLA)
K & R	Kent and Radcliff's Law of New York, Revision of 1801 [A publication] (DLA)
K and R	Kidnaping and Ransom [Insurance policy]
K & W	Kames and Woodhouselee's Folio Dictionary, Scotch Court of Session [A publication] (DLA)
K & W Dic	Kames and Woodhouselee's Folio Dictionary, Scotch Court of Session [A publication] (DLA)
K & Z	Kipp and Zonen Recorders
KANE	New Iberia, LA [AM radio station call letters]
Kaneb	Kaneb Services, Inc. [Associated Press] (SAG)
KANGA	Kangaroo (DSUE)
KANG-FM	Carrington, ND [FM radio station call letters] (RBYB)
KANI	Wharton, TX [AM radio station call letters]
KANJ-FM	Giddings, TX [FM radio station call letters] (RBYB)
KankakB	Kankakkee Bancorp, Inc. [Associated Press] (SAG)
KANL	Elko, NV [Television station call letters] (RBYB)
Kan Law	Kansas Lawyer [A publication] (DLA)
Kan LJ	Kansas Law Journal [A publication] (DLA)
KANM	Winnemucca, NV [Television station call letters] (RBYB)
KANN	Roy, UT [AM radio station call letters]
KANP	St. Charles, MN [FM radio station call letters] (RBYB)
KanPip	Kaneb Pipe Line Partners Ltd. [Associated Press] (SAG)
KanPipSn	Kaneb Pipe Line Partners LP [Associated Press] (SAG)
KANQ	Grand Marais, MN [FM radio station call letters] (RBYB)
KANR	Belle Plaine, KS [FM radio station call letters]
KANr	Kanamycin Resistant [Genetics]
KANS	Kansas (AFM)
Kans	Kansas (ODBW)
Kans	Kansas Reports [A publication] (DLA)
KANS	Larned, KS [AM radio station call letters]
KANS	Osage City, KS [FM radio station call letters] (RBYB)
Kans App	Kansas Appeals Reports [A publication] (DLA)
Kansas LJ	Kansas Law Journal [A publication] (DLA)
Kansas R	Kansas Reports [A publication] (DLA)
Kans BA	Kansas City Bar Journal [A publication] (DLA)
Kan SCC	Kansas State Corporation Commission Reports [A publication] (DLA)
Kan Sess Laws	Session Laws of Kansas [A publication] (DLA)

Kans R......... Kansas Reports [*A publication*] (DLA)
Kans St U.... Kansas State University of Agriculture and Applied Science (GAGS)
Kan Stat...... Kansas Statutes [*A publication*] (DLA)
Kan Stat Ann... Kansas Statutes, Annotated [*A publication*] (DLA)
Kan Stat Ann... Kansas Statutes Annotated [*A publication*] (AAGC)
Kan St LJ..... Kansas State Law Journal [*A publication*] (DLA)
Kan Subject Ann Vernon's... Vernon's Kansas Statutes, Annotated [*A publication*] (DLA)
KANT........... Roseau, MN [*FM radio station call letters*] (RBYB)
KANU........... Kenya African National Union [*Political party*] (PPW)
KANU........... Lawrence, KS [*FM radio station call letters*]
Kan UCC Ann (Vernon)... Vernon's Kansas Statutes, Annotated, Uniform Commercial Code [*A publication*] (DLA)
Kan U Lawy... Kansas University Lawyer [*A publication*] (DLA)
Kan Univ Lawy... Kansas University Lawyer [*A publication*] (DLA)
KANW........... Albuquerque, NM [*FM radio station call letters*]
KANX-FM..... Pine Bluff, AR [*FM radio station call letters*] (RBYB)
KANZ........... Garden City, KS [*FM radio station call letters*]
KANZUS....... Korea, Australia, New Zealand, and the United States
kao.............. Kaolin (BARN)
KAO............. Kappa Alpha Order
KAO............. Kinesthetic Anharmonic Oscillator [*Facetious term for a swing*]
KAO............. Kirtland Area Office [*Department of Energy*]
KAO............. Kirtland Area Office (DOGT)
KAO............. Knee-Ankle Orthosis [*Medicine*] (DAVI)
KAO............. Knights of Aquarius Order (EAIO)
KAO............. Kuiper Airborne Observatory [*NASA*]
KAO............. Kuusamo [*Finland*] [*Airport symbol*] (OAG)
KAOA EXP STN... New Orleans, LA [*Radio expansion station*] (RBYB)
KAOB........... Devils Lake, ND [*FM radio station call letters*] (RBYB)
KAOC........... Cavalier, ND [*FM radio station call letters*] (RBYB)
KAOD........... Babbitt, MN [*FM radio station call letters*] (RBYB)
KAOE........... Hilo, HI [*FM radio station call letters*]
KAOG........... Jonesboro, AR [*FM radio station call letters*] (RBYB)
KAOH-FM..... Lompoc, CA [*FM radio station call letters*] (RBYB)
KAOI............ Kihei, HI [*AM radio station call letters*]
KAOI-FM...... Wailuku, HI [*FM radio station call letters*]
KAOK........... Lake Charles, LA [*AM radio station call letters*]
KAOL........... Carrollton, MO [*AM radio station call letters*]
KAOM........... Kansas Association of Osteopathic Medicine (SRA)
KAOR........... Vermillion, SD [*FM radio station call letters*]
KAOS........... Killer as an Organized Sport [*Campus game*]
KAOS........... Olympia, WA [*FM radio station call letters*]
KAOW-FM..... Fort Smith, AR [*FM radio station call letters*] (RBYB)
KAOX-FM..... Kemmerer, WY [*FM radio station call letters*] (RBYB)
KAOY........... Kealakekua, HI [*FM radio station call letters*]
KAP.............. CapMAC Holdings [*NYSE symbol*] (SAG)
KAP.............. CapMAC Holdings [*NYSE symbol*] (TTSB)
KAP.............. Hyannis Air Service, Inc. [*ICAO designator*] (FAAC)
KAP.............. Kaphearst Resources [*Vancouver Stock Exchange symbol*]
KAP.............. Kids Against Pollution
KAP.............. Kinematical Analysis Program
KAP.............. Knowledge, Attitudes, and Practice [*Sociology*]
KAP.............. Kuwait Action Plan [*Advisory Committee on Pollution of the Sea*]
KAPA........... Kaneohe, HI [*TV station call letters*] (RBYB)
KAPA........... Potassium Aminopropylamide [*Organic chemistry*]
KAPB........... Marksville, LA [*AM radio station call letters*]
KAPB-FM..... Marksville, LA [*FM radio station call letters*]
KAPC-FM..... Butte, MT [*FM radio station call letters*] (RBYB)
KAPCS......... Kansas Association of Private Career Schools (SRA)
KAPE............ Cape Girardeau, MO [*AM radio station call letters*]
KAPE............ Kansas Association of Public Employees (SRA)
KAPE............ Keeping the Army in the Public Eye [*British military*] (DMA)
KAPF-FM..... Taos, NM [*FM radio station call letters*] (RBYB)
KAPI............. Kasatuan Aksi Peladjar Indonesia [*Political party*] (BARN)
KAPI-FM...... Ruston, LA [*FM radio station call letters*] (RBYB)
KAPK-FM..... Grants Pass, OR [*FM radio station call letters*] (RBYB)
KAPL............ Kennedy Approved Parts List [*NASA*] (KSC)
KAPL............ Knolls Atomic Power Laboratory [*Schenectady, NY*] [*Department of Energy*]
KAPL............ Phoenix, OR [*AM radio station call letters*] (RBYB)
KAPM-FM.... Alexandria, LA [*FM radio station call letters*] (RBYB)
K-APN.......... KSC [*Kennedy Space Center*] Automated Payloads Notice [*NASA*] (NASA)
KAPN........... Salt Lake City, UT [*AM radio station call letters*]
KAPO........... Kameradschaftpolizei (BJA)
KAPP........... Key Asset Protection Plan [*National Guard*] (INF)
KAPP........... Knolls Atomic Power Plant
KAPP........... Yakima, WA [*Television station call letters*]
K-APPS........ KSC [*Kennedy Space Center*] Automated Payloads Project Specification [*NASA*] (NASA)
KAPR........... Douglas, AZ [*AM radio station call letters*]
KAPS........... Kawasaki Automatic Power-Drive System [*Kawasaki Motors Corp.*]
KAPS........... Kuopio Atherosclerosis Prevention Study
KAPS........... Mount Vernon, WA [*AM radio station call letters*]
KAPSE......... Kernel APSE [*ADA Program Support Environment*] [*Computer science*]
KapsnSn...... Kapson Senior Quarters Corp. [*Associated Press*] (SAG)
KAPU-FM..... Amarillo, TX [*FM radio station call letters*] (RBYB)
KAPV-FM..... Elma, WA [*FM radio station call letters*] (RBYB)
KAPY........... Port Angeles, WA [*AM radio station call letters*]
KAPZ........... Bald Knob, AR [*AM radio station call letters*]
KAQA-FM..... Kilauea, HI [*FM radio station call letters*] (RBYB)
KAQD-FM..... Abilene, TX [*FM radio station call letters*] (RBYB)
KAQE-FM..... St. Martinville, LA [*FM radio station call letters*] (RBYB)
KAQF-FM..... Clovis, NM [*FM radio station call letters*] (RBYB)
KAQQ........... Spokane, WA [*AM radio station call letters*]
KAQR-FM..... Helena, MT [*FM radio station call letters*] (RBYB)
KAQS........... Shawnee, OK [*TV station call letters*] (RBYB)
KAQU........... Huntington, TX [*FM radio station call letters*]
KAQX-FM..... Bonanza, OR [*FM radio station call letters*] (RBYB)
Kar.............. Indian Law Reports, Karachi Series [*A publication*] (DLA)
KAR............. Kamarang [*Guyana*] [*Airport symbol*] (OAG)
KAR............. Kansas Administrative Regulations [*A publication*]
KAR............. Kap Resources [*Vancouver Stock Exchange symbol*]
KAR............. Karabiner [*Carbine*] [*German military - World War II*]
KAR............. Karachi [*Pakistan*] [*Seismograph station code, US Geological Survey*] (SEIS)
KAR............. Kar-Air OY [*Finland ICAO designator*] (FAAC)
kar.............. Karen [*MARC language code Library of Congress*] (LCCP)
Kar.............. Karolus de Tocco [*Flourished, 13th century*] [*Authority cited in pre-1607 legal work*] (DSA)
KAR............. Kars [*Turkey*] [*Airport symbol*] (AD)
KAR............. Keilschrifttexte aus Assur Religioesen Inhalts [*A publication*] (BJA)
KAR............. Kentucky Administrative Regulations [*A publication*] (AAGC)
KAR............. King's African Rifles [*Military unit*] [*British*]
KAR............. Knot Area Ratio (PDAA)
KAR............. Kodak Automated Retrieval [*Kodak*] [*Microfilm office information system*] (NITA)
Kar.............. Pakistan Law Reports, Karachi Series [*A publication*] (DLA)
KARA........... Santa Clara, CA [*FM radio station call letters*]
KARAC......... Kustoms and Rodders Association of Canada
KARB........... Price, UT [*FM radio station call letters*]
KARD........... West Monroe, LA [*Television station call letters*]
KARE........... Koala Corp. [*NASDAQ symbol*] (SAG)
KARE........... Minneapolis, MN [*Television station call letters*]
KARF........... Washington [*District of Columbia*] [*ICAO location identifier*] (ICLI)
KARI............ Blaine, WA [*AM radio station call letters*]
KARI............ Keilschrifttexte aus Assur Religioesen Inhalts [*A publication*] (BJA)
KARI............ Ketol-Acid Reductoisomerase [*An enzyme*]
KARK........... Little Rock, AR [*Television station call letters*]
KARL........... Karlsruhe Architectural Language [*Computer science*] (CSR)
KARL........... Tracy, MN [*FM radio station call letters*]
KARM........... Visalia, CA [*FM radio station call letters*]
KARN........... Humnoke, AR [*FM radio station call letters*] (RBYB)
KARN........... Little Rock, AR [*AM radio station call letters*]
KARO........... Caldwell, ID [*FM radio station call letters*] (RBYB)
KARP........... Glencoe, MN [*FM radio station call letters*]
KARPEN....... Karyawan Pegawai Negeri [*Indonesia*]
KARQ........... Ashdown, AR [*FM radio station call letters*]
KARR........... Karrington Health, Inc. [*NASDAQ symbol*] (SAG)
KARR........... Kirkland, WA [*AM radio station call letters*]
KarrHlth....... Karrington Health, Inc. [*Associated Press*] (SAG)
KARS........... Belen, NM [*AM radio station call letters*]
KARS........... Kansas Applied Remote Sensing Program [*University of Kansas*] [*Research center*] (RCD)
KARS........... Kennedy Athletic Recreation and Social [*NASA*] (KSC)
KART........... Jerome, ID [*AM radio station call letters*]
KART........... Watertown/International [*New York*] [*ICAO location identifier*] (ICLI)
KARV........... Russellville, AR [*AM radio station call letters*]
KARW........... Longview, TX [*AM radio station call letters*]
KARX........... Claude, TX [*FM radio station call letters*]
KARY........... Grandview, WA [*FM radio station call letters*]
KARY........... Prosser, WA [*AM radio station call letters*]
KARZ........... Burney, CA [*FM radio station call letters*]
KAS.............. Benedictine College, North Campus, Atchison, KS [*Library symbol Library of Congress*] (LCLS)
KAS.............. Kansas [*Obsolete*] (ROG)
Kas.............. Kansas Reports [*A publication*] (DLA)
kas.............. Kashmiri [*MARC language code Library of Congress*] (LCCP)
KAS.............. Kaskada Resources Ltd. [*Vancouver Stock Exchange symbol*]
KAS.............. Kasler Holdings [*NYSE symbol*] (SPSG)
KAS.............. Kastamonu [*Turkey*] [*Seismograph station code, US Geological Survey*] (SEIS)
KAS.............. Katz Adjustment Scales [*Psychology*]
KAS.............. Kenya-Australia Society
KAS.............. Ketoacyl-ACP Synthase [*An enzyme*]
KAS.............. Kingston Air Services [*Canada ICAO designator*] (FAAC)
KAS.............. Knowledge Access System [*Interface*]
KAS.............. Knowledge Acquisition System
KAS.............. Konrad Adenauer Stiftung [*Germany Political party*]
KAS.............. Kroeber Anthropological Society (EA)
KAS.............. Kulanka Afka Somalyed
KASA........... Kentucky Association of School Administrators (SRA)
KASA........... Phoenix, AZ [*AM radio station call letters*]
KASA........... Santa Fe, NM [*Television station call letters*]
KASB........... Bellevue, WA [*FM radio station call letters*]
KASB........... Kansas Association of School Boards (SRA)
KASC........... Knowledge Availability Systems Center [*University of Pittsburgh*]
KASE........... Austin, TX [*FM radio station call letters*]
KASF........... Alamosa, CO [*FM radio station call letters*]
KASH........... Anchorage, AK [*FM radio station call letters*]
Kash............ Kashmir (VRA)
KASH........... Kash n'Karry Food Stores [*NASDAQ symbol*] (TTSB)
KASH........... Kash n Karry Food Stores, Inc. [*NASDAQ symbol*] (SAG)
KASH........... Knowledge, Attitude, Skills, Habits [*Formula*] [*LIMRA*]
Kashmir LJ... Kashmir Law Journal [*India*] [*A publication*] (DLA)
KashrK........ Kash n Karry Food Stores, Inc. [*Associated Press*] (SAG)
KASI............ Ames, IA [*AM radio station call letters*]

KASI............ Kesatuan Aksi Sardjana Indonesia [*Action Front of Indonesian Scholars*]
KASL............ Kansas Association of School Librarians (SRA)
KASL............ Newcastle, WY [*AM radio station call letters*]
Kasler Holding Co.... Kasler Corp. [*Associated Press*] (SAG)
KASM........... Albany, MN [*AM radio station call letters*]
KASM-FM .... Albany, MN [*FM radio station call letters*]
KASN........... Pine Bluff, AR [*Television station call letters*]
KASO........... Minden, LA [*AM radio station call letters*]
KASO-FM..... Minden, LA [*FM radio station call letters*]
KASP .... Kehr-Activated Sludge Process (PDAA)
Kas R........... Kansas Reports [*A publication*] (DLA)
KASR........... Perry, OK [*AM radio station call letters*]
KASR-FM..... Perry, OK [*FM radio station call letters*]
KASS .... Casper, WY [*FM radio station call letters*] (RBYB)
Kass............ Kassinin [*Biochemistry*]
KASS .... Kent Automated Serials System [*Kent State University*] [*Automated library system*] (NITA)
KASSP .... Kentucky Association of Secondary School Principals (SRA)
KAST........... Astoria, OR [*AM radio station call letters*]
KAST........... Kalman Automatic Sequential TMA [*Military*] (CAAL)
KAST........... Kindergarten Auditory Screening Test [*Otorhinolaryngology*] (DAVI)
KAST-FM .... Astoria, OR [*FM radio station call letters*]
KASU........... Jonesboro, AR [*FM radio station call letters*]
KASW .... Phoenix, AZ [*Television station call letters*]
KASY .... Albuquerque, NM [*FM radio station call letters*]
KASY-TV ..... Albuquerque, NM [*Television station call letters*]
KAT............. Asbury Theological Seminary, Wilmore, KY [*OCLC symbol*] (OCLC)
KAT............. Die Keilinschriften und das Alte Testament [*A publication*] (BJA)
KAT............. Kaitaia [*New Zealand*] [*Airport symbol*] (OAG)
KAT............. Kanamycin Acetyltransferase [*An enzyme*]
KAT............. Kappa Alpha Theta [*Sorority*]
kat .... Katal [*Unit of enzyme activity*]
KAT............. Kattegat Air, AS [*Denmark ICAO designator*] (FAAC)
KAT............. Key-to-Address Transformation [*Computer science*] (PDAA)
KAT............. Kizyl-Arvat [*Former USSR Seismograph station code, US Geological Survey*] (SEIS)
KAT............. Kommentar zum Alten Testament [*A publication*] (BJA)
KATA........... Arcata, CA [*AM radio station call letters*]
KATB........... Anchorage, AK [*FM radio station call letters*]
KATC........... Katz Digital Technologies [*NASDAQ symbol*] (TTSB)
KATC........... Katz Digital Technologies, Inc. [*NASDAQ symbol*] (SAG)
KATC........... Korean Army Training Center
KATC........... Lafayette, LA [*Television station call letters*]
KATCA .... Korean-American Technical Cooperation Association
Katch Pr Law... Katchenovsky's Prize Law [*2nd ed.*] [*1867*] [*A publication*] (DLA)
KATD........... Pittsburg, CA [*AM radio station call letters*]
KATE........... Albert Lea, MN [*AM radio station call letters*]
KatechBR..... Katechetische Blaetter [*Berlin-Grunewald*] [*A publication*] (BJA)
KATF........... Dubuque, IA [*FM radio station call letters*]
KATH .... Bozeman, MT [*FM radio station call letters*]
KathM.......... Die Katholischen Missionen (BJA)
KATI .... California, MO [*FM radio station call letters*] (RBYB)
KATJ........... George, CA [*FM radio station call letters*]
KATK........... Carlsbad, NM [*AM radio station call letters*]
KATK-FM .... Carlsbad, NM [*FM radio station call letters*]
KATL........... Atlanta/The William B. Hartsfield Atlanta International [*Georgia*] [*ICAO location identifier*] (ICLI)
KATL........... Miles City, MT [*AM radio station call letters*]
KATM.......... Katmai National Monument
KATM.......... Modesto, CA [*FM radio station call letters*]
KATN .... Fairbanks, AK [*Television station call letters*]
KATO .... Safford, AZ [*AM radio station call letters*]
KATP........... Amarillo, TX [*FM radio station call letters*]
KATQ.......... Plentywood, MT [*AM radio station call letters*]
KATQ-FM..... Plentywood, MT [*FM radio station call letters*]
KATR .... Wray, CO [*FM radio station call letters*]
KATS........... Kennedy Space Center Avionics Test Set [*NASA*] (NASA)
KATS........... Yakima, WA [*FM radio station call letters*]
KatShing..... Katorikku Shingaku [*Catholic Theology*] [*Tokyo*] [*A publication*] (BJA)
KATSI......... Kommentar zum Alten Testament [*E. Sellin*] [*A publication*] (BJA)
KATT........... Oklahoma City, OK [*FM radio station call letters*]
KATU........... Portland, OR [*Television station call letters*]
KATUSA...... Korean Augmentation to the United States Army
KATV.......... Little Rock, AR [*Television station call letters*]
KATW.......... Lewiston, ID [*FM radio station call letters*]
KATY.......... Idyllwild, CA [*FM radio station call letters*]
KatyInd........ Katy Industries, Inc. [*Formerly, Missour-Kansas-Texas R.R. Co., with Wall Street slang name of "Kathy"*] [*Associated Press*] (SAG)
KATYP .... Kallitype (VRA)
KATZ.......... St. Louis, MO [*AM radio station call letters*]
KatzDig....... Katz Digital Technologies, Inc. [*Associated Press*] (SAG)
KatzM......... Katz Media Group, Inc. [*Associated Press*] (SAG)
kau............. Kanuri [*MARC language code Library of Congress*] (LCCP)
KAU .... Kaohsiung [*Takao*] [*Republic of China*] [*Seismograph station code, US Geological Survey*] (SEIS)
KAU .... Kauhava [*Finland*] [*Airport symbol*] (AD)
KAU .... Kenya African Union [*1944*] [*Political party*] (PPW)
KAU .... Keystation Adapter Unit [*Computer science*]
KAU .... Kilo Accounting Units (NASA)
KAU .... King-Armstrong Unit [*Clinical chemistry*]
KaufBH .... Kaufman & Broad Home Corp. [*Associated Press*] (SAG)
KaufHW ...... Kaufman [*H. W.*] Financial Group [*Associated Press*] (SAG)
Kauf Mack ... Kaufmann's Edition of Mackeldey's Civil Law [*A publication*] (DLA)

Kaufm Mackeld Civ Law... Kaufmann's Edition of Mackeldey's Civil Law [*A publication*] (DLA)
KAUG .... Augusta [*Maine*] [*ICAO location identifier*] (ICLI)
KAUI .... Kekaha, HI [*FM radio station call letters*]
KAUM .... Colorado City, TX [*FM radio station call letters*]
KAUR .... Sioux Falls, SD [*FM radio station call letters*]
KAUS .... Austin, MN [*AM radio station call letters*]
KAUS .... Austin/Robert Mueller Municipal [*Texas*] [*ICAO location identifier*] (ICLI)
KAUS-FM..... Austin, MN [*FM radio station call letters*]
KAUZ .... Wichita Falls, TX [*Television station call letters*]
KAV............ Cambourne Resources [*Vancouver Stock Exchange symbol*]
KAV............ Kavieng [*New Ireland*] [*Seismograph station code, US Geological Survey Closed*] (SEIS)
KAV............ Keilschrifttexte aus Assur Verschiedenen Inhalts [*A publication*] (BJA)
KAVA .... Burney, CA [*AM radio station call letters*]
KAVC .... Rosamond, CA [*FM radio station call letters*]
KAVE .... Oakridge, OR [*FM radio station call letters*]
KAVI .... Keilschrifttexte aus Assur Verschiedenen Inhalts [*A publication*] (BJA)
KAVL .... Lancaster, CA [*AM radio station call letters*]
KAVS .... Mojave, CA [*FM radio station call letters*]
KAVU .... Victoria, TX [*Television station call letters*]
KAVV .... Benson, AZ [*FM radio station call letters*]
KAW........... Kawthaung [*Myanmar*] [*Airport symbol*] (OAG)
KAWA .... Floydada, TX [*AM radio station call letters*]
KAWAD .... Karnataka Watersheds Development
KAWB .... Brainerd, MN [*Television station call letters*]
KAWC .... Yuma, AZ [*AM radio station call letters*]
KAWC-FM.... Yuma, AZ [*FM radio station call letters*]
KAWE .... Bemidji, MN [*Television station call letters*]
KAWJ.......... Korrespondenzblatt des Vereins zur Gruendung und Erhaltung der Akademie fuer dieWissenschaft des Judentums [*A publication*] (BJA)
KAWK-FM.... Custer, SD [*FM radio station call letters*] (RBYB)
KAWL .... York, NE [*AM radio station call letters*]
KAWN .... Carswell [*Texas*] [*ICAO location identifier*] (ICLI)
KAWOL .... Knowledge, Absent Without Leave [*Army*] (ADDR)
KAWS .... Hemphill, TX [*AM radio station call letters*]
KAWW .... Heber Springs, AR [*AM radio station call letters*]
KAWW-FM.... Heber Springs, AR [*FM radio station call letters*]
KAWZ .... Twin Falls, ID [*FM radio station call letters*]
KAX............ Kalbarri [*Australia Airport symbol*] (OAG)
KAXE .... Grand Rapids, MN [*FM radio station call letters*]
KAXL .... Green Acres, CA [*FM radio station call letters*]
KAXT .... Hollister, CA [*AM radio station call letters*] (RBYB)
KAXX .... Ventura, CA [*FM radio station call letters*]
KAY............ Katlanovo [*Yugoslavia*] [*Seismograph station code, US Geological Survey*] (SEIS)
Kay............ Kay's English Vice-Chancellors' Reports [*69 English Reprint*] [*A publication*] (DLA)
KAY............ Wakaya [*Fiji*] [*Airport symbol Obsolete*] (OAG)
Kay & J ...... Kay and Johnson's English Vice-Chancellors' Reports [*69, 70 English Reprint*] [*A publication*] (DLA)
Kay & J (Eng)... Kay and Johnson's English Vice-Chancellors' Reports [*69, 70 English Reprint*] [*A publication*] (DLA)
Kay & John... Kay and Johnson's English Vice-Chancellors' Reports [*69, 70 English Reprint*] [*A publication*] (DLA)
Kay & Johns... Kay and Johnson's English Vice-Chancellors' Reports [*69, 70 English Reprint*] [*A publication*] (DLA)
KAYD .... Beaumont, TX [*AM radio station call letters*] (RBYB)
KAYD-FM ..... Beaumont, TX [*FM radio station call letters*]
Kaydon .... Kaydon Corp. [*Associated Press*] (SAG)
KAYE........... Kaye Group [*NASDAQ symbol*] (TTSB)
KAYE........... Kaye Group, Inc. [*NASDAQ symbol*] (SAG)
KAYE........... Tonkawa, OK [*FM radio station call letters*]
KayeGrp...... Kaye Group, Inc. [*Associated Press*] (SAG)
KayeK......... Kaye Kotts Associates, Inc. [*Associated Press*] (SAG)
Kay (Eng).... Kay's English Vice-Chancellors' Reports [*69 English Reprint*] [*A publication*] (DLA)
KAYL .... Storm Lake, IA [*AM radio station call letters*]
KAYL-FM ..... Storm Lake, IA [*FM radio station call letters*]
KAYO-FM ..... Aberdeen, WA [*FM radio station call letters*]
KAYQ .... Warsaw, MO [*FM radio station call letters*]
KAYR .... Van Buren, AR [*AM radio station call letters*]
KAYS .... Hays, KS [*AM radio station call letters*]
KAYSEE...... Kansas City [*Missouri*] [*Slang*]
Kay Ship..... Kay. Shipmasters, and Seamen [*2nd ed.*] [*1894*] [*A publication*] (DLA)
KAYU .... Spokane, WA [*Television station call letters*]
KAYX .... Richmond, MO [*FM radio station call letters*]
KAZ............ Karuizawa [*Also, KRZ*] [*Japan*] [*Seismograph station code, US Geological Survey*] (SEIS)
kaz............ Kazakh [*MARC language code Library of Congress*] (LCCP)
KAZA .... Gilroy, CA [*AM radio station call letters*]
KAZAIR .... Kazakhstan Airlines [*ICAO designator*] (FAAC)
KAZI........... Austin, TX [*FM radio station call letters*]
KAZL .... Castle Rock, WA [*FM radio station call letters*]
KAZM .... Sedona, AZ [*AM radio station call letters*]
KAZN .... Pasadena, CA [*AM radio station call letters*]
KAZQ .... Albuquerque, NM [*Television station call letters*]
KAZR-FM ..... Pella, IA [*FM radio station call letters*] (RBYB)
KazSSR ...... Kazakh Soviet Socialist Republic
KAZU .... Pacific Grove, CA [*FM radio station call letters*]
KAZY-FM ..... Winfield, KS [*FM radio station call letters*] (RBYB)
KAZZ .... Deer Park, WA [*FM radio station call letters*]

KB	Bermuda [*IYRU nationality code*] (IYR)	
KB	Burnthills [*ICAO designator*] (AD)	
KB	English Law Reports, King's Bench Division [*1901-52*] [*A publication*] (DLA)	
KB	Kashin-Bek Disease [*Medicine*] (DMAA)	
KB	Kaufman & Broad, Inc. (MHDW)	
KB	Kauri-Butanol Value [*Measure of relative solvent power*]	
KB	Keel Bending (SSD)	
KB	Keilinschriftliche Bibliothek [*Berlin*] [*A publication*] (BJA)	
KB	Kelly Bushing [*Drilling*] (DICI)	
KB	Ketone Bodies [*Clinical chemistry*]	
KB	Keyboard [*Computer science*]	
KB	Kickback (MHDB)	
kb	Kilobar	
kb	Kilobase	
KB	Kilobaud (IAA)	
kb	KiloBIT [*Binary Digit*] [*Computer science*]	
KB	Kilo BTU [*British Thermal Unit*]	
KB	Kilobyte [*10^3 bytes*] [*Computer science*]	
Kb	Kilobyte (NFD)	
KB	Kincheng Banking Corp. [*Hong Kong*]	
KB	King's Bench [*of law courts*] [*British*]	
KB	King's Bishop [*Chess*]	
KB	Kitchen and Bathroom	
KB	Kitchen Biddy [*Female kitchen worker*] [*Restaurant slang*]	
KB	Kite Balloon [*Air Force*]	
K-B	Kleihauer-Betke [*Stain*] [*Medicine*] (MEDA)	
KB	Knee Bearing [*Prosthesis*]	
KB	Knee Brace [*Technical drawings*]	
KB	Knight Bachelor [*or Knight Companion*] of the Order of the Bath [*British*]	
Kb	Knit into Back [*of Stitch*] [*Knitting*] (BARN)	
Kb	Knit into Back of Stitch [*Knitting*] (BARN)	
KB	Knowledgeability Brief (MCD)	
KB	Knowledge Base [*Computer science*] (IAA)	
KB	Knuckle-Bender Splint [*Orthopedics*] (DAVI)	
KB	Komercni Bank [*Czech Republic Bank*]	
KB	Komercni Banka AS [*Czech Republic*] [*Banking*]	
KB	Kommanditbolaget [*Limited Partnership*] [*German*] (ILCA)	
KB	Koninklijk Besluit [*Royal Decree*] [*Dutch*] (ILCA)	
KB	Kontrabass [*Double Bass*] [*Music*]	
KB	Korpus Bezpieczenstwa (BJA)	
KB	Korrespondenz-Blatt des Verbandes der Deutschen Juden [*A publication*] (BJA)	
KB	Kulturbund	
KB	Kunstgeschichte in Bildern [*A publication*] (OCD)	
KBA	Barbados [*IYRU nationality code*] (IYR)	
KBA	Beni Abbes [*Algeria*] [*Airport symbol*] (AD)	
KBA	Kabala [*Sierra Leone*] [*Airport symbol*] (OAG)	
KBA	Kansas Bankers Association (SRA)	
KBA	Kansas Bar Association (SRA)	
KBA	Kenn Borek Air Ltd. [*Canada ICAO designator*] (FAAC)	
KBA	Kentucky Bar Association (SRA)	
KBA	Kentucky Broadcasters Association (SRA)	
KBA	Ketobutyraldehyde Dimethyl Acetal [*Biochemistry*]	
KBA	Keyboard Assembly (DWSG)	
KBA	Killed by Action [*In reference to the enemy*] [*Vietnam*] (VNW)	
KBA	Killed by Air [*Military*]	
KBA	Killed by Artillery [*In reference to the enemy*] [*Vietnam*] (VNW)	
KBA	Kleinwort Benson Aus [*NYSE symbol*] (TTSB)	
KBA	Kleinwort Benson Australian Income Fund, Inc. [*NYSE symbol*] (SPSG)	
KBA	Knight of St. Benedict of Avis	
KBAB	Marysville/Beale Air Force Base [*California*] [*ICAO location identifier*] (ICLI)	
KBAC	Kennedy Booster Assembly Contractor (MCD)	
KBAC	Las Vegas, NM [*FM radio station call letters*]	
KBAD	Shreveport/Barksdale Air Force Base [*Louisiana*] [*ICAO location identifier*] (ICLI)	
KBAE	Llano, TX [*FM radio station call letters*] (RBYB)	
KBAI	Morro Bay, CA [*AM radio station call letters*]	
KBAK	Bakersfield, CA [*Television station call letters*]	
KBAL	Kimball International, Inc. [*NASDAQ symbol*] (NQ)	
KBAL	Kleine Beitraege zum Assyrischen Lexikon [*A publication*]	
KBAL	San Saba, TX [*AM radio station call letters*]	
KBALB	Kimball Intl CI'B' [*NASDAQ symbol*] (TTSB)	
KBAL-FM	San Saba, TX [*FM radio station call letters*] (RBYB)	
K-BALL	Cannibalize (MCD)	
KBAM	Longview, WA [*AM radio station call letters*]	
KBAQ	Phoenix, AZ [*FM radio station call letters*]	
KBAR	Burley, ID [*AM radio station call letters*]	
KBAR	Kilobar	
KBART	Kings Bay Army Terminal	
KBAS	Bullhead City, AZ [*AM radio station call letters*]	
KBAT	Midland, TX [*FM radio station call letters*]	
KBAU	Big Sandy, TX [*FM radio station call letters*] (RBYB)	
KBAust	Kleinwort Benson Australian Income Fund, Inc. [*Associated Press*] (SAG)	
KBAX	Fallbrook, CA [*FM radio station call letters*]	
KBAY	San Jose, CA [*FM radio station call letters*]	
KBB	Baker University, Baldwin City, KS [*Library symbol Library of Congress*] (LCLS)	
KBB	Bear Stearns Companies, Inc. [*AMEX symbol*] (SAG)	
KBB	Bear Stearns Cos.'CUBS''98 [*AMEX symbol*] (TTSB)	
KBB	King's Bad Bargain [*Undesirable serviceman*] [*Slang British*] (DSUE)	

KBB	Kitchens, Bedrooms, and Bathrooms Equipment Exhibition [*British*] (ITD)	
KBBA	Abilene, TX [*AM radio station call letters*]	
KBBB-FM	Billings, MT [*FM radio station call letters*] (RBYB)	
KBBC	Lake Havasu City, AZ [*FM radio station call letters*]	
KBBE	McPherson, KS [*FM radio station call letters*]	
KBBF	Santa Rosa, CA [*FM radio station call letters*]	
KBBG	Waterloo, IA [*FM radio station call letters*]	
KBBI	Homer, AK [*AM radio station call letters*]	
KBBK	Rupert, ID [*AM radio station call letters*]	
KBBL	Cabot, AR [*AM radio station call letters*]	
KBBL-FM	Cabot, AR [*FM radio station call letters*]	
KBBN	Broken Bow, NE [*FM radio station call letters*]	
KBBO	Yakima, WA [*AM radio station call letters*]	
KBBQ	Fort Smith, AR [*FM radio station call letters*]	
KBBR	North Bend, OR [*AM radio station call letters*]	
KBBS	Buffalo, WY [*AM radio station call letters*]	
KBBT	Portland, OR [*AM radio station call letters*]	
KBBV	Big Bear Lake, CA [*AM radio station call letters*]	
KBBW	Waco, TX [*AM radio station call letters*]	
KBBX	Omaha, NE [*AM radio station call letters*]	
KBBY-FM	Ventura, CA [*FM radio station call letters*]	
KBBZ	Kalispell, MT [*FM radio station call letters*]	
KBC	Bellarmine College, Louisville, KY [*OCLC symbol*] (OCLC)	
KBC	Birch Creek [*Alaska*] [*Airport symbol*] (OAG)	
KBC	K-Band Circulator	
KBC	King's Bench Court [*British*]	
KBC	Kiowa Business Committee [*An association*]	
KBCA	Keystone Bituminous Coal Association	
KBCB	Bellingham, WA [*Television station call letters*]	
KBCD	Newport Beach, CA [*FM radio station call letters*]	
KBCE	Boyce, LA [*FM radio station call letters*]	
KBCH	Kings Beach, CA [*FM radio station call letters*] (RBYB)	
KBCH	Lincoln City, OR [*AM radio station call letters*]	
KBCI	Boise, ID [*Television station call letters*]	
KBCK	Diamondville, WY [*FM radio station call letters*]	
KBCL	Shreveport, LA [*AM radio station call letters*]	
KBCN	Marshall, AR [*FM radio station call letters*]	
KBCO	Boulder, CO [*AM radio station call letters*]	
KBCO-FM	Boulder, CO [*FM radio station call letters*]	
KBCQ	Roswell, NM [*AM radio station call letters*]	
KBCR	Steamboat Springs, CO [*AM radio station call letters*]	
KBCR-FM	Steamboat Springs, CO [*FM radio station call letters*] (RBYB)	
KBCS	Bellevue, WA [*FM radio station call letters*]	
KBCT	Boca Raton [*Florida*] [*ICAO location identifier*] (ICLI)	
KBCT-FM	Waco, TX [*FM radio station call letters*] (RBYB)	
KBCU	North Newton, KS [*FM radio station call letters*]	
KBCY	Tye, TX [*FM radio station call letters*]	
KBD	Kaschin-Beck Disease [*Medicine*]	
KBD	Keyboard	
KBD	King's Bench Division [*of law courts*] [*British*] (ROG)	
KBD	Thousand Barrels per Day [*Also, TBD*]	
KBDC	King's Bench Divisional Court [*British*]	
KBDE	Baudette [*Minnesota*] [*ICAO location identifier*] (ICLI)	
KBDG	Turlock, CA [*FM radio station call letters*]	
KBDI	Broomfield, CO [*Television station call letters*]	
KB Div'l Ct	King's Bench Divisional Court [*England*] (DLA)	
KBDL	Windsor Locks/Bradley International [*Connecticut*] [*ICAO location identifier*] (ICLI)	
KBDN	Bandon, OR [*FM radio station call letters*] (RBYB)	
KBDR	Mirando City, TX [*FM radio station call letters*]	
KBDZ	Perryville, MO [*FM radio station call letters*]	
KBE	Bell Island, AK [*Location identifier FAA*] (FAAL)	
KBE	Berea College, Berea, KY [*OCLC symbol*] (OCLC)	
KBE	Keyboard Encoder [*Computer science*]	
KBE	Keyboard Entry [*Computer science*]	
KBE	Key British Enterprises [*Dun & Bradstreet Ltd.*] [*Information service or system*] (IID)	
KBE	Knight Commander of the [*Order of the*] British Empire	
KBE	Knight of the Black Eagle [*Russia*] [*Obsolete*]	
KBE	Knowledge-Based Engineering [*Expert systems*] [*Computer-aided design*]	
KBEC	Waxahachie, TX [*AM radio station call letters*]	
KBED	Bedford/Laurence G. Hanscom Field [*Massachusetts*] [*ICAO location identifier*] (ICLI)	
KBEE	Modesto, CA [*AM radio station call letters*]	
KBEE	Salt Lake City, UT [*FM radio station call letters*] (RBYB)	
KBEH	Bellevue, WA [*Television station call letters*]	
KBEK	Mora, MN [*FM radio station call letters*]	
KBEL	Idabel, OK [*AM radio station call letters*]	
KBEL-FM	Idabel, OK [*FM radio station call letters*]	
KBEM	Minneapolis, MN [*FM radio station call letters*]	
KBEN	Carrizo Springs, TX [*AM radio station call letters*]	
KBENC	Keyboard Encoder (NITA)	
KB (Eng)	English Law Reports, King's Bench Division [*1901-52*] [*A publication*] (DLA)	
KBEQ	Blue Springs, MO [*AM radio station call letters*]	
KBEQ	Kansas City, MO [*FM radio station call letters*]	
KBER	Ogden, UT [*FM radio station call letters*]	
KBES	Ceres, CA [*FM radio station call letters*]	
KBES	Knowledge-Based Expert System	
KBET	Canyon Country, CA [*AM radio station call letters*]	
KBEW	Blue Earth, MN [*AM radio station call letters*]	
KBEW-FM	Blue Earth, MN [*FM radio station call letters*]	
KBEZ	Tulsa, OK [*FM radio station call letters*]	

KBF............. K-Band Feed

KBF............. Kyburz Flat [*California*] [*Seismograph station code, US Geological Survey*] (SEIS)

KBFC........... Forrest City, AR [*FM radio station call letters*]

KBFC........... Karen Brooks Fan Club (EA)

KBFC........... Kippe Brannon Fan Club [*Defunct*] (EA)

KBFD .... Honolulu, HI [*Television station call letters*]

KBFI............ Bonners Ferry, ID [*AM radio station call letters*]

KBFI............ Seattle Boeing Field/King Country International [*Washington*] [*ICAO location identifier*] (ICLI)

KBFL........... Bakersfield/Meadows Field [*California*] [*ICAO location identifier*] (ICLI)

KBFL........... Buffalo, MO [*FM radio station call letters*]

KBFM........... Edinburg, TX [*FM radio station call letters*]

KBFM........... Mobile/Aerospace [*Alabama*] [*ICAO location identifier*] (ICLI)

KBFS........... Belle Fourche, SD [*AM radio station call letters*]

KBFW........... Bellingham-Ferndale, WA [*AM radio station call letters*]

KBFX........... Anchorage, AK [*FM radio station call letters*]

KBGA-FM..... Missoula, MT [*FM radio station call letters*] (RBYB)

KBGE .... Bellevue, WA [*Television station call letters*] (RBYB)

KBGG........... San Francisco, CA [*FM radio station call letters*] (RBYB)

KBGH........... Filer, ID [*Television station call letters*]

KBGN........... Caldwell, ID [*AM radio station call letters*]

KBGO-FM..... Las Vegas, TX [*FM radio station call letters*] (RBYB)

KBGR .... Bangor/International [*Maine*] [*ICAO location identifier*] (ICLI)

KBGS .... Big Spring/Webb Air Force Base [*Texas*] [*ICAO location identifier*] (ICLI)

KBH .... Kaufman & Broad Home [*NYSE symbol*] (TTSB)

KBH .... Kaufman & Broad Home Corp. [*NYSE symbol*] (SPSG)

KBH .... Killed by Helicopter [*In reference to the enemy*] [*Vietnam*]

KBHB........... Sturgis, SD [*AM radio station call letters*]

KBHC........... Nashville, AR [*AM radio station call letters*]

KBHE .... Rapid City, SD [*FM radio station call letters*]

KBHE-TV ..... Rapid City, SD [*Television station call letters*]

KBHK .... San Francisco, CA [*Television station call letters*]

KBHL .... Osakis, MN [*FM radio station call letters*]

KBHM .... Birmingham [*Alabama*] [*ICAO location identifier*] (ICLI)

KBHP .... Bemidji, MN [*FM radio station call letters*]

KBHR .... Big Bear City, CA [*FM radio station call letters*]

KBHS .... Hot Springs, AR [*AM radio station call letters*]

KBHT .... Crockett, TX [*FM radio station call letters*]

KBHU .... Spearfish, SD [*FM radio station call letters*]

KBHW .... International Falls, MN [*FM radio station call letters*]

KBHZ-FM ..... Willmar, MN [*FM radio station call letters*] (RBYB)

KBI............. Keyboard Immortals [*Recording label*]

KBI............. Key Buying Influence (WDMC)

KBI............. Kribi [*Cameroon*] [*Airport symbol*] (OAG)

KBIA........... Columbia, MO [*FM radio station call letters*]

KBIA........... Kent Barlow Information Associates [*British*] (NITA)

KBIB........... Marion, TX [*AM radio station call letters*]

KBIC........... Raymondville, TX [*FM radio station call letters*] (RBYB)

KBID........... Bakersfield, CA [*AM radio station call letters*]

KBIF........... El Paso/Biggs Air Force Base [*Texas*] [*ICAO location identifier*] (ICLI)

KBIF........... Fresno, CA [*AM radio station call letters*]

KBIG .... Los Angeles, CA [*FM radio station call letters*]

KBIL .... Breckenridge, TX [*AM radio station call letters*]

KBIM........... Keyboard Interface Module (MCD)

KBIM........... Roswell, NM [*AM radio station call letters*]

KBIM-FM ..... Roswell, NM [*FM radio station call letters*]

KBIM-TV ..... Roswell, NM [*Television station call letters*]

KBIN .... Council Bluffs, IA [*Television station call letters*]

KBIQ .... Fountain, CO [*FM radio station call letters*]

KBIQ-FM...... Manitou Springs, CO [*FM radio station call letters*] (RBYB)

KBIS .... Kitchen and Bath Industry Show West (ITD)

KBIT/S .... KiloBITS [*Binary Digits*] per Second [*Transmission rate*] [*Computer science*] (TEL)

KBIU .... Lake Charles, LA [*FM radio station call letters*]

KBIX........... Biloxi/Keesler Air Force Base [*Mississippi*] [*ICAO location identifier*] (ICLI)

KBIX........... Muskogee, OK [*AM radio station call letters*]

KBIZ........... Ottumwa, IA [*AM radio station call letters*]

KBJ............. Kentucky State Bar Journal [*A publication*] (DLA)

KBJJ........... Marshall, MN [*FM radio station call letters*]

KBJM........... Lemmon, SD [*AM radio station call letters*]

KBJR........... Superior, WI [*Television station call letters*]

KBJS........... Jacksonville, TX [*FM radio station call letters*]

KBJT........... Fordyce, AR [*AM radio station call letters*]

KBK............. KBK Capital [*AMEX symbol*] (TTSB)

KBK............. KBK Capital Corp. [*AMEX symbol*] (SAG)

KBK............. Kirkjubaejar [*Iceland*] [*Airport symbol*] (AD)

KBKB .... Fort Madison, IA [*AM radio station call letters*]

KBKB-FM ..... Fort Madison, IA [*FM radio station call letters*]

KBKC .... KBK Capital Corp. [*NASDAQ symbol*] (SAG)

KBK Cap ..... KBK Capital Corp. [*Associated Press*] (SAG)

KBKG .... Corning, AR [*FM radio station call letters*]

KBKK .... Spanish Fork, UT [*FM radio station call letters*] (RBYB)

KBKL .... Grand Junction, CO [*AM radio station call letters*]

KBKO .... Billings, MT [*FM radio station call letters*] (RBYB)

KBKR .... Baker City, OR [*AM radio station call letters*]

KBKS-FM ..... Tacoma, WA [*FM radio station call letters*] (RBYB)

KBKW .... Aberdeen, WA [*AM radio station call letters*] (RBYB)

KBL............. Hebraeisches und Aramaeisches Lexikon zum Alten Testament [*L. Koehler and W. Baumgarther*] [*A publication*] (BJA)

KBL............. Kabul [*Afghanistan*] [*Airport symbol*] (OAG)

KBL............. Kabul [*Afghanistan*] [*Seismograph station code, US Geological Survey*] (SEIS)

KBL............. Keyboard Listener [*Computer science*] (MHDI)

KBL............. Kilusan ng Bangong Lipunan [*New Society Movement*] [*Philippines*] (PD)

KBL............. Kraft Black Liquor [*Pulping technology*]

KBL............. Kredietbank Luxembourgeoise [*Luxembourg*]

KBL............. Lexicon in Veteris Testamenti Libros. Supplementum [*L. Koehler and W. Baumgartner*] [*A publication*] (BJA)

KBLA........... Santa Monica, CA [*AM radio station call letters*]

KBLE........... Seattle, WA [*AM radio station call letters*]

KBLF........... Red Bluff, CA [*AM radio station call letters*]

KBLG........... Billings, MT [*AM radio station call letters*]

KBLH .... Keel Blade Height [*Botany*]

KBLI........... Bellingham/International [*Washington*] [*ICAO location identifier*] (ICLI)

KBLJ........... La Junta, CO [*AM radio station call letters*]

KBLK........... Burnet, TX [*FM radio station call letters*]

KBLL........... Helena, MT [*AM radio station call letters*]

KBLL........... Keel Blade Length [*Botany*]

KBLL-FM ..... Helena, MT [*FM radio station call letters*]

KBLP........... Lindsay, OK [*FM radio station call letters*]

KBLPS .... Knowledge-Based Logistics Planning Shell

KBLQ........... Logan, UT [*FM radio station call letters*]

KBLR........... Paradise, NV [*Television station call letters*]

KBLS........... North Fort Riley, KS [*FM radio station call letters*]

KBLU........... Yuma, AZ [*AM radio station call letters*]

KBLV........... Bellerville/Scott Air Force Base [*Illinois*] [*ICAO location identifier*] (ICLI)

KBLV........... Bellevue, WA [*AM radio station call letters*]

KBLX........... Berkeley, CA [*AM radio station call letters*] (RBYB)

KBLZ........... Kaneohe, HI [*FM radio station call letters*]

KBM........... Kabwum [*Papua New Guinea*] [*Airport symbol*] (OAG)

KBM........... Karissimo Bene Merenti [*To the Most Dear and Well-Deserving*] [*Correspondence*]

KBM........... Keyboard Monitor [*Computer science*]

KBM........... Knowledge Base Machine [*Computer science*]

KBMA........... Bryan, TX [*FM radio station call letters*]

KBMC........... Bozeman, MT [*FM radio station call letters*]

KBME........... Bismarck, ND [*Television station call letters*]

KBMG........... Hamilton, MT [*FM radio station call letters*]

KBMI........... Roma, TX [*FM radio station call letters*]

KBMJ........... Hardin, MT [*FM radio station call letters*]

KBMR........... Bismarck, ND [*AM radio station call letters*]

KBMS........... Knowledge Based Management System

KBMS........... Knowledge Base Management System [*Computer science*]

KBMS........... Vancouver, WA [*AM radio station call letters*]

KBMT........... Beaumont, TX [*Television station call letters*]

KBMT........... Knowledge-Based Machine Translation [*Computer science*]

KBMV........... Birch Tree, MO [*AM radio station call letters*]

KBMV-FM .... Birch Tree, MO [*FM radio station call letters*]

KBMW........... Breckenridge, MN [*AM radio station call letters*]

KBMX........... Eldon, MO [*AM radio station call letters*]

KBMY........... Bismarck, ND [*Television station call letters*]

KBN............. Kill Bad Name [*Marketing*] (WDMC)

KBNA........... El Paso, TX [*AM radio station call letters*]

KBNA........... Nashville/Metropolitan [*Tennessee*] [*ICAO location identifier*] (ICLI)

KBNA-FM .... El Paso, TX [*FM radio station call letters*]

KBNB-AM .... Gilmer, TX [*AM radio station call letters*] (RBYB)

KBND........... Bend, OR [*AM radio station call letters*]

KBNJ........... Corpus Christi, TX [*FM radio station call letters*]

KBNL........... Laredo, TX [*FM radio station call letters*]

KBNO........... Denver, CO [*AM radio station call letters*]

KBNP........... Portland, OR [*AM radio station call letters*]

KBNR........... Brownsville, TX [*FM radio station call letters*]

KBNU-FM .... Uvalde, TX [*FM radio station call letters*] (RBYB)

KBO........... Kabalo [*Zaire*] [*Airport symbol*] (AD)

KBO........... Keep Buggering On [*Perseverance*] [*Slang British*] (DSUE)

KBo........... Keilschrifttexte aus Boghazkoi [*A publication*] (BJA)

KBO........... Kite and Balloon Officer [*Navy*]

KBO........... Kommunistischer Bund Oesterreichs [*Communist League of Austria*] [*Political party*] (PPW)

KBO........... Kuiper Belt Objects [*Planetary science*]

KBO........... Organization for the Management and Development of the Kagera River Basin (EA)

KBOA........... Kennett, MO [*AM radio station call letters*]

KBOA........... Piggott, AR [*FM radio station call letters*] (RBYB)

KBOB........... Muscatine, IA [*FM radio station call letters*]

KBOC........... Bridgeport, TX [*FM radio station call letters*]

KBOE........... Oskaloosa, IA [*AM radio station call letters*]

KBOE-FM ..... Oskaloosa, IA [*FM radio station call letters*]

KBOF........... Washington/Bolling Air Force Base [*District of Columbia*] [*ICAO location identifier*] (ICLI)

KBOI........... Boise/Boise Air Terminal [*Idaho*] [*ICAO location identifier*] (ICLI)

KBOI........... Boise, ID [*AM radio station call letters*]

KBOK........... Malvern, AR [*AM radio station call letters*]

KBOK-FM ..... Malvern, AR [*FM radio station call letters*]

KBOM........... Los Alamos, NM [*FM radio station call letters*]

KBOO........... Portland, OR [*FM radio station call letters*]

KBOP........... Pleasanton, TX [*AM radio station call letters*]

KBOQ........... Carmel, CA [*FM radio station call letters*] (RBYB)

KBOR........... Brownsville, TX [*AM radio station call letters*]

KBOS........... Boston/Logan International [*Massachusetts*] [*ICAO location identifier*] (ICLI)

KBOS........... Tulare, CA [*FM radio station call letters*]

KBOT........... Kansas City Board of Trade

KBOT .... Pelican Rapids, MN [*FM radio station call letters*]
KBOV .... Bishop, CA [*AM radio station call letters*]
KBOW .... Butte, MT [*AM radio station call letters*]
KBOX .... Lompoc, CA [*FM radio station call letters*]
KBOY .... Medford, OR [*FM radio station call letters*]
KBOZ .... Bozeman, MT [*AM radio station call letters*]
KBP .... Kainate-Binding Protein [*Biochemistry*]
KBP .... Kappa Beta Pi [*Society*]
KBP .... Kent-Barlow Publications Ltd. [*Information service or system*] (IID)
KBP .... Keyboard Process [*Computer science*]
KBP .... Kiev Borispol Airport [*Former USSR Airport symbol*] (OAG)
kbp .... Kilobase Pairs [*Genetics*]
KBP .... King's Bishop's Pawn [*Chess*] (IIA)
KBP .... Kite Balloon Pilot
KBP .... Koala Bear Park [*Adelaide*] [*Airport symbol*] (AD)
KBPA .... Knowledge-Based Programming Assistant (PDAA)
KBPAP .... Kidney Bean Purple Acid Phosphatase [*An enzyme*]
KBPI .... Denver, CO [*FM radio station call letters*]
KBPK .... Buena Park, CA [*FM radio station call letters*]
KBPL .... Communist League Proletarian Left [*Netherlands Political party*] (PPW)
KBPR .... Brainerd, MN [*FM radio station call letters*]
KBPRC .... Keyboard and Printer Controller [*Computer science*] (NITA)
kbps .... KiloBITS [*Binary Digits*] per Second [*Transmission rate*] [*Computer science*]
Kbps .... Kilobits per Second [*Computer science*]
KBPS .... Kilobytes Per Second (NITA)
Kbps .... Kilobytes per Second [*Computer science*] (DOM)
KBPS .... Portland, OR [*AM radio station call letters*]
KBPS-FM .... Portland, OR [*FM radio station call letters*]
KBPT .... Beaumont Port-Arthur/Jefferson County [*Texas*] [*ICAO location identifier*] (ICLI)
KBQQ .... Minot, ND [*FM radio station call letters*]
KBR .... Kaaba Resources [*Vancouver Stock Exchange symbol*]
KBR .... Kota Bharu [*Malaysia*] [*Airport symbol*] (OAG)
KBr .... Potassium Bromide [*An anticonvulsant and sedative*] (DAVI)
KBRB .... Ainsworth, NE [*AM radio station call letters*]
KBRB-FM .... Ainsworth, NE [*FM radio station call letters*]
KBRC .... Mount Vernon, WA [*AM radio station call letters*]
KBRD .... Lacey, WA [*AM radio station call letters*] (RBYB)
KBRE .... Cedar City, UT [*AM radio station call letters*]
KBRE-FM .... Cedar City, UT [*FM radio station call letters*]
KBRF .... Fergus Falls, MN [*AM radio station call letters*]
KBRG .... Fremont, CA [*FM radio station call letters*]
KBRH .... Baton Rouge, LA [*AM radio station call letters*]
KBRI .... Brinkley, AR [*AM radio station call letters*]
KBRJ .... Anchorage, AK [*FM radio station call letters*]
KBRK .... Brookings, SD [*AM radio station call letters*]
KBRK-FM .... Brookings, SD [*FM radio station call letters*]
KBRL .... McCook, NE [*AM radio station call letters*]
KBRN .... Boerne, TX [*AM radio station call letters*]
KBRO .... Bremerton, WA [*AM radio station call letters*]
KBRO .... Brownsville/International [*Texas*] [*ICAO location identifier*] (ICLI)
KBRQ .... Hillsboro, TX [*FM radio station call letters*]
KBRR .... Thief River Falls, MN [*Television station call letters*]
KBRS .... Springdale, AR [*FM radio station call letters*]
KBRT .... Avalon, CA [*AM radio station call letters*]
KBRU .... Fort Morgan, CO [*FM radio station call letters*]
KBRV .... Soda Springs, ID [*AM radio station call letters*]
KBRW .... Barrow, AK [*AM radio station call letters*]
KBRW-FM .... Barrow, AK [*FM radio station call letters*] (RBYB)
KBRX .... O'Neill, NE [*AM radio station call letters*]
KBRX-FM .... O'Neill, NE [*FM radio station call letters*]
KBRZ .... Freeport, TX [*AM radio station call letters*]
KBS .... Bo [*Sierra Leone*] [*Airport symbol Obsolete*] (OAG)
KBS .... Gamair Ltd. [*Gambia*] [*ICAO designator*] (FAAC)
kbs .... Kellogg Biological Station [*Michigan State University*]
kbs .... KiloBITS [*Binary Digits*] per Second [*Transmission rate*] [*Computer science*]
KBS .... Kilobytes per Second [*Computer science*]
KBS .... Kinematic Bombing System
KBS .... Kingsbay [*Spitsbergen*] [*Seismograph station code, US Geological Survey*] (SEIS)
KBS .... Kluver-Bucy Syndrome [*Psychiatry*] (DAVI)
KBS .... Knight of the Blessed Sacrament
KBS .... Knowledge-Based System [*Computer model*] [*Computer science*]
KBS .... Korean Broadcasting System [*South Korea*] (FEA)
KBS .... Stites, McElwain & Fowler, Bellarmine College Library, Louisville, KY [*OCLC symbol*] (OCLC)
KBSA .... El Dorado, AR [*FM radio station call letters*]
KBSA .... Kassian Benevolent Society in America (EA)
KBSA .... Knowledge-Based Software Assistant [*Computer science*]
KBSB .... Bemidji, MN [*FM radio station call letters*]
KBSC .... Knowledge-Based Systems Centre [*Polytechnic of the South Bank*] [*British*] (CB)
KBSD .... Ensign, KS [*Television station call letters*]
KBSF .... Springhill, LA [*AM radio station call letters*]
KBSG .... Auburn, WA [*AM radio station call letters*]
KBSG .... Tacoma, WA [*FM radio station call letters*]
KBSH .... Hays, KS [*Television station call letters*]
KBSI .... Cape Girardeau, MO [*Television station call letters*]
KBSL .... Goodland, KS [*Television station call letters*]
KBSM .... Austin/Bergstrom Air Force Base [*Texas*] [*ICAO location identifier*] (ICLI)
KBSM .... McCall, ID [*FM radio station call letters*]

KBSN .... Moses Lake, WA [*AM radio station call letters*]
KBSO .... Corpus Christi, TX [*FM radio station call letters*]
KBSP .... Salem, OR [*Television station call letters*]
KBSR .... Kankakee, Beaverville & Southern Railroad Co. [*AAR code*]
KBSR .... Laurel, MT [*AM radio station call letters*]
KBST .... Big Spring, TX [*AM radio station call letters*]
KBST-FM .... Big Spring, TX [*FM radio station call letters*]
KBSU .... Boise, ID [*AM radio station call letters*]
KBSU-FM .... Boise, ID [*FM radio station call letters*]
KBSV-TV .... Ceres, CA [*TV station call letters*] (RBYB)
KBSW .... Twin Falls, ID [*FM radio station call letters*]
KBSZ .... Wickenburg, AZ [*FM radio station call letters*] (RBYB)
KBTA .... Batesville, AR [*AM radio station call letters*]
KBTC .... Houston, MO [*AM radio station call letters*]
KBTC .... Tacoma, WA [*FM radio station call letters*]
KBTC-TV .... Tacoma, WA [*Television station call letters*]
KBTD .... Knee Board Training Device [*Military*] (MCD)
KBTG .... Keep Britain Tidy Group (DCTA)
KBTM .... Jonesboro, AR [*AM radio station call letters*]
KBTN .... Neosho, MO [*AM radio station call letters*]
KBTN-FM .... Neosho, MO [*FM radio station call letters*] (RBYB)
KBTO .... Bottineau, ND [*FM radio station call letters*]
KBTR .... Baton Rouge/Ryan Field [*Louisiana*] [*ICAO location identifier*] (ICLI)
KBTS .... Big Spring, TX [*FM radio station call letters*]
KBTT .... Bridgeport, TX [*FM radio station call letters*]
KBTU .... Kilo British Thermal Unit (WDAA)
KBTV .... Burlington/International [*Vermont*] [*ICAO location identifier*] (ICLI)
KBTX .... Bryan, TX [*Television station call letters*]
KBU .... Keyboard Unit [*Computer science*] (NASA)
KBU .... Knuckle Buster University [*Facetious term*]
KBU .... Kotabaru [*West Irian, Indonesia*] [*Airport symbol*] (AD)
KBUC .... Pleasanton, TX [*FM radio station call letters*]
KBUC .... Upper Canada King's Bench Reports [*A publication*] (DLA)
KBUE .... Long Beach, CA [*FM radio station call letters*] (RBYB)
KBUF .... Buffalo/Greater Buffalo International [*New York*] [*ICAO location identifier*] (ICLI)
KBUF .... Holcomb, KS [*AM radio station call letters*]
KBUG .... Osceola, MO [*FM radio station call letters*]
KBUK .... La Grange, TX [*FM radio station call letters*]
KBUL .... Carson City, NV [*FM radio station call letters*]
KBUN .... Bemidji, MN [*AM radio station call letters*]
KBUQ-FM .... Paradise Valley, AZ [*FM radio station call letters*] (RBYB)
KBUR .... Burbank/Hollywood-Burbank [*California*] [*ICAO location identifier*] (ICLI)
KBUR .... Burlington, IA [*AM radio station call letters*]
KBUS .... Paris, TX [*FM radio station call letters*]
KBUT .... Crested Butte, CO [*FM radio station call letters*]
KBUX .... Quartzsite, AZ [*FM radio station call letters*]
KBUY .... Ruidoso, NM [*AM radio station call letters*]
KBUY-FM .... Amarillo, TX [*FM radio station call letters*]
KBUZ .... Topeka, KS [*FM radio station call letters*]
KBV .... Kobold Resources Ltd. [*Vancouver Stock Exchange symbol*]
KBV .... Kustbevakningen [*Sweden ICAO designator*] (FAAC)
KBVA .... Bella Vista, AR [*FM radio station call letters*]
KBVI .... Boulder, CO [*AM radio station call letters*] (RBYB)
KBVM .... Portland, OR [*FM radio station call letters*]
KBVR .... Corvallis, OR [*FM radio station call letters*]
KBVU .... Eureka, CA [*Television station call letters*]
KBVV .... Enid, OK [*FM radio station call letters*]
KBW .... Kommunistischer Bund Westdeutschland [*Communist League of West Germany*] [*Political party*] (PPW)
KBWC .... Marshall, TX [*FM radio station call letters*]
KBWD .... Brownwood, TX [*AM radio station call letters*]
KBWI .... Baltimore/Baltimore-Washington International [*Maryland*] [*ICAO location identifier*] (ICLI)
KBWS .... Sisseton, SD [*FM radio station call letters*]
KBXB-FM .... Sikeston, MO [*FM radio station call letters*] (RBYB)
KBXL .... Caldwell, ID [*FM radio station call letters*]
KBXR .... Ashland, MO [*FM radio station call letters*]
KBXX .... Houston, TX [*FM radio station call letters*]
KBXY .... Baker, CA [*FM radio station call letters*]
KBY .... Streaky Bay [*Australia Airport symbol*] (OAG)
KBYB .... El Dorado, AR [*FM radio station call letters*]
KBYE .... Oklahoma City, OK [*AM radio station call letters*]
KBYG .... Big Spring, TX [*AM radio station call letters*]
KBYG .... Coahoma, TX [*FM radio station call letters*]
KBYH .... Blytheville Air Force Base [*Arkansas*] [*ICAO location identifier*] (ICLI)
KBYN .... Arnold, CA [*FM radio station call letters*]
KBYO .... Tallulah, LA [*AM radio station call letters*]
KBYO-FM .... Tallulah, LA [*FM radio station call letters*]
KBYR .... Anchorage, AK [*AM radio station call letters*]
KBYU .... Provo, UT [*FM radio station call letters*]
KBYU-TV .... Provo, UT [*Television station call letters*]
KBYZ .... Bismarck, ND [*FM radio station call letters*]
KBZE .... Berwick, LA [*FM radio station call letters*]
KBZN .... Ogden, UT [*FM radio station call letters*]
KBZO .... Lubbock, TX [*FM radio station call letters*] (RBYB)
KBZQ .... Lawton, OK [*FM radio station call letters*]
KBZR .... Coolidge, AZ [*FM radio station call letters*] (RBYB)
KBZS-AM .... Grand Junction, CO [*AM radio station call letters*] (RBYB)
KBZT .... San Diego, CA [*FM radio station call letters*]
KBZY .... Salem, OR [*AM radio station call letters*]
KBZZ .... La Junta, CO [*AM radio station call letters*]
KC .... Canada [*IYRU nationality code*] (IYR)
KC .... Cook Islands International [*ICAO designator*] (AD)

KC	[*The*] Kanawha Central Railway Co. [*AAR code*]
KC	Kansas City [*Missouri*] [*Slang*]
KC	Kansas City-St. Joseph [*Diocesan abbreviation*] [*Missouri*] (TOCD)
KC	Karman Constant [*Physics*]
KC	Kartell Convent Deutscher Studenten Juedischen Glaubens (BJA)
KC	Kathodal Closing [*Medicine*]
KC	Kennel Club
KC	Keratoconjunctivitis [*Ophthalmology*]
KC	Keratoconus [*Ophthalmology*] (DAVI)
KC	Keratoma Climacterium [*Dermatology*] (DAVI)
KC	Kerr Cell [*Optics*]
KC	Ketocyclazocine [*Biochemistry*]
KC	Keystone Center [*An association*] (EA)
kc	Kilocalorie
KC	Kilocharacter (BUR)
KC	Kilocurie (IAA)
kc	Kilocurie (IDOE)
kc	Kilocycle [*Radio*]
kc	Kilograms per Square Centimeter (DS)
KC	King's Colonials [*British military*] (DMA)
KC	King's Counsel [*British*]
KC	Kings County [*Sussex, New Brunswick*] (DAS)
KC	King's Cross [*British*] (ADA)
KC	Kiting Check [*Investment*] (MHDB)
KC	Knees to Chest [*Position*] [*Medicine*] (DAVI)
KC	Knight Club (EA)
KC	Knight Commander
KC	Knight of the Crescent [*Turkey*]
KC	Knights of Columbus
KC	Knuckle Cracking [*Orthopedics*] (DAVI)
Kc	Koruna [*Czech Coin*] (BARN)
Kc	Kupffer Cell [*Histology*]
KC	Kyle Classification [*Library science*]
KCA	Kansas Chiropractic Association (SRA)
KCA	Kansas Contractors Association (SRA)
KCA	Keeshond Club of America (EA)
KCA	Keesings Contemporary Archives [*A publication Also, an information service or system*]
KCA	Kentucky Callers Association (EA)
KCA	Kentucky Cattlemen's Association (SRA)
KCA	Kentucky Coal Association (SRA)
KCA	Kiowa-Comanche-Apache
KCA	Komondor Club of America (EA)
KCA	Kuvasz Club of America (EA)
KCAB	Dardanelle, AR [*AM radio station call letters*]
KCAC	Camden, AR [*FM radio station call letters*]
KCAD-FM	Dickinson, ND [*FM radio station call letters*] (RBYB)
KCAH	Watsonville, CA [*Television station call letters*]
KCAILUC	Kiowa-Comanche-Apache Intertribal Land Use Committee
kcal	Kilocalorie
KCAL	Redlands, CA [*AM radio station call letters*] (RBYB)
KCAL-FM	Redlands, CA [*FM radio station call letters*]
KCAL-TV	Los Angeles, CA [*Television station call letters*]
KCAM	Glennallen, AK [*AM radio station call letters*]
KCAN	Albion, NE [*Television station call letters*]
KCAO	Kansas City Area Office [*Energy Research and Development Administration*]
KCAP	Helena, MT [*AM radio station call letters*]
KCAQ	Oxnard, CA [*FM radio station call letters*]
KCAR	Caribou [*Maine*] [*ICAO location identifier*] (ICLI)
KCAR	Clarksville, TX [*AM radio station call letters*]
KCAS	Knots Calibrated Airspeed (MCD)
KCAT	Kemptville College of Agricultural Technology [*Canada*] (ARC)
KCAT	Pine Bluff, AR [*AM radio station call letters*]
KCAU	Sioux City, IA [*Television station call letters*]
KCAW	Sitka, AK [*FM radio station call letters*]
KCAY	Russell, KS [*AM radio station call letters*]
KCAZ	Mission, KS [*AM radio station call letters*] (RBYB)
KCB	Kansas City Ballet
KCB	Kartell Convent Blaetter (BJA)
KCB	Keyboard Change Button [*Computer science*]
KCB	Knight Commander of the [*Order of the*] Bath [*British*] (GPO)
KCBA	Salinas, CA [*Television station call letters*]
KCBC	Riverbank, CA [*AM radio station call letters*]
KCBD	Lubbock, TX [*Television station call letters*]
KCBF	Fairbanks, AK [*AM radio station call letters*]
KCBI	Dallas, TX [*FM radio station call letters*]
KCBM	Colombus Air Force Base [*Mississippi*] [*ICAO location identifier*] (ICLI)
KCBN	Reno, NV [*AM radio station call letters*]
KCBQ	San Diego, CA [*AM radio station call letters*]
KCBQ-FM	San Diego, CA [*FM radio station call letters*]
KCBR	Monument, CO [*AM radio station call letters*]
KCBS	Los Angeles, CA [*FM radio station call letters*]
KCBS	San Francisco, CA [*AM radio station call letters*]
KCBS-TV	Los Angeles, CA [*Television station call letters*]
KCBT	Board of Trade of Kansas City, MO (EA)
KCBX	San Luis Obispo, CA [*FM radio station call letters*]
KCBY	Coos Bay, OR [*Television station call letters*]
KCBZ	Cannon Beach, OR [*FM radio station call letters*] (RBYB)
KCC	Centre College of Kentucky, Danville, KY [*OCLC symbol*] (OCLC)
KCC	Coffman Cove, AK [*Location identifier FAA*] (FAAL)
KCC	Kansas City Connecting Railroad Co. [*AAR code*]
KCC	Kansas Co-Operative Council (SRA)
KCC	Kathodal Closure Contraction [*Medicine*]

KCC	Kentucky Chamber of Commerce (SRA)
KCC	Keokuk Community College [*Iowa*]
KCC	Keyboard Common Contact [*Computer science*]
KCC	Key Control Characteristic
KCC	K-III Communications [*NYSE symbol*] (TTSB)
KCC	K-III Communications Corp. [*NYSE symbol*] (SPSG)
KCC	Knapp Communications Corp.
KCC	Knife Collectors Club (EA)
KCC	Knight Commander of the [*Order of the*] Crown [*Belgium*]
KCC	Kona Coffee Council [*Defunct*] (EA)
KCC	Koplar Communications Center [*St. Louis, MO*] [*Telecommunications*] (TSSD)
KCCA	Colorado City, AZ [*FM radio station call letters*]
KCCB	Corning, AR [*AM radio station call letters*]
KCCC	Carlsbad, NM [*AM radio station call letters*]
KCCC	Key Chain Collectors Club (EA)
KCCD	Moorhead, MN [*FM radio station call letters*]
KCCF	Cave Creek, AZ [*AM radio station call letters*]
KCCH	Knight Commander of Court of Honor [*British*]
KCCI	Des Moines, IA [*Television station call letters*]
KCCI	Kansas Chamber of Commerce and Industry (SRA)
KCCK	Cedar Rapids, IA [*FM radio station call letters*]
KCCM	Kupffer Cell Conditioned Medium
KCCM	Moorhead, MN [*FM radio station call letters*]
KCCN	Honolulu, HI [*AM radio station call letters*]
KCCN	Monterey, CA [*Television station call letters*]
KCCN-FM	Honolulu, HI [*FM radio station call letters*]
KCCO	Alexandria, MN [*Television station call letters*]
KCCPr	K-III Commun$2.875SrExPfd [*NYSE symbol*] (TTSB)
KCCQ	Ames, IA [*FM radio station call letters*]
KCCR	Pierre, SD [*AM radio station call letters*]
KCCS	Salem, OR [*AM radio station call letters*]
KCCT	Corpus Christi, TX [*AM radio station call letters*]
KCCT	Kaolin Cephalin Clotting Time (PDAA)
KCCU	Lawton, OK [*FM radio station call letters*]
KCCV	Overland Park, KS [*AM radio station call letters*]
KCCV-FM	Olathe, KS [*FM radio station call letters*]
KCCW	Walker, MN [*Television station call letters*]
KCCY	Pueblo, CO [*FM radio station call letters*]
KCDA	Coeur D'Alene, ID [*FM radio station call letters*]
KCDC	Longmont, CO [*AM radio station call letters*]
KCDD	Hamlin, TX [*FM radio station call letters*]
KCDI	Oro Valley, AZ [*FM radio station call letters*]
KCDL	Cordell, OK [*FM radio station call letters*]
KCDQ	Monahans, TX [*FM radio station call letters*]
KCDR	Turlock, CA [*AM radio station call letters*] (RBYB)
KCDS	Angwin, CA [*FM radio station call letters*]
KCDS	Childress [*Texas*] [*ICAO location identifier*] (ICLI)
KCDT	Coeur D'Alene, ID [*Television station call letters*]
KCDU-FM	Hollister, CA [*FM radio station call letters*] (RBYB)
KCDV-FM	Cordova, KS [*FM radio station call letters*] (RBYB)
KCDX	San Carlos, AZ [*FM radio station call letters*]
KCDY	Carlsbad, NM [*FM radio station call letters*]
KCDZ	Twentynine Palms, CA [*FM radio station call letters*]
KCE	Collinsville [*Australia Airport symbol*] (OAG)
KCE	Key Configuration Element (DNAB)
KCEA	Atherton, CA [*FM radio station call letters*]
KCEC	Denver, CO [*Television station call letters*]
KCED	Centralia, WA [*FM radio station call letters*]
KCEE	Tucson, AZ [*AM radio station call letters*]
KCEF	Chicopee Falls/Westover Air Force Base [*Massachusetts*] [*ICAO location identifier*] (ICLI)
KCEN	Temple, TX [*Television station call letters*]
KCEO	Vista, CA [*AM radio station call letters*]
KCEP	Las Vegas, NV [*FM radio station call letters*]
KCER	Kananaskis Centre for Environmental Research [*University of Calgary*] [*Research center*] (RCD)
KCES	Eufaula, OK [*FM radio station call letters*]
KCET	Los Angeles, CA [*Television station call letters*]
KCEW	Crestview/Bob Sikes [*Florida*] [*ICAO location identifier*] (ICLI)
KCEY	Huntsville, TX [*AM radio station call letters*]
KCEZ	Corning, CA [*FM radio station call letters*]
KCF	Key-Click Filter
KCF	Key Clinical Finding [*Medicine*] (HCT)
KCF	Thousand Cubic Feet
KCFA	Amold, CA [*FM radio station call letters*]
KCFB	St. Cloud, MN [*FM radio station call letters*]
KCFC	Karen Carpenter Fan Club [*Defunct*] (EA)
KCFD	Bryan/Coulter Field [*Texas*] [*ICAO location identifier*] (ICLI)
KCFE	Eden Prairie, MN [*FM radio station call letters*]
KCFF	Korean Cultural and Freedom Foundation (EA)
KCFMC	Kevin Collins Foundation for Missing Children (EA)
KCFN	Wichita, KS [*FM radio station call letters*]
KCFO	Tulsa, OK [*FM radio station call letters*]
KCFP-FM	Pueblo, CO [*FM radio station call letters*] (RBYB)
KCFR	Denver, CO [*FM radio station call letters*]
KCFS	Sioux Falls, SD [*FM radio station call letters*]
KCFV	Ferguson, MO [*FM radio station call letters*]
KCFW	Kalispell, MT [*Television station call letters*]
KCFX	Harrisonville, MO [*FM radio station call letters*]
KCFY	Yuma, AZ [*FM radio station call letters*]
KCG	Chignik, AK [*Location identifier FAA*] (FAAL)
KCG	Key Calling [*Telecommunications*] (IAA)
KCG	Kinetocardiogram [*Cardiology*]
KCGB	Hood River, OR [*FM radio station call letters*]

KCGM .... Scobey, MT [*FM radio station call letters*]
KCGN .... Sioux Falls, SD [*AM radio station call letters*]
KCGN-FM ..... Ortonville, MN [*FM radio station call letters*]
KCGQ .... Cape Girardeau, MO [*AM radio station call letters*]
KCGQ-FM ..... Gordonville, MO [*FM radio station call letters*]
KCGR .... Cottage Grove, OR [*FM radio station call letters*]
KCGS .... Marshall, AR [*AM radio station call letters*]
KCGX .... Broken Bow, OK [*FM radio station call letters*] (RBYB)
KCGY .... Laramie, WY [*FM radio station call letters*]
KCH .... Ketch
kch .... Kilocharacter (MHDB)
KCH .... King's College Hospital
KCH .... Knight Commander of the Guelphic Order of Hanover [*British*]
KCH .... Kuching [*Malaysia*] [*Airport symbol*] (OAG)
KCHA .... Charles City, IA [*AM radio station call letters*]
KCHA .... Chattanooga/Lovell [*Tennessee*] [*ICAO location identifier*] (ICLI)
KCHA-FM ..... Charles City, IA [*FM radio station call letters*]
KCHC-FM ..... Conroe, TX [*FM radio station call letters*] (RBYB)
KCHD .... Chandler/Williams Air Force Base [*Arizona*] [*ICAO location identifier*] (ICLI)
KCHE .... Cherokee, IA [*AM radio station call letters*]
KCHE-FM ..... Cherokee, IA [*FM radio station call letters*]
KCHF .... Santa Fe, NM [*Television station call letters*]
KCHG .... Somerset, TX [*AM radio station call letters*]
KCHI .... Chicago/Metropolitan Area [*Illinois*] [*ICAO location identifier*] (ICLI)
KCHI .... Chillicothe, MO [*AM radio station call letters*]
KCHI-FM ..... Chillicothe, MO [*FM radio station call letters*]
KCHJ .... Delano, CA [*AM radio station call letters*]
KCHK .... New Prague, MN [*AM radio station call letters*]
KCHK-FM ..... New Prague, MN [*FM radio station call letters*]
KCHL .... San Antonio, TX [*AM radio station call letters*]
KCHO .... Chico, CA [*FM radio station call letters*]
KCHQ .... Altamont, OR [*FM radio station call letters*]
KCHR .... Charleston, MO [*AM radio station call letters*]
kchr .... Kilocharacter (MHDB)
KCHS .... Charleston/Municipal and Air Force Base [*South Carolina*] [*ICAO location identifier*] (ICLI)
KCHS .... Kilo Characters per Second (IAA)
KCHS .... Knight Commander of the Holy Sepulchre
KCHS .... Truth or Consequences, NM [*AM radio station call letters*]
KCHT .... Kechabta [*Tunisia*] [*Seismograph station code, US Geological Survey*] (SEIS)
KCHT-AM ..... Selah, WA [*AM radio station call letters*] (RBYB)
KCHU .... Valdez, AK [*AM radio station call letters*]
KCHX .... Midland, TX [*FM radio station call letters*]
KCHZ-FM ..... Ottawa, KS [*FM radio station call letters*] (RBYB)
KCI .... Key Club International (EA)
KCI .... Key Collectors International (EA)
kCi .... Kilocurie (DEN)
KCI .... Kit Collectors International (EA)
KCIA .... Medford, OR [*FM radio station call letters*]
KCIA .... South Korean Central Intelligence Agency [*Later, Agency for National Security Planning*] (PD)
KCIB .... Milan, NM [*AM radio station call letters*] (RBYB)
KCIC .... Grand Junction, CO [*FM radio station call letters*]
KCID .... Caldwell, ID [*AM radio station call letters*]
KCID-FM ..... Caldwell, ID [*FM radio station call letters*]
KCIE .... Dulce, NM [*FM radio station call letters*]
KCIE .... Knight Commander of the [*Order of the*] Indian Empire [*British*]
KCII .... Washington, IA [*AM radio station call letters*]
KCII-FM ..... Washington, IA [*FM radio station call letters*]
KCIJ .... North Fort Polk, LA [*FM radio station call letters*]
KCIL .... Houma, LA [*FM radio station call letters*]
KCIM .... Carroll, IA [*AM radio station call letters*]
KCIN .... Tacoma, WA [*FM radio station call letters*] (RBYB)
KCIO .... King's Commissioned Indian Officer [*British military*] (DMA)
KCIR .... Twin Falls, ID [*FM radio station call letters*]
KCIS .... Edmonds, WA [*AM radio station call letters*]
KCIT .... Amarillo, TX [*Television station call letters*]
KCIV .... Mount Bullion, CA [*FM radio station call letters*]
KCIX .... Garden City, ID [*FM radio station call letters*]
KCIY .... Liberty, MO [*FM radio station call letters*] (RBYB)
KCJB .... Minot, ND [*AM radio station call letters*]
KCJC .... Dardanelle, AR [*FM radio station call letters*] (RBYB)
KCJH .... Stockton, CA [*FM radio station call letters*]
KCJJ .... Iowa City, IA [*AM radio station call letters*]
KCJZ .... Terrell Hills, TX [*FM radio station call letters*] (RBYB)
KCK .... Kansas City, KS [*Location identifier FAA*] (FAAL)
KCKA .... Centralia, WA [*Television station call letters*]
KCKC .... San Bernardino, CA [*AM radio station call letters*]
KCKI .... Henryetta, OK [*FM radio station call letters*]
KCKL .... Malakoff, TX [*FM radio station call letters*]
KCKN .... Roswell, NM [*AM radio station call letters*]
KCKR .... Waco, TX [*FM radio station call letters*]
KCKS .... Concordia, KS [*FM radio station call letters*]
KCKX .... Stayton, OR [*AM radio station call letters*]
KCKY .... Coolidge, AZ [*AM radio station call letters*]
KCL .... Chignik, AK [*Location identifier FAA*] (FAAL)
KCL .... Keystation Control Language [*Computer science*] (MHDI)
KCL .... King's College, London
KCL .... Kirchhoff's Current Law [*Electronics*] (IAA)
KCL .... Kitchen, Company Level
KCL .... Klamath County Library, Klamath Falls, OR [*OCLC symbol*] (OCLC)
KCL .... Knitting Cylinder Lubrication (PDAA)
KCL .... Knudsen Cosine Law [*Physics*]
KCLA .... Pine Bluff, AR [*AM radio station call letters*]
KCLB .... Coachella, CA [*AM radio station call letters*]
KCLB-FM ..... Coachella, CA [*FM radio station call letters*]
KCLC .... Kinder-Care Learning Centers, Inc. [*NASDAQ symbol*] (SAG)
KCLC .... Kinder-Care Learning Ctrs [*NASDAQ symbol*] (TTSB)
KCLC .... St. Charles, MO [*FM radio station call letters*]
KCLCW .... Kinder-Care Lrng Ctr Wrrt [*NASDAQ symbol*] (TTSB)
KCLD .... St. Cloud, MN [*FM radio station call letters*]
KCLE .... Cleburne, TX [*AM radio station call letters*]
KCLE .... Cleveland/Cleveland-Hopkins International [*Ohio*] [*ICAO location identifier*] (ICLI)
KCLE .... Continuing Legal Education, University of Kentucky College of Law (DLA)
KCLE .... Glen Rose, TX [*FM radio station call letters*] (RBYB)
KCLI .... Clinton, OK [*FM radio station call letters*]
KCLI .... Kansas City Life Ins [*NASDAQ symbol*] (TTSB)
KCLI .... Kansas City Life Insurance Co. [*NASDAQ symbol*] (NQ)
KCLI-AM ..... Clinton, OK [*AM radio station call letters*] (RBYB)
KCLJ .... Knight Commander of the Order of St. Lazarus of Jerusalem (DD)
KCLK .... Asotin, WA [*AM radio station call letters*]
KCLK .... Clarkston, WA [*FM radio station call letters*]
KCLL .... College Station/Easterwood Field [*Texas*] [*ICAO location identifier*] (ICLI)
KCLL .... Lompoc, CA [*AM radio station call letters*]
KCLM .... Newport, OR [*FM radio station call letters*]
KCLN .... Clinton, IA [*FM radio station call letters*]
KCLO .... Rapid City, SD [*Television station call letters*]
KCLQ .... Lebanon, MO [*FM radio station call letters*]
KCLR .... Boonville, MO [*FM radio station call letters*]
KCLR .... Ralls, TX [*AM radio station call letters*]
KCLS .... Flagstaff, AZ [*AM radio station call letters*]
KCLS .... Kern County Library System [*Library network*]
KCLS .... Knight Commander of the Lion and the Sun
KCLT .... West Helena, AR [*FM radio station call letters*]
KCLU .... Korean Council of Organization [*South Korea*]
KCLU .... Thousand Oaks, CA [*FM radio station call letters*]
KCLV .... Clovis, NM [*AM radio station call letters*]
KCLV-FM ..... Clovis, NM [*FM radio station call letters*]
KCLW .... Hamilton, TX [*AM radio station call letters*]
KCLX .... Colfax, WA [*AM radio station call letters*]
KCLY .... Clay Center, KS [*FM radio station call letters*]
KCLY .... Kent and County of London Yeomanry [*Military unit*] [*British*]
KCM .... Kam Creed Mines Ltd. [*Vancouver Stock Exchange symbol Toronto Stock Exchange symbol*]
KCM .... Keratinocyte-Conditioned Medium [*Biochemistry*]
KCM .... Key Center for Mines [*University of Wollongong*] [*Australia*]
KCM .... Kilenge Mission [*New Britain*] [*Seismograph station code, US Geological Survey*] (SEIS)
KCM .... Kirchhoff Coda Migration [*For seismic wave imaging*]
KCM .... Kupffer Cell Medium
KCMA .... Holdenville, OK [*FM radio station call letters*] (RBYB)
KCMA .... Kitchen Cabinet Manufacturers Association (EA)
KCM & B ..... Kansas City, Memphis & Birmingham Railroad
KCMB .... Baker City, OR [*FM radio station call letters*]
KCMC .... Texarkana, TX [*AM radio station call letters*]
KCME .... Kuznetsk Commodity and Raw Materials Exchange [*Russian Federation*] (EY)
KCME .... Manitou Springs, CO [*FM radio station call letters*]
KCMG .... Knight Commander of St. Michael and St. George [*Facetiously translated, "Kindly Call Me God"*] [*British*]
KCMG .... Mountain Grove, MO [*AM radio station call letters*]
KCMG-FM ..... Mountain Grove, MO [*FM radio station call letters*]
KCMH .... Columbus/Port Columbus International [*Ohio*] [*ICAO location identifier*] (ICLI)
KCMH .... Mountain Home, AR [*FM radio station call letters*]
KCMI .... Terrytown, NE [*FM radio station call letters*]
KCMJ .... Indio, CA [*FM radio station call letters*]
KCMJ .... Palm Springs, CA [*AM radio station call letters*]
KCMLN .... Kansas City Metropolitan Library Network Council [*Library network*]
KCMN .... Colorado Springs, CO [*AM radio station call letters*]
KCMO .... Kansas City, Mexico & Orient [*AAR code*]
KCMO .... Kansas City, MO [*AM radio station call letters*]
KCMO-FM ..... Kansas City, MO [*FM radio station call letters*]
KCMQ .... Columbia, MO [*FM radio station call letters*]
KCMR .... Mason City, IA [*FM radio station call letters*]
KCMS .... Edmonds, WA [*FM radio station call letters*]
KCMS .... Kodak Color Management System [*Eastman Kodak Co.*] (PCM)
KCMT .... Chester, CA [*FM radio station call letters*]
KCMU .... Seattle, WA [*FM radio station call letters*]
KCMW .... Warrensburg, MO [*FM radio station call letters*]
KCMX .... Ashland, OR [*AM radio station call letters*]
KCMX .... Keyset Central Multiplexer
KCMX-FM ..... Ashland, OR [*FM radio station call letters*]
KCMY .... Sacramento, CA [*Television station call letters*]
KCN .... Chernofski Harbor, AK [*Location identifier FAA*] (FAAL)
KCN .... Intetnational Colin Energy [*NYSE symbol*] (SAG)
KCN .... Intl Colin Energy [*NYSE symbol*] (TTSB)
KCN .... Kids' Clubs Network (AIE)
KCN .... Kit Configuration Notice (MCD)
KCN .... Kit Control Number [*Navy*] (NG)
KCNA .... Cave Junction, OR [*FM radio station call letters*]
KCNA .... Korean Central News Agency [*North Korea*]
KCNC .... Denver, CO [*Television station call letters*]
KCND .... Bismarck, ND [*FM radio station call letters*]
KCNE .... Chadron, NE [*FM radio station call letters*]

KCNF .... Fort Worth [*Texas*] [*ICAO location identifier*] (ICLI)
KCNI .... Broken Bow, NE [*AM radio station call letters*]
KCNM .... Carlsbad/Cavern City Air Terminal [*New Mexico*] [*ICAO location identifier*] (ICLI)
KCNM .... San Jose, Philippines [*AM radio station call letters*]
KCNN .... East Grand Forks, MN [*AM radio station call letters*]
KCNO .... Alturas, CA [*AM radio station call letters*]
KCNO-FM ..... Alturas, CA [*FM radio station call letters*] (RBYB)
KCNQ .... Kernville, CA [*FM radio station call letters*]
KCNR .... Salt Lake City, UT [*AM radio station call letters*]
KCNS .... San Francisco, CA [*Television station call letters*]
KCNT .... Hastings, NE [*FM radio station call letters*]
KCNW .... Fairway, KS [*AM radio station call letters*]
KCNW .... Kelly's Creek & Northwestern Railroad Co. [*AAR code*]
KCNW .... Waco/James Connally [*Texas*] [*ICAO location identifier*] (ICLI)
KCNZ .... Cedar Falls, IA [*AM radio station call letters*] (RBYB)
KCO .... Keep Cost Order [*Telecommunications*] (TEL)
KCOB .... Newton, IA [*AM radio station call letters*]
KCOB-FM ..... Newton, IA [*FM radio station call letters*]
KCOF .... Cocoa/Patrick Air Force Base [*Florida*] [*ICAO location identifier*] (ICLI)
KCOG .... Centerville, IA [*AM radio station call letters*]
KCOH .... Houston, TX [*AM radio station call letters*]
KCOL .... Fort Collins, CO [*AM radio station call letters*]
KColC .... Colby Community College, Colby, KS [*Library symbol Library of Congress*] (LCLS)
KCole .... Kenneth Cole Productions, Inc. [*Associated Press*] (SAG)
KColePd .... Kenneth Cole Productions, Inc. [*Associated Press*] (SAG)
KCOM .... Comanche, TX [*AM radio station call letters*]
KCOMZ .... Korean Communications Zone [*Military*]
KCON .... Conway, AR [*AM radio station call letters*]
KCOP .... Los Angeles, CA [*Television station call letters*]
KCOR .... San Antonio, TX [*AM radio station call letters*]
KCOS .... Colorado Springs/Peterson Field [*Colorado*] [*ICAO location identifier*] (ICLI)
KCOS .... El Paso, TX [*Television station call letters*]
KCOT .... Cotulla/Municipal [*Texas*] [*ICAO location identifier*] (ICLI)
KCOT .... San Augustine, TX [*FM radio station call letters*]
KCOU .... Columbia, MO [*FM radio station call letters*]
KCOW .... Alliance, NE [*AM radio station call letters*]
KCOY .... Santa Maria, CA [*Television station call letters*]
KCOZ .... Point Lookout, MO [*FM radio station call letters*] (RBYB)
KCP .... Kansas City Plant (DOGT)
KCP .... Kansas City Plant [*Department of Energy*] [*Kansas City, MO*] (GAAI)
KCP .... Kansas City Plant
KCP .... Kansas City Public Library, Kansas City, MO [*OCLC symbol*] (OCLC)
KCP .... Keene's Cement Plaster [*Technical drawings*]
KCP .... Kenneth Cole Productions'A' [*NYSE symbol*] (TTSB)
KCP .... Kenneth Cole Productions, Inc. [*NYSE symbol*] (SAG)
KCP .... Keyboard-Controlled Phototypesetter (NITA)
KCP .... Key Crude Prices [*Database*] [*Petroleum Intelligence Weekly*] [*Information service or system*] (CRD)
KCP .... Kirghiz Communist Party [*Political party*]
KCP .... Knight Commander of [*the Order of*] Pius IX
KCP .... Korean Communist Party [*Political party North Korea*] (FEA)
KCPA .... Kaolin Clay Producers Association (DGA)
KCP & G ...... Kansas City, Pittsburgh & Gulf Railroad
KCPB .... Thousand Oaks, CA [*FM radio station call letters*]
KCPC .... Keene's Cement Plaster Ceiling [*Technical drawings*]
KCPCA .... Kansas Committee for Prevention of Child Abuse (EDAC)
KCPI .... Albert Lea, MN [*FM radio station call letters*]
KCPL .... Kansas City Power & Light Co. [*Associated Press*] (SAG)
KCPL .... Olympia, WA [*AM radio station call letters*]
KCPM .... Chico, CA [*Television station call letters*]
KCPQ .... Tacoma, WA [*Television station call letters*]
KCPR .... San Luis Obispo, CA [*FM radio station call letters*]
KCPS .... Burlington, IA [*AM radio station call letters*]
KCPS .... Kansas City Public Service R. R. [*AAR code*]
kcps .... Kilocycles per Second
KCPT .... Kansas City, MO [*Television station call letters*]
KCPW .... Salt Lake City, UT [*FM radio station call letters*]
KCPX .... Centerville, UT [*FM radio station call letters*]
KCPX-AM ..... Centerville, UT [*AM radio station call letters*] (RBYB)
KCQL .... Aztec, NM [*AM radio station call letters*]
KCQQ .... Davenport, IA [*FM radio station call letters*] (RBYB)
KCQV .... Arthur, ND [*FM radio station call letters*]
KCR .... Colorado Creek, AK [*Location identifier FAA*] (FAAL)
KCR .... Kansas City Law Review [*A publication*] (DLA)
KCR .... Key Call Receiver [*Telecommunications*] (TEL)
KCR .... [*The*] Kowloon Canton Railway [*Hong Kong*] (DCTA)
KCR .... Reports Tempore Chancellor King [*A publication*] (DLA)
KCRA .... Sacramento, CA [*Television station call letters*]
KCRB .... Bemidji, MN [*FM radio station call letters*]
KCRC .... Enid, OK [*AM radio station call letters*]
KCRC .... Kansas City Records Center [*Military*]
KCRC .... Kowloon-Canton Railway Corp. [*Commercial firm*] [*Hong Kong*]
KCRCHE .... Kansas City Regional Council for Higher Education [*Library network*]
KCRE .... Crescent City, CA [*FM radio station call letters*]
KCRF .... Korean Conflict Research Foundation [*Defunct*]
KCRF .... Newport, OR [*FM radio station call letters*] (RBYB)
KCRG .... Cedar Rapids, IA [*AM radio station call letters*]
KCRG-TV ..... Cedar Rapids, IA [*Television station call letters*]
KCRH .... Hayward, CA [*FM radio station call letters*]
KCRK .... Colville, WA [*FM radio station call letters*]
KCRL .... Rayne, LA [*FM radio station call letters*]
KCRN .... San Angelo, TX [*AM radio station call letters*]
KCRN-FM ..... San Angelo, TX [*FM radio station call letters*]
KCRO .... Omaha, NE [*AM radio station call letters*]
KCRP .... Corpus Christi/International [*Texas*] [*ICAO location identifier*] (ICLI)
KCRR .... Grundy Center, IA [*FM radio station call letters*] (RBYB)
KCRS .... Midland, TX [*AM radio station call letters*]
KCRS-FM ..... Midland, TX [*FM radio station call letters*]
KCRT .... Keyboard Cathode Ray Tube (MCD)
KCRT .... Trinidad, CO [*AM radio station call letters*]
KCRT-FM ..... Trinidad, CO [*FM radio station call letters*]
KCRU .... Oxnard, CA [*FM radio station call letters*]
KCRV .... Caruthersville, MO [*AM radio station call letters*]
KCRW .... Santa Monica, CA [*FM radio station call letters*]
KCRX .... Roswell, NM [*AM radio station call letters*]
KCRY .... Indio, CA [*FM radio station call letters*]
KCRZ .... Tucson, AZ [*FM radio station call letters*]
KCS .... [*The*] Kansas City Southern Railway Co. [*AAR code*]
KCS .... Kansas City Standard [*Audio tape technology*] (EECA)
KCS .... KCS Energy, Inc. [*Formerly, KCS Group, Inc.*] [*NYSE symbol*] (SPSG)
KCS .... Keratoconjunctivitis Sicca [*Ophthalmology*]
KCS .... Keyboard Configuration Studies (NASA)
KCS .... Keyboard Controlled Sequencer [*Computer science*]
KCS .... Keyboards, Computers, and Software [*A publication*]
KCS .... Key Configuration Studies (NASA)
KCS .... Kilocharacters per Second (IAA)
kcs .... Kilocycles per Second
KCS .... King's College School [*British*]
KCS .... Knight of [*the Order of*] Charles III of Spain
KCS .... Knight of the Order of Charles XIII of Sweden [*Freemasonry*]
KCS .... Korean Chemical Society
KCS .... Thousand Characters per Second
KCSA .... Kerr Center for Sustainable Agriculture [*Research center*] (RCD)
KCSB .... Santa Barbara, CA [*FM radio station call letters*]
KCSC .... Edmond, OK [*FM radio station call letters*]
KCSC .... Kansas City Service Center [*IRS*]
KCSC .... Kansas Cosmosphere and Space Center [*Hutchinson, KS*]
KCSD .... Sioux Falls, SD [*FM radio station call letters*]
KCSD-TV ..... Sioux Falls, SD [*Television station call letters*] (RBYB)
KCSE-FM ..... Ballinger, TX [*FM radio station call letters*] (RBYB)
KCSF .... Stanton Foundation (EA)
KCSG .... Knight Commander of [*the Order of*] St. Gregory [*British*]
KCSI .... Knight Commander of the [*Order of the*] Star of India [*British*]
KCSI .... Red Oak, IA [*FM radio station call letters*]
KCSJ .... Pueblo, CO [*AM radio station call letters*]
KCSM .... San Mateo, CA [*FM radio station call letters*]
KCSM-TV ..... San Mateo, CA [*Television station call letters*]
KCSN .... Northridge, CA [*FM radio station call letters*]
KCSo .... Kansas City Southern Industries, Inc. [*Associated Press*] (SAG)
KCSO .... Modesto, CA [*Television station call letters*]
KCSou .... Kansas City Southern Industries, Inc. [*Associated Press*] (SAG)
KCSP .... Casper, WY [*FM radio station call letters*]
KCSR .... Chadron, NE [*AM radio station call letters*]
KCSS .... Key Center for Statistical Services [*Deakin University*] [*Australia*]
KCSS .... Knight Commander of [*the Order of*] St. Sylvester
KCSS .... Turlock, CA [*FM radio station call letters*]
KCS/SO .... Keyboard Class Select / Statistics Output [*Computer science*] (MHDI)
KCST .... Florence, OR [*AM radio station call letters*]
KCST-FM ..... Florence, OR [*FM radio station call letters*]
KCStJ & CB ... Kansas City, St. Joseph & Council Bluffs Railroad
KCSU .... Fort Collins, CO [*FM radio station call letters*]
KCT .... Kansas City Terminal Railway Co. [*AAR code*]
KCT .... Kaolin Cephalin Time [*Clinical chemistry*]
KCT .... Kaolin Clotting Time [*Clinical chemistry*]
KCT .... Kathodal Closing Tetanus [*Medicine*]
KCT .... Kelvin Circulation Theorem [*Physics*]
KCT .... Knight Commander of the Temple [*Freemasonry*] (ROG)
KCT .... Knox's Cube Test [*Short-term memory and attention span test*]
KCTA .... Corpus Christi, TX [*AM radio station call letters*]
KCTB .... Cut Bank [*Montana*] [*ICAO location identifier*] (ICLI)
KCTC .... Sacramento, CA [*AM radio station call letters*]
KCTE .... Independence, MO [*AM radio station call letters*]
KCTE .... Kathodal Closure Tetanus [*Medicine*]
KCTF .... Waco, TX [*Television station call letters*]
KCTG .... Ozark, MO [*FM radio station call letters*] (RBYB)
KCTI .... Gonzales, TX [*AM radio station call letters*]
KCTI-FM ..... Gonzales, TX [*FM radio station call letters*] (RBYB)
KCTM .... Rio Grande City, TX [*FM radio station call letters*]
KCTMLPCC ... Key Chain Tag and Mini License Plate Collectors Club [*Later, LPKCMLPCC*] (EA)
KCTN .... Garnavillo, IA [*FM radio station call letters*]
KCTO .... Columbia, LA [*AM radio station call letters*]
KCTO-FM ..... Columbia, LA [*FM radio station call letters*]
KCTR-FM ..... Billings, MT [*FM radio station call letters*]
KCTS .... Knight Commander of the Tower and Sword [*Portugal*] (ROG)
KCTS .... Seattle, WA [*Television station call letters*]
KCTT .... Yellville, AR [*FM radio station call letters*]
KCTV .... Kansas City, MO [*Television station call letters*]
KCTX .... Childress, TX [*AM radio station call letters*]
KCTY .... Salinas, CA [*AM radio station call letters*]
KCtyPL .... Kansas City Power & Light Co. [*Associated Press*] (SAG)
KCTZ .... Bozeman, MT [*Television station call letters*]
KCU .... Keyboard Control Unit
KCU .... Kilocurie (IAA)
KCUA .... Coalville, UT [*FM radio station call letters*]

KCUB .... Stephenville, TX [*FM radio station call letters*]
KCUB .... Tucson, AZ [*AM radio station call letters*]
KCUE .... Red Wing, MN [*AM radio station call letters*]
KCUI .... Pella, IA [*FM radio station call letters*]
KCUK .... Chevak, AK [*FM radio station call letters*]
KCUR .... Kansas City, MO [*FM radio station call letters*]
KCUS .... Columbus/Municipal [*New Mexico*] [*ICAO location identifier*] (ICLI)
KCUV .... Englewood, CO
KCUZ .... Clifton, AZ [*AM radio station call letters*]
KCV .... Kancana Ventures Ltd. [*Vancouver Stock Exchange symbol*]
KCVG .... Cincinnati/Greater Cincinnati [*Ohio*] [*ICAO location identifier*] (ICLI)
KCVI .... Blackfoot, ID [*FM radio station call letters*]
KCVL .... Colville, WA [*AM radio station call letters*]
KCVO .... Camdenton, MO [*FM radio station call letters*]
KCVO .... Knight Commander of the Royal Victorian Order [*British*]
KCVP .... Konservativ-Christlichsoziale Volkspartei [*Conservative Christian-Social Party*] [*Switzerland Political party*] (PPE)
KCVR .... Lodi, CA [*AM radio station call letters*]
KCVS .... Clovis/Cannon Air Force Base [*New Mexico*] [*ICAO location identifier*] (ICLI)
KCVS .... Salina, KS [*FM radio station call letters*]
KCVT-FM ..... Silver Lake, KS [*FM radio station call letters*] (RBYB)
KCVU .... Paradise, CA [*Television station call letters*]
KCVW-FM .... Kingman, KS [*FM radio station call letters*] (RBYB)
KCWA .... Arnold, MO [*FM radio station call letters*]
KCWB .... Kansas City Westport Belt [*AAR code*]
KCWB-TV .... Kansas City, MO [*TV station call letters*] (RBYB)
KCWC .... Lander, WY [*Television station call letters*]
KCWC .... Riverton, WY [*FM radio station call letters*]
KCWD .... Harrison, AR [*FM radio station call letters*]
KCWD .... Kaleidoscope: Current World Data [*ABC-CLIO*] [*Information service or system*] (IID)
KCWM .... Hondo, TX [*AM radio station call letters*] (RBYB)
KCWM-FM ... Hondo, TX [*FM radio station call letters*] (RBYB)
KCWN .... New Sharon, IA [*FM radio station call letters*]
KCWR .... Bakersfield, CA [*AM radio station call letters*]
KCWS .... Merkel, TX [*FM radio station call letters*]
KCWT .... Wenatchee, WA [*Television station call letters*]
KCWW .... Tempe, AZ [*AM radio station call letters*]
KCWX .... Columbia Falls, MT [*FM radio station call letters*]
KCXL .... Calexico/International [*California*] [*ICAO location identifier*] (ICLI)
KCXL .... Liberty, MO [*AM radio station call letters*] (RBYB)
KCXX .... Lake Arrowhead, CA [*FM radio station call letters*] (RBYB)
KCXY .... Camden, AR [*FM radio station call letters*]
KCYC .... King's Cheshire Yeomanry Cavalry [*British military*] (DMA)
KCYL .... Lampasas, TX [*AM radio station call letters*]
KCYN-FM .... Moab, UT [*FM radio station call letters*] (RBYB)
KCYS .... Cheyenne [*Wyoming*] [*ICAO location identifier*] (ICLI)
KCYT-FM .... Houston, AK [*FM radio station call letters*] (RBYB)
KCYY .... San Antonio, TX [*FM radio station call letters*]
KCZ .... Kochi [*Japan*] [*Airport symbol*] (OAG)
KCZE .... New Hampton, IA [*FM radio station call letters*]
KCZO .... Carrizo Springs, TX [*FM radio station call letters*]
KCZQ .... Cresco, IA [*FM radio station call letters*]
KCZY .... Osage, IA [*FM radio station call letters*]
KD .... Cathodal Duration [*Medicine*] (DMAA)
Kd .... Coefficient of Soil-Water Absorption (GNE)
K$_d$ .... Dissociation Constant [*Physics*] (DAVI)
K$_d$ .... Distribution Coefficient [*Partition coefficient*] [*Physics*] (DAVI)
KD .... Kallidin [*Biochemistry*]
KD .... Kathodal Duration [*Medicine*]
KD .... Kawasaki Disease [*Also, KS, MLNS*] [*Medicine*]
KD .... Keep It Dark [*Say nothing about it*] [*Slang*]
KD .... Kendell Airlines [*ICAO designator*] (AD)
KD .... Kennnedy Disease [*Medicine*] (DMAA)
KD .... Kentucky Dam [*TVA*]
KD .... Keto-Diastix [*Miles Inc.*] [*Pharmacology*] (DAVI)
KD .... Kettledrum
KD .... Keyboard and Display [*Computer science*] (MHDB)
K/D .... Keyboard/Display (ACRL)
KD .... Key Definition (MHDB)
KD .... Keyed to Differ [*Locks*] (ADA)
KD .... Khaki Drill [*British military*] (DMA)
KD .... Killed (AABC)
KD .... Kiln-Dried [*Lumber*]
kD .... Kilodalton [*Molecular mass measure*]
KD .... Kilter Diagram
KD .... Klinge [*Germany*] [*Research code symbol*]
KD .... Knee Disarticulation [*Medicine*]
KD .... Knitted Dacron (MEDA)
KD .... Knocked Down [*i.e., disassembled*]
KD .... Known-Distance [*Range*] [*Weaponry*] (INF)
KD .... Komitet Domowy. Warsaw Ghetto (BJA)
KD .... Korsakoff's Disease [*Medicine*]
KD .... Kriegs Dekoration [*War Decoration*] [*German*]
KD .... Kuwaiti Dinar [*Monetary unit*] (BJA)
KD .... Pilotless Aerial Target [*Navy*]
KDA .... Kendall Airlines [*Australia ICAO designator*] (FAAC)
kDa .... Kilodalton [*Physics*] [*Chemistry*] (DOG)
KDA .... Kit Design Approach
KDA .... Known Drug Allergies [*Medicine*] (DMAA)
KDA .... Kolda [*Senegal*] [*Airport symbol*] (AD)
KDA .... Kuranda [*Australia Seismograph station code, US Geological Survey Closed*] (SEIS)
KDAA .... Rolla, MO [*FM radio station call letters*] (RBYB)

KDAB .... Prairie Grove, AR [*FM radio station call letters*]
KDAC .... Fort Bragg, CA [*AM radio station call letters*]
KDAE .... Sinton, TX [*AM radio station call letters*]
KDAF .... Dallas, TX [*Television station call letters*]
KDAG .... Farmington, NM [*FM radio station call letters*]
KDAK .... Carrington, ND [*AM radio station call letters*]
KDAL .... Dallas/Dallas-Love Field [*Texas*] [*ICAO location identifier*] (ICLI)
KDAL .... Duluth, MN [*AM radio station call letters*]
KDAL-FM .... Duluth, MN [*FM radio station call letters*]
KDAM .... Monroe City, MO [*FM radio station call letters*]
KDAO .... Marshalltown, IA [*AM radio station call letters*]
KDAO-FM .... Eldora, IA [*FM radio station call letters*]
KDAP .... Douglas, AZ [*AM radio station call letters*]
KDAP-FM .... Douglas, AZ [*FM radio station call letters*]
KDAQ .... Shreveport, LA [*FM radio station call letters*]
KDAR .... Oxnard, CA [*FM radio station call letters*]
KDAT .... Cedar Rapids, IA [*FM radio station call letters*] (RBYB)
KDAT .... Kiln-Dried After Treatment [*Lumber*]
KDAY .... Dayton/James M. Coxdayton Municipal [*Ohio*] [*ICAO location identifier*] (ICLI)
KDAY .... Independence, CA [*FM radio station call letters*]
KDAZ .... Albuquerque, NM [*AM radio station call letters*]
KDB .... Kambalda [*Australia Airport symbol*] (OAG)
KDB .... Keller-Dorian, Berthon [*Method*] [*Photography*]
KDB .... Kelvin Double Bridge [*Physics*]
KDB .... Konedobu [*Papua New Guinea*] [*Seismograph station code, US Geological Survey*] (SEIS)
KDB .... Korea Development Bank
KDB .... Santa Barbara, CA [*FM radio station call letters*]
KDBB .... Bonne Terre, MO [*FM radio station call letters*]
KDBC .... El Paso, TX [*Television station call letters*]
KDBH .... Natchitoches, LA [*FM radio station call letters*]
KDBM .... Dillon, MT [*AM radio station call letters*]
KDBM-FM ... Dillon, MT [*FM radio station call letters*]
KDBR .... Kalispell, MT [*FM radio station call letters*]
KDBS-AM ... Alexandria, LA [*AM radio station call letters*] (RBYB)
KDBX .... Banks, OR [*AM radio station call letters*]
KDc .... Dodge City Public Library, Dodge City, KS [*Library symbol Library of Congress*] (LCLS)
KDC .... Kathodal Duration Contraction [*Medicine*]
KDC .... KD Air Corp. [*ICAO designator*] (FAAC)
KDC .... Keil and Delitzsch Commentaries [*A publication*] (BJA)
KDC .... Key Distribution Center (MCD)
KDC .... Keyed Display Console
KDC .... Kidney Disease Treatment Center (DMAA)
KDC .... Kodiak [*Alaska*] [*Seismograph station code, US Geological Survey*] (SEIS)
KDC .... Kosher Dining Club (BJA)
KDCA .... Washington/National [*District of Columbia*] [*ICAO location identifier*] (ICLI)
KDCC .... Dodge City, KS [*AM radio station call letters*]
KDCC .... Washington [*District of Columbia*] [*ICAO location identifier*] (ICLI)
KDCD .... San Angelo, TX [*FM radio station call letters*]
KDCE .... Espanola, NM [*AM radio station call letters*]
KDCG .... San Diego Coast Guard Air Base [*California*] [*ICAO location identifier*] (ICLI)
KDCL .... Knocked Down, in Carloads
KDCP .... Kidney Disease Control Program [*Public Health Service*]
KDCQ .... Coos Bay, OR [*FM radio station call letters*] (RBYB)
KDCR .... Sioux Center, IA [*FM radio station call letters*]
KDCV .... Blair, NE [*FM radio station call letters*]
KDD .... Kokusai Denshin Denwa Co. Ltd. [*Telegraph & Telephone Corp.*] [*Tokyo, Japan*] [*Telecommunications*]
KDDA .... Dumas, AR [*AM radio station call letters*]
KDDB .... Paso Robles, CA [*FM radio station call letters*]
KDDD .... Dumas, TX [*AM radio station call letters*]
KDDK .... Jacksonville, AR [*FM radio station call letters*]
KDDQ .... Comanche, OK [*FM radio station call letters*]
KDDR .... Oakes, ND [*AM radio station call letters*]
KDDX .... Spearfish, SD [*FM radio station call letters*] (RBYB)
KDDZ-AM ... San Diego, CA [*AM radio station call letters*] (RBYB)
KDe .... Derby Public Library, Derby, KS [*Library symbol Library of Congress*] (LCLS)
KDE .... Keyboard Data Entry
KDE .... Kinetic Depth Effect [*Cognitive science*]
KDE .... Koroba [*Papua New Guinea*] [*Airport symbol Obsolete*] (OAG)
KDEA .... New Iberia, LA [*FM radio station call letters*]
KDEB .... Springfield, MO [*Television station call letters*]
KDEC .... Decorah, IA [*AM radio station call letters*]
KDEC-FM .... Decorah, IA [*FM radio station call letters*]
KDEF .... Albuquerque, NM [*AM radio station call letters*]
KDEL .... Arkadelphia, AR [*FM radio station call letters*]
KDEM .... Deming, NM [*FM radio station call letters*]
KDEM .... Kurzweil Data Entry Machine [*for optical character recognition*]
KDEN .... Denver/Stapleton International [*Colorado*] [*ICAO location identifier*] (ICLI)
KDEN-TV .... Longmont, CO [*TV station call letters*] (RBYB)
KDEO-FM .... Waipahu, HI [*FM radio station call letters*]
KDEP .... Kentucky Department of Environmental Protection
KDEP .... Kentucky Department of Environmental Protection (DOGT)
KDEP .... Smoke Layer Estimated (Feet) Deep [*Meteorology*] (FAAC)
KDEP-FM .... Depoe Bay, OR [*FM radio station call letters*] (RBYB)
KDES .... Palm Springs, CA [*AM radio station call letters*] (RBYB)
KDES-FM .... Palm Springs, CA [*FM radio station call letters*]
KDET .... Center, TX [*AM radio station call letters*]

KDET............ Detroit/Detroit City [*Michigan*] [*ICAO location identifier*] (ICLI)
KDET-FM ..... Center, TX [*FM radio station call letters*]
KDEW .... De Witt, AR [*AM radio station call letters*] (RBYB)
KDEW-FM ..... De Witt, AR [*FM radio station call letters*] (RBYB)
KDEX............ Dexter, MO [*AM radio station call letters*]
KDEX-FM ..... Dexter, MO [*FM radio station call letters*]
KDEZ............ Jonesboro, AR [*FM radio station call letters*]
KDF.............. Kalamein [*Trademark*] Door and Frame
KDF.............. Knob Door Fastener
KDF.............. Knocked Down Flat
KDF.............. Kraft durch Freude [*Strength through Joy Movement*] [*Pre-World War II*] [*German*]
KDFC .... Kenny Dale Fan Club (EA)
KDFC .... Korea Development Finance Corp.
KDFC .... Palo Alto, CA [*AM radio station call letters*]
KDFC .... San Francisco, CA [*FM radio station call letters*]
KDFI .... Dallas, TX [*Television station call letters*]
KDFN .... Doniphan, MO [*AM radio station call letters*]
KDFR .... Des Moines, IA [*FM radio station call letters*]
KDFT .... Ferris, TX [*AM radio station call letters*]
KDFW .... Dallas-Fort Worth/Regional Airport [*Texas*] [*ICAO location identifier*] (ICLI)
KDFW .... Dallas, TX [*Television station call letters*]
KDFX .... Dallas, TX [*AM radio station call letters*] (RBYB)
KDG .... Kedougou [*Senegal*] [*Seismograph station code, US Geological Survey Closed*] (SEIS)
KDG .... King's Dragoon Guards [*Later, QDG*] [*Military unit*] [*British*]
KDGB .... Dodge City, KS [*FM radio station call letters*]
KDGE .... Gainesville, TX [*FM radio station call letters*]
KDGO .... Durango, CO [*AM radio station call letters*]
KDGS .... Andover, KS [*FM radio station call letters*] (RBYB)
KDH .... Kandahar [*Afghanistan*] [*Airport symbol*] (OAG)
KDH .... Key Depression per Hour [*Computer science*] (IAA)
KDH .... Korean Direct Hire
KDH .... Kosher Dining Hall (BJA)
KDHI .... Twentynine Palms, CA [*FM radio station call letters*]
KDHL .... Faribault, MN [*AM radio station call letters*]
KDHN .... Dimmitt, TX [*AM radio station call letters*]
KDHN .... Dothan [*Alabama*] [*ICAO location identifier*] (ICLI)
KDHT .... Dalhart [*Texas*] [*ICAO location identifier*] (ICLI)
KDHX .... St. Louis, MO [*FM radio station call letters*]
KDI .... Kendari [*Indonesia*] [*Airport symbol*] (OAG)
KDI .... Knowledge and Distributed Intelligence
KDI .... Korea Development Institute (ECON)
KDI .... Kuwaiti Dinar [*Monetary unit*] (DS)
KDIA .... Oakland, CA [*AM radio station call letters*]
KDIC .... Grinnell, IA [*FM radio station call letters*]
KDIF .... Riverside, CA [*AM radio station call letters*]
KDIG .... Orland, CA [*FM radio station call letters*]
KDII .... Key Defense Intelligence Issue (MCD)
KDIN .... Des Moines, IA [*Television station call letters*]
KDIO .... Ortonville, MN [*AM radio station call letters*]
KDIU .... Dimmitt, TX [*FM radio station call letters*]
KDIX .... Dickinson, ND [*AM radio station call letters*]
KDIZ-AM ...... Golden Valley, MN [*AM radio station call letters*] (RBYB)
KDJ .... Njdole [*Gabon*] [*Airport symbol*] (AD)
KDJI .... Holbrook, AZ [*AM radio station call letters*]
KDJK .... Oakdale, CA [*FM radio station call letters*]
KDJR .... De Soto, MO [*FM radio station call letters*]
KDJS .... Willmar, MN [*AM radio station call letters*]
KDJS-FM ..... Willmar, MN [*FM radio station call letters*]
KDJW .... Amarillo, TX [*AM radio station call letters*]
KDK .... Khodzhikent [*Former USSR Seismograph station code, US Geological Survey Closed*] (SEIS)
KDK .... Knit de Knit Texturing (IAA)
KDK .... Kodiak [*Alaska*] Municipal Airport [*Airport symbol Obsolete*] (OAG)
KDKA .... Pittsburgh, PA [*First station to broadcast a baseball game, August 5, 192 1*] [*AM radio station call letters*]
KDKA-TV...... Pittsburgh, PA [*Television station call letters*]
KDKB-FM ..... Mesa, AZ [*FM radio station call letters*] (RBYB)
KDKD .... Clinton, MO [*AM radio station call letters*]
KDKD-FM..... Clinton, MO [*FM radio station call letters*]
KDKF .... Klamath Falls, OR [*Television station call letters*]
KDKK .... Park Rapids, MN [*FM radio station call letters*]
KDKO .... Littleton, CO [*AM radio station call letters*]
KDKR-FM..... Decatur, TX [*FM radio station call letters*] (RBYB)
KDKS-FM..... Haughton, LA [*FM radio station call letters*]
KDL .... Kerrisdale Resources Ltd. [*Vancouver Stock Exchange symbol*]
KDL .... Koronadal [*Mindanao, Philippines*] [*Airport symbol*] (AD)
KDL .... Kreisinger Development Laboratory (KSC)
KDLA .... De Ridder, LA [*AM radio station call letters*]
KDLB .... Henryetta, OK [*AM radio station call letters*]
KDLCL .... Knocked Down, in Less than Carloads
KDLF............ Del Rio/Laughlin Air Force Base [*Texas*] [*ICAO location identifier*] (ICLI)
KDLG .... Dillingham, AK [*AM radio station call letters*]
KDLH .... Duluth/International [*Minnesota*] [*ICAO location identifier*] (ICLI)
KDLH .... Duluth, MN [*Television station call letters*]
KDLK .... Del Rio, TX [*AM radio station call letters*] (RBYB)
KDLK-FM ..... Del Rio, TX [*FM radio station call letters*]
KDLL .... Kenai, AK [*FM radio station call letters*] (RBYB)
KDLM .... Detroit Lakes, MN [*AM radio station call letters*]
KDLO .... Watertown, SD [*FM radio station call letters*]
KDLO-TV...... Florence, SD [*Television station call letters*]
KDLP .... Bayou Vista, LA [*AM radio station call letters*]

KDLR .... Devils Lake, ND [*AM radio station call letters*]
KDLS .... Perry, IA [*AM radio station call letters*]
KDLS-FM ..... Perry, IA [*FM radio station call letters*]
KDLT............ Mitchell, SD [*Television station call letters*]
kdlth .... Kodalith (VRA)
KDLX .... Makawao, HI [*FM radio station call letters*]
KDLY .... Lander, WY [*FM radio station call letters*]
KDM............ Kingdom (WGA)
KDM............ Kyrgyzstan Democratic Movement [*Political party*]
KDMA .... Montevideo, MN [*AM radio station call letters*]
KDMA .... Tucson/Davis Monthan Air Force Base [*Arizona*] [*ICAO location identifier*] (ICLI)
KDMD .... Anchorage, AK [*Television station call letters*]
KDMG .... Burlington, IA [*FM radio station call letters*]
KDMI .... Des Moines, IA [*FM radio station call letters*]
KDMI .... Thousands of Delivered Machine Instructions [*Computer science*]
KDMI-AM ..... Des Moines, IA [*AM radio station call letters*] (RBYB)
KDMM .... Herington, KS [*FM radio station call letters*]
KDMM .... Highland Park, TX [*AM radio station call letters*]
KDMN .... Buena Vista, CO [*AM radio station call letters*]
KDMO .... Carthage, MO [*AM radio station call letters*]
KDMS .... El Dorado, AR [*AM radio station call letters*]
KDMS .... Kennedy Space Center Data Management System [*NASA*] (NASA)
KDMX .... Dallas, TX [*FM radio station call letters*]
KDN .... Kaydon Corp. [*NYSE symbol*] (SAG)
K/DN .... Kickdown [*Automotive engineering*]
KDN .... Kinetically Designed Nozzle (NASA)
KdN .... Koninkrijk der Nederlanden [*Kingdom of the Netherlands*] [*Dutch*] (BARN)
KDN .... N'Dende [*Gabon*] [*Airport symbol*] (OAG)
K-DNA .... Deoxyribonucleic Acid - Kinetoplast [*Biochemistry, genetics*]
kDNA .... Kinetoplast DNA[*Deoxyribonucleic Acid*] [*Genetics*] (DOG)
KDNA .... Yakima, WA [*FM radio station call letters*]
KDNE .... Crete, NE [*FM radio station call letters*]
KDNI .... Duluth, MN [*FM radio station call letters*]
KDNK .... Carbondale, CO [*FM radio station call letters*]
KDNL .... St. Louis, MO [*Television station call letters*]
KDNO .... Delano, CA [*FM radio station call letters*]
KDNP .... Keresztenydemokrata Neppart [*Christian Democratic People's Party*] [*Hungary Political party*] (EY)
KDNR........... Los Lunas, NM [*AM radio station call letters*] (RBYB)
KDNS .... Downs, KS [*FM radio station call letters*]
KDNW .... Duluth, MN [*FM radio station call letters*]
KDO .... Ketodeoxyoctonate [*Biochemistry*]
KDO .... Key District Office [*IRS*]
KDOC .... Anaheim, CA [*Television station call letters*]
KDOG .... North Mankato, MN [*FM radio station call letters*]
KDOK .... Tyler, TX [*FM radio station call letters*]
KDOL .... Henderson, NV [*AM radio station call letters*]
KDOM .... Windom, MN [*AM radio station call letters*]
KDOM-FM ..... Windom, MN [*FM radio station call letters*]
KDON........... Salinas, CA [*FM radio station call letters*]
KDOR .... Bartlesville, OK [*Television station call letters*]
KDOS .... Key Display Operating System
KDOS .... Key to Disk Operating System
KDOS .... Laredo, TX [*AM radio station call letters*]
KDOT-FM ..... Reno, NV [*FM radio station call letters*] (RBYB)
KDOV .... Dover Air Force Base [*Delaware*] [*ICAO location identifier*] (ICLI)
KDOV .... Medford, OR [*FM radio station call letters*] (RBYB)
KDP .... Kandep [*Papua New Guinea*] [*Airport symbol Obsolete*] (OAG)
KDP .... Kappa Delta Pi [*Honor society*] (AEE)
KDP .... Keyboard, Display, and Printer [*Computer science*]
KDP .... Key Data Points (MCD)
KDP .... Key Decision Point [*USCG*] (TAG)
KDP .... Key Development Plan [*Telecommunications*] (TEL)
KDP .... Known Datum Point
KDP .... Korean Democratic Party [*North Korea Political party*] (FEA)
KDP .... Kurdish Democratic Party [*Iran*] [*Political party*]
KDP .... Potassium Dideuterium Phosphate
KDP .... Potassium [*Kalium*] Dihydrogen Phosphate [*Inorganic chemistry*]
KDPA .... Knitgoods Dyers and Processors Association
KDPA .... West Chicago/Du Page County [*Illinois*] [*ICAO location identifier*] (ICLI)
KDPI .... Kurdish Democratic Party of Iran [*Political party*] (PPW)
K-DPN.......... KSC [*Kennedy Space Center*] DOD Payloads Notice [*Department of Defense*] [*NASA*] (NASA)
K-DPPS........ KSC [*Kennedy Space Center*] DOD Payloads Projects Specification [*Department of Defense*] [*NASA*] (NASA)
KDPR........... Dickinson, ND [*FM radio station call letters*]
KDPS .... Des Moines, IA [*FM radio station call letters*]
KDPS .... Kurdish Democratic Party of Syria [*Political party*]
KDQN .... De Queen, AR [*AM radio station call letters*]
KDQN-FM ..... De Queen, AR [*FM radio station call letters*]
KDR .... Kandrian [*Papua New Guinea*] [*Airport symbol*] (OAG)
KDR .... Kangeld Resources Ltd. [*Vancouver Stock Exchange symbol*]
KDR .... Kappa Delta Rho [*Fraternity*]
KDR .... Keyboard Data Recorder [*Computer science*]
KDR .... Kidderminster [*British depot code*]
K/DR .... Kitchen/Dining Room [*Classified advertising*] (ADA)
KDR .... Knockdown Resistance [*Pesticide technology*]
KDRE .... North Little Rock, AR [*FM radio station call letters*]
KDRG .... Deer Lodge, MT [*AM radio station call letters*]
KDRH........... Glenwood Springs, CO [*FM radio station call letters*]
KDRK .... Spokane, WA [*FM radio station call letters*]
KDRM........... Moses Lake, WA [*FM radio station call letters*]

KDRO .... Sedalia, MO [*AM radio station call letters*]
KDRQ .... Wishek, ND [*AM radio station call letters*]
KDRS .... Paragould, AR [*AM radio station call letters*]
KDRT .... Del Rio/International [*Texas*] [*ICAO location identifier*] (ICLI)
KDRV .... Medford, OR [*Television station call letters*]
KDRY .... Alamo Heights, TX [*AM radio station call letters*]
KDS .... K2 Del Aire SA de CV [*Mexico ICAO designator*] (FAAC)
KDS .... Kamad Silver Co. Ltd. [*Vancouver Stock Exchange symbol*]
KDS .... Kathode Dark Space
KDS .... Kaufman Developmental Scale [*Child development test*]
KDS .... Kedougou [*Senegal*] [*Seismograph station code, US Geological Survey*] (SEIS)
KDS .... Keel Depth Simulator
KDS .... Keyboard Display Station [*Computer science*] (DA)
KDS .... Key Data Station (NITA)
KDS .... Key Display System [*Computer science*] (MDG)
KDS .... Key to Disc System
KDS .... Kiting Detection System (HGAA)
KDS .... Komma Dimokratikou Sosialismou [*Party for Democratic Socialism*] [*Greek Political party*] (PPE)
KDS .... Kristen Demokratisk Samling [*Christian Democratic Union*] [*Sweden Political party*] (PPE)
KDSD .... Aberdeen, SD [*Television station call letters*]
KDSD .... Pierpont, SD [*FM radio station call letters*]
KDSE .... Dickinson, ND [*Television station call letters*]
kd/sec .... Kilocycles per Second [*Measurement*] (DAVI)
KDSI .... Alice, TX [*AM radio station call letters*]
KDSI .... Thousands of Delivered Source Instructions [*Computer science*]
KDSJ .... Deadwood, SD [*AM radio station call letters*]
KDSL .... Thousands of Delivered Source Lines of Code [*Computer science*]
KDSM .... Des Moines [*Iowa*] [*ICAO location identifier*] (ICLI)
KDSM .... Des Moines, IA [*Television station call letters*]
KDSM .... Keratinizing Desquamative Squamous Metaplasia [*Medicine*]
KDSN .... Denison, IA [*AM radio station call letters*]
KDSN-FM .... Denison, IA [*FM radio station call letters*]
KDSR .... Williston, ND [*FM radio station call letters*]
KDSS .... Ely, NV [*FM radio station call letters*]
KDSS .... Key-to-Disk Subsystem [*Computer science*] (MHDB)
KDST .... Dyersville, IA [*AM radio station call letters*]
KDSU .... Fargo, ND [*FM radio station call letters*]
KDSX .... Denison-Sherman, TX [*AM radio station call letters*]
KDT .... Kammer der Technik
KDT .... Kathodal Duration Tetanus [*Medicine*]
KDT .... Keyboard and Display Test (MCD)
KDT .... Keyboard Display Terminal (MCD)
KDT .... Key Data Terminal
KDT .... Key Definition Table [*Computer science*] (PCM)
KDT .... Key-to-Disk-to-Tape (MCD)
KDTA .... Delta, CO [*AM radio station call letters*]
KDTE .... Kathodal Duration Tetanus [*Medicine*] (ROG)
KDTH .... Dubuque, IA [*AM radio station call letters*]
KDTK .... Prescott Valley, AZ [*FM radio station call letters*]
KDTL-FM .... Lake Village, AR [*FM radio station call letters*] (RBYB)
KDTN .... Denton, TX [*Television station call letters*]
KDTV .... San Francisco, CA [*Television station call letters*]
KDTW .... Detroit/Metropolitan Wayne County [*Michigan*] [*ICAO location identifier*] (ICLI)
KDTX .... Dallas, TX [*Television station call letters*]
KDU .... Christian Democratic Union [*Czechoslavakia*] [*Political party*] (ECON)
KDU .... Keyboard Display Unit (MCD)
KDU .... Skardu [*Pakistan*] [*Airport symbol*] (AD)
KDUC .... Barstow, CA [*FM radio station call letters*]
KDUG .... Douglas/Bisbee International [*Arizona*] [*ICAO location identifier*] (ICLI)
KDUH .... Scottsbluff, NE [*Television station call letters*]
KDUK .... Eugene, OR [*AM radio station call letters*]
KDUK .... Florence, OR [*FM radio station call letters*]
KDUN .... Reedsport, OR [*AM radio station call letters*]
KDUQ .... Ludlow, CA [*FM radio station call letters*]
KDUR .... Durango, CO [*FM radio station call letters*]
KDUS .... Cadus Pharmaceutical Corp. [*NASDAQ symbol*] (SAG)
KDUV .... Visalia, CA [*FM radio station call letters*]
KDUX .... Aberdeen, WA [*FM radio station call letters*]
KDUZ .... Hutchinson, MN [*AM radio station call letters*]
KDV .... Kandavu [*Fiji*] [*Airport symbol*] (OAG)
KdV .... Korteweg-deVries [*Equation*] [*Mathematics*]
kDVC .... Kilovolts, Direct Current (KSC)
KDVE-FM .... Denison-Sherman, TX [*FM radio station call letters*] (RBYB)
KDVL .... Devils Lake, ND [*FM radio station call letters*]
KDVR .... Denver, CO [*Television station call letters*]
KDVS .... Davis, CA [*FM radio station call letters*]
KDVV .... Topeka, KS [*FM radio station call letters*]
KDWA .... Hastings, MN [*AM radio station call letters*]
KDWB .... Richfield, MN [*FM radio station call letters*]
KDWG .... Billings, MT [*AM radio station call letters*] (RBYB)
KDWN .... Las Vegas, NV [*AM radio station call letters*]
KDX .... Klondex Mines [*Vancouver Stock Exchange symbol*]
KDX .... Klondex Mines Ltd [*VS, exchange symbol*] (TTSB)
KDX .... Knock Down Export [*Automotive engineering*]
KDXE .... Sulphur Springs, TX [*AM radio station call letters*]
KDXL .... St. Louis Park, MN [*FM radio station call letters*]
KDXU .... St. George, UT [*AM radio station call letters*]
KDXY-FM .... Lake City, AR [*FM radio station call letters*] (RBYB)
KDY .... Kennedy Resources [*Vancouver Stock Exchange symbol*]
KDYL .... Salt Lake City, UT [*AM radio station call letters*]

KDYN .... Ozark, AR [*AM radio station call letters*]
KDYN-FM.... Ozark, AR [*FM radio station call letters*]
KDYS .... Abilene/Dyess Air Force Base [*Texas*] [*ICAO location identifier*] (ICLI)
KDYS-AM.... Lafayette, LA [*AM radio station call letters*] (RBYB)
KdyWils ...... Kennedy Wilson, Inc. [*Associated Press*] (SAG)
KDZ .... Kurdzhali [*Bulgaria*] [*Seismograph station code, US Geological Survey*] (SEIS)
KDZA .... Pueblo, CO [*AM radio station call letters*]
KDZA-FM .... Pueblo, CO [*FM radio station call letters*] (RBYB)
KDZN .... Glendive, MT [*FM radio station call letters*]
KDZZ .... Albuquerque, NM [*AM radio station call letters*]
Ke .... Exchangeable Body Potassium [*Biochemistry*] (DAVI)
KE .... Kaiser Engineers (NRCH)
Ke .... Keen's English Rolls Court Reports [*48 English Reprint*] [*A publication*] (DLA)
KE .... Kendall's Compound E [*Cortisone*]
ke .... Kenya [*MARC country of publication code Library of Congress*] (LCCP)
KE .... Kenya [*ANSI two-letter standard code*] (CNC)
KE .... Kerr Effect [*Optics*]
KE .... Key Equipment [*Telecommunications*] (TEL)
KE .... Kinetic Energy
KE .... King Edward (ROG)
KE .... Kitchen Exhaust (OA)
KE .... Knight of the Eagle
KE .... Knight of the Elephant [*Denmark*]
KE .... Knights of Equity (EA)
KE .... Knowledge Engineer [*Computer science*]
KE .... Koger Equity [*AMEX symbol*] (TTSB)
KE .... Koger Equity, Inc. [*AMEX symbol*] (CTT)
KE .... Korea Fund [*NYSE symbol*] (TTSB)
KE .... Korean Air [*Airline flight code*] (ODBW)
KE .... Korean Air Lines [*ICAO designator*] (AD)
KEA .... Kanada Esperanto-Asocio [*Canadian Esperanto Association*]
KEA .... Kealakomo [*Hawaii*] [*Seismograph station code, US Geological Survey Closed*] (SEIS)
KEA .... Keane, Inc. [*AMEX symbol*] (SPSG)
KEA .... Kent Executive Aviation Ltd. [*British ICAO designator*] (FAAC)
KEA .... Knitwear Employers Association (EA)
KEAG .... Anchorage, AK [*FM radio station call letters*]
KEAL-FM..... Douglas, AZ [*FM radio station call letters*] (RBYB)
KEAN .... Abilene, TX [*AM radio station call letters*]
Kean C NJ ... Kean College of New Jersey (GAGS)
Keane .... Keane, Inc. [*Associated Press*] (SAG)
Keane & Gr... Keane and Grant's English Registration Appeal Cases [*1854-62*] [*A publication*] (DLA)
Keane & GRC... Keane and Grant's English Registration Appeal Cases [*1854-62*] [*A publication*] (DLA)
KEAN-FM .... Abilene, TX [*FM radio station call letters*]
KEAR .... San Francisco, CA [*FM radio station call letters*]
KEAS .... Eastland, TX [*AM radio station call letters*]
KEAS .... Knots Equivalent Airspeed (MCD)
KEASAT ...... Kinetic Energy Anti-Satellite
KEAS-FM .... Eastland, TX [*FM radio station call letters*]
Keat Fam Sett... Keatinge's Family Settlements [*1810*] [*A publication*] (DLA)
KEAZ .... De Ridder, LA [*FM radio station call letters*]
KEB .... English Bay, AK [*Location identifier FAA*] (FAAL)
KEB .... Keban [*Turkey*] [*Seismograph station code, US Geological Survey*] (SEIS)
Keb .... Keble's English King's Bench Reports [*83, 84 English Reprint*] [*A publication*] (DLA)
KEB .... Korea Exchange Bank (IMH)
KEBC .... Oklahoma City, OK [*FM radio station call letters*]
KEB COLL ... Keble College [*Oxford University*] (ROG)
KEBE .... Jacksonville, TX [*AM radio station call letters*]
KEBI .... Kentucky Enterprise Bancorp [*NASDAQ symbol*] (SAG)
Keb J .... Keble's Justice of the Peace [*A publication*] (DLA)
Kebl .... Keble's English King's Bench Reports [*83, 84 English Reprint*] [*A publication*] (DLA)
Keble .... Keble's English King's Bench Reports [*83, 84 English Reprint*] [*A publication*] (DLA)
Keble (Eng)... Keble's English King's Bench Reports [*83, 84 English Reprint*] [*A publication*] (DLA)
KEBN .... Salem, OR [*Television station call letters*]
KEBR .... North Highlands, CA [*FM radio station call letters*]
KEBR .... Rocklin, CA [*AM radio station call letters*]
Keb Stat ..... Keble's Statutes [*A publication*] (DLA)
KEC .... KDD Engineering and Consulting Inc. (NITA)
KEC .... Kecskemet [*Hungary*] [*Seismograph station code, US Geological Survey*] (SEIS)
KEC .... Klebsiella, Enterobacter, Citrobacter [*Bacteriae*] [*Microbiology*] (DAVI)
KECC .... Miles City, MT [*FM radio station call letters*]
KECG .... El Cerrito, CA [*FM radio station call letters*]
KECG .... Elizabeth City Coast Guard Air Base/Municipal [*North Carolina*] [*ICAO location identifier*] (ICLI)
KECH .... Sun Valley, ID [*FM radio station call letters*]
KECI .... Missoula, MT [*Television station call letters*]
KECME........ Kuzbass Commodity and Raw Materials Exchange [*Russian Federation*] (EY)
KECN-AM .... Blackfoot, ID [*AM radio station call letters*] (RBYB)
KECO .... Elk City, OK [*FM radio station call letters*]
KECP .... Kit Engineering Change Proposal (KSC)
KECR .... El Cajon, CA [*AM radio station call letters*]
KECS .... Gainesville, TX [*FM radio station call letters*] (RBYB)

KECY............	El Centro, CA [*Television station call letters*] (RBYB)
KED............	Kaedi [*Mauritania*] [*Airport symbol*] (OAG)
KED............	Kedougou [*Senegal*] [*Seismograph station code, US Geological Survey Closed*] (SEIS)
KED............	Known Enemy Dead [*Military*]
KEDA............	San Antonio, TX [*AM radio station call letters*]
KEDDS........	Kansas Education Dissemination/Diffusion System (EDAC)
KEDG............	Las Vegas, NV [*FM radio station call letters*]
KEDJ............	Sun City, AZ [*FM radio station call letters*]
KEDM............	Monroe, LA [*FM radio station call letters*]
KEDO	Korea Energy Development Organisation [*A consortium formed by the US, North Korea, and South Korea to finance and build reactors*] (ECON)
KEDO	Longview, WA [*AM radio station call letters*]
KEDP	Las Vegas, NM [*FM radio station call letters*]
KEDR............	Sacramento, CA [*FM radio station call letters*]
KEDT............	Corpus Christi, TX [*FM radio station call letters*]
KEDT-TV	Corpus Christi, TX [*Television station call letters*]
KEDW............	Edwards Air Force Base [*California*] [*ICAO location identifier*] (ICLI)
KEE............	Emporia State University, School of Library Science, Emporia, KS [*OCLC symbol*] (OCLC)
KEE............	Kelle [*Congo*] [*Airport symbol*] (OAG)
KEE............	Kerr Electro-Optical Effect [*Optics*]
KEE............	Keychart Educational Equipment [*for use with an electronic typewriter*]
KEE............	Keystone Air Services Ltd. [*Canada ICAO designator*] (FAAC)
KEE............	Knowledge Engineering Environment [*An artificial intelligence system*]
KEED............	Eugene, OR [*AM radio station call letters*] (RBYB)
KEEE............	Nacogdoches, TX [*AM radio station call letters*]
KEEF............	Los Angeles, CA [*Television station call letters*]
KEEH............	Spokane, WA [*FM radio station call letters*]
KEEL............	Kent European Enterprises Ltd. [*British*]
KEEL............	Shreveport, LA [*AM radio station call letters*]
Keen............	Keen's English Rolls Court Reports [*48 English Reprint*] [*A publication*] (DLA)
KEEN............	Palmer, AK [*FM radio station call letters*] (RBYB)
Keen Ch.......	Keen's English Rolls Court Reports [*48 English Reprint*] [*A publication*] (DLA)
Keen (Eng)...	Keen's English Rolls Court Reports [*48 English Reprint*] [*A publication*] (DLA)
Keener Quasi Contr...	Keener's Cases on Quasi Contracts [*A publication*] (DLA)
Keene St C...	Keene State College (GAGS)
KEEP............	Bandera, TX [*FM radio station call letters*]
KEEP............	Kamehameha Early Education Program [*Hawaii*] (EDAC)
KEEP............	Kentucky Environmental Education Program (EDAC)
KEEP............	Kyosato Education Experiment Project [*Self-help program for Japanese farmers established by Americans in 1948*]
KEEPS........	Kodak Ektaprint Electronic Publishing System [*Hardware and software components*] [*Eastman Kodak Co.*]
KEES............	Gladewater, TX [*AM radio station call letters*]
KEET............	Eureka, CA [*Television station call letters*]
KEEY............	St. Paul, MN [*FM radio station call letters*]
KEEZ............	Mankato, MN [*FM radio station call letters*]
KEF............	Keflavik [*Iceland*] [*Airport symbol*] (AD)
KEF............	Korea Equity Fund [*NYSE symbol*] (SPSG)
KEF............	Reykjavik [*Iceland*] Keflavik Airport [*Airport symbol*] (OAG)
KEFD............	Houston/Ellington Air Force Base [*Texas*] [*ICAO location identifier*] (ICLI)
KEFE............	Los Alamos, NM [*FM radio station call letters*]
KEFM............	Omaha, NE [*FM radio station call letters*]
KEFR............	Le Grand, CA [*FM radio station call letters*]
KEG............	Keg Restaurants Ltd. [*Toronto Stock Exchange symbol Vancouver Stock Exchange symbol*]
KEG............	Key Energy Group [*AMEX symbol*] (SPSG)
KEG............	Key Gap [*Computer science*] (MHDI)
KEGE............	Richfield, MN [*AM radio station call letters*]
KEGE-FM	Minneapolis, MN [*FM radio station call letters*]
KEGG	Daingerfield, TX [*AM radio station call letters*]
KEGG	Kyoto Encyclopedia of Genes and Genomes [*Computer network*]
KEGL	Fort Worth, TX [*FM radio station call letters*]
KEGP	Eagle Pass/Municipal [*Texas*] [*ICAO location identifier*] (ICLI)
KEGR	Red Bluff, CA [*FM radio station call letters*] (RBYB)
KEGS	Kenworth Engine Governing System [*Automotive engineering*]
KEGT	Lake Village, AR [*FM radio station call letters*]
KEGX	Richland, WA [*FM radio station call letters*]
KEH............	King Edward's Horse Regiment [*Military unit*] [*British*]
KEH............	Kurzgefasstes Exegetisches Handbuch zum Alten Testament [*Leipzig*] [*A publication*] (BJA)
KEHK-FM	Brownsville, OR [*FM radio station call letters*] (RBYB)
KEI............	Keithley Instruments [*NYSE symbol*] (TTSB)
KEI............	Keithley Instruments, Inc. [*AMEX symbol*] (SPSG)
KEI............	Kepi [*Indonesia*] [*Airport symbol*] (OAG)
KEI............	Kresge Eye Institute
KEIA............	Korea Economic Institute of America (EA)
Keil............	Keilway's English King's Bench Reports [*72 English Reprint*] [*A publication*] (DLA)
KEIL............	Key Essential Item List [*Defense Supply Agency*]
Keilw............	Keilway's English King's Bench Reports [*72 English Reprint*] [*A publication*] (DLA)
Keilway........	Keilway's English King's Bench Reports [*72 English Reprint*] [*A publication*] (DLA)
Keilw (Eng)...	Keilway's English King's Bench Reports [*72 English Reprint*] [*A publication*] (DLA)
KEIN............	Great Falls, MT [*AM radio station call letters*]

KEIS............	Kentucky Economic Information System [*University of Kentucky*] [*Lexington Database producer*] [*Information service or system*]
Keith Ch PA...	Registrar's Book, Keith's Court of Chancery [*Pennsylvania*] [*A publication*] (DLA)
Keithly........	Keithley Instruments, Inc. [*Associated Press*] (SAG)
KEJC	Modesto, CA [*FM radio station call letters*] (RBYB)
KEJO	Corvallis, OR [*FM radio station call letters*]
KEJS	Lubbock, TX [*FM radio station call letters*]
KEK	Ekwok [*Alaska*] [*Airport symbol*] (OAG)
KEK	Kappa Eta Kappa [*Fraternity*]
KEK	Konferenz Europaeischer Kirchen [*Conference of European Churches - CEC*] (EA)
KEK	Kypriakon Ethnikon Komma [*Cypriot National Party (1944-1960)*] [*Greek Cypriot*] [*Political party*] (PPE)
KEKA...........	Eureka, CA [*FM radio station call letters*]
KEKB...........	Fruita, CO [*FM radio station call letters*]
Ke/Kg	Exchangeable Potassium per Kilogram of Body Weight [*Biochemistry*] (DAVI)
KEL	Karntner Einheitsliste [*Carinthian Unity List*] [*Austria Political party*] (PPE)
KEL	Keles [*Later, TKT*] [*Former USSR Geomagnetic observatory code*]
Kel	Kelim (BJA)
KEL	Kelsey-Hayes Canada Ltd. [*Toronto Stock Exchange symbol*]
KEL	Kelud [*Java*] [*Seismograph station code, US Geological Survey Closed*] (SEIS)
KEL	Known Enemy Location [*Military*]
KEL	Koroska Enotna Lista [*Carinthian Unity List*] [*Austria Political party*] (PPE)
KELA...........	Centralia-Chehalis, WA [*AM radio station call letters*]
Kel An	Kelly's Life Annuities [*1835*] [*A publication*] (DLA)
Kel Cont	Kelly on Contracts of Married Women [*A publication*] (DLA)
KELD...........	El Dorado, AR [*AM radio station call letters*]
KELD...........	El Dorado/Goodwin Field [*Arkansas*] [*ICAO location identifier*] (ICLI)
Kel Draft	Kelly's Draftsman [*14th ed.*] [*1978*] [*A publication*] (DLA)
KELE-AM	Mountain Grove, MO [*AM radio station call letters*] (RBYB)
Kel-f............	Polymonochlorotrifluoroethylene (IDOE)
KELG...........	Elgin, TX [*AM radio station call letters*]
Kel GA	Kelly's Reports [*1-3 Georgia*] [*A publication*] (DLA)
Kelh...........	Kelham's Norman French Law Dictionary [*A publication*] (DLA)
Kelham........	Kelham's Norman French Law Dictionary [*A publication*] (DLA)
Kelh Dict	Kelham's Norman French Law Dictionary [*A publication*] (DLA)
KELI...........	Kristana Esperantista Ligo Internacia [*International Christian Esperanto Association*] (EAIO)
KELI...........	San Angelo, TX [*FM radio station call letters*]
K-ELISA	Kinetic Measurement of Enzyme-Linked Immunosorbant Assay
KELK...........	Elko, NV [*AM radio station call letters*]
Kelk Jud Acts...	Kelke's Judicature Acts [*A publication*] (DLA)
KELL...........	Kellstrom Industries [*NASDAQ symbol*] (TTSB)
KELL...........	Kellstrom Industries, Inc. [*NASDAQ symbol*] (SAG)
Kellen........	Kellen's Reports [*146-55 Massachusetts*] [*A publication*] (DLA)
Kel Life Ann...	Kelly on Life Annuities [*A publication*] (DLA)
KellOG........	Kelley Oil and Gas Corp. [*Associated Press*] (SAG)
Kellogg........	Kellogg Co. [*Associated Press*] (SAG)
KELLW........	Kellstrom Inds Wrrt [*NASDAQ symbol*] (TTSB)
Kellwood	Kellwood Co. [*Associated Press*] (SAG)
Kelly...........	Kelly's Reports [*1-3 Georgia*] [*A publication*] (DLA)
Kelly & C....	Kelly and Cobb's Reports [*4, 5 Georgia*] [*A publication*] (DLA)
Kelly & Cobb...	Kelly and Cobb's Reports [*4, 5 Georgia*] [*A publication*] (DLA)
KellyRus	Kelly Russell Studios, Inc. [*Associated Press*] (SAG)
KellyS..........	Kelly Services, Inc. [*Associated Press*] (SAG)
KELN...........	Kell Negative [*Hematology*] (DAVI)
KELN...........	North Platte, NE [*FM radio station call letters*]
KELO...........	Sioux Falls, SD [*AM radio station call letters*]
KELO-FM	Sioux Falls, SD [*FM radio station call letters*]
KELO-TV	Sioux Falls, SD [*Television station call letters*]
KELP...........	El Paso/International [*Texas*] [*ICAO location identifier*] (ICLI)
KELP...........	El Paso, TX [*AM radio station call letters*]
KELP...........	Kindergarten Evaluation for Learning Potential [*McGraw Hill*]
KELR...........	Chariton, IA [*FM radio station call letters*]
KELS...........	Kohlman Evaluation of Living Skills [*Occupational therapy*]
Kel Sc Fac...	Kelly's Scire Facias [*2nd ed.*] [*1849*] [*A publication*] (DLA)
Kelstr.........	Kellstrom Industries, Inc. [*Associated Press*] (SAG)
Kelstrm.......	Kellstrom Industries, Inc. [*Associated Press*] (SAG)
KELU...........	Kuching Employees and Labourers' Union [*Sarawak*]
Kel Us	Kelly on Usury [*1835*] [*A publication*] (DLA)
KELY...........	Ely, NV [*AM radio station call letters*]
KELY...........	Kelly Services, Inc. [*NASDAQ symbol*] (NQ)
KELYA........	Kelly Services'A' [*NASDAQ symbol*] (TTSB)
KELYB........	Kelly Services'B' [*NASDAQ symbol*] (TTSB)
KELY-FM	Ely, NV [*FM radio station call letters*]
KEm............	Emporia Public Library, Emporia, KS [*Library symbol Library of Congress*] (LCLS)
KEM............	Kemi [*Finland*] [*Airport symbol*] (OAG)
KEM............	Kemper Corp. [*NYSE symbol*] (SPSG)
KEM............	Kinetic Energy Missile (INF)
KEMAR........	Knowles Electronics Manikin for Acoustic Research
KEMB........	Emmetsburg, IA [*FM radio station call letters*]
Kemble Sax...	Kemble's The Saxons in England [*A publication*] (DLA)
KEMC........	Billings, MT [*FM radio station call letters*]
KEmC........	College of Emporia, Emporia, KS [*Library symbol Library of Congress*] (LCLS)
KEMC........	Kemper Corp. (MHDW)
Kemet........	Kemet Corp. [*Associated Press*] (SAG)
KEMM........	Commerce, TX [*FM radio station call letters*]
KEMO........	Kennesaw Mountain National Battlefield Park

Kemo Tx...... Chemical Therapy [or Chemotherapy] [Pharmacology] (DAVI)
Kemper....... Kemper Corp. [Associated Press] (SAG)
KEmT........ Kansas State Teachers College, Emporia, KS [Library symbol Library of Congress Obsolete] (LCLS)
KEmU........ Emporia State University, Emporia, KS [Library symbol Library of Congress] (LCLS)
KEM-V .... Kinetic Energy Missile Vehicle [Army]
KEMV........ Mountain View, AR [Television station call letters]
KEMX........ Locust Grove, OK [FM radio station call letters]
Ken............ Kendall [Record label]
KEN........... Kenema [Sierra Leone] [Airport symbol] (OAG)
KEN........... Kenridge Mineral [Vancouver Stock Exchange symbol]
KEN........... Kentucky
Ken........... Kentucky (ODBW)
KEN........... Kenya [ANSI three-letter standard code] (CNC)
Ken........... Kenya (VRA)
KEN........... Kenyon College, Gambier, OH [OCLC symbol] (OCLC)
Ken........... Kenyon's English King's Bench Reports [A publication] (DLA)
KENA........ Mena, AR [AM radio station call letters]
KENA-FM .... Mena, AR [FM radio station call letters]
Kenan........ Kenan's Reports [76-91 North Carolina] [A publication] (DLA)
Kenan........ Kenan Transportation Co. [Associated Press] (SAG)
KENCLIP ..... Kentucky Cooperative Library and Information Project [Library network]
KENCO .... Kendrick & Co. [Telecommunications service] (TSSD)
KEND .... Enid/Vance Air Force Base [Oklahoma] [ICAO location identifier] (ICLI)
KEND .... Roswell, NM [FM radio station call letters]
Ken Dec ...... Kentucky Decisions (Sneed) [2 Kentucky] [A publication] (DLA)
KENE........... Toppenish, WA [AM radio station call letters]
Kenetech ..... Kenetech Corp. [Associated Press] (SAG)
KENI........... Anchorage, AK [AM radio station call letters]
Ken LR .... Kentucky Law Reporter [A publication] (DLA)
Ken L Re ..... Kentucky Law Reporter [A publication] (DLA)
KENN .... Farmington, NM [AM radio station call letters]
KENN .... Kennecott Co. Railroad [AAR code]
Kenn Ch ...... Kennedy's Chancery Practice [2nd ed.] [1852-53] [A publication] (DLA)
Kenn C Mar... Kennedy on Courts-Martial [A publication] (DLA)
Kennett....... Kennett's Glossary [A publication] (DLA)
Kennett....... Kennett upon Impropriations [A publication] (DLA)
Kennett Gloss... Kennett's Glossary [A publication] (DLA)
Kennett Par Ant... Kennett's Parochial Antiquities [A publication] (DLA)
Kenn Gloss... Kennett's Glossary [A publication] (DLA)
Kenn Imp..... Kennett upon Impropriations [A publication] (DLA)
Kenn Jur ..... Kennedy on Juries [A publication] (DLA)
Kennmtl....... Kennametal, Inc. [Associated Press] (SAG)
Kenn Par Antiq... Kennett's Parochial Antiquities [A publication] (DLA)
Kenn Pr ...... Kennedy's Chancery Practice [2nd ed.] [1852-53] [A publication] (DLA)
KENO .... Las Vegas, NV [AM radio station call letters]
Ken Opin ..... Kentucky Opinions [A publication] (DLA)
Kenora........ Keewatin, Norman, and Rat Portage [Communities that merged to form town in Ontario, Canada]
KENR .... Hudson, TX [AM radio station call letters]
Ken R .... Kenyon Review [A publication] (BRI)
KENS .... Kensington [West London] (ROG)
KENS .... San Antonio, TX [AM radio station call letters]
KenseyN ...... Kensey Nash Corp. [Associated Press] (SAG)
KENS-TV ..... San Antonio, TX [Television station call letters]
KENT.......... Kent Financial Services [NASDAQ symbol] (SPSG)
KENT.......... Kent Financial Svcs [NASDAQ symbol] (TTSB)
Kent.......... Kent's Commentaries on American Law [A publication] (DLA)
KENT.......... Odessa, TX [AM radio station call letters]
Kent & R St... Kent and Radcliff's Law of New York, Revision of 1801 [A publication] (DLA)
Kentch .... Kenetech Corp. [Associated Press] (SAG)
Kent Com..... Kent's Commentaries on American Law [A publication] (DLA)
Kent Comm... Kent's Commentaries on American Law [A publication] (DLA)
Kentekl........ Kentek Information Systems, Inc. [Associated Press] (SAG)
KentEl......... Kent Electronics [Associated Press] (SAG)
KentEnt....... Kentucky Enterprise Bancorp [Associated Press] (SAG)
KENT-FM ..... Odessa, TX [FM radio station call letters]
KentFn......... Kent Financial Services, Inc. [Associated Press] (SAG)
Kent's Commen... Kent's Commentaries on American Law [A publication] (DLA)
Kent St U..... Kent State University (GAGS)
KENU .... Enumclaw, WA [AM radio station call letters]
KENV .... Wendover/Wendover Auxiliary Air Base [Utah] [ICAO location identifier] (ICLI)
KENV-TV...... Elko, NV [TV station call letters] (RBYB)
KENW .... Portales, NM [FM radio station call letters]
KENW-TV...... Portales, NM [Television station call letters]
Ke:nx.......... Connects [Macintosh] [Computer science]
Keny.......... Kenyon's English King's Bench Reports [A publication] (DLA)
Kenya LR..... Kenya Law Reports [A publication] (DLA)
Keny Ch....... Chancery Cases [2 Notes of King's Bench Cases] [England] [A publication] (DLA)
KENZ-FM ..... Orem, UT [FM radio station call letters] (RBYB)
KEO............ Keld'Or Resources, Inc. [Vancouver Stock Exchange symbol]
KEO............ King Edward's Own [British military] (DMA)
KEO............ Odienne [Ivory Coast] [Airport symbol] (OAG)
KEOC .... King Edward's Own Cavalry [British military] (DMA)
KEOJ........... Caney, KS [FM radio station call letters]
KEOK .... Tahlequah, OK [FM radio station call letters]
KEOL........... King Edward's Own Lancers [British military] (DMA)

KEOL........... La Grande, OR [FM radio station call letters]
KEOM......... Mesquite, TX [FM radio station call letters]
KEOR.......... Atoka, OK [AM radio station call letters]
KEOS.......... College Station, TX [FM radio station call letters] (RBYB)
KEP............ Kaneb Energy Partners Ltd. (MHDW)
KEP............ Kellner Eye Piece
KEP............ Key Entry Processing
KEP............ King Edward Point [South Georgia Island] [Seismograph station code, US Geological Survey] (SEIS)
KEP............ Knight of the Eagle and Pelican [Freemasonry]
KEP............ Korea Electric Power ADS [NYSE symbol] (TTSB)
KEP............ Korea Electric Power Corp. [NYSE symbol] (SAG)
KEP............ Nepalganj [Nepal] [Airport symbol] (OAG)
KEPB.......... Eugene, OR [Television station call letters]
KEPC.......... Colorado Springs, CO [FM radio station call letters]
KEPE.......... Kentron Programmatismou kai Oikonomikon Ereunon [Centre of Planning and Economic Research] [Greece]
KEPG.......... Victoria, TX [FM radio station call letters]
KEPI........... Eagle Pass, TX [FM radio station call letters] (RBYB)
KEPOA........ Keep This Office Advised
KEPR.......... Pasco, WA [Television station call letters]
KEPROM...... Keyed-Access, Erasable, Programmable Read-Only Memory [Computer science]
KEPS.......... Eagle Pass, TX [AM radio station call letters]
KEPX.......... Eagle Pass, TX [FM radio station call letters]
KEPZ.......... Kaohsiung Export Processing Zone [Reexport manufacturing complex] [Taiwan]
KEQ............ Kebar [Indonesia] [Airport symbol] (OAG)
KEQU......... Kewaunee Scientific [NASDAQ symbol] (TTSB)
KEQU......... Kewaunee Scientific Corp. [Formerly, Kewaunee Science Equipment] [NASDAQ symbol] (NQ)
Ker............ Indian Law Reports, Kerala Series [A publication] (DLA)
Ker............ Kerithoth (BJA)
KER........... Kerman [Iran] [Airport symbol] (OAG)
KER........... Kermanshah [Iran] [Seismograph station code, US Geological Survey] (SEIS)
KER........... Kerr-Addison Mines [TS, exchange symbol] (TTSB)
KER........... Kerr Addison Mines Ltd. [Toronto Stock Exchange symbol]
KER........... Kerry [County in Ireland] (ROG)
KER........... Kinetic Energy Release
KERA.......... Dallas, TX [FM radio station call letters]
KERA.......... Kentucky Education Reform Act
KERA.......... Kentucky Education Reform Act
Kera.......... Keratitis [Ophthalmology] (DAVI)
KERA.......... KeraVision, Inc. [NASDAQ symbol] (SAG)
Kerala......... All Indian Law Reports, Kerala Series [A publication] (DLA)
Kerala LJ..... Kerala Law Journal [A publication] (DLA)
KERA-TV ..... Dallas, TX [Television station call letters]
KeraVis....... KeraVision, Inc. [Associated Press] (SAG)
KeraVs....... KeraVision, Inc. [Associated Press] (SAG)
KERB.......... Kermit, TX [AM radio station call letters]
KERB-FM ..... Kermit, TX [FM radio station call letters]
KERC .... Marked Tree, AR [FM radio station call letters]
KERD .... Kinetic Energy Release Distribution [Of ions for spectral studies]
KERE .... Atchison, KS [AM radio station call letters]
KERE-FM ..... Horton, KS [FM radio station call letters]
KEREN-OR ... Jerusalem Institutions for the Blind (EA)
KERI........... Wasco, CA [AM radio station call letters]
KERM......... Torrington, WY [FM radio station call letters]
KERMA .... Kinetic Energy Released per Unit Mass (DEN)
KERN......... Bakersfield, CA [AM radio station call letters]
Kern.......... Kernan's Reports [11-14 New York] [A publication] (DLA)
Kern.......... Kern's Reports [100-116 Indiana] [A publication] (DLA)
KERN-FM ..... Bakersfield, CA [FM radio station call letters]
KERO.......... Bakersfield, CA [Television station call letters]
KERO.......... Kerosine [British]
KERP.......... Pueblo, CO [FM radio station call letters]
Kerr............ Kerr Group [Associated Press] (SAG)
KERR.......... Kerrier [England]
Kerr .... Kerr's New Brunswick Reports [A publication] (DLA)
Kerr .... Kerr's Reports [27-29 New York Civil Procedure] [A publication] (DLA)
Kerr .... Kerr's Reports [18-22 Indiana] [A publication] (DLA)
KERR .... Polson, MT [AM radio station call letters]
Kerr Act....... Kerr's Actions at Law [3rd ed.] [1861] [A publication] (DLA)
Kerr Anc L.... Kerr on Ancient Lights [A publication] (DLA)
Kerr Black..... Kerr's Blackstone [12th ed.] [1895] [A publication] (DLA)
Kerr Disc ..... Kerr's Discovery [1870] [A publication] (DLA)
Kerr Ext ...... Kerr on Inter-State Extradition [A publication] (DLA)
Kerr F & M... Kerr's Fraud and Mistake [7th ed.] [1952] [A publication] (DLA)
Kerr Fr .... Kerr's Fraud and Mistake [7th ed.] [1952] [A publication] (DLA)
KerrGp......... Kerr Group [Associated Press] (SAG)
Kerr Inj .... Kerr on Injunctions [A publication] (DLA)
KerrMc........ Kerr McGee Corp. [Associated Press] (SAG)
Kerr (NB).... Kerr's New Brunswick Reports [A publication] (DLA)
Kerr Rec ..... Kerr on Receivers [A publication] (DLA)
Kerr Stu Black... Kerr's Student's Blackstone [A publication] (DLA)
Kerr W & M Cas... Kerr's Water and Mineral Cases [A publication] (DLA)
Kerse.......... Kerse's Manuscript Decisions, Scotch Court of Session [A publication] (DLA)
KERUK-NASI... Kerukunan Nasional [Campaign for National Harmony] [Indonesia]
KERV .... Kentucky Equine Respiratory Virus [Veterinary science] (DMAA)
KERV .... Kerrville, TX [AM radio station call letters]
Kerwin .... Kerwin Shops, Inc. [Associated Press] (SAG)
KERX .... Paris, AR [FM radio station call letters]

KES.............. Key Element Search (MCD)
KES.............. Keystone Consolidated Industries, Inc. [*NYSE symbol*] (SPSG)
KES.............. Keystone Consol Ind [*NYSE symbol*] (TTSB)
KES.............. Knigovedenie: Entsiklopedicheskil Slovar [*A publication*]
KES.............. Knowledge Engineering System [*Software Architecture and Engineering Inc.*] (NITA)
KES.............. Ksar Es Souk [*Seismograph station code, US Geological Survey Closed*] (SEIS)
KES.............. Kvakera Esperantista Societo [*Quaker Esperanto Society - QES*] (EAIO)
KESD .... Brookings, SD [*FM radio station call letters*]
KESD-TV ...... Brookings, SD [*Television station call letters*]
KESE............ Bentonville-Bella Vista, AR [*AM radio station call letters*] (RBYB)
KESF............ Alexandria/Esler Field [*Louisiana*] [*ICAO location identifier*] (ICLI)
KESI............. Kentucky Electric Steel [*NASDAQ symbol*] (TTSB)
KESI............. Kentucky Electric Steel Co. [*NASDAQ symbol*] (SAG)
KESI............. Kurzweil Educational Systems, Inc.
KESM........... El Dorado Springs, MO [*AM radio station call letters*]
KESM-FM ..... El Dorado Springs, MO [*FM radio station call letters*]
KESQ .... Palm Springs, CA [*Television station call letters*]
KESS........... Fort Worth, TX [*AM radio station call letters*]
KESS........... Kesselring Site [*Knolls Atomic Power Laboratory*] (GAAI)
KESS........... Kinetic Energy Storage System
KEST........... Kestrel Energy [*NASDAQ symbol*] (TTSB)
KEST........... Kestrel Energy, Inc. [*NASDAQ symbol*] (SAG)
KEST........... San Francisco, CA [*AM radio station call letters*]
Kestrel........ Kestrel Energy, Inc. [*Associated Press*] (SAG)
KESY........... Omaha, NE [*FM radio station call letters*]
KESZ........... Phoenix, AZ [*FM radio station call letters*]
KET.............. Cat Kargo Hava Tasima, AS [*Turkey*] [*FAA designator*] (FAAC)
KET.............. Kengtung [*Myanmar*] [*Airport symbol*] (OAG)
KET.............. Keravat [*New Britain*] [*Seismograph station code, US Geological Survey Closed*] (SEIS)
KET.............. Ketamine [*An anesthetic*]
Ket.............. Kethuboth (BJA)
KET.............. Kiel Electron Telescope
KET.............. Krypton Exposure Technique (MCD)
KETA........... Oklahoma City, OK [*Television station call letters*]
KETAL......... Kalamazoo Area Library Consortium [*Library network*]
KET BD .... Ketone Bodies [*Endocrinology*] (DAVI)
KETC........... St. Louis, MO [*Television station call letters*]
KETG........... Arkadelphia, AR [*Television station call letters*]
KETH........... Houston, TX [*Television station call letters*]
Keth............ Kethuboth (BJA)
KETK........... Jacksonville, TX [*Television station call letters*]
keto............ Ketosteroid [*Endocrinology*]
KE-TP.......... Kinetic Energy-Training Projectile (MCD)
KETR........... Commerce, TX [*FM radio station call letters*]
KETRI.......... Kenya Trypanosomiasis Research Institute
KETS........... Little Rock, AR [*Television station call letters*]
K'ETTE........ Kitchenette [*Classified advertising*] (ADA)
KETV........... Omaha, NE [*Television station call letters*]
KETX........... Livingston, TX [*AM radio station call letters*]
KETX-FM..... Livingston, TX [*FM radio station call letters*]
KEU.............. Eastern Kentucky University, Richmond, KY [*OCLC symbol*] (OCLC)
KEUN.......... Eunice, LA [*AM radio station call letters*]
KEV.............. Kevo [*Finland*] [*Seismograph station code, US Geological Survey*] (SEIS)
keV............. Kiloelectron Volt
KEV.............. King's Empire Veterans [*British military*] (DMA)
KEV.............. Komisarstvo za Evreiskiie Vuprosi [*Bulgaria*] (BJA)
KEVA........... Evanston, WY [*AM radio station call letters*]
KEVII........... King Edward VII [*British*]
KEVIII.......... King Edward VIII [*British*]
Kevlin......... Kevlin Corp. [*Associated Press*] (SAG)
KEVN.......... Rapid City, SD [*Television station call letters*]
KEVT........... Cortaro, AZ [*AM radio station call letters*]
KEVU.......... Eugene, OR [*Television station call letters*]
KEW............. Kew [*England*] [*Seismograph station code, US Geological Survey Closed*] (SEIS)
KEW............. Kewatin
keW............. Kiloelectron Watt
KEW............. Kinetic Energy Weapons [*Military*] (RDA)
KEWB.......... Anderson, CA [*FM radio station call letters*]
KEWB.......... Kinetic Experiment on Water Boiler [*Nuclear reactor*]
KEWE.......... Oroville, CA [*FM radio station call letters*]
KEWI........... Benton, AR [*AM radio station call letters*]
KEWL.......... New Boston, TX [*FM radio station call letters*] (RBYB)
KEWN .... New Bern/Simmons-Nott [*North Carolina*] [*ICAO location identifier*] (ICLI)
KewnSc....... Kewaunee Scientific Corp. [*Associated Press*] (SAG)
KEWR .... Newark/International [*New Jersey*] [*ICAO location identifier*] (ICLI)
KEWS.......... Koger Equity Wrrt [*AMEX symbol*] (TTSB)
KEWS-FM ... Arlington, TX [*FM radio station call letters*] (RBYB)
KEWU.......... Cheney, WA [*FM radio station call letters*]
KEX............. Kanabea [*Papua New Guinea*] [*Airport symbol*] (OAG)
KEX............. Kirby Corp. [*AMEX symbol*] (SPSG)
KEX............. Portland, OR [*AM radio station call letters*]
KEXL........... Norfolk, NE [*FM radio station call letters*]
KEXO .... Grand Junction, CO [*AM radio station call letters*]
KEXS........... Excelsior Springs, MO [*AM radio station call letters*]
KEXT........... Bosque Farms, NM [*FM radio station call letters*] (RBYB)
KEY............. Key [*Commonly used*] (OPSA)
KEY............. Key Anacon Mines Ltd. [*Toronto Stock Exchange symbol*]
KEY............. KeyCorp [*NYSE symbol*] (SPSG)

Key .... Keyes' New York Court of Appeals Reports [*A publication*] (DLA)
KEYA........... Belcourt, ND [*FM radio station call letters*]
Key & Elph Conv... Key and Elphinstone's Conveyancing [*15th ed.*] [*1953-54*] [*A publication*] (DLA)
KEYB.......... Altus, OK [*FM radio station call letters*]
KEYBD......... Keyboard [*Computer science*]
KEYC........... Mankato, MN [*Television station call letters*]
Key Ch .... Keyes on Future Interest in Chattels [*A publication*] (DLA)
KeyCon .... Keystone Consolidated Industries [*Associated Press*] (SAG)
Keycorp .... Keycorp [*Associated Press*] (SAG)
Keycp.......... Keycorp [*Associated Press*] (SAG)
KEYE........... Perryton, TX [*AM radio station call letters*]
KEYE-FM ..... Perryton, TX [*FM radio station call letters*]
KeyEng .... Key Energy Group [*Associated Press*] (SAG)
Keyes.......... Keyes' New York Court of Appeals Reports [*A publication*] (DLA)
KEYE-TV ..... Austin, TX [*Television station call letters*] (RBYB)
KEYF........... Cheney, WA [*FM radio station call letters*]
KEYF........... Dishman, WA [*AM radio station call letters*]
KeyFn .... Keyston Financial, Inc. [*Associated Press*] (SAG)
KEYG........... Grand Coulee, WA [*AM radio station call letters*]
KEYG-FM .... Grand Coulee, WA [*FM radio station call letters*]
KEYH........... Houston, TX [*AM radio station call letters*]
KEYI........... San Marcos, TX [*FM radio station call letters*]
KeyInt .... Keystone International [*Associated Press*] (SAG)
KEYJ .... Abilene, TX [*FM radio station call letters*]
Keyl .... Keylway's [*or Keilway's*] English King's Bench Reports [*A publication*] (DLA)
KEYL........... Long Prairie, MN [*AM radio station call letters*]
Key Lands ... Keyes on Future Interest in Lands [*A publication*] (DLA)
Keylway...... Keylway's [*or Keilway's*] English King's Bench Reports [*A publication*] (DLA)
KEYMAT...... Keying Material [*Computer science*] (NVT)
KEYN.......... Wichita, KS [*FM radio station call letters*]
KEYPER....... Keywords Permuted (DIT)
KEYPrA....... KeyCorp 10% cm Dep Pfd [*NYSE symbol*] (TTSB)
KeyPrd........ Key Production Co., Inc. [*Associated Press*] (SAG)
KEYQ .... Fresno, CA [*AM radio station call letters*]
KEYR........... Marlin, TX [*FM radio station call letters*]
Key Rem..... Keyes on Remainders [*A publication*] (DLA)
KEYS........... Corpus Christi, TX [*AM radio station call letters*]
KEYS........... Keys [*Commonly used*] (OPSA)
KEYS........... Keystone Automotive Industries, Inc. [*NASDAQ symbol*] (SAG)
KeysAut ...... Keystone Automotive Industries, Inc. [*Associated Press*] (SAG)
KeysHer...... Keystone Heritage Group, Inc. [*Associated Press*] (SAG)
Keys St Ex... Keyser's Stock Exchange [*1850*] [*A publication*] (DLA)
KeystFn....... Keystone Financial [*Associated Press*] (SAG)
KEYSTN ...... Keystone
KEYT........... Santa Barbara, CA [*Television station call letters*]
KeyTech...... Key Technology, Inc. [*Associated Press*] (SAG)
KEYTECT..... Keyword Detection (NITA)
Key Trn....... Key Tronics Corp. [*Associated Press*] (SAG)
KEYV........... Las Vegas, NV [*FM radio station call letters*]
KEYW.......... Key West/Key West International [*Florida*] [*ICAO location identifier*] (ICLI)
KEYW.......... Pasco, WA [*FM radio station call letters*]
KEYY........... Provo, UT [*AM radio station call letters*]
KEYZ........... Williston, ND [*AM radio station call letters*]
KEZA........... Fayetteville, AR [*FM radio station call letters*]
KEZB........... Hempstead, TX [*FM radio station call letters*]
KEZC........... Yuma, AZ [*AM radio station call letters*]
KEZD........... Windsor, CA [*AM radio station call letters*]
KEZE-FM ..... Spokane, WA [*FM radio station call letters*] (RBYB)
KEZF........... Tigard, OR [*AM radio station call letters*]
KEZG........... Lincoln, NE [*FM radio station call letters*]
KEZH........... Hastings, NE [*FM radio station call letters*]
KEZI........... Eugene, OR [*Television station call letters*]
KEZJ .... Twin Falls, ID [*AM radio station call letters*]
KEZJ-FM ..... Twin Falls, ID [*FM radio station call letters*]
KEZK........... St. Louis, MO [*FM radio station call letters*]
KEZL........... Fowler, CA [*FM radio station call letters*]
KEZM........... Sulphur, LA [*AM radio station call letters*]
KEZN........... Palm Desert, CA [*FM radio station call letters*]
KEZO........... Omaha, NE [*AM radio station call letters*]
KEZO-FM .... Omaha, NE [*FM radio station call letters*]
KEZP........... Bunkie, LA [*FM radio station call letters*]
KEZQ .... Little Rock, AR [*AM radio station call letters*] (RBYB)
KEZQ .... Sheridan, AR [*FM radio station call letters*]
KEZR........... San Jose, CA [*FM radio station call letters*]
KEZS........... Cape Girardeau, MO [*FM radio station call letters*]
KEZT........... Ames, IA [*FM radio station call letters*]
KEZU........... Booneville, AR [*FM radio station call letters*]
KEZW.......... Aurora, CO [*AM radio station call letters*]
KEZX........... Seattle, WA [*AM radio station call letters*]
KEZY........... Anaheim, CA [*AM radio station call letters*]
KEZZ........... Aitkin, MN [*FM radio station call letters*]
KF............... Catskill Airways [*ICAO designator*] (AD)
KF............... Fiji [*IYRU nationality code*] (IYR)
kf .... Flocculation Speed in Antigen-Antibody Reactions [*Immunology*] (DAVI)
KF............... Gold Coast Judgments and the Masai Cases, by King-Farlow [*1915-17*] [*Ghana*] [*A publication*] (DLA)
KF............... Karl Fischer [*Reagent*] [*Analytical chemistry*]
KF............... Kenner-Fecal Medium [*Organic chemistry*] (DAVI)
KF............... Kerr-Fourier [*Imaging*]
KF............... Key Field

KF .... Kidney Function [*Nephrology*] (DAVI)
KF .... KIDS Fund (EA)
KF .... Kleine Flote [*Piccolo*] [*German*]
KF .... Klenow Fragment [*Genetics*]
KF .... Klippel-Feil [*Syndrome*] [*Neurology*] (DAVI)
KF .... Knight of Ferdinand [*Spain*]
KF .... Knudsen Flow [*Physics*]
KF .... Koff [*Type of ship*] (DS)
KF .... Koinonia Foundation (EA)
KF .... Konservative Folkeparti [*Conservative People's Party (Commonly called the Conservative Party)*] [*Denmark Political party*] (PPE)
KF .... Kontrafagott [*Double Bassoon*] [*Organ stop Music*]
KF .... Korea Fund, Inc. [*NYSE symbol*] (SPSG)
KF .... Kosciuszko Foundation (EA)
KF .... Kossuth Foundation (EA)
KF .... Rhine Air AG [*Sweden ICAO designator*] (ICDA)
KFA .... Keep Fit Association [*British*]
KFA .... Kelowna Flightcraft Air Charter Ltd. [*Canada ICAO designator*] (FAAC)
KFA .... Kernforschungsanlage [*Julich, Germany*]
KFA .... Kiffa [*Mauritania*] [*Airport symbol*] (OAG)
KFA .... Kinesthetic Figural Aftereffects [*Also, KFAE*] [*Psychometrics*]
KFA .... Krishnamurti Foundation of America (EA)
KFAA .... Rogers, AR [*Television station call letters*]
KFAB .... Kidney-Fixing Antibody [*Immunology*]
KFAB .... Omaha, NE [*AM radio station call letters*]
KFAC .... Santa Barbara, CA [*FM radio station call letters*]
KFAD .... Alexandria, LA [*FM radio station call letters*]
KFAE .... Kinesthetic Figural Aftereffects [*Also, KFA*] [*Psychometrics*]
KFAE .... Richland, WA [*FM radio station call letters*]
KFAED .... Kuwait Fund for Arab Economic Development
KFAI .... Minneapolis, MN [*FM radio station call letters*]
KFAL .... Fulton, MO [*AM radio station call letters*]
KFAM .... Keyed File Access Method [*Computer science*] (PDAA)
KFAM .... North Salt Lake City, UT [*AM radio station call letters*]
KFAN .... Johnson City, TX [*FM radio station call letters*]
KFAN .... Minneapolis, MN [*AM radio station call letters*]
KFAO .... Knee-Foot-Ankel Orthosis [*Orthopedics*] (DAVI)
KFAR .... Fairbanks, AK [*AM radio station call letters*]
KFAS .... Casa Grande, AZ [*AM radio station call letters*]
KFAS .... Keyed File Access System
KFAT .... Corvallis, OR [*FM radio station call letters*]
KFAT .... Fresno/Fresno Air Terminal [*California*] [*ICAO location identifier*] (ICLI)
KFAV .... Warrenton, MO [*FM radio station call letters*]
KFAX .... San Francisco, CA [*AM radio station call letters*]
KFAY .... Bentonville, AR [*FM radio station call letters*] (RBYB)
KFAY .... Farmington, AR [*AM radio station call letters*]
KFB .... Air Botnia OY, AB, Finland [*FAA designator*] (FAAC)
KFB .... Bethany College, Lindsborg, KS [*OCLC symbol*] (OCLC)
KFB .... Kuwait French Bank
KFBB .... Great Falls, MT [*Television station call letters*]
KFBC .... Cheyenne, WY [*AM radio station call letters*]
KFBD .... Waynesville, MO [*FM radio station call letters*]
KFBG .... Fort Bragg/Simons Auxiliary Air Base [*North Carolina*] [*ICAO location identifier*] (ICLI)
KFBH .... Kaufman & Broad Home Corp. [*Associated Press*] (SAG)
KFBI .... Klamath First Bancorp [*NASDAQ symbol*] (TTSB)
KFBI .... Klamath First Bancorp, Inc. [*NASDAQ symbol*] (SAG)
KFBI .... Pahrump, NV [*FM radio station call letters*]
KFBK .... Sacramento, CA [*AM radio station call letters*]
KFBN .... Lincoln, NE [*FM radio station call letters*]
KFBQ .... Cheyenne, WY [*FM radio station call letters*]
KFBT .... Las Vegas, NV [*Television station call letters*]
KFC .... Kajagoogoo Fan Club [*Defunct*] (EA)
KFC .... Katholieke Film-Centrale [*Netherlands*]
KFC .... Kentfield [*California*] [*Seismograph station code, US Geological Survey*] (SEIS)
KFC .... Kentucky Fried Chicken Corp. [*Later, KFC Corp.*] (ADA)
KFC .... Korea Friendship Committee [*British*] (EAIO)
KFCA .... Conway, AR [*AM radio station call letters*]
KFCB .... Concord, CA [*Television station call letters*]
KFCC .... Bay City, TX [*AM radio station call letters*] (RBYB)
KFCF .... Fresno, CA [*FM radio station call letters*]
KFCI .... Knife and Fork Club International (EA)
KFCM .... Cherokee Village, AR [*FM radio station call letters*]
KFCR .... Custer, SD [*AM radio station call letters*]
KFCT .... Fort Collins, CO [*FM radio station call letters*]
KFD .... Key Financial Data (ADA)
KFD .... Kinetic Family Drawing [*Psychology*]
KFD .... Kyasanur Forest Disease
KFDA .... Amarillo, TX [*Television station call letters*]
KFDC .... Washington/National Flight Data Center [*District of Columbia*] [*ICAO location identifier*] (ICLI)
KFDF .... Van Buren, AR [*AM radio station call letters*]
KFDI .... Wichita, KS [*AM radio station call letters*]
KFDI-FM ...... Wichita, KS [*FM radio station call letters*]
KFDM .... Beaumont, TX [*Television station call letters*]
KfdO .... Komitee fuer den Osten (BJA)
KFDT .... Kinetic Family Drawing Test [*Psychology*] (DAVI)
KFDX .... Wichita Falls, TX [*Television station call letters*]
KFE .... Kathode Flicker Effect
KFEA .... Korean Federation of Education Associations
KFEL .... Pueblo, CO [*AM radio station call letters*]
KFEQ .... St. Joseph, MO [*AM radio station call letters*]

KFER .... Santa Cruz, CA [*FM radio station call letters*]
KFEZ .... Kansas City, MO [*AM radio station call letters*]
KFF .... Kvinnenes Frie Folkevalgte [*Women's Freely Elected Representatives*] [*Norway Political party*] (PPE)
KFFA .... Helena, AR [*AM radio station call letters*]
KFFA-FM ..... Helena, AR [*FM radio station call letters*] (RBYB)
KFFB .... Fairfield Bay, AR [*FM radio station call letters*]
KFFG .... Los Altos, CA [*FM radio station call letters*] (RBYB)
KFFLBA .... Konglomerati Florida Foundation for Literature and the Book Arts (EA)
KFFM .... Yakima, WA [*FM radio station call letters*]
KFFN-AM ..... Tucson, AZ [*AM radio station call letters*] (RBYB)
KFFO .... Dayton/Wright-Patterson Air Force Base [*Ohio*] [*ICAO location identifier*] (ICLI)
KFFR .... Eagle River, AK [*AM radio station call letters*]
KFFX .... Emporia, KS [*FM radio station call letters*]
KFGE .... Lincoln, NE [*FM radio station call letters*]
KFGG .... Corpus Christi, TX [*FM radio station call letters*]
KFGI-FM ...... Brainerd, MN [*FM radio station call letters*] (RBYB)
KFGO .... Fargo, ND [*AM radio station call letters*]
KFGO-FM ..... Fargo, ND [*FM radio station call letters*]
KFGQ .... Boone, IA [*AM radio station call letters*]
KFGQ-FM ..... Boone, IA [*FM radio station call letters*]
KFGX-FM ..... Detroit Lakes, MN [*FM radio station call letters*] (RBYB)
KFGY-FM ..... Healdsburg, CA [*FM radio station call letters*] (RBYB)
KFH .... Fort Hays State University, Hays, KS [*OCLC symbol*] (OCLC)
KFH .... Ku-Band Feed Horn
KFH .... Wichita, KS [*AM radio station call letters*]
KFI .... Kinetic Fluid Induction
KFI .... Los Angeles, CA [*AM radio station call letters*]
KFIA .... Carmichael, CA [*AM radio station call letters*]
KFIA .... King Fahd International Airport [*Saudi Arabia*]
KFIE .... Merced, CA [*FM radio station call letters*]
KFIG .... Fresno, CA [*AM radio station call letters*]
KFIL .... Preston, MN [*AM radio station call letters*]
KFIL-FM ...... Preston, MN [*FM radio station call letters*]
KFIN .... Jonesboro, AR [*FM radio station call letters*]
KFIR .... Sweet Home, OR [*AM radio station call letters*]
KFIS .... Soda Springs, ID [*FM radio station call letters*]
KFIT .... Lockhart, TX [*AM radio station call letters*]
KFIT EXP STN ... San Antonio, TX [*Radio expansion station*]
KFIV .... Modesto, CA [*AM radio station call letters*]
KFIX-FM ...... Plainville, KS [*FM radio station call letters*] (RBYB)
KFIZ .... Fond Du Lac, WI [*AM radio station call letters*]
KFIZ-FM ...... Fond du Lac, WI [*FM radio station call letters*] (RBYB)
KFJB .... Marshalltown, IA [*AM radio station call letters*]
KFJC .... Los Altos, CA [*FM radio station call letters*]
KFJM .... Grand Forks, ND [*AM radio station call letters*]
KFJM-FM ..... Grand Forks, ND [*FM radio station call letters*]
KFJY .... Grand Forks, ND [*FM radio station call letters*] (RBYB)
KFJZ .... Fort Worth, TX [*AM radio station call letters*]
KFKA .... Greeley, CO [*AM radio station call letters*]
KFKF .... Kansas City, KS [*FM radio station call letters*]
KFKQ .... New Holstein, WI [*FM radio station call letters*]
KFKX-FM ..... Hastings, NE [*FM radio station call letters*] (RBYB)
KFL .... Kenya Federation of Labour
KFL .... Kenya Flamingo Airways Ltd. [*ICAO designator*] (FAAC)
KFL .... Key Facilities List [*AEC*]
KFL .... University of Kansas, Law Library, Lawrence, KS [*OCLC symbol*] (OCLC)
KFLA .... Scott City, KS [*AM radio station call letters*]
KFIAH .... United States Army Hospital, Fort Leavenworth, KS [*Library symbol Library of Congress*] (LCLS)
KFLD .... Pasco, WA [*AM radio station call letters*] (RBYB)
KFLG .... Bullhead City, AZ [*AM radio station call letters*]
KFLG-FM ..... Bullhead City, AZ [*FM radio station call letters*]
KFIGS .... United States Army, Command and General Staff College Library, Fort Leavenworth,KS [*Library symbol Library of Congress*] (LCLS)
KFLL .... Floydada, TX [*FM radio station call letters*]
KFLL .... Fort Lauderdale/Fort Lauderdale-Hollywood International [*Florida*] [*ICAO location identifier*] (ICLI)
KFLN .... Baker, MT [*AM radio station call letters*]
KFLO .... Florence/Municipal [*South Carolina*] [*ICAO location identifier*] (ICLI)
KFLO .... Shreveport, LA [*AM radio station call letters*]
KFLP-AM ..... Floydada, TX [*AM radio station call letters*] (RBYB)
KFLQ .... Albuquerque, NM [*AM radio station call letters*]
KFLR .... Phoenix, AZ [*FM radio station call letters*]
KFLS .... Klamath Falls, OR [*AM radio station call letters*]
KFLS .... Tulelake, CA [*FM radio station call letters*]
KFLT .... Tucson, AZ [*AM radio station call letters*]
KFLW .... St. Robert, MO [*FM radio station call letters*] (RBYB)
KFLX .... Kachina Village, AZ [*FM radio station call letters*]
KFLY .... Corvallis, OR [*FM radio station call letters*]
KFLZ .... Bishop, TX [*FM radio station call letters*]
KFM .... Klystron Frequency Multiplier
KFM .... Knight of St. Ferdinand and Merit [*Italy*]
KFMA-FM ..... Green Valley, AZ [*FM radio station call letters*] (RBYB)
KFMB .... San Diego, CA [*AM radio station call letters*]
KFMB-FM ..... San Diego, CA [*FM radio station call letters*]
KFMB-TV ..... San Diego, CA [*Television station call letters*]
KFMC .... Fairmont, MN [*FM radio station call letters*]
KFMD .... Delta, UT [*FM radio station call letters*]
KFME .... Fargo, ND [*Television station call letters*]
KFMF .... Chico, CA [*FM radio station call letters*]

KFMG............	Pella, IA [*FM radio station call letters*]
KFMH............	Falmouth/Otis Air Force Base [*Massachusetts*] [*ICAO location identifier*] (ICLI)
KFMI............	Eureka, CA [*FM radio station call letters*]
KFMJ-FM ...	Ketchikan, AK [*FM radio station call letters*] (RBYB)
KFMK............	Winton, CA [*FM radio station call letters*]
KFML............	Kommunistiska Foerbundet Marxist-Leninisterna [*Communist League of Marxist-Leninists*] [*Sweden Political party*] (PPE)
KFML............	Little Falls, MN [*FM radio station call letters*]
KFMM............	Thatcher, AZ [*FM radio station call letters*]
KFMN............	Farmington [*New Mexico*] [*ICAO location identifier*] (ICLI)
KFMN............	Lihue, HI [*FM radio station call letters*]
KFMO............	Park Hills, MO [*AM radio station call letters*]
KFMQ-FM ...	Gallup, NM [*FM radio station call letters*] (RBYB)
KFMR-FM ...	Winslow, AZ [*FM radio station call letters*] (RBYB)
KFMS-FM ...	Las Vegas, NV [*FM radio station call letters*]
KFMT............	Fremont, NE [*FM radio station call letters*]
KFMU............	Oak Creek, CO [*FM radio station call letters*]
KFMV............	Franklin, LA [*FM radio station call letters*]
KFMW............	Waterloo, IA [*FM radio station call letters*]
KFMX............	Lubbock, TX [*FM radio station call letters*]
KFMY............	Fort Myers/Page Field [*Florida*] [*ICAO location identifier*] (ICLI)
KFMY-FM ...	South Bend, WA [*FM radio station call letters*] (RBYB)
KFMZ............	Columbia, MO [*FM radio station call letters*]
KFNA............	El Paso, TX [*AM radio station call letters*]
KFNB............	Casper, WY [*Television station call letters*]
KFNE............	Riverton, WY [*Television station call letters*]
KFNF............	Oberlin, KS [*FM radio station call letters*]
KFNN............	Mesa, AZ [*AM radio station call letters*]
KFNO............	Fresno, CA [*FM radio station call letters*]
KFNR............	Rawlins, WY [*Television station call letters*]
KFNS............	Wood River, IL [*AM radio station call letters*]
KFNV............	Ferriday, LA [*AM radio station call letters*]
KFNV-FM ...	Ferriday, LA [*FM radio station call letters*]
KFNW............	West Fargo, ND [*AM radio station call letters*]
KFNW-FM ...	Fargo, ND [*FM radio station call letters*]
KFNZ-AM ...	Salt Lake, UT [*AM radio station call letters*] (RBYB)
KFO............	Killing Federal Officer
KFO............	King Solomon Resources [*Vancouver Stock Exchange symbol*]
KFO............	Klamath Falls [*Oregon*] [*Seismograph station code, US Geological Survey*] (SEIS)
KFOC............	Kaiser-Frazer Owners Clubs of America [*Later, KFOCI*] (EA)
KFOCI.........	Kaiser-Frazer Owners Club International (EA)
KFOE............	Topeka/Forbes Air Force Base [*Kansas*] [*ICAO location identifier*] (ICLI)
KFOG............	San Francisco, CA [*FM radio station call letters*]
KFOK	West Hampton Beach/Suffolk County [*New York*] [*ICAO location identifier*] (ICLI)
KFON............	Austin, TX [*AM radio station call letters*]
KFOR............	Lincoln, NE [*AM radio station call letters*]
KFOR-TV....	Oklahoma City, OK [*Television station call letters*]
KFOX............	Redondo Beach, CA [*FM radio station call letters*]
KFOX-TV....	El Paso, TX [*Television station call letters*]
KFP............	False Pass [*Alaska*] [*Airport symbol*] (OAG)
KFP............	Konstitutionella Folkpartiet [*Constitutional People's Party*] [*Finland Political party*] (PPE)
KFP............	Korean Fighter Program
KFP............	Pittsburg State University, Pittsburg, KS [*OCLC symbol*] (OCLC)
KFPR............	Redding, CA [*FM radio station call letters*]
KFPW............	Fort Smith, AR [*AM radio station call letters*]
KFQC............	Davenport, IA [*AM radio station call letters*]
KFQD............	Anchorage, AK [*AM radio station call letters*]
KFQX-TV.....	Grand Junction, CO [*TV station call letters*] (RBYB)
KFR............	Kayser-Fleischer Ring [*Medicine*] (DMAA)
KFR............	Keefer Resources, Inc. [*Vancouver Stock Exchange symbol*]
KFRA............	Franklin, LA [*AM radio station call letters*]
KFRB-FM ...	Bakersfield, CA [*FM radio station call letters*] (RBYB)
KFRC............	San Francisco, CA [*AM radio station call letters*]
KFRC-FM....	San Francisco, CA [*FM radio station call letters*]
KFRD............	Bellville, TX [*AM radio station call letters*]
KFRE............	Fresno, CA [*AM radio station call letters*]
KFRG	San Bernardino, CA [*FM radio station call letters*]
KFRL............	Kansas Flight Research Laboratory
KFRM............	Salina, KS [*AM radio station call letters*]
KFRN............	Long Beach, CA [*AM radio station call letters*]
KFRO............	Gilmer, TX [*FM radio station call letters*]
KFRO............	Longview, TX [*AM radio station call letters*]
KFRQ............	Harlingen, TX [*FM radio station call letters*]
KFRQ-FM ...	Harlingen, TX [*FM radio station call letters*]
KFRR............	Woodlake, CA [*FM radio station call letters*]
KFRST.........	Killing Frost [*NWS*] (FAAC)
KFRU............	Columbia, MO [*AM radio station call letters*]
KFRX............	Lincoln, NE [*FM radio station call letters*]
KFS............	Kalitta Flying Service, Inc. [*FAA designator*] (FAAC)
KFS............	Kalman Filtering System
KFS............	Keyed File System [*Computer science*]
KFS............	Klippel-Feil Syndrome [*Medicine*]
KFS............	Kohles, F. S., Montebello CA [*STAC*]
KFS............	University of Kansas, Spencer Library, Lawrence, KS [*OCLC symbol*] (OCLC)
KFSA............	Fort Smith, AR [*AM radio station call letters*]
KFSA............	Keep Fit South Australia
KFSB............	Joplin, MO [*AM radio station call letters*]
KFSD	Keratosis Follicularis Spinulosa Decalvans [*Medicine*] (DMAA)
KFSD	San Diego, CA [*FM radio station call letters*]

KFSG	Los Angeles, CA [*FM radio station call letters*]
KFSH & RC...	King Faisal Specialist Hospital and Research Center [*Saudi Arabia*]
KFSI............	Rochester, MN [*FM radio station call letters*]
KFSK............	Petersburg, AK [*FM radio station call letters*]
KFSM............	Fort Smith, AR [*Television station call letters*]
KFSM............	Fort Smith/Municipal [*Arkansas*] [*ICAO location identifier*] (ICLI)
KFSN............	Fresno, CA [*Television station call letters*]
KFSO............	Visalia, CA [*FM radio station call letters*]
KFSR............	Fresno, CA [*FM radio station call letters*]
KFSR............	Karakul Fur Sheep Registry [*Later, AKFSR*] (EA)
KFST............	Fort Stockton, TX [*AM radio station call letters*]
KFST-FM ...	Fort Stockton, TX [*FM radio station call letters*]
KFT............	Kalman Filter Theory
KFTCIC.......	Kuwait Foreign Trading, Contracting & Investment Co.
KFTE............	Breaux Bridge, LA [*FM radio station call letters*]
KFTG............	Pasadena, TX [*FM radio station call letters*] (RBYB)
KFTH............	Marion, AR [*FM radio station call letters*]
KFTL............	Stockton, CA [*Television station call letters*]
KFTM............	Fort Morgan, CO [*AM radio station call letters*]
KFTS............	Klamath Falls, OR [*Television station call letters*]
KFTU............	Korean Federation of Trade Unions [*North Korea*]
KFTV............	Hanford, CA [*Television station call letters*]
KFTW............	Fort Worth/Meacham [*Texas*] [*ICAO location identifier*] (ICLI)
KFTW............	Fredericktown, MO [*AM radio station call letters*]
KFTX............	Kingsville, TX [*FM radio station call letters*] (RBYB)
KFTY............	Santa Rosa, CA [*Television station call letters*]
KFTZ............	Idaho Falls, ID [*FM radio station call letters*]
KFU............	Friends University, Wichita, KS [*OCLC symbol*] (OCLC)
KFUK	Kristelig Forening for Unge Kvinder [*Young Women's Christian Associations - YWCA*] [*Denmark*]
KFUM............	Kristelig Forening for Unge Maend [*Young Men's Christian Associations - YMCA*] [*Denmark*]
KFUN	Las Vegas, NM [*AM radio station call letters*]
KFUO............	Clayton, MO [*AM radio station call letters*]
KFUO-FM ...	Clayton, MO [*FM radio station call letters*]
KFV............	Quest for Value Dual Fd [*NYSE symbol*] (TTSB)
KFV............	Quest for Value Fund [*NYSE symbol*] (SAG)
KFVE............	Honolulu, HI [*Television station call letters*]
KFVPr.........	Quest For Value Income Shrs [*NYSE symbol*] (TTSB)
KFVR............	Crescent City, CA [*AM radio station call letters*]
KFVS............	Cape Girardeau, MO [*Television station call letters*]
KfW............	Kreditanstalt fur Wiederaufbau [*Finance*] [*Germany*]
KFW............	Wichita Public Library, Wichita, KS [*OCLC symbol*] (OCLC)
KFWB............	Los Angeles, CA [*AM radio station call letters*]
KFWD............	Fort Worth, TX [*Television station call letters*]
KFWH............	Fort Worth/Carswell Air Force Base [*Texas*] [*ICAO location identifier*] (ICLI)
KFWJ............	Lake Havasu City, AZ [*AM radio station call letters*]
KFWU............	Fort Bragg, CA [*Television station call letters*]
KFX............	KFX Inc. [*AMEX symbol*] (TTSB)
KFX............	KFX, Inc. [*AMEX symbol*] (SAG)
KFX............	Korean Foreign Exchange (IMH)
KFXA............	Cedar Rapids, IA [*Television station call letters*] (RBYB)
KFXB............	Dubuque, IA [*Television station call letters*] (RBYB)
KFXD............	Nampa, ID [*AM radio station call letters*]
KFXD-FM ...	Nampa, ID [*FM radio station call letters*]
KFXE............	Cuba, MO [*AM radio station call letters*]
KFXE............	Fort Lauderdale/Executive [*Florida*] [*ICAO location identifier*] (ICLI)
KFXF............	Fairbanks, AK [*Television station call letters*] (RBYB)
KFXI............	KFx, Inc. [*NASDAQ symbol*] (SAG)
KFXI............	Marlow, OK [*FM radio station call letters*]
KFX Inc......	KFx, Inc. [*Associated Press*] (SAG)
KFXJ............	Abilene, TX [*FM radio station call letters*]
KFXK............	Longview, TX [*Television station call letters*]
KFXR............	Chinle, AZ [*FM radio station call letters*] (RBYB)
KFXS............	Rapid City, SD [*FM radio station call letters*] (RBYB)
KFXT............	Sulphur, OK [*FM radio station call letters*]
KFXX............	Hugoton, KS [*FM radio station call letters*]
KFXX............	Oregon City, OR [*AM radio station call letters*]
KFXY............	Morgan City, LA [*FM radio station call letters*]
KFXZ............	Maurice, LA [*FM radio station call letters*]
KFY............	KISS [*Knights in the Service of Satan*] - Flaming Youth [*Defunct*] (EA)
KFYI............	Phoenix, AZ [*AM radio station call letters*]
KFYN............	Bonham, TX [*AM radio station call letters*]
KFYO............	Lubbock, TX [*AM radio station call letters*]
KFYR............	Bismarck, ND [*AM radio station call letters*]
KFYR-TV.....	Bismarck, ND [*Television station call letters*]
KFYV............	Fayetteville/Drake Field [*Arkansas*] [*ICAO location identifier*] (ICLI)
KFYZ............	Bonham, TX [*FM radio station call letters*]
KG............	Catalina Airlines [*ICAO designator*] (AD)
KG............	Center of Gravity above Keel (MCD)
KG............	Kammergericht [*District Court, Berlin*] [*German*] (DLA)
KG............	Kampfgeschwader [*Bombardment wing*] [*German military - World War II*]
KG............	Karmann-Ghia [*Volkswagen model designation*]
KG............	Keg
KG............	Ketoglutarate (DMAA)
KG............	Ketoglutaric [*Biochemistry*]
KG............	Key Generator (MCD)
kG............	Kilogauss
kg............	Kilogram [*Also, k*] [*Symbol SI unit for mass*]
Kg............	Kilogram (AAGC)
KG............	Kilogram (GAVI)
KG............	Kindergarten

KG	Kinder, Gentler [America] [In a George Bush speech during the 1989 Republican Convention]
KG	King
KG	Kininogen [Biochemistry]
KG	Knifemakers Guild (EA)
KG	Knight of [the Order of] the Garter [British]
KG	Known Gambler [Police slang]
KG	Kommanditgesellschaft [Limited Partnership] [German]
KG	Kultusgemeinde (BJA)
KG-1	Koeffler Golde-1 [Cell line] [Cytology] (DAVI)
KG5	HMS King George V [British military] (DMA)
KGA	Kananga [Zaire] [Airport symbol] (OAG)
KGA	King's German Artillery [British military] (DMA)
KGA	Kitchen Guild of America
KGA	Kyrghyzstan Airlines [ICAO designator] (FAAC)
KGA	Spokane, WA [AM radio station call letters]
KGAC	Kentucky Guild of Artists and Craftsmen (SRA)
KGAC	St. Peter, MN [FM radio station call letters]
KGAF	Gainesville, TX [AM radio station call letters]
KGAG	Gage [Oklahoma] [ICAO location identifier] (ICLI)
KgAG	Kurzgefasste Assyrische Grammatik [A publication] (BJA)
KGAK	Gallup, NM [AM radio station call letters]
KGAL	Lebanon, OR [AM radio station call letters] (RBYB)
KGAL/MIN	Kilogallons per Minute (MCD)
KGAN	Cedar Rapids, IA [Television station call letters]
KGAP	Clarksville, TX [AM radio station call letters]
KGAS	Carthage, TX [AM radio station call letters]
KGAS-FM	Carthage, TX [FM radio station call letters]
KGB	Kewaunee, Green Bay & Western R. R. [AAR code]
KGB	Kindly Gunn Bunch [Refers to the Metropolitan Transit Authority of New York City; Gunn is the MTA chairman]
KGB	Komitet Gosudarstvennoi Bezopasnosti [Committee of State Security] [Russian Secret Police Also satirically interpreted as Kontora Grubykh Banditov, or "Office of Crude Bandits"]
KGB	Konge [Papua New Guinea] [Airport symbol] (OAG)
KGB	San Diego, CA [FM radio station call letters]
KGBA	Holtville, CA [FM radio station call letters]
KGbB	Barton County Community College, Great Bend, KS [Library symbol Library of Congress] (LCLS)
KGBC	Galveston, TX [AM radio station call letters]
KGBI	Omaha, NE [FM radio station call letters]
KGbLS	Central Kansas Library System, Great Bend, KS [Library symbol Library of Congress] (LCLS)
KGbMC	Central Kansas Medical Center, Great Bend, KS [Library symbol Library of Congress] (LCLS)
KGBR	Gold Beach, OR [FM radio station call letters]
KGBS	Krypton Gas Bottling Station [Nuclear energy] (NRCH)
KGBT	Harlingen, TX [AM radio station call letters]
KGBT-TV	Harlingen, TX [Television station call letters]
KGBX	Nixa, MO [FM radio station call letters]
KGBY	Sacramento, CA [FM radio station call letters]
KGC	Keflin, Gentamicin, and Carbenicellin [Antibiotics] (DAVI)
kgc	Kilogram-Calorie (IDOE)
KGC	Kingscote [Australia Airport symbol] (OAG)
KGC	Kinross Gold [NYSE symbol] (TTSB)
KGC	Kinross Gold Corp. [NYSE symbol] (SAG)
KGC	Kiwi Growers of California (EA)
KGC	Knight Grand Commander
KGC	Knight of the Golden Circle
KGC	Knight of the Grand Cross
KGC	W. M. Krogman Center for Research in Child Growth and Development [University of Pennsylvania] [Research center] (RCD)
kgcal	Kilogram-Calorie
KGCB	Knight Grand Cross of the [Order of the] Bath [British]
KGCB	Prescott, AZ [FM radio station call letters]
KGCF	Kahlil Gibran Centennial Foundation (EA)
KGCK	Garden City [Kansas] [ICAO location identifier] (ICLI)
KGCR	Goodland, KS [FM radio station call letters]
KGCSG	Knight Grand Cross of the Order of St. Gregory the Great [British] (ADA)
kg/cum	Kilograms per Cubic Meter
KGD	Karaganda [Former USSR Geomagnetic observatory code]
KGDC	Walla Walla, WA [AM radio station call letters] (RBYB)
KGDD	Paris, TX [AM radio station call letters]
KGDE	Lincoln, NE [FM radio station call letters] (RBYB)
KGDN	Pasco, WA [FM radio station call letters]
KGDP	Orcutt, CA [AM radio station call letters]
KGE	King-Errington Resources Ltd. [Vancouver Stock Exchange symbol]
KGE	Klein-Gordon Equation [Physics]
KGE	Knights of the Golden Eagle (EA)
KGEE	Monahans, TX [FM radio station call letters]
KGEG	Spokane/International [Washington] [ICAO location identifier] (ICLI)
KGEM	Boise, ID [AM radio station call letters]
KGEN	Hanford, CA [FM radio station call letters] (RBYB)
KGEN	Tulare, CA [AM radio station call letters]
KGEO	Bakersfield, CA [AM radio station call letters]
KGER	Long Beach, CA [AM radio station call letters]
KGET	Bakersfield, CA [Television station call letters]
KGEZ	Kalispell, MT [AM radio station call letters]
KGF	Keilinschriften und Geschichtsforschung [A publication] (BJA)
KGF	Keratinocyte Growth Factor [Biochemistry]
kg-f	Kilogram-Foot
kgf	Kilogram-Force [Unit of force]
KGF	Knight of the Golden Fleece [Spain and Austria]

KGF	Kriegsgefangener [Prisoner of War] [German]
KGFA	Great Falls/Malmstrom Air Force Base [Montana] [ICAO location identifier] (ICLI)
KGFC-FM	Great Falls, MT [FM radio station call letters] (RBYB)
KGF/CM²	Kilogram Force per Square Centimeter
KGFE	Grand Forks, ND [Television station call letters]
KGFF	Shawnee, OK [AM radio station call letters]
KGFJ	Los Angeles, CA [AM radio station call letters]
KGFK	Grand Forks/International [North Dakota] [ICAO location identifier] (ICLI)
KGFL	Clinton, AR [AM radio station call letters]
KGFM	Bakersfield, CA [FM radio station call letters]
KGF/M	Kilogram Force per Meter
KGF/M²	Kilogram Force per Square Meter
KGFR	Keratinocyte Growth Factor Receptor [Biochemistry]
KGFS	King George's Fund for Sailors [British]
KGFT	Pueblo, CO [FM radio station call letters]
KGFW	Kearney, NE [AM radio station call letters]
KGFX	Pierre, SD [AM radio station call letters]
KGFX-FM	Pierre, SD [FM radio station call letters]
KGFY	Stillwater, OK [FM radio station call letters]
KGG	Consolidated Goldwest [Vancouver Stock Exchange symbol]
KGG	Kedougou [Senegal] [Airport symbol] (OAG)
KgGBAS	Kurzgefasste Grammatik der Biblisch Aramaeischen Sprache [A publication] (BJA)
KGGF	Coffeyville, KS [AM radio station call letters]
KGGG	Longview/Gregg County [Texas] [ICAO location identifier] (ICLI)
KGGG	Sterling, KS [FM radio station call letters] (RBYB)
KGGI	Riverside, CA [FM radio station call letters]
KGGK-FM	Winner, SD [FM radio station call letters] (RBYB)
KGGL	Missoula, MT [FM radio station call letters] (RBYB)
KGGM	Delhi, LA [FM radio station call letters] (RBYB)
KGGN	Gladstone, MO [AM radio station call letters]
KGGO	Des Moines, IA [FM radio station call letters]
KGGR	Dallas, TX [AM radio station call letters]
KGGY	Dubuque, IA [FM radio station call letters]
KGH	Kidney Goldblatt Hypertension Scale
KGH	Knight of the Guelphic Order of Hanover [British]
KGHF	Pueblo, CO [AM radio station call letters]
KGHL	Billings, MT [AM radio station call letters]
KGHO-AM	Olympia, WA [AM radio station call letters] (RBYB)
KGHO-FM	Hoquiam, WA [FM radio station call letters]
KGHP	Gig Harbor, WA [FM radio station call letters]
KG/HR	Kilograms per Hour (WDAA)
KGHR	Tuba City, AZ [FM radio station call letters]
KGHS	International Falls, MN [AM radio station call letters]
KGHT	Kidney Goldblatt Hypertension [Medicine] (DAVI)
KGHT	Sheridan, AR [FM radio station call letters]
KGI	Cryderman Gold, Inc. [Vancouver Stock Exchange symbol]
KGI	Kalgoorlie [Australia Airport symbol] (OAG)
KGI	Kellogg [Idaho] [Seismograph station code, US Geological Survey] (SEIS)
KGII	King George II [British]
KGIM	Aberdeen, SD [AM radio station call letters]
KGIN	Grand Island, NE [Television station call letters]
KGIR-AM	Cape Giradeau, MO [AM radio station call letters] (RBYB)
KGIW	Alamosa, CO [AM radio station call letters]
KGJ	Karonga [Malawi] [Airport symbol] (OAG)
KG/J	Kilograms per Joule
KGJ	King Jack Resources [Vancouver Stock Exchange symbol]
KGK	Kabushiki Goshi Kaisha [Partnership] [Japan]
KGK	Koliganek [Alaska] [Airport symbol] (OAG)
KGKL	San Angelo, TX [AM radio station call letters]
KGKL-FM	San Angelo, TX [FM radio station call letters]
KGL	Kaufel Group Ltd. [Toronto Stock Exchange symbol]
KGL	Kigali [Rwanda] [Airport symbol] (OAG)
KGL	King's German Legion [British military] (DMA)
KGL	Koeniglich [Royal] [German]
KGL	Port-Aux-Francais [Formerly, Kerguelen] [France] [Geomagnetic observatory code]
KGLA	Gretna, LA [AM radio station call letters]
KGLB	Okmulgee, OK [Television station call letters]
KGLC	Miami, OK [FM radio station call letters]
KGLD	Tyler, TX [AM radio station call letters]
KGLE	Glendive, MT [AM radio station call letters]
KGLE	South Lake Tahoe, CA [FM radio station call letters]
KGLF	Robstown, TX [AM radio station call letters]
KGLI	Sioux City, IA [FM radio station call letters]
KGLL	Greeley, CO [FM radio station call letters]
KGLM	Anaconda, MT [FM radio station call letters]
KGLN	Glenwood Springs, CO [AM radio station call letters]
KGLO	Mason City, IA [AM radio station call letters]
KGLP	Gallup, NM [FM radio station call letters]
KGLS	Galveston/Scholes Field [Texas] [ICAO location identifier] (ICLI)
KGLS	Pratt, KS [FM radio station call letters]
KGLT	Bozeman, MT [FM radio station call letters]
KGLW	San Luis Obispo, CA [AM radio station call letters]
KGLX	Gallup, NM [AM radio station call letters]
KGLY	Tyler, TX [FM radio station call letters]
KGM	Keratinocyte Growth Medium [Cell culture]
KGM	Kerr Group [NYSE symbol] (SPSG)
KGM	Key Generator Module
KGM	Kiena Gold Mines Ltd. [Toronto Stock Exchange symbol]
kgm	Kilogram [Also, k, kg] [SI unit for mass] (DAVI)
kg-m	Kilogram-Meter

kgm .... Kilogram-Meter (IDOE)
KGM.............. Kluang [*Malaysia*] [*Seismograph station code, US Geological Survey*] (SEIS)
KG/M² .... Kilograms per Square Meter
KG/M³ .... Kilograms per Cubic Meter
kg/m³ .... Kilograms per Cubic Meter (IDOE)
KGMB .... Honolulu, HI [*Television station call letters*]
KGMC .... Clovis, CA [*Television station call letters*]
KGMD .... Hilo, HI [*Television station call letters*]
KGME .... Glendale, AZ [*AM radio station call letters*]
KGMens .... K & G Mens Center, Inc. [*Associated Press*] (SAG)
KGMI .... Bellingham, WA [*AM radio station call letters*]
KGMN .... Kingman, AZ [*FM radio station call letters*]
KGMO .... Cape Girardeau, MO [*FM radio station call letters*]
KGMS .... Green Valley, AZ [*FM radio station call letters*]
KGMT .... Fairbury, NE [*AM radio station call letters*]
KGMV .... Wailuku, HI [*Television station call letters*]
KGMX .... Lancaster, CA [*FM radio station call letters*]
KGMY .... Aurora, MO [*FM radio station call letters*]
KGMY .... Springfield, MO [*AM radio station call letters*]
KGMZ .... Aiea, HI [*FM radio station call letters*]
KGNB .... New Braunfels, TX [*AM radio station call letters*]
KGNC .... Amarillo, TX [*AM radio station call letters*]
KGNC-FM ..... Amarillo, TX [*FM radio station call letters*]
KGND .... Ketchum, OK [*FM radio station call letters*]
KGNM .... St. Joseph, MO [*AM radio station call letters*]
KGNN .... Cuba, MO [*AM radio station call letters*]
KGNN-FM .... Cuba, MO [*FM radio station call letters*] (RBYB)
KGNO .... Dodge City, KS [*AM radio station call letters*]
KGNS .... Laredo, TX [*Television station call letters*]
KGNT .... Grants/Grants-Milan [*New Mexico*] [*ICAO location identifier*] (ICLI)
KGNU .... Boulder, CO [*FM radio station call letters*]
KGNV .... Gainesville [*Florida*] [*ICAO location identifier*] (ICLI)
KGNV .... Washington, MO [*FM radio station call letters*]
KGNW .... Burien-Seattle, WA [*AM radio station call letters*]
KGNZ .... Abilene, TX [*FM radio station call letters*]
KGO .... Kasongo [*Zaire*] [*Airport symbol*] (AD)
KGO .... King's Gurkha Officer [*British military*] (DMA)
KGO .... San Francisco, CA [*AM radio station call letters*]
KGOE .... Eureka, CA [*FM radio station call letters*]
KGOK .... Pauls Valley, OK [*FM radio station call letters*]
KGOL .... Humble, TX [*AM radio station call letters*]
KGON .... Portland, OR [*FM radio station call letters*]
KGOR .... Omaha, NE [*FM radio station call letters*]
KGOS .... Torrington, WY [*AM radio station call letters*]
KGOT .... Anchorage, AK [*FM radio station call letters*]
KGO-TV .... San Francisco, CA [*Television station call letters*]
KGOU .... Norman, OK [*FM radio station call letters*]
KGOZ .... Gallatin, MO [*FM radio station call letters*]
KGP .... Komma Georgiou Papandreou [*Party of George Papandreou*] [*Greek Political party*] (PPE)
KG/(PA S M²)... Kilograms per Pascal Second Square Meter
KGPL .... Dermott, AR [*AM radio station call letters*]
KGPQ-FM ..... Monticello, AR [*FM radio station call letters*] (RBYB)
KGPR .... Great Falls, MT [*FM radio station call letters*]
kgps .... Kilograms per Second
KGPZ .... Coleraine, MN [*FM radio station call letters*]
KGR .... Kanonengranate [*Shell for a gun*] [*German military - World War II*]
KGR .... Kengate Resources [*Vancouver Stock Exchange symbol*]
KGR .... Key Generator Receiver (MCD)
kgr .... Kilograin (BARN)
kgr .... Kirghiz Soviet Socialist Republic [*MARC country of publication code Library of Congress*] (LCCP)
KGR .... Klydonograph Type Gradient Recorder (IAA)
KGRA .... Jefferson, IA [*FM radio station call letters*]
KGRA .... Known Geothermal Resource Area [*Department of the Interior*]
KGRB .... Greenbay/Austin Straubel [*Wisconsin*] [*ICAO location identifier*] (ICLI)
KGRB .... West Covina, CA [*AM radio station call letters*]
KGRC .... Hannibal, MO [*FM radio station call letters*]
KGRD .... Orchard, NE [*FM radio station call letters*]
KGRE .... Greeley, CO [*AM radio station call letters*]
KGRG .... Auburn, WA [*FM radio station call letters*]
KGRI .... Henderson, TX [*FM radio station call letters*]
KGRK .... Killeen/Robert Gray Army Air Field [*Texas*] [*ICAO location identifier*] (ICLI)
KGRM .... Grambling, LA [*FM radio station call letters*]
KGRN .... Grinnell, IA [*AM radio station call letters*]
KGRO .... Pampa, TX [*AM radio station call letters*]
KGRR .... Epworth, IA [*FM radio station call letters*]
KGRR .... Grand Rapids/Kent County Cascade [*Michigan*] [*ICAO location identifier*] (ICLI)
KGRS .... Burlington, IA [*FM radio station call letters*]
KGRT .... Las Cruces, NM [*AM radio station call letters*]
KGRT-FM ..... Las Cruces, NM [*FM radio station call letters*]
KGRV .... Winston, OR [*AM radio station call letters*]
KGRW .... Friona, TX [*FM radio station call letters*]
KGRZ .... Missoula, MT [*AM radio station call letters*]
KGS .... Kate Greenaway Society (EA)
KGS .... Ketogenic Steroid [*Endocrinology*]
kg/s .... Kilograms per Second
Kgs .... Kings [*Old Testament book*]
KGS .... Kos [*Greece*] [*Airport symbol*] (OAG)
KGSB .... Goldsboro/Seymour-Johnson Air Force Base [*North Carolina*] [*ICAO location identifier*] (ICLI)
KGSP .... Parkville, MO [*FM radio station call letters*]

KGSR .... Bastrop, TX [*FM radio station call letters*]
KGST .... Fresno, CA [*AM radio station call letters*]
kgst .... Kilograms Static Thrust (DOMA)
KGStJ .... Knight of Grace, Order of St. John of Jerusalem
KGT .... Kemper Intermediate Government Trust [*NYSE symbol*] (SPSG)
KGT .... Kemper Interm Gvt Tr [*NYSE symbol*] (TTSB)
KGTF .... Agana, GU [*Television station call letters*]
KGTF .... Great Falls/International [*Montana*] [*ICAO location identifier*] (ICLI)
KGTL .... Homer, AK [*AM radio station call letters*]
KGTM .... Rexburg, ID [*FM radio station call letters*]
KGTO .... Tulsa, OK [*AM radio station call letters*]
KGTR .... Larned, KS [*FM radio station call letters*] (RBYB)
KGTS .... College Place, WA [*FM radio station call letters*]
KGTV .... San Diego, CA [*Television station call letters*]
KGTW .... Ketchikan, AK [*FM radio station call letters*]
KGU .... Honolulu, HI [*AM radio station call letters*]
KGU .... Keningau [*Malaysia*] [*Airport symbol*] (OAG)
KGU .... Kobe Gakuin University [*UTLAS symbol*]
KGUL .... Port Lavaca, TX [*AM radio station call letters*]
KGUM .... Agana, GU [*AM radio station call letters*]
KGUN .... Tucson, AZ [*Television station call letters*]
KGUS .... Peru/Grisson Air Force Base [*Indiana*] [*ICAO location identifier*] (ICLI)
KGV .... King George V [*British*]
KGV .... Knight of Gustavus Vasa [*Sweden*]
KGVA .... Fort Belknap Agency, MT [*FM radio station call letters*] (RBYB)
KGVE .... Grove, OK [*FM radio station call letters*]
KGVL .... Greenville, TX [*AM radio station call letters*]
KGVM .... Gardnerville-Minden, NV [*FM radio station call letters*]
KGVO .... King George the Fifth's Own [*British military*] (DMA)
KGVO .... Missoula, MT [*AM radio station call letters*]
KGVT .... Greenville/Majors Field [*Texas*] [*ICAO location identifier*] (ICLI)
KGVW .... Belgrade, MT [*AM radio station call letters*]
KGVW .... Grandview/Richards-Gebaur Air Force Base [*Missouri*] [*ICAO location identifier*] (ICLI)
KGVY .... Green Valley, AZ [*AM radio station call letters*]
KGW .... Kagi [*Papua New Guinea*] [*Airport symbol*] (OAG)
KGW .... Kreeger, George W., Atlanta GA [*STAC*]
KGW .... Portland, OR [*Television station call letters*]
KGWA .... Enid, OK [*AM radio station call letters*]
KGWB .... Wahpeton, ND [*FM radio station call letters*]
KGWC .... Casper, WY [*Television station call letters*]
KGWC .... Offutt Air Force Base, Omaha [*Nebraska*] [*ICAO location identifier*] (ICLI)
KGWL .... Lander, WY [*Television station call letters*]
KGWN .... Cheyenne, WY [*Television station call letters*]
KGWO .... Greenwood-Leflore [*Mississippi*] [*ICAO location identifier*] (ICLI)
KGWR .... Rock Springs, WY [*Television station call letters*]
KGWT .... Kilogram Weight (IAA)
KGWY .... Gillette, WY [*FM radio station call letters*]
KGX .... Grayling [*Alaska*] [*Airport symbol*] (OAG)
KGXY .... Lenwood, CA [*FM radio station call letters*]
kGy .... Kilo Gray [*Absorbed dose*] [*Radiology*]
KGY .... Kingaroy [*Australia Airport symbol*] (OAG)
KGY .... Olympia, WA [*AM radio station call letters*]
KGY-FM .... McCleary, WA [*FM radio station call letters*]
KGYN .... Guymon, OK [*AM radio station call letters*]
KGZ .... Glacier Creek, AK [*Location identifier FAA*] (FAAL)
KGZC .... Folsom, LA [*FM radio station call letters*]
KGZF .... Emporia, KS [*FM radio station call letters*]
KGZH .... Nyssa, OR [*FM radio station call letters*]
KGZO-FM ..... Shafter, CA [*FM radio station call letters*] (RBYB)
KH .... Cambodia [*ANSI two-letter standard code*] (CNC)
KH .... Cook Islandair [*ICAO designator*] (AD)
KH .... Hong Kong [*IYRU nationality code*] (IYR)
KH .... Hungary [*License plate code assigned to foreign diplomats in the US*]
KH .... Kadosh [*Freemasonry*] (ROG)
KH .... Kawasaki Heavy Industries Ltd. [*Japan ICAO aircraft manufacturer identifier*] (ICAO)
KH .... Kelvin-Helmholtz [*Waves*] [*Meteorology*]
KH .... Keren Hayesod (BJA)
KH .... Kersten Hurik Group [*Commercial firm British*]
KH .... Key Hole [*Reconnaissance satellite series*] (DOMA)
KH .... Keyhole Series [*Optical reconnaissance satellites*]
Kh .... Khirbet (BJA)
KH .... Kilohenry
kH .... Kilohertz
KH .... King's Hussars [*Military unit*] [*British*]
KH .... Kneller Hall [*British military*] (DMA)
KH .... Knight of Honor
KH .... Knight of the Guelphic Order of Hanover [*British*]
KH .... Kramers-Henneberger [*Coordinate frame for electron movement*] [*Physics*]
KH .... Krebs-Henseleit [*Cycle*] [*or Ornithine cycle Analytical biochemistry*] (DAVI)
KH .... Krebs-Henseleit Buffer [*Analytical biochemistry*] (DMAA)
KH .... Kupat Holim (BJA)
KHA .... Kansas Hospital Association (SRA)
KHA .... Khancoban [*Australia Seismograph station code, US Geological Survey*] (SEIS)
kha .... Khasi [*MARC language code Library of Congress*] (LCCP)
KHA .... Killed by Hostile Action [*Military*]
KHA .... Kitty Hawk Airways, Inc. [*ICAO designator*] (FAAC)
KHAC .... Tse Bonito, NM [*AM radio station call letters*]

KHAD .... De Soto, MO [*AM radio station call letters*]
KHAK-FM ..... Cedar Rapids, IA [*FM radio station call letters*]
KHalH .... Hertzler Research Foundation, Halstead, KS [*Library symbol Library of Congress*] (LCLS)
KHAP .... Chico, CA [*FM radio station call letters*]
KHAR .... Anchorage, AK [*AM radio station call letters*]
KHAR .... Harrisburg/Capital City [*Pennsylvania*] [*ICAO location identifier*] (ICLI)
KHAS .... Hastings, NE [*AM radio station call letters*]
KHAS-TV ..... Hastings, NE [*Television station call letters*]
KHAT .... Kurzer Handkommentar zum Alten Testament [*Tuebingen*] [*A publication*] (BJA)
KHAT .... Lincoln, NE [*AM radio station call letters*]
KHAW .... Hilo, HI [*Television station call letters*]
KHAY .... Ventura, CA [*FM radio station call letters*]
KHayF .... Fort Hays State University, Hays, KS [*Library symbol Library of Congress*] (LCLS)
KHayv .... Haysville Community Library, Haysville, KS [*Library symbol Library of Congress*] (LCLS)
KHAZ .... Hays, KS [*FM radio station call letters*]
KHB .... Khabarovsk [*Former USSR Geomagnetic observatory code*]
KHB .... King's Hard Bargain [*British military slang for undesirable sailor or soldier*]
KHB .... Korea Housing Bank (IMH)
KHB .... Krebs-Henseleit Bicarbonate [*A buffer*] [*Analytical biochemistry*]
KHB .... KSC [*Kennedy Space Center*] Handbook [*NASA*] (KSC)
KHB .... Kurzgefasstes Exegetisches Handbuch zum Alten Testament [*Leipzig*] [*A publication*] (BJA)
KHb .... Potassium Hemoglobinate (AAMN)
KHBC .... Hilo, HI [*Television station call letters*]
KHBG .... Healdsburg, CA [*FM radio station call letters*] (RBYB)
KHBM .... Monticello, AR [*AM radio station call letters*]
KHBM-FM ..... Monticello, AR [*FM radio station call letters*]
KHBR .... Hillsboro, TX [*AM radio station call letters*]
KHBR .... Hobart [*Oklahoma*] [*ICAO location identifier*] (ICLI)
KHBS .... Fort Smith, AR [*Television station call letters*]
KHBT .... Humboldt, IA [*FM radio station call letters*]
KHC .... 135 Airways [*FAA designator*] (FAAC)
KHC .... Karen Horney Clinic (EA)
KHC .... Kasperske Hory [*Czechoslovakia*] [*Seismograph station code, US Geological Survey*] (SEIS)
KHC .... Kinetic Hemolysis Curve [*Biochemistry*] (DAVI)
KHC .... King's Honorary Chaplain [*British*]
KHCA .... Wamego, KS [*FM radio station call letters*]
KHCB .... Galveston, TX [*AM radio station call letters*]
KHCB .... Houston, TX [*FM radio station call letters*]
KHCC .... Hutchinson, KS [*FM radio station call letters*]
KHCD .... Kenya High Court Digest [*A publication*] (DLA)
KHCD .... Salina, KS [*FM radio station call letters*]
KHCE .... Khabarovsk Commodity Exchange [*Russian Federation*] (EY)
KHCE .... San Antonio, TX [*Television station call letters*]
KHCK .... Denton, TX [*FM radio station call letters*] (RBYB)
KHCME .... Kharkov Commodity and Raw Materials Exchange [*Ukraine*] (EY)
KHCR .... Potosi, MO [*FM radio station call letters*]
KHCS .... Palm Desert, CA [*FM radio station call letters*]
KHCT .... Great Bend, KS [*FM radio station call letters*]
KHCV .... Seattle, WA [*Television station call letters*]
KHD .... Kinky Hair Disease [*Medicine*] (DMAA)
KHDC .... Chualar, CA [*FM radio station call letters*]
KHDN .... Hardin, MT [*AM radio station call letters*] (RBYB)
KHDS .... King's Honorary Dental Surgeon [*British*]
KHDT .... Caldwell, ID [*Television station call letters*]
KHDX .... Conway, AR [*FM radio station call letters*]
KHDY-FM ..... Plainview, TX [*FM radio station call letters*] (RBYB)
KHE .... Kanfey-Ha'Emek Aviation [*Israel*] [*FAA designator*] (FAAC)
KHE .... Kheis [*Former USSR Seismograph station code, US Geological Survey*] (SEIS)
KHE .... Kherson [*USSR*] [*Airport symbol*] (AD)
KHEP .... Phoenix, AZ [*AM radio station call letters*]
KHER .... Crystal City, TX [*FM radio station call letters*]
KHET .... Honolulu, HI [*Television station call letters*]
KHEY .... El Paso, TX [*AM radio station call letters*]
KHEY-FM ..... El Paso, TX [*FM radio station call letters*]
KHF .... Know How Fund [*European economic development fund*]
KHF .... Korean Hemorrhagic Fever [*Medicine*]
KHFD .... Hartford/Brainard Field [*Connecticut*] [*ICAO location identifier*] (ICLI)
KHFI .... Georgetown, TX [*FM radio station call letters*]
KHFM .... Albuquerque, NM [*FM radio station call letters*]
KHFN .... Los Ranchos de Albuquerque, NM [*AM radio station call letters*] (RBYB)
KHFT .... Hobbs, NM [*Television station call letters*]
KHG .... Kashi [*China*] [*Airport symbol*] (OAG)
KHG .... Keystone Heritage Group [*AMEX symbol*] (TTSB)
KHG .... Keystone Heritage Group, Inc. [*AMEX symbol*] (SAG)
K hgb .... Potassium Hemoglobinate [*Organic chemistry*] (DAVI)
KHGI .... Kearney, NE [*Television station call letters*]
KHH .... Kaohsiung [*Taiwan*] [*Airport symbol*] (OAG)
KHH .... Kirchoff, H. H., St. Paul MN [*STAC*]
KHHK-FM ..... Naches, WA [*FM radio station call letters*] (RBYB)
KHHO-AM ..... Tacoma, WA [*AM radio station call letters*] (RBYB)
KHHT .... Killeen, TX [*FM radio station call letters*]
KHI .... Kakhk [*Iran*] [*Seismograph station code, US Geological Survey*] (SEIS)
KHi .... Kansas State Historical Society, Topeka, KS [*Library symbol Library of Congress*] (LCLS)
KHI .... Karachi [*Pakistan*] [*Airport symbol*] (OAG)
KHI .... Kelvin-Helmholtz Instability (PDAA)
KHI .... Kemper High Income [*NYSE symbol*] (SPSG)
KHIB .... Durant, OK [*FM radio station call letters*]
KHIB .... Hibbing/Chisholm-Hibbing [*Minnesota*] [*ICAO location identifier*] (ICLI)
KHID .... McAllen, TX [*FM radio station call letters*]
KHIF .... Keeping House of Ill Fame
KHIF .... Ogden/Hill Air Force Base [*Utah*] [*ICAO location identifier*] (ICLI)
KHIH-FM ..... Denver, CO [*FM radio station call letters*] (RBYB)
KHII .... Security, CO [*FM radio station call letters*]
KHIL .... Willcox, AZ [*AM radio station call letters*]
KHiIT .... Tabor College, Hillsboro, KS [*Library symbol Library of Congress*] (LCLS)
KHIM-TV ..... Conroe, TX [*TV station call letters*] (RBYB)
KHIN .... Red Oak, IA [*Television station call letters*]
KHIP .... Felton, CA [*FM radio station call letters*]
KHIS .... Bakersfield, CA [*AM radio station call letters*]
KHIS-FM ..... Bakersfield, CA [*FM radio station call letters*]
KHIT .... Reno, NV [*FM radio station call letters*]
KHIT-AM ..... Reno, NV [*AM radio station call letters*] (RBYB)
KHIZ .... Barstow, CA [*Television station call letters*]
KHJJ .... Lancaster, CA [*AM radio station call letters*]
KHJM .... Taft, OK [*FM radio station call letters*]
KHK .... Khark [*Iran*] [*Airport symbol Obsolete*] (OAG)
KHK .... Kurzer Handkommentar zum Alten Testament [*A publication*] (BJA)
KHKC .... Atoka, OK [*FM radio station call letters*]
KHKE .... Cedar Falls, IA [*FM radio station call letters*]
KHKI .... Des Moines, IA [*FM radio station call letters*]
KHKK-FM ..... Modesto, CA [*FM radio station call letters*] (RBYB)
KHKR .... East Helena, MT [*AM radio station call letters*]
KHKR-FM ..... East Helena, MT [*FM radio station call letters*]
KHKS .... Denton, TX [*FM radio station call letters*]
KHKY .... Hickory/Municipal [*North Carolina*] [*ICAO location identifier*] (ICLI)
KHL .... Kennedy-Heaviside Layer [*Electronics*]
KHL .... Keren Hajesod Ljisroel (BJA)
KHL .... Khulna [*Bangladesh*] [*Airport symbol*] (AD)
KHL .... Kupat Holim Le-'Ovdim Le'umiyim [*A publication*] (BJA)
KHLA .... Lake Charles, LA [*FM radio station call letters*]
KHLB .... Burnet, TX [*AM radio station call letters*]
KHLB-FM ..... Burnet, TX [*FM radio station call letters*]
KHLL .... Richwood, LA [*FM radio station call letters*]
KHLO .... Hilo, HI [*AM radio station call letters*]
KHLR .... Cameron, TX [*FM radio station call letters*]
KHLR .... Kahler Corp. [*NASDAQ symbol*] (NQ)
KHLR .... KahlerRealty [*NASDAQ symbol*] (TTSB)
KHLS .... Blytheville, AR [*FM radio station call letters*]
KHLT .... Hallettsville, TX [*AM radio station call letters*] (RBYB)
KHM .... Cambodia [*ANSI three-letter standard code*] (CNC)
KHM .... Khamtis [*Myanmar*] [*Airport symbol*] (OAG)
KHM .... King's Harbour Master [*Obsolete British*]
KH-M .... Yad V'Kidush Hashem, House of Martyrs (EA)
KHMA .... Kentucky Hotel and Motel Association (SRA)
KHMB .... Hamburg, AR [*FM radio station call letters*]
KHMC .... Goliad, TX [*FM radio station call letters*]
KHME .... Winona, MN [*FM radio station call letters*]
KHMG .... Barrigada, GU [*FM radio station call letters*] (RBYB)
KHMN .... Alamogordo/Holloman Air Force Base [*New Mexico*] [*ICAO location identifier*] (ICLI)
KHMO .... Hannibal, MO [*AM radio station call letters*]
KHMS .... Victorville, CA [*FM radio station call letters*]
KHMT .... Hardin, MT [*Television station call letters*] (RBYB)
KHMX .... Houston, TX [*FM radio station call letters*]
KHN .... Knoop Hardness Number
KHN .... Nanchang [*China*] [*Airport symbol*] (OAG)
KHN .... Northern Kentucky University, Highland Heights, KY [*OCLC symbol*] (OCLC)
KHNC .... Johnstown, CO [*AM radio station call letters*]
KHND .... Harvey, ND [*AM radio station call letters*]
KHNE .... Hastings, NE [*FM radio station call letters*]
KHNE-TV ..... Hastings, NE [*Television station call letters*]
KHNL .... Honolulu, HI [*Television station call letters*]
KHNR .... Honolulu, HI [*AM radio station call letters*]
KHNS .... Haines, AK [*FM radio station call letters*]
KHNS .... King's Honorary Nursing Sister [*British*]
KHO .... Khorog [*Former USSR Seismograph station code, US Geological Survey*] (SEIS)
KHO .... Khors Aircompany [*Ukraine*] [*FAA designator*] (FAAC)
kho .... Khotanese [*MARC language code Library of Congress*] (LCCP)
KHOB .... Hobbs/Les County [*New Mexico*] [*ICAO location identifier*] (ICLI)
KHOB .... Hobbs, NM [*AM radio station call letters*]
KHOE .... Fairfield, IA [*FM radio station call letters*]
KHOG .... Fayetteville, AR [*Television station call letters*]
KHOK .... Hoisington, KS [*FM radio station call letters*]
KHOL .... Beulah, ND [*AM radio station call letters*]
KHOM .... Houma, LA [*FM radio station call letters*]
KHON .... Honolulu, HI [*Television station call letters*]
KHOP .... Hopkinsville/Campbell Army Air Field [*Kentucky*] [*ICAO location identifier*] (ICLI)
KHOP .... Modesto, CA [*FM radio station call letters*]
KHOS .... Sonora, TX [*AM radio station call letters*]
KHOS-FM ..... Sonora, TX [*FM radio station call letters*]
KHOT .... Globe, AZ [*FM radio station call letters*] (RBYB)
KHOT .... Madera, CA [*AM radio station call letters*]
KHOU .... Houston, TX [*Television station call letters*]
KHOU .... Houston/William P. Hobby [*Texas*] [*ICAO location identifier*] (ICLI)

KHOW .... Denver, CO [*AM radio station call letters*]
KHOX .... Hoxie, AR [*FM radio station call letters*]
KHOY .... Laredo, TX [*FM radio station call letters*]
KHOZ .... Harrison, AR [*AM radio station call letters*]
KHOZ-FM .... Harrison, AR [*FM radio station call letters*]
KHP .... Honorary Physician to the King [*British*]
KHP .... Koppers Hydrate Process
KHPA .... Hope, AR [*FM radio station call letters*]
KHPE .... Albany, OR [*FM radio station call letters*]
KHPN .... White Plains/Westchester [*New York*] [*ICAO location identifier*]   (ICLI)
KHPQ .... Clinton, AR [*FM radio station call letters*]
KHPR .... Honolulu, HI [*FM radio station call letters*]
KHPY .... Moreno Valley, CA [*AM radio station call letters*]
KHQ .... Spokane, WA [*Television station call letters*]
KHQA .... Hannibal, MO [*Television station call letters*]
KHQN .... Spanish Fork, UT [*AM radio station call letters*]
KHR .... Khazar [*Turkmenistan*] [*ICAO designator*]   (FAAC)
KHR .... Khorongon [*Former USSR Seismograph station code, US Geological Survey Closed*]   (SEIS)
KHRI .... Kresge Hearing Research Institute [*University of Michigan*] [*Research center*]
KHRL .... Harlingen/Industrial Airpack [*Texas*] [*ICAO location identifier*]   (ICLI)
KHRN .... Hearne, TX [*FM radio station call letters*]   (RBYB)
KHRO .... Harrison/Boone County [*Arkansas*] [*ICAO location identifier*]   (ICLI)
KHRR .... Tucson, AZ [*Television station call letters*]
KHRT .... Mary Esther/Eglin Air Field Auxiliary [*Florida*] [*ICAO location identifier*]   (ICLI)
KHRT .... Minot, ND [*AM radio station call letters*]
KHS .... Honorary Surgeon to the King [*British*]
KHS .... Kinky Hair Syndrome [*Medicine*]   (DMAA)
KHS .... Knight of the Holy Sepulchre
KHS .... Knight of the Holy Sepulchre of Jerusalem   (DD)
KHS .... Kushtia [*Bangladesh*] [*Airport symbol*]   (AD)
KHSA .... Kentucky Human Services Association   (SRA)
KHSC .... Ontario, CA [*Television station call letters*]
KHSD .... Lead, SD [*Television station call letters*]
KHSH .... Alvin, TX [*Television station call letters*]
KHSL .... Paradise, CA [*FM radio station call letters*]
KHSL-TV ..... Chico, CA [*Television station call letters*]
KHSN .... Coos Bay, OR [*AM radio station call letters*]
KHSP .... Ashdown, AR [*FM radio station call letters*]
KHSP .... Texarkana, TX [*AM radio station call letters*]
KHSS .... Walla Walla, WA [*FM radio station call letters*]
KHST .... Homestead/Homestead Air Force Base [*Florida*] [*ICAO location identifier*]   (ICLI)
KHST .... Lamar, MO [*FM radio station call letters*]
KHSU .... Arcata, CA [*FM radio station call letters*]
KHSX .... Irving, TX [*Television station call letters*]
KHT .... Kathode Heating Time
KHT .... Khost [*Afghanistan*] [*Airport symbol Obsolete*]   (OAG)
KHTC .... Phoenix, AZ [*FM radio station call letters*]   (RBYB)
KHTH .... Dillon, CO [*AM radio station call letters*]
KHTK .... Sacramento, CA [*AM radio station call letters*]
KHTL .... Albuquerque, NM [*AM radio station call letters*]   (RBYB)
KHTL .... Houghton Lake/Roscommon [*Michigan*] [*ICAO location identifier*]   (ICLI)
KHTN .... Los Banos, CA [*FM radio station call letters*]
KHTO .... Mount Vernon, MO [*FM radio station call letters*]
KHTQ .... Hayden, ID [*FM radio station call letters*]   (RBYB)
KHTR .... Pullman, WA [*FM radio station call letters*]
KHTS .... El Cajon, CA [*FM radio station call letters*]   (RBYB)
KHTT .... Muskogee, OK [*FM radio station call letters*]
KHTTA .... Kanata High Technology Training Association [*Canada*]   (EDAC)
KHTV .... Houston, TX [*Television station call letters*]
KHTX .... Salinas, CA [*AM radio station call letters*]   (RBYB)
KHTY .... Santa Barbara, CA [*FM radio station call letters*]
KHTZ .... Albuquerque, NM [*FM radio station call letters*]   (RBYB)
KHu .... Hutchinson Public Library, Hutchinson, KS [*Library symbol Library of Congress*]   (LCLS)
KHU .... Kahuku [*Hawaii*] [*Seismograph station code, US Geological Survey*]   (SEIS)
KHUB .... Fremont, NE [*AM radio station call letters*]
KHuC .... Hutchinson Community Junior College, Hutchinson, KS [*Library symbol Library of Congress*]   (LCLS)
KHUG .... Rocky Ford, CO [*FM radio station call letters*]
KHUL .... Houlton/International [*Maine*] [*ICAO location identifier*]   (ICLI)
KHUM .... Garberville, CA [*FM radio station call letters*]   (RBYB)
KHUT .... Hutchinson, KS [*FM radio station call letters*]
KHV .... Khabarovsk [*Former USSR Airport symbol*]   (OAG)
KhV .... Khranit' Vechno [*To be Kept in Perpetuity*] [*KGB file status*]
KhV .... Khristianski Vostok   (BJA)
KHVH .... Honolulu, HI [*AM radio station call letters*]
KHVN .... Fort Worth, TX [*AM radio station call letters*]
KHVO .... Hilo, HI [*Television station call letters*]
KHVR .... Havre [*Montana*] [*ICAO location identifier*]   (ICLI)
KHWG-FM .... Kings Beach, CA [*FM radio station call letters*]   (RBYB)
KHWI .... Hilo, HI [*FM radio station call letters*]
KHWK .... Tonopah, NV [*FM radio station call letters*]
KHWO .... Hollywood/North Perry [*Florida*] [*ICAO location identifier*]   (ICLI)
KHWY .... Essex, CA [*FM radio station call letters*]
KHWZ-FM .... Ludlow, CA [*FM radio station call letters*]   (RBYB)
KHX .... Hugo Rizzuto [*ICAO designator*]   (FAAC)
KHXS .... Abilene, TX [*FM radio station call letters*]
KHYB .... Kupat Holim Year Book [*A publication*]   (BJA)
KHYI .... Howe, TX [*FM radio station call letters*]

KHYL .... Auburn, CA [*FM radio station call letters*]
KHYM .... Gilmer, TX [*AM radio station call letters*]
KHYS .... Port Arthur, TX [*FM radio station call letters*]
KHYT-FM .... Tucson, AZ [*FM radio station call letters*]   (RBYB)
KHYZ .... Mountain Pass, CA [*FM radio station call letters*]
kHz .... Kilohertz [*Electronics*]
KHZ .... Kilohertz [*FAA*]   (TAG)
KHZL .... Shingletown, CA [*FM radio station call letters*]   (RBYB)
KI .... Kach International   (EA)
KI .... Kanaanaeische Inschriften [*A publication*]   (BJA)
KI .... Karyopyknotic Index [*Cytology*]   (MAE)
KI .... Karyotype Instability [*Genetics*]
KI .... Keyette International   (EA)
KI .... Key Industry [*Business term*]
KI .... Khmer Insurgents [*Cambodian rebel force*]
KI .... Kilo   (WDAA)
KI .... Kinase Insert
KI .... Kings [*Old Testament book*]
KI .... Kitchen   (AABC)
KI .... Kiwanis International   (EA)
KI .... Knesset Israel   (BJA)
KI .... Know, Inc.   (EA)
KI .... Knowledge Integrity [*Electronic information*]   (IT)
KI .... Kovats [*Retention*] Index
KI .... Kroenig's Isthmus [*Of resonance*] [*Medicine*]
KI .... Potassium Iodide   (AAMN)
KiA .... Die Keilinschriften der Achaemeniden [*A publication*]   (BJA)
KIA .... Kachin Independence Army [*Myanmar*] [*Political party*]   (EY)
KIA .... Kaiapit [*New Guinea*] [*Airport symbol*]   (AD)
KIA .... Kansai International Airport [*Japan*]
KIA .... Kent International Airport [*British*]
KIA .... Killed in Action [*Military*]
KIA .... KIWI International Air Lines, Inc. [*ICAO designator*]   (FAAC)
KIA .... Kligler Iron Agar [*Medium*]
KIA .... Kotoka International Airport [*Ghana*]
KIAA .... Kangaroo Industries Association of Australia
KIAB .... Wichita/McConnell Air Force Base [*Kansas*] [*ICAO location identifier*]   (ICLI)
KIA - BNR ... Killed in Action - Body Not Recovered   (MCD)
KIAC .... Kansai International Airport Co. [*Japan*]
KIAC .... Kerr Industrial Applications Center [*Southeastern Oklahoma State University*] [*Durant*] [*Information service or system*]   (IID)
KIAD .... Washington/Dulles International [*District of Columbia*] [*ICAO location identifier*]   (ICLI)
KIAG .... Niagara Falls/International [*New York*] [*ICAO location identifier*]   (ICLI)
KIAH .... Houston/Intercontinental [*Texas*] [*ICAO location identifier*]   (ICLI)
KIAI .... Mason City, IA [*FM radio station call letters*]
KIAK .... Fairbanks, AK [*AM radio station call letters*]
KIAK-FM ..... Fairbanks, AK [*FM radio station call letters*]
KIAL .... Unalaska, AK [*AM radio station call letters*]
KIAM .... Nenana, AK [*AM radio station call letters*]
KIAQ .... Clarion, IA [*FM radio station call letters*]
KIAR .... Kiwanis International Accredited Representative
KIAR .... Kuzell Institute for Arthritis Research [*Medical Research Institute at Pacific Medical Center*] [*Research center*]   (RCD)
KIAS .... Knots Indicated Airspeed   (MCD)
KIAS .... Korea Advanced Institute of Science
KIB .... Ivanof Bay, AK [*Location identifier FAA*]   (FAAL)
KiB .... Keilinschriftliche Bibliothek [*A publication*]   (BJA)
KIBB-FM ..... Los Angeles, CA [*FM radio station call letters*]   (RBYB)
KIBC .... Burney, CA [*FM radio station call letters*]
KIBG-FM ..... Merced, CA [*FM radio station call letters*]   (RBYB)
KIBIC .... Karolinska Institutets Bibliotek och Informationscentral [*Karolinska Institute Library and Information Center*] [*Sweden Information service or system*]   (IID)
KIBL .... Beeville, TX [*AM radio station call letters*]
KIBN .... Wichita, KS [*FM radio station call letters*]
KIBS .... Bishop, CA [*FM radio station call letters*]
KIBZ .... Lincoln, NE [*FM radio station call letters*]
KIC .... Kansas Information Circuit [*Library network*]
KIC .... Karlsruhe Isochronous Cyclotron
KIC .... Kart Industry Council
KIC .... Ketoisocaproate [*Biochemistry*]
KIC .... Keto Isocaproic Acid   (DMAA)
KIC .... King City, CA [*Location identifier FAA*]   (FAAL)
KIC .... Knight of the Iron Crown [*British*]   (ROG)
KIC .... Kosan Boka [*Ivory Coast*] [*Seismograph station code, US Geological Survey*]   (SEIS)
KICA .... Clovis, NM [*AM radio station call letters*]
KICA .... Farwell, TX [*FM radio station call letters*]
KICB .... Fort Dodge, IA [*FM radio station call letters*]
KICB .... Killed Intracellular Bacteria [*Microbiology*]   (DAVI)
KICD .... Spencer, IA [*AM radio station call letters*]
KICD-FM ..... Spencer, IA [*FM radio station call letters*]
KICE .... Bend, OR [*FM radio station call letters*]
KICI .... Corsicana, TX [*FM radio station call letters*]   (RBYB)
KICI .... Denton, TX [*AM radio station call letters*]   (RBYB)
KICK .... Master Glaziers Karate Intl [*NASDAQ symbol*]   (TTSB)
KICK .... Master Glaziers Karate Intl. [*NASDAQ symbol*]   (SAG)
KICK .... Palmyra, MO [*FM radio station call letters*]
KICKW .... Master Glaziers Karate Wrrt'A' [*NASDAQ symbol*]   (TTSB)
KICKZ .... Master Glaziers Karate Wrrt'B' [*NASDAQ symbol*]   (TTSB)
KICM .... Healdton, OK [*FM radio station call letters*]
KICN .... Idaho Falls, ID [*AM radio station call letters*]

KICO	Calexico, CA [*AM radio station call letters*]
KICR	Oakdale, LA [*AM radio station call letters*]
KICR-FM	Oakdale, LA [*FM radio station call letters*]
KICS	Hastings, NE [*AM radio station call letters*]
KICS	Kansas Individualized Curriculum Sequencing (EDAC)
KICT	Wichita, KS [*FM radio station call letters*]
KICT	Wichita/Mid-Continent [*Kansas*] [*ICAO location identifier*] (ICLI)
KICU	Keyboard Interface Control Unit [*Computer science*]
KICU	San Jose, CA [*Television station call letters*]
KICX	McCook, NE [*FM radio station call letters*]
KICY	Nome, AK [*AM radio station call letters*]
KICY-FM	Nome, AK [*FM radio station call letters*]
KID	Idaho Falls, ID [*AM radio station call letters*]
KID	Kent Infant Development Scale (EDAC)
KID	Keratitis, Ichthyosis, and Deafness Syndrome [*Medicine*] (DMAA)
KID	Keyboard Input Device (MCD)
KID	Key Industry [*Business term*] (DS)
KID	Kiddie
KID	Kidd Resources Ltd. [*Vancouver Stock Exchange symbol*]
Kid	Kiddushin (BJA)
KID	Kidnaping [*FBI standardized term*]
KID	Kidney [*Anatomy*] (DAVI)
KID	Kildare [*County in Ireland*] (ROG)
KID	Kinase-Inducible Domain [*Biochemistry*]
KID	Kristianstad [*Sweden*] [*Airport symbol*] (OAG)
KIDA	Ida Grove, IA [*FM radio station call letters*]
KidAInt	Kiddie Academy International, Inc. [*Associated Press*] (SAG)
KIDC	Kentucky Industrial Development Council (SRA)
KIDC	Kiowa Industrial Development Commission
KIDD	First Yars Inc. (The) [*NASDAQ symbol*] (SAG)
KIDD	First Years [*NASDAQ symbol*] (TTSB)
KIDD	Kiddie Products, Inc. [*NASDAQ symbol*] (NQ)
KIDD	Monterey, CA [*AM radio station call letters*]
KiddAcInt	Kiddie Academy International, Inc. [*Associated Press*] (SAG)
KIDDCOS	Kitchens Design Drawing and Costing [*Kitchens International DMS Electronics Ltd.*] [*Software package*] (NCC)
KIDE	4 Kids Entertainment [*NASDAQ symbol*] (TTSB)
KIDE	For Kids Entertainment, Inc. [*NASDAQ symbol*] (SAG)
KIDE	Hoopa, CA [*FM radio station call letters*]
Kideo	Kideo Productions [*Associated Press*] (SAG)
KID-FM	Idaho Falls, ID [*FM radio station call letters*]
KIDH	Eagle, ID [*AM radio station call letters*]
KIDI	Guadalupe, CA [*FM radio station call letters*]
KIDK	Idaho Falls, ID [*Television station call letters*]
KIDN	Hayden, CO [*FM radio station call letters*]
KIDO	Boise, ID [*AM radio station call letters*]
KIDO	Kideo Productions [*NASDAQ symbol*] (SAG)
KIDQ	New Horizon Kids Quest [*NASDAQ symbol*] (TTSB)
KIDQ	New Horizon Kids Quest, Inc. [*NASDAQ symbol*] (SAG)
KIDR	Phoenix, AZ [*AM radio station call letters*]
KIDS	Children's Comprehensive Services [*NASDAQ symbol*] (SAG)
KIDS	Children's Comp Svcs [*NASDAQ symbol*] (TTSB)
KIDS	Kent Infant Development Scale [*Neonatology*] (DAVI)
KIDS	Kestrel Interactive Development System [*Computer science*]
KIDS	Kindergarten Inventory of Developmental Skills [*Child development test*]
KIDS	Knowledge-Based Integrated Design System (DOMA)
KIDS	Springfield, MO [*AM radio station call letters*]
Kidult	Kid-Adult [*Television viewer aged 12-34*]
KIDWE	Direct Connect Intl Wrrt [*NASDAQ symbol*] (TTSB)
KIDX	Billings, MT [*FM radio station call letters*]
KIDY	San Angelo, TX [*Television station call letters*]
KIE	Kennedy Institute of Ethics, Washington, DC [*OCLC symbol*] (OCLC)
KIE	Kieta [*Papua New Guinea*] [*Airport symbol*] (OAG)
KIE	Kinetic Isotope Effect [*Physical chemistry*]
KIE	Kirklees Information Exchange [*Formerly, Huddersfield and District Information*] (NITA)
KIE	Kodak Image Enhancement
KIEE	Knoxville International Energy Exposition [*1982*]
KIEE	Korean Institute of Electrical Engineers
KI-EF	Kiwanis International - European Federation [*An association*]
KIEI	Kundu Introversion-Extraversion Inventory [*Personality development test*] [*Psychology*]
KIEM	Eureka, CA [*Television station call letters*]
KIET	Korea Institute for Industrial Economics and Trade (ECON)
KIEV	Glendale, CA [*AM radio station call letters*]
KIEZ	Carmel Valley, CA [*AM radio station call letters*]
KIF	Kiwanis International Foundation [*An association*]
KIF	Knitting Industries Foundation [*British*] (DBA)
KIF	Knowledge Interchange Format [*Computer science*]
KIF	Kodak Industrial Film
KIF	Korean Investment Fund [*NYSE symbol*] (SAG)
KIF	Name and Address Key Index File [*IRS*]
KIFG	Iowa Falls, IA [*AM radio station call letters*]
KIFG-FM	Iowa Falls, IA [*FM radio station call letters*]
KIFI	Idaho Falls, ID [*Television station call letters*]
KIFIS	Kollsman Integrated Flight Instrumentation System [*Aviation*]
KIFM	San Diego, CA [*FM radio station call letters*]
KIFO	Pearl City, HI [*AM radio station call letters*]
KIFTSG	Kiftsgate [*England*]
KIFW	Sitka, AK [*AM radio station call letters*]
KIFX	Roosevelt, UT [*FM radio station call letters*]
KIG	Koingnaas [*South Africa*] [*Airport symbol*] (OAG)
KIGC	Oskaloosa, IA [*FM radio station call letters*]
KIGL	Spencer, IA [*FM radio station call letters*]

KIGN-FM	Cheyenne, WY [*FM radio station call letters*] (RBYB)
KIGO	St. Anthony, ID [*AM radio station call letters*]
KIGS	Hanford, CA [*AM radio station call letters*]
KIH	Coast Independent Hi-Tech [*Vancouver Stock Exchange symbol*]
KIH	Kaisar-I-Hind [*Indian medal*]
KIH	Kilometres in the Hour [*Rate of march*] [*Military British*]
KIH	Kish Island [*Iran*] [*Airport symbol*] (OAG)
KIHN	Hugo, OK [*AM radio station call letters*]
KIHR	Hood River, OR [*AM radio station call letters*]
KIHR	Korean Institute for Human Rights (EA)
KIHT	St. Louis, MO [*FM radio station call letters*]
K-II	Karyovirus-II (ECON)
KII	Keystone International, Inc. [*NYSE symbol*] (SPSG)
KII	Kuder Interest Inventory [*Occupational information*] (OICC)
KIIC	Kuwait International Investment Co.
KIII	Corpus Christi, TX [*Television station call letters*]
K-III	K-III Communications Corp. [*Associated Press*] (SAG)
KIIK	Fairfield, IA [*FM radio station call letters*]
KIIM	Tucson, AZ [*FM radio station call letters*]
KIIN	Iowa City, IA [*Television station call letters*]
KIIS	Korean Institute of International Studies
KIIS	Los Angeles, CA [*AM radio station call letters*]
KIIS-FM	Los Angeles, CA [*FM radio station call letters*]
KIIX	Wellington, CO [*AM radio station call letters*]
KIIZ	Killeen, TX [*FM radio station call letters*]
KIJ	Independence Community Junior College, Independence, KS [*Library symbol Library of Congress*] (LCLS)
KIJ	Kawah Idjen [*Java*] [*Seismograph station code, US Geological Survey Closed*] (SEIS)
KIJ	Niigata [*Japan*] [*Airport symbol*] (OAG)
KIJK	Prineville, OR [*FM radio station call letters*]
KIJN	Farwell, TX [*AM radio station call letters*]
KIJN-FM	Farwell, TX [*FM radio station call letters*]
KIJV	Huron, SD [*AM radio station call letters*]
KIK	Kentucky's Individualized Kindergartens (EDAC)
kik	Kikuyu [*MARC language code Library of Congress*] (LCCP)
KIK	Kirkuk [*Iraq*] [*Airport symbol*] (AD)
KIK	Kozawa, Iwatsuru, and Kawaguchi [*Factor involving injection of cancerous gastric juices into rabbits, named for its discoverers*] [*Medicine*]
KIKC	Forsyth, MT [*AM radio station call letters*]
KIKC-FM	Forsyth, MT [*FM radio station call letters*]
KIKF	Garden Grove, CA [*FM radio station call letters*]
KIKI	Honolulu, HI [*AM radio station call letters*]
KIKI-FM	Honolulu, HI [*FM radio station call letters*]
KIKK	Pasadena, TX [*AM radio station call letters*]
KIKK-FM	Houston, TX [*FM radio station call letters*]
KIKM	Sherman, TX [*FM radio station call letters*]
KIKN	Salem, SD [*FM radio station call letters*]
KIKO	Claypool, AZ [*FM radio station call letters*]
KIKO	Miami, AZ [*AM radio station call letters*]
KIKR	Asbury, IA [*FM radio station call letters*]
KIKS	Iola, KS [*FM radio station call letters*]
KIKT	Greenville, TX [*FM radio station call letters*]
KIKU	Honolulu, HI [*Television station call letters*]
KIKV	Alexandria, MN [*FM radio station call letters*]
KIKX	Manitou Springs, CO [*FM radio station call letters*]
KIKY	Hutto, TX [*FM radio station call letters*] (RBYB)
KIKY-FM	Hutto, TX [*FM radio station call letters*] (RBYB)
KIKZ	Seminole, TX [*AM radio station call letters*]
KIL	Keyed Input Language
KIL	Keystone Intl [*NYSE symbol*] (TTSB)
KIl	Kil'aim (BJA)
KIL	Kilderkin [*Unit of measurement*] [*British*] (ROG)
KIL	Kilembe Resources Ltd. [*Vancouver Stock Exchange symbol*]
KIL	Kilogram
KIL	Kilometer
KIL	Krypton Ion LASER
KILA	Las Vegas, NV [*FM radio station call letters*]
KIlb	Kilburn's English Magistrates' Cases [*A publication*] (DLA)
KILD	Kildare [*County in Ireland*] (ROG)
KILD	Kilderkin [*Unit of measurement*] [*British*]
KILE-AM	Port Lavaca, TX [*FM radio station call letters*] (RBYB)
Kilern	Killearn Properties, Inc. [*Associated Press*] (SAG)
KILG	Wilmington/Greater Wilmington [*Delaware*] [*ICAO location identifier*] (ICLI)
KILJ	Mount Pleasant, IA [*AM radio station call letters*]
KILJ-FM	Mount Pleasant, IA [*FM radio station call letters*]
KILK	Kilkenny [*County in Ireland*]
Kilk	Kilkerran's Scotch Court of Session Decisions [*A publication*] (DLA)
Kilkerran	Kilkerran's Scotch Court of Session Decisions [*A publication*] (DLA)
KILLS	Ka-Inertial Launch and Leave System
KILM	Wilmington/New Hannover County [*North Carolina*] [*ICAO location identifier*] (ICLI)
KILN	Kirlin Holding [*NASDAQ symbol*] (TTSB)
KILN	Kirlin Holding Corp. [*NASDAQ symbol*] (SAG)
KILO	Colorado Springs, CO [*FM radio station call letters*]
KILO	Kilogram
KILO	Kilometer
KILOL	Kiloliter
KILOM	Kilometer
kilovar	Kilovolt-Ampere Reactive Hour (BARN)
KILR	Estherville, IA [*AM radio station call letters*]
KILR-FM	Estherville, IA [*FM radio station call letters*]
KILS	Minneapolis, KS [*FM radio station call letters*]

KILT............ Houston, TX [*AM radio station call letters*]
KILT-FM...... Houston, TX [*FM radio station call letters*]
KILU........... Paauilo, HI [*FM radio station call letters*] (RBYB)
KIM............ Keyboard Input Matrix [*Computer science*]
KIM............ Kimberley [*South Africa*] [*Seismograph station code, US Geological Survey*] (SEIS)
KIM............ Kimberley [*South Africa*] [*Airport symbol*] (OAG)
KIM............ Kimco Realty [*NYSE symbol*] (SPSG)
KIM............ Knowledge-Based Integrated Machine [*Computer science*]
KIMA.......... Yakima, WA [*Television station call letters*]
KIMB.......... Kimball, NE [*AM radio station call letters*]
Kimbal........ Kimball International, Inc. [*Associated Press*] (SAG)
KimbClk...... Kimberly Clark [*Associated Press*] (SAG)
Kimc.......... Kimco Realty Corp. [*Associated Press*] (SAG)
Kimco......... Kimco Realty Corp. [*Associated Press*] (SAG)
KIMCODE..... Kimble Method for Controlled Devacuation
KimEnv........ Kimmins Environmental Services [*Associated Press*] (SAG)
KIML.......... Gillette, WY [*AM radio station call letters*]
KIMM.......... Rapid City, SD [*AM radio station call letters*]
KIMMA........ Kongres Indian Muslim Malaysia [*Malaysia Indian Moslem Congress*] [*Political party*] (PPW)
KIMN.......... Fort Collins, CO [*FM radio station call letters*]
KIMO.......... Anchorage, AK [*Television station call letters*]
KIMO.......... Kings Mountain National Military Park
KIMP.......... Mount Pleasant, TX [*AM radio station call letters*]
KIMPrA........ Kimco Rlty 7.75% Sr'A'Dep Pfd [*NYSE symbol*] (TTSB)
KIMPrB........ Kimco Rlty 8.50% Sr'B'Dep Pfd [*NYSE symbol*] (TTSB)
KIMPrC........ Kimco Rlty 8.375% Sr'C'Dep [*NYSE symbol*] (TTSB)
KIMS.......... Kennedy Inventory Management System [*NASA*] (SSD)
KIMS.......... Kodak Image Management System (HGAA)
KIMSA........ Kirsten Murine Sarcoma [*Virus*] [*Oncology*] (DAVI)
KiMSV........ Kirsten Murine Sarcoma Virus
KIMT.......... Mason City, IA [*Television station call letters*]
KI MUSV..... Kirsten Murine Sarcoma Virus
KIMX.......... Laramie, WY [*FM radio station call letters*]
KIMY.......... Watonga, OK [*FM radio station call letters*]
KIN............ Association of Kinsmen Clubs (EA)
KIN............ Kinark Corp. [*AMEX symbol*] (SPSG)
KIN............ Kinescope
kin............ Kinetic (VRA)
KIN............ Kingston [*Jamaica*] [*Airport symbol*] (OAG)
KIN............ Kingston [*Jamaica*] [*Seismograph station code, US Geological Survey*] (SEIS)
Kin............ Kinnim (BJA)
KIN............ Kinross-Shire [*Former county in Scotland*] (WGA)
kin............ Kinyarwanda [*MARC language code Library of Congress*] (LCCP)
KINA.......... Salina, KS [*AM radio station call letters*]
Kinark........ Kinark Corp. [*Associated Press*] (SAG)
KINC.......... Las Vegas, NV [*Television station call letters*] (RBYB)
KIND.......... Independence, KS [*AM radio station call letters*]
KIND.......... Indianapolis/International [*Indiana*] [*ICAO location identifier*] (ICLI)
KIND.......... Kindergarten (WDAA)
KIND.......... Kindness in Nature's Defense [*Elementary school course*]
KINDERGTN... Kindergarten
KIND-FM...... Independence, KS [*FM radio station call letters*]
KINE.......... Honolulu, HI [*FM radio station call letters*]
KINE.......... Kinescope
KINE.......... Kingsville, TX [*AM radio station call letters*] (RBYB)
Kinetic........ Kinetic Concepts, Inc. [*Associated Press*] (SAG)
KINF-AM...... Denton, TX [*AM radio station call letters*] (RBYB)
KING.......... Kinetic Intense Neutron Generator
King.......... King's Reports [*5, 6 Louisiana*] [*A publication*] (DLA)
King.......... Select Cases in Chancery Tempore King, Edited by Macnaghten [*1724-33*] [*England*] [*A publication*] (DLA)
King Cas..... Cases in King's Colorado Civil Practice [*A publication*] (DLA)
King Cas Temp... Select Cases in Chancery Tempore King [*1724-33*] [*England*] [*A publication*] (DLA)
KINGD........ Kingdom
King Dig...... King's Tennessee Digest [*A publication*] (DLA)
King-Farlow... Gold Coast Judgments and the Masai Cases, by King-Farlow [*1915-17*] [*Ghana*] [*A publication*] (DLA)
KING-FM...... Seattle, WA [*FM radio station call letters*]
KINGMAP..... King's Music Analysis Package [*King's College*] [*University of London*] [*British*] (NITA)
Kings.......... Kingsway [*Record label*]
KINGSBR..... Kingsbridge [*England*]
King's Con Cs... King's Conflicting Cases [*Texas*] [*A publication*] (DLA)
King's Conf Ca... King's Conflicting Cases [*Texas*] [*A publication*] (DLA)
KING-TV...... Seattle, WA [*Television station call letters*]
KingWd....... King World Productions [*Associated Press*] (SAG)
KINI.......... Crookston, NE [*FM radio station call letters*]
KINK.......... Portland, OR [*FM radio station call letters*]
KINK.......... Wink/Winkler County [*Texas*] [*ICAO location identifier*] (ICLI)
KINL.......... Eagle Pass, TX [*FM radio station call letters*]
KINL.......... International Falls [*Minnesota*] [*ICAO location identifier*] (ICLI)
KINN.......... Alamogordo, NM [*AM radio station call letters*]
KINN.......... Kinnard Investments [*NASDAQ symbol*] (TTSB)
KINN.......... Kinnard Investments, Inc. [*NASDAQ symbol*] (NQ)
Kinnard....... Kinnard Investments, Inc. [*Associated Press*] (SAG)
Kinney Law Dict & Glos... Kinney's Law Dictionary and Glossary [*A publication*] (DLA)
KINO.......... Winslow, AZ [*AM radio station call letters*]
Kinross........ Kinross Gold Corp. [*Associated Press*] (SAG)
KINS.......... Eureka, CA [*AM radio station call letters*]

KINS........... Indian Springs/Indian Springs Army Air Field [*Nevada*] [*ICAO location identifier*] (ICLI)
KINSA........ Kodak International Newspaper Snapshot Awards
KINSYM....... Kinematic Synthesis (PDAA)
KINT.......... El Paso, TX [*Television station call letters*]
KINT.......... Winston Salem/Smith-Reynolds [*North Carolina*] [*ICAO location identifier*] (ICLI)
KINTB........ Kintbury [*England*]
KINT-FM...... El Paso, TX [*FM radio station call letters*]
KINY.......... Juneau, AK [*AM radio station call letters*]
KINZ-TV...... Arlington, TX [*TV station call letters*] (RBYB)
KIo........... Iola Free Public Library, Iola, KS [*Library symbol Library of Congress*] (LCLS)
KIO........... Kachin Independence Organization [*Myanmar*] [*Political party*] (EY)
KIO........... Kick It Off [*Slang*] (DOMA)
KIO........... Kili [*Marshall Islands*] [*Airport symbol*] (OAG)
KIO........... Kraiaero [*Russian Federation*] [*ICAO designator*] (FAAC)
KIOA.......... Des Moines, IA [*AM radio station call letters*]
KIOA-FM..... Des Moines, IA [*FM radio station call letters*]
KIOC.......... Orange, TX [*FM radio station call letters*]
KIOI.......... San Francisco, CA [*FM radio station call letters*]
KIOK.......... Richland, WA [*FM radio station call letters*]
KIOL.......... Lamesa, TX [*FM radio station call letters*]
KIOO.......... Porterville, CA [*FM radio station call letters*]
KIOPI......... Kienzle Input/Output Peripheral Interface
KIOPI......... Kienzle Input/Output Processor Interface (NITA)
KIOQ.......... Folsom, CA [*AM radio station call letters*]
KIOS.......... Omaha, NE [*FM radio station call letters*]
KIoS.......... Southeast Kansas Library System, Iola, KS [*Library symbol Library of Congress*] (LCLS)
KIOT.......... Los Lunas [*FM radio station call letters*]
KIOU.......... Shreveport, LA [*AM radio station call letters*]
KIOV.......... Payette, ID [*AM radio station call letters*]
KIOW.......... Forest City, IA [*FM radio station call letters*]
KIOX.......... El Campo, TX [*FM radio station call letters*]
KIOZ.......... Oceanside, CA [*FM radio station call letters*]
KIP........... Keyboard Input Processor [*Computer science*] (NASA)
KIP........... Key Indigenous Personnel (MCD)
KIP........... Key Intelligence Position (AFM)
KIP........... Key Intermediary Proteins (DAVI)
KIP........... Kilopound (IAA)
KIP........... Kipapa [*Hawaii*] [*Seismograph station code, US Geological Survey*] (SEIS)
KIP........... Kit, Individual Protection [*British army*] (INF)
KIP........... Knowledge Industry Publications, Inc. [*Telecommunications*]
KIP........... Knowledge Information Processing [*Computer science*]
KIP........... Thousand Pounds
KIPA.......... Hilo, HI [*AM radio station call letters*]
KIP-FT........ Thousand Foot-Pounds
KIPI.......... Knowledge Industry Publications, Inc. [*White Plains, NY*] [*Telecommunications Information service or system*]
KIPL.......... Imperial/Imperial County [*California*] [*ICAO location identifier*] (ICLI)
Kiplinger..... Kiplinger's Personal Finance Magazine [*A publication*] (BRI)
KIPO.......... Honolulu, HI [*FM radio station call letters*]
KIPO.......... Keyboard Input Printout [*Computer science*] (IEEE)
KIPR.......... Pine Bluff, AR [*FM radio station call letters*]
KIPS.......... 10^3 (K) of Instructions Per Second [*Unit of computer processing speed*] (NITA)
KIPS.......... Kaufman Infant and Preschool Scale [*Child development test*] [*Psychology*]
KIPS.......... Key Indicators, Probes, and a Scoring Method [*Health care*] (HCT)
KIPS.......... Kilo-Instructions per Second
KIPS.......... Kilowatt Isotope Power System (IEEE)
KIPS.......... Knowledge Information Processing Systems [*Computer science*]
KIPT.......... Twin Falls, ID [*Television station call letters*]
KIQ........... Key Intelligence Question [*CIA*]
KIQ........... Kira [*Papua New Guinea*] [*Airport symbol*] (OAG)
KIQI.......... San Francisco, CA [*AM radio station call letters*]
KIQK.......... Rapid City, SD [*FM radio station call letters*]
KIQO.......... Atascadero, CA [*FM radio station call letters*]
KIQQ.......... Barstow, CA [*AM radio station call letters*]
KIQS.......... Willows, CA [*AM radio station call letters*]
KIQX.......... Durango, CO [*FM radio station call letters*]
KIQZ.......... Rawlins, WY [*FM radio station call letters*]
KIR........... Key Intelligence Requirement (MCD)
KIR........... Killer-Cell Inhibitory Receptor [*Immunology*]
Kir........... Kirby's Connecticut Reports and Supplement [*1785-89*] [*A publication*]
kir........... Kirghiz [*MARC language code Library of Congress*] (LCCP)
KIR........... Kiruna [*Sweden*] [*Seismograph station code, US Geological Survey*] (SEIS)
KIR........... Kiruna [*Sweden*] [*Geomagnetic observatory code*]
KIR........... Knight's Industrial Reports [*A publication*] (DLA)
Kirb.......... Kirby's Connecticut Reports and Supplement [*1785-89*] [*A publication*] (DLA)
KIRBS........ Korean Institute for Research in the Behavioral Sciences
Kirby......... Kirby Exploration Co., Inc. [*Associated Press*] (SAG)
Kirby......... Kirby's Connecticut Reports and Supplement [*1785-89*] [*A publication*] (DLA)
Kirby's Conn R... Kirby's Connecticut Reports [*A publication*] (DLA)
Kirby's R..... Kirby's Connecticut Reports [*A publication*] (DLA)
Kirby's Rep... Kirby's Connecticut Reports [*A publication*] (DLA)
KIRC.......... Seminole, OK [*FM radio station call letters*]
KirinBr........ Kirin Brewery Co. Ltd. [*Associated Press*] (SAG)
KIRK.......... Kirkcaldy [*Seaport in Scotland*]

KIRK .... Lebanon, MO [*FM radio station call letters*]
KIRKCUDB ... Kirkcudbrightshire [*County in Scotland*]
KIRL .... St. Charles, MO [*AM radio station call letters*]
Kirlin .... Kirlin Holding Corp. [*Associated Press*] (SAG)
KIRO .... Seattle, WA [*AM radio station call letters*]
KIRO-FM ...... Seattle, WA [*FM radio station call letters*]
KIRO-TV ...... Seattle, WA [*Television station call letters*]
KIRP .... Kodak Infrared Phosphor
KIRQ .... Lawton, OK [*FM radio station call letters*] (RBYB)
KIRS .... Kodak Infrared Scope
KIRS .... Sun Valley, NV [*AM radio station call letters*] (RBYB)
KirSeph. ...... Kirjath Sepher [*Jerusalem*] (BJA)
KirSSR .... Kirghiz Soviet Socialist Republic
KIRT .... Mission, TX [*AM radio station call letters*]
Kirt Sur Pr ... Kirtland on Practice in Surrogates' Courts [*A publication*] (DLA)
KIRV .... Fresno, CA [*AM radio station call letters*]
KIRX .... Kirksville, MO [*AM radio station call letters*]
KIS .... Contactair Flugdienst & Co. [*Germany ICAO designator*] (FAAC)
KIS .... Keep It Simple (ADA)
KIS .... Kenny Information Systems [*Database producer*] (IID)
KIS .... Kenya Independent Squadron [*British military*] (DMA)
KIS .... Keyboard Input Simulation [*Computer science*]
KIS .... Kishinev [*Former USSR Seismograph station code, US Geological Survey*] (SEIS)
KIS .... Kisumu [*Kenya*] [*Airport symbol*] (OAG)
KIS .... Kitting Instruction Sheet [*NASA*] (NASA)
KIS .... Kodak Infrared Scope
KIS .... Krankenhaus Information System (DAVI)
KISA .... Honolulu, HI [*AM radio station call letters*]
KISA .... Karaoke International Sing-Along Association (EA)
KISA .... Voluntary International Service Assignments [*of the Society of Friends*]
Kisb Ir Land L.. Kisbey on the Irish Land Law [*A publication*] (DLA)
KISC .... Knowledge Industry Systems Concept [*Publishing and education*] [*Pronounced "kiss"*]
KISC .... Knowledge Information Skills and Curriculum [*Project*] (AIE)
KISC .... Spokane, WA [*FM radio station call letters*]
KISD .... Pipestone, MN [*FM radio station call letters*]
KISE-FM ...... Seaside, CA [*FM radio station call letters*] (RBYB)
KISF .... Lexington, MO [*FM radio station call letters*]
KISI .... Malvern, AR [*AM radio station call letters*]
KISL .... Avalon, CA [*FM radio station call letters*]
KISM-FM ..... Bellingham, WA [*FM radio station call letters*] (RBYB)
KISMIF .... Keep It Simple, Make It Fun
KISN .... Salt Lake City, UT [*AM radio station call letters*]
KISN .... Williston/International [*North Dakota*] [*ICAO location identifier*] (ICLI)
KISN-FM ...... Salt Lake City, UT [*FM radio station call letters*]
KISNOPI ...... Keyboard Input Stimulation Noise Problem Input (IAA)
KISO .... Phoenix, AZ [*AM radio station call letters*]
KISP .... Blair, NE [*FM radio station call letters*]
KISP .... Islip/MacArthur Field [*New York*] [*ICAO location identifier*] (ICLI)
KISR .... Fort Smith, AR [*FM radio station call letters*]
KISS .... Keep It Short and Simple (MCD)
KISS .... Keep It Short and Sweet [*Radio messages*]
KISS .... Keep It Simple, Sir (SAA)
KISS .... Keep It Simple, Stupid [*Bridge bidding term*]
KISS .... Keep It Straight and Simple [*Computer science*]
KISS .... Keyed Indexed Sequential Search
KISS .... Key Integrative Social Systems
KISS .... Knights in the Service of Satan [*Rock music group*]
KISS .... Knowledge Integrating Simulation System
KISS .... Korean Intelligence Support System (DOMA)
KISS .... San Antonio, TX [*FM radio station call letters*]
KISS .... Saturated Solution of Potassium Iodide [*Pharmacology*] (DAVI)
KIST .... Keyword Index to Serial Titles [*A publication*]
KIST .... Korean Institute for Science and Technology
KIST .... Santa Barbara, CA [*AM radio station call letters*]
KISU .... Pocatello, ID [*Television station call letters*]
KiSV .... Kirsten Sarcoma Virus
KISW .... Seattle, WA [*FM radio station call letters*]
KISX .... Whitehouse, TX [*FM radio station call letters*]
KISZ .... Cortez, CO [*FM radio station call letters*]
KISZ .... Kommunista Ifjusagi Szovetseg [*Communist Youth Organization*] [*Hungary*]
KIT .... Kahn Intelligence Test (DMAA)
KIT .... Kaufman Ion Thrustor
KIT .... Keep in Touch [*Slang*] (DNAB)
KIT .... Kent Information Technology Conference (NITA)
KIT .... Kentucky & Indiana Terminal Railroad Co. [*AAR code*]
KIT .... Kermit [*Texas*] [*Seismograph station code, US Geological Survey*] (SEIS)
KIT .... Key Issue Tracking [*Database*]
KIT .... Kitchen (ADA)
Kit .... Kitchin's Retourna Brevium [*4 eds.*] [*1581-92*] [*A publication*] (DLA)
Kit .... Kithira [*Greece*] [*Airport symbol*] (OAG)
Kit .... Kit Manufacturing Co. [*AMEX symbol*] (SPSG)
Kit .... Kit Mfg [*AMEX symbol*] (TTSB)
KIT .... Kittrell Junior College, Kittrell, NC [*Inactive*] [*OCLC symbol*] (OCLC)
KIT .... KWIC Interactive Tagger [*University of Minnesota*] [*Text editing system*] (NITA)
KIT .... Yakima, WA [*AM radio station call letters*]
KITA .... Kesatuan Insaf Tanah Air [*National Consciousness Party*] [*Malaysia*] [*Political party*] (PPW)
KITA .... Kick in the Afterdeck [*Bowdlerized version*]
KITA .... Little Rock, AR [*AM radio station call letters*]

kitch........... Kitchen (BARN)
Kitch .... Kitchin on Jurisdictions of Courts-Leet, Courts-Baron, Etc. [*A publication*] (DLA)
Kitch Courts... Kitchin on Jurisdictions of Courts-Leet, Courts-Baron, Etc. [*A publication*] (DLA)
Kitch Cts...... Kitchin on Courts [*A publication*] (DLA)
Kitchen .... Griqualand West Reports [*Cape Colony, South Africa*] [*A publication*] (DLA)
Kit Ct .... Kitchin on Jurisdictions of Courts-Leet, Courts-Baron, Etc. [*A publication*] (DLA)
KITE .... Kerrville, TX [*FM radio station call letters*]
KITE .... Kinetic Energy Weapon Integrated Test Experiment (MCD)
KITES .... Kinescope Image Test and Evaluation System (MCD)
KITG .... Kiting (ABBR)
KITI .... Centralia-Chehalis, WA [*AM radio station call letters*]
KITI .... Winlock, WA [*AM radio station call letters*] (RBYB)
Kit Jur .... Kitchin on Jurisdictions of Courts-Leet, Courts-Baron, Etc. [*A publication*] (DLA)
Kit Mfg .... Kit Manufacturing Co. [*Associated Press*] (SAG)
KITN .... Kitten (ABBR)
KITN .... Worthington, MN [*FM radio station call letters*] (RBYB)
KITO .... Vinita, OK [*AM radio station call letters*]
KITO-FM ..... Vinita, OK [*FM radio station call letters*]
KITR .... Creston, IA [*FM radio station call letters*]
Kit Rd Trans... Kitchin's Road Transport Law [*19th ed.*] [*1978*] [*A publication*] (DLA)
KITS .... Meridian Diagnostics [*NASDAQ symbol*] (TTSB)
KITS .... San Francisco, CA [*FM radio station call letters*]
KITT .... Kinetic Tree Theory (PDAA)
KITT .... Knight Industries Two Thousand [*Acronym is name of computerized car in TV series "Knight Rider"*]
KITT .... Korean International Telephone & Telegraph
KITT .... Shreveport, LA [*FM radio station call letters*]
KITTY .... Kentucky-Illinois-Tennessee League [*Old baseball league*]
KittyHk........ Kitty Hawk, Inc. [*Associated Press*] (SAG)
KITU .... Beaumont, TX [*Television station call letters*]
KITV .... Honolulu, HI [*Television station call letters*]
KITX .... Hugo, OK [*FM radio station call letters*]
KITZ .... Silverdale, WA [*AM radio station call letters*]
KIU .... Kainantu [*New Guinea*] [*Airport symbol*] (AD)
KIU .... Kallikrein Inactivator Unit [*Analytical biochemistry*]
KIU .... Kallikrein-Inhibiting Unit [*Analytical biochemistry*] (DAVI)
KIUL .... Garden City, KS [*AM radio station call letters*]
KIUN .... Pecos, TX [*AM radio station call letters*]
KIUP .... Durango, CO [*AM radio station call letters*]
KIV .... Air Kiev [*Ukraine*] [*FAA designator*] (FAAC)
KIV .... Kali Venture Corp. [*Vancouver Stock Exchange symbol*]
KIV .... Keep in View
KIV .... Ketoisovalerate [*Biochemistry*]
KIV .... Kiev [*Former USSR Geomagnetic observatory code*]
KIV .... Kishinev [*Former USSR Airport symbol*] (OAG)
KIVA .... Corrales, NM [*AM radio station call letters*]
KIVA .... Workgroup for Indians of North America [*Acronym is based on foreign phrase Netherlands*]
KIVI .... Koninklijk Instituut van Inginieurs [*Netherlands*] (ACII)
KIVI .... Nampa, ID [*Television station call letters*]
KIVV .... Lead, SD [*Television station call letters*]
KIVY .... Crockett, TX [*AM radio station call letters*]
KIVY-FM ...... Crockett, TX [*FM radio station call letters*]
KIW .... Kitwe [*Zambia*] [*Airport symbol*] (OAG)
KIW .... Royal New Zealand Air Force [*FAA designator*] (FAAC)
KIWA .... Keuringsinstituut voor Waterleidingartikelen
KIWA .... Sheldon, IA [*AM radio station call letters*]
KIWA-FM ..... Sheldon, IA [*FM radio station call letters*]
KIWI .... Bakersfield, CA [*FM radio station call letters*]
KIWR .... Council Bluffs, IA [*FM radio station call letters*]
KIWW .... Harlingen, TX [*FM radio station call letters*]
KIXA .... Lucerne Valley, CA [*FM radio station call letters*]
KIXB .... El Dorado, AR [*FM radio station call letters*]
KIXC .... Quanah, TX [*FM radio station call letters*]
KIXE .... Redding, CA [*Television station call letters*]
KIXF .... Baker, CA [*FM radio station call letters*]
KIXF .... Kodak Industrial X-Ray Film
KIXI .... Mercer Island-Seattle, WA [*AM radio station call letters*]
KIXK .... Canton, SD [*FM radio station call letters*] (RBYB)
KIXL .... Del Valle, TX [*AM radio station call letters*]
KIXN .... Hobbs, NM [*FM radio station call letters*] (RBYB)
KIXQ .... Webb City, MO [*FM radio station call letters*]
KIXR .... Ponca City, OK [*FM radio station call letters*]
KIXS .... Victoria, TX [*FM radio station call letters*]
KIXT-FM ...... Grover City, CA [*FM radio station call letters*]
KIXV .... Brady, TX [*FM radio station call letters*]
KIXW .... Apple Valley, CA [*AM radio station call letters*] (RBYB)
KIXW .... Lenwood, CA [*FM radio station call letters*]
KIXX .... Watertown, SD [*FM radio station call letters*]
KIXY .... San Angelo, TX [*FM radio station call letters*]
KIXZ .... Amarillo, TX [*AM radio station call letters*]
KIY .... Kilwa [*Tanzania*] [*Airport symbol*] (OAG)
KIY .... Kiyosumi [*Japan*] [*Seismograph station code, US Geological Survey Closed*] (SEIS)
KIYS .... Jonesboro, AR [*FM radio station call letters*]
KIYU .... Galena, AK [*AM radio station call letters*]
KIYX-FM ...... Sageville, IA [*FM radio station call letters*] (RBYB)
KIZ .... Kanaf-Arkia Airlines Ltd. [*Israel*] [*ICAO designator*] (FAAC)
KIZN .... Boise, ID [*FM radio station call letters*]

KIZZ .... Minot, ND [*FM radio station call letters*]
KJ .... Air Guyane [*ICAO designator*] (AD)
KJ .... Jamaica [*IYRU nationality code*] (IYR)
kJ .... Kilojoule
KJ .... King James [*Version of the Bible*] (WDAA)
KJ .... Kirchenmusikalisches Jahrbuch [*A publication*]
KJ .... Knee Jerk [*Medicine*]
KJ .... Knight of St. Joachim
KJ .... Knights of Jurisprudence
KJA .... Avistar (Cyprus) Ltd. [*ICAO designator*] (FAAC)
KJAA .... Globe, AZ [*AM radio station call letters*]
KJAB .... Mexico, MO [*FM radio station call letters*]
KJAC .... Port Arthur, TX [*Television station call letters*]
KJAE .... Leesville, LA [*FM radio station call letters*]
KJAK .... Slaton, TX [*FM radio station call letters*]
KJAM .... Madison, SD [*AM radio station call letters*]
KJAM-FM .... Madison, SD [*FM radio station call letters*]
KJAN .... Atlantic, IA [*AM radio station call letters*]
KJAN .... Jackson/Allen C. Thompson Field [*Mississippi*] [*ICAO location identifier*] (ICLI)
KJAS-FM .... Jasper, TX [*FM radio station call letters*] (RBYB)
KJAV .... Alamo, TX [*FM radio station call letters*]
KJAX .... Jacksonville/International [*Florida*] [*ICAO location identifier*] (ICLI)
KJAX .... Stockton, CA [*AM radio station call letters*]
KJAY .... Sacramento, CA [*AM radio station call letters*]
KJAZ .... McFarland, CA [*AM radio station call letters*]
KJBC .... Midland, TX [*AM radio station call letters*]
KJBN .... Little Rock, AR [*AM radio station call letters*]
KJBR-FM .... Marked Tree, AR [*FM radio station call letters*] (RBYB)
KJBZ .... Laredo, TX [*FM radio station call letters*]
KJC .... Jefferson Community College, Louisville, KY [*OCLC symbol*] (OCLC)
KJC .... Keystone Junior College [*Pennsylvania*]
KJCB .... Lafayette, LA [*AM radio station call letters*]
KJCC .... Lake Havasu City, AZ [*FM radio station call letters*]
KJCE .... Rollingwood, TX [*AM radio station call letters*]
KJCF .... Festus, MO [*AM radio station call letters*]
KJCK .... Junction City, KS [*AM radio station call letters*]
KJCK-FM .... Junction City, KS [*FM radio station call letters*]
KJCPL .... Koninklijke Java-China-Paketvaart Lijnen
KJCR .... Keene, TX [*FM radio station call letters*]
KJCS .... Nacogdoches, TX [*FM radio station call letters*]
KJCT .... Grand Junction, CO [*Television station call letters*]
KJDJ .... San Luis Obispo, CA [*AM radio station call letters*]
KJDX .... Susanville, CA [*FM radio station call letters*]
KJDY .... John Day, OR [*AM radio station call letters*]
KJDY-FM .... Canyon City, OR [*FM radio station call letters*] (RBYB)
KJEE .... Montecito, CA [*FM radio station call letters*]
KJEF .... Jennings, LA [*AM radio station call letters*]
KJEF-FM .... Jennings, LA [*FM radio station call letters*]
KJEL .... Lebanon, MO [*AM radio station call letters*]
KJEM .... Seligman, MO [*FM radio station call letters*] (RBYB)
KJEO .... Fresno, CA [*Television station call letters*]
KJET .... Hoquiam, WA [*AM radio station call letters*] (RBYB)
KJEZ .... Poplar Bluff, MO [*FM radio station call letters*]
KJF .... Kajaani [*Finland*] [*Seismograph station code, US Geological Survey*] (SEIS)
KJF .... Karl-Jaspers Foundation (EA)
KJF .... Kutta-Joukowski Force
KJFA .... Grass Valley, CA [*FM radio station call letters*]
KJFF-AM .... Festus, MO [*AM radio station call letters*] (RBYB)
KJFK .... New York/John F. Kennedy International [*New York*] [*ICAO location identifier*] (ICLI)
KJFM .... Louisiana, MO [*FM radio station call letters*]
KJFX .... Fresno, CA [*FM radio station call letters*]
KJGM .... Fredonia, KS [*FM radio station call letters*] (RBYB)
KJHK .... Lawrence, KS [*FM radio station call letters*]
KJHY .... Emmett, ID [*FM radio station call letters*]
KJIB .... South Padre Island, TX [*FM radio station call letters*]
KJIL .... Copeland, KS [*FM radio station call letters*]
KJIM .... Sherman, TX [*AM radio station call letters*]
KJIN .... Houma, LA [*AM radio station call letters*]
KJIW .... West Helena, AR [*AM radio station call letters*]
KJIW-FM .... West Helena, AR [*FM radio station call letters*]
KJJ .... Kuhner, J. J., Cleveland OH [*STAC*]
KJJB .... Eunice, LA [*FM radio station call letters*]
KJJC .... Osceola, IA [*FM radio station call letters*]
KJJJ-FM .... Seligman, AZ [*FM radio station call letters*] (RBYB)
KJJK .... Fergus Falls, MN [*AM radio station call letters*]
KJJK-FM .... Fergus Falls, MN [*FM radio station call letters*]
KJJL-AM .... Cheyenne, WY [*AM radio station call letters*] (RBYB)
KJJO .... St. Louis Park, MN [*AM radio station call letters*]
KJJQ .... Volga, SD [*AM radio station call letters*]
KJJR .... Whitefish, MT [*AM radio station call letters*]
KJJY .... Ankeny, IA [*FM radio station call letters*]
KJJZ .... Kodiak, AK [*FM radio station call letters*]
KJKB-FM .... Jacksboro, TX [*FM radio station call letters*] (RBYB)
KJKJ .... Grand Forks, ND [*FM radio station call letters*]
KJKS .... Cameron, TX [*FM radio station call letters*]
KJKT .... Joplin, MO [*FM radio station call letters*]
KJL .... Kenneth J. Lane [*Jewelry designer*]
KJLF .... El Paso, TX [*Television station call letters*]
KJLH .... Compton, CA [*FM radio station call letters*]
KJLO .... Monroe, LA [*FM radio station call letters*]
KJLS .... Hays, KS [*FM radio station call letters*]
KJLT .... North Platte, NE [*AM radio station call letters*]
KJLT-FM .... North Platte, NE [*FM radio station call letters*]
KJLU .... Jefferson City, MO [*FM radio station call letters*]
KJLY .... Blue Earth, MN [*FM radio station call letters*]
KJMB .... Blythe, CA [*FM radio station call letters*]
KJME .... Denver, CO [*AM radio station call letters*]
KJMH .... Burlington, IA [*Television station call letters*]
KJMM .... Bixby, OK [*FM radio station call letters*]
KJMN-FM .... Castle Rock, CO [*FM radio station call letters*] (RBYB)
KJMO .... Jefferson City, MO [*FM radio station call letters*]
KJMS .... Memphis, TN [*FM radio station call letters*]
KJMX .... Tulia, TX [*FM radio station call letters*]
KJMY .... Seaside, CA [*FM radio station call letters*] (RBYB)
KJMZ .... Henderson, NV [*FM radio station call letters*] (RBYB)
KJMZ-FM .... Lawton, OK [*FM radio station call letters*] (RBYB)
KJN .... Kajaani [*Finland*] [*Seismograph station code, US Geological Survey Closed*] (SEIS)
KJNA .... Jena, LA [*AM radio station call letters*]
KJNA-FM .... Jena, LA [*FM radio station call letters*]
KJNO .... Juneau, AK [*AM radio station call letters*]
KJNP .... North Pole, AK [*AM radio station call letters*]
KJNP-FM .... North Pole, AK [*FM radio station call letters*]
KJNP-TV .... North Pole, AK [*Television station call letters*]
KJNT .... Hempsted [*New York*] [*ICAO location identifier*] (ICLI)
KJO .... Kommunistische Jugend Oesterreich [*Communist Youth of Austria*]
KJOC .... Davenport, IA [*AM radio station call letters*]
KJOE .... Slayton, MN [*FM radio station call letters*] (RBYB)
KJOI .... Dinuba, CA [*FM radio station call letters*]
KJOJ .... Conroe, TX [*AM radio station call letters*]
KJOJ-FM .... Freeport, TX [*FM radio station call letters*]
KJOK .... Yuma, AZ [*FM radio station call letters*]
KJOL .... Grand Junction, CO [*FM radio station call letters*]
KJOP .... Lemoore, CA [*AM radio station call letters*]
KJOT .... Boise, ID [*FM radio station call letters*]
KJOV-FM .... Woodward, OK [*FM radio station call letters*] (RBYB)
KJOX-AM .... Yakima, WA [*AM radio station call letters*] (RBYB)
KJOY .... Stockton, CA [*FM radio station call letters*]
KJPN .... Waipahu, HI [*AM radio station call letters*]
KJPW .... Waynesville, MO [*AM radio station call letters*]
KJPW-FM .... Waynesville, MO [*FM radio station call letters*]
KJQY .... San Diego, CA [*FM radio station call letters*]
KJR .... Seattle, WA [*AM radio station call letters*]
KJRB .... Spokane, WA [*AM radio station call letters*]
KJRE .... Ellendale, ND [*Television station call letters*]
KJR-FM .... Seattle, WA [*FM radio station call letters*]
KJRG .... Newton, KS [*AM radio station call letters*]
KJRH .... Tulsa, OK [*Television station call letters*]
KJRR .... Jamestown, ND [*Television station call letters*]
KJRT .... Amarillo, TX [*FM radio station call letters*]
KJS .... Kansas Journal of Sociology
KJS .... Karl-Jaspers Stiftung [*Karl-Jaspers Foundation - KJF*] (EA)
KJS .... Kodak Job Sheet
KJS .... V-Groove on One Side [*Lumber*]
KJSA .... Mineral Wells, TX [*AM radio station call letters*]
KJSK .... Columbus, NE [*AM radio station call letters*]
KJSL .... St. Louis, MO [*AM radio station call letters*]
KJSN .... Modesto, CA [*FM radio station call letters*]
KJSR .... Tulsa, OK [*FM radio station call letters*] (RBYB)
KJStJ .... Knight of Justice, Order of St. John of Jerusalem
KJTA .... Flagstaff, AZ [*FM radio station call letters*]
KJTL .... Wichita Falls, TX [*Television station call letters*]
KJTT .... Oak Harbor, WA [*AM radio station call letters*]
KJTV .... Lubbock, TX [*Television station call letters*]
KJTX .... Jefferson, TX [*FM radio station call letters*]
KJTY .... Topeka, KS [*FM radio station call letters*]
KJU .... Kamiraba [*Papua New Guinea*] [*Airport symbol Obsolete*] (OAG)
KJUD .... Juneau, AK [*Television station call letters*]
KJUG .... Tulare, CA [*AM radio station call letters*]
KJUG-FM .... Tulare, CA [*FM radio station call letters*]
KJUL .... North Las Vegas, NV [*FM radio station call letters*]
KJUN .... Eatonville, WA [*FM radio station call letters*]
KJUN .... Puyallup, WA [*AM radio station call letters*]
KJUS .... Beaumont, TX [*AM radio station call letters*] (RBYB)
KJV .... King James Version [*or Authorized Version of the Bible, 1611*]
KJVC .... Mansfield, LA [*FM radio station call letters*]
KJVD .... Kommunistischer Jugendverband Deutschlands [*Communist Youth Club of Germany*]
KJVH .... Longview, WA [*FM radio station call letters*]
KJVI .... Jackson, WY [*Television station call letters*]
KJWA .... Grand Junction, CO [*Television station call letters*]
KJWL .... Fresno, CA [*FM radio station call letters*]
KJWY-TV .... Jackson, WY [*TV station call letters*] (RBYB)
KJYE .... Grand Junction, CO [*FM radio station call letters*]
KJYL .... Eagle Grove, IA [*FM radio station call letters*]
KJYO .... Oklahoma City, OK [*FM radio station call letters*]
KJZY .... Sebastopol, CA [*FM radio station call letters*] (RBYB)
KJZZ .... Phoenix, AZ [*FM radio station call letters*]
KJZZ-TV .... Salt Lake City, UT [*Television station call letters*]
KK .... Die Welt der Bibel. Kleinkommentare zur Heiligen Schrift [*Duesseldorf*] [*A publication*] (BJA)
KK .... Kabushiki Kaishi [*Joint stock company*] [*Japan*]
KK .... Kahal Kadosh. Holy Congregation (BJA)
KK .... Kaluza-Klein [*Theories*] [*Physics*]
KK .... Kar-Kraft [*Automotive industry supplier*]
KK .... Kenya [*IYRU nationality code*] (IYR)
KK .... Keren Kayemeth (BJA)

KK	Kilokayser
KK	Kilokelvin
KK	Kings
KK	Kingston Korner (EA)
K-K	Kirov-Kiev [Former USSR]
KK	Kleinkaliber [Small Caliber] [German military]
KK	Knee Kick [Neurology]
KK	Kokusai Koryu [Japan Foundation] (EAIO)
KK	Komisja Koordynacyjna. Zydowskie Instytucje Opiekuncze (BJA)
KK	Kosher Kitchen (BJA)
KK	Kremlin Kommandant
KK	Kulutosuuskuntien Keskusliitto [Co-Operative Union] [Finland] (EY)
KK	Kurtis-Kraft [US racecar maker]
KK	Kurzgefasster Kommentar zu den Heiligen Schriften Alten und Neuen Testaments [Munich] [A publication] (BJA)
KKA	Benedictine College, Atchison, KS [OCLC symbol] (OCLC)
KKA	Kitchen Klutzs of America [Inactive] (EA)
KKA	Knights of King Arthur (EA)
KKA	Koyukuk [Alaska] [Airport symbol] (OAG)
KKAA	Aberdeen, SD [AM radio station call letters]
KKAG	Porterville, CA [Television station call letters]
KKAJ-FM	Ardmore, OK [FM radio station call letters]
KKAL	Arroyo Grande, CA [AM radio station call letters]
KKAM	Lubbock, TX [AM radio station call letters]
KKAN	Phillipsburg, KS [AM radio station call letters]
KKAQ	Thief River Falls, MN [AM radio station call letters]
KKAR	Omaha, NE [AM radio station call letters]
KKAS	Silsbee, TX [AM radio station call letters]
KKAT	Ogden, UT [FM radio station call letters]
KKAY	Donaldsonville, LA [FM radio station call letters]
KKAY	White Castle, LA [AM radio station call letters]
KKAZ	Cheyenne, WY [FM radio station call letters]
KKB	Baker University, Baldwin City, KS [OCLC symbol] (OCLC)
KKB	Kitoi [Alaska] [Airport symbol] (OAG)
KKBA	Kingsville, TX [FM radio station call letters] (RBYB)
KKBB	Bakersfield, CA [FM radio station call letters]
KKBC	Baker City, OR [FM radio station call letters]
KKBC	Korea Kuwait Banking Corp.
KKBG	Hilo, HI [FM radio station call letters]
KKBH	San Diego, CA [FM radio station call letters] (RBYB)
KKBI	Broken Bow, OK [FM radio station call letters]
KKBJ	Bemidji, MN [AM radio station call letters]
KKBJ-FM	Bemidji, MN [FM radio station call letters]
KKBL	Monett, MO [FM radio station call letters]
KKBN	Twain Harte, CA [FM radio station call letters]
KKBQ	Houston, TX [AM radio station call letters]
KKBQ	Pasadena, TX [FM radio station call letters]
KKBR	Billings, MT [FM radio station call letters]
KKBS	Guymon, OK [FM radio station call letters]
KKBT	Los Angeles, CA [FM radio station call letters]
KKBY-AM	Puyallup, WA [AM radio station call letters] (RBYB)
KKBY-FM	Eatonville, WA [FM radio station call letters] (RBYB)
KKBZ	Clarinda, IA [FM radio station call letters]
KKc	Kansas City Public Library, Kansas City, KS [Library symbol Library of Congress] (LCLS)
KKC	Kansas City Public Library, Kansas City, KS [OCLC symbol] (OCLC)
KKC	Khon Kaen [Thailand] [Airport symbol] (OAG)
KKCA	Knox College Library, University of Toronto [UTLAS symbol]
KKCA	Fulton, MO [FM radio station call letters]
KKcB	Central Baptist Theological Seminary, Kansas City, KS [Library symbol Library of Congress] (LCLS)
KKCB-FM	Duluth, MN [FM radio station call letters] (RBYB)
KKcBM	Bethany Medical Center, Kansas City, KS [Library symbol Library of Congress] (LCLS)
KKcD	Donnelly College, Kansas City, KS [Library symbol] [Library of Congress] (LCLS)
KKCD	Omaha, NE [FM radio station call letters]
KKCI	Goodland, KS [FM radio station call letters]
KKcJS	Jensen-Salsbery Laboratories, Kansas City, KS [Library symbol Library of Congress] (LCLS)
KKCK	Marshall, MN [FM radio station call letters]
KKCL	Lorenzo, TX [FM radio station call letters]
KKCM	Shakopee, MN [AM radio station call letters]
KKCN	Trumann, AR [FM radio station call letters] (RBYB)
KKCO-TV	Grand Junction, CO [TV station call letters] (RBYB)
KKcP	Providence - Saint Margaret Health Center, Kansas City, KS [Library symbol Library of Congress] (LCLS)
KKcPS	Kansas City Kansas Public Schools, Kansas City, KS [Library symbol] [Library of Congress] (LCLS)
KKCQ	Fosston, MN [AM radio station call letters]
KKCQ-FM	Fosston, MN [FM radio station call letters]
KKCR-FM	Hanalei, HI [FM radio station call letters] (RBYB)
KKCS	Colorado Springs, CO [AM radio station call letters]
KKCS-FM	Colorado Springs, CO [FM radio station call letters]
KKCT	Bismarck, ND [FM radio station call letters]
KKCV	Cedar Falls, IA [FM radio station call letters]
KKCW	Beaverton, OR [FM radio station call letters]
KKCY	Colusa, CA [FM radio station call letters]
KKD	Kokoda [Papua New Guinea] [Airport symbol] (OAG)
KKD	Korintji-Kaba-Dempo [Sumatra] [Seismograph station code, US Geological Survey Closed] (SEIS)
KKDA	Dallas, TX [FM radio station call letters]
KKDA	Grand Prairie, TX [AM radio station call letters]
KKDD	Katalog Kandidatskikh i Doktorskikh Dissertatsii [A bibliographic publication]

KKDD	North Las Vegas, NV [AM radio station call letters] (RBYB)
K K-D-H	Knight Kadosch [Freemasonry]
KKDJ	Fresno, CA [FM radio station call letters]
KKDL	Detroit Lakes, MN [FM radio station call letters]
KKDM	Des Moines, IA [FM radio station call letters]
KKDQ	Thief River Falls, MN [FM radio station call letters]
KKDS	South Salt Lake, UT [AM radio station call letters]
KKDY	West Plains, MO [FM radio station call letters]
KKDZ	Seattle, WA [AM radio station call letters]
KKE	Kerikeri [New Zealand] [Airport symbol] (OAG)
KKE	Kleena Kleene Gold Mines [Vancouver Stock Exchange symbol]
KKE	Kommunistiko Komma Ellados [Communist Party of Greece] [Political party] (PPW)
KKEE	Long Beach, WA [FM radio station call letters]
KKEes	Kommunistiko Komma Ellados - Esoterikou [Communist Party of Greece - Interior] [Political party] (PPE)
KKEex	Kommunistiko Komma Ellados - Exoterikou [Communist Party of Greece - Exterior] [Political party] (PPE)
KKEG	Fayetteville, AR [FM radio station call letters]
KKEL	Hobbs, NM [AM radio station call letters]
KKEQ-FM	Fosston, MN [FM radio station call letters] (RBYB)
KKES	Kommunistiko Komma Ellados - Esoterikou [Communist Party of Greece - Interior] [Political party] (PPW)
KKEX	Preston, ID [FM radio station call letters]
KKEY	Portland, OR [AM radio station call letters]
KKEZ	Fort Dodge, IA [FM radio station call letters]
KKFC	KISS [Knights in the Service of Satan] Konnection Fan Club (EA)
KKFG	Bloomfield, NM [FM radio station call letters]
KKFI	Kansas City, MO [FM radio station call letters]
KKFJ-AM	Alturas, CA [AM radio station call letters] (RBYB)
KKFM	Colorado Springs, CO [FM radio station call letters]
KKFN	Denver, CO [AM radio station call letters]
KKFO	Coalinga, CA [AM radio station call letters]
KKFR	Glendale, AZ [FM radio station call letters]
KKG	Kappa Kappa Gamma [Sorority]
KKG	Konawaruk [Guyana] [Airport symbol Obsolete] (OAG)
KKG	Kootenay King Resources [Vancouver Stock Exchange symbol]
KKG	Thousand Kilograms (EG)
KKGB	Sulphur, LA [FM radio station call letters]
KKGM	Grand Junction, CO [AM radio station call letters] (RBYB)
KKGO	Frazier Park, CA [AM radio station call letters]
KKGO-FM	Los Angeles, CA [FM radio station call letters]
KKH	Kailua-Kona [Hawaii] [Seismograph station code, US Geological Survey] (SEIS)
KKH	Karakoram Highway [Asia]
KKH	Kongiganak [Alaska] [Airport symbol] (OAG)
KKHB-FM	Eureka, CA [FM radio station call letters] (RBYB)
KKHG	Tucson, AZ [FM radio station call letters]
KKHI	San Rafael, CA [AM radio station call letters]
KKHI-FM	San Rafael, CA [FM radio station call letters]
KKHJ	Los Angeles, CA [AM radio station call letters]
KKHK-FM	Denver, CO [FM radio station call letters] (RBYB)
KKHL	Klung Kidney-Heart-Lung [Machine]
KKHQ	Odem, TX [FM radio station call letters]
KKHR	Anson, TX [FM radio station call letters]
KKHT	Conroe, TX [FM radio station call letters] (RBYB)
KKI	Akiachak [Alaska] [Airport symbol] (OAG)
KKI	Karkar Island [Papua New Guinea] [Seismograph station code, US Geological Survey] (SEIS)
KKIC	Boise, ID [AM radio station call letters]
KKID	Sallisaw, OK [AM radio station call letters]
KKIFC	Kris Kristofferson International Fan Club (EA)
KKIK	Temple, TX [FM radio station call letters] (RBYB)
KKIM	Albuquerque, NM [AM radio station call letters]
KKIN	Aitkin, MN [AM radio station call letters]
KKIN-FM	Aitkin, MN [FM radio station call letters] (RBYB)
KKIQ	Livermore, CA [FM radio station call letters]
KKIS	Concord, CA [AM radio station call letters]
KKIS	Soldotna, AK [FM radio station call letters]
KKIT	Taos, NM [AM radio station call letters]
KKIX	Fayetteville, AR [FM radio station call letters]
KKJ	Kita Kyushu [Japan] [Airport symbol Obsolete] (OAG)
KKJG	San Luis Obispo, CA [FM radio station call letters]
KKJI	Gallup, NM [FM radio station call letters]
KKJJ-FM	Ashland, OR [FM radio station call letters] (RBYB)
KKJL	San Luis Obispo, CA [AM radio station call letters] (RBYB)
KKJM	St Joseph, MN [FM radio station call letters]
KKJO	St. Joseph, MO [FM radio station call letters]
KKJQ	Garden City, KS [FM radio station call letters]
KKJT	Hutchison, MN [FM radio station call letters]
KKJT	Joshua Tree, CA [FM radio station call letters]
KKJZ	Lake Oswego, OR [FM radio station call letters]
KKK	Invisible Empire Knights of the Ku Klux Klan (EA)
KKK	Kissel Kar Klub (EA)
KKK	Kolmer, Kline, Kahn [Test for syphilis] [Medicine] (DAVI)
KKK	Kuehnle, Kopp, & Kausch [Auto industry supplier]
KKKK	Odessa, TX [FM radio station call letters]
KKL	Kam-Kotia Mines Ltd. [Toronto Stock Exchange symbol]
KKL	Karluk Lake, AK [Location identifier FAA] (FAAL)
KKL	Keren Kayemeth Leisrael (BJA)
KKL	Kol-Kol Airlines Ltd. [Nigeria] [FAA designator] (FAAC)
KKLA	Los Angeles, CA [FM radio station call letters]
KKLA	San Bernardino, CA [AM radio station call letters] (RBYB)
KKLB	Elgin, TX [FM radio station call letters]
KKLD-FM	Prescott Valley, az [FM radio station call letters] (RBYB)

KKLE............ Winfield, KS [*AM radio station call letters*]
KKLH-FM..... Marshfield, MO [*FM radio station call letters*] (RBYB)
KKLI............ Widefield, CO [*FM radio station call letters*]
KKLL............ Webb City, MO [*AM radio station call letters*]
KKLL-FM..... Webb City, MO [*FM radio station call letters*]
KKLO.......... Leavenworth, KS [*AM radio station call letters*]
KKLQ.......... Oceanside, CA [*AM radio station call letters*] (RBYB)
KKLQ-FM..... San Diego, CA [*FM radio station call letters*]
KKLR.......... Poplar Bluff, MO [*FM radio station call letters*]
KKLS.......... Rapid City, SD [*AM radio station call letters*]
KKLS-FM..... Sioux Falls, SD [*FM radio station call letters*]
KKLT............ Phoenix, AZ [*FM radio station call letters*]
KKLV.......... Honolulu, HI [*FM radio station call letters*]
KKLX.......... Worland, WY [*FM radio station call letters*]
KKLY-FM..... Pecos, TX [*FM radio station call letters*] (RBYB)
KKLZ............ Las Vegas, NV [*FM radio station call letters*]
KKM............ Kota Kinabalu [*Malaysia*] [*Seismograph station code, US Geological Survey*] (SEIS)
KKM............ North Central Kansas Library, Manhattan, KS [*OCLC symbol*] (OCLC)
KKMA.......... Le Mars, IA [*FM radio station call letters*]
KKMC.......... Gonzales, CA [*AM radio station call letters*]
KKMC.......... King Khalid Military City [*Saudi Arabia*] (DOMA)
KKMG.......... Pueblo, CO [*FM radio station call letters*]
KKMI............ Burlington, IA [*FM radio station call letters*]
KKMJ............ Austin, TX [*FM radio station call letters*]
KKMK.......... Rapid City, SD [*FM radio station call letters*]
KKMO.......... Tacoma, WA [*AM radio station call letters*]
KKMV.......... Rupert, ID [*FM radio station call letters*]
KKMX.......... Tri City, OR [*FM radio station call letters*]
KKMY.......... Orange, TX [*FM radio station call letters*]
KKN............ Kansas Newman College, Wichita, KS [*OCLC symbol*] (OCLC)
KKN............ Kirkenes [*Norway*] [*Airport symbol*] (OAG)
KKNB.......... Crete, NE [*AM radio station call letters*]
KKND.......... Tucson, AZ [*AM radio station call letters*] (RBYB)
KKND-FM..... Port Sulphur, LA [*FM radio station call letters*] (RBYB)
KKNG.......... Laramie, WY [*FM radio station call letters*]
KKNN.......... Delta, CO [*FM radio station call letters*] (RBYB)
KKNO.......... Gretna, LA [*AM radio station call letters*]
KKNU .... Springfield-Eugene, OR [*FM radio station call letters*]
KKNX-AM..... Eugene, OR [*AM radio station call letters*] (RBYB)
KKO .... Kaikohe [*New Zealand*] [*Airport symbol Obsolete*] (OAG)
KKO .... National Citizens' Committee [*Poland*] [*Political party*]
KKOA.......... Ottawa University, Ottawa, KS [*OCLC symbol*] (OCLC)
KKOA.......... Kustom Kemps of America (EA)
KKOA.......... Volcano, HI [*FM radio station call letters*]
KKOB.......... Albuquerque, NM [*AM radio station call letters*]
KKOB Exp Stn... Santa Fe, NM [*Radio expansion station*] (RBYB)
KKOB-FM..... Albuquerque, NM [*FM radio station call letters*]
KKOH.......... Reno, NV [*AM radio station call letters*] (RBYB)
KKOJ............ Jackson, MN [*AM radio station call letters*]
KKOK.......... Morris, MN [*FM radio station call letters*]
KKOL .... Hampton, AR [*FM radio station call letters*]
KKON.......... Kealakekua, HI [*AM radio station call letters*]
KKOR.......... Gallup, NM [*FM radio station call letters*]
KKOS-FM..... Palacios, TX [*FM radio station call letters*] (RBYB)
KKOT.......... Columbus, NE [*FM radio station call letters*]
KKOW .... Pittsburg, KS [*AM radio station call letters*]
KKOW-FM..... Pittsburg, KS [*FM radio station call letters*]
KKOY.......... Chanute, KS [*AM radio station call letters*]
KKOY-FM..... Chanute, KS [*FM radio station call letters*]
KKOZ .... Ava, MO [*AM radio station call letters*]
KKOZ-FM..... Ava, MO [*FM radio station call letters*]
KKP............ Canadian Communist Party [*Political party*]
KKP............ Chinese Communist Party [*Political party*]
KKP............ Cuban Communist Party [*Political party*]
KKP............ Cypriot Communist Party [*Political party*]
KKP............ Kappa Kappa Psi [*Society*]
KKP............ Kina Kommunista Partja [*Communist Party of China*] [*Political party*]
KKP............ King's Knight's Pawn [*Chess*] (IIA)
KKP............ University of Kansas, Medical Library, Kansas City, KS [*OCLC symbol*] (OCLC)
KKPC .... Pueblo, CO [*FM radio station call letters*]
KKPC-AM..... Pueblo, CO [*AM radio station call letters*] (RBYB)
KKPL.......... Opportunity, WA [*AM radio station call letters*]
KKPR .... Kearney, NE [*AM radio station call letters*]
KKPR-FM..... Kearney, NE [*FM radio station call letters*]
KKPS.......... Brownsville, TX [*FM radio station call letters*]
KKPT............ Little Rock, AR [*FM radio station call letters*]
KKPZ.......... Portland, OR [*AM radio station call letters*] (RBYB)
KKQ............ Sterling College, Sterling, KS [*OCLC symbol*] (OCLC)
KKQQ.......... Volga, SD [*FM radio station call letters*]
KKQY-FM..... HillCity, KS [*FM radio station call letters*] (RBYB)
KKR............ Emporia State University, Emporia, KS [*OCLC symbol*] (OCLC)
KKR............ Kaukura [*French Polynesia*] [*Airport symbol*] (OAG)
KKR............ Kohlberg Kravis Roberts & Co.
KKR............ Kokanee Resources Ltd. [*Vancouver Stock Exchange symbol*]
KKR............ Kurtis-Kraft Register [*Defunct*] (EA)
KKR............ Kurukshetra [*India*] [*Seismograph station code, US Geological Survey*] (SEIS)
KKRB .... Klamath Falls, OR [*FM radio station call letters*]
KKRC .... Granite Falls, MN [*FM radio station call letters*]
KKRD-FM..... Wichita, KS [*FM radio station call letters*]
KKRF .... Stuart, IA [*FM radio station call letters*]
KKRH.......... Salem, OR [*FM radio station call letters*] (RBYB)

KKRK .... Douglas, AZ [*FM radio station call letters*]
KKRL .... Carroll, IA [*FM radio station call letters*]
KKRN-FM..... Cabot, AR [*FM radio station call letters*] (RBYB)
KKRO .... Anchorage, AK [*FM radio station call letters*]
KKRO .... Koo Koo Roo [*NASDAQ symbol*] (TTSB)
KKRO .... Koo Koo Roo, Inc. [*NASDAQ symbol*] (SAG)
KKRQ .... Iowa City, IA [*FM radio station call letters*]
KKRT .... Wenatchee, WA [*AM radio station call letters*]
KKRV-FM..... Wenatchee, WA [*FM radio station call letters*]
KKRW .... Houston, TX [*FM radio station call letters*]
KKRX .... Lawton, OK [*AM radio station call letters*]
KKRX-FM..... Lawton, OK [*FM radio station call letters*]
KKRZ .... Portland, OR [*FM radio station call letters*]
KKS............ Kansas State University, Farrell Library, Manhattan, KS [*OCLC symbol*] (OCLC)
KKSA .... Keith Keating Society for the Arts [*Defunct*] (EA)
KKSA .... San Angelo, TX [*AM radio station call letters*] (RBYB)
KKSF .... San Francisco, CA [*FM radio station call letters*]
KKSI .... Eddyville, IA [*FM radio station call letters*]
KKSJ .... San Jose, CA [*AM radio station call letters*]
KKSL .... Lake Oswego, OR [*AM radio station call letters*] (RBYB)
KKSM-AM..... Oceanside, CA [*AM radio station call letters*] (RBYB)
KKSN .... Portland, OR [*AM radio station call letters*]
KKSN .... Vancouver, WA [*AM radio station call letters*]
KKSO .... Des Moines, IA [*AM radio station call letters*]
KKSR .... Sartell, MN [*FM radio station call letters*]
KKSS .... Santa Fe, NM [*FM radio station call letters*]
KKSU .... Manhattan, KS [*AM radio station call letters*]
KKSY .... Bald Knob, AR [*FM radio station call letters*]
KKT............ King's Knight [*Chess*]
KKTK-AM..... Waco, TX [*AM radio station call letters*] (RBYB)
KKTO-FM..... Tahoe City, CA [*FM radio station call letters*] (RBYB)
KKTP .... King's Knight's Pawn [*Chess*] (IIA)
KKTR .... Fresno, CA [*AM radio station call letters*]
KKTU .... Cheyenne, WY [*Television station call letters*]
KKTV .... Colorado Springs, CO [*Television station call letters*]
KKTX .... Kilgore, TX [*AM radio station call letters*]
KKTX-FM..... Kilgore, TX [*FM radio station call letters*]
KKTY .... Douglas, WY [*AM radio station call letters*]
KKTY-FM..... Douglas, WY [*FM radio station call letters*]
KKTZ .... Mountain Home, AR [*FM radio station call letters*]
KKU............ Ekuk [*Alaska*] [*Airport symbol*] (OAG)
KKU............ Keanakolu [*Hawaii*] [*Seismograph station code, US Geological Survey*] (SEIS)
KKU............ University of Kansas, Lawrence, KS [*OCLC symbol*] (OCLC)
KKUA .... Wailuku, HI [*FM radio station call letters*]
KKUB .... Brownfield, TX [*AM radio station call letters*]
KKUH .... King Khalid University Hospital [*Saudi Arabia*]
KKUL-FM..... Lincoln, NE [*FM radio station call letters*] (RBYB)
KKUP .... Cupertino, CA [*FM radio station call letters*]
KKUS .... Tyler, TX [*FM radio station call letters*]
KKUZ .... Sallisaw, OK [*FM radio station call letters*]
KKUZ-AM..... Sallisaw, OK [*AM radio station call letters*] (RBYB)
KKV............ Central Kansas Library System, Book Processing Center, Great Bend, KS [*OCLC symbol*] (OCLC)
KKV............ Kinetic-Kill Vehicle [*Military*] (SDI)
KKV............ Kinetic Kill Vehicle (DOMA)
KKVI .... Twin Falls, ID [*Television station call letters*]
KKVO .... Altus, OK [*FM radio station call letters*]
KKVV .... Las Vegas, NV [*AM radio station call letters*]
KKW............ Kainokawa [*Japan*] [*Seismograph station code, US Geological Survey*] (SEIS)
KKW............ Kikwit [*Zaire*] [*Airport symbol*] (OAG)
KKW............ Washburn University of Topeka, Topeka, KS [*OCLC symbol*] (OCLC)
KKWM .... Winfield, KS [*FM radio station call letters*]
KKWQ .... Warroad, MN [*FM radio station call letters*]
KKWS .... Wadena, MN [*FM radio station call letters*]
KKWZ .... Richfield, UT [*FM radio station call letters*]
KKX............ Kikaiga Shima [*Japan*] [*Airport symbol*] (OAG)
KKX............ Southwestern College, Winfield, KS [*OCLC symbol*] (OCLC)
KKXK .... Montrose, CO [*FM radio station call letters*]
KKXL .... Grand Forks, ND [*AM radio station call letters*]
KKXL-FM..... Grand Forks, ND [*FM radio station call letters*]
KKXO .... Eugene, OR [*AM radio station call letters*]
KKXX .... Delano, CA [*FM radio station call letters*]
KKXX .... Paradise, CA [*AM radio station call letters*]
KKYA .... Yankton, SD [*FM radio station call letters*]
KKYC .... Muleshoe, TX [*FM radio station call letters*]
KKYD .... Denver, CO [*AM radio station call letters*]
KKYN .... Plainview, TX [*AM radio station call letters*]
KKYN-FM..... Plainview, TX [*FM radio station call letters*]
KKYR .... Texarkana, AR [*AM radio station call letters*]
KKYR-FM..... Texarkana, AR [*FM radio station call letters*]
KKYS .... Bryan, TX [*FM radio station call letters*]
KKYT .... McCook, NE [*FM radio station call letters*]
KKYX .... San Antonio, TX [*AM radio station call letters*]
KKYY .... Gunnison, CO [*FM radio station call letters*]
KKYZ .... Sierra Vista, AZ [*FM radio station call letters*]
KKZIS.......... Komisja Koordynacyjna Zydowskich Instytucji Spolecznych (BJA)
KKZQ .... Lowell, AR [*FM radio station call letters*]
KKZX .... Spokane, WA [*FM radio station call letters*]
KKZZ .... Santa Paula, CA [*AM radio station call letters*]
KL............... Air Atlantique [*ICAO designator*] (AD)
KL............... Kaliszer Leben (BJA)

KL	Kansalaisvallen Liitto [*League of Civil Power*] [*Finland Political party*] (PPW)
K-L	Kansas State Library, Law Department, Topeka, KS [*Library symbol Library of Congress*] (LCLS)
KL	Karl Lagerfeld [*Fashion designer*]
K-L	Karl-Lorimar Home Video, Inc.
KL	Keel (ROG)
KL	Keller's Language [*1977*] [*Computer science*] (CSR)
KL	Kelvin Law [*Physics*]
KL	Kerley Lines [*Radiology*]
KL	Key Length [*Computer science*] (BUR)
KL	Key Lever (IAA)
KL	Key Locker
KL	Kidney Lobe
kL	Kilolambert
KL	Kiloliter
KL	Klaeger [*Plaintiff*] [*German*] (ILCA)
kl	Klang [*Musical Overtone*] [*German*]
KL	Klebs-Loeffler [*Bacteriology*]
KL	Kleine-Levin [*Syndrome*] [*Medicine*] (DAVI)
KL	Kleinmann-Low [*Astronomy*]
KL	Klemm Flugzeugbau GmbH & Apparatebau Nabern [*Germany ICAO aircraft manufacturer identifier*] (ICAO)
KL	KLM [*Koninklijke Luchtvaart Maatschappij*] Royal Dutch Airlines [*ICAO designator*] (OAG)
KL	Knight of Leopold [*Austria, Belgium*] (ROG)
KL	Knight of [*the Order of*] Leopold of Austria
KL	Knights of Lithuania
KL	Konzentrationslager [*Concentration Camp*] [*German*] (BJA)
KL	Kuala Lumpur [*Malaysia*]
KL	Kullback-Leibler [*Mathematics*]
KLA	Air Lietuva [*Lithuania*] [*ICAO designator*] (FAAC)
KLA	Ka-Ahari Resources [*Vancouver Stock Exchange symbol*]
KLA	Kampala [*Uganda*] [*Airport symbol*] (AD)
KLA	Key Learning Area [*Education*]
KLA	KLA Instruments Corp. [*Associated Press*] (SAG)
KLA	Klystron Amplifier
KLA	Knight of [*the Order of*] Leopold of Austria
KLAA	Tioga, LA [*FM radio station call letters*]
KLAC	KLA Instruments [*NASDAQ symbol*] (TTSB)
KLAC	KLA Instruments Corp. [*NASDAQ symbol*] (NQ)
KLAC	Los Angeles, CA [*AM radio station call letters*]
KLAD	Klamath Falls, OR [*AM radio station call letters*]
KLAD-FM	Klamath Falls, OR [*FM radio station call letters*]
KLAK	Durant, OK [*FM radio station call letters*]
KLAM	Cordova, AK [*AM radio station call letters*]
Klamath	Klamath First Bancorp, Inc. [*Associated Press*] (SAG)
KLAN	Glasgow, MT [*FM radio station call letters*]
KLAN	Lansing/Capital Region [*Michigan*] [*ICAO location identifier*] (ICLI)
KLANSS	Keep That Local Area Network Simple, Stupid [*Telecommunications*]
KLAQ	El Paso, TX [*FM radio station call letters*]
KLAR	Laredo, TX [*AM radio station call letters*]
KLAS	Las Vegas/McCarran International [*Nevada*] [*ICAO location identifier*] (ICLI)
KLAS	Las Vegas, NV [*Television station call letters*]
KLaSH	Larned State Hospital, Larned, KS [*Library symbol Library of Congress*] (LCLS)
Klass Phil Stud	Klassische Philologische Studien [*A publication*] (OCD)
KLAT	Houston, TX [*AM radio station call letters*]
KLAV	Las Vegas, NV [*AM radio station call letters*]
KLaw	Lawrence Free Public Library, Lawrence, KS [*Library symbol Library of Congress*] (LCLS)
KLAW	Lawton, OK [*FM radio station call letters*]
K Law Rep	Kentucky Law Reporter [*A publication*] (DLA)
KLAX	Long Beach, CA [*FM radio station call letters*]
KLAX	Los Angeles/International [*California*] [*ICAO location identifier*] (ICLI)
KLAX-TV	Alexandria, LA [*Television station call letters*]
KLAY	Lakewood, WA [*AM radio station call letters*]
KLAZ	Hot Springs, AR [*FM radio station call letters*]
KLB	Kalabo [*Zambia*] [*Airport symbol*] (OAG)
KLB	Kilopound (MCD)
KLB	Knight of [*the Order of*] Leopold [*Belgium*]
KLBA	Albia, IA [*AM radio station call letters*]
KL Bac	Klebs-Loeffler Bacillus (AAMN)
KLBA-FM	Albia, IA [*FM radio station call letters*]
KLBB	Lubbock/Regional [*Texas*] [*ICAO location identifier*] (ICLI)
KLBB	St. Paul, MN [*AM radio station call letters*]
KLBC	Durant, OK [*FM radio station call letters*]
KLBF	Kilopound-Force (WDAA)
KLBG	Alexandria, LA [*AM radio station call letters*] (RBYB)
KLBJ	Austin, TX [*AM radio station call letters*]
KLBJ-FM	Austin, TX [*FM radio station call letters*]
KLBK	Lubbock, TX [*Television station call letters*]
KLBM	La Grande, OR [*AM radio station call letters*]
KLBN	Auberry, CA [*FM radio station call letters*] (RBYB)
KLBO	Monahans, TX [*AM radio station call letters*]
KLBQ	El Dorado, AR [*FM radio station call letters*]
KLBS	Los Banos, CA [*AM radio station call letters*]
KLBY	Colby, KS [*Television station call letters*]
KLC	Kaolack [*Senegal*] [*Airport symbol*] (AD)
KLC	Kern County Library System, Bakersfield, CA [*OCLC symbol*] (OCLC)
KLC	Kirkland Lake [*Ontario*] [*Seismograph station code, US Geological Survey Closed*] (SEIS)
KLC	KLM Cityhopper BV [*Netherlands ICAO designator*] (FAAC)
KLCB	Libby, MT [*AM radio station call letters*]
KLCC	Eugene, OR [*FM radio station call letters*]
KLCC	Kuala Lumpur City Center [*Malaysia*] (ECON)
KLCCL	Kilocycle (ABBR)
KLCD	Decorah, IA [*FM radio station call letters*]
KLCE	Blackfoot, ID [*FM radio station call letters*]
KLCH	Lake Charles/Lake Charles [*Louisiana*] [*ICAO location identifier*] (ICLI)
KLCI	Nampa, ID [*FM radio station call letters*]
KLCK	Goldendale, WA [*AM radio station call letters*]
KLCK	Rickenbacker Air Force Base [*Ohio*] [*ICAO location identifier*] (ICLI)
KLCL	Lake Charles, LA [*AM radio station call letters*]
KLCM	Lewistown, MT [*FM radio station call letters*]
KLCN	Blytheville, AR [*AM radio station call letters*]
KLCO	Newport, OR [*FM radio station call letters*]
KLCQ	Healdsburg, CA [*FM radio station call letters*]
KLCS	Los Angeles, CA [*Television station call letters*]
KLCV-FM	Lincoln, NE [*FM radio station call letters*] (RBYB)
KLCX	Indio, CA [*FM radio station call letters*] (RBYB)
KLCY	East Missoula, MT [*AM radio station call letters*]
KLCY-FM	Vernal, UT [*FM radio station call letters*]
KLCZ	Corcoran, CA [*FM radio station call letters*]
KLD	Kelly, Douglas & Co. Ltd. [*Toronto Stock Exchange symbol*]
KLD	King's Light Dragoons [*British military*] (DMA)
KLD	Kongres Liberalno-Demokratyczny [*Liberal Democratic Congress*] [*Poland Political party*] (EY)
KLDC	Commerce City, CO [*AM radio station call letters*] (RBYB)
KLDC-AM	Brighton, CO [*AM radio station call letters*] (RBYB)
KLDE	Houston, TX [*FM radio station call letters*]
KLDG	Liberal, KS [*FM radio station call letters*]
KLDI	Laramie, WY [*AM radio station call letters*]
KLDJ-FM	Duluth, MN [*FM radio station call letters*] (RBYB)
KLDN	Lufkin, TX [*FM radio station call letters*]
KLDO	Laredo, TX [*Television station call letters*]
KLDR	Harbeck-Fruitdale, OR [*FM radio station call letters*]
KLDR	Killdeer (ABBR)
KLDSOP	Kaleidoscope (ABBR)
KLDSOPC	Kaleidoscopic (ABBR)
KLDT	Lake Dallas, TX [*Television station call letters*]
KLDZ	Lincoln, NE [*FM radio station call letters*]
KLE	Kaele [*Cameroon*] [*Airport symbol*] (AD)
KLE	Kala Explorations [*Vancouver Stock Exchange symbol*]
KLe	Leavenworth Public Library, Leavenworth, KS [*Library symbol Library of Congress*] (LCLS)
KLEA	Lovington, NM [*AM radio station call letters*]
KLEA-FM	Lovington, NM [*FM radio station call letters*]
KLEB	Golden Meadow, LA [*AM radio station call letters*]
Kleb	Klebsiella [*Genus of microorganisms*] (MAH)
KleBl	Klerusblatt [*Munich*] [*A publication*] (BJA)
Klebs	Klebsiella [*A genus of bacteria*]
KLEE	Ottumwa, IA [*AM radio station call letters*]
KleerVu	Kleer-Vu Industries, Inc. [*Associated Press*] (SAG)
KLEF	Anchorage, AK [*FM radio station call letters*]
KLEH	Anamosa, IA [*AM radio station call letters*]
KLEI	Kailua-Kona, HI [*AM radio station call letters*]
Kleinrt	Kleinert's, Inc. [*Associated Press*] (SAG)
KLEL	San Jose, CA [*FM radio station call letters*]
KLEM	Le Mars, IA [*AM radio station call letters*]
KLEN	Cheyenne, WY [*FM radio station call letters*]
KLEO	Kahaluu, HI [*FM radio station call letters*]
KLEP	Newark, AR [*Television station call letters*]
KLEPTO	Kleptomania (ABBR)
KLER	Orofino, ID [*AM radio station call letters*]
KLER-FM	Orofino, ID [*FM radio station call letters*]
KLeS	Saint Mary College, Leavenworth, KS [*Library symbol Library of Congress*] (LCLS)
KLeVA	United States Veterans Administration Center, Leavenworth, KS [*Library symbol Library of Congress*] (LCLS)
KLEW	Lewiston, ID [*Television station call letters*]
KLEX	Lexington, MO [*AM radio station call letters*]
KLEY	Wellington, KS [*AM radio station call letters*]
KLFA	King City, CA [*FM radio station call letters*]
KLFB	Lubbock, TX [*AM radio station call letters*]
KLFC	Branson, MO [*FM radio station call letters*]
KLFD	Litchfield, MN [*AM radio station call letters*]
KLFE	Seattle, WA [*AM radio station call letters*] (RBYB)
KLFF	San Luis Obispo, CA [*FM radio station call letters*] (RBYB)
KLFI	Hampton/Langley Air Force Base [*Virginia*] [*ICAO location identifier*] (ICLI)
KLFJ	Springfield, MO [*AM radio station call letters*]
KLFK	Lufkin/Angelina County [*Texas*] [*ICAO location identifier*] (ICLI)
KLFM	Great Falls, MT [*FM radio station call letters*]
KLFT	Lafayette/Regional [*Louisiana*] [*ICAO location identifier*] (ICLI)
KLFX	Nolanville, TX [*FM radio station call letters*] (RBYB)
KLFY	Lafayette, LA [*Television station call letters*]
KLG	Kalgoorlie [*Australia Seismograph station code, US Geological Survey*] (SEIS)
KLG	Kalskag [*Alaska*] [*Airport symbol*] (OAG)
KLG	Keto-Laevo-Gulonic Acid [*Organic chemistry*]
KLG	Keto-L-glutonic (Acid) [*Biochemistry*]
KLG	Killing (ABBR)
KLG	Knudsen Leaf Gauge [*Physics*]
KLG	University of Louisville, Louisville, KY [*OCLC symbol*] (OCLC)
KLGA	Algona, IA [*AM radio station call letters*]
KLGA	New York/La Guardia [*New York*] [*ICAO location identifier*] (ICLI)
KLGA-FM	Algona, IA [*FM radio station call letters*]

KLGB	Long Beach [*California*] [*ICAO location identifier*] (ICLI)
KLGM	Kilogram (ABBR)
KLGN	Logan, UT [*AM radio station call letters*]
KLGR	Knight's Local Government Reports [*A publication*] (DLA)
KLGR	Redwood Falls, MN [*AM radio station call letters*]
KLGR-FM	Redwood Falls, MN [*FM radio station call letters*]
KLGT	Buffalo, WY [*FM radio station call letters*]
KLGT-TV	Minneapolis, MN [*Television station call letters*]
KLH	Kapapala Ranch [*Hawaii*] [*Seismograph station code, US Geological Survey*] (SEIS)
KLH	Keyhole Limpet Hemocyanin [*Immunology*]
KLH	KLM Helicopters NV [*Netherlands ICAO designator*] (FAAC)
KLH	Kloss, Low, and Hofmann [*Initialism is name of electronics company and brand name of its products*]
KLH	Knight of the Legion of Honor [*France*]
KLH	Knight of the Legion of Honour (DD)
KLH	Long Akha [*Malaysia*] [*Airport symbol*] (AD)
KLHB-FM	Odem, TX [*FM radio station call letters*] (RBYB)
KLHI	Lahaina, HI [*FM radio station call letters*]
KLHS	Lewiston, ID [*FM radio station call letters*]
KLHT	Honolulu, HI [*AM radio station call letters*]
KLI	Kaliber Resources Ltd. [*Vancouver Stock Exchange symbol*]
KLI	King's Light Infantry [*Military unit*] [*British*]
KLI	Klingon Language Institute
KLI	Kolyma-Avia [*Former USSR*] [*FAA designator*] (FAAC)
Kliatt	Kliatt Young Adult Paperback Book Guide [*A publication*] (BRI)
KLIC	Keyletter-in-Context [*Computer science*]
KLIC	Kulicke & Soffa Ind [*NASDAQ symbol*] (TTSB)
KLIC	Kulicke & Soffa Industries, Inc. [*NASDAQ symbol*] (NQ)
KLIC	Monroe, LA [*AM radio station call letters*]
KLID	Poplar Bluff, MO [*AM radio station call letters*]
KLIF	Dallas, TX [*AM radio station call letters*]
KLIK	Jefferson City, MO [*AM radio station call letters*]
KLIL	Moreauville, LA [*FM radio station call letters*]
KLIM	Limon, CO [*AM radio station call letters*] (RBYB)
KLIN	Lincoln, NE [*AM radio station call letters*]
KLINA	K, Li, and Na [*For the chemical elements potassium, lithium, and sodium*] [*Beckman flame system Trademark*]
KLindB	Bethany College, Lindsborg, KS [*Library symbol Library of Congress*] (LCLS)
KLIP	Monroe, LA [*FM radio station call letters*]
KLIR	Columbus, NE [*FM radio station call letters*]
KLIS	Palestine, TX [*FM radio station call letters*]
KLIT	Little Rock/Adams Field [*Arkansas*] [*ICAO location identifier*] (ICLI)
KLIV	San Jose, CA [*AM radio station call letters*]
KLIX	Twin Falls, ID [*AM radio station call letters*]
KLIX-FM	Twin Falls, ID [*FM radio station call letters*]
KLIZ	Brainerd, MN [*AM radio station call letters*]
KLIZ	Korea Limited Identification Zone
KLIZ	Limestone/Loring Air Force Base [*Maine*] [*ICAO location identifier*] (ICLI)
KLIZ-FM	Brainerd, MN [*FM radio station call letters*]
KLJ	Jewish Hospital, Louisville, KY [*OCLC symbol*] (OCLC)
KLJ	Knight of [*the Order of*] St. Lazarus of Jerusalem [*British*]
KLJ	Knight of the Military and Hospitalier Order of St. Lazarus (DD)
KLJB	Davenport, IA [*Television station call letters*]
KLJC	Kansas City, MO [*FM radio station call letters*]
KLJY	Killjoy (ABBR)
KLJZ	Port Sulphur, LA [*FM radio station call letters*] (RBYB)
KLK	Kealakekua [*Hawaii*] [*Seismograph station code, US Geological Survey Closed*] (SEIS)
KLK	Killick Gold Co. [*Vancouver Stock Exchange symbol*]
KLKC	Parsons, KS [*AM radio station call letters*]
KLKC-FM	Parsons, KS [*FM radio station call letters*]
KLKE	Albion, NE [*Television station call letters*] (RBYB)
KLKI	Anacortes, WA [*AM radio station call letters*]
KLKK	Clear Lake, IA [*FM radio station call letters*]
KLKL	Benton, LA [*FM radio station call letters*]
KLKN-TV	Lincoln, NE [*TV station call letters*] (RBYB)
KLKO	Elko, NV [*AM radio station call letters*]
KLKS	Breezy Point, MN [*FM radio station call letters*]
KLKX	Rosamond, CA [*FM radio station call letters*]
KLKY	Milton-Freewater, OR [*AM radio station call letters*]
KLKY-FM	Milton-Freewater, OR [*FM radio station call letters*] (RBYB)
KLL	Kalltalsperre [*Federal Republic of Germany*] [*Seismograph station code, US Geological Survey*] (SEIS)
KLL	Levelock [*Alaska*] [*Airport symbol*] (OAG)
KLLA	Leesville, LA [*AM radio station call letters*]
KLLB	West Jordan, UT [*AM radio station call letters*]
KLLC-FM	San Francisco, CA [*FM radio station call letters*] (RBYB)
KLLF	Wichita Falls, TX [*AM radio station call letters*]
KLLI	Hooks, TX [*FM radio station call letters*]
KLLK	Fort Bragg, CA [*FM radio station call letters*]
KLLK	Willits, CA [*AM radio station call letters*]
KLLL	Lubbock, TX [*AM radio station call letters*]
KLLL-FM	Lubbock, TX [*FM radio station call letters*]
KLLM	Forks, WA [*FM radio station call letters*]
KLLM	KLLM Transport Services, Inc. [*NASDAQ symbol*] (NQ)
KLLM	KLLM Transport Sv [*NASDAQ symbol*] (TTSB)
KLLN	Newark, AR [*FM radio station call letters*]
KLLR	Amarillo, TX [*FM radio station call letters*] (RBYB)
KLLS	Augusta, KS [*FM radio station call letters*]
KLLT	Vinton, IA [*FM radio station call letters*]
KLLV	Breen, CO [*AM radio station call letters*]
KLLY	Oildale, CA [*FM radio station call letters*]
KLLZ	Walker, MN [*AM radio station call letters*]
KLLZ-FM	Walker, MN [*FM radio station call letters*]
KL/M	Kiloliters per Minute
KLM	Kilometer
KLM	KLM Royal Dutch Air [*NYSE symbol*] (TTSB)
KLM	KLM Royal Dutch Airlines [*Netherlands ICAO designator*] (FAAC)
KLM	KLM [*Koninklijke Luchtvaart Maatschappij*] Royal Dutch Airlines [*NYSE symbol*] (SPSG)
KLM	Koninklijke Luchtvaart Maatschappij [*Royal Dutch Airlines*]
KLM	Kuala Lumpur [*Malaysia*] [*Seismograph station code, US Geological Survey*] (SEIS)
KLM	University of Louisville, School of Music Library, Louisville, KY [*OCLC symbol*] (OCLC)
KLMA	Hobbs, NM [*FM radio station call letters*]
KLMB-FM	Bastrop, LA [*FM radio station call letters*] (RBYB)
KLMC	Knights of Life Motorcycle Club (EA)
KLMJ	Hampton, IA [*FM radio station call letters*]
KLMN	Amarillo, TX [*FM radio station call letters*]
KLMO	Longmont, CO [*AM radio station call letters*]
KLMP	Rapid City, SD [*FM radio station call letters*]
KLMR	Lamar, CO [*AM radio station call letters*]
KLMTR	Kilometer (ABBR)
KLMX-AM	Clayton, NM [*AM radio station call letters*] (RBYB)
KLMY	Seaside, CA [*FM radio station call letters*]
KLN	Kelan Resources [*Vancouver Stock Exchange symbol*]
KLN	Larsen Bay [*Alaska*] [*Airport symbol*] (OAG)
KLN	Norton-Children's Hospital Medical Library, Louisville, KY [*OCLC symbol*] (OCLC)
KLNA	West Palm Beach/Palm Beach County Park [*Florida*] [*ICAO location identifier*] (ICLI)
KLNA-FM	Dunnigan, CA [*FM radio station call letters*] (RBYB)
KLND	Little Eagle, SD [*FM radio station call letters*] (RBYB)
KLNE	Lexington, NE [*FM radio station call letters*]
KLNE-TV	Lexington, NE [*Television station call letters*]
KLNG	Council Bluffs, IA [*AM radio station call letters*]
KLNI	Decorah, IA [*FM radio station call letters*]
KLNK	Lincoln/Municipal [*Nebraska*] [*ICAO location identifier*] (ICLI)
KLNR	Panaca, NV [*FM radio station call letters*]
KLNT	Clinton, IA [*AM radio station call letters*]
KLO	Kalibo [*Philippines*] [*Airport symbol*] (OAG)
KLO	Klystron Oscillator
KLO	Ogden, UT [*AM radio station call letters*]
KLOA	Ridgecrest, CA [*AM radio station call letters*]
KLOA-FM	Ridgecrest, CA [*FM radio station call letters*]
KLOB	Thousand Palms, CA [*FM radio station call letters*]
KLOC	Ceres, CA [*AM radio station call letters*]
KLOC	Kush Locke [*NASDAQ symbol*] (SAG)
KLOC	Kushner-Locke [*NASDAQ symbol*] (TTSB)
KLOC	[*The*] Kushner-Locke Co. [*NASDAQ symbol*] (NQ)
KLOCW	Kushner-Locke Wrrt [*NASDAQ symbol*] (TTSB)
KLOD	Shafter, CA [*FM radio station call letters*]
KLOE	Goodland, KS [*AM radio station call letters*]
KLOF	Kloof Gold Mining Co. Ltd. [*NASDAQ symbol*] (NQ)
KLOFY	Kloof Gold Mining ADR [*NASDAQ symbol*] (TTSB)
KLOG	Kelso, WA [*AM radio station call letters*]
KLOH	Pipestone, MN [*AM radio station call letters*]
KLOK	San Jose, CA [*AM radio station call letters*]
KLOK-FM	Greenfield, CA [*FM radio station call letters*] (RBYB)
KLOL	Houston, TX [*FM radio station call letters*]
KLOM	Lompoc, CA [*AM radio station call letters*]
KLON	Long Beach, CA [*FM radio station call letters*]
KLOO	Corvallis, OR [*AM radio station call letters*]
KloofG	Kloof Gold Mining Co. Ltd. [*Associated Press*] (SAG)
KLOQ	Merced, CA [*AM radio station call letters*]
KLOQ-FM	Winton, CA [*FM radio station call letters*] (RBYB)
KLOR	Ponca City, OK [*FM radio station call letters*]
KLOS	Los Angeles, CA [*FM radio station call letters*]
KLOU	Louisville/Bowman [*Kentucky*] [*ICAO location identifier*] (ICLI)
KLOU	St. Louis, MO [*FM radio station call letters*]
KLOV	Loveland, CO [*AM radio station call letters*]
KLOW	Caruthersville, MO [*FM radio station call letters*]
KLOZ	Eldon, MO [*FM radio station call letters*]
KLP	Korean Labor Party [*Political party*]
KLP	Louisville Free Public Library, Louisville, KY [*OCLC symbol*] (OCLC)
KLP	Redding Aero Enterprises, Inc. [*FAA designator*] (FAAC)
KLPA	Alexandria, LA [*Television station call letters*]
KLPA	Khan-Lewis Phonological Analysis [*Speech evaluation test*]
Kl Pauly	Der Kleine Pauly [*A publication*] (OCD)
KLPB	Lafayette, LA [*Television station call letters*]
KLPI	Ruston, LA [*FM radio station call letters*]
KLPL	Lake Providence, LA [*AM radio station call letters*]
KLPL-FM	Lake Providence, LA [*FM radio station call letters*]
KLPQ	Sherweeod, AR [*FM radio station call letters*]
KLPR-FM	Keamey, NE [*FM radio station call letters*] (RBYB)
KLPTMN	Kleptomania (ABBR)
KLPTMNC	Kleptomaniac (ABBR)
KLPW	Union, MO [*AM radio station call letters*]
KLPW-FM	Union, MO [*FM radio station call letters*]
KLPX	Tucson, AZ [*FM radio station call letters*]
KLPZ	Parker, AZ [*AM radio station call letters*]
KLQB	Oracle, AZ [*FM radio station call letters*]
KLQL	Luverne, MN [*FM radio station call letters*]
KLQP	Madison, MN [*FM radio station call letters*]
KLQZ	Paragould, AR [*FM radio station call letters*]
KLR	Columbus Air Transport, Inc. [*ICAO designator*] (FAAC)

KLR........... Kalmar [*Sweden*] [*Airport symbol*] (OAG)
KLR........... Kathiawar Law Reports [*India*] [*A publication*] (DLA)
KLR........... Kentucky Law Reporter [*A publication*] (DLA)
KLRA......... England, AR [*AM radio station call letters*]
KLRA-FM .... England, AR [*FM radio station call letters*]
KLRB......... Aurora, NE [*AM radio station call letters*]
KLRC......... Siloam Springs, AR [*FM radio station call letters*]
KLRD......... Laredo/International [*Texas*] [*ICAO location identifier*] (ICLI)
KLRD......... Yucaipa, CA [*FM radio station call letters*]
KLRE......... Little Rock, AR [*FM radio station call letters*]
KLRF......... Brownsville, OR [*FM radio station call letters*]
KLRF......... Jacksonville/Little Rock Air Force Base [*Arkansas*] [*ICAO location identifier*] (ICLI)
KLRG......... North Little Rock, AR [*AM radio station call letters*]
KLRK......... Vandalia, MO [*FM radio station call letters*]
KLRN......... San Antonio, TX [*Television station call letters*]
KLRQ......... Clinton, MO [*FM radio station call letters*]
KLRR......... Redmond, OR [*FM radio station call letters*]
KLRS......... Chico, CA [*FM radio station call letters*]
KLRT......... Kleinert's, Inc. [*NASDAQ symbol*] (NQ)
KLRT......... Little Rock, AR [*Television station call letters*]
KLRU......... Austin, TX [*Television station call letters*]
KLRZ......... Larose, LA [*FM radio station call letters*]
KLS............ Faculty of Library and Information Science, University of Toronto [*UTLAS symbol*]
KLS............ Karlskrona [*Sweden*] [*Seismograph station code, US Geological Survey Closed*] (SEIS)
KLS............ Kaskaskia Library System [*Library network*]
KLS............ Kelso Resources [*Vancouver Stock Exchange symbol*]
KLS............ Kelso, WA [*Location identifier FAA*] (FAAL)
KLS............ Key Lock Switch
KLS............ Kidney, Liver, Spleen [*Medicine*]
KLS............ Knight of the Lion and Sun [*Persia*] (ROG)
KLS............ Knotted List Structure (BUR)
KLS............ Kreuzbein Lipomatous Syndrome [*Medicine*] (DMAA)
KLS............ Krypton LASER System
KLSA......... Alexandria, LA [*FM radio station call letters*]
KLSB......... Nacogdoches, TX [*Television station call letters*]
KLSC......... Korean Logistic Service Corps (CINC)
KLSC-FM .... Fayette, MO [*FM radio station call letters*] (RBYB)
KI Schr .... Kleine Schriften [*of various authors*] [*Classical studies*] (OCD)
KLSE......... Kuala Lumpur Stock Exchange
KLSE......... Rochester, MN [*FM radio station call letters*]
KLSIFC........ Kathy Lynn Sacra International Fan Club (EA)
KLSK......... Santa Fe, NM [*FM radio station call letters*]
KLSN......... New London, MO [*FM radio station call letters*] (RBYB)
KLSP......... Angola, LA [*FM radio station call letters*]
KLSQ .... Laughlin, NV [*AM radio station call letters*] (RBYB)
KLSQ EXP STN... East Las Vegas, NV [*Radio expansion station*] (RBYB)
KLSR......... Memphis, TX [*AM radio station call letters*]
KLSR-FM .... Memphis, TX [*FM radio station call letters*]
KLSS-FM .... Mason City, IA [*FM radio station call letters*]
KLST.......... Kindergarten Language Screening Test
KLST.......... San Angelo, TX [*Television station call letters*]
KLSU.......... Baton Rouge, LA [*FM radio station call letters*]
KLSV.......... Las Vegas/Nellis Air Force Base [*Nevada*] [*ICAO location identifier*] (ICLI)
KLSX.......... Los Angeles, CA [*FM radio station call letters*]
KLSY.......... Bellevue, WA [*FM radio station call letters*]
KLSZ.......... Van Buren, AR [*FM radio station call letters*]
KLT............ Kansas City Power & Light Co. [*NYSE symbol*] (SPSG)
KLT............ Kansas City Pwr & Lt [*NYSE symbol*] (TTSB)
KLT............ Karhunen-Loeve Transform [*Mathematics*]
KLT............ Kiloton [*Nuclear equivalent of 1000 tons of high explosives*] (AAG)
KIT............ Kleine Texte fuer Theologische und Philosophische Vorlesungen [*A publication*] (BJA)
KLT............ Klystron Life Test
KLTA.......... Breckenridge, MN [*FM radio station call letters*]
KLTB.......... Boise, ID [*FM radio station call letters*]
KLTC.......... Dickinson, ND [*AM radio station call letters*]
KLTCB........ Korean Long Term Credit Bank
KLTD.......... Temple, TX [*FM radio station call letters*]
KLTE.......... Kirksville, MO [*FM radio station call letters*]
KLTF.......... Little Falls, MN [*AM radio station call letters*]
KLTG.......... Corpus Christi, TX [*FM radio station call letters*]
KLTH.......... Kansas City, MO [*FM radio station call letters*]
KLTI........... Macon, MO [*AM radio station call letters*]
KLTJ.......... Galveston, TX [*Television station call letters*]
KLTK.......... South West City, MO [*AM radio station call letters*]
KLTL.......... Lake Charles, LA [*Television station call letters*]
KLTM.......... Monroe, LA [*Television station call letters*]
KLTN.......... Kiloton (ABBR)
KLTN.......... Port Arthur, TX [*FM radio station call letters*]
KLTO.......... Knurling Tool
KLTO.......... Rosenberg, TX [*FM radio station call letters*] (RBYB)
KLTP-FM .... Galveston, TX [*FM radio station call letters*] (RBYB)
KLTPrA....... Kansas City P&L 3.80% Pfd [*NYSE symbol*] (TTSB)
KLTPrD....... Kansas City P&L 4.35% Pfd [*NYSE symbol*] (TTSB)
KLTPrE....... Kansas City P&L 4.50% Pfd [*NYSE symbol*] (TTSB)
KLTQ.......... Sparta, MO [*FM radio station call letters*]
KLTR.......... Franklin, TX [*FM radio station call letters*]
KLTR.......... Franklin, TX [*FM radio station call letters*] (RBYB)
KLTR.......... Kilter (ABBR)
KLTS.......... Altus Air Force Base [*Oklahoma*] [*ICAO location identifier*] (ICLI)
KLTS.......... Shreveport, LA [*Television station call letters*]

KLTT.......... Brighton, CO [*AM radio station call letters*]
KLTV.......... Tyler, TX [*Television station call letters*]
KLTW-AM .... Sierra Vista, AZ [*AM radio station call letters*] (RBYB)
KLTX.......... Harker Heights, TX [*FM radio station call letters*]
KLTY.......... Fort Worth, TX [*FM radio station call letters*]
KLTZ.......... Glasgow, MT [*AM radio station call letters*]
KLU............ Kaiser Aluminum [*NYSE symbol*] (TTSB)
KLU............ Kaiser Aluminum & Chemical Corp. [*NYSE symbol*] (SPSG)
KLU............ Key and Lamp Units [*Telecommunications*]
KLU............ Klagenfurt [*Austria*] [*Airport symbol*] (OAG)
KLU............ Klutina [*Alaska*] [*Seismograph station code, US Geological Survey*] (SEIS)
KLUA.......... Kailua-Kona, HI [*FM radio station call letters*]
KLUB.......... Bloomington, TX [*FM radio station call letters*]
KLUC-FM .... Las Vegas, NV [*FM radio station call letters*]
KLUE.......... Knowledge Legacy of the Unavailable Expert [*Computer science*] (BTTJ)
KLUE.......... Soledad, CA [*FM radio station call letters*]
KLUF.......... Phoenix/Luke Air Force Base [*Arizona*] [*ICAO location identifier*] (ICLI)
KLUH.......... Poplar Bluff, MO [*FM radio station call letters*]
KLUJ.......... Harlingen, TX [*Television station call letters*]
KLUK.......... Cincinnati/Municipal-Lunken Field [*Ohio*] [*ICAO location identifier*] (ICLI)
KLUK.......... Laughlin, NV [*FM radio station call letters*] (RBYB)
KLUP.......... Terrell Hills, TX [*AM radio station call letters*]
KLUPrD....... Kaiser Alum 8.255% 'PRIDES' [*NYSE symbol*] (TTSB)
KLUR.......... Wichita Falls, TX [*FM radio station call letters*]
KLUV.......... Dallas, TX [*FM radio station call letters*]
KLUX.......... Robstown, TX [*FM radio station call letters*]
KLUZ.......... Albuquerque, NM [*Television station call letters*]
KLV............ Karlovy Vary [*Former Czechoslovakia*] [*Airport symbol*] (OAG)
KLVA.......... Casa Grande, AZ [*FM radio station call letters*] (RBYB)
KLVC.......... Magalia, CA [*FM radio station call letters*]
KLVE.......... Los Angeles, CA [*FM radio station call letters*]
KLVF.......... Las Vegas, NM [*FM radio station call letters*]
KLVG.......... Garberville, CA [*FM radio station call letters*] (RBYB)
KLVI.......... Beaumont, TX [*AM radio station call letters*]
KLVJ.......... Mountain Home, ID [*AM radio station call letters*]
KLVJ-FM .... Mountain Home, ID [*FM radio station call letters*]
KLVK.......... Dimmitt, TX [*FM radio station call letters*] (RBYB)
KLVL.......... Pasadena, TX [*AM radio station call letters*]
KLVM.......... Prunedale, CA [*FM radio station call letters*]
KLVN.......... Chowchilla, CA [*FM radio station call letters*] (RBYB)
KLVO.......... Belen, NM [*FM radio station call letters*] (RBYB)
KLVQ.......... Athens, TX [*AM radio station call letters*]
KLVR.......... Santa Rosa, CA [*FM radio station call letters*]
KLVS.......... Las Vegas [*New Mexico*] [*ICAO location identifier*] (ICLI)
KLVS-FM .... Kingsburg, CA [*FM radio station call letters*] (RBYB)
KLVT.......... Levelland, TX [*AM radio station call letters*]
KLVT-FM .... Levelland, TX [*FM radio station call letters*]
KLVU.......... Haynesville, LA [*AM radio station call letters*]
KLVV.......... Ponca City, OK [*FM radio station call letters*]
KLVW.......... Julian, CA [*FM radio station call letters*] (RBYB)
KLVX.......... Las Vegas, NV [*Television station call letters*]
KLW........... Claw Resources Ltd. [*Vancouver Stock Exchange symbol*]
KLW........... Faculty of Law Library, University of Toronto [*UTLAS symbol*]
KLW........... Klawock [*Alaska*] [*Airport symbol*] (OAG)
KLWJ.......... Umatilla, OR [*AM radio station call letters*]
KLWN.......... Lawrence, KS [*AM radio station call letters*]
KLWT.......... Kilowatt (ABBR)
KLWT.......... Lebanon, MO [*AM radio station call letters*]
KLWY.......... Cheyenne, WY [*Television station call letters*]
KLX........... Kalamata [*Greece*] [*Airport symbol*] (OAG)
KLX........... Kalix Air [*Nigeria*] [*FAA designator*] (FAAC)
KLX........... Kidney and Lung Extract
KLXK.......... Duluth, MN [*FM radio station call letters*]
KLXO.......... El Centro, CA [*Television station call letters*]
KLXQ.......... Hot Springs, AR [*FM radio station call letters*]
KLXR.......... Redding, CA [*AM radio station call letters*]
KLXS.......... Pierre, SD [*FM radio station call letters*]
KLXV.......... San Jose, CA [*Television station call letters*]
KLXX.......... Bismarck-Mandan, ND [*AM radio station call letters*]
KLY........... Kalima [*Zaire*] [*Airport symbol*] (AD)
KLY........... Klyuchi [*Former USSR Seismograph station code, US Geological Survey*] (SEIS)
KLYC.......... McMinnville, OR [*AM radio station call letters*]
KLYD.......... Shafter, CA [*FM radio station call letters*] (RBYB)
KLYF.......... Des Moines, IA [*FM radio station call letters*]
KLYK.......... Longview, WA [*FM radio station call letters*]
KLYN.......... Lynden, WA [*FM radio station call letters*]
KLYQ.......... Hamilton, MT [*AM radio station call letters*]
KLYR.......... Clarksville, AR [*AM radio station call letters*]
KLYR.......... Smoke Layer Aloft [*Meteorology*] (FAAC)
KLYR-FM .... Clarksville, AR [*FM radio station call letters*]
KLYT.......... Albuquerque, NM [*FM radio station call letters*]
KLYV.......... Dubuque, IA [*FM radio station call letters*]
KLYY-FM .... Arcadia, CA [*FM radio station call letters*] (RBYB)
KLZ........... Denver, CO [*AM radio station call letters*]
KLZ........... Kleinzee [*South Africa*] [*Airport symbol*] (OAG)
KLZE.......... Owensville, MO [*FM radio station call letters*]
KLZK.......... Brownfield, TX [*FM radio station call letters*]
KLZR.......... Lawrence, KS [*FM radio station call letters*]
KLZX-FM .... Brigham City, UT [*FM radio station call letters*] (RBYB)
KLZY.......... Powell, WY [*FM radio station call letters*]

KLZZ.......... Waite Park, MN [*FM radio station call letters*]
KM.............. Air Malta [*ICAO designator*] (AD)
KM.............. Comoros [*ANSI two-letter standard code*] (CNC)
KM.............. Draepelin-Morel [*Disease*] [*Psychiatry*] (DAVI)
KM.............. Ha-Kibbuts ha-Me'uhad (BJA)
KM.............. Kabataang Makabayan [*Nationalist Youth*] [*Philippines*]
KM.............. Kanamycin [*Antibacterial compound*]
KM.............. [*The*] Kansas & Missouri Railway & Terminal Co. [*Formerly, KMRT*] [*AAR code*]
kM .... Kilomega
km .... Kilometer
KM.............. Kilometer [*BTS*] (TAG)
KM.............. K-Immunoglobulin Light Chains [*Immunology*] (DAVI)
KM.............. Kinetic Momentum
KM.............. King and Martyr [*Church calendars*]
KM.............. Kingdom
KM.............. King's Medal [*or Medallist*] [*British*]
KM.............. King's Messenger [*British*] (ROG)
KM.............. Kirchoff Method [*Telecommunications*] (OA)
KM.............. Kitchen Mechanic [*Restaurant slang*]
KM.............. Klystron Mount
KM.............. Kmart [*NYSE symbol*] (TTSB)
KM.............. K Mart Corp. [*NYSE symbol*] (SPSG)
KM.............. K mart Financing Trust I [*NYSE symbol*] (SAG)
KM.............. Knight of Malta
KM.............. Knight of the Sovereign and Military Order of Malta (DD)
KM.............. Kraepelin-Morel [*Disease*] [*Psychiatry*] (DAVI)
KM.............. Kubelka-Munk [*Optics*]
KM.............. Kurram Militia [*British military*] (DMA)
KM.............. Manhattan Public Library, Manhattan, KS [*Library symbol Library of Congress*] (LCLS)
Km .... Michaelis-Menten Dissociation Constnat (DAVI)
KM2 .... Kermit [*Texas*] [*Seismograph station code, US Geological Survey*] (SEIS)
km² .... Square Kilometer (CDAI)
km2 .... Square Kilometer
K M²/W .... Kelvin Square Meters per Watt
KM³ .... Cubic Kilometer
KM5 .... Kermit [*Texas*] [*Seismograph station code, US Geological Survey*] (SEIS)
KM6 .... Kermit [*Texas*] [*Seismograph station code, US Geological Survey*] (SEIS)
KM9 .... Kermit [*Texas*] [*Seismograph station code, US Geological Survey*] (SEIS)
KMA............. Kerema [*Papua New Guinea*] [*Airport symbol*] (OAG)
KMA............. Korea Military Academy
KMA............. Ku-Band Multiple Access (MCD)
KMA............. Shenandoah, IA [*AM radio station call letters*]
KMAA........... Kart Marketing Association of America (EA)
KMAC.......... Gainesville, MO [*FM radio station call letters*]
KMAC.......... Kushi Macrobiotic Corp. [*NASDAQ symbol*] (SAG)
KMAC.......... Kushi Macrobiotics [*NASDAQ symbol*] (TTSB)
KMACW....... Kushi Macrobiotics Wrrt [*NASDAQ symbol*] (TTSB)
KMAD.......... Madill, OK [*AM radio station call letters*]
KMAD-FM..... Madill, OK [*FM radio station call letters*]
KMAF.......... Midland/Regional Air Terminal [*Texas*] [*ICAO location identifier*] (ICLI)
KMAG .... Fort Smith, AR [*FM radio station call letters*]
KMAG .... Komag, Inc. [*NASDAQ symbol*] (NQ)
KMAG .... Korea Military Advisory Group [*United States*]
KMAGV .... Korean Military Assistance Group, Vietnam (VNW)
KMAJ.......... Topeka, KS [*AM radio station call letters*]
KMAJ-FM..... Topeka, KS [*FM radio station call letters*]
KMAK.......... Orange Cove, CA [*FM radio station call letters*]
KMAL.......... Malden, MO [*FM radio station call letters*]
KMAM......... Butler, MO [*AM radio station call letters*]
KMAN .... Manhattan, KS [*AM radio station call letters*]
KMAQ .... Marquoketa, IA [*AM radio station call letters*]
KMAQ-FM ... Maquoketa, IA [*FM radio station call letters*]
KMAR .... Winnsboro, LA [*AM radio station call letters*]
KMAR-FM ... Winnsboro, LA [*FM radio station call letters*]
K mart .... K Mart Corp. [*Associated Press*] (SAG)
KmartF .... K mart Financing Trust I [*Associated Press*] (SAG)
KMAS.......... Korean Medical Association of America (EA)
KMAS.......... Shelton, WA [*AM radio station call letters*]
KMAU.......... Wailuku, HI [*Television station call letters*]
KMAV.......... Mayville, ND [*AM radio station call letters*]
KMAV-FM .... Mayville, ND [*FM radio station call letters*]
KMAX.......... Arcadia, CA [*FM radio station call letters*]
KMAX-AM .... Opportunity, WA [*AM radio station call letters*] (RBYB)
KMAY.......... Billings, MT [*AM radio station call letters*]
KMB............. Kimbe [*New Britain*] [*Seismograph station code, US Geological Survey Closed*] (SEIS)
KMB............. Kimberly-Clark [*NYSE symbol*] (TTSB)
KMB............. Kimberly-Clark Corp. [*NYSE symbol*] (SPSG)
KMB............. Koinambe [*Papua New Guinea*] [*Airport symbol*] (OAG)
KMBC.......... Kansas City, MO [*Television station call letters*]
KMBD .... Tillamook, OR [*AM radio station call letters*]
KMBH .... Harlingen, TX [*Television station call letters*]
KMBH-FM .... Harlingen, TX [*FM radio station call letters*]
KMBI........... Spokane, WA [*AM radio station call letters*]
KMBI-FM ..... Spokane, WA [*FM radio station call letters*]
KMBL.......... Junction, TX [*AM radio station call letters*]
KMBO .... Keith Martin Ballet Oregon
KMBQ .... Wasilla, AK [*FM radio station call letters*]

KMBS........... West Monroe, LA [*AM radio station call letters*]
KMBV........... Navasota, TX [*AM radio station call letters*]
KMBY........... Capitola, CA [*AM radio station call letters*] (RBYB)
KMBY-FM ..... Gonzales, CA [*FM radio station call letters*] (RBYB)
KMBZ........... Kansas City, MO [*AM radio station call letters*]
KMC............. Kamloops CableNet [*Vancouver Stock Exchange symbol*]
KMC............. Kernel Migration Coefficient (PDAA)
kMc............. Kilomegacycle
KMC............. Kinetic Monte Carlo [*Simulation*]
KMC............. Korean Marine Corps [*North Korea*]
KMC............. Manhattan Christian College, Manhattan, KS [*Library symbol*] [*Library of Congress*] (LCLS)
KMCC........... Sacremento/McClellan Air Force Base [*California*] [*ICAO location identifier*] (ICLI)
KMCD .... Fairfield, IA [*AM radio station call letters*]
KMCF........... Tampa/MacDill Air Force Base [*Florida*] [*ICAO location identifier*] (ICLI)
KMCH .... Manchester, IA [*FM radio station call letters*]
KMCI........... Kansas City/International [*Missouri*] [*ICAO location identifier*] (ICLI)
KMCI........... Lawrence, KS [*Television station call letters*]
KMCK .... Siloam Springs, AR [*FM radio station call letters*]
KMCL........... McCall, ID [*AM radio station call letters*]
KMCL-FM .... McCall, ID [*FM radio station call letters*]
KMCM.......... Miles City, MT [*FM radio station call letters*]
K-MCM .... Potassium-Containing Minimal Capacitation Medium [*Medicine*] (BABM)
KMCO .... McAlester, OK [*FM radio station call letters*]
KMCO .... Orlando/McCoy Air Force Base [*Florida*] [*ICAO location identifier*] (ICLI)
KMCP........... Kodak Metal Clad Plate (IAA)
KMcpC........ McPherson College, McPherson, KS [*Library symbol Library of Congress*] (LCLS)
kMcps......... Kilomegacycles per Sound [*Measurement*] (DAVI)
KMCQ .... The Dalles, OR [*FM radio station call letters*]
KMCR .... Montgomery City, MO [*FM radio station call letters*]
kMcs.......... Kilomegacycles per Second (AABC)
KMCT.......... West Monroe, LA [*Television station call letters*]
KMCX.......... Ogallala, NE [*FM radio station call letters*]
KMCY.......... Minot, ND [*Television station call letters*]
KMD............ Kamlode Resources, Inc. [*Vancouver Stock Exchange symbol*]
KMDAT .... KeyMath Diagnostic Arithmetic Test
KMDL.......... Kaplan, LA [*FM radio station call letters*]
KMDO .... Fort Scott, KS [*AM radio station call letters*]
KMDT........... Middletown/Harrisburg International-Olmsted Field [*Pennsylvania*] [*ICAO location identifier*] (ICLI)
KMDW .... Chicago/Chicago Midway [*Illinois*] [*ICAO location identifier*] (ICLI)
KME............. Kappa Mu Epsilon [*Society*]
KME............. Kermit [*Texas*] [*Seismograph station code, US Geological Survey Closed*] (SEIS)
KME............. Kerr Magneto-Optical Effect [*Optics*]
KME............. Kraft Mill Effluent [*Pulp and paper processing*]
KME............. Media Center, Audio Visual Library, University of Toronto [*UTLAS symbol*]
KMEB........... Wailuku, HI [*Television station call letters*]
KMED.......... Medford, OR [*AM radio station call letters*]
KMEF.......... Keratin, Myosin, Epidermin, Fibrin [*Biochemistry*]
KMEG........... Sioux City, IA [*Television station call letters*]
KMEIA........ Kodaly Music Education Institute of Australia
KMEL.......... San Francisco, CA [*FM radio station call letters*]
KMEM.......... Lincoln, NE [*AM radio station call letters*]
KMEM.......... Memphis/International [*Tennessee*] [*ICAO location identifier*] (ICLI)
KMEM.......... Memphis, MO [*FM radio station call letters*]
KMEN.......... San Bernardino, CA [*AM radio station call letters*]
KMER.......... Kemmerer, WY [*AM radio station call letters*]
KMER.......... Kodak Metal Etch Resist
KMER.......... Merced/Castle Air Force Base [*California*] [*ICAO location identifier*] (ICLI)
KMET.......... Banning, CA [*AM radio station call letters*]
KMET.......... Kemet Corp. [*NASDAQ symbol*] (SAG)
KMEX.......... Los Angeles, CA [*Television station call letters*]
KMEZ.......... Belle Chasse, LA [*FM radio station call letters*]
KMF............. Kamina [*Papua New Guinea*] [*Airport symbol*] (OAG)
KMF............. Koussevitzky Music Foundation (EA)
KMFA.......... Austin, TX [*FM radio station call letters*]
KMFB.......... Mendocino, CA [*FM radio station call letters*]
KMFC........... Centralia, MO [*FM radio station call letters*]
KMFC........... Kimberly McCullough Fan Club (EA)
KMFE.......... McAllen/Miller International [*Texas*] [*ICAO location identifier*] (ICLI)
KMFM.......... Premont, TX [*FM radio station call letters*]
KMFX.......... Lake City, MN [*FM radio station call letters*]
KMFX.......... Wabasha, MN [*AM radio station call letters*]
KMFY.......... Grand Rapids, MN [*FM radio station call letters*]
KMG............. Kerr-McGee [*NYSE symbol*] (TTSB)
KMG............. Kerr McGee Corp. [*NYSE symbol*] (SAG)
KMG............. Kerr-McGee Corp. [*NYSE symbol Toronto Stock Exchange symbol*] (SPSG)
KMG............. Kumagaya [*Japan*] [*Seismograph station code, US Geological Survey*] (SEIS)
KMG............. Kunming [*China*] [*Airport symbol*] (OAG)
KMGA.......... Albuquerque, NM [*FM radio station call letters*]
KMGC.......... Camden, AR [*FM radio station call letters*] (RBYB)
KMGE.......... Eugene, OR [*FM radio station call letters*]
KMGE.......... Marietta/Dobbins Air Force Base [*Georgia*] [*ICAO location identifier*] (ICLI)
KMGG.......... Monte Rio, CA [*FM radio station call letters*]

KMGH	Denver, CO [*Television station call letters*]
KMGI	Pocatello, ID [*FM radio station call letters*]
KMGK	Glenwood, MN [*FM radio station call letters*]
KMGL	Oklahoma City, OK [*FM radio station call letters*]
KMGM	Montevideo, MN [*FM radio station call letters*]
KMGN	Flagstaff, AZ [*FM radio station call letters*]
KMGO	Centerville, IA [*FM radio station call letters*]
KMGPrD	Kerr Group $1.70 Cv Pfd [*NYSE symbol*] (TTSB)
KMGQ	Goleta, CA [*FM radio station call letters*]
KMGR	Murray, UT [*AM radio station call letters*]
KMGW	Casper, WY [*FM radio station call letters*]
KMGX	Rio Dell, CA [*FM radio station call letters*] (RBYB)
KMGZ	Lawton, OK [*FM radio station call letters*] (RBYB)
kmh	Kilometers per Hour
KMH	Knight of Merit of Holstein
KMHA	Four Bears, ND [*FM radio station call letters*]
KMHD	Gresham, OR [*FM radio station call letters*]
KMHK-FM	Hardin, MT [*FM radio station call letters*] (RBYB)
KMHL	Marshall, MN [*AM radio station call letters*]
KMHM-FM	Lutesville, MO [*FM radio station call letters*] (RBYB)
KM/HR	Kilometers per Hour
KMHR	Sacramento/Mather Air Force Base [*California*] [*ICAO location identifier*] (ICLI)
KMHT	Marshall, TX [*AM radio station call letters*]
kMHZ	Kilomega Hertz (MCD)
KMI	Keilschrifttexte Medizinischen Inhalts [*A publication*] (BJA)
KMI	Kessler Marketing Intelligence [*Information service or system*] (IID)
KMI	KSC [*Kennedy Space Center*] Management Instruction [*NASA*] (KSC)
KMI	Miyazaki [*Japan*] [*Airport symbol*] (OAG)
KMIA	Jasper, TX [*FM radio station call letters*]
KMIA	Miami/International [*Florida*] [*ICAO location identifier*] (ICLI)
KMIB	Minot/Minot Air Force Base [*North Dakota*] [*ICAO location identifier*] (ICLI)
KMID	Midland, TX [*Television station call letters*]
KMIH	Mercer Island, WA [*FM radio station call letters*]
KMiJ	Johnson County Mental Health Center, Mission, KS [*Library symbol Library of Congress*] (LCLS)
KMIL	Cameron, TX [*AM radio station call letters*]
KMIN	Grants, NM [*AM radio station call letters*]
KMIQ	Robstown, TX [*FM radio station call letters*]
KMIR	Palm Springs, CA [*Television station call letters*]
KMIS	New Madrid, MO [*FM radio station call letters*]
KMIS	Portageville, MO [*AM radio station call letters*]
KMIT	Mitchell, SD [*FM radio station call letters*]
KMIV	Millville/Millville [*New Jersey*] [*ICAO location identifier*] (ICLI)
KMIX	Tracy, CA [*FM radio station call letters*] (RBYB)
KMIZ	Columbia, MO [*Television station call letters*]
KMJ	Fresno, CA [*AM radio station call letters*]
KMJ	Knight of Maximilian Joseph [*Bavaria*]
KMJ	Kumamoto [*Japan*] [*Airport symbol*] (OAG)
KMJ	Kume Jima [*Ryukyu Islands*] [*Seismograph station code, US Geological Survey*] (SEIS)
KMJC	Mount Shasta, CA [*AM radio station call letters*] (RBYB)
KMJC-FM	Mount Shasta, CA [*FM radio station call letters*] (RBYB)
KMJE-FM	Gridley, CA [*FM radio station call letters*] (RBYB)
KMJI	Sacramento, CA [*AM radio station call letters*] (RBYB)
KMJJ	Shreveport, LA [*FM radio station call letters*]
KMJK	Buckeye, AZ [*FM radio station call letters*]
KMJM	St. Louis, MO [*FM radio station call letters*]
KMJQ	Houston, TX [*FM radio station call letters*]
KMJX	Conway, AR [*FM radio station call letters*]
KMJY	Newport, WA [*AM radio station call letters*]
KMJY-FM	Newport, WA [*FM radio station call letters*]
KMJZ-FM	St. Louis Park, MN [*FM radio station call letters*] (RBYB)
KMK	Kamakura [*Japan*] [*Seismograph station code, US Geological Survey Closed*] (SEIS)
KMK	Kansas State University, Manhattan, KS [*Library symbol Library of Congress*] (LCLS)
KMK	Keren Mif'alim Konstruktiviyim [*Constructive Enterprises Fund*] (BJA)
KMK	Konyvtartudomanyi es Modszertani Kozpont [*Center for Library Science and Methodology*] [*Hungary*] [*Information service or system*] (IID)
KMK	Makabana [*Congo*] [*Airport symbol*] (AD)
KMKC	Kansas City/Kansas City [*Missouri*] [*ICAO location identifier*] (ICLI)
KMKE	Grand Junction, CO [*FM radio station call letters*]
KMKE	Milwaukee/General Mitchell Field [*Wisconsin*] [*ICAO location identifier*] (ICLI)
KMKF	Manhattan, KS [*FM radio station call letters*]
KMKM	Kansas City [*Missouri*] [*ICAO location identifier*] (ICLI)
KMKO	Muskogee/Davis [*Oklahoma*] [*ICAO location identifier*] (ICLI)
KMKRY	Kvutzat Mesahake Kadur Regel Yehudit (BJA)
KMKS	Bay City, TX [*FM radio station call letters*]
KMK-V	Kansas State University, Veterinary Medicine Library, Manhattan, KS [*Library symbol Library of Congress*] (LCLS)
KMKX	San Diego, CA [*FM radio station call letters*] (RBYB)
KMKZ	Lahoma, OK [*FM radio station call letters*]
KML	Carmel Container Sys [*AMEX symbol*] (TTSB)
KML	Carmel Container Systems Ltd. [*AMEX symbol*] (SPSG)
KML	Kamileroi [*Australia Airport symbol Obsolete*] (OAG)
KML	Kamuela [*Hawaii*] [*Seismograph station code, US Geological Survey Closed*] (SEIS)
KMLA-FM	El Rio, CA [*FM radio station call letters*] (RBYB)
KMLB	Melbourne/Cape Kennedy Regional [*Florida*] [*ICAO location identifier*] (ICLI)

KMLB	Monroe, LA [*AM radio station call letters*]
KMLC	McAlester/Municipal [*Oklahoma*] [*ICAO location identifier*] (ICLI)
KMLE	Chandler, AZ [*FM radio station call letters*]
KMLM	Odessa, TX [*Television station call letters*]
KMLO-FM	Lowry, SD [*FM radio station call letters*] (RBYB)
KMLT	Millinocket/Millinocke [*Maine*] [*ICAO location identifier*] (ICLI)
KMLU	Monroe/Monroe Municipal [*Louisiana*] [*ICAO location identifier*] (ICLI)
KMLW	Moses Lake, WA [*FM radio station call letters*] (RBYB)
KMM	Kamigamo [*Japan*] [*Seismograph station code, US Geological Survey Closed*] (SEIS)
KMM	Kemper Multi-Market Income [*NYSE symbol*] (SPSG)
KMM	Kimam [*Indonesia*] [*Airport symbol*] (OAG)
KMM	Knight of the Order of Military Merit [*Prussia*] (ROG)
KMM	Morehead State University, Morehead, KY [*OCLC symbol*] (OCLC)
KMMA	Knitting Machine Manufacturers Association [*Defunct*] (EA)
KMMC	Kangaroo Marketing and Management Committee [*Australia*]
KMMC	Salem, MO [*FM radio station call letters*]
KMMJ	Grand Island, NE [*AM radio station call letters*]
KMML	Amarillo, TX [*FM radio station call letters*]
KMMM	Madera, CA [*FM radio station call letters*]
KMMO	Marshall, MO [*AM radio station call letters*]
KMMO-FM	Marshall, MO [*FM radio station call letters*]
KMMR	Malta, MT [*FM radio station call letters*]
KMMS	Bozeman, MT [*AM radio station call letters*]
K-MMSEN	KSC [*Kennedy Space Center*] MMSE Notice [*Multiuse Mission Support Equipment*] [*NASA*] (NASA)
K-MMSEPS	KSC [*Kennedy Space Center*] MMSE Project Specification [*Multiuse Mission Support Equipment*] [*NASA*] (NASA)
KMMS-FM	Bozeman, MT [*FM radio station call letters*]
KMMT	Mammoth Lakes, CA [*FM radio station call letters*]
KMMX	Lamesa, TX [*FM radio station call letters*]
KMMY	Muskogee, OK [*FM radio station call letters*]
KMN	Kamina [*Zaire*] [*Airport symbol*] (OAG)
KMN	Kumano [*Japan*] [*Seismograph station code, US Geological Survey*] (SEIS)
KMNC	North Central Kansas Libraries, Manhattan, KS [*Library symbol Library of Congress*] (LCLS)
KMND	Midland, TX [*AM radio station call letters*]
KMNE	Bassett, NE [*FM radio station call letters*]
KMNE-TV	Bassett, NE [*Television station call letters*]
KMNO	Kimono (ABBR)
KMnO	Potassium Permanganate [*Pharmacology*] (DAVI)
KMNR	Rolla, MO [*FM radio station call letters*]
KMNS	Sioux City, IA [*AM radio station call letters*]
KMNT	Centralia, WA [*FM radio station call letters*]
KMNY	Pomona, CA [*AM radio station call letters*]
KMNZ	Oklahoma City, OK [*Television station call letters*]
KMO	Kobe Marine Observatory (BARN)
KMO	Manokotak [*Alaska*] [*Airport symbol*] (OAG)
KMOB	Mobile/Bates Field [*Alabama*] [*ICAO location identifier*] (ICLI)
KMOC	Wichita Falls, TX [*FM radio station call letters*]
KMOD	Tulsa, OK [*FM radio station call letters*]
KMOE	Butler, MO [*FM radio station call letters*]
KMOG	Payson, AZ [*AM radio station call letters*]
KMOH	Kingman, AZ [*Television station call letters*]
KMOJ	Minneapolis, MN [*FM radio station call letters*]
KMOK	Lewiston, ID [*FM radio station call letters*]
KMOL	San Antonio, TX [*Television station call letters*]
KMOM	Monticello, MN [*AM radio station call letters*]
KMON	Great Falls, MT [*AM radio station call letters*]
KMON	Keyboard Monitor [*Digital Equipment Corp.*]
KMON-FM	Great Falls, MT [*FM radio station call letters*]
KMOO-FM	Mineola, TX [*FM radio station call letters*]
KMOQ	Baxter Springs, KS [*FM radio station call letters*]
KMOR	Scottsbluff, NE [*FM radio station call letters*]
KMOS	Sedalia, MO [*Television station call letters*]
KMOT	Minot/International [*North Dakota*] [*ICAO location identifier*] (ICLI)
KMOT	Minot, ND [*Television station call letters*]
KMOU	Roswell, NM [*FM radio station call letters*]
KMOV	St. Louis, MO [*Television station call letters*]
KMOX	St. Louis, MO [*AM radio station call letters*]
KMOZ	Rolla, MO [*AM radio station call letters*]
KMP	Kangaroo Management Program [*Australia*]
KMP	Keetmanshoop [*South-West Africa*] [*Airport symbol*] (OAG)
KMP	Kent Mathematics Project [*British*] (AIE)
KMP	Kilusang Mabubukid ng Pilipinas [*Philippine Peasant Federation*] [*Political party*]
KMP	Kommunistak Magyarorszagi Partja [*Communist Party of Hungary*] [*Political party*] (PPE)
KMP	Policy and Regulations Division, Information Resources Management Service (AAGC)
KMPC	Los Angeles, CA [*AM radio station call letters*]
KMPD	Kingston Military Products Division (SAA)
KMPG	Hollister, CA [*AM radio station call letters*]
KMPH	Hanford, CA [*FM radio station call letters*]
kmph	Kilometers per Hour (AABC)
KMPH	Visalia, CA [*Television station call letters*]
KmpHi	Kemper High Income Trust [*Associated Press*] (SAG)
KmpIGv	Kemper Intermediate Government Trust [*Associated Press*] (SAG)
KMPL	Sikeston, MO [*AM radio station call letters*]
KmpMI	Kemper Multi-Market Income Trust [*Associated Press*] (SAG)
KmpMu	Kemper Municipal Income Fund [*Associated Press*] (SAG)
KMPO	Modesto, CA [*FM radio station call letters*]
KMPP	Kisan Mazdoor Praja Party [*India*] [*Political party*]
KMPQ	Rosenberg-Richmond, TX [*AM radio station call letters*]

KMPR	Minot, ND [*FM radio station call letters*]
KMPS	Kernel Multiple Processing System [*Computer science*]
kmps	Kilometers per Second
KMPS	Seattle, WA [*AM radio station call letters*]
KMPS-FM	Seattle, WA [*FM radio station call letters*]
KmpSInc	Kemper Strategic Income Fund [*Associated Press*] (SAG)
KmpStr	Kemper Strategic Municipal Income Trust [*Associated Press*] (SAG)
KMP-TUCP	Katipunang Manggagawang Pilipino [*Trade Union Congress of the Philippines*] (EY)
KMPV	Montpelier/Edward F. Knapp [*Vermont*] [*ICAO location identifier*] (ICLI)
KMPX	Decatur, TX [*Television station call letters*]
KMQ	Komatsu [*Japan*] [*Airport symbol*] (OAG)
KMQA	West Covina, CA [*FM radio station call letters*]
KMQT	Marquette/Marquette County [*Michigan*] [*ICAO location identifier*] (ICLI)
KMQUT	Kumquat (ABBR)
KMQX	Springtown, TX [*FM radio station call letters*] (RBYB)
KMR	Cambria Resources Ltd. [*Vancouver Stock Exchange symbol*]
KMR	Kafrarian Mounted Rifles [*British military*] (DMA)
KMR	Karimui [*Papua New Guinea*] [*Airport symbol*] (OAG)
KMR	Kremsmuenster [*Austria*] [*Seismograph station code, US Geological Survey*] (SEIS)
KMR	Kwajalein Missile Range (AABC)
KMR	Western Pacific Airlines, Inc. [*FAA designator*] (FAAC)
KMRA	Knitwear Mill Representatives Association [*Defunct*] (EA)
KMRC	Morgan City, LA [*AM radio station call letters*]
KMRE	Dumas, TX [*FM radio station call letters*]
KMRF	Keyswitch Magic Relay Finder (IAA)
KMRF	Marshfield, MO [*AM radio station call letters*]
KMrJ	Johnson County Library, Merriam, KS [*Library symbol Library of Congress*] (LCLS)
KMRJ-FM	Rancho Mirage, CA [*FM radio station call letters*] (RBYB)
KMRK	Odessa, TX [*FM radio station call letters*]
KMRL	Buras, LA [*FM radio station call letters*] (RBYB)
KMRN	Cameron, MO [*AM radio station call letters*]
KMRO	Camarillo, CA [*FM radio station call letters*]
KMRR	South Tucson, AZ [*AM radio station call letters*]
KMRS	Morris, MN [*AM radio station call letters*]
KMrS	Shawnee Mission Medical Center, Merriam, KS [*Library symbol Library of Congress*] (LCLS)
KMRT	Dallas, TX [*AM radio station call letters*]
KMRT	[*The*] Kansas & Missouri Railway & Terminal Co. [*Later, KM*] [*AAR code*]
KMRT-FM	Granbury, TX [*FM radio station call letters*] (RBYB)
KMRV-FM	Blair, NE [*FM radio station call letters*] (RBYB)
KMRY	Cedar Rapids, IA [*AM radio station call letters*]
KMS	Camas Resources Ltd. [*Vancouver Stock Exchange symbol*]
KMS	Kabuki Make-Up Syndrome [*Medicine*] (DMAA)
KMS	Karitane Mothercraft Society [*Australia*]
KMS	Keysort Multiple Selector
km/s	Kilometers per Second
KMS	King's Magnetic Ore Separator (ROG)
KMS	Knowledge Management System [*Computer science*]
KMS	Kumasi [*Ghana*] [*Airport symbol*] (OAG)
KMS	Kwashiorkormarasmus Syndrome [*Medicine*] (DMAA)
KMS	K-Words Times Millions of Seconds [*Unit of measure*] (GFGA)
KMS	Murray State University, Murray, KY [*OCLC symbol*] (OCLC)
KMSA	Grand Junction, CO [*FM radio station call letters*]
KMSB	Tucson, AZ [*Television station call letters*]
KMSC	Sioux City, IA [*FM radio station call letters*]
KMSD	Milbank, SD [*AM radio station call letters*]
KMSG	Sanger, CA [*Television station call letters*]
KMSI	Moore, OK [*FM radio station call letters*]
KMSK	Austin, MN [*FM radio station call letters*]
KMSL	Great Falls, MT [*AM radio station call letters*]
KMSM	Butte, MT [*FM radio station call letters*]
KMSN	Madison/Truax Field [*Wisconsin*] [*ICAO location identifier*] (ICLI)
KMSO	Missoula, MT [*FM radio station call letters*]
KMSP	Minneapolis/Minneapolis-St. Paul International [*Minnesota*] [*ICAO location identifier*] (ICLI)
KMSP	Minneapolis, MN [*Television station call letters*]
KMSR	Sauk Centre, MN [*FM radio station call letters*]
KMSS	Massena/Richards Field [*New York*] [*ICAO location identifier*] (ICLI)
KMSS	Shreveport, LA [*Television station call letters*]
KMSU	Mankato, MN [*FM radio station call letters*]
KMSY	New Orleans/International [*Louisiana*] [*ICAO location identifier*] (ICLI)
KMT	Kennametal, Inc. [*NYSE symbol*] (SPSG)
KMT	Kinomoto [*Japan*] [*Seismograph station code, US Geological Survey Closed*] (SEIS)
KMT	Knight of St. Maria Theresa [*Austria*] (ROG)
KMT	Kuomintang [*Nationalist Party of Taiwan*] [*Political party*] (PD)
KMTA	Miles City, MT [*AM radio station call letters*]
KMTB	Kibris Milli Turk Birligi [*Cypriot National Turkish Union*] (PPE)
KMTB	Murfreesboro, AR [*FM radio station call letters*]
KMTC	Mount Clemens/Selfridge Air Force Base [*Michigan*] [*ICAO location identifier*] (ICLI)
KMTC	Russellville, AR [*Television station call letters*]
KMTH	Maljamar, NM [*FM radio station call letters*]
KMTI	Manti, UT [*AM radio station call letters*]
KMTL	Sherwood, AR [*AM radio station call letters*]
KMTN	Jackson, WY [*FM radio station call letters*]
KMTP	San Francisco, CA [*Television station call letters*]
KMTPS	Key Makers' Trade Protection Society [*A union*] [*British*]
KMTR	Eugene, OR [*Television station call letters*]
KMTS	Glenwood Springs, CO [*FM radio station call letters*]
KMTT	Tacoma, WA [*AM radio station call letters*]
KMTT-FM	Tacoma, WA [*FM radio station call letters*]
KMTV	Omaha, NE [*Television station call letters*]
KMTX	Helena, MT [*AM radio station call letters*]
KMTX-FM	Helena, MT [*FM radio station call letters*]
KMTX-TV	Roseburg, OR [*Television station call letters*]
KMTY-FM	Holdrege, NE [*FM radio station call letters*] (RBYB)
KMTZ	Coos Bay, OR [*Television station call letters*]
KMU	Kamikineusu Station [*Japan*] [*Seismograph station code, US Geological Survey*] (SEIS)
KMU	Kilusang Mayo Uno [*May First Movement*] [*Philippines*] [*Political party*]
KMU	Kismayu [*Somalia*] [*Airport symbol*] (OAG)
KMU	Kit Munition Unit [*Air Force*] (MCD)
KMUD	Garberville, CA [*FM radio station call letters*]
KMUE-FM	Eureka, CA [*FM radio station call letters*] (RBYB)
KMUL	Muleshoe, TX [*FM radio station call letters*]
KMUN	Astoria, OR [*FM radio station call letters*]
KMUO	Mountain Home/Mountain Home Air Force Base [*Idaho*] [*ICAO location identifier*] (ICLI)
KMUS	Burns, WY [*FM radio station call letters*]
KMUS-AM	Muskogee, OK [*AM radio station call letters*] (RBYB)
KMUW	Wichita, KS [*FM radio station call letters*]
KMUZ	Gresham, OR [*AM radio station call letters*] (RBYB)
KMV	Kalemyo [*Myanmar*] [*Airport symbol*] (OAG)
KMV	Keen Mountain [*Virginia*] [*Seismograph station code, US Geological Survey Closed*] (SEIS)
KMV	Killed Measles-Virus Vaccine
KMVC	Marshall, MO [*FM radio station call letters*]
KMVI	Wailuku, HI [*AM radio station call letters*]
KMVI-FM	Pukalani, HI [*FM radio station call letters*]
KMVK	Benton, AR [*FM radio station call letters*]
KMVL	Madisonville, TX [*AM radio station call letters*]
KMVL-FM	Madisonville, TX [*FM radio station call letters*] (RBYB)
KMVR	Mesilla Park, NM [*FM radio station call letters*]
KMVT	Twin Falls, ID [*Television station call letters*]
KMVU	Medford, OR [*Television station call letters*]
KMVX	Jerome, ID [*FM radio station call letters*]
kmw	Kilomegawatt (WGA)
kmwh	Kilomegawatt-Hour (WGA)
KMWL	Mineral Wells [*Texas*] [*ICAO location identifier*] (ICLI)
KMWX	Yakima, WA [*AM radio station call letters*]
KMXA-AM	Aurora, CO [*AM radio station call letters*] (RBYB)
KMXA-FM	Minot, ND [*FM radio station call letters*] (RBYB)
KMXB	Orem, UT [*AM radio station call letters*]
KMXC	Sioux Falls, SD [*FM radio station call letters*]
KMXD	Ankeny, IA [*FM radio station call letters*]
KMXE	Red Lodge, MT [*FM radio station call letters*]
KMXF	Montgomery/Maxwell Air Force Base [*Alabama*] [*ICAO location identifier*] (ICLI)
KMXG	Clinton, IA [*FM radio station call letters*]
KMXI	Chico, CA [*FM radio station call letters*] (RBYB)
KMXJ-FM	Sallisaw, OK [*FM radio station call letters*] (RBYB)
KMXK	Cold Spring, MN [*FM radio station call letters*]
KMXL	Carthage, MO [*FM radio station call letters*]
KMXM-FM	Gooding, ID [*FM radio station call letters*] (RBYB)
KMXN	Santa Rosa, CA [*AM radio station call letters*]
KMXO	Merkel, TX [*AM radio station call letters*]
KMXQ	Socorro, NM [*FM radio station call letters*]
KMXR	Corpus Christi, TX [*FM radio station call letters*]
KMXS	Anchorage, AK [*FM radio station call letters*] (RBYB)
KMXT	Kodiak, AK [*FM radio station call letters*]
KMXU	Manti, UT [*FM radio station call letters*]
KMXV	Kansas City, MO [*FM radio station call letters*]
KMXX	Imperial, CA [*FM radio station call letters*]
KMXY-FM	Grand Junction, CO [*FM radio station call letters*] (RBYB)
KMXZ-FM	Tucson, AZ [*FM radio station call letters*] (RBYB)
KMY	Moser Bay [*Alaska*] [*Airport symbol*] (OAG)
KMYC	Marysville, CA [*AM radio station call letters*]
KMYI	Kirtland, NM [*FM radio station call letters*]
KMYR	Myrtle Beach/Myrtle Beach Air Force Base [*South Carolina*] [*ICAO location identifier*] (ICLI)
KMYX	Taft, CA [*AM radio station call letters*]
KMYX-FM	Taft, CA [*FM radio station call letters*]
KMYY	Monroe, LA [*FM radio station call letters*]
KMYZ	Pryor, OK [*AM radio station call letters*]
KMYZ-FM	Pryor, OK [*FM radio station call letters*]
KMZ	Kangaroo Management Zone
KMZA	Seneca, KS [*FM radio station call letters*]
KMZE	Woodward, OK [*FM radio station call letters*]
KMZN	Farwell, TX [*Television station call letters*]
KMZQ	Henderson, NV [*FM radio station call letters*]
KMZU	Carrollton, MO [*FM radio station call letters*]
KMZX	Lonoke, AR [*FM radio station call letters*]
KN	Air Kentucky [*ICAO designator*] (AD)
KN	GKN Group Services Ltd. [*British ICAO designator*] (ICDA)
KN	Kenya Navy
KN	Khan (ABBR)
kN	Kilonewton
KN	Kinetics of Neutralization [*Chemistry*]
KN	Kings Norton Mint [*British*]
KN	Kitting Notice [*NASA*] (NASA)
KN	Klamath Northern Railway Co. [*Later, KNOR*] [*AAR code*]

Kn	Knapp's Privy Council Appeal Cases [*1829-36*] [*England*] [*A publication*] (DLA)
kn	Knee
KN	Knight (ABBR)
KN	Knot
KN	Known
kn	Known (VRA)
KN	Know-Nothing [*American political party, 1855-60*]
KN	Knudsen Number [*IUPAC*]
KN	Kol Nidre (BJA)
kn	Korea, North [*MARC country of publication code Library of Congress*] (LCCP)
KN	Krone
KN	Kronen (ABBR)
KN	KSC [*Kennedy Space Center*] Notice [*NASA*] (NASA)
KN	St. Christopher-Nevis [*ANSI two-letter standard code*] (CNC)
KN	Temsco Airlines [*ICAO designator*]
KNA	Katholische Nachrichten-Agentur [*Catholic Press Agency*] [*Germany*]
KNA	Kenar Resources [*Vancouver Stock Exchange symbol*]
KNA	Kenya News Agency
KNA	Kex National Association (EA)
KNA	Killed; Not Enemy Action [*Military*]
KNA	Knight Air Ltd. [*Canada ICAO designator*] (FAAC)
KNA	Knogo North America [*AMEX symbol*] (TTSB)
KNA	Knogo North America, Inc. [*AMEX symbol*] (SAG)
KNA	Korean National Airlines
KNA	Korean National Association (EA)
KNA	Kuki National Assembly [*India*] [*Political party*] (PPW)
KNA	Kununurra [*Australia Seismograph station code, US Geological Survey*] (SEIS)
KNA	St. Christopher-Nevis [*ANSI three-letter standard code*] (CNC)
KNAB	Albany/Albany Naval Air Station [*Georgia*] [*ICAO location identifier*] (ICLI)
KNAB	Burlington, CO [*AM radio station call letters*]
KNAB-FM	Burlington, CO [*FM radio station call letters*]
KNAC	Earlimart, CA [*FM radio station call letters*] (RBYB)
Kn AC	Knapp's Privy Council Appeal Cases [*1829-36*] [*England*] [*A publication*] (DLA)
KNAF	Fredricksburg, TX [*AM radio station call letters*]
KNAI	Phoenix, AZ [*FM radio station call letters*]
KNAIR	Kuehne & Nagel Air Cargo Ltd. [*British*]
KNAK	Delta, UT [*AM radio station call letters*]
KNAL	Victoria, TX [*AM radio station call letters*]
Kn & O	Knapp and Ombler's English Election Cases [*A publication*] (DLA)
Kn & Omb	Knapp and Ombler's English Election Cases [*A publication*] (DLA)
KNAP	Knape & Vogt Manufacturing Co. [*NASDAQ symbol*] (NQ)
KNAP	Knape & Vogt Mfg [*NASDAQ symbol*] (TTSB)
KNAP	Knapwell [*England*]
KnapeV	Knape & Vogt Manufacturing Co. [*Associated Press*] (SAG)
Knapp	Knapp's Privy Council Reports [*England*] [*A publication*] (DLA)
Knapp & O	Knapp and Ombler's English Election Cases [*A publication*] (DLA)
KNAQ	Flagstaff, AZ [*FM radio station call letters*] (RBYB)
KNAS	Nashville, AR [*FM radio station call letters*]
KNAT	Albuquerque, NM [*Television station call letters*]
KNAU	Flagstaff, AZ [*FM radio station call letters*]
KNAX	Fresno, CA [*FM radio station call letters*]
KNAZ	Flagstaff, AZ [*Television station call letters*]
KNB	Kanab [*Utah*] [*Seismograph station code, US Geological Survey*] (SEIS)
KNB	Kanab [*Utah*] [*Airport symbol*] (OAG)
KNB	Kanab, UT [*Location identifier FAA*] (FAAL)
KNBA-FM	Anchorage, AK [*FM radio station call letters*] (RBYB)
KNBC	Beaufort/Beaufort Marine Corps Air Station [*South Carolina*] [*ICAO location identifier*] (ICLI)
KNBC	Los Angeles, CA [*Television station call letters*]
KNBE	Dallas/Hensley Field Naval Air Station [*Texas*] [*ICAO location identifier*] (ICLI)
KNBG	New Orleans/Alvin Callender Naval Air Station [*Louisiana*] [*ICAO location identifier*] (ICLI)
KNBJ	Bemidji, MN [*FM radio station call letters*]
KNBL	Knife Blade
KNBO	New Boston, TX [*AM radio station call letters*]
KNBR	Knobbier (ABBR)
KNBR	San Francisco, CA [*AM radio station call letters*]
KNBR-FM	Haltom City, TX [*FM radio station call letters*] (RBYB)
KNBST	Knobbiest (ABBR)
KNBT	New Braunfels, TX [*FM radio station call letters*]
KNBU	Baldwin City, KS [*FM radio station call letters*]
KNBW	Kirin Brewery Co. Ltd. [*NASDAQ symbol*] (NQ)
KNBWY	Kirin Brewery ADS [*NASDAQ symbol*] (TTSB)
KNBY	Knobby (ABBR)
KNBY	Newport, AR [*AM radio station call letters*]
KNC	Canadian Crew Energy [*Vancouver Stock Exchange symbol*]
KNC	Kamerun National Congress
KNC	Kansas Newman College [*Formerly, Sacred Heart College*] [*Wichita*]
KNC	Kingcome Navigation [*AAR code*]
KNCA	Burney, CA [*FM radio station call letters*]
KNCA	Jacksonville/New River Marine Corps Air Station [*North Carolina*] [*ICAO location identifier*] (ICLI)
KNCB	Vivian, LA [*AM radio station call letters*]
KNCB-FM	Vivian, LA [*FM radio station call letters*]
KNCC	Elko, NV [*FM radio station call letters*]
KNCC	Kinetic Concepts [*NASDAQ symbol*] (TTSB)
KNCI	Kinetic Concepts, Inc. [*NASDAQ symbol*] (NQ)
KNCI	Sacramento, CA [*FM radio station call letters*]
KNCIAWPRC	Korean National Committee of the International Association on Water Pollution Research and Control (EAIO)
KNCIAWPRC	Kuwaiti National Committee of the International Association on Water Pollution Research and Control (EAIO)
Kn Civ Proc	Knox on Civil Procedure in India [*A publication*] (DLA)
KNCK	Concordia, KS [*AM radio station call letters*]
KNCKBT	Knockabout (ABBR)
KNCKDN	Knockdown (ABBR)
KNCKKN	Knock-knee (ABBR)
KNCKOT	Knockout (ABBR)
KNCKR	Knocker (ABBR)
KNCM-FM	Appleton, MN [*FM radio station call letters*] (RBYB)
KNCN	Sinton, TX [*FM radio station call letters*]
KNCO	Grass Valley, CA [*AM radio station call letters*]
KNCO	Quonset Point/Quonset Point Naval Air Station [*Rhode Island*] [*ICAO location identifier*] (ICLI)
KNCO-FM	Grass Valley, CA [*FM radio station call letters*]
KNCQ	Redding, CA [*FM radio station call letters*]
KNCR	Paso Robles, CA [*FM radio station call letters*] (RBYB)
Kn Cr Law	Knox on Bengal Criminal Law [*A publication*] (DLA)
KNCT	Belton, TX [*Television station call letters*]
KNCT	Killeen, TX [*FM radio station call letters*]
KnCtyL	Kansas City Life Insurance [*Associated Press*] (SAG)
KNCY	Nebraska City, NE [*AM radio station call letters*]
KNCY-FM	Auburn, NE [*FM radio station call letters*] (RBYB)
KND	Kindu [*Zaire*] [*Airport symbol*] (OAG)
KNDA	Alice, TX [*FM radio station call letters*] (RBYB)
KNDC	Hettinger, ND [*AM radio station call letters*]
KNDD	Seattle, WA [*FM radio station call letters*]
KNDGTN	Kindergarten (ABBR)
KNDHTD	Kindhearted (ABBR)
KNDHTDNS	Kindheartedness (ABBR)
KNDI	Honolulu, HI [*AM radio station call letters*]
KNDK	Langdon, ND [*AM radio station call letters*]
KNDK-FM	Langdon, ND [*FM radio station call letters*]
KNDL	Kindle (ABBR)
KNDLD	Kindled (ABBR)
KNDLES	Kindless (ABBR)
KNDLG	Kindling (ABBR)
KNDLIR	Kindlier (ABBR)
KNDLNS	Kindliness (ABBR)
KNDLST	Kindliest (ABBR)
KNDLY	Kindly (ABBR)
KNDN	Farmington, NM [*AM radio station call letters*]
KNDNS	Kindness (ABBR)
KNDO	Karen National Defense Organization [*Burma*]
KNDO	Yakima, WA [*Television station call letters*]
KNDP	Kamerun National Democratic Party [*Later, UNC*]
KNDR	Kinder (ABBR)
KNDR	Mandan, ND [*FM radio station call letters*]
KNDRD	Kindred (ABBR)
KNDRG	Kindergarten (ABBR)
KNDRGR	Kindergartener (ABBR)
KndrL	Kinder-Care Learning Centers, Inc. [*Associated Press*] (SAG)
KndrLr	Kinder-Care Learning Centers, Inc. [*Associated Press*] (SAG)
KNDST	Kindest (ABBR)
KNDU	Richland, WA [*Television station call letters*]
KNDY	Kindly (ABBR)
KNDY	Marysville, KS [*AM radio station call letters*]
KNDY-FM	Marysville, KS [*FM radio station call letters*]
KNE	KN Energy [*NYSE symbol*] (TTSB)
KNE	KN Energy, Inc. [*NYSE symbol*] (SPSG)
KNE	Knie Resources, Inc. [*Vancouver Stock Exchange symbol*]
KNEA	Brunswick/Glynco Naval Air Station [*Georgia*] [*ICAO location identifier*] (ICLI)
KNEA	Jonesboro, AR [*AM radio station call letters*]
KNEB	Scottsbluff, NE [*AM radio station call letters*]
KNEB-FM	Scottsbluff, NE [*FM radio station call letters*]
KNEB-TV	Ketchikan, AK [*Television station call letters*] (RBYB)
KNECP	Kneecap (ABBR)
KNED	Knife Edge
KNED	McAlester, OK [*AM radio station call letters*]
KNEDP	Kneedeep (ABBR)
KNEI	Waukon, IA [*AM radio station call letters*]
KNEI-FM	Waukon, IA [*FM radio station call letters*]
KNEK	Washington, LA [*AM radio station call letters*]
KNEK-FM	Washington, LA [*FM radio station call letters*]
KNEL	Brady, TX [*AM radio station call letters*]
KNEL	Lakehurst/Lakehurst Naval Air Station [*New Jersey*] [*ICAO location identifier*] (ICLI)
KNEL-FM	Brady, TX [*FM radio station call letters*] (RBYB)
KNELG	Kneeling (ABBR)
KNELR	Kneller (ABBR)
KNEM	Nevada, MO [*AM radio station call letters*]
KNEN	Norfolk, NE [*FM radio station call letters*]
KN Engy	KN Energy, Inc. [*Associated Press*] (SAG)
KNEO	Neosho, MO [*FM radio station call letters*]
KNeo	W. A. Rankin Memorial Library, Neodesha, KS [*Library symbol Library of Congress*] (LCLS)
KNES	Fairfield, TX [*FM radio station call letters*]
KNET	Palestine, TX [*AM radio station call letters*]
KNET-FM	Lincoln, NE [*FM radio station call letters*] (RBYB)
KNEU	Roosevelt, UT [*AM radio station call letters*]
KNEV	Reno, NV [*FM radio station call letters*]
KNEW	New Orleans [*Louisiana*] [*ICAO location identifier*] (ICLI)

KNEW	Oakland, CA [*AM radio station call letters*]
KNF.............	Klein-Nishina Formula [*Physics*]
KNF.............	Knife (ABBR)
KNFD	Knifed (ABBR)
KNFG	Knifing (ABBR)
KNFL	Tremonton, UT [*AM radio station call letters*]
KNFL-FM	Tremonton, UT [*FM radio station call letters*]
KNFLK	Kinfolk (ABBR)
KNFLK	Knifelike (ABBR)
KNFM	Midland, TX [*FM radio station call letters*]
KNFO	Basalt, CO [*FM radio station call letters*] (RBYB)
KNFP	Kellogg National Fellowship Program
KNFR	Opportunity, WA [*FM radio station call letters*]
KNFT	Bayard, NM [*AM radio station call letters*]
KNFT-FM	Bayard, NM [*FM radio station call letters*]
KNFX	Austin, MN [*AM radio station call letters*]
KNFX-FM	Spring Valley, MN [*FM radio station call letters*]
KNG	Kaimana [*Indonesia*] [*Airport symbol*] (OAG)
KNG	Kaliningrad [*Former USSR Geomagnetic observatory code*]
KNG	King Aviation [*British ICAO designator*] (FAAC)
KNG	Kininogen (DMAA)
KNG	Konigsberg [*Kaliningrad*] [*Former USSR Seismograph station code, US Geological Survey Closed*] (SEIS)
KNGA	St. Peter, MN [*FM radio station call letters*]
KNGDM........	Kingdom (ABBR)
KNGDM........	Kinhdom
KNGFSH.......	Kingfish (ABBR)
KNGFSHR ...	Kingfisher (ABBR)
KNGHT........	Knight
KnghtR........	Knight Ridder, Inc. [*Associated Press*] (SAG)
KNGL	McPherson, KS [*AM radio station call letters*]
KNGLNS	Kingliness (ABBR)
KNGLR........	Kinglier (ABBR)
KNGLST	Kingliest (ABBR)
KNGLY	Kingly (ABBR)
KNGM	Emporia, KS [*FM radio station call letters*]
KNGN	McCook, NE [*AM radio station call letters*]
KNGP	Corpus Christi/Corpus Christi Naval Air Station [*Texas*] [*ICAO location identifier*] (ICLI)
KNGPN........	Kingpin (ABBR)
KNGR..........	Kangaroo (ABBR)
KNGS	Coalinga, CA [*FM radio station call letters*]
KngsRd	Kings Road Entertainment, Inc. [*Associated Press*] (SAG)
KNGSZ........	Kingsize (ABBR)
KNGT	Jackson, CA [*FM radio station call letters*]
KNGT	Knight (ABBR)
KNGT	Knight Transportation [*NASDAQ symbol*] (SAG)
KNGTHD	Knighthood (ABBR)
KNGTLY	Knightly (ABBR)
KNGT-RNT ...	Knight-Errant (ABBR)
KNGU	Norfolk/Norfolk Naval Air Station [*Virginia*] [*ICAO location identifier*] (ICLI)
KNGY	Kingly (ABBR)
KNGZ	Alameda/Alameda Naval Air Station [*California*] [*ICAO location identifier*] (ICLI)
KNH	Kipuka Nene [*Hawaii*] [*Seismograph station code, US Geological Survey*] (SEIS)
KNHC	Seattle, WA [*FM radio station call letters*]
KNHK	Patuxent River/Patuxent River Naval Air Station [*Maryland*] [*ICAO location identifier*] (ICLI)
KNHN..........	Kansas City, KS [*AM radio station call letters*]
KNHT	Knight (ABBR)
KNHZ	Brunswick/Brunswick Naval Air Station [*Maryland*] [*ICAO location identifier*] (ICLI)
KNI..............	Kalallit Niuerfiat [*Greenland Trade*] (EY)
KNI..............	Kantorberita Nasional Indonesia [*News service*] [*Indonesia*] (EY)
KNI..............	Koyna Nagar [*India*] [*Seismograph station code, US Geological Survey Closed*] (SEIS)
KNI..............	Kyodo News International, Inc. [*Information service or system*] (IID)
KNIA	Knoxville, IA [*AM radio station call letters*]
KNIC	[*The*] Knickerbocker [*L.L.*] Company, Inc. [*NASDAQ symbol*] (SAG)
Knick	[*The*] Knickerbocker [*L. L.*] Co., Inc. [*Associated Press*] (SAG)
KnickL	[*The*] Knickerbocker [*L. L.*] Company, Inc. [*Associated Press*] (SAG)
KNID	Enid, OK [*FM radio station call letters*]
Knight Mech Dict...	Knight's American Mechanical Dictionary [*A publication*] (DLA)
Knight's Ind...	Knight's Industrial Reports [*A publication*] (DLA)
KnightTr.......	Knight Transportation [*Associated Press*] (SAG)
KNIK	Anchorage, AK [*FM radio station call letters*]
KNIM	Maryville, MO [*AM radio station call letters*]
KNIM-FM	Maryville, MO [*FM radio station call letters*]
KNIN-FM	Wichita Falls, TX [*FM radio station call letters*]
KNIN-TV	Caldwell, ID [*TV station call letters*] (RBYB)
KNIP	Jacksonville/Jacksonville Naval Air Station [*Florida*] [*ICAO location identifier*] (ICLI)
KNIR	Beeville/Chase Field Naval Air Station [*Texas*] [*ICAO location identifier*] (ICLI)
KNIR	New Iberia, LA [*AM radio station call letters*]
KNIS	Carson City, NV [*FM radio station call letters*]
KNIT	Techknits, Inc. [*NASDAQ symbol*] (SAG)
KNITG	Knitting (ABBR)
KNITR	Knitter (ABBR)
KNIX	Phoenix, AZ [*FM radio station call letters*]
KNJ	Kindamba [*Congo*] [*Airport symbol*] (OAG)
KNJK...........	El Centro Naval Air Station [*California*] [*ICAO location identifier*] (ICLI)

KNJO	Thousand Oaks, CA [*FM radio station call letters*]
KNJP	Sargent, NE [*FM radio station call letters*]
KNJU	Raton, NM [*FM radio station call letters*]
KNJY...........	Spokane, WA [*FM radio station call letters*]
KNJZ	Alton, IL [*FM radio station call letters*]
KNK	Kakhonak [*Alaska*] [*Airport symbol*] (OAG)
KNK	Kankakee Bancorp [*AMEX symbol*] (TTSB)
KNK	Kankakee Bancorp, Inc. [*AMEX symbol*] (SAG)
KNK	Knik Glacier [*Alaska*] [*Seismograph station code, US Geological Survey*] (SEIS)
KNKA	Kansas City [*Missouri*] [*ICAO location identifier*] (ICLI)
KNKE	Jasper, TX [*FM radio station call letters*]
KNKL	Knuckle (ABBR)
KNKLD	Knuckled (ABBR)
KNKLG	Knuckling (ABBR)
KNKN	Pueblo, CO [*FM radio station call letters*]
KNKR	Kinkier (ABBR)
KNKRS	Knickers (ABBR)
KNKST	Kinkiest (ABBR)
KNKT	Armijo, NM [*FM radio station call letters*] (RBYB)
KNKT	Cherry Point Marine Corps Air Station [*North Carolina*] [*ICAO location identifier*] (ICLI)
KNKX	Miramar Naval Air Station [*California*] [*ICAO location identifier*] (ICLI)
KNL	Centaur Resources Ltd. [*Vancouver Stock Exchange symbol*]
KNL	Darrow's Solution [*For antidiarrhea potassium therapy*] (DAVI)
KNL	Keller, N. L., Washington DC [*STAC*]
KNL	Kennel (ABBR)
KNL	Kennel
KNL	Knight of the Netherlands Lion
KNL	Knoll (ABBR)
KNL	Knoll
KNLA	Karen National Liberation Army [*Myanmar*] [*Political party*]
KNLA	White Rock, NM [*FM radio station call letters*]
KNLB	Lake Havasu City, AZ [*FM radio station call letters*]
KNLC	Hanford/Lemorre Naval Air Station [*California*] [*ICAO location identifier*] (ICLI)
KNLC	St. Louis, MO [*Television station call letters*]
KNLD	Duluth, MN [*Television station call letters*]
KNLD	Kenneled (ABBR)
KNLE	Round Rock, TX [*FM radio station call letters*]
KNLF	Karen National Liberation Front [*Myanmar*] [*Political party*] (PD)
KNLF	Quincy, CA [*FM radio station call letters*]
KNLG	Kenneling (ABBR)
Kn LGR........	Knight's Local Government Reports [*A publication*] (DLA)
KNLJ	Jefferson City, MO [*Television station call letters*]
KNLR	Bend, OR [*FM radio station call letters*]
KNLS	Knolls (MCD)
KNLS	Knolls
KNLT	Walla Walla, WA [*FM radio station call letters*]
KNLU	Monroe, LA [*FM radio station call letters*]
KNLV	Ord, NE [*AM radio station call letters*]
KNLV-FM	Ord, NE [*FM radio station call letters*]
KNM............	Keene State College, Keene, NH [*OCLC symbol*] (OCLC)
KNM............	Kenya National Museum
KNM............	Mennonite Historical Society, Newton, KS [*Library symbol Library of Congress*] (LCLS)
KNMC	Havre, MT [*FM radio station call letters*]
KNME	Albuquerque, NM [*Television station call letters*]
KNMH	Coast Guard Station, Washington [*District of Columbia*] [*ICAO location identifier*] (ICLI)
KNMI	Farmington, NM [*FM radio station call letters*]
KNML-AM	Los Ranchos de Albuquerque, NM [*AM radio station call letters*] (RBYB)
KNMO	Nevada, MO [*FM radio station call letters*]
KNMT...........	Portland, OR [*Television station call letters*]
KNMTCS	Kinematics
KNMX	Las Vegas, NM [*AM radio station call letters*]
KNMZ-FM	Alamogordo, NM [*FM radio station call letters*] (RBYB)
KNN	Kankan [*Guinea*] [*Airport symbol*] (AD)
KNN	Kenton Natural Resources Corp. [*Vancouver Stock Exchange symbol*]
KNN	K-Nearest-Neighbor [*Algorithm*]
KNnB	Bethel College, North Newton, KS [*Library symbol Library of Congress*] (LCLS)
KNNB	Whiteriver, AZ [*FM radio station call letters*]
KNNC	Georgetown, TX [*FM radio station call letters*]
KNND	Cottage Grove, OR [*AM radio station call letters*]
KNNG	Sterling, CO [*FM radio station call letters*]
KNNK-FM	Dimmitt, TX [*FM radio station call letters*] (RBYB)
KNNN	Central Valley, CA [*FM radio station call letters*]
KNNS	Beverly Hills, CA [*AM radio station call letters*] (RBYB)
Kn NSW.......	Knox's New South Wales Reports [*A publication*] (DLA)
KNNZ	Costa Mesa, CA [*AM radio station call letters*] (RBYB)
KNO	Kano, Nigeria [*Remote site*] [*NASA*] (NASA)
KNO	Keep Needle Open [*Reference to intravenous fluid lines*] (DAVI)
KNO	Knox Ranch [*California*] [*Seismograph station code, US Geological Survey Closed*] (SEIS)
KNO	Koch, Neff, Oetlinger [*Germany*] (NITA)
KNO	Korrespondenzblatt der Nachrichtenstelle fuer den Orient [*A publication*] (BJA)
KNOB..........	San Rafael, CA [*AM radio station call letters*] (RBYB)
KNOBS........	Knowledge-Based System
KNOC	Natchitoches, LA [*AM radio station call letters*]
KNOD	Harlan, IA [*FM radio station call letters*]
KNOE	Monroe, LA [*AM radio station call letters*]

KNOE-FM..... Monroe, LA [*FM radio station call letters*]
KNOE-TV..... Monroe, LA [*Television station call letters*]
KNOF......... St. Paul, MN [*FM radio station call letters*]
KNOG-FM .... Nogales, AZ [*FM radio station call letters*] (RBYB)
KnogNA....... Knogo North America, Inc. [*Associated Press*] (SAG)
KNOL......... Knoll [*Commonly used*] (OPSA)
KNOLL....... Knoll [*Commonly used*] (OPSA)
KNOLLS....... Knolls [*Commonly used*] (OPSA)
KNOM......... Nome, AK [*AM radio station call letters*]
KNOM-FM.... Nome, AK [*FM radio station call letters*]
KNON......... Dallas, TX [*FM radio station call letters*]
KNOP......... North Platte, NE [*Television station call letters*]
KNOR......... Klamath Northern Railway Co. [*AAR code*]
KNOR......... Norman, OK [*AM radio station call letters*]
knork .... Knife and Fork [*Pharmacology*] (DAVI)
KNOS......... Albuquerque, NM [*AM radio station call letters*] (RBYB)
KNOS-FM..... Omaha, NE [*FM radio station call letters*] (RBYB)
KNoSH........ Norton State Hospital, Norton, KS [*Library symbol Library of Congress*] (LCLS)
KNOT......... Prescott, AZ [*AM radio station call letters*]
KNOT-FM..... Prescott, AZ [*FM radio station call letters*]
Know .... Knowledge [*Record label*]
KNOW......... Port Angeles Coast Guard Air Station [*Washington*] [*ICAO location identifier*] (ICLI)
KNOW-FM..... Minneapolis-St. Paul, MN [*FM radio station call letters*]
Knowles....... Knowles' Reports [*3 Rhode Island*] [*A publication*] (DLA)
KNOWLT...... Knowlton [*England*]
KNOW-NET... Knowledege Network of Washington (EDAC)
KNOX......... Grand Forks, ND [*AM radio station call letters*]
Knox .... Knox's New South Wales Reports [*A publication*] (DLA)
Knox & F .... Knox and Fitzhardinge's New South Wales Reports [*A publication*] (DLA)
KNOX-FM..... Grand Forks, ND [*FM radio station call letters*]
KNOZ......... Cameron, MO [*FM radio station call letters*]
KNP .... Katholieke Nationale Partij [*Catholic National Party*] [*Netherlands Political party*] (PPE)
KNP .... Katholisk Nederlands Persbureau [*Catholic Netherlands Press Agency*] [*Netherlands*]
KNP .... Kinetics of Nonhomogeneous Processes
KNP .... King's Knight's Pawn [*Chess*] (BARN)
KNP .... Korea National Party [*South Korea Political party*] (PPW)
KNP .... Koshkonong Nuclear Plant (NRCH)
KNPA......... Pensacola/Pensacola Naval Air Station [*Florida*] [*ICAO location identifier*] (ICLI)
KNPB......... Reno, NV [*Television station call letters*]
Kn PC .... Knapp's Privy Council Appeal Cases [*1829-36*] [*England*] [*A publication*] (DLA)
KNPC .... Kuwait National Petroleum Co.
KNPI......... Kundu's Neurotic Personality Inventory [*Psychology*]
KNPP......... Karenni National Progressive Party [*Myanmar*] [*Political party*] (EY)
KNPP......... Kewaunee Nuclear Power Plant (NRCH)
KNPR......... Las Vegas, NV [*FM radio station call letters*]
KNPSK........ Knapsack (ABBR)
KNPT......... Newport, OR [*AM radio station call letters*]
KNQ .... Kone [*New Caledonia*] [*Airport symbol Obsolete*] (OAG)
KNQI......... Kingsville Naval Air Station [*Texas*] [*ICAO location identifier*] (ICLI)
KNQX......... Key West/Key West Naval Air Station [*Florida*] [*ICAO location identifier*] (ICLI)
KNR .... Kalaallit Nunaata Radioa [*Greenland*] (EY)
KNR .... Kidnap and Ransom [*Insurance terminology*]
KNR .... King's National Roll
KNR .... Klamath Northern Railway (MHDW)
KNR .... Korean National Railroad (DCTA)
KNRB......... Mayport/Mayport Naval Station [*Florida*] [*ICAO location identifier*] (ICLI)
KNRC......... Reno, NV [*AM radio station call letters*] (RBYB)
KNRK......... Camas, WA [*FM radio station call letters*] (RBYB)
KNRK......... Kirsten Sarcoma Virus in Normal Rat Kidney [*Medicine*] (DMAA)
KNRL......... Kernel (ABBR)
KNRL .... Knurl [*Engineering*]
KNRO......... Redding, CA [*AM radio station call letters*]
KNRQ......... Springfield, OR [*AM radio station call letters*] (RBYB)
KNRQ-FM..... Creswell, OR [*FM radio station call letters*] (RBYB)
KNRR......... Pembina, ND [*Television station call letters*]
KNRV-FM..... Harker Heights, TX [*FM radio station call letters*] (RBYB)
KNRX......... Castle Rock, CO [*FM radio station call letters*] (RBYB)
KNRX-FM..... Oklahoma City, OK [*FM radio station call letters*] (RBYB)
KNRY......... Monterey, CA [*AM radio station call letters*]
KNS .... Kazan [*Formerly, Kazanskaya*] [*Former USSR Geomagnetic observatory code*]
KNS .... Kenuz Airlines Ltd. [*Nigeria*] [*ICAO designator*] (FAAC)
KNS .... King Island [*Tasmania*] [*Airport symbol*] (OAG)
KNS .... Knight of [*the Order of*] the Royal Northern Star [*Sweden*]
KNSA......... Unalakleet, AK [*AM radio station call letters*]
KNSCP........ Kinescope (ABBR)
KNSD......... San Diego, CA [*Television station call letters*]
KNSE......... Ontario, CA [*AM radio station call letters*]
KNSF......... Washington Naval Air Facility [*District of Columbia*] [*ICAO location identifier*] (ICLI)
KNSG......... Springfield, MN [*FM radio station call letters*] (RBYB)
KNSHP........ Kinship (ABBR)
KNSI......... San Nicolas Island/San Nicolas Auxiliary Air Base [*California*] [*ICAO location identifier*] (ICLI)
KNSI......... St. Cloud, MN [*AM radio station call letters*]
KNSMN....... Kinsman (ABBR)

KNSN......... Chico, CA [*AM radio station call letters*] (RBYB)
KNSO......... Merced, CA [*Television station call letters*]
KNSP......... Staples, MN [*AM radio station call letters*]
KNSP-FM..... Staples, MN [*FM radio station call letters*]
KNSQ......... Mount Shasta, CA [*FM radio station call letters*]
KNSR......... Collegeville, MN [*FM radio station call letters*]
KNSS......... Wichita, KS [*AM radio station call letters*]
KNST......... Tucson, AZ [*AM radio station call letters*]
KNSU......... Thibodaux, LA [*FM radio station call letters*]
KNSW......... Knife Switch
KNSWMN..... Kinswoman (ABBR)
KNSY......... Kensey Nash [*NASDAQ symbol*] (TTSB)
KNSY......... Kensey Nash Corp. [*NASDAQ symbol*] (SAG)
KNT .... Kent Electronics [*NYSE symbol*] (TTSB)
KNT .... Kent Electronics Corp. [*NYSE symbol*] (SPSG)
KNT .... Knight [*British title*]
KNT .... Knightway Air Charter Ltd. [*British ICAO designator*] (FAAC)
KNT .... Knitting
KNT .... Sanandaj [*Iran*] [*Airport symbol*] (AD)
KNTA......... Santa Clara, CA [*AM radio station call letters*]
KNTB......... Los Alamitos/Los Alamitos Naval Air Station [*California*] [*ICAO location identifier*] (ICLI)
KNTB-FM .... Lakewood, WA [*FM radio station call letters*] (RBYB)
KNTC......... Kinetic (ABBR)
KntckyEl...... Kentucky Electric Steel Co. [*Associated Press*] (SAG)
KNTD......... Knotted (ABBR)
KNTD......... Point Mugu Naval Air Station [*California*] [*ICAO location identifier*] (ICLI)
KNTE......... Lakewood, WA [*AM radio station call letters*]
KNTG......... Knotting (ABBR)
KNTHL........ Knothole (ABBR)
KNTI......... Lakeport, CA [*FM radio station call letters*]
KNTK......... Kentek Information Sys [*NASDAQ symbol*] (TTSB)
KNTK......... Kentek Information Systems, Inc. [*NASDAQ symbol*] (SAG)
KNTL......... Bethany, OK [*FM radio station call letters*]
KNTLK........ Knotlike (ABBR)
KNTLS .... Knotless (ABBR)
KNTN......... Thief River Falls, MN [*FM radio station call letters*]
KNTO......... Livingston, CA [*FM radio station call letters*]
KNTR......... Ferndale, WA [*AM radio station call letters*]
KNTS .... Abilene, TX [*AM radio station call letters*]
KNTTD......... Knitted
KNTU......... Denton, TX [*FM radio station call letters*]
KNTU......... Virginia Beach/Oceana Naval Air Station [*Virginia*] [*ICAO location identifier*] (ICLI)
KNTV......... San Jose, CA [*Television station call letters*]
KNTWR....... Knitwear
KNTY......... Knotty (ABBR)
KNU .... Kanpur [*India*] [*Airport symbol*] (OAG)
KNU .... Karen National Union [*Myanmar*] (PD)
KNU .... Knuckle [*Automotive engineering*]
KNUC......... Smithfield, UT [*FM radio station call letters*]
KNUE......... Tyler, TX [*FM radio station call letters*]
KNUFNS...... Kampuchean National United Front for National Salvation (PD)
KNUI......... Kahului, HI [*AM radio station call letters*]
KNUI-FM..... Kahului, HI [*FM radio station call letters*]
KNUJ......... New Ulm, MN [*AM radio station call letters*]
KNUJ......... Sleepy Eye, MN [*FM radio station call letters*]
KNUP......... Karen National Unity Party [*Burma*]
KNUQ......... Mountain View/Moffett Naval Air Station [*California*] [*ICAO location identifier*] (ICLI)
KNUQ-FM .... Paauilo, HI [*FM radio station call letters*] (RBYB)
KNUS......... Denver, CO [*AM radio station call letters*]
KNUU......... Paradise, NV [*AM radio station call letters*]
KNUW......... Whidbey Island/Whidbey Island Naval Air Station [*Washington*] [*ICAO location identifier*] (ICLI)
KNUW-FM .... Central, NM [*FM radio station call letters*] (RBYB)
KNUZ......... Houston, TX [*AM radio station call letters*]
KNUZ Exp Stn... Houston, TX [*Radio expansion station*]
KNV .... Knave (ABBR)
KNVA......... Austin, TX [*Television station call letters*]
KNVC......... Consolidated Nevada Goldfields Corp. [*NASDAQ symbol*] (SAG)
KNVCF........ Consolidated Nev Goldfields [*NASDAQ symbol*] (TTSB)
KNVH......... Knavish (ABBR)
KNVHLY...... Knavishly (ABBR)
KNVO......... McAllen, TX [*Television station call letters*]
KNVRY....... Knavery (ABBR)
KNW .... Konawaena [*Hawaii*] [*Seismograph station code, US Geological Survey Closed*] (SEIS)
KNW .... New Stuyahok [*Alaska*] [*Airport symbol*] (OAG)
KNWA......... Bellefonte, AR [*AM radio station call letters*]
KNWB......... Hilo, HI [*FM radio station call letters*] (RBYB)
KNWB......... Knowable (ABBR)
KNWC......... Sioux Falls, SD [*AM radio station call letters*]
KNWC-FM..... Sioux Falls, SD [*FM radio station call letters*]
KNWD......... Natchitoches, LA [*FM radio station call letters*]
KNWDV....... Knickerbocker L L Wrrt [*NASDAQ symbol*] (TTSB)
KNWG......... Knowing (ABBR)
KNWGNS..... Knowingness (ABBR)
KNWGY...... Knowingly (ABBR)
KNWHW...... Know-How (ABBR)
KNWL......... Knowledge (ABBR)
KNWLB....... Knowledgeable (ABBR)
KNWLDG..... Knowledge (ABBR)
KNWLDGB ... Knowledgeable (ABBR)

KNWNTHG ... Know-Nothing (ABBR)
KNWO .... Cottonwood, ID [*FM radio station call letters*]
KNWR .... Ellensburg, WA [*FM radio station call letters*] (RBYB)
KNWR .... Knower (ABBR)
KNWS .... Waterloo, IA [*AM radio station call letters*]
KNWS-FM ... Waterloo, IA [*FM radio station call letters*]
KNWS-TV ... Katy, TX [*Television station call letters*]
KNWV-FM ... Clarkston, WA [*FM radio station call letters*] (RBYB)
KNWX .... Seattle, WA [*AM radio station call letters*] (RBYB)
KNWY .... Yakima, WA [*FM radio station call letters*]
KNWZ .... Thousand Palms, CA [*AM radio station call letters*]
KNWZ-FM ... Yucca Valley, CA [*FM radio station call letters*]
KNX .... Knighthawk Air Express Ltd. [*Canada ICAO designator*] (FAAC)
KNX .... Knoxville [*Diocesan abbreviation*] [*Tennessee*] (TOCD)
KNX .... Kununurra [*Australia Airport symbol*] (OAG)
KNX .... Los Angeles, CA [*AM radio station call letters*]
KNXN .... Sierra Vista, AZ [*AM radio station call letters*]
KNXR .... Rochester, MN [*FM radio station call letters*]
KNXT .... Visalia, CA [*Television station call letters*]
KNXV .... Knoxville [*Tennessee*] (ABBR)
KNXV .... Phoenix, AZ [*Television station call letters*]
KNXX .... Willow Grove/Willow Grove Naval Air Station [*Pennsylvania*] [*ICAO location identifier*] (ICLI)
KNY .... Kanoya [*Japan*] [*Geomagnetic observatory code*]
KNY .... Kenergy Resource Corp. [*Vancouver Stock Exchange symbol*]
KNYC .... New York (City) [*New York*] [*ICAO location identifier*] (ICLI)
KNYD .... Broken Arrow, OK [*FM radio station call letters*]
KNYL .... Yuma/Vincent Marine Corps Air Station [*Arizona*] [*ICAO location identifier*] (ICLI)
KNYN .... Santa Fe, NM [*FM radio station call letters*]
KNZ .... Kanozan [*Japan*] [*Geomagnetic observatory code*]
KNZ .... Kenieba [*Mali*] [*Airport symbol*] (OAG)
KNZA .... Hiawatha, KS [*FM radio station call letters*]
KNZJ .... El Toro Marine Corps Air Station [*California*] [*ICAO location identifier*] (ICLI)
KNZR .... Bakersfield, CA [*AM radio station call letters*]
KNZS .... Montecito, CA [*AM radio station call letters*]
KNZW .... South Weymouth/South Weymouth Naval Air Station [*Massachusetts*] [*ICAO location identifier*] (ICLI)
KNZY .... San Diego/North Island Naval Air Station [*California*] [*ICAO location identifier*] (ICLI)
KNZZ .... Grand Junction, CO [*AM radio station call letters*]
Ko .... C. H. Boehringer Sohn, Ingelheim [*Germany*] [*Research code symbol*]
KO .... [*The*] Coca-Cola Co. [*NYSE symbol*] (SPSG)
KO .... Commanding Officer [*Military slang*]
KO .... Contracting Officer [*Also, CO, CONTRO*]
KO .... Kashrut Observance (BJA)
KO .... Kattoo [*Ship's rigging*] (ROG)
KO .... Keep Off [*i.e., avoid assuming the risk on an application, pending further investigation*] [*Insurance*]
KO .... Keep On [*Continue*] [*Medicine*] (DAVI)
K/O .... Keep Open [*Medicine*]
KO .... Kickoff (MSA)
KO .... Killarney Oscillation [*Climatology*]
KO .... Killed Organism [*Medicine*] (DMAA)
KO .... Kilogram (ROG)
KO .... Kilohm (ABBR)
KO .... King's Own [*Military unit*] [*British*]
KO .... Klystron Oscillator
KO .... Knee Orthosis [*Medicine*]
K/O .... Knocked Out [*To write or produce something quickly*] [*Also called knock off*] (WDMC)
KO .... Knockout [*Partly cut out or loosened area which can be easily removed, as in a junction box*] [*Technical drawings*]
KO .... Knockout [*Boxing*]
KO .... Kodiak-Western Alaska Airlines, Inc. [*CAB official abbreviation*]
ko .... Korea, South [*MARC country of publication code Library of Congress*] (LCCP)
KO .... Kraus-Thomson Organization [*Publisher*]
KOA .... Communications on Alternatives in Education [*Defunct*] (EA)
KOA .... Denver, CO [*AM radio station call letters*]
KOA .... Kailua-Kona, HI [*Location identifier FAA*] (FAAL)
KOA .... Kampground Owners Association [*Phoenix, AZ*] (EA)
KOA .... Kampgrounds of America
KOA .... Kentucky Optometric Association (SRA)
KOA .... Knocked-on-Atom
KOA .... Kobuan [*Solomon Islands*] [*Seismograph station code, US Geological Survey Closed*] (SEIS)
KOA .... Kona [*Hawaii*] [*Airport symbol*] (OAG)
KOA .... Kone Air Ltd. [*Finland ICAO designator*] (FAAC)
KOAA .... Pueblo, CO [*Television station call letters*]
KOAB .... Bend, OR [*FM radio station call letters*]
KOAB-TV ... Bend, OR [*Television station call letters*]
KOAC .... Corvallis, OR [*AM radio station call letters*]
KOAC-TV ... Corvallis, OR [*Television station call letters*]
KOAI .... Fort Worth, TX [*FM radio station call letters*]
KOAK .... Oakland/Metropolitan Oakland International [*California*] [*ICAO location identifier*] (ICLI)
KOAK .... Red Oak, IA [*AM radio station call letters*]
KOAL .... Price, UT [*AM radio station call letters*]
KOALA .... Keyfile Open Access Layer [*Workflow automation software*] (PCM)
Koala .... Koala Corp. [*Associated Press*] (SAG)
KOAM .... Korean-American Oil Co.
KOAM .... Pittsburg, KS [*Television station call letters*]

KO & G .... Kansas, Oklahoma & Gulf Railway Co.
KOAQ .... Terrytown, NE [*AM radio station call letters*]
KOAS .... Broken Arrow, OK [*FM radio station call letters*] (RBYB)
KOAT .... Albuquerque, NM [*Television station call letters*]
KOAZ-FM ... Glendale, AZ [*FM radio station call letters*] (RBYB)
KOB .... Albuquerque, NM [*Television station call letters*]
KOB .... King's Own Borderers [*British military*] (DMA)
KOB .... Kob Air Ltd. [*Uganda*] [*ICAO designator*] (FAAC)
KOB .... Kobe [*Japan*] [*Seismograph station code, US Geological Survey*] (SEIS)
KoB .... Koehler and Baumgartner Lexikon in Veteris Testamenti Libros [*Leiden*] [*A publication*] (BJA)
KOB .... Koutaba [*Cameroon*] [*Airport symbol*] (OAG)
KOB .... Kriegsoffizier-Bewerber [*Applicant for Wartime Commission*] [*German military - World War II*]
KOBB .... Bozeman, MT [*AM radio station call letters*]
KOBC .... Joplin, MO [*FM radio station call letters*]
KOBE .... Las Cruces, NM [*AM radio station call letters*]
Kobe UL Rev ... Kobe University. Law Review [*A publication*] (DLA)
KOBF .... Farmington, NM [*Television station call letters*]
KOBI .... Medford, OR [*Television station call letters*]
KOBN .... Honolulu, HI [*Television station call letters*]
KOBO .... Yuba City, CA [*AM radio station call letters*]
KOBOL .... Keystation On-Line Business-Oriented Language [*Computer science*]
KOBR .... Roswell, NM [*Television station call letters*]
Koc .... Coefficient of Organic Carbon Partition (GNE)
KOC .... Kathodal Opening Contraction [*Medicine*]
KOC .... Key Operational Capability [*Military*] (RDA)
KOC .... Knight of the [*Order of the*] Oak Crown
KOC .... Kochi [*Japan*] [*Seismograph station code, US Geological Survey*] (SEIS)
KOC .... Koumac [*New Caledonia*] [*Airport symbol*] (OAG)
KOC .... Kuwait Oil Co.
Koc .... Measure of Soil Absorption (GNE)
KOC .... Occupational and Environmental Health Unit, University of Toronto [*UTLAS symbol*]
KOC .... TCC Beverages Ltd. [*Toronto Stock Exchange symbol*]
KOCB .... Oklahoma City, OK [*Television station call letters*]
KOCC .... Oklahoma City, OK [*FM radio station call letters*]
KOCCCG ...... Kunia Operations Control Center Coordination Group (CINC)
KOCD .... Columbus, KS [*FM radio station call letters*]
KOCE .... Huntington Beach, CA [*Television station call letters*]
KOCE .... Komi Commodity Exchange [*Russian Federation*] (EY)
Koch .... Koch's Supreme Court Decisions [*Ceylon*] [*A publication*] (DLA)
KOCN .... Pacific Grove, CA [*FM radio station call letters*]
KOCO .... Korea Oil Corp.
KOCO .... Oklahoma City, OK [*Television station call letters*]
KOCP .... Camarillo, CA [*FM radio station call letters*] (RBYB)
KOCT .... Carlsbad, NM [*Television station call letters*]
KOCV .... Odessa, TX [*FM radio station call letters*]
KOCV-TV ... Odessa, TX [*Television station call letters*]
KOCY-FM ... Hoxie, AR [*FM radio station call letters*] (RBYB)
KO'd .... Knocked Out [*Boxing*] (DAVI)
KOD .... Kodaikanal [*India*] [*Geomagnetic observatory code*]
KOD .... Kodaikanal [*India*] [*Seismograph station code, US Geological Survey*] (SEIS)
KODA .... Houston, TX [*FM radio station call letters*]
KODC .... Korea Oceanographic Data Center [*Marine science*] (OSRA)
KODCH .... Kodachrome (VRA)
KODCO .... Korean Overseas Development Co. [*Korean government agency*]
KODE .... Joplin, MO [*Television station call letters*]
KODI .... Cody, WY [*AM radio station call letters*]
KODJ .... Salt Lake City, UT [*FM radio station call letters*]
KODL .... The Dalles, OR [*AM radio station call letters*]
KODM .... Odessa, TX [*FM radio station call letters*]
KODR .... King's Overseas Dominions Regiment [*British military*] (DMA)
KODS .... Carnelian Bay, CA [*FM radio station call letters*]
KODY .... North Platte, NE [*AM radio station call letters*]
KODZ .... Eugene, OR [*FM radio station call letters*]
KOE .... Kilograms Oil Equivalent [*Petroleum industry*]
kOe .... Kilooersted
KOE .... Koppel [*Federal Republic of Germany*] [*Seismograph station code, US Geological Survey*] (SEIS)
KOE .... Kupang [*Indonesia*] [*Airport symbol*] (OAG)
KOE .... Northland Aviation, Inc. [*ICAO designator*] (FAAC)
KOEA .... Doniphan, MO [*FM radio station call letters*]
KOEBES .... Koelner Bibliothekserschliessungssystem [*Automated library system*] (NITA)
KOED .... Tulsa, OK [*Television station call letters*]
KOEL .... Oelwein, IA [*AM radio station call letters*]
KOEL-FM ... Oelwein, IA [*FM radio station call letters*]
KOEO .... Key-On Engine-Off [*Automotive engineering*]
KOER .... Key-On Engine-Running [*Automotive engineering*]
KOET .... Eufaula, OK [*Television station call letters*]
KOEX .... Oklahoma City [*Oklahoma*] [*ICAO location identifier*] (ICLI)
KOEZ .... Newton, KS [*FM radio station call letters*]
KOF .... Coca-Cola FEMSA [*NYSE symbol*] (SPSG)
KOF .... Coca-Cola FEMSA ADS [*NYSE symbol*] (TTSB)
KOF .... Knitted Outerwear Foundation (EA)
KOF .... Kofu [*Japan*] [*Seismograph station code, US Geological Survey*] (SEIS)
KOFC .... Fayetteville, AR [*AM radio station call letters*]
K of C .... Knights of Columbus (EA)
KOFE .... St. Maries, ID [*AM radio station call letters*]

KOFF............ Offutt Air Force Base, Omaha [*Nebraska*] [*ICAO location identifier*] (ICLI)
K of H.......... Knight of Hanover
KOFI............ Kalispell, MT [*AM radio station call letters*]
KOFI-FM....... Kalispell, MT [*FM radio station call letters*]
K of L.......... Knights of Labor
K of L.......... Knights of Lithuania (EA)
KOFM.......... Enid, OK [*FM radio station call letters*]
KOFO.......... Ottawa, KS [*AM radio station call letters*]
K of P.......... Knights of Pythias
KOFS.......... Key Officers of Foreign Service Posts [*A publication*]
KOFST......... Korean Federation of Science and Technology
KOFT.......... Gallup, NM [*Television station call letters*]
KOFX.......... El Paso, TX [*FM radio station call letters*]
KOFY.......... San Francisco, CA [*Television station call letters*]
KOFY.......... San Mateo, CA [*AM radio station call letters*]
KOG............ Kansas, Oklahoma & Gulf Railway Co. [*AAR code*]
KOG............ Kindly Old Gentleman [*Slang*]
KOGA.......... Ogallala, NE [*AM radio station call letters*]
KOGA-FM...... Ogallala, NE [*FM radio station call letters*]
KOGC.......... Kelley Oil and Gas Corp. [*NASDAQ symbol*] (SAG)
KogEq......... Koger Equity, Inc. [*Associated Press*] (SAG)
KOGG.......... Wailuku, HI [*Television station call letters*]
KOGM.......... Opelousas, LA [*FM radio station call letters*]
KOGO.......... San Diego, CA [*AM radio station call letters*]
KogrEq........ Koger Equity, Inc. [*Associated Press*] (SAG)
KOGS.......... Ogdensburg [*New York*] [*ICAO location identifier*] (ICLI)
KOGT.......... Orange, TX [*AM radio station call letters*]
KOH............ King's Own Hussars [*British military*] (DMA)
KOH............ Kohala [*Hawaii*] [*Seismograph station code, US Geological Survey*] (SEIS)
Koh............. Kohelet (BJA)
KOH............ Koolatah [*Australia Airport symbol Obsolete*] (OAG)
KOH............ Potassium Hydroxide [*Organic chemistry*]
KOHEPFC..... King of Our Hearts Elvis Presley Fan Club (EA)
KOHI........... St. Helens, OR [*AM radio station call letters*]
KOHL.......... Fremont, CA [*FM radio station call letters*]
Kohls.......... Kohls Corp. [*Associated Press*] (SAG)
KOHM.......... Kilohm (MCD)
KOHM.......... Lubbock, TX [*FM radio station call letters*]
KOHO.......... Honolulu, HI [*AM radio station call letters*]
KohR........... Kohelet Rabbah (BJA)
KOHS.......... Orem, UT [*FM radio station call letters*]
KOHT.......... Marana, AZ [*FM radio station call letters*]
KOHU.......... Hermiston, OR [*AM radio station call letters*]
KOI............. Kennedy Operating Instructions [*NASA*] (KSC)
KOI............. Kirkwall [*Orkney Islands*] [*Airport symbol*] (OAG)
KOI............. KSC [*Kennedy Space Center*] Operation Instruction [*NASA*] (NASA)
KOI............. Ontario Institute for Studies in Education Library [*UTLAS symbol*]
KOIL........... Bellevue, NE [*AM radio station call letters*]
KOIN.......... Portland, OR [*Television station call letters*]
KOIR........... Edinburg, TX [*FM radio station call letters*]
KOIS........... Kuder Occupational Interest Survey [*Aptitude and skills test*]
KOIT........... San Francisco, CA [*AM radio station call letters*]
KOIT-FM....... San Francisco, CA [*FM radio station call letters*]
KOJ............ Kagoshima [*Japan*] [*Airport symbol*] (OAG)
KOJ............ Keen on the Job (ADA)
KOJJ........... East Porterville, CA [*FM radio station call letters*]
KOJM.......... Havre, MT [*AM radio station call letters*]
KOJO.......... Lake Charles, LA [*FM radio station call letters*]
KOK............ Horizon Cargo Transport, Inc. [*ICAO designator*] (FAAC)
KOK............ Kansallinen Kokoomus [*National Coalition Party*] [*Finland*] [*Political party*] (EAIO)
KOK............ Kokkola [*Finland*] [*Airport symbol*] (OAG)
kok............. Konkani [*MARC language code Library of Congress*] (LCCP)
KOKA.......... Shreveport, LA [*AM radio station call letters*]
KOKB.......... Blackwell, OK [*AM radio station call letters*]
KOKC.......... Guthrie, OK [*AM radio station call letters*]
KOKC.......... Oklahoma City/Will Rogers World [*Oklahoma*] [*ICAO location identifier*] (ICLI)
KOKE.......... Giddings, TX [*FM radio station call letters*]
KOKF.......... Edmond, OK [*FM radio station call letters*]
KOKH.......... Oklahoma City, OK [*Television station call letters*]
KOKI........... Tulsa, OK [*Television station call letters*]
KOKK.......... Huron, SD [*AM radio station call letters*]
KOKL.......... Okmulgee, OK [*AM radio station call letters*]
KO-KO......... Kommerzielle Koordination [*Former East German political party*]
KOKO.......... Warrensburg, MO [*AM radio station call letters*]
KOKR.......... Newport, AR [*FM radio station call letters*]
KOKS.......... Poplar Bluff, MO [*FM radio station call letters*]
KOKU.......... Agana, GU [*FM radio station call letters*]
KOKX.......... Keokuk, IA [*AM radio station call letters*]
KOKX-FM...... Keokuk, IA [*FM radio station call letters*]
KOKZ.......... Waterloo, IA [*FM radio station call letters*]
KOL............ King's College, Wilkes-Barre, PA [*OCLC symbol*] (OCLC)
KOL............ Knights of Lithuania (EA)
KOL............ Kollmorgen Corp. [*NYSE symbol*] (SPSG)
KOl............ Olathe Public Library, Olathe, KS [*Library symbol Library of Congress*] (LCLS)
KOLA.......... San Bernardino, CA [*FM radio station call letters*]
KOLD.......... Tucson, AZ [*Television station call letters*]
KOLE.......... Port Arthur, TX [*AM radio station call letters*]
KOIH........... Olathe Community Hospital, Olathe, KS [*Library symbol Library of Congress*] (LCLS)
KOLI........... King's Own Light Infantry [*Military unit*] [*British*]

KOIJL.......... Johnson County Law Library, Olathe, KS [*Library symbol Library of Congress*] (LCLS)
KOLK-FM....... Onawa, IA [*FM radio station call letters*] (RBYB)
KOLL.......... Maumelle, AR [*FM radio station call letters*]
KollRE......... Koll Real Estate Group [*Associated Press*] (SAG)
KollRI......... Koll Real Estate Group [*Associated Press*] (SAG)
KOLM.......... Rochester, MN [*AM radio station call letters*]
KOIMN........ Mid-America Nazarene College, Olathe, KS [*Library symbol Library of Congress*] (LCLS)
Kolmor........ Kollmorgen Corp. [*Associated Press*] (SAG)
KOLN.......... Lincoln, NE [*Television station call letters*]
KOLO.......... Reno, NV [*Television station call letters*]
KOLR.......... Springfield, MO [*Television station call letters*]
KOLS.......... Dodge City, KS [*FM radio station call letters*]
KOLS.......... Nogales/International [*Arizona*] [*ICAO location identifier*] (ICLI)
KOLT.......... Scottsbluff, NE [*AM radio station call letters*]
KOLT-FM....... Santa Fe, NM [*FM radio station call letters*]
KOLU.......... Pasco, WA [*FM radio station call letters*]
KOLV.......... Olivia, MN [*FM radio station call letters*]
KOLX.......... Barling, AR [*FM radio station call letters*]
KOLY.......... Mobridge, SD [*AM radio station call letters*]
KOLY-FM...... Mobridge, SD [*FM radio station call letters*]
Kolze.......... Transvaal Reports, by Kolze [*A publication*] (DLA)
KOM............ Kansas-Oklahoma-Missouri League [*Old baseball league*]
KOM............ Kentucky, Ohio, Michigan [*Medical library network*]
KOM............ Kilometric Wavelength [*Radio astronomy*]
KOM............ Knight of the Order of Malta (WDAA)
KOM............ Komaba [*Japan*] [*Seismograph station code, US Geological Survey Closed*] (SEIS)
KOM............ Komitet Opiekunczy Miejski (BJA)
KOM............ Komo-Manda [*Papua New Guinea*] [*Airport symbol Obsolete*] (OAG)
KoM............ Korea Microforms, Seoul, Korea [*Library symbol Library of Congress*] (LCLS)
KOM............ KSC [*Kennedy Space Center*] Organizational Manual [*NASA*] (NASA)
KOMA.......... Oklahoma City, OK [*AM radio station call letters*]
KOMA.......... Omaha/Eppley Air Field [*Nebraska*] [*ICAO location identifier*] (ICLI)
KOMA-FM...... Oklahoma City, OK [*FM radio station call letters*]
Komag......... Komag, Inc. [*Associated Press*] (SAG)
KOMB.......... Fort Scott, KS [*FM radio station call letters*]
KomBeiANT... Kommentare und Beitraege zum Alten und Neuen Testament [*Duesseldorf*] [*A publication*] (BJA)
KOMC.......... Branson, MO [*AM radio station call letters*]
KOME.......... San Jose, CA [*FM radio station call letters*]
KOMH-AM.... Pawhuska, OK [*AM radio station call letters*] (RBYB)
KOMO.......... Seattle, WA [*AM radio station call letters*]
KOMO-TV..... Seattle, WA [*Television station call letters*]
KOMP.......... Las Vegas, NV [*FM radio station call letters*]
KOMRMLN... Kentucky-Ohio-Michigan Regional Medical Library [*Library network*]
KOMS.......... Poteau, OK [*FM radio station call letters*]
KOMSOMOL... Communist Youth League [*From the Russian*]
KOMU.......... Columbia, MO [*Television station call letters*]
KOMW.......... Omak, WA [*AM radio station call letters*]
KOMW-FM.... Omak, WA [*FM radio station call letters*]
KOMX.......... Pampa, TX [*FM radio station call letters*]
kon............. Kongo [*MARC language code Library of Congress*] (LCCP)
KON............ Kongsberg [*Norway*] [*Seismograph station code, US Geological Survey*] (SEIS)
KON............ Kontum [*South Vietnam*] [*Airport symbol*] (AD)
KONA.......... Kennewick, WA [*AM radio station call letters*]
KONA-FM...... Kennewick, WA [*FM radio station call letters*]
KOND-FM .... Cleveland, TX [*FM radio station call letters*] (RBYB)
KONE.......... Lubbock, TX [*FM radio station call letters*]
KONG.......... Everett, WA [*Television station call letters*]
KONI........... Lanai City, HI [*FM radio station call letters*]
KONO.......... San Antonio, TX [*AM radio station call letters*]
KONO-FM...... Fredricksburg, TX [*FM radio station call letters*]
KONP.......... Port Angeles, WA [*AM radio station call letters*]
KONQ.......... Dodge City, KS [*FM radio station call letters*]
Konst & W Rat App... Konstam and Ward's Rating Appeals [*1909-12*] [*A publication*] (DLA)
Konst Rat App... Konstam's Rating Appeals [*1904-08*] [*A publication*] (DLA)
KONT.......... Ontario/International [*California*] [*ICAO location identifier*] (ICLI)
KONY.......... Washington, UT [*AM radio station call letters*]
KONY-FM..... Kanab, UT [*FM radio station call letters*]
KONZ.......... Arizona City, AZ [*FM radio station call letters*]
KOO............ Kongolo [*Zaire*] [*Airport symbol*] (OAG)
KOOC.......... Belton, TX [*FM radio station call letters*]
KOOD.......... Hays, KS [*Television station call letters*]
KOOG.......... Ogden, UT [*Television station call letters*]
KOOI........... Jacksonville, TX [*FM radio station call letters*]
KOOJ.......... Riverside, CA [*FM radio station call letters*]
KOOKR........ Kookier (ABBR)
KooKR......... Koo Koo Roo, Inc. [*Associated Press*] (SAG)
KOOKST....... Kookiest (ABBR)
KOOL.......... Phoenix, AZ [*AM radio station call letters*]
KOOL.......... Thermagenesis Corp. [*NASDAQ symbol*] (SAG)
KOOL.......... Thermogenesis Corp. [*NASDAQ symbol*] (SAG)
KOOL-FM...... Phoenix, AZ [*FM radio station call letters*]
KOOP.......... Hornsby, TX [*FM radio station call letters*]
KOOQ.......... North Platte, NE [*AM radio station call letters*]
Koor........... Koor Industries Ltd. [*Associated Press*] (SAG)
KOOS.......... North Bend, OR [*FM radio station call letters*]
KOOU.......... Hardy, AR [*FM radio station call letters*]
KOOV.......... Copperas Cove, TX [*FM radio station call letters*]
KOOZ.......... Great Falls, MT [*FM radio station call letters*]

KOP .... Kansallis-Osake-Pankki [*National Capital Stock Bank*] [*Finland*]
KOP .... Kickoff Point [*Diamond drilling*]
KOP .... Kopeck [*Monetary unit in Russia*]
KOP .... Nakhon Phanom [*Thailand*] [*Airport symbol Obsolete*] (OAG)
KOPA .... Scottsdale, AZ [*AM radio station call letters*]
KOPB .... Portland, OR [*FM radio station call letters*]
KOPB-TV ...... Portland, OR [*Television station call letters*]
KOPCC .... Kunzang Odsal Palyul Changchub Choling [*An association*] (EA)
KOPE .... Medford, OR [*AM radio station call letters*]
KOPF .... Miami/Opa Locka [*Florida*] [*ICAO location identifier*] (ICLI)
Kopin .... Kopin Corp. [*Associated Press*] (SAG)
KOPN .... Columbia, MO [*FM radio station call letters*]
KOPN .... Kopin Corp. [*NASDAQ symbol*] (SAG)
KOPR .... Butte, MT [*FM radio station call letters*]
KOPS .... K (10³) Operations Per Second (NITA)
KOPS .... Keep Off Pounds Sensibly [*Club*]
KOPS .... Thousands of Operations per Second (NASA)
KOPY-AM ...... Alice, TX [*AM radio station call letters*] (RBYB)
KOPY-FM ...... Alice, TX [*FM radio station call letters*] (RBYB)
KOQI .... Soquel, CA [*AM radio station call letters*]
KOQL .... Columbia, MO [*FM radio station call letters*]
KOQO .... Clovis, CA [*AM radio station call letters*]
KOQO .... Fresno, CA [*FM radio station call letters*]
KOR .... Air Koryo [*North Korea*] [*ICAO designator*] (FAAC)
KOR .... Contracting Officer
KOR .... King's Own Royal [*Military unit*] [*British*]
KOR .... Klein Offset Rotation [*Typography*] (DGA)
KOR .... Knowledge of Results [*Visual monitoring*]
KOR .... Koala Resources Ltd. [*Vancouver Stock Exchange symbol*]
KOR .... Kodak Ortho Resist
KOR .... Kokoro [*Papua New Guinea*] [*Airport symbol*] (OAG)
KOR .... Koor Indus Ltd ADS [*NYSE symbol*] (TTSB)
KOR .... Koor Industries Ltd. [*NYSE symbol*] (SAG)
KOR .... Koran (ROG)
Kor .... Korea (VRA)
kor .... Korean [*MARC language code Library of Congress*] (LCCP)
KOR .... Koror [*Palau Islands*] [*Seismograph station code, US Geological Survey Closed*] (SEIS)
KOR .... Republic of Korea [*ANSI three-letter standard code*] (CNC)
KOR .... Seaplane [*Russian symbol*]
KOR .... Social Self-Defense Committee [*Also, SSDC*] [*Poland*] (PD)
KORA .... Bryan, TX [*FM radio station call letters*]
KORB .... Bettendorf, IA [*FM radio station call letters*] (RBYB)
KORC .... Waldport, OR [*AM radio station call letters*]
KORD .... Chicago/O'Hare [*Illinois*] [*ICAO location identifier*] (ICLI)
KORD-FM ...... Richland, WA [*FM radio station call letters*]
KORDI .... Korea Ocean Research and Development Institute (USDC)
KORE .... Kinetic Analysis Using Over-Relaxation [*FORTRAN computer program*] [*Physical chemistry*]
KORE .... Springfield-Eugene, OR [*AM radio station call letters*]
Korea .... Korea Fund, Inc. [*Associated Press*] (SAG)
KoreaElc ...... Korea Electric Power Corp. [*Associated Press*] (SAG)
KoreaEqt ...... Korea Equity Fund [*Associated Press*] (SAG)
KoreaInv ...... Korean Investment Fund [*Associated Press*] (SAG)
Korea LR ...... Korea Law Review [*A publication*] (DLA)
KoreaM .... Korea Mobile Telecommunications [*Associated Press*] (SAG)
Korean J Comp L... Korean Journal of Comparative Law [*A publication*] (DLA)
Korean J Int'l L... Korean Journal of International Law [*A publication*] (DLA)
Korean J of Internat L... Korean Journal of International Law [*A publication*] (DLA)
Korean L....... Korean Law [*A publication*] (DLA)
KorEIN .... Korea Electric Power Corp. [*Associated Press*] (SAG)
KORF .... Norfolk/Norfolk Regional Airport [*Virginia*] [*ICAO location identifier*] (ICLI)
KORG .... Anaheim, CA [*AM radio station call letters*]
KORI .... Mansfield, LA [*FM radio station call letters*]
KORK .... Las Vegas, NV [*AM radio station call letters*]
KORL .... Honolulu, HI [*AM radio station call letters*]
KORL .... Orlando [*Florida*] [*ICAO location identifier*] (ICLI)
KORL-FM ...... Honolulu, HI [*FM radio station call letters*] (RBYB)
KORN .... Mitchell, SD [*AM radio station call letters*]
KORO .... Corpus Christi, TX [*Television station call letters*]
KOROC .... Keep Out of Reach of Children (DI)
KORP .... Charles, [*J. W.*] Financial Services [*NASDAQ symbol*] (SAG)
KORP .... Charles (JW) Finl Svcs [*NASDAQ symbol*] (TTSB)
KORQ-FM ...... Abilene, TX [*FM radio station call letters*]
KORR .... American Falls, ID [*FM radio station call letters*] (RBYB)
KORR .... King's Own Royal Regiment [*Military unit*] [*British*]
KORSTIC .... Korea Scientific and Technical Information Centre (NITA)
KORSTIC .... Korea Scientific and Technological Information Center [*INSPEC operator*]
KORT .... Grangeville, ID [*AM radio station call letters*]
KORT-FM ...... Grangeville, ID [*FM radio station call letters*]
KORV .... Oroville, CA [*AM radio station call letters*]
KOS .... Kent University On-Line System [*Computer science*] (PDAA)
KO's .... Knockout Drops [*A drug producing unconsciousness*] [*Slang*]
KOS .... Kosmodemyansk [*Former USSR Seismograph station code, US Geological Survey Closed*] (SEIS)
KOS .... Kosovaair [*Yugoslavia*] [*ICAO designator*] (FAAC)
KOSA .... Odessa, TX [*Television station call letters*]
KOSB .... King's Own Scottish Borderers [*Military unit*] [*British*]
KOSC .... Oscoda/Wurtsmith Air Force Base [*Michigan*] [*ICAO location identifier*] (ICLI)
KOSCO .... Korea Oil Storage Co. (CINC)
KOSCOT .... Cosmetics for the Community of Tomorrow [*Acronym used as brand name*]

KOSE .... Osceola, AR [*AM radio station call letters*]
KOSE-FM ...... Osceola, AR [*FM radio station call letters*]
KOSG .... Camden, AR [*AM radio station call letters*]
KOSH .... Osawatomie State Hospital, Osawatomie, KS [*Library symbol Library of Congress*] (LCLS)
KOSI .... Denver, CO [*FM radio station call letters*]
KOSJ .... Nebraska City, NE [*FM radio station call letters*] (RBYB)
KoSNU .... Seoul National University, Seoul, Korea [*Library symbol Library of Congress*] (LCLS)
KOSO .... Patterson, CA [*FM radio station call letters*]
KOSP .... Willard, MO [*FM radio station call letters*]
KOSR-AM ...... Omaha, NE [*AM radio station call letters*] (RBYB)
KOSS .... Koss Corp. [*NASDAQ symbol*] (SAG)
KOST .... Los Angeles, CA [*FM radio station call letters*]
KOSU .... Stillwater, OK [*FM radio station call letters*]
KoSYU .... Yonsei University, Seoul, Korea [*Library symbol Library of Congress*] (LCLS)
KOSZ .... Vermillion, SD [*AM radio station call letters*]
KOSZ-FM ...... Idaho Falls, ID [*FM radio station call letters*]
KOT .... Knowledge of Occupations Test [*Psychology*] (DAVI)
KOT .... Kotlik [*Alaska*] [*Airport symbol*] (OAG)
KOTA .... Rapid City, SD [*AM radio station call letters*]
KOTA-TV ...... Rapid City, SD [*Television station call letters*]
KOTB .... Evanston, WY [*FM radio station call letters*]
KOTC .... Kennett, MO [*AM radio station call letters*] (RBYB)
KOTD .... Plattsmouth, NE [*AM radio station call letters*]
KOTD-FM ...... Plattsmouth, NE [*FM radio station call letters*]
KOTE .... Eureka, KS [*FM radio station call letters*]
KOTI .... Klamath Falls, OR [*Television station call letters*]
KOTK .... Portland, OR [*AM radio station call letters*] (RBYB)
KOTM .... Ottumwa, IA [*FM radio station call letters*]
KOTN .... Keep on Truckin' News [*A publication*] (EAAP)
KOTN .... Pine Bluff, AR [*AM radio station call letters*]
KOTO .... Telluride, CO [*AM radio station call letters*]
KOTR .... Cambria, CA [*FM radio station call letters*]
KOTRA .... Korea Trade Promotion Center (EA)
KOTS .... Deming, NM [*AM radio station call letters*]
KOTT .... Otterville, MO [*FM radio station call letters*]
KOtU .... Ottawa University, Ottawa, KS [*Library symbol Library of Congress*] (LCLS)
KOTV .... Tulsa, OK [*Television station call letters*]
KOTZ .... Kotzebue, AK [*AM radio station call letters*]
Kotze .... Kotze's Transvaal High Court Reports [*South Africa*] [*A publication*] (DLA)
Kotze & B .... Supreme Court Reports, Transvaal [*1885-88*] [*South Africa*] [*A publication*] (DLA)
Kotze & Barb... Supreme Court Reports, Transvaal [*1885-88*] [*South Africa*] [*A publication*] (DLA)
Kotze & Barber... Transvaal Court Reports [*A publication*] (DLA)
KOU .... Koula Moutou [*Gabon*] [*Airport symbol*] (OAG)
KOU .... Koumac [*New Caledonia*] [*Seismograph station code, US Geological Survey*] (SEIS)
KOUL .... Sinton, TX [*FM radio station call letters*]
KOUT .... Rapid City, SD [*FM radio station call letters*]
KOUU .... American Falls, ID [*FM radio station call letters*]
KOUZ .... Alexandria, LA [*FM radio station call letters*] (RBYB)
KOV .... Key Operated Valve
Kov .... N. A. Kovach, Los Angeles, CA [*Library symbol Library of Congress*] (LCLS)
KOVC .... Valley City, ND [*AM radio station call letters*]
KOVC-FM ...... Valley City, ND [*FM radio station call letters*]
KOVE .... Lander, WY [*AM radio station call letters*]
KOVO .... Provo, UT [*AM radio station call letters*]
KOvpJ .... Johnson County Community College, Overland Park, KS [*Library symbol Library of Congress*] (LCLS)
KovpST .... St. Thomas High School, Overland Park, KS [*Library symbol*] [*Library of Congress*] (LCLS)
KOVR .... Stockton, CA [*Television station call letters*]
KOVT .... Silver City, NM [*Television station call letters*]
Kow .... Coefficient of Octanolwater Partition (GNE)
KOW .... Ghanzhou [*China*] [*Airport symbol*] (OAG)
KOW .... Keen on Waller [*A coterie of women admirers of British stage actor, Lewis Waller (1860-1915)*] (ROG)
KOW .... Knock-Off Wheels [*Automotive accessory*]
KOW .... Kowkash Gold [*Vancouver Stock Exchange symbol*]
KOWB .... Laramie, WY [*AM radio station call letters*]
KOWF .... Escondido, CA [*FM radio station call letters*]
KOWL .... South Lake Tahoe, CA [*AM radio station call letters*]
KOWO .... Waseca, MN [*AM radio station call letters*]
KOWW-AM ..... Blue Springs, MO [*AM radio station call letters*] (RBYB)
KOWZ-FM ...... Blooming Prairie, MN [*FM radio station call letters*] (RBYB)
KOX .... Kokonao [*West Irian, Indonesia*] [*Airport symbol*] (AD)
KOXE .... Brownwood, TX [*FM radio station call letters*]
KOXR .... Oxnard, CA [*AM radio station call letters*]
KOY .... Koyama [*Japan*] [*Seismograph station code, US Geological Survey Closed*] (SEIS)
KOY .... Olga Bay [*Alaska*] [*Airport symbol*] (OAG)
KOY .... Phoenix, AZ [*AM radio station call letters*]
KOYE .... Laredo, TX [*FM radio station call letters*]
KOYLI .... King's Own Yorkshire Light Infantry [*Military unit*] [*British*]
KOYN .... Paris, TX [*FM radio station call letters*]
KOZ .... Kozyrevsk [*Former USSR Seismograph station code, US Geological Survey*] (SEIS)
KOZ .... Ouzinkie, AK [*Location identifier FAA*] (FAAL)
KOZA .... Odessa, TX [*AM radio station call letters*]

KOZE............	Lewiston, ID [*AM radio station call letters*]
KOZE-FM	Lewiston, ID [*FM radio station call letters*]
KOZI.............	Chelan, WA [*AM radio station call letters*]
KOZI-FM	Chelan, WA [*FM radio station call letters*]
KOZJ............	Joplin, MO [*Television station call letters*]
KOZK............	Springfield, MO [*Television station call letters*]
KOZO-FM	Branson, MO [*FM radio station call letters*] (RBYB)
KOZQ...........	Waynesville, MO [*AM radio station call letters*]
KOZT...........	Fort Bragg, CA [*FM radio station call letters*]
KOZX...........	Cabool, MO [*FM radio station call letters*]
KOZY	Grand Rapids, MN [*AM radio station call letters*]
KOZZ...........	Reno, NV [*AM radio station call letters*]
KOZZ-FM	Reno, NV [*FM radio station call letters*]
KP...............	Democratic People's Republic of Korea [*ANSI two-letter standard code*] (CNC)
K-P..............	Kaiser-Permanente [*Diet*]
kp................	Kaliophilite [*CIPW classification*] [*Geology*]
KP...............	Kaufmann-Peterson Base [*Medicine*] (DMAA)
KP...............	Kensington Palace [*British*]
KP...............	Keogh Plan [*Business term*]
KP...............	Keratitic Precipitate [*Ophthalmology*]
KP...............	Keratitis Punctata [*Ophthalmology*]
KP...............	Keskustapuolue [*Center Party of Finland*] [*Political party*] (PPW)
KP...............	Keyboard Perforator
KP...............	Key Personnel
KP...............	Key Production Co. [*NYSE symbol*] (SAG)
KP...............	Key Pulsing
KP...............	Keypunch [*Computer science*]
KP...............	Kickpipe [*Building construction*]
KP...............	Kick Plate
KP...............	Kidney Pore
KP...............	Kidney Protein [*Nephrology*] (DAVI)
KP...............	Kidney Punch [*Medicine*] (DAVI)
KP...............	Kids of Preachers
KP...............	Killed Parenteral [*Vaccine*] [*Immunology*] (DAVI)
KP...............	Kill Probability (MCD)
KP...............	Kilometer Post
KP...............	Kilopond
kp................	Kilopulse
KP...............	Kinetic Percolation
KP...............	Kinetic Potential
KP...............	King Post
KP...............	King's Parade [*British*] (DSUE)
KP...............	King's Pawn [*Chess*] (ADA)
KP...............	King's Pleasure [*British*]
KP...............	King's Proctor [*British*]
KP...............	Kitchen Police [*Kitchen helpers*] [*Military*]
KP...............	Klebsiella Pneumoniae [*Genus of microorganism*] (DAVI)
KP...............	Klein Paradox [*Physics*]
KP...............	Knight of Pius IX
KP...............	Knight of St. Patrick [*British*]
KP...............	Knights of Pythias (EA)
KP...............	Knotty Pine
KP...............	Kodak Process Resist [*Photography*] (DICI)
KP...............	Komma Proodeftikon [*Progressive Party*] [*Greek Political party*] (PPE)
KP...............	Kommunistesch Partei [*Communist Party*] [*Luxembourg*] [*Political party*] (PPE)
KP...............	Kommunistische Partei [*Communist Party*] [*German Political party*]
KP...............	Kurdish Program (EA)
KP...............	Kurie Plot [*Physics*]
KP...............	Papua New Guinea [*IYRU nationality code*] (IYR)
KP...............	Safair [*ICAO designator*] (AD)
KPA.............	Innkeepers USA Trust [*NYSE symbol*] (SAG)
KPA.............	Key Pulse Adapter [*Telecommunications*] (TEL)
KPA.............	Kidney Plasminogen Activator [*Anticlotting agent*]
kPa.............	Kilopascal
KPA.............	Klystron Power Amplifier
KPA.............	Kopiago [*Papua New Guinea*] [*Airport symbol*] (OAG)
KPA.............	Korea Procurement Agency
KPA.............	Kraft Paper Association [*Later, API*] (EA)
KPAC	San Antonio, TX [*FM radio station call letters*]
KPAE...........	Erwinville, LA [*FM radio station call letters*]
KPAE...........	Everett/Snohomish County-Paine Field [*Washington*] [*ICAO location identifier*] (ICLI)
KPAG	Pagosa Springs, CO [*AM radio station call letters*]
KPAL-AM	North Little Rock, AR [*AM radio station call letters*] (RBYB)
KPAM..........	Panama City/Tyndall Air Force Base [*Florida*] [*ICAO location identifier*] (ICLI)
KPAN	Hereford, TX [*AM radio station call letters*]
KP & D	Kick Plate and Drip (AAG)
KPAN-FM	Hereford, TX [*FM radio station call letters*]
KPAR	Granbury, TX [*AM radio station call letters*]
KParSH	Parsons State Hospital, Parsons, KS [*Library symbol Library of Congress*] (LCLS)
KPAS	Fabens, TX [*FM radio station call letters*]
KPAW	Fort Collins, CO [*FM radio station call letters*] (RBYB)
KPAX	Missoula, MT [*Television station call letters*]
KPAY	Chico, CA [*AM radio station call letters*]
KPAZ	Phoenix, AZ [*Television station call letters*]
KPB.............	Kalium [*Potassium*] Phosphate Buffer [*Biochemistry*] (DAVI)
KPB.............	Kenai Peninsula Borough [*Alaska*]
KPB.............	Ketophenylbutazone [*or Kebuzone*] [*An antirheumatic*] (DAVI)
KPB.............	Kommunistische Partij van Belgie [*Communist Party of Belgium*] [*See also PCB*] [*Political party*] (PPE)

KPB.............	Point Baker, AK [*Location identifier FAA*] (FAAL)
KPBA...........	Pine Bluff, AR [*AM radio station call letters*]
KPBC	Garland, TX [*AM radio station call letters*]
KPBF...........	Pine Bluff/Grider Field [*Arkansas*] [*ICAO location identifier*] (ICLI)
KPBG	Plattsburg/Plattsburg Air Force Base [*New York*] [*ICAO location identifier*] (ICLI)
KPBI...........	Greenwood, AR [*AM radio station call letters*]
KPBI...........	West Palm Beach/Palm Beach International [*Florida*] [*ICAO location identifier*] (ICLI)
KPBQ	Pine Bluff, AR [*FM radio station call letters*]
KPBS	San Diego, CA [*Television station call letters*]
KPBS-FM	San Diego, CA [*FM radio station call letters*]
KPBX...........	Spokane, WA [*FM radio station call letters*]
KPC.............	Kappa Resources [*Vancouver Stock Exchange symbol*]
KPC.............	Kentucky Power Co. [*NYSE symbol*] (SAG)
KPC.............	Kentucky Pwr 8.72% Sr'A'Debs [*NYSE symbol*] (TTSB)
KPC.............	Keratinocyte Precursor Cell
KPC.............	Keratoconus Posticus Circumscriptus [*Medicine*] (DMAA)
KPC.............	Keyboard/Printer Control [*Computer science*]
KPC.............	Keyboard Priority Controller [*Computer science*] (HGAA)
KPC.............	Key Personnel Course (MCD)
KPC.............	Key Product Characteristic
KPC.............	Keypunch Cabinet [*Computer science*]
KPC.............	Khapcheranga [*Former USSR Seismograph station code, US Geological Survey*] (SEIS)
kpc..............	Kiloparsec [*Astronomy*]
KPC.............	Kinetic Process Control
KPC.............	Klystron Phase Control
KPC.............	Knights of Peter Claver (EA)
KPC.............	Koblenz Procurement Center [*Federal Republic of Germany*] [*Military*] (NATG)
KPC.............	Kodak Photofabrication Center
KPC.............	Paducah Junior College, Paducah, KY [*OCLC symbol*] (OCLC)
KPC.............	Port Clarence [*Alaska*] [*Airport symbol*] (OAG)
KPC.............	Port Clarence, AK [*Location identifier FAA*] (FAAL)
KPCB-TV	Snyder, TX [*TV station call letters*] (RBYB)
KPCC	Pasadena, CA [*FM radio station call letters*]
KPCH	Dubach, LA [*FM radio station call letters*]
KPCI...........	Key Production [*NASDAQ symbol*] (TTSB)
KPCI...........	Key Production Co., Inc. [*NASDAQ symbol*] (NQ)
KPCK...........	Kopeck (ABBR)
KPCL...........	Farmington, NM [*FM radio station call letters*]
KPCO	Quincy, CA [*AM radio station call letters*]
KPCR	Bowling Green, MO [*AM radio station call letters*]
KPCR-FM	Bowling Green, MO [*FM radio station call letters*]
KPCW	Park City, UT [*FM radio station call letters*]
KPD.............	Kennedy Program Directive [*NASA*] (NASA)
KPD.............	Knowledge-Based Producibility Decision-Maker [*Productivity technology*] (RDA)
KPD.............	Kommunistische Partei Deutschlands [*Communist Party of Germany*] [*Political party*] (PPW)
KPD-ML	Kommunistische Partei Deutschlands/Marxisten-Leninisten [*Communist Party of Germany/Marxists-Leninists*] [*Political party*] (PPW)
KPDQ	Portland, OR [*AM radio station call letters*]
KPDQ-FM	Portland, OR [*FM radio station call letters*]
KPDR	Wheeler, TX [*FM radio station call letters*]
KPDU	Kaffa People's Democratic Union [*Ethiopia*] [*Political party*] (EY)
KPDX...........	Portland/International [*Oregon*] [*ICAO location identifier*] (ICLI)
KPDX...........	Vancouver, WA [*Television station call letters*]
KPE.............	Kelman Phakoemulsification [*Ophthalmology*] (DAVI)
KPE.............	Key Point Error [*Computer science*] (IAA)
KPE.............	Kilman Phacoemulsification [*Medicine*] (MEDA)
kpe..............	Kpelle [*MARC language code Library of Congress*] (LCCP)
KPEJ	Odessa, TX [*Television station call letters*]
KPEK-FM	Albuquerque, NM [*FM radio station call letters*] (RBYB)
KPEL	Lafayette, LA [*AM radio station call letters*]
KPEL-FM	Erath, LA [*FM radio station call letters*]
KPENC	Korean Centre of International PEN (EAIO)
KPEN-FM	Soldotna, AK [*FM radio station call letters*]
KPER	Hobbs, NM [*FM radio station call letters*]
KPET	Lamesa, TX [*AM radio station call letters*]
KPEZ	Austin, TX [*FM radio station call letters*]
KPF.............	Kangaroo Protection Foundation (EA)
KPF.............	Katadyn Pocket Filter
KPF.............	Key Pulse on Front Cord [*Telecommunications*] (TEL)
KPFA	Berkeley, CA [*FM radio station call letters*]
KPFA	Knackery and Pet Food Association [*Australia*]
KPFB	Berkeley, CA [*FM radio station call letters*]
KPFK	Los Angeles, CA [*FM radio station call letters*]
KPFM	Mountain Home, AR [*FM radio station call letters*]
KPFT	Houston, TX [*FM radio station call letters*]
KPFX	Fargo, ND [*FM radio station call letters*]
KPG.............	Keeping
KPG.............	Kurupung [*Guyana*] [*Airport symbol*] (OAG)
KPGE	Page, AZ [*AM radio station call letters*]
KPGR	Pleasant Grove, UT [*FM radio station call letters*]
KPH.............	Kaena Point [*Hawaii*] [*Seismograph station code, US Geological Survey Closed*] (SEIS)
KPH.............	Keystrokes Per Hour (NITA)
kph..............	Kilometers per Hour
KPH.............	Know Problems of Hydrocephalus (EA)
KPH.............	Komunisticka Partija Hrvatske [*Communist Party of Croatia*] [*Political party*]
KPH	Ktav Publishing House, Inc. [*New York*] (BJA)

KPH .... Pauloff Harbor/Sanak Island, AK [*Location identifier FAA*] (FAAL)
KPhA .... Kansas Pharmacists Association (SRA)
KPhA .... Kentucky Pharmacists Association (SRA)
KPHF .... Newport News/Patrick Henry [*Virginia*] [*ICAO location identifier*] (ICLI)
KPHF .... Phoenix, AZ [*FM radio station call letters*]
KPHL .... Philadelphia/International [*Pennsylvania*] [*ICAO location identifier*] (ICLI)
KPHN .... Pittsburg, KS [*AM radio station call letters*]
KPHN .... Port Huron [*Michigan*] [*ICAO location identifier*] (ICLI)
KPHO .... Phoenix, AZ [*Television station call letters*]
KPHR .... Milbank, SD [*FM radio station call letters*]
KPHS-FM .... Plains, TX [*FM radio station call letters*] (RBYB)
KPHT .... Kindred, ND [*FM radio station call letters*] (RBYB)
KPHX .... Phoenix, AZ [*AM radio station call letters*]
KPHX .... Phoenix/Sky Harbor International [*Arizona*] [*ICAO location identifier*] (ICLI)
KPI .... Kapit [*Malaysia*] [*Airport symbol*] (OAG)
KPI .... Karyopyknotic Index [*Cytology*]
KPI .... Kernel Programming Interface [*Computer science*]
KPI .... Key Performance Indicator (TDOB)
KPI .... Killearn Properties, Inc. [*AMEX symbol*] (SPSG)
KPI .... King Pin Inclination [*Automotive engineering*]
kpi .... Kips [*Thousands of Pounds*] per Square Inch
KPI .... Kontron Personal Instrumentation [*Kontron Electronics*] (NITA)
KPI .... Kunitz Protease Inhibitor [*Medicine*]
KPI .... KWIK Products International Corp. [*Vancouver Stock Exchange symbol*]
KPIC .... Key Phrase in Context
KPIC .... Roseburg, OR [*Television station call letters*]
KPIE .... St. Petersburg/Clearwater International [*Florida*] [*ICAO location identifier*] (ICLI)
KPIG .... Freedom, CA [*FM radio station call letters*]
KPIK .... Beebe, AR [*FM radio station call letters*]
KPIN-FM ...... Pinedale, WY [*FM radio station call letters*] (RBYB)
KPIT .... Pittsburgh/Greater Pittsburgh [*Pennsylvania*] [*ICAO location identifier*] (ICLI)
KPIX .... San Francisco, CA [*AM radio station call letters*] (RBYB)
KPIX-FM ...... San Francisco, CA [*FM radio station call letters*] (RBYB)
KPIX-TV ...... San Francisco, CA [*Television station call letters*]
KPJ .... Komunisticka Partija Jugoslavije [*Communist Party of Yugoslavia*] [*Political party*] (PPE)
KPK .... Kanaka Peak [*California*] [*Seismograph station code, US Geological Survey*] (SEIS)
KPK .... Kapok (ABBR)
KPK .... Kappa Phi Kappa [*Fraternity*]
KPK .... Parks [*Alaska*] [*Airport symbol*] (OAG)
KPK .... Parks, AK [*Location identifier FAA*] (FAAL)
KPKE-AM ..... Gunnison, CO [*AM radio station call letters*] (RBYB)
KPKX .... Livingston, MT [*FM radio station call letters*] (RBYB)
KPKY .... Pocatello, ID [*FM radio station call letters*]
KPL .... Copeland Resources [*Vancouver Stock Exchange symbol*]
KPL .... Khao San Pathet Lao [*News agency*] [*Laos*] (FEA)
KPL .... Kick Plate [*Building construction*]
KPL .... Killearn Properties [*AMEX symbol*] (TTSB)
KPL .... Kommunistisch Partei vu Leetzebuerg [*Communist Party of Luxembourg*] [*Political party*] (PPW)
K-PL .... Potassium-Plasma [*Biochemistry*] (DAVI)
KPLA .... Columbia, MO [*AM radio station call letters*] (RBYB)
KPLC .... Lake Charles, LA [*Television station call letters*]
KPLM .... Palm Springs, CA [*FM radio station call letters*]
KPLN-FM .... Plains, TX [*FM radio station call letters*]
KPLO .... Reliance, SD [*FM radio station call letters*]
KPLO-TV ..... Reliance, SD [*Television station call letters*]
KPLR .... St. Louis, MO [*Television station call letters*]
KPLS .... Key Pulsing (MSA)
KPLS .... Orange, CA [*AM radio station call letters*]
KPLT .... Paris, TX [*AM radio station call letters*]
KPLT-FM ..... Paris, TX [*FM radio station call letters*]
KPLU .... Tacoma, WA [*FM radio station call letters*]
KPLV .... Port Lavaca, TX [*FM radio station call letters*]
KPLW-FM .... Wenatchee, WA [*FM radio station call letters*] (RBYB)
KPLX .... Fort Worth, TX [*FM radio station call letters*]
KPLY .... Sparks, NV [*AM radio station call letters*]
KPLZ .... Seattle, WA [*FM radio station call letters*]
KPM .... Kahler Process Model [*Computer science*]
KPM .... Kathode Pulse Modulation
KPM .... Kensington Palace Gardens [*British interrogation center*]
Kpm .... Kilopondmeter
KPM .... King's Police Medal
KPM .... Kronig-Penny Model
KPMB .... Pembina [*North Dakota*] [*ICAO location identifier*] (ICLI)
KPMD .... Palmdale/Air Force Plant No. 42 [*California*] [*ICAO location identifier*] (ICLI)
KPMG .... Klynveld Peat Marwick Goerdeler [*Commercial firm British*]
KPMI .... Kraner Preschool Math Inventory [*Educational test*]
KPMO .... Mendocino, CA [*AM radio station call letters*]
KPMW .... Hallimaile, HI [*FM radio station call letters*]
KPMX .... Sterling, CO [*FM radio station call letters*]
KPN .... Confederation for an Independent Poland (PD)
KPN .... Kipnuk [*Alaska*] [*Airport symbol*] (OAG)
KPN .... Kipnuk, AK [*Location identifier FAA*] (FAAL)
KPN .... Koninklijke PTT Nederland [*Post and telecommunications company*] (ECON)
KPN .... KPN [*NYSE symbol*] (SAG)

KPN .... Kupiano [*Papua New Guinea*] [*Seismograph station code, US Geological Survey*] (SEIS)
KPN .... Royal PTT Nederland ADS [*NYSE symbol*] (TTSB)
KPNC .... Ponca City [*Oklahoma*] [*ICAO location identifier*] (ICLI)
KPNC .... Ponca City, OK [*FM radio station call letters*]
KPND .... Sandpoint, ID [*FM radio station call letters*]
KPNE .... North Platte, NE [*Television station call letters*]
KPNE .... Philadelphia/North Philadelphia [*Pennsylvania*] [*ICAO location identifier*] (ICLI)
KPNE-FM .... North Platte, NE [*FM radio station call letters*]
KPNLF .... Khmer People's National Liberation Front [*Cambodia*] [*Political party*] (PD)
KPNO .... Kitt Peak National Observatory [*Tucson, AZ*] [*National Science Foundation*]
KPNO .... Norfolk, NE [*FM radio station call letters*]
KPNOB .... Kitt Peak National Observatory [*Tucson, AZ*]
KPNS .... Pensacola/Regional [*Florida*] [*ICAO location identifier*] (ICLI)
KPNT-FM .... Ste. Genevieve, MO [*FM radio station call letters*] (RBYB)
KPNW .... Eugene, OR [*AM radio station call letters*]
KPNX-TV ..... Mesa, AZ [*Television station call letters*]
KPNY .... Alliance, NE [*FM radio station call letters*]
KPO .... Keypunch Operator [*Computer science*]
KPO .... King Pin Offset [*Automotive engineering*]
KPO .... Kitt Peak National Observatory, Tucson, AZ [*OCLC symbol*] (OCLC)
KPO .... Kommunistische Partei Oesterreichs [*Communist Party of Austria*] [*Political party*] (PPW)
KPOA .... Lahaina, HI [*FM radio station call letters*]
KPOB .... Fayetteville/Pope Air Force Base [*North Carolina*] [*ICAO location identifier*] (ICLI)
KPOB .... Poplar Bluff, MO [*Television station call letters*]
KPOC .... Key Prep on Campus [*Slang*]
KPOC .... Pocahontas, AR [*AM radio station call letters*]
KPOC-FM .... Pocahontas, AR [*FM radio station call letters*]
KPOD .... Crescent City, CA [*AM radio station call letters*]
KPOD-FM .... Crescent North, CA [*FM radio station call letters*]
KPOF .... Denver, CO [*AM radio station call letters*]
KPOI .... Honolulu, HI [*FM radio station call letters*]
KPOK .... Bowman, ND [*AM radio station call letters*]
KPOM .... Fort Smith, AR [*Television station call letters*]
KPOO .... San Francisco, CA [*FM radio station call letters*]
KPOP .... San Diego, CA [*AM radio station call letters*]
KPOS .... Post, TX [*AM radio station call letters*]
KPOS-FM .... Post, TX [*FM radio station call letters*]
KPOW .... Powell, WY [*AM radio station call letters*]
KPOWU .... Kenya Petroleum and Oil Workers' Union
KPP .... Kaneb Pipeline Partnership LP [*NYSE symbol*] (SPSG)
KPP .... Kaneb Pipe Line PtnrsL.P. [*NYSE symbol*] (TTSB)
KPP .... Keeper of the Privy Purse [*British*]
KPP .... Komunistyczna Partia Polski [*Communist Party of Poland (1925-1938)*] [*Political party*] (PPE)
KPPC .... Pasadena, CA [*AM radio station call letters*]
KPPL .... Colusa, CA [*AM radio station call letters*]
KPPR .... Williston, ND [*FM radio station call letters*]
KPPS .... Kilopackets per Second [*Telecommunications*]
kpps .... Kilopulses per Second
KPPV .... Prescott Valley, AZ [*FM radio station call letters*]
KPQ .... Wenatchee, WA [*AM radio station call letters*]
KPQ-FM ...... Wenatchee, WA [*FM radio station call letters*]
KPQI .... Presque Isle/Presque Isle [*Maine*] [*ICAO location identifier*] (ICLI)
KPQX .... Havre, MT [*FM radio station call letters*]
KPR .... Keeper (ABBR)
KPR .... Key Pulse Rate [*Cardiology*] (DAVI)
KPR .... Keypunch Replacement [*Computer science*] (MHDI)
KPR .... Knight of Polonia Restituta [*British*]
KPR .... Knots per Revolution
KPR .... Kodak Photo Resist
KPR .... Krasnaya Polyana [*Former USSR Seismograph station code, US Geological Survey Closed*] (SEIS)
KPR .... Kuder Preference Record [*Psychology*] (DAVI)
KPR .... Port Williams [*Alaska*] [*Airport symbol*] (OAG)
KPR .... Port Williams, AK [*Location identifier FAA*] (FAAL)
KPRA .... Ukiah, CA [*FM radio station call letters*]
KPRC .... Houston, TX [*AM radio station call letters*]
KPRC-TV ..... Houston, TX [*Television station call letters*]
KPRD .... Hays, KS [*FM radio station call letters*] (RBYB)
KPRD .... KSC [*Kennedy Space Center*] Program Requirements Document [*NASA*] (NASA)
KPRE .... Vail, CO [*FM radio station call letters*] (RBYB)
KPRG .... Agana, GU [*FM radio station call letters*] (RBYB)
KPRI .... Fagaitua, AS [*FM radio station call letters*] (RBYB)
KPRJ .... Jamestown, ND [*FM radio station call letters*]
KPRK .... Livingston, MT [*AM radio station call letters*]
KPRL .... Paso Robles, CA [*AM radio station call letters*]
KPRM .... Park Rapids, MN [*AM radio station call letters*]
KPRN .... Grand Junction, CO [*FM radio station call letters*]
KPRO .... Riverside, CA [*AM radio station call letters*]
KPRP .... Kampuchean [*or Khmer*] People's Revolutionary Party [*Political party*] (PD)
KPR-P .... Kuder Preference Record - Personal [*Psychology*]
KPRQ .... Price, UT [*FM radio station call letters*]
KPRR .... El Paso, TX [*FM radio station call letters*]
KPRS .... Kansas City, MO [*FM radio station call letters*]
KPRT .... Kansas City, MO [*AM radio station call letters*]
KPRV .... Heavener, OK [*FM radio station call letters*]
KPR-V .... Kuder Preference Record - Vocational [*Psychology*] (DAVI)

KPRV .... Poteau, OK [*AM radio station call letters*]
KPRW-FM .... Perham, MN [*FM radio station call letters*] (RBYB)
KPRX .... Bakersfield, CA [*FM radio station call letters*]
KPRY .... Pierre, SD [*Television station call letters*]
KPRZ .... San Marcos, CA [*AM radio station call letters*]
KPRZ-FM ...... Fountain, CO [*FM radio station call letters*] (RBYB)
KPS .... Kempsey [*Australia Airport symbol*] (OAG)
KPS .... Keypunch Performance System [*Computer science*] (PDAA)
KPS .... Kilometers per Second [*NASA*]
KPS .... Kirbati Philatelic Society (EA)
KPS .... Klystron Power Supply
KPS .... Knight of the (Order of the) Polar Star [*Sweden*] (ROG)
KPS .... Knowledge Processing System [*Expert system shell*] (NITA)
KPS .... Kommunistische Partei der Schweiz [*Communist Party of Switzerland*] [*Political party*] (PPE)
KPS .... Kommunistische Partij Suriname [*Communist Party of Surinam*] [*Political party*] (PPW)
KPS .... One Thousand Pulses per Second (KSC)
KPSA ...... Alamogordo, NM [*AM radio station call letters*]
KPSA ...... La Luz, NM [*FM radio station call letters*]
KPSC ...... Palm Springs, CA [*FM radio station call letters*]
KPSD ...... Faith, SD [*FM radio station call letters*]
KPSD-TV ...... Eagle Butte, SD [*Television station call letters*]
KPSI ...... Kip [*Thousands of Pounds*] per Square Inch
KPSI ...... Palm Springs, CA [*AM radio station call letters*]
KPSI-FM ...... Palm Springs, CA [*FM radio station call letters*]
KPSK ...... Keepsake (ABBR)
KPSL ...... Thousand Palms, CA [*AM radio station call letters*]
KPSM ...... Brownwood, TX [*FM radio station call letters*]
KPSM ...... Klystron Power Supply Modulator
KPSM ...... Portsmouth/Pease Air Force Base [*New Hampshire*] [*ICAO location identifier*] (ICLI)
KPSNSW ...... Koala Preservation Society of New South Wales [*Australia*]
KPSO ...... Falfurrias, TX [*AM radio station call letters*]
KPSO-FM ...... Falfurrias, TX [*FM radio station call letters*]
KPSQ ...... Kapson Senior Quarters Corp. [*NASDAQ symbol*] (SAG)
KPSS .... Kommunisticheskaya Partiya Sovietskogo Soyuza [*Communist Party of the Soviet Union*] [*Political party*]
KPST ...... Vallejo, CA [*Television station call letters*]
KPSU ...... Goodwell, OK [*FM radio station call letters*]
KPSX ...... Palacios [*Texas*] [*ICAO location identifier*] (ICLI)
KPT .... Kaena Point Station [*Hawaii*] [*Military*]
KPT .... Kai's Power Tools for Windows [*HSC Software*] (PCM)
KPT .... Karpatair [*Hungary ICAO designator*] (FAAC)
KPT .... Keeprite, Inc. [*Toronto Stock Exchange symbol*]
KPT .... Kidney Punch Test [*or Murphy's test*] (DAVI)
KPT .... Kuder Performance Test [*Psychology*] (DAVI)
KPT .... Pittsburg State University, Pittsburg, KS [*Library symbol Library of Congress*] (LCLS)
KPT3 ...... Kai's Power Tools [*Computer science*]
KPTB ...... Lubbock, TX [*Television station call letters*] (RBYB)
KPTI ...... Kunitz Pancreatic Trypsin Inhibitor [*Medicine*] (MAE)
KPTL ...... Carson City, NV [*AM radio station call letters*]
KPTM ...... Omaha, NE [*Television station call letters*]
KPTS ...... Hutchinson, KS [*Television station call letters*]
KPTT ...... Kaolin Partial Thromboplastin Time [*Clinical chemistry*] (MAE)
KPTV ...... Portland, OR [*Television station call letters*]
KPTX ...... Pecos, TX [*FM radio station call letters*]
KPU .... Kaneb Pipe Line Partners LP [*NYSE symbol*] (SAG)
KPU .... Kaneb Pipe Ln Ptnrs LP Pref Ut [*NYSE symbol*] (TTSB)
KPU .... Khapalu [*Pakistan*] [*Airport symbol*] (AD)
KPU .... Kommunisticheskaia Partiia Ukrainy [*Communist Party of the Ukraine*] [*Political party*]
KPUA ...... Hilo, HI [*AM radio station call letters*]
KPUB ...... Pueblo Memorial [*Colorado*] [*ICAO location identifier*] (ICLI)
KPUC ...... Korean Presidential Unit Citation [*Military award*]
KPUG ...... Bellingham, WA [*AM radio station call letters*]
KPUP ...... Key Personnel Upgrade Program [*National Guard*]
KPUR ...... Amarillo, TX [*AM radio station call letters*]
KPUR-FM ...... Canyon, TX [*FM radio station call letters*]
KPUZ ...... Kommunisticheskaia Partiia Uzbekistana [*Communist Party of Uzbekistan*] [*Political party*]
KPV .... Kid-Powered Vehicle
KPV .... Killed Parenteral Vaccine [*Immunology*] (DAVI)
KPVD ...... Providence/Theodore Francis Greene State [*Rhode Island*] [*ICAO location identifier*] (ICLI)
KPV HMG .... Krupnokalibernyi Pulemyoy Vladimirova Heavy Machine Gun [*Soviet-made weaponry used extensively by the People's Army of North Vietnam*] (VNW)
KPVI ...... Pocatello, ID [*Television station call letters*]
KPVS ...... Hilo, HI [*FM radio station call letters*]
KPVU ...... Prairie View, TX [*FM radio station call letters*]
KPVY ...... Amarillo, TX [*FM radio station call letters*]
KPWA ...... Korean Patriotic Women's Association in America [*Defunct*] (EA)
KPWB ...... Piedmont, MO [*AM radio station call letters*]
KPWB-FM ...... Piedmont, MO [*FM radio station call letters*]
KPWB-TV ...... Sacramento, CA [*Television station call letters*] (RBYB)
KPWM ...... Portland/International Jetport [*Maine*] [*ICAO location identifier*] (ICLI)
KPWR ...... Los Angeles, CA [*FM radio station call letters*]
KPWS ...... Crowley, LA [*AM radio station call letters*]
KPXA ...... Sisters, OR [*FM radio station call letters*]
KPXC ...... Indian Springs, NV [*FM radio station call letters*]
KPXE ...... Liberty, TX [*AM radio station call letters*]
KPXF ...... Lacombe, LA [*FM radio station call letters*]
KPXH ...... Garapan-Saipan, MP [*FM radio station call letters*]

KPXI ...... Mount Pleasant, TX [*FM radio station call letters*]
KPXP ...... Garapan-Saipan, MP [*FM radio station call letters*]
KPXQ-AM ...... Phoenix, AZ [*AM radio station call letters*] (RBYB)
KPY .... Port Bailey [*Alaska*] [*Airport symbol*] (OAG)
KPY .... Port Bailey, AK [*Location identifier FAA*] (FAAL)
KPYK ...... Terrell, TX [*AM radio station call letters*]
KPYN ...... Atlanta, TX [*FM radio station call letters*]
KPZA ...... Espanola, NM [*FM radio station call letters*] (RBYB)
KQ .... Air South, Inc. [*Airline code*]
KQ .... Kenya Airways [*ICAO designator*] (AD)
KQ .... Kenya Airways [*Airline flight code*] (ODBW)
KQ .... Line Squall [*Meteorology*] (WDAA)
KQA ...... Akutan [*Alaska*] [*Airport symbol*] (OAG)
KQA ...... Akutan, AK [*Location identifier FAA*] (FAAL)
KQA ...... Kenya Airways Ltd. [*ICAO designator*] (FAAC)
KQAA ...... Aberdeen, SD [*AM radio station call letters*]
KQAC ...... Amarillo, TX [*FM radio station call letters*]
KQAD ...... Luverne, MN [*AM radio station call letters*]
KQAK ...... Bend, OR [*FM radio station call letters*]
KQAL ...... Winona, MN [*FM radio station call letters*]
KQAM ...... Wichita, KS [*AM radio station call letters*]
KQAY ...... Tucumcari, NM [*FM radio station call letters*]
KQAZ ...... Springerville-Eager, AZ [*FM radio station call letters*]
KQBE ...... Ellensburg, WA [*FM radio station call letters*]
KQBR ...... Davis, CA [*FM radio station call letters*]
KQC .... King's College London [*British*] (IRUK)
KQCA ...... Stockton, CA [*Television station call letters*] (RBYB)
KQCD ...... Dickinson, ND [*Television station call letters*]
KQCL ...... Faribault, MN [*FM radio station call letters*]
KQCP ...... King's and Queen's College of Physicians [*Ireland*]
KQCT ...... Davenport, IA [*Television station call letters*]
KQCV ...... Oklahoma City, OK [*AM radio station call letters*]
KQDI-FM ...... Great Falls, MT [*FM radio station call letters*]
KQDJ ...... Jamestown, ND [*AM radio station call letters*]
KQDJ-FM ...... Valley City, ND [*FM radio station call letters*] (RBYB)
KQDS ...... Duluth, MN [*AM radio station call letters*]
KQDS-FM ...... Duluth, MN [*FM radio station call letters*]
KQDY ...... Bismarck, ND [*FM radio station call letters*]
KQED ...... San Francisco, CA [*FM radio station call letters*]
KQED-TV ...... San Francisco, CA [*Television station call letters*]
KQEG ...... La Crescent, MN [*FM radio station call letters*]
KQEN ...... Roseburg, OR [*AM radio station call letters*]
KQEP ...... Rock Valley, IA [*FM radio station call letters*]
KQEQ ...... Fowler, CA [*AM radio station call letters*] (RBYB)
KQEW ...... Fordyce, AR [*FM radio station call letters*]
KQEX ...... Fortuna, CA [*FM radio station call letters*]
KQF .... Krupp Quick-Firing Gun
KQFC ...... Boise, ID [*FM radio station call letters*]
KQFE ...... Springfield, OR [*FM radio station call letters*]
KQFM ...... Hermiston, OR [*FM radio station call letters*]
KQFN ...... Fargo, ND [*AM radio station call letters*] (RBYB)
KQFX ...... Borger, TX [*FM radio station call letters*]
KQHC-FM ...... Burns, OR [*FM radio station call letters*] (RBYB)
KQHN ...... Nederland, TX [*AM radio station call letters*]
KQHT ...... Crookston, MN [*FM radio station call letters*]
KQIC ...... Willmar, MN [*FM radio station call letters*]
KQID ...... Alexandria, LA [*FM radio station call letters*]
KQIK ...... Lakeview, OR [*AM radio station call letters*]
KQIK-FM ...... Lakeview, OR [*FM radio station call letters*]
KQIL ...... Grand Junction, CO [*AM radio station call letters*]
KQIP ...... Odessa, TX [*FM radio station call letters*]
KQIX ...... Grand Junction, CO [*FM radio station call letters*]
KQIZ ...... Amarillo, TX [*FM radio station call letters*]
KQJM ...... King, Queen, Jack Meld [*Canasta*]
KQKD ...... Redfield, SD [*AM radio station call letters*]
KQKD-FM ...... Redfield, SD [*FM radio station call letters*]
KQKI ...... Bayou Vista, LA [*FM radio station call letters*]
KQKQ ...... Council Bluffs, IA [*FM radio station call letters*]
KQKS ...... Longmont, CO [*FM radio station call letters*]
KQKY ...... Kearney, NE [*FM radio station call letters*]
KQL .... Kol [*Papua New Guinea*] [*Airport symbol*] (OAG)
KQLA ...... Ogden, KS [*FM radio station call letters*]
KQLB ...... Los Banos, CA [*FM radio station call letters*]
KQLL ...... Owasso, OK [*FM radio station call letters*]
KQLL ...... Tulsa, OK [*AM radio station call letters*]
KQLM-FM ...... Odessa, TX [*FM radio station call letters*] (RBYB)
KQLO ...... Reno, NV [*AM radio station call letters*]
KQLS ...... Colby, KS [*FM radio station call letters*]
KQLT ...... Casper, WY [*FM radio station call letters*]
KQLX ...... Lisbon, ND [*AM radio station call letters*]
KQLX-FM ...... Lisbon, ND [*FM radio station call letters*]
KQM .... Kolson Quick Modality Test [*Education*]
KQMA ...... Phillipsburg, KS [*FM radio station call letters*]
KQMB-FM ...... Midvale, UT [*FM radio station call letters*] (RBYB)
KQMC ...... Brinkley, AR [*FM radio station call letters*]
KQMG ...... Independence, IA [*AM radio station call letters*]
KQMG-FM ...... Independence, IA [*FM radio station call letters*]
KQML ...... Knowledge Query and Manipulation Language [*Computer science*]
KQMN ...... Thief River Falls, MN [*FM radio station call letters*]
KQMO-FM ...... Ash Grove, MO [*FM radio station call letters*] (RBYB)
KQMQ ...... Honolulu, HI [*AM radio station call letters*]
KQMQ-FM ...... Honolulu, HI [*FM radio station call letters*]
KQMS ...... Redding, CA [*AM radio station call letters*]
KQMX-FM ...... Clinton, OK [*FM radio station call letters*] (RBYB)
KQNA ...... Prescott Valley, AZ [*AM radio station call letters*]

KQNC .... Quincy, CA [FM radio station call letters]
KQNG .... Lihue, HI [AM radio station call letters]
KQNG-FM .... Lihue, HI [FM radio station call letters]
KQNK .... Norton, KS [AM radio station call letters]
KQNK-FM.... Norton, KS [FM radio station call letters]
KQNN .... Alice, TX [FM radio station call letters]
KQNS .... Lindsborg, KS [FM radio station call letters]
KQNV .... Sparks, NV [FM radio station call letters] (RBYB)
KQOD .... Stockton, CA [FM radio station call letters]
KQOL .... Boulder City, NV [FM radio station call letters] (RBYB)
KQPM .... Ukiah, CA [FM radio station call letters]
KQPR .... Albert Lea, MN [FM radio station call letters]
KQPT .... Sacramento, CA [FM radio station call letters]
KQQK .... Galveston, TX [FM radio station call letters]
KQQL .... Anoka, MN [FM radio station call letters]
KQQQ .... Pullman, WA [AM radio station call letters]
KQR .... Cobequid Resources Ltd. [Vancouver Stock Exchange symbol]
KQR .... Kit Quotation Request (MCD)
KQRC-FM .... Leavenworth, KS [FM radio station call letters]
KQRK .... Ronan, MT [FM radio station call letters]
KQRN .... Mitchell, SD [FM radio station call letters]
KQRS .... Golden Valley, MN [AM radio station call letters]
KQRS-FM.... Golden Valley, MN [FM radio station call letters]
KQRX .... Midland, TX [FM radio station call letters]
KQSB .... Santa Barbara, CA [AM radio station call letters]
KQSC .... Willows, CA [FM radio station call letters]
KQSD .... Lowry, SD [Television station call letters]
KQSK .... Chadron, NE [FM radio station call letters]
KQSS .... Miami, AZ [FM radio station call letters]
KQST .... Sedona, AZ [FM radio station call letters]
KQSW .... Rock Springs, WY [FM radio station call letters]
KQSY .... Nowata, OK [FM radio station call letters] (RBYB)
KQT .... Konkordanz zu den Qumrantexten [A publication] (BJA)
KQTL .... Sahuarita, AZ [AM radio station call letters]
KQTP .... St. Marys, KS [FM radio station call letters]
KQTV .... St. Joseph, MO [Television station call letters]
KQTY .... Borger, TX [AM radio station call letters]
KQTZ .... Hobart, OK [FM radio station call letters]
KQUA .... Lutesville, MO [FM radio station call letters]
KQUE .... Houston, TX [FM radio station call letters]
KQUL .... Lake Ozark, MO [FM radio station call letters]
KQUS .... Hot Springs, AR [FM radio station call letters]
KQUY .... Butte, MT [FM radio station call letters]
KQV .... Pittsburgh, PA [AM radio station call letters]
KQVO .... Calexico, CA [FM radio station call letters]
KQWB .... Moorhead, MN [FM radio station call letters]
KQWC .... Webster City, IA [AM radio station call letters]
KQWC-FM.... Webster City, IA [FM radio station call letters]
KQXC .... Wichita Falls, TX [FM radio station call letters]
KQXI .... Aruada, CO [AM radio station call letters]
KQXL .... New Roads, LA [FM radio station call letters]
KQXR .... Payette, ID [FM radio station call letters] (RBYB)
KQXT .... San Antonio, TX [FM radio station call letters]
KQXX .... McAllen, TX [FM radio station call letters]
KQXY .... Beaumont, TX [FM radio station call letters]
KQYB .... Spring Grove, MN [FM radio station call letters]
KQYN .... Twentynine Palms, CA [FM radio station call letters]
KQYX .... Joplin, MO [AM radio station call letters]
KQZE .... St. Johns, AZ [FM radio station call letters]
KQZZ-FM ..... Devils Lake, ND [FM radio station call letters] (RBYB)
KR .... Contractor [Navy]
KR .... Kallah Rabbati (BJA)
KR .... Kar-Air [ICAO designator] (AD)
KR .... Karat (ABBR)
KR .... Keesom Relationship
K-R .... Kent-Rosanoff Free Association Test [Psychology]
KR .... Kenya Railways
KR .... Ketoaldonate Reductase [An enzyme]
KR .... Ketoreductase [An enzyme]
KR .... Keying Relay
KR .... Key Records [Record label]
KR .... Key Register
KR .... Khmer Rouge (BARN)
kR .... Kilorayleigh
kR .... Kiloroentgen
KR .... Kinetic Reaction
KR .... King's Regiment [Military unit] [British]
KR .... King's Regulations for the Army and the Army Reserves [British]
KR .... King's Remembrancer [British]
KR .... King's Rook [Chess]
KR .... Kipp Relay
KR .... Kirkus Review [A publication] (BRI)
KR .... Knight of the [Order of the] Redeemer [Greece]
KR .... Knight-Ridder
KR .... Knowledge of Results
KR .... Knowledge Representation [Computer science]
KR .... Koloniale Rundschau (BJA)
KR .... Kopper Reppart [Medium] [Biochemistry] (DAVI)
KR .... Kreuzer [Monetary unit] [German]
KR .... Kroger Co. [NYSE symbol] (TTSB)
KR .... Krona [Crown] [Monetary unit Iceland, Sweden] (EY)
KR .... Krone [Crown] [Monetary unit Denmark, Norway] (EY)
K-R .... Krueger-Ringier [Book manufacturer]
Kr .... Krypton [Chemical element]
K-R .... Kuder-Richardson Formula [Education] (AEE)

KR .... Republic of Korea [ANSI two-letter standard code] (CNC)
KRA .... Contractor Responsible Action (MCD)
KRA .... Karenni Revolutionary Army [Myanmar] [Political party] (EY)
KRA .... Kerang [Victoria, Australia] [Airport symbol] (AD)
KRA .... Key Result Area
KRA .... Kickback Racket Act
KRA .... Klinefelter-Reifenstein-Albright [Syndrome] [Medicine] (DAVI)
KRA .... Krakow [Poland] [Seismograph station code, US Geological Survey] (SEIS)
KRAB .... Greenacres, CA [FM radio station call letters]
KRAD .... Kilorad (WDAA)
KRAD .... Portland, TX [FM radio station call letters]
KRAE .... Cheyenne, WY [AM radio station call letters]
KRAF .... Holdenville, OK [AM radio station call letters]
KRAG-JORG... Krag-Jorgensen Rifle
KRAI .... Craig, CO [AM radio station call letters]
KRAI-FM .... Craig, CO [FM radio station call letters]
KR Air .... King's Regulations and Orders for the Royal Canadian Air Force
KRAJ .... Johannesburg, CA [FM radio station call letters]
KRAK-FM ...... Sacramento, CA [FM radio station call letters]
KRAL .... Rawlins, WY [AM radio station call letters]
KRAM .... St. Louis, MO [AM radio station call letters] (RBYB)
KRAN .... Krantor Corp. [NASDAQ symbol] (SAG)
KR & ACI ...... King's Regulations and Air Council Instructions [British military] (DMA)
KR & AI .... King's Regulations and Admiralty Instructions [Navy British]
KR & O (Can)... King's Regulations and Orders for the Royal Canadian Army
Krantor .... Krantor Corp. [Associated Press] (SAG)
Krantr .... Krantor Corp. [Associated Press] (SAG)
KRANW .... Krantor Corp.Wrrt'A' [NASDAQ symbol] (TTSB)
Kranzc .... Kranzco Realty Trust [Associated Press] (SAG)
KRAO .... Colfax, WA [FM radio station call letters]
KRAQ .... Jackson, MN [FM radio station call letters]
KRAS .... Keyworded References to Archaeological Science [Department of Archaeology] [University of Leicester British] [Database] (NITA)
Krause .... Krauses Furniture, Inc. [Associated Press] (SAG)
KrauseF .... Krauses Furniture, Inc. [Associated Press] (SAG)
KRAV .... Tulsa, OK [FM radio station call letters]
KRAY .... Salinas, CA [FM radio station call letters]
KRAZ .... Sutter Creek, CA [FM radio station call letters]
KRB .... Kansas River Basin
KRB .... Kariba [Zimbabwe] [Seismograph station code, US Geological Survey Closed] (SEIS)
KRB .... Karumba [Australia Airport symbol] (OAG)
KRB .... Krebs-Ringer-Bicarbonate [Buffer solution]
KRB .... Krebs-Ringer Bicarbonate Buffer [Biochemistry] (DAVI)
KRB .... MBNA Corp. [NYSE symbol] (SPSG)
KRBA .... Lufkin, TX [AM radio station call letters]
KRBB .... Krebs-Ringer Bicarbonate Buffer [Biochemistry] (DAVI)
KRBB .... Wichita, KS [FM radio station call letters]
KRBC .... Abilene, TX [Television station call letters]
KRBD .... Ketchikan, AK [FM radio station call letters]
KRBE .... Houston, TX [FM radio station call letters]
KRBF .... Bonners Ferry, ID [FM radio station call letters]
KRBFC .... Kenny Roberts and Bettyanne Fan Club [Defunct] (EA)
KRBG .... Canadian, TX [FM radio station call letters]
KRBG .... Krebs-Ringer Bicarbonate Buffer [Containing] Glucose (DAVI)
KRBG .... Krebs-Ringer Bicarbonate Buffer with Glucose [Medicine] (DMAA)
KRB-GA .... Krebs-Ringer-Bicarbonate Glucose-Albumin [Buffer solution]
KRBH-FM....... Hondo, TX [FM radio station call letters] (RBYB)
KRBI .... St. Peter, MN [AM radio station call letters]
KRBI-FM .... St. Peter, MN [FM radio station call letters]
KRBL .... Idalou, TX [FM radio station call letters] (RBYB)
KRBM .... Pendleton, OR [FM radio station call letters]
KRBN .... Boston [Massachusetts] [ICAO location identifier] (ICLI)
KRBO .... Las Vegas, NV [FM radio station call letters]
KRBPrA .... MBNA Corp.7.50% Sr'A'Pfd [NYSE symbol] (TTSB)
KRBR-FM ...... Superior, WI [FM radio station call letters] (RBYB)
KRBS .... Krebs-Ringer Bicarbonate Solution
KRBSG .... Krebs-Ringer Bicarbonate Solution with Glucose
KRBT .... Fresno, CA [FM radio station call letters]
KRBV .... Dallas, TX [FM radio station call letters] (RBYB)
KRBZ .... Reedsport, OR [FM radio station call letters]
KRC .... Keweenaw Research Center [Houghton, MI] [Army Research center] (GRD)
KRC .... King Ranch [California] [Seismograph station code, US Geological Survey Closed] (SEIS)
KRC .... Knight of the Red Cross [Freemasonry]
KRC .... Knowledge Resource Center [Computer-based information delivery system in libraries] [Generic term]
KRC .... Kodak Reflex Camera
KRC .... Regis College Library, University of Toronto [UTLAS symbol]
KRCA .... Rapid City/Ellsworth Air Force Base [South Dakota] [ICAO location identifier] (ICLI)
KRCA .... Riverside, CA [Television station call letters]
KRCB .... Santa Rosa, CA [FM radio station call letters]
KRCB-TV...... Cotati, CA [Television station call letters]
KRCC .... Colorado Springs, CO [FM radio station call letters]
KRCC .... Kingston Regional Cancer Center [Canada] (PDAA)
KRCD .... Chubbuck, ID [AM radio edition call letters]
KRCG .... Jefferson City, MO [Television station call letters]
KRCH .... Rochester, MN [FM radio station call letters]
KRCHF .... Kerchief (ABBR)
KRCI .... Avalon, CA [FM radio station call letters]
KRCK .... Burbank, CA [AM radio station call letters]

KRCL	Salt Lake City, UT [*FM radio station call letters*]
KRCN	King's Regulations and Orders for the Royal Canadian Navy
KRCO	Prineville, OR [*AM radio station call letters*]
KRCQ	Detroit Lakes, MN [*FM radio station call letters*] (RBYB)
KRCR	Redding, CA [*Television station call letters*]
KRCRA	Known Recoverable Coal Resource Area (PDAA)
KRCS	Sturgis, SD [*FM radio station call letters*]
KRCU	Cape Girardeau, MO [*FM radio station call letters*]
KRCW	Royal City, WA [*FM radio station call letters*]
KRCX	Roseville, CA [*AM radio station call letters*]
KRCY	Kingman, AZ [*FM radio station call letters*]
KRD	Kourday [*Former USSR Seismograph station code, US Geological Survey Closed*] (SEIS)
KRD	Krieger Data International Corp. [*Vancouver Stock Exchange symbol*]
KRDC	St. George, UT [*FM radio station call letters*]
KRDD	Roswell, NM [*AM radio station call letters*]
KRDE	Denver [*Colorado*] [*ICAO location identifier*] (ICLI)
KRDF	Spearman, TX [*FM radio station call letters*]
KRDG	Redding, CA [*AM radio station call letters*]
KRDO	Colorado Springs, CO [*AM radio station call letters*]
KRDO-FM	Colorado Springs, CO [*FM radio station call letters*]
KRDO-TV	Colorado Springs, CO [*Television station call letters*]
KRDR	Red River/Grand Forks Air Force Base [*North Dakota*] [*ICAO location identifier*] (ICLI)
KRDS	Tolleson, AZ [*AM radio station call letters*]
KRDS	Wickenburg, AZ [*FM radio station call letters*]
KRDU	Dinuba, CA [*AM radio station call letters*]
KRDU	Raleigh/Raleigh-Durham [*North Carolina*] [*ICAO location identifier*] (ICLI)
KRDZ	Wray, CO [*AM radio station call letters*]
KRE	Aerosucre, SA [*Colombia*] [*FAA designator*] (FAAC)
KRE	Capital Re [*NYSE symbol*] (TTSB)
KRE	Capital Real Estate [*NYSE symbol*] (SPSG)
KRE	Capital Re Corporation1 [*NYSE symbol*] (SAG)
KRE	Consolidated Regal Resources Ltd. [*Vancouver Stock Exchange symbol*]
KRE	Knight of the Red Eagle [*Prussia*]
KRE	Kure [*Japan*] [*Seismograph station code, US Geological Survey Closed*] (SEIS)
KREA	Ontario, CA [*FM radio station call letters*]
KREB	Huntsville, AR [*FM radio station call letters*]
KREC	Brian Head, UT [*FM radio station call letters*]
KRED-FM	Eureka, CA [*FM radio station call letters*]
KREE	Lubbock/Reese Air Force Base [*Texas*] [*ICAO location identifier*] (ICLI)
KREEP	Potassium [*Chemical symbol: K*], Rare-Earth Elements, and Phosphorus [*Acronym used to describe crust material brought from the moon by astronauts*]
KREG	Glenwood Springs, CO [*Television station call letters*]
KREG	Koll Real Estate Group [*NASDAQ symbol*] (SAG)
KREG	Koll Real Estate Grp [*NASDAQ symbol*] (TTSB)
KREGP	Koll Real Estate Cv'A'Pfd [*NASDAQ symbol*] (TTSB)
KREH	Oakdale, LA [*AM radio station call letters*]
KREI	Farmington, MO [*AM radio station call letters*]
Kreislr	Kreisler Manufacturing Co. [*Associated Press*] (SAG)
KREJ	Medicine Lodge, KS [*FM radio station call letters*]
KREK	Bristow, OK [*FM radio station call letters*]
KREL	California, MO [*AM radio station call letters*] (RBYB)
KREM	Spokane, WA [*Television station call letters*]
KREMS	Kiernan Reentry Measurement Site
KREMU	Kenya Rangeland Ecological Monitoring Unit
KREN	Kings Road Entertainment, Inc. [*NASDAQ symbol*] (NQ)
KREN	Kings Road Entmt [*NASDAQ symbol*] (TTSB)
KREN	Reno, NV [*Television station call letters*]
KREP	Belleville, KS [*FM radio station call letters*]
KREPrL	Capital Re LLC'MIPS' [*NYSE symbol*] (TTSB)
KRES	Moberly, MO [*FM radio station call letters*]
KRESS	Kinetic Ring Energy Storage System
Kress	Kress' Reports [*2-12 Pennsylvania Superior Court*] [*166-194 Pennsylvania*] [*A publication*] (DLA)
KREU-FM	Roland, OK [*FM radio station call letters*] (RBYB)
KREUZ	Kreuzer [*Monetary unit*] [*German*] (ROG)
KREV	Lakeville, MN [*FM radio station call letters*]
KREW	Sunnyside, WA [*AM radio station call letters*]
KREW-FM	Sunnyside, WA [*FM radio station call letters*]
KREX	Grand Junction, CO [*Television station call letters*]
KREX	Keel Blade Tip Reflex [*Botany*]
KREY	Montrose, CO [*Television station call letters*]
KREZ	Durango, CO [*Television station call letters*]
KRF	Kathode Ray Furnace
KRF	Kerf Petroleums [*Vancouver Stock Exchange symbol*]
KRF	Knowledge of Results Feedback
KRF	Kramfors [*Sweden*] [*Airport symbol*] (OAG)
KrF	Kristelig Folkpartiet [*Christian People's Party*] [*Norway Political party*] (PPE)
KrF	Kristeligt Folkeparti [*Christian People's Party*] [*Denmark Political party*] (PPE)
KRF	No. 32 (The Royal) Squadron [*British*] [*FAA designator*] (FAAC)
KRFA	Moscow, ID [*FM radio station call letters*]
KRFC	KISS [*Knights in the Service of Satan*] Rocks Fan Club (EA)
KRFE	Lubbock, TX [*AM radio station call letters*] (RBYB)
KRFM..........	Show Low, AZ [*FM radio station call letters*]
KRFN	Knight-Ridder Financial News [*Database*] (IT)
KRFO	Owatonna, MN [*AM radio station call letters*]
KRFO-FM	Owatonna, MN [*FM radio station call letters*]

KRFS	Superior, NE [*AM radio station call letters*]
KRFS-FM	Superior, NE [*FM radio station call letters*]
KRFT	Knowledge of Results Feedback Task (SAA)
KRFW	Fort Worth [*Texas*] [*ICAO location identifier*] (ICLI)
KRFX	Denver, CO [*FM radio station call letters*]
KRG	Karasabai [*Guyana*] [*Airport symbol*] (OAG)
KRG	Kerema [*Papua New Guinea*] [*Seismograph station code, US Geological Survey Closed*] (SEIS)
KRG	Knight of the Redeemer of Greece (ROG)
KRG	Krebs-Ringer-Glucose [*Buffer solution and growth medium*]
KRG	KRG Management, Inc. [*Toronto Stock Exchange symbol*]
KrG	Kriegsgericht [*War Tribunal*] [*German*]
KRG	Krug International Corp. [*AMEX symbol*] (SAG)
KRG	Quantum Restaurant Group, Inc. [*NYSE symbol*] (SPSG)
KRGC	Chicago [*Illinois*] [*ICAO location identifier*] (ICLI)
KRGE	Weslaco, TX [*AM radio station call letters*]
KRGI	Grand Island, NE [*AM radio station call letters*]
KRGI-FM	Grand Island, NE [*FM radio station call letters*]
KRGN	Amarillo, TX [*FM radio station call letters*]
KRGO	Fowler, CA [*AM radio station call letters*]
KRGQ	West Valley City, UT [*AM radio station call letters*]
KRGQ-FM	Roy, UT [*FM radio station call letters*]
KRGS	Rifle, CO [*AM radio station call letters*]
KRGV	Weslaco, TX [*Television station call letters*]
KRH	Redhill [*England*] [*Airport symbol*]
KRHCF	Rich Coast Res Ltd [*NASDAQ symbol*] (TTSB)
KRHCF	Rich Coast Resouces [*NASDAQ symbol*] (SAG)
KRHD	Duncan, OK [*AM radio station call letters*]
KRHD-FM	Duncan, OK [*FM radio station call letters*]
KRHS	Overland, MO [*FM radio station call letters*]
KRHT-AM.....	Concord, CA [*AM radio station call letters*] (RBYB)
KRHV	Big Pine, CA [*FM radio station call letters*] (RBYB)
KRI	Karin Lake Explorations [*Vancouver Stock Exchange symbol*]
KRI	Kikori [*Papua New Guinea*] [*Airport symbol*] (OAG)
KRI	King Research, Inc. [*Computer consultant*] [*Information service or system*] (IID)
KRI	King's Royal Irish [*Military unit*] [*British*]
KRI	Knight-Ridder, Inc. [*NYSE symbol*] (SPSG)
KRI	Krilo [*Former USSR*] [*FAA designator*] (FAAC)
KRIB	Mason City, IA [*AM radio station call letters*]
KRIC	Rexburg, ID [*FM radio station call letters*]
KRIC	Richmond/Richard Evelyn Byrd International [*Virginia*] [*ICAO location identifier*] (ICLI)
KRIG	Nowata, OK [*FM radio station call letters*]
KRIG	Pawhuska, OK [*AM radio station call letters*] (RBYB)
KRIH	King's Royal Irish Hussars [*British military*] (DMA)
KRII	Knight-Ridder Information Inc.
KRIL	Odessa, TX [*AM radio station call letters*]
KRIM	Payson, AZ [*FM radio station call letters*]
KRIN	Waterloo, IA [*Television station call letters*]
KRIO	Floresville, TX [*FM radio station call letters*]
KRIO	McAllen, TX [*AM radio station call letters*]
KRIPES	K-Resolved Inverse Photoelectron Spectroscopy
KRIPO	Kriminalpolizei [*Ordinary Criminal Police*] [*German*]
KRIS	Corpus Christi, TX [*Television station call letters*]
KRISP	Kenya Rift International Seismic Project
KRIV	Houston, TX [*Television station call letters*]
KRIV	Riverside/March Air Force Base [*California*] [*ICAO location identifier*] (ICLI)
KRIZ	Renton, WA [*AM radio station call letters*]
KRJ	Kamimuroga [*Japan*] [*Seismograph station code, US Geological Survey*] (SEIS)
KRJB	Ada, MN [*FM radio station call letters*]
KRJC	Elko, NV [*FM radio station call letters*]
KRJT	Bowie, TX [*AM radio station call letters*]
KRJT-FM	Bowie, TX [*FM radio station call letters*]
KRK	Kirkenes [*Norway*] [*Seismograph station code, US Geological Survey Closed*] (SEIS)
KRK	Krakow [*Poland*] [*Airport symbol*] (OAG)
KRKC	Kansas City [*Missouri*] [*ICAO location identifier*] (ICLI)
KRKC	King City, CA [*AM radio station call letters*]
KRKC-FM	King City, CA [*FM radio station call letters*]
KRKE	Aspen, CO [*AM radio station call letters*]
KRKI	Estes Park, CO [*AM radio station call letters*]
KRKK	Rock Springs, WY [*AM radio station call letters*]
KRKL	Yountville, CA [*AM radio station call letters*]
KRKM	Kremmling, CO [*FM radio station call letters*]
KRKN	Eldon, IA (RBYB)
KRKN	Kraken (ABBR)
KRKO	Everett, WA [*AM radio station call letters*]
KRKQ-FM	Boone, IA [*FM radio station call letters*] (RBYB)
KRKR-FM	Roy, UT [*FM radio station call letters*] (RBYB)
KRKS	Boulder, CO [*FM radio station call letters*]
KRKS	Denver, CO [*AM radio station call letters*]
KRKT	Albany, OR [*AM radio station call letters*]
KRKT-FM	Albany, OR [*FM radio station call letters*]
KRKX	Billings, MT [*FM radio station call letters*]
KRKY	Granby, CO [*AM radio station call letters*]
KRKZ	Altus, OK [*FM radio station call letters*]
KRL	Karlsruhe [*Federal Republic of Germany*] [*Seismograph station code, US Geological Survey*] (SEIS)
KRL	Kathode Ray Lamp
KRL	Kingdom Resources Ltd. [*Vancouver Stock Exchange symbol*]
KRL	Kirchhoff Radiation Law [*Physics*]
KRL	Knowledge Representation Language

KRL............. Korla [China] [Airport symbol] (OAG)
KRL............. Kryla [Ukraine] [FAA designator] (FAAC)
KRLA .... Los Angeles [California] [ICAO location identifier] (ICLI)
KRLA .... Pasadena, CA [AM radio station call letters]
KRLB .... Lubbock, TX [FM radio station call letters]
KRLC .... Lewiston, ID [AM radio station call letters]
KRLD .... Dallas, TX [AM radio station call letters]
KRLF .... Pullman, WA [FM radio station call letters]
KRLI .... Malta Bend, MO [FM radio station call letters]
KRLK .... Cassville, MO [FM radio station call letters]
KRLN .... Canon City, CO [AM radio station call letters]
KRLN-FM .... Canon City, CO [FM radio station call letters]
KRLR .... Las Vegas, NV [Television station call letters]
KRLS .... Keweenaw Rocket Launch Site [University of Michigan]
KRLS .... Knoxville, IA [FM radio station call letters]
KRLT .... South Lake Tahoe, CA [FM radio station call letters]
KRLV .... Las Vegas, NV [AM radio station call letters] (RBYB)
KRLW .... Walnut Ridge, AR [AM radio station call letters]
KRLW-FM ... Walnut Ridge, AR [FM radio station call letters]
KRLX .... Northfield, MN [FM radio station call letters]
KRM............. Karma (ABBR)
KRM............. Klein-Rydberg Method [Physics]
KRM............. Kurmenty [Former USSR Seismograph station code, US Geological Survey] (SEIS)
KRM............. Kurzweil Reading Machine
KRM............. Royal Ontario Museum Library [UTLAS symbol]
KRMA .... Denver, CO [Television station call letters]
KRMB-FM .... Bisbee, AZ [FM radio station call letters] (RBYB)
KRMC .... Douglas, AZ [FM radio station call letters] (RBYB)
KRMC .... Karmic (ABBR)
KRMD .... Shreveport, LA [AM radio station call letters]
KRMD-FM ... Shreveport, LA [FM radio station call letters]
KRME .... Rome/Griffiss Air Force Base [New York] [ICAO location identifier] (ICLI)
KRME-FM ... Shafter, CA [FM radio station call letters] (RBYB)
KRMG .... Tulsa, OK [AM radio station call letters]
KRMJ-FM .... Grand Junction, CO [FM radio station call letters] (RBYB)
KRML .... Carmel, CA [FM radio station call letters]
KRMO .... Monett, MO [AM radio station call letters]
KRMS .... Osage Beach, MO [AM radio station call letters]
KRMT .... Denver, CO [Television station call letters] (RBYB)
KRMX .... Pueblo, CO [AM radio station call letters]
KRMY .... Kileen, TX [AM radio station call letters]
KRN .... Kiruna [Sweden] [Airport symbol] (OAG)
KRN .... Knight Ridder Newspapers [Viewdata Corp.] [Videotex producer] (NITA)
KRNA .... Iowa City, IA [FM radio station call letters]
KRNB .... Decatur, TX [FM radio station call letters] (RBYB)
KRND .... San Antonio/Randolf Air Force Base [Texas] [ICAO location identifier] (ICLI)
KRNE .... Merriman, NE [FM radio station call letters]
KRNE-TV ..... Merriman, NE [Television station call letters]
KRNG .... Fallon, NV [FM radio station call letters] (RBYB)
KRNH .... Comfort, TX [FM radio station call letters]
KRNI .... Mason City, IA [AM radio station call letters]
KRNL .... Kernel (ABBR)
KRNL .... Mount Vernon, IA [FM radio station call letters]
KRNN-AM .... North Little Rock, AR [AM radio station call letters] (RBYB)
KRNO .... Reno/International [Nevada] [ICAO location identifier] (ICLI)
KRNO .... Reno, NV [FM radio station call letters]
KRNQ-FM .... Keokuk, IA [FM radio station call letters] (RBYB)
KRNR .... Roseburg, OR [AM radio station call letters]
KRNT .... Des Moines, IA [AM radio station call letters]
KRNU .... Lincoln, NE [FM radio station call letters]
KRNV .... Reno, NV [Television station call letters]
KRNV-FM .... Reno, NV [FM radio station call letters] (RBYB)
KRNW .... Chillicothe, MO [FM radio station call letters]
KRNY .... Kearney, NE [FM radio station call letters]
KRNY .... New York [New York] [ICAO location identifier] (ICLI)
KRO .... Aliblu Airways SpA [Italy ICAO designator] (FAAC)
KRO .... Kathode Ray Oscilloscope
KRO .... Katholieke Radio Omroep [Catholic Broadcasting Association] [Netherlands]
kro .... Kru [MARC language code Library of Congress] (LCCP)
KROA .... Grand Island, NE [FM radio station call letters]
KROAG .... Committee for the Revolution in Oman and the Arabian Gulf [Denmark]
KROC .... Rochester, MN [AM radio station call letters]
KROC .... Rochester/Rochester-Monroe County [New York] [ICAO location identifier] (ICLI)
KROC-FM .... Rochester, MN [FM radio station call letters]
KROD .... El Paso, TX [AM radio station call letters]
KROE .... Sheridan, WY [AM radio station call letters]
KROE-FM .... Sheridan, WY [FM radio station call letters]
KROF .... Abbeville, LA [AM radio station call letters]
KROF-FM .... Abbeville, LA [FM radio station call letters]
KROG .... Phoenix, OR [FM radio station call letters]
Kroger .... [The] Kroger Co. [Associated Press] (SAG)
KROK .... De Ridder, LA [FM radio station call letters]
KROL .... Las Cruces, NM [FM radio station call letters]
KROM .... San Antonio, TX [FM radio station call letters]
KRON .... Kronos, Inc. [NASDAQ symbol] (SAG)
KRON .... San Francisco, CA [Television station call letters]
Kronos .... Kronos, Inc. [Associated Press] (SAG)
KROO .... Breckenridge, TX [FM radio station call letters]

KROP .... Brawley, CA [AM radio station call letters]
KROQ .... Pasadena, CA [FM radio station call letters]
KROS .... Clinton, IA [AM radio station call letters]
KROU .... Spencer, OK [FM radio station call letters]
KROW .... Mariposa, CA [FM radio station call letters]
KROW .... Roswell/Industrial Air Center [New Mexico] [ICAO location identifier] (ICLI)
KROX .... Crookston, MN [AM radio station call letters]
KROX-FM .... Giddings, TX [FM radio station call letters] (RBYB)
KROY .... Victorville, CA [AM radio station call letters] (RBYB)
KROZ .... Roseburg, OR [Television station call letters]
KRP .... Karapiro [New Zealand] [Seismograph station code, US Geological Survey] (SEIS)
KRP .... Karup [Denmark] [Airport symbol] (OAG)
KRP .... Key Resource People [US Chamber of Commerce]
KRP .... Kinesin-Related Polypeptide [Biochemistry]
KRP .... King's Rook's Pawn [Chess]
KRP .... Known Reference Point
KRP .... Kodak Relief Plate
KRP .... Kolmer [Test with] Reiter Protein [Serology]
KRP .... Krebs-Ringer-Phosphate [Buffer solution]
KRP .... Kurdistan Revolutionary Party [Iraq] [Political party] (PPW)
KRPA .... Rancho Palos Verdes, CA [Television station call letters]
KRPB .... Krebs-Ringer-Phosphate Buffer [Solution]
KRPL .... Moscow, ID [AM radio station call letters]
KRPM .... Tacoma, WA [FM radio station call letters]
KRPM-AM .... Seattle, WA [AM radio station call letters] (RBYB)
KRPQ .... Rohnert Park, CA [FM radio station call letters]
KRPR .... Rochester, MN [FM radio station call letters]
KRPS .... Krebs-Ringer-Phosphate Buffer Solution (MAE)
KRPS .... Pittsburg, KS [FM radio station call letters]
KRPT .... Anadarko, OK [AM radio station call letters]
KRPT-FM .... Anadarko, OK [FM radio station call letters]
KRPV .... Roswell, NM [Television station call letters]
KRPX .... Price, UT [AM radio station call letters]
KRQ .... Crimsonstar Resources [Vancouver Stock Exchange symbol]
KRQC .... Marina, CA [AM radio station call letters]
KRQE .... Albuquerque, NM [Television station call letters]
KRQK .... Lompoc, CA [FM radio station call letters]
KRQQ .... Tucson, AZ [FM radio station call letters]
KRQR .... San Francisco, CA [FM radio station call letters]
KRQS .... Pagosa Springs, CO [FM radio station call letters]
KRQT-FM .... Castle Rock, WA [FM radio station call letters] (RBYB)
KRQU .... Laramie, WY [FM radio station call letters]
KRQX .... Mexia, TX [AM radio station call letters]
KRQZ-FM .... Wagoner, OK [FM radio station call letters] (RBYB)
KRR .... Kansai Research Reactor [Japan]
KRR .... Karoi [Zimbabwe] [Seismograph station code, US Geological Survey] (SEIS)
KRR .... Kettle River Resources Ltd. [Vancouver Stock Exchange symbol]
KRR .... King's Royal Rifles [Military unit] [British]
KRR .... Krasnodar [Former USSR Airport symbol] (OAG)
KRRB .... Dickinson, ND [FM radio station call letters]
KRRC .... King's Royal Rifle Corps [Military unit] [British]
KRRC .... Portland, OR [FM radio station call letters]
KRRD .... Dickinson, ND [FM radio station call letters]
KRRF-AM .... Denver, CO [AM radio station call letters] (RBYB)
KRRG .... Laredo, TX [FM radio station call letters]
KRRK .... Bennington, NE [FM radio station call letters]
KRRM .... Rogue River, OR [FM radio station call letters]
KRRO .... Sioux Falls, SD [FM radio station call letters]
KRRP .... Coushatta, LA [AM radio station call letters]
KRRQ .... Lafayette, LA [FM radio station call letters]
KRRR-FM .... Cheyenne, WY [FM radio station call letters] (RBYB)
KRRS .... Kinetic Resonance Raman Spectroscopy (DAVI)
KRRS .... Santa Rosa, CA [AM radio station call letters]
KRRT .... Kerrville, TX [Television station call letters]
KRRU .... Pueblo, CO [AM radio station call letters]
KRRV .... Alexandria, LA [AM radio station call letters]
KRRV-FM .... Alexandria, LA [FM radio station call letters]
KRRW .... Dallas, TX [FM radio station call letters]
KRRY .... Canton, MO [FM radio station call letters] (RBYB)
KRRZ .... Minot, ND [AM radio station call letters]
KRS .... Kearney State College, Kearney, NE [OCLC symbol] (OCLC)
KRS .... Kentucky Revised Statutes [A publication]
KRS .... Kerato-Refractive Society (EA)
KRS .... Kinematograph Renter's Society
KRS .... Knowledge Retrieval System [KnowledgeSet Corp.]
KRS .... Korsar [Russian Federation] [ICAO designator] (FAAC)
KRS .... Krasnogorka [Former USSR Seismograph station code, US Geological Survey Closed] (SEIS)
KRS .... Kristiansand [Norway] [Airport symbol] (OAG)
KRSA .... Petersburg, AK [AM radio station call letters]
KRSB .... Roseburg, OR [FM radio station call letters]
KRSC .... Claremore, OK [Television station call letters]
KRSC .... Kaiser Resources, Inc. [NASDAQ symbol] (SAG)
KRSC .... Kaiser Ventures [NASDAQ symbol] (TTSB)
KRSC .... Kaiser Ventures, Inc. [NASDAQ symbol] (SAG)
KRSC .... Othello, WA [AM radio station call letters]
KRSC-FM .... Claremore, OK [FM radio station call letters] (RBYB)
KRSD .... Sioux Falls, SD [FM radio station call letters]
KRSE .... Seattle [Washington] [ICAO location identifier] (ICLI)
KRSE .... Yakima, WA [FM radio station call letters]
KRSEN .... Kerosene (ABBR)
KRSH .... Middletown, CA [FM radio station call letters]

KRSI	Garapan-Saipan, MP [*FM radio station call letters*]
KRSI	Kelly Russell Studios, Inc. [*NASDAQ symbol*] (SAG)
KRSI	Kreisler Mfg [*NASDAQ symbol*] (TTSB)
KRSJ	Durango, CO [*FM radio station call letters*]
KRSL	Kreisler Manufacturing Co. [*NASDAQ symbol*] (NQ)
KRSL	Russell, KS [*AM radio station call letters*]
KRSM	Dallas, TX [*FM radio station call letters*]
KRSN	Kerosene (MSA)
KRSN	Los Alamos, NM [*AM radio station call letters*]
KRS-ONE	Knowledge Reigns Supreme Over Nearly Everyone [*Rap recording artist*]
KRSP	Salt Lake City, UT [*FM radio station call letters*]
KRSQ	Laurel, MT [*FM radio station call letters*]
KRSR	Coos Bay, OR [*AM radio station call letters*]
KRSS	Chubbuck, ID [*FM radio station call letters*]
KRST	Albuquerque, NM [*FM radio station call letters*]
KRSTL	Knowledge Representation Systems Trials Laboratory [*Pronounced "crystal"*] [*Artificial intelligence*]
KRSU	Appleton, MN [*FM radio station call letters*]
KRSV	Afton, WY [*AM radio station call letters*]
KRSV-FM	Afton, WY [*FM radio station call letters*]
KRSW	Worthington-Marshall, MN [*FM radio station call letters*]
KRSY	Roswell, NM [*AM radio station call letters*]
KRT	Cretan Airlines SA [*Greece*] [*ICAO designator*] (FAAC)
KRT	Karate
KRT	Kathode Ray Tube (AAG)
KRT	Keratin (DMAA)
KRT	Keravat [*New Britain*] [*Seismograph station code, US Geological Survey Closed*] (SEIS)
KRT	Khartoum [*Sudan*] [*Airport symbol*] (OAG)
KRT	Kranzco Realty Trust [*NYSE symbol*] (SPSG)
KRTA	Medford, OR [*AM radio station call letters*] (RBYB)
KRTE	Karate (ABBR)
KRTH	Los Angeles, CA [*FM radio station call letters*]
KRTI	Grinnell, IA [*FM radio station call letters*]
KRTL	Atlanta [*Georgia*] [*ICAO location identifier*] (ICLI)
KRTM	Temecula, CA [*FM radio station call letters*]
KRTN	Karatin (ABBR)
KRTN	Raton, NM [*AM radio station call letters*]
KRTN-FM	Raton, NM [*FM radio station call letters*]
KRTO	Kathode Ray Tube Oscillograph
KRTO-FM	West Covina, CA [*FM radio station call letters*] (RBYB)
KRTR	Kailua, HI [*FM radio station call letters*]
KRTS	Kathode Ray Tube Shield
KRTS	Seabrook, TX [*FM radio station call letters*]
KRTT	Kathode Ray Tube Tester
KRTU	San Antonio, TX [*FM radio station call letters*]
KRTV	Great Falls, MT [*Television station call letters*]
KRTX	Galveston, TX [*FM radio station call letters*]
KRTY	Los Gatos, CA [*FM radio station call letters*]
KRTZ	Cortez, CO [*FM radio station call letters*]
KRU	Karasu [*Former USSR Seismograph station code, US Geological Survey*] (SEIS)
kru	Kurukh [*MARC language code Library of Congress*] (LCCP)
KRUA	Anchorage, AK [*FM radio station call letters*]
KRUE	Waseca, MN [*FM radio station call letters*]
KRUF-FM	Shreveport, LA [*FM radio station call letters*] (RBYB)
KRUG	KRUG International [*NASDAQ symbol*] (TTSB)
KRUG	KRUG International Corp. [*NASDAQ symbol*] (NQ)
KRUGW	KRUG Intl Wrrt [*NASDAQ symbol*] (TTSB)
KRUI	Iowa City, IA [*FM radio station call letters*]
KRUI	Ruidoso Downs, NM [*AM radio station call letters*]
Krummeck ...	Decisions of the Water Courts [*1913-36*] [*South Africa*] [*A publication*] (DLA)
KRUN	Ballinger, TX [*AM radio station call letters*]
KRUN-FM	Ballinger, TX [*FM radio station call letters*]
KRUP	Dillingham, AK [*FM radio station call letters*] (RBYB)
KRUS	Ruston, LA [*AM radio station call letters*]
KRUU	Boone, IA [*FM radio station call letters*]
KRUX	Las Cruces, NM [*FM radio station call letters*]
KRUZ	Europa Cruises [*NASDAQ symbol*] (TTSB)
KRUZ	Europa Cruises Corp. [*NASDAQ symbol*] (SAG)
KRUZ	Santa Barbara, CA [*FM radio station call letters*]
KRV	Kilham Rat Virus [*Medicine*]
KRV	Kirovabad [*Former USSR Seismograph station code, US Geological Survey*] (SEIS)
KRVA	Cockrell Hill, TX [*AM radio station call letters*]
KRVA	McKinney, TX [*FM radio station call letters*]
KRVC	Medford, OR [*AM radio station call letters*]
KRVE	Brusly, LA [*FM radio station call letters*]
KRVH	Rio Vista, CA [*FM radio station call letters*]
KRVL	Kerrville, TX [*FM radio station call letters*]
KRVM	Eugene, OR [*FM radio station call letters*]
KRVN	Lexington, NE [*AM radio station call letters*]
KRVN-FM	Lexington, NE [*FM radio station call letters*]
KRVR	Copperopolis, CA [*FM radio station call letters*] (RBYB)
KRVS	Lafayette, LA [*FM radio station call letters*]
KRVV	Bastrop, LA [*FM radio station call letters*]
KRVZ	Springerville-Eager, AZ [*AM radio station call letters*]
KRW	Karlsruhe - West [*Federal Republic of Germany*] [*Seismograph station code, US Geological Survey*] (SEIS)
KRWA	Waldron, AR [*FM radio station call letters*]
KRWA	Washington [*District of Columbia*] [*ICAO location identifier*] (ICLI)
KRWB	Roseau, MN [*AM radio station call letters*]
KRWB-FM	Roseau, MN [*FM radio station call letters*] (RBYB)
KRWC	Buffalo, MN [*AM radio station call letters*]
KRWF	Redwood Falls, MN [*Television station call letters*]
KRWG	Las Cruces, NM [*FM radio station call letters*]
KRWG-TV	Las Cruces, NM [*Television station call letters*]
KRWM	Bremerton, WA [*FM radio station call letters*]
KRWN	Farmington, NM [*FM radio station call letters*]
KRWQ	Gold Hill, OR [*FM radio station call letters*]
KRX	Christina Exploration [*Vancouver Stock Exchange symbol*]
KRX	Kar Kar [*Papua New Guinea*] [*Airport symbol*] (OAG)
KRXI	Reno, NV [*Television station call letters*]
KRXK	Rexburg, ID [*AM radio station call letters*]
KRXL	Kirksville, MO [*FM radio station call letters*]
KRXO	Oklahoma City, OK [*FM radio station call letters*]
KRXQ	Roseville, CA [*FM radio station call letters*]
KRXR	Gooding, ID [*AM radio station call letters*]
KRXS	Globe, AZ [*FM radio station call letters*]
KRXT	Rockdale, TX [*FM radio station call letters*]
KRXV	Yermo, CA [*FM radio station call letters*]
KRXX-FM	Kodiak, AK [*FM radio station call letters*] (RBYB)
KRXZ	Ardmore, OK [*FM radio station call letters*] (RBYB)
KRY	Karamay [*China*] [*Airport symbol*] (OAG)
KRYD	Telluride, CO [*FM radio station call letters*]
KRYK	Chinook, MT [*FM radio station call letters*]
KRYL	Gatesville, TX [*FM radio station call letters*]
KRYPN	Krypton (ABBR)
KRYS	Corpus Christi, TX [*AM radio station call letters*]
KRYS	Krystal Co. [*NASDAQ symbol*] (SAG)
KRYS-FM	Corpus Christi, TX [*FM radio station call letters*]
KRYSQ	Krystal Company [*NASDAQ symbol*] (TTSB)
Krystal	Krystal Co. [*Associated Press*] (SAG)
KRZ	Karuizawa [*Japan*] [*Also, KAZ*] [*Seismograph station code, US Geological Survey*] (SEIS)
KRZ	Kiri [*Zaire*] [*Airport symbol*] (OAG)
KRZA	Alamosa, CO [*FM radio station call letters*]
KRZE	Farmington, NM [*AM radio station call letters*]
KRZI	Waco, TX [*AM radio station call letters*]
KRZK	Branson, MO [*FM radio station call letters*]
KRZN	Albuquerque, NM [*FM radio station call letters*]
KRZQ	Tahoe City, CA [*FM radio station call letters*]
KRZR	Hanford, CA [*FM radio station call letters*]
KRZY	Albuquerque, NM [*AM radio station call letters*]
KRZY-FM	Santa Fe, NM [*FM radio station call letters*] (RBYB)
KRZZ	Derby, KS [*FM radio station call letters*]
KS	Kansas [*Postal code*]
KS	Kansas Reports [*A publication*] (DLA)
KS	Kaposi's Sarcoma [*Medicine*]
KS	Kartagener's Syndrome [*Medicine*] (DAVI)
KS	Katoptric System [*Optics*]
KS	Kawasaki Syndrome [*Also, KD, MLNS*]
KS	Keep Type Standing [*Printing*]
KS	Kelly-Springfield Tire Co.
KS	Keltic Society and the College of Druidism (EA)
KS	Ketosteroid [*Endocrinology*]
KS	Key Seated [*Freight*]
KS	Keyset [*Navy*] (NVT)
KS	Key Stage [*Of National Curriculum*] [*British*] (AIE)
KS	Keystone (IAA)
K/S	Kick Stage [*NASA*] (NASA)
KS	Kidney Sac
KS	Kilostere
KS	King Solomon [*Freemasonry*] (ROG)
KS	King's Scholar [*British*]
KS	King's Serjeant [*British*] (ROG)
KS	King's Speech [*British*]
KS	Kipling Society of North America - USA and Canada (EA)
KS	Kirjath Sepher [*Jerusalem*] (BJA)
KS	Kiting Stock [*Investment term*]
KS	Klinefelter's Syndrome [*Medicine*]
KS	Knife Switch
KS	Knight of the Sword [*of Sweden*]
KS	Knock Sensor [*Automotive engineering*]
KS	Knowledge Source (IAA)
KS	Kodak Standard [*Photography*]
KS	Kokoxili Suture [*Paleogeography*]
KS	Kolmogorov - Smirnov Test [*Statistics*]
KS	Konungariket Sverige [*Kingdom of Sweden*] (BARN)
KS	Korea Society (EA)
KS	Korsakoff Syndrome [*Medicine Medicine*] (DMAA)
KS	Kraemer System
KS	Kugel-Stoloff [*Syndrome*] [*Medicine*] (DAVI)
KS	Kurze Sicht [*Short Sight*] [*German*]
Ks	Kush (BJA)
KS	Kveim-Seltzback (Test) [*Medicine*]
KS	Peninsula Airways [*ICAO designator*] (AD)
ks	Potassium Metasilicate [*CIPW classification*] [*Geology*]
KS	Singapore [*IYRU nationality code*] (IYR)
KS	Storm of Drifting Snow [*Meteorology*] (WDAA)
KSA	Kafka Society of America (EA)
KSA	Kansas Motor Carriers Association, Topeka KS [*STAC*]
KSA	Kansas Statutes, Annotated [*A publication*]
KSA	Kitchen Specialists Association [*British*] (DBA)
KSA	Kite-Supported Antenna
KSA	Klinefelter Syndrome and Associates (EA)
KSA	Knight of St. Anne [*Russia*] [*Obsolete*]
KSA	Knowledge, Skills, and Abilities [*Psychology*] (DAVI)

KSA............. Ksara [*Lebanon*] [*Geomagnetic observatory code*]
KSA............. Ksara [*Lebanon*] [*Seismograph station code, US Geological Survey*] (SEIS)
KSA............. Ku-Band Single Access (MCD)
KSA............. Kwajalein Standard Atmosphere
KSA............. St. Augustine's Seminary Library, University of Toronto [*UTLAS symbol*]
KSAA .... Keats-Shelley Association of America (EA)
KSAB .... Robstown, TX [*FM radio station call letters*]
KSAC .... Sacramento/Executive [*California*] [*ICAO location identifier*] (ICLI)
KSAC .... Sutter Creek, CA [*FM radio station call letters*] (RBYB)
KSAE .... Kansas Society of Association Executives (SRA)
KSAE .... Kentucky Society of Association Executives (SRA)
KSAF .... K-Band, Single Access Forward (SSD)
KSAF .... Santa Fe [*New Mexico*] [*ICAO location identifier*] (ICLI)
KSAH .... Universal City, TX [*AM radio station call letters*]
KSAI .... Saipan, MP [*AM radio station call letters*]
KSAJ .... Abilene, KS [*FM radio station call letters*]
KSAK .... Walnut, CA [*FM radio station call letters*]
KSAL .... Salina, KS [*AM radio station call letters*]
KSal............. Salina Public Library, Salina, KS [*Library symbol Library of Congress*] (LCLS)
KSalM.......... Marymount College, Salina, KS [*Library symbol Library of Congress*] (LCLS)
KSalW .... Kansas Wesleyan University, Salina, KS [*Library symbol Library of Congress*] (LCLS)
KSAM .... Huntsville, TX [*AM radio station call letters*]
KSAM .... Keyed Sequential Access Method [*Computer science*] (CMD)
KSAM .... Key Field Sequential Access Method (NITA)
KSAM-FM .... Huntsville, TX [*FM radio station call letters*]
KSAN .... San Diego/International-Lindbergh Field [*California*] [*ICAO location identifier*] (ICLI)
KSAN .... San Francisco, CA [*FM radio station call letters*]
KSAR .... K-Band, Single Access Return (SSD)
KSAR .... Salem, AR [*FM radio station call letters*]
KSAS .... Wichita, KS [*Television station call letters*]
KSAT .... San Antonio/International [*Texas*] [*ICAO location identifier*] (ICLI)
KSAT .... San Antonio, TX [*Television station call letters*]
KSAU .... Nacogdoches, TX [*FM radio station call letters*]
KSAV .... KS Bancorp [*NASDAQ symbol*] (TTSB)
KSAV .... KS Bancorp, Inc. [*NASDAQ symbol*] (SAG)
KSAV .... Savannah/Municipal [*Georgia*] [*ICAO location identifier*] (ICLI)
KSAW .... Gwinn/K. I. Sawyer Air Force Base [*Michigan*] [*ICAO location identifier*] (ICLI)
KSAX .... Alexandria, MN [*Television station call letters*]
KSAY .... Fort Bragg, CA [*FM radio station call letters*]
KSAZ .... Tucson, AZ [*AM radio station call letters*]
KSAZ-TV .... Phoenix, AZ [*Television station call letters*]
KSB............. Kradschuetzen-Bataillon [*Motorcycle Battalion*] [*German military - World War II*]
KSBA .... Coos Bay, OR [*FM radio station call letters*]
KSB Bc .... KSB Bancorp [*Associated Press*] (SAG)
KSBC .... Hot Springs, AR [*FM radio station call letters*]
KS Bcp......... KS Bancorp, Inc. [*Associated Press*] (SAG)
KSBD .... San Bernardino/Norton Air Force Base [*California*] [*ICAO location identifier*] (ICLI)
KSBH .... Coushatta, LA [*FM radio station call letters*]
KSBI .... Oklahoma City, OK [*Television station call letters*]
KSBJ .... Humble, TX [*FM radio station call letters*]
KSBK .... KSB Bancorp [*NASDAQ symbol*] (SAG)
KSBL .... Carpinteria, CA [*FM radio station call letters*]
KSBN .... Spokane, WA [*AM radio station call letters*]
KSBN .... Springdale, AR [*Television station call letters*]
KSBQ .... Santa Maria, CA [*AM radio station call letters*]
KSBR .... Mission Viejo, CA [*FM radio station call letters*]
KSBS .... Pago Pago, AS [*FM radio station call letters*]
KSBS .... Steamboat Springs, CO [*Television station call letters*]
KSBT......... Steamboat Springs, CO [*FM radio station call letters*]
KSBW .... Salinas, CA [*Television station call letters*]
KSBY .... Salisbury/Wicomico County [*Maryland*] [*ICAO location identifier*] (ICLI)
KSBY .... San Luis Obispo, CA [*Television station call letters*]
KSBZ .... Sitka, AK [*FM radio station call letters*]
KSC............. Council of State Governments, Lexington, KY [*OCLC symbol*] (OCLC)
KSC............. Kagoshima Space Center [*Japan*]
KSC............. Kathodal Closing Contraction [*Medicine*] (DAVI)
KSC............. Kennedy Space Center [*NASA*]
KSC............. King's School, Canterbury (ROG)
KSC............. Knight of St. Columba
KSC............. Komunisticka Strana Ceskoslovenska [*Communist Party of Czechoslovakia*] [*Political party*] (PPW)
KSC............. Korean Service Corps
KSC............. Kosice [*Former Czechoslovakia*] [*Airport symbol*] (OAG)
KSCA .... Glendale, CA [*FM radio station call letters*]
KSCAP .... Kennedy Space Center Area Permit [*NASA*] (MCD)
KSCB .... Khe Sanh Combat Base [*Vietnam*] [*Marine Corps*] (VNW)
KSCB .... Liberal, KS [*AM radio station call letters*]
KSCB-FM .... Liberal, KS [*FM radio station call letters*]
KSCE .... El Paso, TX [*Television station call letters*]
KSCF............. Thousand Standard Cubic Feet
KSch (Alt)... Kleine Schriften zur Geschichte de Volkes Israel [*A. Alt*] [*A publication*] (BJA)
KSCI .... San Bernardino, CA [*Television station call letters*]

KSCI............. San Clemente Naval Auxiliary Air Base [*California*] [*ICAO location identifier*] (ICLI)
KSCJ............. Sioux City, IA [*AM radio station call letters*]
KSCK .... Stockton/Stockton Metropolitan [*California*] [*ICAO location identifier*] (ICLI)
KSCL............. Shreveport, LA [*FM radio station call letters*]
KSCN .... Potassium Thiocyanate [*Broth*] [*A reagent*] [*Pharmacology*] (DAVI)
KSCO .... Santa Cruz, CA [*AM radio station call letters*]
KSCQ .... Silver City, NM [*FM radio station call letters*]
KSCR .... Benson, MN [*AM radio station call letters*]
KSCR-FM .... Benson, MN [*FM radio station call letters*]
KSCS .... Fort Worth, TX [*FM radio station call letters*]
KSCU .... Santa Clara, CA [*FM radio station call letters*]
KSC/ULO..... Kennedy Space Center/Unmanned Launch Operations [*NASA*]
KSCV .... Kearney, NE [*FM radio station call letters*]
KSC-WTROD... Kennedy Space Center - Western Test Range Operations Division [*NASA*]
KSCY .... Belgrade, MT [*FM radio station call letters*]
KSD .... C. H. Boehringer Sohn, Ingelheim [*Germany*] [*Research code symbol*]
KSD .... Karlstad [*Sweden*] [*Airport symbol*] (OAG)
KSD .... St Louis, MO [*AM radio station call letters*]
KSDA .... Agat, GU [*FM radio station call letters*]
KSDA .... Korean Securities Dealers' Association (ECON)
KSDB .... Kommunal Statistisk DataBank [*Danmarks Statistik*] [*Denmark Information service or system*] (CRD)
KSDB .... Manhattan, KS [*FM radio station call letters*]
KSD-FM ..... St. Louis, MO [*FM radio station call letters*]
KSDJ .... Brookings, SD [*FM radio station call letters*]
KSDK .... St. Louis, MO [*Television station call letters*]
KSDL .... Sedalia, MO [*FM radio station call letters*]
KSDM .... International Falls, MN [*FM radio station call letters*]
KSDN .... Aberdeen, SD [*AM radio station call letters*]
KSDN-FM .... Aberdeen, SD [*FM radio station call letters*]
KSDO .... San Diego, CA [*AM radio station call letters*]
KSDP .... Sand Point, AK [*AM radio station call letters*]
KSDR .... Watertown, SD [*AM radio station call letters*]
KSDR-FM .... Watertown, SD [*FM radio station call letters*]
KSDS .... Key Sequenced Data Set (CMD)
KSDS .... San Diego, CA [*FM radio station call letters*]
KSDT .... Hemet, CA [*AM radio station call letters*] (RBYB)
KSDZ .... Gordon, NE [*FM radio station call letters*]
KSE .... Karachi Stock Exchange [*Pakistan*]
KSE .... Kasese [*Uganda*] [*Airport symbol*] (OAG)
KSE .... Kids for Saving Earth [*An association*] (EA)
KSE .... Kisbee Air Ltd. [*New Zealand*] [*ICAO designator*] (FAAC)
KSE .... Knight of Saint-Esprit [*France*]
KSE .... Knight of the Star of the East (ROG)
KSE .... Korea Stock Exchange (ECON)
KSEA .... Greenfield, CA [*FM radio station call letters*]
KSEA .... Korean Scientists and Engineers Association in America (EA)
KSEA .... Seattle/Seattle-Tacoma International [*Washington*] [*ICAO location identifier*] (ICLI)
KSEC .... Lamar, CO [*FM radio station call letters*]
KSED .... Sedona, AZ [*FM radio station call letters*]
KSEE .... Fresno, CA [*Television station call letters*]
KSEG .... Sacramento, CA [*FM radio station call letters*]
KSEI .... Pocatello, ID [*AM radio station call letters*]
KSEK .... Girard, KS [*FM radio station call letters*]
KSEL .... Portales, NM [*AM radio station call letters*]
KSEL-FM...... Portales, NM [*FM radio station call letters*]
KSEM .... Selma/Craig Air Force Base [*Alabama*] [*ICAO location identifier*] (ICLI)
KSEM .... Seminole, TX [*FM radio station call letters*]
KSEN .... Shelby, MT [*AM radio station call letters*]
KSEO .... Durant, OK [*AM radio station call letters*]
KSEQ .... Visalia, CA [*FM radio station call letters*]
KSER .... Everett, WA [*FM radio station call letters*]
KSES .... Selma/Selfield [*Alabama*] [*ICAO location identifier*] (ICLI)
KSES-FM ..... Yucca Valley, CA [*FM radio station call letters*] (RBYB)
KSET .... El Paso, TX [*FM radio station call letters*]
KSEV .... Tomball, TX [*AM radio station call letters*]
KSEY .... Seymour, TX [*AM radio station call letters*]
KSEY-FM ..... Seymour, TX [*FM radio station call letters*]
KSEZ .... Sioux City, IA [*FM radio station call letters*]
KSF............. Karen Silkwood Fund (EA)
KSF............. Kassel [*Germany Airport symbol*] (OAG)
KSF............. K-Band Shuttle Forward (SSD)
KSF............. Keel Shock Factor (NATG)
ksf............. Kips [*Thousands of Pounds*] per Square Foot
KSF............. Knight of San Fernando [*Spain*]
KSF............. Knight of St. Ferdinand [*Sicily*] (ROG)
KSF............. Quaker State Corp. [*NYSE symbol*] (SPSG)
KSFA .... Nacogdoches, TX [*AM radio station call letters*]
KSFC .... Keith Sewell Fan Club (EA)
KSFC .... Spokane, WA [*FM radio station call letters*]
KSFF .... Spokane/Felts [*Washington*] [*ICAO location identifier*] (ICLI)
KSFH .... Mountain View, CA [*FM radio station call letters*]
KSFI .... Salt Lake City, UT [*FM radio station call letters*]
KSFM .... Knight of St. Ferdinand and Merit [*Italy*]
KSFM .... Woodland, CA [*FM radio station call letters*]
KSFO .... San Francisco, CA [*AM radio station call letters*]
KSFO .... San Francisco/International [*California*] [*ICAO location identifier*] (ICLI)
KSFR .... Santa Fe, NM [*FM radio station call letters*]

KSFS............ San Francisco Coast Guard Air Station [*California*] [*ICAO location identifier*] (ICLI)
KSFT............ St. Joseph, MO [*AM radio station call letters*]
KSFT-FM...... South Sioux City, NE [*FM radio station call letters*] (RBYB)
KSFUS.......... Korean Student Federation of the United States (EA)
KSFX............ Roswell, NM [*FM radio station call letters*]
KSFY............ Sioux Falls, SD [*Television station call letters*]
KSG .... Harvard University, Kennedy School for Government, Cambridge, MA [*OCLC symbol*] (OCLC)
KSG .... Knight of St. George [*Russia*] [*Obsolete*]
KSG .... Knight of St. Gregory
KSGC............ Tusayan, AZ [*FM radio station call letters*]
KSGI .... Cedar City, UT [*Television station call letters*]
KSGI .... St. George, UT [*AM radio station call letters*]
KSGI-FM....... St George, UT [*FM radio station call letters*]
KSGL .... Wichita, KS [*AM radio station call letters*]
KSGM.......... Chester, IL [*AM radio station call letters*]
KSGN.......... Riverside, CA [*FM radio station call letters*]
KSGS-AM...... St. Louis Park, MN [*AM radio station call letters*] (RBYB)
KSGT.......... Jackson, WY [*AM radio station call letters*]
KSGW.......... Sheridan, WY [*Television station call letters*]
KSH .... K-Band Shuttle (SSD)
KSH .... Kenya Shilling [*Monetary unit*] (IMH)
KSh .... Kenya Shilling [*Monetary unit*] (ODBW)
KSH .... Kermanshah [*Iran*] [*Airport symbol*] (AD)
KSH .... Key Strokes per Hour
KSH .... Knight of St. Hubert [*Bavaria*]
KSH .... Kolel Shomre Hachomos [*An association*] (EA)
KSH .... Kuh Shi [*Republic of China*] [*Seismograph station code, US Geological Survey*] (SEIS)
KSHA............ Redding, CA [*FM radio station call letters*]
KSHB .... Kansas City, MO [*Television station call letters*]
KSHE .... Crestwood, MO [*FM radio station call letters*]
KSHI .... Zuni, NM [*FM radio station call letters*]
KSHL .... Gleneden Beach, OR [*FM radio station call letters*]
KshLc.......... Kush Locke [*Associated Press*] (SAG)
KShm.......... Johnson County Public Library, Shawnee Mission, KS [*Library symbol Library of Congress*] (LCLS)
KSHN .... Liberty, TX [*FM radio station call letters*]
KSHO .... Lebanon, OR [*AM radio station call letters*]
KSHP-AM...... North Las Vegas, Nv [*AM radio station call letters*] (RBYB)
KSHR .... Coquille, OR [*FM radio station call letters*]
KSHR .... Kosher (ABBR)
KSHR .... Kosher
KSH/RMBH.. Kolel Shomre Hachomos/Reb Meir Baal Haness (EA)
KSHU .... Huntsville, TX [*FM radio station call letters*]
KSHV .... Kaposi's Sarcoma Associated Herpesvirus [*Medicine*]
KSHV .... Shreveport, LA [*Television station call letters*] (RBYB)
KSHV .... Shreveport/Regional Airport [*Louisiana*] [*ICAO location identifier*] (ICLI)
KSHY .... Cheyenne, WY [*AM radio station call letters*]
KSI .... Karsanskaya [*Later, TFS*] [*Former USSR Geomagnetic observatory code*]
KSI .... Kemgas Sydney, Inc. [*Vancouver Stock Exchange symbol*]
KSI .... Kilopounds per Square Inch (SAA)
KSI .... Kips [*Thousands of Pounds*] per Square Inch (MCD)
KSI .... Kissidougou [*Guinea*] [*Airport symbol*] (AD)
KSI .... Kleine Schriften zur Geschichte des Volkes Israel [*A. Alt*] [*A publication*] (BJA)
KSI .... Knight of [*the Order of*] the Star of India [*British*]
KSIB .... Creston, IA [*AM radio station call letters*]
KSID .... Sidney, NE [*AM radio station call letters*]
KSID-FM...... Sidney, NE [*FM radio station call letters*]
KSIG .... Basile, LA [*FM radio station call letters*]
KSIG .... Crowley, LA [*AM radio station call letters*]
KSII .... El Paso, TX [*FM radio station call letters*] (RBYB)
KSIIMK .... Kratkie Soobshcheniia o Dokladakh i Polevykh Issledovaniiakh Instituta Istorii Materialnoi Kulturi [*A publication*] (BJA)
K-SIM .... K-Band Simulation (SSD)
KSIM .... Sikeston, MO [*AM radio station call letters*]
KSIN .... Sioux City, IA [*Television station call letters*]
KSIP............ Kent Scientific & Industrial Projects Ltd. [*University of Kent*] [*Research center British*] (IRUK)
KSIQ............ Brawley, CA [*FM radio station call letters*]
KSIR .... Brush, CO [*AM radio station call letters*]
KSIR-FM...... Brush, CO [*FM radio station call letters*]
KSIS .... Sedalia, MO [*AM radio station call letters*]
KSIT .... Rock Springs, WY [*FM radio station call letters*]
KSIV .... Clayton, MO [*AM radio station call letters*]
KSIV-FM...... St. Louis, MO [*FM radio station call letters*] (RBYB)
KSIW .... Woodward, OK [*AM radio station call letters*]
KSIX............ Corpus Christi, TX [*AM radio station call letters*]
KSIZ .... Jacksonville, TX [*FM radio station call letters*]
KSJ .... Kashima [*Japan*] [*Seismograph station code, US Geological Survey*] (SEIS)
KSJ .... Kasos Island [*Greece*] [*Airport symbol*] (OAG)
KSJ .... Knight of St. Januarius [*Naples*]
KSJ .... Knights of St. John (EA)
KSJB .... Jamestown, ND [*AM radio station call letters*]
KSJC .... Stockton, CA [*FM radio station call letters*]
KSJD .... Cortez, CO [*FM radio station call letters*]
KSJE .... Farmington, NM [*FM radio station call letters*]
KSJJ .... Redmond, OR [*FM radio station call letters*]
KSJK .... Talent, OR [*AM radio station call letters*]
KSJL .... San Antonio, TX [*FM radio station call letters*]

KSJM-FM.... Oro Valley, AZ [*FM radio station call letters*] (RBYB)
KSJN............ Minneapolis, MN [*FM radio station call letters*]
KSJO............ San Jose, CA [*FM radio station call letters*]
KSJQ............ Savannah, MO [*FM radio station call letters*]
KSJR............ Collegeville, MN [*FM radio station call letters*]
KSJS............ San Jose, CA [*FM radio station call letters*]
KSJSC.......... Knights of St. John Supreme Commandery (EA)
KSJT............ San Angelo/Mathis Field [*Texas*] [*ICAO location identifier*] (ICLI)
KSJT............ San Angelo, TX [*FM radio station call letters*]
KSJV............ Fresno, CA [*FM radio station call letters*]
KSJX............ San Jose, CA [*AM radio station call letters*]
KSJY............ Lafayette, LA [*FM radio station call letters*]
KSJZ............ Jamestown, ND [*FM radio station call letters*]
KSK............ Kappa Sigma Kappa [*Later, Theta Xi*] [*Fraternity*]
KSK............ Karlskoga [*Sweden*] [*Airport symbol*] (OAG)
KSK............ Kathodenschliessungs-Kontaktion [*or kathodal closing contraction*] [*Medicine*] (DAVI)
KSK............ Kiosk (ABBR)
KSKA............ Anchorage, AK [*FM radio station call letters*]
KSKA............ Spokane/Fairchild Air Force Base [*Washington*] [*ICAO location identifier*] (ICLI)
KSKB............ Brooklyn, IA [*FM radio station call letters*]
KSKD............ Sweet Home, OR [*FM radio station call letters*]
KSKE............ Vail, CO [*AM radio station call letters*]
KSKE-FM...... Vail, CO [*FM radio station call letters*]
KSKF............ Klamath Falls, OR [*FM radio station call letters*]
KSKF............ San Antonio/Kelly Air Force Base [*Texas*] [*ICAO location identifier*] (ICLI)
KSKG............ Salina, KS [*FM radio station call letters*]
KSKI............ Sun Valley, ID [*FM radio station call letters*]
KSKJ............ American Slovenian Catholic Union of the USA (EA)
KSKK............ Staples, MN [*FM radio station call letters*]
KSKL............ Scott City, KS [*FM radio station call letters*]
KSKN............ Spokane, WA [*Television station call letters*]
KSKO............ McGrath, AK [*AM radio station call letters*]
KSKS............ Fresno, CA [*FM radio station call letters*]
KSKU............ Lyons, KS [*FM radio station call letters*]
KSKX-FM...... Security, CO [*FM radio station call letters*] (RBYB)
KSKY............ Balch Springs, TX [*AM radio station call letters*]
KSKY............ Sandusky/Griffing [*Ohio*] [*ICAO location identifier*] (ICLI)
KSKZ............ Leoti, KS [*FM radio station call letters*] (RBYB)
KSL............ Kanadska Slovenska Liga [*Canadian Slovak League - CSL*]
KSL............ Kassala [*Sudan*] [*Airport symbol*] (OAG)
KSL............ Keio University [*EDUCATSS*] [*UTLAS symbol*]
KSL............ Kentucky Department of Libraries, Library Extension Division, Frankfort, KY [*OCLC symbol*] (OCLC)
KSL............ Keyboard Simulated Lateral Telling [*Computer science*]
KSL............ Knight of the Sun and Lion [*Persia*]
KSL............ Salt Lake City, UT [*AM radio station call letters*]
KSLA............ Shreveport, LA [*Television station call letters*]
KSLC............ McMinnville, OR [*FM radio station call letters*]
KSLC............ Salt Lake City/International [*Utah*] [*ICAO location identifier*] (ICLI)
KSLD............ Soldotna, AK [*AM radio station call letters*]
KSLI............ King's Shropshire Light Infantry [*Military unit*] [*British*]
KSLJ............ Knight of [*the Order of*] St. Lazarus of Jerusalem [*British*]
KSLK............ Visalia, CA [*FM radio station call letters*]
KSLM............ Salem, OR [*AM radio station call letters*]
K-SLN............ KSC [*Kennedy Space Center*] Spacelab Notice [*NASA*] (NASA)
KSLO............ Opelousas, LA [*AM radio station call letters*]
K-SLPS .... KSC [*Kennedy Space Center*] Spacelab Project Specification [*NASA*] (NASA)
KSLQ............ Washington, MO [*AM radio station call letters*]
KSLQ-FM...... Washington, MO [*FM radio station call letters*]
KSLR............ San Antonio, TX [*AM radio station call letters*]
KSLS............ Liberal, KS [*FM radio station call letters*]
KSLT............ Spearfish, SD [*FM radio station call letters*]
KSL-TV .... Salt Lake City, UT [*Television station call letters*]
KSLU............ Hammond, LA [*FM radio station call letters*]
KSLV............ Monte Vista, CO [*AM radio station call letters*]
KSLV-FM...... Monte Vista, CO [*FM radio station call letters*]
KSLX............ Scottsdale, AZ [*FM radio station call letters*]
KSLY............ San Luis Obispo, CA [*FM radio station call letters*]
KSM............ Katubsanan sa Mamumio [*Philippine United Labor Congress*]
KSM............ Kemper Strategic Municipal Trust [*NYSE symbol*] (SPSG)
KSM............ Kemper Strategic Muni Tr [*NYSE symbol*] (TTSB)
KSM............ Kooperative Serbaguna Malaysia [*Bank*]
KSM............ Korean Service Medal [*Military decoration*]
K-SM............ KSC [*Kennedy Space Center*] Shuttle Management [*Document*] [*NASA*] (NASA)
KSM............ Saint Mary's [*Alaska*] [*Airport symbol*] (OAG)
KSM............ Saint Mary's, AK [*Location identifier FAA*] (FAAL)
KSM............ Shawnee Medical Center Medical Library, Shawnee Mission, KS [*OCLC symbol*] (OCLC)
KSM............ St. Michael's College Library, University of Toronto [*UTLAS symbol*]
K-SMA............ Keats-Shelley Memorial Association [*British*] (DBA)
KSMA............ Santa Maria, CA [*AM radio station call letters*]
KSM & SG ... Knight of Saint Michael and Saint George [*Ionian Islands*]
KSMB............ Lafayette, LA [*FM radio station call letters*]
KSMC............ Moraga, CA [*FM radio station call letters*]
KSMF............ Ashland, OR [*FM radio station call letters*]
KSMF............ Sacramento/Sacramento Metropolitan [*California*] [*ICAO location identifier*] (ICLI)
KSMG............ Seguin, TX [*FM radio station call letters*]
KSML............ Diboll, TX [*AM radio station call letters*] (RBYB)
KSML............ Kosher Meal [*Airline notation*]

KSMMP........ Kin Seeking Missing Military Personnel [*Organization of parents with sons missing in action with purpose of supplementing US government search for missing personnel*] [*Post-World War II*]
KSMN .... Worthington, MN [*Television station call letters*]   (RBYB)
KSMO .... Kansas City, MO [*Television station call letters*]
KSMO .... Salem, MO [*AM radio station call letters*]
KSMQ .... Austin, MN [*Television station call letters*]
KSMR .... Winona, MN [*FM radio station call letters*]
KSMS .... Point Lookout, MO [*AM radio station call letters*]
KSMS-TV ..... Monterey, CA [*Television station call letters*]
KSMT .... Breckenridge, CO [*FM radio station call letters*]
KSMet .... Kismet   (ABBR)
KSMU .... Komunistycha Spilka Molodi Ukrainy
KSMU .... Springfield, MO [*FM radio station call letters*]
KSMX .... Clovis, NM [*FM radio station call letters*]   (RBYB)
KSN .... Kassan Resources [*Vancouver Stock Exchange symbol*]
KSN .... Kit Shortage Notice
KSN .... Sam Neua [*Laos*] [*Airport symbol*]   (AD)
KSNB .... Superior, NE [*Television station call letters*]
KSNC .... Great Bend, KS [*Television station call letters*]
KSND .... Lincoln City, OR [*FM radio station call letters*]
KSNE-FM ..... Las Vegas, NV [*FM radio station call letters*]   (RBYB)
KSNF .... Joplin, MO [*Television station call letters*]
KSNG .... Garden City, KS [*Television station call letters*]
KSNI .... Santa Maria, CA [*FM radio station call letters*]
KSNK .... McCook, NE [*Television station call letters*]
KSNM .... Truth or Consequences, NM [*FM radio station call letters*]
KSNN .... Arlington, TX [*FM radio station call letters*]
KSNO .... Snowmass Village, CO [*FM radio station call letters*]
KSNOPI....... Keyboard Input Simulation-Noise-Problem Input [*Computer science*]   (SAA)
KSNP .... Burlington, KS [*FM radio station call letters*]
KSNR .... Thief River Falls, MN [*FM radio station call letters*]
KSNT .... Topeka, KS [*Television station call letters*]
KSNW .... Wichita, KS [*Television station call letters*]
KSNY .... Snyder, TX [*AM radio station call letters*]
KSNY-FM ..... Snyder, TX [*FM radio station call letters*]
KSO .... Kastoria [*Greece*] [*Airport symbol*]   (OAG)
KSOC .... Key Symbol Out of Context [*Computer science*]   (DIT)
KSOF .... Caledonia, MN [*FM radio station call letters*]
KSOH .... Wapato, WA [*FM radio station call letters*]
KS/OI .... Kaposi's Sarcoma and Opportunistic Infection [*Infectious disease*]   (DAVI)
KSOK .... Arkansas City, KS [*AM radio station call letters*]
KSOK-FM..... Winfield, KS [*FM radio station call letters*]   (RBYB)
KSOL .... San Francisco, CA [*FM radio station call letters*]
KSOM .... Audubon, IA [*FM radio station call letters*]   (RBYB)
KSON .... San Diego, CA [*AM radio station call letters*]
KSON-FM..... San Diego, CA [*FM radio station call letters*]
KSOO .... Sioux Falls, SD [*AM radio station call letters*]
KSOP .... Salt Lake City, UT [*FM radio station call letters*]
KSOP .... South Salt Lake, UT [*AM radio station call letters*]
KSOR .... Ashland, OR [*FM radio station call letters*]
KSOS .... Brigham City, UT [*AM radio station call letters*]
KSOS-FM..... Brigham City, UT [*FM radio station call letters*]
KSOU-AM..... Sioux Center, IA [*AM radio station call letters*]   (RBYB)
KSOU-FM..... Sioux Center, IA [*FM radio station call letters*]   (RBYB)
KSOX .... Raymondville, TX [*AM radio station call letters*]
KSOX-FM..... Raymondville, TX [*FM radio station call letters*]
KSP............. Karolinska Scales of Personality [*Medicine*]   (DMAA)
KSP............. Kentucky Department of Libraries, Processing Center, Frankfort, KY [*OCLC symbol*]   (OCLC)
KSP............. Keyset Panel
KSP............. Kidney-Specific Protein [*Medicine*]   (DAVI)
KSP............. Knight of St. Stanislaus of Poland
KSP............. Kodak Special Plate
KSP............. Ksiaz [*Poland*] [*Seismograph station code, US Geological Survey*]   (SEIS)
Ksp .... Potassium Solubility Product [*Biochemistry*]   (DAVI)
KSP............. Servicios Aereos Especializados en Transportes Petroleros [*Colombia*] [*ICAO designator*]   (FAAC)
KSPA .... Escondido, CA [*AM radio station call letters*]
KSPB .... Pebble Beach, CA [*FM radio station call letters*]
KSPC .... Claremont, CA [*FM radio station call letters*]
KSPD .... Boise, ID [*AM radio station call letters*]
KSPE........... Santa Barbara, CA [*AM radio station call letters*]
KSPE-FM ..... Ellwood, CA [*FM radio station call letters*]   (RBYB)
KSPG .... Clearwater, KS [*FM radio station call letters*]
KSPG .... St. Petersburg/Albert Whitted [*Florida*] [*ICAO location identifier*]   (ICLI)
KSPI............ Stillwater, OK [*AM radio station call letters*]
KSPI-FM ...... Stillwater, OK [*FM radio station call letters*]
KSPK .... Walsenburg, CO [*FM radio station call letters*]
KSPL-FM ..... Kalispell, MT [*FM radio station call letters*]   (RBYB)
KSPN .... Aspen, CO [*FM radio station call letters*]
K-SPN .... KSC [*Kennedy Space Center*] Shuttle Project Notice [*NASA*]   (NASA)
KSPO .... Spokane, WA [*FM radio station call letters*]
KSPQ .... West Plains, MO [*FM radio station call letters*]
KSPR .... Springfield, MO [*Television station call letters*]
KSPS .... Kilo Symbols per Second   (MCD)
K-SPS......... KSC [*Kennedy Space Center*] Shuttle Project Specification [*NASA*]   (NASA)
KSPS .... Spokane, WA [*Television station call letters*]
KSPS .... Wichita Falls/Sheppard Air Force Base and Municipal [*Texas*] [*ICAO location identifier*]   (ICLI)

K-SPT .... Potassium-Urine [*Spot*] [*Biochemistry*]   (DAVI)
KSPT........... Sandpoint, ID [*AM radio station call letters*]
KSPT-FM .... Sandpoint, ID [*FM radio station call letters*]   (RBYB)
KSPY .... Quincy, CA [*FM radio station call letters*]
KSPZ........... Colorado Springs, CO [*FM radio station call letters*]
KSQA .... Wallace, ID [*FM radio station call letters*]
KSQD .... Lowry, SD [*FM radio station call letters*]
KSQQ .... Morgan Hill, CA [*FM radio station call letters*]
KSQR .... Sacramento, CA [*AM radio station call letters*]   (RBYB)
KSQY .... Deadwood, SD [*FM radio station call letters*]
KSR .... Kaiser   (ABBR)
KSR .... K-Band Shuttle Return   (SSD)
KSR .... Keyboard Send and Receive [*Computer science*]
KSR .... Koster [*South Africa*] [*Seismograph station code, US Geological Survey*]   (SEIS)
KSR .... Sandy River, AK [*Location identifier FAA*]   (FAAL)
KSRA .... Salmon, ID [*AM radio station call letters*]
KSRA-FM.... Salmon, ID [*FM radio station call letters*]
KSRE .... Minot, ND [*Television station call letters*]
KSRF .... Poipu, HI [*FM radio station call letters*]
KSRG .... Ashland, OR [*FM radio station call letters*]   (RBYB)
KSRH .... San Rafael, CA [*FM radio station call letters*]
KSRM .... Soldotna, AK [*AM radio station call letters*]
KSRN .... Sparks, NV [*FM radio station call letters*]
KSRO .... Santa Rosa, CA [*AM radio station call letters*]
KSRQ .... Thief River Falls, MN [*FM radio station call letters*]
KSRR .... Provo, UT [*AM radio station call letters*]
KSRS .... Roseburg, OR [*FM radio station call letters*]
KSR/T .... Keyboard Send/Receive Terminal [*Computer science*]   (MHDI)
KSRV .... Ontario, OR [*AM radio station call letters*]
KSRV-FM.... Ontario, OR [*FM radio station call letters*]
KSRW .... Childress, TX [*FM radio station call letters*]
KSRX .... El Dorado, KS [*AM radio station call letters*]
KSS .... Kearns-Sayre Syndrome [*Ophthalmology*]
KSS .... Kellogg Switchboard and Supply
KSS .... Kent State University, School of Library Science, Kent, OH [*OCLC symbol*]   (OCLC)
KSS .... Keying Switching Station
KSS .... Knee Signature System [*Orthopedics*]
KSS .... Knight of St. Sylvester
KSS .... Knight of the Southern Star [*Brazil*]
KSS .... Knight of the Sword of Sweden
KSS .... Kohl's Corp. [*NYSE symbol*]   (SPSG)
KSS .... Komunisticka Strane Slovenska [*Communist Party of Slovakia*] [*Former Czechoslovakia*] [*Political party*]   (PPW)
KSS .... Korea Stamp Society   (EA)
KSSB .... Calipatria, CA [*FM radio station call letters*]
KSSB .... Kissable   (ABBR)
KSSC .... KSC [*Kennedy Space Center*] Security Steering Committee [*NASA*]   (SSD)
KSSC .... Sumter/Shaw Air Force Base [*South Carolina*] [*ICAO location identifier*]   (ICLI)
KSSD .... Cedar City, UT [*FM radio station call letters*]
KSSI............ China Lake, CA [*FM radio station call letters*]
KSSJ .... Shingle Springs, CA [*FM radio station call letters*]
KSSK .... Honolulu, HI [*AM radio station call letters*]
KSSK .... Waipahu, HI [*FM radio station call letters*]
KSSM.......... Sault Ste. Marie/Sault Ste. Marie Municipal [*Michigan*] [*ICAO location identifier*]   (ICLI)
KSSN .... Little Rock, AR [*FM radio station call letters*]
KSSQ .... Conroe, TX [*AM radio station call letters*]
KSSR .... Kisser   (ABBR)
KSSR .... Santa Rosa, NM [*AM radio station call letters*]
KSSS .... Bismarck, ND [*FM radio station call letters*]
K-SSS......... KSC [*Kennedy Space Center*] Shuttle Project Station Set Specification [*NASA*]   (NASA)
KSST........... Sulphur Springs, TX [*AM radio station call letters*]
KSSU-FM.... Durant, OK [*FM radio station call letters*]   (RBYB)
KST .... Kallistatin   (DMAA)
KST .... Kathodenschilessungs-Tetanus [*or Kathodal closing tetanus*] [*Medicine*]   (DAVI)
KST .... Keilinschriftliche Studien [*A publication*]   (BJA)
KST .... Kemper Strategic Income [*AMEX symbol*]   (TTSB)
KST .... Kemper Strategic Income Fund [*NYSE symbol*]   (SAG)
KST .... Keyseat   (KSC)
KST .... Key Station Terminal [*Computer science*]
KST .... King Solomon's Temple [*Freemasonry*]
KST .... Known Segment Table [*Computer science*]   (IAA)
KST .... Kolcsonos Segito Takarekpenztarak [*Mutual Savings Banks*] [*Hungarian*]
KST .... Kosti [*Sudan*] [*Airport symbol*]   (AD)
KSTA .... Coleman, TX [*AM radio station call letters*]
KSTA-FM ..... Coleman, TX [*FM radio station call letters*]
KSTB-FM ..... Crystal Beach, TX [*FM radio station call letters*]   (RBYB)
KSTC .... Kansas State Teachers College
KSTC .... Sterling, CO [*AM radio station call letters*]
KSTE .... Rancho Cordova, CA [*AM radio station call letters*]
KSteC .... Sterling College, Sterling, KS [*Library symbol Library of Congress*]   (LCLS)
KSTF........... Scottsbluff, NE [*Television station call letters*]
KSTG .... Sikeston, MO [*FM radio station call letters*]
KStJ .... Knight Commander of [*the Order of*] St. John of Jerusalem [*British*]
KStJ .... Knight of the Order of St. John of Jerusalem   (DD)
K St J of J.... Knight of St. John of Jerusalem [*Freemasonry*]   (ROG)
KSTK........... Wrangell, AK [*FM radio station call letters*]

KSTL............ St. Louis/Lambert-St. Louis International [*Missouri*] [*ICAO location identifier*] (ICLI)
KSTL............ St. Louis, MO [*AM radio station call letters*]
KSTM............ Indianola, IA [*FM radio station call letters*]
KSTN............ Keystone Financial [*NASDAQ symbol*] (TTSB)
KSTN............ Keystone Financial, Inc. [*NASDAQ symbol*] (NQ)
KSTN............ Kriegsstaerke-Nachweisung [*Table of Organization*] [*German military - World War II*]
KSTN............ Stockton, CA [*AM radio station call letters*]
KSTN-FM..... Stockton, CA [*FM radio station call letters*]
KSTO............ Agana, GU [*FM radio station call letters*]
K stoff.......... Chloromethyl Chloroformate [*Organic chemistry*] (DAVI)
KSTP............ St. Paul, MN [*AM radio station call letters*]
KSTP-FM...... St. Paul, MN [*FM radio station call letters*]
KSTP-TV...... St. Paul, MN [*Television station call letters*]
KSTQ............ Alexandria, MN [*FM radio station call letters*]
KSTR............ Montrose, CO [*FM radio station call letters*]
KSTRL.......... Kestrel (ABBR)
KSTS............ San Jose, CA [*Television station call letters*]
K-STSM........ KSC [*Kennedy Space Center*] Space Transportation System Management [*Document*] [*NASA*] (NASA)
K-STSN........ KSC [*Kennedy Space Center*] Shuttle Test Station Notice [*NASA*] (GFGA)
K-STSPS...... KSC [*Kennedy Space Center*] Shuttle Test Station Project Specification [*NASA*] (GFGA)
KSTT............ Los Osos-Baywood Park, CA [*FM radio station call letters*]
KSTU............ Salt Lake City, UT [*Television station call letters*]
KSTV............ Stephenville, TX [*AM radio station call letters*]
KSTV............ Ventura, CA [*Television station call letters*]
KSTW............ Tacoma, WA [*Television station call letters*]
KSTX............ San Antonio, TX [*FM radio station call letters*]
KSTY............ Canon City, CO [*FM radio station call letters*]
KSTZ............ Des Moines, IA [*FM radio station call letters*]
ksu.............. Kansas [*MARC country of publication code Library of Congress*] (LCCP)
KSU............. Kansas City So. Ind. [*NYSE symbol*] (TTSB)
KSU............. Kansas City Southern Industries, Inc. [*NYSE symbol*] (SPSG)
KSU............. Kansas State University
KSU............. Kent State University [*Ohio*]
KSU............. Kent State University, Kent, OH [*OCLC symbol*] (OCLC)
KSU............. Key Service Unit (IEEE)
KSU............. Key System Control Unit [*Telecommunications*]
KSU............. Kousour [*Djibouti*] [*Seismograph station code, US Geological Survey*] (SEIS)
KSU............. Kristiansund [*Norway*] [*Airport symbol*] (OAG)
KSU............. Kyoto Sangyo University [*UTLAS symbol*]
KSUA............ College, AK [*FM radio station call letters*]
KSUB............ Cedar City, UT [*AM radio station call letters*]
KSUD............ West Memphis, AR [*AM radio station call letters*]
KSUE............ Susanville, CA [*AM radio station call letters*]
KSUI............ Iowa City, IA [*FM radio station call letters*]
KSUM............ Fairmont, MN [*AM radio station call letters*]
KSUN............ Phoenix, AZ [*AM radio station call letters*]
KSUP............ Juneau, AK [*FM radio station call letters*]
KSUPr.......... Kansas City So. Ind 4% Pfd [*NYSE symbol*] (TTSB)
KSUT............ Ignacio, CO [*FM radio station call letters*]
KSUU............ Cedar City, UT [*FM radio station call letters*]
KSUU............ Fairfield/Travis Air Force Base [*California*] [*ICAO location identifier*] (ICLI)
KSUV-FM..... McFarland, CA [*FM radio station call letters*]
KSUX............ Sioux City [*Iowa*] [*ICAO location identifier*] (ICLI)
KSUX............ Winnebago, NE [*FM radio station call letters*]
KSVA............ Corrales, NM [*FM radio station call letters*]
KSVC............ Richfield, UT [*AM radio station call letters*]
KSVE............ El Paso, TX [*AM radio station call letters*]
KSVI............ Billings, MT [*Television station call letters*]
KSVN............ Ogden, UT [*AM radio station call letters*]
KSVP............ Artesia, NM [*AM radio station call letters*]
KSVR............ Mount Vernon, WA [*FM radio station call letters*]
KSVY............ Opportunity, WA [*AM radio station call letters*]
KSW............. C. H. Boehringer Sohn, Ingelheim [*Germany*] [*Research code symbol*]
KSW............. Wichita State University, Wichita, KS [*OCLC symbol*] (OCLC)
KSWA............ Graham, TX [*AM radio station call letters*]
KSWA............ Swan Islands [*ICAO location identifier*] (ICLI)
KSWB............ Seaside, OR [*AM radio station call letters*] (RBYB)
KSWB-TV..... San Diego, CA [*TV station call letters*] (RBYB)
KSWC............ Winfield, KS [*FM radio station call letters*]
KSWD............ Seward, AK [*AM radio station call letters*]
KSWF............ Newburgh/Stewart [*New York*] [*ICAO location identifier*] (ICLI)
KSWG-FM..... Wickenburg, AZ [*FM radio station call letters*] (RBYB)
KSWH............ Arkadelphia, AR [*FM radio station call letters*]
K Swiss........ K Swiss, Inc. [*Associated Press*] (SAG)
KSWK............ Lakin, KS [*Television station call letters*]
KSWM............ Aurora, MO [*AM radio station call letters*]
KSWO............ Lawton, OK [*AM radio station call letters*]
KSWO-TV..... Lawton, OK [*Television station call letters*]
KSWP............ Lufkin, TX [*FM radio station call letters*]
KSWR............ Clinton, OK [*FM radio station call letters*]
KSWS............ K Swiss, Inc. [*NASDAQ symbol*] (SAG)
KSWS............ K Swiss Inc. 'A' [*NASDAQ symbol*] (TTSB)
KSWS............ Sisseton, SD [*FM radio station call letters*]
KSWT............ Yuma, AZ [*Television station call letters*]
KSWV............ Santa Fe, NM [*AM radio station call letters*]
KSWW............ Raymond, WA [*FM radio station call letters*]

KSXX............ Marysville, CA [*FM radio station call letters*]
KSYC............ Yreka, CA [*AM radio station call letters*]
KSYC-FM..... Yreka, CA [*FM radio station call letters*] (RBYB)
KSYD............ Reedsport, OR [*FM radio station call letters*]
KSYE............ Frederick, OK [*FM radio station call letters*]
KSYG............ Little Rock, AR [*AM radio station call letters*] (RBYB)
KSYG-FM..... Little Rock, AR [*FM radio station call letters*] (RBYB)
KSYL............ Alexandria, LA [*AM radio station call letters*]
KSYM............ San Antonio, TX [*FM radio station call letters*]
KSYM............ Smyrna/Sewart Air Force Base [*Tennessee*] [*ICAO location identifier*] (ICLI)
KSYN............ Joplin, MO [*FM radio station call letters*]
KSYR............ Syracuse/Hancock International [*New York*] [*ICAO location identifier*] (ICLI)
KSYS............ Medford, OR [*Television station call letters*]
KSYV............ Solvang, CA [*FM radio station call letters*]
KSYY-FM..... Fallbrook, CA [*FM radio station call letters*] (RBYB)
KSYZ............ Grand Island, NE [*FM radio station call letters*]
KSZL............ Barstow, CA [*AM radio station call letters*]
KSZL............ Knobnoster/Whiteman Air Force Base [*Missouri*] [*ICAO location identifier*] (ICLI)
KSZZ............ San Bernardino, CA [*AM radio station call letters*] (RBYB)
KT................ British Airtours Ltd. [*British ICAO designator*] (ICDA)
KT................ Canadian-Tech Industries, Inc. [*Vancouver Stock Exchange symbol*]
KT................ Contract [*Navy*]
KT................ Cretaceous-Tertiary [*Geology*]
KT................ Kangmar Thrust [*Geophysics*]
KT................ Karat [*Also, CT*]
KT................ Karuna Trust [*Multinational association based in England*] (EAIO)
KT................ Katy Indus [*NYSE symbol*] (TTSB)
KT................ Katy Industries, Inc. [*Formerly, Missouri-Kansas-Texas R. R. Co., with Wall Street slang name of "Kathy"*] [*NYSE symbol*] (SPSG)
KT................ Keel Torsion (SSD)
KT................ Kentucky & Tennessee Railway [*AAR code*]
KT................ Kermit [*Texas*] [*Seismograph station code, US Geological Survey*] (SEIS)
KT................ Ketamine [*An anesthetic*]
KT................ Keying Time [*Computer order entry*]
KT................ Khaksar Tehrik [*Pakistan*] [*Political party*] (FEA)
KT................ Khotanese Texts (BJA)
KT................ Kidney Transplant [*Surgery*] (DAVI)
KT................ Kidney Transplant [*Medicine*] (DMAA)
kt................ Kiloton [*Nuclear equivalent of 1000 tons of high explosives*]
KT................ Kinetic Theory
KT................ Kinetin [*Plant growth regulator*]
KT................ Kingston-upon-Thames [*Postcode*] (ODBW)
KT................ Kit
KT................ Klippel-Trenaunay [*Syndrome*] [*Medicine*] (DAVI)
KT................ Knight [*British title*]
KT................ Knight [*Chess*]
KT................ Knighted
KT................ Knight of Tabor [*Freemasonry*] (ROG)
KT................ Knight of the Thistle [*British*]
KT................ Knights Templar
KT................ Knots [*Also, K*] [*Nautical speed unit*]
K-T............... Kosterlitz-Thouless Theory [*Physics*]
KT................ Kuder Test [*Psychology*] (DAVI)
KT................ Kungtang [*Labor party*] [*Taiwan*] [*Political party*] (EY)
KT................ Topeka Public Library, Topeka, KS [*Library symbol Library of Congress*] (LCLS)
KT................ Trinidad and Tobago [*IYRU nationality code*] (IYR)
KT................ Turtle Airways [*ICAO designator*] (AD)
KTA.............. Kansas Telecommunications Association (SRA)
KTA.............. Karratha [*Australia Airport symbol*] (OAG)
KTA.............. Kentucky Telephone Association (SRA)
KTA.............. Kentucky Thoroughbred Association (SRA)
KTA.............. Keyboard Teachers Association (EA)
KTA.............. Key Telephone Adapter [*Telecommunications*] (TEL)
KTA.............. Kindergarten Teachers Association (BARN)
KTA.............. Kite Trade Association International (EA)
KTA.............. Knitted Textile Association (EA)
KTA.............. Knots True Airspeed
KTA.............. Korea Tourist Association (EAIO)
KTA.............. Kotzebue [*Alaska*] [*Seismograph station code, US Geological Survey*] (SEIS)
KTA.............. Potassium Turbo-Alternator
KTAA............ Kerman, CA [*FM radio station call letters*]
KTAB............ Abilene, TX [*Television station call letters*]
KTAC............ Ephrata, WA [*FM radio station call letters*] (RBYB)
KTAE............ Taylor, TX [*AM radio station call letters*]
KTAG............ Cody, WY [*FM radio station call letters*]
KTAG............ Korea Trade Advisory Group [*British Overseas Trade Board*] (DS)
KTAI............ Kingsville, TX [*FM radio station call letters*]
KTAI............ Kite Trade Association International [*Later, KTA*] (EA)
KTAJ............ St. Joseph, MO [*Television station call letters*]
KTAK............ Riverton, WY [*FM radio station call letters*]
KTAL............ Texarkana, TX [*Television station call letters*]
KTAL-TV...... Texarkana, TX [*Television station call letters*]
KTAM............ Bryan, TX [*AM radio station call letters*]
KTAN............ Sierra Vista, AZ [*AM radio station call letters*]
KTAO............ Taos, NM [*FM radio station call letters*]
KTAP............ Santa Maria, CA [*AM radio station call letters*]
KTAQ............ Greeneville, TX [*Television station call letters*]
KTAR............ Phoenix, AZ [*AM radio station call letters*]
KTAS............ Knots True Airspeed [*Navy*] (NVT)

KTAT	Frederick, OK [*AM radio station call letters*]
KTAX	Kaye Kotts Associates, Inc. [*NASDAQ symbol*] (SAG)
KTAX	Kay Kotts Assoc [*NASDAQ symbol*] (TTSB)
KTAXW	Kaye Kotts Assoc Wrrt [*NASDAQ symbol*] (TTSB)
KTB	Kosterlitz-Thouless-Berezinskii Layers [*Physics*]
KTB	Kriegstagebuch [*War Diary*] [*German military - World War II*]
KTB	Thorne River, AK [*Location identifier FAA*] (FAAL)
KTBA	Ketothiomethylbutyric Acid [*Organic chemistry*]
KTBA	Tuba City, AZ [*AM radio station call letters*]
Kt Bach	Knight Bachelor
KTBB	Tyler, TX [*AM radio station call letters*]
KTBC	Austin, TX [*Television station call letters*]
KTBI	Ephrata, WA [*AM radio station call letters*]
KTBJ-FM	Festus, MO [*FM radio station call letters*] (RBYB)
KTBL-FM	Albuquerque, NM [*FM radio station call letters*] (RBYB)
KTBN	Santa Ana, CA [*Television station call letters*]
KTBO	Oklahoma City, OK [*Television station call letters*]
KTBQ	Nacogdoches, TX [*FM radio station call letters*]
KTBR	Roseburg, OR [*AM radio station call letters*]
KTBS	Shreveport, LA [*Television station call letters*]
KTBW	Tacoma, WA [*Television station call letters*]
KTBY	Anchorage, AK [*Television station call letters*]
KTBZ	Lake Jackson, TX [*AM radio station call letters*] (RBYB)
KTC	Kellogg Telecommunications Corp. [*Littleton, CO*] [*Telecommunications*] (TSSD)
KTC	Kentucky Tourism Council (SRA)
KTC	Kutchino [*Later, MOS*] [*Former USSR Geomagnetic observatory code*]
KTC	Somerset Community College, Somerset, KY [*OCLC symbol*] (OCLC)
KTC	Trinity College Library, University of Toronto [*UTLAS symbol*]
KTCA	St. Paul, MN [*Television station call letters*]
KTCB	Malden, MO [*AM radio station call letters*]
KTCC	Colby, KS [*FM radio station call letters*]
KTCC	Key Tronic Corp. [*NASDAQ symbol*] (TTSB)
KTCC	Key Tronics Corp. [*NASDAQ symbol*] (NQ)
KTCC	Tucumcari [*New Mexico*] [*ICAO location identifier*] (ICLI)
KTCE	Payson, UT [*AM radio station call letters*]
KTCF	Crosby, MN [*FM radio station call letters*]
KTCH	Wayne, NE [*AM radio station call letters*]
KTCH-FM	Wayne, NE [*FM radio station call letters*]
KTCHN	Kitchen
KTCHP	Ketchup (ABBR)
KTCI	St. Paul, MN [*Television station call letters*]
KTCJ	Minneapolis, MN [*AM radio station call letters*]
KTCK	Dallas, TX [*AM radio station call letters*]
KTCL	Fort Collins, CO [*FM radio station call letters*]
KTCM	Kingman, KS [*FM radio station call letters*]
KTCM	Tacoma/McChord Air Force Base [*Washington*] [*ICAO location identifier*] (ICLI)
KTCN	Eureka Springs, AR [*FM radio station call letters*]
KTCN	Kitchen (ABBR)
KTCNET	Kitchennette (ABBR)
KTCNWR	Kitchenware (ABBR)
KTCO	Duluth, MN [*FM radio station call letters*]
KTCO	Kenan Transport [*NASDAQ symbol*] (TTSB)
KTCO	Kenan Transportation Co. [*NASDAQ symbol*] (NQ)
KTCR	Kennewick, WA [*AM radio station call letters*]
KTCS	Fort Smith, AR [*AM radio station call letters*]
KTCS	Truth Or Consequences/Municipal [*New Mexico*] [*ICAO location identifier*] (ICLI)
KTCS-FM	Fort Smith, AR [*FM radio station call letters*]
KTCU	Fort Worth, TX [*FM radio station call letters*]
KTCV	Kennewick, WA [*AM radio station call letters*]
KTCX-FM	Beaumont, TX [*FM radio station call letters*] (RBYB)
KTCY	Denison, TX [*FM radio station call letters*]
KTCZ	Minneapolis, MN [*FM radio station call letters*]
KTD	Killed Target Detector [*Military*] (PDAA)
KTD	Kita-Daito [*Japan*] [*Airport symbol*] (OAG)
KTDB	Ramah, NM [*FM radio station call letters*]
KTDO	Columbia, CA [*FM radio station call letters*] (RBYB)
KTDR	Del Rio, TX [*FM radio station call letters*]
KTDS	Key to Disk Software
KTDX	Mountain Pine, AR [*FM radio station call letters*] (RBYB)
KTDY	Lafayette, LA [*FM radio station call letters*]
KTE	Kennedy-Thorndike Experiment
KTE	Kermit [*Texas*] [*Seismograph station code, US Geological Survey*] (SEIS)
K-TEA	Kaufman Test of Educational Achievement
KTEB	Teterboro [*New Jersey*] [*ICAO location identifier*] (ICLI)
KTEC	Key Technologies, Inc. [*NASDAQ symbol*] (SAG)
KTEC	Key Technology [*NASDAQ symbol*] (TTSB)
KTEC	Klamath Falls, OR [*FM radio station call letters*]
KTEG	Albuquerque, NM [*FM radio station call letters*] (RBYB)
KTEH	San Jose, CA [*Television station call letters*]
KTEJ	Jonesboro, AR [*Television station call letters*]
KTEK	Alvin, TX [*AM radio station call letters*]
K-TEL	Kives-Television [*In company name K-Tel International. Derived from name of company president and fact that it markets its products on television*]
KTEL	K-Tel International [*NASDAQ symbol*] (TTSB)
K-Tel	K-tel International, Inc. [*Associated Press*] (SAG)
KTEL	K-tel International, Inc. [*NASDAQ symbol*] (SAG)
KTEL	Walla Walla, WA [*AM radio station call letters*]
KTEL-FM	Walla Walla, WA [*FM radio station call letters*]
KTEM	Temple, TX [*AM radio station call letters*]

KTEN	Ada, OK [*Television station call letters*]
KTEO	Wichita Falls, TX [*FM radio station call letters*]
KTEP	El Paso, TX [*FM radio station call letters*]
KTEQ	Rapid City, SD [*FM radio station call letters*]
KTEX	Brownsville, TX [*FM radio station call letters*]
KTF	Kansas Turfgrass Foundation (EA)
KTF	Kauai Test Facility [*AEC*]
KTF	Kemper Municipal Income Fund [*NYSE symbol*] (CTT)
KTF	Kemper Muni Income [*NYSE symbol*] (TTSB)
KTF	Kuwaiti [*Civil Affairs*] Task Force (DOMA)
KTFA	Groves, TX [*FM radio station call letters*]
KTFC	Sioux City, IA [*FM radio station call letters*]
KTFG	Sioux Rapids, IA [*FM radio station call letters*]
KTFH	Conroe, TX [*Television station call letters*]
KTFI	Twin Falls, ID [*AM radio station call letters*]
KTFJ	Dakota City, NE [*AM radio station call letters*]
KTFM	San Antonio, TX [*FM radio station call letters*]
KTFO	Tulsa, OK [*Television station call letters*]
KTFR	Claremore, OK [*AM radio station call letters*]
KTFR	Kodak Thin-Film Resist [*Cathode coating*]
KTFS-AM	Texarkana, TX [*AM radio station call letters*] (RBYB)
KTFX	Sand Springs, OK [*FM radio station call letters*] (RBYB)
KTG	Kap Tobin [*Greenland*] [*Seismograph station code, US Geological Survey*] (SEIS)
KTG	Ketapang [*Indonesia*] [*Airport symbol*] (OAG)
KTGE	Salinas, CA [*AM radio station call letters*]
KTGF	Great Falls, MT [*Television station call letters*]
KTGF	Keratinocyte T-Cell Growth Factor [*Immunology*]
KTGG	Spring Arbor, MI [*AM radio station call letters*]
KTGIFC	Karen Taylor-Good International Fan Club [*Defunct*] (EA)
KTGL	Beatrice, NE [*FM radio station call letters*]
KTGM	Tamuning, GU [*Television station call letters*]
KTGO	Tioga, ND [*AM radio station call letters*]
KTGP-FM	Pawhuska, OK [*FM radio station call letters*] (RBYB)
KTGR	Columbia, MO [*AM radio station call letters*]
KTH	Kungliga Tekniska Hoegskolan [*Royal Institute of Technology*] [*Stockholm, Sweden*] (ARC)
KTHB	Kungliga Tekniska Hogskolans Bibliotek [*Royal Institute of Technology Library*] [*Information service or system*] (IID)
KTHC	Sidney, MT [*FM radio station call letters*] (RBYB)
KTHE	Thermopolis, WY [*AM radio station call letters*]
KTHK	Okmulgee, OK [*FM radio station call letters*]
KTHO	South Lake Tahoe, CA [*AM radio station call letters*]
KTHQ-FM	Eagar, AZ [*FM radio station call letters*] (RBYB)
KTHR-FM	Grants, NM [*FM radio station call letters*] (RBYB)
KTHS	Berryville, AR [*AM radio station call letters*]
KTHS-FM	Berryville, AR [*FM radio station call letters*]
KTHT	Fresno, CA [*FM radio station call letters*]
KTHV	Little Rock, AR [*Television station call letters*]
KTHX	Visalia, CA [*AM radio station call letters*]
KTHX-FM	Carson City, NV [*FM radio station call letters*]
KTI	Kano Transport International Ltd. KATI Air [*Nigeria*] [*ICAO designator*] (FAAC)
KTI	Kinai Technologies, Inc. [*Formerly, Kinai Resources Corp.*] [*Vancouver Stock Exchange symbol*]
KTI	Kirsch Technologies, Inc. [*Software manufacturer*] [*St. Clair, MI*]
KTI	Kitchen Table International [*David D. Busch's vaporware software company*]
KTI	Kratie [*Cambodia*] [*Airport symbol*] (AD)
KTI	KTI, Inc. [*Associated Press*] (SAG)
KTIB	Thibodaux, LA [*AM radio station call letters*]
KTIC	West Point, NE [*AM radio station call letters*] (RBYB)
KTIE	Bakersfield, CA [*FM radio station call letters*]
KTIE	KTI, Inc. [*NASDAQ symbol*] (SAG)
KTIG	Pequot Lakes, MN [*FM radio station call letters*]
KTII	K-Tron International, Inc. [*NASDAQ symbol*] (NQ)
KTII	K-Tron Intl [*NASDAQ symbol*] (TTSB)
KTIJ	Elk City, OK [*FM radio station call letters*]
KTIK	Nampa, ID [*AM radio station call letters*]
KTIK	Oklahoma City/Tinker Air Force Base [*Oklahoma*] [*ICAO location identifier*] (ICLI)
KTIL-FM	Tillamook, OR [*FM radio station call letters*]
KTIM	Wickenburg, AZ [*AM radio station call letters*]
KTIN	Fort Dodge, IA [*Television station call letters*]
KTIP	Porterville, CA [*AM radio station call letters*]
KTIS	Minneapolis, MN [*AM radio station call letters*]
KTIS-FM	Minneapolis, MN [*FM radio station call letters*]
KTIV	Sioux City, IA [*Television station call letters*]
KTIX	Pendleton, OR [*AM radio station call letters*]
KTJC	Rayville, LA [*FM radio station call letters*]
KTJJ	Farmington, MO [*FM radio station call letters*]
KTJN	Mercedes, TX [*FM radio station call letters*]
KTJO	Ottawa, KS [*FM radio station call letters*]
KTJS	Hobart, OK [*AM radio station call letters*]
KTJX	Mission, TX [*FM radio station call letters*]
KTKA	Topeka, KS [*Television station call letters*]
KTKC	Springhill, LA [*FM radio station call letters*]
KTKK	Sandy, UT [*AM radio station call letters*]
KTKN	Ketchikan, AK [*AM radio station call letters*]
KTKO	Beeville, TX [*FM radio station call letters*]
KTKR	San Antonio, TX [*AM radio station call letters*]
KTKS	Versailles, MO [*FM radio station call letters*]
KTKT	Tucson, AZ [*AM radio station call letters*]
KTKU	Juneau, AK [*FM radio station call letters*]
KTKX	Crystal Beach, TX [*FM radio station call letters*]

ktl .... Kai ta Loipa [*And the Rest, And So Forth*]
KTL .... Kettle (ABBR)
KTL .... Key-Edit Terminal Language [*Computer science*] (MHDI)
KTL .... Kitale [*Kenya*] [*Airport symbol*] (AD)
KTL .... K-Tel International, Inc. [*Toronto Stock Exchange symbol*] (SPSG)
KTL .... Kuratorium fuer Technik in der Landwirtschaft
KTLA .... Los Angeles, CA [*Television station call letters*]
KTLB .... Twin Lakes, IA [*FM radio station call letters*]
KTLC .... Oklahoma City, OK [*Television station call letters*]
KTLD .... Pineville, LA [*AM radio station call letters*]
KTLDR .... Kettledrum (ABBR)
KTLE .... Tooele, UT [*FM radio station call letters*]
KTLF .... Colorado Springs, CO [*FM radio station call letters*]
KTLH .... Tallahassee/Dale Mabry Field [*Florida*] [*ICAO location identifier*] (ICLI)
KTLI .... El Dorado, KS [*FM radio station call letters*]
KTLK .... Thornton, CO [*AM radio station call letters*]
KTLN .... Thibodaux, LA [*FM radio station call letters*] (RBYB)
KTLO .... Mountain Home, AR [*AM radio station call letters*]
KTLO-FM .... Mountain Home, AR [*FM radio station call letters*]
KTLQ .... Tahlequah, OK [*AM radio station call letters*]
KTLR .... Terrell, TX [*FM radio station call letters*]
KTLS .... Ada, OK [*FM radio station call letters*]
KTLT .... Wichita Falls, TX [*FM radio station call letters*]
KTLU .... Rusk, TX [*AM radio station call letters*]
KTLV .... Midwest City, OK [*AM radio station call letters*]
KTLW .... Lancaster, CA [*FM radio station call letters*] (RBYB)
KTLX .... Columbus, NE [*FM radio station call letters*]
KTM .... Katmai [*Alaska*] [*Seismograph station code, US Geological Survey*] (SEIS)
KTM .... Katmandu [*Nepal*] [*Airport symbol*] (OAG)
KTM .... Key Transport Module
KTM .... Menninger Clinic Library, Topeka, KS [*Library symbol Library of Congress*] (LCLS)
KTM .... Thomas More College, Fort Mitchell, KY [*OCLC symbol*] (OCLC)
KT MAR SC... Knight Mareschal of Scotland (ROG)
KTMB .... Miami/New Tamiami [*Florida*] [*ICAO location identifier*] (ICLI)
KTMC .... McAlester, OK [*AM radio station call letters*]
KTMC-FM .... McAlester, OK [*FM radio station call letters*]
KTMD .... Galveston, TX [*Television station call letters*]
KTME .... Lompoc, CA [*AM radio station call letters*]
KTMF .... Missoula, MT [*Television station call letters*]
KTMG .... Deer Trail, CO [*AM radio station call letters*]
KTMN .... Los Alamos, NM [*FM radio station call letters*]
KTMO .... Kennett, MO [*FM radio station call letters*]
KTMP .... Heber City, UT [*AM radio station call letters*]
KTMR .... Edna, TX [*AM radio station call letters*]
KTMS .... Knapp Time Metaphor Scale
KTMS .... Santa Barbara, CA [*AM radio station call letters*]
KTMT .... Medford, OR [*FM radio station call letters*]
KTMT .... Phoenix, OR [*AM radio station call letters*]
KTMX .... York, NE [*FM radio station call letters*]
KTN .... Keltic, Inc. [*Toronto Stock Exchange symbol*]
KTN .... Ketchikan [*Alaska*] [*Airport symbol*] (OAG)
KTN .... Ketchikan, AK [*Location identifier FAA*] (FAAL)
KTN .... Kitten (ABBR)
KTN .... Kuratorium fuer die Tagungen der Nobelpreistrager [*Standing Committee for Nobel Prize Winners' Congresses - SCNPWC*] [*Germany*] (EA)
KTN .... Potassium Tantalate Niobate (MCD)
KTNA .... Talkeetna, AK [*FM radio station call letters*]
KTNC .... Falls City, NE [*AM radio station call letters*]
KTNC-TV ...... Concord, CA [*TV station call letters*] (RBYB)
KTND .... Ojai, CA [*FM radio station call letters*] (RBYB)
KTNE .... Alliance, NE [*FM radio station call letters*]
KTNE-TV ...... Alliance, NE [*Television station call letters*]
KTNF .... Kodak Timing Negative Film
KTNH .... Kittenish (ABBR)
KTNI .... Kansas Neurological Institute, Topeka, KS [*Library symbol Library of Congress*] (LCLS)
KTNL .... Sitka, AK [*Television station call letters*]
KTNM .... Tucumcari, NM [*AM radio station call letters*]
KTNN .... Window Rock, AZ [*AM radio station call letters*]
KTNO .... Fort Worth, TX [*AM radio station call letters*]
KTNP-FM .... Bennington, NE [*FM radio station call letters*] (RBYB)
KTNQ .... Los Angeles, CA [*AM radio station call letters*]
KTNR .... Kenedy, TX [*FM radio station call letters*]
KTNS .... Oakhurst, CA [*AM radio station call letters*]
KTNT .... Edmund, OK [*FM radio station call letters*]
KTNT .... Miami/Dade-Collier Training and Transition Airport [*Florida*] [*ICAO location identifier*] (ICLI)
KTNV .... Las Vegas, NV [*Television station call letters*]
KTNW .... Richland, WA [*Television station call letters*]
KTNY .... Libby, MT [*FM radio station call letters*]
KTNZ .... Amarillo, TX [*AM radio station call letters*] (RBYB)
KTO .... Kato [*Guyana*] [*Airport symbol*] (OAG)
KTO .... Kraus-Thomson Organization [*Publishing*]
KtO .... KTO Microform, Millwood, NY [*Library symbol Library of Congress*] (LCLS)
KTO .... Kuwaiti Theatre of Operation [*Operation Desert Storm*]
KTOB .... Petaluma, CA [*AM radio station call letters*]
KTOC .... Jonesboro, LA [*AM radio station call letters*]
KTOC-FM .... Jonesboro, LA [*FM radio station call letters*]
KTOD .... Conway, AR [*FM radio station call letters*]
KTOE .... Mankato, MN [*AM radio station call letters*]

KTOF .... Cedar Rapids, IA [*FM radio station call letters*]
KTOK .... Oklahoma City, OK [*AM radio station call letters*]
KTOL .... Lacey, WA [*AM radio station call letters*]
KTOM .... Salinas, CA [*AM radio station call letters*]
KTOM-FM ... Salinas, CA [*FM radio station call letters*]
KTON .... Belton, TX [*AM radio station call letters*]
KTON .... Ketone [*Organic chemistry*] (ABBR)
KTOO .... Juneau, AK [*FM radio station call letters*]
KTOO-TV .... Juneau, AK [*Television station call letters*]
KTOP .... Topeka, KS [*AM radio station call letters*]
KTOQ .... Rapid City, SD [*AM radio station call letters*]
KTOW .... Sand Springs, OK [*AM radio station call letters*]
KTOW-FM ... Sand Springs, OK [*FM radio station call letters*]
KTOX .... Needles, CA [*AM radio station call letters*]
KTOZ .... Marshfield, MO [*FM radio station call letters*]
KTOZ .... Springfield, MO [*AM radio station call letters*]
KTP .... Kentucky Truck Plant [*Ford Motor Co.*]
KTP .... Keyboard Typing Perforator (NITA)
KTP .... Kingston-Tinson [*Jamaica*] [*Airport symbol*] (OAG)
KT P .... Knight's Pawn [*Chess*] (ROG)
KTP .... Kommunistinen Tyovaenpuolue [*Communist Workers' Party*] [*Finland*] [*Political party*] (EY)
KTPA .... Prescott, AR [*AM radio station call letters*]
KTPA .... Tampa/International [*Florida*] [*ICAO location identifier*] (ICLI)
KTPB .... Kilgore, TX [*FM radio station call letters*]
KTPH .... Tonopah, NV [*FM radio station call letters*]
KTPI .... Kaum-Tani Persatuan Indonesia [*Indonesian Farmers' Party*] [*Surinam*] [*Political party*] (PPW)
KTPI .... Tehachapi, CA [*FM radio station call letters*]
KTPK .... Topeka, KS [*FM radio station call letters*]
KTPR .... Fort Dodge, IA [*FM radio station call letters*]
KTQM .... Clovis, NM [*FM radio station call letters*]
KTQX .... Bakersfield, CA [*FM radio station call letters*]
KTR .... Contractor
KTR .... Helikoptertransport AB [*Sweden ICAO designator*] (FAAC)
KTR .... K-2 Resources, Inc. [*Vancouver Stock Exchange symbol*]
KTR .... Katherine [*Northern Territory, Australia*] [*Airport symbol*] (AD)
KTR .... Katuura [*Japan*] [*Seismograph station code, US Geological Survey Closed*] (SEIS)
KTR .... Katuura [*Japan*] [*Later, HTY*] [*Geomagnetic observatory code*]
KTR .... Keyboard Typing Reperforator [*Computer science*]
KTRA .... Farmington, NM [*FM radio station call letters*]
KTRB .... Modesto, CA [*AM radio station call letters*]
KTRC .... Santa Fe, NM [*AM radio station call letters*]
KTRE-TV ...... Lufkin, TX [*Television station call letters*]
KTRF .... Thief River Falls, MN [*AM radio station call letters*]
KTRG .... Del Rio, TX [*Television station call letters*]
KTRH .... Houston, TX [*AM radio station call letters*]
KTRI .... Mansfield, MO [*FM radio station call letters*]
KTRJ-AM .... Frazier Park, CA [*AM radio station call letters*] (RBYB)
KTRK .... Houston, TX [*Television station call letters*]
KTRN .... Silverton, CO [*FM radio station call letters*]
KTRO .... Port Hueneme, CA [*AM radio station call letters*]
KTron .... K-Tron International, Inc. [*Associated Press*] (SAG)
KTRQ-FM .... Quincy, WA [*FM radio station call letters*] (RBYB)
KTRR .... Loveland, CO [*FM radio station call letters*]
KTRS .... Casper, WY [*FM radio station call letters*]
KTRT .... Claremore, OK [*AM radio station call letters*]
KTRU .... Houston, TX [*FM radio station call letters*]
KTRV .... Nampa, ID [*Television station call letters*]
KTRW .... Spokane, WA [*AM radio station call letters*]
KTRX .... Tarkio, MO [*FM radio station call letters*]
KTRY .... Bastrop, LA [*AM radio station call letters*]
KTRY-FM .... Bastrop, LA [*FM radio station call letters*]
KTRZ .... Riverton, WY [*FM radio station call letters*]
KTS .... Brevig Mission [*Alaska*] [*Airport symbol*] (OAG)
KTS .... Kelvin Temperature Scale
KTS .... Kethoxal Thiosemicarbazone [*An antiviral*] [*Pharmacology*] (DAVI)
KTS .... Key Telephone System [*Telecommunications*] (AAG)
KTS .... Kiersley Temperament Sorter [*Psychiatry*] (DAVI)
KTS .... Klippel-Trenaunay Syndrome [*Medicine*] (DMAA)
KTS .... Knight of the Tower and Sword [*Portugal*]
KTS .... Knots (ADA)
KTS .... Kodiak Tracking Station [*NASA*] (MCD)
KTS .... Kotas Joint Civil Aviation Enterprise [*Former USSR*] [*FAA designator*] (FAAC)
KTS .... Kwajalein Test Site (MCD)
KTS .... Southern Baptist Theological Seminary, Louisville, KY [*OCLC symbol*] (OCLC)
KTS .... Teller Mission, AK [*Location identifier FAA*] (FAAL)
KTSA .... Kahn Test of Symbol Arrangement [*Psychology*]
KTSA .... San Antonio, TX [*AM radio station call letters*]
KTSB .... Sioux Center, IA [*FM radio station call letters*]
KTSC .... Kitsch (ABBR)
KTSC .... Pueblo, CO [*FM radio station call letters*]
KTSC-TV ...... Pueblo, CO [*Television station call letters*]
KTSD .... Reliance, SD [*FM radio station call letters*]
KTSD-TV ...... Pierre, SD [*Television station call letters*]
KTSF .... San Francisco, CA [*Television station call letters*]
KTSG .... Klippel-Trenaunay Support Group (EA)
KTSH .... Tishomingo, OK [*FM radio station call letters*]
KTSH .... Topeka State Hospital, Topeka, KS [*Library symbol Library of Congress*] (LCLS)
KTSJ .... Pomona, CA [*AM radio station call letters*]
KTSL .... Medical Lake, WA [*FM radio station call letters*]

KTSM.......... El Paso, TX [*AM radio station call letters*]
KTSM-FM.... El Paso, TX [*FM radio station call letters*]
KTSM-TV..... El Paso, TX [*Television station call letters*]
KTSN-AM..... Elko, NV [*AM radio station call letters*] (RBYB)
KTSR.......... College Station, TX [*FM radio station call letters*]
KTST.......... Oklahoma City, OK [*FM radio station call letters*] (RBYB)
KTSU.......... Houston, TX [*FM radio station call letters*]
KTSV.......... Stormont-Vail Hospital, Topeka, KS [*Library symbol Library of Congress*] (LCLS)
KTSW.......... San Marcos, TX [*FM radio station call letters*]
KTSY.......... Caldwell, ID [*FM radio station call letters*]
KTT.......... Kermit [*Texas*] [*Seismograph station code, US Geological Survey Closed*] (SEIS)
KTT.......... Kittila [*Finland*] [*Airport symbol*] (OAG)
KTTC.......... Keesler Technical Training Center
KTTC.......... Rochester, MN [*Television station call letters*]
KTTG.......... Mena, AR [*FM radio station call letters*] (RBYB)
KTTI.......... Yuma, AZ [*FM radio station call letters*]
KTTL.......... Alva, OK [*FM radio station call letters*]
KTTL.......... Korea Tactical Target List (MCD)
KTTM.......... Huron, SD [*Television station call letters*]
KTTN.......... Trenton/Mercer County [*New Jersey*] [*ICAO location identifier*] (ICLI)
KTTN.......... Trenton, MO [*AM radio station call letters*]
KTTN-FM...... Trenton, MO [*FM radio station call letters*]
KTTR.......... Rolla, MO [*AM radio station call letters*]
KTTR.......... St. James, MO [*FM radio station call letters*]
KTTS.......... Springfield, MO [*AM radio station call letters*]
KTTS-FM..... Springfield, MO [*FM radio station call letters*]
KTTT.......... Columbus, NE [*AM radio station call letters*]
KTTU.......... Tucson, AZ [*Television station call letters*]
KTTV.......... Los Angeles, CA [*Television station call letters*]
KTTW.......... Sioux Falls, SD [*Television station call letters*]
KTTX.......... Brenham, TX [*FM radio station call letters*]
KTTY.......... Kitty Hawk, Inc. [*NASDAQ symbol*] (SAG)
KTTY.......... San Diego, CA [*Television station call letters*]
KTTZ.......... Ajo, AZ [*FM radio station call letters*]
KTU.......... Key Telephone Unit
KTU.......... Kidney Transplant Unit [*National Health Service*] [*British*] (DI)
KTU.......... Kota [*India*] [*Airport symbol*] (OAG)
KTU.......... Kutaisi [*USSR*] [*Airport symbol*] (AD)
KTU.......... Transylvania University, Lexington, KY [*OCLC symbol*] (OCLC)
KTUC.......... Tucson, AZ [*AM radio station call letters*]
KTUE.......... Tulia, TX [*AM radio station call letters*]
KTUF.......... Kirksville, MO [*FM radio station call letters*]
KTUH.......... Honolulu, HI [*FM radio station call letters*]
KTUI.......... Sullivan, MO [*AM radio station call letters*]
KTUI-FM..... Sullivan, MO [*FM radio station call letters*]
KTUL.......... Tulsa/International [*Oklahoma*] [*ICAO location identifier*] (ICLI)
KTUL.......... Tulsa, OK [*Television station call letters*]
KTUN-FM..... Eagle, CO [*FM radio station call letters*] (RBYB)
KTUO.......... Sonora, CA [*FM radio station call letters*]
KTUR.......... Tooele, UT [*FM radio station call letters*]
KTUS.......... Tucson/International [*Arizona*] [*ICAO location identifier*] (ICLI)
KTUU-TV..... Anchorage, AK [*Television station call letters*]
KTUX.......... Carthage, TX [*FM radio station call letters*]
KTV.......... Kamarata [*Venezuela*] [*Airport symbol*] (OAG)
KTV.......... Kuwait Television
KTVA.......... Anchorage, AK [*Television station call letters*]
KTVA.......... United States Veterans Administration Hospital, Topeka, KS [*Library symbol Library of Congress*] (LCLS)
KTVB.......... Boise, ID [*Television station call letters*]
KTVC.......... Cedar Rapids, IA [*Television station call letters*]
KTVD.......... Denver, CO [*Television station call letters*]
KTVE.......... El Dorado, AR [*Television station call letters*]
KTVF.......... Fairbanks, AK [*Television station call letters*]
KTVG.......... Grand Island, NE [*Television station call letters*]
KTVH.......... Helena, MT [*Television station call letters*]
KTVI.......... St. Louis, MO [*Television station call letters*]
KTVJ.......... Boulder, CO [*Television station call letters*]
KTVK.......... Phoenix, AZ [*Television station call letters*]
KTVL.......... Medford, OR [*Television station call letters*]
KTVM.......... Butte, MT [*Television station call letters*]
KTVN.......... Reno, NV [*Television station call letters*]
KTVO.......... Kirksville, MO [*Television station call letters*]
KTVQ.......... Billings, MT [*Television station call letters*]
KTVR.......... La Grande, OR [*Television station call letters*]
KTVS.......... Sterling, CO [*Television station call letters*]
KTVT.......... Fort Worth, TX [*Television station call letters*]
KTVU.......... Oakland, CA [*Television station call letters*]
KTVW.......... Phoenix, AZ [*Television station call letters*]
KTVX.......... Salt Lake City, UT [*Television station call letters*]
KTVZ.......... Bend, OR [*Television station call letters*]
KTW.......... Katowice [*Poland*] [*Airport symbol*] (OAG)
KTW.......... Klippel-Trenaunay-Weber Syndrome [*Medicine*] (DMAA)
KTW.......... Washburn University of Topeka, Topeka, KS [*Library symbol Library of Congress*] (LCLS)
KTWA.......... Ottumwa, IA [*FM radio station call letters*]
KTWB.......... Sioux Falls, SD [*FM radio station call letters*]
KTWC.......... Glendale, AZ [*FM radio station call letters*]
KTWG.......... Agana, GU [*AM radio station call letters*]
KTWI.......... Warm Springs, OR [*FM radio station call letters*]
KTWK.......... Colorado Springs, CO [*FM radio station call letters*]
KTW-L.......... Washburn University of Topeka, School of Law, Topeka, KS [*Library symbol Library of Congress*] (LCLS)
KTWN.......... Texarkana, TX [*AM radio station call letters*]

KTWN-FM.... Texarkana, AR [*FM radio station call letters*]
KTWO.......... Casper, WY [*AM radio station call letters*]
KTWO.......... K2 Design, Inc. [*NASDAQ symbol*] (SAG)
KTWO-TV..... Casper, WY [*Television station call letters*]
KTWS.......... Bend, OR [*FM radio station call letters*]
KTWS.......... Klippel-Trenaunay-Weber Syndrome [*Medicine*] (DMAA)
KTWU.......... Topeka, KS [*Television station call letters*]
KTWV.......... Los Angeles, CA [*FM radio station call letters*]
KTWY-FM.... Walla Walla, WA [*FM radio station call letters*] (RBYB)
KTX.......... Keith Railway Equipment Co. [*AAR code*]
KTX.......... Kermit [*Texas*] [*Seismograph station code, US Geological Survey*] (SEIS)
KTXA.......... Arlington, TX [*Television station call letters*]
KTXB.......... Beaumont, TX [*FM radio station call letters*]
KTXC.......... Cuero, TX [*AM radio station call letters*] (RBYB)
KTXH.......... Houston, TX [*Television station call letters*]
KTXJ.......... Jasper, TX [*AM radio station call letters*]
KTXK.......... Texarkana/Municipal-Webb Field [*Arkansas*] [*ICAO location identifier*] (ICLI)
KTXK.......... Texarkana, TX [*FM radio station call letters*]
KTXL.......... Sacramento, CA [*Television station call letters*]
KTXN.......... Victoria, TX [*FM radio station call letters*]
KTXQ.......... Fort Worth, TX [*FM radio station call letters*]
KTXR.......... Springfield, MO [*FM radio station call letters*]
KTXS.......... Sweetwater, TX [*Television station call letters*]
KTXT.......... Lubbock, TX [*FM radio station call letters*]
KTXT-TV..... Lubbock, TX [*Television station call letters*]
KTXX.......... Devine, TX [*FM radio station call letters*]
KTXY.......... Jefferson City, MO [*FM radio station call letters*]
KTXZ.......... West Lake Hills, TX [*AM radio station call letters*]
KTY.......... Kitty (ABBR)
KTY.......... Terror Bay [*Alaska*] [*Airport symbol*] (OAG)
KTY.......... Terror Bay, AK [*Location identifier FAA*] (FAAL)
KTYCR.......... Kitty-Corner (ABBR)
KTYD.......... Katydid (ABBR)
KTYD.......... Santa Barbara, CA [*FM radio station call letters*]
KTYL.......... Tyler, TX [*FM radio station call letters*]
KTYM.......... Inglewood, CA [*AM radio station call letters*]
KTYN.......... Minot, ND [*AM radio station call letters*]
KTYR.......... Tyler/Pounds Field [*Texas*] [*ICAO location identifier*] (ICLI)
KTYS.......... Knoxville/McGee Tyson [*Tennessee*] [*ICAO location identifier*] (ICLI)
KTZ.......... Katz Media [*AMEX symbol*] (TTSB)
KTZ.......... Katz Media Group, Inc. [*AMEX symbol*] (SAG)
KTZ.......... Kutztown [*Pennsylvania*] [*Seismograph station code, US Geological Survey*] (SEIS)
KTZA.......... Artesia, NM [*FM radio station call letters*]
KTZR.......... Tucson, AZ [*AM radio station call letters*]
KTZZ.......... Seattle, WA [*Television station call letters*]
KU.......... Kallikrein Unit (DMAA)
KU.......... Kapuskasing Uplift [*Geology*] [*Canada*]
KU.......... Karmen Unit [*Medicine*] (MAE)
KU.......... Keep Up [*Typography*] (DGA)
KU.......... Kentucky University (PDAA)
KU.......... Keyboard Unit [*Computer science*] (NASA)
KU.......... Kilourane (ABBR)
KU.......... Kimbel Unit (AAMN)
KU.......... Kitvei Ugarit (BJA)
KU.......... Knightsbridge University [*Denmark*] (ECON)
K-U.......... Kremers-Urban Co. (DAVI)
KU.......... KU Energy [*NYSE symbol*] (TTSB)
KU.......... KU Energy Co. [*NYSE symbol*] (SPSG)
KU.......... Kurchatovium [*See also Rf*] [*Proposed name for chemical element 104*]
Ku.......... Kurtosis [*The relative degree of flatness in the region about the mode of a frequency curve*]
ku.......... Kuwait [*MARC country of publication code Library of Congress*] (LCCP)
KU.......... Kuwait Airways [*ICAO designator*] (AD)
KU.......... University of Kansas, Lawrence, KS [*Library symbol Library of Congress*] (LCLS)
KUA.......... Kit Upkeep Allowance [*British*]
KUA.......... Kuantan [*Malaysia*] [*Airport symbol*] (OAG)
KUAC.......... Fairbanks, AK [*FM radio station call letters*]
KUAC-TV..... Fairbanks, AK [*Television station call letters*]
KUAD.......... Windsor, CO [*FM radio station call letters*]
KUAF.......... Fayetteville, AR [*FM radio station call letters*]
KUAI.......... Eleele, HI [*AM radio station call letters*]
KUAM.......... Agana, GU [*AM radio station call letters*]
KUAM-FM.... Agana, GU [*FM radio station call letters*]
KUAM-TV.... Agana, GU [*Television station call letters*]
KUAP.......... Pine Bluff, AR [*FM radio station call letters*]
KUAR.......... Little Rock, AR [*FM radio station call letters*]
KUAS.......... Tucson, AZ [*Television station call letters*]
KUAT.......... Tucson, AZ [*AM radio station call letters*]
KUAT-FM.... Tucson, AZ [*FM radio station call letters*]
KUAT-TV.... Tucson, AZ [*Television station call letters*]
KUAU.......... Haiku, HI [*AM radio station call letters*]
KUAZ.......... Tucson, AZ [*AM radio station call letters*]
KUB.......... Keilschrifturkunden aus Boghazkoi [*A publication*] (BJA)
KUB.......... Kidney and Upper Bladder
KUB.......... Kidney, Ureter, Bladder [*X-ray*]
KUB.......... Kubota Corp. ADR [*NYSE symbol*] (SPSG)
KUBA.......... Yuba City, CA [*AM radio station call letters*]
KUBB.......... Mariposa, CA [*FM radio station call letters*]
KUBC.......... Montrose, CO [*AM radio station call letters*]

KUBD .... Denver, CO [Television station call letters]
KUBE .... Seattle, WA [FM radio station call letters]
KUBL .... Salt Lake City, UT [FM radio station call letters] (RBYB)
KUBO .... Calexico, CA [FM radio station call letters]
Kubota .... Kubota Corp. [Associated Press] (SAG)
KUBQ .... La Grande, OR [FM radio station call letters]
KUBR .... San Juan, TX [AM radio station call letters]
KUBS .... Newport, WA [FM radio station call letters]
KUC .... Kucino [Former USSR Seismograph station code, US Geological
                    Survey Closed] (SEIS)
KUC .... Kuria [Kiribati] [Airport symbol] (OAG)
KUCA .... Conway, AR [FM radio station call letters]
KUCB .... Des Moines, IA [FM radio station call letters]
KUCD .... Pearl City, HI [FM radio station call letters]
KUCE .... Kiev Universal Commodity Exchange [Ukraine] (EY)
KUCI .... Irvine, CA [FM radio station call letters]
KUCOG .... Kunia Coordinating Group (SAA)
KUCR .... Riverside, CA [FM radio station call letters]
KUCU-AM ..... Hobbs, NM [AM radio station call letters] (RBYB)
KUCV .... Lincoln, NE [FM radio station call letters]
KUD .... Kudat [Malaysia] [Airport symbol] (OAG)
KUDL .... Kansas City, KS [FM radio station call letters]
KUDU-FM ..... Tok, AK [FM radio station call letters] (RBYB)
KUDY .... Spokane, WA [AM radio station call letters]
KUED .... Kodak Unitized Engineering Data
KUED .... Salt Lake City, UT [Television station call letters]
KUEL .... Fort Dodge, IA [FM radio station call letters]
KU Engy ...... KU Energy Corp. [Associated Press] (SAG)
KUER .... Salt Lake City, UT [FM radio station call letters]
KUET .... Black Canyon, AZ [AM radio station call letters] (RBYB)
KUEZ .... Lufkin, TX [FM radio station call letters]
KUF .... Kidney Ultrafiltration Rate [Nephrology] (DAVI)
KUFM .... Missoula, MT [FM radio station call letters]
KUFM-TV ...... Missoula, MT [Television station call letters]
KUFNCD .... Kampuchean United Front for National Construction and Defence
                    [Political party] (PPW)
KUFN-FM ..... Hamilton, MT [FM radio station call letters] (RBYB)
KUFO .... Portland, OR [FM radio station call letters]
KUFR .... Salt Lake City, UT [FM radio station call letters]
KUFX .... Gilroy, CA [FM radio station call letters]
KUG .... Kupang [Timor] [Seismograph station code, US Geological Survey]
                    (SEIS)
KUGB .... Karate Union of Great Britain
KUGBNC .... Karate Union of Great Britain National Championship
KUGN .... Eugene, OR [AM radio station call letters]
KUGN-FM .... Eugene, OR [FM radio station call letters]
KUGR .... Green River, WY [AM radio station call letters]
KUGS .... Bellingham, WA [FM radio station call letters]
KUGT .... Jackson, MO [AM radio station call letters]
KUH .... Kaapuna [Hawaii] [Seismograph station code, US Geological
                    Survey] (SEIS)
KUH .... Kuhlman Corp. [NYSE symbol] (SPSG)
KUH .... Kushiro [Japan] [Airport symbol] (OAG)
KUHB .... St. Paul Island, AK [FM radio station call letters]
KUHD .... Port Neches, TX [AM radio station call letters]
KUHF .... Houston, TX [FM radio station call letters]
KUHG .... Milford, NE [FM radio station call letters]
KUHL .... Santa Maria, CA [AM radio station call letters]
Kuhlm .... Kuhlman Corp. [Associated Press] (SAG)
KUHM-FM ..... Helena, MT [FM radio station call letters] (RBYB)
KUHT .... Houston, TX [Television station call letters]
KUIC .... Vacaville, CA [FM radio station call letters]
KUID .... Moscow, ID [Television station call letters]
KUIK .... Hillsboro, OR [AM radio station call letters]
KUJ .... Walla Walla, WA [AM radio station call letters]
KUK .... Kasigluk [Alaska] [Airport symbol] (OAG)
KUK .... University of Kentucky, Lexington, KY [OCLC symbol] (OCLC)
KUKA .... San Diego, TX [FM radio station call letters]
KUKI .... Ukiah, CA [AM radio station call letters]
KUKI-FM ...... Ukiah, CA [FM radio station call letters]
KUKL .... Kalispell, MT [FM radio station call letters] (RBYB)
KUKN .... Kelso, WA [FM radio station call letters]
KUKQ .... Tempe, AZ [AM radio station call letters]
KUKU .... Willow Springs, MO [AM radio station call letters]
KUKU-FM .... Willow Springs, MO [FM radio station call letters]
KUL .... Kinjo Gakuin University Library [UTLAS symbol]
KUL .... Kuala Lumpur [Malaysia] [Airport symbol] (OAG)
KUL .... Kulyab [Former USSR Seismograph station code, US Geological
                    Survey] (SEIS)
KUL .... Sterling Central Union List of Serials, Sterling, KS [OCLC symbol]
                    (OCLC)
KU-L .... University of Kansas, School of Law, Lawrence, KS [Library symbol
                    Library of Congress] (LCLS)
KULA .... Maunawili, HI [AM radio station call letters]
KULC .... Ogden, UT [Television station call letters]
Kulcke .... Kulicke & Soffa Industries, Inc. [Associated Press] (SAG)
KULE .... Ephrata, WA [AM radio station call letters]
KULE-FM ..... Ephrata, WA [FM radio station call letters]
KULF .... Brenham, TX [FM radio station call letters]
KULM .... Columbus, TX [FM radio station call letters]
KULP .... El Campo, TX [AM radio station call letters]
Kulp .... Kulp's Luzerne Legal Register Reports [Pennsylvania]
                    [A publication] (DLA)
KULR .... Billings, MT [Television station call letters]
KULS .... Kentucky Union List of Serials [Library network]

KULY .... Ulysses, KS [AM radio station call letters]
KUM .... Kumamoto [Japan] [Seismograph station code, US Geological
                    Survey] (SEIS)
KU-M .... University of Kansas, School of Medicine, Kansas City, KS [Library
                    symbol Library of Congress] (LCLS)
KUM .... University of Kentucky, Medical Center, Lexington, KY [OCLC
                    symbol] (OCLC)
KUM .... Yaku Shima [Japan] [Airport symbol] (OAG)
KUMA .... Pendleton, OR [AM radio station call letters]
KUMA-FM ..... Pendleton, OR [FM radio station call letters]
KUMD .... Duluth, MN [FM radio station call letters]
KUMM .... Morris, MN [FM radio station call letters]
KUMMI .... Kobe University Medical Mission to Indonesia
KUMR .... Rolla, MO [FM radio station call letters]
KUMT .... Centerville, UT [FM radio station call letters]
KUMU .... Honolulu, HI [AM radio station call letters]
KUMU-FM ..... Honolulu, HI [FM radio station call letters]
KUMV .... Wiliiston, ND [Television station call letters]
KU-MW .... University of Kansas, School of Medicine-Witchita, Witchita, KS
                    [Library symbol] [Library of Congress] (LCLS)
KUN .... Kunia, Oahu, HI [Location identifier FAA] (FAAL)
KUN .... Kunming [Republic of China] [Seismograph station code, US
                    Geological Survey] (SEIS)
KUNA .... Indio, CA [AM radio station call letters]
KUNA-FM ..... La Quinta, CA [FM radio station call letters]
KUNC .... Greeley, CO [FM radio station call letters]
KUNI .... Cedar Falls, IA [FM radio station call letters]
KUNM .... Albuquerque, NM [FM radio station call letters]
KUNO .... Corpus Christi, TX [AM radio station call letters]
KUNQ .... Houston, MO [FM radio station call letters]
KUNR .... Reno, NV [FM radio station call letters]
KUNV .... Las Vegas, NV [FM radio station call letters]
KUNY .... Mason City, IA [FM radio station call letters]
KUO .... Kuopio [Finland] [Airport symbol] (OAG)
KUOA .... Siloam Springs, AR [AM radio station call letters]
KUOI .... Moscow, ID [FM radio station call letters]
KUOL .... San Marcos, TX [AM radio station call letters]
KUOM .... Minneapolis, MN [AM radio station call letters]
KUON .... Lincoln, NE [Television station call letters]
KUOO .... Spirit Lake, IA [FM radio station call letters]
KUOP .... Stockton, CA [FM radio station call letters]
KUOR .... Redlands, CA [FM radio station call letters]
KUOW .... Seattle, WA [FM radio station call letters]
KUP .... Kupang [Timor] [Seismograph station code, US Geological Survey
                    Closed] (SEIS)
KUP .... Kupiano [Papua New Guinea] [Airport symbol] (OAG)
KUP .... University of Kentucky, Prestonburg Community College,
                    Prestonburg, KY [OCLC symbol] (OCLC)
KUPD .... Tempe, AZ [FM radio station call letters]
KUPI .... Idaho Falls, ID [AM radio station call letters]
KUPI-FM ...... Idaho Falls, ID [FM radio station call letters]
KUPK-TV ..... Garden City, KS [Television station call letters]
KUPL-FM ..... Portland, OR [FM radio station call letters]
KUPN .... Las Vegas, NV [Television station call letters] (RBYB)
KUPR .... Carlsbad, CA [FM radio station call letters] (RBYB)
KUPS .... Tacoma, WA [FM radio station call letters]
KUQQ-FM ..... Milford, IA [FM radio station call letters] (RBYB)
KUR .... Kit Use Ratio [Statistics]
kur .... Kurdish [MARC language code Library of Congress] (LCCP)
KUR .... Kurilsk [Former USSR Seismograph station code, US Geological
                    Survey] (SEIS)
KUR .... Kyoto University Reactor
KURA .... Ouray, CO [FM radio station call letters]
KURB .... Little Rock, AR [AM radio station call letters]
KURB-FM ..... Little Rock, AR [FM radio station call letters]
KURE-FM ..... Ames, IA [FM radio station call letters] (RBYB)
KURL .... Billings, MT [AM radio station call letters]
KURM .... Rogers, AR [AM radio station call letters]
KURR-FM ..... Bountiful, UT [FM radio station call letters] (RBYB)
KURS .... San Diego, CA [AM radio station call letters]
KURV .... Edinburg, TX [AM radio station call letters]
KURY .... Brookings, OR [AM radio station call letters]
KURY-FM ..... Brookings, OR [FM radio station call letters]
KURZ .... Kurzweil Applied Intelligence, Inc. [NASDAQ symbol] (SAG)
Kurzweil ...... Kurzweil Applied Intelligence, Inc. [Associated Press] (SAG)
KUS .... Kidney, Ureter, and Spleen [Anatomy] (MAH)
KUS .... Kulusuk Island [Greenland] [Airport symbol] (AD)
KUS .... Kursk State Air Enterprise [Former USSR] [FAA designator] (FAAC)
KUS .... Kushiro [Japan] [Seismograph station code, US Geological Survey]
                    (SEIS)
KU-S .... University of Kansas, Kenneth Spencer Research Library, Lawrence,
                    KS [Library symbol Library of Congress] (LCLS)
KUS .... University of Kentucky, Southeast Center, Cumberland, KY [OCLC
                    symbol] (OCLC)
KUSA .... Denver, CO [Television station call letters]
KUSC .... Los Angeles, CA [FM radio station call letters]
KUSD .... Vermillion, SD [AM radio station call letters]
KUSD-FM ..... Vermillion, SD [FM radio station call letters]
KUSD-TV ..... Vermillion, SD [Television station call letters]
KUSF .... San Francisco, CA [FM radio station call letters]
KUSG .... St. George, UT [Television station call letters]
KUSH .... Cushing, OK [AM radio station call letters]
Kush .... Kushan (VRA)
Kushi .... Kushi Macrobiotic Corp. [Associated Press] (SAG)
KushLc .... Kush Locke [Associated Press] (SAG)

KushLc......... [*The*] Kushner-Locke Co. [*Associated Press*] (SAG)
KushLk........ Kush Locke [*Associated Press*] (SAG)
KushLk........ [*The*] Kushner-Locke Co. [*Associated Press*] (SAG)
KUSI .... San Diego, CA [*Television station call letters*]
KUSK .... Prescott, AZ [*Television station call letters*]
KUSM .... Bozeman, MT [*Television station call letters*]
KUSN .... Coffeyville, KS [*FM radio station call letters*]
KUSP .... Ku-Band Signal Processor (MCD)
KUSP .... Ku-Band Single Processor (MCD)
KUSP .... Santa Cruz, CA [*FM radio station call letters*]
KUSR .... Ames, IA [*FM radio station call letters*]
KUSU .... Logan, UT [*FM radio station call letters*]
KUSZ .... Proctor, MN [*FM radio station call letters*] (RBYB)
KUT.............. Austin, TX [*FM radio station call letters*]
KUT.............. Kutahya [*Turkey*] [*Airport symbol*] (AD)
kut .... Kutenai [*MARC language code Library of Congress*] (LCCP)
KUT.............. Kutsu-Ga-Hara [*Japan*] [*Seismograph station code, US Geological Survey*] (SEIS)
Kut.............. Kuttim (BJA)
KUT.............. Lexington Technical Institute, Lexington, KY [*OCLC symbol*] (OCLC)
KUT.............. University of Toronto Union Catalogue Section [*UTLAS symbol*]
KUTA .... Blanding, UT [*AM radio station call letters*]
Kutch .... All India Reporter, Kutch [*1949-56*] [*A publication*] (DLA)
KUTD .... Keep Up to Date (KSC)
KUTGW .... Keep Up the Good Work
KUTI .... Selah, WA [*AM radio station call letters*]
KUTP .... Phoenix, AZ [*Television station call letters*]
KUTQ .... Bountiful, UT [*FM radio station call letters*]
KUTT .... Fairbury, NE [*FM radio station call letters*]
KUTV .... Salt Lake City, UT [*Television station call letters*]
KUTX .... San Angelo, TX [*FM radio station call letters*] (RBYB)
KUTY .... Palmdale, CA [*AM radio station call letters*]
KUTZ .... Lampasas, TX [*FM radio station call letters*]
Kutztown U... Kutztown University of Pennsylvania (GAGS)
KUU .... Kulu [*India*] [*Airport symbol*] (AD)
KUUL .... Davenport, IA [*FM radio station call letters*]
KUUY .... Orchard Valley, WY [*AM radio station call letters*]
KUUZ .... Lake Village, AR [*FM radio station call letters*]
KUVA .... Uvalde, TX [*FM radio station call letters*]
KUVN .... Garland, TX [*Television station call letters*]
KUVO .... Denver, CO [*FM radio station call letters*]
KUVR .... Holdrege, NE [*AM radio station call letters*]
KUVR-FM .... Holdrege, NE [*FM radio station call letters*]
KUW .... Kuwait (ABBR)
Kuw .... Kuwait (VRA)
KUWJ .... Jackson, WY [*FM radio station call letters*]
KUWL .... Fairbanks, AK [*FM radio station call letters*]
KUWR .... Laramie, WY [*FM radio station call letters*]
KUWS .... Superior, WI [*FM radio station call letters*]
KUWZ .... Rock Springs, WY [*FM radio station call letters*]
KUX .... Kumix Resources Corp. [*Vancouver Stock Exchange symbol*]
KUY .... Kuyper [*Indonesia*] [*Later, TNG*] [*Geomagnetic observatory code*]
KUY .... Uyak [*Alaska*] [*Airport symbol*] (OAG)
KUY .... Uyak, AK [*Location identifier FAA*] (FAAL)
KUYO .... Evansville, WY [*AM radio station call letters*]
KUZZ .... Bakersfield, CA [*FM radio station call letters*]
KUZZ-TV ..... Bakersfield, CA [*Television station call letters*]
KV .... British Virgin Island [*IYRU nationality code*] (IYR)
KV .... Kanamycin-Vancomycin [*An antibiotic*] (DAVI)
KV .... Kerr Vector [*Optics*]
KV .... Key Verifier [*Computer science*]
KV .... Kidney Valve
KV .... Killed Vaccine [*Immunology*] (MAE)
KV .... Killed Virus [*Pharmacology*] (DAVI)
KV .... Kill Vehicle
kV .... Kilovolt
KV .... Kinematic Viscosity
KV .... Knights of Vartan (EA)
KV .... Kochel-Verzeichnis [*List of Mozart's works*] (IIA)
KV .... Kriegsverwendungsfaehig [*Fit for Active Service*] [*German military - World War II*]
KV .... K-V Pharmaceutical Co. [*AMEX symbol*] (SPSG)
KV .... Transkei Airways [*ICAO designator*] (AD)
KV1 .... Kalanchoe Virus 1 [*Plant pathology*]
KVA .... Karavia [*Zaire*] [*Geomagnetic observatory code*]
KVA .... Kavala [*Greece*] [*Airport symbol*] (OAG)
kVA .... Kilovolt Ampere
KVAB-FM .... Clarkston, WA [*FM radio station call letters*] (RBYB)
KVAC .... Forks, WA [*AM radio station call letters*]
KVAC .... Kilovolt Alternating Current (IAA)
KVAD .... Valdosta/Moody Air Force Base [*Georgia*] [*ICAO location identifier*] (ICLI)
KVAG-FM .... Rugby, ND [*FM radio station call letters*] (RBYB)
kVAH .... Kilovolt-Ampere Hour
kVAhm .... Kilovolt-Ampere Hour Meter (MSA)
KVAK .... Valdez, AK [*AM radio station call letters*]
KVAL .... Eugene, OR [*Television station call letters*]
kVAM .... Kilovolt-Ampere Meter
KVAN .... Vancouver, WA [*AM radio station call letters*]
kvar .... Kilovar
kVAr .... Kilovolt-Ampere Reactive
KVAR .... Riverside, CA [*FM radio station call letters*]
kvarh .... Kilovar-Hour
kVARh .... [*Reactive*] Kilovolt-Ampere-Hour (IDOE)
KVAS .... Astoria, OR [*AM radio station call letters*]

KVAW .... Eagle Pass, TX [*Television station call letters*]
KVAY .... Lamar, CO [*FM radio station call letters*]
KVAZ .... Henryetta, OK [*FM radio station call letters*]
KVBA .... Kanamycin-Vancomycin Blood Agar [*Microbiology*]
KVBC .... Las Vegas, NV [*Television station call letters*]
KVBC-FM .... Las Vegas, NV [*FM radio station call letters*] (RBYB)
KVBG .... Lompoc/Vandenberg Air Force Base [*California*] [*ICAO location identifier*] (ICLI)
KVBM........... Minneapolis, MN [*Television station call letters*]
KVBR .... Brainerd, MN [*AM radio station call letters*]
KVBR-FM .... Brainerd, MN [*FM radio station call letters*]
KVC .... King Cove [*Alaska*] [*Airport symbol*] (OAG)
KVC .... King Cove, AK [*Location identifier FAA*] (FAAL)
KVCE .... Fallon, NV [*FM radio station call letters*]
KVCI............ Mineola, TX [*AM radio station call letters*]
KVCK .... Wolf Point, MT [*AM radio station call letters*]
KVCK-FM .... Wolf Point, MT [*FM radio station call letters*]
KVCL .... Winnfield, LA [*AM radio station call letters*]
KVCL-FM .... Winnfield, LA [*FM radio station call letters*]
KVCM........... Helena, MT [*FM radio station call letters*]
KVCO .... Concordia, KS [*FM radio station call letters*]
kVCP .... Kilovolt Constant Potential
KVCQ .... Cuero, TX [*FM radio station call letters*] (RBYB)
KVCR .... San Bernardino, CA [*FM radio station call letters*]
KVCR-TV .... San Bernardino, CA [*Television station call letters*]
KVCS .... KXE6S Verein Chess Society (EA)
KVCS-AM .... Perry, OK [*FM radio station call letters*] (RBYB)
KVCS-FM .... Perry, OK [*FM radio station call letters*] (RBYB)
KVCT .... Victoria, TX [*Television station call letters*]
KVCV .... Victorville/George Air Force Base [*California*] [*ICAO location identifier*] (ICLI)
KVCX .... Gregory, SD [*FM radio station call letters*]
KVCY .... Fort Scott, KS [*FM radio station call letters*]
KVDA .... San Antonio, TX [*Television station call letters*]
KVDB .... Sioux Center, IA [*AM radio station call letters*]
kVdc .... Kilovolt Direct Current (IEEE)
KVDL .... Quanah, TX [*AM radio station call letters*]
KVDP .... Dry Prong, LA [*FM radio station call letters*]
KVDT .... Keyboard Visual Display Terminal (MCD)
KVE .... Kaposi's Varicelliform Eruption [*Medicine Medicine*] (DMAA)
KVEA .... Corona, CA [*Television station call letters*]
KVEC .... San Luis Obispo, CA [*AM radio station call letters*]
KVEG .... North Las Vegas, NV [*AM radio station call letters*]
KVEL .... Vernal, UT [*AM radio station call letters*]
KVEN .... Ventura, CA [*AM radio station call letters*]
KVEO .... Brownsville, TX [*Television station call letters*]
KVER .... El Paso, TX [*FM radio station call letters*]
KVET .... Austin, TX [*AM radio station call letters*]
KVET-FM..... Austin, TX [*FM radio station call letters*]
KVEW .... Kennewick, WA [*Television station call letters*]
KVEZ-FM..... Parker, AZ [*FM radio station call letters*] (RBYB)
KVF .... Kent Volunteer Fencibles [*British military*] (DMA)
KVFC .... Cortez, CO [*AM radio station call letters*]
KVFD .... Fort Dodge, IA [*AM radio station call letters*]
KVFM........... Logan, UT [*FM radio station call letters*]
KVFX .... Manteca, CA [*FM radio station call letters*]
KVG .... Kavieng [*Papua New Guinea*] [*Airport symbol*] (OAG)
KVG .... Kavieng [*Papua New Guinea*] [*Seismograph station code, US Geological Survey*] (SEIS)
KVG .... Kavieng [*New Ireland*] [*Airport symbol*] (AD)
KVG .... Keyed Video Generator
KVGB .... Great Bend, KS [*AM radio station call letters*]
KVGB-FM .... Great Bend, KS [*FM radio station call letters*]
KVGO-FM.... Spring Valley, MN [*FM radio station call letters*] (RBYB)
KVHI .... KVH Industries [*NASDAQ symbol*] (TTSB)
KVHI .... KVH Industries, Inc. [*NASDAQ symbol*] (SAG)
KVHInd .... KVH Industries, Inc. [*Associated Press*] (SAG)
KVHP .... Lake Charles, LA [*Television station call letters*]
KVHS .... Concord, CA [*FM radio station call letters*]
KVHT .... Vermillion, SD [*FM radio station call letters*]
KVI .... Carlsbad Ventures [*Vancouver Stock Exchange symbol*]
KVI .... Korean Veterans International (EA)
KVI .... Seattle, WA [*AM radio station call letters*]
KVIA .... El Paso, TX [*Television station call letters*]
KVIC .... Victoria, TX [*FM radio station call letters*]
KVIE .... Sacramento, CA [*Television station call letters*]
KVIH .... Clovis, NM [*Television station call letters*]
KVII .... Amarillo, TX [*Television station call letters*]
KVIK .... Decorah, IA [*FM radio station call letters*] (RBYB)
KVIL-FM ..... Highland Park, TX [*FM radio station call letters*]
KVIP .... Redding, CA [*AM radio station call letters*]
KVIP-FM ..... Redding, CA [*FM radio station call letters*]
KVIQ .... Eureka, CA [*Television station call letters*]
KVIS .... Miami, OK [*AM radio station call letters*]
KVIV .... El Paso, TX [*AM radio station call letters*]
KVJY .... Pharr, TX [*AM radio station call letters*]
KVK .... Kriegsverdienstkreuz [*War Service Cross*] [*German military decoration - World War II*]
KVKI .... Shreveport, LA [*FM radio station call letters*]
KVL .... Kingsvale Resources [*Vancouver Stock Exchange symbol*]
KVL .... Kirchhoff's Voltage Law (PDAA)
KVL .... Kivalina [*Alaska*] [*Airport symbol*] (OAG)
KVL .... Kivalina, AK [*Location identifier FAA*] (FAAL)
KVLA .... Vidalia, LA [*AM radio station call letters*]
KVLBA .... Kanamycin-Vancomycin Labeled Blood Agar [*Microbiology*]

KVLC .... Hatch, NM [*FM radio station call letters*] (RBYB)
KVLD .... Valdez, AK [*AM radio station call letters*]
KVLE .... Gunnison, CO [*FM radio station call letters*]
KVLF .... Alpine, TX [*AM radio station call letters*]
KVLG .... La Grange, TX [*AM radio station call letters*]
KVLH .... Pauls Valley, OK [*AM radio station call letters*]
KVLI .... Lake Isabella, CA [*AM radio station call letters*]
KVLI-FM .... Lake Isabella, CA [*FM radio station call letters*]
KVLL .... Woodville, TX [*AM radio station call letters*]
KVLL-FM .... Woodville, TX [*FM radio station call letters*]
KVLM .... Kevlin Corp. [*NASDAQ symbol*] (NQ)
KVLO-FM .... Sheridan, AR [*FM radio station call letters*] (RBYB)
KVLR .... Twisp, WA [*FM radio station call letters*]
KVLT .... Victoria, TX [*FM radio station call letters*]
KVLU .... Beaumont, TX [*FM radio station call letters*]
KVLV .... Fallon, NV [*AM radio station call letters*]
KVLV-FM .... Fallon, NV [*FM radio station call letters*]
KVLY .... Edinburg, TX [*FM radio station call letters*]
KVLY-TV .... Fargo, ND [*Television station call letters*] (RBYB)
kVM .... Kilovolt Meter
KVM .... Rusaerolizing Airling [*Former USSR*] [*FAA designator*] (FAAC)
KVMA .... Magnolia, AR [*AM radio station call letters*]
KVMA-FM ..... Magnolia, AR [*FM radio station call letters*]
KVMC .... Colorado City, TX [*AM radio station call letters*]
KVMD-TV ...... Twentynine Palms, CA [*TV station call letters*] (RBYB)
KVML .... Sonora, CA [*AM radio station call letters*]
KVMR .... Nevada City, CA [*FM radio station call letters*]
KVMV .... McAllen, TX [*FM radio station call letters*]
KVMX .... Eastland, TX [*FM radio station call letters*]
KVN .... Kaiserville [*Nevada*] [*Seismograph station code, US Geological Survey*] (SEIS)
KVN .... Kimmins Corp. [*NYSE symbol*] (TTSB)
KVN .... Kimmins Environmental Services [*NYSE symbol*] (SPSG)
KVNA .... Flagstaff, AZ [*AM radio station call letters*]
KVNA-FM ...... Flagstaff, AZ [*FM radio station call letters*]
KVNE .... Tyler, TX [*FM radio station call letters*]
KVNF .... Paonia, CO [*FM radio station call letters*]
KVNI .... Coeur D'Alene, ID [*AM radio station call letters*]
KVNO .... Omaha, NE [*FM radio station call letters*]
KVNU .... Logan, UT [*AM radio station call letters*]
KVO .... Keep Vein Open [*Medicine*]
KVO .... Kraftverkehrsordnung fuer den Gueterfernverkehr mit Kraftfahrzeugen [*Regulation for the Carriage of Goods by Motor Vehicles*] [*German Business term*] (ILCA)
KVOA .... Tucson, AZ [*Television station call letters*]
KVOC .... Casper, WY [*AM radio station call letters*]
KVO C D5W ... Keep Vein Open Cum [*with*] Dextrose 5% in Water [*Pharmacology*] (DAVI)
KVOD .... Denver, CO [*FM radio station call letters*]
KVOE .... Emporia, KS [*AM radio station call letters*]
KVOE-FM ...... Emporia, KS [*FM radio station call letters*]
KVOI .... Oro Valley, AZ [*AM radio station call letters*]
KVOK .... Kodiak, AK [*AM radio station call letters*]
KVOL .... Lafayette, LA [*AM radio station call letters*]
KVOL .... Opelousas, LA [*FM radio station call letters*]
KVOM .... Morrilton, AR [*AM radio station call letters*]
KVOM-FM ..... Morrilton, AR [*FM radio station call letters*]
KVON .... Napa, CA [*AM radio station call letters*]
KVOO .... Tulsa, OK [*AM radio station call letters*]
KVOO-FM ...... Tulsa, OK [*FM radio station call letters*]
KVOP .... Plainview, TX [*AM radio station call letters*]
KVOR .... Colorado Springs, CO [*AM radio station call letters*]
KVOS-TV ...... Bellingham, WA [*Television station call letters*]
KVOU .... Uvalde, TX [*AM radio station call letters*]
KVOW .... Riverton, WY [*AM radio station call letters*]
KVOX .... Moorhead, MN [*AM radio station call letters*]
KVOX-FM ...... Moorhead, MN [*FM radio station call letters*]
KVOY .... Mojave, CA [*AM radio station call letters*]
KVOZ .... Laredo, TX [*AM radio station call letters*]
KVP .... Katholieke Volkspartij [*Catholic People's Party*] [*Netherlands Political party*] (PPE)
kVP .... Kilovolt Peak
KVP .... Kodak Vacuum Probe
KVP .... Kodak Versamat Processor
KVPA .... Port Isabel, TX [*FM radio station call letters*]
KVPC .... San Joaquin, CA (RBYB)
KV Ph .... K-V Pharmaceutical Co. [*Associated Press*] (SAG)
KVPI .... Ville Platte, LA [*AM radio station call letters*]
KVPI-FM .... Ville Platte, LA [*FM radio station call letters*]
KVPR .... Fresno, CA [*FM radio station call letters*]
KVPS .... Valparaiso/Eglin Air Force Base [*Florida*] [*ICAO location identifier*] (ICLI)
KVPT .... Fresno, CA [*Television station call letters*]
KVRB .... Vero Beach/Vero Beach [*Florida*] [*ICAO location identifier*] (ICLI)
KVRC .... Arkadelphia, AR [*AM radio station call letters*]
KVRD .... Cottonwood, AZ [*AM radio station call letters*]
KVRD-FM ...... Cottonwood, AZ [*FM radio station call letters*]
KVRE .... Hot Springs Village, AR [*FM radio station call letters*]
KVRG .... Seaside, CA [*FM radio station call letters*]
KVRG .... Soledad, CA [*AM radio station call letters*] (RBYB)
KVRH .... Salida, CO [*AM radio station call letters*]
KVRH-FM ...... Salida, CO [*FM radio station call letters*]
KVRP .... Haskell, TX [*FM radio station call letters*]
KVRP .... Stamford, TX [*AM radio station call letters*]
KVRQ .... Atwater, CA [*FM radio station call letters*]

KVRR .... Fargo, ND [*Television station call letters*]
KVRS .... Lawton, OK [*FM radio station call letters*]
KVRT .... Victoria, TX [*FM radio station call letters*] (RBYB)
KVRW .... Lawton, OK [*FM radio station call letters*]
KVRX .... Austin, TX [*FM radio station call letters*]
KVRY .... Mesa, AZ [*FM radio station call letters*]
KVS .... Kansanvalistusseura [*Society for Culture and Education*] [*Finland*] (EAIO)
KVS .... Kelvin-Varley Slide [*Electronics*]
KVS .... Keyboard/Video Switch [*Computer science*]
KVS .... Kurzweil VoiceSystem [*Voice-recognition computer device*]
KVSA .... McGehee, AR [*AM radio station call letters*]
KVSC .... St. Cloud, MN [*FM radio station call letters*]
KVSF .... Santa Fe, NM [*AM radio station call letters*]
KVSH .... Valentine, NE [*AM radio station call letters*]
KVSI .... Montpelier, ID [*AM radio station call letters*]
KVSL .... Show Low, AZ [*AM radio station call letters*]
KVSN .... Tumwater, WA [*AM radio station call letters*]
KVSO .... Ardmore, OK [*AM radio station call letters*] (RBYB)
KVSP .... Oklahoma City, OK [*AM radio station call letters*]
KVST .... Huntsville, TX [*FM radio station call letters*]
KVST .... Keystone Visual Survey Test [*Ophthalmology*]
KVSV .... Beloit, KS [*AM radio station call letters*]
KVSV-FM ...... Beloit, KS [*FM radio station call letters*]
KVT .... Kavak [*Turkey*] [*Seismograph station code, US Geological Survey*] (SEIS)
KVTF .... Williams, AZ [*FM radio station call letters*]
KVTH .... Hot Springs, AR [*Television station call letters*] (RBYB)
KVTI .... Tacoma, WA [*FM radio station call letters*]
KVTJ-TV .... Jonesboro, AR [*TV station call letters*] (RBYB)
KVTN .... Pine Bluff, AR [*Television station call letters*]
KVTO .... Berkeley, CA [*AM radio station call letters*]
KVTT .... Dallas, TX [*FM radio station call letters*]
KVTV .... Laredo, TX [*Television station call letters*]
KVU .... Kleer-Vu Industries [*AMEX symbol*] (TTSB)
KVU .... Kleer-Vu Industries, Inc. [*AMEX symbol*] (SPSG)
KVU .... Victoria University Library, University of Toronto [*UTLAS symbol*]
KVUE .... Austin, TX [*Television station call letters*]
KVUT .... Little Rock, AR [*Television station call letters*]
KVUU .... Pueblo, CO [*FM radio station call letters*]
KVVA .... Phoenix, AZ [*AM radio station call letters*]
KVVA-FM ...... Apache Junction, AZ [*FM radio station call letters*]
KVVP .... Leesville, LA [*FM radio station call letters*]
KVVQ .... Hesperia, CA [*AM radio station call letters*]
KVVQ .... Victorville, CA [*FM radio station call letters*]
KVVS .... Windsor, CO [*AM radio station call letters*]
KVVU .... Henderson, NV [*Television station call letters*]
KVVV .... Baytoun, TX [*Television station call letters*]
KVW .... Kansas City, Kaw Valley R. R., Inc. [*AAR code*]
KVW .... Kurzweil Voice Writer
KVWC .... Vernon, TX [*AM radio station call letters*]
KVWC-FM ...... Vernon, TX [*FM radio station call letters*]
KVWG .... Pearsall, TX [*AM radio station call letters*]
KVWG-FM ...... Pearsall, TX [*FM radio station call letters*]
KVWM .... Show Low, AZ [*AM radio station call letters*]
KVWM-FM ...... Show Low, AZ [*FM radio station call letters*]
KVY .... CAI [*Compagnia Aeronautica Italiana SpA*] [*Italy ICAO designator*] (FAAC)
KVYE-TV .... El Centro, CA [*TV station call letters*] (RBYB)
KVYF .... Wilson Creek, WA [*FM radio station call letters*]
KVYN .... St. Helena, CA [*FM radio station call letters*]
KVYS .... St. George, UT [*FM radio station call letters*]
KVYY-FM ...... Ventura, CA [*FM radio station call letters*] (RBYB)
KVZK-2 .... Pago Pago, AS [*Television station call letters*]
KVZK-4 .... Pago Pago, AS [*Television station call letters*]
KVZK-5 .... Pago Pago, AS [*Television station call letters*]
K_w .... Dissociation Constant of Water [*Physics*] (DAVI)
KW .... Dorado Wings [*Airline code*]
KW .... Kaiser Wilhelm [*King William*] [*Name of two Prussian kings and emperor of Germany*] (ROG)
KW .... Kaliszer Woch (BJA)
KW .... Kampfwagen [*Tank*] [*German military - World War II*]
KW .... Katabatic Wind
KW .... Keith-Wagener [*Ophthalmology*]
KW .... Kenworth Truck Co.
KW .... Key West [*Florida*]
KW .... Key Word [*Online database field identifier*]
KW .... Killer Weed [*Slang for phencyclidine; also called PCP and Sernyl*] (DAVI)
kW .... Kilohm [*Formerly, K*] [*Unit of electrical resistance*] (DAVI)
kW .... Kilowatt
KW .... Kilowatt (DFIT)
KW .... Kilowatt [*DOE*] (TAG)
KW .... Kiloword (BUR)
KW .... Kimmelstiel-Wilson [*Medicine*]
KW .... Kirkwall, Orkney [*Postcode*] (ODBW)
KW .... Knight of William [*Netherlands*]
KW .... Knight of Windsor (ROG)
KW .... Knitwise [*Knitting*]
KW .... Korean War
KW .... Kraftwagen [*Motor Vehicle*] [*German*]
KW .... Kruskal-Wallis Test [*Fisheries*]
KW .... Kugelberg-Welander Disease (DAVI)
KW .... Kuwait [*ANSI two-letter standard code*] (CNC)
KWA .... Keyword Adapted [*Computer science*]

KWA............ Kwajalein [*Marshall Islands*] [*Airport symbol*] (OAG)
KWA............ Kwantlen College Library [*UTLAS symbol*]
KWA............ Kweiyang [*Republic of China*] [*Seismograph station code, US Geological Survey*] (SEIS)
KWAB........ Big Spring, TX [*Television station call letters*]
KWAC........ Bakersfield, CA [*AM radio station call letters*]
KWAC........ Keyword and Context [*Indexing*] (DIT)
KWAD........ Wadena, MN [*AM radio station call letters*]
KWADE...... Key Word as a Dictionary Entry [*IBM*] [*Indexing system*] (NITA)
KWAI......... Honolulu, HI [*AM radio station call letters*]
KWAJ........ Kwajalein Atoll (AABC)
KWAK........ Stuttgart, AR [*AM radio station call letters*]
KWAK-FM ... Stuttgart, AR [*FM radio station call letters*]
KWAL........ Wallace, ID [*AM radio station call letters*]
KWAL........ Wallops Island/Wallops Station [*Virginia*] [*ICAO location identifier*] (ICLI)
KWAM .... Memphis, TN [*AM radio station call letters*]
KWAN .... Gualala, CA [*FM radio station call letters*]
Kwansei Gak L Rev... Kwansei Gakuin University. Law Review [*A publication*] (DLA)
KWAR........ Waverly, IA [*FM radio station call letters*]
KWAS .... Joplin, MO [*AM radio station call letters*]
KWAT .... Watertown, SD [*AM radio station call letters*]
KWAV .... Monterey, CA [*FM radio station call letters*]
KWAX .... Eugene, OR [*FM radio station call letters*]
KWAY .... Waverly, IA [*AM radio station call letters*]
KWAY-FM ... Waverly, IA [*FM radio station call letters*]
KWAZ .... Needles, CA [*FM radio station call letters*]
KWB............ Keith, Wagener, Barker [*Ophthalmology*]
KWBC........ Navasota, TX [*AM radio station call letters*]
KWBC........ Washington [*District of Columbia*] [*ICAO location identifier*] (ICLI)
KWBE........ Beatrice, NE [*AM radio station call letters*]
KWBF........ Flagstaff, AZ [*Television station call letters*] (RBYB)
KWBF........ Katholische Welt-Bibelfoderation [*World Catholic Federation for the Biblical Apostolate - WCFBA*] (EAIO)
KWBG........ Boone, IA [*AM radio station call letters*]
KWBH........ Rexburg, ID [*FM radio station call letters*]
KWBI......... Morrison, CO [*FM radio station call letters*]
KWBP........ Salem, OR [*Television station call letters*] (RBYB)
KWBR........ Pismo Beach, CA [*FM radio station call letters*]
KWBU........ Waco, TX [*FM radio station call letters*]
KWBW........ Hutchinson, KS [*AM radio station call letters*]
KWBY........ Woodburn, OR [*AM radio station call letters*]
KWC............ K-Band Waveguide Circulator
KWC............ Kentucky Wesleyan College [*Owensboro*]
KWC............ Kierownictwo Walki Cywilnej (BJA)
KWC............ Wycliffe College Library, University of Toronto [*UTLAS symbol*]
KWCB........ Floresville, TX [*FM radio station call letters*]
KWCC-FM ... Muscatine, IA [*FM radio station call letters*] (RBYB)
KWCD........ Bisbee, AZ [*FM radio station call letters*]
KWCH........ Hutchinson, KS [*Television station call letters*]
KWCK........ Searcy, AR [*AM radio station call letters*]
KWCK-FM .... Searcy, AR [*FM radio station call letters*]
KWCL........ Oak Grove, LA [*FM radio station call letters*]
KWCM .... Appleton, MN [*Television station call letters*]
KWCO........ Chickasha, OK [*AM radio station call letters*]
KWCR........ Ogden, UT [*FM radio station call letters*]
KWCV........ Wichita, KS [*Television station call letters*]
KWCW........ Walla Walla, WA [*FM radio station call letters*]
KWCX........ Wilcox, AZ [*FM radio station call letters*]
KWD............ Consolidated Westrex Development [*Vancouver Stock Exchange symbol*]
KWD............ Draco [*Sweden*] [*Research code symbol*]
KWD............ Kellwood Co. [*NYSE symbol*] (SPSG)
KWDA........ White Hall, AR [*FM radio station call letters*]
KWDF........ Ball, LA [*AM radio station call letters*]
KWDK........ Tacoma, WA [*Television station call letters*]
KWDM........ West Des Moines, IA [*FM radio station call letters*]
KWDQ........ Woodward, OK [*FM radio station call letters*]
KWDX........ Silsbee, TX [*FM radio station call letters*]
KWE............ Guiyang [*China*] [*Airport symbol*] (OAG)
KWE............ Keith-Welti-Ernst [*Method*] [*Radiology*] (DAVI)
KWE............ Kilowatt Electric [*DOE*] (TAG)
kWe........... Kilowatts of Electric Energy
KWE............ Knight of the White Eagle [*Poland*]
KWE............ Kweiyang [*China*] [*Airport symbol*] (AD)
KWEB........ Rochester, MN [*AM radio station call letters*]
KWED .... Seguin, TX [*AM radio station call letters*]
KWEI......... Weiser, ID [*AM radio station call letters*]
KWEI-FM .... Fruitland, ID [*FM radio station call letters*] (RBYB)
KWEL........ Midland, TX [*AM radio station call letters*]
KWEN .... Tulsa, OK [*FM radio station call letters*]
KWEO .... Garberville, CA [*FM radio station call letters*]
KWES .... Ruidoso, NM [*FM radio station call letters*]
KWES-TV .... Odessa, TX [*Television station call letters*]
KWET .... Cheyenne, OK [*Television station call letters*]
KWEX........ San Antonio, TX [*Television station call letters*]
KWEY .... Weatherford, OK [*AM radio station call letters*]
KWEY-FM .... Weatherford, OK [*FM radio station call letters*]
KWF............ Waterfall, AK [*Location identifier FAA*] (FAAL)
KWFC........ Kelli Warren Fan Club [*Defunct*] (EA)
KWFC........ Springfield, MO [*FM radio station call letters*]
KWFH........ Parker, AZ [*FM radio station call letters*]
KWFJ......... Roy, WA [*FM radio station call letters*]
KWFL......... Roswell, NM [*FM radio station call letters*]

KWFM........ Kurt Weill Foundation for Music (EA)
KWFM-FM ... Tucson, AZ [*FM radio station call letters*]
KWFR........ San Angelo, TX [*FM radio station call letters*] (RBYB)
KWFS......... Wichita Falls, TX [*FM radio station call letters*]
KWFS-FM .... Wichita Falls, TX [*FM radio station call letters*] (RBYB)
KWFT........ Kilowatt Foot (IAA)
KWFT........ Wichita Falls, TX [*AM radio station call letters*]
KWFX........ Woodward, OK [*FM radio station call letters*]
KWG............ Stockton, CA [*AM radio station call letters*]
KWGDF........ KWG Resources, Inc. [*NASDAQ symbol*] (SAG)
KWGN .... Denver, CO [*Television station call letters*]
KWG Rs ...... KWG Resources, Inc. [*Associated Press*] (SAG)
KWGS .... Tulsa, OK [*FM radio station call letters*]
kWh .... Kilowatt-Hour
KWH .... Kilowatt-Hour (DFIT)
KWH .... Kilowatt Hour [*DOE*] (TAG)
KWHB........ Tulsa, OK [*Television station call letters*]
KWHD........ Castle Rock, CO [*Television station call letters*]
KWHE........ Honolulu, HI [*Television station call letters*]
kWhe.......... Kilowatt-Hour Electric
KWHH........ Hilo, HI [*Television station call letters*]
KWHI......... Brenham, TX [*AM radio station call letters*]
KWHL........ Anchorage, AK [*FM radio station call letters*]
KWHM........ Kilowatt-Hour Meter
KWHM........ Wailuku, HI [*Television station call letters*]
KWHN .... Fort Smith, AR [*AM radio station call letters*]
KWHN .... Haynesville, LA [*FM radio station call letters*]
KWHO........ Weed, CA [*FM radio station call letters*]
KWHQ........ Kenai, AK [*FM radio station call letters*]
KWHR........ Kilowatthour (ABBR)
kWhr.......... Kilowatt-Hour
KWHT........ Pendleton, OR [*FM radio station call letters*]
KWHW........ Altus, OK [*AM radio station call letters*]
KWHY........ Los Angeles, CA [*Television station call letters*]
KWI............ Kosher Wine Institute (EA)
KWI............ Kuwait [*Airport symbol*] (OAG)
KWi............ Wichita Public Library, Wichita, KS [*Library symbol Library of Congress*] (LCLS)
KWiB .... [*The*] Boeing Co., Wichita Division Library, Wichita, KS [*Library symbol Library of Congress*] (LCLS)
KWIC........ Kennedy Wilson, Inc. [*NASDAQ symbol*] (SAG)
KWIC........ Keyword in Context [*Indexing*]
KWIC........ Topeka, KS [*FM radio station call letters*]
KWiF.......... Friends University, Wichita, KS [*Library symbol Library of Congress*] (LCLS)
KWiGS .... Church of Jesus Christ of Latter-Day Saints, Genealogical Society Library, Wichita Branch, Wichita, KS [*Library symbol Library of Congress*] (LCLS)
KWiIL......... Institute of Logopedics, Wichita, KS [*Library symbol Library of Congress*] (LCLS)
KWiK .... Kansas Newman College, Wichita, KS [*Library symbol Library of Congress*] (LCLS)
KWIK .... Pocatello, ID [*AM radio station call letters*]
KWIL.......... Albany, OR [*AM radio station call letters*]
KWIM .... Window Rock, AZ [*FM radio station call letters*]
KWIN .... Lodi, CA [*FM radio station call letters*]
KWIP......... Dallas, OR [*AM radio station call letters*]
KWIP......... Keyword Word in Permutation [*Indexing*] (PDAA)
KWIQ........ Moses Lake, WA [*AM radio station call letters*]
KWIQ-FM .... Moses Lake, WA [*FM radio station call letters*]
KWiSF .... Saint Francis Hospital, Wichita, KS [*Library symbol Library of Congress*] (LCLS)
KWiSJ......... Saint Joseph Hospital, Wichita, KS [*Library symbol Library of Congress*] (LCLS)
KWIT.......... Keyword in Title [*Indexing*]
KWIT.......... Sioux City, IA [*FM radio station call letters*]
KWiU .... Wichita State University, Wichita, KS [*Library symbol Library of Congress*] (LCLS)
KWiVA .... United States Veterans Administration Hospital, Wichita, KS [*Library symbol Library of Congress*] (LCLS)
KWiWC .... Wichita Clinic, Wichita, KS [*Library symbol Library of Congress*] (LCLS)
KWiWM .... Wesley Medical Center, Wichita, KS [*Library symbol Library of Congress*] (LCLS)
KWIX.......... Moberly, MO [*AM radio station call letters*]
KWIZ.......... Santa Ana, CA [*AM radio station call letters*]
KWIZ-FM .... Santa Ana, CA [*FM radio station call letters*]
KWJC.......... Liberty, MO [*FM radio station call letters*]
KWJJ.......... Portland, OR [*AM radio station call letters*]
KWJJ-FM .... Portland, OR [*FM radio station call letters*]
KWJM........ Farmerville, LA [*FM radio station call letters*]
KWJZ.......... Seattle, WA [*FM radio station call letters*] (RBYB)
KWK............ Kampfwagenkanone [*Tank Gun*] [*German military - World War II*]
KWK............ Kwigillingok [*Alaska*] [*Airport symbol*] (OAG)
KWK............ Kwigillingok, AK [*Location identifier FAA*] (FAAL)
KWKA........ Clovis, NM [*AM radio station call letters*]
KWKB-TV .... Iowa City, IA [*TV station call letters*] (RBYB)
KWKH........ Shreveport, LA [*AM radio station call letters*]
KWKH-FM .... Shreveport, LA [*FM radio station call letters*]
KWKK........ Dardanelle, AR [*FM radio station call letters*]
KWKQ........ Graham, TX [*FM radio station call letters*]
KWKT........ Waco, TX [*Television station call letters*]
KWKW........ Los Angeles, CA [*AM radio station call letters*]
KWKY........ Des Moines, IA [*AM radio station call letters*]
KWKZ........ Charleston, MO [*FM radio station call letters*]

KWL............ Guilin [China] [Airport symbol] (OAG)
KWLA.......... Many, LA [AM radio station call letters]
KWLC.......... Decorah, IA [AM radio station call letters]
KWLD .... Plainview, TX [FM radio station call letters]
KWLF.......... Fairbanks, AK [FM radio station call letters]
KWLF.......... Kodak Wratten Light Filter
KWLL.......... Casa Grande, AZ [AM radio station call letters]
KWLM .... Willmar, MN [AM radio station call letters]
KWLO .... Waterloo, IA [AM radio station call letters]
KWLS .... Pratt, KS [AM radio station call letters]
KWLT.......... North Crossett, AR [FM radio station call letters]
KWLV.......... Many, LA [FM radio station call letters]
kWm .... Kilowatt Meter
KWM .... Korean War Memorial (EA)
KWM........... Kowanyama [Australia Airport symbol] (OAG)
KW/M²......... Kilowatts per Square Meter
KWMC .... Del Rio, TX [AM radio station call letters]
KWME .... Wellington, KS [FM radio station call letters]
KWMJ.......... Tulsa, OK [Television station call letters]
KWMQ .... Southwest City, MO [AM radio station call letters]
KWMT .... Fort Dodge, IA [AM radio station call letters]
KWMU .... St. Louis, MO [FM radio station call letters]
KWMW .... Maljamar, NM [FM radio station call letters]
KWMX .... Lakewood, CO [FM radio station call letters]
KWN .... Kenwin Shops [AMEX symbol] (TTSB)
KWN .... Kenwin Shops, Inc. [AMEX symbol] (SPSG)
KWN .... Korean Wideband Network [Communications] [Military] (MCD)
KWN .... Quinhagak [Alaska] [Airport symbol] (OAG)
KWN .... Quinhagak, AK [Location identifier FAA] (FAAL)
KWNA .... Winnemucca, NV [AM radio station call letters]
KWNA-FM .... Winnemucca, NV [FM radio station call letters]
KWNB .... Hayes Center, NE [Television station call letters]
KWNC .... Quincy, WA [AM radio station call letters]
KWND .... Kenetech Corp. [NASDAQ symbol] (SAG)
KWND .... Springfield, MO [FM radio station call letters]
KWNDZ .... KENETECH Cp 8.25% Cv Dep Pfd [NASDAQ symbol] (TTSB)
KWNE .... Ukiah, CA [FM radio station call letters]
KWNG .... Red Wing, MN [FM radio station call letters]
KWNK .... Simi Valley, CA [AM radio station call letters]
KWNN .... Turlock, CA [FM radio station call letters] (RBYB)
KWNO .... Rushford, MN [FM radio station call letters]
KWNO .... Winona, MN [AM radio station call letters]
KWNR .... Henderson, NV [FM radio station call letters]
KWNS .... Winnsboro, TX [FM radio station call letters]
KWNV-TV ..... Winnemucca, NV [TV station call letters] (RBYB)
KWNZ .... Carson City, NV [FM radio station call letters]
KWOA .... Worthington, MN [AM radio station call letters]
KWOA-FM .... Worthington, MN [FM radio station call letters]
KWOC .... Keyword out of Context [Indexing]
KWOC .... Poplar Bluff, MO [AM radio station call letters]
KWOCA......... Key Word Online Catalogue Access
KWOD .... Sacramento, CA [FM radio station call letters]
KWOF .... Waterloo, IA [AM radio station call letters] (RBYB)
KWOM .... Watertown, MN [AM radio station call letters] (RBYB)
KWON .... Bartlesville, OK [AM radio station call letters]
KWOR .... Worland, WY [AM radio station call letters]
KWOS .... Jefferson City, MO [AM radio station call letters]
KWOT .... Keyword out of Title [Indexing]
KWOT .... Kilometer-Wave Orbiting Telescope [NASA]
KWOW .... Clifton, TX [FM radio station call letters]
KWOX .... Woodward, OK [FM radio station call letters]
KWOZ .... Mountain View, AR [FM radio station call letters]
KWP .... Kierowinctwo Walki Podziemnej (BJA)
KWP .... King World Prod'ns [NYSE symbol] (TTSB)
KWP .... King World Productions, Inc. [NYSE symbol] (SPSG)
KWP .... Korean Workers' Party [North Korea Political party] (PD)
KWP .... West Point [Alaska] [Airport symbol] (OAG)
KWP .... West Point, AK [Location identifier FAA] (FAAL)
KWPA-AM .... Pomona, CA [AM radio station call letters] (RBYB)
KWPC .... Muscatine, IA [AM radio station call letters]
KWPM .... West Plains, MO [AM radio station call letters]
KWPN-FM .... West Point, NE [FM radio station call letters]
KWPZ-FM .... Lynden, WA [FM radio station call letters] (RBYB)
KWQC .... Davenport, IA [Television station call letters]
KWQH-FM .... San Luis Obispo, CA [FM radio station call letters] (RBYB)
KWQJ-FM .... Anchorage, AK [FM radio station call letters] (RBYB)
KWQL .... Dishman, WA [FM radio station call letters]
kWr .... Kilowatts Reactive
KWR .... KW Resources Ltd. [Vancouver Stock Exchange symbol]
KWRB .... Bisbee, AZ [FM radio station call letters] (RBYB)
KWRB .... Macon/Robins Air Force Base [Georgia] [ICAO location identifier] (ICLI)
KWRD .... Henderson, TX [AM radio station call letters]
KWRE .... Warrenton, MO [AM radio station call letters]
KWRF .... Warren, AR [FM radio station call letters]
KWRF-FM .... Warren, AR [FM radio station call letters]
KWRI .... Wrightstown/McGuire Air Force Base [New Jersey] [ICAO location identifier] (ICLI)
KWRK .... Window Rock, AZ [FM radio station call letters]
KWRL .... La Grande, OR [FM radio station call letters]
KWRM .... Corona, CA [AM radio station call letters]
KWRN .... Apple Valley, CA [FM radio station call letters] (RBYB)
KWRO .... Coquille, OR [AM radio station call letters]
KWRP .... San Jacinto, CA [FM radio station call letters]
KWRQ .... Clifton, AZ [FM radio station call letters] (RBYB)

KWRR-FM .... Ethete, WY [FM radio station call letters] (RBYB)
KWRRI .... Kansas Water Resources Research Institute [Kansas State University] [Department of the Interior Research center] (RCD)
KWRRI .... Kentucky Water Resources Research Institute [University of Kentucky] [Lexington, KY] [Department of the Interior] [Research center] (RCD)
KWRS .... Spokane, WA [FM radio station call letters]
KWRT .... Boonville, MO [AM radio station call letters]
KWRV .... Sun Valley, ID [AM radio station call letters]
KWRW .... Rusk, TX [FM radio station call letters]
KWS .... Korean Welfare Society [Australia]
KWS .... Southwestern College, Winfield, KS [Library symbol Library of Congress] (LCLS)
KWSA .... West Klamath, OR [AM radio station call letters]
KWSB .... Gunnison, CO [FM radio station call letters]
KWSC .... Wayne, NE [FM radio station call letters]
KWSD .... White Sands/Condron Army Air Field [New Mexico] [ICAO location identifier] (ICLI)
KWSE .... Williston, ND [Television station call letters]
KWSH .... Wewoka, OK [AM radio station call letters]
KWSJ .... Saint John's College, Winfield, KS [Library symbol Library of Congress] (LCLS)
KWSJ-FM .... Haysville, KS [FM radio station call letters] (RBYB)
KWSK-FM .... Daingerfield, TX [FM radio station call letters] (RBYB)
KWSL .... Sioux City, IA [AM radio station call letters] (RBYB)
KWSM .... Sherman, TX [FM radio station call letters]
KWSN .... Sioux Falls, SD [AM radio station call letters]
KWSO .... Warm Springs, OR [FM radio station call letters]
KWSP .... Santa Margarita, CA [FM radio station call letters]
KWST .... Brawley, CA [FM radio station call letters]
KWSU .... Pullman, WA [AM radio station call letters]
KWSU-TV .... Pullman, WA [Television station call letters]
KWSW .... Eureka, CA [AM radio station call letters]
KWSWA .... Kansas Wine and Spirits Wholesalers Association (SRA)
kWt .... Kilowatt, Thermal
KWT .... Kuwait [ANSI three-letter standard code] (CNC)
KWT .... Kwethluk [Alaska] [Airport symbol] (OAG)
KWT .... Kwethluk, AK [Location identifier FAA] (FAAL)
kW(th) .... Kilowatt, Thermal
KWTO .... Springfield, MO [AM radio station call letters]
KWTO-FM .... Springfield, MO [FM radio station call letters]
KWTR .... Georgetown, TX [AM radio station call letters]
KWTS .... Canyon, TX [FM radio station call letters]
KWTV .... Oklahoma City, OK [Television station call letters]
KWTX .... Waco, TX [AM radio station call letters]
KWTX-FM .... Waco, TX [FM radio station call letters]
KWTX-TV .... Waco, TX [Television station call letters]
KWTY .... Cartago, CA [FM radio station call letters]
KWU .... Kansas Wesleyan University [Salina]
KWU .... Kawau Island [New Zealand] [Airport symbol] (AD)
KWU .... Kraftwerksunion [Germany]
KWUA .... Clovis, NM [FM radio station call letters]
KWUC .... Keyword and Universal Decimal Classification (PDAA)
KWUR .... Clayton, MO [FM radio station call letters]
KWVA .... Eugene, OR [FM radio station call letters]
KWVA .... Korean War Veterans Association (EA)
KWVE .... San Clemente, CA [FM radio station call letters]
KWVM .... Korean War Veterans Memorial [Defunct] (EA)
KWVR .... Enterprise, OR [AM radio station call letters]
KWVR-FM .... Enterprise, OR [FM radio station call letters]
KWVV .... Homer, AK [FM radio station call letters]
KWW .... Asbury College, Wilmore, KY [OCLC symbol] (OCLC)
KWWC .... Columbia, MO [FM radio station call letters]
KWWD .... Wildwood/Cape May County [New Jersey] [ICAO location identifier] (ICLI)
KWWF-FM .... West Yellowstone, MT [FM radio station call letters] (RBYB)
KWWJ.......... Baytown, TX [AM radio station call letters]
KWWK .... Rochester, MN [FM radio station call letters]
KWWL .... Waterloo, IA [Television station call letters]
KWWR .... Mexico, MO [FM radio station call letters]
KWWS-FM .... Walla Walla, WA [FM radio station call letters] (RBYB)
KWwUT .... United Telecommunications/U.S. Sprint, Westwood, KS [Library symbol] [Library of Congress] (LCLS)
KWWV .... Morro Bay, CA [FM radio station call letters]
KWWW .... Quincy, WA [FM radio station call letters]
KWWX .... Wenatchee, WA [AM radio station call letters]
KWX .... Kiwai Island [Papua New Guinea] [Airport symbol] (OAG)
KWXA .... Durango, CO [FM radio station call letters]
KWXD .... Asbury, MO [FM radio station call letters]
KWXE .... Glenwood, AR [FM radio station call letters]
KWXH .... Sun City, CA [FM radio station call letters]
KWXI .... Glenwood, AR [AM radio station call letters]
KWXI-AM .... Glenwood, AR [AM radio station call letters] (RBYB)
KWXT .... Dardanelle, AR [AM radio station call letters]
KWXX .... Hilo, HI [FM radio station call letters]
KWXY .... Cathedral City, CA [AM radio station call letters]
KWXY-FM .... Cathedral City, CA [FM radio station call letters]
KWY............ Key Way
KWYB .... Butte, MT [Television station call letters]
KWYD .... Colorado Springs, CO [AM radio station call letters]
KWYI .... Kawaihae, HI [FM radio station call letters]
KWYK .... Aztec, NM [FM radio station call letters]
KWYN .... Wynne, AR [AM radio station call letters]
KWYN-FM .... Wynne, AR [FM radio station call letters]
KWYO .... Sheridan, WY [AM radio station call letters]

KWYO-FM.... Sheridan, WY [*FM radio station call letters*]
KWYR.......... Winner, SD [*AM radio station call letters*]
KWYR-FM.... Winner, SD [*FM radio station call letters*]
KWYS.......... West Yellowstone, MT [*AM radio station call letters*]
KWYX.......... Jasper, TX [*FM radio station call letters*]
KWYZ.......... Everett, WA [*AM radio station call letters*]
KWZ............ Kolwezi [*Zaire*] [*Airport symbol*] (AD)
KX.............. Cayman Airways [*ICAO designator*] (AD)
KX.............. Cayman Airways [*Airline flight code*] (ODBW)
KX.............. [*The*] Holy Bible (1955) [*R.A. Knox*] [*A publication*] (BJA)
KXA............ Kasaan, AK [*Location identifier FAA*] (FAAL)
KXAA.......... Rock Island, WA [*FM radio station call letters*]
KXAC.......... St. James, MN [*FM radio station call letters*]
KXAL.......... Pittsburg, TX [*FM radio station call letters*]
KXAM.......... Mesa, AZ [*AM radio station call letters*]
KXAM-TV.... Llano, TX [*Television station call letters*]
KXAN.......... Austin, TX [*Television station call letters*]
KXAR.......... Hope, AR [*AM radio station call letters*]
KXAR-FM.... Hope, AR [*FM radio station call letters*]
KXAS.......... Fort Worth, TX [*Television station call letters*]
KXAX.......... St. James, MN [*FM radio station call letters*]
KXAZ.......... Page, AZ [*FM radio station call letters*]
KXBJ.......... Victoria, TX [*FM radio station call letters*]
KXBS.......... Santa Paula, CA [*FM radio station call letters*]
KXBT.......... Vallejo, CA [*AM radio station call letters*]
KXBX.......... Lakeport, CA [*AM radio station call letters*]
KXBX-FM.... Lakeport, CA [*FM radio station call letters*]
KXBZ-FM.... Manhattan, KS [*FM radio station call letters*] (RBYB)
KXC............ Keleket X-Ray Corp.
KXCC.......... Rockport, TX [*FM radio station call letters*]
KXCI........... Tucson, AZ [*FM radio station call letters*]
KXCL.......... Yuba City, CA [*FM radio station call letters*]
KXCR.......... El Paso, TX [*FM radio station call letters*]
KXCV.......... Maryville, MO [*FM radio station call letters*]
KXDA.......... Las Cruces, NM [*FM radio station call letters*] (RBYB)
KXDC.......... Carmel, CA [*FM radio station call letters*] (RBYB)
KXDD.......... Yakima, WA [*FM radio station call letters*]
KXDG.......... Webb City, MO [*FM radio station call letters*] (RBYB)
KXDL.......... Browerville, MN [*FM radio station call letters*]
KXEB.......... Sherman, TX [*AM radio station call letters*]
KXED.......... Los Angeles, CA [*AM radio station call letters*]
KXEG.......... Tolleson, AZ [*AM radio station call letters*]
KXEI........... Havre, MT [*FM radio station call letters*]
KXEL.......... Waterloo, IA [*AM radio station call letters*]
KXEM.......... Bakersfield, CA [*AM radio station call letters*] (RBYB)
KXEN.......... Festus-St. Louis, MO [*AM radio station call letters*]
KXEO.......... Mexico, MO [*AM radio station call letters*]
KXEQ.......... Reno, NV [*AM radio station call letters*]
KXEW.......... South Tucson, AZ [*AM radio station call letters*]
KXEX.......... Fresno, CA [*AM radio station call letters*]
KXEZ.......... Los Angeles, CA [*FM radio station call letters*]
KXF............ Kodak X-Ray Film
KXF............ Koro [*Fiji*] [*Airport symbol*] (OAG)
KXFE.......... Dumas, AR [*FM radio station call letters*]
KXFG-FM.... Sun City, CA [*FM radio station call letters*] (RBYB)
KXFM.......... Santa Maria, CA [*FM radio station call letters*]
KXFX.......... Santa Rosa, CA [*FM radio station call letters*]
KXGA.......... Glennallen, AK [*FM radio station call letters*] (RBYB)
KXGF.......... Great Falls, MT [*AM radio station call letters*]
KXGJ.......... Bay City, TX [*FM radio station call letters*]
KXGM.......... Muenster, TX [*FM radio station call letters*]
KXGN.......... Glendive, MT [*AM radio station call letters*]
KXGN-TV..... Glendive, MT [*Television station call letters*]
KXGO.......... Arcata, CA [*FM radio station call letters*]
KXGR.......... Green Valley, AZ [*Television station call letters*]
KXGT-FM.... Jamestown, ND [*FM radio station call letters*] (RBYB)
KXHA.......... Shafter, CA [*FM radio station call letters*]
KXHV.......... Sacramento, CA [*FM radio station call letters*]
KXIA........... Marshalltown, IA [*FM radio station call letters*]
KXIC........... Iowa City, IA [*AM radio station call letters*]
KXII............ Sherman, TX [*Television station call letters*]
KXIO........... Clarksville, AR [*FM radio station call letters*]
KXIT........... Dalhart, TX [*AM radio station call letters*]
KXIT-FM..... Dalhart, TX [*FM radio station call letters*]
KXIX........... Bend, OR [*FM radio station call letters*]
KXJB........... Valley City, ND [*Television station call letters*]
KXJK........... Forrest City, AR [*AM radio station call letters*]
KXJZ........... Sacramento, CA [*FM radio station call letters*]
KXKB.......... Tahoe City, CA [*FM radio station call letters*]
KXKC.......... New Iberia, LA [*FM radio station call letters*]
KXKK.......... Lordsburg, NM [*FM radio station call letters*]
KXKL........... Denver, CO [*AM radio station call letters*]
KXKL-FM..... Denver, CO [*FM radio station call letters*]
KXKM.......... McCarthy, AK [*FM radio station call letters*] (RBYB)
KXKQ.......... Safford, AZ [*FM radio station call letters*]
KXKS.......... Albuquerque, NM [*AM radio station call letters*]
KXKT.......... Atlantic, IA [*FM radio station call letters*]
KXKX.......... Knob Noster, MO [*FM radio station call letters*]
KXKZ.......... Ruston, LA [*FM radio station call letters*]
KXL............ Portland, OR [*AM radio station call letters*]
KXLA.......... Rayville, LA [*FM radio station call letters*]
KXLC.......... La Crescent, MN [*FM radio station call letters*]
KXLE.......... Ellensburg, WA [*AM radio station call letters*]
KXLE-FM..... Ellensburg, WA [*FM radio station call letters*]
KXLF........... Butte, MT [*Television station call letters*]
KXLI........... St. Cloud, MN [*Television station call letters*]
KXLK.......... Haysville, KS [*FM radio station call letters*]
KXLM.......... Oxnard, CA [*FM radio station call letters*]
KXLN.......... Rosenburg, TX [*Television station call letters*]
KXLO.......... Lewistown, MT [*AM radio station call letters*]
KXLP.......... New Ulm, MN [*FM radio station call letters*]
KXLQ.......... Indianola, IA [*AM radio station call letters*] (RBYB)
KXLR.......... Fairbanks, AK [*FM radio station call letters*]
KXLS.......... Alva, OK [*FM radio station call letters*]
KXLT........... Eagle, ID [*FM radio station call letters*]
KXLT-TV..... Rochester, MN [*Television station call letters*]
KXLU.......... Los Angeles, CA [*FM radio station call letters*]
KXLY.......... Spokane, WA [*AM radio station call letters*]
KXLY-FM..... Spokane, WA [*FM radio station call letters*]
KXLY-TV..... Spokane, WA [*Television station call letters*]
KXMA.......... Dickinson, ND [*Television station call letters*]
KXMB.......... Bismarck, ND [*Television station call letters*]
KXMC.......... Minot, ND [*Television station call letters*]
KXMD.......... Williston, ND [*Television station call letters*]
KXMG-AM.... Los Angeles, CA [*AM radio station call letters*] (RBYB)
KXMR.......... Bismarck, ND [*AM radio station call letters*] (RBYB)
KXMS.......... Joplin, MO [*FM radio station call letters*]
KXMX.......... Cedar Rapids, IA [*FM radio station call letters*] (RBYB)
KXNE.......... Norfolk, NE [*FM radio station call letters*]
KXNE-TV..... Norfolk, NE [*Television station call letters*]
KXNO.......... North Las Vegas, NV [*AM radio station call letters*]
KXNP.......... North Platte, NE [*FM radio station call letters*]
KXO............ El Centro, CA [*AM radio station call letters*]
KXOA.......... Sacramento, CA [*AM radio station call letters*]
KXOA-FM..... Sacramento, CA [*FM radio station call letters*]
KXOF.......... Bloomfield, IA [*FM radio station call letters*]
KXO-FM...... El Centro, CA [*FM radio station call letters*]
KXOI........... Crane, TX [*AM radio station call letters*]
KXOJ.......... Sapulpa, OK [*AM radio station call letters*]
KXOJ-FM..... Sapulpa, OK [*FM radio station call letters*]
KXOK.......... Florissant, MO [*FM radio station call letters*]
KXOL.......... Clinton, OK [*AM radio station call letters*]
KXOO.......... Elk City, OK [*FM radio station call letters*] (RBYB)
KXOQ.......... Kennett, MO [*FM radio station call letters*] (RBYB)
KXOR.......... Thibodaux, LA [*FM radio station call letters*]
KXOW.......... Hot Springs, AR [*AM radio station call letters*]
KXOX.......... Sweetwater, TX [*AM radio station call letters*]
KXOX-FM..... Sweetwater, TX [*FM radio station call letters*]
KXOZ.......... Mountain View, MO [*FM radio station call letters*]
KXPA-AM.... Pasadena, CA [*AM radio station call letters*] (RBYB)
KXPC.......... Lebanon, OR [*FM radio station call letters*]
KXPK.......... Evergreen, CO [*FM radio station call letters*]
KXPO.......... Grafton, ND [*AM radio station call letters*]
KXPO-FM..... Grafton, ND [*FM radio station call letters*]
KXPR.......... Sacramento, CA [*FM radio station call letters*]
KXPT.......... Las Vegas, NV [*FM radio station call letters*]
KXPW.......... Belle Plaine, IA [*FM radio station call letters*]
KXPX.......... Stillwater, OK [*FM radio station call letters*] (RBYB)
KXPZ.......... Lytle, TX [*FM radio station call letters*]
KXRA.......... Alexandria, MN [*AM radio station call letters*]
KXRA-FM..... Alexandria, MN [*FM radio station call letters*]
KXRB.......... Sioux Falls, SD [*AM radio station call letters*]
KXRD.......... Victorville, CA [*FM radio station call letters*]
KXRE.......... Manitou Springs, CO [*AM radio station call letters*]
KXRJ.......... Russellville, AR [*FM radio station call letters*]
KXRK.......... Provo, UT [*FM radio station call letters*]
KXRM.......... Colorado Springs, CO [*Television station call letters*]
KXRO.......... Aberdeen, WA [*AM radio station call letters*]
KXRS.......... Hemet, CA [*FM radio station call letters*]
KXRX.......... Walla Walla, WA [*FM radio station call letters*]
KXSA-FM..... Dermott, AR [*FM radio station call letters*]
KXSB.......... Big Bear Lake, CA [*FM radio station call letters*] (RBYB)
KXSM.......... Saint Mary College, Xavier, KS [*Library symbol Library of Congress*] (LCLS)
KXSP.......... Ventura, CA [*AM radio station call letters*] (RBYB)
KXSR.......... Groveland, CA [*FM radio station call letters*]
KXSS.......... Waite Park, MN [*AM radio station call letters*]
KXST-FM..... Oceanside, CA [*FM radio station call letters*] (RBYB)
KXTC.......... Thoreau, NM [*FM radio station call letters*]
KXTD.......... Wagoner, OK [*AM radio station call letters*]
KXTE-FM..... Rahrump, NV [*FM radio station call letters*] (RBYB)
KXTJ........... Beaumont, TX [*FM radio station call letters*]
KXTK-AM.... Des Moines, IA [*AM radio station call letters*] (RBYB)
KXTL........... Butte, MT [*AM radio station call letters*]
KXTN.......... San Antonio, TX [*AM radio station call letters*]
KXTN-FM..... San Antonio, TX [*FM radio station call letters*]
KXTO.......... Reno, NV [*AM radio station call letters*]
KXTP.......... Superior, WI [*AM radio station call letters*]
KXTQ.......... Lubbock, TX [*AM radio station call letters*]
KXTQ-FM..... Lubbock, TX [*FM radio station call letters*]
KXTR.......... Kansas City, MO [*FM radio station call letters*]
KXTV.......... Sacramento, CA [*Television station call letters*]
KXTX.......... Dallas, TX [*Television station call letters*]
KXU............ Kastamonu [*Turkey*] [*Airport symbol*] (AD)
KXU............ Keyword Transformation Unit [*Computer science*] (MHDI)
KXUS.......... Springfield, MO [*FM radio station call letters*]
KXUX.......... Bend, OR [*AM radio station call letters*]
KXVO.......... Omaha, NE [*Television station call letters*] (RBYB)
KXXI........... Gallup, NM [*FM radio station call letters*]
KXXK.......... Chickasha, OK [*FM radio station call letters*]

KXXL............	Crane, TX [*FM radio station call letters*]
KXXO............	Olympia, WA [*FM radio station call letters*]
KXXS............	Toppenish, WA [*FM radio station call letters*]
KXXV..........	Waco, TX [*Television station call letters*]
KXXX...........	Colby, KS [*AM radio station call letters*]
KXXY............	Oklahoma City, OK [*AM radio station call letters*]
KXXY-FM....	Oklahoma City, OK [*FM radio station call letters*]
KXXZ............	Barstow, CA [*FM radio station call letters*]
KXYL............	Brownwood, TX [*AM radio station call letters*]
KXYL-FM.....	Brownwood, TX [*FM radio station call letters*]
KXYQ...........	Milwaukie, OR [*AM radio station call letters*]
KXYZ...........	Houston, TX [*AM radio station call letters*]
KXZZ............	Lake Charles, LA [*AM radio station call letters*]
KY...............	Cayman Islands [*ANSI two-letter standard code*] (CNC)
KY...............	Kabaka Yekka [*The King Alone*] [*Uganda Suspended*] [*Political party*]
KY...............	Kapustin Yar [*Test Facility*] [*US prefix for Soviet-Russian developmental missiles*] (DOMA)
KY...............	Kentucky [*Postal code*] (AFM)
Ky...............	Kentucky (ODBW)
Ky...............	Kentucky Department of Libraries, Frankfort, KY [*Library symbol Library of Congress*] (LCLS)
Ky...............	Kentucky Reports [*A publication*] (AAGC)
KY...............	Kentucky Supreme Court Reports [*1879-1951*] [*A publication*] (DLA)
KY...............	Kent Yeomanry [*Military unit*] [*British*]
KY...............	Key (MCD)
KY...............	Key
KY...............	Keyhole [*United States reconnaissance satellite*] (DOMA)
KY...............	Keying Devices [*JETDS nomenclature*] [*Military*] (CET)
KY...............	Kol Yisroel [*Israeli Broadcasting Service*]
KY...............	Kyrie [*Liturgical*]
KY...............	Sun West [*ICAO designator*] (AD)
KyA.............	Ashland Public Library, Ashland, KY [*Library symbol Library of Congress*] (LCLS)
KYA.............	Konya [*Turkey*] [*Airport symbol*] (AD)
KYA.............	Kyakhta [*Former USSR Seismograph station code, US Geological Survey Closed*] (SEIS)
KYA.............	Yana Air Cargo (Kenya) Ltd. [*ICAO designator*] (FAAC)
KY Admin Reg...	Kentucky Administrative Register [*A publication*] (DLA)
KY Admin Regs...	Kentucky Administration Regulations Service [*A publication*] (DLA)
Ky Admin Regs...	Kentucky Administrative Regulations [*A publication*] (AAGC)
KYAJ...........	Merced, CA [*FM radio station call letters*]
KYAK..........	Anchorage, AK [*AM radio station call letters*]
Ky-Ar..........	Kentucky Department of Libraries and Archives, Kentucky State Archives, Frankfort, KY [*Library symbol*] [*Library of Congress*] (LCLS)
KYAT...........	Keokuk, IA [*FM radio station call letters*]
KYAX..........	Alturas, CA [*FM radio station call letters*]
KYB.............	Kayaba Industry Co. [*Auto industry supplier*]
KYB.............	Know Your Body (DAVI)
KYBA..........	Stewartville, MN [*FM radio station call letters*]
KyBB...........	Berea College, Berea, KY [*Library symbol Library of Congress*] (LCLS)
KYBC-AM....	Cottonwood, AZ [*AM radio station call letters*] (RBYB)
KYBD..........	Copeland, KS [*FM radio station call letters*]
KYBD..........	Keyboard (MSA)
KYBE..........	Frederick, OK [*FM radio station call letters*]
KYBG..........	Aurora, CO [*AM radio station call letters*]
KyBgW.......	Western Kentucky University, Bowling Green, KY [*Library symbol Library of Congress*] (LCLS)
KyBgW-K....	Western Kentucky University, Kentucky Library, Bowling Green, KY [*Library symbol Library of Congress*] (LCLS)
KYBI-FM.....	Huntington, TX [*FM radio station call letters*] (RBYB)
KYBJ...........	Lake Jackson, TX [*FM radio station call letters*] (RBYB)
Ky-BPH......	Kentucky Library for the Blind and Physically Handicapped, Frankfort, KY [*Library symbol Library of Congress*] (LCLS)
KYBRD.......	Keyboard
KYBR-FM....	Espanola, NM [*FM radio station call letters*] (RBYB)
KyBvU........	Union College, Barbourville, KY [*Library symbol Library of Congress*] (LCLS)
KYC............	HCL Aviation, Inc. [*ICAO designator*] (FAAC)
KYC............	Know Your Customer [*Business term*]
KYC............	Know Your Customer [*Investment term*] (DFIT)
KYCA..........	Prescott, AZ [*AM radio station call letters*]
KyCambC....	Campbellsville College, Campbellsville, KY [*Library symbol Library of Congress*] (LCLS)
KyCarD......	Dow Corning Corp., TIS Library, Carrollton, KY [*Library symbol Library of Congress*] (LCLS)
KYCH..........	Convent General of the Knights York Cross of Honour (EA)
KYCK..........	Crookston, MN [*FM radio station call letters*]
KYCN..........	Wheatland, WY [*AM radio station call letters*]
KYCN-FM....	Wheatland, WY [*FM radio station call letters*]
KyColW.......	Lindsey Wilson College, Columbia, KY [*Library symbol Library of Congress*] (LCLS)
KY Comment'r...	Kentucky Commentator [*A publication*] (DLA)
KyCov.........	Kenton County Public Library, Covington, KY [*Library symbol Library of Congress*] (LCLS)
KyCovStE....	Saint Elizabeth Medical Center, Covington, KY [*Library symbol Library of Congress*] (LCLS)
KYCR..........	Golden Valley, MN [*AM radio station call letters*]
KYCS...........	Rock Springs, WY [*FM radio station call letters*]
KYCW..........	Seattle, WA [*FM radio station call letters*]
KYCX...........	Mexia, TX [*FM radio station call letters*]
KYCY...........	San Francisco, CA [*FM radio station call letters*]

KYd.............	Kilo Yard
Kyd.............	Kyd on Bills of Exchange [*A publication*] (DLA)
Kyd Aw.......	Kyd on Awards [*A publication*] (DLA)
Kyd Bills.....	Kyd on Bills of Exchange [*A publication*] (DLA)
KyDC..........	Centre College of Kentucky, Danville, KY [*Library symbol Library of Congress*] (LCLS)
KYDE..........	Pine Bluff, AR [*AM radio station call letters*]
KY Dec.......	Sneed's Kentucky Decisions [*2 Kentucky*] [*A publication*] (DLA)
KYDS...........	Kiloyards (MCD)
KYDS...........	Sacramento, CA [*FM radio station call letters*]
KYDT-FM....	Sundance, WY [*FM radio station call letters*] (RBYB)
KYDZ..........	Cody, WY [*FM radio station call letters*]
KYEA..........	West Monroe, LA [*FM radio station call letters*]
KYEE..........	Alamogordo, NM [*FM radio station call letters*]
KYEG-FM....	Canadian, TX [*FM radio station call letters*] (RBYB)
KyeKtts......	Kaye Kotts Associates, Inc. [*Associated Press*] (SAG)
KYERI.........	Know Your Endorsers - Require Identification [*Advice to businessmen and others who cash checks for the public*]
KyErP.........	Seminary of Saint Pius X, Erlanger, KY [*Library symbol Library of Congress*] (LCLS)
KYES...........	Anchorage, AK [*Television station call letters*]
KYET...........	Williams, AZ [*AM radio station call letters*]
KYEZ...........	Salina, KS [*FM radio station call letters*]
KYF.............	Kentucky First Bancorp [*AMEX symbol*] (TTSB)
KYF.............	Kentucky First Bancorp, Inc. [*AMEX symbol*] (SAG)
KYF.............	Yeelirie [*Australia Airport symbol*] (OAG)
KYFA..........	Amarillo, TX [*FM radio station call letters*]
KYFC..........	Kansas City, MO [*Television station call letters*]
KyFc...........	United States Army, Fort Campbell Post Library (R. F. Sink Memorial Library), Fort Campbell, KY [*Library symbol Library of Congress*] (LCLS)
KyFCE........	Kentucky Council on Higher Education, Frankfort, KY [*Library symbol*] [*Library of Congress*] (LCLS)
KyFkAS.......	United States Army Armor School, Fort Knox, KY [*Library symbol Library of Congress*] (LCLS)
KYFL..........	Monroe, LA [*FM radio station call letters*]
KyFLR.........	Legislative Research Commission, Library, Frankfort, KY [*Library symbol*] [*Library of Congress*] (LCLS)
KYFM..........	Bartlesville, OK [*FM radio station call letters*]
KyFmTM......	Thomas More College, Fort Mitchell, KY [*Library symbol Library of Congress*] (LCLS)
KYFO..........	Ogden, UT [*AM radio station call letters*]
KYFO-FM....	Ogden, UT [*FM radio station call letters*]
KYFR..........	Shenandoah, IA [*AM radio station call letters*]
KYFS..........	San Antonio, TX [*FM radio station call letters*]
KyFSC........	Kentucky State University, Frankfort, KY [*Library symbol Library of Congress*] (LCLS)
KY Fst........	Kentucky First Bancorp, Inc. [*Associated Press*] (SAG)
KY FstB.......	Kentucky First Bancorp, Inc. [*Associated Press*] (SAG)
KYFT..........	Lubbock, TX [*FM radio station call letters*]
KYFW..........	Wichita, KS [*FM radio station call letters*]
KYFX..........	Little Rock, AR [*FM radio station call letters*]
Ky-G..........	Kentucky Department of Libraries and Archives, Kentucky Guide Project, Frankfort, KY [*Library symbol*] [*Library of Congress*] (LCLS)
KyGeC.........	Georgetown College, Georgetown, KY [*Library symbol Library of Congress*] (LCLS)
KYGL..........	Texarkana, AR [*FM radio station call letters*] (RBYB)
KYGO..........	Lakewood, CO [*AM radio station call letters*]
KYGO-FM....	Denver, CO [*FM radio station call letters*]
KyHaHi.......	Harrodsburg Historical Society, Harrodsburg, KY [*Library symbol Library of Congress*] (LCLS)
KyHhN.........	Northern Kentucky University, Highland Heights, KY [*Library symbol Library of Congress*] (LCLS)
KyHhN-L......	Northern Kentucky University, B. P. Chase College of Law, Covington, KY [*Library symbol Library of Congress*] (LCLS)
KyHi...........	Kentucky Historical Society, Frankfort, KY [*Library symbol Library of Congress*] (LCLS)
KYHL..........	Keyhole (ABBR)
KyHopC.......	Hopkinsville Community College, Hopkinsville, KY [*Library symbol*] [*Library of Congress*] (LCLS)
KYHT..........	Yermo, CA [*FM radio station call letters*]
KyHzC.........	Hazard Community College, Hazard, KY [*Library symbol Library of Congress*] (LCLS)
KYIN..........	Mason City, IA [*Television station call letters*]
KYIP..........	Detroit/Willow Run [*Michigan*] [*ICAO location identifier*] (ICLI)
KYIS..........	Oklahoma City, OK [*FM radio station call letters*]
KYIX..........	South Oroville, CA [*FM radio station call letters*] (RBYB)
KYJC-FM.....	Grants Pass, OR [*FM radio station call letters*]
KYJT..........	Yuma, AZ [*FM radio station call letters*] (RBYB)
KYK............	Karluk [*Alaska*] [*Airport symbol*] (OAG)
KYK............	Karluk, AK [*Location identifier FAA*] (FAAL)
KYK............	Kayak (ABBR)
KYK............	Kayak Island [*Alaska*] [*Seismograph station code, US Geological Survey*] (SEIS)
KYK............	Kelley-Kerr Energy [*Vancouver Stock Exchange symbol*]
KYKA..........	Naches, WA [*FM radio station call letters*]
KYKC..........	Byng, OK [*FM radio station call letters*]
KYKD..........	Bethel, AK [*FM radio station call letters*]
KYKF..........	San Fernando, CA [*FM radio station call letters*]
KYKK..........	Hobbs, NM [*AM radio station call letters*]
KYKM..........	Yoakum, TX [*FM radio station call letters*] (RBYB)
KYKN..........	Keizer, OR [*AM radio station call letters*]
KYKN..........	Nephi, UT [*FM radio station call letters*]

KYKN	Pkynocytes [*Hematology*] (DAVI)
KYKR	Beaumont, TX [*FM radio station call letters*]
KYKS	Lufkin, TX [*FM radio station call letters*]
KYKX	Longview, TX [*FM radio station call letters*]
KYKY	St. Louis, MO [*FM radio station call letters*]
KYKZ	Lake Charles, LA [*FM radio station call letters*]
KY L	Kentucky Law Reporter [*A publication*] (DLA)
KYL	Kyle Resources, Inc. [*Vancouver Stock Exchange symbol*]
KY Law Rep	Kentucky Law Reporter [*A publication*] (DLA)
KYLC	Osage Beach, MO [*FM radio station call letters*]
KYLD	San Mateo, CA [*FM radio station call letters*]
KYLE	Bryan, TX [*Television station call letters*]
KyLo	Louisville Free Public Library, Louisville, KY [*Library symbol Library of Congress*] (LCLS)
KyLoB	Bellarmine College, Louisville, KY [*Library symbol Library of Congress*] (LCLS)
KyLoB-M	Bellarmine College, Thomas Merton Studies Center, Louisville, KY [*Library symbol Library of Congress*] (LCLS)
KyLoBW	Brown & Williamson Tobacco Corp., Research Department Library, Louisville, KY [*Library symbol Library of Congress*] (LCLS)
KyLoC	Courier-Journal & Louisville Times Co., Inc., Louisville, KY [*Library symbol Library of Congress*] (LCLS)
KyLoF	Filson Club, Louisville, KY [*Library symbol Library of Congress*] (LCLS)
KyLoJ	Jefferson Community College, Louisville, KY [*Library symbol Library of Congress*] (LCLS)
KyLoL	Louisville Presbyterian Seminary, Louisville, KY [*Library symbol Library of Congress*] (LCLS)
KyLoM	Louisville Medical Library, Louisville, KY [*Library symbol Library of Congress*] (LCLS)
KyLoN	Spalding College, Louisville, KY [*Library symbol Library of Congress*] (LCLS)
KyLoS	Southern Baptist Theological Seminary, Louisville, KY [*Library symbol Library of Congress*] (LCLS)
KyLoU	University of Louisville, Louisville, KY [*Library symbol Library of Congress*] (LCLS)
KyLoU-Ar	University of Louisville, University Archives and Records Center, Louisville, KY [*Library symbol Library of Congress*] (LCLS)
KyLoU-HS	University of Louisville, Health Sciences Library, Louisville, KY [*Library symbol Library of Congress*] (LCLS)
KyLoU-L	University of Louisville, Law Library, Louisville, KY [*Library symbol*] [*Library of Congress*] (LCLS)
KyLoU-Mu	University of Louisville, Dwight Anderson Music Library, Louisville, KY [*Library symbol*] [*Library of Congress*] (LCLS)
KyLoV	United States Veterans Administration Hospital, Louisville, KY [*Library symbol Library of Congress*] (LCLS)
KYLR	Huntsville, TX [*AM radio station call letters*]
KY LR	Kentucky Law Reporter [*A publication*] (DLA)
KY L Rep	Kentucky Law Reporter [*A publication*] (DLA)
KY L Rev	Kentucky Law Review [*A publication*] (DLA)
KY L Rptr	Kentucky Law Reporter [*A publication*] (DLA)
KYLT	Missoula, MT [*AM radio station call letters*]
KyLx	Lexington Public Library, Lexington, KY [*Library symbol Library of Congress*] (LCLS)
KyLxCB	Lexington Theological Seminary, Lexington, KY [*Library symbol Library of Congress*] (LCLS)
KyLxCS	Council of State Governments, State Information Center, Lexington, KY [*Library symbol Library of Congress*] (LCLS)
KyLxI	IBM Corp., Office Products Division, Lexington, KY [*Library symbol Library of Congress*] (LCLS)
KyLxIMM	Institute for Mining and Minerals Research, Lexington, KY [*Library symbol Library of Congress*] (LCLS)
KyLxK	Keeneland Association, Inc., Lexington, KY [*Library symbol Library of Congress*] (LCLS)
KyLxT	Transylvania University, Lexington, KY [*Library symbol Library of Congress*] (LCLS)
KyLxTI	Lexington Technical Institute, Lexington, KY [*Library symbol Library of Congress*] (LCLS)
KyLxV	United States Veterans Administration Hospital, Lexington, KY [*Library symbol Library of Congress*] (LCLS)
KYLZ	Santa Cruz, CA [*FM radio station call letters*]
KYMA	Yuma, AZ [*Television station call letters*]
KyMadC	Madisonville Community College, Media Center, Madisonville, KY [*Library symbol Library of Congress*] (LCLS)
KyMan	Clay County Public Library, Manchester, KY [*Library symbol Library of Congress*] (LCLS)
KYMC	Ballwin, MO [*FM radio station call letters*]
KYMD	Kentucky Medical Insurance Co. [*NASDAQ symbol*] (NQ)
KyMdC	Midway Junior College and Pinkerton High School, Midway, KY [*Library symbol Library of Congress*] (LCLS)
KyMed	Kentucky Medical Insurance Co. [*Associated Press*] (SAG)
KYMG	Anchorage, AK [*FM radio station call letters*]
KYMI	Los Ybanez, TX [*FM radio station call letters*]
KYMN	Northfield, MN [*AM radio station call letters*]
KYMO	East Prairie, MO [*AM radio station call letters*]
KYMO	Kymograph (ABBR)
KYMO-FM	East Prairie, MO [*FM radio station call letters*]
KyMoreU	Morehead State University, Morehead, KY [*Library symbol Library of Congress*] (LCLS)
KYMS	Keep Your Mouth Shut
KYMS	Santa Ana, CA [*FM radio station call letters*]
KyMurT	Murray State University, Murray, KY [*Library symbol Library of Congress*] (LCLS)
KYMV	Kennedya Yellow Mosaic Virus [*Plant pathology*]
KYMX	Sacramento, CA [*FM radio station call letters*]
KyMyC	Maysville Community College, Maysville, KY [*Library symbol*] [*Library of Congress*] (LCLS)
KYN	Kynurenic Acid (DMAA)
KYN	Kynurenine [*Biochemistry*]
KYN	Kyrnair [*France ICAO designator*] (FAAC)
KyNaM	Nazareth Mother House Archives, Nazareth, KY [*Library symbol Library of Congress*] (LCLS)
KYND	Cypress, TX [*AM radio station call letters*]
KYNE	Omaha, NE [*Television station call letters*]
KYNG	Dallas, TX [*FM radio station call letters*]
KYNG	Youngstown [*Ohio*] [*ICAO location identifier*] (ICLI)
KYNO	Fresno, CA [*AM radio station call letters*]
KYNT	Keynote (ABBR)
KYNT	Yankton, SD [*AM radio station call letters*]
KYNTG	Keynoting (ABBR)
KYNU	Jamestown, ND [*FM radio station call letters*]
KYNZ	Lone Grove, OK [*FM radio station call letters*]
KYO	Kyocera Corp. [*NYSE symbol*] (SPSG)
KYO	Kyocera Corp.ADR [*NYSE symbol*] (TTSB)
KYO	Kyoto [*Japan*] [*Seismograph station code, US Geological Survey*] (SEIS)
Kyocer	Kyocera Corp. [*Associated Press*] (SAG)
KYOK	Houston, TX [*AM radio station call letters*]
KYOO	Bolivar, MO [*AM radio station call letters*]
KYOO-FM	Halfway, MO [*FM radio station call letters*]
KY Op	Kentucky Court of Appeals Opinions [*A publication*] (DLA)
KY Opin	Kentucky Opinions [*A publication*] (DLA)
KYOS	Merced, CA [*AM radio station call letters*]
KYOT-FM	Phoenix, AZ [*FM radio station call letters*]
Kyoto L Rev	Kyoto Law Review [*A publication*] (DLA)
KYOU	Wendover, NV [*FM radio station call letters*]
KYOU-TV	Ottumwa, IA [*Television station call letters*]
KyOw	Owensboro-Daviess County Public Library, Owensboro, KY [*Library symbol Library of Congress*] (LCLS)
KyOwB	Brescia College, Owensboro, KY [*Library symbol Library of Congress*] (LCLS)
KyOwC	Owensboro Community College, Owensboro, KY [*Library symbol*] [*Library of Congress*] (LCLS)
KyOwK	Kentucky Wesleyan College, Owensboro, KY [*Library symbol Library of Congress*] (LCLS)
KYP	Kyaukpyu [*Myanmar*] [*Airport symbol*] (OAG)
KYPA-AM	Los Angeles, CA [*AM radio station call letters*] (RBYB)
KyPad	Paducah Public Library, Paducah, KY [*Library symbol Library of Congress*] (LCLS)
KyPadC	Paducah Community College, Paducah, KY [*Library symbol Library of Congress*] (LCLS)
KyParF	John Fox, Jr. Memorial Library, Paris, KY [*Library symbol Library of Congress*] (LCLS)
kyph	Kyphosis [*Orthopedics*] (DAVI)
KyPikC	Pikeville College, Pikeville, KY [*Library symbol Library of Congress*] (LCLS)
KYPL-FM	Yakima, WA [*FM radio station call letters*] (RBYB)
KyPpA	Alice Lloyd College, Pippa Passes, KY [*Library symbol*] [*Library of Congress*] (LCLS)
KyPrbC	Prestonburg Community College, Prestonsburg, KY [*Library symbol*] [*Library of Congress*] (LCLS)
KyPw25	Kentucky Power Co. [*Associated Press*] (SAG)
KYQQ	Arkansas City, KS [*FM radio station call letters*]
KYQX	Weatherford, TX [*FM radio station call letters*] (RBYB)
KY R	Kentucky Reports [*A publication*] (DLA)
KYR	Kyber Resources [*Vancouver Stock Exchange symbol*]
KyRE	Eastern Kentucky University, Richmond, KY [*Library symbol Library of Congress*] (LCLS)
KY Rev Stat	Kentucky Revised Statutes [*A publication*] (DLA)
KY Rev Stat & Rules Serv	Kentucky Revised Statutes and Rules Service (Baldwin) [*A publication*] (DLA)
KY Rev Stat Ann	Baldwin's Kentucky Revised Statutes, Annotated [*A publication*] (DLA)
KYRK-FM	Eunice, NM [*FM radio station call letters*] (RBYB)
KYRO	Potosi, MO [*AM radio station call letters*]
KYRS	Atwater, NM [*FM radio station call letters*]
KYRX	Chaffee, MO [*FM radio station call letters*]
KYS	Kayes [*Mali*] [*Airport symbol*] (OAG)
KYS	Kentucky State University, Frankfort, KY [*OCLC symbol*] (OCLC)
KYS	Keycorp Industries [*Vancouver Stock Exchange symbol*]
KYS	Keys
KYS	Kiyosumi - Telemeter [*Japan*] [*Seismograph station code, US Geological Survey*] (SEIS)
KY SBJ	Kentucky State Bar Journal [*A publication*] (DLA)
KYSC	Yakima, WA [*FM radio station call letters*]
KYSG	Coos Bay, OR [*FM radio station call letters*] (RBYB)
Kyshe	Kyshe's Reports [*1808-90*] [*A publication*] (DLA)
KYSL	Frisco, CO [*FM radio station call letters*]
KYSM	Mankato, MN [*AM radio station call letters*]
KYSM-FM	Mankato, MN [*FM radio station call letters*]
KYSN	East Wenatchee, WA [*FM radio station call letters*]
KySoC	Somerset Community College, Somerset, KY [*Library symbol Library of Congress*] (LCLS)
Kysor	Kysor Industrial Corp. [*Associated Press*] (SAG)
KYSR	Los Angeles, CA [*FM radio station call letters*]
KYSS-FM	Missoula, MT [*FM radio station call letters*]
kyst	Keystone (VRA)
KYST	Texas City, TX [*AM radio station call letters*]
KY St BJ	Kentucky State Bar Journal [*A publication*] (DLA)

KY St Law ... Morehead and Brown. Digest of Kentucky Statute Laws [*A publication*] (DLA)
KYSTN .... Keystone (ABBR)
KYT .... Corporate High Yield Fd II [*NYSE symbol*] (TTSB)
KYT .... Corporate High Yield II [*NYSE symbol*] (SAG)
KYT .... Keystone Explorations [*Vancouver Stock Exchange symbol*]
KYT .... Kyauktaw [*Myanmar*] [*Airport symbol*] (OAG)
KYTC .... Northwood, IA [*FM radio station call letters*]
KYTE .... Newport, OR [*FM radio station call letters*]
KYTN .... Wrightsville, AR [*FM radio station call letters*]
KYTOON....... Kite Balloon [*Air Force*]
KyTrA .... Abbey of Gethsemani, Trappist, KY [*Library symbol Library of Congress*] (LCLS)
KYTT .... Coos Bay, OR [*FM radio station call letters*]
KYTV .... Springfield, MO [*Television station call letters*]
KYTX .... Beeville, TX [*FM radio station call letters*]
kyu .... Kentucky [*MARC country of publication code Library of Congress*] (LCCP)
KYU .... Koyukuk [*Alaska*] [*Airport symbol*] (OAG)
KYU .... Koyukuk, AK [*Location identifier FAA*] (FAAL)
KyU .... University of Kentucky, Lexington, KY [*Library symbol Library of Congress*] (LCLS)
KyU-A .... University of Kentucky, Ashland Community College, Ashland, KY [*Library symbol Library of Congress*] (LCLS)
KyU-ASC..... University of Kentucky, Agricultural Science Center, Lexington, KY [*Library symbol Library of Congress*] (LCLS)
KYUC .... Roland, OK [*FM radio station call letters*]
KyU-C .... University of Kentucky, Southeast Center, Cumberland, KY [*Library symbol Library of Congress*] (LCLS)
KyU-E .... University of Kentucky, Elizabethtown Community College, Elizabethtown, KY [*Library symbol Library of Congress*] (LCLS)
KyU-F .... University of Kentucky, Fort Knox Center, Fort Knox, KY [*Library symbol Library of Congress*] (LCLS)
KYUF .... Uvalde, TX [*FM radio station call letters*]
KyU-H .... University of Kentucky, Northwest Center, Henderson, KY [*Library symbol Library of Congress*] (LCLS)
KYUK .... Bethel, AK [*AM radio station call letters*]
KYUK-TV ..... Bethel, AK [*Television station call letters*]
KyU-L .... University of Kentucky, Law Library, Lexington, KY [*Library symbol Library of Congress*] (LCLS)
KyU-M .... University of Kentucky, Medical Center, Lexington, KY [*Library symbol Library of Congress*] (LCLS)
KYUM .... Yuma/Yuma Marine Corps Air Station, Yuma International [*Arizona*] [*ICAO location identifier*] (ICLI)
KyU-N .... University of Kentucky, Northern Center, Covington, KY [*Library symbol Library of Congress*] (LCLS)
KyU-P .... University of Kentucky, Prestonburg Community College, Prestonburg, KY [*Library symbol Library of Congress*] (LCLS)
KYUS .... Miles City, MT [*Television station call letters*]
KYUU .... Liberal, KS [*AM radio station call letters*]
KYV .... Kibris Turk Hava Yollari Ltd. [*Turkey*] [*FAA designator*] (FAAC)
KYVA .... Gallup, NM [*AM radio station call letters*]
KYVE .... Yakima, WA [*Television station call letters*]
KYW .... Philadelphia, PA [*AM radio station call letters*]
KyWA .... Asbury College, Wilmore, KY [*Library symbol Library of Congress*] (LCLS)
KyWAT .... Asbury Theological Seminary, Wilmore, KY [*Library symbol Library of Congress*] (LCLS)
KyWavH...... Waverly Hills Tuberculosis Sanatorium, Waverly Hills, KY [*Library symbol Library of Congress*] (LCLS)
KY WC Dec... Kentucky Workmen's Compensation Board Decisions [*A publication*] (DLA)
KyWilC........ Cumberland College, Williamsburg, KY [*Library symbol Library of Congress*] (LCLS)
KyWn .... Clark County Public Library, Winchester, KY [*Library symbol Library of Congress*] (LCLS)
KyWnS........ Southeastern Christian College, Winchester, KY [*Library symbol Library of Congress*] (LCLS)
KYW-TV ...... Philadelphia, PA [*Television station call letters*]
KYX .... Yalumet [*Papua New Guinea*] [*Airport symbol*] (OAG)
KYXE .... Selah, WA [*AM radio station call letters*]
KYXK .... Gurdon, AR [*FM radio station call letters*]
KYXS .... Mineral Wells, TX [*FM radio station call letters*]
KYXX .... Ozona, TX [*FM radio station call letters*]
KYXY .... San Diego, CA [*FM radio station call letters*]
KYYA .... Billings, MT [*FM radio station call letters*]
KYYD .... Abilene, TX [*FM radio station call letters*]
KYYI .... Burkburnett, TX [*FM radio station call letters*]
KYYK .... Palestine, TX [*FM radio station call letters*]
KYYS .... Kansas City, MO [*FM radio station call letters*]
KYYT .... Goldendale, WA [*FM radio station call letters*]
KYYX .... Minot, ND [*FM radio station call letters*]
KYYY .... Bismarck, ND [*FM radio station call letters*]
KYYZ .... Williston, ND [*FM radio station call letters*]
KYZ .... Kayseri [*Turkey*] [*Airport symbol*] (AD)
Kyzen......... Kyzen Corp. [*Associated Press*] (SAG)
KYZN .... Kyzen Corp. [*NASDAQ symbol*] (SAG)
KYZN .... Kyzen Corp.'A' [*NASDAQ symbol*] (TTSB)
KYZNW........ Kyzen Corp.Wrrt'A' [*NASDAQ symbol*] (TTSB)
KYZS .... Tyler, TX [*AM radio station call letters*]
KYZX .... Pueblo, CO [*FM radio station call letters*]
KYZZ .... San Angelo, TX [*FM radio station call letters*]
KZ .... Dust/Sand Storm [*Meteorology*] (WDAA)
KZ .... Kaplan-Zuelzer [*Syndrome*] (DAVI)
KZ .... Ketoconazole (DMAA)

KZ.............. Killing Zone [*Military British*]
KZ.............. Kilohertz [*Preferred form is kHz*] [*Electronics*] (MCD)
KZ.............. Konzentrationslager [*Concentration Camp*] [*Initials also used in medicine to indicate a psychiatric syndrome found in surviving victims of the World War II camps*] [*German*]
KZ.............. Kuhns Zeitschrift fuer Vergleichende Sprachforschung [*A publication*] (BJA)
Kz.............. Kwanza [*Monetary Unit*] [*Angola*] (BARN)
KZ.............. Kysor Indl [*NYSE symbol*] (TTSB)
KZ.............. Kysor Industrial Corp. [*NYSE symbol*] (SPSG)
KZ.............. New Zealand [*IYRU nationality code*] (IYR)
KZ.............. Oriens & King [*ICAO designator*] (AD)
KZA............ Kazakhstan Airlines [*ICAO designator*] (FAAC)
KZAB.......... Albuquerque [*New Mexico*] [*ICAO location identifier*] (ICLI)
KZAC.......... Esparto, CA [*FM radio station call letters*] (RBYB)
KZAK.......... Incline Village, NV [*FM radio station call letters*]
KZAL.......... Desert Center, CA [*FM radio station call letters*]
KZAM-FM .... Ganado, TX [*FM radio station call letters*] (RBYB)
KZAP.......... Paradise, CA [*FM radio station call letters*] (RBYB)
KZAR-TV ..... Provo, UT [*FM radio station call letters*] (RBYB)
KZAT.......... Kommentar zum Alten Testament [*A publication*] (BJA)
KZAU .... Chicago, Aurora [*Illinois*] [*ICAO location identifier*] (ICLI)
KZAZ.......... Bellingham, WA [*FM radio station call letters*]
KZB............ Zachar Bay [*Alaska*] [*Airport symbol*] (OAG)
KZB............ Zachar Bay, AK [*Location identifier FAA*] (FAAL)
KZBA.......... Shafter, CA [*FM radio station call letters*]
KZBB.......... Poteau, OK [*FM radio station call letters*]
KZBE.......... Pleasant Hope, MO [*FM radio station call letters*] (RBYB)
KZBK.......... Brookfield, MO [*AM radio station call letters*]
KZBK-FM .... Brookfield, MO [*FM radio station call letters*]
KZBL.......... Natchitoches, LA [*FM radio station call letters*]
KZBN.......... Santa Barbara, CA [*FM radio station call letters*] (RBYB)
KZBQ-FM .... Pocatello, ID [*FM radio station call letters*]
KZBR-FM .... Mountain Pine, AR [*FM radio station call letters*] (RBYB)
KZBW.......... Boston, Nashua [*New Hampshire*] [*ICAO location identifier*] (ICLI)
KZBZ.......... Salina, KS [*FM radio station call letters*]
KZCD.......... Lawton, OK [*FM radio station call letters*]
KZCO-FM .... Oroville, CA [*FM radio station call letters*] (RBYB)
KZCR.......... Fergus Falls, MN [*FM radio station call letters*]
KZDC .... San Antonio, TX [*AM radio station call letters*] (RBYB)
KZDC .... Washington, Leesburg [*Virginia*] [*ICAO location identifier*] (ICLI)
KZDG .... Greeley, CO [*FM radio station call letters*]
KZDV .... Denver, Longmont [*Colorado*] [*ICAO location identifier*] (ICLI)
KZDX .... Burley, ID [*FM radio station call letters*]
KZEE .... Weatherford, TX [*AM radio station call letters*]
KZEL .... Eugene, OR [*FM radio station call letters*]
KZEN .... Central City, NE [*FM radio station call letters*]
KZEP-FM .... San Antonio, TX [*FM radio station call letters*]
KZEY .... Tyler, TX [*AM radio station call letters*]
KZEY-FM .... Marshall, TX [*FM radio station call letters*]
KZEZ .... St. George, UT [*FM radio station call letters*]
KZF............ Kaintiba [*Papua New Guinea*] [*Airport symbol*] (OAG)
KZFM.......... Corpus Christi, TX [*FM radio station call letters*]
KZFN.......... Moscow, ID [*FM radio station call letters*]
KZFO.......... Madera, CA [*FM radio station call letters*]
KZFR.......... Chico, CA [*FM radio station call letters*]
KZFT.......... Merced, CA [*FM radio station call letters*] (RBYB)
KZFW.......... Fort Worth, Euless [*Texas*] [*ICAO location identifier*] (ICLI)
KZGL.......... Cottonwood, AZ [*FM radio station call letters*]
KZGO.......... Glenwood Springs, CO [*FM radio station call letters*] (RBYB)
KZGT.......... Great Falls [*Montana*] [*ICAO location identifier*] (ICLI)
KZGZ.......... Agana, GU [*FM radio station call letters*]
KZHE.......... Stamps, AR [*FM radio station call letters*]
KZHR.......... Dayton, WA [*FM radio station call letters*]
KZHT.......... Provo, UT [*FM radio station call letters*]
KZHU.......... Houston, Humble [*Texas*] [*ICAO location identifier*] (ICLI)
KZI............. Kozani [*Greece*] [*Airport symbol*] (OAG)
KZIA.......... Las Cruces, NM [*Television station call letters*]
KZID.......... Indianapolis [*Indiana*] [*ICAO location identifier*] (ICLI)
KZIG.......... Cave City, AR [*FM radio station call letters*]
KZII.......... Lubbock, TX [*FM radio station call letters*]
KZIM.......... Cape Girardeau, MO [*AM radio station call letters*]
KZIN.......... Shelby, MT [*FM radio station call letters*]
KZIO.......... Superior, WI [*FM radio station call letters*]
KZIP.......... Amarillo, TX [*AM radio station call letters*]
KZIQ.......... Ridgecrest, CA [*AM radio station call letters*]
KZIQ-FM .... Ridgecrest, CA [*FM radio station call letters*]
KZIZ.......... Sumner, WA [*AM radio station call letters*]
KZJC.......... Flagstaff, AZ [*Television station call letters*]
KZJG.......... Longmont, CO [*Television station call letters*]
KZJH.......... Jackson, WY [*FM radio station call letters*]
KZJL.......... Houston, TX [*Television station call letters*]
KZJX.......... Jacksonville Hillard [*Florida*] [*ICAO location identifier*] (ICLI)
KZKC.......... Kansas City Olathe [*Kansas*] [*ICAO location identifier*] (ICLI)
KZKE.......... Seligman, AZ [*FM radio station call letters*] (RBYB)
KZKI.......... San Bernardino, CA [*Television station call letters*]
KZKK.......... Huron, SD [*FM radio station call letters*]
KZKL.......... Rio Rancho, NM [*FM radio station call letters*]
KZKS.......... Rifle, CO [*FM radio station call letters*]
KZKX.......... Seward, NE [*FM radio station call letters*]
KZKZ.......... Greenwood, AR [*FM radio station call letters*]
KZLA.......... Los Angeles, CA [*FM radio station call letters*]
KZLA.......... Los Angeles Palmdale [*California*] [*ICAO location identifier*] (ICLI)
KZLC.......... Salt Lake City [*Utah*] [*ICAO location identifier*] (ICLI)
KZLE.......... Batesville, AR [*FM radio station call letters*]

KZLN............ Othello, WA [*FM radio station call letters*]
KZLO............ Bozeman, MT [*AM radio station call letters*]
KZLS............ Great Bend, KS [*FM radio station call letters*]
KZLT............ East Grand Forks, MN [*FM radio station call letters*]
KZLZ............ Keamy, AZ [*FM radio station call letters*]
KZMA............ Miami [*Florida*] [*ICAO location identifier*] (ICLI)
KZMA............ Poplar Bluff, MO [*FM radio station call letters*]
KZME............ Hudson, IA [*FM radio station call letters*]
KZME............ Memphis [*Tennessee*] [*ICAO location identifier*] (ICLI)
KZMG............ New Plymouth, ID [*FM radio station call letters*]
KZMI............ San Jose, MP [*FM radio station call letters*]
KZMK............ Sierra Vista, AZ [*FM radio station call letters*]
KZMM............ Troy, MO [*FM radio station call letters*]
KZMP............ Minneapolis, Farmington [*Minnesota*] [*ICAO location identifier*] (ICLI)
KZMQ............ Greybull, WY [*AM radio station call letters*]
KZMQ-FM .... Greybull, WY [*FM radio station call letters*]
KZMS............ Patterson, CA [*FM radio station call letters*]
KZMT............ Helena, MT [*FM radio station call letters*]
KZMU............ Moab, UT [*FM radio station call letters*]
KZMX............ Hot Springs, SD [*AM radio station call letters*]
KZMX-FM .... Hot Springs, SD [*FM radio station call letters*]
KZMZ............ Alexandria, LA [*FM radio station call letters*]
KZN............. Kazan [*Former USSR Airport symbol*] (OAG)
KZN............. Kozani [*Greece*] [*Seismograph station code, US Geological Survey*] (SEIS)
KZN............. Zaimische [*Later, KNS*] [*Former USSR Geomagnetic observatory code*]
KZNA............ Hill City, KS [*FM radio station call letters*]
KZNC............ Huron, SD [*FM radio station call letters*]
KZNG............ Hot Springs, AR [*AM radio station call letters*]
KZNM............ Grants, NM [*FM radio station call letters*]
KZNN............ Rolla, MO [*FM radio station call letters*]
KZNO............ Nogales, AZ [*FM radio station call letters*] (RBYB)
KZNY............ New York, Ronkonkoma [*New York*] [*ICAO location identifier*] (ICLI)
KZOA............ KZ Owners' Association [*Defunct*] (EA)
KZOA............ Oakland, Freemont [*California*] [*ICAO location identifier*] (ICLI)
KZOB............ Cleveland, Oberlin [*Ohio*] [*ICAO location identifier*] (ICLI)
KZOE............ Longview, WA [*FM radio station call letters*]
KZOK............ Seattle, WA [*FM radio station call letters*]
KZOL-FM ...... Santa Cruz, CA [*FM radio station call letters*] (RBYB)
KZON............ Phoenix, AZ [*FM radio station call letters*]
KZOO............ Honolulu, HI [*AM radio station call letters*]
KZOQ............ Missoula, MT [*FM radio station call letters*]
KZOR............ Hobbs, NM [*FM radio station call letters*]
KZOT............ Marianna, AR [*AM radio station call letters*]
KZOZ............ San Luis Obispo, CA [*FM radio station call letters*]
KZP............. Kwartalnik dla Historji Zydow w Polsce [*A publication*] (BJA)
KZPA............ Fort Yukon, AK [*AM radio station call letters*]
KZPD............ Ash Grove, MO [*FM radio station call letters*]
KZPE............ Ford City, CA [*FM radio station call letters*]
KZPH............ Cashmere, WA [*FM radio station call letters*]
KZPI-FM ...... Deming, NM [*FM radio station call letters*] (RBYB)
KZPK............ Paynesville, MN [*FM radio station call letters*]
KZPM............ Bakersfield, CA [*AM radio station call letters*]
KZPN............ Bayside, CA [*FM radio station call letters*]
KZPO............ Lindsay, CA [*FM radio station call letters*]
KZPR............ Minot, ND [*FM radio station call letters*]
KZPS............ Dallas, TX [*FM radio station call letters*]
KZQD............ Liberal, KS [*FM radio station call letters*]
kzr............. Kazakh Soviet Socialist Republic [*MARC country of publication code Library of Congress*] (LCCP)
KZR............. Khuzdar [*Pakistan*] [*Airport symbol*] (AD)
KZRA............ Springdale, AR [*AM radio station call letters*]
KZRB............ New Boston, TX [*FM radio station call letters*]
KZRK............ Canyon, TX [*AM radio station call letters*] (RBYB)
KZRK-FM...... Canyon, TX [*FM radio station call letters*] (RBYB)
KZRO............ Dunsmuir, CA [*FM radio station call letters*]
KZRQ............ Santa Fe, NM [*FM radio station call letters*]

KZRR .... Albuquerque, NM [*FM radio station call letters*]
KZS............. Kutztown State College, Kutztown, PA [*OCLC symbol*] (OCLC)
KZSA............ Placerville, CA [*FM radio station call letters*]
KZSC............ Santa Cruz, CA [*FM radio station call letters*]
KZSD............ Martin, SD [*FM radio station call letters*]
KZSD-TV...... Martin, SD [*Television station call letters*]
KZSE............ Rochester, MN [*FM radio station call letters*]
KZSE............ Seattle, Auburn [*Washington*] [*ICAO location identifier*] (ICLI)
KZSF............ Alameda, CA [*FM radio station call letters*] (RBYB)
KZSJ............ San Martin, CA [*AM radio station call letters*] (RBYB)
KZSN............ Hutchinson, KS [*FM radio station call letters*]
KZSN............ Wichita, KS [*AM radio station call letters*]
KZSP............ South Padre Island, TX [*FM radio station call letters*]
KZSQ............ Sonora, CA [*FM radio station call letters*]
KZSR............ Reno, NV [*FM radio station call letters*]
KZSS............ Albuquerque, NM [*AM radio station call letters*]
KZST............ Santa Rosa, CA [*FM radio station call letters*]
KZSU............ Stanford, CA [*FM radio station call letters*]
KZTA............ Yakima, WA [*AM radio station call letters*]
KZTA-FM...... Yakima, WA [*FM radio station call letters*]
KZTB-FM...... Sunnyside, WA [*FM radio station call letters*] (RBYB)
KZTL............ Atlanta, Hampton [*Georgia*] [*ICAO location identifier*] (ICLI)
KZTO............ Ottawa, KS [*FM radio station call letters*]
KZTQ............ Laredo, TX [*FM radio station call letters*]
KZTU............ Eugene, OR [*AM radio station call letters*] (RBYB)
KZTU-AM...... Eugene, OR [*AM radio station call letters*] (RBYB)
KZTV............ Corpus Christi, TX [*Television station call letters*]
KZTW............ Fairview, OR [*AM radio station call letters*] (RBYB)
KZTX............ Refugio, TX [*FM radio station call letters*]
KZTY............ Winchester, NV [*AM radio station call letters*]
KZUA............ Holbrook, AZ [*FM radio station call letters*]
KZUB .... Tahoka, TX [*FM radio station call letters*]
KZUE............ El Reno, OK [*AM radio station call letters*]
KZUL............ Lake Havasu City, AZ [*FM radio station call letters*]
KZUM............ Lincoln, NE [*FM radio station call letters*]
KZUN............ Zuni Pueblo/Blackrock [*New Mexico*] [*ICAO location identifier*] (ICLI)
KZUS............ Toledo, OR [*AM radio station call letters*]
KZUS-FM...... Toledo, OR [*FM radio station call letters*]
KZUU .... Pullman, WA [*FM radio station call letters*]
KZV............. Kartell Zionistischer Verbindungen (BJA)
KZWA............ Lake Charles, LA [*FM radio station call letters*]
KZWC............ Walnut Creek, CA [*FM radio station call letters*]
KZXA............ Santa Fe, NM [*FM radio station call letters*]
KZXB............ Homer, LA [*FM radio station call letters*]
KZXC............ Anchorage, AK [*Television station call letters*]
KZXR............ Prosser, WA [*FM radio station call letters*]
KZXX............ Kenai, AK [*AM radio station call letters*]
KZXY-FM ..... Apple Valley, CA [*FM radio station call letters*]
KZYP............ Pine Bluff, AR [*FM radio station call letters*]
KZYR............ Avon, CO [*FM radio station call letters*]
KZYX............ Philo, CA [*FM radio station call letters*]
KZYZ............ Willits, CA [*FM radio station call letters*] (RBYB)
KZZB............ Beaumont, TX [*AM radio station call letters*]
KZZC-FM...... Tipton, CA [*FM radio station call letters*] (RBYB)
KZZE............ Eagle Point, OR [*FM radio station call letters*] (RBYB)
KZZF-FM...... South Lake Tahoe, CA [*FM radio station call letters*] (RBYB)
KZZI............ Belle Fourche, SD [*FM radio station call letters*] (RBYB)
KZZJ............ Rugby, ND [*AM radio station call letters*] (RBYB)
KZZK-FM...... New London, MO [*FM radio station call letters*] (RBYB)
KZZL............ Pullman, WA [*FM radio station call letters*]
KZZN............ Littlefield, TX [*AM radio station call letters*]
KZZP............ Winner, SD [*FM radio station call letters*] (RBYB)
KZZQ............ Winterset, IA [*FM radio station call letters*] (RBYB)
KZZR............ Burns, OR [*AM radio station call letters*]
KZZT............ Moberly, MO [*FM radio station call letters*]
KZZU............ Spokane, WA [*FM radio station call letters*]
KZZX............ Alamogordo, NM [*FM radio station call letters*]
KZZY............ Devils Lake, ND [*FM radio station call letters*]
KZZZ............ Kingman, AZ [*FM radio station call letters*]

L

By Acronym

L .... Angle
L .... Angular Momentum [*Symbol*] [*IUPAC*]
I----- .... Atlantic Ocean [*MARC geographic area code Library of Congress*] (LCCP)
L .... Avogadro Constant [*Symbol*] [*IUPAC*]
I .... Azimuthal Quantum Number [*or Orbital Angular Momentum Quantum Number*] [*Symbol*]
L .... Azimuthal Quantum Number [*or Orbital Angular Momentum Quantum Number*] - Total [*Symbol*]
L .... Coefficient of Physics [*Physics*] (DAVI)
L .... Concerts and Recitals of Serious Music (Permits) [*Public-performance tariff class*] [*British*]
L .... Countermeasures [*JETDS nomenclature*]
L .... Days before Launch [*Usually followed by a number*] [*NASA*] (KSC)
L .... Difference of Latitude [*Navigation*]
L .... Drizzle [*Meteorology*]
L .... Electrical [*in British naval officers' ranks*]
L .... Electromagnet Radiance [*Astronomy*] (BARN)
L .... Element
L .... Elevated [*Railway*] [*Also, EL*]
L .... Equipped with Search Light [*Suffix to plane designation*] [*Navy*]
L .... Fifty [*Roman numeral*]
I .... Finland [*IYRU nationality code*] (IYR)
L .... Glider Aircraft [*When first letter in Navy aircraft designation*]
L .... Inductance [*Symbol*] (AAG)
L .... Kinetic Potential [*Symbol*]
L .... Labaz [*Belgium, France*] [*Research code symbol*]
L .... Label (MDG)
L .... Labetalol [*Pharmacology*]
L .... Labor
L .... Laboratory
L .... Laboratory Attendant [*Ranking title*] [*British Royal Navy*]
L .... Lactobacillus
L .... Ladestreifen [*Ammunition Clip*] [*German military - World War II*]
L .... Ladinian [*Geology*]
L .... Lady [*or Ladyship*]
L .... Lagrangian Function
L .... Lake [*Maps and charts*]
L .... Lambda (WDAA)
L .... Lambert [*Unit of luminance*] [*Preferred unit is lx, Lux*]
L .... Lambert (IDOE)
L .... Lameness [*Used by immigration officials*] [*Obsolete*]
L .... Laminated
L .... Lamp
L .... Lancashire Flats [*British*] (DCTA)
L .... Lancers
L .... Land
L .... Landing
L .... Landplane
L .... Land Transportation [*FCC*] (NTCM)
L .... Landulfus Acconzaioco [*Flourished, 13th century*] [*Authority cited in pre-1607 legal work*] (DSA)
L .... Lane
L .... Langmuir [*Unit of measure*]
L .... Language
L .... Lansing's New York Supreme Court Reports [*A publication*] (DLA)
L .... Lansing's Select Cases in Chancery [*1824, 1826*] [*New York*] [*A publication*] (DLA)
L .... Lanthanum [*Chemical element; symbol is La*]
L .... Larceny [*FBI standardized term*]
L .... Large [*Size designation for clothing, etc.*]
I .... Large (WDMC)
L .... Larva [*Biology*]
L .... Laser
L .... L-Asparaginase [*Also, A, L-ase, L-asnase, L-Asp*] [*An enzyme, an antineoplastic*]
L .... Lat [*Monetary unit*] [*Latvia*]
L .... Latching [*Electronics*]
L .... Late
L .... Late (WDMC)
L .... Latent Heat
L .... Lateral (IAA)
L .... Latex (DMAA)
L .... Latin
L .... Latitude
L .... Laudatur [*Latin*]

L .... Launch [*or Launcher*]
L .... Laurentius Hispanus [*Deceased, 1248*] [*Authority cited in pre-1607 legal work*] (DSA)
L .... Lavender [*Botany*]
L .... Law
L .... Lawson's Notes of Decisions, Registration [*A publication*] (DLA)
L .... Layer [*Officer's rating*] [*British Royal Navy*]
L .... "Lay" Source (BJA)
L .... Leader (ADA)
L .... Leader Sequence (DMAA)
L .... Lead Sheath (AAG)
L .... Leaf [*Bibliography*] [*Botany*]
L .... Leaflet
L .... League
L .... Learner
L .... Learning [*Denotes learning drivers before they receive their automobile driving licenses*] [*British*]
L .... Leasehold (ROG)
L .... Leather
L .... Leave
L .... Lederle Laboratories [*Research code symbol*]
L .... Leeward
L .... Left [*Politics*]
L .... Left [*Direction*]
I .... Left (WDMC)
L .... Left Eye [*Opthalmology*] (DAVI)
L .... Left Hand [*Music*] (ROG)
L .... Legal Division [*Coast Guard*]
L .... Leges [*Laws*] [*Latin*] (ROG)
L .... Legge [*Law, Act, Statute*] [*Italian*] (ILCA)
L .... Legionella [*A bacteria*] (DAVI)
L .... Legitimate
L .... Leishmania [*Microbiology*] (MAE)
L .... Lek [*Monetary unit*] [*Albania*] (BARN)
L .... Lempira [*Monetary unit*] [*Honduras*]
L .... Lenad Subgroup [*Leucite, nephelite, halite, thenardite*] [*CIPW classification Geology*]
I .... Length [*Symbol*] [*IUPAC*]
L .... Length [*or Lengthwise*]
L .... Lens
L .... Lente Insulin [*Pharmacology*] (DAVI)
L .... Leo (WDAA)
L .... Lepetit [*Italy*] [*Research code symbol*]
L .... Lepidocrocite [*A mineral*]
L .... Leptospira [*A bacteria*] (DAVI)
L .... Leptotrichia [*A bacteria*] (DAVI)
L .... Lesser (DAVI)
L .... Lethal
L .... Letter
L .... Leu [*Monetary unit*] [*Romania*]
L .... Leucine [*One-letter symbol; see Leu*] [*An amino acid*]
L .... Leuconostoc [*An algae*] [*Biochemistry*] (DAVI)
L .... Lev [*Monetary unit*] [*Bulgaria*]
L .... Level (KSC)
L .... Lever
L .... Levo [*or Laevo*] [*Configuration in chemical structure*]
I .... Levorotary [*or Levorotatory*] [*Chemistry*]
L .... Levorotatory [*Optics*] [*Chemistry*] (DOG)
L .... Lewisite [*War gas*] [*Army symbol*]
L .... Lexical Rule [*Linguistics*]
L .... Liaison [*Airplane designation*]
L .... Liber [*Book*] [*Latin*]
L .... Liberal [*Politics*]
L .... Liberty Financial Companies, Inc. [*NYSE symbol*] (SAG)
L .... Liberty Financial Cos. [*NYSE symbol*] (TTSB)
L .... Libra [*Pound*]
L .... Library
L .... Libration [*Space exploration*]
L .... Licenciatus [*Academic Qualification*] [*Latin*]
L .... License
L .... Licensed to Practice [*Medicine*]
L .... Licentiate
L .... Lidocaine [*Topical anesthetic*]
L .... Lidoflazine [*A vasodilator*]
L .... Lies [*Read*] [*German*]
L .... Lieutenant [*Navy British*]

L.................	Life [*Insurance*]
L.................	Lifestyle [*Wire service code*] (NTCM)
L.................	Lift
L.................	Ligament [*or Ligamentum*]
L.................	Ligand [*Chemistry*]
L.................	Light [*Chain*] [*Biochemistry, immunochemistry*]
L.................	Lighting [*As part of a code*]
L.................	Lightning [*Meteorology*]
L.................	Light Sense
L.................	Lignite (WDAA)
L.................	Lilac
L.................	Lilangeni [*Monetary unit*] [*Swaziland*] (BARN)
L.................	Lima [*Phonetic alphabet*] [*International*] (DSUE)
L.................	Lime
L.................	Limen or Threshold [*Psychology*]
L.................	Limes [*Boundary*] [*Pharmacology*] (DAVI)
L.................	Limestone [*Petrology*]
L.................	Limit
L.................	Limited (DLA)
L.................	Line
l.................	Line (WDMC)
L.................	Line Assembly (AAG)
L.................	Linen [*Deltiology*]
L.................	Line (of Print) [*Publishing*] (NTCM)
L.................	Liner [*Nautical*]
L.................	Lines Dose [*Medicine*]
L.................	Lingual [*Dentistry*]
L.................	Link
L.................	Linnaean
L.................	Lip
L.................	Lipoid [*Biochemistry*]
(l)................	Liquid [*Chemistry*]
L.................	Liquidity [*Business term*]
L.................	Liquor (DAVI)
L.................	Lira [*Monetary unit*] [*Italy*]
L.................	List (MSA)
L.................	Listed [*Stock exchange term*]
L.................	Listening Post [*In symbol only*]
L.................	Listeria [*A bacteria*] (DAVI)
L.................	Lit
L.................	Litas [*Monetary unit*] [*Lithuania*]
L.................	Liter [*Also, l*] [*Metric measure of volume*]
l.................	Liter
l.................	Liter (IDOE)
L.................	Literate
L.................	Lithium [*Chemical element*] (ROG)
L.................	Little
L.................	Live [*Wiring code*] [*British*]
L.................	Liver (MAE)
L.................	Liverpool [*Postcode*] (ODBW)
L.................	Living (DAVI)
L.................	Living Room (ROG)
L.................	Livre [*Monetary unit*] [*Obsolete French*]
L.................	Load (MDG)
L.................	Loam [*Agronomy*]
L.................	Lobe [*Of a leaf*] [*Botany*]
L.................	Loblaw Companies Ltd. [*Toronto Stock Exchange symbol Vancouver Stock Exchange symbol*]
L.................	Loblaw Cos. [*TS, exchange symbol*] (TTSB)
l.................	Local (WDMC)
L.................	Local [*Broadcasting program*] (NTCM)
l.................	Locative (Case) [*Linguistics*]
L.................	Locator [*Compass*]
L.................	Locator Beacon
L.................	Loch
L.................	Lockheed Aircraft Corp. [*ICAO aircraft manufacturer identifier*] (ICAO)
L.................	Locking [*Lamp base type*] (NTCM)
L.................	Locus [*Place*] [*Latin*]
L.................	Lodge
L.................	Logarithm [*Mathematics*]
L.................	London [*Phonetic alphabet*] [*Royal Navy World War I Pre-World War II*] (DSUE)
L.................	London [*England*]
L.................	Long
L.................	Longacre [*James B.*] [*Designer's mark, when appearing on US coins*]
L.................	Longitude
L.................	Long, Rolling Sea [*Meteorology*]
L.................	Loop [*Fingerprint description*]
L.................	Looper [*Computer science*] (MDG)
L.................	LORAN [*Long-Range Navigation*] (IAA)
L.................	Lorazepam [*A tranquilizer*]
L.................	Lord [*or Lordship*]
L.................	Lorentz Unit [*Electronics*]
L.................	Lost [*Sports statistics*]
L.................	Lost [*RADAR*]
L.................	Loti [*Monetary unit*] [*Lesotho*] (BARN)
L.................	Lough [*Maps and charts*]
L.................	Louisiana Reports [*A publication*] (DLA)
L.................	Louisiana State Library, Baton Rouge, LA [*Library symbol Library of Congress*] (LCLS)
L.................	Louisville [*Diocesan abbreviation*] [*Kentucky*] (TOCD)
L.................	Love [*Phonetic alphabet*] [*World War II*] (DSUE)
L.................	Low [*or Lower*]
l.................	Low (IDOE)
L.................	Lower Bow [*Music*] (ROG)
l.................	Lower Limit of a Class Interval [*Psychology*]
L.................	Low Season [*Airline fare code*]
L.................	Loyalty
L.................	Lues [*or Syphilis*] [*Medicine*] (DAVI)
L.................	Luitingh [*Holland*]
L.................	Lumbar [*Medicine*]
L.................	Lumen [*Unit of luminous flux*]
l.................	Lumen (IDOE)
L.................	Lumen [*Anatomy*] (DAVI)
L.................	Luminance (DMAA)
L.................	Lunch (CDAI)
L.................	Lung [*Anatomy*] (DAVI)
L.................	Luteolin [*Botany*]
L.................	Luxembourg
L.................	Luxury [*In automobile model name "Cordia L"*]
L.................	Lymph [*A fluid*] [*Biochemistry*] (DAVI)
L.................	Lymphocyte [*Biochemistry*] (DAVI)
L.................	Lymphogranuloma [*Pathology*] (DAVI)
L.................	Lysosome [*Biochemistry*] (DAVI)
l.................	Lyxose [*As substituent on nucleoside*] [*Biochemistry*]
l.................	Mean Free Path [*Symbol*] [*IUPAC*]
l.................	Merck & Co., Inc. [*Research code symbol*]
L.................	Promotional Fare [*Also, K, Q, V*] [*Airline fare code*]
L.................	Quinquaginta [*Fifty*] [*Latin*]
L.................	Radiance [*Symbol*] [*IUPAC*]
L.................	Requires Fuel and Oil [*Search and rescue symbol that can be stamped in sand or snow*]
L.................	Sandoz Pharmaceuticals [*Research code symbol*]
L.................	San Francisco [*Branch in the Federal Reserve regional banking system*] (BARN)
L.................	Searchlight Control [*JETDS nomenclature*]
L.................	Self-Inductance [*Symbol*] [*IUPAC*]
L.................	Shape Descriptor [*Dining el, for example. The shape resembles the letter for which it is named*]
L.................	Silo Launched [*Missile launch environment symbol*]
L.................	Single Acetate (AAG)
L.................	Timber [*Lumber*] [*Vessel load line mark*]
L.................	Time of Launch [*NASA*]
L1...............	First Language (ADA)
L_1..............	First Lumbar Nerve [*Second lumbar nerve is L_2, etc., through L_5*] [*Medicine*] (DAVI)
L_1..............	First Lumbar Vertebra [*Second lumbar vertebra is L_2, etc., through L5*] [*Medicine*]
L1TC...........	Level 1 Trauma Center [*Medicine*] (DMAA)
L/3..............	Lower Third [*Referring to long bones*] [*Orthopedics*] (DAVI)
L3S..............	LNG [*Liquefied Natural Gas*] Seabed Supported System
L4................	Automatic Lockup Four Speed [*DOE*] (TAG)
L5................	Long Quinto [*Pt. 10 of Year Books*] [*A publication*] (DSA)
L-5HTP........	L-5-Hydroxytryptophan [*Pharmacology*] (DAVI)
L6................	Laboratories Low-Level Linked List Language [*Bell Systems*] (DIT)
L-10-W........	Levulose (10 Percent) in Water
L123UA.......	Lotus 1-2-3 Users' Association
LA..............	Concerts and Recitals of Serious Music (Annual Licence) [*Public-performance tariff class*] [*British*]
LA..............	Fighter [*Russian aircraft symbol*]
LA..............	Hoffmann-La Roche, Inc. [*Research code symbol*]
La..............	[*The*] Holy Bible from Ancient Eastern Manuscripts [*G. M. Lamsa*] [*A publication*] (BJA)
LA..............	Lab. Aron [*France*] [*Research code symbol*]
La..............	Labial [*Dentistry*]
LA..............	Labor Arbitration Reports [*A publication*] (DLA)
LA..............	Labor Area
La..............	Laches [*of Plato*] [*Classical studies*] (OCD)
LA..............	Lactalbumin [*Biochemistry*]
LA..............	Lactic Acid [*Biochemistry*]
LA..............	Lag Amplifier
LA..............	Lag Angle (IAA)
LA..............	LA Gear, Inc. [*NYSE symbol*] (CTT)
La..............	Lagulanda (BJA)
LA..............	Laira [*Plymouth*] [*British depot code*]
LA..............	Lake Aircraft [*ICAO aircraft manufacturer identifier*] (ICAO)
LA..............	Lama Foundation (EA)
LA..............	Lambda Alpha
La..............	Lambert [*Unit of luminance*] [*Preferred unit is lx, Lux*] (ADA)
La..............	Lamellar Phase [*Physical chemistry*]
La..............	Lamentations [*Old Testament book*] (BJA)
LA..............	Lancaster [*Postcode*] (ODBW)
LA..............	Lancastrian [*Of the royal house of Lancaster*] [*British*] (ROG)
La..............	Lan Chile [*Airline flight code*] (ODBW)
LA..............	Land Agent [*Ministry of Agriculture, Fisheries, and Food*] [*British*]
L/A..............	Landing Account [*Shipping*]
La..............	Landulfus Acconzaioco [*Flourished, 13th century*] [*Authority cited in pre-1607 legal work*] (DSA)
La..............	Lane
La..............	Lane's English Exchequer Reports [*1605-12*] [*A publication*] (DLA)
La..............	Lanfrancus [*Deceased, 1089*] [*Authority cited in pre-1607 legal work*] (DSA)
La..............	Lanfrancus Cremensis [*Deceased, 1229*] [*Authority cited in pre-1607 legal work*] (DSA)
LA..............	Language [*Online database field identifier*]
LA..............	Language Age [*Score*]
LA..............	Language Arts [*A publication*] (BRI)
La..............	Lanthanum [*Chemical element*]

LA	Laos [or Lao People's Democratic Republic] [ANSI two-letter standard code] (CNC)
La	Lapus de Castiglionchio [Flourished, 1353-81] [Authority cited in pre-1607 legal work] (DSA)
La	Lapus Tatti [Flourished, 14th century] [Authority cited in pre-1607 legal work] (DSA)
LA	Large Amount [Medicine]
LA	Large Aperture [Photography] (ROG)
LA	LASER Altimeter [NASA]
LA	LASER Angioplasty [Cardiology] (DMAA)
LA	LASER [Gyro] Axis (IEEE)
LA	Last [Wool weight]
la	Late (VRA)
LA	Late Abortion [Medicine] (DMAA)
LA	Late Antigen [Biochemistry] (DAVI)
LA	Latex Agglutination [Test] [Clinical chemistry]
LA	Lathe [Division in the county of Kent] [British]
LA	Latin America
LA	Launch Abort [NASA] (KSC)
LA	Launch Aft
LA	Launch Analyst [Aerospace] (AAG)
LA	Launch Area [NASA] (KSC)
LA	Launch Azimuth [NASA] (KSC)
LA	Laureate in Arts
La	Laurentius Hispanus [Deceased, 1248] [Authority cited in pre-1607 legal work] (DSA)
LA	Lava [Maps and charts]
LA	Lavatory (DSUE)
LA	Lavochkin [USSR aircraft type] [World War II]
LA	Law Agent
LA	Lawyers' Reports, Annotated [A publication] (DLA)
LA	Lead Adapter [Electric equipment]
LA	Lead Amplifier
LA	Lead Angle (MSA)
LA	Leading Aircraftsman [RAF] [British]
LA	Leading Article (ROG)
LA	Leaf Abscission [Botany]
LA	Learning Activity (ADA)
LA	Leasehold Area (ADA)
L/A	Leave Address (DNAB)
L/A	Leave Advance [Military]
LA	Lebensalter [Chronological Age] [Psychology]
LA	Ledger Account (ROG)
LA	Ledger Asset
LA	Left Angle
LA	Left Angulation [Orthopedics] (DAVI)
LA	Left Arm [Medicine]
LA	Left Ascension
LA	Left Atrial [or Avricular] Appendage [Cardiology] (DAVI)
LA	Left Atrium [Anatomy]
LA	Left Auricle [Anatomy]
LA	Left Axilla (KSC)
LA	Legal Adviser
LA	Legal Asset [Business term]
LA	Lege Artis [According to the Art] [Pharmacy]
LA	Legislative Affairs
LA	Legislative Assembly
LA	Legislative Assistant [US Congress]
LA	Legitimate Access [British police term]
LA	Legum Allegoriae [Philo] (BJA)
LA	LeMans America (EA)
LA	Lemko Association of US and Canada (EA)
LA	Leschetizky Association (EA)
LA	Lethal Area [Of indirect-fire weapon systems] [Military]
LA	Letter of Activation [Military]
L/A	Letter of Authority
LA	Letters Abroad (EA)
L/A	Lettre d'Avis [Letter of Advice] [French]
LA	Leucine Aminopeptidase [Also, LP, LPAP] [An enzyme]
LA	Leukemia Antigen [Immunochemistry] (DAVI)
LA	Leukoagglutinating [Immunochemistry]
LA	Leukogglutination (DMAA)
LA	Leuprolide Acetate (DMAA)
LA	Levator Ani [Anatomy]
LA	Level Absolute (SSD)
LA	Level Alarm [Engineering]
LA	Level Amplifier (IAA)
LA	Levulinic Acid [Organic chemistry]
LA	Liberal Arts
LA	Liberator Atlanta [An association] (EA)
LA	Libertarian Alliance [British] (EAIO)
LA	Library Association [British]
LA	Library Association [British] (NITA)
LA	Library Automation
LA	Library of Art [A publication]
LA	Licensing Act (DLA)
LA	Licensing Assistant (NRCH)
LA	Licensing Authority (DCTA)
LA	Licentiate in Arts
LA	Lichen Amyloidosis [Dermatology] (DAVI)
LA	Lieutenant-at-Arms [British]
LA	Light Ale (ADA)
LA	Light Alloy
LA	Light Armor [Telecommunications] (TEL)
LA	Light Artillery

LA	Lighter Association (EA)
LA	Lighter-than-Air [Aircraft]
LA	Lightning Arrester
LA	Lightwood-Albright [Syndrome] [Nephrology] (DAVI)
LA	Limited Area
LA	Linea Aerea Nacional de Chile [Chilean airline] [ICAO designator] (OAG)
LA	Line Adapter [Computer science] (CMD)
LA	Line Adaptor (NITA)
LA	Linear Arithmetic [Computer science]
LA	Linear Assembly
LA	Linguoaxial [Dentistry]
LA	Link Address (IAA)
LA	Link Allotter
LA	Link Analysis
LA	Linnaean Society
LA	Linoleic Acid (AAMN)
LA	Liquid Asset [Business term]
LA	Listed Address [Telecommunications] (TEL)
LA	Listing Agent [Classified advertising] (ADA)
LA	Literate in Arts
LA	Live Action (NTCM)
LA	Liverpool Academy [British]
LA	Living Allowance
L/A	Lloyd's Agent
LA	Load Address (IAA)
LA	Load Adjuster (CET)
LA	Load Allocation [Environmental science] (FFDE)
LA	Loan Amount [Dialog] [Searchable field] [Information service or system] (NITA)
LA	Lobuloalveolar [Medicine] (DAVI)
LA	Local Address
LA	Local Agent
LA	Local Alarm (NRCH)
LA	Local Anesthetic [Medicine]
LA	Local Authority
LA	Lock Actuator (MCD)
LA	Locus Allowed (ROG)
LA	Lodging Allowance [British military] (DMA)
LA	Log Analyzer Processor [Computer science]
LA	Logarithmic Amplifier
LA	Logical Address
LA	Loners of America [An association] (EA)
LA	Long-Acting [Pharmacy]
LA	Long-Arm [Cast] [Orthopedics] (DAVI)
LA	Longitudinal Acoustic [Spectroscopy]
LA	Look Ahead (IAA)
LA	Loop Antenna (DEN)
LA	Lord Advocate of Scotland (DLA)
LA	Los Alamos Scientific Laboratory [USAEC] (MCD)
LA	Los Angeles [California] [Slang]
LA	Louisiana [Postal code] (AFM)
LA	Louisiana & Arkansas Railway Co. [AAR code]
LA	Louisiana Reports [A publication] (DLA)
LA	Louisiana Supreme Court Reports [A publication] (DLA)
LA	Low Alcohol [Trademark of Anheuser-Busch, Inc.]
LA	Low Altitude
LA	Low Angle [RADAR] (DEN)
LA	Low Anxiety (MAE)
LA	Lower Arm
LA	Ludwig's Angina [Medicine] (DAVI)
LA	Luscombe Association (EA)
LA	Lymphadenopathy [Medicine]
La	Old Latin Version (BJA)
LAA	Amphibious Assault Ship [Military]
LAA	Jamahiriya Libyan Arab Airlines [ICAO designator] (FAAC)
LAA	Lamar [Colorado] [Airport symbol] (OAG)
LAA	Lamar, CO [Location identifier FAA] (FAAL)
LAA	Laser Association of America [Later, LEMA] (EA)
LAA	LASER Attenuator Assembly
LAA	Lateral Accelerometer Assembly (MCD)
LAA	Launch Area Antenna (MCD)
LAA	Laundrette Association of Australia
LAA	League of Advertising Agencies [New York, NY] (EA)
LAA	Leather Apparel Association (EA)
LAA	Left Atrial Abnormality [Medicine] (MEDA)
LAA	Leukemia-Associated Antigen [Immunochemistry] (DAVI)
LAA	Leukocyte Ascorbic Acid [Clinical chemistry] (AAMN)
LAA	Lieutenant-at-Arms [British] (DMA)
LAA	Life Insurance Advertisers Association [Later, LCA] (EA)
LAA	Light Antiaircraft [Guns]
LAA	Light Army Aircraft
LAA	Lighterage Assembly Area
LAA	Limited Access Authorization [Military] (GFGA)
LAA	Lipizzan Association of America (EA)
LAA	Lithuanian Alliance of America (EA)
LAA	Little America [Antarctica] [Seismograph station code, US Geological Survey Closed] (SEIS)
LAA	Little Athletics Association [Australia]
LAA	Live Assembly Area (MCD)
LAA	Liverpool Academy of Arts [England]
LAA	Local Airport Advisory [Aviation] (FAAC)
LAA	Los Angeles Airways, Inc.
LA A	Louisiana Annual Reports [A publication] (DLA)
LA A	Louisiana Courts of Appeal Reports [A publication] (DLA)

LAA............. Low-Altitude Attack
LAAA.......... Latin American Association of Archives [See also ALA] (EAIO)
LAAAAS ...... Latin American Association for Afro-Asian Studies [Mexico] (EAIO)
LAAAS .... Low-Altitude Airfield Attack System (MCD)
LAAB.......... Landscape Architectural Accreditation Board (GAGS)
LAAB.......... Light Armored Assault Battalion [Marine Corps]
LAABAM ...... Latin American Association of Behavior Analysis and Modification [Uruguay] (EAIO)
LAABF......... Ladies' Auxiliary of the American Beekeeping Federation (EA)
LAAC.......... Library Association's Annual Conference [British]
LAAC.......... Lord Chancellor's Legal Aid Advisory Committee [British] (DLA)
LAACC .... Light Antiaircraft Control Center (NATG)
LAACT......... Legislative Assembly of the Australian Capital Territory
LA Acts........ State of Louisiana: Acts of the Legislature [A publication] (DLA)
LAAD .... Latin American Agribusiness Development Corp.
LAAD .... Los Angeles Aircraft Division [Rockwell International]
LAADBN ...... Low Altitude Air Defense Battalion [Navy] (ANA)
LAADIW....... Latin American Association for the Development and Integration of Women [See also ALADIM] [Chile] (EAIO)
LA Admin Code... Louisiana Administrative Code [A publication] (DLA)
LA Admin Reg... Louisiana Administrative Register [A publication] (DLA)
LAADS .... Los Angeles Air Defense Sector [ADC]
LAADS .... Low-Altitude Air Defense [or Delivery] System
LAADS .... Low-Altitude Air Dropped Stores (MCD)
LAAEMCTS.. Latin American Association of Environmental Mutagens, Carcinogens, and Teratogens Societies [Mexico] (EAIO)
LAAF .... Lawson Army Airfield [Fort Benning, GA] (MCD)
LAAF .... Libby Army Airfield
LAAFS......... Los Angeles Air Force Station
LAAG .... Latin American Anthropology Group (EA)
LAAGOWRNAFE... Local Authority Associations Group of Work Related Non-Advanced Further Education (AIE)
LAAI............ Licentiate of the Institute of Administrative Accountants [British] (DBQ)
LAAIB.......... Latin American Air Intelligence Brief (MCD)
LAAM.......... Large-Animal Anesthesia Machine [Instrumentation]
LAAM.......... Levo-alpha-Acetylmethadol [Drug alternative to methadone]
LAAM.......... Light Antiaircraft Missile
LAAMBN ...... Light Antiaircraft Missile Battalion (MUGU)
LAAMSF....... Latin American Association of Medical Schools and Faculties [See also ALAFEM] [Ecuador] (EAIO)
La An .... Lawyers' Reports, Annotated [A publication] (DLA)
LA & LR ...... Livonia Avon & Lakeville Railroad (MHDB)
LA & M........ Library Administration and Management
LA Ann......... Louisiana Annual Reports [A publication] (DLA)
LA Ann Reps... Louisiana Annual Reports [A publication] (DLA)
LA An R ...... Louisiana Annual Reports [A publication] (DLA)
LA An Rep ... Louisiana Annual Reports [A publication] (DLA)
L A Ant .... Latin America Antiquity [A publication]
LA Ant .... Latin American Antiquity [A publication] (BRI)
LAAO .... L-Amino Acid Oxidase [An enzyme]
LAAO .... Los Alamos Area Office [Energy Research and Development Administration]
LA A (Orleans)... Louisiana Court of Appeals (Parish of Orleans) (DLA)
LAAP.......... Law Association for Asia and the Pacific [Australia]
LAAP.......... Longhorn Army Ammunition Plant (MCD)
LAAP.......... Louisiana Army Ammunition Plant (AABC)
LAAPD .... Los Angeles Air Procurement District
LAAPI.......... Latin American Association of Pharmaceutical Industries [See also ALIFAR] (EAIO)
LA App........ Louisiana Courts of Appeal Reports [A publication] (DLA)
LA App (Orleans)... Louisiana Court of Appeals (Parish of Orleans) (DLA)
LAAPS .... Laptop Automated Aid Positioning System [Coast Guard] [Computer science] (DOMA)
LAAR .... Liquid Air Accumulator Rocket
LAARS .... LASER-Augmented Air-Rescue System (PDAA)
LAAS .... Light Armor Antitank System (MCD)
LAAS .... Los Angeles Air Service, Inc.
LAAS .... Low-Altitude Alerting System
LAASCA ...... Long-Range Antisubmarine Capability Aircraft
LAASL .... Latin American Association for the Study of the Liver [Mexico] (EAIO)
LAASP .... Latin American Association for Social Psychology [Formerly, Latin American Social Psychology Committee] (EA)
LAAT.......... LASER-Augmented Airborne TOW Sight [Army] (MCD)
LAAT.......... LASER-Augmented Airborne Track
LAAT.......... Logistics Assessment and Assistance Team (MCD)
LAAV.......... Light Airborne ASW [Antisubmarine Warfare] Vehicle
LAAW.......... Legal Automated Army-Wide
LAAW.......... Light Assault Antitank Weapon
LAAW.......... Local Antiair Warfare (NVT)
LAAWC .... Local Antiair Warfare Commander (NVT)
Lab .... Labatt's California District Court Reports [1857-58] [A publication] (DLA)
LAB............. Label [or Labelling] (IAA)
LAB............. Lablab [Papua New Guinea] [Airport symbol] (OAG)
LAB............. Labmin Resources Ltd. [Toronto Stock Exchange symbol]
LAB............. Labor
LAB.:.......... Labor Advisory Board [New Deal]
LAB............. Laboratory (AFM)
LAB............. Laboratory
lab .... Laboratory (WDMC)
LAB............. Laboratory for Applied Biophysics [MIT] (MCD)
LAB............. Labour Party [British Political party]
LAB............. Labrador [Canada]
LAB............. Labrador Retriever [Dog breed]

LAB............. Labuan [Island in Malaysia] (ROG)
LAB............. Lactic Acid Bacteria [Food microbiology]
Lab .... Lambertus de Ramponibus [Deceased, 1304] [Authority cited in pre-1607 legal work] (DSA)
LAB............. Latin America Bureau [British] (EAIO)
LAB............. Lead Acid Battery
LAB............. Leave Authorization Balance [Air Force] (AFM)
LAB............. Leisure Activities Blank [Vocational guidance test]
LAB............. Level of Aspiration Board [Psychology]
LAB............. Liber Antiquitatum Biblicarum. Pseudo-Philo (BJA)
LAB............. Licentiate of the Associated Board of Royal Schools of Music [British]
LAB............. Light Assault Bridge [Military program] (INF)
LAB............. Light Attack Battalion (INF)
LAB............. Linear Alkylbenzene [Organic chemistry]
LAB............. Lithosphere-Asthenosphere Boundary [Geology]
LAB............. Live Animals Board [IATA] (DS)
LAB............. Lloyd Aereo Boliviano SA [Lloyd Bolivian Air Line]
LAB............. Local Area Broadcast (NVT)
LAB............. Los Angeles Branch [AEC]
LAB............. Low-Altitude Bombing [Military]
LABA.......... Laboratory Animal Breeders Association (EA)
Lab AC........ Labour Appeal Cases [India] [A publication] (DLA)
LABAC........ Licentiate Member of the Association of Business and Administrative Computing [British] (DBQ)
LABAN........ Lakas ng Bayan [Peoples' Power Movement - Fight] [Philippines] [Political party] (PPW)
Lab & Auto Bull... Labor and Automation Bulletin [A publication] (DLA)
LA Bar .... Louisiana Bar. Official Publication of the Louisiana State Bar Association [A publication] (DLA)
Lab Arb....... Labor Arbitration Reports [Bureau of National Affairs] [A publication] (DLA)
Lab Arb & Disp Settl... Labor Arbitration and Dispute Settlements [A publication] (DLA)
Lab Arb Awards... Labor Arbitration Awards [Commerce Clearing House] [A publication] (DLA)
LaBarg......... La Barge, Inc. [Associated Press] (SAG)
LABB.......... Legal Abbreviations [Database]
LabChile...... Laboratorio Chile SA [Associated Press] (SAG)
LABCOM...... Laboratory Command [Adelphi, MD] [Army] (RDA)
LAB-CO-OP... Labour and Co-Operative Party [British]
LabCp......... Laboratory Corp. of America Holdings [Associated Press] (SAG)
LABE.......... Lava Beds National Monument
LABE.......... Louisiana Association of Business Educators (EDAC)
LABECO ...... Laboratory Equipment Corp. [Auto industry supplier]
LABEL........ Law Students Association for Buyers' Education in Labeling [Student legal action organization]
LABEX......... Laboratory Equipment Exhibition (TSPED)
LABF.......... Latin American Banking Federation [Bogota, Colombia] (EA)
Lab His .... Labour History [A publication]
LABIB......... LASER Bibliography (MCD)
LABIL......... Light Aircraft Binary Information Link
Lab Ind .... Labour and Industry [A publication]
LABIS......... Laboratory Information Systems (DNAB)
Lab J Aust .. Laboratory Journal of Australasia [A publication]
LABK.......... Lafayette American Bank & Trust [NASDAQ symbol] (SAG)
LABK.......... Lafayette American Bk & Tr [NASDAQ symbol] (TTSB)
LABL.......... Australian Co. Secretary's Business Law Manual [A publication]
LABL.......... Multi-Color Corp. [NASDAQ symbol] (NQ)
Lab L Rep ... Labor Law Reporter [Commerce Clearing House] [A publication] (DLA)
LABMIS....... Laboratories Management Information System
LABN .... Lake Ariel Bancorp [NASDAQ symbol] (SAG)
LabOne....... LabOne, Inc. [Associated Press] (SAG)
Labor C....... Labor Code [A publication] (DLA)
LABORDOC. International Labour Documentation [International Labour Office] [Geneva, Switzerland Bibliographic database]
LABORINFO... Labour Information Database [International Labour Office] [Information service or system] (IID)
LABORSTAT... International Labor Organization, Bureau of Statistics Database (GFGA)
LABP.......... Latin American Book Programs [Defunct]
LABP.......... Lethal Aid for Bomber Penetration (MCD)
LABPIE........ Low-Altitude Bombing Position Indicator Equipment [Military]
LABPR .... Local Advisory Board Procedural Regulation (Office of Rent Stabilization) [Economic Stabilization Agency] [A publication] (DLA)
LAB PROC ... Laboratory Procedure [Medicine] (BABM)
LABR .... Laborer
L Abr .... Lilly's Abridgment [England] [A publication] (DLA)
LABRAPS.... Laboratoire de Recherche en Administration et Politique Scolaires [Canada]
Lab Rel Guide (P-H)... Labor Relations Guide (Prentice-Hall, Inc.) [A publication] (DLA)
LABREV ...... Laboratoire de Recherche sur l'Emploi, la Repartition, et la Securite du Revenu [University of Quebec at Montreal] [Research center] (RCD)
LABROC....... Laboratory Rocket
LABS.......... LabOne, Inc. [NASDAQ symbol] (SAG)
LABS.......... Laboratory Admission Baseline Studies
LABS.......... LASER Active Boresight System (PDAA)
LABS.......... Learning about Basic Science [Education program]
LABS.......... Low-Altitude Bombing System [Air Force]
LABSAP....... Laboratoire des Sciences de l'Activite Physique [Laval University] [Canada Research center] (RCD)
LabSpc .... Laboratory Specialists of America, Inc. [Associated Press] (SAG)

LabSpec ...... Laboratory Specialists of America, Inc. [*Associated Press*] (SAG)
LABSTAT ...... Labor Statistics [*Database*] [*Department of Labor*]
LAB TECH .... Laboratory Technologies Corp. (PCM)
LABU .... Latin American Blind Union [*See also ULAC*] [*Uruguay*] (EAIO)
LABUT .... Labor Utilization (MCD)
LAbV .... Vermilion Parish Library, Abbeville, LA [*Library symbol Library of Congress*] (LCLS)
LabVIEW ...... Laboratory Virtual Instrument Engineering Workbench
LABVT .... Left Atrial Ball-Valve Thrombus [*Cardiology*] (DAVI)
LABZ .... Laboratory Specialists Amer [*NASDAQ symbol*] (TTSB)
LABZ .... Laboratory Specialists of America, Inc. [*NASDAQ symbol*] (SAG)
LABZW .... Laboratory Specialists Wrrt [*NASDAQ symbol*] (TTSB)
LAC .... AB Bofors [*Sweden*] [*Research code symbol*]
LAC .... Fort Lewis, WA [*Location identifier FAA*] (FAAL)
LaC .... Labiocervical [*Dentistry*]
LAC .... Labour Appeal Cases [*India*] [*A publication*] (ILCA)
LAC .... Labour Arbitration Cases [*Canada Law Book, Inc.*] [*Information service or system A publication A publication*] (CRD)
LAC .... Laceration [*Medicine*]
Lac .... Lacerta [*Constellation*]
LAC .... Lacquer (WDAA)
lac .... Lacquer (VRA)
LAC .... LaCrosse [*A virus*]
LAC .... La Crosse [*A bunyavirus*]
LAC .... Lactation (WDAA)
LAC .... Lactose [*Cardiology*] (DAVI)
LAC .... Lae-City [*Papua New Guinea*] [*Airport symbol*] (OAG)
LAC .... Landers [*California*] [*Seismograph station code, US Geological Survey*] (SEIS)
LAC .... Large Acrocentric Chromosome [*Medicine*]
LAC .... Large-Area-Counter [*Astronomy*] [*Instrumentation*]
LAC .... Large Area Coverage [*Marine science*] (OSRA)
LAC .... LASER Amplifier Chain
LAC .... Launch Analyst's Console [*Aerospace*] (AAG)
LAC .... Launcher Assignment Console
LAC .... Law-abiding Citizen (BARN)
LAC .... Leading Aircraftsman [*RAF*] [*British*]
LAC .... Learning Assistance Center [*Stanford University*]
LAC .... Left Atrial Contraction [*Cardiology*] (DAVI)
LAC .... Legal Advisory Committee [*of NYSE*]
LAC .... Lemon Administrative Committee (EA)
LAC .... Liberal Academic Complex
LAC .... Liberated Areas Committee [*World War II*]
LAC .... Liberty Amendment Committee of the USA (EA)
LAC .... Library Advisory Council [*Department of Education and Science*] [*British*] (NITA)
LAC .... Library Assistants Certificate [*City and Guilds Institute*] [*British*] (NITA)
LAc .... Licensed Acupuncturist [*Medicine*]
LAC .... Licentiate of the Apothecaries' Company [*British*]
LAC .... Lights Advisory Committee [*General Council of British Shipping*] (DS)
LAC .... Limited Area Coverage [*Data*]
LAC .... Limiting Admissible Concentration
LAC .... Limits to Acceptable Change [*Park tourism management*]
LAC .... Lindamood Auditory Conceptualization Test
LAC .... Lindamood Auditory Conceptualization Test [*Psychology*] (DAVI)
LAC .... Linear Absorption Coefficient
LAC .... Linear Aeronautical Chart (BARN)
LAC .... Linear Amplitude-Continuous (PDAA)
LAC .... Linguoaxiocervical [*Dentistry*]
LAC .... Liposome-Antibody-Complement [*Immunochemistry*]
LAC .... Liquid Affinity Chromatography
LAC .... List of Assessed Contractors [*Military*] (RDA)
LAC .... Lithuanian American Community (EA)
LAC .... Live Action Camera (WDMC)
LAC .... Load Accumulator
LAC .... Local Advisory Council [*British labor*]
LAC .... Local Agency Check (AFM)
LAC .... Local Area Coverage [*Meteorology*]
LAC .... Lockheed Aircraft Corp. [*ICAO designator*] (FAAC)
LAC .... Logistics Area Coordinator (MCD)
LAC .... Long Arm Cast [*Medicine*] (MEDA)
LAC .... Longitudinal Aerodynamic Characteristics
LAC .... Long-Run Average Cost Curve [*Economics*]
LAC .... Low-Altitude Cruise (MCD)
LAC .... Low Amplitude Contraction [*Neurology*] (DAVI)
LAC .... Lunar Aeronautical Chart [*Air Force*]
LAC .... Lunar Atlas Chart [*Aerospace*] (SAA)
LAC .... Lupus Anticoagulant [*Immunochemistry*]
LACA .... Ladies Apparel Contractors Association (EA)
LACA .... Life Agency Cashiers Association of the United States and Canada (EA)
LACA .... Low-Altitude Control Area
LACAC .... Latin American Civil Aviation Commission [*See also CLAC*] (EAIO)
lac & cont ... Lacerations and Contusions [*Medicine*] (DAVI)
LACAP .... Latin American Cooperative Acquisitions Program [*or Project*]
LACAS .... LASER Applications in Close Air Support [*Air Force*]
LACas .... Latin American Casinos, Inc. [*Associated Press*] (SAG)
LACAS .... Lineas Aereas Costarricenses SA [*Costa Rica*] [*ICAO designator*] (FAAC)
LACAS .... Local Authority Catering Advisory Service (AIE)
LACAS .... Low-Altitude Close Air Support [*Military*]
LACASA .... Latin American and Caribbean Solidarity Association (EA)
LACAT .... Legislative Alliance of Creative Arts Therapies [*Defunct*] (EA)
LACATA .... Laundry and Cleaners Allied Trades Association [*Later, TCATA*] (EA)
LACATE .... Lower Atmosphere Composition and Temperature Experiment [*National Science Foundation*]
LACB .... Landing Aids Control Building [*NASA*] (NASA)
LACB .... Look Angles of Celestial Bodies (KSC)
LACBWR ...... LaCrosse Boiling Water Reactor [*Also, LCBWR*]
LACC .... Latin American and Caribbean Center [*Florida International University*] [*Research center*] (RCD)
LACC .... Lloyd's Aviation Claims Centre (AIA)
LACC .... Los Angeles City College [*California*]
l'ACCAB .... L'Association Canadienne des Centres d'Action Benevole (AC)
LACCB .... Latin American Confederation of Clinical Biochemistry [*Colombia*] (EAIO)
LACCSM ...... Latin American and Caribbean Council for Self-Management (EAIO)
LACD .... Limited-Amplitude, Controlled-Decay (PDAA)
LACDL .... Louisiana Association of Criminal Defense Lawyers (SRA)
LACE .... Alpine Lace Brands [*NASDAQ symbol*] (SPSG)
LACE .... Language for ALGOL [*Algorithmic Language*] Compiler Extension [*Computer science*] (CSR)
LACE .... LASER Aerospace Communications Experiment
LACE .... Launch Angle Condition Evaluator
LACE .... Launch Automatic Checkout Equipment
LACE .... Library Advisory Council for England (NITA)
LACE .... [*The*] Lingerie and Corsetry Exhibition [*British*] (ITD)
LACE .... Liquid Air Collection Engine
LACE .... Liquid Air Cycle Engine [*Aerospace plane engine concept*]
LACE .... Local Automatic Circuit Exchange [*Telecommunications*]
LACE .... Low-Power Atmospheric Compensation Experiment [*Strategic Defense Initiative*]
LACE .... Lunar Atmospheric Composition Experiment [*Apollo*] [*NASA*]
LACE .... Luton Analogue Computing Engine [*British*] (DEN)
LACE .... Lysergic Acid Cryptoethelane (IIA)
LACES .... London Airport Cargo Electronic-Data-Processing Scheme
Lacey Dig .... Lacey's Digest of Railroad Decisions [*A publication*] (DLA)
Lach .... Laches [*of Plato*] [*Classical studies*] (OCD)
LACH .... Lightweight Amphibious Container Handler (MCD)
LACI .... Latin Amer Casinos [*NASDAQ symbol*] (TTSB)
LACI .... Latin American Casinos, Inc. [*NASDAQ symbol*] (SAG)
LACI .... Lipoprotein-Associated Coagulation Inhibitor [*Hematology*]
LACIE .... Large Area Crop Inventory Experiment [*NASA*]
LACIM .... Latin American and Caribbean International Moving [*Panama*] (EAIO)
LACIP .... Large Area Crop Inventory Program [*NASA*] (NASA)
LA Civ Code Ann (West)... West's Louisiana Code of Civil Procedure, Annotated [*A publication*] (DLA)
LACIW .... Latin Amer Casinos Wrrt [*NASDAQ symbol*] (TTSB)
L'ACJE .... L'Association Canadienne pour les Jeunes Enfants (AC)
Lacka Leg News... Lackawanna Legal News [*Pennsylvania*] [*A publication*] (DLA)
Lackawanna B... Lackawanna Bar Reporter [*Pennsylvania*] [*A publication*] (DLA)
Lack Bar R... Lackawanna Bar Reporter [*Pennsylvania*] [*A publication*] (DLA)
Lack Co (PA)... Lackawanna County Reports [*Pennsylvania*] [*A publication*] (DLA)
Lack Leg N... Lackawanna Legal News [*Pennsylvania*] [*A publication*] (DLA)
Lack Leg News (PA)... Lackawanna Legal News [*Pennsylvania*] [*A publication*] (DLA)
Lack Leg R... Lackawanna Legal Record [*Pennsylvania*] [*A publication*] (DLA)
Lack Leg Rec... Lackawanna Legal Record [*Pennsylvania*] [*A publication*] (DLA)
Lack LN .... Lackawanna Legal News [*Pennsylvania*] [*A publication*] (DLA)
Lack LR .... Lackawanna Legal Record [*Pennsylvania*] [*A publication*] (DLA)
LACLA .... Latin American Constitutional Law Association [*Argentina*] (EAIO)
LacledeSt ..... Laclede Steel Co. [*Associated Press*] (SAG)
LaclGas .... Laclede Gas Co. [*Associated Press*] (SAG)
LACM .... Latin America Common Market [*Proposed*]
LACM .... Load Accumulator with Magnitude (HGAA)
LACMA .... Latin American and Caribbean Movers Association (EAIO)
LACMA .... Los Angeles County Museum of Art
LACMN .... Leading Aircrewman [*British military*] (DMA)
lac-mRNA ..... Ribonucleic Acid, Messenger - lac operon [*Biochemistry, genetics*]
LACN .... Local Area Communications Network (DMAA)
LACNSW ...... Legal Aid Commission of New South Wales [*Australia*]
LACNT .... Legal Aid Commission of the Northern Territory [*Australia*]
LACO .... LASER Communication (SSD)
LACO .... Los Angeles College of Optometry [*California*]
LA Code Civ Pro Ann... West's Louisiana Code of Civil Procedure, Annotated [*A publication*] (DLA)
LA Code Crim Pro Ann... West's Louisiana Code of Criminal Procedure, Annotated [*A publication*] (DLA)
LAC of AMFC... Library Affairs Committee of the Associated Mid-Florida Colleges [*Library network*]
LACOM .... Low-Altitude Contour Matching (MCD)
LACONIQ ..... Laboratory Computer Online Inquiry
LA Const Art... Louisiana Constitution [*A publication*] (DLA)
LACOTS .... Local Authorities' Coordinating Body on Training Standards [*British*]
LACP .... Lignes Aeriennes Canadiennes Pacifiques
LACQ .... Lacquer
LACQLD .... Legal Aid Commission of Queensland [*Australia*]
Lacr .... Lacerta [*Constellation*]
lacr .... Lacrimal [*Ophthalmology*] (DAVI)
LACR .... Low-Altitude Coverage RADAR
LACRC .... Locally Assigned Convoy Route Carrier Code
LAC REC ...... Lactis Recentis [*New Milk*] [*Pharmacy*] (ROG)
LaCrose .... LaCrosse Footwear, Inc. [*Associated Press*] (SAG)
Lac RR Dig... Lacey's Digest of Railroad Decisions [*A publication*] (DLA)
LACS .... Laboratory Automated Calibration System (MCD)
LACS .... League Against Cruel Sports (EA)
LACS .... Listener Active State (IAA)
LACS .... Lithuanian-American Catholic Services [*Defunct*] (EA)
LACS .... Los Angeles Catalyst Study [*Environmental Protection Agency*]

LACS	Los Angeles Copyright Society (EA)
LACSA	Lineas Aereas Costarricenses Sociedad Anonima [Airline] [Costa Rica]
LACSAB	Local Authorities' Conditions of Service Advisory Board [British] (DCTA)
L'ACSQ	Association Canadienne des Cinq Quilles [Formerly, Canadian Bowling Congress] (AC)
lact	Lactate [or Lactating] (AAMN)
lact	Lactating [Medicine] (MAE)
LACT	Lactic Acid [Biochemistry] (DAVI)
LAC T	Lactose Tolerance [Gastroenterology] (DAVI)
LACT	Lease Automatic Custody Transfer
LACT	Legal Aid Commission of Tasmania [Australia]
LACT	Low-Affinity Choline Transport
LACUS	Linguistic Association of Canada and the United States (EA)
LACUSA	Liberty Amendment Committee of the USA (EA)
LACUSA	Lithuanian-American Community of the USA [Later, LAC] (EA)
LAC/USC	Los Angeles County/University of Southern California Medical Center (DAVI)
LACV	Light Amphibious Cargo Vehicle (MCD)
LACV	Light Armored Combat Vehicle
LACV	Lighter, Air-Cushion Vehicle [Usually used in combination with numerals] [Military] (RDA)
LACV-30	Lighter, Air Cushion Vehicle, 30 Tons [Military] (MCD)
LACW	Leading Aircraft Woman [RAF] [British]
LACWA	Legal Aid Commission of Western Australia
LACYMCA	Latin American Confederation of YMCAs [See also CLACJ] (EAIO)
LAD	Lactate Dehydrogenase [Also, LD, LDH] [An enzyme]
LAD	Lactic Acid Dehydrogenase [See also LDH] [An enzyme]
LAD	Ladder (MSA)
lad	Ladino [MARC language code Library of Congress] (LCCP)
LAD	Ladron Mountain [New Mexico] [Seismograph station code, US Geological Survey] (SEIS)
LAD	Landing Assist Device [Aviation] (NG)
LAD	Language Acquisition Device
LAD	Large Area Detector [Instrumentation]
LAD	Large Area Display
LAD	LASER Acoustic Delay
LAD	LASER Acquisition and Direction
LAD	LASER Acquisition Device (MCD)
LAD	LASER Air Defense
LAD	Last Appearance Datum [Geology]
LAD	Lateral Awareness and Directionality Test [Sensorimotor skills test]
LAD	Latest Arrival Date (AABC)
LAD	Leaf Area Duration [Botany]
LAD	Lebanon Airport Development Corp. [ICAO designator] (FAAC)
LAD	Left Anterior Descending [Artery]
LAD	Left Anterior Digestive [Gland]
LAD	Left Axis Deviation [Medicine]
LAD	Leukocyte Adhesion Deficiency [Medicine]
LAD	Library Administration Division [American Library Association] [Later, LAMA] (EA)
LAD	Ligament Augmentation Device [Sports medicine]
LAD	Light Aid Detachment [Military British]
LAD	Light Area Defense (MCD)
LAD	Linoleic Acid Depression [Clinical chemistry] (AAMN)
LAD	Lipoamide Dehydrogenase [An enzyme]
LAD	Liquid Agent Detector (AABC)
LAD	Lithium Aluminum Deuteride [Inorganic chemistry]
LAD	Lloyd's Aviation Department (AIA)
LAD	Load Address (IAA)
LAD	Location Aid Device (MCD)
LAD	Logical Analysis Device
LAD	Logical Aptitude Device (BUR)
LAD	Logic and Adder (IAA)
LAD	Logistic Approval Data
LAD	Logistics Anchor Desk [Army] (RDA)
LAD	Lookout Assist Device [Navigation] (OA)
LAD	Low-Accuracy Data/Designation [System] (MUGU)
LAD	Low Alcohol Drinking [Rat strain]
LAD	Low-Altitude Dispenser
LAD	Low-Angle Dolly
LAD	Luanda [Angola] [Airport symbol] (OAG)
LAD	Lunar Atmosphere Detector [Aerospace]
LAD	Lymphocyte-Activating Determinant (DAVI)
LAD	Our Lady of Angels College, Aston, PA [OCLC symbol] (OCLC)
LADA	Laboratory Animal Dander Allergy (DAVI)
LADA	Left Acromio-Dorso-Anterior [A fetal position] [Obstetrics]
LADA	Left Anterior Descending Artery [Anatomy] (DAVI)
LADA	Lesson Analysis Design Approach
LADA	Light Air Defense Artillery [Army]
LADA	London Air Defence Area [British military] (DMA)
LADAPT	Lookup Dictionary Adaptor Program (IEEE)
LADAR	LASER Detection and Ranging
LADAR	LASER Doppler RADAR (MCD)
LADB	Laboratory Animal Data Bank [Battelle Memorial Institute] [Columbus, OH No longer available online] [Information service or system] (IID)
LADB	Latin American Data Bank [University of Florida] (IID)
LADB	Latin American Data Base [An association] (EA)
LADC	LASER Advanced Development Center (IAA)
L'ADC	L'Association Dentaire Canadienne (AC)
LADC	Left Anterior Descending Coronary Artery [Anatomy]
LADCA	Left Anterior Descending Coronary Artery [Medicine] (MEDA)
Ladd	Ladd's Reports [59-64 New Hampshire] [A publication] (DLA)

LADD	Left Anterior Descending Diagonal [Branch of coronary artery] [Anatomy] (DAVI)
LADD	Low-Altitude Drogue Delivery (AFM)
LADDER	Language Access to Distributed Data with Error Recovery
LaddFr	Ladd Furniture, Inc. [Associated Press] (SAG)
LADDR	Layered Device Driver Architecture [Microsoft Corp.] [Computer science] (PCM)
LADDS	Laundry and Decontamination Drycleaning System [Military] (DWSG)
LADE	Lineas Aereas del Estada [Argentine Air Force airline]
La de Castigl...	Lapus de Castiglionchio [Flourished, 1353-81] [Authority cited in pre-1607 legal work] (DSA)
LADECO	Linea Aerea del Cobre SA [Chile] (EY)
La de Rampo...	Lambertus de Ramponibus [Deceased, 1304] [Authority cited in pre-1607 legal work] (DSA)
LADF	Ladd Furniture [NASDAQ symbol] (SAG)
LADH	Lactic Acid Dehydrogenase [An enzyme] (DAVI)
LADH	Liver Alcohol Dehydrogenase [An enzyme]
LADIES	Life after Divorce Is Eventually Sane (EA)
LADIES	Los Alamos Digital Image Enhancement Software (PDAA)
LADIES	Low-Altitude Air Defense Identification and Engagement Study
LADIR	Low-Cost Arrays for Detection of Infrared (PDAA)
LADIZ	Leaving Air Defense Identification Zone
LADLE	Librarians Antidefamation League
LAD-LOMS...	Library Administration Division, Library Organization and Management Section [American Library Association] (AEBS)
LADM	Laboratory Automated Data Management
LADME	Liberation, Absorption, Distribution, Metabolism, Excretion [Medicine] (DAVI)
LAD-MIN	Left Axis Deviation Minimal [Cardiology] (DAVI)
LADOG	Low-Altitude Drive on Ground (IAA)
Ladp	Ladyship (BARN)
LADP	Leadership Assessment and Development Program [Army] (INF)
LADP	Left Acromio-Dorso-Posterior [A fetal position] [Obstetrics]
LADPOP	Lethal Agent Disposal Process Optimization Program (MCD)
LADR	Linear Accelerator-Driven Reactor (BARN)
LADRAP	Lethal Area Data Reduction and Plotting (SAA)
LADS	LASER Actuator Director System [DoD]
LADS	LASER Airborne Depth Sounder
LADS	LASER Air Defense System
LADS	Light Area Defense System (MCD)
LADS	Lightweight Air Defense System (MCD)
LADS	Limited Attack Defense System
LADS	Linear Analysis and Design of Structure (IAA)
LADS	Listener Addressed State (IAA)
LADS	Local Area Data Service [Telecommunications] (ACRL)
LADS	Local Area Data Set
LADS	Low-Altitude Defense System (MCD)
LADS	Low-Altitude Detection System [Air Force]
LADS	Low-Altitude Dispensing System [Missiles]
LADSIRLAC...	Liverpool and District Scientific Industrial and Research Library Advisory Council [Library cooperative scheme] [British] (NITA)
LADT	Local Area Data Transport [AT & T]
LADT	Local Area Digital Transmission (WGA)
LADT	Low-Altitude Drop Test [NASA]
LADu	Lobuloalveolar-Ductal [Medicine] (DAVI)
L Adv	Lord Advocate [British] (DAS)
L Advertiser...	Law Advertiser [1823-31] [A publication] (DLA)
LadyLuck	Lady Luck Gaming Corp. [Associated Press] (SAG)
LAE	Lae [Papua New Guinea] [Airport symbol] (OAG)
LAE	Lae [Papua New Guinea] [Seismograph station code, US Geological Survey Closed] (SEIS)
LAE	Launcher Adapter Electronics (MCD)
LAE	Lead Angle Error
LAE	Leadership Ability Evaluation [Psychology]
LAE	Left Arithmetic Element
LAE	Left Atrial Enlargement [Cardiology]
LAE	Lethal Area Estimate
LAE	Linear Alcohol Ethoxylate [Surfactant]
LAE	Lineas Aereas Colombianas Ltd. [Colombia] [ICAO designator] (FAAC)
LAE	"Love Is All" for Enge (EA)
LAECC	Groupe International Laicat et Communaute Chretienne [International Laity and Christian Community Group - ILCCG] [Defunct] (EA)
LAECG	Local Aboriginal Education Consultative Group [Australia]
LAED	Large Area Electronic Display
LAED	Low Angle Electron Diffraction (PDAA)
LAEDP	Large Area Electronic Display Panel
LAEDV	Left Atrial Volume in End Diastole [Medicine] (DMAA)
LAEF	Luso-American Education Foundation (EA)
LAEI	Left Atrial Emptying Index [Medicine] (DMAA)
LAE NOTE	Licensed Aircraft Engineers' Notice (DNAB)
LAEP	Large Area Electronic Panel
LAEPC	Local Aboriginal Employment Promotion Committee [Australia]
LAER	Lowest Achievable Emission Rate [Environmental Protection Agency]
LAERF	Lewisville Aquatic Ecosystem Research Facility [Texas]
LAERF	Lewisville Aquatic Ecosystem Research Facility [Army]
LAET	Limiting Actual Exposure Time (KSC)
LAETRILE...	Laevo-Mandelonitrile-beta-glucuronic Acid [Possible anticancer compound]
LAEV	Laevus [Left] [Pharmacy]
LAF	Lafarge Corp. [NYSE symbol] (SPSG)
LAF	Lafayette [Rhode Island] [Seismograph station code, US Geological Survey Closed] (SEIS)
LAF	Lafayette [Indiana] [Airport symbol] (OAG)
LAF	Lafayette [Diocesan abbreviation] [Louisiana] (TOCD)

LAF .... Lafayette College, Easton, PA [*OCLC symbol*] (OCLC)
LAF .... Lafayette, IN [*Location identifier FAA*] (FAAL)
LAF .... Laminar Airflow (KSC)
LAF .... Landscape Architecture Foundation (EA)
Laf .... Lanfrancus [*Deceased, 1089*] [*Authority cited in pre-1607 legal work*] (DSA)
Laf .... Lanfrancus Cremensis [*Deceased, 1229*] [*Authority cited in pre-1607 legal work*] (DSA)
LAF .... Latin American Female [*Classified advertising*] (DMAA)
LAF .... Left Anterior Fascicle [*Anatomy*]
LAF .... Leukocyte-Activating Factor [*Immunochemistry*]
LAF .... Limited Amplifier Filter
LAF .... Limits and Fits [*System*] [*Precision of tolerance*] [*Automotive engineering*]
LAF .... Live Aid Foundation (EA)
LAF .... Living Arts Foundation (EA)
LAF .... Logistic Availability Factor (CAAL)
LAF .... Long Address Form (NITA)
LAF .... Luteal Angiogenic Factor [*Biochemistry*]
LAF .... Lymphocyte Activating Factor [*Immunology*]
LAF .... Lyophilized Allantoic Fluid [*Endocrinology*]
Lafarge .... Lafarge Corp. [*Associated Press*] (SAG)
Lafay .... Lafayette Industries, Inc. [*Associated Press*] (SAG)
LafayABk .... Lafayette American Bank & Trust [*Associated Press*] (SAG)
Lafaye .... Lafayette Industries, Inc. [*Associated Press*] (SAG)
LAFB .... Langley Air Force Base (MCD)
LAFB .... Left Anterior Fascicular Block [*Cardiology*]
LAFB .... Libyan Arab Foreign Bank
LAFB .... Light Assault Floating Bridge [*British military*] (DMA)
LAFB .... Lincoln Air Force Base
LAFB .... Local Authority Fire Brigade [*British*]
LAFB .... Lowry Air Force Base (SAA)
LAFC .... Latin-American Forestry Commission
LAFC .... Lynn Anderson Fan Club (EA)
LAFF .... Launcher Air Filtration Facility
LAFF .... Luso-American Fraternal Federation (EA)
LAFI .... Lafayette Industries, Inc. [*NASDAQ symbol*] (SAG)
LAFIE .... Lafayette Industries [*NASDAQ symbol*] (TTSB)
LAFIS .... Local Authority Financial Information System (PDAA)
LAFIS .... Local Authority Financial Institution System (AIE)
LAFL .... Latin American Football League [*British*]
LAFM .... Los Alamos Fuel Model [*Department of Energy*] (GFGA)
LA FONT ..... La Fontaine [*French author, 1621-1695*] (ROG)
LAFR .... Laminar Air Flow Room (DMAA)
LaFr .... Laminar Airflow Room [*Medicine*] (DAVI)
LAFTA .... Latin American Association of Freight and Transport Agents [*Paraguay*] (EAIO)
LAFTA .... Latin-American Free Trade Association [*Later, LAIA*]
LAFTC .... Latin American Federation of Thermalism and Climatism [*See also FLT*] [*Argentina*] (EAIO)
LAFTO .... Latin American Confederation of Tourist Organizations [*Argentina*] (EAIO)
LAFTS .... LASER and FLIR [*Forward-Looking Infrared*] Test Set [*Air Force*]
LAFTS .... Los Alamos Fourier Transform Spectrometer [*Department of Energy*] (GRD)
LAFU .... Ladies Amateur Fencing Union [*British*] (DBA)
LAFU .... Laminar Airflow Unit [*Medicine*] (DAVI)
LAFUS .... Latvian Association of Foresters in the United States [*Defunct*] (EA)
LAFV .... Light Armoured Fighting Vehicle [*British military*] (DMA)
LAFWE .... Lafayette Industries Wrrt [*NASDAQ symbol*] (TTSB)
LAG .... Aerovias de Lagos SA de CV [*Mexico ICAO designator*] (FAAC)
LaG .... Labiogingival [*Dentistry*]
Lag .... Lagena [*Flask*] [*Latin*]
LAG .... Lagging [*Engineering*]
LAG .... Lagoon [*Maps and charts*]
LAG .... La Guaira [*Venzuela*] [*Airport symbol*] (AD)
LAG .... LaGuardia Community College Library [*UTLAS symbol*]
LAG .... Langila [*Cape Gloucester*] [*New Britain*] [*Seismograph station code, US Geological Survey*] (SEIS)
LAG .... LASER Absolute Gravimeter
LAG .... Lastenausgleichsgesetz (BJA)
LAG .... Legal Action Group [*British*] (DBA)
LAG .... Librarians Automation Group [*Australia*] (NITA)
LAG .... Liga Armada Gallega [*Armed Galician League*] [*Spain*] (PD)
LAG .... Line of Arrested Growth [*Biology*]
LAG .... Linguoaxiogingival [*Dentistry*]
LAG .... [*A*] Literary Atlas and Gazetteer of the British Isles [*A publication*]
LAG .... Livermore Action Group [*Defunct*] (EA)
LAG .... Load and Go (NITA)
LAG .... Load and Go Assembler (BUR)
LAG .... Logical Applications Group [*Social Security Administration*]
LAG .... London Amusement Guide
LAG .... Lympangiosium [*Medicine*]
LAG .... Lymphangiogram [*or Lymphangiography*]
LAGB .... Linguistics Association of Great Britain
LAGB .... Linhas Aereas da Guine-Bissau [*Airline*] [*Guinea-Bissau*]
LAGE .... Los Angeles Grain Exchange (EA)
LA Gear ...... LA Gear, Inc. [*Associated Press*] (SAG)
LAGEO .... LASER Geodynamic Satellite [*NASA*] (PDAA)
LAGEOS ...... LASER Geodynamic Satellite [*NASA*]
LAGER .... Liberal Action Group for Electoral Reform [*British*] (DI)
LAGG .... Fighter [*Russian aircraft symbol*]
LaGIN .... Louisiana Government Information Network [*Louisiana State Library*] [*Baton Rouge*] [*Information service or system*] (IID)
LAGLG .... Library Association Government Libraries Group (PDAA)

LAGMA .... Lawn and Garden Manufacturers Association [*Defunct*] (EA)
LAGN .... Lagoon [*Board on Geographic Names*]
LAGO .... Light Atomic Gas Oil [*Petroleum product*]
Lagos HCR... Lagos High Court Reports [*A publication*] (DLA)
Lagos R ...... Judgments in the Supreme Court, Lagos [*1884-92*] [*Nigeria*] [*A publication*] (DLA)
LaGrange C... LaGrange College (GAGS)
LAGS .... LASER-Activated Geodetic Satellite [*AFCRL*]
LAGS .... Launch Abort Guide Simulation [*NASA*] (NASA)
LAGUMS ..... LASER-Guided Missile System (MCD)
Lah .... Indian Law Reports, Lahore Series [*A publication*] (DLA)
Lah .... Indian Rulings, Lahore Series [*A publication*] (DLA)
LAH .... Labuha [*Indonesia*] [*Airport symbol*] (OAG)
LAH .... Lactalbumin Hydrolysate [*Biochemistry*] (MAE)
LAH .... LA Helicopter, Inc. [*ICAO designator*] (FAAC)
lah .... Lahnda [*MARC language code Library of Congress*] (LCCP)
LAH .... Lahore [*Pakistan*] [*Seismograph station code, US Geological Survey Closed*] (SEIS)
LAH .... Launch Axis, Horizontal (MCD)
LAH .... Lebanon, NH [*Location identifier FAA*] (FAAL)
LAH .... Left Anterior Hemiblock [*Cardiology*]
LAH .... Left Atrial Hypertrophy [*Cardiology*]
LAH .... Licentiate of the Apothecaries' Hall [*Dublin*]
LAH .... Light-Armed Helicopter [*Military*] (PDAA)
LAH .... Lithium Aluminum Hydride [*Inorganic chemistry*]
LAH .... Logical Analyzer of Hypothesis (IEEE)
LAH .... Low-Altitude Hold [*Military*] (CAAL)
Lah .... Pakistan Law Reports, Lahore Series [*A publication*] (DLA)
LAHA .... Linear Array Hybrid Assembly (PDAA)
LAHAWS ..... LASER Homing and Warning System [*Military*] (PDAA)
LAHB .... Left Anterior Hemiblock [*Medicine*] (MEDA)
LAHB .... Local Authorities Historic Buildings Act [*Town planning*] [*British*]
LAHC .... Low Affinity-High Capacity [*Medicine*] (DMAA)
Lah Cas ...... Lahore Cases [*India*] [*A publication*] (DLA)
LAHCG .... Look Ahead Carry Generator [*Computer science*] (NITA)
LAHF .... Latin American Hospital Federation [*Mexico*] (EAIO)
Lahhs .... Large Hydrofoil Hybrid Ship
LAHIVE .... Low-Altitude/High-Velocity Experiment
Lah LJ .... Lahore Law Journal [*India*] [*A publication*] (DLA)
Lah LT .... Lahore Law Times [*India*] [*A publication*] (DLA)
LAHM .... Limited Area HIBU [*Hydrological Institute and Belgrade University*] (USDC)
Lahore .... All India Reporter, Lahore Series [*A publication*] (ILCA)
Lahore L Times... Lahore Law Times [*India*] [*A publication*] (DLA)
LAHPERD.... Louisiana Association for Health, Physical Education, Recreation, and Dance (SRA)
LAHS .... Local Authority Health Services [*British*]
LAHS .... Low-Altitude, High-Speed
LAHV .... Leukocyte-Associates Herpes Virus [*Medicine*] (DAVI)
LAI .... Labioincisal [*Dentistry*]
LAI .... Lact-Aid International [*Commercial firm*] (EA)
LAI .... LAN [*Linked Access Network*] Automatic Inventory [*Brightwork Development, Inc.*] [*Computer science*] (PCM)
LAI .... Lannion [*France*] [*Airport symbol*] (OAG)
LAI .... Lasir Gold, Inc. [*Vancouver Stock Exchange symbol*]
LAI .... Latex Agglutination-Inhibition (PDAA)
LAI .... Latin American Institute [*University of New Mexico*] [*Research center*] (RCD)
LAI .... Leaf Area Index [*Forestry*]
LAI .... Left Artrial Involvement [*Medicine*] (MEDA)
LAI .... Lesotho Airways Corp. [*ICAO designator*] (FAAC)
LAI .... Lesson Administrative Instructions [*Military*]
LAI .... Leukocyte Adherence Inhibition [*Immunochemistry*]
LAI .... Library Association of Ireland (EAIO)
LAI .... Life Adjustment Inventory [*Psychology*]
LAI .... Light Armored Infantry [*Marine Corps*] (DOMA)
L-A-I .... Linkage, Ability, Interest [*Fundraising term*] (NFD)
LAI .... Load Address Immediate (BUR)
LAI .... Loaded Applicator Impedance
LAI .... Love Attitudes Inventory [*Premarital relations test*] [*Psychology*]
LAI .... Low-Altitude Indicator
LAIA .... Latin American Industrialists Association [*Uruguay*] (EAIO)
LAIA .... Latin American Integration Association [*Formerly, LAFTA*] [*See also ALADI Uruguay*] (EAIO)
LAIC .... Lithuanian-American Information Center [*Defunct*]
LaidlwA ...... Laidlaw, Inc. [*Associated Press*] (SAG)
LaidlwB ...... Laidlaw, Inc. [*Associated Press*] (SAG)
LAIEC .... Latin American Institute of Educational Communication [*Mexico*] (EAIO)
LAIF .... Leukocyte Adherence Inhibition Factor (DAVI)
LAIFS .... Los Angeles International Fern Society (EA)
LAIG .... LA Industrial Group (NITA)
LAIICS .... Latin American Institute for Information and Computer Sciences [*Chile*] (PDAA)
LAILA .... Latin American Indian Literatures Association (EA)
LAIMP .... Lunar-Anchored Interplanetary Monitoring Platform [*Aerospace*] (MCD)
LAINS .... Low-Altitude Inertial Navigation System [*Air Force*]
LAIR .... Letterman Army Institute of Research [*San Francisco, CA*]
LAIR .... Liquid Air (NASA)
LAIRS .... Labor Agreement Information Retrieval System [*Office of Management and Budget*]
LAIRS .... Land-Air Integrated Reduction System (MUGU)
LAIRS .... Lightweight Advanced Inertial Reference Sphere
LAIRTS .... Large Aperture Infrared Telescope System

LAIS............ Labor Arbitration Information System [*LRP Publications*] [*Information service or system*] (CRD)
LAIS............ Labyrinth Air Induction Silencer [*Automotive engineering*]
LAIS............ Labyrinth Air Induction System [*Automotive engineering*]
LAIS............ Leiter Adult Intelligence Scale [*Intelligence test*] [*Psychology*]
LAIS............ Library Acquisitions Information System
LAIS............ Loan Accounting Information System [*Agency for International Development*]
LAISDSS...... Latin American Institute of Social Doctrine and Social Studies [*Chile*] (EAIO)
LAIT............ Latex Agglutination Inhibition Test [*for pregnancy*] [*Medicine*]
LAIT............ Library Association Information Technology Group [*British*] (NITA)
LAIT............ Logistics Assistance and Instruction Team [*Military*] (AABC)
LAITG.......... Library Association Information Technology Group (AIE)
LAITS.......... Latin American Institute for Transnational Studies (EA)
LAIU............ Launch Abort Interface Unit [*NASA*] (MCD)
LAIWS .... Land-Air White Sands (MUGU)
LAJ............. British Mediterranean Airways Ltd. [*FAA designator*] (FAAC)
LAJ............. Lajes [*Brazil*] [*Airport symbol*] (OAG)
LAJ............. London Airtours Ltd. [*British ICAO designator*] (FAAC)
LAJ............. Los Angeles Junction Railway Co. [*AAR code*]
LaJollPh ...... La Jolla Pharmaceutical [*Associated Press*] (SAG)
LaJolP .... La Jolla Pharmaceutical [*Associated Press*] (SAG)
LAJPEL........ Latin American Journal of Politics, Economics, and Law [*A publication*] (DLA)
LAK............ Aklavik [*Canada*] [*Airport symbol*] (OAG)
LAK............ Laker Resources [*Vancouver Stock Exchange symbol*]
LAK............ Lennox Airways [*Kenya*] [*ICAO designator*] (FAAC)
LAK............ Leukocyte-Activated Killer [*Cells*] [*Oncology*] (DAVI)
LAK............ Lightweight Antenna Kit
LAK............ Lymphokine-Activated Killer [*Cells*] [*Immunotherapy*]
LAKE........... Lake [*Commonly used*] (OPSA)
LAKE........... Lakeland Indus [*NASDAQ symbol*] (TTSB)
LAKE........... Lakeland Industries, Inc. [*NASDAQ symbol*] (SAG)
LakeAriel ..... Lake Ariel Bancorp [*Associated Press*] (SAG)
LakehdP ...... Lakehead Pipe Line Partners Ltd. [*Associated Press*] (SAG)
LakeInd........ Lakeland Industries, Inc. [*Associated Press*] (SAG)
LAKES .... Lakes [*Commonly used*] (OPSA)
LakevwF ...... Lakeview Financial Corp. [*Associated Press*] (SAG)
LAKFC .... Los Angeles Kings Fan Club (EA)
LakldFt .... Lakeland First Fianancial Group, Inc. [*Associated Press*] (SAG)
LaL............. Labiolingual [*Dentistry*]
LAL............ Labrador Airways Ltd. [*Canada ICAO designator*] (FAAC)
LAL............ Lakeland [*Florida*] [*Airport symbol*] (AD)
LAL............ Lakeland, FL [*Location identifier FAA*] (FAAL)
LAL............ Lana Gold Corp. [*Vancouver Stock Exchange symbol*]
LAL............ Langley Aeronautical Laboratory [*NASA*]
LAL............ Left Axillary Line [*Medicine*] (DMAA)
LAL............ Limulus Amebocyte Lysate
LAL............ Livonia, Avon & Lakeville Railroad Corp. [*AAR code*]
LAL............ Local Adjunct Language (PDAA)
LAL............ Loudspeaker Acoustical Labyrinth
LAL............ Low Air Loss
LAL............ Lower Acceptance Level
LAL-Ala........ Lysinoalanine [*An amino acid*]
L-Ala.......... L-Alanine [*Biochemistry*] (DAVI)
LALA........... Large Amplitude Late Arrival [*Seismology*]
LALA........... Linoletic Acid-Like Activity (PDAA)
LA(L)A .... Local Authorities (Land) Act [*Town planning*] [*British*]
LALA........... Low-Altitude Alert [*Air traffic control*]
LaLand .... Louisiana Land & Exploration Co. [*Associated Press*] (SAG)
LALD........... Low-Angle Low-Drag
L Alem......... Law of the Alemanni [*A publication*] (DLA)
LALI............ Labiolingual [*Dentistry*]
LALI............ Latin American-Caribbean Labor Institute (EA)
LALI............ Lymphocyte Antibody-Lymphocytolytic Interaction [*Medicine*] (DMAA)
LA LJ .... Louisiana Law Journal [*New Orleans*] [*A publication*] (DLA)
LALLL .... Low-Altitude Low-Light Level
LALLS .... Low-Angle LASER Light Scattering
LALM.......... Limulus Amebocyte Lysate Method
LALO........... Low-Altitude Observation
Lalor........... Lalor's Supplement to Hill and Denio's New York Reports [*A publication*] (DLA)
Lalor Pol Econ... Lalor's Cyclopaedia of Political Science, Political Economy, Etc. [*A publication*] (DLA)
Lalor's Supp.. Lalor's Supplement to Hill and Denio's New York Reports [*A publication*] (DLA)
Lalor's Supp (Hill and Denio)... Lalor's Supplement to Hill and Denio's New York Reports [*A publication*] (DLA)
Lalor Supp... Lalor's Supplement to Hill and Denio's New York Reports [*A publication*] (DLA)
LALP........... Longest Activity from Longest Project
LALR........... Lookahead Left to Right [*Computer science*]
LAIR............ Rapides Parish Library, Alexandria, LA [*Library symbol Library of Congress*] (LCLS)
Lal RP .... Lalor's Law of Real Property [*A publication*] (DLA)
LALS........... LaGuardia Automated Library System [*LaGuardia Community College*] [*Information service or system*] (IID)
LALS........... LASER Alarm Locator System
LALS........... Linkless Ammunition Loading System (MCD)
LALSD .... Language for Automated Logic and System Design [*Computer science*] (CSR)
LALUC .... Local Authority Land Use Classification (PDAA)
LALV........... Lucerne Australian Latent Virus [*Plant pathology*]
Lam .... Lamarck [*Biology*] (BARN)

lam .... Lamba [*MARC language code Library of Congress*] (LCCP)
Lam .... Lambert [*Unit of luminance*] [*Preferred unit is lx, Lux*]
Lam .... Lambertus de Ramponibus [*Deceased, 1304*] [*Authority cited in pre-1607 legal work*] (DSA)
Lam .... Lamentations [*Old Testament book*]
LAM .... Lamina [*Medicine*] (DAVI)
LAM .... Laminate (MSA)
lam .... Laminated (VRA)
lam .... Laminated (WDMC)
LAM .... Laminectomy [*Medicine*]
lam .... Laminogram (MAE)
LAM .... Land Attack Mode [*Navy*] (CAAL)
LAM .... Laramide Resources Ltd. [*Vancouver Stock Exchange symbol*]
LAM .... LASER [*Light Amplification by Stimulated Emission of Radiation*] Aiming Module
LAM .... L-Asparaginase and Methotrexate [*Antineoplastic drug regimen*] (DAVI)
LAM .... Late Ambulatory Monitoring [*Medicine*]
LAM .... Latin America Inv Fd [*NYSE symbol*] (TTSB)
LAM .... Latin America Mission (EA)
LAM .... Latin American Investment Fund [*NYSE symbol*] (SPSG)
LAM .... Latin American Male (DAVI)
LAM .... Latin American Mission [*Air Force*]
LAM .... Leading Air Mechanic [*British military*] (DMA)
LAM .... Learner-Approved Motorcycle
LAM .... Left Anterior Measurement (DAVI)
LAM .... Left Artial Myxoma [*Cardiology*] (DAVI)
LAM .... Liberalium Artium Magister [*Master of the Liberal Arts*]
LAM .... Life Action Ministries (EA)
LAM .... Lightweight Analog Motor (MCD)
LAM .... Limited Area Model [*Marine science*] (OSRA)
LAM .... Limpet Assembly Modular [*Navy*] (CAAL)
LAM .... Linhas Aereas de Mocambique [*Mozambique*] [*ICAO designator*] (FAAC)
LAM .... Lipoarabinomannan [*Biochemistry*]
LAM .... Load Acceptance Module
LAM .... Load Accumulator with Magnitude
LAM .... Lobe Attachment Module [*Computer science*]
LAM .... Lobe Attachment Unit [*Computer science*] (ACRL)
LAM .... Logical Acknowledgement Message [*Aviation*] (DA)
LAM .... London Academy of Music
LAM .... Long Aerial Mine [*Military*]
LAM .... Longitudinal Acoustic [*or Acoustical*] Mode [*Spectroscopy*]
LAM .... Look at Me (IAA)
LAM .... Loop Adder and Multiplier (NITA)
LAM .... Loop Addition and Modification [*Computer science*]
LAM .... Los Alamos [*New Mexico*] [*Airport symbol*] (OAG)
LAM .... Los Alamos, NM [*Location identifier FAA*] (FAAL)
LAM .... Louisiana Motor Freight Bureau [*STAC*]
LAM .... Lousiana Maneuvers [*Military*]
LAM .... Low-Altitude Missile (MCD)
LAM .... Low-Attack Mode (MCD)
LAM .... Lymphangioleiomyomatosis [*Medicine*]
LAM .... Master of Liberal Arts
LAMA .... Laboratory Animal Management Association (EA)
LAMA .... Laminin A (DMAA)
LAMA .... Latin American Manufacturers Association [*Washington, DC*] (EA)
LAMA .... Lead Air Materiel Area [*Air Force*]
LAMA .... Legal Assistant Management Association (EA)
LAMA .... Library Administration and Management Association (EA)
LAMA .... Light Aircraft Manufacturers' Association (EA)
LAMA .... Livestock Auction Markets Association (EA)
LAMA .... Local Automatic Message Accounting [*Telecommunications*] (TEL)
LAMA .... Locomotive and Allied Manufacturers' Association [*British*] (BI)
LAMA BES ... LAMA [*Library Administration and Management Association*] Buildings and Equipment Section
LAMACHA .... Louisiana-Alabama-Mississippi Automated Clearing House Association
LAMA FRFDS... LAMA [*Library Administration and Management Association*] Fund Raising and Financial Development Section
LAMA LOMS... LAMA [*Library Administration and Management Association*] Library Organization and Management Section
LaMan .... LaMan Corp. [*Associated Press*] (SAG)
lam & fus.... Laminectomy and Fusion [*Medicine*] (DAVI)
LAMA PAS ... LAMA [*Library Administration and Management Association*] Personnel Administration Section
LAMA PRS ... LAMA [*Library Administration and Management Association*] Public Relations Section
Lamar......... Lamar's Reports [*25-40 Florida*] [*A publication*] (DLA)
LAMAR .... Large Area Modular Array of Reflectors [*Astronomy*]
LAMAR .... Linear-Elastic Matrix Analysis Routine
LAMARS....... Large Amplitude Multimode Aerospace Research Simulator
Lamar U ...... Lamar University (GAGS)
LAMAS........ Location and Movement Analysis System (MCD)
LAMA SASS... LAMA [*Library Administration and Management Association*] Systems and Services Section
LAMA SS ..... LAMA [*Library Administration and Management Association*] Statistics Section
LAMA SSS ... LAMA [*Library Administration and Management Association*] Systems and Services Section
LA-MAX .... Maximal left Atrial [*Dimension*] [*Cardiology*] (DAVI)
Lamb .... Lambard's Archaionomia [*A publication*] (DLA)
Lamb .... Lambard's Archeion [*1635*] [*A publication*] (DLA)
Lamb .... Lambard's Eirenarcha [*A publication*] (DLA)
Lamb .... Lambard's Explication [*A publication*] (DLA)

LAMB.......... Lambeth [*Degrees granted by Archbishop of Canterbury*] [*British*] (ROG)
LAMB.......... Lambourne [*England*]
Lamb.......... Lamb's Reports [*103-105 Wisconsin*] [*A publication*] (DLA)
LAMB.......... Light Armoured Motor Brigade [*British military*] (DMA)
LAMB.......... Local Area Multiuser Board [*American Micronics*] [*Computer science*]
LAMB.......... Los Alamos Water Boiler (NRCH)
LAMB.......... Low-Altitude Multiburst Code (MCD)
Lamb Arch... Lambard's Archaionomia [*A publication*] (DLA)
Lamb Arch... Lambard's Archeion [*1635*] [*A publication*] (ILCA)
Lamb Archaion... Lambard's Archaionomia [*A publication*] (DLA)
Lamb Const... Lambard's Duties of Constables, Etc. [*A publication*] (DLA)
LAMBDA...... Language for Manufacturing Business and Distribution Activity (IAA)
Lamb de Ramp... Lambertus de Ramponibus [*Deceased, 1304*] [*Authority cited in pre-1607 legal work*] (DSA)
Lamb Dow... Lambert's Law of Dower [*A publication*] (DLA)
Lamb Eir...... Lambard's Eirenarcha [*A publication*] (DLA)
Lamb Eiren... Lambard's Eirenarcha [*A publication*] (DLA)
Lamber de Sal... Lambertus de Salinis [*Flourished, 14th century*] [*Authority cited in pre-1607 legal work*] (DSA)
Lamb Explic... Lambard's Explication [*A publication*] (DLA)
Lam Bk Rpt... Lambda Book Report [*A publication*] (BRI)
LAMBR...... Laminin B Receptor (DMAA)
LAMBS........ Laboratory Animal Management and Business Systems [*Computer science*]
LAMC.......... Laminin C (DMAA)
LAMC.......... Language and Mode Converter [*Computer science*] (TEL)
LAMC.......... Last Maneuver Calculation [*Orbit identification*]
LAMC.......... Letterman Army Medical Center (AABC)
LAMC.......... Lima Army Modification Center (RDA)
LAMC.......... Livestock Auctioneers' Market Committee [*British*] (DBA)
LAMCIS....... Los Angeles Multiple Corridor Identification System (SAA)
LAMCO ...... Liberian American-Swedish Minerals Co.
LAMCS........ Latin American-American Communications Systems (PDAA)
LAMCS....... Latin American Military Communications System
LAMDA ...... [*The*] London Academy of Music and Dramatic Art
LAME.......... Lake Mead National Recreation Area
LAME.......... Licensed Aircraft Maintenance Engineer (ADA)
LAMEF........ Los Alamos Medium Energy Facility
LAMG.......... Laban Art of Movement Guild [*Later, LG*] (EA)
lami.......... Laminotomy [*Medicine*] (DAVI)
Lamin.......... Laminating Technologies, Inc. [*Associated Press*] (SAG)
Laminat...... Laminating Technologies, Inc. [*Associated Press*] (SAG)
LAMIS........ Local Authority Managaement Information System (PDAA)
LAMIT........ Local Authorities' Mutual Investment Trust [*British*]
LAMMA....... LASER Microprobe Mass Analyzer [*Spectrometry*]
LAMMP....... Lower Acceptable Mean Maximum Pressure (SAA)
LAMMR....... Large Antenna Multifrequency Microwave Radiometer (MCD)
LAMMS....... LASER Microprobe Mass Spectrometry [*or Spectroscopy*]
LAMN.......... La Man Corp. [*NASDAQ symbol*] (TTSB)
LAMOPH..... Ladies Auxiliary, Military Order of the Purple Heart, United States of America (EA)
LAMOST ...... Large Area Multi Object Fiber Spectroscopic Telescope [*Proposed, China*]
LAMOST ...... Large Sky Area Multi-Objects Fiber Spectoscopic Telescope [*China*]
LAMP.......... Center for the Study of Legal Authority and Mental Patient Status (EA)
LAMP.......... Lake Acidification Mitigation Project [*Environmental Protection Agency*] (GFGA)
LAMP.......... Lakewide Management Plan [*Great Lakes*] [*Environmental Protection Agency*]
LAMP.......... Lanier Academic Motivational Program [*Military*]
LAMP.......... Laos Ammunition Procedures (CINC)
LAMP.......... Large Advanced Mirror Program [*Military*] (SDI)
LAMP.......... LASER and MASER Patents
LAMP.......... LASER and Mixing Program
LAMP.......... Laser Microbeam Program [*Research center*] (RCD)
LAMP.......... Leap and Stamp [*Dance terminology*]
LAMP.......... Library Addition and Maintenance Program
LAMP.......... Life Agency Management Program [*GAMC*]
LAMP.......... Light Airborne Multipurpose System [*Navy*] (MCD)
LAMP..... Lighthouse Automation and Modernization Project [*US Coast Guard*] (PDAA)
LAMP.......... Logic Analysis for Maintenance Planning (MHDB)
LAMP.......... Logistics Automation Master PLan [*Military*]
LAMP.......... Louis Armstrong Memorial Project
LAMP.......... Low-Altitude Manned Penetrator
LAMP.......... Lunar Analysis and Mapping Program [*NASA*] (IAA)
LAMP.......... Lysosome-Associated Membrane Protein [*Biochemistry*]
LAMPF........ Los Alamos Meson Physics Facility [*Later, Clinton P. Anderson Meson Physics Facility at Los Alamos*] [*Department of Energy*]
LAMP-H...... Lighter, Amphibian Heavy Lift
LAMPP........ Los Alamos Molten Plutonium Program
LAMPRE...... Los Alamos Molten Plutonium Reactor Experiment
LAMPS....... Large Amplitude SLOSH [*Sea, Lake, Overland Surge from Hurricanes*] [*NASA*]
LAMPS....... Light Airborne Multiple Package System
LAMPS....... Light Airborne Multipurpose System [*Navy*]
LAMPS....... Limited Area Mesoscale Prediction System (MCD)
LAMPSOP... Light Airborne Multipurpose System Standard Operating Procedures Manual [*Navy*] (DNAB)
LA/MPSS.... Large Area/Mobile Projected Smoke System [*Military*] (RDA)
LamR.......... Lamentations Rabbah (BJA)
LAMR.......... Large Aperture Microwave Radiometer (SSD)
LAMRL........ Logistic Area Material Readiness List [*Military*] (AFIT)

LamRsch .... Lam Research Corp. [*Associated Press*] (SAG)
LAMRTPI .... Legal Associate Member of the Royal Town Planning Institute [*British*] (DBQ)
LAMS.......... Land Acoustical Monitoring System [*NASA*]
LAMS.......... Land Acquisition and Management Schemes [*British*]
LAMS.......... Large Atypical Mole Syndrome [*Medicine*]
LAMS.......... Load Alleviation and Mode Stabilization
LAMS.......... London Aero Motor Services
LAMS.......... Los Alamos Scientific Laboratory [*USAEC*] (MCD)
LAMSA....... Lineas Aereas Mexicana, Sociedad Anonima
LAMSAC .... Local Authorities' Management Services and Computer Committee [*British*]
LAMSAS..... Linguistic Atlas of the Middle and South Atlantic States
LamSes ...... [*The*] Lamson & Sessions Co. [*Associated Press*] (SAG)
LAMSIM...... Launcher and Missile Simulator
L Am Soc... Law in American Society [*A publication*] (DLA)
L Am Soc'y... Law in American Society [*A publication*] (DLA)
LAMT.......... Laminating Technologies, Inc. [*NASDAQ symbol*] (SAG)
LAmT.......... Tangipahoa Parish Library, Amite, LA [*Library symbol Library of Congress*] (LCLS)
LAMTD........ Laminated
LAMTS........ Launcher Adapter Missile Test Set
LAN.......... Inland [*Aviation code*]
LAN.......... Lanarkshire [*County in Scotland*]
LAN.......... Lancer Corp. [*AMEX symbol*] (SPSG)
LAN.......... Lanchow [*Republic of China*] [*Seismograph station code, US Geological Survey Closed*] (SEIS)
LAN.......... Landing Aid [*Navigation*] (IAA)
Lan .... Landulfus Acconzaioco [*Flourished, 13th century*] [*Authority cited in pre-1607 legal work*] (DSA)
Lan .... Lanfrancus [*Deceased, 1089*] [*Authority cited in pre-1607 legal work*] (DSA)
Lan .... Lanfrancus Cremensis [*Deceased, 1229*] [*Authority cited in pre-1607 legal work*] (DSA)
LAN.......... Langley [*Unit of sun's heat*] (IAA)
lan.......... Langue d'Oc [*MARC language code Library of Congress*] (LCCP)
LAN.......... Lansing [*Michigan*] [*Airport symbol*] (OAG)
LAN.......... Lansing, MI [*Location identifier FAA*] (FAAL)
LAN.......... Lateral Access Network (NITA)
LAN.......... Latin American Newsletters [*British Information service or system*] (IID)
LAN.......... Library Advocacy Now [*American Library Association*]
LAN.......... Library Automation and Networks
LAN.......... Lime-Ammonium-Nitrate [*Fertilizer*]
LAN.......... Linea Aerea Nacional [*National Airline*] [*Chile*]
LAN.......... Linea Aerea Nacional de Chile [*ICAO designator*] (FAAC)
LAN.......... Linked Access Network
LAN.......... Local Apparent Noon [*Navigation*]
LAN.......... Local Area Network [*Telecommunications*]
LAN.......... Local Area Networks [*Information Gatekeepers, Inc.*] [*No longer available online*] [*Information service or system*] (CRD)
LAN.......... Long-Acting Neuroleptic [*Pharmacology*] (DAVI)
LAN.......... Longitude of the Ascending Node
LAN.......... Mesa Public Library, Los Alamos, NM [*OCLC symbol*] (OCLC)
LANA.......... Language Analog [*Project*]
LANA.......... Lithuanian American National Alliance (EA)
LANA.......... Llama Association of North America (EA)
LANA.......... Low-Altitude Night Attack (DOMA)
LANABS ...... Light Attack Navigation and Bombing System (MCD)
LANAC .... Laminar Air Navigation and Anticollision [*Air Force*]
LANAC .... Lawyers Alliance for Nuclear Arms Control [*Later, LAWS*] (EA)
Lan Acon .... Landulfus Acconzaioco [*Flourished, 13th century*] [*Authority cited in pre-1607 legal work*] (DSA)
LANBY .... Large Automatic Navigational Buoy [*Shipping*] (DS)
LANC .... Lancaster [*England*] (ROG)
LANC .... Lancaster Colony [*NASDAQ symbol*] (SAG)
Lanc.......... Lancellottus [*Authority cited in pre-1607 legal work*] (DSA)
LANC .... Lancer [*Military British*] (ROG)
LANC .... Liga Apararii Nationale Crestine [*League of National Christian Defense*] [*Romania*] [*Political party*] (PPE)
LANC .... Local Application Numerical Control [*Sony Corp.*] (DOM)
LANC .... Long-Arm Navicular Cast [*Orthopedics*] (DAVI)
Lancastr ..... Lancaster Colony [*Associated Press*] (SAG)
Lance........ Lance, Inc. [*Associated Press*] (SAG)
LANCE .... Local Area Network Controller for Ethernet [*Mostek*] (NITA)
Lancell Galiaul... Lancellottus Galiaula [*Flourished, 16th century*] [*Authority cited in pre-1607 legal work*] (DSA)
Lancer....... Lancer Corp. [*Associated Press*] (SAG)
LANCET....... Library Association National Council for Educational Technology (NITA)
Lancit......... Lancit Media Productions Ltd. [*Associated Press*] (SAG)
Lanc Law Rev... Lancaster Law Review [*A publication*] (DLA)
Lanc L Rev... Lancaster Law Review [*A publication*] (DLA)
LANCO .... Landscape Nursery Council (EA)
LANCRA...... Landing Craft
LANCRAB.... Landing Craft and Bases [*Military*]
LANCRABEU... Landing Craft and Bases, Europe [*Navy*]
LANCRABNAW... Landing Craft and Bases, Northwest African Waters [*World War II Navy*]
Lan Cre....... Lanfrancus Cremensis [*Deceased, 1229*] [*Authority cited in pre-1607 legal work*] (DSA)
Lanc Rev .... Lancaster Review [*Pennsylvania*] [*A publication*] (DLA)
LANCS .... Lancashire [*County in England*]
LAND .... Land [*Postal Service standard*] (OPSA)
LAND .... Landair Services [*NASDAQ symbol*] (SAG)

LAND .... League Against Nuclear Dangers [*Defunct*] (EA)
LAND .... Local Access Network Directory [*Frye Computer Systems*] [*Telecommunications*] (PCM)
LANDA .... Ladies Auxiliary to the National Dental Association [*Later, ANDA*] (EA)
LANDA .... LAN [*Local Area Network*] Dealers Association (CDE)
L & A .... Landing and Ascent [*NASA*]
L & A .... Leembruggen and Asirvatham's Appeal Court Reports [*Ceylon*] [*A publication*] (DLA)
L & A .... Light and Accommodation [*Optometry*]
L & A .... Light and Accommodation [*Ophthalmology*] (DAVI)
L & A .... Living and Active (DAVI)
L & A .... Louisiana & Arkansas Railway Co.
LANDAC ...... Land Development Accounting System (MHDB)
Landair .... Landair Services [*Associated Press*] (SAG)
Landauer ..... Landauer, Inc. [*Associated Press*] (SAG)
L & B .... Leadam and Baldwin's Select Cases before the King's Council [*England*] [*A publication*] (DLA)
L & B .... Left and Below [*Medicine*]
L & B .... Lothians and Border Horse [*British military*] (DMA)
L & Bank ..... Lawyer and Banker [*A publication*] (DLA)
L & B Bull ... Daily Law and Bank Bulletin [*Ohio*] [*A publication*] (DLA)
L & B Fin..... L & B Financial, Inc. [*Associated Press*] (SAG)
L & B Ins Dig... Littleton and Blatchley's Insurance Digest [*A publication*] (DLA)
LandBnc ...... Landmark Bancshares [*Associated Press*] (SAG)
L & B Prec... Leake and Bullen's Precedents of Pleading [*A publication*] (DLA)
L & BR .... London & Blackwall Railway [*British*] (ROG)
L & C .... Laboratory and Checkout (NASA)
L & C .... Lefroy and Cassel's Practice Cases [*1881-83*] [*Ontario*] [*A publication*] (ILCA)
L & C .... Leigh and Cave's English Crown Cases Reserved [*1861-65*] [*A publication*] (DLA)
L & CCC ..... Leigh and Cave's English Crown Cases Reserved [*1861-65*] [*A publication*] (DLA)
LANDCENT... Allied Land Forces Central Europe [*NATO*]
L & CM .... Lime and Cement Mortar (DAC)
L & Comm... Law and Communication [*A publication*] (DLA)
Land Comp Rep... Land Reports, by Roche, Dillon, and Kehoe [*1881-82*] [*Ireland*] [*A publication*] (DLA)
L & Computer Tech... Law and Computer Technology [*A publication*] (DLA)
Land Com Rep... Land Reports, by Roche, Dillon, and Kehoe [*1881-82*] [*Ireland*] [*A publication*] (DLA)
L & CONTEM PROB... Law and Contemporary Problems [*A publication*] (LWAP)
LANDCRA .... Landing Craft and Bases [*Military*] (AFIT)
LANDCRAB... Landing Craft and Bases [*Military*] (AABC)
L & D .... Labor and Delivery [*Area of a hospital*]
L & D .... Landing and Deceleration [*NASA*] (NASA)
L & D .... Loans and Discounts [*Banking*]
L & D .... Loss and Damage
L & D Conv... Leigh and Dalzell. Conversion of Property [*1825*] [*A publication*] (DLA)
Land Dec ... Land Decisions, United States [*A publication*] (DLA)
L & E .... English Law and Equity Reports [*American Reprint*] [*A publication*] (DLA)
LANDENMARK... Allied Land Forces Denmark [*NATO*]
L & Eq Rep... Law and Equity Reporter [*United States*] [*A publication*] (DLA)
L & E Rep ... English Law and Equity Reports [*American Reprint*] [*A publication*] (DLA)
Land Est C... Landed Estates Court [*England*] (DLA)
LANDEX ...... Landing Exercise [*Navy*] (CAAL)
LANDFAE ..... Large Area Nozzle Delivery of Fuel Air Explosive (RDA)
LANDFOR .... Landing Force [*Military*]
LANDFORASCU... Landing Force Air Support Control Unit [*Navy*]
L & G Temp Plunk... Lloyd and Goold's Irish Chancery Reports Tempore Plunkett [*A publication*] (DLA)
L & G Temp Sugd... Lloyd and Goold's Irish Chancery Reports Tempore Sugden [*1835*] [*A publication*] (DLA)
L & GTP ...... Lloyd and Goold's Irish Chancery Reports Tempore Plunkett [*A publication*] (DLA)
L & GT Plunk... Lloyd and Goold's Irish Chancery Reports Tempore Plunkett [*A publication*] (DLA)
L & GTS ...... Lloyd and Goold's Irish Chancery Reports Tempore Sugden [*1835*] [*A publication*] (DLA)
L & GT Sug... Lloyd and Goold's Irish Chancery Reports Tempore Sugden [*1835*] [*A publication*] (DLA)
L & H .... Lamport & Holt Line [*Steamship*] (MHDB)
L & H .... Laurel and Hardy [*The film comedy team of Stan Laurel and Oliver Hardy*]
L&H .... Lernout & Hauspie [*A speech products manufacturer*] (PCM)
L & HR .... [*The*] Lehigh & Hudson River Railway Co. [*Absorbed into Consolidated Rail Corp.*]
L & HTC ...... Line and Halftone Combined [*Illustration*] (DGA)
L & I .... Launch and Impact (AFM)
L&I............ Liver and Iron (DMAA)
L & ID .... London and India Docks [*Shipping*] [*British*] (ROG)
LANDING ..... Landing [*Commonly used*] (OPSA)
LANDIS .... Low-Approach Navigation Director System [*Aircraft landing aid*] [*Air Force*]
L & J Tr Mar... Ludlow and Jenkyns on the Law of Trade-Marks [*A publication*] (DLA)
LANDJUT..... Allied Land Forces Schleswig-Holstein and Jutland [*NATO*] (NATG)
L & K .... Love and Kisses [*Correspondence*]
L & L .... Latch and Lock (DAC)
L & L .... Leave and Liberty (WDAA)
L & L .... Legislative and Liaison [*Military*]

L&L............ Lerner and Loewe [*Composers*]
L & L .... Lewd and Lascivious
L & L .... Love and Liquor (IIA)
L&L............ Lyrics and Lyricists [*Long running New York show*]
L & LC........ Leeds and Liverpool Canal [*Shipping*] [*British*] (ROG)
L & LC........ Lift and Lift Cruise (MCD)
LANDLD....... Landlord (ROG)
L & Leg GDR... Law and Legislation in the German Democratic Republic [*A publication*] (DLA)
L & Legis in GDR... Law and Legislation in the German Democratic Republic [*A publication*] (DLA)
L & LeM...... Leigh and Le Marchant. Elections [*4th ed.*] [*1885*] [*A publication*] (DLA)
L & Lib....... Law and Liberty [*A publication*] (DLA)
L & M .... Labor and Material Bond
L & M .... Layout and Manuscript [*Advertising*] (WDMC)
L&M.......... Layout and Manuscript [*Publishing*] (WDMC)
L & M .... Legal and Magnanimous Side [*Sarcastic reference to the government of Vietnam and its allies*] (VNW)
L & M .... [*The*] Librarian and the Machine [*A publication*]
L & M .... Lowndes and Maxwell's English Practice Cases [*1852-54*] [*A publication*] (DLA)
L & N .... Louisville & Nashville Railroad Co.
L & NE........ Lehigh & New England Railway Co. [*Absorbed into Consolidated Rail Corp.*]
LANDNON.... Allied Land Forces North Norway [*NATO*] (NATG)
LANDNORTH... Allied Land Forces Northern Europe [*NATO*] (NATG)
LANDNORWAY... Allied Land Forces Norway [*NATO*]
L & NRR...... Louisville & Nashville Railroad Co.
L & OD .... Lester & Orpen Dennys [*Canadian publisher*]
L & Order ... Law and Order [*A publication*] (DLA)
L & P.......... Latch and Plaster (DAC)
L & P.......... Lighting and Power
L & PA .... Lodging and Pay Allowance [*British military*] (DMA)
L & PP........ Lunar and Planetary Program
L & Psychology Rev... Law and Psychology Review [*A publication*] (DLA)
L & Psych Rev... Law and Psychology Review [*A publication*] (DLA)
L & R.......... Lake and Rail
L & R.......... Landing and Recovery (KSC)
L & R.......... Larceny and Receiving
L & R.......... Left and Right
L & R.......... Loring and Russell's Election Cases in Massachusetts [*A publication*] (DLA)
L & R Election Cases... Loring and Russell's Election Cases in Massachusetts [*A publication*] (DLA)
Landrys....... Landrys Seafood Restaurants, Inc. [*Associated Press*] (SAG)
L & S.......... Launch and Servicing (AAG)
L & S.......... Laurinburg & Southern Railroad Co. (IIA)
L & S.......... Laverne and Shirley [*Television program*]
L & S.......... Logistics and Support (NASA)
LANDSAT..... Land Remote Sensing Satellite System (GFGA)
LANDSAT..... Land Satellite (USDC)
LANDSAT..... Land Satellite [*Marine science*] (OSRA)
LANDSC....... Landscape
LANDSCPG... Landscaping
LandsE........ Land's End, Inc. [*Associated Press*] (SAG)
LANDSONOR... Allied Land Forces South Norway [*NATO*] (NATG)
LANDSOUTH... Allied Land Forces Southern Europe [*NATO*]
LANDSOUTHEAST... Allied Land Forces Southeastern Europe [*NATO*]
Landstr........ Landstar Systems, Inc. [*Associated Press*] (SAG)
L & SWR ..... London & South-Western Railway (ROG)
L & T.......... Laboratories and Test (NASA)
L & T.......... Landlord and Tenant [*A publication*] (DLA)
L & T.......... Line and Terminal [*Telecommunications*] (TEL)
L & T.......... Longfield and Townsend's Irish Exchequer Reports [*1841-42*] [*A publication*] (DLA)
L & TH........ Lethality and Target Hardening [*Military*] (SDI)
L & U.......... Loading and Unloading
L & U.......... Lower and Upper [*Anatomy*]
LANDUP....... Alberta Land Use Planning Data Bank [*Alberta Municipal Affairs*] [*Information service or system Defunct*] (IID)
Land U Pl Rep... Land Use Planning Reports [*A publication*] (DLA)
Land Use & Env't L Rev... Land Use and Environment Law Review [*A publication*] (DLA)
L & W.......... Living and Well
L & W.......... Lloyd and Welsby's English Commercial and Mercantile Cases [*1829-30*] [*A publication*] (DLA)
L & Welsb... Lloyd and Welsby's English Commercial and Mercantile Cases [*1829-30*] [*A publication*] (DLA)
LANDZEALAND... Allied Land Forces Zealand [*NATO*] (NATG)
LANE.......... Lane [*Commonly used*] (OPSA)
Lane .... Lane's English Exchequer Reports [*1605-12*] [*A publication*] (DLA)
LANE.......... Local Area Network Emulation [*Telecommunications*] (ACRL)
LANES .... Lane [*Commonly used*] (OPSA)
LANFORTRACOMLANT... Landing Force Training Command, Atlantic [*Navy*]
LANFORTRAU... Landing Force Training Unit [*Marine Corps*] (DNAB)
LANG.......... Langley [*England*]
LANG.......... Language (AFM)
LANG.......... Language
Lang Ca Cont... Langdell's Cases on Contracts [*A publication*] (DLA)
Lang Ca Sales... Langdell's Cases on the Law of Sales [*A publication*] (DLA)
Lang Cont... Langdell's Cases on Contracts [*A publication*] (DLA)
Lang Cont... Langdell's Summary of the Law of Contracts [*A publication*] (DLA)
Langd Cont... Langdell's Cases on Contracts [*A publication*] (DLA)
Langd Cont... Langdell's Summary of the Law of Contracts [*A publication*] (DLA)

Lang Eq Pl... Langdell's Cases in Equity Pleading [*A publication*] (DLA)
Lang Eq Pl... Langdell's Summary of Equity Pleading [*A publication*] (DLA)
Langer......... [*The*] Langer Biomechanics Group, Inc. [*Associated Press*] (SAG)
Lang Sales... Langdell's Cases on the Law of Sales [*A publication*] (DLA)
Lang Soc .... Language in Society [*A publication*] (BRI)
Lang Sum Cont... Langdell's Summary of the Law of Contracts [*A publication*] (DLA)
Lang Tr........ Langley's Trustees' Act [*A publication*] (DLA)
LANH .... Launch (MSA)
LANIC .... LAN [*Local Area Network*] Interface Card (PCM)
LANICA .... Lineas Aereas de Nicaragua, SA [*Nicaraguan airline*]
LANL......... Los Alamos National Laboratory [*Los Alamos, NM*] [*Department of Energy*]
L Ann.......... Louisiana Annual Reports [*A publication*] (DLA)
Lannet .... Lannet Data Communictions Ltd. [*Associated Press*] (SAG)
LANNET ...... Large Artificial Nerve [*or Neuron*] Network
Lanoptic ..... Lanoptics Ltd. [*Associated Press*] (SAG)
LAnP .... Louisiana State Penitentiary, Angola, LA [*Library symbol Library of Congress*] (LCLS)
LANP .... Plaintree Systems Inc. [*NASDAQ symbol*] (SAG)
LAN/PDL ..... Local Area Network / Program Design Language (LAIN)
LANPF .... Plaintree Systems [*NASDAQ symbol*] (TTSB)
LANRES ...... Linked Access Network Resource Extension and Service
LAN/RM ...... Local Area Network Reference Model
Lans .... Lansing's New York Supreme Court Reports [*A publication*] (DLA)
LANS .... Large Atypical Nevus Syndrome [*Medicine*]
LANS .... Lightweight Airborne Navigation System (MCD)
LANS .... Local Area Network System [*Telecommunications*]
LANS .... LORAN Airborne Navigation System (IEEE)
LANSA .... Lineas Aereas Nacionales Consolidadas Sociedad Anonima
LANSCE ...... Los Alamos Neutron Scattering Center
Lans Ch ...... Lansing's Select Cases in Chancery [*1824, 1826*] [*New York*] [*A publication*] (DLA)
Lansg......... New York Supreme Court Reports (Lansing) [*A publication*] (DLA)
LANSHIPRON... Landing Ship Squadron (CINC)
Lansing....... New York Supreme Court Reports (Lansing) [*A publication*] (DLA)
LANSL .... Los Alamos National Scientific Laboratories [*New Mexico*]
Lans Sel Cas... Lansing's Select Cases in Chancery [*1824, 1826*] [*New York*] [*A publication*] (DLA)
LANSW .... Laryngectomee Association of New South Wales [*Australia*]
LANSW .... Legislative Assembly of New South Wales [*Australia*]
LANSW .... Lupus Association of New South Wales [*Australia*]
LANT .... Atlantic
LANT........... Lannet Data Communications Ltd. [*NASDAQ symbol*] (SAG)
LANT........... Legislative Assembly of the Northern Territory [*Australia*]
LANTCOM .... Atlantic Command [*Navy*]
LANTCOMINSGEN... Atlantic Command Inspector General (DNAB)
LANTCOMMBPO... Atlantic Command Military Blood Program Office (DNAB)
LANTCOMOPCONCEN... Atlantic [*Fleet*] Commander Operational Control Center [*Navy*]
LANTCOMOPSUPPFAC... Atlantic Command Operations Support Facility (DNAB)
LANTFAP ..... Allied Command Atlantic Frequency Allocation Panel [*Obsolete NATO*] (NATG)
LANTFAST ... Atlantic Forward Area Support Team [*Military*] (DNAB)
LANTFLEASWTACSCOL... Atlantic Fleet Antisubmarine Warfare Tactical School [*Navy*]
LANTFLT...... Atlantic Fleet
LANTFLTHEDSUPPACT... Atlantic Fleet Headquarters Support Activity [*Navy*] (DNAB)
LANTFLTMATCONOFF... Atlantic Fleet Material Control Office [*Navy*] (DNAB)
LANTFLTPEB... Atlantic Fleet Propulsion Examining Board [*Navy*] (DNAB)
LANTFLTRANSUPPFAC... Atlantic Fleet Training Support Facilities
LANTFLTWPNRAN... Atlantic Fleet Weapons Range [*Later, AFRSF*] [*Navy*]
LANTFLTWPNTRAFAC... Atlantic Fleet Weapons Training Facility [*Navy*] (DNAB)
L Anti.......... Antilles (VRA)
L Anti.......... Lesser Antilles (VRA)
LANTICOMIS... LANTCOM Integrated Command and Control Management Information System (MCD)
LANTINTCEN... Atlantic Intelligence Center [*Navy*]
LANTIRN...... Low-Altitude Navigation and Targeting Infrared [*System*] for Night [*Aviation*]
LANTMS ...... Linked Access Network Transport Management System [*Telecommunications*]
LANTNAVFACENGCOM... Atlantic Division Naval Facilities Engineering Command
LANTOPS..... Atlantic Operations Supply Facilities (MCD)
LANTOPSSUPFAC... Atlantic Operations Supply Facilities
LANTREADEX... Atlantic Readiness Exercise (MCD)
LANTREPCNAVRES... Atlantic Fleet Chief of Naval Reserve Representative (DNAB)
LANTREPCOMNAVSURFRES... Atlantic Representative for Commander Naval Surface Reserve Force (DNAB)
LANTRESFLT... Atlantic Reserve Fleet
LANTSAR..... Atlantic International Air and Surface Search and Rescue Seminar (PDAA)
LANTSOC..... Atlantic Fleet Signals Security Operations Center [*Navy*] (DNAB)
LANTWWMCCS... Atlantic Fleet Worldwide Military Command Control System [*Navy*] (DNAB)
LANV .... LanVision Systems [*NASDAQ symbol*] (TTSB)
LANV .... Left Atrial Neovascularization [*Cardiology*] (DAVI)
LANX .... Local Area Network Exchange
LANZ .... Lancer Orthodontics [*NASDAQ symbol*] (TTSB)
LANZ .... Lancer Orthodontics, Inc. [*NASDAQ symbol*] (SAG)
lao .... Lao [*MARC language code Library of Congress*] (LCCP)
LAO........... Laoag [*Philippines*] [*Airport symbol*] (OAG)
LAO........... Lao Aviaton [*Laos*] [*ICAO designator*] (FAAC)

LAO........... Laos [*or Lao People's Democratic Republic*] [*ANSI three-letter standard code*] (CNC)
LAO............. Large Assembly Order (MCD)
LAO............. Lasa Array [*Montana*] [*Seismograph station code, US Geological Survey*] (SEIS)
LAO............. La Teko Resources Ltd. [*Vancouver Stock Exchange symbol*]
LAO............. Lead Agency Official (MHDB)
LAO............. Left Anterior Oblique [*Cardiology*]
LAO............. Left Anterior Occipital [*Position*] [*Obstetrics*] (DAVI)
LAO............. Left Atrial Overloading [*Cardiology*] (DAVI)
LAO............. Legal Aid Office
LAO............. Legal Assistance Officer
LAO............. Licensing Authorities Office
LAO............. Licentiate in Obstectric Science (DAVI)
LAO............. Licentiate of the Art of Obstetrics [*British*]
LAO............. Logistics Area Officer (MCD)
LAO............. Logistics Assistance Office [*or Officer*] [*Army Materiel Command*]
LAOAR .... Latin American Office of Aerospace Research [*Air Force*]
LAOCIF .... Logistic Assistance Office Command Interest Flasher [*Military*] (AABC)
LAOCP .... Limited Amateur Operator's Certificate of Proficiency [*Radio*]
LAOD .... Los Angeles Ordnance District [*Military*] (AAG)
LAOOC .... Los Angeles Olympic Organizing Committee (EA)
LAOR .... La Teko Resources Ltd. [*NASDAQ symbol*] (SAG)
LAORF .... La Teko Resources Ltd [*NASDAQ symbol*] (TTSB)
LAOS .... Laymen's Overseas Service [*Acronym is now used as official name of the organization*]
LAOSA .... Librarianship and Archives Old Students' Association (DGA)
LAOSC .... Local Authorities Ordnance Survey Committee [*British*]
LAP............. Laboratory Accreditation Program [*Department of Commerce*]
LAP............. Laboratory of Advertising Performance [*McGraw-Hill*]
LAP............. Laboratory of Architecture and Planning [*Massachusetts Institute of Technology*] [*Research center*] (RCD)
LAP............. Lakewood Public Library, Lakewood, OH [*OCLC symbol*] (OCLC)
lap............. Laparoscopy [*Medicine*]
LAP............. Laparotomy [*Medicine*]
LAP............. Laparotomy [*Sponges*] (DAVI)
LAP............. La Paz [*Mexico*] [*Seismograph station code, US Geological Survey*] (SEIS)
LAP............. La Paz [*Mexico*] [*Airport symbol*] (OAG)
LAP............. Lapland
lap............. Lapp [*MARC language code Library of Congress*] (LCCP)
Lap............. Lapus de Castiglionchio [*Flourished, 1353-81*] [*Authority cited in pre-1607 legal work*] (DSA)
LAP............. Large Area Panel
LAP............. Large-Area Processing [*For fabricating multichip modules*]
LAP............. Latin American Parliament [*See also PLA*] [*Colombia*] (EAIO)
LAP............. Lattice Assessment Program [*Civil Defense*]
LAP............. Launch Analyst Panel [*Aerospace*] (AAG)
LAP............. Learning Accomplishment Profile [*Psychology*]
LAP............. Learning Activity Package (EDAC)
LAP............. Learning Activity Packet (AEE)
LAP............. Leased Attached Pallet (SSD)
LAP............. Left Arterial Pressure [*Cardiology*] (DAVI)
LAP............. Left Atrial Pressure [*Cardiology*]
LAP............. Lesson Assembly Program (IEEE)
LAP............. Lethality Assessment Program
LAP............. Leucine Aminopeptidase [*Also, LA, LP*] [*An enzyme*]
LAP............. Leukocyte Alkaline Phosphatase [*An enzyme*]
LAP............. Liberation Action Party [*Trinidad and Tobago*] [*Political party*] (PPW)
LAP............. Library Access Program
LAP............. Library Awareness Program [*FBI*]
LAP............. Line Access Point [*Telecommunications*] (TEL)
LAP............. Linear Arithmetic Processor (IAA)
LAP............. Lineas Aereas Paraguayas [*Paraguay*] [*ICAO designator*] (FAAC)
LAP............. Lingual Antimicrobial Peptide [*Biochemistry*]
LAP............. Lingual Antimicrobial Peptide [*Medicine*]
LAP............. Link Access Procedure [*Telecommunications*] (TEL)
LAP............. Link Access Protocol [*Telecommunications*]
LAP............. List Assembly Programming [*Computer science*]
LAP............. Load, Assemble, Pack [*Army*] (AABC)
LAP............. Loading Assembling and Packing
LAP............. Local Access Port [*Telecommunications*] (ACRL)
LAP............. Local Analysis and Prediction [*Branch*] (USDC)
LAP............. Local Analysis and Prediction [*Marine science*] (OSRA)
LAP............. Location Audit Program [*Navy*] (NG)
LAP............. Logistics Assistance Program
LAP............. Loide Aereo Nacional, SA [*Brazilian airline*]
LAP............. London Airport
LAP............. Lord's Acre Plan (EA)
LAP............. Loudspeaker Acoustical Phase-Inverter
L Ap............ Louisiana Courts of Appeal Reports [*A publication*] (DLA)
LAP............. Low Achievers Project [*Education*] (AIE)
LAP............. Low-Altitude Penetration
LAP............. Low-Altitude Performance
LAP............. Low Atmospheric Pressure (DAVI)
LAP............. Lyophilized Anterior Pituitary [*Endocrinology*]
LAPA .... Latin America Parents Association (EA)
LAPA .... Leukocyte Alkaline Phosphatase Activity [*Biochemistry*]
LAPA .... Lightweight Aggregate Producers Association (EA)
LAPA .... Los Angeles Procurement Agency [*Army*]
LAPAC .... Life Amendment Political Action Committee [*Defunct*] (EA)
LaPac .... Louisiana-Pacific Corp. [*Associated Press*] (SAG)
LAPADS .... Lightweight Acoustic Processing and Display System [*British military*] (DMA)

LAPAM.........	Low-Altitude Penetrating Attack Missile [*Proposed*]
LAPAR.........	Large Phased-Array RADAR
LAPB...........	Laboratories' Applied Physiology Branch [*Army*]
LAPB...........	Link Access Procedure [*or Protocol*] Balanced [*Telecommunications*]
LAPB...........	Link Access Protocol, B Channel [*Telecommunications*]
LAPC...........	Landmarks of American Popular Culture [*A publication*]
LAPC...........	Los Angeles Pacific College [*California*]
LAPD...........	Limited Axial Power Distribution (IEEE)
LAPD...........	Link Access Procedure-D [*Telecommunications*] (DOM)
LAPD...........	Link Access Protocol, D Channel [*Telecommunications*]
LAPD...........	Los Angeles Air Procurement District
Lap Dec.......	Laperriere's Speaker's Decisions [*Canada*] [*A publication*] (DLA)
LAPDOG......	Low-Altitude Pursuit Dive on Ground (MCD)
LAPDRY......	Lapidary
LAPE..........	Lineas Aereas Postales Espanoles [*Airline*] [*Spain*]
LAPERS.......	Labor and Production Effectiveness Reporting System [*DoD*]
LAPES........	Low-Altitude Parachute Extraction System [*Military*]
LAPF...........	Link Access Procedure to Frame Mode Bearer Services [*Telecommunications*] (ACRL)
LAPFO.........	Los Angeles Procurement Field Office
LAPH	Lithium Aluminum Pentahydride (MCD)
lapid	Lapideum [*Stony*] [*Latin*] (MAE)
LAPIS.........	LASER Photoionization Spectroscopy
LAPIS.........	Legislative Authorization Program Information System [*General Accounting Office*] [*Defunct*] (IID)
LAPIS.........	Local Automated Personnel Information System (DNAB)
LAPL..........	Lead Allowance Parts List
LAPL..........	Library Association Publishing Ltd. [*British*]
LAPL..........	Los Angeles Public Library
LaPL..........	Louisiana Power & Light Co. [*Associated Press*] (SAG)
LAPLS........	Lead Allowance Parts List System (DNAB)
LAPM.........	Last Premidcourse Orbit
LAPM.........	Link Access Procedure for MODEMs [*Communications protocol*] [*Computer science*] (PCM)
LAPMS........	Latin American Paper Money Society (EA)
LAPMS........	Long Arm Posterior Molded Splint [*Medicine*] (MEDA)
LAPOCA	L-Asparaginase, Prednisone, Oncovin [*Vincristine*], Cytarabine, Adriamycin [*Antineoplastic drug regimen*]
LAPP..........	Lappish [*Language, etc.*] (ROG)
LAPP..........	Lower Achieving Pupils Project [*British*]
LAPPES.......	Large Power Plant Effluent Study (NRCH)
Lappie	Live-Alone Person [*Lifestyle classification*]
LAPR	Life Assurance Premium Relief [*Business term*]
LAPR..........	Los Alamos Power Reactor
LAPRE	Los Alamos Power Reactor Experiment
LAPS.........	LASER Profile System
LAPS..........	Latin American Philatelic Society (EA)
LAPS.........	Latin American, Portuguese, and Spanish [*Division*] [*Library of Congress*]
LAPS.........	Launcher Avionics Packages (MCD)
LAPS..........	Left Aft Propulsion System [*or Subsystem*] (NASA)
LAPS..........	Light-Addressable Potentiometric Sensor [*Semiconductor*]
LAPS.........	Literary, Artistic, Political, or Scientific [*Value*] [*In obscenity law, a criterion established by the 1973 case of Miller Versus California*]
LAPS..........	Loan Application Processing System
LAPS..........	Local Analysis and Prediction System [*Marine science*] (OSRA)
LAPS..........	Local Analysis and Prediction System (USDC)
LAPS..........	Louis-Allen Power Supply
LAPS..........	Lovelace Aerosol Particle Separator [*Lovelace Foundation for Medical Education and Research*] (PDAA)
LAPS..........	Low-Altitude Proximity Sensor (MCD)
LAPS..........	Low Attaining Pupils in Secondary Schools (AIE)
LAPSA	Lineas Aereas Paraguayas Sociedad Anonima [*Airline*] [*Paraguay*]
LAPSE	Longterm Ambulatory Physiological Surveillance Equipment (PDAA)
LAPSS	LASER Airborne Photographic Scanning System [*Navy*]
LAPSS	Low-Angle Polycrystalline Silicon Sheet [*Photovoltaic energy systems*]
LAPT..........	Library Acquisitions: Practice and Theory [*A publication*]
LAPT..........	Local Apparent Time (MSA)
LAPT..........	Los Angeles Union Passenger Terminal [*AAR code*]
LAPUT	Light-Activated Programmable Unijunction Transistor
LAPW.........	Left Atrial Posterior Wall [*Cardiology*] (DAVI)
LAPW.........	Linear Augmented Plane-Wave [*Physics*]
LAPW.........	Linearized Augmented Plane Wave [*Physical chemistry*]
LAPX..........	Link Access Procedure Half-Duplex [*Telecommunications*] (ACRL)
LAQ...........	Al Bayda [*Libya*] [*Airport symbol*] (AD)
LAQ...........	Beida [*Libya*] [*Airport symbol*] (OAG)
LAQ...........	Lacquer (KSC)
LAQ...........	Latin America Equity Fd [*NYSE symbol*] (TTSB)
LAQ...........	Latin America Equity Fund [*NYSE symbol*] (SPSG)
LAQ...........	Leathercrafters' Association of Queensland [*Australia*]
LAQ...........	Lebanese Air Transport [*ICAO designator*] (FAAC)
LAQ...........	Legislative Assembly of Queensland [*Australia*]
L'AQORCD ..	L'Association Quebecoise des Organismes Regionaux de Concertation et de Developpement (AC)
LAQT..........	Low-Altitude Qualification Test [*Balloon*]
LaQuinta......	La Quinta Motor Inns Ltd. [*Associated Press*] (SAG)
LAR...........	Labor Arbitration Reports [*Bureau of National Affairs*] [*A publication*] (DLA)
LAR...........	Land Registry [*British*]
LAR...........	Laramie [*Wyoming*] [*Seismograph station code, US Geological Survey*] (SEIS)
LAR...........	Laramie [*Wyoming*] [*Airport symbol*] (OAG)
LAR...........	Laramie, WY [*Location identifier FAA*] (FAAL)
LAR...........	Larceny [*Legal shorthand*] (LWAP)

LAR...........	Lariat Oil & Gas Ltd. [*Toronto Stock Exchange symbol*]
LAR...........	Laryngology
lar............	Larynx [*Anatomy*] (DAVI)
LAR...........	LASER-Aided Rocket (MCD)
LAR...........	Late Asthmatic Response [*Medicine*] (DAVI)
LAR...........	Late Reaction [*Medicine*] (DMAA)
LAR...........	Launch Acceptability Region (MCD)
LAR...........	Launch Alert Receiver (DNAB)
LAR...........	Launcher Adapter Rail (MCD)
LAR...........	Lawrence Aviation, Inc. [*ICAO designator*] (FAAC)
LAR...........	Leaf Area Ratio [*Botany*]
LAR...........	Leaflet Artillery Round [*PSYOP*] (RDA)
LAR...........	Left Arm Reclining [*or Recumbent*] [*Medicine*]
LAR...........	Leukocyte Adhesion Receptor [*Immunology*]
LAR...........	Leukocyte Antigen-Related [*Medicine*] (DMAA)
LAR...........	Library Association Record [*A publication*] (BRI)
LAR...........	Life Assurance Relief [*British*]
LAR...........	Light Artillery Rocket (MCD)
LAR...........	Light Attendant Station [*Coast Guard*]
LAR...........	Limit Address Register [*Computer science*]
LAR...........	Linhas Aereas Regionais SA [*Portugal ICAO designator*] (FAAC)
LAR...........	Liquid Air Rocket
LAR...........	Local Acquisition RADAR (CET)
LAR...........	Locus Activation Region [*Genetics*]
LAR...........	Logistics Assistance Representative [*Army*] (DOMA)
LAR...........	Loita Armada Revolucionaria [*Armed Revolutionary Struggle*] [*Spain*] (PD)
LAR...........	Long-Range Aircraft Rocket (NG)
LAR...........	Long-Range Assessments and Research [*Program*] [*Department of State*] [*Washington, DC*]
L-Ar...........	Louisiana Department of State, State Archives and Records, Baton Rouge, LA [*Library symbol Library of Congress*] (LCLS)
LA R	Louisiana Reports [*A publication*] (DLA)
LAR...........	Low-Altitude Release
LAR...........	Low-Angle Reentry [*Aerospace*] (MCD)
LAR...........	Low-Aspect Ratio
LARA.........	Latin American Railways Association (EA)
LARA.........	Light Armed Reconnaissance Aircraft [*Air Force*]
LARA.........	Low-Altitude RADAR Altimeter [*Air Force*]
LARAM	Line Addressable Random Access Memory [*Computer science*] (MDG)
LArB..........	Bienville Parish Library, Arcadia, LA [*Library symbol Library of Congress*] (LCLS)
LArbG	Landesarbeitsgericht [*Provincial Labor Court of Appeal*] [*German*] (ILCA)
LARC	Association for Library Automation Research Communications (EA)
LARC	Lambda Amateur Radio Club (EA)
LARC	Langley Research Center [*NASA*]
LARC	Larceny [*FBI standardized term*]
LARC	Large Automatic Research Computer [*or Calculator*]
LARC	LASER-Activated Recession Compensator (MCD)
LARC	LASER Applications Research Center (RCD)
LARC	Legal Aid Review Committee
LARC	Leukocyte Automatic Recognition Computer [*Blood counting*]
LARC	Library Automation Research and Consulting Association (NITA)
LARC	Library Automation Research and Consulting Services (IAA)
LARC	Libyan-American Reconstruction Commission
LARC	Light Amphibious Resupply Craft
LARC	Lighter, Amphibious, Resupply, Cargo [*Vessel*]
LARC	Lindheimer Astronomical Research Center [*Northwestern University*]
LARC	Livermore Atomic Research Computer
LARC	Local Alcoholism Reception Center
LARC	Locally Assigned Reporting Code [*Munitions reports*] (AFM)
LARC	Loose Actors Revolving Company [*for producing plays; members include actors George C. Scott and Rod Steiger*]
LARC	Low-Altitude Ride Control [*Shock-absorbing system*] [*Aviation*] (MCD)
LARC	Regional Conference for Latin America [*UN Food and Agriculture Organization*]
LARCCH......	Latin America Resource Center and Clearinghouse [*Defunct*] (EA)
LARCF	Lithuanian American Roman Catholic Federation (EA)
LARCT	Last Radio Contact [*Aviation*]
LARC-V.......	Lighter, Amphibious, Resupply, Cargo-Five Ton [*Vessel*] (DNAB)
LARD.........	Load Adjuster Reference Datum (IAA)
LarDav........	Larson-Davis [*Associated Press*] (SAG)
LARDS........	Low-Accuracy RADAR Data Transmission System
LARE.........	Local Asymptotic Relative Efficiency [*Statistics*]
LAREHS	Laboratory of Research in Human and Social Ecology [*University of Quebec at Montreal*] [*Canada Research center*] (RCD)
LA Rep	Louisiana Reports [*A publication*] (DLA)
LA Rev Stat Ann (West)...	West's Louisiana Revised Statutes, Annotated [*A publication*] (DLA)
LARF.........	Lebanese Armed Revolutionary Faction
LARF.........	Low-Altitude RADAR Fuzing (CET)
LARG.........	Largamente [*Easily*] [*Music*]
LARG.........	Largo [*Very Slow*] [*Music*] (ROG)
LARG.........	Library-Anthropology Resource Group
LARGO........	Larghetto [*Slow*] [*Music*] (ROG)
LARGOS.......	LASER-Activated Reflecting Geodetic Optical Satellite
LARIA........	Local Authorities Research and Intelligence Association [*British*]
LARIAT	LASER RADAR Intelligence Acquisition Technology
LARIAT	Long-Range Area RADAR for Intrusion Detection and Tracking
LARIS.........	Low-Altitude RADAR Interface System (MCD)
Larizz.........	Larizza Industries, Inc. [*Associated Press*] (SAG)
LARK	Landmark Bancshares [*NASDAQ symbol*] (SAG)
LARK	Landmark Bancshares [*NASDAQ symbol*] (TTSB)

LARL............	Laurel Cap Group [*NASDAQ symbol*] (TTSB)
LARL............	Laurel Capital Group [*NASDAQ symbol*] (SAG)
LARM..........	Logistics Assets Requirements Model (PDAA)
LARM..........	Low-Angle Re-Entry Maneuvering Re-Entry Vehicle (PDAA)
LARMC........	Landstuhl Army Regional Medical Center [*Germany*]
LARO..........	Latin American Regional Office [*United Nations Food and Agricultural Organization*] (BARN)
LAROO........	Lackland Aircraft Reactors Operations Office (SAA)
LARP..........	Launch and Recovery Platform (DNAB)
LARP..........	Line Automatic Reperforator (CET)
LARP..........	Local and Remote Printing [*Computer science*]
LARP..........	Local Approvals Review Program
LARPS........	Local and Remote Printing Station [*Computer science*]
LARR..........	Large Area Record Reader (IAA)
LARR..........	Linear Accelerator Regenerator Reactor (BARN)
LARRL........	Fort Keogh Livestock and Range Research Laboratory [*Miles City, MT*] [*Department of Agriculture*] (GRD)
LARRS........	Livestock and Range Research Station [*Department of Agriculture*] (GRD)
LARRS........	Low-Altitude Retro Rocket System (DWSG)
LARS..........	Laboratory for Agricultural Remote Sensing
LARS..........	Laboratory for Applications of Remote Sensing [*Purdue University*] [*Research center*] (RCD)
LARS..........	Laminar Angular Rate Sensor [*Navy*]
LARS..........	Language-Structured Auditory Retention Span Test
LARS..........	Larscom Inc. [*NASDAQ symbol*] (SAG)
LARS..........	LASER-Aided Rocket System [*Military*] (CAAL)
LARS..........	LASER Angular Rate Sensor [*or Scanner*]
LARS..........	LASER-Articulated Robotic System
LARS..........	Launch and Recovery System [*NASA*]
LARS..........	Learning and Recognition System [*GTE*]
LARS..........	Left Add, Right Subtract [*Army field artillery technique*] (INF)
LARS..........	Leucyl-Transfer Ribonucleic Acid [*Biochemistry*] (DAVI)
LARS..........	Light Artillery Rocket System (NATG)
LARS..........	Living Aquatic Resources Sector [*Aquaculture*]
LARS..........	Low-Altitude RADAR System (NATG)
LARS..........	Lower Airspace RADAR Advisory Service [*British*] (DA)
LARS..........	Lower Atmosphere Research Satellite (SSD)
LARSA........	Latin American Rural Sociological Association (EAIO)
Larscom	Larscom Inc. [*Associated Press*] (SAG)
LARSI........	Laboratoire de Recherche en Sciences Immobilieres [*University of Quebec at Montreal*] [*Research center*] (RCD)
LA RSIS.......	LA Reference, Special and Information Section [*British*] (NITA)
LARSIS........	Library Association Reference and Special Information Section (PDAA)
LARSP........	Language Assessment Remediation and Screening Procedure [*for the language impaired*]
LARSSYAA..	Laboratory for Applications of Remote Sensing System for Aircraft Analysis [*NASA*] (GFGA)
LART............	Lateral Acceleration Response Time
LARV............	Low-Altitude Research Vehicle (IAA)
LARVA.........	Low-Altitude Research Vehicular Advancements
laryn...........	Laryngeal [*Otorhinolaryngology*] (DAVI)
laryn...........	Laryngitis [*Otorhinolaryngology*] (DAVI)
laryn...........	Laryngoscopy [*Otorhinolaryngology*] (DAVI)
Laryng.........	Laryngology
LARYNGLGST...	Laryngologist
LARYNGLGY...	Laryngology
Laryngol......	Laryngologist (DAVI)
LARYNGOL...	Laryngology
LAS.............	Almirall [*Spain*] [*Research code symbol*]
LAS.............	Label as Such [*Pharmacology*] (CDAI)
LAS.............	Labor Area Summary [*Employment and Training Administration*] [*Department of Labor*]
LAS.............	Laboratories of Applied Sciences [*University of Chicago*] (MCD)
LAS.............	Laboratory Automation System
LAS.............	Laboratory of Atmospheric Sciences [*National Science Foundation*]
LAS.............	Land Agents' Society [*British*] (DI)
LAS.............	Landing Approach Simulator
LAS.............	LANDSAT [*Land Remote Sensing Satellite System*] Sensor [*NASA*] (SSD)
LAS.............	Language Assessment Scales [*Test*]
LAS.............	Lapidus Airfloat System (DAVI)
LAS.............	Large Amplitude Simulator
LAS.............	Large Astronomical Satellite [*ESRO*]
LAS.............	Large-Probe Atmospheric Structure [*NASA*]
LAS.............	La Salle College, Philadelphia, PA [*OCLC symbol*] (OCLC)
LAS.............	LASER Absorption Spectrometer
LAS.............	LASER Antiflash System
LAS.............	LASER Attack System
LAS.............	Laser Indus Ltd, Ord [*AMEX symbol*] (TTSB)
LAS.............	Laser Industries Ltd. [*AMEX symbol*] (SPSG)
LAS.............	Las Vegas [*Nevada*] [*Airport symbol*] (OAG)
LAS.............	Las Vegas, NV [*Location identifier FAA*] (FAAL)
LAS.............	Launch Area Supervisor (AFM)
LAS.............	Launch Auxiliary System
las.............	Laxative [*Medicine*] (DAVI)
LAS.............	Laxative Abuse Syndrome [*Medicine*] (DAVI)
LAS.............	Leader Authenticity Scale [*Psychology*] (EDAC)
LAS.............	Leadership Appraisal Survey [*Interpersonal skills and attitudes test*]
LAS.............	League of Arab States [*Tunis, Tunisia*]
LAS.............	Lebanese-American Society of Greater New York [*Defunct*] (EA)
LAS.............	Left Anterior-Superior [*Anatomy*] (DAVI)
LAS.............	Left Arm Sitting [*Blood pressure and pulse measurement*] [*Cardiology*] (DAVI)
LAS.............	Legal Aid Society (WDAA)
LAS.............	Leipziger Aegyptologische Studien [*A publication*] (BJA)
LAS.............	Leucine Acetylsalicylate [*Biochemistry*] (DAVI)
LAS.............	Library Automation Services [*Oxford University*]
LAS.............	Life Assurance of Scotland [*Commercial firm*]
LAS.............	Light-Activated Switch
LAS.............	Lignes Aerienne Seychelles [*ICAO designator*] (FAAC)
LAS.............	Limited Assignment Status [*Military*]
LAS.............	Limited Assortment Store (WDMC)
LAS.............	Line Apparatus Shop [*Telecommunications*] (OA)
LAS.............	Linear Alkylbenzene Sulfonate [*Surfactant*]
LAS.............	Link Active Scheduler (ACII)
LAS.............	Litha-Alumina-Silicate [*Inorganic chemistry*]
LAS.............	Liturgical Arts Society (EA)
LAS.............	Local Adaptation Syndrome [*Medicine*]
LAS.............	Local Address Space
LAS.............	Local Alignment System [*Optics*]
LAS.............	Local Area Screening
LAS.............	Logical Address Strobe
LAS.............	Logical Compare Accumulator with Storage (SAA)
LAS.............	Logic Analysis System [*Rohde and Schwartz*] [*Germany*] (NITA)
LAS.............	London Appreciation Society
LAS.............	Long-Arm Splint [*Orthopedics*] (DAVI)
LAS.............	Longitudinal Air Spring
LAS.............	Long-Range Assistance Strategy (CINC)
LAS.............	Look-Out Aiming Sight [*Military*] (PDAA)
LAS.............	Loop Actuating Signal (SAA)
LAS.............	Lord Advocate of Scotland
LAS.............	Low Air Speed (MCD)
LAS.............	Low-Alloy Steel
LAS.............	Low-Altitude Satellite
LAS.............	Lower Abdominal Surgery (DAVI)
LAS.............	Lower Airspace (WDAA)
LAS.............	Lunar Alignment System [*Aerospace*]
LAS.............	Lutheran Academy for Scholarship [*Defunct*] (EA)
LAS.............	Lymphadenopathy Syndrome [*Medicine*]
LAS.............	Lysine Acetylsalicylate [*Biochemistry*]
LAS.............	McCarran International Airport [*FAA*] (TAG)
LAS.............	Saskatchewan Libraries Retrospective Conversion [*UTLAS symbol*]
LASA...........	Laboratory Animal Science Association [*British*]
LASA...........	Large Aperture Seismic Array [*Nuclear detection device*]
LASA...........	Large Area Solar Array
LASA...........	LASER Anti-Satellite Weapon (LAIN)
LASA...........	Latin American Studies Association (EA)
LA(SA).........	Latvian Association of South Australia
LASA...........	LIDAR [*Light Detection and Ranging*] Atmospheric Sounder and Altimeter
LASA...........	Linear-Analogue Self Assessment (DMAA)
LaSalle........	La Salle Re Holdings Ltd. [*Associated Press*] (SAG)
LASAM........	LASER Semiactive Missile
LASA-P........	Linear-Analogue Self-Assessment-Pristman (DMAA)
LASAR........	Logic Automated Stimulus and Response (MCD)
LASARS........	Low Probability of Intercept Antijam Secure Airborne Radio System (MCD)
LASAS.........	Latin American Secretariat for Academic Services [*Defunct*]
LASA-S........	Linear-Analogue Self-Assessment-Selby (DMAA)
LASB...........	Lackawaxen & Stourbridge Railroad Corp. [*AAR code*]
LASC...........	Light Armored Squad Carrier
LASCA.........	Large Area Solar Cell Array
LASCAR.......	Language for Simulation of Computer Architecture (CSR)
Lasc H War...	Lascelles' Horse Warranty [*2nd ed.*] [*1880*] [*A publication*] (DLA)
Lasc Juv Off...	Lascelles on Juvenile Offenders [*A publication*] (DLA)
LASCO........	Large Angle and Spectrometric Coronagraph Experiment [*For observation of the sun*]
LASCO........	Large-Angle Spectrometric Coronagraph [*Marine science*] (OSRA)
LASCO........	Large-Angle Spectrometric Coronagraph (USDC)
LASCO........	Large-Angle Spectroscopic Coronagraph [*Instrumentation*]
LASCO........	Latin America Science Cooperation Office (MSC)
LASCODOCS...	Linguistic Analysis of Spanish Colonial Documents
LASCOT.......	Large Screen Color Television System (NASA)
LASCR........	Light-Activated Silicon-Controlled Rectifier
LASCS.........	Light-Activated Silicon-Controlled Switch (MCD)
LASD...........	Labor Agreement Settlement Data [*Cast Metals Association*] [*A publication*]
LASD...........	Latin American Serial Documents
LASE...........	LAMPS Shipboard Element (MCD)
LASE...........	Large Aperture Seismic Experiment [*Geophysical survey*]
LASE...........	Laser Sight, Inc. [*NASDAQ symbol*] (SAG)
LASE...........	Lasersight Inc. [*NASDAQ symbol*] (TTSB)
L-Ase..........	L-Asparaginase [*Also, A, L, L-Asp, L-asnase*] [*An enzyme, an antineoplastic*]
LASE...........	LIDAR [*Light Detection and Ranging*] Atmosphere Sensing Experiment
LASE...........	Logistics Asset Support Estimate
Laser..........	Laser Industries Ltd. [*Associated Press*] (SAG)
LASER.........	League for the Advancement of States' Equal Rights (EA)
LASER.........	Learning Achievement through Saturated Educational Resources
LASER.........	Light Amplification by Stimulated Emission of Radiation [*Acronym was coined in 1957 by scientist Gordon Gould*]
laser..........	Light Amplification by Stimulated Emission of Radiation (WDMC)
LASER.........	London and South Eastern Library Region [*Information service or system*] (IID)
LASERCOM...	LASER Communications (MCD)
LASERCOM...	Light Amplification by Stimulated Emission of Radiation Computer Output Microfilm (EECA)

Lasergte	Lasergate Systems, Inc. [*Associated Press*] (SAG)
LaserSt	Laser Storm, Inc. [*Associated Press*] (SAG)
Lasertech	Laser Technics [*Associated Press*] (SAG)
LA Sess Law Serv	Louisiana Session Law Service [*A publication*] (DLA)
LASFB	Left Anterior-Superior Fascicular Block [*Cardiology*] (DAVI)
LASH	LASER Antitank Semiactive Homing
LASH	Latin American Society of Hepatology [*See also SLH*] (EAIO)
LASH	Left Anterosuperior Hemiblock [*Cardiology*] (DAVI)
LASH	Legislative Action on Smoking and Health (EA)
LASH	Lighter Aboard Ship [*Barge-carrying ship*]
LASHUP	Land-Air Synergic Homogeneous Ultra-Processor (SAA)
LASI	Landing-Site Indicator [*Aviation*]
LASI	Library of Ancient Semitic Inscriptions (BJA)
LASI	Licentiate of the Ambulance Service Institute [*British*] (DBQ)
LASIE	Library Automated Systems Information Exchange [*Australia*] (NITA)
LASIK	Laser Assisted In-Situ Keratomileusis [*Ophthalmology*]
LASIL	Land and Sea Interaction Laboratory [*Environmental Science Services Administration*]
LASIM	LASER Aiming Simulation (PDAA)
LASINT	LASER Intelligence (MCD)
LASL	Los Alamos Scientific Laboratory [*USAEC*]
LASLA	Laboratoire d'Analyse Statistique des Langues Anciennes [*Laboratory for the Statistical Analysis of Ancient Languages*] [*University of Liege, Belgium*]
LASM	Land-Attack Standard Missile
LASM	LASER Semiactive Missile (DNAB)
LASMEC	Local Authorities School Meals Equipment Consortium
Lasmo	Lasmo Ltd. [*Associated Press*] (SAG)
LASMO	London & Scottish Marine Oil [*British*]
L-Asnase	L-Asparaginase [*Also, A, L, L-ase, L-Asp*] [*An enzyme, an antineoplastic*]
LASO	Low-Altitude Search Option [*Search mode of the BOMARC guidance system*]
LASOR	LASER Spillover and Reflectivity (MCD)
LASP	Laboratory for Atmospheric and Space Physics [*University of Colorado*] [*Research center*]
L-Asp	L-Asparaginase [*Also, A, L, L-ase, L-asnase*] [*An enzyme, an antineoplastic*]
LASP	Local Attached Support Processor
LASP	Low-Altitude Space Platform (MCD)
LASP	Low-Altitude Surveillance Platform (MCD)
LASPAC	Landing Gear, Avionics Systems Package (MCD)
LASPAU	Latin American Scholarship Program of American Universities (EA)
LasPMd	Laser Pacific Media Corp. [*Associated Press*] (SAG)
LASR	Laboratories for Astrophysics and Space Research [*University of Chicago*] [*Research center*]
LASR	Letter Writing with Automatic Send-Receive (IAA)
LASR	Low-Altitude Surveillance RADAR
LASR-2	Litton Airborne Search RADAR Mark Two [*Canada*] (PDAA)
LASRAM	Low-Altitude Short-Range Missile
LasrCp	Laser Corp. [*Associated Press*] (SAG)
LASRE	Lightweight Advanced Super-Responsive Engine [*Automotive engineering*]
Lasrgt	Lasergate Systems, Inc. [*Associated Press*] (SAG)
LASRM	Low-Altitude Short-Range Missile
LASRM	Low-Altitude Supersonic Research Missile
LasrmTc	LaserMaster Technologies, Inc. [*Associated Press*] (SAG)
Lasrscp	Laserscope, Inc. [*Associated Press*] (SAG)
Lasrtch	Laser Technics, Inc. [*Associated Press*] (SAG)
LASS	Labile Aggregation-Stimulating Substance [*Hematology*]
LASS	Language and Assembly Language [*Computer science*] (DNAB)
LASS	Large Aircraft Start System (DWSG)
LASS	Large Aperture Solenoid Spectrometer [*Stanford Linear Accelerator Center*]
LASS	Large Area Screening Systems (MCD)
LASS	Large Area Sky Survey
LASS	LASER-Activated Semiconductor Switch (IAA)
LASS	LASER-Activated Silicon Switch (MCD)
LASS	LASER Applications System Study [*Military*]
LASS	Lateral Acceleration Sensing System (PDAA)
LASS	Launch Area Support Ship
LASS	Library Access and Sixth-Form Studies [*British*] (AIE)
LASS	Library Automated Service System (IAA)
LASS	Light-Activated Silicon Switch
LASS	Lighter-than-Air Submarine Simulator
LASS	Line Amplifier and Super Sync Mixer
LASS	Linguistic Analysis of Speech Samples (DAVI)
LASS	Linked Administrative Statistical Sample [*Social Security Administration*] (GFGA)
LASS	Local Area Sensor System [*Military*] (LAIN)
LASS	Local Area Signaling Service [*Bell Laboratories*]
LASS	Local Area Signaling Services [*Telecommunications*] (ACRL)
LASS	Local Authority Social Services [*British*]
LASS	Lockheed Airline System Simulation (PDAA)
LASS	Logistic-Automated Support System (SSD)
LASS	Logistics Analysis Simulation System
LASS	Logistics Automated Supply System
LASS	Low-Angle Silicon Sheet [*Photovoltaic energy systems*]
LASS	Lunar Applications of a Spent Stage [*Aerospace*] (MCD)
LASSA	Licensed Animal Slaughterers and Salvage Association [*British*] (BI)
LASSC	Latin American Social Sciences Council [*Argentina Database producer*] (EA)
LASSII	Low-Altitude Satellite Studies of Ionospheric Irregularities
LASSM	Line Amplifier and Super Sync Mixer (MSA)
LASSO	Landing and Approach System, Spiral-Oriented

LASSO	LASER Search and Secure Observer (CET)
LASSO	LASER Synchronization from Stationary Orbit (IEEE)
LASSO	Library Acquisition Services System Online [*Suggested name for the Library of Cogress computer system*]
LASSO	Light Air-to-Surface Semiautomatic Optical [*French missile*]
LASSO	Light Aviation Special Support Operations
LASSO	Lunar Applications of a Spent Stage in Orbit [*Aerospace*] (MCD)
LASSOS	Library Automation Systems and Services Options Study [*Advisory committee*] (NITA)
LASSP	Laboratory for Atomic and Solid State Physics [*Cornell University*] [*Research center*] (RCD)
LASST	Laboratory for Surface Science and Technology [*University of Maine at Orono*] [*Research center*] (RCD)
LASSV	Land and Approach System for Space Vehicles [*NASA*] (KSC)
LAST	Language and Systems Together [*Programming language*] [*Baytec Bay City, MI*]
LAST	Large Aperture Scanning Telescope (TEL)
LAST	Last Satellite Position [*Navy Navigation Satellite System*] (DNAB)
LAST	Left Anterior Small Thoracotomy [*Medicine*] (DMAA)
LAST	Leukocyte-Antigen Sensitivity Testing [*Medicine*] (MEDA)
LAST	Low-Altitude Supersonic Target (RDA)
LASTE	Low-Altitude Safety and Targeting Equipment (DWSG)
LASU	Local Air Supply Unit [*British military*] (DMA)
LA SUQ	Louisiana State University. Quarterly [*A publication*] (DLA)
LASV	Low-Altitude Supersonic Vehicle [*Formerly, SLAM*] [*Air Force*]
LASV	Low-Altitude Surface Vehicle (WDAA)
LasVDsc	Las Vegas Discount Golf & Tennis, Inc. [*Associated Press*] (SAG)
LasVE	Las Vegas Entertainment Network [*Associated Press*] (SAG)
LasVEE	Las Vegas Entertainment Network [*Associated Press*] (SAG)
LASVEM	Lightly Armored Structure Vulnerability Estimation Methodology (MCD)
LasVEnt	Las Vegas Entertainment Network [*Associated Press*] (SAG)
LasVMaj	Las Vegas Major League Sports [*Associated Press*] (SAG)
LASX	Laser Technics [*NASDAQ symbol*] (SAG)
LASX	Lasertechnics Inc. [*NASDAQ symbol*] (TTSB)
LAT	Aviation Legere de l'Armee de Terre [*France ICAO designator*] (FAAC)
LaT	Lactate Threshold [*Biochemistry*]
LAT	Lae [*Papua New Guinea*] [*Seismograph station code, US Geological Survey*] (SEIS)
LAT	Language Aptitude Test [*Military*] (AFM)
LAT	Large Angle Tagger (MCD)
LAT	Large Angle Torque (MCD)
LAT	LASER Acquisition and Tracking (OA)
LAT	Latch (NASA)
Lat	Latch's English King's Bench Reports [*1625-28*] [*A publication*] (DLA)
LAT	Latent
LAT	Lateral (KSC)
lat	Lateral (VRA)
LAT	Latex Agglutination Test [*Clinical chemistry*]
LAT	Lathwell Resources Ltd. [*Vancouver Stock Exchange symbol*]
LAT	Latin
lat	Latin [*MARC language code Library of Congress*] (LCCP)
LAT	Latitude
LAT	Latitude of Target
LAT	Latrine (DSUE)
LAT	Latus [*Wide*] [*Pharmacy*]
LAT	Latvia
LAT	Learning Ability Test [*Military*] (AFM)
LAT	Left Anterior Thigh [*Medicine*]
LAT	Less Active Tetragonal (PDAA)
LAT	Level above Threshold
LAT	Licensing Appeals Tribunal [*Australia*]
LAT	Light Artillery Tractor [*British military*] (DMA)
LAT	Linear Accelerator Tube
LAT	Linseed Association Terms [*Shipping*]
LAT	Local Apparent Time
LAT	Local Area Transport [*Telecommunications*]
LAT	Lockheed Air Terminal, Inc. [*Subsidiary of Lockheed Aircraft Corp.*]
LAT	Logistics Assistance Team (MCD)
LAT	Long-Acting Theophylline [*Pharmacology*]
LAT	Los Angeles Times [*A publication*]
LAT	Lot Acceptance Test (NASA)
LAT	Low-Altitude Tactics (DOMA)
LAT	Low-Angle Track (CAAL)
LAT	Lowest Astronomical Tide (PDAA)
LAT	Lumbermen's Association of Texas (SRA)
Lat	Valsts Biblioteka [*State Library of Latvia*], Riga, Latvia [*Library symbol Library of Congress*] (LCLS)
LAT-A	Latrunculin-A [*A toxin*]
LATA	Local Access and Transport Area
LATA	Local Access Transport Area [*Telecommunications*]
LATA	Local-Area Telephone Authority [*Telecommunications*]
LATA	London Amenity and Transport Association
LatACas	Latin American Casinos, Inc. [*Associated Press*] (SAG)
LatADis	Latin American Discovery Fund [*Associated Press*] (SAG)
LatADIr	Latin America Dollar Income Fund [*Associated Press*] (SAG)
LAT ADMOV	Lateri Admoveatum [*Let It Be Applied to the Side*] [*Pharmacy*]
LatAEqt	Latin America Equity Fund [*Associated Press*] (SAG)
LATAF	Logistics Activation Task Force [*Air Force*] (MCD)
LATAG	LASER Air-to-Air Gunnery Simulator [*Military*] (CAAL)
LATAG	Latin American Trade Advisory Group [*British Overseas Trade Board*] (DS)
LatAInv	Latin American Investment Fund [*Associated Press*] (SAG)

LATAR	LASER-Augmented Target Acquisition and Recognition System (MCD)
LATAS	LASER-Augmented Target Acquisition System
LAT-B	Latrunculin-B [A toxin]
LATB	Lithium Aluminum Tri-tert-Butoxyhydride [Organic chemistry]
LATBR	Los Angeles Times Book Review [A publication] (BRI)
LATC	Los Angeles Theater Center [California]
LATCC	London Air-Traffic Control Center
Latch	Latch's English King's Bench Reports [1625-28] [A publication] (DLA)
LATCH	Literature Attached to Charts [Nursing program]
LATD	Large Area Transmission Density (MCD)
LATD	Latitude (ADA)
LATDISP	Lateral Dispersion (MCD)
LAT DOL	Lateri Dolente [To the Painful Side] [Pharmacy]
LATE	Late Assessment of Thrombolytic Efficacy [Cardiology study]
LATE	Legal Assistance for the Elderly
LATE	London Association for the Teaching of English [British] (AIE)
La Tech U	Louisiana Tech University (GAGS)
LaTeko	La Teko Resources Ltd. [Associated Press] (SAG)
LATER	Ladies' After Thoughts on Equal Rights [Acronym is used as name of association] [Defunct] (EA)
LATER	[The] Life and Times of Eddie Roberts [TV program]
Later Rom Emp	[The] Later Roman Empire [A publication] (OCD)
Latex	Latex Resources [Associated Press] (SAG)
LATEX	Louisiana-Texas Experiment [Gulf Marine Minerals Management] (USDC)
LATEX	Louisiana-Texas Experiment [Gulf Marine Minerals Management] [Marine science] (OSRA)
LatexRs	Latex Resources [Associated Press] (SAG)
LATF	Legal Aid Task Force
LATF	Lloyd's American Trust Fund (AIA)
LATH	Laos and Thailand Military Assistance
La Th	La Themis [A publication] (DLA)
Lath	Lathrop's Reports [115-145 Massachusetts] [A publication] (DLA)
LATH	Libraries of Affiliated Teaching Hospitals - School of Medicine [Library network]
La Them LC	La Themis (Lower Canada) [A publication] (DLA)
LATHES	LASER Terminal Homing Engagement Simulator (PDAA)
Lathrop	Lathrop's Reports [115-145 Massachusetts] [A publication] (DLA)
Lath Wind L	Latham on the Law of Window Lights [A publication] (DLA)
LATI	Linee Aeree Transcontinentali Italiane
LatinAGr	Latin America Growth Fund, Inc. [Associated Press] (SAG)
LATIS	Lightweight Airborne Thermal Imaging System (MCD)
LATIS	Loop Activity Tracking Information System [Telecommunications] (TEL)
Lat Jus	Latrobe's Justice [A publication] (DLA)
LATK	Local Administrative Tool Kit [AT & T] [Software development and integration tools] (NITA)
LATKWEPSCOLPAC	Light Attack Weapons School, Pacific (DNAB)
LATL	Lateral (MSA)
LATLI	Latin American Tax Law Institute [Uruguay] (EAIO)
lat men	Lateral Meniscectomy [Orthopedics] (DAVI)
LATN	Low-Altitude Tactical Navigation
LATNS	Los Angeles Times News Service
LATO	List of Applicable Technical Orders [Military] (AFIT)
LATOFF	Lowest Astronomical Tide of the Foreseeable Future (PDAA)
LATOM	Lowest Astronomical Tide of the Month (PDAA)
LATOY	Lowest Astronomical Tide of the Year (PDAA)
LATP	League of American Theatres and Producers (EA)
LATP	Left Atrial Transmural Pressure [Medicine] (DMAA)
LATP	Lima Army Tank Plant [Ohio]
LATPT	Left Atrial Transesophageal Pacing Test [Medicine] (DMAA)
LATR	Lateral (DNAB)
Latr	Locator [Compass] (DA)
LA TR	Louisiana Term Reports (Martin) [A publication] (DLA)
LATREC	LASER-Acoustic Time Reversal Expansion and Compression (MCD)
LATRL	Lateral
LA TR (NS)	Louisiana Term Reports, New Series (Martin) [1823-30] [A publication] (DLA)
LATS	L.A. T Sportswear [NASDAQ symbol] (TTSB)
LATS	LA T Sportswear, Inc. [NASDAQ symbol] (SAG)
LATS	LDEF [Long-Duration Exposure Facility] Assembly and Transportation System [NASA] (NASA)
LATS	Leather and Associated Trades Show [British] (ITD)
LATS	Light Armored Turret System (MCD)
LATS	Light Attack Turbofan Single Aircraft [Aviation]
LATS	Lightweight Antenna Seeker
LATS	Long-Acting Thyroid Stimulator [Endocrinology]
LATS-P	Long Acting Thyroid Stimulator-Protector [Endocrinology]
LA T Spt	LA T Sportswear, Inc. [Associated Press] (SAG)
LatSSR	Latvian Soviet Socialist Republic
LATT	LASER Atmospheric Transmission Test
Lattice	Lattice Semiconductor Corp. [Associated Press] (SAG)
Latt Pr C Pr	Lattey's Privy Council Practice [1869] [A publication] (DLA)
LATUF	Latin America Trade Union Federation (NATG)
Latv	Latvia (VRA)
Latv	Latvian
LATWING	Light Attack Wing [Navy] (NVT)
LATX	Latex Res Inc. [NASDAQ symbol] (TTSB)
LATX	Latex Resources, Inc. [NASDAQ symbol] (SAG)
LAU	Lamu [Kenya] [Airport symbol] (OAG)
LAU	Lauder [New Zealand] [Geomagnetic observatory code]
LAU	Laumontite [A zeolite]
LAU	Launcher Aircraft Unit
LAU	Launcher Armament Unit [Navy] (DOMA)
LAU	Laundry (MSA)
LAU	Laurentian University Library [UTLAS symbol]
Lau	Laurentius Hispanus [Deceased, 1248] [Authority cited in pre-1607 legal work] (DSA)
LAU	Line Access Unit (NITA)
LAU	Line Adapter Unit [Computer science]
LAU	Linear Accelerometer Unit (PDAA)
LAU	Lineas Aereas Suramericanas Ltd. [Colombia] [ICAO designator] (FAAC)
lau	Louisiana [MARC country of publication code Library of Congress] (LCCP)
LAU	Lower Arithmetic Unit (IAA)
LAUA	Lloyd's Aviation Underwriters Association [British] (DBA)
LAUD	League of Americans of Ukrainian Descent (EA)
Lau de Pin	Laurentius de Pinu [Deceased, 1397] [Authority cited in pre-1607 legal work] (DSA)
Lauder	Fountainhall's Session Cases [1678-1712] [Scotland] [A publication] (DLA)
LAUK	Library Association of the United Kingdom
LAUM	Linguistic Atlas of the Upper Midwest
LAUNC	Launceston [Municipal borough in England]
LAUP	LASER-Assisted Uvulopalatoplasty [Medicine] (DMAA)
LAUR	Laurel Bancorp, Inc. [NASDAQ symbol] (SAG)
Laur	Laurentian Library [Classical studies] (OCD)
Laur	Laurentius Hispanus [Deceased, 1248] [Authority cited in pre-1607 legal work] (DSA)
Laur	Reports of the High Court of Griqualand [1882-1910] [South Africa] [A publication] (DLA)
LAURA	Low-Altitude Unmanned Reconnaissance Aircraft (DOMA)
Laur de Palat	Laurentius de Pallatis [Flourished, 16th century] [Authority cited in pre-1607 legal work] (DSA)
LaurelBc	Laurel Bancorp, Inc. [Associated Press] (SAG)
Lauren	Laurentius Hispanus [Deceased, 1248] [Authority cited in pre-1607 legal work] (DSA)
Laurence	Laurence's Reports of the High Court of Griqualand [1882-1910] [South Africa] [A publication] (DLA)
Lauren de Rodul	Laurentius de Rodulphis [Flourished, 15th century] [Authority cited in pre-1607 legal work] (DSA)
Laur HC Ca	Lauren's High Court Cases [South Africa] [A publication] (DLA)
LaurlCa	Laurel Capital Group [Associated Press] (SAG)
Laur Prim	Laurence's Primogeniture [1878] [A publication] (DLA)
LAUS	Local Area Unemployment Statistics (OICC)
LAUSC	Linguistic Atlas of the United States and Canada [1930]
Lauss Eq	Laussat's Equity Practice in Pennsylvania [A publication] (DLA)
LAUTRO	Life Assurance and Unit Trust Regulatory Organisation [British]
LAV	Las Vegas [Diocesan abbreviation] [Nevada] (TOCD)
lav	Latvian [MARC language code Library of Congress] (LCCP)
LAV	Launch Axis, Vertical (MCD)
LAV	Lavaliere [Lapel microphone] (NTCM)
LAV	Lavatory (KSC)
lav	Lavender [Philately]
LAV	Law Association of Victoria [Australia]
LAV	Leafhopper A Virus [Medicine] (DMAA)
LAV	Legislative Assembly of Victoria [Australia]
LAV	Lifting Ascent Vehicle
LAV	Light Armored Vehicle [Army] (RDA)
LAV	Linea Aeropostal Venezolana [Venezuela] [ICAO designator] (FAAC)
LAV	Lymphadenopathy-Associated Virus
LAV	Lymphocyte-Associated Virus
LAV	Varah [L. A.] Ltd. [Toronto Stock Exchange symbol]
LAVA	Linear Acoustic Vernier Analyzer (CAAL)
LAVA	Linear Amplifier for Various Applications (IEEE)
LAVA	Local Authority Valuers Association [British] (DBA)
LAVA	Look Ahead Variable Acceleration [Computer science] (MHDB)
LAVA	Low-Frequency Acoustic Vernier Analyzer (NVT)
LAVAC	LASER Atmospheric Visibility and Contamination (PDAA)
LAV/AD	Light Armored Vehicle / Air Defense [Army] (DWSG)
LAV/ADS	Light Armored Vehicle/Air Defense System [Army]
LAV-AF	Light Armored Vehicle, Air Force (LAIN)
LAV-AG	Light Armored Vehicle-Assault Gun [Marine Corps] (DOMA)
LavalTPh	Laval Theologique et Philosophique [Quebec] [A publication] (BJA)
LAV-AT	Light Armored Vehicle - Antitank [Canada]
LAVB	Light Armored Vehicle Battalion [Marine Corps] (DOMA)
LAVc	Local Area Vaxcluster (USDC)
LAVE	Association Vocanologique Europeenne [European Volcanological Association] [Paris, France] (EAIO)
LAVEND	Lavendula [Lavender] [Pharmacology] (ROG)
LAVEPA	Local Administration of Vocational Education and Practical Arts (OICC)
LAVERS	Lake Vessel Reporting System
LAVFWUS	Ladies Auxiliary to the Veterans of Foreign Wars of the United States (EA)
LAVH	Laparoscopically-Assisted Vaginal Hysterectomy [Medicine]
LAVH	Leparoscopically Assisted Vaginal Hysterectomy [Medicine]
LAVI	Lymphadenopathy-Associated Virus (PDAA)
LAVM	LORAN [Long-Range Navigation] Automatic Vehicle Monitoring (PDAA)
LAVM	Low-Altitude Vulnerability Model [Aerospace] (MCD)
LAVO	Lassen Volcanic National Park
LAVO	Lavatory [Slang] (DSUE)
Lav Pall	Lavacrum Palladis [of Callimachus] [Classical studies] (OCD)
LAW	Ladies Against Women (EA)
LAW	Land Authority for Wales
LAW	LASER Absorption Wave (PDAA)

LAW............ Lawrence [*Kansas*] [*Seismograph station code, US Geological Survey*] (SEIS)
LAW............ Lawter International, Inc. [*NYSE symbol*] (SPSG)
LAW............ Lawter Intl [*NYSE symbol*] (TTSB)
LAW............ Lawton [*Oklahoma*] [*Airport symbol*] (OAG)
LAW............ Lawton, OK [*Location identifier FAA*] (FAAL)
LAW............ Lawyer (ADA)
LAW............ Leading Aircraft Woman [*RAF*] [*British*]
LAW............ League of American Wheelmen
LAW............ Left Atrial Wall [*Medicine*] (DMAA)
LAW............ Left Attack Wing [*Women's lacrosse position*]
LAW............ Left-Handers Against the World [*Defunct*] (EA)
LAW............ Legal Advocates for Women (EA)
LAW............ Legal Aid Warranty [*Fund providing legal services in case of arrest*]
LAW............ Library, Amphibious Warfare (DNAB)
LAW............ Light Antiarmor Weapon [*Military*] (RDA)
LAW............ Light Antitank Weapon
LAW............ Light Area Weapon
LAW............ Light Assault Weapon
LAW............ Light Attack Weapon
LAW............ Link Airways of Australia [*Australia ICAO designator*] (FAAC)
LAW............ Local Air Warning
LAW............ Local Air Wing (DNAB)
LAW............ Logistics Action Worksheet
LAW............ Low-Acid Waste [*Nuclear energy*] (NRCH)
LAW............ Low Active Waste [*Nuclear energy*]
LAW............ Low-Altitude Warning (MCD)
LAW............ Loyalist Association of Workers [*Trade union*] [*Northern Ireland*]
LAW............ Lubricant, Arctic, Weapon [*Military*] (INF)
LAW............ Quaere Legal Resources Ltd. [*UTLAS symbol*]
LAW............ United States Supreme Court Library, Washington, DC [*OCLC symbol*] (OCLC)
LAWA.......... Legislative Assembly of Western Australia
Law Advert... Law Advertiser [*1823-31*] [*A publication*] (DLA)
Law Alm ...... Law Almanac [*New York*] [*A publication*] (DLA)
Law Amdt J... Law Amendment Journal [*1855-58*] [*A publication*] (DLA)
Law Am Jour... Law Amendment Journal [*1855-58*] [*A publication*] (DLA)
Law & Bank... Lawyer and Banker [*New Orleans*] [*A publication*] (DLA)
Law & Bank... Lawyers' and Bankers' Quarterly [*A publication*] (DLA)
Law & Banker... Lawyer and Banker and Central Law Journal [*A publication*] (DLA)
Law & Bk Bull... Weekly Law and Bank Bulletin [*Ohio*] [*A publication*] (DLA)
Law & Eq Rep... Law and Equity Reporter [*New York*] [*A publication*] (DLA)
Law & Hist Rev... Law and History Review [*A publication*] (DLA)
Law & Legisl in the German Dem Rep... Law and Legislation in the German Democratic Republic [*A publication*] (DLA)
Law & Lib ... Law and Liberty [*A publication*] (DLA)
Law & Mag... Lawyer and Magistrate Magazine [*1898-99*] [*Dublin*] [*A publication*] (DLA)
Law & Magis Mag... Lawyer's and Magistrate's Magazine [*A publication*] (DLA)
Law & Mag Mag... Lawyer and Magistrate Magazine [*1898-99*] [*Dublin*] [*A publication*] (DLA)
Law & Psychology Rev... Law and Psychology Review [*A publication*] (DLA)
Law & Soc... Law and Social Change [*A publication*] (DLA)
LAWASIA ..... LAWASIA. Journal of the Law Association for Asia and the Western Pacific [*A publication*] (DLA)
LAWASIA HRB... LAWASIA [*Law Association for Asia and the Pacific*] Human Rights Bulletin [*A publication*]
LAWASIA LJ... LAWASIA [*Law Association for Asia and the Pacific*] Law Journal [*A publication*] (DLA)
LAWB.......... Los Alamos Water Boiler [*Nuclear reactor*] (NRCH)
Law Bk Rev Dig... Law Book Review Digest and Current Legal Bibliography [*A publication*] (DLA)
Law Bul & Br... Law Bulletin and Brief [*A publication*] (DLA)
Law Bul IA... Law Bulletin. State University of Iowa [*A publication*] (DLA)
Law Bull ...... Law Bulletin [*Zambia*] [*A publication*] (DLA)
Law Bull ...... Weekly Law Bulletin [*Ohio*] [*A publication*] (DLA)
LAW/BUSA... League of American Wheelman/Bicycle USA (EA)
LAWC.......... Land Air Warfare Committee [*Military*]
Law Cas Wm I... Law Cases, William I to Richard I [*England*] [*A publication*] (DLA)
Law Ch Bdg Soc... Law on Church Building Societies [*A publication*] (DLA)
Law Ch P... Lawes on Charterparties [*1813*] [*A publication*] (DLA)
Law Chr...... Law Chronicle [*England*] [*A publication*] (DLA)
Law Chr...... Law Chronicle [*South Africa*] [*A publication*] (ILCA)
Law Chr & Auct Rec... Law Chronicle and Auction Record [*A publication*] (DLA)
Law Chr & Jour Jur... Law Chronicle and Journal of Jurisprudence [*A publication*] (DLA)
Law Ch Ward... Law on Church Wardens [*A publication*] (DLA)
Law Cl .... Law Clerk (DLA)
Law Cl Rec... Law Clerk Record [*1910-11*] [*A publication*] (DLA)
Law Com ..... Law Commission (DLA)
Law Com ..... Law Commission Report [*A publication*] (DLA)
Law Committee News... Lawyers' Committee News [*A publication*] (DLA)
Law Con ...... Lawson on Contracts [*A publication*] (DLA)
Law Dept Bull... Law Department Bulletin, Union Pacific Railroad Co. [*A publication*] (DLA)
LAWDS........ LORAN-Aided Weapons Delivery System
LAWEB........ Lake Warning [*or Weather*] Bulletin [*National Weather Service*] [*A publication*]
Law Ecc Law... Law's Ecclesiastical Law [*2nd ed.*] [*1844*] [*A publication*] (DLA)
Law Ed ...... Lawyer's Edition, United States Supreme Court Reports [*A publication*] (DLA)
Law Ed 2d ... United States Supreme Court Reports, Lawyers' Edition, Second Series [*A publication*] (DLA)
Law Ed Adv Op... United States Supreme Court Reports, Lawyers' Edition, Advance Opinions [*A publication*] (DLA)

Lawes Ch..... Lawes on Charterparties [*1813*] [*A publication*] (DLA)
Lawes Pl ..... Lawes on Pleading [*A publication*] (DLA)
Law Ex J..... Law Examination Journal [*A publication*] (DLA)
Law Ex Rep... Law Examination Reporter [*A publication*] (DLA)
Law Fr Dict... Law French Dictionary [*A publication*] (DLA)
LAWG .... Latin American Working Group [*Canada*] (CROSS)
Law Gaz ...... Law Gazette [*A publication*] (DLA)
Law Guild M... Lawyers Guild Monthly [*A publication*] (DLA)
Law in Cont... Law in Context [*A publication*]
Law Int ...... Law Intelligencer [*United States*] [*A publication*] (DLA)
Law J........ Law Journal Reports [*A publication*] (DLA)
Law J Ch ... Law Journal, New Series, Chancery [*A publication*] (DLA)
Law J Exch... Law Journal, New Series, Exchequer [*A publication*] (DLA)
Law Jour ..... Law Journal Reports [*A publication*] (DLA)
Law Jour (M & W)... Morgan and Williams' Law Journal [*London*] [*A publication*] (DLA)
Law JPD ...... Law Journal, Probate Division [*A publication*] (DLA)
Law JPD & A.. Law Journal Reports, New Series, Probate, Divorce, and Admiralty [*1875-1946*] [*A publication*] (DLA)
Law JQB ...... Law Journal, New Series, English Queen's Bench [*A publication*] (DLA)
Law Jr QB ... Law Journal, New Series, English Queen's Bench [*A publication*] (DLA)
Law Jur ...... Law's Jurisdiction of the Federal Courts [*A publication*] (DLA)
Law Lat Dic... Law Latin Dictionary [*A publication*] (DLA)
Law Lib N.... Law Library News [*A publication*] (DLA)
Law Lib NS... Law Library, New Series [*Philadelphia, PA*] [*A publication*] (DLA)
Law LJ .... Lawrence Law Journal [*A publication*] (DLA)
LAW M .... Law Magazine and Review [*A publication*] (ROG)
LawM.......... Lawrence Microfilming Service, Fuquay-Varina, NC [*Library symbol Library of Congress*] (LCLS)
LAWM......... Light All-Weather Missile (MCD)
Law Mag .... Law Magazine [*A publication*] (DLA)
Law Mag & Law Rev... Law Magazine and Law Review [*A publication*] (DLA)
Law Mag & R... Law Magazine and Review [*A publication*] (DLA)
Law Mag & Rev... Law Magazine and Review [*A publication*] (DLA)
Law Mo ...... Western Law Monthly (Reprint) [*Ohio*] [*A publication*] (DLA)
Law N .... Law News [*A publication*] (DLA)
LAWN .... Local Area Wireless Network [*O'Neill Communications, Inc.*] [*Computer science*] (PCM)
Law of Trusts Tiff & Bul... Tiffany and Bullard on Trusts and Trustees [*A publication*] (DLA)
Law Pat....... Law's United States Patent Cases [*A publication*] (DLA)
Law Pat Dig... Law's Digest of United States Patent Cases [*A publication*] (DLA)
Law Pl........ Lawes' Pleading in Assumpsit [*1810*] [*A publication*] (DLA)
Law Pl........ Lawes' Pleading in Civil Actions [*1806*] [*A publication*] (DLA)
Law Pr........ Law's Practice in United States Courts [*A publication*] (DLA)
Law Q Rev... Law Quarterly Review [*A publication*] (BRI)
Lawr.......... Lawrence High Court Reports [*Griqualand*] [*A publication*] (DLA)
LAWRC........ Limited Air Weather Reporting Certificate (IAA)
Law Rec ..... Ceylon Law Recorder [*A publication*] (DLA)
Law Rec ..... Irish Law Recorder [*1827-38*] [*A publication*] (ILCA)
Law Rec ..... Law Recorder [*1827-31*] [*Ireland*] [*A publication*] (DLA)
Law Rec (NS)... Law Recorder, New Series [*Ireland*] [*A publication*] (DLA)
Law Rec (OS)... Law Recorder, First Series [*Ireland*] [*A publication*] (DLA)
Law Ref Com... Law Reform Committee (DLA)
Law Ref Cttee... Law Reform Committee (DLA)
Law Reg ..... American Law Register [*Philadelphia*] [*A publication*] (DLA)
Law Reg ...... Law Register, Chicago [*A publication*] (DLA)
Law Reg Cas... Lawson's Registration Cases [*England*] [*A publication*] (DLA)
Lawrence.... Lawrence's Reports [*20 Ohio*] [*A publication*] (DLA)
Lawrence Comp Dec... Lawrence's First Comptroller's Decisions [*United States*] [*A publication*] (DLA)
Lawrence Compt Dec... Lawrence's First Comptroller's Decisions [*United States*] [*A publication*] (DLA)
Law Rep...... Law Reporter [*England*] [*A publication*] (DLA)
Law Rep...... Law Reporter (Ramsey and Morin) [*Canada*] [*A publication*] (DLA)
Law Rep...... Law Reports [*England*] [*A publication*] (DLA)
Law Rep...... Louisiana Reports [*A publication*] (DLA)
Law Rep...... New Zealand Law Reports [*A publication*] (DLA)
Law Rep...... Ohio Law Reporter [*A publication*] (DLA)
Law Rep A & E... Law Reports, Admiralty and Ecclesiastical Cases [*1865-75*] [*A publication*] (DLA)
Law Rep App Cas... Law Reports, Appeal Cases [*England*] [*A publication*] (DLA)
Law Rep CC... Law Reports, Crown Cases [*A publication*] (DLA)
Law Rep Ch... Law Reports, Chancery Appeal Cases [*England*] [*A publication*] (DLA)
Law Rep Ch App... Law Reports, Chancery Appeal Cases [*England*] [*A publication*] (DLA)
Law Rep Ch D... Law Reports, Chancery Division [*A publication*] (DLA)
Law Rep CP... Law Reports, Common Pleas [*England*] [*A publication*] (DLA)
Law Rep CPD... Law Reports, Common Pleas Division [*England*] [*A publication*] (DLA)
Law Rep Dig... Law Reports Digest [*A publication*] (DLA)
Law Rep Eq... Law Reports, Equity Cases [*A publication*] (DLA)
Law Rep Ex... Law Reports, Exchequer [*A publication*] (DLA)
Law Rep Ex D... Law Reports, Exchequer Division [*England*] [*A publication*] (DLA)
Law Rep HL... Law Reports, House of Lords, English and Irish Appeal Cases [*A publication*] (DLA)
Law Rep HL Sc... Law Reports, Scotch and Divorce Appeal Cases, House of Lords [*A publication*] (DLA)
Law Rep Ind App... Law Reports, Indian Appeals [*A publication*] (DLA)
Law Rep Ir... Law Reports, Irish [*A publication*] (DLA)
Law Rep Misc D... Law Reports, Miscellaneous Division [*A publication*] (DLA)
Law Rep NS... Law Reports, New Series [*New York*] [*A publication*] (DLA)

Law Repos... Carolina Law Repository [North Carolina] [A publication] (DLA)
Law Rep P... Law Reports, Probate [A publication] (DLA)
Law Rep P & D... Law Reports, Probate and Divorce Cases [A publication] (DLA)
Law Rep PC... Law Reports, Privy Council, Appeal Cases [England] [A publication] (DLA)
Law Rep QB... Law Reports, Queen's Bench [A publication] (DLA)
Law Rep QBD... Law Reports, Queen's Bench Division [A publication] (DLA)
Law Repr..... Law Reporter (Ramsey and Morin) [Canada] [A publication] (DLA)
Law Rep (Tor)... Law Reporter (Toronto) [A publication] (DLA)
Law Rev & Qu J... Law Review and Quarterly Journal [London] [A publication] (DLA)
Law Rev J... Law Review Journal [A publication] (DLA)
Law Rev Qu... Law Review Quarterly [Albany, NY] [A publication] (DLA)
Law Rev U Det... Law Review. University of Detroit [A publication] (DLA)
LawrG......... Lawrence Insurance Group, Inc. [Associated Press] (SAG)
LAWRS........ Limited Aviation Weather Reporting Station [FAA] (TAG)
LAWRS........ Limited Aviation Weather Reporting Station (FAAC)
LawrSB........ Lawrence Savings Bank [Associated Press] (SAG)
Lawr Wh... Lawrence's Edition of Wheaton on International Law [A publication] (DLA)
LAWS.......... Land and Water Systems [Michigan]
LAWS.......... LASER Atmospheric Wind Sounder [NASA]
LAWS.......... Lawson Products [NASDAQ symbol] (SAG)
LAWS.......... Lawyers Alliance for World Security (EA)
LAWS.......... Leadership and World Society [Defunct]
LAWS.......... Light Antitank Weapon System (LAIN)
LAWS........ Low-Altitude Warning System (NVT)
Law School Rec... Law School Record [Chicago] [A publication] (DLA)
Law School Rev... Law School Review. Toronto University [A publication] (DLA)
Laws Cont ... Lawson on Contracts [A publication] (DLA)
Law Ser MO Bull... University of Missouri. Bulletin. Law Series [A publication] (DLA)
Lawsn.......... Lawson Products, Inc. [Associated Press] (SAG)
LAWSO........ Lockheed Antisubmarine Warfare Systems Organization
Law Soc ACT NL... Law Society of the Australian Capital Territory. Newsletter [A publication]
Law Soc G... Law Society. Gazette [A publication]
Law Soc Jo... Law Society of Massachusetts. Journal [A publication] (DLA)
Law Soc Tas NL... Law Society of Tasmania. Newsletter [A publication]
Law Soc'y Scotl... Law Society of Scotland. Journal [A publication] (DLA)
Lawson Exp Ev... Lawson on Expert and Opinion Evidence [A publication] (DLA)
Lawson Pres Ev... Lawson on Presumptive Evidence [A publication] (DLA)
Lawson Rights Rem & Pr... Lawson on Rights, Remedies, and Practice [A publication] (DLA)
Lawson Usages & Cust... Lawson on the Law of Usages and Customs [A publication] (DLA)
Laws Reg Cas... Lawson's Registration Cases, Irish [1885-1914] [A publication] (DLA)
Law Stud ..... Law Student [A publication] (ILCA)
Law Stud Mag... Law Students' Magazine [A publication] (DLA)
Law Stud Mag NS... Law Students' Magazine. New Series [A publication] (DLA)
Law Stu H ... Law Students' Helper [A publication] (ILCA)
Law Stu Mag... Law Students' Magazine [A publication] (DLA)
Laws Wom... Laws of Women [A publication] (DLA)
Law T .... Law Times Reports [A publication] (DLA)
Law Tchr...... Law Teacher [A publication] (DLA)
Law Tenn Rep... Tennessee Reports [A publication] (DLA)
Lawter .... Lawter International, Inc. [Associated Press] (SAG)
Law Times (NS)... Law Times. New Series [Pennsylvania] [A publication] (DLA)
Law Times (OS)... Law Times, Old Series [Luzerne, PA] [A publication] (DLA)
Law T NS..... Law Times. New Series [Pennsylvania] [A publication] (DLA)
Law T NS..... Law Times Reports, New Series [England] [A publication] (DLA)
Law Tr......... Law Tracts [A publication] (DLA)
Law T Rep NS... Law Times Reports, New Series [England] [A publication] (DLA)
Law T Rep OS... Law Times Reports, Old Series [England] [A publication] (DLA)
Law US Cts... Law's Practice in United States Courts [A publication] (DLA)
LAWV.......... [The] Lorain & West Virginia Railway Co. [AAR code]
Law V & S... Lawrence's Visitation and Search [A publication] (DLA)
Law W .... Law Weekly [A publication] (DLA)
Law Wheat... Lawrence's Edition of Wheaton on International Law [A publication] (DLA)
Lawy........... Lawyer (DLA)
Lawyer & Banker... Lawyer and Banker and Central Law Journal [A publication] (DLA)
Lawyers Co-Op... Lawyers Co-Operative Publishing Co. (DLA)
Lawyers' Rep Ann... Lawyers' Reports, Annotated [A publication] (DLA)
Lawyers' Rep Annotated... Lawyers' Reports, Annotated [A publication] (DLA)
Lawyers' Rev... Lawyers' Review [A publication] (DLA)
Lawy Mag.... Lawyers' Magazine [A publication] (DLA)
Lawy Rep Ann... Lawyers' Reports, Annotated [A publication] (DLA)
Lawy Rev..... Lawyers' Review [A publication] (DLA)
LAX............. Bahia De Los Angeles [Mexico] [Seismograph station code, US Geological Survey] (SEIS)
LAX............. Lacrosse [British] (ROG)
LAX............. Laurel Explorations Ltd. [Vancouver Stock Exchange symbol]
lax.............. Laxative [Pharmacy]
LAX............. Los Angeles [California] [Airport symbol] (OAG)
LAX............. Los Angeles [California]
LAXRAY...... Large X-Ray Survey Experiment (PDAA)
LAXS.......... Low-Angle X-Ray Scattering (MCD)
LAY............. Ladysmith [South Africa] [Airport symbol] (OAG)
LAY............. Lanyu [Republic of China] [Seismograph station code, US Geological Survey] (SEIS)
Lay............. Lay's English Chancery Reports [A publication] (DLA)
LAYB.......... Library Association Year Book [A publication] (DGA)

LAYDET....... Layer Detection (SAA)
LAYGEN ..... Layout Generator [Ergonomics]
LAYN .... Layne Christensen Co. [NASDAQ symbol] (SAG)
LAYN .... Layne Christensen Co. [NASDAQ symbol] (TTSB)
LAYN .... Layne, Inc. [NASDAQ symbol] (SAG)
Layne......... Layne Christensen Co. [Associated Press] (SAG)
Layne......... Layne, Inc. [Associated Press] (SAG)
Layos........ Layos, Hollywood [Record label]
LAZ............ Balkan-Bulgarian Airlines [ICAO designator] (FAAC)
LAZ............ Bom Jesus Da Lapa [Brazil] [Airport symbol] (OAG)
LAZ............ La Luz Mines Ltd. [Toronto Stock Exchange symbol]
LaZ Boy...... La-Z Boy Chair Co. [Associated Press] (SAG)
LazKap...... Lazare Kaplan International, Inc. [Associated Press] (SAG)
LAZR.......... Laser Storm [NASDAQ symbol] (TTSB)
LAZRG........ Laser Storm, Inc. [NASDAQ symbol] (SAG)
LAZRU........ Laser Storm Unit [NASDAQ symbol] (TTSB)
LAZRW....... Laser Storm Wrrt [NASDAQ symbol] (TTSB)
LB............. Baccalaureus Literarum [Bachelor of Literature] [Latin]
LB............. Farbwerke Hoechst AG [Germany] [Research code symbol]
LB............. Graduate in Letters
LB............. LaBarge, Inc. [AMEX symbol] (SPSG)
LB............. Laboratory (MAE)
LB............. Laboratory Bulletin
LB............. Labrador [Postal code] [Canada]
LB............. Lactose Broth [Microbiology]
LB............. Ladies of Bethany (TOCD)
LB............. Lady Boss
LB............. Lag Bolt [Technical drawings]
LB............. Lamellar Body [Physiology]
LB............. Land Based
LB............. Landing Barge
LB............. Landing Beach [Navy]
L/B............. Landing Book [Tea trade] (ROG)
LB............. Lane Bryant, Inc.
LB............. Langmuir-Blodgitt Technique [Optics] (EECA)
LB............. Large Bowel [Anatomy]
LB............. Lasa B Ring [Montana] [Seismograph station code, US Geological Survey] (SEIS)
LB............. Last Brochure
LB............. Late Babylonian (BJA)
LB............. Late Bronze [Age] (BJA)
LB............. Launch Boost (MCD)
LB............. Launch Bunker (MUGU)
LB............. Launch Bus (NASA)
LB............. Laurentian Bank of Canada [Toronto Stock Exchange symbol]
LB............. Lavatory Basin
LB............. Lebanon [ANSI two-letter standard code] (CNC)
LB............. Lectori Benevolo [To the Kind (or Gentle) Reader] [Latin]
LB............. Lecture Bottle [Shipment of gas products] [Union Carbide Corp.]
LB............. Left Back [Football] (WDAA)
LB............. Left Base [Aviation] (FAAC)
LB............. Left Border [Genetics]
LB............. Left Breast [Medicine] (DMAA)
LB............. Left Bundle [Cardiology] (DMAA)
LB............. Left Buttock [Medicine]
LB............. Left Fullback [Soccer]
LB............. Left on Base [Baseball]
LB............. Legal Bond [Investment term]
LB............. Leg Bye [Cricket]
LB............. Legum Baccalaureus [Bachelor of Laws]
LB............. Leiomyoblastoma [Medicine]
L/B............. Length/Beam Ratio (DNAB)
Lb............. Leptosphaerulinia briosiana [A fungus]
LB............. Letter Box
LB............. Levobunolol [Also, LBUN] [Biochemistry]
LB............. Liaison Branch [BUPERS]
lb............. Liberia [MARC country of publication code Library of Congress] (LCCP)
lb............. Libra [Pound] [Latin] (AAG)
LB............. Library Bookseller (NITA)
LB............. Library Bulletin
L-B............. Liebermann-Burchard [Reaction] [Medicine] (MEDA)
LB............. Lifeboat (AAG)
LB............. Lifeboat Station [Coast Guard]
LB............. Ligand Binding Domain [Genetics]
LB............. Light Battalion [British military] (DMA)
LB............. Light Bombardment [Air Force]
LB............. Light Bomber [Air Force]
LB............. Light Bracket (AAG)
LB............. Lighted Buoy [USCG] (TAG)
LB............. Limited Base [Air Force] (AFM)
LB............. Limited Benefits [Unemployment insurance] (OICC)
LB............. Limited Partner in Brokers Firm [London Stock Exchange]
LB............. Linebacker [Football]
LB............. Line Buffer [Computer science]
LB............. Line Busy
LB............. Link Babler [Telecommunications] (ECII)
LB............. Linoleum Base [Technical drawings]
LB............. Lipid Body [Biochemistry] (MAE)
LB............. Lithium Bromide (DNAB)
LB............. Litterarum Baccalaureus [Bachelor of Letters or Literature] [Latin]
LB............. Litter Bearer (AABC)
LB............. Live Birth
LB............. Living Bank (EA)
LB............. Lloyd Aereo Boliviano [ICAO designator] (AD)

LB	Load Bank [*Computer science*] (KSC)
LB	Local Batch (IAA)
LB	Local Battery [*Radio*]
LB	Local Board
LB	Logan Brothers Book Co.
LB	Log Book
LB	Logical Block
LB	London Borough [*England*]
LB	London Bridge
LB	Long Bill [*Business term*]
LB	Long Binh [*Vietnam*]
LB	Loose Body [*Medicine*]
LB	Low Back [*Disorder*] [*Medicine*]
LB	Low Band (AAG)
LB	Low Bay (KSC)
LB	Lower Bearing
LB	Lower Bound [*Computer science*]
LB	Lower Brace (MCD)
LB	Lunch Break
LB	Luria Broth [*For cultivation of cells*]
LB	Photographic Laboratory Specialist [*Navy*]
lb	Pound [*Libra*] [*Unit of weight*]
LBA	Lahr/Bader Area [*Germany*]
LBA	LASER Beam Analyzer (IAA)
LBA	Leeds/Bradford [*England*] [*Airport symbol*] (OAG)
LBA	Left Basal Artery [*Medicine*] (DMAA)
LBA	Lifting-Body Airship (PDAA)
LBA	Ligand-Binding Assay [*Analytical biochemistry*]
LBA	Lima Bean Agar [*Microbiology*]
LBA	Limas Bulgarian Airlines [*ICAO designator*] (FAAC)
LBA	Limit of Basic Aircraft (MCD)
LBA	Linear-Bounded Automaton
LBA	Little Books on Art [*A publication*]
LBA	Load-Bearing Axis
LBA	Local Battery Apparatus
LBA	Local Bus Adapter [*Computer science*]
LBA	Local Bus Adaptor (NITA)
LBA	Logical Block Address [*Computer science*]
LBA	London Boroughs Association [*British*] (DCTA)
LBA	Longbow Apache [*Helicopter*] [*Army*] (RDA)
LBA	Louisiana Bankers Association (SRA)
LBA	Lutheran Benevolent Association (EA)
LBA	Luxembourg Brotherhood of America (EA)
LBAB	Lima Bean Advisory Board [*Superseded by California Dry Bean Advisory Board*] (EA)
LBAD	Lexington-Blue Grass Army Depot [*Kentucky*] (AABC)
LBAF	Line Width, Black-to-White-Ratio, Area, Fixation Point
LBAK	Lightweight Broadband Antenna Kit
lb ap	Apothecaries' Pound (BARN)
LBAT	Late Babylonian Astronomical and Related Texts (BJA)
LBA-TESS	Longbow Apache-Tactical Engagement Simulation System
lb av	Pound Avoirdupois (BARN)
LBB	Lancaster Bible College, Lancaster, PA [*OCLC symbol*] (OCLC)
LBB	Left Breast Biopsy (DAVI)
LBB	Left Bundle-Branch [*Cardiology*] (DAVI)
LBB	Left Bundle Branch [*Cardiology*] (AAMN)
Lbb	Leishmania braziliensis braziliensis [*Microbiology*]
LBB	Life Blower Bearing
LBB	Linear Ball Bushing
LBB	[*The*] Little Black Book [*Cygnet Technologies, Inc.*] [*Database software*]
LBB	Low Back Bending (DMAA)
LBB	Lubbock [*Texas*] [*Airport symbol*] (OAG)
LBB	Lubbock, TX [*Location identifier FAA*] (FAAL)
LBBA	London Bacon Buyers' Association Ltd. [*British*]
LBBB	Left Bundle Branch Block [*Cardiology*]
LBBG	Burgas [*Bulgaria*] [*ICAO location identifier*] (ICLI)
LBBM	Ludlow Bone Bed Member [*England*] [*Geology*]
LBBP	Laboratory of Blood and Blood Products [*Public Health Service*]
LBBSB	Left Bundle Branch System Block [*Cardiology*]
LBBX	Left Breast Biopsy Examination [*Medicine*] (AAMN)
LBBY	Lobby
LBC	Albanian Airline Co. [*ICAO designator*] (FAAC)
LBC	Laboratoires Bruneau & Cie [*France*] [*Research code symbol*]
LBC	Laboratorio Chile ADS [*NYSE symbol*] (TTSB)
LBC	Laboratorio Chile SA [*NYSE symbol*] (SAG)
LBC	Land Bank Commission
LBC	Large Bore Cannon (MCD)
LBC	LASER Beam Cutting [*Welding*]
LBC	Layman's Bible Commentary [*London*] [*A publication*] (BJA)
LBC	Left Book Club [*Founded in the 1930's by publisher Victor Gollancz*] [*Defunct British*]
LBC	Left Bounded Context [*Computer science*] (MHDB)
LBC	Levesque, Beaubien & Co. [*Toronto Stock Exchange symbol*]
LBC	Liberty Baptist College [*Virginia*]
LBC	Liberty Bell Communications, Inc. [*Detroit, MI*] [*Telecommunications*] (TSSD)
LBC	Lidocaine Blood Concentration (DMAA)
LBC	Lilliputian Bottle Club (EA)
LBC	Line Balance Converter
LBC	Load Bus Contactor [*Aviation*]
LBC	Local Baggage Committee [*IATA*] (DS)
LBC	Local Bus Controller
LBC	Logistical Base Command [*Korea*]
LBC	London Ballet Circle

LBC	London Bankruptcy Court
LBC	London Broadcasting Co.
LBC	Loose Bladder Construction [*Ball*] (DICI)
LBC	Lothian and Berwick Cavalry [*British military*] (DMA)
LBC	Lowband Color [*Broadcasting*] (NTCM)
LBC	Lubudi [*Zaire*] [*Seismograph station code, US Geological Survey*] (SEIS)
LBC	Lummer-Brodhun Cube [*Physics*]
LBC	Lymphadenosis Benigna Cutis [*Medicine*] (DMAA)
LBC-A	LASER Beam Cutting - Air
LB CAL	Pound Calorie (WDAA)
LBCC	Long Beach City College [*California*]
LBC/CML	Lymphoid Blast Crisis of Chronic Myeloid Leukemia [*Oncology*]
LBCD	Left Border Cardiac Dullness [*Cardiology*]
LBC-EV	LASER Beam Cutting - Evaporative
LBCF	Laboratory Branch Complement Fixation [*Clinical chemistry*]
LBCI	Liberty Bancorp, Inc. [*NASDAQ symbol*] (SAG)
LBC-IG	LASER Beam Cutting - Inert Gas
LBCL	Louisville Behavior Check List [*Psychology*]
LBCL	Lymphoblastoid B-Cell Line [*Genetics*]
LBCM	Locator at Back Course Marker (PDAA)
LBCO	Lanthanum-Barium-Copper-Oxide [*Inorganic chemistry*]
LBC-O	LASER Beam Cutting - Oxygen
LBcS	Belle Chasse State School, Belle Chasse, LA [*Library symbol Library of Congress*] (LCLS)
LBD	Large Bile Duct [*Medicine*] (DMAA)
LBD	Left Border of Dullness [*Cardiology*]
LBD	Licensed Beverage Distributors (SRA)
LBD	Lifting Body Development
LBD	Ligand-Binding Domain [*Biochemistry*]
LBD	Light Beam Deflection
LBD	Little Black Devils [*Nickname given to the 90th Battalion of the Winnipeg Rifles during the Northwest Rebellion in 1885*]
LBD	Little Black Dress [*Women's fashions*]
LBD	Logic Block Diagram (IAA)
LBD	Lower Back Disability [*Medicine*]
LBDA	Lexington Bluegrass Depot Activity [*Kentucky*] [*Army*]
LBDQ	Leader Behavior Description Questionnaire [*Psychology*]
L/Bdr	Lance-Bombardier [*British military*] (DMA)
LBDS	Leiden-Berkeley Deep Survey [*Astronomy*]
LBDT	Low Bay Dolly Tug (NASA)
LBE	Lakewood Board of Education, Lakewood, OH [*Inactive*] [*OCLC symbol*] (OCLC)
LBE	Lance-Bubbling-Equilibrium [*Steelmaking*]
LBE	Land-Bearing Equipment [*Military*] (INF)
LBE	Landing Barge, Emergency Repair
LBE	Latrobe [*Pennsylvania*] [*Airport symbol*] (OAG)
LBE	Latrobe, PA [*Location identifier FAA*] (FAAL)
LBE	Libra Energy, Inc. [*Vancouver Stock Exchange symbol*]
LBE	Load-Bearing Equipment (INF)
LBE	Location-Based Entertainment
LBE	Long Bill of Exchange [*Business term*] (MHDW)
LBEA	Lutheran Braille Evangelism Association (EA)
LBeB	Bossier Parish Library, Benton, LA [*Library symbol Library of Congress*] (LCLS)
LBEB	Laboratory of Brain Evolution and Behavior [*National Institute of Mental Health*]
LBEF	Land-Based Evaluation Facility [*Military*] (CAAL)
LBEFM	Low Background Epifluorescence Microscopy
LBEI	Licentiate of the Institution of Body Engineers [*British*] (DBQ)
LBEN	Low-Byte Enable
Lber	Literaturbericht (BJA)
LBES	Laboratory of Biomedical and Environmental Sciences [*Research center*] (RCD)
LBETV	Les Brown's Encyclopedia of Television [*A publication*]
LB Eur	Lehman Brothers, Inc. [*Associated Press*] (SAG)
LBF	Lactobacillus bulgaricus Factor [*Biochemistry*]
LBF	Landing Barge Flak [*British military*] (DMA)
LBF	Latin America Dollar Inc.Fd [*NYSE symbol*] (TTSB)
LBF	Latin America Dollar, Inc. Fund [*NYSE symbol*] (SPSG)
LBF	Les Buteaux [*France*] [*Seismograph station code, US Geological Survey*] (SEIS)
LBF	Limb Blood Flow (AAMN)
LBF	Liver Blood Flow [*Physiology*]
LBF	Load Bit Field [*Computer science*] (IAA)
LBF	London Book Fair [*England*]
LBF	Louis Braille Foundation for Blind Musicians [*Defunct*] (EA)
LBF	Lyme Borreliosis Foundation (EA)
LBF	North Platte [*Nebraska*] [*Airport symbol*] (OAG)
LBF	North Platte, NE [*Location identifier FAA*] (FAAL)
LBF	Pounds, Force (MCD)
LBFA	Official Martin Landau-Barbara Bain Fan Association (EA)
LBFC	Lane Brody Fan Club (EA)
LBFC	Laura Branigan Fan Club (EA)
LBFC	Lauralee Bell Fan Club (EA)
LBFCR	Longbow Fire Control RADAR (DWSG)
LBFI	L & B Financial, Inc. [*NASDAQ symbol*] (SAG)
LBF/IN²	Pound-Force per Square Inch (WDAA)
LBFL	L&B Financial [*NASDAQ symbol*] (TTSB)
LBF-S	Pound-Force per Second
LBF S/FT²	Pound-Force Seconds per Square Foot
LB/FT	Pounds per Foot
LB/FT²	Pounds per Square Foot
LB/FT³	Pounds per Cubic Foot
LB/(FT H)	Pounds per Foot-Hour

LB/(FT S)..... Pounds per Foot-Second
LBG............ Le Bourget Airport [France]
LBG............ Left Buccal Ganglion [Medicine]
LBG............ Locust Bean Gum (OA)
LBG............ Low BTU Gas (MCD)
LBG............ Lucky Break Gold [Vancouver Stock Exchange symbol]
LB/GAL ...... Pounds per Gallon
LBGO.......... Gorna Orechovitsa [Bulgaria] [ICAO location identifier] (ICLI)
LBH............ Laker Airways (Bahamas) Ltd. [ICAO designator] (FAAC)
LBH............ Leased Bachelor Housing [Military] (DNAB)
LBH............ Length, Breadth, Height
LBH............ Local Board of Health [British]
LBH............ Lyman-Birge-Hopfield [System] [Physics] (MUGU)
LB/H.......... Pounds per Hour
LBH............ Sydney [Australia Airport symbol] (OAG)
LBHA.......... Little Big Horn Associates (EA)
LBHB.......... Low-Barrier Hydrogen Bond [Enzymology]
LB/(HP H) .... Pounds per Horsepower-Hour
LBHS.......... Longbow Hellfire Seeker (DWSG)
LBI............ Albi [France] [Airport symbol] (OAG)
LBI............ Last Byte In (ECII)
LBI............ Leo Baeck Institute (EA)
LBI............ Liberte Investors [Formerly, Lomas & Nettleton Mortgage Investors] [NYSE symbol] (SPSG)
LBI............ Libra Industries, Inc. [Vancouver Stock Exchange symbol]
LBI............ Library Bibliographies and Indexes [A publication]
LBI............ Library Binding Institute (EA)
LBI............ Licensed Beverage Industries [Later, DISCUS] (EA)
LBI............ Lima Bean (trypsin) Inhibitor [Biochemistry]
LBI............ Lloyds & BOLSA [Bank of London & South America] International Bank Ltd. [British]
LBI............ Lloyds Bank International (ADA)
LBI............ Long-Baseline Interferometer [or Interferometry] (PDAA)
LBI............ Lost by Inventory (DNAB)
LBI............ Low Back Injury [Medicine] (DMAA)
LBI............ Low Serum-Bound Iron (MAE)
LBibel........ Im Lande der Bibel [Berlin-Dahlem] [A publication] (BJA)
LBIC.......... Licensed Beverage Information Council (EA)
LBIMS........ Laban/Bartenieff Institute of Movement Studies (EA)
LBIN.......... Pound-Force per Inch (MSA)
LB/IN²....... Pounds per Square Inch
LB/IN³....... Pounds per Cubic Inch
LBIPP........ Licentiate of the British Institute of Professional Photography (DBQ)
LBIR.......... LASER Beam Image Reproducer
LBIST........ Licentiate of the British Institute of Surgical Technologists (DBQ)
LBJ............ Lady Bird Johnson [Mrs. Lyndon Baines Johnson]
LBJ............ Little Brown Job [Unidentified bird, to a bird watcher]
LBJ............ Load Bank and Jump [Computer science]
LBJ............ Long Binh Jail [Vietnam]
LBJ............ Lower Ball Joint [Automotive engineering]
LBJ............ Lyndon Baines Johnson [US president, 1908-1973]
LBJL.......... Lyndon B. Johnson Library
LBJSC........ Lyndon B. Johnson Space Center (MSC)
LBK............ Landing Barge, Kitchen
LBK............ Left Bank
LBL............ Label (MSA)
LBL............ Label
LBL............ Labeled Lymphoblast [Oncology] (DMAA)
LBL............ Laminar Boundary Layer
LBL............ Lawrence Berkeley Laboratory [Berkeley, CA] [Department of Energy] (GRD)
LBL............ Left Buttock Line (MCD)
LBL............ Liberal [Kansas] [Airport symbol] (OAG)
LBL............ Liberal, KS [Location identifier FAA] (FAAL)
LBL............ Limited Broadcasting License [Australia]
LBL............ Lymphoblastic Lymphoma [Oncology]
LBLG.......... Large Blast Load Generator (PDAA)
LBLS.......... Laminar Boundary-Layer Separation
LBLTY........ Liability
LBM........... LASER Beam Machine (IAA)
LBMI.......... Lean Body Mass [Exercise]
LBM........... Left Buffer Memory (GFGA)
LBM........... Liberty-Bell Mines, Inc. [Vancouver Stock Exchange symbol]
LBM........... Liquid Boost Module
LBM........... Little Butte [Montana] [Seismograph station code, US Geological Survey Closed] (SEIS)
LBM........... Load Buffer Memory [Computer science]
LBM........... Local Board Memoranda
LBM........... Locator Back Marker [Aviation] (DA)
LBM........... Logic Bus Monitor [Computer science] (CET)
LBM........... Loose Bowel Movement [Medicine] (CPH)
LBM........... Lowband Monochrome [Broadcasting] (NTCM)
LBM........... Lunar Breaking Module [NASA] (IAA)
LBM........... Lung Basement Membrane [Medicine] (DMAA)
LBM........... Morehouse Parish Library, Bastrop, LA [Library symbol Library of Congress] (LCLS)
LBM........... Pounds, Mass (MCD)
LB/M.......... Pounds per Minute (AAG)
LBMA.......... London Bullion Market Association
LBMC.......... Liberty Bell Matchcover Club (EA)
LBMCTX...... Local Battery Magneto Call Telephone Exchange (IAA)
LBMI.......... Lease Base Machine Inventory (MHDB)
LB/MIN ...... Pounds per Minute
LBMM.......... Lifetime Book of Money Management [A publication]
LBMP.......... Land-Based Marine Pollution

LBMS.......... Learmonth & Burchett Management Systems [British] (NITA)
LBM/S-IN2 ... Pounds of Mass per Second per Square Inch
LBMSY........ Learmouth & Burchett Management Systems, Inc. [NASDAQ symbol] (SAG)
LBMSY........ Learmouth & Burchett Mgt ADS [NASDAQ symbol] (TTSB)
LbN............ Labial Nerve [Anatomy]
LBN............ Lebanon [ANSI three-letter standard code] (CNC)
LBN............ Letter Box Number [Viet Cong equivalent to the US APO]
LBN............ Lewis x Brown Norway [Rat strain]
LBN............ Liberty Broadcasting Network [Cable-television system]
LBN............ Line Balancing Network [Telecommunications] (TEL)
LBN............ Logic Bucket Number (NITA)
LBNA.......... Liberty Bancorp, Inc., Oklahoma [NASDAQ symbol] (SAG)
LBNA.......... Liberty Bancorp(OK) [NASDAQ symbol] (TTSB)
LBNP.......... Lower Body Negative Pressure [Boots] [Space flight equipment] [NASA]
LBNPD........ Lower Body Negative Pressure Device [Space flight equipment] [NASA]
LBNS.......... Long Beach Naval Shipyard (DNAB)
LBNSY........ Long Beach Naval Shipyard (MUGU)
LBO............ Landing Barge Oiler [British military] (DMA)
LBO............ Large Bowel Obstruction [Medicine]
LBO............ Lebanon, MO [Location identifier FAA] (FAAL)
LBO............ Leveraged Buy-Out
LBO............ Light Beam Oscillograph
LBO............ Line Building Out
LBO............ Lithium Boron Oxide [Inorganic chemistry]
LBocNS....... Northwest State School, Bossier City, LA [Library symbol Library of Congress] (LCLS)
L Book Adviser... Law Book Adviser [A publication] (DLA)
LBP............ Land-Based Plant (NRCH)
LBP............ Laser Beam Printer (NITA)
LBP............ Length Between Perpendiculars [Technical drawings]
LBP............ Leucine-Binding Protein [Biochemistry]
LBP............ Light Beam Pickup
LBP............ Line Binder Post (IAA)
LBP............ Lipopolysaccharide-Binding Protein [Biochemistry]
LBP............ Low-Back Pain [Medicine]
LBP............ Low Blood Pressure [Medicine]
LBP............ Lumbar Back Pain [Medicine] (DMAA)
LBP............ Personnel Landing Boat [Navy symbol Obsolete]
LBPD.......... Plovdiv [Bulgaria] [ICAO location identifier] (ICLI)
LBPF.......... Long Bone or Pelvic Fracture [Medicine] (DMAA)
LBPH.......... Libraries for the Blind and Physically Handicapped [Automated system]
L-BPH......... Louisiana State Library, Department for the Blind and Physically Handicapped, Baton Rouge, LA [Library symbol Library of Congress] (LCLS)
LBPI.......... LASER Beam Position Indicator
LBPIS........ LASER Beam Position Indicator System
LBPO.......... Lifting Body Program Office [NASA]
LBPQ.......... Low Back Pain Questionnaire [Medicine] (DMAA)
LBPR.......... Lumped Burnable Poison Rod [Assembly] [Nuclear energy] (NRCH)
LBQ............ Lambarene [Gabon] [Airport symbol] (OAG)
LBQS.......... Large Bright Quasar Survey [Astronomy]
LBr............ East Baton Rouge Parish Public Library, Baton Rouge, LA [Library symbol Library of Congress] (LCLS)
Lbr............ Labor
LBR............ Laborer
LBR............ Labrea [Brazil] [Airport symbol] (AD)
LBR............ LASER Beam Recorder [or Recording]
LBR............ LASER Beam Rider (RDA)
LBR............ L-Band Radiometer (MCD)
LBR............ Liberia [ANSI three-letter standard code] (CNC)
LBR............ Librarian (WDAA)
LBR............ Line of Bomb Release (NATG)
LBR............ Little Bear Resources [Vancouver Stock Exchange symbol]
LBR............ Little Books on Religion [A publication]
LBR............ Living Benefits Rider [Insurance] (WYGK)
LBR............ Local Base Rescue [Air Force] (AFM)
LBR............ Low Birth Rate
LBR............ Low BIT [Binary Digit] Rate [Computer science] (MCD)
LBR............ Lower Burma Rulings [India] [A publication] (DLA)
LBR............ Low Rurning Rate (KSC)
LBR............ [The] Lowville & Beaver River Railroad Co. [AAR code]
LBR............ Lumber (KSC)
LBRA.......... Laboratory of Biochemical Risk Analysis (GNE)
LBrAg......... Louisiana State Department of Agriculture, Research Library, Baton Rouge, LA [Library symbol Library of Congress] (LCLS)
LBRC.......... Loft Bomb Release Computer (MCD)
LBrC.......... Louisiana Commerce Department, Research Library, Baton Rouge, LA [Library symbol Library of Congress] (LCLS)
LBrCJIS...... Commission on Law Enforcement and Criminal Justice, Criminal Justice InformationSystem, Baton Rouge, LA [Library symbol Library of Congress] (LCLS)
LBrcTI........ Louisiana Training Institute, Bridge City Library, Bridge City, LA [Library symbol Library of Congress] (LCLS)
LBrE.......... Ethyl Corp., Chemical Development Library, Baton Rouge, LA [Library symbol Library of Congress] (LCLS)
LBrEd......... Louisiana Education Department, Baton Rouge, LA [Library symbol Library of Congress] (LCLS)
LBRF.......... Louse-Borne Relapsing Fever [Medicine] (AAMN)
LBRF.......... Lower Branchial Filament
LBrG.......... Gulf South Research Institute, Baton Rouge, LA [Library symbol Library of Congress] (LCLS)

LBRG	LASER Beam Rider Guidance (MCD)
LBrGS	Church of Jesus Christ of Latter-Day Saints, Genealogical Society Library, BatonRouge Branch, Baton Rouge, LA [*Library symbol Library of Congress*] (LCLS)
LBrHR..........	Louisiana Department of Health and Human Resources, Policy Planning and Evaluation Office, Baton Rouge, LA [*Library symbol Library of Congress*] (LCLS)
LBrHR-Y	Louisiana Department of Health and Human Resources, Office of Youth Services, Baton Rouge, LA [*Library symbol Library of Congress*] (LCLS)
LBrIPA	Louisiana Information Processing Authority, Baton Rouge, LA [*Library symbol Library of Congress*] (LCLS)
LBrJ	Louisiana Justice Department, Huey P. Long Library, Baton Rouge, LA [*Library symbol Library of Congress*] (LCLS)
LBrJS...........	Jimmy Swaggart Bible College Library, Baton Rouge, LA [*Library symbol Library of Congress*] (LCLS)
LBrL	Labor Department, Research Library, Baton Rouge, LA [*Library symbol Library of Congress*] (LCLS)
LBrLAS	Louisiana Arts and Science Center, Baton Rouge, LA [*Library symbol Library of Congress*] (LCLS)
LBrLC...........	Louisiana Legislative Council, Reference Division, Baton Rouge, LA [*Library symbol Library of Congress*] (LCLS)
LBrLH	Earl K. Long Hospital, Medical Library, Baton Rouge, LA [*Library symbol Library of Congress*] (LCLS)
LBRM...........	Large Basin Runoff Model [*Marine science*] (OSRA)
LBRM...........	Large Basin Runoff Model (USDC)
LBrNR..........	Natural Resources Department, Research and Development Library, Baton Rouge, LA [*Library symbol Library of Congress*] (LCLS)
LBrNR-F.......	Natural Resources Department, Office of Forestry, Baton Rouge, LA [*Library symbol Library of Congress*] (LCLS)
LBrPS	Public Service Commission, Baton Rouge, LA [*Library symbol Library of Congress*] (LCLS)
LBrR	Louisiana Revenue Department, Research Department, Baton Rouge, LA [*Library symbol Library of Congress*] (LCLS)
LBRS	Rousse [*Bulgaria*] [*ICAO location identifier*] (ICLI)
LBrSP	State Planning Office, Library, Baton Rouge, LA [*Library symbol Library of Congress*] (LCLS)
LBRT............	Liberty
LBrTD-Av	Department of Transportation and Development, Aviation Office, Baton Rouge, LA [*Library symbol Library of Congress*] (LCLS)
LBrTD-H.......	Department of Transportation and Development, Office of Highways, Research and Development Library, Baton Rouge, LA [*Library symbol Library of Congress*] (LCLS)
LBrTD-Pw	Department of Transportation and Development, Office of Public Works, Baton Rouge, LA [*Library symbol Library of Congress*] (LCLS)
LBRTY	Liberty
LBrUC...........	Department of Urban and Community Affairs, Office of Planning and Technical Assistance, Baton Rouge, LA [*Library symbol Library of Congress*] (LCLS)
LBRV	Lifting Body Research Vehicle
LBRV	Low BIT [*Binary Digit*] Rate Voice [*Telecommunications*]
LBrWF-S	Department of Wildlife and Fisheries, Louisiana Stream Control Commission, BatonRouge, LA [*Library symbol Library of Congress*] (LCLS)
LBRY	Library (MSA)
LBRY	Library
LBS	Labasa [*Fiji*] [*Airport symbol*] (OAG)
LBS	Lactobacillus Selector [*Microbiology*] (DAVI)
LBS	Laminar Boundary-Layer Separation
LBS	Land-Based Sources [*of Marine Pollution*] [*Marine science*] (OSRA)
LBS	Land-Based Sources of Marine Pollution (USDC)
LBS	Landing Boat, Support [*Navy symbol*]
LBS	Large Blast Simulator
LBS	Large Bulb Ship
LBS	LASER Beam Surgery
LBS	LASER Bombing System
LBS	Launch Base Support [*Air Force*]
LBS	Launch Blast Simulator (MUGU)
LBS	Lead Belly Society (EA)
LBS	Lecithin Bile State [*Medicine*]
LBS	Lectori Benevolo Salutem [*To the Kind (or Gentle) Reader, Greeting*] [*Latin*]
LBS	Liberation Broadcasting Station (CINC)
LBS	Light Bomber Strike [*Air Force*] (NATG)
LBS	Line Buffer System [*Computer science*]
LBS	Lithuanian Boy Scouts (EA)
LBS	Load Balance System [*Telecommunications*] (TEL)
LBS	Load-Bearing Surface (MCD)
LBS	Load Bearing System
LBS	Local Battery Signaling [*Telecommunications*] (IAA)
LBS	Local Battery Supply [*Telecommunications*] (IAA)
LBS	Local Battery Switchboard [*Telecommunications*] (IAA)
LBS	Local Battery System [*Telecommunications*] (IAA)
LBS	Loire Base Section [*World War II*]
LBS	London Business Aviation [*British ICAO designator*] (FAAC)
LBS	London Business School [*England*]
LBS	Low Back Strain (DAVI)
LBS	Low Back Syndrome [*Medicine*] (DMAA)
LBS	Lumbar Back Strain [*Medicine*] (DMAA)
LB/S	Lysine-Binding Site [*Hematology*]
LB/S	Pounds per Second
LBSA	Libraries Board of South Australia
LBSA	Lipid-Bound Sialic Acid [*Analytical biochemistry*]
LBSA	Long Binh Subarea [*Vietnam*]

LBSC..........	Licentiate of the British Society of Commerce (DBQ)
LBSCR	London, Brighton & South Coast Railway [*British*]
LBSD	Lightweight Battlefield Surveillance Device
LBSF	Lions Blind Sports Foundation (EA)
LBSF	Little Brothers of Saint Francis (TOCD)
LBSF	Sofia [*Bulgaria*] [*ICAO location identifier*] (ICLI)
LBSG	Letter Box Study Group [*British*] (DBA)
LBSS	Local Boards of the Selective Service System
lbst	Pounds [*Libra in Latin*] Static Thrust (DOMA)
LBSTR	Lobster
LBSZ	Stara Zagora [*Bulgaria*] [*ICAO location identifier*] (ICLI)
LBT	Air Liberte Tunisie [*Tunisia*] [*ICAO designator*] (FAAC)
LBT	Chemical Laboratory Technician [*or Technology*] [*Navy*]
LBT	Labatt [*John*] Ltd. [*Toronto Stock Exchange symbol Vancouver Stock Exchange symbol*]
LBT	Labete [*Solomon Islands*] [*Seismograph station code, US Geological Survey*] (SEIS)
LBT	Land-Based Tanker [*Aircraft*] (DOMA)
LBT	Large Binocular Telescope
LBT	L-Band Tetrode
LBT	L-Band Transmitter
LBT	Lean Best Torque [*Automotive engineering*]
lbt	Librettist [*MARC relator code*] [*Library of Congress*] (LCCP)
LBT	Light-Beam Transmissometer (PDAA)
LBT	Linear Beam Tube
LBT	Listen before Talk (IAA)
LBT	Local Battery Telephone [*Telecommunications*] (IAA)
LBT	Long-Baseline Tiltmeter [*For earthquake study*]
LBT	Low Back Tenderness [*Medicine*] (DMAA)
LBT	Low Bandpass Transformer
LBT	Low BIT [*Binary Digit*] Test [*Computer science*] (IEEE)
LBT	Lumberton, NC [*Location identifier FAA*] (FAAL)
LBT	Lutheran Bible Translators (EA)
LBT	Pounds Thrust [*NASA*] (KSC)
LBT	Pound Troy
LBT CBS	Local-Battery Talking, Common-Battery Signaling [*Telecommunications*] (TEL)
LBTF	Land-Based Test Facility (DNAB)
LBTF	Long Beach Test Facility [*Missiles*]
LBTI	Long-Burning Target Indicator [*British military*] (DMA)
LBTMA	Listen Before Transmission Multiple Access (PDAA)
LBTS	Land-Based Test Site
LBTS	Local Battery Telephone Set [*Telecommunications*] (IAA)
LBTS	Local Battery Telephone Switchboard [*Telecommunications*] (IAA)
LbtTrm	Liberty Term Trust [*Associated Press*]
LBTX	Local Battery Telephone Exchange [*Telecommunications*] (IAA)
LBTY..........	Tele-Communications Class A [*NASDAQ symbol*] (SAG)
LBTYA	Tele-Comm Inc. 'A' Liberty Media [*NASDAQ symbol*] (TTSB)
LbtyASE	Liberty All-Star Equity [*Associated Press*] (SAG)
LbtyASG	Liberty All Star Growth [*Associated Press*] (SAG)
LBTYB.........	Tele-Comm'B'Liberty Media [*NASDAQ symbol*] (TTSB)
LbtyBc	Liberty Bancorp, Inc. [*Associated Press*] (SAG)
LbtyH	Liberty Homes, Inc. [*Associated Press*] (SAG)
LBU	Labuan [*Malaysia*] [*Airport symbol*] (OAG)
LBU	Large Base Unit [*Telecommunications*]
LBU	Launcher Booster Unit
LBUN	Levobunolol [*Also, LB*] [*Biochemistry*]
LBuP...........	Plaquemines Parish Library, Buras, LA [*Library symbol Library of Congress*] (LCLS)
LBV	La Belle, FL [*Location identifier FAA*] (FAAL)
LBV	Landing Boat, Vehicle [*Navy symbol Obsolete*]
LBV	Left Brachial Vein [*Cardiology*] (DAVI)
LBV	Libreville [*Gabon*] [*Airport symbol*] (OAG)
LBV	Load-Bearing Vest [*Military*] (INF)
LBV	Local Bus Video
LBV	Luminous Blue Variables [*Astronomy*]
LBW	Landing Barge Water [*British military*] (DMA)
LBW	LASER Beam Welding
LBW	Lean Body Weight [*Medicine*] (DMAA)
LBW	Leg before Wicket [*Cricket*]
LBW	Long Bawan [*Indonesia*] [*Airport symbol*] (OAG)
LBW	Low Birth Weight [*Obstetrics*]
LBW	Low Body Weight
LBW	Low-Speed Black and White [*Photography*]
LBW	Lutheran Braille Workers (EA)
LBWBUZCALTX...	Local Battery with Buzzer Calling Telephone Exchange [*Telecommunications*] (IAA)
LBWI	Low-Birth-Weight Infant [*Obstetrics*] (MAE)
LBWMABCTX...	Local Battery with Magneto and Buzzer Calling Telephone Exchange [*Telecommunications*] (IAA)
LBWN	Varna [*Bulgaria*] [*ICAO location identifier*] (ICLI)
LBWOC	Level Bombing Wind Offset Computer [*Military*] (IAA)
LBWR	Lung-Body Weight Ratio [*Medicine*] (MAE)
LBX	Lake Jackson, TX [*Location identifier FAA*] (FAAL)
LBY	Hattiesburg, MS [*Location identifier FAA*] (FAAL)
LBY	La Baule [*France*] [*Airport symbol*] (AD)
LBY	Libbey, Inc. [*NYSE symbol*] (SPSG)
LBY	Libya [*ANSI three-letter standard code*] (CNC)
LB/YD^2	Pounds per Square Yard
LB/YD^3	Pounds per Cubic Yard
LBYR	Labyrinth [*Engineering*]
LBYRPK	Labyrinth [*Engineering*]
LC	Ewell's Leading Cases on Infancy, Etc. [*A publication*] (DLA)
L/C	Inductance/Capacitance (AAG)
LC	Label Clause

LC	Laboratory Craftsman (ADA)
LC	Labor Cases [A publication] (DLA)
LC	Labor Code (DNAB)
LC	Labour Canada [See also TRAVC]
LC	Labour Corps [British military] (DMA)
LC	La Crosse [Diocesan abbreviation] [Wisconsin] (TOCD)
LC	Lactation Consultant [Medicine] (MEDA)
LC	Laennec's Cirrhosis [Medicine] (MAE)
LC	Lagonda Club, US Section (EA)
LC	Lake Central Airlines
LC	Lakey Clinic Medical Center [Burlington, MA]
LC	Lamb Committee (EA)
LC	Lancaster & Chester Railway Co. [AAR code]
LC	Lance Corporal
LC	Land Commission [British]
LC	Land Court [Legal] [British]
LC	Landing Craft
LC	Langerhans' Cells [Medicine]
LC	Langmuir Circulation [Geophysics]
LC	Language Code [Online database field identifier]
LC	Large Case [Indicator] [IRS]
LC	Large Cell [Lymphoma classification]
LC	Larval Chamber [Botany]
LC	Lasa C Ring [Montana] [Seismograph station code, US Geological Survey] (SEIS)
LC	Last Card
LC	Late Clamped [Umbilical cord]
LC	Late Commitment [Reason for missed interception] [Military]
LC	Lateral Component
LC	Launch Center
LC	Launch Complex
LC	Launch Conference [Aerospace] (AAG)
L/C	Launch Control [Aerospace] (AAG)
LC	Launch Coordinator [NASA]
LC	Launch Corridor [Aerospace] (AAG)
LC	Launch Cost [Aerospace]
LC	Launch Count [NASA] (KSC)
LC	Launch Countdown [NASA] (NASA)
LC	Launch Critical (MCD)
LC	Launching Control [Military]
LC	Laundry Chute (MSA)
LC	Laureate of Arts
LC	Laureate of Letters
LC	Law Commission (DLA)
LC	Law Courts
LC	Lead Covered [or Coated]
LC	Leading Cases (DLA)
LC	League of Communists [Former Yugoslavia]
LC	League of Composers (EA)
LC	League of the Cross [Roman Catholic religious order] (ROG)
LC	Learning Curve (MSA)
LC	Least Count
LC	Leesona Corp. (KSC)
LC	Left Center [A stage direction]
LC	Left Chest [Medicine] (KSC)
LC	Left Circumflex (Artery) [Anatomy]
LC	Left Ear, Cold Stimulus [Medicine] (MEDA)
LC	Legal Committee (MCD)
LC	Legal Currency (ADA)
LC	Legionaries of Christ [Roman Catholic men's religious order]
lc	Legionaries of Christ (TOCD)
LC	Legislative Council [British]
LC	Legitimate Child
LC	Leisure Counseling [Medicine] (MEDA)
LC	Length of Chord (MSA)
LC	Lethal Concentration
L/C	Lettera di Credito [Letter of Credit] [Italian Business term]
LC	Letter Contract
LC	Letter of Credit
L/C	Letter of Credit (DFIT)
LC	Letters and Cards [US Postal Service]
LC	Lettre de Credit [Letter of Credit] [Business term] [French]
lc	Leucite [CIPW classification] [Geology]
LC	Level Control
LC	Level Crossing
LC	Leverage Contract [Business term]
LC	Leydig's Cells [Endocrinology]
LC	Leyland Cars [Leyland Daf Ltd.]
LC	Liaison-Cargo [Air Force]
LC	Liberal Conservative
LC	Liberalt Centrum [Liberal Center] [Denmark Political party] (PPE)
LC	Liberty Corp. [NYSE symbol] (SPSG)
LC	Library of Congress
LC	Library of Congress Card Number (NITA)
LC	Library of Congress Classification
LC	Licensing Country [Dialog] [Searchable field] [Information service or system] (NITA)
LC	Lieutenant Commander
LC	Life Care [Medicine] (BABM)
LC	Light Car [British]
LC	Light Case [Military] (NATG)
LC	Light Chain [Immunoglobulin]
LC	Light Company [British military] (DMA)
LC	Light Control [Technical drawings]
LC	Light Current (IAA)
LC	Lightly Canceled
LC	Limited Coordinating (NG)
LC	Limp Cloth [Bookbinding] (DGA)
LC	Linear Combination
LC	Line-Carrying
LC	Line Circuit [Telecommunications]
LC	Line Collector
LC	Line Concentrator
LC	Line Connection
LC	Line Connector (NITA)
LC	Line Construction Tools [JETDS nomenclature] [Military] (CET)
LC	Line Contractor (MCD)
LC	Line Control
LC	Line Crosser [Deserter] [Military]
LC	Line Length Ciceros [Typography] (DGA)
LC	Line of Communication [Military]
LC	Line of Contact [Military]
L/C	Line of Credit [Business term]
LC	Linguocervical [Dentistry]
LC	Link Circuit
LC	Link Control [Telecommunications] (OSI)
LC	Links and Chargers (NATG)
LC	Lipid Cytosome [Biochemistry] (MAE)
LC	Liquid Capacity
LC	Liquid Chromatography
LC	Liquid Crystal
LC	Literature Criticism from 1400 to 1800 [A publication]
LC	Lithocholate [Biochemistry]
LC	Liturgical Conference (EA)
LC	Liver Cirrhosis [Medicine]
LC	Living Children
LC	Load Carrier
LC	Load Cell
LC	Load Center (MSA)
LC	Load-Compensating (MSA)
LC	Load Computer [or Controller] (MCD)
LC	Load Contactor
LC	Loading Coil [Telecommunications] (TEL)
LC	Loan Capital [Business term]
LC	Loan Crowd [Investment term]
LC	Local Call [Followed by telephone number]
LC	Local Channel (CET)
LC	Localization Code (IAA)
LC	Localized Corrosion (PDAA)
LC	Location Counter [Computer science]
LC	Locked Closed
LC	Loco Citato [In the Place Cited] [Latin]
LC	Locus Ceruleus [Brain anatomy]
LC	Locus of Control [Psychology]
LC	Loganair [ICAO designator] (AD)
LC	Logical Channel (PDAA)
LC	Logic Cell (IAA)
LC	Logic Corp.
LC	Logistics Command (IAA)
LC	London Clause [Business term]
LC	London Club (EA)
LC	Long-Chain [Triglyceride] [Biochemistry] (MAE)
L/C	Loop Check (MUGU)
LC	Loose Coupler
LC	Lord Chamberlain [British]
LC	Lord Chancellor [British]
LC	Los Californianos (EA)
LC	Loss of Contact (IAA)
LC	Lotta Continua [Continuous Struggle] [Italy Political party] (PPE)
LC	Loud and Clear
LC	[A] Lover's Complaint [Shakespearean work]
LC	Low Calorie (AAMN)
LC	Low Carbon [Content, as low-carbon steel]
L/C	Low Compression [Automotive engineering]
LC	Low Conditioners [Psychology]
LC	Low Cost Color [Computer science] (CDE)
LC	Lower California
LC	Lower Canada
L/C	Lowercase [i.e., small letters] [Typography]
lc	Lowercase (WDMC)
LC	Lower Character (IAA)
LC	Lower Control (IAA)
LC	Lower Cylinder
LC	LOX [Liquid Oxygen] Clean
LC	Lubrication Chart
LC	Luminosity Class [Astronomy] (IAA)
LC	Lutheran Council [British] (DBA)
LC	Lyman Continuum [Spectroscopy] (OA)
LC	Lymphocyte-Mediated Cytotoxicity [Also, LMC] [Immunology]
LC	Lytic Capacity [Clinical chemistry]
LC	Scottish Land Court Reports [A publication] (DLA)
L/C	Single Acetate Single Cotton [Wire insulation] (AAG)
LC	St. Lucia [ANSI two-letter standard code] (CNC)
LC$_{50}$	Lethal Concentration, Median [Lethal for 50% of test group]
LCA	Lacana Mining Corp. [Toronto Stock Exchange symbol]
LCA	Lake Carriers' Association (EA)
LCA	Lake Central Airlines
LCA	Lamborghini Club America (EA)
LCA	Laminate Council of America [Defunct] (EA)
LCA	Land Compensation Act [Town planning] [British]

LCA	Landing Craft, Armored [*Used in Vietnam by the French to transport their engineer units*] (VNW)
LCA	Landing Craft, Assault [*Navy ship symbol*]
LCA	Larnaca [*Cyprus*] [*Airport symbol*] (OAG)
LCA	Launch Control Amplifier [*NASA*] (NASA)
LCA	Launch Control Analyst [*NASA*] (AAG)
LCA	Launch [*or Launcher*] Control Area [*Missiles*]
LCA	Lead Contractors Association [*British*] (EAIO)
LCA	Leadership Councils of America (EA)
LCA	Leading Cases, Annotated [*A publication*] (DLA)
LCA	Leading Catering Accountant [*British military*] (DMA)
LCA	Leber's Congenital Amaurosis [*Medicine*] (DAVI)
LCA	LeConte Airlines [*ICAO designator*] (FAAC)
LCA	Left Carotid Artery [*Cardiology*] (DAVI)
LCA	Left Coronary Artery [*Cardiology*]
LCA	Lesson Content Analysis
LCA	Leukocyte Common Antigen [*Immunochemistry*]
LCA	Leveling Control Amplifier
LCA	Library Club of America [*Defunct*] (EA)
LCA	Library-College Associates [*Defunct*] (EA)
LCA	Library of Congress Authority File [*Source file*] [*UTLAS symbol*]
LCA	Licensed Company Auditor [*British*]
LCA	Life Communicators Association [*Des Moines, IA*] (EA)
LCA	Life Cycle Analysis [*or Assessment*] [*Environmental science*]
LCA	Light Combat Aircraft [*Military*]
LCA	Lighting Control Assembly [*NASA*] (KSC)
LCA	Line Clearance Airdrome [*Air Force*]
LCA	Line Control Adapter
LCA	Liquid Crystal Analog
LCA	Lithocholic Acid [*Biochemistry*]
LCA	Lithuanian Catholic Alliance (EA)
LCA	Living Centers of America [*NYSE symbol*] (SAG)
LCA	Load-Carrying Ability (IAA)
LCA	Load Controller Assembly (NASA)
LCA	Local Communications Adapter [*IBM Corp.*]
LCA	Local Communications Area (KSC)
LCA	Local Cooperation Agreement [*Army Corps of Engineers*]
LCA	Local Core Alignment [*Telecommunications*] (NITA)
LCA	Log Cabin [*Alabama*] [*Seismograph station code, US Geological Survey*] (SEIS)
LCA	Logic Cell Array (IAA)
LCA	Logistic Control Activity (AABC)
LCA	Logistics Control Area (IAA)
LCA	London City Airport [*British*]
LCA	Longitudinal Chromatic Aberration
LCA	Louisiana Cattlemen's Association (SRA)
LCA	Louisiana Chemical Association (SRA)
LCA	Low-Cost Automation (WDAA)
LCA	Lowercase Alphabet
lca	Lowercase-Alphabet Length [*Typesetting*] (WDMC)
LCA	Lussazione Congenita dell'Anca [*Congenital Hip Dislocation*] [*Italian Medicine*]
LCA	Lutheran Church in America [*Later, ELCA*]
LCA	Lutheran Collegiate Association [*Defunct*] (EA)
LCA	St. Lucia [*ANSI three-letter standard code*] (CNC)
LCAA	Licensed Clubs Association of Australia
LCAACT	Licensed Clubs Association of the Australian Capital Territory
LCAAJ	Language and Culture Atlas of Ashkenazic Jewry [*A publication*] (BJA)
LCAAP	Lake City Army Ammunition Plant (AABC)
LCABLS Bull	Law Council of Australia. Business Law Section. Bulletin [*A publication*]
LCaC	Cameron Parish Library, Cameron, LA [*Library symbol Library of Congress*] (LCLS)
LCAC	Landing Craft, Air Cushion [*Navy symbol*]
LCAC	Library of Congress Classification - Additions and Changes [*A publication*]
LCAC	Listed Company Advisory Committee [*of NYSE*]
LCAC	Low-Cost Automation Centre [*British*]
LCACCC	Laymen's Commission of the American Council of Christian Churches (EA)
LCACT	Law Council of the Australian Capital Territory
LCAD	Logistics Cost Analysis Data (MCD)
LC-ADD	Library of Congress - American Doctoral Dissertations [*A bibliographic publication*]
LCAF	Lutheran Church in America Foundation
LCA(FT)	Landing Craft, Assault (Flamethrower) [*British military*] (DMA)
LCA(H)	Landing Craft, Assault (Hedgerow)
LCAH	London and Continental Advertising Holdings [*British*]
LCAL	Lower Conformance Altitude (SAA)
LCAM	Liver Cell Adhesion Molecule [*Cytology*]
LC & M Gaz	Lower Courts and Municipal Gazette [*Canada*] [*A publication*] (DLA)
LCANSW	Landscape Contractors' Association of New South Wales [*Australia*]
LCANSW	Licensed Clubs Association of New South Wales [*Australia*]
LCAO	Leadership Council of Aging Organizations (EA)
LCAO	Limited Configuration Atomic Orbital (MCD)
LCAO	Linear Combination of Atomic Orbitals [*Physical chemistry*]
LCA(OC)	Landing Craft, Assault (Obstacle Clearance) [*British military*] (DMA)
LCAofGB	Lightweight Cycle Association of Great Britian (DBA)
LCAO-MO-SCF	Linear Combination of Atomic Orbitals to Form Molecular Orbitals by a Self-Consistent Field [*Quantum mechanics*]
LCAP	Local Combat Air Patrol
LCAP	Loop Carrier Analysis Program [*Bell System*]
LCAR	Late Cutaneous Anaphylactic Reaction [*Immunology*]
LCAR	Launch Complex Assessment Report [*NASA*] (KSC)

LCAR	Lotus Cortina of America Register [*Defunct*] (EA)
LCAR	Low-Cost Attack RADAR
LCAR	Low-Coverage Acquisiton RADAR (PDAA)
LCar	United States Public Health Service Hospital, Carville, LA [*Library symbol Library of Congress*] (LCLS)
LCAS	Lithuanian Catholic Academy of Sciences (EA)
LCASA	Licensed Clubs Association of South Australia
LCAT	Lecithin-Cholesterol Acyltransferase [*An enzyme*]
LCAT	Licensed Clubs Association of Tasmania [*Australia*]
LCAT	Lifts and Cranes Appeals Tribunal [*Australia*]
LCATA	Laundry and Cleaners Allied Trades Association [*Later, TCATA*]
LCAUE	Liaison Committee of the Architects of United Europe [*EC*] (ECED)
LCAUS	Latvian Choir Association of the US (EA)
LCAV	Landscape Contractors Association of Victoria [*Australia*]
LCAV	LCA-Vision [*NASDAQ symbol*] (TTSB)
LCAVAT	Landing Craft and Amphibious Vehicle Assignment Table
LCAX	Landing Craft, Assault, Experimental [*Navy ship symbol*]
LCB	Landing Craft, Vehicle [*Navy symbol*]
LCB	Launch Control Building [*NASA*]
LCB	Least-Common Bigram [*Computer science*] (BYTE)
LCB	Least Common BIT [*Binary Digit*] (MCD)
LCB	Left Cornerback [*Football*]
LCB	Liefdezusters van de H. Carolus Borromeus [*Sisters of Charity of St. Charles Borromeo - SCSCB*] (EAIO)
LCB	Limited Capability Buoy
LCB	Line Control Block [*Computer science*]
LCB	Liquor Control Board [*Canada*]
LCB	Living Country Blues [*A publication*]
LCB	Logic Control Block
LCB	London Centre for Biotechnology [*British*] (IRUK)
LCB	Long-Chain Branching [*Organic chemistry*]
LCB	Longitudinal Position of Center of Buoyancy
LCB	Lord Chief Baron [*British*]
LCBA	Loyal Christian Benefit Association [*Erie, PA*] (EA)
LCBB	"Life Can Be Beautiful" [*Old radio program; nicknamed "Elsie Beebee"*]
LCBF	Local Cerebral Blood Flow [*Medicine*]
LCBM	Lifecore Biomedical [*NASDAQ symbol*] (TTSB)
LCBM	LifeCore Biomedical, Inc. [*NASDAQ symbol*] (SAG)
LCBO	Linear Combination of [*Semi-localized*] Band Orbitals [*Atomic physics*]
LCBS	London Classification of Business Studies [*Library classification scheme*] [*British*] (NITA)
LCBWR	LaCrosse Boiling Water Reactor [*Also, LACBWR*]
LCBX	Large Computerized [*Private*] Branch Exchange (MHDI)
LCC	Amphibious Command Ship [*Formerly, AGC*] [*Navy symbol*]
LCC	Charles A. Lindbergh Collectors Club (EA)
LCC	Labor Case Comments [*Cast Metals Association*] [*A publication*]
LCC	Labor Class Code (DNAB)
LCC	Labour Coordinating Committee [*British*]
LCC	Lactose Coliform Count [*Medicine*] (BABM)
LCC	Land Capability Classes [*Agriculture*]
LCC	Land Component Commander (MCD)
LCC	Land Court Cases [*New South Wales*] [*A publication*] (DLA)
LCC	Landing Control Center
LCC	Landing Craft, Control
LCC	Langley Complex Coordination [*Device*] [*NASA*]
LCC	Language for Conversational Computing (MDG)
LCC	Large Capacity Cassette [*Electronic printing*] (DGA)
LCC	Large Cavitation Channel [*Pressurized water tunnel to test submarines and ship models*] [*Navy*]
LCC	Large Compressor Colorimeter (MCD)
LCC	Last Clear Chance [*Legal shorthand*] (LWAP)
LCC	Late Choice Call (NITA)
LCC	Launch Command and Control
LCC	Launch Commit Criteria (MCD)
LCC	Launch Control Center [*NASA*]
LCC	Launch Control Console
LCC	Leach's English Crown Cases [*1730-1815*] [*A publication*] (DLA)
LCC	Lead-Coated Copper (OA)
LCC	Lead Covered Cable [*Telecommunications*] (TEL)
LCC	Leadless Chip Carrier [*Motorola, Inc.*]
LCC	Le Cercle Concours d'Elegance (EA)
LCC	Ledger Card Computer (MHDB)
LCC	Left Circumflex Coronary Artery [*Medicine*] (DMAA)
LCC	Legacy Coordinating Council [*Australia*]
LCC	Legalise Cannabis Campaign [*British*] (DBA)
LCC	Lesser of Costs or Charges [*Medicine*] (GFGA)
LCC	Levo-Carnitine Chloride [*Biochemistry*]
LCC	Liang-Chow [*Republic of China*] [*Seismograph station code, US Geological Survey Closed*] (SEIS)
LCC	Libertarian Council of Churches [*Defunct*] (EA)
LCC	Libraries Consultative Committee [*Australia*]
LCC	Libraries Copyright Committee [*Australia*]
LCC	Library of Congress Classification
LCC	Life-Cycle Costing [*or Costs*] [*DoD*]
LCC	Lignin-Carbohydrate Complex [*Organic chemistry*]
LCC	Ligue Canadienne des Composeurs [*Canadian League of Composers - CLC*]
LCC	Limited Capability Configuration [*Army*] (DOMA)
LCC	Lincoln Capital Corp. [*Toronto Stock Exchange symbol*]
LCC	Linear Cutting Cord [*Aircraft escape technology*] (PDAA)
LCC	Linecaster Control (DGA)
LCC	Link Control Standard Controller [*Telecommunications*] (ECII)
LCC	Liquid Crystal Cell (IEEE)

LCC............ Liquid-Cushion Electroplating Cell [Steel production]
LCC............ Liquor Control Commission
LCC............ Lithophane Collectors Club (EA)
LCC............ Little Carter Cay [NASA] (KSC)
LCC............ Load Controlling Crewman [Helicopter] [Navy]
LCC............ Loading Coil Case [Telecommunications] (TEL)
LCC............ Local Communications Complex
LCC............ Local Communications Console
LCC............ Local Control Console (CAAL)
LCC............ Local Coordinating Committee
LCC............ Lockheed-California Co. [Division of Lockheed Aircraft Corp.]
LCC............ Logistic Control Code [Military] (AABC)
LCC............ Logistics Control Center [Military] (INF)
LCC............ Logistics Coordination Center [NATO]
LCC............ London Chamber of Commerce [British] (DAS)
LCC............ London Communications Committee [World War II]
LCC............ London County Council [or Councillor] [Later, GLC]
LCC............ Lost Calls Cleared [Telecommunications] (NITA)
LCC............ Lost Chord Clubs (EA)
LCC............ Low-Cement Castable [Ceramics]
LCC............ Low-Cost Classifier (MCD)
LCC............ Lundy Collectors Club (EA)
LCCA.......... Late Cortical Cerebellar Atrophy [Neurology]
LCCA.......... Lawyers Committee on Central America [Defunct] (EA)
LCCA.......... Left Circumflex Coronary Artery [Anatomy]
LCCA.......... Left Common Carotid Artery [Cardiology] (DAVI)
LCCA.......... Leukocytoelastic Angitis [Cardiology] (DAVI)
LCCA.......... Life Cycle Cost Analysis (MCD)
LCCA.......... Lionel Collectors Club of America (EA)
LCCA.......... Lithuanian Chamber of Commerce of America (EA)
LCCA.......... Load Current Contacting Aiding
LCCA.......... London Church Choir Association
LCCA.......... Low-Cost Computer Attachment (IAA)
LCCB.......... Local Change Control Board (MCD)
LCCB.......... Local Configuration Control Board (AABC)
LCCB.......... Low-Cost Controllable Booster (MCD)
LCCC.......... Leadless Ceramic Chip Carrier [Electronics]
LCCC.......... Library of Congress Catalogue Card (WDAA)
LCCC.......... Library of Congress Computer Catalog (NITA)
LCCC.......... Lower Canada Civil Code [A publication] (DLA)
LCCC.......... Luzerne County Community College [Nanticoke, PA] (TSSD)
LCCC.......... Nicosia [Cyprus] [ICAO location identifier] (ICLI)
LCCCN........ Library of Congress Catalog Card Number (NITA)
LCCD.......... Launch Commit Criteria Document [NASA] (NASA)
LCCD.......... Low Complexity Color Display [Video technology] (EECA)
LCC/DTC...... Life Cycle Cost / Design to Cost
LCCE.......... Lee County Central Electric [AAR code]
LCCE.......... Life-Cycle Cost Estimate (AABC)
LCCEB........ London Chamber of Commerce Examinations Board [British] (AIE)
LCCEP........ Logistics Civilian Career Enhancement Program [Military]
LCCFC........ Launch Control Complex Facility Console [NASA] (IAA)
LCCI.......... London Chamber of Commerce and Industry [British] (DCTA)
LCCID .... Life Cycle Cost in Design [Computer program released by US Army Construction Engineering Research Laboratory] (RDA)
LCCM.......... LanClient Control Manager [Computer science]
LCCM.......... Late Choice Call Meter [Telecommunications] (NITA)
LCCMARC... Library of Congress Current MARC [Machine-Readable Catalog] File (NITA)
LCCMS........ Launch Control Center Measuring Station [NASA] (KSC)
LCCN .... Library of Congress Catalog-Card Number
LCCO.......... Landing Craft Control Officer [Military]
LCCO .... Leadership Career Counseling Officer (DNAB)
LCCO .... Life Cycle Cost of Ownership (MCD)
LCCOGA...... Liaison Committee of Cooperating Oil and Gas Associations (EA)
LC Cont....... Langdell's Cases on Contracts [A publication] (DLA)
LCCP.......... Landing Craft Control Primary [Military]
LCCP.......... LASER Code Control Panel (MCD)
LCCP.......... Launch Captain's Control Panel [Navy] (CAAL)
LCCP.......... Lower Canada Civil Procedure [A publication] (DLA)
LCC-PDR...... League of Communists of Croatia - Party of Democratic Reform [Political party]
LCCPT........ Low-Cost Cockpit Procedures Trainer (MCD)
LCCR .... Laboratory for Computer and Communications Research [Simon Fraser University] [Canada Research center] (RCD)
LCCR .... Leadership Conference on Civil Rights (EA)
LCCRUL...... Lawyers' Committee for Civil Rights under Law (EA)
LCCS.......... Large Capacity Core Storage [Computer science] (MDG)
LCCS.......... Launch Checkout and Countdown System [Aerospace] (IAA)
LCCS.......... Launch Control and Checkout System [Aerospace] (IAA)
LCCS.......... Launcher Captain Control System [Military] (NVT)
LCCS.......... Library of Congress Classification Schedules [A publication]
LCCS.......... Logistics Control Center System
LCCS.......... Low Cervical Caesarean Section
LCCTS........ Life Cycle Cost Tracking System [Social Security Administration]
LCCU.......... Lightweight Crewman Communication Umbilical (MCD)
LCCV.......... Large-Component Cleaning Vessel [Nuclear energy] (NRCH)
LCCW.......... Low-Cost Composite Weapon (MCD)
LCD............ Language for Computer Design (CSR)
LCD............ Launch Control Design [NASA] (AAG)
LCD............ Launch Countdown [NASA] (NASA)
LCD............ Least [or Lowest] Common Denominator [or Divisor] [Mathematics]
LCD............ Letter Carrier Depot (DD)
LCD............ Lightweight Ceramic Dome
LCD............ Line Current Disconnect (HGAA)
LCD............ Liquid Crystal Digital [Battery-powered wristwatch]

LCD............ Liquid Crystal Diode
LCD............ Liquid Crystal Display
LCD............ Liquor Carbonis Detergens [Coal tar solution] [Medicine]
LCD............ List of Chosen Descriptors (PDAA)
LCD............ Liver Cell Dysplasia [Medicine]
LCD............ LM [Lunar Module] Change Directive [NASA] (KSC)
LCD............ Local Climatological Data [A publication]
LCD............ Localized Collagen Dystrophy [Medicine] (DAVI)
LCD............ Logistics Communications Division [Military]
LCD............ London College of Divinity
LCD............ Lord Chancellor's Department [British]
LCD............ Loss of Clock Detector
LCD............ Louis Trichardt [South Africa] [Airport symbol] (OAG)
LCD............ Low Cost Drifter [Marine science] (OSRA)
LCD............ Lumped Constant Dispersion
LCD............ Ohio Lower Court Decisions [A publication] (DLA)
LCDC .... Laboratory Centre for Disease Control [Canada]
LCDD .... Light Chain Deposition Disease [Medicine] (DMAA)
LCDDS .... Leased Circuit Digital Data Service [British Telecom] (EECA)
LCDHWIU ... Laundry, Cleaning, and Dye House Workers' International Union [Later, Textile Processors, Service Trades, Health Care, Professional, and Technical Employees International Union] (EA)
LCDOSEM .... Local Civil Defense Operating Systems Evaluation Model (PDAA)
LCDR .... Lieutenant Commander (AAG)
LCDR .... London, Chatham & Dover Railway [British]
LCDS .... Lefschetz Center for Dynamical Systems [Brown University] [Research center] (RCD)
LCDS .... Liquid-Crystal Displays [Computer science]
LCDS .... Low-Cost Development System [National Semiconductor Corp.]
LCDT.......... London Contemporary Dance Theatre
LCDT.......... London Contemporary Dance Theatre [Defunct]
LCDTL......... Load-Compensated Diode Transistor Logic [Computer science]
LCDTL......... Low Current Diode Transistor Logic [Electronics] (IAA)
LCE............ La Ceiba [Honduras] [Airport symbol] (OAG)
LCE............ Lance (WGA)
LCE............ Land-Covered Earth (OA)
LCE............ Landing Craft, Emergency Repair
LCE............ Latest Cost Estimate (NATG)
LCE............ Launch Complex Engineer [NASA] (KSC)
LCE............ Launch Complex Equipment
LCE............ Launch Control Equipment (AAG)
LCE............ Launch Countdown Exercise [NASA] (AFM)
LCE............ Left Center Entrance [Theater] (WDMC)
LCE............ Legal Counsel for the Elderly (EA)
LCE............ Licentiate in Civil Engineering (WDAA)
LCE............ Load-Carrying Equipment (MCD)
LCE............ Load Circuit Efficiency
LCE............ Logistic Capability Estimate (MCD)
LCE............ Lone Star Indus [NYSE symbol] (TTSB)
LCE............ Lone Star Industries, Inc. [Formerly, Lone Star Cement Corp.] [NYSE symbol] (SPSG)
LCE............ Low-Cost Expendable [Refers to payload type] [NASA]
LCE............ Lyapunov Characteristic Exponent [Mathematics]
LCEA.......... Licentiate of the Association of Cost and Executive Accountants [British] (DBQ)
LCEAPL....... Lawyers Committee for the Enforcement of Animal Protection Law (EA)
LCEB.......... Launch Control Equipment Building (AFM)
LCEBM........ Liaison Committee of European Bicycle Manufacturers [Belgium] (EAIO)
LCEC.......... Liquid Chromatographs with Electrochemical Detection
LCED.......... Low-Cost Encryption Device [Military] (GFGA)
LCEE.......... Louisiana Council on Economic Education (EDAC)
LCEECSTI..... Liaison Committee of the European Economic Community Steel Tube Industry [Defunct] (EAIO)
LCEHV .... Low-Cost Expendable Harassment Vehicle [Air Force] (MCD)
LCEM.......... Leading Control Electrical Mechanic [British military] (DMA)
LCEMM........ Liaison Committee of European Motorcycle Manufacturers [Belgium] (EAIO)
LCEOP .... Landing Craft, Engine Overhaul Parties
LCEP.......... Lower Critical End Points [Supercritical extraction]
LCEPS......... Labor Cooperative Educational and Publishing Society [Defunct] (EA)
LC Eq.......... White and Tudor's Leading Cases in Equity [A publication] (DLA)
LCER.......... Labour Campaign Electoral Reform [British] [An association] (DBA)
LCES.......... Least Cost Estimating and Scheduling (IAA)
LCE.WS .... Lone Star Indus Wrrt [NYSE symbol] (TTSB)
LCEWS........ Low-Cost Electronic Warfare Suite (NVT)
LCF............ Landing Craft, Flak
LCF............ Language Central Facility [Computer science] (IEEE)
LCF............ Last Chance Filter (MCD)
LCF............ Last Chance Forever (EA)
LCF............ Latent Cancer Fatalities (PDAA)
LCF............ Launch Control Facility
LCF............ Law Centres Federation [British] (DBA)
LCF............ Lawyers Christian Fellowship (EA)
LCF............ Learning Curve Factor
LCF............ Least [or Lowest] Common Factor [Mathematics]
LCF............ Least Cost Feed Formulation System (ADA)
LCF............ Lederberg-Coxeter-Frucht [Notation] [Graph theory, mathematics]
LCF............ Left Circumflex Artery [Anatomy]
LCF............ Left Common Femoral [Artery] [Anatomy] (DAVI)
LCF............ Level Control Function [Computer science]
LCF............ Librarians' Christian Fellowship [British] (DBA)
LCF............ Library of Congress Films [Source file] [UTLAS symbol]

LCF.............. Lime, Cement, and Flyash (PDAA)
LCF.............. Lincomycin Cosynthetic Factor [Biochemistry]
LCF.............. Liquid, Complex Fertilizer (PDAA)
LCF.............. Little City Foundation (EA)
LCF.............. Living Church Foundation (EA)
LCF.............. Local Control Facility [FAA] (TAG)
LCF.............. Local Cycle Fatigue (IEEE)
LCF.............. Log Cabin Federation (EA)
LCF.............. Logical Channel Fill
LCF.............. Longitudinal Position of Center of Flotation
LCF.............. Low Cab Forward [Automotive engineering]
LCF.............. Low Cab Forward [Truck configuration]
LCF.............. Low-Carbon Ferrochrome [Metallurgy]
LCF.............. Low Coefficient of Friction [Aerodynamics]
LCF.............. Low-Cycle Fatigue [Rocket engine]
LCF.............. Lymphocyte Chemoattractant Factor [Biochemistry]
LCFA............ Lithuanian Catholic Federation Ateitis (EA)
LCFA............ Long-Chain Fatty Acids [Organic chemistry]
LCFC............ Launch Complex Facility Console [NASA] (IAA)
LCFC............ Leslie Charleson Fan Club (EA)
LCFC............ Living Colour Fan Club (EA)
LCFC............ Low-Cycle Fatigue Counter (PDAA)
LC(FF).......... Landing Craft, Infantry (Flotilla Flagship) [Navy symbol]
LCFLOLS...... Laterally Compounded Fresnel Lens Optical Landing System
LCFLOTSPAC... Landing Craft, Flotilla, Pacific Fleet
LCFNM......... Lawyers' Campaign to Free Nelson Mandela [Defunct] (EA)
LCFS............ Last-Come, First-Served
LCFS............ Launch Control Facility Simulator [NASA] (IAA)
LCFSPR ...... Last Come, First Served Preemptive Resume (PDAA)
LCFU............ Laboratory Configured Fire Units (MCD)
LCG............. La Coruna [Spain] [Airport symbol] (OAG)
LCG............. Landing Craft Gun (MCD)
LCG............. Landing Craft, Gunboat
LCG............. Langerhans' Cell Granule [Anatomy]
LCG............. Langerhans' Cell Granulomatosis [Oncology]
LCG............. Lead Computing Gyro (MCD)
LCG............. Left Cerebral Ganglion [Medicine]
LCG............. Leon Cerro Gordo [Mexico] [Seismograph station code, US
              Geological Survey] (SEIS)
LCG............. Liquid-Cooled Garment [Spacesuit]
LCG............. Load Classification Group (DA)
LCG............. Loads Control Group [Prepares supplies to be airlifted] [Military]
LCG............. Logistics Control Group [Air Materiel Command] (AAG)
LCG............. Longitudinal Position of Center of Gravity
LCG............. Lookahead Carry Generator [Computer science] (IAA)
LCG............. Low Center of Gravity [Tractor engineering]
LCG............. Low-Cost Generator
LCG............. Lower Courts Gazette [Ontario] [A publication] (DLA)
LCG............. Wayne, NE [Location identifier FAA] (FAAL)
LCGB .... Letzeburger Chreschtliche Gewerkschaftsbond [Confederation of
              Christian Trade Unions of Luxembourg]
LCGB .... Locomotive Club of Great Britain (BI)
LCGF .... Longitudinal Ciliated Groove of Filament
LCGIL.......... Libera Confederazione Generale Italiana dei Lavoratori [Free Italian
              General Confederation of Workers]
LCG(L)......... Landing Craft, Gun (Large)
LCG(M)........ Landing Craft, Gun (Medium)
LCGME........ Liaison Committee on Graduate Medical Education
LCGN .... Logical Channel Group Number [Telecommunications] (OSI)
LCGO .... Linear Combination of Gaussian Orbitals [Atomic physics]
LCGP .... Landing Craft, Group
LCG(S)......... Landing Craft, Gun (Small) [British military] (DMA)
LCGS .... Lead Computing Gun Sight
LCGT .... Listening Comprehension Group Test
LCGT/IGS..... Low-Cost Graphics Terminal/Interactive Graphics System (PDAA)
LCGU .... Lead Computing Gyroscope Unit (MCD)
LCGU .... Local Cerebral Glucose Utilization [Biochemistry]
LCH............. Lake Charles [Louisiana] [Airport symbol] (OAG)
LCH............. Lake Charles, LA [Location identifier FAA] (FAAL)
LCH............. Landing Craft Headquarters [British military] (DMA)
LCH............. Landing Craft (Heavy) (ADA)
LCH............. Landing Craft Hospital [British military] (DMA)
LCH............. Larch Resources Ltd. [Vancouver Stock Exchange symbol]
LCH............. Latch (MSA)
LCH............. Launch
LCH............. Launching Charging Header
LCh............. Licentiate of the Institute of Chiropodists [British]
L Ch............ Licentiatus Chirurgiae [Licentiate in Surgery]
LCH............. Life Cycle Hypothesis [Economics]
LCH............. Load Channel (IAA)
LCH............. Local City Hospital (DAVI)
LCH............. Logical Channel Queue [Computer science]
L CH .... Lord Chancellor [British] (ROG)
LCH............. Lost Calls Held [Telecommunications] (NITA)
Lch.............. Lunch
LCHA .... Lynch Flying Service, Inc. [ICAO designator] (FAAC)
LCHA .... Love Canal Homeowners Association (EA)
LChaMC....... Louisiana Universities Marine Consortium, Chauvin, LA [Library
              symbol] [Library of Congress] (LCLS)
LCHE........... Luton College of Higher Education (AIE)
LCHP .... Local Control Hydraulic Panel
LCHQ .... Local Command Headquarters [NATO] (NATG)
LCHR .... Launcher (AAG)
L Chr .... Law Chronicle [England] [A publication] (DLA)
LCHR .... Lawyers Committee for Human Rights (EA)

LChr............ Liberte Chretienne [A publication] (BJA)
L Chron........ Law Chronicle [England] [A publication] (DLA)
L Chron & L Stud Mag... Law Chronicle and Law Students' Magazine
              [A publication] (DLA)
L Chron & L Stud Mag (NS)... Law Chronicle and Law Students' Magazine (New
              Series) [A publication] (DLA)
LCHS .... Large Component Handling System [Nuclear energy] (NRCH)
LChSt........... Saint Bernard Parish Library, Chalmette, LA [Library symbol Library
              of Congress] (LCLS)
LCHTF......... Low-Cycle High-Temperature Fatigue [Rocket engine]
LCI.............. Laboratory of Cellular Immunology [University of Arizona] [Research
              center] (RCD)
LCI.............. Labor Cost Index
LCI.............. Laconia [New Hampshire] [Airport symbol] (OAG)
LCI.............. Laconia, NH [Location identifier FAA] (FAAL)
LCI.............. Lafarge Canada, Inc. [Toronto Stock Exchange symbol]
LCI.............. Landing Craft, Infantry [Obsolete]
LCI.............. Launch Complex Instrumentation (IAA)
LCI.............. Launcher Control Indicator [Missiles] (AABC)
LCI.............. LCI International [NYSE symbol] (SAG)
LCI.............. Learner-Centered Instruction (PDAA)
LCI.............. Legally Correct Interpretation [of the ABM treaty]
LCI.............. Life Cycle Inventory [Environmental engineering]
LCI.............. Liga Comunista Internacionalista [International Communist League]
              [Portugal Political party] (PPE)
LCI.............. Lions Clubs International (EA)
LCI.............. Liquid Crystal Institute [Kent State University] (PDAA)
LCI.............. Literary Criticism Index [A publication]
LCI.............. Livestock Conservation Institute (EA)
LCI.............. Locus of Control Interview [Psychology]
LCI.............. Low-Cost Inertial
LCI.............. Lummus Crest, Inc. [Telecommunications service] (TSSD)
LCI.............. United States Central Intelligence Agency, McLean, VA [OCLC
              symbol] (OCLC)
LCI(A)......... Landing Craft, Infantry (Ammunition)
LCIA........... London Court of International Arbitration
LCIB........... Library of Congress. Information Bulletin [A publication]
LCIC........... Leisure Concepts [NASDAQ symbol] (SAG)
LCICD .... Liquid Crystal Induced Circular Dichroism [Spectroscopy]
LCI(D).......... Landing Craft, Infantry (Demolition) [British military] (DMA)
LCIDIV .... Landing Craft, Infantry, Division
LCIFC.......... Lou Christie International Fan Club (EA)
LCIFLOT...... Landing Craft, Infantry, Flotilla [Obsolete]
LCI(G).......... Landing Craft, Infantry, Gunboat [Obsolete]
LCIGB .... Locomotive and Carriage Institution of Great Britain and Eire (BI)
LCIGRP........ Landing Craft, Infantry, Group
LCIGS .... Low-Cost Inertial Guidance Subsystem (MCD)
LCIHR .... Lawyers Committee for International Human Rights (EA)
LCI Int .... LCI International [Associated Press] (SAG)
LCIL........... Landing Craft, Infantry, Large [Obsolete]
LCILFLOT...... Landing Craft, Infantry, Large, Flotilla [Obsolete]
LCI(M)......... Landing Craft, Infantry (Medium) [British military] (DMA)
LCI(M)......... Landing Craft, Infantry (Mortar Ship) [Obsolete]
LC Intl .... LCI International [Associated Press] (SAG)
LCIOB .... Licentiate of the Chartered Institute of Building [British] (DI)
LCIPr........... LCI Intl 5% Cv Exch Pfd [NYSE symbol] (TTSB)
LCI(R).......... Landing Craft, Infantry (Rocket Ship) [Obsolete]
LC/IR........... Liquid Chromatography/Infrared
LCI(S).......... Landing Craft, Infantry (Small) [British military] (DMA)
LCIS........... Lighter Collectors' International Society [Defunct] (EA)
LCIS........... Lobular Carcinoma in Situ [Medicine] (AAMN)
LCJ............. Lawyers for Civil Justice (EA)
LCJ............. Lord Chief Justice [British]
LCJ............. Low Cost Junction [Optical fibre equipment] (NITA)
LCJ............. Lower Canada Jurist, Montreal [1848-91] [A publication] (DLA)
LC Jur .... Lower Canada Jurist [A publication] (DLA)
LCK............. Columbus, OH [Location identifier FAA] (FAAL)
LCK............. Landing Craft, Kitchen
L Ck............ Leading Cook [British military] (DMA)
LCK............. Legion of Christ the King [Defunct] (EA)
LCK............. Library Construction Kit [Microsoft Corp.] [Computer science] (PCM)
LCK............. Lock
LCK............. Lock [Postal Service standard] (OPSA)
LCKR........... Locker
LCKR........... Locker (DNAB)
LCKS........... Locks
LCKS........... Locks
LCKY........... Lucky
LCL............. Labor Congress of Liberia
LCL............. Lambert Cosine Law [Physics]
LCL............. Landing Craft, Logistic [British military] (DMA)
LCL............. Lateral Collateral Ligament [Anatomy]
LCL............. Leading Catholic Layman
LCL............. Lens Culinaris Lectin
LCL............. Less-than-Carload [Under 60,000 pounds]
LCL............. Less-than-Carload Lot (DFIT)
LCL............. Less-than-Container Load [Shipping]
LCL............. Levinthal-Coles-Lillie Bodies [Microbiology]
LCL............. Liberal Country League [Australia] (BARN)
LCL............. Library Control Language (OA)
LCL............. Library of Congress, Interlibrary Loan Department [UTLAS symbol]
LCL............. Licentiate of Canon Law [British]
LCL............. Licentiate of Civil Law
LCL............. Lifting Condensation Level [Meteorology]
LCL............. Light Center Length

LCL............. Limited Channel Logout
LCL............. Linkage Control Language [Computer science] (BUR)
LCL............. Local (AFM)
LCL............. Local
LCLi............ Localizer (CET)
LCL............. Loeb Classical Library. Harvard University Press [A publication] (BJA)
LCL............. Logical Comparative LOFAR
LCL............. Loose Container Load [Shipping] (IMH)
LCL............. Lot-Car Load
LCL............. Low-Capacity Link [Telecommunications] (OA)
LCL............. Lower Confidence Limit [Statistics]
LCL............. Lower Control Limit [QCR]
LCL............. Lower of Cost or Market (TDOB)
LCL............. Lymphoblastoid Cell Line
LCL............. Lymphocytic Leukemia (MAE)
LCL............. Lymphocytic Lymphosarcoma [Oncology]
LCL............. Lymphoma Cell Line [Oncology]
LCL............. Mala Services Ltd. [British] [FAA designator] (FAAC)
LCLA.......... Lutheran Church Library Association (EA)
LCLAA........ Labor Council for Latin American Advancement (EA)
LCLC.......... Large Cell Lung Carcinoma [Oncology] (DAVI)
LCL/CI........ Limited Calendar Life, Controlled Item
LCLD.......... Laclede Steel [NASDAQ symbol] (TTSB)
LCLD.......... Laclede Steel Co. [NASDAQ symbol] (SAG)
LCLi............ Audubon Regional Library, Clinton, LA [Library symbol Library of Congress] (LCLS)
LCLJ.......... Lower Canada Law Journal [A publication] (DLA)
LCL Jo........ Lower Canada Law Journal [A publication] (DLA)
LCLK.......... Larnaca [Cyprus] [ICAO location identifier] (ICLI)
LCLM.......... Low-Cost Lightweight Missile (MCD)
LCLo............ Lethal Concentration Low (ERG)
LCLS.......... Lewis and Clark Library System [Library network]
LCLSC........ Life-Cycle Logistic Support Cost (PDAA)
LCLU.......... Landing Control Logic Unit [Aviation] (OA)
LCLV.......... Liberace Club of Las Vegas (EA)
LCLV.......... Lilac Chlorotic Leafspot Virus [Plant pathology]
LCLV.......... Liquid-Crystal Light Valve (IEEE)
LCLV.......... Low-Cost Launch Vehicle [NASA] (KSC)
LCLZR........ Localizer (IAA)
LCM........... Laboratory Contract Manager (MCD)
LCM........... La Cumbre [Argentina] [Airport symbol] (AD)
LCM........... Lake Champlain & Moriah Rail Road Co. [AAR code]
LCM........... Land Combat Missile
LCM........... Landing Craft, Mechanized [Navy symbol]
LCM........... Landing Craft, Medium [Navy]
LCM........... Large-Core Memory [Computer science]
LCM........... Laser Capture Microdissection [Biochemistry]
LCM........... LASER Cloud Mapper
LCM........... LASER Countermeasure
LCM........... Last Calls Meter [Telecommunications] (NITA)
LCM........... Late Change Message [Aviation] (DA)
LCM........... Launch Control Monitor (MCD)
LCM........... Launch Crew Member (AAG)
LCM........... Lead-Coated Metal [Technical drawings]
LCM........... Least Common Multiple [Mathematics]
LCM........... Least Concave Majorant [Statistics]
LCM........... Left Costal Margin [Medicine]
LCM........... Legis Comparativae Magister [Master of Comparative Law] [Latin] (WGA)
LCM........... Leukocyte-Conditioned Medium [Microbiology]
LCM........... Library of Congress Maps [Source file] [UTLAS symbol]
LCM........... Life Cycle Manager (MCD)
LCM........... Lightning Creek Mines Ltd. [Vancouver Stock Exchange symbol]
LCM........... Line Concentrator Module
LCM........... Line Control Module [Telecommunications] (TEL)
LCM........... Liquid Composite Molding [Materials science]
LCM........... Liquid Curing Medium
LCM........... Little Company of Mary, Nursing Sisters [Roman Catholic religious order]
LCM........... LOCA [Loss-of-Coolant Accident] Core Melt [Nuclear energy] (NRCH)
LCM........... Loer, C. M., Reno NV [STAC]
LCM........... London City Mission
LCM........... London College of Music (ROG)
LCM........... Longhaul Customer Modem [Telecommunications] (NITA)
LCM........... Loose Cubic Meter (DAC)
LCM........... Lost Circulation Material [Oil well drilling]
LCM........... Low Cost Module (IAA)
LCM........... Lower of Cost or Market
LCM........... Lowest Common Multiple [Mathematics]
LCM........... Lymphocyte Conditioned Medium [Hematology]
LCM........... Lymphocytic Choriomeningitis [Medicine]
LCM(2)........ Landing Craft, Mechanized, MKII [Navy symbol]
LCM(3)........ Landing Craft, Mechanized, MKIII [Navy symbol]
LCM6.......... Landing Craft, Mechanized, MKVI [Navy symbol]
LCM8.......... Landing Craft, Mechanized, MKVIII [Navy symbol]
LCMA.......... Lightweight Cycle Manufacturers Association [British] (DBA)
LCMA.......... Longhaul Customer Modem Adapter [Telecommunications] (NITA)
LCMA.......... Lutheran Campus Ministry Association [Defunct] (EA)
LCMA.......... Lutheran Church Men of America
LC MARC...... Library of Congress Machine Readable Catalog [Washington, DC] [Bibliographic database] [Library of Congress]
LCMARC ...... Library of Congress MARC [Machine-Readable Catalog] Files (NITA)

LCMCFC...... Liaison Committee for Mediterranean Citrus Fruit Culture [See also CLAM] [Madrid, Spain] (EAIO)
LCMCS........ Liquid Conditioned Microclimate System [Army] (RDA)
LCMD.......... Low-Cost Motor Demonstration (MCD)
LCME.......... Large Climate-Moderating Envelope [Energy-conserving form of architecture]
LCME.......... Liaison Committee on Medical Education (EA)
LCM(G)........ Landing Craft, Mechanised (Gun) [British military] (DMA)
LCMG.......... Long-Chain Monoglyceride [Biochemistry] (MAE)
LCMH.......... Lake Charles Memorial Hospital [Lake Charles, LA]
LCMI........... Licentiate of Cost and Management Institute [British]
LCML.......... Library of Congress Minimal Level Cataloguing [Source file] [UTLAS symbol]
LCML.......... Low-Capacity Microwave Link
LC(ML)C...... Ligue Communiste (Marxiste-Leniniste) du Canada [Canadian Communist League (Marxist-Leninist)]
LCMM.......... Life-Cycle Management Model (AABC)
LCMM.......... Life Cycle Material Manager (MCD)
LCMO.......... Lanthanum/Calcium/Manganese/Oxygen [Inorganic chemistry]
LCMP.......... Launcher Control and Monitoring Panel
LCMP.......... Life Cycle Management Planning [Army]
LCMP.......... Local Commandant, Military Police [British military] (DMA)
LCM-PDR...... League of Communists of Macedonia - Party for Democratic Reform [Political party]
LCM(R)........ Landing Craft, Mechanised (Rocket) [British military] (DMA)
LCMRGlc..... Local Cerebral Metabolic Rate for Glucose [Brain research]
LCMS.......... LASER Countermeasure System [Military] (INF)
LCMS.......... Launch Control and Monitoring System [NASA] (AAG)
LCMS.......... Library Collection Management System (NITA)
LCMS.......... Life-Cycle Management System
LC/MS.......... Liquid Chromatography/Mass Spectrometry
LCMS.......... Logistics Command Management System
LCMS.......... Longshore Case Management System [Department of Labor] (GFGA)
LCMS.......... Low-Cost Modular Spacecraft [NASA]
LCMS.......... Lutheran Church - Missouri Synod
LCMSO........ Landing Craft, Material Supply Officer
LCMT.......... London Centre for Marine Technology [British] (IRUK)
LCMV.......... Lymphocytic Choriomeningitis Virus
LC-MY.......... League of Communists - Movement for Yugoslavia [Political party]
LCN............ La Cosa Nostra [Our Thing]
LCN............ Landing Craft, Navigation [Obsolete]
LCN............ Large Co-Ops Network [British]
LCN............ Left Caudate Nucleus [Medicine] (DMAA)
LCN............ Liaison Change Notice
LCN............ Library of Congress Number (MCD)
LCN............ Lineas Aereas Canarias SA [Spain ICAO designator] (FAAC)
LCN............ Linked Cluster Network [Chemistry]
LCN............ Load Classification Number (AFM)
LCN............ Local Civil Noon (ADA)
LCN............ Local Communication Network (ACRL)
LCN............ Local Communications Network (GAVI)
LCN............ Local Computer Network
LCN............ Local Control Number (MCD)
LCN............ Logical Channel Number [Computer science] (TNIG)
LCN............ Logistics Control Number (MCD)
LCN............ Loosely Coupled Network [Telecommunications] (OSI)
LCNA .... Lewis Carroll Society of North America (EA)
LC/NA.......... Lutherans Concerned/North America (EA)
LCNADE....... Liquid-Cooled Naturally Aspirated Diesel Engine
LCNC .... Local Cartage National Conference [Later, LSHCNC]
LCNC .... Nicosia [Cyprus] [ICAO location identifier] (ICLI)
LC NGO-EC... Liaison Committee of Development Non-Governmental Organizations to the European Communities [Belgium] (EAIO)
LCNN .... Land Commander, North Norway [NATO] (NATG)
LCNP .... Lawyers' Committee on Nuclear Policy (EA)
LCNP .... Licentiate of the National Council of Psychotherapists [British]
LCNR .... Liquid Core Nuclear Rocket
LCNSD........ Licensed
LCNSW .... Labor Council of New South Wales [Australia]
LCNSW .... Legislative Council of New South Wales [Australia]
LCNT........... Link Celestial Navigation Trainer
LCNTR .... Location Counter [Computer science]
LC/NUC....... Library of Congress and National Union Catalog Author Lists, 1942-1962 [A publication]
LCNVA .... Low-Cost Night Vision Aid (MCD)
LCNVG .... Low-Cost Night Vision Goggles (MCD)
LCO............ Landing Craft Officer [British] (ADA)
LCO............ Launch Control Operation (MCD)
LCO............ Launching Control Office [or Officer] [Military]
LCO............ Light Cycle Oil [Petrochemical technology]
LCO............ Limiting Conditions for Operation [Nuclear energy] (NRCH)
LCO............ Linea Aerea del Cobre Ltda. [Chile] [ICAO designator] (FAAC)
LCO............ Lipo-Chitooligosaccharide [Botany]
LCO............ Logistics Control Office [Military] (AABC)
LCO............ Lord Chancellor's Office [British] (DLA)
LCO............ Low Cardiac Output [Cardiology]
LCO............ Lowest Cost of Ownership
LCOA.......... Logistics Control Office, Atlantic [Military]
LCOC.......... Launch Control Officer's Console (AAG)
LCOC.......... Lincoln Continental Owners Club (EA)
LCOCC........ Atlantic [Fleet] Commander Operational Control Center [Navy]
LCOCU........ Landing Craft, Obstruction Clearance Unit
LC OFC........ Linear Crystal Oxygen Free Copper [Cable component] (NITA)
L/COH........ Lance-Corporal of Horse [British military] (DMA)
LCOL........... Lieutenant Colonel

LCoIC........... Caldwell Parish Library, Columbia, LA [*Library symbol Library of Congress*] (LCLS)
LCoIfG .... Grant Parish Library, Colfax, LA [*Library symbol Library of Congress*] (LCLS)
LCOLNT .... Low Coolant
LCOM .... Local Committee Operations Manual [*A publication*] (EAAP)
LCOM .... Logic Control Output Module (MCD)
LCOM .... Logistics Composite Model
LCOMM........ Library Council of Metropolitan Milwaukee [*Wisconsin*] [*Library network*]
L Comment... Law Commentary [*A publication*] (DLA)
L Comment'y... Law Commentary [*A publication*] (DLA)
L COMP RAM... Licentiate in Composition, Royal Academy of Music [*British*] (ROG)
L/COMPT ..... Luggage Compartment [*Automotive engineering*]
LCOP .... Launch Control Officer's Panel (AAG)
LCOP .... Logistics Control Office, Pacific [*Military*] (AABC)
LCOR .... Lincoln Cosmopolitan Owners Registry [*Defunct*] (EA)
L-CORP....... Lance-Corporal [*Military British*] (ROG)
LCOS .... Lead Computing Optical Sight
LCOS .... Low Cardiac Output Syndrome [*Medicine*] (DMAA)
LCOS .... Lycos Inc. [*NASDAQ symbol*] (TTSB)
LCOSE .... Launch Complex Operational Support Equipment
LCOSS .... Lead Computing Optical Sighting System (MCD)
LCOT........... Lower Critical Ordering Transition [*Polymer physics*]
LCouRR .... Red River Parish Library, Coushatta, LA [*Library symbol Library of Congress*] (LCLS)
LCovD .... Delta Regional Primate Research Center, Science Information Service, Covington, LA [*Library symbol Library of Congress*] (LCLS)
LCovSt .... Saint Tammany Parish Library, Covington, LA [*Library symbol Library of Congress*] (LCLS)
LCP............. Galbraith Lake Camp, AK [*Location identifier FAA*] (FAAL)
LCP............. Landing Craft, Personnel
LCP............. Language Conversion Program [*Computer science*] (BUR)
LCP............. Large Coil Program [*Physics*]
LCP............. Large Computer Project (IAA)
LCP............. Last Card Program Start (IAA)
LCP............. Last Complete Program (WDAA)
LCP............. Lateral Choroid Plexus (PDAA)
LCP............. Launch Control Panel
LCP............. Launch Control Post (MCD)
LCP............. Laws for Construction of Programs (MHDB)
LCP............. Lawyers Co-Operative Publishing Co. [*Rochester, NY*]
LCP............. Leader, Company Procurement [*Military*] (AFIT)
LCP............. League of Canadian Poets [*Canada*] (EAIO)
LCP............. Left Circular Polarization
L-C-P........... Leg-Calve-Perthes Disease [*Medicine*]
LCP............. Legislative Council for Photogrammetry [*Later, MAPPS*] (EA)
LCP............. Lehndorff Canadian Prop. [*Limited Partnership Units*] [*Toronto Stock Exchange symbol*]
LCP............. Letter Carrier Presort [*Canadian postal term*] (NFD)
LCP............. Liberal Country Party [*Australia*] (BARN)
LCP............. Licensed Clinical Psychologist
LCP............. Licentiate of the College of Preceptors [*British*]
LCP............. Light Compact Performance [*Filtration systems*] [*Automotive engineering*]
LCP............. Link Control Procedure [*Telecommunications*]
LCP............. Link Control Protocol [*Telecommunications*] (ACRL)
LCP............. Liquid-Crystal Polymer [*Organic chemistry*]
LCP............. Liquid Cyclone Process [*for making high-protein edible cottonseed flour*]
LCP............. Little Computer Person [*Activision computer game*]
LCP............. Load Cell Platform
LCP............. Loading Control Program (IAA)
LCP............. Local Calibration Procedure
LCP............. Local Collaborative Projects [*Between business and education*] [*British*]
LCP............. Local Control Panel (CAAL)
LCP............. Local Control Point [*Telecommunications*] (TEL)
LCP............. Logistic Capability Plan [*Navy*]
LCP............. London College of Printing
LCP............. Long-Chain Polysaturated Fatty Acid [*Biochemistry*] (MAE)
LCP............. Lost Cause Press, Louisville, KY [*Library symbol Library of Congress*] (LCLS)
LCP............. Low-Calcium Pyroxene [*Mineralogy*]
LCP............. Low-Cost Production (WDAA)
LCP............. Lower Cost Processor (MCD)
LCP............. Lymphocyte Cytosol Polypeptide [*Medicine*] (DMAA)
LCPA........... Lincoln Center for the Performing Arts (EA)
LC-PAD .... Liquid Chromatography plus Pulsed Amperometric Detection [*Analytical chemistry*]
LCP & SA .... Licentiate of Physicians and Surgeons of America
LCPC........... Liquid Cyclone Processed Cottonseed Flour
LCPC........... Low-Cost-to-Produce Classifier (MCD)
LCP-FY........ Logistic Capability Plan - Fiscal Year [*Navy*] (NG)
LCPG .... Logic Clock Pulse Generator [*Computer science*]
LCPH........... Paphos [*Cyprus*] [*ICAO location identifier*] (ICLI)
LCPIS......... Low-Cost Propulsion Integration Study (MCD)
LCPL........... Lance Corporal
LCPL........... Landing Craft, Personnel, Large [*Navy symbol*]
LCPL........... Left Circularly Polarized Light
LCPL........... Leon-Jefferson Library System [*Library network*]
LCPLR .... Landing Craft, Personnel Leader
LCP(M)........ Landing Craft, Personnel (Medium)

LCP(N)........ Landing Craft, Personnel (Nested) [*Obsolete*]
LCPO .... Leading Chief Petty Officer (DNAB)
LCP(P)........ Landing Craft, Personnel (Plastic)
LCPR .... Landing Craft, Personnel, Ramped [*Navy symbol*]
LCPRC .... Liquid Crystalline Polymer Research Center [*University of Connecticut*] [*Research center*] (RCD)
LCP(S)........ Landing Craft, Personnel (Small) [*British military*] (DMA)
LCPS .... Large Cloud Particle-Size Spectrometer
LCPS .... Licentiate of the College of Physicians and Surgeons [*British*]
LCPS .... Lithuanian Catholic Press Society (EA)
LCP(SY)....... Landing Craft, Personnel (Survey)
LCPT........... Lightweight Collapsible Pillolo Tank
LCPTT .... Low-Cost Part Task Trainer (MCD)
LCP(U)........ Landing Craft, Personnel (Utility) [*British military*] (DMA)
LCQ............ Launch Crew Quarters (AFM)
LCQ............ Learning Climate Questionnaire [*Medicine*] (DMAA)
LCQ............ Liquid Crystal Quartz (WGA)
LCQ............ Logical Channel Queue [*Computer science*] (BUR)
LCR............ Inductance-Capacitance-Resistance (CET)
LCR............ La Lucha [*Costa Rica*] [*Seismograph station code, US Geological Survey*] (SEIS)
LCR............ Land Compensation Reports [*A publication*] (ILCA)
LCR............ Landing Craft, Raiding [*British*]
LCR............ Landing Craft, Rocket [*British military*] (DMA)
LCR............ Landing Craft, Rubber
LCR............ Las Cruces, NM [*Location identifier FAA*] (FAAL)
LCR............ Late Cutaneous Reaction [*Immunology*]
LCR............ Launch Control Room (MCD)
LCR............ Least-Cost Routing [*Telecommunications*]
LCr............. Letter of Credit
L/CR.......... Lettre de Credit [*Letter of Credit*] [*French*]
LCR............ Leurocristine [*Oncovin, Vincristine*] [*Also, O, V, VC, VCR*] [*Antineoplastic drug*]
LCR............ Level Crossing Rate (IAA)
LCR............ Level Crossing Resonance [*Physical chemistry*]
LCR............ Libyan Arab Company for Air Cargo [*ICAO designator*] (FAAC)
LCr............. Lieutenant Commander [*Navy British*]
LCR............ Ligase Chain Reaction [*Genetics*]
LCR............ Light Chopping Reticle
LCR............ Ligue Communiste Revolutionnaire [*Revolutionary Communist League*] [*France Political party*] (PPW)
LCR............ Limit Control Register [*Navy Navigation Satellite System*] (DNAB)
LCR............ Liquid Chromatographic Reactor
LCR............ Liquide Cephalo-Rachidien [*Cerebrospinal Fluid*] [*French*]
LCR............ Liquido Cefaloraquideo [*Cerebrospinal Fluid*] [*Spanish*]
LCR............ Load Complement Register (IAA)
LCR............ Locus Control Region [*Genetics*]
LCR............ Logarithmic Correlators Ratiometer (PDAA)
LCR............ Log Count Rate [*Nuclear energy*] (NRCH)
LCR............ Logistic Change Report [*Military*] (AFM)
LCR............ Low Compression Ratio [*Automotive engineering*] (IAA)
LCR............ Low Cost Range
LCR............ Low-Cost Reusable [*Refers to payload type*] [*NASA*]
LCR............ Low Count Range [*Nuclear energy*] (NUCP)
LCR............ Low Cross Range
LCR............ Lower Canada Reports [*A publication*] (DLA)
LCR............ Lower Circulating Reflux [*Chemical engineering*]
LCR............ Lucero Resources Corp. [*Vancouver Stock Exchange symbol*]
LCR............ Lung Configuration Recorder
LCR............ Lutheran Churches of the Reformation
LCrA........... Acadia Parish Library, Crowley, LA [*Library symbol Library of Congress*] (LCLS)
LCRA .... Akrotiri [*Cyprus*] [*ICAO location identifier*] (ICLI)
LCRA .... Labour Cost Research Associates Ltd. [*British*] (ECON)
LCRA .... Lithuanian Catholic Religious Aid (EA)
LCRA .... Lower Colorado River Authority
LCRC .... Lake Champlain Research Consortium [*Marine science*] (OSRA)
LCRC .... Lake Champlain Research Consortium (USDC)
LCRC .... Laotian Cultural and Research Center (EA)
LCRC .... Lenawee County Railroad Co., Inc. [*AAR code*]
LCRE........... Lithium Cooled Reactor Experiment
LC Rep S Qu... Lower Canada Seignorial Questions Reports [*A publication*] (DLA)
LCRES .... Letter Carrier Route Evaluation System [*Postal Service*]
LCRF........... L'Association Canadienne des Ludotheques et des Centres de Ressources pour la Famille [*Canadian Association of Toy Libraries and Parent Resource Centers*] [*See also TLRC*] (EAIO)
LCRIS .... Loop Cable Record Inventory System (MCD)
LCR(L)......... Landing Craft, Rubber (Large) [*Obsolete*]
LCRL........... Lewis and Clark Regional Library [*Library network*]
LCRM.......... Launch Control Room (AAG)
LCRM.......... Linear Count Rate Meter (NRCH)
LCRO.......... Episkopi [*Cyprus*] [*ICAO location identifier*] (ICLI)
LCRO.......... Linear Combination of Rydberg Orbitals [*Atomic physics*]
LCRO.......... Low Cross-Range Orbiter (KSC)
LCR(R)........ Landing Craft, Rubber (Rocket)
LCRR........... Low-Cost Risk Reduction (PDAA)
LCRR........... Nicosia [*Cyprus*] [*ICAO location identifier*] (ICLI)
LCR(S)........ Landing Craft, Rubber (Small) [*Obsolete*]
LCRS........... Low-Cost Readout Station [*NASA*]
LCRSMEEC... Liaison Committee of the Rice Starch Manufacturers of the EEC [*Belgium*] (EAIO)
LCRT........... Low-Contrast Resolution Test [*Optics*]
LCRU .... Landing Craft, Recovery Unit
LCRU .... Lunar Communications Relay Unit [*Apollo*] [*NASA*]
LCRV .... Length of Curve (MSA)

LCRY .... LeCroy Corp. [NASDAQ symbol] (SAG)
LCS .... Laboratory-Certifying Scientist [Analytical chemistry]
LCS .... Laboratory for Computational Statistics [Stanford University] (PDAA)
LCS .... Laboratory for Computer Science [Massachusetts Institute of Technology] [Research center] (RCD)
LCS .... Lancaster Resources [Vancouver Stock Exchange symbol]
LCS .... Land Combat System
LCS .... Landing Craft, Support
LCS .... Lane Control Signal
LCS .... Large Capacity [or Core] Storage [Computer science]
LCS .... Large Core Storage [Computer science] (OA)
LCS .... LASER Communications System
LCS .... LASER Crosswind System (RDA)
LCS .... Last Cast Syndrome [Fictitious fishing malady]
LCS .... Lateral Channel Stop (IAA)
LCS .... Lateral Control System (MUGU)
LCS .... Lathe Control System
LCS .... Launch Complex Set
LCS .... Launch Control Sequence (AAG)
LCS .... Launch Control Simulator
LCS .... Launch Control Station
LCS .... Launch Control System [or Subsystem]
LCS .... Law of Corresponding States [Physics]
LCS .... LCS Industries, Inc. [Associated Press] (SAG)
LCS .... League Championship Series [Baseball]
LCS .... Leakage Collection System [Nuclear energy] (NRCH)
LCS .... Leak Control System [Nuclear energy] (NRCH)
LCS .... Learning Classifier System [Computer science]
LCS .... Leveling Control System
LCS .... Liaison Call Sheet
LCS .... Library Cat Society (EA)
LCS .... Library Computer System [University of Illinois] [Library network]
LCS .... Library Control System [Ohio State Library] [Columbus] [Information service or system] (IID)
LCS .... Lichen Chronicus Simplex [Dermatology] (DAVI)
LCS .... Life Care Services
LCS .... Life-Cycle Survivability (MSA)
LCS .... Light Cruiser Squadron [British military] (DMA)
LCS .... Lincoln Calibration Sphere
LCS .... Linear Collision Sequence (MCD)
LCS .... Line Coding Storage
LCS .... Link Control Station [Telecommunications] (ECII)
LCS .... Linked Cross Sectional (PDAA)
LCS .... Liquid Controlled Solid (KSC)
LCS .... Liquid Cooling System
LCS .... Liquid Crystal Shutter [Epson] [Printer technology]
LCS .... List of Command Signals (MCD)
LCS .... Lithuanian Cultural Society [Defunct] (EA)
LCS .... Litton Computer Services [Information service or system] (IID)
LCS .... Lladro Collectors Society (EA)
LCS .... Loadable Control Storage [Computer science] (NITA)
LCS .... Local Communications Services [British]
LCS .... London Controlling Section [British military] (DMA)
LCS .... Loop Control System [Nuclear energy] (NRCH)
LCS .... LOPO [Local Post] Collectors Society (EA)
LCS .... Lottery Collectors Society (EA)
LCS .... Loudness Contour Selector
LCS .... Low Constant [or Continuous] Suction [Surgical procedure] (DAVI)
LCS .... Low-Cost LASER Seeker (MCD)
LCS .... Low-Cost Sonobuoy (DOMA)
LCS .... Statewide Library Computer System [University of Illinois] [Information service or system] (IID)
LCSA .... Legislative Council of South Australia
LCSA .... Lewis and Clark Society of America (EA)
LCSA .... Lotteries Commission of South Australia
LC Sales ...... Langdell's Cases on the Law of Sales [A publication] (DLA)
LCSB .... Launch Control Support Building [Missiles]
LCSCU .... Launch Coolant System Control Unit (AAG)
LCSE .... LASER Communication Satellite Experiment [NASA]
LCSE .... Life-Cycle Software Engineering [Army] (RDA)
LCSEC .... Life-Cycle Software Engineering Center [Army]
LCSEFE .... Labor Committee for Safe Energy and Full Employment [Defunct] (EA)
LCSH .... Library of Congress Subject Headings [Formerly, SHDC] [A publication]
LCSI .... Launch Critical Support Items [NASA] (KSC)
LCSI .... LCS Industries [NASDAQ symbol] (SAG)
LCSI .... Licentiate of the Construction Surveyors' Institute [British] (DBQ)
LCSI .... Logistic Control Shipping Instruction (AAG)
LCSIE .... Liquid-Cooled Spark Ignition Engine
LCS/IS .... Local Communications Services/Information Services (NITA)
LCS(L) .... Landing Craft, Support (Large) [Obsolete]
LCSLT .... Low-Cost Solid Logic Technology (IAA)
LCS(M) .... Landing Craft, Support (Medium)
LCSM .... Launch Control and Status Monitor
LCSMM .... Life-Cycle Systems Management Model
LCSN .... Local Circuit Switched Network
LCSO .... Launch Complex Safety Officer (IAA)
LCSO .... Launch Control Safety Officer (MCD)
LCSO .... Local Communications Service Order
LCSO .... Low-Cost Systems Office [NASA] (PDAA)
LCSP .... Logical Channels Switching Program (MHDB)
LCS-PDR ..... League of Communists of Slovenia - Party of Democratic Reform [Political party]
LCSPL .... Launch Critical Spare Parts List [NASA] (KSC)

LCSR .... Laboratory for Computer Science Research [Rutgers University] [Research center] (RCD)
LCS(R) .... Landing Craft, Support (Rocket)
LCSR .... Landing Craft, Swimmer Reconnaissance [Navy symbol]
LCSR .... Large Caliber Soft Recoil [Weaponry] (MCD)
LCSR(L) ...... Landing Craft, Swimmer Recovery (Light) [Navy symbol] (NVT)
LCSRM .... Loop Current Step Response Method (IEEE)
LCSS .... Land Combat Support Set (NATG)
LCSS .... Land Combat Support System (DWSG)
LCSS .... Land Combat Support Systems
LCSS .... Land Combat System Study (AFIT)
LCS(S) .... Landing Craft, Support (Small), MKI [Navy symbol Obsolete]
LCSS .... Launch Control and Sequencer System
LCSS .... Launch Control System Simulator [NASA] (IAA)
LCSS .... Life Cycle Software Support
LCSS .... Lightweight Camouflage Screen System (MCD)
LCSS .... London Council of Social Service
LCSSAP .... Low-Cost Silicon Solar Array Project
LCSSC .... Life-Cycle Software Support Center [Army]
LCSSE .... Life-Cycle Software Support Environment [Army]
LCSSP .... Laboratory of Chemical and Solid-State Physics [MIT] (MCD)
LCST .... Licentiate of the College of Speech Therapists [British]
LCST .... Lower Critical-Solution-Temperature
LCSU .... Lao Civil Servants' Union
LCSU .... Local Concentrator Switching Unit [Telecommunications] (TEL)
LCSVF .... Logistics Combat Support Vehicle Family (MCD)
LCSW .... Latch Checking Switch (MSA)
LCSW .... Licensed Clinical Social Worker (MEDA)
LCSW .... Licensed Clinical Social Worker [Medicine]
LCT .... Landing Craft, Tank [Navy symbol]
LCT .... Laplace-Carson Transform [Mathematics]
LCT .... Last Card Total (IAA)
LCT .... Latest Closing Time
LCT .... Launch Control Trailer
LCT .... Launch Countdown [NASA] (NASA)
L Ct .... Law Court (DLA)
LCT .... Legislative Council of Tasmania [Australia]
LCT .... Lencourt Ltd. [Toronto Stock Exchange symbol]
LCT .... Less than Truckload Lot [Under 24,000 pounds] (MHDW)
LCT .... Licensing Commission of Tasmania [Australia]
LCT .... Life Component Tester
LCT .... Light Capital Technology (PDAA)
LCT .... Ligue Communiste des Travailleurs [Communist Workers' League] [Senegal] [Political party] (PPW)
LCT .... Linear Combination Technique [Nuclear science] (OA)
LCT .... Linkage Control Table [Telecommunications] (IAA)
LCT .... Liquid Crystal Thermography
LCT .... Liver Cell Tumor [Medicine] (DMAA)
LCT .... Local Civil Time
LCT .... Local Correlation-Tracking [Instrumental technique]
LCT .... Locate (MSA)
LCT .... Location, Command, and Telemetry (IAA)
LCT .... Locust (MSA)
LCT .... Logical Channel Termination
LCT .... Logical Channel Termination (NITA)
LCT .... Long Calcined Ton [Bauxite, etc.]
LCT .... Long-Chain Triglyceride [Biochemistry]
LCT .... Louis Comfort Tiffany [Signature on the art glass designed by Tiffany]
LCT .... Low Cervical Transverse [Position] [Obstetrics] (DAVI)
LCT .... Low-Cost Technology (PDAA)
LCT .... Low Cost Terminal [Telecommunications] (LAIN)
LCT .... Luscher Color Test [Psychology] (DAVI)
LCT .... Lymphocytotoxicity [Medicine] (DMAA)
LCT .... Lymphocytotoxicity Test [Hematology]
LCT-1 .... Lunar Cycle Test One [Aerospace]
LCTA .... Land Condition-Trend Analysis [Army] (RDA)
LCT(A) .... Landing Craft, Tank (Armored)
LCTA .... London Corn Trade Association
LCTA .... Lymphocytotoxic Antibodies [Immunochemistry]
LCTB .... Launch Control Training Building [NASA] (IAA)
LC/TC .... Livonia Career/Technical Center
LCTCDE .... Liquid-Cooled Turbocharged Diesel Engine
LCTD .... Located (AFM)
LCTF .... Large Coil Test Facility (MCD)
LCTF .... Lloyd's Canadian Trust Fund (AIA)
LCT(H) .... Landing Craft, Tank (Hospital) [British military] (DMA)
LCTHF .... Lewis and Clark Trail Heritage Foundation (EA)
LCTI .... Large Components Test Installation [Nuclear energy] (NRCH)
LCTL .... Large Component Test Loop [Nuclear energy]
LCTMP .... Little Change in Temperature [NWS] (FAAC)
LCTN .... Location
LCTN .... Location
LCTP .... Launcher Control Test Panel
LCT(R) .... Landing Craft, Tank (Rocket)
LCTR .... Locator
LCT(S) .... Landing Craft, Tank (Slow)
LCTS .... LASER Coherence Techniques Section
LCTSU .... Launch Control Transfer Switching Unit [Aerospace] (AAG)
LCTT .... Launch Complex Telemetry Trailer
LCU .... Lac-Coated Urea Fertilizer
LCU .... Landing Craft, Utility [Navy symbol]
LCU .... Large Close-Up (ADA)
LCU .... LASER Cooling Unit (MCD)
LCU .... Launch Control Unit (MCD)

LCU............ Library of Congress Music [Source file] [UTLAS symbol]
LCU............ Life Change Unit [Psychometrics]
LCU............ Line Control Unit [Data communications]
LCU............ Line Coupling Unit (NASA)
LCU............ Link Control Unit [Telecommunications] (TEL)
LCU............ Local Control Unit (IAA)
LCU............ Lower Control Unit (WDAA)
LCU............ Lucin, UT [Location identifier FAA] (FAAL)
LCUC......... Letter Carriers' Union of Canada
LCuC.......... Liver Copper Concentration [Physiology]
LCUG......... Liquid-Cooled Undergarment (MCD)
LC/USA...... Lutheran Council in the USA [Defunct] (EA)
LCUT.......... Lifetime Hoan [NASDAQ symbol] (TTSB)
LCUT.......... Lifetime Hoan Corp. [NASDAQ symbol] (SAG)
LCV............ La Cueva [New Mexico] [Seismograph station code, US Geological Survey] (SEIS)
LCV............ Landing Craft, Vehicle [Navy symbol]
LCV............ Large Compound Vesicle [Biochemistry]
LCV............ LASER Compatible Vidicon
LCV............ League of Conservation Voters (EA)
LCV............ Legislative Council of Victoria [Australia]
LCV............ Level Control Valve (MCD)
LCV............ Light Commercial Vehicle
LCV............ Llymphocryptovirus
LCV............ Load Control Valve [Engineering]
LCV............ Local Control Valve [Nuclear energy] (NRCH)
LCV............ Longer Combination Vehicle [Trucks hauling multiple trailers]
LCV............ Lorry Command Vehicle [British military] (DMA)
LCV............ Low Calorific Value [of a fuel]
LCV............ Low Cervical Vertical [Incision] [Obstetrics] (DAVI)
LCVA.......... Light Commercial Vehicle Association (EA)
LCVAO........ Linear Combination of Virtual Atomic Orbitals [Physical chemistry]
LCVASI....... Low-Cost Visual-Approach Slope Indicator (DNAB)
LCVD.......... Laser-Assisted Chemical Vapor Deposition [Coating technology]
LCVD.......... LASER Chemical Vapor Deposition [Coating technology]
LCVD.......... Least Coincidence Voltage Detection (MDG)
LCVG.......... Liquid Cooling and Ventilation Garment [NASA] (NASA)
LCVIP......... Licensee Contractor Vendor Inspection Report Program [Nuclear energy] (NRCH)
LCVM......... Log Conversion Voltmeter
LCVP.......... Landing Craft, Vehicle, Personnel [Navy symbol NATO]
LCW........... Limited Conventional War [Description of Vietnam War] [DoD] (VNW)
LCW........... Line Control Word
LCW........... Lithuanian Catholic Women (EA)
LCW........... Lutheran Church Women [Defunct] (EA)
LCWA.......... Legislative Council of Western Australia
LCWA.......... Lotteries Commission of Western Australia
LCWDS........ Low-Cost Weapon Delivery System (MCD)
LCWF.......... Launch Complex Work Flow (IAA)
LCWHN....... Latin American and Caribbean Women's Health Network (EAIO)
LCWI.......... Left Ventricular Cardiac Work Index [Physiology]
LCWIO........ Liaison Committee of Women's International Organisations [British] (DI)
LCWP......... Law Commission Working Paper [A publication] (DLA)
LCWR......... Leadership Conference of Women Religious of the USA (EA)
LCWSL........ Large Caliber Weapon Systems Laboratory [ARRADCOM] (RDA)
LCX........... Higginsville, MO [Location identifier FAA] (FAAL)
LCX........... Launch Complex
LCX........... Left Circumflex Coronary Artery [Cardiology] (DAVI)
LCXT.......... Large Cosmic X-Ray Telescope (PDAA)
LCY............ Guthrie, OK [Location identifier FAA] (FAAL)
LCY............ League of Communists of Yugoslavia [Savez Komunista Jugoslavije] [Political party] (PPW)
LCY............ Loose Cubic Yard (DAC)
LCZ............ Laws of the Canal Zone [A publication] (DLA)
LCZR.......... Localizer
LD.............. Decisions Lost [Boxing]
LD.............. Doctor of Letters
LD.............. Lab. Dausse [France] [Research code symbol]
LD.............. Label Definition (IAA)
LD.............. Labor and Delivery [Obstetrics] (DAVI)
LD.............. Laboratory Data (MAE)
LD.............. Labor Daily [A publication]
LD.............. Labor Department
LD.............. Labor Dispute (DLA)
LD.............. Labyrinthine Defect [Physiology] (MAE)
LD.............. Lactate Dehydrogenase [Also, LAD, LDH] [An enzyme]
LD.............. Lady Day [March 25, the Feast of the Annunciation] [British]
LD.............. Lamina Densa [Dermatology]
LD.............. Lamp Driver
LD.............. Land
LD.............. Landing Distance [Aviation] (IAA)
LD.............. Land Office Decisions, United States [A publication] (DLA)
LD.............. Large Dollar [Indicator] [IRS]
LD.............. Lasa D Ring [Montana] [Seismograph station code, US Geological Survey] (SEIS)
LD.............. LASER Desorption [of ions for analysis]
LD.............. LASER Diode
LD.............. LASER Discectomy [Spinal surgery]
LD.............. Lateral Direction (MCD)
LD.............. Lateral Dorsal [Anatomy]
LD.............. Lateral Drift
LD.............. Lateralis Dorsalis [Neuroanatomy]
LD.............. Launch Director [NASA] (KSC)
LD.............. Launching Division [Missiles] (MUGU)

LD.............. Laus Deo [Praise to God] [Latin]
LD.............. Law Dictionary [A publication] (DLA)
LD.............. Layer Depth
LD.............. Lead [or Leads] [Publishing]
ld.............. Lead (WDMC)
ld.............. Leading (WDMC)
LD.............. Leading (MSA)
LD.............. Leading Edge Delay [Aviation] (IAA)
LD.............. Leak Detection [Nuclear energy] (IAA)
LD.............. Learning Disabilities/Differences
LD.............. Learning Disability [or Learning-Disabled]
LD.............. Least Depth [Nautical charts]
LD.............. Lectio Divina [Paris] [A publication] (BJA)
LD.............. Left Defense
LD.............. Left Deltoid [Medicine]
LD.............. Left Door [Theater]
LD.............. Legal Deposit (ADA)
LD.............. Legal Discriminator (MCD)
LD.............. Legionnaire's Disease
LD.............. Legislative Department [Generic term] (ROG)
L-D........... Leishman-Donovan (Bodies) [Microbiology]
LD.............. Length-Diameter Ratio
LD.............. Lepide Dictum [Wittily Said] [Latin] (ADA)
LD.............. Letdown [Nuclear energy] (NRCH)
LD.............. Lethal Dose
LD.............. Let's Discuss
LD.............. Letter Description (PDAA)
L/D........... Letter of Deposit [Banking]
LD.............. Level Detector
LD.............. Level Discriminator
LD.............. Levodopa [Obstetrics] (DAVI)
LD.............. Library of Devotion [A publication]
LD.............. Libyan Dinar [Monetary unit] (BJA)
LD.............. Licentiate in Dentistry [British] (ROG)
LD.............. Licentiate in Divinity (DAS)
LD.............. Lifeboat Deck
L:D........... Lift-Drag [Ratio]
LD.............. Light-Dark [Cycles]
L/D........... Light-Dark [Ratio] [Ophthalmology] (DAVI)
LD.............. Light Difference [Difference between amounts of light perceptible to the two eyes] [Ophthalmology]
LD.............. Light Dragoons [Military unit] [British]
LD.............. Light Driver (IAA)
L/D........... Light Duty [Automotive engineering]
LD.............. Lighting Designer (NTCM)
LD.............. Lighting Director (NTCM)
LD.............. Light on Dark
LD.............. Limited
LD.............. Limited Disease [Medicine]
LD.............. Limited Partner in Dual Capacity Firm [London Stock Exchange]
LD.............. Linear Decision
LD.............. Linear Dichroism [Spectra]
LD.............. Line Dolly (MCD)
LD.............. Line Drawing (MSA)
LD.............. Line Driver
LD.............. Line of Departure [Military]
LD.............. Line of Duty [Military]
LD.............. Linguodistal [Dentistry]
LD.............. Linkage Disequilibrium [Genetics]
LD.............. Linker Directive [Telecommunications] (TEL)
LD.............. Linz and Donawetz [Furnace] [Metallurgy Named after two plant sites in Austria]
LD.............. Liquid Drop
LD.............. List Down
LD.............. List of Drawings [USN] (MCD)
LD.............. Litera Dominicalis [Sunday Letter]
LD.............. Litterarum Doctor [Doctor of Letters or Literature] [Latin] (ROG)
lD.............. Liver Disease [Gastroenterology] (DAVI)
LD.............. Living Donor [Medicine]
LD.............. Load [or Loader] (AAG)
LD.............. Load Draught (IAA)
LD.............. Loaded Deployability [Posture] [Military] (DOMA)
LD.............. Loading Dock (MCD)
LD.............. Loading Dose
LD.............. Local Delivery
LD.............. Local Director (DCTA)
LD.............. Local Directory (ACRL)
LD.............. Loft Dried Paper (DGA)
LD.............. Logical Design
LD.............. Logic Driver [Computer science]
LD.............. Logistics Demonstration (MCD)
LD.............. Logistics Document (MCD)
LD.............. Lombard-Dowell [Broth medium] [Microbiology]
LD.............. London Docks
LD.............. Long Day [Botany]
LD.............. Long Delay
LD.............. Long Distance
LD.............. Long Duration
LD.............. Longitudinal Diameter
LD.............. Longitudinal Division [Cytology]
LD.............. Loop Diagram
LD.............. Loop-Disconnect [Telecommunications] (TEL)
LD.............. Lord
LD.............. Loss and Damage (IAA)
LD.............. Louis Dreyfus Natural Gas [NYSE symbol] (TTSB)

LD.............. Louis Dreyfus Natural Gas Holdings Corp. [*NYSE symbol*] (SPSG)
LD.............. Low Density
LD.............. Low Dispersion [*Optics*]
LD.............. Low Door (WDAA)
LD.............. Low Dose [*Medicine*]
LD.............. Low Drag
LD.............. Low Dust
LD.............. Low Dutch [*Language, etc.*]
LD.............. Low Dynamic
LD.............. Lower Deck
LD.............. Luminescence Detector (SSD)
LD.............. Luminescence Diode (IAA)
LD.............. Lunar Day (KSC)
LD.............. Lunar Docking [*NASA*] (IAA)
LD.............. Lunar Drill [*NASA*] (KSC)
LD.............. Lyme Disease [*Medicine*]
LD.............. Lymphocyte Defined [*Immunology*]
LD.............. Lymphocyte Depletion [*Hematology*]
LD.............. Lymphocytical Determined [*Hematology*] (DAVI)
LD.............. Vietnam [*License plate code assigned to foreign diplomats in the US*]
LD$_{50}$........ Lethal Dose, Median [*Also, MLD*] [*Lethal for 50% of test group*]
LDA............ Ascension Parish Library, Donaldsonville, LA [*Library symbol Library of Congress*] (LCLS)
LDA............ Laboratory Designated Area (AFIT)
LDA............ Labor Developments Abroad [*A publication*]
LDA............ Land Development Aircraft (PDAA)
LDA............ Landing Directional Aid [*FAA*] (TAG)
LDA............ Landing Distance Available [*FAA*] (TAG)
LDA............ Landing Distance Available [*ICAO*] (FAAC)
LDA............ LASER Doppler Anemometry
LDA............ Last Day of Attendance
LDA............ Late-Differentiation Antigen [*Immunology*]
LDA............ Lauda Air [*Austria ICAO designator*] (FAAC)
LDA............ Lauryl Diethanolamide [*Also, LDE*] [*Organic chemistry*]
LDA............ Lead Development Association [*British*] (EAIO)
LDA............ Learning Disabilities Association of America (EA)
LDA............ Left Dorso-Anterior [*A fetal position*] [*Obstetrics*]
LDA............ Legitimacy Declaration Act [*British*] (ROG)
LDA............ Lesson Design Approach (MCD)
LDA............ Limited Depository Account
LDA............ Limiting Dilution Analyses [*Analytical biochemistry*]
LDA............ Linear Discriminant Analysis
LDA............ Linear Displacement Analysis (DAVI)
LDA............ Linear Dynamic Analyzer (IAA)
LDA............ Line Driving Amplifier
LDA............ Lithium Diisopropylamide [*Organic chemistry*]
LDA............ Local Data Administrator
LDA............ Local-Density (Functional) Approximation [*Physical chemistry*]
LDA............ Local Design Agency (MCD)
LDA............ Local Display Adapter (MHDB)
LDA............ Localizer Directional Aid [*Aviation*]
LDA............ Locate Drum Address (CET)
LDA............ Logical Device Address [*Computer science*] (IBMDP)
LDA............ Lord's Day Alliance of the United States (EA)
LDA............ Low-Density Amorph [*Materials science*]
LDA............ Lower-Deck Attitude [*British military*] (DMA)
LDA............ Lowest Designated Assembly
LDA............ Lutheran Deaconess Association (EA)
LDA............ Lymphocyte-Dependent Antibody [*Immunology*]
LDAC .... Learning Disabilities Association of Canada (EAIO)
LDAC .... Lunar Surface Data Acquisition Camera [*Aerospace*]
LDAK .... Lidak Pharmaceuticals [*NASDAQ symbol*] (SAG)
LDAKA .... LIDAK Pharmaceuticals 'A' [*NASDAQ symbol*] (TTSB)
LDAM......... Local Damage Assessment Model (PDAA)
LDAO......... Lauryldimethylamine Oxide [*Detergent*]
LDAP .... Lightweight Directory Access Protocol [*Computer science*]
LDAP .... Lightweight Directory Access Protocol [*Computer science*]
LDAP .... Lightweight Directory Access Protocol [*Computer utility tool*] (PCM)
LDAP .... Lightweight Directory Access Protocol [*Computer science*]
LDAPS .... Long-Duration Auxiliary Power System (NG)
LDAQ .... Association Quebecoise pour les Troubles d'Apprentissage (AC)
LDAQ .... Learning Disabilities Association of Quebec (AC)
LDAR .... Latex Direct Agglutination Reaction [*Medicine*] (DMAA)
LDAR .... Leak Detection and Repair [*Chemical engineering*]
LDAR .... Lightning Detection and Ranging System [*Meteorology*]
LDAS .... LASER Detection and Analysis System (MCD)
LDASE .... Large Deployable Antenna Shuttle Experiment [*NASA*] (PDAA)
LdB............ Das Land der Bibel (BJA)
LDB............ Lamb Dysentery Bacillus [*Medicine*] (DMAA)
LDB............ Launch Data Bus [*Computer science*] (MCD)
LDB............ Leader Dogs for the Blind (EA)
LDB............ Legionnaires Disease Bacillus [*Medicine*] (DMAA)
LDB............ Legionnaire's Disease Bacterium
LDB............ Legislative Data Base [*Department of Energy*] [*Information service or system*] (IID)
LDB............ Leisure Diagnostic Battery [*Psychology*] (EDAC)
LDB............ Lexington Development Branch (SAA)
LDB............ Light Distribution Box (AAG)
LDB............ Limited Data Block (KSC)
LDB............ Load Determining Bolt
LDB............ Local Data Buffer (IAA)
LDB............ Logical Database
LDB............ Logistics Data Bank (NASA)
LDB............ Londrina [*Brazil*] [*Airport symbol*] (OAG)
LDB............ Low-Drag Bomb

LDBE........... London Diocesan Board of Education
Ld Birk .... Lord Birkenhead's Judgments, House of Lords [*England*] [*A publication*] (DLA)
LDBLC .... Low-Drag Boundary Layer Control [*Military*]
LDBOS........ LASER Designation Battlefield Obscuration Simulator (RDA)
Ld Br Sp ..... Lord Brougham's Speeches [*A publication*] (DLA)
LDBS .... Local Data Base System (MHDI)
LDC............ Laboratory Data Control [*Commercial firm*]
LDC............ Labor Data Collection (MCD)
LDC............ Labor Day Committee [*Australia*]
LDC............ Ladeco Cargo, SA [*Chile*] [*FAA designator*] (FAAC)
LDC............ Large Diameter Core (SAA)
LDC............ LASER Discharge Capacitor (IAA)
LDC............ Latitude Data Computer
LDC............ Laundry and Dry Cleaning International Union
LDC............ Learning Disability Center
LDC............ Learning Disordered Children
LDC............ Less Developed Country
LDC............ Leukocyte Differential Count [*Medicine*] (MEDA)
LDC............ Level Decision Circuit
LDC............ Libertarian Defense Caucus [*Defunct*] (EA)
LDC............ Library Development Center [*Columbia University*]
LDC............ Library Development Consultants, Inc. [*Information service or system*] (IID)
LDC............ Light Direction Center [*Military*]
LDC............ Lightweight Deployable Communications System [*Army*]
LDC............ Limiting Dilution Cloning [*Biochemistry*]
LDC............ Lindeman Island [*Australia Airport symbol*]
LDC............ Linear Detonating Cord (MSA)
LDC............ Line Directional Coupler
LDC............ Line-Drop Compensator (MSA)
LDC............ Linguistic Data Consortium [*Defense Advanced Research Projects Agency*]
LDC............ Linguistics Documentation Center [*University of Ottawa*] [*Database*] [*Canada*] (NITA)
LDC............ Load Drawer Computer (MCD)
LDC............ Local Damping Control [*Automotive engineering*]
LDC............ Local Data Concentrator [*Telecommunications*]
LDC............ Local Defense Center
LDC............ Local Departmental Committee [*British labor*]
LDC............ Local Development Company
LDC............ Local Display Controller
LDC............ Local Distribution Company
LDC............ Logistics Data Center [*Army*] (AABC)
LDC............ London Dumping Convention [*Sets standards for disposal of wastes in oceans*]
LDC............ Long Day Care
LDC............ Long-Distance Call
LDC............ Long-Distance Communications
LDC............ Lower Dead Center
LDC............ Low-Speed Data Channel
LDC............ Lutheran Deaconess Conference (EA)
LDCA .... Land Development Contractors' Association [*Australia*]
LDCC .... Large Diameter Component Cask [*Nuclear energy*] (NRCH)
LDCC .... Lectin-Dependent Cell-Mediated Cytoxicity [*Biochemistry*]
LDCF .... Lymphocyte Derived Chemotactic Factor [*Biochemistry*]
LDCM.......... LANDesk Client Manager Technology [*Intel*] [*Computer science*]
LDCO .... Laundry and Dry Cleaning Operations [*Military*]
LDCP .... Landing Dynamics Computer Program [*NASA*]
L(D)CRS ...... Leachate (Detection) Collection and Removal System (GNE)
LDCS .... Long-Distance Control System (IEEE)
LDCT .... Late Distal Cortical Tubule [*Medicine*] (DMAA)
LDCT .... Linear Discriminant Classification Tree [*Mathematics*]
LDCV .... Large Dense-Core Vesicle [*Neurobiology*]
LDD .... LASER Detector Diode
LDD .... LASER Diode Driver
LDD .... Letter of Determination of Dependency
LDD .... Light-Dark Discrimination [*Ophthalmology*]
LDD .... Light-Dependent Diode [*Instrumentation*]
LDD .... Lightly Doped Drain (MCD)
LDD .... Little Diomede Island, AK [*Location identifier FAA*] (FAAL)
LDD .... Loaded
LDD .... Local Data Distribution
LDD .... Local Development District
LDD .... Logical Database Designer [*Computer science*]
LDD .... Logic Design Data [*Telecommunications*] (TEL)
LDD .... Long-Distance Dispersal [*Botany*]
LDD .... Low-Density Data (KSC)
LDD .... Luminaire Dirt Depreciation [*Floodlighting*]
LDD .... Lunar Dust Detector [*NASA*]
LDDC .... Least-Developed Developing Country [*Trade status*]
LDDC .... London Docklands Development Corp. [*British*] (ECON)
LDDC .... Long-Distance Dialing Center (IAA)
LDDCS .... Laundry and Decontamination Drycleaning System [*Military*] (DWSG)
LDDI .... Local Distributed Data Interface [*Telecommunications*]
LDDL .... Logical Data Definition Language (IAA)
LDDO .... Long-Distance Diesel Oil (PDAA)
LDDS .... Light Division Direct Support [*Artillery system*] (MCD)
LDDS .... Limited Distance Data Service [*Telecommunications*]
LDDS .... Limited Distance Data Set [*Modem*] (NITA)
LDDS .... Local Dentist (DAVI)
LDDS .... Local Digital Distribution Subsystem
LDDS .... Local Doctor of Dental Surgery (MAE)
LDDS .... Long-Distance Discount Service [*Telecommunications*]
LDDS .... Low-Density Data System

LDDT	Light-Duty Diesel Truck [*Automotive emissions*]
LDDV	Light Duty Diesel Vehicle [*VDOT*] (TAG)
LDE	Lagrange Differential Equation
LDE	Laminar Defect Examination (IEEE)
LDE	Lauryl Diethanolamide [*Also, LDA*] [*Organic chemistry*]
LDE	Les Dames d'Escoffier (EA)
LDE	Lighting Director Engineer (NTCM)
LDE	Linear Differential Equation
LDE	Lineas Aereas del Estado [*Argentina ICAO designator*] (FAAC)
LDE	Local Dynamics Experiment [*Marine science*] (MSC)
LDE	Long-Delayed Echo
LDE	Long-Duration Exposure
LDE	Lourdes/Tarbes [*France*] [*Airport symbol*] (OAG)
LDeB	Beauregard Parish Library, DeRidder, LA [*Library symbol Library of Congress*] (LCLS)
L Dec	Land Office Decisions, United States [*A publication*] (DLA)
LDEC	Lunar Docking Events Controller [*NASA*] (MCD)
LDEF	Long-Duration Exposure Facility [*NASA*]
LDEG	Laus Deo et Gloria [*Praise and Glory Be to God*] [*Latin*]
LDERRY	Londonderry [*County in Ireland*] (ROG)
LDET	Level Detector (MSA)
LDEX	Landing Exercise [*Navy*] (NVT)
LD-EYA	Lombard-Dowell Egg Yolk Agar [*Microbiology*]
LDF	Land Disposal Facility
LDF	Landed Duty Free
LDF	Latin American Discovery Fd [*NYSE symbol*] (TTSB)
LDF	Latin American Discovery Fund [*NYSE symbol*] (SPSG)
LDF	Light Digital FACSIMILE [*Machine*]
LDF	Light Distillate Feedstock (PDAA)
LDF	Linear Discriminant Function [*Mathematics*]
LDF	Linear Driving Force
LDF	Load Division Fault
LDF	Load Factor (IAA)
LDF	Local Defense Forces
LDF	Local-Density Functional Equation (MCD)
LDF	Local Density Functional Theory [*Chemistry*]
LDF	London Diocesan Fund
LDF	Lyme Disease Foundation
LDF	NAACP [*National Association for the Advancement of Colored People*] Legal Defense and Educational Fund (EA)
LDFC	Lew DeWitt Fan Club [*Defunct*] (EA)
LDFSTN	Landing Direction Finding Station [*Aviation*] (IAA)
LDG	Lactic Dehydrogenase (DMAA)
LDG	Lading (WDAA)
LDG	Landing [*Maps and charts*] (AFM)
LDG	Leading
LDG	Left Digestive Gland
LDG	Lexington Design Group (SAA)
LDG	Libyan Desert Glass [*Archeology*]
LDG	Linear Displacement Gauge
LDG	Lingual Developmental Groove (DMAA)
LDG	Loading
LDG	Lodge [*or Lodging*] (MCD)
LDG	Lodge
LDG	Longs Drug Stores [*NYSE symbol*] (TTSB)
LDG	Longs Drug Stores Corp. [*NYSE symbol*] (SPSG)
LDG	Low-Density Gas
Ldg & Dly	Landing and Delivery [*Shipping*] (DS)
LDGE	LEM [*Lunar Excursion Module*] Dummy Guidance Equipment [*NASA*] (KSC)
LDGE	Lodge [*Commonly used*] (OPSA)
LDGLT	Leading Light [*Navigation signal*]
L-DGO	Lamont-Doherty Geological Observatory [*Formerly, LGO*] [*Columbia University*]
LDGO	Lamont Doherty Geological Observatory [*Marine science*] (OSRA)
LDGP	Low-Drag General Purpose (MCD)
LDGPS	Local DGPS [*Differential*] [*Global Positioning System*] (GAVI)
LDGSPTBN	Landing Support Battalion (DNAB)
Ld Gt	Land Grant (MHDB)
Ldg Tel	Leading Telegraphist
LDGV	Light-Duty Gasoline Vehicle
LDH	Lactate Dehydrogenase [*Also, LAD, LD*] [*An enzyme*]
L d'H	Legion d'Honneur [*French decoration*]
LDH	Ligue des Droits de l'Homme [*France*]
LDH	Limiting Dome Height [*Automotive metal stamping*]
LDH	Lord Howe Island [*Australia Airport symbol*] (OAG)
LDHC	Lactic Dehydrogenase-C (DMAA)
LDHC	Locker Door Hydraulic Cylinder
LDHD	Lymphocyte-Depletion Hodgkin's Disease [*Medicine*]
LDHI	Lactic Dehydrogenase Isoenzymes (DAVI)
LDHK	Lactic Dehydrogenase-K (DMAA)
LDHM	London Diocesan Home Mission [*or Missionary*]
LDHRR	League for the Defense of Human Rights in Romania [*Paris, France*] (EAIO)
LDI	Landing Direction Indicator [*ICAO*] (FAAC)
LDI	LASER Desorption Ionization [*Spectroscopy*]
LDI	Lauda Air [*Italy ICAO designator*] (FAAC)
LDI	Life Detection Instrument
LDI	Lindi [*Tanzania*] [*Airport symbol*] (OAG)
LDI	Linear Displacement Indicator
LDI	Load Indicator
LDI	Lockheed DataPlan, Inc. [*Information service or system*] (IID)
LDI	Loredi Resources Ltd. [*Vancouver Stock Exchange symbol*]
LDI	Lossless Digital Integrator (IAA)
LDI	Low-Density Indication (MCD)

LDIC	LDI Corp. [*NASDAQ symbol*] (SAG)
LDI Cp	LDI Corp. [*Associated Press*] (SAG)
L Dict	Law Dictionary [*A publication*] (DLA)
LDIH	Left Direct Inguinal Hernia [*Medicine*] (DMAA)
LDII	Larson-Davis [*NASDAQ symbol*] (SAG)
LDII	Larson Davis [*NASDAQ symbol*] (TTSB)
LDIM	Luminescence Digital Imaging Microscopy
LDIN	Lead-In Lighting [*or Lights*] [*Aviation*]
LDIN	Lead-in-Light System [*FAA*] (TAG)
L-Dink	Lower Class - Double [*or Dual*] Income, No Kids [*Lifestyle classification*]
LDIP	Laboratory Data Integrity Program [*Environmental Protection Agency*] (GFGA)
L-DISC	Late Direct Injection Stratified Charge
LDISCR	Level Discriminator (MSA)
LD Is FFD	Line of Departure Is Friendly Forward Disposition [*Army*] (AABC)
LDISO	Lactic Dehydrogenase Isoenzymes (DAVI)
LD Is PPOS	Line of Departure Is Present Positions [*Military*] (AABC)
LDIU	Launch Data Interface Unit (MCD)
L Div	Law Division (DLA)
L Div	Licentiate in Divinity
LDJ	Linden, NJ [*Location identifier FAA*] (FAAL)
LDJ	Load D-Bank and Jump [*Computer science*]
LDJU	Luvers of David Jones United (EA)
LDK	Lower Deck
Ld Ken	Lord Kenyon's English King's Bench Reports [*1753-59*] [*A publication*] (DLA)
Ld Kenyon	Lord Kenyon's English King's Bench Reports [*1753-59*] [*A publication*] (DLA)
Ld Kenyon (Eng)	Lord Kenyon's English King's Bench Reports [*1753-59*] [*A publication*] (DLA)
LDL	Landing Direction Light [*Aviation*] (IAA)
LDL	Language Description Language [*Computer science*]
LDL	Learned Doctor of Laws
LDL	Lighting Design Lumen (PDAA)
LDL	Liquid Delay Line
LDL	Logical Data Language [*Computer science*] (IAA)
LDL	Logical Display List (MCD)
LDL	Long Distance Love [*An association*] (EA)
LDL	Loudness Discomfort Level (MAE)
LDL	Low-Density Lipoprotein [*Biochemistry*]
LDL	Lower Detectable Limit [*Chemical analysis*]
LDL	Lower Deviation Level (AABC)
LDL	Lydall, Inc. [*NYSE symbol*] (SPSG)
LDL	University of Nebraska, Lincoln, Lincoln, NE [*OCLC symbol*] (OCLC)
LDLA	Limited Distance Line Adapter
LDLA	Low-Density Lipoprotein Apheresis [*Medicine*] (DMAA)
LD/LC	Line of Departure/Line of Contact [*Army*] (ADDR)
LDL-C	Low-Density Lipoprotein-Cholesterol [*Biochemistry*]
LDLE	Light-Duty Lathe Engine
LdLew	Lewisville Public Library, Lewisville, ID [*Library symbol*] [*Library of Congress*] (LCLS)
LD-LISC	Ligand-Driven Light-Induced Spin Changes [*Physics*]
LD LMT	Load Limit (WDAA)
LD^{Lo}	Lethal Dose Low (ERG)
LDLP	Low Density Lipoprotein [*Biochemistry*]
LDLR	Land Development Law Reporter [*A publication*] (DLA)
LDLR	Low-Density Lipoprotein Receptor [*Biochemistry*]
Ldlw COO	Laidlaw One, Inc. [*Associated Press*] (SAG)
Ldlw000	Laidlaw One, Inc. [*Associated Press*] (SAG)
LDM	Laidlaw Transportation Ltd. [*Toronto Stock Exchange symbol*]
LDM	LASER Drilling Machine
LDM	Last Day of the Month (AFM)
LDM	Lee, David M., Los Angeles CA [*STAC*]
LDM	Libby Dam [*Montana*] [*Seismograph station code, US Geological Survey*] (SEIS)
LDM	Licentiate of Dental Medicine
LDM	Limited-Distance MODEM [*Computer science*]
LDM	Linear Delta Modulation
LDM	Load Distribution Matrix (IAA)
LDM	Local Data Manager
LDM	Long-Delay Monostable [*Circuitry*]
LDM	Lord Mayor
LDM	Low-Density Microsome [*Cytology*]
LDM	Ludington, MI [*Location identifier FAA*] (FAAL)
LDMA	London Discount Market Association [*British*] (MHDW)
LDME	LASER Distance Measuring Equipment (DNAB)
LDMI	LASER Distance Measuring Instrument
LDMK	Landmark (KSC)
LdmkBc	Landmark Bancorp [*Associated Press*] (SAG)
LdmkGph	Landmark Graphics Corp. [*Associated Press*] (SAG)
LDMOS	Lateral Double-Diffused Metal-Oxide Semiconductor (MCD)
LD-MPT	Ligue Democratique - Mouvement pour le Parti des Travailleurs [*Democratic League - Movement for the Workers' Party*] [*Senegal*] [*Political party*] (PPW)
LDMS	Laboratory Data Management System [*IBM Corp.*]
LDMS	LASER Desorption Mass Spectrometry
LDMS	LASER Distance Measuring System
LDMS	Lunar Distance Measuring System [*Aerospace*]
LDMWR	Limited Depot Maintenance Work Requirements
LDMX	Local Digital Message Exchange (AABC)
LDN	Lamidanda [*Nepal*] [*Airport symbol*] (OAG)
LDN	Lightning Detection Network [*Electric Power Research Institute*]
LDN	Linden, VA [*Location identifier FAA*] (FAAL)
LDN	Listed Directory Number [*Bell System*]

LDN .... Locally Defined Neighborhood
LDN .... London [Ontario] [Seismograph station code, US Geological Survey] (SEIS)
LDN .... London [England]
LDN .... London Silver Corp. [Vancouver Stock Exchange symbol]
LDNA .... Long-Distance Navigation Aid
LD-NEYA ..... Lombard-Dowell Neomycin Egg Yolk Agar [Microbiology]
LDNG .... Loading
LDNS .... Lightweight Doppler Navigation System (MCD)
LDO .... Ladouanie [Suriname] [Airport symbol] (OAG)
LDO .... Laminated Diatom Ooze [Oceanography]
LDO .... Launch Division Officer [Missiles] (MUGU)
LDO .... Light Diesel Oil (IAA)
LDO .... Limited Duty Officer [Navy]
LDO .... Linear Diophantine Object
LDO .... Local Dental Officer
LDO .... Logical Device Order [Computer science] (IBMDP)
LDO .... Long-Distance Oil [Service mark] [Amoco Oil Co.]
LDO .... Low-Density Oil [Petroleum industry]
LDO .... Low-Density Overlay [Plywood]
LDO .... Low Drop Out
LDO .... St. Mary's Dominican College, New Orleans, LA [OCLC symbol] (OCLC)
LDOCE .... Longman's Dictionary of Contemporary English [A publication]
LDOM .... Lorenz Domination [Statistics]
L-DOPA .... Levo-Dihydroxyphenylalanine [Pharmacology]
LDOS .... Leather Dressers' Old Society [A union] [British]
LDOS .... Local Density of Electron States [Physical chemistry]
LDOS .... Local Density of States [Solid state physics]
LDOS .... Lord's Day Observance Society [British]
LDP .... Laban ng Demokratikong Pilipino [Democratic Filipino's Struggle] [Political party]
LDP .... Laboratory Data Processor (IAA)
LDP .... Laboratory Distribution Panel
LDP .... Ladyship [or Lordship]
LDP .... Landed Duty Paid [Military]
LDP .... Langmuir Diffusion Pump [Engineering]
LDP .... Language Data Processing (MSA)
LDP .... Large Developmental Plant [Project] [Department of Energy]
LDP .... Leadership Development Projects [National Science Foundation]
LDP .... Leaflet Dispensing Pod
LDP .... League for Democracy and Peace [Myanmar] [Political party] (EY)
LDP .... Left Dorso-Posterior [A fetal position] [Obstetrics]
LDP .... Liberal Democratic Party [Slovenia] [Political party] (EY)
LDP .... Liberal-Democratic Party of Japan [Jiyu-Minshuto] [Political party] (PPW)
LDP .... Liberal Demokratische Partei [Liberal Democratic Party] [Germany Political party] (PPE)
LDP .... Lietuviy Demokraty Partija [Lithuanian Democratic Party] [Political party] (PPE)
L/DP .... Living/Dying Project (EA)
LDP .... Local Data Package (KSC)
LDP .... Local Data Processor (AABC)
LDP .... Logistics Data Package
LDP .... Logistics Development Program (DOMA)
LDP .... Lomas Data Products [Marlboro, MA] [Computer manufacturer]
LDP .... London Daily Price [British]
LDP .... Long-Day Plant [Botany]
LDP .... Lordship [British]
LDP .... Lorentz Doppler Profile [Physics]
LDP .... Lung Damaging Particle
LDPD .... Liberal-Demokratische Partei Deutschlands [Liberal Democratic Party of Germany] [Political party] (PPW)
LDPE .... Low-Density Polyethylene [Polymer]
LDPN .... Low-Density Phenolic Nylon [Polymer]
LDPS .... L-Band Digital Phase Shifter
LDQ .... Leaders Equity Corp. [Vancouver Stock Exchange symbol]
LDQ .... Lobe-Dominated Quasar [Astronomy]
LDR .... Aero Lider SA de CV [Mexico ICAO designator] (FAAC)
LDR .... Labor, Delivery, Recovery Room [Medicine]
LDR .... Landauer, Inc. [AMEX symbol] (SPSG)
LDR .... Land Disposal Restrictions [Environmental Protection Agency]
LDR .... Landmark Resources Ltd. [Vancouver Stock Exchange symbol]
LDR .... Large Deployable Reflector [Astronomy]
LDR .... LASER Designator Range (MCD)
LDR .... Leader (AFM)
LDR .... Leader
LDR .... Leading Deep Recess [Rotary automotive engine]
LDR .... Ledger (ADA)
LDR .... Length-Diameter Ratio
LDR .... Level Distribution Recorder
LDR .... Liberal, Democratic, and Reformist Group [European political movement] (ECON)
LDR .... Light Dependent Resistor
LDR .... Light-to-Dark Ratio
LDR .... Limiting Drawing Ratio (MCD)
LDR .... Linear Decision Rule
LDR .... Linear Dynamic Range
LDR .... Line Driver-Receiver [Computer communication] (TEL)
LDR .... Liquid Droplet Radiator (MCD)
LDR .... Llandore [Welsh depot code]
LDR .... Loader (MSA)
LDR .... Lodar [South Arabia] [Airport symbol] (AD)
LDR .... Log Dose Response [Biochemical analysis]
LDR .... Lorentz Double Refraction [Physics]

L/DR .... Lounge/Dining Room [Classified advertising] (ADA)
LDR .... Low Data Rate [RADAR]
LDR .... Low Data Register [Computer science]
LDR .... Low-Density, Recorder
LDR .... Low Dose Rate [Medicine]
LDRA .... Low Data Rate Auxiliary [RADAR]
Ld Ray .... Lord Raymond's King's Bench and Common Pleas Reports [1694-1732] [A publication] (DLA)
Ld Raym...... Lord Raymond's King's Bench and Common Pleas Reports [1694-1732] [A publication] (DLA)
LDRC .... Libel Defense Resource Center (EA)
LDRC .... Lumber Dealers Research Council [Defunct] (EA)
LDRDA .... Long Distance Running Directors Association (EA)
LDRER .... Launderer
LDRF .... Long-Distance Range Finder (SSD)
LDRG .... Liberal, Democratic and Reformist Group [See also GLDR] (EAIO)
LDRI .... Learning Disabilities Research Institute [University of Virginia] (EDAC)
LDRI .... Low Data Rate Input [RADAR]
LDRIACS..... Low Data Rate Integrated Acoustic Communications System [Military] (CAAL)
LDRM .... LASER Designator Rangefinding Module (RDA)
LDRP .... Labor, Delivery, Recovery, Post-Partum [Medicine] (MEDA)
LDRP .... Learning Disability Rating Procedure [Educational test]
LDRPS .... Labor-Delivery-Recovery-Postpartum Suite (HCT)
LDRRIM....... Low-Density Reinforced Reaction Injection Molding [Plastics]
LD-RRIM...... Low Density-Reinforced Reaction Injection Molding
LDRS .... Labor-Delivery-Recovery Suite (HCT)
LDRS .... LASER Discrimination RADAR System
L/DRS .... Level and Density Recorder Switch [Nuclear energy] (NRCH)
LDRSHP....... Leadership
LDRSP .... Leadership (AFM)
LDRT .... [The] Lake Front Dock & Railroad Terminal Co. [Formerly, LDT] [AAR code]
LDRT .... Low Data Rate [RADAR] (IAA)
LDRTF .... Land Disposal Restrictions Task Force [Environmental Protection Agency] (GFGA)
LDRY .... Landry's Seafood Restaurants [NASDAQ symbol] (TTSB)
LDRY .... Landrys Seafood Restaurants, Inc. [NASDAQ symbol] (SAG)
LDRY .... Laundry (AFM)
LDryNG....... Louis Dreyfus Natural Gas [Associated Press] (SAG)
LDS............. Havre, MT [Location identifier FAA] (FAAL)
LDS............. Landing/Deceleration Subsystem [NASA] (NASA)
LDS............. Landing, Deservicing, and Safing [NASA] (KSC)
LDS............. Langmuir Dark Space [Electronics]
LDS............. Large Disk Storage [Computer science] (IEEE)
LDS............. LASER Deep Space
LDS............. LASER Designator System [Rangefinder] (MCD)
LDS............. Laser Detection System
LDS............. LASER Drilling System
LDS............. Last Data Sample (IAA)
LDS............. Latter-Day Saints [Mormons]
LDS............. Launch Data System [NASA] (KSC)
LDS............. Launch Detection Satellite [Former USSR]
LDS............. Laus Deo Semper [Praise to God Always] [Latin]
LDS............. Layered Defense System (MCD)
LDS............. Lead Design Supervisor [Engineering]
LDS............. Leader Development Study [Army]
LDS............. Leak Detection System [Nuclear energy] (NRCH)
LDS............. Lethal Defense System (MCD)
LDS............. Lexington Developmental Scales [Child development test]
LDS............. Licentiate in Dental Surgery
LDS............. Lietuviu Darbininku Susivienijimas [Association of Lithuanian Workers] (EA)
LDS............. Ligating and Dividing Stapler [Used surgical procedures] (DAVI)
LDS............. Light Distillate Spirit (PDAA)
LDS............. Lightweight Decontamination System (INF)
LDS............. Linear Dynamic System
LDS............. Liquid, Diesel-Cycle, Supercharged
LDS............. Loads [Military]
LDS............. Local Digital Switch [Telecommunications] (TEL)
LDS............. Local Distribution Service [Cable TV network] (NITA)
LDS............. Local Distribution System [or Service] [Cable television] (MDG)
LDS............. Locked Door Seclusion [Medicine] (DMAA)
LDS............. Logistics Data Sheet
LDS............. Long Distance Savers
LDS............. Long Distance Swimmer
LDS............. Longitudinal Direct Substitution Imputation Procedure [Bureau of the Census] (GFGA)
LDS............. Lunar Drill System [NASA]
LDSA .... Logistics Doctrine and Systems Agency [Army] (MCD)
LDSc........... Licentiate in Dental Science [British]
ldscp........... Landscape (VRA)
LDSD .... Lookdown/Shootdown (MCD)
LDSD .... Low Dimensional Structures and Devices [British]
LDSI .... Licentiate in Dental Surgery (Ireland)
LDSJ .... Little Daughters of St. Joseph [Roman Catholic religious order]
LDSO .... Logistics Doctrine and Systems Office [Army]
LDSP .... Lietuvos Socialdemokratu Partija [Social Democratic Party of Lithuania] [Political party] (EAIO)
LDSR .... League of Distilled Spirits Rectifiers [Defunct]
LDSRA......... Logistics Doctrine Systems and Readiness Agency [Army] (AABC)
LDSRCPS Glas... Licentiate in Dental Surgery of the Royal College of Physicians and Surgeons of Glasgow [British]

LDSRCS.......	Licentiate in Dental Surgery of the Royal College of Surgeons [*British*]
LDSRCSEd...	Licentiate in Dental Surgery of the Royal College of Surgeons of Edinburgh (DI)
LDSRCS Edin...	Licentiate in Dental Surgery of the Royal College of Surgeons of Edinburgh [*British*]
LDSRCS Eng...	Licentiate in Dental Surgery of the Royal College of Surgeons of England
LDSRCS Irel...	Licentiate in Dental Surgery of the Royal College of Surgeons in Ireland
LD-SRIM......	Low-Density Structural Reaction Injection Molding [*Plastics*]
LDSS	LASER Designator Search System
LDSS	Lunar Deep Seismic Sounding [*Aerospace*] (MCD)
LDSSIG........	Learning Disabled Student SIG [*Special Interest Group*] (EA)
LDST...........	Letdown Storage Tank [*Nuclear energy*] (NRCH)
LDSU	Local Distribution Service Unit (IAA)
LDT.............	[*The*] Lake Front Dock & Railroad Terminal Co. [*Later, LDRT*] [*AAR code*]
LDT.............	Language Dependent Translator
LDT.............	LASER Discharge Tube
LDT.............	Lateral Dorsal Tract [*Neuroanatomy*]
LDT.............	L-DOPA Test [*Endocrinology*]
LDT.............	Left Dorsotransverse [*Medicine*] (DMAA)
LDT.............	Level Delay Time
LDT.............	Level Detector (KSC)
LDT.............	Library Development Team
LDT.............	Licensed Deposit-Taking Institution [*British*]
LDT.............	Light Displacement Ton [*MARAD*] (TAG)
LDT.............	Light-Duty Truck
LDT.............	Linear Differential Transformer
LDT.............	Linear Displacement Transduced (MCD)
LDT.............	Local Daylight Saving Time
LDT.............	Local Descriptor Table [*Computer science*]
LDT.............	Logical Design Translator [*NITA*]
LDT.............	Logical Device Table (IAA)
LDT.............	Logic Design Translator [*Computer science*]
LDT.............	Logistic Delay Time (CAAL)
LDT.............	London Dipole Theory
LDT.............	Long Distance Transmission (BUR)
LDT.............	Long Dry Ton
LDT.............	Lubbock, TX [*Location identifier FAA*] (FAAL)
LDTA...........	Leak Detection Technology Association (EA)
LDTC...........	Lawndale Transportation Co. [*AAR code*]
LDTC...........	Learning Disabilities Teacher Consultant
LD/TE..........	Line Driver/Terminal Equipment (MCD)
LDTEL.........	Long Distance Telephone [*Telecommunications*] (IAA)
LDTF..........	Light of Divine Truth Foundation (EA)
LDTM..........	Lander Dynamic Test Model [*NASA*]
LDTOF	LASER Desorption Time-of-Flight [*Spectrometry*]
LDTR	Long Dwell Time RADAR (NATG)
LDTTY.........	Landing Line Teletype
LDU	Lahad Datu [*Malaysia*] [*Airport symbol*] (OAG)
LDU	Lamp Dimmer Unit (MCD)
LdU............	Landesring der Unabhaengigen [*Independent Party*] [*Switzerland Political party*] (PPE)
LDU	Leather Dressers' Union [*British*]
LDU	Line Driver Unit [*Computer communication*] (MCD)
LDUB	Long Double Upright Brace [*Medicine*]
LDUH..........	Low-Dose Unfractionated Heparin [*Medicine*] (DMAA)
LD/USA........	Long Distance/USA, Inc. [*Honolulu, HI*] [*Telecommunications*] (TSSD)
LDV.............	Lactic Dehydrogenase Virus
LDV.............	Large Dense-Cored Vesicle [*Medicine*] (DMAA)
LDV.............	LASER Doppler Velocimeter
LDV.............	Leadville [*Nevada*] [*Seismograph station code, US Geological Survey Closed*] (SEIS)
LDV.............	League of Disabled Voters (EA)
LDV.............	Lectus Developments Ltd. [*Vancouver Stock Exchange symbol*]
LDV.............	Light-Duty Vehicle
LDV.............	Linear Differential Vector
LDV.............	Local Defence Volunteers [*Later called Home Guards*] [*British World War II*]
LDV.............	Low-Dollar Value
LDVA...........	Lodi District Vintners Association (EA)
LDVE...........	Linear Differential Vector Equation
LDW............	Laidlaw Inc. [*NYSE symbol*] (SAG)
LDW............	Left Defense Wing [*Women's lacrosse position*]
LDW............	Liability Damage Waiver [*Insurance*]
LDW............	Licensed Driver's Waiver (BARN)
LDWA..........	Long Distance Walkers Association [*British*] (DBA)
LDWSS	LASER Designator Weapon System Simulation (RDA)
LDX.............	Long-Distance Xerography [*Xerox Corp.*] [*Communications facsimile system*]
LDY.............	Laundry
LDY.............	Leicestershire and Derbyshire Yeomanry [*Military unit*] [*British*]
LDY.............	Londonderry [*Northern Ireland*] [*Airport symbol*] (OAG)
LDZ.............	Lodz [*Poland*] [*Airport symbol*] (AD)
LDZ.............	St. Louis, MO [*Location identifier FAA*] (FAAL)
LE	Antenna Effective Length for Electric-Field Antennas (IEEE)
LE	Eunice Public Library, Eunice, LA [*Library symbol Library of Congress*] (LCLS)
LE	Laboratory Evaluation (MUGU)
LE	Laboratory of Electronics [*Rockefeller University*] [*Research center*] (RCD)
LE	Labor Exchange

LE	Lactate Extraction [*Medicine*] (DMAA)
LE	Lands' End [*NYSE symbol*] (SPSG)
LE	LAN [*Local Area Network*] Emulation [*Computer science*]
LE	Large End (OA)
LE	LASER Electronics (MCD)
LE	Lateral Element
LE	Lateral Epicondyle [*Anatomy*]
LE	Latest Estimate [*Business term*]
LE	Launch Eject
LE	Launch Electronics
L/E	Launch Encounter [*NASA*] (KSC)
LE	Launch Escape [*NASA*] (KSC)
LE	Launching Equipment
LE	Law Enforcement
LE	Laws of Eshnunna (BJA)
LE	Lawyers' Edition, United States Supreme Court Reports [*A publication*] (DLA)
LE	Lead Engineer (AAG)
LE	Leading Edge [*Aerospace*]
LE	Lease
LE	Leave Edge (DGA)
le	Lebanon [*MARC country of publication code Library of Congress*] (LCCP)
LE	Lector
Le	Ledge
LE	Lee-Enfield [*British military*] (DMA)
LE	Left Ear (DMAA)
LE	Left End
LE	Left Extremity
LE	Left Eye
LE	Leg Exercise [*Sports medicine*]
LE	Length (IAA)
Le	Leonard [*Unit for cathode rays*]
LE	Leone [*Monetary unit*] [*Sierra Leone*]
LE	Less than or Equal
LE	Leucine Enkephalin [*Biochemistry*]
LE	Leucocyte Elastase [*An enzyme*]
LE	Leukemia [*Oncology*]
LE	Leukoerythrogenetic (MAE)
LE	Levy Industries Ltd. [*Toronto Stock Exchange symbol*]
Le	Lewis [*Blood group*]
Le	Lewis Number [*IUPAC*]
LE	Library Edition (ADA)
LE	Lifting Eye
LE	Light Equipment
LE	Limited Edition (ADA)
LE	Limits of Error
LE	Linear Expansion [*Physics*]
LE	Line Equipment [*Telecommunications*] (TEL)
LE	Linkage Editor (IAA)
LE	Linkage Equilibrium [*Genetics*]
LE	Local Exchange [*Telecommunications*] (TEL)
LE	Locally Engaged
LE	Locally Excited [*Physical chemistry*]
LE	Logic Element
LE	Logistic Effectiveness (CAAL)
LE	Logistic Evaluation
LE	Long-Evans Rat
LE	Loop Extender [*Telecommunications*] (TEL)
LE	Louisiana Eastern Railroad [*AAR code*]
LE	Low Efficiency
LE	Low Energy (CAAL)
LE	Low Entry [*Truck cab*]
LE	Lower Epidermis [*Botany*]
LE	Lower Extremity [*Medicine*]
LE	Low Explosive [*Military*]
LE	Lugalbanda and Enmerkar (BJA)
LE	Lugalbanda Epos (BJA)
LE	Lunar Ephemeris
LE	Lupus Erythematosus [*Hematology*]
LE	Magnum Airlines [*ICAO designator*] (AD)
Le	[*The*] Twenty-Four Books of the Holy Scriptures (1853) [*I. Leeser*] (BJA)
LE 2d	Lawyer's Edition, United States Supreme Court Reports, Second Series [*A publication*] (DLA)
LEA	Landes-Entschaedigungsamt (BJA)
LEA	Language Experience Approach [*Education*]
LEA	Latest Epicardial Activation [*Cardiology*]
LEA	Launch Enable Alarm (MCD)
LEA	Launch Escape Assembly [*NASA*] (KSC)
LEA	Law Enforcement Agencies (DOMA)
LEA	Law Enforcement Assistance Program (EA)
LEA	Lead [*South Dakota*] [*Seismograph station code, US Geological Survey Closed*] (SEIS)
LEA	Lead Air Jet Service [*France ICAO designator*] (FAAC)
LEA	Leader Resources, Inc. [*Vancouver Stock Exchange symbol*]
LEA	League [*Unit of measurement*]
LEA	League
LEA	Lear Corp. [*NYSE symbol*] (TTSB)
LEA	Learmonth [*Australia Airport symbol*] (OAG)
LEA	Learning Experience Approach [*Education*] (EDAC)
LEA	Lear Seating Co. [*NYSE symbol*] (SAG)
Lea	Lea's Tennessee Reports [*A publication*] (DLA)
LEA	Leather
lea	Leather (VRA)

LEA............	Leave
LEA............	Letter Enjoyers Association (EA)
LEA............	Light-Emitting Array
LEA............	Linear Embedding Algorithm (PDAA)
LEA............	Line Equalizing Amplifier (AFM)
LEA............	Load Effective Address [Computer science]
LEA............	Local Education Agency [School district] [HEW] (OICC)
LEA............	Local Education Authority [British]
LEA............	Local Employment Act [Town planning] [British]
LEA............	Logistic Evaluation Agency [Army]
LEA............	Logistics Engineering Analysis (NASA)
LEA............	Logistics Evaluation Activity [Army]
LEA............	Long-Endurance Aircraft
LEA............	Longitudinally Excited Atmosphere [LASER technology] (EECA)
LEA............	Loop Extension Amplifier
LEA............	Loss Executives Association [Parsippany, NJ] (EA)
LEA............	Lower Excess Air [Combustion technology]
LEA............	Lower Extremity Amputation [Medicine] (DMAA)
LEA............	Low-Excess-Air [Combustion technology]
LEA............	Lutheran Education Association (EA)
LEAA.........	Lace and Embroidery Association of America [Later, Lace Importers Association] (EA)
LEAA.........	Law Enforcement Assistance Act
LEAA.........	Law Enforcement Assistance Administration [Closed, functions transferred to Office of Justice Assistance, Research, and Statistics] [Department of Justice]
LEAA Legal Op...	Law Enforcement Assistance Administration. Legal Opinions [A publication] (DLA)
LEAB.........	Albacete [Spain ICAO location identifier] (ICLI)
LEA/BZ......	Vessel Leased to Brazil [Navy]
LEAC.........	Levelized Energy Adjustment Clause (NRCH)
LEAC.........	Madrid [Spain ICAO location identifier] (ICLI)
Leach........	Leach's English Crown Cases [1730-1815] [A publication] (DLA)
LEA/CH......	Vessel Leased to China [Navy]
Leach CC....	Leach's Crown Cases, King's Bench [England] [A publication] (DLA)
Leach CL....	Leach's Cases in Crown Law [A publication] (DLA)
Leach Cl Cas...	Leach's Club Cases [London] [A publication] (DLA)
Leach Cr Cas...	Leach's English Crown Cases [1730-1815] [A publication] (DLA)
LEAD.........	Law Students Exposing Advertising Deceptions [Student legal action organization]
LEAD.........	Leader Effectiveness and Adaptability Description [Test]
Lead..........	Leader Law Reports [Ceylon] [A publication] (DLA)
LEAD.........	Leadership and Excellence in Alzheimer's Disease Award Program [Department of Health and Human Services] (GFGA)
LEAD.........	Leadership, Education, and Development [US Army Corps of Engineers]
LEAD.........	Leadership for Environment and Development Institute [Non-profit organization] (ECON)
LEAD.........	Leadership in Educational Administration Development
LEAD.........	Leadville Corp. [NASDAQ symbol] (SAG)
LEAD.........	Learn, Execute, and Diagnose
LEAD.........	Lens Electronic Automatic Design (IAA)
LEAD.........	Letterkenny Army Depot [Pennsylvania] (AABC)
Leadam......	Leadam's Select Cases before King's Council in the Star Chamber [Selden Society Publications, Vols. 16, 25] [A publication] (DLA)
Leadam Req...	Select Cases in the Court of Requests, Edited by I. S. Leadam [Selden Society Publications, Vol. 12] [A publication] (DLA)
Lead Cas Am...	American Leading Cases, Edited by Hare and Wallace [A publication] (DLA)
Lead Cas Eq...	Leading Cases in Equity, by White and Tudor [A publication] (DLA)
Lead Cas in Eq...	Leading Cases in Equity, by White and Tudor [A publication] (DLA)
Lead Cas in Eq (Eng)...	Leading Cases in Equity, by White and Tudor [England] [A publication] (DLA)
LEADER	Lehigh Automatic Device for Efficient Retrieval [Center for Information Sciences, Lehigh University] [Bethlehem, PA] [Computer science]
LEADER	Logistics Echelons above Division in Europe (MCD)
LEADERMART...	LEADER Mechanical Analysis and Retrieval of Text (NITA)
LEADEX.......	Lead Experiment [Marine science] (OSRA)
LEADEX.......	Lead Experiment (USDC)
Lead LR......	Leader Law Reports [South Africa] [A publication] (DLA)
LEADR........	Lawyers Engaged in Alternative Dispute Resolution [Australia An association]
LeadrFn	Leader Financial Corp. [Associated Press] (SAG)
LEADS	Law Enforcement Automated Data System (IEEE)
LEADS	Library Experimental Automated Demonstration System [Computer science]
LEADS	Line Equipment Assignment and Display System [GTE Corp.]
LEAD USA...	Leadership Education and Development USA (EA)
Leadvle.......	Leadville Corp. [Associated Press] (SAG)
LEA/EC.......	Vessel Leased to Ecuador [Navy]
LEAF..........	Interleaf, Inc. [Cambridge, MA] [NASDAQ symbol] (NQ)
LEAF..........	Land Educational Associates Foundation [Defunct] (EA)
LEAF..........	Law Enforcement Access Field [Telecommunications]
LEAF..........	Legal Environmental Assistance Foundation (EA)
LEAF..........	Liberal Education for Adoptive Families (EA)
LEAF..........	LISP Extended Algebraic Facility
LEAF..........	Lotus Extended Applications Facility
LEAF..........	Women's Legal Education and Action Fund [Canada]
LEA/FR.......	Vessel Leased to France [Navy]
LEAFS........	LASER-Excited Atomic Fluorescent Spectrometry
LEAG..........	Legislative Extended Assistance Group [University of Iowa] [Research center] (RCD)
LEA/GR.......	Vessel Leased to Greece [Navy]
LEAGUE	Lesbian, Bisexual, and Gay United Employees at AT & T
League of Nations Off J...	League of Nations. Official Journal [A publication] (DLA)
League of Nations OJ...	League of Nations. Official Journal [A publication] (DLA)
League of Nations OJ Spec Supp...	League of Nations. Official Journal. Special Supplement [A publication] (DLA)
LEAH..........	Lulov, Esrog, Arrovos, Hadassim (BJA)
LEAHS.........	Lifetime Evaluation and Analysis of Heterogeneous System (PDAA)
LEAK..........	Leak-X Environmental [NASDAQ symbol] (TTSB)
LEAK..........	Leak-X Environmental Corp. [NASDAQ symbol] (SAG)
LEAK..........	Liposome-Encapsulated Amikacin [Bactericide]
Leake.........	Leake on Contracts [1861-1931] [A publication] (DLA)
Leake.........	Leake's Digest of the Law of Property in Land [A publication] (DLA)
Leake Cont...	Leake on Contracts [1861-1931] [A publication] (DLA)
Leake Land...	Leake's Digest of the Law of Property in Land [A publication] (DLA)
LEAKW........	Leak-X Environmental Wrrt [NASDAQ symbol] (TTSB)
LeakX........	Leak-X Environmental Corp. [Associated Press] (SAG)
LEAL..........	Alicante [Spain ICAO location identifier] (ICLI)
LEAM..........	Almeria [Spain ICAO location identifier] (ICLI)
LEAM..........	Lunar Ejecta and Meteorites [Experiment] [NASA]
Leam & Spic...	Leaming and Spicer's Laws, Grants, Concessions, and Original Constitutions [New Jersey] [A publication] (DLA)
LEA/MX......	Vessel Leased to Mexico [Navy]
Le & Ca.....	Leigh and Cave's English Crown Cases Reserved [1861-65] [A publication] (DLA)
LEA/NE.......	Vessel Leased to Netherlands [Navy]
LEA/NO.......	Vessel Leased to Norway [Navy]
LEANON.......	Lupus Erythematosus Anonymous (EA)
LEANS	Lehigh Analog Simulator (IAA)
LEAO..........	Almagro [Spain ICAO location identifier] (ICLI)
LEAP..........	Laboratory Education Advancement Program [Department of Labor]
LEAP..........	Laboratory Evaluation and Accreditation Program
LEAP..........	Laboratory Evening Academic Program (SAA)
LEAP..........	Labor Education Advancement Program
LEAP..........	Language for Expressing Associative Procedures [Computer science]
LEAP..........	Large Einsteinium Activation Program
LEAP..........	Large Experimental Aquifer Program [Oregon Graduate Institute of Science and Technology] [Research center] (RCD)
LEAP..........	Leadership and Education for Advancement of Phoenix [Arizona]
LEAP..........	Leading Edge Airborne PANAR
LEAP..........	Leap Group, Inc. (The) [NASDAQ symbol] (SAG)
LEAP..........	Legal and Educational Aid to the Poor [Center]
LEAP..........	Lewis Expandable Adjustable Prosthesis [Orthopedics]
LEAP..........	Lifetime Element Advancing Program
LEAP..........	Lift-Off Elevation and Azimuth Programmer
LEAP..........	Light Exo-Atmospheric Projectile [Formerly, Lightweight] (DOMA)
LEAP..........	Lightweight Exoatmospheric Advanced Projectile [Military] (SDI)
LEAP..........	Linear-Elastic Analysis Program [SIA Computer Services] [Software package] (NCC)
LEAP..........	Liquid Engine Air-Augmented Package (MCD)
LEAPW........	Loaned Executives Assignment Program [American Association of Advertising Agencies lobbying group]
LEAP..........	Local Education Authorities Project for School Management Training (AIE)
LEAP..........	Lockheed Electronics Assembly Program
LEAP..........	Logistic Element Action Proposal (MCD)
LEAP..........	Logistic Element Alternatives Process (MCD)
LEAP..........	Logistic Event and Assessment Program
LEAP..........	Logistics Efficiencies to Increase Army Power (MCD)
LEAP..........	Long-Term Equity Anticipations [Business term]
LEAP..........	Low-Energy All-Purpose (Collimator) [Radiology]
LEAP..........	Lower Eastside Action Project [New York City]
LEAP..........	Lower-Extremity Amputation Protocol [Orthopedics]
LEAP..........	Lunar Escape Ambulance Pack [Aerospace]
LEA/PA.......	Vessel Leased to Panama [Navy]
LEA/PE.......	Vessel Leased to Peru [Navy]
LEA/PG.......	Vessel Leased to Paraguay [Navy]
LeapGrp.......	Leap Group, Inc. (The) [Associated Press] (SAG)
Leap Rom Civ L...	Leapingwell on the Roman Civil Law [A publication] (DLA)
LEAPS.........	LASER Electro-Optical Alignment Pole for Surveying [NASA]
LEAPS.........	LASER Engineering and Application of Prototype System (MCD)
LEAPS.........	Local Exchange Area Planning Simulation [Bell Laboratories]
LEAPS.........	Long-Term Equity Anticipation Securities [Investment term] (DFIT)
LEAR..........	Learn [Database]
LEAR..........	Logistics Evaluation and Review
LEAR..........	Low-Energy Antiproton Ring [Particle physics]
LEAR..........	Low Erucic Acid Rapeseed [Plant variety]
LearBur........	Learmouth & Burchett Management Systems, Inc. [Associated Press] (SAG)
LEARN	Learnng
LEARN	Los Angeles Educational Alliance for Restructuring Now [Education-reform project] (ECON)
Learn & L....	Learning and the Law [A publication] (DLA)
Learn & Law...	Learning and the Law [A publication] (DLA)
Learnl........	LeaRonal, Inc. [Associated Press] (SAG)
LEARS	Long [Term] Equity Anticipation Securities [Finance]
LearSeat......	Lear Seating Co. [Associated Press] (SAG)
LEARSYN......	Logistics Evaluation and Review Synchronization (IAA)
LEA/RU.......	Vessel Leased to Russia [Navy]
LEAS..........	Aviles/Asturias [Spain ICAO location identifier] (ICLI)
LEAS..........	Lease Electronic Accounting System (IEEE)
LEAs..........	Local Education Agencies (PAZ)
LEAS..........	Local Education Authorities (ECON)
LEAS..........	Lower Echelon Automatic Switchboard
LEAS..........	Pride Automotive Gp [NASDAQ symbol] (TTSB)
LEAS..........	Pride Automotive Group, Inc. [NASDAQ symbol] (SAG)

LEASAT........	Leased Satellite (NITA)
LEASAT........	Leased Satellite Communications (NVT)
LEASE..........	Leasing
LeasEd.........	Leasing Edge Corp. [*Associated Press*] (SAG)
LEAS-FACS...	Lease-Financial Accounting Control System (MHDB)
LEASIB........	Local Education Authorities and Schools Item Banking [*Project*] (AIE)
L East Eur....	Law in Eastern Europe [*A publication*] (DLA)
LEASW........	Pride Automotive Gp Wrrt [*NASDAQ symbol*] (TTSB)
LEATGS........	Local Education Authority Training Grants Scheme (AIE)
LEATH..........	Leather (ROG)
LEATH..........	Leatherhead [*City in England*]
LeathFac......	Leather Factory, Inc. [*Associated Press*] (SAG)
LEA/UK	Vessel Leased to United Kingdom [*Navy*]
LEA/UR	Vessel Leased to Uruguay [*Navy*]
LEAVERATS...	Leave Rations [*Military*]
LEB	East Baton Rouge Parish Public Library, Baton Rouge, LA [*OCLC symbol*] (OCLC)
LEB	Lateral Efferent Bundle [*Neuroanatomy*]
LEB	Lebanon [*New Hampshire*] [*Airport symbol*] (OAG)
Leb	Lebanon (VRA)
LEB	Lebanon, NH [*Location identifier FAA*] (FAAL)
LEB	Lebap [*Turkmenistan*] [*ICAO designator*] (FAAC)
LEB	Local Ethernet Bridge [*RAD Network Devices, Inc.*]
LEB	London Electricity Board
LEB	Low-Emissions Bus
LEB	Lower Equipment Bay [*Apollo*] [*NASA*]
LEBA	Cordoba [*Spain ICAO location identifier*] (ICLI)
LEBA	Long Endurance Breathing Apparatus (PDAA)
Lebanon	Lebanon County Legal Journal [*Pennsylvania*] [*A publication*] (DLA)
Lebanon Co LJ (PA)...	Lebanon County Legal Journal [*Pennsylvania*] [*A publication*] (DLA)
LeBAU	American University of Beirut, Beirut, Lebanon [*Library symbol Library of Congress*] (LCLS)
LEBB	Bilbao [*Spain ICAO location identifier*] (ICLI)
LEBC	Letchworth Indep Bancshares [*NASDAQ symbol*] (TTSB)
LEBC	Letchworth Independent Bancshares Corp. [*NASDAQ symbol*] (SAG)
LEBCW	Letchworth Indep Bcshs Wrrt [*NASDAQ symbol*] (TTSB)
LEBG	Burgos [*Spain ICAO location identifier*] (ICLI)
LEBL	Barcelona [*Spain ICAO location identifier*] (ICLI)
LEBNAP	Lebanese Kidnap [*Victims*] [*American hostages held in Beirut*]
LEBR...........	Bardenas Reales [*Spain ICAO location identifier*] (ICLI)
LebSeels	Lebendige Seelsorge (BJA)
LEBT	Betera [*Spain ICAO location identifier*] (ICLI)
LEBU	Large Eddy Breakup Device [*Aerodynamics*]
LEBZ	Badajoz/Talavera La Real [*Spain ICAO location identifier*] (ICLI)
LEC	Lake Erie College [*Painesville, OH*]
LEC	Lake Erie College, Painesville, OH [*OCLC symbol*] (OCLC)
LEC	LAMPS [*Light Airborne Multipurpose System*] Element Coordinator [*Navy*] (CAAL)
LEC	Landed Estates Courts Commission [*England*] (DLA)
LEC	LAN [*Local Area Network*] Emulation Client [*Telecommunications*] (ACRL)
LEC	LANTCOM ELINT Center (MCD)
LEC	LASER Electronic Computer
LEC	Launch Escape Control [*NASA*] (KSC)
LEC	Lec Refrigeration Ltd. [*British ICAO designator*] (FAAC)
LEC	Lecture
LEC	Levelized Energy Cost
LEC	Library of English Classics [*A publication*]
LEC	Light-Emitting Chemical Compound [*Marking agent for equipment used in night operations*] [*Military*] (VNW)
LEC	Light-Emitting Electrochemical Cell [*Chemistry*]
LEC	Light Energy Converter [*Telecommunications*] (TEL)
LEC	Limited Editions Club
LEC	Liquid Encapsulated Czochralski [*Crystal growing technique*] (IEEE)
LEC	List Execution Condition (IAA)
LEC	Livestock Equipment Council [*Defunct*] (EA)
LEC	Local Employment Committee [*Department of Employment*] [*British*]
LEC	Local Engineering Change [*DoD*]
LEC	Local Exchange Carrier [*Telecommunications*] (PCM)
LEC	Local Export Control [*British*] (DS)
LEC	Lockheed Electronics Corp. [*Subsidiary of Lockheed Aircraft Corp.*]
LEC	London Education Classification [*Library classification system*] (NITA)
LEC	Low-Echo-Centroid [*Geology*]
LEC	Low Emitter Concentration (PDAA)
LEC	Lower Epidermal Cell [*Botany*]
LEC	Lumped Element Circulator
LEC	Lunar Equipment Conveyor [*Aerospace*]
LECA	Landed Estate Companies Association [*British*] (BI)
LECA	Launch Escape Control Area [*NASA*] (KSC)
LECA	Lehman Caves National Monument
LECA	Light European Combat Aircraft (PDAA)
LECA	Light-Expanded Clay Aggregate (DAC)
LECA	Madrid [*Spain ICAO location identifier*] (ICLI)
LECAM........	Lectin Adhesion Molecule [*Biochemistry*]
LECAM........	Lectin-Cellular Adhesion Molecule [*Biochemistry*]
LECAPSR	Llano Estacado Center for Advanced Professional Studies and Research [*Eastern New Mexico University*] [*Research center*] (RCD)
LECB	Barcelona [*Spain ICAO location identifier*] (ICLI)
LECC	Lake Erie Cleanup Committee [*Defunct*] (EA)
LECC	Linear Error Correcting Code (IAA)
LECCAM......	Leukocyte Endothelial Cell-Cell Adhesion Molecule [*Cytology*]
LECE..........	Leasing Edge [*NASDAQ symbol*] (TTSB)
LECE..........	Leasing Edge Corp. [*NASDAQ symbol*] (SAG)
LECEL	Leasing Edge Wrrt'B' [*NASDAQ symbol*] (TTSB)
LECEP	Leasing Edge cm Cv'A'Pfd [*NASDAQ symbol*] (TTSB)
LECEZ	Leasing Edge Wrrt'A' [*NASDAQ symbol*] (TTSB)
LECH..........	Calamocha [*Spain ICAO location identifier*] (ICLI)
LECH..........	Lechters, Inc. [*NASDAQ symbol*] (SAG)
Lechters	Lechters, Inc. [*Associated Press*] (SAG)
LECL	Valencia [*Spain ICAO location identifier*] (ICLI)
LECM..........	Madrid [*Spain ICAO location identifier*] (ICLI)
LECNA	Lutheran Educational Conference of North America (EA)
LECO..........	La Coruna [*Spain ICAO location identifier*] (ICLI)
LECO..........	Lincoln Electric [*NASDAQ symbol*] (TTSB)
LECO..........	[*The*] Lincoln Electric Co. [*NASDAQ symbol*] (SAG)
LECO..........	Local Engineering Control Office [*Telecommunications*] (TEL)
LECOA	Lincoln Electric 'A' [*NASDAQ symbol*] (TTSB)
LEconSc......	License Economic Sciences [*Canada*] (DD)
LECOS	Lunar-Environment Construction and Operations Simulator [*NASA*] (IAA)
LECP	Low-Energy Charged Particle [*Atomic physics*]
LECP	Palma [*Spain ICAO location identifier*] (ICLI)
LeCroy........	LeCroy Corp. [*Associated Press*] (SAG)
LECS	LAN [*Local Area Network*] Emulation Configuration Server [*Telecommunications*] (ACRL)
LECS	Launching Equipment Checkout Set
LECS	Local Economic Consequences Study [*Military*]
LECS	Local Enterprise Companies [*Scotland*] (ECON)
LECS	Sevilla [*Spain ICAO location identifier*] (ICLI)
LECT	League for the Exchange of Commonwealth Teachers (EA)
LECT	LecTec Corp. [*NASDAQ symbol*] (SAG)
LECT	Lectern (ROG)
LECT	Lecture [*or Lecturer*]
LECT	Lecture
Lectec.........	LecTec Corp. [*Associated Press*] (SAG)
Lect LSUC ...	Special Lectures. Law Society of Upper Canada [*A publication*] (DLA)
lectn	Lectionary (VRA)
LECTO.........	Lectotype
LECTR.........	Lecturer
LECTR.........	Lecturer
Lect y V......	Lectura y Vida [*A publication*]
LECV	Colmenar Viejo [*Spain ICAO location identifier*] (ICLI)
LED	Large Electronic Display
LED	Law Enforcement Division [*National Park Service*]
L Ed	Lawyers' Edition, United States Supreme Court Reports [*A publication*] (DLA)
LED	Leaded
LED	League for Ecological Democracy (EA)
LED	Ledger
LED	Leningrad [*Former USSR Airport symbol*] (OAG)
LED	Library Education Division [*American Library Association*] [*Defunct*]
LED	Light-Emitting Diode [*Display component*]
LED	Line Embossing Device [*Computer science*]
LED	Liquid Element Display
LED	Logical Error Detection
LED	Logistics Engineering Directorate [*ARRCOM*] (RDA)
LED	Longitudinal Establishment Data [*Bureau of the Census*] (GFGA)
LED	Low-Energy Detector
LED	Low-Energy Diffraction
LED	Lower Emissions Dispatch [*Environmental Protection Agency*]
LED	Lowest Emitting Dose [*Medicine*] (DMAA)
LED	Lupus Erythematosus Disseminatus [*Medicine*]
LED	North Platte, NE [*Location identifier FAA*] (FAAL)
L Ed 2d	Lawyers' Edition, United States Supreme Court Reports, Second Series [*A publication*] (DLA)
LEDA...........	LANDSAT Earthnet Data Availability [*ESA-Earthnet Programme Office*] [*Database*]
LEDA...........	Low-Energy Deasphalting [*Petroleum refining*]
L Ed (Adv Ops)...	United States Supreme Court Reports, Lawyers' Edition, Advance Opinions [*A publication*] (DLA)
LEDC...........	League for Emotionally Disturbed Children
LEDC...........	Local Economic Development Corp.
LEDC...........	Logistics Executive Development Course [*Army*]
LEDC...........	Low-Energy Detonating Cord (SAA)
LEDD...........	Light-Emitting Diode Display
LEDET.........	Law Enforcement Detachment [*Coast Guard*]
LED FO	Ledger Folio (ROG)
LEDI...........	Local Employment Development Initiative [*Australia*]
LEDM..........	Valladolid [*Spain ICAO location identifier*] (ICLI)
LEDO..........	Long-Term Effects of Dredging Operations [*Coastal Engineering Research Center*]
LEDP..........	Large Electronic Display Panel
LEDR..........	Laboratory for Environmental Data Research [*National Oceanic and Atmospheric Administration*]
LEDR..........	Light-Emitting Diode Recorder (MCD)
LEDS	Law Enforcement Data System
LEDS	Liquid Effluents Data System [*Environmental Protection Agency*] (GFGA)
LEDSHP	Leadership
LEDT	Limited Entry Decision Table
L Ed (US)....	Lawyers' Edition, United States Supreme Court Reports [*A publication*] (DLA)
L Ed US......	Supreme Court Reports, Lawyer's Edition [*A publication*] (NTCM)
LEE	[*The*] Lake Erie & Eastern Railroad Co. [*AAR code*]
LEE	LASER Energy Evaluator (PDAA)
LEE	Launch Electronics Equipment
LEE	Leading Edge Environment

LEE .... Leeds [*Utah*] [*Seismograph station code, US Geological Survey*] (SEIS)
LEE .... Lee Enterprises [*NYSE symbol*] (TTSB)
LEE .... Lee Enterprises, Inc. [*NYSE symbol*] (SPSG)
LEE .... Leesburg, FL [*Location identifier FAA*] (FAAL)
Lee .... Lee's English Ecclesiastical Reports [*A publication*] (DLA)
Lee .... Lee's Reports [*9-12 California*] [*A publication*] (DLA)
LEE .... Logistics Evaluation Exercise
LEEA .... Lifting Equipment Engineers Association [*British*] (EAIO)
Lee Abs ..... Lee's Abstracts of Title [*1843*] [*A publication*] (DLA)
Lee & H ...... Lee's English King's Bench Reports Tempore Hardwicke [*1733-38*] [*A publication*] (DLA)
Lee Bank .... Lee's Law and Practice of Bankruptcy [*3rd ed.*] [*1887*] [*A publication*] (DLA)
LEEBI .... Low-Energy Electron Beam Irradiation [*Physics*]
LEEC .... LASER-to-Electric Energy Conversion (SSD)
LEEC .... Sevilla-El Copero Base [*Spain ICAO location identifier*] (ICLI)
Lee Cap ...... Lee on Captures [*A publication*] (DLA)
LEED .... LASER-Energized Explosive Device
LEED .... Longitudinal Employer-Employee Data File [*Social Security Administration*]
LEED .... Low-Energy Electron Diffraction [*Spectroscopy*]
Lee Dict ...... Lee's Dictionary of Practice [*A publication*] (DLA)
LeedsFdl ..... Leeds FSB [*Associated Press*] (SAG)
LEEE .... Madrid [*Spain ICAO location identifier*] (ICLI)
Lee Eccl ...... Lee's English Ecclesiastical Reports [*A publication*] (DLA)
LeeEnt .... Lee Enterprises, Inc. [*Associated Press*] (SAG)
LE-EIA .... Leukocyte Esterase Enzyme Immunoassay
LEEIXS .... Low-Energy-Electron-Induced X-Ray Spectrometry
LEEM .... Low-Energy Electron Microscopy
LEEP .... Law Enforcement Education Program [*Department of Justice*]
LEEP .... Law Enforcement Explorer Post [*Boy Scouts*]
LEEP .... Library Education Experimental Project [*Syracuse University*]
LEEP .... Loop Electrosurgical Excision Procedure [*Medicine*]
LeePhr .... Lee Pharmaceuticals [*Associated Press*] (SAG)
LEER .... Low-Energy Electron Reflection (IEEE)
LEERS .... Long-Endurance Experimental Research Submarine (SAA)
LEES .... Laboratory for Electromagnetic and Electronic Systems [*Massachusetts Institute of Technology*] [*Research center*] (RCD)
LEES .... Lake Erie Environmental Studies
LEES .... Launch Equipment Evaluation Set (MCD)
Leese .... Leese's Reports [*26 Nebraska*] [*A publication*] (DLA)
Lee Ship ..... Lee's Laws of Shipping [*A publication*] (DLA)
LEET .... Limiting Equivalent Exposure Time (MUGU)
Lee T Hard .. Lee's English King's Bench Cases Tempore Hardwicke [*1733-38*] [*England*] [*A publication*] (DLA)
Lee T Hardw .. Lee's English King's Bench Cases Tempore Hardwicke [*1733-38*] [*England*] [*A publication*] (DLA)
LEF .... Lake Erie, Franklin & Clarion Railroad Co. [*AAR code*]
LEF .... Landpower Education Fund
LEF .... LASER Excited Fluorescence
LEF .... Leading Edge Flap [*Aviation*]
LEF .... Left-In Telephone [*Telecommunications*] (TEL)
LEF .... Leukokinesis-Enhancing Factor [*Medicine*] (DMAA)
LEF .... Licentiate in Economics and Finance
LEF .... Life Extension Foundation (EA)
LEF .... Light-Emitting Film (IEEE)
LEF .... Lincoln Educational Foundation [*Defunct*] (EA)
LEF .... Linear-Energy Spectrophotofluorometry
LEF .... Line Expansion Function
LEF .... Liquid Expanded Film
LEF .... Lobby Europeen des Femmes [*European Women's Lobby*] [*Belgium*] (EAIO)
LEF .... Loss Entry Form [*Insurance*]
LEF .... Lupus Erythematosus Factor [*Medicine*] (DMAA)
LEF .... Lymphoid-Enhanced Binding Factor [*Medicine*] (DMAA)
LEF .... Lymphoid Enhancer Factor [*Biochemistry*]
Lef & Cas ... Lefroy and Cassel's Practice Cases [*1881-83*] [*Ontario*] [*A publication*] (DLA)
LEFC .... L-Band Electronic Frequency Converter
Lef Cr L ...... Lefroy's Irish Criminal Law [*A publication*] (DLA)
LEFCS .... Leading Edge Flap Control System [*Aviation*]
Lef Dec .... Lefevre's Parliamentary Decisions, by Bourke [*England*] [*A publication*] (DLA)
LEFE .... Linear Electric Field Effect (PDAA)
LEFM .... Linear-Elastic Fracture Mechanics
LEFO .... Land's End for Order [*Shipping*]
Lefroy .... Lefroy's Railroad and Canal Cases [*England*] [*A publication*] (DLA)
LEFU .... Light Ends Fractionating Unit [*Petroleum technology*]
LEFW .... Lake Erie & Fort Wayne Railroad Co. [*AAR code*]
LEG .... Aleg [*Mauritania*] [*Airport symbol*] (AD)
Leg .... De Legibus [*of Cicero*] [*Classical studies*] (OCD)
LEG .... Language of Functions and Graphs (AIE)
LEG .... Law Enforcement Group (WDAA)
LEG .... Legal (AFM)
LEG .... Legate
Leg .... Legatio ad Gaium [*of Philo Judaeus*] [*Classical studies*] (OCD)
LEG .... Legato [*Smoothly and Connectedly*] [*Music*]
LEG .... Legend [*Numismatics*]
Leg .... Leges [*Laws*] [*Latin*] (ILCA)
LEG .... Leggett & Platt [*NYSE symbol*] (TTSB)
LEG .... Leggett & Platt, Inc. [*NYSE symbol*] (SPSG)
LEG .... Legislation [*or Legislature*]
LEG .... Legislative Library of British Columbia [*UTLAS symbol*]

LEG .... Legit [*He, or She, Reads*] [*Latin*]
LEG .... Legunt [*They Read*] [*Latin*] (ADA)
LEG .... Library Education Group of the Library Association (NITA)
LEG .... Liquefied Energy Gas
LEG .... Logistical Expediting Group
LEG .... Logistic Evaluation Group
LEGA .... Granada/Armilla [*Spain ICAO location identifier*] (ICLI)
Legacy .... Legacy: A Journal of American Women Writers [*A publication*] (BRI)
Leg Adv ...... Legal Adviser [*Chicago*] [*A publication*] (DLA)
Leg Agr .... De Lege Agraria [*of Cicero*] [*Classical studies*] (OCD)
LEGAL .... League for Equitable General Aviation Legislation (EA)
Legal Adv ... Legal Advertiser [*Chicago*] [*A publication*] (DLA)
Legal Adv ... Legal Adviser [*Denver*] [*A publication*] (DLA)
Legal Asp Med Prac... Legal Aspects of Medical Practice [*A publication*] (DLA)
Leg Alfred ... Leges Alfredi [*Laws of King Alfred*] [*Latin A publication*] (DLA)
Legal Gaz (PA)... Legal Gazette (Pennsylvania) [*A publication*] (DLA)
Legal Int ..... Legal Intelligencer [*A publication*] (DLA)
Legal Intel ... Legal Intelligencer [*A publication*] (DLA)
Legal Intell .. Legal Intelligencer [*A publication*] (DLA)
Legal Obser ... Legal Observer [*London*] [*A publication*] (DLA)
Legal Observer... New York Legal Observer [*A publication*] (DLA)
LegalR .... Legal Research Center, Inc. [*Associated Press*] (SAG)
Legal Rep .... Legal Reporter [*Australia A publication*]
Legal Rep .... Legal Reporter, New Series [*Tennessee*] [*A publication*] (DLA)
Legal Resp Child Adv Protection... Legal Response; Child Advocacy and Protection [*A publication*] (DLA)
Leg & Ins R .. Legal and Insurance Reporter [*Pennsylvania*] [*A publication*] (DLA)
Leg & Ins Rep... Legal and Insurance Reporter [*Philadelphia, PA*] [*A publication*] (DLA)
Leg & Ins Rept... Legal and Insurance Reporter [*Philadelphia, PA*] [*A publication*] (DLA)
Legat .... De Lagatione ad Caium [*Philo*] (BJA)
LEGAT .... Legal Attache [*FBI agent posted at an American embassy*]
Legato .... Legato Systems, Inc. [*Associated Press*] (SAG)
Leg Bibl ...... Legal Bibliography [*A publication*] (DLA)
Leg Canut ... Leges Canuti [*Laws of King Canute or Knut*] [*Latin A publication*] (DLA)
Leg Ch Forms... Leggo's Chancery Forms [*Ontario*] [*A publication*] (DLA)
Leg Ch Pr ... Leggo's Chancery Practice [*Ontario*] [*A publication*] (DLA)
Leg Chron ... Legal Chronicle Reports, Edited by Foster [*Pennsylvania*] [*A publication*] (DLA)
Leg Chron Rep... Legal Chronicle Reports [*Pottsville, PA*] [*A publication*] (DLA)
Legco .... Legislative Council [*Hong Kong*] (ECON)
LEG COM ..... Legally Committed (BABM)
legd .... Legend
LEGE .... Gerona/Costa Brava [*Spain ICAO location identifier*] (ICLI)
Leg Edm ..... Leges Edmundi [*Laws of King Edmund*] [*Latin A publication*] (DLA)
LEGEN .... Liposome-Encapulated Gentamicin [*Bactericide*]
LEGEND ...... Legal Electronic Network and Database (IID)
Legend .... Legend Properties, Inc. [*Associated Press*] (SAG)
Leg Ethel .... Leges Ethelredi [*Laws of King Ethelred*] [*Latin A publication*] (DLA)
Leg Exam .... Legal Examiner [*London or New York*] [*1831-35; 1862-68; 1869-72*] [*A publication*] (DLA)
Leg Exam & LC... Legal Examiner and Law Chronicle [*London*] [*A publication*] (DLA)
Leg Exam & Med J... Legal Examiner and Medical Jurist [*London*] [*A publication*] (DLA)
Leg Exam NS... Legal Examiner, New Series [*England*] [*A publication*] (DLA)
Leg Exam WR... Legal Examiner Weekly Reporter [*A publication*] (DLA)
Leg Exch ...... Legal Exchange [*Des Moines, IA*] [*A publication*] (DLA)
LEGG .... Launch Eject Gas Generator
Leg G .... Legal Guide [*A publication*] (DLA)
Legg .... Leggett's Reports [*India*] [*A publication*] (DLA)
LEGG .... Leggiero [*Light and Rapid*] [*Music*]
Leg Gaz ...... Legal Gazette [*A publication*] (DLA)
Leg Gaz R ... Campbell's Legal Gazette Reports [*Pennsylvania*] [*A publication*] (DLA)
Leg Gaz Re ... Campbell's Legal Gazette Reports [*Pennsylvania*] [*A publication*] (ILCA)
Leg Gaz Rep... Campbell's Legal Gazette Reports [*Pennsylvania*] [*A publication*] (DLA)
Legg Bills L... Leggett on Bills of Lading [*A publication*] (DLA)
LeggMas ..... Legg Mason, Inc. [*Associated Press*] (SAG)
Leggo .... Leggiero [*Light and Rapid*] [*Music*]
Legg Out ..... Legge on Outlawry [*A publication*] (DLA)
LEGGS .... Loyal Escorts of the Green Garters (EA)
Leg HI .... Laws of King Henry the First [*A publication*] (DLA)
Leg Inf Bul ... Legal Information Bulletin [*A publication*] (DLA)
Leg Inq .... Legal Inquirer [*London*] [*A publication*] (DLA)
Leg Int .... Legal Intelligencer [*A publication*] (DLA)
Leg Intel ..... Legal Intelligencer [*A publication*] (DLA)
Leg Intell .... Legal Intelligencer [*A publication*] (DLA)
Leg Intl ...... Legal Intelligencer [*A publication*] (DLA)
LEGIS .... Legislative [*or Legislature*]
LEGIS .... Legislative Information and Status System [*for House of Representatives*]
LEGISL .... Legislative (ADA)
LEGISLN ...... Legislation
LEGISN .... Legislation [*Legal shorthand*] (LWAP)
LEGISNET .... National Legislative Network [*National Conference of State Legislatures*] [*Information service or system*] (IID)
LEGISOR ..... Legislator [*Legal shorthand*] (LWAP)
Legis Stud Q... Legislative Studies Quarterly [*A publication*] (DLA)
Leg Issues ... Legal Issues of European Integration [*A publication*] (ILCA)
LEGISURE .... Legislature [*Legal shorthand*] (LWAP)

LEGISV .... Legislative [*Legal shorthand*] (LWAP)
LEGIT......... Legitimate (DSUE)
LEGIW .... Co. Counsel Inc. Wrrt [*NASDAQ symbol*] (TTSB)
Leg J .... Pittsburgh Legal Journal [*Pennsylvania*] [*A publication*] (DLA)
Leg Jour ...... Pittsburgh Legal Journal [*Pennsylvania*] [*A publication*] (DLA)
LEGL.......... Co-Counsel, Inc. [*NASDAQ symbol*] (SAG)
LEGM.......... Low-Energy Gamma Monitor
Leg Misc ...... Legal Miscellany [*Ceylon*] [*A publication*] (DLA)
Leg Misc & Rev... Legal Miscellany and Review [*India*] [*A publication*] (DLA)
Leg News .... Legal News [*Canada*] [*A publication*] (DLA)
Leg Notes.... Legal Notes on Local Government [*New York*] [*A publication*] (DLA)
LEGO .... Leg Godt [*Play Well*] [*Acronym is brand of child's building toy*]
     [*Denmark*]
Leg Obs....... Legal Observer [*London*] [*A publication*] (DLA)
Leg Obs....... Legal Observer and Solicitor's Journal [*London*] [*A publication*] (DLA)
LEGOL .... Legally Oriented Language [*Programming language project*]
     [*British*] (NITA)
Leg Oler ..... Laws of Oleron [*Maritime law*] [*A publication*] (DLA)
Leg Op........ Legal Opinion [*Pennsylvania*] [*A publication*] (DLA)
Leg Ops (PA)... Legal Opinion [*Pennsylvania*] [*A publication*] (DLA)
Leg Out........ Legge on Outlawry [*A publication*] (DLA)
LegPlat........ Leggett & Platt, Inc. [*Associated Press*] (SAG)
Leg Port ...... Leges Portuum [*A publication*] (DLA)
Leg Pract & Sol J... Legal Practitioner and Solicitor's Journal [*1846-47, 1849-51*]
     [*A publication*] (DLA)
LEGR .... Granada [*Spain ICAO location identifier*] (ICLI)
Leg R .... Legal Record Reports [*Pennsylvania*] [*A publication*] (DLA)
Leg Rec....... Legal Record [*Detroit, MI*] [*A publication*] (DLA)
Leg Rec Rep... Legal Record Reports [*Pennsylvania*] [*A publication*] (DLA)
Leg Ref....... Legal Reformer [*1819-20*] [*A publication*] (DLA)
Leg Rem....... Legal Remembrancer [*Calcutta*] [*A publication*] (DLA)
Leg Rep....... Legal Reporter [*1840-43*] [*Ireland*] [*A publication*] (DLA)
Leg Rep (Ir)... Legal Reporter, Irish Courts [*A publication*] (DLA)
Leg Rep SL... Legal Reporter Special Leave Supplement [*A publication*] (DLA)
Leg Rev....... Legal Review [*1812-13*] [*London*] [*A publication*] (DLA)
Leg R (Tenn)... Legal Reporter Parallel to Shannon Cases [*Tennessee*]
     [*A publication*] (DLA)
LEGS.......... Lateral Electronic Guidance System [*Automotive engineering*]
LEGS.......... Learning Experience Guides for Nursing Students [*Series of films,*
     games, slides, etc.]
LEGS.......... Legacies (ROG)
LEGS.......... Lethality End Game Simulation (MCD)
LEGS.......... Lighter Electronics Guidance System (MCD)
LEGS.......... Logistic Engine Generator Set (DWSG)
LEGT.......... Lycee d'Enseignement General et Technologique [*High School for*
     General and Technical Studies] [*French*] (BARN)
LEGT.......... Madrid/Getafe [*Spain ICAO location identifier*] (ICLI)
Leg T Cas.... Legal Tender Cases [*A publication*] (DLA)
Legul.......... Leguleian [*1850-65*] [*A publication*] (DLA)
LEG (UN) ..... Department of Legal Affairs of the United Nations
Legve.......... Legislative
Leg W........ Legal World [*India*] [*A publication*] (DLA)
Leg Wisb..... Laws of Wisby [*Maritime law*] [*A publication*] (DLA)
LEG WT ...... Legal Weight (WDAA)
LEGY.......... Legacy (ROG)
Leg YB....... Legal Year Book [*London*] [*A publication*] (DLA)
LEH........... Launch/Entry Helmet (MCD)
LEH........... Leeds Central Helicopters [*British*] [*FAA designator*] (FAAC)
LEH........... Le Havre [*France*] [*Airport symbol*] (OAG)
Leh........... Lehigh County Law Journal [*Pennsylvania*] [*A publication*] (DLA)
LEH........... Lehman Br Holdngs [*NYSE symbol*] (TTSB)
LEH........... Lehman Brothers [*NYSE symbol*] (SAG)
LEH........... Liposome Encapsulated Hemoglobin [*Biochemistry*]
LehAMGN.... Lehman Brothers Holdings, Inc. [*Associated Press*] (SAG)
LehBr35...... Lehman Brothers [*Associated Press*] (SAG)
LEHC.......... Huesca [*Spain ICAO location identifier*] (ICLI)
Leh Co LJ (PA)... Lehigh County Law Journal [*Pennsylvania*] [*A publication*] (DLA)
LehGTel...... Lehman Brothers, Inc. [*Associated Press*] (SAG)
LEHI.......... Hinojosa Del Duque [*Spain ICAO location identifier*] (ICLI)
Lehigh........ Lehigh Valley Law Reporter [*Pennsylvania*] [*A publication*] (DLA)
Lehigh Co LJ... Lehigh County Law Journal [*Pennsylvania*] [*A publication*] (DLA)
LehighGp..... Lehigh Group, Inc. [*Formerly, LUI Group*] [*Associated Press*] (SAG)
Lehigh LJ ..... Lehigh County Law Journal [*Pennsylvania*] [*A publication*] (DLA)
Lehigh U...... Lehigh University (GAGS)
Lehigh Val Law Rep... Lehigh Valley Law Reporter [*Pennsylvania*] [*A publication*]
     (DLA)
Lehigh Val LR... Lehigh Valley Law Reporter [*Pennsylvania*] [*A publication*] (DLA)
Lehigh Val L Rep... Lehigh Valley Law Reporter [*Pennsylvania*] [*A publication*]
     (DLA)
LeHK.......... Lehman Brothers, Inc. [*Associated Press*] (SAG)
Leh LJ .... Lehigh County Law Journal [*A publication*] (DLA)
Lehman C (CUNY)... Herbert H. Lehman College of The City University of New
     York (GAGS)
LehmBr....... Lehman Brothers [*Associated Press*] (SAG)
LEHMIC....... Lumped Element Hybrid Microwave Integrated Circuit [*Electronics*]
     (LAIN)
LehMU........ Lehman Brothers, Inc. [*Associated Press*] (SAG)
LehORCL..... Lehman Brothers Holdings, Inc. [*Associated Press*] (SAG)
LEHPZ........ Lower Esophageal High Pressure Zone [*Gastroenterology*] (DAVI)
LEHR .... Laboratory for Energy-Related Health Research [*University of*
     California-D avis] [*Department of Energy*] (GRD)
LehRgBk...... Lehman Brothers, Inc. [*Associated Press*] (SAG)
LehSTc .... Lehman Brothers [*Associated Press*] (SAG)
Leh VLR (PA)... Lehigh Valley Law Reporter [*Pennsylvania*] [*A publication*] (DLA)
LEI .... Air UK (Leisure) Ltd. [*British ICAO designator*] (FAAC)

LEI .... Almeria [*Spain*] [*Airport symbol*] (OAG)
LEI .... LASER-Enhanced Ionization [*Spectrometry*]
LEI .... Leading Economic Indicator
LEI .... Lehigh Group [*NYSE symbol*] (TTSB)
Lei .... Leijona [*Record label*] [*Finland*]
LEI .... Leipzig [*German Democratic Republic*] [*Seismograph station code,*
     US Geological Survey Closed] (SEIS)
LEI .... Libertarian Education Institute (EA)
LEI .... Library Equipment Institute [*American Library Association*]
LEI .... Life Events [*or Expectancy*] Inventory
LEI .... Literacy and Evangelism International (EA)
LEI .... Local Engineering Instruction (DNAB)
LEI .... Locher Evers International Ltd.
LEI .... Raleigh, NC [*Location identifier FAA*] (FAAL)
LEIA .... Luminescence Enzyme Immunoassay [*Clinical chemistry*]
LEIB .... Ibiza [*Spain ICAO location identifier*] (ICLI)
LEIC .... Leicestershire [*County in England*] (ROG)
LEICS .... Leicestershire [*County in England*]
LEICSC....... Legal Education Institute, United States Civil Service Commission
     (DLA)
LEID .... Limit of Error on Inventory Difference
LEID .... Low-Energy Ion Detector
LEIDS .... Logistics Electronic Information Delivery System
LeIF .... Leukocyte Interferon [*Genetics*]
LEIFS .... Lake Erie Information Forecasting System [*Marine science*] (OSRA)
LEIFS .... Lake Erie Information Forecasting System (USDC)
Leigh .... Leigh's Virginia Supreme Court Reports [*1829-42*] [*A publication*]
     (DLA)
Leigh .... Ley's English King's Bench Reports [*1608-29*] [*A publication*] (DLA)
Leigh Abr..... Leigh's Abridgment of the Law of Nisi Prius [*1838*] [*A publication*]
     (DLA)
Leigh & C.... Leigh and Cave's English Crown Cases Reserved [*1861-65*]
     [*A publication*] (DLA)
Leigh & CCC... Leigh and Cave's English Crown Cases Reserved [*1861-65*]
     [*A publication*] (DLA)
Leigh & D Conv... Leigh and Dalzell. Conversion of Property [*1825*]
     [*A publication*] (DLA)
Leigh & LM Elec... Leigh and Le Marchant. Elections [*4th ed.*] [*1885*]
     [*A publication*] (DLA)
Leigh GA .... Leigh's Game Act [*A publication*] (DLA)
Leigh NP .... Leigh's Abridgment of the Law of Nisi Prius [*1838*] [*A publication*]
     (DLA)
Leigh (VA)... Leigh's Virginia Supreme Court Reports [*1829-42*] [*A publication*]
     (DLA)
LEIM .... Law Enforcement Information Management Section [*An*
     association] (EA)
LEIN .... Law Enforcement Information Network
LEINS R....... Leinster Regiment [*Military unit*] [*British*] (ROG)
leio .... Leiomyoma [*Gynecology*] (DAVI)
LEIP .... Leipzig [*City in East Germany*] (ROG)
LEIP .... Link Eleven Improvement Program (DOMA)
Leipz Stud ... Leipziger Studien zur Klassischen Philosophie [*A publication*] (OCD)
LEIS .... Lander Electrical Interface Simulator [*NASA*]
Le Is .... Leeward Islands (BARN)
LEIS .... LeisureLine [*Footscray Institute of Technology Library*] [*Database*]
     [*Information service or system*] (IID)
LEIS .... Low-Energy Ion Scattering [*For study of surfaces*]
LeisMkt....... Leisureways Marketing [*Associated Press*] (SAG)
LEISS .... Low-Energy Ion Scattering Spectroscopy
LEIT .... Leitrim [*County in Ireland*] (ROG)
LEIT .... Light Emission via Inelastic Tunnelling (IAA)
Leith Black... Leith. Blackstone on Real Property [*2nd ed.*] [*1880*] [*A publication*]
     (DLA)
Leith R Pr.... Leith's Real Property Statutes [*Ontario*] [*A publication*] (DLA)
LEITR........ Leitrim [*County in Ireland*] (ROG)
LEIU .... Law Enforcement Intelligence Units [*An association*] (EA)
LEIX .... Lowrance Electronics [*NASDAQ symbol*] (SAG)
LEJ .... Leipzig [*Germany Airport symbol*] (OAG)
LEJ .... Longitudinal Expansion Joint [*Technical drawings*]
LEJR .... Jerez [*Spain ICAO location identifier*] (ICLI)
LeJY .... Lehman Brothers, Inc. [*Associated Press*] (SAG)
LEK .... Labe [*Guinea*] [*Airport symbol*] (AD)
LEK .... Laiko Enotiko Komma [*Populist Union Party*] [*Greece*] [*Political*
     party] (PPE)
LEK .... LASER Experimental Package
LEK .... Lexington [*Kentucky*] [*Seismograph station code, US Geological*
     Survey] (SEIS)
LEK .... Liquid Encapsulated Kyropoulos [*Crystal growing technique*]
LEKOTEK..... Leksaker, Bibliotek [*Program providing meaningful toys for mentally*
     disturbed children; operates on the same principle as a lending
     library.] [*Name formed from Swedish words for "playthings" and*
     "library"]
lekyt........... Lekythos (VRA)
LEL .... Lake Evella [*Australia Airport symbol*] (OAG)
LEL .... Lancashire Enterprise Ltd. [*British*] (ECON)
LEL .... Large Engineering Loop [*NASA*] (NRCH)
LEL .... Laureate in English Literature
LEL .... League of Empire Loyalists [*British*]
LEL .... Learning Expectancy Level [*Education*]
LEL .... Lens-End-Lamp
LEL .... Letitia Elizabeth Landon [*English poet and novelist, 1802-1839*]
LEL .... Link-Edit Language [*Computer science*]
LEL .... Low Energy LASER [*Light Amplification by Stimulated Emission of*
     Radiation] [*Military*]
LEL .... Lower Earnings Limit (MHDB)

LEL .... Lower Electrical Limit (NRCH)
LEL .... Lower Explosive Limit [of fuel vapor]
LEL .... Lowest Effect Level [Toxicology]
LELC .... Murcia/San Javier [Spain ICAO location identifier] (ICLI)
LELL .... Sabadell [Spain ICAO location identifier] (ICLI)
LELN .... Leon [Spain ICAO location identifier] (ICLI)
LELO .... Logrono [Spain ICAO location identifier] (ICLI)
LELS .... Low-Energy LASER System
LELTS .... Lightweight Electronic Locating and Tracking System
LELU .... Launch Enable Logic Unit
LELU .... Lugo [Spain ICAO location identifier] (ICLI)
Lely & F Elec... Lely and Foulkes' Elections [3rd ed.] [1887] [A publication] (DLA)
Lely & F Jud Acts... Lely and Foulkes' Judicature Acts [4th ed.] [1883] [A publication] (DLA)
Lely & F Lic Acts... Lely and Foulkes' Licensing Acts [3rd ed.] [1887] [A publication] (DLA)
Lely Railw... Lely's Regulation of Railway Acts [1873] [A publication] (DLA)
LEM .... Antenna Effective Length for Magnetic-Field Antennas (IEEE)
LEM .... Laboratory Environment Model (MCD)
LEM .... Laboratory of Electro-Modeling [Former USSR]
LEM .... Lake Exploration Module [University of Wisconsin]
LEM .... LASER Energy Monitor
LEM .... LASER Exhaust Measurement
LEM .... Lateral Eye Movement
LEM .... Launch Enclosure Maintenance [Aerospace] (IAA)
LEM .... Launcher Electronic Module [Military] (RDA)
LEM .... Launch Escape Monitor (MCD)
LEM .... Launch Escape Motor [NASA]
LEM .... Law Enforcement Manual [IRS]
LEM .... Leading Electrical Mechanician
LEM .... Legacy Encapsulation Methodology
LEM .... Leibovitz-Emory Medium [Microbiology]
LEM .... Lembang [Java] [Seismograph station code, US Geological Survey] (SEIS)
LEM .... Lemmon, SD [Location identifier FAA] (FAAL)
lem .... Lemon [Philately]
LEM .... Length of Effectiveness for Magnetic-Field Antennae
LEM .... Leukocytic Endogenous Mediator [Immunochemistry]
LEM .... Leukoencephalomalacia [Veterinary medicine]
LEM .... Light Effector Mediator System [Plant physiology]
LEM .... Light Equipment Maintenance (MCD)
LEM .... Linear Electric Motor [Magnetic rapid-transit car] (PS)
LEM .... Liquid Emulsion Membrane [Separation technology]
LEM .... Logical End of Media
LEM .... Logic Enhanced Memory
LEM .... Logistic Element Manager
LEM .... Luminescences Emission Monitor
LEM .... Lunar Excursion Module [Later, LM] [NASA]
LEM .... Lunar Exploration Module [NASA] (IAA)
LEMA .... Laser and Electro-Optics Manufacturers' Association (EA)
LEM(A) ...... Leading Electrical Mechanic (Air) [British military] (DMA)
LEMA .... Lifting Equipment Manufacturers Association [British] (BI)
LEMA .... Lighting Equipment Manufacturers' Association (DAC)
LEMAC ...... Leading Edge Mean Aerodynamic Chord
LEMAR ...... Legalize Marijuana [Acronym is used for name of an organization]
Le Mar ...... Le Marchant's Gardner Peerage Case [A publication] (DLA)
LEM(AW) ... Leading Electrical Mechanic (Air Weapon) [British military] (DMA)
LEMCO ...... Light Equipment Maintenance Co. (MCD)
LEMD .... Madrid/Barajas [Spain ICAO location identifier] (ICLI)
LEMDA ...... Lighting-Electrical Materials Distributors Association (EA)
LEMDE ...... Lunar Excursion Module Descent Engine [NASA] (MCD)
LEMES ...... Low-Energy Magnetic Electron Spectrum (IAA)
LEMF .... Labour Exchange Managers' Federation [A union] [British]
LEMF .... Law Enforcement Memorial Foundation (EA)
LEMF .... Local Effective Mole Fraction [Chemistry]
LEMG .... Malaga [Spain ICAO location identifier] (ICLI)
LEMH .... Mahon/Menorca [Spain ICAO location identifier] (ICLI)
LEML & AIA... Locomotive Engineers Mutual Life and Accident Insurance Association (EA)
LEMM .... Madrid [Spain ICAO location identifier] (ICLI)
LEMO .... Local Emergency Management Officer
LEMO .... Lowest Empty Molecular Orbital [Medicine] (DMAA)
LEMO .... Sevilla/Moron [Spain ICAO location identifier] (ICLI)
LEMPA ...... Low-Energy Magnetospheric Particle Analyzer [Atomic physics]
LEMRAS ... Law Enforcement Manpower Resources Allocation [IBM program product]
LEMRP ...... Law Enforcement Memorial Research Project (EA)
LEMS .... Linear Econometric Modeling System (BUR)
LEMS .... Low-Energy Molecular Scattering (MCD)
LEMSIP........ Laboratory for Experimental Medicine and Surgery in Primates [New York University] [Research center]
LEMT .... Lunar Excursion Module Track [NASA] (IAA)
LEMUF ...... Limits of Error on Material Unaccounted For
LEN .... [The] Lake Erie & Northern Railway Co. [AAR code]
LEN .... Large Extension Node [Telecommunications] (LAIN)
LEN .... Length
LEN .... Leninakan [Former USSR Seismograph station code, US Geological Survey] (SEIS)
LEN .... Lennar Corp. [NYSE symbol] (SPSG)
LEN .... Lenora Explorations Ltd. [Toronto Stock Exchange symbol]
LEN .... Lentini Aviation, Inc. [ICAO designator] (FAAC)
LEN .... Leon [Mexico] [Airport symbol] (OAG)
LEN .... Library of Early Novelists [A publication]
LEN .... Light-Emitting Numerics

LEN .... Ligue Europeenne de Natation [European Swimming Federation] [Sweden] (EAIO)
LEN .... Linear Electrical Network
LEN .... Load Equalization Net [Aircraft arresting barrier] [Trademark]
LEN .... Local Employment Network (AIE)
LEN .... Local Entry Network (NITA)
LEN .... Low Entry Networking (MCD)
LEND .... Credit Depot [NASDAQ symbol] (TTSB)
LEND .... Credit Depot Corp. [NASDAQ symbol] (SAG)
L en D .... Licencie en Droit [Licentiate in Law] [French]
LEND .... Lockheed Engineers for National Deployment (SAA)
LENGTH ..... Length
LENGTHD ... Lengthened (ROG)
LENIT.......... Leniter [Gently] [Pharmacy]
Lennar ...... Lennar Corp. [Associated Press] (SAG)
LENS .... Concord Camera [NASDAQ symbol] (TTSB)
LENS .... Concord Camera Corp. [NASDAQ symbol] (NQ)
LENS .... LASER-Engineered Net Shaping
LENS .... LASER Enhanced NMR [Nuclear Magnetic Resonance] Spectroscopy
LEntA .... London Enterprise Agency
LENTO ...... Lentando [With Increasing Slowness] [Music] (ROG)
LENWID ..... Length to Width Ratio [Of a leaf] [Botany]
LEO .... Dreyfus Strategic Municipals [NYSE symbol] (SPSG)
LEO .... Law Enforcement Officer (MCD)
LEO .... Lear Oil & Gas Corp. [Vancouver Stock Exchange symbol]
Leo .... Leonard's King's Bench Reports [1540-1615] [England] [A publication] (DLA)
Leo .... Leonardus [Authority cited in pre-1607 legal work] (DSA)
LEO .... Leoncito [Argentina] [Seismograph station code, US Geological Survey] (SEIS)
LEO .... Leopair SA [Switzerland ICAO designator] (FAAC)
LEO .... Liaison Engineering Order
LEO .... Library Entrance Online
LEO .... Librating Equidistant Observer
LEO .... Littoral Environment Observation [Program] [Oceanography]
LEO .... Local Elected Official (OICC)
LEO .... Low Earth Orbit
LEO .... Lunar Exploration Office [NASA]
LEO .... Lyon's Electronic Office
LEO .... Lyons Electronic Office [J. Lyons & Co] [British] (NITA)
Leoc .... Against Leocrates [of Lycurgus] [Classical studies] (OCD)
LEOC.......... Local Emergency Operations Controller
LEOC.......... Ocana [Spain ICAO location identifier] (ICLI)
LEOD .... Lens Extraction, Oculus Dexter [Right eye] [Ophthalmology] (DAVI)
LEOMA....... LASER and Electro-Optics Manufacturers' Association
LEOMA....... LASER/Electro/Optic Measurement Alignment System
Leon .... Leonard's King's Bench, Common Pleas, and Exchequer Reports [England] [A publication] (DLA)
Leon LA Dig... Leonard's Louisiana Digest of United States Cases [A publication] (DLA)
Leon Prec... Leonard's Precedents in County Courts [1869] [A publication] (DLA)
LEOPARD..... Lentigines, EKG Abnormalities, Ocular Hypertelorism, Pulmonary Stenosis, Abnormalities of Genitalia, Retardation of Growth, and Deafness Syndrome [Medicine] (DMAA)
LEOPCID ..... Local Elected Officials Project of the Center for Innovative Diplomacy [Defunct] (EA)
LEOS.......... IEEE [Institute of Electrical and Electronics Engineers] LASERS and Electro-Optics Society (EA)
LEOS.......... Loral Electro-Optical Systems Corp.
LEOS.......... Low Earth Orbit Satellite (MCD)
LEOS.......... Low Earth Orbit Satellites (ACRL)
LEOT.......... Left-End-of-Tape
LEOV.......... Oviedo [Spain ICAO location identifier] (ICLI)
LEP .... Air West Airlines, Inc. [ICAO designator] (FAAC)
LEP .... Laboratory Evaluation Program [Environmental Protection Agency] (GFGA)
LEP .... Large Electronic Panel
LEP .... Large Electron-Positron [Accelerator] [in Europe]
LEP .... Least Energy Principle
Lep .... Lepidoptera [Entomology]
Lep .... Lepus [Constellation]
LEP .... Library of Exact Philosophy
LEP .... Light-Emitting Polymer
LEP .... Light Evaluation Plan (MCD)
LEP .... Lightning-Induced Electron Precipitation [Atmospheric physics]
LEP .... Limited English Proficiency
LEP .... Lipoprotein Electrophoresis [Biochemistry]
LEP .... List of Effective Pages (NVT)
LEP .... Local Enterprise Program
LEP .... Local Field Potential [Neurobiology]
LEP .... Locally Enlisted Personnel [British military] (DMA)
LEP .... Low Egg Passage [Rabies vaccine]
LEP .... Low Emissions Partnership
LEP .... Lower End Plug (IEEE)
LEP .... Lowest Effective Power
LEP .... Low-Frequency Prediction [Marine science] (OSRA)
LEP .... Lupus Erythematosus Preparation [Hematology] (DAVI)
LEP .... Lycee d'Enseignement Professionel [Professional Secondary School for AdvancedStudies] [French] (BARN)
LEPA .... Laboratoire d'Etudes Politiques et Administratives [Universite Laval, Quebec] [Canada]
LEPA.......... Palma De Mallorca [Spain ICAO location identifier] (ICLI)
LEPC.......... Law Enforcement Planning Commission
LEPC.......... Local Emergency Planning Committee [Hazardous waste]

LEPC	Local Emergency Planning Committee [*For hazard analysis*]
LEPC	Low Emissions Paint Consortium
LEPD	Legal Enforcement Policy Division [*Environmental Protection Agency*] (GFGA)
LEPD	Low-Energy Photon Detector [*Environmental Protection Agency*]
LEPEDEA	Low-Energy Proton-Electron Differential Energy Analyzer [*NASA*]
LEPG	Lep Group Ltd. [*NASDAQ symbol*] (SAG)
LE/PH	Local Exchange/Packet Handler (ACRL)
LEPI	Litton Educational Publishing, Inc.
LEPMA	Lithographic Engravers and Plate Makers Association (EA)
LEPO	Pollensa [*Spain ICAO location identifier*] (ICLI)
LEPOR	Long-Term and Expanded Program of Oceanic Exploration and Research
LEPORE	Long-Term and Expanded Program of Oceanic Research and Exploration (BARN)
LEPP	Pamplona/Noain-Pamplona [*Spain ICAO location identifier*] (ICLI)
LEPR	LASER Electron Paramagnetic Resonance
LEPRA	British Leprosy Relief Association (IRUK)
LEPRA	Leprosy Relief Association [*British*] (DI)
LE Prep	Lupus Erythematosus Preparation [*Hematology*] (CPH)
LEPS	Launch Escape Propulsion System [*NASA*]
Leps	Lepus [*Constellation*]
LEPS	London-Eyring-Polanyi-Sato Method [*Reaction dynamics*]
LEPSOC	Lepidopterists' Society (EA)
Lept	Against Leptines [*of Demosthenes*] [*Classical studies*] (OCD)
LEPT	Leptocytes [*Biochemistry*] (DAVI)
Lept	Leptospira [*Genus of bacteria*]
LEPT	Long-Endurance Patrolling Torpedo
LEPT	Low-Energy Particle Telescope
LEPTOS	Leptospirosis Agglutinins [*Biochemistry*] (DAVI)
LEPW	Longitudinal Electric Pressure Wave
LEQ	Lehman Br Hldg 8.30%'QUICS' [*NYSE symbol*] (TTSB)
LEQ	Lehman Brothers [*NYSE symbol*] (SAG)
LEQ	Level Equivalent (SSD)
LEQ	Life Events Questionnaire [*Psychology*] (EDAC)
LEQ	Line Equipped [*Telecommunications*] (TEL)
LEQ	Line of Equipment [*Telecommunications*] (TEL)
Leq	Loudness Equivalent [*Medicine*] (DMAA)
LER	Land Equivalent Ratio [*Agriculture*]
LER	Launcher Equipment Room [*Missiles*]
LER	Leading Edge Radius (MSA)
LER	Lease Expenditure Request (MCD)
LER	Leinster [*Australia Airport symbol*] (OAG)
LER	Lerwick [*United Kingdom*] [*Geomagnetic observatory code*]
LER	Licensee Event Report [*Nuclear energy*] (NRCH)
LER	Light Efficiency Radiator [*General Motors Corp.*] [*Automotive engineering*]
LER	Light-Emitting Resistor [*Computer hacker terminology*] (NHD)
LER	London Electric Railway
LER	Long Eye Relief (MCD)
LER	Loss Exchange Ratio (MCD)
LERA	Limited Employee Retirement Account (IEEE)
LERB	Line Error Recording Block (MCD)
LERC	Language for Export Research Center [*University of Western Sydney*] [*Australia*]
LERC	Laramie Energy Research Center [*Department of Energy*]
LERC	Lewis Research Center [*NASA*] (KSC)
LERF	Laboratory Experimental Research Facility [*Army*] (RDA)
LERI	Murcia/Alcantarilla [*Spain ICAO location identifier*] (ICLI)
LERIS	Low-Energy Recoil Ion Spectroscopy
LERK	LASER Experimental Research Kit
LERMISTOR	Learning Materials Information Store (PDAA)
LERN	Learning Resources Network (EA)
LERP	Labor Education and Research Project (EA)
LERP	Linear Interpolation [*Computer science*] (NHD)
LERS	Reus [*Spain ICAO location identifier*] (ICLI)
LERSC	Location Evaluation Recognition and Statistical Comparison (PDAA)
LERSO	Low Erucic Acid Rapeseed Oil (PDAA)
LERT	Lockheed Emergency Reset Timer (IAA)
LERT	Rota [*Spain ICAO location identifier*] (ICLI)
LERTCON	Alert Condition [*Military*] (AABC)
LERX	Leading Edge Root Extension [*Aviation*]
L-ERX	Leukoerythroblastic Reaction [*Biochemistry*] (DAVI)
LES	Automotors Salta SACYF [*Argentina ICAO designator*] (FAAC)
LES	Laboratory for Environmental Studies [*Ohio State University*] [*Research center*] (RCD)
LES	Lambert-Eaton Myasthenic Syndrome [*Medicine*]
LES	LAN [*Local Area Network*] Emulation Server [*Telecommunications*] (ACRL)
LES	Large Eddy Simulation [*For modelling fluid flow*]
LES	LASER Excitation Spectroscopy
LES	Lateral Epithelial Space [*Anatomy*] (DAVI)
LES	Launch Effects Simulator
LES	Launch Enabling System
LES	Launch/Entry Suit [*NASA*]
LES	Launch Environmental Simulator (MCD)
LES	Launch Equipment Shop (MCD)
LES	Launch Escape System [*or Subsystem*] [*NASA*]
LES	Law Enforcement Squadron
LES	Lawrence Experiment Station [*Agar*] [*Medicine*] (BABM)
LES	Leading Edge Slats (MCD)
LES	Leave and Earnings Statement [*Military*] (AABC)
LES	Lesbian (DSUE)
LES	Lesobeng [*Lesotho*] [*Airport symbol*] (OAG)

LES	Lesozavodsk [*Former USSR Seismograph station code, US Geological Survey Closed*] (SEIS)
LES	Licensing Executives Society (EA)
LES	Life Experiences Survey [*Psychology*]
LES	Light-Emitting Switch [*Electronics*] (OA)
LES	Light Experimental Supercruiser (MCD)
LES	Light Exposure Speed [*Photography*] (OA)
LES	Lilliput Edison Screw
LES	Limited Early Site [*Nuclear energy*] (NRCH)
LES	Limited English Speaking (OICC)
LES	Lincoln Experimental Satellite [*Lincoln Laboratory, MIT*]
LES	Loaded Equipment Section
LES	Local Engineering Specifications [*DoD*]
LES	Local Engineering Standard (IAA)
LES	Local Excitatory State
LES	Locally Engaged Staff
LES	Locke Egg Serum [*Medicine*] (MAE)
LES	Loop Error Signal
LES	Low-Energy Sputter
LES	Lower Esophageal Sphincter [*Medicine*]
LES	Lunar Escape System [*NASA*]
LES	Lupus Erythematosus, Systemic [*Medicine*] (MAE)
LES	Support Landing Boat [*Navy symbol Obsolete*]
LESA	Lake Erie Steam Association [*Defunct*]
LESA	Land Evaluation and Site Assessment System [*Department of Agriculture*]
LESA	Lunar Exploration System for Apollo [*NASA*]
LESA	Salamanca [*Spain ICAO location identifier*] (ICLI)
LESAP	Law Enforcement Security Access Position
LESAT	Leased Satellite [*Military*] (CAAL)
LESC	Launch Escape System Control [*NASA*] (KSC)
LESC	LE [*Lupus Erythematosus*] Support Club (EA)
LESC	Light-Emitting Switch Control [*Electronics*] (OA)
LESC	Lunar-Environment Sample Container [*Apollo*] [*NASA*]
Lesco	Lesco, Inc. [*Associated Press*] (SAG)
LESCS	Launch Escape Stabilization and Control System [*NASA*] (IAA)
LESD	Letterer-Siwe Disease [*Medicine*] (DMAA)
LESG	Late Effects Study Group [*for Hodgkins disease*]
Lesh	Leshonenu [*Jerusalem*] (BJA)
LESI	Leif Ericson Society International (EA)
LESJ	Son San Juan Air Force Base [*Spain ICAO location identifier*] (ICLI)
LESL	Law Enforcement Standards Laboratory [*National Institute of Standards and Technology*]
LESL	Leslies Poolmart [*NASDAQ symbol*] (SAG)
LESL	Leslie's Poolmart [*NASDAQ symbol*] (TTSB)
L es L	Licencie es Lettres [*Licentiate in Letters*] [*French*] (EY)
LESM	Longman's Elementary Science Manuals [*A publication*]
LESM	Murcia [*Spain ICAO location identifier*] (ICLI)
Les Miz	Les Miserables [*Musical based on Victor Hugo's novel*]
LESNW	Lesnwith [*England*]
LESO	San Sebastian [*Spain ICAO location identifier*] (ICLI)
LESOC	Lincoln Experimental Satellite Operations Center (MCD)
LESOP	Leveraged Employee Stock Ownership Plan [*Procter & Gamble Co.*]
LESP	Law Enforcement Standards Program [*National Institute of Law Enforcement and Criminal Justice*]
LESP	Lower Esophageal Sphincter Pressure [*Medicine*]
LESP	Madrid [*Spain ICAO location identifier*] (ICLI)
LesPol	Leslie's Poolmart, Inc. [*Associated Press*] (SAG)
L'Esprit	L'Esprit Createur [*A publication*] (BRI)
LESR	Limited Early Site Review [*Nuclear energy*] (NRCH)
LESS	LASER-Excited Shpol'skii Spectrometry
LESS	Lateral Electrical Spine Stimulation [*Orthopedics*] (DAVI)
LESS	Launch Escape System Simulator [*NASA*] (IAA)
LESS	Law Encounter Severity Scale [*Personality development test*] [*Psychology*]
LESS	Leading Edge Structure Subsystem [*Aviation*] (NASA)
LESS	Least-Cost Estimating and Scheduling System
LesS	Licencie es Sciences [*Licentiate in Science*] [*French*] (BARN)
L/ESS	Loads/Environmental Spectra Survey (MCD)
LESS	Lunar Escape System Simulator [*NASA*]
L es SC	Licencie es Sciences [*Licentiate of Sciences*] [*French*]
lessy	lesbian [*Psychology*] (DAVI)
LEST	Large Earth-Based [*formerly, European*] Solar Telescope
LEST	Large Earth Survey Telescope
LEST	Launch Electronics System Test
LEST	Launch Enable System Turret (IAA)
Lest	Licencie es Lettres [*Licentiate in Letters*] [*French*] (BARN)
LEST	Low-Energy Speech Transmission
LEST	Santiago [*Spain ICAO location identifier*] (ICLI)
Lest & But	Lester and Butler's Supplement to Lester's Georgia Reports [*A publication*] (DLA)
Lester	Lester's Reports [*31-33 Georgia*] [*A publication*] (DLA)
Lester & B	Lester and Butler's Supplement to Lester's Georgia Reports [*A publication*] (DLA)
Lester Supp	Lester and Butler's Supplement to Lester's Georgia Reports [*A publication*] (DLA)
Lest PL	Lester's Decisions in Public Land Cases [*A publication*] (DLA)
LESTR	Leukocyte-Expressed Seven-Transmembrane-Domain Receptor [*Biochemistry*]
LESU	Law Enforcement Study Unit [*of the American Topical Association*] (EA)
LESU	Seo De Urgel [*Spain ICAO location identifier*] (ICLI)
LET	Aerolineas Ejecutivas SA [*Mexico ICAO designator*] (FAAC)
LET	Laboratory Electronics Technician (IAA)
LET	Launch Effects Trainer [*Weaponry*] (MCD)

LET	Launch Eject Test
LET	Launch Equipment Test
LET	Launch Escape Tower [*NASA*] (MCD)
LET	Leader Effectiveness Training [*A course of study*]
LET	Leading Edge Tracker
LET	Learning Efficiency Test [*Educational test*]
LET	Legacy Encapsulation Technology
LET	Leticia [*Colombia*] [*Airport symbol*] (OAG)
LET	Letter
LET	Lettish [*Latvian*] (ROG)
LET	Lidocaine, Epinephrine, and Tetracaine Solution [*Medicine*] (DMAA)
LET	Life Environmental Testing (IAA)
LET	Light Equipment Transporter (MCD)
LET	Limited Environmental Test (MCD)
LET	Lincoln Experimental Terminal [*NASA*]
LET	Linear Energy Transfer [*Radiology*]
LET	Lithium Excretion Test [*Clinical chemistry*]
LET	Live Environment Testing
LET	Live Environment Training [*Military*] (ADDR)
LET	Local Enterprise Trust [*British*]
LET	Logical Equipment Table
LET	Logistic Escape Trunk (CAAL)
LET	London and Edinburgh Trust [*British*]
LET	Low-Emissions Truck
LET	Low-End Torque [*Automotive engineering*]
LET	Low-Energy Telescope [*Geophysics*]
LET	Lux e Tenebris [*Light Out of Darkness*] [*Freemasonry*] [*Latin*]
LETA	Latvian Telegraph Agency (EY)
LETA	Sevilla/Tablada [*Spain ICAO location identifier*] (ICLI)
LETATA	Light Edge Tool and Allied Trades Association [*British*] (BI)
LETB	Local Exchange Test Bed [*Telecommunications*] (TEL)
LETC	Laramie Energy Technology Center [*Department of Energy*] (GRD)
Letch	Letchworth Independent Bancshares Corp. [*Associated Press*] (SAG)
LetchInd	Letchworth Independent Bancshares Corp. [*Associated Press*] (SAG)
LETCS	Launch Escape Tower Canard System [*NASA*] (IAA)
Let D	Doctor of Letters
LETD	Lowest Effective Toxic Dose [*Medicine*] (DMAA)
LE-TE	Leading Edge - Trailing Edge [*Aerodynamics*]
LETEC	London East Training and Enterprise Council [*British*] (AIE)
LETF	Launch Equipment Test Facility [*NASA*] (NASA)
LETFO	Letter Follows (NOAA)
leth	Lethal [*Pharmacology*] (DAVI)
LETHR	Leather
LETIS	Leicestershire Technical Information Service [*British*] (NITA)
LETM	Lake Evaporation and Thermodynamics Model [*Marine science*] (OSRA)
LETM	Lake Evaporation and Thermodynamics Model (USDC)
LETN	Law Enforcement Television Network
LETO	Madrid/Torrejon [*Spain ICAO location identifier*] (ICLI)
LETS	Large, External Transformation Sensitive [*Glycoprotein*] [*Also known as CSP Cytochemistry*]
LETS	Launch Equipment Test Set (MCD)
LETS	Law Enforcement Teletype [*or Teletypewriter*] Service [*Phoenix, AZ*]
LETS	Leading Edge Tracker System
LETS	Learning Experience for Technical Students [*NASA*]
LETS	Linear-Energy Transfer Spectrometer [*Radiology*] (KSC)
LETS	Linear-Energy Transfer System [*Radiology*]
LETS	Live Environment Testing with SAGE (MCD)
LETS	Low-Energy Telescope System [*Geophysics*]
LETS	Lunar Experiment Telemetry System [*Aerospace*]
LETT	Letters
LETT	Lettish [*Latvian*] (ROG)
LEU	Emory University, Division of Librarianship, Atlanta, GA [*OCLC symbol*] (OCLC)
LEU	Launch Enable Unit
LEU	Launcher Electronic Unit (MCD)
Leu	Leucine [*Also, L*] [*An amino acid*]
leu	Leucine [*An amino acid*] (DOG)
LEU	Leucovorin (DMAA)
LEU	Leukocyte Equivalent Unit (DMAA)
LEU	Lewis, IN [*Location identifier FAA*] (FAAL)
LEU	License to Export Uranium (NRCH)
LEU	Lions-Air, AG [*Switzerland*] [*FAA designator*] (FAAC)
LEU	Low-Enriched Uranium [*Nuclear energy*]
LEU	Seo De Urgel [*Spain*] [*Airport symbol*] (OAG)
LEUC	Leucotomy [*European term for lobotomy*] (DSUE)
LeucNtl	Leucadia National Corp. [*Associated Press*] (SAG)
Leuk	Leukemia [*Medicine*]
LEUK	Leukocyte [*Biochemistry*] (DAVI)
LEUKAP	Leukocyte Alkaline Phosphatase [*Biochemistry*] (DAVI)
leuko	Leukocyte [*Hematology*]
LEUP	Leuprlide [*Antineoplastic drug*] (CDI)
LEV	Bureta [*Fiji*] [*Airport symbol*] (OAG)
LEV	Grand Isle, LA [*Location identifier FAA*] (FAAL)
LEV	Launch Escape Vehicle [*NASA*]
LEV	Leibovitz-Emory Medium for Viral Cultures [*Microbiology*]
LEV	Leichtverwundet; Leichtverwundeter [*Slightly wounded; minor casualty*] [*German military - World War II*]
LEV	Levamisole [*Antineoplastic drug*] (CDI)
LEV	Levant
lev	Levator [*Muscle*] [*Medicine*] (MEDA)
LEV	Level
LEV	Lever
LEV	Leviathan Gas PL Partners Ltd. [*NYSE symbol*] (SPSG)
LEV	Leviathan Gas PLPtnrs LP [*NYSE symbol*] (TTSB)

Lev	Levinz's King's Bench and Common Pleas Reports [*1660-97*] [*England*] [*A publication*] (DLA)
LEV	Levis [*Light*] [*Pharmacy*]
Lev	Leviticus [*Old Testament book*]
lev	Levorotatory [*Optics*] [*Chemistry*] (DOG)
LEV	Lev Scientific Industries Ltd. [*Vancouver Stock Exchange symbol*]
LEV	Levyne [*A zeolite*]
LEV	Lifting Entry Vehicle
LEV	Loader/Editor/Verifier [*Telecommunications*] (TEL)
LEV	Local Exhaust Ventilation [*Hazardous material control*]
LEV	Logistics Entry Vehicle
LEV	Lolium Enation Virus [*Plant pathology*]
LEV	Low-Emissions Vehicle
LEV	Loyal Edinburgh Volunteers [*British military*] (DMA)
LEV	Lunar Escape Vehicle (IAA)
LEV	Lunar Excursion Vehicle [*Aerospace*]
LEVC	Valencia [*Spain ICAO location identifier*] (ICLI)
LEVCB	Low-Emission Vehicle Certification Board [*Terminated, 1980*] [*Environmental Protection Agency*]
LEVD	Valladolid [*Spain ICAO location identifier*] (ICLI)
LevelOne	Level One Communications, Inc. [*Associated Press*] (SAG)
Lev Ent	Levinz's Entries [*England*] [*A publication*] (DLA)
LevGas	Leviathan Gas Pipeline [*Associated Press*] (SAG)
LE-VGF	Liquid Encapsulation-Vertical Gradient Freeze (PDAA)
Levi Com L	Levi's International Commercial Law [*2nd ed.*] [*1863*] [*A publication*] (DLA)
Levi Merc L	Levi's Mercantile Law [*1854*] [*A publication*] (DLA)
LEVIT	Leviter [*Lightly*] [*Pharmacy*]
LEVIT	Leviticus [*Old Testament book*] (ROG)
Levitz	Levitz Furniture, Inc. [*Associated Press*] (SAG)
Lev JP	Levinge's Irish Justice of the Peace [*A publication*] (DLA)
LEVL	Level One Communications [*NASDAQ symbol*] (TTSB)
LEVL	Level One Communications, Inc. [*NASDAQ symbol*] (SAG)
LEVM	Valencia [*Spain ICAO location identifier*] (ICLI)
LEVMETR	Levelometer
LevR	Leviticus Rabbah (BJA)
LEVS	Leaves
LEVS	Madrid/Cuatro Vientos [*Spain ICAO location identifier*] (ICLI)
LEVT	Left Extremity Venous Tracing [*Cardiology*] (DAVI)
LEVT	Lower Extremity Venous Tracing [*Cardiology*] (DAVI)
LEVT	Vitoria [*Spain ICAO location identifier*] (ICLI)
LEVTAB	Level Table (MHDB)
LEVVA	Lunar Extravehicular Visor Assembly [*NASA*] (KSC)
LEVX	Vigo [*Spain ICAO location identifier*] (ICLI)
Levy WTM	Woerterbuch ueber die Talmudim und Midraschim [*J. Levy*] [*A publication*] (BJA)
LEW	Auburn-Lewiston [*Maine*] [*Airport symbol*] (AD)
LEW	Auburn-Lewiston, ME [*Location identifier FAA*] (FAAL)
Lew	Lewin's English Crown Cases Reserved [*1822-38*] [*A publication*] (DLA)
LEW	Lewis [*Rat strain*]
Lew	Lewis' Reports [*Nevada*] [*A publication*] (DLA)
Lew	Lewis' Reports [*Missouri*] [*A publication*] (DLA)
LEW	Lewiston [*Maine*] [*Airport symbol*] (OAG)
Lew App	Lewin's Apportionment [*1869*] [*A publication*] (DLA)
Lew B & S	Lewis on Bonds and Securities [*A publication*] (DLA)
Lew CC	Lewin's English Crown Cases [*A publication*] (DLA)
Lew CL	Lewis' Criminal Law [*A publication*] (DLA)
Lew Conv	Lewis' Principles of Conveyancing [*A publication*] (DLA)
Lew Dig Cr L	Lewis' Digest of United States Criminal Law [*A publication*] (DLA)
Lew Elec	Lewis' Election Manual [*A publication*] (DLA)
Lew Eq Dr	Lewis on Equity Drafting [*A publication*] (DLA)
Lewin	Lewin on Trusts [*A publication*] (DLA)
Lewin CC	Lewin's English Crown Cases Reserved [*1822-38*] [*A publication*] (DLA)
Lewin CC (Eng)	Lewin's English Crown Cases [*A publication*] (DLA)
Lewin Cr Cas	Lewin's English Crown Cases Reserved [*A publication*] (DLA)
Lew Ind Pen	Lewis' East India Penal Code [*A publication*] (DLA)
Lewis	Lewis' Appeals Reports [*29-35 Missouri*] [*A publication*] (DLA)
Lewis	Lewis' Kentucky Law Reporter [*A publication*] (DLA)
Lewis	Lewis' Reports [*Nevada*] [*A publication*] (DLA)
Lewis & Clark C	Lewis and Clark College (GAGS)
Lewis Em Dom	Lewis on Eminent Domain [*A publication*] (DLA)
Lewis Perp	Lewis' Law of Perpetuities [*A publication*] (DLA)
Lew L Cas	Lewis' Leading Cases on Public Land Law [*A publication*] (DLA)
Lew LT	Lewis on Land Titles in Philadelphia [*A publication*] (DLA)
LEWP	Line Echo Wave Pattern
Lew Perp	Lewis' Law of Perpetuities [*A publication*] (DLA)
Lew St	Lewis on Stocks, Bonds, Etc. [*A publication*] (DLA)
Lew Tr	Lewin on Trusts [*A publication*] (DLA)
LEWU	Lanka Estate Workers' Union [*Ceylon*]
Lew US Cr L	Lewis' Digest of United States Criminal Law [*A publication*] (DLA)
LEX	Cary Memorial Library, Lexington, MA [*OCLC symbol*] (OCLC)
LEX	Land Exercise [*Marine Corps*]
LEX	Leading Edge Extension [*Aviation*]
LEX	Letter Exchange (EA)
Lex	Lexical (BJA)
LEX	Lexicographer (ABBR)
LEX	Lexicon
LEX	Lexington [*Virginia*] [*Seismograph station code, US Geological Survey Closed*] (SEIS)
LEX	Lexington [*Diocesan abbreviation*] [*Kentucky*] (TOCD)
LEX	Lexington/Frankfort [*Kentucky*] [*Airport symbol*] (OAG)
LEX	L'Express, Inc. [*ICAO designator*] (FAAC)
LEX	Line Exchange [*Telecommunications*]

LEX	Listing Exchange
LEx	Liver Extract [Protein/lipid substance] [Immunology]
LexBLF	Lexington B & L Financial Corp. [Associated Press] (SAG)
LexCrpP	Lexington Corporate Properties [Associated Press] (SAG)
Lex Cust	Lex Custumaria [Latin A publication] (DLA)
LEXD	Lexden [England]
LexGlbl	Lexington Global Asset Managers, Inc. [Associated Press] (SAG)
LEXI	Lexical (ABBR)
LEXICO	Lexicographer (ABBR)
LEXICOG	Lexicography
LEXIS	Legal Research Service [Registered service mark] (IID)
LEXIS	Lexicography Information Service [Germany Computer science]
LEXJ	Santander [Spain ICAO location identifier] (ICLI)
Lex Man	Lex Maneriorum [Latin A publication] (DLA)
Lex Mer Am	Lex Mercatoria Americana [Latin A publication] (DLA)
Lex Mess	Lexicon Messanense [Classical studies] (OCD)
Lexmrk	Lexmark International Group [Associated Press] (SAG)
LEXN	Lexicon (ABBR)
LEXOG	Lexicology (ABBR)
LEXOGL	Lexicological (ABBR)
LEXOGT	Lexicologist (ABBR)
LEXP	Language Experience
Lex Parl	Lex Parliamentaria [Latin A publication] (DLA)
LEXPHR	Lexicographer (ABBR)
LEXPHY	Lexicography (ABBR)
LEXSWG	Lunar Exploration Science Working Group [NASA]
LexSyr	Lexicon Syriacum [A publication] (BJA)
L/EXT	Lower Extremity [Medicine]
Ley	Ley's English Court of Wards Reports [A publication] (DLA)
Ley	Ley's English King's Bench Reports [1608-29] [A publication] (DLA)
LEY	Liberal European Youth
LEYD	Leyden [Netherlands] (ROG)
Ley Wards	Ley's English Court of Wards Reports [A publication] (DLA)
LEZ	Lunar Equatorial Zone [Army Map Service]
LEZA	Zaragoza [Spain ICAO location identifier] (ICLI)
LEZG	Zaragoza [Spain ICAO location identifier] (ICLI)
LEZL	Sevilla [Spain ICAO location identifier] (ICLI)
LEZOR	Liquid Encapsulation Zone-Refining (PDAA)
LF	Lacrimatory Factor [Food technology]
LF	Lacrosse Foundation (EA)
LF	Lactoferrin [Biochemistry]
LF	La Fosse Platinum Group, Inc. [Toronto Stock Exchange symbol]
LF	Lama Foundation (EA)
LF	[The] Lancashire Fusiliers [Military unit] [British]
LF	Land Forces [Military British]
LF	Landing Force [Navy] (NVT)
LF	Largest Frame (ACRL)
LF	Laryngofissure (MAE)
LF	Latex Fixation [Test] [Medicine]
LF	Lathe Fixture (MCD)
LF	Laucks Foundation (EA)
LF	Launch Facility
LF	Launch Forward
LF	Law French (DLA)
LF	Lawn Faucet (MSA)
LF	Lead-Free
lf	Leaf (VRA)
LF	Leaf [Bibliography] (ROG)
LF	Leaflet (WGA)
LF	League of Friendship [Defunct] (EA)
LF	Leapfrog Configuration [Circuit theory] (IEEE)
LF	Least Frequent (AEBS)
LF	Lebanese Forces
LF	Lederer Foundation (EA)
LF	Ledger Folio
LF	Left (ECII)
LF	Left Field [or Fielder] [Baseball]
LF	Left Foot
LF	Left Forward [Football]
LF	Left Front
LF	Left Fullback [Soccer]
LF	Legion of Frontiersmen [British military] (DMA)
LF	Lettering Faded
LF	Liberty Federation (EA)
LF	Liederkranz Foundation (EA)
LF	Life (ABBR)
LF	Life Float
LF	Lifeline Foundation (EA)
LF	Lifting Fan [Hovercraft]
LF	Lightface [Type]
lf	Lightface Type (WDMC)
LF	Light Fastness Ink (DGA)
LF	Ligue de Foyer [Salvation Army Home League - SAHL] (EAIO)
LF	Limiting Fragmentation [Physics] (OA)
LF	Limit of Flocculation
LF	Lineal Feet
LF	Linear File [Computer file] (NITA)
LF	Linear Filter
LF	Linear Foot
LF	Line Feed [Control character] [Computer science]
LF	Line Feed [Computer science] (DOM)
LF	Line Finder [Teletype]
L/F	Linen-Faced Paper (DGA)
LF	Linjeflyg [ICAO designator] (AD)
LF	Linoleum Floor [Technical drawings]
LF	Lisle Fellowship (EA)
LF	Listener Function (IAA)
LF	Lituanus Foundation (EA)
LF	Live Fire
LF	Live Flying (NATG)
LF	Load Factor
LF	Loaf
LF	Loaf
LF	Loan Forgiveness (DICI)
LF	Local Film
LF	Local Force [Viet Cong combat force]
LF	Locally Funded (AFM)
LF	Lock Forward
LF	Logical File [Computer science] (BUR)
LF	Logic Function
LF	Lost on Foul [Boxing]
LF	Lovelace Foundation for Medical Education and Research [Reorganized to form Lovelace Medical Foundation and Lovelace Biomedical and Environmental Research Institute]
LF	Low Fat [Diet]
LF	Low Flange (DICI)
LF	Low-Fluence [Physics]
LF	Low Foliage Forager [Ecology]
LF	Low Food Density [Ecology]
LF	Low Force
LF	Low Forceps [Delivery] [Obstetrics]
LF	Low Frequency
lf	Low Frequency (WDMC)
lf	Low Rate Forward [Ecology]
LF	Siebelwerke ATG GmbH [Germany ICAO aircraft manufacturer identifier] (ICAO)
LFA	Air Alfa Hava Yollari Ve Tec, AS [Turkey] [FAA designator] (FAAC)
LFA	Klamath Falls, OR [Location identifier FAA] (FAAL)
LFA	Land Force Adriatic [British Royal Marines] [World War II]
LFA	Land Force, Airmobility [NATO] (NATG)
LFA	Landing Force Aviation
LFA	Language Foundation of Australia
LFA	Large Families of America [Defunct] (EA)
LFA	Last Field Address (IAA)
LFA	Leading Field Activity (MCD)
LFA	Left Femoral Artery [Anatomy]
LFA	Left Frontal Craniotomy [Medicine] (DMAA)
LFA	Left Frontoanterior [A fetal position] [Obstetrics]
LFA	Leukocyte Function-Associated Antigen [Immunology]
LFA	Leukotactic Factor Activity [Medicine] (DMAA)
LFA	Light Freight Agent (ADA)
LFA	Lime Fly Ash [Aggregate] (DICI)
LFA	Littlefield, Adams [AMEX symbol] (TTSB)
LFA	Littlefield, Adams & Co. [AMEX symbol] (SPSG)
LFA	Local Flying Area [Aviation] (DA)
LFA	Local Freight Agent
LFA	Low Flow Alarm (IEEE)
LFA	Low Frequency Active (DOMA)
LFA	Low Friction Arthroplasty [Orthopedics] (DAVI)
LFA	Low Functioning Autism
LFA	Lupus Foundation of America (EA)
LFA	Lutheran Fraternities of America (EA)
LFA	Luther Family Association
LFA	Lymphocyte Function-Associated Antigen [Immunochemistry]
LFAA	Ambleteuse [France ICAO location identifier] (ICLI)
LFAAV	Landing Force Assault Amphibious Vehicle (MCD)
LFAB	Dieppe/Saint-Aubin [France ICAO location identifier] (ICLI)
LFAC	Calais/Dunkerque [France ICAO location identifier] (ICLI)
LFACS	Light Future Armored Combat System [Tank]
LFAD	Compiegne/Margny [France ICAO location identifier] (ICLI)
LFAE	Eu-Mers/Le Treport [France ICAO location identifier] (ICLI)
LFAF	Laon/Chambry [France ICAO location identifier] (ICLI)
LFAF	Low-Frequency Accelerometer Flutter (MCD)
LFAG	Leafage (ABBR)
LFAG	Peronne/Saint-Quentin [France ICAO location identifier] (ICLI)
LFAH	Soissons/Cuffies [France ICAO location identifier] (ICLI)
LFAI	Lifting Fair Air Intake [Hovercraft]
LFAI	Nangis/Les Loges [France ICAO location identifier] (ICLI)
LFAJ	Argentan [France ICAO location identifier] (ICLI)
LFAK	Dunkerque-Ghyvelde [France ICAO location identifier] (ICLI)
LFAL	La Fleche/Thoree-Les-Pins [France ICAO location identifier] (ICLI)
LFAM	Berck-Sur-Mer [France ICAO location identifier] (ICLI)
LFAM	Low-Frequency Accelerometer Modes (MCD)
LFAN	Conde-Sur-Noireau [France ICAO location identifier] (ICLI)
LFAO	Bagnole-De-L'Orne [France ICAO location identifier] (ICLI)
LFAP	Low-Frequency Accelerometer POGO [Polar Orbiting Geophysical Observatory] [NASA] (NASA)
LFAP	Rethel-Perthes [France ICAO location identifier] (ICLI)
LFAQ	Albert/Bray [France ICAO location identifier] (ICLI)
LFAR	Last Frame Address Register
LFAR	Libertarians for Animal Rights (EA)
LFAR	Montdidier [France ICAO location identifier] (ICLI)
LFAS	Falaise-Monts-D'Eraines [France ICAO location identifier] (ICLI)
LFAS	League of Finnish-American Societies (EAIO)
LFAS	Low-Frequency Active Sonar (DOMA)
LFASV	Landing Force Amphibious Support Vehicle (SAA)
LFAT	Le Touquet/Paris-Plage [France ICAO location identifier] (ICLI)
LFATDS	Light Field Artillery Tactical Data System (GFGA)
LFaU	Union Parish Library, Farmerville, LA [Library symbol Library of Congress] (LCLS)

LFAU............ Vauville [*France ICAO location identifier*] (ICLI)
LFAV............ Valenciennes/Denain [*France ICAO location identifier*] (ICLI)
LFAW............ Villerupt [*France ICAO location identifier*] (ICLI)
LFAX............ Mortagne-Au-Perche [*France ICAO location identifier*] (ICLI)
LFAY............ Amiens/Glisy [*France ICAO location identifier*] (ICLI)
LFB............ Lafayette, TN [*Location identifier FAA*] (FAAL)
LFB............ Landing Force Bulletin [*Marine Corps*]
LFB............ Lateral Forebrain Bundle
LFB............ Left Fullback [*Soccer*]
LFB............ Licensed Fishing Boat
LFB............ Light Field Battery [*British military*] (DMA)
LFB............ Limited Frequency Band
LFB............ London Festival Ballet
LFB............ London Fire Brigade
LFB............ Longview Fibre [*NYSE symbol*] (TTSB)
LFB............ Longview Fibre Co. [*NYSE symbol*] (CTT)
LFB............ Loop Fluidized Bed [*Chemical engineering*]
LFB............ Low-Frequency Beacon
LFB............ Luxol Fast Blue [*Biological stain*]
LFB2............ London Festival Ballet's Ensemble Group
LFBA............ Agen/La Garenne [*France ICAO location identifier*] (ICLI)
LFBA............ Licentiate of the Corporation of Executives and Administrators [*British*] (DBQ)
LFBB............ Bordeaux [*France ICAO location identifier*] (ICLI)
LFBC............ Cazaux [*France ICAO location identifier*] (ICLI)
LFBD............ Bordeaux/Merignac [*France ICAO location identifier*] (ICLI)
LFBD............ Letters of the First Babylonian Dynasty [*A publication*] (BJA)
LFBD............ Lifeblood (ABBR)
LFBE............ Bergerac/Roumaniere [*France ICAO location identifier*] (ICLI)
LFBF............ Louisiana Farm Bureau Federation (SRA)
LFBF............ Toulouse/Francazal [*France ICAO location identifier*] (ICLI)
LFBG............ Cognac/Chateau Bernard [*France ICAO location identifier*] (ICLI)
LFBH............ La Rochelle/Laleu [*France ICAO location identifier*] (ICLI)
LFBI............ Little Falls Bancorp [*NASDAQ symbol*] (TTSB)
LFBI............ Poitiers/Biard [*France ICAO location identifier*] (ICLI)
LFBJ............ Saint-Junien [*France ICAO location identifier*] (ICLI)
LFBK............ Montlucon-Gueret [*France ICAO location identifier*] (ICLI)
LFBL............ Limoges/Bellegarde [*France ICAO location identifier*] (ICLI)
LFBM............ Mont-De-Marsan [*France ICAO location identifier*] (ICLI)
LFBN............ Niort/Souche [*France ICAO location identifier*] (ICLI)
LFBO............ Toulouse/Blagnac [*France ICAO location identifier*] (ICLI)
LFBP............ Pau/Pont-Long-Uzein [*France ICAO location identifier*] (ICLI)
LFBQ............ Toulouse [*France ICAO location identifier*] (ICLI)
LFBR............ LASER Fusion Breeder Reactor
LFBR............ Liquid Fluidized Bed Reactor
LFBR............ Muret/Lherm [*France ICAO location identifier*] (ICLI)
LFBR-CX............ Liquid Fluidized Bed Reactor Critical Experiment
LFBS............ Biscarosse/Parentis [*France ICAO location identifier*] (ICLI)
LFBT............ Lifeboat (ABBR)
LFBT............ Tarbes/Ossun-Lourdes [*France ICAO location identifier*] (ICLI)
LFBU............ Angouleme/Brie-Champniers [*France ICAO location identifier*] (ICLI)
LFBV............ Brive/La Roche [*France ICAO location identifier*] (ICLI)
LFBW............ Mont-De-Marsan [*France ICAO location identifier*] (ICLI)
LFBX............ Perigeux/Bassillac [*France ICAO location identifier*] (ICLI)
LFBY............ Dax/Seyresse [*France ICAO location identifier*] (ICLI)
LFBZ............ Biarritz-Bayonne/Anglet [*France ICAO location identifier*] (ICLI)
LFC............ Aero Control Air Ltd. [*Canada ICAO designator*] (FAAC)
LFC............ Concordia Parish Library, Ferriday, LA [*Library symbol Library of Congress*] (LCLS)
LFC............ Lafayette Flying Corps [*World War I*]
LFC............ Lake Forest College [*Illinois*]
LFC............ Lake Fork Canyon [*New Mexico*] [*Seismograph station code, US Geological Survey*] (SEIS)
LFC............ Laminar Flow Control [*Aerodynamics*]
LFC............ Lands and Forests Commission [*Australia*]
LFC............ Large Format Camera [*Space exploration*]
LFC............ Lateral Femoral Condyle [*Anatomy*]
LFC............ L-Band Frequency Converter
LFC............ Level of Free Convection [*Meteorology*]
LFC............ Light Fighter Course [*Army*]
LFC............ Liquids from Coal
LFC............ Live Fire Component (MCD)
LFC............ Living Female Child [*Medicine*] (DMAA)
LFC............ Load Frequency Control (IEEE)
LFC............ Local Files Check
LFC............ Local Forms Control [*Computer science*] (CMD)
LFC............ Logic Flow Chart [*Computer science*]
LFC............ Logo Forum on Compuserve [*Defunct*] (EA)
LFC............ Lomas Financial Corp. [*NYSE symbol*] (SPSG)
LFC............ Loverboy Fan Club (EA)
LFC............ Low Fat and Cholesterol Diet (DMAA)
LFC............ Low-Frequency Choke (DEN)
LFC............ Low-Frequency Correction (CET)
LFC............ Low-Frequency Current
LFC............ Lunar Facsimile Capsule [*NASA*] (KSC)
LFC............ Lunar Farside Chart [*Air Force*]
LFC............ Lutheran Free Church (WDAA)
LFCA............ Chatellerault/Targe [*France ICAO location identifier*] (ICLI)
LFCB............ Bagneres De Luchon [*France ICAO location identifier*] (ICLI)
LFCB............ Legal Fees and Costs Board [*Australia*]
LFCC............ Cahors/Lalbenque [*France ICAO location identifier*] (ICLI)
LFCD............ Andernos-Les-Bains [*France ICAO location identifier*] (ICLI)
LFCE............ Gueret/Saint-Laurent [*France ICAO location identifier*] (ICLI)
LFCF............ Figeac/Livernon [*France ICAO location identifier*] (ICLI)
LFCG............ Saint-Girons/Antichan [*France ICAO location identifier*] (ICLI)
LFCH............ Arcachon/La Teste De Buch [*France ICAO location identifier*] (ICLI)
LFCI............ Albi/Le Sequestre [*France ICAO location identifier*] (ICLI)
LFCI............ Licentiate of the Faculty of Commerce and Industry [*British*] (DBQ)
LFCJ............ Jonzac/Neulles [*France ICAO location identifier*] (ICLI)
LFCK............ Castres/Mazamet [*France ICAO location identifier*] (ICLI)
LFCL............ Less Than Full Container Load
LFCL............ Toulouse/Lasbordes [*France ICAO location identifier*] (ICLI)
LFCM............ Low-Frequency Cross-Modulation [*Electronics*] (OA)
LFCM............ Millau/Larzac [*France ICAO location identifier*] (ICLI)
LFCN............ Nogaro [*France ICAO location identifier*] (ICLI)
LFCO............ Oloron/Herrere [*France ICAO location identifier*] (ICLI)
LFCP............ Pons/Avy [*France ICAO location identifier*] (ICLI)
LFCQ............ Graulhet/Mondragon [*France ICAO location identifier*] (ICLI)
LFCR............ Rodez/Marcillac [*France ICAO location identifier*] (ICLI)
LFCS............ Bordeaux/Saucats [*France ICAO location identifier*] (ICLI)
LFCS............ Land Forces Classification System (AABC)
LFCS............ LASER Fire Control System
LFCS............ Licentiate of the Faculty of Secretaries [*British*] (DBQ)
LFCT............ Leader Financial [*NASDAQ symbol*] (TTSB)
LFCT............ Leader Financial Corp. [*NASDAQ symbol*] (SAG)
LFCT............ Thouars [*France ICAO location identifier*] (ICLI)
LFCU............ Ussel/Thalamy [*France ICAO location identifier*] (ICLI)
LFCV............ Villefranche-De-Rouergue [*France ICAO location identifier*] (ICLI)
LFCW............ Villeneuve-Sur-Lot [*France ICAO location identifier*] (ICLI)
LFCX............ Castelsarrasin/Moissac [*France ICAO location identifier*] (ICLI)
LFCY............ Royan/Medis [*France ICAO location identifier*] (ICLI)
LFCZ............ Mimizan [*France ICAO location identifier*] (ICLI)
LFD............ Lactose-Free Diet
LFD............ Latest Finish Date
LFD............ Launch and Flight Division [*Ballistic Research Laboratory*] (RDA)
LFD............ Least Fatal Dose
LFD............ Line Fault Detector [*Telecommunications*] (TEL)
LFD............ Litchfield, MI [*Location identifier FAA*] (FAAL)
LFD............ Local Frequency Distribution
LFD............ Longford [*County in Ireland*] (ROG)
LFD............ Low-Fat Diet
LFD............ Low-Forceps Delivery [*Obstetrics*]
LFD............ Low-Frequency Decoy
LFD............ Low-Frequency Disturbance
LFD............ Lutheran Foundation for Religious Drama (EA)
LFDA............ Aire-Sur-L'Addour [*France ICAO location identifier*] (ICLI)
LFDA............ Land and Facilities Development Administration [*HUD*]
LFDB............ Montauban [*France ICAO location identifier*] (ICLI)
LFDC............ Montendre/Marcillac [*France ICAO location identifier*] (ICLI)
LFDE............ Egletons [*France ICAO location identifier*] (ICLI)
LFDF............ Low-Frequency Direction Finder (MCD)
LFDF............ Sainte-Foy-La-Grande [*France ICAO location identifier*] (ICLI)
LFDG............ Gaillac/Lisle Sur Tarn [*France ICAO location identifier*] (ICLI)
LFDH............ Auch/Lamothe [*France ICAO location identifier*] (ICLI)
LFDI............ Libourne/Artiques De Lussac [*France ICAO location identifier*] (ICLI)
LFDJ............ Pamiers/Les Pujols [*France ICAO location identifier*] (ICLI)
LFDK............ Soulac-Sur-Mer [*France ICAO location identifier*] (ICLI)
LFDL............ Loudun [*France ICAO location identifier*] (ICLI)
LFDM............ Low Flyer, Defense Mode
LFDM............ Marmande/Virazeil [*France ICAO location identifier*] (ICLI)
LFDN............ Rochefort/Saint-Agnant [*France ICAO location identifier*] (ICLI)
LFDO............ Bordeaux/Souge [*France ICAO location identifier*] (ICLI)
LFDP............ Saint-Pierre D'Oleron [*France ICAO location identifier*] (ICLI)
LFDQ............ Castelnau-Magnoac [*France ICAO location identifier*] (ICLI)
LFDR............ La Reole/Floudes [*France ICAO location identifier*] (ICLI)
LFDS............ Sarlat/Domme [*France ICAO location identifier*] (ICLI)
LFDT............ Tarbes/Laloubere [*France ICAO location identifier*] (ICLI)
LFDU............ Lesparre/St. Laurent Du Medoc [*France ICAO location identifier*] (ICLI)
LFDV............ Couhe/Verac [*France ICAO location identifier*] (ICLI)
LFDW............ Chauvigny [*France ICAO location identifier*] (ICLI)
LFDX............ Fumel/Montayral [*France ICAO location identifier*] (ICLI)
LFDY............ Bordeaux-Yvrac [*France ICAO location identifier*] (ICLI)
LFDZ............ Condat-Sur-Vezere [*France ICAO location identifier*] (ICLI)
LFE............ Brotherhood of Locomotive Firemen and Enginemen [*Later, United Transportation Union*] [*AFL-CIO*]
LFE............ Laboratory for Electronics (DNAB)
LFE............ Laminar Flow Element [*Engineering*]
LFE............ Large Flight Envelope (MCD)
LFE............ Logarithmic Feedback Element [*Computer science*]
LFEA............ Delle-Ile [*France ICAO location identifier*] (ICLI)
LFEB............ Dinan/Trelivan [*France ICAO location identifier*] (ICLI)
LFEB............ Launch Facility Equipment Building [*Missiles*]
LFEC............ Ouessant [*France ICAO location identifier*] (ICLI)
Lfecore............ LifeCore Biomedical, Inc. [*Associated Press*] (SAG)
LFED............ Leeds Federal Svgs Bk [*NASDAQ symbol*] (TTSB)
LFED............ Leeds FSB [*NASDAQ symbol*] (SAG)
LFED............ Pontivy [*France ICAO location identifier*] (ICLI)
LFEE............ Reims [*France ICAO location identifier*] (ICLI)
LFEF............ Amboise/Dierre [*France ICAO location identifier*] (ICLI)
LFEG............ Argenton-Sur-Creuse [*France ICAO location identifier*] (ICLI)
LFEH............ Aubigny-Sur-Nere [*France ICAO location identifier*] (ICLI)
LFEI............ Briare/Chatillon [*France ICAO location identifier*] (ICLI)
LFEJ............ Chateauroux/Villers [*France ICAO location identifier*] (ICLI)
LFEK............ Issoudun/Le Fay [*France ICAO location identifier*] (ICLI)
LFEL............ Le Blanc [*France ICAO location identifier*] (ICLI)
LfelneS............ Lifeline Systems, Inc. [*Associated Press*] (SAG)
LFEM............ Montargis/Vimory [*France ICAO location identifier*] (ICLI)
LfeMd............ Life Medical Sciences [*Associated Press*] (SAG)
LfeMed............ Life Medical Sciences [*Associated Press*] (SAG)

LFEN............	Laboratorio de Fisica e Engenharia Nucleores [*Portugal*]
LFEN............	Tours/Sorigny [*France ICAO location identifier*] (ICLI)
LFEO............	Saint-Malo/Saint-Servan [*France ICAO location identifier*] (ICLI)
LFEP............	Pouilly-Maconge [*France ICAO location identifier*] (ICLI)
LFEQ............	Quiberon [*France ICAO location identifier*] (ICLI)
LfeQst..........	LifeQuest Medical, Inc. [*Associated Press*] (SAG)
LFER............	Linear Free Energy Relationship
LFER............	Redon/Bains-Sur-Oust [*France ICAO location identifier*] (ICLI)
LFES............	Guiscriff-Scaer [*France ICAO location identifier*] (ICLI)
LFET............	Til-Chatel [*France ICAO location identifier*] (ICLI)
LfeTch..........	Life Technologies, Inc. [*Associated Press*] (SAG)
LFETS..........	Live Fire Evasive Target System [*Army*] (INF)
LFEU............	Bar-Le-Duc [*France ICAO location identifier*] (ICLI)
LfeUSA........	Life USA Holding, Inc. [*Associated Press*] (SAG)
LFEV............	Gray-Saint-Adrien [*France ICAO location identifier*] (ICLI)
LFEW............	Saulieu-Liernais [*France ICAO location identifier*] (ICLI)
LF-EX...........	Life Expectancy [*Military*]
LFEX............	Nancy-Azelot [*France ICAO location identifier*] (ICLI)
LFEY............	Ile-D'Yeu/Le Grand Phare [*France ICAO location identifier*] (ICLI)
LFEZ............	Nancy-Malzeville [*France ICAO location identifier*] (ICLI)
LFF	La Frestal [*France*] [*Seismograph station code, US Geological Survey*] (SEIS)
LFF	Large Formation Flyer (SSD)
LFF	Light Filter Factor
LFF	Limited Fanout-Free (MHDB)
LFF	Logistic Factors File (DOMA)
LFF	London Film Festival
LFF	Low-Frequency Filter (IAA)
LFFA............	CORTA (Orly Ouest) [*France ICAO location identifier*] (ICLI)
LFFB............	Buno-Bonnevaux [*France ICAO location identifier*] (ICLI)
LFFC............	Mantes-Cherence [*France ICAO location identifier*] (ICLI)
LFFD............	Saint-Andre-De L'Eure [*France ICAO location identifier*] (ICLI)
LFFE............	Enghien-Moisselles [*France ICAO location identifier*] (ICLI)
LFFET..........	Low-Frequency Field-Effect Transistor [*Electronics*] (OA)
LFFF............	Paris [*France ICAO location identifier*] (ICLI)
LFFG............	La Ferte-Gaucher [*France ICAO location identifier*] (ICLI)
LFFH............	Chateau-Thierry-Belleau [*France ICAO location identifier*] (ICLI)
LFFI............	Ancenis [*France ICAO location identifier*] (ICLI)
LFFJ............	Joinville-Mussey [*France ICAO location identifier*] (ICLI)
LFFK............	Fontenay-Le-Conte [*France ICAO location identifier*] (ICLI)
LFFL............	Bailleau-Armenonville [*France ICAO location identifier*] (ICLI)
LFFM............	La Motte-Beuvron [*France ICAO location identifier*] (ICLI)
LFFN............	Brienne-Le-Chateau [*France ICAO location identifier*] (ICLI)
LFFO............	Tonnerre-Moulins [*France ICAO location identifier*] (ICLI)
LFFP............	LASER Fusion Feasibility Project [*Nuclear fusion*]
LFFP............	Pithiviers [*France ICAO location identifier*] (ICLI)
LFFQ............	La Ferte-Alais [*France ICAO location identifier*] (ICLI)
LFFR............	Bar-Sur-Seine [*France ICAO location identifier*] (ICLI)
LFFS............	Suippes [*France ICAO location identifier*] (ICLI)
LFFT............	Left Front Fluid Temperature [*Brake system*] [*Automotive engineering*]
LFFT............	Neufchateau-Roucaux [*France ICAO location identifier*] (ICLI)
LFFU............	Chateauneuf-Sur-Cher [*France ICAO location identifier*] (ICLI)
LFFV............	Vierzon-Mereau [*France ICAO location identifier*] (ICLI)
LFFW............	Montaigu-Saint-Georges [*France ICAO location identifier*] (ICLI)
LFFX............	Tournus-Cuisery [*France ICAO location identifier*] (ICLI)
LFFY............	Etrepagny [*France ICAO location identifier*] (ICLI)
LFFZ............	Sezanne-Saint-Remy [*France ICAO location identifier*] (ICLI)
LFG.............	Landfill Gas
LFG.............	Lead-Free Glass
LFG.............	Lexical Functional Grammar [*Artificial intelligence*]
LFG.............	Low-Frequency Generator
LFGA............	Colmar/Houssen [*France ICAO location identifier*] (ICLI)
LFGB............	Mulhouse/Habsheim [*France ICAO location identifier*] (ICLI)
LFGC............	Strasbourg/Neuhof [*France ICAO location identifier*] (ICLI)
LFGD............	Arbois [*France ICAO location identifier*] (ICLI)
LFGE............	Avallon [*France ICAO location identifier*] (ICLI)
LFGF............	Beaune/Challanges [*France ICAO location identifier*] (ICLI)
LFGG............	Belfort/Chaux [*France ICAO location identifier*] (ICLI)
LFGG............	Low-Frequency Gravity Gradiometer
LFGH............	Cosne-Sur-Loire [*France ICAO location identifier*] (ICLI)
LFGI............	Dijon/Val Suzon [*France ICAO location identifier*] (ICLI)
LFGJ............	Dole/Tavaux [*France ICAO location identifier*] (ICLI)
LFGK............	Joigny [*France ICAO location identifier*] (ICLI)
LFGL............	Lons Le Saunier/Courlaoux [*France ICAO location identifier*] (ICLI)
LFGM............	Montceau Les Mines/Pouilloux [*France ICAO location identifier*] (ICLI)
LFGN............	Paray Le Monial [*France ICAO location identifier*] (ICLI)
LFGO............	Pont-Sur-Yonne [*France ICAO location identifier*] (ICLI)
LFGP............	Saint-Florentin/Cheu [*France ICAO location identifier*] (ICLI)
LFGQ............	Semur-En-Auxois [*France ICAO location identifier*] (ICLI)
LFGR............	Doncourt-Les-Conflans [*France ICAO location identifier*] (ICLI)
LFGRD..........	Lifeguard (ABBR)
LFGS............	Longuyon/Villette [*France ICAO location identifier*] (ICLI)
LFGT............	Sarrebourg/Buhl [*France ICAO location identifier*] (ICLI)
LFGU............	Sarreguemines/Neunkirch [*France ICAO location identifier*] (ICLI)
LFGV............	Thionville/Yutz [*France ICAO location identifier*] (ICLI)
LFGW............	Verdun/Rozelier [*France ICAO location identifier*] (ICLI)
LFGX............	Champagnole/Crotenay [*France ICAO location identifier*] (ICLI)
LFGY............	Saint-Die/Remoneix [*France ICAO location identifier*] (ICLI)
LFGZ............	Nuits-Saint-Georges [*France ICAO location identifier*] (ICLI)
LFH.............	Left Femoral Hernia [*Medicine*]
LFH.............	Lower Fascial Height [*Medicine*]
LFH.............	Lunar Far Horizon (KSC)
LFHA............	Issoire/Le Broc [*France ICAO location identifier*] (ICLI)
LFHB............	Moulins/Avermes [*France ICAO location identifier*] (ICLI)
LFHC............	Perouges/Meximieux [*France ICAO location identifier*] (ICLI)
LFHD............	Pierrelatte [*France ICAO location identifier*] (ICLI)
LFHE............	Romans/Saint-Paul [*France ICAO location identifier*] (ICLI)
LFHF............	Ruoms [*France ICAO location identifier*] (ICLI)
LFHG............	Saint-Chamond/L'Horme [*France ICAO location identifier*] (ICLI)
LFHH............	Vienne/Reventin [*France ICAO location identifier*] (ICLI)
LFHI............	Morestel [*France ICAO location identifier*] (ICLI)
LFHJ............	Lyon/Corbas [*France ICAO location identifier*] (ICLI)
LFHK............	Camp De Canjuers [*France ICAO location identifier*] (ICLI)
LFHL............	Langogne/L'Esperon [*France ICAO location identifier*] (ICLI)
LFHL............	Low-Frequency Hearing Loss (DMAA)
LFHM............	Megeve [*France ICAO location identifier*] (ICLI)
LFHN............	Bellegarde/Vouvray [*France ICAO location identifier*] (ICLI)
LFHO............	Aubenas-Vals-Lanas [*France ICAO location identifier*] (ICLI)
LFHP............	Le Puy/Loudes [*France ICAO location identifier*] (ICLI)
LFHQ............	Saint-Flour/Coltines [*France ICAO location identifier*] (ICLI)
LFHR............	Brioude-Beaumont [*France ICAO location identifier*] (ICLI)
LFHS............	Bourg/Ceyreziat [*France ICAO location identifier*] (ICLI)
LFHT............	Ambert-Le-Poyet [*France ICAO location identifier*] (ICLI)
LFHU............	L'Alpe D'Huez [*France ICAO location identifier*] (ICLI)
LFHV............	Villefrance/Tarare [*France ICAO location identifier*] (ICLI)
LFHW............	Belleville-Villie-Morgon [*France ICAO location identifier*] (ICLI)
LFHX............	Lapalisse-Perigny [*France ICAO location identifier*] (ICLI)
LFHY............	Moulins/Montbeugny [*France ICAO location identifier*] (ICLI)
LFHZ............	Sallanches-Mont-Blanc [*France ICAO location identifier*] (ICLI)
LFI	Hampton, VA [*Location identifier FAA*] (FAAL)
LFI	Last Frame Indicator
LFI	Let's Face It [*Later, AFLFI*] [*An association*] (EA)
LFI	Levitz Furniture [*NYSE symbol*] (TTSB)
LFI	Levitz Furniture, Inc. [*NYSE symbol*] (SPSG)
LFI	Licensed Financial Institution
LFI	Lifting Fan Intake [*Hovercraft*]
LFI	Linear Function Interpolator
L-FI	Live-Free, Inc. [*An association*] (EA)
LFI	Long Fiber Injection
LFI	Low-Frequency Inductor
LFIA............	Luminescence and Fluorescence Immunoassay [*Clinical chemistry*]
LFIB	Belves-Saint-Pardoux [*France ICAO location identifier*] (ICLI)
LFIC	Cross Corsen [*France ICAO location identifier*] (ICLI)
LFIC	Landing Force Intelligence Center [*Navy*] (DNAB)
LFICS	Landing Force Integrated Communications System [*Marine Corps*]
LFID	Condom-Valence-Sur-Baise [*France ICAO location identifier*] (ICLI)
LFIE	Cross Etel [*France ICAO location identifier*] (ICLI)
LFIF	Saint-Afrique-Belmont [*France ICAO location identifier*] (ICLI)
LFIG	Cassagnes-Begonhes [*France ICAO location identifier*] (ICLI)
LFIH	Chalais [*France ICAO location identifier*] (ICLI)
LFIINST........	Life Fellow Imperial Institute [*British*] (ROG)
LFIJ	Cross Jobourg [*France ICAO location identifier*] (ICLI)
LFIK	Riberac-Saint-Aulaye [*France ICAO location identifier*] (ICLI)
LFIL	Rion-Des-Landes [*France ICAO location identifier*] (ICLI)
LFILIE..........	Libera Federazione Italiana Lavoratori Industrie Estrattive [*Free Italian Federation of Workers in Mining Industries*]
LFIM	Low-Frequency Instruments and Measurement (MCD)
LFIM	Saint Gaudens Montrejeau [*France ICAO location identifier*] (ICLI)
LFIN	Cross Gris-Nez [*France ICAO location identifier*] (ICLI)
LFINT...........	Low-Frequency Intersection
LFIP	Peyresourde-Balestas [*France ICAO location identifier*] (ICLI)
LFIPA...........	Laminated Fiberglass Insulation Producers Association [*Defunct*] (EA)
LFIR	Revel-Montgey [*France ICAO location identifier*] (ICLI)
LFIRSS.........	Louis Finkelstein Institute for Religious and Social Studies (EA)
LFISWB........	Loyal, Free, Industrious Society of Wheelwrights and Blacksmiths [*A union*] [*British*]
LFIT	Toulouse-Bourg-Saint-Bernard [*France ICAO location identifier*] (ICLI)
LFIV	Vendays-Montalivet [*France ICAO location identifier*] (ICLI)
LFIX	Itxassou [*France ICAO location identifier*] (ICLI)
LFIY	Saint-Jean-D'Angely [*France ICAO location identifier*] (ICLI)
LFJ.............	Local Feed Junctor [*Telecommunications*] (NITA)
LFJ.............	Low-Frequency Jammer
LFJG	Cross La Garde [*France ICAO location identifier*] (ICLI)
LFJV	Low Frequency Jet Ventilation [*Medicine*]
LFK.............	Lufkin/Nacogdoches [*Texas*] [*Airport symbol*] (OAG)
LFK.............	Lufkin, TX [*Location identifier FAA*] (FAAL)
LFKA............	Albertville [*France ICAO location identifier*] (ICLI)
LFKB............	Bastia/Poretta, Corse [*France ICAO location identifier*] (ICLI)
LFKC............	Calvi/Sainte-Catherine, Corse [*France ICAO location identifier*] (ICLI)
LFKD............	Sollieres-Sardieres [*France ICAO location identifier*] (ICLI)
LFKE............	Saint-Jean-En-Royans [*France ICAO location identifier*] (ICLI)
LFKF............	Figari, Sud-Corse [*France ICAO location identifier*] (ICLI)
LFKG............	Ghisonaccia-Alzitone [*France ICAO location identifier*] (ICLI)
LFKH............	Saint-Jean-D'Avelanne [*France ICAO location identifier*] (ICLI)
LFKJ............	Ajaccio/Campo Dell'Oro, Corse [*France ICAO location identifier*] (ICLI)
LFKL............	Lyon-Brindas [*France ICAO location identifier*] (ICLI)
LFKM............	Saint-Galmier [*France ICAO location identifier*] (ICLI)
LFKO............	Propriano [*France ICAO location identifier*] (ICLI)
LFKP............	La Tour-Du-Pin-Cessieu [*France ICAO location identifier*] (ICLI)
LFKS............	Solenzara, Corse [*France ICAO location identifier*] (ICLI)
LFKT............	Corte [*France ICAO location identifier*] (ICLI)
LFKY............	Belley-Peyrieu [*France ICAO location identifier*] (ICLI)
LFKZ............	Saint-Claude-Pratz [*France ICAO location identifier*] (ICLI)
LFL	LASER Flash Lamp
LFL	League for Liberty (EA)
LFL	Left Frontolateral [*Medicine*] (DMAA)

LFL .... Length of Flowering Period [*Botany*]
LFL .... Lesbian Feminist Liberation (EA)
LFL .... Leukocyte Feeder Layer [*Medicine*] (DMAA)
LFL .... Libertarians for Life (EA)
LFL .... Linear Field Line
LFl .... Long Flashing Light [*Navigation signal*]
LFL .... Lower Flammable Limit
LFL .... Lutherans for Life (EA)
LFLA .... Auxerre/Moneteau [*France ICAO location identifier*] (ICLI)
LFLA .... Landing Force Logistics Afloat (MCD)
LFlAA .... Laut-und Formenlehre des Aegyptisch-Aramaeisch [*A publication*] (BJA)
LFLB .... Chambery/Aix-Les-Bains [*France ICAO location identifier*] (ICLI)
LFLC .... Clermont-Ferrand/Aulnat [*France ICAO location identifier*] (ICLI)
LFLD .... Bourges [*France ICAO location identifier*] (ICLI)
LFLE .... Chambery/Challes-Les-Eaux [*France ICAO location identifier*] (ICLI)
LFLEN .... Leaf Length [*Botany*]
LFLF .... Orleans [*France ICAO location identifier*] (ICLI)
LFLG .... Grenoble/Le Versoud [*France ICAO location identifier*] (ICLI)
LFLGTH .... Leaf Length [*Botany*]
LFLH .... Chalon/Champforgeuil [*France ICAO location identifier*] (ICLI)
LFLI .... Annemasse [*France ICAO location identifier*] (ICLI)
LFLJ .... Courchevel [*France ICAO location identifier*] (ICLI)
LFLK .... Lifelike (ABBR)
LFLK .... Oyonnax/Arbent [*France ICAO location identifier*] (ICLI)
LFLL .... Lyon/Satolas [*France ICAO location identifier*] (ICLI)
LFLM .... Macon/Charnay [*France ICAO location identifier*] (ICLI)
LFLN .... Lifeline (ABBR)
LFLN .... Saint-Yan [*France ICAO location identifier*] (ICLI)
LFLO .... Roanne/Renaison [*France ICAO location identifier*] (ICLI)
LFLOW .... Linearized High-Resolution Wind-Field Flow [*Model*] [*Marine science*] (OSRA)
LFLOW .... Linearized High-Resolution Wind-Field Flow [*Model*] (USDC)
LFLP .... Annecy/Meythet [*France ICAO location identifier*] (ICLI)
LFLPU .... Libyan Federation of Labor and Professional Unions
LFLQ .... Montelimar/Ancone [*France ICAO location identifier*] (ICLI)
LFLR .... Saint-Rambert-D'Albon [*France ICAO location identifier*] (ICLI)
LFLS .... Grenoble/Saint-Geoirs [*France ICAO location identifier*] (ICLI)
LFLS .... Leafless (ABBR)
LFLSY .... Lifelessly (ABBR)
LFLT .... Left Front Lining Temperature [*Brake system*] [*Automotive engineering*]
LFLT .... Montlucon/Domerat [*France ICAO location identifier*] (ICLI)
LFLU .... Valence/Chabeuil [*France ICAO location identifier*] (ICLI)
LFLV .... Vichy/Charmeil [*France ICAO location identifier*] (ICLI)
LFLW .... Aurillac [*France ICAO location identifier*] (ICLI)
LFLWP .... Land Forces Logistics Working Party (MCD)
LFLX .... Chateauroux/Deols [*France ICAO location identifier*] (ICLI)
LFLY .... Lyon/Bron [*France ICAO location identifier*] (ICLI)
LFLZ .... Feurs/Chambeon [*France ICAO location identifier*] (ICLI)
LFM .... Franklin and Marshall College, Lancaster, PA [*OCLC symbol*] (OCLC)
LFM .... Landing Force Manual [*Marine Corps, Navy*]
LFM .... LASER Feedback Microscope
LFM .... LASER Force Microscope
LFM .... Lateral Force Microscopy [*Morphology*]
LFM .... Launch First Motion
LFM .... Lieutenant Field Marshal
LFM .... Limited-Area Fine-Mesh Model (USDC)
LFM .... Limited-Area Fine-Mesh Model [*Marine science*] (OSRA)
LFM .... Limited Fine Mesh
LFM .... Linear Feet per Minute
LFM .... Linear Frequency Modulation (CAAL)
LFM .... Local File Manager
LFM .... Longitudinal Field Modulator
LFM .... Loss Frequency Method [*Insurance*]
LFM .... Lower Figure of Merit
LFM .... Low-Field Magnetometer [*Instrumentation*]
LFM .... Low-Frequency Magnetic [*Field*]
LFM .... Low-Frequency Modulation
LFM .... Low-Powered Fan Marker (MUGU)
LFM .... Lubrecht Forest [*Montana*] [*Seismograph station code, US Geological Survey Closed*] (SEIS)
LFMA .... Aix-Les-Milles [*France ICAO location identifier*] (ICLI)
LFMA .... Laminated Foil Manufacturers' Association [*Defunct*]
LFMB .... Aix-En-Provence [*France ICAO location identifier*] (ICLI)
LFMC .... Le Luc/Le Cannet [*France ICAO location identifier*] (ICLI)
LFMD .... Cannes/Mandelieu [*France ICAO location identifier*] (ICLI)
LfMd .... Life Medical Sciences [*Associated Press*] (SAG)
LFME .... Nimes/Courbessac [*France ICAO location identifier*] (ICLI)
LFMER .... Lovelace Foundation for Medical Education and Research [*Reorganized to form Lovelace Medical Foundation and Lovelace Biomedical and Environmental Research Institute*] (MCD)
LFMF .... Fayence [*France ICAO location identifier*] (ICLI)
LF/MF .... Low Frequency, Medium Frequency
LFMG .... La Montagne Noire [*France ICAO location identifier*] (ICLI)
LFMH .... Saint-Etienne/Boutheon [*France ICAO location identifier*] (ICLI)
LFMI .... Istres/Le Tube [*France ICAO location identifier*] (ICLI)
LFMJ .... Nice/Mont Agel [*France ICAO location identifier*] (ICLI)
LFMK .... Carcassonne/Salvaza [*France ICAO location identifier*] (ICLI)
LFML .... Little Flower Mission League (EA)
LFML .... Marseille/Marignane [*France ICAO location identifier*] (ICLI)
LFMM .... Aix-En-Provence [*France ICAO location identifier*] (ICLI)
LFMN .... Nice/Cote D'Azur [*France ICAO location identifier*] (ICLI)
LFMO .... Orange/Caritat [*France ICAO location identifier*] (ICLI)
LFMOP .... Linear Frequency Modulation on Pulse (MCD)
LFMP .... Perpignan/Rivesaltes [*France ICAO location identifier*] (ICLI)
LFM/PD .... Local Flow Management/Profile Descent
LFMQ .... Le Castellet [*France ICAO location identifier*] (ICLI)
LFMR .... Barcelonnette/Saint-Pons [*France ICAO location identifier*] (ICLI)
LFMR .... Low-Frequency Microwave Radiometer
LFMS .... Ales/Deaux [*France ICAO location identifier*] (ICLI)
LFMS .... Laminated Ferrite Memory System (MCD)
LFMT .... Montpellier/Frejorgues [*France ICAO location identifier*] (ICLI)
LFMU .... Beziers/Vias [*France ICAO location identifier*] (ICLI)
LFMV .... Avignon/Caumont [*France ICAO location identifier*] (ICLI)
LFMW .... Castelnaudary/Villeneuve [*France ICAO location identifier*] (ICLI)
LFMX .... Chateau-Arnoux/Saint-Auban [*France ICAO location identifier*] (ICLI)
LFMY .... Salon [*France ICAO location identifier*] (ICLI)
LFMZ .... Lezignan-Corbieres [*France ICAO location identifier*] (ICLI)
LFN .... Lactoferrin [*Biochemistry*] (MAE)
LFN .... Logical File Name
LFN .... Logical File Number [*Computer science*] (MCD)
LFN .... Long Filename (PCM)
LFN .... Louisburg, NC [*Location identifier FAA*] (FAAL)
LFNA .... Gap/Tallard [*France ICAO location identifier*] (ICLI)
LFNB .... Mende/Brenoux [*France ICAO location identifier*] (ICLI)
LFNC .... Mont-Dauphin/Saint-Crepin [*France ICAO location identifier*] (ICLI)
LFND .... Pont-Saint-Esprit [*France ICAO location identifier*] (ICLI)
LFNE .... Salon/Eyguieres [*France ICAO location identifier*] (ICLI)
LFNF .... Vinon [*France ICAO location identifier*] (ICLI)
LFNG .... Montpellier/L'Or [*France ICAO location identifier*] (ICLI)
LFNGFT .... Landing Force Naval Gunfire Team
LFNH .... Carpentras [*France ICAO location identifier*] (ICLI)
LFNI .... Conqueyrac [*France ICAO location identifier*] (ICLI)
LFNJ .... Aspres-Sur-Buech [*France ICAO location identifier*] (ICLI)
LFNK .... Vars-Les-Crosses-Et-Les-Tronches [*France ICAO location identifier*] (ICLI)
LFNL .... Saint-Martin-De-Londres [*France ICAO location identifier*] (ICLI)
LFNM .... La Mole [*France ICAO location identifier*] (ICLI)
LFNO .... Florac-Sainte-Enimie [*France ICAO location identifier*] (ICLI)
LFNP .... Pezenas-Nizas [*France ICAO location identifier*] (ICLI)
LFNQ .... Mont-Louis-La-Quillane [*France ICAO location identifier*] (ICLI)
LFNR .... Berre-La-Fare [*France ICAO location identifier*] (ICLI)
LFNS .... Leafiness (ABBR)
LFNS .... Low-Frequency Navigation System (NG)
LFNS .... Sisteron-Theze [*France ICAO location identifier*] (ICLI)
LFNT .... Avignon-Pujaut [*France ICAO location identifier*] (ICLI)
LFNT .... Low Frequency Intersection (FAAC)
LFNU .... Uzes [*France ICAO location identifier*] (ICLI)
LFNV .... Valreas-Visan [*France ICAO location identifier*] (ICLI)
LFNW .... Puivert [*France ICAO location identifier*] (ICLI)
LFNX .... Bedarieux-La-Tour-Sur-Orb [*France ICAO location identifier*] (ICLI)
LFNY .... Saint-Etienne-En-Devoluy [*France ICAO location identifier*] (ICLI)
LFNZ .... Le Mazet-De-Romanin [*France ICAO location identifier*] (ICLI)
LFO .... Large Follow-On
LFO .... LASER/Fiber-Optic (MCD)
LFO .... Light Fuel Oil (BARN)
LFO .... Low-Frequency Oscillator
LFOA .... Avord [*France ICAO location identifier*] (ICLI)
LFOA .... Last Frame of Action [*Cinematography*] (WDMC)
LFOB .... Beauvais/Tille [*France ICAO location identifier*] (ICLI)
LFOC .... Crateaudun [*France ICAO location identifier*] (ICLI)
LFOC .... Landing Force Operation Center [*Navy*] (CAAL)
LFOC .... Lea-Francis Owners Club [*British*] (EAIO)
LFOD .... Saumur/Saint-Florent [*France ICAO location identifier*] (ICLI)
LFOE .... Evreux/Fauville [*France ICAO location identifier*] (ICLI)
LFOF .... Alencon/Valframbert [*France ICAO location identifier*] (ICLI)
LFOG .... Flers/Saint-Paul [*France ICAO location identifier*] (ICLI)
LFOH .... Le Havre/Octeville [*France ICAO location identifier*] (ICLI)
LFOI .... Abbeville [*France ICAO location identifier*] (ICLI)
LFOJ .... Orleans/Bricy [*France ICAO location identifier*] (ICLI)
LFOK .... Chalons/Vatry [*France ICAO location identifier*] (ICLI)
LFOL .... L'Aigle/Saint-Michel [*France ICAO location identifier*] (ICLI)
LFOM .... Lessay [*France ICAO location identifier*] (ICLI)
LFOM .... Low-Frequency Outer Marker (MSA)
LFON .... Dreux/Vernouillet [*France ICAO location identifier*] (ICLI)
LFOO .... Les Sables D'Olonne/Talmont [*France ICAO location identifier*] (ICLI)
LFOP .... Landing and Ferry Operations Panel [*NASA*] (NASA)
LFOP .... Rouen/Boos [*France ICAO location identifier*] (ICLI)
LFOQ .... Blois/Le Breuil [*France ICAO location identifier*] (ICLI)
LFOR .... Chartres/Champhol [*France ICAO location identifier*] (ICLI)
LFORM .... Landing Force Operational Reserve Material [*Navy*] (NVT)
LFOS .... Launch and Flight Operations System
LFOS .... Saint-Valery/Vittefleur [*France ICAO location identifier*] (ICLI)
LFOT .... Tours/Saint-Symphorien [*France ICAO location identifier*] (ICLI)
LFOU .... Cholet/Le Pontreau [*France ICAO location identifier*] (ICLI)
LFOV .... Large Field of View [*Radiology*] (DAVI)
LFOV .... Laval/Entrammes [*France ICAO location identifier*] (ICLI)
LFOW .... Saint-Quentin/Roupy [*France ICAO location identifier*] (ICLI)
LFOX .... Etampes/Mondesir [*France ICAO location identifier*] (ICLI)
LFOY .... Le Havre/Saint-Romain [*France ICAO location identifier*] (ICLI)
LFOZ .... Orleans/Saint-Denis-De-L'Hotel [*France ICAO location identifier*] (ICLI)
LFP .... Labor-Force Participation
LFP .... Large Flat Plate
LFP .... Late Flight Plan
LFP .... Left Frontoposterior [*A fetal position*] [*Obstetrics*]
LFP .... LFP Holdings, Inc. [*Toronto Stock Exchange symbol*]

LFP............	Liberala Folkpartiet [Liberal People's Party] [Finland Political party] (PPE)
LFP.............	Libraries for Prisons [An association] (EA)
LFP.............	Listen for Pleasure [Audio books]
LFP.............	Livestock Feed Program
LFP.............	Local Field Potential [Electrophysiology]
LFP.............	Low-Frequency Prediction (USDC)
LFPA.........	Persan-Beaumont [France ICAO location identifier] (ICLI)
LFPAG	Live Firing Program Analysis Group [Military] (CAAL)
LFPB.........	Paris/Le Bourget [France ICAO location identifier] (ICLI)
LFPC.........	Creil [France ICAO location identifier] (ICLI)
LFPD.........	Bernay/Saint-Martin [France ICAO location identifier] (ICLI)
LFPE.........	Meaux/Esbly [France ICAO location identifier] (ICLI)
LFPEF........	Low-Frequency Pulsed Electromagnetic Field
LFPER........	Leaf Persistence [Botany]
LFPF.........	Beynes/Thiverval [France ICAO location identifier] (ICLI)
LFPG.........	Paris/Charles-De-Gaulle [France ICAO location identifier] (ICLI)
LFPH.........	Chelles/Le Pin [France ICAO location identifier] (ICLI)
LFPI..........	Paris/Issy-Les-Moulineaux [France ICAO location identifier] (ICLI)
LFPJ.........	Taverny [France ICAO location identifier] (ICLI)
LFPK.........	Coulommiers/Voisins [France ICAO location identifier] (ICLI)
LFPL.........	Lewis Flight Propulsion Laboratory [NASA]
LFPL.........	Lognes/Emerainville [France ICAO location identifier] (ICLI)
LFPM........	Melun/Villaroche [France ICAO location identifier] (ICLI)
LFPN........	Toussus-Le-Noble [France ICAO location identifier] (ICLI)
LFPO........	Paris/Orly [France ICAO location identifier] (ICLI)
LFPP.........	Le Plessis-Belleville [France ICAO location identifier] (ICLI)
LFPPV........	Low-Frequency Positive Pressure Ventilation [Medicine] (DMAA)
LFPQ.........	Fontenay-Tresigny [France ICAO location identifier] (ICLI)
LFPR.........	Guayancourt [France ICAO location identifier] (ICLI)
LFPRL........	Lewis Flight Propulsion Research Laboratory [NASA] (MUGU)
LFPS.........	Licentiate of the Faculty of Physicians and Surgeons [British]
LFPS.........	Low-Frequency Phase Shifter [Telecommunications]
LFPS.........	Paris [France ICAO location identifier] (ICLI)
LFPSG	Licentiate of the Faculty of Physicians and Surgeons, Glasgow (ROG)
LFPT.........	Pontoise/Cormeilles-En-Vexin [France ICAO location identifier] (ICLI)
LFPU.........	Moret/Episy [France ICAO location identifier] (ICLI)
LFPUB	Leaf Pubescence [Botany]
LFPV.........	Villacoublay/Velizy [France ICAO location identifier] (ICLI)
LFPW........	Low-Frequency Plasma Wave
LFPW........	Paris, Centre Meteorologique [France ICAO location identifier] (ICLI)
LFPX.........	Chavenay/Villepreux [France ICAO location identifier] (ICLI)
LFPY.........	Bretigny-Sur-Orge [France ICAO location identifier] (ICLI)
LFPZ.........	Saint-Cyre-L'Ecole [France ICAO location identifier] (ICLI)
LFQ..........	Light Foot Quantizer
LFQ..........	Limited Flying Quality
LFQA.........	Reims/Prunay [France ICAO location identifier] (ICLI)
LFQB.........	Troyes/Barberey [France ICAO location identifier] (ICLI)
LFQC.........	Luneville/Croismare [France ICAO location identifier] (ICLI)
LFQD.........	Arras/Roclincourt [France ICAO location identifier] (ICLI)
LFQE.........	Etain/Rouvres [France ICAO location identifier] (ICLI)
LFQF.........	Autun/Bellevue [France ICAO location identifier] (ICLI)
LFQG.........	Nevers/Fourchambault [France ICAO location identifier] (ICLI)
LFQH.........	Chatillon-Sur-Seine [France ICAO location identifier] (ICLI)
LFQI..........	Cambrai/Epinoy [France ICAO location identifier] (ICLI)
LFQJ.........	Maubeuge/Elesmes [France ICAO location identifier] (ICLI)
LFQK.........	Chalons/Ecury-Sur-Coole [France ICAO location identifier] (ICLI)
LFQL.........	Lens/Benifontaine [France ICAO location identifier] (ICLI)
LFQM	Besancon-La-Veze [France ICAO location identifier] (ICLI)
LFQN	Saint-Omer/Wizernes [France ICAO location identifier] (ICLI)
LFQO.........	Lille/Marcq-En-Baroeul [France ICAO location identifier] (ICLI)
LFQP.........	Phalsbourg/Bourscheid [France ICAO location identifier] (ICLI)
LFQQ.........	Lille/Lesquin [France ICAO location identifier] (ICLI)
LFQR.........	Romilly-Sur-Seine [France ICAO location identifier] (ICLI)
LFQS.........	Vitry-En-Artois [France ICAO location identifier] (ICLI)
LFQT.........	Merville/Calonne [France ICAO location identifier] (ICLI)
LFQU.........	Sarre-Union [France ICAO location identifier] (ICLI)
LFQV.........	Charleville/Mezieres [France ICAO location identifier] (ICLI)
LFQW........	Vesoul-Frotey [France ICAO location identifier] (ICLI)
LFQY.........	Saverne-Steinbourg [France ICAO location identifier] (ICLI)
LFQZ.........	Dieuze-Gueblange [France ICAO location identifier] (ICLI)
L FR..........	Franc [Monetary unit] [Luxembourg]
LFR...........	Inshore Fire Support Ship [Navy symbol]
LFR...........	Laboratory Facilities Request (MCD)
LFR...........	La Fria [Venezuela] [Airport symbol] (OAG)
LFR...........	Laminar-Flow Reactor [Engineering]
LFR...........	LASERgraphics Film Recorder (PCM)
L Fr...........	Law French (DLA)
LFR...........	Leafier (ABBR)
LFR...........	Lifer (ABBR)
LFR...........	Linear Flow Reactor [Chemical engineering]
LFR...........	Line Frequency Rejection (IAA)
LFR...........	Lowest Fare Routing [Travel industry]
LFR...........	Low-Flux Reactor
LFR...........	Low Frequency Radio Range (TAG)
LFR...........	Low-Frequency Range (MCD)
LFr...........	Saint Mary Parish Library, Franklin, LA [Library symbol Library of Congress] (LCLS)
LFRA..........	Angers/Avrille [France ICAO location identifier] (ICLI)
LFRA..........	League of Federal Recreation Associations (EA)
LFRA..........	Leatherhead Food Research Association [British] (ARC)
LFRAP	Long Feeder Route Analysis Program [Bell System]
LFRB..........	Brest/Guipavas [France ICAO location identifier] (ICLI)
LFRC..........	Cherbourg/Maupertus [France ICAO location identifier] (ICLI)
LFRC..........	Latex Foam Rubber Council [Defunct] (EA)
LFRC..........	Laurentian Forest Research Center [Canadian Forestry Service] [Research center] (RCD)
LFRC..........	Library Fundraising Resource Center [American Library Association]
LFRD..........	Dinard/Pleurtuit-Saint-Malo [France ICAO location identifier] (ICLI)
LFRD..........	Lot Fraction Reliability Deviation [Quality control]
LFRE..........	La Baule/Escoublac [France ICAO location identifier] (ICLI)
LFRED	Liquid-Fueled Ramjet Engine Demonstration [Navy] (MCD)
LFRF..........	Granville [France ICAO location identifier] (ICLI)
LFRG..........	Deauville/Saint-Gatien [France ICAO location identifier] (ICLI)
LFRH..........	Lorient/Lann-Bihoue [France ICAO location identifier] (ICLI)
LFRI...........	La Roche-Sur-Yon/Les Ajoncs [France ICAO location identifier] (ICLI)
LFRJ..........	Landivisiau [France ICAO location identifier] (ICLI)
LFRJ..........	Liquid-Fueled Ramjet [Navy] (MCD)
LFRK..........	Caen/Carpiquet [France ICAO location identifier] (ICLI)
LFRL..........	Lanveoc/Poulmic [France ICAO location identifier] (ICLI)
LFRM..........	Le Mans/Arnage [France ICAO location identifier] (ICLI)
LFRN..........	Rennes/Saint-Jacques [France ICAO location identifier] (ICLI)
LFRO..........	Lannion/Servel [France ICAO location identifier] (ICLI)
LFRP..........	Ploermel-Loyat [France ICAO location identifier] (ICLI)
LFRQ..........	Quimper/Pluguffan [France ICAO location identifier] (ICLI)
LFRR..........	Brest [France ICAO location identifier] (ICLI)
LFRR..........	Low-Frequency Radio Range (MCD)
LFRS..........	Nantes/Chateau Bougon [France ICAO location identifier] (ICLI)
LFRSB	Loose Fuel-Rod Shipping Basket (GAAI)
LFRT..........	Saint-Brieuc Armor [France ICAO location identifier] (ICLI)
LFrtW........	Washington Parish Library, Franklinton, LA [Library symbol Library of Congress] (LCLS)
LFRU..........	Morlaix/Ploujean [France ICAO location identifier] (ICLI)
LFRV..........	Vannes/Meucon [France ICAO location identifier] (ICLI)
LFRW..........	Avranches/Le Val Saint-Pere [France ICAO location identifier] (ICLI)
LFRX..........	Brest [France ICAO location identifier] (ICLI)
LFRY..........	Cherbourg [France ICAO location identifier] (ICLI)
LFRZ..........	Saint-Nazaire/Montoir [France ICAO location identifier] (ICLI)
LFS...........	Amphibious Fire Support Ship [Navy symbol]
LFS...........	Labour Force Survey [Canada]
LFS...........	Lancaster Finishing School [British military] (DMA)
LFS...........	LASER Fluorescence Spectroscopy
LFS...........	Launch Facility Simulator
LFS...........	League of Filipino Students
LFS...........	Leather Finishers' Society [A union] [British]
LFS...........	Libertarian Futurist Society (EA)
LFS...........	Licentiate of the Faculty of Architects and Surveyors [British] (DBQ)
LFS...........	Li-Fraumeni Syndrome [Oncology]
LFS...........	Liquid Filtration System
LFS...........	Liquid Flow System
LFS...........	Liver Function Series [Clinical chemistry]
LFS...........	Local Format Storage
LFS...........	Logical File Structure [Computer science] (OA)
LFS...........	Logical File System (IAA)
LFS...........	Logic Fault Simulator [Computer science]
LFS...........	Logistics Feasibility System
LFS...........	Logistics/Ferry Station
LFS...........	Loop Feedback Signal
LFS...........	Low-Frequency Stimulation [Neurophysiology]
LFS...........	Low-Frequency Stimulation [Neurophysiology]
LFS...........	Luftfahrzeug Service - Aircraft Service [Austria ICAO designator] (FAAC)
LFSA..........	Besancon/Thise [France ICAO location identifier] (ICLI)
LFSA..........	Logistical Force Structure Assessment (MCD)
LFSB..........	Bale/Mulhouse [France/Switzerland] [ICAO location identifier] (ICLI)
LFSB..........	LFS Bancorp [NASDAQ symbol] (SAG)
LFS Bcp	LFS Bancorp [Associated Press] (SAG)
LFSC..........	Colmar/Meyenheim [France ICAO location identifier] (ICLI)
LFSC..........	Limited First-Strike Capability
LFSC..........	Louisville Fear Survey for Children [Psychology]
LFSCWW	Live Food Singles Club - World Wide [Defunct] (EA)
LFSD..........	Dijon/Longvic [France ICAO location identifier] (ICLI)
LFSE..........	Epinal/Dogneville [France ICAO location identifier] (ICLI)
LFSF..........	Metz/Frescaty [France ICAO location identifier] (ICLI)
LFSG..........	Epinal/Mirecourt [France ICAO location identifier] (ICLI)
LFSH..........	Haguenau [France ICAO location identifier] (ICLI)
LFSI...........	Saint-Dizier/Robinson [France ICAO location identifier] (ICLI)
LFSID	Local Form Session Identifier (ACRL)
LFSJ..........	Sedan/Douzy [France ICAO location identifier] (ICLI)
LFSK..........	Vitry-Le-Francois/Vauclerc [France ICAO location identifier] (ICLI)
LFSL..........	Toul/Rosieres [France ICAO location identifier] (ICLI)
LFSM..........	Montbeliard/Courcelles [France ICAO location identifier] (ICLI)
LFSMT/S.....	Liquid Fuel Systems Maintenance Technician/Specialist [Aerospace] (AAG)
LFSN..........	Nancy/Essey [France ICAO location identifier] (ICLI)
LFSO..........	Nancy/Ochey [France ICAO location identifier] (ICLI)
LFSP..........	Landing Force Support Party [Navy] (ANA)
LFSP..........	Pontarlier [France ICAO location identifier] (ICLI)
LFSQ..........	Belfort/Fontaine [France ICAO location identifier] (ICLI)
LFSR..........	Linear Feedback Shift Register
LFSR..........	Reims/Champagne [France ICAO location identifier] (ICLI)
LFSS..........	Landing Force Support Ship [Navy]
LFSS..........	Launch Facility Security System [NASA] (KSC)
LFST..........	Largest Feasible Steerable Telescope
LFST..........	Lifestyle (ABBR)
LFST..........	Strasbourg/Entzheim [France ICAO location identifier] (ICLI)
LFSTK.........	Leafstalk (ABBR)
LFSU..........	Rolampont [France ICAO location identifier] (ICLI)
LFSV..........	Landing Force Support Vehicle (MCD)

LFSV .... Lifesaver (ABBR)
LFSV .... Pont-Saint-Vincent [*France ICAO location identifier*] (ICLI)
LFSW .... Epernay/Plivot [*France ICAO location identifier*] (ICLI)
LFSW .... Landing Force Support Weapon
LFSX .... Luxeuil/Saint-Sauveur [*France ICAO location identifier*] (ICLI)
LFSY .... Chaumont-La Vendue [*France ICAO location identifier*] (ICLI)
LFSZ .... Lifesize (ABBR)
lf sz .... Life Size (VRA)
LFSZ .... Vittel/Champ De Courses [*France ICAO location identifier*] (ICLI)
LFT .... Aerolift Philippines Corp. [*ICAO designator*] (FAAC)
LFT .... Ladd-Franklin Theory [*Color vision*]
LFT .... Lafayette [*Louisiana*] [*Airport symbol*] (OAG)
LFT .... Lafayette [*Diocesan abbreviation*] [*Indiana*] (TOCD)
LFT .... Lafayette, LA [*Location identifier FAA*] (FAAL)
LFT .... Laminar Flow Torch [*For plasma generation*]
LFT .... LASER Flash Tube
LFT .... Late Finish Time
LFT .... Latest Finish Time
LFT .... Latex Fixation Test [*Medicine*]
LFT .... Latex Flocculation Test [*Clinical chemistry*]
LFT .... Launch Facility Trainer
LFT .... Law Foundation of Tasmania [*Australia*]
LFT .... Leafiest (ABBR)
LFT .... Leaflet (ADA)
LFT .... Leap-Frog Test
LFT .... Left (ABBR)
lft .... Left (VRA)
LFT .... Left Frontotransverse [*A fetal position*] [*Obstetrics*]
LFT .... Left Half Indicators, Off Test (SAA)
LFT .... Lifting (MSA)
LFT .... Ligand-Field Theory [*Physical chemistry*]
LFT .... Light Fire Team [*Military*] (CINC)
LFT .... Linear Flash Tube
LFT .... Linear Foot (ADA)
LFT .... Live Fire Test
LFT .... Liver Function Test [*Medicine*]
LFT .... Long-Fiber Thermoplastic
LFT .... Low-Frequency Tetanus [*Medicine*] (DMAA)
LFT .... Low-Frequency Transduction
L/FT² .... Lumens per Square Foot (WDAA)
LFTA .... Low-Frequency Timing Assembly (IAA)
LFT & E .... Live Fire Test and Evaluation [*Required testing for major weapon system and munition programs*] [*Military*] (RDA)
LFT & E .... Live Fire Test and Evaluation (DOMA)
LFTC .... Landing Force Training Command [*Navy*] (NVT)
LFTC .... Toulon [*France ICAO location identifier*] (ICLI)
LFTCPAC ..... Landing Force Training Command, Pacific [*Navy*] (DNAB)
LFTDWP .... Land Force Tactical Doctrine Working Party [*NASA*] (MCD)
LFTEG .... Liquid-Fuelled Thermo-Electric Generator (PDAA)
LFTF .... Cuers/Pierrefeu [*France ICAO location identifier*] (ICLI)
LFTF .... Liftoff (ABBR)
LFTH .... Hyeres/Le Palyvestre [*France ICAO location identifier*] (ICLI)
LFTHDD .... Lefthanded (ABBR)
LFTHDY .... Lefthandedly (ABBR)
LFTINS .... Loftiness (ABBR)
LFTIR .... Loftier (ABBR)
LFTIT .... Loftiest (ABBR)
LFTM .... Lifetime (ABBR)
LFTN .... La Grand'Combe [*France ICAO location identifier*] (ICLI)
LFTOV .... Leftover (ABBR)
LFtp .... Library Program, Cataloging Department, Recreation Service, Fort Polk, LA [*Library symbol Library of Congress*] (LCLS)
LFTPR .... Long Fiber Thermoplastic Resin
LFTR .... Toulon/Saint-Mandrier [*France ICAO location identifier*] (ICLI)
LFTS .... Toulon [*France ICAO location identifier*] (ICLI)
LFTT .... Leftist (ABBR)
LFTU .... Frejus/Saint-Raphael [*France ICAO location identifier*] (ICLI)
LFTU .... Landing Force Training Unit [*Marine Corps*]
LFTW .... Nimes/Garons [*France ICAO location identifier*] (ICLI)
LFTWF .... Luftwaffe (ABBR)
LFTWG .... Leftwing (ABBR)
LFTWR .... Leftwinger (ABBR)
LFTY .... Lofty (ABBR)
LFU .... Least Frequency Unit (NITA)
LFU .... Least Frequently Used [*Computer science*]
LFU .... Leonhartsberger Flugunternchmen GmbH [*Austria ICAO designator*] (FAAC)
LFU .... LFU Leonhartsberger Flugunternehmen Gesellschaft MbH [*Austria*] [*FAA designator*] (FAAC)
LFU .... Lunar Flying Unit [*NASA*]
LFUS .... Littelfuse, Inc. [*NASDAQ symbol*] (SAG)
LFUSS .... Landing Force Organizational Systems Study
LFUSW .... Littelfuse Inc. Wrrt'A' [*NASDAQ symbol*] (TTSB)
LFV .... Large Field of View [*Radiology*] (DAVI)
LFV .... Lassa-Fever Virus
LFV .... Low-Frequency Vibration
LFV .... Lunar Flying Vehicle [*NASA*]
LFV .... Northhampton, MA [*Location identifier FAA*] (FAAL)
LFVLF .... Low Frequency, Very Low Frequency (IAA)
LFVM .... Miquelon [*France ICAO location identifier*] (ICLI)
LFVO .... Library Foundation for Voluntary Organizations [*Defunct*] (EA)
LFVP .... Saint-Pierre, Saint-Pierre-Et Miquelon [*France ICAO location identifier*] (ICLI)
LFW .... Linear Friction Welding [*Environmental science*]
LFW .... Lome [*Togo*] [*Airport symbol*] (OAG)

LFW .... Looking for Work
LFWB .... Sccom Sud-Ouest [*France ICAO location identifier*] (ICLI)
LFWID .... Length of Leaf at Widest Portion [*Botany*]
LFWK .... Lifework (ABBR)
LFX .... Live Fire Exercise [*Army*] (INF)
LFX .... Live-Fire Exercises [*Army*] (INF)
LFXA .... Amberieu [*France ICAO location identifier*] (ICLI)
LFXB .... Saintes/Thenac [*France ICAO location identifier*] (ICLI)
LFXC .... Contrexeville [*France ICAO location identifier*] (ICLI)
LFXD .... Doullens/Lucheux [*France ICAO location identifier*] (ICLI)
LFXE .... Camp De Mourmelon [*France ICAO location identifier*] (ICLI)
LFXF .... Limoges/Romanet [*France ICAO location identifier*] (ICLI)
LFXG .... Camp De Bitche [*France ICAO location identifier*] (ICLI)
LFXH .... Camp Du Valdahon [*France ICAO location identifier*] (ICLI)
LFXI .... Apt/Saint-Christol [*France ICAO location identifier*] (ICLI)
LFXJ .... Bordeaux [*France ICAO location identifier*] (ICLI)
LFXK .... Camp De Suippes [*France ICAO location identifier*] (ICLI)
LFXL .... Mailly-Le-Camp [*France ICAO location identifier*] (ICLI)
LFXM .... Mourmelon [*France ICAO location identifier*] (ICLI)
LFXN .... Narbonne [*France ICAO location identifier*] (ICLI)
LFXO .... Tours/Cinq-Mars La Pile [*France ICAO location identifier*] (ICLI)
LFXP .... Camp De Sissonne [*France ICAO location identifier*] (ICLI)
LFXQ .... Camp De Coetquidan [*France ICAO location identifier*] (ICLI)
LFXR .... Rochefort/Soubise [*France ICAO location identifier*] (ICLI)
LFXS .... Camp De La Courtine [*France ICAO location identifier*] (ICLI)
LFXT .... Camp De Caylus [*France ICAO location identifier*] (ICLI)
LFXU .... Les Mureaux [*France ICAO location identifier*] (ICLI)
LFXV .... Lyon/Mont-Verdun [*France ICAO location identifier*] (ICLI)
LFXW .... Camp Du Larzac [*France ICAO location identifier*] (ICLI)
LFY .... Leafy (ABBR)
LFYA .... Drachenbronn [*France ICAO location identifier*] (ICLI)
LFYD .... Damblain [*France ICAO location identifier*] (ICLI)
LFYF .... Centre Meteorologique de Concentration et de Diffusion, French Air Force [*France ICAO location identifier*] (ICLI)
LFYG .... Cambrai/Niergnies [*France ICAO location identifier*] (ICLI)
LFYH .... Broye-Les-Pesmes [*France ICAO location identifier*] (ICLI)
LFYL .... Lure/Malbouhans [*France ICAO location identifier*] (ICLI)
LFYM .... Marigny-Le-Grand [*France ICAO location identifier*] (ICLI)
LFYO .... Villacoublay [*France ICAO location identifier*] (ICLI)
LFYR .... Romorantin/Pruniers [*France ICAO location identifier*] (ICLI)
LFYS .... Sainte-Leocadie [*France ICAO location identifier*] (ICLI)
LFYT .... Saint-Simon/Clastres [*France ICAO location identifier*] (ICLI)
LFYX .... Paris [*France ICAO location identifier*] (ICLI)
LFZ .... Laminar Flow Zone
LG .... Guidotti & C. [*Italy*] [*Research code symbol*]
LG .... Laban Guild [*Formerly, LAMG*] (EA)
LG .... Laboratory of Genetics (GNE)
LG .... Laclede Gas [*NYSE symbol*] (TTSB)
LG .... Laclede Gas Co. [*NYSE symbol*] (SPSG)
LG .... Lady [*of the Order of the*] Garter (BARN)
LG .... Lagoon [*Maps and charts*] (ROG)
LG .... Landed Gentry
LG .... Landgericht [*Regional Court*] [*German*] (ILCA)
L/G .... Land Grant (DLA)
LG .... Landing Gear [*Aircraft*]
LG .... Landing Ground [*Navy*]
LG .... Landing Group [*Navy*] (NVT)
LG .... Lane Grader [*Slang for an army instructor*] (VNW)
LG .... Language [*Online database field identifier*]
LG .... Large
LG .... Large Grain
LG .... Laryngectomy [*Medicine*] (MAE)
LG .... LASER Gyro (MCD)
LG .... Lateral Gastrocnemius
LG .... Launcher Group [*Army*]
LG .... Law Glossary (DLA)
LG .... Leathercraft Guild (EA)
LG .... Left Gluteus [*Medicine*]
LG .... Left Guard [*Football*]
LG .... Leg (IAA)
LG .... Leichtgeschuetz [*Light gun for airborne operations*] [*German military - World War II*]
LG .... Length (MSA)
LG .... Level Gauge
LG .... Lewis Gun
LG .... Lieutenant General [*British*] (ROG)
LG .... Life Guards [*Military unit*] [*British*]
LG .... Light Green
LG .... Light Gun
LG .... Linear Gate
LG .... Line Generator [*Computer science*]
LG .... Line Graph (OA)
LG .... Line-to-Ground (IAA)
LG .... Linguogingival [*Dentistry*]
LG .... Lining
LG .... Linkage Group [*Genetics*] (OA)
LG .... Liquid Gas
LG .... [*The*] Literary Guild
LG .... Little Guides [*A publication*]
LG .... Local Government (ADA)
LG .... Loganiar Ltd. [*British*]
LG .... Logistics Group [*Military*]
LG .... Long (KSC)
LG .... Longold Resources, Inc. [*Vancouver Stock Exchange symbol*]
LG .... Longwood Gardens [*Kennett Square, PA*]

LG .... Loop Gain
LG .... Low German [Language, etc.]
LG .... Low Glucose [Medicine]
LG .... Lumen Gentium [Dogmatic Constitution on the Church] [Vatican II document]
LG .... Lymph Glands [Medicine]
LGA .... Elgaz [Poland ICAO designator] (FAAC)
LGA .... LaGuardia Airport [New York] (CDAI)
LGA .... Large for Gestational Age [Pediatrics]
LGA .... LGA: Local Government Administration [A publication]
LGA .... Light-Gun Amplifier
LGA .... Local Government Administration
LGA .... Local Government Area (ADA)
LGA .... Local Government Audit [British]
LgA .... Lodging Allowance [British military] (DMA)
LGA .... Low-Gain Antenna
LGA .... New York [New York] La Guardia [Airport symbol] (OAG)
LGAANSW .... Local Government Auditors' Association of New South Wales [Australia]
LGAB .... Local Government Advisory Board [Tasmania, Australia]
LGAB .... Local Government Auditors' Board [Queensland, Australia]
LGAC .... Athinai [Greece] [ICAO location identifier] (ICLI)
LgacySft ...... Legacy Software, Inc. [Associated Press] (SAG)
LGAD .... Andravida [Greece] [ICAO location identifier] (ICLI)
LGAES .... Lesbian and Gay Associated Engineers and Scientists [Later, NOGLSTP] (EA)
LGAF .... Light Ground-Attack Fighter
LGAG .... Agrinion [Greece] [ICAO location identifier] (ICLI)
LGAG .... Luggage (ABBR)
LGAL .... Alexandroupolis [Greece] [ICAO location identifier] (ICLI)
LGAM .... Amphiali [Greece] [ICAO location identifier] (ICLI)
LGAM .... Lexington Global Asset Managers, Inc. [NASDAQ symbol] (SAG)
LGAM .... Lexington Global Assets Mgrs [NASDAQ symbol] (TTSB)
LGANSW ...... Local Government Association of New South Wales [Australia]
LGANT .... Local Government Association of the Northern Territory [Australia]
LGAR .... Ladies of the Grand Army of the Republic (EA)
LGAS .... Louisville Gas & Electric Co. [NASDAQ symbol] (SAG)
LGAS .... Low-G Accelerometer System [NASA]
LGASA .... Local Government Association of South Australia
LGASP .... Louiseville G&E 5% Pfd [NASDAQ symbol] (TTSB)
LGAT .... Athinai [Greece] [ICAO location identifier] (ICLI)
LGAX .... Alexandria [Greece] [ICAO location identifier] (ICLI)
L Gaz .... Law Gazette [A publication] (DLA)
LGB .... Landry-Guillain-Barre (Syndrome) [Medicine]
LGB .... LASER-Guided Bomb
LGB .... Lateral Geniculate Body
LGB .... Legible (ABBR)
LGB .... Local Government Board
LGB .... Long Beach [California] [Airport symbol] (OAG)
LGB .... Long Beach, CA [Location identifier FAA] (FAAL)
LGBA .... Lesbian and Gay Bands of America (EA)
LGBC .... Local Government Boundaries Commission [New South Wales, Australia]
LGBCE .... Local Government Boundary Commission for England
LGBL .... Nea Anghialos [Greece] [ICAO location identifier] (ICLI)
LGBO .... Local Government Board Office [British]
LGBPM .... Lesbian, Gay, and Bisexual People in Medicine (EA)
LGBR .... Loganberry (ABBR)
LGBRU .... Lugubrious (ABBR)
LGBRUY .... Lugubriously (ABBR)
LGBS .... Landry-Guillain-Barre Syndrome [Medicine] (DMAA)
LGBT .... Legibility (ABBR)
LGBY .... Legibly (ABBR)
LGC .... Laboratory of the Government Chemist [Research center British] (IRC)
LGC .... La Grange, GA [Location identifier FAA] (FAAL)
LGC .... Lakewood Golf Course [California] [Seismograph station code, US Geological Survey] (SEIS)
LGC .... Large Diameter Gravity Corer [Nuclear energy] (NUCP)
LGC .... Large-Probe Gas Chromatograph [NASA]
LGC .... Launch Guidance Computer
LGC .... Laurentian Group Corp. [Toronto Stock Exchange symbol]
LGC .... Leafy Greens Council (EA)
LGC .... Line Group Controller (ACRL)
LGC .... LM [Lunar Module] Guidance Computer [NASA]
LGC .... Local Government Center [Database producer] (EA)
LGC .... Local Government Chronicle [1855] [A publication] (DLA)
LGC .... Local Government Commission [Victoria, Australia]
LGC .... Local Government Council
LGC .... Logic (MSA)
LGC .... Logic
LGC .... Lord Great Chamberlain [British A publication] (DLA)
LGC .... Lorry with Gas Containers [British]
LGC .... Lunar Gas Chromatograph
LGC .... Lunar Geological Camera [NASA] (KSC)
LGCA .... Land-Grant College of Agriculture
LGCA .... Late Great Chevrolet Association (EA)
LGCA .... Local Government Clerks' Association [Australia]
LGCA .... London Gregorian Choral Association
LGCANSW .... Local Government Clerks' Association of New South Wales [Australia]
LGCB .... Local Government Clerks' Board [Queensland, Australia]
LGCC .... Local Government Clerks' Certificate
LGCL .... Licentiate of the Guild of Cleaners and Launderers [British] (DBQ)
LGCL .... Logical (ABBR)

LGCL .... Logical
LGCLT .... Logicality (ABBR)
LGCLY .... Logically (ABBR)
LGCN .... Logician (ABBR)
LGCOMB ..... Large Combatant (DNAB)
LGCP .... Lexical-Graphical Composer Printer [Photocomposition]
LGCPHW ..... Lesbian and Gay Caucus of Public Health Workers (EA)
LGCY .... Legacy (ABBR)
LGCY .... Legacy Software [NASDAQ symbol] (TTSB)
LGCY .... Legacy Software, Inc. [NASDAQ symbol] (SAG)
LGD .... Compagnie Aerienne du Languedoc [France ICAO designator] (FAAC)
LGd .... Dorsal Lateral Geniculate Nucleus [Also, dLGN] [Anatomy]
LGD .... La Grande, OR [Location identifier FAA] (FAAL)
LGD .... Lambda Gamma Delta [Society]
LGD .... Large Group Display (MCD)
LGD .... Leaderless Group Discussion
lgd .... Legend (VRA)
LGD .... Low-Grade Dysplasia [Medicine]
LGDA .... National Lawn and Garden Distributors Association (EA)
LGDHC .... Ligue Guineenne des Droits de l'Homme [Guinea] [Political party] (EY)
LGDM .... LASER-Guided Dispenser Munition (PDAA)
LGDMN .... Legerdemain (ABBR)
LGDR .... Labor of Genetic Disease Research [National Institutes of Health]
LGE .... Landing Ground, Emergency [British military] (DMA)
LGE .... Large (MSA)
LGE .... League (WDAA)
LGE .... LEM [Lunar Excursion Module] Guidance Equipment [NASA] (KSC)
LGE .... LG & E Energy [NYSE symbol] (SPSG)
LGE .... Local Government Engineer
LGE .... Logic Gate Expander [Computer science]
LGE .... Lunar Geological Equipment [NASA]
LGEANSW .... Local Government Electricity Association of New South Wales [Australia]
LGEANSW .... Local Government Engineers' Association of New South Wales [Australia]
LGEC .... Lunar Geological Exploration Camera (PDAA)
LGEEQC .... Local Government Electrical Engineering Qualifications Committee [Australia]
LGEL .... Elefsis [Greece] [ICAO location identifier] (ICLI)
LGEME .... Legion of Greeks from Egypt and the Middle East [Australia An association]
LGEMP .... Local Government Energy Management Program
LGen .... Lieutenant General [Navy British]
LGEQC .... Local Government Engineering Qualifications Committee [Australia]
LGER .... Low German [Language, etc.] (ROG)
LGF .... Yuma/Yuma Proving Ground, AZ [Location identifier FAA] (FAAL)
LGFA .... Lattice Girder Floor Association [British] (DBA)
LGFC .... Lesley Gore Fan Club (EA)
LGFS .... Local Government Financial System (MHDB)
LGFSTF .... Liquified Gaseous Fuels Spill Test Facility [Department of Energy]
LGFSTP .... Liquefied Gaseous Fuels Spill Test Facility (USDC)
LGG .... Legging (ABBR)
LGG .... Liege [Belgium] [Airport symbol] (OAG)
LGG .... Light Gas Gun
LGG .... Light-Gun Pulse Generator
LGGBFC .... Larry Gatlin and the Gatlin Brothers Fan Club (EA)
LGGBIFC ...... Larry Gatlin and the Gatlin Brothers International Fan Club (EA)
LGGC .... Local Government Grants Commission
LGGG .... Athinai [Greece] [ICAO location identifier] (ICLI)
LGGR .... Logger (ABBR)
LGGRHD ...... Loggerhead (ABBR)
LGH .... Lactogenic Hormone [Also, LTH, PR, PRL] [Endocrinology]
LGH .... Lansing General Hospital [Michigan]
LGH .... Laugh (ABBR)
LGH .... Leigh Creek [Australia Airport symbol] (OAG)
LGH .... Length
LGH .... Logarithmic Histogram Scanning [Mass spectrometry]
LGHB .... Laughable (ABBR)
LGHBY .... Laughably (ABBR)
LGHCS .... Lutheran General Health Care System (EA)
LGHD .... Laughed (ABBR)
LGHET .... Larghetto (ABBR)
LGHG .... Laughing (ABBR)
LGHGY .... Laughingly (ABBR)
LGHI .... Khios [Greece] [ICAO location identifier] (ICLI)
LGHL .... Porto Heli [Greece] [ICAO location identifier] (ICLI)
LGHN .... Leghorn (ABBR)
LGHP .... Large Group Health Plan [Department of Health and Human Services] (GFGA)
LGHR .... Laugher (ABBR)
LGHTR .... Laughter (ABBR)
LGHTR .... Lighter
LGI .... Deadman's Cay [Bahamas] [Airport symbol] (OAG)
LGI .... Large Glucagon Immunoreactivity [Immunochemistry]
LGI .... Lateral Giant Interneuron [Neurobiology]
LGI .... Linear Gate and Integrator (MHDB)
LGI .... Locally Generated Income (MCD)
LGI .... Lunar Geology Investigation [NASA]
LGIEE .... Liaison Group for International Educational Exchange (EA)
LGIO .... Ioannina [Greece] [ICAO location identifier] (ICLI)
LGIR .... Iraklion [Greece] [ICAO location identifier] (ICLI)
LGITIT .... Legitimist (ABBR)
LGITIZ .... Legitimize (ABBR)

LGITIZD ...... Legitimized (ABBR)
LGITIZG ...... Legitimizing (ABBR)
LGITMA .... Legitimate (ABBR)
LGITMAD ..... Legitimated (ABBR)
LGITMAG ..... Legitimating (ABBR)
LGITMC .... Legitmacy (ABBR)
LGITMY .... Legitimately (ABBR)
LGIU .... LASER Gyro Interface Unit (NASA)
LGIU .... Local Government Information Unit [British]
LGJ .... Local Government Journal [A publication] (ROG)
LGK .... Langkawi [Malaysia] [Airport symbol] (OAG)
LGk .... Late Greek [or Low Greek] [Language] (BARN)
LGKA .... Kastoria [Greece] [ICAO location identifier] (ICLI)
LGKC .... Kithira [Greece] [ICAO location identifier] (ICLI)
LGKF .... Kefallinia [Greece] [ICAO location identifier] (ICLI)
LGKJ .... Kastelorizo [Greece] [ICAO location identifier] (ICLI)
LGKL .... Kalamata [Greece] [ICAO location identifier] (ICLI)
LGKM .... Kavala/Amigdhaleon [Greece] [ICAO location identifier] (ICLI)
LGKO .... Kos [Greece] [ICAO location identifier] (ICLI)
LGKP .... Karpathos [Greece] [ICAO location identifier] (ICLI)
LGKR .... Kerkira [Greece] [ICAO location identifier] (ICLI)
LGKS .... Kasos [Greece] [ICAO location identifier] (ICLI)
LGKV .... Kavala/Khrisoupolis [Greece] [ICAO location identifier] (ICLI)
LGKZ .... Kozani [Greece] [ICAO location identifier] (ICLI)
LGL .... Labioglossolaryngeal [Dentistry] (DAVI)
LGL .... La Gloria [Colombia] [Airport symbol] (AD)
LGL .... Large Granular Leukocyte [Hematology]
LGL .... Large Granular Lymphocyte [Hematology]
LGL .... Legal (ABBR)
LGL .... Legal
LGL .... Local Government Library [A publication]
LGL .... Local Graphics Library [Cambridge Computer Graphics Ltd.] [Software package] (NCC)
LGL .... Long Lellang [Malaysia] [Airport symbol] (OAG)
LGL .... Lown-Ganong-Levine [Syndrome] [Medicine]
LGL .... Luxair-Societe Luxembourgeoise de Navigation Aerienne SA [Germany ICAO designator] (FAAC)
LGL .... Lynch Corp. [AMEX symbol] (SPSG)
LGLA .... Legislate (ABBR)
LGLAD .... Legislated (ABBR)
LGLAG .... Legislating (ABBR)
LGLAN .... Legislation (ABBR)
LGLAR .... Legislator (ABBR)
LGLAR .... Legislature (ABBR)
LGLAY .... Legislative (ABBR)
LGLC .... Libertarians for Gay and Lesbian Concerns (EA)
LGLE .... Leros [Greece] [ICAO location identifier] (ICLI)
LGLM .... Legalism (ABBR)
LGLR .... Larissa [Greece] [ICAO location identifier] (ICLI)
LGLST .... Legalist (ABBR)
LGLSTC .... Legalistic (ABBR)
LGLSTCY ...... Legalistically (ABBR)
LGLT .... Legality (ABBR)
LGLTC .... Legalistic (ABBR)
LGLY .... Legally (ABBR)
LGLZ .... Legalize (ABBR)
LGLZD .... Legalized (ABBR)
LGLZG .... Legalizing (ABBR)
LGLZN .... Legalization (ABBR)
LGM .... LASER Ground Mapper
LGM .... LASER-Guided Munition
LGM .... Last Glacial Maximum [Climatology]
LGM .... Liberty Godparent Ministry (EA)
LGM .... Little Green Men [British term for space signals]
LGM .... Little Green Mountain [Idaho] [Seismograph station code, US Geological Survey Closed] (SEIS)
LGM .... Local Government Management [A publication]
LGM .... Logistic Guidance Memorandum
LGM .... Logistics Module [Simulation games] [Army] (SSD)
LGM .... Loop Ground Multiplexer (MCD)
LGMA .... Lesbian and Gay Medical Association [Defunct] (EAIO)
LGMB .... Local Government Management Board (AIE)
LGMD .... Limb Girdle Muscular Dystrophy [Medicine]
LGMD .... Lobular Giant Movement Detector (PDAA)
LGMG .... Megara [Greece] [ICAO location identifier] (ICLI)
LGMK .... Mikonos [Greece] [ICAO location identifier] (ICLI)
LGML .... Milos [Greece] [ICAO location identifier] (ICLI)
LGMN .... Ligament (ABBR)
LGMR .... Marathon [Greece] [ICAO location identifier] (ICLI)
LGMS .... LASER Ground Mapping System
LGMT .... Mitilini [Greece] [ICAO location identifier] (ICLI)
LGN .... Lagoon (ADA)
LGN .... Lagunillas [Venezuela] [Seismograph station code, US Geological Survey] (SEIS)
LGN .... Lateral Geniculate Nucleus
LGN .... Left Green Network [An association] (EA)
LGN .... Legion (ABBR)
LGN .... Legion
LGN .... Legion Resources Ltd. [Vancouver Stock Exchange symbol]
LGN .... Line Gate Number [Computer science]
LGN .... Lobular Glomerulonephritis [Medicine] (MAE)
LGN .... Logical Group Number [Computer science] (IBMDP)
LGN .... Logicon, Inc. [NYSE symbol] (SPSG)
LGNAP .... Lagniappe (ABBR)
LGNAR .... Legionaire (ABBR)

LGNBRY .... Loganberry (ABBR)
LGND .... Lateral Geniculate Nucleus Dorsal [Neuroanatomy]
LGND .... Legend (ABBR)
LGND .... Ligand Pharmaceuticals 'B' [NASDAQ symbol] (TTSB)
LGND .... Ligand Pharmaceuticals, Inc. [NASDAQ symbol] (SAG)
LGNDY .... Legendary (ABBR)
LGNMVTE ...... Lignum Vitae [Botany]
LGNS .... Largeness (ABBR)
LGNS .... Leggoons Inc. [NASDAQ symbol] (TTSB)
LGNY .... Legionary (ABBR)
LGO .... Lamont Geological Observatory [Later, L-DGO] [Columbia University]
LGO .... Largo (ABBR)
LGO .... Light Gas Oil [Fuel technology]
LGO .... Local Government Office
LGO .... Logo Resources Ltd. [Vancouver Stock Exchange symbol]
LGO .... Low Gravity Orbit
LGO .... Lunar Geoscience Observer (MCD)
LGOC .... London General Omnibus Co. [British] (DCTA)
LGOFC .... Linda Gray's Official Fan Club (EA)
LGON .... Lagoon (ABBR)
LGOR .... Langor (ABBR)
LGORU .... Langorous (ABBR)
LGORU .... Local Government Operational Research Unit [British] (DI)
LGORUY .... Langorously (ABBR)
LGP .... Labioglossopharyngeal [Dentistry] (DAVI)
LGP .... Laboratory Graduate Participation [Oak Ridge National Laboratory]
LGP .... LASER-Guided Projectile (MCD)
LGP .... Legaspi [Philippines] [Seismograph station code, US Geological Survey] (SEIS)
LGP .... Legaspi [Philippines] [Airport symbol] (OAG)
LGP .... Low Ground Pressure
LGP .... Lummer-Gehreke Plate [Physics]
LGPA .... Paros [Greece] [ICAO location identifier] (ICLI)
LGPANSW ..... Livestock and Grain Producers' Association of New South Wales [Australia]
LGPIM .... Lesbian and Gay People in Medicine [Later, LGBPM] (EA)
LGPN .... International Leather Goods, Plastic, and Novelty Workers' Union (EA)
LGPZ .... Preveza [Greece] [ICAO location identifier] (ICLI)
LGQ .... Lago Agrio [Ecuador] [Airport symbol] (OAG)
LGQB .... Local Government Qualifications Board [Victoria, Australia]
LGR .... Knight's Local Government Reports [A publication] (DLA)
LGR .... Lager (ABBR)
LGR .... Laird Group, Inc. [Toronto Stock Exchange symbol]
LGR .... Larger (WGA)
LGR .... Leasehold Ground Rent (ROG)
LGR .... Lethal Ground Range (MCD)
LGR .... Letter of General Representation (PDAA)
LGR .... Light-Water-Cooled, Graphite-Moderated Reactor (NRCH)
LGR .... Local Government Reorganization [British]
LGR .... Local Government Reports [England] [A publication] (DLA)
LGR .... Localized Gain Region (PDAA)
LGR .... Logrono [Spain] [Seismograph station code, US Geological Survey] (SEIS)
LGR .... London Grand Rank [Freemasonry]
LGR .... Longer (WGA)
LGR .... Loop Gap Resonator [Spectrometry]
LGR .... Low Greek [Language, etc.]
LGR .... Low Group Receiving Unit
LGra .... Grambling State University, Grambling, LA [Library symbol Library of Congress] (LCLS)
LGRD .... Laggard (ABBR)
LGRD .... Rodos/Maritsa [Greece] [ICAO location identifier] (ICLI)
LGR (Eng) .... Local Government Reports [England] [A publication] (DLA)
LGRF .... Loan Guaranty Revolving Fund
LGrJ .... Jefferson Parish Public Library, Gretna, LA [Library symbol Library of Congress] (LCLS)
LGRMG .... Lesbian/Gay Rights Monitoring Group (EA)
LGRP .... Rodos/Paradisi [Greece] [ICAO location identifier] (ICLI)
LGRX .... Araxos [Greece] [ICAO location identifier] (ICLI)
LGS .... Grambling State University, Grambling, LA [OCLC symbol] (OCLC)
LGS .... Lagoons [Maps and charts] (ROG)
LGS .... Landing Guidance System [Aerospace]
LGS .... Large Gray Ship [Slang Navy]
LGS .... Large Green Soft [Stool] [Gastroenterology] (DAVI)
LGS .... LASER Guidance System (MCD)
LGS .... Late Glacial Stage [Paleontology]
LGS .... Lega dei Giovani Somali [Somali Youth League]
LGS .... Limerick Generation Station [Nuclear energy] (NRCH)
LGS .... Liquid Asset and Government Securities (ADA)
LGS .... Lithogenic Grain Size [An indicator of wind intensity]
LGS .... Litton Graphics Standard (MCD)
LGS .... Lower Group Stop (NRCH)
LGS .... Lunar Geophysical Surface
LGS .... Lunar Gravity Simulator [Aerospace]
LGSA .... Khania/Souda [Greece] [ICAO location identifier] (ICLI)
LGSB .... Local Government Services Bureau [South Australia]
LGSB .... Local Government Superannuation Board [Queensland, Australia]
LGSC .... Large Scale (ABBR)
LGSD .... Sedes [Greece] [ICAO location identifier] (ICLI)
L/GSE .... Launch and Ground Support Equipment
LGSK .... Skiathos [Greece] [ICAO location identifier] (ICLI)
LGSL .... Lugsail (ABBR)
LGSM .... Licentiate of Guildhall School of Music [British]
LGSM .... Light Ground Station Module

LGSM.......... Samos [Greece] [ICAO location identifier] (ICLI)
LGSP.......... Sparti [Greece] [ICAO location identifier] (ICLI)
LGSR.......... Santorini [Greece] [ICAO location identifier] (ICLI)
LGsSH .... Greenwell Springs State Hospital, Greenwell Springs, LA [Library symbol Library of Congress] (LCLS)
LGST.......... Sitia [Greece] [ICAO location identifier] (ICLI)
LGSTC......... Logistic (ABBR)
LGSTCL........ Logistical (ABBR)
LGSTCN........ Logistician (ABBR)
LGSV.......... Stefanovikion [Greece] [ICAO location identifier] (ICLI)
LGSY.......... Skyros [Greece] [ICAO location identifier] (ICLI)
LGT.......... Langat Encephalitis [Medicine]
LGT.......... Largest (ABBR)
LGT.......... Late Generalized Tuberculosis [Medicine]
LGT.......... Legate (ABBR)
LGT.......... Liechtenstein Global Trust
LGT.......... Light
LGT.......... Light
LGT.......... Liquid Gas Tank
LGT.......... Local Geomagnetic Time
LGT.......... Logistec Corp. [Toronto Stock Exchange symbol]
LGT.......... Low Gelling Temperature [Analytical biochemistry]
LGT.......... Low Group Transmitting Unit
LGTA.......... Ligue Generale des Travailleurs Angolais [General League of Angolan Workers in Exile]
LGTB.......... Local Government Training Board [British]
LGTD.......... Lighted
LGTE.......... Legatee (ABBR)
LGTFGR .... Lightfingered (ABBR)
LGTFTD....... Lightfooted (ABBR)
LGTFTY....... Lightfootedly (ABBR)
LGTG.......... Lighting (ABBR)
LGTG.......... Tanagra [Greece] [ICAO location identifier] (ICLI)
LGTH.......... Length (AFM)
lgth.......... Length (VRA)
LGTH .... Lexington Group in Transportation History (EA)
LGTH .... Lightning Hole [Electronics]
LGTHCOLM... Length of Column [Military] (GFGA)
LGTHD......... Lightheaded (ABBR)
LGTHDY....... Lightheadedly (ABBR)
LGTHIY .... Lengthily (ABBR)
LGTHN........ Lengthen (ABBR)
LGTHND....... Lengthened (ABBR)
LGTHNG...... Lengthening (ABBR)
LGTHNS...... Lengthiness (ABBR)
LGTHR .... Lengthier (ABBR)
LGTHRTD..... Lighthearted (ABBR)
LGTHRTNS... Lightheartedness (ABBR)
LGTHRTY..... Lightheartedly (ABBR)
LGTHS........ Lighthouse (ABBR)
LGTHT .... Lengthiest (ABBR)
LGTHWS..... Lengthwise (ABBR)
LGTHY .... Lengthy (ABBR)
LGTI.......... Lower Genital Tract Infection [Medicine] (DMAA)
LGTIC.......... Logistic (ABBR)
LGTICL......... Logistical (ABBR)
LGTL.......... Kasteli [Greece] [ICAO location identifier] (ICLI)
LGTMDD...... Lightminded (ABBR)
LGTMDY ..... Lightmindedly (ABBR)
LGTN.......... Legation (ABBR)
LGTN.......... Lighten (ABBR)
LG TN.......... Long Ton [2240 pounds] (WDAA)
LGTNG......... Lightning (ABBR)
LGTO .... Legato (ABBR)
LGTO .... Legato Systems [NASDAQ symbol] (TTSB)
LGTO .... Legato Systems, Inc. [NASDAQ symbol] (SAG)
LGTP.......... Tripolis [Greece] [ICAO location identifier] (ICLI)
LGTPB......... Local Government Town Planners' Board [Queensland, Australia]
LG TPR....... Long Taper (WDAA)
LGTR.......... Ligature (ABBR)
LGTR.......... Lightener (ABBR)
LGTRD .... Ligatured (ABBR)
LGTRG......... Ligaturing (ABBR)
LGTS.......... Lights
LGTS.......... Lights [Postal Service standard] (OPSA)
LGTS.......... Thessaloniki [Greece] [ICAO location identifier] (ICLI)
LGTT.......... Dekeleia/Tatoi [Greece] [ICAO location identifier] (ICLI)
LGTUD .... Longitude (ABBR)
LGTUDL....... Longitudinal (ABBR)
LGTUDY...... Longitudinally (ABBR)
LGTWT........ Lightweight (ABBR)
LGTY.......... Lightly (ABBR)
LGTYR .... Lightyear (ABBR)
LGU .... Ladies Golf Union
LGU .... Land-Grant University
LGU .... League (ABBR)
LGU .... Legume (ABBR)
LGU .... Local Glucose Utilization [Physiology]
LGU .... Logan [Utah] [Airport symbol] (OAG)
LGU .... Logan, UT [Location identifier FAA] (FAAL)
L Guard .... Law Guardian [A publication] (DLA)
LGUD .... Leagued (ABBR)
LGUG .... Leaguing (ABBR)
LGUNU......... Leguminous (ABBR)
LGV .... Large Granular Vesicle (OA)

LGV.............. Lymphogranuloma Venereum [Medicine]
LGVC.............. Local Government Valuers' Committee [New South Wales, Australia]
LGVD .... Large Group View Display (MCD)
LGVHD......... Lethal Graft-Versus-Host Disease [Medicine] (DMAA)
LGVO .... Volos [Greece] [ICAO location identifier] (ICLI)
LGW.............. Landing Gear Warning
LGW.............. Laser-Guided Weapon (DOMA)
LGW.............. London-Gatwick [England] [Airport symbol] (OAG)
LGW.............. Love Games Won [Tennis]
LGW.............. Lufttarhtgesellschaft Walter GmbH [Germany ICAO designator] (FAAC)
LGWCM......... LASER-Guided Weapons Counter-Measure (PDAA)
LGWF.............. Libyan General Workers' Federation
LGWS.............. LASER-Guided Weapons Systems (IEEE)
LGWV .... Long Wave (FAAC)
LGWX.............. Logic Works [NASDAQ symbol] (TTSB)
LGWX.............. Logic Works, Inc. [NASDAQ symbol] (SAG)
LGX.............. Lovington, NM [Location identifier FAA] (FAAL)
LGY.............. Lagunillas [Venezuela] [Airport symbol] (AD)
LGY.............. Largely (ABBR)
LGY.............. Leggy (ABBR)
LGZA.............. Zakinthos [Greece] [ICAO location identifier] (ICLI)
LH.............. Deutsche Lufthansa AG [Germany] [ICAO designator] (OAG)
LH.............. Laboratory Corp. Amer Hldgs Wrrt [NYSE symbol] (TTSB)
LH.............. Laboratory Corp. of America Holdings [NYSE symbol] (SAG)
LH.............. Labor Historians [Defunct] (EA)
LH.............. Labor Hour [In contract work]
LH.............. Laetolil Hominid
LH.............. Lamphole (ABBR)
LH.............. Langmuir-Hinshelwood Mechanism [Chemistry]
LH.............. Large Heavy Seeds [Botany]
LH.............. Larval Heart
LH.............. Las Hermanas [Later, LH-USA] (EA)
LH.............. Last Half [of month] [Business term] (DS)
LH.............. Last Harvest [An association] (EA)
LH.............. Last Hope [Facetious name for Chrysler's 1993 sedans]
LH.............. Late Helladic (BJA)
LH.............. Latent Heat (IAA)
LH.............. Lateral Hypothalamic [or Hypothalamus]
LH.............. Learning Handicapped
L/H.............. Leasehold [Legal term] (DLA)
LH.............. Left Half (WDAA)
LH.............. Left Halfback [Soccer]
LH.............. Left Hand
LH.............. Left Hyperphoria [Ophthalmology]
LH.............. Legal Holiday (MHDW)
LH.............. Legion d'Honneur [French decoration]
LH.............. Lewisite-Mustard Gas Mix [for land mines] [Army symbol]
LH.............. L. Hungerford [Record label] [Great Britain]
lh.............. Liechtenstein [MARC country of publication code Library of Congress] (LCCP)
LH.............. Lighthawk [An association] (EA)
LH.............. Light Helicopter [Military] (RDA)
LH.............. Light Horse [Cavalry]
LH.............. Lighthouse [Maps and charts]
LH.............. Lightly Hinged [Philately]
LH.............. Limited Hold
LH.............. Linear Hybrid
LH.............. Link Header (ACRL)
LH.............. Link House Books [Publisher] [British]
LH.............. Lipid Hydrocarbon [Biochemistry]
LH.............. Liquid Helium (IAA)
LH.............. Liquid Hydrogen
LH.............. Litter Hook
LH.............. Load-High [Computer science] (PCM)
LH.............. Local Horizontal
LH.............. Locating Head [Engineering] (OA)
LH.............. Loch's Horse [British military] (DMA)
LH.............. Lower Half
LH.............. Lower Hemispherical (MCD)
LH.............. Lower Hold [Shipping]
LH.............. Low Head [Nuclear energy] (NRCH)
L/H.............. Low-to-High (MDG)
LH.............. Lues Hereditaria [Medicine]
LH.............. Lufthansa (ABBR)
LH.............. Lufthansa German Airlines [ICAO designator] (AD)
LH.............. Luteinizing-Hormone [Also, ICSH, LSH] [Endocrinology]
LH$_2$.............. Liquid Hydrogen [NASA]
LHA.............. Amphibious Assault Carrier [or Ship] (Landing Helicopter Assault Ship) [Navy symbol]
LHA.............. Ladies' Hermitage Association (EA)
LHA.............. Landing Helicopter Assault
LHA.............. Lanham Housing Act (DLA)
LHA.............. Lateral Hypothalamic Area
LHA.............. Lay Helpers' Association [British]
LHA.............. Left Heart Assistance [Cardiology]
LHA.............. Left Hepatic Artery [Medicine] (DMAA)
LHA.............. Leisure & Hotel Appointments [Recruitment for the hotel, leisure, and travel industries] [British]
LHA.............. Lhasa [Tibet] [Seismograph station code, US Geological Survey Closed] (SEIS)
LHA.............. Libertarian Humanist Association (EA)
LHA.............. Licentiate of the Institute of Health Service Administrators [British] (DBQ)
LHA.............. Light Helicopter, Attack [Computer test vehicle]

LHA	Lincoln Highway Association [*Motoring history organization*]
LHA	Livestock Husbandry Adviser [*Ministry of Agriculture, Fisheries, and Food*] [*British*]
LHA	Local Health Authority [*British*]
LHA	Local Hour Angle [*Navigation*]
LHA	Local Housing Authority
LHA	Lord High Admiral [*British*]
LHA	Lower-Half Assembly
LHA	Lower Hour Angle [*Navigation*]
LHA	Lutheran Hospital Association of America (EA)
LHA	McNeese State University, Lake Charles, LA [*OCLC symbol*] (OCLC)
LHAA	Budapest [*Hungary*] [*ICAO location identifier*] (ICLI)
LHAAP	Longhorn Army Ammunition Plant (AABC)
L/Hadr	Lance Havidar [*Military British*]
LHAL	Lethal (ABBR)
LHAMS	Local Hour Angle of Mean Sun
LHAR	London, Havre, Antwerp, Rouen [*Shipping route*] (ROG)
LHAR	London, Hull, Antwerp, or Rotterdam [*Shipping route*]
LHAR	Lothario (ABBR)
LHarC	Catahoula Parish Library, Harrisonburg, LA [*Library symbol Library of Congress*] (LCLS)
LHAS	Luteinizing Hormone Antiserum [*Endocrinology*]
LHaSC	Saint Charles Parish Library, Hahnville, LA [*Library symbol Library of Congress*] (LCLS)
LHAT	League of Historic American Theatres (EA)
LHATS	Local Hour Angle of True Sun
LHAW	Liquid High Activity Waste [*Nuclear energy*] (NUCP)
LHB	Bachelor of Humane Letters [*or Bachelor of Literature or Bachelor of the More Humane Letters*]
LHB	Laboratory Hazards Bulletin [*Royal Society of Chemistry*] [*Information service or system*] (IID)
LHB	Late Heavy Bombardment [*Planetary history*]
LHb	Lateral Habenular (Nucleus) [*Neuroanatomy*]
LHB	Left Halfback [*Soccer*]
LHB	Lost Heartbeat [*An attractive girl*] [*Slang*]
LHBANA	Log House Builder's Association of North America (EA)
LHBMA	Let's Have Better Mottoes Association [*A mythical association*] (EA)
LHBP	Budapest/Ferihegy [*Hungary*] [*ICAO location identifier*] (ICLI)
LHC	Arlington, TN [*Location identifier FAA*] (FAAL)
LHC	Heavy Salvage Ship [*Navy symbol*] (VNW)
LHC	Lakehead University [*Thunder Bay*] [*Ontario*] [*Seismograph station code, US Geological Survey*] (SEIS)
LHC	Large Hadron Collider [*Nuclear physics*] (ECON)
LHC	Left-Hand Chain (MHDI)
LHC	Left-Hand Circular [*Polarization*] (IEEE)
LHC	Left Hypochondrium [*Medicine*]
LHC	Light Harvesting Complex
LHC	Light Hydrocarbon [*Organic chemistry*]
LHC	Lignin-Hemicellulose-Cellulose [*A complex found in plants*]
LHC	Lined Hollow Charge
LHC	Liquid Hydrogen Container
LHC	LNH Real Estate Investment Trust (SPSG)
LHC	LNH REIT, Inc. [*NYSE symbol*] (SAG)
LHC	Local Health Councils [*Scotland*] (DAVI)
LHC	Log Homes Council (EA)
LHC	Lord High Chancellor [*British*]
LHC	Loretto Heights College [*Denver, CO*]
LHC	Louis, Holland, Callaway [*Advertising agency*]
LHC	Lovers of the Holy Cross Sisters (TOCD)
LHC	Lutheran Historical Conference (EA)
LHCA	Longshoremen's and Harbor Workers' Compensation Act (DLA)
LHCC	Budapest [*Hungary*] [*ICAO location identifier*] (ICLI)
LHCIMA	Licentiate of the Hotel, Catering, and Institutional Management Association [*British*] (DBQ)
LHCP	Left-Hand Circularly Polarized [*LASER waves*]
LHCTL	Left-Hand Control (IAA)
LHD	Anchorage, AK [*Location identifier FAA*] (FAAL)
LHD	Doctor of Humane Letters (DD)
LHD	Doctor of Literature (DD)
LHD	Doctor of the Humanities (DD)
LHD	Lakehead University Library [*UTLAS symbol*]
LHD	Lateral Head Displacement [*Sperm*] [*Medicine*] (DMAA)
LHD	Left-Hand Drive [*AEC*]
LHD	Licentiate in Health, Dublin (ROG)
LHD	Litterarum Humaniorum Doctor [*Doctor of Humane Letters*] [*Latin*]
LHD	Load, Haul, Dump [*Mining*]
LHD	Multipurpose Amphibious Assault Ship
LHDA	Lesotho Highlands Development Authority (ECON)
LHDC	Debrecen [*Hungary ICAO location identifier*] (ICLI)
LHDC	Lateral Homing Depth Charge
LHDDE	Light Heavy-Duty Diesel Engine [*Motor vehicle specifications*]
LHDR	Left-Hand Drive [*AEC*]
LHDS	LASER Hole Drilling System
LHE	Lagrange-Helmholtz Equation
LHE	Lahore [*Pakistan*] [*Airport symbol*] (OAG)
LHE	Liquid Helium
LHEA	Laboratory for High Energy Astrophysics [*Greenbelt, MD*] [*NASA*] (GRD)
L HEB	Late Hebrew (WDAA)
LHEB	Left-Hand Equipment Bay [*NASA*] (KSC)
LHEF	Lesbian Herstory Educational Foundation (EA)
LHEG	Local Healthcare Executive Group (HCT)
LHeT	Liquid Helium Temperature (PDAA)
LHF	Labor Heritage Foundation (EA)
LHF	Lamp Heat Flux

LHF	Left Heart Failure [*Medicine*]
LHF	Lighthouse, Fixed [*Maps and charts*] (ROG)
LHF	List Handling Facility
LHFA	Lung Hageman Factor Activator [*Medicine*] (DMAA)
LHFC	Laura Hendler Fan Club (EA)
LHFCS	Long Haul Fuel Conservation System
LHFEB	Left-Hand Forward Equipment Bay [*NASA*] (KSC)
LHFI	Lighthouse, Floating [*Maps and charts*] (ROG)
LHFS	Ligand Hyperfine Structure
LHFT	Light Helicopter Fireteam [*Navy*] (NVT)
LHG	Left Hand Grip (DMAA)
LHG	Licentiate of the Institute of Heraldic and Genealogical Studies [*British*] (DBQ)
LHG	Local Hemolysis in Gel (PDAA)
LHGR	Linear Heat Generation Rate [*Nuclear energy*] (NRCH)
LHH	League of Home Help [*Australia An association*]
LHH	Left-Hand Head
LHH	Lower Hybrid Resonance Heating (MCD)
LHHS	Lutheran Hospitals and Homes Society of America (EA)
LHHW	Langmuir-Hinshelwood-Hougen-Watson Rate Equation [*Chemical kinetics*]
LHI	Fort Lauderdale, FL [*Location identifier FAA*] (FAAL)
LHI	Lefthanders International (EA)
LHI	Leigh Instruments Ltd. [*Toronto Stock Exchange symbol*]
LHI	Lighthouse, Intermittent [*Maps and charts*] (ROG)
LHI	Lipid Hydrocarbon Inclusions [*Biochemistry*] (DAVI)
LHi	Louisiana Historical Society, New Orleans, LA [*Library symbol Library of Congress*] (LCLS)
LHID	Logical Hardware Interface Description [*Computer science*]
LHL	Left Hemisphere Lesion [*Neurology*] (DAVI)
LHL	Left Hepatic Lobe [*Anatomy*]
LHL	Line and Half Line [*Illustration*] (DGA)
LHLW	Liquid High Level Waste [*Nuclear energy*] (NUCP)
LHM	Lake Helena [*Montana*] [*Seismograph station code, US Geological Survey Closed*] (SEIS)
LHM	Left-Hand Circularly Polarized Mode (IAA)
LHM	Licensed Hotel Motel
LHM	Lisuride Hydrogen Maleate [*Pharmacology*]
LHM	Loop Handling Machine [*Nuclear energy*] (NRCH)
LHM	Master of Humane Letters [*or Master of the More Humane Letters*]
LHMC	London Hospital Medical College [*British*] (DI)
LHME	LASER HELLFIRE Missile Evaluation (MCD)
LHMEL	LASER-Hardened Materials Evaluation Laboratory
LHMM	Laymen's Home Missionary Movement (EA)
LHMP	Life Health Monitoring Program (BABM)
LHMU	Ladies' Home Mission Union [*British*] (BI)
LHN	Express One International, Inc. [*ICAO designator*] (FAAC)
LHN	Lillehammer [*Norway*] [*Seismograph station code, US Geological Survey*] (SEIS)
LHN	Localized Hypertrophic Neuropathy [*Medicine*]
LHN	Long-Haul Network (RDA)
LHNCBC	Lister Hill National Center for Biomedical Communications [*National Library of Medicine*] [*Information service or system*] (IID)
LHO	Local Head Office [*British*] (DCTA)
LHOB	Longworth House Office Building
LHoC	Clairborne Parish Library, Homer, LA [*Library symbol Library of Congress*] (LCLS)
LHOLD	Leasehold (ROG)
LHON	Leber's Hereditary Optic Neuropathy [*Ophthalmology*]
LHO ratio	Library Holdings Ratio per Inhabitant
LHOTS	Long-Haul Optical Transmission Set [*Telecommunications*] (EECA)
LHouT	Terrebonne Parish Library, Houma, LA [*Library symbol Library of Congress*] (LCLS)
LHOX	Low- and High-Pressure Oxygen
LHP	Lakehead Pipe Line Partners Ltd. [*NYSE symbol*] (SPSG)
LHP	Lakehead Pipe Line Ptrs L.P. [*NYSE symbol*] (TTSB)
LHP	Lamp of Hope Project [*An association*] (EA)
LHP	Larval Hemolymph Protein [*Entomology*]
LHP	Late Hyperpolarizing Potential [*Neurophysiology*]
LHP	Launcher Handling Procedure
LHP	Left Half Plane (IAA)
LHP	Left-Handed Pitcher [*Baseball*]
LHP	Left-Hand Page (DGA)
lhp	Left-Hand Page (WDMC)
LHP	Left-Hand Panel
LHP	Left Hemiparesis [*Medicine*] (MEDA)
LHP	Lehu [*Papua New Guinea*] [*Airport symbol*] (OAG)
LHPC	Light-Harvesting Chlorophyll Protein Complex [*Botany*]
LHPG	LASER-Heated Pedestal Growth [*Crystal growing technology*]
LHPS	Lead Hydrogen Purge System [*Nuclear energy*] (IEEE)
LHQ	Allied Land Headquarters [*World War II*]
LHQ	Lancaster, OH [*Location identifier FAA*] (FAAL)
LHQ	Life History Questionnaire [*Psychology*] (DAVI)
LHR	Left-Hand Rule
LHR	[*The*] Lehigh & Hudson River Railway Co. [*Absorbed into Consolidated Rail Corp.*] [*AAR code*]
LHR	Leukocyte Histamine Release [*Test*]
LHR	Lighthouse, Revolving [*Maps and charts*] (ROG)
LHR	Liquid-Holding Recovery [*of bacterial cells*]
LHR	London-Heathrow [*England*] [*Airport symbol*] (OAG)
LHR	Long-Term Heart Rate (PDAA)
LHR	Lower Hybrid Resonance
LHR	Low-Heat-Rejection Engine [*Mechanical engineering*] (RDA)
LHR	Low heat Release [*Adiabatic engines*] [*Automotive engineering*]
LHR	Lumen Hour (ADA)

LHRAA.........	Lutheran Human Relations Association of America (EA)
LHRBI.........	Luteinizing Hormone Receptor Binding Inhibitor [Endocrinology]
LHRE.........	Low Heat Rejection Engine [Mechanical engineering]
LH-RF.........	Luteinizing-Hormone Releasing Factor [Also, GnRF, GnRH, LH-RH, LH-RH/FSH-RH, LRF, LRH] [Endocrinology]
LHRH.........	Left Hand, Right Hand (IAA)
LH-RH.........	Luteinizing-Hormone Releasing Hormone [Also, GnRF, GnRH, LH-RF, LH-RH/FSH-RH, LRF, LRH] [Endocrinology]
LH-RH/FSH-RH...	Luteinizing-Hormone Releasing Hormone/Follicle-Stimulating Hormone Releasing Hormone [Also, GnRF, GnRH, LH-RF, LH-RH, LRF, LRH] [Endocrinology]
LHRS.........	Life History Recorder Set [or System] (MCD)
LHRT.........	Library History Round Table [American Library Association]
LHS.........	Lake Hughes, CA [Location identifier FAA] (FAAL)
LHS.........	Layered Half Space
LHS.........	Left-Hand Side
LHS.........	Left Heart Strain [Medicine]
LHS.........	Liberty Hill [South Carolina] [Seismograph station code, US Geological Survey] (SEIS)
LHS.........	Library History Seminar
LHS.........	Lightweight Hydraulic System [Navy aviation]
LHS.........	Loop Handling System [Nuclear energy] (NRCH)
LHS.........	Lunar Horizon Sensor [Aerospace]
LHS.........	Southeastern Louisiana University, Hammond, LA [Library symbol Library of Congress] (LCLS)
LHSC.........	Left-Hand Side Console [NASA] (KSC)
LHSC.........	Liquid Hydrogen System Complex [NASA] (KSC)
LHSC.........	Luther Hospital Sentence Completions [Nursing school test]
LHSI.........	Low-Head Safety Injection [Nuclear energy] (NRCH)
LHSLG.........	Lincoln Health Sciences Library Group [Library network]
LHSP.........	Lernout & Hauspie Speech Products [NASDAQ symbol] (SAG)
LHSPF.........	Lernout & Hauspie Speech Pds [NASDAQ symbol] (TTSB)
LHSSC.........	Left-Hand Side Storage Container [NASA] (KSC)
LHSV.........	Liquid Hourly Space Velocity [Fluid dynamics]
LHT.........	Left Hypertropia [Ophthalmology]
LHT.........	Library Hi Tech [Pierian Press, Inc.] [Information service or system A publication] (IID)
LHT.........	Light (ABBR)
LHT.........	Lighthouse Tender
LHT.........	Line and Halftone [Illustration] (DGA)
LHT.........	Line-Haul Tractor (DOMA)
LHT.........	Lord High Treasurer [British]
LHT.........	Lunar Hand Tool [NASA]
LHTD.........	Lighted (ABBR)
LHTEC.........	Light Helicopter Turbine Engine Co. [US Army contractor]
LHTEN.........	Lighten (ABBR)
LHTEND.........	Lightened (ABBR)
LHTENG.........	Lightening (ABBR)
LHTF.........	Lincoln Heritage Trail Foundation (EA)
LHTG.........	Lighting (ABBR)
LHTH.........	Left-Hand Thread
L-HTL.........	L-Histidinol [Biochemistry]
LHTN.........	Library Hi Tech News [A publication]
LHTNG.........	Lightning (ABBR)
LHTR.........	Lighter (ABBR)
LHTR.........	Lighthouse Transmitter Receiver (IAA)
LHTST.........	Lightest (ABBR)
LHTY.........	Lightly (ABBR)
LHU.........	Lake Havasu City [Arizona] [Airport symbol] (OAG)
LH-USA.........	Las Hermanas-United States of America (EA)
LHUSA.........	Likud-Herut USA (EA)
LHV.........	Light Horse Volunteers [British military] (DMA)
LHV.........	Liquid Hydrogen Vessel
LHV.........	Lock Haven [Pennsylvania] [Airport symbol] (AD)
LHV.........	Lock Haven, PA [Location identifier FAA] (FAAL)
LHV.........	Low Heat [or Heating] Value (MCD)
LHV.........	Luchtvaart Historische Vereniging [Society of Aeronautical Historians] [Netherlands Defunct] (EAIO)
LHW.........	Hinesville, GA [Location identifier FAA] (FAAL)
LHW.........	Lanzhou [China] [Airport symbol] (OAG)
LHW.........	Lees-Hromas-Webb [Theory]
LHW.........	Left Half Word
LHW.........	Left Hand World [British] [An association] (DBA)
LHW.........	Lehman Brothers, Inc. [AMEX symbol] (SAG)
LHW.........	Lower High-Water [Tides and currents]
LHWCA.........	Longshore and Harbor Workers' Compensation Act (AAGC)
LHWI.........	Lower High-Water Interval [Tides and currents]
LHWP.........	Lesotho Highlands Water Project (ECON)
LH.WS.........	Laboratoy Corp. Amer Hldgs Wrrt [NYSE symbol] (TTSB)
LHX.........	La Junta [Colorado] [Airport symbol] (AD)
LHX.........	La Junta, CO [Location identifier FAA] (FAAL)
LHX.........	Light Helicopter, Experimental [Army] (RDA)
LHX.........	Light Helicopters [Army] (RDA)
LHX.........	Lochiel Exploration Ltd. [Toronto Stock Exchange symbol]
LHY.........	Lancashire Hussars Yeomanry [British military] (DMA)
LHY.........	Lohame Herut Yisrael (BJA)
L Hy.........	Registered Hypnotist
LHY.........	Wilkes-Barre, PA [Location identifier FAA] (FAAL)
LI.........	Labeling Index [Measurement of cell labeling]
L/I.........	Labindustries [Commercial firm]
LI.........	Labor Intensive (MHDW)
LI.........	Land Institute [An association] (EA)
LI.........	Landscape Institute [British]
LI.........	Late Iron [Age] (BJA)
LI.........	Launch Instructions (SAA)
LI.........	Lawn Institute (EA)
LI.........	(Laws of) Lipit-Ishtar (BJA)
LI.........	Leadership Institute (EA)
LI.........	Leakage of Information [British World War II]
LI.........	Learned Information [Database originator and marketer] (NITA)
LI.........	Leeward Islands (BARN)
LI.........	Left in Place [Telecommunications] (TEL)
LI.........	Legal Intelligencer [A publication] (DLA)
LI.........	Legislative Instrument [Ghana] [1960-] [A publication] (ILCA)
LI.........	Leitender Ingenieur [Chief Engineer] [German military - World War II]
LI.........	Length Indicator [Computer science] (TNIG)
L/I.........	Letter of Indemnity (DS)
LI.........	Letter of Intent
L/I.........	Letter of Intent (DFIT)
LI.........	Letter of Introduction (ADA)
LI.........	Level Indicator
LI.........	Liability [Insurance]
LI.........	Liberal International [World Liberal Union] [British] (EAIO)
LI.........	Liberia (ABBR)
LI.........	Libertarian International (EA)
LI.........	License Inquiry [Police]
LI.........	Licentiate of Instruction [or Licentiate Instructor]
LI.........	Liechtenstein [ANSI two-letter standard code] (CNC)
LI.........	Lifegain Institute (EA)
LI.........	Lifting Index [Ergonometrics]
LI.........	Liga International (EA)
LI.........	Light Infantry
LI.........	Lightly Included [Colored gemstone grade]
LI.........	Ligue Internationale de la Representation Commerciale [International League of Commercial Travelers and Agents - ILCTA] (EAIO)
LI.........	Lilac (ROG)
LI.........	Lilly Industries 'A' [NYSE symbol] (TTSB)
LI.........	Lilly Industries, Inc. [NYSE symbol] (SAG)
LI.........	Lincoln's Inn [London] [One of the Inns of Court]
LI.........	Linear Interpolator (IAA)
LI.........	Line Item (AABC)
li.........	Lines per Vertical Inch (WDMC)
LI.........	Linguoincisal [Dentistry]
LI.........	Link
LI.........	Lions International [Later, LCI] (EA)
LI.........	Liquid Ionization [Spectrometric instrumentation]
LI.........	Litchfield Institute (EA)
LI.........	Liter [Metric measure of volume] (MCD)
Li.........	Lithium [Chemical element]
LI.........	Lithograph [or Lithography] (WDAA)
LI.........	Lithographer [Navy rating]
LI.........	Load Index [Tires] [Automotive engineering]
LI.........	Local Interneuron [Neuroanatomy]
LI.........	Location Identifier (IAA)
LI.........	Logistic Index (CAAL)
LI.........	Logistics Instructions [Military]
LI.........	Loglan Institute (EA)
LI.........	Loitering with Intent [British] (DSUE)
LI.........	London International [Record label] [Great Britain, USA, etc.]
LI.........	Long Island
LI.........	[The] Long Island Rail Road Co. [AAR code]
LI.........	Longitudinal Interval (ADA)
LI.........	Loop of Intestine
LI.........	Lot Indices
LI.........	Low Impulsiveness (MAE)
LI.........	Low Intensity
LI.........	Lubrication Instructions [Marine Corps]
LI.........	Lubricity Index (IAA)
LI.........	Lues I [Primary syphilis] [Infectious diseases] (DAVI)
LI.........	Luteinization Inhibitor [Endocrinology]
LI.........	Lymphoid Cellular Infiltration [Oncology]
LI1.........	Lithographer, First Class [Navy rating]
LI2.........	Lithographer, Second Class [Navy rating]
LI3.........	Lithographer, Third Class [Navy rating]
LIA.........	International Union of Life Insurance Agents
LIA.........	Label Information Area (CMD)
LIA.........	Land Information and Analysis [Program] [Department of the Interior]
LIA.........	Laser Institute of America (EA)
LIA.........	Lead Industries Association [New York, NY] (EA)
LIA.........	Leather Industries of America (EA)
LIA.........	Lebanese International Airways
LIA.........	Leeward Islands Air Transport (1974) Ltd. [Antigua and Barbuda] [ICAO designator] (FAAC)
LIA.........	Leukemia-Associated Inhibiting Activity [Medicine]
LIA.........	Leukemia Cell-Derived Inhibitory Activity [Hematology] (DAVI)
LIA.........	Level Indicating Alarm [Engineering]
LIA.........	Liaison
LIA.........	Licensing Industry Association [Later, ILMA] (EA)
LIA.........	Licentiate in Accountancy (DD)
LIA.........	Life Insurance Act [Australia]
LIA.........	Life Insurance Association [British] (DBA)
LIA.........	Lima [Ohio] [Airport symbol] (OAG)
LIA.........	Limited Intelligent Agent [Virtual reality technology] (PS)
LIA.........	Limiting Interval Availability
LIA.........	Linear Induction Accelerator (MCD)
LIA.........	Liposome Immunoassay [Clinical chemistry]
LIA.........	Lithographic Institute of Australia
LIA.........	Little Ice Age [Geoscience]
LIA.........	Liver Infusion Agar [Germination medium]
LIA.........	Localized Induction Approximation [Mathematics]

LIA .... Lock-In Amplifier (MAE)
LIA .... Loop Interface Address
LIA .... Low-Impact Aerobics
LIA .... Luminescence Immunoassay [Clinical chemistry]
LIA .... Lymphocyte-Induced Angiogenesis [Immunology]
LIA .... Lysine Iron Agar [Microbiology]
LIAA .... Life Insurance Association of America [Later, ACLI] (EA)
LIAA .... Louisiana Independent Administrators Association (SRA)
LIAB .... Liability
LIAB .... Life Insurance Adjustment Bureau [Defunct] (EA)
LIABT .... Liability (ABBR)
LIAC .... Legal Industry Advisory Council (EA)
LIAC .... Liberian International American Corporation [New York]
LIAC .... Light-Induced Absorbance Change
LIAC .... Local Industry Advisory Committee [Civil defense]
LIADA .... Liga Ibero-Americana de Astronomia [Ibero-American Astronomy League] (EAIO)
LIADA .... Louisiana Independent Automobile Dealers Association (SRA)
LIAFI .... Late Infantile Amaurotic Familial Idiocy [Medicine] (MAE)
LIAI .... Love in Action International (EA)
LIAMA .... Life Insurance Agency Management Association [Later, LIMRA]
LIAR .... Lexicon of Inconspicuously Ambiguous Recommendations [Term coined by Robert J. Thornton of Lehigh University]
LIAS .... Library Information Access System [Pennsylvania State University Libraries] [University Park] [Information service or system] (IID)
LIASAR .... LASER Inertial Aided Synthetic Aperture RADAR (MCD)
LIASE .... Linking Industry and School Education (AIE)
LIAT .... Leeward Islands Air Transport Services Ltd. [Humorous interpretation: Luggage in Another Town] [Airline]
LIB .... Air Liberte [France ICAO designator] (FAAC)
LIB .... Federal Liberal Agency of Canada Library [UTLAS symbol]
LIB .... Laboratory Information Bulletin (GNE)
LIB .... Left Inboard (MCD)
LIB .... Left in Bottle (MAE)
LIB .... Liber [Book] [Latin]
LIB .... Liberal
LIB .... Liberation
LIB .... Liberator Bomber Aircraft [British] (DSUE)
Lib .... Liberia
LIB .... Liberty [Geographical division] [British]
LIB .... Liberty, NC [Location identifier FAA] (FAAL)
LIB .... Libra [Pound]
Lib .... Libra [Constellation]
LIB .... Librarian (DLA)
LIB .... Library (AFM)
LIB .... Library [A publication] (BRI)
LIB .... Libretto [Music]
LIB .... Light Ion Beam (PDAA)
LIB .... Line Interface Base [Telecommunications]
LIBA .... Amendola [Italy ICAO location identifier] (ICLI)
LIBA .... Licentiate of the Institute of Business Administration
LIBA .... Long Island Biological Association
LIBACC .... Library Acquisition Program [Computer program]
Lib & Cult ... Libraries & Culture [A publication] (BRI)
LIB & SL ..... Libel and Slander [Legal term] (DLA)
Lib Ass ...... Liber Assisarum [Book of Assizes, or pleas of the crown] [Pt. 5 of Year Books] [A publication] (DLA)
LIBB .... Brindisi [Italy ICAO location identifier] (ICLI)
Libbey .... Libbey, Inc. [Associated Press] (SAG)
LIBC .... Crotone [Italy ICAO location identifier] (ICLI)
LIBC .... Latent Iron-Binding Capacity [Clinical chemistry]
LIBC .... Liberty National Bank [NASDAQ symbol] (SAG)
LIBC .... Lloyd's Insurance Brokers Committee (AIA)
LIB CAT ...... Library Catalogue (WDAA)
LIBCEPT ...... LIBRIS Intercept [Sweden] (NITA)
Lib Colon .... Libri Coloniarum [Classical studies] (OCD)
LIBCON .... Libertarian Conservative
LIBCON .... Library of Congress
LIBCON/E .... Library of Congress/English [Database on English language monographs] (NITA)
LIB CONG ... Library of Congress (WDAA)
Lib Cong Q . Library of Congress. Quarterly Journal [A publication] (DLA)
LI Bcp .... Long Island Bancorp, Inc. [Associated Press] (SAG)
LIBD .... Bari/Palese Macchie [Italy ICAO location identifier] (ICLI)
LIBE .... Library Editor (MHDI)
LIBE .... Ligo Internacia de Blindaj Esperantistoj [International League of Blind Esperantists - ILBE] (EAIO)
LIBE .... Monte S. Angelo [Italy ICAO location identifier] (ICLI)
LIBEC .... Light Behind Camera [Photographic technique]
LIBEDIT ...... Library Editor (MHDI)
Lib Ent .... Old Books of Entries [A publication] (DLA)
Liber .... Liberia (VRA)
LIBER .... Ligue des Bibliotheques Europeennes de Recherche [League of European Research Libraries] (EAIO)
LIBERD .... Liberated (ABBR)
LIBERG .... Liberating (ABBR)
LIBERN .... Liberation (ABBR)
LIBERR .... Liberator (ABBR)
Liberte .... Liberte Investors, Inc. [Associated Press] (SAG)
LIBF .... Foggia [Italy ICAO location identifier] (ICLI)
Lib Feud ..... Liber Feudorum [Book of Feuds] [At the end of the Corpus Juris Civilis] [A publication] (DLA)
LibFin .... Liberty Financial Companies, Inc. [Associated Press] (SAG)
LIBG .... Grottaglie [Italy ICAO location identifier] (ICLI)

LIBGIS .... Library General Information Survey [of the National Center for Educational Statistics]
LIBH .... Liberty Homes, Inc. [NASDAQ symbol] (SAG)
LIBH .... Marina Di Ginosa [Italy ICAO location identifier] (ICLI)
LIBHA .... Liberty Homes CI'A' [NASDAQ symbol] (TTSB)
LIBHB .... Liberty Homes CI'B' [NASDAQ symbol] (TTSB)
LIBI .... Vieste [Italy ICAO location identifier] (ICLI)
LIBID .... London Interbank Bid Rate [Finance British]
LibInt(BG) .... Liberal International (British Group) [World Liberal Union] (EAIO)
LIBISAC .... Livres Bibliotheque Saclay Database [Commissariat a l'Energie Atomique] [France Information service or system] (CRD)
LIBJ .... Vibo Valentia [Italy ICAO location identifier] (ICLI)
LIBK .... Caraffa Di Catanzaro [Italy ICAO location identifier] (ICLI)
LIBL .... Liable (ABBR)
LIBL .... Liberal
LIBL .... Palascia [Italy ICAO location identifier] (ICLI)
LIB LAB ...... Liberal-Labour Alliance [British] (DSUE)
Lib L & Eq ... Library of Law and Equity [A publication] (DLA)
LIBLZG .... Liberalizing (ABBR)
LIBM .... Grottammare [Italy ICAO location identifier] (ICLI)
LIBMAN .... Library Management (MHDB)
LIBMAS .... Library Master File [FORTRAN program]
LIBMISH ...... Liberia Military Mission [US]
LIBMRG .... Library Merge Program [Computer program]
LIBN .... Lecce [Italy ICAO location identifier] (ICLI)
LIBN .... Librarian (WGA)
LIBNAT .... Library Network Analysis Theory
LibNBk .... Liberty National Bank [Huntington Beach, CA] [Associated Press] (SAG)
LIBO .... Lincoln Boyhood National Memorial
LIBO .... London Interbank Offered [Rate] [Reference point for syndicated bank loans]
LIBO .... Ortanova [Italy ICAO location identifier] (ICLI)
LIB/OL .... Librarian/Online [Database] (MHDI)
LIBOL .... Litton Business-Oriented Language (IAA)
LIBOR .... London Interbank Offered Rate [Reference point for syndicated bank loans]
LIBORS .... LASER Ionization Based on Resonant Saturation [Physics]
LIBP .... Pescara [Italy ICAO location identifier] (ICLI)
Lib Plac ...... Lilly's Assize Reports [1688-93] [A publication] (DLA)
LIBQ .... Monte Scuro [Italy ICAO location identifier] (ICLI)
LIBR .... Brindise/Casale [Italy ICAO location identifier] (ICLI)
Libr .... Libra [Constellation]
LIBR .... Librarian (EY)
LIBR .... Library
libr .... Library (VRA)
LIBR .... Librium [Pharmacology] (DAVI)
Lib Reg .... Register Book [A publication] (DLA)
LIBRI .... Literary Information Bases for Research and Instruction [American Philological Association] [An association] (NITA)
LIBRIS .... Library Information Service [or System] [The Royal Library Database] [Information service or system] (IID)
LIBRLZ .... Liberalize (ABBR)
LIBRN .... Librarian
LIBRN .... Librarian
LibrtyTc .... Liberty Technologies, Inc. [Associated Press] (SAG)
LIBRY .... Library (ABBR)
LIBS .... Campobasso [Italy ICAO location identifier] (ICLI)
LIBS .... LASER-Induced Breakdown Spectroscopy
LIBS .... Library Internet Browsing Software
LIBSET .... Library Set [Computer program]
LibSIG .... Libertarian SIG [Special Interest Group] (EA)
LIBSOFT ...... Library Software Archives [Computer science] (TNIG)
LIBSTAD ...... Working Party on Library and Book Trade Relations [British]
LIBSYS .... Library System [Computer program]
LIBT .... Liability (ABBR)
LIBT .... Liberty (ABBR)
LIBT .... Liberty Technologies [NASDAQ symbol] (TTSB)
LIBT .... Liberty Technologies, Inc. [NASDAQ symbol] (SAG)
LIBT .... Termoli [Italy ICAO location identifier] (ICLI)
LibtProp .... Liberty Property Trust [Associated Press] (SAG)
LibtyCp .... Liberty Corp. [Associated Press] (SAG)
LIBU .... Latronico [Italy ICAO location identifier] (ICLI)
LIB (UN) ...... Headquarters Library of the United Nations
LIBV .... Gioia Del Colle [Italy ICAO location identifier] (ICLI)
LibVT .... Libri Veteris Testamenti (BJA)
LIBW .... Bonifati [Italy ICAO location identifier] (ICLI)
LIBX .... Martina Franca [Italy ICAO location identifier] (ICLI)
LIBY .... Santa Maria Di Leuca [Italy ICAO location identifier] (ICLI)
LIBZ .... Potenza [Italy ICAO location identifier] (ICLI)
LIC .... Chief Lithographer [Navy rating]
LIC .... Lacquer Insulating Compound
LIC .... Lamto [Ivory Coast] [Seismograph station code, US Geological Survey] (SEIS)
LIC .... Language Identity Code [Army] (INF)
LIC .... Large Integrated Circuit [Electronics]
LIC .... LASER Image Converter
LIC .... LASER-Induced Chemistry (RDA)
LIC .... LASER Intercept Capability [Military] (CAAL)
LIC .... Last Instruction Cycle (IAA)
LIC .... Launcher Interchange Circuit (IAA)
LIC .... Law in Context [Australia A publication]
LIC .... Lawson, I. C., St. Paul MN [STAC]
LIC .... League International for Creditors (DCTA)
LIC .... Least Incompatible [Laboratory science] (DAVI)

LIC	Lecturer in Charge (ADA)
LIC	Left Iliac Crest [*Anatomy*] (DAVI)
LIC	Left Internal Carotid [*Artery*] [*Anatomy*] (DAVI)
LIC	Leisure-Interest Class (MEDA)
LIC	Less Industrialized Country (MHDW)
LIC	Level Indicator Controller (NRCH)
LIC	Library Information Center [*Lunar and Planetary Institute*] [*Information service or system*] (IID)
LIC	License (KSC)
LIC	Licentiate
LIC	Life Insurers Conference [*Richmond, VA*] (EA)
LIC	Limiting Isorrheic Concentration [*Medicine*]
LIC	Limon, CO [*Location identifier FAA*] (FAAL)
LIC	Linear Integrated Circuit
LIC	Lineas Aereas del Caribe [*Colombia*] [*ICAO designator*] (FAAC)
LIC	List of Instruments and Controls (DNAB)
LIC	Lithuanian Information Center [*Defunct*] (EA)
LIC	Load Interface Circuit (MCD)
LIC	Local Import Control [*British*] (DS)
LIC	Local Indigenous Civilian [*Military*]
LIC	Local Interstellar Cloud [*Astronomy*]
LIC	Logistics Indoctrination Course [*Military*] (DNAB)
LIC	London International College [*British*]
LIC	Loop Insertion Cell [*Nuclear energy*] (NRCH)
LIC	Louisiana Insurers' Conference (SRA)
LIC	Low Income Country
LIC	Low Inertia Clutch
LIC	Low-Intensity Conflict [*Military*]
LIC	Lunar Instrument Carrier [*NASA*] (KSC)
LICA	Lamezia/Terme [*Italy ICAO location identifier*] (ICLI)
LICA	Land Improvement Contractors of America (EA)
LICA	Left Internal Carotid Artery [*Anatomy*] (DAVI)
LICA	Ligue Internationale Contre le Racisme et l'Antisemitism [*International League Against Racism and Antisemitism*]
LICA	Lithium Isopropylcyclohexylamide [*Organic chemistry*]
LicAc	Licentiate in Acupuncture [*British*]
Lic Agro	Licentiate in Agronomy [*British*]
LICALM	LORAN Inertial Command Air-Launched Missile
LICAP	LASER-Induced Cut and Patch
LICB	Comiso [*Italy ICAO location identifier*] (ICLI)
LICB	Licensable (ABBR)
LICC	Catania/Fontanarossa [*Italy ICAO location identifier*] (ICLI)
LICC	League for Innovation in the Community College (EA)
LICC	Local Interagency Coordinating Council
LICCD	Ligue Internationale Contre la Concurrence Deloyale [*International League Against Unfair Competition*] (EAIO)
LICD	Lampedusa [*Italy ICAO location identifier*] (ICLI)
LICD	Licensed (ROG)
LICE	Enna [*Italy ICAO location identifier*] (ICLI)
LICE	LASER Interface Control Electronics (MCD)
LICE	License (ROG)
LIC ECON	Licentiate in Economic Sciences (WDAA)
Lic en Der	Licenciado en Derecho [*Licentiate in Law*] [*Spanish*]
Lic en Fil	Licenciado en Filosofia [*Licentiate in Philosophy*] [*Spanish*]
LICET	Library of Industrial and Commercial Education and Training
LICF	Laser-Induced Chlorophyll Fluorescence [*Analytical biochemistry*]
LICF	Messina [*Italy ICAO location identifier*] (ICLI)
LICG	Licensing (ABBR)
LICG	Pantelleria [*Italy ICAO location identifier*] (ICLI)
LICGS	Lightweight Intermediate Caliber Gun System (MCD)
LICH	Capo Spartivento [*Italy ICAO location identifier*] (ICLI)
LICH	Lichfield [*City in England*] (ROG)
LICI	Finale [*Italy ICAO location identifier*] (ICLI)
LICIT	Labor-Industry Coalition for International Trade [*Washington, DC*] (EA)
LICITA	Life Insurance Co. Income Tax Act of 1959
LICJ	Palermo/Punta Raisi [*Italy ICAO location identifier*] (ICLI)
LICK	Lightweight Communication Kit (MCD)
LICL	Gela [*Italy ICAO location identifier*] (ICLI)
LICM	Calopezzati [*Italy ICAO location identifier*] (ICLI)
LICM	Left Intercostal Margin [*Anatomy*]
LICM	Master Chief Lithographer [*Navy rating*]
Lic Med	Licentiate in Medicine
LICND	Life Insurance Committee for a Nuclear Disarmament (EA)
LICNWF	Life Insurance Committee for a Nuclear Weapons Freeze [*Later, LICND*] (EA)
LICO	Cozzo Spadaro [*Italy ICAO location identifier*] (ICLI)
LICO	Low Income Cut-Off [*Canada*]
LiCO₃	Lithium Carbonate [*Pharmacology*] (DAVI)
LICOF	Land Lines Communications Facilities (FAAC)
LICOR	Lightning Correlation
LICP	Lead Inventory Control Point (NG)
LICP	Palermo/Boccadifalco [*Italy ICAO location identifier*] (ICLI)
Lic Phil	Licentiate in Philosophy [*British*]
LICR	Reggio Calabria [*Italy ICAO location identifier*] (ICLI)
LICRA	Ligue Internationale Contre le Racisme et l'Antisemitisme [*France*]
LICROSS	League of International Red Cross Societies
LiCrOx	Lithium/Chromium-Oxide [*Type of battery*]
LICS	Left Intercostal Space [*Cardiology*] (MAE)
LICS	Lotus International Character Set [*Printer technology*] (PCM)
LICS	Sciacca [*Italy ICAO location identifier*] (ICLI)
LICS	Senior Chief Lithographer [*Navy rating*]
LICT	Trapani/Birgi [*Italy ICAO location identifier*] (ICLI)
LICTA	Life Insurance Co. Tax Act of 1955
Lic Tech	Licentiate in Technology [*British*]

Lic Theol	Licentiate in Theology [*British*]
LICU	League of IBM [*International Business Machines Corp.*] Employee Credit Unions (EA)
LICU	Ustica [*Italy ICAO location identifier*] (ICLI)
LICVD	LASER-Induced Chemical Vapor Deposition [*Photovoltaic energy systems*]
LICW	Licentiate of the Institute of Clerks of Works of Great Britain, Inc. (DBQ)
LICX	Prizzi [*Italy ICAO location identifier*] (ICLI)
LICZ	Sigonella [*Italy ICAO location identifier*] (ICLI)
LID	Alidaunia SRL [*Italy ICAO designator*] (FAAC)
LID	Laboratory of Infectious Diseases [*Later, Laboratory of Viral Diseases*] [*NIAID*]
LID	Labor Information Database [*International Labor Office*] [*Information service or system*] (IID)
LID	LASER Image Display (MCD)
LID	LASER Injection Diode
LID	LASER Intrusion Detector
LID	LASER Intrusion Device (MCD)
LID	LASER Isotope Dating
LID	Leadless Inverted Device
LID	League for Industrial Democracy (EA)
LID	Letters in Digit Strings [*Psychology*]
LID	Library Issue Document (NVT)
LID	Lidco Industries, Inc. [*Toronto Stock Exchange symbol*]
LID	Lift Improvement Device (MCD)
LID	Light Infantry Division [*Army*] (INF)
LID	Limited Instrument Departure (MCD)
LID	Linear Imaging Device (MCD)
LID	Line Isolation Device [*Telecommunications*] (NITA)
LID	Line Item Description (MCD)
LID	Liquid Immersion Development [*Reprography*]
LID	Liquid Interface Diffusion
LID	Literaturdienst Medizin und Umwelt [*Literature Service in Medicine and Environment*] [*Austrian National Institute for Public Health*] [*Information service or system*] (IID)
LID	Local Issue Data [*Telecommunications*] (TEL)
LID	Locked-In Device (MSA)
LID	Logical Identification (MCD)
LID	Logistics Identification Document (NASA)
LID	Low-Iodine Diet [*Medicine*]
LID	Lunar Ionosphere Detector (PDAA)
LIDA	Ligue Internationale des Droits de l'Animal [*International League for Animal Rights*] (EAIO)
LIDA	Lodzer Idishe Dramatishe Aktyorn (BJA)
Lidak	Lidak Pharmaceuticals [*Associated Press*] (SAG)
LIDAR	Atmospheric Light Detection and Ranging Facility [*Los Alamos, NM*] [*Los Alamos National Laboratory*] [*Department of Energy*] (GRD)
LIDAR	LASER Infrared RADAR (IEEE)
LIDAR	LASER Intensity Direction and Ranging (IEEE)
LIDAR	Light Detection and Ranging
LIDAS	Laboratory Instrument Data Acquisition
LIDB	Line Information Database [*Telecommunications*] (ACRL)
LIDB	Logistics Intelligence Data Base (AABC)
LIDC	Lead Industries Development Council [*British*] (DAS)
LIDC	Ligue Internationale du Droit de la Concurrence [*International League for Competition Law*] [*Paris, France*] (EA)
LIDC	Low Intensity - Direct Current
LIDF	Line Intermediate Distributing Frame
LIDIA	Learning in Dialog (PDAA)
LIDIA	Liaison Internationale des Industries de l'Alimentation [*International Liaison for the Food Industries*]
LIDO	Logic In, Documents Out (PDAA)
LIDO	Logistics Inventory Disposition Order (AAG)
LIDOC	Lidocaine [*Topical anesthetic*] (WDAA)
LIDS	Laboratory for Information and Decision Systems [*Massachusetts Institute of Technology*] [*Research center*] (RCD)
LIDS	LASER Illumination Detection System
LIDS	LASER Infrared Countermeasures Demonstration System [*Air Force*]
LIDS	Listener Idle State (IAA)
LIDS	Lithium Ion Drift Semiconductor
LIDS	Logistics Item Data Systems [*DoD*]
LIDT	LASER-Induced Damage Testing
LIDUS	Liberal-Demokratische Union der Schweiz [*Liberal Democratic Union of Switzerland*] [*Political party*] (PPE)
LIE	Left Inboard Elevon [*Aviation*] (MCD)
LIE	Lessio Intellectuale Europeo [*Research Institute*] [*Consiglio Nazionale delle Richerche*] [*Italy*] (NITA)
LIE	Libenge [*Zaire*] [*Airport symbol Obsolete*] (OAG)
LIE	Liechtenstein [*ANSI three-letter standard code*] (CNC)
LIE	Limited Information Estimation
LIE	Line Islands Experiment [*National Science Foundation*]
LIE	Line Islands Experiment [*Marine science*] (OSRA)
LIE	Long Island Expressway (BARN)
LIEA	Alghero [*Italy ICAO location identifier*] (ICLI)
LIEA	Low Income Energy Assistance [*Later, LIHEAP*] [*Block grant*]
LIEB	Capo Bellavista [*Italy ICAO location identifier*] (ICLI)
Lieber Civ Lib	Lieber on Civil Liberty and Self Government [*A publication*] (DLA)
Lieb Herm	Lieber's Hermeneutics [*A publication*] (DLA)
LIEC	Capo Carbonara [*Italy ICAO location identifier*] (ICLI)
LIECH	Liechtenstein (ABBR)
Liecht	Liechtenstein
LIECU	League of IBM [*International Business Machines Corp.*] Employee Credit Unions [*Later, LICU*] (EA)
LIED	Decimomannu [*Italy ICAO location identifier*] (ICLI)

LIED............ LASER Initiating Explosive Device
LIED............ Linkage Editor [Computer science]
LIEE............ Cagliari/Elmas [Italy ICAO location identifier] (ICLI)
LIEE............ Law in Eastern Europe [A publication] (DLA)
LIEF............ Capo Frasca [Italy ICAO location identifier] (ICLI)
LIEF............ Launch Information Exchange Facility [NASA]
LIEFC.......... Long Island Early Fliers Club (EA)
LIEG............ Guardiavecchia [Italy ICAO location identifier] (ICLI)
LIEH............ Capo Caccia [Italy ICAO location identifier] (ICLI)
LIEL............ Capo S. Lorenzo [Italy ICAO location identifier] (ICLI)
LIEM............ Macomer [Italy ICAO location identifier] (ICLI)
LIEN............ Fonni [Italy ICAO location identifier] (ICLI)
LIENS.......... Ligue Europeenne pour une Nouvelle Societe [European League for
                a New Society - ELNS] [Paris, France] (EAIO)
LIEO............ Olbia/Costa Smeralda [Italy ICAO location identifier] (ICLI)
LIEP............ LORAN Integrated Engineering Program
LIEP............ Perdasdefogu [Italy ICAO location identifier] (ICLI)
LIEPS.......... LORAN Integrated Engineering Program, Shed Light
LIES............ Library Information and Enquiry System
LIESST........ Light-Induced Excited Spin State Trapping [Physics]
LIETS.......... Land Integrated Equipment for Tactical Systems (MCD)
LIEUT.......... Lieutenant (EY)
LIEUTC........ Lieutenancy (ABBR)
Lieut-Col...... Lieutenant-Colonel [British military] (DMA)
LIEUTE........ Lieutenancy (ABBR)
Lieut-Gen..... Lieutenant-General [British military] (DMA)
Lieut Jg....... Lieutenant Junior Grade [Navy]
LIF............. LASER-Induced Fluorescence [Physical chemistry]
LIF............. LASER Interference Filter
LIF............. Layaway of Industrial Facilities (AABC)
LIF............. Left Iliac Fossa [Medicine]
LIF............. Leukemia Inhibitory Factor [Oncology]
LIF............. Leukocyte Inhibition Factor [Hematology]
LIF............. Leukocytosi-Inducing Factor [Hematology] (DAVI)
LIF............. Lief (ABBR)
LIF............. Lifu [Loyalty Islands] [Airport symbol] (OAG)
LIF............. Lighting Industry Federation [British] (DBA)
LIF............. Logistics Intelligence File (AABC)
LIF............. Lone Indian Fellowship [Later, Lone Indian Fellowship and Lone
                Scout Alumni] (EA)
LIF............. Low-Ionization Filament Component [Galactic science]
LIFA........... Licentiate of the International Faculty of Arts [British]
LIFB........... Life Bancorp [NASDAQ symbol] (TTSB)
LIFB........... Life Bancorp, Inc. [NASDAQ symbol] (SAG)
LIFC........... Lifecell Corp. [NASDAQ symbol] (SAG)
LIFE........... Laboratory for International Fuzzy Engineering Research [Japan]
LIFE........... Language Improvement to Facilitate Education of Hearing-Impaired
                Children [A project of NEA]
LIFE........... LASER-Induced Fluorescence Emission
LIFE........... League for International Food Education [Defunct] (EA)
LIFE........... Lear Integrated Flight Equipment (MCD)
LIFE........... Learning in a Free Environment [Education program]
LIFE........... Less Infant Fatality Everywhere [In association name, Project LIFE]
LIFE........... Let's Improve Future Environment
LIFE........... Liberia International Foundation for Elevation
LIFE........... Life Issues in Formal Education (EA)
LIFE........... Lifeline Systems [NASDAQ symbol] (SAG)
LIFE........... Lifeline Systems [NASDAQ symbol] (TTSB)
LIFE........... Lifetime [Cable television channel]
LIFE........... Living in Family Environments
LIFE........... Logistics Evaluation and Review Integrated Flight Equipment
                [Aviation] (IAA)
LIFE........... Logistics Intelligence File Europe
LIFE........... Longitudinal Interval Follow-Up Evaluation (MEDA)
LIFE........... Love Is Feeding Everyone (EA)
LIFE........... Low Income Family Emancipation Society
LIFE........... Low Income Family Emergency Center
LIFE........... Lung-Imaging Fluorescent Endoscope [Medicine] (ECON)
Life and Acc Ins R... Bigelow's Life and Accident Insurance Reports
                [A publication] (DLA)
Life Bcp...... Life Bancorp, Inc. [Associated Press] (SAG)
Life C......... Life (Health and Accident) Cases [Commerce Clearing House]
                [A publication] (DLA)
Life Cas...... Life (Health and Accident) Cases [Commerce Clearing House]
                [A publication] (DLA)
Life Cas 2d... Life (Health and Accident) Cases, Second Series [Commerce
                Clearing House] [A publication] (DLA)
Lifecell....... Lifecell Corp. [Associated Press] (SAG)
LifeHoan..... Lifetime Hoan Corp. [Associated Press] (SAG)
LIFEL......... Limited Functional English Literacy
LIFEMAN..... Live Fire Evaluation Manikin [Perceptronics, Inc.] [Military]
LifePart...... Life Partners [Associated Press] (SAG)
LIFER......... Language Interface Facility with Ellipsis and Recursion [Computer
                science] (MHDI)
LifeRe........ Life Re Corp. [Associated Press] (SAG)
LifeRte....... LifeRate Systems, Inc. [Associated Press] (SAG)
LIFES......... LASER-Induced Fluorescence and Environmental Sensing [NASA]
LifeSpir...... [The] Life of the Spirit [London] [A publication] (BJA)
LIFESTA...... Lifeboat Station [Coast Guard]
Lifeway...... Lifeway Foods, Inc. [Associated Press] (SAG)
LIFF.......... Lifschultz Inds [NASDAQ symbol] (TTSB)
LIFF.......... Lifschultz Industries, Inc. [NASDAQ symbol] (SAG)
LIFFE......... London International Financial Futures Exchange Ltd. [London,
                England]
LiFHAS....... Libertarian Foundation for Human Assistance (EAIO)

LIFLSA....... Lone Indian Fellowship and Lone Scout Alumni (EA)
LIFMOP....... Linearly Frequency-Modulated Pulse
LIFO.......... Last In, First Out [Queuing technique] [Accounting]
LIFO.......... Life Orientation (Survey)
LIFPL......... Ligue Internationale de Femmes pour la Paix et la Liberte [Women's
                International League for Peace and Freedom - WILPF] (EAIO)
LIFPL/SF..... Ligue Internationale de Femmes pour la Paix et la Liberte, Section
                Francaise (EAIO)
LIFR.......... Leukemia Inhibitory Factor Receptor [Biochemistry]
LIFRAM....... Liquid-Fueled Ramjet [Navy] (MCD)
LIFS.......... LASER-Induced Fluorescence Spectroscopy
LIFS.......... London International Furniture Show [British] (ITD)
Lifschlt....... Lifschultz Industries, Inc. [Associated Press] (SAG)
LIFSUM....... Airlift Summary Report [Air Force]
LIFT.......... Bereavement Services & Community Education (AC)
LIFT.......... Labor Investing for Tomorrow [Department of Labor]
LIFT.......... Lead-In Flight Training [Air Force] (DOMA)
LIFT.......... Link Intellectual Functions Tester
LIFT.......... Logically Integrated FORTRAN Translator [UNIVAC]
LIFT.......... London International Festival of Theatre [British]
LIFT.......... London International Freight Terminal (DS)
LIFT.......... Lower Inventory for Tomorrow [A program of the Canadian
                government to bring heavy stocks of wheat into line with demand
                by paying farmers not to produce]
LIFT.......... Low Interfacial Tension [Physical chemistry]
LIFTG........ Lifting (ABBR)
LIFU.......... Liquid Fuel
LIG........... LASER Image Generator (MCD)
LIG........... LASERS in Graphics (DGA)
LIG........... Last Interglacial Period [Climatology]
LIG........... Leichte Infanteriegeschuetz [Light Infantry Howitzer] [German military
                - World War II]
LIG........... Liege (ABBR)
LIG........... Ligament [or Ligamentum]
LIG........... Ligament [Anatomy] (DAVI)
LIG........... Ligated [or Ligation] [Medicine]
LIG........... Ligature (DGA)
LIG........... Limoges [France] [Airport symbol] (OAG)
LIG........... London Industrial Group [British]
Lig........... Pro Ligario [of Cicero] [Classical studies] (OCD)
LIGA.......... Liquid Granule Applicator [Device used to disperse pesticides]
LIGA.......... Lithographic Galvanoforming Abformung [Materials science]
Ligand....... Ligand Pharmaceuticals, Inc. [Associated Press] (SAG)
LIGCM........ Licentiate of the Incorporated Guild of Church Musicians [British]
                (ROG)
Lig Dig...... Ligon's Digest [Alabama] [A publication] (DLA)
LIGG.......... Ligaments [or Ligamenti]
ligg.......... Ligature [Surgery] (DAVI)
LIGHT........ Light [Commonly used] (OPSA)
LIGHT........ Light Industrial Gas Heat Transfer
LIGHT........ Lighting (ABBR)
LIGHT........ Lighting
LIGHT........ Lightning (ABBR)
LIGHTEX..... Searchlight Illumination Exercise [Also, LITEX] [Military] (NVT)
LightP........ LightPath Technologies, Inc. [Associated Press] (SAG)
LIGHTPHOTORON... Light Photographic Squadron
LIGHTS....... Lights [Commonly used] (OPSA)
LightSav..... Light Savers USA, Inc. [Associated Press] (SAG)
Lign.......... Lignum [Wood] [Latin]
LIGO.......... LASER Interferometry Gravitational Wave Observatory [Proposed]
LIH........... LASER Interferometric Holography
LIH........... Left Inguinal Hernia [Medicine]
LIH........... Letters and Inscriptions of Hammurabi [A publication] (BJA)
LIH........... Light Intensity High
LIH........... Lihue [Hawaii] [Airport symbol] (OAG)
LIH........... Line Interface Handler
LIHA.......... Low Impulsiveness, High Anxiety (MAE)
LIHDC........ Low Income Housing Development Corp. [North Carolina] (EA)
LIHE.......... Lutheran Institute of Human Ecology (EA)
LIHEAP....... Low Income Home Energy Assistance Program [Formerly, LIEA]
                [Block grant]
LIHG.......... Ligue Internationale de Hockey sur Glace [International Ice Hockey
                Federation]
LihirGld...... Lihir Gold Ltd. [Associated Press] (SAG)
LIHIS......... Low Income Housing Information Service (EA)
LIHM.......... Licentiate of the Institute of Housing Managers [British] (DI)
LIHN.......... Hieronymi Liber Interpretationis Hebraicorum Nominum (BJA)
LIHPRHA..... Low Income Housing Preservation and Resident Homeownership Act
                of 1990
LIHRY........ Lihir Gold ADS [NASDAQ symbol] (TTSB)
LIHRY........ Lihir Gold Ltd. [NASDAQ symbol] (SAG)
LII........... Flight Research Institute, M. Gromov [Former USSR] [FAA
                designator] (FAAC)
LII........... Larizza Industries, Inc. [AMEX symbol] (SPSG)
LII........... Life Insurance Index [A publication]
LII........... Livestock Industry Institute (EA)
LII........... Lues II [or Secondary syphilis] [Infectious diseases] (DAVI)
LII........... Mulia [Indonesia] [Airport symbol] (OAG)
LIIA.......... Italy International NOTAM Office [Italy ICAO location identifier] (ICLI)
LIIB.......... Roma [Italy ICAO location identifier] (ICLI)
LIIC.......... Italy Military International NOTAM Office [Italy ICAO location
                identifier] (ICLI)
LIIG.......... Logistics Item Identification Guide [Military] (AFM)
LIII.......... Lues III [Teritiary syphilis] [Infectious diseases] (DAVI)
LIII.......... Roma [Italy ICAO location identifier] (ICLI)

LIIP LASER-Induced Infrared Photochemistry
LIIR Italian Agency for Air Navigation Services [*Italy ICAO location identifier*] (ICLI)
LIJ Lawyers for an Independent Judiciary [*Defunct*] (EA)
LIJ Left Internal Jugular Vein [*Medicine*] (DMAA)
LIJJ Roma [*Italy ICAO location identifier*] (ICLI)
LIK Leichte Infanteriekolonne [*Light Infantry Supply Column*] [*German military - World War II*]
LIK Likiep [*Marshall Islands*] [*Airport symbol*] (OAG)
LIL Laboratory Interface Language [*Programming language*]
LIL Large Immersion Lens
LIL Large-Ion Lithophile
LIL Law of the Iterated Logarithm (PDAA)
LIL Lead-In Light-System [*Aviation*]
LIL Light Intensity Low
LIL Lilac (ROG)
LIL Lille [*France*] [*Airport symbol*] (OAG)
LIL Lille [*France*] [*Seismograph station code, US Geological Survey Closed*] (SEIS)
LIL Lilliputian (ABBR)
Lil Lilly's English Assize Reports [*1688-93*] [*A publication*] (DLA)
LIL Lincoln's Inn Library [*A publication*] (DLA)
LIL Lithuanian Airlines [*ICAO designator*] (FAAC)
LIL Little (ABBR)
LIL Live-In Lover [*Slang*] (DSUE)
LIL Log-Inject-Log [*Petroleum technology*]
LIL Long Island Light'g [*NYSE symbol*] (TTSB)
LIL Long Island Lighting Co. [*Formerly, LLT*] [*NYSE symbol*] (SPSG)
LIL Low-Input Landscaping
LIL Lunar International Laboratory
LILA Ligue Internationale de la Librairie Ancienne [*International League of Antiquarian Booksellers - ILAB*] (EAIO)
LILA Low Impulsiveness, Low Anxiety (MAE)
Lil Abr Lilly's Abridgment [*England*] [*A publication*] (DLA)
LILAC Low-Intensity Large Area [*Headlight*]
LILACS Latin American and Caribbean Health Sciences Literature (IID)
LILAM Licentiate of the Institute of Leisure and Amenity Management [*British*] (DBQ)
LILCo Long Island Lighting Co. [*Associated Press*] (SAG)
Lil Conv Lilly's Conveyancer [*A publication*] (DLA)
LILE Large Ion Lithophile Element [*Geochemistry*]
Lill Ent Lilly's Entries [*England*] [*A publication*] (DLA)
Lilly Lilly [*Eli*] and Co. [*Associated Press*] (SAG)
Lilly Lilly's Reports and Pleadings of Cases in Assize [*170 English Reprint*] [*1688-93*] [*A publication*] (DLA)
Lilly Abr Lilly's Abridgment [*England*] [*A publication*] (DLA)
Lilly Assize Lilly's Reports and Pleadings of Cases in Assize [*170 English Reprint*] [*1688-93*] [*A publication*] (DLA)
Lilly Assize (Eng) Lilly's Reports and Pleadings of Cases in Assize [*170 English Reprint*] [*1688-93*] [*A publication*] (DLA)
LillyE Lilly [*Eli*] & Co. [*Associated Press*] (SAG)
LillyEli Lilly [*Eli*] [*Associated Press*] (SAG)
LillyInd Lilly Industries, Inc. [*Associated Press*] (SAG)
LILO Last-In, Last-Out [*Accounting*]
LILO Link Loader (IAA)
LILOC Light Lyne Optical Correlation (MCD)
LILPrA Long Island Ltg 7.95% Pfd [*NYSE symbol*] (TTSB)
LILPrB Long Island Ltg 5% B Pfd [*NYSE symbol*] (TTSB)
LILPrC Long Island Ltg 7.66% Pfd [*NYSE symbol*] (TTSB)
LILPrE Long Island Ltg 4.35% Cv E Pfd [*NYSE symbol*] (TTSB)
LILPrI Long Island Ltg, 5.75% Cv I Pfd [*NYSE symbol*] (TTSB)
LILPrQ Long Island Ltg 7.05% Pfd [*NYSE symbol*] (TTSB)
LILRC Long Island Library Resources Council [*Bellport, NY*] [*Library network*]
Lil Reg Lilly's Practical Register [*A publication*] (ILCA)
LilVern Lillian Vernon Corp. [*Associated Press*] (SAG)
LIM BVBA Lucorp [*Belgium*] [*FAA designator*] (FAAC)
LIM Compass Locator of Inner Marker Site
LIM Laboratory Institute of Merchandising [*New York, NY*]
LIM Language Interface Module (NITA)
LIM Language Interpretation Module
LIM Latent Image Memory
LIM Leg-Inducing Membrane [*Entomology*]
LIM Leningrad Institute of Metals [*Former USSR*] (MCD)
LIM Light Intensity Medium
LIM Lima [*Peru*] [*Airport symbol*] (OAG)
LIM Lima [*Peru*] [*Seismograph station code, US Geological Survey*] (SEIS)
LIM Lima Public Library, Lima, OH [*OCLC symbol*] (OCLC)
LIM Limber (MSA)
LIM Limerick [*County in Ireland*] (ROG)
lim Limes [*Limit*] [*Latin*]
LIM Limit
LIM Limiter [*Electronics*] (ECII)
LIM Limonene [*Organic chemistry*]
LIM Linear Induction Motor [*Magnetic rapid-transit car*]
LIM Line Insulation Monitor (PDAA)
LIM Line Interface Module
LIM Liquid Injection Molding
LIM Liquid Injection Molding
LIM Locator Inner Marker [*Aviation*] (DA)
LIM Losing Inventory Manager [*Army*] (AABC)
LIM Lotus/Intel/Microsoft [*Computer science*]
LIM Lower Inlet Module [*Nuclear energy*] (NRCH)
LIMA LASER-Induced Ion-Mass Analyzer [*Instrumentation*]
LIMA Left Internal Mammary Artery [*Anatomy*] (AAMN)
LIMA Licentiate of the Institute of Mathematics and Its Applications [*British*] (DBQ)
LIMA Logic-in-Memory Array
LIMA Torino [*Italy ICAO location identifier*] (ICLI)
LIMAC Large Integrated Monolithic Array Computer (MCD)
LIM ACT Limitation of Action [*Legal term*] (DLA)
LIMAS Lightweight Marking System [*British Army*]
LIMB Library Instruction Materials Bank [*Loughborough University of Technology*] [*Information service or system*] (IID)
LIMB Limestone Injection/Multistage Burner
LIMB Limestone-Injection, Multi-Stage Burner (GNE)
LIMB Liquid Metal Breeder [*Reactor*]
LIMB Milano/Bresso [*Italy ICAO location identifier*] (ICLI)
LIMC Milano/Malpensa [*Italy ICAO location identifier*] (ICLI)
LIMD Grigna Settentrionale [*Italy ICAO location identifier*] (ICLI)
LIMD Limited (ROG)
LIMDAT Limiting Date
LIMDIS Limited Distribution [*Military*] (AFIT)
LIMDOW Light Intensity Modulation Direct OverWrite [*Computer science*]
LIMDU Limited Duty (MCD)
LIME Bergamo/Orio Al Serio [*Italy ICAO location identifier*] (ICLI)
LIME Low-Iron, Manganese-Enriched [*Meteorite*]
LIMEA Low-Iron-Content Monoethanolamine
LIMEAN London Interbank Median Average Rate
LIM-EMS Lotus-Intel-Microsoft Expanded Memory Specification [*Computer science*] (BTTJ)
limest Limestone [*Petrology*]
LIMF Licentiate of the Institute of Metal Finishing [*British*] (DBQ)
LIMF Torino/Caselle [*Italy ICAO location identifier*] (ICLI)
LIMFAC Limiting Factor (MCD)
LIMG Albenga [*Italy ICAO location identifier*] (ICLI)
LIMH Pian Rosa [*Italy ICAO location identifier*] (ICLI)
LIMI Colle Del Gigante [*Italy ICAO location identifier*] (ICLI)
LIMI Leningrad International Management Institute [*Joint Venture between Bocconi University, Italy and Leningrad University*] (ECON)
LIMIRIS LASER-Induced Modulation of Infrared in Silicon
LIMIT Leicester Intravenous Magnesium Intervention Trial [*Cardiology study*]
LIMIT Lot-Size Inventory Management Interpolation Technique (BUR)
Limitd [*The*] Limited, Inc. [*Associated Press*] (SAG)
LIMJ Genova/Sestri [*Italy ICAO location identifier*] (ICLI)
LIMK Torino/Bric Della Croce [*Italy ICAO location identifier*] (ICLI)
LIML Limited Information Maximum Likelihood [*Econometrics*]
LIML Milano/Linate [*Italy ICAO location identifier*] (ICLI)
LIMM Milano [*Italy ICAO location identifier*] (ICLI)
LIMN Cameri [*Italy ICAO location identifier*] (ICLI)
LIMNOL Limnology
LIMO Least Input for the Most Output [*Business term*]
LIMO Limousine (DSUE)
LIMO Limousine
LIMO Limousine Industry Manufacturers Organization (EA)
LIMO Monte Bisbino [*Italy ICAO location identifier*] (ICLI)
LIMON Limonis [*Of Lemon*] [*Pharmacy*] (ROG)
LIMOS Laser Intensity Modulation System [*Computer science*]
LIMOSO Limitation of Supplies Order [*World War II*]
LIMP Language-Independent Macro Processor (PDAA)
LIMP Louis XIV, James II, Mary, Prince of Wales [*Jacobite toast*]
LIMP Lunar-Anchored Interplanetary Monitoring Platform [*Aerospace*]
LIMP Lunar Interplanetary Monitoring Probe (IAA)
LIMP Parma [*Italy ICAO location identifier*] (ICLI)
LIMPS Linear Induction Motor Propulsion System
LIMQ Govone [*Italy ICAO location identifier*] (ICLI)
LIMR Limiter
LIMR Novi Ligure [*Italy ICAO location identifier*] (ICLI)
LIMRA Life Insurance Marketing and Research Association [*Hartford, CT*] (EA)
LIMRC LRU [*Line Replaceable Unit*] Identification and Maintenance Requirements Catalog (NASA)
LIMRF Life Insurance Medical Research Fund [*Defunct*]
LIMRV Linear Induction Motor Research Vehicle [*Magnetic rapid-transit car*]
LIMS Laban Institute of Movement Studies [*Later, LBIMS*] (EA)
LIMS Laboratory Information Management System
LIMS LASERInduced Microgrough Structures [*Surface Technology*]
LIMS Library Information Management System [*University of Maryland*]
LIMS Limb Infrared Monitor of the Stratosphere
LIMS Limb-Motion Sensor [*System*]
LIMS Limb Sounder (SSD)
LIMS Lithium Metal Sulfide
LIMS Logistic Inventory Management System [*North American Rockwell*]
LIMS Piacenza/San Damiano [*Italy ICAO location identifier*] (ICLI)
LIMSS Logistics Information Management Support System [*Military*]
LIMSW Limit Switch (NRCH)
LIMT Passo Della Cisa [*Italy ICAO location identifier*] (ICLI)
LIMTV Linear Induction Motor Test Vehicle [*Magnetic rapid-transit car*]
LIMU Capo Mele [*Italy ICAO location identifier*] (ICLI)
LIMU LASER Inertial Measurement Unit (MCD)
LIMV Lilac Mottle Virus [*Plant pathology*]
LIMV Passo Dei Giovi [*Italy ICAO location identifier*] (ICLI)
LIMW Aosta [*Italy ICAO location identifier*] (ICLI)
LIMY Monte Malanotte [*Italy ICAO location identifier*] (ICLI)
LIMZ Levaldigi [*Italy ICAO location identifier*] (ICLI)
LIN Law Institute News [*Australia A publication*]
LIN Linair-Hungarian Regional Airlines [*FAA designator*] (FAAC)
LIN Lincoln [*Diocesan abbreviation*] [*Nebraska*] (TOCD)

LIN.............	Lincoln [*Nebraska*] [*Seismograph station code, US Geological Survey Closed*] (SEIS)
Lin	Linden [*Record label*]
LIN	Linden, CA [*Location identifier FAA*] (FAAL)
LIN	Line (WDAA)
LIN	Lineal (MSA)
LIN	Linear (KSC)
LIN	Line Item Number (AABC)
LIN	Linen (ADA)
LIN	Linen
lin	Linen (VRA)
LIN	Liniment
LIN	Liquid Nitrogen (AFM)
LIN	Massachusetts Institute of Technology, Lincoln Laboratory, Lexington, MA [*OCLC symbol*] (OCLC)
LIN	Milan [*Italy*] Forlanini-Linate [*Airport symbol*] (OAG)
LINA	Liberian News Agency (EY)
LINA	Literaturnachweise [*Literature Compilations Database*] [*Fraunhofer Society*] (IID)
LINABOL	Lineas Navieras Bolivianas [*Shipping line*] [*Bolivia*] (EY)
LINAC	Linear [*Electron*] Accelerator
LINAS	LASER Inertial Navigation Attack System (IAA)
LINAS	LASER-Integrated Navigation/Attack System (MCD)
LINC	Laboratory Instrument Computer [*Medical analyzer*]
LINC	Language Information Network Coordination [*Education*] (AIE)
LINC	Learning Institute of North Carolina
LINC	Legislative Information Network Corp. [*Information service or system*] (IID)
LINC	Library & Information Consultants Ltd. [*Information service or system*] (IID)
LINC	Lincolnshire [*County in England*]
LINC	Lindas Diversified Holdings [*NASDAQ symbol*] (SAG)
LINC	Lucas Industries Noise Centre [*Research center British*] (IRUK)
LINCA	Linda's Flame Roasted Chicken [*NASDAQ symbol*] (TTSB)
L'INCA	L'Institut National Canadien pour les Aveugles (AC)
Lincare	Lincare Holdings, Inc. [*Associated Press*] (SAG)
LINCE	LASER-Improved Naval Combat Equipment (PDAA)
LincEl	[*The*] Lincoln Electric Co. [*Associated Press*] (SAG)
LincEIA	Lincoln Electric Co. (The) [*Associated Press*] (SAG)
LINCLOE	Lightweight Individual Combat Clothing and Equipment (AABC)
LinCMOS	Linear CMOS [*Complementary Metal Oxide Semiconductor*] [*Texas Instruments*] (NITA)
LINCMOS	Linear Complementary Metal-Oxide Semiconductor [*Electronics*] (EECA)
LincN	Lincoln National Corp. [*Associated Press*] (SAG)
LincN	Lincoln National Corp. Capital I [*Associated Press*] (SAG)
LincN	Lincoln National Corp. Capital II [*Associated Press*] (SAG)
LincNatl	Lincoln National Corp. [*Associated Press*] (SAG)
LincNIF	Lincoln National Income Fund, Inc. [*Associated Press*] (SAG)
LINCO	Linear Composition (PDAA)
LINCO	Linearly Organized Chemical Code for Use in Computer Systems (DIT)
Lincoln U	Lincoln University (GAGS)
LINCOMPEX...	Linked Compressor and Expander (NATG)
LINCOS	Lingua Cosmica [*Artificial language consisting of radio signals of varying lengths and frequencies*]
LINCOTT	Liaison, Interface, Coupling, Technology Transfer
LINCS	Language Information Network and Clearinghouse System [*Center for Applied Linguistics*] [*Washington, DC*]
LINCS	Leased Interfacility Nas Communications System [*FAA*] (TAG)
LINCS	Lincolnshire [*County in England*]
LincSB	Lincoln Savings Bank [*Associated Press*] (SAG)
LincSnk..........	Lincoln Snacks Co. [*Associated Press*] (SAG)
LINCT	Linctus [*Tincture*] [*Pharmacy*] (ROG)
LincTel	Lincoln Telecommunications Co. [*Associated Press*] (SAG)
LINCW	Linda's Flame Rstd Ckn Wrrt'A' [*NASDAQ symbol*] (TTSB)
LINCZ	Linda's Flame Rstd Ckn Wrrt'B' [*NASDAQ symbol*] (TTSB)
LIND	Lindberg Corp. [*NASDAQ symbol*] (SAG)
Linda	Lindas Flame Roasted Chicken, Inc. [*Associated Press*] (SAG)
Linda	Lindasw Diversified Holdings [*Associated Press*] (SAG)
LINDA	Line Drawing Analyzer [*Cybernetics*]
LindasCh	Lindas Flame Roasted Chicken, Inc. [*Associated Press*] (SAG)
LindasDiv	Lindas Diversified Holdings [*Associated Press*] (SAG)
Lindbrg	Lindberg Corp. [*Associated Press*] (SAG)
LINDI	Line-to-Disk [*Computer science*] (MHDI)
Lind Jur	Lindley's Study of Jurisprudence [*A publication*] (DLA)
Lindl Copartn...	Lindley on Partnership [*A publication*] (DLA)
Lindley	Lindley's Law of Companies [*A publication*] (DLA)
Lindley Comp...	Lindley's Law of Companies [*A publication*] (DLA)
Lindley P	Lindley on Partnership [*A publication*] (DLA)
Lindley Part...	Lindley on Partnership [*A publication*] (DLA)
LindlH..........	Lindal Cedar Homes, Inc. [*Associated Press*] (SAG)
Lindl Partn...	Lindley on Partnership [*A publication*] (DLA)
Lind Part	Lindley on Partnership [*A publication*] (DLA)
Lind Pr	Lindewoode's Provincials [*A publication*] (DLA)
Lind Prob.....	Lindsay on Probates [*A publication*] (DLA)
Lindsy	Lindsay Manufacturing [*Associated Press*] (SAG)
lindwd	Lindenwood (VRA)
LINE	Lightweight Inertial Northseeking Equipmet (SAA)
LINE	Long Interspersed Element Sequence [*Genetics*]
LINE	Long Interspersed Nuclear Element [*Genetics*]
LinearT..........	Linear Technology Corp. [*Associated Press*] (SAG)
L in Eastern Eur...	Law in Eastern Europe [*A publication*] (DLA)
LINED	Line Editor [*Computer science*] (MHDI)
LINEII..........	Logic and Information Network Compiler II [*Computer science*] (HGAA)
LINER	Low-Ionization Nuclear Emission-Line Region [*Spectroscopy*]
LINES..........	Library Information Network Exchange Services [*Australia A publication*]
LINEs..........	Long Interspersed Nuclcotide Elements [*Genetics*]
LINES..........	Long-Interspersed Repeated Segments [*of DNA*] [*Genetics*] (DAVI)
Linfield C....	Linfield College (GAGS)
LINFT	Linear Foot
Ling	De Lingua Latina [*of Varro*] [*Classical studies*] (OCD)
LING	Learning Independence Through Computers, Inc.
LING	Linguistics
LINGUA..........	Linguistic Analysis System (ECII)
LINIM	Liniment
Lin Ins	De Lineis Insecabilibus [*of Aristotle*] [*Classical studies*] (OCD)
Linium	Linium Technology Corp. [*Associated Press*] (SAG)
LINJET	Liquid Injection Electric Thruster [*NASA*] (NASA)
LINK	Interlink Electronics [*NASDAQ symbol*] (TTSB)
LINK	Interlink Electronics, Inc. [*NASDAQ symbol*] (SAG)
LINK	Lambeth Information Network [*Information service or system*] [*British*] (NITA)
LINK	Library and Information Network [*Planned Parenthood Federation of America, Inc.*] [*Information service or system*] (IID)
LINK	Literature in Nursing Kardex
LINKW	Interlink Electrs Wrrt [*NASDAQ symbol*] (TTSB)
LINLOG	Linear-Logarithmic (IEEE)
LINMH	Linear Meters per Hour (IAA)
LINN	Linnaeus
Linn Ind.......	Linn's Index of Pennsylvania Reports [*A publication*] (DLA)
Linn Laws Prov PA...	Linn on the Laws of the Province of Pennsylvania [*A publication*] (DLA)
LINO	Liaison Officer [*Military*]
lino	Linocut (VRA)
LINO	Linoleum
Lino	Linotronic [*Computer science*]
LINO	Linotype
LINOL	Linoleum (MSA)
LINOSCO..........	Libraries in North Staffordshire and South Cheshire in Cooperation [*British*] (NITA)
LINQ	Literature in North Queensland [*A publication*]
LINS	Labrador Institute of Northern Studies [*Memorial University of Newfoundland*] [*Canada Research center*] (RCD)
LINS..........	LASER Inertial Navigation System (MCD)
LINS..........	Lightweight Inertial Navigation System [*Air Force*]
LINS..........	LORAN Inertial System
L in Soc'y	Law in Society [*A publication*] (DLA)
LInstBB..........	Licentiate of the Institute of British Bakers (DBQ)
LInstBCA..........	Licentiate of the Institute of Burial and Cremation Administration [*British*] (DBQ)
L Inst P..........	Licentiate of the Institute of Physics [*British*]
LInstPRA..........	Licentiate of the Institute of Park and Recreation Administration [*British*] (DI)
LinTelev	Lin Television Corp. [*Associated Press*] (SAG)
L Intell..........	Law Intelligencer [*United States*] [*A publication*] (DLA)
L in Trans J...	Law in Transition Journal [*A publication*] (DLA)
L in Trans Q...	Law in Transition Quarterly [*A publication*] (DLA)
LINUS	Local Information Network for Universal Service [*Telecommunications service*] (TSSD)
LINUS	Logical Inquiry and Update System
LINZ	Lindsay Manufacturing [*NASDAQ symbol*] (SAG)
LINZ	Lindsay Mfg [*NASDAQ symbol*] (TTSB)
LIO.............	Air Charter Ltd. (Leiguflug Isleifs Ottesen) [*Iceland*] [*FAA designator*] (FAAC)
LIO.............	Left Inferior Oblique [*Anatomy*] (DAVI)
LIO.............	Lesser Included Offense
LIO.............	Liberian Iron Ore Ltd. [*Toronto Stock Exchange symbol*]
LIO.............	Limon [*Costa Rica*] [*Airport symbol*] (OAG)
LiO.............	Liottite [*A zeolite*]
LiO.............	Lithium Organic Battery
LIO.............	Local Interconnect Option [*Wang Laboratories, Inc.*] (BYTE)
LIO.............	National Restaurant Association Large Independent Operators [*Defunct*] (EA)
LIOAS	LASER-Induced Optoacoustic Spectroscopy
LIOC..........	Lighted Independent of Computer
LIOCS	Logical Input/Output Control System [*Computer science*]
LIOD	Lightweight Optronic Director (MCD)
LIODD	LASER In-Flight Obstacle Detection Device
LiOH	Lithium Hydroxide (NASA)
LIOL	Legal Information On-Line [*Ministry of Labour*] [*Hamilton, ON*] [*Information service or system*] (IID)
LION	Fidelity National [*NASDAQ symbol*] (TTSB)
LION	Fidelity National Corp. [*NASDAQ symbol*] (SAG)
LION	Lehman Investment Opportunity Note
LION	Library Information OnLine [*International Atomic Energy Agency*] [*United Nations*] (DUND)
LION	Local Input/Output Nozzle [*Computer science*]
LI/ON	Logicon Input/Output Network
LION	Lunar International Observer Network [*NASA*]
LionBrw..........	Lion Brewery, Inc. (The) [*Associated Press*] (SAG)
LIONS	Library Information and On-Line Network Service [*New York Public Library*] [*Information service or system*] (IID)
LIOP..........	Life in One Position [*Telecommunications*] (TEL)
LIOP..........	Limited Initial Operating Production (MCD)
LIP.............	Boston, MA [*Location identifier FAA*] (FAAL)
LIP.............	Large Internet Packet [*Computer science*] (PCM)

LIP	LASER-Induced Plasma [*Spectroscopy*]
LIP	Latent Information Parameter
LIP	Lateral Intraparietal Area [*Anatomy*]
LIP	Launch in Process [*NASA*] (IAA)
LIP	Legal Inverse Path [*Physics*]
LIP	Letter Input Procesing [*Printing*] (DGA)
LIP	Library Information Plan (AIE)
LIP	Life Insurance Policy
LIP	Limited Implementation Program [*FAA*] (TAG)
lip	Lipemic [*Cardiology*] (DAVI)
LIP	Lipkovo [*Yugoslavia*] [*Seismograph station code, US Geological Survey*] (SEIS)
Lip	Lipoate [*Also called Lipoic acid*] [*Biochemistry*] (DAVI)
LIP	Local Initiatives Program [*Canada*]
LIP	Low Internal Phase [*Emulsion chemistry*]
LIP	Lunar Impact Probe [*Aerospace*]
LIP	Lymphoid Interstitial Pneumonitis [*Medicine*]
LIPA	Aviano [*Italy ICAO location identifier*] (ICLI)
LIPA	Labor Institute of Public Affairs (EA)
LIPA	Lauric [*or Lauroyl or Lauryl*] Isopropanolamide [*Also, LPA*] [*Organic chemistry*]
LIPA	List of Interchangeable Parts and Assemblies
LIPA	Louisiana Independent Physicians Association, Inc.
LIPAD	Ligue Patriotique pour le Developpement [*Burkina Faso*] [*Political party*] (EY)
LIPAS	LASER-Induced Photoacoustic Spectroscopy
LIPB	Bolzano [*Italy ICAO location identifier*] (ICLI)
LIPB	Lipase B (DMAA)
LIPB	Lloyd's International Private Banking [*Finance*]
Lip Bib Jur	Lipenius' Bibliotheca Juridica [*A publication*] (DLA)
LIPC	Cervia [*Italy ICAO location identifier*] (ICLI)
LIPC	Levenson's Internal, Powerful Others, and Chance Scales (EDAC)
LIPC	Livestock Industry Promotion Council [*Australia*]
LIPD	Lipase D (DMAA)
LIPD	Udine/Campoformido [*Italy ICAO location identifier*] (ICLI)
LIPE	Bologna/Borgo Panigale [*Italy ICAO location identifier*] (ICLI)
LIPF	Ferrara [*Italy ICAO location identifier*] (ICLI)
LIPF	LASER-Induced Photodissociation and Fluorescence [*Coal technology*]
LIPG	Gorizia [*Italy ICAO location identifier*] (ICLI)
LIPH	Treviso/San Angelo [*Italy ICAO location identifier*] (ICLI)
LIPHE	Life Interpersonal History Enquiry [*Test*] [*Psychology*]
LIPI	Indonesian Institute of Sciences [*Marine science*] (OSRA)
LIPI	Rivolto [*Italy ICAO location identifier*] (ICLI)
LIPID	Logical Page Identifier
LIPJ	Bassano Del Grappa [*Italy ICAO location identifier*] (ICLI)
LIPK	Forli [*Italy ICAO location identifier*] (ICLI)
LIPL	Ghedi [*Italy ICAO location identifier*] (ICLI)
LIPL	Linear Information Processing Language [*High-order programming language*] [*Computer science*] (IEEE)
LIPN	Verona/Boscomantico [*Italy ICAO location identifier*] (ICLI)
LIPO	Liposome Co. [*NASDAQ symbol*] (SAG)
LIPO	Montichiari [*Italy ICAO location identifier*] (ICLI)
Liposm	[*The*] Liposome Co., Inc. [*Associated Press*] (SAG)
LIPOZ	Liposome $1.9375 Cv Dep'A'Pfd [*NASDAQ symbol*] (TTSB)
LIPP	LASER-Induced Pressure Pulse [*Medicine*] (DMAA)
LIP P	Lipid Profile [*Cardiology*] (DAVI)
LIPP	Padova [*Italy ICAO location identifier*] (ICLI)
Lipp Cr L	Lippitt's Massachusetts Criminal Law [*A publication*] (DLA)
LIPQ	Ronchi De'Legionari [*Italy ICAO location identifier*] (ICLI)
LIPR	Rimini [*Italy ICAO location identifier*] (ICLI)
LIPS	Laboratory Interface Peripheral Subsystem [*Computer science*]
LIPS	Lanthanide Ion Probe Spectroscopy
LIPS	Leiter International Performance Scale [*Psychology*]
LIPS	Library and Information Plans [*British*]
LIPS	Litton Industries Privacy System
LIPS	Logical Inferences per Second [*Processing power units*] [*Computer science*]
LIPS	Logic Inference per Second (IAA)
Lips	Low Income, Parents Supporting [*Lifestyle classification*]
LIPS	Treviso/Istrana [*Italy ICAO location identifier*] (ICLI)
Lipsm	[*The*] Liposome Co., Inc. [*Associated Press*] (SAG)
LIPT	Leiter International Performance Test [*Psychology*] (DAVI)
LIPT	Vicenza [*Italy ICAO location identifier*] (ICLI)
LIPU	Padova [*Italy ICAO location identifier*] (ICLI)
LIPV	Venezia/San Nicolo [*Italy ICAO location identifier*] (ICLI)
LIPX	Villafranca [*Italy ICAO location identifier*] (ICLI)
LIPY	Ancona/Falconara [*Italy ICAO location identifier*] (ICLI)
LIPZ	Venezia/Tessera [*Italy ICAO location identifier*] (ICLI)
LIQ	Athens, TX [*Location identifier FAA*] (FAAL)
LIQ	Liquest International Marketing [*Vancouver Stock Exchange symbol*]
liq	Liqueur [*Solution*] [*Pharmacy*]
LIQ	Liquid (AAG)
LIQ	Liquidation (MCD)
LIQ	Liquor
LIQ	Lisala [*Zaire*] [*Airport symbol*] (OAG)
LIQ	Lower Inner Quadrant [*Anatomy*]
LIQB	Arezzo [*Italy ICAO location identifier*] (ICLI)
LIQB	Liqui-Box Corp. [*NASDAQ symbol*] (SAG)
LIQC	Capri [*Italy ICAO location identifier*] (ICLI)
LIQD	Liquid (ECII)
LIQD	Passo Della Porretta [*Italy ICAO location identifier*] (ICLI)
LIQDTE	Liquidate (ROG)
LIQFRKT	Liquid Fuel Rocket (IAA)
LIQI	Gran Sasso [*Italy ICAO location identifier*] (ICLI)

LIQJ	Civitavecchia [*Italy ICAO location identifier*] (ICLI)
LIQK	Capo Palinuro [*Italy ICAO location identifier*] (ICLI)
LIQM	Rifredo Mugello [*Italy ICAO location identifier*] (ICLI)
LIQN	Rieti [*Italy ICAO location identifier*] (ICLI)
LIQO	Monte Argentario [*Italy ICAO location identifier*] (ICLI)
LIQOR	Liquidator (ROG)
LIQP	Palmaria [*Italy ICAO location identifier*] (ICLI)
LIQQ	Monte Cavo [*Italy ICAO location identifier*] (ICLI)
LIQR	Radicofani [*Italy ICAO location identifier*] (ICLI)
LIQS	Siena [*Italy ICAO location identifier*] (ICLI)
LIQSS	Liquid Steady State (PDAA)
LIQT	Circeo [*Italy ICAO location identifier*] (ICLI)
LIQT	Liquid Transient (PDAA)
LiquiBox	Liqui-Box Corp. [*Associated Press*] (SAG)
LIQUID	Liquidus [*Liquid*] [*Pharmacy*] (ROG)
LIQUON	Liquidation
Liquor Cont L Serv (CCH)	Liquor Control Law Service (Commerce Clearing House) [*A publication*] (DLA)
LIQV	Volterra [*Italy ICAO location identifier*] (ICLI)
LIQW	Sarzana/Luni [*Italy ICAO location identifier*] (ICLI)
LIQZ	Ponza [*Italy ICAO location identifier*] (ICLI)
LIR	Dover, DE [*Location identifier FAA*] (FAAL)
LIR	Laboratory for Insulation Research [*MIT*] (MCD)
LIR	Leader Internode Ratio [*Botany*]
LIR	Left Iliac Region [*Medicine*] (MAE)
LIR	Left Inferior Rectus [*Muscle*] [*Ophthalmology and surgery*] (DAVI)
LIR	Level Indicator Recorder [*Electronics*] (ECII)
LIR	Liberia [*Costa Rica*] [*Airport symbol*] (OAG)
LIR	Library and Information Resources (NITA)
LIR	Licentiate of the Institute of Population Registration [*British*] (DBQ)
LIR	Limiting Interval Reliability
LIR	Line Integral Refractometer
LIR	Lionair SA [*Luxembourg*] [*ICAO designator*] (FAAC)
lir	Lira [*Monetary unit*] [*Italy*]
lir	Lithuanian Soviet Socialist Republic [*MARC country of publication code Library of Congress*] (LCCP)
LIR	Load-Indicating Relay (IAA)
LIR	Load-Indicating Resistor (IAA)
LIR	Longitude Independent Reset
LIR	Lost Item Replacement (MCD)
LIRA	Lambeg Industrial Research Association [*British*] (IRUK)
LIRA	Liberal Industrial Relations Association [*British*]
LIRA	Linen Industry Research Association [*British*] (BI)
LIRA	Little Italy Restoration Association
LIRA	Roma/Ciampino [*Italy ICAO location identifier*] (ICLI)
LIRB	Vigna Di Valle [*Italy ICAO location identifier*] (ICLI)
LIRBM	Liver, Iron, Red Bone Marrow
LIRC	Centocelle [*Italy ICAO location identifier*] (ICLI)
LIRC	Lebanese Information and Research Center (EA)
LIRC	Level Indicator Recorder Controller [*Electronics*] (ECII)
LIRC	Ligue Internationale de la Representation Commerciale [*International League of Commercial Travelers and Agents - ILCTA*] (EAIO)
LIRC	Low Interest Rate Currency (MHDW)
LIRE	Lincoln Institute for Research and Education (EA)
LIRE	Pratica Di Mare [*Italy ICAO location identifier*] (ICLI)
LIRES	Literature Retrieval System [*Computer science*]
LIRES-MC	Literature Retrieval System - Multiple Searching, Complete Text [*Computer science*]
LIRF	Low-Intensity Reciprocity Failure [*Of photographic emulsions*]
LIRF	Roma/Fiumicino [*Italy ICAO location identifier*] (ICLI)
LIRG	Guidonia [*Italy ICAO location identifier*] (ICLI)
LIRG	Landesverband der Israelitischen Religionsgemeinde (BJA)
LIRG	Library and Information Research Group [*Bristol Polytechnic Library*] [*British Information service or system*] (IID)
LIRH	Frosinone [*Italy ICAO location identifier*] (ICLI)
LIRI	Salerno/Pontecagnano [*Italy ICAO location identifier*] (ICLI)
LIRIC	Language Instruction for Recent Immigrants through Computer Technology (EDAC)
LIRJ	Marina Di Campo [*Italy ICAO location identifier*] (ICLI)
LIRK	Monte Terminillo [*Italy ICAO location identifier*] (ICLI)
LIRL	Latina [*Italy ICAO location identifier*] (ICLI)
LIRL	Low Intensity Runway Edge Lights [*FAA*] (TAG)
LIRL	Low-Intensity Runway Lighting
LIRLY	Load-Indicating Relay (MSA)
LIRM	Grazzanise [*Italy ICAO location identifier*] (ICLI)
LIRMA	London Insurance and Reinsurance Market Association (ECON)
LIRN	Library and Information for the Northwest [*Program of the Fred Meyer Charitable Trust*]
LIRN	Library and Information Research News [*A publication*] (NITA)
LIRN	Napoli/Capodichino [*Italy ICAO location identifier*] (ICLI)
LIROC	Last Instruction Readout Cycle (IAA)
LIRP	Pisa [*Italy ICAO location identifier*] (ICLI)
LIRQ	Firenze [*Italy ICAO location identifier*] (ICLI)
LIRR	[*The*] Long Island Rail Road Co.
LIRR	Roma [*Italy ICAO location identifier*] (ICLI)
LIRS	Grosseto [*Italy ICAO location identifier*] (ICLI)
LIRS	Lance Information Retrieval System
LIRS	Legal Information and Reference Services [*General Accounting Office*] (IID)
LIRS	Level Indicator Recording Switch (NRCH)
LIRS	Library Information Retrieval Service [*Oregon State University*] [*Information service or system*]
LIRS	Library Information Retrieval System [*California Institute of Technology*] [*Pasadena, CA*]
LIRS	Low Impact Resistant Supports [*FAA*] (TAG)

LIRS............	Lutheran Immigration and Refugee Service (EA)
LIRSH.........	List of Items Requiring Special Handling
LIRT............	Library Instruction Round Table [American Library Association]
LIRT............	Low Input Reduced Tillage [Cropping systems] (GNE)
LIRT............	Trevico [Italy ICAO location identifier] (ICLI)
LIRTS..........	Large Infrared Telescope
LIRU...........	Roma/Urbe [Italy ICAO location identifier] (ICLI)
LIRV...........	Viterbo [Italy ICAO location identifier] (ICLI)
LIRZ...........	Perugia [Italy ICAO location identifier] (ICLI)
LIS..............	Airlis SA [Spain ICAO designator] (FAAC)
LIS..............	Laboratory Information Systems
LIS..............	Language Implementation System (IAA)
LIS..............	Lanthanide-Induced Shift [Spectroscopy]
LIS..............	Lanthanide-Ion Induced Chemical Shift [Spectroscopy]
LIS..............	LARC Instruction Simulator
LIS..............	Large Interactive Surface [Automated drafting table that serves as a computer input and output device]
LIS..............	LASER Illuminator System
LIS..............	LASER-Induced Separation (MCD)
LIS..............	LASER Interferometer System
LIS..............	LASER Isotope Separation
LIS..............	Lateral Intercellular Space (PDAA)
LIS..............	Launch Instant Selector
LIS..............	Laurentide Ice Sheet [Climatology]
LIS..............	Left Intercostal Space [Cardiology]
LIS..............	Legislative Information Service [New Jersey State Legislature] [Trenton] [Information service or system] (IID)
LIS..............	Legislative Information System [National Conference of State Legislatures] [Information service or system] (IID)
LIS..............	Libertarian Information Service [An association] (EA)
LIS..............	Library and Information Science
LIS..............	Library and Information Service
LIS..............	Library and Information Services [Institution of Mining and Metallurgy] [British Information service or system] (IID)
LIS..............	Library Information System [Georgetown University] [Information service or system]
LIS..............	Licensing Information Service (IID)
LIS..............	Licensure Information System [Public Health Service] [Georgetown University Medical Center] (IID)
LIS..............	Line Information Store [Telecommunications] (TEL)
LIS..............	Line Isolation Switch [Reactor level switch] (IEEE)
LIS..............	Link Information Sciences (BUR)
LIS..............	Liposome Immunosensor [Electrochemistry]
LIS..............	Lisbon [Portugal] [Seismograph station code, US Geological Survey] (SEIS)
LIS..............	Lisbon [Portugal] [Airport symbol] (OAG)
LIS..............	List and Index Society [British] (NITA)
LIS..............	Lithium Diodosalicylate [Organic chemistry]
LIS..............	LM [Lunar Module] Interface Control Specification [NASA] (KSC)
LIS..............	Load I-Bank and Jump [Computer science]
LIS..............	Lobular in Situ [Medicine]
LIS..............	Locate in Scotland [Investment group] (ECON)
LIS..............	Lockheed Information Systems (NITA)
LIS..............	Loop Input Signal
LIS..............	Loss Information Service [Insurance]
LIS..............	Low-Impact Switch (MCD)
LIS..............	Low Inductance Stripline (IAA)
LIS..............	Low-Intensity Sonication [Chemistry]
LIS..............	Low Intermittent Suction [Medicine] (MEDA)
LIS..............	Lutheran Immigration Service [Later, LIRS] (EA)
LIS..............	Luxembourg Income Study [Economics]
LISA............	Laboratory for Information Science in Agriculture [Research center Defunct] (RCD)
LISA............	LARC Instruction Assembly
LISA............	LASER Indirect Fire Semiactive
LISA............	Lead-in-Steel Analyser (PDAA)
LISA............	Leather Industry Suppliers Associates [British] (DBA)
LISA............	Library Systems Analysis
LISA............	Licht Sammler [Light Collector] [Fluorescent plastic used in commercial displays] [German]
LISA............	Life Insurance Society of America (EA)
LISA............	Linear Systems Analysis
LISA............	Line Impedance Stabilization Network
LISA............	Linked Indexed Sequential Access
LISA............	Locally Integrated Software Architecture [Apple microcomputer] [Computer science]
LISA............	London and International School of Acting [British]
LISA............	Low-Input Sustainable Agriculture
LISA............	Seaman Apprentice, Lithographer, Striker [Navy rating]
LISARD........	Latest Information Selected and Abstracted for Researchers and Decision-Makers [Database]
LISARD........	Library and Information Service Automated Retrieval of Data (NITA)
LISARD........	Library Information Search and Retrieval Data System [US Navy] (NITA)
LISB...........	Lithium Ion Storage Battery (PCM)
LISB...........	Long Island Bancorp [NASDAQ symbol] (TTSB)
LISB...........	Long Island Bancorp, Inc. [NASDAQ symbol] (SAG)
LISC...........	Library and Information Services Council [British]
LISC...........	Lions International Stamp Club (EA)
LISC...........	Local Initiatives Support Corp. (EA)
LISD...........	Latest Information Selected and Abstracted for Researchers and Decision-Makers [Database]
LISD...........	Library and Information Services Division [National Oceanic and Atmospheric Administration] (NITA)

LISDOK........	Literaturinformationssystem [Literature Information System] [North Rhine-Westphalia Institute for Air Pollution Control] [Information service or system] (IID)
LISDP..........	LOAD [Low-Altitude Defense] Interceptor Subsystem Development Plan
LISE...........	Librarians of Institutes and Schools of Education [British] (DBA)
LISFA..........	Lost in Space Fannish Alliance (EA)
LISH...........	Last In, Still Here [Accounting] (ADA)
LISI............	Library Interface Systems, Inc. [Information service or system] (IID)
LISIC..........	Library and Information Service to Industry and Commerce (NITA)
LISK...........	Liskeard [Municipal borough in England]
LISM..........	Licentiate, Institute of Sales and Marketing Executives (ADA)
LISM..........	Licentiate of the Incorporated Society of Musicians (ROG)
LISN...........	Library Services Network [Library network]
LISN...........	Line Impedance Stabilization Network
LISN...........	Load Impedance Stabilization Network [Electrical engineering]
LISN...........	Long Island Sports Network [Cable-television system]
LISN...........	Seaman, Lithographer, Striker [Navy rating]
LISNY.........	Life Insurance Society of New York (SRA)
LISP...........	LASER Isotope Separation Program
LISP...........	Library and Information Software Package (PDAA)
LISP...........	Lightweight Individual Special Purpose [Weaponry]
LISP...........	Liquid Injector Spray Pattern (MCD)
LISP...........	List Processing [Programming language] [Facetious translation: "Lots of Insane, Stupid Parentheses"] [Computer science]
LISP...........	List Processor [Standard programming language] [1958] [Computer science]
LISPB..........	Lithospheric Seismic Profile in Britain (PDAA)
LISPER........	Limited Speech Recognition (PDAA)
LISR...........	Line Information Storage and Retrieval [Information service or system] (NITA)
LISRB..........	Life Insurance Sales Research Bureau [Later, LIMRA]
LISREL........	Linear Structural Relationships (NITA)
LISS...........	Lightweight Integrated Shelter System (DWSG)
LISS...........	Linear/Imaging Self-Scanner Sensor (MCD)
LISS...........	Los-Ionic-Strength Saline Solution [Medicine] (MEDA)
LISS...........	Low-Ionic-Strength Saline [Medicine] (DMAA)
LISSADA......	Library and Information Science Students Attitudes, Demographics, and Aspirations Survey [American Libraries Association]
LISST..........	Library and Information Scholarship Today [A publication]
LIST...........	Last In, Still There [Accounting]
LIST...........	Library and Information Science Trends
LIST...........	Library and Information Services, Tees-Side (IEEE)
LIST...........	Library and Information Services Today [A publication]
LIST...........	Library Index Search and Transcribe
LIST...........	Low Isotonic Strength Titrator
LISTAR........	Lincoln Information Storage and Associative Retrieval System [Lincoln Laboratory] [Massachusetts Institute of Technology] (NITA)
LISTAR........	Lincoln Information Storage and Retrieval [MIT]
LISTD..........	Licentiate of the Imperial Society of Teachers of Dancing [British]
LISTS..........	Library Information System Time-Sharing
LISU...........	Library and Information Statistics Unit (AIE)
LISV...........	Loyal Independent Sheffield Volunteers [British military] (DMA)
LISWG........	Land Interface Sub-Working Group [NATO] (NATG)
LIT..............	Adams Field [FAA] (TAG)
LIT..............	Air Littoral [France ICAO designator] (FAAC)
LIT..............	Language Imitation Test
LIT..............	Language Inventory for Teachers [Child development test]
LIT..............	Lawrence Institute of Technology [Later, Lawrence Technological University]
LIT..............	Lead-In Training [Air Force] (DOMA)
LIT..............	Librarians Inquiry Terminal (IT)
Lit..............	Lietuvos TSR Valstybine Respublikine Biblioteka [National Library of Lithuania], Vilnius, Lithuania [Library symbol Library of Congress] (LCLS)
LIT..............	Life Insurance Trust (DLA)
LIT..............	Light Interface Technology [Signal transmission]
LIT..............	Light Intratheater Transport [Air Force]
LIT..............	Light Ion Trough
LIT..............	Line Insulation Test [Telecommunications]
LIT..............	Liquid Injection Technique (IEEE)
Lit..............	Lire Italiane [Italian Lire] [Monetary unit]
LIT..............	Litany (ROG)
LIT..............	Liter [Metric measure of volume]
LIT..............	Literacy
LIT..............	Literal
LIT..............	Literary
LIT..............	Literature
lit..............	Literature (WDMC)
lit..............	Lithuanian [MARC language code Library of Congress] (LCCP)
LIT..............	Lithuanian Apostolate for Lithuanian Catholics [Diocesan abbreviation] (TOCD)
Lit..............	Littell's Kentucky Reports [A publication] (DLA)
LIT..............	Litter (WDAA)
LIT..............	Litterae [Letters] [Latin] (ADA)
Lit..............	Little
LIT..............	Little Rock [Arkansas] [Airport symbol] (OAG)
Lit..............	Littleton's English Common Pleas Reports [A publication] (DLA)
Lit..............	Littleton's Tenures [A publication] (DLA)
LIT..............	Litton Indus [NYSE symbol] (TTSB)
LIT..............	Litton Industries, Inc. [NYSE symbol] (SPSG)
LIT..............	Liturgy
LIT..............	Local Inclusive Tour (DCTA)
LIT..............	Local Income Tax (PDAA)

LIT .... Location/Identification Transmitter [*NASA*]
LIT .... London Investment Trust [*British*]
LIT .... Low-Impedance Transmission
LITA .... Library and Information Technology Association (EA)
LITA .... LIbrary and Information Technology Associaton of the ALA (NITA)
Lit & Bl Dig... Littleton and Blatchley's Insurance Digest [*A publication*] (DLA)
LITAS .... Low Intensity Two-Color Approach Slope Indicator [*Aviation*] (DA)
LITASTOR .... Light Tapping Storage (IAA)
Lit B .... Litterarum Baccalaureus [*Bachelor of Letters or Literature*] [*Latin*]
Lit Brooke.... Brooke's New Cases, English King's Bench [*1515-58*]
             [*A publication*] (DLA)
LitchFin .... Litchfield Financial Corp. [*Associated Press*] (SAG)
Lit Crit .... Literary Criticism (WGA)
LITD .... Laser-Induced Thermal Desorption
Lit D .... Litterarum Doctor [*Doctor of Letters or Literature*] [*Latin*]
LitDokAB...... Literaturdokumentation zur Arbeitsmarkt- und Berufsforschung
             [*Deutsche Bundesanstalt fuer Arbeit*] [*Germany Information
             service or system*] (CRD)
LITE .... LASER Illuminator Targeting Equipment
LITE .... LASER In-Space Technology Experiment
LITE .... Legal Information Through Electronics [*Air Force*]
LITE .... Let's Improve Today's Education [*Newsletter*]
Litelfuse ...... Littelfuse, Inc. [*Associated Press*] (SAG)
LITES .... LASER Initiated Transfer Energy Subsystem [*Detonator, developed
             by US Navy*]
LITES .... LASER Intercept and Technical Exploitation System (MCD)
LITEX .... Searchlight Illumination Exercise [*Also, LIGHTEX*] [*Military*] (NVT)
LitfldAd....... Littlefield, [*Adams*] & Co. [*Associated Press*] (SAG)
Litfse .... Littelfuse, Inc. [*Associated Press*] (SAG)
LITFUND...... Fund for the Relief of Russian Writers and Scientists in Exile (EA)
litg .... Liturgy (VRA)
LITH .... Lithium [*Pharmacy*] (DAVI)
lith............ Lithograph (WDMC)
LITH .... Lithograph [*or Lithography*] (ROG)
lith............ Lithographic (WDMC)
lith............ Lithography (WDMC)
Lith .... Lithuania (VRA)
LITH .... Lithuania (ROG)
LITH .... Lithuanian [*Language, etc.*]
LITH BRO..... Lithium Bromide (DNAB)
LITHD .... Lithographed (ROG)
LITHO .... Lithograph (AABC)
LITHO .... Lithograph
litho .... Lithograph (VRA)
litho .... Lithograph (WDMC)
litho .... Lithographic (WDMC)
litho .... Lithography (WDMC)
litho .... Lithotripsy [*Medicine*] (DAVI)
LITHOC .... Lithographic
lithog .... Lithograph (WDMC)
lithog .... Lithographic (WDMC)
LITHOG .... Lithographing
LITHOG .... Lithography
lithog .... Lithography (WDMC)
lithol.......... Lithology (BARN)
LITHOR .... Lithographer
LITHOT .... Lithotomy [*Medicine*]
LITHOY .... Lithography
LithSSR....... Lithuanian Soviet Socialist Republic
LITHUAN ..... Lithuanian
LIT HUM ..... Litterae Humaniores [*Classic literature*] [*Latin*] (ROG)
Litig........... Litigation [*A publication*] (DLA)
LITIGON ...... Litigation (ROG)
LITINT........ Literacy International
LITINT........ Literature Intelligence (MCD)
LITIR.......... Literary Information and Retrieval [*Computer science*]
LITIR.......... Literature Information and Retrieval [*Database on Victorian studies
             literature*] [*University of Alberta*] [*Canada*] (NITA)
LIT-LIT........ Committee on World Literacy and Christian Literature [*Later,
             Intermedia*] (EA)
Lit M.......... Master of Literature
LitMo .... Liturgie und Moenchtum [*A publication*] (BJA)
LITPrB .... Litton Indus,$2 B Pfd [*NYSE symbol*] (TTSB)
LITR........... Low-Cost Indirect-Fire Training Round [*Army*] (INF)
LITR........... Low-Intensity Test Reactor [*ORNL*]
Lit Sel Ca .... Littell's Select Kentucky Cases [*A publication*] (DLA)
Litt............ Littell's Kentucky Supreme Court Reports [*1822-24*] [*A publication*]
             (DLA)
LITT........... Litterateur [*French*] (ROG)
Litt............. Littleton's English Common Pleas Reports [*A publication*] (DLA)
Litt & S St Law... Littell and Swigert's Digest of Statute Law [*Kentucky*]
             [*A publication*] (DLA)
Litt B .... Litterarum Baccalaureus [*Bachelor of Letters or Literature*] [*Latin*]
Litt Comp Laws... Littell's Statute Law [*Kentucky*] [*A publication*] (DLA)
Litt D .... Litterarum Doctor [*Doctor of Letters or Literature*] [*Latin*]
LittD(Econ).. Doctor of Letters in Economic Studies (ADA)
Littell........ Littell's Kentucky Reports [*A publication*] (DLA)
LittHD .... Doctor of Hebrew Letters (BJA)
Litt (KY) ...... Littell [*Kentucky*] [*A publication*] (DLA)
Litt L.......... Licentiate in Letters
Little Brooke... Brooke's New Cases, English King's Bench [*1515-58*]
             [*A publication*] (DLA)
Littleton...... Littleton's English Common Pleas and Exchequer Reports
             [*A publication*] (DLA)
Litt M.......... Master of Letters

Litton .... Litton Industries, Inc. [*Associated Press*] (SAG)
Litt Rep .... Littleton's English Common Pleas and Exchequer Reports
             [*A publication*] (DLA)
LITTS .... Large Inventory Top-Tier Site [*Industrial hazard designation*] [*British*]
Litt Sel Cas.. Littell's Select Kentucky Cases [*A publication*] (DLA)
Litt Ten ...... Littleton's Tenures [*A publication*] (DLA)
LITTY .... Libraries of Idaho Teletype Network - Academics [*Library network*]
LITURG....... Liturgies (ROG)
LITVC......... Liquid Injection Thrust Vector Control
LITW .... Longitudinally in Homogeneous Traveling Waves (MCD)
LITZ .... Litzendraht [*Wire*] [*German*]
LIU .... Library and Information Unit
LIU .... Line Interface Unit [*Data communications*]
LIU .... Line Isolation Unit [*Electronics*]
LIU .... Link Interface Unit [*Telecommunications*] (ECII)
LIU .... Littlefield, TX [*Location identifier FAA*] (FAAL)
LIU .... Long Island University [*Brooklyn, NY*]
LIU .... Long Island University (Brooklyn Campus) (GAGS)
LIU .... Wood, Wire, and Metal Lathers' International Union [*Later, UBC*]
LIUNA .... Laborers' International Union of North America (EA)
LIUP.......... Long Island University Press (DGA)
Liuski......... Liuski International, Inc. [*Associated Press*] (SAG)
LIV .... Law of Initial Value [*Joseph Wilder*]
LIV .... Left Innominate Vein [*Medicine*] (MAE)
LIV .... Legislative Indexing Vocabulary
LIV .... Light Infantry Volunteers [*Military unit*] [*British*]
LIV .... Linear, Invariant (PDAA)
LIV .... Line Item Value
LIV .... Lived [*or Living*]
LIV .... Livengood, AK [*Location identifier FAA*] (FAAL)
LIV .... Liver Battery Test [*Gastroenterology*] (DAVI)
LIV .... Liverpool (ROG)
LIV .... Living (DAVI)
LIV .... Livingstone Energy [*Vancouver Stock Exchange symbol*]
Liv .... Livingston's Mayor's Court Reports [*New York*] [*A publication*] (DLA)
LIV .... Livorno [*Italy*] [*Seismograph station code, US Geological Survey
             Closed*] (SEIS)
LIV .... Livraison [*Delivery*] [*French*]
LIV .... Livre [*Book or Pound*] [*French*]
LIV .... Livy [*Roman historian, c. 10BC*] (ROG)
LIV .... Low-Input Voltage (KSC)
LIV .... Low Investment Vehicle
LIV .... Lunar and Interplanetary Vehicle [*Aerospace*] (AFM)
Liv Ag......... Livermore on Principal and Agent [*A publication*] (DLA)
LIVB.......... Passo Del Brennero [*Italy ICAO location identifier*] (ICLI)
LIV-BP .... Leucine, Isoleucine, and Valine Binding Protein [*Biochemistry*]
             (DMAA)
LIVC.......... Low-Input Voltage Converter
LIVC.......... Monte Cimone [*Italy ICAO location identifier*] (ICLI)
Liv Cas ...... Livingston's Cases in Error [*New York*] [*A publication*] (DLA)
LIVCR .... Low-Input Voltage Conversion and Regulation
LIVD.......... Dobbiaco [*Italy ICAO location identifier*] (ICLI)
Liv Dis........ Livermore's Dissertation on the Contrariety of Laws [*A publication*]
             (DLA)
LIVE........... Learning through Industry and Voluntary Educators [*Community
             education program*]
LIVE........... Live Entertainment [*NASDAQ symbol*] (TTSB)
LIVE........... Lunar Impact Vehicle [*NASA*] (KSC)
LIVE........... Passo Resia [*Italy ICAO location identifier*] (ICLI)
LiveEn .... LIVE Entertainment, Inc. [*Associated Press*] (SAG)
LiveEnt .... LIVE Entertainment, Inc. [*Associated Press*] (SAG)
Livent .... Livent, Inc. [*Associated Press*] (SAG)
LIVEP......... Live Entmt cm Cv'B' Pfd [*NASDAQ symbol*] (TTSB)
Liverm Ag..... Livermore on Principal and Agent [*A publication*] (DLA)
Livermore Ag... Livermore on Principal and Agent [*A publication*] (DLA)
LIVEX .... Live Exercise [*Military exercise in which live forces participate*]
             (NATG)
LIVF.......... Frontone [*Italy ICAO location identifier*] (ICLI)
LIVG........... Monte Grappa [*Italy ICAO location identifier*] (ICLI)
Livingston U... Livingston University (GAGS)
Liv Jud Cas... Livingston's Judicial Opinions [*New York*] [*A publication*] (DLA)
Liv Judic Op... Livingston's Judicial Opinions [*New York*] [*A publication*] (DLA)
Liv Jud Op... Livingston's Judicial Opinions [*New York*] [*A publication*] (DLA)
Liv La Cr Code... Livingston's Louisiana Criminal Code [*A publication*] (DLA)
Liv Law Mag... Livingston's Law Magazine [*New York*] [*A publication*] (DLA)
Liv L Mag... Livingston's Law Magazine [*New York*] [*A publication*] (DLA)
Liv L Reg... Livingston's Law Register [*New York*] [*A publication*] (DLA)
LIVM.......... Marino Di Ravenna [*Italy ICAO location identifier*] (ICLI)
LivngCtr...... Living Centers of America, Inc. [*Associated Press*] (SAG)
LIVO.......... Tarvisio [*Italy ICAO location identifier*] (ICLI)
LIVP........... Paganella [*Italy ICAO location identifier*] (ICLI)
LIVR.......... Low-Input Voltage Regulation
LIVR.......... Passo Rolle [*Italy ICAO location identifier*] (ICLI)
liv rm......... Living Room (BARN)
LIVT........... Trieste [*Italy ICAO location identifier*] (ICLI)
Liv US Pen Co... Livingston's System of United States Penal Codes
             [*A publication*] (DLA)
LIVV........... Monte Venda [*Italy ICAO location identifier*] (ICLI)
LIW .... Letters in Words [*Psychology*]
LIW .... Lightweight Individual Weapon (PDAA)
LIW .... Loikaw [*Myanmar*] [*Airport symbol*] (OAG)
LIW .... Long Instruction Word [*Teraplex*] [*Computer science*]
LIW .... Loss in Weight
LIWB.......... Livermore Water Boiler [*Nuclear reactor*] [*Dismantled*]
LIWMS........ Laura Ingalls Wilder Memorial Society (EA)

LIX	Liquid Crystal *(IDOE)*
LIXISCOPE	Low-Intensity X-Ray Imaging Scope
LIY	Leicestershire Imperial Yeomanry [*British military*] *(DMA)*
LIY	Limay [*Nicaragua*] [*Seismograph station code, US Geological Survey*] *(SEIS)*
LIYP	Legacy International Youth Program [*Later, LIYTP*] *(EA)*
LIYTP	Legacy International Youth Training Program *(EA)*
LIYV	Lettuce Infectious Yellows Virus
LIYW	Aviano [*Italy ICAO location identifier*] *(ICLI)*
LIZ	Limestone, ME [*Location identifier FAA*] *(FAAL)*
LIZ	Lizard *(MSA)*
LIZ	Liz Claiborne [*NYSE symbol*] *(TTSB)*
LIZ	Liz Claiborne, Inc. [*NYSE symbol*] *(SAG)*
LIZARDS	Library Information Search and Retrieval Data System *(IEEE)*
Lizars	Lizar's Scotch Exchequer Cases [*A publication*] *(DLA)*
LizClab	Claiborne [*Liz*], Inc. [*Associated Press*] *(SAG)*
Liz Sc Exch	Lizar's Scotch Exchequer Cases [*A publication*] *(DLA)*
LJ	British Guiana Limited Jurisdiction (Official Gazette) [*1899-1955*] [*A publication*] *(DLA)*
LJ	Hall's American Law Journal [*A publication*] *(DLA)*
LJ	House of Lords Journals [*England*] [*A publication*] *(DLA)*
LJ	Jennings Public Library, Jennings, LA [*Library symbol Library of Congress*] *(LCLS)*
LJ	Joullie [*France*] [*Research code symbol*]
LJ	Law Journal Newspaper [*1866-1965*] [*A publication*]
LJ	Law Judge *(DLA)*
LJ	Lawson & Jones Ltd. [*Toronto Stock Exchange symbol*]
LJ	Lennard-Jones [*Physical chemistry*]
LJ	Library Journal [*A publication*] *(BRI)*
LJ	Life Jacket
LJ	Limited Partner in Jobbers Firm [*London Stock Exchange*]
LJ	Line Judge [*Football*]
LJ	Little Joe [*Early developmental spacecraft*] [*NASA*]
LJ	Little John [*Rocket*] [*Military*] *(AABC)*
LJ	Long Jump
LJ	Lord Justice
L-J	Lowenstein-Jensen [*Growth medium*]
LJ	Lower Canada Law Journal [*A publication*] *(DLA)*
LJ	Sierra Leone Airways [*ICAO designator*] *(AD)*
LJA	Lady Jockeys Association [*British*] *(DBA)*
LJA	Lodja [*Zaire*] [*Airport symbol*] *(OAG)*
LJA	Lord Justice of Appeal
LJaD	Dixon Correctional Institute, Jackson, LA [*Library symbol Library of Congress*] *(LCLS)*
LJ Adm	Law Journal, New Series, Admiralty [*A publication*] *(DLA)*
LJ Adm NS	Law Journal Reports, Admiralty, New Series [*1865-75*] [*A publication*] *(DLA)*
LJ Adm NS (Eng)	Law Journal Reports, New Series, Admiralty [*England*] [*A publication*] *(DLA)*
LJ App	Law Journal Reports, New Series, Appeals [*A publication*] *(DLA)*
LJ Bank	Law Journal Reports, Bankruptcy [*A publication*] *(DLA)*
LJ Bank NS	Law Journal Reports, New Series, Bankruptcy [*A publication*] *(DLA)*
LJ Bankr	Law Journal Reports, Bankruptcy [*A publication*] *(DLA)*
LJ Bankr NS (Eng)	Law Journal Reports, New Series, Bankruptcy [*England*] [*A publication*] *(DLA)*
LJ Bcy	Law Journal Reports, New Series, Bankruptcy [*A publication*] *(DLA)*
LJ Bk	Law Journal Reports, Bankruptcy [*A publication*] *(DLA)*
LJC	La Jolla [*California*] [*Seismograph station code, US Geological Survey Closed*] *(SEIS)*
LJC	Laredo Junior College [*Texas*]
LJC	Lasell Junior College [*Newton, MA*]
LJC	Law Journal Reports, New Series, Common Pleas [*England*] [*A publication*] *(DLA)*
LJC	Lees Junior College [*Jackson, KY*]
LJC	London Juvenile Court *(DAS)*
LJC	Lord Jesus Christ *(ROG)*
LJC	Loretto Junior College [*Kentucky*]
LJC	Louisville, KY [*Location identifier FAA*] *(FAAL)*
LJCC	Law Journal, County Courts Reporter [*A publication*] *(DLA)*
LJCC	Local Joint Consultative Committee [*British*] *(DCTA)*
LJCCA	Law Journal Newspaper, County Court Appeals [*England*] [*A publication*] *(DLA)*
LJCCR	Law Journal Reports, New Series, Crown Cases Reserved [*England*] [*A publication*] *(DLA)*
LJCCR (NS)	Law Journal Reports, New Series, Crown Cases Reserved [*England*] [*A publication*] *(DLA)*
LJ Ch	Law Journal Reports, New Series, Chancery [*A publication*] *(DLA)*
LJ Ch (Eng)	Law Journal Reports, New Series, Chancery [*England*] [*A publication*] *(DLA)*
LJ Ch NS (Eng)	Law Journal Reports, New Series, Chancery [*England*] [*A publication*] *(DLA)*
LJ Ch (OS)	Law Journal Reports, Chancery, Old Series [*1822-31*] [*England*] [*A publication*] *(DLA)*
LJCP	Law Journal Reports, Common Pleas Decisions [*England*] [*A publication*] *(DLA)*
LJCPD	Law Journal Reports, Common Pleas Decisions [*England*] [*A publication*] *(DLA)*
LJCP (Eng)	Law Journal Reports, Common Pleas Decisions [*England*] [*A publication*] *(DLA)*
LJCP NS	Law Journal Reports, Common Pleas Decisions, New Series [*1831-75*] [*A publication*] *(DLA)*
LJCP NS (Eng)	Law Journal Reports, Common Pleas, New Series [*England*] [*A publication*] *(DLA)*
LJCP (OS)	Law Journal Reports, Common Pleas, Old Series [*England*] [*A publication*] *(DLA)*

LJCRF	La Jolla Cancer Research Foundation [*Research center*] *(RCD)*
LJCS	Lord Justice Clerk of Scotland *(DAS)*
LJD	Doctor of Letters of Journalism
LJD & M	Law Journal Reports, New Series, Divorce and Matrimonial [*England*] [*A publication*] *(DLA)*
LJDFC	Lacy J. Dalton Fan Club *(EA)*
LJE	Local Job Entry
LJ Ecc	Law Journal Reports, New Series, Ecclesiastical Cases [*A publication*] *(DLA)*
LJ Eccl	Law Journal Reports, New Series, Ecclesiastical Cases [*A publication*] *(DLA)*
LJED	Large Jet Engine Department [*NASA*] *(KSC)*
LJeL	LaSalle Parish Library, Jena, LA [*Library symbol Library of Congress*] *(LCLS)*
LJ Eq	Law Journal Reports, Chancery, New Series [*1831-1946*] [*A publication*] *(DLA)*
LJEWU	Lanka Jatika Estate Workers' Union [*Ceylon National Estate Workers' Union*]
LJ Ex	Law Journal Reports, New Series, Exchequer Division [*England*] [*A publication*] *(DLA)*
LJ Exch	Law Journal Reports, New Series, Exchequer Division [*England*] [*A publication*] *(DLA)*
LJ Exch (Eng)	Law Journal Reports, New Series, Exchequer Division [*England*] [*A publication*] *(DLA)*
LJ Exch in Eq (Eng)	English Law Journal. Exchequer in Equity [*A publication*] *(DLA)*
LJ Exch NS	Law Journal Reports, New Series, Exchequer [*1831-75*] [*A publication*] *(DLA)*
LJ Exch NS (Eng)	Law Journal Reports, New Series, Exchequer Division [*England*] [*A publication*] *(DLA)*
LJ Exch (OS)	Law Journal Reports, Exchequer, Old Series [*A publication*] *(DLA)*
LJ Ex D	Law Journal Reports, New Series, Exchequer Division [*England*] [*A publication*] *(DLA)*
LJ Ex Eq	Law Journal, Exchequer in Equity [*England*] [*A publication*] *(DLA)*
LJFC	Leon Jordan Fan Club *(EA)*
LJG	Levend Joods Geloof (Liberaal Joodse Gemeente) *(BJA)*
LJG	Lord Justice General [*British*]
LJHL	Law Journal Reports, New Series, House of Lords [*England*] [*A publication*] *(DLA)*
LJI	Legal Journals Index [*Information service or system*] *(IID)*
LJI	Library of Jewish Information *(BJA)*
LJI	List of Journals Indexed *(DMAA)*
LJIFS	Law Journal, Irish Free State [*1931-32*] [*A publication*] *(DLA)*
LJ Ir	Law Journal, Irish [*1933-34*] [*A publication*] *(DLA)*
LJJ	Jefferson Davis Parish Library, Jennings, LA [*Library symbol Library of Congress*] *(LCLS)*
LJJ	Lords Justices
LJK	Ashland, VA [*Location identifier FAA*] *(FAAL)*
LJKB	Law Journal Reports, King's Bench [*A publication*] *(DLA)*
LJKB (Eng)	Law Journal Reports, King's Bench [*England*] [*A publication*] *(DLA)*
LJKB NS	Law Journal Reports, King's Bench, New Series [*A publication*] *(DLA)*
LJKB NS (Eng)	Law Journal Reports, King's Bench, New Series [*England*] [*A publication*] *(DLA)*
LJKB OS	Law Journal, King's Bench, Old Series [*England*] [*A publication*] *(DLA)*
LJL	Lateral Joint Line [*Orthopedics*] *(DAVI)*
LJL	Little John Launcher [*Military*]
LJLC	Law Journal (Lower Canada) [*A publication*] *(DLA)*
LJLT	Law Journal (Law Tracts) [*England*] [*A publication*] *(DLA)*
LJLV	Little Joe Launch Vehicle [*NASA*]
LJM	Limited Joint Mobility [*Medicine*] *(DMAA)*
LJM	Lowenstein-Jensen Growth Medium *(MAE)*
LJ Mag	Law Journal, New Series, Common Law, Magistrates Cases (Discontinued) [*A publication*] *(DLA)*
LJ Mag Cas	Law Journal Reports, Magistrates' Cases [*1822-31*] [*A publication*] *(DLA)*
LJ Mag Cas (Eng)	Law Journal Reports, Magistrates' Cases [*England*] [*A publication*] *(DLA)*
LJ Mag Cas NS	Law Journal Reports, Magistrates' Cases, New Series [*1831-96*] [*A publication*] *(DLA)*
LJ Mag Cas NS (Eng)	Law Journal Reports, Magistrates' Cases, New Series [*England*] [*A publication*] *(DLA)*
LJM & W	Morgan and Williams' Law Journal [*London*] [*A publication*] *(DLA)*
LJ Mat	Law Journal, Matrimonial [*England*] [*A publication*] *(DLA)*
LJ Mat Cas	Law Journal, New Series, Divorce and Matrimonial [*England*] [*A publication*] *(DLA)*
LJ Mat (Eng)	Law Journal, Matrimonial [*England*] [*A publication*] *(DLA)*
LJMC	Law Journal Reports, New Series, Magistrates' Cases [*England*] [*A publication*] *(DLA)*
LJM Cas	Law Journal Reports, New Series, Magistrates' Cases [*England*] [*A publication*] *(DLA)*
LJMCOS	Law Journal Reports, Old Series, Magistrates' Cases [*England*] [*A publication*] *(DLA)*
LJMPA	Law Journal Reports, Matrimonial, Probate, and Admiralty [*England*] [*A publication*] *(DLA)*
LJN	Lake Jackson [*Texas*] [*Airport symbol*] *(OAG)*
LJNC	Law Journal, Notes of Cases [*A publication*] *(DLA)*
LJNCCA	Law Journal Newspaper, County Court Appeals [*England*] [*A publication*] *(DLA)*
LJNCCR	Law Journal Newspaper, County Court Reports [*England*] [*A publication*] *(DLA)*
LJNC (Eng)	Law Journal, Notes of Cases [*England*] [*A publication*] *(DLA)*
LJ News	Law Journal Newspaper [*1866-1965*] [*A publication*] *(DLA)*
LJ News (Eng)	Law Journal Newspaper [*England*] [*A publication*] *(DLA)*

LJ Newsp..... Law Journal Newspaper [1866-1965] [A publication] (DLA)
LJ NS........... Law Journal, New Series [England] [A publication] (DLA)
LJo........... Jackson Parish Library, Jonesboro, LA [Library symbol Library of Congress] (LCLS)
L Jo........... Law Journal Newspaper [England] [A publication] (DLA)
LJ of the Marut Bunnag Internat L Off... Law Journal. Marut Bunnag International Law Office [A publication] (DLA)
L Jo NC Law Journal, Notes of Cases [England] [A publication] (DLA)
LJ OS......... Law Journal, Old Series [1822-31] [London] [A publication] (DLA)
LJ OS Ch..... Law Journal, Old Series, Chancery [1822-23] [A publication] (DLA)
LJ OS CP..... Law Journal, Old Series, Common Pleas [1822-31] [A publication] (DLA)
LJ OS Ex..... Law Journal, Old Series, Exchequer [1830-31] [A publication] (DLA)
LJ OS KB..... Law Journal, Old Series, King's Bench [1822-31] [A publication] (DLA)
LJOSMC...... Law Journal, Old Series, Magistrates' Cases [1826-31] [A publication] (ILCA)
LJP............ Law Journal Reports, New Series, Privy Council [England] [A publication] (DLA)
LJP............ Law Journal Reports, Probate, Divorce, and Admiralty [England] [A publication] (DLA)
LJP............ Liquid Junction Potential
LJP............ Localized Juvenile Periodontitis [Dentistry]
LJP............ Local Job Processing (IAA)
LJP & M...... Law Journal, Probate and Matrimonial [England] [A publication] (DLA)
LJPC........... La Jolla Pharmaceutical [NASDAQ symbol] (SAG)
LJPC........... Law Journal Reports, Privy Council [England] [A publication] (DLA)
LJ PC (Eng)... Law Journal Reports, Privy Council [England] [A publication] (DLA)
LJ PC NS.... Law Journal Reports, New Series, Privy Council [England] [A publication] (DLA)
LJPCW........ La Jolla Pharmaceutical Wrrt [NASDAQ symbol] (TTSB)
LJPD & A..... Law Journal Reports, New Series, Probate, Divorce, and Admiralty [1875-1946] [A publication] (DLA)
LJPD & Adm... Law Journal Reports, New Series, Probate, Divorce, and Admiralty [England] [A publication] (DLA)
LJPM & A.... Law Journal Reports, New Series, Probate, Matrimonial, and Admiralty [England] [A publication] (DLA)
LJ Prob........ Law Journal Reports, New Series, Probate and Matrimonial [1858-59, 1866-75] [A publication] (DLA)
LJ Prob & Mat... Law Journal, Probate and Matrimonial [England] [A publication] (DLA)
LJ Prob (Eng)... Law Journal, Probate and Matrimonial [England] [A publication] (DLA)
LJ Prob NS... Law Journal Reports, New Series, Probate and Matrimonial [1858-59, 1866-75] [A publication] (DLA)
LJ Prob NS (Eng)... Law Journal, Probate and Matrimonial, New Series [England] [A publication] (DLA)
LJQB........... Law Journal Reports, New Series, Queen's Bench [England] [A publication] (DLA)
LJQBD .... Law Journal Reports, New Series, Queen's Bench Division [England] [A publication] (DLA)
LJQBD NS.... Law Journal Reports, New Series, Queen's Bench Division [England] [A publication] (DLA)
LJQB (Eng)... Law Journal Reports, New Series, Queen's Bench [England] [A publication] (DLA)
LJQB NS...... Law Journal Reports, New Series, Queen's Bench [1831-1946] [A publication] (DLA)
LJQB NS (Eng)... Law Journal Reports, Queen's Bench, New Series [England] [A publication] (DLA)
LJR .... Law Journal Reports [A publication]
LJR .... Lead Joint Runner
LJR .... Little John Rocket [Military]
LJR .... Lone Jack Resources Ltd. [Vancouver Stock Exchange symbol]
LJR .... Low Jet Route (ADA)
LJR (Eng) .... Law Journal Reports [England] [A publication] (DLA)
LJ Rep .... Law Journal Reports [A publication] (DLA)
LJ Rep NS ... Law Journal Reports, New Series [A publication] (DLA)
LJS .... Lap Joint Strength
LJ Sm......... Smith's Law Journal [London] [A publication] (DLA)
LJSU .... Local Junction Switching Unit [Telecommunications] (TEL)
LJU .... Ljubljana [Slovenia] [Seismograph station code, US Geological Survey] (SEIS)
LJU .... Ljubljana [Slovenia] [Airport symbol] (OAG)
LJU .... Oscoda, MI [Location identifier FAA] (FAAL)
LJUC .... Law Journal of Upper Canada [A publication] (DLA)
LJWG .... Logistic Joint Work Group [DoD]
LJZ .... Lajes [Brazil] [Airport symbol] (AD)
LK .... Arawak Airlines (OAG)
LK .... Laiko Komma [Populist Party] [Greece] [Political party] (PPE)
LK .... Lake [Board on Geographic Names] (MCD)
LK .... Lake
LK .... Leak (KSC)
LK .... Left Kidney [Medicine]
LK .... Lek [Monetary unit] [Albania]
Lk .... Leptosphaeria korrea [A fungus]
LK .... Letaba Airways [ICAO designator] (AD)
LK .... Lichenoid Keratosis [Medicine] (DMAA)
LK .... Liederkranz [Type of cheese] (BJA)
L-K .... Linguistic-Kinesic [Psychiatry]
LK .... Link (KSC)
LK .... Lock [Automotive engineering]
LK .... Looking for Party [Telecommunications] (TEL)
LK .... Lord Keeper [of the Great Seal] [British] (ROG)
LK .... Lowenfeld Kaleidoblocs [Psychological testing]

LK .... Low-Priority Key [Computer science]
Lk .... Luke [New Testament book]
LK .... Lymphokine [Immunochemistry]
LK .... Sri Lanka [ANSI two-letter standard code] (CNC)
LK1 .... Ladies' Kayak, Single Person (ADA)
LK2 .... Ladies' Kayak, Two Person (ADA)
LK4 .... Ladies' Kayak, Four Person (ADA)
LKA .... Alkair Flight Operations APS [Denmark ICAO designator] (FAAC)
LKA .... Amphibious Cargo Ship [Navy symbol]
LKA .... Attack Cargo Ship [Navy symbol]
LKA .... Ladies Kennel Association [British] (BI)
LKA .... Larantuka [Indonesia] [Airport symbol] (OAG)
LKA .... Last Known Address (LAIN)
LKA .... Lighthouse Keepers Association (EA)
LKA .... Literarische Keilschrifttexte aus Assur [A publication] (BJA)
LKA .... Miraloma, CA [Location identifier FAA] (FAAL)
LKA .... Sri Lanka [ANSI three-letter standard code] (CNC)
LKAA .... Ladies Kennel Association of America (EA)
LKAA .... Praha [Former Czechoslovakia] [ICAO location identifier] (ICLI)
LK & PRR .... Lahaina-Kaanapali & Pacific Railroad [Hawaii]
LKA of A ..... Ladies Kennel Association of America (EA)
LKartB .... Landeskartellbehoerde [Provincial Cartel Authority] [German] (DLA)
LKB .... Lakeba [Fiji] [Airport symbol] (OAG)
LKBB .... Bratislava [Former Czechoslovakia] [ICAO location identifier] (ICLI)
LKC .... Lake Chabot [California] [Seismograph station code, US Geological Survey] (SEIS)
LKC .... Lake Charles [Diocesan abbreviation] [Louisiana] (TOCD)
LKC .... Lancaster County Library, Lancaster, PA [OCLC symbol] (OCLC)
LKC .... Lekana [Congo] [Airport symbol] (OAG)
LKCL .... LASER Kit Combination Lock
LKD .... Locked (KSC)
LKDP .... Lietuviu Krikscioniu Demokratu Partija [Lithuanian Christian Democratic Party] [Political party] (PPE)
LKF .... Linear Kalman Filter
LKG .... League of the Kingdom of God [Church of England]
LKG .... Leakage (MSA)
LKG .... Linking (IAA)
LKG .... Locking (KSC)
LKG .... Looking (MSA)
LKG .... Loop Key Generator (MCD)
LKGABKG...... Leakage and Breakage (IAA)
LKG & BKG... Leakage and Breakage (WDAA)
LKGE .... Linkage (MSA)
LKHO .... Holesov [Former Czechoslovakia] [ICAO location identifier] (ICLI)
LKI .... Duluth, MN [Location identifier FAA] (FAAL)
LKI .... Lazare Kaplan International, Inc. [AMEX symbol] (SPSG)
LKI .... Lazare Kaplan Intl [AMEX symbol] (TTSB)
LKI .... Loki Gold Corp. [Vancouver Stock Exchange symbol]
LKIB .... Bratislava/Ivanka [Former Czechoslovakia] [ICAO location identifier] (ICLI)
LKID .... Left Kidney [Anatomy] (DAVI)
LKJ .... Linton Kwesi Johnson [British musician]
LKK .... Kulik Lake, AK [Location identifier FAA] (FAAL)
LKK .... Lake Shore Mines Ltd. [Toronto Stock Exchange symbol]
LKKV .... Karlovy Vary [Former Czechoslovakia] [ICAO location identifier] (ICLI)
LKKZ .... Kosice [Former Czechoslovakia] [ICAO location identifier] (ICLI)
LKL .... Lakeland Aviation [ICAO designator] (FAAC)
LKL .... Lakselv [Norway] [Airport symbol] (OAG)
LKLY .... Likely (FAAC)
LKM .... Lafayette, LA [Location identifier FAA] (FAAL)
LKM .... Liver-Kidney Microsomal [Antibody] [Medicine] (DMAA)
LKM .... Locke Rich Minerals [Vancouver Stock Exchange symbol]
LKM .... Low-Key Maintenance
LKM .... Nekempt [Ethiopia] [Airport symbol] (AD)
LKMT .... Ostrava [Former Czechoslovakia] [ICAO location identifier] (ICLI)
LKN .... Leknes [Norway] [Airport symbol] (OAG)
LKN .... Lock-In
LK-NDV....... Newcastle Disease Virus, L-Kansas Strain
LKNPOS....... Last Known Position (MCD)
LKNPT .... Last Known Port (MCD)
LKNT .... Locknut (MSA)
LKO .... Billings, MT [Location identifier FAA] (FAAL)
LKO .... Lucknow [India] [Airport symbol] (OAG)
LKP .... Lake Placid, NY [Location identifier FAA] (FAAL)
LKP .... Lamellar Keratoplasty [Ophthalmology]
LKP .... Landelijke Knokplogen [Netherlands Regional Action Groups] [World War II]
LKP .... Last Known Position [Aviation] (NVT)
LKP .... Liberaalinen Kansanpuolue [Liberal People's Party] [Finland Political party] (PPE)
LKP .... Lietuvos Komunisty Partija [Communist Party of Lithuania] [Political party] (PPE)
LKPP .... Piestany [Former Czechoslovakia] [ICAO location identifier] (ICLI)
LKPR .... Praha/Ruzyne [Former Czechoslovakia] [ICAO location identifier] (ICLI)
LKQ .... Like Kind and Quality (Metal) [Auto repair]
LKQCPI........ Licentiate of the King's and Queen's College of Physicians of Ireland
LKR .... Lake Air Helicopters Ltd. [British ICAO designator] (FAAC)
LKR .... Lancaster, SC [Location identifier FAA] (FAAL)
LKR .... Left Knee Right [Guitar playing]
LKR .... LK Resources Ltd. [Toronto Stock Exchange symbol]
LKR .... Locker (KSC)
LKROT .... Locked Rotor
LKRT .... Loyal Knights of the Round Table (EA)

LKS	Lakes
LKS	Lakes [Commonly used] (OPSA)
LKS	Lakeside Aviation Ltd. [British ICAO designator] (FAAC)
LKS	Lambda Kappa Sigma (EA)
LKS	Liberation Kanake Socialiste [Socialist Kanak Liberation] [New Caledonia] (PD)
LKS	Liver, Kidneys, and Spleen (DAVI)
LKS	Liver, Kidney, Spleen [Medicine]
LKS	Logan-Keck-Stickney [Method]
LKS	Louisville, KY [Location identifier FAA] (FAAL)
LKS	Lucky 7 Exploration [Vancouver Stock Exchange symbol]
LKSB	Liver, Kidney, Spleen, Bladder [Medicine] (DMAA)
LKSCR	Lockscrew
LKSL	Sliac [Former Czechoslovakia] [ICAO location identifier] (ICLI)
LKS NP	Liver, Kidneys, and Spleen Not Palpable [On physical examination] (DAVI)
LKT	Locket (ROG)
LKT	Lookout (MSA)
LKT	Salmon, ID [Location identifier FAA] (FAAL)
LKTT	Poprad/Tatry [Former Czechoslovakia] [ICAO location identifier] (ICLI)
LKTYP	Like Type (FAAC)
LKU	Literarische Keilschrifttexte aus Uruk [A publication] (BJA)
LKUP	Lockup
LKV	Laked Kanamycin-Vancomycin [Agar] [Microbiology]
LKV	Lake Ventures Ltd. [Vancouver Stock Exchange symbol]
LKV	Lakeview, OR [Location identifier FAA] (FAAL)
LKV	Left Knee Vertical [Guitar playing]
LKV	Lengyel-Kerman-Vargar [Rating] [Psychology] (DAVI)
LKVY	Lykens Valley Railroad Co. [AAR code]
LKW	Lake Wisdom [Papua New Guinea] [Seismograph station code, US Geological Survey] (SEIS)
LKW	Lakewood Mining [Vancouver Stock Exchange symbol]
LKW	Larkana [Pakistan] [Airport symbol] (AD)
LK/WA	Lock Washer [Automotive engineering]
LKWASH	Lock Washer [Automotive engineering]
LKX	La Pryor, TX [Location identifier FAA] (FAAL)
LKY	Lucky Strike Resources [Vancouver Stock Exchange symbol]
LKZ	Letaba Airways [South Africa ICAO designator] (FAAC)
LL	All Is Well [Search and rescue symbol that can be stamped in sand or snow]
LL	Bell-Air [ICAO designator] (AD)
LL	Double-Loop Magnetic Mine Sweep [Navy British]
LL	Lab. Lafon [France] [Research code symbol]
LL	Labor Letter [Cast Metals Association] [A publication]
LL	Lamina Lucida [Dermatology]
LL	Landline [Aviation]
LL	Land-Line [Telecommunications] (TEL)
LL	Land Locomotion Division [Army Tank-Automotive Command] [Warren, MI]
LL	Land Locomotion Laboratory [Army]
LL	Landlord [Legal shorthand] (LWAP)
ll	Lapis Lazuli (VRA)
LL	Large Letter
LL	Large Light Seeds [Botany]
LL	Large Lymphocyte [Medicine]
LL	Last (ROG)
LL	Late Latin [Language, etc.]
LL	Latent Lethality [Radiation casualty criterion] [Army]
LL	Lateral Lemniscus [Neuroanatomy]
LL	Lateral Line [Invertebrate zoology]
LL	Lateral Lip
L/L	Latitude/Longitude (IEEE)
LL	Laugh Lovers (EA)
LL	Launch and Landing [NASA] (NASA)
LL	Launch Left (MCD)
LL	Laurentian Life Insurance Co., Inc. [Toronto Stock Exchange symbol]
LL	Law Latin
L-L	Law Library of Louisiana, New Orleans, LA [Library symbol Library of Congress] (LCLS)
LL	Law List (ILCA)
LL	Laws (ROG)
LL	Laymen's League (EA)
LL	League (ROG)
LL	Lean Line (EA)
LL	Leased Line [Private telephone or Teletype line] [Telecommunications]
LL	Lease or Loan
LL	Leaves [Bibliography]
LL	Lederle Laboratories [Research code symbol]
LL	Left Lateral [Anatomy] (DAVI)
LL	Left Leg (MAE)
LL	Left Lower [Medicine]
LL	Left Lung [Medicine]
LL	Lega Lombarda [Italy] [Political party] (ECED)
LL	Leges [Laws] [Latin]
LL	Legislative Liaison
LL	Legum [Of Laws] [Latin] (ADA)
L/L	Leigh Light [British military] (DMA)
LL	Lending Library
LL	Lend-Lease [Bill] [World War II]
LL	Lepromatous-Type Leprosy [Animal pathology]
LL	Lessons Learned
LL	Lever Lock (MCD)
LL	Liberty Lobby (EA)

L/L	Library Labels [Antiquarian book trade]
LL	License in Civil Law
LL	Lighterage Limits
LL	Light Line [Military]
LL	Light Load (AAG)
LL	Light Lock
LL	Light Lorry [British]
LL	Limited Liability [Finance]
LL	Limiting Level
LL	Lincoln Laboratory [MIT] (MCD)
LL	Lincoln Library of Essential Information
L/L	Line for Line [Typesetting] (WDMC)
LL	Line Leg [Telegraph] [Telecommunications] (TEL)
LL	Line Link (IAA)
LL	Lines
ll	Lines (WDMC)
LL	Lines Layout (MCD)
L-L	Line-to-Line (MCD)
LL	Linking Loader (MCD)
LL	Link Level [Telecommunications]
LL	Liquid Level (ECII)
LL	Liquid Limit (IEEE)
L/L	Liquid/Liquid Extraction [Laboratory procedure]
LL	Liquor Law
LL	Literary Lives [A publication]
LL	Litre (ROG)
LL	Little League [Baseball]
LL	Live Load
LL	Load Line [Shipping] (DS)
LL	Load List (MSA)
LL	Local Lesion [Pathology]
LL	Local Line [Telecommunications]
LL	Local Linearization
LL	Local Loopback (MHDB)
LL	Locator Lists [Army]
LL	Loco Laudato [In the Place Quoted] [Latin]
LL	Lodges [Freemasonry] (ROG)
LL	Loft Line (MSA)
LL	Long Lead (NASA)
LL	Long Line [Telecommunications] (MCD)
LL	Loose Leaf
LL	Lord Lieutenant
LL	Lords
LL	Loudness Level
LL	Lower Laterals [Botany]
LL	Lower Left
LL	Lower Leg
LL	Lower Lid [Ophthalmology]
LL	Lower Limb [Lower edge of sun, moon, etc.] [Navigation]
LL	Lower Limen [Psychology]
LL	Lower Limit
LL	Lower Lip [Anatomy] (DAVI)
LL	Lower Lobe [Medicine]
LL	Low Latin [Language, etc.]
LL	Low Level
LL	Low Load [Finance]
LL	Lumbar Length [Anatomy] (DAVI)
LL	Lunar Landing [NASA] (KSC)
LL	Luther League [Defunct] (EA)
LL	Lutlag [Limited Company] [Norwegian]
LL	Lymphoblastic Lymphoma [Oncology] (DAVI)
L/L	Lymphoma/Leukemia [Oncology]
LL	Lysolecithin [Biochemistry]
LLA	Lady Licentiate of Arts [Scotland]
LLA	Lady Literate in Arts [British]
LLA	Latin Liturgy Association (EA)
LLA	Laubach Literacy Action (EA)
LLA	Leased Line Adapter [Telecommunications]
LLA	Leased Line Adaptor (NITA)
LLA	Lend-Lease Administration [Defunct]
LLA	Lesotho Liberation Army (PD)
LLA	Limited Locus Allowed [Legal] (ROG)
LLA	Limiting Lines of Approach [Navy] (NVT)
LLA	Limulus Lysate Assay (DMAA)
LLA	Literary Landmarks Association (EA)
LLA	Little Library [À publication]
LLA	Llanada [California] [Seismograph station code, US Geological Survey] (SEIS)
LLA	Lower Left Abdomen [Injection Site]
LLA	Low-Level Analog (MCD)
LLA	Low Low Alarm (ECII)
LLA	Lulea [Sweden] [Airport symbol] (OAG)
LLA	Luther League of America [Later, LL]
LLA	Servicio Leo Lopez SA de CV [Mexico ICAO designator] (FAAC)
LLA	White Lake, LA [Location identifier FAA] (FAAL)
LLAA	Israel Airports Authority Headquarters [Israel] [ICAO location identifier] (ICLI)
LLAAII	Leurs Altesses Imperiales [Their Imperial Highnesses] [French]
LLAARR	Leurs Altesses Royales [Their Royal Highnesses] [French]
LLAD	Ben Gurion [Israel] [ICAO location identifier] (ICLI)
LLAD	Low-Level Air Defence [Navy British]
LLafL	Lafayette Public Library, Lafayette, LA [Library symbol Library of Congress] (LCLS)
LLafS	University of Southwestern Louisiana, Lafayette, LA [Library symbol Library of Congress] (LCLS)

LL Alfredi .... Leges Alfredi [*Laws of King Alfred*] [*Latin A publication*] (DLA)
Llam .... Lumbar Laminectomy [*Medicine*] (DAVI)
LLAMA .... Low-Level Acceleration Measurement Apparatus
LLAN .... Llandaff (ROG)
LL & B .... Latch, Lock, and Bolt (DAC)
LI & GTP .... Lloyd and Goold's Irish Chancery Reports Tempore Plunkett
               [*A publication*] (DLA)
LI & GT PI ... Lloyd and Goold's Irish Chancery Reports Tempore Plunkett
               [*A publication*] (DLA)
LI & GTS .... Lloyd and Goold's Irish Chancery Reports Tempore Sugden [*1835*]
               [*A publication*] (DLA)
LL & N .... Language, Literacy and Numeracy Skills Taskforce [*Australia*]
LI & W .... Lloyd and Welsby's English Mercantile Cases [*A publication*] (DLA)
LI & Wels .... Lloyd and Welsby's English Commercial Cases [*A publication*] (DLA)
LLAP .... LocalTalk Link Access Protocol [*Computer science*] (ACRL)
LLap .... Saint John Parish Library, La Place, LA [*Library symbol Library of
               Congress*] (LCLS)
LLAR .... Local Loop Access Ring [*Telecommunications*] (ACRL)
LLAT .... Law Latin
LLAT .... Lawrence Lowery Apperception Test
LLAT .... Left Lateral [*Radiology*] (DAVI)
LL Athelst .... Laws of Athelstan [*A publication*] (DLA)
LLATIS .... Low Light and Thermal Imaging System (PDAA)
LLAW .... Liquid Low Activity Waste [*Nuclear energy*] (NUCP)
LLB .... Bachelor of Laws (DD)
LL B .... Bachelor of Laws (PGP)
LLB .... Computrac, Inc. [*AMEX symbol*] (SPSG)
LLB .... Lawyers' Law Books [*1977*] [*A publication*] (ILCA)
LLB .... Left Lateral Border [*Medicine*] (DMAA)
LLB .... Left Linebacker (WGA)
LLB .... Legum Baccalaureus [*Bachelor of Laws*] [*Latin*]
LLB .... Liquor Licensing Board [*Australian Capital Territory*]
LLB .... Little League Baseball (EA)
LLB .... Lloyd Aereo Boliviano SA [*Bolivia*] [*ICAO designator*] (FAAC)
LLB .... Long Leg Brace [*Orthopedics*]
LLB .... Long-Leg Brace (DMAA)
LLB .... Lower Leg Brace [*Medicine*]
LLB .... Luluabourg [*Zaire*] [*Airport symbol*] (AD)
LLBA .... Language and Language Behavior Abstracts [*Sociological Abstracts*]
               [*Database*] (NITA)
LLBAM .... Lincoln Laboratory Boolean Algebra Minimizer (IAA)
LLBBMA .... Loose Leaf and Blank Book Manufacturers Association [*Later,
               ABPM*] (EA)
LLBC .... Liquid Large-Bore Cannon (MCD)
LLBCD .... Left Lower Border of Cardiac Dullness [*Cardiology*]
LLBD .... Meteorological Service [*Israel*] [*ICAO location identifier*] (ICLI)
LLBG .... Tel Aviv/D. Ben Gurion [*Israel*] [*ICAO location identifier*] (ICLI)
LLBS .... Beersheba/Teyman [*Israel*] [*ICAO location identifier*] (ICLI)
LLBS .... Low-Level Bombsight (NATG)
LL Burgund ... Laws of Burgundians [*A publication*] (DLA)
LLc .... Lake Charles Public Library, Lake Charles, LA [*Library symbol
               Library of Congress*] (LCLS)
LLC .... Lakeland Library Cooperative [*Library network*]
LLC .... La Lucha Farm [*Costa Rica*] [*Seismograph station code, US
               Geological Survey*] (SEIS)
LLC .... Lankalink Aircargo (Pvp) Ltd. [*Sri Lanka*] [*FAA designator*] (FAAC)
LLC .... Law Certificate
LLC .... Left Line Contactor (MCD)
LLC .... Light Salvage Ship [*Navy symbol*] (VNW)
LLC .... Lightweight Leader Computer [*Army*] (INF)
LLC .... Limited Liability Company
LLC .... Limited Life Component (MCD)
LLC .... Liquid Level Control
LLC .... Liquid Level Controller (ECII)
LLC .... Liquid-Liquid Chromatography
LLC .... Local Level Control [*Electronics*]
LLC .... Logical Link Control [*Telecommunications*]
LLC .... Logic Link Control [*Network interfacing*] (NITA)
LLC .... Long Leg Cast [*Orthopedics*]
LLC .... Long Lines Coordination (NATG)
LLC .... Long-Linking Carbon
LLC .... Low Liquid Cutoff
LLC .... Loyola University, Career Information Center, New Orleans, LA
               [*OCLC symbol*] (OCLC)
LLC .... Luneberg Lens Commutator [*Physics*]
LLC .... Lymphocytic Leukemia, Chronic (MAE)
LLC .... Lyotropic Liquid Crystals [*Physical chemistry*]
LL Canuti R ... Laws of King Canute [*or Knut*] [*A publication*] (DLA)
LLcC .... Calcasieu Parish Public Library, Lake Charles, LA [*Library symbol
               Library of Congress*] (LCLS)
LI CC Pr .... Lloyd's County Courts Practice [*A publication*] (DLA)
LLCF .... Launch and Landing Computational Facilities [*NASA*] (NASA)
LLCFR .... Lobbyists and Lawyers for Campaign Finance Reform (EA)
LLCM .... Licentiate of the London College of Music [*British*] (DBQ)
LLCM .... Master of Comparative Law (DLA)
LLCM .... Master of Comparative Law (GAGS)
LLcM .... McNeese State University, Lake Charles, LA [*Library symbol Library
               of Congress*] (LCLS)
LLCM(TD) .... Licentiate of the London College of Music (Teacher's Diploma)
               [*British*]
LLCO .... Licentiate of the London College of Osteopathy
LI Comp .... Lloyd's Compensation for Lands, Etc. [*6th ed.*] [*1895*]
               [*A publication*] (DLA)
LL COOL J ... Ladies Love Cool James [*Rap recording artist, James Todd Smith*]
LLCS .... Link Level Communications Subsystem [*NCR Corp.*]

LLCS .... Liquid Level Control Switch
LLCS .... Low-Level Compaction Station [*Nuclear energy*] (NRCH)
LLCSC .... Lower Level Computer Software Component
LLCUNAE ..... Law Library of Congress United Association of Employees
LLD .... Doctor of Laws (DD)
LL D .... Doctor of Laws (PGP)
LLD .... Doctor of Laws (GAGS)
LLD .... Lactobacillus Lactis Dorner Factor [*Vitamin B$_{12}$*] [*Also, APA, APAF,
               EF*]
LLD .... Lamp Lumen Depreciation
LLD .... LASER Light Detector
LLD .... Launcher Load Dolly
LLD .... Law and Legal Information Directory [*A publication*]
LLD .... Left Lateral Decubitus [*Medicine*] (AAMN)
LLD .... Leg Length Discrepancy [*Orthopedics*] (DAVI)
LLD .... Legum Doctor [*Doctor of Laws*] [*Latin*]
LLD .... Live Letter-Drop [*Espionage*]
LLD .... Logic Level Driver [*Computer science*] (MCD)
LLD .... Long-Lasting Depolarization [*Neurophysiology*]
LLD .... Lower Limit of Detection [*Spectrometry*]
LLD .... Low-Level Detector (IEEE)
LLD .... Low-Level Dose [*Nuclear energy*] (NRCH)
LLDEF .... Lambda Legal Defense and Education Fund (EA)
LLDH .... Liver Lactate Dehydrogenase [*An enzyme*] (DAVI)
LLDL .... Low-Level Differential Logic (IAA)
LLDPE .... Linear Low-Density Polyethylene [*Plastics technology*]
LLDR .... Lightweight LASER [*Light Amplification by Stimulated Emission of
               Radiation*] Designator Range Finder [*DoD*]
LLDS .... Low-Level Weapons Delivery System (MCD)
LLDV .... Luc-Luong Dac-Viet [*Vietnamese special forces*]
LLE .... Laboratory for LASER Energetics [*University of Rochester*] [*Research
               center*]
LLE .... Large Local Exchange [*Telecommunications*] (TEL)
LLE .... Left Lower Extremity [*Medicine*]
LLE .... Lightning Loss Exclusion [*Insurance*]
LLE .... Liquid-Liquid Equilibria [*Physical chemistry*]
LLE .... Liquid-Liquid Extraction
LLE .... Long Line Effect
LLE .... Long Line Equipment [*Telecommunications*] (TEL)
LLE .... West Bend, WI [*Location identifier FAA*] (FAAL)
LL Edw Conf ... Laws of Edward the Confessor [*A publication*] (DLA)
LLEE .... Leurs Eminences [*Their Eminences*] [*French*]
LLEE .... Leurs Excellences [*Their Excellencies*] [*French*]
LLEIS .... Lower Level End Item Subdivision [*Army*] (AABC)
LLE Ry .... LL & E Royalty Trust [*Associated Press*] (SAG)
LLES .... Eyn-Shemer [*Israel*] [*ICAO location identifier*] (ICLI)
LLeS .... Leesville State School, Leesville, LA [*Library symbol Library of
               Congress*] (LCLS)
LLET .... Elat/J. Hozman [*Israel*] [*ICAO location identifier*] (ICLI)
L LETT .... Licentiate of Letters (WDAA)
LLETZ .... Large Loop Excision of the Transformation Zone [*Medicine*]
LLeV .... Vernon Parish Library, Leesville, LA [*Library symbol Library of
               Congress*] (LCLS)
LLF .... Fibrin-Stabilizing Factor [*Hematology*] (DAVI)
LLF .... Lag Line Filter
LLF .... Laki-Lorand Factor [*Factor XIII*] [*Also, FSF Hematology*]
LLF .... Land Level Facility [*Navy*]
LLF .... Latin American Growth Fd [*NYSE symbol*] (TTSB)
LLF .... Laubach Literacy Fund [*Later, LLI*] (EA)
LLF .... Left Lateral Femoral [*Site of injection*] [*Medicine*]
LLF .... Left Lateral Flexion [*Medicine*] (DMAA)
LL F .... Lehman Brothers Latin American Growth Fund [*NYSE symbol*]
               (SAG)
LLF .... Light Loss Factor [*Floodlighting*]
LLF .... Line Link Frame [*Telecommunications*] (TEL)
LLF .... Little League Foundation (EA)
LLF .... Load List File (AFIT)
LLFA .... Low-Low Frequency Acoustics (DOMA)
LLFC .... Laryssa Lauret Fan Club (EA)
LLFC .... Loretta Lynn Fan Club (EA)
LLFET .... Linear-Load Field Effect Transistor [*Electronics*] (PDAA)
LLFM .... Land Line Frequency Modulation (AAG)
LLFM .... Low-Level Flux Monitor [*Nuclear energy*] (NRCH)
LLFPB .... Linear, Lumped, Finite, Passive, Bilateral
LLG .... Chillagoe [*Australia Airport symbol Obsolete*] (OAG)
LLG .... Line-to-Line to Ground (IAA)
LLG .... Logical Language Group [*An association*] (EA)
LLG .... Logical Line Group [*Computer science*] (IBMDP)
LLGc .... Luggage and Leather Goods Salesmen's Association of America
               (EA)
LLGA .... Leadless Land Grid Array [*Electronics*] (EECA)
LLGAF .... Leslie-Lohman Gay Art Foundation (EA)
LLGDS .... Landlocked and Geographically Disadvantaged States [*Developing
               countries*]
LLGF .... Leather, Leather Goods, Fur [*Department of Employment*] [*British*]
LLGL .... Low-Level Graphical Language (PDAA)
LLGMA .... Luggage and Leather Goods Manufacturers of America (EA)
LL-GXT .... Low-Level Graded Exercise Test [*Cardiology*] (DAVI)
LLH .... Ladies Left Handed
LLH .... Lahore Light Horse [*British military*] (DMA)
LLH .... Library of Literary History [*A publication*]
LLH .... Low-Level Heating [*Nuclear energy*] (OA)
LLHA .... Haifa/U. Michaeli [*Israel*] [*ICAO location identifier*] (ICLI)
LL Hen I ...... Laws of Henry I [*A publication*] (DLA)
LLHZ .... Herzlia [*Israel*] [*ICAO location identifier*] (ICLI)

LLI .... Lalibella [Ethiopia] [Airport symbol] (OAG)
LLI .... Language-Based Learning Impairment [Neurology]
LLI .... Late Latent Infection [Medicine]
LLI .... Latitude and Longitude Indicator
LLI .... Laubach Literacy International (EA)
LLI .... Life Line International (EA)
LLI .... Ligula Length Index
LLI .... Limited Life Item (MCD)
LLI .... Link Layer Interface [Computer science] (PCM)
LLI .... Lipari [Lipari Islands] [Seismograph station code, US Geological
                    Survey] (SEIS)
LLI .... Liquid Level Indicator
LLI .... Logical Link Identifier (ACRL)
LLI .... Longitude and Latitude Indicator
LLI .... Long Lead Item (MUGU)
LLI .... Lord Lieutenant of Ireland
LLI .... Low-Level Interface
LLIB .... Load Module Librarian (MHDB)
LLIB .... Rosh Pina/Mahanaim-I. Ben-Yaakov [Israel] [ICAO location
                    identifier] (ICLI)
LLIBC .... Lotus Lantern International Buddhist Center [South Korea] (EAIO)
LLIL .... Long Lead Item List
LLIL .... Long Lead Time Items List (NASA)
LLiLi .... Livingston Parish Library, Livingston, LA [Library symbol Library of
                    Congress] (LCLS)
LL Inse .... Laws of Ina [A publication] (DLA)
LLIT .... Liquid-Like Intermediate Transistory
LLIU .... Launch and Landing Interface Unit (MCD)
LLIV .... Low-Level Input Voltage
LLJ .... Challis, ID [Location identifier FAA] (FAAL)
LLJ .... Lahore Law Journal [India] [A publication] (DLA)
LLJ .... Lalmonirhat [Bangladesh] [Airport symbol] (AD)
LLJ .... LaTrobe Library Journal [A publication]
LLJ .... Low-Level Jet (USDC)
LLJ .... Low-Level Jet [Marine science] (OSRA)
LLJJ .... Lords Justices
LLJM .... Ministry of Transport [Israel] [ICAO location identifier] (ICLI)
LI Jud Act.... Lloyd's Supreme Court of Judicature Acts [1875] [A publication]
                    (DLA)
LLK .... Liberator Lake, AK [Location identifier FAA] (FAAL)
LLK .... Little Lake Resources Ltd. [Vancouver Stock Exchange symbol]
LLK .... Louis Leakey - Korongo [Anthropological skull]
LLL .... La Leche League [Local affiliates of LLLI] (EA)
LLL .... Land Locomotion Laboratory [Army]
LLL .... Lawrence Livermore Laboratory [Also, LLNL] [University of
                    California]
LLL .... Lawyers, Layers, and Limos [Television broadcasting industry]
LLL .... Left Lower Eyelid [Medicine]
LLL .... Left Lower Limb [Anatomy] (DAVI)
LLL .... Left Lower Lobe [of lung] [Medicine]
LLL .... Liberte, Liberation, et Liberation Nationale [French resistance
                    movement] [World War II]
LLL .... Licentiate in Laws
LLL .... Light Living Library (EA)
LLL .... Lillooet [British Columbia] [Seismograph station code, US Geological
                    Survey Closed] (SEIS)
LLL .... Long Lead List (MCD)
LL/L .... Long Leadtime/Items List
LLL .... Long Line Loiter [Aircraft]
LLL .... Loose Leaf Ledger
LLL .... Love's Labour's Lost [Shakespearean work]
LLL .... Lower Lip Length [Medicine]
LLL .... Low Level Language [Computer programming] (NTCM)
LLL .... Low-Level Logic
LLL .... Low Light Level
LLL .... Low Liquid Level [Engineering]
LLL .... Loyal Lusitanian League [British military] (DMA)
LLL .... Lutheran Laymen's League [Later, ILLL] (EA)
LLL .... University of Nebraska, Lincoln College of Law, Lincoln, NE [OCLC
                    symbol] (OCLC)
LLLB .... Left Long Leg Brace [Medicine]
LLLGB .... Low-Level-LASER Guided Bomb
LLLI .... La Leche League International (EA)
LI List LR ... Lloyd's List Law Reports [England] [A publication] (DLA)
LLLLL .... Laboratories Low Level Linked List (NITA)
LLLLLL ...... Laboratories Low-Level Linked List Language [Bell Systems] (MCD)
LI LLR .... Lloyd's List Law Reports [England] [A publication] (DLA)
LLLO .... Lend-Lease Liaison Office [World War II]
LL Longobard... Laws of the Lombards [A publication] (DLA)
LI L Pr Cas... Lloyd's List Prize Cases Reports [England] [A publication] (DLA)
LI LR .... Lloyd's List Law Reports [England] [A publication] (DLA)
LI L Rep ..... Lloyd's List Law Reports [England] [A publication] (DLA)
LLLT .... Low-Light-Level Television [Night vision device] [Military] (RDA)
LLLTV .... Low-Level LASER Television
LLLTV .... Low-Light-Level Television [Night vision device] [Military]
LLLTV .... Low-Light-Level Television [Military] (DOMA)
LLLW .... Liquid Low Level Waste [Nuclear energy] (NUCP)
LLLW .... Low Level Liquid Waste [Nuclear energy] (NUCP)
LLLWT .... Low-Level Liquid Waste Tank [Nuclear energy] (NRCH)
LLM .... Launcher Loader Module
LLM .... Lawyers Linked by MODEM [Computer bulletin board system] [FIDO]
LLM .... Legum Magister [Master of Laws] [Latin]
LLM .... Limb Load Monitor
LLM .... Linear Learning Machine [Data analysis]
LLM .... Load Line Method

LLM .... Localized Leukocyte Mobilization
LLM .... Long Lama [Malaysia] [Airport symbol] (AD)
LLM .... Low-Level Multiplexer
LLM .... Loyola University, New Orleans, LA [OCLC symbol] (OCLC)
LLM .... Lunar Landing Mission [NASA]
LLM .... Lunar Landing Module [NASA] (MCD)
LLM .... Master of Law (GAGS)
LLM .... Master of Laws
LL M .... Master of Laws (PGP)
LLMA .... Leavers Lace Manufacturers of America [Defunct] (EA)
LL Malcom R Scott... Laws of Malcolm, King of Scotland [A publication] (DLA)
LI Mar LN .... Lloyd's Maritime Law Newsletter [A publication] (DLA)
LLM (CL) .... Master of Laws in Comparative Law
LLM Com.... Master of Commercial Law
LLME .... Leuo Leucine Methylester [Biochemistry]
LLMFC .... Laura Lee McBride Fan Club (EA)
LLMH .... Loyal Legion of the Medal of Honor (EA)
LLMI .... Local Labour Market Information/Intelligence [British] (AIE)
LLM (Int L).. Master of Laws in International Law
LLMM .... Leurs Majestes [Their Majesties] [French]
LLMPP .... Liquid Level Monitor Port Plug [Nuclear energy] (NRCH)
LLMR .... Mitzpe-Ramon [Israel] [ICAO location identifier] (ICLI)
LLMZ .... Metzada/I. Bar Yehuda [Israel] [ICAO location identifier] (ICLI)
LLN .... Language, Literacy and Numeracy
LLN .... League for Less Noise
LLN .... Levelland, TX [Location identifier FAA] (FAAL)
LLN .... Line Link Network [Bell System]
LLN .... Local Line Network [Telecommunications] (NITA)
LLNL .... Lawrence Livermore National Laboratory [Also, LLL] [Livermore, CA]
                    [Department of Energy] (GRD)
LLNO .... Low-Level Night Operations [Aviation]
LL NS .... Law Library, New Series [Philadelphia Reprint of English Treatises]
                    [A publication] (DLA)
LLO .... Eliadamello SPA [Italy ICAO designator] (FAAC)
LLO .... Legionella-Like Organisms [Medicine]
LLO .... Legislative Liaison Office (AAGC)
LLO .... Llano, TX [Location identifier FAA] (FAAL)
LLO .... Local Lockout (IAA)
LLO .... Low Lunar Orbit
LLOC .... Land Line of Communications [Military]
LLOD .... Lowe Limit of Detection [Also, LLD] [Analytical chemistry]
LLOS .... Landmark Line of Sight (KSC)
LLOV .... Low-Level Output Voltage
LLOV .... Ovda [Israel] [ICAO location identifier] (ICLI)
Lloyd & Goold (T Plunkett) (Ir)... Lloyd and Goold's Irish Chancery Reports
                    Tempore Plunkett [A publication] (DLA)
Lloyd & Goold (T Sugden) (Ir)... Lloyd and Goold's Irish Chancery Reports
                    Tempore Sugden [A publication] (DLA)
Lloyd & W... Lloyd and Welsby's English Mercantile Cases [A publication] (DLA)
Lloyd LR .... Lloyd's List Law Reports [England] [A publication] (DLA)
Lloyd Pr Cas... Lloyd's List Prize Cases Reports [England] [A publication] (DLA)
Lloyd Pr Cas NS... Lloyd's List Prize Cases Reports, Second Series [1939-53]
                    [A publication] (DLA)
Lloyd's List LR... Lloyd's List Law Reports [England] [A publication] (DLA)
Lloyd's Mar LN... Lloyd's Maritime Law Newsletter [A publication] (DLA)
Lloyd's Pr Cas... Lloyd's List Prize Cases Reports [England] [A publication] (DLA)
Lloyd's Prize Cas... Lloyd's List Prize Cases Reports [London] [A publication]
                    (DLA)
Lloyd's Rep... Lloyd's List Law Reports [England] [A publication] (DLA)
LLP .... Lambda Limiting Process
LLP .... LASER Light Pump
LLP .... Launch and Landing Project [NASA] (NASA)
LLP .... Law and Liberty Project [Defunct] (EA)
LLP .... Leased Long Lines Program (NATG)
LLP .... Liberian Liberal Party [Political party] (EY)
LLP .... Linear Log Potentiometer
LLP .... Line Link Pulsing [Telecommunications]
LLP .... Literacy and Learning Program
LLP .... Live Load Punch
LLP .... Lloyd's of London Press [British]
LLP .... Local Language Program
LLP .... Lollipop Daycare [Vancouver Stock Exchange symbol]
LLP .... London Labour Party [British Political party]
LLP .... Long Lead Part
LLP .... Lunar Landing Program [NASA]
LLP .... Lyman Laboratory of Physics [Harvard] (MCD)
LLPA .... Low Level Waste Policy Act [1980] (NUCP)
LLPDD .... Late Luteal Phase Dysphoric Disorder [Gynecology]
LLPE .... Labor's League for Political Education [AFL] [Later merged into
                    Committee on Political Education of AFL-CIO]
LLpEC .... East Carroll Parish Library, Lake Providence, LA [Library symbol
                    Library of Congress] (LCLS)
LLPI .... Linen and Lace Paper Institute [Later, SSI] (EA)
LLPL .... Low Low Pond Level (IEEE)
LLPMS .... Long Leg Posterior Molded Splint [Medicine] (MEDA)
LLPN .... Lumped, Linear, Parametric Network
LLPO .... Launch and Landing Project Office [NASA] (NASA)
LI Pr .... Lloyd on Prohibition [1849] [A publication] (DLA)
LI Pr Cas ... Lloyd's List Prize Cases Reports [England] [A publication] (DLA)
LI Pr Cas NS... Lloyd's List Prize Cases Reports, New Series [1939-53]
                    [A publication] (DLA)
LLPS .... Low-Level Pumping Station (ADA)
LL-PTC .... Liquid Liquid Phase Transfer Catalysis [Physical chemistry]
LLQ .... Left Lower Quadrant [of abdomen] [Medicine]
LLQA .... Limiting Lines of Quiet Approach [Navy] (NVT)

LLR	High Court of Lagos Law Reports [*Nigeria*] [*A publication*] (ILCA)
LLR	Lancaster Law Review [*A publication*] (DLA)
LLR	Large Local Reaction [*Medicine*] (DMAA)
LLR	Leader Law Reports [*South Africa*] [*A publication*] (DLA)
LLR	Left Lateral Rectus [*Eye muscle*] (BABM)
LLR	Left Lateral Rotation [*Medicine*]
LLR	Left Lumbar Region [*Medicine*] (MAE)
LLR	Lender of Last Resort
LLR	Leukemia-Like Reaction [*Hematology*]
LLR	Liberian Law Reports [*A publication*] (ILCA)
LLR	Line Length Remainder [*Graphic arts*] (DGA)
LLR	Line of Least Resistance
LLR	Load-Limiting Resistor
LLR	LOFT [*Loss-of-Fluid Test*] Lead Rod (GAAI)
LLR	Log-Likelihood Ratio (PDAA)
LLR	Long Latency Response [*Neurology*]
LLR	Long Length Record (IAA)
LLR	Low-Level Radiation
LLR	Low-Level Resistance [*to disease*]
LLR	Lunar LASER Ranging [*Aerospace*]
LLRA	LapLink Remote Access [*Traveling Software, Inc.*] [*Computer science*] (PCM)
LLRC	Luneberg Lens Rapid Commutator [*Physics*]
LLRDS	Long Life Recording and Data Storage (MCD)
Ll Rep	Lloyd's List Law Reports [*England*] [*A publication*] (DLA)
LLRES	Load-Limiting Resistor (MSA)
LLRF	Low-Level Radio Frequency
LLRF	Lunar Landing Research Facility [*Aerospace*]
LLRF	Lunar LASER Range-Finder [*Aerospace*]
LLRI	Low-Level-Run-In (MCD)
LLRM	Low-Level Radio Modulator
LLRP	Long Lead Repair Part
Ll R Pr Cas	Lloyd's List Prize Cases Reports, Second Series [*1939-53*] [*A publication*] (DLA)
LLRR	Log-Likelihood Ratio Representation (MHDB)
LLRR	Lowest Level Remove-Replace (SAA)
LLRS	LASER Lightning Rod System (PDAA)
LLRT	Local Leak Rate Test [*Nuclear energy*] (NRCH)
LLRT	Low-Level Reactor Test (IEEE)
LLRV	Lunar Landing Research Vehicle [*Aerospace*]
LLRW	Low-Level Radiological Waste [*U.S. Army Corps of Engineers*]
LLRWPA	Low-Level Radioactive Waste Policy Act of 1980 (GAAI)
LLRWPAA	Low-Level Radioactive Waste Policy Amendments Act of 1985 (GAAI)
LLS	Land Laws Service [*Australia A publication*]
LLS	LASER Light Scattering [*Physical chemistry*]
LLS	LASER Light Source
LLS	LASER Line Scanner
LLS	Launch and Landing Site (MCD)
LLS	Lazy Leukocyte Syndrome [*Medicine*]
LLS	Linear Least Squares [*Mathematics*]
LLS	Liquid Level Sensor
LLS	Liquid Level Switch (IAA)
LLS	Local Library System [*OCLC*]
LLS	Long Left Shift (SAA)
LLS	Long Leg Splint [*Orthopedics*] (DAVI)
LLS	Louisiana State University, Graduate School of Library Science, Baton Rouge, LA [*OCLC symbol*] (OCLC)
LLS	Low-Level Sensor (KSC)
LLS	Low-Level Service [*Computer science*]
LLS	Low-Level Solid [*Nuclear energy*] (NRCH)
LLS	Lunar Landing Simulator [*Aerospace*] (AAG)
LLS	Lunar Logistics System [*NASA*]
LLS	Lyman Limit System [*Spectroscopy*]
LLSA	Land Lines Assembly [*Ground Communications Facility, NASA*]
LLSA	Latin Languages Speaking Allergists [*See also GAILL*] (EAIO)
LLSA	Limiting Lines of Surfaced Approach [*Navy*] (NVT)
LLSAC	LASER Line Scanner Aerial Camera
LLSAGW	Low-Level Surface-to-Air Guided Weapon (IAA)
LLSB	Left Lower Scapular Border [*Medicine*] (DMAA)
LLSB	Left Lower Sternal Border [*Anatomy*] (DAVI)
LLSC	Israel South Control Area Control Center Unit [*Israel*] [*ICAO location identifier*] (ICLI)
LLSD	Tel Aviv/Sde Dov [*Israel*] [*ICAO location identifier*] (ICLI)
LLSIL	Lower Living Standard Income Level [*CETA*] [*Department of Labor*]
LLSNA	Limiting Lines of Snorkel Approach [*Navy*] (NVT)
LLSPT	Licentiateship of the London School of Polymer Technology [*British*] (DBQ)
LLSS	LASER Light Scattering Spectroscopy
LLSS	LASER Light Source Station
LLSS	Long Life Space System (IAA)
LLSS	Low-Level Sounding System [*for measuring weather conditions*]
Ll St	Lloyd's Statutes of Practical Utility [*A publication*] (DLA)
LLSU	Low-Level Signaling Unit [*Telecommunications*] (TEL)
LLSUA	Limiting Lines of Submerged Approach [*Navy*] (NVT)
Ll Suc	Lloyd on Succession Laws [*1877*] [*A publication*] (DLA)
LLSV	Low-Level Storage Vault [*Nuclear energy*] (NRCH)
LLSV	Lunar Logistics Supply Vehicle [*NASA*] (IAA)
LLSV	Lunar Logistics System Vehicle [*NASA*]
LLSWV	Low-Level Solid Waste Storage Vault [*Nuclear energy*] (NRCH)
LLT	Lahore Law Times [*India*] [*A publication*] (DLA)
LLT	Lander Local Time [*NASA*]
LLT	Land-Line Teletypewriter [*Military*] (IAA)
LLT	Left Lateral [*Anatomy*] (DAVI)
LLT	Left Lateral Thigh [*Medicine*]

LLT	Library of Living Thought [*A publication*]
LLT	London Landed Terms [*Shipping*]
LLT	Long Lead Time
LLT	Low-Level Terminal
LLT	Low-Level Turbulence
LLT	Low-Light Television
LLT	Loyola University, Law Library, New Orleans, LA [*OCLC symbol*] (OCLC)
LLT	Lysolecithin (DMAA)
LLTA	Tel Aviv [*Israel*] [*ICAO location identifier*] (ICLI)
LLTC	Linear Technology Corp. [*NASDAQ symbol*] (TTSB)
LLTCS	Low-Limit Temperature Control Systems
LLTD	Lightweight LASER Target Designator
LLTDS	Launch Landing Test Data System (MCD)
LLTI	Long Lead Time Items (AAG)
LLTIL	Long Lead Time Items List [*Military*] (CAAL)
LLTM	Long Lead Time Material (DNAB)
LLTR	Large Leak Test Rig [*Nuclear energy*] (NRCH)
LLTR	Low-Level Transit Time
Ll Tr M	Lloyd on Trade-Marks [*A publication*] (DLA)
LLTT	Landline Teletypewriter [*Military*]
LLTTY	Landline Teletypewriter [*Military*]
LLTV	Low-Light-Level Television [*Night vision device*] [*Military*]
LLTV	Lunar Landing Training Vehicle [*Aerospace*]
LLTWP	Low-Level Tritiated Water Processing Subsystem (MCD)
LLU	Lamar, MO [*Location identifier FAA*] (FAAL)
LLU	Lending Library Unit
LLU	Loma Linda University, Loma Linda, CA [*OCLC symbol*] (OCLC)
LLu	Saint James Parish Library, Lutcher, LA [*Library symbol Library of Congress*] (LCLS)
LLV	Long Life Valve
LLV	Long Life Vehicle [*Automotive engineering*]
LLV	Lonicera Latent Virus [*Plant pathology*]
LLV	Loyal London Volunteers [*British military*] (DMA)
LLV	Lunar Landing Vehicle [*NASA*]
LLV	Lunar Logistics Vehicle [*NASA*]
LLV	Lymphocytic Leukemia Virus
LLVIR	Long Line Voice Interface Rack (SSD)
LLVP	Left Lateral Ventricular Preexcitation [*Medicine*] (DMAA)
LLVPG	Large Launch Vehicle Planning Group [*NASA*]
LLW	Lilongwe [*Malawi*] [*Airport symbol*] (OAG)
LLW	Lower Low Water [*Tides and currents*]
LLW	Low-Level Radioactive Waste
LLW	Low-Level Waste [*Nuclear energy*] (NRCH)
LLW	Low-Level Waste
LLWAS	Low-Level Windshear Alert System [*Marine science*] (OSRA)
LLWAS	Low-Level Windshear Alert System (USDC)
LLWAS	Low Level Wind Shear Alert System [*Aviation*] (FAAC)
LLWAS	Low Level Windshear Alert System
LLWC	Long-Leg Walking Cast [*Orthopedics*] (DAVI)
LLWDDD	Low-Level Waste Disposal Development and Demonstration
LLWI	Lower Low-Water Interval [*Tides and currents*]
LL Wisegotho	Laws of the Visigoths [*A publication*] (DLA)
LL Wm Conq	Laws of William the Conqueror [*A publication*] (DLA)
LL Wm Noth	Laws of William the Bastard [*A publication*] (DLA)
LLWMP	Low-Level Waste Management Program (GAAI)
LLWS	Low Level Wind Shear [*Aviation*] (FAAC)
LLWSV	Low-Level Waste Storage Vault [*Nuclear energy*] (NRCH)
LLX	Louisiana Land & Exploration Co. [*NYSE symbol Toronto Stock Exchange symbol*]
LLX	Louisiana Land/Exp [*NYSE symbol*] (TTSB)
LLX	Lyndonville, VT [*Location identifier FAA*] (FAAL)
LLY	Lilly [*Eli*] & Co. [*NYSE symbol*] (SPSG)
LLY	Lilly (Eli) [*NYSE symbol*] (TTSB)
LLY	Llanelly [*Welsh depot code*]
LLYP	Long Leaf Yellow Pine [*Lumber*]
LLZ	Left Lower Zone [*Medicine*] (DMAA)
LLZ	Localizer [*ICAO designator*] (CET)
LM	Labiomental [*Lip and chin*] [*Dentistry*] (DAVI)
LM	Laboratory Manager
LM	Laboratory Microscope
LM	Laboratory Module (MCD)
LM	Labour Mobility [*British*]
LM	Lactic Acid Mineral (DMAA)
LM	Lactose Malabsorption [*Gastroenterology*]
LM	Lacus Mortis [*Lunar area*]
LM	Lamentations [*Old Testament book*]
LM	Landmark (KSC)
LM	Land Mine [*Military*]
LM	Land Mobile
LM	Large Memory [*Computer science*]
LM	Large Mouth Bass [*Pisciculture*]
LM	Laryngeal Mask [*Medicine*] (DMAA)
LM	Laryngeal Muscle (BABM)
LM	LASER Machine (IAA)
LM	Late Model [*Class of racing cars*]
LM	Lateral Malleolus [*Anatomy*]
LM	Lateral Meniscus [*Anatomy*]
LM	Laufenden Monats [*Of the Current Month*] [*German*]
LM	Launch Module
LM	Launch Mount (AFM)
LM	Leading Mechanician
LM	Leave Message [*Word processing*]
LM	Lee-Metford [*British military*] (DMA)
LM	Left Male (MSA)

LM	Left Mid (NASA)
LM	Legal Medicine
LM	Legg Mason, Inc. [*NYSE symbol*] (SPSG)
LM	Legion of Merit [*Military decoration*]
LM	Leg Multiple [*Telegraph*] [*Telecommunications*] (TEL)
LM	Lentigo Maligna [*Oncology*]
LM	Leprosy Mission [*Australia An association*]
LM	Leptomeningeal Metastasis
LM	Lethal Material
LM	Level Meter
LM	Liability Management (TDOB)
LM	Licentiate in Medicine
LM	Licentiate in Midwifery
LM	Licentiate in Music (WDAA)
LM	Light Machine Gun
LM	Light Maintenance
LM	Light Metal
LM	Light Microscope
LM	Light Minimum [*Medicine*]
LM	Light Music [*Canadian Broadcasting Corp. record series prefix*]
LM	Lime Mortar (DAC)
LM	Limit (IAA)
LM	Limitation [*Dialog*] [*Searchable field*] [*Information service or system*] (NITA)
LM	Lincoln Mercury [*Division of Ford Motor Co.*]
LM	Linear Meter
LM	Linear Modulation
LM	Line Mark (IAA)
L/M	Lines per Minute [*Computer science*]
l/m	Lines per Minute (IDOE)
l/m	Linguomesial [*Dentistry*]
LM	Link Manager
LM	Lipid Mobilizing Hormone [*Endocrinology*]
LM	Liquidity-Money Supply [*Economics*]
LM	Liquid Membrane
LM	Liquid Metal
Lm	[*Maltese*] Lira [*Monetary Unit*] [*Malta*] (BARN)
LM	Listeria Monocytogenes [*Microorganism*]
LM	List of Material [*DoD*]
L/M	List of Materials (AAG)
LM	Litchfield & Madison [*AAR code*]
L/M	Liters per Minute
LM	Liturgie und Moenchtum [*A publication*] (BJA)
LM	Load Module (IID)
LM	Load Multiple [*Computer command*] (PCM)
LM	Local Manufacture (AAG)
LM	Local Memory
LM	Local Militia [*British military*] (DMA)
LM	Locus Monumenti [*Place of the Monument*] [*Latin*]
LM	Logical Module (NITA)
LM	Logic Module [*Computer science*] (MCD)
LM	Logistics Manager (MCD)
LM	Logistics Module [*Simulation games*] [*Army*] (SSD)
LM	Longitudinal Muscle [*Anatomy*]
LM	Long Measure (ROG)
LM	Long Meter [*Music*]
LM	Long Module (MCD)
LM	Loop Multiplexer
LM	Lord Mayor
LM	Loss Margin (IAA)
LM	Louisiana Midland Railway Co. (IIA)
L-M	Louisiana State Museum, New Orleans, LA [*Library symbol Library of Congress*] (LCLS)
LM	Lower Magazine [*Typography*]
LM	Lower Motor [*Neurology*]
LM	Low Meaningfulness [*Psychology*]
L/M	Low/Medium (MCD)
LM	Low-Melting (OA)
LM	Low Molecular [*Chemistry*]
LM	Luftmine [*Aerial mine*] [*German military - World War II*]
LM	Lumen [*Symbol*] [*SI unit of luminous flux*]
lm	Lumen (IDOE)
L/M	Luminosity to Mass [*Ratio*] [*Astronomy*]
LM	Lunar Mission
LM	Lunar Module [*Formerly, LEM*] [*NASA*]
LM	Maestretti [*Italy*] [*Research code symbol*]
LM	Middle Latitude [*Navigation*]
LM1A	Late Minoan 1A [*Archaeology*]
LM1B	Late Minoan 1B [*Archaeology*]
LM2	Lima [*Magdalena*] [*Peru*] [*Seismograph station code, US Geological Survey*] (SEIS)
LM2	Liver Microsomal Band 2
L/(M² D)	Liters per Square Meter Day
LMA	Labor Market Area
LMA	Lake Minchumina [*Alaska*] [*Airport symbol*] (OAG)
LMA	Laminating Materials Association [*Oradell, NJ*] (EA)
LMA	Land Mammal Ages [*Paleontology*]
LMA	Large Model Access (MCD)
LMA	LASER Microspectral Analysis
LMA	Last Manufacturers Association [*Defunct*] (EA)
LMA	Leading Medical Assistant [*British military*] (DMA)
LMA	League for Mutual Aid [*Defunct*] (EA)
LMA	Leased Management Agreement [*Radio*] [*Television*] (WDMC)
LMA	Lebanese Moslem Association [*Australia*]
LMA	Left Mentoanterior [*A fetal position*] [*Obstetrics*]

LMA	Licensed Merchandisers' Association [*Later, ILMA*] (EA)
LMA	Lingerie Manufacturers Association [*Later, IAMA*] (EA)
LMA	Liquor Merchants' Association [*Australia*]
LMA	Liver Membrane Autoantibody [*Immunochemistry*]
LMA	Livestock and Meat Authority [*Queensland, Australia*]
LMA	Livestock Marketing Association (EA)
LMA	Local Marshalling Areas (MCD)
LMA	Lock Museum of America (EA)
LMA	Logsplitter Manufacturers Association [*Defunct*] (EA)
LMA	Low Moisture Activity [*Brake system*] [*Automotive engineering*]
LMA	Lunar Meteoroid Analyzer [*NASA*]
LMA	Lunar Module Adapter [*NASA*] (MCD)
LMAA	Liquor Merchants' Association of Australia
LMAA	Logistics Management Association of Australia
LMAB	London Munitions Assignments Board [*World War II*]
LMAC	Labor-Management Advisory Committee [*Terminated, 1974*] [*Cost of Living Council*] (EGAO)
LMAC	Labor Market Advisory Councils [*Department of Labor and Department of Health, Education, and Welfare*] [*Terminated, 1982*] (EGAO)
LMaD	DeSoto Parish Library, Mansfield, LA [*Library symbol Library of Congress*] (LCLS)
LMAD	Let's Make a Deal [*TV program*]
LMAE	Lunar Module Ascent Engine [*NASA*]
LMAF	Live Missile Assembly Facility
LMAFS	Lookout Mountain Air Force Station
LM-Ag	Liver Membrane Antigen [*Immunochemistry*]
L Mag & LR	Law Magazine and Law Review [*A publication*] (DLA)
L Mag & Rev	Law Magazine and Review [*A publication*] (DLA)
LMAL	Langley Memorial Aeronautical Laboratory [*NASA*] (AAG)
LMAMA	Louisa May Alcott Memorial Association (EA)
LmAN	Limited Area Networks (NITA)
LM & LR	Law Magazine and Law Review [*A publication*] (DLA)
LM & P	Lowndes, Maxwell, and Pollock's English Bail Court Practice Reports [*1850-51*] [*A publication*] (DLA)
LM & Sc R	London, Midland & Scottish Railway [*British*] (DCTA)
LManyS	Sabine Parish Library, Many, LA [*Library symbol Library of Congress*] (LCLS)
LMAQ	Liquor Merchants Association of Queensland [*Australia*]
LMAQ	Livestock and Meat Authority of Queensland [*Australia*]
LMarA	Avoyelles Parish Library, Marksville, LA [*Library symbol Library of Congress*] (LCLS)
LMARS	Library Management and Retrieval System [*Navy Information service or system*] (IID)
LM/ATM	Lunar Module Apollo Telescope Mount [*NASA*] (MCD)
LMAV	LASER Maverick (MCD)
LMAW	Liquid Medium Active Waste (NUCP)
LMB	Laboratory of Molecular Biophysics (GNE)
LMB	Labor Market Bulletin (OICC)
LMB	Laurence-Moon-Biedl [*Medicine*]
LMB	Left Main-Stem Bronchus [*Medicine*] (MEDA)
LMB	Left Most BIT [*Binary Digit*] [*Computer science*] (MHDB)
LMB	Leiomyblastoma [*Pathology*] (DAVI)
LMB	Linear Motion Bearing
LMB	Local Message Box (NATG)
LMB	Low-Maintenance Battery (MCD)
LMBB	Laurence-Moon-Bardet-Biedl Syndrome [*Medicine*] (DMAA)
LMBBS	Laurence-Moon-Bardet-Biedl Syndrome [*Medicine*]
LMBBSN	Laurence-Moon-Bardet-Biedl Syndrome Network [*An association*] (EA)
LMBC	Lady Margaret Boat Club [*of St. John's College, Cambridge*] [*British*]
LMBC	Landmark Bancorp [*NASDAQ symbol*] (SAG)
LMBC	Liverpool Marine Biological Committee [*British*] (BARN)
LMBF	Low and Medium Bleeding Frequency [*Medicine*]
LMBI	Local Memory Bus Interface [*Computer science*]
LMBO	Leveraged Management Buy-Out
LMBR	Lumber
LMBS	Laurence-Moon-Biedl Syndrome [*Medicine*]
LMC	Cleveland-Marshall College of Law, Cleveland, OH [*OCLC symbol*] (OCLC)
LMC	Laboratory of Molecular Carcinogensis (GNE)
LMC	Labor Market Characteristics (OICC)
LMC	Lamacarena [*Colombia*] [*Airport symbol Obsolete*] (OAG)
LMC	Lamina Monopolar Cell [*Cytology*]
LMC	Lamocks [*Republic of China*] [*Seismograph station code, US Geological Survey*] (SEIS)
LMC	Lancia Motor Club [*Ledbury, Herefordshire, England*] (EAIO)
LMC	Large Magellanic Cloud [*Astronomy*]
LMC	Large Monopolar Cell [*Anatomy*]
LMC	LASER Mirror Coating
LMC	Lateral Motor Column [*of the spinal cord*] [*Neurobiology*]
LMC	Latex-Modified Concrete (PDAA)
LMC	Launch Monitor Console [*or Control*] [*NASA*] (IAA)
LMC	Least Material Condition (MSA)
LMC	Ligue Monarchiste du Canada [*Monarchist League of Canada*] (EAIO)
LMC	Lime-Magnesium Carbonate
LMC	Liquid Media Concentrate [*Cell culture*]
LMC	Liquid Metal Cycle
LMC	Living Male Child [*Medicine*] (DMAA)
LMC	Lloyd's Machinery Certificate [*Shipping*]
LMC	Local Management Committee
LMC	Local Mate Competition [*Entomology*]
LMC	Local Medical Committee [*British*]
LMC	Logistic Movement Center [*Military*] (CAAL)

LMC .... Logistics Management Center [*Army*] (MCD)
LMC .... London Montessori Centre [*British*] (AIE)
LMC .... Long-Run Marginal Cost Curve [*Economics*]
LMC .... Lon Morris College [*Texas*]
LMC .... Loss of Mesodermal Competence [*Developmental biology*]
LMC .... Louisville Municipal College [*Kentucky*]
LMC .... Low Middling Clause [*Business term*]
LMC .... Low-Pressure Molding Compound (MCD)
LMC .... Lymphocyte-Mediated Cytotoxicity [*Also, LC*] [*Immunology*]
LMC .... Lymphomyeloid Complex [*Medicine*]
LMc .... Morgan City Public Library, Morgan City, LA [*Library symbol Library of Congress*] (LCLS)
LMCA........... Laboratory Materiel Control Activity (AFIT)
LMCA........... Left Main Coronary Artery [*Anatomy*]
LMCA........... Left Middle Cerebral Artery [*Medicine*] (MAE)
LMCA........... Logistics Management Course for Auditors [*Army*]
LMCA........... Logistics Material Control Activity [*Military*]
LMCA........... Lorry-Mounted Crane Association [*British*] (BI)
LMCAD .... Left Main Coronary Artery Disease
LMCC........... Land Mobile Communications Council (EA)
LMCC........... Licentiate of Medical Council of Canada
LMCC........... Licentiate of the Medical College of Canada (DD)
LMCC........... Logistic Movement Coordination Center [*Navy*] (ANA)
LMCC........... Low-Mintage Coin Club (EA)
LMCD........... Liquid Metal Cooled Demonstration (IAA)
LMCLQ......... Lloyds Maritime and Commercial Law Quarterly [*A publication*] (DLA)
LM/CM² .... Lumens per Square Centimeter
LMCMS........ Licentiate Ministers and Certified Mediums Society (EA)
LMCN.......... Launch Maintenance Conference Network [*Aerospace*] (AAG)
LMCN.......... Launch Missile Control Network (IAA)
LMCP........... Laboratory Module Computer Program
LMCR........... Liquid Metal Cooled Reactor
LMCSS......... Letter Mail Code Sort System [*Postal Service*]
LMCT........... Ligand-to-Metal Charge Transfer [*Physical chemistry*]
LMD .... Laboratory Management Division
LMD .... Labor Mobility Demonstration
LMD .... Lamda Airlines [*Greece*] [*ICAO designator*] (FAAC)
LMD .... LASER Microwave Division [*Army*]
LMD .... Leaf-Mold (ROG)
LMD .... Left Medial Deltoid [*Injection Site*]
LMD .... Licensed Motor Dealer
LMD .... Liquid Metal Detector
L/(M D) .... Liter per Meter Day
LMD .... Local Medical Doctor
LMD .... Logistics Management Data [*Military*] (MCD)
LMD .... Long Meter Double [*Music*]
LMD .... Louisiana Midland Railway Co. [*Later, LMT*] [*AAR code*]
LMD .... Low Modulus Direction [*Mechanical testing*]
LMD .... Low-Molecular-Weight Dextran [*Medicine*]
LMD .... Lunar Meteoroid Detector [*NASA*]
LMDA.......... Lee's Multidifferential Agar [*Brewery bacteria culture medium*]
LMDA.......... Lunar Meteoroid Detector-Analyzer [*NASA*]
LMDC.......... Leadership and Management Development Center [*Maxwell Air Force Base, AL*]
LMDE.......... Lunar Module Descent Engine [*NASA*]
LMDM......... Little Mission for the Deaf-Mute [*See also PMS*] [*Rome, Italy*] (EAIO)
LMDS.......... Local Multipoint Distribution Service [*Telecommunications*]
LMDS.......... Local Multipoint Distribution System [*Telecommunications*] (ACRL)
LMDS.......... Local Multipoint Distribution Systems [*Broadcasting term*]
LM/DUP ...... Launch Module / Defense Unit Platform
LMDX.......... Low-Molecular-Weight Dextran (MAE)
LME .... Labor Market Exposure [*Work Incentive Program*]
LME .... Lambda Mercantile Corp. [*Toronto Stock Exchange symbol*]
LME .... Large Marine Ecosystem
LME .... Launch Monitor Equipment [*NASA*] (KSC)
LME .... Layer Management Entity [*Telecommunications*]
LME .... Left Mediolateral Episiotomy [*Obstetrics*] (MAE)
LME .... Light Mitochondrial Extract (OA)
LME .... Link Monitor Equipment (MCD)
LME .... Liquid Membrane Extraction [*Separation science and technology*]
LME .... Liquid Mercury Engine
LME .... Liquid Metal Embrittlement (MCD)
LME .... Locally Manufactured Equipment
LME .... Logistics Management Engineering, Inc. [*Annapolis, MD*] [*Telecommunications*] (TSSD)
LME .... London Metal Exchange
LME .... Lunar Module Engine [*NASA*]
LME .... Lysine Methyl Ester [*Biochemistry*]
LMEC .... Line Map Editing Console
LMEC .... Liquid Metal Engineering Center [*Energy Research and Development Administration*]
LMed & Ch.. Licentiate in Medicine and Surgery (DAVI)
LMEE .... Left Middle Ear Exploration [*Otorhinolaryngology*] (DAVI)
LMEE .... Light Military Electronics Equipment
LMEIC .... Life Member of Engineering Institute of Canada
LMER.......... Land Margin Ecosystem Research (USDC)
LMER.......... Land Margin Ecosystem Research [*Marine science*] (OSRA)
LMES .... Laboratory for Meteorology and Earth Sciences [*NASA*]
LMES .... Lockheed Martin Energy Systems, Inc. (GAAI)
LMET .... Leadership and Management Education and Training [*Navy*]
LMetJ.......... Jefferson Parish Library, Metairie, LA [*Library symbol Library of Congress*] (LCLS)
LMetR.......... Jefferson Parish Recreation Department, Metairie, LA [*Library symbol Library of Congress*] (LCLS)
LMF .... Lack of Moral Fibre [*British military*] (DMA)

LMF .... Lake Michigan Federation (EA)
LMF .... Language Media Format (CET)
LMF .... Large Myelinated Fiber [*Neuroanatomy*]
LMF .... Large-Scale Melt Facility [*Nuclear reactor test unit*]
LMF .... Last Meal Furnished
LMF .... Last Month's Forecast (MCD)
LMF .... Left Middle Finger (DMAA)
LMF .... Le Mans [*France*] [*Seismograph station code, US Geological Survey Closed*] (SEIS)
LMF .... Leukeran [*Chlorambucil*], Methotrexate, Fluorouracil [*Antineoplastic drug regimen*]
LMF .... Leukocyte Mitogenic Factor [*Medicine*]
LMF .... Linear Matched Filter (IEEE)
LMF .... Linear Multistep Formula (PDAA)
LMF .... Liquid Metal Fuel
LMF .... Low and Medium Frequency
LMF .... Lower Mid Fuselage (NASA)
LMF .... Lymphocyte Mitogenic Factor [*Endocrinology, hematology*]
LMFA .... Light Metal Founders Association [*British*] (DBA)
LMFA .... Lucky Mee Family Association (EA)
LMFBR........ Liquid Metal Fast Breeder Reactor
LMFC .... Leigh McCloskey Fan Club (EA)
LMFC .... Liza Minnelli Fan Club (EA)
LMFC .... Louise Mandrell Fan Club (EA)
LMFE .... London Meat Futures Exchange [*British*]
LMFR .... Liquid Metal Fueled Reactor
LMFRE .... Liquid Metal Fueled Reactor Experiment
LM/FT² .... Lumen per Square Foot (WDAA)
lm/ft² .... Lumens per Square Foot (IDOE)
LMG .... Laboratory of Molecular Genetics (GNE)
LMG .... Lamington [*Papua New Guinea*] [*Seismograph station code, US Geological Survey*] (SEIS)
LMG .... LASER Milling Gauge
LMG .... Lauerer Markin Gibbs, Inc. [*Maumee, OH*] [*Telecommunications*] (TSSD)
LMG .... Left Main Gear (MCD)
LMG .... Light Machine Gun
LMG .... Liquid Methane Gas
LMG .... Louisiana Mining Corp. [*Vancouver Stock Exchange symbol*]
LMGC .... Lunar Module Guidance Computer [*NASA*] (KSC)
LMGEN .... Load Module Generator (IAA)
LMGR .... Liberation Movement of the German Reich [*An association*] (EAIO)
LMGSM........ Latin and Mediterranean Group for Sport Medicine (EA)
LMH .... Lady Margaret Hall [*Oxford University*]
LMH .... Lewis, M. H., Winchester VA [*STAC*]
LMH .... Light Metal Hydride
LMH .... Light Military Hovercraft (PDAA)
LMH .... Lipid Mobilizing Hormone [*Endocrinology*]
LMH .... Lumen Hour (IAA)
LMHA .... Lay Mission-Helpers Association (EA)
LMHF .... Lauritz Melchior Heldentenor Foundation (EA)
LMHI .... Liga Medicorum Homoeopathica Internationalis [*International Homoeopathic Medical League*] (EA)
LMHR .... Lumen Hour (IAA)
lm-hr .... Lumen-Hour (IDOE)
LMHS .... Lancaster Mennonite Historical Society (EA)
LMHX.......... Liquid Metal Heat Exchanger (NRCH)
LMI .... Labor Market Information [*Department of Labor*]
LMI .... Lawn Mower Institute [*Later, OPEI*]
LMi .... Leo Minor [*Constellation*]
LMI .... Leukocyte Migration Inhibition [*Hematology*]
LMI .... Life Management Institute [*Life Office Management Association*]
LMI .... Link Management Interface [*Computer science*]
LMI .... Liquid Mercury Isolator
LMI .... Liquid Metal Ionization [*Spectrometry*]
LMI .... Livestock Merchandising Institute [*Later, LII*] (EA)
LMI .... Loaded Motional Impedance
LMI .... Local Management Interface [*Telecommunications*] (ACRL)
LMI .... Local Memory Image
LMI .... Logistics Management Institute [*Bethesda, MD*] [*Research center*] (AFM)
LMI .... Low-Molecular-Weight Inhibitor [*of protease activity*]
LMI .... Lumi [*Papua New Guinea*] [*Airport symbol*] (OAG)
LMI .... Luthiers Mercantile International [*Healdsburg, CA*] [*Commercial firm*]
LMI .... Lymphocyte Migration Index
LMIA .... Louisiana Meat Industry Association (SRA)
LMIAA......... Licentiate Architect Member of the Incorporated Association of Architects and Surveyors [*British*] (DAS)
LMIAS......... Licentiate Surveyor Member of the Incorporated Association of Architects and Surveyors [*British*] (DAS)
LMI-ATS ...... Labor Market Information - Analytical Table Series [*Department of Labor - Employment and Training Administration*] (OICC)
LMIB .... Light Motorized Infantry Battalion (INF)
LMIC .... Liberty Mutual Insurance Co.
LMIC .... Liquid Metals Information Center [*AEC*]
LMIC .... Lower Middle Income Country
LMIF .... Leukocyte Migration Inhibition Factor [*Hematology*] (DMAA)
LMIG .... Liquid Metal Ion Gun [*Surface analysis*]
LMIN .... Laboratory of Molecular and Integrative Neuroscience (GNE)
LMin .... Leo Minor [*Constellation*]
L/MIN .... Liters per Minute
LMIS .... Labor Market Information System [*Department of Labor*]
LMIS .... Liquid Metal Ion Source
LMIS .... Lloyd's Maritime Information Services Ltd. [*Information service or system*] (IID)

LMIS............ Logistics Management Information System [*Marine Corps*] (GFGA)
LMIT............ Lockheed Martin Idaho Technologies (GAAI)
LMiW............ Webster Parish Library, Minden, LA [*Library symbol Library of Congress*] (LCLS)
LMJ............ Greer, SC [*Location identifier FAA*] (FAAL)
LMK............ Landmark (NASA)
LMK............ Landmark Corp. [*Toronto Stock Exchange symbol*]
LML............ Lae [*Marshall Islands*] [*Airport symbol*] (OAG)
LML............ Large and Medium Lymphocytes [*Medicine*]
LML............ Lean Misfire Limb (PDAA)
LML............ Lean Misfire Limit [*Automotive engine testing*]
LML............ Leesona Moos Laboratory
LML............ Left Mediolateral [*Episiotomy*] [*Obstetrics*]
LML............ Left Mentolateral [*Episiotomy*] [*Obstetrics*]
LML............ Left Middle Lobe [*of lung*] (DAVI)
LML............ Logical Memory Level
LML............ Lookout Mountain Laboratories [*California*] (SAA)
LML............ Lowest Maintenance Level (MCD)
LMLA............ Leisureways Marketing [*NASDAQ symbol*] (SAG)
LMLAF............ Leisureways Marketing Ltd [*NASDAQ symbol*] (TTSB)
LMLE............ Local Maximum Likelihood Estimates [*Statistics*]
LMLE............ Long Magazine Lee-Enfield [*British military*] (DMA)
LMLR............ Load Memory Lockout Register
LM/LRV............ Lunar Module/Lunar Roving Vehicle [*NASA*]
LMLV............ Lockheed Martin Launch Vehicle
LMLW............ Liquid Medium Level Waste [*Nuclear energy*] (NUCP)
LMM............ Lactobacillus Maintenance Medium [*Microbiology*]
LMM............ Lemming Resources, Inc. [*Vancouver Stock Exchange symbol*]
LMM............ Lentigo Maligna Melanoma [*Oncology*]
LMM............ Library Microfilm & Materials Co.
LMM............ Light Meromyosin [*Biochemistry*]
LMM............ Lights Monitor Module [*Automotive engineering*]
LMM............ Linear Multi-Step Method (PDAA)
LMM............ Lines per Millimeter (AAG)
LMM............ Liquid Money Market [*Banking*]
LMM............ Living Masters of Music [*A publication*]
LMM............ Llanelly & Mynydd Mawr Railway [*Wales*]
LMM............ Locator at Middle Marker [*Aviation*]
LMM............ Los Mochis [*Mexico*] [*Airport symbol*] (OAG)
LMM............ Lourenco Marques [*Mozambique*] [*Seismograph station code, US Geological Survey*] (SEIS)
LMM............ Lumbar Motion Monitor [*Ergonometrics*]
LM/M²............ Lumen per Square Meter (WDAA)
lm/m²............ Lumens per Square Meter (IDOE)
LMMA............ Lutheran Medical Mission Association [*Defunct*] (EA)
LMMCI............ Labor Management Maritime Committee, Inc. (EA)
LMMF............ Lisa Madonia Memorial Fund [*An association*] (EA)
LMMF............ Local Maintenance and Management of Facilities [*Military*] (AABC)
LMMFHR............ Letelier-Moffitt Memorial Fund for Human Rights [*Later, LMMFHR/IPS*] (EA)
LMMFHR/IPS... Letelier-Moffitt Memorial Fund for Human Rights/Institute for Policy Studies (EA)
LMMHD............ Liquid Metal Magnetohydrodynamics
LMML............ Malta/Luqa [*Malta*] [*ICAO location identifier*] (ICLI)
LMMM............ Malta [*Malta*] [*ICAO location identifier*]
LMMS............ LASER Microprobe Mass Spectrometry [*or Spectroscopy*]
LMMS............ Library Materials Management System
LMMS............ Lightweight Multipurpose Missile System (MCD)
LMMS............ Local Message Metering Service [*Telecommunications*] (TEL)
LMMU............ Latin Mediterranean Medical Union [*See also UMML*] [*Mantua, Italy*] (EAIO)
LMMV............ Lamium Mild Mosaic Virus [*Plant pathology*]
LMN............ Lamoni, IA [*Location identifier FAA*] (FAAL)
LMN............ Lanthanum Magnesium Double Nitrate
LMN............ Lateral Mesencephalic Nucleus [*Brain anatomy*]
LMN............ Lateral Motoneuron [*Neurobiology*]
LMN............ Library Management Network, Inc. [*Information service or system*] (IID)
LMN............ Library Micromation News (NITA)
LMN............ Limbang [*Malaysia*] [*Airport symbol*] (OAG)
LMN............ Lineman (AABC)
LMN............ Load Matching Network
LMN............ Locomotor Neuron [*Neurology*]
LMN............ Lornex Mining Corp. [*Vancouver Stock Exchange symbol*]
LMN............ Lost Music Network [*Defunct*] (EA)
LMN............ Lower Motor Neuron [*Anatomy*]
LMN............ Northeast Louisiana University, Monroe, LA [*Library symbol Library of Congress*] (LCLS)
LMNA............ Label Manufacturers National Association [*Defunct*]
LMNA............ Land-Based Multimission Naval Aircraft (MCD)
LMNA............ Long-Range Multipurpose Naval Aircraft (HGAA)
LMNDF............ Lesbian Mothers National Defense Fund (EA)
LMNED............ Laboratories for Molecular Neuroendocrinology and Diabetes [*Tulane University*] [*Research center*] (RCD)
LMNL............ Lower Motor Neuron Lesion [*Medicine*]
LMNT............ Laminate
LMNTNG...... Laminating
LMO............ LASER Master Oscillator
LMO............ Lasmo Canada, Inc. [*Toronto Stock Exchange symbol*]
LMO............ Lens-Modulated Oscillator
LMO............ Linear Master Oscillator
LMO............ Living Modified Organism
LMO............ Logistics Management Office [*Army*]
LMO............ Lookout Mountain Observatory [*California*] [*Seismograph station code, US Geological Survey Closed*] (SEIS)

LMO............ Ouachita Parish Public Library, Monroe, LA [*Library symbol Library of Congress*] (LCLS)
LMOA............ Locomotive Maintenance Officers' Association (EA)
LMOI............ Labor Market and Occupational Information (OICC)
LMOS............ Loop Maintenance Operations System [*Formerly, MLR*] [*Bell System*]
LMP............ Labor Mobility Project [*Department of Labor*]
LMP............ Lamap [*New Hebrides*] [*Seismograph station code, US Geological Survey*] (SEIS)
LMP............ Laminated Metal Part
LMP............ Lampedusa [*Italy*] [*Airport symbol*] (OAG)
LMP............ Large Multifunctional Protease [*Medicine*] (DMAA)
LMP............ Last Menstrual Period [*Medicine*]
LMP............ Latent Membrane Potential [*Medicine*] (DMAA)
LMP............ Latent Membrane Protein [*Genetics*]
LMP............ Lawson Mardon Group Ltd. [*Toronto Stock Exchange symbol*]
LMP............ Layered Metal Phosphates [*Physical chemistry*]
LMP............ Left Mentoposterior [*A fetal position*] [*Obstetrics*]
LMP............ Library Material Processed
LMP............ Light Marching Pack [*Military*]
LMP............ Light Metal Products
LMP............ Linguistic Minorities Project [*Education*] (AIE)
LMP............ Liquid Metal Plasma Valve (IAA)
LMP............ Liquid Monopropellant
LMP............ Liquid Oxygen Maintenance Panel (AAG)
LMP............ List of Measurement Points (NASA)
LMP............ Literary Market Place [*A publication*]
LMP............ LM [*Lunar Module*] Mission Programmer [*NASA*] (KSC)
LMP............ Longitudinal Muscles of Pinnule
LMP............ Low Melting Point
LMP............ Low-Molecular-Weight Polypeptide [*Biochemistry*]
LMP............ Lumbar Puncture [*Medicine*]
LMP............ Lunar Module Pilot [*Apollo*] [*NASA*]
LMPA............ Qualified Member of the Master Photographers Association [*British*] (DBQ)
LMPBLK............ Lampblack
LMPCR............ Ligation-Mediated Polymerase Chain Reaction [*Genetics*]
LMPG............ Light Mobile Protected Gun (INF)
LMPM............ Library Material Preservation Manual
LMPRT............ Locally Most Powerful Rank Test [*Statistics*]
LMPS............ Lunar Module Procedures Simulator [*NASA*]
LMPT............ Logistics and Material Planning Team (NATG)
LMQ............ La Malbaie [*Quebec*] [*Seismograph station code, US Geological Survey*] (SEIS)
LMQ............ Marsa Brega [*Libya*] [*Airport symbol*] (AD)
LMR............ Labor-Management Relations
LMR,............ La Mourre [*France*] [*Seismograph station code, US Geological Survey*] (SEIS)
LMR............ Land Mobile Radio (NITA)
LMR............ LASER Magnetic Resonance (MCD)
LMR............ Launch Mission Rules [*NASA*] (KSC)
LMR............ Launch Monitor Room [*NASA*] (MCD)
LMR............ Left Medial Rectus [*Eye muscle*] (BABM)
LMR............ Library Maintenance Routine (IAA)
LMR............ Licensed Motor Repairer
LMR............ Light Modulation Recording
LMR............ Ligue Marxiste Revolutionnaire [*Revolutionary Marxist League*] [*Switzerland Political party*] (PPW)
LMR............ Linear Multiple Regression (IAA)
LMR............ Line Monitor/Recorder (MCD)
LMR............ Lipman Management Resources Ltd. (NITA)
LMR............ Liquid Metal Reactor
LMR............ Liquid Molding Resin [*Organic chemistry*]
LMR............ Literary Magazine Review [*A publication*] (BRI)
LMR............ Living Marine Resource [*Marine science*] (OSRA)
LMR............ Living Marine Resource (USDC)
LMR............ Localized Magnetic Resonance (DAVI)
LMR............ Longmoor Military Railway [*British military*] (DMA)
LMR............ Lowest Maximum Range
LMR............ Lymphocytic Meningpolyradiculitis [*Medicine*] (DMAA)
LMR............ St. Louis, MO [*Location identifier FAA*] (FAAL)
LMRA............ Labor-Management Relations Act [*1947*]
LMRCP............ Licenciate in Midwifery of the Royal College of Physicians [*British*]
LMRD............ Launch Mission Rules Document [*NASA*] (NASA)
LMRDA............ Labor-Management Reporting and Disclosure Act [*1959*]
LMRDA-IM... Labor-Management Reporting and Disclosure Act - Investigative Matter [*FBI standardized term*]
LMRDFS...... Lightweight Man-Transportable Radio Direction-Finding System [*Army*]
LMRK............ Landmark Graphics [*NASDAQ symbol*] (SAG)
LMRP............ Lunar Module Replaceable Package [*NASA*] (KSC)
LMRPC............ Linear-Motor Resonant-Piston Compressor [*Navy*]
LMRR............ Lunar Module Rendezvous RADAR [*NASA*]
LMRS............ Labor-Management Relations Service of the US Conference of Mayors (EA)
LMRS............ Labor-Management Relations Staff [*Department of Agriculture*] (GFGA)
LMRS............ Lockheed Maintenance Recording System
LMRS............ Lunar Module Rendezvous Simulator [*NASA*] (IAA)
LMRSH............ Licentiate Member of the Royal Society of Health [*British*]
LMRTPI...... Legal Member of the Royal Town Planning Institute [*British*] (DBQ)
LMRU............ Library Management Research Unit (NITA)
LMS............ Laboratory for Mathematics and Statistics [*University of California at San Diego*] [*Research center*] (RCD)
LMS............ Laboratory of Molecular Structure [*Massachusetts Institute of Technology*]

LMS .... Lamsn & Sessions [*NYSE symbol*] (TTSB)
LMS .... [*The*] Lamson & Sessions Co. [*NYSE symbol*] (SPSG)
LMS .... Land Mass Simulator
LMS .... Land Mobile Service (DA)
LMS .... LASER Bank Management System [*Computer science*]
LMS .... LASER Magnetic Stage
LMS .... LASER Magnetic Storage International
LMS .... LASER Mapping System
LMS .... LASER Mass Spectrometer
LMS .... Latin Mass Society (EAIO)
LMS .... Laurence-Moon Syndrome [*Medicine*]
LMS .... Least Mean Square (IEEE)
LMS .... Leiomyosarcoma [*Oncology*]
LMS .... LEM [*Lunar Excursion Module*] Mission Simulator [*NASA*]
LMS .... Level Measuring Set [*for test signals*] [*Telecommunications*] (TEL)
LMS .... Library Maintenance System (PDAA)
LMS .... Library Management System
LMS .... Licentiate in Medicine and Surgery [*British*]
LMS .... Lightning Mapper Sensor [*NASA*]
LMS .... Limestone [*Technical drawings*]
LMS .... Limited Mass Search [*Chromatography*]
LMS .... Linear Measuring System
LMS .... Liquid Measuring System
LMS .... Liquid Metal System
LMS .... List Management System
LMS .... Literature Management System
LMS .... Loadmaster Systems, Inc. [*Vancouver Stock Exchange symbol*]
LMS .... Load Matching Switch
LMS .... Load Measurement System (NASA)
LMS .... Local Management of Schools [*British*]
LMS .... Local Measured Service [*Telecommunications*] (TEL)
LMS .... Local Missile Selector (IAA)
LMS .... Lockheed Missile System (MCD)
LMS .... Logistics Management Specialist (MCD)
LMS .... Logistics Master Schedules (MCD)
LMS .... Lomas Helicopters Ltd. [*British ICAO designator*] (FAAC)
LmS .... London Microfilming Services Ltd., London, ON, Canada [*Library symbol Library of Congress*] (LCLS)
LMS .... London, Midland & Scottish Railway [*British*]
LMS .... London Missionary Society
LMS .... Lookout Mountain Observatory [*California*] [*Seismograph station code, US Geological Survey*] (SEIS)
LMS .... Louisville, MS [*Location identifier FAA*] (FAAL)
LM/S .... Lumens per Second (MCD)
LMS .... Lunar Mass Spectrometer [*NASA*]
LMS .... Lunar Measuring System [*Aerospace*]
LMS .... Lunar Module Simulator [*NASA*] (SSD)
LMS .... Lutheran Mission Societies (EA)
LMSA .... Labor-Management Services Administration [*Department of Labor*]
LMSA .... Large Metoscale Area (PDAA)
LMSC .... Let Me See Correspondence [*Business term*]
LMSC .... Liquid Metals Safety Committee [*AEC*] (MCD)
LMSC .... Little Missionary Sisters of Charity (TOCD)
LMSC .... Lockheed Missiles & Space Corp. [*Subsidiary of Lockheed Aircraft Corp.*]
LMSC .... Logistics Management Systems Center [*Military*]
LMSD .... Lockheed Missile and Space Division (IAA)
LMSE .... Laboratory Module Simulation Equipment
LMSE .... Liquid Metal Slip Ring
LMSEC .... Lumen Second (IAA)
LMSG .... Low Magnetic Saturation Garnet
LMSI .... Association of Lithuanian Foresters in Exile [*Defunct*] (EA)
LMSN .... Local Message Switched Network
LMSQFT ...... Lumen per Square Foot (IAA)
LMSR .... Large, Medium Speed RO/RO [*Roll On/Roll Off*] [*Navy*]
LMSR .... London, Midland & Scottish Railway [*British*]
LMSS .... Land Mobile Satellite Service [*Rockwell International Corp.*]
LMSS .... Lunar Mapping and Survey System [*NASA*] (MCD)
LMSSA .... Licentiate in Medicine and Surgery of the Society of Apothecaries [*British*]
LMST .... Learning of Middle Size Task [*Psychology*]
lmst .... Limestone (VRA)
LMSWA .... Land Management Society of Western Australia
LMT .... Air Limousin TA [*France ICAO designator*] (FAAC)
LMT .... Klamath Falls [*Oregon*] [*Airport symbol*] (OAG)
LMT .... Large Millimeter Telescope [*US-Mexico project*] [*Proposed, 1994*]
LMT .... LASER Marksmanship Trainer (MCD)
LMT .... Launch Motor Test
LMT .... Leadership and Management Training [*Navy*] (NVT)
LMT .... Learning Methods Test [*Mills*] [*Education*]
LMT .... Left Mentotransverse [*A fetal position*] [*Obstetrics*]
LMT .... Lemonthyme [*Tasmania*] [*Seismograph station code, US Geological Survey Closed*] (SEIS)
LMT .... Length, Mass, Time [*Physics*]
LMT .... Length of Mean Turn
LMT .... Levtech Medical Technologies Ltd. [*Vancouver Stock Exchange symbol*]
LMT .... Licensed Massage Therapist [*Medicine*]
LMT .... Lifetime Medical Television
LMT .... Limit (AFM)
LMT .... Limit
LMT .... Local Mean Time (AFM)
LMT .... Lockheed Martin [*NYSE symbol*] (TTSB)
LMT .... Lockheed Martin Corp. [*NYSE symbol*] (SAG)
LMT .... Logical Mapping Table

LMT .... Logic Master Tape (IAA)
LMT .... Logistic Management of the Turnaround (MCD)
LMT .... Logistics Management Team [*Navy*]
LMT .... Log Mean Temperature
LMT .... Louisiana Midland Transport [*AAR code*]
LMT .... Lowenfeld Mosaic Test [*Psychology*]
LMTA .... Language Modalities Test for Aphasia [*Psychology*]
LMTA .... Library/Media Technical Assistant
LMTA .... Light Microscopy Trace Analysis
LMTA .... Louisiana Motor Transport Association (SRA)
LMTBR .... Liquid Metal Thorium Breeder Reactor
LMTBS .... Lightweight Multifunction Tactical Beacon System (MCD)
LMTC .... Launcher Maintenance Trainer Course
lmtd .... Limited (AAMN)
LMTD .... Logarithmic Mean Temperature Difference
LMTDNS ...... Launch Environment, Mission, Type, Design Number, and Series [*Missiles*] (AFM)
LMTG .... Limiting (MSA)
LMTI .... Louisiana Training Institute, Monroe, LA [*Library symbol Library of Congress*] (LCLS)
LMTLSS .... Limitless
LMTN .... Labor Market Training Needs
LMTN .... Leamington [*British depot code*]
LMTO .... Linear Combination of Muffin Tin Orbitals [*Atomic physics*]
LMTPI .... Legal Member of the Town Planning Institute [*British*] (DLA)
LMTR .... Limiter [*Electronics*]
LMTS .... LaserMaster Technologies [*NASDAQ symbol*] (TTSB)
LMTS .... LaserMaster Technologies, Inc. [*NASDAQ symbol*] (SAG)
LMTV .... Light Medium Tactical Vehicle [*Army*] (RDA)
LMU .... Lake Mountain [*Utah*] [*Seismograph station code, US Geological Survey*] (SEIS)
LMU .... Latin Monetary Union [*Established in 1865*]
LMU .... Lincoln Memorial University [*Tennessee*]
LMU .... Line Monitor Unit
LMU .... Loyola Marymount University [*Los Angeles, CA*]
LMU .... University of Missouri, Law School, Columbia, MO [*OCLC symbol*] (OCLC)
LMUA .... Lloyd's Motor Underwriters Association [*British*] (DBA)
LMus .... Licentiate of Music
LMusLCM ..... Licentiate in Music of the London College of Music [*British*] (DBQ)
LMusTCL ..... Licentiate in Music, Trinity College of Music, London [*British*] (DBQ)
LMV .... Lettuce Mosaic Virus
LMV .... Long Market Value [*Investment term*]
LMV .... Low Mass Vehicle
LMVD .... Lower Mississippi Valley Division [*Army Engineers*]
LMVE .... Linear, Minimum Variance Estimation (PDAA)
LMW .... Ladd Mountain [*Washington*] [*Seismograph station code, US Geological Survey*] (SEIS)
LMW .... LASER Microwelder
LMW .... Lower Midwest
LMW .... Low-Molecular Weight [*Chemistry*]
LMW .... Low Molecular Weight
lm/W .... Lumens per Watt
lmwd .... Limewood (VRA)
LMWD .... Low-Molecular-Weight Dextran [*Medicine*] (AAMN)
LMWH .... Low-Molecular-Weight Heparin [*Biochemistry*]
LMWHC .... Low-Molecular-Weight Hydrocarbon (MCD)
LMWK .... Low Molecular-Weight Kininogen [*Biochemistry*]
LMWP .... Labor-Management Welfare-Pension [*Reports*] [*Department of Labor*]
LMWP .... Low-Molecular-Weight Proteinuria [*Medicine*]
LMX .... Aerolineas Mexicanas JS SA de CV [*Mexico ICAO designator*] (FAAC)
LMX .... LMX Resources Ltd. [*Vancouver Stock Exchange symbol*]
LMX .... L-Type Multiplex [*Telecommunications*] (TEL)
LMXB .... Low-Mass X-Ray Binary [*Star system*]
LMY .... Lake Murray [*Papua New Guinea*] [*Airport symbol*] (OAG)
LN .... Background Noise Level (CAAL)
ln .... Central and Southern Line Islands [*gb (Gilbert Islands) used in records cataloged after October 1978*] [*MARC country of publication code Library of Congress*] (LCCP)
LN .... Labionasal [*lip and nose*] [*Otorhinolaryngology*] (DAVI)
LN .... Lane (MCD)
LN .... Lane
Ln .... Lanthanide [*Chemical element*] (WGA)
LN .... Large-Probe Nephelometer [*NASA*]
LN .... LASER Nephelometry [*Analytical biochemistry*]
LN .... Lateen [*Ship's rigging*] (ROG)
LN .... Lateral Neuropil [*Neurology*]
LN .... Law Notes, American Bar Association Section of General Practice [*A publication*] (DLA)
LN .... Law Notes, London [*A publication*] (DLA)
LN .... Leading Note [*Music*] (ROG)
LN .... League of Nations [*1919-1946*]
LN .... Legal News [*Canada*] [*A publication*] (DLA)
LN .... Legal Notice (OICC)
LN .... Legal Notification [*Ghana*] [*A publication*] (DLA)
LN .... Lepista Nuda [*A fungus*]
L-N .... Lesch-Nyhan [*Medicine*]
LN .... Lesion Number [*Pathology*]
L/N .... Letter-Numerical [*system*] (DAVI)
LN .... Liaison (AFM)
LN .... Liber Niger [*Black Book*] [*A publication*] (DLA)
LN .... Libyan Arab Airlines [*ICAO designator*] (AD)
LN .... Licensed Nurse
LN .... Lien

LN	Line (AAG)
ln	Line (VRA)
LN	Link Number (MHDB)
LN	Lip Nerve
LN	Liquid Nitrogen
LN	Lira Nuova [Monetary unit] [Italy] (ROG)
LN	Load Number
LN	Loan
LN	Local National
ln	Logarithm (Natural) [Mathematics]
LN	Lot Number
LN	Love Notes [An association] (EA)
LN	Low Foliage Nester [Ecology]
LN	Low Noise (IAA)
LN	Luminometer Number [Hydrocarbon fuel rating]
LN	Lupus Network (EA)
LN	Lymph Node [Medicine]
LN	New Orleans Public Library, New Orleans, LA [Library symbol Library of Congress] (LCLS)
ln----	North Atlantic Ocean [MARC geographic area code Library of Congress] (LCCP)
LN₂	Liquid Nitrogen [NASA] (NASA)
LNA	Airlen [Russian Federation] [ICAO designator] (FAAC)
LNA	Lahu National Army [Myanmar] [Political party] (EY)
LNA	Launch Numerical Aperture [Telecommunications] (TEL)
LNA	Leading National Advertiser
LNA	League for National Advancement [Papua New Guinea] [Political party] (EY)
LNA	League of the Norden Associations (EA)
LNA	Leucine Nitroanilide [Biochemistry]
LNA	Liberation News Agency [Vietnam]
LNA	Lithium Nitrate Ammoniate [Inorganic chemistry]
LNA	Lithographers National Association
LNA	Lithuanian Numismatic Association (EA)
LNA	Local Navy Authority
LNA	Local Numbering Area [Telecommunications] (TEL)
LnA	London Allowance [British military] (DMA)
LNA	Love-N-Addiction [An association] (EA)
LNA	Low-Noise Amplifier [Satellite communications]
LNA	Low-Noise Antenna
LNA	Lunar Resources Ltd. [Vancouver Stock Exchange symbol]
LNA	New Orleans City Archives, New Orleans, LA [Library symbol Library of Congress] (LCLS)
LNA	West Palm Beach, FL [Location identifier FAA] (FAAL)
LNAC	Amistad Research Center Library, New Orleans, LA [Library symbol] [Library of Congress] (LCLS)
LNAC	Librarians for Nuclear Arms Control [Defunct] (EA)
LNAC	Limited National Agency Check (AFM)
LNAC	Louisville, New Albany & Corydon Railroad Co. [AAR code]
LNADW	Lower North Atlantic Deep Water [Oceanography]
LNAH	League of Night Adoration in the Home [Later, NAH] (EA)
LNaN	Northwestern State University of Louisiana, Natchitoches, LA [Library symbol Library of Congress] (LCLS)
LNaNa	Natchitoches Parish Library, Natchitoches, LA [Library symbol Library of Congress] (LCLS)
LNAP	Low Nonessential Air Pressure (IEEE)
LNapA	Assumption Parish Library, Napoleonville, LA [Library symbol Library of Congress] (LCLS)
LNAPL	Light Non-Aqueous Phase Liquids
LNAV	Lateral Navigation [Provides computer description of aircraft's planned lateral flight path] (GAVI)
lnaz--	Azores Islands [MARC geographic area code Library of Congress] (LCCP)
LNB	Lamen Bay [Vanuata] [Airport symbol] (OAG)
LNB	Large Navigation Buoy [Marine science] (MSC)
LNB	Lithium Niobate (PDAA)
LNB	Local Name Base [Computer science]
LNB	Louisiana National Bank [Baton Rouge] (TSSD)
LNB	Low Nitrogen Oxide Burner [Combustion technology]
LNB	Low-Noise Block [Satellite communications]
LNB	Lymph Node Biopsy [Surgical procedure] (DAVI)
LNB	New Orleans Baptist Theological Seminary, New Orleans, LA [Library symbol Library of Congress] (LCLS)
LNBA	Bell Aerospace Co., New Orleans, LA [Library symbol Library of Congress] (LCLS)
LNBA	Laymen's National Bible Association (EA)
LNBC	Laymen's National Bible Committee [Formerly, LNC] [Later, LNBA] (EA)
LNBD	Lens Board [Mechanical engineering]
LNBF	Low-Noise Block Feed [Satellite communications]
lnbm--	Bermuda [MARC geographic area code Library of Congress] (LCCP)
LNBS	Lesotho National Broadcasting Service [South Africa]
LNC	Lancaster, TX [Location identifier FAA] (FAAL)
LNC	Lance
LNC	Lancer Resources [Vancouver Stock Exchange symbol]
LNC	Landscape Nursery Council (EA)
LNC	Laymen's National Committee [Later, LNBC] (EA)
LNC	Lincoln National Corp. [NYSE symbol] (SPSG)
LNC	Lincoln National Corp. Capital I [NYSE symbol] (SAG)
LNC	Lincoln National Corp. Capital II [NYSE symbol] (SAG)
LNC	Lincoln Natl Corp. [NYSE symbol] (TTSB)
LNC	Local Naval Commander
LNC	LORAN Navigation Chart [Air Force]
LNC	Low-Noise Cable
LNC	Low-Noise Converter [Satellite communications]
LNC	Lunacharskoye [Former USSR Seismograph station code, US Geological Survey Closed] (SEIS)
LNC	Lymph Node Cell [Medicine]
LNC	New Orleans Public Library, New Orleans, LA [OCLC symbol] (OCLC)
lnca--	Canary Islands [MARC geographic area code Library of Congress] (LCCP)
LNCE	Lance, Inc. [NASDAQ symbol] (SAG)
LNCFS	Low Nitric Oxide [Combustion technology]
LNCH	Launch (AAG)
LNCHR	Launcher
LncNtC	Lincoln National Convertible Securities Fund, Inc. [Associated Press] (SAG)
L-NCP	Liberal-National Country Party [Australia Political party] (PPW)
LNCPr	Lincln Natl $3.00 Cv Pfd [NYSE symbol] (TTSB)
LNCR	Lincare Holdings [NASDAQ symbol] (TTSB)
LNCR	Lincare Holdings, Inc. [NASDAQ symbol] (SAG)
LncrOrt	Lancer Orthodontics, Inc. [Associated Press] (SAG)
LNCRT	Licentiate of the National College of Rubber Technology [British] (DI)
LNCT	Lancit Media Productions [NASDAQ symbol] (TTSB)
LNCT	Lancit Media Productions Ltd. [NASDAQ symbol] (SAG)
lncv--	Cape Verde [Islands] [MARC geographic area code Library of Congress] (LCCP)
LNCY	Lunacy [FBI standardized term]
LND	Dillard University, New Orleans, LA [Library symbol Library of Congress] (LCLS)
LND	Lander, WY [Location identifier FAA] (FAAL)
LND	Lawyers for Nuclear Disarmament [Defunct] (EAIO)
LND	Limiting Nose Dive [Aerospace]
LND	Lincoln National Income Fund, Inc. [Formerly, Lincoln National Direct Placement Fund, Inc.] [NYSE symbol] (SPSG)
LND	Lincoln Natl Income Fd [NYSE symbol] (TTSB)
LND	Lined
LND	Local Number Dialed [Telecommunications] (TEL)
LND	Local Number Dialling [Telecommunications] (NITA)
LND	London [Ontario] [Seismograph station code, US Geological Survey] (SEIS)
LND	Lymph Node Dissection [Medicine]
LND	Skargardsflyg, AB, Finland [FAA designator] (FAAC)
LNDC	Delgado Community College, New Orleans, LA [Library symbol Library of Congress] (LCLS)
LNDC	Landec Corp. [NASDAQ symbol] (TTSB)
LNDC	Lesotho National Development Corp.
LNDCF	Locally-Normalized Discrete Correlation Function [Mathematics]
LNDFLL	Landfill
LNDG	Landing
LNDG	Landing [Maps and charts] (KSC)
LNDH	Local Nationals, Direct Hire [Military] (AABC)
LNDL	Least Negative Down Level (IAA)
LNDL	Lindal Cedar Homes [NASDAQ symbol] (SAG)
LNDMRK	Landmark
LNDNG	Landing [Commonly used] (OPSA)
LNDO	Local Neglect of Differential Overlap [Physical chemistry]
LNDRMT	Laundromat
LNDRY	Laundry
LNDSCP	Landscape
LndsPc	Landsing Pacific Fund [Associated Press] (SAG)
LNDSPTPLT	Landing Support Platoon [Navy] (DNAB)
LNE	Lehigh & New England Railway Co. [Absorbed into Consolidated Rail Corp.] [AAR code]
LNE	Liquid Nitrogen Evaporator
LNE	Local Network Emulator
LNE	Lonorore [Vanuata] [Airport symbol] (OAG)
LNE	Lymph Node Enlargement [Medicine] (DMAA)
LNE	Northeast Louisiana University, Monroe, LA [OCLC symbol] (OCLC)
LNEP	Low-Noise Emission Product (GFGA)
LNER	London & North Eastern Railway [British]
LNERG	London & North Eastern Railway Group [British]
LNESC	LULAC [League of United Latin American Citizens] National Educational Service Centers (EA)
LneSStk	Lone Star Steakhouse & Saloon, Inc. [Associated Press] (SAG)
LNET	LodgeNet Entertainment [NASDAQ symbol] (TTSB)
LNET	Lodgenet Entertainment Corp. [NASDAQ symbol] (SAG)
LNewr	Pointe Coupee Parish Library, New Roads, LA [Library symbol Library of Congress] (LCLS)
LNF	Latvian National Foundation [Stockholm, Sweden] (EAIO)
LNF	Leon's Furniture Ltd. [Toronto Stock Exchange symbol]
LNF	Linfen [Republic of China] [Seismograph station code, US Geological Survey] (SEIS)
LNF	Liposoluble Neutral Fraction (OA)
LNF	Lithuanian National Foundation (EA)
LNF	Little-Known Fan [of science fiction or fantastic literature] [See also BNF]
LNF	Local National Forces [SEATO] (CINC)
LNF	London Flights (Biggin Hill) Ltd. [British ICAO designator] (FAAC)
LNF	Low-Noise Feed [Satellite communications]
LNFC	Leonard Nimoy Fan Club (EA)
LNFCS	Leonard Nimoy Fan Club, Spotlight (EAIO)
LNFM	Louisiana Masonic Grand Lodge, New Orleans, LA [Library symbol Library of Congress] (LCLS)
LNG	Lateral Nasal Gland [Anatomy]
LNG	Length (IAA)
LNG	Lese [Papua New Guinea] [Airport symbol] (OAG)
LNG	Lining (MSA)
LNG	Liquefied Natural Gas

LNG .... Liquid Natural Gas [*BTS*] [*DOE*] (TAG)
LNG .... Liste de Noms Geographiques [*A publication*] (BJA)
LNG .... Long
LNG .... Lounge
LNG .... Luning [*Nevada*] [*Seismograph station code, US Geological Survey Closed*] (SEIS)
Lnge .... Lounge [*Classified advertising*] (ADA)
LNGR .... Lingerie
LngStk .... Longhorn Steaks, Inc. [*Associated Press*] (SAG)
LNH .... Large Number Hypothesis [*Medicine*] (DMAA)
LNH .... Lengeh [*Iran*] [*Airport symbol*] (AD)
LNH .... LNH REIT [*Real Estate Investment Trust*], Inc. [*Associated Press*] (SAG)
LNH .... Lunar Near Horizon [*NASA*] (KSC)
LNHA .... Louisiana Historical Association, Memorial Hall, New Orleans, LA [*Library symbol Library of Congress*] (LCLS)
LNHiC .... [*The*] Historic New Orleans Collection, New Orleans, LA [*Library symbol Library of Congress*] (LCLS)
LNI .... Inland Library System, Redlands, CA [*OCLC symbol*] (OCLC)
LNI .... Log Neutralization Index [*Microbiology*]
LNI .... Lonely, AK [*Location identifier FAA*] (FAAL)
LNIAC .... Los Ninos International Adoption Center (EA)
LNIB .... Loch Ness Investigation Bureau [*Inactive*] (EA)
LNiI .... Iberia Parish Library, New Iberia, LA [*Library symbol Library of Congress*] (LCLS)
LNIS .... Atlantic Naval Intelligence Summary (MCD)
LNIT .... Local Nasal Immunotherapy
lnjn-- .... Jan Mayen [*MARC geographic area code Library of Congress*] (LCCP)
LNK .... Airlink Airlines (Pty) Ltd. [*South Africa ICAO designator*] (FAAC)
L/Nk .... Lance-Naik [*British military*] (DMA)
LNK .... Lenkoran [*Former USSR Seismograph station code, US Geological Survey*] (SEIS)
LNK .... Lincoln [*Nebraska*] [*Airport symbol*] (OAG)
LNK .... Link
LNKEDT ...... Linkage Editor [*Computer science*] (IAA)
LNL .... Land O'Lakes [*Wisconsin*] [*Airport symbol*] (AD)
LNL .... Land O' Lakes, WI [*Location identifier FAA*] (FAAL)
LNL .... Law Library of Louisiana, New Orleans, LA [*OCLC symbol*] (OCLC)
LNL .... Let Nicaragua Live [*An association Defunct*] (EA)
LNL .... Loyola University, New Orleans, LA [*Library symbol Library of Congress*] (LCLS)
LNL .... Lymph Node Lymphocyte [*Medicine*] (DMAA)
LNLA .... Lithuanian National League of America (EA)
LNLI .... League for National Labor in Israel (EA)
LNL-L .... Loyola University, Law Library, New Orleans, LA [*Library symbol Library of Congress*] (LCLS)
LNLM .... Linoleum
LNLM .... Low-Noise Level Margin
LNLM .... United States Bureau of Land Management, New Orleans Outer Continental Shelf Office, New Orleans, LA [*Library symbol Library of Congress*] (LCLS)
LNL-Phar ..... Loyola University, Pharmacy Library, New Orleans, LA [*Library symbol Library of Congress*] (LCLS)
LNM .... Langimar [*Papua New Guinea*] [*Airport symbol*] (OAG)
LNM .... LAN [*Linked Access Network*] Network Manager
LNM .... Lansdowne Minerals [*Vancouver Stock Exchange symbol*]
LNM .... Lebanese National Movement [*Political party*] (PPW)
LNM .... Leon [*Mexico*] [*Seismograph station code, US Geological Survey*] (SEIS)
LNM .... Level of No Motion [*Oceanography*]
LNM .... Library Cooperative of Macomb [*Library network*]
LNM .... Lithium Nuclear Microprobe
LNM .... Local Notice to Mariners
LNM .... Logical Network Machine (MHDB)
LNM .... Lymph Node Metastases [*Oncology*]
LNM .... Margaret C. Hanson Normal School, New Orleans, LA [*Library symbol Library of Congress Obsolete*] (LCLS)
lnma-- .... Madeira Islands [*MARC geographic area code Library of Congress*] (LCCP)
LNMA .... New Orleans Museum of Art, New Orleans, LA [*Library symbol Library of Congress*] (LCLS)
LNMC .... Monaco [*Monaco*] [*ICAO location identifier*] (ICLI)
LNME .... Mobil Exploration and Producing U.S., Inc., New Orleans, LA [*Library symbol*] [*Library of Congress*] (LCLS)
LNMMS .... McMain Magnet Secondary School, New Orleans, LA [*Library symbol*] [*Library of Congress*] (LCLS)
LNMP .... Last Normal Menstrual Period [*Medicine*]
LNMRB .... Laboratory of Nuclear Medicine and Radiation Biology
LNMS .... Large-Probe Neutral Mass Spectrometer [*NASA*]
LNN .... Leningrad [*Former USSR Seismograph station code, US Geological Survey Closed*] (SEIS)
LNN .... Leningrad [*Former USSR Geomagnetic observatory code*]
LNN .... Lincoln Resources, Inc. [*Vancouver Stock Exchange symbol*]
LNN .... Linear Nearest Neighbor (MHDB)
LNN .... Willoughby, OH [*Location identifier FAA*] (FAAL)
LNNB .... Luria-Nebraska Neuropsychological Battery
LNND .... Notre Dame Seminary, New Orleans, LA [*Library symbol Library of Congress*] (LCLS)
LNO .... Laona & Northern Railway Co. [*AAR code*]
LNO .... Leonora [*Australia Airport symbol*] (OAG)
LNO .... Liaison Officer [*Military*]
LNO .... Limited Nuclear Option [*Military*] (MCD)
LNOC .... Libya National Oil Co.
LNOP .... Lanoptics Ltd. [*NASDAQ symbol*] (SAG)

LNOP .... Orleans Parish Medical Society, New Orleans, LA [*Library symbol Library of Congress*] (LCLS)
LNOPF .... LanOptics Ltd [*NASDAQ symbol*] (TTSB)
L Notes .... Law Notes, England [*A publication*] (DLA)
L Notes Gen Pract... Law Notes for the General Practitioner [*A publication*] (DLA)
LNP .... Bibliotheca Parsoniana, New Orleans, LA [*Library symbol Library of Congress Obsolete*] (LCLS)
LNP .... Chieftain Aviation PC [*South Africa ICAO designator*] (FAAC)
LNP .... Large Neuronal Polypeptide [*Medicine*] (DMAA)
LNP .... Least Newtonian Path (IAA)
LNP .... Leg Negative Pressure (PDAA)
LNP .... Liberal/National Party [*Political party Australia*]
LNP .... Libertarian Party [*Australia Political party*]
LNP .... Liquefied Natural Petroleum
LNP .... Liquid Nitrogen Processing
LNP .... Loss of Normal Power (IEEE)
LNP .... Low Needle Position [*on dial*]
LNP .... Lunar Neutron Probe [*NASA*] (KSC)
LNP .... Lunping [*Taiwan*] [*Geomagnetic observatory code*]
LNP .... Wise, VA [*Location identifier FAA*] (FAAL)
LNP & W ...... Laramie, North Park & Western Railroad (IIA)
LNPF .... Lebanese National Patriotic Forces [*Political party*]
LNPF .... Lymph Node Permeability Factor [*Immunology*]
LNPIB .... Loch Ness Phenomena Investigation Bureau [*Later, LNIB*]
LNPo .... Polyanthos, New Orleans, LA [*Library symbol Library of Congress*] (LCLS)
LNQ .... Longest Queue
LNR .... Lagos Notes and Records [*A publication*]
LNR .... Linamar Machine Ltd. [*Toronto Stock Exchange symbol*]
LNR .... Liner
LNR .... Liquid Natural Rubber
LNR .... Liquid Nitrogen Refrigeration
LNR .... Local Nature Reserve (PDAA)
LNR .... Lone Rock, WI [*Location identifier FAA*] (FAAL)
LNR .... Lonorore [*New Hebrides*] [*Seismograph station code, US Geological Survey*] (SEIS)
LNR .... Louisiana Numerical Register [*Louisiana State Library*] [*Baton Rouge, LA*] [*Library network*]
LNR .... Low-Noise Receiver
LNR .... Luftnachrichten-Regiment [*Air forces signal regiment*] [*German military - World War II*]
LNR .... Lymph Node Region [*Medicine*] (DAVI)
LNRA .... Sky Liners Air Services Ltd. [*Suriname*] [*ICAO designator*] (FAAC)
LNRA .... Linear Nested Region Analysis (PDAA)
LNRC .... Little Nash Rambler Club (EA)
LNRS .... Limited Night Recovery System (PDAA)
LNS .... Laboratory for Nuclear Science [*MIT*] (MCD)
LNS .... Lancaster [*Pennsylvania*] [*Airport symbol*] (OAG)
LNS .... Land Navigation System
LNS .... Lansco Resources [*Vancouver Stock Exchange symbol*]
LNS .... Lanslevillard [*France*] [*Seismograph station code, US Geological Survey*] (SEIS)
LNS .... LASER Night Sensor
LNS .... Lateral Nuclear Stratum [*Medicine*] (DMAA)
LNS .... Lesch-Nyhan Syndrome [*Medicine*]
LNS .... Liberation News Service (EA)
LNS .... London Normal School
LNS .... Long Normal Superchron [*Geology*]
LNS .... Lutheran News Service [*Lutheran Church in America*] [*Information service or system*] (IID)
LNS .... Nicholls State University, Ellender Memorial Library, Thibodaux, LA [*OCLC symbol*] (OCLC)
LNSA .... Local Navy Supervising Activity
lnsb-- .... Svalbard and Jan Mayen [*MARC geographic area code Library of Congress*] (LCCP)
lnsd .... Linseed Oil (VRA)
LNSF .... Light Night Striking Force [*British military*] (DMA)
LNSL .... Liberia National Shipping Line (EY)
LNSL .... Southeast Louisiana Library Network Cooperative (SEALLING), New Orleans, LA [*Library symbol Library of Congress*] (LCLS)
LNSM .... Saint Mary's Dominican College, New Orleans, LA [*Library symbol Library of Congress*] (LCLS)
LNSN .... Local Non-Switched Network
LNSO .... Shell Oil Co., New Orleans, LA [*Library symbol Library of Congress*] (LCLS)
LNSP .... Lens Speed [*Mechanical engineering*]
LnStr .... Lone Star Industries [*Associated Press*] (SAG)
LnStrInd ...... Lone Star Industries [*Associated Press*] (SAG)
LNSU .... Library Network of SIBIL Users (EAIO)
LNSU .... United States Department of Agriculture, Southern Utilization and Development Division, Agricultural Research Service, New Orleans, LA [*Library symbol Library of Congress*] (LCLS)
LNT .... Aerolineas Internacionales, SA de CV [*Mexico*] [*FAA designator*] (FAAC)
LNT .... Launch Network Test
LNT .... Linear No-Threshold [*Risk model*]
LNT .... Liquid Nitrogen Temperature (IAA)
LNT .... Millinocket, ME [*Location identifier FAA*] (FAAL)
LNT .... Tulane University, New Orleans, LA [*Library symbol Library of Congress*] (LCLS)
LNT-BA .... Tulane University, Graduate School of Business Administration, New Orleans, LA [*Library symbol Library of Congress*] (LCLS)
LNTC .... International House, Cunningham Library, New Orleans, LA [*Library symbol Library of Congress*] (LCLS)
LNTC .... Lymph Node T Cells [*Immunology*]

LNTex .... Texas, Inc., New Orleans, LA [*Library symbol*] [*Library of Congress*] (LCLS)
LNTL .... Lintel
LNT-L .... Tulane University, Law Library, New Orleans, LA [*Library symbol Library of Congress*] (LCLS)
LNT-M .... Tulane University, Medical Library, New Orleans, LA [*Library symbol Library of Congress*] (LCLS)
LNT-MC .... Greater New Orleans Microform Cooperative, Tulane University, New Orleans, LA [*Library symbol Library of Congress*] (LCLS)
LNTO .... Lento [*Very Slow*] [*Music*] (ROG)
LNTP .... New Orleans Times-Picayune, New Orleans, LA [*Library symbol Library of Congress*] (LCLS)
LNTS .... League of Nations Treaty Series [*A publication*] (DLA)
LNTS .... Liquid Nitrogen Transfer System
LNTV .... Lin Television Corp. [*NASDAQ symbol*] (SAG)
LNTWA .... Low-Noise Traveling Wave Amplifier
LNTWTA .... Low-Noise Traveling Wave Tube Amplifier (IAA)
LNU .... Last Name Unknown
LNU .... League of Nations Union
LNU .... University of New Orleans, New Orleans, LA [*Library symbol Library of Congress OCLC symbol*] (LCLS)
LNUCA .... United States Circuit Court of Appeals, Fifth Circuit Law Library, New Orleans, LA [*Library symbol Library of Congress*] (LCLS)
LNUrs .... Ursuline Academy, New Orleans, LA [*Library symbol Library of Congress*] (LCLS)
LNV .... Lincln Natl Cv Sec [*NYSE symbol*] (TTSB)
LNV .... Lincoln National Convertible Securities Fund, Inc. [*NYSE symbol*] (SPSG)
LNV .... Londolovit [*Papua New Guinea*] [*Airport symbol Obsolete*] (OAG)
LNV .... Longovilo [*Chile*] [*Seismograph station code, US Geological Survey*] (SEIS)
LNV .... Lonvest Corp. [*Toronto Stock Exchange symbol Vancouver Stock Exchange symbol*]
LNVA .... United States Veterans Administration Hospital, New Orleans, LA [*Library symbol Library of Congress*] (LCLS)
LNVT .... Launch Network Verification Test (IAA)
LNW .... [*The*] Louisiana & North West Railroad Co. [*AAR code*]
LNWR .... London & North Western Railway [*British*]
LNX .... Lenex [*Poland ICAO designator*] (FAAC)
LNX .... London Executive Aviation Ltd. [*British*] [*FAA designator*] (FAAC)
LNX .... Xavier University, New Orleans, LA [*Library symbol Library of Congress OCLC symbol*] (LCLS)
LNY .... Lanai City [*Hawaii*] [*Airport symbol*] (OAG)
LNY .... Laws of New York [*A publication*] (DLA)
LNYD .... Lanyard
LNYL .... Leksikon fun der Nayer Yidisher Literatur [*New York*] [*A publication*] (BJA)
LNYT .... League of New York Theatres [*Later, LNYTP*] (EA)
LNYTP .... League of New York Theatres and Producers (EA)
LNYV .... Lettuce Necrotic Yellows Virus
LNZ .... Linz [*Austria*] [*Airport symbol*] (OAG)
LNZ .... Litag K.G. [*Austria*] [*FAA designator*] (FAAC)
LO .... Laboratory Outfitting (SSD)
LO .... Lamp Oil
LO .... Landelijke Organistatie [*Netherlands underground organization*] [*World War II*]
LO .... Landsorganisasjonen i Norge [*Norwegian Federation of Trade Unions*]
LO .... Landsorganisationen i Sverige [*Swedish Federation of Trade Unions*]
LO .... Larval Operculum
LO .... Lateral Oblique [*X-ray view*] (DAVI)
LO .... Launch Operations [*or Operator*] [*NASA*]
LO .... Law Observer [*1872*] [*India*] [*A publication*] (DLA)
LO .... Law Officer
LO .... Law Opinions [*A publication*] (DLA)
LO .... Lay Observer (ILCA)
LO .... Layout [*Graphic arts*]
LO .... Learning Objective
LO .... Left Outboard (MCD)
LO .... Legal Observer [*British*]
LO .... Legal Officer
LO .... Legal Opinion [*1870-73*] [*A publication*] (DLA)
LO .... Lenticular Opacity [*Ophthalmology*] (DAVI)
lo .... Lesotho [*MARC country of publication code Library of Congress*] (LCCP)
L/O .... Letter of Offer
LO .... Letter Orders
LO .... Level Off
LO .... Liaison Office [*or Officer*]
LO .... Licensed Officer [*US Merchant Marine*]
LO .... [*The*] Lifestyles Organization (EA)
LO .... Lift-Off (AAG)
LO .... Limerent Object [*One who is the object of obsessional romantic love*]
LO .... Limited Order [*Business term*]
LO .... Line Occupancy
LO .... Line Office (USDC)
LO .... Line Office [*Marine science*] (OSRA)
LO .... Linguoocclusal [*Dentistry*]
LO .... Liquid Oxygen
LO .... Loam [*Type of soil*] (ROG)
Lo .... Local [*Navy*]
LO .... Local Office
LO .... Local Order
LO .... Local Origination [*Television programming*]
LO .... Local Oscillator [*Electronics*]

LO .... Locator File [*Information retrieval*]
LO .... Locked Open [*Technical drawings*]
LO .... Locked Oscillator
LO .... Lock-On
LO .... Lock-Out
LO .... Loco [*Place*] [*Latin*]
LO .... Loco [*As Written*] [*Music*]
LO .... Logical Operation (AAG)
LO .... Logistics Offensive
LO .... London Office
LO .... Longitude
LO .... Longitudinal Optic
LO .... Look-Out [*Navy British*]
Lo .... Lord (WGA)
Lo .... Lotarius [*Flourished, 1191-1212*] [*Authority cited in pre-1607 legal work*] (DSA)
LO .... Louisville Orchestra [*Record label*]
LO .... Louth [*County in Ireland*] (ROG)
LO .... Love Object
LO .... Low (KSC)
lo .... Low (IDOE)
LO .... Lowest Offer [*Business term*]
LO .... Low Loaders (DCTA)
LO .... Low Oblique [*Aerospace*]
LO .... Low Observable (DOMA)
LO .... Low Order [*Computer science*] (OA)
LO .... Low Ordinary (IAA)
LO .... Lubricating Oil
LO .... Lubrication Order
LO .... Lunar Orbiter [*Aerospace*] (MCD)
LO .... Lutte Ouvriere [*Workers' Struggle*] [*France Political party*] (PPW)
LO .... Lysyl Oxidase [*An enzyme*]
LO .... Opelousas-Eunice Public Library, Opelousas, LA [*Library symbol Library of Congress*] (LCLS)
LO .... Solicitor's Law Opinion, United States Internal Revenue Bureau [*A publication*] (DLA)
LO₂ .... Liquid Oxygen [*Also, LOX*] [*NASA*] (KSC)
LO2 .... Pahute Mesa [*Nevada*] [*Seismograph station code, US Geological Survey Closed*] (SEIS)
LOA .... Landing Operations Area [*NASA*] (NASA)
LOA .... LASER Opto-Acoustic
LOA .... Launch on Assessment [*Military*]
LOA .... Launch on Attack [*Military*]
LOA .... Launch Operations Agency [*NASA*] (KSC)
LOA .... Launch Operations Area (MCD)
LOA .... Leave of Absence
LOA .... Left Occipitoanterior [*A fetal position*] [*Obstetrics*]
LOA .... Length Over-All [*Technical drawings*]
LOA .... Leona, TX [*Location identifier FAA*] (FAAL)
LOA .... Letter of Acceptance
LOA .... Letter of Agreement
LOA .... Letter of Authorization
LOA .... Letter of Offer and Acceptance (MCD)
LOA .... Level of Authority [*Military*] (AFIT)
LOA .... Life Offices' Association [*British*] (DCTA)
LOA .... Light Observation Aircraft
LOA .... Limit of Advance [*Army*] (DOMA)
LOA .... Line of Assurance
LOA .... Local Overseas Allowance [*British military*] (DMA)
LOA .... Log-Out Analysis (NITA)
LOA .... London Orphan Asylum (ROG)
LOA .... Lorcan Resources Ltd. [*Vancouver Stock Exchange symbol*]
LOA .... Lorraine [*Australia Airport symbol Obsolete*] (OAG)
LOA .... Los Alamos [*New Mexico*] [*Seismograph station code, US Geological Survey*] (SEIS)
LOA .... Low Oil Agglomeration [*Coal processing*]
LOA .... Low-Speed Output Adapter (MHDB)
LOAA .... Letter of Agreement and Acceptance
LOAC .... Low Accuracy
LOAD .... LASER Optoacoustic Detection
LOAD .... Low-Altitude Defense (MCD)
LOADEX .... Loading Exercise [*Military*] (NVT)
LOADS .... Lifting of Aerodynamic Decelerators (PDAA)
LOADS .... Low-Altitude Defense System
LOAEL .... Lowest Observed Adverse Effect Level (EG)
LOAF .... Large Open-Area Floor
LOAF .... Loaf [*Commonly used*] (OPSA)
LOAL .... Lock-On after Launch [*Weaponry*] (CAAL)
LOAM .... List of Applicable Material (MCD)
LOAMP .... Logarithmic Amplifier (IEEE)
LOAN .... Horizon Bancorp, Inc. (TX) [*NASDAQ symbol*] (SAG)
LOAN .... Horizon Bancorp(TX) [*NASDAQ symbol*] (TTSB)
LOAN .... Local Officials' Administration Network [*An association*]
LOAN/A .... Vessels Loaned to Army [*Navy*]
LOAN/C .... Vessels Loaned to Coast Guard [*Navy*]
LO & DS .... London Operatic and Dramatic Society (ROG)
LOAN/M .... Vessels Loaned to Miscellaneous Activities [*US Maritime Academy, etc.*] [*Navy*]
LOAN/S .... Vessels Loaned to States [*Navy*]
LOAN/W .... Vessels Loaned to War Shipping Administration [*Terminated, 1946*] [*Navy*]
LOAP .... Length of Adjacency Process (MHDB)
LOAP .... List of Applicable Publications [*Air Force*]
LOAPS .... Large Order Assembly Planning System (MCD)
LOAS .... Lift-Off Acquisition System

LOAS .... List of Assessed Spares (MCD)
LOAS .... Loyal Order of Ancient Shepherds [British] (BI)
LOAT .... Trausdorf [Austria ICAO location identifier] (ICLI)
LOAV .... Lift Owners' Association of Victoria [Australia]
LOAV .... Voslau [Austria ICAO location identifier] (ICLI)
LOB .... Laboratory Office Building
LOB .... [The] Land of the Bible: A Historical Geography [A publication] (BJA)
LOB .... Launch Operations Branch [NASA]
LOB .... Launch Operations Building [NASA]
LOB .... Left of Baseline
LOB .... Left on Base [Baseball]
LOB .... Left Outboard (MCD)
LOB .... Left Out of Battle [British]
LOB .... Limited Operating Base (AFM)
LOB .... Line of Balance
LOB .... Line of Bearing [Navy] (NVT)
LOB .... Line of Business [Used in corporate reports to Federal Trade Commission]
LOB .... Lobito [Angola] [Airport symbol] (AD)
LOB .... Location of Offices Bureau [British]
LOB .... Logistics Operating Base
LOB .... Logistics-over-the-Beach Base [Military] (VNW)
LOB .... Loyal Order of the Boar (EA)
LObA .... Allen Parish Library, Oberlin, LA [Library symbol Library of Congress] (LCLS)
LOBA .... Last Offer Binding Arbitration [Labor negotiations]
LOBAR .... Long Baseline RADAR
LOBI .... Library Orientation/Bibliographic Instruction [Florida Library Association caucus]
Lobin .... Lobingier's Extra-Territorial Cases [United States Court for China] [A publication] (DLA)
LOBL .... Lock-On Before Launch [Missile] (DOMA)
LOBSTER .... Long-Term Ocean Bottom Settlement Test for Engineering Research [Navy project]
LOBTP .... League of Off-Broadway Theatres and Producers [Later, OBL] (EA)
LOC .... Landing Operations Center (MCD)
LOC .... Large Optical Cavity [LASER design]
LOC .... Launch Operations Center [NASA]
LOC .... Launch Operations Complex
LOC .... Launch Operations Control
LOC .... Launch Operator's Console [Aerospace] (AAG)
LOC .... Laverda Owner's Club (EA)
LOC .... Laxative of Choice [Medicine]
LOC .... Le Groupe Opus Communications, Inc. [Vancouver Stock Exchange symbol]
LOC .... LeMoyne-Owen College, Memphis, TN [OCLC symbol] (OCLC)
LOC .... Letter of Comment
LOC .... Letter of Compliance [Program] [Coast Guard]
LOC .... Letter of Consent
LOC .... Letterpress to Offset Conversion (DGA)
LOC .... Letters of Credit
LOC .... Level of Care [Medicine] (GFGA)
LOC .... Level of Concern [Environmental Protection Agency] (ERG)
LOC .... Level of Consciousness [Medicine]
LOC .... Liaison Officer Coordinator [Air Force] (AFM)
LOC .... Libraries and Our Civilizations [A publication]
LOC .... Library of Congress
LOC .... Light-Off Catalyst [Exhaust emissions] [Automotive engineering]
LOC .... Limitation of Cost (AAGC)
LOC .... Limited Operational Capability (CET)
LOC .... Limiting Oxygen Concentration [For ignition]
LOC .... Lincoln Owners Club (EA)
LOC .... Lincoln School [California] [Seismograph station code, US Geological Survey] (SEIS)
LOC .... Line of Code
LOC .... Line of Communication [Military]
LOCL .... Line of Contact (MCD)
LOC .... Line of Correction
LOC .... Linked Object Code (TEL)
LOC .... Linked Operational Capability (DOMA)
LOC .... Liquid Organic Compound
LOC .... Load Overcurrent
LOC .... Local
LOC .... Localizer (MSA)
LOC .... Localizer Line of Sight
LOC .... Local Original Channel [Cable television broadcasting]
LOC .... Locate (MSA)
LOC .... Location (AFM)
loc .... Location (VRA)
LOC .... Location Counter [Computer science]
LOC .... Locative (Case) [Linguistics]
LOC .... Locavia 49 [France ICAO designator] (FAAC)
LOC .... Lock-On Completed (MCD)
LOC .... Loco [Place] [Latin] (WGA)
LOC .... Loctite Corp. [NYSE symbol] (SPSG)
LOC .... Logistic Operation Center [Military]
LOC .... Lord of Creation
LOC .... Loss of Consciousness [Medicine]
LOC .... Loss of Coolant (GAAI)
LOCA .... Late Onset Cerebellar Ataxia [Medicine]
LOCA .... Loss-of-Coolant Accident [Nuclear energy]
LOCA .... Low-Cost Computer Attachment (IAA)
LOCA .... Low Osmolar Contrast Agent [Medicine]
LOCAAS .... Low-Cost Anti-Armor Submunitions [Military]
LOCAL .... Laboratory Program for Computer-Assisted Learning (IAA)

LOCAL .... Load On-Call [Computer science]
lo cal .... Low Calorie (MAE)
lo calc .... Low Calcium [Diet] (DAVI)
Local Ct & Mun Gaz... Local Courts and Municipal Gazette [Toronto, ON] [A publication] (DLA)
Local Gov.... Local Government and Magisterial Reports [England] [A publication] (DLA)
Local Gov R Aust... Local Government Reports of Australia [A publication] (DLA)
Local Gov't... Local Government and Magisterial Reports [England] [A publication] (DLA)
Local Govt Jl WA... Local Government Journal of Western Australia [A publication]
LOCALS .... Low-Cost Alternate LASER Seeker (MCD)
LOCAM .... Logistics Cost Analysis Model (MCD)
LOCAP .... Low Capacitance [Cable] [Bell System]
LOCAP .... Low [Altitude] Combat Air Patrol (NVT)
LOCAS .... Local Cataloguing Service (NITA)
LOCAT .... Location (DAVI)
LOCAT .... Low-Altitude Clear-Air Turbulence (MCD)
LOCAT .... Low-Cost Air Target (MCD)
LOCATE .... Library of Congress Automation Techniques Exchange
LOCATE .... List of Common Abbreviations in Training and Education (AIE)
LOCATE .... Local Area Telecommunications, Inc. [Digital microwave carrier] [New York, NY] (TSSD)
LOCATE .... LORAN/OMEGA Course and Tracking Equipment (MCD)
LOCATS .... Lockheed Optical Communications and Tracking System
LOCC .... Launcher Order and Capture Computer (MCD)
LOCC .... Launch Operations Control Center
LOCC .... Limitation of Cost Clause (AAGC)
Locc .... Loccenius. De Jure Maritimo [A publication] (DLA)
LOCC .... Logistical Operations Control Center [Army]
loc cit .... In the Place Cited [Loco citato] [Latin] (WDMC)
LOC CIT .... Loco Citato [In the Place Cited] [Latin]
LOCCOZO .... Line of Communication Combat Zone [Military]
LOCCS .... Letter of Credit Control System [Department of Housing and Urban Development] (GFGA)
Loc Ct Gaz... Local Courts and Municipal Gazette [Toronto, ON] [A publication] (DLA)
LOCD .... Lines of Communication Designators (MCD)
LOCD .... Local Disease
LOC DOL .... Loco Dolenti [To the Painful Spot] [Pharmacy]
LOCE .... Limited Operational Capability for Europe [DoD]
LOCE .... Loss-of-Coolant Experiment [Nuclear energy]
LOCF .... Location File (MCD)
LOCF .... Loss-of-Coolant Flow [Nuclear energy] (NRCH)
Loc Gov Chron... Local Government Chronicle [London, England] [A publication] (DLA)
Loc Govt Chr & Mag Rep... Local Government Chronicle and Magisterial Reporter [London] [A publication] (DLA)
LOCI .... Ligue des Originaires de Cote d'Ivoire [League of Ivory Coast Natives]
LOCI .... List of Cancelled Items
LOCI .... Local Course Improvement [National Science Foundation] (EDAC)
LOCI .... Logarithmic Computing Instrument
LOCI .... Low-Cost Interceptor (MCD)
LOCID .... Location Identifier [FAA] (TAG)
LOCIG .... Limited-Overs Cricket Information Group [British] (DBA)
LOCIS .... Library of Congress Information System [Library of Congress Information service or system] (IID)
LO CIT .... Loco Citato [In the Place Cited] [Latin]
LOCK .... Lock [Commonly used] (OPSA)
LOCK .... Logistical Operational Control Key [Army] (AABC)
Lock GL .... Locke's Game Laws [5th ed.] [1866] [A publication] (DLA)
LockhM .... Lockheed Martin Corp. [Associated Press] (SAG)
Lock Rev Ca... Lockwood's Reversed Cases [New York] [A publication] (DLA)
Lock Rev Cas... Lockwood's Reversed Cases [New York] [A publication] (DLA)
LOCKS .... Locks [Commonly used] (OPSA)
LOCL .... Loyal Order of Catfish Lovers (EA)
LOC LAUD ... Loco Laudato [In the Place Quoted] [Latin]
LOCLED .... Low-Operating Current Light-Emitting Diode
LOC LF .... Local Line Feed [Telecommunications] (DNAB)
LOCMOS .... Locally-Oxidized Complementary Metal-Oxide Semiconductor (PDAA)
LOCN .... Location
LOCO .... Locomotion (WDAA)
LOCO .... Locomotive (AABC)
LOCO .... Long Core [Drilling program]
LOCOM .... Local Community (ADA)
LOCOM .... Locomotive
LOCOR .... Local Coordinator (FAAC)
LOCOS .... Local Oxidation of Silicon [Transistor technology]
LOCOSS .... Logic of Computers Operating System (MCD)
LOCO TAC .... Low-Cost Tactical RADAR (DNAB)
LOCP .... Launcher Operation Control Panel
LOCP .... Loss-of-Coolant Protection [Nuclear energy] (NRCH)
LOCPOD .... Low-Cost Powered Dispenser
LOCPORT .... Lines of Communications Ports (AABC)
Loc Primo Cit... Loco Primo Citato [In the Place First Cited] [Latin] (ILCA)
LOC PRIUS CIT... Loco Prius Citato [In the Place First Cited] [Latin] (ADA)
LOCPURO .... Local Purchase Order
LOCS .... Land-Ocean-Climate Satellite [Marine science] (OSRA)
LOCS .... Librascope Operations Control System
LOCS .... Logic and Control Simulation (NITA)
LOCS .... Logic and Control Simulator [Computer science] (BUR)
LOCT .... Lockheed Command and Tracking (IAA)
Loctite .... Loctite Corp. [Associated Press] (SAG)
LOCTRACS... Lockheed Tracking and Control System

LOCUSP......	Low Cost Uncooled Sensor Prototype [Army]
Locus Standi..	Locus Standi Reports [England] [A publication] (DLA)
LOD	Large Organic Debris [Pisciculture]
LOD	Launch Operations Directive [or Director] [NASA]
LOD	Launch Operations Division [NASA] (KSC)
LOD	Law Officers' Department [British]
LOD	Leading Ones Detector [Computer science]
LOD	Length of Day
LOD	Level of Detail (MCD)
LOD	Light-Off Detector [Military] (CAAL)
LOD	Limit of Detection
LOD	Line of Dance
LOD	Line of Departure [Military] (AFM)
LOD	Line of Direction
LOD	Line of Duty [Military]
LOD	List of Drawings
LOD	Little Oxford Dictionary [A publication]
LOD	Locally One-Dimensional [Engineering] (OA)
LOD	Location Dependent
LOD	Lodi Metals, Inc. [Vancouver Stock Exchange symbol]
LOD	Logarithm of the Odds
lod	Logarithm of the Odds [Favoring linkage] [Genetics] (DOG)
LOD	Longana [Vanuatu] [Airport symbol] (OAG)
LOD	Low Density (IAA)
LODACS	Longitudinal Fame Developing and Conducting System (PDAA)
LODACS	Low-Dispersion Automatic Cannon System
LODC	Local Defense District Craft
LODCS	Lunar Orbiter Data Conversion System [Aerospace]
LODE	Comstock Bank [NASDAQ symbol] (SAG)
LODE	Cornstock Bk Carson City Nev [NASDAQ symbol] (TTSB)
LODE	Large Optics Demonstration Experiment [DoD]
LODEM	Loading Dock Equipment Manufacturers Association (EA)
LODESMP	Logistics Data Element Standardization and Management Process (IEEE)
LODESTAR	Logically Organized Data Entry, Storage, and Recording
LODG	Lodge [Commonly used] (OPSA)
LODG	Sholodge, Inc. [NASDAQ symbol] (SAG)
LODGE	Lodge [Commonly used] (OPSA)
LodgEnt	Lodgenet Entertainment Corp. [Associated Press] (SAG)
LODI	List of Deleted Items (NG)
LODIF	Long Distance Infrared Flash Camera (PDAA)
LODISNAV	Long Distance Navigation (FAAC)
LODOR	Loaded, Waiting Orders or Assignment [Navy]
LODP	Lunar Orbiter Data Printer [Aerospace]
LODR	Loader
LODTM	Large Optics Diamond Turning Machine (SDI)
LODUS	Low Data Rate UHF [Ultra-High Frequency] Satellite [RADAR] (MCD)
LODYC	Laboratoire d'Oceanographie Dynamique et de Climatologie [France] [Marine science] (OSRA)
LOE	Left Outboard Elevon [Aviation] (MCD)
LOE	Letter of Evaluation
LOE	Letter of Execution (MCD)
LOE	Level of Effort (KSC)
LOE	Light-Off Examination [Navy] (NVT)
LOE	Line of Effort (MCD)
LOE	Line Oriented Evaluation (GAVI)
LOE	Loei [Thailand] [Airport symbol Obsolete] (OAG)
LOE	Loeser, Luftfahrtgesellschaft GmbH [Germany ICAO designator] (FAAC)
LOEAT	Lowest Temperature Equaled for All Time [NWS] (FAAC)
LOEC	List of Effective Cards (NVT)
LOEC	Lowest Observed Effect Concentration [Environmental Technology]
LOEFM	Lowest Temperature Equaled for the Month [NWS] (FAAC)
LOEH	Loehmann's Inc. [NASDAQ symbol] (TTSB)
LOEL	Lowest-Observed-Effect Level [Environmental science] (FFDE)
LOEL	Lowest Observed Effect Level [Toxicology]
LOEM(A)	Leading Ordnance Electrical Mechanic (Air) [British military] (DMA)
LOEP	List of Effective Pages (NVT)
LOEP	Loss of Electric Power
LOERO	Large Orbiting Earth Resources Observatory (IEEE)
LOESE	Lowest Temperature Equaled So Early [NWS] (FAAC)
LOESL	Lowest Temperature Equaled So Late [NWS] (FAAC)
Loewen	Loewen Group, Inc. [Associated Press] (SAG)
LoewenG	Loewen Group Capital LP [Associated Press] (SAG)
Loews	Loew's Corp. [Formerly, Loew's Theatres, Inc.] [Associated Press] (SAG)
LOEX	Library Orientation/Instruction Exchange [Library network]
LOF	Lack of Fusion
LOF	Lecherous Old Fool [Slang]
LOF	Letter of Finding (GFGA)
LOF	Libbey-Owens-Ford Glass Co. [Auto industry supplier]
LOF	Limitation of Funds (AAGC)
LOF	Line of Fire
LOF	Line-of-Flight (MCD)
LOF	Line of Force
LOF	Local Oscillator Filter [Electronics]
LOF	Local Oscillator Frequency [Electronics]
LOF	Lofexidine (DMAA)
LOF	London and Overseas Freighter
LOF	Longest Operation First
LOF	Look Ahead on Fault [Computer science] (MHDB)
LOF	Loss of Feedwater [Nuclear energy] (NRCH)
LOF	Loss of Flow [Nuclear energy] (NRCH)
LOF	Loss of Fluid (BARN)

LOF	Lowest Operating Frequency (IEEE)
LOF	Low Outlet Forceps [Delivery] [Obstetrics] (DAVI)
LOF	Lube and Oil Filter
LOF	Lube, Oil, and Filter [Automobile servicing]
LOF	Trans States Airlines, Inc. [ICAO designator] (FAAC)
LOFA	Leisure and Outdoor Furniture Association [British] (DBA)
LOFA	Loss of Flow Accident [Nuclear energy] (NRCH)
LOFAAD	Low-Altitude Forward Area Air Defense (AABC)
LOFAADS	Low-Altitude Forward Area Anti-Aircraft Defense System [Army]
LOFADS	Low-Altitude Forward Air Defense System (PDAA)
LOFAR	Low-Frequency Acquisition and Ranging
LOFAR	Low-Frequency Analysis and Recording [Sonobuoys] [Navy]
LOFAT	Low-Flying Aerial Target [Military] (CAAL)
L of C	Library of Congress
LOFC	Loss of Forced Circulation [Nuclear energy] (NRCH)
LOFES	Load Factor Error Sensor (MCD)
LOFEZ	Low Fighter Engagement Zone (PDAA)
LOFF	Leakoff [Mechanical engineering]
L Off Econ & Mgt...	Law Office Economics and Management [A publication] (DLA)
Lofft	Lofft's English King's Bench Reports [1772-74] [A publication] (DLA)
Lofft Append..	Lofft's Maxims, Appended to Lofft's Reports [A publication] (DLA)
Lofft Lib	Lofft on the Law of Libels [A publication] (DLA)
Lofft Max	Maxims Appended to Lofft's Reports [A publication] (DLA)
Lofft's Rep..	Lofft's English King's Bench Reports [1772-74] [A publication] (DLA)
Lofft Un L	Lofft's Elements of Universal Law [A publication] (DLA)
L of N	League of Nations [1919-1946]
LOFO	Low-Frequency Oscillation (MCD)
L of P	Lodge of Perfection [Freemasonry] (DAS)
LOFRECO	Low Front End Cost [Engineering]
LOFS	London & Overseas Freightliners [NASDAQ symbol] (SAG)
LOFSY	London & Overseas Freight ADS [NASDAQ symbol] (TTSB)
LOFT	Line Oriented Flight Training (MCD)
Loft	Lofft's English King's Bench Reports [1772-74] [A publication] (DLA)
LOFT	Loss of Flow [or Fluid] Test Facility [Nuclear energy]
LOFT	Loss-of-Fluid Test (GAAI)
LOFT	Low-Frequency Telescope [NASA]
LOFTI	Low-Frequency Transionospheric Satellite
LOFTPS	Lube Oil Fill, Transfer, and Purification System (DNAB)
LOFW	Loss of Feedwater [Nuclear energy] (NRCH)
LOG	Labor Old Guard [Australia An association]
LOG	Lawn-O-Gram [A publication] (EAAP)
LOG	Legion of Guardsmen (EA)
LOG	Logan [Utah] [Seismograph station code, US Geological Survey Closed] (SEIS)
LOG	Loganair Ltd. [British ICAO designator] (FAAC)
LOG	Logan Mines Ltd. [Vancouver Stock Exchange symbol]
LOG	Logarithm [Mathematics]
log	Logarithm (IDOE)
log	Loggia (VRA)
LOG	Logging
LOG	Logic
LOG	Logistician
LOG	Logistics (KSC)
log	Logogram (BJA)
log	Logographic (BJA)
LOG	Pago Pago, AQ [Location identifier FAA] (FAAL)
LOG	Rayonier Timberlands CI'A' [NYSE symbol] (TTSB)
LOG	Rayonier Timberlands LP [NYSE symbol] (SPSG)
LOGACS	Low-G Accelerometer Calibration System [NASA]
LOGAIR	Logistics Airlift [Military]
LOGAIRNET..	Logistics Air Network [Air Force]
LOGAIS	Logistics Automated Information System [Marine Corps] (DOMA)
LOGAL	Logical Algorithmic Language [Computer science] (CSR)
LogalEd	Logal Educational Software & Systems Ltd. [Associated Press] (SAG)
LOGALGOL	Logical Algorithmic Language [Computer science]
LOGAM	Logistics Analysis Model [Army] (RDA)
LOGAMP	Logarithmic Amplifier (IAA)
LOGAMP	Logistics and Acquisition Management Program [Army] (RDA)
LOGANDS	Logical Commands
Logans	Logan's Roadhouse, Inc. [Associated Press] (SAG)
LOGATAK	Logistics Attack Model [BDM Corp.] (MCD)
LOGBALNET..	Logistics Ballistic Missile Network [Air Force]
LOGC	Logic Devices [NASDAQ symbol] (TTSB)
LOGC	Logic Devices, Inc. [NASDAQ symbol] (SAG)
LOGC	Logistics Center [Army]
LOGCAB	Logistics Center Advisory Board (MCD)
LOGC-AMIP..	Logistics Center Involvement in Army Model Improvement Program
LOGCAP	Logistic and Command Assessment of Projects [Army]
LOGCAP	Logistics Capability
LOGCAP	Logistics Civil Augmentation Program [Army]
LOGCCIS	Logistics Command Central Information System [British]
LOGCEN	Logistics Center (MCD)
LOGCMD	Logistical Command
LOGCOM	Logistic Communications (CET)
LOGCOM	Logistics Command (MCD)
LOGCOMD	Logistical Command
Log Comp...	Logan's Compendium of Ancient Law [A publication] (DLA)
LOGCON	Logistics Readiness Condition System [DARCOM] (MCD)
LOGCOR	Logistics Coordination (NVT)
LOGCOST	Logistics Cost Model (PDAA)
LOG CTR...	Logistic Center [Army]
LOGDB	Logistics Database
LOGDEC	Logarithmic Decrement (IAA)

LOGDESMAP... Logistics Data Element Standardization and Management Program [*DoD*] (AABC)
LOGDESMO... Logistics Data Element Standardization and Management Office [*DoD*] (AABC)
LOGDIV....... Logistics Division [*Supreme Headquarters, Allied Powers Europe*] (NATG)
log$_e$.......... Logarithm to the Base e [*Mathematics*] (DAVI)
LOGEL .... Logic Generating Language [*Computer science*]
LOGEST....... Annual Logistic Estimate (NATG)
LOGEX .... Logistical Exercise [*Army*] (AABC)
LOGFED...... Log File Editor (NITA)
LOGFED...... Log File Editor Processor [*Computer science*]
LOGFOR...... Logistics Force [*Military*]
LOGFTC ...... Logarithmic Fast Time Constant
LOGHELO .... Logistics Helicopter (NVT)
LOGI .... Logarithmic Computing Instrument (HGAA)
LOGIC .... LASER Optical Guidance Integration Concept [*Missile guidance*]
LOGIC .... Level of Greatest Item Control [*DoD*]
LOGIC .... Local Government Information Center
Logic .... Logic Works, Inc. [*Associated Press*] (SAG)
LogicD .... Logic Devices, Inc. [*Associated Press*] (SAG)
LOGICOM... Logical Communications, Inc. [*East Norwalk, CT*] [*Telecommunications*] (TSSD)
Logicon........ Logicon Corp. [*Associated Press*] (SAG)
LOGIFAMP... Logarithmic Intermediate Frequency Amplifier (IAA)
LOGIK .... Logical Organizing and Gathering of Information Knowledge (MHDI)
LOGIMP ...... Logistic Improvement Program [*Military*]
LOGIN .... Local Government Information Network [*Information service or system*]
LOGIPAC...... Logical Processor and Computer
LOGISTC ..... Logistic
LOGIT .... Logical Inference Tester [*NASA*]
LOGK .... Kapfenberg [*Austria ICAO location identifier*] (ICLI)
LOGL .... Logal Educational Software & Systems Ltd. [*NASDAQ symbol*] (SAG)
LOGLAN....... Logical Language
LOGLAND..... Logistics Transport by Land [*Military*]
LOGLF .... Logal Educational Softwr&Sys [*NASDAQ symbol*] (TTSB)
LOGLISP...... Prolog and List Processing
LOGMAP...... Logistics System Master Plan [*Army*]
LOGMAPS.... Logistics Master Planning System
LOGMARS.... Logistic Applications of Automated Marking and Reading Symbols [*DoD*]
LOGMET ...... Logistics Management Engineering Team [*Military*]
LOGMIS ...... Logistics Management Information System [*USACC*]
LOGMOD...... Logic Model [*Fault isolation device*] [*Army*] (MCD)
LOGMOD...... Logistics Module [*Simulation games*] [*Army*] (INF)
LOGMTD...... Logarithmic Mean Temperature Difference (IAA)
LOGN .... Logansort Financial [*NASDAQ symbol*] (TTSB)
LOGN .... Logansport Financial Corp. [*NASDAQ symbol*] (SAG)
LOGNET ...... Logistics Network (MCD)
Lognspt........ Logansport Financial Corp. [*Associated Press*] (SAG)
LOGO .... Limitation of Government Obligation (MCD)
LOGO .... Logotype [*Advertising*] (DSUE)
LOGOIS....... Logistics Operating Information System (AABC)
LOGP .... Logistics Plans
LOGPAC...... Logistics Package [*Army*] (INF)
LOGPARS .... Logistics Planning and Requirements Simplification System [*Army*] (RDA)
LOG PLAN ... Logistics System Plan [*Navy DoD*]
LOGR .... Logistical Ratio [*Army*]
LOGRAM...... Logical Program
LOGREC....... Log Recording [*Computer science*]
LOGREP...... Logistics Replenishment (NVT)
LOGREP...... Logistics Representative [*Navy*] (NVT)
LOGREQ...... Logistics Requirements (NVT)
LOGS .... Labor's Old Guard Socialists [*Australia An association*]
LOGS .... Logistics Supportability (AABC)
LOGSACS.... Logistics Structure and Composition System (AABC)
LOGSAFE..... Logistics Sustainability Analysis Feasibility Estimator (DOMA)
LOGSAM..... Logistics Support Alternative [*or Analysis*] Model (MCD)
LOGSAR...... Logistics Storage and Retrieval System (MCD)
LOGSAT...... Logistics Special Assistance Team (MCD)
LOGSEA...... Logistics Transport by Sea [*Military*]
LOGSS .... Logistics Support Squadron [*Military*]
LOGSTAT..... Logistical Status Report [*Military*] (INF)
LOGSTCN.... Logistician
LOGSUM..... Logistics Summary (NVT)
LOGSUP...... Logistics Support
LOGSVC...... Logistics Service [*Military*] (NVT)
LOGTAB...... Logic Tables (IEEE)
LOGTANBG... Logarithm Tangent Bearing (IAA)
LOgWC ...... West Carroll Parish Library, Oak Grove, LA [*Library symbol Library of Congress*] (LCLS)
LOH .... "Lady of the House" [*Advertising*] (DOAD)
loh .... Lady of the House [*Telephone marketing*] (WDMC)
LOH .... League of Housewives [*Also known as HOW*]
LOH .... Length of Hospitalization
LOH .... Light Observation Helicopter
LOH .... Line Overhead (ACRL)
LOH .... Local Osteolytic Hypercalcemia [*Endocrinology*]
LOH .... Loja [*Ecuador*] [*Airport symbol*] (OAG)
LOH .... Loop of Henle [*Medicine*] (DMAA)
LOH .... Loss of Heterozygosity [*Genetics*]
LOHAC .... Loading and Handling Corrective Action Program

LOHAP .... Light Observation Helicopter Avionics Package (MCD)
LOHET .... Linear Output Hall Effect Transducer
LOHO .... Longhorn Steaks [*NASDAQ symbol*] (TTSB)
LOHO .... Longhorn Steaks, Inc. [*NASDAQ symbol*] (SAG)
LOHS .... Loss of Heat Sink [*Nuclear energy*] (NRCH)
LOHTADS..... Light Observation Helicopter Target Acquisition Designation System (MCD)
LOI .... Laboratory Operating Instructions (MCD)
LOI .... Laredo [*Texas*] [*Airport symbol*] (AD)
LOI .... Laredo, TX [*Location identifier FAA*] (FAAL)
LOI .... Letter of Instruction
LOI .... Letter of Intent (MCD)
LOI .... Letter of Interest (NG)
LOI .... Letter of Introduction
LOI .... Level of Incompetence (DMAA)
LOI .... Level of Injury [*Neurology*] (DAVI)
LOI .... Limiting Oxygen Index
LOI .... Limit of Impurities
LOI .... Line of Induction
LOI .... List of Items (AABC)
LOI .... Lock-On Initiated (MCD)
LOI .... Lodge of Instruction [*Freemasonry*]
LOI .... Loss of Imprinting [*Genetics*]
LOI .... Loss on Ignition [*Analytical chemistry*]
LOI .... Lunar Orbit Insertion [*NASA*]
LOICZ .... Land-Ocean Interaction in the Costal Zone [*International Geosphere Biosphere Programme*]
LOID .... Location Identifiers [*A publication FAA*]
LOIH .... Hohenems-Dornbirn [*Austria ICAO location identifier*] (ICLI)
LOIH .... Left Oblique Inguinal Hernia [*Medicine*] (DMAA)
LOIJ .... St. Johann, Tirol [*Austria ICAO location identifier*] (ICLI)
LOIS............ Langsam Library Online Information Services [*University of Cincinnati*] (OLDSS)
LOIS............ Legal Office Information System
LOIS............ Library Online Information Services [*Morehead State University*] (OLDSS)
LOIS............ Library Order Information System [*Computer system*] [*Library of Congress Obsolete*]
LOIS............ Loss of Interim Status [*Environmental Protection Agency*]
Lois Batim... Lois des Batiments [*A publication*] (DLA)
Lois Rec ..... Lois Recentes du Canada [*A publication*] (DLA)
LOIT .... Loitering [*FBI standardized term*]
LOIUSA....... Loyal Orange Institution of United States of America (EA)
LOIV........... Loyal Orange Institution of Victoria [*Australia*]
LoJack......... Lo-Jack Corp. [*Associated Press*] (SAG)
LOJN........... LoJack Corp. [*NASDAQ symbol*] (SAG)
LOK............. Lockwood Petroleum, Inc. [*Vancouver Stock Exchange symbol*]
LOKSMTH .... Locksmith
LOKTAL........ Locked Octal (IAA)
LOL............. Laughing Out Loud
LOL............. Laugh Out Loud [*Internet language*] [*Computer science*]
LOL............. League of Lefthanders [*Defunct*] (EA)
LOL............. Left Occipitolateral [*A fetal position*] [*Obstetrics*]
LOL............. Length of Lead [*Actual*] [*Technical drawings*]
LOL............. Limited Operating Life
LOL............. Limit of Liability (MCD)
LOL............. Line of Launch [*Navy*] (CAAL)
LOL............. Little Old Lady [*Slang*]
lol.............. Lolo (Bantu) [*MARC language code Library of Congress*] (LCCP)
LOL............. London-Oiseau-Lyre [*Record label*] [*Great Britain, USA, etc.*]
LOL............. Longitude of Launch
LOL............. Lovelock [*Nevada*] [*Airport symbol Obsolete*] (OAG)
LOL............. Loyal Orange Lodge
LOLA........... Layman-Oriented Language (IAA)
LOLA........... Library On-Line Acquisitions [*Washington State University*] [*Data processing system*]
LOLA........... Light Observation Light-Armored Aircraft
LOLA........... London Online Local Authorities (NITA)
LOLA........... Long Line Azimuth [*Survey*]
LOLA........... Lower Leg Artery [*Anatomy*]
LOLA........... Low-Level Oil Alarm (IAA)
LOLA........... Lunar Orbit and Landing Approach [*Simulator*] [*NASA*]
LOLAD......... Low-Altitude LASER Air Defense System
LOLAS......... Location of Launching Site [*Army*]
LOLEX......... Low-Level Extraction [*Military aviation*]
LOLI........... Limited Operational-Life Items [*NASA*] (NASA)
LOLI........... Loyal Orange Ladies Institution (EA)
LOLITA........ Language for the On-Line Investigation and Transformation of Abstractions [*Computer science*]
LOLITA........ Library On-Line Information and Text Access [*Oregon State University*] [*Corvallis, OR Data processing system*]
LOLITS........ Little Old Ladies in Tennis Shoes [*Facetious reference to minor league baseball*]
LO/LO......... Lift-On/Lift-Off
LOLP........... Loss of Load Probability [*Nuclear energy*] (IEEE)
LOLV........... Lower Leg Vein [*Anatomy*]
LOLVE......... Lower Leg Venule [*Anatomy*]
LOLW.......... Laid Off, Lack of Work [*Unemployment insurance and the Bureau of Labor Statistics*] (OICC)
LOLW.......... Wels [*Austria ICAO location identifier*] (ICLI)
LOM........... Laminated Object Manufacturing [*Desktop manufacturing*]
LOM........... LASER Optical Modulator
LOM........... Launch Operations Manager [*NASA*]
LOM........... League of Mercy [*Salvation Army*]
LOM........... Left Otitis Media [*Medicine*] (CPH)

LOM............	Legion of Merit [*Military award*]
LOM............	Level of Maintenance (MCD)
LOM............	Light-Optic Microscope (MSA)
LOM............	Limitation of Motion [*Neurology*] (DAVI)
LOM............	Limitation of Movement
LOM............	List of Materials (CET)
LOM............	List of Modifications (AFM)
LOM............	Little Old Man [*Slang*] (DAVI)
LOM............	Locator at Outer Marker [*Aviation*]
LOM............	Loewen, Ondaatje, McCutcheon, Inc. [*Toronto Stock Exchange symbol Vancouver Stock Exchange symbol*]
LOM............	Lome [*Togo*] [*Seismograph station code, US Geological Survey*] (SEIS)
LOM............	Loss of Motion [*Medicine*]
LOM............	Low-Frequency Outer Marker
LOM............	Low-Order Memory (CET)
LOM............	Loyal Order of Moose (EA)
LOM............	Lunar Orbital Map [*Air Force*]
LOM............	Lunar Orbital Mission [*NASA*] (KSC)
LOM............	SERTEL [*Servicios Telereservacios SA de CV*] [*ICAO designator*] (FAAC)
LOMA..........	Life Office Management Association [*Atlanta, GA*] (EA)
LOMA..........	Literature on Modern Art
LOMA..........	Lutheran Outdoors Ministry Association [*Later, NLOMA*] (EA)
LOMAC........	Logistic Management Advisory Committee
LOMAD........	Low-to-Medium-Altitude Air Defense (AABC)
LOMAH........	Location of Miss and Hit [*Marksmanship training*] [*Army*] (INF)
Lomak	Lomak Petroleum, Inc. [*Associated Press*] (SAG)
Loma Linda U...	Loma Linda University (GAGS)
LOMAR........	Local Manual Attempt Recording (TEL)
LOMAR........	Logistics, Maintenance, and Repair (IAA)
LOMAS........	Law Office Managemnt and Accounting System (HGAA)
Lomax Ex'rs...	Lomax on Executors [*A publication*] (DLA)
LOMB..........	Lockheed Missile Beacon (IAA)
LOMC..........	Logistics Management Committee (AAGC)
Lom CH Rep...	Lomas's City Hall Reporter [*New York*] [*A publication*] (DLA)
Lom Dig	Lomax's Digest of Real Property [*A publication*] (DLA)
Lom Ex	Lomax on Executors [*A publication*] (DLA)
LOMF..........	Loss of Main Feedwater [*Nuclear energy*] (NRCH)
LOMI..........	Letter of Moral Intent [*Business term*]
LOMI..........	Low Oxidation State Metallic Ion [*Nuclear energy*] (NUCP)
LOMIS	Locator Map in Source (IAA)
LOMK..........	Lomak Petroleum [*NASDAQ symbol*] (TTSB)
LOMK..........	Lomak Petroleum, Inc. [*NASDAQ symbol*] (SAG)
LOMMIS.......	Land Ordnance Maintenance Management Information System (PDAA)
LOMO..........	London Overseas Mail Office
LOMOR........	Long-Distance Medium Frequency Omni Range (IAA)
LOMP..........	Local Office Microcomputer Project (NITA)
LOMS..........	Library Organization and Management Section [*Library Administration Division of ALA*]
LOMSA	Left Otitis Media Suppurative Acute [*Medicine*]
LOMSACh	Left Otitis Media Suppurative, Chronic [*Medicine*] (MEDA)
LOMSCH......	Left Otitis Media Suppurative Chronic [*Medicine*]
LOMUSS.......	Lockheed Multiprocessor Simulation System (IEEE)
LOMV..........	Lolium Mottle Virus [*Plant pathology*]
LON	Avilond, TAC [*Ukraine*] [*FAA designator*] (FAAC)
LON	Letter of Notification
LON	Line of Nodes
LON	London [*England*] [*Airport symbol*] (OAG)
Lon	London [*Record label*] [*Export issues of English Decca - mainly USA, Canada, etc.*]
LON	London European Airways PLC [*British ICAO designator*] (FAAC)
LON	Longitude (KSC)
LON	Longmire [*Washington*] [*Seismograph station code, US Geological Survey*] (SEIS)
LON	Tupelo, MS [*Location identifier FAA*] (FAAL)
LON	University College, London, England [*OCLC symbol*] (OCLC)
LoNa..........	Low Sodium [*Dietetics*] (DAVI)
LONAL	Local Off-Net Access Line [*Telecommunications*] (TEL)
LOND..........	London
Lond..........	London Encyclopedia [*A publication*] (DLA)
LOND..........	London International Group Ltd. [*NASDAQ symbol*] (SAG)
LondInt.......	London International Group PLC [*Associated Press*] (SAG)
Lond Jur......	London Jurist Reports [*England*] [*A publication*] (DLA)
Lond Jur NS...	London Jurist, New Series [*A publication*] (DLA)
Lond LM......	London Law Magazine [*A publication*] (DLA)
LondonP......	London Pacific Group Ltd. [*Associated Press*] (SAG)
LondOvr......	London & Overseas Freightliners [*Associated Press*] (SAG)
LONDY........	London Intl Group plc ADS [*NASDAQ symbol*] (TTSB)
LONESHS.....	Limited- or Non-English Speaking Handicapped Student
LoneStar.....	Lone Star Technologies [*Associated Press*] (SAG)
LoneStr.......	Lone Star Technologies, Inc. [*Associated Press*] (SAG)
LONEX........	Laboratory Office Network Experiment [*DoD*]
LONF	London Financial [*NASDAQ symbol*] (TTSB)
Long	Longford [*County in Ireland*] (WGA)
LONG..........	Longitude (AFM)
LONG..........	Longus [*Long*] [*Pharmacy*]
Long & R.....	Long and Russell's Election Cases [*Massachusetts*] [*A publication*] (DLA)
Long & T.....	Longfield and Townsend's Irish Exchequer Reports [*1841-42*] [*A publication*] (DLA)
Long Beach B Bull...	Long Beach Bar Bulletin [*A publication*] (DLA)
LongDr........	Longs Drug Stores Corp. [*Associated Press*] (SAG)
LongDrg.......	Longs Drug Stores [*Associated Press*] (SAG)

LONGF........	Longford [*County in Ireland*] (ROG)
Longf & T....	Longfield and Townsend's Irish Exchequer Reports [*1841-42*] [*A publication*] (DLA)
LONGFD......	Longford [*County in Ireland*]
Longf Dist....	Longfield on Distress and Replevin [*A publication*] (DLA)
Long Irr	Long on Irrigation [*A publication*] (DLA)
longit	Longitudinal (VRA)
LONGN........	Longeron [*Aerospace engineering*]
Long Q........	Long Quinto [*Pt. 10 of Year Books*] [*A publication*] (DLA)
Long Quinto...	Year Books, Part X [*5 Edw. 4, 1465*] [*A publication*] (DLA)
Long S........	Long on Sales of Personal Property [*A publication*] (DLA)
LONGT........	Longtree [*England*]
LONGV........	Longevity (AFM)
LongvF........	Longview Fibre Co. [*Associated Press*] (SAG)
Longwood C..	Longwood College (GAGS)
LONO	Letter of No Objection [*FDA*]
LONO	Low Noise
Lon R Bks...	London Review of Books [*A publication*] (BRI)
LONS	Laboratory Office Network System [*DoD*]
LONS	Light of the Night Sky [*Galaxy*]
LONS	Local Online Network System
Lons Cr L....	Lonsdale's Statute Criminal Law [*A publication*] (DLA)
LOO	Laghouat [*Algeria*] [*Airport symbol*] (AD)
LOO	Leave One Out at a Time [*Data analysis*]
LOO	Loumic Resources Ltd. [*Vancouver Stock Exchange symbol*]
LOOM	Light Opera of Manhattan
LOOM	Loyal Order of Moose (EA)
LOOP	Long-Range Open Ocean Patrol [*Navy*] (NVT)
LOOP	Loop [*Postal Service standard*] (OPSA)
LOOP	Loss of Offsite Power [*Nuclear energy*] (NRCH)
LOOP	Louisiana Offshore Oil Port [*Group of major oil companies*]
LOOPS	Local Office Online Payment System [*Unemployment insurance*]
LOOPS	Loop [*Commonly used*] (OPSA)
LOOW	Lake Ontario Ordnance Works
LOP...........	Lake Ontario Cement Ltd. [*Toronto Stock Exchange symbol*]
LOP...........	Last Operation Completed [*Computer science*]
LOP...........	Launch Operations [*or Operator's*] Panel [*NASA*]
LOP...........	Learning Opportunity [*Education*]
LOP...........	Least Objectionable Program [*Television*]
LOP...........	Leave on Pass
LOP...........	Left Occipitoposterior [*A fetal position*] [*Obstetrics*]
LOP...........	Left Outside Position [*Dancing*]
LOP...........	Letter of Promulgation [*Navy*] (NVT)
LOP...........	Letter of Proposal [*Military*] (AFM)
LOP...........	Levels-of-Processing [*Psychology*]
LOp...........	Lex Operator Gene
LOP...........	Life of Program
LOP...........	Line of Position [*Electronics*]
LOP...........	Line of Power (WDAA)
LOP...........	Line-Oriented Protocol
LOP...........	Linton-on-Ouse FTU [*British ICAO designator*] (FAAC)
LOP...........	Loanda [*Brazil*] [*Airport symbol*] (AD)
LOP...........	Locally-Originated Program [*Broadcasting*] (NTCM)
LOP...........	Local Office Project [*Department of Health and Social Security*] [*British*]
LOP...........	Local Operating Procedures (AFM)
LOP...........	Local Operational Plot
LOP...........	Logic Processor (IAA)
LOP...........	Logistics Officer Program [*Army*]
LOP...........	Lookout Post (IAA)
LOP...........	Loss of Offsite Power [*Nuclear energy*] (NRCH)
LOP...........	Low-Order Position [*Military*] (AFIT)
LOP...........	Lubricating Oil Pump (MSA)
LOP...........	Lunar Orbit Plane [*NASA*] (IAA)
LOPA	Layout of Passenger Accommodation (MCD)
LOPA	Local Payment of Airline (MCD)
LOPAC	Load Optimization and Passenger Acceptance Control [*Airport computer*]
LOPAD	Logarithmic Outline [*or Online*] Processing System for Analog Data (IEEE)
LOPAIR.......	Long Path Infrared
LOP & G......	Live Oak, Perry & Gulf Railroad (IIA)
LOPAR........	Long Baseline Position and Rates [*Guidance and tracking system*] [*Air Force*]
LOPAR........	Low-Power Acquisition RADAR
LOPC	Lunar Orbital Photocraft [*NASA*] (IAA)
LOPC	Lunar Orbit Plane Change [*NASA*]
LOPG	Launch Operations Planning Group
LOP-GAP.....	Liquid Oxygen Petrol, Guided Aircraft Projectile
LOPI..........	Loss of Pipe Integrity [*Nuclear energy*] (NRCH)
LOPKGS......	Loose or in Packages [*Freight*]
LOPO	Local Post (EA)
LOPO	Low-Power Boiler [*US reactor*]
LOPOS	Local Oxidation of Polysilicon over Silicon [*Transistor technology*]
LOPP	Lunar Orbiter Photographic Project [*Aerospace*]
LOPPLAR.....	LASER Doppler RADAR (IAA)
LOPRA	Low-Power Reactor Assembly [*University of Illinois*] (NRCH)
LO-PRO.......	Low-Profile
LOPRPr.......	Santander Overseas Bk'A' Pfd [*NYSE symbol*] (TTSB)
LOPS	Length of Patient Stay [*Medicine*] (AABC)
LOPS	Lunar Orbiting Photographic System [*Aerospace*]
LOPT..........	Line Output Transformer (IAA)
LOPU.........	Logistics Organization Planning Unit
LOQ	Leadership Opinion Questionnaire [*Test*]
LOQ..........	Limit of Quantitation [*Analytical chemistry*]

LOQ .... Lobatsi [Botswana] [Airport symbol] (AD)
LOQ .... Loquitur [He, or She, Speaks] [Latin]
LOQ .... Lower Outer Quadrant [Anatomy]
LO-QG........ Locked Oscillator-Quadrature Grid [Computer science]
LOR .... Ladies of Retreads (EA)
LOR .... Large Optical Reflector
LOR .... Letter of Request (AFIT)
LOR .... Level of Repair
LOR .... Light Output Ratio (WDAA)
LOR .... Likely Operational Range [Navy] (ANA)
LOR .... Lockout Relay (MCD)
LOR .... Long Open Reading [Frame] [Genetics]
LOR .... Loral Corp. [NYSE symbol] (SPSG)
LOR .... Loral Space Communications [NYS] (TTSB)
LOR .... Lorazepam [A tranquilizer]
LOR .... Lorcha [Ship's rigging] (ROG)
LOR .... Loricrin (DMAA)
LOR .... Lormes [Somee] [France] [Seismograph station code, US Geological Survey] (SEIS)
LOR .... Loss of Righting Reflex [Medicine] (DMAA)
LOR .... Lower Operator Rate [Telecommunications British]
LOR .... Low-Frequency Omnidirectional Radio Range
LOR .... Lunar Orbit [or Orbital] Rendezvous [NASA]
LOR .... Ozark, Fort Rucker, AL [Location identifier FAA] (FAAL)
LORA .... Lecturer-Oriented Response Analysis (PDAA)
LOR/A .... Letter of Repair/Analysis (AAGC)
LORA .... Level of Repair Analysis (MCD)
LORA .... Long-Range Adaption (MCD)
LORA .... Long-Range Addition (NVT)
LORA .... Low Out of Range Alarm (ECII)
LORAAS ...... Long-Range Airborne ASW [Antisubmarine Warfare] System (MCD)
LORAC........ Long-Range Accuracy [RADAR]
LORAD........ Long-Range Active Detection
LORAD........ Long-Range Air Defense (AABC)
LORADAC.... Long-Range Active Detection and Communications System
LORADS...... LASER Optical Ranging and Designation System
LORAE .... Long-Range Attitude and Event [Instrumentation system]
LORAH .... Long-Range Area Homing
LORA-HOJ ... Long-Range - Home on Jam
Loral .... Loral Corp. [Associated Press] (SAG)
LORAM .... Level of Repair for Aeronautical Material (PDAA)
LORAMS ..... Long-Range Automatic Measuring Station [Meteorology]
LORAN....... Long-Range Aid to Navigation [Military] (DOMA)
LORAN....... Long-Range Navigation
loran.......... Long-Range Navigation (IDOE)
LORAN....... Long-Range Radio Navigation (ACRL)
LORAN D .... Long-Range Navigation Doppler Inertial (DNAB)
LORAN DM... Long-Range Navigation Double Master
Lor & Russ... Loring and Russell's Election Cases in Massachusetts [A publication] (DLA)
LORAN DS .. Long-Range Navigation Double Slave
LORAN M..... Long-Range Navigation Master
LORAN S ..... Long-Range Navigation Slave
LORAP........ Level of Repair Analysis Program
LORAPH...... Long-Range Passive Homing System
LORAPL ...... Long-Range Planning Task Group [Oversaw military strategy in Vietnam] (VNW)
LORAS .... Linear Omnidirectional Airspeed System (PDAA)
LORAS .... Low-Range Airspeed System (MCD)
Loras C........ Loras College (GAGS)
LORBAS....... Large Off-Line Retrieval Text Base Access System
LORBI .... Locked-On RADAR Bearing Indicator
LORC .... Lockheed Radio Command (MUGU)
LORCS .... League of Red Cross Societies
LORD .... Licensing Online Retrieval Data (NRCH)
LORD .... List of Required Documents (NVT)
LORD .... Long-Range and Detection RADAR (NATG)
LORD .... Lordosis [Medicine]
LORDS........ Licensing On-Line Retrieval Data System (NRCH)
Lords Jour ... Journals of the House of Lords [England] [A publication] (DLA)
LORE .... Land Ordnance Engineering Branch [Canada Military] (PDAA)
LOREC .... Long-Range Earth Current Communications
LORELCO .... Lower Elevated Serum Cholesterol [Acronym is trade name of Dow Chemical]
LORELEI ..... Long-Range Echo Level Indicator
LORENDAS... Long-Range Energy Development and Supply (PDAA)
Lorenz .... Lorenz's Ceylon Reports [A publication] (DLA)
Lorenz App R... Lorenz's Appeal Reports [Ceylon] [A publication] (DLA)
Lorenz Rep... Lorenz's Ceylon Reports [A publication] (ILCA)
LOREORS ... Long-Range, Electro-Optical Reconnaissance System
LORES .... Long-Route Engineering Study [Bell System]
LO-RES ...... Low Resolution [Computer science]
LORI .... Limited Operational Readiness Inspection (MCD)
LoriCp......... Lori Corp. [Associated Press] (SAG)
Loring & Russel El Cases... Loring and Russell's Election Cases in Massachusetts [A publication] (DLA)
Loring & Russell... Loring and Russell's Election Cases in Massachusetts [A publication] (DLA)
Lor Inst....... Lorimer. Institutes of Law [A publication] (ILCA)
LORL .... Large Orbital Research Laboratory [NASA]
LORMODS ... Long-Range Metal Object Detection System (MCD)
LORMONSTA... LORAN Monitor Station
LORO .... Lobe-On Receive Only [Electronic counter-countermeasures]
Loronix .... Loronix Information Systems, Inc. [Associated Press] (SAG)
LOROP......... Long-Range Oblique Photography

LORPGAC ... Long-Range Proving Ground Automatic Computer (IEEE)
L or RC....... Leather or Rubber Covered [Freight]
LORRE .... Laboratory of Renewable Resources Engineering [Purdue University]
LORS .... Labor Organization Reporting System [Department of Labor] (GFGA)
LORS .... LM [Lunar Module] Optical Rendezvous System [NASA]
LORS .... Long-Range SONAR
LORS .... Lunar Orbiting Reconnaissance System [Aerospace]
LORSA .... Long-Range Steerable Antenna (MCD)
LORSAC....... Long-Range Submarine Communications (AAG)
Lor Sc L ...... Lorimer's Handbook of Scotch Law [A publication] (DLA)
LORS-I........ Level of Rehabilitation Scale-I [Medicine] (DAVI)
LORSTA....... LORAN Transmitting Station
LORSU .... Long-Range Special Unit [Military]
LORT .... League of Resident Theaters (EA)
LORTAN....... Long-Range and Tactical Navigation System
LORTRAP.... Long-Range Training and Rotation Plan
LORV .... Low-Observability Reentry Vehicle
LORW .... Light Output Ratio Working (PDAA)
LORX .... Loronix Information Systems, Inc. [NASDAQ symbol] (SAG)
LORX .... Loronix Info Systems [NASDAQ symbol] (TTSB)
LOS .... Laboratory Operating System [NASA]
LOS .... Lagos [Nigeria] [Airport symbol] (OAG)
LOS .... Land Observation Satellite (PDAA)
LOS .... Land Ownership Survey
LOS .... Latin Old Style (ADA)
LOS .... Launcher Operation Station (MCD)
LOS .... Launch on Search [Navy] (CAAL)
LOS .... Launch Operations System [NASA] (KSC)
LOS .... Launch Optional Selector (IAA)
LOS .... Law of the Sea [United Nations] (ASF)
LOS .... Length of Service
LOS .... Length of Stay
LOS .... Level of Service [BTS] (TAG)
LOS .... Liaison Office Support
LOS .... Licentiate in Obstetrical Science
LOS .... Lift-Off Simulator [NASA] (NASA)
LOS .... Limited Operational Strategy
LOS .... Limit Order Switching (PDAA)
LOS .... Line of Scrimmage [Football]
LOS .... Line of Sight
LOS .... Line of Supply
LOS .... Line-Oriented Simulation (GAVI)
LOS .... Line Out of Service [Telecommunications] (TEL)
LOS .... Live Oak Society (EA)
LOS .... Local Operating Station (DNAB)
LOS .... Local Operating System (IAA)
LOS .... Logistic Operation - Streamline [Military] (AABC)
LOS .... Logistic Oriented Schools [Army]
LOS .... Loop Output Signal (CET)
LOS .... Lossiemouth FTU [British ICAO designator] (FAAC)
LOS .... Loss of Sight
LOS .... Loss of Signal
LOS .... Loss of Synchronization
LOS .... Low Output Syndrome (MAE)
LOS .... Lunar Orbiting Satellite [or Spacecraft] [Aerospace] (MCD)
LOS .... Midwestern Baptist Theological Seminary, Kansas City, MO [OCLC symbol] (OCLC)
LOS-AD....... Line-of-Sight - Air Defense [DoD]
LOSAM....... Low-Altitude Surface-to-Air Missiles (NATG)
Los Angeles BAB... Los Angeles Bar Association. Bulletin [A publication] (DLA)
Los Angeles L Rev... Los Angeles Law Review [A publication] (DLA)
LOSARP....... Line-of-Sight - Repeater Placement Program (IAA)
LOSAT .... Language-Oriented System Analysis Table (IAA)
LOS-AT .... Line-of-Sight - Antitank [DoD]
LOSC .... Laboratory Operations Support Center [NASA] (SSD)
LOSC .... Law of the Sea Conference [United Nations] (MSC)
LOSC .... Law of the Sea Convention [Australia]
LOSC .... Local On-Scene Commander [Military] (DNAB)
LOSD .... League of St. Dymphna (EA)
LOSE........... Let Others Share Equally [Slogan opposing President Gerald R. Ford's anti-inflation WIN campaign]
LOSE........... Let's Omit Superfluous Expenses [Slogan opposing President Gerald R. Ford's anti-inflation WIN campaign]
LOSE........... Line-of-Sight Expendables (DNAB)
LOS-F......... Line-of-Sight - Forward [DoD]
LOS-FH....... Line-of-Sight - Forward Heavy [DoD]
LOS-FL....... Line of Sight-Forward Light [DoD]
LOSIS .... Law of the Sea Information System (GNE)
LOSL.......... Saint Landry Parish Library, Opelousas, LA [Library symbol Library of Congress] (LCLS)
LOSM.......... Launch Operations Simulation Model
LOS of NA ... Ladies Oriental Shrine of North America (EA)
LOSOS .... Local Oxidation of Silicon on Sapphire [Transistor technology] (IAA)
LOSP .... Loss of Offsite Power [Nuclear energy] (NRCH)
LOSP .... Loss of System Pressure [Nuclear energy] (NRCH)
LOS(P)........ Lower O-Esophageal Sphincter Pressure [Medicine] (DMAA)
LOSR .... Limit of Stack Register
LOSR .... Line-of-Sight Rate (MCD)
LOS-R......... Line-of-Sight - Rear [DoD]
LOSREP ...... Loss Report [Aircrew/aircraft]
LOSS .... Landing Observer Signal System (MSA)
LOSS .... LAPS Observing System Simulation (USDC)
LOSS .... LAPS [Local Analysis and Prediction System] Observing System Stimulation [Marine science] (OSRA)
LOSS .... Large Object Salvage System [Navy]

LOSS .... Lunar Orbital Survey System [*NASA*] (KSC)
LOSS .... Lunar Orbit Space Station [*NASA*]
Loss & Dam Rev... Loss and Damage Review [*A publication*] (DLA)
Loss Sec Reg... Loss' Security Regulations [*A publication*] (DLA)
LOSSYS ...... Landing Observer Signal System
LOST .... Law of the Sea Treaty (MCD)
LOST .... Linear One-Step Transition [*Mathematical model for social grouping*]
LOST .... Lommel and Steinkopf [*German name for mustard gas, taken from two of the chemists who helped develop it as a chemical warfare agent*]
LOST .... Lube Oil Storage Tank (NRCH)
LOST/A ...... Vessels Lost by Accident, Collision, or Similar Methods [*Navy*]
LOST/E ...... Vessels Lost through Enemy Action [*Navy*]
LOSTF .... Line-of-Sight Test Fixture
LOSTFC ...... Line-of-Sight Task Force Communications [*Military*] (CAAL)
LOSTFCS .... Line-of-Sight Task Force Communications System [*Military*]
LOST/P ...... Vessels Lost Due to Weather, Perils of the Sea, or Similar Reasons [*Navy*]
LOSTW .... Lostwithiel [*Municipal borough in England*]
LOT .... Laminated Overlay Transistor [*Electronics*] (IAA)
LOT .... Lapped Orthogonal Transform [*Telecommunications*]
LOT .... Large Orbiting Telescope (MCD)
LOT .... Lateral Olfactory Tract
LOT .... Leak-Off Test
LOT .... Left Occipitotransverse [*A fetal position*] [*Obstetrics*]
LOT .... Left Outer Thigh [*Injection site*]
LOT .... Letter of Transmittal (MCD)
LOT .... Life of Type (AFIT)
LOT .... Lift-Off Time [*Aerospace*] (MCD)
LOT .... Light-Off Temperature [*For steady-state combustion*]
LOT .... Light-Off Time [*Exhaust emissions*] [*Automotive engineering*]
LOT .... Light Operated Typewriter
LOT .... Limited Operational Test
LOT .... Linear Optical Trajectory [*Vision*]
LOT .... List on Tape (IAA)
LOT .... Load on Top [*Oil tankers*]
LOT .... Lock on Track
LOT .... Lodestar Energy, Inc. [*Vancouver Stock Exchange symbol*]
Lot .... Lotarius Rosario de Cremona [*Deceased, 1227*] [*Authority cited in pre-1607 legal work*] (DSA)
LOT .... Lotio [*Lotion*] [*Pharmacy*]
LOT .... Lotru [*Romania*] [*Seismograph station code, US Geological Survey*] (SEIS)
LOT .... Lower Outer Tube
LOT .... Low-Observable Technology (MCD)
LOT .... Polskie Linie Lotnicze [*Poland*] [*ICAO designator*] (FAAC)
LOT .... Romeoville, IL [*Location identifier FAA*] (FAAL)
LOTADS ...... Long-Term Worldwide Air Defense Study [*Army*] (AABC)
LOTAS .... Large Optical Tracker - Aerospace
LOTAWS ..... LASER Obstacle Terrain Avoidance Warning System
LOTC .... London Over-the-Counter Market [*Information service or system*] (IID)
LOTCIP .... Long-Term Communications Improvement Plan (NATG)
LOTE .... Languages Other than English
LOTE .... Lesser of Two Evils [*Politics*]
LOTH R .... Lotharian Regiment [*Military British*] (ROG)
LOTIS .... Logical Structure: The Timing and the Sequencing of Synchronous/Asynchronous Machines [*Computer science*] (CSR)
LOTIS .... Logical Timing Sequencing (NITA)
LOTMP .... Lowest Temperature [*NWS*] (FAAC)
LOTO .... Lottery Enterprises [*NASDAQ symbol*] (TTSB)
LOTON .... Long Tons Discharged or Loaded
LOTOS .... Language of Temporal Ordering of Specifications [*Computer science*]
LOTR .... [*The*] Lord of the Rings [*A trilogy*]
LOTS .... Large Overland Transporter System (MCD)
LOTS .... Launch Operations Television System
LOTS .... Launch Optical Trajectory System [*NASA*] (IAA)
LOTS .... LEM [*Lunar Excursion Module*] Optical Tracking System [*NASA*] (KSC)
LOTS .... Lighter, Over-the-Shore [*Missions*] [*For air-cushion vehicles*] (RDA)
LOTS .... Load over the Side
LOTS .... Logistics over the Shore [*Military*]
LOTS .... LORAN Operational Training School
LOTSS .... Libraries of the Social Sciences [*Australia An association*]
LotteryE ...... Lottery Enterprises, Inc. [*Associated Press*] (SAG)
LottoW .... Lotto World, Inc. [*Associated Press*] (SAG)
LOTUS .... Long-Term Upper Ocean Study
LOTV .... Launch Operations and Test Vehicle [*NASA*] (KSC)
LOTW .... Loaded on Trailers or Wagons [*Freight*]
LOU .... Letter of Understanding [*Nuclear energy*] (NRCH)
LOU .... Letters of Undertaking [*RSPA*] (TAG)
LOU .... Line Output Unit [*Printing*] (DGA)
LOU .... Linomatic Operating Unit [*Printing*] (DGA)
LOU .... Louisiana
LOU .... Louisville, KY [*Location identifier FAA*] (FAAL)
Lou .... Louth [*County in Ireland*] (WGA)
LouG .... Louisville Gas & Electric Co. [*Associated Press*] (SAG)
LouG 5 .... Louisville Gas & Electric Co. [*Associated Press*] (SAG)
LOUH .... Light Observation Utility Helicopter (NATG)
LOUISA ...... Lunar Optical-UVIR [*Ultraviolet Infrared*] Synthesis Array [*NASA*]
Louisiana Ann... Louisiana Annual Reports [*A publication*] (DLA)
Louisiana Ann Rep... Louisiana Annual Reports [*A publication*] (DLA)
Louisiana Rep... Louisiana Reports [*A publication*] (DLA)
Louis Rep... Louisiana Reports [*A publication*] (DLA)
Lou Leg N ... Louisiana Legal News [*A publication*]

Lou LJ .... Louisiana Law Journal [*New Orleans*] [*A publication*] (DLA)
Lou L Jour... Louisiana Law Journal [*A publication*] (DLA)
LOUO .... Limited Official Use Only [*Military*]
Lou R .... Louisiana Reports [*A publication*] (DLA)
Lou Rep NS... Martin's Louisiana Reports, New Series [*A publication*] (DLA)
Lou Reps.... Louisiana Reports [*A publication*] (DLA)
LOV .... Large Opaque Vesicle [*Medicine*] (DMAA)
LOV .... Limit of Visibility
LOV .... London Flight Centre (Stansted) Ltd. [*British ICAO designator*] (FAAC)
LOV .... Loss of Vehicle (KSC)
LOV .... Loss of Visibility (NASA)
LOV .... Loss of Vision (DAVI)
LOV .... Lovo [*Sweden*] [*Geomagnetic observatory code*]
LOV .... Monclova [*Mexico*] [*Airport symbol*] (AD)
LOV .... Societe Miniere Louvem, Inc. [*Toronto Stock Exchange symbol*]
LOVA .... Low Vulnerability Ammunition [*Military*] (RDA)
Lov Arb ...... Lovesy on Arbitration [*1867*] [*A publication*] (DLA)
LOVE .... Language Organization Voicing Esperanto
LOVE .... Linguistics of Visual English [*Sign language system for the hearing impaired*]
Love Bank ... Lovesy's Bankruptcy Act [*1869, 1870*] [*A publication*] (DLA)
LOVER .... Lunar Orbiting Vehicle for Emergency Rescue (PDAA)
LOVISIM ..... Low-Visibility Landing Simulation [*Program*] [*Air Force*]
LOVL .... Laugh Out Very Loud [*Internet language*] [*Computer science*]
LOVV .... Wien [*Austria ICAO location identifier*] (ICLI)
LOW .... Launch on Warning [*Missiles*]
LOW .... Laws of War (MCD)
LOW .... Link Orderwire Project
LOW .... Loners on Wheels (EA)
LOW .... Low Core Threshold (NITA)
Low........... Lowell's District Court Reports [*United States, Massachusetts District*] [*A publication*] (DLA)
low........... Lower (VRA)
LOW .... Lowe's Companies, Inc. [*NYSE symbol*] (SPSG)
LOW .... Lowe's Cos. [*NYSE symbol*] (TTSB)
LOW .... West Yellowstone, MT [*Location identifier FAA*] (FAAL)
LOWBI .... Low-Birth-Weight Infant [*Obstetrics*]
Low Can ..... Lower Canada Reports [*A publication*] (DLA)
Low Can Jur... Lower Canada Jurist [*A publication*] (DLA)
Low Can Jurist... Lower Canada Jurist [*A publication*] (DLA)
Low Can LJ... Lower Canada Law Journal [*A publication*] (DLA)
Low Can R... Lower Canada Reports [*A publication*] (DLA)
Low Can Rep... Lower Canada Reports [*A publication*] (DLA)
Low Can Rep SQ... Lower Canada Seignorial Questions Reports [*A publication*] (DLA)
Low C Seign... Lower Canada Seignorial Questions Reports [*A publication*] (DLA)
Low Dec (F)... Lowell's Decisions [*A publication*] (DLA)
Low Dis ...... Lowell's District Court Reports [*United States, Massachusetts District*] [*A publication*] (DLA)
Low-E .... Low-Elevation (CAAL)
LOW-E .... Low-Emissivity [*Glass*]
Lowell .... Lowell's District Court Reports [*United States, Massachusetts District*] [*A publication*] (DLA)
Lower Can Jur... Lower Canada Jurist [*A publication*] (DLA)
Lower Can SQ... Lower Canada Seignorial Questions Reports [*A publication*] (DLA)
Lower Ct Dec... Ohio Lower Court Decisions [*A publication*] (DLA)
Lowes .... Lowe's Companies, Inc. [*Associated Press*] (SAG)
LOWESS ...... Locally-Weighted Scatterplot Smoother [*Medicine*]
LOWFAR ...... Low-Frequency Analysis and Recording (MCD)
LOWG .... Graz [*Austria ICAO location identifier*] (ICLI)
LOWG .... Landing Operations Working Group [*NASA*] (NASA)
LOWI .... Innsbruck [*Austria ICAO location identifier*] (ICLI)
LOWK .... Klagenfurt [*Austria ICAO location identifier*] (ICLI)
LOWL .... Linz [*Austria ICAO location identifier*] (ICLI)
LOWL .... Low-Level Language [*Computer programming*]
LOWM .... Wien [*Austria ICAO location identifier*] (ICLI)
Lown & M ... Lowndes and Maxwell's English Bail Court Reports [*1852-54*] [*A publication*] (DLA)
Lownd & M... Lowndes and Maxwell's English Bail Court Reports [*1852-54*] [*A publication*] (DLA)
Lownd Av... Lowndes' General Average [*10th ed.*] [*1975*] [*A publication*] (DLA)
Lownd Col... Lowndes on Collisions at Sea [*A publication*] (DLA)
Lownd Cop... Lowndes on Copyright [*A publication*] (DLA)
Lowndes & M... Lowndes and Maxwell's English Bail Court Reports [*1852-54*] [*A publication*] (DLA)
Lowndes & M (Eng)... Lowndes and Maxwell's English Bail Court Reports [*1852-54*] [*A publication*] (DLA)
Lowndes M & P... Lowndes, Maxwell, and Pollock's English Bail Court Reports [*1850-51*] [*A publication*] (DLA)
Lownd Ins... Lowndes on Insurance [*A publication*] (DLA)
Lownd Leg... Lowndes on Legacies [*A publication*] (DLA)
Lownd M & P... Lowndes, Maxwell, and Pollock's English Bail Court Reports [*1850-51*] [*A publication*] (DLA)
LownInST... P. W. Lown Institute. Brandeis University. Studies and Texts (BJA)
Lown Leg..... Lowndes on Legacies [*A publication*] (DLA)
Lown M & P... Lowndes, Maxwell, and Pollock's English Bail Court Reports [*1850-51*] [*A publication*] (DLA)
Low Pr Code... Lower Provinces Code [*India*] [*A publication*] (DLA)
LOWR .... Lower
Lowranc...... Lowrance Electronics, Inc. [*Associated Press*] (SAG)
LOWS .... Salzburg [*Austria ICAO location identifier*] (ICLI)
LOWW .... Wien/Schwechat [*Austria ICAO location identifier*] (ICLI)
LOWZ.......... Zell Am See [*Austria ICAO location identifier*] (ICLI)
LOX .... Liquid Oxygen [*Also, LO_2*]

LOX	Liquid Oxygen Expert System (NITA)
LO-X	Low Thermal Expansion [Synthetic ceramic]
LOXA	Aigen/Ennstal [Austria ICAO location identifier] (ICLI)
LOXAT	Lowest Temperature Exceeded for All Time [NWS] (FAAC)
LOXFM	Lowest Temperature Exceeded for the Month [NWS] (FAAC)
LOXG	Graz [Austria ICAO location identifier] (ICLI)
LOXK	Klagenfurt [Austria ICAO location identifier] (ICLI)
LOXL	Horsching [Austria ICAO location identifier] (ICLI)
LOX/LH	Liquid Oxygen and Liquid Hydrogen
LOXN	Wiener Neustadt [Austria ICAO location identifier] (ICLI)
Lox-PLD	Loxoseles reclusus - Phospholipase D [An enzyme]
LOXS	Schwaz, Tirol [Austria ICAO location identifier] (ICLI)
LOXSE	Lowest Temperature Exceeded So Early [NWS] (FAAC)
LOXSL	lowest Temperature Exceeded So Late [NWS] (FAAC)
LOXT	Langenlebarn [Austria ICAO location identifier] (ICLI)
LOXT	Large Orbital X-Ray Telescope [NASA]
LOXZ	Zeltweg [Austria ICAO location identifier] (ICLI)
LOY	Loyalty (AABC)
LOY	Loyola - Notre Dame Library, Inc., Baltimore, MD [OCLC symbol] (OCLC)
LOYC	Loyola Capital [NASDAQ symbol] (SAG)
Loy Con Prot J	Loyola Consumer Protection Journal [Los Angeles] [A publication] (DLA)
Loy Dig	Loyola Digest [A publication] (DLA)
Loy Law	Loyola Lawyer [A publication] (DLA)
Loy LJ	Loyola Law Journal [New Orleans] [1920-32] [A publication] (DLA)
Loyola	Loyola Capital Corp. [Associated Press] (SAG)
Loyola C (Md)	Loyola College (Maryland) (GAGS)
Loyola Dig	Loyola Digest [A publication] (DLA)
Loyola LJ	Loyola Law Journal [A publication] (DLA)
Loyola Marymount U	Loyola Marymount University (Los Angeles) (GAGS)
Loyola U Chicago	Loyola University of Chicago (GAGS)
Loyola U (La)	Loyola University (Louisiana) (GAGS)
Loyola ULJ (Chicago)	Loyola University. Law Review (Chicago) [A publication] (DLA)
Loyola Univ L Rev	Loyola University. Law Review [Chicago] [A publication] (DLA)
LOZ	Liquid Ozone
LOZ	London [Kentucky] [Airport symbol] (OAG)
LOZ	Lovozero [Former USSR Geomagnetic observatory code]
LOZ	Lozenge [Pharmacy] (DAVI)
LP	Air Alpes [ICAO designator] (AD)
LP	Laboratory Procedure
LP	Labour Party of South Africa [Political party] (PPW)
L/P	Lactate/Pyruvate [Ratio]
LP	Ladyship [or Lordship]
LP	Laminated Polyethylene Film
LP	Lamp [Automotive engineering]
LP	Landing Point [British military] (DMA)
LP	Land Plane
LP	Large-Paper Edition [of a book]
LP	Large Particle
LP	Large Post
LP	Laryngeal Pharyngeal [Medicine]
LP	Last Paid [Military]
LP	Last Performance
LP	Last Post (WDAA)
LP	Latent Period [Physiology]
LP	Lateral Pyloric [Neuron]
LP	Launching Platoon [Army]
LP	Launch Pad (KSC)
LP	Launch Panel
LP	Launch Platform
LP	Laureate of Philosophy
LP	Law Pamphlet (ROG)
LP	Lay Preacher
LP	Leadership Project [Defunct] (EA)
LP	Leaf Protein [Food industry]
LP	Leathery Pocket [of pineapple]
LP	Left Pectoral Fin [Fish anatomy]
LP	Left Traffic Pattern [Aviation] (FAAC)
LP	Legal Process [British]
LP	Legal Procurator (WDAA)
LP	Legislative Proposal (GFGA)
LP	Lempira [Monetary unit] [Honduras]
LP	Lesson Plan
LP	Lettering Piece (ROG)
L/P	Letterpress (ADA)
LP	Letters Patent (ROG)
LP	Leucine Aminopeptidase [Also, LA, LAP] [An enzyme]
LP	Leucocyte Pyrogen [Immunology]
LP	Leukocyte-Poor [Hematology]
LP	Liability Policy [Information service or system] (DOAD)
LP	Liberal Party [Canada] (PPW)
LP	Liberator Party [Guyana] [Political party] (PPW)
LP	Libertarian Party (EA)
LP	Library of Parliament [Canada]
LP	Library of Philosophy [A publication]
L/P	Life Policy [Insurance]
LP	Lighting Panel (IAA)
LP	Light Pen
LP	Light Perception [Ophthalmology]
LP	Lightproof [Technical drawings]
LP	Light Pulse [Embryology]
LP	Limited Partnership

LP	Limited Planning (MCD)
LP	Limited Procurement
LP	Limited Production (AABC)
LP	Limited Proprietorship [Business term]
LP	Limit of Proportionality [Mechanics] (IAA)
LP	Limp [Binding] [Publishing]
LP	Linear Phase
LP	Linear Polarization
LP	Linear Prediction [Computer science]
LP	Linear Programming [Computer science]
LP	Linear Programming Language (NITA)
LP	Linen Press (ADA)
lp	Line Pair [Philately]
LP	Line Pressure
LP	Line Printer [Computer science]
LP	Linguistic Problems
LP	Linguopulpal [Dentistry]
LP	Linker Polypeptide [Biochemistry]
LP	Linkport [Electronics] (ECII)
LP	Link Printer (ACRL)
Lp	Lipoprotein [Biochemistry]
LP	Liquefied Petroleum [Gas]
LP	Liquidity Preference [Economics]
LP	Liquid Phase [Chemistry]
LP	Liquid Propellant
LP	Listening Post
LP	List of Publications [National Institute of Standards and Technology]
LP	List Price (BARN)
LP	List Processor [Standard programming language] [1958] [Computer science] (BUR)
LP	Lists of Parts (NATG)
LP	Litter Patient
LP	Livens Projector [Military]
LP	Liver Protein [Medicine]
LP	Liver to Plasma Concentration Ratio (MAE)
LP	Load Point (BUR)
LP	Local-Pair [Superconductivity]
LP	Local Pastors [British]
LP	Local Procurement [Military]
LP	Local Purchase (AFM)
LP	Locating Point [Optical tooling]
LP	Lodge-Pole Pine [Utility pole] [Telecommunications] (TEL)
LP	Loewenthal Papers [Shanghai/Washington, DC] [A publication] (BJA)
LP	Logic Probe
LP	Log Periodic [Antenna] (NATG)
LP	Lollipop Power [An association] (EA)
LP	London Particular [Marsala]
LP	Longest Path
LP	Longest Perpendicular [IOR] [Yacht racing]
LP	Longitudinal Parity [Telecommunications] (TEL)
LP	Long-Pass [Absorption cell]
LP	Long Period
LP	Long Persistence
LP	Long Picot
LP	Long Play [VHS recorder mode] (NTCM)
LP	Long Playing [Phonograph record]
LP	Long Position [Investment term]
LP	Long Primer
LP	Long Provost
LP	Loop [Knitting]
LP	Lord President of the Court of Session, Scotland (DLA)
LP	Lord Provost [British]
LP	Lorentz-Polarization [Optics]
LP	Losing Pitcher [Baseball]
LP	Loss of Pay [Court-martial sentence] [Marine Corps]
LP	Lost Planes [An association] (EA)
LP	Love Project (EA)
LP	Lower Panel (IAA)
LP	Lower Peninsula [Michigan]
LP	Low Pass [Electronics]
LP	Low Performance
LP	Low Point
LP	Low Power [Microscopy]
LP	Low Pressure
LP	Low-Pressure Cylinder [Especially, a locomotive cylinder]
LP	Low Primary (IAA)
LP	Low Protein [Nutrition]
LP	Lumbar-Peritoneal [Shunt] (DAVI)
LP	Lumbar Puncture [Medicine]
LP	Lunar and Planetary [Aerospace] (IAA)
LP	Luster Paper [Photography] (DGA)
L/P	Lymphocyte to Polymorph Ratio [Hematology]
LP	Lymphoid Plasma [Hematology] (MAE)
LP	Lymphoid Predominance [Medicine] (AAMN)
L/P	Lymph-Plasma [Ratio] [Laboratory science] (DAVI)
LP	Lymph-Plasma Ratio [Hematology] (MAE)
LP	Lythway Press [British]
LP	Popular Concerts [Public-performance tariff class] [British]
LP-28	Ligas Populares de 28 de Febrero [February 28 Popular Leagues] [El Salvador] (PD)
LPA	Amphibious Transport [Navy ship symbol]
LPA	Labor Policy Association (EA)
LPA	La Plata [Argentina] [Seismograph station code, US Geological Survey] (SEIS)
LPA	LASER Printer Adapter

LPA............. Las Palmas [*Canary Islands*] [*Airport symbol*] (OAG)
LPA............. Latex Particle Agglutination [*Immunochemistry*] (DAVI)
LPA............. Launcher Plant Assembly (IAA)
LPA............. Launch Phase Analyst
LPA............. Lauric [*or Lauroyl or Lauryl*] Isopropanolamide [*Also, LIPA*] [*Organic chemistry*]
LPA............. Leaky Pipe Antenna
LPA............. Leather Producers' Association for England, Scotland, and Wales (BI)
LPA............. Left Pulmonary Artery [*Anatomy*]
LPA............. Light Pulser Array
LPA............. Limited Period Appointment [*Short-term employment*] [*British*]
LPA............. Limited Purpose Agency (OICC)
LPA............. Linear Power Amplifier
LPA............. Link Pack Area [*Computer science*] (MCD)
LpA............. Lipoprotein A [*Biochemistry*]
LPA............. Liquid Propellant Analysis
LPA............. Literature Primers [*A publication*]
LPA............. Lithium Perchlorate Ammoniate [*Inorganic chemistry*]
LPA............. Little People of America (EA)
LPA............. Local Pay Authority (AIE)
LPA............. Local Planning Assistance (OICC)
LPA............. Local Planning Authority [*British*] (DCTA)
LPA............. Local Processing Agency [*Department of Housing and Urban Development*] (GFGA)
LPA............. Local Public Agency
LPA............. Logarithmic Periodic Antenna (MCD)
LPA............. Logistics Pipeline Analysis [*Military*] (MCD)
LPA............. Log Periodic Antenna
LPA............. Louisiana Pharmacists Association (SRA)
LPA............. Louisiana Press Association (SRA)
LPA............. Louisiana Psychological Association (SRA)
LPA............. Low-Power Amplifier (CET)
LPA............. Low-Pressure Alarm (IEEE)
LPA............. Lysophosphatidic Acid [*Biochemistry*]
LPA............. PAL Aerolineas SA de CV [*Mexico ICAO designator*] (FAAC)
LPAA........... League of Pace Amendment Advocates (EA)
LPAA........... Log Periodic Array Antenna
LPAAT......... Lysophosphatidic Acid Acyltransferase [*An enzyme*]
LPAB........... Legal Practitioners' Admission Board [*Australia*]
LPAC........... Labor Policy Advisory Committee for Multilateral Trade Negotiations [*Terminated, 1980*] (EGAO)
LPAC........... Laser Pacific Media Corp. [*NASDAQ symbol*] (SAG)
LPAC........... Laser-pac Media [*NASDAQ symbol*] (TTSB)
LPAC........... Libertarian Party Abolitionist Caucus (EA)
LPAI........... Ligue Populaire Africaine pour l'Independance [*African People's League for Independence*] [*Djibouti*]
LPAM.......... Lisboa [*Portugal ICAO location identifier*] (ICLI)
L-PAM .... L-Phenylalanine Mustard [*Melphalan*] [*Also, A, M, MPH, MPL*] [*Antineoplastic drug*]
L-PAM .... L-Phenylalanin, Procarbazine, Adriamycin, Methotrexate [*Antineoplastic drug regimen*] (DAVI)
LP & KTF.... London Printing and Kindred Trades Federation (DGA)
LP & M........ Liverpool Post and Mercury [*A publication*] (ROG)
LP & P........ Logistics Policy and Procedures for Contingency Operations [*DARCOM*] (CINC)
LPAR .... Alverca [*Portugal ICAO location identifier*] (ICLI)
LPAR .... Large Phased-Array RADAR
LPARM....... Liquid Propellant Applied Research Motor
LPAS.......... Luciano Pavarotti Appreciation Society [*British*] (DBA)
LPASA........ Linear Pulse-Height Analyzer Spectrum Analysis (PDAA)
L/PAT........ Legislative/Political Action Team
L/PAT........ Letters Patent (ROG)
LPATS........ Lightning Position and Tracing System (MCD)
LPAV.......... Aveiro [*Portugal ICAO location identifier*] (ICLI)
LPAZ.......... Santa Maria, Santa Maria Island [*Portugal ICAO location identifier*] (ICLI)
LPB............. La Paz [*Bolivia*] [*Seismograph station code, US Geological Survey*] (SEIS)
LPB............. La Paz [*Bolivia*] [*Airport symbol*] (OAG)
LPB............. Lighted Pushbutton (ECII)
LpB............. Lipoprotein B [*Biochemistry*]
LPB............. Lithium Polymer Battery
LPB............. Loan Policy Board [*of SBA*] [*Abolished, 1965*]
LPB............. Lollipop Power Books (EA)
LPB............. [*The*] Louisiana & Pine Bluff Railway Co. [*AAR code*]
LPB............. Low-Level Penetration Bomb
LPB............. Low-Probability Behavior
LPB............. Lunar and Planetary Bibliography [*Lunar and Planetary Institute*] [*Information service or system*] (IID)
LPB............. Paper Book of Laurence, J., in Lincoln's Inn Library [*A publication*] (DLA)
LPBA.......... Lawyer-Pilots Bar Association (EA)
LPBBA........ Log Periodic Broadband Antenna
LPBE.......... Beja [*Portugal ICAO location identifier*] (ICLI)
LPBE.......... Linear Poisson-Boltzmann Equation [*Physical chemistry*]
LPBG.......... Braganca [*Portugal ICAO location identifier*] (ICLI)
LPBJ.......... Beja [*Portugal ICAO location identifier*] (ICLI)
LPBP.......... Low-Profile Bioprosthesis [*Medicine*] (DMAA)
LPBR.......... Braga [*Portugal ICAO location identifier*] (ICLI)
LPBT.......... Ladies Professional Bowlers Tour (EA)
LPC............. Laboratory Precision Connector (IAA)
LPC............. Laboratory Pulse Compression
LPC............. La Cumbre Peak [*California*] [*Seismograph station code, US Geological Survey*] (SEIS)

LPC............. Lamina Precursor Cell [*Neurology*]
LPC............. Landmarks Preservation Commission [*New York City*]
LPC............. Land Protection Council [*Victoria, Australia*]
LPC............. Laser Photocoagulation [*Ophthalmology*] (DAVI)
LPC............. Late Positive Component (MAE)
LPC............. Launch Pod Container [*General Support Rocket System*] (MCD)
LPC............. Laurylpyridinium Chloride [*Also, DPC*] [*Organic chemistry*]
LPC............. Leader Preparation Course
LPC............. Leaf Protein Concentrate [*Food industry*]
LPC............. League of Professional Craftsmen [*British*] (DBA)
LPC............. Least-Preferred Co-Worker [*Management term*]
LPC............. Leather Personnel Carriers [*i.e., boots*] [*Slang Army*]
LPC............. Less Prosperous Country
LPC............. Leukocyte Particle Counter [*Instrumentation*]
LPC............. Licensed Professional Counselor
LPC............. Light Patrol Car [*British*]
LPC............. Linear Power Controller
LPC............. Linear Prediction Code
LPC............. Linear Predictive Coding [*Digital coding technique*] [*Telecommunications*]
LPC............. Linkport Controller [*Electronics*] (ECII)
LPC............. Link Priority Change [*NASA*] (KSC)
LPC............. Lipocortin (DMAA)
LpC............. Lipoprotein C [*Biochemistry*]
LPC............. Livestock Publications Council (EA)
LPC............. Lockheed Propulsion Co. [*Division of Lockheed Aircraft Corp.*] (KSC)
LPC............. Lompoc, CA [*Location identifier FAA*] (FAAL)
LPC............. Longitudinal Parity Check [*Telecommunications*] (IAA)
LPC............. Longitudinal Primary Care [*Medicine*] (DMAA)
LPC............. Loop-Control [*Relay*] (IEEE)
LPC............. Loop Preparation Cask [*Nuclear energy*] (NRCH)
LPC............. Lord President's Committee [*British*]
LPC............. Lords of the Privy Council Lower Provinces Code [*India*] [*A publication*] (DLA)
LPC............. Lottery Promotion Co. [*British*] (ECON)
LPC............. Lower Pump Cubicle (IEEE)
LPC............. Low-Power Channel (IAA)
LPC............. Low-Power Counter
LPC............. Low-Pressure Chamber Technician [*Navy*]
LPC............. Low-Pressure Composite
LPC............. Low-Pressure Compressor
LPC............. Lumped-Parameter Calorimeter [*Heat measure*]
LPC............. Lysophosphatidylcholine [*Also, Lyso-PC*] [*Biochemistry*]
LPCA.......... Louisiana Pest Control Association (SRA)
LPCA.......... Louisiana Primary Care Association (SRA)
LPCA.......... Lunar Pyrotechnic Control Assembly [*Aerospace*]
LPCAT........ Laboratory for Pest Control Application Technology [*Ohio State University*] [*Research center*] (RCD)
LPCC.......... Legal Practitioners Complaints Committee [*South Australia*]
LPCC.......... Low-Pressure Combustion Chamber
LPCG.......... LASER Planning and Coordination Group [*Energy Research and Development Administration*]
LPCH .... Chaves [*Portugal ICAO location identifier*] (ICLI)
LPCH .... Local Process Control Host (IAA)
LPCI........... Low-Pressure Coolant Injection [*Nuclear energy*] (NRCH)
LPCIS......... Low-Pressure Coolant Injection System [*Nuclear energy*] (NRCH)
LPCL.......... Laboratory Pulse Compression Loop
LPCM.......... Linear Phase Code Modulation
LPCM.......... Linear Pulse-Code Modulation [*Computer science*]
LPCM.......... Low Placed Conus Medullaris [*Medicine*] (DMAA)
LPCO.......... Coimbra [*Portugal ICAO location identifier*] (ICLI)
LPCO.......... Low-Pressure Cut-Off [*Air conditioning system*] [*Automotive engineering*]
LPCP........... Launcher Preparation Control Panel
LPCRS........ Low-Pressure Coolant Recirculation System [*Nuclear energy*] (IEEE)
LPCS.......... Cascais [*Portugal ICAO location identifier*] (ICLI)
LPCS.......... Laterally to the Pedunculus Cerebellaris Superior [*Medicine*]
LPCS.......... Local Post Collectors Society (EA)
LPCS.......... Low-Pressure Core Spray System [*Nuclear energy*] (NRCH)
LPCV.......... Covilha [*Portugal ICAO location identifier*] (ICLI)
LPCVD .... Liquid Phase Chemical Vapor Deposition [*Photovoltaic energy systems*]
LPCVD .... Low-Pressure Chemical Vapor Deposition [*Semiconductor technology*]
LP-CW .... Long Pulse - Continuous Wave (NG)
LPD............. Amphibious Transport Dock [*Landing Platform, Dock*] [*Navy ship symbol*]
LPD............. Labelled Plan Display (PDAA)
LPD............. Labour Party of Dominica [*Political party*] (EY)
LPD............. Landing Platform, Dock
LPD............. Landing Point Designator [*Apollo*] [*NASA*]
LPD............. Language Processing and Debugging [*Computer science*] (BUR)
LPD............. La Pedrera [*Colombia*] [*Airport symbol*] (OAG)
LPD............. Laredo Petroleums [*Vancouver Stock Exchange symbol*]
LPD............. LASER Polarization Detector
LPD............. Lateral Photoelectric Detector (PDAA)
LPD............. Launch Platform Detected [*Navy*] (CAAL)
LPD............. Launch Point Determination
LPD............. Launch Procedure Document [*NASA*] (KSC)
LPD............. Least Perceptible Difference [*Psychology*]
LPD............. Lighting-Power Density
LPD............. Linear Phasing Device [*Telecommunications*] (OA)
LPD............. Line Printer Daemon (PCM)
LpD............. Lipoprotein D [*Biochemistry*]
LPD............. Liquid-Protein Diet

LPD............ Liters per Day (KSC)
LPD............ Local Power Density (NRCH)
LPD............ Local Procurement Direct [Military]
LPD............ Log Periodic Dipole
LPD............ Low-Performance Drone
LPD............ Low Period Dipole
LPD............ Low-Power Difference (IEEE)
LPD............ Low-Pressure Difference (IEEE)
LPD............ Low Protein Diet
LPD............ Luteal Phase Defect [Gynecology] (DAVI)
LPD............ Lymphoproliferative Disease [Oncology]
LPDA......... Linear Photodiode Array [Instrumentation]
LPDA......... Log Periodic Dipole Antenna [Military] (CAAL)
LPDA......... Log Periodic Dipole Array
LPDC......... LASER Plasmadynamic Converter
LPDC......... London Parcels Delivery Co.
LPDF.......... Lipoprotein-Deficient Fraction [Medicine] (DMAA)
LpDH.......... Lysopine Dehydrogenase [An enzyme]
LPDM......... List of Physical Dimensions (NASA)
LPDM......... Lao People's Democratic Republic
LPDR......... Local Public Document Room (GFGA)
LPDS......... Lipoprotein Deficient Human Serum
LPDT.......... Legal Practitioners Disciplinary Tribunal [South Australia]
LPDT.......... Low Power Distress Transmitter [Aviation] (DA)
LPDTL........ Low-Power Diode Transistor Logic [Electronics] (IAA)
LPDU .... Link Layer Protocol Data Unit [Telecommunications] (OSI)
LPE............ Launch Preparation Equipment (AABC)
LPE............ Layer Primitive Equation (MHDI)
LPE............ Lead Piping Engineer
LPE............ Limited Paperback Editions
LPE............ Linear Parameter Estimation [Physical chemistry]
LPE............ Linear Polyethylene [Organic chemistry]
LPE............ Linkport Extension [Electronics] (ECII)
LpE............ Lipoprotein E [Biochemistry]
LPE............ Lipoprotein Electrophoresis [Biochemistry]
LPE............ Liquid Phase Epitaxy [Magnetic film]
LPE............ London Press Exchange
LPE............ Loop Preparation Equipment [Nuclear energy] (NRCH)
LPE............ Low Probability of Exploitation (PDAA)
LPE............ Lunar and Planetary Ephemerides Assembly [Space Flight
              Operations Facility, NASA]
LPE............ Lysophosphatidylethanolamine [Biochemistry]
LPEA.......... Luis Palau Evangelistic Association (EA)
LPEC.......... Launch Preparation Equipment Compartment (AABC)
LPEM.......... Launch Preparation Equipment Monitor (MCD)
LPEO.......... Local Public Employment Office
LPerc......... Light Perception [Ophthalmology]
LPERE........ Linear Phase with Equal Ripple Error (IAA)
LPES.......... Launch Preparation Equipment Set (AABC)
LPEV.......... Evora [Portugal ICAO location identifier] (ICLI)
LPEV.......... Launch Preparation Equipment Vault (MCD)
LPF............ Landsing Pacific Fund [AMEX symbol] (CTT)
LPF............ Latvian Popular Front [Political party Defunct] (EAIO)
LPF............ Leach-Precipitate Float (BARN)
LPF............ League for Programming Freedom (EA)
LPF............ Left Posterior Fascicle [Anatomy]
LPF............ Le Pertre [France] [Seismograph station code, US Geological
              Survey] (SEIS)
LPF............ Leukocytosis-Promoting Factor [Hematology]
LPF............ Life Probability Function
LPF............ Light Patrol Frigate (ADA)
LPF............ Liquid Pressure Filter
LPF............ Localized Plaque Formation [Dentistry] (MAE)
LPF............ Logically Passive Function
LPF............ Lowest Possible Airfare
LPF............ Low-Pass Filter [Electronics]
LPF............ Low-Power Field [Microscopy]
LPF............ Low-Profile Flange
LPF............ Lutheran Peace Fellowship (EA)
LPF............ Lymphocytosis-Promoting Factor [Hematology] (DAVI)
LPF............ Pop Festivals [Public-performance tariff class] [British]
LPFA.......... Laminated Plastics Fabricators Association [British] (BI)
LPFA.......... London Potato Futures Association [London Stock Exchange]
LPFB.......... Left Posterior Fascicular Block [Cardiology]
LPFGEN...... Linear Programming File Generator [Computer science] (IAA)
LPFL.......... Flores, Flores Island [Portugal ICAO location identifier] (ICLI)
LPFL.......... Lowpass Filter (MSA)
LPFM......... Low-Powered Fan Marker (MSA)
LPFO.......... London Procurement Field Office
LPFP.......... Low-Pressure Fuel Pump (KSC)
LPFR.......... Faro [Portugal ICAO location identifier] (ICLI)
LPFR.......... Liquid Phase Flow Reactor (KSC)
LPFRT........ Limited Preliminary Flight Rating Test
LPFSSB...... Lone Parents' Family Support Service - Birthright [Australia]
LPFT.......... Low-Pressure Fuel Turbopump
LPFTP........ Low-Pressure Fuel Turbopump (NASA)
LPFU.......... Funchal, Madeira Island [Portugal ICAO location identifier] (ICLI)
LPG............ Lake Ponask Gold Corp. [Toronto Stock Exchange symbol]
LPG............ Langage de Programmation et de Gestion [French computer
              language]
LPG............ La Plata [Argentina] [Airport symbol] (OAG)
LPG............ Lapping [Electricity]
LPG............ Last Page Generator (NASA)
LPG............ Launch Preparations Group [NASA]
LPG............ Le Parti de la Guadeloupe [Political party] (EY)

LPG............ Licentiate of the Physicians Guild [British]
LPG............ Life Partners Group [NYSE symbol] (TTSB)
LPG............ Life Partners Group, Inc. [NYSE symbol] (SPSG)
LPG............ Lipophosphoglycan [Biochemistry]
LPG............ Liquefied Petroleum Gas
LPG............ Liquid Propane Gas
LPG............ Liquid Propane-Gas Shutoff [NFPA pre-fire planning symbol] (NFPA)
LPG............ Liquid Propellant Gun (NASA)
LPG............ List Program Generator (IAA)
LPG............ Long Path Gas [Spectroscopy]
LPG............ Lousy Paying Guest [Hotel slang]
LPG............ Low-Pressure Gas (NRCH)
LPGA .... Ladies Professional Golf Association (EA)
LPGA .... Living Plant Growers Association (EA)
LPGA .... Louisiana Pecan Growers' Association (EA)
LPGE.......... LEM [Lunar Excursion Module] Partial Guidance Equipment
              [NASA] (KSC)
LPGG......... Liquid Propellant Gas Generator
LPGITA....... Liquefied Petroleum Gas Industry Technical Association [British]
LPGITC ...... Liquified Petroleum Gas Industry Technical Committee
LPGL.......... London Pacific Group Ltd. [NASDAQ symbol] (SAG)
LPGLY........ London Pacific Grp ADS [NASDAQ symbol] (TTSB)
LPGM......... Last Pinedale Glacial Maximum [Climatology]
LPGR......... Graciosa, Graciosa Island [Portugal ICAO location identifier] (ICLI)
LPGS......... Liquid Pathway Generic Study [Nuclear energy] (NRCH)
LPGS......... Liquified Petroleum Gas Report [American Petroleum Institute]
              [Database]
LPGTC .... Liquified Petroleum Gas Industry Technical Committee (MCD)
LPH............ Amphibious Assault Ship (Landing Platform, Helicopter) [Navy
              symbol]
LPH............ Assault Hospital Ship [Navy symbol] (VNW)
LPH............ Laboratory of Physiological Hygiene [University of Minnesota]
              [Research center] (RCD)
LPH............ Landing Personnel Helicopter [British] (NATG)
LPh............ Late Phoenician (BJA)
LPH............ Lee Pharmaceuticals [AMEX symbol] (SPSG)
LPH............ Left Posterior Hemiblock [Cardiology]
LPH............ Legrest Pin Handle
LPh............ Licentiate of Philosophy
LPH............ Lines per Hour [Printing]
LPH............ Lipotropin Hormone [Endocrinology]
LPH............ Liters per Hour (KSC)
LPH............ Lochgilphead [Scotland] [Airport symbol] (OAG)
LPHB.......... Low-Pressure Heating Boiler
LPHLDR...... Lampholder
LPHR......... Horta, Faial Island [Portugal ICAO location identifier] (ICLI)
LPHS......... Lunar and Planetary Horizon Scanner [Aerospace]
LPHSW ...... Last Pass Heat Sink Welding [Nuclear energy] (NUCP)
LPI............ Colorado Springs, CO [Location identifier FAA] (FAAL)
LPI............ Latent Photographic Image
LPI............ Launching Position Indicator
LPI............ Leaf Plastochron Index [Botany]
LPI............ Learning Preference Inventory
LPI............ Left Posterior-Inferior [Medicine] (DMAA)
LPI............ Lightning Protection Institute (EA)
LPI............ Linear Partial Information (PDAA)
LPI............ Lines per Inch [Printing]
LPI............ Linkoeping [Sweden] [Airport symbol] (OAG)
LPI............ Linus Pauling Institute of Science and Medicine [Research center]
              (RCD)
LPI............ List per Inch (IAA)
LPI............ Logistics Performance Indicator (PDAA)
LPI............ Lomond Publications, Inc. [Telecommunications service] (TSSD)
LPI............ Longitudinally Applied Paper Insulation [Telecommunications] (TEL)
LPI............ Louisiana Polytechnic Institute
LPI............ Low-Power Illuminator (NATG)
LPI............ Low-Power Injection [Nuclear energy] (NRCH)
LPI............ Low-Power Interrupt (MCD)
LPI............ Low-Pressure Index
LPI............ Low-Pressure Injection [Nuclear energy] (NRCH)
LPI............ Low Probability of Intercept (NVT)
LPI............ Low Probability of Interest
LPI............ Lunar and Planetary Institute [University Space Research
              Association] [Research center] (RCD)
LPI............ Lysinuric Protein Intolerance [Medicine] (DMAA)
LPIA.......... Label Printing Industries of America (EA)
LPIA.......... Launch Pad Interface Assembly
LPIA.......... Liquid Propellant Information Agency [Johns Hopkins Univeristy]
LPIB.......... Law and Policy in International Business [ABA] [A publication]
              (AAGC)
LPIBSS ...... Lunar and Planetary Institute Bibliographic Search Service [University
              Space Research Association] [Information service or system]
              (IID)
LPiC.......... Central Louisiana State Hospital, Medical Library, Pineville, LA
              [Library symbol Library of Congress] (LCLS)
LPICBM...... Liquid Propellant Intercontinental Ballistic Missile [Military] (IAA)
LPID.......... Logical Page Identifier (BUR)
LPiL.......... Louisiana College, Pineville, LA [Library symbol Library of
              Congress] (LCLS)
LPIN.......... Espinho [Portugal ICAO location identifier] (ICLI)
LPIR.......... Limited Partnership Investment Review [Information service or
              system] (IID)
LPIR.......... Low-Probability Intercept RADAR
LPIS.......... Low-Pressure Injection System [Nuclear energy] (NRCH)
LPISS........ Low-Power Illuminator Signal Source (MCD)

LPIU............	Lithographers and Photoengravers International Union [*Later, Graphic Arts International Union*]
LPJF............	Leiria [*Portugal ICAO location identifier*] (ICLI)
LPJO............	Alijo [*Portugal ICAO location identifier*] (ICLI)
LPK.............	Lao Pen Kang [*Laotian Neutralist Party*] (CINC)
LPK.............	Liver Pyruvate Kinase [*Medicine*] (DMAA)
LPKCMLPCC...	License Plate, Key Chain, and Mini License Plate Collectors Club (EA)
LPL.............	Entergy Louisiana, Inc. [*NYSE symbol*] (SAG)
LPL.............	Entergy Louisiana, Inc. Capital I [*NYSE symbol*] (SAG)
LPL.............	Laborers Political League (EA)
LPL.............	Labour Protection League [*A union*] [*British*]
LPL.............	Lamina Propria Lymphocyte [*Hematology*]
LPL.............	Lamp-Pumped LASER (MCD)
LPL.............	LASER-Pumped-LASER
LPL.............	Lawton Public Library, Lawton, OK [*OCLC symbol*] (OCLC)
LPL.............	Lease-A-Plane International [*ICAO designator*] (FAAC)
LPL.............	Lethbridge Public Library [*UTLAS symbol*]
LPL.............	Lichen Planus-Like Lesion [*Medicine*] (DMAA)
LPL.............	Lightproof Louver [*Technical drawings*]
LPL.............	Linear Programming Language [*Intertechnique*] [*French Computer science*]
LPL.............	Lipoprotein Lipase [*An enzyme*]
LPL.............	List Processing Language [*Computer science*] (IEEE)
LPL.............	Liverpool [*England*] [*Airport symbol*] (OAG)
LPL.............	LM [*Lunar Module*] Plan [*NASA*] (KSC)
LPL.............	Local Processor Link
LPL.............	Long Pulse LASER
LPL.............	Louisiana Power & Light Co. [*NYSE symbol*] (SPSG)
LPL.............	Low Polar Latitude [*Geophysics*]
LPL.............	Low-Power Logic
LPL.............	Lunar and Planetary Laboratory [*University of Arizona*] [*Research center*] (MCD)
LPL.............	Lunar Projects Laboratory
LPL.............	Lysophospholipase [*An enzyme*]
LPLA............	Lajes, Terceira Island [*Portugal ICAO location identifier*] (ICLI)
LPLA............	Lao Peoples Liberation Army (CINC)
LPLA............	Lipoprotein Lipase Activity [*Medicine*] (DMAA)
LPLA............	Log-Periodic Loop Antenna (PDAA)
LPlaI...........	Iberville Parish Library, Plaquemine, LA [*Library symbol Library of Congress*] (LCLS)
LPLG...........	Lagos [*Portugal ICAO location identifier*] (ICLI)
LPLG...........	Left Pleural Ganglion [*Medicine*]
LPLIS..........	Lipoprotein Lipase Inactivation System [*Biochemistry*] (DAVI)
LPLM...........	Lowest Planned Level of Maintenance (SAA)
LPLNG.........	Low-Pressure Liquefied Natural Gases (NRCH)
LPLPr..........	Entergy Louisiana 12.64% cmPfd [*NYSE symbol*] (TTSB)
LPLPrA........	Entergy Louisiana 9.68% cm Pfd [*NYSE symbol*] (TTSB)
LPLR...........	Lock Pillar (AAG)
LPL?TMC......	Low-Pressure Low-Temperature Molding Compound
LPLWS........	Launch Pad Lightning Warning System [*NASA*] (KSC)
LPM............	Lamap [*Vanuatu*] [*Airport symbol*] (OAG)
LPM............	Lane Photograph Method
LPM............	LASER Particle Monitor (PDAA)
LPM............	LASER Phase Macroscope
LPM............	LASER Precision Microfabrication (IAA)
LPM............	Lateral Pterygoid Muscle (DMAA)
LPM............	Leading Patrolman [*Navy British*] (DI)
lpm............	Letters Per Minute (WDMC)
LPM............	Licensing Project Manager [*Nuclear energy*] (NRCH)
LPM............	Light Pulser Matrix
LPM............	Linearly Polarized Mode [*Telecommunications*] (TEL)
LPM............	Lines per Millimeter (WDAA)
LPM............	Lines per Minute [*Computer science*]
lpm............	Lines per Minute (IDOE)
LPM............	Liquid Phase Methanation [*Fuel chemistry*]
LPM............	Liters per Minute (MCD)
LPM............	Liver Plasma Membrane
LPM............	Local Processor Memory (IAA)
LPM............	Long Particular [*or Peculiar*] Metre [*Music*]
LPM............	Los Pinos Mountain [*New Mexico*] [*Seismograph station code, US Geological Survey*] (SEIS)
LPM............	Lunar Payload Module [*Aerospace*] (MCD)
LPM............	Lunar Portable Magnetometer [*Apollo*] [*NASA*]
LPMA...........	Lead Pencil Manufacturers Association [*Later, Pencil Makers Association*] (EA)
LPMA...........	Loose-Parts-Monitor Assembly [*Nuclear energy*] (NRCH)
LPMAD........	Living Personnel Management Authorization Document [*DoD*]
LPMATGEN...	Linear Programming Matrix Generation (IAA)
LPMC...........	Low-Pressure Molding Compound [*Environmental science*]
LPMC...........	Low-Pressure Molding Compound
LPMES.........	Logistics Performance Measurement and Evaluation System (AABC)
LPMF...........	Monfortinho [*Portugal ICAO location identifier*] (ICLI)
LPMG...........	Lisboa [*Portugal ICAO location identifier*] (ICLI)
LPMI...........	Mirandela [*Portugal ICAO location identifier*] (ICLI)
LPMOSS......	Linear Programming Mathematical Optimization Subroutine System (IAA)
LPMR...........	Monte Real [*Portugal ICAO location identifier*] (ICLI)
LPM/S.........	Liquid Phase Methanation/Shift Reaction [*Fuel chemistry*]
LPMS...........	Lock Performance Monitoring System [*DOD*] [*COE*] (TAG)
LPMS...........	Logistics Program Management System [*Air Force*] (AFIT)
LPMS...........	Loose-Parts Monitoring System [*Nuclear energy*] (NRCH)
LPMT...........	Montijo [*Portugal ICAO location identifier*] (ICLI)
LPN.............	Alpenair GmbH & Co. KG [*Austria ICAO designator*] (FAAC)
LPN.............	Licensed Practical Nurse

LPN.............	Logical Page Number (BUR)
LPN.............	Long Part Number
LPN.............	Longview, Portland & Northern Railway Co. [*AAR code*]
LPN.............	Low-Pass Network [*Electronics*]
LPN.............	National Federation of Licensed Practical Nurses
LPNA...........	Lithographers and Printers National Association [*Later, PIA*] (EA)
LPNAF.........	Licensed Practical Nurses Association of Florida (SRA)
LPNGP........	Low-Pressure Noble Gas Processing (NRCH)
LPO.............	La Porte [*Indiana*] [*Airport symbol*] (OAG)
LPO.............	Laramie Project Office [*Laramie, WY*] [*Department of Energy*] (GRD)
LPO.............	Late Pleistocene Origins [*Ecology*]
LPO.............	Lateral Preoptic [*Brain anatomy*]
LPO.............	Lattice-Preferred Orientation [*Geophysics*]
LPO.............	Lauroyl Peroxide [*Organic chemistry*]
LPO.............	Left Posterio Occipital [*A fetal position*] (DAVI)
LPO.............	Left Posterior Oblique [*Cardiology*] (MAE)
LPO.............	Le Pouchou [*France*] [*Seismograph station code, US Geological Survey*] (SEIS)
LPO.............	Liberale Partei Oesterreichs [*Liberal Party of Austria*] [*Political party*] (PPE)
LPO.............	Liberal Party Organization [*British*]
LPO.............	Light Perception Only [*Ophthalmology*]
LPO.............	Limited Production Option [*Automotive engineering*]
LPO.............	Liquid Phase Oxidation [*Chemical processing*]
LPO.............	Loan Production Office [*Banking*]
LPO.............	Lobus Parolfactorius (PDAA)
LPO.............	Local Purchase Order
LPO.............	London Philharmonic Orchestra
LPO.............	Low Power Output (MSA)
LPO.............	Low-Pressure Oxygen
LPO.............	Lunar Parking Orbit [*Apollo*] [*NASA*]
LPO.............	Lunar Polar Orbiter [*NASA*]
LPO.............	Lunar Program Office [*NASA*] (IAA)
LPOC...........	Labile Particulate Organic Carbon [*Environmental science*]
LPOF...........	Low-Pressure Oil-Filled [*Cable*] (DICI)
LpOH...........	Lysopine Dehydrogenase (BABM)
L/POL.........	Life Policy [*Insurance*] (DCTA)
L'POOL........	Liverpool (ROG)
LPOP...........	Low-Pressure Oxidizer Turbopump (NASA)
L POST........	Left Posterior [*Medicine*] (MEDA)
LPOT...........	Low-Pressure Oxidizer Turbopump (MCD)
LPOT...........	Ota [*Portugal ICAO location identifier*] (ICLI)
LPOTP.........	Low-Pressure Oxidizer Turbopump (NASA)
LPOX...........	Low-Pressure Oxygen (AFM)
LPP.............	Laboratory of Pulmonary Pathobiology (GNE)
LPP.............	Labor Protection Plan
LPP.............	Labour Progressive Party [*Canadian communist party*]
LPP.............	Lanka Prajatantrawadi Party [*Ceylon*]
LPP.............	Lappeenranta [*Finland*] [*Airport symbol*] (OAG)
LPP.............	Large Paper Proofs
LPP.............	LASER-Produced Plasma
LPP.............	Lateral Pterygoid Plate [*Medicine*] (DMAA)
LPP.............	Launcher Preparation Control Panel
LPP.............	Leader Preparation Program
LPP.............	Lebowa People's Party [*South Africa*] [*Political party*] (PPW)
LPP.............	Length of Perpendiculars
LPP.............	Liberian People's Party [*Political party*] (EY)
LPP.............	Lightweight Presentation Protocol [*Telecommunications*] (ACRL)
LPP.............	Linear Photopolymerization [*Organic chemistry*]
LPP.............	Lines per Page
LPP.............	Link Peripheral Processor (ACRL)
LPP.............	Lipoprotein Lipase [*An enzyme*] (DAVI)
LPP.............	Liquid Phase Processing [*Chemistry*]
LPP.............	Local Patching Panel
LPP.............	Long Periodic Perturbation
LPP.............	Long-Period Pulses [*Volcanology*]
LPP.............	Low-Power Physics (IEEE)
LPP.............	Low-Pressure-Pipe System [*Waste water treatment*]
LPP.............	Lunar Precepts Positioner [*Aerospace*]
LPPA...........	Licensed Pearl Producers' Association [*Australia*]
LPPC...........	Lisboa [*Portugal ICAO location identifier*] (ICLI)
LPPC...........	Load Point Photocell
LPPD...........	Ponta Delgada, Sao Miguel Island [*Portugal ICAO location identifier*] (ICLI)
LPPH...........	Late Postpartum Hemorrhage [*Medicine*] (DMAA)
LPPH...........	Leningrad Prison Psychiatric Hospital [*Later, LSPH*]
LPPI...........	Pico, Pico Island [*Portugal ICAO location identifier*] (ICLI)
LPPM...........	Low Pressure Permanent Mould (PDAA)
LPPM...........	Portimao [*Portugal ICAO location identifier*] (ICLI)
LPPMUL	Lawyers Protecting People from Malicious and Unjustified Lawsuits (EA)
LPPO...........	Santa Maria [*Portugal ICAO location identifier*] (ICLI)
LPPR...........	Porto [*Portugal ICAO location identifier*] (ICLI)
LPPS...........	Low-Pressure Plasma Sprayed [*Thermal barrier coating*]
LPPS...........	Porto Santo, Porto Santo Island [*Portugal ICAO location identifier*] (ICLI)
LPPT...........	Lisboa [*Portugal ICAO location identifier*] (ICLI)
LPPT...........	Low Pressurization Pressure Test Transmitter (IEEE)
LPPTS.........	[*The*] Library of the Palestine Pilgrims' Text Society (BJA)
LPPV...........	Praia Verde [*Portugal ICAO location identifier*] (ICLI)
LPQ.............	Luang Prabang [*Laos*] [*Airport symbol*] (AD)
LPR.............	Amphibious Transport (Small) [*Navy ship symbol*]
LPR.............	Lactate-Pyruvate Ratio (MAE)
LPR.............	Lanpar Technologies, Inc. [*Toronto Stock Exchange symbol*]

LPR.............. La Peregrina [*Puerto Rico*] [*Seismograph station code, US Geological Survey*] (SEIS)
LPR.............. Late Phase Reaction [*or Response*] [*Medicine*]
LPR.............. Late Position Report [*Report of a flight which is off flight plan*]
LPR.............. Late Procurement Request [*Air Force*] (AFM)
LPR.............. Lawful Permanent Resident [*Department of Justice*]
LPR.............. Leadership Potential Rating [*Army*] (AABC)
LPR.............. Licensed Preacher
LPR.............. License Plate Reader
LPR.............. Lilly's Practical Register [*A publication*] (DLA)
LPR.............. Linea Aerea Privadas Argentina [*ICAO designator*] (FAAC)
LPR.............. Linear Polarization Resistance (MCD)
LPR.............. Line Printer [*Computer science*] (NASA)
LPR.............. Line Printer Remote (PCM)
LPR.............. Liquid Propellant Rocket [*Air Force*]
LPR.............. Local Payment Receipt (AABC)
LPR.............. London Property Register [*London Research Centre*] [*British Information service or system*] (IID)
LPR.............. Long-Playing Record (IAA)
LPR.............. Long-Playing Rocket [*Aerospace*]
LPR.............. Looper Position Regulator
LPRI.............. Lymphocyte Proliferative Response [*Immunology*]
LPR.............. Lynchburg Pool Reactor
LPR-5.............. Lease Production Revenue System - 5 File [*Petroleum Information Corp.*] [*Information service or system*] (CRD)
LPR-10.............. Lease Production Revenue System - 10 File [*Petroleum Information Corp.*] [*Information service or system*] (CRD)
LPRA .... Laws of Puerto Rico Annotated [*A publication*]
LPRA .... Lost Parts Replacement Authorization (MCD)
LPRB.............. Loaded Program Request Block [*Computer science*] (BUR)
LPRC.............. Launch Pitch Rate Control
LPRC .... Library Public Relations Council (EA)
LPRCO.............. Logistics Planning and Reporting Code [*Military*]
LPRD.............. Launch Program Requirement Document [*NASA*] (IAA)
LPRE.............. Liquid Propellant Rocket Engine [*Air Force*]
LPRF.............. Low-Power Radio Frequency (MCD)
LPRF.............. Low Pulse Recurrence Frequency (MCD)
LPRI.............. Licentiate of the Plastics and Rubber Institute [*British*] (DBQ)
LPRINT........ Lookup Dictionary Print Program (IEEE)
LPRL.............. Lentz Peace Research Laboratory (EA)
LPRM.............. Local Power Range Monitor (NRCH)
LPRM.............. Low-Power Range Monitor [*Nuclear energy*] (NRCH)
LPRO .... Legend Properties, Inc. [*NASDAQ symbol*] (SAG)
LProj.............. Light Projection [*Ophthalmology*]
LPRP.............. Lao People's Revolutionary Party [*Phak Pasason Pativat Lao*] [*Political party*] (PPW)
LPRPrB........ Santander Overseas Bk 'B'Pfd [*NYSE symbol*] (TTSB)
LPRR .... Low-Power Research Reactor
LPRS .... Local Primary Reference Source
LPRS .... Low-Pressure Recirculation System (NRCH)
LPRSVR........ Life Preserver
LPRT.............. Low Power Relay Transmitter
LPS.............. Laboratory Peripheral System
LPS.............. Laboratory Program Summary (MCD)
LPS.............. Landing Performance Score (MCD)
LPS.............. Language for Programming-in-the-Small [*Computer science*] (MHDI)
LPS.............. Lanterman-Petris-Short Act [*Psychology*] (DAVI)
LPS-T.............. La Palma [*El Salvador*] [*Seismograph station code, US Geological Survey*] (SEIS)
LPS.............. Large Pointing System (MCD)
LPS.............. LASER Particulate Spectrometer [*NASA*]
LPS.............. LASER Power Supply
LPS.............. Laser Printing System (NITA)
LPS.............. Last Papanicolaou Smear [*Gynecology*] (DAVI)
LPS.............. Last Period Satisfied [*IRS*]
LPS.............. Laterality Preference Schedule [*Psychology*]
LPS.............. Lateral Premotor System (DMAA)
LPS.............. Launch Phase Simulator [*NASA*]
LPS.............. Launch Processing System [*NASA*] (KSC)
LPS.............. L-Band Phase Shifter
LPS.............. Levator Palpebrae Superioris [*Muscle*] [*Anatomy*] (AAMN)
LPS.............. Liberale Partei der Schweiz [*Liberal Party of Switzerland*] [*Political party*] (PPE)
LPS.............. Liberian Philatelic Society [*Defunct*] (EA)
LPS.............. Library Processes System [*Educomp*] [*Information service or system*] (IID)
LPS.............. Life-Cycle Productivity System
LPS.............. Lightning Protection System [*Boating*]
LPS.............. Lightproof Shade [*Technical drawings*]
LPS.............. Linear Profile Scan [*Medicine*] (DMAA)
LPS.............. Linear Programming System [*Computer science*]
LPS.............. Linear Pulse Sector (OA)
LPS.............. Line Procedure Specifications (CMD)
LPS.............. Line Program Selector (IAA)
LPS.............. Lines per Second [*Computer science*]
LPS.............. Lipase (MAE)
LPS.............. Lipopolysaccharide [*Biochemistry*]
LPS.............. Liquid-Phase Sintering (MCD)
LPS.............. Liters per Second (KSC)
LPS.............. Loan Production System [*Department of Veterans Affairs*]
LPS.............. Local Process Specification (NG)
LPS.............. Logicon Products [*Vancouver Stock Exchange symbol*]
LPS.............. Logistic Policy Statement [*Navy*]
LPS.............. Logistics Planning Study (MCD)
LPS.............. London & Port Stanley Railway Co. [*AAR code*]

LPS.............. London Press Service
LPS.............. Longfellow Poetry Society (EA)
Lps.............. Loops [*Military decoration*] (AABC)
LPS.............. Lopez Island [*Washington*] [*Airport symbol*] (OAG)
LPS.............. Lord Privy Seal [*British*]
LPS.............. Low-Power Schottky [*Electronics*]
LPS.............. Low-Pressure Sand [*Casting*] [*Automotive engineering*]
LPS.............. Low-Pressure Scram [*Nuclear energy*] (IEEE)
LPS.............. Low-Pressure Separator [*Chemical engineering*]
LPS.............. Low-Pressure Sodium
LPS.............. Lunar Penetrometer System [*Aerospace*]
LPS.............. Lunar Pilotage System [*Aerospace*]
LPSA.............. Lithographic Preparatory Services Association [*Later, GPA*] (EA)
LPSA.............. Log Periodic Scattering Array
LPSC.............. Luxembourg Philatelic Study Club [*Defunct*] (EA)
LPSC.............. Santa Cruz [*Portugal ICAO location identifier*] (ICLI)
LPS/CDS.............. Launch Processing System / Central Data Subsystem [*Military*]
LPSCU.............. Ladies Pennsylvania Slovak Catholic Union (EA)
LPSD .... Logically Passive Self-Dual
LPSF .... Lens-Pinhole Spatial Filter (PDAA)
LPSG .... Live Oak, Perry & South Georgia Railway Co. [*AAR code*]
LPSI.............. Low-Pressure Safety Injection [*Nuclear energy*] (NRCH)
LPSI.............. Sines [*Portugal ICAO location identifier*] (ICLI)
LPSIP.............. Low-Pressure Safety Injection Pump [*Nuclear energy*] (NRCH)
LPSJ.............. Sao Jorge, Sao Jorge Island [*Portugal ICAO location identifier*] (ICLI)
LPSN.............. Local Packet Switched Network
LPSNY.............. Lithuanian Philatelic Society of New York (EA)
LPSO.............. Laboratory Procurement Supply Office
LPSO .... Lloyd's Policy Signing Office [*Lloyd's of London*]
LPSOL.............. Linear Programming Solution (IAA)
LPSS.............. Amphibious Transport Submarine [*Landing Platform, Submarine*] [*Navy ship symbol*]
LPSS.............. Law and Political Science Section [*Association of College and Research Libraries*]
LPSS.............. Line Protection Switching System [*Bell System*]
LPSS.............. Local Population Studies Society [*British*]
LPSSNJ.............. Low-Power Self-Screening Noise Jammer [*Military*] (CAAL)
LPSSR.............. Low-Power Spread Spectrum RADAR (PDAA)
LPST.............. Sintra [*Portugal ICAO location identifier*] (ICLI)
LPSTTL.............. Low-Power Schottky Transistor-Transistor Logic [*Electronics*] (IAA)
LPSV.............. Low-Pressure Solenoid Valve
LPSVD.............. Linear Prediction with Singular Value Decomposition [*Computer science*]
LPSW.............. Load Program Status Word (IAA)
LPSW.............. Low-Pressure Service Water [*Nuclear energy*] (NRCH)
LPT.............. Lampang [*Thailand*] [*Seismograph station code, US Geological Survey*] (SEIS)
LPT.............. Lampang [*Thailand*] [*Airport symbol*] (OAG)
LPT.............. Language Proficiency Test [*Military*] (AFM)
LPT.............. Largest-Processing Time First [*Computer science*] (MHDB)
LPT.............. LASER Propulsion Test (SSD)
LPT.............. LASER Pyrolysis Technique [*Inorganic synthesis*]
LPT.............. Latest Recommended Posting Times [*Business term*] (DCTA)
LPT.............. Leading Physical Trainer [*British military*] (DMA)
LPT.............. Licensed Physical Therapist
LPT.............. Light Pen Tracking (MCD)
LPT.............. Limited Procurement Test
LP-T.............. Limited Production - Test (AABC)
LPT.............. Line Printer [*Computer science*]
LPT.............. Line Printer [*Computer science*] (DOM)
LPT.............. Lipotropin (DMAA)
LPT.............. Liquid Penetrant Testing [*or Examination*] [*Nuclear energy*] (NRCH)
LPT.............. Listed Property Trust
LPT.............. Local Public Transportation
LPT.............. Lock Pointer Table
LPT.............. Long-Period Tremor [*Volcanology*]
LPT.............. Low Point [*Technical drawings*]
LPT.............. Low-Power Test
LPT.............. Low-Pressure Test
LPT.............. Low-Pressure Transducer
LPT.............. Low-Pressure Turbine [*Nuclear energy*] (NRCH)
LPT.............. Low Pressure Turbocharger
LPT.............. Luminescent Pigment Tattooing
LPtaW.............. West Baton Rouge Parish Library, Port Allen, LA [*Library symbol, Library of Congress*] (LCLS)
LPTB.............. London Passenger Transport Board
LPTB.............. Low-Pressure Turbine [*on a ship*] (DS)
LPTD.............. Linear Programmed Thermal Degradation [*Instrumentation*]
LPTD.............. Long Play Talkdown
LPTD-MS.............. Linear Programmed Thermal Degradation - Mass Spectroscopy [*Instrumentation*]
LPTF.............. Low-Power Test Facility [*Nuclear energy*]
LPTH.............. LightPath Technologies, Inc. [*NASDAQ symbol*] (SAG)
LPTHA.............. LightPath Technologes'A' [*NASDAQ symbol*] (TTSB)
LPTHU.............. LightPath Technologies Unit [*NASDAQ symbol*] (TTSB)
LPTHW.............. LightPath Technol Wrrt 'A' [*NASDAQ symbol*] (TTSB)
LPTHZ.............. LightPath Technol Wrrt 'B' [*NASDAQ symbol*] (TTSB)
LPTIS.............. Laguna Peak Tracking and Injection Station
LPTN.............. Tancos [*Portugal ICAO location identifier*] (ICLI)
LPTR.............. Line Printer [*Computer science*] (MSA)
LPTR.............. Livermore Pool Type Reactor
LPTS.............. Louisiana Presbyterian Theological Seminary
LPTTL.............. Low-Power Transistor-Transistor Logic
LPTTP.............. League of Professional Theatre Training Programs [*Defunct*] (EA)
LPTV.............. Large Payload Test Vehicle [*Air Force*]

LPTV............ Low-Power Television
LPTW........... Lake Providence, Texarkana & Western R. R. [AAR code]
LPU............. Language Processor Unit
LPu............. Late Punic (BJA)
LPU............. League of Prayer for Unity [Defunct] (EA)
LPU............. Least Publishable Unit [of research data]
LPU............. Legal Practices Update [A publication]
LPU............. Life Preserver Unit
LPU............. Limited Procurement, Urgent (MCD)
LP-U............ Limited Production - Urgent (AABC)
LPU............. Line Processing Unit
LPU............. Lions Philatelic Unit (EA)
LPU............. Liquid Processing Unit
LPU............. Low Pay Unit [British]
LPU............. Low-Power Unit (CAAL)
LPUG........... Lasers in Publishing Users Group (EA)
LPUL........... Least Positive Uplevel (IAA)
LPUU........... Linear Programming under Uncertainty [Computer science]
LPV............. Houston, TX [Location identifier FAA] (FAAL)
LPV............. Landing Platform Vehicle [Navy British]
LPV............. Landing Pontoon Vehicle [Military]
LPV............. Laser-Protective Visor (DOMA)
LPV............. Launching Point Vertical (NATG)
LPV............. Left Pulmonary Vein [Anatomy]
LPV............. Light Pen Value (IAA)
LPV............. Lightproof Vent [Technical drawings]
LPV............. Limiting Pressure Velocity (PDAA)
LPV............. Log Periodic V [Antenna]
LPV............. Lymphopathia Venereum (MAE)
LPV............. Lymphotropic Papovavirus
LPVP........... Left Posterior Ventricular Preexcitation [Medicine] (DMAA)
LPVR........... Vila Real [Portugal ICAO location identifier] (ICLI)
LPVS........... Link Packetized Voice Subsystem [Telecommunications] (ACRL)
LPVT........... Large Print Video Terminal
LPVZ........... Viseu [Portugal ICAO location identifier] (ICLI)
LPW............ Lateral Pharyngeal Wall [Medicine] (DMAA)
LPW............ Liberal Party of Wales [Political party]
LPW............ Linear Polarized Wave
LPW............ Local Point Warning [Military]
LPW............ Longitudinal Pressure Wave
lp/W........... Lumens per Watt (CET)
LPWA........... Local Public Works Act (OICC)
LPWG........... Lunar and Planetary Working Group [Aerospace] (IAA)
Lp-X........... Lipoprotein-X [Biochemistry] (MAE)
LPX............. Louisiana Pacific [NYSE symbol] (TTSB)
LPX............. Louisiana-Pacific Corp. [NYSE symbol] (SPSG)
LPYS........... Labour Party Young Socialists [British Political party]
LPZ............. La Paz [San Calixto] [Bolivia] [Seismograph station code, US Geological Survey] (SEIS)
LPZ............. Leipzig [City and district in East Germany] (ROG)
LPZ............. Low Population Zone (NRCH)
LPZ............. Ruston, LA [Location identifier FAA] (FAAL)
LQ............. Inland Empire Airlines [ICAO designator] (AD)
LQ............. Last Quarter [Moon phase]
LQ............. Laterality Quotient [Neuropsychology]
LQ............. Learning Quotient
LQ............. Lege Quaeso [Please Read] [Latin]
LQ............. Lens Quality [Optics]
LQ............. Letter Quality (PCM)
LQ............. Library Quarterly [A publication] (BRI)
LQ............. Limiting Quality (IAA)
LQ............. Linear Quadratic [Mathematics]
lq............. Liquid
LQ............. Longevity Quotient [Demography]
LQ............. Lordosis Quotients [Medicine]
Lq............. Love Wave [Earthquakes]
LQ............. Lowest Quadrant
LQ............. Lowest Quadrille
LQA............ La Quiaca [Argentina] [Seismograph station code, US Geological Survey Closed] (SEIS)
LQA............ La Quiaca [Argentina] [Geomagnetic observatory code]
LQA............ Link Quality Analysis (PDAA)
LQA............ Living Quarters Allowance [Air Force] (AFM)
LQD............ Liquid
LQD............ Liquid
LQD............ Lowest Quantity Determinable [Analytical chemistry]
LQDR........... Liquidator
LQFD........... Liquefied
LQG............ Linear Quadratic Gaussian (MCD)
LQG............ Lorain, OH [Location identifier FAA] (FAAL)
LQGLS......... Liquid in Glass
LQI............. La Quinta Inns [NYSE symbol] (SAG)
LQIV........... Linear, Quasi Invariant (PDAA)
LQK............ Pickens, SC [Location identifier FAA] (FAAL)
LQL............ Willoughby, OH [Location identifier FAA] (FAAL)
LQM........... Puerto Leguizamo [Colombia] [Airport symbol] (OAG)
LQMD.......... LifeQuest Medical [NASDAQ symbol] (TTSB)
LQMD.......... LifeQuest Medical, Inc. [NASDAQ symbol] (SAG)
LQMETR....... Liquidometer
LQN........... Boston, MA [Location identifier FAA] (FAAL)
LQN........... Qala-Nau [Afghanistan] [Airport symbol Obsolete] (OAG)
LQP........... Fort Collins, CO [Location identifier FAA] (FAAL)
LQP........... Letter Quality Printer [Computer science]
LQP........... Linear Quadratic Problem [Mathematics]
LQQ........... Chicago, IL [Location identifier FAA] (FAAL)

LQR............ Larned, KS [Location identifier FAA] (FAAL)
LQR............ Liquor
LQR............ Liquor
LQR............ Local Qualitative Radio [Ratings] (NTCM)
LQRR........... Low-Quality Recruiting Report (DNAB)
LQS............. Les Quatre Saisons [Record label] [France]
LQS............. Lock Haven State College, Lock Haven, PA [OCLC symbol] (OCLC)
LQST........... Leadership Q-Sort Test [Psychology]
LQT............ Linear Quantizer (IAA)
LQT............ Liverpool Quay Terms (DS)
LQT............ Los Queltehues [Chile] [Seismograph station code, US Geological Survey] (SEIS)
lqtx........... Liquitex (VRA)
LQU............ Quilmes Ind(Quinsa)ADS [NYSE symbol] (TTSB)
LQUT........... Queensland Unit and Group Titles Law and Practice [Australia A publication]
LQV............ Pennington Gap, VA [Location identifier FAA] (FAAL)
LQX............ Lehighton, PA [Location identifier FAA] (FAAL)
LQY............ Springfield, IL [Location identifier FAA] (FAAL)
LR.............. Dealer
Lr.............. King Lear [Shakespearean work]
LR.............. Labeled Release [Mars life detection experiment]
LR.............. Laboratory Reactor
LR.............. Laboratory Reagent
LR.............. Laboratory Reference (MAE)
LR.............. Laboratory Report
LR.............. Labor Reports (OICC)
LR.............. Labor Review [A publication]
LR.............. Labor Room [Obstetrics]
LR.............. Lactated Ringer [Medicine]
LR.............. Ladder Rung (AAG)
LR.............. Lady's Realm [A publication] (ROG)
Lr.............. Lancer [Military British] (DMA)
LR.............. Landing RADAR
LR.............. Landing Report (WDAA)
LR.............. Land Registry (DLA)
LR.............. Lapse Ratio [Insurance]
LR.............. Large Ring
LR.............. LASER-RADAR (MCD)
LR.............. Last Record (IAA)
LR.............. Last Renewal
LR.............. Latency Relaxation
LR.............. Lateral Rectus [Muscle] [Anatomy]
LR.............. Lateral Reversal [Typography] (DGA)
LR.............. Lateral Root [Botany]
IR.............. Laufend Rechnung [Current Account] [German Business term]
L/R............. Launch/Reentry (MCD)
LR.............. Launch Reliability (MCD)
LR.............. Launch Right (MCD)
LR.............. Lawesson Reagent [Organic chemistry]
LR.............. Law Record [1911-12] [India] [A publication] (DLA)
LR.............. Law Recorder [1827-38] [Ireland] [A publication] (DLA)
LR.............. Law Register [1880-1909] [A publication] (DLA)
Lr.............. Lawrencium [Original symbol, Lw, changed in 1963] [Chemical element]
LR.............. Law Reporter [1821-22] [A publication] (DLA)
LR.............. Layer Rating [British military] (DMA)
LR.............. Lay Reader (ROG)
LR.............. Leaching Rate [Nuclear energy] (NUCP)
LR.............. Leaders of Religion [A publication]
LR.............. Leaf Rust [Plant Pathology]
LR.............. Lear [ICAO aircraft manufacturer identifier] (ICAO)
LR.............. Leave Rations [Military]
LR.............. Leave to Appeal Refused [Legal term] (ADA)
LR.............. Ledger (ROG)
L - R.......... Left minus Right [Stereo signals] (NTCM)
L + R.......... Left plus Right [Stereo signals] (NTCM)
LR.............. Left Rear
LR.............. Left Rudder (MCD)
L-R............. Left to Right
LR.............. Left to Right (MAE)
L-R............. Left to Right (DMAA)
L/R............. Left to Right [Ratio] (DAVI)
LR.............. Legal Reserve (MHDW)
LR.............. Leicestershire Regiment [Military unit] [British]
LR.............. Lending Rate [Banking] (MHDW)
LR.............. Lent Reading (ROG)
LR.............. Lesion Expansion Rate [Pathology]
LR.............. Letter [Online database field identifier]
LR.............. Letter Report
LR.............. Letter Requirement
LR.............. Level Recorder
LR.............. Level Regulator (NRCH)
LR.............. Leviticus Rabbah (BJA)
LR.............. Liaison Report (AAG)
LR.............. Liaison Request (AAG)
LR.............. Liberia [ANSI two-letter standard code] (CNC)
LR.............. Library Review [A publication] (BRI)
LR.............. Licensing Registration [British]
L/R............. Life/Revisit [NASA] (KSC)
LR.............. Lifespan Resources [An association] (EA)
LR.............. Light Reaction (MAE)
LR.............. Light Reflex [Medicine] (AAMN)
LR.............. Likelihood Ratio [Statistics]
Lr.............. Limes Reacting Dose of Diphtheria Toxin [Medicine] (DMAA)

LR	Limited Recoverable (IEEE)
LR	Limit Register
LR	Lincoln Red [*Livestock terminology*]
LR	Lindblad Resonance [*Planetary science*]
LR	Linear Regression [*Mathematics*]
LR	Lineas Aereas Costarricenses, Sociedad Anonima (LACSA) [*Costa Rica*] [*ICAO designator*] (ICDA)
LR	Line Receiver
LR	Line Relay
LR	Link Resources, Inc. [*Vancouver Stock Exchange symbol*]
LR	Liquid Rocket
LR	Listing Requirement [*Investment term*]
LR	Little Rock [*Diocesan abbreviation*] [*Arkansas*] (TOCD)
LR	Living Room
LR	Lloyd's Register of Shipping
LR	Loading Ramp
LR	Load Ratio
LR	Load Rejection (NRCH)
LR	Load-Resistor Relay (MSA)
LR	Loan Rate [*Banking*]
L/R	Local/Remote [*Telecommunications*] (TEL)
LR	Lock Rail
LR	Lock Range (IAA)
L/R	Locus of Radius
LR	Logical Record
LR	Logistical Reassignment [*Military*] (AFIT)
LR	Logistical Requirement
LR	Logistic Regression [*Medicine*]
LR	Log Run [*Lumber*]
LR	London Rank [*Freemasonry*]
LR	Long Range
LR	Long Rifle
LR	Long Run [*Economics*]
LR	Louisiana Register [*A publication*] (AAGC)
LR	Louisiana Reports [*A publication*] (DLA)
LR	Lower (ADA)
LRAT	Lower Rail [*Typography*]
LR	Lower Right
LR	Lower Rule
lr	Low Rate Reverse [*Ecology*]
LR	Low Reduction (NITA)
LR	Low Register (IAA)
LR	Low Resistance (IAA)
LR	Low Risk
LR	Loyal Regiment [*Military British*]
LR	Lugger [*Ship's rigging*] (ROG)
LR	New Zealand Law Reports [*A publication*] (DLA)
LR	Ohio Law Reporter [*A publication*] (DLA)
LR	Radiolocation Land Station [*ITU designation*]
Lr	Rayleigh Wave [*Earthquakes*]
LR3	LASER Ranging Retroreflection [*Also, LRRR*] [*Initialism pronounced "LR-cubed" Apollo 11 experiment*] [*NASA*]
LR³	Logistics Readiness Rating Report [*DoD*]
LRA	Labor Research Association (EA)
LRA	Lace Research Association [*British*]
LRA	Lagged Reserve Accounting [*Banking*]
LRA	Landing Rights Airport [*US Customs*]
LRA	Larissa [*Greece*] [*Airport symbol*] (OAG)
LRA	LASER [*Gyro*] Reference Axis (IEEE)
LRA	Last Return Amount [*IRS*]
LRA	Launcher Relay Assembly [*Navy*] (CAAL)
LRA	Lawyers' Reports, Annotated [*A publication*] (DLA)
LRA	Lease Rental Agreement (MHDB)
LRA	Least Restrictive Alternative [*For the education of the handicapped*]
LRA	left Renal Artery [*Anatomy*] (DAVI)
LRA	Libertarian Republican Alliance (EA)
LRA	Library of Romance [*A publication*]
LRA	Light Replaceable Assemblies
LRA	Line Receiving Amplifier (MSA)
LRA	Lithuanian Regeneration Association (EA)
LRA	Little Red Air Service [*Canada ICAO designator*] (FAAC)
LRA	Little Rock [*Arkansas*] [*Seismograph station code, US Geological Survey Closed*] (SEIS)
LRA	Load Real Address (HGAA)
LRA	Load Reference Axis
LRA	Locked-Rotor Amperes (MSA)
LRA	Logical Record Access [*Computer science*] (MHDB)
LRA	Logical Record Address (NITA)
LRA	Long-Range Aviation [*Army*] (AABC)
LRA	Lord Ruthven Assembly [*An association*] (EA)
LRA	Louisiana Realtors Association (SRA)
LRA	Louisiana Restaurant Association (SRA)
LRA	Louisiana Retailers Association (SRA)
LRA	Lower Right Abdomen [*Injection site*]
LRA	Low Right Atrium [*Anatomy*]
LRA	North Carolina Union List of Serials for Community Colleges [*Library network*]
LRAA	Long-Range Air Army [*Former USSR*] (MCD)
LRAACA	Long-Range Air Antisubmarine Warfare Capable Aircraft (MCD)
LRAAM	Long Range Air-to-Air Missile [*Air Force*]
LRA & E	English Law Reports, Admiralty and Ecclesiastical [*A publication*] (DLA)
LRAAS	Long-Range Airborne ASW [*Antisubmarine Warfare*] System (MCD)
LRAC	English Law Reports, Appeal Cases [*A publication*] (DLA)
LRAC	Long-Run Average Costs [*Marketing*]
LRAD	Licentiate of the Royal Academy of Dancing [*British*]
LRADM	Long-Range Air Defense Missile (MCD)
LR Adm & Ecc	Law Reports, Admiralty and Ecclesiastical Cases [*1865-75*] [*A publication*] (DLA)
LR Adm & Eccl	Law Reports, Admiralty and Ecclesiastical Cases [*1865-75*] [*A publication*] (DLA)
LR Adm & Eccl (Eng)	Law Reports, Admiralty and Ecclesiastical Cases [*England*] [*A publication*] (DLA)
LRADP	Long-Range Active Duty Program [*Army*]
LRAF	Long-Range Air Force
LRALS	Long-Range Approach and Landing System (PDAA)
LRAM	Licentiate of the Royal Academy of Music [*British*] (EY)
LRAN	Local Regional Access Node (MCD)
LR Ann	Lawyers' Reports, Annotated [*A publication*] (DLA)
LRA NS	Lawyers' Reports, Annotated, New Series [*A publication*] (DLA)
LRAO	Logistics Review and Analysis Office [*US Army Defense Ammunition Center and School*]
LRAOP	Long-Range Aerospace Observation Platform
LRAP	Leucine-Rich Amelogenin Polypeptide [*Biochemistry of dental enamel*]
LRAP	Long-Range Acoustic Propagation
LR App	English Law Reports, Appeal Cases, House of Lords [*A publication*] (DLA)
LRAPP	Long-Range Acoustic Propagation Project
LR App Cas	English Law Reports, Appeal Cases, House of Lords [*A publication*] (DLA)
LR App Cas (Eng)	English Law Reports, Appeal Cases, House of Lords [*A publication*] (DLA)
LRAR	Arad [*Romania*] [*ICAO location identifier*] (ICLI)
LRaR	Richland Parish Library, Rayville, LA [*Library symbol Library of Congress*] (LCLS)
LRAS	Logistics Requirements Allocation Sheet (SSD)
LRAS	Long-Range Autonomous Submersible
LRAS	Lunar Module Replaceable Assembly [*NASA*] (IAA)
LRASM	Long-Range Air-to-Surface Missile (MCD)
LRASV	Long-Range Air-to-Surface Vessel (IAA)
LRAT	Lecithin-Retinol Acyltransferase [*An enzyme*]
LRAT	Long-Range Antitank [*Army*] (INF)
LRATC	Long-Run Average Total Costs [*Economics*]
LRATGW	Long-Range Antitank Guided Weapon [*British military*] (DMA)
LRB	Labour Relations Board [*Canada*]
LRB	Level Reference Base
LRB	Lissamine Rhodamine B [*Fluorescent dye*]
LRB	Load Request Block (IAA)
LRB	Local Reference Beam [*Holography*]
LRB	London Rifle Brigade [*Military unit*] [*British*]
LRB	Loyalty Review Board [*Abolished, 1953*] [*Civil Service Commission*]
LRBB	Bucuresti [*Romania*] [*ICAO location identifier*] (ICLI)
LRBC	Bacau [*Romania*] [*ICAO location identifier*] (ICLI)
LRBC	Lift-Right Bounded-Context [*Computer science*] (MHDI)
LRBC	Lloyd's Registry Building Certificate
LRBF	Longitudinal Ridge of Basal Fold
LRBFM	National Labor Relations Board Field Manual
LRBG	Law Reports, British Guiana [*1890-1955*] [*A publication*] (DLA)
LRBM	Baia Mare/Tauti Magherusi [*Romania*] [*ICAO location identifier*] (ICLI)
LRBM	Long-Range Ballistic Missile
LRBR	Long-Range Ballistic Rocket
LRBR	Long-Range Bombardment Round
LRBS	Bucuresti/Baneasa [*Romania*] [*ICAO location identifier*] (ICLI)
LRBS	LASER Ranging Bombing System
LR Burm	Law Reports, British Burma [*A publication*] (DLA)
LR Burma	Law Reports, British Burma [*A publication*] (DLA)
LRC	Labour Representation Committee [*Northern Ireland*] (PPW)
LRC	Labrador Retriever Club (EA)
LRC	Langley Research Center [*NASA*]
LRC	Launch/Recovery Visual Landing Aid Change (MCD)
LRC	Law Reform Commission [*Canada*]
LRC	Law Reform Committee (DLA)
LRC	Leaders Reaction Course [*Military training*] (INF)
LRC	Lead Resistance Compensator
LRC	Learning Resource Center
LRC	Lenoir Rhyne College [*Hickory, NC*]
LRC	Lesbian Resource Center (EA)
LRC	Level Recording Controller
LRC	Lewis Research Center [*NASA*]
LRC	Liberia Refining Co.
LRC	Library Research Center [*University of Illinois*] (IID)
LRC	Light Rapid Comfortable [*Train system*]
LRC	Light Reflective Capacitor [*Electronics*] (DA)
LRC	Light Repair Car [*British*]
LRC	Limnological Research Center [*University of Minnesota*] [*Research center*] (RCD)
LRC	Linear Responsibility Charting (PDAA)
LRC	Lineas Aereas Costarricenses SA [*Costa Rica*] [*ICAO designator*] (FAAC)
LRC	Line Rectifier Circuit
LRC	Linguistics Research Center [*University of Texas at Austin*] [*Research center*] (RCD)
LRC	Lionel Railroader Club (EA)
LRC	Lipid Research Center [*Washington University*] [*Research center*] (RCD)
LRC	Lipid Research Clinics
LRC	Load Ratio Control (MSA)
LRC	Locomotor Respiratory Coupling [*Physiology*]

LRC............	Lode Resources Corp. [*Vancouver Stock Exchange symbol*]
LRC............	Logistics Readiness Center [*Air Force*]
LRC............	Logistics to Relay Converter (MCD)
LRC............	London Rowing Club
LRC............	Lone Oak Road [*California*] [*Seismograph station code, US Geological Survey*] (SEIS)
LRC............	Longitudinal Redundancy Check [*Computer science*]
LRC............	Long-Range Climb (MCD)
LRC............	Long Range Communications (NTCM)
LRC............	Long-Range Cruise [*Aircraft speed*]
LRC............	Lori Corp. [*AMEX symbol*] (SPSG)
LRC............	Lower Rib Cage [*Anatomy*]
LRC............	Luneberg Rapid Commutator [*Physics*]
LRC............	Lung Rate Counter
LRC............	Lutheran Resources Commission (EA)
LRCA.........	Law Reports, Court of Appeals of New Zealand [*A publication*] (DLA)
LRCA.........	Lithuanian Roman Catholic Alliance of America [*Later, LCA*] (EA)
LRCA.........	Long-Range Combat Aircraft
LRCA.........	Lop Rabbit Club of America (EA)
LRCC	English Law Reports, Crown Cases Reserved [*2 vols.*] [*1865-75*] [*A publication*] (DLA)
LRCC	Library Resources Coordinating Committee of the University of London (NITA)
LRCC	Longitudinal Redundancy Check Character [*Telecommunications*] (TEL)
LRCC (Eng)...	English Law Reports, Crown Cases Reserved [*2 vols.*] [*1865-75*] [*A publication*] (DLA)
LRCCM	Long-Range Conventional Cruise Missile (MCD)
LRCCPPT	Lipid Research Clinics Coronary Primary Prevention Trial [*Cardiology*]
LRCCR	Law Reports, Crown Cases Reserved [*England*] [*A publication*] (DLA)
LRCD	Linear Rule of Cumulative Damage (PDAA)
LRCE	LASER Relay Communication Equipment
LRCE...........	Little Rock Cotton Exchange [*Defunct*]
LRCFA	Lithuanian Roman Catholic Federation of America (EA)
LR Ch	Law Reports, Chancery Appeal Cases [*England*] [*A publication*] (DLA)
LR Ch App ...	Chancery Appeal Cases [*1865-75*] [*A publication*] (DLA)
LR Ch D	English Law Reports, Chancery Division [*A publication*] (DLA)
LR Ch D (Eng)...	Law Reports, Chancery Division, English Supreme Court of Judicature [*A publication*] (DLA)
LR Ch Div (Eng)...	Law Reports, Chancery Division, English Supreme Court of Judicature [*A publication*] (DLA)
LR Ch (Eng)...	Law Reports, Chancery Appeal Cases [*England*] [*A publication*] (DLA)
LRCI............	Legal Research Center [*NASDAQ symbol*] (TTSB)
LRCI............	Legal Research Center, Inc. [*NASDAQ symbol*] (SAG)
LRCK	Constanta/M. Kogalniceau [*Romania*] [*ICAO location identifier*] (ICLI)
LRCL...........	Cluj-Napoca/Someseni [*Romania*] [*ICAO location identifier*] (ICLI)
LRCL...........	Long-Range Chemical LASER (MCD)
LRCM..........	Licentiate of the Royal College of Music [*British*]
LRCM..........	Long-Range Cruise Missile [*Navy*]
LRCNSW......	Law Reform Commission of New South Wales [*Australia*]
LRCO..........	Limited Remote [*or Radio*] Communication Outlet
LRCO..........	Long-Range Capability Objective [*Air Force*]
LRCP	Laboratory Research Cooperative Program [*Scientific Services Program*] [*Army*] (RDA)
LRCP	Law Reports, Common Pleas [*1865-75*] [*England*] [*A publication*] (DLA)
LRCP	Licentiate of the Royal College of Physicians [*British*]
LRCP	Long-Range Construction Program [*Military*]
LRCP & S ...	Licentiate of the Royal College of Physicians and the College of Surgeons of Edinburgh, and of the Faculty of Physicians and Surgeons of Glasgow (ROG)
LRCP & SI ...	Licentiate of the Royal College of Physicians and Surgeons of Ireland (AAMN)
LRCPD	English Law Reports, Common Pleas Division [*A publication*] (DLA)
LRCP Div.....	Law Reports, Common Pleas Division [*England*] [*A publication*] (DLA)
LRCP Div (Eng)...	English Law Reports, Common Pleas Division [*A publication*] (DLA)
LRCPE	Licentiate of the Royal College of Physicians (Edinburgh)
LRCP (Eng)...	Law Reports, Common Pleas [*England*] [*A publication*] (DLA)
LRCPI	Licentiate of the Royal College of Physicians of Ireland
LRCP Irel.....	Licentiate of the Royal College of Physicians of Ireland
LRCPLA	Lithuanian Roman Catholic Priests' League of America (EA)
LRCPSGlasg...	Licentiate of the Royal College of Physicians and Surgeons of Glasgow (DI)
LRCR	Longitudinal Redundancy Check Register [*Telecommunications*] (IAA)
LR Cr Cas Res...	Law Reports, Crown Cases Reserved [*England*] [*A publication*] (DLA)
LRCS	Caransebes/Caransebes [*Romania*] [*ICAO location identifier*] (ICLI)
LRCS	LASER RADAR Cross Section
LRCS	League of Red Cross and Red Crescent Societies [*Switzerland*] (EA)
LRCS	League of Red Cross Societies
LRCS	Licentiate of the Royal College of Surgeons [*British*]
LRCS	Lincoln Red Cattle Society [*British*] (DBA)
LRCS	Load Relief Control System
LRCSA	Lincoln Red Cattle Society of Australia
LRCSE	Licentiate of the Royal College of Surgeons (Edinburgh)
LRCS (Edin)...	Licentiate of the Royal College of Surgeons (Edinburgh) (DI)
LRCSI	Licentiate of the Royal College of Surgeons in Ireland
LRCS Irel.....	Licentiate of the Royal College of Surgeons in Ireland

LRCSOW......	Long-Range Conventional Standoff Weapon [*Military*]
LRCSW	Long-Range Conventional Standoff Weapon (MCD)
LRCT	Licentiate of the Royal Conservatory of Toronto [*Canada*]
L/RCU	Local/Remote Control Unit
LRCU	Logic Refresh Control Unit
LRCV	Craiova [*Romania*] [*ICAO location identifier*] (ICLI)
LRCVS	Licentiate of the Royal College of Veterinary Surgeons [*British*]
LRC-W.........	Lutheran Resources Commission - Washington [*Later, LRC*] (EA)
LRCX	Lam Research [*NASDAQ symbol*] (TTSB)
LRCX	Lam Research Corp. [*NASDAQ symbol*] (SAG)
LRD	Labelled RADAR Display (PDAA)
LRD	Labour Research Department [*Trade union*] [*British*]
LRD	Landing and Recovery Division [*NASA*]
LRD	Laredo [*Texas*] [*Airport symbol*] (OAG)
LRD	Laredo Air, Inc. [*ICAO designator*] (FAAC)
LRD	LASER Ranger and Designator (MCD)
LRD	Launch Readiness Demonstration [*NASA*] (KSC)
LRD	Lightning and Radio-Emission Detector [*Instrumentation*]
LRD	Living Related Donor [*Medicine*]
LRD	Living Renal Donor [*Nephrology*] (DAVI)
LRD	Logistics Requirements Determination (MCD)
LRD	Long-Range Data [*RADAR*]
LRD	Long-Reach Detonator [*Explosive*]
LRD	Lord River Gold [*Vancouver Stock Exchange symbol*]
LRD	Lysinated Rhodamine Dextran [*Cytology*]
LRDC	Land Resources Development Centre [*British*] (ARC)
LRDC	Learning Research and Development Center [*University of Pittsburgh*] [*Research center*]
LRDCT	Linear Rotary Differential Capacitance Transducer [*Instrumentation*]
LRDD	Limited Rights to Delivered Data
LRDE	Long-Run Deal Effect [*Marketing*]
LRDG	Learning Resources Development Group [*British*] (DBA)
LRDG	Long Range Desert Group [*British Army*] [*World War II*]
LR Dig	Law Reports Digest [*A publication*] (DLA)
LRDL	Longitudinal Ridge of Dorsal Lip
LRDMM	Long-Range Dual-Mission Missile (MCD)
LRDP	Long-Range Development Program (IAA)
LRDR	Last Revision Date Routine
LRDS	LASER Ranging and Designation System [*Military*] (CAAL)
LRDSB	Left Minus Right Double Sideband (IAA)
LRDT	Laboratory of Reproductive and Developmental Toxicology (GNE)
LRDT	Living Related Donor Transplant [*Medicine*] (DMAA)
LRDU	Long-Range Development Unit
LRE	Lafayette Radio Electronics Corp.
LRE	Latest Revised Estimate (MCD)
LRE	Law-Related Education (AEE)
LRE	Least Restrictive Environment [*For the education of the handicapped*]
LRE	Leukemic Reticuloendotheliosis [*Medicine*] (AAMN)
LRE	Library Resources Exhibition [*British*]
LRE	Licentiate in Religious Education
LRE	Life Re [*NYSE symbol*] (TTSB)
LRE	Life Real Estate [*NYSE symbol*] (SPSG)
LRE	Light Responsive Element [*Chemistry*]
LRE	Liquid Rocket Engine
LRE	Local Resource Enhancement [*Biology*]
LRE	Logistics Readiness Elements (MCD)
LRE	Longreach [*Australia Airport symbol*] (OAG)
LRE	Lossless Reciprocal Embedding (IAA)
LRE	Low Rate Encoding [*Telecommunications*] (LAIN)
LRE	Lunar Retrograde Engine [*NASA*] (KSC)
LREA..........	Law Reports, East Africa [*A publication*] (DLA)
LRE & I App ...	Law Reports, House of Lords, English and Irish Appeals [*1866-75*] [*A publication*] (DLA)
LREB..........	London Regional Examining Board [*British*] (AIE)
L Rec	Law Recorder [*Dublin, Ireland*] [*A publication*] (DLA)
LREC..........	Liaison Residency Endorsement Committee [*RRCEM*] [*Superseded by*] (EA)
LRECL.........	Logical Records of Fixed Length (MCD)
L Rec NS	Law Recorder, New Series [*Ireland*] [*A publication*] (DLA)
L Record......	Law Recorder [*Dublin, Ireland*] [*A publication*] (DLA)
L Rec OS	Law Recorder, First Series [*Ireland*] [*A publication*] (DLA)
LREDA........	Liberal Religious Educators Association (EA)
LREE	Light Rare Earth Elements [*Chemistry*]
LREG	Leading Regulator [*British*]
LREH	Low-Renin Essential Hypertension [*Medicine*]
LREI...........	Life Role Expectations Inventory (EDAC)
LREM(A)	Leading Radio Electrical Mechanic (Air) [*British military*] (DMA)
LR Eng & Ir App...	Law Reports, English and Irish Appeals [*1866-75*] [*A publication*] (DLA)
L Rep..........	Carolina Law Repository (Reprint) [*North Carolina*] [*A publication*] (DLA)
L Rep Mont...	Law Reporter, Montreal [*A publication*] (DLA)
L Repos.......	Law Repository [*A publication*] (DLA)
LR Eq	English Law Reports, Equity [*1866-75*] [*A publication*] (DLA)
LR Eq (Eng)...	English Law Reports, Equity [*1866-75*] [*A publication*] (DLA)
L-RERP	Long-Range Effects Research Program [*Marine science*] (OSRA)
L-RERP	Long-Range Effects Research Program (USDC)
LRES	Letters
LRES..........	Linear Rocket Engine System (PDAA)
LRES..........	Long-Range Earth Sensor
LRES..........	Low Rigid Frame
L Rev & Quart J...	Law Review and Quarterly Journal [*London*] [*A publication*] (DLA)
L Rev Dig	Law Review Digest [*A publication*] (DLA)
L Rev U Detroit...	Law Review, University of Detroit [*A publication*] (DLA)

LREW........... Long-Range Early Warning (NATG)
LREWP .... Long-Range Electronic Warfare Plan [Military] (CAAL)
LREWS .... Long-Range Early Warning System (NATG)
LR Ex........... English Law Reports, Exchequer [1866-75] [A publication] (DLA)
LR Ex Cas... English Law Reports, Exchequer [1866-75] [A publication] (DLA)
LR Exch ...... English Law Reports, Exchequer [1866-75] [A publication] (DLA)
LR Exch D .... English Law Reports, Exchequer Division [A publication] (DLA)
LR Exch Div.. Law Reports, Exchequer Division [England] [A publication] (DLA)
LR Exch Div (Eng)... English Law Reports, Exchequer Division [A publication]
                 (DLA)
LR Exch (Eng)... English Law Reports, Exchequer [1866-75] [A publication] (DLA)
LR Ex D .... Law Reports, Exchequer Division [England] [A publication] (DLA)
LR Ex Div .... English Law Reports, Exchequer Division [A publication] (DLA)
LRF.............. Jacksonville, AR [Location identifier FAA] (FAAL)
LRF.............. Ladle Refining Furnace [Nuclear energy] (NUCP)
LRF.............. LASER RADAR Fuze
LRF.............. LASER Range-Finder
LRF.............. Last Return Filed [IRS]
LRF.............. Late Renal Failure [Medicine]
LRF.............. Latex and Resorcinol Formaldehyde
LRF.............. Launch Rate Factor
LRF.............. Lepidoptera Research Foundation (EA)
LRF.............. Lincoln Resign Formulation
LRF.............. Liquid Rocket Fuel (MCD)
LRF.............. Liver Residue Factor [Molybdenum] [Medicine]
LRF.............. London Regional Federation [League of Nations Union]
LRF.............. Long-Range Facility [Telecommunications] (TEL)
LRF.............. Long-Range Flight
LRF.............. Low Refraction Layer
LRF.............. Lumber Recovery Factor
LRF.............. Luteinizing-Hormone Releasing Factor [Also, GnRF, GnRH, LH-RF,
                 LH-RH, LH-RH/FSH-RH, LRH] [Endocrinology]
LRFAX .... Low-Resolution Facsimile [Telecommunications] (TEL)
LRFC............ LASER Range-Finder Controller (MCD)
LRF/D.......... LASER Range-Finder/Designator (MCD)
LRFG .... Low-Range Force Gauge
LRFI............. League for Religious Freedom in Israel [Later, American Friends of
                 Religious Freedom in Israel] (EA)
LRF/MTR ..... LASER Range-Finder and Marked Target Receiver (MCD)
LRFPS .... Licentiate of the Royal Faculty of Physicians and Surgeons [British]
LRFPS(G)..... Licentiate of the Royal Faculty of Physicians and Surgeons, Glasgow
LRFS........... Long-Range Forecasting System (TEL)
LRF/SSC ..... LASER Ranger Finder/Solid State Computer (MCD)
LRFT............ Left Rear Fluid Temperature [Brake system] [Automotive
                 engineering]
LRG .... Land Resources Group
LRG .... Landscape Research Group [Lutterworth, Leicestershire, England]
                 (EAIO)
LRG .... Leucine-Rich Glycoprotein
LRG .... License Review Group [Nuclear energy] (NRCH)
LRG .... Lincoln, ME [Location identifier FAA] (FAAL)
LRG .... Liquefied Refinery Gas
LRG .... Logistic Review Group [Military] (CAAL)
LRG .... Long Range
LRG .... Long-Range Guidance (MCD)
LRG .... Lorgues [France] [Seismograph station code, US Geological
                 Survey] (SEIS)
LRGB .... Long-Range Guided Bomb (MCD)
LRGPP .... Long-Range Generation Planning Problem [Energy]
LRH .... La Rochelle [France] [Airport symbol] (OAG)
LRh .... Liquid Rheostat
LRH .... Luteinizing-Hormone Releasing Hormone [Also, GnRF, GnRH, LH-
                 RF, LH-RH, LH-RH/FSH-RH, LRF] [Endocrinology]
LRHL .... Law Reports, English and Irish Appeals and Peerage Claims, House
                 of Lords [England] [A publication] (DLA)
LRHL (Eng)... Law Reports, English and Irish Appeals and Peerage Claims, House
                 of Lords [England] [A publication] (DLA)
LRHL Sc ...... English Law Reports, House of Lords, Scotch and Divorce Appeal
                 Cases [1866-75] [A publication] (DLA)
LRHL Sc App Cas... Law Reports, House of Lords, Scotch and Divorce Appeal
                 Cases [1866-75] [A publication] (DLA)
LRHL Sc App Cas (Eng)... English Law Reports, House of Lords, Scotch and
                 Divorce Appeal Cases [1866-75] [A publication] (DLA)
LRHS .... Large Radioisotope Heat Source [NASA] (IAA)
LRHS .... Longitudinal Retirement History Survey [Social Security
                 Administration] (GFGA)
LRHSC......... Large Radioisotope Heat Source Capsule [NASA] (KSC)
LRI.............. Big Lost River [Idaho] [Seismograph station code, US Geological
                 Survey Closed] (SEIS)
LRI.............. Lawndale Railway & Industrial Co. [Terminated AAR code]
LRI.............. Learning Resources Institute (EA)
LRI.............. LeaRonal, Inc. [NYSE symbol] (SPSG)
LRI.............. Left-Right Indicator
LRI.............. Legal Resource Index [Information Access Corp.] [Bibliographic
                 database] [Information service or system] (IID)
LRI.............. Library Resources, Inc. [Subsidiary of Encyclopaedia Britannica]
Lrl.............. Library Resources, Incorporated, Chicago, IL [Library symbol Library
                 of Congress] (LCLS)
LRI.............. Lighting Research Institute (EA)
LRI.............. Limited Range Intercept [Telecommunications Navy] (ANA)
LRI.............. Literature and Religion of Israel [A publication]
LRI.............. Longboat Resources, Inc. [Vancouver Stock Exchange symbol]
LRI.............. Long-Range Indicator
LRI.............. Long-Range Input (CET)
LRI.............. Long-Range Inspector

LRI.............. Long-Range Interceptor
LRI.............. Long-Range International (DOMA)
LRI.............. Long-Range RADAR Input
LRI.............. Lorica [Colombia] [Airport symbol] (AD)
LRI.............. Lower Respiratory Infection [Medicine]
LRIA............ English Law Reports, Indian Appeals [A publication] (DLA)
LRIA............ Iasi [Romania] [ICAO location identifier] (ICLI)
LRIA............ Level Removable Instrument Assembly [Nuclear energy] (IEEE)
LRIBA .... Licentiate of the Royal Institute of British Architects
LRIC .... Licentiate of the Royal Institute of Chemistry [British]
LRIC .... Long-Run Incremental Cost [Business term] (ADA)
LRIM .... Long-Range Input Monitor [RADAR]
LR Ind App... English Law Reports, Indian Appeals [A publication] (DLA)
LR Ind App Supp... English Law Reports, Indian Appeals, Supplement
                 [A publication] (DLA)
LR Indian App... English Law Reports, Indian Appeals [A publication] (DLA)
LR Indian App (Eng)... English Law Reports, Indian Appeals [A publication] (DLA)
LRINF .... Longer-Range Intermediate-Range Nuclear Forces
LRIP............ Language Research in Progress (DIT)
LRIP............ Liberia Research and Information Project (EA)
LRIP............ Long-Range Impact Point (MUGU)
LRIP............ Low-Rate Initial Production (RDA)
L Ripuar ...... Law of the Ripuarians [A publication] (DLA)
LRIr............ Law Reports, Ireland [1878-1893] [A publication]
LR Ir .... Law Reports, Irish [A publication] (DLA)
LRIR .... Limb Radiance Inversion Radiometer
LRIR .... Low-Resolution Infrared Radiometer
LRIRR .... Low-Resolution Infrared Radiometer (MSA)
LRIS .... Low Resolution Imaging Spectrograph [Instrumentation]
LRIS .... Low Resolution Imaging Spectrograph [Instrumentation]
LRJ .... Lemars, IA [Location identifier FAA] (FAAL)
LRK .... Kenya Law Reports [A publication] (DLA)
LRK .... LASER Research Kit
LRKB .... English Law Reports, King's Bench Division [1901-52]
                 [A publication] (DLA)
LRKB .... Quebec Official Reports, King's Bench [A publication] (ILCA)
LRL .... Lawrence Radiation Laboratory [Livermore] [Later, Lawrence
                 Livermore Laboratory University of California]
LRL .... Leakage Resistance Limit
LRL .... Light Railway Loads [British]
LRL .... Limited Raman LASER
LRL .... Lincoln Research Laboratory
LRL .... Linguistics Research Laboratory [Gallaudet College] [Research
                 center] (RCD)
LRL .... Linking Relocating Loader
LRL .... Livermore Research Laboratory [University of California] (KSC)
LRL .... Logical Record Length
LRL .... Logical Record Location
LRL .... Lunar Receiving Laboratory [NASA]
LRL .... Lunar Research Laboratory [NASA] (DAVI)
LRL .... Tulane University, Law Library, New Orleans, LA [OCLC symbol]
                 (OCLC)
LR/LD .... Line Receiver/Line Driver (MCD)
LRLEI .... League for Religious Labor in Eretz Israel (EA)
LRLF........... Local Radio Luminosity Function [Cosmology]
LRLG .... Long-Range Logistics Guidance [Air Force]
LRL-L......... Lawrence Radiation Laboratory, Livermore [Later, Lawrence
                 Livermore Laboratory] [University of California]
LRLL .... Longitudinal Ridge of Lateral Lip
LRLM........... Lower Reject Limit Median (SAA)
LRLT........... Left Rear Lining Temperature [Brake system] [Automotive
                 engineering]
LRLTRAN ..... Lawrence Radiation Laboratory FORTRAN [Programming language]
                 [1961] (CSR)
LRLTRAN ..... Lawrence Radiation Laboratory Translator (IEEE)
LRM............ Labor Relations Reference Manual [A publication] (DLA)
LRM............ Land Resources Management (MCD)
LRM............ La Rassegna Musicale [A publication]
LRM............ La Romana [Dominican Republic] [Airport symbol] (OAG)
LRM............ Latching Relay Matrix
LRM............ Lead Reactor Manufacturer (NRCH)
LRM............ Leaflet Rolling Machine [PSYOP] (RDA)
LRM............ Least Recently Used Master [Computer science]
LRM............ Left Radical Mastectomy [Medicine] (MAE)
LRM............ Lightweight Ramjet Missile (MCD)
LRM............ Limited Register Machine
LRM............ Line Replacement Module
LRM............ Liquid Reaction Molding
LRM............ Liquid Rocket Motor (KSC)
LRM............ Logarithmic Radiation Monitor (NRCH)
LRM............ Logarithmic Ratio Module
LRM............ Long-Range Missile Launcher
LRM............ Lower Reject Limit Median
LRM............ Lunar Reconnaissance [or Rendezvous] Mission [Aerospace]
LRM............ Lunar Reconnaissance Module [Aerospace]
LR Mad........ Indian Law Reports, Madras Series [A publication] (DLA)
LRMC.......... Lloyd's Refrigerating Machinery Certificate
LRMC.......... Long-Run Marginal Costs
LRMG .... Hughes Lockless Rifle/Machine Gun (MCD)
LR Misc D ... Law Reports, Miscellaneous Division [A publication] (DLA)
LRML........... Long-Range Missile Launcher [Military] (IAA)
LRMP.......... Last Regular Menstrual Period [Gynecology] (DMAA)
LRMP.......... Legacy Resource Management Program (DOMA)
LRMP.......... Long-Range Maritime Patrol [Aircraft] (NATG)
LRMS.......... Library Routine Management System

LRMTS.........	LASER Range-Finder and Marked Target Seeker (MCD)
LRMV.........	Lilac Ring Mottle Virus [*Plant pathology*]
LRN	Long-Range Navigation
LRN	Long Reference Number
LRN	LORAN [*Long-Range Aid to Navigation*]
LRNA	Laws Relating to the Navy Annotated [*Military law*]
LRNAV	Long Range Navigation [*FAA*] (TAG)
LRNBA	La Raza National Bar Association (EA)
LRNC	Long Reference Number Code
LRND	Left Radical Neck Dissection [*Surgical procedure*] (DAVI)
LRNG	Learning
LRNG	Learning Co. [*NASDAQ symbol*] (SAG)
LrngCo.......	Learning Co. [*Associated Press*] (SAG)
LrnHaus......	Lernout & Hauspie Speech Products [*Associated Press*] (SAG)
LRNOD........	Long-Range Night Observation Device [*Army*] (AABC)
LRNR	Low-Resolution Non-Scanning Radiometer (MCD)
LRNS	Long-Range Navigation System [*Aviation*]
LRNS	Nova Scotia Law Reports [*A publication*] (DLA)
LRNSW.......	Law Reports, New South Wales Supreme Court [*A publication*] (DLA)
LrnTree.......	Learning Tree International, Inc. [*Associated Press*] (SAG)
LRNZ	Law Reports, New Zealand [*A publication*] (DLA)
LRO	Laboratory Review Office [*Army*] (RDA)
LRO	Large Radio Observatory (KSC)
LRO	Lathrop, CA [*Location identifier FAA*] (FAAL)
LRO	Leading Radio Operator [*British military*] (DMA)
LRO	Logistics Readiness Officer [*Military*] (AABC)
LRO	Long-Range Objectives [*Navy*]
LRO	Long-Range Order
LRO	Low-Resistance Ohmmeter
LROA	Land Rover Owners Association (EA)
LROA USA ...	Land Rover Owners Association, USA (EA)
LROC	Libertarian Republican Organizing Committee [*Defunct*] (EA)
LROD	Long-Range Overwater Diffusion [*Experiment*] [*Marine science*] (OSRA)
LROD	Long-Range Overwater Diffusion [*Experiment*] (USDC)
LROD	Oradea [*Romania*] [*ICAO location identifier*] (ICLI)
LRO(G)	Leading Radio Operator (General) [*British military*] (DMA)
LROG	Long-Range Objectives Group [*Navy*] (MCD)
LROI	Legal Rate of Interest [*Business term*]
LROL	Laboratoire de Recherches en Optique et Laser [*Laval University*] [*Canada Research center*] (RCD)
LROP	Bucuresti/Otopeni [*Romania*] [*ICAO location identifier*] (ICLI)
LROP	Lower Radicular Obstetrical Paralysis [*Medicine*] (DMAA)
LROR	Low-Resolution Omnidirectional Radiometer (MCD)
LRO(W).......	Leading Radio Operator (Warfare) [*British military*] (DMA)
LRP	English Law Reports, Probate Division [*A publication*] (DLA)
LRP	Lancaster, PA [*Location identifier FAA*] (FAAL)
LRP	Large Repairs to Hull
LRP	Large Rotating Plug [*Nuclear energy*] (NRCH)
LRP	LASER Retinal Photocoagulator
LRP	Late Receptor Potential [*Photoreceptor*] [*Physiology*]
LRP	Latest Reporting Period [*Business term*]
LRP	Launching Reference Point
LRP	LDI [*Low Density Lipoprotein*] Receptor-Related Protein [*Biochemistry*]
LRP	League for the Revolutionary Party (EA)
LRP	Lebanese Revolutionary Party [*Political party*] (PD)
LRP	Lesbian Rights Project [*Later, NCLR*] (EA)
LRP	Lichen Ruber Planus (DMAA)
LRP	Limited Rate Production
LRP	Limited Reaction Processing [*Semiconductor technology*]
LRP	Liporotein Receptor-Related Protein [*Biochemistry*]
LRP	LM [*Lunar Module*] Replaceable Package [*NASA*]
LRP	Loan Repayment Program [*Department of Health and Human Services*] (GFGA)
LRP	Logical Record Processor (IAA)
LRP	Logistics Release Point [*Army*] (INF)
LRP	Long-Range Path (IEEE)
LRP	Long-Range Patrol [*Pronounced "lurp"*] [*Formerly, LRRP*] [*Army*] (AABC)
LRP	Long-Range Penetration
LRP	Long-Range Plans (NVT)
LRP	Low Rate Production (RDA)
LRP	Low Rigging Penalty [*IOR*] [*Yacht racing*]
LRPA	Little Rock Port Railroad [*AAR code*]
LRPA	Long-Range Patrol Aircraft (MCD)
LRP & D	Probate and Divorce Cases [*1865-75*] [*England*] [*A publication*] (DLA)
LRP & M	Law Reports, Probate and Matrimonial [*1866-75*] [*A publication*] (DLA)
LRPC	English Law Reports, Privy Council, Appeal Cases [*1866-75*] [*A publication*] (DLA)
LRPC	Lightweight Remote Procedure Call [*Computer science*]
LRPC	London Regional Passengers Committee [*British*] (ECON)
LRPC (Eng)...	English Law Reports, Privy Council, Appeal Cases [*1866-75*] [*A publication*] (DLA)
LRPD	Law Reports, Probate Division [*A publication*] (DLA)
LRP Div	English Law Reports, Probate, Divorce, and Admiralty Division [*A publication*] (DLA)
LRPDS	Long-Range Position-Determining System [*Army*] (RDA)
LRPE	Long-Range Procurement Estimate (PDAA)
LRPE	Long-Run Price Effect [*Marketing*]
LRPF	Liberal Religious Peace Fellowship (EA)
LRPG	Long-Range Penetration Group [*Military World War II*]
LRPG	Long-Range Proving Ground [*Air Force*]

LRPGD.........	Long-Range Proving Ground Division [*Air Force*]
LRPGR.........	Long-Range Planning Ground Rules (AAG)
LRP/GWU ...	Logistics Research Project, George Washington University
LRPL	Liquid Rocket Propulsion Laboratory [*Army*] (IEEE)
LRPLS	Long-Range Passive Location System (PDAA)
LRPP	Long-Range Propulsion Plan (MCD)
LRPPD	Long-Range Planning Purpose Document
LR Prob & M (Eng)...	English Law Reports, Probate, Divorce, and Admiralty Division [*A publication*] (DLA)
LR Prob Div...	English Law Reports, Probate, Divorce, and Admiralty Division [*A publication*] (DLA)
LR Prob Div (Eng)...	English Law Reports, Probate, Divorce, and Admiralty Division [*A publication*] (DLA)
LRPS	Licentiate of the Royal Photographic Society [*British*] (DBQ)
LRPS	Long-Range Planning Service [*Stanford Research Institute*] [*Assists businesses in investment activities*] (IID)
LRPS	Long-Range Positioning System
LRPSI	Long-Range Planning for School Improvement [*Pennsylvania*] (EDAC)
LRPT...........	Large Repair Parts Transporter (MCD)
LRPT...........	Longest Remaining Processing Time (PDAA)
LRQ	Lower Right Quadrant (MAE)
LRQB	English Law Reports, Queen's Bench Division [*1865-75*] [*A publication*] (DLA)
LRQB	Quebec Queen's Bench Reports [*Canada*] [*A publication*] (DLA)
LRQBD	English Law Reports, Queen's Bench Division [*1865-75*] [*A publication*] (DLA)
LRQB Div.....	English Law Reports, Queen's Bench Division [*1865-75*] [*A publication*] (DLA)
LRQB Div (Eng)...	English Law Reports, Queen's Bench Division [*1865-75*] [*A publication*] (DLA)
LRQB (Eng)...	English Law Reports, Queen's Bench Division [*1865-75*] [*A publication*] (DLA)
LR-QR	Letter Requirement - Quick Reaction [*Army*]
LRR	Labyrinthine Righting Reflex [*Physiology*]
LRR	Lagged Reserve Requirement [*Finance*]
LRR	Land-Rover Register 1947-1951 [*Petersfield, Hampshire, England*] (EAIO)
LRR	LASER Radiation Receiver
LRR	Launch Readiness Report [*or Review*] [*NASA*] (KSC)
LRR	Leucine-Rich Repeat [*Biochemistry*]
LRR	Leucine-Rich Repeats [*Genetics*]
LRR	Logistic Readiness Review [*Navy*]
LRR	Long-Range RADAR
LRR	Long-Range Reconnaissance (MCD)
LRR	Long-Range Requirements [*Navy*]
LRR	Long-Range Rocket (MUGU)
LRR	Longreach Resources Ltd. [*Vancouver Stock Exchange symbol*]
LRR	Long Reduced Rate [*Taxation*] (WDAA)
LRR	Long Regulatory Region [*Genetics*]
LRR	Loop Regenerative Repeater
LRR	Loss of Righting Reflex [*Medicine*]
LRR	Lot Rejection Report
LRR & MF	Long-Range Resource and Management Forecast
LRRC	Labor Relations and Research Center [*University of Massachusetts*]
LRRC	Land Resource Research Centre [*Canada*] (IRC)
LRRD	Long-Range Reconnaissance Detachment
LRRDAP.......	Long-Range Research, Development, and Acquisition Plan (RDA)
LRRI	Land Resources Research Institute [*Agriculture Canada*] [*Formerly, Soil Research Institute*] [*Research center*] (RCD)
LRRI	Long-Range Reference Retroreflectance Instrument [*Bicycle test*] [*National Institute of Standards and Technology*]
LRRM	Labor Relations Reference Manual [*Bureau of National Affairs*] [*A publication*] (DLA)
LRRM	Loss Ratio Reserve Method [*Insurance*]
lrRNA	Ribonucleic Acid, Light Ribosomal [*Biochemistry, genetics*]
LRRO	Land Revenue Records and Enrollments Office [*British*]
LRRP	Law Reports, Restrictive Practices Cases [*1958-72*] [*A publication*] (DLA)
LRRP	Long-Range Reconnaissance Patrol [*Pronounced "lurp"*] [*Later, LRP*] [*Army*] (AABC)
LRRP	Lowest Required Radiated Power
LRRPC	Restrictive Practices Cases [*1958-72*] [*England*] [*A publication*] (DLA)
LRRR	LASER Ranging Retroreflection [*Also, LR3*] [*Pronounced "LR-cubed" Apollo 11 experiment*] [*NASA*]
LRRS	Library Reports & Research Service, Inc. [*Information service or system*] (IID)
LRRS	Limited Remaining Radiation Service [*Unit*] [*Military*]
LRRS	Long-Range RADAR Site (OA)
LRRSA	Light Railway Research Society of Australia
LRRT	Library Research Round Table [*American Library Association*]
LRRT	Light Rail Rapid Transit [*TRB*] (TAG)
LR/RT	Long-Range Radiotelephone (DNAB)
LRS.............	Laboratory Recoil Simulator (MCD)
LRS.............	Laboratory Release System (MCD)
LRS.............	Labor Relations Specialist (AAGC)
LRS.............	Lactated Ringer's Solution [*Intravenous solution*]
LRS.............	Lake Reporting Service
LRS.............	Lamb-Retherford Shift [*Physics*]
LRS.............	Lander Radio Subsystem [*NASA*]
LRS.............	Lanyard Release Switch
LRS.............	Larder Resources, Inc. [*Toronto Stock Exchange symbol*]
LRS.............	Lares [*Puerto Rico*] [*Seismograph station code, US Geological Survey*] (SEIS)

LRS............ Large Ring Sparger [*Engineering*]
LRS............ LASER Raman Scattering
LRS............ LASER Raman Spectroscopy
LRS............ LASER Ranging System
LRS............ LASER Raster Scanner
LRS............ LASER Reflectance Spectrometer (SSD)
LRS............ Launch Recoil Simulator
LRS............ Laurinburg & Southern Railroad Co. [*AAR code*]
LRS............ Lawyer Referral Service
LRS............ League of Religious Settlements (EA)
LRS............ Legislative Reference Service [*Later, Congressional Research Service*] [*Library of Congress*]
LRS............ Level Recording Switch (NRCH)
LRS............ Library Reproduction Service, Microfilm Co. of California, Los Angeles, CA [*Library symbol Library of Congress*] (LCLS)
L/R/S .... Library Rubber Stamps [*Antiquarian book trade*]
LRS............ Lifetime Reproductive Success [*Demographics*]
LRS............ Light Radiation Sensor
LRS............ Light Repair Section [*British military*] (DMA)
LRS............ Light's Retention Scale [*Test*]
LRS............ Lightweight RADAR Set
LRS............ Limited Resources Specialty (AFM)
LRS............ Linear Referencing System [*FHWA*] (TAG)
LRS............ Linguistics Research System
LRS............ Liquid RADWASTE System (NRCH)
LRS............ Lloyd's Register of Shipping
LRS............ Logistics Requirements System [*Navy*]
LRS............ London Record Society [*British*] (ILCA)
LRS............ Long-Range Schedule (SAA)
LRS............ Long-Range Search
LRS............ Long-Range Study
LRS............ Long-Range Surveillance [*Military*] (INF)
LRS............ Lateral Reversed Superchron [*Geology*]
LRS............ Long Right Shift
LRS............ Low-Rate Station
LRSA .... Laboratoire de Recherche en Sciences de l'Administration [*Laval University*] [*Canada Research center*] (RCD)
LRSAGW...... Long-Range Surface-to-Air Guided Weapon (IAA)
LRSAM .... Long-Range Surface-to-Air Missile (NATG)
LRS & D App... Law Reports, Scotch and Divorce Appeals [*1866-75*] [*A publication*] (DLA)
LRS & TP .... Long-Range Science and Technology Plan [*Army*]
LRSB .... Sibiu/Turnisor [*Romania*] [*ICAO location identifier*] (ICLI)
LRSC .... Law Reports, New Zealand Supreme Court [*A publication*] (DLA)
LRSC .... Licentiate of the Royal Society of Chemistry [*British*] (DBQ)
LRSC .... Long-Range Surveillance Co. [*Military*] (INF)
LRSCA .... Land Remote Sensing Commercialization Act [*1984*]
LRSCA .... Large Retractable Solar Cell Array
LR Sc & D... English Law Reports, House of Lords, Scotch and Divorce Appeal Cases [*1866-75*] [*A publication*] (DLA)
LR Sc & D App... Scottish and Divorce Appeals [*1866-75*] [*A publication*] (DLA)
LR Sc & D App... Scottish and Divorce Cases before the House of Lords [*A publication*] (DLA)
LR Sc & Div... Scotch and Divorce Appeals [*1866-75*] [*A publication*] (DLA)
LR Sc App ... Law Reports, Scotch Appeals [*A publication*] (DLA)
LR Sc Div App... Law Reports, Scotch Appeals [*A publication*] (DLA)
LRSD .... Long-Range Surveillance Detachment [*Military*] (INF)
LRSDC .... Lakes Region Sled Dog Club (EA)
LR Sess Cas... English Law Reports, Sessions Cases [*A publication*] (DLA)
LRSF.......... Lactating Rat Serum Factor [*Immunology*]
LRSF.......... Liver Regenerating Serum Factor [*Medicine*] (DMAA)
LRSF.......... Long-Range Systems Forecast
LRSI.......... LifeRate Systems [*NQS*] (TTSB)
LRSI.......... LifeRate Systems, Inc. [*NASDAQ symbol*] (SAG)
LRSI.......... Long-Range SOF [*Special Operation Force*] Insertion (DOMA)
LRSI.......... Low-Temperature Reusable Surface Insulation (NASA)
LRSIFC .... Lori Robin Smith International Fan Club (EA)
LRSK .... Long-Range Station Keeping (NG)
LRSL .... Law Reports, Sierra Leone Series [*A publication*] (DLA)
LRSL .... Long-Range Surveillance Leader [*Military*] (INF)
LRSLA .... Long-Range Service Life Analysis (MCD)
LRSLP .... Lietuvos Revoliuciniu Socialistu Liaudininkai Partija [*Revolutionary Socialist Populists Party of Lithuania*] [*Political party*] (PPE)
LRSM........ Laboratory for Research on the Structure of Matter [*University of Pennsylvania*]
LRSM........ Licentiate of the Royal School of Music, London [*British*]
LRSM........ Long-Range Seismograph Measurements (MCD)
LRSM........ Satu Mare [*Romania*] [*ICAO location identifier*] (ICLI)
LRSO .... Long-Range Surveillance Outpost (MCD)
LRSOM .... Long-Range Stand-Off Missile
LRSOW .... Long-Range Conventional Standoff Weapon
LRSP .... Long-Range Strategic Planning (PDAA)
LRSR .... Liquid Redox Sulfur Recovery [*Processes for removing hydrogen sulfide from gases*]
LRSR .... Long-Range Sniper Rifle (PDAA)
LRSS .... Long-Range Strategic Studies [*Military*] (AFIT)
LRSS .... Long-Range Survey System [*Military*]
LR Stat .... English Law Reports, Statutes [*A publication*] (DLA)
LRSTPP .... Long-Range Scientific Technical Planning Program (NG)
LRSU .... Long-Range Surveillance Unit [*Military*] (INF)
LRSUBRS .... Long-Range Surveillance Unit Base Radio Station [*Military*] (INF)
LRSV .... Lychnis Ringspot Virus [*Plant pathology*]
LRSV .... Suceava/Salcea [*Romania*] [*ICAO location identifier*] (ICLI)
LRT............ LASER Range-Finder Theodolite
LRT............ Last Resort Target [*Military*]

LRT............ Launch, Recovery, and Transport [*Vehicle*]
LRT............ Lawrenceburg, TN [*Location identifier FAA*] (FAAL)
LRT............ Light Rail Transit
LRT............ Light Repair Truck [*British*]
LRT............ Likelihood Ratio Test [*Statistics*]
LRT............ LL&E Royalty Tr UBI [*NYSE symbol*] (TTSB)
LRT............ LL & E Royalty Trust UBI [*NYSE symbol*] (SPSG)
LRT............ Load Ratio Transformer (IAA)
LRT............ Local Leak Rate Test [*Nuclear energy*] (IEEE)
LRT............ Local Radiotherapy
LRT............ Loki Ranging Transponder
LRT............ London Reading Test [*Educational test*]
LRT............ London Regional Transport
LRT............ Long-Range Radiotelephone
LRT............ Long-Range Transport [*Navy British*]
LRT............ Long-Range Typhon [*Navy*] (NG)
LRT............ Long Ring Timer
LRT............ Lorentz Reciprocal Theorem
LRT............ Lorient [*France*] [*Airport symbol*] (OAG)
LRT............ Lower Respiratory Tract [*Medicine*]
LRTA........... Lath Renders' Trade Association [*A union*] [*British*]
LRTA........... Leisure, Recreation, and Tourism Abstracts [*Database*] [*Commonwealth Agricultural Bureaux International*] [*Information service or system*] (CRD)
LRTA........... Light Rail Transit Association [*Milton, Keynes, England*] (EAIO)
LRTAP......... Long-Range Transport of Atmospheric Pollutants
LRTC.......... Law Reform Commission of Tasmania [*Australia*]
LRTC.......... Tulcea/Cataloi [*Romania*] [*ICAO location identifier*] (ICLI)
LRTF.......... Linear Radial Transmission Filter [*Photography*]
LRTF.......... Long-Range Technical Forecast (IEEE)
LRTG......... Logistics Reassignment Task Group [*DoD*] (MCD)
LRTGT........ Last Resort Target [*Military*]
LRThD........ Lateral Reach-Through Device (PDAA)
LRTI.......... Lower Respiratory Tract Illness (DAVI)
LRTI.......... Lower Respiratory Tract Infection [*Medicine*] (ADA)
LRTL.......... Light Railway Transport League [*British*] (DCTA)
LRTM.......... Long-Range Training Mission [*Military*]
LRTM.......... Tirgu Mures/Vidrasau [*Romania*] [*ICAO location identifier*] (ICLI)
LRTNF........ Long-Range Theater Nuclear Force [*Military*]
LRTNW........ Long-Range Theater Nuclear Weapons [*Military*]
LRTP.......... Long-Range Technical Plan (PDAA)
LRTP.......... Long-Running Thermal Precipitation (DICI)
LRTR.......... Timisoara/Giarmata [*Romania*] [*ICAO location identifier*] (ICLI)
LRTRO........ Loaded Radial Tire Run-Out [*Automotive engineering*]
LRTS.......... LASER Ranging and Tracking System (RDA)
LRTS........... Library Resources & Technical Services [*Association for Library Collections and Technical Services*] [*American Library Association*]
LRTx .... Living Related Renal Transplantation [*Medicine*]
LRU .... Las Cruces [*New Mexico*] [*Airport symbol*] (OAG)
LRU .... Las Cruces, NM [*Location identifier FAA*] (FAAL)
LRU .... Least Recently Used [*Replacement algorithm*] [*Computer science*]
LRU .... Least Repairable Unit
LRU .... Least Replaceable Unit (IAA)
LRU .... Less than Release Unit [*Army*] (AABC)
LRU .... Line Removable Unit
LRU .... Line Replaceable Unit (AFM)
LRU .... Link Retraction Unit (KSC)
LRU .... Little Rock University [*Merged with University of Arkansas*]
LRU .... Lone Replaceable Unit (MCD)
LRU .... Lowest Repairable Unit (MCD)
LRU .... Lowest Replacement Unit (MCD)
LRU .... Tulane University, New Orleans, LA [*OCLC symbol*] (OCLC)
LRuL........ Louisiana Technical University, Ruston, LA [*Library symbol Library of Congress*] (LCLS)
LRuLP........ Lincoln Parish Library, Ruston, LA [*Library symbol Library of Congress*] (LCLS)
LRUP .... La Raza Unida Party (EA)
LRUPS........ Line Replaceable Unit Power Supply (MCD)
LRV.......... Lanarkshire Rifle Volunteers [*British military*] (DMA)
LRV.......... Lancashire Rifle Volunteers [*British military*] (DMA)
LRV.......... Launch Readiness Verification [*NASA*] (NASA)
LRV.......... Left Renal Vein [*Anatomy*] (DAVI)
LRV.......... Leirvogur [*Iceland*] [*Geomagnetic observatory code*]
LRV.......... Lifting Reentry Vehicle (MCD)
LRV.......... Light Rail Vehicle
LRV.......... Light Reconnaissance Vehicle [*Military*]
LRV.......... Light Recreational Vehicle [*Mitsubishi minivan*]
LRV.......... Little Rabbit Valley [*California*] [*Seismograph station code, US Geological Survey*] (SEIS)
LRV.......... Long-Range Video (MCD)
LRV.......... Lunar Rover [*or Roving*] Vehicle [*NASA*]
LRVEP........ League of Rural Voters Education Project (EA)
LRW.......... Labor Relations Week [*Bureau of National Affairs*] [*Information service or system*] (CRD)
LRW.......... London Radio Workshop [*Independent Local Radio*] [*British*]
LRWRO........ Loaded Radial Wheel Run-Out [*Automotive engineering*]
LRY.......... Lady Robyn Resources, Inc. [*Vancouver Stock Exchange symbol*]
LRY.......... Latching Relay (IAA)
LRY.......... Liberal Religious Youth
LRY.......... Liberty Property Trust [*NYSE symbol*] (SAG)
LS............ Labologists Society [*Farnborough, Hampshire, England*] (EAIO)
LS............ Laboratory System
LS............ Labor Service [*Military*]
L/S............ Lactose/Sucrose [*Ratio*]

LS	Lacus Somniorum [Lunar area]
LS	Lamellar Strip [Botany]
LS	Landesschuetzeneinheit [Regional defense force] [German military - World War II]
LS	Landing Ship
LS	Landing Side [Air Force]
LS	Landing Site (KSC)
LS	Land Service
LS	Land Surveying Program [Association of Independent Colleges and Schools specialization code]
LS	Land Surveyor
LS	Lange Sicht [Long Sight] [German]
LS	Language Specification (IEEE)
LS	Lantern Slide [Photography]
Is	Laos [MARC country of publication code Library of Congress] (LCCP)
LS	Lapped Seam (DNAB)
LS	Lasallian Sisters (Vietnam) (TOCD)
LS	LASER System
LS	Lastensegler; Lastensegelflugzeug [Cargo transport glider] [German military - World War II]
LS	Latch Side
LS	Lateral Septum
LS	Lateral Subsylvian Cortex [Neuroanatomy]
LS	Lateral Suspensor [Ligament] [Anatomy] (DAVI)
LS	Late Scramble [Reason for missed interception] [Military]
LS	Late Shock [Medicine]
LS	Launching System
LS	Launch Sequence (MCD)
LS	Launch Service
LS	Launch Set
LS	Launch Simulator (MUGU)
LS	Launch Site [NASA] (MCD)
LS	Launch Station (MCD)
LS	Law Society (WDAA)
LS	Law Student (DLA)
LS	Leaders of Science [A publication]
LS	Leading Seaman [Navy British]
LS	Leading Stoker
LS	Lead Sheet [Military]
LS	Leaf Spring [Automotive engineering]
L-S	Leap-Second
LS	Learning Step
LS	Lease
LS	Lease [Legal shorthand] (LWAP)
LS	Least Significant (IEEE)
LS	Least Squares [Mathematical statistics]
L/S	Lecithin/Sphingomyelin [Ratio] [Clinical chemistry]
LS	Lectori Salutem [Latin]
LS	Left Sacrum [Medicine] (KSC)
LS	Left Safety [Football] (DICI)
LS	Left Shift
LS	Left Side
LS	Left Sign (IAA)
LS	Legally Separated (MAE)
LS	Legal Scroll
LS	Le Gros Scouts [British military] (DMA)
LS	Leiomyosarcoma [Medicine]
LS	Length of Stroke
LS	Lepidopterists' Society
LS	Lesotho [ANSI two-letter standard code] (CNC)
LS	Less
LS	Lessing Society (EA)
LS	Letter Service
LS	Letter Signed [Manuscript descriptions]
Is	Letter Signed [Handwritten signature] (WDMC)
LS	Letter Stock
LS	Leukemia Society of America
LS	Level Setter
LS	Level Switch
LS	Library Science
LS	Library Search
LS	Library Services
LS	Licensed Surveyor [British] (ADA)
LS	Licentiate in Science
LS	Licentiate in Surgery
LS	Lifesaving Service [Coast Guard]
LS	Life Science (NASA)
LS	Life Support (AAG)
LS	Life System (MCD)
LS	Lighthouse Service [Coast Guard]
LS	Lighting Supervisor [Television]
LS	Lighting System
LS	Lightning Sensor [Aviation]
LS	Light Ship
LS	Light Source
LS	Light Sussex [Poultry]
LS	Light Switch
LS	Lignosulfonate [Pulp and paper processing]
LS	Like-Sexed
LS	Limbic System [Brain anatomy]
LS	Limestone [Petrology] (AAG)
LS	Liminal [or Least] Sensation [Psychology]
LS	Limit Switch [Electronics]
LS	Line Scan (DEN)
LS	Line-Sequential (IAA)

LS	Line Speed
L/S	Lines per Second (WDAA)
LS	Line Stretcher
LS	Line Switch [Telecommunications] (TEL)
LS	Linker Scanning [Mutants] [Genetics]
LS	Linksozialisten [Left Socialists] [Austria Political party] (PPE)
LS	Link State (ACRL)
LS	Linnean Society [Australia]
LS	Liquid Scintillation [Chemical analysis]
LS	Liquid Sensor (AAG)
LS	Listed Securities
LS	List of Specifications (NATG)
LS	List Total [Banking]
LS	Literature Search
l/s	Liters per Second [SI symbol]
LS	Little Stock (MHDW)
LS	Liver and Spleen [Medicine]
LS	Livestock (DCTA)
LS	Loading Splice [Telecommunications] (TEL)
L/S	Load System (MCD)
LS	Lobe Switching (IAA)
LS	Local Store
LS	Local Sunset
LS	Local Sunset Time (WDMC)
LS	Loca Sancta [A publication] (BJA)
LS	Locked Shut (NRCH)
LS	Lockheed Standards
LS	Locus Sepulchri [Place of the Sepulchre] [Latin]
LS	Locus Sigilli [Place of the Seal] [Legal term Latin]
LS	Logical Sum [Computer science]
LS	Logistical Support [Army]
LS	Logistics Squadron [Military]
LS	Log-Skidder [Tires] (DICI)
LS	London Scottish [Army regiment]
LS	[The] London Sinfonietta
Ls	Longear Sunfish [Ichthyology]
LS	Longitudinal Section
LS	Longitudinal Staggering (IAA)
LS	Long Service (ADA)
LS	Long Shot [A photograph or motion picture sequence taken from a distance]
LS	Long Sight (WDAA)
LS	Long Sleeves [Dressmaking]
LS	Loose Shot
LS	Lost Seska [Defunct] (EA)
LS	Loudspeaker
LS	Lovat Scouts [British military] (DMA)
LS	Lower Sprocket (ECII)
LS	Lower Structure
LS	Low-Power Schottky [Electronics]
LS	Low Salt [Dietetics]
LS	Low Secondary (IAA)
LS	Low Similarity [Psychology]
LS	Low-Sodium Diet (DMAA)
LS	Low-Speed
LS	Lumbar Spine [Medicine] (DMAA)
LS	Lumbosacral [Medicine]
LS	Lump Sum
LS	Lunar Surface (KSC)
LS	Lung Sounds [Medicine]
LS	Luteinization Stimulator [Endocrinology]
LS	Lute Society [Harrow, England] (EAIO)
LS	Luxury Sport [In automobile model name "Cordia LS"]
LS	Lymphosarcoma [Medicine]
LS	Marco Island Airways [ICAO designator] (AD)
ls----	South Atlantic Ocean [MARC geographic area code Library of Congress] (LCCP)
LS	Sudanese Pound (IMH)
LS	Summer [Vessel load line mark]
LS3	London Specialist Software Systems (NITA)
LSA	Labor Services Agency (AABC)
LSA	Labor Surplus Area
LSA	Labour Staff Association [National Coal Board] [British]
LSA	Lamesa, TX [Location identifier FAA] (FAAL)
LSA	Landing Ship, Assault [Navy British]
LSA	Landing Supply Activity
LSA	Land Service Assistant [Ministry of Agriculture, Fisheries, and Food] [British]
LSA	Land Settlement Association [British]
LSA	Language Sampling and Analysis [Educational test]
LSA	Large Science Aperture [Spectrometer]
LSA	Large Space Antenna (SSD)
LSA	Large Spherical Array
LSA	LASER-Supported Absorption (PDAA)
LSA	Lateral Spherical Aberration
LSA	Late Stone Age
LSA	Launch Services Agreement (MCD)
LSA	Law and Society Association (EA)
LSA	Law Services Association [British] (DBA)
LSA	Layton School of Art [Wisconsin]
LSA	Leading Stores Accountant [British military] (DMA)
LSA	Leading Supply Assistant (WDAA)
LSA	Lead Spring Assembly
LSA	League for Socialist Action [Canada]
LSA	Leaving Scene of an Accident [Traffic offense charge]

LSA	Left Sacroanterior [*A fetal position, the breech position*] [*Obstetrics*]
LSA	Left Subclavian Artery [*Anatomy*] (AAMN)
LSA	Leisure Studies Association [*British*]
LSA	Leukemia Society of America (EA)
LSA	Level Shift Amplifier
LSA	Lhasa [*Tibet*] [*Seismograph station code, US Geological Survey*] (SEIS)
LSA	Library Science Abstracts [*A publication*]
LSA	Library Services Act [*1956*]
LSA	Licentiate in Agricultural Science
LSA	Licentiate of the Society of Apothecaries [*British*]
LSA	Lichen Sclerosis et Atrophicus [*Dermatology*]
LSA	Life Saving Appliance [*or Apparatus*] (DS)
LSA	Life Style Analysis [*Psychology*]
LSA	Light Strike Aircraft [*Military*] (PDAA)
LSA	Limited Space-Charge Accumulation [*Electronics*]
LSA	Linea Aerea Nacional (Lansa) [*Dominican Republic*] [*ICAO designator*] (FAAC)
LSA	Linear Servo Actuator
LSA	Line Sensing Amplifier (IAA)
LSA	Line-Sharing Adapter
LSA	Line Sharing Adaptor (NITA)
LSA	Linguistic Society of America (EA)
LSA	Lipid-Bound Sialic Acid [*Biochemistry*] (DAVI)
LSA	Liquid Scintillation Analyzer [*Chemistry*]
LSA	List of Sections Affected (AAGC)
LSA	Lithuanian Scouts Association (EA)
LSA	Lithuanian Students Association (EA)
LSA	Little Sisters of the Assumption [*See also PSA*] [*France*] (EAIO)
LSA	Livestock Agent
LSA	Local Supervising Authority
LSA	Locksmith Security Association (EA)
LSA	Logic State Analyzer (IAA)
LSA	Logistics Supply Area
LSA	Logistics Support Analysis
LSA	Logistic Support Agreement [*Military*] (CAAL)
LSA	Logistic Support Aircraft (MCD)
LSA	Logistic Support Analysis
LSA	Logistic Support Area (NVT)
LSA	Logistic System Analysis [*Navy*]
LSA	Longitudinal Spherical Aberration
LSA	Losuia [*Papua New Guinea*] [*Airport symbol*] (OAG)
LSA	Loudspeaker Amplifier (DWSG)
LSA	Louisiana Statutes, Annotated [*A publication*] (DLA)
LSA	Low-Cost Solar Array (IEEE)
LSA	Lowe's Syndrome Association (EA)
LSA	Low Specific Activity [*Radioisotope*]
LSA	Low-Speed Adapter (IAA)
LSA	Lubricant, Small Arms [*Weaponry*] [*Military*] (VNW)
LSA	Lute Society of America (EA)
LSa	Lymphosarcoma [*Medicine*]
LSA	University of Arizona, Graduate Library School, Tucson, AZ [*OCLC symbol*] (OCLC)
LSAA	Library Services Authority Act (NITA)
LSAA	Linen Supply Association of America [*Later, TRSA*] (EA)
LSAAP	Lone Star Army Ammunition Plant (AABC)
LSAB	Learning Systems and Access Branch [*Education*] (AIE)
LSAC	Labor Sector Advisory Committee [*Terminated, 1980*] (EGAO)
LSAC	Law School Admission Council (EDAC)
LSAC	London Small Arms Co. [*Military*]
LSAC	Low-Pressure Suction Air Conveyor (PDAA)
LSAC	Low-Speed Access to a Computer (PDAA)
LSAC/LSAS	Law School Admission Council/Law School Admission Services (EA)
LSACN	Logistic Support Analysis Control Number (MCD)
LSAD	Launch Safe-and-Arm Device
LSAG	Geneve [*Switzerland ICAO location identifier*] (ICLI)
LSAH	Launch Site Accommodations Handbook [*NASA*] (NASA)
lsai--	Ascension Island [*MARC geographic area code Library of Congress*] (LCCP)
LSAL	Left Salivary [*Gland*]
L Salic	Salic Law [*A publication*] (DLA)
LSA/LSAR	Logistic Support Analysis/Logistic Support Analysis Record [*Army*] (RDA)
LSALT	Lowest Safe Altitude [*Aviation*] (DA)
LSAM	Launcher System Angles Matched [*Navy*] (CAAL)
LSAM	Logistics Support Alternative [*or Analysis*] Model (MCD)
LSAM	Lumped Shell Analysis Method
LSA mode	Limited Space Charge Accumulation Mode [*Telecommunications*] (NITA)
LSANA	Leukocyte-Specific Antinuclear Antibody [*Hematology*] (DMAA)
LS & GCM	Long Service and Good Conduct Medal [*Military decoration British*]
LS & MS	Lake Shore & Michigan Southern Railway
LS and MS	Less Sleep and More Speed [*Hobo slang*]
LSANSW	Limbless Soldiers' Association of New South Wales [*Australia*]
LSANSW	Liquor Stores Association of New South Wales [*Australia*]
LSAO	Line Station Assembly Order (MCD)
LSAP	Laboratory Space Allocation Plan (MCD)
LSAP	Launch Sequence Applications Program (MCD)
LSAP	Letzeburger Sozialistesch Arbechter Partei [*Socialist Workers' Party of Luxembourg*] [*Political party*] (PPE)
LSAP	Linear Systems Analysis Program [*Statistics*]
LSAP	Link Layer Service Access Point
LSAP	Local Service Access Point [*Telecommunications*] (OSI)
LSAP	Logistic Support Analysis Plan [*or Program*] [*Army*]
LSAP	Logistic Support Analysis Process [*Navy*]

LSAPT	Lunar Sample Analysis Planning Team [*NASA*]
LSAQ	Limbless Soldiers' Association of Queensland [*Australia*]
LSAR	Local Storage Address Register (IAA)
LSAR	Logistic Support Analysis Record (RDA)
LSAR	Lymphosarcoma Cell [*Oncology*] (DAVI)
LSA/RCS	Lymphosarcoma - Reticulum Cell Sarcoma [*Oncology*] (MAE)
LSARS	West's Louisiana Revised Statutes [*A publication*] (DLA)
LSAS	Law School Admission Services (EDAC)
LSAS	Longitudinal Stability Augmentation System [*Aviation*] (DA)
LSASA	Limbless Soldiers' Association of South Australia
LSAT	Law School Admission Test
LSAT	Law School Aptitude Test (GAGS)
LSAT	Legal Scholastic Aptitude Test (HGAA)
LSAT	Leveling/Sharpening Aggressions Test [*Psychology*] (EDAC)
LSAT	Logistic Shelter Air Transportable
LSAV	Limbless Soldiers' Association of Victoria [*Australia*]
LSAV	Liquor Stores' Association of Victoria [*Aerospace*]
LSAW	LASER-Supported Absorption-Wave (PDAA)
LSAWA	Liquor Stores' Association of Western Australia
LSAY	Longitudinal Study of American Youth [*Northern Illinois University*] [*Education*]
LSAZ	Zurich [*Switzerland ICAO location identifier*] (ICLI)
LSB	Bachelor of Life Science
LSB	Labour Supply Board [*British*]
LSB	Landing Ship, Bombardment
LSB	La Sacra Bibbia (BJA)
LSB	Launcher Support Building
LSB	Launch Service Building
LSB	Learned Society Board (ACII)
LSB	Leased Spacecraft Bus (SSD)
LSB	Least Significant BIT [*or Byte*] [*Data compaction*]
LSB	Left Sternal Border
LSB	Lensibavia [*Former USSR*] [*FAA designator*] (FAAC)
LSB	Library of Standard Biographies [*A publication*]
LSB	Life Safety Box
LSB	Lifestyle Beverage Corp. [*Vancouver Stock Exchange symbol*]
LSB	Line Segment Block [*Computer science*]
LSB	List of Successful Bidders [*DoD*]
LSB	Logistics Sustaining Base [*Military*] (RDA)
LSB	Logistic Support Base (NVT)
LSB	London School Board
LSB	Longitudinal Studies Branch [*Department of Education*] (GFGA)
LSB	Lordsburg, NM [*Location identifier FAA*] (FAAL)
LSB	Lower Sideband [*Data transmission*]
LSB	Low Silhouette Blade [*Aircraft*]
LSB	Low-Speed Breaker Relay (IEEE)
LSB	Low-Speed Buffer (CET)
LSB	Low-Surface-Brightness [*Galaxies - astronomy*]
LSB	LSB Industries [*NYSE symbol*] (TTSB)
LSB	LSB Industries, Inc. [*NYSE symbol*] (SAG)
LSB	Lucas-Sumitomo Brakes [*Auto industry supplier*]
LSB	Lunar Surface Base [*NASA*] (KSC)
LSB	Southern University, Library, Baton Rouge, LA [*OCLC symbol*] (OCLC)
LSBA	Leading Sick Bay Attendant [*Navy British*]
LSBC	[*The*] La Salle & Bureau County Railroad Co. [*AAR code*]
LSB Fn	LSB Financial Corp. [*Associated Press*] (SAG)
LSB Fncl	LSB Financial Corp. [*Associated Press*] (SAG)
LSBI	LSB Financial [*NASDAQ symbol*] (TTSB)
LSBI	LSB Financial Corp. [*NASDAQ symbol*] (SAG)
LSB Ind	LSB Industries, Inc. [*Associated Press*] (SAG)
LSB NC	LSB Bancshares, Inc. of North Carolina [*Associated Press*] (SAG)
LSBPHF	Library Service to the Blind and Physically Handicapped Forum [*Association of Specialized and Cooperative Library Agencies*]
LSBPrC	LSB Ind $3.25 Cv Exch Pfd [*NYSE symbol*] (TTSB)
LS BPS	Laparoscopic Bilateral Partial Salpingectomies [*Gynecology*] (DAVI)
LSBR	Large Seed-Blanket Reactor
LSBR	Liquid Strand Burning Rate (MCD)
LSBRT	Library Service to the Blind Round Table
lsbv--	Bouvet Island [*MARC geographic area code Library of Congress*] (LCCP)
LSBX	Lawrence Savings Bank [*NASDAQ symbol*] (SAG)
LSBY	Least Significant Byte [*Data compaction*] [*Computer science*]
LSC	Labor Socialist Committee [*Australia*]
LSC	Labor Studies Center [*AFL-CIO*]
LSC	Lake Survey Center [*National Oceanic and Atmospheric Administration*]
LSC	Landing Ship Carrier [*British military*] (DMA)
LSC	Language and Society Centre [*Monash University*] [*Australia*]
LSC	Languages Services Centre [*South Australia*]
LSC	Large-Scale Computer
LSC	Large Single Copy Region [*Of a chromosome*] [*Genetics*]
LSC	Large Solar Concentrator (SSD)
LSC	Large Submetacentric Chromosome [*Medicine*]
LSC	Las Cruces [*Diocesan abbreviation*] [*New Mexico*] (TOCD)
LSC	La Serena [*Chile*] [*Airport symbol*] (AD)
LSC	LASER Spectral Control
LSC	LASER-Supported Combustion (MCD)
LSC	Last Significant Character (ECII)
LSC	Late Systolic Click [*Cardiology*] (DAVI)
LSC	Launch Sequence Control
L/SC	Launch/Storage Container
L Sc	Laureate of Science
LSC	Law of the Sea Conference [*United Nations*]

LSC............ Learning Skills Center Reading and Study Skills Program [*Cornell University*] [*Research center*] (RCD)
LSC............ Least Significant Character (IEEE)
LSC............ Least Square Center (IAA)
LSC............ Least Squares Circle [*Manufacturing term*]
LSC............ Least-Squares Collocation [*Mathematics*]
LSC............ Left-Sided Colon Cancer [*Oncology*]
LSC............ Left Stage Center [*A stage direction*]
LSC............ Legal Services Corp. [*Government agency*]
LSC............ Legal Services for Children (EA)
LSC............ Legislative Service Center [*Washington State Legislature*] [*Information service or system*] (IID)
LSC............ Lens Sign Convention
LSC............ Liberian Shipowners Council (EA)
LSC............ Library Services Center, Midwestern Regional Library System [*UTLAS symbol*]
LSC............ Library Services Center of Missouri [*Library network*]
LSc............. Licentiate in Science (DD)
LSC............ Lid, Sclera, and Conjunctiva [*Opthalmology*] (DAVI)
LSC............ Life Safety Code
LSC............ Limit Signaling Comparator
LSC............ Lincoln Sesquicentennial Committee [*Terminated, 1960*] [*Government agency*]
LSC............ Linear Sequential Circuit
LSC............ Linear-Shaped Charge
LSC............ Linear Slope Controlled (PDAA)
LSC............ Liquid Scintillation Cocktail [*Analytical chemistry*]
LSC............ Liquid Scintillation Counter [*or Counting*]
LSC............ Liquid Smoke Condensate
LSC............ Liquid Solid Chromatography
LSC............ Liquids Solids Contact
LSC............ Little Sisters of Carmel
LSC............ LOAD [*Low Altitude Defense*] Simulation Center
LSC............ Load Standardization Crew (MCD)
LSC............ Lobbyist Systems Corp. [*Information service or system*] (IID)
LSC............ Local Supercluster [*Cosmology*]
LSC............ Local Switching Centre [*Telecommunications*] (NITA)
LSC............ Loco Sub Citato [*In the Place Cited Below*] [*Latin*] (ROG)
LSC............ Loco Supra Citato [*In the Place Cited Above*] [*Latin*]
LSC............ Logistical Support Center [*Army*]
LSC............ Logistic Support Cadre (MCD)
LSC............ London Salvage Corps
LSC............ Loop Station Connector (MHDB)
LSC............ Low-Speed Concentrator
LSC............ LSI Logic Corp. of Canada, Inc. [*Toronto Stock Exchange symbol*]
LSC............ Luminescent Solar Concentrator
LSC............ Luminescent Stamp Club [*Defunct*] (EA)
LSC............ Lump-Sum Contract
LSC............ Luxury Sport Coupe
LSC............ Shopco Laurel Centre L.P. [*AMEX symbol*] (TTSB)
LSC............ Shopco Laurel Centre Ltd. [*AMEX symbol*] (SPSG)
LSC............ Southern University, Law Library, Baton Rouge, LA [*OCLC symbol*] (OCLC)
LScA.......... Left Scapuloanterior [*A fetal position*] [*Obstetrics*]
LSCA.......... Left Subclavian Artery [*Anatomy*] (DAVI)
LSCA.......... Library Services and Construction Act [*1963*]
LSCA.......... Logistics Support Cost Analysis (NASA)
LScAdmin.... Licence in Administration [*Canada*] (DD)
LSCC.......... Lattice Semiconductor [*NASDAQ symbol*] (TTSB)
LSCC.......... Lattice Semiconductor Corp. [*NASDAQ symbol*] (SAG)
LSCC.......... Liberty Seated Collectors Club (EA)
LScC.......... Licentiate in Commercial Science (DD)
LSCC.......... Line-Sequential Color Composite (IEEE)
LSCC.......... Local Servicing Control Center [*Telecommunications*] (TEL)
LSCC.......... London Scottish Cadet Corps [*British military*] (DMA)
LScCom....... Licentiate in Commercial Science
LScComm..... Licentiate in Commercial Science (DD)
LScCompt.... Licencie en Sciences Comptables [*Licentiate of Accounting*] (DD)
L Sc D........ Doctor of the Science of Law
LSCD.......... Leading Seaman Clearance Diver
LSCE.......... Launch Sequence and Control Equipment
LSCE.......... Least Square Complex Exponential [*Mathematics*]
LScEco........ Licence in Economics [*Canada*] (DD)
LSc(Econ)... Licence in Science (Economics) [*British*] (DI)
LSCG.......... Law School Computer Group [*Defunct*] (EA)
LSCI........... Large-Scale Compound Integration
LSCI........... Lymphosarcoma Cell Leukemia [*Medicine*] (DMAA)
LSCL.......... Limit Switch Closed [*Electronics*] (IAA)
LSCL.......... Lower Surface Center Line
LSCM.......... LASER-Scan Confocal Microscope
LSCM.......... LASER Scanning Confocal Microscopy
LSCM.......... Logistic Support Coordination Meeting [*Military*] (MCD)
LSCO.......... Lanthanum Strontium Copper Oxide [*Inorganic chemistry*]
LSCO.......... Lesco, Inc. [*NASDAQ symbol*] (SAG)
LScO.......... Licence in the Science of Optometry [*Canada*] (DD)
LSCP.......... Laserscope [*NASDAQ symbol*] (SAG)
LScP.......... Left Scapuloposterior [*A fetal position*] [*Obstetrics*]
LSCP.......... Logistic Support Control Point [*Military*] (AFM)
LSCP.......... Low-Speed Card Punch [*Computer science*] (AABC)
LSCP(Assoc).. Associate of the London and Counties Society of Physiologists [*British*] (DBQ)
LScRel........ Licentiate in Religion (DD)
LSCRRC...... Law Students Civil Rights Research Council (EA)
LSCS.......... Lower Segment Caesarean Section [*Medicine*]

LScS.......... Southern University, Scotlandville, Baton Rouge, LA [*Library symbol Library of Congress*] (LCLS)
LScS-N....... Southern University at New Orleans, New Orleans, LA [*Library symbol Library of Congress*] (LCLS)
LScSoc....... Licence in Social Science [*British*]
LSCT.......... LASER Spectral Control Technique
LSCT.......... Loevinger Sentence Completion Test (EDAC)
LSCT.......... Low-Speed Compound Terminal (CET)
LSCU.......... Local Servicing Control Unit [*Telecommunications*] (TEL)
LSCV.......... Left Subclavian Vein [*Anatomy*] (DAVI)
LSD........... Amphibious Ship, Dock
LSD........... Doctor of Library Science
LSD........... Doctor of Life Science
LSD........... Landing Ship Deck
LSD........... Landing Ship, Dock [*Navy symbol*]
LSD........... Landing-Site Determination [*NASA*] (KSC)
LSD........... Landing, Storage, Delivery [*Business term*]
LSD........... Language for Systems Development
LSD........... Large Screen Display
LSD........... Large Shallow-Draught [*Bulk carrier*] (PDAA)
LSD........... Large Steel Desk [*Position given to ex-astronauts*]
LSD........... Laryngeal Sound Discrimination [*Medicine*] (DMAA)
LSD........... LASER-Selective Demagnetization [*Analytical technique*]
LSD........... LASER Signal Device
LSD........... LASER-Supported Detonation Waves (MCD)
LSD........... Last Safe Date [*Marine insurance*] (DS)
LSD........... Latching Semiconductor Diode
LSD........... Latest Start Date
LSD........... Launch Support Division [*NASA*] (KSC)
LSD........... Launch Systems Data
LSD........... Law Student Division [*American Bar Association*] (BARN)
LSD........... Leadless Sealed Device (PDAA)
LSD........... Lead Sulfide Detection
LSD........... League of Safe Drivers [*British*] (BI)
LSD........... Leased (WGA)
LSD........... Least Significant Decade (IAA)
LSD........... Least Significant Difference [*Statistics*]
LSD........... Least Significant Digit [*Data compaction*] (MUGU)
LSD........... Lesson Specification Document (MCD)
LSD........... Level Sensor Demonstration
LSD........... Lexington, KY [*Location identifier FAA*] (FAAL)
LSD........... Library Service to the Disadvantaged Committee
LSD........... Life, Sport, and Drama [*A publication British*]
LSD........... Lightermen, Stevedores, and Dockers
LSD........... Light-Sensing Device (IAA)
LSD........... Lime Juice, Scotch, Drambuie [*A cocktail*] (IIA)
LSD........... Limited Saturation Device (PDAA)
LSD........... Limited-Slip Differential [*Automotive engineering*]
LSD........... Limited Space-Charge Drift [*Electronics*] (IAA)
LSD........... Limitswitch Down [*Electronics*] (IAA)
LSD........... Line-Sharing Device
LSD........... Line Signal Detector
LSD........... Linkage System Diagnostic (IAA)
LSD........... Local Spin Density [*Physics*]
LSD........... Logarithmic Series Distribution [*Statistics*]
LSD........... Logistics Systems Division [*Air Force*]
LSD........... Log-Slope Difference [*Statistics*]
LSD........... Lomir Shoyn Davenen (BJA)
LSD........... Long Side
LSD........... Long, Slow Distance [*Training method for runners*]
LSD........... Lowest Significant Dose [*Toxicology*]
LSD........... Low-Sodium Diet (DMAA)
LSD........... Low-Speed Data
LSD........... Low-Sulfur Diesel Fuel [*Petroleum marketing*]
LSD........... Lump-Sum Distribution [*Banking*]
LSD........... Lunar Surface Drill [*Aerospace*]
LSD........... Lysergic Acid Diethylamide [*or Lysergsaeure Diethylamid*] [*Hallucinogenic drug*]
LSDA.......... Licentiate of the Speech and Drama Association (ADA)
LSDA.......... Louisiana Soft Drink Association (SRA)
LSDAS........ Law School Data Assembly Service (GAGS)
LSDF.......... Large Sodium Disposal Facility [*Nuclear energy*] (NRCH)
LSDF.......... Library Service to the Deaf Forum [*Association of Specialized and Cooperative Library Agencies*]
LSDG.......... Latitudinal Species-Diversity Gradient [*Biodiversity*]
LSDH.......... Ligue Suisse des Droits de l'Homme [*Switzerland*]
LSDM.......... Lagrangian Stochastic Dispersion Model [*Marine science*] (OSRA)
LSDM.......... Lagrangian Stochastic Dispersion Model (USDC)
LSDM.......... Logical Systems Design Methodology (NITA)
LSDP.......... Lietuvos Socialdemokratu Partija [*Lithuanian Social Democratic Party*] [*Political party*] (PPE)
LSDP.......... Lump-Sum Death Payment
LSDR.......... Local Store Data Register
LSDRM....... Logistic Support Data Responsibility Matrix (MCD)
LSDS.......... Large-Scale Dynamical System (PDAA)
LSDS.......... Large Screen Display System
LSDS.......... Low-Speed Data Service [*RCA Global Communications, Inc.*] [*Piscataway, NJ*] [*Telecommunications*] (TSSD)
LSDS.......... Low-Speed Digital System
LSDSP........ Latvijas Socialdemokratiska Stradnieku Partija [*Latvian Social Democratic Workers' Party*] [*Political party*] (EAIO)
LSDT.......... Local Sidereal Time (MSA)
LSDU.......... Link Layer Service Data Unit
LSE........... Laboratory Support Equipment (SSD)
LSE........... La Crosse [*Wisconsin*]/Winona [*Minnesota*] [*Airport symbol*] (OAG)

LSE............ Landing Ship, Emergency Repair
LSE............ Landing Signal Enlisted [*Military*]
LSE............ Large-Scale Equipment (MCD)
LSE............ Lattice Screen Editor [*Program editor*]
LSE............ Launch Sequencer Equipment [*NASA*]
LSE............ Launch Station Equipment
LSE............ Launch Support Equipment [*NASA*] (AAG)
LSE............ Lease (ROG)
LSE............ Least Squares Estimator [*Statistics*]
LSE............ Left Second Entrance [*Theater*]
LSE............ Left Sternal Edge [*Cardiology*]
LSE............ Legal Services for the Elderly (EA)
lse............ Licensee [*MARC relator code*] [*Library of Congress*] (LCCP)
LSE............ Life Science Experiment (MUGU)
LSE............ Life Support Equipment (KSC)
LSE............ Life Support Evaluator (SAA)
LSE............ Limited Signed Edition (ADA)
LSE............ Liquid-Solid Extraction [*Chemistry*]
LSE............ Living Skin Equivalent [*Synthetic organ*]
LSE............ Local Side Effects [*Pharmacology*] (DAVI)
LSE............ Logistics Support Element
LSE............ Logistics Support Equipment [*Military*] (MCD)
LSE............ London School of Economics
LSE............ London Stock Exchange
LSE............ Longitudinal-Section Electric (IEEE)
LSE............ Loose
LSE............ Louisiana Sugar Exchange (EA)
LSE............ Lower Sternal Edge [*Cardiology*]
LSE............ Low-Speed Encoder (IAA)
LSE............ Low-Styrene Emission
LSE............ Lunar Support Equipment [*Aerospace*] (IAA)
LSE............ Lunar Surface Experiment [*NASA*]
LSE............ Luxembourg Stock Exchange
LSE............ Luxury Sport Euro [*Automobile model designation*] [*General Motors Corp. - Cadillac*]
LSE............ Queen's Bench Library [*Alberta*] [*UTLAS symbol*]
LSEC.......... Australian Company Secretary's Practice Manual [*A publication*]
LSEC.......... Life-Cycle Software Engineering Center [*Army*]
l/sec.......... Liters per Second [*Respiration*] [*Medicine*] (DAVI)
LSECS........ Life Support and Environmental Control System (IEEE)
LsEd.......... Leasing Edge Corp. [*Associated Press*] (SAG)
LSEED........ Launch Support Equipment - Engineering Division [*NASA*] (KSC)
LSEG.......... Low Styrene Emission Gelcoat
LSELR........ Low-Styrene-Emission Laminating Resin
LSEP.......... Legal Services for the Elderly Poor [*Later, LSE*] (EA)
LSEP.......... Lifetime Sports Education Project [*of Lifetime Sports Foundation*]
LSEP.......... Lunar Surface Experiment Package [*NASA*]
LSEQ.......... Launch Sequencer [*Navy*] (CAAL)
LSER.......... Laser Corp. [*NASDAQ symbol*] (SAG)
LSER.......... Linear Solvation Energy Relationship [*Physical chemistry*]
LSER.......... Raron [*Switzerland ICAO location identifier*] (ICLI)
LSES.......... Large Surface Effect Ship (PDAA)
LSES.......... Life Support and Environmental System (IAA)
LSE SKDS.... Loose or on Skids [*Freight*]
LSET.......... Logistics Supportability Evaluation Team [*Military*] (AFIT)
LSEV.......... Lunar Surface Exploration Vehicle [*Aerospace*]
LSEZ.......... Zermatt [*Switzerland ICAO location identifier*] (ICLI)
LSF............ Fort Benning (Columbus), GA [*Location identifier FAA*] (FAAL)
LSF............ Laboratory Simulation Facility (MCD)
LSF............ Lande Splitting Factor
LSF............ Landing Ship, Fighter Direction [*British military*] (DMA)
LSF............ Language System FORTRAN [*Computer science*]
LSF............ La Souterraine [*France*] [*Seismograph station code, US Geological Survey*] (SEIS)
LSF............ Launch Support Facility [*NASA*] (KSC)
LSF............ Least Square Fit
LSF............ Lightship Screen File [*Computer science*]
LSF............ Lightweight Strike Fighter [*NATO Air Forces*]
LSF............ Limit Switch Forward [*Electronics*] (IAA)
LSF............ Line Spread Function (MCD)
LSF............ Line Switch Frame [*Telecommunications*] (TEL)
LSF............ Liquid-State Submerged Fermentation [*Biochemistry*]
LSF............ Literary Society Foundation (EA)
LSF............ Lloyd Shaw Foundation (EA)
LSF............ Load Sheet Fuel [*Aviation*] (DA)
LSF............ Logistic Support Force [*Military*]
LSF............ Loss Factor [*Electronics*] (IAA)
LSF............ Lower Side Frequency [*Electronics*] (ECII)
LSF............ Low Saturated Fat [*Diet*] (DAVI)
LSF............ Lumped Selection Filter [*Telecommunications*] (OA)
LSF............ Lunar Scientific Facility [*NASA*] (KSC)
LSF............ Lymphocyte-Stimulating Factor [*Biochemistry*]
LSFA.......... Logistic System Feasibility Analysis (AABC)
LSFAE........ Low-Speed Fuel Air Explosive
LSFC.......... Lennon Sisters Fan Club (EA)
LSFE.......... Life Sciences Flight Experiment [*NASA*] (NASA)
LSFF.......... Landing Ship, Flotilla Flagship [*Navy symbol Obsolete*]
LSFFAR...... Low-Spin Folding Fin Aircraft Rocket (IEEE)
lsfk--.......... Falkland Islands [*MARC geographic area code Library of Congress*] (LCCP)
LSFN.......... List of Selected File Numbers (AABC)
LSFO.......... Logistics Support Field Office [*Federal disaster planning*]
LSFO.......... Low-Sulfur Fuel Oil
LSFR.......... Large-Probe Solar Net Flux Radiometer [*NASA*]
LSFR.......... Local Storage Function Register

LSFS.......... Lateral Separation Focus Sensor (PDAA)
LSFS.......... Light Sequence Flasher System (DWSG)
LSFT.......... Low Steamline Flow Test (IEEE)
LSG............ Laminated Safety Glass [*Automotive engineering*]
LSG............ Landing Ship, Gantry
LSG............ Landing Ship, Gun [*British military*] (DMA)
LSG............ Language Structure Group [*CODASYL*]
LSG............ Large-Scale Geostrophic [*Marine science*] (OSRA)
LSG............ Lateral Superior Geniculate Artery [*Anatomy*]
LSG............ Legal Services Group
LSG............ Legislative Strategy Group [*Reagan administration*]
LSG............ Level Sensor Gradiometer
LSG............ Ligo Samseksamaj Geesperantistoj [*Richmond, Surrey, England*] (EAIO)
LSG............ Limited Subgroup (NATG)
LSG............ Little Sisters of the Gospel (France) (TOCD)
LSG............ Logistics Support Group (AAG)
LSG............ Loh's Sinfully Good Ice Cream & Cookies, Inc. [*Vancouver Stock Exchange symbol*]
LSG............ Low-Stress Grinding (DICI)
LSG............ Lunar Surface Gravimeter [*Apollo*] [*NASA*]
LSGA.......... Laminators Safety Glass Association (EA)
LSGC.......... Les Eplatures [*Switzerland ICAO location identifier*] (ICLI)
LSGC.......... Long Service and Good Conduct (ADA)
LSGD.......... Lymphocyte Specific Gravity Distribution [*Medicine*]
LSGE.......... Ecuvillens [*Switzerland ICAO location identifier*] (ICLI)
LSGG.......... Geneve/Cointrin [*Switzerland ICAO location identifier*] (ICLI)
LSGK.......... Saanen [*Switzerland ICAO location identifier*] (ICLI)
LSGL.......... Lausanne/Blecherette [*Switzerland ICAO location identifier*] (ICLI)
LSG/LSU..... Landing Support Group/Logistics Support Unit (DNAB)
LSGN.......... Neuchatel [*Switzerland ICAO location identifier*] (ICLI)
LSGP.......... La Cote [*Switzerland ICAO location identifier*] (ICLI)
LSGP.......... Large-Scale General Purpose
LSGP.......... Lateral Simulated Ground Plane [*Aerodynamics*]
LSGR.......... Loose Granular Snow [*Skiing condition*]
LSGS.......... Left Stellate Ganglion Stimulation [*Physiology*]
LSGS.......... Sion [*Switzerland ICAO location identifier*] (ICLI)
LsgSolu...... Leasing Solutions, Inc. [*Associated Press*] (SAG)
LSGT.......... Gruyeres [*Switzerland ICAO location identifier*] (ICLI)
L/Sgt......... Lance Sergeant [*British military*] (DMA)
LSGT.......... Lasergate Systems [*NASDAQ symbol*] (TTSB)
LSGT.......... Lasergate Systems, Inc. [*NASDAQ symbol*] (SAG)
LSGTW....... Lasergate Sys Wrrt [*NASDAQ symbol*] (TTSB)
LSGU.......... Local Spinal Glucose Utilization [*Medicine*]
LSH............ Landing Ship, Headquarters
LSH............ Landing Ship, Heavy
LSH............ Lashio [*Myanmar*] [*Airport symbol*] (OAG)
LSH............ Library Services to the Handicapped, Alberta Culture [*UTLAS symbol*]
LSH............ Light Ship (IAA)
LSH............ London School of Hygiene
LSH............ Lowland-Southern Hybrid [*Hemoglobin phenotype of Rana pipiens*]
LSH............ Low Section Height [*Automotive engineering*]
LSH............ Loyal Suffolk Hussars [*British military*]
LSH............ Lutein-Stimulating Hormone [*Also, ICSH, LH*] [*Endocrinology*]
LSH............ Lymphocytosis-Stimulating Hormone [*Endocrinology*]
LSh............ Shreve Memorial and Caddo Parish Extension Library, Shreveport, LA [*Library symbol Library of Congress*] (LCLS)
LSH............ Southeastern Louisiana University, Hammond, LA [*OCLC symbol*] (OCLC)
LSHA.......... Gstaad-Inn Grund [*Switzerland ICAO location identifier*] (ICLI)
LShC.......... Centenary College of Louisiana, Shreveport, LA [*Library symbol Library of Congress*] (LCLS)
LSHC.......... Light-Saturated Hydrocarbon [*Organic chemistry*]
LShCa........ Caddo Parish Library, Shreveport, LA [*Library symbol Library of Congress*] (LCLS)
LSHCNC...... Local and Short Haul Carriers National Conference (EA)
LSHG.......... Gampel [*Switzerland ICAO location identifier*] (ICLI)
LSHG.......... Lashing [*Engineering*]
LSHI.......... Large-Scale Hybrid Integration
LSHIP......... Leadership
LSH(L)........ Landing Ship, Headquarters (Large)
LSHLD........ Leasehold
LSH/LSF..... Landing Ship, Helicopter/Landing Ship, Fighter Direction (DNAB)
LShN.......... R. W. Norton Art Foundation, Shreveport, LA [*Library symbol Library of Congress*] (LCLS)
LSHQ.......... Landing Ship, Headquarters [*British military*] (DMA)
LSH(S)........ Landing Ship, Headquarters (Small)
LSHS.......... Low Sulphur Heavy Stock (PDAA)
LSHS.......... Sezegnin [*Switzerland ICAO location identifier*] (ICLI)
LShTE........ Texas Eastern Transmission Corp., Shreveport, LA [*Library symbol Library of Congress*] (LCLS)
LSHTM........ London School of Hygiene and Tropical Medicine (DAVI)
LShUG........ United Gas Corp., Shreveport, LA [*Library symbol Library of Congress*] (LCLS)
LsHUP........ Pennzoil United, Inc., Shreveport, LA [*Library symbol Library of Congress*] (LCLS)
LSHV.......... Laminated Synthetic High Voltage
LSI............ Alis [*Former USSR*] [*FAA designator*] (FAAC)
LSI............ Labour Supply Inspector [*British*]
LSI............ Lake Superior & Ishpeming Railroad Co. [*AAR code*]
LSI............ Landing Ship, Infantry [*Navy symbol*]
LSI............ Large-Scale Integration [*of circuits*] [*Electronics*]
LSI............ Largest Single Item (AFM)
LSI............ LASER Surface Interaction

LSI............. Lateral Shear Interferometer (PDAA)
LSI............. Launch Success Indicator
LSI............. Law of the Sea Institute (EA)
LSI............. Laws of the State of Israel (BJA)
LSI............. Lead Systems Integration
LSI............. Learning Style Inventory [Occupational therapy]
LSI............. Learning Systems Institute [Florida State University] [Research center] (RCD)
LSI............. Lear Siegler Inc. (NITA)
LSI............. Legal Support Inspection [Clean Water Act] [Environmental Protection Agency] (EPA)
LSI............. Lerwick [Scotland] [Airport symbol] (OAG)
LSI............. Life Satisfaction Index [Medicine] (DMAA)
LSI............. Life Space Interviewing [Teaching technique]
LSI............. Light Scatter Index
LSI............. Listing Site Inspection [Environmental science] (FFDE)
LSI............. Little Sitkin Island [Alaska] [Seismograph station code, US Geological Survey Closed] (SEIS)
LSI............. Logistic Supportability Index
LSI............. Logistic Support Impact
LSI............. LSI Logic [NYSE symbol] (TTSB)
LSI............. LSI Logic Corp. [NYSE symbol] (SPSG)
LSI............. Lumbar Spine Index [Medicine] (DMAA)
LSI............. Lunar Science Institute [Houston]
LSI............. Lunar Surface Instrument [Aerospace]
LSIA........... Lamp and Shade Institute of America [Defunct] (EA)
LSIA........... Licentiate of the Society of Industrial Artists [British]
LSIB........... London Stage Information Bank [Lawrence University] [Information service or system] (IID)
LSIC........... Large-Scale Integrated Circuit [Electronics] (KSC)
LSIC........... Large-Scale Integration Computer
LSIC........... Little Servant Sisters of the Immaculate Conception (TOCD)
LSICA......... Liquid and Solid Industrial Control Association (EA)
LSID........... Large Scale Integration Development
LSID........... Launch Sequence and Interlock Document [NASA] (NASA)
LSID........... Local Session Identification [Computer science] (IBMDP)
LSidFW...... United States Fish and Wildlife Service, Sidell, LA [Library symbol Library of Congress] (LCLS)
LSIEF......... Library Service to the Impaired Elderly Forum [Association of Specialized and Cooperative Library Agencies]
LSI(G)........ Landing Craft, Infantry (Gunboat) [Navy symbol Obsolete]
LSIG........... Least Significant (IAA)
LSIG........... Line Scan Image Generator (OA)
LSI(H)........ Landing Ship, Infantry (Hand-Hoisted Boats) [British]
LSI Ind...... LSI Industries, Inc. [Associated Press] (SAG)
LSI Inds...... LSI Industries, Inc. [Associated Press] (SAG)
LSIL........... Land and Sea Interaction Laboratory [Environmental Science Services Administration] (NOAA)
LSI(L)........ Landing Ship, Infantry (Large) [Obsolete]
LSIL........... Low-Grade Squamous Intraepithelial Lesion [Medicine]
LSI Log...... LSI Logic Corp. [Associated Press] (SAG)
LSI(M)....... Landing Craft, Infantry (Mortar) [Navy symbol Obsolete]
LSI(M)....... Landing Ship, Infantry (Medium) [British]
LSIMS........ Liquid Secondary Ion Mass Spectrometry
LSIO.......... Lumbosacroiliac Orthosis [Medicine]
LSI-P......... Learning Styles Inventory-Primary Version [Occupational therapy] (EDAC)
LSI(R)........ Landing Craft, Infantry (Rocket) [Navy symbol Obsolete]
LSIR........... Limb-Scanning Infrared Radiometer
LSIR........... Low-Ship Impact Ranging [Navy] (CAAL)
LSI(S)........ Landing Ship, Infantry (Small)
LSIS........... LASER Scan Inspection System (PDAA)
LSIS........... LASER Shutterable Image Sensor
LSIS........... League of Shut-In Sodalists (EA)
LSIS........... Learning Style Identification Scale [Educational test]
LSIT........... Large-Scale Integration Technology (IAA)
LSIT........... Linear Strip Ion Thruster
LSITT......... Let's Stick It to Them [Acronym used as book title]
LSITV......... Liquid Secondary Injection Thrust Vector Control (PDAA)
LSJ............ La Societe Jersiaise (EAIO)
LSJ............ Liddell and Scott [Greek-English Lexicon, 9th ed., revised by H. Stuart Jones] [A publication] (OCD)
LSJ............ Little Sisters of Jesus [See also PSJ] [Italy] (EAIO)
LSJM......... Laus Sit Jesu et Mariae [Praise Be to Jesus and Mary] [Latin]
LSJM......... Little Sisters of Jesus and Mary (TOCD)
LSK........... Leucosulfakinin [Biochemistry]
LSK........... Liquid Sample Kit
LSK........... Liuski International [NASDAQ symbol] (TTSB)
LSK........... Liver, Spleen, Kidney [Medicine]
LSK........... Lusk, WY [Location identifier FAA] (FAAL)
LSKI.......... Liuski International, Inc. [NASDAQ symbol] (SAG)
LSKM........ Liver-Spleen-Kidney Megaly [Medicine]
LSL........... Ladder Static Logic
LSL........... Landing Ship, Logistic [British]
LSL........... Lateral Superlattice [Physics]
LSL........... Left Sacrolateral [A fetal position] [Obstetrics]
LSL........... Life Sciences Laboratory (AAG)
LSL........... Link and Selector Language
LSL........... Link Support Layer
LSL........... Linnaean Society of London
LSL........... Litton Systems Ltd. (MCD)
LSL........... Logical Shift Left [Computer science]
LSL........... Logistics Spares List (KSC)
LSL........... Logistics Systems Laboratory
LSL........... Long Service Leave (ADA)

LSL........... Los Chiles [Costa Rica] [Airport symbol] (OAG)
LSL........... Louisiana State Library, Baton Rouge, LA [OCLC symbol] (OCLC)
LSL........... Lower Specified Limit
LSL........... Low Sight Lobe
LSL........... Low-Speed Logic (IAA)
LSL........... Lump-Sum Leave Payment [Military] (DNAB)
LSLA.......... Low Speed Line Adaptor (NITA)
LSLB.......... Land Surveyors' Licensing Board [Western Australia]
LSLB.......... Left Short Leg Brace [Medicine]
LSLBP........ Lump-Sum Leave Payment, Basic Pay [Military] (DNAB)
LSLDP........ Lietuvos Socialistu Liaudininkai Demokratu Partija [Socialist Populists Democratic Party of Lithuania] [Political party] (PPE)
LSLI.......... Large-Scale Linear Integration (IAA)
LSLP.......... Lietuvos Socialistu Liaudininkai Partija [Socialist Populists Party of Lithuania] [Political party] (PPE)
LSLP.......... Lump-Sum Leave Payment [Air Force] (AFM)
LSL PMA .... Lump-Sum Leave Payment, Personal Money Allowance [Military] (DNAB)
LSL QTRS... Lump-Sum Leave Payment, Quarters [Military] (DNAB)
LSL SUBS... Lump-Sum Leave Payment, Subsistence [Military] (DNAB)
LSLT.......... League to Save Lake Tahoe (EA)
LSM........... Laboratory for the Structure of Matter [Navy] (PDAA)
LSM........... Lakeside & Marblehead R. R. [AAR code]
LSM........... Landing Ship, Medium [Navy symbol]
LSM........... Large Solid Motor [Aerospace]
LSM........... LASER Scanning Microscope
LSM........... LASER Slicing Machine
LSM........... Late Systolic Murmur (MAE)
LSM........... Launcher Status Multiplexer (MSA)
LSM........... Launching System Module
LSM........... Launch Site Maintenance [NASA] (IAA)
LSM........... Layered Synthetic Microstructure [For optical instruments]
LSM........... Learning Systems Model (EDAC)
LSM........... Least Square Mean [Mathematical statistics]
LSM........... Letter Sorting Machine [US Postal Service]
LSM........... Liberation Support Movement Information Center (EA)
LSM........... Life Science Module [NASA] (NASA)
LSM........... Linear Select Memory
LSM........... Linear Sequential Machine
LSM........... Linear Synchronous Motor (IAA)
LSM........... Linear Synchronous Motor [TRB] (TAG)
LSM........... Line-Scanning Mode [Microscopy]
LSM........... Line Selection Module [Telecommunications] (TEL)
LSM........... Line Select Module (NITA)
LSM........... Litera Scripta Manet [The Written Word Remains] [Latin] (ADA)
LSM........... Little Skull Mountain [Nevada] [Seismograph station code, US Geological Survey] (SEIS)
LSM........... Local Service for Mobiles [Computer science]
LSM........... Logistic Support Manager
LSM........... Longitudinal Section Magnetic [Electronics] (OA)
LSM........... Long Semado [Malaysia] [Airport symbol] (OAG)
LSM........... Loop Sampling Module
LSM........... Louisiana State Library, Processing Center, Baton Rouge, LA [OCLC symbol] (OCLC)
LSM........... Low-Speed MODEM (IAA)
LSM........... Low-Sulfate Medium [Microbiology]
LSM........... Lunar Surface Magnetometer [NASA]
LSM........... Lymphocyte Separation Medium [Medicine]
LSM........... Lysergic Acid Morpholide
LSM........... Master of Life Science
LSMA.......... Low-Speed Multiplexer Arrangement
LSMC.......... Launching System Module Console [Navy] (CAAL)
LSMD.......... Dubendorf [Switzerland ICAO location identifier] (ICLI)
LSME.......... Emmen [Switzerland ICAO location identifier] (ICLI)
LSME.......... Logistic Support Maintenance Equipment (MCD)
LSME.......... London Society of Music Engravers [British] (DGA)
LS/MFT...... Lucky Strike Means Fine Tobacco [Advertising slogan]
LSMHT........ List of Standard/Modified Hand Tools (MCD)
LSMI.......... Logistics Support Management Information [NASA] (NASA)
LSMITH...... Locksmith
LSMLC........ Low-Speed Multiline Controller (MHDB)
L/Smn....... Leading Seaman [Navy British] (DMA)
LSMP.......... Logistic Support and Mobilization Plan [Military] (NVT)
LSMP.......... Payerne [Switzerland ICAO location identifier] (ICLI)
LSM(R)...... Landing Ship, Medium (Rocket) [Later, LFR] [Navy symbol]
LSMR.......... Rocket Ship [Navy symbol]
LSMS.......... Living Standards Management Study [International Monetary Fund]
LSMS.......... Louisiana State Medical Society (SRA)
LSMSO........ Landing Ship, Material Supply Officer
LSMT.......... Land Site Marshalling Team [Military]
LSMTP........ ListServ Simple Mail Transport Protocol [L-Soft International, Inc.] [Computer science]
LSMU.......... LASERcom Space Measurement Unit (IEEE)
LSM-USA.... Lutheran Student Movement - USA (EA)
LSMV.......... Lettuce Speckles Mottle Virus [Plant pathology]
LSMW.......... London School of Medicine for Women (ROG)
LSN........... Life Services Network of Illinois (SRA)
LSN........... Linear Sequential Network (MUGU)
LSN........... Line Stabilization Network
LSN........... Load Sharing Network
LSN........... Local Stock Number
LSN........... Los Banos, CA [Location identifier FAA] (FAAL)
LSND.......... Liquid Scintillator Neutrino Detector [Physics]
LSNLIS........ Lunar Science Natural Language Information System (PDAA)
LSNSR........ Line of Bearing Sensor

LSNSW .... Law Society of New South Wales [*Australia*]
LSNT .... Law Society of the Northern Territory [*Australia*]
LSNY .... Linnaean Society of New York (EA)
LSO .... Aerolineas del Sol, SA de CV [*Mexico*] [*FAA designator*] (FAAC)
LSO .... Kelso, WA [*Location identifier FAA*] (FAAL)
LSO .... Landing Safety Officer (MCD)
LSO .... Landing Signal Officer
LSO .... Landing Support Officer [*Navy*]
LSO .... Large Solar Observatory [*NASA*]
LSO .... LASMO pic ADS [*NYSE symbol*] (TTSB)
LSO .... Lasmo PLC [*NYSE symbol*] (SAG)
LSO .... Last Standing Order
LSO .... Lateral Superior Olive [*Brain anatomy*]
LSO .... Launch/Safety Officer [*NASA*]
LSO .... Law Schools On-Line (AAGC)
LSO .... Left Salpingo-Oophorectomy [*Gynecology*] (CPH)
LSO .... Lesotho [*ANSI three-letter standard code*] (CNC)
lso .... Licensor [*MARC relator code*] [*Library of Congress*] (LCCP)
LSO .... Life Systems Officer [*NASA*] (KSC)
LSO .... Line Stabilized Oscillator
LSO .... Linseed Oil (PDAA)
LSO .... Logistics Studies Office [*Army*] (RDA)
LSO .... London Symphony Orchestra
LSO .... Lost Lake Resources Ltd. [*Vancouver Stock Exchange symbol*]
LSO .... Louisiana Southern Railway Co. [*AAR code*]
LSO .... Lumbosacral Orthosis [*Medicine*]
LSO .... Lutetium, Silicon, and Oxygen [*Inorganic chemistry*]
LSOA .... Longitudinal Study of the Aging [*Department of Health and Human Services*] (GFGA)
LSOAD .... Life Sciences Organizations and Agencies Directory [*A publication*]
LSOC .... Launch Support Operations Contractor (SSD)
LSOC .... Lockheed Space Operations Co.
LSOC .... Logistical Support Operations Center [*Army*]
LSOCE .... Linear Stochastic Optimal Control and Estimation [*Computer program*]
LSOMT .... Large-Scale Operations Management Test (RDA)
LSOP .... Limit Switch Open [*Electronics*] (IAA)
LSOP .... L-Serine-O-Phosphate [*Biochemistry*]
LSOP .... Lunar Surface Operations Planning [*NASA*] (KSC)
LSOPrA .... LASMO plc Sr'A'Pref ADS [*NYSE symbol*] (TTSB)
LSOT .... Landing Signal Officer Trainer [*Navy*]
LSOV .... Linguistic Survey of the Ottawa Valley [*Carleton University*] [*Canada Research center*] (RCD)
LSP .... Landing Ship Personnel [*British military*] (DMA)
LSP .... Land Surface Parmeterization [*Environmental science*]
LSP .... Las Mesas [*Puerto Rico*] [*Seismograph station code, US Geological Survey*] (SEIS)
LSP .... Las Piedras [*Venezuela*] [*Airport symbol*] (OAG)
LSP .... Launcher Status Panel (MCD)
LSP .... Launch Sequence Plan [*NASA*] (IAA)
LSP .... Least Significant Portion (MCD)
LSP .... Least Significant Position (CMD)
LSP .... Left Sacroposterior [*A fetal position, the breech position*] [*Obstetrics*]
LSp .... Left Span (MAE)
LSP .... Level Set Point (NRCH)
LSP .... Levitated Spherator (PDAA)
LSP .... Liberale Staatspartij [*Liberal State Party*] [*Netherlands Political party*] (PPE)
LSP .... Liberal Socialist Party [*Egypt*] [*Political party*] (PPW)
LSP .... Library Software Package (ADA)
LSp .... Life Span
LSP .... Life Support Package [*Diving apparatus*]
LSP .... Light Scattering Photometer
LSP .... Lincoln Society of Philately [*Defunct*] (EA)
LSP .... Linear Selenium Photocell
LSP .... Line Spectrum Pair (IAA)
LSP .... Line Synchronizing Pulse
LSP .... Linked Systems Project [*of the Library of Congress*]
LSP .... Linked Systems Protocol [*Computer science*] (TNIG)
LSP .... Link State Packet [*Telecommunications*]
lsp .... Liters per Second per Person (ECON)
LSP .... Little Sisters of the Poor [*Roman Catholic religious order*]
LSP .... Liver-Specific [*Membrane*] Lipoprotein (DAVI)
LSP .... Liver-Specific Protein
LSP .... LM [*Lunar Module*] Specification [*NASA*] (KSC)
LSP .... Local Store Pointer
LSP .... Logical Signal Processor (IAA)
LSP .... Logistics Support Plan
LSP .... Lot Sensitive Plan (PDAA)
LSP .... Lower Sequential Permissive (NRCH)
LSP .... Lower Solution Point
LSP .... Low-Salinity Plume [*Oceanography*]
LSP .... Low-Speed Printer
LSP .... Low Support Program (OICC)
LSP .... Lucas-Sargent Proposition [*Economics*]
LSP .... Lumbar Spine [*Medicine*] (DHSM)
LSP .... Lunar Spectral Photometrics [*Aerospace*]
LSP .... Lunar Surface Probe [*Aerospace*]
LSP .... Lunar Survey Probe [*NASA*] (IAA)
LSPA .... Amlikon [*Switzerland ICAO location identifier*] (ICLI)
LSPA .... Lithuanian State Privatisation Agency
LSPAFRO ..... Lump-Sum Payment to Air Force Reserve Officers
LSPBP .... Large-Solid Propellant Booster Program [*Aerospace*] (IAA)
LSPBV .... Load-Sensing Proportioning and Bypass Valve
LSPC .... Legal Services for Prisoners with Children (EA)

LSPC .... Lewis Space Flight Center (MCD)
LSPC .... Linear Selenium Photocell
LSPC .... Living Stream Prayer Circle (EA)
LSPC .... Logistics Systems Policy Committee [*Navy*]
LSPC .... Louisiana Sweet Potato Commission
LSPD .... Dittingen [*Switzerland ICAO location identifier*] (ICLI)
LSPDF .... Life Science Payloads Development Facility (MCD)
LSPDS .... Lunar Survey Probe Delivery System [*NASA*] (SAA)
LSPE .... Lunar Seismic Profiling Experiment [*NASA*]
LSPET .... Lunar Sample Preliminary Examination Team [*NASA*]
LSPF .... Least Square Polynomial Fit (IAA)
LSPF .... Library Service to Prisoners Forum [*Association of Specialized and Cooperative Library Agencies*]
LSPF .... Schaffhausen [*Switzerland ICAO location identifier*] (ICLI)
LSPH .... Leningrad Special Psychiatric Hospital [*Formerly, LPPH*]
LSPH .... Winterthur [*Switzerland ICAO location identifier*] (ICLI)
LSPK .... Hasenstrick [*Switzerland ICAO location identifier*] (ICLI)
LSPK .... Loudspeaker (TEL)
LSPL .... Langenthal [*Switzerland ICAO location identifier*] (ICLI)
LSPN .... Triengen [*Switzerland ICAO location identifier*] (ICLI)
LSPO .... Lunar Surface Project Office [*NASA*] (KSC)
LSPP .... Step-by-Step Precedents and Procedures. Companies, Trusts, Superannuation Funds [*Australia A publication*]
LSPPO .... Lead Screw Position Pick-Off
LSPPS .... Logistic Support Plan for Preoperational Support (MCD)
LSPR .... Low-Speed Pulse Restorer (MCD)
LSPS .... Limited Serial Project Slip
LSPS .... Local Service Planning System [*Telecommunications*] (TEL)
LSPS .... Logistic Support Plan Summary
LSPSD .... Low-Speed Packet Switched Data [*Computer science*] (ACRL)
LSPT .... London School of Polymer Technology [*British*] (AIE)
LSPTP .... Low-Speed Paper Tape Punch [*Telecommunications*] (AABC)
LSPTR .... Low-Speed Paper Tape Reader [*Telecommunications*] (TEL)
LSPUD .... Lietuvos Socialdemokratu Partijos Uzsienio Delegatura [*Lithuanian Social Democratic Party*] (EAIO)
LSPV .... Wangen-Lachen [*Switzerland ICAO location identifier*] (ICLI)
LSPVPD .... Library Service to People with Visual or Physical Disabilities Forum [*Association of Specialized and Cooperative Library Agencies*] [*American Library Association*]
LSPZ .... Luzern-Beromunster [*Switzerland ICAO location identifier*] (ICLI)
LSQ .... Line Squall [*ICAO*] (FAAC)
LSQ .... L'Octogone, Bibliotheque Municipale de LaSalle, Quebec [*UTLAS symbol*]
LSQ .... Newark, NJ [*Location identifier FAA*] (FAAL)
LSQA .... Local System Queue Area [*Computer science*] (BUR)
LSQCP .... Logistic System Quality Control Program [*Military*] (AFIT)
LSR .... Alsair Societe [*France ICAO designator*] (FAAC)
LSR .... Laboratory for Space Research [*Netherlands*]
LSR .... Landing Ship, Rocket (NATG)
LSR .... Land Sea Rescue (NASA)
LSR .... Land Speed Record [*Auto racing*]
LSR .... Lanthanide Shift Reagent [*Spectroscopy*]
LSR .... Large Ship Reactor
LSR .... Laser
lsr .... Laser (VRA)
LSR .... Laser Technology [*AMEX symbol*] (TTSB)
LSR .... Laser Technology, Inc. [*AMEX symbol*] (SPSG)
LSR .... Last Speed Rating [*of a horse*]
LSR .... Launch Signal Responder (AAG)
LSR .... Launch Site Recovery [*NASA*] (KSC)
LSR .... Launch Support Requirement [*NASA*] (KSC)
LSR .... League for Socialist Reconstruction [*Later, IUP*] (EA)
LSR .... Lecithin/Sphingomyelin Ratio [*Medicine*] (DMAA)
LSR .... Left Superior Rectus [*Muscle*] [*Medicine*] (DMAA)
LSR .... Life Science Research Ltd. [*British*] (IRUK)
LSR .... Lighthouse Resources, Inc. [*Vancouver Stock Exchange symbol*]
LSR .... Light-Scattering Response [*Biology*]
LSR .... Light-Sensitive Relay
LSR .... Light-Sensitive Resistor
LSR .... Light Stopping Reticle
LSR .... Light, Straight Run [*Petroleum technology*]
LSR .... Limited Style Run
LSR .... Limited to Searches (MCD)
LSR .... Limit Switch Reverse [*Electronics*] (IAA)
LSR .... LINAC Stretcher Ring [*Design for an electron accelerator*]
LSR .... Linear Seal Ring
LSR .... Linear Sedimentation Rate [*Geology*]
LSR .... Line Source Range (IAA)
LSR .... Lingual Skills Required [*Civil service*]
LSR .... Liquid Slip Ring
LSR .... Liver/Spleen Ratio [*Medicine*] (DMAA)
LSR .... Load Shifting Resistor (MSA)
LSR .... Load Storage Register
LSR .... Local Shared Resources [*Computer science*] (IBMDP)
LSR .... Local Standard of Rest [*Galactic science*]
LSR .... Local Storage Register (NITA)
LSR .... Local Sunrise
LSR .... Location Stack Register
LSR .... Locus Standi Reports [*A publication*] (DLA)
LSR .... Logical Shift Right [*Computer science*]
LSR .... Logistics Support Requirements (NG)
LSR .... Logistic Status Review
LSR .... Loop Shorting Relay (MCD)
LSR .... Loose Snow on Runway [*NWS*] (FAAC)
LSR .... Lost River, AK [*Location identifier FAA*] (FAAL)

LSR............. Lovers of the Stinking Rose (EA)
LSR............. Low-Speed Reader
LSR............. Low Stocking Rate [*Agriculture*] (OA)
LSR............. Luftschutzraum [*Air-Raid Shelter*] [*German military - World War II*]
LSR............. Lunar Surface Rendezvous [*NASA*] (KSC)
LSR............. Lynchburg Source Reactor
LSRA.......... Logistic Support Requirement Analysis (MCD)
LSRB.......... Linear Sound Ranging Base (PDAA)
LSRC........... Launch Site Recovery Commander [*NASA*] (KSC)
LSRC........... Logistics Systems Review Committee [*DARCOM*] (MCD)
LSRC........... Lunar Surface Return Container [*NASA*] (KSC)
LSRD........... Logistic Support Readiness Date
LSRE........... Leisure
LSREF......... LaSalle Re Holdings Ltd. [*NASDAQ symbol*] (SAG)
LSREF......... LaSall Re Holdings [*NASDAQ symbol*] (TTSB)
LSRF........... LASER Submarine Range-Finder
LSRF........... Logistic Support Resource Funds [*Army*]
LSRI............ Large Screen RADAR Indicator
LSRM.......... Life Science Research Module (MCD)
LSRO........... Life Sciences Research Office [*NASA*] (KSC)
LSRP........... Local Switching Replacement Planning [*Telecommunications*] (TEL)
LSR-P......... Loose Snow on Runway-Patchy [*Aviation*] (DNAB)
LSRS........... LOAD [*Low Altitude Defense*] System Requirements Simulation
LsrSght....... Laser Sight, Inc. [*Associated Press*] (SAG)
LsrTc.......... Laser Technology, Inc. [*Associated Press*] (SAG)
LsrTech....... Laser Technology, Inc. [*Associated Press*] (SAG)
LsrV........... Laser Video Network, Inc. [*Associated Press*] (SAG)
LSRV........... London and Scottish Rifle Volunteers [*Military British*] (ROG)
LSRV........... Lunar Surface Roving Vehicle [*Aerospace*]
LsrVd.......... Laser Video Network, Inc. [*Associated Press*] (SAG)
LsrVide....... Laser Video Network, Inc. [*Associated Press*] (SAG)
LsrVis........ Laser Vision Centers, Inc. [*Associated Press*] (SAG)
LsrVs.......... Laser Vision Centers, Inc. [*Associated Press*] (SAG)
LSR.WS..... Laser Technology Wrrt [*AMEX symbol*] (TTSB)
LSS............. Exec Express II, Inc. [*ICAO designator*] (FAAC)
LSS............. Laboratory for Surface Studies [*University of Wisconsin, Milwaukee*] [*Research center*] (RCD)
LSS............. Laboratory Support Service
LSS............. Ladies Shoemakers' Society [*A union*] [*British*]
LSS............. Landing, Separation Simulator (MCD)
LSS............. Landing Ship Sternchute [*British military*] (DMA)
LSS............. Landing Ship, Support (NATG)
LSS............. Landing-Site Supervisor
LSS............. Lane Sensing System [*Automotive engineering*]
LSS............. Language for Symbolic Simulation
LSS............. Language Support System (IAA)
LSS............. Large-Scale Standard (IAA)
LSS............. Large-Scale Structure [*Cosmology*]
LSS............. Large Space Structure (IEEE)
LSS............. Large Space System (IEEE)
LSS............. Lateral Series Servo (MCD)
LSS............. Launcher Support Structure [*Navy*] (CAAL)
LSS............. Launch Sequence Simulator
LSS............. Launch Signature Simulator (MCD)
LSS............. Launch Status Summarizer
LSS............. Launch Support Section [*NASA*]
LSS............. Launch Support System [*NASA*] (KSC)
LSS............. Law Society of Scotland
LSS............. Leipziger Semitische Studien [*A publication*] (BJA)
LSS............. Leopold Stokowski Society (EA)
LSS............. Les Saintes [*Guadeloupe*] [*Airport symbol*] (OAG)
LSS............. Licensing Support System [*Department of Energy*] (EGAO)
LSS............. Life Saving Service (WDAA)
LSS............. Lifesaving Station [*Nautical charts*]
LSS............. Life Services System [*For the disabled*]
LSS............. Life-Span Study [*Environmental science*] (FFDE)
LSS............. Life Support System [*or Subsystem*]
LSS............. Light Spot Scanner
LSS............. Limited Storage Site (AABC)
LSS............. Line Scanner System
LSS............. Linking Segment Subprogram
LSS............. Liquid Scintillation Spectrometer
LSS............. Liver-Spleen Scan [*Medicine*] (MEDA)
LSS............. Local Synchronization Subsystem [*Telecommunications*] (TEL)
LSS............. Logistic Support Squadron (AAG)
LSS............. Logistic Support System (AABC)
LSS............. Longitudinal Static Stability
LSS............. Loop Switching System [*Telecommunications*]
LSS............. LOT [*Limited Operational Test*] Support Services [*Military*] (DWSG)
LSS............. Lumbosacral Spine [*Medicine*] (MEDA)
LSS............. Lunar Soil Stimulant [*NASA*] (KSC)
LSS............. Lunar Surveying System [*Aerospace*]
LSS............. Lunar Survey Sensor [*NASA*] (KSC)
LSS............. Lung Serum Simulant (PDAA)
LSSA........... Lutheran Social Service System [*An association*]
LSSA........... Law Society of South Australia
LSSA........... Leopold Stokowski Society of America (EA)
LSSA........... Lipid Soluble Secondary Antioxidants [*Biochemistry*]
LSSA........... Lithuanian Student Scout Association [*Later, Lithuanian Scouts Association College Division*] (EA)
LSSA........... Logistic System Support Activity [*Army*]
LSSA........... Logistic System Support Agency
LSSAS......... Longitudinal Static Stability Augmentation System (MCD)
LSSB........... Bern Radio [*Switzerland ICAO location identifier*] (ICLI)

LSSB........... Legal Support Services Branch [*General Accounting Office*] [*Information service or system*] (IID)
LSSB........... Light SEAL [*Sea, Air, and Land*] Support Boat [*Navy*] (DNAB)
LSSC........... Lake Superior State College [*Sault Ste. Marie, MI*]
LSSc........... Licentiate in Sacred Scriptures
LSSC........... Licentiate in Sanitary Science [*British*] (ROG)
LSSC........... Light SEAL [*Sea, Air, and Land*] Support Craft [*Navy symbol*]
LSSC........... Logistic Support System Characteristics (AAG)
LSSC........... Logistic System Support Center [*Army*]
LSSC........... Lower-Sideband Suppressed Carrier (IDOE)
LSSD........... Level Sensitive Scan Design (MCD)
LSSD........... Lower-Speed Service-Deriving [*Telecommunications*] (TSSD)
LSSD........... Lunar Surface Sampling Device [*Aerospace*]
LSSDDPMAG... Library Service to Developmentally Disabled Persons Membership Activity Group [*Association of Specialized and Cooperative Library Agencies*] [*American Library Association*]
LSSDPF....... Library Service to the Developmentally Disabled Persons Forum [*Association of Specialized and Cooperative Library Agencies*] [*American Library Association*]
LSSE........... Licentiate in Social, Economic, & Political Sciences (DD)
LSSF........... Land Special Security Force [*Army*] (AABC)
LSSF........... Life Sciences Support Facility [*NASA*] (NASA)
LSSF........... Limited Service Storage Facility
LSSG........... Logistics Studies Steering Group (AABC)
LSSGR......... Local Switching System General Requirement [*Telecommunications*]
LSSI........... Leasing Solutions [*NASDAQ symbol*] (TTSB)
LSSI........... Leasing Solutions, Inc. [*NASDAQ symbol*] (SAG)
LSSI........... Library Systems and Services, Inc. [*Information service or system*] (IID)
LSSL........... Landing Ship Support, Large [*Military*] (VNW)
LSSL........... Life Sciences Space Laboratory [*NASA*] (NASA)
LSSL........... Support Landing Ship (Large) MK III
LSSM.......... Launch Site Support Manager [*NASA*] (NASA)
LSSM.......... Local Scientific Survey Module [*NASA*]
LSSM.......... Lunar Surface Scientific Module [*NASA*]
LSSO........... Bern. Office Federal de l'Air [*Switzerland ICAO location identifier*] (ICLI)
LSSO........... Library Science Student Organization
LSSP........... Lanka Sama Samaja Party [*Sri Lanka Equal Society Party*] [*Political party*] (PPW)
LSSP........... Latest Scram Set Point (NRCH)
LSSP........... Launch Site Support Plan (MCD)
LSSP........... Lunar Surveying System Program [*Aerospace*]
LSSPO......... Life Support Systems Project Office [*NASA*] (MCD)
LSSPS......... Libraries Serving Special Populations Section [*Association of Specialized and Cooperative Library Agencies*]
LSSPSC....... Life Sciences Strategic Planning Study Committee [*NASA*]
LSSR........... Amphibious Coastal Reconnaissance Ship [*Navy symbol*]
LSSR........... Berne/Radio Suisse SA [*Switzerland ICAO location identifier*] (ICLI)
LSSR .... Lessor
LSSRC......... Life Sciences Shuttle Research Centrifuge [*NASA*] (NASA)
LSSS........... Geneve [*Switzerland ICAO location identifier*] (ICLI)
LSSS........... LASER Source Signature Simulator
LSSS........... Lightweight Ship SATCOM Set [*Navy*] (CAAL)
LSSS........... Lime-Sulphur-Synthetic-Solution [*Hydrometallurgy*]
LSSS........... Limiting Safety System Setting [*Nuclear energy*] (NRCH)
LSST........... Launch Site Support Team (MCD)
lsst............. Lead-Sheathed Steel-Taped
LS/ST......... Light Shield/Star Tracker (NASA)
LSST........... List of Specifications and Standards (MSA)
LSST........... Lone Star Technologies [*NASDAQ symbol*] (SAG)
LSSTA......... Low Supersonic Transport (PDAA)
LSSTA......... Lunar Space Tug (PDAA)
LSSU .... Lake Superior State University [*Michigan*]
LSSW.......... Zurich [*Switzerland ICAO location identifier*] (ICLI)
LST............. Amphibious Ship, Tank
LST............. Lakewood Forest Products Ltd. [*Vancouver Stock Exchange symbol*]
LST............. Laminated SONAR Transistor
LST............. Landing Ship, Tank [*Navy symbol*]
LST............. Landing Ship Transport (MCD)
LST............. Laplace-Stieltjes Transform
LST............. Large Space Telescope [*Later, Space Telescope*] [*NASA*]
LST............. Large Stellar Telescope (KSC)
LST............. Large Subsonic Tunnel [*NASA*]
LST............. LASER Spot Tracker (MCD)
LST............. Last (BUR)
LST............. Lateral Sinus Thrombophlebitis [*Medicine*] (MEDA)
LST............. Lateral Spinothalamic Tract [*Neurology*] (DAVI)
LST............. Late Start Time
LST............. Launceston [*Tasmania*] [*Airport symbol*] (OAG)
LST............. Launch Support Team [*NASA*] (KSC)
LST............. Lauryl Sulfate Tryptose [*Growth medium*]
LST............. Law Society of Tasmania [*Australia*]
LST............. Left Sacrotransverse [*A fetal position*] [*Obstetrics*]
LST............. Left Store (SAA)
LST............. Licentiate in Sacred Theology [*British*]
LST............. Life-Sustaining Treatment [*Medicine*] (DMAA)
LST............. Light-Sensitive Tube
LST............. Line Scan Tube
LST............. Liquid Oxygen Start Tank (AAG)
LST............. Liquid Storage Tank (AAG)
LST............. Listing of a Program in a File [*Computer science*]
LST............. Living Structures Tank (WDAA)
LST............. Local Sidereal Time
LST............. Local Solar Time

LST............. Local Standard Time
LST............. Local Summer Time [Astronomy] (IAA)
LST............. Lone Star [Missouri] [Seismograph station code, US Geological Survey] (SEIS)
LST............. Lone Star, TX [Location identifier FAA] (FAAL)
LST............. Long-Term Stability Test [Chemistry]
LST............. Loud Speaking Telephone (NITA)
LST............. Low-Solvent Technology (GNE)
LST............. Lunar Surface Telescope [NASA]
LST............. Lunar Surface Transponder [Aerospace]
LSTAR......... Limited Scientific and Technical Aerospace Reports [NASA] (MCD)
LSTAT......... Life Support for Trauma And Transport [Northrop Grumman] (PS)
LSTB........... Bellechasse [Switzerland ICAO location identifier] (ICLI)
LSTB........... Long Shoot Terminal Bud [Botany]
LStBA.......... Saint Joseph's Abbey, St. Benedict, LA [Library symbol Library of Congress] (LCLS)
LST/CAM...... LASER Spot Tracker/Strike Camera (MCD)
LSTD.......... Leading Steward [British military] (DMA)
LSTD.......... Lunar Satellite Tracking Data [NASA] (KSC)
lstd--......... Tristan da Cunha Island [MARC geographic area code Library of Congress] (LCCP)
LSTE.......... Large Structure Technology Experiment (SSD)
LSTE.......... Launch Site Transportation Equipment [NASA] (NASA)
LSTF.......... Lead Sulfide Thin Film
LST-G......... Large Steam Turbine-Generator
LStgH.......... Hunt Correctional Center (Louisiana Correctional Institute for Women), St. Gabriel, LA [Library symbol Library of Congress] (LCLS)
LST(H)........ Landing Ship, Tank (Casualty Evacuation) [Navy symbol Obsolete]
LST(H)........ Landing Ship, Tank (Hospital) [British military] (DMA)
LStjT.......... Tensas Parish Library, St. Joseph, LA [Library symbol Library of Congress] (LCLS)
LSTL.......... Laparoscopic Tubal Ligation [Gynecology] (DAVI)
LSTM.......... Lander Static Test Model [NASA]
LSTM.......... Large-Sample Scanning Tunneling Mode [Microscopy]
LSTM.......... Low Steam
LStmSM...... St. Martin Parish Library, St. Martinville, LA [Library symbol Library of Congress] (LCLS)
LSTN.......... Light Station [Coast Guard] (IAA)
LSTNG........ Lasting
LSTO.......... Motiers [Switzerland ICAO location identifier] (ICLI)
LSTR.......... Landstar System [NASDAQ symbol] (TTSB)
LSTR.......... Landstar System, Inc. [NASDAQ symbol] (SAG)
LSTR.......... Montricher [Switzerland ICAO location identifier] (ICLI)
LSTS.......... Landing Ship (Utility) [Navy symbol]
LSTS.......... Launch Station Test Set (MCD)
LSTS.......... Low-Pressure Side Temperature Sensor [Air conditioning system] [Automotive engineering]
LSTS.......... Lunar Surface Thermal Simulator [NASA] (KSC)
LST/SCAM... LASER Spot Tracker / Strike Camera
LSTSRFA .... Launch Station Test Set Radio Frequency Adapter (MCD)
LSTT.......... Lake Superior Terminal & Transfer Railway Co. [AAR code]
LSTTL........ Low-Power Schottky Transistor-Transistor Logic [Electronics]
L Stud H...... Law Students' Helper [A publication] (DLA)
L Stud Helper... Law Students' Helper [A publication] (DLA)
L Stud J...... Law Students' Journal [A publication] (DLA)
L Stu Mag ... Law Students' Magazine [A publication] (DLA)
L Stu Mag NS... Law Students' Magazine. New Series [A publication] (ILCA)
L Stu Mag OS... Law Students' Magazine. Old Series [A publication] (ILCA)
lstwx......... Lost Wax (VRA)
LSTX.......... Bex [Switzerland ICAO location identifier] (ICLI)
LSTY.......... Yverdon [Switzerland ICAO location identifier] (ICLI)
LSU............. Institute of Continuing Legal Education, Louisiana State University Law Center (DLA)
LSU............. Labor Service Unit [Military]
LSU............. Lactose Saccharose Urea [Cell growth medium]
LSU............. Lamentation over the Destruction of Sumer and Ur (BJA)
LSU............. Landing Ship, Utility [Navy symbol Obsolete]
LSU............. Launcher Selector Unit
LSU............. Launcher Switching Unit [Navy] (CAAL)
LSU............. Law Society of Upper Canada [UTLAS symbol]
LSU............. Leading Signal Unit [Telecommunications] (TEL)
LSU............. Liberalsoziale Union [Liberal Social Union] [Germany Political party] (PPW)
LSU............. Library Storage Unit
LSU............. Life Support Umbilical [NASA]
LSU............. Life Support Unit [NASA] (KSC)
LSU............. Lighthouse Study Unit (EA)
LSU............. Limit Switch Up [Electronics] (IAA)
LSU............. Line Selection Unit [Telecommunications] (IAA)
LSU............. Line-Sharing Unit
LSU............. Livestock Unit
LSU............. Load Storage Unit [Computer science]
LSU............. Local Storage Unit [Computer science]
LSU............. Local Switching Unit [Telecommunications] (TEL)
LSU............. Local Synchronization Utility [Telecommunications] (TEL)
LSU............. Logistics Support Unit [Military] (NVT)
LSU............. Lone Signalling Unit (NITA)
LSU............. Lone Signal Unit [Telecommunications] (TEL)
LSU............. Long Sukang [Malaysia] [Airport symbol] (OAG)
LSU............. Louisiana State University
LSU............. Louisiana State University and Agricultural and Mechanical College (GAGS)
LSU............. Southern University at New Orleans, New Orleans, LA [OCLC symbol] (OCLC)

LSU Med Cent... Louisiana State University Medicine Center (GAGS)
LSUNO......... Louisiana State University in New Orleans [Later, University of New Orleans]
L Sup............ Lake Superior (BARN)
LSUP............ Loader Storage Unit Support Program [Computer science] (MHDI)
L Sup H & D... Lalor's Supplement to Hill and Denio's New York Reports [A publication] (DLA)
LSUR............ Leisure
LSU Shreveport... Louisiana State University Shreveport (GAGS)
LSUV............ Lunar Surface Ultraviolet [Camera] [NASA]
LSUV............ Luxury Sport Utility Vehicle
LSV............ Alak [Former USSR ICAO designator] (FAAC)
LSV............ Landing Ship, Vehicle [Navy symbol]
LSV............ Las Vegas, NV [Location identifier FAA] (FAAL)
LSV............ Left Subclavian Vein [Anatomy]
LSV............ Lily Symptomless Virus [Plant pathology]
LSV............ Linear Shift-Varying (PDAA)
LSV............ Linear Sweep Voltammograms [Electrochemistry]
LSV............ Line Status Verifier [Telecommunications] (TEL)
LSV............ Logistics Support Vessel [Military]
LSV............ Low-Signature Vehicle [Hazardous materials control]
LSV............ Lunar Shuttle Vehicle [Aerospace] (AAG)
LSV............ Lunar Surface Vehicle [Aerospace]
LSV............ Lunar Survey Viewfinder [Aerospace]
LSVC............ Lunar Surface Vehicle Communications [Aerospace]
LSVG............ Lifesaving (MSA)
LSVI............ Little Switzerland [NASDAQ symbol] (TTSB)
LSVI............ Little Switzerland, Inc. [NASDAQ symbol] (SAG)
LSVP............ Landing Ship, Vehicle and Personnel [Navy symbol]
LSW............ Detroit, MI [Location identifier FAA] (FAAL)
LSW............ Labrador Sea Water [Oceanography]
LSW............ Landslide [Washington] [Seismograph station code, US Geological Survey Closed] (SEIS)
LSW............ LASER Spot Welder
LSW............ Least Significant Word (MCD)
LSW............ Licensed Shorthand Writer
LSW............ Lifshitz-Slyozov-Wagner Theory of Mineral Recrystallization
LSW............ Light Support Weapon (MCD)
LSW............ Limit Switch [Electronics]
LSW............ Line Switch [Telecommunications] (IAA)
LSWA............ Large-Amplitude, Slow Wave Activity [Encephalography]
LSWA............ Law Society of Western Australia
LSWMA....... Lutheran Society for Worship, Music, and the Arts [Later, Liturgical Conference]
LSWP............ Lump-Sum Wage Payments (MCD)
LSWR............ London & South-Western Railway (ROG)
LSWT............ Low-Speed Wind Tunnel (MCD)
LSX............ Landing Ship, Experimental
LSXB............ Balzers/FL [Switzerland ICAO location identifier] (ICLI)
LSXD............ Domat-Ems [Switzerland ICAO location identifier] (ICLI)
LSXE............ Erstfeld [Switzerland ICAO location identifier] (ICLI)
LSXH............ Holziken [Switzerland ICAO location identifier] (ICLI)
lsxj--........... St. Helena [MARC geographic area code Library of Congress] (LCCP)
LSXL............ Lauterbrunnen [Switzerland ICAO location identifier] (ICLI)
LSXM............ St. Moritz [Switzerland ICAO location identifier] (ICLI)
LSXO............ Gossau SG [Switzerland ICAO location identifier] (ICLI)
LSXS............ Schindellegi [Switzerland ICAO location identifier] (ICLI)
LSXT............ Trogen [Switzerland ICAO location identifier] (ICLI)
LSXU............ Untervaz [Switzerland ICAO location identifier] (ICLI)
LSXV............ San Vittore [Switzerland ICAO location identifier] (ICLI)
LSXW............ Wurenlingen [Switzerland ICAO location identifier] (ICLI)
LSY............ Lindsay Aviation, Inc. [ICAO designator] (FAAC)
LSY............ Lismore [Australia Airport symbol] (OAG)
LSYC............ League of Socialist Youth of Croatia [Political party]
LSZA............ Lugano [Switzerland ICAO location identifier] (ICLI)
LSZB............ Bern/Belp [Switzerland ICAO location identifier] (ICLI)
LSZC............ Bad Ragaz [Switzerland ICAO location identifier] (ICLI)
LSZD............ Ascona [Switzerland ICAO location identifier] (ICLI)
LSZE............ Bad Ragaz [Switzerland ICAO location identifier] (ICLI)
LSZF............ Birrfeld [Switzerland ICAO location identifier] (ICLI)
LSZG............ Grenchen [Switzerland ICAO location identifier] (ICLI)
LSZH............ Zurich [Switzerland ICAO location identifier] (ICLI)
LSZI............ Fricktal-Schupfart [Switzerland ICAO location identifier] (ICLI)
LSZJ............ Courtelary [Switzerland ICAO location identifier] (ICLI)
LSZK............ Speck-Fehraltorf [Switzerland ICAO location identifier] (ICLI)
LSZL............ Locarno [Switzerland ICAO location identifier] (ICLI)
LSZM............ Bale [Switzerland ICAO location identifier] (ICLI)
LSZN............ Hausen Am Albis [Switzerland ICAO location identifier] (ICLI)
LSZP............ Biel/Kappelen [Switzerland ICAO location identifier] (ICLI)
LSZR............ Altenrhein [Switzerland ICAO location identifier] (ICLI)
LSZS............ Samedan [Switzerland ICAO location identifier] (ICLI)
LSZT............ Lommis [Switzerland ICAO location identifier] (ICLI)
LSZU............ Buttwil [Switzerland ICAO location identifier] (ICLI)
LSZV............ Sitterdorf [Switzerland ICAO location identifier] (ICLI)
LSZW............ Thun [Switzerland ICAO location identifier] (ICLI)
LSZX............ Schanis [Switzerland ICAO location identifier] (ICLI)
LSZY............ Porrentruy [Switzerland ICAO location identifier] (ICLI)
LSZZ............ Collective address for NOTAM and SNOWTAM [Switzerland ICAO location identifier] (ICLI)
LT............ Fixed Light [USCG] (TAG)
LT............ Great Sierra [ICAO designator] (AD)
LT............ Heat-labile Enterotoxin [Biochemistry] (DAVI)
LT............ Laboratory Test (IAA)
LT .... [The] Lake Terminal Railroad Co. [AAR code]

LT	Laminated TEFLON
LT	Landed Terms
LT	Landing Team
LT	Lands Tribunal [Legal] [British]
LT	Language Translation [Computer science]
LT	Laplace Transform [Mathematics]
LT	Lapped Transform [Telecommunications]
LT	Laptop [Computer] (BARN)
LT	Large Tug [Army]
LT	Larsen and Toubro Ltd. [India] [Commercial firm]
LT	LASER Trimming (PDAA)
LT	Last (ROG)
LT	Last Telecast (NTCM)
LT	Last Telecast (WDMC)
LT	Lateral Tooth
LT	Lateral Triceps Brachii [Medicine]
LT	Latest Time [Business term]
LT	Laughter Therapy (EA)
LT	Launch Test [NASA] (IAA)
LT	Laundry Tray
LT	Lawn Tennis
LT	Law Times Journal [A publication] (DLA)
LT	Law Times Newspaper [A publication] (DLA)
LT	Law Times Reports [British]
LT	Layout Template (MCD)
L/T	Leading Telegraphist
LT	Leading Torpedoman [Navy British]
LT	Lead Time (NG)
LT	League of Tarcisians (EA)
LT	Left
LT	Left Tackle [Football]
LT	Left Thigh
LT	Left Triceps [Anatomy] (DAVI)
LT	Legal Tender [Currency]
LT	Legal Title [Business term]
lt	Legal Training [Navy British]
Lt	Leptosphaerulina Trifolii [A fungus]
LT	Less Than (IBMDP)
LT	Letter
LT	Letter of Transmittal (MCD)
LT	Letter Telegram
LT	Leukotriene [Clinical pharmacology]
LT	Level Transmitter (NRCH)
LT	Level Trigger
LT	Levin Tube [Medicine]
LT	Levothyroxine [Pharmacy]
LT	Library Talk [A publication] (BRI)
LT	Licentiate in Teaching [British]
LT	Licentiate in Theology
LT	Lid Tank
LT	Lieutenant (EY)
LT	Lieutenant
LT	Light (AAG)
lt	Light (WDMC)
lt	Light (VRA)
LT	Light Tank
LT	Light Terminal (PDAA)
LT	Light Test (IAA)
LT	Light Trap
LT	Light Truck [British]
LT	Limit (DEN)
LT	Limited Term Employee (OICC)
L/T	Line Telecommunications
L/T	Line Telegraphy
LT	Line Terminator
LT	Linked Term [Online database field identifier]
LT	Link Terminal [Telecommunications] (TEL)
LT	Link Testing (NITA)
LT	Link Trainer Instructor
LT	Liquid Toned [Copier] [Reprography]
LT	Lira Toscana [Tuscany Pound] [Monetary unit] [Italian] (ROG)
LT	Lira Turca [Turkish Pound] [Monetary unit] [Italian] (ROG)
LT	Liter (ECII)
LT	Loader Trainer (MCD)
LT	Loader-Transporter [British military] (DMA)
L/T	Load Test (MCD)
LT	Local Time
LT	Locum Tenens [In the Place Of] [Latin]
LT	Logic Theorist [or Theory] [Computer science]
LT	Logic Tree
LT	London-Ducretet-Thomson [Record label] [Great Britain, USA, etc.]
LT	London Transport
LT	Long Term
LT	Long-Term Stay [in hospital] [British]
LT	Long Throw [Speaker system]
LT	Long Ton [2240 pounds]
LT	Long Tour [Military] (GFGA)
LT	Long Treble [Crocheting] (ROG)
LT	Lookthrough (LAIN)
L/T	Loop Test [Aerospace] (AAG)
LT	Lot
LT	Lo Ta'aseh (BJA)
LT	Lot Time (SAA)
LT	Lower Torso
LT	Low Temperature

LT	Low Tension
LT	Low Torque
LT	Low Transverse [incision] [Obstetrics] (DAVI)
LT	Lucis Trust (EA)
LT	Lug Terminal
LT	Lumbar Traction [Orthopedics] (DAVI)
LT	Luxury Tax (MHDB)
LT	Lymphocyte Transformation [Hematology]
LT	Lymphoid Tissue [Biology]
LT	Lymphotoxin [Immunochemistry]
LT	Turn Left after Takeoff [Aviation] (FAAC)
LTA	Land Trust Alliance (EA)
LTA	Large Transport Airplane
LTA	Launch Test Area
LTA	Lawn Tennis Association (EAIO)
LTA	Lead Tetraacetate [Organic chemistry]
LTA	Leave Travel Allowance
LTA	Legionarios del Trabajo in America (EA)
LTA	Leisure Time Activity
LTA	LEM Test Article (MCD)
LTA	Lettera di Transporto Aereo [Air Waybill] [Italian Business term]
LTA	Lettre de Transport Aerien [Air Waybill] [French Business term]
LTA	Leucotriene A [Clinical pharmacology]
LTA	Leveling Torquer Amplifier
LTA	Library Technical Assistant
LTA	Lighter-than-Air [Aircraft]
LTA	Linea Aerea Tama [Chile] [ICAO designator] (FAAC)
LTA	Linen Trade Association (EA)
LTA	Lipoate Transacetylase [An enzyme]
LTA	Lipoteichoic Acid [Biochemistry]
LTA	Living Together Arrangement
LTA	LM [Lunar Module] Test Article [NASA]
LTA	Local Training Area (MCD)
LTA	Logical Transient Area
LTA	Logic Time Analyzer (IAA)
LTA	Long-Term Arrangements [Department of State]
LTA	Long-Term Average (CAAL)
LTA	Lower Torso Assembly [Aerospace] (MCD)
LTA	Low Temperature Aftercooled [Automotive engineering]
LTA	Low-Temperature Ashing [Analytical chemistry]
LTA	South Lake Tahoe, CA [Location identifier FAA] (FAAL)
LTA	Tzaneen [South Africa] [Airport symbol] (OAG)
LTAA	Ankara [Turkey ICAO location identifier] (ICLI)
LTAB	Guvercinlik [Turkey ICAO location identifier] (ICLI)
LTAB	League to Abolish Billionaires [Fictitious organization mentioned in Donald Duck comic by Carl Barks]
LTAC	Ankara/Esenboga [Turkey ICAO location identifier] (ICLI)
LTAC	Literary Translators Association of Canada (EAIO)
LTACFIRE	Lightweight Tactical Fire Direction System [Artillery] [Army] (INF)
LTAD	Ankara/Etimesgut [Turkey ICAO location identifier] (ICLI)
LTADL	Launcher Tube Azimuth Datum Line
LTAE	Ankara/Murted [Turkey ICAO location identifier] (ICLI)
LTAF	Adana/Sakirpasa [Turkey ICAO location identifier] (ICLI)
LTAG	Adana/Incirlik [Turkey ICAO location identifier] (ICLI)
LTAH	Afyon [Turkey ICAO location identifier] (ICLI)
LTAI	Antalya [Turkey ICAO location identifier] (ICLI)
LTAJ	Gaziantep [Turkey ICAO location identifier] (ICLI)
LTAK	Iskenderun [Turkey ICAO location identifier] (ICLI)
LTAL	Kastamonu [Turkey ICAO location identifier] (ICLI)
LTAL	Lower Transition Altitude (SAA)
LTALT	Light Alternating (IAA)
LTAM	Kayseri [Turkey ICAO location identifier] (ICLI)
LTaM	Madison Parish Library, Tallulah, LA [Library symbol Library of Congress] (LCLS)
LTAN	Konya [Turkey ICAO location identifier] (ICLI)
LT & D	Love, Togetherness, and Devotion [Rock music group]
LT & S	London, Tilbury & Southend Railway [British]
LT & SR	London, Tilbury & Southend Railway [British] (ROG)
LTAO	Malatya/Erhac [Turkey ICAO location identifier] (ICLI)
LTAP	Merzifon [Turkey ICAO location identifier] (ICLI)
LTAQ	Samsun [Turkey ICAO location identifier] (ICLI)
LTAR	Sivas [Turkey ICAO location identifier] (ICLI)
LTAS	Lead Tetraacetate-Schiff (Reaction) [Clinical chemistry]
LTAS	Lighter than Air Society [An association] (PDAA)
LTAS	Zonguldak [Turkey ICAO location identifier] (ICLI)
LTAT	Malatya/Erhac [Turkey ICAO location identifier] (ICLI)
LTAU	Kayseri/Erkilet [Turkey ICAO location identifier] (ICLI)
LTAV	Sivrihisar [Turkey ICAO location identifier] (ICLI)
LTAVD	Low-Temperature Arc Vapor Deposition [Coating technology]
LTB	Acute Laryngotracheobronchitis [Commonly known as croup] (PAZ)
Li B	Bachelor of Literature
LTB	Laparoscopic Tubal Banding [Ligation] (DAVI)
LTB	Laryngo-Tracheal Bronchitis
LTB	Last Trunk Busy [Telecommunications] (TEL)
LTB	Lawrence Traffic Bureau Inc., Kansas City MO [STAC]
LTB	Law Times Bankruptcy Reports [United States] [A publication] (DLA)
LTB	Leucotriene B [Clinical pharmacology]
LTB	Light Bay [Horse racing]
LTB	Limited Test Ban [Nuclear testing]
LTB	Line Term Buffer [Computer science] (AABC)
LTB	London Tourist Board [British] (DCTA)
LTB	London Transport Board [British]
LT(B)	Low-Tension (Battery) (DEN)
LTBA	Die Lexikalischen Tafelserien der Babylonier und Assyrer in den Berliner Museen [A publication] (BJA)

LTBA .... Istanbul/Yesilkoy [*Turkey ICAO location identifier*] (ICLI)
LTBA .... Louisiana Thoroughbred Breeders Association (SRA)
LTBB .... Istanbul [*Turkey ICAO location identifier*] (ICLI)
LTBC .... Alasehir [*Turkey ICAO location identifier*] (ICLI)
LTBC .... Lawn Tennis Ball Convention [*British*] (BI)
LTBD .... Aydin [*Turkey ICAO location identifier*] (ICLI)
LTBE .... Bursa [*Turkey ICAO location identifier*] (ICLI)
LTBF .... Balikesir [*Turkey ICAO location identifier*] (ICLI)
LTBG .... Bandirma [*Turkey ICAO location identifier*] (ICLI)
LTBH .... Canakkale [*Turkey ICAO location identifier*] (ICLI)
LTBI .... Eskisehir [*Turkey ICAO location identifier*] (ICLI)
LTBJ .... Izmir/Cumaovasi [*Turkey ICAO location identifier*] (ICLI)
LTBK .... Izmir/Gaziemir [*Turkey ICAO location identifier*] (ICLI)
LTBL .... Izmir/Cigli [*Turkey ICAO location identifier*] (ICLI)
LtBl .... Light Blend [*Horticulture*]
LTBM .... Isparta [*Turkey ICAO location identifier*] (ICLI)
LTBMC .... Long-Term Bone Marrow Culture [*Cell culture*]
LTBN .... Kutahya [*Turkey ICAO location identifier*] (ICLI)
LTBO .... Linear Time Base Oscillator
LTBO .... Usak [*Turkey ICAO location identifier*] (ICLI)
LTBP .... London Tanker Broker Panel
LTBP .... Yalova [*Turkey ICAO location identifier*] (ICLI)
LTBQ .... Topel [*Turkey ICAO location identifier*] (ICLI)
LTBR .... Yenisehir [*Turkey ICAO location identifier*] (ICLI)
LTBS .... Dalaman [*Turkey ICAO location identifier*] (ICLI)
LTBT .... Akhisar [*Turkey ICAO location identifier*] (ICLI)
LTBT .... Limited Test Ban Treaty [*Signed in 1963; prohibits testing of nuclear devices in certain environments*]
LTC .... Lafferty Transportation [*AAR code*]
LTC .... Lai [*Chad*] [*Airport symbol*] (AD)
LTC .... Land Tenure Center [*University of Wisconsin*] [*Research center*]
LTC .... Land Transport Corps [*British military*] (DMA)
LTC .... Land Trust Commission (BARN)
LTC .... Language Testing Center [*University of Melbourne*] [*Australia*]
LTC .... Large Transformed Cell [*Medicine*] (DMAA)
LTC .... Last Telecast (WDMC)
LTC .... Latcharter [*Latvia*] [*FAA designator*] (FAAC)
LTC .... Lattice (MSA)
LTC .... Launceston Technical College [*Australia*]
LTC .... Launch Vehicle Test Conductor [*NASA*] (KSC)
LTC .... Lawn Tennis Club [*British*]
LTC .... Lead Telluride Crystal [*Photoconductor*]
LTC .... Lead to Come [*Publishing*] (WDMC)
LTC .... Left to Count (DAVI)
LTC .... Lesotho Telecommunications Corp. [*Ministry of Transport and Communications*] [*Lesotho*] (TSSD)
LTC .... Less than Truckload Cargo (MCD)
LTC .... Letdown Terrain Clearance (DNAB)
LTC .... Leukotriene C [*Clinical pharmacology*]
LTC .... Liberia Telecommunications Corp. (IMH)
LTC .... Liberty to the Captives [*Later, ACAT*] (EA)
LTC .... Library Technical Centre [*Polytechnic of Central London*] (NITA)
LTC .... Lidocaine Tissue Concentration [*Medicine*] (DMAA)
LTC .... Lieutenant Colonel (AABC)
LTC .... Lieutenant Commander (GFGA)
LTC .... Lightly Treated Coated [*Papermaking*]
LTC .... Light Terminal Complexes
LTC .... Linear Transformation Converter (IAA)
LTC .... Linear Transmission Channel
LTC .... Line Terminal Control (IAA)
LTC .... Line Time Clock
LTC .... Line Traffic Coordinator (CET)
LTC .... Living Tree Center (EA)
LTC .... Livros Tecnicos e Cientificos Editora Ltda. [*Brazil*]
LTC .... Load Tap Changing
LTC .... Local Telephone Circuit [*Telecommunications*] (TEL)
LTC .... Local Terminal Controller
LTC .... Lockwood Torday & Carlisle Ltd. [*British*]
LTC .... Longitudinal Time Code (NTCM)
LTC .... Longitudinal Time Constant
LTC .... Long-Term Care [*Medicine*]
LTC .... Long-Term Contract (ADA)
LTC .... Long Term Costing [*Military*] (RDA)
LTC .... Long Time Constant (IEEE)
LTC .... Loop Test Conference [*Aerospace*] (AAG)
LTC .... Lotus Cosmetics International Ltd. [*Vancouver Stock Exchange symbol*]
LTC .... Low-Tar Content [*of cigarettes*]
LTC .... Low-Temperature Carbonization
LTC .... Low-Temperature Catalyst
LTC .... Low-Temperature Coefficient
LTC .... Low-Temperature Cooling
LTC .... Low-Tension Current (IAA)
LTC .... LTC Properties [*NYSE symbol*] (TTSB)
LTC .... LTC Properties, Inc. [*NYSE symbol*] (SPSG)
LTC .... Lunar Terrain [*or Topographic*] Camera [*NASA*]
LTC .... Lynchburg Technology Center (GAAI)
L(TC) .... Tax Cases Leaflets [*Legal*] [*British*]
LTCA .... Elazig [*Turkey ICAO location identifier*] (ICLI)
LTCB .... Agri [*Turkey ICAO location identifier*] (ICLI)
LTCB .... Long Term Credit Bank [*Japan*] (ECON)
LTCB .... Long-Term Credit Bank of Japan, Ltd. (ECON)
LTCC .... Diyarbakir [*Turkey ICAO location identifier*] (ICLI)
LTCC .... Language Testing and Curriculum Center [*Griffith University*] [*Australia*]

LTCC .... Long-Term Care Campaign (EA)
LTCCM .... Loading Training Captive Carry Missile (MCD)
LTCD .... Erzincan [*Turkey ICAO location identifier*] (ICLI)
LTCDA .... Low Temperature Coal Distillers Association [*British*] (DBA)
LTCDR .... Lieutenant Commander
LTCE .... Erzurum [*Turkey ICAO location identifier*] (ICLI)
LTCF .... Kars [*Turkey ICAO location identifier*] (ICLI)
LTCF .... Long-Term Care Facility [*Medicine*]
LTCF .... Long-Term Care Facility [*Medicine*] (DAVI)
LTCG .... Long-Term Capital Gain
LTCG .... Trabzon [*Turkey ICAO location identifier*] (ICLI)
LTCH .... Litchfield Financial [*NASDAQ symbol*] (TTSB)
LTCH .... Litchfield Financial Corp. [*NASDAQ symbol*] (SAG)
LTCH .... Urfa [*Turkey ICAO location identifier*] (ICLI)
LTCI .... Van [*Turkey ICAO location identifier*] (ICLI)
LTCJ .... Batman [*Turkey ICAO location identifier*] (ICLI)
LTCL .... Licentiate of Trinity College of Music, London [*British*]
LTCL .... Long-Term Capital Loss
LTCM .... Licentiate of the Toronto Conservatory of Music [*Canada*]
LTCMDS .... Long-Term Care Minimum Data Set [*Department of Health and Human Services*] (GFGA)
LTCOL .... Lieutenant Colonel
LTCOM .... Lieutenant Commander (DNAB)
LT COMDR .... Lieutenant Commander (DNAB)
Lt-Comm .... Lieutenant-Commander [*British military*] (DMA)
LT/COR/WR .... Light Corner Wear [*Deltiology*]
LTC Prp .... LTC Properties, Inc. [*Associated Press*] (SAG)
LT/CR .... Light Crease [*Deltiology*]
LTCS .... Low Transverse Cesarean Section [*Medicine*] (MEDA)
LTCSB .... Long-Term Care Statistics Branch [*Department of Health and Human Services*] (GFGA)
LTCT .... Lower Thermal Comfort Threshold [*Environmental heating*]
LTD .... Ghadames [*Libya*] [*Airport symbol*] (OAG)
LTD .... Land Titles Division [*South Australia*]
LTD .... Language Training Detachment [*Defense Language Institute*] (DNAB)
LTD .... Laron-Type Dwarfism [*Medicine*]
LTD .... LASER Target Designator
LTD .... Launch Test Directive [*NASA*] (KSC)
LTD .... Letdown [*Nuclear energy*] (NRCH)
LTD .... Leukotriene D [*Clinical pharmacology*]
LTD .... Lift-Drag [*Ratio*] (MCD)
LTD .... Lightweight Target Designator
LTD .... Limited [*British corporation*] (EY)
Ltd .... Limited (DD)
LTD .... Limited
ltd .... Limited (DAVI)
Ltd .... Limited (NFD)
LTD .... [*The*] Limited, Inc. [*NYSE symbol*] (SPSG)
LTD .... Limit to Topographic Development [*Of hillsides*] [*Geology*]
LTD .... Linear Transport Drive
LTD .... Linear Tumor Diameter [*Oncology*]
LTD .... Line Transfer Device
LTD .... Litchfield, IL [*Location identifier FAA*] (FAAL)
LTD .... Live Test Demonstration
LTD .... Local Test Desk [*Telecommunications*] (KSC)
LTD .... Logistic Technical Data [*Navy*]
LTD .... Long Tank Delta
LTD .... Long-Term Depression [*Neurophysiology*]
LTD .... Long-Term Disability
LTD .... Low-Temperature Drying
LTD .... Lumber Transfer and Distribution
LTDA .... Licensed Taxi Drivers' Association [*British*] (DBA)
LTD ED .... Limited Edition [*Publishing*]
LTDI .... Learning Technology Dissemination Initiative (AIE)
LTDL .... Life Test Data Logger (CAAL)
LTDM .... Light Transmittance Difference Meter
LTDP .... Long-Term Defense Program [*NATO*] (MCD)
LTDQ .... Limited Quantity [*Refers to a test performed on a scanty specimen*] [*Biochemistry*] (DAVI)
LTD/R .... LASER Target Designator/Ranger (DWSG)
LTDR .... LASER Target Designator Receiver
LTDS .... LASER Target Designator System (MCD)
LTDS .... Launch Tracking [*or Trajectory*] Data System
LTDSS .... LASER Target Designator Scoring System (MCD)
LTDSTD .... Limited Standard (IAA)
LTDT .... Langley Transonic Dynamics Tunnel [*NASA*] (KSC)
LTD(U) .... Land Treatment Demonstration [*or Unit*] (GNE)
LTE .... Land Trust Exchange [*Later, LTA*] (EA)
LTE .... Laplace Transformation Estimator
LTE .... Large Table Electroplotter [*Computer science*]
LTE .... Large Terminal Repeats [*Genetics*] (DAVI)
LTE .... Large Thrust per Element
LTE .... Launch to Eject
LTE .... Letter to the Editor
LTE .... Leucotriene E [*Clinical pharmacology*]
LT(E) .... Lieutenant (Engineer)
LTE .... Limited Technical Evaluation (MCD)
LTE .... Limited Test Equipment
LTE .... Linear Threshold Element [*Computer science*]
LTE .... Line Terminating Equipment (ACRL)
LTE .... Line Termination Equipment [*Telecommunications*] (TEL)
LTE .... Local Telephone Exchange (NITA)
LTE .... Local Thermal Equilibrium [*Physical chemistry*]
LTE .... Local Thermodynamic Equilibrium [*or Equivalent*] [*Astronautics, astrophysics*]

LTE .... London Transport Executive
LTE .... Long-Term Effect
LTE .... Long-Term Enhancement [*Neurophysiology*]
LTE .... Long-Term Equilibration [*Analytical chemistry*]
LTE .... Low-Thrust Engine
LTE .... LTE International Airways SA [*Spain*] [*FAA designator*] (FAAC)
LTEA .... Leaf Tobacco Exporters Association (EA)
LTEC .... Lincoln Telecmmun [*NASDAQ symbol*] (TTSB)
LTED .... Long-Term Economic Deterioration [*Department of Commerce*]
LT/ED/WR .... Light Edge Wear [*Deltiology*]
Ltee .... Limitee [*Limited*] [*French*]
LTEK .... Life Technologies [*NASDAQ symbol*] (TTSB)
LTEMP .... Low Temperature
L T (Eng) ..... Law Times Journal (England) [*A publication*] (DLA)
LTEP .... Long-Term Equipment Plan [*Military*] (RDA)
LTER .... Long Term Ecological Research [*National Science Foundation*]
LTER .... Long-Term Ecological Research
LTERR .... Lunar Terrestrial Age
LTF .... Landline Telephony [*Aviation*] (DA)
LTF .... LASER Terrain Follower
LTF .... Latvijas Tautas Fronte [*Popular Front of Latvia*] [*Political party*] (EY)
LTF .... Layman Tithing Foundation (EA)
LTF .... Leucotriene F [*Clinical pharmacology*]
LTF .... Ligand-Responsive Transcription Factor [*Genetics*]
LTF .... Light-Float [*Navigation*]
LTF .... Lightning Training Flight [*British military*] (DMA)
LTF .... Lipotropic Factor [*Choline*] [*Biochemistry*]
LTF .... Liquid Thermal Flowmeter
LTF .... Lithographic Technical Foundation [*Later, GATF*] (MSA)
LTF .... Local Training Flight
LTF .... Logical Twin Forward Pointer (MHDI)
LTF .... Lymphocyte Transforming Factor [*Immunology*]
LTF .... Nicholls State University, Thibodaux, LA [*Library symbol Library of Congress*] (LCLS)
LTFC .... Landing Traffic [*Aviation*] (FAAC)
LTFC .... Low-Temperature Fuel Cell [*Energy source*]
LTFCS .... LASER Tank Fire Control System
LTFD .... Logic and Test Function Drawer [*Computer science*] (MCD)
LT/FM .... Long-Term/Frequency Modulation
LTFRD .... Lot Tolerance Fraction Reliability Deviation [*Quality control*]
LTFS .... LASER Terrain Following System
LTFT .... Low-Temperature Flow Test [*Lubricant technology*]
LTFV .... Less Than Fair Value [*Business term*]
LTG .... Catalina Lighting [*NYSE symbol*] (SAG)
LTG .... Legal Technology Group [*Information service or system*] (IID)
LTG .... Lettering (ADA)
LTG .... Lieutenant General (AABC)
LTG .... Lightening
LTG .... Lighting
LTG .... Lightning [*Meteorology*]
LTG .... Lightning Minerals [*Vancouver Stock Exchange symbol*]
LTG .... Linear Tangent Guidance (MCD)
LTG .... Line Trunk Group [*Telecommunications*]
LTG .... Line Trunk Group [*Telecommunications*] (ACRL)
ltg .... Lithographer [*MARC relator code*] [*Library of Congress*] (LCCP)
LTG .... Little Theatre Guild [*British*] (DBA)
LTG .... Local Tactical Grid [*Military*] (NVT)
LTG .... Long-Term Goals (DAVI)
LTG .... Lunar Traverse Gravimeter [*Experiment*] [*NASA*]
LTGA .... Left [*or Levo*] Transposition of the Great Arteries [*Also called corrected transposition*] [*Cardiology*] (DAVI)
LTGC .... Lieutenant Grand Commander [*Freemasonry*]
LTGCA .... Lightning Cloud-to-Air [*NWS*] (FAAC)
LTGCC .... Lightning Cloud-to-Cloud [*NWS*] (FAAC)
LTGCCCG .... Lightning Cloud-to-Cloud, Cloud-to-Ground [*NWS*] (FAAC)
LTGCG .... Lightning Cloud-to-Ground [*NWS*] (FAAC)
LTGCW .... Lightning Cloud-to-Water [*NWS*] (FAAC)
LTGE .... Lighterage
LTGEN .... Lieutenant General
LTGF Newl.. Lawyers' Title Guaranty Funds Newsletter [*A publication*] (DLA)
LTGH .... Lightening Hole [*Engineering*]
LTGIC .... Lightning in Clouds [*NWS*] (FAAC)
LTGL .... Lee-Tse-Goldberg-Lowe [*Theory*]
LT Gov .... Lieutenant Governor (WGA)
LTH .... Enterprise Thesaurus [*Database*]
LTH .... Laboratory Test Handbook
LTH .... Lactogenic Hormone [*Also, LGH, PR, PRL*] [*Endocrinology*]
L Th .... La Themis [*Lower Canada*] [*A publication*] (DLA)
LTH .... Leather [*Automotive advertising*]
LTH .... Less than Honorable Discharge [*Military*] (VNW)
L Th .... Licentiate in Theology
LTH .... Light Training Helicopter (WDAA)
LTH .... Logical Track Header
LTH .... London Teaching Hospitals [*National Health Service*] [*British*] (DI)
LTH .... Long-Term Holiday (MHDB)
LTH .... Low-Temperature Herschel (OA)
LTH .... Low-Temperature Holding
LTH .... Low Turret Half
LTH .... Luteotrophic Hormone [*Also, PR, PRL*] [*Endocrinology*]
Lth .... Martin Luther's German Version of the Bible [*A publication*] (BJA)
LTHA .... Long-Term Heat Aging
LTHG .... Lathing
LTHO .... Lighthouse
LTHR .... Leather (KSC)
LTHR .... Leather

LTHV .... Lucke Tumor Herpesvirus
LTI .... Aerotaxis Latinoamericanos SA de CV [*Mexico ICAO designator*] (FAAC)
LTI .... Land Training Installations (NATG)
LTI .... Lawyers Tile [*NYSE symbol*] (TTSB)
LTI .... Lawyers Title Corp. [*NYSE symbol*] (SAG)
LTI .... Licentiate of the Textile Institute [*British*] (DBQ)
LTI .... Light Transmission Index
LTI .... Limited to Interrogations (MCD)
LTI .... Linear Technology, Inc. [*Toronto Stock Exchange symbol*]
LTI .... Linear Time Invariant (IAA)
LTI .... Lingua Tertii Imperii [*A study of the abuse of language under Nazism by Viktor Klemperer*]
LTI .... Long-Term Integration (CAAL)
LTI .... Lost Time Injury [*Industrial plant safety*]
LTI .... Lowell Technological Institute [*Massachusetts*]
LTI .... Low-Temperature Isomerization [*Organic chemistry*]
LTI .... Low-Temperature Isotope
LTI .... Lupus-Type Inclusions [*Medicine*] (DMAA)
LTIB .... Lead Technical Information Bureau [*British*] (BI)
LTIC .... Language Teaching Information Centre [*British*] (CB)
LTID .... LASER Target Interface Device (RDA)
LTID .... Light-Intensity Detector (MSA)
Lt Inf .... Light Infantry [*British military*] (DMA)
LTIOV .... Latest Time Information of Value [*Military*] (AFM)
LTIP .... Long-Term Incentive Plan
LTIRF .... Lowell Technological Institute Research Foundation (MCD)
LTIS .... LASER Target Interface System
LTIV .... Lunar Trajectory Injection Vehicle [*NASA*] (KSC)
LTJ .... Law Times Journal [*A publication*] (DLA)
LTJ .... Lutheran Theological Journal [*A publication*] (APTA)
LTJC .... Lyons Township Junior College [*Illinois*]
LTJG .... Lieutenant Junior Grade [*Navy*]
LT Jo (Eng)... Law Times Journal (England) [*A publication*] (DLA)
LTK .... Latakia [*Syria*] [*Airport symbol*] (OAG)
LTK .... Lead To Come [*Copyediting*] (WDMC)
LTK .... Leukocyte Tyrosine Kinase [*An enzyme*]
LTK1 .... Ladies' Touring Kayak, Single Person (ADA)
LTL .... Lafourche Parish Library, Thibodaux, LA [*Library symbol Library of Congress*] (LCLS)
LTL .... Laparoscopic Tubal Ligation [*Gynecology*] (DAVI)
LTL .... Lastourville [*Gabon*] [*Airport symbol*] (OAG)
LTL .... Latvian Airlines [*ICAO designator*] (FAAC)
LTL .... Learning Through Listening [*Recording for the blind*]
LTL .... Learning to Look
LTL .... Less than Lethal (INF)
LTL .... Less than Truckload [*Under 24,000 pounds*]
LTL .... Line-to-Line
LTL .... Lintel [*Technical drawings*]
LTL .... Listing-Time Limit (MSA)
LTL .... Little
LTL .... Little
LTL .... Lot-Truck Load
LTL .... Lytton Minerals Ltd. [*Toronto Stock Exchange symbol Vancouver Stock Exchange symbol*]
LTLA .... Launcher Tube Longitudinal Axis
LTLA .... Louisiana Trial Lawyers Association (SRA)
lt lat .... Left Lateral [*Medicine*] (MAE)
LTLCG .... Little Change (FAAC)
LTLS .... Lincoln Trail Libraries System [*Library network*]
LTLS .... Long-Term Lapse Survey [*LIMRA*]
LTLT .... Long Time Low Temperature [*Food processing*]
LTM .... Laici per il Terzo Mondo [*Italy*]
LTM .... LASER Target Marker (RDA)
LTM .... LASER Transfer Module [*Telecommunications*] (LAIN)
LTM .... Leading Torpedoman [*Navy British*]
LTM .... Lead Time Matrix (MCD)
LTM .... Leave Trapping Mode (SAA)
LTM .... Lethem [*Guyana*] [*Airport symbol*] (OAG)
LTM .... Leverage Transaction Merchant (MHDI)
LTM .... Licentiate in Tropical Medicine [*British*]
LTM .... Lient Trief Mixed [*Cement*]
LTM .... Life Test Model
LTM .... Limits-to-Throughput Model [*Environmental science*]
LTM .... Line Transition Monitoring (NITA)
LTM .... Line Type Modulation [*Radio*]
LTM .... Little Maria Mountains [*California*] [*Seismograph station code, US Geological Survey*] (SEIS)
LTM .... Live Traffic Model [*Telecommunications*] (TEL)
LTM .... Load Ton Mile (IAA)
LTM .... Logic Theory Machine (SAA)
LTM .... Long-Term Memory
LTM .... Low Thermal Mass (PDAA)
LTM .... Low-Trajectory Missiles (NRCH)
LTM1 .... Lunar Tele-Operations Model 1 [*Mooncolony modeling*]
LTMAC .... Lauryltrimethylammonium Chloride [*Organic chemistry*]
LTMC .... Lymphoid Tissue Mononuclear Cell [*Physiology*]
LTMED .... Low-Temperature Multieffect Distillation [*Chemical engineering*]
LTMFM .... Low-Temperature Magnetic Force Microscope
LTMR .... LASER Target Marker Ranger [*Aviation*] (OA)
LTMR .... Long-Term Multilineage Reconstituting [*Cytology*]
LTMRSC ...... Long-Term Multilineage Reconstituting Stem Cell [*Cytology*]
LTMS .... Lubricant Test Monitoring System [*Automotive engineering*]
LTMS .... Lunar Terrain Measuring System [*Aerospace*]
LTN .... Aerolineas Latinas CA [*Venezuela*] [*ICAO designator*] (FAAC)

LTN............. Alaska Legislative Teleconference Network [*Alaska State Legislative Affairs Agency*] [*Juneau, AK*] [*Telecommunications service*] (TSSD)
LTN............. Liberty Tree Network [*An association*] (EA)
LTN............. Lightning (ADA)
LTN............. Linear Time-Varying Network
LTN............. Listen (IAA)
LTN............. Long-Term Nephelometer [*Instrumentation*]
LTN............. Luton [*England*] [*Airport symbol*] (OAG)
LTNG.......... Lightning [*Meteorology*]
LTNGARR .... Lightning Arrester (IAA)
LTNGP......... Low-Temperature Noble Gas Process [*Nuclear energy*] (NRCH)
LTNIF.......... Low-Temperature Neutron Irradiation Facility [*Oak Ridge, TN*] [*Oak Ridge National Laboratory*] [*Department of Energy*] (GRD)
LTNP.......... Long-Term Nonprogressor [*Of the human immune deficiency virus*]
LT NS .... Law Times. New Series [*Pennsylvania*] [*A publication*] (DLA)
LT NS .... Law Times Reports, New Series [*England*] [*A publication*] (DLA)
LTNS.......... Long Time, No See [*Computer science*] (DOM)
LT NS (Eng)... Law Times. New Series [*England*] [*A publication*] (DLA)
LTO............. Landing and Takeoff
LTO............. Leading Torpedoman [*Navy British*] (DMA)
LTO............. Lead-Tin Overlay [*Automotive engineering*]
LTO............. Local Tax Office [*British*]
LTO............. Loreto [*Mexico*] [*Airport symbol*] (OAG)
LTO............. Lot Time Order
LTO............. Low-Temperature Orthorhombic [*Crystallography*]
LTO............. Low Temperature Oxidation [*Physical chemistry*]
LTOC.......... Lowest Total Overall Cost (MHDI)
LTOE.......... Living Table of Organization and Equipment [*Army*] (INF)
LTOF.......... Low-Temperature Optical Facility
LTOM.......... London's Traded Options Market [*British*] (ECON)
LTON.......... Long Ton [*2240 pounds*]
LTOOR........ Light Truck On-Off Road
LTOP.......... Lease to Ownership Plan
LTOS.......... Law Times, Old Series [*British*]
LT OS .... Law Times Reports, Old Series [*England*] [*A publication*] (DLA)
LTOS.......... Long to Short [*Computer utility tool*] (PCM)
LTOT.......... Latest Time over Target (AFM)
LT-P........... Large Transmitter Coated with Paraffin
LTP............. Latpass [*Latvia*] [*FAA designator*] (FAAC)
LTP............. Leader Training Program [*Army*]
LTP............. Lead, Test, Probe (DWSG)
LTP............. LEM [*Lunar Excursion Module*] Test Procedure [*NASA*] (KSC)
LTP............. Let's Tax Plutocrats [*Humorous interpretation of LTP - Limit on Tax Preferences*]
LTP............. Letterpress
LTP............. Library Technology Program [*Formerly, Library Technology Project*] [*ALA*] [*Defunct*]
LTP............. Lient Trief Pure [*Cement*]
LTP............. Limit on Tax Preferences
LTP............. Linear Time Plot (MUGU)
LTP............. Line-Throwing Projectile (NG)
LTP............. Line Type Processor [*Radio*] (IAA)
LTP............. Lipid Transfer Protein [*Biochemistry*]
LTP............. Living Together Partner [*Lifestyle classification*]
LTP............. Local Tourism Plan
LTP............. Local Training Plan [*Job Training and Partnership Act*] (OICC)
LTP............. Long-Tailed Pair [*Electronics*] (OA)
LTP............. Long-Term Potentiation [*Neurophysiology*]
LTP............. Long Term Projections [*Townsend-Greenspan & Co., Inc.*] [*Database*]
LTP............. Lower Trip Point
LTP............. Low-Temperature Passivation (PDAA)
LTP............. Low-Temperature Phase (PDAA)
LTP............. Low-Temperature Phosphorimetry [*Analytical chemistry*]
LTP............. Low-Temperature Physics
LTP............. Low-Temperature Polymer (IAA)
LTP............. Lunar Tidal Perturbation
LTPA.......... Louisiana Travel Promotion Association (SRA)
LTPB.......... Lactone Terminated Polybutadiene [*Organic chemistry*] (MCD)
LTPD.......... Lot Tolerance Percent Defective [*Quality control*] (MSA)
LTPE.......... Long-Term Public Expenditure [*British*]
LTPHOTORON... Light Photographic Squadron
LTPL.......... Long-Term Procedural Language
LTPN.......... Long-Term Parenteral Nutrition (PDAA)
LTPO.......... LASER Technology Program Office [*Navy*]
LTPP.......... Lipothiamide-Pyrophosphate
LTPP.......... Long-Term Pavement Performance [*FHWA*] (TAG)
LTPR.......... Lightproof [*Technical drawings*] (IAA)
LTPR.......... Long Taper
LTPR.......... Long-Term Prime Rate [*Finance*]
LTPS.......... Lateral Transitional Phase Shift [*Optics*]
LTPS.......... Lincoln Tube Process Specification (SAA)
LTPT.......... Low-Turbulence Pressure Tunnel [*NASA*]
LTPWG .... LOAD [*Low Altitude Defense*] Test Planning Working Group
LTPWS........ Low Tire-Pressure Warning System [*Automotive engineering*]
LTQ............ Le Touquet [*France*] [*Airport symbol*] (OAG)
LTQ............ Local Track Quality (NVT)
LTQ............ Low Torque
LTQC.......... Long-Term Quality-Control [*Analytical chemistry*]
LTR............. AS Lufttransport [*Norway ICAO designator*] (FAAC)
LTR............. Lander Trajectory Reconstruction [*Program*] [*NASA*]
LTR............. Lands Tribunal Rules [*Town planning*] [*British*]
LTR............. LASER Tank Range-Finder
LTR............. LASER Target Recognition [*Military*] (CAAL)

LTR............. Lattice Test Reactor
LTR............. Law Times Reports, New Series [*England*] [*A publication*] (DLA)
LTR............. [*The*] Learning Tree [*UTLAS symbol*]
LTR............. Left Test Register (IAA)
LTR............. Letter (AFM)
LTR............. Letter
LTR............. Library Technology Reports [*American Library Association*]
L-TR........... Licensing Technical Review [*Nuclear energy*] (NRCH)
LTR............. Lighter
LTR............. Light Tactical Raft
LTR............. Liquid Test Rig [*Apollo*] [*NASA*]
LTR............. List Test Resister (PDAA)
LTR............. Living Together Relationship
LTR............. Load Task Register [*Computer science*] (PCM)
LTR............. Location Transactivating Region [*Medicine*] (DMAA)
LTR............. Lockheed Training Reactor
LTR............. Loew's Corp. [*Formerly, Loew's Theatres, Inc.*] [*NYSE symbol*] (SPSG)
LTR............. Lone Tree Road [*California*] [*Seismograph station code, US Geological Survey*] (SEIS)
LTR............. Longitudinal Triangular Ripples [*Oceanography*]
LTR............. Long Terminal Repeat [*or Redundancy*] [*Genetics*]
LTR............. Long-Term Reserve [*British military*] (DMA)
LTR............. Long-Term Revitalization (OA)
LTR............. Long Treble [*Knitting*]
LTR............. Long-Tube Recirculation [*Evaporator*]
LTR............. Lord Treasurer's Remembrancer [*British*]
LTR............. Low-Temperature Reactor [*Chemical engineering*]
LTRA.......... Lands Tribunal Rating Appeals [*Legal*] [*British*]
LTRA.......... Leukotriene Receptor Antagonist [*Biochemistry*]
L-TRAN....... Lesson Translator (NVT)
L Trans Q .... Law in Transition Quarterly [*A publication*] (DLA)
LTRC.......... Louisiana Transportation Research Center [*Louisiana State University*] [*Research center*] (RCD)
LTRCA........ Lawn Tennis Registered Coaches Association [*British*] (BI)
LTRE.......... Learning Tree Intl. [*NASDAQ symbol*] (TTSB)
LTren.......... Left Trendelenburg [*Position*] [*Surgery*] (DAVI)
LT Rep........ Law Times Reports, New Series [*England*] [*A publication*] (DLA)
LT Rep NS ... Law Times Reports, New Series [*England*] [*A publication*] (DLA)
LTRF.......... LASER Tank Range-Finder
LTRF.......... Low Temperature Research Facility [*NASA*]
LTRI........... Lightning and Transients Research Institute [*St. Paul, MN*] (MCD)
LTRN .... Lantern (MSA)
LTRN .... Lantern Slide (VRA)
LTR NS .... Law Times Reports, New Series [*England*] [*A publication*] (DLA)
LTRO .... Lateral Tire Run-Out [*Automotive engineering*]
LTROM .... Linear Transformer Read Only Memory [*Computer science*] (IAA)
LTRP.......... Long-Term Requirement Plan (NATG)
LTRPRS ...... Letterpress
LTRPRS ...... Letterpress
LTRS.......... LASER Target Recognition System
LTRS.......... Letters Shift [*Teleprinters*]
LTRS.......... Low Temperature Research Station [*British*]
LT Rulings... Land Tax Rulings [*Australia A publication*]
LTS............. Altus, OK [*Location identifier FAA*] (FAAL)
LTS............. Laboratory Test Set
LTS............. Labor Turnover Statistics (OICC)
LTS............. Landfall Technique School [*Navy*]
LTS............. Language Teaching System
LTS............. Language Translation System
LTS............. LASER Target Simulator (MCD)
LTS............. LASER Test Set (MCD)
LTS............. LASER Time Sharing (PDAA)
LTS............. LASER-Triggered Switch (MCD)
LTS............. Lateral Test Simulator (IAA)
LTS............. Launch Telemetry Station
LTS............. Launch Telemetry System
LTS............. Launch Test Set
LTS............. Launch Tracking Station
LTS............. Launch Tracking System
LTS............. Library Technical Services [*Library network*]
LTS............. Lifetrends Behavioral Systems, Inc. [*Vancouver Stock Exchange symbol*]
LTS............. Lift-Off Transmission Subsystem (IAA)
LTS............. Lighting Test Set (KSC)
LTS............. Light Tactile Stimulation [*Neurology*] (DAVI)
LTS............. Linearity Test Set
LTS............. Line Transient Suppression
LTS............. Link Terminal Simulator
LTS............. Linomatic Tape System [*Typography*] (DGA)
LTS............. Llantrisant [*Welsh depot code*]
LTS............. Load Transfer Switch
LTS............. Logistics Test Squadron [*Military*]
LTS............. Long-Term Stability
LTS............. Long-Term Standard [*Lamp for spectrometry*]
LTS............. Long-Term Storage [*Memory*] [*Computer science*]
LTS............. Long-Term Survival [*Medicine*] (DMAA)
LTS............. Love Token Society (EA)
LTS............. Low-Frequency Transmit System (DWSG)
LTS............. Low-Temperature Separation
LTS............. Low-Temperature Smoking (PDAA)
LTS............. Low Threshold Spike [*Neurochemistry*]
LTS............. LTU [*Lufttransport Unternehmen Sud*] GmbH [*Germany ICAO designator*] (FAAC)
LTS............. Lufttransport-Sud [*Airline*] [*Germany*]

LTS.............	Lunar Touchdown System [*NASA*] (IAA)
LTS.............	Trinity Lutheran Seminary, Columbus, OH [*OCLC symbol*] (OCLC)
LTSC...........	Licentiate in the Technology of Surface Coatings [*British*] (DBQ)
LTSC...........	Low-Temperature Semiconductor [*Electronics*]
LTSDE.........	Low-Temperature Superconducting Device Electronics (DOMA)
LTSEM........	Low-Temperature Scanning Electron Microscopy
LTSF...........	Lid Tank Shielding Facility [*Nuclear energy*] (NRCH)
LTSG...........	LASER-Triggered Spark Gap
LTSH...........	League of Tarcisians of the Sacred Heart [*Later, LT*] (EA)
LTSM...........	Long-Range Tactical Strike Missile (MCD)
LT(Sp)........	Lieutenant (Special)
LTSPC.........	L'Union Territoriale des Syndicats Professionelles Caledoniens [*Territorial Federation of New Caledonian Unions of Private Employees*]
LT-SR	Large Transmitter Coated with Silicon Rubber
LTSR...........	Line Trunk Scanner Register [*Computer science*] (IAA)
LTSS...........	Long-Term Scientific Study [*NATO Defense Research Group*] (MCD)
LTSTA.........	Light Station [*Coast Guard*]
LTSV...........	Light Savers USA [*NASDAQ symbol*] (TTSB)
LTSV...........	Light Savers USA, Inc. [*NASDAQ symbol*] (SAG)
LTSV...........	Lucerne Transient Streak Virus [*Plant pathology*]
LTSW..........	Light Switch
LtSwtz........	Little Switzerland, Inc. [*Associated Press*] (SAG)
LTT	Landline Teletypewriter [*Military*]
LTT	Land Title Trust (DLA)
LTT	LASER Target Tracker
LTT	Latakia Type Tobacco [*Shipping*]
LTT	Less than Truckload [*Under 24,000 pounds*] (WGA)
LTT	Leucine Tolerance Test [*Clinical chemistry*] (AAMN)
LTT	Liberty Term Trust-1999 [*NYSE symbol*] (SPSG)
LT T	Lieutenant of Treasury [*British*]
LTT	Light Tactical Transport (MCD)
LTT	Light-Travel-Time [*Astronomy*]
LTT	Limited Treadmill Test [*Medicine*] (DMAA)
LTT	Liquid Toner Transfer [*Typography*] (DGA)
LTT	Lithium Thallium Tartrate [*Inorganic chemistry*]
LTT	Long-Term Training (MCD)
LTT	Long-Term Trend [*Finance*] (MHDI)
LTT	Louis Trichardt [*South Africa*] [*Seismograph station code, US Geological Survey*] (SEIS)
LTT	Low Temperature Teatment [*Materials science*]
LTT	Low-Temperature Test
LTT	Low-Temperature Tetragonal [*Crystallography*]
LTT	Lunar Test Table [*Aerospace*]
LTT	Lymphoblastic Transformation Test [*Biochemistry*] (DAVI)
LTT	Lymphocyte Transformation Test [*Medicine*]
LTTA	Logic Tree Trouble-Shooting Aid (PDAA)
LTTA	Long Tank Thrust-Augmented (PDAA)
LTTAD........	Long Tank Thrust-Augmented Delta (PDAA)
LTTAS........	Light Tactical Transport Aircraft System [*Helicopter*] [*Military*] (RDA)
LTTAT........	Long Tank Thrust-Augmented Thor
LTTB..........	Listen to the Band (EA)
LTTBT........	Low-Threshold Test Ban Treaty [*Proposed*]
LTTC...........	Lowry Technical Training Center [*Air Force*] (AFM)
LTTD...........	Letter-Type Technical Directive [*Navy*] (NG)
LTTE	Liberation Tigers of Tamil Eelam [*Sri Lanka*]
LTTL...........	Low-Power Transistor-Transistor Logic (IEEE)
LTTMT........	Low-Temperature Thermomechanical Treatment
LTTO...........	Lotto World [*NASDAQ symbol*] (TTSB)
LTTO...........	Lotto World, Inc. [*NASDAQ symbol*] (SAG)
LTTR...........	Latter
LTTR...........	Long-Term Tape Recorder
LTU	Land Treatment Unit [*Waste disposal*]
LTU	Lawrence Technological University
LTU	Less Than
LTU	Lift-Off Time and Update
LTU	Line Terminating Unit (CET)
LTU	Line Termination Unit (NITA)
LTU	Little Mountain [*Utah*] [*Seismograph station code, US Geological Survey*] (SEIS)
LTU	Long-Term Unemployed
LTU	Long Ton Unit
LTU	Lufttransport Unternehmen GmbH [*Germany ICAO designator*] (FAAC)
LTU	Spencer, IA [*Location identifier FAA*] (FAAL)
LTUS...........	Garden Fresh Restaurant [*NASDAQ symbol*] (TTSB)
LTUS...........	Garden Fresh Restaurant Corp. [*NASDAQ symbol*] (SAG)
LTUSA	La Trobe University Staff Association [*Australia*]
LTV	Land Transport Vehicle (NVT)
LTV	Large Test Vessel [*Nuclear energy*] (NRCH)
LTV	Launch Test Vehicles
LTV	Life Test Vehicle
LTV	Light-Vessel [*Navigation*]
LTV	Ling-Temco-Vought Co.
LTV	Load Threshold Value (DA)
LTV	Loan-to-Value Ratio [*Finance*]
LTV	Long-Term Vibration
LTV	Long Tube Vertical
LTV	LTV Corp. [*Formerly, Ling-Temco-Vought, Inc.*] [*NYSE symbol*] (SPSG)
LTV	Lunar Excursion Module Test Vehicle [*NASA*] (IAA)
LTVC...........	Launcher Tube Vertical Centerline
LTW	League of Tasmanian Wheelmen [*Australia*]
LTW	Leydig-Cell Tumor in Wistar Rat [*Medicine*] (DMAA)
LTW	Long-Term Waviness [*Metal surface finish*]
LTW.............	Los Trancos Woods [*California*] [*Seismograph station code, US Geological Survey*] (SEIS)
LTW.............	Low-Tension Winding (IAA)
LTW.............	NV Luchtvaartmaatschappij Twente [*Netherlands ICAO designator*] (FAAC)
LTWA.........	Lawn Tennis Writers' Association of America [*Later, USTWA*] (EA)
LTWA.........	Long Trailing Wire Antenna (MCD)
LTWG.........	Launch Test Working Group
LTWT	Lightweight
LTX	Lap-Top Expansion [*Computer science*]
ltx	Latex (VRA)
LTX	Leo Taxi Aereo SA de CV [*Mexico ICAO designator*] (FAAC)
LTX	Lintronics International Ltd. [*Vancouver Stock Exchange symbol*]
LTX	LTX Corp. [*Associated Press*] (SAG)
LTXRD........	Low-Temperature X-Ray Diffraction [*Instrumentation*]
LTXW.........	Latex Resources Wrrt [*NASDAQ symbol*] (TTSB)
LTXX	LTX Corp. [*NASDAQ symbol*] (SAG)
LTYR	Light Year
Lu	H. Lundbeck [*Denmark*] [*Research code symbol*]
LU	Labor Union (OICC)
LU	Lamentations over the Destruction of Ur (BJA)
LU	Laws of Ur Nammu (BJA)
LU	Left Unity Group [*European political movement*] (ECON)
LU	Left Upper [*Medicine*]
LU	Liberal-Unionist [*British*] (ROG)
LU	Libraries Unlimited [*Library network*]
LU	Library Utility [*Computer science*]
LU	Ligue Universelle [*Esperantiste*]
LU	Line Unit (IAA)
LU	Line-Up
LU	List Up
LU	Load Unit
LU	Lock Up (ADA)
LU	Logical Unit [*Computer science*]
LU	Logistical Unit (NATG)
LU	Looking Up [*An association*] (EA)
LU	Loudness Unit
LU	Louisiana State University, Baton Rouge, LA [*Library symbol Library of Congress*] (LCLS)
LU	Lucent Technologies [*NYSE symbol*] (TTSB)
LU	Lucent Technologies, Inc. [*NYSE symbol*] (SAG)
LU	Lues [*Syphilis*] [*Latin*] (WDAA)
Lu	Lumbar [*Anatomy*] (DAVI)
Lu	Lumen [*Anatomy*]
Lu	Lutetium [*Chemical element*]
Lu	Lutheran [*Blood group*]
LU	Luxembourg [*ANSI two-letter standard code*] (CNC)
lu	Luxembourg [*MARC country of publication code Library of Congress*] (LCCP)
LU	St. Luke's Gospel [*New Testament book*] (ROG)
LU	Theron Airways [*ICAO designator*] (AD)
LU	Upper Limen [*Psychology*]
LUA	Launch under Attack [*Nuclear warfare option*]
LUA	Left Upper Arm [*Medicine*]
LUA	Library Users of America (EA)
LUA	Liverpool Underwriters Association (DS)
LUA	Lloyd's Underwriters' Association [*British*] (DBA)
LU-A	Louisiana State University in Alexandria, Alexandria, LA [*Library symbol Library of Congress*] (LCLS)
LUA	Luanda [*Angola*] [*Seismograph station code, US Geological Survey Closed*] (SEIS)
LUA	Luanda Belas [*Angola*] [*Geomagnetic observatory code*]
LUA	Lukla [*Nepal*] [*Airport symbol*] (OAG)
LUA	Luray, VA [*Location identifier FAA*] (FAAL)
LUAC	Life Underwriters Association of Canada
LUAMC	Leading Underwriters' Agreement for Marine Cargo Business (DS)
LUAMH	Leading Underwriters' Agreement for Marine Hull Business (DS)
LUAP	Land Use Adjustment Program
LUAR	Liga de Uniao e Acao Revolucionaria [*Portugal*]
LU-Ar	Louisiana State University, Department of Archives and Manuscripts, Baton Rouge,LA [*Library symbol Library of Congress*] (LCLS)
LUB.............	Least [*or Lowest*] Upper Bound
LUB.............	Left Upper Lobe Bronchus [*Anatomy*]
LUB.............	Logical Unit Block [*Computer science*]
lub	Luba [*MARC language code Library of Congress*] (LCCP)
LUB.............	Lubbock [*Texas*] [*Seismograph station code, US Geological Survey*] (SEIS)
LUB.............	Lubricant (WDAA)
LUB.............	Lubricate [*or Lubrication*] (AAG)
LUB.............	Luby's Cafeterias [*NYSE symbol*] (TTSB)
LUB.............	Luby's Cafeterias, Inc. [*NYSE symbol*] (SPSG)
LUB.............	Lusiana [*Czechoslovakia*] [*ICAO designator*] (FAAC)
LUBA	Limited Underwater Breathing Apparatus (NG)
LUBE..........	Lubricate (ADA)
LUBEE.........	Lubrication
Lube Eq	Lube on Equity Pleading [*A publication*] (DLA)
Lube PL	Lube on Equity Pleading [*A publication*] (DLA)
LUBO..........	Lubricating Oil
LUBR	Lubricant
LUBR	Lubricate (ADA)
Lubrizol	[*The*] Lubrizol Corp. [*Associated Press*] (SAG)
LUBS	Large Undisturbed-Bottom Sampler (PDAA)
LUBT	Lubricant (MSA)
Lubys..........	Luby's Cafeterias, Inc. [*Associated Press*] (SAG)

LUC............	Land Use Concurrence [*Acquisition of real estate for the use of US forces on a rent-free basis*] [*Vietnam*]
LUC............	Large Unstained Cells [*Cytology*]
LUC............	Laucala Island [*Fiji*] [*Airport symbol*] (OAG)
LUC............	League of Ukrainian Catholics of America (EA)
LUC............	Living under Canvas [*British military*] (DMA)
LU-C............	Louisiana State University, Chemistry Library, Baton Rouge, LA [*Library symbol Library of Congress*] (LCLS)
LUC............	Louisiana Union Catalog [*Library network*]
Luc............	Lucan [*39-65AD*] [*Classical studies*] (OCD)
Luc............	Lucas: an Evangelical History Review [*A publication*] (APTA)
Luc............	Lucas' Reports [*Modern Reports, Part X*] [*A publication*] (DLA)
LUC............	Lucifer (WDAA)
Luc............	Luciferase [*An enzyme*]
Luc............	Lucullus [*of Plutarch*] [*Classical studies*] (OCD)
Luc............	Lucullus or Academica Posteriora [*of Cicero*] [*Classical studies*] (OCD)
LUC............	Lukens, Inc. [*NYSE symbol*] (SPSG)
Luc............	[*The*] Rape of Lucrece [*Shakespearean work*]
LUCALOX......	Translucent Aluminum Oxide [*Ceramic*]
LUCAS........	Line Utilization Cable Assignment System (MCD)
Lucas..........	Lucas' Reports [*Modern Reports, Part X*] [*A publication*] (DLA)
LucasV........	Lucasvarity PLC [*Associated Press*] (SAG)
LUCC...........	Land Use and Cover Change [*Environmental studies*] (ECON)
LUCC	Lehigh University Computing Center [*Pennsylvania*] [*Research center*] (RCD)
Lucent	Lucent Technologies, Inc. [*Associated Press*] (SAG)
LUCF..........	Load, Unload, Cool, Fracture (PDAA)
LUCHIP........	Lutheran Church and Indian People [*An association Defunct*] (EA)
LUCID	Language for Utility Checkout and Instrumentation Development
LUCID	Language Used to Communicate Information System Design
LUCID	Loughborough University Computerized Information and Drawings Project [*British*]
Lucil	Lucilius [*Second century BC*] [*Classical studies*] (OCD)
Lucile	Lucille Farms, Inc. [*Associated Press*] (SAG)
LucileFr.......	Lucille Farms, Inc. [*Associated Press*] (SAG)
Luck	Indian Law Reports, Lucknow Series [*A publication*] (DLA)
LUCK	Lady Luck Gaming'A' [*NASDAQ symbol*] (TTSB)
LUCK	Lady Luck Gaming Corp. [*NASDAQ symbol*] (SAG)
LUCK	Logical Unit and Checker (NITA)
LUCKN.........	Lucknow [*City in India*] (ROG)
Luck Ser	Indian Law Reports, Lucknow Series [*A publication*] (DLA)
LUCO	Lloyd's Underwriters Claims Office (AIA)
LUCOLA.......	Lutheran Coalition on Latin America (EA)
LUCOM	Lunar Communication [*System*] [*Aerospace*]
Lucor..........	Lucor, Inc. [*Associated Press*] (SAG)
LUCP	League to Uphold Congregational Principles [*Defunct*] (EA)
LUC PRIM....	Luce Primo [*At Daybreak*] [*Pharmacy*]
LUCR	Lucor, Inc. [*NASDAQ symbol*] (SAG)
LUCR	Lucor Inc.'A' [*NASDAQ symbol*] (TTSB)
Lucr	[*The Rape of*] Lucrece [*Shakespearean Work*] (BARN)
LUCR	Lucretius [*Roman poet, 96-55BC*] [*Classical studies*] (ROG)
LUCRE	Lower Unit Costs and Related Earnings (MHDB)
LUCS	London University Computer Services (IAA)
LUCY	Lucille Farms [*NASDAQ symbol*] (TTSB)
LUCY	Lucille Farms, Inc. [*NASDAQ symbol*] (SAG)
LUCYW	Luclle Farm Wrrt [*NASDAQ symbol*] (TTSB)
LUD	Land Use Designation [*US Forest Service*]
LUD	Lift-Up Door [*Technical drawings*]
LUD	Luderitz [*South-West Africa*] [*Airport symbol*] (OAG)
LUD	Lundin Explorations [*Vancouver Stock Exchange symbol*]
LUDA	Land Use Data
Lud & J Tr M...	Ludlow and Jenkyns on Trade-Marks [*A publication*] (DLA)
Lud Bolog....	Ludovicus Bologninus [*Deceased, 1508*] [*Authority cited in pre-1607 legal work*] (DSA)
Ludd	Ludden's Reports [*43, 44 Maine*] [*A publication*] (DLA)
Ludden	Ludden's Reports [*43, 44 Maine*] [*A publication*] (DLA)
Lud de Ro ...	Ludovicus Pontanus de Roma [*Deceased, 1439*] [*Authority cited in pre-1607 legal work*] (DSA)
Lud EC	Luder's Election Cases [*England*] [*A publication*] (DLA)
Lud El Cas...	Luder's Election Cases [*England*] [*A publication*] (DLA)
Luder Elec Cas...	Luder's Election Cases [*England*] [*A publication*] (DLA)
Luders Elec Cas (Eng)...	Luder's Election Cases [*England*] [*A publication*] (DLA)
ludes	Quaaludes [*Methaqualone*] [*Pharmacology*] (DAVI)
Lud Gozad ...	Ludovicus Gozzadini [*Deceased, 1536*] [*Authority cited in pre-1607 legal work*] (DSA)
Ludo	Ludovicus Pontanus de Roma [*Deceased, 1439*] [*Authority cited in pre-1607 legal work*] (DSA)
Ludo Bolog...	Ludovicus Bologninus [*Deceased, 1508*] [*Authority cited in pre-1607 legal work*] (DSA)
Ludo Ro.......	Ludovicus Pontanus de Roma [*Deceased, 1439*] [*Authority cited in pre-1607 legal work*] (DSA)
LUE............	Dallas, TX [*Location identifier FAA*] (FAAL)
LUE............	Left Upper Entrance [*Theater*]
LUE............	Left Upper Extremity [*Medicine*]
LUE............	Left Upper Extremity [*Anatomy*] (DMAA)
LUE............	Linear Unbiased Estimator [*Statistics*]
LUE............	Link Utilization Efficiency
LU-E...........	Louisiana State University in Eunice, Eunice, LA [*Library symbol Library of Congress*] (LCLS)
LU-ECT	Louisiana State at Baton Rouge, Eighteenth Century Short Title Catalogue, Baton Rouge, LA [*Library symbol Library of Congress*] (LCLS)
LUEV...........	Lucerne Enation Virus [*Plant pathology*]
LUF............	Glendale, AZ [*Location identifier FAA*] (FAAL)

LUF............	Lift Unit Frame [*Shipping*] (DS)
LUF............	Limiting System Utilization Factor (MHDB)
LUF............	Local Utah Freight Bureau, Omaha NE [*STAC*]
LUF............	Lowest Usable [*or Useful*] Frequency [*Radio*]
LUF............	Luteinized Unruptured Follicle [*Medicine*] (DMAA)
LUFK..........	Lufkin Industries [*NASDAQ symbol*] (TTSB)
LUFK..........	Lufkin Industries, Inc. [*NASDAQ symbol*] (SAG)
Lufkin	Lufkin Industries, Inc. [*Associated Press*] (SAG)
LUFO	Least Used, First Out [*Computer science*]
LUFS..........	Luteinized Unruptured Follicle Syndrome [*Medicine*] (DMAA)
LUG	Lesbian Until Graduation
LUG	Lewisburg, TN [*Location identifier FAA*] (FAAL)
LUG	Light Utility Glider
LUG	LOCAS Users Group (NITA)
LUG	Lock-Up Garage
lug	Luganda [*MARC language code Library of Congress*] (LCCP)
LUG	Lugano [*Switzerland*] [*Airport symbol*] (OAG)
LUG	Lugano Resources Ltd. [*Vancouver Stock Exchange symbol*]
LUG	Luganville [*New Hebrides*] [*Seismograph station code, US Geological Survey*] (SEIS)
LUG	Luggage
LUG	Lugger [*Boat*]
LUG BAT......	Lugdunum Batavorum [*Leyden*] [*Imprint*] (ROG)
LUGD..........	Lugdunum [*Lyons*] [*Imprint*] (ROG)
LUGG	Luggage
LUGL	Lumen and Glare Calculations [*Facet Ltd.*] [*Software package*] (NCC)
LUGS	Land Use Game Simulation
LUH	Lumen Hour
LUHF	Lowest Usable [*or Useful*] High-Frequency [*Radio*]
LUI............	La Union [*Honduras*] [*Airport symbol Obsolete*] (OAG)
LUI............	Load Upper Immediate [*Computer science*]
LUI............	Logical Unit of Information (IAA)
LUI............	London United Investments [*British*]
lui	Luiseno [*MARC language code Library of Congress*] (LCCP)
LUIE..........	Leeds University Institute of Education [*British*] (AIE)
LUIS...........	Library User Information System [*Detroit, MI*] [*Library network*]
LUIS...........	Low-Dose Urea in Invert Sugar (AAMN)
LUJ............	Big Lake, TX [*Location identifier FAA*] (FAAL)
LUJ............	Lesotho Union of Journalists (EAIO)
LUJB..........	Left Umbilical Junction Box [*Aerospace*] (AAG)
LUK...........	Cincinnati, OH [*Location identifier FAA*] (FAAL)
LUK...........	Leucadia National [*NYSE symbol*] (TTSB)
LUK...........	Leucadia National Corp. [*NYSE symbol*] (SPSG)
Lukens.........	Lukens, Inc. [*Associated Press*] (SAG)
LukMed........	Lukens Medical Corp. [*Associated Press*] (SAG)
LUKN	Lukens Med [*NASDAQ symbol*] (TTSB)
LUKN	Lukens Medical Corp. [*NASDAQ symbol*] (SAG)
LUL............	Language, Unseamanlike [*Slang Military*] (DNAB)
LUL............	Laurel, MS [*Location identifier FAA*] (FAAL)
LUL............	Left Upper Eyelid [*Medicine*]
LUL............	Left Upper Limb [*Medicine*]
LUL............	Left Upper Lobe [*of lung*] [*Medicine*]
LUL............	London Underground Ltd. [*British*] (ECON)
LU-L...........	Louisiana State University, Law Library, Baton Rouge, LA [*Library symbol Library of Congress*] (LCLS)
LULA..........	Loyola University of Los Angeles [*Later, Loyola Marymount University*]
LULAC.........	League of United Latin American Citizens (EA)
LULOP	London Union List of Periodicals
LULS..........	Lunar Logistics System [*NASA*]
LULU	Locally Unwanted Land Use [*i.e. garbage incinerators, prisons, roads, etc.*]
LULU	Logical Unit to Logical Unit
LUM............	Bellingham, WA [*Location identifier FAA*] (FAAL)
LUM............	Launch Utility Mode
LUM............	Living Utility Module [*NASA*] (KSC)
LUM............	Local Urgent Mail [*British*]
LU-M...........	Louisiana State University, Medical Center, New Orleans, LA [*Library symbol Library of Congress*] (LCLS)
LUM............	Lumbago (WDAA)
LUM............	Lumbar [*Medicine*] (WDAA)
LUM............	Lumber (WDAA)
Lum	Lumen [*Record label*] [*France*]
LUM............	Lumex, Inc. [*AMEX symbol*] (SPSG)
LUM............	Luminous (MSA)
LUM............	Lumonics, Inc. [*Toronto Stock Exchange symbol*]
LUM............	Maputo [*Mozambique*] [*Airport symbol*]
LUM............	University of Maryland, School of Law, Baltimore, MD [*OCLC symbol*] (OCLC)
Lum Ann......	Lumley on the Law of Annuities [*A publication*] (DLA)
LUMAS	Lunar Mapping System [*Aerospace*]
lumb	Lumbar [*Medicine*] (MAE)
Lum Bast.....	Lumley on Bastardy [*A publication*] (DLA)
Lum BL	Lumley on Bye-Laws [*A publication*] (DLA)
LUMCON......	Louisiana Universities Marine Consortium
LUME..........	Light Utilization More Efficient (MCD)
Lumex.........	Lumex, Inc. [*Associated Press*] (SAG)
LUMF..........	Lockheed Underwater Missile Facility (AAG)
LUMI..........	Lumisys, Inc. [*NASDAQ symbol*] (SAG)
LUMIS	Land Use Management Information System [*NASA*]
Lumisys.......	Lumisys, Inc. [*Associated Press*] (SAG)
Lumley PLC...	Lumley's Poor Law Cases [*1834-42*] [*A publication*] (DLA)
LUMO	Lowest Unoccupied Molecular Orbital [*Atomic physics*]
Lum Parl Pr...	Lumley's Parliamentary Practice [*A publication*] (DLA)

Lumpkin	Lumpkin's Reports [59-77 Georgia] [A publication] (DLA)
Lum PLC......	Lumley's Poor Law Cases [1834-42] [A publication] (DLA)
Lum PL Cas...	Lumley's Poor Law Cases [1834-42] [A publication] (DLA)
Lumps	Life-Giving Unselfish Middle-Class Parent Survivors [Facetious term coine d by columnist Erma Bombeck to describe the Yuppies' progenitors] [Lifestyle classification]
Lum Pub H...	Lumley's Public Health Acts [12th ed.] [1950-55 and supplements] [A publication] (DLA)
Lum Sett.....	Lumley on the Law of Settlements [A publication] (DLA)
LUN	Logical Unit Number
LUN	Ludington & Northern Railway [AAR code]
LUN	Lunar (KSC)
LUN	Lund [Sweden] [Seismograph station code, US Geological Survey Closed] (SEIS)
LUN	Lunette
lun	Lunette (VRA)
LUN	Lusaka [Zambia] [Airport symbol] (OAG)
LUNA	Language for Users' Needs and Aims (NITA)
Lunar	Lunar Corp. [Associated Press] (SAG)
LUNARG	Lunar Gravity Simulator [Aerospace] (MCD)
LUNCO	Lloyd's Underwriters Non-Marine Claims Office (AIA)
LUND	Lund International [NASDAQ symbol] (TTSB)
LUND	Lund International Holdings, Inc. [NASDAQ symbol] (SAG)
LundInt	Lund International Holdings, Inc. [Associated Press] (SAG)
Lund Pat	Lund on Patents [A publication] (DLA)
LUNK	Line/Trunk (MCD)
LUNN	Lunn Industries [NASDAQ symbol] (SAG)
LunnI	Lunn Industries, Inc. [Associated Press] (SAG)
LUNR	Lunar Corp. [NASDAQ symbol] (SAG)
LUO	Laboratory Unit Operation
LUO	Left Ureteral Orifice [Medicine]
LUO	Luena [Angola] [Airport symbol] (OAG)
LUO	Luogo [As Written] [Music]
LUOQ	Left Upper Outer Quadrant [of abdomen] [Medicine]
LUOTC	London University Officers Training Corps [British military] (DMA)
LUP	Kalaupapa [Hawaii] [Airport symbol] (OAG)
LUP	Land Use and Planning [British]
LUP	Laying-Up Position [British military] (DMA)
LUP	Liberia Unification Party [Political party]
LUP	Lupenga Air Charters [Zambia] [ICAO designator] (FAAC)
Lup	Lupus [Constellation]
LUPAC	Life Underwriters Political Action Committee
LUPF	Linear Utility Prediction Function [Mathematics]
Lupi	Lupus [Constellation]
LUPS	Logistics Unit Productivity Study [or System] [Army]
LUPUL	Lupulus [Hops] [Pharmacy] (ROG)
LUPWT	Langley Unitary Plan Wind Tunnel [NASA] (KSC)
LUQ	Left Upper Quadrant [of abdomen] [Medicine]
LUQ	San Luis [Argentina] [Airport symbol] (OAG)
LUR	Cape Lisburne [Alaska] [Airport symbol] (OAG)
LUR	Laurasia Resources Ltd. [Toronto Stock Exchange symbol]
LUR	Laureate [Numismatics]
LUR	Lineas Aereas Latur SA de CV [Mexico ICAO designator] (FAAC)
LUR	London Underground Railway
LUR	Luria [L.] & Sons, Inc. [NYSE symbol] (SAG)
LUR	Luria (L)& Son [NYSE symbol] (TTSB)
LURE	Lunar Ranging Experiment [Aerospace]
Luria	Luria [L.] & Sons, Inc. [Associated Press] (SAG)
LURS	Land Use and Requirements Study (MCD)
LURS	Logistic Unit Productivity System [Army]
LURTx..........	Living Unrelated Renal Transplantation [Medicine]
LUS	Land Utilization Survey (WDAA)
LUS	Laparoscopic Ultrasonography [Medicine]
LUS	Large Ultimate Size [Telecommunications] (TEL)
LUS	Latch Up Screen
LUS	Laws of the United States [A publication] (DLA)
LUS	Library of Useful Stories [A publication]
LUS	Liquid Upper Stage (NASA)
LUS	Load, Update, Subset
LUS	Lock-Up Solenoid [Automotive engineering]
LUS	Louisiana State University in Shreveport, Library, Shreveport, LA [OCLC symbol] (OCLC)
LU-S	Louisiana State University in Shreveport, Shreveport, LA [Library symbol Library of Congress] (LCLS)
LUS	Lusaka [Zambia] [Seismograph station code, US Geological Survey] (SEIS)
LUS	Lusitanair-Transportes Aereos Comercials SA [Portugal ICAO designator] (FAAC)
lus	Lustre (VRA)
LUSA	Life USA Holding, Inc. [NASDAQ symbol] (SAG)
LUSA	Life USA Holdings [NASDAQ symbol] (TTSB)
LUSB	Left Upper Sternal Border [Anatomy] (DAVI)
LUSCC	Latymer Upper School Cadet Corps [British military] (DMA)
LUSEX	Lunar Surface Explorer Simulation Program [Aerospace] (MCD)
Lush.............	Lushington's English Admiralty Reports [1859-62] [A publication] (DLA)
Lush Adm	Lushington's English Admiralty Reports [1859-62] [A publication] (DLA)
Lush Pr........	Lush's Common Law Practice [A publication] (DLA)
Lush Pr L....	Lushington on Prize Law [A publication] (DLA)
LUSI............	Lunar Surface Inspection [Aerospace]
LUSING........	Lusingando [Coaxingly] [Music]
LUSL	Loyola University School of Law (DLA)
LU-SM	Louisiana State University in Shreveport, Medical Center Library, Shreveport, LA [Library symbol Library of Congress] (LCLS)

LUSOLT	Lakehead University School of Library Technology [Canada]
LUST	Latrine Urinal Shower Toilet [A unit of mobility equipment] [Military]
LUST	Leaking Underground Storage Tank [Environmental chemistry]
LUST	List Updated Sort and Total (PDAA)
LUST	Lustrous (WDAA)
LUST	Wanderlust Interactive [NASDAQ symbol] (TTSB)
LUST	Wanderlust Interactive, Inc. [NASDAQ symbol] (SAG)
LUSTER	Lunar Dust and Earth Return [NASA] (IAA)
LUSTW	Wanderlust Interactive Wrrt [NASDAQ symbol] (TTSB)
LUSURF	Lunar Surface (PDAA)
LUSVC	Logical Unit Services Manager (MHDB)
LUT	Launch Umbilical Tower [NASA]
LUT	Laura Station [Australia Airport symbol Obsolete] (OAG)
LUT	Limited User Test [Military] (RDA)
LUT	Line Unit [Computer science] (BUR)
LUT	Lining Up Table (DGA)
LUT	Local User Terminal
LUT	Lookup Table [Computer science] (BYTE)
LUT	Loughborough University of Technology [British] (IRUK)
LUT	Luteum [Yellow] [Latin]
LUT	Miri [Malaysia] [Airport symbol] (AD)
LUTC	Life Underwriter Training Council [Washington, DC] (EA)
LUTC	Life Underwriter Training Course
LUTCAM	Language Used to Conceal Actual Meaning
LUTE	Language Understander Translator and Editor (NITA)
Lut Elec Cas...	Lutwyche's English Election Cases [A publication] (DLA)
Lut Ent........	Lutwyche's Entries [1704; 1718] [A publication] (DLA)
LUTET	Lutetia Parisiorum [Paris] [Imprint] (ROG)
LUTFCSUSTC...	Librarians United to Fight Costly, Silly, Unnecessary Serial Title Changes [Defunct] (EA)
LUTH	Lutheran
LUTH	Lutheran
LUTH	Luther Medical Products [NASDAQ symbol] (SAG)
LUTH	Luther Med Products [NASDAQ symbol] (TTSB)
LuthMed	Luther Medical Products, Inc. [Associated Press] (SAG)
LUTIRO........	Life and Unit Trust Intermediaries Regulatory Organisation [British]
LUTIS	Luton Information Service (NITA)
LUTOM	Land Use Trade Off Model (DICI)
LUTP	Land Use and Transport Planning [British]
LUT PAR.....	Lutetia Parisiorum [Paris] [Imprint] (ROG)
Lut RC	Lutwyche's English Registration Appeal Cases [1843-45] [A publication] (DLA)
LUTS	Light Units, Times Square [Electronics]
LUTT	Launcher Umbilical Tower Transporter [NASA] (KSC)
Lutw E	Lutwyche's English Common Pleas Reports [A publication] (DLA)
Lutw Reg Cas...	Lutwyche's English Registration Cases [A publication] (DLA)
LUU	Illumination Unit (MCD)
LUU	Laura [Australia Airport symbol Obsolete] (OAG)
LUU	Louisiana State University, Baton Rouge, LA [OCLC symbol] (OCLC)
LUV	Langgur [Indonesia] [Airport symbol] (OAG)
LUV	Large Unilamellar Vesicle [Pharmacy Biochemistry]
LUV	Light Utility Vehicle [Pickup truck]
LU-V	Louisiana State University, School of Veterinary Medicine, Medical Library, Baton Rouge, LA [Library symbol Library of Congress] (LCLS)
LUV	Southwest Airlines [NYSE symbol] (TTSB)
LUV	Southwest Airlines Co. [NYSE symbol] (SPSG)
LUVO	Lunar Ultraviolet Observatory [NASA]
LUW	Logical Units of Work [Computer science] (BYTE)
LUW	Luwuk [Indonesia] [Airport symbol] (OAG)
LUX	Laurens, SC [Location identifier FAA] (FAAL)
LUX	Lincoln Airlines, Inc. [ICAO designator] (FAAC)
LUX	Luxembourg [Seismograph station code, US Geological Survey] (SEIS)
LUX	Luxembourg [Airport symbol] (OAG)
LUX	Luxembourg [ANSI three-letter standard code] (CNC)
Lux.............	Luxembourg (VRA)
LUX	Luxottica Group ADS [NYSE symbol] (SPSG)
LUX	Luxury [or Luxurious] [Classified advertising] (ADA)
Luxem	Luxembourg
LuxLBN........	Bibliotheque Nationale de Luxembourg, Service du Pret, Luxembourg, Luxembourg [Library symbol Library of Congress] (LCLS)
Luxottca........	Luxottica Group [Associated Press] (SAG)
Luxtec........	Luxtec Corp. [Associated Press] (SAG)
LUXY	Cinemastar Luxury Theaters [NASDAQ symbol] (TTSB)
LUXY	CinemaStar Luxury Theaters, Inc. [NASDAQ symbol] (SAG)
LUXYW	Cinemastar Luxry Theaters Wrrt [NASDAQ symbol] (TTSB)
LUY	Lushoto [Tanzania] [Airport symbol] (AD)
LUZED	Luzon Engineer District [Army World War II]
Luzerne Leg Obs (PA)...	Luzerne Legal Observer [Pennsylvania] [A publication] (DLA)
Luzerne Leg Reg R (PA)...	Luzerne Legal Register Reports [Pennsylvania] [A publication] (DLA)
Luzerne LJ (PA)...	Luzerne Law Journal [Pennsylvania] [A publication] (DLA)
Luz Law T....	Luzerne Law Times [Pennsylvania] [A publication] (DLA)
Luz Leg Obs...	Luzerne Legal Observer [Pennsylvania] [A publication] (DLA)
Luz Leg Reg Rep...	Luzerne Legal Register Reports [Pennsylvania] [A publication] (DLA)
Luz LJ	Luzerne Law Journal [Pennsylvania] [A publication] (DLA)
Luz LO	Luzerne Legal Observer [Pennsylvania] [A publication] (DLA)
Luz L Reg Rep...	Luzerne Legal Register Reports (Continuation of Kulp) [Pennsylvania] [A publication] (DLA)
Luz LT (NS)...	Luzerne Law Times. New Series [Pennsylvania] [A publication] (DLA)

Luz LT (OS)... Luzerne Law Times. Old Series [*Pennsylvania*] [*A publication*] (DLA)
LV............. Laboratory Vehicle (MCD)
LV............. Lacrosse Victoria [*Australia An association*]
LV............. Lactobacillus Viridescens [*Biochemistry*] (DAVI)
LV............. Lancastrian Volunteers [*British military*] (DMA)
LV............. Landing Vehicle
LV............. Land Value (ADA)
LV............. Largest Vessel [*British*] (ADA)
LV............. LASER Velocimeter
LV............. LaserVision [*Videodisc system*]
LV............. Last Vehicle [*Railroads*] (ROG)
LV............. Latent Variable [*Data analysis*]
LV............. Lateral Ventricle [*Neuroanatomy*]
LV............. Lateral Vestibular Nucleus [*Neuroanatomy*]
LV............. Launch Vehicle (MCD)
LV............. Launch Verification [*NASA*] (IAA)
LV............. Lava (WGA)
LV............. Laverda SpA [*Italy ICAO aircraft manufacturer identifier*] (ICAO)
LV............. Laws of Virginia [*A publication*] (DLA)
LV............. Leaky Valve [*Nuclear energy*] (NRCH)
LV............. Leave (AFM)
LV............. Leeds Volunteers [*British military*] (DMA)
LV............. Left Ventral Fin [*Fish anatomy*]
LV............. Left Ventricle [*Cardiology*]
LV............. Legal Volt
LV............. Lehigh Valley Railroad Co. [*Absorbed into Consolidated Rail Corp.*] [*AAR code*]
LV............. Leukemia Virus [*Hematology*] (MAE)
LV............. Lev [*Monetary unit*] [*Bulgaria*]
LV............. Level of Study [*Online database field identifier*]
Lv............. Leviticus [*Old Testament book*]
LV............. Licensed Victualer
LV............. Lift Vector (NASA)
LV............. Light and Variable [*Referring to wind*]
LV............. Light Value [*Photography*] (DICI)
LV............. Light Variegated Maize
LV............. Light Vehicle [*British military*] (DMA)
LV............. Light-Vessel [*Navigation*]
LV............. Limited Visibility Study (MCD)
LV............. Limit Value
LV............. Linear Velocity
LV............. Livery
LV............. Live Vaccine [*Medicine*]
LV............. Live Virus [*Medicine*] (MAE)
LV............. Livre [*Monetary unit*] [*Obsolete French*] (ROG)
LV............. Loading Valve (MCD)
LV............. Load Vertical
L/V............. Local Vertical (KSC)
LV............. Louis Vuitton [*Initials used as a pattern on Vuitton luggage, handbags, etc.*]
LV............. Low in Volatiles [*Commercial grading*]
LV............. Low Velocity [*British military*] (DMA)
LV............. Low Voltage
LV............. Low Volume
LV............. Lumbar Vertebra [*Medicine*]
LV............. Luncheon Voucher [*British*]
LV............. Lung Volume (MAE)
LV............. Valda [*France*] [*Research code symbol*]
LVA............. Lancashire Volunteer Artillery [*British military*] (DMA)
LVA............. Landing Vehicle, Airfoil
LVA............. Landing Vehicle, Assault [*Navy symbol*]
LVA............. Large Vertical Aperture Antenna [*Aviation*]
LVA............. Launch Vehicle Availability [*NASA*]
LVA............. Lava Capital Corp. [*Toronto Stock Exchange symbol*]
LVA............. Left Ventricular Aneurysm [*Cardiology*]
LVA............. Left Ventricular Assistance [*Cardiology*]
LVA............. Left Visual Acuity [*Medicine*]
LVA............. Literacy Volunteers of America (EA)
LVA............. Local Virtual Address
LVA............. Logarithmic Video Amplifier (IAA)
LVA............. Low-Velocity Anomaly [*Seismology*]
LVA............. Low Vision Aid [*Ophthalmology*]
LVA............. Low-Voltage Activated [*Neurochemistry*]
LVA............. Low-Voltage Avalanche [*Electronics*] (IAA)
LVA............. Lucasvarity PLC [*NYSE symbol*] (SAG)
LV (A) (2).... Landing Vehicle, Tracked (Armored) (Mark II) [*"Water Buffalo," Canopy Type*]
LVAD........... Left Ventricle Assist Device [*Cardiology*]
LVAD........... Low Velocity Air Drop [*Military vehicle specifications*]
LVAIC........... Lehigh Valley Association of Independent College Libraries [*Library network*]
L-VAM........ Lupron, Vinblastine, Adriamycin, Mutamycin [*Antineoplastic drug*] (CDI)
LVAP............ Launch Vehicle and Propulsion [*NASA*] (IAA)
LVAR............ Launch Vehicle Assessment Report [*or Review*] [*NASA*] (KSC)
LVAR............ Lithuanian Veterans Association Ramove (EA)
LVAS............ Launch Vehicle Alarm System [*NASA*] (IAA)
LVAS............ Left Ventricle Assist System [*Cardiology*]
LVAS............ Light-Vehicle Animation Simulation [*Accident reconstruction*] [*Automotive engineering*]
LVB............. Left Ventricular Bypass [*Cardiology*]
LVB............. Liquid-Vapor Bubble [*Chemical engineering*]
LVB............. Livramento [*Brazil*] [*Airport symbol*] (OAG)
LVB............. Low-Voltage Bias
LVBR........... Land Valuation Boards of Review [*Australia*]

LVC............. Decisions of the Lands Tribunal (Rating) [*A publication*] (DLA)
LVC............. Enid, OK [*Location identifier FAA*] (FAAL)
LVC............. Large Vacuum Chamber [*Army*]
LVC............. Lebanon Valley College [*Pennsylvania*]
LVC............. Lebanon Valley College, Annville, PA [*OCLC symbol*] (OCLC)
LVC............. Lillian Vernon [*AMEX symbol*] (TTSB)
LVC............. Lillian Vernon Corp. [*AMEX symbol*] (SPSG)
LVC............. Log Voltmeter Converter
LVC............. Low-Voltage Capacitor
LVC............. Low-Voltage Cutoff [*Battery*]
LVC............. Lutheran Volunteer Corps (EA)
LVCD.......... Least Voltage Coincidence Detector
LVCD.......... Liquid Volume Charge Density [*Automotive fuel systems*]
LVCI............ Laser Vision Centers [*NASDAQ symbol*] (TTSB)
LVCI............ Laser Vision Centers, Inc. [*NASDAQ symbol*] (SAG)
LVCM.......... Licentiate of the Victoria College of Music [*London*] (ROG)
LVCP........... Laboratory Vehicle Checkout Procedure
LVCT........... Low-Voltage Circuit Tester (MCD)
LVD............. Laboratory Vehicle Development
lvd............. Leaved
LVD............. Left Ventricular Assist Device [*An artificial organ*]
LVD............. Left Ventricular Dysfunction [*Cardiology*] (DAVI)
LVd............. Left Ventricular End-Diastolic Pressure [*Cardiology*] (MAE)
LVD............. Level Island, AK [*Location identifier FAA*] (FAAL)
LVD............. Light Valve Display
LVD............. Liquid Crystal Visual Display [*Electronics*] (EECA)
LVD............. Louvered Door (AAG)
LVD............. Low-Velocity Detonation [*or Drop*]
LVD............. Low-Voltage Drop (CET)
LVDA........... Launch Vehicle Data Adapter [*NASA*]
LVDA........... Launch Vehicle Deployment Assembly [*NASA*] (MCD)
LVDC........... Launch Vehicle Data Center [*NASA*] (KSC)
LVDC........... Launch Vehicle Digital Computer [*NASA*]
LVDC........... Low-Voltage Direct Current
LVDd........... Left Ventricular Dimension in Enddiastole [*Cardiology*] (DMAA)
LVDG........... Las Vegas Disc Golf & Tennis [*NASDAQ symbol*] (TTSB)
LVDG........... Las Vegas Discount Golf & Tennis [*NASDAQ symbol*] (SAG)
LVDI............ Left Ventricular Dimension [*Cardiology*] (DMAA)
LVDIFC........ Leroy Van Dyke International Fan Club (EA)
LVDL........... Licensed Victuallers' Defence League of England and Wales (BI)
LVDP........... Left Ventricular Developed Pressure [*Medicine*] (DMAA)
LVDP........... Left Ventricular Diastolic Pressure [*Cardiology*]
LV dp/dt...... First Derivation of Left Ventricular Pressure [*Cardiology*] (DAVI)
LVDS.......... Light-Vehicle Dynamics Simulation [*Accident reconstruction*] [*Automotive engineering*]
LVDS.......... Liquid, Vee, Diesel-Cycle, Supercharged
LVDT........... Linear Variable Differential Transformer
LVDT........... Linear Variable Displacement Transducer
LVDT........... Linear Velocity Displacement Transformer (IEEE)
LVDT........... Linear Voltage Differential Transformer (NASA)
LVDT-PRIM... Linear Variable Differential Transformer - Primary
LVDT-SEC... Linear Variable Differential Transformer - Secondary
LVDV........... Left Ventricular Diastolic Volume [*Cardiology*] (MAE)
LVE............. Launch Vehicle Engine (IAA)
LVE............. Leave (WGA)
LVE............. Left Ventricular Ejection [*Medicine*] (DMAA)
LVE............. Left Ventricular Enlargement [*Cardiology*]
LVE............. Linear Vector Equation
LVE............. Liquid Vapor Equilibrium
LVED........... Left Ventricular End-Diastolic [*Cardiology*]
LVEDC........ Left Ventricular End-Diastolic Circumference [*Cardiology*] (MAE)
LVEDD........ Left Ventricular End-Diastolic Dimension [*Cardiology*]
LVEDP........ Left Ventricular End-Diastolic Pressure [*Cardiology*]
LVEDV........ Left Ventricular End-Diastolic Volume [*Cardiology*]
LVEF........... Left Ventricular Ejection Fraction [*Time*] [*Cardiology*]
LVEN........... Las Vegas Entertainment Network [*NASDAQ symbol*] (SAG)
LVEN........... Las Vegas Entmt Ntwk [*NASDAQ symbol*] (TTSB)
LVEndo....... Left Ventricular Endocardial Half [*Cardiology*] (DAVI)
LVENW........ Las Vegas Entmt Ntwk Wrrt'A' [*NASDAQ symbol*] (TTSB)
LVENZ......... Las Vegas Entmt Ntwk Wrrt'B' [*NASDAQ symbol*] (TTSB)
LVEP........... Left Ventricular End-Diastolic Pressure [*Cardiology*] (MAE)
LVEpi.......... Left Ventricular Epicardial Half [*Cardiology*] (DAVI)
LVER........... Liver Fraction Elevated [*Gastroenterology*] (DAVI)
LVER........... Local Veterans Employment Representative [*Department of Labor*]
LVES........... Low-Voltage Electrical Stimulation [*Meat treatment*]
LVET........... Left Ventricular Ejection Time [*Cardiology*]
LVET........... Low Volume Eye Test (DMAA)
LVETI.......... Left Ventricular Ejection Time Index [*Cardiology*]
LVF............. Dallas, TX [*Location identifier FAA*] (FAAL)
LVF............. Left Ventricular Failure [*Cardiology*]
LVF............. Left Visual Field [*Psychometrics*]
LVF............. Linear Vector Function
LVF............. Low-Voltage Fast [*Electronics*]
LVF............. Low-Voltage Foci (MAE)
LVFA........... Low Velocity Friction Apparatus (PDAA)
LVFC........... Launch Vehicle Flight Control
LVFCS......... Launch Vehicle Flight Control System
LVFP........... Left Ventricular Filling Pressure [*Cardiology*]
LVFS........... Large Volume Filtration System [*Environmental chemistry*]
LVG............. Lauro/Viceroy/Global Joint Service [*Shipping*] (DS)
LVG............. Leaving
LVG............. Left Ventral Gluteal [*Injection site*]
LVG............. Left Ventriculography [*Medicine*]
LVG............. Left Ventrogluteal [*Anatomy*] (DAVI)
LVG............. Left Visceral Ganglion [*Medicine*]

LVG............ Levengood Oil & Gas, Inc. [*Vancouver Stock Exchange symbol*]
LVGC.......... Launch Vehicle Guidance Computer [*NASA*]
LVGO.......... Light Vacuum Gas Oil [*Petroleum technology*]
LVGSE .... Launch Vehicle Ground Support Equipment [*NASA*] (KSC)
LVH............ Landing Vehicle, Hydrofoil
LVH............ Large Vessel Hematocrit (MAE)
LVH............ Left Ventricular Hypertrophy [*Cardiology*]
LVHF.......... Low Very High Frequency (IAA)
LVHV.......... Low-Volume High-Velocity (IEEE)
LVHX .... Landing Craft, Hydrofoil, Experimental [*Navy symbol*]
LVI............. Laus Verbo Incarnato [*Praise to the Incarnate Word*] [*Latin*]
LVI............. Lavalin Industries, Inc. [*Toronto Stock Exchange symbol*]
LVI............. Left Ventricular Insufficiency [*Cardiology*] (MAE)
LVI............. Left Ventricular Ischemia [*Medicine*] (DMAA)
LVI............. Lehigh Group, Inc. [*Formerly, LUI Group*] [*NYSE symbol*] (SAG)
LVI............. Liquid Vapor Interface
LVI............. Livingstone [*Zambia*] [*Airport symbol*] (OAG)
LVI............. Local Veterinary Inspector [*British*]
LVI............. Low-Viscosity Index (IAA)
LVIA.......... Lay Volunteers International Association
LVID.......... Left Ventricle Internal Diameter [*Cardiology*]
LVID.......... Left Ventricular Internal Dimension [*Cardiology*] (DAVI)
LVIDP........ Left Ventricular Initial Diastolic Pressure [*Cardiology*] (AAMN)
L-VIS......... LASER Viewdata Information Service (NITA)
LVIS........... Launch Vehicle Instrumentation Systems [*NASA*] (KSC)
LVIT.......... Linear Variable Inductance Transducer
LVJ............ Cleveland, OH [*Location identifier FAA*] (FAAL)
LVK........... Livermore, CA [*Location identifier FAA*] (FAAL)
LVK........... Lovelock [*Nevada*] [*Seismograph station code, US Geological Survey Closed*] (SEIS)
LVL........... Laminated-Veneer Lumber
LVL........... Lawrenceville, VA [*Location identifier FAA*] (FAAL)
LVL........... Left Vastus Lateralis [*Anatomy*] (DAVI)
lvl............. Level (VRA)
LVL........... Level (AAG)
LVL........... Levelland Energy [*Vancouver Stock Exchange symbol*]
LVL........... Lex Vehicle Leasing [*British*]
LVL........... Long Vertical Left
LVL........... Low-Velocity Layer [*Geophysics*] (OA)
LVL........... Universite Laval, Bibliotheque [*UTLAS symbol*]
LVLB......... Land Valuers' Licensing Board [*Western Australia*]
LVLG......... Left Ventrolateral Gluteal [*Site of injection*] [*Medicine*]
LVLH......... Local Vertical/Local Horizontal (NASA)
LVLO......... Local Vehicle Licensing Office [*British*]
LVLOF....... Level Off [*Aviation*] (FAAC)
LVLP......... Large Virus-Like Particle
LVLSH .... Level Shifter (NITA)
LVM.......... LaSallian Volunteer Movement (EA)
LVM.......... Launch Vehicle Material (MCD)
LVM.......... Launch Vehicle Monitor
LVM.......... Left Ventricular Mass [*Cardiology*]
LVM.......... Light Vehicle Mine [*Military*]
LVM.......... Line Voltage Monitor
LVM.......... Livingston, MT [*Location identifier FAA*] (FAAL)
LVM.......... Localized Vibrational Mode (PDAA)
LVM.......... Low-Value Materiel (MCD)
LVMA........ Louisiana Veterinary Medical Association (SRA)
LVMC........ Low-Variation Medical Condition
LVMH........ Louis Vuitton Moet-Hennessy [*Commercial firm*] [*Belgium*]
LVMH........ LVMH Moet Hennessey Louis Vuitton [*NASDAQ symbol*] (SAG)
LVMH........ LVMH Moet Hennessey Louis Vuitton [*Associated Press*] (SAG)
LVMHY ...... LVMH Most Henn Lou Vttn ADS [*NASDAQ symbol*] (TTSB)
LVMM........ Left Ventricular Muscle Mass [*Cardiology*] (DAVI)
LVMP........ Launch Vehicle Mission Peculiar
LVMS......... LEG [*Liquefied Energy Gas*] Volume Measuring System
LVMS......... Limb Volume Measuring System
LVMTAS..... Low-Visibility, Moving Target Acquisition and Strike [*Military*]
LVN.......... Carnegie Public Library, Las Vegas, NM [*OCLC symbol*] (OCLC)
LVN.......... Lakeville, MN [*Location identifier FAA*] (FAAL)
LVN.......... Las Vegas [*Nevada*] [*Seismograph station code, US Geological Survey*] (SEIS)
LVN.......... Lateral Vestibular Nucleus [*Medicine*] (DMAA)
LVN.......... Levon Resources Ltd. [*Toronto Stock Exchange symbol Vancouver Stock Exchange symbol*]
LVN.......... Library Video Network [*Video producer*]
LVN.......... Licensed Visiting Nurse
LVN.......... Licensed Vocational Nurse
LVN.......... Light Virgin Naphtha (PDAA)
LVN.......... Limiting Viscosity Number
LVN.......... Low-Voltage Neon
LVNAT .... Licensed Vocational Nurses Association of Texas (SRA)
LVND......... LASER Variable Neutral Density
LVNDL....... Licensed Victuallers' National Defence League [*British*] (DI)
LVNG .... Living
LVNI.......... Laser Video Network [*NASDAQ symbol*] (SAG)
LVNI.......... Laser Video Network [*NASDAQ symbol*] (TTSB)
LVNIW....... Laser Video Network Wrrt'A' [*NASDAQ symbol*] (TTSB)
LVNIZ........ Laser Video Network Wrrt'B' [*NASDAQ symbol*] (TTSB)
LVNJ.......... Long Valley [*New Jersey*] [*Seismograph station code, US Geological Survey*] (SEIS)
LVNTE........ Livent Inc. [*NASDAQ symbol*] (TTSB)
LVNTF........ Livent, Inc. [*NASDAQ symbol*] (SAG)
LVO........... Launch Vehicle Operations
LVO........... Laverton [*Australia Airport symbol*] (OAG)
LVO........... Left Ventricle Outflow [*Medicine*] (DMAA)

LVO............ left Ventricular Overactivity [*Cardiology*] (DAVI)
LVO............ Lieutenant of the Victorian Order [*Canada*] (DD)
LVO............ Lithiated Vanadium Oxide [*Battery technology*]
LVO............ Louver Opening
LVOA.......... Left Ventricular Overactivity [*Cardiology*] (DAVI)
LVOD.......... Launch Vehicle Operations Division [*NASA*] (IAA)
LVOP.......... Local Vertical and Orbit Plane
LVOR.......... Low-Powered, Very-High-Frequency Omnirange
LVOT.......... Left Ventricular Outflow Tract [*Cardiology*] (CPH)
LVP............ Large Volume Parenterals [*Medicine*]
LVP............ Left Ventricular Pressure [*Cardiology*]
LVP............ Left Ventricular Pump [*Cardiology*]
LVP............ Light Valve Projector
LVP............ Low-Value Product
LVP............ Low-Voltage Plate
LVP............ Low-Voltage Protection [*Electronics*]
LVP............ Lysine Vasopressin [*Antidiuretic hormone*]
LVPD.......... Launch Vehicle Pressure Display [*NASA*] (KSC)
LVpE.......... Evangeline Parish Library, Ville Platte, LA [*Library symbol Library of Congress*] (LCLS)
LVPFR .... Left Ventricular Peak Filling Rate [*Cardiology*] (DMAA)
LVPG.......... Launch Vehicle Planning Group [*Aerospace*] (AAG)
LVPL.......... Liverpool [*England*]
LVPP.......... Launch Vehicle and Propulsion Program [*NASA*]
LVPS.......... Laboratory Vehicle Procedure Simulator
LVPS.......... Low-Voltage Power Supply
LVPTG........ Lateral Vascularized Patellar Tendon Graft [*Orthopedics*]
LVPW......... Left Ventricular Posterior Wall [*Cardiology*] (DMAA)
LVPWT....... Left Ventricular Posterior Wall Thickness [*Cardiology*] (DAVI)
LVR........... Laboratory of Virology and Rickettsial Diseases
lvr............ Latvian Soviet Socialist Republic [*MARC country of publication code Library of Congress*] (LCCP)
LVR........... Lever (MSA)
LVR........... Lever
LVR........... Line Voltage Regulator
LVR........... Liverpool [*England*] [*Seismograph station code, US Geological Survey Closed*] (SEIS)
LVR........... London Volunteer Regiment [*British military*] (DMA)
LVR........... Longitudinal Video Recording
LVR........... Long Vertical Right
LVR........... Louver (MSA)
LVR........... Low-Voltage Rack
LVR........... Low-Voltage Relay
LVR........... Low-Voltage Release [*Electronics*]
LVR........... Low-Volume Ramjet (MCD)
LVRATS ...... Leave Rations [*Military*] (DNAB)
LVRATS SL... Leave Rations, Sick Leave [*Military*] (DNAB)
LVRATS SPEC... Leave Rations, Special Leave [*Military*] (DNAB)
LVRC .... Lamoille Valley Railroad Co. [*AAR code*]
LVR(CE)...... Low-Voltage Release (Continuous Effect) [*Electronics*] (DNAB)
LVRE.......... Low-Voltage Release Effect [*Electronics*] (MSA)
LV Rep .... Lehigh Valley Law Reporter [*Pennsylvania*] [*A publication*] (DLA)
LVRIS .... Low-Volume Ramjet Inlet System
LVRJ.......... Low-Volume Ramjet
LVRJ.......... Low-Volume Ramjet
LVRLSE....... Low-Voltage Release [*Electronics*]
LV-ROM...... LASER Vision Read-Only Memory
LVRR .... Lehigh Valley Railroad Co. [*Absorbed into Consolidated Rail Corp.*]
LVRS .... Launch Vehicle Recovery System [*NASA*] (IAA)
LVRS .... Lightweight Video Reconnaissance System [*Military*] (INF)
LVRT.......... Land and Valuation Review Tribunal [*Northern Territory, Australia*]
LV/RVV .... Local Vertical/Relative Velocity Vector
LVS........... Las Vegas, NM [*Location identifier FAA*] (FAAL)
LVS........... Launch Vehicle Simulator [*NASA*] (IAA)
LVS........... Leaves (MSA)
LVS........... Left Ventricular Strain [*Cardiology*]
LVS........... Left Ventricular Strain [*Cardiology*] (DAVI)
LVs........... Left Ventricular Systolic Pressure Mean [*Cardiology*] (MAE)
LVS........... Light Value System [*Photography*] (BARN)
LVS........... Logistical Vehicle System
LVS........... Logistics Vehicle System
LVS........... Low-Velocity Scanning
LVSB.......... Lakeview Financial [*NASDAQ symbol*] (TTSB)
LVSB.......... Lakeview Financial Corp. [*NASDAQ symbol*] (SAG)
LVSC.......... London Voluntary Service Council [*British*]
LVSE.......... Launch Vehicle Systems Engineer [*NASA*] (SAA)
LVSEMI....... Left Ventricular Subendocardia Lischemia [*Cardiology*] (DMAA)
LVSF.......... Laboratory Vehicle Support Facility
LVSG.......... Launch Vehicle Study Group [*NASA*] (KSC)
LVS/ITS...... LASER Vibration Sensor Inspection Test System [*Army*] (RDA)
LVSP.......... Left Ventricular Systolic Pressure [*Cardiology*]
LVSS.......... Laboratory Vehicle System Segment
LVSS.......... LASER Vector Scoring System (DWSG)
LVSSTS....... Launch Vehicle Safety System Test Set [*NASA*] (IAA)
LVST.......... Lateral Vestibulospinal Tract [*Medicine*] (DMAA)
LVST.......... Longitudinal Velocity Sorting Tube
LVSTCK....... Livestock
LVSTK........ Livestock
LVSV.......... Left Ventricular Stroke Volume [*Cardiology*]
LVSW......... Left Ventricular Septal Wall [*Cardiology*] (DAVI)
LVSW......... Left Ventricular Stroke Work [*Cardiology*]
LVSWI........ Left Ventricular Stroke Work Index [*Cardiology*]
LVT........... Landing Vehicle, Tracked (Unarmored) [*Navy symbol*]
LVT........... Left Ventricular Tension [*Cardiology*] (MAE)

LVT.............. Lexicon Hebraicum et Aramaicum Veteris Testamenti [*Rome*] [*A publication*] (BJA)
LVT.............. Licensed Veterinary Technician
LVT.............. Linear Velocity Transducer
LVT.............. Livingston, TN [*Location identifier FAA*] (FAAL)
LVT.............. Low-Voltage Tubular
LVT.............. Lysine Vasotonin [*Adrenergic agent*]
LVT (1)........ Landing Vehicle, Tracked (Unarmored) (Mark I) ["*Alligator*"] [*Navy symbol*]
LVT (2)........ Landing Vehicle, Tracked (Unarmored) (Mark II) ["*Water Buffalo*"] [*Navy symbol*]
LVT (3)........ Landing Vehicle, Tracked (Unarmored) (Mark III) [*Navy symbol*]
LVT (4)........ Landing Vehicle, Tracked (Unarmored) (Mark IV)
LVT (A)........ Landing Vehicle, Tracked (Armored) [*Turret Type*]
LVTA........... London Vintage Taxi Association - American Section (EA)
LVT (A) (1)... Landing Vehicle, Tracked (Armored) (Mark I) ["*Water Buffalo*," Turret Type]
LVT (A) (4)... Landing Vehicle, Tracked (Armored) (Mark IV)
LVT (A) (5)... Landing Vehicle, Tracked (Armored) (Mark V)
LVTC.......... Landing Vehicle, Tracked, Command (NVT)
LVTC.......... Launch Vehicle Test Conductor [*NASA*] (KSC)
LVTCX......... Landing Vehicle, Tracked, Command, Experimental (MCD)
LVTD.......... Las Vegas Mjr League Sports [*NASDAQ symbol*] (TTSB)
LVTE.......... Landing Vehicle, Tracked, Engineer [*Model 1*]
LVTH.......... Landing Vehicle, Tracked, Howitzer [*Model 6*]
LVTL.......... Lexicon in Veteris Testamenti Libros [*A publication*] (BJA)
LVTP.......... Landing Vehicle, Tracked, Personnel (AABC)
LVTP-CMD ... Landing Vehicle, Tracked Personnel, Command [*Marine Corps*] (VNW)
LVTPX........ Landing Vehicle, Tracked, Personnel, Experimental (MCD)
LVTR.......... Landing Vehicle, Tracked, Retriever (NVT)
LVT(R)........ Landing Vehicle, Tracked (Rocket) [*British military*] (DMA)
LVTR.......... Low-VHF [*Very-High-Frequency*] Transmitter-Receiver
LVTRX........ Landing Vehicle, Tracked, Recovery, Experimental (MCD)
LVTU.......... Landing Vehicle, Tracked (Unarmored)
LVUPK........ Leave and Upkeep Period [*Military*] (NVT)
LVUSA........ Legion of Valor of the United States of America (EA)
LVV........... Delavan, WI [*Location identifier FAA*] (FAAL)
LVV........... Left Ventricular Volume [*Cardiology*]
LVV........... Lvov [*Ukraine*] [*Seismograph station code, US Geological Survey*] (SEIS)
LVVC.......... Lincolnshire Vintage Vehicle Club [*British*] (DCTA)
LVVP.......... Chlorambucil, Vinblastine, Vincristine, Prednisone [*Antineoplastic drug regimen*] (DAVI)
LVW........... Landing Vehicle, Wheeled
LVW........... Las Vegas [*Nevada*] [*Seismograph station code, US Geological Survey*] (SEIS)
LVW........... Left Ventricular Wall [*Anatomy*]
LVW........... Left Ventricular Work [*Cardiology*]
LVW........... Linked Vertical Well [*Coal gastification*] (DICI)
LVW........... Loaded Vehicle Weight [*Automotive engineering*]
LVWI.......... Left Ventricular Work Index [*Cardiology*]
LVWT.......... Left Ventricular Wall Thickness [*Cardiology*] (DMAA)
LVX........... Lily Virus X [*Plant pathology*]
LVY........... La Verendrye Management Corp. [*Toronto Stock Exchange symbol*]
LVY........... Levy [*Alaska*] [*Seismograph station code, US Geological Survey*] (SEIS)
LVZ........... Low-Viscosity Zone
LW............. Air Nevada [*ICAO designator*] (AD)
LW............. Griechische und Lateinische Lehnwoerter im Talmud, Midrasch und Targum [*A publication*] (BJA)
LW............. Lab. Wander [*France*] [*Research code symbol*]
LW............. Lacerated Wound
LW............. Landsteiner-Wiener [*Serum*]
L-W........... Landsverk-Wollan [*Radiation survey meter*]
LW............. Langwelle [*Long Wave*] [*German*] (MCD)
LW............. Last Word (IAA)
LW............. Lateral Wall [*Image on transesophageal echocardiography*] [*Cardiology*] (DAVI)
LW............. Late Warning
LW............. Launch Window [*Aerospace*] (AAG)
LW............. Lawrence Welk
Lw............. Lawrencium [*Symbol changed, 1963, to Lr*] [*Chemical element*]
LW............. Law Weekly [*A publication*] (DLA)
LW............. Leave Word [*Telecommunications*] (TEL)
LW............. Lee-White Method [*Hematology*] (MAE)
LW............. Left Ear, Warm Stimulus [*Medicine*] (MEDA)
LW............. Left Wing
LW............. Lethal Weapon [*A motion picture*]
LW............. Light Wall
LW............. Light Warning
LW............. Light Weight [*Technical drawings*]
LW............. Lightweight RADAR (NATG)
LW............. Limited War
LW............. Literatures of the World [*A publication*]
LW............. Lives With (ADA)
lw............. Loan Word (BJA)
LW............. Logical Weakness [*Used in correcting manuscripts, etc.*]
LW............. Logistics Wing [*Military*]
LW............. Long Wave [*Radio*]
LW............. Lotus West (EA)
LW............. Louisville & Wadley Railway Co. [*AAR code*]
Lw............. Low [*Automotive advertising*]
Lw............. Lower Hold [*Shipping*] (DS)
LW............. Low Water [*Tides and currents*]

LW............. Low Wave (WDAA)
LW............. Low Wing [*Aviation*] (AIA)
LW............. Lumens per Watt (ADA)
I/W........... Lumens per Watt (IDOE)
LW............. Lung Water
LW............. United States Law Week [*A publication*] (NTCM)
LWA........... Last Word Address
LWA........... Liberian World Airlines, Inc. [*ICAO designator*] (FAAC)
LWA........... Lightly Wounded in Action
LWA........... Lightweight Armor
LWA........... Limited Work Authorizations [*Nuclear energy*]
LWA........... Local Welfare Authority [*British*]
LWA........... Long Wire Antenna
LWA........... University of Southwestern Louisiana, Lafayette, LA [*OCLC symbol*] (OCLC)
LWAAM....... Light-Weight Air-to-Air Missile (MCD)
LWAR......... Lightweight Attack and/or Reconnaissance (NATG)
LWASV........ Lightweight Aircraft-to-Surface Vessel [*Military*]
LW/AW .... Light Weight / Air Warning
LWAY......... Lifeway Foods [*NASDAQ symbol*] (SAG)
LWB........... Greenbrier [*West Virginia*] [*Airport symbol*] (OAG)
LWB........... Laboratory Workbench
LWB........... Lewisburg, WV [*Location identifier FAA*] (FAAL)
LWB........... Light-Water Breeder [*Reactor*]
LWB........... Long Wheelbase
LWB........... Lower Bound [*Computer science*]
LWBR......... Light-Water Breeder Reactor
LWBS......... Loyal Wheelwrights' and Blacksmiths' Society [*A union*] [*British*]
LWC........... Lawrence [*Kansas*] [*Airport symbol*] (OAG)
LWC........... League of Women Composers [*Later, ILWC*] (EA)
LWC........... Lightweight Coated [*Paper*]
LWC........... Lightweight Concrete [*Technical drawings*]
LWC........... Lindsey Wilson College [*Columbia, KY*]
LWC........... Liquid Water Content
LWC........... Lithuanian World Community (EA)
LWC........... Little Way Circle [*An association*] (EA)
LWC........... Living with Cancer [*An association*] (EA)
LWCA......... Light-Water Critical Assembly [*Nuclear reactor*] [*Japan*]
LWCA......... Longwave Club of America (EA)
LWCF......... Land and Water Conservation Fund [*Department of the Interior*]
LWCF......... Land and Water Conservation Fund (GNE)
LWCG......... Lightweight Coated Gravure [*Paper*] (DGA)
LWCH......... Lightweight Container Handler (MCD)
LWCHW....... Light-Water-Cooled, Heavy-Water-Moderated Reactor (NRCH)
LWCMD .... Licentiate of the Welsh College of Music and Drama [*British*] (DBQ)
LWCMS....... Lightweight Company Mortar System
LWCO......... Lightweight Coated Offset [*Paper*] (DGA)
LW-COIN...... Limited War - Counterinsurgency
LWCS......... Limited War Capabilities Study
LWCSS .... Lightweight Camouflage Screen System (MCD)
LWCT........ Lachar-Wrobel Critical Items [*Psychology*] (DAVI)
LWCT........ Lee-White Clotting Time [*Hematology*]
LWD........... Larger Word [*Computer science*]
LWD........... Large Woody Debris [*Pisciculture*]
LWD........... LASER Welder/Driller (PDAA)
LWD........... Launch Window Display [*Aerospace*] (MCD)
LWD........... Left Wing Down [*Aviation*]
LWD........... Long-Working Distance [*Microscopy*]
LWD........... Loomis-Wood Diagram [*Physics*]
LWD........... Low-Water Data [*Marine science*] (OSRA)
LWD........... Low-Water Data (USDC)
LWD........... Low-Water Datum
LWD........... Worldwide Airline Services, Inc. [*ICAO designator*] (FAAC)
LWDG......... Lightweight Director Group [*Military*] (CAAL)
LWE........... Allwe [*Former USSR*] [*FAA designator*] (FAAC)
LWE........... Lawrence Mining [*Vancouver Stock Exchange symbol*]
LWE........... Liquid Whole Egg
LWECS........ Low-Wind Energy Conversion System (PDAA)
LWeJ.......... Welsh Public Library, Welsh, LA [*Library symbol Library of Congress*] (LCLS)
LWF........... Lightweight Fighter [*Air Force*]
LWF........... Local Welfare Authority Full Time [*British*]
LWF........... Luminous Wall Firing (DICI)
LWF........... Lutheran World Federation [*See also FLM*] [*Geneva, Switzerland*] (EAIO)
LWF & C..... Low Water Full and Change [*Tides and currents*]
LWFC......... Lloyd Wood Fan Club [*Defunct*] (EA)
LWFCS........ Lightweight Fire Control System [*Military*] (CAAL)
LWFJTF........ Lightweight Fighter Joint Test Force [*Air Force*]
LWFUSANC... Lutheran World Federation United States of America National Committee (EA)
LWG........... Corvallis, OR [*Location identifier FAA*] (FAAL)
LWG........... Lightweight Gun (NG)
LWG........... Logistic Work Group [*NATO*] (NATG)
LWG........... Longwood Gardens Library, Kennett Square, PA [*OCLC symbol*] (OCLC)
LWGCR .... Light-Water Moderated, Gas-Cooled Reactor (IAA)
LWGM........ Lightweight Gun Mount [*Military*] (CAAL)
LWGR......... Light-Water-Cooled, Graphic-Moderated (IAA)
LWH........... Lawn Hill [*Australia Airport symbol Obsolete*] (OAG)
LWHS......... Lightweight Headset [*Apollo*] [*NASA*]
LWHVR....... Lightweight High-Velocity Rifle
LWI........... LASER without Inversion
LWI........... Load Wear Index
LWI........... Long Wavelength Infrared (MCD)

LWI............. Low-Water Interval
LWI............. Lwiro [*Zaire*] [*Seismograph station code, US Geological Survey*] (SEIS)
LWIC........... Lightweight Insulating Concrete [*Technical drawings*]
LWII........... Long Wavelength Infrared Illuminator
LWinF.......... Franklin Parish Library, Winnsboro, LA [*Library symbol Library of Congress*] (LCLS)
LWIR .... Long Wavelength Infrared
LWIRC .... Limited Warfare Intelligence Reduction Complex
LWIU .... Laundry, Dry Cleaning, and Dye House Workers' International Union [*Later, Textile Processors, Service Trades, Health Care, Professional, and Technical Employees International Union*]
LWIU .... Leather Workers International Union of America (EA)
LWiW.......... Winn Parish Library, Winnfield, LA [*Library symbol Library of Congress*] (LCLS)
LWJ .... Lucas, William J., Albuquerque NM [*STAC*]
LWK .... Large White Kidney [*Medicine*] (DMAA)
LWK .... Lerwick [*Scotland*] Tingwall Airport [*Airport symbol*] (OAG)
LWL .... Lambair Ltd. [*Canada ICAO designator*] (FAAC)
LWL .... Land Warfare [*formerly, Limited War*] Laboratory [*Army*]
LWL .... Length [*of a boat*] at Waterline
LWL .... Lightweight Launcher (MCD)
LWL .... Limited War Laboratory [*Military*] (IIA)
LWL .... Load Waterline
LWL .... Low Waterline
LWL .... Waterline Length [*Navy*]
LWL .... Wells [*Nevada*] [*Airport symbol Obsolete*] (OAG)
LWLC.......... Light-Weight Low-Cost (PDAA)
LWLD.......... Lightweight LASER Designator
LWM .... Larrimore, William M., San Francisco CA [*STAC*]
LWM .... Lawrence [*Massachusetts*] [*Airport symbol*] (AD)
LWM .... Lawrence, MA [*Location identifier FAA*] (FAAL)
LWM .... Leonard Wood Memorial [*American Leprosy Foundation*] (EA)
LWM .... Liquid Waste Monitor [*Nuclear energy*] (IEEE)
LWM .... Low Watermark
LWMB .... Local Works Managing Budget [*British Armed Forces*]
LWMEL........ Leonard Wood Memorial for the Eradication of Leprosy [*Later, LWM*] (EA)
LWML.......... Lutheran Women's Missionary League [*Later, ILWML*] (EA)
LWMS......... Liquid Waste Management System [*Nuclear energy*] (NRCH)
LWN........... Loewen Group Capital Ltd. [*NYSE symbol*] (SAG)
LWN........... Loewen Group, Inc. [*Toronto Stock Exchange symbol*]
LWNA .... Lumber [*Timber*], Winter, North Atlantic [*Vessel load line mark*]
LWNGF........ Loewen Group [*NASDAQ symbol*] (TTSB)
LWNPr......... Loewen Group Cap Ser'A' 'MIPS' [*NYSE symbol*] (TTSB)
LWO........... Layout Work Order (MCD)
LWO........... Limited Warning Operation
LWO........... Limited War Office [*Air Force*] (MCD)
LWO........... Long-Wavelength Oscillation [*Astrophysics*]
LWO........... Lubavitch Women's Organization (EA)
LWO........... Lwow [*Former USSR Airport symbol*] (OAG)
LWOFC .... Lindsay Wagner's Official Fan Club (EA)
LWOP .... Lease with Option to Purchase (AAGC)
LWOP .... Leave without Pay
L-word .... Liberal [*Especially in negative political context*]
LWOS .... Low-Water Ordinary Spring [*Tides*]
LWOST .... Low-Water Ordinary Spring Tides
LWP .... Langley Working Paper [*NASA*]
LWP .... Leave with Pay (KSC)
LWP .... Limited War Plan
LWP .... Liquid Waste Processing [*Nuclear energy*] (NRCH)
LWP .... Liquid-Water Path [*Meteorology*]
LWP .... Load Water Plane
LWP .... Low Waterplane (PDAA)
LWPF .... Long-Wave Pass Filter (PDAA)
LWPS.......... Liquid Waste Processing System [*Nuclear energy*] (NRCH)
LWQ .... Low-Water Quadrature
LWQ .... Walnut Ridge, AR [*Location identifier FAA*] (FAAL)
LWR........... LASER Warning Receiver (MCD)
LWR........... Launch Warning Receiver [*Electronic countermeasure device*] [*Military*] (VNW)
LWR........... Lawrence Ins. Group [*AMEX symbol*] (TTSB)
LWR........... Lawrence Insurance Group [*AMEX symbol*] (SPSG)
LWR........... Light-Water Reactor
LWR........... Limited War Capability (AAG)
LWR........... Liquid Waste Release [*Nuclear energy*] (IEEE)
LWR........... Local Wage Rate
LWR........... Long Wavelength Redundant [*Camera for spectra*]
LWR........... Long-Wave Radiation
LWR........... Lower (AAG)
LWR........... Lutheran World Relief (EA)
LWRECCE .... Lightweight Reconnaissance Aircraft (NATG)
LWRENAM... Leading WREN [*Women's Royal Naval Service*] Air Mechanic [*British military*] (DMA)
LWRENCINE... Leading WREN [*Women's Royal Naval Service*] Cinema Operator [*British military*] (DMA)
LWRENDHYG... Leading WREN [*Women's Royal Naval Service*] Dental Hygienist [*British military*] (DMA)
LWRENDSA... Leading WREN [*Women's Royal Naval Service*] Dental Surgery Assistant [*British military*] (DMA)
LWRENEDUC... Leading WREN [*Women's Royal Naval Service*] Education Assistant [*British military*] (DMA)
LWRENMET... Leading WREN [*Women's Royal Naval Service*] Meteorologist [*British military*] (DMA)

LWRENMT ... Leading WREN [*Women's Royal Naval Service*] Motor Transport Driver [*British military*] (DMA)
LWRENPHOT... Leading WREN [*Women's Royal Naval Service*] Photographer [*British military*] (DMA)
LWRENQA.... Leading WREN [*Women's Royal Naval Service*] Quarters Assistant [*British military*] (DMA)
LWRENREM... Leading WREN [*Women's Royal Naval Service*] Radio Electrical Mechanic [*British military*] (DMA)
LWRENRO(M)... Leading WREN [*Women's Royal Naval Service*] Radio Operator (Morse) [*British military*] (DMA)
LWRENS(C)... Leading WREN [*Women's Royal Naval Service*] Stores Assistant (Clothes) [*British military*] (DMA)
LWRENS(S)... Leading WREN [*Women's Royal Naval Service*] Stores Assistant (Stores) [*British military*] (DMA)
LWRENSTD.. Leading WREN [*Women's Royal Naval Service*] Steward [*British military*] (DMA)
LWRENS(V)... Leading WREN [*Women's Royal Naval Service*] Stores Assistant (Victualling) [*British military*] (DMA)
LWRENTEL... Leading WREN [*Women's Royal Naval Service*] Telephonist [*British military*] (DMA)
LWRENTSA... Leading WREN [*Women's Royal Naval Service*] Training Support Assistant [*British military*] (DMA)
LWRENWA... Leading WREN [*Women's Royal Naval Service*] Weapon Analyst [*British military*] (DMA)
LWRENWTR(G)... Leading WREN [*Women's Royal Naval Service*] Writer (General) [*British military*] (DMA)
LWRENWTR(P)... Leading WREN [*Women's Royal Naval Service*] Writer (Pay) [*British military*] (DMA)
LWRENWTR(S)... Leading WREN [*Women's Royal Naval Service*] Writer (Shorthand) [*British military*] (DMA)
LWRM .... Lightweight RADAR Missile (MCD)
LWRO .... Lateral Wheel Run-Out [*Automotive engineering*]
LWRRI........ Louisiana Water Resources Research Institute [*Louisiana State University*] [*Department of the Interior*] [*Research center*] (RCD)
LWRS .... Lightweight Weather RADAR Set
LWRU .... Lightweight RADAR Unit (NATG)
LWS .... LASER Weapon System (MCD)
LWS .... Lewiston [*Idaho*] [*Airport symbol*] (OAG)
LWS .... Library Wholesale Services [*Information service or system*] (IID)
LWS .... Lightning Warning Set [*Air Force*]
LWS .... Lightning Warning System [*NASA*] (NASA)
LWS .... Light-Warning RADAR Set (NATG)
LWS .... Lightweight Sight
LWS .... Lightweight Sports [*Concept car*] [*Automotive engineering*]
LWS .... Lightweight System
LWS .... Low Water of Spring Tide
LWS .... Low-Water Sensitivity [*Brake fluid designation*]
LWS .... Lutheran Welfare Services [*Australia*]
LWSD .... LASER Weapon System Demonstrator [*Military*]
LWSF .... Lightweight Strike Fighter [*NATO Air Forces*]
LWSR .... Lightweight Search RADAR (IAA)
LWSR .... Lightweight Strike and Reconnaissance Aircraft (NATG)
LWSR(R) ..... Lightweight Strike and Reconnaissance Aircraft (Reconnaissance Role) (NATG)
LWSR(S)..... Lightweight Strike and Reconnaissance Aircraft (Strike Role) (NATG)
LWSS .... Letter-Writing Support System (PDAA)
LWST .... Light Waste Storage Tank (IEEE)
LWST.......... Lowest (MSA)
LW(STA)...... Light Warning (Station)
LWSTC........ Liquid Waste and Sludge Transporter Council (EA)
Lw Stu H ..... Law Students' Helper [*A publication*] (DLA)
LW-SWC..... Light Weight Sheet Molding Compound
LWT........... Amphibious Warping Tug [*Navy symbol*]
LWT........... Lamb Weather Type [*Meteorology*]
LWT........... Lewistown [*Montana*] [*Airport symbol*] (OAG)
LWT........... Lightweight Torpedo [*Now Mk 50*] (DOMA)
LWT........... Lightweight Transponder
LWT........... Lightweight Type [*Anchor gear*]
LWT........... Liquid Waste Treatment (MCD)
LWT........... Listen While Talk
LWT........... Local Winter Time [*Astronomy*] (IAA)
LWT........... London Weekend Television [*England*]
LWTA......... LASER Window Test Apparatus [*Air Force*]
LWTF......... Low-Water-Tolerant Brake Fluid [*Automotive engineering*]
LWTMA...... Listen While Transmission Multiple Access [*Telecommunications*] (PDAA)
LWTR........ Leading Writer [*British military*] (DMA)
LWTS......... Laundry Waste Treatment System [*Nuclear energy*] (NRCH)
LWTT......... Liquid Waste Test Tank [*Nuclear energy*] (IEEE)
LWU.......... LASER Welder Unit
LWU.......... Leather Workers International Union of America
LWUI........ Longshoremen's and Warehousemen's Union International
LWULT....... Least Widely Used and Least Taught Languages (AIE)
LWV.......... Lackawanna & Wyoming Valley Railway Co. [*Absorbed into Consolidated Rail Corp.*] [*AAR code*]
LWV.......... Landwirtschaftsversorgungsamt [*German Land Economic Supply Office*] [*Post-World War II*]
LWV.......... Lawrenceville [*Illinois*] [*Airport symbol Obsolete*] (OAG)
LWV.......... League of Women Voters of the United States
LWV.......... Light-Weight Van
LWVEF....... League of Women Voters Education Fund (EA)
LWVUS ...... League of Women Voters of the United States (EA)
LWVV........ League of Women Voters of Victoria [*Australia*]
LWW.......... Launch Window Width [*Aerospace*]
LWW.......... Lightweight Weapon

LWWS	Lightweight Weapons Sight
LWX	LAN [*Linked Access Network*]/WAN Exchange [*Wide Area Network*] [*Telecommunications*]
LWY	Lawas [*Malaysia*] [*Airport symbol*] (OAG)
LWYACC	Lithuanian World Youth Association Communications Center [*Defunct*] (EA)
LWYR	Lawyer
LwyrTitl	Lawyers Title Corp. [*Associated Press*] (SAG)
LX	Crossair [*ICAO designator*] (AD)
LX	La Crosse, WI
LX	Liver Extract [*Protein/lipid substance*] [*Immunology*]
LX	Local Irradiation (MAE)
LX	Lower Extremity [*Anatomy*] (DMAA)
LX	Low Index [*NWS*] (FAAC)
lx	Lux [*Symbol*] [*SI unit of luminance*]
LX	Lux [*Light*] [*Latin*]
LXA	Lhasa [*China*] [*Airport symbol*] (OAG)
LXA	Lipoxin A [*Biochemistry*]
LXA	Load Index from Address
LXAD	Lexington Army Depot [*Kentucky*] (AFIT)
LXB	Lipoxin B [*Biochemistry*]
LXB	Pittsburgh, PA [*Location identifier FAA*] (FAAL)
LXBK	LSB Bancshares, Inc. North Carolina [*NASDAQ symbol*] (SAG)
LXBK	LSB Bancshares(NC) [*NASDAQ symbol*] (TTSB)
LXC	Liquid-Ion Exchange Chromatography (PDAA)
LXD	LASER Transceiver Device
LXD	Load Index from Decrement
LXE	LXE, Inc. [*Associated Press*] (SAG)
LXEI	LXE, Inc. [*NASDAQ symbol*] (SAG)
LXFT	Linear Xenon Flash Tube
LXG	Luong Namtha [*Laos*] [*Airport symbol*] (AD)
LXGB	Gibraltar/North Front [*Gibraltar*] [*ICAO location identifier*] (ICLI)
LXK	Lexmark International Group [*NYSE symbol*] (SAG)
LXK	Lexmark Intl Group'A' [*NYSE symbol*] (TTSB)
LXL	Little Falls, MN [*Location identifier FAA*] (FAAL)
LXM	Lintex Minerals [*Vancouver Stock Exchange symbol*]
LXMAR	Load External Memory Address Register
LXMO	Lexington B & L Financial Corp. [*NASDAQ symbol*] (SAG)
LXN	Lexington, NE [*Location identifier FAA*] (FAAL)
LXN	Lexington Resources Ltd. [*Vancouver Stock Exchange symbol*]
LXP	Lexington Corporate Prop [*NYSE symbol*] (TTSB)
LXP	Lexington Corporate Properties [*NYSE symbol*] (SAG)
LXP	Lorain Public Library, Lorain, OH [*OCLC symbol*] (OCLC)
LXR	Airluxor Ltda. [*Portugal ICAO designator*] (FAAC)
LXR	Luxor [*Egypt*] [*Airport symbol*] (OAG)
LXR	LXR Biotechnology [*AMEX symbol*] (TTSB)
LXR	LXR Biotechnology, Inc. [*AMEX symbol*] (SAG)
LXRBiot	LXR Biotechnology, Inc. [*Associated Press*] (SAG)
LXS	Lemnos [*Greece*] [*Airport symbol*] (OAG)
LX S	Lux Second
LXT	Left Exotropia [*Ophthalmology*]
LXT	Linear Xenon Tube
LXU	Lukulu [*Zambia*] [*Airport symbol*] (AD)
LXU	Luxtec Corp. [*AMEX symbol*] (SAG)
LXV	Leadville, CO [*Location identifier FAA*] (FAAL)
LXX	Septuagint [*Version of the Bible*]
LXY	Mexia, TX [*Location identifier FAA*] (FAAL)
LY	El Al Israel Airlines [*ICAO designator*] (AD)
LY	Lactoalbumin-Yeastolate [*Cell growth medium*]
LY	Langley [*Unit of sun's heat*]
LY	Last Year's Model [*Merchandising slang*]
LY	League for Yiddish [*Later, LYI*] (EA)
LY	Leicestershire Yeomanry (Prince Albert's Own) [*British military*] (DMA)
LY	Lethal Yellowing [*Plant pathology*]
LY	Libya [*ANSI two-letter standard code*] (CNC)
ly	Libya [*MARC country of publication code Library of Congress*] (LCCP)
LY	Light Year
LY	Linear Yard (AFM)
LY	Lucifer Yellow [*A dye*] [*Organic chemistry*]
Ly	Lyman [*Spectrography*]
LY	Lynngold Resources, Inc. [*Toronto Stock Exchange symbol*]
LY	Queen's Own Lowland Yeomanry [*Military unit*] [*British*]
LYA	Lynch, Young & Associates [*Newport Beach, CA*] [*Telecommunications*] (TSSD)
LYA	Lyon Air [*France ICAO designator*] (FAAC)
LYB	Little Cayman [*West Indies*] [*Airport symbol*] (OAG)
LYBA	Beograd [*Former Yugoslavia*] [*ICAO location identifier*] (ICLI)
LYBB	Beograd [*Former Yugoslavia*] [*ICAO location identifier*] (ICLI)
LYBE	Beograd [*Former Yugoslavia*] [*ICAO location identifier*] (ICLI)
LYBK	Banja Luka [*Former Yugoslavia*] [*ICAO location identifier*] (ICLI)
LYBNT	Last Year but Not This [*Fundraising*]
LYC	Leicestershire Yeomanry Cavalry (Prince Albert's Own) [*British military*] (DMA)
LYC	Lycoming College, Williamsport, PA [*OCLC symbol*] (OCLC)
Lyc	Lycurgus [*of Plutarch*] [*Fourth century BC*] [*Classical studies*] (OCD)
Lycoming	Lycoming Reporter [*Pennsylvania*] [*A publication*] (DLA)
Lycoming R (PA)	Lycoming Reporter [*Pennsylvania*] [*A publication*] (DLA)
Lycoph	Lycophron [*Third century BC*] [*Classical studies*] (OCD)
Lycurg	Lycurgus [*of Plutarch*] [*Fourth century BC*] [*Classical studies*] (OCD)
LYD	Houston, TX [*Location identifier FAA*] (FAAL)
LYD	Lydney [*British depot code*]
Lydall	Lydall, Inc. [*Associated Press*] (SAG)
LYDMA	Lymphocyte Determined Membrane Antigen [*Immunology*]

Lydnbg	Lydenburg Platinum Ltd. [*Associated Press*] (SAG)
LYDPY	Lydenburg Platinum Ltd ADR [*NASDAQ symbol*] (TTSB)
LYDU	Dubrovnik [*Former Yugoslavia*] [*ICAO location identifier*] (ICLI)
LYE	Lyneham, FTU [*British*] [*FAA designator*] (FAAC)
LYES	Liver Yang Exuberance Syndrome [*Medicine*] (DMAA)
LYF	Lutheran Youth Fellowship (EA)
LYFT	Low-Yield Fallout Trajectory (DNAB)
LYG	Lymphomatoid Granulomatosis [*Medicine*]
LYH	Lynchburg [*Virginia*] [*Airport symbol*] (OAG)
LYI	League for Yiddish, Inc. (EA)
LYI	Libby, MT [*Location identifier FAA*] (FAAL)
LYL	League of Young Liberals [*British*] (ROG)
LYL	Lima, OH [*Location identifier FAA*] (FAAL)
LYLJ	Ljubljana [*Former Yugoslavia*] [*ICAO location identifier*] (ICLI)
LYM	Last Year's Model [*Marketing*] (WDAA)
LYM	Lymph [*or Lymphatic*] (WDAA)
LYM	Lymphocyte
LYM	Lympne [*England*] [*Airport symbol*] (AD)
LYMB	Maribor [*Former Yugoslavia*] [*ICAO location identifier*] (ICLI)
LYMBS	Lodzer Young Men's Benevolent Society (EA)
LYMO	Mostar [*Former Yugoslavia*] [*ICAO location identifier*] (ICLI)
LYMPH	Lymphocyte
Lymphos	Lymphocytes [*Medicine*] (BABM)
LYN	Atlanta, GA [*Location identifier FAA*] (FAAL)
LYN	Lehman Brothers, Inc. [*AMEX symbol*] (SAG)
LYN	Lynton Aviation [*British ICAO designator*] (FAAC)
Lyn	Lynx [*Constellation*]
Lynchburg C	Lynchburg College (GAGS)
LynchC	Lynch Corp. [*Associated Press*] (SAG)
Lynd	Lyndwood's Provinciales [*A publication*] (DLA)
Lynd Prov	Lyndwood's Provinciales [*A publication*] (DLA)
Lyndw Prov	Lyndwood's Provinciales [*A publication*] (DLA)
Lyne Lea	Lyne's Irish Chancery Cases (Wallis) [*1766-91*] [*A publication*] (DLA)
Lyne Lea	Lyne on Leases for Lives [*A publication*] (DLA)
Lyne on Renew	Lyne on Renewals [*A publication*] (DLA)
Lyne (Wall)	Wallis' Select Cases, Edited by Lyne [*1766-91*] [*Ireland*] [*A publication*] (DLA)
LYO	Lubavitch Youth Organization (EA)
LYO	Lyondell Petrochem [*NYSE symbol*] (TTSB)
LYO	Lyondell Petrochemical [*NYSE symbol*] (SPSG)
LYO	Lyons, KS [*Location identifier FAA*] (FAAL)
LYO	Lyophilized [*Medicine*] (DMAA)
LYOH	Ohrid [*Former Yugoslavia*] [*ICAO location identifier*] (ICLI)
LYON	Liquid-Yield Option Note [*Merrill Lynch & Co.*] [*Finance*]
Lyon & R BS	Lyon and Redman on Bills of Sale [*A publication*] (DLA)
Lyondl	Lyondell Petrochemical Co. [*Associated Press*] (SAG)
Lyon Ind L	Lyon on the Laws of India [*A publication*] (DLA)
Lyon Just	Lyon's Institutes of Justinian [*A publication*] (DLA)
LYOS	Osijek [*Former Yugoslavia*] [*ICAO location identifier*] (ICLI)
lyot	Layout (VRA)
LYP	Faisalabad [*Pakistan*] [*Airport symbol*] (OAG)
LYP	Lactose, Yeast, and Peptone Agar [*Medicine*] (DMAA)
LYP	Lower Yield Point [*Medicine*] (DMAA)
LYP	Lyallpur [*Pakistan*] [*Airport symbol*] (AD)
Lyp	Lymphosarcoma [*Medicine*] (AAMN)
LYpAS	Logicheskii Yazyk dlia Predstavleniya Algoritmov Sinteza Releinykh Ustroistv [*A Programming Language for Logic and Coding Algorithm*] [*Book title*]
LYPL	Pula [*Former Yugoslavia*] [*ICAO location identifier*] (ICLI)
LYPR	Pristina [*Former Yugoslavia*] [*ICAO location identifier*] (ICLI)
LYPW	Legion of Young Polish Women (EA)
LYPZ	Portoroz [*Former Yugoslavia*] [*ICAO location identifier*] (ICLI)
LYR	Lancashire & Yorkshire Railway [*British*]
LYR	Layer (MSA)
LYR	Layer Cloud [*Meteorology*] (DA)
LYR	Longyear [*Norway*] [*Airport symbol*] (OAG)
Lyr	Lyra [*Constellation*]
LYR	Lyric [*or Lyrical*]
Lyr	Lyrichord [*Record label*]
lyr	Lyricist [*MARC relator code*] [*Library of Congress*] (LCCP)
LYRI	Rijeka [*Former Yugoslavia*] [*ICAO location identifier*] (ICLI)
LYRIC	Language for Your Remote Instruction by Computer [*Computer science*] (MDG)
Lys	De Lysia [*of Dionysius Halicarnassensis*] [*Classical studies*] (OCD)
LYS	Light of Yoga Society (EA)
LYS	Lycksele [*Sweden*] [*Geomagnetic observatory code*]
LYS	Lyon [*France*] [*Airport symbol*] (OAG)
Lys	Lysander [*of Plutarch*] [*Classical studies*] (OCD)
LYS	Lysander Gold [*Vancouver Stock Exchange symbol*]
Lys	Lysias [*Fifth century BC*] [*Classical studies*] (OCD)
Lys	Lysine [*Also, K*] [*An amino acid*]
LYS	Lysine (DMAA)
lys	Lysine [*An amino acid*] (DOG)
Lys	Lysistrata [*of Aristophanes*] [*Classical studies*] (OCD)
LYS	Lysodren (DMAA)
LYS	Lysosome [*Cytology*]
LYS	Lysozyme [*Also, LZM*] [*An enzyme*]
LYS	Lysyl [*Enzymology*]
LYS	Lytes Electrolytes [*Medicine*] (DMAA)
LYS	Olean, NY [*Location identifier FAA*] (FAAL)
LYSA	Sarajevo [*Former Yugoslavia*] [*ICAO location identifier*] (ICLI)
LYSK	Skopje [*Former Yugoslavia*] [*ICAO location identifier*] (ICLI)
Lyso-PC	Lysophosphatidylcholine [*Also, LPC*] [*Biochemistry*]
LYSP	Split [*Former Yugoslavia*] [*ICAO location identifier*] (ICLI)
LYSV	Leek Yellow Stripe Virus [*Plant pathology*]

LYT .... Layout (MSA)
LYTBT .... Low-Yield Test Ban Treaty
Lytes .... Electrolytes [*Medicine*] (BABM)
LYTI .... Titograd [*Former Yugoslavia*] [*ICAO location identifier*] (ICLI)
LYTS .... LSI Industries [*NASDAQ symbol*] (TTSB)
LYTS .... LSI Industries, Inc. [*NASDAQ symbol*] (SAG)
LYTT .... Lytta [*A Blistering Fly*] [*Pharmacy*] (ROG)
LYTV .... Tivat [*Former Yugoslavia*] [*ICAO location identifier*] (ICLI)
LYU .... Lehigh University, Bethlehem, PA [*OCLC symbol*] (OCLC)
LYV .... Legume Yellows Virus [*Plant pathology*]
LYVR .... Vrsac [*Former Yugoslavia*] [*ICAO location identifier*] (ICLI)
LYW .... Lyman [*Washington*] [*Seismograph station code, US Geological Survey*] (SEIS)
LYX .... Atlantic Rich 9% Exch Nts'97 [*NYSE symbol*] (TTSB)
LYX .... Atlantic Richfield Co. [*NYSE symbol*] (SAG)
LYX .... Lydd [*England*] [*Airport symbol*]
LYX .... Lynx-Canada Explorations Ltd. [*Toronto Stock Exchange symbol*]
Lyx .... Lyxose [*Also, l*] [*A sugar*]
LYY .... Batesville, AR [*Location identifier FAA*] (FAAL)
LYYY .... Beograd [*Former Yugoslavia*] [*ICAO location identifier*] (ICLI)
LYZ .... Lysozyme [*Medicine*] (DMAA)
LYZA .... Zagreb [*Former Yugoslavia*] [*ICAO location identifier*] (ICLI)
LYZB .... Zagreb [*Former Yugoslavia*] [*ICAO location identifier*] (ICLI)
LYZD .... Zadar [*Former Yugoslavia*] [*ICAO location identifier*] (ICLI)
LZ .... Balkan [*ICAO designator*] (AD)
LZ .... Landing Zone
LZ .... Left Zero (IAA)
LZ .... Lempel Zev [*Computer science*]
LZ .... Leucine Zipper [*Protein structure*]
LZ .... Live Zero (IAA)
LZ .... Loading Zone
LZ .... [*The*] Lubrizol Corp. [*NYSE symbol*] (SPSG)
LZ1 .... Luftschiff Zeppelin 1

LZA .... Labor Zionist Alliance (EA)
LZB .... La-Z Boy Chair [*NYSE symbol*] (TTSB)
LZB .... La-Z Boy Chair Co. [*NYSE symbol*] (SPSG)
LZCC .... Landing Zone Control Center [*Air Force*] (IAA)
LZCO .... Landing Zone Control Officer [*Air Force*] (AFM)
LZD .... Launch Zone Display
LZDF .... Launch Zone Display Flag
LZEEBE .... Long-Term Zonal Earth Energy Budget Experiment [*Spacecraft*] [*NASA*]
LZF .... Launch Zone Flag
LZGF .... Lewis Zero Gravity Facility
LZH .... Lanchow [*Republic of China*] [*Seismograph station code, US Geological Survey*] (SEIS)
LZIF .... Lyudmila Zhivkova International Foundation (EAIO)
LZL .... Landing Zone Locator
LZL .... Launcher, Zero Length [*British military*] (DMA)
LZM .... Lysozyme [*An enzyme*]
LZO .... Launch Zone Override
LZOA .... Labor Zionist Organization of America - Poale Zion [*Later, LZA*] (EA)
LZOC .... Lincoln Zephyr Owner's Club (EA)
LZP .... Latvian Green Party [*Political party*] (EY)
LZP .... Left Zero Print (IAA)
LZP .... Lorazepam [*Also, L, LOR*] [*Antiepileptic drug*]
LZPC .... Lead-Zinc Producers Committee (EA)
LZR .... Lazurus Distributors [*Vancouver Stock Exchange symbol*]
LZR .... Lizard Island [*Australia Airport symbol*] (OAG)
LZT .... Lead Zirconate Titanate [*Ferroelectric material*]
LZT .... Local Zone Time
LZU .... Lincoln University, Lincoln University, PA [*OCLC symbol*] (OCLC)
LZV .... Lazarev [*Later, NVL*] [*Former USSR Geomagnetic observatory code*]
LZW .... Lempel-Zev-Welch [*Compression*] [*Computer science*] (PCM)
LZW .... Olney-Noble, IL [*Location identifier FAA*] (FAAL)
LZY .... Greensboro, NC [*Location identifier FAA*] (FAAL)
LZZ .... Lampasas, TX [*Location identifier FAA*] (FAAL)

M
By Acronym

M .... Absolute Magnitude [*Astronomy*]
M .... All India Reporter, Madras Series [*A publication*] (ILCA)
M .... Angular Momentum [*Symbol*] [*Physics*]
M .... Bending Moment [*Aerospace*] (AAG)
M .... Days before Move Operation [*Usually followed by a number*] [*NASA*] (KSC)
m .... Em [*Printing*] (WDMC)
M .... Em [*Printing*] (WDMC)
M .... Emma [*Phonetic alphabet*] [*In use in 1904 and 1914*] (DSUE)
M .... Field Goals Missed [*Football, basketball*]
M .... First Sergeant [*Army skill qualification identifier*] (INF)
M .... Ground, Mobile [*JETDS nomenclature*]
M .... Human Being Movement [*Rorschach*] [*Psychology*]
M .... Hungary [*IYRU nationality code*] (IYR)
M .... Imperial Chemical Industries [*Great Britain*] [*Research code symbol*]
M .... Indian Law Reports, Madras Series [*A publication*] (DLA)
M .... Instrumental Magnitude [*Earthquakes*]
M .... Intensity of Magnetization [*Symbol*] (DEN)
m----- .... Intercontinental Areas (Eastern Hemisphere) [*MARC geographic area code Library of Congress*] (LCCP)
M .... J. F. Macfarlan & Co. [*Scotland*] [*Research code symbol*]
M .... Macerare [*Macerate*] [*Pharmacy*]
M .... Machine
M .... Mach Number
M .... MacNeil [*Herman A.*] [*Designer's mark, when appearing on US coins*]
M .... Macpherson's Scotch Session Cases [*1862-73*] [*A publication*] (DLA)
M .... Magenta (WDMC)
m .... Magenta (WDMC)
M .... Magister [*Master*] [*Latin*]
M .... Magistrate
M .... Magnaflux
M .... Magnetic
M .... Magnetic Moment [*Symbol*] (DEN)
M .... Magnetic Polarization [*Symbol*] (DEN)
m .... Magnetic Quantum Number [*Atomic physics*] [*Symbol*]
M .... Magnetron (MDG)
M .... Magnification (NTCM)
M .... Magnitude
M .... Maiden
M .... Mail
M .... Main
m .... Main [*Menu*] [*Computer science*] [*Telecommunications*]
M .... Maintainability [*or Maintenance*] (MCD)
M .... Maintenance and Test Assemblies [*JETDS nomenclature*]
M .... Majesty
M .... Major [*Cycle*]
M .... Make
M .... Male [*Electronics*]
m .... Male (DD)
M .... Male
M .... Malignant [*Medicine*]
M .... Maloti [*Plural of Loti*] [*Monetary Unit*] [*Lesotho*] (BARN)
M .... Man
M .... Mandatory (KSC)
M .... Mandatory
M .... Mane [*Morning*] [*Pharmacy*]
M .... Maneuvering Ship [*In speed triangle of relative movement problems*]
M .... Manichaean Middle Persian
M .... Manila [*Rope*]
M .... Manipulus [*A Handful*] [*Pharmacy*]
M .... Mannitol [*Organic chemistry*]
M .... Mano [*Hand*] [*Spanish*]
M .... Mantissa [*Decimal portion of a logarithm*]
M .... Manual
M .... Map
M .... March
M .... Mare [*Thoroughbred racing*]
m .... Marginal Propensity to Import [*Economics*]
M .... Maria [*Mary*]
M .... Marine [*Insurance*]
M .... Marine [*FCC*] (NTCM)
M .... Marine Corps [*When used as prefix with plane designation*]
M .... Marinus de Caramanico [*Flourished, 1269-85*] [*Authority cited in pre-1607 legal work*] (DSA)
M .... Maritus [*Bridegroom*] [*Latin*]

M .... Mark [*Monetary unit*] [*German*] (GPO)
M .... Marker [*Beacon*] (AFM)
M .... Markka [*Monetary unit*] [*Finland*]
M .... Marksman [*British military*] (DMA)
M .... Marquis [*or Marquess*]
M .... Married
M .... Mars
M .... Marshal
M .... Martin Co. Division [*Martin-Marietta Corp.*] [*ICAO aircraft manufacturer identifier*] (ICAO)
M .... Martinus Gosia [*Authority cited in pre-1607 legal work*] (DSA)
M .... Martinus Zamorensis [*Flourished, 13th century*] [*Authority cited in pre-1607 legal work*] (DSA)
M .... Martyr
M .... Marxist [*Politics*]
M .... Masculine
M .... Masochism (CDAI)
M .... Mason (ROG)
m .... Mass [*Symbol*] [*IUPAC*]
M .... Massachusetts State Library, Boston, MA [*Library symbol Library of Congress*] (LCLS)
M .... Massage
M .... Masseur [*Ranking title*] [*British Royal Navy*]
M .... Massive [*Agriculture*]
M .... Master
M .... Mate [*of a ship*]
M .... Mater [*Mother*] [*Latin*]
M .... Mathematics [*Secondary school course*] [*British*]
M .... Matinee
M .... Matins [*Early morning prayers*]
M .... Matrix
M .... Matrix
M .... Matron [*British military*] (DMA)
M .... Mature
M .... Mature Audiences [*Movie rating*] [*Replaced by GP*]
M .... Matured Bonds [*Investment term*] (DFIT)
M .... Mauthner [*Cell*] [*Neurology*]
M .... Maximal [*or Maximum*] [*Medicine*]
M .... Maximum Value [*Electronics*]
M .... Maxwell [*Electronics*] (DEN)
M .... May
M .... Mean [*Arithmetic average*]
M .... Mean Active Maintenance Downtime [*Computer science*]
M .... Meaningfulness [*Psychology*]
M .... Mean Square
M .... Measure [*Music*]
M .... Measured Ceiling [*Aviation*]
M .... Mechanical
M .... Mechlorethamine [*Also, HN, HN2, MBA, NM*] [*Mustargen, nitrogen mustard*] [*Antineoplastic drug*]
M .... Medal (ADA)
M .... Media [*Laboratory*] (AAMN)
M .... Medial (DAVI)
(M) .... Median
M .... Mediator
M .... Medical
M .... Medicinae [*Of Medicine*] [*Latin*]
M .... Medicine
M .... Medieval
M .... Medium [*Size designation for clothing, etc.*]
m .... Medium [*Spectral*]
M .... Medium [*or 2-engine*] Plane
M .... Mega [*A prefix meaning multiplied by one million*] [*Symbol*]
M .... Megabyte [*Data storage capacity*] [*Computer science*]
M .... Megohm (AAG)
M .... Melendus [*Flourished, 1188-1209*] [*Authority cited in pre-1607 legal work*] (DSA)
M .... Melittin [*Bee venom*]
M .... Melphalan [*Also, A, L-PAM, MPH, MPL*] [*Antineoplastic drug*]
M .... Melts At ____ [*Followed by a temperature*]
M .... Member
M .... Membrana [*Membrane*] [*Anatomy*]
M .... Memorandum
M .... Memoria [*Memory*] [*Latin*]
M .... Memorial; Journal Officiel du Grand Duche de Luxembourg [*A publication*] (ILCA)

M .... Memory
M .... Mensura [By Measure] [Pharmacy] (ROG)
M .... Mentum [Chin]
M .... Menzies' Cape Colony Supreme Court Reports [A publication] (DLA)
M .... Meperidine [Also, MEP] [An analgesic]
M .... Mercaptopurine [Purinethol] [Also, MP, P] [Antineoplastic drug]
M .... Mercury [Chemical symbol is Hg] (KSC)
M .... Mercury
M .... Merehurst [Publisher] [British]
M .... Merge [Computer science] (IBMDP)
M .... Merides [Latin] [Noon] (WDMC)
m .... Meridian (Lower Branch)
M .... Meridian (Upper Branch)
M .... Meridies [Noon] [Latin]
M .... Meridional Part [Navigation]
M .... Mesangium [Anatomy]
M .... Mesh
M .... Mesial [Dentistry]
M .... Mesomeric [Organic chemistry]
M .... Mesophyll [Botany]
m .... Meta [Chemistry]
M .... Metabolite
M .... Metacenter
M .... Metal
M .... Metalsmith [Navy]
M .... Metamorphosis [Phylogeny]
M .... Metaproterenol [Pharmacology]
M .... Metastasis [Oncology]
M .... Meteorological [JETDS nomenclature]
m .... Meter [SI unit of length]
M .... Meter (WDMC)
M .... Methionine [One-letter symbol; see Met]
M .... Method
M .... Methodist
M .... Methotrexate [Antineoplastic drug]
m .... Methyl [As substituent on nucleoside] [Biochemistry]
M .... Metoclopramide [An antiemetic]
M .... Metronome
M .... Metropolitan
M .... Mews
M .... Mezzo [Moderate] [Music]
M .... Michaelmas Term [British Legal term] (ILCA)
m .... Micro (WGA)
M .... Micrococcus [Genus of bacteria]
M .... Micrometer
M .... Microphones [JETDS nomenclature] [Military] (CET)
M .... Microprocessor
M .... Microsporum [Genus of fungi]
M .... Microtubule [Cytology]
M .... Midazolan [An anesthetic]
M .... Midday (ADA)
M .... Middle
M .... Middle
M .... Middle School [British]
M .... Middle Term of a Syllogism [Logistics] (WDAA)
M .... Midfield [Men's lacrosse position]
M .... Midline
M .... Midnight (ROG)
m .... Midship [Shipping] (DS)
M .... Midwest Stock Exchange [Chicago, IL]
M .... Mike [Phonetic alphabet] [International] [World War II] (DSUE)
M .... Mil [Monetary unit] [Cyprus]
m .... Mil[thousand] (DAVI)
M .... Mild (DAVI)
M .... Mile (WDMC)
m .... mile (WDMC)
M .... Miles
M .... Miles' Pennsylvania Reports [A publication] (DLA)
M .... Military
M .... Militia
M .... Milk (ROG)
M .... Mill
M .... Mille [Thousand] [Roman numeral]
m .... Milli- [A prefix meaning divided by 1000] [SI symbol]
M .... Milli (DFIT)
M .... Millime [Monetary unit] [Tunisia]
M .... Millimicrometer (IAA)
M .... Millimicron (IAA)
M .... Million
M .... Mine
M .... Minesweeper [Navy]
M .... Miniature [Horticulture]
M .... Minim
M .... Minimum (ADA)
M .... Ministry
M .... Minor
M .... Mint [Condition] [Numismatics, etc.]
M .... Minus
M .... Minute
M .... Miotic [Biology]
M .... Mira [A star] [Astronomy] (OA)
M .... Mired (IAA)
M .... Misce [Mix] [Pharmacy]
M .... Miscellaneous
M .... Miscible

M .... Mishnah [Basis of the Talmud] (BJA)
M .... Missile [Air Force]
M .... Missile Carrier Aircraft [Designation for all US military aircraft]
M .... Missing [Data]
M .... Missing (Weather Reports Only) [NWS] (FAAC)
M .... Mission
M .... Mist [Meteorology]
M .... Mistura [Mixture] [Pharmacy]
M .... Mitic Subgroup [Magnetite, chromite, hematite, ilmenite, titanite, perofskite, rutile] [CIPW classification Geology]
M .... Mitochondrion [Cytology]
M .... Mitomycin [Also, MC, MT] [Antineoplastic drug]
M .... Mitosis [Cytology]
M .... Mitte [Send] [Latin]
M .... Mix [or Mixture]
M .... Mixed School [British]
M .... Mobile [Missile launch environment symbol] [Biology]
M .... Mobilization [as in M-Day] [Military] (AABC)
M .... Modal (Verb) [Linguistics]
M .... Mode
M .... Model [in military nomenclature]
M .... MODEM [Computer science]
M .... Moderate
M .... Moderate Sea or Swell [Meteorology]
M .... Modern [Post-1920] [Deltiology]
M .... Modification [FCC] (NTCM)
m .... Modified [Regulation or order modified] [Used in Shepard's Citations] [Legal term] (DLA)
m .... Modulation Coefficient (IDOE)
M .... Modulation Depth [Broadcasting]
M .... Modulator (IAA)
M .... Modulus
M .... Moisture
M .... Mol [or Mole] [Measurement] (DAVI)
m .... Molal [Solute concentration by weight] [Chemistry]
M .... Molar [Permanent] [Dentistry]
M .... Molar [Solute concentration by volume] [Chemistry]
m .... Molar [Tooth, deciduous] [Dentistry] (DAVI)
M .... Molar Mass [Symbol] [IUPAC]
M .... Mole
M .... Molecular Weight [Also, MOL WT, MW]
M .... Moment
M .... Moment of Force [Symbol] [IUPAC]
M .... Monastery
M .... Monday
M .... Money
M .... Monitor (MDG)
M .... Monitor
M .... Monkey [Phonetic alphabet] [Royal Navy World War I Pre-World War II] (DSUE)
M .... Monochrome (IAA)
M .... Monoclonal [Biochemistry]
M .... Monocyte [Hematology]
M .... Monograph
M .... Monophage [Biology]
M .... Monoplane
M .... Monotype (DGA)
M .... Monsieur [Mister] [French]
M .... Monsoon
M .... Mont [Monte, etc.] [Italy and Sicily only]
M .... Montana (DLA)
M .... Montavit Co. [Austria] [Research code symbol]
M .... Month
m .... Month (WDMC)
M .... Monthly
M .... Montmorillonite [A mineral]
M .... Montreal Stock Exchange
M .... Monumentum [Monument] [Latin]
M .... Moon
M .... Morgan [George T.] [Designer's mark, when appearing on US coins]
M .... Morison's Dictionary of Decisions, Scotch Court of Session [1540-1808] [A publication] (DLA)
M .... Morning
m .... Morning (WDMC)
m .... Morpha [Form] [Biology]
M .... Morphine [Slang]
M .... Morphological Rule [Linguistics]
M .... Morphometric Analysis [Botany]
M .... Mort [Dead] [French] (ROG)
M .... Mortar
M .... Mortgage
M .... Mortis [Of Death] [Latin]
M .... Motel
M .... Mother
m .... Motile [Sperm] (MAE)
M .... Motivational Ability
M .... Motor
M .... Motorship (DS)
M .... Motorway [Traffic sign] [British]
M .... Moulder [Navy rating British]
M .... Mound (MSA)
M .... Mountain
M .... Mouth
M .... Move Being Made [Computer science]
M .... Movement [Neurology]

M	*[Time in Days Before]* Move Operations	
M	Mu *[Twelfth letter of the Greek alphabet]* (DAVI)	
M	Mucoid	
M	Mucoid Colony *[Biochemistry]* (DAVI)	
M	Mud	
M	Muddy *[Track condition]* *[Thoroughbred racing]*	
M	Muddy *[Quality of the bottom]* *[Nautical charts]*	
M	Multipara (MAE)	
M	Multiplier	
M	Municipal Premises *[Public-performance tariff class]* *[British]*	
M	Murmur *[Heart]* *[Medicine]*	
M	Musculus *[Muscle]* *[Anatomy]*	
M	Music *[Films, television, etc.]*	
M	Mustard Gas *[Also, H, HD, HS, HT]* *[Poison gas US Chemical Corps symbol]*	
M	Muster	
M	Mutitas *[Dullness]* *[Latin]*	
M	Mutual Companies	
M	Mutual Inductance *[Symbol]* *[IUPAC]*	
M	Mycelium *[Biology]*	
M	Mycobacterium *[Genus of microorganisms]*	
M	Mycoplasma *[Medicine]* (MAE)	
M	Myopia	
M	Myosin *[Muscle physiology]*	
M	New York Miscellaneous Reports *[A publication]* (DLA)	
M	Nomina *[Names]* *[Probably a misprint for NN, by some supposed to denote St. Mary, patron saint of girls]* *[Latin]* (ROG)	
M	Noon *[Meridies]*	
M	Ohio Miscellaneous Reports *[A publication]* (DLA)	
M	One Thousand *[Roman numeral]*	
M	Ordered Multistate *[Botany]*	
M	Queen Mary (DLA)	
M	Radiant Exitance *[Symbol]* *[IUPAC]*	
M	Reckitt & Sons Ltd. *[Great Britain]* *[Research code symbol]*	
M	Red Star of Prominent Titanium Oxide Intensity *[Astronomy]* (BARN)	
M	Refractive Modulus (IDOE)	
m	Response to Human Being Movement *[Rorschach]* *[Psychology]*	
M	Strength of Pole *[Chemistry]* (DAVI)	
M	Thioinosine *[One-letter symbol; see SIno, Sno]*	
/M	Thousand	
M	Time of Maneuver	
M/0/0/S	Minutes Zero Zero Seconds *[Aerospace]* (AAG)	
M/1	Method 1 (NITA)	
M_1	Mitral First Sound *[Cardiology]*	
M_1	Money Supply of a Country, Consisting of Currency and Demand Deposits *[Economics]*	
M_1	Sight Dullness *[on Auscultation]* *[Medicine]* (DAVI)	
M1S	Matte One Side *[Aluminum]*	
M_2	Insular Segment of Middle Cerebral Artery *[Cardiology]* (DAVI)	
M_2	Marked Dullness *[on Auscultation]* *[Medicine]* (DAVI)	
M2	Masterspec 2 *[Production Systems for Architects & Engineers, Inc.]* *[Information service or system]* (IID)	
M_2	Mitral Second Heart Sound *[Cardiology]* (DAVI)	
M_2	Money Supply of a Country, Including M_1 and Commercial Time Deposits *[Economics]*	
M^2	Square Meter	
m^2	Square Meter (IDOE)	
m2	Square Meter	
M2C	Massachusetts Microelectronics Center *[Research center]* (RCD)	
M^2C^2	Multi-Media Communication Control (DOMA)	
M^2FCS	Multi-Microprocessor Flight Control System (PDAA)	
M2FM	Modified Modified Frequency Modulation	
M^{2H2}	Mary Hartman, Mary Hartman *[Initialism is shortened form of television program title]* *[Also, MH2]*	
M2M	Manager-to-Manager (ACRL)	
M2M	May Second Movement *[1960s Yale University war protest]* (VNW)	
M2S	Matte Two Sides *[Aluminum]*	
M^2/S	Square Meters per Second	
M_3	Absolute Dullness *[on Auscultation]* *[Medicine]* (DAVI)	
M^3	Cubic Meter	
m3	Cubic Meter	
m^3	Cubic Meter (IDOE)	
M/3	Middle Third *[of long bones]* *[Orthopedics]* (DAVI)	
M3	Military Manpower Models	
M_3	Money Supply of a Country, Including M_2, Savings and Loan Association Deposits, and Certificates of Deposit *[Economics]*	
M-3 APD	Military Manpower Models Airborne Personnel Detector *[Device used to collect and test air samples to identify enemy sites]* *[Vietnam]* (VNW)	
M^3/D	Cubic Meters per Day	
M^3/J	Cubic Meters per Joule	
M^3/KG	Cubic Meters per Kilogram	
$M^3/(M A)$	Cubic Meters per Meter Year	
$M^3/(M D)$	Cubic Meters per Meter Day	
M^3/MIN	Cubic Meters per Minute	
M^3/S	Cubic Meters per Second	
M-3 TAP	Military Manpower Models Toxicological Agents Protective Suit *[Provided protection from chemical agents]* (VNW)	
M-3V	Movimiento 3V *[Nicaragua]* *[Political party]* (EY)	
M_4	Cortical Segment of Middle Cerebral Artery *[Cardiology]* (DAVI)	
M4	Message from Multiple Media Maximizes *[Communications]* (WDMC)	
M5	Manual Five Speed *[DOE]* (TAG)	
M/10	Tenth Molar *[Solute concentration by volume]* *[Chemistry]* (DAVI)	
M12	M12 *[Hawaii]* *[Seismograph station code, US Geological Survey Closed]* (SEIS)	

M-18-X	Movimiento 18 de Octubre de Accion Revolucionaria Astra *[Astra 18th October Movement of Revolutionary Action]* *[Ecuador]* *[Political party]* (PD)	
M-20	Movimiento-20 *[Panama]* *[Political party]* (EY)	
M50	Mean of 1950 *[Coordinate system]* *[NASA]* (NASA)	
M85	85 Percent/15 Percent Unleaded Gasoline *[BTS]* (TAG)	
M/100	Hundredth Molar *[Solute concentration by volume]* *[Chemistry]* (DAVI)	
MA	Aircraft Stations *[ITU designation]* (CET)	
MA	Amherst College, Amherst, MA *[Library symbol Library of Congress]* (LCLS)	
ma----	Arab States *[MARC geographic area code Library of Congress]* (LCCP)	
Ma	Ma'arbae (BJA)	
Ma	Ma'aserot (BJA)	
MA	Machine Accountant *[Navy]*	
Ma	Mach Number *[IUPAC]*	
MA	Macronutrient Additives *[Fat substituted for food]*	
MA	Madras Artillery *[British military]* (DMA)	
MA	Magister Artium *[Master of Arts]* *[Latin]*	
MA	Magma Arizona Railroad Co. *[Later, MAA]* *[AAR code]*	
MA	Magnesium Association *[Later, IMA]* (EA)	
MA	Magnetic Amplifier	
MA	Mahogany Association (EA)	
MA	Maids of Athena (EA)	
MA	Main Alarm (IAA)	
MA	Main Amplifier (OA)	
MA	Maintenance	
MA	Maintenance	
MA	Maintenance Ability (KSC)	
MA	Maintenance Actions	
M/A	Maintenance Analysis (KSC)	
MA	Maintenance Area *[Military British]*	
MA	Maintenance Availability	
MA	Major (DSUE)	
Ma	Male (DAVI)	
M/A	Male, Altered Animal (DMAA)	
MA	Maleic Anhydride *[Also, MAH]* *[Organic chemistry]*	
MA	Malignant Angioendotheliomatosis *[Oncology]*	
MA	Malignant Arrhythmia *[Medicine]* (DMAA)	
MA	Malonaldehyde *[Organic chemistry]*	
MA	Malpractice Association (EA)	
MA	Malvalic Acid (PDAA)	
MA	Mamma (DSUE)	
MA	Management Administration *[Department of Labor Statistics]* (OICC)	
MA	Management Adviser	
MA	Manager of Aviation	
MA	Manager's Assistant (DCTA)	
MA	Mandelic Acid *[Organic chemistry]* (AAMN)	
MA	Manifest Achievement (AAMN)	
MA	Manifest Anxiety	
MA	Maniilaq Association (EA)	
MA	Manpower Administration *[Later, Employment and Training Administration]* *[Department of Labor]*	
MA	Manual	
M/A	Manual or Automatic (NRCH)	
MA	Manufacturing Assembly	
MA	Manure (ROG)	
MA	Manx Airlines Ltd.	
MA	Map Analysis	
MA	March	
Ma	March's Action for Slander and Arbitrament *[A publication]* (DLA)	
MA	Margin Account *[Investment term]*	
MA	Marine Class	
MA	Maritime Administration *[Also, MARAD, MARITADMIN]* *[Department of Transportation]*	
ma	Maritime Antarctic *[Air Mass]* *[Meteorology]* (BARN)	
MA	Mark *[Coin]* (ROG)	
MA	Market Administration (HCT)	
MA	Market Average *[Investment term]*	
MA	Marketing Assistance (MCD)	
MA	Marriage Analysis *[Psychology]*	
Ma	Marsh *[Maps and charts]*	
MA	Marshaling Area *[Military]*	
MA	Martingana *[Ship's rigging]* (ROG)	
Ma	Martinus de Caramanico *[Flourished, 1269-85]* *[Authority cited in pre-1607 legal work]* (DSA)	
Ma	Martinus Gosia *[Authority cited in pre-1607 legal work]* (DSA)	
MA	Massachusetts *[Postal code]*	
MA	Massachusetts Reports *[A publication]* (DLA)	
MA	Mass Analyzer	
M_a	Mass Flow of Air *[Aviation]* (DA)	
MA	Mast Aerial (IAA)	
MA	Master (MSA)	
MA	Master	
MA	Master Alarm	
MA	Master Assistant *[British military]* (DMA)	
MA	Master-at-Arms *[Navy]*	
MA	Master of Arts	
MA	Masurium	
MA	Matched Angle (OA)	
MA	Mater *[Mother]* *[Latin]* (ADA)	
MA	Material Authorization (KSC)	
MA	Material Authorization	
MA	Mathematical Association *[British]* (BI)	

Ma	Matheus de Mathesillanis [*Flourished, 1381-1402*] [*Authority cited in pre-1607 legal work*] (DSA)
MA	Matrix Antigen [*Biochemistry*]
MA	Matt Art [*Paper*] (DGA)
Ma	Mattes [*Quality of the bottom*] [*Nautical charts*]
MA	Maturational Age [*Also, Development Age*] [*Medical term*] (PAZ)
MA	Mature Adult [*Film and video classification*]
MA	Mature Australia [*An association*]
MA	May
MA	May Department Stores Co. [*NYSE symbol*] (SPSG)
MA	May Dept Stores [*NYSE symbol*] (TTSB)
MA	Mazdaznan Association (EA)
MA	Mean Arterial Blood Pressure [*Medicine*] (MAE)
MA	Measurement Accuracy
MA	Mechanical Accessories (MCD)
MA	Mechanical Advantage
MA	Mechanical Ambush (VNW)
MA	Mechanically Alloyed [*Metallurgy*]
MA	Mechanician Apprentice [*British military*] (DMA)
MA	Mechanoacoustic
MA	Media Alliance (EA)
MA	Medicaid (DLA)
MA	Medical Abbreviation (AAMN)
MA	Medical Assistance [*HEW*]
MA	Medical Assistant (DAVI)
MA	Medical Audit (MAE)
MA	Medical Authority
MA	Medical Authorization (DAVI)
M/A	Mediterranean/Adriatic [*Shipping*] (DS)
MA	Mediterranean Area
MA	Medium Artillery
MA	Mega [*A prefix meaning multiplied by one million*]
Ma	Megaannum (DOG)
MA	Megampere (IEEE)
MA	Melanesian Alliance [*Papua New Guinea*] [*Political party*] (FEA)
MA	Melodious Accord (EA)
MA	Membrane Antigen [*Immunology*]
MA	Memory Address [*Computer science*]
MA	Memory Available [*Computer science*] (IAA)
MA	Menorah Association [*Defunct*] (EA)
MA	Menstrual Age [*Medicine*]
MA	Mental Age [*Psychology*]
MA	Mentum Anterior [*In reference to the chin*]
MA	Mercenary Association (EA)
MA	Mercer Associates (EA)
MA	Mercury Arc (MSA)
MA	Mercury-Atlas [*Spacecraft*] [*NASA*]
MA	Message Assembler
M/A	Mess Attendant
MA	Messies Anonymous [*Commercial firm*] (EA)
MA	Messing Allowance [*British military*] (DMA)
MA	Metabolic Activity
MA	Metabolic Analyzer
MA	Metal Anchor (AAG)
MA	Metallurgistes Unis d'Amerique [*United Steelworkers of America*] (EAIO)
MA	Meteorological Applications [*Branch*] [*Marine science*] (OSRA)
MA	Meteorological Applications [*Branch*] [*Forecast Systems Laboratory*] (USDC)
MA	Meter Amplifier
MA	Meter Angle
M/A	Meters per Year
MA	Methamphetamine [*Pharmacology*]
MA	Methoxylamine [*Organic chemistry*]
MA	Methyl Acrylate [*Organic chemistry*]
MA	Methyl Anthranilate [*Organic chemistry*]
MA	Methylanthranilic Acid
MA	Metric Association [*Later, USMA*] (EA)
MA	Mexican-American
MA	Michigan Amber [*Variety of wheat*]
MA	Microagglutination [*Immunochemistry*] (DAVI)
MA	Microalloy
MA	Microfilm Address (NITA)
MA	Microphone Amplifier
MA	Microscopic Agglutination [*Medicine*] (DMAA)
MA	Microwave Associates, Inc. [*Later, M/A-Com*] (AAG)
MA	Middeck Act
MA	Middeck Aft (MCD)
MA	Middle Ages
MA	Middle Assyrian [*Language, etc.*] (BJA)
MA	Midmarch Associates (EA)
MA	Midwest Academy (EA)
MA	Mike Amplifier (NASA)
MA	Mike Amplifier
MA	Mikes of America (EA)
MA	Mileage Allowance
MA	Miles Laboratories, Inc. [*Research code symbol*]
MA	Military Academy
MA	Military Accountant [*British military*] (DMA)
MA	Military Administration
MA	Military Aircraft
MA	Military Assistance [*or Assistant*]
MA	Military Attache [*Diplomacy*]
MA	Military Aviator
MA	Mill Annealed
MA	Miller-Abbot (Tube) [*Medicine*]
MA	Milliammeter (IAA)
mA	Milliampere [*or Milliamperage*]
MA	Milliampere
MA	Milliangstrom [*Unit of wavelength of light*] (WGA)
Ma	Million Years Ago
MA	Mind Association (EA)
MA	Minimum Aircraft [*Powered hang gliders, replicas of early flying machines, etc.*] [*British*]
MA	Ministry of Aviation [*British*]
MA	Minnesota [*Obsolete*] (ROG)
MA	Miscellaneous at Anchor [*Navy*] (NVT)
MA	Miss Angle
MA	Missed Appointment
MA	Missed Approach
MA	Missile Airframe (AAG)
MA	Missile Away
MA	Mission Accomplished [*Air Force*]
MA	Mission Analysis (MCD)
MA	Missionarius Apostolicus [*Missionary Apostolic*] [*Latin*]
MA	Missouri Appeal Reports [*A publication*] (DLA)
MA	Mistresses Anonymous (EA)
MA	Mitomycin-C and Adriamycin [*Antineoplastic drug regimen*] (DAVI)
MA	Mitotic Apparatus [*Cytology*]
MA	Mitral Annulus [*Cardiology*] (DAVI)
MA	Mobile Airlock (MCD)
MA	Mobilization Augmentee [*Military*] (AFM)
MA	Mobilization for Animals [*Defunct*] (EA)
MA	Moderately Advanced (MAE)
MA	Modern Age [*A publication*] (BRI)
MA	Modified Atmosphere [*Food technology*]
MA	Modify Address (IEEE)
MA	Monarchist Alliance (EA)
MA	Monarticular Arthritis [*Medicine*]
M/A	Monetary Allowance
MA	Monitoring Agency
MA	Monoamine [*Chemistry*]
MA	Monoclonal Antibody [*Medicine*] (DMAA)
MA	Monte Carlo Resources [*Vancouver Stock Exchange symbol*]
MA	Months After
M/A	Mood and/or Affect [*Psychology*] (DAVI)
MA	Moored Alongside [*Navy*] (NVT)
MA	Moral Alternatives [*An association*] (EA)
MA	Moreshet Archives [*Jerusalem*] (BJA)
MA	Morning After (IIA)
MA	Morocco [*IYRU nationality code*] [*ANSI two-letter standard code*] (CNC)
MA	Mortuary Affairs [*Army*] (INF)
MA	Mother's Aide [*Red Cross Nursing Services*]
MA	Mothers of Asthmatics (EA)
MA	Mountain Artillery
MA	Mountaineering Association [*British*] (BI)
MA	Moving Average [*Statistics*]
MA	Multiple Access (NASA)
MA	Multiple Application [*Military*] (AFIT)
MA	Munitionsanstalt [*Ammunition Depot*] [*German military - World War II*]
MA	Munitions Tribunals Appeals, Great Britain High Court of Justice [*A publication*] (DLA)
MA	Muscle Activity (MAE)
MA	Musical Appreciation [*Record label*]
MA	Music Alliance [*Defunct*] (EA)
MA	Muslim Almanac [*A publication*]
MA	Mutagenic Activity
MA	Mutual Age
MA	My Account [*Business term*]
MA	Myanma Airways (EY)
ma	Myria [*A prefix meaning multiplied by 10⁴*]
MA	United States Military Academy (AAGC)
MA1	Machine Accountant, First Class [*Navy*]
MA2	Machine Accountant, Second Class [*Navy*]
MA3	Machine Accountant, Third Class [*Navy*]
MAA	Aerotransportes Mas de Carga SA de CV [*Mexico ICAO designator*] (FAAC)
MAA	Maastrichtial [*Paleontology*]
MAA	Macroaggregated Albumin [*Medicine*]
MAA	Madras [*India*] [*Airport symbol*] (OAG)
MAA	Magma Arizona Railroad Co. [*AAR code*]
MAA	Major Aircraft Accident (MCD)
MAA	Manantiales [*Argentina*] [*Seismograph station code, US Geological Survey*] (SEIS)
MAA	Mandatory Advertising Association [*Automotive retailing*]
MAA	Manitoba Association of Architects [*1914*] [*Canada*] (NGC)
MAA	Manufacturers' Agents Association of Great Britain and Ireland (BI)
MAA	Manufacturers Aircraft Association [*Supersedes AMA*] [*Defunct*] (EA)
MAA	Marina Association of America [*Defunct*] (EA)
MAA	Marineartillerieabteilung [*Naval Coast Artillery Battalion*] [*German military - World War II*]
MA A	Massachusetts Appeals Court Reports [*A publication*] (DLA)
MAA	Master Army Aviator
MAA	Master-at-Arms [*Navy*]
MAA	Master of Administrative Arts (GAGS)
MAA	Master of Aeronautics and Astronautics (GAGS)
MAA	Master of Applied Art (GAGS)
MAA	Master of Applied Arts

MAA............ Material Access Area [Nuclear energy] (NRCH)
MAA............ Mathematical Association of America (EA)
MAA............ Mature Age Allowance
MAA............ Maximum Authorized Altitude [Aviation]
MAA............ Mecca Minerals Ltd. [Vancouver Stock Exchange symbol]
MAA............ Mechanical Arm Assembly (NASA)
MAA............ Mechanical Arm Assembly
MAA............ Mediaeval Academy of America (EA)
MAA............ Medical Administrative Assistant (DAVI)
MAA............ Medical Artists Association of Great Britain (PDAA)
MAA............ Medical Assistance for the Aged
MAA............ Medium Antiaircraft Weapon (NATG)
MAA............ Melanoma-Associated Antigen [Oncology]
MAA............ Menthoxyacetic Acid [Organic chemistry]
MAA............ Methacrylic Acid [Organic chemistry]
MAA............ Methanearsonic Acid [Organic chemistry]
MAA............ Methyl Acetoacetate [Organic chemistry]
MAA............ Microlight Aircrafts Association [British] (DI)
MAA............ Mid-Amer Apart Communities [NYSE symbol] (TTSB)
MAA............ [The] Mid-America Apartment Communities [NYSE symbol] (SPSG)
MAA............ Mission Area Analysis (MCD)
MAA............ Mobilization Automation Appraisal (MCD)
MAA............ Modeling Association of America [Later, MAAI]
MAA............ Moderate Angle of Attack
MAA............ Modified Ames Assay [For toxicology]
MAA............ Monarticular Arthritis [Orthopedics] (DAVI)
MAA............ Moped Association of America [Defunct] (EA)
MAA............ Motel Association of America [Later, National Innkeeping Association]
MAA............ Motor Agents' Association [British]
MAA............ Mouvement Anti-Apartheid [France]
MAA............ Municipal Arborist Association [Later, MAUFS] (EA)
MAAA .... Master of Arts in Arts Administration (PGP)
MAAA .... Member of the American Academy of Actuaries
MAAA .... Metropolitan Area Apparel Association (EA)
MAAAA .... Mid-Am Antique Appraisers Association (EA)
MAAB .... Maintenance Air Abort [Air Force] (AFIT)
MAAB .... Materials Application Advisory Board [NASA] (NASA)
MAABR .... Maintenance Air Abort Rate [Air Force] (AFIT)
MAABS .... Master of Arts in Applied Behavioral Sciences (GAGS)
MAAC.......... Mastic Asphalt Advisory Council [British] (BI)
MAAC.......... Maximum Allowable Actual Charge [Medicare]
MAAC.......... Medical Assistants Advisory Council (DAVI)
MAAC.......... Mid-Atlantic Area Council [Regional power council]
MAAC.......... Military Assistance Advisory Command (DOMA)
MAAC.......... Milliampere Alternating Current (IAA)
MAAC.......... Mutual Assistance Advisory Committee
MAACBA ..... Middle Atlantic Association of Colleges of Business Administration
MAACL........ Multiple Affect Adjective Check List [of Educational and Industrial Testing Service] [Psychology]
MAACP .... Mediterranean Area Airlift Command Post (AFM)
MAACS .... Multi Address Asynchronous Communication System
MA ADAM .... Master of Arts in Alcoholism and Drug Abuse Ministry (PGP)
MAADMA .... Methylaminoacetaldehyde Dimethyl Acetal [Organic chemistry]
MAAE .... Master of Aeronautical and Astronomical Engineering (GAGS)
MAAE .... Master of Arts in Applied Economics (GAGS)
MAAF.......... Mediterranean Allied Air Force
MAAF.......... Mediterranean Army Air Forces
MAAF.......... Michael Army Air Field (MCD)
MAAF.......... Museum Association of the American Frontier (EA)
MAA-FDI ..... Museum of African Art - Frederick Douglass Institute [Smithsonian Institution] (EA)
MAAG .... Military Assistance Advisory Group [Merged with US Military Assistance Command]
MAAGB .... Medical Artists Association of Great Britain (DAVI)
MAAGI .... Military Assistance Advisory Group, Indochina [Later, MAAGV] (VNW)
MAAGV .... Military Assistance Advisory Group, Vietnam [Formerly, MAAGI] (VNW)
MAAH .... Museum of African American History (EA)
MAAH .... Museum of Afro-American History (EA)
MAAI........... Modeling Association of America International (EA)
MAAK.......... Movement for All-Macedonian Action [Political party]
MAAL.......... Monthly Adjustment Acceptance List [Military] (AFIT)
MAALOX ..... Magnesium-Aluminum Hydroxide [Commercial antacid]
MAALT........ Multiple Aircraft Approach and Landing Techniques (MCD)
MAAM........ Medium Antiaircraft Missile
MAAMA....... Middletown Air Materiel Area (SAA)
MAAmSt ..... Master of Arts in American Studies (GAGS)
MAAN .... Methyleneaminoacetonitrile [Organic chemistry]
MAAN .... Mutual Advertising Agency Network [Grand Forks, ND] (EA)
MA & D ...... Mission Analysis and Design
MA & E....... Mission Analysis and Engineering [NASA]
MA & P....... Maintenance Analysis and Planning (NASA)
MA & T....... Manufacturing Assembly and Test (MCD)
MA and T.... Missile Assembly and Test [Building] (NATG)
MAANPI ...... Mutual Aid Association of the New Polish Immigration (EA)
MAAOM ...... Master of Arts in Applied Organizational Management (PGP)
MAAP......... Maintenance and Administration Panel [Bell System]
MAAP......... Material Access Authorization Program [Nuclear energy] (NRCH)
MAAP......... Milan Army Ammunition Plant (AABC)
MAAPA .... Massachusetts Aggregates and Asphalt Pavement Association (SRA)
MAAPS .... Massachusetts Association of 766 Approved Private Schools (SRA)
MAAR .... Mandatory Annual Audit Requirement (AAGC)
MAAR .... Monthly Associate Administrator's Review [NASA]
MAAR .... Monthly Associate Administrator's Review [NASA] (NASA)

MAARA .... Midlands Asthma and Allergy Research Association [British] (DBA)
MAARC .... Magnetic Annular Arc (IEEE)
MA Arch ..... Master of Arts in Architecture
MAARM ...... Memory-Aided Antiradiation Missile (MCD)
MAARP .... Medium Attack Advanced Readiness Program [Navy] (DOMA)
Ma'as .... Ma'asroth (BJA)
MAAS.......... Manpower Allocation and Accounting Subsystem [Air Force] (AFM)
MAAS.......... Michigan Association of Ambulance Services (SRA)
MAAS.......... Muhammad Ali Amateur Sports
MAAS.......... Multiple Array Avionics Subsystem
MA-ASE ...... Multiple Association Application Service Element [Telecommunications] (OSI)
MA(AsianStudies)... Master of Arts (Asian Studies)
MAASL........ Military Assistance Article and Service List (AFIT)
MAASLA ..... Movimiento Argentino Antiimperialista de Solidaridad Latinoamericana
Ma'asSh .... Ma'aser Sheni (BJA)
MAAT.......... MAC [McDonnell Aircraft Corporation] Acquisition and Attack Trainer (MCD)
MAAT.......... Management of Advanced Automation Technology Center [Worcester Polytechnic Institute] [Research center] (RCD)
MAAT.......... Master of Arts in Applied Theology (PGP)
MAAT.......... Master of Arts in Art Therapy (GAGS)
MAAT.......... McCormick Affective Assessment Technique [Teacher evaluation test]
MAAT.......... Member of the Association of Accounting Technicians [British] (DCTA)
MAATAG ..... Mission Area Analysis Test Advisory Group [Army]
MAATC....... Mobile Antiaircraft Training Center
MAAU .... Mexican-American Affairs Unit [Office of Education]
MAAW .... Medium Antitank Assault Weapon
MAAWS ...... Middle Atlantic Association of Women Sailors
MAB........... Macroaddress Bus
MAB........... Magazine Advertising Bureau [of MPA]
MAB........... Magnetic Amplifier Bridge
MAB........... Mainly about Books [A publication]
MAB........... Malfunction Analysis Branch [NASA]
MAB........... Man and the Biosphere Program [UNESCO] [Paris, France]
MAB........... Manganese Alkaline Battery
MAB........... Manhay [Belgium] [Geomagnetic observatory code]
MAB........... Manual d'Archeologie Biblique [A publication] (BJA)
MAB........... Maraba [Brazil] [Airport symbol] (OAG)
MAB........... Marine Air Base
MAB........... Marine Amphibious Brigade
MAB........... Master Acquisition Bus [Computer science] (MCD)
MAB........... Master of Arts in Business (PGP)
MAB........... Material Applications Board
MAB........... Materials Advisory Board [Later, NMAB] [NAS-NRC]
MAB........... Materials Applications Board (MCD)
MAB........... Maximum Androgen Blockade [Oncology]
MAB........... Mechanical Automation Breadboard (KSC)
MAB........... Medical Advisory Board
MAB........... Member, Advisory Board
MAB........... Memorial Advisory Bureau [British] (CB)
MAB........... Menswear Association of Britain (PDAA)
MAB........... Methylaminoazobenzene [Organic chemistry]
MAB........... Metropolitan Asylums Board [British]
MAB........... Mid-America Bancorp [AMEX symbol] (SPSG)
MAB........... Millardair Ltd. [Canada ICAO designator] (FAAC)
MAB........... Missile Activation Building [NWA]
MAB........... Missile Assembly Building (MCD)
MAB........... Mission Analysis Branch [Manned Spacecraft Center]
MAB........... Mobile Assault Bridge [Army]
MAb........... Monoclonal Antibody [Immunochemistry]
MAB........... Multibase Arithmetic Block (ADA)
MAB........... Munitions Assignment Board [Anglo-American] [World War II]
MAB........... Mutual Air Board [Canada World War II]
MABA.......... Meta-Aminobenzoic Acid [Organic chemistry]
MABA.......... (Methylamino) Benzoic Acid [Organic chemistry]
MABAC .... Member of the Association of Business and Administrative Computing [British] (DBQ)
MABB.......... Maximum Achievable Body Burden (PDAA)
MABCGT ..... Mutual Adjustment Bureau of Cloth and Garment Trades [Defunct] (EA)
MABDG....... Marine Aircraft Base Defense Group
MABDW ...... Marine Air Base Defense Wing
MABE.......... Master of Agricultural Business and Economics (WGA)
MABE.......... Master of Arts in Business Education
MABE.......... Member of the Association of Business Executives (DCTA)
MABE.......... Mobile Assault Bridge Equipment (SAA)
MABF.......... Master of Agricultural Business and Finance
MABF.......... Mobile Assault Bridge/Ferry [Army] (RDA)
MABFEX ..... Marine Amphibious Brigade Field Exercise (NVT)
MABL.......... Mass Addition Boundary Layer Program [NASA]
MABLE........ Miniature Autonetics Baseline Equipment
MABLEX...... Marine Amphibious Brigade Landing Exercise (NVT)
MABM........ Master of Agribusiness Management (PGP)
MABM........ Multilayer Absorbing Bottom Layer
MABNET ..... Global Network for Monitoring the Biosphere [Marine science] (MSC)
MABO .... Marianas-Bonins Group
MABOP...... Mustargen [Nitrogen mustard], Adriamycin, Bleomycin, Oncovin , Prednisone [Vincristine] [Antineoplastic drug regimen]
MABOPA..... Malaysian Book Publishers' Association (EAIO)
MABP.......... Mean Arterial Blood Pressure [Medicine]
MABPD .... Military Assistance Basic Planning Document (CINC)

MABRON......	Marine Air Base Squadron
MABS..........	Maltese-American Benevolent Society (EA)
MABS..........	Marine Air Base Squadron
MABS..........	Maritime Application Bridge System (OA)
MABS..........	Master of Arts in Behavior Science (GAGS)
MABS..........	Master of Arts in Biblical Studies (PGP)
MABS..........	Mixed Air Battle Simulation
MABS..........	Moored Acoustic Buoy System [*Marine science*] (MSC)
MABU..........	Maschinengewehr-Eisenbeton-Unterstand [*Machine-Gun-Iron-Reinforced Concrete Emplacement*] [*German "pill box," battlefield redoubts World War I*]
MABUS........	Multi-Access Broadcast Unit System (PDAA)
MABX..........	American Biogenetic Sciences, Inc. [*NASDAQ symbol*] (SAG)
MABXA.......	Amer Biogenetic Sciences'A' [*NASDAQ symbol*] (TTSB)
MAC............	Chief Machine Accountant [*Later, DPC*] [*Navy rating*]
MAC............	Macadam (ADA)
MAC............	Macalester College, Weyerhaeuser Library, St. Paul, MN [*OCLC symbol*] (OCLC)
MAC............	MacAndrew [*Alcoholism scale*]
Mac............	Macassey's New Zealand Reports [*A publication*] (DLA)
MAC............	Macau [*ANSI three-letter standard code*] (CNC)
Mac............	Macbeth [*Shakespearean work*]
MAC............	Maccabees [*Old Testament book*] [*Roman Catholic canon*] (ROG)
MAC............	MacConkey [*Agar*] [*Microbiology*]
mac............	Macedonian [*MARC language code Library of Congress*] (LCCP)
MAC............	Macerare [*Macerate*] [*Pharmacy*]
MAC............	Macerich Co. [*NYSE symbol*] (SAG)
MAC............	Machine-Aided Cognition [*Computer project*] [*Massachusetts Institute of Technology*]
Mac............	Macintosh [*Computer science*] (WDMC)
MAC............	Mackerel [*Pimp*] [*Slang*] (DSUE)
MAC............	Mackintosh (DSUE)
Mac............	Maclean's [*A publication*] (BRI)
Mac............	Macnaghten's English Chancery Reports [*A publication*] (DLA)
MAC............	Macon, GA [*Location identifier FAA*] (FAAL)
MAC............	Magistrates' Appeal Cases [*A publication*] (DLA)
MAC............	Magnetic Attitude Control
MAC............	Magnetic Automatic Calculator (DEN)
MAC............	Main Display Console
MAC............	Maintenance Advisory Committee [*NSIA*]
MAC............	Maintenance Allocation Chart [*Military*]
MAC............	Maintenance Analysis Center [*FAA*]
MAC............	Maintenance and Construction [*Computer science*] (IAA)
MAC............	Major Activity Center
MAC............	Major Air Command [*Later, MAJCOM*]
MAC............	Major Ambulatory Categories [*Patient classification system*] (DAVI)
MAC............	Malignancy-Associated Changes [*Cancer*]
MAC............	Malta Air Charter Co. Ltd. [*ICAO designator*] (FAAC)
MAC............	Mammary Carcinoma [*Oncology*]
MAC............	Management Advisory Committee [*Environmental Protection Agency*] (GFGA)
MAC............	Man and Computer (DIT)
MAC............	Maneuver Analysis and Command
MAC............	Maneuver Area Command [*Army*]
MAC............	Manpower Advisory Committee (OICC)
MAC............	Marine Affairs Council [*Marine science*] (MSC)
MAC............	Marine Amphibious Corps
MAC............	Maritime Advisory Committee [*Terminated, 1968*]
MAC............	Maritime Air Command [*Canada NATO*] (NATG)
MAC............	Marker and Cell [*Computing technique*] [*NASA*]
MAC............	Mark West Springs [*California*] [*Seismograph station code, US Geological Survey*] (SEIS)
MAC............	Martial Arts Commission [*British*] (DI)
MAC............	Mass Absorption Coefficient
MAC............	Massive Algebraic Computation [*Programming language*] [*1958*] [*Computer science*] (CSR)
MAC............	Master Acoustical Console [*Army*]
M Ac........	Master Control (MCD)
M Ac........	Master of Accounting
M Ac........	Master of Acupuncture (PGP)
MAC............	Master of Arts in Communication (GAGS)
MAC............	Master of Arts in Counseling (PGP)
MAC............	Material Availability Commitment (AAG)
MAC............	Materials Analysis Co.
MAC............	Materials and Coatings (SSD)
MAC............	Maximum Acid Concentration [*Clinical chemistry*]
MAC............	Maximum Admissible [*or Allowable*] Concentration
MAC............	Maximum Allowable Concentration [*Toxicology*]
MAC............	Maximum Allowable Cost [*Medicare, Medicaid*]
MAC............	Maximum Atmospheric Concentration
MAC............	McDonnell Aircraft Co. [*Later, McDonnell Douglas Corp.*] (MCD)
MAC............	McLeod Aerating Cardiac
MAC............	McMaster University [*Hamilton, ON*] (DSUE)
MAC............	Mean Aerodynamic Center
MAC............	Mean Aerodynamic Chord
MAC............	Measurement and Analysis Center [*Telecommunications*] (TEL)
MAC............	Measurement and Control [*A publication*] (IAA)
MAC............	Mechanical Advantage Changer
MAC............	Mechanical Analog Computer (DEN)
MAC............	Media Access Control [*Telecommunications*]
MAC............	Media Action Coalition [*Defunct*] (EA)
MAC............	Media Assistance Center (DNAB)
MAC............	Medical Administrative Corps [*Army World War II*]
MAC............	Medical Advisory Committee [*IATA*] (DS)
MAC............	Medical Alert Center

MAC............	Mediterranean Air Command [*Military*]
MAC............	Medium Access Control [*Telecommunications*]
MAC............	Membrane Affinity Chromatography
MAC............	Membrane Applications Centre [*University of Bath*] [*British*] (CB)
MAC............	Membrane Attack Complex [*Biochemistry*]
MAC............	Memory Access Command [*Computer science*] (IAA)
MAC............	Memory Access Controller
MAC............	Memory-Address Counter [*Computer science*] (IAA)
MAC............	Men after Christ Band [*R & B recording group*]
MAC............	Merchant Aircraft Carrier [*A ship carrying a cargo of oil or grain and provided with a flight deck for the operation of antisubmarine aircraft*] [*British World War II*]
MAC............	Message Act Concellation (DA)
MAC............	Message Authentication Code
MAC............	Message Authenticity Check [*Computer science*]
MAC............	Metabolic and Analytical Chemistry
MAC............	Metacarpal Ash per Centimeter
MAC............	Metal Arc Cutting [*Welding*]
MAC............	Methotrexate, Actinomycin D, Cyclophosphamide [*Antineoplastic drug regimen*]
MAC............	Methyl Acetamido Cinnamate [*Organic chemistry*]
MAC............	Methyl Allyl Chloride [*Organic chemistry*]
MAC............	Michigan Apple Committee (EA)
MAC............	Microcystic Adnexal Carcinoma [*Oncology*]
MAC............	Microfilm Aperture Card
MAC............	Microwave-Assisted Curing [*Chemical engineering*]
MAC............	Midair Collision (IIA)
MAC............	Mid-American Conference [*College football*]
MAC............	Midarm Circumference
MAC............	Middle Atlantic Conference, East Riverdale MD [*STAC*]
MAC............	Midwest Archives Conference (EA)
MAC............	Military Aid to the Community [*British military*] (DMA)
Mac............	Military Aircraft Command [*Airline call sign*]
MAC............	Military Airlift Command [*Formerly, Military Air Transport Service*]
MAC............	Military/Allied Commission [*World War II*]
MAC............	Military Armistice Commission (KSC)
MAC............	Military Assistance Command (CINC)
MAC............	Mine Advisory Committee [*NAS-NRC*] (MCD)
MAC............	Mineralogical Association of Canada
MAC............	Mini-Accommodation Center [*In MAC-1, a low-cost, plastic sleeping module promoted by Texas businessman Charles McLaren*]
MAC............	Minimal Alveolar Concentration [*Anesthesiology*]
MAC............	Minimal Auditory Capability Test [*Medicine*]
MAC............	Minimum Alveolar Concentration [*Physiology*]
MAC............	Mining Association of Canada
MAC............	Missile Activation Circuit
MAC............	Missile Advisory Committee [*Pacific Missile Range*] (MUGU)
MAC............	Mission Assignment Code (NATG)
MAC............	Mitomycin C, Adriamycin, Cyclophosphamide [*Antineoplastic drug regimen*]
MAC............	Mitral Annular Calcification [*Cardiology*]
MAC............	MIUW [*Mobile Inshore Undersea Warfare*] Attack Craft [*Navy symbol*]
MAC............	Mixed Armistice Commission [*Arab-Israel borders*] (BJA)
MAC............	Mobile Inshore Undersea Warfare Attack Craft [*Navy*] (MCD)
MAC............	Model Airplane Club
MAC............	Model Algorithmic Control [*Chemical engineering*] [*Computer science*]
MAC............	Modern Arts Criticism [*A publication*]
MAC............	Modern Authors Checklist [*Publication series*]
MAC............	Monitor and Control [*Computer science*] (IAA)
MAC............	Monitored Anesthesia Care [*Medicine*] (DAVI)
MAC............	Monthly Availability Charge (BUR)
MAC............	Months after Contract Award
MAC............	Morning-After Call [*Sales*]
MAC............	Mosaic Resources Ltd. [*Vancouver Stock Exchange symbol*]
MAC............	Motion Analysis Camera
MAC............	Motor Ambulance Convoy
MAC............	MOUT [*Military Operations on Urbanized Terrain*] Assault Course (INF)
MAC............	Movimiento Amplio Colombiano [*Broad-Based Movement of Colombia*] [*Political party*] (PPW)
MAC............	Movimiento Autentico Cristiano [*El Salvador*] [*Political party*] (EY)
MAC............	Movimiento de Autenticidad Colorada [*Paraguay*] [*Political party*] (EY)
MAC............	Mudiad Amdyffyn Cymru [*Welsh Defense Movement*]
MAC............	Multi-Access Computing (NITA)
MAC............	Multiaction Computer
MAC............	Multi-Analyzer Configuration (IAA)
MAC............	Multi-Application Computer (IAA)
MAC............	Multifunctional Automobile Communication System [*Automotive engineering*]
MAC............	Multiple Access Computer
MAC............	Multiple Access Control [*Computer science*] (DIT)
MAC............	Multiple Address Code
MAC............	Multiple Address Computer (IAA)
MAC............	Multiple Array Correlation (CAAL)
MAC............	Multiplexed Analog Component [*Satellite television*] [*British*]
MAC............	Multiplexed Analog Components [*Satellite television system*]
MAC............	Multiply and Accumulate [*Computer science*] (PCM)
MAC............	Multipurpose Arthritis Center [*Medical University of South Carolina*] [*Research center*]
MAC............	Multipurpose Arthritis Center [*Brigham and Women's Hospital*] [*Research center*] (RCD)
MAC............	Municipal Assistance Corp. [*New York*] [*Also known as "Big Mac"*]

MAC............ Munitions Assignments Committee [*World War II*]
MAC............ Museum Association of the Caribbean (EAIO)
MAC............ Museums Association of Canada
MAC............ Musiciens Amateurs du Canada [*Canadian Amateur Musicians*] (EAIO)
MAC............ Mycobacterium Avium Complex
MAC............ Mycobacterium Avium-Intracellulare Complex [*Bacteriology*]
MAc............ Russell Memorial Library, Acushnet, MA [*Library symbol*] [*Library of Congress*] (LCLS)
MACA......... Mammoth Cave National Park
MACA......... Management Assistance Corporation of America (AAGC)
MACA..... Maritime Air Control Authority [*NATO*] (NATG)
MACA..... Master of Arts in Communication Arts
MACA..... Master of Arts in Computer Applications (GAGS)
MAcA......... Master of the Acupuncture Association [*British*] (DBQ)
MAcA......... Member of the Acupuncture Association [*British*]
MACA..... Mental After Care Association [*British*] (EAIO)
MACA..... Mexican-American Correctional Association (OICC)
MACA..... Michigan Association of Children's Alliances (SRA)
MACA..... Military Airlift Clearance Authority (AABC)
MACA..... Mini-America's Cup Association (EA)
MAC(A)...... Munitions Assignments Committee (Air) [*World War II*]
MACABRE.... Material Ablation with Chemically Active Boundary Layers in Reentry [*NASA*]
MACADS...... MAC Automated Deployment Reporting System [*Military*] (GFGA)
MACAF........ Mediterranean Allied Coastal Air Forces
MACAL........ Military Airlift Command Airlift Operations Report
Macalp Mon L... Macalpin on Money Lenders [*A publication*] (DLA)
MACAM...... Military Airlift Command Automated Management
Mac & G...... Macnaghten and Gordon's English Chancery Reports [*A publication*] (DLA)
Mac & H...... Cox, Macrae, and Hertslet's Reports, Crown Cases [*1847-58*] [*England*] [*A publication*] (DLA)
Mac & I...... Macrae and Hertslet's English Insolvency Cases [*1847-52*] [*A publication*] (DLA)
Mac & Rob... Maclean and Robinson's Scotch Appeal Cases [*1839*] [*A publication*] (DLA)
MACAP .... Major Appliance Consumer Action Panel (EA)
Mac A Pat Cas... MacArthur's Patent Cases [*District of Columbia*] [*A publication*] (DLA)
MAC-API...... Mordechai Anielewicz Circle of Americans for Progressive Israel (EA)
MacAr......... MacArthur's Patent Cases [*A publication*] (DLA)
MacAr......... MacArthur's Reports [*8-10 District of Columbia*] [*A publication*] (DLA)
MacAr & M... MacArthur and Mackey's District of Columbia Supreme Court Reports [*A publication*] (DLA)
MacAr & Mackey... MacArthur and Mackey's District of Columbia Supreme Court Reports [*A publication*] (DLA)
MacAr Pat Cas... MacArthur's Patent Cases [*District of Columbia*] [*A publication*] (DLA)
MACARS...... Microfilm Aperture Card Automated Retrieval System
MacArth...... MacArthur's Patent Cases [*A publication*] (DLA)
MacArth...... MacArthur's Reports [*8-10 District of Columbia*] [*A publication*] (DLA)
MacArth & M... MacArthur and Mackey's District of Columbia Supreme Court Reports [*A publication*] (DLA)
MacArth & M (Dist Col)... MacArthur and Mackey's District of Columbia Supreme Court Reports [*A publication*] (DLA)
MacArth Ct Mar... MacArthur on Courts-Martial [*A publication*] (DLA)
MacArth Pat Cas... MacArthur's Patent Cases [*United States*] [*A publication*] (DLA)
MacArthur.... MacArthur's Patent Cases [*A publication*] (DLA)
MacArthur.... MacArthur's Reports [*8-10 District of Columbia*] [*A publication*] (DLA)
MacArthur & M... MacArthur and Mackey's District of Columbia Supreme Court Reports [*A publication*] (DLA)
MacArthur Pat Cas... MacArthur's Patent Cases [*United States*] [*A publication*] (DLA)
Macas......... Macassey's New Zealand Reports [*A publication*] (DLA)
MACAS .... Magnetic Capability and Safety System (NVT)
Macask Ex... Macaskie on Executors, Etc. [*A publication*] (DLA)
MACAT........ Master of Arts in Counseling Psychology: Art Therapy (PGP)
MA(C)AT...... Motor Accidents (Compensation) Appeal Tribunal [*Northern Territory, Australia*]
Macaulay Hist Eng... Macaulay's History of England [*A publication*] (DLA)
Macb .... Macbeth [*Shakespearean work*] (BARN)
MACB .... Martial Arts Control Board [*Victoria, Australia*]
MACB.......... Missile Assembly Control Building
MACBAA ..... Maine/Anjou Cattle Breeders' Association of Australia
MACBANK.... Machining Data Bank [*PERA*] [*Software package*] (NCC)
MACBASIC ... Measurement and Control BASIC [*Programming language developed by Analog Devices*]
Macc............ Maccabees [*Old Testament book*] [*Roman Catholic canon*]
MACC.......... MACC Private Equities [*NASDAQ symbol*] (TTSB)
MACC.......... MACC Private Equities, Inc. [*NASDAQ symbol*] (SAG)
MACC.......... Macro-Ovalocyte [*Biochemistry*] (DAVI)
MACC.......... Madison Academic Computing Center [*University of Wisconsin - Madison*] [*Information service or system Research center*]
MACC.......... Malaysian-American Chamber of Commerce [*Later, AAACC*]
M Acc .... Master of Accountancy [*or Accounting*]
MAcc .... Master of Accounting (GAGS)
MACC.......... Methotrexate, Adriamycin [*Doxorubicin*], Cyclophosphamide [*Cytoxan*], CCNU [*Lomustine*] (DAVI)
MACC.......... Methotrexate, Adriamycin, Cyclophosphamide, CCNU [*Lomustine*] [*Antineoplastic drug regimen*]
MACC.......... Methotrexate, Adriamycin, Cytoxan, CCNU [*Lomustine*] [*Antineoplastic drug*] (CDI)
MACC.......... Micro Asynchronous Communications Controller (MHDI)

MACC.......... MidAmerican Communications Corp. [*Telecommunications service*] (TSSD)
MACC.......... Military Aid to Civil Community [*British*]
MACC.......... Military Assistant to the Civil Community
MACC.......... Mobility-Affect-Cooperation-Communication [*Psychiatry*]
MACC.......... Modified Air Control Center [*Air Force*] (DOMA)
MACC.......... Modular Alter and Compose Console [*Computer science*]
MACC.......... Multiple Applications Control Center (SSD)
MACC.......... Multiple Architecture Control Console (MCD)
MacCarthy ... MacCarthy's Irish Land Cases [*A publication*] (DLA)
Mac CC........ MacGillivray's Copyright Cases [*1901-49*] [*A publication*] (DLA)
Macc Cas... Maccala's Breach of Promise Cases [*A publication*] (DLA)
Maccl.......... Maccala's Reports [*Modern Reports, Part X*] [*1710-25*] [*A publication*] (DLA)
Maccl Tr...... Macclesfield's Trial (Impeachment) [*1725*] [*London*] [*A publication*] (DLA)
Mac CM....... Macomb on Courts-Martial [*A publication*] (DLA)
M Acco .... Master of Accounting
M-Accounts... Merged Accounts (AAGC)
MACCS .... Manufacturing and Cost Control System (IAA)
MACCS .... Manufacturing Cost Collection System
MACCS .... Marine Air Command and Control System (NVT)
M Accs .... Master of Accounts
MACCS .... Molecular Access System [*Computer program*]
MAccSc....... Master in Accounting Science (DD)
M Acct .... Master of Accountancy (PGP)
M Acct .... Master of Accounting (PGP)
MACCT........ Master of Arts in Community College Teaching (GAGS)
MACCT........ Multiple Assembly Cooling Cask Test [*Nuclear energy*] (NRCH)
M ACCUR..... Misce Accuratissime [*Mix Thoroughly*] [*Pharmacy*]
M Accy .... Master of Accountancy (PGP)
MACD .... MacDermid, Inc. [*NASDAQ symbol*] (NQ)
MacD.......... MacDevitt's Irish Land Commissioner's Reports [*A publication*] (DLA)
MACDAC..... Machine Communication with Digital Automatic Computer
MACDAC..... Man Communication and Display for an Automatic Computer (PDAA)
MACDAC...... McDonnell Douglas Corp. (KSC)
MACDACsys... MACDAC system (NITA)
MACDATA .... Materials and Components Development and Testing Association [*Paisley College of Technology*] [*British*] (IRUK)
MACDC .... Military Assistance Command Director of Construction
MacDermott Commission... Commission on the Isle Of Man Constitution. Report [*1959*] [*A publication*] (DLA)
MacDev ...... MacDevitt's Irish Land Cases [*1882-84*] [*A publication*] (DLA)
Macd Jam ... Macdougall's Jamaica Reports [*A publication*] (DLA)
MacDrmd..... MacDermid, Inc. [*Associated Press*] (SAG)
MACDS .... Monitor and Control Display System (MCD)
MACE .... Mace Security International [*NASDAQ symbol*] (SAG)
MACE .... Mace Security Intl [*NASDAQ symbol*] (TTSB)
MACE .... Machine-Aided Composition and Editing
MACE .... Maintenance Analysis Checkout Equipment
MACE .... Management Applications in a Computer Environment (IEEE)
MACE .... Managing Company Expansion [*Manpower Services Commission*] [*British*]
MACE........... Marginal Absolute Certainty Equivalent [*Statistics*]
MACE........... Master Control Executive (IAA)
MACE........... Master of Air Conditioning Education (NADA)
MACE........... Master of Air Conditioning Engineering
MACE........... Master of Arts in Christian Education (PGP)
MACE........... Master of Arts in Civil Engineering
MACE........... Master of Arts in Computer Education (PGP)
MACE........... Mechanical Antenna Control Electronics (MCD)
MACE........... Member of the Association of Conference Executives [*British*] (DBQ)
MACE........... Methylchloroform Chloroacetophenone [*Riot-control gas*]
MACE........... Metropolitan Architectural Consortium for Education (AIE)
MACE........... Mid-America Commodity Exchange [*Chicago, IL*]
MACE........... Military Air Cargo Export [*Subsystem*]
MACE........... Military Airlift Capability Estimator
MACE........... Military Airlift Center, Europe (MCD)
MACE........... Minority Advisory Committee on Energy [*Terminated, 1982*] (EGAO)
Maced .... Macedonia
MACED .... Macedonian
MACEF........ Mastic Asphalt Council and Employers Federation [*British*] (DBA)
MAC Eng..... Master of Air Conditioning Engineering
MACER .... Macerare [*Macerate*] [*Pharmacy*]
Macerich ..... Macerich Co. [*Associated Press*] (SAG)
MaceSec..... Mace Security International [*Associated Press*] (SAG)
MacF .... MacFarlane's Scotch Jury Court Reports [*1838-39*] [*A publication*] (DLA)
MacF .... MacFarlane's Scotch Jury Trials [*A publication*] (DLA)
MACF .... Mulitple Association Control Function [*Telecommunications*] (OSI)
MacFar........ MacFarlane's Scotch Jury Court Reports [*1838-39*] [*A publication*] (DLA)
MacFarl .... MacFarlane's Scotch Jury Trials [*A publication*] (DLA)
MacFarlane... MacFarlane's Scotch Jury Trials [*A publication*] (DLA)
Macf Cop ..... Macfie on Copyright [*A publication*] (DLA)
Macf Min ..... Macfarland's Digest of Mining Cases [*A publication*] (DLA)
MacF Pr...... MacFarlane's Practice of the Court of Sessions [*A publication*] (DLA)
MacFrug...... MacFrugals Bargains Close Outs [*Associated Press*] (SAG)
MACG .... MacGregor Sports & Fitness [*NASDAQ symbol*] (TTSB)
MacG .... MacGregor Sports & Fitness, Inc. [*Associated Press*] (SAG)
MACG .... MacGregor Sports & Fitness, Inc. [*NASDAQ symbol*] (SAG)
MACG .... Maneuver Analysis and Command Group
MACG .... Marine Air Control Group
MACG .... Marshaling Area Control Group [*Military*] (AABC)
MAC(G)........ Munitions Assignments Committee (Ground) [*World War II*]

MacG CC ..... MacGillivray's Copyright Cases [1901-49] [*A publication*] (DLA)
MacGillivray & Parkington... MacGillivray and Parkington's Insurance Law [*6th ed.*] [*1975*] [*A publication*] (DLA)
MacG S........ MacGregor Sports & Fitness, Inc. [*Associated Press*] (SAG)
MacG Sp....... MacGregor Sports & Fitness, Inc. [*Associated Press*] (SAG)
MACGW .... MacGregor Sports&Fitness Wrrt [*NASDAQ symbol*] (TTSB)
MACH .... Machabees [*Old Testament book*] [*Douay version*]
MACH .... Machine [*or Machinery*]
MACH .... Machine
MACH .... Machine
MACH .... Machinist (WDAA)
MACH .... Master of Arts in Church History (PGP)
MACH .... Military Air Command Hunter [*In MACH 3, a video game by Mylstar Electronics*]
MACH .... Modular Automated Container Handling [*Shipping*] (DS)
MACH .... Multilayer Actuator Head [*Epson America, Inc.*] [*Computer science*] (PCM)
MACHA .... Michigan Automated Clearing House Association
MACHA .... Mid-Atlantic Clearinghouse Association [*Maryland, Virginia, and Washington, DC*]
MACHA .... Midwest Automated Clearing House Association
MACHA .... Military Armistice Commission Headquarters Area (INF)
MACHALT ..... Machinery Alteration
MACH D........ Machine Direction Paper (DGA)
MACHDC........ Machinability Data Center [*Computerized search services*] [*Metcut Research Associates, Inc.*]
Macheez .... Macheezmo Mouse Restaurants, Inc. [*Associated Press*] (SAG)
MA Chem ...... Master of Applied Chemistry
MACHG .... Machining
MACHGR...... Machine Group
MACH III...... Maintenance Aided Computer-HAWK-[*Homing All The Way Killer*]-Intelligence/Institutional/Instructor [*Military*]
MA(ChildLit/Reading)... Master of Arts in Children's Literature and Reading
MACHO........ Machismo [*Spanish*] (DSUE)
MACHO........ Massive Compact Halo Object [*Astrophysics*]
MACHO........ Massive Compact Halo Object [*Cosmology*]
MACHO........ Massive Compact Halo Objects [*Astronomy*]
Macho .... Movimiento Anticomunista Hondureno [*Honduran Anti-Communist Movement*] [*Political party*] (PD)
MACHR........ Machiner
MACH R....... Machine Ruling (DGA)
m-AChr .... Muscarinic Acetylcholine Receptor [*Biochemistry*]
MACHST .... Machinist
MACHY .... Machinery
MACHY .... Machinery (ROG)
MACI........... Member of the American Concrete Institute
MACI........... Military Adaptation of Command [*or Commercial*] Items [*DoD*] (AABC)
MACI........... Monitor, Access, and Control Interface (NASA)
MAC II .... Mica and Chessy [*Acronym is name of interior decorating firm and is taken from first names of owners Mica Ertegun and Chessy Rayner*]
MACII.......... Missouri Aptitude and Career Information Inventory [*Vocational guidance test*]
MACIMS ...... Military Airlift Command Integrated Management System
MACIS .... Management and Contracts Information Service
MACK.......... Mackenzie
MAC(K)........ Military Armistice Commission (Korea)
Mack & F Jud A... Mackeson and Forbes' Judicature Acts [*A publication*] (DLA)
Mack BL ...... Mackenzie on Bills of Lading [*A publication*] (DLA)
Mack CL ...... Mackeldey on Modern Civil Law [*A publication*] (DLA)
Mack Crim... Mackenzie's Treatise on Criminal Law [*4 eds.*] [*1678-1758 Scotland*] [*A publication*] (DLA)
Mack Cr L... Mackenzie's Treatise on Criminal Law [*4th ed.*] [*1678-1758 Scotland*] [*A publication*] (DLA)
Mack Ct Sess... Mackay. Court of Session Practice [*A publication*] (ILCA)
Mackeld........ Mackeldey on Modern Civil Law [*A publication*] (DLA)
Mackeld........ Mackeldey on Roman Law [*A publication*] (DLA)
Mackeld Civil Law... Mackeldey on Modern Civil Law [*A publication*] (DLA)
Mackeld Rom Law... Mackeldey on Roman Law [*A publication*] (DLA)
Mackey........ Mackey's District of Columbia Reports [*12-20 District of Columbia*] [*A publication*] (DLA)
MackFn........ Mackenzie Financial Corp. [*Associated Press*] (SAG)
Mackie........ Mackie Designs, Inc. [*Associated Press*] (SAG)
Mack Inst..... Mackenzie's Institutes of the Law of Scotland [*9 eds.*] [*1684-1758*] [*A publication*] (DLA)
Mack Law of Prop... Mackay's Law of Property [*1882*] [*A publication*] (DLA)
Mack Nat..... Mackintosh's Law of Nature and Nations [*5th ed.*] [*1835*] [*A publication*] (DLA)
Mack Obs .... Mackenzie's Observations on Acts of Parliament [*1675, etc.*] [*Scotland*] [*A publication*] (DLA)
Mack Rom Law... Mackenzie's Studies in Roman Law [*A publication*] (DLA)
MacI........ Maclaren on Wills and Successions [*A publication*] (DLA)
MacI........ Maclaurin's Scotch Criminal Decisions [*A publication*] (DLA)
MACL.......... Master of Arts in Classroom Psychology (PGP)
MACL.......... Maximum Approximate Conditional Likelihood [*Statistics*]
MACL.......... Minimum Acceptable Compliance Level (IAA)
MACL.......... Mood Adjective Check List [*Psychometrics*]
MacI & R..... Maclean and Robinson's Scotch Appeal Cases [*9 English Reprint*] [*A publication*] (DLA)
MacI & Rob... Maclean and Robinson's Scotch Appeal Cases [*9 English Reprint*] [*A publication*] (DLA)
MacI Bank ... Macleod's Theory and Practice of Banking [*A publication*] (DLA)
Maclean & R... Maclean and Robinson's Scotch Appeal Cases [*9 English Reprint*] [*A publication*] (DLA)

Maclean & R (Sc)... Maclean and Robinson's Scotch Appeal Cases [*9 English Reprint*] [*A publication*] (DLA)
maclib .... Macrolibrary (MHDI)
MAC LLC ..... Media Access Control Logical Link Control [*Computer science*]
MacI Rem Cas... Maclaurin's Remarkable Cases [*1670-1773*] [*Scotland*] [*A publication*] (DLA)
MacI Sh....... Maclachlan on Merchant Shipping [*A publication*] (DLA)
MacI Shipp... Maclachlan on Merchant Shipping [*A publication*] (DLA)
MACM.......... Master Chief Machine Accountant [*Later, DPCM*] [*Navy rating*]
MACM.......... Master of Arts in Christian Ministries (PGP)
MACM.......... Master of Arts in Church Music (PGP)
MACM.......... Military Aid to Civil Ministries [*British military*] (DMA)
MA/CM.......... Milliamperes per Centimeter
MACM.......... Motorized Air Cycle Machine (MCD)
MACMA........ Military and Aerospace Connector Manufacturers Association (EA)
MACMA........ Mutual Aid Centre Managing Agency [*British*] (CB)
MACMH .... Altona Community Memorial Health Centre, Manitoba [*Library symbol National Library of Canada*] (NLC)
MACMIS ...... Maintenance and Construction Management Information System [*Computer science*]
MACMIS ...... Major Army Command Management Information System
MACMOL ..... Macromolecular
MACMS .... Miniature Arms Collectors/Makers Society (EA)
Macn .... Macnaghten's Hindu Law Cases [*India*] [*A publication*] (DLA)
Macn .... Macnaghten's Nizamut Adalat Cases [*1805-50*] [*Bengal, India*] [*A publication*] (DLA)
Macn .... Macnaghten's Select Cases in Chancery Tempore King [*A publication*] (DLA)
Macn .... Macnaghten's Select Cases, Sadr Diwani Adalat [*1791-1858*] [*Bengal, India*] [*A publication*] (DLA)
MAC(N)........ Munitions Assignments Committee (Navy) [*World War II*]
Macn & G...... Macnaghten and Gordon's English Chancery Reports [*A publication*] (DLA)
Macn & G (Eng)... Macnaghten and Gordon's English Chancery Reports [*A publication*] (DLA)
Macn CM..... Macnaghten on Courts-Martial [*A publication*] (DLA)
Macn Cr Ev... Macnaghten's Criminal Evidence [*A publication*] (DLA)
Macn El Hind L... Macnaghten's Elements of Hindu Law [*A publication*] (DLA)
Macn Ev ...... Macnally's Rules of Evidence on Pleas of the Crown [*A publication*] (DLA)
MACNIMAATZ... MacArthur, Nimitz, and Spaatz [*Nickname for World War II command structure of Douglas MacArthur, Chester W. Nimitz, and Carl A. Spaatz*]
Macn NA Beng... Macnaghten's Nizamut Adalat Reports [*Bengal, India*] [*A publication*] (DLA)
Macn Nul...... Macnamara's Nullities and Irregularities in Law [*1842*] [*A publication*] (DLA)
MacNSc....... [*The*] MacNeal-Schwendler Corp. [*Associated Press*] (SAG)
Macn SDA ... Macnaghten's Select Cases, Sadr Diwani Adalat [*1791-1858*] [*Bengal, India*] [*A publication*] (DLA)
Macn Sel Cas... Select Cases in Chancery Tempore King, Edited by Macnaghten [*1724-33*] [*A publication*] (DLA)
MACNYC...... Men's Apparel Club of New York City (EA)
Mac NZ........ Macassey's New Zealand Reports [*A publication*] (DLA)
MACO .... Major Assembly Checkout [*NASA*] (NASA)
MAC(O)........ Management Analysis Course (Class O) [*Navy*] (DNAB)
MACO .... Marshaling Area Control Officer [*Military*] (AABC)
MACO .... Master of Arts in Counseling (PGP)
MACOI .... MACV [*Military Assistance Command, Vietnam*] Office of Information (VNW)
MACOM .... Maintenance Assembly and Check-Out Model (PDAA)
MACOM .... Major Army Command (AABC)
M Ac OM ..... Master of Arts in Acupuncture and Oriental Medicine (PGP)
Macomb CM... Macomb on Courts-Martial [*A publication*] (DLA)
MA Comm ... Master of Arts in Communication (PGP)
MACOMTELNET... Military Airlift Command Teletype Network (SAA)
MACON .... Maintenance Console (MCD)
MACON .... Matrix Connector Punched Card Programmer [*Computer science*] (IEEE)
MACONS....... Mid-Atlantic Continental Shelf
MACOP........ Methotrexate, Ara-C, Cyclophosphamide, Oncovin [*Vincristine*], Prednisone [*Antineoplastic drug regimen*]
MACOPS...... Military Airlift Command Operational Phone System (AFM)
MACOPT....... Machining Optimisation [*PERA*] [*Software package*] (NCC)
Mac OS .... Macintosh Operating System [*Computer science*] (CDE)
MACOS .... Man - A Course of Study [*Title of social-studies course*] [*National Science Foundation*]
MACOS .... Military Airlift Combat Operations Staff
MACOV .... Mechanized and Army Combat Operations Vietnam (AABC)
MACP.......... Macro Control Processor [*Computer science*] (IAA)
macp .... Macroprocessor (MHDB)
MACP.......... Master of Arts in Community Psychology (PGP)
MACP.......... Master of Arts in Counseling Psychology (PGP)
MACP.......... Michigan Association of Cherry Producers (EA)
MACP.......... Michigan Association of Chiefs of Police (SRA)
MACP.......... Military Aid to the Civil Power [*British military*] (DMA)
MACP.......... Mission Analysis Computer Program
MACP.......... Mortuary Affairs Collection Point [*Army*] (INF)
MACPA........ Maryland Association of Certified Public Accountants (SRA)
MACPA........ Michigan Association of Certified Public Accountants (SRA)
MACPA........ Mid America Crop Protection Association (SRA)
MAC-PAC..... Manufacturing, Planning, and Control [*Arthur Anderson & Co.*] [*Software package*] (NCC)
Mac-Paps .... Mackenzie-Papineau Battalion [*Canada*]
Mac Pat Cas... Macrory's Patent Cases [*England*] [*A publication*] (DLA)

Mac PC....... Macrory's Patent Cases [*England*] [*A publication*] (DLA)
Macph .... Macpherson, Lee, and Bell's Scotch Session Cases [*A publication*] (DLA)
Macph .... Macpherson's Scotch Court of Session Cases [*1862-73*] [*A publication*] (DLA)
Macph Inf .... Macpherson on Infancy [*A publication*] (DLA)
Macph Jud Com... Macpherson's Practice of the Judicial Committee of the Privy Council [*A publication*] (DLA)
Macph L & B... Macpherson, Lee, and Bell [*Scotland*] [*A publication*] (DLA)
Macph Pr C... Macpherson's Practice of the Judicial Committee of the Privy Council [*2nd ed.*] [*1873*] [*A publication*] (DLA)
Macph Priv Counc... Macpherson's Privy Council Practice [*A publication*] (DLA)
Macq .... Macqueen's Scotch Appeal Cases, House of Lords [*A publication*] (DLA)
Macq D........ Macqueen's Debates on Life-Peerage Questions [*A publication*] (DLA)
Macq Div ...... Macqueen's Marriage, Divorce, and Legitmacy [*2nd ed.*] [*1860*] [*A publication*] (DLA)
Macq H & W... Macqueen's Rights and Liabilities of Husband and Wife [*4th ed.*] [*1905*] [*A publication*] (DLA)
Macq HL Cas... Macqueen's Scotch Appeal Cases, House of Lords [*A publication*] (DLA)
Macq Mar.... Macqueen's Marriage, Divorce, and Legitimacy [*2nd ed.*] [*1860*] [*A publication*] (DLA)
Macq Sc App Cas... Macqueen's Scotch Appeal Cases, House of Lords [*A publication*] (DLA)
Mac R....... Macdougall's Jamaica Reports [*A publication*] (DLA)
Mac R....... Maclean and Robinson's Scotch Appeal Cases [*1839*] [*A publication*] (DLA)
Macr .... Macrobii [*of Lucian*] [*Classical studies*] (OCD)
Macr .... MacroChem Corp. [*Associated Press*] (SAG)
MACR .... Macrocytosis [*Hematology*] (DAVI)
MACR .... Macromedia, Inc. [*NASDAQ symbol*] (SAG)
Macr .... Macrory's Patent Cases [*England*] [*A publication*] (DLA)
MACR .... Member of the American College of Radiology
MACR .... Methacrolein [*Also, MAL*] [*Organic chemistry*]
MACR .... Minneapolis, Anoka & Cuyuna Range Railroad Co. [*AAR code*]
MACR .... Missing Air Crew Report
MACR .... Multiply, Accumulate, and Round
Macr & H.... Macrae and Hertslet's English Insolvency Cases [*1847-52*] [*A publication*] (DLA)
Macrch .... MacroChem Corp. [*Associated Press*] (SAG)
MACRI .... Mercantile Atlantic Coastal Routing Instructions
MACrimStudies... Master of Arts in Criminological Studies
MACRIT .... Manpower Authorization Criteria [*Army*]
Macrmd .... Macromedia, Inc. [*Associated Press*] (SAG)
MACRO .... Macroassembler (MHDI)
MACRO .... Macrocytosis [*Hematology*] (DAVI)
MACRO .... Macroinstruction (ECII)
MACRO .... Macroprocessor (MHDI)
MACRO .... Massachusetts Association of Community Rehabilitation Organizations (SRA)
MACRO .... Merge and Correlate Recorded Output [*Computer science*] (NASA)
MACRO .... Monopole, Astrophysics and Cosmic Ray Observatory [*Italy*]
Macrob .... Macrobius [*Late fourth and early fifth century AD*] [*Classical studies*] (OCD)
MACROCAL... [*Enhanced*] Macro Version of Common Assembler Language [*Interdata*] (NITA)
MacroCh ..... MacroChem Corp. [*Associated Press*] (SAG)
MACROL ...... Macro-Based Display Oriented Language [*Raytheon Co.*]
Macr Pat Cas... Macrory's Patent Cases [*England*] [*A publication*] (DLA)
Macr P Cas... Macrory's Patent Cases [*England*] [*A publication*] (DLA)
MACRS .... Modified Accelerated Cost Recovery System [*IRS*]
MacS .... MacSweeney on Mines, Quarries, and Minerals [*5 eds.*] [*1884-1922*] [*A publication*] (DLA)
MACS........... Mainline Automated Clearance System [*Interstate trucking*] [*Highway safety*]
MACS........... Management Administration Control System
MACS........... Management & Computer Services, Inc. [*Information service or system*] (IID)
MACS........... Manned Air Combat Simulation (MCD)
MACS........... Marine Air Control Squadron
MACS........... Mass and Charge Spectroscopy
MACS........... Mastoid Air Cell System [*Anatomy*]
MACS........... McDonnell Automatic Checkout System [*McDonnell Douglas Corp.*]
MACS........... Media Account Control System (PDAA)
MACS........... Medium-Altitude Communications Satellite
MACS........... Member of the American Chemical Society
MACS........... Merchant Airship Cargo Satellite (PDAA)
MACS........... Metering and Accounting System (NITA)
MACS........... Michigan Association of Christian Schools (SRA)
MACS........... Michigan Association of Convenience Stores (SRA)
MACS........... Microwave Attitude Control Sensor
MACS........... Migrant Advisory Committee
MACS........... Military Aeronautical Communications Service
MACS........... Military Airlift Command Service (NATG)
MACS........... Missile Air-Conditioning System
MACS........... Mississippi Association of Convenience Stores (SRA)
MACS........... Mobile Acoustic Communications System
MACS........... Mobile Air Conditioning Society (EA)
MACS........... Monitoring and Control Station
MACS........... Multi-Access Computer Switch [*Telecommunications*] (TSSD)
MACS........... Multicenter AIDS [*Acquired Immune Deficiency Syndrome*] Cohort Study [*National Institutes of Health*]
MACS........... Multiline Automatic Calling System (HGAA)

MACS........... Multiple Access Communications System [*West German and Dutch*]
MACS........... Multiple Application Connector System
MACS........... Multiple-Technique Analytical Computer System
MACS........... Multiproject Automated Control System
MACS........... Multipurpose Acquisition and Control System (IAA)
MACS........... Multipurpose Arcade Combat Simulator [*Marksmanship training*] [*Army*] (INF)
MACS........... Senior Chief Machine Accountant [*Later, DPCS*] [*Navy rating*]
MACSAT ...... Multiple Access Commercial Satellite (DOMA)
MACSCO ...... Metropolitan Academic Consultants Sales Corp.
MACSEA ...... Military Assistance Command, Southeast Asia
MAC/SM ...... Maintenance Allocation Chart and System Maintenance (MCD)
MACSOG ...... Military Assistance Command Studies and Observation Group (CINC)
MACSQ .... Marine Air Control Squadron
MACSRRPCC... Maxwellian Averaged Cross Section Reactor Physics Computer Code [*Electronics*] (IAA)
MACSS .... Master of Arts in Church Social Services (PGP)
MACSS .... Medium-Altitude Communications Satellite System
MACSV .... Multipurpose Airmobile Combat-Support Vehicle (SAA)
MACSYM ..... Measurement and Control System (MHDB)
MACSYMA ... MAC [*Massive Algebraic Computation*] Symbolic Manipulator [*Programming language*] [*1969*] (CSR)
MACT.......... Master of Arts in College Teaching
MACT.......... Maximum Achievable [*or Available*] Control Technology [*Environmental chemistry*]
MACT.......... Military Assistance Command, Thailand (VNW)
MACT.......... Moral Action Choice Test (EDAC)
MACTEC...... MAC Technical Services Co. (GAAI)
MACTELNET... Military Airlift Command Teletype Network (AFM)
MacTEP ...... Mac [*Apple's Mackintosh computer*] Terminal Emulation Program
MACTM....... Master of Applied Communication Theory and Methodology (PGP)
MACTRAC ... Military Airlift Command Traffic Reporting and Control System
MACTU .... Mines and Countermeasures Technical Unit [*Navy*]
MACU .... Monitor and Control Unit [*Aerospace*] (IAA)
MACUL .... Michigan Association for Computer Users in Learning (EDAC)
MACV .... Military Assistance Command, Vietnam
MACV......... Multipurpose Airmobile Combat-Support Vehicle
MACVD .... Microwave-Assisted Chemical Vapor Deposition [*Coating technology*]
MACVNAG... Military Assistance Command, Vietnam Naval Advisory Group (VNW)
MACVSOG.... Military Assistance Command Vietnam Special Operations Group (INF)
MACV-SOG.... Military Assistance Command, Vietnam Studies and Observations Group (VNW)
MACW .... Missionary Association of Catholic Women [*Defunct*] (EA)
M Acy .... Master of Accountancy (PGP)
MACY......... Master of Arts in Accountancy (PGP)
Mad .... All India Reporter, Madras [*A publication*] (DLA)
Mad .... Indian Law Reports, Madras Series [*A publication*] (DLA)
Mad .... Indian Rulings, Madras Series [*A publication*] (DLA)
MAD........... Machine Analysis Display
MAD........... Machine ANSI Data
Mad .... Madagascar
MAD........... Madam
MAD........... Madang [*Papua New Guinea*] [*Seismograph station code, US Geological Survey*] (SEIS)
Mad .... Maddock's English Chancery Reports [*56 English Reprint*] [*1815-22*] [*A publication*] (DLA)
Mad .... Maddock's Reports [*9-18 Montana*] [*A publication*] (DLA)
MAD........... Madeco SA [*NYSE symbol*] (SPSG)
MAD........... Madeco S.A. ADS [*NYSE symbol*] (TTSB)
MAD........... Madison [*Diocesan abbreviation*] [*Wisconsin*] (TOCD)
MAD........... Madison, CT [*Location identifier FAA*] (FAAL)
Mad .... Madras High Court Reports [*India*] [*A publication*] (DLA)
MAD........... Madrid [*Spain*] [*Airport symbol*] (OAG)
MAD........... Madrid [*Spain*]
MAD........... Magnetic Airborne Detector [*Navy*]
MAD........... Magnetic Anomaly Detection [*or Detector*]
MAD........... Magnetic Azimuth Detector (MCD)
MAD........... Main Assembly Drawing
MAD........... Maintenance Alert Directive [*Aviation*]
MAD........... Maintenance Analysis Data [*or Diagram*] (MCD)
MAD........... Maintenance, Assembly, and Disassembly
MAD........... Major Air Disaster (PDAA)
MAD........... Management Analysis Division [*NASA*] (MCD)
MAD........... Manhunter Assignment Device [*Computer science*]
MAD........... Manufacturing Assembly Drawing
MAD........... Maple Air Services Ltd. [*Canada ICAO designator*] (FAAC)
MAD........... Marine Air [*or Aviation*] Detachment
MAD........... Marine Air Detection (AFIT)
MAD........... Mass Analyzer Detector
MAD........... Master Accession Document [*Computer science*] (BUR)
MAD........... Master Air Data [*Computer*]
M Ad........... Master of Administration (PGP)
MAd........... Master of Arts Administration (GAGS)
MAD........... Material Analysis Data
MAD........... Material Assistance Designated [*Report*] (MCD)
MAD........... Material Availability Date (CET)
MAD........... Materials for the Assyrian Dictionary (BJA)
MAD........... Materiel Acquisition and Delivery [*Military*]
MAD........... Mathematical Analysis of Downtime (DNAB)
MAD........... Maximum Acceptable Deviation
MAD........... Maximum Acid Output [*Biochemistry*] (DAVI)
MAD........... Maximum Applicable Dose [*Environmental chemistry*]
MAD........... Mean Absolute Deviation [*Statistics*]
MAD........... MeCCNU [*Semustine*], Adriamycin [*Antineoplastic drug regimen*]

MAD............ Media Access Device [*Telecommunications*]
MAD............ Median Absolute Deviation [*Statistics*]
MAD............ Memory Access Director [*Computer science*] (IAA)
MAD............ Methylacridone [*Organic chemistry*]
MAD............ Methylandrostenediol [*Methandriol*] [*Endocrinology*]
MAD............ Michigan Algorithmic Decoder [*IBM Corp.*] [*University of Michigan Programming language 1961*]
MAD............ Mileage Accumulation Dynamometer
MAD............ Militarischer Abschirmdienst [*Military counterintelligence*] [*Germany*]
MAD............ Military Air Distress (LAIN)
MAD............ Mind-Altering Drug
MAD............ Mine Assembly Depot [*Navy*]
MAD............ Mini-Attack Drone
MAD............ Minimal Aural Dose
MAD............ Minimum Absolute Deviation [*Statistics*]
MAD............ Minimum Approach Distance (SAA)
MAD............ Missile Assembly Data
MAD............ Mission Analysis Division [*NASA*] (KSC)
MAD............ Mission Area Deficiency [*Army*]
MAD............ Mitotic Arrest-Deficient [*Cytology*]
MAD............ Mixed Analog and Digital [*Telecommunications*] (TEL)
MAD............ Model A Drivers (EA)
MAD............ More After Dark [*Screen-saver computer program from Berkeley Systems*] (PCM)
MAD............ Morse Automatic Decoder (IAA)
MAD............ Mortar Air Delivery System [*Military*] (VNW)
MAD............ Mosquito Abatement District (DICI)
MAD............ Motor Assembly and Disassembly
MAD............ Motorsport Advanced Display [*Auto racing*]
MAD............ Multiple Access Device
MAD............ Multiple Access Drive (NITA)
MAD............ Multiple-Aperture Device (MUGU)
MAD............ Multiple Audio Distribution [*Communications*]
MAD............ Multiple-Wavelength Anomalous Dispersion [*Crystallography*]
MAD............ Multiply and Add
MAD............ Multiwavelength Anomalous Diffraction [*Physics*]
MAD............ Music and Dance [*American Dance Festival project*]
MAD............ Mutual Ability for Defense [*Pentagon defense policy*]
MAD.!.......... Mutual Assured Destruction [*Nuclear warfare*]
MAD............ Myoadenylate Deaminase [*An enzyme*]
MADA .... Multiple Access Demand Assignment (MCD)
MADA .... Multiple Access - Discrete Address [*Navy tactical voice communication*]
MADAEC ...... Military Application Division of the Atomic Energy Commission
MADAG........ Madagascar (ROG)
Madag .... Madagascar [*Malagasy Republic*] (VRA)
Madag .... Malagasy Republic (VRA)
MADAIR...... Magnetic Anomaly Detection and Identification Ranging (MCD)
MADALINE... Multi-Adaptive Linear Neuron (PDAA)
MADAM .... Maintenance Diagnostic Assistance Module [*Military*] (CAAL)
MADAM .... Manchester Automatic Digital Machine [*Manchester University*] [*British*] (DEN)
MADAM .... Marine Air-Droppable Area Marker (MCD)
MADAM .... Moderately Advanced Data Management [*Computer science*]
MADAM .... Multipurpose Automatic Data Analysis Machine
Mad & B .... Maddox and Bach's Reports [*19 Montana*] [*A publication*] (DLA)
Mad & Gel... Maddock and Geldart's English Chancery Reports [*A publication*] (DLA)
MADAP .... Maastricht Automatic Data Processing and Display System [*Air traffic control*]
MADAR........ Malfunction Analysis, Detection, and Recording [*Computer science*]
MADAR........ Malfunction and Data Recorder [*Computer science*] (IAA)
MADARS...... Maintenance Analysis, Detection, and Reporting System [*Computer science*] (AFM)
MADARS...... Malfunction Analysis, Detection, and Recording Subsystem [*Computer science*]
MADARTS.... Malfunction Detection Analysis, Recording, and Training System
MADB .... Madison Bancshares Group [*NASDAQ symbol*] (SAG)
MADB .... Madison Bancshares Group [*NASDAQ symbol*] (TTSB)
Mad Bar ..... Madox's Barona Anglia [*A publication*] (DLA)
MADC .... Machine-Assisted Detection and Classification (NVT)
MADC .... Milliampere Direct Current [*Electronics*] (IAA)
MADC .... Multiplexer Analog-to-Digital Converter (MCD)
MADCAP...... Mammoth Decimal Arithmetic Program [*NASA*] (KSC)
MADCAP...... Mobilization and Deployment Capability Assurance Concept [*Military*]
MADCAP...... Model of Advection, Diffusion, and Chemistry for Air Pollution [*Environmental Protection Agency*] (GFGA)
MADCAR...... Management Data Charting and Review (IAA)
Mad Ch Pr... Maddock's English Chancery Practice [*3rd ed.*] [*1837*] [*A publication*] (DLA)
MADCK .... Marine Aide-de-Camp to the King [*British Admiralty*]
Mad Co....... Madras Code [*India*] [*A publication*] (DLA)
MAD/CO...... Mid-America Dance Company [*St. Louis, MO*]
Madd .... Maddock's English Chancery Reports [*A publication*] (DLA)
Madd .... Maddox's Reports [*9-18 Montana*] [*A publication*] (DLA)
MADD .... Module for Automatic Dock and Detumble [*Orbital rescue*] [*NASA*]
MADD .... Mothers Against Drunk Driving (EA)
MADD .... Multichannel Analog-to-Digital Data Decoder (IAA)
MADDAM ..... Macromodule and Digital Differential Analyzer Machine [*Computer science*]
MADDAM..... Multiplexed Analog to Digital, Digital to Analog Multiplexed [*Computer science*]
Madd & B... Maddox and Bach's Reports [*19 Montana*] [*A publication*] (DLA)
Madd & G.... Maddock and Geldart's English Chancery Reports [*A publication*] (DLA)

Madd & Gel... Maddock and Geldart's English Chancery Reports [*A publication*] (DLA)
Madd Ch...... Maddock's English Chancery Reports [*56 English Reprint*] [*1815-22*] [*A publication*] (DLA)
Madd Ch (Eng)... Maddock's English Chancery Reports [*56 English Reprint*] [*A publication*] (DLA)
Madd Ch Pr... Maddock's English Chancery Practice [*A publication*] (DLA)
MADDDC.... Manufacturers of Aerial Devices and Digger-Derricks Council (EA)
Madden ...... Madden Steven Ltd. [*Associated Press*] (SAG)
MADDIDA .... Magnetic Drum Digital Differential Analyzer
MADDWU .... Mechanics' Assistants' and Dry Dock Workers' Union [*British*]
MADE......... Magnetic Device Evaluator [*Computer science*]
MADE......... Manufacturing and Automated Design Engineering
MADE......... Master of Agricultural Development Economics
MADE......... Microalloy Diffused Electrode
MADE......... Minimum Airborne Digital Equipment
MADE......... Multichannel Analog-to-Digital Data Encoder
Madeco....... Madeco SA [*Associated Press*] (SAG)
M Ad Ed .... Master of Adult Education (PGP)
MAdEd........ Master of Arts in Adult Education (GAGS)
Ma de Ma.... Matheus de Mathesillanis [*Flourished, 1381-1402*] [*Authority cited in pre-1607 legal work*] (DSA)
Ma de Math... Matheus de Mathesillanis [*Flourished, 1381-1402*] [*Authority cited in pre-1607 legal work*] (DSA)
MADEPSQ.... Marine Air Depot Squadron
MADER .... Management of Atmospheric Data for Evaluation and Research (USDC)
MADER .... Management of Atmospheric Data for Evaluation and Research [*Marine science*] (OSRA)
MADERI....... Mexican-American Documentation and Educational Research Institute
MaderSin..... Maderas y Sinteticos Sociedad Anonima [*Associated Press*] (SAG)
MADEX .... Magnetic Anomaly Detection Exercise (NVT)
Mad Exch.... Madox's History of the Exchequer [*A publication*] (DLA)
MADF......... Maintenance Action Data Form [*Military*] (CAAL)
Mad Fir Burg... Madox's Firma Burgi [*A publication*] (DLA)
Mad Form.... Madox's Formulare Anglicanum [*A publication*] (DLA)
Mad Form Angl... Madox's Formulare Anglicanum [*A publication*] (DLA)
MADG .... Madge NV [*NASDAQ symbol*] (SAG)
Madge .... Madge NV [*Associated Press*] (SAG)
MadGE........ Madison Gas & Electric Co. [*Associated Press*] (SAG)
MADGE........ Microwave Aircraft Digital Guidance Equipment [*Helicopters*]
MadgeNt...... Madge NV [*Associated Press*] (SAG)
MADGF........ Madge Networks N.V. [*NASDAQ symbol*] (TTSB)
MADH .... Master of Applied Development and Health (PGP)
MADH .... Methylamine Dehydrogenase [*An enzyme*]
Mad HC ..... Madras High Court Reports [*India*] [*A publication*] (DLA)
Mad Hist Exch... Madox's History of the Exchequer [*A publication*] (DLA)
Madh Pra.... All India Reporter, Madhya Pradesh [*A publication*] (DLA)
MADI......... Madison Group Assoc [*NASDAQ symbol*] (TTSB)
MADI......... Master Data Index
MADICA...... Massachusetts Acoustical Drywall-Interior Contractors Association (SRA)
MADIS .... Burda-MarketingInfoSystem [*Burda GmbH, Marketing Service Department*] [*Information service or system*] (IID)
MADIS .... Manual Aircraft Data Input System (MCD)
MADIS .... Manual Aircraft Display Information System [*Military*] (CAAL)
MADIS .... Millivolt Analog-Digital Instrumentation System
Mad Isls ..... Madeira Islands
MADIZ .... Military Air Defense Identification Zone (MCD)
M/ADJ........ Manual Adjusting [*Automotive engineering*]
Mad Jur ..... Madras Jurist [*India*] [*A publication*] (DLA)
MADL......... Microwave Acoustic Delay Line
Mad Law Rep... Madras Law Reporter [*India*] [*A publication*] (DLA)
MADLR........ Major Assembly Direct Labor Reporting (MCD)
Mad L Rep... Madras Law Reporter [*India*] [*A publication*] (DLA)
Mad LT....... Madras Law Times [*India*] [*A publication*] (DLA)
Mad LW....... Madras Law Weekly [*India*] [*A publication*] (DLA)
MADM .... Maintenance Automated Data Management
MADM .... Manchester Automatic Digital Machine [*Manchester University*] [*British*]
M Adm .... Master of Administration
MADM .... Medium Atomic Demolition Munition [*Military*] (AABC)
MADMAN.... Magnetic Anomaly Detector Contact Man (NVT)
MADMAN.... Master Activity Data Management (DNAB)
M Adm E ..... Master of Administrative Engineering
MAdmin....... Master of Administration
M Admin...... Master of Administration (PGP)
M Admin...... Master of Administrative Studies
M Adm J..... Master in Administration of Justice (PGP)
M Adm Mgt... Master of Administration Management (PGP)
Madn .... Madden Steven Ltd. [*Associated Press*] (SAG)
MADN......... Metropolitan Area Digital Network (NTCM)
MAD-N....... Mid-America Dance Network [*Kansas City, MO*]
MADN......... Mid-American Dance Network
MADO........ Mulliken Approximation for Differential Overlap [*Physics*]
MADOC....... Medical Analysis of Days of Care [*Report*]
MADOM....... Magnetic Acoustic Detection of Mines (DOMA)
Madox .... Madox's Formulare Anglicanum [*A publication*] (DLA)
Madox .... Madox's History of the Exchequer [*A publication*] (DLA)
MADP......... Main Air Display Plot
MADP .... Major Acquisition Decision Point [*Military*] (MCD)
MADP .... Material Acquisition Decision Process [*Military*] (MCD)
MADP .... Mission Area Development Plan [*DoD*]

MADPA........	Medicaid Antidiscriminatory Drug Pricing [*and Patient Benefit Restoration*]Act
MADPAC......	Materiel Deterioration Prevention and Control [*Program*] [*Army*] (RDA)
Mad Papers...	James Madison's Papers [*A publication*] (DLA)
MADR.........	Madras [*India*] (ROG)
MADR.........	Madritum [*Madrid*] [*Imprint*] [*Latin*] (ROG)
MADR.........	Master of Arts in Dispute Resolution (PGP)
MADR.........	Materiel Acquisition Decision Review [*Army*]
MADR.........	Microprogram Address Register
MAD-R.........	Multiapertured Device-Resistance (DNAB)
MA(Drama)..	Master of Arts (Drama)
Madras LJ ...	Madras Law Journal and Reports [*India*] [*A publication*] (DLA)
MADRE.......	Magnetic Drum RADAR Equipment
MADRE.......	Magnetic Drum Receiving Equipment
MADRE.......	Manufacturing Data Retrieval System (NASA)
MADRE.......	Manufacturing Data Retrieval System
MADRE.......	Martin Automatic Data-Reduction Equipment
MADREC.....	Malfunction Detection and Recording [*Checkout system for aircraft*] [*Air Force*]
Mad Reg.....	Madden on Registration of Deeds [*A publication*] (DLA)
MADS.........	Machine-Aided Drafting System (IEEE)
MADS.........	Maintenance and Diagnosis System [*Military*] (CAAL)
MADS.........	Mars Atmosphere Density Sensor
MADS.........	Meteorological Airborne Data System
MADS.........	Missile Attitude Determination System [*LASER device*] [*Air Force*]
MADS.........	Mission Area Deficiency Statement [*Army*] (RDA)
MADS.........	Mobile Airborne Defense Station Concept [*Air Force*]
MADS.........	Mobile Air Defense System
MADS.........	Modular Air Defense System (MCD)
MADS.........	Modular Army Demonstration System (MCD)
MADS.........	Modular Auxiliary Data System
MADS.........	Modular Auxiliary Data Systems (NASA)
MADS.........	Multiple Access Digital System [*Computer science*] (IAA)
MadsBn	Madison Bancshares Group [*Associated Press*] (SAG)
Mad SDAR...	Madras Sadr Diwani Adalat Reports [*India*] [*A publication*] (DLA)
Mad Sel Dec...	Madras Select Decrees [*A publication*] (DLA)
Mad Ser	Indian Law Reports, Madras Series [*A publication*] (DLA)
MAD-SMS....	Movement for Autonomous Democracy-Society for Moravia and Silesia [*Former Czechoslovakia*] [*Political party*] (EY)
MADSPM	Mobilization Against the Draft and Student Peace Mobilization [*An association*] (EA)
MADT..........	Mean Administrative Delay Time
MADT..........	Micro-Alloy Diffused Base Transistor (NITA)
MADT..........	Microalloy Diffused Transistor (MUGU)
MADU	Methylaminodeoxyuridine [*Pharmacology*]
M Ad VE	Master of Administration in Vocational Education (PGP)
MADVEC.....	Magnetic Anomaly Detector Vectoring [*Military*] (CAAL)
MADW	Military Air Defense Warning Network
Mad WN	Madras Weekly Notes [*A publication*] (DLA)
MADWN......	Military Air Defense Warning Network (IAA)
Mad WNCC...	Madras Weekly Notes, Criminal Cases [*India*] [*A publication*] (DLA)
MAE...........	Madera, CA [*Location identifier FAA*] (FAAL)
MAE...........	Maebashi [*Japan*] [*Seismograph station code, US Geological Survey*] (SEIS)
MAE...........	Maersk Commuter IS [*Netherlands ICAO designator*] (FAAC)
Mae...........	Maestro [*Record label*] [*Belgium, etc.*]
MAE...........	Maine Association of Engineers (SRA)
MAE...........	Maintenance Engineer
MAE...........	Malignant Angioendotheliomatosis [*Oncology*]
MAE...........	Master Electric (IAA)
MAE...........	Master of Aeronautical Engineering (WDAA)
M Ae...........	Master of Aeronautics
MAE...........	Master of Aerospace Engineering (PGP)
MAE...........	Master of Agricultural Economics (PGP)
MAE...........	Master of Agricultural Education (PGP)
MAE...........	Master of Agricultural Engineering (GAGS)
MAE...........	Master of Agricultural Extension (GAGS)
MAE...........	Master of Art Education
MAE...........	Master of Arts in Education
MAE...........	Master of Arts in English (PGP)
MAE...........	Master of Automotive Engineering (PGP)
MA E...........	Master of Engineering (WDAA)
MAE...........	Material and Equipment [*Nuclear energy*] (IAA)
MAE...........	Matrix Arithmetic Expression
MAE...........	McDonnell Airborne Evaluator [*McDonnell Douglas Corp.*] (MCD)
MAE...........	Mean Absolute Error
MAE...........	Mean Area of Effectiveness (CINC)
MAE...........	Mechanical and Electrical (IAA)
MAE...........	Medical Air Evacuation
MAE...........	Medium Altitude Endurance (RDA)
MAE...........	Memory Address Register (NITA)
MAE...........	(Methylamino)ethanol [*Organic chemistry*]
MAE...........	Metropolitan Area Exchange [*Telecommunications*] (ACRL)
MAE...........	Micro Aided Engineering (NITA)
MAE...........	Miramar Energy Corp. [*Vancouver Stock Exchange symbol*]
MAE...........	Missile Airborne Equipment (IAA)
MAE...........	Missile Assembly Equipment (IAA)
MAE...........	Mission Accomplishment Estimate [*DoD*]
MAE...........	Mississippi Association of Educators (SRA)
MAE...........	Mobile Ammunition Evaluation
MAE...........	Modified Anglia Engine [*Cosworth racing engines*]
MAE...........	Motion Aftereffect
MAE...........	Movement After-Effect (PDAA)
MAE...........	Moves All Extremities [*Medicine*] (MAE)
MAE............	Multilingual Aphasia Examination [*Speech and language therapy*] (DAVI)
MAE............	Mutual Assistance, Executive [*Military appropriation*] (NG)
MAEB	Material Application Evaluation Board [*NASA*] (MCD)
MAEBR	Management of Enlisted Bonus Recipients
MAEC.........	Manufacturing Analysis of Engineering Change (MCD)
MAEC.........	Master of Arts in Economics
MA Ec	Master of Arts in Economics (PGP)
MAEC.........	Minimum Adverse Effect Concentration [*Pollution technology*]
MAEC.........	Missile Attack Emergency Conference (MCD)
MAECAM.....	Micro-Aided Engineering/Computer Aided Manufacturing [*Micro-Aided Engineering Ltd. and Digital Microsystems Ltd.*] [*Software package*] (NCC)
MAECO	NRA [*National Restaurant Association*] Multi-Unit Architects, Engineers, and Construction Officers (EA)
MA (Econ) ...	Master of Arts in Economic and Social Studies [*University of Manchester*] [*British*]
MA (Econ) ...	Master of Arts in Economic Studies [*Universities of Newcastle and Sheffield*] [*British*]
MAECON.....	Mid-America Electronics Conference
MA Ed.........	Master of Arts in Education
MAED..........	Micro Area Electron Diffraction [*Surface analysis*]
MAEDOS	Micro-Aided Engineering/Drawing Office System [*Micro-Aided Engineering Ltd.*] [*Software package*] (NCC)
MA EdU	Master of Arts in Education (PGP)
MAEE..........	Marine Aircraft Experimental Establishment
M Ae E	Master of Aeronautical Engineering
MAEE..........	Mid-Atlantic Electrical Exhibition (ITD)
M Ae Eng.....	Master of Aeronautical Engineering
MAEEW.......	Moves All Extremities Equally Well [*Neurology*] (DAVI)
MAEF..........	Mastic Asphalt Employers' Federation [*British*] (BI)
MAEI..........	Malaysian-American Electronics Industry
MAEL..........	Marine Aircraft Experimental Laboratory [*British*]
MAELU........	Mutual Atomic Energy Liability Underwriters [*Chicago, IL*] (EA)
MAENF........	Miramar Mining [*NASDAQ symbol*] (TTSB)
MAENF........	Miramar Mining Corp. [*NASDAQ symbol*] (SAG)
MAEO..........	Months after Exercise of Option
MAEP..........	Measure of Adult English Proficiency (EDAC)
MAEP..........	Minimum AUTOLAND [*Automatic Landing*] Entry Point (NASA)
MAEPS........	Model Adoption Exchange Payment System (EDAC)
MAER..........	Maximum Allowable Emission Rate [*Environmental Protection Agency*] (ERG)
MAER..........	Mechanical and Electrical Room (IAA)
MAER..........	Mobile Ammunition and Reconditioning Unit [*Military*]
M Aero E	Master of Aeronautical Engineering
M Aero E	Master of Aerospace Engineering (PGP)
M Aero Eng...	Master of Aeronautical Engineering
MAEROSPOPNSMGT...	Masters Aerospace Operations Management [*Air Force*]
MAERP........	Mutual Atomic Energy Reassurance Pool
MAERU	Mobile Ammunition Evaluation and Reconditioning Unit
Maes	Maestoso [*Majestic*] [*Music*]
MAES..........	Maine Agriculture Experiment Station [*University of Maine at Orono*] [*Research center*] (RCD)
MAES..........	Manufacturing and Engineering Support (IAA)
M Ae S	Master of Aeronautical Science
MAES..........	Master of Arts in Environmental Sciences (PGP)
MAES..........	Medical Aid for El Salvador (EA)
MAES..........	Mexican-American Engineering Society (EA)
MAES..........	Michigan Agricultural Experiment Station [*Michigan State University*] [*Research center*] (RCD)
MAESA........	Measurement for Assessing the Effects of Stratospheric Aircraft [*Marine science*] (OSRA)
MAESA........	Measurements for Assessing the Effects of Stratospheric Aircraft (USDC)
M Ae Sc	Master of Aeronautical Science
MAESON......	Marxist All-Ethiopian Socialist Movement [*Political party*] (PD)
MAESTO	Maestoso [*Majestic*] [*Music*]
MAESTRO	Machine-Assisted Educational System for Teaching by Remote Operation (IEEE)
MAESTRO	Mission Analysis Evaluation and Space Trajectory Operations [*NASA*]
MAET..........	Master of Arts in English Teaching (PGP)
MAET..........	Microwave Amplifier Electron Tube
MAET..........	Missile Accident Emergency Team (AFM)
MAETS........	Medical Air Evacuation Transport Squadron [*Army World War II*]
MAEVIS.......	Micro-Aided Engineering 3D Visualisation [*Micro-Aided Engineering Ltd. and Micro-Aided Engineering Digital Microsystems Ltd.*] [*Software package*] (NCC)
MAEW..........	Moves All Extremities Well [*Medicine*] (MEDA)
MAF...........	Front Militant Autonome [*Autonomous Militant Front*] [*French*] (PD)
MAF...........	Macrophage Activating Factor [*Biochemistry*]
MAF...........	Magnetic Anisotropy Field
MAF...........	Maintenance Action Form
MAF...........	Major Academic Field
MAF...........	Manpower Authorization File
MAF...........	Manual Authority File
MAF...........	Marine Air Facility
MAF...........	Marine Amphibious Force (AABC)
MAF...........	Marriage Adjustment Form [*Psychology*]
MAF...........	Mass Air Flow [*Automotive engineering*]
MAF...........	Mass Air Flow
MAF...........	Master Address File [*US Census Bureau*]
MAF...........	Master Appraisal File [*Real estate*]
MAF...........	Master Audit File (SSD)
MAF...........	Master Facility Tool (MCD)

MAF............ Master of Arts in Finance (PGP)
MAF............ Maximum Amplitude Filter
MAF............ Medical Awareness Foundation [*Commercial firm*] (EA)
MAF............ Michoud Assembly Facility [*NASA*] (MCD)
MAF............ Midland/Odessa [*Texas*] [*Airport symbol*] (OAG)
MAF............ Million Acre Feet [*Hydrology*]
MAF............ Minimum Audible Field
MAF............ Minister of Armed Forces (NATG)
MAF............ Ministry of Agriculture and Fisheries [*British*]
MAF............ Missile Assembly Facility
MAF............ Mission Aviation Fellowship [*Indonesia*] [*ICAO designator*] (FAAC)
MAF............ Mixed Amine Fuel
MAF............ Mobile Air Force (NATG)
MAF............ Mobile Assault Ferry [*Army*]
MAF............ Moisture and Ash Free
MAF............ Morris Animal Foundation (EA)
MAF............ Movable Appendage Factor [*IOR*] [*Yacht racing*]
MAF............ Movement Aftereffect [*Optics*]
MAF............ Multiple Access Facility [*Computer science*]
MAF............ Multiple Access Forward (SSD)
MAF............ Municipal Advantage Fund [*NYSE symbol*] (SAG)
MAFA.......... Manchester Academy of Fine Arts [*British*]
MAFA.......... Middle Atlantic Fisheries Association (EA)
MAFAC........ Marine Fisheries Advisory Committee [*Department of Commerce Washington, DC*] (EGAO)
MAFAP........ Minimum Altitude over FAcility on Final Approach Course [*Aviation*] (FAAC)
MAFAS........ Marine Automated Flowcharting Analysis System
MAFAs........ Movement-Associates Fetal [*Heart rate*] Accelerations [*Obstetrics*] (DAVI)
MAFASA...... Marine Amphibious Force Air Support Airfield (MCD)
MAFB.......... MAF Bancorp [*NASDAQ symbol*] (SPSG)
MAFB.......... Malmstrom Air Force Base [*Montana*] (KSC)
MAFB.......... Mitchell Air Force Base
MAF Bcp..... MAF Bancorp, Inc. [*Associated Press*] (SAG)
MAFC.......... MAGTF [*Marine Air Ground Task Force*] All-Source Fusion Center (DOMA)
MAFC.......... Major Army Field Command (AABC)
MAFC.......... Master of Arts in Family Counseling (GAGS)
MAFC.......... Mel Anderson Fan Club [*Defunct*] (EA)
MAFC.......... Mythadventures Fan Club (EA)
MAFCA........ Model A Ford Club of America (EA)
MAFCC........ Model A Ford Cabriolet Club (EA)
Mafco........ Mafco Consolidated Group [*Associated Press*] (SAG)
MAFCO........ Magnetic Field Code
MAFD.......... Minimum Acquisition Flux Density
MAFE.......... Maintenance of Air/FMF [*Fleet Marine Force*] Expeditionary Equipment (NG)
MAFES........ Mississippi Agricultural and Forestry Experiment Station [*Mississippi State University*] [*Research center*] (RCD)
MAFF.......... Ministry of Agriculture, Fisheries, and Food [*British*]
MAFF.......... Ministry of Agriculture, Forestry and Fisheries [*Japan*] (ECON)
MAFFC........ Munsters and the Addams Family Fan Club (EA)
MAFFEX...... Marine Amphibious Force Field Exercise [*Military*] (NVT)
Maffies....... Middle-Aged Affluent Folks [*Lifestyle Classification*]
MAFFS........ Modular Airborne Fire Fighting System [*Air Force*]
MAFH.......... Macroaggregated Ferrous Hydroxide [*Medicine*] (MAE)
MA/FH........ Maintenance Actions per Flight Hour (MCD)
MAFH.......... Multicentric Angiofollicular (Lymph Node) Hyperplasia [*Oncology*]
MAFH.......... Museum of American Financial History (EA)
MAFI.......... Medic Alert Foundation International [*Also known as Medic Alert*] (EA)
MAFIA........ Marimba and Fife Inspectors Association [*Women's tongue-in-cheek organization*] [*Defunct*]
MAFIA........ Morte alla Francia Italia Anelo [*Death to the French is Italy's Cry*] [*When used in reference to the secret society often associated with organized crime, "Mafia" is from the Sicilian word for boldness or lawlessness*]
MAFIA........ Multiaccess Executive with Fast Interrupt Acceptance [*Computer science*] (MHDI)
MAFIS........ Malaysian Aquatic Sciences and Fisheries Information System [*Marine science*] (OSRA)
MAFIS........ Management Farm Information Service (PDAA)
MAFIS........ Master of Accountancy and Financial Information Systems (PGP)
MAFIS........ Mobile Automated Field Instrumentation System [*TRADOC*] (RDA)
MAFL.......... Manual of Air Force Law [*British*]
MAFL.......... Multiaperture Ferrite Logic
MAFLA........ Mississippi, Alabama, and Florida [*Oil industry*]
MAFLEX...... Marine Amphibious Force Landing Exercise [*Military*] (NVT)
MAFLIR...... Modified Advanced Forward-Looking Infrared
MAFLL........ Master of Arts in Foreign Language and Literature (PGP)
MAFMIC...... Minnesota Association of Farm Mutual Insurance Companies (SRA)
MAFOG........ Mediterranean Area Fighter Operations Grid
MAFOR....... Marine Forecast [*Pronounced "mayfor"*]
MAFP.......... Military and Air Force Police [*British military*] (DMA)
MAFPA........ Mid-America Food Processors Association (SRA)
MAFR.......... Merged Accountability and Fund Reporting [*Air Force*] (AFM)
mafr........... Missionaries of Africa (TOCD)
MAfr........... Missionaries of Africa (TOCD)
MAFR.......... Modified Anarchy Flood Routing (PDAA)
MAfr........... Society of Missionaries of Africa (EAIO)
MAFRC........ Middle Atlantic Fisheries Research Center [*National Oceanic and Atmospheric Administration*]
MAFS.......... Memoirs. American Folklore Society [*A publication*]
MAFS.......... Mexico-Albania Friendship Society (EAIO)

MAFS.......... Mobilization Air Force Specialty
MAFSC........ Mobilization Air Force Specialty Code
MAFSI........ Marketing Agents for Food Service Industry (EA)
MAFSS........ Multipoint Airfield Fuel Support System
MAFT.......... Modified-Adopted-Fernald Technique (EDAC)
MAF/TDC..... Maintenance Action Form / Technical Directives Compliance [*Military*] (DNAB)
MAFTEP...... Method for Analysis of Fleet Tactical Effectiveness Performance [*Navy*] (PDAA)
MAFV.......... Mean Ambient Flow Vector [*Geology*]
MAFVA........ Miniature Armoured Fighting Vehicle Association (EA)
MAG........... Air Margarita [*Venezuela*] [*ICAO designator*] (FAAC)
MAG........... Macrogenerator [*SEMIS*]
MAG........... Madang [*Papua New Guinea*] [*Airport symbol*] (OAG)
MAG........... Magadan [*Former USSR Seismograph station code, US Geological Survey*] (SEIS)
mag .... Magahi [*MARC language code Library of Congress*] (LCCP)
MAG........... Magazine (AFM)
MAG........... Magazine
mag .... Magazine [*Slang*] (WDMC)
mag .... Magazine (VRA)
MAG........... Magazine
MAG........... Magenta (ROG)
MAG........... Maggie Mines [*Vancouver Stock Exchange symbol*]
Mag .... [*The*] Magistrate [*London*] [*A publication*] (DLA)
Mag .... [*The*] Magistrate [*Australia A publication*] (ILCA)
Mag .... Magistrate and Municipal and Parochial Lawyer [*London*] [*A publication*] (DLA)
MAG........... Magnesium [*Chemical symbol is Mg*]
MAG........... MagneTek, Inc. [*NYSE symbol*] (SPSG)
MAG........... Magnetic (AFM)
mag .... Magnetic (WDMC)
MAG........... Magneto (KSC)
MAG........... Magnetometer [*or Magnetometry*]
MAG........... Magnetron (CET)
MAG........... Magnification
MAG........... Magnitude (AFM)
MAG........... Magnitude
MAG........... Magnum (WDAA)
MAG........... Magnus [*Large*] [*Pharmacy*]
Mag .... Magruder's Reports [*1, 2 Maryland*] [*A publication*] (DLA)
MAG........... Magyar [*Language, etc.*] (ROG)
MAG........... Main Armament Group
MAG........... Management Advisory Group [*Environmental Protection Agency*] (GFGA)
MAG........... Management Assistance Group [*Washington, DC*] (EA)
MAG........... Marine Aircraft [*or Aviation*] Group
MAG........... Marine Air Group (VNW)
MAG........... Maritime Action Group [*Non-carrier naval task group*] (DOMA)
MAG........... Maritime Air Group [*Canada*]
MAG........... Marker-Adder Generator
MAG........... Marketing Aids Group
M Ag .... Master of Agriculture
MAG........... Master of Applied Geography (PGP)
MAG........... Maximum Available Gain (IAA)
MAG........... Medical Association of Georgia (SRA)
MAG........... Military Advisory Group
MAG........... Military Airlift Group [*Air Force*]
MAG........... Minnesota Attorney General's Office, St. Paul, MN [*OCLC symbol*] (OCLC)
MAG........... Mississippi Air National Guard [*FAA designator*] (FAAC)
MAG........... Mittelassyrisches Gesetz (BJA)
MAG........... Monoammonium Glutamate [*Organic chemistry*]
MAG........... Motorcycle Action Group [*British*] (DBA)
MAG........... Myelin-Associated Glycoprotein [*Biochemistry*]
MAGA......... Medium-Accuracy Gyro Assembly
Magal......... Magal Security Systems [*Commercial firm Associated Press*] (SAG)
Magalog ..... Magazine-Catalog [*Advertising*]
MAGAMP.... Magnetic Amplifier
magamp...... Magnetic Amplifier (IDOE)
Mag & Con... Magistrate and Constable [*A publication*] (DLA)
Mag & Const... Magistrate and Constable [*A publication*] (DLA)
Mag & E Comp... Magnus and Estrin on Companies [*5th ed.*] [*1978*] [*A publication*] (DLA)
Mag & M & PL... Magistrate and Municipal and Parochial Lawyer [*A publication*] (DLA)
Mag Antiq.... Magazine Antiques [*A publication*] (BRI)
Mag Arch.... Magister Architecturae [*Master of Architecture*] [*Latin*]
MAGARLM... Military Assistance Advisory Group, Army Branch, Logistics-Medical (CINC)
MAGB......... Maltsters Association [*British*] (DBA)
MAGB......... Masectomy Association of Great Britain
MAGB......... Microfilm Association of Great Britain
Mag Bl....... Magical Blend [*A publication*]
Mag Bl....... Magical Blend [*A publication*] (BRI)
MAGBNT..... Museums and Art Galleries Board of the Northern Territory [*Australia*]
MAGBRG..... Magnetic Bearing [*Navigation*] (DNAB)
MAG BRIT... Magna Britannia [*Great Britain*] [*Latin*] (ROG)
MagC......... Magma Copper Co. [*Associated Press*] (SAG)
MAGCAP..... Magazine Capacity [*Military*]
MAGCARD.... Magnetic Card [*Electronics*] (ECII)
Mag Cas .... Bittleston, Wise, and Parnell's Magistrates' Cases [*England*] [*A publication*] (DLA)
Mag Cas ..... Magisterial Cases [*England*] [*A publication*] (DLA)

Mag Cas......	Magistrates' Cases [*Reprinted from Law Journal Reports*] [*1892-1910*] [*A publication*] (DLA)
Mag Char.....	Magna Charta [*or Carta*] [*Great Charter*] [*Latin*] [*A publication*] (DLA)
MAGCI........	Magnetic Cast Iron (IAA)
mag cit........	Magnesium Citrate [*Pharmacy*]
MAGCON......	Magnetized Concentration [*Lunar*]
MagCp........	Magnetech Corp. [*Associated Press*] (SAG)
MAGCS........	Magnetic Cast Steel (IAA)
Mag Ct........	Magistrates' Court (DLA)
MAGD.........	Magdalen College [*Oxford University*] (ROG)
MAGD.........	Magdalene College, Cambridge University [*England*] (ROG)
MAGDARR....	Magnavox Doppler and Ranging RADAR (NG)
MAgDevEc....	Master of Agricultural Development Economics (ADA)
Mag Dig......	Magrath's South Carolina Digest [*A publication*] (DLA)
Magdl.........	Magdalenian (VRA)
MAGE.........	Marine Aerosol and Gas Exchange (USDC)
MAGE.........	Marine Aerosol and Gas Exchange [*Marine science*] (OSRA)
MAGE.........	Mechanical Aerospace Ground Equipment (TEL)
M Ag Ec......	Master of Agricultural Economics
M Ag Ed......	Master of Agricultural Education
MagelPt.......	Magellan Petroleum Corp. [*Associated Press*] (SAG)
MagelRst.....	Magellan Restauraunt System [*Associated Press*] (SAG)
MAGEN........	Matrix Generating and Reporting System [*Computer science*] (PDAA)
MAGERT.......	Map and Geography Round Table [*American Library Association*]
MAGES........	Magnitude Estimation Scaling (MCD)
MAgExt........	Master of Agricultural Extension (GAGS)
MAGFET.......	Magnetic Metal-Oxide-Semiconductor Field-Effect Transistor (PDAA)
MAGG..........	Maggiore [*Major*] [*Music*]
MAGG..........	Modular Alphanumeric Graphics Generator (IEEE)
MAGGE........	Medium-Altitude Gravity Gradient Experiment
MAggF.........	Macrophage Agglutination Factor [*Biochemistry*] (MAE)
MAGGI.........	Million Ampere Generator [*British*] (DEN)
MagGp........	Magna Group, Inc. [*Associated Press*] (SAG)
MAGGS........	Modular Advanced Graphics Generation System (IEEE)
Magh..........	Maghreb (BJA)
MAGI..........	Mackenzie Art Gallery [*University of Regina*] [*Canada Research center*] (RCD)
MAGI..........	Magna Group, Inc. [*NASDAQ symbol*] (NQ)
MAGI..........	Maryland Automated Geographic Information System [*Maryland State Department of State Planning*] [*Information service or system*] (IID)
MAGI..........	Master Group Information System [*AT & T*]
MAGI..........	Mathematical Applications Group, Inc. (MCD)
MAGI..........	Military Gamma Irradiator
MAGI..........	Multiarray Gamma Irradiator
MAGIC.........	Machine-Aided Graphics for Illustration and Composition [*Bell Telephone*]
MAGIC.........	Machine for Automatic Graphics Interface to a Computer
MAGIC.........	Madison Avenue General Ideas Committee [*New York City*]
MAGIC.........	Magnetic and Germanium Integer Calculator (DEN)
MAGIC.........	Magnetic Immunochemistry [*Laboratory analysis*]
MAGIC.........	Manual Assisted Gaming of Integrated Combat (PDAA)
MAGIC.........	Marine Corps Air-Ground Intelligence Center (MCD)
MAGIC.........	Market Analysis Guide - Intercity Communications [*AT & T*]
MAGIC.........	Marketing and Advertising General Information Centre [*Datasolve Ltd.*] [*British Information service or system*]
MAGIC.........	Matrix Algebra General Interpretive Coding (IEEE)
MAGIC.........	Method for Asynchronous Graphics Integral Control [*Computer science*] (PDAA)
MAGIC.........	Michigan Automatic General Integrated Computation (MCD)
MAGIC.........	Microprobe Analysis Generalized Intensity Corrections
MAGIC.........	Microprocessor Application of Graphic with Interactive Communication
MAGIC.........	Modern Analytical Generator of Improved Circuits [*Computer science*]
MAGIC.........	Modified Action Generated Input Control
MAGIC.........	Modular Area Graphics Illustrations Composition (DGA)
MAGIC.........	Monodisperse Aerosol Generation Interface [*Physics*]
MAGIC.........	Motorola Automatically Generated Integrated Circuits
MAGIC.........	Mozambique, Angola, and Guine Information Center [*British*]
MAGIC.........	Multipurpose and Generalized Interface to COBOL [*Computer science*]
MAGICS.......	Multiphase Model for Air, Groundwater, Immiscible Contaminant and Solute Transport [*Computer program for testing water flow*]
MAGID........	Magnetic Intrusion Detector (NVT)
MAGIE........	Midwest Agri Industries Expo [*Illinois Fertilizer and Chemical Association*] (TSPED)
MAGIIC.......	Mobile Army Ground Imagery Interpretation Center (MCD)
Mag Ins......	Magen on Insurance [*A publication*] (DLA)
MAGIS........	Magistrate
MAGIS........	Marine Air Ground Intelligence System
MAGIS........	Megawatt Air-to-Ground Illumination System (MCD)
MAGIS........	Municipal Automated Geographic Information System [*District of Columbia Office of the Mayor*] [*Information service or system*] (IID)
Magis & Const (PA)...	Magistrate and Constable [*Pennsylvania*] [*A publication*] (DLA)
Magis Ct......	Magistrates' Court (DLA)
MAGL..........	Magna-Lab, Inc. [*NASDAQ symbol*] (SAG)
MAGL..........	Material Acquisition Guidance Letter (MCD)
MAGLA........	Magna-Lab 'A' [*NASDAQ symbol*] (TTSB)
MAGLAD.......	Marksmanship and Gunnery LASER Device (RDA)
MAGLATCH...	Magnetic Latch (MUGU)
MAG-LEV.....	Magnetically-Levitated [*High-speed ground transportation*]
MAGLL........	Magna-Lab Wrrt 'E' [*NASDAQ symbol*] (TTSB)
MAGLOC......	Magnetic Logic Computer

MAGLU........	Magna-Lab Unit [*NASDAQ symbol*] (TTSB)
MAGLW........	Magna-Lab Wrrt 'A' [*NASDAQ symbol*] (TTSB)
MAGLZ........	Magna-Lab Wrrt 'B' [*NASDAQ symbol*] (TTSB)
Magmc	Magma Copper Co. [*Associated Press*] (SAG)
Mag (MD).....	Magruder's Reports [*1, 2 Maryland*] [*A publication*] (DLA)
MAGMOD......	Magnetic Modulator
Mag Mor......	Magna Moralia [*of Aristotle*] [*Classical studies*] (OCD)
Mag Mun Par Law...	Magistrate and Municipal and Parochial Lawyer [*A publication*] (DLA)
MAGN.........	Magainin Pharmaceuticals [*NASDAQ symbol*] (SPSG)
MAGN.........	Magnetic (ROG)
MAGN.........	Magnetron [*Electricity*]
MAGN.........	Magnus [*Great*] [*Latin*] (ADA)
MAGN.........	Monoaminoguanidine Nitrate [*Organic chemistry*]
Magna	Magna-Lab, Inc. [*Associated Press*] (SAG)
MagnaBb	Magna Bancorp [*Associated Press*] (SAG)
Magnal........	Magna International, Inc. [*Associated Press*] (SAG)
MagnaL.......	Magna-Lab, Inc. [*Associated Press*] (SAG)
Magna Rot Pip...	Magnus Rotulus Pipae [*Great Roll of the Pipe*] [*Latin A publication*] (DLA)
MAGNA-SID...	Magnetic Sensing Intrusion Device [*Remote sensor*] [*Also, M-SID*] [*Military*] (VNW)
MAGNETTOR...	Magnetic Modulator (SAA)
magnif........	Magnification
MAGNOX.......	Magnesium Oxide [*Magnesium-based alloy*]
MagnPet.......	Magnum Petroleum [*Associated Press*] (SAG)
magns	Magnesium (VRA)
MAGNT........	Museums and Art Galleries of the Northern Territory [*Australia*]
Magntk	Magnatek, Inc. [*Associated Press*] (SAG)
MAGOX........	Magnesium Oxide [*Acronym is trademark of Basic Chemicals*]
MagP...........	Magnum Petroleum [*Associated Press*] (SAG)
MAGP..........	Master of Arts in Gerontological Psychology (PGP)
MAGP..........	Microfibrillar-Associated Glycoprotein [*Biochemistry*]
MAGp..........	Military Airlift Group [*Air Force*] (AFM)
MagPet........	Magnum Petroleum [*Associated Press*] (SAG)
Mag Pharm...	Magister Pharmaciae [*Master of Pharmacy*] [*Latin*]
Mag Phil......	Magister Philosophiae [*Master of Philosophy*] [*Latin*]
Mag Phil Fac Theol...	Magister Philosophiae Facultatis Theologicae [*Latin*]
MagPhr........	Magainin Pharmaceuticals [*Associated Press*] (SAG)
MAGPIE	Machine Automatically Generating Production Inventory Evaluation [*Computer science*] (IEEE)
MAGPIE	Magazine Page Interactive Editor (DGA)
MAGPIE	Markov Game Planar Intercept-Evasion Package [*Computer science*]
MAGPIE	Mega-Ampere Generator for Plasma Implosion Experiments [*Astrophysics*] (ECON)
MagPt	Magnum Petroleum [*Associated Press*] (SAG)
M Agr	Master of Agriculture
MAgrDevEc...	Master of Agricultural Development Economics
M Agr E	Master of Agricultural Engineering
MAgrEc........	Master of Agricultural Economics
M Agr Eng ...	Master of Agricultural Engineering
Mag Rer Nat...	Magister Rerum Naturalium [*Latin*]
Mag Rer Soc Oec...	Magister Rerum Socialium Oeconomicarumque [*Latin*]
M Agric........	Master of Agriculture
MAGROCV	Military Advisory Group, Government of the Republic of China, Vietnam
Mag Rot	Magnus Rotulus [*Great Roll of the Exchequer*] [*Latin A publication*] (DLA)
M Agr S	Master of Agricultural Science
M Agr Sc	Master of Agricultural Science
MAgrSci.......	Master of Agricultural Science
MAgrSt........	Master of Agricultural Studies (ADA)
Magruder.....	Magruder's Reports [*1, 2 Maryland*] [*A publication*] (DLA)
MAGS	Magal Security Systems [*NASDAQ symbol*] (SAG)
MAGS	Magistrates (ROG)
MAGS	Multiple Aminoglycosides [*Antibacterial agents*]
MAGSAT	Magnetic Field Satellite [*NASA*] (MCD)
MAGSAT	Magnetometer Satellite (NASA)
MAgSc	Master of Agricultural Science (ADA)
MAgSci	Master of Agricultural Science
MAGSF	Magal Security Systems Ltd [*NASDAQ symbol*] (TTSB)
MagSft........	Magic Software Enterprises [*Associated Press*] (SAG)
MAGSI	Minimum Altitude at Glide Slope Intersection Inbound [*Aviation*] (FAAC)
MAGSIM	Magnetic Shield Simulator (PDAA)
MAgSt.........	Master of Agricultural Studies
MAGSTR	Magistrate
mag sulf	Magnesium Sulfate [*Pharmacology*] (DAVI)
MAGTAF	Marine Air-Ground Task Force (AFM)
MAGTC	Magnetic Tape Controller (NITA)
MagTch........	Magnetics Technology [*Associated Press*] (SAG)
MAGTD	Magnitude
MAGTF........	Marine Air-Ground Task Force (NVT)
Mag Theol....	Magister Theologiae [*Master of Theology*] [*Latin*]
MAG-THOR...	Magnesium-Thorium [*Inorganic chemistry*]
MAGTOP......	Management of Traffic Operations [*Federal Highway Administration*]
MAGTRAC....	Magnetic Tracker (MUGU)
MAGW........	Maximum Alternate Gross Weight
Magy..........	Magyar Muza [*Record label*] [*Hungary*]
Magz..........	Magazine
MAH...........	Collection des Tablettes Cuneiformes du Musee d'Art et d'Histoire de Geneve (BJA)
MAH...........	Findlay, OH [*Location identifier FAA*] (FAAL)
MAH...........	Hampshire College, Amherst, MA [*Library symbol Library of Congress*] (LCLS)

MAH............	Hanna [*M. A.*] Co. [*NYSE symbol*] (SPSG)
MAH............	Magnesium Aspartate Hydrochloride [*Antihypertensive*]
MAH............	Mahableshwar [*India*] [*Seismograph station code, US Geological Survey Closed*] (SEIS)
MAH............	Mahogany (MSA)
mah	Mahogany (VRA)
MAH............	Mahommedanism (ROG)
MAH............	Mahon [*Spain*] [*Airport symbol*] (OAG)
MAH............	Maleic Anhydride [*Also, MA*] [*Organic chemistry*]
MAH............	Malev-Hungarian Airlines [*ICAO designator*] (FAAC)
MAH............	Malignancy-Associated Hypercalcemia [*Oncology*]
MAH............	Massachusetts Historical Society, Boston, MA [*OCLC symbol*] (OCLC)
MAH............	Master of Arts in Humanities (GAGS)
mAH............	Milliampere Hour
MAH............	Mothers at Home [*An association*] (PAZ)
MAHA	Metropolitan Association of Handwriting Analysts (EA)
MAHA	Microangiopathic Hemolytic Anemia [*Medicine*]
Mah & DRT...	Mahaffy and Dodson's Road Traffic [*3rd ed.*] [*1961*] [*A publication*] (DLA)
Maharashtra LJ...	Maharashtra Law Journal [*India*] [*A publication*] (DLA)
Mahaska......	Mahaska Investment Co. [*Associated Press*] (SAG)
MAHC	Maximum Allowable Housing Cost [*Army*] (AABC)
MAHCD........	Master of Applied Human and Community Development (PGP)
MAHE	Master of Arts in Hebrew Education (BJA)
MAHE	Master of Arts in Human Ecology (GAGS)
MAHE&FE.....	Master of Arts in Home Economics and Family Ecology (GAGS)
MAHEFE	Master of Arts in Home Economics and Family Ecology (PGP)
MAHH	Malignancy-Associated Humoral Hypercalcemia [*Medicine*] (DMAA)
MAHi	Amherst Historical Society, Amherst, MA [*Library symbol Library of Congress*] (LCLS)
MAHI	Monarch Avalon [*NASDAQ symbol*] (TTSB)
MAHI	Monarch Avalon, Inc. [*NASDAQ symbol*] (NQ)
MAHL	Master of Arts in Hebrew Letters (PGP)
MAHL	Master of Hebrew Literature (BJA)
Mah LJ	Maharashtra Law Journal [*India*] [*A publication*] (DLA)
MAHMA	Midwest Assisted Housing Management Association (SRA)
MAHMO	Maryland Association of Health Maintenance Organizations (SRA)
MAHOC	Manual for Administration of the Hands-On Component (MCD)
MAHOG.......	Mahogany (DSUE)
MA(Hons)	Master of Arts with Honours (ADA)
MAHP	Member of the Association of Hypnotists and Physiotherapists [*British*]
MAHRM	Master of Arts in Human Resource Management (GAGS)
MAHS	Master of Human Services (GAGS)
MAHSM	Master of Arts in Human Service Management (GAGS)
MAHT.........	Master of Arts in History Teaching (PGP)
MAI............	Air Moravia [*Czechoslovakia*] [*ICAO designator*] (FAAC)
MAI............	Machine-Aided Index (NITA)
MAI............	Machine-Aided Indexing (KSC)
MAI............	Magister in Arte Ingeniaria [*Master of Engineering*]
Mai	Maine's Reports [*A publication*] (DLA)
mai	Maithili [*MARC language code Library of Congress*] (LCCP)
MAI............	Maius [*May*] [*Latin*]
MAI............	Maizuru [*Japan*] [*Seismograph station code, US Geological Survey Closed*] (SEIS)
MAI............	Mantle Arm Index
MAI............	Mapper Application Interface [*Computer science*]
MAI............	Marianna [*Florida*] [*Airport symbol*] (AD)
MAI............	Marianna, FL [*Location identifier FAA*] (FAAL)
MAI............	Marriage Adjustment Inventory [*Psychology*]
MAI............	Master of Fine Arts International [*British*]
MAI............	Material Annex Item [*Military*]
MAI............	Maximum Allowable Increase [*Environmental Protection Agency*]
MAI............	Mean Annual Increment
MAI............	Media Associates International [*An association*] (EA)
MAI............	Medical Aid for Indochina [*An association*] (EA)
MAI............	Medical Aid for Iraq
MAI............	Member, Appraisal Institute [*American Institute of Real Estate Appraisers of the National Association of Realtors*] [*Designation awarded by*]
MAI............	Member of the Anthropological Institute [*British*]
MAI............	Metropolitan Action Institute [*Formerly, SAI*] (EA)
MAI............	Micanite and Insulators (IAA)
MAI............	Military Assistance Institute [*Air Force*]
MAI............	Minimum Annual Income (WDAA)
MAI............	Ministerium fuer Aussenhandel und Innerdeutschen Handel [*Ministry for Foreign Trade and Domestic German Trade*] [*See also MfAl*]
MAI............	Monash Asia Institute [*Monash University*] [*Australia*]
MAI............	Multiple Access Interface
MAI............	Multiple Address Instruction
MAI............	Music Association of Ireland (DBA)
MAI............	Mycobacterium Avium-Intracellulare [*Medicine*]
MAIA	Magnetic Antibody Immunoassay
MAIA	Master of Arts in Industrial Arts (PGP)
MAIA	Master of Arts in International Affairs (GAGS)
MAIA	Member of the American Institute of Appraisers
MAIAA	Member of the American Institute of Aeronautics and Astronautics [*Formerly, MIAS*]
MAIADA	Massachusetts Independent Auto Dealers Association (SRA)
Mai Anc L....	Maine's Ancient Law [*A publication*] (DLA)
MAIB..........	Motor Accidents Insurance Board [*Tasmania, Australia*]
MAIBC	Member of the Architectural Institute of British Columbia [*Canada*] (DD)
MAIBL.........	Midland & International Banks Ltd. [*British*]

MAIC...........	MAIC Holdings [*NASDAQ symbol*] (TTSB)
MAIC...........	MAIC Holdings, Inc. [*NASDAQ symbol*] (SAG)
MAIC...........	Maine Aquaculture Innovation Center [*University of Maine*] [*Research center*] (RCD)
MAIC...........	Major Analytical Instrumentation Center [*University of Florida*] [*Research center*] (RCD)
MAIC...........	Michigan Association of Insurance Companies (SRA)
MAIC...........	Mid-America International Agricultural Consortium
MAICE.........	Member of the American Institute of Consulting Engineers
MAIChE	Member of the American Institute of Chemical Engineers
MAIC Hld.....	MAIC Holdings, Inc. [*Associated Press*] (SAG)
MAICS	Master of Arts in Intercultural Studies (PGP)
MAICYA	Major Authors and Illustrators for Children and Young Adults [*A publication*]
MAID	Magnetic Anti-Intrusion Detector (PDAA)
MAID	Maidstone [*Municipal borough in England*]
MAID	Maintenance Automatic Integration Director [*Computer science*]
MAID	Manual Intervention and Display
MAID	Market Analysis and Information Database [*MAID Systems Ltd.*] [*British Information service or system*] (IID)
MAID	Master Area Interest Decks (MCD)
MAID	Master of Arts in Interior Design (GAGS)
MAID	Master of Arts in International Diplomacy (GAGS)
MAID	Merger Acquisition Improved Decision [*Computer science*]
MAID	Monroe Automatic Internal Diagnosis [*Computer science*]
MAID	Multiple Aircraft Identification Display (PDAA)
MAIDA	Multi-Attribute Identification and Analysis Program [*Jointly developed by Georgia Tech Research Institute and the US Air Force*]
MAID/MILES...	Magnetic Anti-Intrusion Detector/Magnetic Intrusion Line Sensor (MCD)
MAIDS	Machine-Aided Information and Dissemination Systems
MAIDS	Management Automated Information Display System (KSC)
MAIDS	Multipurpose Automatic Inspection and Diagnostic Systems [*Army*]
MAIDS	Murine-Acquired Immunodeficiency Syndrome [*Animal pathology*]
MAIDY	M.A.I.D. ADS [*NASDAQ symbol*] (TTSB)
MAIE	Member of the British Association of Industrial Editors (DBQ)
MAIEE	Member of the American Institute of Electrical Engineers
MAIF	Major Analytical Instruments Facility [*Case Western Reserve University*] [*Research center*] (RCD)
MAIIC.........	Master of Arts in International Communications (PGP)
Mai Inst......	Maine's History of Institutions [*A publication*] (DLA)
MAIL	Mail Boxes Etc. [*NASDAQ symbol*] (NQ)
MAIL	MILES [*Multiple Integrated LASER Engagement System*] Action Item Log [*Army*]
MailBx	Mail Boxes Etc. [*Associated Press*] (SAG)
MAILS	Materiel Acquisition and Integrated Logistics Support
MAILS	Mid-America Interlibrary Services [*Library network*]
MAILS	Mississippi Automated Interlibrary Loan System [*Mississippi State Library Commission*] [*Information service or system*] (IID)
MailWell.....	Mail-Well, Inc. [*Associated Press*] (SAG)
Maim	Moses Maimonides [*Spanish Talmudist, 1135-1204*] (BJA)
MAIME........	Member of the American Institute of Mining and Metallurgical Engineers
MAIN	Main St. & Main [*NASDAQ symbol*] (TTSB)
MAIN	Main St. & Main, Inc. [*NASDAQ symbol*] (SAG)
MAIN	Maintenance (NASA)
MAIN	Maintenance
MAIN	Material Automated Information System
MAIN	Material Automated Inventory Network (MCD)
MAIN	Medical Automation Intelligence [*System*]
MAIN	Mid-America Interconnected Network [*Regional power council*]
MAIN	Midwest Alliance in Nursing (SRA)
MAIN	Military Authorization Identification Number
MAIN	Multiple Access Internal Network [*Computer science*]
MA in Comm...	Master of Arts in Communications
MAIND........	Master of Arts in Interior Design (PGP)
MainDta.......	Mainstream Data, Inc. [*Associated Press*] (SAG)
Maine	Maine Reports [*A publication*] (DLA)
Maine Anc Law...	Maine's Ancient Law [*A publication*] (DLA)
Maine PUR...	Maine Public Utilities Commission Reports [*A publication*] (DLA)
Maine R	Maine Reports [*A publication*] (DLA)
Maine Rep...	Maine Reports [*A publication*] (DLA)
Mainlobe	Major Investigation for Low-Frequency Ocean Bottom Loss Experiments [*Marine science*] (MSC)
MAINS	Marine-Aided Inertial Navigation System (PDAA)
MAINSITE	Modular Automated Integrated Systems / Interoperability Test and Evaluation (PDAA)
MainSt........	Main St. & Main, Inc. [*Associated Press*] (SAG)
MainStB......	Main Street BankGroup, Inc. [*Associated Press*] (SAG)
MAINT	Maintenance (AFM)
MA/INT	Maintenance Actions per Interval (MCD)
MAINTBN	Maintenance Battalion (DNAB)
MAINTCE	Maintenance (ROG)
maintd	Maintained
MAINTN	Maintenance [*Automotive advertising*]
MAINTNCE ..	Maintenance [*Freight*]
MAINTRAIN...	Maintenance and Training [*in complex equipment*]
MAINTSUPOFC...	Maintenance Supply Office (DNAB)
MAINTSUPP...	Maintenance and Support (DNAB)
MAINTSUPPOFF...	Maintenance Support Office [*Navy*]
MA in Urb Pl...	Master of Arts in Urban Planning
MAIO	Mashhad [*Iran*] [*Seismograph station code, US Geological Survey*] (SEIS)
MAIP..........	Matrix Algebra Interpretive Program (IEEE)
MAIPP.........	Mid-Atlantic Independent Power Producers (SRA)

MAIR	Manufacturing and Inspection Record (KSC)
MAIR	Manufacturing and Inspection Record
MAIR	Master of Arts in Industrial Relations
MAIR	Master of Arts in International Relations (GAGS)
MAIR	Mesaba Holdings [NASDAQ symbol] (TTSB)
MAIR	Mesaba Holdings, Inc. [NASDAQ symbol] (SAG)
MAIR	Modular Airborne Intercept RADAR (IAA)
MAIR	Molecular Airborne Intercept RADAR
MAIREASTLANT...	Maritime Air, Eastern Atlantic (DNAB)
MAIRMAR...	Marine Air Depot, Miramar [California]
MAIRMED...	Maritime Air Forces Mediterranean [NATO] (DNAB)
MAIRS	Military Air Integrated Reporting System (MCD)
MAIRU	Mobile Aircraft Instrument Repair Unit
MAIS	Maintenance Information System [Military] (NVT)
MAIS	Management Audit Information System
MAIS	Master of Accounting Information Systems (PGP)
MAIS	Master of Arts in Interdisciplinary Studies (GAGS)
MAIS	Master of Arts in International Studies (GAGS)
MAIS	Mechanical Aids for the Individual Soldier [Army]
MAIS	Mediterranean Association of International Schools (EA)
MAIS	Microfilm Alpha Index System
MAIS	Minnesota Adaptive Instructional System (EDAC)
MAIS	Mobile Automated Instrumentation Suite (DWSG)
MAIS	Mycobacterium Avium-Intracellulare-Scrofulaceum [Bacteriology]
MAISA	Middle Atlantic Intercollegiate Sailing Association
MAISA	Multiple Analytical Isoelectrofocusing Scanning Apparatus
MAISARC....	Major Automated Information System Review Council [Army]
MAISRC	Major Automated Information Systems Review Council [Army]
MAI Sy	MAI Systems Corp. [Associated Press] (SAG)
MAI Sys....	MAI Systems Corp. [Associated Press] (SAG)
MAIT	Maintenance Assistance and Instruction Team [Army] (AABC)
Mait	Maitland's Select Pleas of the Crown [A publication] (DLA)
MAIT	Matrix Analysis of Insider Threat [Nuclear energy] (NRCH)
MAIT	Methotrexate and Cytosine Arabinoside [Antineoplastic drug regimen] (DAVI)
MAIT	Minimum Autoignition Temperature
MAITA	Marine and Allied Industries Training Association (AIE)
Mait GI	Maitland's Pleas of the Crown, County of Gloucester [A publication] (DLA)
Maitland	Maitland's Manuscript Session Cases [Scotland] [A publication] (DLA)
Maitland	Maitland's Pleas of the Crown [1221] [England] [A publication] (DLA)
Maitland	Maitland's Select Pleas of the Crown [A publication] (DLA)
MAIWO	Member of the Austrlaian Institute of Welfare Officers
MAJ	Jones Library, Amherst, MA [Library symbol Library of Congress] (LCLS)
MAJ	Majestic Airlines, Inc. [ICAO designator] (FAAC)
MAJ	Majestic Electronic Stores, Inc. [Toronto Stock Exchange symbol]
MAJ	Majolica [Ceramics] (ROG)
maj	Majolica (VRA)
MAJ	Major [Military] (AABC)
MAJ	Majority (KSC)
MAJ	Majuro [Marshall Islands] [Airport symbol] (OAG)
MAJ	Maron [Java] [Seismograph station code, US Geological Survey Closed] (SEIS)
MAJ	Master of Arts in Journalism (GAGS)
MAJ	Michael Anthony Jewelers [AMEX symbol] (TTSB)
MAJ	Michael Anthony Jewelers, Inc. [AMEX symbol] (SPSG)
MAJ	Model Air Jet
MAJAC	Maintenance Antijam Console [Air Force]
MAJC	Master of Arts in Journalism and Communication (PGP)
MAJC	Mount Aloysius Junior College [Pennsylvania]
MAJC	Mutual Association of Journeymen Coopers [A union] [British]
MAJCOM....	Major Command [Formerly, Major Air Command] [Military]
MAJCON	Major Air Command Controlled [Units]
MAJCS	Master of Arts in Jewish Communal Service (BJA)
MAJCSSW ...	Master of Arts in Jewish Communal Studies and Social Work (BJA)
MAJE	Master of Arts in Jewish Education (BJA)
MAJ Ed	Master of Arts in Jewish Education (PGP)
MAJ GEN	Major General (AFM)
MAJI	Magestic Agency for Joint Intelligence
MAJI	Majority Agency for Joint Intelligence
MAJIC	Maji Controlled [A security classification]
MAJO	Matsushiro [Japan] [Seismograph station code, US Geological Survey] (SEIS)
MAJR	Major Realty [NASDAQ symbol] (TTSB)
MAJR	Major Realty Corp. [NASDAQ symbol] (SAG)
MajRty	Major Realty Corp. [Associated Press] (SAG)
MAJS	Master of Arts in Jewish Studies (PGP)
MAJS	Master of Arts in Judaic Studies (BJA)
MAJSR	Major State Register (MHDB)
MAJY	Majority (ROG)
MAK	Makedonski Aviotrnasport-Macedonian Airline [FAA designator] (FAAC)
MAK	Makhachkala [Former USSR Seismograph station code, US Geological Survey] (SEIS)
MAK	Making
MAK	Makkoth (BJA)
MAK	Malakal [Sudan] [Airport symbol] (OAG)
MAK	Maliair Ltd. [British ICAO designator] (FAAC)
MAK	Manual Abell-Kendall [Clinical chemistry]
mAk	Maritime Arctic [Cold Air] [Meteorology] (BARN)
MAK	Markway Resources Ltd. [Vancouver Stock Exchange symbol]
MAK	Medical Accessories Kit [Apollo] [NASA]
MAK	Methyl Amyl Ketone [Organic chemistry]

MAK	Methylated Albumin Kieselguhr [Chromatography]
MAK	Monopulse Antenna Kit
MAKA	Major Karyotypic Abnormalities [Medicine]
MAKETRANS...	Make Necessary Transfer [Military] (DNAB)
Makhsh	Makhshirin (BJA)
MAKHU	Moskovsky Akademichesky Khoreografichesky Uchilishche
Makita	Makita Corp. [Associated Press] (SAG)
MAKL	Markel Corp. [NASDAQ symbol] (NQ)
makm	Makimono (VRA)
MAKO	Mako Marine International, Inc. [NASDAQ symbol] (SAG)
MAKo	Mako Marine Intl. [NASDAQ symbol] (TTSB)
MakoM	Mako Marine International, Inc. [Associated Press] (SAG)
MAKOU	Mako Marine Intl. 'Unit' [NASDAQ symbol] (TTSB)
MAKRO	Management Analysis of Key Resource Operations [Military]
Maks	Makhshirin (BJA)
MAKS	Multipurpose Aero-Space Plane [Russian delta-wing orbiter]
Maksh	Makhshirin (BJA)
MAKSUTSUB...	Make Suitable Substitution
MAL	Macroassembly Language [Computer science] (BUR)
MAL	Mad Art Lover
MAL	Magnetic Armature Loudspeaker
MAL	Maintain at Least (Altitude) [Aviation] (FAAC)
Mal	Malachi [Old Testament book]
MAL	Malachias [Old testament book] [Douay version]
MAL	Malaga [Spain] [Seismograph station code, US Geological Survey] (SEIS)
MAL	Malan Realty Investors [NYSE symbol] (SAG)
MAL	Malariology Technician [Navy]
MAL	Malaspina College Learning Resources Centre [UTLAS symbol]
MAL	Malate
MAL	Malay (WDAA)
mal	Malayalam [MARC language code Library of Congress] (LCCP)
MAL	Malayan (AABC)
MAL	Malayan Airways Ltd.
MAL	Malaysia (WDAA)
MAL	Malaysian Air Lines
Mal	Maleyl [Biochemistry]
MAL	Malfunction (KSC)
MAL	Malfunction
MAL	Malicious [FBI standardized term]
MAL	Malleable (MSA)
mal	Malonate [Organic chemistry]
MAL	Malone [New York] [Airport symbol] (AD)
MAL	Malone College, Canton, OH [OCLC symbol] (OCLC)
MAL	Malone, NY [Location identifier FAA] (FAAL)
MAL	Malta (WDAA)
mal	Malum [III] [Latin] (MAE)
MAL	Man and LASER (MCD)
MAL	Marco Resources [Vancouver Stock Exchange symbol]
MAL	Master Authorization List
MAL	Materiel Allowance List [Military]
MAL	Maximal Acceptable Load (PDAA)
MAL	McAlpine Aviation Ltd. [British ICAO designator] (FAAC)
MAL	Medullary Thick Ascending Limb [Anatomy]
MAL	Memory Access Logic
MAL	Mercury Arc Lamp
MAL	Meta Assembly Language
MAL	Methacrolein [Also, MACR] [Organic chemistry]
MAL	Midaxillary Line [Medicine]
MAL	Middle Assyrian Laws (BJA)
MAL	Mobile Airlock (MCD)
MAL	Modern American Law [A publication] (DLA)
MAL	Multiairline [Type of British pole line construction]
MAL	Multiple Address Letter (NOAA)
MALA	Malarial Parasites [Infectious diseases Laboratory and respiratory] (DAVI)
MALA	Manpower and Logistics Analysis (MCD)
MALA	Master of Arts in Liberal Arts (PGP)
MALA	Master of Arts in Liturgical Arts (PGP)
MAL-AAACE...	Media and Adult Learning Section of the American Association for Adult and Continuing Education (EA)
MALAC	Malacology
MALAD	Maladjusted Child [Social Work] [British] (DSUE)
MALAGOC...	Mutual Assistance of the Latin American Government Oil Companies G2 [See also ARPEL] (EA)
Malag Rep...	Malagasy Republic
MalanR	Malan Realty Investors [Associated Press] (SAG)
MALAR	Malaria [Infectious diseases] (DAVI)
MALAS	Master of Arts in Latin American Studies (PGP)
MALAS	Midwestern Association for Latin American Studies
Malay	Malaysia (VRA)
Malaysa	Malaysia Fund, Inc. [Associated Press] (SAG)
Mal-BSA	Maleated Bovine Serum Albumin [Medicine] (DMAA)
MALC	Madison Area Library Council [Library network]
MALC	Management of Acquisition Logistics Course (AAGC)
MALCAP	Maryland Academic Library Center for Automated Processing (NITA)
MALCAP	Maryland Library Center for Automated Processing [Library network]
MALCD	Matrix-Addressed Liquid Crystal Display
MALCM	Mercantile Adjuster and the Lawyer and Credit Man [A publication] (DLA)
Malcolm Ethics...	Malcolm's Legal and Judicial Ethics [A publication] (DLA)
MALCS	Mujeres Activas en Letras y Cambio Social (EA)
MALD	Master of Arts in Law and Diplomacy
MALD	Master of Arts in Law and Diplomacy (GAGS)

MA(LD) .... Master of Arts (Landscape Design), University of Manchester [*British*] (DBQ)
MALD .... Modular Analysis of Learning Difficulties (OICC)
MALDEF .... Mexican American Legal Defense and Educational Fund (EA)
MALDI .... Matrix-Assisted LASER Desorption Ionization [*Spectroscopy*]
Mald Isls ..... Maldive Islands
MALDMS ..... Matrix-Assisted LASER Desorption Mass Spectrometry
MALDT .... Mean Administrative and Logistics Downtime [*Quality control*] (MCD)
MALE .... Multiaperture Logic Element
MALER .... Master of Arts in Labor and Employment Relations (PGP)
Malerei u Zeichn... Malerei und Zeichnung [*A publication*] (OCD)
MALF .... Malfunction (KSC)
MALF .... Mobile Aerobee Launch Facility
MALI .... Material Annex Line Item [*Military*]
MALI .... Matrix-Assisted Laser Ionizaion [*Spectrometry*]
MALI .... Michigan Accident Location Index [*Michigan State Police*] [*Information service or system*] (IID)
MALIB .... Math Analysis Library (MCD)
MA(LibSc) ... Master of Arts (Library Science)
malig .... Malignant [*Medicine*]
MALIMET ..... Master List of Medical Indexing Terms
Malinc .... Mallinckrodt Group [*Formerly, IMCERA Group*] [*Associated Press*] (SAG)
Malinckr ...... Mallinckrodt Group [*Formerly, IMCERA Group*] [*Associated Press*] (SAG)
MALIPR .... Material Annex Line Item Progress Report [*Military*] (NG)
MALIS .... Master of Arts in Library and Information Science (PGP)
MALL .... Creative Computers [*NASDAQ symbol*] (TTSB)
MALL .... Creative Computers, Inc. [*NASDAQ symbol*] (SAG)
MALL .... Mall [*Postal Service standard*] (OPSA)
MALL .... Malleable (KSC)
MALL .... Malleable
MALL .... Master of Arts in Liberal Learning (PGP)
MALL .... Minnesota Association of Law Libraries [*Library network*]
MALLAR ..... Manned Lunar Landing and Return [*NASA*]
Mal Law M... Malynes' Ancient Law Merchant [*A publication*] (DLA)
Mall Ent...... Mallory's Modern Entries [*A publication*] (DLA)
Mal Lex Merc... Malynes' Lex Mercatoria [*3 eds.*] [*1622-36*] [*A publication*] (DLA)
Mallon .... Mallon Resources Corp. [*Associated Press*] (SAG)
Mallory .... Mallory's Irish Chancery Reports [*A publication*] (DLA)
Mal L Rev ... Malaya Law Review [*A publication*] (DLA)
MALLS .... Multiangle LASER Light-Scattering [*Instrumentation*]
MALM .... Maryknoll Associate Lay Missioners (EA)
MALMARC ... Malaysian MARC (NITA)
MAL MISCH... Malicious Mischief [*Legal term*] (DLA)
MALN .... Minimum Air Low Noise (PDAA)
MALN .... Mouvement Africain de Liberation Nationale [*African Movement for National Liberation*]
MALODES .... Modern Army Logistics Data Exchange System
MALOF .... Minimum Accepted Level of Fill [*Military*]
Malone .... Editor, 6, 9, and 10, Heiskell's Tennessee Reports [*A publication*] (DLA)
MALOR .... Mortar and Artillery Location RADAR (RDA)
MALOS .... Maintenance and Logistics Space [*System*]
MALP .... Major Assembly Labor and Performance (MCD)
MALPAS ...... Malvern Program Analysis System (NITA)
MAL PROS... Malicious Prosecution [*Legal term*] (DLA)
MALR .... Mortar/Artillery Locating RADAR (PDAA)
MALS .... Master of Arts in Liberal Studies
MALS .... Master of Arts in Library Science
MALS .... Master of Arts in Library Service (NADA)
MALS .... Medium-Intensity Approach Lighting System [*Aviation*]
MALS .... Members of an Amalgamated Society [*Slang British*] (DSUE)
MALSCE .... Massachusetts Association of Land Surveyors and Civil Engineers (SRA)
MALSF .... Medium-Intensity Approach Lighting System with Sequenced Flashers [*Aviation*]
MALSF .... Medium Intensity Approach Light System with Sequenced Flashing Lights [*FAA*] (TAG)
MALSR :....... Medium-Intensity Approach Lighting System with Runway Alignment Indicator Lights [*Aviation*]
MALSR .... Medium Intensity Approach Light System with Rail [*FAA*] (TAG)
MALS/RAIL... Minimum-Approach Lighting System with Runway Alignment Indicator Lights [*Aviation*] (DNAB)
MALT .... Lion Brewery [*NASDAQ symbol*] (TTSB)
MALT .... Lion Brewery, Inc. (The) [*NASDAQ symbol*] (SAG)
MALT .... Macosa-Associated Lymphoid Tissue [*Medicine*]
MALT .... Male, Altered Animal (DMAA)
MALT .... Maltese (DSUE)
MALT .... Master of Arts in Language Teaching (GAGS)
MALT .... Military Adviser's Language Text
MALT .... Military Assistance Language Training
MALT .... Mnemonic Assembly Language Translator [*Computer science*] (IEEE)
MALT .... Monetary Allowance in Lieu of Transportation [*DoD*]
MALT .... Mucosa-Associated Lymphoid Tissue [*Anatomy*]
MALTA .... Middle Atlantic Lawn Tennis Association
Malt CM ...... Maltby on Courts-Martial [*A publication*] (DLA)
MALU .... Maine Association of Life Underwriters (SRA)
MALU .... Massachusetts Association of Life Underwriters (SRA)
MALU .... Michigan Association of Life Underwriters (SRA)
MALU .... Minnesota State Association of Life Underwriters (SRA)
MALU .... Mississippi Association of Life Underwriters (SRA)
MALU .... Missouri Association of Life Underwriters (SRA)
MALU .... Mode Annunciator and Logic Unit (PDAA)
MALV .... Malva [*Mallow*] [*Pharmacy*] (ROG)

Malynes....... Malynes' Lex Mercatoria [*3 eds.*] [*1622-36*] [*A publication*] (DLA)
MAm .... Amesbury Public Library, Amesbury, MA [*Library symbol Library of Congress*] (LCLS)
M + Am .... Compound Myopic Astigmatism [*Ophthalmology*]
MAM .... Joint II March-May Study [*Coastal Upwelling Ecosystems Analysis*] (MSC)
MAM .... Madam (DSUE)
MAM .... Maintenance Assist Module
MAM .... Maintenance Assumes Monitor [*Aviation*] (FAAC)
MAM .... Mambajao [*Philippines*] [*Seismograph station code, US Geological Survey Closed*] (SEIS)
MAM .... Management Analysis Memorandum [*DoD*] (MCD)
MAM .... Management and Administration Manual (NRCH)
MAM .... Marquis Academic Media [*Publisher*]
MAM .... Mars Aeronomy Mission (MCD)
MAM .... Master Model (MCD)
MAM .... Master of Agriculture and Management (PGP)
MAM .... Master of Animal Medicine (GAGS)
MAM .... Master of Applied Mechanics (PGP)
MAM .... Master of Arts in Management
MAM .... Master of Arts Management (PGP)
MAM .... Master of Arts - Ministry (PGP)
MAM .... Master of Association Management (PGP)
MAM .... Master of Avian Medicine (PGP)
MAM .... Master of Aviation Management (GAGS)
MAM .... Matamoros [*Mexico*] [*Airport symbol*] (OAG)
MAM .... Material Acquisition Manager [*Army*] (AAGC)
MAM .... Materiel Acquisition Management Program [*Army*] (RDA)
MAM .... Matter-Anti-Matter (PDAA)
MAM .... Maxxim Medical [*NYSE symbol*] (TTSB)
MAM .... Maxxim Medical, Inc. [*NYSE symbol*] (SPSG)
MAM .... Medium-Altitude Missile (MCD)
MAM .... Medium Automotive Maintenance
MAM .... Memory Access Multiplexer (NITA)
MAM .... Memory Allocation Manager
MAM .... Mercury Asset Management [*Commercial firm British*]
MAM .... Message Access Method [*Honeywell, Inc.*]
MAM .... Meta Aviotransport-Macedonia [*Yugoslavia*] [*ICAO designator*] (FAAC)
MAM .... Methylazoxymethanol Acetate [*Organic chemistry*]
MAM .... Microwave Attenuator Monitor (IAA)
MAM .... Military Air Movement
MAM .... Military Assistance Manual (AFM)
MAM .... Milliammeter
MAM .... Milliampere Minutes
MAM .... Missile Alarm Monitor
MAM .... Missile Assembly and Maintenance [*NASA*] (IAA)
MAM .... Mission Air Ministries [*Defunct*] (EA)
MAM .... Mission Area Manager [*Army*]
MAM .... Monoacetylmorphine [*Organic chemistry*]
MAM .... Mot a Mot [*Word for Word*] [*French*]
MAM .... Multiapplication Monitor
MAM .... Multiple Access to Memory [*Computer science*] (IEEE)
M+Am.......... Myopic Astigmatism [*Ophthalmology*] (DAVI)
MAM .... Society of Automotive Engineers, Inc. (AAGC)
MAMA .... Management Accounting Maintenance Advertising, Inc.
MAMA .... Manual-Automatic Multipoint Apparatus (MCD)
MAMA .... Material Acquisition Management Application [*Suggested name for the Library of Congress computer system*]
MAMA .... Meet-a-Mum Association [*British*] (DI)
MAMA .... Middletown Air Materiel Area [*Air Force*]
MAMA .... Mobile Automated Metabolic Analyzer [*Aerospace*]
MAMA .... Monoammonium Methanearsonate
MAMA .... Monoclonal Antimalignant Antibody [*Immunochemistry*]
MAMA .... Movement for All-Macedonian Action [*Political party*]
MAMA .... Multi-Anode Microchannel Array (PDAA)
MAM Ac....... Methylazoxymethanol Acetate [*Organic chemistry*] (DMAA)
MAMB .... Master of Applied Molecular Biology (PGP)
MAMB .... Military Acquisition Management Branch [*Army*] (RDA)
MAMB .... Military Advisory Mission, Brazil
MAMB .... Missile Assembly and Maintenance Building [*NASA*] (IAA)
MAMBO .... Mediterranean Association for Marine Biology and Oceanology [*ICSU*] (EAIO)
MAMBO .... Minuteman Assembly-Maintenance Building, Ogden (SAA)
MAMC .... Altona Medical Centre Library, Manitoba [*Library symbol National Library of Canada*] (NLC)
MAMC .... Madigan Army Medical Center (AABC)
MAMC .... Master of Arts in Mass Communication (PGP)
MAMC .... Midarm Muscle Circumference [*Myology*]
MAMDC .... Multipurpose Arthritis and Musculoskeletal Diseases Center [*University of Alabama, Birmingham*] [*Research center*] (RCD)
MAME .... Master of Arts in Missions/Evangelism (PGP)
MAME .... Missile and Munitions Evaluation (MCD)
MAME .... Mobile America [*NASDAQ symbol*] (TTSB)
MAME .... Mobile America Corp. [*NASDAQ symbol*] (NQ)
MA Mech ..... Master of Applied Mechanics
MAMEE .... Meyer Ammunition Module - Emerson Electric
MAMFC .... Master of Arts in Marriage and Family Counseling (GAGS)
MAMFCC ...... Master of Arts in Marriage, Family, and Child Counseling (PGP)
MAMFT .... Master of Arts in Marriage and Family Therapy (PGP)
MAMGRAPHY... Mammography
MA Mgt........ Master of Arts in Management (PGP)
MAmHi .... Amesbury Historical Society, Amesbury, MA [*Library symbol Library of Congress*] (LCLS)
MAMI .... Machine-Aided Manufacturing Information [*Computer science*]

MAMI	Modified Alternate Mark Inversion [*Telecommunications*] (TEL)
MAMI	Multiple Association Management Institute [*Later, IAMC*] (EA)
MAMIE	Magnetic Amplification of Microwave Integrated Emissions (IEEE)
MAMIE	Minimum Automatic Machine for Interpolation and Extrapolation
M Am IMME	Member of the American Institute of Mining and Metallurgical Engineers
MA Min	Master of Arts in Ministry (PGP)
Ma-Min	Milliampere-Minute
MAMIS	Mandatory Modification and Inspection Summary [*Aviation*] (DA)
MA Missions	Master of Arts in Missions (PGP)
MAML	Master of Arts in School Media Librarianship (PGP)
MAMM	Master of Arts in Ministry Management (PGP)
MAMMA	Men Against the Maxi-Midi Atrocity [*Klosters, Switzerland, group opposing below-the-knee fashions introduced in 1970*]
MAMMAX	Machine-Made and Machine-Assisted Index [*Computer science*] (IAA)
mammo	Mammography [*Gynecology*] (DAVI)
MAMO	Advanced Mammography Sys [*NASDAQ symbol*] (TTSB)
MAMO	Advanced Mammography Systems [*NASDAQ symbol*] (SAG)
MAMOE	Medical Administration and Miscellaneous Operating Expenses [*Veterans Administration*]
MAMOS	Marine Automatic Meteorological Observing Station [*Automatic system*]
MAMOS	Missouri Associated Migrant Opportunities Services (EA)
MaMP	Maine State Planning Office, Augusta, ME [*Library symbol Library of Congress*] (LCLS)
MAMP	Mainz Army Maintenance Plant (MCD)
MAMP	Materiel Acquisition Management Plan
MAMP	Michigan Army Missile Plant (MCD)
MAMP	Millampere [*or Milliamperage*] (IAA)
MAMP	Mission Area Materiel Plan [*Army*]
MAMRD	Master of Agricultural Management and Resource Development (GAGS)
MAMRON	Marine Aircraft Maintenance Squadron
MAMS	Maintenance Activity Management System [*Military*]
MAMS	Maintenance Assist Modules (MCD)
MAMS	Marine Meteorological Services [*Marine science*] (MSC)
MAMS	Master of Applied Mathematical Sciences (PGP)
MAMS	Master of Associated Medical Sciences (PGP)
MAMS	Materiel Acquisition Management System
MAMS	Medical Administrative Management System
MAMS	Member of the Association of Medical Secretaries, Practice Administrators, and Receptionists [*British*] (DBQ)
MAMS	Military Aircraft Marshaling System
MAMS	MIRCOM [*Missile Material Readiness Command*] Automated Microfilm System [*Army*] (IID)
MAMS	Missile Altitude Measurement System
MAMS	Missile Assembly and Maintenance Shop [*NASA*]
MAMS	Missile Assistance Maintenance Structure (IAA)
MAMS	Modern Army Maintenance System
MAMS	Multiple Access to Memory System [*Computer science*]
m-AMSA	Acridinyl Ansidide [*Antineoplastic drug*] (DAVI)
m-AMSA	Amsacrine [*Antineoplastic drug*] [*Also, AMSA*] (CDI)
MAMSA	Managing and Marketing Sales Association [*British*] (DBA)
MAM Sc	Master of Applied Mathematical Science (PGP)
M Am Soc CE	Member of the American Society of Civil Engineers
MAMSPAR	Member of the Association of Medical Secretaries, Practice Administrators, and Receptionists [*British*] (DI)
MAMSS	Machine Augmented Manual Scheduling System (MCD)
MAMT	Mean Active Maintenance Time (MCD)
MAMTF	Mobile Automated Microwave Test Facility (PDAA)
MAMTR	Milliammeter
MA (Mus)	Master of Arts in Music
MAMV	Maclura Mosaic Virus [*Plant pathology*]
MAmW	Whittier Home Association, Amesbury, MA [*Library symbol Library of Congress*] (LCLS)
MAN	Magnetic Automatic Navigation [*System*] (RDA)
MAN	Magnocellular Nucleus [*of anterior neostriatum*] [*Neurology*] (DAVI)
MAN	Mailorder Association of Nurserymen [*Defunct*] (EA)
MAN	Mainly about Nature [*A publication*]
MAN	Maintenance Alert Network [*RCA*]
MAN	Management (WDAA)
MAN	Manager [*or Managing*] (EY)
man	Managing (DD)
Man	Mancando [*Dying Away*] [*Music*]
MAN	Manchester [*England*] [*Airport symbol*] (OAG)
MAN	Mandato de Accion y Unidad Nacional [*Mandate of Action and National Unity*] [*Bolivia*] [*Political party*] (PPW)
man	Mandingo [*MARC language code Library of Congress*] (LCCP)
MAN	Mane [*Morning*] [*Pharmacy*]
MAN	Manege [*Horsemanship*] [*French*]
MAN	Manhattan
MAN	Manifest (AABC)
MAN	Manila [*Philippines*] [*Seismograph station code, US Geological Survey*] (SEIS)
MAN	Manilla (ADA)
man	Manipulate [*Medicine*] (MAE)
MAN	Manipulus [*A Handful*] [*Pharmacy*]
MAN	Manitoba [*Canadian province*]
Man	Manitoba [*Canada*] (DD)
Man	Manitoba Law Reports [*Canada*] [*A publication*] (DLA)
Man	Manning's Reports [*1 Michigan*] [*A publication*] (DLA)
Man	Manning's Reports, English Revision Court [*1832-35*] [*A publication*] (DLA)
MAN	Mannion Air Charter, Inc. [*ICAO designator*] (FAAC)

MAN	Mann Oil Resources, Inc. [*Vancouver Stock Exchange symbol*]
Man	Mannose [*A sugar*]
MAN	Manpower, Inc. [*NYSE symbol*] (SPSG)
MAN	Mansfield State College, Mansfield, PA [*OCLC symbol*] (OCLC)
Man	Manson's English Bankruptcy Cases [*A publication*] (DLA)
MAN	Manual (KSC)
man	Manual [*A handbook*] (WDMC)
MAN	Manuel Antonio Noriega [*Military commander and de facto ruler of Panama*]
MAN	Manufacture
MAN	Manufacturer (WDAA)
MAN	Maschinenfabrik Augsburg-Nuernburg [*Manufacturer of diesel engines*]
MAN	Meaningful Assistance in the Neighborhood [*of Legal Aid Bureau of George Washington University Law School*] (EA)
MAN	Metropolitan Area Network [*Telecommunications*]
MAN	Microwave Aerospace Navigation
MAN	Military Aviation Notice [*Air Force*]
MAN	Molecular Anatomy
MAN	Molesters Anonymous (EA)
MAN	Mouvement pour une Alternative Non-Violente [*Movement for a Nonviolent Alternative*] [*France Political party*] (PPE)
MAN	Movementu Antiyas Nobo [*New Antilles Movement*] [*Netherlands Political party*] (EAIO)
MAN	Movimentu Antiyas Nobo [*New Antilles Movement*] [*Political party*] (EY)
MAN	Movimiento de Accion Nacionalista [*National Action Movement*] [*Uruguay*] [*Political party*] (EY)
MAN	University of Manitoba Library [*UTLAS symbol*]
MAN-6-P	Mannose-6-Phosphate [*Chemistry*] (DAVI)
MANA	Manassas National Battlefield Park
MANA	Manatron, Inc. [*NASDAQ symbol*] (NQ)
MANA	Manufacturers Agents National Association (EA)
MANA	Mexican American Women's National Association (EA)
MANA	Midwives Alliance of North America (EA)
MANA	Music Advisers' National Association [*British*]
MANA	Musicians Against Nuclear Arms [*Defunct*] (EA)
MAN-AEDS	Manitoba Association for Educational Data Systems [*Canada*] (EDAC)
MANAG	Manage
MANAM	Manual Amendment
Man & G	Manning and Granger's English Common Pleas Reports [*A publication*] (DLA)
Man & R	Manning and Ryland's English King's Bench Reports [*1827-30*] [*A publication*] (DLA)
Man & R	Manning and Ryland's English Magistrates' Cases [*1827-30*] [*A publication*] (DLA)
Man & Ry	Manning and Ryland's English King's Bench Reports [*1827-30*] [*A publication*] (DLA)
Man & Ry	Manning and Ryland's English Magistrates' Cases [*1827-30*] [*A publication*] (DLA)
Man & Ry KB	Manning and Ryland's English King's Bench Reports [*1827-30*] [*A publication*] (ILCA)
Man & Ry Mag	Manning and Ryland's English Magistrates' Cases [*1827-30*] [*A publication*] (DLA)
Man & Ry Mag Cas	Manning and Ryland's English Magistrates' Cases [*1827-30*] [*A publication*] (DLA)
Man & Ry MC	Manning and Ryland's English Magistrates' Cases [*1827-30*] [*A publication*] (DLA)
Man & S	Manning and Scott's English Common Bench Reports, Old Series [*IX*] [*A publication*] (DLA)
Man & Sask Tax Rep (CCH)	Manitoba and Saskatchewan Tax Reporter (Commerce Clearing House) [*A publication*] (DLA)
Man & Sc	Manning and Scott's English Common Bench Reports, Old Series [*IX*] [*A publication*] (DLA)
MANAV	Maneuvering and Navigation System [*Military*] (IAA)
ManBagel	Manhattan Bagel Co., Inc. [*Associated Press*] (SAG)
Manb Coke	Manby's Abridgement of Coke's Reports [*A publication*] (DLA)
Manb Fines	Manby on Fines [*A publication*] (DLA)
Man B News	Manitoba Bar News [*A publication*] (ILCA)
MANC	Mancando [*Decreasing in Loudness*] [*Music*]
MANCAN	Man-Carried Automatic Navigator (MCD)
Man Cas	Manumission Cases in New Jersey, by Bloomfield [*A publication*] (DLA)
MANCH	Manchester [*England*]
Manch	Manchuria
MANCO	Mancando [*Decreasing in Loudness*] [*Music*]
MANCUN	Mancunium [*Signature of the Bishops of Manchester*] (ROG)
Mand	Mandaic (BJA)
MAND	Mandamus [*We Command*] [*Latin*] (ADA)
MAND	Mandatory (AABC)
mand	Mandibar [*Dentistry*] (DAVI)
MAND	Mandible
MAND	Mandolin [*Music*]
M & A	Maintenance and Assembly (MCD)
M & A	Management and Administration
M & A	Mergers and Acquisitions
M&A	Mergers and Acquisitions (TDOB)
M & A	Mergers & Acquisitions Data Base [*MLR Publishing Co.*] [*Information service or system*] (CRD)
M & A	Mississippi & Alabama Railroad (IIA)
M & A	Missouri & Arkansas Railway Co.
M & A	Money and Advice
M & A	Montagu and Ayrton's English Bankruptcy Reports [*1833-38*] [*A publication*] (DLA)

M & ABL...... Montagu and Ayrton's Bankrupt Laws [*A publication*] (DLA)
MANDATE.... Multiline Automatic Network Diagnostic and Transmission Equipment
M & AW ...... Mountain and Arctic Warfare [*British military*] (DMA)
M & Ayr....... Montagu and Ayrton's English Bankruptcy Reports [*1833-38*]
    [*A publication*] (DLA)
M & B......... Marianna & Blountstown [*Railroad*] (MHDB)
M & B......... Marianna & Blountstown Railroad Co. (IIA)
M & B......... Matched and Beaded
M & B......... Mild and Bitter [*Beer*]
M & B......... Montagu and Bligh's English Bankruptcy Reports [*1832-33*]
    [*A publication*] (DLA)
M & BR ...... Meridian & Bigbee River Railroad Co. (IIA)
M & C......... Maintenance and Checkout (NASA)
M & C......... Maintenance and Cure [*Legal shorthand*] (LWAP)
M & C......... Manufacturers and Contractors
M&C .... Measurement and Control [*The Journal of InstMC*] (ACII)
M & C......... Monitor and Control Panel [*Computer science*] (NASA)
M & C......... Montagu and Chitty's English Bankruptcy Reports [*1838-40*]
    [*A publication*] (DLA)
M & C......... Morphine and Cocaine [*Mixture*] [*Slang*]
M & C......... Mylne and Craig's English Chancery Reports [*A publication*] (DLA)
M & C Bills... Miller and Collier on Bills of Sale [*A publication*] (DLA)
M & Chit Bankr... Montagu and Chitty's English Bankruptcy Reports [*1838-40*]
    [*A publication*] (DLA)
M & Cht Bankr... Montagu and Chitty's English Bankruptcy Reports [*1838-40*]
    [*A publication*] (DLA)
M & C Partidas... Moreau-Lislet and Carleton's Laws of Las Siete Partidas in
    Force in Louisiana [*A publication*] (DLA)
M & CSq...... Mapping and Charting Squadron [*Air Force*]
M & CU ...... Monitor and Control Unit [*Aerospace*] (AAG)
M and CW ... Maternity and Child Welfare [*Medicine British*]
M & D .... Maidstone & District Motor Services Ltd. [*British*] (DCTA)
M & D .... McCormack & Dodge (NITA)
M & D .... Medicine and Duty [*Marked on a medical report and implying a
    suspicion of malingering*] [*Military British*]
M & D .... Mergers and Divestures
M & DOD..... Mission and Data Operations Directorate (MCD)
M & DV .... Map and Data Viewer [*NASA*] (KSC)
M & E......... Maintenance and Equipment (NATG)
M & E......... Maneuvers and Exercises (NATG)
M & E......... Material and Equipment [*Nuclear energy*] (NRCH)
M & E......... Mechanical and Electrical Room (AAG)
M & E......... Monitoring and Evaluation (ECON)
M & E......... Morning and Evening (WDMC)
M & E......... Music and Effects [*Television*]
M & E......... Music and Sound Effects (WDMC)
M and E...... Music and Sound Effects (WDMC)
MANDEC...... Maneuvering Decoy (MCD)
Man Dem..... Mansel on Demurrer [*1828*] [*A publication*] (DLA)
M & ER....... Mechanical and Electrical Room (AAG)
M & F......... Male and Female [*Components, as of connecting devices*]
M & F......... Materials and Facilities (MCD)
M & F......... Mother and Father
MANDFHAB... Male and Female Homosexual Association of Great Britain
M & G .... Macnaghten and Gordon's English Chancery Reports
    [*A publication*] (DLA)
M & G .... Maddock and Geldart's English Chancery Reports [*1815-22*]
    [*A publication*] (DLA)
M & G .... Manning and Granger's English Common Pleas Reports
    [*A publication*] (DLA)
M & G .... Mapping and Geodesy [*Army*] (AABC)
M & Gel ...... Maddock and Geldart's English Chancery Reports [*1815-22*]
    [*A publication*] (DLA)
M & GN ...... Midland and Great Northern Joint Line [*Railway*] [*British*] (ROG)
M & Gord .... Macnaghten and Gordon's English Chancery Reports
    [*A publication*] (DLA)
M & H .... Murphy and Hurlstone's English Exchequer Reports [*1836-37*]
    [*A publication*] (DLA)
M & HDA..... Medical and Hospital Department, Army
M & I.......... Manpower and Immigration [*Canada*]
M & I.......... Marine & Industrial
M & I.......... Marshall & Ilsley Bank
M & I.......... Minnesota & International Railway
M & I.......... Modernization and Improvement (AABC)
M & I.......... Modification and Installation (KSC)
M & I.......... Moisture and Impurities [*In fats*]
M & I.......... Movements and Identification [*Military*] (AFM)
M & I.......... Municipal and Industrial [*Users of water*]
M & IR .... Manufacturing and Inspection Record (KSC)
M & K......... Mylne and Keen's English Chancery Reports [*A publication*] (DLA)
M and L....... Management and Logistics [*NATO*] (NATG)
mandl......... Mandorla (VRA)
M&L........... Matched and Lost [*Investment term*] (DFIT)
M & L......... Matched and Lost [*Business term*]
M & LA .... Manpower and Logistics Analysis
M & M........ Make and Mend
M & M........ Manchester & Milford Railway [*Wales*]
M & M........ Martha and the Muffins [*Musical group*]
M & M........ Materials and Maintenance (NASA)
M & M........ Merchants and Manufacturers Association (EA)
M & M........ Metals and Minerals Research Services [*British*]
M & M........ Milk and Molasses [*Enema*] [*Medicine*]
M&M.......... Mining & Metallurgy Divisions (ACII)
M & M........ Montagu and MacArthur's English Bankruptcy Reports
    [*A publication*] (DLA)

M & M......... Moody and Malkin's English Nisi Prius Reports [*A publication*] (DLA)
M & M'A..... Montagu and MacArthur's English Bankruptcy Reports
    [*A publication*] (DLA)
M & McA ..... Montagu and MacArthur's English Bankruptcy Reports
    [*A publication*] (DLA)
M & M's ...... Mass and Meals [*Refers to nuns who appear only at these activities*]
M & N .... May and November [*Denotes semiannual payments of interest or
    dividends in these months*] [*Business term*]
M & N .... Medical and Nursing [*Red Cross Disaster Services*]
M & N .... Morning and Night [*Medicine*]
M & NA ...... Missouri & North Arkansas Railroad [*Nickname: May Never Arrive*]
M & NE ...... Manistee & Northeastern Railroad (IIA)
M & NW ..... Minnesota & Northwestern Railroad
M & O .... Machinery and Optics
M & O .... Maintenance and Operation (MCD)
M & O .... Maintenance and Overhaul
m & o .... Maintenance and Overhaul (AD)
m & o .... Management and Organization (AD)
M & O .... Management and Organization
MANDO........ Mancando [*Decreasing in Loudness*] [*Music*] (ROG)
M & O .... Manpower and Organization [*Military*]
M & O .... Materials and Others
M & O .... Mobile & Ohio Railroad
M & O .... Muscat and Oran (AD)
M & OB ...... Maintenance and Operations Branch [*BUPERS*]
M & OC ...... Monitor and Operations Control System [*Space Flight Operations
    Facility, NASA*]
M & P......... Maryland & Pennsylvania Railroad Co. (IIA)
M & P......... Material and Process
m & p .... Materials and Processes (AD)
M & P......... Moore and Payne's English Common Pleas Reports [*A publication*]
    (DLA)
M & PE....... Materials and Process Engineering (MCD)
M & PP....... Manitou & Pike's Peak Railway
M & PP....... Materials and Plant Protection [*Nuclear energy*] (NRCH)
M & P Sh ... Maude and Pollock's Law of Merchant Shipping [*A publication*] (DLA)
M&Q .... Mines and Quarries (AD)
M & R .... Maclean and Robinson's Scotch Appeal Cases [*1839*]
    [*A publication*] (DLA)
m & r .... Maintainability and Reliability (AD)
m & r .... Maintainability and Repairs (AD)
M & R .... Maintenance and Refurbishment (NASA)
M & R .... Maintenance and Repair
M & R .... Manning and Ryland's English King's Bench Reports [*1827-30*]
    [*A publication*] (DLA)
M&R .... Martini & Rossi
M & R .... Measure and Record
M & R .... Moody and Robinson's English Nisi Prius Reports [*1830-44*]
    [*A publication*] (DLA)
M & RA ...... Manpower and Reserve Affairs
M & RDET ... Maintenance and Repair Detachment
M & RE....... Money and Real Estate [*Newspaper section*] (ADA)
M & R I & O... Measure and Record Intake and Output [*Fluid measurement*]
    [*Medicine*] (CPH)
M & RMC .... Manning and Ryland's English Magistrates' Cases [*1827-30*]
    [*A publication*] (DLA)
MANDRO ..... Mechanically-Alterable Nondestructive Read Out [*Computer
    science*] (IAA)
M & Rob...... Maclean and Robinson's Scotch Appeal Cases [*1839*]
    [*A publication*] (DLA)
M & Rob...... Moody and Robinson's English Nisi Prius Reports [*A publication*]
    (DLA)
M & S......... Bureau of Medicine and Surgery [*Navy*]
M & S......... Maintenance and Supply
MANDS........ Maintenance and Supply
M & S......... Maintenance and Supply (AD)
M & S......... Manning and Scott's English Common Bench Reports [*IX*]
    [*A publication*] (DLA)
M & S......... March and September [*Denotes semiannual payments of interest or
    dividends in these months*] [*Business term*]
M&S........... Marketing & Sales Division (ACII)
M & S......... Marks & Spencer [*English department store chain*]
M & S......... Marshall and Swift Cost Index (DICI)
M & S......... Materials and Services [*NASA*] (KSC)
M & S......... Materials and Structures (SDI)
M&S........... Maternity and Surgical (AD)
M & S......... Maule and Selwyn's English King's Bench Reports [*A publication*]
    (DLA)
M & S......... McClelland & Stewart [*Canadian publisher*]
M & S......... Media and Status [*Code*] [*DoD*]
M&S........... Medical and Surgical (AD)
M & S......... Medicine and Surgery (AD)
M & S......... Methods and Standards
M & S......... Microculture and Sensitivity [*Laboratory*] (DAVI)
M & S......... Milwaukee & Superior Railroad
M & S......... Model and Series (AAG)
m & s .... Model and Series (AD)
M & S......... Modeling and Simulation
M & S......... Moore and Scott's English Common Pleas Reports [*1831-34*]
    [*A publication*] (DLA)
m & s .... Mud and Snow (AD)
M & S......... Mud and Snow Tire [*Automotive engineering*]
M & SC....... Missile and Space Council [*Defunct*] (EA)
M & Sc....... Moore and Scott's English Common Pleas Reports [*1831-34*]
    [*A publication*] (DLA)

M & Scott....	Moore and Scott's English Common Pleas Reports [1831-34] [A publication] (DLA)
MANDSD......	Mean and Standard Deviation
M & SS........	Mapping and Survey System (KSC)
M & SSq.....	Maintenance and Supply Squadron [Air Force]
M & StP.......	Milwaukee & St. Paul Railway
M & T.........	Maintenance and Test (AAG)
M and T.......	Movements and Transports (NATG)
M & TE........	Measurement and Test Equipment (KSC)
M & TP.......	Manufacturing and Testing Process (KSC)
M & U	Middletown & Unionville Railroad [Nickname: Miserable and Useless]
M and V	Meat-and-Vegetable [A canned ration] [Military]
M & W	Meeson and Welsby's English Exchequer Reports [A publication] (DLA)
M & WAA	Movers' and Warehousemen's Association of America [Defunct]
M & W Abr...	Marshall and Wood's Abridgment [A publication] (DLA)
M & W Cas...	Mining and Water Cases, Annotated [United States] [A publication] (DLA)
M & WH	Missile and Warhead Magazines
M & W Law Dic...	Mozley and Whiteley's Law Dictionary [A publication] (ILCA)
M & X	Microscope and X-Ray Inspection
M & Y.........	Martin and Yerger's Tennessee Reports [8 Tennessee] [1825-28] [A publication] (DLA)
M and Yerger's Rep...	Martin and Yerger's Tennessee Reports [8 Tennessee] [1825-28] [A publication] (DLA)
M & YR	Martin and Yerger's Tennessee Reports [8 Tennessee] [1825-28] [A publication] (DLA)
MAN ED.......	Managing Editor (DGA)
Man El Cas...	Manning's English Election Cases (Court of Revision) [A publication] (DLA)
M Anesth Ed...	Master of Anesthesiology Education (PGP)
MANEX	Management Experten-Nachweis [Management Experts Data Base] [Society for Business Information] [Information service or system] (IID)
Man Exch Pr...	Manning's English Exchequer Practice [A publication] (DLA)
MANF..........	Manifold (KSC)
MANF..........	Manifold
MANF..........	Manufacturer (WGA)
MANF..........	May, August, November, and February [Denotes quarterly payments of interest or dividends in these months] [Business term]
MANFG	Manufacturing (ROG)
MANFIST	Maneuver and Fire Support Team (MCD)
Man For......	Management Forum [A publication]
MANFOR.......	Manpower Force Packaging [Military]
MANFORCE...	Manpower for a Clean Environment [Water Pollution Control Federation]
MANFR	Manufacturer
MANFRD.......	Manufactured
MANFRG.......	Manufacturing
MANFST	Manifest
MANG	Management
Man G & S...	Manning, Granger, and Scott's English Common Bench Reports, Old Series [I-VIII] [A publication] (DLA)
Man Gaz......	Manitoba Gazette [A publication] (DLA)
MANGR.......	Manager
Man Gr & S...	Manning, Granger, and Scott's English Common Bench Reports, Old Series [I-VIII] [A publication] (DLA)
MANGRSS ...	Manageress (ROG)
MANGT	Management (ROG)
Manhattan C...	Manhattan College (GAGS)
Manhattan Sch Music...	Manhattan School of Music (GAGS)
Manhattanville C...	Manhattanville College (GAGS)
MANHC........	Madras Army Native Hospital Corps [British military] (DMA)
MAnHi	Andover Historical Society, Andover, MA [Library symbol Library of Congress] (LCLS)
ManhLfe	Manhattan Life Insurance Co. [Associated Press] (SAG)
MA-NHP.......	Massachusetts Natural Heritage Program [Massachusetts State Division of Fisheries and Wildlife] [Information service or system] (IID)
MANI	Manifold [Automotive engineering]
MANIAC.......	Mathematical Analyzer, Numerical Integrator and Computer
MANIAC.......	Mechanical and Numerical Integrator and Computer (IEEE)
MANICOM.....	Manned Information and Communications Facility (SAA)
MANIF	Manifest
manif.........	Manifesto (VRA)
manifest......	Manifestation [Medicine]
MAnimSc.....	Master of Animal Science, University of Liverpool [British] (DBQ)
Man Int Law...	Manning's Commentaries on the Law of Nations [A publication] (DLA)
Manip	All India Reporter, Manipur [A publication] (DLA)
manip.........	Manipulation [Medicine]
Manip	Manipulus [A Handful] [Pharmacy]
MANIP	Manual Input [Computer science]
MANIS	Modified Atlantic Naval Intelligence Summary
MANIT	Manitoba [Canadian province]
Manitoba	Armour. Queen's Bench and County Court Reports Tempore Wood [Manitoba] [A publication] (DLA)
Manitoba	Manitoba Law Reports [Canada A publication] (DLA)
Manitoba L (Can)...	Manitoba Law Reports [Canada] [A publication] (DLA)
Manitw	[The] Manitowoc Co., Inc. [Associated Press] (SAG)
MANIX	Machine Aids to Nike-X [Army] (AABC)
Mankato St U...	Mankato State University (GAGS)
MANL..........	Manual (IAA)
Man Lim......	Mansel on Limitations [1839] [A publication] (DLA)
Man LR........	Manitoba Law Reports [Canada A publication] (DLA)

Man LS Chron...	Manchester Law Students' Chronicle [A publication] (DLA)
Man LSJ	Manchester Law Students' Journal [A publication] (DLA)
MANM	Methylated Albumin-Nitrocelluse Membrane [Analytical biochemistry]
MANMAM	Manufacturing Management (PDAA)
MANMAN	Manufacturing Management (MHDI)
MANMED	Manual of the Medical Department [Navy]
MANMEDDEPT...	Manual of the Medical Department [Navy]
MANN	Manna [Pharmacy] (ROG)
Mann	Manning's Digest of the Nisi Prius Reports [England] [A publication] (DLA)
Mann	Manning's English Court of Revision Reports [A publication] (DLA)
Mann	Manning's Reports [1 Michigan] [A publication] (DLA)
MANN	Mannlicher Rifle
ManNac.......	N-Acetylmannosamine [Biochemistry]
Mann & G (Eng)...	Manning and Granger's English Common Pleas Reports [A publication] (DLA)
Mann & R....	Manning and Ryland's English King's Bench Reports [1827-30] [A publication] (DLA)
Mann & R....	Manning and Ryland's English Magistrates' Cases [1827-30] [A publication] (DLA)
Mann & R (Eng)...	Manning and Ryland's English King's Bench Reports [1827-30] [A publication] (DLA)
Mann Bills...	Manning on Bills and Notes [A publication] (DLA)
Mann Com...	Manning's Commentaries on the Law of Nations [A publication] (DLA)
Mann EC......	Manning's Revision Cases [1832-35] [A publication] (DLA)
Mann Ex Pr...	Manning's English Exchequer Practice [A publication] (DLA)
Mann G & S...	Manning, Granger, and Scott's English Common Bench Reports [135-39 English Reprint] [1845-56] [A publication] (DLA)
Mann G & S (Eng)...	Manning, Granger, and Scott's English Common Bench Reports, Old Series [I-VIII] [A publication] (DLA)
Manning	Manning's Reports [1 Michigan] [A publication] (DLA)
Manning	Manning's Unreported Cases [Louisiana] [A publication] (DLA)
Manning LA...	Manning's Unreported Cases [Louisiana] [A publication] (DLA)
Manning's UC...	Manning's Unreported Cases [Louisiana] [A publication] (DLA)
Manning's Unrep Cases...	Manning's Unreported Cases [Louisiana] [A publication] (DLA)
Mann Nat.....	Manning's Commentaries on the Law of Nations [A publication] (DLA)
Mann Unrep Cas...	Manning's Unreported Cases [Louisiana] [A publication] (DLA)
MANO	Manometer
MANOP........	Manganese Nodule Program [For sampling on ocean floor]
MANOP........	Manual of Operations
MANOR........	Manor [Commonly used] (OPSA)
ManorCr	Manor Care, Inc. [Associated Press] (SAG)
MANORS......	Manors [Commonly used] (OPSA)
MANOVA......	Multivariate Analysis of Variance [Statistics]
MANOVA......	Multiway Analysis of Variance (MCD)
MAnP.........	Phillips Academy, Andover, MA [Library symbol Library of Congress] (LCLS)
MANPAD......	Man-Portable Air Defense (AABC)
MANPADS....	Man-Portable Air Defense System (MCD)
MAN PR	Mane Primo [Early in the Morning] [Pharmacy]
MANPRINT...	Manpower and Personnel Integration [Military] (RDA)
Manpwl........	Manpower, Inc. [Associated Press] (SAG)
MANPWR......	Manpower (KSC)
MANR	Manager (ROG)
Man R	Manitoba Reports [Maritime Law Book Co. Ltd.] [Information service or system A publication A publication] (DLA)
Man Ray......	Emmanuel Radnitsky [American artist, 1890-1976]
Man Rev Stat...	Manitoba Revised Statutes [Canada] [A publication] (DLA)
MANRRDC....	Manpower Resources Research and Development Center [Army] (RDA)
Man RT Wood...	Manitoba Reports Tempore Wood [Canada] [A publication] (DLA)
Mans	Mansfield's Reports [49-52 Arkansas] [A publication] (DLA)
MANS	Mansiones
MANS	Mansions
Mans	Manson's English Bankruptcy and Winding-Up Cases [A publication] (DLA)
MANS	Map Analysis System [Computer science]
MANS	Mathematics Applied to novel Situations Test (EDAC)
MANSA	Man-Made Soling Association Ltd. [British] (BI)
MAN/SAFE....	Manual/Automatic Separation and Flotation Equipment (DNAB)
MANSAT	Manned Satellite
Mans Dem...	Mansel on Demurrer [1828] [A publication] (DLA)
Mansf Dig...	Mansfield's Digest of Statutes [Arkansas] [A publication] (DLA)
Mansfield U...	Mansfield University of Pennsylvania (GAGS)
MANSH........	Manshead [England]
Mans Lim.....	Mansel on Limitations [1839] [A publication] (DLA)
Manson........	Manson's English Bankruptcy and Winding-Up Cases [A publication] (DLA)
Manson Bankr Cas...	Manson's English Bankruptcy and Winding-Up Cases [A publication] (DLA)
Mans on C...	Mansel on Costs [A publication] (DLA)
Manson (Eng)...	Manson's English Bankruptcy Cases [A publication] (DLA)
Man Stat......	Manitoba Statutes [Canada] [A publication] (DLA)
MANSWG......	Manpower Systems Work Group
M Ant	Marcus Antoninus [of Scriptores Historiae Augustae] [Classical studies] (OCD)
MANT.........	Master of Arts in New Testament (PGP)
MANTAPS	Maneuver Arms Tactical Protective System [Army] (RDA)
MANTECH....	Manufacturing Technology
MANTIS	Manpack Tactical Intelligence System
MANTRAC....	Manual Angle Tracking Capability

MANTRAP.... Management Training Program [*of Center for Research in Business and Economics, University of Houston*]
MANTRAPERS... Manpower, Training, and Personnel (MCD)
Mantrn......... Manatron, Inc. [*Associated Press*] (SAG)
Man T Wood... Manitoba Reports Tempore Wood [*Canada*] [*A publication*] (DLA)
manu............ Manufacture (DAVI)
MANU .... Manugistics Group [*NASDAQ symbol*] (TTSB)
MANU .... Manugistics Group, Inc. [*NASDAQ symbol*] (SAG)
MANU .... Mozambique African National Union [*Later, FRELIMO*]
MANUF .... Manufacturer [*or Manufacturing*] (ROG)
Manufacturing Mgmt... Manufacturing and Management [*A publication*]
MANUFD..... Manufactured (ROG)
MANUFG..... Manufacturing (ADA)
ManufHm.... Manufactured Home Communities, Inc. [*Associated Press*] (SAG)
Manugist ..... Manugistics Group, Inc. [*Associated Press*] (SAG)
Manum Cas... Bloomfield's Manumission (or Negro) Cases [*New Jersey*] [*A publication*] (DLA)
Manum Cases... Bloomfield's Manumission (or Negro) Cases [*New Jersey*] [*A publication*] (DLA)
Man Unr Cases.. Manning's Unreported Cases [*Louisiana*] [*A publication*] (DLA)
Man Unrep Cas... Manning's Unreported Cases [*Louisiana*] [*A publication*] (DLA)
Man Unrep Cas (LA)... Manning's Unreported Cases [*Louisiana*] [*A publication*] (DLA)
MANUPACS... Manufacturing Planning and Control System (PDAA)
MANUV....... Maneuvering (KSC)
Manvl .... Manville Corp. [*Associated Press*] (SAG)
Manvlle .... Manville Corp. [*Associated Press*] (SAG)
MANVOS..... Manual Visas for Overseas System [*Australia*]
Manw......... Manwood's Forest Laws [*1592, 1598, 1615*] [*A publication*] (DLA)
Manw For Law... Manwood's Forest Laws [*1592, 1598, 1615*] [*A publication*] (DLA)
Manwood..... Manwood's Forest Laws [*1592, 1598, 1615*] [*A publication*] (DLA)
MANX .... Mannion Air Charter, Inc. [*Air carrier designation symbol*]
MAO............ MAC Aviation SL [*Spain ICAO designator*] (FAAC)
MAO............ Magnetic Amplifier Output
MAO............ Mailing Address Only [*Military*] (AABC)
MAO............ Maintenance and Operation [*Army*] (AFIT)
MAO............ Major Attack Option [*Military*] (MCD)
MAO............ Manaus [*Brazil*] [*Airport symbol*] (OAG)
MAO............ Manned Apollo Operations [*NASA*] (KSC)
mao............ Maori [*MARC language code Library of Congress*] (LCCP)
MAO............ Marion, SC [*Location identifier FAA*] (FAAL)
MAO............ Mars Aeronomy Orbiter (MCD)
MAO............ Massive Attack Option (MCD)
MAO............ Master of Art of Oratory
MAO............ Master of the Art of Obstetrics
MAO............ Matair Ltd. [*British ICAO designator*] (FAAC)
MAO............ Material Adjustment Order (MCD)
MAO............ Maximum [*or Minimum*] Acid Output [*Clinical chemistry*]
MAO............ Mechanization of Algebraic Operations (PDAA)
MAO............ Medial Ankle Orthosis [*Orthopedics*] (DAVI)
MAO............ Medical Assistance Only (GFGA)
MAO............ Methylaluminoxane [*Organic chemistry*]
MAO............ Methyl Aluminoxane Cocatalyst
MAO............ Military Assistance Officer [*Army*]
MAO............ Monoamine Oxidase [*An enzyme*]
MAO............ Monoamin Oxidase Inhibitors [*An antidepressant*]
MAO............ Movement to Arrest Oppressors (EA)
MAO............ Muhammadan Anglo-Oriental
MAOA......... Meteorological Aspects of Ocean Affairs [*Marine science*] (MSC)
MAOA......... Meyers Aircraft Owners Association (EA)
MAOA......... Monoamine Oxidase A [*An enzyme*]
MAOA......... Panel of Meteorological Aspects of Ocean Affairs [*Marine science*] (OSRA)
MAO-B........ Monoamine Oxidase B [*An enzyme*]
MAODP........ Medic Alert Organ Donor Program (EA)
MAOE......... Master of Adult and Occupational Education (PGP)
MAOF......... Mexican-American Opportunity Foundation (EA)
MAOI......... Monoamine Oxidase Inhibitor [*Biochemistry*]
MAOM .... Master of Aerospace Operations Management (GAGS)
MAOP......... Maximum Allowable Operating Pressure [*In pipelines*]
MAOS......... Magnetic Amplifier Output Stage
MAOS......... Metal-Alumina-Oxide Semiconductor [*Computer science*] (IAA)
MAOS......... Metal-Aluminum-Oxide Silicon (MSA)
MAOS......... Minimum Airfield Operating Surface [*Military*]
MAOT......... Master of Arts in Occupational Therapy
MAOT......... Master of Arts in Old Testament (PGP)
MAOT......... Maximum Allowable Operating Time (NASA)
MAOT......... Medium Aperture Optical Telescope (PDAA)
MAOT......... Member, Association of Occupational Therapists [*British*]
MAOT......... Military Assistance Observer Team
MAOT......... Missile Auxiliary Output Tester
MAOT......... Mobile Air Operations Team [*Military*]
MAOU......... Member of the American Ornithologists' Union
MAP........... Machine Analyzer Package (PDAA)
MAP........... Macro Arithmetic Processor [*Computer science*] (MDG)
MAP........... Macroassembly Program [*Computer science*]
MAP........... Madeira Abyssal Plain [*Geology*]
MAP........... Maghreb-Arabe Presse [*Maghreb Arab Press Agency*] [*Morocco*]
MAP........... Magnetic-Acoustic-Pressure (NVT)
MAP........... Main Arithmetic Processor (IAA)
MAP........... Maine Public Service [*AMEX symbol*] (TTSB)
MAP........... Maine Public Service Co. [*AMEX symbol*] (SPSG)
MAP........... Mainly about People [*A publication*]
MAP........... Maintenance Administration Panel (ACRL)
MAP........... Maintenance Analysis Procedure [*Computer science*]

MAP........... Maintenance Analysis Program [*NASA*] (KSC)
MAP........... Maitre en Administration Publique [*Master of Public Administration*]
map........... Malayo-Polynesian [*MARC language code Library of Congress*] (LCCP)
MAP........... Mamai [*Papua New Guinea*] [*Airport symbol*] (OAG)
MAP........... Management Analysis [*or Assessment*] Program
MAP........... Management and Planning Committee [*Library of Congress*]
MAP........... Management and Programming (IAA)
MAP........... Management Application Protocol (ACRL)
MAP........... Management Assistance for Profits
MAP........... Manifold Absolute Pressure
MAP........... Manifold Air Pressure
MAP........... Manpower [*A publication*]
MAP........... Manpower Absorption Plan [*Department of Labor*]
MAP........... Manpower Analysis Paper
MAP........... Manpower Assistance Project [*Department of Labor*]
MAP........... Manufacturers' Assistance Program [*Michigan State Department of Commerce*] [*Lansing, MI*] [*Information service or system*] (IID)
MAP........... Manufacturing Activity Projection
MAP........... Manufacturing Automation Protocol [*Data communications standards*]
MAP........... MAP [*Medical Assistance Programs*] International (EA)
MAP........... Maples, MO [*Location identifier FAA*] (FAAL)
MAP........... Mapping (MSA)
MAP........... Marine Advisory Program [*Marine science*] (MSC)
MAP........... Marketing Action Planner [*National Association of Printers and Lithographers*] [*A publication*]
MAP........... Marketing Assistance Program [*Department of Agriculture*]
MAP........... Mars Atmosphere Probe
MAP........... Master Activity Programming
MAP........... Master Air Pilot
MAP........... Master Attack Plan [*Military*] (DOMA)
MAP........... Master of Applied Psychology (PGP)
MAP........... Master of Arts in Planning (PGP)
MAP........... Material Acquisition Process [*or Program*] (MCD)
MAP........... Materiel Acquisition Plan [*Army*]
MAP........... Mathematical Analysis without Programming [*Computer science*]
MAP........... Maximal Aerobic Power [*Laboratory*] (DAVI)
MAP........... Maximum A Posteriori [*Statistics*]
MAP........... Maximum Average Price
MAP........... Mean Airway Pressure [*Medicine*] (DMAA)
MAP........... Mean Aortic Pressure [*Medicine*]
MAP........... Mean Arterial Pressure [*Medicine*]
MAP........... Measurement Assurance Program [*National Institute of Standards and Technology*]
MAP........... Measure of Academic Progress [*Educational test*]
MAP........... Mecury All Position (IAA)
MAP........... Media Access Project (EA)
MAP........... Media Analysis Project (EA)
MAP........... Media and People [*Information service or system*] (IID)
MAP........... Medical Aid Post
MAP........... Medical Audit Program [*Computerized system of abstracted medical record information*]
MAP........... Medicare Advocacy Project
MAP........... Megaloblastic Anemia of Pregnancy [*Obstetrics*] (MAE)
MAP........... Melphalan, Adriamycin, Prednisone [*Antineoplastic drug regimen*]
MAP........... Memory Allocation and Protection
MAP........... Memory Allocation Processor (NITA)
MAP........... Mercapturic Acid Pathway [*Biochemistry*]
MAP........... Mesenteric Arterial Pressure [*Medicine*]
MAP........... Message Acceptance Pulse [*Aerospace communications*]
MAP........... Meta-Aminophenol [*Organic chemistry*]
MAP........... Meta-Aminopyrimethamine [*Biochemistry*]
MAP........... Methionyl Aminopeptidase [*An enzyme*]
MAP........... Methyl Acceptor Protein [*Biochemistry*] (DAVI)
MAP........... Methylacetoxyprogesterone [*Also, MPA*] [*Endocrinology*]
MAP........... Methylacetylene Propadiene [*Organic chemistry*]
MAP........... Methyl(acetylenyl)putrescine [*Biochemistry*]
MAP........... Methyl(amino)propanediol [*Organic chemistry*]
MAP........... Methylaminopurine (MAE)
MAP........... Microelectronics Application Programme (AIE)
MAP........... Microelectronics Application Project [*British*] (DCTA)
MAP........... Microprocessor Application Project [*In manufacturing industry*] [*Department of the Interior*]
MAP........... Microprogrammed Array Processor
MAP........... Microtubule-Associated Protein [*Cytology*]
MAP........... Microwave Anisotropy Probe [*NASA*]
MAP........... Microwave Anisotropy Probe [*NASA*]
MAP........... Middle Atmosphere Programme [*International Council of Scientific Unions*]
MAP........... Migrant Action Program (OICC)
MAP........... Milestone Analysis Procedure
MAP........... Military Airport Plan [*FAA*] (TAG)
MAP........... Military Assistance Program [*DoD*]
MAP........... Military Association of Podiatrists [*Later, FSPMA*] (EA)
MAP........... Military Audit Project
MAP........... Military Awards Profile [*Information service or system*] (IID)
MAP........... Miller Assessment for Preschoolers
MAP........... Minimum Acceptable Performance [*Telecommunications*] (TEL)
MAP........... Minimum Annual Premium (MHDW)
MAP........... Minimum Association Price (WDAA)
MAP........... Minimum Attack Parameter [*Military*]
MAP........... Minimum Audible Pressure
MAP........... Ministry of Aircraft Production [*British*]
MAP........... Minorities Advancement Plan
MAP........... Missed Approach Point [*Aviation*] (AFM)

MAP............	Missed Approach Procedure [Aviation]
MAP............	Missile and Package Tester
MAP............	Missile Application Propulsion
MAP............	Missile Assignment Program (SAA)
MAP............	Mission Application Program (NASA)
MAP............	Mitogen-Activated Protein [Biochemistry]
MAP............	Mixed Aniline Point
MAP............	Model and Program [Computer science]
MAP............	Modification Application Plan [Army]
MAP............	Modified American Plan [Travel]
MAP............	Modified Atmospheric Packaging [Food industry]
MAPK..........	Modular Acoustic Panel
MAP............	Modular Analysis Processor [Applied Data Research, Inc.]
MAP............	Modular Application System [Computer science]
MAP............	Modular Assembly Prosthesis [Medicine]
MAP............	Monitoring Attitudes of the Public [ACLI]
MAP............	Monoammonium Phosphate [Inorganic chemistry]
MAP............	Monophasic Action Potential [Electrophysiology] (AAMN)
MAP............	Mothers of AIDS [Acquired Immune Deficiency Syndrome] Patients (EA)
MAP............	Mouse Antibody Production [Test for virus]
MAP............	Movement of the Assemblies of People [Grenada]
MAP............	Multi-Access Pointer (PCM)
MAP............	Multibus Accounting Package (PDAA)
MAP............	Multichannel Astrometric Photometer [Astronomy]
MAP............	Multicoverage Account Program [Insurance]
MAP............	Multicultural Australia Papers [A publication]
MAP............	Multifunction Adaptive Processor (NITA)
MAP............	Multiple Address Processing
MAP............	Multiple Aim Point [ICBM]
MAP............	Multiple Allocation Procedure [PERT]
MAP............	Multiple Array Processor
MAP............	Municipal Airport (MCD)
MAP............	Muscle Action Potential
MAP............	Museum Assessment Program [National Foundation on the Arts and the Humanities]
MAP............	Musical Aptitude Profile
MAP............	Mutamycin, Adriamycin, Platinol [Antineoplastic drug] (CDI)
MAP............	Mutual African Press Agency
MAP............	Mutual Assistance Pact
MAP............	Mutual Assistance Plan (NATG)
MAP............	Mutual Assistance Program
MAP............	National Oceanic and Atmospheric Administration [ICAO designator] (FAAC)
MAP3S........	Multistate Atmospheric Power Production Pollution Study [Department of Energy]
MAPA..........	Master of Arts in Public Administration (GAGS)
MAPA..........	Master of Arts in Public Affairs (GAGS)
MAPA..........	Mexican-American Political Association
MAPA..........	Mooney Aircraft Pilots Association (EA)
MAPAD........	Military Assistance Program Address Directory
MAPAF.........	Military Assistance Program Address File
MAPAG........	Military Assistance Program Advisory Group
MAPAG........	Multi-Association Policy Advisory Group [An association]
MAPAI.........	Mifleget Po'alei Eretz-Yisrael (BJA)
MAPAM........	Mifleget Po'alim Me'uhedet (BJA)
MAPAR........	Materials and Processes Acceptance Requirement
MAPAS........	Master of Arts in Public Administration in Spanish (PGP)
MAPC..........	Master of Arts in Pastoral Counseling (PGP)
MAPC..........	Maximum Allowable Pevailing Charge [Medicine]
MAPC..........	Migrating Action Potential Complex [Electrophysiology]
MAPCC........	Master of Arts in Pastoral Care and Counseling (PGP)
MAPCC........	Military Assistance Program Country Code (AFM)
MAPCHE......	Mobile Automatic Programmed Checkout Equipment
MAP/CIO......	Military Assistance Program/Common Item Order
MAPCO........	MAPCO, Inc. [Associated Press] (SAG)
MAPCO........	Mid-American Pipeline Co.
MAPCON......	Microprocessor Applications Consultancy (NITA)
MAPD..........	Master Part Dimensioned (MCD)
MAPD..........	Maximum Allowable Percent Defective (PDAA)
MAPDA........	Mid-America Periodical Distributors Association
MAPDFA......	Media-Advertising Partnership for a Drug-Free America [Later, DFA] (EA)
MAPDU........	Management Application Protocol Data Unit [Telecommunications] (OSI)
MAPE..........	Master of Arts in Physical Education (GAGS)
MAPE..........	Master of Arts in Political Economy (PGP)
MAPE..........	Maximum Absolute Percentage Error [Statistics]
MAPE..........	Mean Absolute Percentage Error [Statistics]
MAPE..........	Microcomputers and Primary Education
MAPETT.......	Military Assistance Program Evaluation Team, Thailand (CINC)
MAPEX........	Map Exercise [Military] (INF)
MAPEX........	Mid-America Payment Exchange
MAPEX........	Military Articles Pacific Excesses (AFIT)
MAPF..........	Microatomized Protein Food (MAE)
MAPF..........	Mobile Aerial Port Flight [Air Force]
MAPG..........	Maximum Available Power Gain (MSA)
MAP-GA.......	Military Assistance Program - Grant Aid
MAPGEN......	Map Generator (MHDI)
MAPHILINDO..	Malaya-Philippines-Indonesia
MAPI..........	Machinery and Allied Products Institute (MHDI)
MAPI..........	Mail Application Programming Interface [Computer science] (PCM)
MAPI..........	Mail Applications Program Interface [Microsoft Corp.]
MAPI..........	Manufacturers Alliance for Productivity and Innovation (EA)

MAPI..........	Messaging API [Application Programming Interface] [Computer science]
MAPI..........	Millon Adolescent Personality Inventory [Personality development test] [Psychology]
MAPI..........	Mitsubishi Atomic Power Industries (IAA)
MAPICS.......	Manufacturing, Accounting and Product Information Central System (NITA)
MAPICS.......	Manufacturing, Accounting, and Production Information Control System [IBM Corp.]
MAPID........	Machine-Aided Program for Preparation of Instruction Data
MapInfo.......	Mapinfo Corp. [Associated Press] (SAG)
MAPK.........	Mitogen Activated Protein Kinase [An enzyme]
MAPL.........	Manufacturing Assembly Parts List
MAPL.........	Master Allowance Parts List [Military] (CAAL)
MAPL.........	Military Acquisition Position List (RDA)
MAPLA.......	Military Assistance Program Logistics Agency [Merged with Defense Supply Agency]
MAPLE.......	Marketing and Product Line Evaluation (PDAA)
MAPLE.......	Minor Atomic Prolonged Life Equipment (PDAA)
MAPLHGN...	Maximum Average Planar Linear Heat-Generator [Nuclear energy] (IAA)
MAPLHGR...	Maximum Average Planar Linear Heat-Generation Rate [Nuclear energy] (NRCH)
MAPM........	Master of Arts in Pastoral Ministry (PGP)
MAPM........	Master of Arts in Pastoral Music (PGP)
M Ap Ma.....	Master of Applied Mathematics (PGP)
MAP Min.....	Master of Arts in Pastoral Ministry (PGP)
MAPMIS......	Manpower and Personnel Management Information System [Navy]
MAPMISMAN...	Manpower and Personnel Management Information System Manual [Navy] (DNAB)
MAPMOPP...	Marine Pollution [or Petroleum] Monitoring Pilot Project [Marine science] (MSC)
MAPNY.......	Maritime Association of the Port of New York [Later, MAPONY/NJ] (EA)
MAPOLE......	Magnetic Dipole Spark Transmitter (NASA)
MAPOM......	Military Assistance Program Owned Materiel (AFM)
MAP/One....	Manufacturing Automation Protocol/One [Local area network] [Industrial Networking, Inc.]
MAPONY.....	Maritime Association of the Port of New York
MAPONY/NJ...	Maritime Association of the Port of New York/New Jersey (EA)
MAPORD.....	Methodology Approach to Planning and Programming Air Force Operational Requirements, Research and Development (IEEE)
MAP/OSP....	Military Assistance Program Offshore Procurement (DNAB)
MAPP.........	Manpower and Personnel Plan [Army] (AABC)
MAPP.........	Manpower and Production Projections [LIMRA]
MAPP.........	Masking Parameter Printout [Computer science]
MAPP.........	MasterCard Automated Point-of-Sale Program
MAPP.........	Master of Arts in Public Policy (GAGS)
MAPP.........	Mathematical Analysis of a Perception and Preference
MAPP.........	Methyl Acetyl Propadrine and Propane (MCD)
MAPP.........	Mid-Continent Area Power Pool [Electric power]
MAPP.........	Mission Analysis and Performance Program
MAPP.........	Modern Aids to Planning Program [Military] (GFGA)
MApp..........	Musical Appreciation [Record label]
MAppEpidem..	Master of Applied Epidemiology
MAPPER......	Maintaining, Preparing, and Processing Executive Reports [Computer science] (CDE)
MAPPER......	Maintaining, Preparing and Producing Executive Reports (NITA)
MAPPEX......	Magazine and Periodical Publishers Exhibition (NITA)
MAPPLE......	Macro-Associative Processor Programming Language [Computer science] (PDAA)
MAppLing....	Master of Applied Linguistics
MApplLit......	Master of Applied Literature (GAGS)
MApplM......	Master of Applied Mathematics (GAGS)
M Appl Stat...	Master of Applied Statistics (PGP)
MAppPsych...	Master of Applied Psychology
MAPPS.......	Management Association of Private Photogrammetric Surveyors (EA)
MAppSc......	Master of Applied Science
MAppSc-BltEnvir...	Master of Applied Science - Built Environment
MAppSci.....	Master of Applied Science
MAppSc-MedPhys...	Master of Applied Science - Medical Physics
MAppSc(SocEcol)...	Master of Applied Science in Social Ecology
MAPR.........	Manufacturing Aids Program Requirements (AAG)
MAPRAT.....	Maximum Power Ratio (IEEE)
MAPRC.......	Mediterranean Allied Photographic Reconnaissance Command
MAPRES.....	Mini Air Passenger Reservation System
MAPRIAL....	Mezhdunarodnaja Assotsiatsija Professorov Russkogo Jazyka i Literatury [International Association of Teachers of Russian Language and Literature] (EAIO)
MAPROS.....	Maintain Production Schedules
MAPRP......	Mesoscale Atmospheric Processes Research Program [National Oceanic and Atmospheric Administration]
MAPRS......	Master of Arts in Pacific Rim Studies (GAGS)
MAPS.........	Machine Automated Parts System (MCD)
MAPS.........	Maintenance Analysis and Procedures System [Computer science]
MAPS.........	Major Assembly Performance System (MCD)
MAPS.........	Make-a-Picture Story [Psychological testing]
MAPS.........	Management Accounting and Payroll System (NITA)
MAPS.........	Management Accounting and Performance System
MAPS.........	Management Analysis and Planning System
MAPS.........	Manifold Air Pressure Sensor [Automotive engineering]
MAPS.........	Manpower Analysis and Planning Society (EA)
MAPS.........	Manpower and Production Survey [LIMRA]
MAPS.........	Manpower Area Planning System [Under CAMPS]
MAPS.........	Mapinfo Corp. [NASDAQ symbol] (SAG)

MAPS............	Market-Auction Preferred Stock
MAPS............	Marketing, Advertising, and Promotions Solutions Exhibition [*British*] (ITD)
MAPS............	Master Activation Phasing Schedule (IAA)
MAPS............	Master of Arts in Pastoral Studies (PGP)
MA Ps...........	Master of Arts in Psychology (PGP)
MAPS............	Master of Arts in Public Service
MAPS............	McGill Action Planning System
MAPS............	Measurement of Air Pollution from Satellites
MAPS............	Measurement of Air [*or Atmospheric*] Pollution from Satellites
MAPS............	Measuring Air Pollution from Space (USDC)
MAPS............	Measuring Air Pollution from Space [*Marine science*] (OSRA)
MAPS............	Mesoscale Analysis and Prediction System [*Marine science*] (OSRA)
MAPS............	Mesoscale Analysis and Prediction System (USDC)
MAPS............	Meteorological Applied Problem Solving
MAPS............	Methyl(deazaisoalloxazine)propanesulfonic Acid [*Organic chemistry*]
MAPS............	Metropolitan Air Post Society (EA)
MAPS............	Microprogramable Arithmetic Processor System (PDAA)
MAPS............	Middle Atlantic Planetarium Society (EA)
MAPS............	Migratory Animal Pathological Survey (PDAA)
MAPS............	Military Applications of Photovoltaic Systems
MAPS............	Military Aviation Preservation Society (EA)
MAPS............	Million Adds per Second
MAPS............	Miniature Air Pilot System
MAPS............	Minnesota Analysis and Planning System [*University of Minnesota*] [*Research center*] (RCD)
MAPS............	Missile Application Propulsion Study
MAPS............	Mission Analysis and Planning System (MCD)
MAPS............	Mobile Aerial Port Squadron [*Air Force*]
MAPS............	Mobility Analysis Planning System (MCD)
MAPS............	Mobilization Asset Planning System [*Army*]
MAPS............	Modern Accounts Payable System (MHDW)
MAPS............	Modular Acoustic Processing System (MCD)
MAPS............	Modular Azimuth Position System [*Army*] (RDA)
MAPS............	Monetary and Payments System [*Committee*] [*American Bankers Association*]
MAPS............	Monitoring of Air Pollution by Satellites (KSC)
MAPS............	Monoclonal Antibody Purification System
MAPS............	Monopropellant Accessory Power Supply [*Aerospace*] (AAG)
MAPS............	Muhammad Ali Professional Sports [*Commercial firm*]
MAPS............	Multicolor Automatic Projection System (IEEE)
MAPS............	Multi-jurisdictional Automated Pre-clearance System
MAPS............	Multiple Address Processing System
MAPS............	Multiple Agency Processing System
MAPS............	Multiple Aim-Point System
MAPS............	Multiple Application Phototypesetting System (DGA)
MAPS............	Multiple Automated Printing Systems (MCD)
MAPS............	Multisatellite Attitude Program System [*NASA*]
MAPS............	Multitarget Automatic Plotting System
MAPS............	Multivariate Analysis and Prediction of Schedules
MAPS............	Multivariate Analysis, Participation, and Structure
MAPSAC.....	Machine-Aided Planning, Scheduling, and Control
MAPSAD.....	Military Assistance Property Sales and Disposal (AFM)
MAPS/ALPS...	Multiple Aim Point System / Alternate Launch Point System (PDAA)
MAP/SAMSR...	Joint Army-Air Force Master Plan for the Satisfaction of Army Meteorological Support Requirements (MCD)
MAPSAS	Member of APSAS [*Association of Public Service Administrative Staff*] [*British*]
MApSc.........	Master of Applied Science (GAGS)
MAPSE.........	Minimal APSE [*Ada Program Support Environment*] [*Computer science*]
MAPSE.........	Minimum Implementation ADA Programming Support Environment (NITA)
MAPSEP	Mission Analysis Program for Solar Electric Propulsion [*Computer science NASA*]
MAPSIM	Mesoscale Air Pollution Simulation Model [*Environmental Protection Agency*] (GFGA)
MAPSq.........	Mobile Aerial Port Squadron [*Air Force*]
M Ap Stat	Master of Applied Statistics (PGP)
MA Psych	Master of Arts in Psychology (PGP)
MAPsych.....	Master of Arts in Psychology (GAGS)
MAPT..........	Military Assistance Program Training (AFM)
MAPT..........	Military Assistance Program Transfer (AFM)
MAPT..........	Missed Approach Point [*Aviation*] (FAAC)
MAPT..........	More Advanced Petrol Tractors [*Germany*]
MAPT..........	Mothers Are People Too [*Defunct*] (EA)
MAPTAC	Methacrylamidopropyltrimethylammonium Chloride [*Organic chemistry*]
MAPTEL......	Maplin Telecommunications (NITA)
MAPTIS.......	Manpower Personnel and Training Information System [*Navy*]
MAP-TOE....	Management Practices in TOE Units [*Military*] (GFGA)
MAP/TOP....	Manufacturing Automation Protocol / Technical Office Protocol (BTTJ)
MAPU	Memory Allocation and Protection Unit (MSA)
MAPU	Movimiento de Accion Popular Unida [*Unified Popular Action Movement*] [*Chile*] [*Political party*] (PD)
MAPU	Multiple Address Processing Unit [*Military*] (AABC)
MAPUC.......	Member of the Association for Promoting the Unity of Christendom [*British*]
MAPUC.......	Modified Area Production Urgency Committee [*World War II*]
MAPW	Master of Arts in Professional Writing (PGP)
MAPW	Medical Association for the Prevention of War [*British*] (DBA)
MAQ............	MAC Aviation, S.L. [*Spain*] [*FAA designator*] (FAAC)
maq............	Maquette (VRA)
M Aq...........	Master of Aquaculture (PGP)
MAq............	Master of Aquacultures (GAGS)

MAQ............	Maximum Acceptance Quantity
MAQ............	Measures for Air Quality [*Program*] [*National Institute of Standards and Technology*]
MAQ............	Monetary Allowance in Lieu of Quarters
MAQ............	Sena Maduereira [*Brazil*] [*Airport symbol*] (AD)
MAR............	Macroaddress Register
MAR............	Magnetic Amplifier Relay
MAR............	Maintainability Action Request (MCD)
MAR............	Maintenance Action Request
MAR............	Maintenance Analysis Report (MCD)
MAR............	Maintenance and Refurbishment (MCD)
MAR............	Maintenance and Repair
MAR............	Major Aircraft Review [*Navy*]
MAR............	Major Assembly Release [*Military*] (AABC)
MAR............	Malfunction Array RADAR
MAR............	Managed Approach Reservoir [*FAA*] (TAG)
MAR............	Management Analysis Report [*DoD*] (MCD)
MAR............	Management Assessment Report (MCD)
MAR............	Management Assessment Review (MCD)
MAR............	Manistee & Repton R. R. [*AAR code*]
MAR............	Manufacturing Action Request (MCD)
MAR............	Manufacturing Assembly Report (IAA)
MAR............	Maracaibo [*Venezuela*] [*Airport symbol*] (OAG)
mar............	Marathi [*MARC language code Library of Congress*] (LCCP)
MAR............	March (AFM)
MAR............	March Helicopters Ltd. [*British ICAO designator*] (FAAC)
Mar............	March's English King's Bench Reports [*1639-42*] [*A publication*] (DLA)
MAR............	Margin (DAVI)
MAR............	Mar-Gold Resources [*Vancouver Stock Exchange symbol*]
MAR............	Marian Minerals [*Vancouver Stock Exchange symbol*]
MAR............	Marimba [*Music*]
MAR............	Marine (MSA)
Mar............	Marion Laboratories, Inc.
MAR............	Maritime
MAR............	Maritime Administration Report [*Department of Commerce*]
MAR............	Maritime Central Airways
Mar............	Marius [*of Plutarch*] [*Classical studies*] (OCD)
MAR............	Market
mar............	Maroon [*Philately*]
MAR............	Marquette [*Diocesan abbreviation*] [*Michigan*] (TOCD)
MAR............	Married
MAR............	Marriott International [*NYSE symbol*] (SPSG)
MAR............	Marseilles [*France*] [*Seismograph station code, US Geological Survey Closed*] (SEIS)
MAR............	Marshal (ROG)
Mar............	Marshall and Sevestre's Appeals [*1862-64*] [*Bengal, India*] [*A publication*] (DLA)
Mar............	Marshall's Circuit Court Reports [*United States*] [*A publication*] (DLA)
Mar............	Marshall's Reports [*Ceylon*] [*A publication*] (DLA)
Mar............	Marshall's Reports [*Bengal*] [*A publication*] (DLA)
Mar............	Marshall's Reports [*Kentucky*] [*A publication*] (DLA)
MAR............	Martial [*Roman poet of the first century AD*] (ROG)
Mar............	Martin's Louisiana Reports [*A publication*] (DLA)
Mar............	Martin's North Carolina Reports [*1 North Carolina*] [*A publication*] (DLA)
Mar............	Marvel's Reports [*Delaware*] [*A publication*] (DLA)
Mar............	Mary (Queen of England) (DLA)
MAR............	Mass Accumulation Rate [*Geology*]
MAR............	Massachusetts College of Art, Boston, MA [*OCLC symbol*] (OCLC)
M-Ar	Massachusetts Secretary of State, Archives Division, Boston, MA [*Library symbol Library of Congress*] (LCLS)
MAR............	Master Angular Reference (IAA)
M Ar	Master of Architecture
MAR............	Master of Arts in Religion
MAR............	Master of Arts in Religion (GAGS)
MAR............	Master of Arts in Research (GAGS)
MA(R)........	Master of Arts (Research) (PGP)
MAR............	Material Availability Report [*NASA*] (KSC)
MAR............	Material Availability Request
MAR............	Matrix Attachment Region [*Genetics*]
MAR............	Medication Administration Record [*Medicine*]
MAR............	Memory-Address Register [*Computer science*]
MAR............	Mercury Arc Rectifier (IAA)
MAR............	Microanalytical Reagent
MAR............	Microprogram Address Register
MAR............	Mid-Air Retrieval (MCD)
MAR............	Mid-Atlantic Ridge [*of sea floor*]
MAR............	Minimal Angle Resolution
MAR............	Minimally Attended RADAR (MCD)
MAR............	Minimum Acceptable Rate of Return (MHDW)
MAR............	Minimum Acceptable Reliability
MAR............	Minimum Angle of Resolution (MCD)
MAR............	Miscellaneous Apparatus Rack (IAA)
MAR............	Mission Analysis Representative
MAR............	Mississippi-Atchafalaya River [*System*] (USDC)
MAR............	Mississippi-Atchafalaya River [*Marine science*] (OSRA)
MAR............	Monoclonal Antibody Resistant [*Immunochemistry*]
MAR............	Montana Administrative Register [*A publication*] (AAGC)
MAR............	Morocco [*ANSI three-letter standard code*] (CNC)
MAR............	Movimiento di Azione Rivoluzionaria [*Revolutionary Action Movement*] [*Italian*] (PD)
MAR............	Movimiento de Accion Revolucionaria [*Revolutionary Action Movement*] [*Mexico*] (PD)
MAR............	Multi-Adversity Resistance [*to root rot*] [*Plant pathology*]

MAR............ Multifunction Array RADAR
MAR............ Multiple Aberration Region [*Genetics*]
MAR............ Multiple Access Relay
MAR............ Multiple Access Return (SSD)
MAR............ Multiple Array RADAR (IAA)
MAR............ Municipal Association Record [*A publication*]
MAR............ Muscarinic Acetylcholine Receptor [*Biochemistry*]
MaR............ Myth and Ritual. Essays on the Myth and Ritual of the Hebrews in Relation to theCulture Pattern of the Ancient East [*A publication*] (BJA)
MAR............ Mythology of All Races [*A publication*]
MAr............ Robbins Public Library, Arlington, MA [*Library symbol Library of Congress*] (LCLS)
MAR............ Tacoma, WA [*Location identifier FAA*] (FAAL)
MARA........ Majority Rule Association (EA)
MARA........ Midget Auto Racing Association [*Sanctioning organization*]
MARAAWEX... Marine Antiair Warfare Exercise (NVT)
MARAD........ Maritime Administration [*Also, MA, MARITADMIN*] [*Department of Transportation*]
MArAd........ Master of Archive Administration, University of Liverpool [*British*] (DBQ)
MARADVU ... Marine Advisory Unit
MARAIRMED... Maritime Air Forces Mediterranean [*NATO*] (NATG)
MARAIRWING... Marine Aircraft Wing
MARALLWEAFITRARON... Marine All Weather Fighter Training Squadron
Mar & Yer ... Martin and Yerger's Tennessee Reports [*8 Tennessee*] [*1825-28*] [*A publication*] (DLA)
MARAS........ Middle Airspace RADAR Advisory Service [*Military*] (DA)
Mar Av........ Marvin on General Average [*A publication*] (DLA)
marb............ Marble (VRA)
MARB.......... Marbled [*Edges or sides of cover*] [*Bookbinding*] (ROG)
MARB.......... Materiel Acquisition Review Board [*Army*]
MARBA........ Mid-America Regional Bargaining Association
MARBARGE... Maritime Maintenance Barge
MARBASSCOL... Marine Corps Basic School
MarbFn........ Marble Financial Corp. [*Associated Press*] (SAG)
MARBI........ Machine-Readable Form of Bibliographic Information [*American Library Association*]
Mar Bills ..... Marius on Bills of Exchange [*A publication*] (DLA)
MARBKS...... Marine Barracks
MARBO........ Marianas-Bonins Command
Mar Br........ March's Brooke's New Cases [*1651*] [*England*] [*A publication*] (DLA)
MARBRIG .... Marine Brigade
MARC.......... Hruska Meat Animal Research Center [*Department of Agriculture*] (GRD)
MARC.......... Maastricht Referendum Campaign [*British*] (ECON)
MARC.......... Machine-Readable Cards
MARC.......... Machine-Readable Catalog (NITA)
MARC.......... Machine-Readable Cataloging [*Library of Congress*]
MARC.......... Machine-Readable Code (IAA)
MARC.......... Magnetic Abrasion Resistant Coating (IAA)
MARC.......... Manpower Allocation Requirement Criteria [*Military*] (RDA)
MARC.......... Manpower Authorization Request for Change [*Air Force*]
MARC.......... Manpower Requirements Criteria [*Army*]
MARC.......... Manufacturing Resource Control System [*Deritend Computer Bureau Ltd.*] [*Software package*] (NCC)
MARC.......... Marcato [*Emphasized*] [*Music*]
Marc............ Marcellus [*of Plutarch*] [*Classical studies*] (OCD)
MARC.......... MARC, Inc. [*NASDAQ symbol*] (SAG)
MARC.......... M/A/R/C INC. [*NASDAQ symbol*] (TTSB)
Marc............ Marcus [*of Scriptores Historiae Augustae*] [*Classical studies*] (OCD)
M/A/R/C .... Marketing And Research Counselors Inc. [*Irving, TX*] (WDMC)
MARC.......... Maryland Automotive Reclamation Corp. [*Automotive materials recycling project*]
MARC.......... Master of Arts in Religious Communication (PGP)
MARC.......... Matador Automatic RADAR Command
MARC.......... Material Accountability Recoverability Code
MARC.......... Materiel Acquisition Resource Committee [*Military*]
MARC.......... Media Action Research Center (EA)
MARC.......... Methodist Archives and Research Centre [*John Rylands University Library of Manchester*] [*British*] (CB)
MARC.......... Methodology for Assessing Radiological Consequences (PDAA)
MARC.......... Metropolitan Administration for Review and Comment [*Program using regional councils of government to serve as clearinghouses for Federal grants*]
MARC.......... Metropolitan Applied Research Center (BARN)
MARC.......... Micronesian Area Research Center [*University of Guam*] [*Research center*] (RCD)
MARC.......... Mid-America Regional Council [*Information service or system*] (IID)
MARC.......... Mining and Reclamation Council of America (EA)
MARC.......... Minority Access to Research Careers [*Program*] [*Public Health Service Bethesda, MD*]
MARC.......... Missions Advanced Research and Communication Center (EA)
MARC.......... Model "A" Restorers Club (EA)
MARC.......... Modified Azimuth RADAR Correlator
MARC.......... Monitor and Results Computer (IAA)
MARC.......... Monitoring and Assessment Research Centre [*Marine science*] (MSC)
MARC.......... Monitoring and Risk Assessment Centre [*British*]
MARC.......... Moore Automatic Remote Control
MARC.......... Mortgage Account Report Compiler (IAA)
MARC.......... Mouvement d'Action pour la Resurrection du Congo [*Action Movement for the Resurrection of the Congo*] [*Zaire*] (PD)

MARC .... Movimiento Agrario Revolucionario del Campesinado Boliviano [*Revolutionary Movement of Bolivian Indian Peasants*] [*Political party*] (PPW)
MARC .... Multiaxial Radial Circuit (IAA)
MARC .... Multifocal and Recurrent Choroidopathy [*Medicine*] (DMAA)
MARC .... Mutliple Access Remote Computing (PDAA)
MA(RCA)..... Master of Arts, Royal College of Art (Photography) [*British*] (DBQ)
MARCA .... Mid-Continent Area Reliability Coordination Agreement [*Regional power council*]
MARCAD ..... Marine Corps Aviation Cadet
Marcam ...... Marcam Corp. [*Associated Press*] (SAG)
MARCAMP .. Marine Corps Accrued Military Pay System (NG)
MARCAN ..... Maneuvering Reentry Control and Ablation Studies
MarCap ...... Marion Capital Holdings, Inc. [*Associated Press*] (SAG)
MARCAS ..... Maneuvering Reentry Control and Ablation Studies (MCD)
Mar Cas ..... Maritime Cases, by Crockford and Cox [*1860-71*] [*A publication*] (DLA)
MARCCO ..... Master Real-Time Circulation Controller (PDAA)
MARCE .... Materiel Asset Redistribution Center Europe [*Military*]
Marcell .... Pro Marcello [*of Cicero*] [*Classical studies*] (OCD)
MARCEP ..... Maintainability and Reliability Cost-Effectiveness Program (IEEE)
MARCH....... Marchioness
March .... March's English King's Bench and Common Pleas Reports [*A publication*] (DLA)
March .... March's Translation of Brooke's New Cases, English King's Bench [*82 English Reprint*] [*A publication*] (DLA)
MArch .... Master of Architectural Engineering (GAGS)
M Arch .... Master of Architecture
MARCH....... Melt-Down Accident Response Characteristics [*Nuclear energy*] (NRCH)
MARCHA..... Methodists Associated Representing the Cause of Hispanic Americans [*An association*]
M Arch Des... Master of Architectural Design
M Arch E .... Master of Architectural Engineering
M Arch Eng... Master of Architectural Engineering
M Arch H .... Master of Architectural History (PGP)
MArchH...... Master of Architectural History (GAGS)
M Arch in CP... Master of Architecture in City Planning
MArchivAdmin... Master of Archives Administration (ADA)
March N ...... March's New Cases, English King's Bench and Common Pleas Reports [*A publication*] (DLA)
March NC .... March's New Cases, English King's Bench [*1639-42*] [*A publication*] (DLA)
March NC .... Translation of Brook's New Cases [*1515-58*] [*A publication*] (DLA)
March NR ... March's New Cases, English King's Bench [*1639-42*] [*A publication*] (DLA)
M Arch Studies... Master of Architectural Studies (PGP)
M Arch UD... Master of Architecture in Urban Design (PGP)
MArchUD..... Master of Architecture in Urban Design (GAGS)
MARCIA ...... Mathematical Analysis of Requirements for Career Information Appraisal
MARC IS..... MARC Israel (NITA)
MARCIVE ..... MARC Five (NITA)
MARCKS..... Myristoylated Alanine-Rich C-Kinase Substrate [*Biochemistry*]
MARC(LC).... MARC Library of Congress (NITA)
Marc Mant... Marcus Mantua Benavidius [*Deceased, 1582*] [*Authority cited in pre-1607 legal work*] (DSA)
MarcNG...... Marcum Natural Gas Services, Inc. [*Associated Press*] (SAG)
MARCO....... Machine Referenced and Coordinated Outline
MARCO....... Mid-American Research Corp.
MARCOGAZ... Union of the Gas Industries of the Common Market Countries [*Defunct*] (EAIO)
MARCOM..... Maritime Command [*Canada, since 1964*]
MARCOM..... Microwave Airborne Communications Relay (IEEE)
MARCOMM... Maritime Commission (DNAB)
MARCOMMDET... Marine Communications Detachment (DNAB)
MARCOMNAVADGRU... Marine Corps Component Navy Advisory Group (CINC)
MARCON..... Mars Consortium
MARCON..... Micro Archives and Records Online [*Developed by AirS, Inc.*]
MARCONFOR... Maritime Contingency Force [*NATO*] (NATG)
MARCONFORLANT... Maritime Contingency Forces, Atlantic [*NATO*] (NATG)
MARCONP .. Maritime Contingency Plans (NATG)
Mar Conv..... Marcy's Epitome of Conveyancing [*1881*] [*A publication*] (DLA)
Mar Conv St... Marcy's Conveyancing Statutes [*5th ed.*] [*1893*] [*A publication*] (DLA)
MARCOR..... Marine Corps
MARCORABSCOLLUNIT... Marine Corps Absentee Collection Unit (DNAB)
MARCORADMINDET... Marine Corps Administrative Detachment (DNAB)
MARCORASBCOLLUNITDET... Marine Corps Absentee Collection Unit Detachment (DNAB)
MARCORDISBOF... Marine Corps Disbursing Office
MARCOREP... Marine Corps Representative (DNAB)
MARCORESTRACEN... Marine Corps Reserve Training Center
MARCORHISTCEN... Marine Corps Historical Center (DNAB)
MARCORMAN... Marine Corps Manual
MARCORPERSMAN... Marine Corps Personnel Manual
MARCORPS... Marine Corps
MARCORSUPDEP... Marine Corps Supply Depot
MARCORSYSCOM... Marine Corps Systems Command
MARCORSYSCOM... Marine Corps Systems Command (DOMA)
MARCOT...... Maritime Command Operational Team Training [*Canadian Navy*]
Mar Crp G ... Marine Corps Gazette [*A publication*] (BRI)
MARC-S...... Machine-Readable Cataloging - Serials (ADA)
MARC(S)..... MARC Serials (NITA)
MARCS .... Marine Computer System (PDAA)

MARCS .... Melcom All Round Adaptive Consolidated Software [*Japan*]
MARCS .... MELCOM All Round Adaptive Consolidated Software (NITA)
MARC(UK) ... MARC (United Kingdom) (NITA)
Marcus .... [*The*] Marcus Corp. [*Associated Press*] (SAG)
Marcus An ... Marcus Antonius Blancus [*Deceased, 1548*] [*Authority cited in pre-1607 legal work*] (DSA)
Marcus Anto... Marcus Antonius Blancus [*Deceased, 1548*] [*Authority cited in pre-1607 legal work*] (DSA)
MARD .... Marine Assessment Research Division [*Now Ocean Environmental Research Division*] (USDC)
MARD .... Marine Assessment Research Division [*Marine science*] (OSRA)
MA-RD .... Maritime Administration Office of Research and Development [*Washington, DC*]
MARD .... Military Aeronautical Research and Development (PDAA)
MARDAC ..... Manpower Research and Data Analysis Center [*DoD*] (NVT)
MARDAN...... Marine Differential Analyzer
MARDATA.... Maritime Data Network [*Lloyd's Maritime Data Network Ltd.*] [*Stamford, CT Database*]
Mar de Lau... Martinus Caratti de Laude [*Flourished, 1438-45*] [*Authority cited in pre-1607 legal work*] (DSA)
MARDET ...... Marine Detachment
MARDEZ ...... Maritime Defense Zone [*Navy*] [*Coast Guard*] (DOMA)
MARDIS....... Modernized Army Research and Development Information System
MARDIV ...... Marine Division
MARDO........ Months after Receipt of Delivery Order (MCD)
MarDrl .... Marine Drilling Co. [*Associated Press*] (SAG)
MARDS........ Medium Artillery Delivered Sensor [*Army*]
MARE.......... Major Accident Response Exercise (MCD)
MARE.......... Major Account Response Evaluation (MCD)
MARE.......... Maritime Engineering [*Canadian Navy*]
MARE.......... Master of Arts in Religious Education (PGP)
MARE.......... Months after Receipt of Equipment [*Navy*]
MAREA .... Member of the American Railway Engineering Association
MAREA .... Middle Leaf Area [*Botany*]
MARECEBO... Manned Research on Celestial Bodies Committee [*International Academy of Astronautics*]
MARECS ..... Marine Communications Satellites (NITA)
MARECS ..... Maritime Communications Satellite
MARED .... Materiel Acquisition and Readiness Executive Development [*Program*] [*Army*] (RDA)
Ma Reg........ Massachusetts Register [*A publication*] (AAGC)
MAREGSQ.... Marine Air Regulating Squadron
MAREMIC.... Maintenance Repair and Minor Construction [*Program*] [*Air Force*]
Mar Eng....... Marine Engineer (PGP)
MARENTS ..... Modified Advanced Research Environmental Test Satellite [*Air Force*]
MAREP .... Marine Environmental Prediction Task Group [*US government*] [*Terminated, 1969*]
MARES .... Marine Corps Automated Readiness Evaluation System
MARES/FORSTAT... Marine Corps Automated Readiness Evaluation System/Status of Forces
MARESTNG... Marine Corps Reserve Training (NVT)
MARF.......... Master Area Reference File [*Bureau of the Census*] (GFGA)
MARF........... Master Availability Reference File [*Army Electronics Command*]
Mar Fa........ Martinus de Fano [*Deceased circa 1275*] [*Authority cited in pre-1607 legal work*] (DSA)
MARFAIR..... Marine Fleet Air
MARFAIRWEST... Marine Fleet Air, West Coast
Mar Fan....... Martinus de Fano [*Deceased circa 1275*] [*Authority cited in pre-1607 legal work*] (DSA)
MARFINCEN... Marine Corps Finance Center (DNAB)
MARFIREX... Marine Firing Exercise (NVT)
MARFOR...... Marine Forces [*Element of a Joint Task Force*]
MARFS .... Multienvironment Active RF [*Radio Frequency*] Seeker
MARG .... Margarine
MARG .... Margin [*or Marginal*]
marg .... Margin (WDMC)
MARG .... Marine Amphibious Ready Group (MCD)
MARG .... Market Analysis Report Generator [*Computer science*]
MARG .... Mediterranean Amphibious Ready Group (MCD)
MARGARFOR... Marine Garrison Force
Margate....... Margate Ventures [*Associated Press*] (SAG)
MARGE .... Margarine (ADA)
MARGEN...... Management Report Generator [*Randolph Data Services, Inc.*] [*Software package*] [*Computer science*] (IEEE)
MARGIE....... Memory Analysis, Response Generation, and Interference in English
MARGILSAREA... Marshalls-Gilberts Area
MARGL .... Marginal (ROG)
Margo......... Margo Nursery Farms [*Associated Press*] (SAG)
MARHELILEX... Marine Helicopter Landing Exercise (NVT)
MARI .... Marijuana Cigarette [*Slang*] (DSUE)
Mari............ Marinus de Caramanico [*Flourished, 1269-85*] [*Authority cited in pre-1607 legal work*] (DSA)
MARI .... Medicare Administrative Reform Initiative [*Health Care Financing Administration*]
MARI .... Mercantile Atlantic Routing Instructions
MARI .... Microelectronics Applications Research Institute [*Newcastle-Upon-Tyne, England*]
MARI .... Motivator and Response Indicator
MARIA .... Macroaggregated Radioiodinated Albumin [*Radiology*] [*Pharmacy*] (DAVI)
Maria Soci... Marianus Socinus [*Authority cited in pre-1607 legal work*] (DSA)
MARIC .... Marine Resources Information Center [*Massachusetts Institute of Technology*] (NOAA)
MARID........ Mica-Amphibole-Rutile-Ilmenite-Diopside [*Geology*]
MARIDAS..... Maritime Data System (IAA)

Mariet......... Marietta Corp. [*Associated Press*] (SAG)
Marijuana Rev... Marijuana Review [*A publication*] (DLA)
MARINE....... Management Analysis Reporting Information on the Naval Environment System (NG)
Marine Ct R... Marine Court Reporter (McAdam's) [*New York*] [*A publication*] (DLA)
MarinerH ..... Mariner Health Group, Inc. [*Associated Press*] (SAG)
MARINEX..... Marine Express (AABC)
Marin Frecc... Marinus Freccia [*Flourished, 16th century*] [*Authority cited in pre-1607 legal work*] (DSA)
MARINTRARON... Marine Instrument Training Squadron
MARIP .... Maintenance And Repair Inspection Program [*Military*] (DNAB)
MARIS .... Materials and Resources Information Service (NITA)
MarisaC....... Marisa Christina, Inc. [*Associated Press*] (SAG)
MARISAT .... Maritime Satellite System [*COMSAT*]
MARISP ...... Maritime Strike Plan
MARIT .... Maritime
MARITA ...... Maritime Airfield (NATG)
MARITADMIN... Maritime Administration [*Also, MA, MARAD*] [*Department of Transportation*] (MUGU)
MARITCOM... Maritime Commission
Maritimes L Rep (CCH)... Maritimes Law Reporter (Commerce Clearing House) [*A publication*] (DLA)
Maritrn........ Maritrans, Inc. [*Associated Press*] (SAG)
MARITZ........ Maritzburg (ROG)
Marius........ Marius. Concerning Bills of Exchange [*4 eds.*] [*1651-84*] [*A publication*] (DLA)
MARK .... Maintenance and Reliability Kit [*Military*] (NVT)
Mark .... Market
mark .... Market (VRA)
MARK .... Mechanized Assignment and Record Keeping [*Database management system*]
MARK .... Mid-Atlantic Ridge Kane
MARKAR...... Mapping and Reconnaissance Ku-Band Airborne RADAR
MarkCtr....... Mark Centers Trust [*Associated Press*] (SAG)
Mark El........ Markby's Elements of Law [*6th ed.*] [*1905*] [*A publication*] (DLA)
Markel......... Markel Corp. [*Associated Press*] (SAG)
Markerl........ Marker International [*Associated Press*] (SAG)
MarkIV........ Mark IV Industries, Inc. [*Associated Press*] (SAG)
MARKS .... Modern Army Record Keeping System (INF)
Marks & Sayre... Marks and Sayre's Reports [*108 Alabama*] [*A publication*] (DLA)
Marks & Sayre's... Marks' and Sayre's Reports [*108 Alabama*] [*A publication*] (DLA)
MarksBr....... Marks Bros. Jewelers, Inc. [*Associated Press*] (SAG)
MARKSIM..... [*A*] Marketing Decision Simulation [*Game*]
MarkSol....... Mark Solutions, Inc. [*Associated Press*] (SAG)
MARKSTRAT... Marketing Strategy [*Simulation package developed by Professors Jean-Claude Larreche and Hubert Gatignon*]
MarkVII........ Mark VII, Inc. [*Associated Press*] (SAG)
MarkWst...... MarkWest Hydrocarbon, Inc. [*Associated Press*] (SAG)
MARL.......... Marlboro [*Vermont*] [*Seismograph station code, US Geological Survey*] (SEIS)
MARL.......... Master of Arts and Letters
MARL.......... Master of Arts in Religious Leadership (PGP)
MARL.......... Mobile Acoustics Research Laboratory (MCD)
Marl........... Statute of Marlborough [*A publication*] (DSA)
Mar LA........ Martin's Louisiana Reports [*A publication*] (DLA)
MARLAB ..... Mobile Air Research Laboratory (PDAA)
MARLAGS..... Marine Life and Geochemical Studies [*Marine science*] (MSC)
MARLB .... Marlborough (ROG)
Mar LC .... Maritime Law Cases, by Crockford [*1860-71*] [*A publication*] (DLA)
Mar L Cas (NS)... Maritime Law Cases (New Series), by Aspinall [*1870-1940*] [*A publication*] (DLA)
Mar LC NS... Maritime Law Cases, New Series, by Aspinall [*1870-1940*] [*England*] [*A publication*] (DLA)
Mar Leg Bib... Marvin's Legal Bibliography [*A publication*] (DLA)
MARLEX....... Marine Corps Reserve Landing Exercise (NVT)
MAR LIC ..... Marriage License (WDAA)
MARLIN .... Middle Atlantic Regional Information Network
MARLIS .... Multi-Agent Research Linkage Information System (NITA)
MARLIS .... Multiaspect Relevance Linkage Information System
Mar LJ .... Maryland Law Journal and Real Estate Record [*A publication*] (DLA)
MARLNO...... Marine Liaison Office (DNAB)
MARLO........ Marine Liaison Officer (DOMA)
MARLOG...... Marine Logistical Command (VNW)
Mar LR .... Maritime Law Cases, First Series, by Crockford [*1860-71*] [*A publication*] (DLA)
Mar LR .... Maritime Law Cases, New Series, by Aspinall [*1870-1940*] [*A publication*] (DLA)
Mar L Rec ... Maryland Law Record [*A publication*] (DLA)
MARLSR ...... Manufacturers Association of Robes, Leisurewear, Shirts, and Rainwear [*Defunct*] (EA)
Marlton........ Marlton Technologies, Inc. [*Associated Press*] (SAG)
MarM.......... Marine Midland Banks, Inc. [*Associated Press*] (SAG)
MARM .... Microprocessor Arithmetic Model
MARM .... Middle Atlantic Regional Meeting [*of American Chemical Society*]
MARM .... Moving Average Rating Method [*Insurance*]
Mar Mant..... Marcus Mantua Benavidius [*Deceased, 1582*] [*Authority cited in pre-1607 legal work*] (DSA)
MARMAP..... Marine Resources Monitoring, Assessment, and Prediction [*National Oceanic and Atmospheric Administration*]
Mar Mech E... Marine Mechanical Engineer
MARMETS ... Marine Meteorological Service
Marm Par .... Marmor Parium [*Classical studies*] (OCD)
MAR/MSR.... Multifunction Array RADAR / Missile Site RADAR (SAA)

MARN	Marion Capital Holdings [*NASDAQ symbol*] (NQ)
MARNA	Marine Navigation (NITA)
MARNAF	Marquardt Navair Fuel [*A boron slurry propellant for spacecraft*]
Mar N & Q	Maritime Notes and Queries [*1873-1900*] [*A publication*] (DLA)
MarNB	Marine National Bank (California) [*Associated Press*] (SAG)
MarNBk	Marine National Bank (California) [*Associated Press*] (SAG)
Mar NC	March's New Cases, English King's Bench [*1639-42*] [*A publication*] (DLA)
Mar NC	Martin's North Carolina Reports [*1 North Carolina*] [*A publication*] (DLA)
MarnLP	Marine Ltd. [*Associated Press*] (SAG)
MarnLP	Marine Ltd. Partnership [*Associated Press*] (SAG)
Mar NR	March's New Cases [*1639-42*] [*A publication*] (DLA)
Mar NS	Martin's Louisiana Reports, New Series [*A publication*] (DLA)
MARO	Maritime Air Radio Organization [*NATO*] (NATG)
MAROPS	Maritime Operations
MAROTS	Maritime Orbital Test Satellite
MARP	Manpower Allocation/Requirements Plan [*Navy*]
MARP	Marine Petroleum Trust [*NASDAQ symbol*] (NQ)
MARP	Maximum Authorized for Repair Parts (DNAB)
MARP	Mobilization Augmentee Revitalization Program [*Military*]
MARP	Months after Receipt of Problem [*Navy*] (NG)
MARPAC	Headquarters, Department of the Pacific [*Marine Corps*]
MARPAC	Maritime Command Pacific [*Canada, since 1964*]
MARPAC/ORT	Maritime Forces Pacific Operational Research Team [*Canada*]
MARPDA	Mid-America Periodical Distributors Association (EA)
MARPEP	Marine Physical Environmental Prediction
MarPet	Marine Petroleum Trust [*Associated Press*] (SAG)
MARPEX	Management of Repair Parts Expenditure [*Army*] (PDAA)
MARPIC	Marine Pollution Information Centre [*Marine Biological Association of the United Kingdom*] (IID)
Marpie	Middle-Aged Rural Professional [*Lifestyle classification*]
MARPOL	International Convention for the Prevention of Pollution from Ships [*1973*]
MARPOL	Maritime Pollution Convention [*1978*] (DS)
MARPOLMON	Sub-Group of Experts on Marine Pollution Monitoring [*Marine science*] (MSC)
MARPRO	Marine Profile Data Base (GNE)
Mar Prov	Maritime Provinces Reports [*Canada*] [*A publication*] (DLA)
MARPS	Mechanized Accounting Reserve Pay System
marq	Marquetry (VRA)
MARQ	Marquette Electronics, Inc. [*NASDAQ symbol*] (SPSG)
MARQ	Marquette Medical Systems, Inc. [*NASDAQ symbol*] (SAG)
MARQ	Marquis [*or Marquess*]
MARQA	Marquette Electronics'A' [*NASDAQ symbol*] (TTSB)
MarqEl	Marquette Electronics, Inc. [*Associated Press*] (SAG)
MarqG	Marquee Group, Inc. (The) [*Associated Press*] (SAG)
MarqGrp	Marquee Group, Inc. (The) [*Associated Press*] (SAG)
MarqMed	Marquette Medical Systems, Inc. [*Associated Press*] (SAG)
Marqst	Marquest Medical Products, Inc. [*Associated Press*] (SAG)
Marquette Bus Rev	Marquette Business Review [*A publication*] (DLA)
Marquette U.	Marquette University (GAGS)
MARQUIS	Master Remote Query Interface System [*Computer science*]
Marr	Hay and Marriott's English Admiralty Reports [*A publication*] (DLA)
MARR	Marine Accidents Requiring Rescue (OA)
Mar R	Maritime Law Reports [*A publication*] (DLA)
Marr	Marrack's European Assurance Cases [*England*] [*A publication*] (DLA)
Marr	Marriage (DLA)
MARR	Maximum Annual Rate of Return [*Finance*]
MARR	Minimum Attractive Rate of Return [*Economics*]
Marr Adm	Marriott's English Admiralty Reports [*A publication*] (DLA)
MARRC	Multi-Channel Automatic Remote Recording
MARRCS	Manpower Requirements and Resources Control System [*Navy*] (NVT)
MARRD	Married (ROG)
MARRE	Manual RADAR Reconnaissance Exploitation (MCD)
MARRE	Marriage (ROG)
Mar Rec B	Martin's Recital Book [*A publication*] (DLA)
Mar Reg	Mitchell's Maritime Register [*England*] [*A publication*] (DLA)
MARRES	Manual RADAR Reconnaissance Exploitation System [*Air Force*]
Marr Form	Marriott's Formulare Instrumentorum [*Admiralty Court*] [*1802*] [*A publication*] (DLA)
MarriotI	Marriott International [*Associated Press*] (SAG)
MARRS	Mechanized Ammunition Recording and Reporting System
MARR SETTL	Marriage Settlement [*Legal term*] (DLA)
MARS	Machine-Aided Realization System
MARS	Machine-Assisted Reference Section [*American Library Association*] [*Information service or system*] (IID)
MARS	Machine-Assisted Reference Service [*St. Paul Public Library*] (OLDSS)
MARS	Machine Automated Realty Service
MARS	Machine Retrieval System
MARS	Magnetic Airborne Recording System
MARS	Maintenance Activities and Resources Simulation [*Computer science*]
MARS	Maintenance Analysis and Recording Systems
MARS	Maintenance Analysis Repair Set
MARS	Maintenance Assistance and Repair System [*Military*]
MARS	Major Accident Reporting System [*Engineering*]
MARS	Management Action Reporting System (MCD)
MARS	Management Analysis Reporting System [*Computer science*]
MARS	Management and Administrative Reporting Subsystem [*Department of Health and Human Services*] (GFGA)
MARS	Management Reports and Statistics
MARS	Manhour Accounting and Reporting System

MARS	Man-Hour Accounting and Reporting System [*Military*] (MCD)
MARS	Manned Aerodynamic Reusable Spaceship
MARS	Manned Astronautical Research Station [*Space laboratory*]
MARS	Marconi Automatic Relay System (IEEE)
MARS	Marine Account Reconciliation Service
MARS	Marine Aircraft Repair Squadron
MARS	Marine Reporting Station [*National Weather Service*]
MARS	Maritime Surface and Subsurface [*Canadian Navy*]
MARS	Market Analysis and Reference System [*Vancouver stock exchange computer system*] [*Canada*]
MARS	Marketing and Advertising Reference Service (NITA)
Mars	Marsden's Select Pleas in the Court of Admiralty [*Selden Society Publications, Vols. 6, 11*] [*A publication*] (DLA)
MARS	Marsh Supermarkets, Inc. [*NASDAQ symbol*] (NQ)
MARS	Martin Automatic Reporting System
MARS	Master Attitude Reference System
MARS	Master of Arts in Religious Studies (PGP)
MARS	Material Action Reporting System (MCD)
MARS	Material Response Study
MARS	Materiel Acquisition Resource System [*Military*]
MARS	Mathematics Anxiety Rating Scale [*Psychology*]
MARS	Maximum Asset Return Strategy [*Allingham, Anderson, Roll & Ross*] [*British*] (ECON)
MARS	Measuring Accuracy and Repeatability Study
MARS	Mechanical Accessory Repair Shop (MCD)
MARS	Media Alert and Response System [*Public relations project devised by Pharmaceutical Manufacturers Association*]
MARS	Memory-Address Register Storage [*Computer science*]
MARS	Meteorological Automatic Reporting Station [*Canada*]
MARS	Mevinolin Atherosclerosis Regression Study (MEDA)
MARS	Midair Recovery [*or Retrieval*] System [*Rescue by helicopter*] [*Military*]
MARS	Migration Agents' Registration Scheme [*Australia*]
MARS	Military Affiliated Radio System [*or Stations*] [*Amateur-operated radio stations*]
MARS	Military Airborne RADAR System [*Air Force*] (IAA)
MARS	Military Amateur Radio System (IAA)
MARS	Military Amphibious Reconnaissance System (RDA)
MARS	Millimeter Wave Amplification by Resonance Saturation (IAA)
MARS	Miniature Attitude Reference System
mars	Minimum-Altitude Release and Strafe (MCD)
MARS	Minolta Automatic Retrieval System (NITA)
MARS	Mirror Advanced Reactor Study (MCD)
MARS	Mission Maintenance and Reliability Simulation (MCD)
MARS	Mobile Atlantic Range Stations [*Tracking stations*] (MUGU)
MARS	Mobile Automatic Reporting System (MCD)
MARS	Model Annotation Search and Retrieval System [*Geological program*]
MARS	Modular Airborne Recorder System (MCD)
MARS	Modular Attack RADAR System (MCD)
MARS	Monitor and Replenisher System
MARS	Monitoring Accounting Reporting and Statistical System [*Aviation*]
MARS	Monthly Aerial Reconnaissance Summary (MCD)
MARS	Motorola Aerial Remote Sensing [*Flying laboratory*]
MARS	Multiaperture Reluctance Switch [*Data storage unit*]
MARS	Multicast Address Resolution Service [*Computer science*]
MARS	Multiple Access Retrieval System [*Control Data Corp.*]
MARS	Multiple Action Raid Simulation [*France*]
MARS	Multiple Aerial Refueling System (PDAA)
MARS	Multiple Artillery Rocket System [*Army*]
MARS	Multiuser Archival and Retrieval System [*Computer science*]
MARS	Multivariate Analysis, Retrieval, and Storage [*System*] [*NASA*]
MARS	PTS Marketing and Advertising Reference Service [*Predicasts, Inc.*] [*Cleveland, OH*] [*Information service or system*] (IID)
MARSA	Marsh Supermkts'A' [*NASDAQ symbol*] (TTSB)
MARSA	Military Accepts Responsibility for Separation of Aircraft (AFM)
Mars Adm	Marsden's English Admiralty [*A publication*] (DLA)
Mar Sal	Marius Salomonius [*Deceased, 1557*] [*Authority cited in pre-1607 legal work*] (DSA)
MARSAM	Multiple Airborne Reconnaissance Sensors Assessment Model (MCD)
MARSAS	Marine Search and Attack System (PDAA)
MARSAT	Maritime Satellite [*COMSAT*]
MARSATS	Maritime Satellite System [*COMSAT*]
MARSB	Marsh Supermkts'B' [*NASDAQ symbol*] (TTSB)
M Ar Sc	Master of Arts and Sciences
MArSci	Master of Arts and Sciences (NADA)
Mars Coll	Marsden's Collisions at Sea [*11th ed.*] [*1961*] [*A publication*] (DLA)
MARSD	Minimal Attended RADAR Station Display (DWSG)
MARSEN	Maritime Remote Sensing (MCD)
Marsh	Marshall and Sevestre's Appeals [*1862-64*] [*Bengal, India*] [*A publication*] (DLA)
Marsh	Marshall's Circuit Court Decisions [*United States*] [*A publication*] (DLA)
Marsh	Marshall's English Common Pleas Reports [*1814-16*] [*A publication*] (DLA)
Marsh	Marshall's High Court Reports [*Bengal*] [*A publication*] (DLA)
Marsh	Marshall's Reports [*Ceylon*] [*A publication*] (DLA)
Marsh	Marshall's Reports [*4 Utah*] [*A publication*] (DLA)
Marsh	Marshall's Reports [*Kentucky*] [*A publication*] (DLA)
MARSH	Matching Aid to Restore States Habitat (GNE)
Marshall	Marshall's Reports [*Bengal*] (DLA)
Marshall	Reports of Cases on Appeal [*Calcutta*] [*A publication*] (DLA)
Marshall U.	Marshall University (GAGS)
Marsh Beng	Marshall's Reports [*Bengal*] [*A publication*] (DLA)
Marsh Calc	Marshall's Reports [*Calcutta*] [*A publication*] (DLA)

Marsh Car ...   Marshall on Railways as Carriers [A publication]   (DLA)
Marsh Ceylon...   Marshall's Ceylon Reports [A publication]   (DLA)
Marsh Costs...   Marshall on the Law of Costs [A publication]   (DLA)
Marsh CP....   Marshall's English Common Pleas Reports [A publication]   (DLA)
Marsh Dec....   Marshall on the Federal Constitution [A publication]   (DLA)
Marsh Dec....   Marshall's Circuit Court Decisions, by Brockenbrough [United States] [A publication]   (DLA)
Marsh (Eng)...   Marshall's English Common Pleas Reports [A publication]   (DLA)
MarshFn ......   Marshalltown Financial Corp. [Associated Press]   (SAG)
MarshI ......   Marshall & Isley Corp. [Associated Press]   (SAG)
MarshIIs ......   Marshall & Isley Corp. [Associated Press]   (SAG)
Marsh Ins ......   Marshall on Marine Insurance [A publication]   (DLA)
Marsh (KY)...   Marshall's Reports [Kentucky] [A publication]   (DLA)
MARSHL ......   Marshal   (ROG)
Marsh Op.....   Marshall's Constitutional Opinions [A publication]   (DLA)
Marsh Ry.....   Marshall on Railways as Carriers [A publication]   (DLA)
Marsh Ry.....   Marshall's Duties and Obligations of Railway Companies [A publication]   (DLA)
Mar Sill ......   Martinus Sillimanus [Flourished, 13th century] [Authority cited in pre-1607 legal work]   (DSA)
MARSIM .....   International Conference on Marine Simulation   (PDAA)
MARSL ....   Machine-Readable Shelf List [Carleton University] [Canada]   (NITA)
MARSO ....   Marine Corps Shipping Order   (NG)
MA/RSO ......   Mobilization Augmentee/Reserve Supplement Officer [Air Force]   (AFM)
MARSPTBN...   Marine Support Battalion   (DNAB)
MARSREPSYS...   Military Affiliate Radio System Repeater System   (DNAB)
MARSTA ......   Marital Status [Army]   (AABC)
MARSTELSYS...   Military Affiliate Radio System Teletypewriter Relay System   (DNAB)
MARSTSIC...   Marst on Sicca [England]
MARSYAS....   Marshall System for Aerospace Simulation [Programming language] [1966-68]   (CSR)
MART..........   Maintenance Analysis Review Technique
Mart..........   Martial [Roman poet, 40-104AD] [Classical studies]   (OCD)
MART..........   Martinique [West Indies]   (WDAA)
Mart..........   Martin's Louisiana Term Reports [1809-30] [A publication]   (DLA)
Mart..........   Martin's North Carolina Reports [1 North Carolina] [A publication]   (DLA)
Mart..........   Martinus Gosia [Authority cited in pre-1607 legal work]   (DSA)
MART..........   Martius [March] [Latin]
MART..........   Martyr
MART..........   Master of Arts in Religion and Theology   (PGP)
MART..........   Mathematical Modeling and Reliability Transducer   (MCD)
MART..........   Mean Active Repair Time   (IEEE)
MART..........   Missile Automation Radiation Test   (IAA)
MART..........   Mobile Automatic Radiation Tester
MARTA ....   Metropolitan Atlanta Rapid Transit Authority [FTA]   (TAG)
MARTAC .....   Martin Automatic Rapid Test and Control
Mart & Y ....   Martin and Yerger's Tennessee Reports [8 Tennessee] [1825-28] [A publication]   (DLA)
Mart & Yer..   Martin and Yerger's Tennessee Reports [8 Tennessee] [1825-28] [A publication]   (DLA)
Mart & Yerg...   Martin and Yerger's Tennessee Reports [8 Tennessee] [1825-28] [A publication]   (DLA)
Mart & Y (Tenn)...   Martin and Yerger's Tennessee Reports [8 Tennessee] [1825-28] [A publication]   (DLA)
Mart Ark .....   Martin's Decisions in Equity [Arkansas] [A publication]   (DLA)
MARTC ....   Marine Air Reserve Training Command
MartCol.......   Martin Color-Fi, Inc. [Associated Press]   (SAG)
MARTCOM....   Marine Air Reserve Training Command
Mart Cond LA...   Martin's Condensed Louisiana Reports [A publication]   (DLA)
Mart Conv....   Martin's Practice of Conveyancing [A publication]   (DLA)
MARTD ....   Marine Air Reserve Training Detachment
Mart Dec .....   United States Decisions in Martin's North Carolina Reports [A publication]   (DLA)
MARTEC ......   Martin Thin-Film Electronic Circuit
Martek........   Martek Biosciences, Inc. [Associated Press]   (SAG)
MARTEL ......   Missile Antiradiation Television [Military]   (CAAL)
Marten........   Marten Transport Ltd. [Associated Press]   (SAG)
Mart Ex......   Martin on Executors [A publication]   (DLA)
Mart GA......   Martin's Reports [21-30 Georgia] [A publication]   (DLA)
Marth W Ca...   Martha Washington Cases [A publication]   (DLA)
MARTI ....   Maneuverable Reentry Technology Investigation
Martin........   Martin's Louisiana Reports [A publication]   (DLA)
Martin..........   Martin's North Carolina Reports [1 North Carolina] [A publication]   (DLA)
Martin..........   Martin's Reports [21-30, 54-70 Georgia] [A publication]   (DLA)
Mart Ind ......   Martin's Reports [54-70 Indiana] [A publication]   (DLA)
MARTINI......   Massive Analog Recording Technical Instrument for Nebulous Indications
Martin Index...   Martin's Index to Virginia Reports [A publication]   (DLA)
Martin (Lou) NS...   Martin's Louisiana Reports, New Series [A publication]   (DLA)
Martin's Chy...   Martin's Chancery Decisions [Arkansas] [A publication]   (DLA)
Martin's LA Rep...   Martin's Louisiana Reports [A publication]   (DLA)
Martin's LA Rep NS...   Martin's Louisiana Reports, New Series [A publication]   (DLA)
Martin's Louisiana R...   Martin's Louisiana Reports [A publication]   (DLA)
Martin's NS...   Martin's Louisiana Reports, New Series [A publication]   (DLA)
Martin's R NS...   Martin's Louisiana Reports, New Series [A publication]   (DLA)
MartIs........   Martyrdom of Isaiah [Pseudepigrapha]   (BJA)
MartIsa........   Martyrdom of Isaiah [Pseudepigrapha]   (BJA)
Mart LA ....   Martin's Louisiana Reports, Old and New Series [A publication]   (DLA)

Mart Laud....   Martinus Caratti de Laude [Flourished, 1438-45] [Authority cited in pre-1607 legal work]   (DSA)
Mart Law Nat...   Martens' Law of Nations [A publication]   (DLA)
Mart MC ......   Martin's Mining Cases [Canada] [A publication]   (DLA)
MartMM ......   Martin Marietta Materials [Associated Press]   (SAG)
Mart NC ......   Martin's North Carolina Reports [1 North Carolina] [A publication]   (DLA)
MartnIn ......   Martin Industries, Inc. [Associated Press]   (SAG)
MartnL ......   Martin Lawrence Ltd. [Associated Press]   (SAG)
Mart NS......   Martin's Louisiana Reports, New Series [A publication]   (DLA)
Mart NS (LA)...   Martin's Louisiana Reports, New Series [A publication]   (DLA)
MARTOS......   Multiaccess Real-Time Operating System [AEG Telefunken] [Germany]
Mart OS (LA)...   Martin's Louisiana Reports, Old Series [A publication]   (DLA)
MARTRA & REPLCOMS...   Marine Training and Replacement Commands
M Art (RCA)...   Master of Art, Royal College of Art
Mart Rep .....   Martin's Louisiana Reports [A publication]   (DLA)
Mart Rep NS...   Martin's Louisiana Reports, New Series [A publication]   (DLA)
MARTS ......   Master RADAR Tracking Station
MARTS ......   Master RADAR Training System
MARTS ......   Mobile Automatic Radio Telephone System   (MCD)
MARTS ......   Monthly Advance Retail Trade Survey [Bureau of the Census]   (GFGA)
Mart USCC...   Martin's Circuit Court Reports [1 North Carolina] [A publication]   (DLA)
MARU ......   Medical Architecture Research Unit [Polytechnic of North London] [British]   (IRC)
MARU ......   Middle America Research Unit
MARUNET...   Maruzen Online Network [Maruzen Co. Ltd.] [Japan Telecommunications]
MARUNITNG...   Marine Unit Training   (NVT)
MARV ......   Maneuverable AntiRADAR Vehicle   (MCD)
MARV ......   Maneuverable Reentry Vehicle   (AABC)
MARV ......   Marvelous   (DSUE)
Marv ......   Marvel's Reports [15-16 Delaware] [A publication]   (DLA)
MARV ......   Mobile Acoustic Recording Vehicle   (MCD)
MARV ......   Mobile Armored Reconnaissance/Operational Vehicle   (MCD)
MARV ......   Multi-Element Articulated Research Vehicle [Engineering]   (OA)
Marv Av......   Marvin on General Average [A publication]   (DLA)
Marv (Del)...   Marvel's Reports [15-16 Delaware] [A publication]   (DLA)
MARVEL ......   Machine-Assisted Realization of the Virtual Electronic Library [Information service or system Library of Congress]
Marvel........   Marvel Entertainment Corp. [Associated Press]   (SAG)
Marvel........   Marvel's Reports [15-16 Delaware] [A publication]   (DLA)
MARVEL ......   Mississippi Aerophysics Research Vehicle with Extended Latitude
Marv Leg Bib...   Marvin's Legal Bibliography [A publication]   (DLA)
MARVLS .....   MARC Video Disc Library System   (NITA)
Marv Wr & S...   Marvin on Wreck and Salvage [A publication]   (DLA)
Mar Wr & S...   Marvin on Wreck and Salvage [A publication]   (DLA)
MARX ....   Mark Aero [Air carrier designation symbol]
Mary ....   Maryland Reports [A publication]   (DLA)
MARY ....   Saint Mary Land & Exploration [NASDAQ symbol]   (SAG)
Marygrove C...   Marygrove College   (GAGS)
Maryland .....   Maryland Reports [A publication]   (DLA)
Maryland Ch Dec...   Maryland Chancery Decisions [A publication]   (DLA)
Maryville U...   Maryville University of St. Louis   (GAGS)
Marywood C...   Marywood College   (GAGS)
MAS..........   Lithuanian Catholic Youth Association Ateitis   (EA)
MAS..........   MacDonald Agricultural Services Ltd. [British]
MAS..........   Machine Accounting School
MAS..........   Macintosh Application System [Computer science]   (CDE)
MAS..........   Macroassembler
MAS..........   Madang Air Services [Australia]
MAS..........   Magic Angle Spinning [Spectroscopy]
MAS..........   Magnesia-Alumina-Silicate [Inorganic chemistry]
MAS..........   Maintenance and Services   (AFIT)
MAS..........   Maintenance and Supply   (AFIT)
MAS..........   Malaysian Airline System [ICAO designator]   (FAAC)
MAS..........   Management Accounting System
MAS..........   Management Advisory Services
MAS..........   Management and Administrative Statistics   (OICC)
MAS..........   Management Appraisal Survey [Test]
MAS..........   Maneuvering Attack System   (MCD)
MAS..........   Manifest Anxiety Scale [Psychology]
MAS..........   Manned Aerial Surveillance
MAS..........   Manual A1 Simplex [Aviation]
MAS..........   Manufacturing Advisory Service   (DCTA)
MAS..........   Manufacturing Assembly Specification
MAS..........   Manus [Papua New Guinea] [Airport symbol]   (OAG)
MAS..........   Manus Island [Bismarck Archipelago] [Airport symbol]   (AD)
MAS..........   MAP [Manufacturing Automation Protocol]/One Applications Services [Software] [Automotive engineering]
MAS..........   Marine Acoustical Services
MAS..........   Marine Advisory Service [See also NMAS] [National Oceanic and Atmospheric Administration Information service or system]   (IID)
MAS..........   Maritime Air Superiority   (NVT)
MAS..........   Market Advisory Service [British Overseas Trade Board]   (DS)
MAS..........   Mars Approach Sensor
mas ....   Masai [MARC language code Library of Congress]   (LCCP)
MAS..........   Masco Corp. [NYSE symbol]   (SPSG)
MAS..........   Masculine
MAS..........   Mason [or Masonry]   (ROG)
MAS..........   Mason Butte [Idaho] [Seismograph station code, US Geological Survey Closed]   (SEIS)
mas ....   Masonry   (VRA)

Mas	Mason's United States Circuit Court Reports [*A publication*] (DLA)
Mas	Masorah (BJA)
Mas	Massachusetts Reports [*A publication*] (DLA)
MAS	Massachusetts State Library, Boston, MA [*OCLC symbol*] (OCLC)
Mas	Masseketh (BJA)
MAS	Master (DSUE)
MAS	Master Activation Schedule (AAG)
MAS	Master Analysis Scheme [*Monitoring technique*]
MAS	Master of Accounting Science
MAS	Master of Actuarial Science
MAS	Master of Administrative Science (PGP)
MAS	Master of Administrative Studies (ADA)
MAS	Master of Aeronautical Science (GAGS)
MAS	Master of Applied Science
MAS	Master of Applied Spirituality (PGP)
MASC	Master of Applied Statistics (GAGS)
MAS	Master of Archival Studies (GAGS)
MAS	Master of Archival Studies
MAS	Material Activity Schedule
MAS	Material Application Service [*NASA*] (IAA)
MAS	Material Availability Schedule
MAS	Mathematics Attitude Scale (EDAC)
MAS	Mature Age Student (ADA)
MAS	Maximum Aerobic Speed [*Biology*]
MAS	McMaster University Library [*UTLAS symbol*]
MAS	Meconium Aspiration Syndrome [*Medicine*]
MAS	Media Advisory Service [*British*]
MAS	Medical Administrative Service (DAVI)
MAS	Medical Advisory Service [*British*]
MASB	Medical Audit Statistics (PDAA)
MAS	Medical Audit Study (HCT)
MAS	Meiosis-Activating Sterol [*Cytology*]
MAS	Member of the Arundel Society [*British*]
MAS	Memory and Auxiliary Storage Subsystem [*Space Flight Operations Facility, NASA*]
MAS	Mercury Analyzer System [*Perkin-Elmer Co. instrument designation*]
MAS	Merged Area Schools (OICC)
MAS	Merseyside Aviation Society [*British*] (DBA)
MAS	Mesoatrial Shunt [*Medicine*] (DMAA)
MAS	Metal-Alumina Semiconductor (IAA)
MA S	Metal-Alumina-Silicon (IEEE)
MAS	Metal Anchor Slots [*Technical drawings*]
MAS	Metastable Atomic State
MAS	Methods and Standards (MCD)
MAS	Methods of Air Sampling and Analysis [*Air Pollution Control Association*]
MAS	Mezhdunarodnaya Assotsiatsiya Sudovladeltsev [*International Shipowners' Association*] [*Poland*] (EAIO)
MAS	Micro-Alloyed Steel [*Metallurgical engineering*]
MAS	Micro Automation System
MAS	Microbeam Analysis Society (EA)
MAS	Microprogram Automation System [*Computer science*] (IAA)
MAS	Midcourse Active System (MCD)
MAS	Middle Air Space (PDAA)
MAS	Military Agency for Standardization [*Brussels, Belgium*] [*NATO*]
MAS	Military Airlift Squadron [*Air Force*] (CINC)
MAS	Military Assistance Sales (MCD)
MAS	Milk-Alkali Syndrome [*Medicine*] (DMAA)
mAs	Milliampere-Second
MAS	Ministry of Aviation Supply [*British*]
MAS	Minnesota Academy of Science
MAS	Missile Alignment Set
MAS	Missile Assembly Site (NATG)
MAS	Missile Assigned Switch
MAS	Missile Auxiliaries System
MAS	MMICS Administration Subsystem (AFIT)
MAS	Mobile Arm Support [*Orthopedics*] (DAVI)
MAS	Mobile Atmospheric Spectrometer (USDC)
MAS	Mobile Atmospheric Spectrometer [*Marine science*] (OSRA)
MAS	Model Assignment Sheet (MCD)
MAS	Modern Army Supply
MAS	Modern Army System
MAS	Modular Accounting System [*Computer science*] (IAA)
MAS	Modular Application Systems [*Martin Marietta Data Systems*]
MAS	Monaco Group, Inc. [*Toronto Stock Exchange symbol*]
MAS	Monetary Allowance in Lieu of Subsistence
MAS	Monitor and Alarm System (MCD)
MAS	Monmouth Antiquarian Society (EA)
MAS	Monoacetoxylscirpenol [*Organic toxin*]
MAS	Mount Angel Seminary [*Oregon*]
MAS	Movement Alarm System [*Gynecology*]
MAS	Movimiento al Socialismo [*Movement towards Socialism*] [*Argentina Political party*] (PPW)
MAS	Movimiento al Socialismo [*Movement towards Socialism*] [*Venezuela Political party*] (PPW)
MAS	Movimiento de Accion Socialista [*Peru*] [*Political party*] (EY)
MAS	Movimiento para Accion y Solidaridad [*Guatemala*] [*Political party*] (EY)
MAS	Muerte a los Secuestradores [*Death to Kidnappers*] [*Colorado*] (PD)
MAS	Mujeres en Accion Sindical [*Organizes national and international conferences on women in the economy*] [*Mexico*] (CROSS)
MAS	Multiaspect Signaling (IEEE)
MAS	Multiple Address System [*Telecommunications*] (CDE)
MAS	Multiple Aim Structure (MCD)
MAS	Multiple Award Schedule [*Government contracting*]

MAS	Municipal Analysis Services, Inc. [*Information service or system*] (IID)
MAS	Mutually Assured Survival
MASA	Mail Advertising Service Association International [*Bethesda, MD*]
MASA	Marine Accessories and Services Association [*Later, NAMPS*] (EA)
MASA	Master of Advanced Studies in Architecture (PGP)
MASA	Mathematical Association of South Australia
MASA	Medical Acronyms, Symbols & Abbreviations [*A publication*]
MASA	Men Against Sexual Assault [*Australia*]
MASA	Merged Area Schools Administrators Association (OICC)
MASA	Military Accessories Service Association (EA)
MASA	Military Automotive Supply Agency
MASA	Modular Avionics Systems Architecture (MCD)
MASA	Multiple Anodic Stripping Analyzer (PDAA)
MASA	Music and Arts Society of America (EA)
MASAC	Master of Arts in Substance Abuse Counseling (PGP)
MASAD	Mission Analysis and Systems Acquisition Division (AAGC)
MASAE	Member of the American Society of Agricultural Engineering
MASAF	Mediterranean Allied Strategic Air Force
MASAI	Mail Advertising Service Association International (EA)
MASAL	Michigan Academy of Science, Arts, and Letters
MASAP	Michigan Association of Single Adoptive Parents (EA)
MASAQUE	Major Action Significantly Affecting the Quality of the Human Environment (DNAB)
MASAR	Management Assurance of Safety, Adequacy, and Reliability (MHDB)
MASAR	Microwave Accurate Surface Antenna Reflector (PDAA)
MASAR	Multimode Airborne Solid-State Array RADAR System [*Military*] (PDAA)
MASB	Main Array Signal Band
MASB	MASSBANK Corp. [*NASDAQ symbol*] (NQ)
MA/SB	Motor Antisubmarine Boat [*Obsolete British*]
MASC	Magazine Advertising Sales Club (EA)
MASC	Magnetic Attitude Spin Coil
MASC	MAGTF [*Marine Air-Ground Task Force*] Automated Services Center (GFGA)
MASC	Maintenance Support Concept Model (MCD)
MASC	Management Systems Concept (PDAA)
MASC	Masculine
masc	Mass Concentration [*Medicine*] (MAE)
MASc	Master of Agricultural Science (DD)
MA Sc	Master of Applied Science
MASC	Methylaluminum Sesquichloride [*Organic chemistry*]
MASC	Microsoft Access Script Command [*Computer language*]
MASC	Middletown Air Service Command [*Air Force*]
MASC	Military Automotive Supply Center (MCD)
MASC	Model to Evaluate Maintenance Support Concepts (MCD)
MASC	Mountain Administrative Support Center (USDC)
MASC	Mountain Administrative Support Center [*Marine science*] (OSRA)
MASC	Multilayer Aluminium Oxide-Silicon-Dioxide Combination (IAA)
MASC	Multiple Award Schedule Contract [*Government contracting*]
MASCA	Museum Applied Science Center for Archeology [*University of Pennsylvania*]
MASCDCS	Madison Avenue Sports Car Driving and Chowder Society (EA)
MASCE	Member of the American Society of Civil Engineers
MASCO	Maintenance Schedule Code (PDAA)
Masco	Masco Corp. [*Associated Press*] (SAG)
MASCO	Mead Access Systems Co.
MASCO	Microprogrammed and Simulated Computer Organization
MASCOM	Master Communications (PDAA)
MASCON	Mass Concentration [*of gravitational pull*]
MASCOT	Management Advisory System using Computerized Optimization Techniques (PDAA)
MASCOT	Manned Shuttle Comprehensive Optimization and Targeting [*NASA*]
Mascot	Mascotech [*Commercial firm Associated Press*] (SAG)
MASCOT	Meteorological Auxiliary Sea Current Observation Transmitter
MASCOT	Military Air-Transportable Satellite Communications Terminal
MASCOT	Mobile Air-Transportable Satellite Communications Terminal [*Military*] (IAA)
MASCOT	Modern Approach to Software Construction, Operation and Test [*Ministry of Defence*] [*British*]
MASCOT	Modular Approach to Software Construction Operation and Test (NITA)
MASCOT	Modular Approach to System Construction Operation and Test (MCD)
MASCOT	Motorola Automatic Sequential Computer Operated Tester
Mascotch	Mascotech [*Commercial firm Associated Press*] (SAG)
MasCp	MassMutual Corporate Investors, Inc. [*Associated Press*] (SAG)
MASCP	Multicultural and Cross-Cultural Supplementation Program [*Australia*]
MASCS	Marriage Adjustment Sentence Completion Survey [*Psychology*]
MASCU	Marine Air Support Control Unit
MASD	Mach Aids to Surface-to-Air Missile Development (IAA)
MASD	Master of Arts in Spiritual Direction (PGP)
MASD	Mobile Air and Space Defense [*Air Force*]
MASDC	Military Aircraft Storage and Disposition Center
MASDR	Measurement and Signature Data Requirements (MCD)
MasdSec	Masada Security Holdings, Inc. [*Associated Press*] (SAG)
MASE	McDonnell Airborne Sidewinder Evaluator [*McDonnell Douglas Corp.*] (MCD)
MASE	Medical and Scientific Equipment
MASE	Military Assistance Service Fund (AAGC)
MASE	Moore School Air Space Simulation Effort (MCD)
MASEA	Midwest Association of Student Employment Administrators [*Formerly, MAUSED*] (EA)
MASEC	Multi-Access Systems Control Terminal (PDAA)
MASEE	Member of the Association of Supervisory and Executive Engineers [*British*] (DBQ)

MASEFI....... Mass Air Sequential Electronic Fuel Injection [*Automotive engineering*]

MASER .... Microwave [*or Molecular*] Amplification by Stimulated Emission of Radiation

maser .... Microwave Amplification by Stimulated Emission of Radiation (WDMC)

MASER .... Molecular Application by Stimulated Emission of Radiation [*Organic chemistry*] (DAVI)

MASES .... Microcomputer Advice and Selection Expert System (PDAA)

MASEX........ Maritime Air Superiority Exercise (NVT)

MASF .... Marconi Advanced Sample Facility (NITA)

MASF .... Military Assistance Service Funded

MASF .... Mobile Aeromedical Staging Facility

MASF .... Multiracial American Scholarship Fund

MASFET....... Metal-Alumina-Silicon Field Effect Transistor (IAA)

MASFM .... Maintenance and Supply Facility Management (AFIT)

MAS/FS ...... Mohawk Aerial Surveillance/Flight Simulator (MCD)

MASG .... Marine Air Support Group

MASG .... Military Airlift Support Group [*Air Force*]

MASG .... Missile Auxiliary Signal Generator

MASG .... Monitor and Alarm Subsystem Group (MCD)

MASGC .... Mississippi-Alabama Sea Grant Consortium [*Sea Grant College*] [*Research center*] (RCD)

MASGP .... Military Airlift Support Group [*Air Force*]

MASH .... Manned Antisubmarine Helicopter

MASH .... Medical Aid for Sick Hippies [*Volunteer medical group*]

MASH .... Melting-Assimilation-Storage-Homogenization [*Geology*]

MASH .... Michigan Area Serial Holdings Consortium [*Library network*]

MASH .... Micro-Analytic Simulation of Households (PDAA)

MASH .... Mobile Army Surgical Hospital [*Acronym also used as title of a satirical film, 1970, and a TV series*]

MASH .... Multiple Accelerated Summary Hearing [*Deportation of illegal aliens*] [*Immigration and Naturalization Service*]

MASH .... Multiple Automated Sample Harvester [*for culture systems*]

MASH .... Mutual Aid Self-Help Group

MASHONLD... Mashonaland (ROG)

M/ASI.......... Mach/Airspeed Indicator (GAVI)

MASI .... Multilevel Academic Skills Inventory [*Educational test*]

MASID .... Marine Science Division [*Instrument Society of America*] (MSC)

MASINT ...... Measurement and Signature Intelligence (MCD)

MASIS .... Management and Scientific Information System [*Air Force*]

MASIS .... Maruzen Scientific Information Service Center [*Maruzen Co. Ltd.*] [*Japan Telecommunications*]

MASIS .... Mercury Abort Sensing Instrumentation System [*NASA*] (AAG)

MASK.......... Align-Rite International, Inc. [*NASDAQ symbol*] (SAG)

MASK.......... Align-Rite Intl. [*NASDAQ symbol*] (TTSB)

MASK........ Maneuvering and Seakeeping

MASK........ Mobile Armored Strike Kommand [*Game*]

MASK........ Multilevel Amplitude Shift Keying

maskon........ Mass Concentration (BARN)

MAsl .... Ashland Public Library, Ashland, MA [*Library symbol Library of Congress*] (LCLS)

MASL .... MA [*Military Assistance*] Articles and Services List [*DoD*]

masl .... Meters above Sea Level

MASL .... Military Articles and Services List

MASL .... Military Assistance Article and Service List (MCD)

Masland ...... Masland Corp. [*Associated Press*] (SAG)

MASLIG ...... Association of Management Analysts in State and Local Government (EA)

MASLPI........ Mexican American State Legislators Policy Institute (CROSS)

MASM.......... Macro Assembler [*Computer language*] (PCM)

MASM.......... Master of Arts in Sacred Music (BJA)

MASM.......... Meta-Assembler (NITA)

MASM.......... Meta-Assembler Language [*Sperry UNIVAC computer language*]

MASM.......... Military Assistance and Sales Manual (AFIT)

MASM.......... Motorized Antenna Switching Matrix

MASME .... Member of the American Society of Mechanical Engineers

MAS/MILS ... Minerals Availability System/Minerals Industry Location Subsystem [*Bureau of Mines*] [*Database*]

MASMOD..... Mass Model [*Computer program*]

MASMR .... Multidimensional Attitude Scale on Mental Retardation (EDAC)

MASN .... Machine Accountant, Seaman [*Navy*]

masn .... Masonite (VRA)

MASN .... Maximum Aggregate Student Number [*Higher Education Funding Council*] (AIE)

MASNC .... Minerals Availability System [*Bureau of Mines*] [*Information service or system*] (IID)

Mas NE Pr... Mason's New England Civil Practice [*A publication*] (DLA)

MASNMR.... Magic Angle Spinning Nuclear Magnetic Resonance [*Spectroscopy*]

MASO .... Military Assistance Sales Order (CINC)

MASO .... Munition Accountable Supply Officer [*Air Force*] (AFM)

MASOA .... Master and Slave Oscillator Array (PDAA)

MA (Social Studies)... Master of Arts (Social Studies)

MA(SocSci)... Master of Arts (Social Sciences), University of Glasgow [*British*] (DBQ)

MASocStud... Master of Arts in Social Studies (NADA)

MASON .... Masonry

Mason .... Mason's United States Circuit Court Reports [*A publication*] (DLA)

Mason CCR... Mason's United States Circuit Court Reports [*A publication*] (DLA)

Mason Circt Ct R... Mason's United States Circuit Court Reports [*A publication*] (DLA)

MasonDix... Mason-Dixon Bancshares, Inc. [*Associated Press*] (SAG)

Mason R...... Mason's United States Circuit Court Reports [*A publication*] (DLA)

Mason's Code... Mason's United States Code, Annotated [*A publication*] (DLA)

Mason's R ... Mason's United States Circuit Court Reports [*A publication*] (DLA)

Mason's Rep... Mason's United States Circuit Court Reports [*A publication*] (DLA)

Mason US... Mason's United States Circuit Court Reports [*A publication*] (DLA)

Mason US Circ Ct Rep... Mason's United States Circuit Court Reports [*A publication*] (DLA)

Mason USR... Mason's United States Circuit Court Reports [*A publication*] (DLA)

MASP.......... Microaerophilus Stationary Phase [*Biochemistry*] (DAVI)

MASP.......... Modular Atmosphere Simulation Program [*NASA*] (KSC)

MASPAC .... Microfilm Advisory Service of the Public Archives of Canada (PDAA)

MAS PIL ... Massa Pilularum [*A Pill Mass*] [*Pharmacy*]

MasPrt........ MassMutual Participation Investors [*Associated Press*] (SAG)

MASPS .... Minimum Aviation System Performance Standards [*FAA*] (TAG)

MASPSq ...... Military Airlift Special Squadron [*Air Force*]

MASPTSq .... Military Airlift Support Squadron [*Air Force*]

MASq .... Military Airlift Squadron [*Air Force*] (AFM)

Mas R .... Massachusetts Reports [*A publication*] (DLA)

MASR .... Memory-Address Select Register [*Computer science*] (IAA)

MASR .... Microwave Atmosphere Sounding Radiometer (PDAA)

MASR .... Multiple-Antenna Moving-Target Surveillance RADAR

MASRC .... Major Automated System Review Council [*Military*]

MASRC .... Mexican American Studies and Research Center [*University of Arizona*] [*Research center*] (RCD)

Mas Rep..... Massachusetts Reports [*A publication*] (DLA)

MASRT .... Marine Air Support RADAR Teams (IEEE)

MASRU .... Marine Air Support RADAR Unit [*DoD*]

MASS......... Magic Angle Sample Spinning [*Spectroscopy*]

MASS......... Manned Activity Scheduling System [*NASA*]

MASS......... MARC [*Machine-Readable Cataloging*] Automated Serials System (PDAA)

MASS......... MARC-Based Automated Serials System (NITA)

MASS......... Marine Air Support Squadron

MASS......... Maritime Anti-Standing SONAR System (DNAB)

MASS......... Massa [*A Mass*] [*Pharmacy*]

MASS......... Massachusetts (AFM)

MASS......... Massachusetts Bay (GAAI)

Mass......... Massachusetts Supreme Judicial Court Reports [*A publication*] (DLA)

MASS......... Massage

MA(SS)........ Master of Arts in Social Science (ADA)

MASS......... Master of Arts in Special Studies (PGP)

M As S .... Master of Association Science

MASS......... Materials Acquisition Sub-System [*Computer science*]

MASS......... Matrix Analysis Subsystem (MCD)

MASS......... Mechanically Accelerated Sabot System [*Generation of high-density molecular beams*]

MASS......... Membrane Affinity Separation System

MASS......... Memorandum Accounts Statement System (DCTA)

MASS......... MICAP [*Mission Critical Parts*] Asset Sourcing System (DOMA)

MASS......... Michigan Automatic Scanning System (IEEE)

MAss......... Middle Assyrian [*Language, etc.*] (BJA)

MASS......... Military Airlift Support Squadron [*Air Force*]

MASS......... Missile and Space Summary (MCD)

MASS......... Missiles/Ammunition System Study

MASS......... Mobility Analysis Support System [*Air Force*]

MASS......... Modern Army Supply System

MASS......... Modular Adaptive Signal Sorter

MASS......... Monitor and Assembly System [*or Subsystem*] [*Computer science*] (BUR)

MASS......... Multiple Access Sequential Selection [*Computer science*] (BUR)

MASS......... Multiple Access Switching System (NITA)

Mass Acts... Acts and Resolves of Massachusetts [*A publication*] (DLA)

Mass AD..... Massachusetts Appellate Decisions [*A publication*] (DLA)

Mass Admin Code... Code of Massachusetts Regulations [*A publication*] (DLA)

Mass Admin Reg... Massachusetts Register [*A publication*] (DLA)

Mass ADR... Massachusetts Appellate Division Reports [*A publication*] (DLA)

Mass Adv Legis Serv... Massachusetts Advance Legislative Service [*Lawyers Co-Operative Publishing Co.*] [*A publication*] (DLA)

Mass Adv Sh... Massachusetts Advance Sheets [*A publication*] (DLA)

Mass Adv Sheets... Massachusetts Advance Sheets [*A publication*] (DLA)

Mass Ann Laws... Annotated Laws of Massachusetts [*A publication*] (DLA)

Mass App Ct... Massachusetts Appeals Court Reports [*A publication*] (DLA)

Mass App Ct Adv Sh... Massachusetts Appeals Court Advance Sheets [*A publication*] (DLA)

Mass App Dec... Massachusetts Appellate Decisions [*A publication*] (DLA)

Mass App Div... Massachusetts Appellate Division Reports [*A publication*] (DLA)

Mass App Rep... Massachusetts Appeals Court Reports [*A publication*] (DLA)

MASSAR ..... Multimode Airborne Solid State Array RADAR

Mass BC & A... Massachusetts Board of Conciliation and Arbitration Reports [*A publication*] (DLA)

Massbnk ..... Massbank Corp. [*Associated Press*] (SAG)

MASSBUS.... Memory Bus [*Digital Equipment Corp.*]

massc.......... Mass Concentration [*Medicine*] (DMAA)

M As Sc....... Master of Association Science

MASSCAL .... Mass Casualties [*Military*] (AABC)

Mass C Art... Massachusetts College of Art (GAGS)

Mass Cont Election Cushing S & J... Massachusetts Controverted Election Cases [*A publication*] (DLA)

Mass C Pharmacy... Massachusetts College of Pharmacy (GAGS)

MASSDATA.... Modular Analysis, Speedup, Sampling, and Data Reduction

MASSDATA... Mark Sense Source Data Automation Test and Analysis (MCD)

MASSDET .... Marine Air Support Squadron Detachment (DNAB)

Mass DIA..... Massachusetts. Department of Industrial Accidents. Bulletin [*A publication*] (DLA)

Mass Dr Com... Masse. Le Droit Commercial [*A publication*] (DLA)

Mass EC L & R... Loring and Russell's Election Cases in Massachusetts [*A publication*] (DLA)

Mass Elec Ca... Massachusetts Election Cases [*A publication*] (DLA)

Mass Elec Cas... Massachusetts Election Cases [*A publication*] (DLA)
Mass Election Cases... Loring and Russell's Election Cases in Massachusetts [*A publication*] (DLA)
Mass Election Cases... Russell's Contested Election Cases [*Massachusetts*] [*A publication*] (DLA)
Mass Gen Laws... Massachusetts General Laws [*A publication*] (DLA)
Mass Gen Laws Ann (West)... Massachusetts General Laws, Annotated (West) [*A publication*] (DLA)
MassHe ...... Massachusetts Health & Education Tax Exempt Trust [*Associated Press*] (SAG)
MASS HFD... Multi-Additional SCSI [*Small Computer System Interface*] Subsystem Hot Fix Device [*Computer science*]
Mass IAB ..... Massachusetts Industrial Accident Board Reports of Cases [*A publication*] (DLA)
MASSIIS ...... Maintenance Analysis and Structural Integration Information System
Mass LRC Dec... Massachusetts Labor Relations Commission Decisions [*A publication*] (DLA)
MASSOP...... Multi-Automatic System for Simulation and Operational Planning (PDAA)
Mass Pil ..... Massa Pilularum [*A Pill Mass*] [*Pharmacy*]
MASSPO...... Manned Space Flight Support Project Office [*NASA*] (IAA)
MASSq........ Military Airlift Support Squadron [*Air Force*] (AFM)
Mass R........ Massachusetts Reports [*A publication*] (DLA)
Mass Rep .... Massachusetts Reports [*A publication*] (DLA)
Mass St BC & A... Massachusetts State Board of Conciliation and Arbitration Reports [*A publication*] (DLA)
Mass Supp... Massachusetts Reports Supplement [*A publication*] (AAGC)
MASST........ Major Shipboard SATCOM Terminal (MCD)
MASST........ Major Ship Satellite Terminal
MASSTER .... Mobile Army Sensor System Test, Evaluation, and Review
MASSTER .... Modern Army Selected System Test, Evaluation, and Review
Mass UCC Op... Massachusetts Unemployment Compensation Commission Opinions [*A publication*] (DLA)
Mass UC Dig... Massachusetts Division of Unemployment Compensation Digest of Board of Review Decisions [*A publication*] (DLA)
Mass UC Ops... Massachusetts Division of Unemployment Compensation Opinions [*A publication*] (DLA)
Mass WCC... Massachusetts Workmen's Compensation Cases [*A publication*] (DLA)
MAST........... Machine Automated Speech Transcription (PDAA)
MAST........... Magnetic Annular Shock Tube
MAST........... Marine Stable Element
MAST........... Market Structures and Trends on Italy [*Databank Ltd.*] [*British*] (ECON)
MAST........... Mastech Corp. [*NASDAQ symbol*] (SAG)
MAST........... Mastectomy [*Medicine*] (AAMN)
MAST........... Master (ROG)
Mast .... Master's Supreme Court Reports [*25-28 Canada*] [*A publication*] (DLA)
MAST........... Mastoid [*Medicine*]
MAST........... Measurement and Stimuli System (SSD)
MAST........... Medical Anti-Shock Trousers [*Military*]
MAST........... Michigan Alcoholism Screening Test
MAST........... Midlevel Positions in Administrative, Staff, and Technical Services [*Civil Service Commission*]
MAST........... Military Antishock Trousers [*Medicine*]
MAST........... Military Assistance to Safety and Traffic [*Project*] [*Army*] (RDA)
MAST........... Minimum Abbreviations of Serial Titles [*A publication*]
MAST........... Missile Automatic Supply Technique
MAST........... Mobile Assembly Sterilizer for Testing
MAST........... Model Assembly Sterilizer for Testing [*NASA*]
MAST........... Multilevel Academic Survey Test [*Educational test*]
MAST........... Multiple-Aircraft Simulation Terminal (DA)
MAST........... Multiple Applications Storage Tube
MAST........... Munitions Assistance and Standardization Team (MCD)
MASTA........ Medical Advisory Services for Travellers Abroad [*London School of Hygiene andTropical Medicine*] [*Information service or system*] (IID)
MastAcftCrmnBad... Master Aircraft Crewman Badge [*Military decoration*] (AABC)
MASTACS .... Maneuverability Augmentation System for Tactical Air Combat Simulation (PDAA)
MASTAP ...... Master System Tape (IAA)
MASTARAV... Master Army Aviator (AABC)
Mast AR Av Bad... Master Army Aviator Badge [*Military decoration*]
MASTARS .... Mechanical and Structural Testing and Referral Service [*National Institute of Standards and Technology*]
MAStat........ Master of Applied Statistics
Mast Div Bad... Master Diver Badge [*Military decoration*]
MAST-E....... Multicenter Acute Stroke Trial-Europe [*Neurology*]
Mastec........ Mastec, Inc. [*Associated Press*] (SAG)
Mastech....... Mastech Corp. [*Associated Press*] (SAG)
Mast El .... Masterman's Parliamentary Elections [*1880*] [*A publication*] (DLA)
MASTER ...... Matching Available Student Time to Educational Resources [*Computer science*]
MASTER ...... Miniaturized Sink-Rate Telemetering RADAR
MASTER ...... Multiple Access Shared Time Executive Routine [*Control Data Corp.*] [*Computer science*]
MASTER KEY... Managership of Soldier Training, Education, and Readiness with Knowledge and Excellence Year-Round [*Army*] (INF)
MASTICH ..... Mastiche [*Mastic*] [*Pharmacy*] (ROG)
MASTIF....... Multi-Axis Spin Test Inertia Facility [*Training device for astronauts*]
MASTIFF...... Modular Automated System to Identify Friend from Foe [*Military*] (PDAA)
MASTIR ...... Microfilmed Abstract System for Technical Information Retrieval [*Illinois Institute of Technology*] (IID)

MastPrchtBad... Master Parachutist Badge [*Military decoration*] (AABC)
MASTS......... Marine Associated Services Technology Systems Exposition [*Canada*] (ITD)
MAstS.......... Member of the Astronomical Society
MASTU .... Mobile Antisubmarine Training Unit [*British*]
MASU .... Machined Surface
MASU .... Mesoamerican Archaeology Study Unit [*American Topical Association*] (EA)
MASU .... Metal Alloy Separation Unit
MASU .... Mobile Army Surgical Unit
MASU .... Multiple Acceleration Sensor Unit (PDAA)
MASUA .... Mid-America State Universities Association [*Defunct*] (EA)
MASURCA... Marine Surface Contre Avions (SAA)
MASW .... Master of Arts in Social Work
MASW .... Master Switch (IAA)
MASW .... Military Airlift Support Wing [*Air Force*]
MASWEP .... Medium Active Solid Waste Encapsulation Plant [*Nuclear energy*] (NUCP)
MASWg....... Military Airlift Support Wing [*Air Force*] (AFM)
MASWSP .... Manager, Antisubmarine Warfare Systems Project [*Navy*]
MASWSPO... Manager, Antisubmarine Warfare Systems Project Office [*Navy*]
MASWT........ Mobile Antisubmarine Warfare Target (MCD)
MASX .... Mastec, Inc. [*NASDAQ symbol*] (SAG)
MAT .... Machine-Aided Translation (NITA)
MAT .... Machine Analysis Table (IAA)
MAT .... Machine-Assisted Translation
MAT .... Machine Available Time [*Computer science*]
MAT .... Maine Aviation Corp. [*ICAO designator*] (FAAC)
MAT .... Maintainability of Software Analysis Tool (MCD)
MAT .... Maintenance Access Terminal [*Aviation*]
MAT .... Maintenance Appraisal Team (MCD)
MAT .... Mammary Ascites Tumor [*Oncology*]
MAT .... Management Advisory Team (NRCH)
MAT .... Manifold Air Temperature [*Automotive engineering*]
MAT .... Manual Arts Therapist
MAT .... Marine Air Temperature [*Meteorology*]
MAT .... Maritime, Aviation, and Transport Insurance (DLA)
MAT .... Marketing Assistance Test
MAT .... Master Account Title [*Office of Management and Budget*]
MAT .... Master of Arts in Teaching
MA(T) .... Master of Arts in Teaching (PGP)
MAT .... Master of Arts in Theology (PGP)
MAT .... Master Operational Recording Tape Address Table (IAA)
MAT .... Matachewan Consolidated Mines Ltd. [*Toronto Stock Exchange symbol*]
MAT .... Matadi [*Zaire*] [*Airport symbol Obsolete*] (OAG)
MAT .... Matching Abacus Test [*Parapsychology*]
MAT .... Material (AFM)
mat............. Material (VRA)
MAT .... Materials Department [*David W. Taylor Naval Ship Research and Development Center*] [*Annapolis, MD*]
MAT .... Materiel [*Military*] (AFM)
MAT .... Maternity
MAT .... Mathematical Automata Theory
MAT .... Matinee
MAT .... Matins (ROG)
MAT .... Matrix (MSA)
MAT .... Matrix
MAT .... Matrix Analogies Test [*Intelligence test*]
MAT .... Matsushiro [*Japan*] [*Seismograph station code, US Geological Survey*] (SEIS)
MAT .... Mattel, Inc. [*NYSE symbol*] (SPSG)
Mat .... Mattheus de Mathesillanis [*Flourished, 1381-1402*] [*Authority cited in pre-1607 legal work*] (DSA)
MAT .... Matthew [*New Testament book*]
MAT .... Matured
MAT .... Maturity
MAT .... Matutinal (ADA)
MAT .... Mean Annual Temperature [*Climatology*]
MAT .... Measurement of Atmospheric Turbulence
MAT .... Mechanical Aptitude Test
MAT .... Mechanical Assembly Technique (IAA)
MAT .... Mechanically Agitated Tank [*Engineering*]
MAT .... Medial Axes Transformation (MHDI)
MAT .... Medial Axis Transformation (MHDB)
MAT .... Medical Assessment Tribunal [*Queensland, Australia*]
MAT .... Medium Artillery Tractor [*British military*] (DMA)
MAT .... Medium Assault Transport (MCD)
MAT .... Memory Access Table [*Computer science*]
MAT .... Memory-Address Test
MAT .... Memory Address Translator (NITA)
MAT .... Mercury Amalgamation Trap [*Analytical chemistry*]
MAT .... Meteorological Atmospheric Turbulence (MCD)
MAT .... Methionine Adenosyltransferase [*An enzyme*]
MAT .... Metropolitan Achievement Test
MAT .... Metropolitan Area Trunk [*Telecommunications*] (TEL)
MAT .... Microactivity Testing [*Catalysis technology*]
MAT .... Microalloy Transistor
MAT .... Microtray Agglutination Test [*Clinical chemistry*]
MAT .... Microwave Antenna Tower
MAT .... Military Aircraft Types
MAT .... Military Air Transport
MAT .... Miller-Abbott Tube [*Surgery*] [*Medicine*] (DAVI)
MAT .... Miller Analogies Test (GAGS)
MAT .... Miller Analogies Test [*Psychology*]

MAT............	Mine Assembly Team [*Navy*] (NVT)
MAT............	Minimal Aversion Threshold [*to noise*]
MAT............	Minimum Allowable Threshold [*Chemistry*]
MAT............	Missile Acceptance Team (AAG)
MAT............	Missile Acceptance Test
MAT............	Missile Acquisition and Track
MAT............	Missile Adapter Tester
MAT............	Missile Airframe Technology (MCD)
MAT............	Missile Antitank
MAT............	Mobile Advisor Team [*Vietnamese team trained by US Army advisors*] (VNW)
MAT............	Mobile Aerial Target (AAG)
MAT............	Mobile Arming Tower (KSC)
MAT............	Mobile Assistance Team [*Federal disaster planning*]
MAT............	Mobile Mine Assembly Team
MAT............	Modular Allocation Technique (PDAA)
MAT............	Modular Assembly Technique (IAA)
MAT............	Molecular Analysis Team
MAT............	Monoamine Transporter [*Biochemistry*]
MAT............	Monocyto-Angiotropin [*Biochemistry*]
MAT............	Motivation Analysis Test [*Psychology*]
MAT............	Motor Ambulance Trolley [*British*]
MAT............	Moving Annual Total [*Statistics*] (DCTA)
MAT............	Multiallelic Mating-Type Regulatory Gene
MAT............	Multifocal Atrial Tachycardia [*Cardiology*]
MAT............	Multimedia Access Terminals [*Philips*] [*Electronics*]
MAT............	Multiple Access Test
MAT............	Multiple Access Time [*Telecommunications*] (ECII)
MAT............	Multiple Actuator Test (MCD)
MAT............	Multiple Address Telegrams
MAT............	Multiple Aptitude Test [*Education*] (AEBS)
MATA..........	Military Assistance Training Advisor
MATA..........	Motorcycle and Allied Trades Association [*Later, MIC*] (EA)
MATA..........	Multiple Answering Teaching Aid (PDAA)
MATA..........	Musical Arena Theatres Association [*Later, PAMI*] (EA)
MATABE......	Multiple-Weapon Automatic Target and Battery Evaluator (SAA)
MATACQ......	Material Acquisition (NG)
MATADOR....	Mobile and Three-Dimensional Air Defense Operations RADAR [*Military*] (PDAA)
MATAF........	Mediterranean Allied Tactical Air Force
MATB..........	Military Air Transport Board
MATB..........	Missile Auxiliary Test Bench
MATC..........	Maximum Acceptable Tolerance Concentration (GNE)
MATC..........	Maximum Acceptable Toxicant Concentration
MATC..........	Military Air Transport Command (MUGU)
MATC..........	Milwaukee Area Technical College (PCM)
MATC..........	Missile Auxiliaries Test Console
MATC..........	Mobilization Army Training Center
MATC..........	Mountain Artillery Training Centre [*British military*] (DMA)
MATCALS....	Marine Air Traffic Control and Landing System [*Navy*]
MATCALS....	Mobile Air Traffic Control and All-Weather Landing System (MCD)
MATCAT......	Material Category
MATCH........	Manned Attack Torpedo Carrying Helicopter (PDAA)
MATCH........	Manpower and Talent Clearinghouse
MATCH........	Matching Alcoholism Treatments to Client Heterogeneity
MATCH........	Materials and Activities for Teachers and Children
MATCH........	Medium-Range Antisubmarine Torpedo Carrying Helicopter (NATG)
MATCH........	Mothers Apart from Their Children [*British*] (DI)
MATCH........	MTMC [*Military Traffic Management Command*] Automated Transportation Scheduler (GFGA)
MATCH........	Multielement Assured Tracking Chopper
MATCM........	Master of Acupuncture and Traditional Chinese Medicine (PGP)
MATCO........	Materials Analysis, Tracking, and Control [*Johnson Space Center data system*] [*NASA*] (NASA)
MATCO........	Military Air Traffic Coordinating Office [*or Officer*] [*Air Force*] (AFM)
MATCOM......	Materiel Command [*Army*] (AABC)
MATCOMEUR..	Materiel Command, Europe
MATCON......	Microwave Aerospace Terminal Control [*Air Force*]
MATCONOFF...	Material Control Officer (MCD)
MatCo-Ord(N)...	Material Co-Ordination Division (Naval) [*British*]
MATCS........	Marine Air Traffic Control Squadron (DNAB)
MATCSDET...	Marine Air Traffic Control Squadron Detachment (DNAB)
MATCU........	Marine Air Tactical [*later, Traffic*] Control Unit [*Marine Corps*]
MATCU........	Military Air Traffic Coordinating Unit [*MTMC*] (TAG)
MATCV........	Mobile Air Traffic Control Vehicle [*Military*]
MATD..........	Mine and Torpedo Detector [*SONAR*] [*Navy*]
MATDA........	Methylene-bis-(aminothiadiazole) [*Pesticide*]
MATDEV......	Materiel Developer
MATE..........	Machine-Aided Translation Editing (PDAA)
MATE..........	Manual Adaptive TMA [*Target Motion Analysis*] Estimator [*Navy*] (ANA)
MATE..........	Manually Aided Tracking Enhancement (MCD)
MATE..........	Marital Attitude Evaluation [*Psychology*]
MATAN........	Married Americans for Tax Equality
MATE..........	Master of Arts in the Teaching of English
Mat E..........	Materials Engineer
MATE..........	Matewan BancShares [*NASDAQ symbol*] (TTSB)
MATE..........	Matewan Bancshares, Inc. [*NASDAQ symbol*] (SAG)
MATE..........	Matrix Automation through EMATS [*Military*] (MCD)
MATE..........	McDonnell Airborne Trainer and Evaluator [*McDonnell Douglas Corp.*] (MCD)
MATE..........	Measuring and Test Equipment (IEEE)
MATE..........	Memory-Assisted Terminal Equipment (PDAA)
MATE..........	Meteorological Analog Test and Evaluation (PDAA)
MATE..........	MICOM [*Missile Command*] Automated Test Equipment
MATE..........	Microprocessor Automatic Testing [*ASMAP Electronics Ltd.*] [*Software package*] (NCC)
MATE..........	Missile/Aircraft Test Equipment
MATE..........	Mission Analysis Technique for Experiments
MATE..........	Mobilization and Training Equipment (MCD)
MATE..........	Modular Automatic Test Equipment
MATE..........	Montana Agri-Trade Exposition [*Jerry Hanson and Associates, Inc.*] (TSPED)
MATE..........	Multiband Automatic Test Equipment
MATE..........	Multiple-Access Time-Division Experiment (IEEE)
MATE..........	Multiple Advanced Technique Evaluation [*Military*] (CAAL)
MATE..........	Multipurpose Automatic Test Equipment
MATE..........	Multisystem Automatic Test Equipment [*British*]
MATEC........	Maintenance Technician (NOAA)
Matec.........	MATEC Corp. [*Associated Press*] (SAG)
MA (T Ed).....	Master of Arts in Teacher Education
MAT-EF.......	Matrix Analogies Test - Expanded Form [*Intelligence test*]
MATELO.......	Maritime Air Telecommunications Organization [*NATO*] (NATG)
MATEM........	Manual Templating Model (MCD)
MATEP........	Matewan Bancshrs 7.5% Cv'A'Pfd [*NASDAQ symbol*] (TTSB)
MATER........	Material
MATERN......	Maternal (WDAA)
MATERN......	Maternity (WDAA)
MATES........	Medium Attack Tactical Employment School [*Military*] (CAAL)
MATES........	Mobilization and Training Equipment Site [*Military*] (AABC)
MATESL.......	Master of Arts in Teaching English as a Second Language (PGP)
MATESOL.....	Master of Arts in Teaching English to Speakers of Other Languages (PGP)
MA(TESOL)...	Master of Arts in Teaching English to Speakers of Other Languages
Matewan......	Matewan BancShares, Inc. [*Associated Press*] (SAG)
MATEX........	Macrotext Editor (MHDB)
MATEX........	Master of Arts in Textiles (PGP)
MATEX........	Material Expediting [*Program*] (DNAB)
MATFL........	Master of Arts in Teaching Foreign Language (PGP)
Math..........	Adversus Mathematicos [*of Sextus Empiricus*] [*Classical studies*] (OCD)
MA(Th).......	Master of Arts in Theology
MA Th........	Master of Arts in Theology (PGP)
MATH..........	Master of Arts in Therapy (PGP)
MATH..........	Mathematics (EY)
Math..........	Mathematics (DD)
MATH..........	Mathematics Abstracts [*Fachinformationszentrum Karlsruhe GmbH*] [*Information service or system*]
Math..........	Matheus de Mathesillanis [*Flourished, 1381-1402*] [*Authority cited in pre-1607 legal work*] (DSA)
Math..........	Mathieu's Quebec Reports [*A publication*] (DLA)
MATH..........	Mathsoft, Inc. [*NASDAQ symbol*] (SAG)
MATH..........	Mobile, Air-Transportable Hospital [*Military*]
Math D........	Doctor of Mathematics
MATHDI.......	Mathematical Didactics [*Fachinformationszentrum Energie, Physik, Mathematik GmbH*] [*Database*]
Mathe de Afflicti...	Matthaeus de Afflictis [*Deceased, 1528*] [*Authority cited in pre-1607 legal work*] (DSA)
MA Theol.....	Master of Arts in Theology
MATHL........	Mathematical
MATHLAB.....	Mathematical Laboratory [*Programming language*] (CSR)
MATHN........	Mathematician (AFM)
Math N........	Matthaeus Nerutius [*Flourished, 16th century*] [*Authority cited in pre-1607 legal work*] (DSA)
MATHP........	Medium Artillery Terminal Homing Projectile
MATHPAC....	Mathematical Package (IAA)
Math Pres Ev...	Mathews on Presumptive Evidence [*A publication*] (DLA)
MATHS........	Mathematics
Mathsft.......	Mathsoft, Inc. [*Associated Press*] (SAG)
Math T........	Mathematics Teacher [*A publication*] (BRI)
MATI..........	Maldives Association of the Tourism Industry (EY)
MATIC........	Multiple Area Technical Information Center
MATICO.......	Machine Applications to Technical Information Center Operations
MATIF........	Marche a Terme des Instruments Financiere [*French stock exchange*]
MATIF........	Marche a Terme des Instruments Financiers [*French Financial Futures Market*]
MATILDA.....	Microwave Analysis Threat Indication and Launch Direction Apparatus [*Military*]
MATINSP.....	Material Inspection [*Navy*] (NVT)
MATK..........	Martek Biosciences, Inc. [*NASDAQ symbol*] (SAG)
MATL..........	Master of Arts in Teaching of Languages (PGP)
MATL..........	Material (KSC)
MATL..........	Materiel [*Military*]
MATL..........	Materiel
MATL..........	Middle Atlantic
MATLAB......	Matrix Laboratory [*Computer science*]
Matlack.......	Matlack Systems, Inc. [*Associated Press*] (SAG)
MATLAN......	Matrix Language [*Computer science*] (IEEE)
Mat L & T.....	Mathews on Landlord and Tenant [*A publication*] (DLA)
MATL REQ....	Material Requisition
MATL RR....	Material Receiving Report
MATM..........	Master of Arts in Teaching of Mathematics (PGP)
MATMO........	Medical Advanced Technology Management Office
MATMO........	Military Advanced Technology Management Office (RDA)
MATMOP......	Materiel Management Optimization Program [*DoD*]
MATMU........	Mobile Aircraft Torpedo Maintenance Unit
MATNO........	Material Requested Is Not Available
MATO..........	Military Air Traffic Operations [*British military*] (DMA)
MATP..........	Masking Template [*Tool*] (AAG)

MATP.........	Military Assistance Training Program (AABC)
MATP.........	Missile Auxiliary Test Position
Mat Par	Matthew Paris. Historia Minor [*A publication*] (DLA)
Mat Paris....	Matthew Paris. Historia Minor [*A publication*] (DLA)
Mat Part....	Mathews on the Law of Partnership [*A publication*] (DLA)
MA-TPM	Maritime Administration Transport Planning Mobilization [*Federal emergency order*]
Mat Por	Mathews on the Law of Portions [*A publication*] (DLA)
MATPS.........	Machine-Aided Technical Processing System [*Yale University Library*] [*New Haven, CT*] [*Computer science*]
MATR.........	Management Access to Records
MATR.........	Matriculate (ROG)
MATR.........	Matron
MATRAC	Military Air Traffic Control System
MatrCap.......	Matrix Capital Corp. [*Associated Press*] (SAG)
MATRD	Materiel Release Denial [*Army*] (AABC)
MATRE	Material Requested
MATRED	Material Redistribution [*Program*] (DNAB)
MATRIC	Matriculation
MATRIC	Midwest Agribusiness Trade Research and Information Center [*Iowa State University of Science and Technology*] [*Research center*] (RCD)
MATRIS	Manpower and Training Research Information System [*DoD Information service or system*] (IID)
MATRIS	Medical Manpower and Training Information Service [*British*] (DAVI)
Matritch	Matritech, Inc. [*Associated Press*] (SAG)
MATRIX	Management Trial Exercise [*Career orientation simulation*]
MATRIX	Market Trend Index [*Associated Equipment Distributors program*]
Matrl...........	Material
MATRL.........	Matrimonial (ROG)
MATRS	Mattress
MATRS	Military Airlift Training Squadron [*Air Force*]
MATRS	Miniature Airborne Telemetry Receiving Station
Matrtc.........	Matritech, Inc. [*Associated Press*] (SAG)
MATRW.......	Military Airlift Training Wing [*Air Force*]
MatrxPh.......	Matrix Pharmaceutical, Inc. [*Associated Press*] (SAG)
MatrxSv.......	Matrix Service Co. [*Associated Press*] (SAG)
MatrxSv.......	Matrix Service Co. [*Associated Press*] (SAG)
MATS.........	Maintenance Analysis Task Sheet
MATS.........	Maintenance Analysis Test Set
MATS.........	Manual Versus Automatic Transmission Study (MCD)
MATS.........	Master of Arts in Teaching of Science (PGP)
MATS.........	Master of Arts in Theological Studies (PGP)
MATS.........	Material and Toxicology System
MATS.........	Materiel Squadron
MATS.........	Matrimonial Matters [*Slang*] (DSUE)
Mats	Matson's Reports [*22-24 Connecticut*] [*A publication*] (DLA)
MATS.........	Mechanical Accounting for Telephone Service (IAA)
MATS.........	Mechanical Anti-Theft System [*Automotive engineering*]
MATS.........	Mediterranean Air Transport Service
MATS.........	Midcourse Airborne Target Signature [*Military*] (PDAA)
MATS.........	Military Air Transport Service [*Later, Military Airlift Command*]
MATS.........	Missile Auxiliaries Test Set
MATS.........	Mission Analysis and Trajectory Simulation (MCD)
MATS.........	Mobile Automatic Telephone System [*Telecommunications*]
MATS.........	Mobile Automatic Test Set (MCD)
MATS.........	Model Aircraft Target System [*British military*] (DMA)
MATS.........	Monitoring and Test Subsystem
MATS.........	Multiple-Access Time Sharing [*Computer science*] (IAA)
MATS.........	Multipurpose Automatic Test System (IAA)
MATSA.........	Managerial, Administrative, Technical, and Supervisory Association [*British*] (DCTA)
MATSB.........	Mobile Advance Tactical Support Base [*Navy*] (VNW)
MATSC.........	Middletown Air Technical Service Command [*Air Force*]
MatSci.........	Material Sciences Corp. [*Associated Press*] (SAG)
MATSCO.........	Management and Technical Services Company (AAGC)
MAT-SF.........	Matrix Analogies Test - Short Form [*Intelligence test*]
MATSG.........	Marine Aviation Training Support Group (DNAB)
MATSO.........	Material Requested Being Supplied [*Military*]
Matson.........	Matson's Reports [*22-24 Connecticut*] [*A publication*] (DLA)
MATSR.........	Military Air Transport Service [*later, Military Airlift Command*] Regulation
MATSS.........	Marine Aviation Training Support Squadron (DNAB)
MATSS.........	Midwest Automated Technical Services Systems [*Information service or system*] (IID)
MATSTAT......	Materiel Status [*Military*]
Matsu	Matsushita Electric Industrial Co. Ltd. [*Associated Press*] (SAG)
MAtt...........	Attleboro Public Library, Attleboro, MA [*Library symbol Library of Congress*] (LCLS)
Matt.............	Matthew [*New Testament book*]
MATT...........	Matthews Studio Equipment Group [*NASDAQ symbol*] (NQ)
MATT...........	Missile ASW [*Antisubmarine Warfare*] Torpedo Target (MCD)
MATT...........	Mobile Acoustic Torpedo Target (NG)
MATT...........	Multimission Advanced Tactical Terminal (DWSG)
Mattel.........	Mattel, Inc. [*Associated Press*] (SAG)
Matth Com ...	Matthews' Guide to Commissioner in Chancery [*A publication*] (DLA)
Matth Cr L ...	Matthews' Digest of Criminal Law [*A publication*] (DLA)
Matthe de Affli...	Matthaeus de Afflictis [*Deceased, 1528*] [*Authority cited in pre-1607 legal work*] (DSA)
Matthews.....	Matthews' Reports [*6-9 West Virginia*] [*A publication*] (DLA)
Matthews.....	Matthews' Reports [*75 Virginia*] [*A publication*] (DLA)
Matth Exe	Matthews' Executors and Administrators [*2nd ed.*] [*1839*] [*A publication*] (DLA)
Matth Gribal...	Matthaeus Gribaldus [*Deceased, 1564*] [*Authority cited in pre-1607 legal work*] (DSA)
Matth Part ...	Matthews on Partnership [*A publication*] (DLA)
Matth Pr Ev...	Matthews on Presumptive Evidence [*A publication*] (DLA)
MatthwInt	Matthews International Corp. [*Associated Press*] (SAG)
MatthwSt	Matthews Studio Equipment Group [*Associated Press*] (SAG)
MATTS.........	Multiple Airborne Target Trajectory System
Mattson	Mattson Technology, Inc. [*Associated Press*] (SAG)
MATU.........	Marine Air Traffic Unit
MATUT.........	Matutinus [*In the Morning*] [*Pharmacy*]
MATV.........	Master Antenna Television
MATV.........	Matav-Cable Systems Media Ltd. [*NASDAQ symbol*] (SAG)
MatvCab	Matav-Cable Systems Media Ltd. [*Associated Press*] (SAG)
MATW.........	Matthews International Corp. [*NASDAQ symbol*] (SAG)
MATW.........	Matthews Intl. 'A' [*NASDAQ symbol*] (TTSB)
MATW.........	Metal Awning Type Window
MATWAS......	Marine Automatic Telephone Weather Answering Service [*Marine science*] (MSC)
MATWING....	Medium Attack Wing (NVT)
MATX.........	Matrix Pharmaceutical [*NASDAQ symbol*] (TTSB)
MATX.........	Matrix Pharmaceutical, Inc. [*NASDAQ symbol*] (SAG)
MATZ.........	Military Aerodrome Traffic Zone
MAU.........	Air Mauritius Ltd. [*ICAO designator*] (FAAC)
MAU.........	Maintenance Analysis Unit
MAU.........	Maintenance Augmenting Unit (NG)
MAU.........	Marine Advisory Unit [*Marine Corps*]
MAU.........	Marine Amphibious Unit (NVT)
mau.........	Massachusetts [*MARC country of publication code Library of Congress*] (LCCP)
MAU.........	Master Augmentation Unit [*Navy*] (DOMA)
MAU.........	Mastung [*Pakistan*] [*Airport symbol*] (AD)
MAU.........	Math Acceleration Unit (NITA)
MAU.........	Mathematical Advisory Unit [*Ministry of Transport*] [*British*]
MAU.........	Matua [*Former USSR Seismograph station code, US Geological Survey*] (SEIS)
MAU.........	Maupiti [*French Polynesia*] [*Airport symbol*] (OAG)
Mau.........	Mauricius [*Authority cited in pre-1607 legal work*] (DSA)
MAU.........	Mauritius (ROG)
MAU.........	Media Access Unit [*Telecommunications*]
MAU.........	Medical Assistance Unit [*HEW*]
MAU.........	Medium Access Unit [*Computer science*] (BYTE)
MAU.........	Medium Attachment Unit [*Computer science*] (TNIG)
MAU.........	Memory Access Unit
mAU.........	Milliabsorbance Unit [*Spectroscopy*]
MAU.........	Million Accounting Units (NASA)
MAU.........	Miscellaneous Armament Unit
MAU.........	Modern American Usage [*A publication*]
MAU.........	Mount Allison University [*New Brunswick, Canada*]
MAU.........	Multiattribute Utility (IEEE)
MAU.........	Multiple Access Unit
MAU.........	Multistation Access Unit [*Telecommunications*] (PCM)
MAUA	Master of Arts in Urban Affairs (GAGS)
Mau & Pol Sh...	Maude and Pollock's Law of Merchant Shipping [*A publication*] (DLA)
Mau & Sel...	Maule and Selwyn's English King's Bench Reports [*A publication*] (DLA)
MAUD	Manually-Assisted Universal Deviator
MAUD	Master of Arts in Urban Design (GAGS)
MAud	Master of Audiology
MAUD	Ministry of Aircraft Uranium Development [*British World War II*]
MAUD	Movimento Academico pela Uniao Democrata [*Academic Movement for Democratic Union*] [*Portugal Political party*] (PPE)
MAUDE	Morse Automatic Decoder
Maude & P...	Maude and Pollock's Law of Merchant Shipping [*A publication*] (DLA)
Maude & P Mer Shipp...	Maude and Pollock's Law of Merchant Shipping [*A publication*] (DLA)
Maude & P Shipp...	Maude and Pollock's Law of Merchant Shipping [*A publication*] (DLA)
MAUDEP......	Metropolitan Association of Urban Designers and Environmental Planners (EA)
Maud Ment Res...	Maudsley on Mental Responsibility [*A publication*] (DLA)
M Au E.........	Master of Automobile Engineering
M Au Eng.....	Master of Automobile Engineering
MAUF.........	Multiattribute Utility Function
MAUFS.........	Municipal Arborists and Urban Foresters Society (EA)
MAUG	MicroNet Apple User's Group [*CompuServe*] [*Database*]
Maug Att.....	Maugham's Attorneys, Solicitors, and Agents [*1825*] [*A publication*] (DLA)
Maug Att.....	Maugham's Statutes Relating to Attorneys, Etc. [*1839*] [*A publication*] (DLA)
Maug Cr L ...	Maugham's Outlines of Criminal Law [*2nd ed.*] [*1842*] [*A publication*] (DLA)
Maugh Lit Pr...	Maugham's Literary Property [*1828*] [*A publication*] (DLA)
Maugh RP ...	Maugham's Outlines of Real Property Law [*1842*] [*A publication*] (DLA)
Maug Jur ...	Maugham's Outlines of the Jurisdiction [*1838*] [*A publication*] (DLA)
Maug Law ...	Maugham's Outlines of Law [*1837*] [*A publication*] (DLA)
Maul & Sel...	Maule and Selwyn's English King's Bench Reports [*A publication*] (DLA)
Maule & S...	Maule and Selwyn's English King's Bench Reports [*A publication*] (DLA)
MAULEX	Marine Amphibious Unit Landing Exercise (NVT)
MauLoa	Mauna Loa Macadamia Partners Ltd. [*Associated Press*] (SAG)
MAULT........	Manual or Automatic Ultrasonic Laboratory Test
Maur...........	Mauritania
Maur...........	Mauritius

Maur Dec..... Mauritius Decisions [*A publication*] (DLA)
Maurit......... Mauritania
MAURP........ Master of Arts in Urban and Regional Planning (GAGS)
Maurti......... Mauritania (VRA)
MAUS .... Mauser Rifle
MAUS .... Messensch Afteliche Autonome Experiment Unter Schewerelosigkeit
MAUS .... Mobile Automated Scanner
MAUS .... Movimiento de Accion y Unidad Socialista [*Socialist Movement for Action and Unity*] [*Mexico Political party*] (PPW)
MAUSED...... Midwest Association of University Student Employment Directors [*Later, MASEA*] (EA)
mauso .... Mausoleum (VRA)
MAUTEL....... Microminiaturized Autonetics Telemetry
MauU.......... University of Mauritius, Reduit, Mauritius [*Library symbol Library of Congress*] (LCLS)
MAUV .... Multiple Autonomous Vehicle
MAUW .... Modified Advanced Underwater Weapons (MCD)
MAV........... Macrosiphum avenae Virus
MAV........... Magyar Allamvasutak [*Hungarian State Railways*]
MAV........... Maintenance Assistance Vehicle (MCD)
MAV........... Maloelap [*Marshall Islands*] [*Airport symbol*] (OAG)
MAV........... Manpower Authorization Voucher
MAV........... Mars Ascent Vehicle [*NASA*]
MAV........... Massive Resources Ltd. [*Vancouver Stock Exchange symbol*]
MAV........... Mavesa SA ADS [*NYSE symbol*] (SAG)
MAV........... Max-Aviation [*Canada ICAO designator*] (FAAC)
MAV........... Maximum Allowable Variation [*Net weight labeling*]
MAV........... Mean Absolute Value [*Statistics*]
MAV........... MeCCNU [*Semustine*], Adriamycin, Vincristine [*Antineoplastic drug regimen*]
MAV........... Mechanical Auxiliary Ventricle (PDAA)
MAV........... Military Aerospace Vehicle
mA/V.......... Milliamperes per Volt (DEN)
MAV........... Minimum Acceptable Value (MCD)
MAV........... Minute Alveolar Volume [*Medicine*] (DAVI)
MAV........... Moscavia [*Former USSR*] [*FAA designator*] (FAAC)
MAV........... Motor Ambulance Van [*British*]
MA(V)......... Motorcycling Australia (Victoria) [*Australia An association*]
MAV........... Multi-Appeal Vehicle
MAV........... Myeloblastosis-Associated Virus
MAV........... Transmembrane Activation Voltage [*Biochemistry*] (DAVI)
MAVA......... Moored Acoustic Vertical Array
MAVAR .... Microwave Amplification by Variable Reactance (IAA)
MAVAR .... Mixer Amplification by Variable Reactance (IAA)
MAVAR .... Modulating Amplifier Using Variable Resistance
MAVCC .... Mid-America Vocational Curriculum Consortium (OICC)
MAVE .... Model for Articulated Vocational Education (EDAC)
MAVE .... Multiple Aerial Vehicle Expert [*Army*]
MAV Ed....... Master of Administration in Vocational Education (PGP)
MAVERICK.. Manufacturers Assistance in Verifying, Identification in Cataloging
MAVES........ Manned Mars and Venus Exploration Studies
Mavesa........ Mavesa SA ADS [*Associated Press*] (SAG)
MAVI .... Microwave Automatic Vehicle Identification (MCD)
MAVICA ...... Magnetic Video Camera [*Sony Corp.*]
MAVICA ...... Magnetic Video Card (NITA)
MAVIN .... Machine-Assisted Vendor Information Network
MAVIN .... Multiple Angle, Variable Interval, Nonorthogonal [*Magnetic resonance imaging*]
MAVIS .... Master Vision Screener (PDAA)
MAVIS .... McDonnell Douglas Automated Voice Information System (MCD)
MAVIS .... Microprocessor-Based Audio Visual Information System (PDAA)
MAVIS .... Mobile Armored Vehicle Indigo System [*Radio-controlled tank*]
MAVK .... Maverick Tube [*NASDAQ symbol*] (TTSB)
MAVK......... Maverick Tube Corp. [*NASDAQ symbol*] (SAG)
MAVPE....... Metal Alkyl Vapor-Phase Epitaxy [*Semiconductor technology*]
MAVS........ Manned Aerial Vehicle for Surveillance (MCD)
MavTube...... Maverick Tube Corp. [*Associated Press*] (SAG)
MAVU .... Modular Audio Visual Unit (PDAA)
MAVWC...... Military Aircraft Voice Weather Code (NATG)
MAW......... Machinists and Aerospace Workers (DICI)
MAW......... Malden, MO [*Location identifier FAA*] (FAAL)
MAW......... Marine Air Wing
mAw......... Maritime Arctic Warm [*Air Mass*] [*Meteorology*] (BARN)
MAW......... Master of Arts in Worship (PGP)
MAW......... Master of Arts in Writing (GAGS)
MAW......... Mawson [*Antarctica*] [*Seismograph station code, US Geological Survey*] (SEIS)
MAW......... Maximum Allowable Weight [*Military*] (INF)
MAW......... Mechanically Aimed Warhead
MAW......... Medium Active Waste [*Nuclear energy*]
MAW......... Medium Antiarmor Weapon (INF)
MAW......... Medium Antitank Weapon
MAW......... Medium Assault Weapon
MAW......... Microsoft At Work [*Computer software*] (PCM)
MAW......... Mid-American Waste Sys [*NYSE symbol*] (TTSB)
MAW......... Mid-American Waste Systems, Inc. [*NYSE symbol*] (SPSG)
MAW......... Military Airlift Wing [*Air Force*] (MCD)
MAW......... Minor Assist Work
MAW......... Mission Adaptive Wing (MCD)
MAW......... Mustique Airways [*Barbados*] [*ICAO designator*] (FAAC)
MAWA........ Maltese American Women's Association
MAWA .... Matehematical Association of Western Australia
MAWA .... Missile Attack Warning and Assessment [*Military*] (PDAA)
MAWB .... Master Air Waybill [*Shipping*] (DS)
MAWC .... Marine Air West Coast

MAWCS .... Mobile Air Weapons Control System [*ESD*]
MAWD .... Mars Atmospheric Water Detection [*NASA*]
MA/WD .... Material Annex/Weapons Dictionary [*Military*]
MAWEC....... Maritime Aircraft Weather Code (NATG)
MAWg......... Military Airlift Wing [*Air Force*] (AFM)
MAWIA .... Mexican American Workers Importation Act
MAWL......... Magnetic Aircraft Weapons Link
MAWLOGS... Models of the [*US*] Army Worldwide Logistics System (AABC)
MAWP .... Marine Air Wing Pacific
MAWP .... Maximum Allowable Working Pressure (PDAA)
MAWS .... Marine Air Warning Squadron
MAWS .... Minimum Additive Waste Stabilization System [*Department of Energy*]
MAWS .... Missile Approach Warning System (DOMA)
MAWS .... Mobile Aircraft Weighing System (OA)
MAWS .... Modular Automated Weather System
MAWste ...... Mid-American Waste Systems, Inc. [*Associated Press*] (SAG)
MAWTS....... Marine Aviation Weapons and Tactics Squadron
MAWTU ...... Marine Air Weapons Training Unit (MCD)
MAX........... Cinemax [*Cable television channel*]
MAX........... Madrid, Spain [*Spaceflight Tracking and Data Network*] [*NASA*]
MAX........... Magic Answer Extractor [*Database*]
max .... Manx [*MARC language code Library of Congress*] (LCCP)
MAX........... Matam [*Senegal*] [*Airport symbol*] (OAG)
MAX........... Max-Aviation [*Canada*] [*FAA designator*] (FAAC)
MAX........... Maxilla [*Jawbone*]
MAX........... Maxim (ROG)
MAX........... Maxima (WDAA)
MAX........... Maximilian Numismatic and Historical Society (EA)
Max........... Maximinus [*of Scriptores Historiae Augustae*] [*Classical studies*] (OCD)
MAX........... Maximum
max........... Maximum (WDMC)
MAX........... Maxwell [*Unit of Magnetic Flux*] [*Electronics*] (IAA)
MAX........... Mediterranean Airlines SA [*Greece*] [*ICAO designator*] (FAAC)
MAX........... Mercury Air Group [*AMEX symbol*] (TTSB)
MAX........... Mercury Air Group, Inc. [*AMEX symbol*] (SPSG)
MAX........... Metropolitan Area Express [*Railway*] [*Portland, OR*] (ECON)
MAX........... Minerex Resources Ltd. [*Vancouver Stock Exchange symbol Toronto Stock Exchange symbol*]
MAX........... Mobile Automatic Exchange [*Telecommunications*] (NITA)
MAX........... Mobile Automatic X-Ray (PDAA)
MAX........... Modular Applications Executive [*Modular Computer Systems*]
Maxam .... Maxxam Corp. [*Associated Press*] (SAG)
MAXC......... Maxco, Inc. [*NASDAQ symbol*] (NQ)
MAXC......... Multiple Access Xerox Computer (NITA)
MAX CLB .... Maximum Engine Thrust for Two-Engine Climb (GAVI)
Maxco......... Maxco, Inc. [*Associated Press*] (SAG)
MAXCO .... Maximum Dynamic Pressure (NASA)
MAXCOL ..... Maximum Column [*Computer science*] (PCM)
MAXCOM .... Modular Applications Executive for Communications [*Modular Computer Systems*]
MaxcrHlt...... Maxicare Health Plans, Inc. [*Associated Press*] (SAG)
MAX CRZ.... Maximum Engine Thrust for Two-Engine Cruise (GAVI)
Max Dig....... Maxwell's Nebraska Digest [*A publication*] (DLA)
MAXE......... Max & Erma's Restaurants [*NASDAQ symbol*] (TTSB)
MAXE......... Max & Erma's Restaurants, Inc. [*NASDAQ symbol*] (NQ)
Max EP....... Maximal Esophageal Pressure [*Medicine*] (MAE)
MaxEr........ Max & Erma's Restaurants, Inc. [*Associated Press*] (SAG)
MAXG........ Maximum Girth [*Pisciculture*]
MAXI......... Maxicare Health Plans [*NASDAQ symbol*] (TTSB)
MAXI......... Maxicare Health Plans, Inc. [*NASDAQ symbol*] (NQ)
MAXID........ Maximize Indefinite Delivery Contracts (AFM)
Maxim........ Maxim Integrated Products, Inc. [*Associated Press*] (SAG)
MaximGp..... Maxim Group [*Associated Press*] (SAG)
MaximPh...... Maxim Pharmaceuticals, Inc. [*Associated Press*] (SAG)
Max Int Stat... Maxwell on the Interpretation of Statutes [*A publication*] (DLA)
Maxis......... Maxis, Inc. [*Associated Press*] (SAG)
MAXIT........ Maximum Interference Threshold [*Telecommunications*] (TEL)
MAX/IT........ Modular, Adaptable, Expandable, Intelligent Terminal [*Link Technologies, Inc.*] (PCM)
Max LD....... Maxwell's Law Dictionary [*A publication*] (DLA)
MAXM........ Maxim Group [*NASDAQ symbol*] (SAG)
MAXMAR ..... Maximum Mobile Army
Max Mar L... Maxwell's Marine Law [*A publication*] (DLA)
MAX/MIN .... Maximum Disclosure / Minimum Delay (DNAB)
MaxmP........ Maxim Pharmaceuticals, Inc. [*Associated Press*] (SAG)
MAXNET ..... Modular Application Executive for Computer Networks (PDAA)
MAXNET ..... Modular Applications Executive Network (NITA)
MAXNOR..... Maximum Number of Runs (MCD)
MAXPAR ..... Maximum Pain Relief [*Medicine*]
MAXPAX ..... Maxwell House Coffee Package [*Vendor-machine system for Maxwell House coffee*]
MAXPEN ..... Maximum Penalty
MAXPID ...... Maximum Pain Intensity Difference [*Medicine*]
MAXS......... Maxwell Shoe'A' [*NASDAQ symbol*] (TTSB)
MAXS......... Maxwell Shoe Company, Inc. [*NASDAQ symbol*] (SAG)
MAXSECOM.. Maximum Security Communications (IAA)
MAXSECON.. Maximum Security Communications
Maxserv...... Maxserv, Inc. [*Associated Press*] (SAG)
MAXTOP...... Maximum Total Duration Penalty
Maxtor........ Maxtor Corp. [*Associated Press*] (SAG)
MAXTTR ..... Maximum Time to Repair [*Navy*] (CAAL)
MAXTWK .... Maximum Total Work Content
Maxu .... Maxus Energy Corp. [*Associated Press*] (SAG)

MAXUPO......	Maximum Undistorted Power Output (IAA)
Maxus.........	Maxus Energy [Associated Press] (SAG)
Maxw Cr Proc...	Maxwell's Treatise on Criminal Procedure [A publication] (DLA)
Maxwel......	Maxwell Laboratories, Inc. [Associated Press] (SAG)
Maxwell......	Irish Land Purchase Cases [1904-11] [A publication] (DLA)
Maxwell......	Maxwell on the Interpretation of Statutes [A publication] (DLA)
Maxw Interp St...	Maxwell on the Interpretation of Statutes [A publication] (DLA)
MaxwllSh	Maxwell Shoe Co., Inc. [Associated Press] (SAG)
MaxwllT......	Maxwell Technologies, Inc. [Associated Press] (SAG)
Maxxim.......	Maxxim Medical, Inc. [Associated Press] (SAG)
may	Malay [MARC language code Library of Congress] (LCCP)
MAY...........	Malye Karmakuly [Former USSR Geomagnetic observatory code]
MAY...........	Mangrove Cay [Bahamas] [Airport symbol] (OAG)
MAY...........	Maya Airways Ltd. [Belize] [ICAO designator] (FAAC)
MAY...........	Maybelline, Inc. [NYSE symbol] (SPSG)
MAY...........	May Department Stores Co., Corporate Information Center, St. Louis, MO [OCLC symbol] (OCLC)
MAY...........	Mayfield [Washington] [Seismograph station code, US Geological Survey Closed] (SEIS)
MAY...........	Maynard Energy, Inc. [Toronto Stock Exchange symbol]
MAY...........	Mayor (ROG)
MAY...........	Mayor
MAYA........	Most Advanced, Yet Acceptable [Industrial design]
May Act......	Mayhew's Action at Law [1828] [A publication] (DLA)
Maybel	Maybelline, Inc. [Associated Press] (SAG)
MAYC........	Methodist Association of Youth Clubs [British] (BI)
May Const Hist...	May's Constitutional History of England [A publication] (DLA)
May Crim Law...	May's Criminal Law [A publication] (DLA)
May Dam.....	Mayne on the Law of Damages [A publication] (DLA)
MayDS........	May Department Stores Co. [Associated Press] (SAG)
MayflCo	Mayflower Co-Operative Bank [Associated Press] (SAG)
May Fr Conv...	May's Fraudulent Conveyances [3rd ed.] [1908] [A publication] (DLA)
May Ins	May on Insurance [A publication] (DLA)
May Just......	Mayo's Justice [A publication] (DLA)
May LR.......	Mayurbhani Law Report [India] [A publication] (DLA)
May Merg....	Mayhew on Merger [1861] [A publication] (DLA)
Mayn	Maynard's English Reports, Exchequer Memoranda of Edward I, and Year Books of Edward II [A publication] (DLA)
MaynOil	Maynard Oil Co. [Associated Press] (SAG)
Mayo & Moul...	Mayo and Moulton's Pension Laws [A publication] (DLA)
Mayo Just....	Mayo's Justice [A publication] (DLA)
Mayo Med Sch...	Mayo Medicine School (GAGS)
May Parl......	May's Parliamentary Practice [A publication] (ILCA)
May Parl Law...	May's Parliamentary Law [A publication] (DLA)
May Parl Pr...	May's Parliamentary Practice [A publication] (DLA)
May PL	May's Parliamentary Practice [A publication] (DLA)
MAYPOLE	May Polarization Experiment [RADAR storm sensing]
MAYS.........	Mays [J. W.], Inc. [NASDAQ symbol] (NQ)
MAYS.........	Mays (JW) [NASDAQ symbol] (TTSB)
MaysJ........	Mays [J. W.], Inc. [Associated Press] (SAG)
MaySpeh	May & Speh, Inc. [Associated Press] (SAG)
Maytag	Maytag Corp. [Associated Press] (SAG)
MAYW	Maywood & Sugar Creek [AAR code]
MAZ...........	Mayaguez [Puerto Rico] [Airport symbol] (OAG)
MAZ...........	Mazatlan [Mexico] [Seismograph station code, US Geological Survey] (SEIS)
MAZ...........	Mazzite [A zeolite]
MAZ...........	Mines Air Service Zambia Ltd. [ICAO designator] (FAAC)
MAZ...........	Missed Approach Azimuth [Aviation]
MAZ...........	Mounting Azimuth [Weaponry] (INF)
MazelSt	Mazel Stores, Inc. [Associated Press] (SAG)
MAZH.........	Missile Azimuth Heading [Air Force]
MAZI.........	Movement for the Advancement of the Zionist Idea [Israel] [Political party] (EY)
MAZL.........	Mazel Stores, Inc. [NASDAQ symbol] (SAG)
MAZO.........	Missile Azimuth Orientation [Air Force] (IAA)
MB.............	All India Reporter, Madhya Bharat [1950-57] [A publication] (DLA)
MB.............	Bachelor of Medicine [Other than from Oxford]
MB.............	Bachelor of Music (WDAA)
mb----	Black Sea and Area [MARC geographic area code Library of Congress] (LCCP)
MB.............	Boston Public Library and Eastern Massachusetts Regional Public Library System, Boston, MA [Library symbol Library of Congress] (LCLS)
MB.............	Countrywide [ICAO designator] (AD)
MB.............	Machine Bolt [Technical drawings]
MB.............	MacMillan Bloedel Ltd. [Associated Press] (SAG)
MB.............	Magnetic Bearing [Navigation]
MB.............	Magnetic Brake [Industrial control] (IEEE)
MB.............	Magnetron Branch [Electronics] (OA)
MB.............	Mailbox (AAG)
MB.............	Main Ballast
MB.............	Main Base [Air Force] (AFM)
MB.............	Main Battery [Guns]
MB.............	Main Bus (MCD)
MB.............	Maintenance Busy [Telecommunications] (TEL)
M-B...........	Make-Break
MB.............	Mallory Body [Medicine]
MB.............	Management Baseline (NASA)
MB.............	Management Board (ACII)
MB.............	Manitoba [Canadian province] [Postal code]
MB.............	March-Bender Factor [Physiology]
MB.............	Margin Buccal [Medicine] (MAE)
MB.............	Marine Barracks
MB.............	Marine Base
MB.............	Marine Board (EA)
MB.............	Mark of the Beast [Disparaging term for 19th century Protestant clerical waistcoats that had Catholic influences]
MB.............	Marks Banco (ROG)
MB.............	Marsh-Bender [Factor] [Muscle tissue]
MB.............	Mass Balance
MB.............	Material Balance
MB.............	May & Baker Ltd. [Great Britain] [Research code symbol]
MB.............	MBB-UV, MBB-UD [Messerschmitt-Boelkow-Blohm], und Pneuma-Technik [Germany ICAO aircraft manufacturer identifier] (ICAO)
MB.............	Measurement Base [Military]
MB.............	Mechanized Battalion [Army]
MB.............	Medal of Bravery
MB.............	Medial Bilateral (Neuron) [Neuroanatomy]
MB.............	Median Bundle [Botany]
MB.............	Medical Board
MB.............	Medical Bulletin
MB.............	Medicare Bureau [Health Care Financing Administration - Social Security Administration] (OICC)
MB.............	Medicinae Baccalaureus [Bachelor of Medicine] [Latin]
MB.............	Medium Bomber
MB.............	Medium Bronze [Numismatics]
MB.............	Megabar
Mb.............	Megabase [A unit of molecular size]
MB.............	Megabit [Binary Digit] [Computer science]
Mb.............	Megabit [Computer science] (WDMC)
Mb.............	Megabit [Marine science] (OSRA)
MB.............	Megabuck [Defense industry colloquialism for one million dollars] (AAG)
MB.............	Megabyte [Data storage capacity] [Computer science]
MB.............	Melt Back
MB.............	Memorandum Book (ROG)
MB.............	Memory Bank
MB.............	Memory Buffer [Computer science]
MB.............	Memory Bus
MB.............	Mercedes-Benz [Automobile]
MB.............	Merchant Bank
MB.............	Meridian & Bigbee Railroad Co. [Later, MBRR] [AAR code]
MB.............	Mesiobuccal [Dentistry]
MB.............	Message Buffer (ACRL)
MB.............	Message Business
MB.............	Messages of the Bible [A publication]
MB.............	Metabisulfite [Inorganic chemistry]
MB.............	Metal Box [Commercial firm British]
MB.............	Methyl Bromide [Organic chemistry]
MB.............	Methylene Blue [Organic chemistry]
MB.............	Metrication Board [British]
MB.............	Metric Board (OICC)
MB.............	Microbeam [Physics]
MB.............	Microbiological Assay [Biochemistry] (DAVI)
MB.............	Microbody
MB.............	Microelectronics Bibliography [A publication]
MB.............	Midbody
MB.............	Middle Babylonian [Language, etc.] (BJA)
MB.............	Middle Bronze Age (BJA)
MB.............	Middle of Bow [Music] (ROG)
MB.............	Militia Bureau [Superseded in 1933 by National Guard Bureau]
mb.............	Millibar [Unit of pressure]
MB.............	Millibar
mb.............	Millibarn [Area of nuclear cross-section]
mb.............	Millibyte [Computer science]
MB.............	Million Bytes [Computer science] (BUR)
MB.............	Milton Bradley Ltd. [British]
MB.............	Minimum Bid [Philately]
MB.............	Misce Bene [Mix Well] [Pharmacy]
MB.............	Miscellaneous Branch, Internal Revenue Bureau [United States] (DLA)
MB.............	Missed Byte [Computer science] (ECII)
MB.............	Missile Base [Military]
MB.............	Missile Body
MB.............	Missile Bomber
MB.............	Mixed Bed [Nuclear energy] (NRCH)
MB.............	Mixing Box (OA)
MB.............	Mobile Base (DEN)
MB.............	Model Block (MSA)
MB.............	Module Balance [Computer science]
MB.............	Mohelbuch (BJA)
MB.............	Moisture Balance
MB.............	Molecular Biosystems [NYSE symbol] (TTSB)
MB.............	Molecular Biosystems, Inc. [NYSE symbol] (SPSG)
MB.............	Molybdenum [Chemical element] (ROG)
MB.............	Monthly Breakdown [Used in atmospheric studies]
MB.............	Monthly Bulletin of Decisions of the High Court of Uganda [A publication] (DLA)
MB.............	Months Before
MB.............	Montpelier & Barre Railroad Co. [AAR code]
MB.............	Mooring Buoy
MB.............	Morale Branch [Military]
MB.............	Morrell's English Bankruptcy Reports [A publication] (DLA)
MB.............	Mortar Board (EA)
MB.............	Motor Barge (ADA)
MB.............	Motor Boat
MB.............	Mountain Battery [British military] (DMA)
MB.............	Multiband (DEN)

MB .... Municipal Bond
MB .... Municipal Borough
MB .... Munitions Board [*Abolished 1953, functions transferred to Department of Defense*]
MB .... Museum of Broadcasting
MB .... Mushroom Body [*Nerve center in insects*]
MB .... Musicae Baccalaureus [*Bachelor of Music*]
MB .... Music for the Blind [*Defunct*] (EA)
MB .... Must Be [*Sold*] [*Classified advertising*]
MB .... Myocardial Band [*Cardiology*]
Mb .... Myoglobin [*Biochemistry, medicine*]
Mb .... Myoglobin Tritium [*Hematology*] (DAVI)
MB .... Western Airlines [*ICAO designator*] (AD)
MB-2 .... Model Boiler-Two [*Nuclear energy*] (GFGA)
MBA .... American Academy of Arts and Sciences, Boston, MA [*Library symbol Library of Congress*] (LCLS)
MBA .... Automobilvertriebs Aktiengesellschaft [*Austria ICAO designator*] (FAAC)
MBA .... Main Battle Area (AABC)
MBA .... Main-Belt Asteroid [*Astronomy*]
MBA .... Make-or-Buy Authorization (AAG)
MBA .... Makers of British Art [*A publication*]
MBA .... Male Bonding Alert [*Screenwriter's lexicon*]
MBA .... Male Bowhunter Aided [*International Bowhunting Organization*] [*Class equipment*]
MBA .... Mantle Bouguer Anomaly [*Geology*]
MBA .... Manufactured Buildings Association [*Defunct*] (EA)
MBA .... Many-Body Alloy [*Metallurgy*]
MBA .... Marching Bands of America (EA)
MBA .... Marine Biological Association [*British*]
MBA .... Mass Balance Area (NUCP)
MBA .... Master Bakers' Association [*Australia*]
MBA .... Master of Business Administration
MBA .... Master of Business Administration (GAGS)
MBA .... Master of the British Arts Association (DBQ)
MBA .... Material Balance Area [*Nuclear energy*]
MBA .... Maximum Benefit Amount [*Unemployment insurance*]
MBA .... Merion Bluegrass Association [*Defunct*] (EA)
MBA .... Methyl Benzyl Alcohol [*Organic chemistry*]
MBA .... Methylbis(beta-chloroethyl)amine [*Nitrogen mustard*] [*Also, HN, NM Antineoplastic; war-gas base*]
MBA .... Methylenebisacrylamide [*Organic chemistry*]
MBA .... Microbiological Associates, Inc.
MBA .... Migratory Bird Act
MBA .... Military Base Agreement (CINC)
MBA .... Military Benefit Association (EA)
MBA .... Milk Bars Association of Great Britain and Ireland Ltd. (BI)
MBa .... Miniature Ball [*Horticulture*]
MBA .... Minimum Burst Altitude (AABC)
MBA .... Minor Basic Allergens [*Immunology*]
MBA .... Mombasa [*Kenya*] [*Airport symbol*] (OAG)
MBA .... Monument Builders of America [*Later, MBNA*]
MBA .... Mortar Box Assembly
MBA .... Mortgage Bankers Association of America [*Washington, DC*] (EA)
MBA .... Motorized Bicycle Association [*Later, MAA*] (EA)
MBA .... Mount Bingar [*Australia Seismograph station code, US Geological Survey Closed*] (SEIS)
MBA .... Multibeam Antenna
MBA .... Multiple Berthing Adaptor (SSD)
MBA .... Multiple Birth Association [*Australia*]
MBA .... Rural Municipality of Argyle Public Library, Baldur, Manitoba [*Library symbol National Library of Canada*] (NLC)
MBAA .... Master Brewers Association of the Americas (EA)
MBAA .... Master of Business Administration in Aviation (PGP)
MBAA .... Messinian Benevolent Association "Aristomenis" (EA)
MBAA .... Methylene Bisacrylamide (PDAA)
MBAA .... Mini Bike Association of America (EA)
MBAA .... Mortgage Brokers' Association of Australia
MBAA .... Motel Brokers Association of America [*Later, AHMB*] (EA)
MBAAS ...... Master of Business Administration in Actuarial Science
MBab .... Middle Babylonian [*Language, etc.*] (BJA)
MBABS ...... Synod Office, Diocese of Brandon, Anglican Church of Canada, Manitoba [*Library symbol National Library of Canada*] (NLC)
MBAC .... Assiniboine Community College, Brandon, Manitoba [*Library symbol National Library of Canada*] (NLC)
MBAC .... Marshall Booster Assembly Contractor (MCD)
MBAC .... Member of the British Association of Chemists (DAS)
MBACFM ..... American Board of Commissioners for Foreign Missions, Boston, MA [*Library symbol Library of Congress*] (LCLS)
M-BACOD .... Methotrexate (High-Dose) (with Citrovorum Factor Rescue), Bleomycin, Adriamycin, Cyclophosphamide, Oncovin [*Vincristine*], Dexamethasone [*Antineoplastic drug regimen*]
M-BACOP .... Myelosuppressive Bleomycin, Adriamycin, Cyclophosphamide, Oncovin [*Vincristine*], Prednisone [*Antineoplastic drug regimen*]
M-BACOS .... Bleomycin, Adriamycin, Cytoxan, Oncovin, Methotrexate with Leucovorin Rescue [*Antineoplastic drug*] (CDI)
MBACT .... Medical Board of the Australian Capital Territory
MBAD .... Medical Badge
MB Adm ..... Master of Business Administration
MBAE .... Master of Biological and Agricultural Engineering (PGP)
MBAE .... Master of Biosystems and Agricultural Engineering (PGP)
MBAE .... Member of the British Association of Electrolysis (DI)
MBA-EP ..... Master of Business Administration - Experienced Professionals (PGP)
MBAG .... Modulated Bayard-Alpert Gauge

MBAG .... Research Station, Agriculture Canada [*Station de Recherches, Agriculture Canada*] Brandon, Manitoba [*Library symbol National Library of Canada*] (NLC)
MBAI .... Mosquito Biting Activity Index [*Canada*]
MBAIB .... Master of Business Administration in International Business (GAGS)
MBAIT .... Master of Business Administration in International Trade (PGP)
MBAJ .... Magna Bibliotheca Anglo-Judaica (BJA)
MBAM .... Main Beam Avoidance Maneuver
MBAMT ...... Methyl(benzylideneamino)mercaptotriazole [*Reagent*]
MBANSW .... Master Butchers' Association of New South Wales [*Australia*]
MBANSW .... Medical Benevolent Association of New South Wales [*Australia*]
MBAOT ...... Member of the British Association of Occupational Therapists (DI)
MBA-PE ..... Master of Business Administration - Physician's Executive (PGP)
mbar .... Millibar [*Unit of pressure*]
MBAR .... Multibeam Acquisition RADAR (MCD)
MBAR .... Myocardial Beta Adrenergic Receptor [*Cardiology*] (DMAA)
MBARI .... Monterey Bay Aquarium Research Institute [*California*]
MBarL .... Barnstable Law Library, Barnstable, MA [*Library symbol*] [*Library of Congress*] (LCLS)
MBAS .... Methylene Blue Active Substance [*Organic chemistry*]
MBAS .... Mutual Benefit and Aid Society [*Later, WBF*] (EA)
MBASA ...... Medical Benevolent Association of South Australia
MBASW ..... Member of the British Association of Social Workers
MBAt .... Boston Athenaeum, Boston, MA [*Library symbol Library of Congress*] (LCLS)
MBATM ...... Master of Business in Telecommunication Management (PGP)
MBAUK ...... Marine Biological Association of the United Kingdom (ARC)
MBAV .... Main Battle Air Vehicle [*Military*] (PDAA)
MBAWS ..... Marine Base Air Warning System
MBB .... Brandeis University, Waltham, MA [*OCLC symbol*] (OCLC)
MBB .... Make-before-Break
MBB .... Marble Bar [*Australia Airport symbol*] (OAG)
MBB .... Maurer, B. B., Chicago IL [*STAC*]
MBB .... Messerschmitt-Boelkow-Blohm GmbH [*West German aircraft company*]
MBB .... Miniature Brushless Blower
MBB .... Mortgage-Backed Bonds
MBB .... MSB Bancorp, Inc. [*AMEX symbol*] (SAG)
MBBA .... Boston Bar Association, Boston, MA [*Library symbol Library of Congress*] (LCLS)
MBBA .... Methoxybenzylidene Butylaniline [*Organic chemistry*]
MBBA .... (Methozybenzylidene)butylaniline [*Organic chemistry*]
MBBA .... Military Benefit Base Amounts
MBBAQ ...... Master Boat Builders' Association of Queensland [*Australia*]
MBBC .... Monterey Bay Bancorp [*NASDAQ symbol*] (TTSB)
MBBC .... Monterey Bay Bancorp, Inc. [*NASDAQ symbol*] (SAG)
MBBI .... Babson College, Babson Park, MA [*Library symbol Library of Congress*] (LCLS)
MBBI .... Multiple-Bit Binary Input
MBBL .... Massachusetts Bureau of Library Extension, Boston, MA [*Library symbol Library of Congress*] (LCLS)
MBBL .... Thousand Barrels (EG)
MBBLS ...... Thousands of Barrels (MCD)
MBbM .... Massachusetts Maritime Academy, Buzzards Bay, MA [*Library symbol Library of Congress*] (LCLS)
MBBO .... Multiple-Bit Binary Output
MBBR .... Brokenhead River Regional Library, Beausejour, Manitoba [*Library symbol National Library of Canada*] (NLC)
MBBS .... Bostonian Society, Boston, MA [*Library symbol Library of Congress*] (LCLS)
MBBSC ...... Bachelor of Medicine and Bachelor of Science [*British*] (ROG)
MBC .... American Congregational Association, Boston, MA [*Library symbol Library of Congress*] (LCLS)
MBC .... Brandon University, Manitoba [*Library symbol National Library of Canada*] (NLC)
MBC .... Magnetic Bias Coil (IIA)
MBC .... Magnetic Bias Control (DNAB)
MBC .... Mailbox Club [*Later, MCI*] (EA)
MBC .... Main Beam Clutter
MBC .... Malwa Bhil Corps [*British military*] (DMA)
MBC .... Manhattan Bible College [*Kansas*]
MBC .... Manhattan Bowery Corp. (EA)
mbc .... Manitoba [*MARC country of publication code Library of Congress*] (LCCP)
MBC .... Manual Battery Control (AAG)
MBC .... Marine Biomedical Center [*Duke University*] [*Research center*] (RCD)
MBC .... Mary Baldwin College [*Virginia*]
MBC .... Master Bus Controller [*Computer science*]
MBC .... Master of Beauty Culture
MBC .... Master of Building Construction (PGP)
MBC .... Maximum Breathing Capacity
MBC .... M'Bigou [*Gabon*] [*Airport symbol*] (OAG)
MBC .... McLaughlin-Buick Club of Canada (EAIO)
MBC .... Mediterranean Bombardment Code
MBC .... Megabar Diamond Cell [*For high-pressure measurements*]
MBC .... Memory Bus Controller
MBC .... Mercantile Bank of Canada [*Toronto Stock Exchange symbol Vancouver Stock Exchange symbol*]
MBC .... Metastatic Breast Cancer [*Medicine*]
MBC .... Meteor Burst Communications [*Military*]
MBC .... Methotrexate, Bleomycin, Cisplatin [*Antineoplastic drug*] (CDI)
MBC .... Methyl Benzimidazolecarbamate [*Organic chemistry*]
MBC .... Methylthymol Blue Complex (BABM)
MBC .... Metropolitan Borough Council [*British*]
MBC .... Mewar Bhil Corps [*British military*] (DMA)

MBC............	Military Budget Committee [*NATO*] (NATG)
MBC............	Miniature Bayonet Cap
MBC............	Miniaturized Ballistic Computer
MBC............	Minimum Bactericidal Concentration
MBC............	Minnesota Bible College [*Rochester*]
MBC............	Modified Brequet Cruise [*SST*]
MBC............	Monkees Buttonmania Club [*Defunct*] (EA)
MBC............	Mononuclear Blood Cell [*Hematology*]
MBC............	Morris Brown College [*Atlanta, GA*]
MBC............	Morris Brown College, Atlanta, GA [*OCLC symbol*] (OCLC)
MBC............	Mortar Ballistic Computer [*Formerly, MFCC*] [*Army*] (INF)
MBCS..........	Mother and Baby Care [*Red Cross Nursing Services*]
MBC............	Motorboat Crew [*British military*] (DMA)
MBC............	Mould Bay [*Northwest Territories*] [*Seismograph station code, US Geological Survey*] (SEIS)
MBC............	Mountain Bike Club [*British*] (DBA)
MBC............	Multiple Basic Channel
MBC............	Multiple Board Computer (IAA)
MBC............	Multiple Burst Correcting
MBCA..........	Archives, Brandon University, Manitoba [*Library symbol National Library of Canada*] (BIB)
MBCA..........	Mechanical Bank Collectors of America (EA)
MBCA..........	Mercedes-Benz Club of America (EA)
MBCA..........	Merchant Bank of Central Africa Ltd.
MBCA..........	Munitions Board Cataloging Agency
MBCAM.......	Commonwealth Air Training Plan Museum, Inc., Brandon, Manitoba [*Library symbol National Library of Canada*] (NLC)
MBCC..........	Massachusetts Bay Community College [*Wellesley*]
MBCC..........	McLaughlin-Buick Club of Canada (EA)
MBCC..........	Medical Benefits Consultative Committee
MBCC..........	Migratory Bird Conservation Commission [*A federal government body*]
MBCD	Modified Binary-Coded Decimal
MBCG	Department of Geography, Brandon University, Manitoba [*Library symbol National Library of Canada*] (NLC)
MBCK..........	Mallory Body Cytokeratin [*Medicine*]
MBCM..........	Baccalaureus Medicinae, Chirurgiae Magister [*Bachelor of Medicine, Master of Surgery*]
MBCM..........	New England Conservatory of Music, Boston, MA [*Library symbol Library of Congress*] (LCLS)
MBCMA.......	Metal Building Component Manufacturers' Association (EA)
MBCMC.......	Milk Bottle Crate Manufacturers Council [*Defunct*] (EA)
MBCNT.......	Multilingual Broadcasting Council of the Northern Territory [*Australia*]
MBCo...........	Countway Library of Medicine, Boston, MA [*Library symbol Library of Congress*] (LCLS)
MBCO	Member of the British College of Ophthalmic Opticians [*British*] (DBQ)
MbCO...........	Myoglobin, Carboxy [*Biochemistry, medicine*]
MBCS..........	Medium Bandwidth Compression System
MBCS..........	Member of the British Computer Society (DCTA)
MBCS..........	Meteor Burst Communication System
MBCS..........	Motion Base Crew Station [*NASA*] (NASA)
MBCU..........	Mobile Bombardment Communications Unit [*Military*] (IAA)
MBd............	Bedford Free Public Library, Bedford, MA [*Library symbol Library of Congress*] (LCLS)
MBD............	Episcopal Diocese of Massachusetts, Boston, MA [*Library symbol Library of Congress*] (LCLS)
MBD............	Macroblock Design
MBD............	Magnetic-Bubble Domain Device [*Computer science*] (IEEE)
MBD............	Manual Board [*Telecommunications*] (NITA)
MBD............	Manual Burst Disable (AABC)
MBD............	Materials-by-Design [*Chemical engineering*]
MBD............	Meander Belt Deposit [*Geology*]
MBD............	Methotrexate, Bleomycin, Diamminedichloroplatinum [*Cisplatin*] [*Antineoplastic drug regimen*]
MBD............	Methoxybenzylaminonitrobenzoxadiazole [*Fluorescent probe*] [*Biochemistry*]
MBD............	Methylbutenedial [*Organic chemistry*]
MBD............	Methylene Blue Dye [*Organic chemistry*] (MAE)
MBD............	Million Barrels Daily
MBD............	Minimal Brain Damage [*or Dysfunction*]
MBD............	Minimal Brain Dysfunction [*Neurology*] (DAVI)
MBD............	Minimal Brain Dysfunction
MBD............	Mission Baseline Description [*NASA*] (KSC)
MBD............	Morquio-Brailsford Disease [*Medicine*] (DMAA)
MBD............	Motor Belt Drive (MSA)
MBD............	Muzzle Boresight Device [*Army*] (INF)
MBDA	Metal Building Dealers Association [*Later, Systems Builders Association*] (EA)
MBDA	Minority Business Development Agency [*Formerly, OMBE*] [*Department of Commerce*]
MBDAACC....	Milling and Baking Division of American Association of Cereal Chemists (EA)
MBdAF........	United States Air Force, Cambridge Research Center, Bedford, MA [*Library symbol Library of Congress*] (LCLS)
MBDC	Minority Business Development Center [*Minority Business Development Administration*]
MBdD...........	Document Research Center, Bedford, MA [*Library symbol Library of Congress*] (LCLS)
MBDET.......	Mobile Boarding Detachment [*Coast Guard*]
MBDG	Marine Base Defense Group
MBdgSc	Master of Building Science
MBDI	Major Business Development Initiative
MBDio	Diocesan Library, Boston, MA [*Library symbol Library of Congress*] (LCLS)

MBDL...........	Missile Battery Data Link (MCD)
MBdM	Middlesex Community College, Bedford, MA [*Library symbol Library of Congress*] (LCLS)
MBdMi........	Mitre Corps., Bedford, MA [*Library symbol Library of Congress*] (LCLS)
MBDOE	Million Barrels per Day Oil Equivalent (MHDB)
MBDP	Minority Bank Deposit Program [*Treasury Department*]
MB(DP)AC ...	Medical Benefits (Dental Practitioners) Advisory Committee
MBDR..........	Make-or-Buy Data Record (KSC)
MBdR...........	Raytheon Co., Missile Systems Division Library, Bedford, MA [*Library symbol Library of Congress*] (LCLS)
MBDS	Modular Building Distribution System [*Telecommunications*] (TEL)
MBdV..........	United States Veterans Administration Hospital, Bedford, MA [*Library symbol Library of Congress*] (LCLS)
MBE............	Bethany Lutheran College, Mankato, MN [*OCLC symbol*] (OCLC)
MBE............	Emerson College, Boston, MA [*Library symbol Library of Congress*] (LCLS)
MBE............	Mail Boxes Etc. USA [*San Diego, CA*] [*Telecommunications*] (TSSD)
MBE............	Management by Exception
MBE............	Martin-Baker Ltd. [*British ICAO designator*] (FAAC)
MBE............	Mary Baker Eddy [*Founder of Christian Science*]
MBE............	Master of Bilingual Education (PGP)
MBE............	Master of Business Economics
MBE............	Master of Business Economics (GAGS)
MBE............	Master of Business Education (GAGS)
MBE............	Master of Business Education
MBE............	May Be Elevated [*Medicine*] (DAVI)
MBE............	Member of the [*Order of the*] British Empire [*Facetious translation: "My Bloody Efforts"*]
MBE............	Mennonite Board of Education (EA)
MBE............	Metals-Based Engineering
MBE............	Minority Business Enterprise (MCD)
MBE............	Missile-Borne Equipment
MBE............	Molecular Beam Epitaxy [*Crystallography*]
MBE............	Monbetsu [*Japan*] [*Airport symbol*] (OAG)
MBE............	Monumenta Biblica et Ecclesiastica [*Rome*] [*A publication*] (BJA)
MBE............	Mountasia Entertainment Intl., Inc. [*AMEX symbol*] (SAG)
MBE............	Moving Boundary Electrophoresis [*Analytical biochemistry*]
MBE............	Multiple-Beam Experiment [*In MBE-4, a heavy-ion accelerator at the Lawrence Berkeley Laboratory*]
MBE............	Multistate Bar Examination
MBEA..........	Missouri Business Education Association (EDAC)
MBE-ARMS...	Multiple Business Entity - Accounts Receivable Management System (MHDB)
MBED..........	Episcopal Diocese of Massachusetts, Diocesan Library and Archives, Boston, MA [*Library symbol*] [*Library of Congress*] (LCLS)
MB Ed.........	Master of Business Education
MBehaviouralSc..	Master of Behavioural Sciences (ADA)
MBEI...........	Member of the Institute of Body Engineers [*British*] (DBQ)
MBEI...........	Minnesota Business Educators, Inc (EDAC)
MBELDEF....	Minority Business Enterprise Legal Defense and Education Fund (EA)
MBelm.........	Belmont Memorial Library, Belmont, MA [*Library symbol Library of Congress*] (LCLS)
MBelmM......	McLean Hospital, Belmont, MA [*Library symbol Library of Congress*] (LCLS)
MBEmm.......	Emmanuel College, Boston, MA [*Library symbol Library of Congress*] (LCLS)
MBEnv	Master of the Built Environment (ADA)
MBEP..........	Metals-Based Engineering Program
MBEPA........	United States Environmental Protection Agency, Region I Library, Boston, MA [*Library symbol Library of Congress*] (LCLS)
MBER..........	Member
MBER..........	Molecular Beam Electric Resonance [*Physics*]
MBES..........	Member of the Bureau of Engineer Surveyors [*British*] (DBQ)
MBES..........	Mezhdunarodnyi Bank Ekonomicheskovo Sotrudnichestva [*International Bank for Economic Co-Operation - IBEC*] [*Moscow, USSR*] (EAIO)
MBev	Beverly Public Library, Beverly, MA [*Library symbol Library of Congress*] (LCLS)
MBev-F........	Beverly Farms Public Library, Beverly, MA [*Library symbol Library of Congress*] (LCLS)
MBevHi........	Beverly Historical Society, Beverly, MA [*Library symbol Library of Congress*] (LCLS)
MBevN........	North Shore Community College, Beverly, MA [*Library symbol Library of Congress*] (LCLS)
MBevT........	Beverly Times, Beverly, MA [*Library symbol Library of Congress*] (LCLS)
MBF............	Main Boundary Fault [*Geophysics*]
MBF............	Master Bibliographic File (ADA)
MBF............	Master Builders Federation [*British*] (BI)
MBF............	Materials Business File [*American Society for Metals, The Institute for Metals*] [*Information service or system*] (IID)
MBF............	MBF USA, Inc. [*Associated Press*] (SAG)
MBF............	Meat Base Formula [*Medicine*] (MEDA)
MBF............	Military Banking Facility
MBF............	Milk Bottlers Federation
MBF............	Missile Beacon Filter
MBF............	Modulator Band Filter (IAA)
MBF............	Molecular Beam Facility [*NASA*]
MBF............	Moving-Bed Filter [*Waste*] (DICI)
MBdF...........	Musicians Benevolent Fund [*British*] (BI)
MBF............	Myocardial Blood Flow [*Cardiology*]
MBF............	Thousand Board Feet [*Lumber*]

MBFA............ Fellowes Athenaeum, Boston, MA [*Library symbol Library of Congress*] (LCLS)
MBFA............ MBF USA, Inc. [*NASDAQ symbol*] (SAG)
MBFC............ Moe Bandy Fan Club (EA)
MBFL............ Mid-Bergen Federation of Public Libraries [*Library network*]
MBFLB.......... Monaural Bifrequency Loudness Balance [*Audiology*] (MAE)
MBFM........... Massachusetts Grand Lodge, F & AM, Boston, MA [*Library symbol Library of Congress*] (LCLS)
MBFN........... Multiple Beam Forming Network [*Military*] (LAIN)
MBFo............ Forsyth Dental Center, Boston, MA [*Library symbol Library of Congress*] (LCLS)
MBFP........... Manufacturing, Build, and Flow Plan (NASA)
MBFR........... Federal Reserve Bank of Boston, Boston, MA [*Library symbol Library of Congress*] (LCLS)
MBFR........... More Better for Russia [*Facetious translation of MBFR - Mutual and Balanced Force Reduction*]
MBFR........... Mutual and Balanced Force Reduction [*Proposed reduction of forces in central Europe by NATO and Warsaw Pact nations*]
MBFUSA....... MBF USA, Inc. [*Associated Press*] (SAG)
MBG............. Gardner Museum, Boston, MA [*Library symbol Library of Congress*] (LCLS)
MBG............. Missouri Botanical Garden
MBG............. Mobridge, SD [*Location identifier FAA*] (FAAL)
MBG & H...... Magna Brittannia, Gallia, et Hibernia [*Great Britain, France, and Ireland*] [*Latin*] (ROG)
MBGE........... Missile-Borne Guidance Equipment (AFM)
MBGH.......... Library Services, Brandon General Hospital, Manitoba [*Library symbol National Library of Canada*] (NLC)
MBGi........... Gillette Co., Boston R and D Laboratory, Boston, MA [*Library symbol Library of Congress*] (LCLS)
MBGiI.......... Gillette Co., Boston R and D Laboratory, Boston, MA [*Library symbol*] [*Library of Congress*] (LCLS)
MBGS.......... Missile-Borne Guidance Set (MCD)
MBGT.......... General Theological Library, Boston, MA [*Library symbol Library of Congress*] (LCLS)
MBGT.......... Grand Turk [*Turks and Caicos Islands*] [*ICAO location identifier*] (ICLI)
MBGTS........ Missile-Borne Guidance Test Set (AABC)
MBH............. Manual Bomb Hoist
MBH............. Maryborough [*Australia Airport symbol*] (OAG)
MBH............. Massachusetts Horticultural Society, Boston, MA [*Library symbol Library of Congress*] (LCLS)
MBH............. Massive Black Hole [*Galactic science*]
MBH............. Mediobasal Hypothalamus [*Brain anatomy*]
MBH............. Minard, Bryant H., Pennsauken NJ [*STAC*]
mbH............. Mit Beschraenkter Haftung [*With Limited Liability*] [*German*] (EG)
MBH............. Movimiento de Bases Hayistas [*Movement of Hayista Bases*] [*Peru*] [*Political party*] (PPW)
MBH............. Thousands of BTU per Hour
MBH2........... Reduced Methylene Blue [*Medicine*] (DMAA)
MBHA.......... Member of the British Hypnotherapy Association (DBQ)
MBHC.......... Boissevain Health Centre, Manitoba [*Library symbol National Library of Canada*] (NLC)
MBHCM....... Master of Behavioral Health Care Management (PGP)
MBHE.......... Ministries to Blacks in Higher Education (EA)
MBHH.......... Handel and Haydn Society, Boston, MA [*Library symbol Library of Congress*] (LCLS)
MBHI........... Member of the British Horological Institute (DBQ)
MBHI........... Millon Behavioral Health Inventory [*Personality development test*] [*Psychology*]
MBHINST..... Member of the British Horological Institute (ROG)
MBHM......... Harvard Musical Association, Boston, MA [*Library symbol Library of Congress*] (LCLS)
MBHoM........ Houghton Mifflin Co., Boston, MA [*Library symbol Library of Congress*] (LCLS)
MBHPFC...... [*The*] Monkees, Boyce and Hart Photo Fan Club (EA)
MBI............... Insurance Library Association of Boston, Boston, MA [*Library symbol Library of Congress*] (LCLS)
MBI............... Management by Initiative [*Management technique*]
MBI............... Marine Biomedical Institute [*University of Texas*] [*Research center*] (RCD)
MBI............... Maritime Bank of Israel (BJA)
MBI............... Maslach Burnout Inventory
MBI............... Master of Biological Illustration (GAGS)
MBI............... May Be Issued
MBI............... Mbeya [*Tanzania*] [*Airport symbol Obsolete*] (OAG)
MBI............... MBIA, Inc. [*NYSE symbol*] (SPSG)
MBI............... Memory Bank Interface
MBI............... Menan Buttes [*Idaho*] [*Seismograph station code, US Geological Survey Closed*] (SEIS)
MBI............... Metal Belt Institute [*Defunct*] (EA)
MBI............... Methylene Blue Installation [*Medicine*] (DAVI)
MBI............... Michigan Biotechnology Institute [*Michigan State University*] [*Research center*] (RCD)
MBI............... Middle Bronze I [*Age*]
MBI............... Military Board Instruction
MBI............... Minimal Baryonic Isocurvature [*Galactic science*]
MBI............... Miscellaneous Babylonian Inscriptions [*A publication*] (BJA)
MBI............... Molecular Biosystems, Inc.
MBI............... Multibus Interface [*Computer science*] (MCD)
MBIA............ Malting Barley Improvement Association (EA)
MBIA............ MBIA, Inc. [*Associated Press*] (SAG)
MBIA............ Merchants Bancorp [*NASDAQ symbol*] (SAG)
MBIA............ Municipal Bond Insurance Association (EA)
MBIAC......... Missouri Basin Inter-Agency Committee

MBIBTC........ Malting and Brewing Industry Barley Technical Committee [*Australia*]
MBIC............ Michigan Bigfoot Information Center [*Later, MCBIC*] (EA)
MBIC............ Monmouth Biomedical Information Consortium [*Library network*]
M Bi Ch....... Master of Biological Chemistry
MBiChem...... Master of Biological Chemistry (NADA)
MBID........... Member of the British Institute of Interior Design (DBQ)
M Bi E......... Master of Biological Engineering
MBIE........... Member of the British Institute of Embalmers (DBQ)
MBiEng........ Master of Biological Engineering (NADA)
MBIFCT....... Mgahinga and Bwindi Inpenetrable Forest Conservation Trust (ECON)
MBII............ Minority Business Information Institute [*Defunct*] (EA)
MBiIC.......... Cabot Corp., Technical Information Center, Billerica, MA [*Library symbol Library of Congress*] (LCLS)
MBiIHi......... Billerica Historical Society, Billerica, MA [*Library symbol Library of Congress*] (LCLS)
MBIM.......... Member of the British Institute of Management [*Formerly, MIIA*]
MBIO........... Microprogrammable Block Input/Output
M Bio E....... Master of Bioengineering (PGP)
MBioEth....... Master of Bioethics
M Biomath.... Master of Biomathematics (PGP)
MBiomedE.... Master of Biomedical Engineering (ADA)
M Biorad..... Master of Bioradiology
MBiotech..... Master of Biotechnology
M Bi Phy..... Master of Biological Physics
M Bi S........ Master of Biological Sciences
MBIS........... Master of Business Information Systems
MB (IT)....... Master of Business (Information Technology)
MBIT........... MegaBIT [*Binary Digit*] [*Computer science*] (MDG)
MBIU........... Multiplex Bus Interface Unit (MCD)
MBJ............. Montego Bay [*Jamaica*] [*Airport symbol*] (OAG)
MBJ............. Multiple Blinking Jammer (MCD)
MBJI............ Marks Bros Jewelers [*NASDAQ symbol*] (TTSB)
MBJI............ Marks Bros. Jewelers, Inc. [*NASDAQ symbol*] (SAG)
MBJT........... Grand Turk [*Turks and Caicos Islands*] [*ICAO location identifier*] (ICLI)
MBK............ Bank of Mitsubishi Ltd. [*NYSE symbol*] (SAG)
MBK............ Bank of Tokyo-MitsubishiADS [*NYSE symbol*] (TTSB)
MBK............ Madchen-Bibel-Kreise [*Bible Reading Circles*] [*German*]
MBK............ Make-Break Keying (IAA)
MBK............ Medications and Bandage Kit (MCD)
MBK............ Methyl Butyl Ketone [*Organic chemistry*]
MBK............ Missing, Believed Killed (ADA)
MBK............ Mitsubishi Bank Ltd. ADS [*NYSE symbol*] (SPSG)
MBK............ Multibanc Financial Corp. [*Toronto Stock Exchange symbol*]
MBK............ Multiple Beam Klystron
MBL............ Main Battle Line [*Military*] (IAA)
MBL............ Manistee [*Michigan*] [*Airport symbol*] (OAG)
MBL............ Mannan-Binding Lectin [*Immunology*]
MBL............ Marble Bar [*Australia Seismograph station code, US Geological Survey*] (SEIS)
MBL............ Marine Biological Laboratory
MBL............ Marine Boundary Layer [*Oceanography*]
MBL............ Master Bidders List (NG)
MBL............ Maximum Benefit Level [*Health insurance*] (GHCT)
MBL............ Measured Blood Loss [*Physiology*]
MBL............ Mechanical Boundary Layer [*Geology*]
MBL............ Medium Brown Loose [*Stool*] [*Gastroenterology*] (DAVI)
MBL............ Menstrual Blood Loss [*Medicine*]
MBL............ Miniature Button Light
MBL............ Minimal Bactericidal Level
MBL............ Missile Baseline
MBL............ Mobile (AFM)
MBL............ Mobile
MBL............ Model Breakdown List
MBL............ Monterey Bay Area Cooperative Library System, Salinas, CA [*OCLC symbol*] (OCLC)
MBL............ Movimiento Bolivia Libre [*Political party*] (EY)
MBL............ Multiples of Background Level [*Of environmental contaminants*]
MBLA.......... MBLA Financial Corp. [*Associated Press*] (SAG)
MBLA.......... Methylbenzyllinoleic Acid [*Organic chemistry*]
MBLA.......... Mouse Specific Bone-Marrow-Derived Lymphocyte Antigen [*Immunology*]
MBLA.......... National Mercantile Bancorp [*NASDAQ symbol*] (NQ)
MBLC.......... Lahey Clinic Foundation, Boston, MA [*Library symbol Library of Congress*] (LCLS)
MBLC.......... Microbore Liquid Chromatography
MBldg......... Master of Building (ADA)
MBldgSc...... Master of Building Science (ADA)
MBldSc........ Master of Building Science
MBLE.......... Mobile Gas Service [*NASDAQ symbol*] (TTSB)
MBLE.......... Mobile Gas Service Corp. [*NASDAQ symbol*] (NQ)
MBLF.......... MBLA Financial [*NASDAQ symbol*] (TTSB)
MBLF.......... MBLA Financial Corp. [*NASDAQ symbol*] (SAG)
MBLM.......... MobileMedia Corp. [*NASDAQ symbol*] (SAG)
MBLR.......... Madhya Bharat Law Reports [*India*] [*A publication*] (DLA)
MblTel......... Mobile Telecommunications & Technology Corp. [*Associated Press*] (SAG)
MBLY.......... Mobley Environmental Services [*NASDAQ symbol*] (SPSG)
MBM........... Magnetic Bubble Memory [*Computer science*]
MBM........... Mambone [*Mozambique*] [*Airport symbol*] (AD)
MBM........... Market Buy Market [*Information service or system*] (IID)
MBM........... Market-by-Market Allocation [*Business term*] (DOAD)
MBM........... Master of Brand Management (GAGS)
MBM Ch...... Master of Building Management (ADA)

MBM............ Master of Business Management
MBM............ Meat and Bone Meal
MBM............ Metal-Barrier-Metal (IEEE)
MBM............ Mineral Basal Medium [Microbiology]
MBM............ Modern Black Men [Johnson Publishing Co., Inc.] [A publication]
MBM............ Mother's Breast Milk [Neonatology] (DAVI)
MBM............ Multibuoy Mooring [Oil platform]
MBM............ Thousand Feet Board Measure [Lumber] (GPO)
MBM............ University of Massachusetts, Joseph P. Healy Library, Boston, MA [Library symbol] [Library of Congress] (LCLS)
MBMA.......... Metal Building Manufacturers Association (EA)
MBMA.......... Military Boot Manufacturers Association (EA)
MBMC.......... Middle Caicos [Turks and Caicos Islands] [ICAO location identifier] (ICLI)
MBMCC........ Mercedes-Benz Model Car Club
MBMetE........ Metcalf & Eddy, Inc., Boston, MA [Library symbol Library of Congress] (LCLS)
MBMF.......... Multibeam Multifrequency (CAAL)
MBMG .... Montana Bureau of Mines and Geology [Montana College of Mineral Science and Technology] [Research center] (RCD)
MBMGH-T.... Massachusetts General Hospital, Treadwell Library, Boston, MA [Library symbol Library of Congress] (LCLS)
MBMH .... Brandon Mental Health Centre, Manitoba [Library symbol National Library of Canada] (NLC)
MBMI.......... Mean Body Mass Index
MBMI.......... Micro Bio-Medics [NASDAQ symbol] (TTSB)
MBMI.......... Micro Bio-Medics, Inc. [NASDAQ symbol] (NQ)
MBMI.......... Mind/Body Medical Institute
MBMS.......... Bachelor of Medicine, Master of Surgery
MBMS.......... Model Base Management Software [Computer science] (IAA)
MBMSA........ Massachusetts College of Art, Boston, MA [Library symbol Library of Congress] (LCLS)
MBMSE........ Master of Business Management and Software Engineering (PGP)
MBMU .... Mobile Base Maintenance Unit
MBMu .... Museum of Fine Arts, Boston, MA [Library symbol Library of Congress] (LCLS)
MBMU .... University of Massachusetts, Boston, MA [Library symbol Library of Congress] (LCLS)
MBN............ Boston Museum of Science, Boston, MA [Library symbol Library of Congress] (LCLS)
MBN............ Metal Building News [A publication] (APTA)
MBN............ Methylbenzylnitrosamine [Organic chemistry]
MBN............ Metrobank NA [AMEX symbol] (SPSG)
MBN............ Mixed Base Notation
MBN............ Mombo [Tanzania] [Airport symbol] (AD)
MBN............ Mutual Black Network (NTCM)
MBNA .... MBNA Corp. [Associated Press] (SAG)
MBNA .... Mercedes Benz of North America
MBNA .... Methyl(butyl)nitrosamine [Organic chemistry]
MBNA .... Monument Builders of North America (EA)
MBNAD........ Marine Barracks, Naval Ammunition Depot
MBNAS........ Marine Barracks, Naval Air Station
MBNC .... North Caicos [Turks and Caicos Islands] [ICAO location identifier] (ICLI)
MBNECO...... New England College of Optometry, Boston MA [Library symbol Library of Congress] (LCLS)
MBNEH .... New England Historic Genealogical Society, Boston, MA [Library symbol Library of Congress] (LCLS)
MBNEL........ New England School of Law, Boston, MA [Library symbol Library of Congress] (LCLS)
MBNEN .... New England Nuclear Corp., Boston, MA [Library symbol Library of Congress] (LCLS)
MBnet......... [The] Manitoba Network [Canada] [Computer science] (TNIG)
MBNMD....... Marine Barracks, Naval Mine Depot
MBNMHi...... New England Methodist Historical Society, Inc., Boston, MA [Library symbol Library of Congress] (LCLS)
MBNOA........ Member of the British Naturopathic and Osteopathic Association
MBNOB........ Marine Barracks, Naval Operating Base
MBNQA....... Malcolm Baldrige National Quality Award [Department of Commerce]
MBNS .... Marine Barracks, Naval Station
MBNU .... Northeastern University, Boston, MA [Library symbol Library of Congress] (LCLS)
MBNU-L....... Northeastern University, Law School, Boston, MA [Library symbol Library of Congress] (LCLS)
MBNY .... Merchants Bank of New York [NASDAQ symbol] (NQ)
MBNY .... Merchants New York Bancorp [NASDAQ symbol] (SAG)
MBNY .... Merchants NY Bancorp [NASDAQ symbol] (TTSB)
MBNYD........ Marine Barracks, Navy Yard
MBO............ Madison, MS [Location identifier FAA] (FAAL)
MBO............ Mamburao [Philippines] [Airport symbol] (OAG)
MBO............ Management and Budget Office (MCD)
MBO............ Management Buy-Out
MBO............ Management Buy-Out
MBO............ Management by Objectives [Management technique] [Facetious translations: "Management by Oblivion," and "Management by Others"]
MBO............ M'Bour [Senegal] [Seismograph station code, US Geological Survey] (SEIS)
MBO............ Meacham Bridge Oscillator [Electronics]
MBO............ Mesiobucco-Occlusal [Dentistry]
MBO............ Mobil Oil Ltd. [Canada ICAO designator] (FAAC)
MBO............ Moist Burn Ointment [Medicine]
MBO............ Monostable Blocking Oscillator [Electronics]
MBO............ Motor Burnout (AABC)
MBO............ Moving Base Operator

MBO$_2$ .... Myoglobin, Oxy [Biochemistry, medicine]
MBOA .... Methoxybenzoxazolinone [Biochemistry]
MBOC .... Middle Bay Oil [NASDAQ symbol] (TTSB)
MBOC .... Middle Bay Oil Co., Inc. [NASDAQ symbol] (SAG)
MBOC .... Minority Business Opportunity Committee [Federal interagency group]
MBOCA .... Methylenebis(ortho-chloroaniline) [Also, MOCA] [Organic chemistry]
MBOH .... Minimum Break-Off Height
MBOL .... Motor Burnout Locking (AABC)
MBOM .... Boissevain and Morton Regional Library, Boissevain, Manitoba [Library symbol National Library of Canada] (NLC)
M-Bone........ Multicast Backbone [Internet]
Mbone......... Multicast Backbone [Internet terminology] (CDE)
M-bone .... Multicast Backbone [Computer science] (DOM)
MBOR .... Management by Objectives and Results [Management technique] (MCD)
MBOS .... Missile Base Operations Supervisor [Air Force] (IAA)
MBOS .... Multi-User Business Operating System (NITA)
MBou .... Jonathan Bourne Public Library, Bourne, MA [Library symbol] [Library of Congress] (LCLS)
MBOU .... Member of the British Ornithologists Union (EY)
MBP............ Magneto-Dynamic Positioning
MBP............ Major Basic Protein
MBP............ Maltose-Binding Protein [Biochemistry]
MBP............ Manhattan Bowery Project (EA)
MBP............ Manpack Battery Pack
MBP............ Massachusetts College of Pharmacy, Boston, MA [Library symbol Library of Congress] (LCLS)
MBP............ Master Buy Plan (AAGC)
MBP............ Maximum Boiling Point
MBP............ MB Brand Present [Cardiology] (DAVI)
MBP............ Mean Blood Pressure [Medicine]
MBP............ Mean Brachial Artery Pressure [Medicine]
MBP............ Mechanical Balance Package (OA)
MBP............ Mechanical Booster Pump
MBP............ Melitensis, Bovine, Porcine [Antigen] (AAMN)
MBP............ Mesiobuccopulpal [Dentistry]
MBP............ Mid-Boiling Point
MBP............ Monodibutyl Phosphate [Organic chemistry] (NUCP)
MBP............ Myelin Basic Protein [Neurology]
MBPA.......... Master of Business and Public Administration
MBPA.......... Military Blood Program Agency (AABC)
MBPAS .... Monthly Bulk Petroleum Accounting Summary [Army] (AABC)
MBP-C......... Mannose-Binding Protein C [Biochemistry]
MBPC.......... Munitions Board Petroleum Committee
MBPD.......... Million Barrels per Day
MBPDA........ Metropolitan Bag and Paper Distributors Association (EA)
MBPI........... Pine Cay [Turks and Caicos Islands] [ICAO location identifier] (ICLI)
MBPKN .... Perry Normal School, Boston, MA [Library symbol Library of Congress] (LCLS)
MBPM.......... Master of Business and Public Management
MBPO.......... Military Blood Program Office (AABC)
MBPP.......... Movimiento Blanco Popular y Progresista [National Action Movement] [Uruguay] [Political party] (EY)
MBPRE .... Multitype Branching Process in a Random Environment [Computer science]
MBPS.......... Mechanical Booster Pump System
MBPS.......... MegaBITS [Binary Digits] per Second [Transmission rate] [Computer science]
MBPS.......... Million BITs [Binary Digits] per Second [Data transmission speed] [Computer science] (NASA)
MBPS.......... Multigated Blood Pool Scanning [Medicine] (DMAA)
MBPT.......... Many-Body Perturbation Theory [Physics]
MBPV.......... Providenciales [Turks and Caicos Islands] [ICAO location identifier] (ICLI)
MBPXL........ MBPXL Corp. [Formerly, Missouri Beef Packers - Kansas Beef Industries]
MBQ............ Marine Board of Queensland [Australia]
MBQ............ Mbarara [Uganda] [Airport symbol] (OAG)
MBQ............ Medical Board of Queensland [Australia]
MBQ............ Modified Biquinary Code [Computer science]
MBR............ Maladapted Behavior Record [Personality development test] [Psychology]
MBR............ Management by Results [Management technique]
MBR............ Marker Beacon Receiver
MBR............ Master Bedroom [Real estate]
MBR............ Master Beneficiary Record [Social Security Administration]
MBR............ Master Boot Record [Computer science] (PCM)
MBR............ Material Balance Report [Nuclear energy]
MBR............ Maximum Base Rent
MBR............ Mbout [Mauritania] [Airport symbol] (AD)
MBR............ Mechanical Bag Retriever [Garbage collector]
MBR............ Mechanical Buffer Register [Computer science]
MBR............ Member (AFM)
mbr............ Member (DD)
MBR............ Member
MBR............ Membrane Bioreactor [Chemical engineering]
MBR............ Membrane-Bound Ribosomes [Cytology]
MBR............ Memory Base Register
MBR............ Memory Buffer Register [Computer science]
MBR............ Metal Bulletin Research [Commercial firm British] (ECON)
MBR$_2$........... Methylene Blue Reduced
MBR............ Microwave Background Radiation [Physics]
MBR............ Mini Badge Reader (IAA)
MBR............ Mission Briefing Room [NASA] (KSC)

MBR............ Modified Bitumen, Reinforced
MBR............ Montebello Resources Ltd. [*Vancouver Stock Exchange symbol*]
MBR............ Motivation by Rotation
MBR............ Moving Belt Radiator
MBR............ Multibomb Rack
MBr............ Public Library of Brookline, Brookline, MA [*Library symbol Library of Congress*] (LCLS)
MBRA .... Marathon Boat Racers Association
MBRA .... Multibeam Radiometer Antenna
MBradJ....... Bradford Junior College [*Later, BC*], Bradford, MA [*Library symbol Library of Congress*] (LCLS)
MBRC .... Marine Biology Research Centre [*University of Moncton*] [*Canada*] (IRC)
MBRDC....... Medical Bioengineering Research and Development Command [*Army*] (PDAA)
MBRDL .... Medical Bioengineering Research and Development Laboratory [*Army*] (MCD)
MBre........... Brewster Ladies Library, Brewster, MA [*Library symbol*] [*Library of Congress*] (LCLS)
MBRE.......... Memory Buffer Register, Even [*Computer science*]
MBreC .... Cape Cod Museum of Natural History, Brewster, MA [*Library symbol*] [*Library of Congress*] (LCLS)
MBRET........ Middle Breton [*Language, etc.*]
MBRF.......... Midbrain Reticular Formation [*Anatomy*]
MBRG .... Ropes & Gray, Boston, MA [*Library symbol*] [*Library of Congress*] (LCLS)
MBrH .... Hebrew College, Brookline, MA [*Library symbol*] [*Library of Congress*] (LCLS)
MBrHC .... Hellenic College of Arts and Sciences and Holy Cross Greek Orthodox Theological School, Brookline, MA [*Library symbol Library of Congress*] (LCLS)
MBridT........ Bridgewater State College, Bridgewater, MA [*Library symbol Library of Congress*] (LCLS)
M Brit IRE ... Member of the British Institution of Radio Engineers [*Later, MIERE*]
M/BRK .... Manual Brake [*Automotive engineering*]
MBRK .... Meadowbrook Rehab Grp'A' [*NASDAQ symbol*] (TTSB)
MBRK .... Meadowbrook Rehabilitation Group [*NASDAQ symbol*] (SAG)
MBRL.......... Multiple Ballistic Rocket Launcher
MBRM .... Membrane
MBRO .... Memory Buffer Register, Odd [*Computer science*]
MBrock .... Brockton Public Library, Brockton, MA [*Library symbol Library of Congress*] (LCLS)
MBrockV ..... United States Veterans Administration Hospital, Brockton, MA [*Library symbol Library of Congress*] (LCLS)
MBRR .... Meridian & Bigbee Railroad Co. [*Formerly, MB*] [*AAR code*]
MBRS .... MemberWorks, Inc. [*NASDAQ symbol*] (SAG)
MBRS .... Minority Biomedical Research Support Program [*Bethesda, MD*] [*National Institutes of Health*] (GRD)
MBRSHP...... Membership
MBRT.......... Methylene Blue Reduction Time
MBRUU........ May Be Retained until Unserviceable
MBRV .... Maneuverable Ballistic Reentry Vehicle
MBRW .... Minnesota Brewing [*NASDAQ symbol*] (TTSB)
MBRW .... Minnesota Brewing Co. [*NASDAQ symbol*] (SAG)
MBrZ........... Zion Research Library, Brookline, Boston, MA [*Library symbol*] [*Library of Congress*] (LCLS)
MBS............ Bay City-Midland-Saginaw [*Michigan*] [*Airport symbol*] (AD)
MBS............ Bethany Lutheran Theological Seminary, Mankato, MN [*OCLC symbol*] (OCLC)
MBS............ Magnetron Beam Switching
MBS............ Main "Bang" Suppressor
MBS............ Main Buffer Storage (IAA)
MBS............ Maleimidobenzoyl N-Hydroxysuccinimide [*Organic chemistry*]
MBS............ Management by System [*Management technique*] (IAA)
MBS............ Manchester Business School [*England*]
MBS............ Market Basket Survey [*Business term*]
MBS............ Master Bibliographic System (ADA)
MBS............ Master of Basic Science
MBS............ Master of Behavioral Science (GAGS)
MBS............ Master of Building Science (GAGS)
MBS............ Medborgerlig Samling [*Citizens Rally*] [*Sweden Political party*] (PPE)
MBS............ Mediterranean Base Section [*Army World War II*]
MBS............ Medium Bomber Strike (NATG)
MBS............ MedQuist, Inc. [*AMEX symbol*] (SAG)
MB/S.......... MegaBITS [*Binary Digits*] per Second [*Transmission rate*] [*Computer science*]
MB/S.......... Megabits per Second
MBS............ Megabits Per Second (NITA)
MBS............ Megabytes Per Second (NITA)
MBS............ Member of the Bibliographical Society (ROG)
MBS............ Menorah Book Service (BJA)
MBS............ Methacrylate Butadiene Styrene [*Plastics technology*]
MBS............ Methionyl Bovine Somatotropin [*Biochemistry*]
MBS............ Methodist Boys' School
MBS............ Micro Business Systems (NITA)
MBS............ Miniature Book Society (EA)
MBS............ Mission Budget Statement [*Army*]
MBS............ Mobile-Base Simulator (PDAA)
MBS............ Modular Banking System (PDAA)
MBS............ Monobutyl Sulfate [*Organic chemistry*]
MBS............ Monumental Brass Society (EA)
MBS............ Morpholine-Based Sulfenamide [*Chemistry*]
MBS............ Mortgage-Backed Securities Information Services [*The Bond Buyer, Inc.*] [*New York, NY*] [*Information service or system*] (IID)
MBS............ Mortgage-Backed Security (DFIT)

MBS............ Mortgage-Backed Security Program [*Government National Mortgage Association*]
MBS............ Motion Base Simulator (MCD)
MBS............ Motor Bus Society (EA)
MBS............ Multibit Shifter (IAA)
MBS............ Multiblade Slurry Saw [*Semiconductor technology*]
MBS............ Multiblock Synchronization Signal Unit [*Telecommunications*] (TEL)
MBS............ Multicore Bar Solder
MBS............ Multilingual Biblioservice of Alberta, Alberta Culture [*UTLAS symbol*]
MBS............ Multiple Batch Station [*Computer science*]
MBS............ Multiple Business System
MBS............ Music Broadcasting Society (NADA)
MBS............ Mutual Broadcasting System
MBS............ Muzzle Bore Sight [*British military*] (DMA)
MBS............ Saginaw [*Michigan*] [*Airport symbol*] (OAG)
MBS............ Saginaw, MI [*Location identifier FAA*] (FAAL)
MBS............ Social Law Library, Boston, MA [*Library symbol Library of Congress*] (LCLS)
MBSA......... Main Bus-Switching Assembly (SSD)
MBSA......... Maleylated Bovine Serum Albumin [*Biochemistry*]
MBSA......... Manual Business Systems Association [*British*] (DBA)
MBSA......... Medical Board of South Australia
MBSA......... Methylated Bovine Serum Albumin
MBSA......... Model-Based System Analysis (PDAA)
MBSA......... Modular Building Standards Association (EA)
MBSA......... Municipal Board Standards Association (NADA)
MBSA......... Munitions Board Standards Agency
MBSA......... Museum Board of South Australia
MBSB......... Marine Barracks, Submarine Base
MBSC......... Boston State College, Boston, MA [*Library symbol Library of Congress*] (LCLS)
MBSc.......... Master of Behavioural Science
MB Sc.......... Master of Business Science
MBSC......... Modular Building Systems Council (EA)
MBSC......... South Caicos [*Turks and Caicos Islands*] [*ICAO location identifier*] (ICLI)
MBSCC .... Mortgage-Backed Securities Clearing Corp. (EMRF)
MBSCSDD... Master of Back Stabbin', Cork Screwin', and Dirty Dealin' [*Self-conferred degree held by Mordecai Jones in 1967 movie "The Flim-Flam Man"*]
MBSD......... Multi-Barrel Smoke Discharger [*Military*] (PDAA)
MBSI.......... Master of Business Information Science (PGP)
MBSI.......... Member of the Boot and Shoe Industry [*British*] (DAS)
MBSI.......... Missile Battery Status Indicator
MBSI.......... Musical Box Society, International (EA)
MBSi.......... Simmons College, Boston, MA [*Library symbol Library of Congress*] (LCLS)
MB-SL .... British Museum - Sloan Herbarium [*London*]
MBSL.......... Mouse Biochemical Specific Locus [*Test for mutagenesis*]
MBSL.......... Multiple-Bubble Sonoluminescence [*Physics*]
MBSM......... Maize Bushy Stunt Mycoplasm [*Plant pathology*]
MBSM......... Mexican Border Service Medal
MBSOGB..... Musical Box Society of Great Britain
MBSP......... Main Bang Synchronization Pulse (IAA)
MBSP......... Mitchell Bancorp, Inc. [*NASDAQ symbol*] (SAG)
MBSpnea.... Society for the Preservation of New England Antiquities, Boston, MA [*Library symbol Library of Congress*] (LCLS)
MBSQ .... Music Broadcasting Society of Queensland [*Australia*]
MBSS .... Main Beach Signal Station (IAA)
MBSSM....... Maxfield-Buchholz Scale of Social Maturity [*Psychology*]
MBST......... Motor Behavior Screening Test [*Physical education*]
MBST......... Multiple Beam Switching Tube
MBSuf........ Suffolk University, Boston, MA [*Library symbol Library of Congress*] (LCLS)
MBSufC....... Suffolk County Court House, Boston, MA [*Library symbol Library of Congress*] (LCLS)
MBSY......... Salt Cay [*Turks and Caicos Islands*] [*ICAO location identifier*] (ICLI)
MBT........... Main Ballast Tank
MBT........... Main Battle Tank
MBT........... Main Boundary Thrust [*Geology*]
MBT........... Many-Body Theory [*Physics*] (BARN)
MBT........... Marble Bar - Town [*Australia Seismograph station code, US Geological Survey Closed*] (SEIS)
MBT........... Marianna & Blountstown Railroad Co. [*AAR code*]
MBT........... Masbate [*Philippines*] [*Airport symbol*] (OAG)
MBT........... Master of Business and Technology
MBT........... Master of Business Taxation (GAGS)
MBT........... Mean Body Temperature (WDAA)
MBT........... Mechanical Bathythermograph
MBT........... Memory Block Table [*Computer science*] (HGAA)
MBT........... Mercaptobenzothiazole [*Organic chemistry*]
MBT........... Mercury Bombardment Thrustor
MBT........... Metal-Base Transistor [*Electronics*] (IEEE)
MBT........... Metal Bond Tape
MBT........... Methylenebisthiocyanate [*Antimicrobial agent*]
MBT........... Methylene Blue Test [*Analytical chemistry*]
MBT........... Metropolitan Ballet Theatre [*Detroit*]
MBT........... Midblastula Stage [*Embryology*]
MBT........... Mid-Blastula Transition [*Developmental biology*]
MBT........... Minimum Best Torque
MBT........... Mixed Bacterial Toxin
MBT........... Mobile Boarding Team
MBT........... Modified Boiling Test (PDAA)
MBT........... Motor Burning Time
MBT........... Murfreesboro, TN [*Location identifier FAA*] (FAAL)

MBT............	Vias Aereas Manabitas CIA Ltds. [Ecuador] [FAA designator] (FAAC)
MBTA..........	Massachusetts Bay Transportation Authority [Formerly, MTA]
MBTA..........	Metropolitan Boston Transit Authority (BARN)
MBTA..........	Migratory Bird Treaty Act (GNE)
MBTC..........	Mercedes-Benz Truck Co.
MBTCA........	Miniature Bull Terrier Club of America (EA)
MBTD/RP.....	Main Battle Tank Distribution/Redistribution Plan (MCD)
MBTFA........	Methylbistrifluoroacetamide [Organic chemistry]
MBTH..........	Methylbenzothiazolinone Hydrazone [Organic chemistry]
MbThSt........	Marburger Theologische Studien (BJA)
MBTI...........	Boston Theological Institute, Learning Development Program, Boston, MA [Library symbol Library of Congress] (LCLS)
MBTI...........	Manpower Business Training Institute
MBTI...........	Myers-Briggs Type Indicator [Psychology]
MBTI:AV......	Myers-Briggs Type Indicator: Abbreviated Version [Personality development test] [Psychology]
MBTS..........	Mercaptobenzothiazole Disulfide [Organic chemistry]
MBTS..........	Meteorological Balloon Tracking System
MBTS..........	Missile Battery Test Set [Military] (IAA)
MBtS...........	Saint John's Seminary, Brighton, MA [Library symbol Library of Congress] (LCLS)
MBTT..........	Marine Builders Training Trust (AIE)
MBtu...........	Million British Thermal Units
MBTWK.......	Multiple Beam Traveling Wave Klystron
MBU............	Boston University, Boston, MA [Library symbol Library of Congress] (LCLS)
MBU............	Boston University, School of Medicine, Boston, MA [OCLC symbol] (OCLC)
MBU............	Hayward Map, CA [Location identifier FAA] (FAAL)
MBU............	Magnetic Bubble Unit (NITA)
MBU............	Mbambanakira [Solomon Islands] [Airport symbol] (OAG)
MBU............	Memory Buffer Unit [Computer science]
MBU............	MIRA [Multifunctional Inertial Reference Assembly] Basic Unit [Air Force] (MCD)
MBU............	Mission Briefing Unit
MBU-E.........	Boston University, School of Education, Boston, MA [Library symbol Library of Congress] (LCLS)
MBUF..........	United Fruit Co., Boston, MA [Library symbol Library of Congress] (LCLS)
MBuild........	Master of Building (ADA)
MBUK	Mercedes-Benz (United Kingdom)
MBU-L	Boston University, School of Law, Boston, MA [Library symbol Library of Congress] (LCLS)
MBU-M	Boston University, School of Medicine, Boston, MA [Library symbol Library of Congress] (LCLS)
MBUMA	Mean Time between Unscheduled Maintenance Actions
MBUMR	MIRA [Multifunctional Inertial Reference Assembly] Basic Unit Mounting Rack [Air Force] (MCD)
MBurPRM	P. R. Mallory & Co., Burlington, MA [Library symbol Library of Congress] (LCLS)
MBus	Master of Business (ADA)
MBus-Accy..	Master of Business - Accountancy
MBusAd	Master of Business Administration (ADA)
MBus-Comn..	Master of Business - Communication
M Bus Ed.....	Master of Business Education
MBus-Mgt....	Master of Business - Management
MBU-T	Boston University, School of Theology, Boston, MA [Library symbol Library of Congress] (LCLS)
MBUUC........	Minnesota Business Utility Users Council [An association] (TSSD)
MBV............	Main Base Visit (NASA)
MBV............	Marine Board of Victoria [Australia]
MBV............	Medical Board of Victoria [Australia]
MBV............	Mexican Border Veterans (EA)
MBV............	Minimum Breakdown Voltage
MBV............	United States Veterans Administration Hospital, Boston, MA [Library symbol Library of Congress] (LCLS)
MBV-O........	United States Veterans Administration, Outpatients Clinic, Boston, MA [Library symbol Library of Congress] (LCLS)
MBVP..........	Mechanical Booster Vacuum Pump
MBVPS........	Mechanical Booster Vacuum Pump System
MBVT..........	Merchants Banchares, Inc. [NASDAQ symbol] (NQ)
MBVT..........	Merchants Bancshares [NASDAQ symbol] (SAG)
MBVT..........	Merchants Bancshares (VT) [NASDAQ symbol] (TTSB)
MBW...........	Mean Body Weight
MBW...........	Medicine Bow, WY [Location identifier FAA] (FAAL)
MBW...........	Medium Black and White [Film] (KSC)
MBW...........	Metropolitan Board of Works [British]
MBW...........	Microbiological Warfare
MBW...........	Moorabbin [Airport symbol]
MBW...........	Mount Baker [Washington] [Seismograph station code, US Geological Survey] (SEIS)
MBW...........	Movement for a Better World (EA)
MBW...........	Munitions Assignment Board (Washington) [World War II]
MBW...........	Western Manitoba Regional Library, Brandon, Manitoba [Library symbol National Library of Canada] (NLC)
MBWA.........	Management by Walking About [or Wandering Around] [Facetious translation of MBO - Management by Objectives]
MBWI..........	Wentworth Institute of Technical, Boston, MA [Library symbol Library of Congress] (LCLS)
MBWO	Microwave Backward Wave Oscillator
MBWS	Wheelock College, Boston, MA [Library symbol Library of Congress] (LCLS)
MBX............	Management by Exception [Management technique] (IAA)
MBX............	Maribor [Former Yugoslavia] [Airport symbol] (OAG)
MBY............	Make Busy (IAA)

MBY............	Middleby Corp. [AMEX symbol] (SPSG)
MBY............	Moberly, MO [Location identifier FAA] (FAAL)
MBY & D	Maintenance, Bureau of Yards and Docks [Budget category] [Obsolete; see FEC] [Navy]
MBZ............	Magnesia-Buffered Zinc Oxide (PDAA)
MBZ............	Mandatory Broadcast Zone [Telecommunications] (DA)
MBZ............	Maues [Brazil] [Airport symbol] (AD)
MBZ............	Menxel Bouzelfa [Tunisia] [Seismograph station code, US Geological Survey] (SEIS)
MBZ............	Middle Border Zone [Geology]
MBZ............	Must Be Zero (IAA)
MC.............	Aermacchi SpA [Italy ICAO aircraft manufacturer identifier] (ICAO)
MC.............	CAA Flying Unit [British ICAO designator] (ICDA)
MC.............	Cambridge Public Library, Cambridge, MA [Library symbol Library of Congress] (LCLS)
MC.............	Chemists' Club [Formerly, Mining Club] (EA)
MC.............	Consolata Missionary Sisters [Roman Catholic religious order]
Mc	Maccabees [Old Testament book] [Roman Catholic canon]
M-C	MacDonald-Cartier Highway [Canada]
M/C	Machine (ROG)
MC.............	Machine Cancellation [Philately]
MC.............	Machine Check [Computer science] (IAA)
MC.............	Machine Code (IAA)
MC.............	Machine Console
MC.............	Machine Cycle (IAA)
MC.............	Machinery Certificate [Shipping]
MC.............	Magic Circle [An association] (EA)
MC.............	Magister Chirurgiae [Master of Surgery]
MC.............	Magistrates Cases [Legal term British]
MC.............	Magnesium Chlorate [Inorganic chemistry]
MC.............	Magnetic Card [Word processing]
MC.............	Magnetic Clutch
MC.............	Magnetic Core
MC.............	Magnetic Course [Navigation]
M-C	Magovern-Cromie [Prosthesis] (AAMN)
MC.............	Mail Chute (DAC)
MC.............	Main Cabin
M/C	Main Chamber [NASA] (KSC)
MC.............	Main Channel
MC.............	Main Chute (KSC)
MC.............	Main Cock
MC.............	Main Color [Crocheting]
MC.............	Main Condenser [Nuclear energy] (NRCH)
MC.............	Main Coolant (MSA)
M/C	Maintenance and Calibration
MC.............	Maintenance Center (MCD)
MC.............	Maintenance Command [Obsolete Air Force British]
MC.............	Maintenance Console
MC.............	Maintenance Cycle (MCD)
MC.............	Major Component
MC.............	Major Cycle
MC.............	Makers of Canada [A publication]
MC.............	Making Capacity (IAA)
MC.............	Malayan Cases [1908-58] [A publication] (DLA)
M/C	Male, Castrated Animal (DMAA)
MC.............	Managed Care [Insurance] (WYGK)
MC.............	Managed Competition
MC.............	Management Committee (IAA)
MC.............	Management Contents [Information Access Co.] [Information service or system] (IID)
M/C	Manchester (ROG)
MC.............	Manganese Centre (EA)
MC.............	Manhole Cover
MC.............	Manned Core (SSD)
MC.............	Manpower Commission (NADA)
MC.............	Mantle Cavity
MC.............	Mantle Collar
MC.............	Manual Code (NITA)
MC.............	Manual Control
MC.............	Manufacturing Change (IAA)
MC.............	Mapping Camera
MC.............	Maps and Charts [Interservice] [NATO]
MC.............	Mare Crisium [Sea of Crises] [Lunar area]
MC.............	Marginal Check [Computer]
MC.............	Marginal Checking (NITA)
MC.............	Marginal Cost [Business term]
M/C	Marginal Credit [Business term]
M/C	Marginal Credit (DFIT)
MC.............	Margin Call [Banking, investments]
MC.............	Marine Corps
MC.............	Marine Craft [British military] (DMA)
MC.............	Maritime Commission [of Department of Commerce] [Merged with Federal Maritime Commission]
MC.............	Mark Cross [Initials often used as pattern on Mark Cross leather goods]
MC.............	Marked Capacity [Freight cars]
MC.............	Market Capacity (ADA)
MC.............	Marketing Center [Veterans Administration]
MC.............	Mark of the Craft [Freemasonry]
MC.............	Marmon Club (EA)
MC.............	Marque de Commerce [Trademark]
MC.............	Marriage Certificate
MC.............	Married Couple (ADA)
MC.............	Martin Co. (MCD)
MC.............	Maryheart Crusaders (EA)

MC.............. Mass Communication (NTCM)
MC.............. Mast Cell
MC.............. Mast Controller (DNAB)
MC.............. MasterCard [*Credit card*]
MC.............. Mastercard International [*New York, NY*] (EA)
MC.............. Master Change (IAA)
MC.............. Master Clock (IAA)
MC.............. Master Commandant
MC.............. Master Commander [*Navy British*] (ROG)
MC.............. Master Control
MC.............. Master of Ceremonies
MC.............. Master of Ceremonies (WDMC)
MC.............. Master of Chemistry
MC.............. Master of Classics
MC.............. Master of Commerce (GAGS)
MC.............. Master of Communication (GAGS)
MC.............. Master of Congress [*British*] (DAS)
MC.............. Master of Counseling (GAGS)
MC.............. Matara Cases [*Ceylon*] [*A publication*] (DLA)
MC.............. Material Code (MCD)
MC.............. Material Control (AAG)
MC.............. Materials Committee (MCD)
MC.............. Materiel Change [*Military*]
MC.............. Materiel Command [*Air Force*]
MC.............. Materiel Concept [*Army*]
MC.............. Mathematical Center (IAA)
MC.............. Matsushita Electric Industrial Co. Ltd. [*NYSE symbol*] (SPSG)
MC.............. Matsushita El Ind ADR [*NYSE symbol*] (TTSB)
MC.............. Maury Center for Ocean Science [*Washington, DC*]
MC.............. Maximum Concentration
MC.............. Maximum Count Output (IAA)
MC.............. Mayor's Court (DLA)
MC.............. Measure Code (NITA)
MC.............. Mechanical Council (EA)
MC.............. Media Coalition [*Later, MC/ACF*] (EA)
MC.............. Medical Care, Civilian Source (DNAB)
MC.............. Medical Center
MC.............. Medical Certificate (ADA)
MC.............. Medical Consultant [*Social Security Administration*] (OICC)
MC.............. Medical Corps [*Navy*]
MC.............. Medicine Cabinet [*Technical drawings*] (NFPA)
M-C.............. Medico-Chirurgical
MC.............. Medium Capacity [*or Charge*] [*Bomb*]
MC.............. Medium-Chain [*Triglycerides*] [*Biochemistry*] (MAE)
MC.............. Medium Curing [*Asphalt grade*]
MC.............. Medullary Cystic Disease [*Medicine*] (AAMN)
Mc.............. Megacurie
Mc.............. Megacycle
mc.............. Megacycle (IDOE)
MC.............. Megacycles per Second (IAA)
MC.............. Melamine Council [*Defunct*] (EA)
MC.............. Member of Congress
MC.............. Member of Council
MC.............. Memorandum Club [*Defunct*] (EA)
MC.............. Memorandum of Conditions
MC.............. Memorial Commission [*Federal body*]
MC.............. Memory Charts
MC.............. Memory Clear [*Computer science*] (PCM)
MC.............. Memory Configuration [*Computer science*] (MCD)
MC.............. Memory-Constrained [*Computer science*]
MC.............. Memory Control [*Unit*] [*Computer science*]
MC.............. Mercury Club [*Defunct*] (EA)
MC.............. Mercury Contact (IAA)
MC.............. Merkel Cell [*Anatomy*]
MC.............. Mesenteric Collateral [*Cardiology*] (DAVI)
MC.............. Mesiocervical [*Dentistry*]
MC.............. Message Center
MC.............. Message Change (MCD)
MC.............. Message$_c$heck (EA)
MC.............. Message Composer [*Communications, data processing*]
MC.............. Mess Call [*Military*]
MC.............. Metacarpal [*or Metacarpus*] [*Anatomy*]
MC.............. Metal Carbide
MC.............. Metal Case [*Bullet*] (DICI)
MC.............. Metal Clad (IAA)
MC.............. Metaling Clause [*Marine insurance*]
M/C.............. Metallic Currency (ROG)
MC.............. Metatarsocuneiform [*Orthopedics*] (DAVI)
MC.............. Meter-Candle
mc.............. Meter-Candle (IDOE)
MC.............. Methacholine Challenge [*Medicine*]
MC.............. Methodist Chaplain
MC.............. Methodist Church (WDAA)
MC.............. Methyl Carbamate [*Organic chemistry*]
MC.............. Methylcellulose [*Organic chemistry*]
MC.............. Methylchloroform [*Organic chemistry*]
MC.............. Methylcholanthrene [*Also, MCA*] [*Organic chemistry*]
MC.............. Methylcystyosine [*Biochemistry*]
MC.............. Methylene Chloride [*Organic chemistry*]
MC.............. Metric Carat [*200 milligrams*]
MC.............. Metropolitan Counties [*British*]
MC.............. Michigan Central Railroad [*Absorbed into Consolidated Rail Corp.*] [*AAR code*]
MC.............. Michigan Chemical Corp.
MC.............. Microcarrier [*Cell culture technology*]

MC.............. Microcephaly [*Medicine*] (AAMN)
MC.............. Microchromatographic
MC.............. Microcomputer (IAA)
MC.............. Microcontrol
MC.............. Microminiature Circuit (IAA)
MC.............. Micronesia Coalition [*Defunct*] (EA)
MC.............. Midcourse
MC.............. Midcourse Correction (SAA)
MC.............. Middle Chamber [*Freemasonry*]
MC.............. Middle Creek Railroad (IIA)
MC.............. Miles on Course
MC.............. Military Characteristics
MC.............. Military College [*British*] (ROG)
MC.............. Military Committee [*NATO*]
MC.............. Military Computer (IEEE)
MC.............. Military Construction (AFM)
MC.............. Military Coordination [*British*]
MC.............. Military Cross [*World War I nickname: Maconochie Cross*] [*British*]
MC.............. Mill Cutter [*Tool*] (MCD)
mC.............. Millicoulomb (MAE)
mC.............. Millicurie [*Also, mCi*]
mc.............. Millicurie (IDOE)
MC.............. Millicycle [*Also, as millihertz*] (WGA)
MC.............. Millipore Corp. [*Bedford, MA*]
MC.............. Mine Clearance [*British military*] (DMA)
M-C.............. Mineralo-Corticoid [*Endocrinology*]
m/c.............. Minha Carta [*My Respects*] [*Correspondence*] [*Portuguese*]
m/c.............. Minha Conta [*My Regards*] [*Correspondence*] [*Portuguese*]
MC.............. Minimum Call [*Television studio on standby*]
MC.............. Mining Club (EA)
MC.............. Minor Construction (AFIT)
MC.............. Minorities in Cable [*Defunct*] (EA)
MC.............. Mirror Coil (MCD)
MC.............. Miscarriage [*Obstetrics*] (DAVI)
MC.............. Misionaras Clarisas [*Poor Clare Missionary Sisters*] [*Roman Catholic religious order*]
MC.............. Missile Car (SAA)
MC.............. Missile Checkout
MC.............. Missile Code (MUGU)
MC.............. Missile Command [*Army*]
MC.............. Missile Compartment
MC.............. Missile Container
MC.............. Missile Control
MC.............. Missionaries of Charity [*Roman Catholic women's religious order*]
MC.............. Missionaries of Charity (TOCD)
MC.............. Missionary Catechists of the Sacred Hearts of Jesus and Mary [*Violetas*] [*Roman Catholic women's religious order*]
MC.............. Missionary Church (EA)
MC.............. Mission Capability [*NASA*] (NASA)
MC.............. Mission Completion (MCD)
MC.............. Mission Computer (MCD)
MC.............. Mission Continuation (MCD)
MC.............. Mission Control [*NASA*]
MC.............. Mississippi Central [*Railroad*] (MHDB)
MC.............. Mississippi Central Railroad (IIA)
MC.............. Mitochondrial Complementation
MC.............. Mitomycin [*Also, M, MT*] [*Antineoplastic drug*]
MC.............. Mitotic Cycle [*Biochemistry*] (DAVI)
MC.............. Mitoxantrone, Cytarabine [*Antineoplastic drug*] (CDI)
MC.............. Mitral Valve Closure [*Cardiology*]
MC.............. Mixed Cell [*Lymphoma classification*]
MC.............. Mixed Cellularity [*Biochemistry*] (DAVI)
MC.............. Mixed Condition [*Deltiology*]
MC.............. Mixed Cryoglobulinemia [*Medicine*]
MC.............. Mixing Chamber
M/C.............. Mixture Control [*Automobile fuel technology*]
MC.............. Mnemonic Code (AAG)
MC.............. Mobile Control (DEN)
MC.............. Mobile Crane (DCTA)
MC.............. Mode Change (CET)
MC.............. Mode Code
MC.............. Mode Control (IAA)
MC.............. Mode Counter
MC.............. Model Cities (OICC)
MC.............. Modem Controller [*Telecommunications*] (IAA)
MC.............. Modular Computer
MC.............. Moisture Content
MC.............. Molded Components (IEEE)
MC.............. Molecular Contamination [*of Clean rooms*]
MC.............. Momentary Contact [*Electronics*]
mc.............. Monaco [*MARC country of publication code Library of Congress*] (LCCP)
MC.............. Monaco [*ANSI two-letter standard code*] (CNC)
MC.............. Moneda Corriente [*Current Money*] [*Spanish*]
MC.............. Monetary Committee
MC.............. Monetary Contact
MC.............. Monitor and Control [*Computer science*] (BUR)
MC.............. Monitor Call [*Computer science*] (IBMDP)
MC.............. Monkey Cells
MC.............. Monkey Complement [*Immunology*]
MC.............. Monocomponent Highly Purified Port Insulin [*Endocrinology*] [*Pharmacology*] (DAVI)
MC.............. Monocoupe Club (EA)
MC.............. Mononuclear Cell [*Clinical chemistry*] [*Also, MNC*]
MC.............. Monopolies Commission [*British*] (DCTA)

MC	Monotype Caster (DGA)
MC	Monte Carlo [Calculation technique] [Nuclear energy] (NUCP)
MC	Montessori Center [Education]
MC	Morse Code
MC	Morse Code - Barry Morse Fan Club (EA)
MC	Mortar Carrier [British]
MC	Mortgage Constant (DICI)
MC	Mortgage Credit Condition (EMRF)
MC	Mothercraft Certificate [British] (ADA)
MC	Motor Car (IAA)
MC	Motor Carrier
MC	Motor Chain
MC	Motor Coaches [Public-performance tariff class] [British]
MC	Motor Contact (WGA)
MC	Motor Converter (IAA)
MC	Motor Cortex [Neuroanatomy]
MC	Motorcycle
MC	Motorcycle Driver [British military] (DMA)
MC	Movement Control [of troops]
MC	Moving Coil [Electronics] (DEN)
MC	Muan Chon [Mass Party] [Political party]
MC	Mucous Cell
MC	Multichip [Circuit] [Electronics]
MC	Multichromatic
MC	Multicomputing (IAA)
MC	Multiconfiguration [Quantum mechanics]
MC	Multipartisan Coalition (EA)
MC	Multiple Choice
MC	Multiple Contact
MC	Multiplex Channel (IAA)
MC	Munitions Command [Later, Armaments Command] [Army]
MC	Mushroom Caucus (EA)
MC	Mycelial [of fungi] (AAMN)
MC	Myelocytomatosis [Avian disease]
MC	Myocarditis [Medicine]
MC	Myotonia Congenita [Medicine]
MC	Poor Clare Missionary Sisters (TOCD)
MC	Rapidair [ICAO designator] (AD)
MC	Submarine Chaser [Navy symbol]
MC5	Motor City Five [Rock music group]
MCA	Arthur D. Little, Inc., Cambridge, MA [Library symbol Library of Congress] (LCLS)
MCA	Macenta [Guinea] [Airport symbol] (AD)
MCA	Magic Collectors' Association (EA)
MCA	Magnetocrystalline Anisotropy [Physics]
MCA	Mail Control Authority (AFM)
MCA	Main Console Assembly [NASA] (KSC)
MCA	Main Coronary Artery [Cardiology] (DAVI)
MCA	Maintenance Capability Audit [Military] (CAAL)
MCA	Major Coronary Arteries [Cardiology]
MCA	Malaysian Chinese Association [Political party] (PPW)
MCA	Management and Command Ashore (NVT)
MCA	Management Consultants Association [British] (DCTA)
MCA	Management Control Activity
MCA	Management Control Authority (NVT)
MCA	Manning Control Authority (MCD)
MCA	Mannlicher Collectors Association (EA)
MCA	Manufacturers' Consumer Advertising
MCA	Manufacturing Change Analysis (MCD)
MCA	Manufacturing Chemists Association [Later, CMA] (EA)
MCA	Marine Corps Association (EA)
MCA	Marine Cranking Amperes [Battery] [Automotive engineering]
MCA	Maritime Control Area
MCA	Market Research Corp. of America
MCA	Marky Cattle Association (EA)
MCA	Master Carvers Association [British] (DBA)
MCA	Master Clock Assembly
MCA	Master Community Antenna
MCA	Master Control Assembly [NASA] (NASA)
MCA	Master Control Assembly
MCA	Master Craftsmen's Association [British] (DBA)
MCA	Master of Commercial Arts
MCA	Master of Commercial Aviation (PGP)
MCA	Master of Communication Arts (PGP)
MCA	Master of Creative Arts
MCA	Mastiff Club of America (EA)
MCA	Material Control Adjustment
MCA	Material Control and Accountability (NRCH)
MCA	Material Control Area (AAG)
MCA	Material Coordinating Agency
MCA	Maternity Center Association (EA)
MCA	Matrix Case Arrangement (DGA)
MCA	Maximal Credible Accident [Nuclear technology]
MCA	Maximum Ceiling Absolute [Aerospace] (AAG)
MCA	Maximum Credible Accident [Nuclear energy] (NRCH)
MCA	Maximum Crossing Altitude (MCD)
MCA	Maximum Crossing Altitude
MCA	McDonnell Douglas Automation Co., McAuto Campus Library, St. Louis, MO [OCLC symbol] (OCLC)
MCA	Mechanical Contractors Association of America
MCA	Mechanization Control Area (AAG)
MCA	Media Credit Association (EA)
MCA	Medical Correctional Association [Defunct] (EA)
MCA	Medical Council on Alcoholism [British]
MCA	Medicines Control Agency [British] (ECON)

MCA	Metal Construction Association (EA)
MCA	Methyl Cation Affinity [Physical chemistry]
MCA	Methylcholanthrene [Also, MC] [Biochemistry]
MCA	Methyl Cyanoacrylate [Organic chemistry]
MCA	Metropolitan Club of America (EA)
MCA	Microcentrifugal Analyzer [Instrumentation]
MCA	Micro Channel [Computer science] (CDE)
MCA	Microchannel Analyzer [Instrumentation]
MCA	Micro Channel Architecture [Computer hardware]
MCA	Microfilm Corporation of America (NITA)
MCA	Microfilming Corp. of America [Information service or system] (IID)
McA	Microfilming Corp. of America, Glen Rock, NJ [Library symbol Library of Congress] (LCLS)
MCA	Microwave Communications Association (EA)
MCA	Microwave Control Assembly
MCA	Midcontinent Airlines, Inc. [ICAO designator] (FAAC)
MCA	Mid-Continental Airlines
MCA	Middle Cerebral Aneurysm [Cardiology] [Neurology] (DAVI)
MCA	Middle Cerebral Artery [Anatomy]
MCA	Mid-West Compensation Association [Superseded by ACA] (EA)
MCA	Midwest Curling Association [Defunct] (EA)
MCA	Military Chaplains Association of the USA (EA)
MCA	Military Civic Action (DOMA)
MCA	Military Construction Appropriation [or Authorization] (AFM)
MCA	Military Construction Army (AFIT)
MCA	Military Coordinating Activity (MCD)
MCA	Millinery Credit Association [Defunct] (EA)
MCA	Minimum Crossing Altitude [Aviation]
MCA	Ministry of Civil Aviation [Later, MTCA] [British]
MCA	Missing Children of America (EA)
MCA	Mississippi Code, Annotated [A publication] (DLA)
MCA	Mistral Class Association (EA)
MCA	Mitsubishi Clean Air [Automotive engineering]
MCA	Model Cities Administration [HUD]
MCA	Modified Cost Approach Document [Department of Housing and Urban Development]
MCA	Mohair Council of America (EA)
MCA	Monetary Compensation Amount [European Community]
MCA	Monitoring and Control Assembly [NASA] (NASA)
MCA	Monitoring and Control Assembly
MCA	Monochloroacetic Acid [Also, MCAA] [Organic chemistry]
MCA	Monoclonal Antibodies [Microbiology] (DAVI)
MCA	Montana Code, Annotated [A publication] (DLA)
MCA	Motor Carriers Traffic Association Inc., Greensboro NC [STAC]
MCA	Motor Control Assembly (MCD)
MCA	Motorcycle Accident (DAVI)
MCA	Motor Cycle Industry Association of Great Britain (EAIO)
MCA	Movement Control Agency [Army]
MCA	Movers Conference of America
MCA	Multichannel Analyzer
MCA	Multiple Classification Analysis [Aviation]
MCA	Multiple Communications Adapter (DGA)
MCA	Multiple Congenital Anomaly [Syndrome] [Medicine]
MCA	Multiplexing Channel Adapter [Telecommunications] (IAA)
MCA	Multiprocessor Communications Adapter
MCA	MuniYield CA Insured Fund II [NYSE symbol] (TTSB)
MCA	MuniYield California Insured Fund II [NYSE symbol] (SPSG)
MCA	Musical Corp. of America (NADA)
MCA	Music Critics Association (EA)
MCA	Musicians Club of America (EA)
MCA	Mustang Club of America (EA)
MCAA	Marine Corps Aviation Association (EA)
MCAA	Mason Contractors Association of America (EA)
MCAA	Mechanical Contractors Association of America (EA)
MCAA	Messenger Courier Association of America (EA)
MCAA	Military Civil Affairs Administration (NADA)
MCAA	Military Construction Appropriations Act (AAGC)
MCAA	Monochloroacetic Acid [Also, MCA] [Organic chemistry]
MCAAAC	Medium Caliber Antiarmor Automatic Cannon
MCAAC	Medium Caliber Antiarmor Automatic Cannon (MCD)
MCAAF	Marine Corps Auxiliary Air Facility
MCAAP	McAlester Army Ammunition Plant [Oklahoma] (AABC)
MCAAS	Marine Corps Auxiliary Air Station
MCAB	Marine Corps Air Base
MCAB	Monoclonal Antibody [Immunochemistry]
MCABM	Manner Common among Business Men
MCAC	Machine Accessory [Tool] (AAG)
MCAC	Military Common Area Control
MC/ACF	Media Coalition/Americans for Constitutional Freedom (EA)
MCACS	Marine Centralized Automatic Control System (PDAA)
MCAD	Marine Corps Air Depot
MCAD	Mechanical Computer-Aided Design
MCAD	Military Contracts Administration Department
MCAD	Minneapolis College of Art and Design
McAdam Landl & T...	McAdam on Landlord and Tenant [A publication] (DLA)
MCAE	Mechanical Computer-Aided Engineering
MCAE	Mechanical Computer-Aided Engineering
MCAE	Mining, Construction, and Agricultural Equipment
MCAF	Marine Corps Air Facility
MCAF	Marine Corps Air Facility (DOMA)
MCAF	Marine Corps Air Field
MCAF	McAfee Associates [NASDAQ symbol] (SAG)
MCAF	Mediterranean Coastal Air Force Headquarters
MCAF	Military Construction, Air Force
MCAFB	McConnell Air Force Base [Kansas]

McAfee .... McAfee Associates [*Associated Press*] (SAG)
MCA/FYP ..... Military Construction, Army / Five Year Plan
MCAG .... Mapping, Charting, and Geodesy [*Activity*] (MCD)
MCAGCC ...... Marine Corps Air-Ground Combat Center [*Twenty-nine Palms, Calif.*] (DOMA)
MCAGCTC ... Marine Corps Air Ground Combat Training Center (MCD)
MCAG/MGI... Mapping, Charting, and Geodesy/Military Geography Information [*DoD*] (MCD)
MCAI........... Maximum Calling Area Indicator (DNAB)
MCAI........... Microcomputer-Assisted Instruction (NITA)
MCAIR .... McDonnell Aircraft Co. [*Later, McDonnell Douglas Corp.*]
MCAL........... Arthur D. Little, Inc., Cambridge, MA [*Library symbol*] [*Library of Congress*] (LCLS)
McAl .... McAllister's United States Circuit Court Reports [*A publication*] (DLA)
McA L & Ten... McAdam on Landlord and Tenant [*A publication*] (DLA)
MCALF........ Marine Corps Auxiliary Landing Field
McAll........... McAllister's United States Circuit Court Reports [*A publication*] (DLA)
McAll (Cal)... McAllister's United States Circuit Court Reports [*California*] [*A publication*] (DLA)
McAllister US Circ Court R... McAllister's United States Circuit Court Reports [*A publication*] (DLA)
MCALS........ Minnesota Computer-Aided Library System [*University of Minnesota*]
MCAM......... Marcam Corp. [*NASDAQ symbol*]
MCAM......... Marine Corps Achievement Medal [*Military decoration*]
MCAM......... Member of the Communication, Advertising, and Marketing Education Foundation [*British*] (DBQ)
McA Mar Ct... McAdam's Marine Court Practice [*A publication*] (DLA)
MCA/MR ...... Multiple Congenital Anomalies/Mental Retardation Syndrome [*Medicine*] (DMAA)
Mcan .... J. S. Canner & Co., Boston, MA [*Library symbol Library of Congress*] (LCLS)
MC&A .... Material Control and Accountability
MC & A....... Material Control and Accounting [*Nuclear energy*] (NRCH)
MC & B....... Michigan Contractor & Builder [*A publication*]
MC & C....... Measurement, Command, and Control (NASA)
MC & G....... Mapping, Charting, and Geodesy [*Air Force*] (AFM)
MC & G/MGI.. Mapping, Charting, and Geodesy/Military Geography Information [*DoD*]
MC & R....... Manufacturing Controls and Requirements
MC & W...... Master Caution and Warning [*NASA*] (KSC)
MC&W....... Master Caution and Warning
M Can L....... Master of Canon Law
MCANSW.... Medical Consumers' Association of New South Wales [*Australia*]
MCANW...... Medical Campaign against Nuclear Weapons (PDAA)
MCAP.......... Medical Commission on Accident Prevention (PDAA)
MCAP.......... [*The*] MicroCap Fund [*NASDAQ symbol*] (SAG)
MCAP.......... Microwave Circuit Analysis Package (PDAA)
MCAP.......... Military Construction Authorized Program
MCAP.......... Minority Contractors Assistance Project [*Jamaica, NY*] (EA)
MCAP.......... Multiple Channel Analysis Program
MCAPI .... Mid-Continent Association of the Pet Industry
MCAR .... Machine Check Analysis and Recording (BUR)
MCAR .... Machining Arbor [*Tool*] (AAG)
McAr........... McArthur's District of Columbia Reports [*A publication*] (DLA)
MCAR .... Military Construction, Army Reserve (AABC)
MCAR .... Minnesota Code of Agency Rules [*A publication*]
MCAR .... Mixed Cell Agglutination Reaction [*Immunology*]
MCAR .... Multichannel Acoustic Relay [*Navy*] (ANA)
MCARNG...... Military Construction, Army National Guard (AABC)
MCARQUALS... Marine Carrier Qualifications (NVT)
McArth & M... MacArthur and Mackey's District of Columbia Reports [*A publication*] (DLA)
MCAS.......... Marine Corps Air Station
MCAS.......... Minuteman Configuration Accountability System [*Air Force*] (IAA)
MCASA .... Master Cleaners' Association of South Australia [*Australia*]
MCAS(H)..... Marine Corps Air Station (Helicopter) (FAAC)
MCASP .... Multiple Constraint Alternative Selector Program [*Bell System*]
MCAT.......... Maritime Central Analysis Team [*NATO*] (NATG)
MCAT.......... Master of Creative Arts in Therapy (PGP)
MCAT.......... Medical College Admissions Test (GAGS)
MCAT.......... Medical College Admission [*or Aptitude*] Test
MCAT.......... Midwest Council on Airborne Television
MCATA........ Management Council of the American Trucking Association [*Defunct*] (EA)
MCATS........ Marine Corps Automated Test System (DWSG)
M-CATS ...... Municipal Certificates of Accrual on Tax-Exempt Securities [*Investment term*] (DFIT)
MCAU .... Main Carrier Acquisition Unit (MCD)
M CAUTE ..... Misce Caute [*Mix Cautiously*] [*Pharmacy*]
MCAUTO ...... McDonnell Douglas Automation Co. [*Robotics*]
MCAWW ...... Methods for Chemical Analysis of Water and Wastes [*Environmental Protection Agency*]
MCB............ Boyne Regional Library, Carman, Manitoba [*Library symbol National Library of Canada*] (NLC)
MCB............ Machine Coated Board (DGA)
MCB............ Main Control Board (NRCH)
MCB............ Malaysian Cocoa Butter
MCB............ Managing Civilians to Budget [*Army*]
MCB............ Marine Construction Battalion
MCB............ Marine Corps Base
MCB............ Markings Center Brief (MCD)
MCB............ Master Car Builder
MCB............ Master Cell Bank [*Cell line*]
MCB............ Master of Clinical Biochemistry
MCB............ Material Classification Board (DNAB)

MCB............ Matheson, Coleman & Bell [*Commercial firm*]
MCB............ MC Beverages [*Vancouver Stock Exchange symbol*]
McB............ McBurney's [*Point*] [*Medicine*]
MCB............ McComb, MS [*Location identifier FAA*] (FAAL)
MCB............ Mechanically Controllable Break [*Junction*] [*In microstructures*]
MCB............ Membranous Cytoplasmic Body
MCB............ Message Control Block [*Computer science*] (CET)
MCB............ Metal Corner Bead [*Technical drawings*]
MCB............ Methodist College, Belfast [*Northern Ireland*]
MCB............ Methylamino(chloro)benzophenone [*Organic chemistry*]
MCB............ Metric Conversion Board (NADA)
MCB............ Metric Conversion Bureau (NADA)
MCB............ Metropolitan Cemeteries Board [*Western Australia*]
MCB............ Miami City Ballet
MCB............ Microcomputer Board
MCB............ Millwork Cost Bureau [*Later, AWI*]
MCB............ Miniature Circuit Breaker
MCB............ Missouri Concert Ballet
MCB............ Mobile Construction Battalion [*Navy*]
MCB............ Modular Controllable Booster (MCD)
MCB............ Module Control Block (KSC)
MCB............ Monochlorinated Biphenyl [*Organic chemistry*]
MCB............ Monochlorobenzene [*Organic chemistry*]
MCB............ Moose Creek [*Alaska*] [*Seismograph station code, US Geological Survey Closed*] (SEIS)
MCB............ Mortgage Collateralized Bond
MCB............ Moscow Classical Ballet
MCB............ Motor Cargo Boat
MCB............ Motor Carriers Tariff Bureau Inc., Cleveland OH [*STAC*]
MCB............ Multilateral Control Board (SSD)
MCB............ Myocardial Bridging [*Cardiology*]
MCBA......... Magnesite and Chrome Brickmakers Association [*British*] (DBA)
MCBA......... Master Car Builders' Association [*Later, CDOA*]
MCBA......... Member of the Certified Bailiffs Association [*British*] (DI)
MCBETH ...... Military Computer Basic Environment for Test Handling
MCBF .... Mean Countdown Between Failures
MCBF .... Mean Cycles between Failures [*Quality control*]
MCBIC .... Michigan/Canadian Bigfoot Information Center (EA)
MCBL......... Motor Cargo Boat (Large) [*Coast Guard*] (DNAB)
MCBM......... Marine Corps Brevet Medal
MCBM......... Muscle Capillary Basement Membrane [*Medicine*]
MCBN......... Mid-Coast Bancorp [*NASDAQ symbol*] (TTSB)
MCBN......... Mid-Coast Bancorp, Inc. [*NASDAQ symbol*] (NQ)
MCBOMF..... Mean Cycles between Operational Mission Failures [*Quality control*]
MCBP.......... Mean Cycles between Premature Removals [*Quality control*] (MCD)
MCBP.......... Melphalan, Cyclophosphamide, BCNU [*Carmustine*], Prednisone [*Antineoplastic drug regimen*]
MCBP.......... Methylchlorobiphenyl [*Organic chemistry*]
MCBP.......... Muscle Calcium Binding Parvalbumin [*Biochemistry*]
McB Pt........ McBurney's Point [*Medicine*] (CPH)
MCBR .... Master Car Builders' Rules
MCBR .... Minimum Concentration of Bilirubin [*Medicine*] (MAE)
McBride....... McBride's Reports [*1 Missouri*] [*A publication*] (DLA)
MCBS.......... Micro Computer Business Services
MCBS.......... Mid Continent Bancshares [*NASDAQ symbol*] (TTSB)
MCBS.......... Mid Continent Bancshares, Inc. [*NASDAQ symbol*] (SAG)
MCBS.......... Mine-Clearing Blade System [*Military*] (INF)
MCBS.......... Missionary Congregation of the Blessed Sacrament (TOCD)
mcbs.......... Missionary Congregation of the Blessed Sacrament (TOCD)
MCBS.......... Multicomponent Boot System [*Army*] (INF)
MCBU .... Microconfined Bed Unit [*Chemical engineering*]
MCBW .... Amalgamated Meat Cutters and Butcher Workmen of North America [*Later, UFCWIU*]
MCC............ MacGillivray's Copyright Cases [*1901-49*] [*A publication*] (DLA)
MCC............ Magdalene College, Cambridge University [*England*] (ROG)
MCC............ Mail Classification Center (DNAB)
MCC............ Main Combustion Chamber (NASA)
MCC............ Main Communications Center
MCC............ Main Control Circuit (IAA)
MCC............ Main Control Console [*Diving apparatus*]
MCC............ Maintenance Control Center [*Telecommunications*] (AFM)
MCC............ Maintenance Control Circuit (IAA)
MCC............ Maintenance of Close Contact
MCC............ Major Category Code (MCD)
MCC............ Major City Code [*IRS*]
MCC............ Majority Congress Committee [*Defunct*] (EA)
MCC............ Management Communication Consultants, Inc. [*Cincinnati, OH*] (TSSD)
MCC............ Management Control Center [*Computer science*] (BUR)
MCC............ Mandarin Capital Corp. [*Vancouver Stock Exchange symbol*]
MCC............ Manhattan Chess Club (EA)
MCC............ Manipulative Communications Cover [*Military*] (ADDR)
MCC............ Manned Control Car [*Nuclear energy*]
MCC............ Manual Combat Center [*Air Force*]
MCC............ Manual Control Center [*Air Force*]
MCC............ Map Collectors' Circle [*Defunct*] (EA)
MCC............ Marine Corps Commandant
MCC............ Maritime Coordination Center
MCC............ Marked Contraction [*Medicine*]
MCC............ Martin's Mining Cases [*British Columbia*] [*A publication*] (DLA)
MCC............ Maryland Committee for Children (EDAC)
MCC............ Marylebone Cricket Club [*Governing body for cricket*]
MCC............ Master Change Committee
MCC............ Master Control Card [*IRS*]
MCC............ Master Control Center (NATG)

MCC............. Master Control Console
MCC............. Matchbox Collectors Club [*Defunct*] (EA)
MCC............. Material Category Code (MCD)
MCC............. Material Characterization Center [*For nuclear wastes*]
MCC............. Material Control Code
MCC............. Material Control Coordinator (MCD)
MCC............. Maui Community College [*Hawaii*]
MCC............. Maxwell Communication Corp. [*Formerly, BPCC*] [*British*]
McC............. McCarthy [*Panendoscope*] [*Medicine*] (BABM)
McC............. McCoy [*Antibodies*] [*Immunology*]
MCC............. Mean Cell [*or Corpuscular*] Hemoglobin Concentration [*Hematology*]
MCC............. Mechanical Chemical Codes
MCC............. Mechanically Compensated Crystal
MCC............. Media Center for Children (EA)
MCC............. Media Club of Canada [*Formerly, Canadian Women's Press Club*]
MCC............. Media Commentary Council [*Defunct*] (EA)
MCC............. Media Conversion Center [*Space Flight Operations Facility, NASA*]
MCC............. Medical Council of Canada
MCC............. Member of the County Council [*British*]
MCC............. Memory Control Circuit [*Computer science*] (IAA)
MCC............. Mennonite Central Committee (EA)
MCC............. Mercury Control Center
MCC............. Mesoscale Convective Complex [*Meteorology*]
MCC............. Mestek, Inc. [*NYSE symbol*] (SPSG)
MCC............. Metacerebral Cell [*Neurobiology*]
MCC............. Metamorphic Core Complex [*Geology*]
MCC............. Metrology and Calibration Center [*Army*] (MCD)
MCC............. Metropolitan County Council [*British*]
MCC............. Mica Creek [*British Columbia*] [*Seismograph station code, US Geological Survey Closed*] (SEIS)
MCC............. Microclimatic Conditioning
MCC............. Microclimatic Cooling System [*Army*]
MCC............. Microcrystalline Cellulose [*Organic chemistry*]
MCC............. Microcrystalline Chitin
MCC............. Microelectronics and Computer Technology Corp.
McC............. Micro Library Canisianum, Maastricht, Holland [*Library symbol Library of Congress*] (LCLS)
MCC............. Midcourse Correction
MCC............. Middlesex Community College [*Bedford, MA*]
MCC............. Midwest Climate Center [*Marine science*] (OSRA)
MCC............. Midwest Climate Center (USDC)
MCC............. Migrating Combustion Chamber [*Increases fuel efficiency*]
MCC............. Military Climb Corridor [*Aviation*]
MCC............. Military Code of Conduct (VNW)
MCC............. Military Colonization Company [*British ranch in the Calgary area of Canada*]
MCC............. Military Communications Center, Inc. [*Minneapolis, MN*] (TSSD)
MCC............. Military Comptrollership Course (MCD)
MCC............. Military Cooperation Committee [*US-Canada*]
MCC............. Military Coordinating Committee
MCC............. Mine Countermeasures Command and Support Ship [*Navy*]
MCC............. Miniature Center Cap
MCC............. Miniaturized Cassegranian Concentration [*Instrumentation*]
MCC............. Mini Car Club, USA (EA)
MCC............. Mini-Channel Communications Control (NITA)
MCC............. Minimum Circumscribed Circle [*Manufacturing term*]
MCC............. Minimum Complete-Killing Concentration (MAE)
MCC............. Mining Commissioner's Cases [*Canada*] [*A publication*] (DLA)
MCC............. Ministerial Committee on Military Coordination [*British World War II*]
MCC............. Ministerial Council for Corporations [*Australia*]
MCC............. Minuteman Change Committee [*Air Force*] (IAA)
MCC............. Miscellaneous Common Carrier
MCC............. Missile Capability Console (MCD)
MCC............. Missile Change Committed (SAA)
MCC............. Missile Checkout Console (SAA)
MCC............. Missile Combat Crew (AAG)
MCC............. Missile Command Coder (AAG)
MCC............. Missile Compensating Control
MCCJ............ Missile Control Center [*Air Force*]
MCC............. Missile Control Console
MCC............. Missing in Colon Cancer [*Genetics*]
MCC............. Mission Control Center [*NASA*] (MCD)
MCC............. Mission Control Complex [*Air Force*]
MCC............. Mississippi College, Law Library, Clinton, MS [*OCLC symbol*] (OCLC)
MCC............. Mixing Cross-Bar Connector [*Telecommunications*] (OA)
MCC............. Mobile Command Center
MCC............. Modern Cereal Chemistry (OA)
MCC............. Modified Close Control [*Air Force*]
MCC............. Modified Continuous Cooking [*Pulp and paper technology*]
MCC............. Modulation with Constant Control
MCC............. Monitor Control Console (CAAL)
MCC............. Monitored Command Code [*Marine Corps*]
MCC............. Moody's English Crown Cases Reserved [*1824-44*] [*A publication*] (DLA)
MCC............. Morgan Car Club (EA)
MCC............. Morrison Commemorative Stamp Committee (EA)
MCC............. Mortgage Credit Certificate (EMRF)
MCC............. Motor Carrier Cases [*ICC*]
MCC............. Motor Control Center
MCC............. Motor Control Center [*NASA*]
MCC............. Motor Cycle Club [*British*]
MCC............. Motorcycle Combination [*British*]
MCC............. Movement Control Center [*Army*]
MCC............. Multicell Compound Tire [*Automotive engineering*]
MCC............. Multichannel Communications Controller

MCC............. Multicomponent Circuits
MCC............. Multiple-Chip Carrier [*Computer technology*]
MCC............. Multiple Communications Control (BUR)
MCC............. Multiple Computer Complex
MCC............. Municipal Corporation's Chronicle [*Privately Printed*] [*A publication*] (DLA)
MCC............. Munitions Carriers Conference (EA)
MCC............. Muskegon Community College [*Michigan*]
MCC............. Mutated in Colorectal Cancer [*Genetics*]
MCC............. Mutual Capital Certificate
MCC............. Ontario Ministry of Culture and Communications (TSSD)
MCCJ............ Royal Military College Certificate (Senior Department) [*British*] (ROG)
MCC............. Sacramento, CA [*Location identifier FAA*] (FAAL)
MCCA........... Conference of the Methodist Church in the Caribbean and the Americas (EAIO)
MCCA........... Manufacturers Council on Color and Appearance [*Defunct*] (EA)
MCCA........... Media Conversion Computer Assembly [*Space Flight Operations Facility, NASA*]
MCCA........... Medicare Catastrophic Coverage Act [*1988*]
MCCA........... Minor Counties Cricket Association [*British*] (DBA)
MCCA........... Model Car Collectors Association (EA)
MCCA........ Motor Car Collectors of America (EA)
McCah........ McCahon's Kansas Reports [*1858-68*] [*A publication*] (DLA)
McCahon ..... McCahon's Kansas Reports [*1858-68*] [*A publication*] (DLA)
McCall Nee... McCall's Needlework [*A publication*] (BRI)
McCall Pr .... McCall's Precedents [*A publication*] (DLA)
McCanless... McCanless' Tennessee Reports [*A publication*] (DLA)
McCar........ McCarter's New Jersey Equity Reports [*A publication*] (DLA)
McCart........ McCarter's New Jersey Equity Reports [*A publication*] (DLA)
McCart........ McCarty's New York Civil Procedure Reports [*A publication*] (DLA)
McCarter..... McCarter's New Jersey Chancery Reports [*A publication*] (DLA)
McCartney .. McCarty's New York Civil Procedure Reports [*A publication*] (DLA)
McCarty ...... McCarty's New York Civil Procedure Reports [*A publication*] (DLA)
McCarty Civ Proc... McCarty's New York Civil Procedure Reports [*A publication*] (DLA)
MC Cas....... Municipal Corporation Cases, Annotated [*11 vols.*] [*A publication*] (DLA)
MCCC........... Macomb County Community College [*Michigan*]
MCCC........... Ministerial Consultative Committee on Curriculum [*Queensland, Australia*]
MCCC........... Missile Combat Crew Commander
MCCC........... Mission Control and Computing Center [*NASA*] (NASA)
MCCCA........ Marine Corps Combat Correspondents Association (EA)
McC Cl Ass... McCall's Clerk's Assistant [*A publication*] (DLA)
MCCD........... Marine Corps Clothing Depot
MCCD .... Mechanical Compatibility Control Drawing (MCD)
MCCD .... Message Cryptographic Check Digits
MCCD .... Multispectral Close Combat Decoy (DWSG)
MCCDC........ Marine Corps Combat Development Command [*Quantico, VA*] (GRD)
MCC-DoD..... Mission Control Center - Department of Defense [*NASA*] (NASA)
MCCDPA...... Marine Corps Central Design and Programming Activity (DNAB)
MCCDS .... Modified Central Computer Display Set (DNAB)
MCCE........... Montana Council for Computers in Education (EDAC)
MCCEd......... Member of the College of Craft Education [*British*] (DI)
MCCES......... Marine Corps Communications Electronics School (DNAB)
MCCF........... Master Class Code File (MCD)
McC F .... McCall's Forms [*A publication*] (DLA)
MCCF........... Michigan Coalition for Clean Forests
M/CCFLS..... Manitowoc Calumet Counties Library System [*Library network*]
MCC-H......... Mission Control Center - Houston [*NASA*] (MCD)
McCl .... Micro-Copy, Inc., Rochester, NY [*Library symbol*] [*Library of Congress*] (LCLS)
MCCI........... MIDCOM Communications [*NASDAQ symbol*] (TTSB)
MCCI........... Midcom Communications, Inc. [*NASDAQ symbol*] (SAG)
MCCISWG ... Military Command, Control, and Information Systems Working Group (NATG)
mccj........... Comboni Missionaries of the Heart of Jesus (TOCD)
MCCJ........... Comboni Missionaries of the Heart of Jesus (Verona) (TOCD)
McC Just .... McCall's New York Justice [*A publication*] (DLA)
MCC-K .... Mission Control Center - Cape Kennedy [*NASA*] (KSC)
MCCL........... Mason City & Clear Lake R. R. [*AAR code*]
MCCL........... McClain Industries [*NASDAQ symbol*] (TTSB)
MCCL........... McClain Industries, Inc. [*NASDAQ symbol*] (NQ)
McCl .... McClelland's English Exchequer Reports [*A publication*] (DLA)
McClain Cr Law... McClain's Criminal Law [*A publication*] (DLA)
McClain's Code... McClain's Annotated Code and Statutes [*Iowa*] [*A publication*] (DLA)
McCl & Y.... McClelland and Younge's English Exchequer Reports [*1824-25*] [*A publication*] (DLA)
McClat........ McClatchy Newspapers, Inc. [*Associated Press*] (SAG)
McClatN...... McClatchy Newspapers [*Associated Press*] (SAG)
McCl Dig .... McClellan's Florida Digest [*A publication*] (DLA)
McCle .... McClelland's English Exchequer Reports [*A publication*] (DLA)
McCle & Yo... McClelland and Younge's English Exchequer Reports [*1824-25*] [*A publication*] (DLA)
McClel........ McClelland's English Exchequer Reports [*A publication*] (DLA)
McClel Dig... McClellan's Digest of Laws [*Florida*] [*A publication*] (DLA)
McClell....... McClelland's English Exchequer Reports [*A publication*] (DLA)
McClell & Y... McClelland and Younge's English Exchequer Reports [*1824-25*] [*A publication*] (DLA)
McCl Ex ...... McClellan's Manual for Executors [*A publication*] (DLA)
McCl IA Co... McClain's Iowa Code [*A publication*] (DLA)
McCl Mal.... McClelland on Civil Malpractice [*A publication*] (DLA)
McCln.......... McClain Industries, Inc. [*Associated Press*] (SAG)

MCCLPHEI ...   Mass Conference of Chief Librarians of Public Higher Educational Institutions [*Library network*]

McCl Pr ......   McClellan's Probate Practice [*A publication*]   (DLA)

MCCM..........   Mexican Chamber of Commerce of US

MCCN..........   Midwest Curriculum Coordination Network   (OICC)

MCC-NASA...   Mission Control Center - National Aeronautics and Space Administration   (NASA)

MCCNSW.....   Mini Car Club of New South Wales [*Australia*]

MCCNU ....   Methyl-(Chloroethyl)-Cyclohexyl-Nitrosourea [*Antineoplastic drug regimen*]   (DAVI)

MCCO ....   Monaco Coach [*NASDAQ symbol*]   (TTSB)

MCCO ....   Monaco Coach Corp. [*NASDAQ symbol*]   (SAG)

MCCOEES ....   Michigan Community College Occupational Education Evaluation System   (EDAC)

McCook........   McCook's Reports [*1 Ohio*] [*A publication*]   (DLA)

MCCOPO.......   Mennonite Central Committee Overseas Peace Office   (EA)

McCor..........   McCormick & Co., Inc. [*Associated Press*]   (SAG)

MCCOR ....   Motion Compensation - Coherent on Receive

McCord........   McCord's South Carolina Law Reports [*1821-28*] [*A publication*]   (DLA)

McCord Ch...   McCord's South Carolina Equity Reports [*1825-27*] [*A publication*]   (DLA)

McCord Eq...   McCord's South Carolina Chancery Reports [*1825-27*] [*A publication*]   (DLA)

McCork ....   McCorkle's Reports [*65 North Carolina*] [*A publication*]   (DLA)

McCorkle ....   McCorkle's Reports [*65 North Carolina*] [*A publication*]   (DLA)

MCCP..........   Maintenance Console Control Panel

MCCP..........   Manufacturing Cost Control Program [*DoD*]

MCCP..........   Marine Corps Capabilities Plan   (DOMA)

MCCP..........   Meta-Chlorophenylpiperazine [*Biochemistry*]

MCCP..........   Microwave Circuit Control Program [*Computer science*]

MCCP..........   Mission Control Computer Program [*NASA*]

MCC/PS ....   Microclimate Conditioning / Power Subsystem [*Army*]   (RDA)

MCCQE ....   Medical Council of Canada's Qualifying Examination

MCCR ....   Master Change Compliance Record

McCr..........   McCrary's United States Circuit Court Reports [*A publication*]   (DLA)

MCCR ....   Medical Committee for Civil Rights [*Defunct*]   (EA)

MCCR ....   Memory Data Capture Cash and Credit Register [*Datacap Systems, Inc.*]

MCCR ....   Mission-Critical Computer Resource [*Computer science*]

MCCR ....   Molded Case Circuit Breaker

MCCRA ....   Medicare Catastrophic Coverage Repeal Act of 1989   (WYGK)

McCrary.......   McCrary's United States Circuit Court Reports [*A publication*]   (DLA)

McCrary Elect...   McCrary's American Law of Elections [*A publication*]   (DLA)

McCrary's Rep...   McCrary's United States Circuit Court Reports [*A publication*]   (DLA)

McCr Elect...   McCrary's American Law of Elections [*A publication*]   (DLA)

MCCRES ....   Marine Corps Combat Readiness Evaluation System

MCCRK ....   McCormick & Co. [*NASDAQ symbol*]   (TTSB)

MCCRK ....   McCormick & Co., Inc. [*NASDAQ symbol*]   (NQ)

MCCRTG ....   Marine Corps Combat Readiness Training Group

MCCS..........   Machine Centralized Control System   (DWSG)

MCCS..........   Master Calendar Control System [*New York City courts' speedup system*]

MCCS..........   Mechanized Calling Card Service [*Formerly, ABC*] [*Telecommunications*]

MCCS..........   Military Committee in Chiefs of Staff Session [*NATO*]   (NATG)

MCCS..........   Missile Critical Circuit Simulator

MCCS..........   Mission Control Center Simulation [*NASA*]   (NASA)

MCCS..........   Mission Critical Computer System   (DOMA)

MCCS..........   Mobile Command and Control System   (MCD)

MCCSD ....   Charles Stark Draper Laboratory, Inc., Technical Information Center, Cambridge, MA [*Library symbol Library of Congress*]   (LCLS)

MCCSL........   Marconi Command and Control Systems Ltd.   (NITA)

MCCSP ....   Ministerial Council on Common Services Provision [*Australia*]

MCCT..........   Multistrip Cesium Contact Thrustor

MCCTA........   Manufacturing Confectioners' Commercial Travellers Association [*British*]   (BI)

MCCTP........   Manpower and Community College Counselor Training Program (OICC)

MCCU ....   Mobile Coronary Care Unit [*Medicine*]

MCCU ....   Multiple Channel Control Unit

MCCU ....   Multiple Communications Control Unit [*Computer science*]

McCul Dict...   McCullough's Commercial Dictionary [*A publication*]   (DLA)

McCul Pol Econ...   McCulloch's Political Economy [*A publication*]   (DLA)

MCCUSCUSRPG...   Military Coordinating Committee, United States Element, Canada-United States Regional Planning Group   (AABC)

MCD............   Air Medical Ltd. [*British ICAO designator*]   (FAAC)

MCD............   Doctor of Comparative Medicine

MCD............   Dynatech Research/Development Co., Cambridge, MA [*Library symbol Library of Congress*]   (LCLS)

MCD............   Magistrates' Court Decisions [*New Zealand*] [*A publication*]   (DLA)

MCD............   Magna Carta Dames, National Society   (EA)

MCD............   Magnetic Circular Dichroism

MCD............   Magnetic Crack Definer [*Aviation*]

MCD............   Maintenance Control Department [*Military*]   (DNAB)

MCD............   Malaria Control Detachment [*Army World War II*]

MCD............   Manipulative Communications Deception [*Military*]   (NVT)

MCD............   Manual Control Device

MCD............   Manufacturing Construction Document   (SAA)

MCD............   Marginal Checking and Distribution

MCD............   Marine Corps District   (DNAB)

MCD............   Maritime Commission Decisions

MCD............   Marr, Cahalan & Dunn [*Law firm*]

MCD............   Mast Cell Degranulating [*or Destroying*] Peptide [*Biochemistry*]

MCD............   Master Clerical Data [*Management system*]

MCD............   Master of Civic Design

MCD............   Master of Communication Disorders   (GAGS)

MCD............   Mathematics and Computer Division [*Supreme Headquarters Allied Powers Europe*]   (NATG)

MCD............   McDonald's Corp. [*NYSE symbol Toronto Stock Exchange symbol*]   (SPSG)

MCD............   McDonnell Douglas Corp.

MCD............   Mean Cell [*or Corpuscular*] Diameter [*Hematology*]

MCD............   Mean of Consecutive Differences   (MAE)

MCD............   Median Control Death

MCD............   Medical Care Development, Inc. [*Augusta, ME*]   (TSSD)

MCD............   Medical Crew Director

MCD............   Medium Corpuscular Density [*Cardiology*]   (DAVI)

MCD............   Medullary Cystic Disease [*Medicine*]   (MAE)

MCD............   Megawatt Cassegrain Diplexer

MCD............   Member of the College of Dentists [*British*]

MCD............   Memory Control Data

MCD............   Mercy College of Detroit [*Michigan*]

MCD............   Metabolic Coronary Dilation [*Medicine*]   (AAMN)

MCD............   Metacarpal Cortical Density [*Anatomy*]

MCD............   Metal-Covered Door [*Technical drawings*]

MCD............   Metals and Ceramics Division [*Air Force*]

MCD............   Metaphyseal Chondrodysplasia [*Medicine*]

MCD............   Microbial Coal Desulfurization

MCD............   Microelectronic Circuits Division   (AAGC)

MCD............   Mid-Central District [*ATSC*]

MCD............   Military Contracts Department

MCD............   Military Coordination Detachment   (NATG)

MCD............   Millicandela

mcD............   Millicurie-Destroyed

MCD............   Mines, Countermines, and Demolitions [*Military*]   (RDA)

MCD............   Mine Warfare and Clearance Diving [*Navy British*]

MCD............   Minimal Cerebral Dysfunction

MCD............   Minimal Change Disease [*Nephrology*]

MCD............   Minimum Cost Design   (MCD)

MCD............   Minor Civil Division [*Bureau of Census*]

MCD............   Missile Countermeasure Device   (DWSG)

MCD............   Mission Communication Display   (MCD)

MCD............   Mission Control Directorate [*NASA*]

MCD............   Modification of Contract Documents   (AAGC)

MCD............   Monitor Criteria Data [*Space Flight Operations Facility, NASA*]

MCD............   Months for Cyclical Dominance [*Economics*]

MCD............   Movimiento por el Cambio Democratico [*Mexico Political party*]   (EY)

MCD............   Multiple Carboxylase Deficiency [*Medicine*]

MCD............   Multiple Concrete Duct [*Telecommunications*]   (TEL)

MCD............   Municipal Construction Division [*Environmental Protection Agency*] (GFGA)

MCDA ....   Manpower and Career Development Agency

MCDARS.....   Mechanized Cost Distribution and Reporting System   (MCD)

MCDAS........   Metropolitan Cities Drug Association Secretaries   (EA)

MC-DAS......   Multiple Channel Data Acquisition System   (NITA)

MCDB ....   Master Code Database

MCDB ....   Minimum Cost Design Booster   (KSC)

MCDB ....   Molecular Cellular, and Developmental Biology [*A discipline division*]

MCDBSU.....   Master Control and Data Buffer Storage Unit

MCDC.........   McDonnell Douglas Corp.

MCDC.........   Mobilization Concepts Development Center [*Washington, DC DoD*] (MCD)

MCDD ....   Monochlorodioxin [*Organic chemistry*]

MCDE.........   Microcide Pharmaceuticals [*NASDAQ symbol*]   (TTSB)

MCDE.........   Microcide Pharmaceuticals, Inc. [*NASDAQ symbol*]   (SAG)

MCDE.........   Monochlorodimethyl Ether [*Organic chemistry*]

MCDEC.......   Marine Corps Development and Education Command

McDerI........   McDermott International, Inc. [*Associated Press*]   (SAG)

McDerJ........   McDermott [*J. Ray*] SA [*Associated Press*]   (SAG)

McDer Land L...   McDermot's Irish Land Laws [*A publication*]   (DLA)

McDevitt......   McDevitt's Irish Land Commissioner's Reports [*A publication*]   (DLA)

MCDF..........   Methyltrichlorodibenzofuran [*Organic chemistry*]

MCDF..........   Missile Defense [*or Alert*] System Control and Display Facility [*Air Force*]   (IAA)

MCDF..........   Mobile Combustion Diagnostic Fixture   (MCD)

MCDG ....   Monitor Criteria Data Set Generation Processor Assembly [*Space Flight Operations Facility, NASA*]

MCDH ....   Master of Community Dental Health, University of Birmingham [*British*]   (DBQ)

MCDI ....   Minnesota Child Development Inventory [*Child development test*] [*Psychology*]

McDInv ....   McDonald & Co. Investment, Inc. [*Associated Press*]   (SAG)

MCDM ....   Multiple Criteria Decision Making

McDn..........   McDonald's Corp. [*Associated Press*]   (SAG)

McDn25.......   McDonalds Corp. [*Associated Press*]   (SAG)

McDn36.......   McDonalds Corp. [*Associated Press*]   (SAG)

McDnD........   McDonnell Douglas Corp. [*Associated Press*]   (SAG)

McDnlds .....   McDonald's Corp. [*Associated Press*]   (SAG)

McDon Jus...   McDonald's Justice [*A publication*]   (DLA)

McDonnell ...   McDonnell's Sierra Leone Reports [*A publication*]   (DLA)

McDow Inst...   McDowall's Institutes of the Law of Scotland [*A publication*]   (DLA)

MCDP..........   Microprogrammed Communication Data Processor   (MCD)

MCDP..........   Missionary Catechists of Divine Providence [*Roman Catholic women's religious order*]

MCDP..........   Missionary Catechists of Divine Providence, San Antonio, TX   (TOCD)

MCDPrE.......   McDonald's Corp. 7.72% Dep Pfd [*NYSE symbol*]   (TTSB)

McDr..........   McDermott, Inc. [*Associated Press*]   (SAG)

MCDR .... Multichannel DIFAR [*Directional Frequency Analysis and Recording System*] Relay (NVT)
MCDS .... Maintenance Control and Display System [*NASA*] (NASA)
MCDS .... Management Communications and Data System (SSD)
MCDS .... Management Control Data System [*Computer science*] (IAA)
MCDS .... Mission-Critical Defense System [*Army*]
MCDS .... Modular Cargo Delivery System [*MARAD*] (TAG)
MCDS .... Multicommand Data System
MCDS .... Multifunction CRT [*Cathode-Ray Tube*] Display System (NASA)
MCDSH .... Management Communications and Data System Hardware (SSD)
MCD/SLV .... Minimum Cost Design/Space Launch Vehicle [*NASA*] (KSC)
MCDSP .... Master Combat Data System Plan [*Military*] (CAAL)
MCDT .... Mast Cell Degranulation Test [*Medicine*] (DAVI)
MCDT .... Mean Corrective Downtime [*Computer science*]
MCDU .... Multifunction CRT [*Cathode-Ray Tube*] Display Unit (NASA)
MCDU .... Multifunction CRT [*Cathode Ray Tube*] Display Unit
MCDU .... Multipurpose Control Display Unit (GAVI)
MCDV .... Maize Chlorotic Dwarf Virus [*Plant pathology*]
MCDY .... Microdyne Corp. [*NASDAQ symbol*] (NQ)
MCE .... Episcopal Divinity School, Cambridge, MA [*Library symbol Library of Congress*] (LCLS)
MCE .... MacNeill Industrial, Inc. [*Vancouver Stock Exchange symbol*]
MCE .... Maintenance Cleaning Equipment (MCD)
MCE .... Mandatory Continuing Education
MCE .... Manufacturing Cycle Effectiveness
MCE .... Marginal Cost Efficiency [*Marketing*]
MCE .... Maritime Commission, Emergency Ship
MCE .... Marshall of Cambridge (Engineering) Ltd. [*British ICAO designator*] (FAAC)
MCE .... Master of Chemical Engineering (GAGS)
MCE .... Master of Christian Education
MCE .... Master of Civil Engineering
MCE .... Master of Civil Engineering (GAGS)
MCE .... Maximum Capability Envelope
MCE .... MCN Corp. [*NYSE symbol*] (SAG)
MCE .... MCN Corp. 8.75%'PRIDE' [*NYSE symbol*] (TTSB)
MCE .... Mean Chance Expectation [*Parapsychology*]
MCE .... Media Conversion Equipment [*Space Flight Operations Facility, NASA*]
MCE .... Medical Care Evaluation
MCE .... Medicare Code Editor (MEDA)
MCE .... Melbourne Corn Exchange [*Australia*]
MCE .... Memphis Cotton Exchange (EA)
MCE .... Merced [*California*] [*Airport symbol*] (AD)
MCE .... Merced, CA [*Location identifier FAA*] (FAAL)
McE .... Microcard Editions, Inc., Englewood, CO [*Library symbol Library of Congress*] (LCLS)
MCE .... Microscopically Controlled Excision [*Medicine*]
MCE .... Military Characteristics Equipment
MCE .... Military Corrective Establishment
MCE .... Missile Compensating Equipment
MCE .... Mission Control Equipment [*NASA*]
MCE .... Mixed Cellulose Esters Membrane Filters
MCE .... Mobile Command Element (NATG)
MCE .... Modular Control Element (MCD)
MCE .... Modular Control Equipment [*DoD*]
MCE .... Montgomery Cotton Exchange [*Defunct*] (EA)
MCE .... Moscow Commodity Exchange [*Russian Federation*] (EY)
MCEA .... Madison Center for Educational Affairs (EA)
MCEAC .... Marine Corps Emergency Actions Center
MCEB .... Marine Corps Equipment Board
MCEB .... Military Communications-Electronics Board [*DoD Washington, DC*]
MCEC .... Marine Corps Education Center
MCED .... Episcopal Divinity School, Cambridge, MA [*Library symbol*] [*Library of Congress*] (LCLS)
MC Ed .... Master of Commercial Education
MCED .... Master of Community Economic Development (PGP)
MC Ed .... Master of Continuing Education (PGP)
MC/EDS ..... Mission Control/Electronic Display System (MCD)
M Ce Eng ... Master of Cement Engineering
MCEF .... Mixed Cellulose Ester Filter (GNE)
MCEI .... Marketing Communications Executives International [*Dallas, TX*] (EA)
MCEL .... Machine Check Extended Logout
McEM .... Microfilming Executors & Methods Organization Ltd., Dublin, Ireland [*Library symbol Library of Congress*] (LCLS)
MCE(Melb)... Master of Civil Engineering (Melbourne University)
MCEMS .... Marine Corps Environmentally Controlled Medical System (MCD)
MCen .... Centerville Public Library, Centerville, MA [*Library symbol*] [*Library of Congress*] (LCLS)
MCEN .... Modified Current Expendable Launch Vehicle [*NASA*] (KSC)
MC Eng ...... Master of Civil Engineering
MCEP .... Maneuver Criteria Evaluation Program [*Army*]
MCEPEN ..... Midwest Continuing Education Professional Nurses (DHSM)
MCER .... Massachusetts Central [*AAR code*]
M Cer E ...... Master of Ceramic Engineering
MCES .... Main Condenser Evacuation System [*Nuclear energy*] (NRCH)
MCES .... Major City Earth Stations [*Telecommunications*] (TSSD)
MCES .... Medical Care Evaluation Study (HCT)
MCES .... Multiple Cholesterol Emboli Syndrome [*Medicine*]
MCESS .... Marine Corps Expeditionary Shelter System (MCD)
MCEU .... Mobile Civil Emergency Unit
MCEWG ...... Multinational Communication-Electronics Working Group [*Formerly, SGCEC*] [*NATO*] (NATG)
MCF .... Macrophage Chemotactic Factor [*Immunochemistry*] (MAE)
MCF .... Magnetic Confinement Fusion [*Physics*]

MCF .... Magyar Communion of Friends (EA)
MCF .... Maintenance and Checkout Facility [*NASA*] (KSC)
MCF .... Maintenance Condemnation Factor (MCD)
MCF .... Master Code File
MCF .... Master Control File
MCF .... Matched Crystal Filters
MCF .... Maximal Contraction Force [*Myology*]
MCF .... McFinley Red Lake Mines Ltd. [*Toronto Stock Exchange symbol*]
MCF .... Mean Carrier Frequency [*Radio*] (IAA)
MCF .... Measurement Compensation Factor (PDAA)
MCF .... Medical Cybernetics Foundation (EA)
MCF .... Medium Corpuscular Fragility [*Hematology*]
MCF .... Merced County Free Library, Merced, CA [*OCLC symbol*] (OCLC)
MCF .... Meta Content File [*Netscape*] [*Computer science*]
MCF .... Metroplex Control Facility [*FAA*] (TAG)
MCF .... Microcomplement Fixation [*Immunochemistry*]
MCF .... Migrant Children's Fund [*Absorbed by NCEMC*]
MCF .... Military Computer Family (MCD)
MCF .... Milled Carbon Fiber
MCF .... Million Cubic Feet
MCF .... Mink Cell Focus-Inducing [*Virus*]
MCF .... Mission Control Facility (MCD)
MCF .... Mission-Critical Function (PDAA)
MCF .... Mobile Calibration Facility
MCF .... Mode Change Flag
MCF .... Modular Combustion Facility (SSD)
MCF .... Monolithic Crystal Filter
MCF .... Mononuclear Cell Factor [*Cytology*]
MCF .... Multichannel Fixed
MCF .... Multilateral Clearing Facility [*Caribbean Community and Common Market*] (EY)
MCF .... Multiple Cassegrain Feed [*Deep Space Instrumentation Facility, NASA*]
MCF .... Multiple Cost Factor
MCF .... Museum Communication Format (NITA)
MCF .... Mutual Coherence Function
MCF .... Myocardial Contractile Force [*Cardiology*]
MCF .... Tampa, FL [*Location identifier FAA*] (FAAL)
MCF .... Taurus MuniCalif Hldgs [*NYSE symbol*] (TTSB)
MCF .... Taurus Municipal California Holdings [*NYSE symbol*] (SPSG)
MCF .... Thousand Cubic Feet
MCF-7 .... Michigan Cancer Foundation - Seventh Sample [*Strain of rapid-growing breast cancer cells used world-wide in cancer research*]
MCFA .... Medium-Chain Fatty Acids [*Organic chemistry*]
MCFA .... Mitsubishi Caterpillar Forklift America
MCFA .... Monosegmented Continuous Flow Analysis [*Analytical chemistry*]
McFar .... McFarlane's Jury Court Reports [*Scotland*] [*A publication*] (DLA)
McFarl .... McFarland Energy, Inc. [*Associated Press*] (SAG)
MCFC .... Mary Jo Cattlett Fan Club (EA)
MCFC .... Molten Carbonate Fuel Cell [*Energy source*]
MCFC .... Motley Crue Fan Club (EA)
MCFD .... Modular Chaff/Flare Dispenser (PDAA)
MCFD .... Thousand Cubic Feet per Day
MCFE .... McFarland Energy [*NASDAQ symbol*] (TTSB)
MCFE .... McFarland Energy, Inc. [*NASDAQ symbol*] (NQ)
MCFF .... Moving Call for Fire [*Military*]
MCFH .... Thousand Cubic Feet per Hour
MCFIM .... Microfilm
MCFL .... Master Civilian Facilities Listing [*DoD*]
MCFLM .... Microfilm (AAG)
MCFO .... Marine Corps Freight Office
MCFP .... Member of the College of Family Physicians [*British*]
MCFR .... Microframe, Inc. [*NASDAQ symbol*] (SAG)
MCFS .... Maneuver Control Functional Segment [*Army*] (RDA)
MCFS .... Master Container Freight [*MARAD*] (TAG)
MCFSA .... Minority Caucus of Family Service America (EA)
MCFSAA ..... Minorities Caucus of Family Service Association of America [*Later, MCFSA*] (EA)
MCFSHE ..... Microfische
McFx .... Microfax, Universal Information System, Paramus, NJ [*Library symbol*] [*Library of Congress*] (LCLS)
MCG .... Magazine Cartoonists Guild [*Later, CG*] (EA)
MCG .... Magnetic Compensator Group
MCG .... Magnetocardiogram
MCG .... Magnetocardiograph (IDOE)
MCG .... Magneto Cumulative Generator (MCD)
MCG .... Mains Cable Group [*British*] (DBA)
MCG .... Man Computer Graphics [*Computer science*] (MCD)
MCG .... Marine Corps Gazette [*A publication*] (DOMA)
MCG .... Master Control Gauge (IAA)
MCG .... Master of Clinical Gerontology (PGP)
MCG .... McGill University, Graduate School of Library Science, Montreal, PQ, Canada [*OCLC symbol*] (OCLC)
McG .... McGloin's Louisiana Court of Appeal Reports [*A publication*] (DLA)
MCG .... McGrath [*Alaska*] [*Airport symbol*] (OAG)
MCG .... McGrath, AK [*Location identifier FAA*] (FAAL)
MCG .... Medical College of Georgia [*Augusta*]
MCG .... Memory Character Generator
MCG .... Memory Controller Group (DWSG)
MCG .... Metric Coordinating Group (MCD)
MCG .... Microgram [*One millionth of a gram*]
MCG .... Microwave Command Guidance
MCG .... Midbrain Central Gray [*Brain anatomy*]
MCG .... Mid-Canada Gold & Copper [*Vancouver Stock Exchange symbol*]
MCG .... Midcourse Guidance [*Navy*] (CAAL)

MCG............ Millimeter Wave Contrast Guidance [*Munitions*] (MCD)
MCG............ Minimally-Cleaned, Coal-Derived Gas
MCG............ Mobile Command Guidance
MCG............ Mobile Communications Group [*Air Force*] (MCD)
mCG............ Monkey Chorionic Gonadotrophin [*Endocrinology*]
MCG............ Monoclonal Gammopathy [*Immunochemistry*] (DMAA)
MCG............ Moving Coil Galvanometer [*Electronics*]
MCGA .... Memory Controller Gate Array [*Computer science*]
MCGA .... Multicolor Graphics Adapter [*Computer technology*]
MCGA .... Multicolor /Graphics Array [*Computer science*]
MCGC .... Michigan Consolidated Gas Co. [*Associated Press*] (SAG)
McGC .... Micro Graphic Corp., Garfield, NJ [*Library symbol*] [*Library of Congress*] (LCLS)
MCGCIS ...... Marine Corps Ground-Controlled Interceptor Squadron (IAA)
MCGCM ...... Marine Corps Good Conduct Medal
MCGF .... Myeloma Cell Growth Factor [*Biochemistry*]
MCGFP .... Maraschino Cherry and Glace Fruit Processors (EA)
MCGH .... Marine Corps Gun Howitzer (MCD)
McGill........ McGill's Manuscript Decisions, Scotch Court of Session [*A publication*] (DLA)
McGl............ McGloin's Louisiana Courts of Appeal Reports [*A publication*] (DLA)
McGl Al ...... McGlashan. Aliment [*Scotland*] [*A publication*] (DLA)
McGl (LA)... McGloin's Louisiana Courts of Appeal Reports [*A publication*] (DLA)
McGloin...... McGloin's Louisiana Courts of Appeal Reports [*A publication*] (DLA)
McGloin Rep (LA)... McGloin's Louisiana Courts of Appeal Reports [*A publication*] (DLA)
McGl Sh ...... McGlashan's Sheriff Court Practice [*Scotland*] [*A publication*] (DLA)
MCGN .... Mesangiocapillary Glomerulonephritis [*Medicine*] (AAMN)
MCGN .... Minimal-Change Glomerular Nephritis [*Minimal-change glomerulonephritis*] [*Nephrology*] (DAVI)
MCGN .... Mixed Cryoglobulinemia-Associated Glomerulonephritis [*Medicine*]
MCGP .... Member of the College of General Practitioners [*British*]
MCGp........ Mobile Communications Group [*Air Force*] (AFM)
MCGPPC ..... Manual on the Control of Government Property in the Possession of Contractors
McGrath...... McGrath's Mandamus Cases [*Michigan*] [*A publication*] (DLA)
McGrH .... McGraw-Hill, Inc. [*Associated Press*] (SAG)
McGrth .... McGrath Rent Corp. [*Associated Press*] (SAG)
MCGS .... Microwave Command Guidance System [*RADC*]
MCGW .... Maximum Certificated Gross Weight (MCD)
MCH............ Churchill Public Library, Manitoba [*Library symbol National Library of Canada*] (NLC)
MCH............ Machala [*Ecuador*] [*Airport symbol*] (OAG)
MCH............ Machine Channel Handler (ECII)
MCH............ Machine Check Handle (NITA)
MCH............ Machine-Check Handler [*Computer science*] (MCD)
MCH............ Machynlleth [*Welsh depot code*]
M Ch........... Magister Chirurgiae [*Master of Surgery*] [*Latin*]
MCH............ Mail Chute (AAG)
MCH............ March
MCH............ Masachapa [*Nicaragua*] [*Seismograph station code, US Geological Survey*] (SEIS)
MCH............ Massachusetts Council for the Humanities [*Defunct*] (EA)
MCH............ Master of Community Health (GAGS)
MCH............ Maternal and Child Health Services [*Generic term*] (DHSM)
MCH............ McAlpine Helicopters Ltd. [*British ICAO designator*] (FAAC)
MCH............ Mean Cell [*or Corpuscular*] Hemoglobin [*Hematology*]
MCH............ Mean Corpuscular Hemoglobin and Red Cell Indices [*Hematology*] (DAVI)
MCH............ Melanin-Concentrating Hormone [*Endocrinology*]
M-Ch........... Memory Channel
MCH............ Methacholine [*A cholinergic*]
MCH............ Methylcyclohexane [*Organic chemistry*]
MCH............ Methylcyclohexanol [*Organic chemistry*]
MCH............ Methylcyclohexenone [*Organic chemistry*]
MCH............ Methylenecyclohexadiene [*Organic chemistry*]
MCH............ Micham Explorations, Inc. [*Vancouver Stock Exchange symbol*]
Mch .... Michigan Reports [*A publication*] (DLA)
McH............ Microeditions Hachette, Paris, France [*Library symbol Library of Congress*] (LCLS)
MCH............ Microfibrillar Collagen Hemostat [*Medicine*] (MEDA)
MCH............ Millenium Chemicals, Inc. [*NYSE symbol*] (SAG)
mch .... Millicurie Hour
MCH............ Mission Chapel [*Church of England*]
MCH............ Muscle Contraction Headache [*Medicine*] (CPH)
MCha .... Eldredge Public Library, Chatham, MA [*Library symbol*] [*Library of Congress*] (LCLS)
MCHAN ...... Multichannel (AABC)
MChB.......... Boston College, Chestnut Hill, MA [*Library symbol Library of Congress*] (LCLS)
MCHb......... Mean Corpuscular Hemoglobin [*Hematology*] (DAVI)
MCHbC .... Mean Corpuscular Hemoglobin Concentration [*Hematology*] (DAVI)
MCHbC .... Mean Corpuscular Hemoglobin Count [*Hematology*] (DAVI)
MCHBG .... Maternal and Child Health Block Grant [*Department of Health and Human Services*] (GFGA)
MChB-WO.... Boston College, Weston Observatory, Weston, MA [*Library symbol Library of Congress*] (LCLS)
MCHC .... Mean Cell [*or Corpuscular*] Hemoglobin Concentration [*Hematology*]
MCHC .... Mean Corpuscular Hemoglobin Concentration and Red Cell Indices [*Hematology*] (DAVI)
MCHC .... Mean Corpuscular Hemoglobin Count [*Hematology*] (DAVI)
MCHC .... Mean Corpusclsar Hemoglobin Concentration [*Physiology*]
MCHC .... Missing Children...Help Center (EA)
MCHCL .... Mechanically Cooled
M Ch D .... Magister Chirurgiae Dentalis [*Master of Dental Surgery*]

MCHE.......... Eskimo Museum, Churchill, Manitoba [*Library symbol National Library of Canada*] (NLC)
M Ch E .... Master of Chemical Engineering
MChelm....... Adams Library (Chelmsford Public Library), Chelmsford, MA [*Library symbol Library of Congress*] (LCLS)
MChels .... Chelsea Public Library, Chelsea, MA [*Library symbol Library of Congress*] (LCLS)
MChem....... Master of Chemistry (ADA)
MChemA..... Master in Chemical Analysis
M Chem E ... Master of Chemical Engineering
MCHF......... Marine Corps Historical Foundation (EA)
MCHFR .... Minimum Critical Heat Flux Rates [*Nuclear energy*] (NRCH)
MCHFR .... Minimum Critical Heat Flux Ratio [*Nuclear energy*] (NRCH)
MCHg......... Mean Corpuscular Hemoglobin [*Hematology*] (DAVI)
MCHgb....... Mean Corpuscular Hemogobin [*Hematology*] (DAVI)
MCHGD....... Mott Center for Human Growth and Development (EA)
MChi........... Chicopee Public Library, Chicopee, MA [*Library symbol Library of Congress*] (LCLS)
MChiD........ Dow Jones & Co., Inc., Chicopee, MA [*Library symbol Library of Congress*] (LCLS)
MChiL......... College of Our Lady of the Elms, Chicopee, MA [*Library symbol Library of Congress*] (LCLS)
M Chir .... Magister Chirurgiae [*Master of Surgery*]
MCHL.......... Mayo Clinic Health Letter [*A publication*]
MCHL.......... Mean Corpuscular Hemoglobin [*Count*] [*Hematology*] (DAVI)
MCHM .... MacroChem Corp. [*NASDAQ symbol*] (NQ)
MCHMAS ..... Michaelmas [*Feast of St. Michael the Archangel, September 29*] (ROG)
MCHML....... Macrochem Corp. Wrrt'A' [*NASDAQ symbol*] (TTSB)
MCHMM ..... Macrochem Corp. Wrrt'AA' [*NASDAQ symbol*] (TTSB)
MCHMN ..... Macrochem Corp. Wrrt'X' [*NASDAQ symbol*] (TTSB)
MCHN .... Machine
MCHND....... Machined
M Ch Orth.... Master of Orthopaedic Surgery
M Ch Otol.... Master of Oto-Rhino-Laryngological Surgery
MCHP.......... (Methylcinnamylhydrazono)propionate [*Biochemistry*]
MCHP.......... Microchip Technology [*NASDAQ symbol*] (TTSB)
MCHP.......... Microchip Technology, Inc. [*NASDAQ symbol*] (SAG)
MChP.......... Pine Manor College, Chestnut Hill, MA [*Library symbol Library of Congress*] (LCLS)
M'CHR .... Manchester [*County in England*] (ROG)
MCHR .... Medical Committee for Human Rights [*Defunct*]
mchr .... Millicurie Hour (MAE)
M Chr Ed ..... Master of Christian Education
MCHRF .... Mechanically Refrigerated
MChrom....... Master of Chromatics [*British*]
MCHRY .... Machinery (MSA)
MCHS .... Maternal and Child Health Service (EA)
MChS .... Member of the Society of Chiropodists
M chs .... Thousands (10^3) of Characters (NITA)
MCHSM....... Mechanism
MCHST .... Machinist (MSA)
MCHT.......... Merchant
MCHTR .... Maintenance Channel Transmit Receiver Register (MHDI)
M'CHTR ...... Manchester [*County in England*] (ROG)
MCHY .... Machinery (ROG)
Mchy fwd .... Machinery Forward (DS)
MCI............. Kansas City [*Missouri*] [*Airport symbol*] (OAG)
MCI............. Kansas City, MO [*Location identifier FAA*] (FAAL)
MCI............. Machine Check Interrupt (NITA)
MCI............. Machine Check Interruption [*Computer science*] (BUR)
MCI............. Major Capital Improvement [*Justification for rent increase*]
MCI............. Malicious Call Identification [*Telecommunications*] (TEL)
MCI............. Malleable Cast Iron
MCI............. Managed Cost Improvement (NRCH)
MCI............. Management Consultants International, Inc. [*Information service or system*] (IID)
MCI............. Manual of Clinical Immunology [*A publication*]
MCI............. Marine Corps Institute
MCI............. Marketing Concepts, Inc. [*New York, NY*] [*Telecommunications*] (TSSD)
MCI............. MassMutual Corp. Inv [*NYSE symbol*] (TTSB)
MCI............. MassMutual Corporate Investors [*NYSE symbol*] (SPSG)
MCI............. Master Configuration Index (MCD)
MCI............. Material Concept Investigation (MCD)
MCI............. Materials Cost Index
MCI............. Maya Carga Internacional SA de CV [*Mexico ICAO designator*] (FAAC)
MCI............. MCI Communications Corp. [*Associated Press*] (SAG)
MCI............. Meal, Combat, Individual [*Military*] (AABC)
MCI............. Mean Cardiac Index
MCi............. Media Control Interface
MCi............. Megacurie
MCI............. Member of the Credit Institute
MCI............. Member of the Institute of Commerce [*British*] (DBQ)
MCI............. Meridian Control Integrator
MCI............. Mexican Coffee Institute (EA)
Mcl............. Microfilm Center, Incorporated, Dallas, Texas [*Library symbol Library of Congress*] (LCLS)
Mcl............. Microplex, Inc., Dallas, TX [*Library symbol*] [*Library of Congress*] (LCLS)
MCI............. Microwave Communications Inc. (NITA)
MCI............. Microwave Communications of America, Inc.
MCI............. Milk Can Institute [*Defunct*]
mCi............. Millicurie [*Also, mC*]

MCI	Ministry of Commerce and Industry [*Korea*]
MCI	Minnesota Counseling Inventory [*Psychology*]
MCI	Mission Change Indicator [*Air Force*] (AFIT)
MCI	Monte Cassino [*Italy*] [*Seismograph station code, US Geological Survey Closed*] (SEIS)
MCI	Mother and Child International [*Switzerland*] (EAIO)
MCI	Motorcycle Industry Association of Great Britain (EAIO)
MCI	Mottled Cast Iron
MCI	Multichip Integration [*Computer science*] (PDAA)
MCIA	Methyl Chloride Industry Association (EA)
MCIA	MicroComputer Investors Association [*Database producer*] (EA)
MCIBS	Member of the Chartered Institution of Building Services [*British*] (DBQ)
MCIC	Machine Check Interruption Code [*Computer science*]
MCIC	Marine Corps Intelligence Center (DOMA)
MCIC	MCI Communications [*NASDAQ symbol*] (TTSB)
MCIC	MCI Communications Corp. [*NASDAQ symbol*] (NQ)
MCIC	Medical Care Insurance Commission [*Canada*]
MCIC	Member of the Chemical Institute of Canada
MCIC	Metals and Ceramics Information Center [*Battelle Memorial Institute*] [*DoD Information service or system*] (IID)
McIC	Micro Industrial Corp., Bayville, NJ [*Library symbol*] [*Library of Congress*] (LCLS)
MCID	Malicious Call Identification [*Telecommunications*] (DOM)
MCID	Multipurpose Concealed Intrusion Detector [*Army*] (RDA)
McIDAS	Man-Computer Interactive Data Access System
MCIF	Member of the Canadian Institute of Forestry
mCihr	Millicurie Hour (MAE)
MCIM	Member Canadian Institute of Mining and Metallurgy (DD)
MCIM	Member of the Canadian Institute of Mining
MCIMM	Member of the Canadian Institute of Mining and Metallurgy
McIn & E Jud Pr	McIntyre and Evans' Judicature Practice [*A publication*] (DLA)
McInc	MAICO Micrographics, Inc., Wormleysburg, PA [*Library symbol*] [*Library of Congress*] (LCLS)
McInc	Microcomfax, Incorporated, Camp Hill, PA [*Library symbol Library of Congress*] (LCLS)
MCINS	Minimal Change Idiopathic Nephrotic Syndrome [*Medicine*] (DMAA)
McInt	McIntosh Music [*Record label*]
MCIOB	Member of the Chartered Institute of Building [*British*] (DBQ)
MCIP	Mated Cast Iron Pair
MCIRA	Microelectronic Replacement Assembly (NG)
MCIS	Maintenance Control Information System (IEEE)
MCIS	Map and Chart Information System (MHDB)
MCIS	Master of Computer and Information Science (PGP)
MCIS	Master of Computer Information Systems (GAGS)
MCIS	Materials Compatibility in Sodium [*Nuclear energy*] (NRCH)
MCIS	Materials Control Information System (MHDB)
MCIS	Multichannel Initial System (MCD)
MCIS	Multiple Corridor Identification System [*Air Force*]
MCIT	Institute of Traditional Science, Cambridge, MA [*Library symbol Library of Congress*] (LCLS)
MCIT	Member of the Chartered Institute of Transport [*British*] (DCTA)
MCIU	Manipulator Controller Interface Unit (NASA)
MCIU	Master Control and Interface Unit [*NASA*] (NASA)
MCIU	Mission Control and Interface Unit [*NASA*] (NASA)
MCIU	Mission Control and Interface Unit
M Civil E	Master of Civil Engineering (PGP)
MCJ	Maicao [*Colombia*] [*Airport symbol*] (OAG)
MCJ	Master of Comparative Jurisprudence
MCJ	Master of Criminal Justice (GAGS)
MCJ	Memory Control J Bus
MCJ	Michigan Civil Jurisprudence [*A publication*] (DLA)
MCJ	Model Car Journal Association [*Publishing company*] (EA)
MCJA	Master of Criminal Justice Administration (GAGS)
MCJC	Maryknoll Center for Justice Concerns (EA)
MCJC	Mason City Junior College [*Iowa*]
MCJR	Multichannel Jezebel [*Sonobuoy System*] Relay [*Military*] (NG)
MCK	Maintenance Check (FAAC)
MCK	Manson Creek Resources Ltd. [*Vancouver Stock Exchange symbol*]
MCK	Master Cook [*Navy*]
MCK	McCook [*Nebraska*] [*Airport symbol*] (OAG)
MCK	McCook, NE [*Location identifier FAA*] (FAAL)
MCK	McKesson Corp. [*Formerly, SP Ventures*] [*NYSE symbol*] (SPSG)
MCK	McKinley [*Alaska*] [*Seismograph station code, US Geological Survey*] (SEIS)
MCK	Mission/Communication Keyboard (MCD)
MCK	Modification Change Kit
MCK	Muscle Creatine Kinase [*An enzyme*]
MCKA	Metal Cutting Knife Association (EA)
McK Consol Laws	McKinney's Consolidated Laws of New York [*A publication*] (DLA)
MCKD	Multicystic Kidney Disease [*Medicine*]
MCKEES	Marine Corps Key Experiences Evaluation System (MCD)
McKelvey Ev	McKelvey on Evidence [*A publication*] (DLA)
McKesson	McKesson Corp. [*Associated Press*] (SAG)
McKin Jus	McKinney's Justice [*A publication*] (DLA)
McKin Phil Ev	McKinnon's Philosophy of Evidence [*A publication*] (DLA)
MCL	Intervega - Movement for Compassionate Living the Vegan Way (EAIO)
MCL	Lesley College, Cambridge, MA [*Library symbol Library of Congress*] (LCLS)
MCL	Maintenance Checkoff List
M-CL	Managment List - Consolidated (IID)
MCL	Manufacturing Control Language [*Computer science*] (MCD)
MCL	Marine Corps League (EA)

MCL	Mass Change Log (MCD)
MCL	Master Change Log
MCL	Master Clear Line (IAA)
MCL	Master Component List (MCD)
MCL	Master Configuration List
MCL	Master Control List
MCL	Master of Canon Law (PGP)
MCL	Master of Civil Law
MCL	Master of Comparative Law
MCL	Mathematics Computation Laboratory [*General Services Administration*]
MCL	Maximum Contaminant Level
MCL	Maximum Contaminant Levels
MCL	McClellan Central Laboratory (MCD)
M'Cl	McClelland's English Exchequer Reports [*A publication*] (DLA)
McL	McLaren Micropublishing, Toronto, ON, Canada [*Library symbol Library of Congress*] (LCLS)
Mc L	McLean's United States Circuit Court Reports [*A publication*] (DLA)
MCL	McNeil River [*Alaska*] [*Seismograph station code, US Geological Survey*] (SEIS)
MCL	Medial Collateral Ligament [*Anatomy*]
MCL	Medial Cruciate Ligament [*Anatomy*]
MCL	Medical Aviation Services Ltd. [*British ICAO designator*] (FAAC)
MCL	Medical College of Ohio at Toledo, Toledo, OH [*OCLC symbol*] (OCLC)
MCL	Memory Control and Logging [*Hewlett-Packard Co.*]
MCL	Message Control Language [*Computer science*]
MCL	Metal Crystal Lattice
MCL	Michigan Compiled Laws (AAGC)
MCL	Microcomputer Center and Library [*Wisconsin State Department of Public Instruction*] [*Information service or system*] (IID)
MCL	Microcomputer Language [*Computer science*] (ECII)
MCL	Microprogram Control Logic [*Computer science*] (MDG)
MCL	Microwave Cavity Laboratory (IAA)
MCL	Mid-Canada Line [*RADAR warning chain of fence across Canada; sometimes called the McGill Fence*]
MCL	Midclavicular Line [*Medicine*]
MCL	Midcostal Line [*Medicine*]
MCL	Mineral Constitution Laboratories [*Pennsylvania State University*] [*Research center*] (RCD)
MCL	Miniature Cartridge Light
MCL	Mini Circuits Laboratory (IAA)
MCL	Minimal Computer Load
MCL	Ministering Children's League [*Australia*]
MCL	Minority Carrier Lifetime [*Solar cell technology*]
MCL	Missile Continuity Loop (MCD)
MCL	Modified Chest Lead [*Medicine*]
MCL	Molten-Caustic-Leaching [*Coal technology*]
MCL	Moore Corp. Ltd. [*NYSE symbol Toronto Stock Exchange symbol*] (SPSG)
MCL	Most Comfortable Level [*Referring to sound level*] [*Otorhinolaryngology*] (DAVI)
MCL	Most Comfortable Loudness Test [*Audiometry*]
MCL	Moving Coil Loudspeaker [*Electronics*]
MCL	Mucocutaneous Leishmaniasis [*Medicine*]
MCL	Multicolor LASER
MCL	Mushroom Canners League (EA)
MCLA	Marine Corps League Auxiliary (EA)
MCLA	Medical Contact Lens Association [*British*]
MCLA	Michigan Compiled Laws, Annotated [*A publication*] (DLA)
MCLA	Microcoded Communications Line Adapter
MCLA	Micro-Coded Communications Link Adaptor (NITA)
MCLA	Motor Carrier Lawyers Association (EA)
MCLAA	Minnesota Computer Literacy and Awareness Assessment (EDAC)
MCLAMS	Measurement, Control, LEID [*Limit of Error of the Inventory Difference*], and MUF Inventory Difference Simulation [*Material Unaccounted For*] [*Nuclear energy*] (NRCH)
McL & R	McLean and Robinson's Scotch Appeal Cases [*1839*] [*A publication*] (DLA)
M'Cl & Y	McClelland and Younge's English Exchequer Reports [*1824-25*] [*A publication*] (DLA)
M'Cl & Yo	M'Clelland and Younge's English Exchequer Reports [*148 English Reprint*] [*A publication*] (DLA)
McLar Tr	McLaren's Trusts in Scotland [*A publication*] (DLA)
McLar W	McLaren's Law of Wills [*Scotland*] [*A publication*] (DLA)
M-CLASS	Mobile CLASS [*Cross-Chain Long-Range Navigation Atmospheric Sounding System*] (USDC)
MCLB	Marine Corps Logistics Base (DOMA)
MCIBiochem	Master of Clinical Biochemistry
MCLC	Lesley College, Cambridge, MA [*Library symbol*] [*Library of Congress*] (LCLS)
MCLC	Mine Clearing Line Charge [*Army*]
M CI D	Master of Clinical Dentistry (PGP)
MCLD	Multicolor LASER Display
MCLE	Mandatory Continuing Legal Education [*Australia A publication*]
M'Cle	M'Clelland's English Exchequer Reports [*148 English Reprint*] [*A publication*] (DLA)
McLean	McLean's United States Circuit Court Reports [*A publication*] (DLA)
M'Cle & Yo	M'Clelland and Younge's English Exchequer Reports [*148 English Reprint*] [*A publication*] (DLA)
McLean's CCR	McLean's United States Circuit Court Reports [*A publication*] (DLA)
McLean's Rep	McLean's United States Circuit Court Reports [*A publication*] (DLA)

M'Clel.......... M'Clelland's English Exchequer Reports [*148 English Reprint*] [*A publication*] (DLA)

M'Clel & Y... M'Clelland and Younge's English Exchequer Reports [*148 English Reprint*] [*A publication*] (DLA)

M'Clel & Y (Eng)... M'Clelland and Younge's English Exchequer Reports [*148 English Reprint*] [*A publication*] (DLA)

M'Clel (Eng)... McClelland's English Exchequer Reports [*A publication*] (DLA)

MCLFDC ...... Marine Corps Landing Force Development Center

MCLG.......... Major Caliber Lightweight Gun [*Navy*] (MCD)

MCLG.......... Maximum Contaminant Level Goal [*Environmental Protection Agency*]

MCLI.......... Meiklejohn Civil Liberties Institute (EA)

MClinPsych... Master of Clinical Psychology

MClinPsychol... Master of Clinical Psychology (ADA)

MClinSc...... Master of Clinical Science (ADA)

MCLJ.......... Mifflin County Legal Journal [*Pennsylvania*] [*A publication*] (DLA)

MCLK.......... Master Clock

MCLL.......... Metrocall, Inc. [*NASDAQ symbol*] (SAG)

MCLL.......... Missile Compartment, Lower Level

MCLL.......... Most Comfortable Loudness Level [*On audiometry*] [*Otorhinolaryngology*] (DAVI)

MCLN.......... Mouvement Centrafricain de Liberation Nationale [*Central African Movement for National Liberation*] (PD)

MCLNS....... Mucocutaneous Lymph Node Synrome [*Kawasaki's disease*] (DAVI)

MCLO.......... Medical Construction Liaison Office [*or Officer*] [*Air Force*] (AFM)

MCLOF........ Market Center Limit Order File [*Investment term*] (DICI)

MCLong....... Longfellow House, Longfellow National Historic Site, Cambridge, MA [*Library symbol Library of Congress*] (LCLS)

MCLORA ...... Marine Corps Level of Repair Analysis

MCLOS........ Manual Command-to-Line-of-Sight [*Missile guidance system*] (INF)

MCLP.......... Military Committee Representative Liaison Paper to the International Staff [*North Atlantic Council*] (NATG)

MCLR.......... Midwest Center for Labor Research (EA)

MCLR.......... Minimum Critical Leaching Rate

MCLS.......... Maintenance Contractor Logistic Support [*Army*]

MCLS.......... Metropolitan Cooperative Library System [*Library network*]

MCLS.......... Monroe County Library System [*Library network*]

MCLS.......... Mucocutaneous Lymph Node Syndrome [*Medicine*]

MCLSBLANT... Marine Corps Logistic Support Base, Atlantic (MCD)

MCLSBPAC... Marine Corps Logistic Support Base, Pacific (MCD)

MCISc.......... Master of Clinical Science (ADA)

M Cl Sc .... Master of Clinical Science (PGP)

MCISci........ Master Clinical Science (DAVI)

MCLT.......... Maximum Cruise Level Thrust (MCD)

MCLWG........ Major Caliber Lightweight Gun [*Navy*] (NG)

MCM.......... Circular Mils, Thousands

MCM.......... Controladora Comercial Mexicana SA de CV [*NYSE symbol*] (SAG)

MCM.......... Cordi-Marian Missionary Sisters [*Roman Catholic religious order*]

MCM.......... Cordi Marian Sisters (TOCD)

MCM.......... Heli-Air-Monaco [*ICAO designator*] (FAAC)

MCM.......... Mac-Am Resources Corp. [*Vancouver Stock Exchange symbol*]

MCM.......... Machine Control Medium (MCD)

MCM.......... Machines for Coordinated Multiprocessing

MCM.......... Macon, MO [*Location identifier FAA*] (FAAL)

MCM.......... Magnetic Card Memory [*Computer science*] (IAA)

MCM.......... Magnetic Core Memory [*Computer science*]

MCM.......... Maintenance Control Manual [*Canadian Airlines International*]

MCM.......... Maintenance Control Module [*Telecommunications*] (TEL)

MCM.......... Manned Circumlunar Mission

MCM.......... Mannes College of Music [*New York, NY*]

MCM.......... Manual Communication Module [*Telecommunication device for the deaf*]

MCM.......... Manual Computer Makeready (DGA)

MCM.......... Manual for Courts-Martial

MCM.......... Manual of Clinical Microbiology [*A publication*]

MCM.......... Marine Corps Manual

MCM.......... Massachusetts Institute of Technology, Cambridge, MA [*Library symbol Library of Congress*] (LCLS)

MCM.......... Mass Control Module

MCM.......... Master Control Module

MCM.......... Master of Christian Ministry (PGP)

MCM.......... Master of Church Management (PGP)

MCM.......... Master of Church Music

MCM.......... Master of Clinical Microbiology (PGP)

MCM.......... Master of Construction Management (PGP)

MCM.......... Materiel Change Management

MCM.......... McCarthy, Crisanti & Maffei, Inc. [*Information service or system*] (IID)

MCM.......... McMurdo Sound [*Antarctica*] [*Seismograph station code, US Geological Survey Closed*] (SEIS)

MCM.......... Mechanical Current Meter [*Marine science*] (OSRA)

MCM.......... Medical Corps, Merchant Marine [*USNR officer designation*]

MCM.......... Mega Cisterna Magna [*Medicine*]

MCM.......... Megawatt Cassegrain Monopulse

MCM.......... Member of the College of Musicians [*British*]

MCM.......... Memory Control Module

MCM.......... Merged Charge Memory [*Computer science*] (IAA)

MCM.......... Microchip Module

MCM.......... Microcircuit Module

MCM.......... Microcomputer Machine (IAA)

McM.......... Micromedia Ltd., Toronto, ON, Canada [*Library symbol Library of Congress*] (LCLS)

MCM.......... Microwave Circuit Module [*Computer science*] (IAA)

MCM.......... Military Characteristics Motor Vehicles

MCM.......... Military Committee Memorandum [*NATO*] (NATG)

MCM.......... Milli Circular Mil (IAA)

MCM.......... Million Centimeters (MCD)

MCM.......... Mine Countermeasures (NG)

MCM.......... Minichromosome Maintenance [*Cytology*]

MCM.......... Minneapolis College of Music

MCM.......... Miscellaneous Contract Material

MCM.......... Missile Carrying Missile (AAG)

MCM.......... Missile Control Module (NVT)

MCMS.......... Mission Communications Manager (SSD)

MCM.......... Mission Control Module

MCM.......... Mississippi College, Clinton, MS [*OCLC symbol*] (OCLC)

MCM.......... Mobile Cinetheodolite Mounts (SAA)

MCM.......... Mode Control Message (MCD)

MCM.......... Monolithic Circuit Mask

MCM.......... Monte Carlo [*Monaco*] [*Airport symbol*] (OAG)

MCM.......... Monte Carlo Method [*Computer science*]

MCM.......... Moving Coil Microphone [*Electronics*]

MCM.......... Moving Coil Motor [*Electronics*] (IAA)

MCM.......... Multichip Module [*Computer science*]

MCM.......... Multilayer Ceramic Multichip [*Electronics*]

MCM.......... Multinational Computer Models, Inc. [*Information service or system*] (IID)

MCM.......... Multiple Connected Motor

MCM.......... Multiple Contact Miscible [*Physical chemistry*]

MCM.......... Municipal Court of Montreal (DLA)

MCM.......... Thousand Circular Mils

MCMA.......... Machine Chain Manufacturers Association (EA)

MCMA.......... Marine Corps Mustang Association (EA)

MCMA.......... Metal Cookware Manufacturers Association [*Later, CMA*] (EA)

MCMAI.......... Milton Clinical Multi-Axial Inventory [*Psychology*] (DAVI)

McMas RR... McMaster's New York Railroad Laws [*A publication*] (DLA)

MCMB.......... Multiple Conductor, Marker Buoy (IAA)

MCMC.......... Marine Corps Memorial Commission

MCMC.......... MCM Corp. [*NASDAQ symbol*] (NQ)

MCMC.......... McM Corp. [*NASDAQ symbol*] (TTSB)

MCMC.......... Medicine Cabinet Manufacturers Council (EA)

MCMC.......... Midwest Committee for Military Counseling (EA)

MCMC.......... Military Construction, Marine Corps (DNAB)

MCMCAT..... Mine Countermeasures Catamaran [*Military*]

MCMCC....... Marine Corps Movement Coordination Center (DNAB)

McM Com Cas... McMaster's United States Commercial Cases [*A publication*] (DLA)

McM Com Dec... McMaster's Commercial Decisions [*A publication*] (DLA)

MCM Cp ...... MCM Corp. [*Associated Press*] (SAG)

McMdL........ Micromedia Ltd., Toronto, ON, Canada [*Library symbol Library of Congress*] (LCLS)

MCMES........ Member of the Civil and Mechanical Engineering Society

MCM-F........ Massachusetts Institute of Technology, University Film Study Center, Cambridge, MA [*Library symbol Library of Congress*] (LCLS)

MCMFA........ Meeting of Consultation of Ministers of Foreign Affairs

MCMFE........ Membrane-Covered Mercury Film Electrode [*Electrochemistry*]

MCMG........ Man-Carrying Motion Generator [*Space-flight simulation*]

MCMG........ Military Committee Meteorological Group [*NATO*] (NATG)

MCM-H........ Massachusetts Institute of Technology, Francis Russell Hart Nautical Museum, Cambridge, MA [*Library symbol Library of Congress*] (LCLS)

MCMH .... Mine Counter-Measures Hovercraft [*Military*] (PDAA)

MCMHA ...... Metropolitan College Mental Health Association (EA)

MCMHC ...... Mine Countermeasures Helicopter Controller (MCD)

MCMI.......... Malleable Chain Manufacturers Institute [*Later, American Chain Association*]

MCMI.......... Millon Clinical Multiaxial Inventory [*Psychology*]

MCMI.......... Minneapolis Center for Microbiological Investigations [*Public Health Service*] (GRD)

MCMIS........ Motor Carrier Management Information System [*BTS*] [*MM*] (TAG)

MCM-L........ Massachusetts Institute of Technology, Lincoln Laboratory, Lexington, MA [*Library symbol Library of Congress*] (LCLS)

MCML.......... Missile Compartment, Middle Level

MCMM........ Management Control - Material Management (IEEE)

MCMOPS..... Mine Countermeasures Operations [*Military*] (NVT)

McMoRn...... McMoRan Oil and Gas Co. [*Associated Press*] (SAG)

MCMOS ...... Motorola Complementary Metal-Oxide Semi-Conductor [*Electronics*] (IAA)

MCMOV....... Maize Chlorotic Mottle Virus [*Plant pathology*]

MCMP.......... Multi-Channel Multi-Port [*Telecommunications*]

MCMR .... Medical Corps, Merchant Marine, General Service [*USNR officer designation*]

MC/MR .... Minimum Change/Minimum Risk [*Mask design concept*] [*Army*] (INF)

MCMS.......... Medical Corps, Merchant Marine, Special Service [*USNR officer designation*]

MCMS.......... Midwest Center for Mass Spectrometry [*University of Nebraska - Lincoln*] [*Research center*] (RCD)

M-CM-S....... Mobility, Countermobility, and Survivability

MCMS.......... Multichannel Memory System [*Computer science*] (AAG)

MCMS.......... Multiple Countermeasure System

MCMU .... Mass Core Memory Unit (MCD)

McMul .... McMullan's South Carolina Law Reports [*A publication*] (DLA)

McMul Eq .... McMullan's South Carolina Equity Reports [*A publication*] (DLA)

McMull Eq (SC)... McMullan's South Carolina Equity Reports [*A publication*] (DLA)

McMull L (SC)... McMullan's South Carolina Law Reports [*A publication*] (DLA)

MCMUS ...... Manual of Courts-Martial, United States

MCMV.......... Maize Chlorotic Mottle Virus [*Plant pathology*]

MCMV.......... Mine Countermeasures Vessel [*or Vehicle*] (NATG)

MCMV.......... Mine Counter-Measure Vessel

MCMV.......... Murine Cytomegalovirus

MCMWTC .... Marine Corps Mountain Warfare Training Center [*Bridgeport, CA*]

MCN............	Mac Dan Aviation Corp. [*ICAO designator*] (FAAC)
MCN............	Macon [*Georgia*] [*Airport symbol*] (OAG)
MCN............	Maintenance Communications Net (MCD)
MCN............	Maintenance Control Number
MCN............	Management Change Notice (MCD)
MCN............	Management Control Number [*Army*] (AABC)
MCN............	Manual Control Number
MCN............	Manufacturing Change Notice
MCN............	Manufacturing Control Number
MCN............	Mapping Cylinder Neighborhood
MCN............	Master Change Notice (KSC)
MCN............	Master Control Number
MCN............	Master of Clinical Nutrition
MCN............	Material Change Notice (MCD)
MCN............	Material Complaint Notice
MCN............	MCN Corp. [*Formerly, Michigan Consolidated Gas Co.*] [*Associated Press*] (SAG)
McN............	McNeil Laboratories, Inc. [*Research code symbol*]
MCN............	McNeil Mantha, Inc. [*Toronto Stock Exchange symbol*]
MCN............	MCN Financing [*NYSE symbol*] (SAG)
MCN............	MCN Michigan LP [*NYSE symbol*] (SAG)
MCN............	Mercury [*Nevada*] [*Seismograph station code, US Geological Survey Closed*] (SEIS)
MCN............	Micro Cellular Network [*Computer science*]
MCN............	Micrococcal Nuclease [*Also, MN*] [*An enzyme*]
MCN............	Midcourse Navigation [*Navy*] (IAA)
MCN............	Military Construction, Navy
MCN............	Minimal Change Nephropathy [*Medicine*] (DMAA)
MCN............	Missing Children Network [*Defunct*] (EA)
MCN............	Molecular and Cellular Neuroscience [*A publication*]
MCN............	Mouvement Congolais National [*Zaire*] [*Political party*] (EY)
MCN............	Movimiento de Conciliacion Nacional [*National Conciliation Movement*] [*Dominican Republic*] [*Political party*] (PPW)
MCN............	Museum Computer Network
MCN............	Museum Computer Network, Inc. [*American Association of Museums*] [*Research center*] (RCD)
McNagh.......	Macnaghten's Select Cases in Chancery Tempore King [*A publication*] (DLA)
McNal Ev.....	Macnally's Rules of Evidence [*A publication*] (DLA)
MCNC.........	Carberry/North Cypress Library, Carberry, Manitoba [*Library symbol National Library of Canada*] (NLC)
MCNC.........	Microcomputer Numerical Control (IAA)
MCNC.........	Microelectronics Center of North Carolina [*Research center*] (RCD)
McNeese St U...	McNeese State University (GAGS)
MCN F.........	MCN Financing [*Associated Press*] (SAG)
MCNG.........	Military Construction, National Guard
McN-JR.......	McNeil Laboratories, Inc. [*Research code symbol*]
MCNL.........	Military Committee of National Liberation [*Mali*] [*Political party*] (PPW)
MCNMI.......	MCN Michigan Ltd. [*Associated Press*] (SAG)
MCNPB.......	Marine Corps - Navy Publicity Bureau (SAA)
MCNPrT.......	MCN Mich L.P.9.375% Pfd [*NYSE symbol*] (TTSB)
MCNR.........	Military Construction, Naval Reserves
MCNRF.......	Military Construction, Naval Reserve Facilities
MCNRS.......	Meal Card Number Recording System (MCD)
MCNS.........	Minimal Change Nephrotic Syndrome [*Medicine*] (DMAA)
MCNY.........	Museum of the City of New York
MCO...........	Aerolineas Marcos SA de CV [*Mexico ICAO designator*] (FAAC)
MCo...........	Concord Free Public Library, Concord, MA [*Library symbol Library of Congress*] (LCLS)
MCO...........	Magnetron Cutoff
MCO...........	Main Civilian Occupation
MCO...........	Maintenance Checkoff
MCO...........	Manged Care Organization
MCO...........	Manual Change Order (MSA)
MCO...........	Marine Corps Officer
MCO...........	Marine Corps Order
MCO...........	Massachusetts College of Optometry
M Co...........	Master of Cosmology
MCO...........	Medicare Carve-Out [*Insurance*] (WYGK)
MCO...........	Merrill Lyn 6.00%'STRYPES' [*NYSE symbol*] (TTSB)
MCO...........	Merrill Lynch & Co. [*NYSE symbol*] (SAG)
MCO...........	Metal Catalyzed Oxidation [*Chemistry*]
MCO...........	Military City Online [*Computer program*]
MCO...........	Mill Culls Out [*Lumber*]
MCO...........	Minneapolis Community College, Minneapolis, MN [*OCLC symbol*] (OCLC)
MCO...........	Miscellaneous Charges Order [*Business term*]
MCO...........	Missile Checkout (NG)
MCO...........	Missile Control Officer
MCO...........	Mission Control Operation [*NASA*]
MCO...........	Monaco [*ANSI three-letter standard code*] (CNC)
MCO...........	Morocco Leather [*Bookbinding*] (DGA)
MCO...........	Movement Control Officer [*Army*]
MCO...........	Multi Column Option (DGA)
MCO...........	Multiple Channel Oscilloscope
MCO...........	Orlando, FL [*Location identifier FAA*] (FAAL)
MCO...........	Orlando [*Florida*] International [*Airport symbol*] (OAG)
MCOA........	Mastiff Club of America (EA)
MCOA........	Music Center Opera Association [*Los Angeles*]
MCOAG.......	Marine Corps Operations Analysis Group
MCOAM.......	Material Control Order Additional Material
MCOA/P......	Multi-Company Accounts Payable (MHDB)
MCODA.......	Motor Cab Owner Drivers' Association [*British*] (BI)
M-COFT.......	Mobile Conduct of Fire Trainer [*Combat simulator*]

MCOG.........	Member of the British College of Obstetricians and Gynaecologists (DAS)
MCOGA.......	Mid-Continent Oil and Gas Association (EA)
MCogSc.......	Master of Cognitive Science
MCOHM......	Military Community Oral Health Managers [*Army*]
MCOI.........	Minority Centers of Influence (DNAB)
MCOLF........	Marine Corps Outlying Landing Field
MColIP........	Member of the College of Preceptors [*British*] (DBQ)
M Com........	Master of Commerce
MCOM........	Mathematics of Computation (IEEE)
MCOM........	Metricom, Inc. [*NASDAQ symbol*] (SAG)
MCOM........	Missile Command [*Army*] (MCD)
M Com Adm...	Master of Commercial Administration
MComm.......	Master of Commerce (ADA)
M Comm......	Master of Commerce and Administration (ROG)
MCOMM......	Minimize Communications
M Comm H...	Master of Community Health
MCommSc...	Master in Commercial Science (DD)
MCommun...	Master in Communication (DD)
M Comp.......	Master of Computing
M Comp E ...	Master of Computer Engineering (PGP)
M Comp L ...	Master of Comparative Law
MCompLaw..	Master of Comparative Law (NADA)
M Com Sc ...	Master of Commercial Science
MComSc......	Master of Computer Science
MCON.........	EMCON [*NASDAQ symbol*] (TTSB)
MCON.........	EMCON Associates [*NASDAQ symbol*] (NQ)
MCON.........	Military Construction
MCON.........	Moment Connections [*Computer Services Consultants Ltd.*] [*Software package*] (NCC)
MConsE......	Member of the Association of Consulting Engineers [*British*] (EY)
MCOP........	Major Command Orientation Program [*Air Force*] (AFM)
MCOP........	Marine Corps Ordnance Publication
mCOP........	Measured Colloidal Osmotic Pressure [*Clinical chemistry*]
MCOP........	Mission Control Operations Panel [*NASA*] (KSC)
MCOP........	Multiple Conductor, Oil-Resistant, Portable [*Cable*]
MCOPR.......	Major Command of Primary Responsibility [*Air Force*] (AFM)
MCOQ........	Multiple Choice Objective Question (DA)
MCOR........	Methodist Committee for Overseas Relief [*Later, UMCOR*] (EA)
MC/ORB......	Maritime Command Operational Research Branch [*Canada*]
MC/ORD......	Maritime Command Operational Research Division [*Canada*]
M'Cord Eq (SC)...	M'Cord's South Carolina Equity Reports [*A publication*] (DLA)
M'Cord L (SC)..	M'Cord's South Carolina Law Reports [*A publication*] (DLA)
MCOS........	Microprogrammable Computer Operating System
MCoS.........	Military College of Science [*British military*] (DMA)
MCot..........	Cotuit Library, Cotuit, MA [*Library symbol*] [*Library of Congress*] (LCLS)
MCOT........	Missile Checkout Trailer
MCOT........	Missile Control Officer, Trainer (NG)
MCOTEA......	Marine Corps Operational Test and Evaluation Activity (CAAL)
Mcoul........	Millicoulomb
M Coun.......	Master of Counseling (PGP)
MCouns(Ed)...	Master of Counselling (Education) (ADA)
MCOV........	Main Chamber Oxidizer Valve [*NASA*] (KSC)
MCOW........	Medical College of Wisconsin
MCoW........	Wayside [*Minute Man National Historical Park*], Concord, MA [*Library symbol Library of Congress*] (LCLS)
MCOY........	Military Citizen of the Year (DNAB)
MCP...........	Bear Stearns Companies, Inc. [*AMEX symbol*] (SAG)
MCP...........	Bear Sterns 5.50%'MRK'CHIPS' [*AMEX symbol*] (TTSB)
MCP...........	Macapa [*Brazil*] [*Airport symbol*] (OAG)
MCP...........	Macrophage-Capping Protein [*Biochemistry*]
MCP...........	Main Call Process [*Telecommunications*] (TEL)
MCP...........	Main Condensate Pump [*Navy*] (CAAL)
MCP...........	Main Coolant Pump (NVT)
MCP...........	Maintenance Control Panel [*Navy*] (CAAL)
MCP...........	Maintenance Control Point (NG)
MCP...........	Malawi Congress Party [*Nyasaland*] [*Political party*] (PPW)
MCP...........	Malayan Communist Party [*Political party*]
MCP...........	Male Chauvinist Pig [*Feminist term*]
MCP...........	Management Control Plan
MCP...........	Manual Control Panel
MCP...........	Manufacturing Change Point
MCP...........	Marcana Petroleum Ltd. [*Vancouver Stock Exchange symbol*]
MCP...........	Marine Corps Capabilities Plan (MCD)
MCP...........	Martinique Communist Party [*Political party*]
MCP...........	Mary Cheney Library, Manchester, CT [*OCLC symbol*] (OCLC)
MCP...........	Massachusetts College of Pharmacy [*Boston*]
MCP...........	Master Change Proposal (KSC)
MCP...........	Master Computer Program [*NASA*] (KSC)
MCP...........	Master Control Program [*Burroughs Corp.*]
M Cp..........	Master of Chiropody
MCP...........	Master of City Planning
MCP...........	Master of City Planning (GAGS)
MCP...........	Master of Community Planning (GAGS)
MCP...........	Master of Community Psychology (PGP)
MCP...........	Master of Counseling Psychology (GAGS)
MCP...........	Materials Control Plan (NASA)
MCP...........	Materiel Command Procedure [*Military*]
MCP...........	Maximum Continuous Power
MCP...........	Measurements Control Procedure (KSC)
MCP...........	Medical College of Pennsylvania
MCP...........	Medical Continuation Pay [*Military*] (AABC)
MCP...........	MEECN [*Minimum Essential Emergency Communications Network*] Communication Plan (MCD)

MCP	Melphalan, Cyclophosphamide, Prednisone [*Antineoplastic drug regimen*]
MCP	Member of the College of Preceptors [*British*]
MCP	Member of the Colonial Parliament [*British*]
MCP	Membrane Cofactor Protein [*Biochemistry*]
MCP	Memory-Centered Processing [*or Processor*] [*System*] [*Computer science*]
MCP	Message Control Program [*Computer science*]
MCP	Metacarpophalangeal [*Anatomy*]
MCP	Meta-Cresol Purple [*Organic chemistry*]
MCP	Metal Case Profile [*Ammunition*]
MCP	Metal Casting Pattern (MSA)
MCP	Meteacarpophalangeal [*Joint*] [*Anatomy*] (DAVI)
MCP	Methyl-Accepting Chemotaxis Proteins [*Biochemistry*]
MCP	Methylchlorophenoxyacetic Acid [*Also, MCPA*] [*Herbicide*]
MCP	Methylcyclopentane [*Organic chemistry*]
MCP	Microchannel Plate [*Computer science*]
MCP	Microcrystalline Polymer [*Plastics technology*]
McP	Micro Photo Division, Bell & Howell Co., Wooster, OH [*Library symbol Library of Congress*] (LCLS)
MCP	Microwave Coupled Plasma [*Spectroscopy*]
MCP	Military Construction Plan
MCP	Military Construction Program (AFIT)
MCP	Militia Career Program [*DoD*]
MCP	Missile Control Panel
MCP	Missile Control Point (NATG)
MCP	Mission Concept Paper (MCD)
MCP	Mission Control Programmer [*NASA*] (KSC)
MCP	Missioneras Catequestas de los Pobres (TOCD)
MCP	Mitotic-Control Protein [*Cytology*] (MAE)
MCP	Moca [*Puerto Rico*] [*Seismograph station code, US Geological Survey*] (SEIS)
MCP	Mode Control Panel
MCP	Model Cities Program
MCP	Monitoring and Control Panel (NASA)
MCP	Monocalcium Phosphate [*Inorganic chemistry*] [*Food additive*]
MCP	Monocyte Chemotactic Protein [*Biochemistry*]
MCP	Monte Capellino [*Italy*] [*Later, ROB*] [*Geomagnetic observatory code*]
MCP	Mouvement Chretien pour la Paix [*Christian Movement for Peace - CMP*] [*Brussels, Belgium*] (EAIO)
MCP	Movimiento Civico Popular [*Panama*] [*Political party*] (EY)
MCP	Multicatalytic Proteinase [*An enzyme*]
MCP	Multichannel Communications Program (IEEE)
MCP	Multicomponent Plasma
MCP	Multiple-Chip Package
MCP	Multiple Comparison Procedure [*Statistics*]
MCP	Multiple Control Program [*Computer science*]
MCP	Municipal Compliance Plan [*Environmental Protection Agency*] (GFGA)
MCP	Mutation as Cellular Process
MCP	Polaroid Corp., Cambridge, MA [*Library symbol Library of Congress*] (LCLS)
MCPA	Member of the Canadian Psychological Association
MCPA	Member of the College of Pathologists Australasia
MCPA	Memory Clock Pulse Amplifier
MCPA	Methylchlorophenoxyacetic Acid [*Also, MCP*] [*Herbicide*]
MCPA	Methylenecyclopropylacetic Acid [*Organic chemistry*]
McPA	Microfilm Corp. of Pennsylvania, Pittsburgh, PA [*Library symbol Library of Congress*] (LCLS)
MCPA	Midwest College Placement Association
MCPAC	Military Construction Programs Advisory Committee (AFM)
MCP/AS	Master Control Program / Advanced System (HGAA)
MC Path	Member of the College of Pathologists [*British*]
MCPBA	Meta-Chloroperoxybenzoic Acid [*Organic chemistry*]
MCPC	Manipulator Controller Power Conditioner (MCD)
MCPC	Musee Canadien de la Photographie Contemporaine [*Canadian Museum of Contemporary Photography - CMCP*]
MCPC	Parks Canada [*Parcs Canada*] Churchill, Manitoba [*Library symbol National Library of Canada*] (NLC)
MCPC	Polaroid Corp. Library, Cambridge, MA [*Library symbol*] [*Library of Congress*] (LCLS)
MCPD	Marine Corps Procurement District
MCPDM	Marine Corps Program Decision Meeting (DOMA)
MCPDP	Meander Channels Plasma Display Panel (IAA)
MCPE	Modular Collective Protection Equipment (RDA)
MCPER	Multiple Critical-Pole Equal-Ripple Rational (MCD)
MCPESCF	Multiconfiguration Paired Excitation Self-Consistent Field [*Physics*]
MCPF	Modular Containerless Processing Facility (SSD)
MCPF	Multichannel Peak Factor (IAA)
MCPG	Media Conversion Program Generator
MCPG	Methycarboxyphenglycine [*Biochemistry*]
MCPH	Metacarpophalangeal [*Anatomy*]
MCPH	Ministry of Concern for Public Health (EA)
McPherson	McPherson, Lee, and Bell's Scotch Session Cases [*A publication*] (DLA)
MCPI	Medical Consumer Price Index (DHSM)
MCPL	Magnetic Circularly Polarized Luminescence [*Spectroscopy*]
MCPL	Members of Congress for Peace through Law [*An association*]
MCPL	Multiple-Cue Probability Learning [*Psychology*]
MCPM	Marine Corps Personnel Manual (SAA)
MCPM	Member of the Confederation of Professional Management [*British*] (DBQ)
MCPM	Moncalcium Phosphate Monohydrate [*Inorganic chemistry*]
MCPO	Master Chief Petty Officer [*Navy*]

MCPO	Military Committee Representative Communication to the Private Office of the NATO Secretary General (NATG)
MCPOC	Master Chief Petty Officer of Command [*Navy*]
MCPOF	Master Chief Petty Officer of the Fleet [*or Force*] (DNAB)
MCPON	Master Chief Petty Officer of the Navy
mCPP	M-Chlorophenylpiperazine [*Organic chemistry*]
MCPP	Mecoprop [*Herbicide*]
MCPPR	Marine Corps Program Progress Report
MCPQ	Municipal Code of the Province of Quebec [*A publication*] (DLA)
MCPR	Maximum Critical Power Ratio [*Nuclear energy*] (NRCH)
MCPR	Minimum Critical Power Ratio [*Nuclear energy*] (NRCH)
MC/PRI	Major Claimant/Priority Rating Indicator (MCD)
MCPS	Major Cost Proposal System (MCD)
MCPS	Mechanical Copyright Protection Society [*British*]
MCPS	Megachips per Second (MCD)
MCPS	Megacycles per Second [*Megahertz*] [*See also MC/S, MCS, MH, MHz*]
MCPS	Member of the Cambridge Philosophical Society (ROG)
MCPS	Member of the College of Physicians and Surgeons [*British*]
MCPS	Military Committee in Permanent Session [*NATO*] (NATG)
MCPS	Mini Core Processing Subsystem (TEL)
MCPS	Missouri Children's Picture Series [*Child development test*] [*Psychology*]
MCPT	Maritime Central Planning Team [*NATO*] (NATG)
MCPTM	Monte Carlo Particle Trajectory Model [*Physics*]
MCPU	Master Controller Processor Unit (MCD)
MCPU	Multiple Central Processing Unit
MCQ	Macquarie Island [*Australia Seismograph station code, US Geological Survey*] (SEIS)
Mcq	Macqueen's Scotch Appeal Cases, House of Lords [*A publication*] (DLA)
MCQ	Memory Call Queue [*Computer science*] (IAA)
MCQ	Multiple Choice Questions (ADA)
MCQC	Musicassette Quality Committee (NTCM)
MCQP	Milk Carton Quality Performing Council (EA)
McQuillin Mun Corp	McQuillin on Municipal Corporations [*A publication*] (DLA)
MCR	Magistrates' Court Reports [*New Zealand*] [*A publication*] (DLA)
MCR	Magnetic Card Reader [*Computer science*]
MCR	Magnetic Character Reader [*Computer science*] (IEEE)
MCR	Magnetic Character Recognition [*Computer science*] (BUR)
MCR	Magnetic Confinement Reactor
MCR	Main Control Room (IEEE)
MCR	Maintenance Control Report
MCR	Management Coaching Relations Test
MCR	Management Control Review (AAGC)
MCR	Manpower Control Report
MCR	Manual Change Request (MSA)
MCR	Manufacturing Change Request
MCR	Marine Corps Representative (SAA)
MCR	Marine Corps Reserve
MCR	Master Change Record
MCR	Master Change Record (AAGC)
MCR	Master Clock Receiver
MCR	Master Control Record System (AABC)
MCR	Master Control Register
MCR	Master Control Relay [*Manufacturing term*]
MCR	Master Control Room (MCD)
MCR	Master Control Routine
MCR	Master of Comparative Religion
M Cr	Master of Criminology
MCR	Matrimonial Causes Rules [*A publication*] (DLA)
MCR	Maximum Combat Readiness [*Military*]
MCR	Maximum Continuous Rating [*Also, MC(S)R*] [*Mechanical engineering*]
MCR	McCloud River Railroad Co. [*AAR code*]
MCR	Medical Corps, General Service [*USNR officer designation*]
MCR	Medical Corps Reserve [*Military*] (DAVI)
MCR	Mediterranean Communications Region [*Air Force*] (MCD)
MCR	Melanocortin Receptor [*Biochemistry*]
MCR	Memory Control Register
MCR	Mercer [*Alaska*] [*Seismograph station code, US Geological Survey Closed*] (SEIS)
MCR	Message Competition Ratio (MAE)
MCR	Metabolic Clearance Rate
MCR	Methodists for Church Renewal
MCR	Metronome-Conditioned Relaxation
MCR	MFS Charter Income Tr [*NYSE symbol*] (TTSB)
MCR	MFS Charter Income Trust [*NYSE symbol*] (SPSG)
McR	Micrecord Sales Corp., Chicago, IL [*Library symbol Library of Congress*] (LCLS)
MCR	Micro
MCR	Microcarbon Residue [*Petroleum analysis*]
MCR	Micrographic Catalog Retrieval
MCR	Micron Industries Ltd. [*Vancouver Stock Exchange symbol*]
MCR	Military Characteristics Requirement (MCD)
MCR	Military Command Region (MCD)
MCR	Military Compact Reactor
MCR	Mine Clearing Roller [*Military*] (INF)
MCR	Minimum Cell Rate [*Telecommunications*] (ACRL)
MCR	Minuteman Change Request [*Air Force*] (IAA)
MCR	Missed Contact Rate (CAAL)
MCR	Missile Clock Receiver
MCR	Missile Computer Room
MCR	Mission Control Room [*Space Flight Operations Facility, NASA*]
MCR	Mission Control Routine [*NASA*]

MCR............	Mobile Control Room (DEN)
MCR............	Mobilization Contracting Requirement (AFIT)
MCR............	Modified Community Rating
MCR............	Monacair-Agusta [Monaco] [ICAO designator] (FAAC)
MCR............	Montreal Condensed Reports [A publication] (DLA)
MCR............	Mother-Child Relationship [Psychology]
MCR............	Multichannel Receiver
MCR............	Multi-Contact Relay (IAA)
MCR............	Multispectral Cloud Radiometer (MCD)
MCR............	Radcliffe College, Cambridge, MA [Library symbol Library of Congress] (LCLS)
MCR............	University of Minnesota Technical College, Crookston, MN [OCLC symbol] (OCLC)
MCRA.........	Member of the College of Radiologists Australasia
MCRA.........	Mitomycin C Resistance Protein A
McRae........	McRae Industries, Inc. [Associated Press] (SAG)
MCR-Ar.......	Radcliffe College, Archives, Cambridge, MA [Library symbol Library of Congress] (LCLS)
MCRB.........	Magnetic Compass Record Book
MCRB.........	Market Compilation and Research Bureau, Inc. [North Hollywood, CA] [Information service or system] (IID)
MCRB.........	Military Cost Review Board (MCD)
MCRB.........	Motor Carrier Rate Bureau
MCRBBS.....	Marine Corps Reserve Bulletin Board System (DOMA)
MCRBIO......	Microbiology
MCRBLGY....	Microbiology
M Cr C........	Madras Criminal Cases [A publication] (DLA)
MCRC........	Marine Corps Recruiting Command
MCRC........	Marketing Communications Research Center [Later, CMC]
MCRC........	Master Component Rework Capability (MCD)
McRC.........	Microfilm Recording Co., Weston, ON, Canada [Library symbol Library of Congress] (LCLS)
MCRD........	Marine Corps Recruit Depot
MCRD........	Marine Corps Requirements Document (MCD)
MCRDAC.....	Marine Corps Research, Development, and Acquisition Command [Quantico, VA] (GRD)
MCRDEP......	Marine Corps Recruit Depot
MCRDT.......	Microdata
McRe.........	Micrecord Sales Corp., Lombard, IL [Library symbol] [Library of Congress] (LCLS)
MCRE.........	Mother-Child Relationship Evaluation [Psychology]
MCREGIS....	Motor Carrier Regulation Information System [BTS] (TAG)
MCREL........	Mid-Continent Regional Educational Laboratory [Aurora, CO] [Department of Education]
MCRELCTRNC...	Microelectronic
MCREP........	Military Committee Representative [to the North Atlantic Council] (AABC)
MCRF.........	Master Cross-Reference File
MCRFCH.....	Microfiche
MCRH........	Main Control Room Habitability [Nuclear energy] (NRCH)
MCRHS.......	Main Control Room Habitability System [Nuclear energy] (NRCH)
MCRHS.......	Mid-Continent Railway Historical Society (EA)
MCRI..........	Cambridge Research Institute, Inc., Cambridge, MA [Library symbol Library of Congress] (LCLS)
MCRI	Marine Craft Radio Installation
MCRI	Microcirculation Research Institute [Texas A & M University] [Research center] (RCD)
MCRI	Monarch Casino & Resort [NASDAQ symbol] (SAG)
MCRIB........	Naval Communications Improvement Review Board (DNAB)
MCrim........	Master of Criminology (GAGS)
MCRL.........	Mapping and Charting Research Laboratory [Ohio State University] (MCD)
MCRL.........	Marine Corrosion Research Laboratory [Navy] (PDAA)
MCRL.........	Master Component Repair List
MCRL.........	Master Cross-Reference List
MCRL.........	Material Cross-Reference List (MCD)
MCRL.........	Micrel, Inc. [NASDAQ symbol] (SAG)
MCRML.......	Midcontinental Regional Medical Library Program [University of Nebraska] [Library network] (IID)
MCRMLP	Midcontinental Regional Medical Library Program [McGoogan Library of Medicine] [Information service or system] (IID)
MCRN.........	Macaroni
MCRN.........	Micronics Computers [NASDAQ symbol] (SPSG)
MCRN.........	Moscow City Relay Network
MCR (NZ).....	Magistrates' Court Reports (New Zealand) [A publication] (ILCA)
MCROA.......	Marine Corps Reserve Officers Association (EA)
MCROC.......	Marine Corps Recruit Option Center
MCROSCPY...	Microscopy
MCRP.........	Maritime Coal, Railway & Power Co. Ltd. [AAR code]
MCRP.........	Master of City and Regional Planning (GAGS)
MCRR.........	Machine Check Recording and Recovery [Computer science]
MCRR.........	Maine Central Road Railroad (MHDB)
MCRR.........	Marine Corps Reserve Ribbon
MCRR.........	[The] Monongahela Connecting Railroad Co. [AAR code]
MCRRCMPTR...	Microcomputer
MCRRD.......	Marine Corps Reserve/Recruitment District
MCRS.........	Maintenance Computing and Recording System
MCRS.........	Marine Corps Recruiting Station
MCRS.........	Material Condition Reporting System
MCRS.........	Micrographic Catalog Retrieval System
MCRS.........	Micros Systems, Inc. [NASDAQ symbol] (NQ)
MCR-S.........	Radcliffe College, Schlesinger Library, Cambridge, MA [Library symbol Library of Congress] (LCLS)
MCRSC.......	Marine Corps Reserve Support Center
MCRSS.......	Marine Corps Recruiting Substation
MCRT.........	Mean Cell Retention Time (GNE)
MCRT.........	Multichannel Rotary Transformer [Electronics]
MCRU.........	Medical Care Research Unit [University of Sheffield] [British] (ECON)
MCRU.........	Mobile Control and Reporting Unit (IAA)
MCRV.........	Manned Command/Reconnaissance Vehicle
Mcrvsn.......	Microvision, Inc. [Associated Press] (SAG)
MCRWV	Microwave (AAG)
MCRWV	Microwave
MCS............	Harvard University, Monographic Cataloging Support Service, Cambridge, MA [OCLC symbol] (OCLC)
MCS............	MacCartney Clan Society (EA)
MCS............	Machine Cancel Society (EA)
MCS............	Macmillan's Commercial Series [A publication]
MCS............	Madras Civil Service [British]
MCS............	Magnetic Card Selecting (DNAB)
MCS............	Magnetic Coupling System (MCD)
MCS............	Main Compution System
MCS............	Main Control Station [Nuclear energy] (IAA)
MCS............	Maintenance and Checkout Station [NASA] (NASA)
MCS............	Maintenance Control Section [DCE]
MCS............	Maintenance Control System [NASA] (IAA)
MCS............	Maintenance Cost System (MCD)
MCS............	Major Component Schedule (AAG)
MCS............	Management Control System (MCD)
MCS............	Maneuver Control System [Computer science]
MCS............	Manpower Consultative Service [Canada] (PDAA)
MCS............	Manufacturing and Consulting Services (PCM)
MCS............	Manufacturing Control System
MCS............	Mapping Camera System
MCS............	[The] Marcus Corp. [NYSE symbol] (SPSG)
MCS............	Marcus Island [Japan] [Seismograph station code, US Geological Survey] (SEIS)
MCS............	Marine Casualty Statistics (OA)
MCS............	Marine Conservation Society [British]
MCS............	Marine Cooks and Stewards Union
MCS............	Marine Corps School [Quantico, VA]
MCS............	Marine Corps Station
MCS............	Marine Corps Supply Activity [Obsolete]
MCS............	Maritime Communication Subsystem [INTELSAT/INMARSAT]
MCS............	Mass Casualty Supplement [Military]
MCS............	Mast Check System
MCS............	Mast Connection System (SAA)
MCS............	Master Circuit System
MCS............	Master Composite Specification (MCD)
MCS............	Master Control Set (IAA)
MCS............	Master Control Station (NRCH)
MCS............	Master Control System [or Subsystem]
MCS............	Master of Clinical Science (PGP)
MCS............	Master of Commercial Science
MCS............	Master of Communication Studies (PGP)
MCS............	Master of Computer Science (WGA)
MCS............	Master of Computer Science (GAGS)
MCS............	Mathematical Code System
MCS............	Maximal Compatible Set (PDAA)
MCS............	McChip Resources, Inc. [Toronto Stock Exchange symbol]
MCS............	Mean Crew Size (MCD)
MCS............	Measurements Calibration System (KSC)
MCS............	Mechanical Control System [Aviation]
MCS............	Mechanized Characteristics Screening
MCS............	Medical Computer Services (IEEE)
MCS............	Medical Consultant Staff [Social Security Administration] (OICC)
MCS............	Medical Corps, Special Service [USNR officer designation]
MCS............	Medium Close Shot [Photography] (ADA)
MCS............	Megacycles per Second [Megahertz] [See also MCPS, MH, MHz]
MCS............	Meridian Control Signal
MCS............	Mesocaval Shunt [Medicine] (DMAA)
MCS............	Mesoscale Convective System [Meteorology]
MCS............	Message Control Supervisor [Computer science] (MHDI)
MCS............	Message Control System [Burroughs Corp.] [Computer science] (BUR)
MCS............	Meter-Candle Second
MCS............	Method of Constant Stimuli [Psychophysics]
MCS............	Metropolitan Communications Squadron [British military] (DMA)
MCS............	Microclimatic Cooling System [Army] (DWSG)
MCS............	Microcomputer System
MCS............	Microculture and Sensitivity [Microbiology] (DAVI)
McS............	Micromation Systems, Inc., Feasterville, PA [Library symbol Library of Congress] (LCLS)
MCS............	Microprocessor Communications System (MCD)
MCS............	Microprogram Certification System (MHDB)
MCS............	Microsoft Consulting Services (CDE)
MCS............	Microwave Carrier Supply
MCS............	Microwave Communication System
MCS............	Milestone Car Society (EA)
MC's...........	Military Characteristics [Technical specification document for nuclear bombs and warheads]
MCS............	Military Communications Stations
MCS............	Miller Communications Systems Ltd. [Telecommunications service] (TSSD)
MCS............	Mine Countermeasures Ship [Navy symbol]
MCS............	Mine Countermeasure Support [Obsolete Military]
MCS............	Mini-Computer Systems Inc. (NITA)
MCS............	Mini Conference System (PDAA)
MCS............	Minimal Cut Set [Engineering]
MCS............	Minimum Chi-Square

MCS............. Missile Calibration Station
MCS-F.......... Missile Checkout Set (AAG)
MCS............. Missile Checkout Station
MCS............. Missile Commit Sequence (AAG)
MCS............. Missile Compensating System
MCS............. Missile Controller Set
MCS............. Missile Control System
MCS............. Missionary Sisters of the Sacred Side (TOCD)
MCS............. Mission Control Segment (SSD)
MCS............. Mitochondrial Capsule Selenoprotein [*Biochemistry*]
MCS............. Mixture Control Solenoid [*Automotive engineering*]
MCS............. Mobile Calibration Station (IAA)
MCS............. Mobile Checkout Station (AAG)
MCS............. Mobile Communications System (MCD)
MCS............. Mobile Computer System
MCS............. Model-Controlled System [*NASA*]
MCS............. Modular Composition System [*Diskettes*]
MCS............. Modular Computer System (IEEE)
MCS............. Modulation-Controlled Synchronization (IAA)
MCS............. Monitor and Control Software [*FAA*] (TAG)
MCS............. Monitor and Control Subsystem
MCS.......:..... Monitor and Control System [*Deep Space Instrumentation Facility, NASA*]
MCS............. Monte Carlo Simulation [*Computer science*] (IAA)
MCS............. Monte Caseros [*Argentina*] [*Airport symbol*] (AD)
MCS............. Motor Circuit Switch
MCS............. Movements Control Section [*British military*] (DMA)
MCS............. Multi-Channel Communications Software (NITA)
MCS............. Multichannel Communication System (IAA)
MCS............. Multichannel Scaling [*Mode*]
MCS............. Multichannel Seismology [*Geophysics*]
MCS............. Multichannel Switch (IAA)
MCS............. Multichannel System (IAA)
MCS............. Multi-Console System (NITA)
MCS............. Multidirectional Category System
MCS............. Multimedia Conference Service [*Telecommunications*] (CDE)
MCS............. Multiple Character Set (CMD)
MCS............. Multiple Chemical Sensitivities [*Medicine*]
MCS............. Multiple Column Selector (IAA)
MCS............. Multiple Compression Shear (OA)
MCSG........... Multiple Computer System
MCS............. Multiple Console Support [*Fujitsu Ltd.*] [*Computer science*] (MCD)
MCS............. Multiplexer Computer Systems (MCD)
MCS............. Multiprogrammed Computer System (IEEE)
MCS............. Multipurpose Communications and Signaling
MCS............. Multivendor Customer Service [*Computer science*] (CDE)
MCS............. Music Construction Set [*Computer program designed by Will Harvey and published by Electronic Arts*]
MCS............. Myocardial Contractile State [*Cardiology*] (MAE)
MCS............. Residential Model Conservation Standard [*Pacific Northwest Electric Power and Conservation Planning Council*] [*Portland, OR*] (EGAO)
MCSA.......... Marble Collectors Society of America (EA)
MCSA.......... Marine Corps Supply Activity [*Obsolete*] (NVT)
MCSA.......... Meritorious Civilian Service Award
MCSA.......... Methuen's Commercial Series [*A publication*]
MCSA.......... Metropolitan Church Schoolmasters' Association [*A union*] [*British*]
MCSA.......... Microcomputer Software Association - of ADAPSO [*Association of Data Processing Service Organizations*] (EA)
MCSA.......... Midwest Collegiate Sailing Association
MCSA.......... Military Construction Supply Agency [*Later, Defense Construction Supply Center*]
MCSA.......... Minimal Cross-Sectional Area [*Radiology*] (DAVI)
MCSA.......... Moloney Cell Surface Antigen [*Medicine*] (DMAA)
MCSA.......... Moscow, Camden & San Augustine Railroad [*AAR code*]
MCSA.......... Motor Carrier Safety Act of 1984 [*FHWA*] (TAG)
MCSA.......... Multichannel Spectrum Analyzer [*Instrumentation*]
MCS-A........ Multi-Functional Communications System - Asynchronous (HGAA)
MCSA.......... Smithsonian Institution, Astrophysical Observatory, Cambridge, MA [*Library symbol Library of Congress*] (LCLS)
MCSAP........ Motor Carrier Safety Assistance Program [*Department of Transportation*]
MCSB.......... Motor Carriers Service Bureau
MCSC.......... Magdalen College School Cadets [*British military*] (DMA)
MCSC.......... Marine Corps Supply Center
MC Sc.......... Master of Commercial Science
MC Sc.......... Master of Computer Science (PGP)
MCSC.......... Materiel Category Structure Code [*Military*]
MCSC.......... Medical College of South Carolina
MCSC.......... Miami Computer Supply Corp. [*NASDAQ symbol*] (SAG)
MCSC.......... Model Codes Standardization Council [*Defunct*]
MCSC.......... Movement Control Sub-Committee [*IATA*] (DS)
MCSCF........ Multiconfigurational Self-Consistent Field [*Chemical physics*]
MCSCF........ Multiconfiguration Self-Consistent Field [*Physical chemistry*]
MCS/CHS..... Maneuver Control System / Common Hardware System [*Computer science*]
MCSD .... Marine Corps Supply Depot (MUGU)
MCSDS........ Marlowe-Crowne Social Desirability Scale [*Medicine*] (DMAA)
MC Se......... Master of Commercial Service
MCSE.......... Master of Computer Science and Engineering (GAGS)
MCSE.......... Minimum Critical Size of Ecosystem [*Project*]
MCSEE........ Member of the Canadian Society of Electrical Engineers (DI)
M-CSF......... Macrophage-Colony Stimulating Factor [*Biochemistry*]
MCSF.......... Marine Corps Security Force (DNAB)
MCSF.......... Mobile Cryptologic Support Facility (DOMA)

MCSG .... Mildly Context-Sensitive Grammar [*Artificial intelligence*]
MCSH .... Maryville College of the Sacred Heart [*Missouri*]
MC Shp....... MC Shipping, Inc. [*Associated Press*] (SAG)
MCSI.......... Mark Solutions [*NASDAQ symbol*] (TTSB)
MCSI.......... Mark Solutions, Inc. [*NASDAQ symbol*] (SAG)
MCSI.......... Member of the Construction Surveyors' Institute [*British*] (DBQ)
MCSJM........ Congregation of Missionary Catechists of the Sacred Heart of Jesus and Mary (TOCD)
MCSL.......... Management Control Systems List [*DoD*]
MCSL.......... Marine Corps Stock [*or Supply*] Lists
MCSM.......... Master of Construction Science/Management (PGP)
MCSMAW .... Marine Corps Shoulder-Launched Multipurpose Assault Weapon (MCD)
MCSO .... Marine Corps Special Orders (SAA)
MCSOII........ Multiple-Cause, Systems-Oriented Incident Investigation [*Engineering*]
MCSP.......... Maintenance Control and Statistics Process [*Telecommunications*] (TEL)
MCSP.......... Member of the Chartered Society of Physiotherapists [*British*]
MCSP.......... Mission Completion Success Probability (MCD)
MCSP.......... Multiple Conductor, Shielded, Pressure-Resistant [*Cable*]
McSPI......... Multicenter Study of Perioperative Ischemia
MCSR .... Material Condition Status Report [*Military*]
MC(S)R........ Maximum Continuous (Service) Rating [*Also, MCR*] [*Mechanical engineering*]
MCSR .... Motor Carrier Safety Regulations [*Department of Transportation*]
MCSRP .... Management Control Systems Research Project (SAA)
MCSS .... Marine Climatological Summaries Scheme [*World Meteorological Organization*] [*United Nations*] (DUND)
MCSS.......... Mechanical Circulatory Support System
MCSS.......... Microscopic Camera Subsystem (KSC)
MCSS.......... Military Clothing Sales Store
MCSS.......... Military Communications Satellite System
MCSS.......... Mine Countermeasure Support Ship [*Military*] (PDAA)
MCSS.......... Missile Checkout System Selector
MCSS.......... Monitor and Control Subsystem [*Deep Space Instrumentation Facility, NASA*]
MCSSCCJM.... Missionary Catechists of the Sacred Hearts of Jesus and Mary (TOCD)
MCSSD .... Mobile Combat Service Support Detachment (DOMA)
MCSSG .... Military Committee Special Study Group [*NATO*] (NATG)
MCSSQT ...... Modified Combat System Ship Qualification Trial [*Navy*] (CAAL)
MCSST........ Multichannel Sea Surface Temperature [*Algorithms for oceanography*]
MCSST........ Multi-Channel Sea-Surface Temperature [*Marine science*] (OSRA)
MCSST........ Multi-Channel SST [*Sea Surface Temperature*] (USDC)
MC/ST........ Magnetic Card Selectric Typewriter (NITA)
MCST.......... Magnetic Card "Selectric" Typewriter [*IBM Corp.*]
MCST.......... Member of the College of Speech Therapists [*British*]
MCST.......... Ministerial Committee on Science and Technology [*South Africa*]
MCSTB........ Motor Carriers Service Tariff Bureau
MCSTSC ...... Military Communications System Technical Standards Committee [*Army*] (AABC)
MCSU .... Management Consultation Services Unit [*LIMRA*]
MCSU .... Maximum Card Study Unit (EA)
MCSW .... Mining Club of the Southwest (EA)
MCSW .... Motor Circuit Switch (MSA)
MCSWG ...... Multinational Command Systems Working Group (NATG)
MCSX.......... Managed Care Solutions [*NQS*] (TTSB)
MCSX.......... Managed Care Solutions, Inc. [*NASDAQ symbol*] (SAG)
MCSY.......... Medic Computer Systems [*NASDAQ symbol*] (TTSB)
MCSY.......... Medic Computer Systems, Inc. [*NASDAQ symbol*] (SAG)
MCSYSCOM... Marine Corps System Command (DOMA)
MCT........... Magnetically-Coupled Transformer (IAA)
MCT........... Magnetic Card and Tape Unit (IAA)
MCT........... Magnetic Character Typewriter (PDAA)
MCT........... Magnetic Compass Table (DNAB)
MCT........... Magnetic Core Tape
MCT........... Magnetic Core Tester
MCT........... Main Central Thrust [*Geophysics*]
MCT........... Main Control Tank (MSA)
MCT........... Mainstream Corporation Tax
MCT........... Managed Change Technique [*Management*]
MCT........... Manifold Charge Temperature [*Automotive engineering*]
MCT........... MANPRINT [*Manpower and Personnel Integration*] Coordination Team [*Army*]
MCT........... Mark Centers Trust [*NYSE symbol*] (SPSG)
MCT........... Mass Culturing Technique [*Microbiology*]
MCT........... Master of Christian Training
MCT........... Mathematical Cuneiform Texts [*A publication*] (BJA)
MCT........... Maximum Climb Thrust (NASA)
MCT........... Maximum Continuous Thrust [*Aviation*]
MCT........... Maxwell Color Triangle
MCT........... Mean Cell [*or Corpuscular*] Thickness [*Hematology*]
MCT........... Mean Cell [*or Corpuscular*] Threshold [*Hematology*] (MAE)
MCT........... Mean Circulation Time [*Medicine*]
MCT........... Mean Corpuscular Thickness [*Hematology*] (CPH)
MCT........... Mean Corrective-Maintenance Time (MCD)
MCT........... Mean Correct Time
MCT........... Mechanical Comprehension Test
MCT........... Medium-Chain Triglyceride [*Biochemistry*]
MCT........... Medullary Cancer of the Thyroid [*Medicine*]
MCT........... Medullary Carcinoma of the Thyroid [*Medicine*] (AAMN)
MCT........... Medullary Collecting Tubules [*Anatomy*]
MCT........... Memory Cycle Time [*Computer science*] (MCD)

MCT	Mercury Cadmium Telluride [*Photodetector*]
MCT	Message Control Task [*Computer science*]
MCT	Metabolic Control Theory [*Biochemistry*]
MCT	Meta-Chlorotoluene [*Organic chemistry*]
MCT	Metric Color Tag [*Computer science*] (PCM)
MCT	Metrizamide Computed Tomography
MCT	Micro Component Technology Inc. (NITA)
MCT	Microstat Development Corp. [*Vancouver Stock Exchange symbol*]
MCT	Microwave Ceramic Triode
MCT	Mid-Cycle Test [*Army training*] (INF)
MCT	Military Command Technology (AAG)
MCT	Minimum Competency Test [*Education*]
MCT	Minimum Connecting Time [*Travel industry*]
MCT	Minnesota Clerical Test
MCT	Missile Compensating Tank
MCT	Mission Control Table (MCD)
MCT	Mobile Communication Terminal
MCT	Mobile Communication Terminal
MCT	Mobile Contact Teams [*Military*] (AABC)
MCT	Mode Coupling Theory [*Physics*]
MCT	Modified Clinical Technique [*Medicine*]
MCT	Moment to Change Trim (DS)
MCT	Monochlorotriazine [*Organic chemistry*]
MCT	Mouse Colon Tumor [*Pathology*]
MCT	Movable Core Transformer [*Nuclear energy*]
MCT	Movement Control Team [*Air Force*] (AFM)
MCT	Mucociliary Transport [*Physiology*]
MCT	Multicell Test (MCD)
MCT	Multiple Compressed Tablet [*Pharmacy*]
MCT	Multistrip Cesium Thrustor
MCT	Muscat [*Oman*] [*Airport symbol*] (OAG)
MCT	United States Department of Transportation, Technical Information Center, Cambridge, MA [*Library symbol Library of Congress*] (LCLS)
MCTA	Metropolitan Commuter Transportation Authority [*Greater New York City*] [*Later, Metropolitan Transportation Authority*]
MCTA	Motor Carriers Tariff Association
MCTA	Motor Carriers Traffic Association
MCTA	Multiple-Cycle Transient Analysis [*Chemistry*]
MCTAS	Military/Commercial Transport Aircraft Simulation (PDAA)
MCTB	Motor Carriers Tariff Bureau (EA)
MCTC	Maritime Cargo Transportation Conference [*of MTRB*]
MCTC	Metrizamide Computed Tomography Cisternography [*Medicine*] (DMAA)
MCTC	Movimiento Campesino Tupaj Catari [*Bolivia*] [*Political party*] (PPW)
MCTD	Medium Capacity Bomb with Temporary Delay Fuse [*British military*] (DMA)
MCTD	Mixed Connective Tissue Disease [*Medicine*]
MCTFIST	Marine Corps Tank Full-Crew Interactive Simulator Trainer
MCTFL	Minnesota Council on the Teaching of Foreign Languages (EDAC)
MCTG	Model Change Training Guide
MCTH	MedCath, Inc. [*NASDAQ symbol*] (SAG)
MCTI	Metal Cutting Tool Institute (EA)
MCTI	Micro Component Tech [*NASDAQ symbol*] (TTSB)
MCTI	Micro Component Technology, Inc. [*NASDAQ symbol*] (SAG)
MCTL	Mediterranean Contingency Target List (MCD)
MCTL	Microtel Franchise&Development [*NASDAQ symbol*] (TTSB)
MCTL	Microtel Franchise & Development Corp. [*NASDAQ symbol*] (NQ)
MCTL	Microtel International, Inc. [*NASDAQ symbol*] (SAG)
MCTL	Militarily Critical Technology List [*DoD*]
MCTLA	Motor Car Traders' Licensing Authority [*Victoria, Australia*]
MCTNS	Manportable Cannon Thermal Night Sight (MCD)
MCTP	Missile Control Test Panel
MCTR	Mackinac Transportation Co. [*AAR code*]
MCTR	Message Center
MCTRAP	Mechanized Customer Trouble Report Analysis Plan [*Telecommunications*] (TEL)
MCTS	Master Central Timing System [*NASA*]
MCTS	Ministerial Correspondence Tracking System [*Australia*]
MCTS	Motor Carriers Tariff Service (EA)
MCTSA	Military Clothing and Textile Supply Agency [*Merged with Defense Supply Agency*] [*Army*]
MCTSE	Marine Corps Test Support Element (MCD)
MCTSSA	Marine Corps Tactical Systems and Support Activity [*Camp Pendleton, CA*] (GRD)
MCTT	Metal-Ceramic Transmitting Tube
MCTV	Man-Carrying Test Vehicle (MCD)
MCTV	Manhattan Cable TV, Inc. [*New York, NY*] [*Telecommunications*] (TSSD)
MCU	Machine Control Unit
MCU	Machine Tool Control Unit (IAA)
MCU	Magma Copper Co. [*NYSE symbol*] (SPSG)
MCU	Magnetic Card Unit [*Computer science*] (IAA)
MCU	Main Control Unit (IAA)
MCU	Maintenance Control Unit [*Computer science*]
MCU	Major Crime Unit [*Elite police squad on television series "Crime Story"*]
MCU	Malaria Control Unit [*Army World War II*]
MCU	Management Control Unit (PDAA)
MCU	Manual Control Unit
MCU	Marble Collectors Unlimited (EA)
MCU	Master Clock Unit
MCU	Master Control Unit
MCU	Maximum Care Unit [*Medicine*]
MCU	Measurement Control Unit (IAA)

MCU	Median Control Unit (WDAA)
MCU	Mediterranean Coordination Unit (GNE)
MCU	Medium Close Up [*A photograph or motion picture sequence taken from a relatively short distance*]
MCU	Memory Control Unit
MCU	Message Construction Unit
MCU	Microcomputer Control Unit
MCU	Microcontroller Unit (CDE)
MCU	Micro-Control Unit (NITA)
MCU	Microprocessor Control Unit
MCU	Microprogram Control Unit (NITA)
MCU	Microprogrammed Control Unit [*Navy*]
mcU	Microunit
MCU	Micturating Cystourethrography [*Medicine*] (DMAA)
MCU	Millicurie [*Also, mC, mCI*] (IAA)
MCU	Miniature Command Unit
MCU	Minicomputer Unit (IAA)
MCU	Mission Control Unit (MCD)
MCU	Mobile Care Unit [*Emergency medicine*] (DAVI)
MCU	Modern Churchmen's Union [*British*]
MCU	Modular Concept Unit (DA)
MCU	Monte Cristo Peak [*Utah*] [*Seismograph station code, US Geological Survey*] (SEIS)
MCU	Mosquito Conversion Unit [*British military*] (DMA)
MCU	Mountain Commando Units (CINC)
MCU	Multicoupler Unit [*Antenna*] [*Telecommunications*] (TEL)
MCU	Multiplexer Control Unit
MCU	Multipoint Control Unit [*Telecommunications*]
MCU	Multiprocessor Communications Unit
MCU	Multi-System Communications Unit (NITA)
MCU	Rochester, NY [*Location identifier FAA*] (FAAL)
MCUAF	Multi-Corp. [*NASDAQ symbol*] (TTSB)
MCUAF	Multi-Corp, Inc. [*NASDAQ symbol*] (SAG)
MCUB	Marine Corps Uniform Board [*Washington, DC*] (EGAO)
MCUG	Military Computers Users Group
MCUIS	Master Control and User Interface Software Subsystem [*Space Flight Operations Facility, NASA*]
MCUL	Missile Compartment, Upper Level
MCUMP	Multidisciplinary Center for Urban and Minority Problems [*Florida State University*] [*Research center Defunct*] (RCD)
MCUPA	Medical Committee Under the Poisons Act [*Australia*]
MCurrSt	Master of Curriculum Studies
MCurrStud	Master of Curriculum Studies
MCUSR	Memory Control Unit Special Register [*Computer science*] (MHDB)
MCV	Magnetic Cushion Vehicle (IEEE)
MCV	Manifold Control Valve [*Automotive engineering*]
MCV	Manufacturing Council of Victoria [*Australia*]
MCV	Maritime Commission, Victory Ship
MCV	Mean Cell [*or Corpuscular*] Volume [*Hematology*]
MCV	Mean Clinical Value (AAMN)
MCV	Mean Corpuscular Volume [*Physiology*]
MCV	Measles-Containing Vaccine
MCV	Mechanised Combat Vehicle [*British military*] (DMA)
MCV	Medical Center of Virginia [*University of Virginia*]
MCV	Mercury [*Nevada*] [*Seismograph station code, US Geological Survey*] (SEIS)
MCV	Mesabi Community College, Virginia, MN [*OCLC symbol*] (OCLC)
MCV	Mesoscale Convectively-Generated Vortices [*Marine science*] (OSRA)
MCV	Mesoscale Convectively-Generated Vortices (USDC)
MCV	Method of Composition Velocity [*Physical chemistry*]
MCV	Microbial Check Valve (PDAA)
MCV	Molluscum Contagiosum Virus
MCV	Movable Closure Valve (NRCH)
MCV	Muerto Canyon Virus [*Hantavirus strain*]
MCVD	Modified Chemical Vapor Deposition [*Telecommunications*]
McVey Dig	McVey's Ohio Digest [*A publication*] (DLA)
MCVF	Multichannel Voice Frequency [*Telecommunications*]
MCVFT	Multichannel Voice Frequency Telegraphy [*Telecommunications*] (TEL)
MC-V(G)	Medical Officers (Qualified for General Detail) [*USNR designation*]
MCVG	Memory Character Vector Generator
MCVP	Materials Control and Verification Program [*NASA*] (NASA)
MCVS	Management and Cost Visibility System (SSD)
MC-V(S)	Medical Officers (Qualified for Specialist Duties) [*USNR designation*]
MCW	Central Missouri State University, Warrensburg, MO [*OCLC symbol*] (OCLC)
MCW	Mallinckrodt Chemical Works [*Later, Mallinckrodt, Inc.*]
MCW	Mason City [*Iowa*] [*Airport symbol*] (OAG)
MCW	Mason City, IA [*Location identifier FAA*] (FAAL)
MCW	McDonalds Corp. [*NYSE symbol*] (SAG)
MCW	Medical Corps, Women's Reserve [*USNR officer designation*]
MCW	Memory Card Writer [*Telecommunications*] (TEL)
MCW	Metal Casement Window [*Technical drawings*]
MCW	Metro-Cammell Weymaua Ltd. [*British*] (DCTA)
MCW	Mills, Clarence W., Laurel MD [*STAC*]
MCW	Modified Continuous Wave [*Telecommunications*] (IAA)
MCW	Modulated Carrier Wave [*Telecommunications*] (IAA)
MCW	Modulated Continuous Wave [*Radio signal transmission*]
MCW	Mount Constitution [*Washington*] [*Seismograph station code, US Geological Survey*] (SEIS)
MCW	Weston School of Theology, Cambridge, MA [*Library symbol Library of Congress*] (LCLS)
MCWA	Malaria Control in War Areas [*Later, Centers for Disease Control*]
MCWA	Mid Continent Wildcatters Association [*Defunct*] (EA)

MCWCS	Ministerial Conference of West and Central African States on Maritime Transportation [*See also CMEAOC*] [*Abidjan, Ivory Coast*] (EAIO)
McWhrtr	McWhorter Technologies, Inc. [*Associated Press*] (SAG)
McWillie	McWillie's Reports [*73-76 Mississippi*] [*A publication*] (DLA)
MCWM........	Military Committee Working Memorandum (NATG)
MCWR	Marine Corps Women's Reserve
MCWU	Military Committee of Western European Union (NATG)
MCX............	Marine Corps Exchange
MCX............	MC Shipping [*AMEX symbol*] (TTSB)
MCX............	MC Shipping, Inc. [*AMEX symbol*] (SPSG)
MCX............	Michelin Capital Ltd. [*Toronto Stock Exchange symbol*]
MCX............	Minimum-Cost Expediting
MCX............	Monticello, IN [*Location identifier FAA*] (FAAL)
MCXD	Magnetic Circular X-Ray Dichroism [*Light polarization*]
MCXM........	Marine Corps Exchange Manual (SAA)
MCXO	Microprocessor-Controlled Crystal Oscillator [*Hughes Aircraft Co.*] (ECON)
MCXSERV	Marine Corps Exchange Service Branch (DNAB)
MCY............	Machinery (IAA)
MCY............	Maroochydore [*Australia Airport symbol*] (OAG)
MCY............	Mercury General [*NYSE symbol*] (SAG)
MCY............	Mercury, NV [*Location identifier FAA*] (FAAL)
MCY............	Mount Calvery Resources Ltd. [*Vancouver Stock Exchange symbol*]
M/CYL	Master Cylinder [*Automotive engineering*]
MCZ............	Maceio [*Brazil*] [*Airport symbol*] (OAG)
MCZ............	Magnetic Czochralski Process [*Crystallization*]
MCZ............	McDonald' Corp. 8.35% 'QUIDS' [*NYSE symbol*] (TTSB)
MCZ............	McDonalds Corp. [*NYSE symbol*] (SAG)
MCZ............	Museum of Comparative Zoology [*Harvard University*] [*Research center*]
MCZ............	Williamston, NC [*Location identifier FAA*] (FAAL)
MCZDO	Multicenter Zero Differential Overlap [*Physics*]
MCZNE........	Minimum When Control Zone Effective (FAAC)
MD............	Air Madagascar [*ICAO designator*] (AD)
MD............	Application for Writ of Mandamus Dismissed for Want of Jurisdiction [*Legal term*] (DLA)
MD............	Delalande [*France*] [*Research code symbol*]
MD............	Doctor of Medicine (PGP)
MD............	Doctor of Medicine (WDMC)
MD............	La Maison-Dieu [*Paris*] [*A publication*] (BJA)
MD............	Machine Dried Paper (DGA)
MD............	Macro Data (IAA)
MD............	Macro Directory [*Computer science*] (IAA)
MD............	Macular Degeneration [*Ophthalmology*]
Md............	Madinhae (BJA)
MD............	Madres de los Desamparados [*Mothers of the Helpless*] [*Roman Catholic religious order*]
MD............	Magnesium Deficiency [*Medicine*] (DMAA)
MD............	Magnetic Deflection [*Cathode-ray tube*] (DEN)
MD............	Magnetic Disk [*Computer science*] (BUR)
MD............	Magnetic Drum
MD............	Main Deck [*Naval engineering*]
MD............	Main Droite [*With the Right Hand*] [*Music*]
MD............	Main Drum (CET)
MD............	Main Duct
MD............	Maintainability Demonstration (MCD)
M/D............	Maintenance/Development [*Effort ratio*]
MD............	Maintenance Documentation [*Bell System*] (IAA)
MD............	Maintenance Dose [*Medicine*]
M-D............	Maiz Dulce [*Race of maize*]
MD............	Make Directory [*Computer science*]
MD............	Malate Dehydrogenase [*Also, MDH*] [*An enzyme*]
MD............	Male Treated with DOC [*Deoxycorticosterone*]
MD............	Malfunction Detection (NASA)
MD............	Malic Dehydrogenase [*An enzyme*] (MAE)
MD............	Management Data (MCD)
MD............	Management Directive
MD............	Management Division [*Environmental Protection Agency*] (GFGA)
MD............	Managing Director
MD............	Managment Domain [*Telecommunications*] (OSI)
M/D............	Man Day
MD............	Manic-Depressive
MD............	Mano Destra [*With the Right Hand*] [*Music*]
MD............	Mantoux Diameter (MAE)
MD............	Manual Damper (OA)
MD............	Manual Data
MD............	Manual Direct (NASA)
MD............	Manual Disconnect (MCD)
MD............	Manu Dextra [*With the Right Hand*] [*Latin*]
MD............	Map Distance (ADA)
MD............	Marchand [*Merchant, Trader*] [*French*]
MD............	Marek's Disease [*Avian pathology*]
MD............	Marine Detachment
MD............	Market Day [*British*]
MD............	Marque Deposee [*Trademark*]
MD............	Married
MD............	Maryland [*Postal code*]
MD............	Maryland Reports [*A publication*] (DLA)
Md............	Maryland State Library, Annapolis, MD [*Library symbol Library of Congress*] (LCLS)
MD............	Master Diagram (MCD)
MD............	Master Dimension (NASA)
MD............	Master Directory [*NASA Information service or system*] (IID)
MD............	Master's Decisions (Patents) [*A publication*] (DLA)
MD............	Match Dissolve [*Cinematography*] (WDMC)
MD............	Materiel Developer [*Army*]
MD............	Maternal Deprivation (MAE)
MD............	Matrimonio Duxit [*Led into Matrimony*] [*Latin*] (ROG)
MD............	Maturity Date [*Banking*]
MD............	Maximum Degree Allowed to Fit
MD............	Maximum Demand (IAA)
MD............	Maximum Design Meter
MD............	McDonnell Douglas [*NYSE symbol*] (TTSB)
MD............	McDonnell Douglas Corp. [*NYSE symbol*] (SPSG)
MD............	Mean Deviation
MD............	Measured Depth [*Diamonds*]
MD............	Measured Discard [*Nuclear energy*] (NRCH)
MD............	Measured Drilling [*Diamonds*]
MD............	Mechanical Diode [*Mechanical power transmission*]
Md............	Median
MD............	Medical Department [*Army*]
MD............	Medical Discharge [*from military service*]
MD............	Medicinae Doctor [*Doctor of Medicine*] [*Latin*]
M/D............	Medicines/Drugs
MD............	Mediodorsal [*Anatomy*]
MD............	Medium Dosage [*Pharmacology*] (MAE)
MD............	Medium Duty
MD............	Megadalton
MD............	Memorandum of Deposit [*Business term*]
MD............	Memory Data Register (DNAB)
MD............	Memory Decrement (MHDB)
Md............	Mendelevium [*Preferred form, but also see Mv*] [*Chemical element*]
MD............	Meniere's Disease [*Medicine*] (DMAA)
MD............	Mentally Deficient
MD............	Mentally Disabled (OICC)
md............	Mercedarious Descalzos (TOCD)
MD............	Mesiodistal [*Dentistry*]
Md............	Mesoderm [*Botany*]
MD............	Message Data
MD............	Message Digest (ACRL)
MD............	Message-Dropping [*Military*]
MD............	Messages per Day
MD............	Mess Deck [*Naval*]
MD............	Metal Deactivator
MD............	Metal Dome [*Watchmaking*] (ROG)
MD............	Metals Disintegrating
MD............	Metaphors Dictionary [*A publication*]
MD............	Meteorology Department [*Navy*]
M/D............	Meters per Day
MD............	Methyldichloroarsine [*Poison gas*]
MD............	Methyldopa [*Also, AMD*] [*Antihypertensive compound*]
MD............	Metropolitan District [*British*]
MD............	Microalloy Diffused
MD............	Microdot (KSC)
MD............	Microdot
MD............	Microsoft DoubleSpace [*Computer science*] (PCM)
MD............	Microwave Desorber [*Instrumentation*]
MD............	Middle Deltoid [*Myology*]
MD............	Middle Distillate [*Fuel technology*]
MD............	Middle District (DLA)
MD............	Middle Door [*Theater*]
MD............	Middle Dutch [*Language, etc.*]
MD............	Midnight Dumping (MHDW)
MD............	Migrant with English Language Difficulty
MD............	Mildly Diabetic
MD............	Military District [*Former USSR*] (NATG)
mD............	Millidarcy
MD............	Millwall Dock [*British*]
MD............	Mine Depot [*Naval*]
MD............	Mine Disposal
MD............	Mini Disk [*Audio/video technology*]
MD............	Minimum Dosage [*Medicine*]
MD............	Minute Difference
MD............	Miscellaneous Direct (MCD)
MD............	Miscellaneous Document
MD............	Miss Distance [*Military*]
MD............	Missile Division (AAG)
MD............	Missile Driver
MD............	Mission Day
MD............	Mission Dependent
MD............	Mission Deviation (MCD)
MD............	Mission Director [*NASA*] (KSC)
MD............	Mitral Disease [*Medicine*]
MD............	Mixed Diet (DMAA)
MD............	Mobile Depot [*Air Force*] (MCD)
MD............	Mode [*Grammar*] (ROG)
MD............	Moderate Dose [*Medicine*]
MD............	Moderately Differentiated
MD............	Modification Document (MCD)
MD............	Modified Design [*Cordite*] [*British military*] (DMA)
MD............	Modular Design
M-D............	Modulation-Demodulation (HGAA)
M/D............	Modulator-Demodulator [*Telecommunications*] (CET)
MD............	Modulators [*JETDS nomenclature*] [*Military*] (CET)
MD............	Molecular Diameter
MD............	Molecular Dynamics
MD............	Money Down
MD............	Monitor Displays [*Computer science*] (BUR)
MD............	Monocular Deprivation [*Optics*]

MD............ Monroe Doctrine
MD............ Months after Date [*or Month's Date*] [*Business term*]
MD............ Mood [*Grammar*] (ROG)
MD............ More Dicto [*As Directed*] [*Pharmacy*]
M/D............ Mother/Daughter [*Apartment*] (BARN)
MD............ Mothers of the Helpless (TOCD)
MD............ Motor Direct
MD............ Motor Drive
MD............ Movement Directive
MD............ Movement Disorder (MAE)
MD............ Multidimensional
MD............ Multidomain [*Grains in rocks*] [*Geophysics*]
MD............ Multinomial Distribution [*Statistics*]
MD............ Multiple Dialyzer [*Chemical analysis*]
MD............ Multiple Dissemination
MD............ Multiply-Divide (IAA)
MD............ Multipurpose Display (MCD)
MD............ Municipal Docks Railway of the Jacksonville Port Authority [*AAR code*]
MD............ Muscular Dystrophy [*Medicine*]
MD............ Musicae Doctor [*Doctor of Music*] (ROG)
MD............ Musical Director
MD............ Music Director (NTCM)
MD............ Myocardial Damage [*Cardiology*] (MAE)
MD............ Myocardial Disease [*Cardiology*]
MD............ Myotonic Dystrophy [*See also MyMD*] [*Medicine*]
MDA............ Magen David Adom [*Israel's Red Cross Service*]
MDA............ Magic Dealers Association [*Later, IMDA*]
MDA............ Magnetic Deflection Amplifier
MDA............ Main Distribution Assembly (NASA)
MDA............ Main Distribution Assembly
MDA............ Maintainability Design Approach
MDA............ Maintenance Data Analysis (MCD)
MDA............ Maintenance Depot Assistance [*Air Force*] (AFM)
MDA............ Maintenance Design Approach
MDA............ Malfunction Detector Analyzer (PDAA)
MDA............ Malondialdehyde [*Biochemistry*]
MDA............ Management Development Adviser (AIE)
MDA............ Mandarian Airlines [*ICAO designator*] (FAAC)
MDA............ Manic-Depressive Association (EA)
MDA............ Manual Dilation of the Anus (AAMN)
MDA............ Manufacturing Defect Analyzer [*Automotive engineering*]
MDA............ MAPCO, Inc. [*NYSE symbol*] (SPSG)
MDA............ Marking Device Association (EA)
MD A............ Maryland Appellate Reports [*A publication*] (DLA)
MDA............ Master Design Award
MDA............ Master Diversion Airfield (AIA)
MDA............ Master Drawings Association (EA)
MDA............ Master Dyers Association (EA)
MDA............ Master of Development Adminstration (PGP)
MDA............ Master of Dramatic Art
MDA............ Material Data Administrator (DNAB)
MDA............ Material Disposal Authority
MDA............ Maximum Deficit Amount [*Office of Management and Budget*] (GFGA)
MDA............ Maximum Demographic Appeal [*Objective of commercial television programming*]
MDA............ Maximum Detachable Activity [*Nuclear energy*] (NUCP)
MDA............ McDonnell-Designed Assembly
MDA............ McDonnell-Douglas Aerospace (GAVI)
MDA............ Measurement, Decision, and Actuation [*Computer science*]
MDA............ Mechanically Despun Antenna (KSC)
MDA............ Mechanized Directory Assistance [*Telecommunications*] (TEL)
MDA............ Menthanediamine [*Organic chemistry*]
MDA............ Mento-Dextra Anterior [*A fetal position*] [*Obstetrics*]
MDA............ Mesocyclone Detection Algorithm (USDC)
MDA............ Mesocyclone Detection Algorithm [*Marine science*] (OSRA)
MDA............ Metal Deactivator [*Fuel technology*]
MDA............ Meteoroid Detector-Analyzer
MDA............ Methyl Diamphetamine
MDA............ Methyldopamine [*Biochemistry*]
MDA............ Methylenedianiline [*Also, DAPM, DDM*] [*Organic chemistry*]
MDA............ Methylenedioxyamphetamine [*Biochemistry*]
MDA............ Microprocessor Development Aid
MDA............ Middeck Assembly (MCD)
MDA............ Milestone Decision Authority
MDA............ Military Damage Assessment
MDA............ Millinery Distributors Association [*British*] (BI)
MDA............ Minimum Decision Altitude (SAA)
MDA............ Minimum Descent Altitude [*Aviation*]
MDA............ Minimum Detectable Activity [*Nuclear energy*] (NRCH)
MDA............ Minimum Detectable Amount [*of radiation*] [*Analytical chemistry*]
MDA............ Minnesota Department of Agriculture, St. Paul, MN [*OCLC symbol*] (OCLC)
MDA............ Miscellaneous Defense Activities (AAGC)
MDA............ Missilized Driver Assembly (MCD)
MDA............ Mission Doctors Association (EA)
MDA............ Mixed Distribution Analysis [*Mathematics*]
MDA............ Mobile Depot Activities [*Air Force*]
MDA............ Modified Diffusion Approximation (PDAA)
MDA............ Monoalythic Design Automation (IAA)
MDA............ Monochrome Display Adapter [*Computer technology*]
MDA............ Monodehydroascorbate [*Biochemistry*]
MDA............ Mothers for Decency in Action [*Group opposing sex education in schools*]

MDA............ Motorcycling Doctors Association (EA)
MDA............ Motor Discriminative Acuity [*Psychology*]
MDA............ Motor Drive Amplifier
MDA............ Mouvement pour la Democratie en Algerie [*Algeria*] [*Political party*] (MENA)
MDA............ Multidimensional Access
MDA............ Multidimensional Analysis (IEEE)
MDA............ Multidimensional Array
MDA............ Multidocking Adapter (IAA)
MDA............ Multiple Digit Absorbing [*Telecommunications*] (TEL)
MDA............ Multiple Discriminant Analysis [*Statistics*]
MDA............ Multiple Docking Adapter [*Apollo*] [*NASA*]
MDA............ Multivariant Discriminant Analysis [*Medicine*] (DMAA)
MDA............ Muscular Dystrophy Association (EA)
MDA............ Museum Documentation Association [*British*] (DBA)
MDA............ Music Distributors Association (EA)
MDA............ Mutual Defense Agency (NADA)
MDA............ Mutual Defense Assistance
MDA............ San Antonio, TX [*Location identifier FAA*] (FAAL)
MdAA............ Hall of Records Commission, Annapolis, MD [*Library symbol Library of Congress*] (LCLS)
MDAA............ Muscular Dystrophy Associations of America (EA)
MDAA............ Mutual Defense Assistance Act
MdAAC............ Public Library of Annapolis and Anne Arundel County, Annapolis, MD [*Library symbol Library of Congress*] (LCLS)
MDaAr............ Danvers Archival Center, Peabody Institute, Danvers, MA [*Library symbol Library of Congress*] (LCLS)
MDAC............ McDonnell Douglas Aircraft Corp.
MDAC............ Medical Data Acquisition System
MDAC............ Methyl(ciethylamino)coumarin [*Organic chemistry*]
MDAC............ Multi-Channel Digital Audio Codec [*Intraplex, Inc.*]
MDAC............ Multiplying Digital-to-Analog Converter [*Computer science*] (IEEE)
MDAC............ Muscular Dystrophy Association of Canada
MDAC............ Mutual Defense Assistance, General Area of China
MdaCad............ ModaCad, Inc. [*Associated Press*] (SAG)
MDACC............ Management of Defense Acquisition Contracts Course [*DoD*] (RDA)
MdaCd............ ModaCad, Inc. [*Associated Press*] (SAG)
MDAD............ Mineral Dust Airway Disease [*Medicine*] (DMAA)
MDAD............ Monitoring and Data Analysis Division [*Environmental Protection Agency*] (GFGA)
MD Admin Code... Code of Maryland Regulations [*A publication*] (DLA)
MdAEPA............ United States Environmental Protection Agency, Annapolis Field Office, AnnapolisScience Center, Annapolis, MD [*Library symbol Library of Congress*] (LCLS)
MDAERP............ Medical Devices Adverse Experience Reporting Project
MDAF............ Memoires. Delegation Archeologique Francaise [*A publication*] (BJA)
MDAFWP............ Motor-Driven Auxiliary Feedwater Pump (IEEE)
MDAGT............ Mutual Defense Assistance, Greece and Turkey
MDAH............ M. D. Anderson Hospital and Tumor Institute [*Houston, TX*]
MDAI............ Multidisciplinary Accident Investigation [*National Accident Sampling System*]
MDAIKP............ Mutual Defense Assistance, Iran, Republic of Korea, and Philippines
MDAIS............ McDonnell Douglas Aerospace Information Services [*Formerly, MCATO*] (MCD)
MD Ala............ United States District Court for the Middle District of Alabama (DLA)
MDAN............ Angelina, Cotui [*Dominican Republic*] [*ICAO location identifier*] (ICLI)
MdAN............ United States Naval Academy, Annapolis, MD [*Library symbol Library of Congress*] (LCLS)
MDANAA............ Mutual Defense Assistance, North Atlantic Area
MD & D............ Montagu, Deacon, and De Gex's English Bankruptcy Reports [*1840-44*] [*A publication*] (DLA)
MD & DeG... Montagu, Deacon, and De Gex's English Bankruptcy Reports [*1840-44*] [*A publication*] (DLA)
MD & S............ Macon, Dublin & Savannah Railroad (IIA)
MdANE............ United States Navy, Naval Ship Research and Development Laboratory, Annapolis, MD [*Library symbol Library of Congress*] (LCLS)
MD Ann Code... Annotated Code of Maryland [*A publication*] (DLA)
MDANSW............ Muscular Dystrophy Association of New South Wales [*Australia*]
MDAO............ Mutual Defense Assistance Office (DOMA)
MDAP............ Machover Draw-A-Person Test [*Psychology*]
MDAP............ Major Defense Acquisition Program (AAGC)
MDAP............ Materiel Deployment/Acceptance Plan (MCD)
MDAP............ Morphological Dictionary Adaptor Program (PDAA)
MDAP............ Mutual Defense Assistance Pact [*or Program*]
MDaP............ Peabody Institute, Danvers, MA [*Library symbol Library of Congress*] (LCLS)
MdApg............ United States Army, Technical Library, Aberdeen Proving Ground, Aberdeen, MD [*Library symbol Library of Congress*] (LCLS)
MdApgC............ United States Army, Chemical Systems Laboratory, Aberdeen Proving Ground, Aberdeen, MD [*Library symbol Library of Congress*] (LCLS)
MdApgO............ United States Army, Ordnance School, Aberdeen Proving Ground, Aberdeen, MD [*Library symbol Library of Congress*] (LCLS)
MdApgOB ... United States Army, Ordnance Board, Aberdeen Proving Ground, Aberdeen, MD [*Library symbol Library of Congress*] (LCLS)
MdApgP............ United States Army, Post Library, Aberdeen Proving Ground, Aberdeen, MD [*Library symbol Library of Congress*] (LCLS)
MD App ... Maryland Appellate Reports [*A publication*] (DLA)
MDAR............ Malfunction Detection Analysis and Recording [*NASA*] (KSC)
MDAR............ Minimum Daily Adult Requirement
MDAR............ Mobile Detection Assessment Response System [*USA*]
MDar 1 .... Dartmouth Public Library, Darmouth, MA [*Library symbol*] [*Library of Congress*] (LCLS)

MDarHi........ Old Dartmouth Historical Society, Dartmouth, MA [*Library symbol Library of Congress*] (LCLS)
MDARS........ Military Damage Assessment Reporting System (MCD)
MDARS........ Mobile Detection, Assessment, and Response System
MDAS.......... Manpower Data Automated System (DNAB)
MDAS.......... Medical Data Acquisition System (KSC)
MDAS.......... Meteorological Data Acquisition System [*NASA*] (KSC)
MDAS.......... Meteorological Data Acquisition System
MDAS.......... Miniature Data Acquisition System
MDAS.......... Mission Data Acquisition System [*NASA*] (NASA)
MDAS.......... Modular Data Acquisition System (NITA)
MdAS.......... Saint John's College, Annapolis, MD [*Library symbol Library of Congress*] (LCLS)
MDASA........ Muscular Dystrophy Association of South Australia
MDAVG........ Mission Duration, Average (MCD)
M (Day)........ Mobilization Day [*Military*] (AFM)
M (Days)..... Metrication Days [*Sponsored by the Metrication Board to educate merchants and public on metric system*] [*British*]
MDB............ Bren Del Win Centennial Library, Deloraine, Manitoba [*Library symbol National Library of Canada*] (NLC)
MDB............ Enoch Pratt Free Library, Baltimore, MD [*OCLC symbol*] (OCLC)
MDB............ Maintenance Data Bank
MDB............ Management Database (ACRL)
MDB............ Master Database (MCD)
MDB............ Master Distribution Box [*Missile system*] [*Army*]
MDB............ Material Distribution Board (DNAB)
MDB............ MDI Mobile Data International, Inc. [*Toronto Stock Exchange symbol Vancouver Stock Exchange symbol*]
MDB............ Memory-Data Bank
MDB............ Mersey Dock Board [*British*] (DAS)
MDB............ Message Database (MCD)
MDB............ Methylenedioxybenzene [*Organic chemistry*]
MDB............ Metrology Data Bank [*GIDEP*]
MDB............ Minimally Distinct Border [*Color perception*]
MDB............ Mission Data Book [*NASA*] (NASA)
MDB............ Mission Display Board Assembly [*Space Flight Operations Facility, NASA*]
MDB............ Mitglied des Deutschen Bundestages [*Member of the German Federal Parliament*]
MDB............ Mojave Desert Block [*Geology*]
MDB............ Movimento Democratico Brasileiro [*Brazilian Democratic Movement*] [*Political party*] (PPW)
MDB............ Multilateral Development Bank
MDB............ Multiple Drive Block
MDB............ Multiplex Data Bus [*Computer science*] (MCD)
MDB............ Mutual Defense Board [*US-Philippines*] (CINC)
MDB............ Professional Bancorp [*AMEX symbol*] (SPSG)
MdBAE........ United States Army, Corps of Engineers, Baltimore, MD [*Library symbol Library of Congress*] (LCLS)
MdBaH........ Harford Community College, Bel Air, MD [*Library symbol Library of Congress*] (LCLS)
MdBaHC...... Harford County Library, Bel Air, MD [*Library symbol Library of Congress*] (LCLS)
MdBAS........ Armco, Inc., Advanced Materials Division, Research Library, Baltimore, MD [*Library symbol Library of Congress*] (LCLS)
MdBASI....... Allied Signal, Inc., Baltimore, MD [*Library symbol*] [*Library of Congress*] (LCLS)
MdBASI-C... Allied Signal, Inc., Communications Diviaion, Baltimore, MD [*Library symbol*] [*Library of Congress*] (LCLS)
MdBB.......... Baltimore Bar Library, Baltimore, MD [*Library symbol Library of Congress*] (LCLS)
MdBb.......... United States Naval Training Center, Bainbridge, MD [*Library symbol Library of Congress*] (LCLS)
MdBBC........ Baltimore Conference, Inc., United Methodist Historical Society, Baltimore, MD [*Library symbol Library of Congress*] (LCLS)
MdBBJC...... Community College of Baltimore, Baltimore, MD [*Library symbol Library of Congress*] (LCLS)
MdBbN........ US Naval Training Center, Bainbridge, MD [*Library symbol*] [*Library of Congress*] (LCLS)
MdBBO .... [*The*] Baltimore & Ohio Railroad Co., Employees' Library, Baltimore, MD [*Library symbol Library of Congress Obsolete*] (LCLS)
MdBBR .... Bendix Corp., Baltimore, MD [*Library symbol Library of Congress*] (LCLS)
MdBBS........ Bon Secours Medical Library, Baltimore, MD [*Library symbol Library of Congress*] (LCLS)
MdBCC........ Catonsville Community College, Learning Resources Division, Baltimore, MD [*Library symbol Library of Congress*] (LCLS)
MdBCH........ Baltimore City Court House, Baltimore, MD [*Library symbol Library of Congress*] (LCLS)
MdBCIC....... Counter Intelligence Center Corps School, Fort Holabird, Baltimore, MD [*Library symbol Library of Congress*] (LCLS)
MdBCP........ Baltimore County Public Library, Towson, MD [*Library symbol Library of Congress*] (LCLS)
MdBCPM...... Chemical Pigment Co., Metals Division, Baltimore, MD [*Library symbol Library of Congress*] (LCLS)
MdBCS........ Coppin State College, Baltimore, MD [*Library symbol Library of Congress*] (LCLS)
MDBDF .... March of Dimes Birth Defects Foundation (EA)
MdBDH .... United States Department of Health and Human Services, Health Care Financing Administration, Office of Research Demonstrations and Statistics, Baltimore, MD [*Library symbol Library of Congress*] (LCLS)
MdBE.......... Enoch Pratt Free Library, Baltimore, MD [*Library symbol Library of Congress*] (LCLS)

MdBeCA...... Concepts Analysis Agency, Bethesda, MD [*Library symbol Library of Congress*] (LCLS)
MdBeCI....... Congressional Information Service, Bethesda, MD [*Library symbol Library of Congress*] (LCLS)
MdBEs .... Essex Community College, Baltimore, MD [*Library symbol Library of Congress*] (LCLS)
MdBeU........ Uniform Services University of the Health Sciences, Bethesda, MD [*Library symbol Library of Congress*] (LCLS)
MDBF.......... Mean Distance between Failures [*Quality control*] (MCD)
MdBFamP.... Family Planning Training Institute, Baltimore, MD [*Library symbol Library of Congress*] (LCLS)
MdBFH........ Fort Holabird Post Library, Baltimore, MD [*Library symbol Library of Congress*] (LCLS)
MdBFM........ Grand Lodge of Ancient Free and Accepted Masons of Maryland, Masonic Library, Baltimore, MD [*Library symbol Library of Congress*] (LCLS)
MdBFr.......... Friends Meeting, Stony Run, Baltimore, MD [*Library symbol Library of Congress*] (LCLS)
MdBG.......... Goucher College, Baltimore, MD [*Library symbol Library of Congress*] (LCLS)
MdBGM-E.... Martin Marietta Corp., Science and Technology Library, Baltimore, MD [*Library symbol Library of Congress*] (LCLS)
MdBGM-N.... Martin Marietta Corp., RIAS Library, Baltimore, MD [*Library symbol Library of Congress*] (LCLS)
MdBH.......... Baltimore City Hospitals, Doctors' Library, Baltimore, MD [*Library symbol Library of Congress*] (LCLS)
MDBH.......... Barahona [*Dominican Republic*] [*ICAO location identifier*] (ICLI)
MdBHC........ Baltimore Hebrew College, Baltimore, MD [*Library symbol Library of Congress*] (LCLS)
MDBI .... Mean Days between Injuries
MDBI .... Murray Darling Basin Initiative [*Australia*]
MdBJ.......... Johns Hopkins University, Baltimore, MD [*Library symbol Library of Congress*] (LCLS)
MdBJ-A........ Johns Hopkins University, Applied Physics Laboratory, Silver Spring, MD [*Library symbol Library of Congress*] (LCLS)
MdBJ-AIS ... Johns Hopkins University, School of Advanced International Studies, Washington, DC [*Library symbol Library of Congress*] (LCLS)
MdBJ-C........ Johns Hopkins university, Alan Chesney Medical Archives, Baltimore, MD [*Library symbol*] [*Library of Congress*] (LCLS)
MdBJ-G........ Johns Hopkins University, John Work Garrett Library, Baltimore, MD [*Library symbol Library of Congress*] (LCLS)
MdBJ-H........ Johns Hopkins University, School of Hygiene and Public Health, Maternal and Child Health-Population Dynamics Library, Baltimore, MD [*Library symbol Library of Congress*] (LCLS)
MdBJ-P........ Johns Hopkins University, George Peabody Library, Baltimore, MD [*Library symbol Library of Congress*] (LCLS)
MdBJ-W....... Johns Hopkins University, William H. Welch Medical Library, Baltimore, MD [*Library symbol Library of Congress*] (LCLS)
MDBK.......... Madin-Darby Bovine Kidney [*Cell line*]
MDBK.......... Medford Savings Bank [*NASDAQ symbol*] (SAG)
MdbkIns...... Meadowbrook Insurance Group [*Associated Press*] (SAG)
MDBL.......... Maintainability Data Baseline (MCD)
MDBL.......... Maintainability Design Baseline (MCD)
MdBLH........ Lutheran Hospital of Maryland, Baltimore, MD [*Library symbol Library of Congress*] (LCLS)
MdBLN........ Loyola - Notre Dame Library, Inc., Baltimore, MD [*Library symbol Library of Congress*] (LCLS)
MdBM.......... Medical and Chirurgical Faculty of the State of Maryland, Baltimore, MD [*Library symbol Library of Congress*] (LCLS)
MDBM.......... MULTICS Data Base Manager
MdBMA........ Baltimore Museum of Art, Baltimore, MD [*Library symbol Library of Congress*] (LCLS)
MdBMC........ Morgan State College [*Later, Morgan State University*] Baltimore, MD [*Library symbol Library of Congress*] (LCLS)
MDBMC........ Murray-Darling Basin Ministerial Council [*Australia*]
MdBMH........ Mercy Hospital, McGlannan Memorial Library, Baltimore, MD [*Library symbol Library of Congress*] (LCLS)
MdBMH-N.... Mercy Hospital, School of Nursing, Baltimore, MD [*Library symbol Library of Congress*] (LCLS)
MdBMI........ Maryland Institute, School of Fine and Applied Arts, Baltimore, MD [*Library symbol Library of Congress*] (LCLS)
MDBMS .... Medical Data Base Management System (SSD)
MdBMStA .... Mount Saint Agnes College, Baltimore, MD [*Library symbol Library of Congress*] (LCLS)
MdBNA........ National Institute on Aging, Gerontology Research Center, Baltimore, MD [*Library symbol Library of Congress*] (LCLS)
MdBo.......... Bowie State College, Bowie, MD [*Library symbol Library of Congress*] (LCLS)
MdBOAS ...... United States Social Security Administration, Baltimore, MD [*Library symbol Library of Congress*] (LCLS)
MdBP.......... Enoch Pratt Free Library, George Peabody Branch, Baltimore, MD [*Library symbol Library of Congress*] (LCLS)
MDBP .... Mechanically Deboned Broiler Product [*Food technology*]
MDBPB........ Microsoft DoubleSpace BIOS [*Basic Input-Output System*] Parameter Block [*Computer science*] (PCM)
MdBPC........ Peabody Conservatory of Music, Baltimore, MD [*Library symbol Library of Congress*] (LCLS)
MdBPH........ United States Public Health Service Hospital, Baltimore, MD [*Library symbol Library of Congress*] (LCLS)
MdBPM........ Peale Museum, Baltimore, MD [*Library symbol Library of Congress*] (LCLS)
MdBR.......... Research Institute for Advanced Study, Baltimore, MD [*Library symbol Library of Congress*] (LCLS)
MdBREC .... Engineering Society of Baltimore, Baltimore, MD [*Library symbol Library of Congress*] (LCLS)

MdbrkRe......	Meadowbrook Rehabilitation Group [Associated Press] (SAG)
MDBS	Micro Data Base Systems (NITA)
MDBS	Mobile Database Station [Telecommunications] (ACRL)
MdBS...........	Saint Mary's Seminary and University, Baltimore, MD [Library symbol Library of Congress] (LCLS)
MdBSAr	Sulpician Archives Baltimore, Baltimore, MD [Library symbol Library of Congress] (LCLS)
MdBSet........	Seton Psychiatric Institute, Baltimore, MD [Library symbol Library of Congress] (LCLS)
MdBSH	Sinai Hospital, Staff Library, Baltimore, MD [Library symbol Library of Congress] (LCLS)
MdBS-P	Saint Mary's Seminary and University, Philosophy Library, Baltimore, MD [Library symbol Library of Congress] (LCLS)
MdBSP........	Sheppard-Pratt Hospital, Baltimore, MD [Library symbol Library of Congress] (LCLS)
MdBSp.........	Sunpapers Library, Baltimore, MD [Library symbol Library of Congress] (LCLS)
MdBSt..........	Saint Agnes Hospital, Baltimore, MD [Library symbol Library of Congress] (LCLS)
MdBSTS.......	Space Telescope Science Institute, Baltimore, MD [Library symbol] [Library of Congress] (LCLS)
MdBSup.......	Sunpapers Library, Baltimore, MD [Library symbol] [Library of Congress] (LCLS)
MdBT	Towson State University, Baltimore, MD [Library symbol Library of Congress] (LCLS)
MdBU...........	University of Baltimore, Baltimore, MD [Library symbol Library of Congress] (LCLS)
MdBU-L	University of Baltimore, Law Library, Baltimore, MD [Library symbol Library of Congress] (LCLS)
MdBUM........	Union Memorial Hospital, Finney Medical Library, Baltimore, MD [Library symbol Library of Congress] (LCLS)
MdBV...........	United States Veterans Administration Hospital, Baltimore, MD [Library symbol Library of Congress] (LCLS)
MdBWA........	Walters Art Gallery, Baltimore, MD [Library symbol Library of Congress] (LCLS)
MdBWe........	Westinghouse Defense and Space Center, Baltimore, MD [Library symbol Library of Congress] (LCLS)
MdBWesE	Western Electric Co., Inc., Baltimore, MD [Library symbol Library of Congress] (LCLS)
MdBwiNA.....	National Aeronautics and Space Administration, Scientific and Technical Information Facility, Baltimore/Washington International Airport, MD [Library symbol] [Library of Congress] (LCLS)
MDC............	Atlantic Aero, Inc. [ICAO designator] (FAAC)
MDC............	Boston, MA [Location identifier FAA] (FAAL)
MDC............	Dow Chemical Co., Library, Midland, MI [OCLC symbol] (OCLC)
MDC............	Machinability Data Center [Computerized search service] [Metcut Research Associates, Inc.] (IID)
MDC............	Machinery Diagnostic Consultant [Software program]
MDC............	Main Display Console
MDC............	Maintenance Data Center (MCD)
MDC............	Maintenance Data Collection [Military] (AFM)
MDC............	Maintenance Dependency Chart (IEEE)
MDC............	Major Diagnostic Categories [Medicine]
MDC............	Management Development Course (MCD)
MDC............	Manhattan Drug Co.
MDC............	Manual Direction Center [Air Force] (AFM)
MDC............	Master Data Center, Inc. [Information service or system] (IID)
MDC............	Master Direction Center [Air Force]
MDC............	Materials Dissemination Center [Institute for Development of Educational Activities]
MDC............	Maximum Deductible Contribution [Superannuation]
MDC............	Maximum Dependable Capacity [Nuclear energy] (NRCH)
MDC............	Maximum Depth of Colonization [Botany]
MDC............	McDonnell Douglas Corp. (MCD)
MDC............	MDC Corp. [Associated Press] (SAG)
MDC............	M.D.C Hldgs [NYSE symbol] (TTSB)
MDC............	MDC Holdings, Inc. [NYSE symbol] (SPSG)
MDC............	Mead Data Central, Inc. [Dayton, OH]
MDC............	Mead Data Control (NITA)
MDC............	Mechanically Deboned Chicken [Food technology]
MDC............	Memory Disk Controller
MDC............	Menado [Indonesia] [Airport symbol] (OAG)
MDC............	Message Display Console (MCD)
MDC............	Message Distribution Center (NATG)
MDC............	Meteorological Data Collection
MDC............	Metropolitan District Commission
MDC............	Metropolitan District Council [British]
MDC............	Microprocessor Development Center [American Microsystems Inc. US] (NITA)
MDC............	Mild Detonating Cord (MCD)
MDC............	Military District Commander
MDC............	Million Dollar Contract [File] [Military]
MDC............	Milwaukee-Downer College [Later, Lawrence University] [Wisconsin]
MDC............	Mine Dispatch Control
MDC............	Miniature Detonating Cord (MCD)
MDC............	Minimobile Data Center [Military]
MDC............	Minimum Detectable Concentration [Analytical chemistry]
MDC............	Ministere des Communications [Department of Communications] [Canada]
MDC............	Missile Development Center [Air Force]
MDC............	Missile Direction Center
MDC............	Mission Director Center [NASA] (KSC)
MDC............	Mission Duty Cycle [NASA] (KSC)
MDC............	Mobile Defence Corps [British military] (DMA)
MDC............	Mobile Distress Call

MDC............	Modification Detection Code (HGAA)
MDC............	Mongoloid Development Council [Later, NADS] (EA)
MDC............	Montreal Diocesan College [Quebec]
MDC............	Montreux Development [Vancouver Stock Exchange symbol]
MDC............	More Developed Country
MDC............	Mother's Day Council (EA)
MDC............	Motor Dealers' Council [New South Wales, Australia]
MDC............	Motor Direct-Connected
MDC............	Mount Diablo [California] [Seismograph station code, US Geological Survey] (SEIS)
MDC............	Movement Designator Code
MDC............	Muller Data Corp. [Information service or system] (IID)
MDC............	Multidimensional Concept [Combines robotic combat vehicles with other unmanned systems] [Army] (RDA)
MDC............	Multilayer Dielectric Coating
MDC............	Multiple Delay Code (AFIT)
MDC............	Multiple Device Controller
MDC............	Multiple Drone Control (MCD)
MDC............	Multistage Depressed Collector (IAA)
MDCA	Main Distribution Control Assembly (MCD)
MDCA	Manufacturing Design Change Analysis
MDCA	Mind Development and Control Association (EA)
MDCAC	Manufacturing Department Change Analysis Commitment (SAA)
MdCam	Dorchester County Public Library, Cambridge, MD [Library symbol Library of Congress] (LCLS)
MdCatSG	Spring Grove State Hospital, Catonsville, MD [Library symbol Library of Congress] (LCLS)
MDCB	Moisture Detector Control Box
MDCC	Master Data Control Console
MDCC	Molecular Devices [NASDAQ symbol] (TTSB)
MDCC	Molecular Devices Corp. [NASDAQ symbol] (SAG)
MDCC	Monaural Detection with Contralateral Cue (PDAA)
MDCD	Meridian Data [NASDAQ symbol] (TTSB)
MDCD	Meridian Data, Inc. [NASDAQ symbol] (SAG)
MdCe	Queen Anne's County Free Library, Centreville, MD [Library symbol Library of Congress] (LCLS)
MDCEF........	Medical-Dental Committee on Evaluation of Fluoridation [Defunct] (EA)
MDCGC	Multidimensional Capillary Gas Chromatography
MD Ch	Maryland Chancery Reports, by Johnson [4 vols.] [A publication] (DLA)
MDCH	MDC Holdings, Inc. (MCD)
MDCH	Middlesex, Duke of Cambridge's Hussars [Military unit] [British]
MD Chan	Maryland Chancery Decisions [A publication] (DLA)
MD Chan Dec....	Maryland Chancery Decisions [A publication] (DLA)
MD Ch D....	Maryland Chancery Decisions [A publication] (DLA)
MD Ch Dec...	Maryland Chancery Decisions [A publication] (DLA)
MdChW........	Washington College, Chestertown, MD [Library symbol Library of Congress] (LCLS)
MDCI	Medical Action Industries [NASDAQ symbol] (TTSB)
MDCI	Medical Action Industries, Inc. [NASDAQ symbol] (NQ)
MDCI	Multidisciplinary Counterintelligence (MCD)
MDCK	Madin-Darby Canine Kidney [Cell line]
MDCL.........	Medical Control [NASDAQ symbol] (SAG)
MDCL.........	MedicalControl Inc [NASDAQ symbol] (TTSB)
MDCLW.......	MedicalControl Wrrt [NASDAQ symbol] (TTSB)
MDCM	Doctor of Medicine and Master of Surgery (DD)
MDCM	Medicinae Doctor Chirurgia Magister [Doctor of Medicine and Master of Surgery]
MDCMA	Melvil Dui Chowder and Marching Association [Later, MDMCA] (EA)
MDCO	Consuelo, San Pedro De Macoris [Dominican Republic] [ICAO location identifier] (ICLI)
MDCO	Marine Drilling [NASDAQ symbol] (TTSB)
MDCO	Marine Drilling Co. [NASDAQ symbol] (NQ)
MdCoA........	Arctec, Inc., Columbia, MD [Library symbol Library of Congress] (LCLS)
MD Code Ann...	Annotated Code of Maryland [A publication] (DLA)
MdCoG........	W. R. Grace & Co., Research Library, Columbia, MD [Library symbol Library of Congress] (LCLS)
MdCoH........	Hittman Associates, Inc., Columbia, MD [Library symbol Library of Congress] (LCLS)
MdConn	Mid-Conn Bank [Associated Press] (SAG)
MD Const.....	Maryland Constitution [A publication] (DLA)
Mdcore	Medicore, Inc. [Associated Press] (SAG)
MdCpM........	United States Bureau of Mines, College Park Research Center, College Park, MD [Library symbol Library of Congress] (LCLS)
MDCPZ	Monodesmethylchlorpromazine [Biochemistry]
MDCR	Cabo Rojo [Dominican Republic] [ICAO location identifier] (ICLI)
MDCR	Maintenance Data Collection Report (MCD)
MDCR	Medcross, Inc. [NASDAQ symbol] (NQ)
MDCR	Miller-Dieker Chromosomal Region [Genetics]
MDCRS	Meteorological Data Collection and Reporting System [FAA] (TAG)
MDCS	Maintenance Data Collection System [or Subsystem] [Navy]
MDCS	Malfunction Display and Control System (MCD)
MDCS	Manufacturing and Distribution Control System
MDCS	Master Data Control System [Computer science] (IAA)
MDCS	Master Digital Command System
MDCS	Material Data Collection System [NASA] (KSC)
MDCS	Metering and Directional Control System
MDCS	Mission Data Collection Sheets (CINC)
MDCS	Mutual Defense Control Staff [Department of State]
MDCS	Santo Domingo [Dominican Republic] [ICAO location identifier] (ICLI)
MDCSC	McDonnell Douglas Computer Systems Co. [Formerly, MICRODATA] (MCD)
MDC/SS	Multiple Drone Control Strike System (MCD)

MD/CSU...... Motor Drive Cassette Support Unit
MDCT.......... Mechanical Draft Cooling Tower [*Nuclear energy*] (NRCH)
MDCT.......... Median Corrective Maintenance Time (MCD)
MDCT.......... Multidimensional Compensatory Task
MdCtr.......... Medical Control [*Associated Press*] (SAG)
MdCu .... Allegany County Library, Cumberland, MD [*Library symbol Library of Congress*] (LCLS)
MDCU .... Magnetic Disk Control Unit
MDCU .... Mobile Dynamic Checkout Unit (AAG)
MdCuAC...... Allegany Community College, Cumberland, MD [*Library symbol Library of Congress*] (LCLS)
MdCvH........ Crownsville State Hospital, Crownsville, MD [*Library symbol Library of Congress*] (LCLS)
MDCZ.......... Constanza [*Dominican Republic*] [*ICAO location identifier*] (ICLI)
MdD............ Caroline County Public Library, Denton, MD [*Library symbol Library of Congress*] (LCLS)
MDD .... Doctor of Dental Medicine
MDD .... Machine Dependent Data (OA)
MDD .... Madrid [*Spain*] [*Seismograph station code, US Geological Survey Closed*] (SEIS)
MDD .... Magnetic Disk Drive
MDD .... Maintenance Design Disclosure
MDD .... Maintenance Due Date (NVT)
MDD .... Major Depressive Disorder [*Psychiatry*]
MdD............ Mandaic Dictionary [*Oxford*] [*A publication*] (BJA)
MDD .... Marijuana Detection Dog (DNAB)
MDD .... Mate/Demate Device [*NASA*] (NASA)
MDD .... McDonald & Co. Invest [*NYSE symbol*] (TTSB)
MDD .... McDonald & Co. Investments, Inc. [*NYSE symbol*] (SPSG)
MDD .... Mean Daily Difference [*Medicine*]
MDD .... Mean Daily Dose
MdD............ Median Deviation [*Statistics*]
MDD .... Median Droplet Diameter
MDD .... Meteorological Data Distribution
MDD .... Midland, TX [*Location identifier FAA*] (FAAL)
MDD .... Milligrams per Square Decimeter per Day
MDD .... Million-Dollar Deal
MDD .... Million Dollar Directory [*Dun's Marketing Services*] [*Parsippany, NJ Database*]
MDD .... Mission Data Display
MDD .... Mission Description Document (SSD)
MDD .... Mouvement Democratique Dahomeen [*Dahomean Democratic Movement*] [*Political party*]
MDD .... Multichannel Demultiplexer and Distributor
MDD .... Multidimensional Database
MDD .... Puerto Maldonado [*Peru*] [*Airport symbol*] (AD)
MDDA.......... Manic Depressive and Depressive Association [*Later, NDMDA*] (EA)
MDDA.......... Mechanicsburg Defense Depot Activity [*AEC*]
MDDC.......... Management Decisions Development Corporation [*Canada*] (NITA)
MDDC.......... Manhattan District Declassified Code [*AEC*]
MDDC.......... Motor Dealers' Disputes Council [*Australia*]
MDDCS........ Memorial Dose Distribution Computation Service [*Memorial Sloan-Kettering Cancer Center*] [*Information service or system*] (IID)
MDDD.......... Merrill-Demos DD Scale [*Drug abuse and delinquent behavior test*]
MDDE.......... Maryland & Delaware Railroad Co. [*AAR code*]
MDDF.......... Minimum Delay Data Format (MCD)
MDDJ.......... Dajabon [*Dominican Republic*] [*ICAO location identifier*] (ICLI)
MDDPC........ Methyl Dimethyldihydropyrancarboxylate [*Organic chemistry*]
MDDPM........ Magnetic Drum Data Processing Machine (IAA)
MDDR.......... Mimimum Distance Decoding Rule (IAA)
MDDS.......... Maintainability Design Data Sheets (MCD)
MDDS.......... Material Directory Data Sheet (MCD)
MDDT.......... Master Digital Data Tape (PDAA)
MDDX.......... Middlesex [*Region of London*]
MDE............ Cincinnati, OH [*Location identifier FAA*] (FAAL)
MDE............ Madame (ROG)
MDE............ Magnetic Decision Element [*Computer science*] (BUR)
MDE............ Main Distribution Equipment (IAA)
MDE............ Major Defense Equipment (MCD)
MDE............ Master of Developmental Economics (PGP)
MDE............ Master of Distance Education (PGP)
MDE............ Master of Domestic Economy (NADA)
MDE............ Matrix Difference Equation
MDE............ McDermott, Inc. [*Formerly, Offshore Pipelines*] [*NYSE symbol*] (SAG)
MDE............ Mechanical Design Environment
MDE............ Medeea Ltd. [*Romania*] [*FAA designator*] (FAAC)
MDE............ Medellin [*Colombia*] [*Airport symbol*] (OAG)
MDE............ Meteoroid Detection Experiment (KSC)
MDE............ Metina Development [*Vancouver Stock Exchange symbol*]
MDE............ Military Damage Expectancy
MDE............ Mindy Explorations Ltd. [*Vancouver Stock Exchange symbol*]
MDE............ Minnesota State Department of Education, Professional Library, St. Paul, MN [*OCLC symbol*] (OCLC)
MDE............ Missile Display Equipment
MDE............ Mission Defendent Experiment
MDE............ Mission Dependent Elements [*NASA*] (KSC)
MDE............ Mission Dependent Equipment [*NASA*] (KSC)
MDE............ Mission Dependent Experiment [*NASA*] (NASA)
MDE............ Mission Display Equipment
MDE............ Mobile District Engineer (AAG)
MDE............ Mobile Telemetering Station [*ITU designation*] (DEN)
MDE............ Modern Drug Encyclopedia [*A publication*]
MDE............ Modular Design of Electronics (MCD)
MDE............ Modular Display Electronics (MCD)
MDE............ Mooring Dynamics Experiment [*Marine science*] (MSC)

MdE............ Mount St. Mary's College, Emmitsburg, MD [*Library symbol Library of Congress*] (LCLS)
MDE............ National Library of Medicine [*Source file*] [*UTLAS symbol*]
MDEA.......... Marketing and Distributive Education Association [*Later, MEA*] (EA)
MDEA.......... Methyldiethanolamine [*Organic chemistry*]
MDEA.......... Methylenedioxyethamphetamine [*Biochemistry*]
MdEa.......... Talbot County Free Library, Easton, MD [*Library symbol Library of Congress*] (LCLS)
M Dec S ...... Master of Decision Sciences (PGP)
MdEdgA ...... United States Army, Technical Library, Army Chemical Center, Edgewood, MD [*Library symbol Library of Congress*] (LCLS)
MDedHi ...... Dedham Historical Society, Dedham, MA [*Library symbol Library of Congress*] (LCLS)
MDee.......... Dickinson Library, Deerfield, MA [*Library symbol Library of Congress*] (LCLS)
MDeeD .... Deerfield Academy, Deerfield, MA [*Library symbol Library of Congress*] (LCLS)
MDeeH .... Historic Deerfield, Inc., Deerfield, MA [*Library symbol Library of Congress*] (LCLS)
MDeeP........ Pocumtuck Valley Memorial Association, Deerfield, MA [*Library symbol Library of Congress*] (LCLS)
MDefStudies... Master of Defence Studies
MDEFWP .... Motor-Driven Emergency Feedwater Pump [*Nuclear energy*] (NRCH)
MDEL.......... Major Defense Equipment List
M-DEMO...... Maintenance Demonstration [*DoD*]
MDEN.......... Enriquillo [*Dominican Republic*] [*ICAO location identifier*] (ICLI)
MDEN.......... Males, Density Of [*Ecology*]
MDENDET.... Mobile Dental Detachment [*Coast Guard*]
M Dent Sc ... Master of Dental Science [*British*]
MDEP.......... Maine Department of Environmental Protection
MDEP.......... Maine Department of Environmental Protection (DOGT)
MDEP.......... Management Decision Package [*DoD*]
MDEPrA ...... McDermott Inc $2.20 cm Cv A Pfd [*NYSE symbol*] (TTSB)
MDEPrB ...... McDermott Inc. $2.60 cm Pfd [*NYSE symbol*] (TTSB)
MDERDA ...... Maximum Degree of Emissions Reduction Deemed Achievable [*Environmental Protection Agency*]
M Des.......... Master of Design
MDes.......... Mercedarios Descalzos (TOCD)
MDES.......... Multiple Data Entry System
M Des (RCA)... Master of Design, Royal College of Art
M Des S ...... Master of Design Studies (PGP)
MDesS.......... Master of Design Studies (GAGS)
MDesSt.......... Master of Design Studies
MDET.......... Militarized Digital Element Tester (MCD)
MDEU.......... Material Delivery Expeditor Unit (DNAB)
MDEX.......... Medex, Inc. [*NASDAQ symbol*] (NQ)
MDF............ Macrodefect Free [*Materials science*]
MDF............ Magnetic Direction Finding [*Meteorology*]
MDF............ Magyar Demokrata Forum [*Hungarian Democratic Forum*] [*Political party*] (EY)
MDF............ Main Distributing Frame [*Bell System*]
MDF............ Main Distribution Frame (NITA)
MDF............ Maintenance Depot Fabrication
MDF............ Manipulator Deployment Facility (MCD)
MDF............ Manipulator Development Facility [*NASA*] (NASA)
MDF............ Manual Direction Finder [*Radio*]
MdF............ Manufacturer's Designated Fuel [*Automotive engineering*]
MDF............ Master Data File (AFIT)
MDF............ Master Directory File [*Computer science*]
MDF............ Master Distribution Frame [*Electronics*] (ECII)
MDF............ Master Document File [*Computer science*]
MDF............ Mate/Demate Facility [*NASA*] (NASA)
MDF............ Mean Dominant Frequency (MAE)
MDF............ Median Demagnetizing Field [*Geophysics*]
MDF............ Medium Density Fiberboard
MDF............ Medium-Frequency Direction Finder [*or Finding*]
MDF............ Metals Datafile [*Materials Information*] [*Information service or system*] (IID)
MDF............ Metric Data Facility (MCD)
MDF............ Microcomputer Development Facilities (IEEE)
MDF............ Micro Defect Free
MDF............ Micro-Dose-Focusing [*Electron microscopy*]
MDF............ Midland Doherty Financial Corp. [*Toronto Stock Exchange symbol*]
MDF............ Midtfly Aps [*Denmark ICAO designator*] (FAAC)
MDF............ Mild Detonating Fuse
MDF............ Mixed Dipterocarp Forest
MDF............ Modify
MDF............ Mooreland, OK [*Location identifier FAA*] (FAAL)
MDF............ Multiband Direction Finder
MDF............ Myocardial Depressant Factor
MDF/1.......... Metals Data File/1 (NITA)
MDFAT.......... Microsoft DoubleSpace File Allocation Table (PCM)
MDFC.......... Mason Dixon International Fan Club (EA)
MDFC.......... Matt Dillon Fan Club (EA)
MDFC.......... McDonnell Douglas Finance Corp. Ltd. [*British*]
MdFdBc ...... Maryland Federal Bancorp, Inc. [*Associated Press*] (SAG)
MdFdM .... United States Army Medical Intelligence and Information Agency, Fort Detrick, MD [*Library symbol Library of Congress*] (LCLS)
MdFhV .... United States Veterans Administration Hospital, Fort Howard, MD [*Library symbol Library of Congress*] (LCLS)
MD Fla .... United States District Court for the Middle District of Florida (DLA)
MDFLT.......... Multi-Directional Forklift Truck (MCD)
MdFmA .... United States Army, Fort George G. Meade Post Recreation Services Library, Fort George G. Meade, MD [*Library symbol Library of Congress*] (LCLS)

MdFmN....... National Security Agency, Fort George G. Meade, MD [*Library symbol Library of Congress*] (LCLS)

MDFMR ...... M-Day Force Materiel Requirement

MDFNA .... Maximum Density Fuming Nitric Acid

MDFP......... Mission Data Formats Project [*NASA*] (SSD)

MDFR .... Make Descent From [*Aviation*] (FAAC)

MdFre......... Frederick County Public Library, Frederick, MD [*Library symbol*] [*Library of Congress*] (LCLS)

MdFreCR .... Frederick Cancer Research Center, Frederick, MD [*Library symbol Library of Congress*] (LCLS)

MdFreD...... Fort Detrick Technical Library, Frederick, MD [*Library symbol Library of Congress*] (LCLS)

MdFreFC..... Frederick Community College, Frederick, MD [*Library symbol Library of Congress*] (LCLS)

MdFreH...... Hood College, Frederick, MD [*Library symbol Library of Congress*] (LCLS)

MdFreHi ..... [*The*] Historical Society of Frederick County, Inc., Frederick, MD [*Library symbol Library of Congress*] (LCLS)

MdFreSD .... Maryland School for the Deaf, Frederick, MD [*Library symbol*] [*Library of Congress*] (LCLS)

MdFroS....... Frostburg State College, Frostburg, MD [*Library symbol Library of Congress*] (LCLS)

MDFRR .... Mission Directors Flight Readiness Review [*NASA*] (KSC)

MDG .... Air Madagascar, Societe Nationale Malgache de Transports Aeriens [*ICAO designator*] (FAAC)

MDG .... Machinery Defective, Government-Furnished (DNAB)

MDG .... Machining-Intensive Durable Goods [*Manufacturing*]

MDG .... Madagascar [*ANSI three-letter standard code*] (CNC)

MDG .... Madang [*Papua New Guinea*] [*Seismograph station code, US Geological Survey*] (SEIS)

MDG .... Marina Development Group [*Commercial firm*] [*British*]

MDG .... Medical Director-General [*Navy British*]

MDG .... Metal Density Gauge

MDG .... Metasystems Design Group, Inc. [*Arlington, VA*] [*Telecommunications service*] (TSSD)

MDG .... Molecular Drag Gauge [*Instrumentation*]

MDG .... Multiplier Decoder Gate [*Computer science*]

MDG .... Multipurpose Display Group (MCD)

MDG .... Valdosta, GA [*Location identifier FAA*] (FAAL)

MDGA .... Guerra [*Dominican Republic*] [*ICAO location identifier*] (ICLI)

MD GA .... United States District Court for the Middle District of Georgia (DLA)

MDGC......... Multidimensional Gas Chromatography

MDGD .... Mercury Doped Germanium Detector

MDGF .... Macrophage Derived Growth Factor [*Biochemistry*]

MDG(N)...... Medical Director-General (Navy) [*British*]

MDGP......... Medgroup Inc. Calif [*NASDAQ symbol*] (TTSB)

MDGR......... Multi-Differential GPS Receiver

MDGT .... Midget (MSA)

MDH .... Carbondale [*Illinois*] [*Airport symbol*] (OAG)

MDH .... Carbondale/Murphysboro, IL [*Location identifier FAA*] (FAAL)

MDH .... Madison Holdings Ltd. [*Vancouver Stock Exchange symbol*]

MDH .... Magnetic Drum Head

MDH .... Malate Dehydrogenase [*Also, MD*] [*An enzyme*]

MDH .... Maneuver Director Headquarters [*Military*]

MDH .... Maximum Diameter Heat [*Nuclear science*] (OA)

MDH .... Mean Dominant Height

MDH .... Medullary Dorsal Horn [*Anatomy*]

MDH .... Minimum Descent Height [*Aviation*] (FAAC)

MDH .... Month-Day-Hour [*Automotive manufacturing*]

MDH .... Multidirectional Harassment (PDAA)

MDHA......... Masters Deerhounds Association [*British*] (DBA)

MdHag......... Washington County Free Library, Hagerstown, MD [*Library symbol Library of Congress*] (LCLS)

MDHBA....... Medical-Dental-Hospital Bureaus of America (EA)

MDHC......... McDonnell Douglas Helicopter Co. [*Formerly, HHI*] (MCD)

MDHC......... Mersey Docks and Harbour Co. [*British*]

MDHE .... Herrera [*Dominican Republic*] [*ICAO location identifier*] (ICLI)

MdHeH .... Henryton State Hospital, Henryton, MD [*Library symbol Library of Congress*] (LCLS)

MdHi........... Maryland Historical Society, Baltimore, MD [*Library symbol Library of Congress*] (LCLS)

MDHJ......... Methyl Dihydrojasmonate [*Organic chemistry*]

MDHL......... Modified Hodges-Lehmann Estimator [*Statistics*]

MDHR......... Methyl Dihydroretinoate [*Biochemistry*]

MDHR......... Mini-Decay Heat Removal [*Nuclear energy*] (NRCH)

MDHS .... McDonnell Douglas Helicopter Systems

MDHTSNAGEJTR... Movement of Dependents and Household Goods to Temporary Station[*s*] Not Authorized at Government Expense, Except as Prescribed in Joint Travel Regulations [*Army*] (AABC)

MDHV .... Marek's Disease Herpesvirus [*Medicine*] (DMAA)

MDHY......... Higuey [*Dominican Republic*] [*ICAO location identifier*] (ICLI)

MdHyD........ De Sales Hall School of Theology, Hyattsville, MD [*Library symbol Library of Congress*] (LCLS)

MdHyP........ Prince George's County Memorial Library, Hyattsville, MD [*Library symbol Library of Congress*] (LCLS)

MDI............. Bemidji, MN [*Location identifier FAA*] (FAAL)

MDI............. Magnetic Detection Indicator (IAA)

MDI............. Magnetic Direction Indicator

MDI............. Makurdi [*Nigeria*] [*Airport symbol*] (OAG)

MDI............. Management Development Institute (MCD)

MDI............. Manic Depression Interval [*Course*]

MDI............. Manic Depressive Illness

MDI............. Manual Data Input [*SAGE*]

MDI............. Market Decisions, Inc. [*Information service or system*] (IID)

MDI............. Market Development Index [*Business term*] (DOAD)

MDI............. Master Dimension Information

MDI............. Master Direction Indicator

MDI............. Master of Didactics

MDI............. Material Departmental Instruction

MDI............. Mechanical Dynamics Inc. (NITA)

MDI............. Media Directions, Inc.

MDI............. Medium Dependent Interface [*Computer science*] (CDE)

MDI............. Memotec Data, Inc. [*Toronto Stock Exchange symbol*]

MDI............. Mental Development Index [*Bayley Scales of Infant Development*] [*Psychometrics*]

MDI............. Meridian Diagnostics, Inc.

MDI............. Metered Dose Inhaler [*Medicine*]

MDI............. Methylenebis (Phenylisocyanate) (GNE)

MDI............. Methylene Diisocyanate [*Organic chemistry*]

MDI............. Methylene Diphenyl Diisocyanate [*Organic chemistry*]

MDI............. Methylenediphenyl Isocyanate [*Organic chemistry*]

MDI............. Michelson Doppler Imager [*Biochemistry*]

MDI............. Michelson Doppler Imager [*Instrumentation*]

MDI............. Microdosimetric Instrumentation

MDI............. Mid America Realty, Inc. [*Formerly, Dial REIT*] [*NYSE symbol*] (SAG)

MDI............. Mid-America Realty Inv [*NYSE symbol*] (TTSB)

MDI............. Military Decision Items (AFIT)

MDI............. Mineral Deposit Inventory Database [*Ontario Geological Survey*] [*Information service or system Canada*] (CRD)

MDI............. Minimum Discrimination Information [*Statistics*]

MDI............. Miss-Distance Indicator [*Missiles*] (MUGU)

MDI............. Mission Dependent Interface

MDI............. Mission to the Deaf, International (EA)

MDI............. Mobilization Day Increment [*Military*]

MDI............. Mobilization Day Index [*Military*] (NG)

MDI............. Monopulse Display Improvement (IAA)

MDI............. Monthly Debit Industrial [*Insurance*]

MDI............. Mouvement pour la Democratie et l'Independance [*Movement for Democracy and Independence*] [*Central Africa*] (PD)

MDI............. Multiple Display Indicator

MDI............. Multiple Document Interface [*Computer science*] (PCM)

MDIB .... Minimum Distribution Incidental Benefit [*Finance*]

MDIBL .... Mount Desert Island Biological Laboratory [*Salsbury Cove, ME*] [*Research center*]

MDIC .... Microwave Dielectric Integrated Circuit (IEEE)

MDIC .... Multi-Disciplinary Counter Intelligence

MDIC .... Multilateral Disarmament Information Centre [*British*]

MDICP .... McDonnell Douglas Industrial Control Products (MCD)

M DICT .... More Dicto [*As Directed*] [*Pharmacy*]

M Dict .... Morison's Dictionary of Decisions, Scotch Court of Session [*1540-1808*] [*A publication*] (DLA)

M Dict .... Morrison's Dictionary of Decisions, Scotch Court of Session [*A publication*] (DLA)

M Did .... Master of Didactics

M Di E......... Master of Diesel Engineering

MDIE .... Mother-Daughter Ionosphere Experiment

M Di Eng .... Master of Diesel Engineering

MDIF .... Manual Data Input Function [*Computer science*]

MDIF & W ... Maine Department of Inland Fisheries and Wildlife, Fishery Research Management Division [*Research center*] (RCD)

MDII............ Mechanical Dynamics [*NASDAQ symbol*] (TTSB)

MDII............ Mechanical Dynamics, Inc. [*NASDAQ symbol*] (SAG)

MDIN.......... Medalist Indus [*NASDAQ symbol*] (TTSB)

MDIN.......... Medalist Industries, Inc. [*NASDAQ symbol*] (NQ)

Md Inst C Art... Maryland Institute College of Art (GAGS)

MDIO.......... Maine Debris Information Office [*National Oceanic and Atmospheric Administration*]

M Dip .... Master of Diplomacy

M-DIRT........ Miss-Distance-Indicator Radioactive Tests [*Missiles*] (MUGU)

MDIS .... Manual Data Input Section [*Computer science*]

MDIS .... Manual Data Input System [*Computer science*]

M Dis.......... Marriage Dissolved

MDIS .... McDonnell Douglas Information Services

MDIS .... Medical Digital Imaging Support (RDA)

MDISC .... McDonnell Douglas International Sales Corp. (MCD)

MDISE .... Merchandise

MDIU .... Manned Data Insertion Unit (KSC)

MDIU .... Manual Data Input Unit [*Computer science*]

M Div .... Master of Divinity

MDJ............ Jaro International SA [*Romania*] [*ICAO designator*] (FAAC)

MdJC.......... Maryland House of Corrections, Jessup, MD [*Library symbol Library of Congress*] (LCLS)

MDJCS........ Memorandum by the Director, Joint Staff for the Joint Chiefs of Staff (MCD)

Md J Int'l L & Trade... Maryland Journal of International Law and Trade [*A publication*] (DLA)

MDJM.......... Jainamosa [*Dominican Republic*] [*ICAO location identifier*] (ICLI)

MDK............ Mbandaka [*Zaire*] [*Airport symbol*] (OAG)

MDK............ Mechanical Disconnect Kit

MDK............ Medicore, Inc. [*AMEX symbol*] (SPSG)

MDK............ Multimedia Development Kit [*Microsoft Corp.*] [*Computer science*]

MDL............ Macro Description Language [*Computer science*] (BUR)

MDL............ Madill [*S.*] Ltd. [*Vancouver Stock Exchange symbol*]

MDL............ Magnetic Delay Line

MDL............ Magnetic Double Layer

MDL............ Main Defense Line (IAA)

MDL............ Maintenance and Diagnostic Logic Display [*Burroughs*] (NITA)

MDL............ Maintenance Diagnostic Logic [*Computer science*] (BUR)

MDL............ Management Data List (AABC)

MDL............ Manager's Discretionary Limit (DCTA)

MDL............ Mandala Airlines PT [*Indonesia*] [*ICAO designator*] (FAAC)
MDL............ Mandalay [*Myanmar*] [*Airport symbol*] (OAG)
MDL............ Mandalay [*Burma*] [*Airport symbol*] (AD)
MDL............ Man Days Lost (NUCP)
MDL............ Master Data Library [*NASA*]
MDL............ Master Drawing List
MDL............ Master of Divine Literature
MDL............ Material Deviation List [*Military*]
MDL............ Medulloblastoma [*A type of brain cancer*] (CDI)
MDL............ Mercury Delay Line
MDL............ Method Detection Limit [*Analytical chemistry*]
MDL............ Microprocessor Development Lab (MHDI)
MDL............ MicroStation Development Language [*Intergraph Corp.*] (PCM)
MDL............ Microstation Development Language
MDL............ Microwave Delay Line
MDL............ Microwave Development Laboratories
MDL............ Middle (MSA)
MDL............ Military Demarcation Line (CINC)
MDL............ Mine Defense Laboratory [*Panama City, Florida*] [*Navy*]
MDL............ Miniature Display Light
MDL............ Minimum Detection Limit [*Chemistry*]
MDL............ Model (ADA)
MDL............ Model
MDL............ Modular Design Language [*Computer science*] (CSR)
MDL............ Modular Dummy Load
MDL............ Module (MSA)
MDL............ Morris Dam Laboratory
MDL............ Motor Distal Latency [*Medicine*]
MDL............ Muddle [*A computer language*]
MDL............ Multipurpose Data Link (GAVI)
MDL............ S Madill Ltd. [*Vancouver Stock Exchange symbol*]
MDL............ University of Baltimore, Law Library, Baltimore, MD [*OCLC symbol*] (OCLC)
MD LA......... United States District Court for the Middle District of Louisiana (DLA)
MdLaD........ Divine Saviour Seminary, Lanham, MD [*Library symbol Library of Congress*] (LCLS)
MdLapC....... Charles County Community College, La Plata, MD [*Library symbol Library of Congress*] (LCLS)
MD Laws..... Laws of Maryland [*A publication*] (DLA)
MDLB.......... Municipal Development and Loan Board [*Canada*]
MDLC.......... Materiel Development and Logistic Command [*Army - replaced Ordnance, Engineer, Signal, Chemical and Quartermaster Overall Commands*]
MDLC.......... Mutliple Data Link Controller
MDLD.......... Midland Financial Group [*NASDAQ symbol*] (SAG)
MDLF.......... Mobile Drydock Launch Facility
MDLI........... MDL Information Sys [*NASDAQ symbol*] (TTSB)
MDLI........... MDL Information Systems, Inc. [*NASDAQ symbol*] (SAG)
MDL Info .... MDL Information Systems, Inc. [*Associated Press*] (SAG)
Md-LL........ Maryland State Law Library, Annapolis, MD [*Library symbol Library of Congress*] (LCLS)
MDLLE........ Mademoiselle
MDLLS........ Mediastinal Diffuse Large-Cell Lymphoma with Sclerosis [*Oncology*]
MDLND....... Midland
MDLP.......... Mobile Dryer Loan Program
MdLP.......... United States Department of the Interior, Patuxent Wildlife Research Center, Laurel, MD [*Library symbol Library of Congress*] (LCLS)
MDLR .... La Romana [*Dominican Republic*] [*ICAO location identifier*] (ICLI)
Md-LR .... Maryland Department of Legislative Reference, Baltimore, MD [*Library symbol Library of Congress*] (LCLS)
MDLRC .... Mental Disability Legal Resource Center [*Later, MPDLRSDB*] (EA)
MD L Rec.... Maryland Law Record [*Baltimore*] [*A publication*] (DLA)
MD L Rep.... Maryland Law Reporter [*Baltimore*] [*A publication*] (DLA)
MDLS.......... Marine Data Logger System
MdLuW........ Maryland College for Women, Lutherville, MD [*Library symbol Library of Congress*] (LCLS)
MDLX.......... Military Demarcation Line Extended (MCD)
MdLxp .... Lexington Park Library, Lexington Park, MD [*Library symbol Library of Congress*] (LCLS)
Mdm............ Madam (WGA)
MDM............ Magnetic Disc Memory
MDM............ Magnetic Drum Memorex [*Computer science*] (IAA)
MDM............ Magneto-Optical Display Memory
MDM............ Maintenance Depot Material Control
MDM............ Maize Dwarf Mosaic Virus [*Plant pathology*]
MDM............ Manipulator Deployment Mechanism (MCD)
MDM............ Manpower Determination Model [*Military*]
MDM............ Marking Diagram Master (MCD)
MDM............ Marshall Drummond McCall, Inc. [*Toronto Stock Exchange symbol*]
MDM............ Mass Democratic Movement [*Political coalition*] [*South Africa*]
MDM............ Master of Development Management
MDM............ Maternal Diabetes Mellitus [*Medicine*]
MDM............ Maximum Design Meter (MSA)
MDM............ Mechanically Deboned Meat [*Food technology*]
MDM............ Medical Monitor (MCD)
MDM............ Medium (AABC)
MDM............ Medium-Depth Mine (MCD)
MDM............ MedPartners/Mullikin [*NYSE symbol*] (TTSB)
MDM............ Metal-Dielectric-Metal [*Filter*]
MDM............ Metal Disintegration Machining [*Nuclear energy*] (NRCH)
MDM............ Methylenedioxymethamphetamine [*A hallucinogenic drug, also known as "Ecstasy," banned in 1985*] [*Also, MDMA*]
MDM............ Michigan-Dartmouth-Massachusetts Institute of Technology [*Observatory*]
MDM............ Microdensitometer (IAA)

MDM............ Midas Minerals, Inc. [*Toronto Stock Exchange symbol*]
MDM............ Mid-Diastolic Murmur [*Medicine*]
MDM............ Minor Determinant Mixture [*Medicine*]
MDM............ Mixed Dark Matter [*Cosmology*]
MDM............ Mobile Depot Maintenance [*Air Force*] (AFM)
MDM............ Modified Diffusion Method (NRCH)
MDM............ Modular Data Module (HGAA)
MDM............ Monolithic Diode Matrix
MDM............ Movement for a Democratic Military (EA)
MDM............ Movimento Democratico de Mocambique [*Democratic Movement of Mozambique*] (AF)
MDM............ Multiplexer/Demultiplexer (NASA)
MDM............ Multiprocessor Diagnostic Monitor (IAA)
MDMA .... M-Day Materiel Assets (AFIT)
MDMA .... Methylenedioxymethamphetamine [*A hallucinogenic drug, also known as "Ecstasy," banned in 1985*] [*Also, MDM*]
MDMAA ...... Mess Deck Master-at-Arms (DNAB)
MDMAF....... Mekong Delta Mobile Afloat Force [*Vietnam*]
Mdmarco..... Medmarco, Inc. [*Associated Press*] (SAG)
MDMC .... Medmarco, Inc. [*NASDAQ symbol*] (SAG)
MDMC .... Monte Cristy [*Dominican Republic*] [*ICAO location identifier*] (ICLI)
MDMCA ...... Melvil Dui Marching and Chowder Association (EA)
MdMC-G ..... Montgomery College, Germantown Campus, Germantown, MD [*Library symbol Library of Congress*] (LCLS)
MdMC-R ..... Montgomery College, Rockville Campus, Rockville, MD [*Library symbol Library of Congress*] (LCLS)
MdMC-T...... Montgomery College, Takoma Park Campus, Takoma Park, MD [*Library symbol Library of Congress*] (LCLS)
MDMCW ..... Medmarco Inc. Wrrt'A' [*NASDAQ symbol*] (TTSB)
MDMCZ....... Medmarco Inc. Wrrt'B' [*NASDAQ symbol*] (TTSB)
mDMD .... Mouse Duchenne Muscular Dystrophy [*Medicine*]
MDME......... Madame
Md-MH .... Maryland Department of Mental Hygiene, Baltimore, MD [*Library symbol Library of Congress*] (LCLS)
MDMH........ Methylol Dimethylhydantoin [*Organic chemistry*]
MDML......... Modified Maximum Likelihood [*Statistics*]
MDMN........ Modified Posterior Mean [*Statistics*]
MDMR........ M-Day Materiel Requirement (AFIT)
MDMR........ M-Day Mobilization Requirement
MDMS .... Maintenance Data Management Schedule
MDMS .... Marketing Data Management System [*British*]
MDMS .... Microbiology Data Management System
MDMS .... Miss-Distance Measuring System
MDMS .... Moore Data Management Services [*Information service or system*] (IID)
MDMS .... Multiple Database Management System (NITA)
MDMV .... Maize Dwarf Mosaic Virus [*Plant pathology*]
MdMwH ...... Mount Wilson State Hospital, Mount Wilson, MD [*Library symbol Library of Congress*] (LCLS)
MDN .... Madison, IN [*Location identifier FAA*] (FAAL)
MDN .... Maiden Race [*Horse racing*]
MDN .... Managed Data Network
MdN .... Mandibular Nerve [*Anatomy*]
MDN .... Manufacturing Day Number (MCD)
MDN .... Mark der Deutschen Notenbank [*Mark of the German Bank of Issue*] [*Later, M*] (EG)
MDN .... Median (MSA)
MDN .... Meridian Industrial Trust [*NYSE symbol*] (TTSB)
MDN .... Meridian Industrial Trust, Inc. [*AMEX symbol*] (SAG)
MDN .... Ministere de la Defense Nationale [*Department of National Defense*] [*Canada*]
MDN .... Mobilisation pour le Developpement National [*Haiti*] [*Political party*] (EY)
MDN .... Movimiento Democratico Nacionalista [*Nationalist Democratic Movement*] [*Guatemala*] [*Political party*]
MDN .... Movimiento Democratico Nicaraguense [*Nicaraguan Democratic Movement*] [*Political party*] (PPW)
MDN .... Universair [*Spain ICAO designator*] (FAAC)
MDNA .... Machinery Dealers National Association (EA)
MDNA .... Maximum Density Nitric Acid
MDNA .... Mobilehome Dealers National Association (EA)
MDNB .... Mean Daily Nitrogen Balance [*Medicine*]
MDNB .... Meta-Dinitrobenzene [*Organic chemistry*]
MD/NC .... Mechanical Drafting/Numerical Control (IEEE)
MDNC .... United States District Court for the Middle District of North Carolina (DLA)
MDNF .... Minimal Disjunctive Normal Form (MHDB)
MDNIS .... Machinery Dealers' National Information System
MDNMNA.... Moorish Divine and National Movement in North America (EA)
MDNP .... Methyl Dinitropentanoate [*An explosive*]
Md-NR .... Maryland State Department of Natural Resources, Annapolis, MD [*Library symbol Library of Congress*] (LCLS)
MDNR .... Minnesota Department of Natural Resources
MDNR .... Missouri Department of Natural Resources (DOGT)
MDNS .... Managed Data Network Services (NITA)
MDNT .... Midnight
MDN.WS..... Meridian Indl Tr Wrrt [*AMEX symbol*] (TTSB)
MDNX......... Modern Air Transport [*Air carrier designation symbol*]
MDO .... Macedonia AS [*Yugoslavia*] [*ICAO designator*] (FAAC)
MDO .... Maintenance Development Officer (MCD)
MDO .... MARC Development Office (NITA)
MDO .... Marine Diesel Oil
MdO .... Masoreten des Ostens (BJA)
MDO .... Massive Dark Object [*Galactic science*]
MDO .... Mechanized Desert Operations [*Military*] (MCD)

MDO	Medium Density Overlay [Plywood]
MDO	Membrane-Derived Oligosaccharide [Biochemistry]
MDO	Methylenedioxyphenyl [Organic chemistry]
MDO	Middleton Island, AK [Location identifier FAA] (FAAL)
MDO	Mobile District Office [Army Corps of Engineers]
MDO	Monthly Debit Ordinary [Insurance]
MdO	Ruth Enlow Library of Garrett County, Oakland, MD [Library symbol Library of Congress] (LCLS)
MDOA	Material Date of Arrival (DNAB)
MDOC	Missouri Department of Conservation
MdOdN	National Plastics Products Co., Odenton, MD [Library symbol Library of Congress Obsolete] (LCLS)
MdOdS	Saran Yarn Co., Odenton, MD [Library symbol Library of Congress Obsolete] (LCLS)
MDOF	Multiple Degree of Freedom [Acoustics]
MdOmR	Rosewood Center, Owing Mills, MD [Library symbol Library of Congress] (LCLS)
MDOP	Malicious Destruction of Property
MDOP	Maximum Design Operating Pressure [NASA]
MDOPA	Methyldopamine [Biochemistry]
MDOS	Motorola Disk Operating System
MDOSIS	Management Data Online Status/Inquiry System (MCD)
MDOT	Michigan Department of Transportation
MDOT	Modular Digital Output Timer
MDovC	Chickering House, Dover, MA [Library symbol Library of Congress] (LCLS)
MDovS	Saint Stephen's College, Dover, MA [Library symbol Library of Congress] (LCLS)
MDP	Coppin State College, Parlett L. Moore Library, Baltimore, MD [OCLC symbol] (OCLC)
MDP	Ferrocarril Mexicano del Pacifico [Mexican Pacific Railroad Co., Inc.] [AAR code]
MDP	Magyar Dolgozok Partja [Hungarian Workers' Party] [Political party] (PPE)
MDP	Main Data Path
MDP	Main Display Panel (SAA)
MDP	Maintainability Demonstration Plan (MCD)
MDP	Maintenance Data Program (MCD)
MDP	Madras Depot Production
MDP	Maintenance Diagnostic Processor (NITA)
MDP	Maintenance Diagnostic Program [Computer science] (IAA)
MDP	Maintenance Display Panel (MCD)
MDP	Malfunction Detection Package
MDP	Malicious Destruction of Property
MDP	Management Development Programme [British] (DCTA)
MDP	Managing Director Posts [British] (DCTA)
MDP	Manic Depressive Psychosis
MDP	Manpower Development Program [Department of Labor]
MDP	Master Decommissioning Plan [Nuclear energy] (NRCH)
MDP	Master Design Plan (MCD)
MDP	Master Display Panel (KSC)
MDP	Maximum Diastolic Potential [Physiology]
MDP	Mean Datum Plane
MDP	Mean Designation Point (CAAL)
MDP	Mechanically Deboned Poultry [Food technology]
MDP	Menthyldiphenyphosphine [Organic chemistry]
MDP	Mento-Dextra Posterior [A fetal position] [Obstetrics]
MDP	Meredith Corp. [NYSE symbol] (SPSG)
MDP	Message Discrimination Process [Telecommunications] (TEL)
MDP	Meteorological Datum Plane
MDP	Methyldichlorophosphine [Organic chemistry]
MDP	Methylene Diphosphonate [Organic chemistry]
MDP	Methylenediphosphonic Acid [Organic chemistry]
MDP	Microprocessor Debugging Program [Computer science] (IAA)
MDP	Milliyetci Demokrasi Partisi [Nationalist Democracy Party] [Turkey Political party] (EY)
MDP	Mindiptana [Indonesia] [Airport symbol] (OAG)
MDP	Minimum Discernible Pulse (MCD)
MDP	Missile Data Processor (OA)
MDP	Mode Products, Inc. [Vancouver Stock Exchange symbol]
MDP	Moslem Democratic Party [Philippines] [Political party] (PPW)
MDP	Most Dispensable Program [Television]
MDP	Motorola Data Processor [Computer science] (IAA)
MDP	Mouvement Democratique et Populaire [Popular Democratic Movement] [Senegal] [Political party] (PPW)
MDP	Mouvement Democratique Populaire [Popular Democratic Party] [The Comoros] [Political party] (EY)
MDP	Mouvement des Democrates Progressistes [Burkina Faso] [Political party] (EY)
MDP	Movimento Democratico Portugues [Portuguese Democratic Movement] [Political party] (PPE)
MDP	Movimiento Democratico del Pueblo [Paraguay] [Political party] (EY)
MDP	Movimiento Democratico Peruano [Peruvian Democratic Movement] [Political party]
MDP	Movimiento Democratico Popular [Popular Democratic Movement] [Ecuador] [Political party] (PPW)
MDP	Movimiento Democratico Popular [Popular Democratic Movement] [Chile] [Political party] (PPW)
MDP	Moving Deformable Barrier [NHTSA] (TAG)
MDP	Multidomain Polymer [Biology]
MDP	Muramyl Dipeptide [Immunochemistry]
MDP	Parkland Regional Library, Dauphin, Manitoba [Library symbol National Library of Canada] (NLC)
MD PA	United States District Court for the Middle District of Pennsylvania (DLA)
MdPa	United States Naval Air Station, Patuxent River, MD [Library symbol Library of Congress] (LCLS)
MDPC	Mount Diablo Peace Center (EA)
MDPC	Punta Cana [Dominican Republic] [ICAO location identifier] (ICLI)
MDPD	Medical Director
MDPF	Methoxy(diphenyl)furanone [Organic chemistry]
MDPG	Magnetic Digital-Pulse Generator
MDPHI	Media Development Project for the Hearing Impaired (NITA)
MDPI	Mathematics Diagnostic/Prescriptive Inventory (EDAC)
MDPM	Maintenance Douglas Process Manual
MDPM	Mechanically Deboned Poultry Meat [Food technology]
MdPM	University of Maryland, Eastern Shore, Princess Anne, MD [Library symbol Library of Congress] (LCLS)
MDPN	Midshipman
MDPP	Puerto Plata/La Union [Dominican Republic] [ICAO location identifier] (ICLI)
MDPPQ	Mouvement pour la Defense des Prisonniers Politiques du Quebec [Movement for the Defense of Political Prisoners of Quebec]
MdPpV	United States Veterans Administration Hospital, Perry Point, MD [Library symbol Library of Congress] (LCLS)
MDPR	Madrid Predict [Orbit identification]
MDPR	Manufacturing Development and Process Request (AAG)
MDPS	Metric Data Processing System [Air Force]
MDPS	Mission Data Preparation System [Military] (CAAL)
MDPS	Mobilization and Deployment Planning System [Army]
MDPS	Mouvement pour la Democratie et le Progres Social [Benin] [Political party] (EY)
MDPT	Median Preventive Maintenance Time (MCD)
MDPVM	Missionary Daughters of the Most Pure Virgin Mary (TOCD)
MDQ	Mar Del Plata [Argentina] [Airport symbol] (OAG)
MDQ	MDC Communication CI'A' [AMEX symbol] (TTSB)
MDQ	MDC Corp. [AMEX symbol] (SAG)
MDQ	MDE Explorations [Vancouver Stock Exchange symbol]
MDQ	Minimum Detectable Quantity
MDQL	Multidimensional Query Language [Computer science]
MDQS	Management Data Query System [Computer science]
MDR	Compania Mexicana de Aeroplanos SA [Mexico ICAO designator] (FAAC)
MDR	Madras [India] [Seismograph station code, US Geological Survey] (SEIS)
MDR	Magnetic Dipole Radiation
MDR	Magnetic Disc Recorder (NTCM)
MDR	Magnetic Document Reader (IAA)
MDR	Magnetic Drum Recorder
MDR	Magnetic Field Dependent Resistor (IAA)
MDR	Maintainability Demonstration Report (MCD)
MDR	Maintenance Data Report [Army] (AABC)
MDR	Maintenance Demand Rate (NASA)
MDR	Maintenance Design Requirement
MDR	Major Design Review (KSC)
MDR	Manual Data Room
MDR	Mark Document Reader [Trademark] [Bell & Howell]
MDR	Market Data Retrieval [Westport, CT] [Information service or system] (IID)
MD R	Maryland Reports [A publication] (DLA)
MDR	Master Data Record (NG)
MDR	Master Discrepancy Report (AAG)
MDR	Master of Dispute Resolution (PGP)
MDR	Material Deficiency Reports [Program]
MDR	McDermott International, Inc. [NYSE symbol] (SPSG)
MDR	McDermott Intl. [NYSE symbol] (TTSB)
MDR	MD Review [Social Security Administration] (OICC)
MDR	Mechanical Development Report (MCD)
MDR	Medfra, AK [Location identifier FAA] (FAAL)
MDR	Median Detection Range (NVT)
MDR	Medical Device Register, Inc. (IID)
MDR	Medical Device Reporting System
MDR	Medium Data Rate (DOMA)
MDR	Medium Deep Recess [Automotive engineering]
MDR	Memory-Data Register
MDR	Message Detail Recording [Later, SMDR] [Telecommunications]
MDR	Metropolitan District Railway [London]
MDR	Microwave Device Reliability (MCD)
MDR	Milestone Decision Review (MCD)
MDR	Military Defense Readiness (SAA)
MDR	Minimum Daily Requirement [of a vitamin, etc.] [Later, Recommended Daily Requirement FDA]
MDR	Minor Discrepancy Repair [NASA] (KSC)
MDR	Minor Discrepancy Review [NASA] (GFGA)
MDR	Missile Deviation Report (AAG)
MDR	Missing Data Report (NASA)
MDR	Mission Data Reduction
MDR	Mock-Up Discrepancy Report [Aerospace] (AAG)
MDR	Monthly Director's Review [NASA] (NASA)
MDR	Monthly Directors' Review [NASA]
MDR	Morphine-Dependent Rate
MDR	Morphology Dependent Resonance [Physics]
MDR	Motion Detection Radar [Hughes Electronics]
MDR	Motor-Driven Relay [or Roter]
MDR	Multichannel Data Recorder
MDR	Multi Disc Reader [Computer science] (DGA)
MDR	Multi-Disc Reader [Floppy discs] (NITA)
MDR	Multidrug Resistance [Medicine]
MDR	Munition Data Requirement
MDRA	Multidrug-Resistance Associated [Genetics]

MDRAF .... Mekong Delta Riverine Assault Force [*Vietnam*]
MDRAM .... Multibank DRAM [*Computer science*]
MDRC .... Manual Data Relay Center (MCD)
MDRC .... Materiel Development and Readiness Command [*Formerly, AMC*] [*See also DARCOM*] [*Army*]
MDRD .... Mission Data Requirements Document [*NASA*] (KSC)
MDRE .... Mass Driver Reaction Engine [*Aerospace*]
MD Rep .... Maryland Reports [*A publication*] (DLA)
MdRFD .... United States Food and Drug Administration, Rockville, MD [*Library symbol Library of Congress*] (LCLS)
MDRL .... Mandrel [*Mechanical engineering*]
MDRM .... Mouvement Democratique de Renovation Malgache [*Democratic Movement Malagasy Restoration*]
MdRMC .... Montgomery County Department of Public Libraries, Rockville, MD [*Library symbol Library of Congress*] (LCLS)
MdRNIO ...... National Institute for Occupational Safety and Health, Rockville, MD [*Library symbol Library of Congress*] (LCLS)
MDROC .... Mission Design Requirements, Objectives, and Constraints
MDROF .... Managing Director of Royal Ordnance Factories [*British*] (RDA)
MDRP .... Migrant Dropout Reconnection Program [*Board of Cooperative Educational Services Geneseo Migrant Center*] (EA)
MDRP .... Movimiento Democratico Reformista Peruano [*Peruvian Democratic Reformist Movement*] [*Political party*] (PPW)
MDRS .... Management Data Reporting System (MCD)
MDRS .... Manpower Data Relay Station (IAA)
MDRS .... Manufacturing Data Retrieval System (NASA)
MDRS .... Manufacturing Data Retrieval System
MDRS .... Mattis Dementia Rating Scale [*Medicine*] (DMAA)
MDRS .... Mission Data Retrieval System [*NASA*]
MDRS .... Mobilization Designation Reserve Section
MDRS .... Mylar Diaphragm Rupture System
MDRSF .... Multi-Dimensional Random Sea Facility [*Hydraulics Research Station*] (PDAA)
MDRSV .... Maize Dwarf Ringspot Virus [*Plant pathology*]
MDRT .... Million Dollar Round Table [*Des Plaines, IL*] (EA)
MDRTB .... Multidrug-Resistant Tuberculosis [*Medicine*]
MDRTC .... Diabetes Research and Training Center [*University of Michigan*] [*Research center*] (RCD)
MDRUS .... Miniature Donkey Registry of the United States (EA)
MDRX .... Medicis Pharmaceutical 'A' [*NASDAQ symbol*] (TTSB)
MDRX .... Medicis Pharmaceutical Corp. [*NASDAQ symbol*] (SAG)
MDRY .... Madison Railway Co., Inc. [*AAR code*]
MDS .... Macintosh Development System [*Computer science*]
MDS .... Madison [*Wisconsin*] [*Seismograph station code, US Geological Survey Closed*] (SEIS)
MDS .... Madison, SD [*Location identifier FAA*] (FAAL)
Mds .... Madrepores [*Quality of the bottom*] [*Nautical charts*]
MDS .... Madrona Resources, Inc. [*Vancouver Stock Exchange symbol*]
MDS .... Magnetic Detection of Submarines [*British military*] (DMA)
MDS .... Magnetic Disk Storage [*Computer science*] (IAA)
MDS .... Magnetic Drum Storage [*Computer science*] (IAA)
MDS .... Magnetic Drum System
MDS .... Mail Distribution Schedule [*Air Force*] (AFM)
MDS .... Mail Distribution Scheme [*Army*]
MDS .... Main Device Scheduler (IAA)
MDS .... Main Dressing Station
MDS .... Maintenance Data System (MCD)
MDS .... Maintenance Diagnostic System (MCD)
MDS .... Maintenance Documentation System [*Bell System*]
MDS .... Malfunction Detection System [*Gemini*] [*NASA*]
MDS .... Management Data System (NASA)
MDS .... Manual Data Supervisor [*Computer science*] (IAA)
MDS .... Marine Distress Signal (IAA)
MDS .... Market Data System [*NYSE*]
MDS .... Market Decision System (HGAA)
MDS .... Mass Digital Storage
MDS .... Master Delivery Schedule (AAG)
MDS .... Master Development Schedule (KSC)
MDS .... Master Dimension Specification (MSA)
MDS .... Master Drum Sender
MDS .... Master of Decision Sciences (GAGS)
MDS .... Master of Dental Science (GAGS)
MDS .... Master of Dental Surgery
MDS .... Materiel Deployment Schedule
MDS .... Maternal Deprivation Syndrome [*Medicine*] (DMAA)
MDS .... Mechanized Documentation System
MDS .... Medical Documentation Service [*College of Physicians of Philadelphia*] [*Information service or system*] (IID)
MDS .... Medical Dressing Station
MDS .... Megawatt Demand Setter (NRCH)
MDS .... Memory Disk System [*Computer science*] (IEEE)
MDS .... Mennonite Disaster Service (EA)
MDS .... Message Distribution Systems
MDS .... Message-Dropping Station [*Military*] (IAA)
MDS .... Metal-Dielectric Semiconductor [*Electronics*] (PDAA)
MDS .... Metastable-Atom De-excitation Spectroscopy
MDS .... Meteoroid Detection Satellite [*NASA*]
MDS .... Meteorological Data System
MDS .... Methods Development Survey [*Bureau of the Census*] (GFGA)
MDS .... Metrofiber Multi-Megabit Data Service [*Metropolitan Fiber Systems, Inc.*]
MDS .... Metropolitan Dairymen's Society [*British*] (BI)
MDS .... "Micky the D" Show [*Later, MDS/MMFC*] [*An association*] (EA)
MDS .... Microcomputer Development System (IAA)
MDS .... Microprocessor Development System [*Motorola, Inc.*]

MDS .... Microsurgery Drill System (DAVI)
MDS .... Microwave Doppler Speed [*Electronic engineering*]
MDS .... Microwave Multipoint Distribution Systems (EDAC)
MDS .... Middle Caicos [*British West Indies*] [*Airport symbol*] (OAG)
MDS .... Middle Distance Swimmer
MDS .... Milford Docks Air Services Ltd. [*British ICAO designator*] (FAAC)
MDS .... Milk Drinker's Syndrome [*Medicine*] (DMAA)
MDS .... Miller-Dieker Lissencephaly Syndrome [*Medicine*]
MDS .... Miller-Dieker Syndrome [*Medicine*] (DMAA)
MDS .... Mine Detection Set
MDS .... Minerals Data System [*Database*]
MDS .... Minimum Data Set [*Computer science*]
MDS .... Minimum Detectable Signal
MDS .... Minimum Discernable System
MDS .... Minimum Discernible Signal [*Radio*]
MDS .... Minimum Discernible System (NASA)
MDS .... Minuteman Defense Study [*DoD*]
MDS .... Minuteman Defense System [*DoD*]
MDS .... Mission Design and Series [*Military*] (AFM)
MDS .... Mission Development Simulator [*NASA*] (NASA)
MDS .... Mission Display System [*Navy*] (DOMA)
MDS .... Mobile Data Service (DA)
MDS .... Mobile Dental Services
MDS .... Mobile Distribution System (AFM)
MDS .... Model Designation and Series [*Military*] (AFIT)
MDS .... Modern Data Systems (IEEE)
MDS .... Modular Data System
MDS .... Modular Decontamination System (DWSG)
MDS .... Modular Disc Storage (NITA)
MDS .... Modular Distribution System
MDS .... Modulate-Demodulate Subsystem
MDS .... Mohawk Data Sciences [*Computer science*] (IAA)
MDS .... Mohawk Data Systems Corporation (NITA)
MDS .... Molybdenum Disulfide [*Inorganic chemistry*]
MDS .... Monitor Distribution System [*Television*]
MDS .... Montant de Soutien [*Amount of Support*] [*A trade negotiating plan EC*]
MDS .... Mouvement Democrate Socialiste [*Democratic Socialist Movement*] [*France Political party*] (PPW)
MDS .... Mouvement des Democrates Socialistes [*Movement of Socialist Democrats*] [*Tunisia*] [*Political party*] (PPW)
MDS .... Mouvement pour la Democratie Sociale [*Burkina Faso*] [*Political party*] (EY)
MDS .... Movement for a Democratic Slovakia [*Former Czechoslovakia*] [*Political party*] (EY)
MDS .... Multidimensional Scaling [*Statistics*]
MDS .... Multiple Dataset System
MDS .... Multiple Deployment System [*Military*] (IAA)
MDS .... Multipoint Distribution Service [*Educational television*]
MDS .... Multipoint Distribution Services (ACRL)
MDS .... Multipoint Distribution System [*Line-of-sight relay system for electronic signals*]
MDS .... Multiprocessor Distributed System [*Raytheon*] (NITA)
MDS .... Municipal Data Service [*International City Management Association*] [*Information service or system*] (IID)
MDS .... Myelodysplasia [*Medicine*]
MDS .... Myelodysplastic Syndrome [*Medicine*]
MDS .... Myocardial Depressant Substance [*Cardiology*] (DAVI)
MDS .... St. Mary's College of Maryland, St. Mary's City, MD [*OCLC symbol*] (OCLC)
MdSalS .... Salisbury State College, Salisbury, MD [*Library symbol Library of Congress*] (LCLS)
MdSalW .... Wicomico County Free Library, Salisbury, MD [*Library symbol Library of Congress*] (LCLS)
MDSB .... Message Digest Signature Block (HGAA)
MDSC .... Management Data Service Center
MD Sc .... Master of Dental Science [*British*]
MDSC .... Modular Digital Scan Converter (MCD)
MDSCB .... Model Data Set Control Block (NITA)
MDSCC .... Madrid Deep Space Communications Complex
MDSD .... Magnetic Disk Storage Device [*Computer science*]
MDSD .... Mate/Demate Stiff Leg Derrick (MCD)
MDSD .... Mate/Demate Stiffleg Derrick
MDSD .... Monitoring and Data Support Division [*Environmental Protection Agency*] (GFGA)
MDSD .... Santo Domingo/De las Americas Internacional [*Dominican Republic*] [*ICAO location identifier*] (ICLI)
MDSE .... Merchandise (AFM)
mdse .... Merchandise (DD)
MDSE .... Merchandise
MDSF .... Mass Data Storage Facility
MDSF .... Mission for Deep Sea Fishermen [*British*] (DI)
MDSF .... Mouvement Democrate Socialiste de France [*Democratic Socialist Movement of France*] [*Political party*] (PPE)
MDSG .... Merchandising
mdsg .... Merchandising (DD)
MDSHPMN... Midshipman
MDSI .... Manufacturing Data Systems Inc. (NITA)
MDSI .... San Isidro [*Dominican Republic*] [*ICAO location identifier*] (ICLI)
MDSIA .... MDS [*Multipoint Distribution System*] Industry Association [*Telecommunications*] (EA)
MDSIC .... Metal-Dielectric-Semiconductor Integrated Circuit [*Electronics*] (PDAA)
MdSim .... Howard County Library, Simpsonville, MD [*Library symbol Library of Congress*] (LCLS)

MDSJ.........	San Juan [*Dominican Republic*] [*ICAO location identifier*] (ICLI)
MDSL.........	Medis E Ltd. [*NASDAQ symbol*] (SAG)
MDSL.........	Moderate Speed Digital Subscriber Line [*Telecommunications*] (ACRL)
MDSLD.......	Mate/Demate Stiff Leg Derrick
MDSLF.......	Medis El Ltd [*NASDAQ symbol*] (TTSB)
MDS/MMFC...	"Micky the D" Show/Metal Micky Fan Club (EA)
MDS-MPOLL...	Mail Distribution Scheme / Military Post Office Location List (DNAB)
MDSN.........	Madisn Gas & Elec [*NASDAQ symbol*] (TTSB)
MDSN.........	Madison Gas & Electric Co. [*NASDAQ symbol*] (NQ)
MDSN.........	Maximum Dissolved Solids Nebulizer [*Product of Applied Research Laboratories*]
MDSNG.......	Merchandising
MdSnW.......	Worcester County Public Library, Snow Hill, MD [*Library symbol*] [*Library of Congress*] (LCLS)
MDSO.........	Medical and Dental Supply Office [*Military*]
MDSO.........	Mentally Disordered Sex Offender
MDSOR.......	Monthly Depot Space and Operating Report
Md-SP........	Maryland State Planning Commission, Baltimore, MD [*Library symbol Library of Congress*] (LCLS)
MDSP.........	San Pedro De Macoris [*Dominican Republic*] [*ICAO location identifier*] (ICLI)
MDSPR.......	Mode Suppressor (KSC)
MDSS.........	Magnetic Drum Storage System
MDSS.........	MAGTF [*Marine Air-Ground Task Force*] Decision-Support System (DOMA)
MDSS.........	Maintenance Decision Support System
MDSS.........	Mass Digital Storage System
MDSS.........	McDonnell Douglas Support Services (MCD)
MDSS.........	Meteorological Data Sounding System (IEEE)
MDSS.........	Microprocessor Development Support System
MDSS.........	Mission Data Support System [*NASA*] (KSC)
MDSS.........	Multidimensional Switching System [*Instrumentation*]
MdSsD.......	Library of Dianetics and Scientology, Silver Spring, MD [*Library symbol Library of Congress*] (LCLS)
MdSsFD.......	United States Food and Drug Administration, Bureau of Medical Services, Silver Spring, MD [*Library symbol Library of Congress*] (LCLS)
MdSsGS.......	Church of Jesus Christ of Latter-Day Saints, Genealogical Society Library, Silver Spring Branch, Silver Spring, MD [*Library symbol Library of Congress*] (LCLS)
MDSS-PCT...	Multidimensional Switching System - Packed Column Trap [*Instrumentation*]
MdSsV........	Vitro Laboratories, Silver Spring Laboratory Library, Silver Spring, MD [*Library symbol Library of Congress*] (LCLS)
MdSsW.......	Washington Theological Coalition, Silver Spring, MD [*Library symbol Library of Congress*] (LCLS)
MdSsX........	Xaverian College, Silver Spring, MD [*Library symbol Library of Congress*] (LCLS)
MDST.........	Mountain Daylight Saving Time (SSD)
MDST.........	Santiago [*Dominican Republic*] [*ICAO location identifier*] (ICLI)
MdStm........	St. Mary's College of Maryland, St. Mary's City, MD [*Library symbol Library of Congress*] (LCLS)
MdSuFR.......	Washington National Records Center, General Services Administration, Suitland, MD [*Library symbol Library of Congress*] (LCLS)
MDSV........	Manned Deep Space Vehicle
MdsxWat.....	Middlesex Water Co. [*Associated Press*] (SAG)
MdSyH........	Springfield State Hospital, Sykesville, MD [*Library symbol Library of Congress*] (LCLS)
MDT..........	Compagnie Air Mediterrannee [*France ICAO designator*] (FAAC)
MDT..........	Harrisburg [*Pennsylvania*] [*Airport symbol*] (OAG)
MDT..........	Maintenance Demand Time (MCD)
MDT..........	Maintenance Downtime (MCD)
MDT..........	Mandatory Date of Transportation [*Military*]
MDT..........	Manual Data Technician [*Computer science*] (IAA)
MDT..........	Manufacturers Delegated Testing (NITA)
MDT..........	Maximum Dive Time
MDT..........	Mean Death Time
MDT..........	Mean Delay Time (CAAL)
MDT..........	Mean Detonating Time (NASA)
MDT..........	Mean Downtime [*Computer science*]
MDT..........	Measurement Descriptor Table (NASA)
MDT..........	Mechanically Deboned Turkey [*Food technology*]
MDT..........	Median Detection Threshold (MAE)
MDT..........	Median Dorsal Tract [*Anatomy*]
MDT..........	Medium Data Technique [*Computer science*] (IAA)
MDT..........	Med-Tech Systems, Inc. [*Vancouver Stock Exchange symbol*]
MDT..........	Medtronic, Inc. [*NYSE symbol*] (SPSG)
MDT..........	Mento-Dextra Transversa [*A fetal position*] [*Obstetrics*]
MDT..........	Merchant Deposit Transmittal
MDT..........	Mercury Dynamic Test
MDT..........	Message Direction Table (MCD)
MDT..........	Message Display Terminal (MCD)
MDT..........	Middletown, PA [*Location identifier FAA*] (FAAL)
MDT..........	Mini Disc Terminal [*Computer science*] (DGA)
MDT..........	Minnesota Dance Theatre
MDT..........	Mobile Data Terminal (MCD)
MDT..........	Mobile Display Terminal [*Vehicle navigation systems*]
MDT..........	Moderate (AFM)
MDT..........	Modified Data Tag [*Computer science*] (IAA)
MDT..........	Modular Display Tactical
MDT..........	Most Demands to Be Traded [*Baseball*]
MDT..........	Mountain Daylight Time
MDT..........	Moviment de Defensa de la Terra [*Spain Political party*] (EY)
MDT..........	Multidimensional Tasking [*Honeywell, Inc.*]
MDT..........	Multidisciplinary Team
MDT..........	Munitions Disposal Technician (SAA)
MDT..........	Mutual Defense Treaty
MDT2.........	Martin Marietta, Diehl, Thorn-EMI, Thomson [*Army*]
MDTA.........	Manpower Development and Training Act [*1962*] [*Later, CETA Department of Labor*]
MDTA.........	McDonald Deep Test of Articulation [*Speech and language therapy*] (DAVI)
MDTA.........	Modulation, Demodulation, Terminal, and Associated Equipment
MDTB.........	Milk Distribution Trade Board [*British*] (DAS)
MDTC.........	MDT Corp. [*NASDAQ symbol*] (NQ)
MDT Cp......	MDT Corp. [*Associated Press*] (SAG)
MD Tenn.....	United States District Court for the Middle District of Tennessee (DLA)
MDTF.........	Macular Degeneration Task Force [*Medicine*]
MDTI.........	Missile Director Train Indicator
MDTI.........	Multiple Director Train Indicator (MCD)
MDTL.........	Modified Diode Transistor Logic [*Electronics*] (IAA)
MDTM.........	Mechanically Deboned Turkey Meat [*Food technology*]
MDTP.........	Materiel Developer's Test Program [*Military*]
MDTP.........	Multidisciplinary Treatment Plan [*Medicine*] (DAVI)
MDTR.........	Mean Diameter-Thickness Ratio (MAE)
MDTS.........	MegaBIT [*Binary Digit*] Digital Troposcatter Subsystem [*Communications*] (MCD)
MDTS.........	Mobile Doppler Tracking Station
MDTS.........	Modular Data Transaction System
MDTS.........	Multiple Dealer Trading System [*Investment term*] (DICI)
MDTU.........	Mobile Dockside Transfer Unit
MdTW.........	Washington Missionary College, Tacoma Park, MD [*Library symbol Library of Congress Obsolete*] (LCLS)
MDTWN......	Midtown
MDU.........	Maintenance Data Unit (MCD)
MDU.........	Maintenance Diagnostic Unit
mdu	Maryland [*MARC country of publication code Library of Congress*] (LCCP)
MDU	Master Driver Unit
MDU	MDU Resources Group [*NYSE symbol*] (TTSB)
MDU	MDU Resources Group, Inc. [*NYSE symbol*] (SPSG)
MDU	Medical Defence Union Ltd. [*British*] (BI)
MDU	Mendi [*Papua New Guinea*] [*Airport symbol*] (OAG)
MDU	Message Decoder Unit
MDU	Middle Dutch [*Language, etc.*]
MDU	Mid-North Resources [*Vancouver Stock Exchange symbol*]
MDU	Mine Disposal Unit
MDU	Missile Design Unit (SAA)
MDU	Mobile Demonstration Unit
MDU	Mobile Development Unit [*Military*] (GFGA)
MDU	Mobile Dynamic Unit (AAG)
MDU	Moral Development Unit [*Prisoner reform program*]
MDU	Motion Detection Unit [*Nuclear energy*] (NRCH)
MDU	Multidimensional Unfolding [*Model*] [*Statistics*]
MDU	University of Maryland, Baltimore, Health Sciences Library, Baltimore, MD [*OCLC symbol*] (OCLC)
MdU...........	University of Maryland, College Park, MD [*Library symbol Library of Congress*] (LCLS)
MdU-A	University of Maryland, Art Library, College Park, MD [*Library symbol Library of Congress*] (LCLS)
MdU-Ar	University of Maryland, Architecture Library, College Park, MD [*Library symbol Library of Congress*] (LCLS)
MdU-BC	University of Maryland, Baltimore County Campus, Baltimore, MD [*Library symbol Library of Congress*] (LCLS)
MdU-C	University of Maryland, Chemistry Library, College Park, MD [*Library symbol Library of Congress*] (LCLS)
MdU-E	University of Maryland, Engineering and Physical Sciences Library, College Park, MD [*Library symbol Library of Congress*] (LCLS)
MdU-H	University of Maryland, Health Sciences Library, Baltimore, MD [*Library symbol Library of Congress*] (LCLS)
MDuHi	Duxbury Rural and Historical Society, Duxbury, MA [*Library symbol Library of Congress*] (LCLS)
MdU-I	International Piano Archives at Maryland, University of Maryland, College Park, MD [*Library symbol Library of Congress*] (LCLS)
MdU-L	University of Maryland, School of Law, Baltimore, MD [*Library symbol Library of Congress*] (LCLS)
MDUO.........	Myocardial Disease of Unknown Origin [*Cardiology*]
MdU-U........	University of Maryland, Undergraduate Library, College Park, MD [*Library symbol Library of Congress*] (LCLS)
MDV..........	Baltimore, MD [*Location identifier FAA*] (FAAL)
MDV..........	Doctor of Veterinary Medicine
MDV..........	Maldives [*ANSI three-letter standard code*] (CNC)
MDV..........	Map and Data Viewer [*NASA*] (KSC)
MDV..........	Marek's Disease Virus [*Avian pathology*]
MDV..........	Master of Veterinary Medicine
MDV..........	Maxim Development Ltd. [*Vancouver Stock Exchange symbol*]
MDV..........	Medeva [*AMEX symbol*] (SPSG)
MDV..........	Medeva ADR [*AMEX symbol*] (TTSB)
MDV..........	Medium-Dollar Value
MDV..........	Medouneu [*Gabon*] [*Airport symbol*] (OAG)
MDV..........	Middlebury [*Vermont*] [*Seismograph station code, US Geological Survey*] (SEIS)
MDV..........	Midivariant [*Genetics*]
MDV..........	Mine-Dispensing Vehicle [*Army*]
MDV..........	Minimum Detectable Velocity [*Physics*]
MDV..........	Minimum Domian Velocity (IAA)
MDV..........	Moldavian Airlines [*Macedonia*] [*FAA designator*] (FAAC)

MDV	Mouvement Democratique Voltaique [*Upper Volta Democratic Movement*]
MDV	Mucosal Disease Virus
MDV	Multiple Dose Vial [*Pharmacy*]
M-DVD	Magnetic Digital Versatile Disc
MDVL	Medeva plc [*LO, exchange symbol*] (TTSB)
mdvl	Medieval (VRA)
MDW	Chicago [*Illinois*] Midway [*Airport symbol*] (OAG)
MDW	Delta Waterfowl Research Station, Manitoba [*Library symbol National Library of Canada*] (NLC)
MDW	Fort Myer Library System and Fort McNair Post Library, Fort Myer, VA [*OCLC symbol*] (OCLC)
MDW	Mars Departure Window [*Aerospace*]
MdW	Masoreten des Westens (BJA)
MDW	Mass Destruction Weapons
MDW	Meadow
MDW	Meadow [*Postal Service standard*] (OPSA)
MDW	Meadow Mountain [*Vancouver Stock Exchange symbol*]
MDW	Measured Daywork [*Payment system*]
MDW	Midway [*Washington*] [*Seismograph station code, US Geological Survey*] (SEIS)
MDW	Midway Aviation, Inc. [*ICAO designator*] (FAAC)
MDW	Military Defence Works [*British*]
MDW	Military District of Washington [*DC*]
MDW	Mine Disposal Weapon (NATG)
MDW	Minnesota, Dakota & Western Railway Co. [*AAR code*]
MDW	Multidimensional Warfare [*Military*] (CAAL)
MDW	Multipair Distribution Wire
MDW	Multiple Drop Wire [*Telecommunications*] (TEL)
MD WCC	Maryland Workmen's Compensation Cases [*A publication*] (DLA)
MdWem	Carroll County Public Library, Westminster, MD [*Library symbol Library of Congress*] (LCLS)
MdWemC	Western Maryland College, Westminster, MD [*Library symbol Library of Congress*] (LCLS)
MdWemHi	Carroll County Historical Society, Westminister, MD [*Library symbol*] [*Library of Congress*] (LCLS)
MdwEx	Midwest Exprss Holding [*Associated Press*] (SAG)
MDWF	Midwife
MdwFdl	Midwest Federal Financial [*Associated Press*] (SAG)
MDWFY	Midwifery
MDWS	Meadows (MCD)
MDWS	Meadows
MdWst	Med Waste [*Associated Press*] (SAG)
MDWST	Midwest
MDWSTRN	Midwestern
MDWV	Medwave, Inc. [*NASDAQ symbol*] (SAG)
MDWY	Midway
MDX	Medical Data Exchange [*Los Altos, CA*] [*Commercial firm*]
MDX	Mercedes [*Argentina*] [*Airport symbol*] (OAG)
MDX	Merritech Development [*Vancouver Stock Exchange symbol*]
MDX	Middlesex [*County in England*]
MDX	University of Maryland, College of Library and Information Services, College Park, MD [*OCLC symbol*] (OCLC)
MDXDCR	Mode Transducer (KSC)
MDXR	Medar, Inc. [*NASDAQ symbol*] (NQ)
MDY	Magnetic Deflection Yoke
MDY	Middlebury College, Middlebury, VT [*OCLC symbol*] (OCLC)
MDY	Midland Gold Corp. [*Formerly, Midland Energy Corp.*] [*Vancouver Stock Exchange symbol*]
MDY	Midway [*Midway Islands*] [*Seismograph station code, US Geological Survey Closed*] (SEIS)
MDY	Month, Date, Year
MDY	Standard & Poor's MidCap 400 Depository Receipts [*AMEX symbol*] (SAG)
MDY	Standard & Poor's MidCap Dep Rc [*AMEX symbol*] (TTSB)
MDYN	Molecular Dynamics, Inc. [*NASDAQ symbol*] (SAG)
MDZ	Maritime Defense Zone [*Program for drug interdiction*]
MDZ	MDC Corp. [*Toronto Stock Exchange symbol*]
MDZ	Medford, WI [*Location identifier FAA*] (FAAL)
MDZ	Mendoza [*Argentina*] [*Airport symbol*] (OAG)
MDZ	Mendoza [*Argentina*] [*Seismograph station code, US Geological Survey*] (SEIS)
MDZ	Middle Zero (IAA)
MDZ	Missile Danger Zone (NVT)
Me	C. H. Boehringer Sohn, Ingelheim [*Germany*] [*Research code symbol*]
me----	Eurasia [*MARC geographic area code Library of Congress*] (LCCP)
M/E	Machine (ROG)
M/E	Macrocytic/Normochromic [*Anemia*] [*Hematology*] (DAVI)
ME	Macular Edema [*Ophthalmology*] (DAVI)
ME	Magic Eye (DEN)
ME	Magnetic Estimation (OA)
ME	Magnetoelastic
ME	Magneto-Electronic (PDAA)
ME	Magnitude Estimation
ME	Maine [*Postal code*]
ME	Main Engine (KSC)
ME	Main Entry [*Library Science*] [*Online database field identifier*]
Me	Maine Reports (AAGC)
Me	Maine State Library, Augusta, ME [*Library symbol Library of Congress*] (LCLS)
ME	Maine Supreme Judicial Court Reports [*A publication*] (DLA)
ME	Maintenance Equipment
ME	Maintenance Evaluation (MCD)
ME	Maitre [*Barrister, Advocate*] [*French*] (ROG)

ME	Majestic Eagles (EA)
ME	Male Equivalents [*Entomology*]
ME	"Malic" Enzyme
ME	Malt Extract [*Microbiology*]
ME	Management Engineering (KSC)
ME	Management Evaluation [*Food Stamp Program*] [*Department of Agriculture*] (GFGA)
ME	Managing Editor
ME	Man-Hours Earned
ME	Manpower Estimate (AAG)
ME	Manson Evaluation [*Psychology*]
ME	Manufacturing Engineering (MCD)
ME	Marbled Edges [*Bookbinding*]
ME	Marche de l'Europe [*March of Europe*] (EAIO)
ME	Marine Engine
ME	Marine Engineer
ME	Marriage Encounter
ME	Marriage Evaluation [*Marital relations test*]
M-E	Martini-Enfield [*Rifle*]
ME	Master Equatorial
ME	Master of Education
ME	Master of Elements
ME	Master of Engineering
ME	Materials Evaluation (PDAA)
ME	Math Error [*IRS*]
ME	Mature Equivalent (OA)
ME	Maximum Effort
ME	Maximum Energy
ME	Meal
ME	Measurement Engine (IAA)
ME	Measuring Element
ME	Mechanical Efficiency
M/E	Mechanical/Electrical (AAG)
ME	Mechanical Engineer [*or Engineering*]
ME	Mechanical Equipment
ME	Medial Epicondyle [*Medicine*]
Me	Median
ME	Median Eminence [*of hypothalamus*] [*Anatomy*]
ME	Medical Education (MAE)
ME	Medical Examiner
ME	Medium Electroendosmosis [*Analytical biochemistry*]
ME	Medium Energy
ME	Megacycle (IAA)
Me	Me'ilah (BJA)
Me	Melendus [*Flourished, 1188-1209*] [*Authority cited in pre-1607 legal work*] (DSA)
ME	Memory Element [*Computer science*]
ME	Memory Error (WDAA)
ME	Mercaptoethanol [*Biochemistry*]
ME	Message Element [*Telecommunications*] (TEL)
ME	Messerschmitt AG [*Germany ICAO aircraft manufacturer identifier*] (ICAO)
ME	Metabolic and Electrolyte Disorders [*Medicine*] (MEDA)
ME	Metabolizable Energy
ME	Metal Evaporated [*Videotape*]
ME	Metalsmith [*Navy*]
ME	Meters [*JETDS nomenclature*] [*Military*] (CET)
ME	Methionine Enkephalin [*Biochemistry*]
ME	Methodist
ME	Methodist Episcopal
ME	Methods Engineering (NG)
ME	Methoxyethanol [*Organic chemistry*]
Me	Methyl [*Organic chemistry*]
ME	Microelectronic
M-E	Microencapsulated
ME	Micrometeoroid Explorer [*Satellite*]
ME	Microsoft Editor [*Computer program*] (PCM)
ME	Middle Ear
ME	Middle East [*or Middle Eastern*]
ME	Middle East Airlines [*ICAO designator*] (AD)
ME	Middle English [*Language, etc.*]
ME	Mid-Engine [*Automotive engineering*]
ME	Military Electronics (MCD)
ME	Military Engineer
ME	Mill Edge (ADA)
ME	Milliequivalent [*or Milligram Equivalent*] [*Also, MEQ*]
ME	Mining Engineer
ME	Minneapolis Eastern Railway
ME	Miscellaneous Equipment (KSC)
ME	Missile Electrician
ME	Missionary Ecumenical (Rome) (TOCD)
ME	Mission Capital Ltd. [*NYSE symbol*] (SAG)
ME	Mission Envelope (AAG)
ME	Mistress of English
ME	Miter End [*Technical drawings*]
ME	Mobility Equipment [*Military*] (AFM)
ME	Modular Electronics (IAA)
ME	Modulation Efficiency
ME	Moessbauer Effect (OA)
ME	Molecular Electronics
ME	Moment Estimator (PDAA)
ME	Moneta Porcupine Mines, Inc. [*Toronto Stock Exchange symbol*]
ME	Morristown & Erie Railroad Co. [*AAR code*]
ME	Most Eminent [*Freemasonry*] (ROG)
ME	Most Excellent [*In titles*]

ME	Mottled Edges [*Bookbinding*] (DGA)
ME	Mouse Embryo [*Medicine*] (DMAA)
ME	Mouse Encephalitis
ME	Mouse Epithelial [*Cells*] [*Hematology*] (DAVI)
ME	Mouvement Europeen [*European Movement*]
ME	Movie Editor
ME	Muhammadan Era
ME	Multiengine
ME	Municipal Engineering and Environmental Technology [*A publication British*]
ME	Munitions Effectiveness
ME	Muzzle Energy
ME	Myalgic Encephalomyelitis [*Medicine*]
ME	Mycobacterial Extracts [*Biochemistry*]
M:E	Myeloid:Erythroid [*Ratio*] [*Hematology*]
ME	Myoepithelium [*Cytology*]
ME3	Minority Engineering Education Effort [*Later, NACME*]
MEa	Eastham Public Library, Eastham, MA [*Library symbol*] [*Library of Congress*] (LCLS)
MEA	Macae [*Brazil*] [*Airport symbol*] (OAG)
MEA	Magnetic Engineering Associates, Inc.
MEA	Main Electronics Assembly (MCD)
MEA	Maine State Library, Augusta, ME [*OCLC symbol*] (OCLC)
MEA	Maintenance Engineering Analysis
MEA	Malt Extract Agar [*Culture media*]
MEA	Manufacturing Engineering Analysis
MEA	Marine Engineering Artificer [*Navy rating British*]
MEA	Marine Engineers' Association [*A union*] [*British*]
MEA	Marine Environmental Activities [*Marine science*] (MSC)
MEA	Maritime Employers Association (NADA)
MEA	Marketing Education Association (EA)
MEA	Master of Engineering Administration
MEA	Master of Engineering Architecture (GAGS)
MEA	Material Experiment Analysis
MEA	Materials Experiment Assembly
MEA	[*The*] Mead Corp. [*NYSE symbol*] (SPSG)
MEA	Meanook [*Canada*] [*Geomagnetic observatory code*]
MEA	Measurements (NATG)
MEA	Meat Extract Agar [*Microbiology*]
MEA	Meath [*County in Ireland*] (ROG)
MEA	Medical Equestrian Association [*British*] (DBA)
MEA	Medical Exhibitors Association [*Later, HCEA*] (EA)
MEA	Memory Inspection Ending Address (MHDB)
MEA	Mercaptoethylamine [*Pharmacology*]
MEA	Metal Edge Amplifier (MCD)
MEA	Metopon Ethnikis Adadimiourgias [*National Regeneration Front*] [*Greece*] [*Political party*] (PPE)
MEA	Metropolitan Economic Area
MEA	Metropolitan Entertainers' Association [*British*] (BI)
MEA	Middle East Airlines - Air Liban [*Lebanon*]
MEA	Middle East Association [*British*] (EAIO)
MEA	Minimum Energy Absorbed
MEA	Minimum Enroute Altitude
MEAS	Minimum en Route IFR Altitude [*FAA*] (TAG)
MEA	Minister, External Affairs (CINC)
MEA	Ministry of External Affairs, Library Services Division [*UTLAS symbol*]
MEA	Missionary Evangelical Alliance [*See also AME*] [*Switzerland*] (EAIO)
MEA	Modular Engine Analyzer [*Automotive engineering*]
MEA	Moisture Evaluation Analysis (PDAA)
MEA	Monoethanolamine [*Organic chemistry*]
MEA	Monoethylamine [*Organic chemistry*]
MEA	Monteagle [*Australia Seismograph station code, US Geological Survey Closed*] (SEIS)
MEA	Multimode Error Analysis
MEA	Multiple Endocrine Abnormalities [*Medicine*]
MEA	Multiple Endocrine Adenomas [*Oncology*]
MEA	Multiple Endocrine Adenopathy [*Endocrinology*] (DAVI)
MEA	Municipal Employees Association (NADA)
MEA	Munitions Effectiveness Assessment (DOMA)
MEA	Musical Educators Association (NADA)
MEA	Music Editors Association (EA)
MEA	Myalgic Encephalomyelitis Association [*British*] (DBA)
MEAB	Maintenance Engineering Analysis Board
MEAC	Manufacturing Engineering Applications Center [*Worchester Polytechnic Institute*] [*Research center*] (RCD)
MEAC	Mid-Eastern Athletic Conference
MEACE	Military Engineering Applications of Commercial Explosives [*Army*] (PDAA)
MEACN	Maintenance Engineering Analyses Control Number [*DoD*]
MEACON	Masking Beacon (IAA)
MEACONING	Measuring and Confusing (DNAB)
ME Acts	Acts, Resolves, and Constitutional Resolutions of the State of Maine [*A publication*] (DLA)
MEAD	Maintenance Engineering Analysis Data
Mead	[*The*] Mead Corp. [*Associated Press*] (SAG)
MEAD	Memphis Army Depot (AABC)
MEAD	Microbial Evaluation Analysis Device (PDAA)
Mead-J	Mead Johnson [*Commercial firm*] [*Pharmacology*] (DAVI)
MEADOW	Meadow [*Commonly used*] (OPSA)
MEADOWS	Meadows [*Commonly used*] (OPSA)
MEADS	Maintenance Engineering Analysis Data System
MEADS	Medium [*Range*] Extended Air Defense System [*USA-Europe*]
MEAF	Middle East Air Force [*British*]
MEAFSA	Middle East/Southern Asia and Africa South of the Sahara [*Military*]
MeAIB	(Methylamino)isobutyric Acid [*Biochemistry*]

MEAL	Master Equipment Allowance [*or Authorization*] List [*Military*]
MEAL	Media Expenditure Analysis Ltd. [*Database producer*]
MEA(L)	Mission of Economic Affairs in London [*World War II*]
MEAL	Mobile Equipment Allowance List (MCD)
MEAM	Advisory Committee for Mechanical Engineering and Applied Mechanics [*Washington, DC*] [*Terminated, 1985*] [*National Science Foundation*] (EGAO)
MeAM	Augusta Mental Health Institute, Augusta, ME [*Library symbol Library of Congress*] (LCLS)
MeAMH	Maine State Department of Human Services, Augusta, ME [*Library symbol Library of Congress*] (LCLS)
MeAMM	Maine State Museum, Augusta, ME [*Library symbol Library of Congress*] (LCLS)
MeAMP	Maine State Planning Office, Augusta, ME [*Library symbol*] [*Library of Congress*] (LCLS)
MEAN	Manganese-Enhanced Austenitic Nitrogen Steel
MEAN	Microcomputer Education Application Network [*Commercial firm*] (EA)
MEANINGEX	Meaning Extraction [*Programming language*] [*1971*] (CSR)
Means	Mean's Kansas Reports [*A publication*] (DLA)
MEANT	Meat Exporters' Association of the Northern Territory [*Australia*]
MEAP	Maintenance Engineering Analysis Program
MEAP	Michigan Educational Assessment Program
MEAP	Military Economic Advisory Panel (MCD)
MEAPL	Manufacturing and Engineering Assembly Parts List [*File*]
MEAPS	Method of Ensemble Average of Periodic Systems
MEAR	Maintenance Engineering Analysis Record [*or Report*]
MEAR	Maintenance Engineering Analysis Request [*NASA*] (NASA)
MEARS	Multi-User Engineering Change Proposal Automated Review System (RDA)
Mears Just	Mears' Edition of Justinian and Gaius [*A publication*] (DLA)
MEAS	Measure (AABC)
MEAS	Measurement (ROG)
MEAS	Measuring
MEASAT	Malaysia East Asia Satellite
MEASCAL	Measure Calibrate (IAA)
Meas Control (1962-64)	Measurement and Control (1962-64) [*A publication*]
Meas Spcl	Measurement Specialities, Inc. [*Associated Press*] (SAG)
MEASURE	Metrology Automated System for Uniform Recall and Reporting [*Navy*]
MEAT	Manpower Employment Assistance Training [*Act*] [*Pennsylvania*]
MEAT	Meat Exporters' Association of Tasmania [*Australia*]
MEAT	Multiedge Adaptive Tracker (MCD)
MEATR	Materials, Engineering, and Advanced Test Reactor (SAA)
MeAu	Auburn Public Library, Auburn, ME [*Library symbol Library of Congress*] (LCLS)
MeAU	University of Maine at Augusta, Augusta, ME [*Library symbol Library of Congress*] (LCLS)
MeAub	Auburn Public Library, Auburn, ME [*Library symbol*] [*Library of Congress*] (LCLS)
MEAV	Meat Exporters' Association of Victoria [*Australia*]
MeaVlly	Meadow Valley Corp. [*Associated Press*] (SAG)
MeaVly	Meadow Valley Corp. [*Associated Press*] (SAG)
MEAWS	Maintenance Engineering Analysis Work Sheet (DNAB)
Me B	Bachelor of Metaphysics
MEB	Bangor Mental Health Institute, Bangor, ME [*OCLC symbol*] (OCLC)
MeB	Bowdoin College, Brunswick, ME [*Library symbol Library of Congress*] (LCLS)
MEB	Main Electronics Box (NASA)
MEB	Main Electronics Box
MEB	Maine Motor Rate Bureau, Portland ME [*STAC*]
MEB	Manufacturing Evaluation Board (MCD)
MEB	Marine Expeditionary Brigade
MEB	Master Electronics Board
MEB	Maxton, NC [*Location identifier FAA*] (FAAL)
MEB	Mechanical Engineering Bulletin [*A publication*] (GFGA)
MEB	Medial Efferent Bundle [*Neuroanatomy*]
MEB	Medical Board
MEB	Medical Evaluation Board [*Military*] (DAVI)
MEB	Melbourne [*Australia Airport symbol*] (OAG)
MEB	Mercury Electron Bombardment
MeB	Methylene Blue [*Organic chemistry*]
MEB	Midlands Electricity Board [*British*]
MEB	Military Early Bird
MEB	Modem Evaluation Board (NITA)
MEB	Moderate Environment Buoy [*Marine science*] (MSC)
MeBa	Bangor Public Library, Bangor, ME [*Library symbol Library of Congress*] (LCLS)
MEBA	Marine Engineers' Beneficial Association
MeBaH	Husson College, Bangor, ME [*Library symbol Library of Congress*] (LCLS)
MeBaHi	Bangor Historical Society, Bangor, ME [*Library symbol Library of Congress*] (LCLS)
MeBarhJ	Jackson Laboratory, Bar Harbor, ME [*Library symbol Library of Congress*] (LCLS)
MeBaT	Bangor Theological Seminary, Bangor, ME [*Library symbol Library of Congress*] (LCLS)
MeBath	Patten Free Library, Bath, ME [*Library symbol Library of Congress*] (LCLS)
MeBathM	Maine Maritime Museum, Bath, ME [*Library symbol*] [*Library of Congress*] (LCLS)
MEBBAS	Mission Essential Bare Base Augmentation Sets [*Air Force*]
MeBC	Captain John Curtis Memorial Library, Brunswick, ME [*Library symbol*] [*Library of Congress*] (LCLS)
MEBD	Medical Evaluation Board [*Military*] (GFGA)

MEBE............ Middle East Basic Encyclopedia [*A publication*] (MCD)
MEBES......... Manufacturing Electron Beam Exposure System (IAA)
MEBFEX....... Marine Expeditionary Brigade Field Exercise (NVT)
MEBLEX....... Marine Expeditionary Brigade Landing Exercise
MEBO........... Main Engine Burnout (NASA)
MeBP........... Pejepscot Historical Society, Brunswick, ME [*Library symbol Library of Congress*] (LCLS)
Me-BPH....... Maine State Library Service for the Blind and Physically Handicapped, Augusta, ME [*Library symbol Library of Congress*] (LCLS)
MEBS........... Marketing, Engineering, and Business Services [*Telecommunications*] (TEL)
MEBS........... Multicore Extruded Bar Solder
MeBSA......... Methylated Bovine Serum Albumin [*Biochemistry*]
MEBU........... Maschinengewehr-Eisenbeton-Unterstand [*Machine-Gun-Iron-Concrete-Emplacement*] [*German "pill box," battlefield redoubts World War I*]
MEBU........... Mission Essential Backup (MCD)
MEC............. Maine Central Railroad Co. [*AAR code*]
MEC............. Main Engine Console (AAG)
MEC............. Main Engine Controller [*NASA*] (NASA)
MEC............. Main Engine Cutoff [*Aerospace*] (AAG)
MEC............. Main Evaluation Center (NVT)
MEC............. Major Events Committee [*Victoria, Australia*]
MEC............. Manta [*Ecuador*] [*Airport symbol*] (OAG)
MEC............. Manual Emergency Controls [*Aerospace*] (KSC)
MEC............. Manufacturing Engineering Council (EA)
MEC............. Map Editing Console
MEC............. Marginal Efficiency of Capital [*Economics*]
MEC............. Marine Expeditionary Corps (NVT)
MEC............. Maritime Electric Co. Ltd. [*Toronto Stock Exchange symbol*]
MEC............. Market Economy Country
MEC............. Master Evaluation Center (MCD)
MEC............. Master Event Controller [*NASA*] (NASA)
M Ec........... Master of Economics
MEC............. Master of Engineering Chemistry
MEC............. Materials Engineering Code
MEC............. Maximum Endurable Concentration (NATG)
MEC............. Mechernich [*Federal Republic of Germany*] [*Seismograph station code, US Geological Survey Closed*] (SEIS)
MEC............. Meconium [*Gynecology*]
MEC............. Medical Examination Centre [*British World War II*]
MEC............. Medicines Evaluation Committee [*Australia*]
MEC............. Member of Executive Council [*British*]
MEC............. Mercado Comune Europeo [*European Common Market*] [*Spanish*] (DLA)
MEC............. Mercury Aircourier Service [*ICAO designator*] (FAAC)
MEC............. Merrimack Education Center [*Chelmsford, MA*] [*Information service or system*]
MEC............. Meteorological Equipment Change (MCD)
MEC............. Meteorology Engineering Center [*Navy*] (MCD)
MEC............. Methodist Episcopal Church
MEC............. Metrolina Educational Consortium [*North Carolina*] (EDAC)
MEC............. Microelectronics Center
MEC............. Microencapsulation [*Chemical engineering*]
MEC............. Microwave Electronics Corp.
MEC............. MidAmerican Energy [*NYSE symbol*] (TTSB)
MEC............. Mid American Energy Co. [*NYSE symbol*] (SAG)
MEC............. Middle Ear Cell (BABM)
MEC............. Middle East Centre [*University of Cambridge*] [*British*] (CB)
MEC............. Middle East Command [*Military*]
MEC............. Military Equipment Code (DNAB)
MEC............. Military Essentiality Class [*or Code*]
MEC............. Minimum Effective Concentration [*Medicine*]
MEC............. Minimum Energy Curve (IAA)
MEC............. Minimum Essential Criteria (MCD)
MEC............. Minimum Explosive Concentration [*Safety*]
MEC............. Missile Engagement Console [*Military*] (CAAL)
MEC............. Missile Engagement Controller [*Military*] (CAAL)
MEC............. Missile Equipment Code
MEC............. Mission Events Controller [*NASA*] (MCD)
MEC............. Mobile Examination Center [*Department of Health and Human Services*] (GFGA)
MEC............. Mobility Equipment Command [*Later, TROSCOM*] [*Army*]
MEC............. Molecular Exclusion Chromatography
MEC............. Monetary and Economic Council (NADA)
MEC............. Monethylcholine [*Biochemistry*]
MEC............. Most Excellent Companion [*Freemasonry*] (ROG)
MEC............. Movimiento Emergente de Concordia [*Emerging Movement for Harmony*] [*Guatemala*] [*Political party*] (PPW)
MEC............. Multimedia European Center
MECA.......... Macedonian Educational and Cultural Association [*Australia*]
MECA.......... Main Engine Controller Assembly [*NASA*] (NASA)
MECA.......... Maintainable Electronics Component Assembly
MECA.......... Malfunctioned Equipment Corrective Action
MECA.......... Manufacturers of Emission Controls Association (EA)
MECA.......... Map Exercise Computer Assistance (MCD)
MECA.......... Mars: Evolution of Its Climate and Atmosphere [*Planetary science project*]
MECA.......... Matsushita Electric Corp. of America (IAA)
MECA.......... Measure of Elementary Communication Apprehension (EDAC)
MECA.......... Medical Emergency Calling Aid (MCD)
MECA.......... Mercury Evaporation and Condensation Analysis [*NASA*]
MECA.......... Micro Education Corp. of America
MECA.......... Military Educators and Counselors Association (EA)

MECA.......... Missile Electronics and Computer Assembly [*Military*] (PDAA)
MECA.......... Molecular Emission Cavity Analysis [*Flame spectrophotometry*]
MECA.......... Multielement Centrifugal Aerowindow
MECA.......... Multielement Component Array
MECA.......... Multivalue Electronic Circuit Analysis (IAA)
MECAB........ Regional Bureau of the Middle East Committee for the Affairs of the Blind [*Saudi Arabia*] (EAIO)
MECACON.... Middle East Civil Aviation Conference (PDAA)
Mecano....... Mechanotherapy [*Physical therapy*] (DAVI)
MECAP........ Medical Examiners and Coroners Alert Program [*Consumer Product Safety Commission*]
MECAR .... Metropolitan Engineers Council on Air Resources
MECAS........ Middle East Center for Arab Studies
MECAS........ Multienergy Californium Assay System [*Nuclear energy*] (NRCH)
MeCasM....... Maine Maritime Academy, Castine, ME [*Library symbol Library of Congress*] (LCLS)
MECAssn ..... Medical Eye Centre Association [*British*] (DBA)
MECC.......... Micellar Electrokinetic Capillary Chromatography
MECC.......... Middle East Council of Churches (EA)
MECC.......... Minnesota Educational Computing Corp. [*NASDAQ symbol*] (SAG)
MECC.......... Muslim Education Co-Ordinating Council (AIE)
MECCA........ Manufacturing Engineering and Cost Control Applications (NITA)
MECCA........ Master Electrical Common Connector Assembly (MCD)
MECCA........ Mechanized Catalog (IEEE)
MECCA........ Milwaukee Exposition and Convention Center and Arena
MECCA........ Missile Environment Computer Control Analysis (MCD)
MECCA........ Missionary and Ecumenical Council of the Church Assembly [*Church of England*]
MECCA........ Modular Electron Column Control and Automation
MECCAS ..... Microbial Exchanges and Coupling in Coastal Atlantic Systems
MeCCNU...... Methyl(chloroethyl)cyclohexylnitrosourea [*Semustine*] [*Antineoplastic drug*]
MECD.......... Military Equipment Characteristics Document (RDA)
MEcDev .... Master of Economics of Development
MECE.......... Master of Electrical and Computer Engineering (PGP)
MECE.......... Master of Electrochemical Engineering
MECE.......... Micellar Electrokinetic Capillary Electrophoresis [*Analytical chemistry*]
MECE.......... Movement, Ethyl Chloride, and Elevation [*Medicine*]
MECEA........ Mutual Educational and Cultural Exchange Act of 1961
MEC-ECR .... Management Engineering Steering Committee for Embedded Computer Resources (MCD)
MECEd........ Master of Early Childhood Education
MECEP........ Marine Corps Enlisted Commissioning Education Program (DNAB)
MECF.......... Main Engine Computational Facilities [*NASA*] (NASA)
MECF.......... Micks External Compression Fixator [*Instrumentation*]
MECG.......... Material Electrocardiogram (MCD)
MECG.......... Maternal Electrocardiogram [*Cardiology*] [*Obstetrics*] (DAVI)
MECH.......... Mechanic [*or Mechanics*] (AFM)
MECH.......... Mechanic
Mech .... Mechanica [*of Aristotle*] [*Classical studies*] (OCD)
mech .... Mechanical (DD)
MECH.......... Mechanics Savings Bank [*NASDAQ symbol*] (SAG)
MECH.......... Mechanism [*Automotive engineering*]
Mech .... Mechanized (VNW)
MECH.......... Mechanized (DOMA)
MECH.......... Methodist Episcopal Church
MECHBAD..... Mechanic Badge
MECHBAT..... Mechanized Battalion [*Army*]
MechDy....... Mechanical Dynamics, Inc. [*Associated Press*] (SAG)
ME Ch E ..... Master of Electrochemical Engineering
Mech E .... Mechanical Engineer (PGP)
ME(Chem)..... Master of Engineering (Chemical) (ADA)
Mechem ...... Mechem on Agency [*A publication*] (DLA)
Mechem ...... Mechem on Partnership [*A publication*] (DLA)
Mechem Ag... Mechem on Agency [*A publication*] (DLA)
Mechem Pub Off... Mechem on Public Offices and Officers [*A publication*] (DLA)
MECHEN ...... Mechanical Engineering (NITA)
Mech Eng .... Mechanical Engineer
MECHENGR... Mechanical Engineer
MECH/HYD... Mechanical/Hydraulic
MECH I/C .... Mechanic in Charge (DCTA)
MECHINF ..... Mechanized Infantry [*Army*]
MECHL........ Mechanical
MECH L .... Mechanic's Lien [*Legal term*] (DLA)
MECHN........ Mechanician [*Navy British*]
MECHNL ...... Mechanical
MECHSFIL ... Mechanized Sandbag Filler and Sealer (MCD)
MECHSIM .... Mechanical Simulation [*of a computer-based directory assistance system*]
MECHSM ..... Mechanism
MechSv....... Mechanics Savings Bank [*Associated Press*] (SAG)
MECHTRAM.. Mechanization of Selected Transportation Movement
MECI.......... Member of the Institute of Employment Consultants [*British*] (DBQ)
MECI.......... Mission Essential Contingency Item [*Military*]
MECK.......... Mecklermedia Corp. [*NASDAQ symbol*] (SAG)
Mecklm....... Mecklermedia Corp. [*Associated Press*] (SAG)
MECL.......... Motorola Emitter-Coupled Logic (IEEE)
MECL.......... Multiemitter-Coupled Logic (IAA)
MECM.......... Meridional Elementary Circulation Mechanism
MECN.......... Mecon Inc. [*NASDAQ symbol*] (TTSB)
MECO.......... Main Engine Cutoff [*Aerospace*]
MECO.......... Manual Equipment Checkout (NG)
MECOBO....... Military Export Cargo Offering and Booking Office
MECOM........ Marine Engine Condition Monitor (PDAA)
MECOM........ Middle East Command [*Military*]

MECOM.......	Middle East Electronic Communications Show and Conference [*Arabian Exhibition Management WLL*] [*Manama, Bahrain*]
MECOM.......	Mobility Equipment Command [*Later, TROSCOM*] [*Army*]
MECOMSAG...	Mobility Equipment Command Scientific Advisory Group (MCD)
MEcon	Master of Economics
M Econ	Master of Economics (PGP)
MEconS	Master of Economic Science (ADA)
MEconSt	Master of Economic Studies (ADA)
MeCP..........	Methyl-CCNU, Cytoxan, Prednisone [*Antineoplastic drug*] (CDI)
MECP	Multielliptical Cavity Pump
MECPr	MidAmer Energy $1.7375 Pfd [*NYSE symbol*] (TTSB)
MECR	Maintenance Engineering Change Request (MCD)
MEc(Reg Plan)...	Master of Economics in Regional Planning (ADA)
MECS..........	Manufacturing Energy Consumption Survey [*Department of Energy*] (GFGA)
MECS..........	Maximal Electroconvulsive Seizure [*Neurophysiology*]
MECS..........	Medicus Systems Corp. [*NASDAQ symbol*] (SAG)
MECS..........	Medicus Systems Softwr [*NASDAQ symbol*] (TTSB)
MECT	Mission Endurance Cycle Test
MECU	Master Engine Control Unit
MECU	Member of the English Church Union
MECU	Municipal Employees Credit Union (NADA)
MECWB.......	Middle East Committee for the Welfare of the Blind (EA)
MECY..........	Methotrexate, Cyclophosphamide [*Antineoplastic drug regimen*]
MECZ..........	Mechanize (AAG)
MED...........	Chicago, IL [*Location identifier FAA*] (FAAL)
MED...........	Macro Editor/Debugger [*Personics Corp.*] [*Computer science*] (PCM)
MED...........	Maine Department of Transportation, Augusta, ME [*OCLC symbol*] (OCLC)
MED...........	Manhattan Engineer District [*Developed atomic bomb; dissolved, 1946*]
MED...........	Manipulative Electronics Deception (MCD)
MED...........	Manual Electron Device
MED...........	Manual Entry Device
MED...........	Manufacturing Engineering Document (SAA)
M Ed	Master of Education
MED...........	Master of Education of the Deaf (GAGS)
MED...........	Master of Elementary Didactics
MED...........	Master of English Divinity
MED...........	Master of Environmental Design (GAGS)
MED...........	Mechanical Equipment Design
MED...........	Medal [*Numismatics*]
med...........	Medal (VRA)
MED...........	Medallion Explorations Ltd. [*Vancouver Stock Exchange symbol*]
MED...........	Medallist [*British*] (ROG)
MED...........	Medan [*Sumatra*] [*Seismograph station code, US Geological Survey Closed*] (SEIS)
Med	Medea [*of Euripides*] [*Classical studies*] (OCD)
MED...........	Media
med...........	Medial [*Medicine*]
MED...........	Median (AFM)
MED...........	Median Effective Dose [*Medicine*]
MED...........	Median Erythrocyte Diameter [*Medicine*]
Med	Mediator [*Legal term*] (DLA)
MED...........	Medical (AFM)
MED...........	Medical
MED...........	Medical Engineering Development (IIA)
MED...........	Medicamenta [*Medicaments*] [*Pharmacy*] (ROG)
MED...........	Medication
MED...........	Medicine (AABC)
MED...........	Medieval
MEdR..........	Medina [*Saudi Arabia*] [*Airport symbol*] (OAG)
MED...........	MEDIQ, Inc. [*AMEX symbol*] (SPSG)
MED...........	Meditation (ROG)
MED...........	Mediterranean (AFM)
MED...........	Mediterranean Engineer Division [*Army Engineers*]
MED...........	Medium (AFM)
MEDA..........	Message Entry Device
MED...........	Microelectronic Device
MED...........	Microwave Emission Detector [*Instrumentation*]
MED...........	Military Energy Depot (SAA)
MED...........	Minimal Effective Dose [*Medicine*]
MED...........	Minimal Erythema Dose [*Medicine*]
MED...........	Minimum Engineering Development (MCD)
MED...........	Minority Enterprise Development
MED...........	Mobile Energy Depot
MED...........	Modem Equivalent Device (ACRL)
MED...........	Modular Evolutionary Development (MCD)
MED...........	Molecular Electronic Device
MED...........	Monitor Execution Dump [*Computer science*]
MED...........	Multieffect Distillation [*Chemical engineering*]
MED...........	Multiformat Electroluminescent Display (PDAA)
MED...........	Multiple Epiphyseal Dysplasia [*Medicine*] (CPH)
MEDA..........	Medaphis Corp. [*NASDAQ symbol*] (SPSG)
MEDA..........	Mennonite Economic Development Associates (EA)
MEDA..........	(Mercaptoethyl)dimethylammonium Chloride [*Organic chemistry*]
MEDA..........	Military Emergency Diversion Aerodrome (DA)
MEDA..........	Multiplex Electronic Doppler Analyzer
MEDAB........	Middle East Database (IID)
MEDAC	Medical Accounting and Billing Process]
MEDAC	Medical Electronic Data Aquisition and Control
MEDAC	Medical Equipment Display and Conference (IAA)
MEDAC	Military Electronic Data Advisory Committee [*NATO*] (NATG)
MEDAC	Mouvement de l'Evolution Democratique de l'Afrique Centrale [*Central African Democratic Evolution Movement*]

MEDAC	Multiple, Endocrine Deficiency - Addison's Disease - Candidiasis [*Syndrome*] [*Endocrinology*] (DAVI)
MEDAC	Multiple Endocrine Deficiency, Autoimmune-Candidiasis [*Syndrome*] [*Medicine*]
MEDACS	Medical Administrative Control System (IAA)
MedAct	Medical Action Industries, Inc. [*Associated Press*] (SAG)
MEdAd	Master of Educational Administration (ADA)
MEdAdm	Master of Educational Administration (ADA)
Med Adm C..	Medical Administrative Corps [*Army World War II*]
MEdAdmin	Master of Educational Administration
MEDAL........	Medallion [*Automotive engineering*]
MEDAL........	Micromechanized Engineering Data for Automated Logistics
MEDALS	Modular Engineering Drafting and Library System (IAA)
MEDALSA	Mediterranean Algeria-Sahara Zone [*NATO*] (NATG)
Medalst	Medalist Industries, Inc. [*Associated Press*] (SAG)
Medamic	Medamicus, Inc. [*Associated Press*] (SAG)
Medaph	Medaphis Corp. [*Associated Press*] (SAG)
Medar.......	Medar, Inc. [*Associated Press*] (SAG)
Medarex	Medarex, Inc. [*Associated Press*] (SAG)
Medarx	Medarex, Inc. [*Associated Press*] (SAG)
MEDAS	Medical Emergency Decisions Assistance System (MCD)
MEDAS	Meteorological Data Acquisition System [*NASA*] (KSC)
MEDAS	Microfilm Enhanced Data System (PDAA)
MEDAUG	Medical Augmentation (MCD)
MEDAX	Message Data Exchange Terminal (MCD)
MEDBAD	Medical Badge
MEDBN	Medical Battalion [*Marine Corps*]
MEDBO	Mediterranean Shipping Board [*World War II*]
MEDBR	Medical Branch
MEDC..........	[*The*] Med-Design Corp. [*NASDAQ symbol*] (SAG)
MEDC..........	Microelectronics Educational Development Centre [*Paisley College*] [*British*] (CB)
MEDC..........	Moessbauer Effect Data Center [*University of North Carolina*] [*Information service or system*] (IID)
MEdCA........	Master of Education in Creative Arts
MEDCAP.......	Patrol [*or Assistance*] [*or Program*] [*Military*]
MEDCASE	Medical Care Support Equipment (AABC)
MEDCAT	Medical Civic Action Teams
MEDCAT	Medium Altitude Clear-Air Turbulence (MCD)
MEDCAT	Medium-Altitude Critical Atmospheric Turbulence (MCD)
MedCath.......	MedCath, Inc. [*Associated Press*] (SAG)
MEDCEN	Medical Center [*Army*] (AABC)
MEDCENT	Central Mediterranean Area [*NATO*]
Med C Georgia...	Medical College of Georgia (GAGS)
MEDCL........	Medical
MEDCMNT	Medicament
MedCmp	Medic Computer Systems, Inc. [*Associated Press*] (SAG)
MEDCN	Medicine
Med C Ohio...	Medical College of Ohio at Toledo (GAGS)
MEDCOM.....	Medical Command (MCD)
MEDCOM.....	Mediterranean Communications [*Military*] (AFM)
MEDCOMP...	Medical Early Direct Commissioning Program (MCD)
MEDCOMPLAN...	Mediterranean Communications Plans [*NATO*] (NATG)
MEDCON	Medical Contingency Report [*Air Force*]
MEDCOOP....	Medical Continuity of Operations Plan [*Army*] (AABC)
MEDCORE....	Medical Resources Consortium of Central New Jersey [*Library network*]
MEDCORPS...	Medical Corps [*Air Force*]
MEDCOS	Mediterranean Chiefs of Staff [*British World War II*]
Med C Penn...	Medicine College of Pennsylvania (GAGS)
MedcR........	Medco Research, Inc. [*Associated Press*] (SAG)
Medcross......	Medcross, Inc. [*Associated Press*] (SAG)
MedCtrl........	Medical Contol [*Associated Press*] (SAG)
Med C Wis...	Medicine College of Wisconsin (GAGS)
Medd	Meddaugh's Reports [*13 Michigan*] [*A publication*] (DLA)
MEDD	Medical Device Technol [*NASDAQ symbol*] (TTSB)
MEDD	Medical Device Technologies, Inc. [*NASDAQ symbol*] (SAG)
MEDDA	Mechanized Defense Decision Anticipation [*AFSC*]
MEDDAC......	Medical Department Activity [*Army*] (AABC)
MEDDARS...	Medical Display Analysis and Recording System
Meddaugh ...	Meddaugh's Reports [*13 Michigan*] [*A publication*] (DLA)
MED-DENT...	Medical Dental Division [*Air Force*]
Med Devices Rep (CCH)...	Medical Devices Reports (Commerce Clearing House) [*A publication*] (DLA)
MedDevT	Medical Device Technologies, Inc. [*Associated Press*] (SAG)
MEDDF	Master Engineering Drawing Data File System
MEdDHi	Dukes County Historical Society, Edgartown, MA [*Library symbol Library of Congress*] (LCLS)
MEDDIC	Medical Evidence Disaggregated Direct Input of Costs Database [*Social Security Administration*] (GFGA)
MEDDOC......	Medical Documentation Systems [*Eli Lilly & Co.*] [*Information service or system*] (IID)
MEDDPERSA...	Medical Department Personnel Support Agency [*Army*] (MCD)
MEDDS	Medical Data Specialist (AABC)
MedDsg	[*The*] Med-Design Corp. [*Associated Press*] (SAG)
MedDv.......	Medical Device Technologies, Inc. [*Associated Press*] (SAG)
MedDvt........	Medical Device Technologies, Inc. [*Associated Press*] (SAG)
MEDDY	Mediterranean Eddy [*Oceanography*]
MedDyn.......	Medical Dynamics, Inc. [*Associated Press*] (SAG)
MEDEA........	Masters Degree in Energy and Environmental Management and Economics (ECON)
MEDEA........	Measurements of Earth Data for Environmental Analysis [*Marine science*] (OSRA)
MEDEA........	Multidiscipline Engineering Design, Evaluation, and Analysis (RDA)
MEDEAST	Eastern Mediterranean Area [*NATO*] (NATG)

MEd(Ed/Psych)... Master of Education (Educational Psychology), University of Birmingham [*British*] (DBQ)
MEDEMG .... Medical Emergencies [*Computerized management course*]
MEDes .... Master of Environmental Design (DD)
Medeva .... Medeva Ltd. [*Associated Press*] (SAG)
MEDEVAC .... Medical Evacuation Team [*Army*]
MEDEVAL ...... Medical Evaluation [*Military*] (AABC)
MEDEX .... Medecin Extension [*Doctors' Aides, or Medics*] [*French*]
Medex .... Medex, Inc. [*Associated Press*] (SAG)
MEDF .... Maximum Energy Distribution Function
MEDF .... Midexpiratory Dynamic Flow Rate [*Medicine*] (DAVI)
MedfdSv .... Medford Savings Bank [*Associated Press*] (SAG)
MEDFLY .... Mediterranean Fruit Fly
MEDGP .... Medical Group [*Air Force*]
MedGr .... Medical Graphics Corp. [*Associated Press*] (SAG)
MEd(Guid&Coun)... Master of Education in Guidance and Counselling
MEDH .... Maintainability Engineering Design Handbook
MEDI .... Marine Environmental Data Information Referral System [*UNESCO*] [*Paris, France*]
medi .... Media (VRA)
MEDI .... Medicine (DSUE)
MEDI .... MedImmune, Inc. [*NASDAQ symbol*] (SPSG)
MEDI .... Missile Error Data Integration [*Military*] (IAA)
MEDI .... Moessbauer Effect Data Index
MEDIA .... Magnavox Electronic Data Image Apparatus
MEDIA .... Man's Environments - Display Implication and Applications (PDAA)
MEDIA .... Manufacturers Educational Drug Information Association
MEDIA .... Measures for Encouraging the Development of the Audiovisual Production Industry [*EC*] (ECED)
Media .... Media General, Inc. [*Associated Press*] (SAG)
MEDIA .... Missile Era Data Integration Analysis
MEDIA .... Modular Electronic Digital Instrumentation Assemblies (PDAA)
MEDIA .... Move to End Deception in Advertising [*Student legal action organization*]
MediaArt...... Media Arts Group, Inc. [*Associated Press*] (SAG)
Media L & P... Media Law and Practice [*A publication*] (DLA)
MediaLog .... Media Logic, Inc. [*Associated Press*] (SAG)
Media M ...... Media and Methods [*A publication*] (BRI)
MEDIA/M ..... Media/Medicine (NITA)
MEDIC .... Mechanized Design and Integrated Control
MEDIC .... Medical Electronic Data Interpretation and Correlation (IAA)
Medic .... Medicamina Faciei [*of Ovid*] [*Classical studies*] (OCD)
MEDICAID ... Medical Aid [*Federal program providing financial assistance for medical expenses of individual needy citizens*]
MEDICARE ... Medical Care [*Federal program providing financial assistance for medical expenses of individual senior citizens*]
MEDICI .... Melodic Dictation Computerized Instruction (EDAC)
Medicis........ Medicis Pharmaceutical Corp. [*Associated Press*] (SAG)
MEDICO .... Medical Information Cooperation (DAVI)
MEDICO .... Medical International Cooperation
MEDICO .... Model Experiment in Drug Indexing by Computer [*Rutgers University*]
MEDICOM ..... Medical Communications
MEDICOR..... Centre for Offshore and Remote Medicine [*Memorial University of Newfoundland*] [*Research center*] (RCD)
MEDICOS ..... Mediterranean Instructions to Convoys [*World War II*]
MEDICS .... Majors Electronic Data Interchange Communications System [*Computer science*]
MEDICS .... Medical Information and Career Service [*British*] (DAVI)
MEDICS .... Medical Information and Communications System (NITA)
MEDICS .... Medical Information Computer System (NASA)
MEDICS ...... Michael E. DeBakey International Cardiovascular Society [*Later, MEDISS*] (EA)
Medicus....... Medicus Systems Corp. [*Associated Press*] (SAG)
MEDIEV........ Medieval
MEDIF.......... Medical Information Form [*British*]
medi gen ...... Media Generated (VRA)
MEDIHC ...... Military Experience Directed into Health Careers [*DoD/HEW project*]
MedImun ..... MedImmune, Inc. [*Associated Press*] (SAG)
MedInd .... Medical Industries of America [*Associated Press*] (SAG)
MedIndA ...... Medical Industries of America [*Associated Press*] (SAG)
MEDINET ..... Medical Information Network [*GTE Telenet Communications Corp.*] [*Telecommunications*]
MEDINFO..... Medical Informatics
MedInn .... Medical Innovations, Inc. [*Associated Press*] (SAG)
MEDINSP..... Medical Inspection [*Military*] (NVT)
MEDINT .... Medical Intelligence (MCD)
MEDIOC .... Mediocris [*Middling*] [*Pharmacy*] (ROG)
MEDIOL .... Mediolanum [*Milan*] [*Imprint*] (ROG)
MEDIPHOR... Monitoring and Evaluation of Drug Interactions in a Pharmacy-Oriented Reporting System [*National Center for Health Services Research*] (DHSM)
MEDIPP .... Medical District Initiated Program Planning [*Veterans Administration*]
MEDIPRO..... Medical District Initiated Peer Review Organization [*Veterans Administration*] (GFGA)
Mediq .... Mediq, Inc. [*Associated Press*] (SAG)
MEDIS .... Message Diversion Relay System (IAA)
MedisE .... Medis E Ltd. [*Associated Press*] (SAG)
MediSens .... MediSense, Inc. [*Associated Press*] (SAG)
MEDI-SOTA LIBR... Medi-Sota Library Consortium [*Library network*]
MEDISS .... Michael E. DeBakey International Surgical Society (EA)
MEDISTAT ... Banque de Donnees Socio-Economiques des Pays Mediterraneens [*Socioeconomic Data Bank on the Mediterranean Countries*] [*International Center for Advanced Mediterranean Agronomic Studies*] [*Information service or system*] (IID)
MEDIT.......... Mediterranean

MEDITEC...... Dodumentation Medizinische Technik [*Medical Technology Documentation*] [*TechnicalInformation Center*] [*Germany*] [*Information service or system*] (IID)
Meditr.......... Meditrust [*Associated Press*] (SAG)
MEDIUM ..... Missile Era Data Integration - Ultimate Method
Mediwre ...... Mediware Information Systems, Inc. [*Associated Press*] (SAG)
M Ed J .... Music Educators Journal [*A publication*] (BRI)
MED JUR ..... Medical Jurisprudence (ADA)
MEDL.......... Marconi Electronic Devices Ltd. [*British*] (IRUK)
MEDL.......... Materials Evaluation and Development Laboratory [*General Services Administration*]
MEDL.......... Medical
MEDLA........ Molecular Electron Density Lego Assembler [*Modeling technique*] [*Organic chemistry*]
Med L & P... Media Law and Practice [*1980*] [*A publication*] (DLA)
Med L & Pub Pol... Medicine, Law, and Public Policy [*A publication*] (DLA)
MEDLARS .... Medical Literature Analysis and Retrieval System [*National Library of Medicine*] [*Bethesda, MD Database*]
Med Lat...... Medieval Latin [*Language*]
Med-Legal J... Medico-Legal Journal [*A publication*] (DLA)
Med-Legal Soc'y Trans... Medico-Legal Society. Transactions [*A publication*] (DLA)
Med Leg Pap... Medico-Legal Papers [*A publication*] (DLA)
Med Leg Soc Trans... Transactions. Medico-Legal Society [*A publication*] (ILCA)
Med Leg Vic Proc... Medico-Legal Society of Victoria. Proceedings [*A publication*]
MEDLI.......... Motoring Experience for the Disabled by Lions International [*British*]
MEDLINE ...... Medical Information Online (NITA)
MEDLINE ..... MEDLARS [*Medical Literature Analysis and Retrieval System*] On-Line [*National Library of Medicine*] [*Bibliographic database*]
MEDList....... Master Enumeration District List [*Bureau of Census*]
medln.......... Medallion (VRA)
Med LN........ Medico-Legal News [*A publication*] (DLA)
MEDLOC...... Mediterranean Lines of Communication [*Military*] (IAA)
MEDLOC...... Mediterranean Location [*Navy*]
Med LP........ Medico-Legal Papers [*A publication*] (DLA)
Med L Rptr... Media Law Reporter [*A publication*] (NTCM)
M Ed LS ..... Master of Education in Library Science
M ED L SC... Master of Education in Library Science (WDAA)
MEDM.......... Medamicus, Inc. [*NASDAQ symbol*] (SAG)
MEDM.......... Medium
Medm.......... Medmarco, Inc. [*Associated Press*] (SAG)
MEDMAF..... Mekong Delta Mobile Afloat Force [*Vietnam*] [*Military*] (VNW)
MEDMAILCOORD... Mediterranean Mail Coordinating Office (DNAB)
MEDMAL...... Medical Malpractice Lawsuit Filings [*Medical Malpractice Verdicts, Settlements & Experts*] [*Information service or system*] (CRD)
MEd(Maths)... Master of Education (Mathematics)
MEDMATS ... Medical Materiel Management System [*Army*]
med men...... Medial Meniscectomy [*orthopedics*] (DAVI)
med men ...... Medial Meniscus [*Orthopedics*] (DAVI)
MEDMER ..... Medical Emergency Report [*Air Force*]
MedMgt....... Medical Management, Inc. [*Associated Press*] (SAG)
MEDMIS ...... Medical Management Information System [*Army*]
Mednet .... Mednet MPC Corp. [*Associated Press*] (SAG)
MEDNOREAST... Northeast Mediterranean Area [*NATO*] (NATG)
MEDNTPS... Mediterranean Near-Term Prepositioned Ship
MEDO .... Middle East Defense Organization (NATG)
MEDO .... Multipole Expansion of Diatomic Overlap [*Physics*]
MEDOC....... Medical Documents [*Eccles Health Sciences Library - University of Utah*] [*Salt Lake City, UT Bibliographic database*]
MEDOC....... Mediterranean Oceanographic Project [*1969*]
MEDOC........ Western Mediterranean Area [*NATO*] (NATG)
MEDOCHAN... Mary Ellen, Dorothy, Chuck, Ann [*Famous Canadian resort, named for the owners' children*]
MEDOFCOM... Medical Officer-in-Command [*Military*]
MEDOL .... Medically Oriented Language
MEDOWS...... Meadows [*Commonly used*] (OPSA)
MEDP.......... Medium Port
MEDP.......... MedPlus, Inc. [*NASDAQ symbol*] (SAG)
MedPAC...... Medicare Payment Advisory Commission
MEDPAR ..... Medicare Provider Analysis and Review (GFGA)
MedPart....... MedPartners, Inc. [*Associated Press*] (SAG)
MedPlus...... MedPlus, Inc. [*Associated Press*] (SAG)
MEDPr........ MEDIQ Inc. Cv Pfd [*AMEX symbol*] (TTSB)
MEDPRO...... Medical Education Resources Program (MEDA)
MEdPsych... Master of Educational Psychology (ADA)
MEDQ .... MedQuist Inc. [*NASDAQ symbol*] (TTSB)
MedQst....... MedQuist, Inc. [*Associated Press*] (SAG)
MedRA........ Medical Resource Companies of America [*Associated Press*] (SAG)
MEDRAMS ... Medical Readiness Assemblage Medical System [*Air Force*] (GFGA)
MEDRC....... Medical Reserve Corps [*Military*] (WDAA)
MEDRED ...... Medical Unit Readiness Report [*Air Force*]
MedResc ..... Medical Resources, Inc. [*Associated Press*] (SAG)
MEDRESCO... Medical Research Council (NADA)
MEDRETES... Medical Readiness Training Exercises [*Army*]
MEDREX ...... Medical Readiness Exercise (MCD)
medRNA ...... Ribonucleic Acid, Mini-Exon-Derived [*Biochemistry, genetics*]
MEd(RuralEd)... Master of Education in Rural Education
MEDS.......... Marine Ecological Database System [*Marine science*] (OSRA)
MEDS.......... Marine Ecological Database System (USDC)
MEDS.......... Marine Environmental Data Service [*Canada*] (NOAA)
MEDS.......... Master of Environmental Design Studies (PGP)
MEDS.......... Mechanized Embarkation Data System [*Military*] (NVT)
MEDS.......... Medical Electronics and Data Society [*Later, MES*] (EA)
MEDS.......... Medical Evaluation Data System (IEEE)
Meds .... Medications [*or Medicines*]
MEDS.......... Medstone International, Inc. [*NASDAQ symbol*] (SAG)

MEDS.......... Medstone Intl. [*NASDAQ symbol*] (TTSB)
MEDS.......... Meteorological and Environmental Data Services (USDC)
MEDS.......... Meteorological Environmental Data Services [*Marine science*] (OSRA)
MEDS.......... Multifunction Electronic Display System [*NASA*]
MEDSAC...... Medical Service Activity [*Army*] (AABC)
MEDSARS.... Maintenance Engineering Data Storage and Retrieval System (NG)
Med Sc D .... Doctor of Medical Science [*or the Science of Medicine*]
MEDSCH...... Medical School (ADA)
MedSch(N)... Institute of Naval Medicine [*British*]
MEDSERV..... Medical Service Corps [*Military*] (MCD)
MEDSERVC... Medical Service Corps [*Military*]
MEDSERVWRNT... Medical Service Warrant
MEDSOM...... Medical Supply, Optical, and Maintenance [*Army*] (RDA)
MEDSOUEAST... Southeast Mediterranean Area [*NATO*] (NATG)
MEDSPECC... Medical Specialist Corps [*Military*]
MEd(SpecEd)... Master of Education (Special Education)
MEd(SpEd).. Master of Education in Special Education (ADA)
MEDSS .... Multiple Echelon Direct Support System (MCD)
MEdSt......... Master of Educational Studies (ADA)
MEDSTAR .... Medical Staffing and Training to Augment Readiness (MCD)
MEDSTAT .... Medicaid Statistical Reporting and Analysis System (GFGA)
med stern ... Median Sternotomy (CPH)
MEDSTOC.... Medical Stock Control System [*Army*]
Medstone..... Medstone International, Inc. [*Associated Press*] (SAG)
MEdStud...... Master of Educational Studies
MEDSUPDEP... Medical Supply Depot
MedSurg...... Medicine and Surgery (DAVI)
M Ed T........ Master of Education in Teaching (PGP)
MEDT.......... Mean Elapsed Downtime [*Computer science*] (MCD)
MedT.......... Medical Technology Systems, Inc. [*Associated Press*] (SAG)
MEDT.......... Military Equipment Delivery Team
MEDTC........ Military Equipment Delivery Team Cambodia (VNW)
med tech .... Medical Technician [*or Technologist*] (AAMN)
Med Tech .... Medical Technology (DAVI)
MedTech...... Medical Technology Systems, Inc. [*Associated Press*] (SAG)
MEDTRAIN... Medical Literature Training File (NITA)
Medtrnc...... Medtronic, Inc. [*Associated Press*] (SAG)
Medusa....... Medusa Corp. [*Associated Press*] (SAG)
MEDUSA .... Multiple Element Directional Universally Steerable Antenna
Med U So Car... Medical University of South Carolina (GAGS)
MedVat....... MediVators, Inc. [*Associated Press*] (SAG)
MEDW .... Mediware Information Sys [*NASDAQ symbol*] (TTSB)
MEDW .... Mediware Information Systems, Inc. [*NASDAQ symbol*] (SAG)
Medwve...... Medwave, Inc. [*Associated Press*] (SAG)
MEDX.......... Medarex, Inc. [*NASDAQ symbol*] (SPSG)
MEDXW....... Medarex Inc. Wrrt [*NASDAQ symbol*] (TTSB)
MEDY.......... Medial Dynamics [*NASDAQ symbol*] (TTSB)
MEDYN .... Medical Dynamics, Inc. [*NASDAQ symbol*] (NQ)
MEE .... Maine Office of Energy Resources Library, Augusta, ME [*OCLC symbol*] (OCLC)
MEE .... Maintenance Engineering Evaluation (MCD)
MEE .... Mare [*Loyalty Islands*] [*Airport symbol*] (OAG)
MEE .... Mass Energy Equivalent
MEE .... Master of Electrical Engineering
MEE .... Mechanical, Electrical, and Electronic (MCD)
MEE .... Mechanical Evaluation Equipment
MEE .... Meerut [*India*] [*Seismograph station code, US Geological Survey Closed*] (SEIS)
MEE .... Merrill Lynch & Co., Inc. [*NYSE symbol*] (SAG)
MEE .... Methyl Ethyl Ether [*Organic chemistry*]
MEE .... Middle Ear Effusion [*Medicine*]
MEE .... Military Essential Equipment (CINC)
MEE .... Minimum Essential Equipment
MEE .... Mission Essential Equipment [*NASA*] (KSC)
MEE .... Muskogee, OK [*Location identifier FAA*] (FAAL)
MEECN........ Minimum Essential Emergency Communications Network [*Military*]
MEED.......... Medium-Energy Electron Diffraction
MEED.......... Microbial Ecology Evaluation Device [*NASA*] (KSC)
ME-EE........ Mechanical Engineer and Electrical Engineer [*Academic degree*]
MEEF .... Manufacturing Engineering Education Foundation
MEEF .... Mobile Equipment Employment File [*Air Force*] (AFM)
MEEL .... Mission Equipment Essentiality List
MeEl .... William Fogg Memorial Library, Eliot, ME [*Library symbol Library of Congress*] (LCLS)
ME(Elec)..... Master of Engineering (Electrical) (ADA)
MEEM .... Master of Environmental Engineering and Management (PGP)
MEEM .... Metastable Electron Emission Microscopy
ME Eng....... Master of Electrical Engineering
MEEP .... Management and Equipment Evaluation Program
MEER .... Mechanical/Electrical Equipment Room (MCD)
MEERS........ Maximum Effective Echo Ranging Speed (NVT)
MEES .... Marine-Estuarine-Environmental Sciences (PDAA)
MEES .... Middle East Economic Survey [*A publication*]
MEES .... Multipurpose Electromagnetic Environment Simulator (MCD)
Mees & Ros... Meeson and Roscoe's English Exchequer Reports [*A publication*] (DLA)
Mees & W ... Meeson and Welsby's English Exchequer Reports [*A publication*] (DLA)
Mees & Wels... Meeson and Welsby's English Exchequer Reports [*A publication*] (DLA)
MEET .... Minimum Essential Equipment for Training
MEETA......... Maximum Improvement in Electronics Effectiveness through Advanced Techniques

MEETAT ...... Maximum Improvement in Electronics Effectiveness through Advanced Techniques
MEEV .... Maintenance and Electricity Equipment Vault (MCD)
MEF .... Emerging Mexico Fund [*NYSE symbol*] (SPSG)
MEF .... Maintenance Efficiency Factor
MEF .... Major Emitting Facility [*Environmental Protection Agency*]
MEF .... Major Equipment File (MCD)
MEF .... Management Engineering Flight [*Air Force*]
MEF .... Marine Expeditionary Force
MEF .... Maximal Expiratory Flow [*Medicine*]
MEF .... Mechanized Engineering File
MEF .... Median Energy of Fission (NRCH)
MEF .... Mediterranean Expeditionary Force [*World War I*] [*British*]
MEF .... Melfi [*Chad*] [*Airport symbol*] (AD)
MEF .... Mesopotamian Expeditionary Force [*British*]
MEF .... Middle Ear Fluid
MEF .... Middle East Forces [*British*]
MEF .... Middle East Forum [*Lebanon*] (BJA)
MEF .... Mideast File [*Tel-Aviv University*] [*Israel*] [*Information service or system*] (IID)
MEF .... Midexpiratory Flow [*Medicine*] (DMAA)
MEF .... Migration Enhancement Factor [*Biochemistry*]
MEF .... Minimum Essential Force (CINC)
MEF .... Ministry for Environment and Forests [*India*]
MEF .... Mission Equipment Facility (MCD)
MEF .... Mortality Enhancing Factors [*Chemical and biological warfare*]
MEF .... Mouse Embryo Fibroblast
MEF .... Multiple Effect Flash [*Evaporator*] [*Seawater conversion system*]
MEF .... Multi-Purpose Electric Furnace (PDAA)
MEF .... Muscle Enhancer Factor [*Genetics*]
MEF .... Musicians Emergency Fund (EA)
MEF .... Myocyte Enhancing Factor [*Genetics*]
MEFA .... Metal Etching and Fabricating Association [*Later, National Association of Name Plate Manufacturers*] (EA)
MEFA .... Methyl-CCNU 5-Fluorouracil, Adriamycin [*Antineoplastic drug regimen*] (DAVI)
MeFarGS .... Church of Jesus Christ of Latter-Day Saints, Genealogical Society Library, Augusta Branch, Farmingdale, ME [*Library symbol Library of Congress*] (LCLS)
MeFarU........ University of Maine at Farmington, Farmington, ME [*Library symbol Library of Congress*] (LCLS)
MEFC .... Maximum Economic Finding Cost
MEFC .... Mister Ed Fan Club (EA)
MEFEX .... Middle East Food and Equipment Exhibition [*Arabian Exhibition Management*]
M-EFF......... Myocardial Efficiency [*Cardiology*]
MEFFEX....... Marine Expeditionary Force Field Exercise (NVT)
MEFLEX....... Marine Expeditionary Force Landing Exercise (NVT)
MEFPAK...... Manpower and Equipment Force Packaging [*Military*]
MEFR.......... Maximum Expiratory Flow Rate [*Medicine*]
MEFR.......... Maximum Midexpiratory Flow Rate [*Medicine*] (DAVI)
MEFS .... Midterm Energy Forecasting System [*Department of Energy*] (GFGA)
ME/FS......... Missing/Embryo Fetus Syndrome
MEFSR......... Maximal Expiratory Flow Static Recoil Curve [*Medicine*] (MAE)
MeFtkU .... University of Maine at Fort Kent, Fort Kent, ME [*Library symbol Library of Congress*] (LCLS)
MEFTL .... Middle East Force Target List (MCD)
MEFV.......... Maintenance Equipment Floor Valve (NRCH)
MEFV.......... Maximal Expiratory Flow Volume [*Medicine*] (AAMN)
MEG........... Madly Enthusiastic about Grapes
MEG........... Magnetoencephalogram [*Medicine*]
MEG........... Magnetoencephalography [*Medicine*] (ECON)
MEG........... Malange [*Angola*] [*Airport symbol*] (OAG)
MEG........... Management Evaluation Group [*Department of State*]
MEG........... Media General, Inc. [*AMEX symbol*] (SPSG)
MEG........... Mega [*A prefix meaning multiplied by one million*] (AAG)
MEG........... Megacycle (NTCM)
Meg........... Megakaryocyte [*Hematology*]
meg........... Megaloblastic [*Cytology*] (AAMN)
meg........... Megaron (VRA)
MEG........... Megaton (WDAA)
MEG........... Megawatt (WDAA)
Meg........... Megiddo (BJA)
MEG........... Megillah (BJA)
MEG........... Megohm (AAG)
meg........... Megohm (IDOE)
MEG........... Megohm
Meg........... Megone's Companies Acts Cases [*1888-90*] [*England*] [*A publication*] (DLA)
MEG........... Mercaptoethylguanidine [*Biochemistry*] (AAMN)
MEG........... Message Entry Generator (NVT)
MEG........... Message Expediting Group (IEEE)
MEG........... Methyl(ethyl)glycine [*Biochemistry*]
MEG........... Midlands Examining Group [*British*] (AIE)
MEG........... Miniature Electrostatic Gyro
MEG........... Monoethylene Glycol [*Chemicals*]
MEG........... Multifocal Eosinophilic Granuloma [*Medicine*] (DMAA)
MEG........... Multimedia Environmental Goals [*Environmental Protection Agency*]
MEG........... NRA [*National Restaurant Association*] Marketing Executives Group [*Chicago, IL*] (EA)
MEGA.......... Megaampere (IAA)
MEGA.......... Megakaryocyte [*Hematology*] (DAVI)
MEGA.......... Military Evaluation of Geographic Areas
mega-......... Millions (10^6) (IDOE)
MEGA.......... Molecular Evolutionary Genetics Analysis [*Computer software*]

MEGACE ...... Megestrol Acetate [*Antineoplastic drug*]
MEGAFLOPS... Millions of Floating Point Operations per Second (PDAA)
Me-GAG .... Methylglyoxalbis(guanylhydrazone) [*Mitoguazone*] [*Also, MGBG*] [*Antineoplastic drug*]
MeGar .... Gardiner Public Library, Gardiner, ME [*Library symbol Library of Congress*] (LCLS)
Megarry .... Megarry's The Rent Acts [*A publication*] (DLA)
MEGAS .... Multienergy Gamma Assay System [*Nuclear energy*] (NRCH)
MEGASTAR... Meaning of Energy Growth: An Assessment of Systems, Technologies, and Requirements [*NASA*]
Megatest ..... Megatest Corp. [*Associated Press*] (SAG)
MEGC .... Megacycle (IAA)
MEGC .... Megacycle per Second [*Megahertz*] (IAA)
mEGF .... Mouse Epidermal Growth Factor
mEGF-URO... Mouse Epidermal Growth Factor - Urogastrone [*Endocrinology*]
MEGG .... Merging (FAAC)
Megg Ass .... Meggison's Assets in Equity [*1832*] [*A publication*] (DLA)
Meg-GPA ..... Megakaryocyte Growth-Promoting Activity [*Hematology*]
MEGHP .... Most Excellent Grand High Priest [*Freemasonry*]
MEGI .... Missile Exhaust Gas Ingestion (MCD)
MEGLUMINE... N-Methylglucamine [*USAN*] [*Organic chemistry*]
MEGM .... Most Eminent Grand Master [*Freemasonry*] (ROG)
MEGO .... Mego Financial [*NASDAQ symbol*] (TTSB)
MEGO .... Mego Financial Corp. [*NASDAQ symbol*] (SAG)
MEGO .... Megohm (MSA)
MEGO .... My Eyes Glaze Over [*An article, written about an important subject, that resists reader interest and has a soporific effect*] [*Journalistic slang*]
MegoFin ...... Mego Financial Corp. [*Associated Press*] (SAG)
MegoFinl ..... Mego Financial [*Associated Press*] (SAG)
MegoMrt ...... Mego Mortgage Corp. [*Associated Press*] (SAG)
Megone .... Megone's Companies Acts Cases [*1888-90*] [*England*] [*A publication*] (DLA)
Me Gov't Reg... Maine Government Register [*A publication*] (AAGC)
MEGS .... Male Electronic Genital Stimulator [*Developed by Biosonics, Inc.*]
MEGS .... Market Entry Guarantee Scheme [*Board of Trade*] [*British*] (DI)
MEGS .... Megasecond (AAG)
MEGS .... Missile End-Game Scoring System (DWSG)
MEGSSS ...... Mathematics Education for Gifted Secondary School Students Project (EDAC)
MEGT .... Megatest Corp. [*NASDAQ symbol*] (SAG)
MEGT .... Megaton [*Nuclear equivalent of one million tons of high explosive*] (AAG)
MegTa'an .... Megillat Ta'anit (BJA)
MEGV .... Megavolt (AAG)
MEGW .... Megawatt [*Also, MW*]
MEGWH .... Megawatt-Hour
MEGX .... Megacards Inc. [*NASDAQ symbol*] (TTSB)
MEGX .... Monoethylglycine Xylidide [*Biochemistry*]
MEH .... Maine State Department of Human Services, Augusta, ME [*OCLC symbol*] (OCLC)
MEH .... Meacham, OR [*Location identifier FAA*] (FAAL)
MEH .... Mehamn [*Norway*] [*Airport symbol*] (OAG)
MEH .... Midwest Express Holdings [*NYSE symbol*] (SAG)
MEH .... Multi-Engined Helicopter (MCD)
Meharry Med C... Meharry Medicine College (GAGS)
MEHDHQ ...... Medical Embarkment and Hospital Distribution Headquarters [*World War II*]
MeHi .... Maine Historical Society, Portland, ME [*Library symbol Library of Congress*] (LCLS)
MEHL .... Mehl Biophile International Corp. [*NASDAQ symbol*] (SAG)
MehlBio .... Mehl Biophile International Corp. [*Associated Press*] (SAG)
MEHP .... Mean Effective Horsepower (IAA)
MEHP .... Monoethylhexyl Phthalate [*Organic chemistry*]
MEHQ .... Monomethyl Ether of Hydroquinone [*Organic chemistry*]
MEHT .... Minimum Eye Height over Threshold [*Aviation*] (FAAC)
MEI .... Main Economic Indicators (NITA)
MEI .... Main Engine Ignition [*Aerospace*]
MEI .... Maintenance and Engineering Inspection
MEI .... Maintenance Effectiveness Inspection (MCD)
MEI .... Maintenance Engineering Investigation [*DoD*]
MEI .... Maintenance Evaluation Inspection (MCD)
MEI .... Major End Item
MEI .... Management Education Institute [*Arthur D. Little, Inc.*]
MEI .... Management Effectiveness Inspection
MEI .... Manpower Education Institute (EA)
MEI .... Manual of Engineering Instructions
MEI .... Marginal Efficiency of Investment
MEI .... Marketing Economics Institute Ltd. [*New York, NY*]
MEI .... Maximally Exposed Individual
MEI .... Maximum Exposed Individual [*Health risk assessment*] [*Environmental Protection Agency*]
MEI .... Maximum Exposed Individual (GNE)
Mel .... Meconium Ileus [*Medicine*]
MEI .... Medicare Economic Index
Mei .... Meiji Seika Kaisha Ltd. [*Japan*]
MEI .... Meres et Enfants Internationale [*Switzerland*] (EAIO)
MEI .... Meridian [*Mississippi*] [*Airport symbol*] (OAG)
MEI .... Meridian, MS [*Location identifier FAA*] (FAAL)
MEI .... Metals Engineering Institute (EA)
MEI .... Middle East Information Service (BJA)
MEI .... Middle East Institute (EA)
MEI .... Military Engineering Item (MCD)
MEI .... [*The*] Ministry of Electronics Industry [*China*]
MEI .... Minority Educational Institution

MEI .... Mission Essential Item [*Army*]
MEI .... Morpholinoethylisocyanide [*Organic chemistry*]
MEI .... Most Exposed Individual [*Environmental science*] (FFDE)
MEI .... Myocardial Efficiency Index [*Cardiology*]
MEIA .... Member of the Institution of Engineers Australia
MEIA .... Microparticle Enzyme Immunoassay
MEIC .... Member of the Engineering Institute of Canada
MEIC .... Middle East Intelligence Center [*World War II*]
Meid .... Against Meidias [*of Demosthenes*] [*Classical studies*] (OCD)
MEIDL .... Manually Entered Identification Library (CAAL)
MEIDS .... Military [*or Miniaturized*] Electronic Information Delivery System (MCD)
MEIE .... Microcomputer Electronic Information Exchange [*Institute for Computer Science and Technology*]
MEIF .... Mobile Equipment Information File [*Air Force*] (AFM)
MEIG .... Main Engine Ignition [*Aerospace*] (KSC)
MEIGN .... Main Engine Ignition [*Aerospace*]
Meigs .... Meigs' Tennessee Supreme Court Reports [*1838-39*] [*A publication*] (DLA)
Meigs Dig.... Meigs' Digest of Decisions of the Courts of Tennessee [*A publication*] (DLA)
Meigs' R...... Meigs' Tennessee Reports [*A publication*] (DLA)
Me'il .... Me'ilah (BJA)
MEIM .... Minuteman Engineering Instruction Manual (SAA)
MEIMN .... Multiend Item Modification Notice [*NASA*] (KSC)
MEIN .... Medium-Energy Intense Neutron
MEIP .... Mean Effective Injection Pressure [*Diesel engines*]
MEIR .... Mideast Information Resource (BJA)
MEIR .... Ministere Federal de l'Expansion Industrielle Regionale [*Department of Regional Industrial Expansion - DRIE*] [*Canada*]
MEIS .... Medium Energy Ion Scattering (MCD)
MEIS .... Middle East Information Service (BJA)
MEIS .... Military Entomology Information Service
MEISR .... Minimum Essential Improvement in System Reliability (MCD)
MEIT .... Momentum/Energy Integral Technique (MCD)
MEITS .... Mission Effective Information Transmission System
MEIU .... Main Engine Interface Unit (MCD)
MEIU .... Middle East Interpretation Unit [*British*]
MEIU .... Mobile Explosives Investigation Unit
MEJ .... Maine Criminal Justice Academy, Waterville, ME [*OCLC symbol*] (OCLC)
MEJ .... Marman Expansion Joint
MEJ .... Maximum Economic Justification
MEJ .... Meade, KS [*Location identifier FAA*] (FAAL)
MEJ .... Medjet International, Inc. [*ICAO designator*] (FAAC)
MEJ .... Middle East Journal [*A publication*] (BRI)
MEJ .... Movement for Economic Justice (EA)
MEJC .... Miniature Excitatory Junction Potential [*Neurophysiology*]
MEK .... Maine State Library, Bookmobiles, Augusta, ME [*OCLC symbol*] (OCLC)
MEK .... Med-Trans of Florida, Inc. [*ICAO designator*] (FAAC)
MEK .... Meekatharra [*Australia Seismograph station code, US Geological Survey*] (SEIS)
Mek .... Mekhilta (BJA)
MEK .... Meknes [*Morocco*] [*Airport symbol*] (AD)
MEK .... Methyl Ethyl Ketone [*Organic chemistry*]
MEK .... Salomon, Inc. [*AMEX symbol*] (SPSG)
MEK .... Salomon Inc. 5% MSFI'ELKA' [*AMEX symbol*] (TTSB)
MEKC .... Micellar Electrokinetic Chromatography
MeKh .... Mekhilta (BJA)
MEKO .... Methyl Ethyl Ketoxime [*Organic chemistry*]
MEKP .... Methyl Ethyl Ketone Peroxide [*Organic chemistry*]
MEKTS .... Modular Electronic Kay Telephone System (IAA)
MeL .... Lewiston Public Library, Lewiston, ME [*Library symbol Library of Congress*] (LCLS)
MEL .... Magnesium Elektron Ltd. [*British*] (IRUK)
MEL .... Maintenance Expenditure Limit (MCD)
MEL .... Maneuvering Element [*Military*] (AABC)
MEL .... Many-Element LASER
MEL .... Marchwood Engineering Laboratories [*Research center British*] (IRUK)
MEL .... Marine Engineering Laboratory [*Navy*]
MEL .... Master Equipment List [*Military*] (NG)
M El .... Master of Elements
MEL .... Master of English Language (PGP)
MEL .... Master of English Literature
MEL .... Material Engineering Laboratory
MEL .... Materials Evaluation Laboratory (MCD)
MEL .... Maximum Engagement Line [*Military*] (INF)
MEL .... Maximum Excess Loss
MEL .... Maximum Expenditure Limit (MCD)
MEL .... Maximum Exposure Limit [*Hazardous material control*]
MEL .... Mean Ear Location [*Automotive engineering*]
MEL .... Melamine
MEL .... Melanoma [*Oncology*]
MEL .... Melbourne [*Australia Airport symbol*] (OAG)
MEL .... Melbourne [*Australia Seismograph station code, US Geological Survey*] (SEIS)
MEL .... Melbourne [*Later, TOO*] [*Australia Geomagnetic observatory code*]
mel .... Melena [*Gastroenterology*] (DAVI)
Mel .... Melendus [*Flourished, 1188-1209*] [*Authority cited in pre-1607 legal work*] (DSA)
MEL .... Mellis [*Of Honey*] [*Pharmacy*] (ROG)
MEL .... Mellon Bank Corp. [*NYSE symbol*] (SPSG)
MEL .... Melody

Mel	Melphalan [Antineoplastic drug] (DAVI)
MEL	Melrose Resources Ltd. [Vancouver Stock Exchange symbol]
MEL	Metabolic Equivalent Level [Medicine]
MEL	Microenergy Logic (IAA)
MEL	Military Education Level (INF)
MEL	Minimum Earnings Level
MEL	Minimum Equipment List
MEL	Mistress of English Literature
MEL	Mobile Erector Launcher [Military]
MEL	Moslem Electoral Lobby [Australia]
MEL	Mouse Erythroleukemia
MEL	Multiengine Land [Pilot rating] (AIA)
MEL	Murine Erythroleukemia [Oncology]
MEL	Music Education League [Defunct] (EA)
MEL	Muzika Esperanto Ligo [Esperantist Music League] (EAIO)
ME L	University of Maine. Law Review [A publication] (DLA)
MEL-A	Marine Engineering Laboratory - Annapolis [Navy] (DNAB)
MELA	Middle East Librarians' Association (EA)
MELAB	Mechanical Engineering Laboratory [NASA] (KSC)
MELAB	Michigan English Language Assessment Battery (GAGS)
MELABS	Microwave Engineering Laboratories, Inc. (MCD)
Melami	Melamine Chemicals, Inc. [Associated Press] (SAG)
MELAN	Melanesia (ROG)
MELAN	Melanin [Pigmentation] (DAVI)
Melanges d'Arch	Melanges d'Archeologie et d'Histoire. Ecole Francaise de Rome [A publication] (OCD)
MELAS	Mitochondrial Myopathy, Encephalopathy, Lactic Acidosis, and Stroke-Like Episod es [Medicine]
MeLB	Bates College, Lewiston, ME [Library symbol Library of Congress] (LCLS)
MELB	Mission Enhancement-Little Bird [Military] (RDA)
MELBA	Multipurpose Extended Lift Blanket Assembly (IEEE)
Melb Rpt	Melbourne Report [A publication]
Melb Stud Ed	Melbourne Studies in Education [A publication]
MELC	Melcombe [England]
MELC	Mouse Erythroleukemia Cell
MELCO	Mitsubishi Electric Corp. [Japan]
MELCOM	Middle East Libraries Committee
MELCU	Multiple External Line Control Unit
MeLDL	Methylated Low-Density Lipoprotein [Biochemistry]
MELDOS	Melioidosis [Dermatology] (DAVI)
MELEC	Microelectronics (IEEE)
M Elec E	Master of Electrical Engineering (PGP)
ME Legis Serv	Maine Legislative Service [A publication] (DLA)
MELEM	Microelement (IEEE)
MELF	Metal Electrode Face Bonding (IAA)
MELF	Middle East Land Forces [British] (NATG)
MELG	Middle East Liaison Group [Military] (AABC)
MELH	Missile Elevation Heading (IAA)
MELI	Master Equipment List Identification [Military] (IAA)
MELI	Master Equipment List Index [Military] (KSC)
MELI	Minimum Equipment List Index (NASA)
MELIOS	Miniature Eyesafe LASER Infrared Observation Set [A rangefinder]
MELISS	Mitsubishi Electric Corp. Literature and Information Search Service
MELKONG	Mechanical Electric Kong [Robot]
MELL	Mellis [Of Honey] [Pharmacy] (ROG)
MellonBk	Mellon Bank Corp. [Associated Press] (SAG)
MellonP	Mellon Participating Mortgage Trust Commercial Property Series [Associated Press] (SAG)
Mell Parl Pr	Mell's Parliamentary Practice [A publication] (DLA)
MELM	Middle East Lutheran Ministry [Lebanon] (EAIO)
MELM	Minimum Equipment List Manual
Mel Masp	Melanges Maspero [A publication] (OCD)
Meln	Mellon Bank Corp. [Associated Press] (SAG)
M Elo	Master of Elocution
MELO	Minimum Expected Loss [Statistics]
Melon	Mellon Bank Corp. [Associated Press] (SAG)
MELP	Measure of Language Proficiency (EDAC)
MELP	Mid-European Law Project
MELPrJ	Mellon Bk 8.50% 'J'Pfd [NYSE symbol] (TTSB)
MELPrK	Mellon Bk 8.20% 'K' Pfd [NYSE symbol] (TTSB)
MELPrI	Mellon Bk 9.60% 'I' Pfd [NYSE symbol] (TTSB)
Me-LR	Law and Legislative Reference Library, Augusta, ME [Library symbol Library of Congress] (LCLS)
MELS	Microwave and Electronic System (IAA)
MELS	Molecularly Engineered Layered Structure
MELSA	Metropolitan Library Service Agency [Library network]
MELSOR	Marx, Engels, Lenin, Stalin, October Revolution [Given name popular in Russia after the Bolshevik Revolution]
MELT	Minimum Equipment Level for Training (MCD)
MELUS	Society for the Study of Multi-Ethnic Literature of the United States (BARN)
MELV	Melilotus Latent Virus [Plant pathology]
MELVA	Military Electronic Light Valve
Melvile	Melville Corp. [Formerly, Melville Shoe Corp.] [Associated Press] (SAG)
Melv Tr	Melvill's Trial (Impeachment) [London] [A publication] (DLA)
MELVYL	Melvil Dewey [Public access online catalog, University of California] (NITA)
Mem	De Memoria [of Aristotle] [Classical studies] (OCD)
MEM	Macrophage Electrophoretic Migration [Clinical chemistry] (AAMN)
MEM	Macrophage Electrophoretic Mobility Test (MAE)
MEM	Magnetic Electron Multiplier (PDAA)
MEM	Magyar Elet Mozgalma [Movement of Hungarian Life] [Political party] (PPE)

MEM	Maine State Museum, Augusta, ME [OCLC symbol] (OCLC)
MEM	Marine Engineering Mechanic [Navy rating British]
MEM	Mars Excursion Mission [NASA] (IAA)
MEM	Mars Excursion Module
MEM	Master of Ecosystem Management (PGP)
MEM	Master of Educational Ministry (PGP)
MEM	Master of Engineering Management
MEM	Master of Engineering Management (GAGS)
MEM	Master of Environmental Management (PGP)
Me M	Master of Metaphysics
MEM	Maximum Entropy Method [Geomagnetism] [Computer science]
MEM	Mediterranean Air Ambulance, SL [Spain] [FAA designator] (FAAC)
MEM	Membach [Belgium] [Seismograph station code, US Geological Survey] (SEIS)
MEM	Member (EY)
mem	Member (WDMC)
MEM	MEM Co. [AMEX symbol] (TTSB)
MEM	MEM Co., Inc. [AMEX symbol] (SPSG)
MEM	Memento
MEM	Memoir
mem	Memoir (WDMC)
Mem	Memorabilia [of Xenophon] [Classical studies] (OCD)
MEM	Memorandum
mem	Memorandum (WDMC)
mem	Memorial (WDMC)
MEM	Memorial
MEM	Memory (MSA)
MEM	Memory
MEM	Memphis [Tennessee] [Airport symbol] (OAG)
MEM	Meteoroid Exposure Module (MCD)
MEM	Methoxyethoxymethyl [Organic chemistry]
MEM	Middle-Ear Muscle [Anatomy]
MEM	Minimum Essential Medium [Culture medium]
MEM	Mirror Electron Microscope (PDAA)
MEM	Missile Engagement Mechanism (MCD)
MEM	Model Emission Model [Environmental Protection Agency] (GFGA)
MEM	Module Exchange Mechanism [NASA] (NASA)
MEM	Molecular Exciton Microscopy
MEM	Mondpaca Esperantista Movado [Esperantist Movement for World Peace - EMWP] [Tours, France] (EAIO)
MEM	Most Efficient/Effective Method [DoD]
MEM	Most Excellent Master [Freemasonry]
MEM	Mount Emily Exploration Ltd. [Vancouver Stock Exchange symbol]
MEM	Multienvironmental Electron Microscope
MEMA	Marine Engine Manufacturers Association [Formerly, OMMA] (EA)
MEMA	Microelectronic Modular Assembly
MEMA	Middle-Ear Muscle Activity
MEMA	Motor and Equipment Manufacturers Association (EA)
MEMAC	Middle East Medical Advisory Committee [World War II]
MeMacU	University of Maine at Machias, Machias, ME [Library symbol Library of Congress] (LCLS)
MEMA/TTC	Motor and Equipment Manufacturers Association's Technical Training Council
MEMB	Member
MEMB	Membranaceous Vellum [Manuscripts] (ROG)
MEMB	Membrane (MSA)
MEMBERS	Microprogrammed Experimental Machine with a Basic Executive for Real-Time Systems (PDAA)
MEMBIS	Member Budget Information System [for House of Representatives]
MEMBLE	Memorable (ROG)
MEMC	MEMC Electronic Materials, Inc. [Associated Press] (SAG)
MEMC	Memco Software Ltd. [NASDAQ symbol] (SAG)
MEMC	Methoxyethylmercuric Chloride
Mem Comm Solar Observ Aust	Memoirs. Commonwealth Solar Observatory. Australia [A publication]
MEMCON	Memorandum of Conversation
MemcoSf	Memco Software Ltd. [Associated Press] (SAG)
MEMDA	Memoranda (ROG)
MEMDB	Medieval and Early Modern Data Bank [Information service or system] (IID)
MEMDUM	Memorandum (ROG)
MEME	Magnetic Environment Measuring Equipment (CAAL)
MEME	Multiple Entry Multiple Exit
MEME	Multitasking Extensible Messaging Environment
MEMEC	Memory and Electronic Components [Commercial firm British]
ME(Mech)	Master of Engineering (Mechanical) (ADA)
MEM ERR	Memory Error [Information retrieval]
Mem Geol Survey Vic	Memoirs. Geological Survey of Victoria [Australia A publication]
MEMI	Master Equipment Management Index [Air Force] (AFM)
MeMi	Millinocket Memorial Library, Millinocket, ME [Library symbol Library of Congress] (LCLS)
MEMIC	Medical Microbiology Interdisciplinary Committee [International Council of Scientific Unions]
MEMIC	Mobile Eletromagnetic Incompatibility (PDAA)
MEMISTOR	Memory Resistor (DEN)
MEML	Master Equipment Management List [Air Force] (AFM)
MEML	Memorial
MEML	Memorial (FAAC)
MEML	Molecular Engineering and Materials Laboratory [MIT] (MCD)
MEMLACTV	Memorial Activities [Military] (AABC)
Mem LJ	Memphis Law Journal [Tennessee] [A publication] (DLA)
MEMLZ	Memorialize (ABBR)
MEMLZD	Memorialized (ABBR)
MEMLZG	Memorializing (ABBR)

MEMLZN...... Memorialization (ABBR)
MEMLZR...... Memorializer (ABBR)
MEMMA...... Mining Electromechanical Maintenance Association (IAA)
MEMMDLE... Memory Module (IAA)
MEMO...... Marine Environmental Management Office [*Marine science*] (MSC)
MEMO...... Medical Equipment Management Office [*Air Force*] (AFM)
MEMO...... Memorandum (AFM)
MEMO...... Memorandum
memo...... Memorandum (WDMC)
MEMO...... Middle East Money [*London-Beirut*] (BJA)
MEMO...... Minnesota Educational Media Organization (EDAC)
MEMO...... Mission Essential Maintenance Only (MCD)
MEMO...... Mission Essential Maintenance Operation (MCD)
MEMO...... Model for Evaluating Missile Observation
MEMO...... More Education - More Opportunities (DNAB)
MEMO...... Voice It Worldwide [*NASDAQ symbol*] (TTSB)
MEMO...... Voice It Worldwide, Inc. [*NASDAQ symbol*] (SAG)
MEMOCS .... Mitsubishi Electric Corp. Multiterm Out-of-Context System
Memo Mgmt... Memo to Management [*Australian Institute of Management, Queensland Division*] [*A publication*]
Memorex..... Memorex Telex NV [*Associated Press*] (SAG)
MEMOREX .. Memory Excellence [*Brand name*]
MEMOS...... Manufacturing Engineering Management Operations System (MCD)
MEMP......... Maximization of Expected Maximum Profit [*Econometrics*]
Memphis LJ... Memphis Law Journal [*Tennessee*] [*A publication*] (DLA)
Memphis St U... Memphis State University (GAGS)
Memp LJ ..... Memphis Law Journal [*Tennessee*] [*A publication*] (DLA)
MEMPP....... Morpholinoethylmethylphenylpyridazone [*An analgesic*]
MEMPT....... Memory Point
MEMQ........ Married Enlisted Men's Quarters
ME (MR)..... Medical Evidence (Medical Report or Record) (OICC)
MEMR........ Memory Read [*Computer science*] (MHDI)
MEMR........ Multiple Exostoses-Mental Retardation Syndrome [*Medicine*] (DMAA)
MEMRA....... Mechanical Equipment Manufacturers Representatives Association (EA)
MEMRAC ..... Mission Essential Material Readiness and Condition (MCD)
memrl......... Memorial (VRA)
MEMS......... Master of Emergency Medical Service (PGP)
MEMS......... Master of Engineering in Manufacturing Systems (GAGS)
MEMS......... Microbial Ecological Monitoring System [*Apollo*] [*NASA*]
MEMS......... Microelectromechanical System [*Materials science and technology*]
MEMS......... Micro-Electro-Mechanical Systems
MEMS......... Micro Electro Mechanical Systems
MEMS......... Mineral Economics and Management Society
MEMS......... Missile Equipment Maintenance Sets (MUGU)
MEMS......... Modular Engine Management System [*Automotive engineering*]
MEMS......... Multieffect, Multistage
MEMSEL ...... Memory Select [*Computer science*] (MHDI)
Mem St UL Rev... Memphis State University. Law Review [*A publication*] (DLA)
Memtec....... Memtec Ltd. [*Associated Press*] (SAG)
MEMU........ Manned Extravehicular Manipulating Unit (MCD)
MEMW........ Memory Write [*Computer science*] (MHDB)
MemWks .... MemberWorks, Inc. [*Associated Press*] (SAG)
MEMX........ Memorex Telex NV [*NASDAQ symbol*] (SAG)
MEMXY....... Memorex Telex ADS [*NASDAQ symbol*] (TTSB)
MEMY........ Memory (ROG)
MEN........... Master Equipment Number [*Military*] (NG)
M En .... Master of English
Men........... Menaechmi [*of Plautus*] [*Classical studies*] (OCD)
Men........... Menahot (BJA)
Men .... Menander [*Fourth century BC*] [*Classical studies*] (OCD)
men .... Mende [*MARC language code Library of Congress*] (LCCP)
MEN........... Mendoza [*Argentina*] [*Seismograph station code, US Geological Survey Closed*] (SEIS)
MEN........... Mennonite (ABBR)
MEN........... Meno [*Slower*] [*Music*]
MEN........... Menology
Men........... Menorah: Australian Journal of Jewish Studies [*A publication*] (APTA)
Men........... Mensa [*Constellation*]
MEN........... Mense [*or Menses*] (ABBR)
MEN........... Men's Equality Now International (EA)
MEN........... Menstruation (ABBR)
MEN........... Mensuration (ABBR)
MEN........... Mention
Men .... Menzies' Cape Of Good Hope Reports [*1828-49*] [*A publication*] (DLA)
MEN........... Mistozen Electronic Nebulizer
MEN........... Multiple Earthed Neutral (IAA)
MEN........... Multiple Endocrine Neoplasia [*Medicine*]
MEN........... Multiple Event Network
MEN........... MuniEnhanced Fund [*NYSE symbol*] (SPSG)
MENA........ Middle East and North Africa [*A publication*]
MENA........ Middle East News Agency
MENA........ Mission Element Need Analysis (MCD)
MENA........ Mitsubishi Engine North America
MENA........ Mitsubishi Engine North America, Inc.
MENC........ Music Educators National Conference (EA)
MENCAP ..... Royal Society for Mentally Handicapped Children & Adults [*England*]
Mence Lib ... Mence's Law of Libel [*1824*] [*A publication*] (DLA)
MEND........ Massive Economic Neighborhood Development [*New York City*]
MEND........ Maximum Entropy Noise Deconvolution [*Statistics*]
MEND........ Medical Education for National Defense
MEND........ Mendelism
MEND........ Mothers Embracing Nuclear Disarmament [*An association*] (EA)
MENEV....... Menevensis [*Signature of the Bishops of St. David's*] [*British*] (ROG)

MENEX........ Maintenance Engineering Exchange
Menex .... Menexemus [*of Plato*] [*Classical studies*] (OCD)
M Eng .... Master of Engineering
M Eng .... Master of English
MENG .... Meaning (ABBR)
M Eng .... Mechanical Engineer
M-ENG .... Multiengined
M Eng & PA... Master in Engineering and Public Administration
MENGF .... Meaningful (ABBR)
MENGFY ..... Meaningfully (ABBR)
MENGLS ...... Meaningless (ABBR)
MENGLSY ..... Meaninglessly (ABBR)
M Eng Mgt... Master of Engineering Management (PGP)
MEngPA...... Master of Engineering and Public Administration (NADA)
M Engr........ Master of Engineering (PGP)
MEngS .... Master of Engineering Science
M Eng Sc... Master of Engineering Science
MEngSt....... Master of Engineering Studies (ADA)
ME(NI)........ Ministry of Education (Northern Ireland)
MENI.......... Multiple Endocrine Neoplasia Type I [*Medicine*] (DMAA)
MENIT........ Mennonite
MENJ.......... Menley & James, Inc. [*NASDAQ symbol*] (SPSG)
Menken........ Menken's Civil Procedure Reports [*30 New York*] [*A publication*] (DLA)
MenleyJ....... Menley & James, Inc. [*Associated Press*] (SAG)
Menn .... Menninger [*Karl Augustus*] [*American psychiatrist*] (DAVI)
MENNON...... Mennonite (ABBR)
MENNS .... Meanness (ABBR)
MENO .... Menopause (DSUE)
MENO .... Menorrhoea (ABBR)
MENP.......... Menopause (ABBR)
MENPL........ Menopausal (ABBR)
Men Rel ...... Menandri Reliquiae [*A publication*] (OCD)
MENS.......... K&G Men's Center [*NQS*] (TTSB)
MENS.......... K & G Mens Center, Inc. [*NASDAQ symbol*] (SAG)
M En S .... Master of Environmental Science (PGP)
Mens .... Mensa [*Constellation*]
Mens .... Mensis [*Month*] [*Latin*]
MENS.......... Mensura [*By Measure*] [*Pharmacy*]
MENS.......... Middle East Neurosurgical Society (EAIO)
MENS.......... Missile Element Need Statement
MENS.......... Mission Element Needs Statement (MCD)
Men's J .... Men's Journal [*A publication*] (BRI)
menst .... Menstrual [*or Menstruate*] (AAMN)
MENSTD ..... Menstruated (ABBR)
MENSTG ...... Menstruating (ABBR)
MENSTL....... Menstrual (ABBR)
MENSTN ...... Menstruation (ABBR)
MENSUR...... Mensuration (ROG)
M Ent.......... Master of Entomology
MENT.......... Mental
MENT.......... Mentalis (ABBR)
MENT.......... Mentioned
MENT.......... Mentor Graphics [*NASDAQ symbol*] (TTSB)
MENT.......... Mentor Graphics Corp. [*NASDAQ symbol*] (NQ)
Mental & Physical Disab L Rep... Mental and Physical Disability Law Reporter [*A publication*] (DLA)
MENTD .... Mentioned
MentGr .... Mentor Graphics Corp. [*Associated Press*] (SAG)
MENTH .... Mentha [*Mint*] [*Pharmacy*] (ROG)
Ment Hlth Aust... Mental Health in Australia [*A publication*]
MentInc .... Mentor Income Fund [*Associated Press*] (SAG)
MENTL........ Mental
MentlHlt ...... Mental Health Management, Inc. [*Associated Press*] (SAG)
MENTLY....... Mentally
MENTN .... Mention (ROG)
MENTNB ..... Mentionable (ABBR)
MENTND ..... Mentioned (ABBR)
MENTNG ..... Mentioning (ABBR)
MENTNR..... Mentioner (ABBR)
Mentor........ Mentor Corp. [*Associated Press*] (SAG)
MENTOR...... Mobile Electrical Network Testing, Observation, and Recording (PDAA)
MENTOR...... [*A*] Programming Language [*1963*] (CSR)
MENTT........ Mentality (ABBR)
MENTY........ Mentally (ABBR)
M Env .... Master of Environment (PGP)
MEnv .... Master of Environmental Studies (DD)
M Env Des ... Master of Environmental Design (PGP)
M Env E....... Master of Environmental Engineering (PGP)
MENVEGR... Master of Environmental Engineering (PGP)
M Envir E...... Master of Environmental Engineering (PGP)
MEnvPlan ... Master of Environmental Planning
MEnvS .... Master of Environmental Science
MEnvS .... Master of Environmental Science (GAGS)
MEnvS .... Master of Environmental Studies
MEnvSc........ Master of Environmental Science (ADA)
M Env Sc ... Master of Environmental Science (PGP)
MEnvSt........ Master of Environmental Studies (ADA)
MEnvStud ... Master of Environmental Studies (ADA)
MEnvStudies... Master of Environmental Studies
MenWre........ Mens Warehouse [*Associated Press*] (SAG)
MeNwS........ Saint Joseph's College, North Windham, ME [*Library symbol Library of Congress*] (LCLS)

Menz............	Menzies' Cape Of Good Hope Reports [1828-49] [A publication] (DLA)
Menz Conv...	Menzies' Conveyancing [A publication] (DLA)
Menzies......	Menzies' Cape Of Good Hope Reports [1828-49] [A publication] (DLA)
MEO............	Jefferson City, MO [Location identifier FAA] (FAAL)
MEO............	Maintenance Engineering Order [NASA] (KSC)
MEO............	Major Engine Overhaul
MEO............	Manned Earth Orbit
MEO............	Manned Extravehicular Operation
MEO............	Marine Engineer Officer [British]
MEO............	Mass in Earth Orbit [NASA]
MEO............	Medical Emergency Officer (DAVI)
MEO............	Medium Earth Orbit (SSD)
MEO............	Military Equal Opportunity (MCD)
MEO............	Mining Engineering Officer [British military] (DMA)
MEO............	Montello Resources Ltd. [Vancouver Stock Exchange symbol]
MEO............	Most Efficient/Effective Organization [DoD]
MEO............	Scandinavian Aviation Center AS [Denmark ICAO designator] (FAAC)
MEOC.........	Marine Emergency Operations Center [Western Australia]
MEOC.........	Marine Environmental Quality Committee [Marine science] (OSRA)
MEOER........	Member of the European Osteopathic Register
MEOF..........	Marine Environmental Observation and Forecasting (NOAA)
MEOH.........	Methanex Corp. [NASDAQ symbol] (SAG)
MEOH.........	Methyl Alcohol
MEOHF........	Methanex Corp. [NASDAQ symbol] (TTSB)
MEOL.........	Manned Earth Orbit Laboratory (IAA)
MEOM........	Manned Earth Orbit Mission
MEOOW......	Marine Engineer Officer of the Watch [British]
MEOP.........	Maximum Engine Operating Pressure
MEOP.........	Maximum Expected Operating Pressure
MEOR.........	Microbial Enhanced Oil Recovery [Petroleum technology]
MEOS.........	Medium Earth Orbit Satellites (ACRL)
MEOS.........	Microsomal Ethanol-Oxidizing System [Biochemistry]
MEOS.........	Mode/Energy Offset
MEOSAB	Missile Explosive Ordnance Safety Advisory Board [Pacific Missile Range] (MUGU)
MEOTBF.......	Mean Engine Operating Time between Failures [Quality control]
MEOV.........	Maximum Expected Operating Value [FCC]
MEOW........	Marine Engineer Officer's Writer [British military] (DMA)
MEOW........	[The] Moral Equivalent of War [Phrase used by President Jimmy Carter to describe his energy bill]
MEOWS......	Multimode Electro-Optical Weapon System
MEP...........	Magnetic Energy Product
MEP...........	Magyar Elet Partja [Party of Hungarian Life] [Political party] (PPE)
MEP...........	Mahajana Eksath Peramuna [People's United Front] [Sri Lanka] [Political party] (PPW)
MEP...........	Main Engine Propellant (MCD)
MEP...........	Main Entry Point (NASA)
MEP...........	Main Entry Point
MEP...........	Maintainability Evaluation Process (MCD)
MEP...........	Major Electronics Procurement
MEP...........	Major Extinction Position [Polarizer-Analyzer]
MEP...........	Management Engineering Program [Air Force] (AFM)
MEP...........	Management Evaluation Program (AAG)
MEP...........	Manual Entry Panel [Military] (CAAL)
MEP...........	Manuals of Engineering Practice [ASCE]
MEP...........	Manufacturing Engineering Plan
MEP...........	Manufacturing Extension Partnership [National Institute for Science and Technology]
MEP...........	Mars Entry Probe
MEP...........	Master Evaluation Plan [Army]
MEP...........	Master of Engineering Physics
MEP...........	Master of Environmental Planning (GAGS)
MEP...........	Maximum Economic Potential
MEP...........	Maximum Entropy Principle (PDAA)
MEP...........	Maximum Escape Performance [Ejection seat] (MCD)
MEP...........	Maxwell Electronic Publishing [Information service or system] (IID)
MEP...........	Mean Effective Pressure
MEP...........	Medical Education Program [Air Force]
MEP...........	Member of the European Parliament
MEP...........	Meperidine [Also, M] [An analgesic]
MEP...........	Mersing [Malaysia] [Airport symbol] (OAG)
MEP...........	Methanol Environmental Performance [Automotive engineering]
MEP...........	Methods Engineering Program [Navy] (NVT)
MEP...........	Methyl(ethyl)pyridine [Organic chemistry]
MEP...........	Methyl Parathion [Also, MP, MPN] [Pesticide]
MEP...........	Microcircuit Emulation Program
MEP...........	Micro-Electronics Education Programme (NITA)
MEP...........	Microelectronics Programme [British]
MEP...........	Microfile Enlarger Printer (NITA)
MEP...........	Middle East Policy [A publication] (BRI)
MEP...........	Midwest Express Airlines, Inc. [ICAO designator] (FAAC)
MEP...........	Minimum Energy Path [Physical chemistry]
MEP...........	Minimum Entry Point (MCD)
MEP...........	Minority Entrepreneurship Program [Small Business Administration]
MEP...........	Minuteman Education Program [Air Force] (AFM)
MEP...........	Mission Effects Projector [Lunar exploration]
MEP...........	Mission Equipment Package
MEP...........	Mobile Electric Power (NG)
MEP...........	Mobil Exploration & Producing Services, Inc., Dallas, TX [OCLC symbol] (OCLC)
MEP...........	Mogul End Prong [Lamp base] (NTCM)
MEP...........	Molecular Electrostatic Potentials [Physical chemistry]
MEP............	Moon-Earth-Plane (SAA)
MEP............	Motor End Plate
MEP............	Motor-Evoked Potential (OA)
MEP............	Mouvement d'Ecologie Politique [Ecology Political Movement] [France Political party] (PPW)
MEP............	Movimiento Electoral del Pueblo [People's Electoral Movement] [Venezuela] [Political party] (PPW)
MEP............	Movimiento Electoral del Pueblo [People's Electoral Movement] [Netherlands Antilles] [Political party] (PPW)
MEP............	Mucoid Exopolysaccharide [Biochemistry]
MEP............	Multielliptical Pump
MEP............	Multimodality Evoked Potential [Neurophysiology]
MEP............	Multiple-Exposure Photography
MEP............	Multiple Extraction Procedure (GNE)
MEP............	Paris Foreign Mission Society (TOCD)
mep...........	Paris Foreign Mission Society (TOCD)
MeP............	Portland Public Library, Portland, ME [Library symbol Library of Congress] (LCLS)
MEP............	Societas Parisiensis Missionum ad Exteros [Paris Foreign Missions Society] [Roman Catholic men's religious order]
MEP-91.......	Mesoscale Evolution Project-1991 (USDC)
MEP-91.......	Mesoscale Evolution Project-1991 [Marine science] (OSRA)
MEPA.........	Marine and Estuarine Protected Area
MEPA.........	Master in Engineering and Public Administration
MEPARC	Middle East Policy and Research Center (EA)
MEPC.........	Marine Environment Protection Committee [IMCO] (MSC)
MEPC.........	Maritime Environment Protection Committee (NADA)
MEPC.........	Master of Environmental Pollution Control (GAGS)
MEPC.........	MEPC International Capital LP [Associated Press] (SAG)
MEPC.........	Miniature End Plate Current
MEPCOM	Military Enlistment Processing Command [DoD]
MEPD.........	Master of Education - Professional Development (PGP)
MEPDP.......	Meander Electrodes Plasma Display Panel (IAA)
MEPED.......	Medium-Energy Proton and Electron Detector
MEPES.......	Medical Planning and Execution System (DOMA)
MEPES.......	Medical Planning and Execution System (Model)
MEPF.........	Multiple Experiment Processing Furnace
MEPGS......	Mobile Electric Power Generator Set (MCD)
MEPH.........	Master of Public Health Engineering (NADA)
MEPH.........	Mephobarital [A sedative and anticonvulsant] [Pharmacology] (DAVI)
MEPHISTO..	Mephistopheles [Foreman] [Slang British] (DSUE)
ME Phy......	Master of Engineering Physics
MePM.........	Maine Charitable Mechanic Association, Portland, ME [Library symbol Library of Congress] (LCLS)
MEPM........	Medium-Term Energy Policy Model
MePMC.......	Maine Medical Center, Portland, ME [Library symbol Library of Congress] (LCLS)
MEPOL.......	Metropolitan Police Officers [British]
MePosS	United Society of Shakers, Shaker Library, Poland Spring, ME [Library symbol Library of Congress] (LCLS)
MEPP.........	Marine Electric Power Plant (PDAA)
MEPP.........	Middle East Peace Project (EA)
MEPP.........	Miniature End Plate Potential
MEPrA........	Mobile Electric Power Plant (NG)
MEPrA........	Mission Capital 9.875%'MIPS' [NYSE symbol] (TTSB)
MEPrB........	Mission Capital 8.50% 'MIPS' [NYSE symbol] (TTSB)
MePriU	University of Maine at Presque Isle, Presque Isle, ME [Library symbol Library of Congress] (LCLS)
MEPROB.....	Meprobamate [Mythyl propyltrimethylene carbamate] [Tranquilizer] (DAVI)
MEPROBAMATE...	Methyl Propyltrimethylene Carbamate [Tranquilizer]
MEPRS.......	Military Entrant-Processing and Reporting System (GFGA)
MEPRS/DDS...	Medical Expense and Performance Reporting System/Dental Data System [Air Force] (GFGA)
MePS.........	Maine Public Service Co. [Associated Press] (SAG)
MEPS........	Means-End Problem-Solving Procedure [or Test] [Psychology]
MEPS........	Medium-Energy Particle Spectrometer (MCD)
MEPS........	Members of the European Parliament (ECON)
MEPS........	Message Editing and Processing System (MCD)
MEPS........	Military Entrance and Processing Station
MEPS........	Modular Electrical Power Station
MEPSA.......	Monochrome Electronic Prepress Systems (DGA)
MEPSA.......	Middle East Peace and Stability Act [1957]
mEPSC.......	Miniature Excitory Postsynaptic Currents [Neurobiology]
MEPSCAT	Military Entrance Physical Strength Capacity Test (INF)
MEPSDU	Module Experimental Process System Development Unit [Photovoltaic energy systems]
MEPSI........	Mexico-Elmhurst Philatelic Society, International (EA)
MEPSP.......	Miniature Excitatory Postsynaptic Potential [Neurophysiology]
MEPU.........	Monofuel Emergency Power Unit
MEQ..........	Marine Environmental Quality [Marine science] (MSC)
MEQ..........	Married Enlisted Quarters
MEQ..........	Middle East Quarterly [A publication] (BRI)
meq..........	Milliequivalent [Gram equivalent weight] (DOG)
MEQ..........	Milliequivalent [or Milligram Equivalent] [Also, ME]
MEQA........	Mechanized Equipment Assignment [AT & T]
MEQC........	Medicaid Eligibility Quality Control (GFGA)
MEQ/L........	Milliequivalent per Liter
MER..........	Ethamoxytriphetol [An antiestrogen] (DAVI)
MER..........	Madras European Regiment [British military] (DMA)
MER..........	Magneto-Elastic Resonance (PDAA)
MER..........	Main Engine Room [Navy] (CAAL)
MER..........	Maine State Department of Environmental Protection and Department of Conservation, Augusta, ME [OCLC symbol] (OCLC)
MER..........	Maintenance Engineering Report (MCD)

MER............	Management Expense Ratio
MER............	Manned Earth Reconnaissance [*Naval Air Electronic Systems Command project*]
MER............	Manpower Estimate Report (AAGC)
MER............	Manpower Estimating Relationships (MCD)
MER............	Manpower Evaluation Report [*Military*]
MER............	Marine Environmental Response [*USCG*] (TAG)
MER............	Market Exchange Rates [*Monetary conversion rate*] (ECON)
MER............	Mass Energy Relationship
MER............	Master Employee Record [*DoD*]
MER............	Master of Energy Resources (GAGS)
MERln..........	Maximum Effective Range
MER............	Maximum Efficient Rate [*Oil*]
MER............	Maximum Energy Recovery [*Chemical engineering*]
MER............	Mean Ejection Rate [*Medicine*]
MER............	Mechanical Equipment Room (DAC)
MER............	Mechanics, Electrical, and Radio (MCD)
MER............	Mercantile
MER............	Merced, CA [*Location identifier FAA*] (FAAL)
MERCN........	Merchandise (ADA)
MER............	Merchant (AFM)
MER............	Mercurial (WDAA)
MER............	Mercury (ADA)
Mer............	Mercury [*Record label*]
MER............	Merida [*Mexico*] [*Seismograph station code, US Geological Survey*] (SEIS)
MER............	Meridian (KSC)
MER............	Meridian
MER............	Meridional [*Geology*]
Mer............	Merivale's English Chancery Reports [*A publication*] (DLA)
MER............	Merlinoite [*A zeolite*]
MER............	Merrell-National Laboratories [*Research code symbol*]
MER............	Merrill Lynch [*NYSE symbol*] (TTSB)
MER............	Merrill Lynch & Co. [*NYSE symbol*] (SAG)
MER............	Merrill Lynch & Co. Preferred Capital Trust I [*NYSE symbol*] (SAG)
MER............	Metal Etch Resist
MERDL........	Metal Evaporated Resistor
MER............	Methanol Extraction [*or Extruded*] Residue [*Immunology*]
MER............	Methow Aviation, Inc. [*ICAO designator*] (FAAC)
MER............	Middle East Record [*A publication*] (BJA)
MER............	Minimum Energy Requirements
MER............	Mission Evaluation Room [*NASA*] (NASA)
MER............	Mitteleuropaeisches Reisebuero [*Middle European Travel Bureau*] [*German*]
MER............	Monthly Energy Review [*Department of Energy*] [*Database*]
MER............	Most Economical Rating
MER............	Multielement RADAR
MER............	Multiple Ejector Rack (NG)
MER............	Museum Education Roundtable (EA)
MER............	Myeloid-Erythrocyte [*or Erythroid*] [*Hematology*] (DAVI)
MER-29........	Triparanol [*Pharmacology*] [*A cholesterol biosynthesis inhibitor removed from market due to side effects*] (DAVI)
MERA..........	Maeventec Employers Rated Almanac [*Maeventec*] [*Information service or system*] (CRD)
MERA..........	Microelectronics for RADAR Application (MCD)
MERA..........	Molecular Electronics for RADAR Applications (IEEE)
MERA..........	Mormons for ERA (EA)
MERADCOM...	Mobility Equipment Research and Development Command [*Army*]
MERADO......	Mechanical Engineering Research and Development Organisation
MERALCO....	Manila Electric Railroad & Light Company [*Still known by acronym, although official name now Manila Electric Company*]
MERALT.......	Meridian Altitude [*Navigation*]
Mer & St Corp...	Merewether and Stephen's Municipal Corporations [*A publication*] (DLA)
MERB..........	Medical Examiniation and Review Board [*DoD*] (DAVI)
MerBkNY......	Merchants New York Bancorp [*Associated Press*] (SAG)
MerBNY.......	Merchants New York Bancorp [*Associated Press*] (SAG)
MERC..........	Meat Export Research Center [*Iowa State University*] [*Research center*] (RCD)
MERC..........	Mercantile (ROG)
Merc	Mercator [*of Plautus*] [*Classical studies*] (OCD)
MERC..........	Mercedes [*Automobile*] (DSUE)
MERC..........	[*A*] Mercenary
MERC..........	Mercurial (ABBR)
MERC..........	Mercury
MERC..........	Mercury
MERC..........	Mercury Project [*NASA*] (KSC)
MERC..........	Middle-Atlantic Educational and Research Center
MERC..........	Middle East Resource Center [*Defunct*] (EA)
MERC..........	Minimum Electrical Resistance Condition (PDAA)
MERC..........	Minority Economic Resource Center [*Howard University, Washington, DC*]
MERC..........	Mobile Equipment Replacement Cask [*Nuclear energy*] (NUCP)
MERC..........	Multi-Racial Education Resources Centre [*British*] (AIE)
MERC..........	Music Education Research Council (EA)
Merc Ad & Law & Credit Man...	Mercantile Adjuster and Lawyer and Credit Man [*A publication*] (DLA)
MercAir.......	Mercury Air Group, Inc. [*Associated Press*] (SAG)
MERCASREP...	Merchant Ship Casualty Report [*Navy*] (NVT)
MERCAST	Merchant Ship Broadcast [*Navy*]
MERCASUM...	Merchant Ship Casualty Summary [*Navy*] (NVT)
MercBcp.......	Mercantile Bancorp [*Associated Press*] (SAG)
Merc Cas.....	Mercantile Cases [*A publication*] (DLA)
MERCE........	Mercedes [*Automobile*] (DSUE)
Mercer........	Mercer County Law Journal [*Pennsylvania*] [*A publication*] (DLA)

Mercer........	Mercer International [*Associated Press*] (SAG)
Mercer Beasley L Rev...	Mercer Beasley Law Review [*A publication*] (DLA)
Mercer BL Rev...	Mercer Beasley Law Review [*A publication*] (DLA)
Mercer U	Mercer University (GAGS)
MercFn........	Mercury Finance Co. [*Associated Press*] (SAG)
MercGn........	Mercury General Corp. [*Associated Press*] (SAG)
MERCH........	Merchantable
Merch Dict....	Merchants' Dictionary [*A publication*] (DLA)
Merc (Hob)...	Mercury (Hobart) [*A publication*]
MERCHT.......	Merchant
Merch V.......	[*The*] Merchant of Venice [*Shakespearean work*] (BARN)
MercInt........	Mercury Interactive Corp. [*Associated Press*] (SAG)
Merck..........	Merck & Co., Inc. [*Associated Press*] (SAG)
Merc LJ.......	Mercantile Law Journal [*New York or Madras*] [*A publication*] (DLA)
MERCM.......	Mercantilism (ABBR)
MERCO........	Mercantile Communications [*Shipping*]
MERCO........	Merchant Ship Control [*Navy*]
MERCOFORM...	Merchant Ship Communications Formatted (MCD)
MERCOMMS...	Merchant Marine Communications System (DNAB)
MERCON.......	Universal Transversal Mercator Converter [*Computer program*]
MERCOS.......	Merchant Codes [*Shipping*]
MERCPAC	Mercury Enthusiast Restorer Custom Performance Auto Club (EA)
MERCRy.......	Mercury [*Chemistry*] (DAVI)
MERCS........	Mercer International SBI [*NASDAQ symbol*] (SPSG)
MERCS........	Mercer Intl. SBI [*NASDAQ symbol*] (TTSB)
MercSt........	Mercantile Stores Co., Inc. [*Associated Press*] (SAG)
MERCT........	Mercantilist (ABBR)
MERCTL.......	Mercantile
MerctlBk......	Mercantile Bankshares Corp. [*Associated Press*] (SAG)
MERCY........	Medical Emergency Relief Care for Youth
MERDC........	Mobility Equipment Research and Development Center [*Army*] (MCD)
MERDI.........	Montana Energy and Magneto-Hydrodynamics Research Institute [*Later, Montana Energy Research and Development Institute*] [*Research center*]
MERDIFF......	Meridian Difference
MerdIns	Meridian Insurance Group, Inc. [*Associated Press*] (SAG)
MERDL........	Medical Equipment Research and Development Laboratory [*Army*]
MerdrNt.......	Meridian National Corp. [*Associated Press*] (SAG)
Merdth........	Meredith Corp. [*Associated Press*] (SAG)
MEREA........	Member of the American Electrical Railway Engineering Association
MERECEN ...	Movimiento Estable Republicano Centrista [*El Salvador*] [*Political party*] (EY)
MEREP........	Merchant Ship Arrival and/or Departure Report (NATG)
MEREP........	Merchant Ship Report [*Navy*]
ME(Res).......	Master of Engineering (Research)
MERES........	Matrix of Environmental Residuals for Energy Systems [*Computerized information system*]
ME Rev Stat...	Maine Revised Statutes [*A publication*] (DLA)
ME Rev Stat Ann...	Maine Revised Statutes, Annotated [*A publication*] (DLA)
Me Rev Stat Ann...	Maine Revised Statutes Annotated [*West*] [*A publication*] (AAGC)
MERF..........	Medical Education Research Foundation [*San Diego*]
MERGE........	Mechanized Retrieval for Greater Efficiency [*Computer science*]
MERGV........	Martian Exploratory Rocket Glide Vehicle
MERI..........	Medical Education Research and Information Database
MERI..........	Meritrust Federal Savings Bank [*NASDAQ symbol*] (SAG)
MERI..........	Meritrust Fed Svg Bk Morgan [*NASDAQ symbol*] (TTSB)
MERI..........	Mineral Exploration Research Institute [*See also IREM*] [*Canada Research center*] (RCD)
MERI..........	Mining and Excavation Research Institute [*Research center*] (RCD)
MERIC	Michigan Education Resources Information Center [*Michigan State Library*] [*Information service or system Defunct*] (IID)
MERID.........	Meridian (ABBR)
MeridDia	Meridian Diagnostics, Inc. [*Associated Press*] (SAG)
MeridDta	Meridian Data, Inc. [*Associated Press*] (SAG)
MeridI.........	Meridian Industrial Trust, Inc. [*Associated Press*] (SAG)
Meridn........	Meridian [*A publication*]
MeridSpt......	Meridian Sports, Inc. [*Associated Press*] (SAG)
MERIE........	Magnetically Enhanced Reactive Ion Etching [*By plasmas*]
MeriFdl	Meritrust Federal Savings Bank [*Associated Press*] (SAG)
MerilCp.......	Merrill Corp. [*Associated Press*] (SAG)
MERINT	Merchant Intelligence Report [*Navy*]
MERINT	Merchant Ship Intelligence (NVT)
MERINTREP...	Merchant Ship Arrival and/or Departure Intermediate Report (NATG)
MERIONS.....	Merionethshire [*County in Wales*]
MERIP	Middle East Research and Information Project (EA)
MERIS	Medium Resolution Imaging Spectrometer (SSD)
Merisel........	Merisel, Inc. [*Associated Press*] (SAG)
MerisL........	Meris Laboratories, Inc. [*Associated Press*] (SAG)
MERIT.........	Maastricht Economic Research Institute on Innovation and Technology
MERIT.........	Medicl Relief International (NADA)
MERIT.........	Method to Extend Research in Time [*National Institutes of Health*]
MERIT.........	Michigan Educational Research Information Triad, Inc.
MERIT.........	Monitor the Earth Rotation and Intercompare Techniques [*by means of radio telescope measurements*]
MERIT.........	Multiple RADAR-Integrated Tracking [*Military*] (PDAA)
MERIT.........	[*The*] The Michigan Educational Research Network [*Computer science*] (TNIG)
MeritH	Merit Holding Corp. [*Associated Press*] (SAG)
MERITOC......	Meritocracy (ABBR)
MERITOC......	Meritocrat (ABBR)
Meriv..........	Merivale's English Chancery Reports [*A publication*] (DLA)
Meriv (Eng)...	Merivale's English Chancery Reports [*A publication*] (DLA)
Merix Cp......	Merix Corp. [*Associated Press*] (SAG)

MERL..........	Marine Ecosystem Research Laboratory [University of Rhode Island] [Research center]
MERL.......	Materials Engineering Research Laboratory [NASA] (NASA)
MERL.......	Materials Engineering Research Laboratory Ltd. [British] (IRC)
MERL.......	Materials Equipment Requirements List (NASA)
MERL.......	Materials Equipment Requirements List
MerL.......	Merrill Lynch & Co., Inc. [Associated Press] (SAG)
MerL.......	Merrill Lynch & Co. Preferred Capital Trust I [Associated Press] (SAG)
MERL..........	Municipal Environmental Research Laboratory [Environmental Protection Agency] (GRD)
MerLEur.....	Merrill Lynch & Co., Inc. [Associated Press] (SAG)
MERLIN	Machine Readable Library Information [British Library] [Information service or system] (IID)
MERLIN	Management of Expenditure and Resident-Linked Information Network [Computer science]
MERLIN	Medium-Energy Reactor Light-Water Industrial Neutron [British] (DEN)
MERLIN	Multielement Radio-Linked Interferometer Network [Astronomy]
Mer LJ........	Mercantile Law Journal [Madras, India] [A publication] (DLA)
MERM..........	Masters of Earth Resources Management (PGP)
MERM..........	Material Evaluation Rocket Motor
MERM..........	Multilateral Exchange Rate Model (ADA)
Mermic........	Merrimac Industries, Inc. [Associated Press] (SAG)
MERMLS.....	Mid-Eastern Regional Medical Library Service [Library network]
MERMUT	Mobile Electronic Robot Manipulator and Underwater Television (IEEE)
MERP..........	Miniature Electronic Repair Program (DNAB)
MerP6........	Meridian Point Realty Trust VI Co. [Associated Press] (SAG)
MERPASS......	Meridian Passage [Navigation]
MERPL........	Mission Essential Repair Parts List (MCD)
MerPnt 8......	Meridian Point Realty Trust VIII [Associated Press] (SAG)
MERPrA	Merrill Lynch 9% Sr'A'Dep Pfd [NYSE symbol] (TTSB)
MERPS........	Multiple Event Record and Playback System (NTCM)
MerPt4........	Meridian Point Realty Trust IV [Associated Press] (SAG)
MerPt6........	Meridian Point Realty Trust VI [Associated Press] (SAG)
MerPt7........	Meridian Point Realty Trust VII [Associated Press] (SAG)
MerPt 8	Meridian Point Realty Trust VIII Co. [Associated Press] (SAG)
MerPt83......	Meridian Point Realty Trust 1983 [Associated Press] (SAG)
MERQ	Mercury Interactive [NASDAQ symbol] (TTSB)
MERQ	Mercury Interactive Corp. [NASDAQ symbol] (SAG)
MerR	Mercuric Ion Receptor [Biochemistry]
MERR	Minor Equipment Relocations, Replacements (DNAB)
MERRA	Middle East Relief and Rehabilitation Administration [World War II]
Merr Att	Merrifield on Attorneys [1830] [A publication] (DLA)
MERRC	Middle Eastern Regional Radioisotope Centre for the Arab Countries [Cairo, Egypt] (WND)
Merr Costs....	Merrifield's Law of Costs [A publication] (DLA)
MERRECT ...	Mercury Rectifier (IAA)
MERRF	Myoclonic Epilepsy Associated with Ragged Red Fibres [Medicine]
Merrimack....	Smith's New Hampshire Reports [A publication] (DLA)
MerrLyn	Merrill Lynch & Co., Inc. [Associated Press] (SAG)
Merry W	[The] Merry Wives of Windsor [Shakespearean work] (BARN)
MERS..........	Medical Equipment Reporting System [Veterans Administration]
MERS..........	Meris Laboratories [NASDAQ symbol] (SPSG)
MERS..........	Mobile Emergency Response Support
MERS..........	Mobility Environmental Research Studies
MERS..........	Most Economical Route Selection [Also, ARS] [Bell System] [Telecommunications]
MERS..........	Movimiento de Estudiantes Revolucionarios Salvadorenos [Revolutionary Movement of Salvadoran Students] (PD)
MERS..........	Multielement Radiometer System
MERSAP	Merchant Ship Auxiliary Program (DNAB)
MERSAR	Merchant Ship Search and Rescue (PDAA)
MERSAT	Meteorology and Earth Observation Satellite (NASA)
MERSEX	Merchant Ship Code Systems [NATO] (NATG)
Mersey	Merseyside [County in England] (WGA)
MERSHIP....	Merchant Ship [Navy] (NVT)
MERSIGS.....	Merchant Signals [Shipping]
MERT..........	Maintenance Engineering Review Team [Navy] (NG)
Mert...........	Merten's Law of Federal Income Taxation [A publication] (DLA)
MERT..........	Merton College [Oxford University] (ROG)
MERT..........	Milwaukee Electric Railway & Transport Co. [AAR code]
MERT..........	Modified Effective-Range Theory (PDAA)
MER/TER	Multiple Ejection Rack/Triple Ejection Rack (MCD)
MertMd.......	Merit Medical Systems, Inc. [Associated Press] (SAG)
MERTS........	Micropound Extended Range Thrust Stand [NASA]
MERU.........	Milliearth Rate Unit [NASA] (KSC)
MERX..........	Mercer Enterprises [Air carrier designation symbol]
MERX..........	Merix Corp. [NASDAQ symbol] (SAG)
MeryL........	Merry Land & Investment Co., Inc. [Associated Press] (SAG)
MeryLd........	Merry Land & Investment Co., Inc. [Associated Press] (SAG)
MERZONE ...	Merchant Shipping Control Zone [NATO] (NATG)
MES............	Maharashtra Ekikaran Samithi [India] [Political party] (PPW)
MES............	Main Engine Start [NASA] (KSC)
MES............	Main Equipment Supplier (NATG)
MES............	Maine State Planning Office, Augusta, ME [OCLC symbol] (OCLC)
MES............	Mainly English-Speaking
MES............	Maintenance Electrolyte Solution [Physiology]
MES............	Management Engineering Squadron [Air Force]
MES............	Manned Exploration Site (MCD)
MES............	Manual Entry System [or Subsystem] (IEEE)
MES............	Manuals of Elementary Science [A publication]
MES............	Manufaturing Execution System [Engineering]
MES............	Marketable Equity Securities [Investment term] (DICI)
MES............	Mass Expulsion System (MCD)
MES............	Master Erection Schedule (DNAB)
MES............	Master of Engineering Sciences
MES............	Master of Engineering Studies
MES............	Master of Environmental Science (DD)
MES............	Master of Environmental Studies (PGP)
MES............	Master of Special Education (PGP)
MES............	Mated Elements [or Events] Simulator [NASA] (MCD)
MES............	Mated Elements Simulator
MES............	Mated Events Simulator
MES............	Maximal Electroshock [Physiology]
MES............	Maximum Electroshock Seizure [Medicine]
MES............	Medan [Indonesia] [Airport symbol] (OAG)
MES............	Medical Electronics Society [Defunct] (EA)
MES............	Medium Energy Source Program [Air Force]
MES............	Medsource Systems, Inc. [Vancouver Stock Exchange symbol]
MES............	Melville Corp. [Formerly, Melville Shoe Corp.] [NYSE symbol] (SPSG)
MES............	Mesaba Aviation [ICAO designator] (FAAC)
MES............	Mesozoic [Period, era, or system] [Geology]
MES............	Message Entry System (MCD)
MES............	Messina [Italy] [Seismograph station code, US Geological Survey] (SEIS)
MES............	Mesylate [Organic chemistry]
ME(S)	Methodist Episcopal, South
MES............	Mexican Epigraphic Society (EA)
MES............	Military Engineer Services [British]
MES............	Minerals Engineering Society [British]
MES............	Miniature Edison Screw
MES............	Minimum Efficiency Scale
MES............	Miscellaneous Equipment Specification (HGAA)
MES............	Missile Electrical Simulator
MES............	Missile Engineering Station
MES............	Mission Events Sequence (MCD)
MES............	Mobile Earth Station (DA)
M-ES..........	Mobile End System (ACRL)
MES............	Moessbauer Emission Spectroscopy
MES............	MOL [Manned Orbiting Laboratory] Environmental Shelter
MES............	Monitoring Energy Systems
MES............	More Effective Schools [Program] [Defunct]
MES............	Morpholinoethanesulfonic Acid [A buffer]
MES............	Motor End Support
MES............	Movimento de Esquerda Socialista [Movement of the Socialist Left] [Portugal Political party] (PPE)
MES............	Moving Earth Simulator (MCD)
MES............	Multiengine Sea [Pilot rating] (AIA)
MES............	Multilinear Events Sequencing [Engineering]
MES............	Multiple Earning Statement [Banking] (MHDW)
MES............	Multiple Endocrine Syndrome [Endocrinology]
MES............	Myoelectric Signal
MESA..........	Maintenance Engineering Support Analysis [Military] (CAAL)
MesA........	Maitre es Arts [Master of Arts] [French]
MESA..........	Malaria Eradication Special Account
MESA..........	Manned Environmental Systems Assessment [NASA]
MESA..........	Marine Ecosystems Analysis [Pollution-monitoring project]
MESA..........	Maximum Entropy Spectrum Analysis
MESA..........	Mechanics Educational Society of America (EA)
MESA..........	Medium Power-Switching Application (IAA)
MESA..........	Men to End Spouse Abuse (EA)
MESA..........	Mesa Air Group [NASDAQ symbol] (TTSB)
MESA..........	Mesa Air Group, Inc. [NASDAQ symbol] (SAG)
MESA..........	Mesa Airlines, Inc. [NASDAQ symbol] (NQ)
MESA..........	Microsurgical Epididymal Sperm Aspiration
ME/SA........	Middle East/Southern Asia
MESA..........	Middle East Studies Association of North America (EA)
MESA..........	Miniature Electrostatically Suspended Accelerometer (MCD)
MESA..........	Minimum Essential Support Analysis (MCD)
MESA..........	Mining Enforcement and Safety Administration [Terminated, 1978; functions transferred to Mine Safety and Health Administration, Department of Labor]
MESA..........	Mobile Entertainments, Southern Area [British military] (DMA)
MESA..........	Model Experimental Systems Analysis [An in-depth study of sewage outfall in the New York Bight] [Defunct] (USDC)
MESA..........	Model Experimental Systems Analysis [In-depth study of sewage outfall in the New York Bight] [Inactive] (OSRA)
MESA..........	Modularized Equipment Storage [or Stowage] Area [or Assembly] [Apollo] [NASA]
MESA..........	Multiple Engagement Simulation Analyzer [Military]
MESA..........	Music Editor, Scorer, and Arranger [Computer program] (PCM)
MesaAir......	Mesa Air Group, Inc. [Associated Press] (SAG)
MesaAr.......	Mesa Airlines, Inc. [Associated Press] (SAG)
MESAB........	Medical Education for South African Blacks [An association] (EA)
Mesab........	Mesabi Trust [Associated Press] (SAG)
Mesaba.......	Mesaba Holdings, Inc. [Associated Press] (SAG)
MesabaH......	Mesaba Holdings, Inc. [Associated Press] (SAG)
MeSaco.......	Dyer Library, Saco, ME [Library symbol Library of Congress] (LCLS)
MeSacoT	Thornton Academy, Saco, ME [Library symbol Library of Congress] (LCLS)
MesaInc......	Mesa, Inc. [Associated Press] (SAG)
MesaLb.......	Mesa Laboratories, Inc. [Associated Press] (SAG)
MESAN........	Mouvement de l'Evolution Sociale de l'Afrique Noire [Black African Social Evolution Movement]
MesaR........	Mesa Royalty Trust [Associated Press] (SAG)
MESAR........	Multifunction Electric Scan Adaptive RADAR [Military British]
MESB..........	Michigan Environmental Science Board

MESBIC....... Minority Enterprise Small Business Investment Company
MESC......... Marine Environmental Sciences Consortium [*Library network*]
MESC......... Master Event Sequence Controller (KSC)
ME Sc......... Master of Engineering Science
MESC......... Mescaline
MESC......... Middle East Service Command [*Army World War II*]
MESC......... Middle East Supercomputer Centre [*Bahrain Centre for Studies and Research*] (ECON)
MESC......... Middle East Supply Center [*World War II*]
MESC......... Middle East Supply Council [*World War II*]
MESC......... Miniature Excitatory Synaptic Current [*Neurophysiology*]
MESC......... Mission Events Sequence Controller [*NASA*] (KSC)
MESCH....... Multi-Environment Scheme [*Medicine*] (DMAA)
MESCO....... Message Electronic Switching Computer (IAA)
MESCPL..... Mess Corporal [*Marine Corps*]
MESC(W).... Middle East Supply Committee (Washington) [*World War II*]
MESD......... Mesdames [*Plural of Mrs.*] [*France*]
MeSepPM.... Penobscot Marine Museum, Searsport, ME [*Library symbol Library of Congress*] (LCLS)
MESF......... Minimum Engineered Safety Features (NRCH)
MESF......... Mobile Earth Station Facility
MESFET...... Metal-Semiconductor Field-Effect Transistor
MESG......... Maximum Experimental Safe Gap (IEEE)
MESG......... Mediterranean Shipping Group [*NATO*] (NATG)
MESG......... Microelectrostatic Gyro
MESGA....... Microelectrostatic Gyro-Accelerometer
MESGE....... Message (ABBR)
MESGER..... Messenger (ABBR)
MESH......... Marine Aspects of Earth System History [*Research programs*]
MESH......... Medical Subject Headings (NITA)
MeSH......... Medical Subject Headings Vocabulary File [*National Library of Medicine*] [*Information service or system*] (CRD)
MESH......... Multiple Electronically Synopsing Hierarchy (RDA)
MESH......... Museum Exchange for System's Help [*National Museum of Natural History*] (IID)
MESI.......... Modified, Exclusive, Shared, and Invalid Data (PCM)
MESIM........ Mission Essential Subsystem Inoperative Maintenance
MeSk......... Skowhegan Free Public Library, Skowhegan, ME [*Library symbol Library of Congress*] (LCLS)
MeSkS........ Margaret Chase Smith Library Center, Skowhegan, ME [*Library symbol*] [*Library of Congress*] (LCLS)
MESL......... Marine Environment Studies Laboratory [*Marine science*] (OSRA)
MESL......... Membrane-Enveloped Soil Layer
MESL......... Merchants' Exchange of St. Louis (EA)
MESL......... Microwave Electronic Systems Ltd.
MESL......... Mission Essential Subsystems List (NVT)
MESM......... Master of Environmental Science (PGP)
MESM......... Mission Essential Subsystem Matrix [*Navy*] (ANA)
MESM......... Multiechelon Supply Model (AABC)
MesoAm...... Meso American (VRA)
Mesol......... Mesolithic (VRA)
Mesop........ Mesopotamia (VRA)
MESOP....... Mesopotamia
MESP......... Minuteman Extended Survivable Power (DWSG)
MesPGN..... Mesangial Proliferative Glomerulonephritis [*Nephrology*] (DMAA)
MESPOT..... Mesopotamia (DSUE)
MeSprN...... Nasson College, Springvale, ME [*Library symbol Library of Congress*] (LCLS)
MESq......... Management Engineering Squadron [*Air Force*]
MESRF....... Middle East Special Requirement Fund
MESROM.... Materials-Evaluation Subcaliber Rocket Motor (SAA)
Mesrx........ Measurex Corp. [*Associated Press*] (SAG)
MESS......... Magnetic Emulsion Spectrometer
MESS......... Master of Exercise and Sport Sciences (PGP)
MESS......... Maximum Effective SONAR Speed (NVT)
MESS......... Maximum Efficiency Structural System (IAA)
MESS......... Mechanical Electronic Subassembly Simulator
MESS......... Messenger (MSA)
MESS......... Messerschmitt [*German fighter aircraft*] (DSUE)
MESS......... Misalignment Estimation Software System (MCD)
MESS......... Mixed Evolutionarily Stable Strategy [*Breeding selection*]
MESS......... Monitor Event Simulation System (IEEE)
MESSAGE... Modular Electronic Solid-State Aerospace Ground Equipment
MESSCPL... Mess Corporal [*Marine Corps*]
MESSE....... Messuage (ROG)
MESSER..... Messerschmitt [*German fighter aircraft*] (DSUE)
MESSR...... Multispectrum Electronic Self-Scanning Radiometer (MCD)
MESSRS..... Messieurs [*Plural of Mister*] [*French*]
MESSSGT... Mess Sergeant [*Marine Corps*]
MESST....... Eucharistic Missionaries of the Most Holy Trinity (TOCD)
MEST......... Eucharistic Missionaries of St. Theresa (Mexico) (TOCD)
MEST......... Maintenance Engineering Support Team (MCD)
MEST......... Mestizo (ABBR)
MEST......... Ministere d'Etat, Sciences et Technologie [*Ministry of State for Science and Technology - MOSST*] [*Canada*]
MEST......... Missile Electrical System Test (NG)
MEST......... Mouse Ear Swelling Test [*Analytical biochemistry*]
MESTA....... Marine Ecosystem Study in Tropical Areas [*Marine science*] (MSC)
Mestek....... Mestek, Inc. [*Associated Press*] (SAG)
MESTS....... Missile Electric System Test Set [*Military*] (PDAA)
MESU........ Microelectronics Support Unit [*for the Microelectronics Education Programme*] [*British*]
MESUCORA.. Measurement, Control Regulation, and Automation (IEEE)
MESUCORA... [*Association for*] Measurement, Control, Regulation and Automation (ECII)

MESUR....... Mars Environmental Survey [*NASA*]
MESW....... Meta-Software [*NASDAQ symbol*] (TTSB)
MESW....... Meta-Software, Inc. [*NASDAQ symbol*] (SAG)
MET.......... East Tennessee State University, Medical Library, Johnson City, TN [*OCLC symbol*] (OCLC)
MET.......... Magic Eye Tube
MET.......... Maintenance Engineering Technique
MET.......... Maintenance Evaluation Team
MET.......... Management Engineering Team [*Air Force*] (AFM)
MET.......... Manufacturer's Excise Tax
MET.......... Master Events Timer (MCD)
MET.......... Master of Education in Teaching (GAGS)
MET.......... Mean Elapsed Time (MCD)
met.......... Measurement (DS)
MET.......... Mechanical Engineering Technician
MET.......... Medium Equipment Transporter (MCD)
MET.......... Memphis [*Tennessee*] [*Seismograph station code, US Geological Survey*] (SEIS)
MET.......... Metabolic Equivalent [*Medicine*]
MET.......... Metal [*or Metallic*] (AAG)
MET.......... Metallic [*Automotive advertising*]
met.......... Metallic [*Referring to breath sounds*] [*Medicine*] (DAVI)
MET.......... Metallurgical
MET.......... Metalore Resources Ltd. [*Toronto Stock Exchange symbol*]
Met.......... Metamorphoses [*of Apuleius*] [*Classical studies*] (OCD)
Met.......... Metamorphoses [*of Ovid*] [*Classical studies*] (OCD)
MET.......... Metaphor
MET.......... Metaphysics
MET.......... Metastasis [*Medicine*]
MET.......... Metatarsus [*Flamenco dance term*]
Met.......... Metcalfe's Reports [*58-61 Kentucky*] [*A publication*] (DLA)
Met.......... Metcalf's Reports [*Rhode Island*] [*A publication*] (DLA)
Met.......... Metcalf's Reports [*Massachusetts*] [*A publication*] (DLA)
MET.......... Meteorological Broadcast (IAA)
MET.......... Meteorological Office [*British*] (DSUE)
MET.......... Meteorological Research Flight [*British ICAO designator*] (FAAC)
MET.......... Meteorology (AFM)
Met.......... Methionine [*Also, M*] [*An amino acid*]
met.......... Methionine [*An amino acid*] (DOG)
MET.......... Metronome [*Music*]
MET.......... Metropolis (ROG)
MET.......... Metropolitan (AAG)
MET.......... Metropolitan Electric Tramways [*British*] (ROG)
MET.......... Metropolitan Music Hall [*London*] [*British*] (DSUE)
Met.......... [*New York*] Metropolitan Opera House
MET.......... [*The*] Metropolitan Railway [*British*] (ROG)
MET.......... Metropolitan Realty [*AMEX symbol*] (TTSB)
MET.......... Metropolitan Realty Corp. [*AMEX symbol*] (CTT)
MET.......... Metuchen [*Diocesan abbreviation*] [*New Jersey*] (TOCD)
MET.......... Micro-Electronic Technology (ADA)
MET.......... Midexpiratory Time [*Medicine*]
MET.......... Midshipman Embarkation Team [*Navy*]
MET.......... Minimum Energy Trajectory
MET.......... Minimum Essentials Test [*Educational test*]
MET.......... Minimum Exposure Time
MET.......... Minor Expendable Tool (MCD)
MET.......... Missile Electrical Technician [*Aerospace*] (IAA)
MET.......... Missile Escort Team [*Air Force*] (AFM)
MET.......... Mission Elapsed Time [*NASA*] (KSC)
MET.......... Mission Entry Time
MET.......... Mission Environment Tape
MET.......... Mission Event Timer [*NASA*] (KSC)
MET.......... Mobile Engineering Team [*Navy*]
MET.......... Mobile Equipment Transporter [*NASA*]
MET.......... Modesto & Empire Traction Co. [*Formerly, METC*] [*AAR code*]
MET.......... Modified Expansion Tube (IEEE)
MET.......... Modular Equipment Transporter [*NASA*]
MET.......... Molecular Electronic Technique
MET.......... Mond Excavation at Thebes [*London*] [*A publication*] (BJA)
MET.......... Motorola Environmental Telemetry
MET.......... Multibutton Electronic Telephone (NITA)
MET.......... Multiemitter Transistor
MET.......... Multi-Environment Trainer (MCD)
MET.......... Multiple Employer Trust [*Insurance*]
META........ Computer series [*Digital Scientific*]
META........ Maritime Education and Training Act of 1980
META........ Megachannel Extraterrestrial Array [*For receiving possible radio signals from non-earth civilizations*]
meta.......... Metacarpal [*Anatomy*] (DAVI)
META........ metamyelocyte [*Hematology*] (DAVI)
meta.......... Metatarsal [*Anatomy*] (DAVI)
META........ Metatec Corp. [*NASDAQ symbol*] (SAG)
META........ Methods of Extracting Text Automatically [*Programming language*] [*General Electric Co.*] [*Computer science*] (IEEE)
META........ Metropolitan Educational Television Association [*Canada*]
META........ Model Engineering Trade Association [*British*] (BI)
META 1....... Metabolic Profile 1 [*Biochemistry*] (DAVI)
METAB....... Metabolism
METABC..... Metabolic (ABBR)
METABZ..... Metabolize (ABBR)
METABZD... Metabolized (ABBR)
METABZG... Metabolizing (ABBR)
METAC....... Medium Tactical Transport Aircraft [*Military*]
METAC....... Methacryloyloxyethyltrimethylammonium Chloride [*Organic chemistry*]

METADEX .... Metal Abstracts Index Data Base [*Bibliographic database*] [*British*] (IID)
METADEX .... Metals Abstracts Inex (NITA)
METADS ..... Meteorological Acquisition and Display System (PDAA)
METAF......... Meteorological Terminal Aviation Weather Forecast [*FAA*] (TAG)
METAG........ Meteorological Advisory Group [*ICAO*] (DA)
MetaGp........ Meta Group, Inc. [*Associated Press*] (SAG)
METAL........ Metallurgy
METAL........ Militarily Significant Emergent Technologies Awareness List [*Proposed*] [*DoD*]
MetalcId ...... Metaclad Corp. [*Associated Press*] (SAG)
MetalcId ...... Metalclad Corp. [*Associated Press*] (SAG)
METALL....... Metallurgy
METALLOG... Metallography (DGA)
MetalR........ Metallica Resources, Inc. [*Associated Press*] (SAG)
META M....... Metaphysical Magazine [*A publication*] (ROG)
MET & E ...... Medical Equipment Test and Evaluation [*Army Medical Material Agency*] (PDAA)
METAPH ...... Metaphorical (ROG)
Metaph .... Metaphysica [*of Aristotle*] [*Classical studies*] (OCD)
METAPH ...... Metaphysical [*or Metaphysics*] (ROG)
METAPH ...... Metaphysician (ABBR)
metaph .... Metaphysics [*Parapsychology*] (DAVI)
METAPHYS... Metaphysic (ABBR)
METAPLAN... Methods of Extracting Text Automatically Programming - Language [*General Electric Co.*] [*Computer science*] (IEEE)
METAR........ Aviation Routine Weather Report [*ICAO*] (FAAC)
METAR........ Meteorological Terminal Aviation Routine Weather Report [*FAA*] (TAG)
METAS........ Metastasize [*Medicine*]
MetaSft........ Meta-Software, Inc. [*Associated Press*] (SAG)
METASYMBOL... Metalanguage Symbol
Metatec ...... Metatec Corp. [*Associated Press*] (SAG)
METATH ...... Metathesis
METB .... Metal Base
METB .... MetroBanCorp [*NASDAQ symbol*] (SAG)
METB .... Metropolitan Borough
METC .... Medesto & Empire Traction Co. (MHDB)
METC .... Metal Curb (AAG)
Metc .... Metcalfe's Reports [*58-61 Kentucky*] [*A publication*] (DLA)
Metc .... Metcalf's Reports [*Rhode Island*] [*A publication*] (DLA)
Metc .... Metcalf's Reports [*Massachusetts*] [*A publication*] (DLA)
METC .... Military Equipment Test Center (CAAL)
METC .... Modesto & Empire Traction Co. [*Later, MET*] [*AAR code*]
METC .... Monthly Estimate to Completion (MCD)
METC .... Morgantown Energy Technology Center [*Morgantown, WV*] [*Department of Energy*] (GRD)
METC .... Mouse Embryo Tissue Culture
METCA .... Merchant Token Collectors Association (EA)
METCAL....... Metrology and Calibration [*Air Force*] (AFIT)
METCAN ...... Metal Matrix Composite Analyzer [*Organic chemistry*]
MET-CAR ..... Metallo-Carbohedrene [*Organic chemistry*]
Metc Cont .... Metcalf on the Law of Contracts [*A publication*] (DLA)
Metc KY...... Metcalfe's Reports [*58-61 Kentucky*] [*A publication*] (DLA)
Metc Mass... Metcalf's Reports [*Massachusetts*] [*A publication*] (DLA)
METCO........ Meteorological Coordination Officer (MUGU)
METCO........ Metropolitan Council for Educational Opportunity (EA)
METCO........ Mobile Engine Tester, Computer-Operated (DNAB)
MetCoil....... Met Coil Systems Corp. [*Associated Press*] (SAG)
METCON ...... Metropolitan Consortium for Minorities in Science and Engineering (USDC)
Metc Yelv .... Metcalf's Edition of Yelverton [*A publication*] (DLA)
METD.......... Management Education Training and Development (AIE)
METD.......... Mean Effective Temperature Difference [*Refrigeration*]
METD.......... Metal Door
METD.......... Metastatic Disease [*Oncology*]
METDLGY .... Methodology
Met E .... Metallurgical Engineer
Mete .... Meteorologica [*of Aristotle*] [*Classical studies*] (OCD)
METE .... Multiple ECM [*Electronic Countermeasures*] Threat Environment [*Military*] (CAAL)
METE .... Multiple Engagement Test Environment [*Military*] (PDAA)
METE .... Multiple Environment Threat Emitter (MCD)
METEC........ Meteoroid Technology [*Satellite*] [*NASA*]
METEC........ Meteorologist Technician (NOAA)
MetEC........ Metropolitan Edison Capital Ltd. [*Associated Press*] (SAG)
MetEng........ Metallurgical Engineering (DD)
METEOR ...... Manned Earth-Satellite Terminal Evolving from Earth-to-Orbit Ferry Rockets (SAA)
METEOR ...... Marine Environmental Testing and Electro-Optical Radiation (MCD)
METEOR ...... Meteorological Satellite [*Former USSR*]
METEOR ...... Meteorology
METEORIT ... Meteoritical
METEOROL... Meteorology
METEOROLO... Meteorology (ABBR)
METEOSAT... Meteorological Satellite [*European Space Agency*]
METEPA...... Tris(methylethylene)phosphoric Triamide [*Organic chemistry*]
METER........ Machine Examination Teaching, Evaluation, and Re-education (PDAA)
METF .... Metal Flashing
MetFACS..... Metropolitan Life Insurance Co. Financial and Administrative Customer Services System (HGAA)
METG.......... META Group [*NASDAQ symbol*] (TTSB)
METG.......... Meta Group, Inc. [*NASDAQ symbol*] (SAG)
METG.......... Metal Grill

METG.......... Middle East Task Group (DNAB)
METGL........ Meteorological (WGA)
MetGlob....... Metro Global Media, Inc. [*Associated Press*] (SAG)
Meth .... Mercaptoethanol [*Organic chemistry*]
METH.......... Methadone (ABBR)
METH.......... Methamphetamine (ABBR)
METH.......... Methane (AAG)
Meth .... Methaphetamine Hydrochloride [*An amphetamine, commonly known as speed*] (VNW)
Meth .... Methedrine [*Stimulant*]
METH.......... Methicillin [*An antibiotic*]
METH.......... Method (ROG)
METH.......... Method
METH.......... Methode Electronics, Inc. [*NASDAQ symbol*] (NQ)
METH.......... Methodist
meth .... Methyl [*Organic chemistry*] (DAVI)
METH.......... Methylated (ADA)
METH.......... Methylated Spirit (DSUE)
METH.......... Methylmeth (ABBR)
METH.......... Methyprylon (ABBR)
METHA........ Methode Electronics 'A' [*NASDAQ symbol*] (TTSB)
Methanx ...... Methanex Corp. [*Associated Press*] (SAG)
MetHb........ Methemoglobin [*Biochemistry, medicine*]
METHB........ Methode Electronics 'B' [*NASDAQ symbol*] (TTSB)
METHC........ Methodic (ABBR)
MethCh .... Methodist Chaplain [*Navy British*]
MeThCh ...... Methylthiocholine [*Biochemistry*]
Meth Ch Ca... Report of Methodist Church Cases [*A publication*] (DLA)
Methd .... Methode Electronics, Inc. [*Associated Press*] (SAG)
METHDST .... Methodist
MeTHF........ Methyltetrahydrofolic Acid [*Biochemistry*]
met hgh ...... Methemoglobin [*Biochemistry*] (DAVI)
METHIMAZOLE... Methylmercaptoimidazole [*Also, MMI*] [*Thyroid inhibitor*]
METHO .... Methodology (ABBR)
METHOG ..... Methodology (ABBR)
METHOGL .... Methodological (ABBR)
METHS........ Methylated Spirits (ADA)
methyl-CCNU... Methyl-1-(2-chloroethyl)-3-cyclohexyl-1 Nitrosourea [*Antineoplastic drug regimen*] (DAVI)
methyl-GAG... methyl-Glyoxal Bisguanylhydrazone [*Antineoplastic drug*] (DAVI)
Methyl-GAG... Methylglyoxal-bis-guanylhydrazone [*Antineoplastic drug*] (CDI)
METHZ........ Methodize (ABBR)
METHZD ..... Methodized (ABBR)
METI .... Major Engineering Test Item (AAG)
METI .... Medical Education Technologies, Inc.
METIC......... Meticulous (ABBR)
METIMP...... Meteorological Equipment Improvement Program (NG)
METJ.......... Metal Jalousie
METJET........ Meteorological Sounding Rocket, Ramjet-Powered [*NASA*] (SAA)
METL.......... Materials and Ecological Testing Laboratory [*Research center*] (RCD)
METL.......... Metal
METL.......... Metal
METL.......... Metallica Resources, Inc. [*NASDAQ symbol*] (SAG)
METL.......... Mission Essential Task List [*Army*] (INF)
Met Lab ...... Metabolic Laboratory [*Colorado State University*] (RCD)
METLC......... Metallic
METLLRGCL... Metallurgical
METLLRGST... Metallurgist
METLO......... Metrological Equipment and Technical Liaison Officer [*Navy*] (NG)
METM .... Master of Engineering and Technology Management (PGP)
METM .... Metal Mold
MET/M......... Missile Engine Technician/Mechanic (AAG)
Metmail....... Metromail Corp. [*Associated Press*] (SAG)
metMb........ Metmyoglobin [*Medicine*] (MEDA)
M et N........ Mane et Nocte [*Morning and Night*] [*Pharmacy*]
m et n .... Mane et Nocte [*Morning and night*] [*Latin*] [*Pharmacy*] (DAVI)
METO .... Maximum Engine Takeoff [*Power*] [*Air Force*]
METO .... Maximum Except during Takeoff
METO .... Meteorological Office [*or Officer*] [*Air Force*]
METO .... Metro Capital Corp. [*NASDAQ symbol*] (SAG)
METO .... Middle East Treaty Organization
METOB........ Meteorologist Observation (NOAA)
METOF........ Meteorological Office
Met Off .... Meteorological Office [*British*] (AIA)
METOFOR ... Methodology for Total Force Concept [*Military*]
METON .... Measured Tons Discharged or Loaded [*Shipping*]
METON .... Metonymy
METOP........ Maximum Expected Takeoff Power (AFM)
Metopera..... Metropolitan Opera Association (EA)
MeToV........ United States Veterans Administration Center, Togus, ME [*Library symbol Library of Congress*] (LCLS)
METOXI....... Military Effectiveness in a Toxin Environment (AABC)
METP .... Metal Partition
METP .... Metal Portion
MetPro........ Met-Pro Corp. [*Associated Press*] (SAG)
metpt......... Metalpoint (VRA)
METR .... Metal Roof
METR .... Meteorology (NG)
METR .... Metropolitan
MetR .... Metropolitan Railway [*British*]
METR .... Minimum Essential Training Requirements
METRA........ Metal RADAR
METRA........ Multiple-Event Time Recording Apparatus (PDAA)
MetraB........ Metra Biosystems [*Associated Press*] (SAG)
MetrBcp...... MetroBancorp [*Associated Press*] (SAG)

Metrbk	Metrobank North America [*Associated Press*] (SAG)
MetrCap	Metro Capital Corp. [*Associated Press*] (SAG)
Metrcm	Metricom, Inc. [*Associated Press*] (SAG)
METREX	Metropolitan Centrex [*Telephone network*]
METRI	Military Essentiality through Readiness Indices
METRIA	Metropolitan Tree Improvement Alliance (EA)
METRIC	Multiechelon Technique for Recoverable Item Control (MCD)
MetrisCo	Metris Companies, Inc. [*Associated Press*] (SAG)
METRL	Meteorology (NG)
METRL	Metrology Requirements List [*DoD*]
METRLGST	Meteorologist
MetRlt	Metropolitan Realty Corp. [*Associated Press*] (SAG)
MetrNet	Metro Networks, Inc. [*Associated Press*] (SAG)
METRO	Materiel Essential to Reconstitution Operations [*Air Force*] (AFM)
METRO	Messenger Transport Organizer [*Developmental biology*]
METRO	Meteorological Equipment Terminal and Representative Observation (MCD)
METRO	Meteorology
METRO	Meteorology
METRO	Metering and Traffic Recording with Offline Processing (PDAA)
Metro	Metro-Goldwyn-Mayer (WDMC)
METRO	Metropolitan [*Subway system*] (DSUE)
METRO	Metropolitan
METRO	Metropolitan Collegiate Athletic Conference (EA)
METRO	Michigan Effectuation, Training, and Research Organization [*Computer-programmed simulation game*]
METRO	New York Metropolitan Reference and Research Library Agency [*Brooklyn, NY*] [*Library network*]
MetroBcp	Metropolitan Bancorp [*Associated Press*] (SAG)
METROC	Meteorological Rocket
Metrocall	Metrocall, Inc. [*Associated Press*] (SAG)
MetroFn	Metro Financial Corp. [*Associated Press*] (SAG)
Metrogs	Metrogas SA [*Associated Press*] (SAG)
METROL	Metrology
Metrolog	Metrologic Instruments, Inc. [*Associated Press*] (SAG)
Metromda	Metromedia International Group [*Associated Press*] (SAG)
METROMEX	Metropolitan Meteorological Experiment
METROP	Metropol (WDAA)
METROP	Metropolis (ADA)
METROP	Metropolitan
METROPOL	Metropolis [*or Metropolitan*] (ABBR)
Metrotrn	Metrotrans Corp. [*Associated Press*] (SAG)
MetroV	MetroVision of North America, Inc. [*Associated Press*] (SAG)
METRRA	Metal Re-Radiation RADAR [*Mine detection system*] [*Army*] (RDA)
MetRS	Methionyl-Transfer Ribonucleic Acid Synthetase [*An enzyme*]
MetrTl	Metro-Tel Corp. [*Associated Press*] (SAG)
MetrV	MetroVision of North America, Inc. [*Associated Press*] (SAG)
METS	Maintainability Evaluation and Tracking System (MCD)
METS	Mechanized Export Traffic System [*Army*] (AABC)
METS	Metal Strip
Mets	Metastasis [*Oncology*] (MAE)
METS	Met-Coil Systems [*NASDAQ symbol*] (TTSB)
METS	Met-Coil Systems Corp. [*NASDAQ symbol*] (NQ)
MET/S	Missile Electrical Technician/Specialist (AAG)
METS	Missile Environmental Testing Study
METS	Mobile Electronic Test Set (MCD)
METS	Mobile Engine Test Stand
METS	Modified Engineered Time Standards
METS	Modular Engine Test System (MCD)
METS	Modularized Equipment Transport System [*NASA*]
METS	Multiple Exposure Testing System [*Advertising analysis*]
METSAAT	Meteorological Satellite (USDC)
MET/SAT	Meteorological Satellite
METSATT	Meteorological Satellite [*Marine science*] (OSRA)
m et sig	Misce et Signa [*Mix and write a label*] [*Latin*] [*Pharmacy*] (DAVI)
M et Sig	Misce et Signa [*Mix and Label*] [*Pharmacy*]
METT	Manned, Evasive Target Tank [*Army*]
METRlt	Microwave Energy Transmission Test (SSD)
METT	Mission, Enemy, Terrain and Weather, Troops and Firepower Available
METTM	Mission, Enemy, Terrain and Weather, Troops and Firepower Available, and Maneuver Space (MCD)
Met Tr J	Metal Trades Journal [*A publication*]
METT-T	Mission, Enemy, Terrain and Weather, Troops and Firepower Available and Time (INF)
METTW	Mission, Enemy, Terrain, Tactics, Weather [*Criteria for establishing military strategy*] [*Army*] (VNW)
METU	Marine Electronic Technical Unit (MUGU)
METU	Mobile Electronics Technical Unit
METU	Mobile Electronics Training Unit
METVC	Main Engine Thrust Vector Control (MCD)
METW	Military Emergency Travel Warrant [*MTMC*] (TAG)
METW	Municipality of East Troy, Wisconsin [*AAR code*]
metwk	Metalwork (VRA)
Metz	Metzenbaum [*Instruments*] [*Surgery*] (DAVI)
meu	Maine [*MARC country of publication code Library of Congress*] (LCCP)
MEU	Main Electronic Unit (INF)
MEU	Marine Expeditionary Unit
MEU	Marromeu [*Mozambique*] [*Airport symbol*] (AD)
MEU	Memory Expansion Unit
MEU	Message Encoder Unit
MEU	Methylumbelliferone [*Biochemistry*]
MEU	Mind Extension University [*Cable television channel*]
MEU	Modern English Usage (WDAA)
MEU	Multiplexer Encoder Unit
MEU	Municipal Electricity Undertaking
MeU	University of Maine, Orono, ME [*Library symbol Library of Congress*] (LCLS)
MEUA	Million European Units of Account (PDAA)
MEUF	Micellar-Enhanced Ultrafiltration [*Chemical engineering*]
MEUG	Major Energy Users' Group [*British*]
MeU-G	University of Maine at Portland/Gorham, Gorham, ME [*Library symbol Library of Congress*] (LCLS)
MeU-L	University of Maine, Law Library, Portland, ME [*Library symbol Library of Congress*] (LCLS)
MEULEX	Marine Expeditionary Unit Landing Exercise (NVT)
MeUmb	Methylumbelliferyl [*Biochemistry*]
MeU-P	University of Maine at Portland/Gorham, Portland, ME [*Library symbol Library of Congress*] (LCLS)
MEV	Manned Entry Vehicle
MEV	Medical Evacuation Vehicle (MCD)
MeV	Mega-Electronvolt (ODBW)
MeV	Megaelectronvolt (IDOE)
MEV	Mega [*or Million*] Electron Volts
MEV	Million Electron Volts (MCD)
MEV	Minden, NV [*Location identifier FAA*] (FAAL)
MEvA	Avco-Everett Research Laboratory, Everett, MA [*Library symbol Library of Congress*] (LCLS)
MEVE	Mesa Verde National Park
MeVEMsJ	Mercury, Venus, Earth, Mars, Jupiter (PDAA)
MEvP	Parlin Memorial Library, Everett, MA [*Library symbol Library of Congress*] (LCLS)
MEW	Manitoba Department of Environment, Workplace Safety, and Health [*UTLAS symbol*]
MEW	Manufactures Empty Weight (MCD)
MEW	Marine Early Warning
MEW	Mean Equivalent Wind [*Meteorology*] (DA)
MEW	Measure of Economic Welfare
MEW	Microwave Early Warning [*Radio*] [*Air Force*]
MEW	Middle East Watch [*An association*] (EA)
MEW	Minimum Envelope Weight (MCD)
MEW	Ministry of Economic Warfare [*British*]
MEW	Missionaries of the Eternal Word [*Formerly, CFMA*] (EA)
MEW	Mobile Early Warning
MEW	Modern English Writers [*A publication*]
MeW	Waterville Public Library, Waterville, ME [*Library symbol Library of Congress*] (LCLS)
MEWA	Ministry of Education, Western Australia
MEWA	Motor and Equipment Wholesalers Association [*Later, ASIA*]
MEWA	Multiple Employer Welfare Arrangement
MEWA	Multiple-Employer Welfare Association (WYGK)
MeWC	Colby College, Waterville, ME [*Library symbol Library of Congress*] (LCLS)
MEWC	Middle East Section of the War Cabinet [*British World War II*]
MEWC	Middle East War Council [*British military*] (DMA)
MEWD	Missile Electronic Warfare Division [*White Sands Missile Range*] (AAG)
MeWe	Wells Public Library, Wells, ME [*Library symbol Library of Congress*] (LCLS)
MeWebr	Walker Memorial Library, Westbrook, ME [*Library symbol Library of Congress*] (LCLS)
MEWG	Maintenance Engineering Working Group [*NASA*] (NASA)
MEWO	Manufacturing Engineering Work Order (MCD)
MEWS	Mews [*Postal Service standard*] (OPSA)
Mews	Mews' Digest of English Case Law [*A publication*] (DLA)
MEWS	Microwave Electronic Warfare System
MEWS	Missile Early Warning Station (AFM)
MEWS	Missile Electronic Warfare System [*Army*]
MEWS	Mission Essential Weapon System [*Military*] (CAAL)
MEWS	Mobile Electronic Warfare Simulator (MCD)
MEWS	Modular Electronic Warfare Simulator [*Navy*]
Mews	[*The*] Reports [*1893-95*] [*England*] [*A publication*] (DLA)
Mews Dig	Mews' Digest of English Case Law [*A publication*] (DLA)
MEWSG	Multiservice Electronic Warfare Support Group [*Originally Maritime Electronic Warfare Support Group*] [*NATO*] (DOMA)
MEWSS	Mobile Electronic Warfare Support System [*Military*] (LAIN)
MEWT	Matrix Electrostatic Writing Technique
MEWT	Microelectronic Weld Tester
MEWTA	Missile Electronic Warfare Technical Area [*White Sands Missile Range*] (AABC)
MEX	Mariner Explorations [*Vancouver Stock Exchange symbol*]
M Ex	Master of Expression
MEx	Mekhilta Exodus (BJA)
MEX	Memorex Corp., Memorex Technical Information Library, Santa Clara, CA [*OCLC symbol*] (OCLC)
MEX	Metro Express II, Inc. [*ICAO designator*] (FAAC)
MEX	Mexican (ROG)
MEX	Mexican
MEX	Mexico [*ANSI three-letter standard code*] (CNC)
Mex	Mexico (VRA)
MEX	Mexico City [*Mexico*] [*Later, TEO*] [*Geomagnetic observatory code*]
MEX	Mexico City [*Mexico*] [*Airport symbol*] (OAG)
MEX	Military Engineering Experimental Establishment [*British*]
MEX	Military Exchange
MEX	Mississippi Export Railroad (IIA)
MEX	Mobile Exercise
MEX	MODEM Executive [*Computer telecommunications program*]
MEX	Temporary Rank [*Army slang*]
MExB	Motor Explosive Boat [*British military*] (DMA)

MEXE	Military Engineering Experimental Establishment [*British*]
MexEqt	Mexico Equity & Income Fund [*Associated Press*] (SAG)
MexFd	[*The*] Mexico Fund, Inc. [*Associated Press*] (SAG)
MEXH	Multi-Energy X-Ray Holography [*Physics*]
MexP	Mexican Pharmacopoeia [*A publication*]
MExSt	Master of Experimental Statistics (GAGS)
MEXT	Maximal Exercise Testing
M Ext Ed	Master of Extension Education (PGP)
MExtEd	Master of Extension Education (GAGS)
MEY	Mapleton, IA [*Location identifier FAA*] (FAAL)
MEY	Maximum Economic Yield [*Fishery management*] (MSC)
MEY	Meghauli [*Nepal*] [*Airport symbol*] (OAG)
Meyer Des Inst Judiciares	Meyer's Des Institutiones Judiciares [*A publication*] (DLA)
MeYoO	Old York Historical Society, York, ME [*Library symbol*] [*Library of Congress*] (LCLS)
MEZ	Augusta Mental Health Institute, Augusta, ME [*OCLC symbol*] (OCLC)
MEZ	Mena, AR [*Location identifier FAA*] (FAAL)
MEZ	Merces [*Brazil*] [*Airport symbol*] (AD)
Mez	Mezuzah (BJA)
MEZ	Mezzo [*Moderate*] [*Music*]
mez	Mezzotint (VRA)
MEZ	Mezzotinto [*Medium Tint, Half Tone*] [*Engraving*] (ROG)
MEZ	Missile Engagement Zone (NVT)
MEZ	Mittel Europaeische Zeit [*Central European Time*] [*German*]
MEZN	Mezzanine (ABBR)
mezn	Mezzanine (VRA)
MEZT	Mezzotint [*Printing*] (ABBR)
MEZZ	Mezzanine (KSC)
MEZZ	Mezzotint [*Printing*] (ABBR)
MEZZO	Mezzosoprano (ABBR)
MEZZO	Mezzotint [*Printing*] (ROG)
MF	5-Methyltetrahydrofolate [*Biochemistry*] (DAVI)
MF	Fall River Public Library, Fall River, MA [*Library symbol Library of Congress*] (LCLS)
MF	Le Maitre Phonetique [*A publication*] (BJA)
MF	Machine Finish [*Paper*]
mf	Machine-Finish Paper (WDMC)
MF	Magazines for Friendship [*An association*] (EA)
MF	Magnetic Field
MF	Magnetic Fluid [*Physics*]
MF	Magnetic Focus [*of cathode-ray tube*] (DEN)
MF	Magneto [*or Magnetic*] Field Generators [*JETDS Nomenclature*] [*Military*] (CET)
MF	Magnetomotive Force (KSC)
MF	Main Feed [*Technical drawings*]
MF	Main Force [*Military*]
M/F	Mainframe (NITA)
MF	Maintenance Factor
MF	Maintenance Float [*Military*]
MF	Maintenance Fuel
M/F	Maintenance to Flight [*Ratio*]
MF	Major Facilitator [*Biochemistry*]
MF	Major Function (MCD)
M/F	Make From (SAA)
MF	Malaysia Fund [*NYSE symbol*] (TTSB)
MF	Malaysia Fund, Inc. [*NYSE symbol*] (SPSG)
MF	Male to Female [*Ratio*]
MF	Mali Franc [*Monetary unit*]
MF	MAM Aviation Ltd. [*British ICAO designator*] (ICDA)
MF	Mandatory Frequency (DA)
MF	Mantle Floor
MF	Manufacture (WGA)
MF	Mare Feccunditatis [*Sea of Fertility*] [*Lunar area*]
M/F	Marked For
MF	Mark Forward [*Papers*] [*British*]
MF	Martinus de Fano [*Deceased circa 1275*] [*Authority cited in pre-1607 legal work*] (DSA)
MF	Masculinity-Femininity (AEBS)
M$_f$	Mass Flow of Fuel [*Aviation*] (DA)
MF	Massora Finalis (BJA)
M/F	Master File
MF	Master Frame
MF	Master of Finance
MF	Master of Forestry
MF	Mastic Floor [*Technical drawings*]
MF	Matching Funds (OICC)
MF	Mate and Ferry [*NASA*] (NASA)
MF	Mate and Ferry
MF	Material Factor
MF	Maurice-Farman [*British military*] (DMA)
mf	Mauritius [*MARC country of publication code Library of Congress*] (LCCP)
MF	Maximum Flowering Day [*Botany*]
MF	Measurement Facility [*Computer science*] (IBMDP)
MF	Meat Free [*Diet*]
MF	Mechanical Flap [*Aviation*]
MF	Meclofenamate [*Organic chemistry*]
MF	Medal of Freedom [*Military decoration*]
MF	Media Filter (ACRL)
MF	Media Forum (EA)
MF	Medical Foundation [*Australia*]
MF	Medium Frequency [*Radio electronics*]
mf	Medium Frequency (WDMC)
MF	Medium Frequency [*300-3000 Kilohertz*]
MF	Melamine-Formaldehyde [*Plastics technology*]
MF	Melomanes Francais [*Record label*] [*France*]
MF	Membrane Filter
MF	Merck Frosst Laboratories [*Canada*]
MF	Merthiolate-Formaldehyde [*Solution*]
MF	Message Format (ECII)
MF	Metal Factor [*Geophysical measurement*]
MF	Metallic Film
MF	Methotrexate, Fluorourcil, Calcium Leucovorin Rescue [*Antineoplastic drug*] (CDI)
MF	Methyl Farnesoate [*Organic chemistry*]
MF	Methyl Formate [*Organic chemistry*]
MF	Methylfuran [*Organic chemistry*]
MF	Mezzo Forte [*Moderately Loud*] [*Music*] (ROG)
MF	Microfarad
MF	Microfiche [*Sheet microfilm*]
Mf	Microfilariae
MF	Microfilm
MF	Microfiltration
MF	Microflocculation [*Biochemistry*] (DAVI)
MF	Microform
MF	Microscopic Factor
MF	Midcavity Forcep [*Medicine*] (DMAA)
MF	Middeck Forward (MCD)
MF	Middle Fork [*AAR code*]
MF	Middle French [*Language, etc.*]
MF	Middling Fair (IAA)
mf	Mid-Frequency (IDOE)
MF	Midfuselage (NASA)
MF	Mid Fuselage
MF	Mi Favor [*My Favor*] [*Spanish*]
MF	Mike Force [*Indigenous personnel trained and commanded jointly by US and Vietnamese forces, and used as a reaction and/or reinforcing unit*]
MF	Milk Foundation [*National Dairy Council*] (EA)
MF	Millard Filmore [*US president, 1800-1874*]
MF	Mill Finish
MF	Mill Fixture (MCD)
MF	Millifarad (GPO)
mF	Millifarad (IDOE)
MF	Millipore Filter [*Intravenous therapy*] (CPH)
MF	Mind Freedom
MF	Minister [*or Ministry*] of Food [*British*]
M/F	Minorities/Females
MF	Missile Failure (AAG)
MF	Mitogenic Factor [*Cytology*]
MF	Mitomycin, Fluorouracil [*Antineoplastic drug regimen*]
MF	Mitotic Figure [*Genetics*]
MF	Mixed Flow (AAG)
MF	Mobile Facility (MCD)
MF	Modern Fiction
MF	Modifying Factor [*Toxicology*]
MF	Modulation Factor
MF	Molecular Formula (NITA)
MF	Mole Fraction [*Chemistry*]
M-F	Monday through Friday (CDAI)
MF	More Follows [*Newspaper copy*] (DGA)
mf	More Follows [*Copyediting*] (WDMC)
MF	More Fragments (ACRL)
MF	Morningstar Foundation (EA)
MF	Morphogenetic Furrow [*Cell differentiation*]
MF	Morris Foundation [*British*] (DBA)
MF	Mossy Fiber [*Neuroanatomy*]
MF	Mother Fooler [*Bowdlerized version*]
MF	Motor Field
MF	Motor Freight
MF	Multifrequency [*Telecommunications*]
MF	Multifunctional (MCD)
MF	Multiplying Factor [*Microscopy*]
MF	Muscle Fiber
MF	Musicians Foundation (EA)
MF	Mutation Frequency [*Medicine*] (DMAA)
MF	Mutual Fund [*Business term*]
MF	Mycosis Fungoides [*Dermatology*]
MF	Myelinated Fiber [*Neuroanatomy*]
MF	Myelin Figure [*Medicine*]
M/F	My Favor (ADA)
MF	Myocardial Fibrosis [*Cardiology*]
MF	Myofibrillar [*Anatomy*]
MF	Red Carpet Flying Service [*ICAO designator*] (AD)
MF	Royal Munster Fusiliers [*Military unit*] (DMA)
MF	SAAB-Scania AB [*Sweden ICAO aircraft manufacturer identifier*] (ICAO)
MF	Spofa Ltd. [*Czechoslovakia*] [*Research code symbol*]
MF/1	Measurement Frequency/1 [*IBM*] (NITA)
MF^{2}K	Medical Force 2000 [*Army*] (DOMA)
MFA	Mafia Islands [*Tanzania*] [*Airport symbol*] (OAG)
MFA	Malfunction Alert [*Computer science*] (BUR)
MFA	Malicious False Alarm [*Firefighting*]
MFA	Malta Fencible Artillery [*British*]
MFA	Manned Flight Awareness [*NASA*] (NASA)
MFA	Marconi-Franklin Antenna
M Fa	Martinus de Fano [*Deceased circa 1275*] [*Authority cited in pre-1607 legal work*] (DSA)

MFA............ Master Fencers Association (NADA)
MFA............ Master File Activities [Computer science]
MFA............ Master of Fine Arts
MFA............ Material Fielding Agreement [Army]
MFA............ Mauritius Freeport Authority
MFA............ Menningar- og Fraedslusamband Althydu [Workers' Educational Association] [Iceland] (EY)
MFA............ Men's Fashion Association of America (EA)
MFA............ Mercantile Fleet Auxiliary [British]
MFA............ Metal Finishing Association [British] (DBA)
MFA............ Methyl Fluoracetate [Organic chemistry]
MFA............ Miami, FL [Location identifier FAA] (FAAL)
MFA............ Microelectronics for All Kit (NITA)
MFA............ Military Flying Area [Canadian]
MFA............ Military Functions Appropriation (AABC)
MFA............ Minimum Flight Altitude [Aviation] (DA)
MFA............ Minister for Foreign Affairs [British]
MFA............ Mitchell Field [Alaska] [Seismograph station code, US Geological Survey Closed] (SEIS)
MFA............ Mobilization for Animals (EA)
MFA............ Monofluoroacetate [Organic chemistry]
MFA............ Motor Factors Association [British] (BI)
MFA............ Movement for Federation of the Americas (EA)
MFA............ Movimento das Forcas Armadas [Armed Forces Movement] [Portugal Political party] (PPE)
MFA............ Multi-Fiber Arrangement [International trade]
MFA............ Multifocal Functional Autonomy [Medicine] (DMAA)
MFA............ Multifunctional Acrylate [Organic chemistry]
MFA............ Multifunction Antenna
MFA............ Multiple Filer Audit Program
MFA............ Museum of Fine Arts [Boston] (BJA)
MFAA.......... Masters of Foxhounds Association of America [Later, American Master of Foxhounds Association] (EA)
MFA & A...... Monuments, Fine Arts, and Archives [SHAEF] [World War II]
MFAB.......... Museum of Fine Arts, Boston
MFAB-F....... Mobile Floating Assault Bridge-Ferry [Military]
MFAC.......... Magnetic Fusion Advisory Committee [Department of Energy] [Washington, DC]
MFAC.......... Market Facts [NASDAQ symbol] (TTSB)
MFAC.......... Market Facts, Inc. [NASDAQ symbol] (NQ)
MFAD.......... Maneuver Force Air Defense
MFai........... Millicent Library, Fairhaven, MA [Library symbol Library of Congress] (LCLS)
MFAIRWEST... Marine Fleet Air, West Coast
MFal........... Falmouth Public Library, Falmouth, MA [Library symbol Library of Congress] (LCLS)
MFalHi........ Falmouth Historical Society, Falmouth, MA [Library symbol Library of Congress] (LCLS)
MFAMUS .... Master of Fine Arts in Music (WDAA)
MFAMW...... Modern Free and Accepted Masons of the World (EA)
MF & P....... Materials Finishes and Processes (MCD)
MF & R....... Manpower Forces and Readiness [Military]
MF & S....... Magazine Flooding and Sprinkling
MFANSW .... Master Farriers' Association of New South Wales [Australia]
MFAP.......... Manned Flight Awareness Program [NASA] (KSC)
MFAR.......... Modernized Fleet Accounting and Reporting
MFAR.......... Multi-Function Array RADAR (MCD)
MFARS........ Defense Mapping Agency Federal Acquisition Regulation Supplement [A publication] (AAGC)
MFAS.......... Master of Fisheries and Aquatic Science (PGP)
MFAT.......... Multifocal Atrial Tachycardia [Cardiology] (DAVI)
MFAW......... Master of Fine Arts in Writing (PGP)
MFB............ Bristol Community College, Fall River, MA [Library symbol Library of Congress] (LCLS)
MFB............ Mass Fraction Burn [Automotive engine combustion analysis]
MFB............ Master of Finance and Banking (PGP)
MFB............ Medial Forebrain Bundle [Medicine]
MFB............ Message from Base
MFB............ Metallic Foreign Body
MFB............ Metropolitan Fire Brigade [British]
MFB............ MFB Mutual Insurance Co. [from Manufacturers Mutual Fire Insurance Co., Firemen's Mutual Insurance Co., Blackstone Mutual Insurance Co.]
MFB............ Mill Fixture Base (MCD)
MFB............ Mixed Functional Block (IEEE)
MFB............ Moisture Free Basis
MFB............ Motional Feedback
MFB............ Motor Freight Tariff Bureau, Springfield IL [STAC]
MFBAR .... Multifunction Band Airborne Radio
MFBB.......... Mexican Food and Beverage Board (EA)
MFBC.......... MFB Corp. [NASDAQ symbol] (SAG)
MFB Cp....... MFB Corp. [Associated Press] (SAG)
MFBF.......... Mean Flights between Failures [Military] (CAAL)
MFBF.......... Minimum Film Boiling Flux
MFBI.......... Major Fuel Burning Installation (GFGA)
MFBM........ Thousand Feet Board Measure [Lumber]
MFBMP....... Project Manager, Fleet Ballistic Missile [Navy]
MFBP.......... Main Feed Booster Pump (NVT)
MFBP.......... Manufacturing Flow and Building Plan (NASA)
MFBS......... Marine and Freshwater Biomedical Science (GNE)
MFC............ Magnesium Flat Cell
MFC............ Magnetic Film Counter
MFC............ Magnetic Tape Field Scan [Computer science]
MFC............ Main Fuel Control (MCD)
MFC............ Manual Frequency Control

MFC............ Maritime Fruit Carriers [Steamship] (MHDW)
MFC............ Mass Flow Controller [Engineering]
MFC............ Master File Copy [Computer science] (KSC)
MFC............ Master Flow Controller [Nuclear energy] (NRCH)
MFC............ Master of Forest Conservation (PGP)
MFC............ Mastership in Food Control [British] (DBQ)
MFC............ Median Femoral Condyle [Anatomy]
MFC............ Medicated Face Conditioner [Brand manufactured by Mennen]
MFC............ Membrane Fecal Coliform (PDAA)
MFC............ Merrell's Fan Club (EA)
MFC............ Metal-Finishing Category (GNE)
MFC............ Microfilm Frame Card
MFC............ Microfunctional Circuit
MFC............ Microsoft Foundation Classes [Computer science] (PCM)
MFC............ Microsoft Foundation Class Library [Computer science] (PCM)
MFC............ Military Frequency Changer
MFC............ Minimal Flight Forecasting Charts [Air Force]
MFC............ Mirinda's Friendship Club (EA)
MFC............ Missile Fire Control (MCD)
MFC............ Modern Foods Council [Defunct] (EA)
MFC............ Moncton Flying Club [Canada ICAO designator] (FAAC)
MFC............ Morrison Fresh Cooking [NYSE symbol] (TTSB)
MFC............ Morrison Fresh Cooking, Inc. [NYSE symbol] (SAG)
MFC............ Mortar Fire Controller [British]
MFC............ Mortgage Funding Corp. [British]
MFC............ Most-Favored Customer (AAGC)
MFC............ Motor Freight Controller [National Accounting and Finance Council] [A publication]
MFC............ Motorized Flow Control
MFC............ Movimiento Familiar Cristiano (EA)
MFC............ Multi-Frequency Code [Telecommunications] (DA)
MFC............ Multifrequency Signaling, Compelled [Telecommunications] (TEL)
MFC............ Multiple File Concept (DNAB)
MFC............ Multiple Flight Computer (NASA)
MFC............ Multiple Flight Controller (NASA)
MFC............ Municipal Financial Corp. [Toronto Stock Exchange symbol]
MFCA.......... Master File Change Activity [Computer science] (MCD)
MFCA.......... Miniature Figure Collectors of America (EA)
MFCA.......... Multi-Function Communications Adaptor (NITA)
MFCAE........ Mutlifunction Communications Adapter
MFCAE........ Masters of Foxhounds Club of America and England [Defunct] (EA)
MFCB.......... Michigan Financial Corp. [NASDAQ symbol] (SAG)
MFCB.......... Michigan Finl Corp. [NASDAQ symbol] (TTSB)
MFCC.......... Marriage and Family Counseling Certificate (PGP)
MFCC.......... Marriage, Family, and Child Counseling (PGP)
MFCC.......... Marriage, Family, and Child Counselor [Psychology] (DAVI)
MFCC.......... Minimum Functional Combat Capability
MFCC.......... Missile Fire Control Computer [Military] (CAAL)
MFCC.......... Missile Flight Caution Corridor (AFM)
MFCC.......... Mortar Fire Control Calculator [Later, MBC] [Military] (INF)
MFCC.......... Mortar Fire Direction Center Data Calculator [Army]
MFCD.......... Modular Flare Chaff Dispenser [Military] (PDAA)
MFCF.......... Multinational Fuel Cycle Facility
MFCI.......... Molten Fuel Coolant Interaction [Nuclear energy] (NRCH)
MFCL.......... Master Fund Control List [Air Force] (AFM)
MFC/LB....... Multi-Frequency / Local Battery [Telecommunications] (DA)
MFCM......... Member of the Faculty of Community Medicine [British]
MFCM......... Multifunction Card Machine (BUR)
MFCMA....... Magnuson Fishery Conservation and Management Act [1976] [Also, FCMA]
MFCO.......... Manual Fuel Cutoff (AAG)
MFCO.......... Microwave Filter [NASDAQ symbol] (TTSB)
MFCO.......... Microwave Filter Co., Inc. [NASDAQ symbol] (NQ)
MFCP.......... Multifunction Control/Panel (MCD)
MFCS.......... Magnetic Field Calibration System
MFCS.......... Manual Flight Control System [NASA]
MFCS.......... Master of Family and Consumer Sciences (PGP)
MFCS.......... Mathematical Foundation of Computer Science (PDAA)
MFCS.......... Maximum Flat Control System
MFCS.......... Medical Function Control System (PDAA)
MFCS.......... Microprocessor Flight Control System (DOMA)
MFCS.......... Missile Fire Control System (NG)
MFCS.......... Mortar Fire Control System [Military] (INF)
MFCT.......... Major Fraction Thereof
MFCU.......... Multifunction Card Unit
MFCV.......... Modulating Flow Control Valve (MCD)
MFCX.......... Marshalltown Financial [NASDAQ symbol] (TTSB)
MFCX.......... Marshalltown Financial Corp. [NASDAQ symbol] (SAG)
MFD............ Canadian Department of Fisheries and Oceans, Marine Fish Division [Research center] (RCD)
MFD............ Magic Foods, Inc. [Vancouver Stock Exchange symbol]
MFD............ Magnetic Frequency Detector
MFD............ Magnetofluiddynamic
MFD............ Main Feed (MCD)
MFD............ Malfunction Detection (NASA)
MFD............ Malfunctioning Display (DA)
MFD............ Manifold [Paper] (DGA)
MFD............ Mansfield [Ohio] [Airport symbol] (OAG)
MFD............ Mansfield, OH [Location identifier FAA] (FAAL)
MFD............ Manufactured
MFD............ Master File Directory [Computer science]
MFD............ Maximum Frequency Difference [Statistics]
MFD............ Mechanical-Front-Drive [Tractor]
MFD............ Memory-for-Designs [Test] [Psychology]
MFD............ Message Format Designator

MFD .... Metal Floor Deck [*Technical drawings*]
MFD .... Microfarad
MFD .... Midforceps Delivery [*Obstetrics*]
MFD .... Military Forwarding Depot [*British military*]   (DMA)
MFD .... Millifarad   (MCD)
MFD .... Minimum Fatal Dose
MFD .... Minimum Focusing Distance [*Optics*]
MFD .... Multifunction Display   (MCD)
MFD .... Multiple Family Dwelling [*Real estate*]
MFD .... Multistage Flash Distillation   (PDAA)
MFD .... Multivariable Frequency Domain
MFD .... Municipal Facilities Division [*Environmental Protection Agency*]   (GFGA)
MFDC .... Morzen Mortar Fire Data Computer [*Military British*]   (INF)
MFDC .... Mouvement des Forces Democratiques de la Casamance [*Senegal*] [*Political party*]
MFDCC ...... Marine Fire Detection Control Center
MF/DF .... Medium-Frequency Direction Finder [*or Finding*]   (NVT)
MFDO .... Member of the Faculty of Dispensing Opticians [*British*]   (DBQ)
MFDP .... Maintenance Float Distribution Point [*Computer science*]   (NATG)
MFDP .... Mississippi Freedom Democratic Party
MFDS .... Modular Fuel Delivery Station [*Shipboard installation*] [*Navy*]   (DOMA)
MFDSG .... Multifunction Display Symbol Generator   (MCD)
MFDSUL ...... Multifunction Data Set Utility Language
MFDT .... Memory-for-Designs Test [*Psychology*]
MFDU .... Multifunction Display Unit [*Aviation*]
MFE .... Machinery and Fixed Equipment [*British*]
MFE .... Magnetic Field Energy
MFE .... Magnetic Field Explorer [*NASA*]
MFE .... Magnetic Fusion Energy
MFE .... Maison de la Fondation Europeenne   (EAIO)
MFE .... Major Fleet Escort
MFE .... Manual of Field Engineering [*British military*]   (DMA)
MFE .... Master of Financial Economics   (PGP)
MFE .... Master of Forest Engineering
MFE .... McAllen [*Texas*] [*Airport symbol*]   (OAG)
MFE .... McAllen, TX [*Location identifier FAA*]   (FAAL)
MFE .... Mean Fibre Extent   (PDAA)
MFE .... Mercury Film Electrode [*Electrochemistry*]
MFE .... Microabrasion Foil Experiment [*For cosmic dust retrieval*]
MFE .... Mid-Frequency Execution
MFE .... Mid-Frequency Executive   (NASA)
MFE .... Mischief Enterprises Ltd. [*Vancouver Stock Exchange symbol*]
MFE .... Moire Fringe Effect   (PDAA)
MFE .... Mouvement Federaliste Europeen [*European Federalist Movement*] [*France*]
MFEA .... Magnetic Fusion Engineering Act
MFED .... Manned Flight Engineering Division [*NASA*]
MFED .... Maximum Flat Envelope Delay
MFed .... Miners' Federation of Great Britain   (DAS)
MFEIP .... Ministry of Food Education and Information Practice [*British*]
MFEM .... Maximal Forced Expiratory Maneuver [*Medicine*]   (DAVI)
MFENET ...... Magnetic Fusion Energy Research Network [*Department of Energy*]
MF Eng .... Master of Forest Engineering
MFEQ .... Mechanical Facilities and Equipment   (SAA)
MFES .... Main Fixed Earth Station [*NASA*]   (PDAA)
MFES .... Major Fleet Escort Study [*Navy*]   (CAAL)
MFF .... Flin Flon Public Library, Manitoba [*Library symbol National Library of Canada*]   (NLC)
MFF .... Magnetic Flip-Flop [*Computer science*]
MFF .... Mariposa Folk Foundation   (EAIO)
MFF .... Master Freight File
MFF .... Match Flip Flop [*Computer science*]   (MHDI)
MFF .... Matching Familiar Figures [*Psychology*]
MFF .... MDM [*Manipulator Deployment Mechanism*] Flight Forward [*NASA*]   (GFGA)
MFF .... Melbourne Film Festival [*Australia*]
MFF .... Mezzo Fortissimo [*Rather Loud*] [*Music*]   (ADA)
MFF .... Military Free Fall [*Parachute jump*]   (MCD)
MFF .... Moanda [*Gabon*] [*Airport symbol*]   (OAG)
MFF .... Munitions Filling Factory   (ADA)
MFF .... St. Martin Du Fouilloux [*France*] [*Seismograph station code, US Geological Survey*]   (SEIS)
MFFC .... Milton Federal [*NASDAQ symbol*]   (TTSB)
MFFC .... Milton Federal Financial Corp. [*NASDAQ symbol*]   (SAG)
MFFGH .... Flin Flon General Hospital, Manitoba [*Library symbol National Library of Canada*]   (NLC)
MFF/HALO ... Military Free Fall / High Altitude Low Opening Parachute
MFFHB .... Hudson Bay Mining & Smelting Co. Ltd., Flin Flon, Manitoba [*Library symbol National Library of Canada*]   (NLC)
MFFLR .... Muffler [*Automotive advertising*]
MFFR .... Modified Field Fire Range   (MCD)
MFFT .... Matching Familiar Figures Test [*Education*]
MFFT .... Minimum Film Formation Temperature [*Coating technology*]
MFG .... Major Functional Group [*NASA*]   (KSC)
MFG .... Manufacturing   (AFM)
mfg .... Manufacturing   (DD)
MFG .... Manufacturing
MFG .... Message Flow Graph
MFG .... Milk Fat Globule
MFG .... Modified Heat-Degraded Gelatin [*Medicine*]   (MEDA)
MFG .... Molded Fiberglass
MFG .... Multi-Function Generator   (NITA)
MFG .... Munitions Family Group
MFGA .... Master Furriers Guild of America   (EA)

MFGM .... Milk Fat Globule Membrane
MFGR .... Manufacturer
MFH .... Magnetic Film Handler   (CMD)
MFH .... Malignant Fibrous Histiocytoma [*Oncology*]
MFH .... Markel Financial Holdings Ltd. [*Toronto Stock Exchange symbol*]
MFH .... Master of Fox Hounds
MFH .... Master of the Fox Hunt   (DD)
MFH .... Membrane-Free Hemolystate [*Hematology*]   (DAVI)
MFH .... Military Family Housing   (AFM)
MFH .... Mobile Field Hospital
MFHA .... Masters of Foxhounds Association [*British*]   (BI)
MFHA .... Medal for Humane Action [*Berlin Airlift, 1948-9*] [*Military decoration*]
MFHBF .... Mean Flight Hours between Failures [*Quality control*]   (MCD)
MFHBMA .... Mean Flight Hours between Maintenance Actions [*Quality control*]   (NVT)
MFHBUMA ... Mean Flight Hour between Unscheduled Maintenance Actions [*Quality control*]   (MCD)
MFHC .... Missile Flight Hazard Corridor   (AFM)
MFHD .... My First Hard Drive [*Computer science*]
MFHFS .... Multifunction High-Frequency SONAR   (MCD)
MF Hom ...... Member of the Faculty of Homoeopathy [*British*]
MFHR .... Media Fund for Human Rights   (EA)
m/f/h/v .... Male, Female, Handicapped, Veteran   (BARN)
MFi .... Fitchburg Public Library and Regional Center for Central Massachusetts, RegionalLibrary System, Fitchburg, MA [*Library symbol Library of Congress*]   (LCLS)
MFI .... MacFrugal's Bargains [*Formerly, Pic'n'Save Corp.*] [*NYSE symbol*]   (SPSG)
MFI .... MacFrugals Bargains Closeouts [*NYSE symbol*]   (TTSB)
MFI .... Magazines for Industry [*An association*]
MFI .... Magnetic Field Indicator
MFI .... Magnetic Field Intensity
MFI .... Major Force Issues [*Army*]   (AABC)
MFI .... Marketfax Infoservices Ltd. [*Vancouver Stock Exchange symbol*]
MFI .... Marketing Freedom Index [*OPEC*] [*Business term*]
MFI .... Marshfield [*Wisconsin*] [*Airport symbol*]   (OAG)
MFI .... Marshfield, WI [*Location identifier FAA*]   (FAAL)
MFI .... Master Facility Inventory [*Department of Health and Human Services*]   (GFGA)
MFI .... Mean Flourescence Intensity [*Biochemistry*]
MFI .... Melt-Flow Index [*of plastics*]
MFI .... Metal Fabricating Institute   (EA)
MFI .... Metal-Finishing Industy
MFI .... Military Financial Instruction
MFI .... Mobile Fuel Irradiator   (IEEE)
MFI .... Multi-point Fuel Injection
MFI .... Multiport Fuel Injection [*Automotive technology*]
MFI .... Myofibril Fragmentation Index [*Food technology*]
MFIA .... Member, Fundraising Institute-Australia, Inc.   (NFD)
MFIC .... Microfluidics International [*NASDAQ symbol*]   (TTSB)
MFIC .... Microfluidics International Corp. [*NASDAQ symbol*]   (SAG)
MFIC .... Military Flight Information Center
MFIC .... Mutual Federation of Independent Cooperatives [*Later, Northeast Dairy Cooperative Federation*]   (EA)
MFID .... Multiple-Electrode Flame Ionization Detector
MFIE .... Magnetic-Field Integral Equation   (PDAA)
MF-IFGR ...... Michael Fund (International Foundation for Genetic Research)   (EA)
MFin .... Master of Finance
M Fin .... Master of Finance   (PGP)
MFIN .... Metro Financial Corp. [*NASDAQ symbol*]   (SAG)
MFinStud .... Master of Financial Studies
MFIP .... Microforms in Print [*Database*]
MFIS .... Magnetic Field-Induced Superconductivity
MFisc.......... Maitrise en Fiscalite   (DD)
MFISH .... Multiplex Fluorescence in Situ Hybridization
MFiT .... Fitchburg State College, Fitchburg, MA [*Library symbol Library of Congress*]   (LCLS)
MFIT .... Manual Fault Isolation Test
MFIT .... Modified Flight Intersection Tape   (SAA)
MFIV .... Mainwater Feed Isolation Valve [*Nuclear energy*]   (NRCH)
MFJ .... Moala [*Fiji*] [*Airport symbol*]   (OAG)
MFJ .... Modified Final Judgment [*Telecommunications*]
MFJ .... Movement for Freedom and Justice [*Ghana*] [*Political party*]   (EY)
MFJC .... Memorial Foundation for Jewish Culture   (EA)
MFJSA .... Mass Finishing Job Shops Association   (EA)
MFK .... Mafeking [*South Africa*] [*Airport symbol*]   (OAG)
MFK .... Mill Fixture Key [*Tool*]
MFKP .... Multifrequency Key Pulsing
MFKT .... Mobile Field Kitchen Trailer   (MCD)
MFKY .... Maxey Flats, Kentucky [*Commercial waste site*]   (GAAI)
MFL .... Magnetic Field Line
MFL .... Main Feedwater Line [*Nuclear energy*]   (NRCH)
MFL .... Maintain Flight Level [*Aviation*]
MFL .... Maintenance-Free Lifetime   (PDAA)
MFL .... Master Force List [*DoD*]
MFL .... Master of Family Life
MFL .... Matrimonial and Family Law [*New York, NY A publication*]
MFL .... Matrimonial and Family Life [*A publication*]
MFL .... Maximum Foreseeable Loss [*Insurance*]
MFL .... Methodists for Life [*Defunct*]   (EA)
MfL .... Microfile (Pty.) Ltd., Johannesburg, South Africa [*Library symbol Library of Congress*]   (LCLS)
MFL .... Missile Firing Laboratory   (KSC)
MFL .... Mobile Field Laboratory
MFL .... Mobile Field Laundry [*Military*]

MFL	Modern Foreign Language
MFL	Motor Freight Line
MFL	Multiple Fragment Laceration [Shrapnel wound] [Military] (VNW)
MFLA	Midwest Federation of Library Associations
m flac	Membrana Flaccida [Flaccid Membrane] [Latin Medicine] (MAE)
MFLB	Motor Fuel Licensing Board [Australia]
MFLD	Male-Female Longevity Difference
MFLD	Manifold (KSC)
MFLD	Message Field [Computer science]
MFlem	Middle Flemish [Language] (BARN)
MFLFd	MuniVest Florida Fund [Associated Press] (SAG)
MFLIC	Modified Fluid in Cell [Automotive engine combustion analysis]
MFLOP	Mega-Floating Point Operation
MFLOP	Mega Floating-Point Operations per Second [Computer science]
MFLOPS	Million Floating-Point Operations per Second [Processing power units] [Computer science]
Mflops	Million Floating-Point Operations per Second [Computer science] (ODBW)
MFLOPS	Millions of Floating Point Operations Per Second [Telecommunications] (ACRL)
MFLP	Multifile Linear Programming
MFLR	Mayflower Co-Operative Bank [NASDAQ symbol] (NQ)
MFLR	Mayflower Cooperative Bank [NASDAQ symbol] (TTSB)
MFLT	Mathematics Functional Literacy Test (EDAC)
MFLT	Mean Fault Location Time (DNAB)
MFLT	Mean First Lesions Time [Immunochemistry]
MFLZ	Mejdunarodna Fondatzia Lyudmila Zhivkova [Lyudmila Zhivkova International Foundation] (EAIO)
MFm	Framingham Town Library, Framingham, MA [Library symbol Library of Congress] (LCLS)
MFM	Glenair [British] [FAA designator] (FAAC)
MFM	Magnetic-Field Modulation [Computer science] (PCM)
MFM	Magnetic Field Monitor [NASA]
MFM	Magnetic Force Microscope
MFM	Magnetic Forming Machine
MFM	Magnetofluid Mechanic
MFM	Master File Maintenance [Computer science]
MFM	Master of Financial Management (ADA)
MFM	Materials Flow Management [Manufacturing]
MFM	Maximally Flat Magnitude
MFM	Meals for Millions Foundation [Later, MFM/FFH] (EA)
MFM	MFC Mining Finance Corp. [Toronto Stock Exchange symbol Vancouver Stock Exchange symbol]
MFM	MFS Municipal Income Trust [NYSE symbol] (SPSG)
MFM	MFS Municipal Inc. Tr [NYSE symbol] (TTSB)
MFM	Micrometer Frequency Meter
MFM	Minced Fish Meat [Food technology]
MFM	Mine Firing Mechanism
MFM	Miniature Fluxgate Magnetometer
MFM	Minneapolis-St. Paul [Minnesota] [Seismograph station code, US Geological Survey] (SEIS)
MFM	Missile Farm Monitor [Army] (AABC)
MFM	Missile Fatigue Monitor
MFM	Mississippi State University, Mississippi State, MS [OCLC symbol] (OCLC)
MFM	Modified Frequency Modulation [Electronics]
MFM	Morrissey, Fernie & Michel Railway [AAR code]
MFM	Mouvement pour le Pouvoir Proletarien [or aux Petits] [Movement for Proletarian Power Malagasy] [Political party] (PPW)
MFM	Movable Fine Mesh
MFM	Multi-Faith Meal [Army] (INF)
MFM	Multifunctional Monomer [Organic chemistry]
MFM	Multistage Frequency Multiplexer
MFMA	Maple Flooring Manufacturers Association (EA)
MFMA	Metal Findings Manufacturers Association (EA)
MFMA	Metal Framing Manufacturers Association (EA)
MFMA	Midwest Feed Manufacturers Association [Later, AFMA] (EA)
MFMA	Monolithic Ferrite Memory Array
MFMANSW	Master Fish Merchants' Association of New South Wales [Australia]
MFMBARS	Multi-Function, Multi-Band Airborne Radio System (PDAA)
MFmcM	Marist College and Seminary, Framingham Center, MA [Library symbol Library of Congress] (LCLS)
MFM/FFH	Meals for Millions/Freedom from Hunger Foundation (EA)
MFMH	Monofluoromethylhistidine [Antineoplastic drug]
MFmHi	Framingham Historical society, Framingham, MA [Library symbol] [Library of Congress] (LCLS)
MFMI	Men for Missions International (EA)
MFMM	Microwave Frequency Measurement Module
MFMR	Multifrequency Microwave Radiometer (MCD)
MFmT	Framingham State College, Framingham, MA [Library symbol Library of Congress] (LCLS)
MFMT	Maryland Functional Mathematics Test (EDAC)
MFMT	Microwave Frequency Modulation Transmitter
MF/MWS	Male/Female - Married/Widow [or Widower]/Single
MFN	MDC Financial, Inc. [Vancouver Stock Exchange symbol]
MFN	Mercury Finance [NYSE symbol] (TTSB)
MFN	Mercury Finance Co. [NYSE symbol] (SPSG)
MFN	Metabolic Fecal Nitrogen (PDAA)
MFN	Milford Sound [New Zealand] [Airport symbol] (OAG)
MFN	Most-Favored-Nation [Trading status]
MFN	Muffin (ABBR)
MFNG	Motion for a Finding of Not Guilty
MFNS	Millard Fillmore National Society [Defunct] (EA)
MFO	Mafco Consolidated Group [NYSE symbol] (SAG)
MFO	Major Function Overlay (MCD)

MFO	Marine Fuel Oil
MFO	Master Frequency Oscillator (NG)
MFO	Material Fielding Operations (MCD)
MFO	Military Forwarding Officer
MFO	Military Forwarding Organization
MFO	Missile Field Office (AAG)
MFO	Missile Firing Order
MFO	Mixed-Function Oxidase [Biochemistry]
MFO	Multinational Force and Observers [Eleven-nation peace-keeping force for the Sinai]
MFO	Multiple Facility Organization
MFOA	Municipal Finance Officers Association of US and Canada [Later, GFOA] (EA)
MFOC	Military and Government Fiber Optics and Communications [Conference] (TSSD)
MFOD	Manned Flight Operations Directive [NASA] (KSC)
MFOE	Mixed-Function Oxidase Enzyme System
MFOI	Major Force Oriented Issue [Military] (AFM)
MFOM	Master, Faculty of Occupational Medicine (DAVI)
MFON	Missile Firing Order Normal [Military] (CAAL)
MFOPP	Missile Firing Order Patch Panel
MFor	Master of Forestry
MForSc	Master of Forest Science (ADA)
MFOT	Mean Forced Outage Time (PDAA)
MFOW	Pacific Coast Marine Firemen, Oilers, Watertenders, and Wipers Association
MFP	Franciscan Missionaries Our Lady of Peace (TOCD)
MFP	Magnetic Field Perturbation
MFP	Main Feed Power [Nuclear energy] (NRCH)
MFP	Main Feed Pump (NVT)
MFP	Main Feedwater Pump [Nuclear energy] (NRCH)
MFP	Main Force Patrol [In movie "Mad Max"]
MFP	Major Force Program [Air Force] (AFIT)
MFP	Management Framework Plan
MFP	Master File Program [Computer science]
MFP	Matched Filter Performance
MFP	Materiel Fielding Plan
MFP	Maximum Fluoride Protection [Colgate-Palmolive Co.]
MFP	Maximum Freezing Point
MFP	Mean Free Path
MFP	Meat, Fish and Poultry
MFP	Melphalan, Fluorouracil, Farlutal (Medroxyprogesterone acetate) [Antineoplastic drug regimen]
MF(P)	Microfiche (Positive)
MFP	Middle Free Path
MFP	Minimal Flight Path
MFP	Ministry of Fuel and Power [British]
MFP	Mixed Fission Products [Nuclear energy]
MFP	Mobile Flux Platform (USDC)
MFP	Mobile Flux Platform [Marine science] (OSRA)
MFP	Moca [Fernando Poo] [Equatorial Guinea] [Seismograph station code, US Geological Survey] (SEIS)
MFP	Molecular Free Path
MFP	Monofluorophosphate [Inorganic chemistry]
MFP	Movement for a Free Philippines (EA)
MFP	Multi-Factor Productivity
MFP	Multiform Printer
MFP	Multifrequency Pulsing (MSA)
MFP	Multifunction Peripheral [Chip] [Computer science]
MFP	Multifunction Polis
MFP	Multifunction Printers (PS)
MFP	Myofascial Pain [Medicine]
MFPA	Monolithic Focal Plane Array (PDAA)
MFPB	Mineral Fiber Products Bureau
MFPC	Man-Made Fibres Producers Committee [British] (DBA)
MFPC	Multifunction Protocol Converter
MFPD	Modern Federal Practice Digest [A publication] (DLA)
MFPE	Minimum Final Prediction Error (MHDI)
MFPF	Minefield Planning Folder [Navy] (DOMA)
MFPG	Mechanical Failures Prevention Group
MFPG	Mixed Fission Products Generator [Nuclear energy]
MFPh	Member of the Faculty of Physiotherapists [British]
MFPhys	Member of the Faculty of Physiatrists [British]
MFPK	Multifunction Program Keyboard (MCD)
MFP/MTP	Materiel Fielding Plan/Materiel Transfer Plan [Army] (RDA)
MFPS	Member of the Faculty of Physicians and Surgeons [Glasgow]
MFPS	Mobile Field Photographic Section (NATG)
MFPS	Modular Force Planning System (MCD)
MFPT	Machinery Failure Prevention Technology (RDA)
MFPT	Main Feedwater Pump Turbine [Nuclear energy] (NRCH)
MFPT	Mean First-Passage Time [Biochemistry]
MFPTC	Main Feed Pump Turbine Condenser [Nuclear energy] (NRCH)
MFP-UK	Mothers for Peace - UK (EAIO)
MFPUL	Mississippi Forest Products Utilization Laboratory [Mississippi State University] [Research center] (RCD)
MFPVC	Multifocal Premature Ventricular Contractions [Medicine] (MEDA)
MFQ	Maradi [Niger] [Airport symbol] (OAG)
M'F R	MacFarlane's Scotch Jury Court Reports [1838-39] [A publication] (DLA)
MFR	Macfie Resources [Vancouver Stock Exchange symbol]
MFR	Mail File Requirement [Code] [Computer science]
MFR	Malfunction Rate
MFR	Malfunction Receiver
MFR	Manipulator Foot Restraint (NASA)
MFR	Manipulator Foot Restraint

MFR	Manufacture [or Manufacturer] (AFM)
mfr	Manufacture (DD)
MFR	Manufacture
MFr	Mare Frigoris [Sea of Cold] [Lunar area]
MFR	Marine Fishery Reserve
MFR	Master Facility Register [Nuclear energy]
MFR	Master Frame Recognize (MCD)
MFR	Master Frequency Record [FCC list] (NTCM)
MFR	Master of Forest Resources (GAGS)
M Fr	Master of French (PGP)
MFR	Maximum Flight Rate (NASA)
MFR	Mean Firing Rate [Neurophysiology]
MFR	Medford [Oregon] [Airport symbol] (OAG)
MFR	Medford, OR [Location identifier FAA] (FAAL)
MFr	Melomanes Francais [Record label] [France]
MFR	Melt-Flow Rate [of plastics]
MFR	Memorandum for Record [Military]
MfR	Microform Review, Inc., Weston, CT [Library symbol Library of Congress] (LCLS)
MFR	Middle French [Language, etc.]
MFR	Mid-Forceps Rotation [Obstetrics] (DAVI)
MFR	Military Field Representative (SAA)
MFR	Missile Firing Range (AAG)
MFR	Model Form and Record
MFR	Mucus Flow Rate (MAE)
MFR	Multifrequency Receiver [Telecommunications]
MFR	Multifunctional Receiver (NASA)
MFR	Multifunctional Receiver
MFR	Multifunctional Review (NASA)
MFR	Multifunction RADAR
MFR	Mutual Force Reductions
MFran	Ray Memorial Library, Franklin, MA [Library symbol Library of Congress] (LCLS)
MFRC	Maritimes Forest Research Centre [Research center] (RCD)
MFRC	Master of Forest Resources and Conservation (PGP)
MFRD	Manufactured (ABBR)
MFRE	Manufacture (ADA)
MFREA	Multiple Food Retailers Employers' Association [British]
MFRF	Mean-Family Replacement Factor
MFRG	Manufacturing
MFRG	Medical Functional Requirements Group (MCD)
MFRI	MFRI, Inc. [NASDAQ symbol] (SPSG)
MFRI	Migratory Fish Research Institute [University of Maine] [Research center] (RCD)
MFRN	Manufacturers Number
MFRP	Midwest Fuel Recovery Plant [AEC]
MFRP	Multigrade Functional Rehabilitation Platform [Medicine]
MFRPA	Maxey Flats Radioactive Protective Association (EA)
MFRR	Manufacturer (ABBR)
MFRS	Master File Replacement System [Computer science]
MFRS	Multifunction Receiver System
MFRT	Maryland Functional Reading Test (EDAC)
MFRT	Modulated Frequency Radio Telephone (PDAA)
MFRY	Manufactory (ABBR)
MFS	Fleet Minesweeper (Steel-Hulled) [Navy symbol]
MFS	Frostburg State College, Library, Frostburg, MD [OCLC symbol] (OCLC)
MFS	Macintosh File System [Computer science]
MFS	Magnetic Field Strength
MFS	Magnetic Tape Field Search [Computer science]
MFS	Malleable Founders' Society [Later, Iron Castings Society - ICS]
MFS	Maltese Falcon Society [Defunct] (EA)
MFS	Manned Flying System (MCD)
MFS	Manufactures
MFS	Marble Falls, TX [Location identifier FAA] (FAAL)
MFS	Marfan Syndrome [Medicine]
MFS	Marine-Finish Slate (MSA)
MFS	Massachusetts Financial Services
MFS	Master Fabrication Schedule (DNAB)
MFS	Master of Family Studies (GAGS)
MFS	Master of Food Science
MFS	Master of Foreign Service
MFS	Master of Foreign Study
MFS	Master of Forensic Science (GAGS)
MFS	Master of Forest Science (GAGS)
MFS	Master of Forest Studies (PGP)
MFS	Master of French Studies (PGP)
MFS	Material False Statement [Nuclear energy] (NUCP)
MFS	Maxillofacial Surgery [Medical specialty] (DHSM)
MFS	McCloud Flat South [California] [Seismograph station code, US Geological Survey] (SEIS)
MFS	Medal Field Service [Canada]
MFS	Medicare Fee Schedule
MFS	Mercury Feed System
MFS	Message Format Service
MFS	Metropolitan Fiber Systems, Inc.
MfS	Microfilm Systems, Colorado Springs, CO [Library symbol Library of Congress] (LCLS)
MFS	Microfuel Systems [Vancouver Stock Exchange symbol]
MFS	Military Flight Service
MFS	Miller Flying Services, Inc. [ICAO designator] (FAAC)
MfS	Ministerium fuer Staatssicherheit [Ministry for State Security] [See also MISTAI, MSS] [Germany] (EG)
MFS	Minnesota Follow-Up Study Rehabilitation Rating Scale
MFS	Miraflores [Colombia] [Airport symbol] (OAG)

MFS	Missile Firing Simulator (NATG)
MFS	Missile Firing Station [Army]
MFS	Missile Fuse Set Servo
MFS	Missing from Shelf (ADA)
MFS	Missouri Followback Survey [Department of Health and Human Services] (GFGA)
MFS	Mitral First Sound [Cardiology] (CPH)
MFS	Modern Fiction Studies [A publication] (BRI)
MFS	Modified Filing System [Computer science] (PCM)
MFS	Modified Full Spray
MFS	Modular Flexible Scheduling [Education]
MFS	Multi-Frequency Signalling [Telecommunications] (NITA)
MFS	Multifunction Sensor (MCD)
MFS	Multi-Function Switch [Automotive engineering]
MFS	Multiple-Frequency Synthesizer
MFS	Multiple Sclerosis Foundation (EA)
MFS	Municipal Ferrous Scrap
MFS	National Mobilization for Survival (EA)
MFSA	Master Floor Sanders Association (NADA)
MFSA	Metal Finishing Suppliers' Association (EA)
MFSA	Methodist Federation for Social Action (EA)
MFSB	Mother, Father, Sister, Brother [Musical group]
MFSB	Mutual Bancompany [NASDAQ symbol] (TTSB)
MFSB	Mutual Bancompany, Inc. [NASDAQ symbol] (SAG)
MFSc	Master of Fisheries Science
MFS C	MFS Communication Co. [Associated Press] (SAG)
MFSC	Missile Flight Safety Center [Pacific Missile Range] (MUGU)
MFS Cm	MFS Communication Co. [Associated Press] (SAG)
MFSE	Main Fire Support Element (AABC)
MFSF	Magazine of Fantasy and Science Fiction [A publication] (BRI)
MFSFU	Matt-Finish Structural Facing Units [Technical drawings]
MFSG	Missile Firing Safety Group (MUGU)
MFSK	Multiple-Frequency Shift Keying
MFSL	Maryland Fed Bancorp [NASDAQ symbol] (TTSB)
MFSL	Maryland Federal Bancorp, Inc. [NASDAQ symbol] (NQ)
MFSL	Mathematical and Functional Subroutine Library (MHDB)
MFSO	Missile Flight Safety Officer
MFSOA	Missile Flight Safety Officer Assistant (MUGU)
MFSOC	Missile Flight Safety Officer Console (MUGU)
MF SOL	Merthiolate-Formaldehyde [Stock] Solution (BABM)
MFSOP	Missile Flight Safety Operations Plan
MFSR	Magnetic Film Strip Recorder
MFSS	Medical Field Service School [Army]
MFSS	Missile Flight Safety System (AAG)
MFSS	Multi-Frequency Signalling System [Telecommunications] (EECA)
MFST	Manifest
MFST	Medical Field Service Technician (BABM)
MFST	MFS Communiations [NASDAQ symbol] (TTSB)
MFST	MFS Communication Co. [NASDAQ symbol] (SAG)
MFST	Mobile Fire Safety Team
MFSTB	Manifestable (ABBR)
MFSTD	Manifested (ABBR)
MFSTG	Manifesting (ABBR)
MFSTN	Manifestation (ABBR)
MFSTO	Manifesto (ABBR)
MFSTP	MFS Commun 8% Cv Dep'A'Pfd [NASDAQ symbol] (TTSB)
MFSU	Mobile Field Service Unit
MFSW	Membrane-Filtered Sea Water
MFT	Drury Military Extension, Springfield, MO [OCLC symbol] (OCLC)
MFT	Magnetic Flow Transmitter
MFT	Mail for Tots (EA)
MFT	Mainframe Termination [Telecommunications] (TEL)
MFT	Major Fraction Thereof
MFT	Manufacturing Fit Test
MFT	Marconi Fast Tuning (MCD)
MFT	Marriage and Family Therapist [Psychology]
MFT	Master File Tax [Code] [IRS]
MFT	Master Fitness Trainer [Army] (INF)
MFT	Master of Family Therapy (GAGS)
MFT	Master of Foreign Trade
MFT	Materiel Fielding Team [Army] (RDA)
MFT	Materiel Field Test (MCD)
MFT	Mean Flight Time (KSC)
MFT	Mean Flight Time
MFT	Mean Free Time
MFT	Mechanized Flame Thrower
MFT	Medical Field Service Technician [Navy]
MFT	Meson Field Theory
MFT	Metal Film Resistor
MFT	Metallic Facility Terminal [Telecommunications] (TEL)
MFT	Meter Fix Time/Slot Time [FAA] (TAG)
MFT	Mine Fuse Train
MFT	Minimum Film-Forming Temperature [Wax polishes]
MFT	Missile Flight Time
MFT	Mission Flight Trainer [Navy]
M FT	Mistura Fiat [Let a Mixture Be Made] [Pharmacy]
MFT	Mobile Foot Restraint (SSD)
MFT	Molecular Field Theory [Physical chemistry]
MFT	Monolayer Formation Time [Physical chemistry] (OA)
MFT	Morgan Financial Corp. [Toronto Stock Exchange symbol]
MFT	Most-Favorable Term (MHDW)
MFT	Motor Freight Tariff [Business term] (ADA)
MFT	Motor Freight Terminal
MFT	Multifocal Atrial Tachycardia [Cardiology] (DMAA)
MFT	Multilingual Forestry Terminology

MFT	Multiposition Frequency Telegraphy [*Telecommunications*] (OA)
MFT	Multiprogramming (NITA)
MFT	Multiprogramming with a Finite Amount of Trouble [*Computer science*]
MFT	Multiprogramming with Fixed Number of Tasks [*Computer science*] (BUR)
MFT	MuniYield FL Insured Fund [*NYSE symbol*] (TTSB)
MFT	MuniYield Florida Insured Fund [*NYSE symbol*] (SPSG)
MFT	Muscle Function Test
MFTA	Managed Futures Trade Association (EA)
MFTA	Multiduct Fuel Test Assembly [*Nuclear energy*] (NRCH)
MFTAD	Master Flight Test Assignment Document (NASA)
MFTAD	Master Flight Test Assignments Document [*NASA*]
MFTB	Motor Freight Tariff Bureau
MFTC	Metalworking Fair Trade Coalition [*Later, MTC*] (EA)
MFTCom	Member of the Faculty of Teachers in Commerce [*British*] (DBQ)
MFTD	Mobile Field Training Detachment [*Military*] (AFM)
MFTDMA	Multiple Frequency Time Division Multiple Access (LAIN)
MFTF	Mirror Fusion Test Facility [*For study of new energy source*]
MFTF	Missionary Flight Training Foundation [*Defunct*]
MFTGS	Midcourse Fix and Terminal Guidance System (MCD)
MFTHBA	Missouri Fox Trotting Horse Breed Association (EA)
MFT L	Millifoot Lamberts (DEN)
MFTL	My Favorite Toy Language [*Computer hacker terminology*] (NHD)
M FT M	Misce Fiat Mistura [*Mix to Make a Mixture*] [*Pharmacy*]
MFTP	Modified Federal Test Procedure [*EPA engine test*]
MFTRS	Magnetic Flight Test Recording System
MFTS	Medial Femorotibial Space [*Anatomy*]
MFT/S	Missile Facilities Technician/Specialist (AAG)
MFTU	Macao Federation of Trade Unions
MFTV	Mechanical Fit Test Vehicle
MFTVP	Motor-Free Test of Visual Perception [*Psychology*] (DAVI)
MFU	Magnetic Force Upset [*Metals*]
MFU	Marine Forecast Unit [*National Weather Service*]
MFU	Mfuwe [*Zambia*] [*Airport symbol*] (OAG)
MFU	Military Foul-Up [*Bowdlerized version*] (DSUE)
MFU	MIRA [*Multifunctional Inertial Reference Assembly*] Fighter Unit [*Air Force*] (MCD)
MFU	Myoclonus Families United (EA)
MFU	Pacific Coast Marine Firemen, Oilers, Watertenders, and Wipers Association [*Also known as Marine Firemen's Union*] (EA)
MFUA	Medical Follow-Up Agency [*National Research Council*]
MFUI	Mechanics Friendly Union Institution [*British*]
MFUMR	MIRA [*Multifunctional Inertial Reference Assembly*] Fighter Unit Mounting Rack [*Air Force*] (MCD)
MFUN	Morgan Funshares [*NASDAQ symbol*] (TTSB)
MFUN	Morgan Funshares, Inc. [*NASDAQ symbol*] (SAG)
Mfurers Mon	Manufacturers' Monthly [*A publication*]
MFUSYS	Microfiche File Update System [*Computer science*] (PDAA)
MFUW	Magnetic Force Upset Welding [*Metals*]
MFV	Forward Visibility More than ___ Miles [*Aviation*] (FAAC)
MFV	Magnetic Field Vector
MFV	Main Feedwater Valve [*Nuclear energy*] (NRCH)
MFV	Main Fuel Valve (KSC)
MFV	Maintenance Floor Valve (NRCH)
MFV	Mars Flyby Vehicle [*Aerospace*]
MFV	Melfa, VA [*Location identifier FAA*] (FAAL)
MFV	Methanol-Fueled Vehicle [*Automotive engineering*]
MFV	MFS Special Value Trust [*NYSE symbol*] (SPSG)
MFV	Microfilm Viewer
MFV	Military Flight Vehicles
MFV	Motor Fishing Vessel [*British military*] (DMA)
MFVD	Maximum Forward Voltage Drop
MFVP	Mauler Feasibility Validation Program
MFVPT	Motor-Free Visual Perception Test
mfVSG	Membrane Form of Variant Surface Glycoprotein [*Biochemistry*]
MFW	Main Feedwater [*Nuclear energy*] (NRCH)
MFW	Maritime Federation of the World (NADA)
MFW	Metres of Fresh Water
MFW	Migrant Farm Worker (OICC)
MFW	Milton-Freewater [*Oregon*] [*Seismograph station code, US Geological Survey*] (SEIS)
MFW	Ms. Foundation for Women (EA)
MFW	Multiple Fragment Wound (MAE)
MFWC	Marine Fleet Air, West Coast
MFWD	Mechanical Front Wheel Drive [*Off-highway equipment*]
MFWLB	Main Feedwater Line Break [*Nuclear energy*] (NRCH)
MFWP	Maryland Functional Writing Program (EDAC)
MFWV	Main Feedwater Valve [*Nuclear energy*] (NRCH)
MFX	Mirror Fusion Experiment [*Nuclear energy*]
MFXT	Meter Fix Time [*Aviation*] (FAAC)
MFY	Manufactory (ABBR)
MFY	Mobilization for Youth
MFY	Music for Youth
MFZ	Mezzo Forzando [*Music*]
MFZ	Missile Firing Zone
MFZ	Mofaz Air [*Malawi*] [*FAA designator*] (FAAC)
MG	Geometric Mean [*Psychology*]
mg	Guadalupe Missioners (TOCD)
MG	Gudalupe Missioners (TOCD)
MG	Machine-Glazed [*Poster paper*]
MG	Machine Gun (MUGU)
MG	Machine Gunner [*British military*] (DMA)
MG	Machinery of Government [*British*]
MG	Madagascar [*ANSI two-letter standard code*] (CNC)

mg	Mafic Granulite [*Geology*]
MG	Magenta (ROG)
MG	Maggioni & C. [*Italy*] [*Research code symbol*]
Mg	Maghemite [*A mineral*]
MG	Magna International, Inc. [*Toronto Stock Exchange symbol*]
Mg	Magnesium [*Chemical element*]
MG	Magnetic Armature (MSA)
MG	Maharashtrawadi Gomantak [*India*] [*Political party*] (PPW)
MG	Main Gauche [*With the Left Hand*] [*Music*]
MG	Main Generator (IAA)
MG	Major General
MG	Make Good
MG	Malachite Green [*A dye*]
mg	Malagasy Republic [*Madagascar*] [*MARC country of publication code Library of Congress*] (LCCP)
MG	Mammary Gland [*Anatomy*]
MG	Managerial Grid
MG	Manager's Guide
Mg	Mangrove [*Maps and charts*]
MG	Manual Group (NRCH)
MG	Manufacturing
MG	Maof Airlines [*Israel*] [*ICAO designator*] (ICDA)
MG	Marcus Gunn [*Pupil*] [*Ophthalmology*]
MG	Margin (DAVI)
MG	Marginal (AAG)
MG	Marine Gunner
MG	Martinus Gosia [*Authority cited in pre-1607 legal work*] (DSA)
MG	Master-General [*Military British*]
MG	Master Generator [*Telecommunications*] (OA)
MG	Matrix Glass [*Geology*]
MG	Meaning (ROG)
MG	Medal for Gallantry
MG	Media General Financial Services [*Information retrieval*]
MG	Medial Gastrocnemius [*Anatomy*]
MG	Medium Grain [*Lumber*]
MG	Megagram
MG	Membranous Glomerulopathy [*Nephrology*]
MG	Menopausal Gonadotropin [*Endocrinology*]
MG	Mesiogingival [*Dentistry*]
MG	Message Generator
MG	Metal Glass (IAA)
MG	Metal Goods [*Department of Employment*] [*British*]
MG	Metallgesellschaft [*German commodities and futures contractor*] (ECON)
MG	Metallurgical Grade
MG	Meteorological Group [*Range Commanders Council*] [*White Sands Missile Range, NM*]
MG	Methylene Glutamine
MG	Methylglucoside [*Organic chemistry*]
MG	Methylglyoxal [*Also, MGLY*] [*Organic chemistry*]
MG	Methyl Green [*A dye*]
MG	MG Car Club (EA)
MG	MGM Grand Air [*ICAO designator*] (AD)
MG	Michaelis-Gutmann Bodies (MAE)
mg	Microgram (DAVI)
MG	Microwave Generator
MG	Middle Gimbal
MG	Middle Gimbal [*Yaw*]
M/G	Miles per Gallon
MG	Military Government [*or Governor*]
MG	Millennium Guild (EA)
MG	Mill Glazed [*Paper*]
MG	Milligauss (ABBR)
mg	Milligram
mg	Milligram
MG	Millwright Group (EA)
MG	Minnesota Groundswell (EA)
MG	Minority Group
MG	Miracle of Grace [*Pseudonym used by William Smith*]
MG	Misioneros de Guadalupe [*Missionaries of Guadelupe*] [*Mexico*] (EAIO)
MG	Missile Gas
MG	Missile Guidance
MG	Mixed Grain
MG	[*The*] Mobile & Gulf Railroad Co. [*Formerly, MGU*] [*AAR code*]
MG	Mobile Generator (KSC)
MG	Modified Guaranteed [*Securities trading*]
MG	Moeso-Gothic [*Language, etc.*] (ROG)
MG	Monoglyceride [*An enzyme*] (MAE)
MG	Morgan Group [*AMEX symbol*] (TTSB)
MG	[*The*] Morgan Group, Inc. [*AMEX symbol*] (SAG)
MG	Morning
MG	Morris Garages [*British automobile manufacturer; initialism used as name of sports car it produces*]
MG	Motion for Mandamus Granted [*Legal term*] (ILCA)
MG	Motor Generator
MG	Mug (ABBR)
MG	Multigauge
MG	Muncie-Getrag [*Refers to an automotive transmission designed by Getrag, a West German company, and built by General Motors in Muncie, IN*]
MG	Muscle Group (MAE)
MG	Myasthenia Gravis [*Medicine*]
MG	Myasthenia Gravis Foundation (EA)
MG	Myoglobin [*Medicine*] (DMAA)

MG............. Myriagram [Ten Thousand Grams] (ROG)
MG............. Pompano Airways [ICAO designator] (AD)
Mg/₁........... Milligrams per Liter (GNE)
MGA........... Magna International, Inc. [NYSE symbol] (SPSG)
MGA........... Major-General in Charge of Administration [British]
MGA........... Managing General Agent [Insurance]
MGA........... Managua [Nicaragua] [Airport symbol] (OAG)
MGA........... Marble and Granite Association [British] (BI)
MGA........... Martin Goffman Associates (IID)
MGA........... Master Gemology Association (EA)
MGA........... Master of Government Administration (GAGS)
MGA........... Matrox Graphics Architecture [Matrox Eletronics Systems Ltd.] (PCM)
MGA........... Medium-Gain Antenna
MGA........... Megaline Resources [Vancouver Stock Exchange symbol]
MGA........... Melengestrol Acetate [Endocrinology]
MGA........... Mercantile Gold [Vancouver Stock Exchange symbol]
MGA........... Middle Gimbal Angle (NASA)
MGA........... Middle Gimbal Assembly (KSC)
MGA........... Middle Gimbal Axis (KSC)
MGA........... Milagra Ridge [California] [Seismograph station code, US Geological Survey] (SEIS)
MGA........... Military Government Association
MGA........... Module Generator Assembly (DWSG)
MGA........... Monochrome Graphics Adapter [Hercules] [Computer science] (PCM)
MGA........... [The] Monongahela Railway Co. [AAR code]
MGA........... Mother Guardian Allowance
MGA........... Multimedia Graphics Architecture [Computer science] (PCM)
MGA........... Multiple Gas Analyzer
MGA........... Mushroom Growers Association [Commercial firm] (EA)
MGA........... Mushroom Growers Cooperative Association [Defunct] (EA)
MGAA .... Medium-Gain Autotrack Antenna
MGAA .... Miniature Golf Association of America (EA)
MGAB .... Maintenance Ground Abort [Air Force] (AFIT)
MGABR ...... Maintenance Ground Abort Rate [Air Force] (AFIT)
MGAD .... Machine-Gun Artillery Division [Former USSR]
mgal .... Milligal [Unit of acceleration]
MGAL......... Thousand Gallons (EG)
MGAL/D ...... Million Gallons per Day
MGALS .... Milligals (ABBR)
MGAM .... Member Get a Member [Prodigy Services Co.]
MGAM .... Morgan Grenfell Asset Management [Investment management firm] [British]
MGAM .... Multimedia Games [NASDAQ symbol] (TTSB)
MGAM .... Multimedia Games, Inc. [NASDAQ symbol] (SAG)
MGaMW ..... Mount Wachusett Community College, Gardner, MA [Library symbol Library of Congress] (LCLS)
MG & L .... Measurement of Gains and Losses (DICI)
MG & S .... Manning, Granger, and Scott's English Common Pleas Reports [1845-56] [A publication] (DLA)
MGAO .... Minority Graphic Arts Organization (EA)
MGAP .... Magnetic Attitude Prediction
MGAP .... Micro-Grain Array Processor [Electronics]
MGAS .... Marcum Natural Gas Service, Inc. [NASDAQ symbol] (SAG)
MGAS .... Marcum Natural Gas Svcs [NASDAQ symbol] (TTSB)
MGAS .... Motor Gasoline [Military]
MGAT .... Manchester General Ability Test [Education] (AEBS)
MGAWA ...... Market Gardeners' Association of Western Australia
MGAWD ...... Make Good All Works Distributed [Legal term] (BARN)
MGB............ Main Gear Box (MCD)
MGB............ Manageable (ABBR)
MGB............ Medium-Girder Bridge (RDA)
MGB............ Ministerstvo Gosudarstvennoy Bezopasnosti [Ministry of State Security] [Former USSR] (LAIN)
MGB............ Mobile Garbage Bin
MGB............ Morgan Stan Global Opt Bd Fd [NYSE symbol] (TTSB)
MGB............ Morgan Stanley Global Opportunities Bond Fund, Inc. [NYSE symbol] (SAG)
MGB............ Motor Gunboat [British]
MGB............ Mount Gambier [Australia Airport symbol] (OAG)
MGBC......... Maranatha Gospel Bottle Crusade [Later, CEM] (EA)
MGBCS....... Murray Grey Beef Cattle Society [Australia]
MGBG .... Methylglyoxalbis(guanylhydrazone) [Mitoguazone] [Also, Me-GAG] [Antineoplastic drug]
MGBN .... Bananera [Guatemala] [ICAO location identifier] (ICLI)
MGBT.......... Manageability (ABBR)
MGBY.......... Manageably (ABBR)
MGC............ Machine-Gun Car [or Carrier] [British]
MGC............ Machine-Gun Co. [or Corps]
MGC............ Machine-Gun Combination [British]
MGC............ Magec Aviation Ltd. [British ICAO designator] (FAAC)
MGC............ Magic (ABBR)
MGC............ Magic
MgC............ Magnocellular Neuroendocrine Cell [Medicine] (DMAA)
MGC............ Major Gain Control
MGC............ Major General Commandant [Marine Corps]
MGC............ Management Group Codes (MCD)
MGC............ Manual Gain Control
MGC............ Marriage Guidance Council [British]
MGC............ Metacerebral Giant Cell [Cytology]
MGC............ Metallized Glass Coil
MGC............ Michigan City [Indiana] [Airport symbol] (OAG)
MGC............ Michigan City, IN [Location identifier FAA] (FAAL)
MGC............ Midcourse Guidance and Control
MGC............ Middle Georgia College [Cochran]
MGC............ Minimal Glomerular Change [Nephrology]

MGC............ Minimum Gelling Concentration [Hematology]
MGC............ Missile Guidance and Control
MGC............ Missile Guidance Computer (MCD)
MGC............ Montgomery County Community College, Blue Bell, PA [OCLC symbol] (OCLC)
MGC............ Morgan Grenfell Smallcap [NYSE symbol] (TTSB)
MGC............ Morgan Grenfell Smallcap Fund, Inc. [NYSE symbol] (SPSG)
MGC............ Movers Association of Greater Chicago, Chicago, IL [STAC]
MGC............ Museums and Galleries Commission [Government body] [British]
MGCA .... Men's Garden Clubs of America (EA)
MGCA .... Mobile Ground-Controlled Approach [Aviation]
MGCA .... Mushroom Growers Cooperative Association [Defunct]
MGCB .... Coban [Guatemala] [ICAO location identifier] (ICLI)
MGCC .... Medical Graphics [NASDAQ symbol] (TTSB)
MGCC .... Medical Graphics Corp. [NASDAQ symbol] (NQ)
MGCC .... MG [Morris Garage] Car Club
MGCC .... Missile Guidance and Control Computer
MGCD .... Maximum Gapless Coverage Distance (NG)
MGCI .... Master Ground-Controller Interception RADAR (NATG)
MGCL.......... Magical (ABBR)
MGCLY .... Magically (ABBR)
MGCN .... Magician (ABBR)
MGCO .... Mars Geoscience/Climatology Orbiter
MGCR .... Carmelita [Guatemala] [ICAO location identifier] (ICLI)
MGCR .... Maritime Gas-Cooled Reactor
MGCRB .... Medicare Geographic Classification Review Board
MGCR-CX ... Maritime Gas-Cooled Reactor Critical Experiment
MGCS .... Meteosat Ground Computer System [Aviation] (DA)
MGCS .... Missile Guidance and Control System (MCD)
MGCS .... Missile Guidance Cooling System (DWSG)
MGCT.......... Coatepeque [Guatemala] [ICAO location identifier] (ICLI)
MGCYL .... Megacycle (ABBR)
MGD .... Machine Gaming Division [Queensland, Australia]
MGD .... Magadan [Later, FUR] [Former USSR Geomagnetic observatory code]
MGD .... Magadan 1 [Former USSR Seismograph station code, US Geological Survey] (SEIS)
MGD .... Magnetogasdynamic
MGD .... Managed
MGD .... Master of Graphic Design (PGP)
MGD .... Maximal Glucose Disposal [Medicine] (DMAA)
MGD .... Mean Gain Deviation (IEEE)
MG/D .... Megagrams per Day
MGD .... Mercury Germanium Detector
MGD .... Miehle-Goss-Dexter [Rockwell International Corp.]
MGD .... Military Geographic Documentation (AABC)
mg/d .... Milligrams per Deciliter
MGD .... Million Gallons per Day
MGD .... Minority Group Designator [Office of Personnel Management] (GFGA)
MGD .... Mixed Gonadal Dysgenesis [Medicine]
MGD .... Molybdopterin Guanine Dinucleotide [Biochemistry]
MGD .... Mouse Genome Database
MGD .... Mugged (ABBR)
MGD .... Murgold Resources, Inc. [Toronto Stock Exchange symbol]
MGD .... North-East Cargo Airlines [Russian Federation] [ICAO designator] (FAAC)
MgdCare ..... Managed Care Solutions, Inc. [Associated Press] (SAG)
MGDF .... Modified Granular Diffusion Flame [Propellant]
MgdHi......... Managed High-Income Income Portfolio [Associated Press] (SAG)
MgdMun ..... Managed Municipals Portfolio [Associated Press] (SAG)
MgdMun2 .... Managed Municipals Portfolio II [Associated Press] (SAG)
MGDSRCS Eng... Membership in General Dental Surgery, Royal College of Surgeons of England [British] (DBQ)
MGE........... Evergreen Regional Library, Gimli, Manitoba [Library symbol National Library of Canada] (NLC)
MGE........... Maintenance Ground Equipment [Formerly, GSF]
MGE........... Manage (ABBR)
MGE........... Marge Enterprises [Vancouver Stock Exchange symbol]
MGE........... Marietta, GA [Location identifier FAA] (FAAL)
MGE........... Master of Geological Engineering (NADA)
MGE........... Master of Geological Engineering (GAGS)
MGE........... Message (ADA)
MGE........... Milwaukee Grain Exchange [Defunct]
MGE........... Minneapolis Grain Exchange (EA)
MGE........... Missile Guidance Element
MGE........... Modular Geographic Environment
MGEB.......... Manageable (ABBR)
MGEBT........ Manageability (ABBR)
MGEBY........ Manageably (ABBR)
MGED.......... Managed (ABBR)
M Ge E .... Master of Geological Engineering
M Ge Eng ... Master of Geological Engineering
MGEG.......... Managing (ABBR)
mg-el.......... Milligram-Element (MAE)
MGEM.......... Modern Gun Effectiveness Model (MCD)
M GEN .... Major General
MGEN .... Micro General [NASDAQ symbol] (TTSB)
MGEN .... Micro General Corp. [NASDAQ symbol] (NQ)
M Gen E ..... Master of General Engineering (PGP)
MGenStud.... Master of General Studies (ADA)
MGENT........ Management (ABBR)
M Geo E ..... Master of Geological Engineering (PGP)
M Geol E ..... Master of Geological Engineering
MGeolEng.... Master of Geological Engineering (NADA)

MGER	Manager (ABBR)
MGERL	Managerial (ABBR)
MGES	Esquipulas [*Guatemala*] [*ICAO location identifier*] (ICLI)
MGES	Maintenance Ground Equipment Section
MGEUS	Maintenance Ground Equipment Utilization Sheets
Mgf	Free Magnesium
MGF	Macrophage Growth Factor (PDAA)
MGF	Magnify (MSA)
MGF	Maringa [*Brazil*] [*Airport symbol*] (OAG)
MGF	Mast-Cell Growth Factor [*Cytology*]
MGF	Maternal Grandfather (AAMN)
MGF	MFS Government Markets Income Trust [*NYSE symbol*] (SPSG)
MGF	MFS Gvt Mkts Income Tr [*NYSE symbol*] (TTSB)
MGF	Missionary Gospel Fellowship (EA)
MGF	Mobile Guerrilla Force [*Vietnam*]
MGF	Moment-Generating Function [*Mathematics*]
MGF	Motor-Generator Flywheel (MCD)
MGF	Myasthenia Gravis Foundation
MGF	Myoblast Growth Factor [*Biochemistry*]
MGF	Myxoma Growth Factor [*Biochemistry*]
MGFC	Mickey Gilley Fan Club [*Defunct*] (EA)
MGFE	Moment-Generating Function Estimator
MGFEL	Master Government-Furnished Equipment List (NVT)
MGFG	Magnifying
MGFL	Flores [*Guatemala*] [*ICAO location identifier*] (ICLI)
MGFS	Media General Financial Services, Inc. [*Information service or system*] (IID)
MGFZB	Mein Gott, Fueg Es zum Besten [*My God, Order It for the Best*] [*Motto of Sophie, consort of Georg Friedrich, Margrave of Brandenburg-Anspach (1563-1639)*] [*German*]
MGG	Machine Gun Guards [*British military*] (DMA)
MGG	Managing (ABBR)
MGG	May-Gruenwald-Giemsa [*A stain*] [*Hematology*]
MGG	Mega Gold Resources Ltd. [*Vancouver Stock Exchange symbol*]
MGG	Memory Gate Generator [*Computer science*]
MGG	MGM Grand [*NYSE symbol*] (TTSB)
MGG	MGM Grand, Inc. [*NYSE symbol*] (SPSG)
MGG	Missile Guidance Group
MGG	Monopropellant Gas Generator (PDAA)
MGG	Mouse Gamma-Globulin
MGG	Mugging (ABBR)
MGG	Musik in Geschichte und Gegenwart [*A publication*]
MGGB	Modular Guided Glide Bomb (MCD)
MGGH	Methylglyoxal Guanylhydrazone [*Antineoplastic drug*] (MAE)
MGGM	Mars General Circulation Model [*For planetary weather study*]
MGGS	Major General, General Staff
MGGT	Guatemala/La Aurora [*Guatemala*] [*ICAO location identifier*] (ICLI)
MGH	Margate [*South Africa*] [*Airport symbol*] (OAG)
MGH	Massachusetts General Hospital (DAVI)
MGH	Massachusetts General Hospital, Treadwell Library, Boston, MA [*OCLC symbol*] (OCLC)
mgh	Milligram Hour [*Pharmacy*]
MGH	Monoglyceride Hydrolase [*An enzyme*] (MAE)
MGH	Morden & Helwig Group, Inc. [*Toronto Stock Exchange symbol*]
MGH	Museum of Garden History [*British*]
MgHiYld	Managed High Yield Fund [*Associated Press*] (SAG)
MGHT	Huehuetenango [*Guatemala*] [*ICAO location identifier*] (ICLI)
MGI	Gillam Municipal Library, Manitoba [*Library symbol National Library of Canada*] (NLC)
MGI	Macrophage and Granulocyte Inducer [*Biochemistry*]
MGI	Magnetics International Ltd. [*Toronto Stock Exchange symbol*]
MGI	Management Games Institute [*Raytheon Co.*]
MGI	Marine Geological Institute [*Indonesia*] [*Marine science*] (OSRA)
MGI	Matagorda Island, TX [*Location identifier FAA*] (FAAL)
MGI	Mavtech Holdings, Inc. [*Toronto Stock Exchange symbol*]
MGI	Medial Giant Interneuron [*Neurobiology*]
MGI	Member of the Gas Institute [*British*]
MGI	Member of the Institute of Certificated Grocers [*British*]
MGI	Metal Grating Institute [*Defunct*]
MGI	MGI Properties [*NYSE symbol*] (SPSG)
MGI	Military Geographic Information [*or Intelligence*] (MCD)
MGI	Mobile Gamma Irradiator [*Nuclear energy*]
MGI	Multigraphic Interface [*XOR Systems*]
MGIB	Management and Graduate Item Bank [*Reasoning skills test*]
MGIB	Montgomery GI Bill (INF)
MGIC	Magic Software Enterprises, Inc. [*NASDAQ symbol*] (SAG)
MGIC	MGIC Investment Co. [*Associated Press*] (SAG)
MGIC	Mortgage Guaranty Insurance Corp. [*Subsidiary of MGIC Investment Corp.*]
MGICF	Magic Software Enterprises [*NASDAQ symbol*] (TTSB)
MGID	Military Geographic Information and Documentation (AABC)
MGIKQ	Magic Restaurants [*NASDAQ symbol*] (TTSB)
MGIN	Margin (ROG)
MGINS	Mugginess (ABBR)
MGI Phr	MGI PHARMA, Inc. [*Associated Press*] (SAG)
MGI Prp	MGI Properties [*Associated Press*] (SAG)
MGIR	Motor Glider Instructor Rating [*Aviation*] (DA)
MGIWQ	Magic Restaurants Wrrt [*NASDAQ symbol*] (TTSB)
MGJ	Montgomery, NY [*Location identifier FAA*] (FAAL)
MGK	Michele Gold Mountain Ltd. [*Vancouver Stock Exchange symbol*]
MGk	Middle Greek [*Language*]
MGK	Modern Greek [*Language, etc.*]
mg/kg	Milligrams per Kilogram (AAMN)
MGl	Gloucester Lyceum and Sawyer Free Public Library, Gloucester, MA [*Library symbol Library of Congress*] (LCLS)

MGL	Machine Gun LASER (MCD)
MGL	Magalia [*California*] [*Seismograph station code, US Geological Survey*] (SEIS)
MGL	Magellan Health Svcs [*AMEX symbol*] (TTSB)
MGL	Magnanimous Green Leprechaun
MGL	Malachite Green Leucocyanite (OA)
MGL	Marginal (MSA)
MGL	Matrix Generator Language [*Computer science*] (BUR)
MG/L	Milligrams per Liter
MGL	Mingle (ABBR)
MGL	Missouri Gravity Low [*Geology*]
MGL	Mogul
MGL	Mongolian Airlines [*ICAO designator*] (FAAC)
MGL	Mongrel (ABBR)
MGL	Mono Gold Mines, Inc. [*Vancouver Stock Exchange symbol*]
MGL	Monteagle, TN [*Location identifier FAA*] (FAAL)
MGL	Move-Grow-Learn [*Program for visual perception development*]
MGLA	Massachusetts General Laws Annotated [*A publication*]
M GLAM	Mid Glamorgan [*County in Wales*]
MGLC	Misty Mountain Gold Ltd. [*NASDAQ symbol*] (SAG)
MGLD	Mild General Learning Disability
MGLD	Mingled (ABBR)
MGLG	Mingling (ABBR)
MGIHi	Cape Ann Historical Association, Gloucester, MA [*Library symbol Library of Congress*] (LCLS)
MGLL	La Libertad [*Guatemala*] [*ICAO location identifier*] (ICLI)
MGLMNA	Megalomania (ABBR)
MGLMNAC ...	Megalomaniac (ABBR)
MGLP	Methylglucose Lipopolysaccharide [*Biochemistry*]
MGLPS	Megalopolis (ABBR)
MGLY	Methylglyoxal [*Also, MG*] [*Organic chemistry*]
MGM	Mailgram
MGM	Master Group Multiplexer
MGM	Maternal Grandmother (AAMN)
MGM	Mayer's Ganz Mispocheh [*Mayer's Whole Family*] [*A Yiddish nickname for Metro-Goldwyn-Mayer, it reflects the tendency of early studio chiefs to hire their relatives and friends*]
MGM	Mechanics of Granular Materials
MGM	Medical Group Missions of the Christian Medical and Dental Society (EA)
MGM	Member-Get-a-Member [*Marketing*] (WDMC)
MGM	Metro-Goldwyn-Mayer [*Record label*] [*USA, Great Britain, etc.*]
MGM	MGM Grand Air, Inc. [*ICAO designator*] (FAAC)
mgm	Milligram
MGM	Milligram (DFIT)
MGM	Mobile-Launched Ground-Attack Missile
MGM	Molecular and Genetic Medicine
MGM	Montgomery [*Alabama*] [*Airport symbol*] (OAG)
MGM	Morgain Minerals, Inc. [*Vancouver Stock Exchange symbol*]
MG/M²	Mother's Grandmother (MAE)
MG/M²	Megagrams per Square Meter
MG/M³	Megagrams per Cubic Meter
mg/m₃	Milligrams of Material per Cubic Meter of Air (GNE)
MGMA	Magma (ABBR)
MGMA	Medical Group Management Association (EA)
MGMA	Metro Global Media [*NASDAQ symbol*] (TTSB)
MGMA	Metro Global Media, Inc. [*NASDAQ symbol*] (SAG)
MGMC	Multiple Gun Motor Carriage
MGMD	Ministerial Group on the Misuse of Drugs [*British*]
MGMG	MGM Grand, Inc. [*Associated Press*] (SAG)
MGMGMG	Milwaukee and Greatlakes MG [*Morris Garage*] Motorcar Group
MGMIS	Medical Group Management Information Service [*Medical Group Management Association*] (DHSM)
MGML	Malacatan [*Guatemala*] [*ICAO location identifier*] (ICLI)
MGMM	Melchor De Mencos [*Guatemala*] [*ICAO location identifier*] (ICLI)
MGMNT	Management
MGMR	Ministry of Geology and Mineral Resources [*China*]
MGMT	Make Good a Magnetic Track of (Degrees) [*Aviation*] (FAAC)
MGMT	Management
MGMT	Management (KSC)
mgmt	Management (DD)
MGMT	Management
Mgmt Forum ...	Management Forum [*A publication*]
MGN	Magangue [*Colombia*] [*Airport symbol*] (AD)
MGN	Magazine (ABBR)
MGN	Magneto [*Generator*]
MGN	Margin [*Accounting*]
MGN	Medial Geniculate Nucleus [*Medicine*]
MGN	Membranous Glomerulonephritis [*Nephrology*]
MGN	Mendial Geniculate Nucleus (PDAA)
MGN	Mengen [*Turkey*] [*Seismograph station code, US Geological Survey*] (SEIS)
MGN	Micrograin (ABBR)
MGN	Mirror Group Newspapers [*British*]
MGN	Morgan Aviation Services Ltd. [*Nigeria*] [*ICAO designator*] (FAAC)
MGN	Morgan Products Ltd. [*NYSE symbol*] (SPSG)
MGN	Multigrounded Neutral [*Telecommunications*] (TEL)
Mgna	Magna-Lab, Inc. [*Associated Press*] (SAG)
MGNAN	Margination (ABBR)
MGNES	Metal Goods Not Elsewhere Specified [*Department of Employment*] [*British*]
MGNETC	Magnetic (ABBR)
MGNETCY	Magnetically (ABBR)
MGNETMTR ..	Magnetometer (ABBR)
MGNETSM ...	Magnetism (ABBR)

MGNETZ	Magnetization (ABBR)
MGNETZ	Magnetize [or Magnetized] (ABBR)
MGNFI	Magnify (ABBR)
MGNFIB	Magnifiable (ABBR)
MGNFID	Magnified (ABBR)
MGNFIG	Magnifying (ABBR)
MGNFIN	Magnification (ABBR)
MGNFIR	Magnifier (ABBR)
MGNFNC	Magnificence (ABBR)
MGNFNT	Magnificent (ABBR)
MGNFTY	Magnificently (ABBR)
MGNIA	Marginalia (ABBR)
MGNL	Magna Bancorp [NASDAQ symbol] (SAG)
MGNLT	Marginality (ABBR)
MGNLY	Marginally (ABBR)
MGNMT	Magnanimity (ABBR)
MGNMU	Magnanimous (ABBR)
MGNSM	Magnesium [Chemical symbol is Mg]
MGNT	Magnate (ABBR)
MGNT	Magnet (ABBR)
MGNTC	Magnetic
MGNTO	Magneto
MGNTUD	Magnitude (ABBR)
MGNTZD	Magnetized
MGO	Machine Gun Officer [British military] (DMA)
MGO	Management by Goals and Objectives (MCD)
MGO	Master General of the Ordnance [Army British]
MGO	Master of Gynaecology and Obstetrics (ADA)
MGO	Mato Grosso [Brazil] [Airport symbol] (AD)
MGO	Megagauss-Oersted [Magnetic field strength]
MGO	Military Government Officer
MGO	Million Gauss Oersted [Unit of energy density]
MGO	Mortgage Insurance Co. of Canada [Toronto Stock Exchange symbol]
MGOCC	Morris Garage Octagon Car Club [British] (EAIO)
MGOe	Megagauss-Oersted [Also, MGO] [Magnetic field strength]
MGOS	Metal-Glass-Oxide-Silicon (PDAA)
MGOT	Maggot (ABBR)
M GOTH	Moeso-Gothic [Language, etc.] (ROG)
MGP	Application for Mandamus Granted in Part [Legal term] (DLA)
MGP	Macarthur Gruen Party [Political party Australia]
MG(P)	Machinery of Government, Parliamentary Procedure [British]
MGP	Maguayo [Puerto Rico] [Seismograph station code, US Geological Survey] (SEIS)
MGP	Maintenance Ground Point
MGP	Manga [Papua New Guinea] [Airport symbol] (OAG)
MGP	Manufactured Gas Plant [Environmental biotechnology]
MGP	Marginal Granulocyte Pool [Hematology]
MGP	Mary Glawgow Publications [Publisher] [British]
MGP	Merchants Group [AMEX symbol] (TTSB)
MGP	Merchants Group, Inc. [AMEX symbol] (SPSG)
MGP	Methylglucose Polysaccharide [Biochemistry]
MGP	Methyl Green Pyronine [A stain]
MGP	Micro-G Physics and Chemistry Experiments Group [NASA] (SSD)
MGP	Monochrome Graphics Printer [Computer science] (CDE)
MGP	Morrison-Grey Enterprises [Vancouver Stock Exchange symbol]
MGP	Mountain Gorilla Project (EA)
MGP	Mouvement Gaulliste Populaire [Popular Gaullist Movement] [France Political party] (PPW)
MGP	Mucous Glycoproteins [Biochemistry]
MGP	Multiple Goal Programming
MGP	Museum of the Great Plains [Lawton, OK]
MGPB	Puerto Barrios [Guatemala] [ICAO location identifier] (ICLI)
MGPC	Grandview Personal Care Home, Manitoba [Library symbol National Library of Canada] (NLC)
MGPCU	Missile Ground Power Control Unit (AAG)
M-GPD	Million US Gallons per Day [AEC, OSW]
MGPF	Multiprogram General-Purpose Facilities [Oak Ridge National Laboratory]
MGPGP	Master of Group Process and Group Psychotherapy (PGP)
MGPHN	Megaphone (ABBR)
MGPL	Marine Gene Probe Laboratory [Dalhousie University] [Canada]
MGPP	Poptun [Guatemala] [ICAO location identifier] (ICLI)
MGPPL	Motor Glider Private Pilot's Licence [British] (AIA)
MGPR	M.G. Products [NASDAQ symbol] (TTSB)
MGPR	MG Products, Inc. [NASDAQ symbol] (SAG)
MG Prod	MG Products, Inc. [Associated Press] (SAG)
MGQ	Mogadishu [Somalia] [Airport symbol] (OAG)
MGQC	Quiche [Guatemala] [ICAO location identifier] (ICLI)
MGQZ	Quezaltenango [Guatemala] [ICAO location identifier] (ICLI)
MGR	Machine Gun Regiment [British military] (DMA)
mgr	Magister [Master] [Latin]
MGR	Manager (AFM)
mgr	Manager (DD)
Mgr	Manager (ODBW)
MGR	Manager
MGR	Manager
MGR	Marrow Granulocyte Reserves [Hematology]
MGR	Medieval Greek [Language, etc.]
MGR	Metal Glaze Resistor
MGR	Method of Generated Responses [Psychology]
MGR	Micro-Graphic Reporting (PDAA)
MGR	Middlegate Resources, Inc. [Vancouver Stock Exchange symbol]
M GR	Middle Greek [Language, etc.] (ROG)
MGR	Mixed Gas Rebreather

MGR	Mobile-Launched Ground-Attack Rocket
MGR	Modified Gain Ratio [Medicine] (MAE)
MGR	Modular Gas-Cooled Reactor [Developed by MIT] [Nuclear energy]
MGR	Monsignor
Mgr.	Monsignor (ODBW)
MGR	Moraga Resources Ltd. [Vancouver Stock Exchange symbol]
MGR	Moultrie, GA [Location identifier FAA] (FAAL)
MGR	Moultrie/Thomasville [Georgia] [Airport symbol] (OAG)
MGR	Mouvement de la Gauche Reformatrice [Movement of the Reformist Left] [France Political party] (PPW)
MGR	Mugger (ABBR)
MGR	Murmurs, Gallops, or Rubs [Cardiology] (DAVI)
MGRA	Major-General, Royal Artillery [Army British]
MGRA	Migrate (ABBR)
MGRAD	Migrated (ABBR)
MGRAG	Migrating (ABBR)
MGRAN	Migration (ABBR)
MGranbyS	Saint Hyacinth College and Seminary, Granby, MA [Library symbol Library of Congress] (LCLS)
MGRATR	Migrator (ABBR)
MGRATRY	Migratory (ABBR)
MGRC	McGrath RentCorp [NASDAQ symbol] (NQ)
MGRC	Melbourne Greyhound Racing Club [Australia]
mgrd	Middleground (VRA)
MGREC	Magnetic Recorder [or Recording] (IAA)
MGrefC	Greenfield Community College, Greenfield, MA [Library symbol Library of Congress] (LCLS)
MGRESS	Manageress (ROG)
MGRGT	Modular Gas-Cooled Reactor Gas Turbine [Developed by MIT] [Nuclear energy]
MGRHS	May God Rest His Soul
MGRI	Mobile Ground Radio Installation
MGRL	Managerial (ABBR)
MGRL	Managerial
MGRM	Major-General, Royal Marines [British military] (DMA)
MGRM	Metallgesellschaft Refining & Marketing [American subsidiary of the German commodities and futures contractor] (ECON)
MGRM	Milligram (ROG)
MGRN	Migration (ABBR)
MGRNL	Migrational (ABBR)
MGRP	Minimum-Gradient Reaction Path [Chemical kinetics]
MGRS	Ferrocarriles Nacionales de Mexico [AAR code]
MGrS	Groton School, Groton, MA [Library symbol Library of Congress] (LCLS)
MGRS	Meter Gauge Rolling-Stock [British]
MGRS	Military Grid Reference System (AABC)
MGRT	Migrant (ABBR)
MGRT	Retalhuleu [Guatemala] [ICAO location identifier] (ICLI)
MGRTY	Migratory (ABBR)
MGRW	Matrix Generator and Report Writer [Computer science]
MGRY	Milgray Electronics [NASDAQ symbol] (TTSB)
MGRY	Milgray Electronics, Inc. [NASDAQ symbol] (NQ)
MGS	Machine Gun School [British military] (DMA)
MGS	Magellan Resources Corp. [Vancouver Stock Exchange symbol]
MGS	Mangaia [Cook Islands] [Airport symbol] (OAG)
MGS	Marine Geophysical Survey [NOO]
MGS	Mars Global Surveyor [NASA]
MGS	Master Gemology Society [Defunct] (EA)
MGS	Master of General Studies (GAGS)
MGS	Master of Gerontological Studies (GAGS)
MG's	Memphis Group [In name of singing group "Booker T and the MG's"]
MGS	Metal Gravel Stop
MGS	Metre-Gram-Second
MGS	Metrogas SA [NYSE symbol] (SAG)
MGS	MetroGas S.A. CI'B'ADS [NYSE symbol] (TTSB)
MGS	Microcomputer Graphic System
MGS	Middleton Gardens [South Carolina] [Seismograph station code, US Geological Survey] (SEIS)
MGS	Midwestern Gilbert and Sullivan Society (EA)
MGS	Military Government Section [World War II]
MGS	Missile Guidance Section [or Set, or System]
MGS	Mission Ground Station (MCD)
MGS	Mobile Ground System
MGS	Moment Gyro System
MGS	Motor Generator Set (CAAL)
MGSA	Marriage Guidance South Australia
MGSA	Melanoma Growth Stimulatory Activity [Biochemistry]
MGSA	Military General Supply Agency [Merged with Defense General Supply Center]
MGSA	Modern Greek Studies Association (EA)
MGSC	Missile Guidance Set Control
MGSCD	Martha Graham School of Contemporary Dance [New York, NY]
MGSE	Maintenance Ground Support Equipment
MGSE	Mechanical Ground Support Equipment
MGSE	Missile Ground Support Equipment
MGSE	Mobile Ground Support Equipment
MGSE-ECM	Maintenance Ground Support Equipment-Environmental Controls and Mechanisms (SAA)
MGSGT	Master Gunnery Sergeant [Marine Corps] (DNAB)
MGSIUF	Marquis Giuseppe Scicluna International University Foundation (EA)
MGSJ	San Jose [Guatemala] [ICAO location identifier] (ICLI)
MGSM	San Marcos [Guatemala] [ICAO location identifier] (ICLI)
MGSpS	Guadalupan Missionaries of the Holy Spirit (TOCD)
MGSS	Manned Geosynchronous Spacecraft Servicer (SSD)

MGST.........	Miles [*Multiple Integrated Laser Engagement System*] Gunnery Skills Test [*USA*]
MGST.........	Military Geography Specialist Team
MGSTL.......	Magisterial (ABBR)
MGSTRA.....	Magistrate (ABBR)
MGT...........	Magenta Development Corp. [*Vancouver Stock Exchange symbol*]
MGT...........	Major Ground Test (NASA)
MGT...........	Management (AFM)
MGT...........	Margate Air Services [*South Africa ICAO designator*] (FAAC)
MGT...........	Master-Group Translator [*Telecommunications*] (TEL)
MGT...........	Master of Gas Technology (GAGS)
MGT...........	Megaton [*Nuclear equivalent of one million tons of high explosive*] (AAG)
MGT...........	Meteorological and Geoastrophysical Titles
MGT...........	Millingimbi [*Airport symbol*]
MGT...........	Mobile [*Truck-Mounted*] Ground Terminal
MGT...........	Movie Going Time
MGTANALYSO...	Management Analysis Officer [*Air Force*]
MGTAV.......	Modern Greek Teachers' Association of Victoria [*Australia*]
MGTENGR....	Management Engineer [*Air Force*]
MGTI.........	Member of the Gymnastic Teachers' Institute [*British*] (ROG)
MGTIR.......	Mightier (ABBR)
mgtis.........	Meningitis [*Medicine*] (MAE)
MGTIST......	Mightiest (ABBR)
MGTMTR....	Magnetometer
MGTNS......	Mightiness (ABBR)
MGTO........	Mexican Government Tourism Office (EA)
MgtTch......	Management Technologies, Inc. [*Associated Press*] (SAG)
MGTY........	Mighty (ABBR)
MGU.........	Main-Group Ureilite [*Meteorite component*]
MGU.........	MGM Resources Corp. [*Vancouver Stock Exchange symbol*]
MGU.........	Midcourse Guidance Unit [*Navy*] (CAAL)
MGU.........	Military Government Unit
MGU.........	[*The*] Mobile & Gulf Railroad Co. [*Later, MG*] [*AAR code*]
MGU.........	Moskovskiy Gosudarstvenniy Universitet [*Moscow State University*] [*Former USSR*] (MSC)
MGUN........	Marine Gunner
MGUS........	Monoclonal Gammopathies of Undetermined Significance [*Medicine*] (DMAA)
MGV.........	Mechanically-Guided Vehicle
MGV.........	Miniature Gate Valve
MGV.........	Monogram Oil & Gas, Inc. [*Vancouver Stock Exchange symbol*]
MGVC........	Manual Governing Valve Control [*Nuclear energy*] (NRCH)
MGVT........	Mated Ground Vibration Test (NASA)
MGVT........	Montgomery [*Vermont*] [*Seismograph station code, US Geological Survey*] (SEIS)
MGW.........	Magnesium Sulfate, Glycerine, and Water (Enema) [*Medicine*]
MGW.........	Maximum Gross Weight (WDAA)
MGW.........	Mission Gross Weight
MGW.........	Morgantown [*West Virginia*] [*Airport symbol*] (OAG)
MGW.........	Morgantown, WV [*Location identifier FAA*] (FAAL)
MGWA........	Marriage Guidance Western Australia
MGWR........	Midland Great Western Railway [*British*] (ROG)
MGWS........	Modular Guided Weapon System (MCD)
MGX.........	Moabi [*Gabon*] [*Airport symbol*] (OAG)
MGX.........	Mossimo Inc. [*NYSE symbol*] (TTSB)
MGX.........	Mossimo, Inc. [*NYSE symbol*] (SAG)
MGXI........	Micrografx, Inc. [*NASDAQ symbol*] (SAG)
M-GXT.......	Multistage Graded Exercise Test [*Cardiology*] (DAVI)
MGY.........	Dayton, OH [*Location identifier FAA*] (FAAL)
MGY.........	Mega-Dyne Industrial Corp. [*Vancouver Stock Exchange symbol*]
MGY.........	Muggy (ABBR)
MGYSGT.....	Master Gunnery Sergeant [*Marine Corps*]
MGZ.........	Maschinengewehr-Zieleinrichtung [*Machine-Gun Sighting Mechanism*] [*German military - World War II*]
MGZ.........	Mayaguez [*Diocesan abbreviation*] [*Puerto Rico*] (TOCD)
MGZ.........	Mergui [*Myanmar*] [*Airport symbol*] (OAG)
MGZF........	Maschinengewehr-Zielfernrohr [*Machine-Gun Telescopic Sight*] [*German military - World War II*]
MH...........	Air-Cushion Vehicle built by Mitsubishi [*Japan*] [*Usually used in combination with numerals*]
MH...........	[*A*] Grammar of Masoretic Hebrew [*A publication*] (BJA)
MH...........	Ha-Mo'atsah ha-Hakla'it (BJA)
MH...........	Harvard University, Cambridge, MA [*Library symbol Library of Congress*] (LCLS)
mh...........	Macao [*MARC country of publication code Library of Congress*] (LCCP)
MH...........	Magnetic Head [*or Heading*]
MH...........	Magnetite-Hematite [*Geology*]
MH...........	Mail Handler [*Computer science*]
MH...........	Main Hatch
MH...........	Maintenance Handbook
MH...........	Maintenance Hemodialysis [*Nephrology*] (CPH)
MH...........	Makkabi Hazair (BJA)
MH...........	Malaysia Airlines [*Airline flight code*] (ODBW)
MH...........	Malaysian Airline System [*ICAO designator*] (AD)
MH...........	Malden Hospital [*Malden, MA*]
MH...........	Maleic Hydrazide [*Plant growth regulator*]
MH...........	Malignant Histiocytosis [*Medicine*]
MH...........	Malignant Hyperpyrexia [*Medicine*]
MH...........	Malignant Hyperthermia [*Medicine*]
MH...........	Malt House
MH...........	Mammotropic Hormone [*Endocrinology*]
MH...........	Manhole (AAG)
MH...........	Man-Hour (MCD)
MH...........	Manual Hold [*Telecommunications*]
MH...........	Mare Humorum [*Sea of Moisture*] [*Lunar area*]
MH...........	Marital History
MH...........	Marshall Islands [*ANSI two-letter standard code*] (CNC)
M-H...........	Martini-Henry [*Rifle*]
MH...........	Masonic Hall (ROG)
MH...........	Master Herbalist
MH...........	Master Hosts [*An association Defunct*] (EA)
MH...........	Master of Hamburgerology [*McDonald's Corp. Hamburger University*]
MH...........	Master of Health (GAGS)
MH...........	Master of Horticulture
MH...........	Master of Hounds [*British*]
MH...........	Master of Humanics
MH...........	Master of Humanities (GAGS)
MH...........	Master of Hygiene
MH...........	Master of the Horse [*British*] (ROG)
MH...........	Master of the Hunt
MH...........	Materials Handling (NATG)
MH...........	Maximum Height [*Ballistics*]
M-H...........	McGraw-Hill (NITA)
MH...........	Mechanical Handling [*Describes type of produce; for example, MH-1 refers to a kind of tomato*]
MH...........	Medal of Honor [*Often erroneously called Congressional Medal of Honor*] [*Military decoration*]
MH...........	Medical History
MH...........	Megahertz [*Megacycles per second*] [*See also MCPS, MCS, MC/S, MHZ*] (NATG)
Mh...........	Mehri (BJA)
MH...........	Melanophore Hormone [*Also, MSH*] [*Endocrinology*]
MH...........	Mended Hearts (EA)
MH...........	Menstrual History [*Medicine*]
MH...........	Mental Health
MH...........	Mentally Handicapped (AIE)
MH...........	Merchants Haulage (DS)
MH...........	Mercurihematoporphyrin [*Pharmacology*]
MH...........	Meristem Height [*Botany*]
MH...........	MeSH Heading [*Online database field identifier*]
MH...........	Message Handler [*Computer science*]
MH...........	Metal Halide (MCD)
M/H...........	Meters per Hour
M/H...........	Microcytic/Hypochromic [*Anemia*] [*Hematology*] (DAVI)
MH...........	Microhematuria [*Medicine*]
MH...........	Middlesex Hussars (Duke of Cambridge's) [*British military*] (DMA)
M/H...........	Miles per Hour [*Also, MPH*]
MH...........	Military History (AABC)
MH...........	Military Hospital (ADA)
mH...........	Millihenry (GPO)
mH...........	Millihour [*One-thousandth of an hour*] (AAG)
MH...........	Ministry of Health [*British*]
M-H...........	Minneapolis-Honeywell Regulator Co. [*Later, HON*]
MH...........	Miscellaneous Hardware
MH...........	Mishnaic Hebrew [*Language, etc.*] (BJA)
MH...........	Mitsubishi Heavy Industries Ltd. [*Japan ICAO aircraft manufacturer identifier*] (ICAO)
MH...........	Mobile High-Power [*Reactor*] [*Proposed*] (NRCH)
MH...........	Mobile Home (WGA)
MH...........	Mobility Haiti (EA)
MH...........	Molting Hormone [*Endocrinology, entomology*]
MH...........	Monosymptomatic Hypochondriasis [*Medicine*] (DMAA)
MH...........	Most High [*Freemasonry*]
MH...........	Most Honorable
MH...........	Mount Hood Railway Co. [*AAR code*]
M-H...........	Mueller-Hinton [*Agar*] [*Microbiology*]
MH...........	Mulberry Heart (OA)
MH...........	Multihandicapped
MH...........	Murine Hepatitis
MH...........	Music Hall [*Record label*]
MH...........	Mutant Hybrid [*Medicine*] (DMAA)
MH...........	Muzzle Hatch
MH2...........	Mary Hartman, Mary Hartman [*Initialism is shortened form of television program title*] [*Also, M^{2H2}*]
MHA...........	Hamline University, St. Paul, MN [*OCLC symbol*] (OCLC)
MH-A...........	Harvard University, Arnold Arboretum, Cambridge, MA [*Library symbol Library of Congress*] (LCLS)
MHa...........	Haverhill Public Library, Haverhill, MA [*Library symbol Library of Congress*] (LCLS)
MHA...........	Machinery Haulers Association Agent, Saint Paul MN [*STAC*]
MHA...........	Madonna House Apostolate [*Combermere, ON*] (EAIO)
MHA...........	Mahdia [*Guyana*] [*Airport symbol*] (OAG)
MHA...........	Maintenance Hazard Analysis (MCD)
MHA...........	Man-Hour Accounting (NVT)
MHA...........	Manila Hemp Association [*British*] (DBA)
MHA...........	Mansion House Association on Transport, Inc. [*British*] (BI)
MHA...........	Marine Historical Association [*Later, MSM*] (EA)
MHA...........	Master of Health Administration
MHA...........	Master of Hospital Administration
MHA...........	Material Handling Area
MHA...........	Maximum Hypothetical Accident [*Nuclear energy*] (IEEE)
MHA...........	Mean Horizontal Acceleration
MHA...........	Meat Hygiene Authority [*Australia*]
MHA...........	Medal for Humane Action [*Berlin Airlift, 1948-9*] [*Military decoration*]
MHA...........	Member of House of Assembly [*British*]
MHA...........	Mennonite Health Association (EA)
MHA...........	Mental Health Abstracts [*Database*] [*IFI/Plenum Data Co.*] [*Information service or system*] (CRD)

MHA............	Mental Health Administration [*Later, ADAMHA*]
MHA............	Mental Health Analysis [*Psychology*] (AEBS)
MHA............	Mental Health Association [*Later, NMHA*] (EA)
MHA............	Mental Health Authority (NADA)
MHA............	Methemalbumin [*Medicine*] (MAE)
MHA............	Methionine Hydroxy Analog [*Poultry feed*]
MHA............	Methodist Homes for the Aged [*British*] (BI)
MHA............	Microangiopathic Hemolytic Anemia [*Medicine*]
MHA............	Microhemagglutination [*Test for Syphilis*] [*Immunochemistry*] (DAVI)
MHA............	Military Health Affairs (DOMA)
MHA............	Minehunter, Auxiliary [*Navy symbol Obsolete*]
MHA............	Minimum Holding Altitude [*Aviation*]
MHA............	Mixed Hemadsorption Assay [*Clinical chemistry*]
MHA............	Modified Handling Authorized [*Air Force*]
MHA............	Mormon History Association (EA)
MHA............	Mountain High Aviation [*ICAO designator*] (FAAC)
MHA............	Mueller Hinton Agar [*Microbiology*] (OA)
MHA............	Multiple Handicapped Association (NADA)
MHA............	Mutual Households Associations Ltd. [*British*] (BI)
MH-AA........	Harvard University, Afro-American Studies, Lamont Undergraduate Library, Cambridge, MA [*Library symbol Library of Congress*] (LCLS)
MHAC..........	Man-Hour Accounting Card
MHAC..........	Multifrequency High-Gain Antenna Configuration (SSD)
MHadP........	Porter-Phelps-Hunting Foundation, Hadley, MA [*Library symbol*] [*Library of Congress*] (LCLS)
MH-AH........	Harvard University, Andover-Harvard Theological Library, Cambridge, MA [*Library symbol Library of Congress*] (LCLS)
MHAM	Amapala [*Honduras*] [*ICAO location identifier*] (ICLI)
MHAMS	Master of Historical Administration and Museum Studies (GAGS)
MHaNE	Northern Essex Community College, Haverhill, MA [*Library symbol Library of Congress*] (LCLS)
MHansAF	United States Air Force Research Library, Hanscom Air Force Base, Hanscom, MA [*Library symbol Library of Congress*] (LCLS)
MH-AO........	Harvard University, Oakes Ames Orchid Library, Cambridge, MA [*Library symbol Library of Congress*] (LCLS)
MHAQ	Material Handling Association of Quebec (AC)
MHar..........	Brooks Free Library, Harwich, MA [*Library symbol*] [*Library of Congress*] (LCLS)
MH-Ar.........	Harvard University Archives, Cambridge, MA [*Library symbol Library of Congress*] (LCLS)
MH-AS	Harvard University, George R. Agassiz Station, Cambridge, MA [*Library symbol Library of Congress*] (LCLS)
MHAS	Man-Hour Accounting System (DNAB)
MHathD	Danvers State Hospital, Hathorne, MA [*Library symbol Library of Congress*] (LCLS)
MHA-TP	Microhemagglutination Assay Treponema Pallidum [*Immunochemistry*]
MHAUS........	Malignant Hyperthermia Association of the United States (EA)
MHAWA	Master Hairdressers' Association of Western Australia
MHB............	Maintenance Handbook
MHB............	Mary Hardin-Baylor College, Belton, TX [*OCLC symbol*] (OCLC)
MHB............	Master Horizontal Bomber
MHB............	Maximum Hospital Benefit [*Medicine*] (DMAA)
MHb............	Medial Habenular [*Neuroanatomy*]
MHB............	Methemoglobin [*Biochemistry, medicine*]
MHB............	Methemoglobin [*Immunochemistry*] (DAVI)
MHB............	Military History Branch [*USMACV*]
MHB............	Mine-Hauling Bogie [*Mining engineering*]
MHB............	Mueller-Hinton Broth [*Cell growth medium*]
MHb............	Myohemoglobin [*Hematology*]
MH-BA	Harvard University, Graduate School of Business Administration, Boston, MA [*Library symbol Library of Congress*] (LCLS)
MHBA	Morgan Horse Breeders Association [*Defunct*] (EA)
MH-BH........	Harvard University, Blue Hill Meteorological Observatory, Cambridge, MA [*Library symbol Library of Congress*] (LCLS)
MH-BL	Harvard University, Biological Laboratories, Cambridge, MA [*Library symbol Library of Congress*] (LCLS)
MH-BM	Harvard University, George David Birkhoff Mathematics Library, Cambridge, MA [*Library symbol Library of Congress*] (LCLS)
MHBM	Modern Heavy Ballistic Missile (ADA)
MHBN	Mothers' Home Business Network (EA)
MH-BR	Harvard University, Busch-Reisinger Museum of Germanic Culture, Cambridge, MA [*Library symbol Library of Congress*] (LCLS)
MH-BS	Harvard University, Biochemical Sciences Tutorial Library, Cambridge, MA [*Library symbol Library of Congress*] (LCLS)
MHBSS	Modified Hank's Balanced Salt Solution [*Cell culture*]
MH-C	Harvard University, Chemistry Library, Cambridge, MA [*Library symbol Library of Congress*] (LCLS)
MHC............	Historical Committee of the Mennonite Church (EA)
MHC............	MAD [*Magnetic Anomaly Detector*] Hunting Circle (NVT)
MHC............	Madras High Court Reports [*India*] [*A publication*] (DLA)
MHC............	Major Histocompatibility Complex [*Immunology*]
MHC............	Manipulator Handset Controller (MCD)
MHC............	Manufactured Home Communities [*NYSE symbol*] (SPSG)
MHC............	Mars Hill College [*North Carolina*]
MHC............	Mary Holmes College, West Point, MS [*OCLC symbol*] (OCLC)
MHC............	Material Handling Crane [*Autocrane*] (MCD)
MHC............	Mean Horizontal Candle [*Aerospace*]
MHC............	Mechanical-Hydraulic Control [*Nuclear energy*] (NRCH)
MHC............	Mental Health Care [*British*] (DAVI)
MHC............	Mental Health Center (MEDA)
MHC............	Mental Health Clinic (DAVI)
MHC............	Mental Health Course [*British*]
MHC............	Mild Hydrocracking [*Petroleum technology*]
MHC............	Minehunter, Coastal [*Navy symbol*]
MHC............	Mobile Housing Carriers Conference Inc., Arlington VA [*STAC*]
MHC............	Modified Huffman Coding (NITA)
MHC............	Moisture Holding Capacity
MHC............	Morgan Horse Club [*Later, American Morgan Horse Association*] (EA)
MHC............	Morris Harvey College [*West Virginia*]
MHC............	Mount Hamilton [*Lick Observatory*] [*California*] [*Seismograph station code, US Geological Survey*] (SEIS)
MHC............	Mount Holyoke College [*South Hadley, MA*]
MHC............	Multiphasic Health Checkup [*Medicine*] (AAMN)
MHC............	Myosin Heavy Chain [*Muscle biology*]
MHCA	Catacamas [*Honduras*] [*ICAO location identifier*] (ICLI)
MHCA	Master of Health Care Administration (GAGS)
MHC & W	Mississippi, Hill City & Western Railroad
MHCAT........	Minehunter Catamaran [*Military*]
MHCC..........	Mobile Housing Carriers Conference [*Defunct*] (EA)
MHCC..........	Multipak Heliax Coaxial Cable
MH-CE	Harvard University, Commission on Extension Courses, Cambridge, MA [*Library symbol Library of Congress*] (LCLS)
MH-CE	Materials Handling and Construction Equipment (DNAB)
MHCG..........	Comayagua [*Honduras*] [*ICAO location identifier*] (ICLI)
MHCH..........	Choluteca [*Honduras*] [*ICAO location identifier*] (ICLI)
MH-CI	Harvard University, Center for International Affairs, Semitic Museum, Cambridge, MA [*Library symbol Library of Congress*] (LCLS)
MHCI	Master of Human-Computer Interaction (PGP)
MHCIMA	Member of the Hotel, Catering, and Institutional Management Association [*British*] (DBQ)
MH-CL	Harvard University, Career Reference Library, Cambridge, MA [*Library symbol Library of Congress*] (LCLS)
MH-CM	Harvard University, Child Memorial and English Tutorial Library, Cambridge, MA [*Library symbol Library of Congress*] (LCLS)
MHCO..........	Marquette & Huron Mountain Railroad Co., Inc. [*AAR code*]
MHCO..........	Mine-Hunting Control Officer (NATG)
MHCO..........	Moore-Handley, Inc. [*Birmingham, AL*] [*NASDAQ symbol*] (NQ)
MHCOA........	Motor, Hearse, and Car Owners Association (EA)
MH-CP........	Harvard University, Center for Population Studies, Boston, MA [*Library symbol Library of Congress*] (LCLS)
MHCP..........	Mean Horizontal Candlepower
MHCR..........	Madras High Court Reports [*India*] [*A publication*] (DLA)
MH-CS	Harvard University, Godfrey Lowell Cabot Science Library, Cambridge, MA [*Library symbol Library of Congress*] (LCLS)
MHCS..........	Mental Hygiene Consultation Service
M/hct.........	Microhematocrit [*Clinical chemistry*]
MHCT..........	Puerto Castilla [*Honduras*] [*ICAO location identifier*] (ICLI)
MHCU..........	Mental Health Care Unit [*Medicine*]
MHD............	Magnetohydrodynamic [*Simulation*] [*Marine science*] (OSRA)
MHD............	Magnetohydrodynamics [*Electric power*]
MHD............	Maintenance Hemodialysis [*Medicine*] (DMAA)
MHD............	Mashhad [*Iran*] [*Airport symbol*] (OAG)
MHD............	Master of Human Development (PGP)
MHD............	Masthead (MSA)
MHD............	Mean Hemolytic Dose [*Pharmacology*] (MAE)
MHD............	Mechanized Hebrew Dictionary [*A publication*] (BJA)
MHD............	Medical Holding Detachment
MHD............	Medium Hard Drawn (MSA)
MHD............	Mental Health Department [*Medicine*]
MHD............	Mental Health Digest
MHD............	Meshed [*Iran*] [*Airport symbol*] (AD)
MHD............	Meter Heading Differential
MHD............	Military History Detachment
MHD............	Minimum Hamming Distance [*Computer science*]
MHD............	Minimum Hemolytic Dose
MHD............	Movable Head Disc (NITA)
MHD............	Moving Head Disk [*Computer science*] (TEL)
MHD............	Multihead Disk (NASA)
MHD............	Multiple Head Disc (NITA)
MHDA	Modified High-Density Acid (MCD)
MHDC..........	Magnetohydrodynamic Conversion [*Nuclear energy*] (NRCH)
MHDDE........	Medium Heavy-Duty Diesel Engine [*Motor vehicle specifications*]
MHDF..........	Medium- and High-Frequency Direction-Finding Station
MHDG..........	Magnetohydrodynamic Generator (PDAA)
MHDI	Morgan Horse Development Institute [*Defunct*] (EA)
MH-DJ	Harvard University, Documentation Center on Contemporary Japan, Cambridge, MA [*Library symbol*] [*Library of Congress*] (LCLS)
MHDL..........	Magnetohydrodynamic LASER (PDAA)
MHDNA........	Mobile Home Dealers National Association [*Defunct*]
MH-DO........	Harvard University, Harvard University Development Office, Cambridge, MA [*Library symbol*] [*Library of Congress*] (LCLS)
MHDPA........	Monohexadecylphosphoric Acid [*Organic chemistry*]
MHDSRIP	May His Departed Soul Rest in Peace (BJA)
MHDU..........	Medical Hemodialysis Unit [*Nephrology*] (DAVI)
MHE............	Maintenance and Handling Equipment
MHE............	Manufactured Home Estates
MHE............	Mass Health & Education Tax-Exempt [*AMEX symbol*] (SPSG)
MHE............	Mass Hlth & Edu Tax-Exempt Tr [*AMEX symbol*] (TTSB)
MHE............	Master of Health Education (GAGS)
MHE............	Master of Higher Education (GAGS)
MHE............	Master of Highway Engineering (NADA)
MHE............	Master of Home Economics (GAGS)
MHE............	Master of Home Economics
MHE............	Master of Home Economics Engineering (NADA)
MHE............	Master of Human Ecology (PGP)
MHE............	Materials Handling Equipment [*Military*] (AFM)
MHE............	Materiel Handling Equipment [*Army*] (INF)

MHE............ Mean Hook Extent (PDAA)
MHE............ Mechanical Handling Equipment (MCD)
MHE............ Mental Health Enquiry [*Medical/computing registers*] [*British*]
MHE............ Missile Handling Equipment
MHE............ Mitchell [*South Dakota*] [*Airport symbol*] (OAG)
MHE............ Mitchell, SD [*Location identifier FAA*] (FAAL)
MHE............ Multiple Headspace Extraction [*Analytical chemistry*]
MHE............ Munitions Handling Equipment (MCD)
MHE............ Muzzle Hatch Electrical
MH-EA .... Harvard University, East Asian Research Center, Cambridge, MA
                [*Library symbol Library of Congress*] (LCLS)
MHEA......... Mechanical Handling Engineers' Association [*British*] (BI)
MHealthAdmin... Master of Health Administration (ADA)
MHEANA...... Masonic Homes Executives' Association of North America (EA)
MH-EB .... Harvard University, Oakes Ames Library of Economic Botany,
                Cambridge, MA [*Library symbol Library of Congress*] (LCLS)
MHeb......... Middle Hebrew [*Language, etc.*] (BJA)
MH Ec......... Master of Home Economics (PGP)
MHEC......... Muzzle Hatch Electrical Control
MH-Ed .... Harvard University, Graduate School of Education, Cambridge, MA
                [*Library symbol Library of Congress*] (LCLS)
MHEd......... Master of Health Education (GAGS)
MHEd......... Master of Higher Education
MHEDA .... Material Handling Equipment Distributors Association (EA)
MHEE......... Master of Home Economics Education (NADA)
MHEEd......... Master of Home Economics Education (NADA)
MHE Ed...... Master of Home Economics Education
MHEF........... Milton H. Erickson Foundation (EA)
MHEO......... Migrant Health Education Officer [*Australia*]
MH-ER .... Harvard University, East Asian Studies Reading Room, Cambridge,
                MA [*Library symbol Library of Congress*] (LCLS)
MH-ES .... Harvard University, Center for European Studies, Cambridge, MA
                [*Library symbol Library of Congress*] (LCLS)
MHET......... Monolithic Hot Electron Transistor (NITA)
MHEX......... Methohexital [*An anesthetic*]
MH-F .... Harvard University, Farlow Reference Library, Cambridge, MA
                [*Library symbol Library of Congress*] (LCLS)
MHF............ Master History File
MHF............ Medium-High Frequency
MHF............ Meridian House Foundation [*Later, MHI*]
MHF............ Microsillon et Haute-Fidelite [*Record label*] [*France*]
MHF............ Mixed Hydrazine Fuel
MHF............ Municipal High Care [*NYSE symbol*] (TTSB)
MHF............ Municipal High Income Fund, Inc. [*NYSE symbol*] (CTT)
MHF............ Myosin Head Fragment [*Biochemistry*]
MHF............ Smith Point, TX [*Location identifier FAA*] (FAAL)
MH-FA .... Harvard University, Fine Arts Library, Cambridge, MA [*Library symbol
                Library of Congress*] (LCLS)
MHFA......... Multiple Conductor, Heat and Flame Resistant, Armor [*Cable*]
MHFB......... Mental Health Film Board (EA)
MHFC......... Merle Haggard Fan Club (EA)
MH/FH .... Man-Hours per Flying Hour [*Air Force*] (DNAB)
MHFPR .... Maximum Hypothetical Fission Product Release [*Nuclear energy*]
                (NRCH)
MHFR .... Maximum Hypothetical Fission Product Release [*Nuclear energy*]
                (NRCH)
MHF(V)......... Mental Health Foundation (Victoria) [*Australia*]
MHFWPR...... Mental Health Fieldwork Performance Report [*Occupational therapy*]
MH-G .... Harvard University, Gray Herbarium, Cambridge, MA [*Library symbol
                Library of Congress*] (LCLS)
MHG .... Mahogany (WGA)
MHG .... Malartic Hygrade Gold Mines Ltd. (MHDW)
MHG .... Mannheim [*Germany Airport symbol*] (OAG)
MHG .... MDS Health Group Ltd. [*Toronto Stock Exchange symbol*]
MHG .... Message Header Generator (PDAA)
MHG .... Middle High German [*Language, etc.*]
MHG .... Midrash ha-Gadol (BJA)
mHg .... Millimeters of Mercury [*A measurement of pressure*] (MAE)
MHG .... Miniature Hydrogen Generator
MHG .... Modern High German [*Language, etc.*] (ROG)
MH-GG......... Harvard University, Committee on Experimental Geology and
                Geophysics, Hoffman Laboratory, Cambridge, MA [*Library symbol
                Library of Congress*] (LCLS)
MH-GI.......... Harvard University, Hamilton A. R. Gibb Islamic Seminar, Cambridge,
                MA [*Library symbol Library of Congress*] (LCLS)
MH-GM .... Harvard University, Gordon McKay Library, Cambridge, MA [*Library
                symbol Library of Congress*] (LCLS)
MH-GS......... Harvard University, Geological Sciences Library, Cambridge, MA
                [*Library symbol Library of Congress*] (LCLS)
MH-H .... Harvard University, Houghton Library, Cambridge, MA [*Library
                symbol Library of Congress*] (LCLS)
MHH .... Mandala Holistic Health [*Defunct*] (EA)
MH-H .... Mare Humorum-Helmet [*Lunar area*]
MHH .... Marsh Harbour [*Bahamas*] [*Airport symbol*] (OAG)
MH-HD......... Harvard University, History Department Library, Cambridge, MA
                [*Library symbol Library of Congress*] (LCLS)
MH-HF .... Harvard University, Harvard Forest Library, Petersham, MA [*Library
                symbol Library of Congress*] (LCLS)
MHHFC .... Machine and Hull History File Card (DNAB)
MH-Hi .... Harvard University, Hilles Library of Radcliffe College, Cambridge,
                MA [*Library symbol Library of Congress*] (LCLS)
MHHI .... Multihandicapped Hearing-Impaired
MH-HJ .... Harvard University, Arnold Arboretum, Horticultural Library, Jamaica
                Plain, MA [*Library symbol Library of Congress*] (LCLS)

MH-HO......... Harvard University, Lucien Howe Library of Ophthalmology, Boston,
                MA [*Library symbol Library of Congress*] (LCLS)
MH-HP......... Harvard University, Center for Analysis of Health Practices,
                Cambridge, MA [*Library symbol Library of Congress*] (LCLS)
MHHPA........ Methylhexahydrophthalic Anhydride [*Organic chemistry*]
MH-HS......... Harvard University, History of Science Library, Cambridge, MA
                [*Library symbol Library of Congress*] (LCLS)
MHHS......... Medal of Honor Historical Society (EA)
MHHW......... Mean Higher High Water [*Tides and currents*]
MHHWS....... Mean Higher High-Water Springs [*Tides and currents*]
MH-HY......... Harvard University, Harvard-Yenching Library, Cambridge, MA
                [*Library symbol Library of Congress*] (LCLS)
MHI............ Manufactured Housing Institute (EA)
MHI............ Marine Hydrophysical Institute
MHI............ Mashhad [*Iran*] [*Seismograph station code, US Geological Survey*]
                (SEIS)
MHi............ Massachusetts Historical Society, Boston, MA [*Library symbol Library
                of Congress*] (LCLS)
MHI............ Material Handling Institute (EA)
MHI............ Mental Health Institute (OICC)
MHI............ Meridian House International (EA)
MHI............ Military Health Institute
MHI............ Military History Institute [*Army*] (MCD)
MHI............ Mitsubishi Heavy Industries
MHI............ Mitsubishi Heavy Industries Ltd.
MHI............ Morgan Hydrocarbons, Inc. [*Toronto Stock Exchange symbol*]
MHI............ Morrison Health Care, Inc. [*NYSE symbol*] (SAG)
MHIA......... Mitsubishi Heavy Industries America, Inc.
MH-IC......... Harvard University, Collection of Historic Scientific Instruments
                Collection, Cambridge, MA [*Library symbol*] [*Library of
                Congress*] (LCLS)
MHIC .... Islas Del Cisne O Santanilla [*Honduras*] [*ICAO location identifier*]
                (ICLI)
MH-ID......... Harvard University, Harvard Institute for International Development,
                Cambridge, MA [*Library symbol*] [*Library of Congress*] (LCLS)
MHID .... Medical and Health Information Directory [*A publication*]
MHIDAS....... Major Hazard Incident Data Service [*Atomic Energy Authority*] [*British
                Information service or system*] (IID)
M Hi E......... Master of Highway Engineering
M Hi Eng .... Master of Highway Engineering
MHIFC......... Michael Harding International Fan Club (EA)
MHIFM......... Milton Helpern Institute of Forensic Medicine (EA)
MHILC......... Hampshire Inter-Library Center, Inc., Amherst, MA [*Library symbol
                Library of Congress Obsolete*] (LCLS)
MHingM........ Hingham Marine Museum, Hingham, MA [*Library symbol Library of
                Congress*] (LCLS)
MHIP .... Missile Homing Improvement Program (DWSG)
MHJ .... Microwave Hybrid Junction
MHJU......... Juticalpa [*Honduras*] [*ICAO location identifier*] (ICLI)
MHK............ Manhattan [*Kansas*] [*Seismograph station code, US Geological
                Survey*] (SEIS)
MHK............ Manhattan [*Kansas*] [*Airport symbol*] (OAG)
MHK............ Manhattan, KS [*Location identifier FAA*] (FAAL)
MHK............ Master of Human Kinetics (GAGS)
MHK............ Member of the House of Keys [*Isle Of Man*] [*British*]
MHK............ Military History of Korea
MHK............ Morgan Stanley Group, Inc. [*AMEX symbol*] (SAG)
MH-KG......... Harvard University, Kennedy School of Government, Cambridge, MA
                [*Library symbol Library of Congress*] (LCLS)
MH-KM .... Harvard University, Kennedy Inter-Faculty Program in Medical Ethics,
                Cambridge, MA [*Library symbol Library of Congress*] (LCLS)
MHKVLY....... Mohawk Valley (FAAC)
MHL............ Hamline University, School of Law, St. Paul, MN [*OCLC symbol*]
                (OCLC)
MH-L......... Harvard University, Law School, Cambridge, MA [*Library symbol
                Library of Congress*] (LCLS)
M (HL)......... House of Lords' Appeals, in Macpherson's Court of Sessions Cases,
                Third Series [*1862-73*] [*Scotland*] [*A publication*] (DLA)
MHL............ March Resources [*Vancouver Stock Exchange symbol*]
MHL............ Marshall Islands [*ANSI three-letter standard code*] (CNC)
MHL............ Marshall, MO [*Location identifier FAA*] (FAAL)
MHL............ Master of Hebrew Letters (BJA)
MHL............ Master of Hebrew Literature
MHL............ Master of Humane Letters
MHL............ Mast Hull Loop
MHL............ Metastable Helium Level
MHL............ Microprocessor Host Loader [*Electronics*]
MHL............ Minimum Helium Loss [*System*]
MHI............ Morrison Health Care [*NYSE symbol*] (TTSB)
MHLA......... McGraw-Hill Learning Architecture
MHLC......... La Ceiba/Goloson Internacional [*Honduras*] [*ICAO location
                identifier*] (ICLI)
MHLC......... Multidimensional Health Locus of Control [*Diagnostic scale*]
MHLE......... La Esperanza [*Honduras*] [*ICAO location identifier*] (ICLI)
MHLH......... Myogenic Helix-Loop-Helix [*Genetics*]
MH-Li .... Harvard University, Linguistics Library, Cambridge, MA [*Library
                symbol Library of Congress*] (LCLS)
MHLLDA....... Mobile Home Landscapers and Landscape Designers Association
                (EA)
MH-Lm .... Harvard University, Lamont Undergraduate Library, Cambridge, MA
                [*Library symbol Library of Congress*] (LCLS)
MHLM......... San Pedro Sula/La Mesa Internacional [*Honduras*] [*ICAO location
                identifier*] (ICLI)
MHLP......... Mental Health Law Project (EA)
MHLS......... Metabolic Heat Load Simulator

MHLS..........	Mid-Hudson Library System [*Library network*]
MHLTA........	Men's Hat Linings and Trimmings Association [*Defunct*] (EA)
MHLW	Mean Higher Low Water [*Tides and currents*]
MHM	Master of Hotel Management (PGP)
MHM	Mental Health Management [*AMEX symbol*] (SPSG)
MHM	Metal-Hydrogen-Metal [*Chemical bond*]
MHM	MHM Services [*AMEX symbol*] (SAG)
MHM	MHM Services [*AMEX symbol*] (TTSB)
mhm	Mill Hill Missionaries (TOCD)
MHM	Mill Hill Missionaries [*Roman Catholic men's religious order*]
MHM	Minchumina, AK [*Location identifier FAA*] (FAAL)
MHM	Minimum Hardware Modification [*Aircraft landing*]
MHM	Mount Hope Mineral Railroad Co. [*Absorbed into Consolidated Rail Corp.*] [*AAR code*]
MHM	Muzzle Hatch Mechanical
MHMA	Marcala [*Honduras*] [*ICAO location identifier*] (ICLI)
MHMA	Master House Movers' Association [*Australia*]
MHMA	Mobile Home Manufacturers Association [*Later, Manufactured Housing Institute*]
MHMC	Mental Health Materials Center (EA)
MH-ME	Harvard University, Center for Middle Eastern Studies, Cambridge, MA [*Library symbol Library of Congress*] (LCLS)
MHME..........	More Heart More Edge [*Screenwriter's lexicon*]
MHMey........	Meyerson [*M.H.*] & Co. [*Associated Press*] (SAG)
MHMeyer......	Meyerson [*M.H.*] & Co. [*Associated Press*] (SAG)
MH-MH	Harvard University, John Peabody Monks Library, Cambridge, MA [*Library symbol Library of Congress*] (LCLS)
MH-ML	Harvard University, Ticknor Library of Modern Languages, Cambridge, MA [*Library symbol Library of Congress*] (LCLS)
MH/MR	Mental Health and Mental Retardation (DAVI)
MHMS	Master of Health Management Systems (PGP)
MHMS	Master of Human Movement Studies (ADA)
MHMS	Material Handling and Management Society (EAIO)
MHMS	Modular Hydrologic Modeling System [*Marine science*] (OSRA)
MHMS	Modular Hydrologic Modeling System (USDC)
MHM Serv ...	MHM Services [*Associated Press*] (SAG)
MH-Mu	Harvard University, Music Library, Cambridge, MA [*Library symbol Library of Congress*] (LCLS)
MHMY	Meyerson [*M.H.*] & Co. [*NASDAQ symbol*] (SAG)
MHMY	M.H. Meyerson & Co. [*NASDAQ symbol*] (TTSB)
MHMYW	M H Meyerson & Co. Wrtt [*NASDAQ symbol*] (TTSB)
MHN	Manhattan Mineral [*Vancouver Stock Exchange symbol*]
MHN	Mannitol Hexanitrate [*Organic chemistry*]
MHN	Massive Hepatic Necrosis [*Medicine*] (MAE)
MHN	McGraw-Hill News [*Database*] (IT)
MHN	Mullen, NE [*Location identifier FAA*] (FAAL)
MHNAMT	Methyl(hydroxylnaphthalamino)mercaptotriazole [*Organic chemistry*]
MH-NE........	Harvard University, Near Eastern Languages and Literatures Library, Cambridge, MA [*Library symbol Library of Congress*] (LCLS)
MHNGS........	Marble Hill Nuclear Generating Station (NRCH)
MHNJ..........	Guanaja [*Honduras*] [*ICAO location identifier*] (ICLI)
MH-NJ	Harvard University, Nieman Collection of Contemporary Journalism, Cambridge, MA [*Library symbol Library of Congress*] (LCLS)
MHNPS	Marble Hill Nuclear Power Station (NRCH)
MHNV	Nuevo Ocotepeque [*Honduras*] [*ICAO location identifier*] (ICLI)
MH-O	Harvard University, Harvard College Observatory, Cambridge, MA [*Library symbol Library of Congress*] (LCLS)
MHO	Manchester Resources Corp. [*Vancouver Stock Exchange symbol*]
MHO	Millhouse Developments Ltd. [*British ICAO designator*] (FAAC)
MHO	Minehunter Ocean [*Navy*] (ANA)
MHO	M/I Schottenstein Homes, Inc. [*NYSE symbol*] (SPSG)
MHO	Mohanbari [*India*] [*Airport symbol*] (AD)
MHO	Mount Hopkins Observatory [*Later, FLWO*] [*Smithsonian Institution*] (GRD)
mho	Reciprocal Ohm [*Unit of conductance*]
MHOA	Mutual Help and Occupancy Agreement [*Department of Housing and Urban Development*] (GFGA)
MHOA	Olanchito [*Honduras*] [*ICAO location identifier*] (ICLI)
M Ho Ec	Master of Household Economy
MHOF	Mobile Home Owners Federation [*NFMHO*] [*Superseded by*] (EA)
MH/OH	Man Hours per Operating Hour [*Maintenance*] (RDA)
MHoly	Holyoke Public Library, Holyoke, MA [*Library symbol Library of Congress*] (LCLS)
MHolyC........	Holyoke Community College, Holyoke, MA [*Library symbol Library of Congress*] (LCLS)
M Hor	Master of Horticulture
MHort(RHS)...	National Diploma in Horticulture (Royal Horticultural Society) [*British*] (DBQ)
MHortSc	Master of Horticultural Science
M Ho Sc	Master of Household Science
MH-P	Harvard University, Peabody Museum, Cambridge, MA [*Library symbol Library of Congress*] (LCLS)
MHp	Harwich Port Library Association, Harwich Port, MA [*Library symbol Library of Congress*] (LCLS)
MHP	Maclean Hunter Ltd. [*Toronto Stock Exchange symbol*]
MHP	Master of Health Planning (ADA)
MHP	Master of Health Professions (PGP)
MHP	Master of Heritage Preservation (GAGS)
MHP	Master of Historical Preservation (GAGS)
MHP	Master of Humanities in Philosophy (PGP)
MHP	McGraw-Hill Companies [*NYSE symbol*] (TTSB)
MHP	McGraw-Hill, Inc. [*NYSE symbol*] (SPSG)
MHP	Medium-High Pressure (MSA)
MHP	Mental Health Project
MHP..........	Mercurihydroxypropane [*Clinical chemistry*]
MHP	Message Handling Processor
MHP..........	Metabolic Heat Production [*Physiology*]
MHP..........	Military Health Plan [*DoD*]
MHP..........	Milli Hedef Partisi [*National Goal Party*] [*Turkish Cyprus*] [*Political party*] (PPE)
MH-PA........	Harvard University, Littauer Library of the Kennedy School of Government, Cambridge, MA [*Library symbol Library of Congress*] (LCLS)
MHPA	Palmerola [*Honduras*] [*ICAO location identifier*] (ICLI)
MH-PC........	Harvard University, Palaeography Library, Cambridge, MA [*Library symbol Library of Congress*] (LCLS)
MHPD	Masonite Hydropress Die (MSA)
MHPE	Master of Health Professions Education (PGP)
MHPE	Methoxy-Hydroxyphenylethanol [*Organic chemistry*] (MAH)
MHPE	Progreso [*Honduras*] [*ICAO location identifier*] (ICLI)
MH PE & R...	Master of Health, Physical Education, and Recreation
MHPE Conj...	Methoxy-Hydroxyphenylethanol Conjugate [*Organic chemistry*] (DAVI)
MHPEd..........	Master of Health Personnel Education (ADA)
MHPG	(Methoxyhydroxyphenyl)ethyleneglycol [*Also, MOPEG*] [*Organic chemistry*]
MHPG Conj...	Methoxyhydropheny Gylcol Conjugate [*Organic chemistry*] (DAVI)
MHPH	Man-Hours per Flying Hour [*Air Force*] (AFIT)
MH-PL	Harvard University, Milman Parry Collection of Oral Literature, Cambridge, MA [*Library symbol Library of Congress*] (LCLS)
MHPL	Puerto Lempira [*Honduras*] [*ICAO location identifier*] (ICLI)
MH-PO........	Harvard University, Personnel Office Library, Cambridge, MA [*Library symbol Library of Congress*] (LCLS)
MH-PP........	Harvard University, Public Policy Program, Cambridge, MA [*Library symbol Library of Congress*] (LCLS)
MH-PR........	Harvard University, Physics Research Library, Cambridge, MA [*Library symbol Library of Congress*] (LCLS)
MH-Ps	Harvard University, Psychology Research Library, Cambridge, MA [*Library symbol Library of Congress*] (LCLS)
MHPU	Puerto Cortes [*Honduras*] [*ICAO location identifier*] (ICLI)
MH-Pv	Harvard University, Preservation Center, Cambridge, MA [*Library symbol*] [*Library of Congress*] (LCLS)
MHQ	Mariehamn [*Finland*] [*Airport symbol*] (OAG)
MHQ	Maritime Headquarters (NVT)
MH-R	Harvard University, Russian Research Center, Cambridge, MA [*Library symbol Library of Congress*] (LCLS)
MHR	Major Histocompatibility Region [*Immunology*]
MHR	Major Homology Region [*Biochemistry*]
MHR	Malignant Hyperthermia Resistance [*Medicine*] (DMAA)
MHR	Man-Hour
MHR	Master of Human Resources (GAGS)
MHR	Maximum Heart Rate
MHR	McGraw-Hill Ryerson Ltd. [*Toronto Stock Exchange symbol*]
MHR	Measurement Handicap Rule [*Sailing*]
MHR	Medical Humanities Review [*A publication*] (BRI)
MHR	Member of the House of Representatives
MHR	Methemoglobin Reductase [*Hematology and laboratory*] (DAVI)
MHR	Microwave Hologram RADAR
MHR	Miniature Helium Refrigerator
MHR	Missile Hazard Report (AFM)
MHR	Mount Hamilton Road [*California*] [*Seismograph station code, US Geological Survey*] (SEIS)
MHr	Myohemerythrin [*Biochemistry*]
MHR	Sacramento, CA [*Location identifier FAA*] (FAAL)
MHR	United States Army Military History Institute, Carlisle Barracks, PA [*OCLC symbol*] (OCLC)
MH-RA........	Harvard University, Harvard Radio Astronomy Center, Fort Davis, TX [*Library symbol Library of Congress*] (LCLS)
MHRA	Modern Humanities Research Association, American Branch [*Defunct*] (EA)
MHRA	Morab Horse Registry of America (EA)
MHRAC	Mine Health Research Advisory Committee [*National Institute for Occupational Safety and Health*] [*Morgantown, WV*] (EGAO)
MH-RB........	Harvard University, Rubel Asiatic Research Bureau, Fogg Art Museum, Cambridge, MA [*Library symbol Library of Congress Obsolete*] (LCLS)
MHRB	Mental Health Review Board [*Victoria, Australia*]
MH-RC........	Harvard University, Fred N. Robinson Celtic Seminar, Cambridge, MA [*Library symbol Library of Congress*] (LCLS)
MHRD	Master in Human Resource Department (PGP)
MH-RI..........	Harvard University, RISM-US Project Center, Cambridge, MA [*Library symbol*] [*Library of Congress*] (LCLS)
MHRI	Mental Health Research Institute [*University of Michigan*] [*Research center*]
MHRIM	Master of Hotel, Restaurant, and Institutional Management (PGP)
MHRIR	Master of Human Resources and Industrial Relations (PGP)
MHRp	Master of Human Resources Management (PGP)
MHRM	Microcomputers in Human Resource Management [*Advanced Personnel Systems*] [*Information service or system*] (CRD)
MHROD	Master of Human Resources and Organization Development (PGP)
MH-RP........	Harvard University, Robbins Library of Philosophy, Cambridge, MA [*Library symbol Library of Congress*] (LCLS)
MHRS	Magnetic Heading Reference System
MHRST	Medical and Health Related Sciences Thesaurus [*A publication*] (IEEE)
MHRT	Mental Health Review Tribunal [*British*]
MHRTA	Masters in Hotel, Restaurant, Tourism, and Administration (PGP)
MHRU	Ruinas De Copan [*Honduras*] [*ICAO location identifier*] (ICLI)
MHRV	Movement for Human Rights in Vietnam [*Defunct*] (EA)

MH-S .... Harvard University, Statistics Library, Cambridge, MA [*Library symbol Library of Congress*] (LCLS)
MHS............. Machined Hemispherical Shell
MHS............. Magnetic Heading System (AAG)
MHS............. Magnetomotive Hammer System
MHS............. Maher, Inc. [*Toronto Stock Exchange symbol*]
MHS............. Mail Handling System [*Computer science*]
MHS............. Major Histocompatibility System [*Immunology*]
MHS............. Malignant Hyperthermia Susceptible [*Medicine*]
MHS............. Malignant Hypothermia Susceptible [*Patients*] [*Emergency medicine*] (DAVI)
MHS............. Mammoth Hot Springs [*Wyoming*] [*Seismograph station code, US Geological Survey*] (SEIS)
MHS............. Man-Hours per Sortie [*Air Force*] (AFIT)
MHS............. Marine Hospital Service [*Public Health Service*]
MHS............. Master Hotel Supplier [*Educational Institute of the American Hotel and M otel Association*] [*Designation awarded by*]
MHS............. Master of Health Sciences (PGP)
MHS............. Master of Health Services (GAGS)
MHS............. Master of Hispanic Studies (PGP)
MHS............. Master of Humane Studies (PGP)
MHS............. Master of Human Services (GAGS)
MHS............. Maximum Histalog Stimulation [*Gastroenterology*] (DAVI)
MHS............. McMaster University Health Sciences Library [*UTLAS symbol*]
MHS............. Measurement Handicapping System [*Yacht racing*]
MHS............. Mechanical Handling System
MHS............. Member of the Historical Society
MHS............. Message Handling Service [*Telecommunications*] (PCM)
MHS............. Message Handling System [*Computer science*]
MHS............. Methylhydrazine Sulfate [*Organic chemistry*]
M/H/S .... Miles per Hour per Second
MHS............. Military Historical Society [*Defunct*] (EA)
MHS............. Ministry of Home Security [*British*]
MHS............. Minnesota Historical Society, St. Paul, MN [*OCLC symbol*] (OCLC)
MHS............. Missile Hazard Space (AFM)
MHS............. Moravian Historical Society (EA)
MHS............. Mount Shasta, CA [*Location identifier FAA*] (FAAL)
MHS............. Multiple Hospital System
MHS............. Multiple Host Support
MHS............. Musical Heritage Society [*Commercial firm*] (EA)
MHS............. Sisters of the Most Holy Sacrament [*Roman Catholic religious order*]
MHSA .... Master of Health Services Administration (DD)
MHSA .... Master of Health Services Administration (GAGS)
MHSA .... Master of Human Services Administration (PGP)
MH-SC .... Harvard University, Herbert Weir Smyth Classical Library, Cambridge, MA [*Library symbol Library of Congress*] (LCLS)
MHSC .... Manipulator Handset Controller (MCD)
MH Sc .... Master of Health Sciences (PGP)
MHSC .... Mental Health Study Center [*National Institute of Mental Health*] (GRD)
MHSCP .... Mean Hemispherical Candlepower
MH-SD .... Harvard University, Graduate School of Design, Cambridge, MA [*Library symbol Library of Congress*] (LCLS)
MHSDC .... Multiple High-Speed Data Channel
MHSE .... Master of Health Science Education (PGP)
MH-SF .... Harvard University, Schering Foundation Library, Boston, MA [*Library symbol Library of Congress*] (LCLS)
MHSH .... Mental Health Services for the Homeless [*Department of Health and Human Services*] (GFGA)
MHSH .... Mission Helpers of the Sacred Heart [*Roman Catholic women's religious order*]
MH-SI .... Harvard University, Program for Science and International Affairs Library, Cambridge, MA [*Library symbol Library of Congress*] (LCLS)
MHSIP .... Mental Health Statistics Improvement Program [*Department of Health and Human Services*] (GFGA)
MH-SL .... Harvard University, Sanskrit Library, Cambridge, MA [*Library symbol Library of Congress*] (LCLS)
MHSLN .... Midwest Health Science Library Network [*Library network*]
MHSM .... Mason & Hanger-Silas Mason Co., Inc. (RDA)
MHSO .... Masada, the Holocaust Survivors Organization (EA)
MHSO .... Minehunter Sweeper Ocean [*Navy*] (ANA)
MH-SP .... Harvard University, Science and Public Police Program Library, Cambridge, MA [*Library symbol Library of Congress*] (LCLS)
MHSP .... Municipal Health Services Program [*Department of Health and Human Services*] (GFGA)
MHSP .... San Pedro Sula [*Honduras*] [*ICAO location identifier*] (ICLI)
MH-SR........ Harvard University, Social Relations Library, Cambridge, MA [*Library symbol Library of Congress*] (LCLS)
MHSR .... Santa Rosa De Copan [*Honduras*] [*ICAO location identifier*] (ICLI)
MHSS .... Materials Handling Support System [*Military*] (AFM)
MHSS .... Mental Health Special Interest Section [*American Occupational Therapy Association*]
MHSS .... Message Handling System Service (NITA)
MHSS .... Military Health Service System
MHSS(NI) .... Ministry of Health and Social Services (Northern Ireland)
MHSSRI....... Michigan Health and Social Security Research Institute [*Detroit, MI*] [*Research center*] (RCD)
MHST.......... Multiphasic Health Screen Test (DAVI)
MHSTB .... Mental Handicap Staff Training Board [*British*]
MHSV .... Multipurpose High-Speed Vehicle (MCD)
MHSZ.......... Santa Barbara [*Honduras*] [*ICAO location identifier*] (ICLI)
MHT............. Maghemite, Inc. [*Vancouver Stock Exchange symbol*]
MHT............. Main Himalayan Thrust [*Geology*]
MHT............. Manchester [*New Hampshire*] [*Airport symbol*] (OAG)

MHT............. Manchester, NH [*Location identifier FAA*] (FAAL)
MHT............. Manhattan [*Kansas*] [*Seismograph station code, US Geological Survey Closed*] (SEIS)
MHT............. Manufacturers Hanover Trust Co. [*of Manufacturers Hanover Corp.*] [*Nickname: "Manny Hanny"*]
MHT............. Mean High Tide [*Tides and currents*]
MHT............. Methyl(hydroxyethyl)thiazole [*Organic chemistry*]
MHT............. Meyer Hydraulic Theory
MHT............. Mild Heat Treatment (IEEE)
MHT............. Missile Handling Trailer (AAG)
MHT............. Museum of History and Technology [*Smithsonian Institution*]
MHTA.......... Molten High-Temperature Alloy
MHTE.......... Tela [*Honduras*] [*ICAO location identifier*] (ICLI)
MHTF.......... Manufactured Housing Task Force [*Defunct*] (EA)
MHTG.......... Marine Helicopter Training Group (NVT)
MHTG.......... Tegucigalpa/Toncontin Internacional [*Honduras*] [*ICAO location identifier*] (ICLI)
MHTGR........ Modular High-Temperature Gas Reactor [*Nuclear energy*]
MHTJ.......... Trujillo [*Honduras*] [*ICAO location identifier*] (ICLI)
MHTL.......... Motorola High-Threshold Logic
MHTS.......... Main Heat Transport System [*Nuclear energy*] (NRCH)
MHTTA........ Member of the Highway and Traffic Technicians Association [*British*] (DBQ)
MHTV.......... Manned Hypersonic Test Vehicle (MCD)
M Hu .... Master of Humanities
MHU........... Material Handling Unit (AFIT)
MHUD......... Monocular Heads-Up Display [*Aviation*]
MHuGH....... John H. Glenn High School, Huntington, NY [*Library symbol Library of Congress*] (LCLS)
M Hum .... Master of Humanities
M Hum Svcs... Master of Human Services (PGP)
MH-UR........ Harvard University, Ukrainian Research Institute Reference Library, Cambridge, MA [*Library symbol Library of Congress*] (LCLS)
MHV........... Magnetic Heart Vector [*Cardiology*]
MHV........... Manned Hypersonic Vehicle
MHV........... Mean Horizontal Velocity
MHV........... Miniature Homing Vehicle [*Missile*]
MHV........... Mojave, CA [*Location identifier FAA*] (FAAL)
MHV........... Mouse Hepatitis Virus
MHV........... Murine Hepatitis Virus
MHVD......... Marek's Herpesvirus Disease [*Avian pathology*] (MAE)
MHVDF........ Medium-, High-, and Very-High-Frequency Direction-Finding Station
MHVPS........ Manual High-Voltage Power Supply
MHW.......... Mean High Water [*Tides and currents*]
MHW.......... Medial Heel Wedge [*Orthopedics*] (DAVI)
MHW.......... Merrill Lynch & Co. [*AMEX symbol*] (SAG)
MHW.......... Ministry of Health and Welfare [*Japan*] (ECON)
MHW.......... Morgan, H. W., Los Angeles CA [*STAC*]
MHW.......... Multihundred Watt
MH-WA........ Harvard University, Charles Warren Center for Studies in American History, Cambridge, MA [*Library symbol Library of Congress*] (LCLS)
MHWI......... Mean High-Water Lunitidal Interval [*Tides and currents*]
MHWLR....... Mobile Hostile Weapon Locating RADAR (NATG)
MHWN........ Mean High-Water Neap [*Tides and currents*]
MHW-RTG ... Multi-Hundred-Watt Radioisotope Thermoelectric Generator (PDAA)
MHWS......... Mean High-Water Springs [*Tides and currents*]
M Hx .... Medical History (MAE)
MHX........... Mine Hunter Experimental
MHy .... Hyannis Public Library, Hyannis, MA [*Library symbol Library of Congress*] (LCLS)
MHY........... Managed High Income Portfolio [*NYSE symbol*] (SPSG)
MHY........... Managed High Inc. Portfolio [*NYSE symbol*] (TTSB)
M Hy .... Master of Hygiene
MHY........... Morehead [*Papua New Guinea*] [*Airport symbol*] (OAG)
M Hyg .... Master of Hygiene
MHyT.......... State Teachers' College, Hyannis, MA [*Library symbol Library of Congress Obsolete*] (LCLS)
MH-Z .... Harvard University, Museum of Comparative Zoology, Cambridge, MA [*Library symbol Library of Congress*] (LCLS)
MHz .... Megahertz [*Megacycles per Second*] [*See also MCPS, MCS, MC/S, MH*]
MHz .... Megahertz [*Megacycles per Second*]
MHZ............ Millihertz (WDAA)
MI .... Lab. Miquel [*Spain*] [*Research code symbol*]
MI .... Mach Indicated
MI .... Machine Independent
MI .... Machine Intelligence (RDA)
MI .... Mackey International Airlines [*ICAO designator*] (AD)
MI .... Mackey International, Inc. [*USA*] [*ICAO designator*] (OAG)
MI .... Madras Infantry [*British*]
MI .... Magazine Index [*Information Access Corp.*] [*Information service or system*] (IID)
MI .... Maintenance Instruction (AAG)
MI .... Major Issue (MCD)
MI .... Major Item [*Military*]
MI .... Malachi [*Old Testament book*] (BJA)
MI .... Malleable Iron
MI .... Management Information (CAAL)
MI .... Management Intern
MI .... Manual Individual [*Nuclear energy*] (NRCH)
MI .... Manual Input [*Computer science*]
MI .... Manufacturing Index (MCD)
MI .... Manufacturing Industries [*Department of Employment*] [*British*]
MI .... Manufacturing Inspector (FAAC)

MI	Manufacturing Instruction (MSA)
MI	Marconi Industries [General Electric Co.] [British]
MI	Mare Imbrium [Sea of Showers] [Lunar area]
MI	Mare Island, California [Site of naval base]
MI	Marginal Income [Economics]
MI	Marine Insurance
MI	Marine Investigation (LAIN)
MI	Market Identifiers [Dun's Marketing Services] [Database]
MI	Market Investigation [Army]
MI	Marshall Indus [NYSE symbol] (TTSB)
MI	Marshall Industries [NYSE symbol] (SPSG)
MI	Marshall Islands
MI	Master Index
MI	Master Item (MSA)
MI	Master of Instruction (PGP)
MI	Master of Insurance (GAGS)
MI	Match Institute [Defunct] (EA)
MI	Material Inspection [Navy]
MI	Maturation Index (MAE)
MI	Meat Inspection Division [of ARS, Department of Agriculture]
MI	Mechanical Impedance
M/I	Mechanical Impulse (KSC)
MI	Meconium Ileus [Medicine]
MI	Medical Illustrator
MI	Medical Improvement [Social Security Administration]
MI	Medical Inspection
MI	Medium Intensity (MSA)
MI	Melanophore Index [Biology]
MI	Mellon Institute [Carnegie-Mellon University] [Research center] (RCD)
MI	Meloidogyne incognita [A nematode]
MI	Melt Inclusions [Geology]
MI	Memorial Inscription
MI	Memory Interface
MI	Mensa International [British] (EAIO)
MI	Menstrual Induction [Medicine]
MI	Mental Illness
MI	(Mercaptoethyl)trimethylammonium Iodide [Pharmacology]
MI	Mercaptoimidazole [Organic chemistry] (MAE)
MI	Merit Increase (MHDW)
MI	Merritt Island [Florida] [NASA] (KSC)
MI	Mesha Inscription (BJA)
MI	Mesioincisal [Dentistry]
MI	Meso-Inositol [or Myoinositol] [Organic chemistry]
MI	Metabolic Index
MI	Metal-to-Insulator [Transition]
MI	Metastases below the Head and Neck [Oncology]
MI	Method Index [British police term]
MI	Methods Instruction (DNAB)
MI	Methylindole [Organic chemistry]
M-I	Metro-International Program Services of New York (EA)
Mi	Mica [A mineral]
Mi	Micah [Old Testament book]
MI	Michelson Interferometer (PDAA)
MI	Michigan [Postal code]
MI	Michigan Reports [A publication] (DLA)
Mi	Michigan State Library, Lansing, MI [Library symbol Library of Congress] (LCLS)
MI	Microbiological Inputs [Canning] (DICI)
MI	Microinch (IAA)
MI	Microinstruction [Computer science]
MI	Micru International (EA)
MI	Middle Initial
MI	Middle Iron Age (BJA)
MI	Migration Index [Immunology]
MI	Migration Inhibition [Cytology]
MI	Mil [Former USSR ICAO aircraft manufacturer identifier] (ICAO)
MI	Mile
mi	Mile
MI	Mile
MI	Military Institute
MI	Military Intelligence [Army]
MI	Military Internee
MI	Military Item
MI	Militia Mariae Immaculatae [Militia of the Immaculate] (EAIO)
MI	Mill
MI	Miller Integrator
MI	Mineral Insulated [Cable] (NRCH)
MI	Miniaturized Instrumentation (MCD)
M/I	Minimum Impulse (KSC)
MI	Ministry of Information [British World War II]
MI	Minor (ROG)
MI	Minority Institution
MI	Minority Interest [Business term]
MI	Minute (ADA)
MI	Miscellaneous Income (MHDW)
MI	Mishnah [Basis of the Talmud] (BJA)
MI	Missed Interception [Military]
MI	Missile (CINC)
MI	Missile Industry (AAG)
MI	Missionary Internship [An association] (EA)
MI	Mission Independent [NASA]
MI	Mississippi [Obsolete] (ROG)
MI	Missouri-Illinois Railroad Co. [AAR code]
Mi	Mitomycin C [Also, MMC, MTC] [Antineoplastic drug]

MI	Mitotic Indices [Cytology]
MI	Mitral Incompetence [Cardiology]
MI	Mitral Insufficiency [Cardiology]
MI	Mixed Income
MI	Mobility Impairment (NVT)
MI	Mobility International (EA)
MI	Mode Indicator (HGAA)
MI	Moderately Included [Colored gemstone grade]
MI	Modification Instructions (KSC)
MI	Moment of Inertia
MI	Monetary Incentive
MI	Money Stock [British] (DCTA)
MI	Monitoring Information (NITA)
MI	Monitor Inspection (AFM)
MI	Monitor International (ASF)
MI	Monument Inscription [Genealogy]
MI	Moose, International (EAIO)
MI	Morphologic Index [Volume of trunk divided by length of limbs]
MI	[The] Mortgage Index [Hale Systems, Inc.] [Information service or system] (CRD)
MI	Mortgage Insurance (EMRF)
MI	Motility Index [Of intestine] [Gastroenterology]
MI	Motorola Interconnect [Electronics]
MI	Mounted Infantry
MI	Move In (WDMC)
MI	Movement Instruction [British military] (DMA)
MI	Multi-Industry Interest
MI	Multiple Instruction (HGAA)
MI	Murphy International Transport [Commercial firm British]
MI	Muskies, Inc. (EA)
MI	Mutual Inductance
MI	Mutual Interference
MI	Myocardial Infarction [Cardiology]
MI	Myo-Inositol [Chemistry] [Dietetics] (DAVI)
MI	Writ of Mandamus Will Issue [Legal term] (DLA)
mi²	Square Mile (CDAI)
MI³MS	Minolta Integrated Information and Image Management System [Optical disc] (IT)
MI5	Military Intelligence [State security] [British] (ODBW)
MI6	Military Intelligence [Espionage] [British] (ODBW)
MiA	Alma Public Library, Alma, MI [Library symbol Library of Congress] (LCLS)
MIA	AMI (Air Mercury International) [Belgium ICAO designator] (FAAC)
MIA	[An] Introduction to the Apocrypha [B. Metzger] [A publication] (BJA)
MIA	Manchester International Airport [British] (DS)
MIA	Manila International Airport
MIA	Marble Institute of America (EA)
MIA	Maritime Information Association [British] (EAIO)
MIA	Master of Industrial Arts
MIA	Master of Intercultural Administration (PGP)
MIA	Master of Internal Affairs (NADA)
MIA	Master of International Administration (PGP)
MIA	Master of International Affairs (GAGS)
MIA	Master of International Affairs
MIA	Medical Indemnity of America, Inc. (DHSM)
MIA	Medically Indigent Adult (MEDA)
MIA	Medically Indigent Adult (DAVI)
MIA	Member of the Institute of Arbitrators [British]
MIA	Metal Interface Amplifier
MIA	Methylisatoic Anhydride [Organic chemistry]
MIA	Miami [Florida] [Seismograph station code, US Geological Survey Closed] (SEIS)
MIA	Miami [Florida] [Airport symbol] (OAG)
MIA	Miami University, Oxford, OH [OCLC symbol] (OCLC)
MIA	Mica Industry Association [Defunct] (EA)
MIA	Military Inspection Agency (NATG)
MIA	Military Intelligence Agency (MCD)
MIA	Millinery Institute of America [Later, MIB] (EA)
MIA	Minimum IFR Altitude [FAA] (TAG)
MIA	Minimum Instrument Altitude [Aviation] (AFM)
MIA	Missile Intelligence Agency (AABC)
MIA	Missing in Action [Military]
MIA	Mission-Independent Area [NASA]
MIA	Monoiodoacetic Acid [Organic chemistry]
MIA	Moore's Indian Appeals [A publication] (DLA)
MIA	"Mouse in Able" Program
MIA	Multiflex Interface Adapter
MIA	Multiplexer Interface Adapter (NASA)
MIA	Multiplex Interface Adapter (NASA)
MIA	Murrumbidgee Irrigation Area [Australia] (BARN)
MIA	Music Industries Association [British] (DBA)
MIA	Mutual Improvement Association [Mormon Youth Movement] (BARN)
MIA	Mythmaking in America [A publication]
MiAa	Ann Arbor Public Library, Ann Arbor, MI [Library symbol Library of Congress] (LCLS)
MIAA	Medical Industry Association of Australia
MIAA	Meetings Industry Association of Australia
MIAA	Member of the Incorporated Association of Architects and Surveyors [British] (DBQ)
MIAA	Member of the Institute of Affiliate Accountants (ADA)
MIAA	Member of the Institute of Automobile Assessors [British]
MIAA	Miniatures Industry Association of America
MIAA	Mutual Insurance Advisory Association [Defunct] (EA)
MiAaC	Concordia Lutheran College, Ann Arbor, MI [Library symbol Library of Congress] (LCLS)

MiAaE........... Environmental Research Institute of Michigan, Ann Arbor, MI [*Library symbol Library of Congress*] (LCLS)

MiAaF......... Gerald R. Ford Library, Ann Arbor, MI [*Library symbol*] [*Library of Congress*] (LCLS)

MiAaFL....... Great Lakes Fisheries Laboratory, Ann Arbor, MI [*Library symbol Library of Congress*] (LCLS)

MiAaI........... Inter-University Consortium for Political and Social Research, Ann Arbor, MI [*Library symbol*] [*Library of Congress*] (LCLS)

MiAaK......... KMS Fusion, Inc., Ann Arbor, MI [*Library symbol Library of Congress*] (LCLS)

MiAaP......... Parke, Davis & Co., Research Library, Ann Arbor, MI [*Library symbol Library of Congress*] (LCLS)

MIA(APS)..... Meat Inspectors' Association (Australian Public Service)

MiAaW......... Washtenaw County Library, Ann Arbor, MI [*Library symbol Library of Congress*] (LCLS)

MiAaWC...... Washtenaw Community College, Ann Arbor, MI [*Library symbol Library of Congress*] (LCLS)

MIAB........... Magnetically Impelled Arc Butt [*Welding*] (MCD)

MIAB........... Modular Interchangeable Ambulance Body [*Military British*]

MiAC........... Alma College, Alma, MI [*Library symbol Library of Congress*] (LCLS)

MIAC........... Manufacturing Industries Advisory Council (NADA)

MIAC........... Material Identification Accounting Code

MIAC........... Metals Information Analysis Center (IID)

MIAC........... Minimum Automatic Computer (IEEE)

MIAC........... Multipoint Interactive Audio-Visual Communication (NITA)

MIACF........ Meander Inverted Autocorrelated Function

MIACS........ Manufacturing Information and Control System

MiAd........... Adrian Public Library, Adrian, MI [*Library symbol Library of Congress*] (LCLS)

MiAdC......... Adrian College, Adrian, MI [*Library symbol Library of Congress*] (LCLS)

MiAdL......... Lenawee County Library, Adrian, MI [*Library symbol Library of Congress*] (LCLS)

MIADS........ Map Information Assembly and Display System

MIADS........ Minot Air Defense Sector [*ADC*]

MiAdS......... Siena Heights College, Adrian, MI [*Library symbol Library of Congress*] (LCLS)

MIAE........... Member of the Institution of Automobile Engineers [*British*]

MIAEA......... Member of the Institute of Automotive Engineer Assessors [*British*] (DBQ)

MI Ae E...... Member of the Institute of Aeronautical Engineers [*British*]

MIAEF......... Missed Interception Due to Airborne Equipment Failure [*Air Force*]

MIAeS......... Member of the Institute of Aeronautical Sciences

MIAESR....... Melbourne Institute of Applied Economic and Social Research [*Australia*]

MIAFTR........ Motor Insurance Anti-Fraud and Theft Register [*Database*] [*British*]

MIAG.......... Management Information and Analysis Group (MCD)

MIAgrE....... Member of the Institution of Agricultural Engineers [*British*]

MiAhO .... Oakland Community College, Auburn Heights, MI [*Library symbol Library of Congress*] (LCLS)

MIAIF.......... Meteorological Information for Aircraft in Flight

MIAK........... Methyl Isoamyl Ketone [*Organic chemistry*]

MiAlb.......... Albion Public Library, Albion, MI [*Library symbol Library of Congress*] (LCLS)

MiAlbC........ Albion College, Albion, MI [*Library symbol Library of Congress*] (LCLS)

MiAlbW....... Woodlands Library Cooperative, Albion, MI [*Library symbol Library of Congress*] (LCLS)

MiAld.......... Helena Township Public Library, Alden, MI [*Library symbol Library of Congress*] (LCLS)

MiAll........... Allendale Township Library, Allendale, MI [*Library symbol Library of Congress*] (LCLS)

MiAlle......... Allegan Public Library, Allegan, MI [*Library symbol Library of Congress*] (LCLS)

MiAllG .... Grand Valley State College, Allendale, MI [*Library symbol Library of Congress*] (LCLS)

MiAlmo....... Henry Stephens Memorial Library, Almont, MI [*Library symbol Library of Congress*] (LCLS)

MiAln.......... Alanson Public Library, Alanson, MI [*Library symbol Library of Congress*] (LCLS)

MiAlp.......... Alpena County Library, Alpena, MI [*Library symbol Library of Congress*] (LCLS)

MiAlpC........ Alpena Community College, Alpena, MI [*Library symbol Library of Congress*] (LCLS)

MIALS......... Medium Intensity Approach Light System [*Aviation*] (DA)

MIAM.......... Major Items Automated Management (AAGC)

MIAM.......... MID Am Inc. [*NASDAQ symbol*] (TTSB)

MIAM.......... Mid-Am, Inc. [*NASDAQ symbol*] (NQ)

MIAMA........ Member of the Incorporated Advertising Managers' Association [*British*] (DAS)

MIAME........ Member of the Institute of Automotive Mechanical Engineers (ADA)

MIAMI......... Metoprolol in Acute Myocardial Infarction [*Cardiology study*]

MIAMI......... Microwave Ice Accretion Measurement Instrument (MCD)

MiamiCm..... Miami Computer Supply Corp. [*Associated Press*] (SAG)

Miami LQ .... Miami Law Quarterly [*A publication*] (DLA)

Miami L Rev... Miami Law Review [*Florida*] [*A publication*] (DLA)

Miami U (Ohio)... Miami University (Ohio) (GAGS)

MIAMP........ Mid Am $1.8125 Cv'A'Pfd [*NASDAQ symbol*] (TTSB)

MiamSb....... Miami Subs Corp. [*Associated Press*] (SAG)

MIAMSI....... Mouvement International d'Apostolat des Milieux Sociaux Independants [*International Movement of Apostolate in the Independent Social Milieux*] [*Vatican City*] (EAIO)

MI & RR...... Material Inspection and Receiving Report [*Military*] (KSC)

MIAO .... Master Index Assembly Outline [*Paper*]

MiAp........... Allen Park Public Library, Allen Park, MI [*Library symbol Library of Congress*] (LCLS)

MIAP........... Member of the Institution of Analysts and Programmers [*British*] (DBQ)

MIAP........... Military Incentive Analysis Program (MCD)

MIAPD........ Mid-Central Air Procurement District

MiApDB ...... Detroit Baptist Divinity School, Allen Park, MI [*Library symbol Library of Congress*] (LCLS)

MIAPL......... Master Index of Allowable Parts Lists [*Navy*]

MiApV......... United States Veterans Administration Hospital, Allen Park, MI [*Library symbol Library of Congress*] (LCLS)

MIAQ .... Music Industry Association of Queensland [*Australia*]

MIAR.......... Microaddress Register [*Computer science*] (MHDI)

M I Arch ..... Master of Interior Architecture

MI Arch....... Master of Interior Architecture (PGP)

M I Arch Eng... Master of Interior Architectural Engineering

MiArm .... Armada Free Public Library, Armada, MI [*Library symbol Library of Congress*] (LCLS)

MIARS......... Maintenance Information Automated Retrieval System [*DoD*]

MIARS......... Microfilm Information and Retrieval System (DNAB)

MIAS.......... Maintenance Information Authorizing System (MCD)

MIAS.......... Major Item Automated System [*Army Materiel Command*] (AABC)

MIAS.......... Marine Information and Advisory Service [*Institute of Oceanographic Sciences*] [*Databank*] [*British*] (IID)

MIAS.......... Member of the Incorporated Association of Architects and Surveyors [*British*] (DBQ)

MIAS.......... Member of the Institute of Aeronautical Science [*Later, MAIAA*]

MIAS.......... Monroe Institute of Applied Sciences [*Later, TMI*] (EA)

MIAS.......... Muhyiddin Ibn Arabi Society

MIASA........ Motorcycle Industry Association of South Australia

MIAT.......... Mean Interarrival Time (MHDB)

MIAT.......... Member of the Institute of Asphalt Technology [*British*] (DBQ)

MiAt........... Montmorency County Public Library, Atlanta, MI [*Library symbol Library of Congress*] (LCLS)

MIAT.......... Music Industry Association of Tasmania [*Australia*]

MIATA......... Murrumbidgee Irrigation Area Tourist Association [*Australia*]

MIATCO ...... Mid-America International Agri-Trade Council

MiAth......... Athens Township Library, Athens, MI [*Library symbol Library of Congress*] (LCLS)

MiAu.......... Augusta-Ross Township District Library (McKay Library), Augusta, MI [*Library symbol Library of Congress*] (LCLS)

MIAX........... McCulloch International Airlines [*Air carrier designation symbol*]

MIB............ Management Improvement Board (AAG)

MIB............ Management Information Base

MIB............ Management Information Block [*Computer science*]

MIB............ Manual Input Buffer [*Computer science*]

MIB............ Marine Index Bureau

MIB............ Maritime Index Bureau (NADA)

MIB............ Marketing of Investments Board [*Finance British*]

MIB............ Master Instruction Book

MIB............ Master Interconnect Board (MCD)

MIB............ Master of International Business (GAGS)

MIB............ Mechanized Infantry Battalion (MCD)

MIB............ Medical Impairment Bureau [*Insurance*]

MIB............ Medical Information Bureau [*Databank*]

MIB............ Medium Industry Bank [*South Korea*] (IMH)

MIB............ Men in Black [*UFO mythology*]

MIB............ Mexican Investment Board [*Public relations and investor assistance*] [*Mexico*] (CROSS)

MIB............ Mezhdunarodnyi Investitsionnyi Bank [*International Investment Bank - IIB*] [*Moscow, USSR*] (EAIO)

MIB............ Michigan Intra-State Motor Tariff Bureau Inc., Lansing MI [*STAC*]

MIB............ Microinstruction Bus [*Computer science*]

MIB............ Midland Bancorp [*NYSE symbol*] (SPSG)

MIB............ Midland Bank PLC [*NYSE symbol*] (SAG)

MIB............ Military Intelligence Battalion (MCD)

MIB............ Military Intelligence Board (MCD)

MIB............ Millinery Information Bureau (EA)

MIB............ Minimum Impulse BIT [*Binary Digit*] [*Computer science*] (MCD)

MIB............ Minot, ND [*Location identifier FAA*] (FAAL)

MIB............ Mint in the Box [*Doll collecting*]

MIB............ Missionary Information Bureau

MIB............ Motor Inspection Building

MIB............ Motor Insurers' Bureau Ltd. [*British*] (ILCA)

MIB............ Mouvement d'Insoumission Bretonne [*Breton Insubordination Movement*] [*France*] (PD)

MIB............ Multibanc NT Financial Corp. [*Toronto Stock Exchange symbol*]

MIB............ Multilayer Interconnection Board

MIB............ Mustard Information Bureau (EA)

MIB............ Mutual Inductance Bridge

MiBa.......... Bad Axe Public Library, Bad Axe, MI [*Library symbol Library of Congress*] (LCLS)

MIBA.......... Malta International Business Authority (EY)

MIBA.......... Master of International Business Administration (GAGS)

MIBA.......... Member of the Institute of British Architects (ROG)

MIBA.......... Metropolitan Intercollegiate Basketball Association (EA)

MIBA.......... Miniere de Bakwanga [*Zaire*]

MiBal......... Pathfinder Community Library, Baldwin, MI [*Library symbol Library of Congress*] (LCLS)

MiBar......... Barryton Public Library, Barryton, MI [*Library symbol Library of Congress*] (LCLS)

MiBar......... Burr Oak Township Library, Burr Oak, MI [*Library symbol Library of Congress*] (LCLS)

MIBAR .... Multi-Channel In-Band Airborne Relay (PDAA)

MIBARS ...... Military Intelligence Battalion Aerial Reconnaissance and Support [*Army*] (AFM)

MiBat .... Battle Creek Public School, Battle Creek, MI [*Library symbol Library of Congress*] (LCLS)

MiBatC .... Battle Creek College, Battle Creek, MI [*Library symbol Library of Congress Obsolete*] (LCLS)

MiBatK .... Kellogg Community College, Battle Creek, MI [*Library symbol Library of Congress*] (LCLS)

MiBatV .... United States Veterans Administration Hospital, Battle Creek, MI [*Library symbol Library of Congress*] (LCLS)

MiBatW .... Willard Public Library, Battle Creek, MI [*Library symbol Library of Congress*] (LCLS)

MiBay .... Bay City Public Library, Bay City, MI [*Library symbol Library of Congress*] (LCLS)

MiBayM .... Bay Medical Center, Bay City, MI [*Library symbol Library of Congress*] (LCLS)

MiBayS .... Bay County Library System, Bay City, MI [*Library symbol Library of Congress*] (LCLS)

MiBayS-A .... Bay County Library System, Auburn Branch Library, Auburn, MI [*Library symbol Library of Congress*] (LCLS)

MiBayS-B .... Bay County Library System, Broadway Branch Library, Bay City, MI [*Library symbol Library of Congress*] (LCLS)

MiBayS-L .... Bay County Library System, Linwood Branch Library, Linwood, MI [*Library symbol Library of Congress*] (LCLS)

MiBayS-P .... Bay County Library System, Pinconning Branch Library, Pinconning, MI [*Library symbol Library of Congress*] (LCLS)

MiBayS-S .... Bay County Library System, Sage Branch Library, Bay City, MI [*Library symbol Library of Congress*] (LCLS)

MIBB .... Missouri & Illinois Bridge & Belt Railroad [*AAR code Terminated*]

MIBC .... Methyl Cap. Isobutyl Carbinol [*Also, MIC*] [*Organic chemistry*]

MIBCO .... Member of the Institution of Building Control Officers [*British*] (DBQ)

MiBeiM .... Beaver Island Mormon Colony Library, St. James, Beaver Island, MI [*Library symbol Library of Congress Obsolete*] (LCLS)

MiBel .... Bellevue Township Library, Bellevue, MI [*Library symbol Library of Congress*] (LCLS)

MiBela .... Bellaire Public Library, Bellaire, MI [*Library symbol Library of Congress*] (LCLS)

MiBen .... Benzonia Public Library, Benzonia, MI [*Library symbol Library of Congress*] (LCLS)

MiBes .... Bessemer Public Library, Bessemer, MI [*Library symbol Library of Congress*] (LCLS)

MiBeu .... Beulah Public Library, Beulah, MI [*Library symbol Library of Congress*] (LCLS)

MIBF .... Member of the Institute of British Foundrymen

MIBF .... Montreal International Book Fair

MIBG .... Meta-Iodobenzylguanidine [*Biochemistry*]

MiBh .... Benton Harbor Public Library, Benton Harbor, MI [*Library symbol*] [*Library of Congress*] (LCLS)

MiBhL .... Lake Michigan College, Benton Harbor, MI [*Library symbol Library of Congress*] (LCLS)

MiBhW .... Whirlpool Corp., Technical Information Center, Benton Harbor, MI [*Library symbol Library of Congress*] (LCLS)

MiBicr .... Thomas Fleschner Memorial Library, Birch Run, MI [*Library symbol Library of Congress*] (LCLS)

MI Biol ...... Member of the Institute of Biology [*British*] (EY)

MiBir .... Baldwin Public Library, Birmingham, MI [*Library symbol Library of Congress*] (LCLS)

MIBK .... Methyl Isobutyl Ketone [*Also, MIK*] [*Organic chemistry*]

MiBla .... Rolland Township Library, Blanchard, MI [*Library symbol Library of Congress*] (LCLS)

MiBloA .... Cranbrook Academy of Art, Bloomfield Hills, MI [*Library symbol Library of Congress*] (LCLS)

MiBloC .... Cranbrook Institute of Science, Bloomfield Hills, MI [*Library symbol Library of Congress*] (LCLS)

MiBloCAr .... Cranbrook Educational Community, Archives and Historical Collections, Bloomfield Hills, MI [*Library symbol*] [*Library of Congress*] (LCLS)

MiBloGS ...... Church of Jesus Christ of Latter-Day Saints, Genealogical Society Library, Bloomfield Hills Branch, Bloomfield Hills, MI [*Library symbol Library of Congress*] (LCLS)

MIBOC .... Marketing of Investments Board Organising Committee [*British*]

MIBOR ...... Madrid Interbank Offered Rate (MHDW)

MiBoy .... Boyne City Public Library, Boyne City, MI [*Library symbol Library of Congress*] (LCLS)

MiBoyf .... Boyne Falls Public Library, Boyne Falls, MI [*Library symbol Library of Congress*] (LCLS)

MIBPA .... Methyliminobispropylamine [*Organic chemistry*]

Mi-BPH ...... Michigan Department of Education, State Library Services, Blind and Physically Handicapped Library, Lansing, MI [*Library symbol Library of Congress*] (LCLS)

MIBPrA .... Midland Bank A1/A2 Unit ADS [*NYSE symbol*] (TTSB)

MIBPrB .... Midland Bank B1/B2 Unit ADS (TTSB)

MIBPrC .... Midland Bank C1/C2 Unit ADS [*NYSE symbol*] (TTSB)

MiBr .... Big Rapids Community Library, Big Rapids, MI [*Library symbol Library of Congress*] (LCLS)

MIBRAG ...... Mitteldeutschen Brunkohle (ECON)

MiBrc .... Brown City Public Library, Brown City, MI [*Library symbol Library of Congress*] (LCLS)

MiBre .... Howe Memorial Library, Breckenridge, MI [*Library symbol Library of Congress*] (LCLS)

MiBrF .... Ferris State College, Big Rapids, MI [*Library symbol Library of Congress*] (LCLS)

MiBrid .... Bridgeport Public Library, Bridgeport, MI [*Library symbol Library of Congress*] (LCLS)

MiBridm ...... Bridgman Public Library, Bridgman, MI [*Library symbol Library of Congress*] (LCLS)

MiBrig .... Brighton City Library, Brighton, MI [*Library symbol Library of Congress*] (LCLS)

MIBritE ...... Member of the Institute of British Engineers (EY)

MIBritishE ... Member of the Institute of British Engineers

MIBs .... Management Information Bases [*Compaq*] [*Computer science*]

MIBS .... Master of International Business Studies

MIBS .... Miami International Boat Show and Sailboat Show (ITD)

MiBs .... Sparks Memorial Library, Berrien Springs, MI [*Library symbol Library of Congress*] (LCLS)

MiBsA .... Andrews University, Berrien Springs, MI [*Library symbol Library of Congress*] (LCLS)

MIBT .... Methyl Isatin-beta-thiosemicarbazone

MiBu .... Taymouth Township Library, Burt, MI [*Library symbol Library of Congress*] (LCLS)

MiBur .... Burr Oak Township Library, Burr Oak, MI [*Library symbol*] [*Library of Congress*] (LCLS)

MiBurl .... Burlington Township Library, Burlington, MI [*Library symbol Library of Congress*] (LCLS)

MIBURN ...... Mississippi Burning [*Code name of FBI investigation*]

MIBWG ...... Military Intelligence Board Working Group

MIC .... Aerolineas de Michoacan [*Mexico ICAO designator*] (FAAC)

MIC .... Congregatio Clericorum Regularium Immaculatae ConceptionisBeatae Mariae Virginis [*Marian Fathers*] [*Roman Catholic religious order*]

mic .... Congregation of Marians of the Immaculate Conception (TOCD)

MIC .... Congregation of Marians of the Immaculate Conception (TOCD)

MIC .... IEEE Medical Imaging Committee (EA)

MIC .... Itasca Community College, Grand Rapids, MN [*OCLC symbol*] (OCLC)

MIC .... Machinery Installation Certificate

MIC .... Made in Canada [*Business term*]

MIC .... Magnesium Industry Council [*British*] (BI)

MIC .... Magnetic Ink Character [*Computer science*] (HGAA)

MIC .... Maintenance Identification Code [*Military*] (CAAL)

MIC .... Maintenance Index Code (DNAB)

MIC .... Maintenance Information Center [*Navy*] (NG)

MIC .... Maintenance Information Chart [*DoD*]

MIC .... Maintenance Inventory Center [*Air Force*] (AFIT)

MIC .... Major Immunogene Complex [*Genetics*] (DOG)

MIC .... Malaysian Indian Congress [*Political party*] (PPW)

MIC .... Management & Industrial Consultants

MIC .... Management Indicator Code (MCD)

MIC .... Management Information Center

MIC .... Management Information Corp. [*Cherry Hill, NJ*] [*Information service or system*] (IID)

MIC .... Management Integration Consortium

MIC .... Marine Information Centre [*Information service or system*] (IID)

MIC .... Market Impact Clearance

MIC .... Marketing Intelligence Corp. [*Information service or system*] (IID)

MIC .... Marketing International Corp. [*Washington, DC*] (TSSD)

MIC .... Maruman Integrated Circuits

MIC .... Maruzen International Co., Inc. [*Information service or system*] (IID)

MIC .... Masonry Industry Committee (EA)

MIC .... Master Interrupt Control [*Computer science*] (OA)

MIC .... Match Indicator Code (MCD)

MIC .... Material Identification and Control (DNAB)

MIC .... Material Inventory Control

MIC .... Materials Irradiation Chamber

MIC .... Maternal and Infant Care [*Medicine*]

MIC .... Maximum Inscribed Circle [*Manufacturing term*]

MIC .... Meat Importers' Council [*Later, MICA*] (EA)

MIC .... Meat Industry Council [*Australia*]

MIC .... Mechanized Information Center [*Information service or system*]

MIC .... Medical Industrial Complex

MIC .... Medical Information Centre (NITA)

MIC .... Medical Intensive Care

MIC .... Medical Interfraternity Conference (EA)

MIC .... Medium-Intensity Conflict [*Military*]

MIC .... Medium Interface Connector [*Optics*] (CDE)

MIC .... Medugorje Information Center (EA)

MIC .... Mellonics Information Center [*Information service or system*] (IID)

MIC .... Mellon InvestData Corp. [*New York, NY Information service or system*] (IID)

MIC .... Memory Interface Connection [*Computer science*]

MIC .... Merseyside Innovation Centre Ltd. [*Research center British*] (CB)

MIC .... Message Identification Code [*Computer science*] (BUR)

MIC .... Meteorological Information Committee [*NATO*] (NATG)

MIC .... Meteorologist-in-Charge (USDC)

MIC .... Meteorologist-In-Charge [*Marine science*] (OSRA)

MIC .... Methylisobutyl Carbinol [*Also, MIBC*] [*Organic chemistry*]

MIC .... Methyl Isocyanate [*Organic chemistry*]

MIC .... Metro Industrial [*Vancouver Stock Exchange symbol*]

Mic .... Micah [*Old Testament book*]

MIC .... Michigan Information Center [*Michigan State Department of Management and Budget*] [*Information service or system*] (IID)

MIC .... Michigan Instructional Computer

MIC .... Michilla [*Chile*] [*Seismograph station code, US Geological Survey*] (SEIS)

mic .... Micmac [*MARC language code Library of Congress*] (LCCP)

MIC .... Microbiologically-Influenced Corrosion [*Metallurgical engineering*]

MIC .... Microbiologically Influenced Corrosion

MIC .... Microcomputer Index [*Information service or system*] (IID)

MIC .... Microcytosis [*Biochemistry*] (DAVI)

MIC.............. Microelectronic Integrated Circuit (MCD)
MIC.............. Micrometer [A "mike"]
mic .... Micrometer (WDMC)
mic .... Microphone (WDMC)
MIC.............. Microphone (AABC)
MIC.............. Microscopic (DAVI)
MIC.............. Microscopic Findings in Centrifugal Urinary Sediment [Biochemistry] (DAVI)
Mic .... Microscopium [Constellation]
MIC.............. Microscopy
MIC.............. Microwave Integrated Circuitry
MIC.............. Microwave Integrated Circuits (NITA)
MIC.............. Microwave Interference Coordination
MIC.............. Middle Income Country [Category of developing country]
MIC.............. Mid-Intensity Conflict [Military] (INF)
MIC.............. Military Indoctrination Center
M-IC............. Military-Industrial Complex
MIC.............. Military Information Center [Defunct] (EA)
MIC.............. Military Introductory Letter
MIC.............. Millicm International Cellular S.A. [Commercial firm] [Luxembourg]
MIC.............. Mineral Industries Census
MIC.............. Minimal [or Minimum] Inhibitory Concentration
MIC.............. Minimal Isorrheic Concentration [Medicine]
MIC.............. Minimum Ignition Current (IEEE)
MIC.............. Minimum Inhibitory Concentration [Bactericidal characteristic]
MIC.............. Minneapolis, MN [Location identifier FAA] (FAAL)
MIC.............. Minocycline [Antibiotic compound] (AAMN)
MIC.............. Minor Care Clinic [Medicine]
MIC.............. Missile Identification Code [Military] (CAAL)
MIC.............. Missing Interruption Character (NITA)
MIC.............. Missing Interruption Checker (MCD)
MIC.............. Missionary Sisters of the Immaculate Conception [Roman Catholic religious order]
MIC.............. Missionary Sisters of the Immaculate Conception (Canada) (TOCD)
MIC.............. Mississippi Industrial College [Holly Springs]
MIC.............. Mobile Information Center [An association]
MIC.............. Mobile Intensive Care [Medicine] (DHSM)
MIC.............. Model Immune Complex [Medicine] (DMAA)
MIC.............. Monitoring, Identification, and Correlation
MIC.............. Monolithic Integrated Circuit
MIC.............. Morphology-Immunology-Cytogenetics [Classification of Leukemias]
MIC.............. Mortgage Insurance Certificate (EMRF)
MIC.............. Mortgage Insurance Co.
MIC.............. Motorcycle Industry Council (EA)
MIC.............. Mountain Instructor's Certificate [British] (DI)
MIC.............. Movimiento de Integracion Colorada [Paraguay] [Political party] (EY)
MIC.............. Multichip Integrated Circuit (NITA)
MIC.............. Multimedia Interactive Control
MIC.............. Multinational Intelligence Cell (MCD)
MIC.............. Multiperil Insurance Conference
MIC.............. MuniYield CA Insured Fund [NYSE symbol] (TTSB)
MIC.............. MuniYield California Insured Fund [NYSE symbol] (SPSG)
MIC.............. Music Industry Conference (EA)
MIC.............. Music Industry Council [Later, Music Industry Conference] (EA)
MIC.............. Mutual Improvement Class [British railroad term]
MIC.............. Mutual Interference Chart (IEEE)
MiCa............ Indianfields Public Library, Caro, MI [Library symbol Library of Congress] (LCLS)
MICA............ Macroinstruction Compiler Assembler [Computer science]
MICA............ Major Incidents Computer Application (PDAA)
MICA............ Meat Importers' Council of America (EA)
MICA............ Mentally Ill Chemical Abuser
MICA............ MicroAge, Inc. [NASDAQ symbol] (SAG)
MICA............ Mobile Industrial Caterers' Association (EA)
MICA............ Mortgage Insurance Companies of America (EA)
MiCac .... Rawson Memorial Library, Cass City, MI [Library symbol Library of Congress] (LCLS)
MiCad .... Cadillac-Wexford Public Library, Cadillac, MI [Library symbol Library of Congress] (LCLS)
MICAD .... Multipurpose Integrated Chemical Agent Alarm [Army] (DOMA)
MiCadCS...... Cadillac Public School, Cadillac, MI [Library symbol] [Library of Congress] (LCLS)
MiCadM....... Mid-Michigan Library League, Cadillac, MI [Library symbol Library of Congress] (LCLS)
MiCadPS...... Wexford Public Schools, Cadillac, MI [Library symbol Library of Congress] (LCLS)
MICAF......... Measuring Improved Capability of Army Forces
MiCal........... Calumet Public-School Library, Calumet, MI [Library symbol Library of Congress] (LCLS)
MICALL....... Microprocedure Call [Computer science] (MHDB)
MiCam........ Camden Township Library, Camden, MI [Library symbol Library of Congress] (LCLS)
MICAM........ Microammeter [Electronics]
MICAM........ Micro Camera (NITA)
MICAM........ Micro-Connection Assembly Method
MICAM........ Mid-Function Integral Control Alarm Module [Electronics systems] [Automotive engineering]
MICAP .... Measuring Improved Capability [Army]
MICAP .... Mission Capability
MICAP .... Mission Incapable, Awaiting Parts (MCD)
MICAPS ...... Mine/Countermine Casualty Assessment Producing System (MCD)
MICAS .... Military Intelligence Co., Aerial Surveillance (MCD)
MiCassC...... Cass County Library, Cassopolis, MI [Library symbol Library of Congress] (LCLS)
MICB........... Meck Island Control Building [Army] (AABC)

MICBM......... Mobile Intercontinental Ballistic Missile
MiCc .... Carson City Public Library, Carson City, MI [Library symbol Library of Congress] (LCLS)
MICC........... Metal Interconnect Cascade Cell [Photovoltaic energy systems]
MICC........... Military Information Control Committee (CINC)
MICC........... Millicom International Cellular [NASDAQ symbol] (SAG)
MICC........... Mineral Insulated, Copper Covered [Cable]
MICCF......... Mortgage Insurance Co. of Canada
MICCF......... Millicom Intl Cellular S.A. [NASDAQ symbol] (TTSB)
MICCI......... Malaysia International Chamber of Commerce and Industry (EAIO)
MICCLE....... Michigan Interorganizational Committee on Continuing Library Education (EDAC)
MICCO........ Model Inner City Community Organization [Washington, DC]
MICCS .... Minuteman Integrated Command and Control System [Missiles]
Mic D.......... Doctor of Microbiology
MICD.......... Mechanical, Thermal, and Optical Interface Control Document (MCD)
MICDS .... Movable In-Core Detector System [Nuclear energy] (NRCH)
MICE.......... Management Information Capability for Enforcement [Environmental Protection Agency] (GFGA)
MICE.......... Man's Impact on Coastal and Estuarine Ecosystems [Marine science] [United Nations] (OSRA)
MICE.......... Material Transfer, Information Transfer, Control Transfer, Energy Transfer
MICE.......... Member of the Institution of Civil Engineers [Formerly, AMICE] [British]
MICE.......... Microelectronic Integrated Checkout Equipment
MICE.......... Money, Ideology, Compromise, Ego [CIA acronym for possible explanations for spy defections]
MICE.......... Mutual Insurance Council of Editors [Later, PICA] (EA)
MiCe .... Nottawa Township Library, Centerville, MI [Library symbol Library of Congress] (LCLS)
MiCeG .... Glen Oaks Community College, Centreville, MI [Library symbol Library of Congress] (LCLS)
MICEI......... Member of the Institution of Civil Engineers of Ireland
MICELEM..... Microphone Element (IEEE)
MiCen .... Leslie R. Foss Public Library, Center Line, MI [Library symbol Library of Congress] (LCLS)
MiCenl......... Central Lake Township Library, Central Lake, MI [Library symbol Library of Congress] (LCLS)
MiCES......... Microcomputer-Controlled Electroanalysis System [Interactive Microwave]
MiCf........... Crystal Falls Community Library, Crystal Falls, MI [Library symbol Library of Congress] (LCLS)
MicFocu....... Micro Focus Group PLC [Associated Press] (SAG)
Micfrm........ Microframe, Inc. [Associated Press] (SAG)
MICG .... Management Information Coordinating Group [Navy]
MICG .... Mercury Iodide Crystal Growth
MICG ...... Microfield Graphics [NASDAQ symbol] (TTSB)
MICG ...... Microfield Graphics, Inc. [NASDAQ symbol] (TTSB)
MICH .... Michaelmas [Feast of St. Michael the Archangel, September 29]
Mich .... Michaelmas Term [British Legal term] (DLA)
MICH .... Michaels [J.], Inc. [NASDAQ symbol] (NQ)
MICH .... Michaels J [NASDAQ symbol] (TTSB)
MICH .... Micheas [Old Testament book] [Douay version]
MICH .... Michigan
Mich .... Michigan (ODBW)
Mich .... Michigan Supreme Court Reports [A publication] (DLA)
MiCha......... Chase Public Library, Chase, MI [Library symbol Library of Congress] (LCLS)
Mich Admin Code... Michigan Administrative Code [A publication] (DLA)
Mich Adv .... Michigan Reports Advanced Sheets [A publication] (DLA)
MichAnt...... Michael Anthony Jewelers, Inc. [Associated Press] (SAG)
Mich App .... Michigan Court of Appeals Reports [A publication] (DLA)
MiChar........ Charlotte Public Library, Charlotte, MI [Library symbol Library of Congress] (LCLS)
Mich Att'y Gen Biennial Rep... Biennial Report of the Attorney General of the State of Michigan [A publication] (DLA)
MichBr........ Michigan Brewery, Inc. [Associated Press] (SAG)
MichBrw ..... Michigan Brewery, Inc. [Associated Press] (SAG)
Mich Calidon... Michael Calidonius [Flourished, 16th century] [Authority cited in pre-1607 legal work] (DSA)
Mich CCR .... Michigan Circuit Court Reporter [A publication] (DLA)
Mich Comp L Ann... Michigan Compiled Laws, Annotated [A publication] (DLA)
Mich Comp Laws... Michigan Compiled Laws [A publication] (DLA)
Mich Comp Laws... Michigan Compiled Laws Annotated [West] [A publication] (AAGC)
Mich Comp Laws Ann... Michigan Compiled Laws, Annotated [A publication] (DLA)
Mich Cr Ct Rep... Michigan Circuit Court Reporter [A publication] (DLA)
Mich Ct Cl ... Michigan Court of Claims (AAGC)
Mich Ct Cl ... Michigan Court of Claims Reports [A publication] (DLA)
MiChe......... Cheboygan Area Public Library, Cheboygan, MI [Library symbol Library of Congress] (LCLS)
MiChel........ McKune Memorial Library, Chelsea, MI [Library symbol Library of Congress] (LCLS)
MIChemE..... Member of the Institution of Chemical Engineers [British] (EY)
MiChes........ Chesaning Public Library, Chesaning, MI [Library symbol Library of Congress] (LCLS)
MichFncl...... Michigan Financial Corp. [Associated Press] (SAG)
Michie's GA Repts Ann... Georgia Reports, Annotated [A publication] (DLA)
Michie's Jur... Michie's Jurisprudence of Virginia and West Virginia [A publication] (DLA)
MichJ........... Michaels [J.], Inc. [Associated Press] (SAG)
Mich Jur ...... Michigan Jurisprudence [A publication] (DLA)
Mich L......... Michigan Lawyer [A publication] (DLA)
Mich Legis Serv... Michigan Legislative Service [A publication] (DLA)

Mich Leg News... Michigan Legal News [*A publication*] (DLA)
MichIF .... Michael Foods, Inc. [*Associated Press*] (SAG)
Mich LJ .... Michigan Law Journal [*A publication*] (DLA)
Mich Nisi Prius... Brown's Michigan Nisi Prius Reports [*A publication*] (DLA)
Mich NP ...... Brown's Michigan Nisi Prius Reports [*A publication*] (DLA)
Mich Pub Acts.. Public and Local Acts of the Legislature of the State of Michigan [*A publication*] (DLA)
Mich PUC Ops... Michigan Public Utilities Commission Orders and Opinions [*A publication*] (DLA)
Mich R......... Michigan Reports [*A publication*] (DLA)
Mich RC Dec... Michigan Railroad Commission Decisions [*A publication*] (DLA)
MICHS .... Michaelmas [*Feast of St. Michael the Archangel, September 29*]
Mich SBA Jo.. Michigan State Bar Association. Journal [*A publication*] (DLA)
Mich Stat Ann.. Michigan Statutes, Annotated [*A publication*] (DLA)
MichStr....... Michael Stores [*Associated Press*] (SAG)
Mich St U .... Michigan State University (GAGS)
Mich Supr Ct Rep... Michigan Reports [*A publication*] (DLA)
Mich T........ Michaelmas Term [*British Legal term*] (DLA)
Mich Tech U... Michigan Technological University (GAGS)
MiChv .... Charlevoix Public Library, Charlevoix, MI [*Library symbol Library of Congress*] (LCLS)
Mich Vac .... Michaelmas Vacation [*British Legal term*] (DLA)
Mich WCC ... Michigan Industrial Accident Board, Workmen's Compensation Cases [*A publication*] (DLA)
MICIS.......... Material Information Control and Information System (MCD)
MICIS.......... Material Inventory Control and Inventory System (NASA)
MICIS.......... Microbial Culture Information Service [*Department of Trade and Industry*] [*British Information service or system*]
MICIS.......... Midwestern Climate Information System (USDC)
MICIS.......... Midwestern Climate Information System [*Marine science*] (OSRA)
MICK.......... Manufacturers Item Correlation Key
MICL.......... Missile In-Commission Level
MiCla.......... Garfield Memorial Public Library, Clare, MI [*Library symbol Library of Congress*] (LCLS)
MICLE.......... Institute of Continuing Legal Education, University of Michigan (DLA)
MICLIC........ Mine Clearing Line Charge [*Army*] (INF)
MiClin.......... Clinton Public Library, Clinton, MI [*Library symbol Library of Congress*] (LCLS)
MICLO.......... Management Information Control Liaison Officers (MCD)
MICM.......... Associate Member of the Institute of Credit Management [*British*] (DBQ)
MICM.......... MICOM Communications [*NASDAQ symbol*] (TTSB)
MICM.......... Micom Communications Corp. [*NASDAQ symbol*] (SAG)
MICM.......... Monolithic Integrated Circuit Mask
MICMD.......... Milwaukee Contract Management District (SAA)
MICMPTR........ Microcomputer (MSA)
MICN .... Medical Intensive Care Nurse (DAVI)
MICN .... Micrion Corp. [*NASDAQ symbol*] (SAG)
MICN .... Mobile Intensive Care Nurse [*Emergency Medicine*] (DAVI)
MICNS .... Modular Integrated Communications and Navigation System (RDA)
MICO .... Management Information Systems Control Officer (MCD)
MICO .... Mankato Industrial Corp. [*Automotive industry supplier*]
MICO .... Member of the Institute of Careers Officers [*British*] (DBQ)
MICO .... Midland Continental R. R. [*AAR code Obsolete*]
MICO .... MLV Integration and Checkout (MCD)
MICOFT......... Mutual Insurance Committee on Federal Taxation (EA)
MiCol.......... Coloma Public Library, Coloma, MI [*Library symbol Library of Congress*] (LCLS)
MiCole........ Coleman Area Library, Coleman, MI [*Library symbol Library of Congress*] (LCLS)
MiColo......... Colon Township Library, Colon, MI [*Library symbol Library of Congress*] (LCLS)
MiCom........ Comstock Township Library, Comstock, MI [*Library symbol Library of Congress*] (LCLS)
MICOM .... Missile Command [*Redstone Arsenal, AL*] [*Army*]
MICOM .... US Army Missile Command (AAGC)
MicomC........ Micom Communications Corp. [*Associated Press*] (SAG)
MICOM-RDEC... Missile Command Research, Development, and Engineering Center [*Army*] (RDA)
MICOMS ...... Maintenance Information Concerning [*the repair and operation of*] Missile Systems
MiCon........ Constatine Township Library, Constatine, MI [*Library symbol Library of Congress*] (LCLS)
MICON .... Military Construction Program (MUGU)
micon .... Motion Icon [*Computer science*] (WDMC)
MICONEX.... Multinational Instrumentation Conference and Exposition [*China Instrument Society*]
MiCoop........ Coopersville District Library, Coopersville, MI [*Library symbol Library of Congress*] (LCLS)
MI-COPICS... Management Information for COPICS [*Communications Oriented Production Information and Control System*] Users [*IBM Corp.*]
MICorrST..... Member of the Institute of Corrosion Science and Technology [*British*] (DBQ)
MICOS .... Mini Computer Systems (NITA)
MICP........... Management and Investment Companies Program
MICP........... Military Inventory Control Point (MCD)
MICPAC .... Microelectronic Integrated Circuit Package (MCD)
MICPAK .... Modular Integrated Circuit Package
MIC PAN .... Mica Panis [*Crumb of Bread*] [*Pharmacy*]
MicPwr....... Microwave Power Devices, Inc. [*Associated Press*] (SAG)
MICR .... Magnetic Ink Character Recognition [*Banking*] [*Computer science*]
MICR .... Management Improvement and Cost Reduction Project Reporting System
MICR .... Microenergy, Inc. [*NASDAQ symbol*] (SAG)
MICR .... Microscope (MSA)

Micr............ Microscopium [*Constellation*]
MICRA .... Medical Injury Compensation Reform Act
MICRA .... Miniature Insulated Contact Range (PDAA)
MICRAD...... Microwave Radiometry (MCD)
MICRADS...... Microwave Radiation System (PDAA)
MICRAM...... Microminiature Individual Components Reliable Assembled Modules
MicrBi......... Micro Bio-Medics, Inc. [*Associated Press*] (SAG)
Micrdy .... Microdyne Corp. [*Associated Press*] (SAG)
Micrel......... Micrel, Inc. [*Associated Press*] (SAG)
Micrenr........ Microenergy, Inc. [*Associated Press*] (SAG)
MicrFlt........ Microwave Filter Co., Inc. [*Associated Press*] (SAG)
Micrgfx....... Micrografx, Inc. [*Associated Press*] (SAG)
MicrGn....... Micro General Corp. [*Associated Press*] (SAG)
Micrion....... Micrion Corp. [*Associated Press*] (SAG)
Micrl.......... Microleague Multimedia, Inc. [*Associated Press*] (SAG)
Micrleag....... Microleague Multimedia, Inc. [*Associated Press*] (SAG)
MICR/MIMR... Magnetic Ink Character Recognition / Magnetic Ink Mark Recognition (BTTJ)
MIC-RN....... Mobile Intensive Care Registered Nurse [*Emergency medicine*] (DAVI)
Micrnics....... Micronics Computers, Inc. [*Associated Press*] (SAG)
MicrnT........ Micron Technology [*Associated Press*] (SAG)
micro.......... Extremely Small (IDOE)
MICRO .... Microcomputer
MICRO .... Microelectronics Innovation and Computer Science Research Program [*University of California*] [*Research center*] (RCD)
MICRO .... Microprocessor
micro .... Microscopic
MICRO .... Multiple Indexing and Console Retrieval Operations (NITA)
MICRO .... Multiple Indexing and Console Retrieval Options [*Information retrieval Computer science*]
MICROACE... Microminiature Automatic Checkout Equipment
MicroAge..... MicroAge, Inc., [*Associated Press*] (SAG)
MICROBIOL... Microbiological [*or Microbiology*]
MicroCap..... [*The*] MicroCap Fund [*Associated Press*] (SAG)
MICROCAT... Micro-Catalogue (NITA)
Microchip ... Microchip Technology, Inc. [*Associated Press*] (SAG)
Microcm...... Microcom, Inc. [*Associated Press*] (SAG)
MICROCON... Microcomputer Based Services for Retrospective Conversions (NITA)
microcryst ... Microcrystalline (BARN)
MicroCSI...... MicroStation Customer Support Library [*Intergraph Corp.*] (PCM)
MicroCT....... Micro Component Technology, Inc. [*Associated Press*] (SAG)
MICRODIS ... Microform Document of Information System (MCD)
MICRO-DISC... Microcomputer-Videodisc
MICRODOC... Council for Microphotography and Document Reproduction [*British*]
Microfd....... Microfield Graphics, Inc. [*Associated Press*] (SAG)
MicrofdG...... Microfield Graphics, Inc. [*Associated Press*] (SAG)
Microflu....... Microfluidics International Corp. [*Associated Press*] (SAG)
MICROG....... Microgram [*One millionth of a gram*]
MicroIntg..... Micro-Integration Corp. [*Associated Press*] (SAG)
MICROLAB... Microfabrication Laboratory [*University of California, Berkeley*] [*Research center*] (RCD)
MicroIg....... Microlog Corp. [*Associated Press*] (SAG)
MicroLin...... Micro Linear Corp. [*Associated Press*] (SAG)
MICROM..... Microinstruction Read-Only Memory [*Computer science*]
MICROMIN... Microminiature (IEEE)
MICRON...... Micronavigator [*Air Force*]
MicronEl...... Micron Electronics, Inc. [*Associated Press*] (SAG)
MICRONET... Microcomputer Network (NITA)
Micront....... Micronetics, Inc. [*Associated Press*] (SAG)
Microp .... Micropolis Corp. [*Associated Press*] (SAG)
MICROPAC... Micromodule Data Processor and Computer (IEEE)
MicroPh....... Microcide Pharmaceuticals, Inc. [*Associated Press*] (SAG)
MICROPSI... Microcomputer Printed Subject Indexes (NITA)
MICROS ..... Microscopy
Micros .... Micros Systems, Inc. [*Associated Press*] (SAG)
MICROSECS... Microfilm Sequential Coding System [*Bell System*]
Microsft...... Microsoft Corp. [*Associated Press*] (SAG)
MICROSID ... Small Seismic Intrusion Detector (PDAA)
MicroSIFT... Microcomputer Software and Information for Teachers [*Northwest Regional Educational Laboratory*] [*Information service or system*] (IID)
MICROSIM... Microinstruction Simulator [*Computer science*] (MHDI)
Microsoft.... Microsoft Corp. [*Associated Press*] (SAG)
MicrosTo ..... Micros-To Mainframe, Inc. [*Associated Press*] (SAG)
Microtel ...... Microtel International, Inc. [*Associated Press*] (SAG)
Microtl ...... Microtel Franchise & Development Corp. [*Associated Press*] (SAG)
MicroTo ...... Micros-To Mainframe, Inc. [*Associated Press*] (SAG)
MICRO TR ... Microwave Tower [*Nautical charts*]
MICRO-VERS... Microcomputer Vocational Education Reporting System (EDAC)
MicroWre..... Micro Warehouse, Inc. [*Associated Press*] (SAG)
MicrPck....... Microelectronic Packaging, Inc. [*Associated Press*] (SAG)
MICRS .... Main Instrument Console and Readout Stations (NATG)
MicrtcRs...... Microtec Research, Inc. [*Associated Press*] (SAG)
Micrtek....... Microtek Medical, Inc. [*Associated Press*] (SAG)
Micrtest ...... Microtest, Inc. [*Associated Press*] (SAG)
MICRU .... MICRU International (EA)
Micrvisn...... Microvision, Inc. [*Associated Press*] (SAG)
MICS .... Maintenance Inventory Control System [*Bell System*]
MICS .... Management Information and Control System [*Navy*]
MICS .... Management Integrated Control System
MICS .... Manned Interactive Control Stations (MCD)
MICS .... Manufacturing Information and Control System (OA)
MICS.......... Material Inventory Control System [*NASA*] (SSD)
MICS.......... Medical Instrument Calibration System (PDAA)

MICS...........	Microprocessor Inertia and Communication System
MICS...........	Military Integrated Communications System (CINC)
MICS...........	Mineral-Insulated Copper-Sheathed [*Cable*] (IEEE)
MICS...........	Missile Inspection Completion Sheet (MCD)
MICS...........	Mitsubishi Intelligent Cockpit System [*Automotive engineering*]
MICS...........	Multiplex Interior Communications (NG)
MICS...........	Museum of the International College of Surgeons (NADA)
MICS...........	MVS Integrated Control System (NITA)
MICSA.......	Maine Indian Claims Settlement Act [*1980*]
MicSem.......	Microsemi Corp. [*Associated Press*] (SAG)
Micsft.........	Microsoft Corp. [*Associated Press*] (SAG)
MICTAR.......	Minnesota Center for Twin and Adoption Research (ECON)
MictchS.......	Microtouch Systems, Inc. [*Associated Press*] (SAG)
MictchSy.......	Microtouch Systems, Inc. [*Associated Press*] (SAG)
MICU	Medical Intensive Care Unit [*Medicine*]
MICU	Mobile Intensive Care Unit [*Medicine*]
MICU(N).......	Mobile Intensive Care Unit [*or Nurse*] (GNE)
MICV..........	Mechanized Infantry Combat Vehicle [*Army*]
MICV-FPW...	Mechanized Infantry Combat Vehicle - Firing Port Weapon (MCD)
MICVS	Mechanized Infantry Combat Vehicle Systems [*Army*] (RDA)
MiCw	Coldwater Public Library, Coldwater, MI [*Library symbol Library of Congress*] (LCLS)
MICW..........	Member of the Institute of Clerks of Works of Great Britain, Inc. (DBQ)
Micware	Microware Systems Corp. [*Associated Press*] (SAG)
MiCwB.........	Branch County Library, Coldwater, MI [*Library symbol Library of Congress*] (LCLS)
MiD.............	Detroit Public Library, Detroit, MI [*Library symbol Library of Congress*] (LCLS)
MID.............	Magnetically Insulated Diode [*Physics*]
MID.............	Maintenace Index Page (DNAB)
MID.............	Manpower Information Division [*Navy*]
MID.............	Mare Island Division [*San Francisco Bay Naval Shipyard, Vallejo, CA*]
MID.............	Marginally Indigent Defendant
MID.............	Master of Industrial Design
MID.............	Master of Interior Design (GAGS)
MID.............	Maximum Inhibiting Dilution [*Medicine*] (MAE)
MID.............	Maximum Inhibiting Duration [*Medicine*] (DAVI)
MID.............	Measure of Intellectual Development (EDAC)
MID.............	Meat Inspection Division [*of ARS, Department of Agriculture*]
MID.............	Median Infective Dose [*Bacteriology*]
MID.............	Mentioned in Dispatches (ADA)
MID.............	Merida [*Mexico*] [*Airport symbol*] (OAG)
MID.............	Mesioincisodistal [*Dentistry*]
MID.............	Message Identification [*Computer science*]
MID.............	Message Identifier (ACRL)
MID.............	Message Input Description
MID.............	Message Input Device (AABC)
MID.............	Mid Airways [*France*] [*FAA designator*] (FAAC)
MID.............	Midbody
MID.............	Midbody (NASA)
MID.............	Midcon Oil & Gas Ltd. [*Toronto Stock Exchange symbol*]
MID.............	Middle (AFM)
MID.............	Middle
mid	Middle (VRA)
MID.............	Middleton Island [*Alaska*] [*Seismograph station code, US Geological Survey*] (SEIS)
MID.............	Middling Space [*Typesetting*] (DGA)
Mid..............	Middoth (BJA)
MID.............	Midland [*Topography*] (ROG)
MID.............	MIDLNET [*Midwest Regional Library Network*], St. Louis, MO [*OCLC symbol*] (OCLC)
MID.............	Midnight
Mid..............	Midrash [*Interpretation of Old Testament writings*] (BJA)
MID.............	Midshipman [*Navy*]
MID.............	Midway Railroad Co. [*AAR code*]
MID.............	Midwest Stock Exchange [*Chicago, IL*] (CDAI)
MID.............	Midwifery (ROG)
MID.............	Military Intelligence Detachment (AABC)
MID.............	Military Intelligence Division [*War Department*] [*World War II*]
MID.............	Minimal Inhibiting Dose [*Medicine*]
MID.............	Minimum Infective Dose [*Bacteriology*]
MID.............	Ministerstvo Inostrannykh Del [*Ministry of Foreign Affairs*] [*Former USSR*]
MID.............	Missile Intelligence Directorate [*Army*] (AABC)
MID.............	Missile Intelligence Directory
MID.............	Modified Ionization Detector (MCD)
MID.............	Mortgage Interest Differential
MID.............	Movimiento de Integracion Democratica [*Democratic Integration Movement*] [*Dominican Republic*] [*Political party*] (PPW)
MID.............	Movimiento Independiente Democratico [*Independent Democratic Movement*] [*Panama*] [*Political party*] (PPW)
MID.............	Multi-Information Display [*Automotive engineering*]
MID.............	Multiple Infant Dementia [*Neurology*] (CPH)
MID.............	Multiple Infarct Dementia [*Neurology*]
MID.............	Multiple Ion Detection
MID.............	Multiplexing Identifier [*Telecommunications*] (ACRL)
MID.............	Munitions Inventions Department [*British military*] (DMA)
MID.............	Musically Intelligent Device [*Electronic musical instruments*]
MiDA	Detroit Institute of Arts, Detroit, MI [*Library symbol Library of Congress*] (LCLS)
MIDA	Major Items Data Agency [*Military*]
MIDA	Message Interchange Distributed Application [*Telecommunications*] (OSI)
MIDA	Mid-American International Development Association [*Nigeria*]
MIDA	Moviemiento de Integracion Democratica [*The Dominican Republic*] [*Political party*] (EY)
MiDAA.........	Catholic Archdiocese of Detroit, Archives, Detroit, MI [*Library symbol*] [*Library of Congress*] (LCLS)
MidAApt.......	Mid America Apartment Communities, Inc. [*Associated Press*] (SAG)
MidABc.......	Mid-America Bancorp [*Associated Press*] (SAG)
MIDAC.........	Management Information for Decision and Control
MIDAC.........	Michigan [*University of*] Digital Automatic Computer
MiDACI.......	American Concrete Institute, Detroit, MI [*Library symbol Library of Congress*] (LCLS)
MIDADE.......	Mouvement International d'Apostolat des Enfants [*International Movement of Apostolate of Children*] [*France*]
MidAE.........	Mid American Energy Co. [*Associated Press*] (SAG)
MidAg.........	Midrash Aggadah (BJA)
Mid-Am........	Mid-America: An Historical Review [*A publication*] (BRI)
MIDAM........	Midamerica Commodity Exchange (EA)
MidAm........	Mid-Am, Inc. [*Associated Press*] (SAG)
MiDAMA	Automobile Manufacturers' Association, Inc., Detroit, MI [*Library symbol Library of Congress*] (LCLS)
MidAmEn.....	Mid American Energy Co. [*Associated Press*] (SAG)
MidAmIn.......	Mid-Am, Inc. [*Associated Press*] (SAG)
MidAmR	Mid America Realty, Inc. [*Formerly, Dial REIT*] [*Associated Press*] (SAG)
MIDAN........	Microprocessor Data Analyzer [*Instrumentation*]
MIDANET.....	Mortgage Information Direct Access Network [*FHLMC*] (EMRF)
MidAp........	Mid America Apartment Communities [*Associated Press*] (SAG)
MIDAR	Microwave Detection and Ranging
MIDAR	Motion Indicating RADAR (MCD)
MID-ARK......	Mid-Arkansas Regional Library [*Library network*]
MIDARM.......	Microdynamic Angle and Rate Monitoring System
MIDAS	Mainline Information Display and Automation System [*Salford Electrical Instruments*] (NITA)
MIDAS	Maintenance Integrated Data Access System (MCD)
MIDAS	Management Information and Development Aids System (SSD)
MIDAS	Management Integrated Data Accumulating System
MIDAS	Man-Machine Integration Design and Analysis System (GAVI)
MIDAS	Maritime Industrial Development Area [*Navy*]
MIDAS	Materiel Inventory Data Acquisition System
MIDAS	Measurement Information Data Analysis System [*or Subsystem*] (IEEE)
MIDAS	Mechanism Integration Design and Analysis System [*Computer-assisted engineering*]
MIDAS	Medical Information Dissemination Using ASSASSIN (NITA)
MIDAS	Memory Implemented Data Acquisition Systems
MIDAS	Meteorological Information and Dose Acquisition System [*Nuclear energy*] (NRCH)
MIDAS	Meteorological Integrating Data Acquisition System [*Marine science*] (MSC)
MIDAS	Microcomputer-Interfaced Data Acquisition System [*Computer science*]
MIDAS	Micro-Diagnostics for Analysis and Repair (NITA)
MIDAS	Microimaged Data Addition System [*CAPS Equipment Ltd.*]
MIDAS	Microprogrammable Integrated Data Acquisition System
MIDAS	Microprogramming Design Aided System [*RCA*]
MIDAS	Microscopic Image Digital Acquisition System (PDAA)
MIDAS	Mine Detection and Avoidance System (MCD)
MIDAS	Miniature Data Acquisition System
MIDAS	Missile Defense Alarm [*or Alert*] System [*Air Force*]
MIDAS	Missile Detection and Alarm System [*Army*] (AABC)
MIDAS	Missile Detection and Surveillance (CAAL)
MIDAS	Missile Intercept Data Acquisition System
MIDAS	Model for Interheater Deployment by Air and Sea [*DoD*]
MIDAS	Modified Integration Digital Analog Simulator [*Computer science*] (MCD)
MIDAS	Modular Integrated Design Automated System
MIDAS	Modular Interactive Data Acquisition System [*National Institute of Standards and Technology*]
MIDAS	Modular International Dealing and Accounting System (NITA)
MIDAS	Modulator Isolation Diagnostic Analysis System (IEEE)
MIDAS	Monopoly Information and Data Analysis System
MIDAS	Multicenter Isradipine Diuretic Atherosclerosis Study
MIDAS	Multi-Discipline Data Analysis System (GAVI)
MIDAS	Multi-Mode International Data Acquisition Service (NITA)
MIDAS	Multioptional Interactive Display and Analytic System (MCD)
MIDAS	Multiple Index Data Access System [*Prime Computer, Inc.*]
MIDAS	Multiple Input Data Acquisition System [*Bell System*]
MIDAS	Multiple Integrated Document Assembly System [*Computer science*] (BYTE)
MIDAS	Multitier Distributed Application Services [*Computer science*]
MID/ASIA....	Middle East/Asia Region [*USTTA*] (TAG)
MIDATA	Marconi Integrated Design and Test Automation [*Marconi Industries*] [*Telecommunications British*]
MIDATL........	Mid-Atlantic (DNAB)
MidAtlan.......	Mid-Atlantic Medical Services, Inc. [*Associated Press*] (SAG)
MidatRty.......	Midatlantic Realty Trust [*Associated Press*] (SAG)
MiDb...........	Dearborn Public [*Henry Ford Centennial*] Library, Dearborn, MI [*Library symbol Library of Congress*] (LCLS)
MiDB	Detroit Bar Association, Detroit, MI [*Library symbol Library of Congress*] (LCLS)
MiD-B	Detroit Public Library, Burton Historical Collection, Detroit, MI [*Library symbol Library of Congress*] (LCLS)
MIDB	Misr Iran Development Bank
MiDBA	Detroit Bar Association, Detroit, MI [*Library symbol*] [*Library of Congress*] (LCLS)

MidBay .... Middle Bay Oil Co., Inc. [*Associated Press*] (SAG)

MiDbEI .... Edison Institute [*Henry Ford Museum and Greenfield Village*] Library, Dearborn, MI [*Library symbol Library of Congress*] (LCLS)

MiDbF .... Ford Motor Co., Dearborn, MI [*Library symbol Library of Congress*] (LCLS)

MiDbGS .... Church of Jesus Christ of Latter-Day Saints, Genealogical Society Library, Dearborn Stake Branch, LDS Chapel, Dearborn, MI [*Library symbol Library of Congress*] (LCLS)

MiDbHi .... Dearborn Historical Museum, Dearborn, MI [*Library symbol Library of Congress*] (LCLS)

MidBk .... Midland Bank PLC [*Associated Press*] (SAG)

MiDbME .... Society of Manufacturing Engineers, Dearborn, MI [*Library symbol*] [*Library of Congress*] (LCLS)

MidbO .... Oakwood Hospital, Dearborn, MI [*Library symbol*] [*Library of Congress*] (LCLS)

MiDbU .... University of Michigan, Dearborn Campus, Dearborn, MI [*Library symbol Library of Congress*] (LCLS)

MiDC .... Detroit Chancery [*Catholic Church*] Archives, Detroit, MI [*Library symbol Library of Congress*] (LCLS)

MIDC .... MidConn Bank [*NASDAQ symbol*] (NQ)

MIDC .... Movement for an Independent and Democratic Cuba (EA)

MiDCh .... Children's Hospital of Michigan, Detroit, MI [*Library symbol Library of Congress*] (LCLS)

MiDChryE ..... Chrysler Corp., Engineering Division, Detroit, MI [*Library symbol Library of Congress*] (LCLS)

MiDCL .... Detroit College of Law, Detroit, ME [*Library symbol*] [*Library of Congress*] (LCLS)

Midcom .... Midcom Communications, Inc. [*Associated Press*] (SAG)

MidContB ..... Mid Continent Bancshares, Inc. [*Associated Press*] (SAG)

MIDCRU ...... Midshipman Cruise [*Navy*] (NVT)

MidCst .... Mid-Coast Bancorp, Inc. [*Associated Press*] (SAG)

MidcstE .... Midcoast Energy Resources, Inc. [*Associated Press*] (SAG)

MIDD .... Middleby Corp. [*NASDAQ symbol*] (TTSB)

MIDDLE .... Microprogram Design Description Language [*1977*] [*Computer science*] (CSR)

Middlebury C... Middlebury College (GAGS)

MiDDS .... Duns Scotus College, Detroit, MI [*Library symbol Library of Congress*] (LCLS)

MIDDX .... Middlesex [*County in England*]

Middx .... Middlesex [*County in England*] (ODBW)

Middx Sit ..... Sittings for Middlesex at Nisi Prius [*A publication*] (DLA)

MIDEASTFOR... Middle East Force [*Military*] (AABC)

MIDEASTFOR... Middle East Force (DOMA)

Mid East L Rev... Middle East Law Review [*A publication*] (DLA)

MIDEAST MI LIB... Mideastern Michigan Library Cooperative [*Library network*]

MiDec .... Van Buren County Library, Decatur, MI [*Library symbol Library of Congress*] (LCLS)

MiDecD .... Decatur Township Library, Webster Memorial Library Building, Decatur, MI [*Library symbol Library of Congress*] (LCLS)

MiDeck .... Deckerville Public Library, Deckerville, MI [*Library symbol Library of Congress*] (LCLS)

MiDecV .... Van Buren County Library, Webster Memorial Library Building, Decatur, MI [*Library symbol Library of Congress*] (LCLS)

MiDEd .... Detroit Edison Co., Detroit, MI [*Library symbol Library of Congress*] (LCLS)

MIDEF .... Microprocedure Definition

MIDEFO .... Mission Debrief Forms (CINC)

MiDelD .... Delton District Library, Delton, MI [*Library symbol Library of Congress*] (LCLS)

MIDES .... Missile Detection System

MiDet .... De Tour Area School and Public Library, De Tour Village, MI [*Library symbol Library of Congress*] (LCLS)

MiDew .... De Witt Public Library, De Witt, MI [*Library symbol Library of Congress*] (LCLS)

MiDex .... Dexter District Library, Dexter, MI [*Library symbol Library of Congress*] (LCLS)

MIDF .... Major Item Data File (AABC)

MIDF .... Multiple Input Describing Function (PDAA)

MiDG .... Gale Research Co., Detroit, MI [*Library symbol Library of Congress*] (LCLS)

Mid G .... Graduate Midwife

MiDGH .... Detroit General Hospital, Medical Library, Detroit, MI [*Library symbol Library of Congress*] (LCLS)

MiDGM-L ...... General Motors World Headquarters, General Motors Law Library, Detroit, MI [*Library symbol Library of Congress*] (LCLS)

MiDGrH .... Grace Hospital, Detroit, MI [*Library symbol Library of Congress*] (LCLS)

MIDH .... Middletown & Hummelstown Railroad Co. [*AAR code*]

MIDH .... Mouvement pour l'Instauration de la Democratie en Haiti [*Political party*] (EY)

MidHag .... Midrash ha-Gadol (BJA)

MiDHF .... Henry Ford Hospital, Detroit, MI [*Library symbol Library of Congress*] (LCLS)

MiDHH .... Harper Hospital, Department of Libraries, Detroit, MI [*Library symbol Library of Congress*] (LCLS)

MiDHi .... Detroit Historical Society, Detroit, MI [*Library symbol Library of Congress*] (LCLS)

MIDI .... Midisoft Corp. [*NASDAQ symbol*] (SAG)

MIDI .... Minnesota Infant Development Inventory [*Child development test*] [*Psychology*]

MIDI .... Miss Distance Indicator (MCD)

MIDI .... Musical Instrument Digital Interface [*Port*] [*Socket on an electronic synthesizer that permits a direct computer connection*]

MiDi .... Windsor Township Library, Dimondale, MI [*Library symbol Library of Congress*] (LCLS)

MIDIRS .... Midwives Information and Resource Service [*British*] (EAIO)

Midisoft .... Midisoft Corp. [*Associated Press*] (SAG)

MIDIST .... Mission Interministerielle de l'Information Scientifique et Technique [*Interministerial Mission for Scientific and Technical Information*] [*France Information service or system*] (IID)

MiDIT .... Detroit Institute of Technology, Detroit, MI [*Library symbol Library of Congress*] (LCLS)

MidIwa .... Mid Iowa Financial Corp. [*Associated Press*] (SAG)

MIDIZ .... Mid-Canada Identification Zone

MidJob .... Midrash Job (BJA)

MidJonah ..... Midrash Jonah (BJA)

MiDL .... Michigan Library Consortium, Wayne State University, Detroit, MI [*Library symbol Library of Congress*] (LCLS)

MIDL .... Midland [*English dialect*] (ROG)

MIDL .... Midlantic Corp. [*NASDAQ symbol*] (NQ)

MIDLAT........ Middle Latitude [*Navigation*]

MidlBk .... Midland Bank PLC [*Associated Press*] (SAG)

Midlby .... Middleby Corp. [*Associated Press*] (SAG)

MidlCp .... Midlantic Corp. [*Associated Press*] (SAG)

MidLekTov..... Midrash Lekah Tov (BJA)

MidlFn .... Midland Financial Group [*Associated Press*] (SAG)

MIDLIS .... Multifamily Insurance and Direct Loan Information System [*Department of Housing and Urban Development*] (GFGA)

MidInd .... Midland Co. [*Associated Press*] (SAG)

MIDLNET ...... Midwest Regional Library Network

MidlRs .... Midland Resources, Inc. [*Associated Press*] (SAG)

MiDM .... Marygrove College, Detroit, MI [*Library symbol Library of Congress*] (LCLS)

MiDMC .... Mercy College of Detroit, Detroit, MI [*Library symbol Library of Congress*] (LCLS)

MiDMch .... Mariners' Church, Detroit, MI [*Library symbol Library of Congress*] (LCLS)

MID-MO....... Mid-Month [*Amount of pay to be received by payee on the 15th day of the month*] (AABC)

MiDMP .... Merrill-Palmer Institute, Detroit, MI [*Library symbol Library of Congress*] (LCLS)

MIDMS .... Machine Independent Data Management System [*Defense Intelligence Agency*] (MCD)

MiDMtC .... Mount Carmel Mercy Hospital, Medical Library, Detroit, MI [*Library symbol Library of Congress*] (LCLS)

MIDN .... Midshipman [*Navy*]

MIDNET .... Midland Network (NITA)

MIDnet........ [*The*] Midwest Network [*Computer science*] (TNIG)

midnoc .... Midnight (DAVI)

MiDo .... Dorr Township Library, Dorr, MI [*Library symbol Library of Congress*] (LCLS)

MIDOC .... Mildew-Induced Defacement of Organic Coatings

MidOcn .... Mid Ocean Ltd. [*Associated Press*] (SAG)

MiDolb .... Osceola Township Public and School Library, Dollar Bay, MI [*Library symbol Library of Congress*] (LCLS)

MIDOP .... Missile Doppler

MIDOR .... Miss Distance Optical Recorder [*Military*] (PDAA)

MIDOT .... Multiple Interferometer Determination of Trajectories

MiDow .... Dowagiac Public Library, Dowagiac, MI [*Library symbol Library of Congress*] (LCLS)

MIDP .... Major Item Distribution Plan (AABC)

MIDP .... Microbiology and Infectious Diseases Program [*Bethesda, MD*] [*National Institute of Allergy and Infectious Diseases*] [*Department of Health and Human Services*] (GRD)

MIDP .... Motor Industry Development Program

MiDP .... Providence Hospital, School of Nursing, Detroit, MI [*Library symbol Library of Congress*] (LCLS)

MIDPAC .... Mid-Pacific

MIDPAC .... US Army Forces, Middle Pacific [*Name commonly used for AFMIDPAC*] [*World War II*]

MiDPD .... Parke, Davis & Co., Detroit, MI [*Library symbol Library of Congress*] (LCLS)

MIDPM .... Member of the Institute of Data Processing Management [*British*] (DCTA)

MidProv .... Midrash Proverbs (BJA)

MidPs .... Midrash Tehillim [*or The Midrash on Psalms*] (BJA)

MIDPT .... Midpoint (FAAC)

MIDR .... Mandatory Incident and Defect Reporting (NATG)

MidR .... Midland Resources, Inc. [*Associated Press*] (SAG)

Midr .... Midrash [*Interpretation of Old Testament writings*] (BJA)

MID-RATS..... Midnight Rations [*Navy*]

MiDRI .... Rehabilitation Institute, Detroit, MI [*Library symbol*] [*Library of Congress*] (LCLS)

MidrR .... Midrash Rabbah (BJA)

MidrSong..... Midrash to the Song of Songs (BJA)

MiDry .... Dryden Township Library, Dryden, MI [*Library symbol Library of Congress*] (LCLS)

MIDS .... Management Information and Data Systems (NVT)

MIDS .... Management Information Display System (MCD)

MIDS .... Marketing Information Data Systems, Inc. [*Information service or system*] (IID)

MIDS .... Matrix Information and Directory Services, Inc.

MIDS .... Mid-South Insurance Co. [*NASDAQ symbol*] (NQ)

MIDS .... Miniature Integrated Data System (MCD)

MIDS .... Miscarriage Infant Death Stillbirth Support Group

MIDS .... Missile Ignition and Destruct Simulator

MIDS .... Movable Information Drive System [*Nuclear energy*] (NRCH)

MIDS .... Movement Information Distribution Station

MIDS .... Multifunctional Information Distribution System [*NATO*] (MCD)

MIDS .... Multi-functional Information Distribution System

MIDS .... Multimode Information Distribution System

Midsag .... Midsagittal [Medicine]

MidSam .... Midrash Samuel (BJA)

MIDSD .... Management Information and Data Systems Division [Environmental Protection Agency] (GFGA)

MiDSH .... Sacred Heart Seminary, Detroit, MI [Library symbol Library of Congress] (LCLS)

MIDSIM .... Maxwell International Development Simulation

MiDSn .... Sinai Hospital, Detroit, MI [Library symbol Library of Congress] (LCLS)

Mids ND ...... [A] Midsummer Night's Dream [Shakespearean work] (BARN)

MidSou .... Mid-South Insurance Co. [Associated Press] (SAG)

MIDSR .... Midsummer (ROG)

MidStat .... Mid-States PLC [Associated Press] (SAG)

Midsth .... Midsouth Bancorp, Inc. [Associated Press] (SAG)

MidsthB .... Midsouth Bancorp, Inc. [Associated Press] (SAG)

MIDTA .... Member of the International Dance Teachers' Association [British] (DBQ)

MidTan .... Midrash Tanna'im on Deuteronomy (BJA)

Mid'Tehil ..... Midrash Tehillim [or The Midrash on Psalms] (BJA)

Mid Tenn St U... Middle Tennessee State University (GAGS)

MIDTRARON... Midshipman Training Squadron [Navy] (NVT)

MIDU .... Malfunction Insertion and Display Unit [Aviation]

MiDU .... University of Detroit, Detroit, MI [Library symbol Library of Congress] (LCLS)

MiDU-C........ University of Detroit, Colombiere Campus, Clarkston, MI [Library symbol Library of Congress] (LCLS)

MiDU-D........ University of Detroit, Dental Library, Detroit, MI [Library symbol Library of Congress] (LCLS)

MiDU-L........ University of Detroit, Law Library, Detroit, MI [Library symbol Library of Congress] (LCLS)

MIDW .... Midwestern (AFM)

MiDW .... Wayne State University, Detroit, MI [Library symbol Library of Congress] (LCLS)

MiDW-AL..... Wayne State University, Walter P. Reuther Library of Labor and Urban Affairs, Archivesof Labor History and Urban Affairs, Detroit, MI [Library symbol] [Library of Congress] (LCLS)

MidwBn .... Midwest Bancshares [Associated Press] (SAG)

MiDWc......... Wayne County Records, Court House, Wayne County, Detroit, MI [Library symbol Library of Congress] (LCLS)

MiDWcC ...... Wayne County Community College, Detroit, MI [Library symbol Library of Congress] (LCLS)

MIDWEEK .... Manager Integrated Dictionary Week [Manager Software Products] (EA)

MIDWESTNAVFACENGCOM... Midwest Division Naval Facilities Engineering Command

Midwest S U... Midwestern State University (GAGS)

MidwGm....... Midway Games, Inc. [Associated Press] (SAG)

MidwGr........ Midwest Grain Products, Inc. [Associated Press] (SAG)

MiDW-L....... Wayne State University, Law Library, Detroit, MI [Library symbol Library of Congress] (LCLS)

MiDW-M...... Wayne State University, Medical Library, Detroit, MI [Library symbol Library of Congress] (LCLS)

MiDW-Mi..... Wayne State University, Miles Manuscript Collection, Detroit, MI [Library symbol Library of Congress Obsolete] (LCLS)

MiDW-P....... Wayne State University, School of Pharmacy, Detroit, MI [Library symbol Library of Congress] (LCLS)

MidwRE....... Midwest Real Estate Shopping Centers Ltd. [Associated Press] (SAG)

MiDW-S....... Wayne State University, Kresge-Hooker Science Library, Detroit, MI [Library symbol Library of Congress] (LCLS)

MIE .... Aero Premier de Mexico, SA de CV [Mexico] [FAA designator] (FAAC)

MiE .... East Lansing Public Library, East Lansing, MI [Library symbol Library of Congress] (LCLS)

MIE .... European Federation for Medical Informatics [Sweden] (EAIO)

MIE .... Magnetic Isotope Effect [Physics]

MIE .... Magnetron Ion Etching [Semiconductor technology]

MIE .... Major Items of Equipment

MIE .... Management Improvement and Evaluation

MIE .... Management Information Element [Telecommunications] (OSI)

MIE .... Maserati Information Exchange (EA)

MIE .... Mass Inertia Excitation

MIE .... Master of Industrial Engineering

MIE .... Master of Industrial Engineering (GAGS)

MIE .... Master of Irrigation Engineering

MIE .... Merrill Lynch & Co. "MITTS" 98 [NYSE symbol] (SPSG)

MIE .... Merrill Lynch & Co'MITTS'98 [NYSE symbol] (TTSB)

MIE .... Meteor Ionizing Efficiency

Mi-E........... Michigan State Library, Escanaba Branch, Escanaba, MI [Library symbol Library of Congress] (LCLS)

MiE .... Minimum Effect [Pharmacology]

MIE .... Minimum Ignition Energy

MIE .... Mission-Independent Equipment [NASA]

MIE .... Mobile Inspection Equipment (SAA)

MIE .... Muncie [Indiana] [Airport symbol] (OAG)

MIE .... Muncie, IN [Location identifier FAA] (FAAL)

MIEA.......... Music Industry Educators Association (EA)

MiEad .... East Detroit Memorial Library, East Detroit, MI [Library symbol Library of Congress] (LCLS)

MiEat .... Eaton Rapids Public Library, Eaton Rapids, MI [Library symbol Library of Congress] (LCLS)

MIEAWA ...... Meat Industries Employers' Association of Western Australia

MIEC .... Branche Africaine du Mouvement International des Etudiants Catholiques [African International Movement of Catholic Students - AIMCS] (EAIO)

MiEc .... Eau Claire District Library, Eau Claire, MI [Library symbol Library of Congress] (LCLS)

MIEC .... Meteorological Information Extraction Center

MIEC .... Military Intelligence Exchange Center (CINC)

MIEC .... Mixed Ionic and Electronic Conducting [Polymers]

MIEC .... [Meteorological Information Extraction Center] Operator Guide

MIEC .... Pax Romana, Mouvement International des Etudiants Catholiques [Pax Romana, International Movement of Catholic Students - IMCS] [Paris, France] (EAIO)

MIED .... Member of the Institution of Engineering Designers [British] (DBQ)

MIEE .... Mechanical, Instrument, and Electrical Engineering [Department of Employment] [British]

MIEE .... Member of the Institution of Electrical Engineers [Formerly, AMIEE] [British] (EY)

MIEEE .... Member of the Institute of Electrical and Electronic Engineers

MIEETAT ..... Major Improvements in Electronic Effectiveness through Advanced Technology (MCD)

MIEF .... Master Imagery Exchange Format (MCD)

MIEI .... Member of the Institution of Engineering Inspection [British]

MIE(Ind) ...... Member of the Institution of Engineers, India

MiEIb .... Elberta Public Library, Elberta, MI [Library symbol Library of Congress] (LCLS)

MIEIecIE ...... Corporate Member of the Institution of Electrical and Electronics Incorporated Engineers [British] (DBQ)

MiEIk .... Elk Rapids District Library, Elk Rapids, MI [Library symbol Library of Congress] (LCLS)

MiEm.......... Glen Lake Community Library, Empire, MI [Library symbol Library of Congress] (LCLS)

MIEM .... Master in International Economics and Management (ECON)

MIEM .... Master Member of the Institute of Executives and Managers [British] (DBQ)

MIEM .... Masters Degree in International Economics and Management (ECON)

MiEM .... Michigan State University, East Lansing, MI [Library symbol Library of Congress] (LCLS)

MIE Mgmt... Master of Industrial Engineering Management (PGP)

MiEmp .... Glen Lake Community Library, Empire, MI [Library symbol] [Library of Congress] (LCLS)

MI Eng........ Master of Industrial Engineering

MIER.......... Management-Initiated Early Retirement (ADA)

MIERE......... Member of the Institution of Electronic and Radio Engineers [Formerly, M Brit IRE] [British]

MIERS .... Modernized Imagery Exploitation and Reporting System (MCD)

MIES .... Member of the Institution of Engineers and Shipbuilders, Scotland

MiEsc.......... Escanaba Public Library, Escanaba, MI [Library symbol Library of Congress] (LCLS)

MiEscB .... Bay De Noc Community College, Escanaba, MI [Library symbol Library of Congress] (LCLS)

MIESR .... Matrix Isolation and Electron Spin Resonance [Analytical chemistry]

MiEv .... Evart Public Library, Evart, MI [Library symbol Library of Congress] (LCLS)

MiEw .... McMillan Township Library, Ewen, MI [Library symbol Library of Congress] (LCLS)

MI Ex .... Member of the Institute of Export [British]

MIExE .... Member of the Institute of Executive Engineers and Officers [British] (DBQ)

MIEx(Grad)... Member of the Institute of Export [British] (DBQ)

MIExpE .... Member of the Institute of Explosives Engineers [British] (DBQ)

MIF .... Macrophage Inhibitory Factor [Immunology]

MIF .... Maker Interchange Format [Computer science] (CDE)

MIF .... Malfunction Investigations File (MCD)

MIF .... Management Information File [Computer science] (PCM)

MIF .... Management Information Format [Computer science]

MIF .... Manual Intervention Facility

MIF .... MARC [Machine-Readable Cataloging] International Format

MIF .... Maritime Interception Force (DOMA)

MIF .... Master Index File

MIF .... Master Inventory File (AFIT)

MIF .... Master Item File (MCD)

MIF .... Maximal Inspiratory Flow [Medicine]

MIF .... Medina, OH [Location identifier FAA] (FAAL)

MIF .... Melanocyte-Inhibiting Factor [Endocrinology]

MIF .... Melanocyte-Stimulating-Hormone Release Inhibiting Factor [Also, MRIF] [Endocrinology]

MIF .... Melanotropin Inhibiting Factor [Biochemistry]

MIF .... Melbourne International Festival [Australia]

MIF .... Membrane Immunofluorescence [Analytical biochemistry]

MIF .... Merthiolate-Iodine-Formaldehyde [Technique]

MIF .... Mesoderm-Inducing Factor [Embryology]

MIF .... Midinspiratory Flow [Medicine] (DMAA)

MIF .... Migration Inhibition [or Inhibitory] Factor [Cytology]

MIF .... Milk Industry Foundation (EA)

MIF .... Milk in First [Tea-pouring procedure]

MIF .... Miners' International Federation [See also FIM] [Brussels, Belgium] (EAIO)

MIF .... Missile-in-Flight

MIF .... Mixed Immunofluorescence [Medicine] (MAE)

MIF .... Mobile Instrument Facility

MIF .... Module Integration Facility (SSD)

MIF .... Monopulse Interference Filter

MIF .... Mortgage Indemnity Fund [Veterans Administration]

MIF .... Multisource Intelligence File (MCD)

MIF .... MuniInsured Fund Inc. [AMEX symbol] (SPSG)

MIF	MunInsred Fund [*AMEX symbol*] (TTSB)
MIF	Myocardial Infarction [*Cardiology*] (DHSM)
MIFA	Mitomycin C, Fluorouracil, Adriamycin [*Antineoplastic drug regimen*]
MIFACS	Medical Institutions' Financial Accounting System
MI-FA-MI	Misery, Famine, Misery [*Said to be "earth's song," in theory that all planets emit musical sounds governed by their paths around the sun*]
MIFAS	Mechanized Integrated Financial Accounting System [*Department of State*]
MIFASS	Marine Integrated Fire and Air Support System
MiFaw	Farwell Public Library, Farwell, MI [*Library symbol Library of Congress*] (LCLS)
MIFC	Madonna International Fan Club [*Defunct*] (EA)
MIFC	Merthiolate-Iodine Formalin Concentration
MIFC	Mid Iowa Financial Corp. [*NASDAQ symbol*] (SAG)
MIFC	Mid-Iowa Finl [*NASDAQ symbol*] (TTSB)
MIFD	Material Information Flow Device [*Military*] (AFM)
MIFE	Minimum Independent Failure Element
MIFF	Management Information Format File [*Computer science*]
MIFF	Member of the Institute of Freight Forwarders [*British*] (ODBW)
MiFg	Fairgrove Township Library, Fairgrove, MI [*Library symbol Library of Congress*] (LCLS)
MIFG	Micro Focus Group Ltd. [*NASDAQ symbol*] (SAG)
MIFG	Patches of Shallow Fog not Deeper Than Two Meters [*NWS*] (FAAC)
MIFGY	Micro Focus Grp ADS [*NASDAQ symbol*] (TTSB)
MIFI	Missile In-Flight Indicator
MiFil	Fife Lake Public Library, Fife Lake, MI [*Library symbol Library of Congress*] (LCLS)
MIFIR	Microwave Instantaneous Frequency Indication Receiver (MCD)
MIFirE	Member of the Institution of Fire Engineers [*British*] (DCTA)
MIFireE	Member of the Institution of Fire Engineers [*British*] (EY)
MIFL	Master International Frequency List
MiFli	Flint Public Library, Flint, MI [*Library symbol Library of Congress*] (LCLS)
MiFliACS	AC Spark Plug Co., General Motors Corp., Flint, MI [*Library symbol Library of Congress*] (LCLS)
MiFliC	University of Michigan at Flint, and Charles Stewart Mott Community College, Flint, MI [*Library symbol Library of Congress*] (LCLS)
MiFliG	GMI Engineering and Management Institute, Flint, MI [*Library symbol Library of Congress*] (LCLS)
MiFos	Watertown Township Library, Fostoria, MI [*Library symbol Library of Congress*] (LCLS)
MiFow	Fowlerville Public Library, Fowlerville, MI [*Library symbol Library of Congress*] (LCLS)
MIFR	Master International Frequency Register
MIFR	Maximal Inspiratory Flow Rate [*Medicine*]
MIFR	Monitored International Frequency Register (NITA)
MIFR	Multiband Infrared Filter Radiometer
MiFra	Frankfort City Library, Frankfort, MI [*Library symbol Library of Congress*] (LCLS)
MiFram	James E. Wickson Memorial Library, Frankenmuth, MI [*Library symbol Library of Congress*] (LCLS)
MiFras	Fraser Public Library, Fraser, MI [*Library symbol Library of Congress*] (LCLS)
MiFrem	Fremont Public Library, Fremont, MI [*Library symbol Library of Congress*] (LCLS)
MIFS	Material Information Flow System [*Military*] (AFM)
MIFS	Multiplex Interferometric Fourier Spectroscopy
MIFSA	Missile In-Flight Safety Approval (MUGU)
MIFT	Manchester International Freight Terminal [*British*] (DS)
Mig	De Migratione Abrahami [*Philo*] (BJA)
MIG	Magnetic Injection Gun (IEEE)
MIG	Magnetized Ionized Gas
MIG	Malaria Immune Globulin
MIG	Management Information Guide [*Reference series*]
MIG	Mars Investigation Group [*Defunct*] (EA)
MIG	Meadowbrook Insurance Group [*NYSE symbol*] (SAG)
MIG	Meadowbrook Insurance Grp [*NYSE symbol*] (TTSB)
MIG	Measles Immune Globulin [*Immunology*]
MIG	Meat Innovation Grant
MIG	Medial Inferior Geniculate Artery [*Anatomy*]
MIG	Medicare Insured Group (HCT)
M-Ig	Membrane Immunoglobulin [*Immunology*]
MIG	Metal-Inert-Gas [*Underwater welding*]
MIG	Methane Inert Gas (MCD)
Mig	Mignon [*Horticulture*]
MIG	Mikoyan and Gurevich [*Acronym used as designation for a Russian aircraft and is formed from the names of the aircraft's designers*]
MIG	Military Intelligence Group (MCD)
MIG	Military Intelligence Guide (MCD)
MIG	Millington, TN [*Location identifier FAA*] (FAAL)
MIG	Ming Mines Ltd. [*Vancouver Stock Exchange symbol*]
MIG	Miniature Integrating Gyroscope
MIG	Moody's Investment Grade
MIG	Multilevel Interconnect Generator
MIG-1	Moody's Investment Grade (DFIT)
MIGA	Multilateral Investment Guarantee Agency [*World Bank*]
MiGal	Galesburg Memorial Library, Galesburg, MI [*Library symbol Library of Congress*] (LCLS)
MI/GAL	Miles per Gallon (WDAA)
MiGali	Galien Township Public Library, Galien, MI [*Library symbol Library of Congress*] (LCLS)
MIGasE	Member of the Institution of Gas Engineers [*British*]
MiGay	Gaylord-Otsego County Public Library, Gaylord, MI [*Library symbol Library of Congress*] (LCLS)

MIGB	Millinery Institute of Great Britain (BI)
MiGc	Garden City Public Library, Garden City, MI [*Library symbol Library of Congress*] (LCLS)
MIGCAP	MIG [*Mikoyan and Gurevich*] Combat Air Patrol (DNAB)
MIGD	Member of the Institute of Grocery Distribution [*British*] (DBQ)
MIGeol	Member of the Institution of Geologists [*British*] (DBQ)
MIGET	Miniature Interface General-Purpose Economy Terminal [*Computer science*] (MHDB)
MIgG	Monkey Immunoglobulin G [*Immunology*]
MiGh	Loutit Library, Grand Haven, MI [*Library symbol Library of Congress*] (LCLS)
MIGI	Meridian Insrance Gp [*NASDAQ symbol*] (TTSB)
MIGI	Meridian Insurance Group, Inc. [*NASDAQ symbol*] (NQ)
MiGl	Gladstone Public Library, Gladstone, MI [*Library symbol Library of Congress*] (LCLS)
MiGlad	Gladwin County Library, Gladwin, MI [*Library symbol Library of Congress*] (LCLS)
MiGlad-B	Gladwin County Library, Beaverton Branch Library, Beaverton, MI [*Library symbol Library of Congress*] (LCLS)
MIGN	Michigan Northern Railway Co., Inc. [*AAR code*]
MiGp	Grosse Pointe Public Library, Grosse Pointe, MI [*Library symbol Library of Congress*] (LCLS)
MiGr	Grand Rapids Public Library, Grand Rapids, MI [*Library symbol Library of Congress*] (LCLS)
MiGrA	Aquinas College, Grand Rapids, MI [*Library symbol Library of Congress*] (LCLS)
MiGran	Grant Public Library, Grant, MI [*Library symbol Library of Congress*] (LCLS)
MiGray	Crawford County Library, Grayling, MI [*Library symbol Library of Congress*] (LCLS)
MiGrB	Grand Rapids Baptist College, Grand Rapids, MI [*Library symbol Library of Congress*] (LCLS)
MiGrC	Calvin College and Seminary, Grand Rapids, MI [*Library symbol Library of Congress*] (LCLS)
MiGre	Greenville Public Library, Greenville, MI [*Library symbol] [Library of Congress*] (LCLS)
MiGrJC	Grand Rapids Junior College, Grand Rapids, MI [*Library symbol Library of Congress*] (LCLS)
MiGrl	Grand Ledge Public Library, Grand Ledge, MI [*Library symbol Library of Congress*] (LCLS)
MiGrL	Grand Rapids Law Library, Grand Rapids, MI [*Library symbol Library of Congress*] (LCLS)
MiGrlP	Grand Ledge Public Library, Grand Ledge, MI [*Library symbol] [Library of Congress*] (LCLS)
MiGrMtM	Mount Mercy Academy, Grand Rapids, MI [*Library symbol Library of Congress*] (LCLS)
MiGrW	Western Michigan Genealogical Society, Grand Rapids, MI [*Library symbol Library of Congress*] (LCLS)
MIGS	Miniature Infrared Guidance Sensor
MIGS	Music Industries Golfing Society [*British*] (BI)
MiGw	Forsythe Township Public Library, Gwinn, MI [*Library symbol Library of Congress*] (LCLS)
MIH	Brownsville, TX [*Location identifier FAA*] (FAAL)
MIH	Master of Industrial Health
MIH	Melanocyte-Stimulating Hormone-Inhibitory Hormone [*Endocrinology*] (DAVI)
MIH	Member of the Institute of Housing [*British*] (DBQ)
MIH	Member of the Institute of Hygiene [*British*]
MIH	Migraine with Interparoxysmal Headache [*Neurology*] (DAVI)
MIH	Miles in the Hour [*Rate of military march*]
MIH	Minimal Intermittent [*Dosage of*] Heparin [*Pharmacology*] (DAVI)
MIH	Missing Interruption Handler [*Computer science*] (IBMDP)
MIH	Molecule-Induced Homolysis [*Chemistry*]
MIH	Molt Inhibitory Hormone
MIH	Multiplex Interface Handler
MiHa	Hart Public Library, Hart, MI [*Library symbol Library of Congress*] (LCLS)
MIHA	Move-In Housing Allowance
MiHaf	Hartford Public Library, Hartford, MI [*Library symbol Library of Congress*] (LCLS)
MiHal	Cromaine Library, Hartland, MI [*Library symbol Library of Congress*] (LCLS)
MiHam	Hamtramck Public Library, Hamtramck, MI [*Library symbol Library of Congress*] (LCLS)
MiHamb	Hamburg Township Library, Hamburg, MI [*Library symbol Library of Congress*] (LCLS)
MiHan	Hancock Public-School Library, Hancock, MI [*Library symbol Library of Congress*] (LCLS)
MiHanS	Suomi College, Hancock, MI [*Library symbol Library of Congress*] (LCLS)
MiHars	Harrison Public Library, Harrison, MI [*Library symbol Library of Congress*] (LCLS)
MiHarsM	Mid-Michigan Community College, Harrison, MI [*Library symbol Library of Congress*] (LCLS)
MiHarv	Alcona County Library, Harrisville, MI [*Library symbol Library of Congress*] (LCLS)
MiHas	Hastings Public Library, Hastings, MI [*Library symbol Library of Congress*] (LCLS)
MiHb	Harbor Beach Public Library, Harbor Beach, MI [*Library symbol Library of Congress*] (LCLS)
Mi-HC	Michigan Historical Commission, State Archives Library, Lansing, MI [*Library symbol Library of Congress*] (LCLS)
MIHC	M. I. Hummel Club (EA)
MiHe	Hesperia Public Library, Hesperia, MI [*Library symbol Library of Congress*] (LCLS)

MIHE............ Member of the Institute of Health Education [*British*]

MIHEc........... Member of the Institute of Home Economics [*British*] (DBQ)

MiHem.......... Mary C. Rauchholz Memorial Library, Hemlock, MI [*Library symbol Library of Congress*] (LCLS)

MiHil .... Mitchell Public Library, Hillsdale, MI [*Library symbol Library of Congress*] (LCLS)

MiHilC......... Hillsdale College, Hillsdale, MI [*Library symbol Library of Congress*] (LCLS)

MiHilm .... Hillman Public Library, Hillman, MI [*Library symbol Library of Congress*] (LCLS)

MiHl............ Houghton Lake Public Library, Houghton Lake, MI [*Library symbol Library of Congress*] (LCLS)

MIHM........... Master of International Health Management (PGP)

MiHM........... Michigan Technological University, Houghton, MI [*Library symbol Library of Congress*] (LCLS)

MIHO .... Miles Homes [*NASDAQ symbol*] (TTSB)

MIHO .... Miles Homes, Inc. [*NASDAQ symbol*] (SAG)

MiHol.......... Herrick Public Library, Holland, MI [*Library symbol Library of Congress*] (LCLS)

MiHolH .... Hope College, Holland, MI [*Library symbol Library of Congress*] (LCLS)

MiHolW .... Western Theological Seminary, Holland, MI [*Library symbol Library of Congress*] (LCLS)

MiHom .... Homer Public Library, Homer, MI [*Library symbol Library of Congress*] (LCLS)

MiHow .... Howell Carnegie Library, Howell, MI [*Library symbol Library of Congress*] (LCLS)

MiHp........... McGregor Public Library, Highland Park, MI [*Library symbol Library of Congress*] (LCLS)

MiHP .... Portage Lake District Library, Houghton, MI [*Library symbol Library of Congress*] (LCLS)

MiHpDH....... Detroit Osteopathic Hospital, Highland Park, MI [*Library symbol Library of Congress*] (LCLS)

MIHPED....... Microwave-Induced Helium Plasma Emission Detection (NATG)

MiHPL......... Portage Lake District Library, Houghton, MI [*Library symbol*] [*Library of Congress*] (LCLS)

MIHT........... Member of the Institution of Highways and Transportation [*British*] (DBQ)

MiHu.......... Hudson Public Library, Hudson, MI [*Library symbol Library of Congress*] (LCLS)

MiHudv........ Hudsonville Public Library, Hudsonville, MI [*Library symbol Library of Congress*] (LCLS)

MIHVE .... Member of the Institution of Heating and Ventilating Engineers [*British*]

MII.............. Caddo Mills, TX [*Location identifier FAA*] (FAAL)

MII.............. Management Interest Inventory [*Test*]

MII.............. Manufacturing Impact Item (MCD)

MII.............. Marilia [*Brazil*] [*Airport symbol*] (OAG)

MI/I............. Microinches per Inch (KSC)

MII.............. Military Intelligence Interpreter

MII.............. Military Intelligence Interrogation

MII.............. Mineral Information Institute (EA)

MII.............. Minnesota Interlibrary Telecommunications Exchange, Minneapolis, MN [*OCLC symbol*] (OCLC)

MII.............. Morton International [*NYSE symbol*] (TTSB)

MII.............. Morton International, Inc. [*NYSE symbol*] (SPSG)

MII.............. Motorists Information, Inc. [*Defunct*] (EA)

MIIAc.......... Medical Intelligence and Information Agency [*Formerly, MIO*] [*DoD*]

MIIA........... Member of the Institute of Industrial Administration [*Later, MBIM*] [*British*]

MIIA........... Merritt Island Industrial Area [*NASA*] (KSC)

MIIA........... Mine Inspectors' Institute of America (EA)

MIIC........... Pax Romana, Mouvement International des Intellectuels Catholiques [*Pax Romana, International Catholic Movement for Intellectual and Cultural Affairs - ICMICA*] [*Geneva, Switzerland*] (EAIO)

MIICS.......... Master Item Identification Control System

MiIld.......... Idlewild Public Library, Idlewild, MI [*Library symbol*] [*Library of Congress*] (LCLS)

MIID........... Media Institutes for Institute Directors

MIIDS .... Missile Interior Intrusion Detection System (DWSG)

MIIF........... Master Item Intelligence File

MIIL........... Master Item Identification List

MIIM........... Master of International and Intercultural Management (PGP)

MIIM........... Member of the Institution of Industrial Managers [*British*] (DCTA)

MI Inf Sc .... Member of the Institute of Information Scientists [*British*]

MiInr.......... Indian River Public Library, Indian River, MI [*Library symbol Library of Congress*] (LCLS)

MI insuf...... Mitral Insufficiency [*Cardiology*] (DAVI)

MiInt.......... Interlovhen Public Library, Interlochen, MI [*Library symbol*] [*Library of Congress*] (LCLS)

MiIrmD .... Dickinson County Library, Iron Mountain, MI [*Library symbol Library of Congress*] (LCLS)

MiIrmD-N .... Dickinson County Library, Norway Branch, Norway, MI [*Library symbol Library of Congress*] (LCLS)

MiIrmM....... Mid-Peninsula Library Federation Headquarters, Iron Mountain, MI [*Library symbol Library of Congress*] (LCLS)

MiIrmV .... United States Veterans Administration Hospital, Iron Mountain, MI [*Library symbol Library of Congress*] (LCLS)

MiIrr.......... West Iron District Library, Iron River, MI [*Library symbol Library of Congress*] (LCLS)

MiIrw .... Ironwood Carnegie Library, Ironwood, MI [*Library symbol Library of Congress*] (LCLS)

MiIsh.......... Ishpeming Carnegie Library, Ishpeming, MI [*Library symbol Library of Congress*] (LCLS)

MIIS............ Miscellaneous Inputs Information Subsystem [*Computer science*]

MIIS............ Monterey Institute of International Studies (ECON)

MIISA.......... Management Information and Instructional Systems Activity (DNAB)

MIISADET .... Management Information and Instructional Systems Activity Detachment (DNAB)

MIISAU .... Management Information and Instructional Systems Activity Unit (DNAB)

MIISE.......... Member of the International Institute of Social Economics [*British*] (DBQ)

MIISec......... Member of the Institute of Industrial Security [*British*] (DBQ)

MIIT........... Manned Interceptor Integration Team (SAA)

Milt........... Thompson Home Library, Ithaca, MI [*Library symbol Library of Congress*] (LCLS)

MIJ .... Dugway/Tooele, UT [*Location identifier FAA*] (FAAL)

MIJ .... Maatschappij [*Joint Stock Company*] [*Netherlands*]

MIJ .... Master of International Journalism (PGP)

MIJ .... Member of the Institution of Journalists

MIJ .... Metal Insulator Junction

MIJ .... Mili [*Marshall Islands*] [*Airport symbol*] (OAG)

MiJa .... Jackson Public Library, Jackson, MI [*Library symbol Library of Congress*] (LCLS)

MiJaC .... Jackson County Library, Jackson, MI [*Library symbol Library of Congress*] (LCLS)

MiJaCc .... Jackson Community College, Jackson, MI [*Library symbol Library of Congress*] (LCLS)

MiJaCP .... Consumers Power Co., Parnall Technical Library, Jackson, MI [*Library symbol*] [*Library of Congress*] (LCLS)

MiJam .... Jamestown Township Library, Jamestown, MI [*Library symbol Library of Congress*] (LCLS)

MIJARC....... Mouvement International de la Jeunesse Agricole et Rurale Catholique [*International Movement of Catholic Agricultural and Rural Youth - IMCARY*] [*Louvain, Belgium*] (EAIO)

MIJC........... Mouvement International des Juristes Catholiques, Pax Romana [*France*]

MiJen .... Georgetown Township Library, Jenison, MI [*Library symbol Library of Congress*] (LCLS)

MIJI........... Meaconing, Intrusion, Jamming, Interference [*Military*] (NVT)

MIJO........... Missile Joint Optimization

MiK............ Kalamazoo Public Library, Kalamazoo, MI [*Library symbol Library of Congress*] (LCLS)

MIK............ Meerblick, SA [*Spain*] [*FAA designator*] (FAAC)

MIK............ Methyl Isobutyl Ketone [*Also, MIBK*] [*Organic chemistry*]

MIK............ Mikkeli [*Finland*] [*Airport symbol*] (OAG)

Mik............ Mikva'ot (BJA)

MIK............ Minitrack [*Alaska*] [*Seismograph station code, US Geological Survey Closed*] (SEIS)

MIK............ More in the Kitchen [*Family dinner-table expression*]

MiKa........... Kalkaska County Library, Kalkaska, MI [*Library symbol Library of Congress*] (LCLS)

MIKA.......... Minor Karyotypic Abnormalities [*Medicine*]

MIKADOS..... Mini Instant Keyboard Assembler, Debug, and Operating System [*Computer science*] (MHDI)

Mikasa........ Mikasa, Inc. [*Associated Press*] (SAG)

MiKB........... Borgess Hospital, Medical Library, Kalamazoo, MI [*Library symbol Library of Congress*] (LCLS)

MiKC........... Kalamazoo College, Kalamazoo, MI [*Library symbol Library of Congress*] (LCLS)

MiKCS .... Institute of Cistercian Studies, Western Michigan University, Kalamazoo, MI [*Library symbol Library of Congress*] (LCLS)

MIKE.......... Manipulator Interactive Kinematics Evaluator (SSD)

MIKE.......... Mass-Analyzed Ion Kinetic Energy

MIKE.......... Measurement of Instantaneous Kinetic Energy (IEEE)

MIKE.......... Michael Stores [*NASDAQ symbol*] (SAG)

MIKE.......... Micro Interpreter for Knowledge Engineering [*Computer science*]

MIKE.......... Microphone (CET)

mike.......... Microphone (IDOE)

MIKE.......... Multiwave Italian Key System (NITA)

MIKER .... Microbalance Inverted Knudsen Effusion Recoil

MIKES........ Mass-Analyzed Ion Kinetic Energy Spectrometry

MikGed........ Mikra'ot Gedolot (BJA)

MiKin.......... Kingston Community Public Library, Kingston, MI [*Library symbol Library of Congress*] (LCLS)

MiKins........ Kingsley Public Library, Kingsley, MI [*Library symbol Library of Congress*] (LCLS)

MIKK.......... Medjunarodni Institut za Kucnu Knjizevnost [*International Institute for Home Literature - IIHL*] [*Belgrade, Yugoslavia*] (EAIO)

MiKL.......... Kalamazoo Library System, Kalamazoo, MI [*Library symbol Library of Congress*] (LCLS)

MIKL.......... Michael Foods [*NASDAQ symbol*] (TTSB)

MIKL.......... Michael Foods, Inc. [*NASDAQ symbol*] (NQ)

MIKN .... Mikohn Gaming [*NASDAQ symbol*] (TTSB)

MIKN .... Mikohn Gaming Corp. [*NASDAQ symbol*] (SAG)

Mikohn........ Mikohn Gaming Corp. [*Associated Press*] (SAG)

MiKPSc........ Kalamazoo Public School District, Kalamazoo, MI [*Library symbol Library of Congress*] (LCLS)

MIKR.......... Mikron Instr [*NASDAQ symbol*] (TTSB)

MIKR.......... Mikron Instrument Co., Inc. [*NASDAQ symbol*] (NQ)

Mikron........ Mikron Instrument Co., Inc. [*Associated Press*] (SAG)

MiKUp........ Upjohn Co., Kalamazoo, MI [*Library symbol Library of Congress*] (LCLS)

MiKUp_B .... Upjohn Co., Business Library, Kalamazoo, MI [*Library symbol*] [*Library of Congress*] (LCLS)

MIKV.......... Kalamazoo Valley Community College, Kalamazoo, MI [*Library symbol Library of Congress*] (LCLS)

Mikv.......... Mikva'ot (BJA)

MiKW.......... Western Michigan University, Kalamazoo, MI [*Library symbol Library of Congress*] (LCLS)

MiKWUp ...... W. E. Upjohn Institute for Employment Research, Kalamazoo, MI [*Library symbol Library of Congress*] (LCLS)

miky............ Milky [*Philately*]

MiL.............. Lansing Public Library, Lansing, MI [*Library symbol Library of Congress*] (LCLS)

MIL.............. Magnetic Indicator Loop (NVT)

MIL.............. Malfunction Indicator Light [*Automotive engineering*]

MIL.............. Malfunction Investigation Laboratory

MIL.............. Marine Instrumentation Laboratory [*Marine science*] (OSRA)

MIL.............. Marine Instrumentation Laboratory (USDC)

MIL.............. Master Index List (MCD)

MIL.............. Master Instrumentation List

MIL.............. Master Item Identification List (AABC)

MIL.............. Material

MIL.............. Member of the Institute of Linguists [*British*]

MIL.............. Mensa International [*British*] (EAIO)

MIL.............. Merritt Island Tracking Station [*Florida*]

MIL.............. Microimplementation Language [*Burroughs Corp.*]

MIL.............. Milan [*Italy*] [*Seismograph station code, US Geological Survey Closed*] (SEIS)

MIL.............. Milan [*Italy*] [*Airport symbol*] (OAG)

MIL.............. Mileage

Mil............... Miles' Pennsylvania Reports [*A publication*] (DLA)

MIL.............. Military (EY)

MIL.............. Military Instrumentation List

MIL.............. Military Specification [*Followed by a single capital letter and numbers*] (IEEE)

MIL.............. Militia

Mil............... Miller's Reports [*1-5 Louisiana*] [*A publication*] (DLA)

Mil............... Miller's Reports [*3-18 Maryland*] [*A publication*] (DLA)

MIL.............. Millieme [*Monetary unit*] [*Egypt, Sudan*]

mil............... Milli-Inch

MIL.............. Milliliter

MIL.............. Milling

MIL.............. Million

MIL.............. Millipore Corp. [*NYSE symbol*] (SPSG)

Mil............... Mills' New York Surrogate's Court Reports [*A publication*] (DLA)

Mil............... Mill's South Carolina Constitutional Reports [*A publication*] (DLA)

MIL.............. Milwaukee [*Wisconsin*]

MIL.............. Minnesota Instructional Language [*Computer science*] (CSR)

MIL.............. Missile Industry Liaison (SAA)

MIL.............. Module Interconnection Language

MIL.............. Mothers-in-Law Club International (EA)

MIL.............. Movimiento Iberico Libertario [*Spain Political party*]

MIL.............. Moving Inspection Lot

MIL.............. Office of Public Library and Interlibrary Cooperation, St. Paul, MN [*OCLC symbol*] (OCLC)

Mil............... Pro Milone [*of Cicero*] [*Classical studies*] (OCD)

MILA........... Merritt Island Launch Area [*NASA*]

Mila........... Militia [*British military*] (DMA)

MILAA........ Milastar Corp. [*NASDAQ symbol*] (NQ)

MiLac......... Missaukee County Library, Lake City, MI [*Library symbol Library of Congress*] (LCLS)

MiLacES ..... Lake City Elementary School, Lake City, MI [*Library symbol*] [*Library of Congress*] (LCLS)

MiLacHS...... Lake City High School, Lake City, MI [*Library symbol*] [*Library of Congress*] (LCLS)

MILAD .... Military Advisor [*SEATO or ANZUS Council*] (CINC)

MILADGOVT... Military Advisory Government

MILADGRU... Military Advisory Group

MILADREP... Military Advisors Representative (CINC)

MiLai.......... Laingsburg Public Library, Laingsburg, MI [*Library symbol Library of Congress*] (LCLS)

MiLakv........ Cato Township Public Library, Lakeview, MI [*Library symbol Library of Congress*] (LCLS)

MiLal.......... Lake Linden-Hubbell Public School Library, Lake Linden, MI [*Library symbol Library of Congress*] (LCLS)

MiLan .... L'Anse Township School and Public Library, L'Anse, MI [*Library symbol Library of Congress*] (LCLS)

MILAN .... Missile d'Infanterie Leger Antichar

MILAN .... Missile, Infantry Light Antiarmor [*Antitank system*] (INF)

Mil & Vet C... Military and Veterans Code [*A publication*] (DLA)

MILAS......... Micrometer Low-Approach System

Mil Av......... Military Aviator [*Army*]

MiLaw .... Lawton Public Library, Lawton, MI [*Library symbol Library of Congress*] (LCLS)

MILBA........ Military Base Agreement (CINC)

MiLC.......... Lansing Community College, Lansing, MI [*Library symbol Library of Congress*] (LCLS)

MILC.......... Metal Ion Liquid Chromatography

MILC.......... Midwest Interlibrary Center [*Later, CRL*]

MILC.......... Military Characteristics

MILCAP...... Military Civic Action Program

MILCAP...... Military Standard Contract Administration Procedures [*DoD*]

MILCEST..... Military Communications Electronic Systems Technology (MCD)

MilcmIn....... Millicom International Cellular [*Associated Press*] (SAG)

MILCOM...... Military Command (DNAB)

MILCOM ..... Military Committee Communication [*NATO*]

MILCOMP .... Military Computer

MILCOMSAT... Military Communications Satellite

MILCON...... Military Construction

MILCON-DA... Military Construction, Defense Agencies

MILCONF ..... Military Confinement

MILCS......... Metropolitan Interlibrary Cooperative System [*New York Public Library*] [*Information service or system*]

MILDAT....... Military Damage Assessment Team (AABC)

MILDDU...... Military-Industry Logistics Data Development Unit

MILDEC...... Military Decision (NATG)

MILDEPS..... Military Departments (AABC)

MILDEPT..... Military Department

MILDET...... Military Detachment

MILDIP ...... Military-Industry Logistics Data Interchange Procedures

MILDIS ...... Military-Industry Logistics Data Interchange System

MILDOC...... Military Document (AAGC)

MiLe.......... Leland Township Public Library, Leland, MI [*Library symbol Library of Congress*] (LCLS)

MILE.......... Minuteman Integrated Life Extension [*Telecommunications*] (LAIN)

MIL-E-CON... Military Electronic Conference

MileH......... Miles Homes, Inc. [*Associated Press*] (SAG)

MileHme...... Miles Homes, Inc. [*Associated Press*] (SAG)

MilePr .... Milestone Properties [*Associated Press*] (SAG)

MiLer......... LeRoy Public Library, LeRoy, MI [*Library symbol Library of Congress*] (LCLS)

MILES........ Magnetic Intrusion Line Sensor (PDAA)

Miles .... Miles' District Court Reports [*1825-41*] [*Philadelphia, PA*] [*A publication*] (DLA)

MILES........ Military Implications of LASER Employment by the Soviets

MILES........ Multiple Integrated LASER Engagement Simulation [*or System*] [*Army*]

MILES/AGES... Multiple-Integrated LASER Engagement Simulation / Air Ground Engagement Simulator

Miles (PA)... Miles' Pennsylvania Reports [*A publication*] (DLA)

Miles R....... Miles' Pennsylvania Reports [*A publication*] (DLA)

Miles R & O... Miles' Rules and Orders [*A publication*] (DLA)

Miles Rep.... Miles' Pennsylvania Reports [*A publication*] (DLA)

MilestnSci ... Milestone Scientific, Inc. [*Associated Press*] (SAG)

MiLew .... Lewiston Public Library, Lewiston, MI [*Library symbol Library of Congress*] (LCLS)

MiLex .... Moore Public Library, Lexington, MI [*Library symbol Library of Congress*] (LCLS)

MILF .... Moro Islamic Liberation Front [*Philippines*] [*Political party*]

MiLG.......... Great Lakes Bible College, Lansing, MI [*Library symbol Library of Congress*] (LCLS)

MILGA .... Member of the Institute of Local Government Administrators [*British*] (ODBW)

MiLGH .... Lansing General Hospital Library, Lansing, MI [*Library symbol*] [*Library of Congress*] (LCLS)

MILGP .... Military Group

Milgray .... Milgray Electronics, Inc. [*Associated Press*] (SAG)

MILGRP ...... Military Group (DNAB)

MILGRU ...... Military Group (DNAB)

MiLGS .... Church of Jesus Christ of Latter-Day Saints, Genealogical Society Library, Lansing Branch, Stake Center, Lansing, MI [*Library symbol Library of Congress*] (LCLS)

MIL-HDBK... Military Handbook

MIL-I.......... Military Instruction (AAGC)

MIL-I........... Military Specification on Interference (IEEE)

MILI........... Multilevel Informal Language Inventory [*Test*]

MILIC .... Microwave Insular Line Integrated Circuit (IEEE)

MILIC .... Millimeter Insular Line Integrated Circuit (PDAA)

MILIC .... Ministerial Libraries and Information Centers

MiLIM .... Ingham Medical Center, John W. Chi Memorial Library, Lansing, MI [*Library symbol*] [*Library of Congress*] (LCLS)

MILINREP .... Military Incident Report (MCD)

MILIRAD ..... Millimeter RADAR (MCD)

MILIRAD ..... Millimeter Wave RADAR Fuze (MCD)

MILIS .... Multicenter Investigation of the Limitation of Infarct Size (MEDA)

MiLit........... Litchfield District Library, Litchfield, MI [*Library symbol Library of Congress*] (LCLS)

MILIT .... Military

Military LJ.. Military Law Journal [*A publication*] (DLA)

MILITRAN .... Military in Transition Database [*Information service or system*] (IID)

MiLivM .... Madonna College, Livonia, MI [*Library symbol Library of Congress*] (LCLS)

MiLivPS....... Livonia Public Schools, Livonia, MI [*Library symbol Library of Congress*] (LCLS)

Mil Jur Cas & Mat... Military Jurisprudence, Cases and Materials [*A publication*] (DLA)

MILJUSDOCFILE... Military Justice Docket File (DNAB)

MILL .... Mill [*Commonly used*] (OPSA)

MILL .... Miller Industries, Inc. [*NASDAQ symbol*] (SAG)

Mill............. Miller's Reports [*1-5 Louisiana*] [*A publication*] (DLA)

Mill............. Miller's Reports [*3-18 Maryland*] [*A publication*] (DLA)

MILL .... Million

Mill............. Mills' New York Surrogate's Court Reports [*A publication*] (DLA)

Mill............. Mill's South Carolina Constitutional Reports [*A publication*] (DLA)

Mill & C Bills... Miller and Collier on Bills of Sale [*A publication*] (DLA)

Mill & F Pr... Miller and Field's Federal Practice [*A publication*] (DLA)

Mill & V Code... Milliken and Vertrees' Tennessee Code [*A publication*] (DLA)

Mill Civ L .... Miller's Civil Law of England [*1825*] [*A publication*] (DLA)

Mill Code.... Miller's Iowa Code [*A publication*] (DLA)

Mill Const.... Mill's South Carolina Constitutional Reports [*A publication*] (DLA)

Mill Const (SC)... Mill's South Carolina Constitutional Reports [*A publication*] (DLA)

Mill Dec ..... Miller's Circuit Court Decisions (Woolworth) [*United States*] [*A publication*] (DLA)

Mill Dec ..... Miller's United States Supreme Court Decisions [*Condensed, Continuation of Curtis*] [*A publication*] (DLA)

Mill El .... Miller's Elements of the Law of Insurances [*A publication*] (DLA)

MillenCh...... Millenium Chemicals, Inc. [Associated Press] (SAG)
Millenia...... Millenia, Inc. [Associated Press] (SAG)
Mill Eq M ... Miller's Equitable Mortgages [1844] [A publication] (DLA)
Miller........... Miller's Reports [1-5 Louisiana] [A publication] (DLA)
Miller........... Miller's Reports [3-18 Maryland] [A publication] (DLA)
Miller Const... Miller on the Constitution of the United States [A publication] (DLA)
MillerIn........ Miller Indusries, Inc. [Associated Press] (SAG)
Miller's Code... Miller's Revised and Annotated Code [Iowa] [A publication] (DLA)
Millersville U... Millersville University of Pennsylvania (GAGS)
MILLIE...... Maximum Interchange of the Latest Logistic Information Is Essential
milli IU/ml... Milli-International Unit per Milliliter (DAVI)
Millin........... Petty Sessions Cases [1875-98] [Ireland] [A publication] (DLA)
Mill Ins....... Miller's Elements of the Law of Insurances [A publication] (DLA)
Millipore...... Millipore Corp. [Associated Press] (SAG)
Millipre....... Millipore Corp. [Associated Press] (SAG)
millisec....... Millisecond
Mill LA ...... Miller's Reports [1-5 Louisiana] [A publication] (DLA)
Mill Log....... Mill's Logic [A publication] (DLA)
Mill MD ...... Miller's Reports [3-18 Maryland] [A publication] (DLA)
Mill Op .... Miller's Circuit Court Decisions (Woolworth) [United States] [A publication] (DLA)
Mill Part...... Miller on Partition [A publication] (DLA)
MillPhar...... Millennium Pharmaceuticals, Inc. [Associated Press] (SAG)
Mill Pl & Pr... Miller's Iowa Pleading and Practice [A publication] (DLA)
MillrHr........ Miller [Herman], Inc. [Associated Press] (SAG)
MILLS.......... Mills [Commonly used] (OPSA)
Mills........... Mills' New York Surrogate's Court Reports [A publication] (DLA)
Mills Ann St... Mills' Annotated Statutes [Colorado] [A publication] (DLA)
Mills C........ Mills College (GAGS)
MillsCp....... Mills Corp. [Associated Press] (SAG)
Mills Em D... Mills on Eminent Domain [A publication] (DLA)
Mills Em Dom... Mills on Eminent Domain [A publication] (DLA)
Mills (NY).... Mills' New York Surrogate's Court Reports [A publication] (DLA)
Mills' Surr Ct... Mills' New York Surrogate's Court Reports [A publication] (DLA)
MIL-M......... Military Manual (MCD)
MILMO......... Military Motorcycle [Army] (INF)
MILNET........ Military Network
MILNRY........ Millinery
MILNRY........ Millinery
MILO........... Mainframe Interface to Libraries Online [Illinois Library Computer Systems Office online union catalog]
MILO........... Maryland Interlibrary Loan (NITA)
MILO........... Maryland Interlibrary Organization [Information service or system] (IID)
MILO........... Miami Valley Library Organization [Library network]
MILO........... Most Input for the Least Output [Business term]
MILOC......... Military Oceanography (PDAA)
MILocoE....... Member of the Institution of Locomotive Engineers [British] (EY)
MIL OPS...... Military Operations [USCG] (TAG)
MIL/OS........ Military/Ordnance Specification (MCD)
Mil P .... Military Post
MILP.......... Mixed Integer Linear Program [Statistics]
MILPAC....... Military Personnel Accounting Activity [Army] (AABC)
MILPAS....... Miscellaneous Information Listing Program Apollo Spacecraft [NASA] (KSC)
MILPERCEN... Military Personnel Center [Alexandria, VA] [Army] (AABC)
MILPERS ..... Military Personnel
MILPERSINS... Military Personnel Information System
MILPERSINST... Military Personnel Instructions (MCD)
MILPERSIS... Military Personnel Information Subsystem (MCD)
MILPHAP..... Military Provincial Health Assistance Program (AABC)
MILPINS...... Military Police Information System (DNAB)
MILPO........ Military Personnel Office (AABC)
MILPOD....... Mixed Integer and Linear Programming Open Deck (PDAA)
MilPr.......... Milestone Properties [Associated Press] (SAG)
MILR.......... Maintenance Incident Log Report [Navy] (CAAL)
MILR.......... Master of Industrial and Labor Relations
MilrBld....... Miller Building Systems, Inc. [Associated Press] (SAG)
MILREP....... Military Representative (NATG)
Mil Rep ...... Militia Reporter [Boston] [A publication] (DLA)
Mil Rev....... Military Review [A publication] (BRI)
MILRIS .... Military Routing Identifier System
MILS.......... Marine Integrated Logistics System
MILS.......... Master of Information and Library Science (GAGS)
MILS.......... Medication Information Leaflet for Seniors [Medicine] (DMAA)
MILS.......... Member of the Incorporated Law Society [British]
MILS.......... Microcomputer Integrated Library System
MILS.......... Microwave Instrument Landing System
MILS.......... Military Standard Logistics System (MCD)
MILS.......... Milliradians (KSC)
MILS.......... Mineral Industry Location System [Bureau of Mines] [Information service or system] (IID)
MILS.......... Missile Impact Locating [or Location] System
MiLS.......... Sparrow (E.W.) Hospital Library, Lansing, MI [Library symbol] [Library of Congress] (LCLS)
MILSAT....... Military Satellite
MILSATCOM... Military Satellite Communications [Systems]
MILSBILLS... Military Standard Billing System
MILSCAP..... Military Standard Contract Administration Procedures [DoD]
MILSICCS .... Military Standard Item Characteristics Coding Structure (SAA)
MILSIMDS ... Military Standard Item Management Data System
MILSIMS..... Military Standard Inventory Management System
MILSO........ Military Standard Logistics Systems Office [DoD] (MCD)
MILS/PAC ... Missile Impact Location System, Pacific (SAA)
MILSPEC...... Military Specification

MILSPEC...... Military Specifications (GAVI)
MILSPETS..... Military Standard Petroleum System (MCD)
MIL SPOT ... Military Standard Procurement Operations Technique
MILSPOT .... Military Standard Purchase Operating Technique
MILSPRED ... Military Standard for Providing Research and Exploratory Development Data
MILSTAAD ... Military Standard Activity Address Directory
MILSTAC...... Military Staff Communication (NATG)
MILSTAG..... Military Standardization Agreement (CINC)
MILSTAM..... International Military Staff Memorandum [NATO] (NATG)
MILSTAMP... Military Standard Transportation and Movement Procedure
MILSTAN .... Military Agency for Standardization [NATO]
MILSTAR .... Military Strategic and Tactical Relay System [Satellite communications]
MILSTARAP... Military Standard Transportation Action Report and Accounting Procedures (MCD)
MILSTD....... Military Standard
MILSTEP...... Military Standard Evaluation Procedure
MILSTEP...... Military Supply and Transportation Evaluation Procedures (AFM)
MILSTICC .... Military Standard Item Characteristics Coding
MILSTICCS ... Military Standard Item Characteristics Coding Structure
MILSTIICS ... Military Standard Item Identification Coding System
MiLStL........ Saint Lawrence Hospital Medical Library, Lansing, MI [Library symbol] [Library of Congress] (LCLS)
MILSTRAMP... Military Standard Transportation and Movement Procedure
MILSTRAP ... Military Standard Requisition and Accounting Procedures (MCD)
MILSTRAP ... Military Standard Transaction Reporting and Accounting Procedures
MILSTRIP ... Military Standard Requisitioning and Issue Procedure
MILSVC........ Military Services
MILT .... Milton [England]
MILT .... Miltope Group [NASDAQ symbol] (TTSB)
MILT .... Miltope Group, Inc. [NASDAQ symbol] (NQ)
MILTAG........ Military Technical Assistance Group
MILTAM....... Misrad Isre'eli Li-tevi'ot Mi-Germanyah (BJA)
MiLTC......... Thomas M. Cooley Law School, Lansing, MI [Library symbol Library of Congress] (LCLS)
MILTELCOMM... Military Telecommunications
MiltonF....... Milton Federal Financial Corp. [Associated Press] (SAG)
MILTOP....... Man-in-the-Loop Trajectory Optimization Program [NASA]
Miltope....... Miltope Group, Inc. [Associated Press] (SAG)
MILTOSS .... Military Transportation of Small Shipments (NVT)
MIL TRA ..... Military Training [USCG] (TAG)
MiLud........ Ludington Public Library, Ludington, MI [Library symbol Library of Congress] (LCLS)
MiLut.......... Luther Public Library, Luther, MI [Library symbol] [Library of Congress] (LCLS)
MILVAN ...... Military Van (MCD)
MILW......... Chicago, Milwaukee, St. Paul & Pacific Railroad Co. [AAR code]
Milw.......... Milward's Irish Ecclesiastical Reports [1819-43] [A publication] (DLA)
Milw.......... Milwaukee [Wisconsin]
Milwaukee Law... Milwaukee Lawyer [A publication] (DLA)
Milwau Sch Eng... Milwaukee School of Engineering (GAGS)
Milw Ir Ecc Rep... Milward's Irish Ecclesiastical Reports [1819-43] [A publication] (DLA)
MilwLnd ...... Milwaukee Land Co. [Associated Press] (SAG)
MiLy........... Lyons Public Library, Lyons, MI [Library symbol Library of Congress] (LCLS)
MIM .... Magnetic Interaction Mechanism
MIM .... Maintenance Instructions Manual [DoD]
MIM .... Maintenance Interface Machine (NITA)
MIM .... Manufacturing Information Memorandum
MIM .... Marine Information Management [Marine science] (MSC)
MIM .... Master of Industrial Management
MIM .... Master of International Management
MIM .... Master of International Management (DD)
MIM .... Member of the Institute of Management (DD)
MIM .... Member of the Institution of Metallurgists [British] (DBQ)
MIM .... Mendelian Inheritance in Man [Genetics]
MIM .... Merimbula [Australia Airport symbol] (OAG)
MIM .... Message Input Module [Telecommunications] (TEL)
MIM .... Metal Injection Molding [Metal fabrication]
MIM .... Metal Insulator Metal [Light detector]
MIM .... Microion Mill
MIM .... Microwave Interface Module
MIM .... Mid Mountain Mining [Vancouver Stock Exchange symbol]
MIM .... Military Iranian Mission [World War II]
MIM .... Milo [Maine] [Seismograph station code, US Geological Survey] (SEIS)
Mim.......... Mimeograph (AAGC)
MIM .... Mimeographed (ADA)
MIM .... Mimino [Former USSR] [FAA designator] (FAAC)
MIM .... Mindanao Independence Movement [Philippines] [Political party]
MIM .... Minimum (DA)
MIM .... Minorities in Media (EA)
MIM .... Minorities in Medicine [Eastern Michigan University Macy Scholarship]
MIM .... Misappropriation, Interference and Misrepresentation
MIM .... Missile Identification Module [Military] (CAAL)
MIM .... Mobile-Launched Interceptor Missile
MIM .... MODEM Interface Modules [Computer science]
MIM .... Modified Index Method (IEEE)
MIM .... Montagu Investments Management [Commercial firm British]
MIM .... Morality in Media (EA)
MIM .... Mouvement Independantiste Martiniquais [Martinique Independence Movement] [Political party] (PD)

MIM............	Multilateral Initiative in Malaria
MIM............	Multilayer Interference Mirror [*Optical instrumentation*]
MIM............	Multiple Ion Monitoring [*Mass spectrometry*]
Mim............	United States Internal Revenue Bureau, Commissioner's Mimeographed Published Opinions [*A publication*] (DLA)
MIMA.........	Mineral Insulation Manufacturers Association (EA)
MIMA.........	Minor Machine Accessory (MCD)
MIMA.........	Minute Man National Historical Park
MIMA.........	Music Industry Manufacturers Association [*Defunct*] (EA)
MIMAA.......	Motor Inn, Motel and Accommodation Association [*Australia*]
MiMaci.......	Mackinac Island Public Library, Mackinac Island, MI [*Library symbol Library of Congress*] (LCLS)
MiMack.......	Mackinaw City Public Library, Mackinaw City, MI [*Library symbol Library of Congress*] (LCLS)
MIMAF.......	Musicians International Mutual Aid Fund
MiMan........	Manchester Township Library, Manchester, MI [*Library symbol Library of Congress*] (LCLS)
MiManc......	Mancelona Township Library, Mancelona, MI [*Library symbol Library of Congress*] (LCLS)
MIManf.......	Member of the Institute of Manufacturing [*British*] (DBQ)
MiMani.......	Manistee County Library, Manistee, MI [*Library symbol Library of Congress*] (LCLS)
MiMant.......	Manton Public Library, Manton, MI [*Library symbol Library of Congress*] (LCLS)
MiMar........	M. Alice Chapin Memorial Library, Marion, MI [*Library symbol Library of Congress*] (LCLS)
MiMarc.......	Marcellus Township Library, Marcellus, MI [*Library symbol Library of Congress*] (LCLS)
MIMarE......	Member of the Institute of Marine Engineers [*British*] (EY)
MiMarl.......	Marlette Township Library, Marlette, MI [*Library symbol Library of Congress*] (LCLS)
MiMaRP	Maple Rapids Public Library, Maple Rapids, MI [*Library symbol*] [*Library of Congress*] (LCLS)
MiMarq.......	Peter White Public Library, Marquette, MI [*Library symbol Library of Congress*] (LCLS)
MiMarqAS ..	Marquette-Alger Intermediate School District, Learning Materials Center, Marquette, MI [*Library symbol Library of Congress*] (LCLS)
MiMarqHi	Marquette County Historical Society, John M. Longyear Memorial Library, Marquette, MI [*Library symbol Library of Congress*] (LCLS)
MiMarqN	Northern Michigan University, Marquette, MI [*Library symbol Library of Congress*] (LCLS)
MiMarqNA ..	Northern Michigan University, University Archives and Historical Collections, Marquette, MI [*Library symbol*] [*Library of Congress*] (LCLS)
MiMarqS......	Superiorland Library Cooperative System, Marquette, MI [*Library symbol Library of Congress*] (LCLS)
MiMars.......	Marshall Public Library, Marshall, MI [*Library symbol Library of Congress*] (LCLS)
MiMary.......	Marysville Public Library, Marysville, MI [*Library symbol Library of Congress*] (LCLS)
MiMas	Ingham County Library, Mason, MI [*Library symbol Library of Congress*] (LCLS)
MIMAS.......	Magnetically Insulated Macroparticle Accelerator System
MiMay	Mayville District Public Library, Mayville, MI [*Library symbol Library of Congress*] (LCLS)
MIMBM......	Member of the Institute of Municipal Building Management [*British*] (DBQ)
MIMC........	Management Inventory on Managing Change [*Test*]
MimC........	Maxwell International Microforms Corporation, Fairview Park, Elmsford, NY [*Library symbol Library of Congress*] (LCLS)
MIMC........	Member of the Institute of Management Consultants
MIMC........	Microforms International Marketing Corp. [*Pergamon*]
MIMC........	Multivariable Internal Model Control [*Control engineering*]
MIMCO	McGraw-Hill Information Management Co. [*Database producer*] (IID)
MiMD.........	Dorsch Memorial Public Library, Monroe, MI [*Library symbol Library of Congress*] (LCLS)
MIMD.........	Multiple Instruction/Multiple Data (NITA)
MIMD.........	Multiple Instruction Stream, Multiple Data Stream (MCD)
MIME........	Member of the Institute of Mining Engineers
MIME........	Member of the Institution of Mechanical Engineers [*Formerly, AMIMechE*] [*British*]
MIME........	Microcomputers in Mathematics Education (AIE)
MIME........	Ministry of Information Middle East [*British World War II*]
MIME........	Minor Machine Equipment (MCD)
MIME........	Multipurpose Internet Mail Extension [*Computer science*]
MIME........	Multipurpose Internet Mail Extensions [*Computer science*] (ACRL)
MiMe	Spies Public Library, Menominee, MI [*Library symbol Library of Congress*] (LCLS)
MiMec	Morton Township Library, Mecosta, MI [*Library symbol Library of Congress*] (LCLS)
MIMechE	Member of the Institution of Mechanical Engineers [*Formerly, AMIMechE*] [*British*] (EY)
MiMen........	Mendon Township Library, Mendon, MI [*Library symbol Library of Congress*] (LCLS)
MIMEO.......	Mimeographed (ADA)
MIMEO.......	Multiple Input Memo Engineering Order (MCD)
MiMer........	Merrill District Library, Merrill, MI [*Library symbol Library of Congress*] (LCLS)
MiMes	Mesick Public Library, Mesick, MI [*Library symbol Library of Congress*] (LCLS)
MIMEX.......	Major Item Material Excess [*Air Force*] (AFIT)
MIMF..........	Member of the Institute of Metal Finishing [*British*] (DBQ)

MIMGTechE...	Member of the Institution of Mechanical Engineers and General Technician Engineers [*British*] (DBQ)
MIMH.........	Member of the Institute of Materials Handling [*British*] (DBQ)
MIMI..........	Member of the Institute of Motor Industry [*British*]
MIMI..........	Micro Miniature Compact Harness
MIMIC........	Measure and Inspection Masks for Integrated Circuits (MCD)
MIMIC........	Method of Micromolding in Capillaries [*Materials science*]
MIMIC........	Microfilm Information Master Image Converter (PDAA)
MIMIC........	Micromoulding in Capillaries [*Plastics technology*]
MIMIC........	Microwave and Millimeter-Wave Monolithic Integrated Circuits Project [*DoD*]
MIMIC........	Microwave Monolithic Integrated Circuit [*Used in wireless communication*]
MIMIC/CUS...	Michigan Metropolitan Information Center/Center for Urban Studies [*Wayne State University*] [*Information service or system*] (IID)
MIMICS.......	Micromodule Microprogrammed Computer System (PDAA)
MiMid.........	Grace A. Dow Memorial [*Public*] Library, Midland, MI [*Library symbol Library of Congress*] (LCLS)
MiMidD........	Dow Chemical Co., Midland, MI [*Library symbol Library of Congress*] (LCLS)
MiMidDC	Dow Corning Corp., Midland, MI [*Library symbol Library of Congress*] (LCLS)
MiMidDG	Dow Gardens, Midland, MI [*Library symbol*] [*Library of Congress*] (LCLS)
MiMidGS	Church of Jesus Christ of Latter-Day Saints, Genealogical Society Library, Midland Stake Branch, Midland, MI [*Library symbol Library of Congress*] (LCLS)
MiMidN........	Northwood Institute, Midland, MI [*Library symbol Library of Congress*] (LCLS)
MiMil..........	Milan Public Library, Milan, MI [*Library symbol Library of Congress*] (LCLS)
MiMill..........	Millington Township Library, Millington, MI [*Library symbol Library of Congress*] (LCLS)
MI MIN........	Miles per Minute (WDAA)
MIMinE........	Member of the Institution of Mining Engineers [*British*] (EY)
MiMio..........	Oscoda County Public Library, Mio, MI [*Library symbol Library of Congress*] (LCLS)
MIMIT........	Member of the Institute of Musical Instrument Technology [*British*] (DBQ)
MIMJ	Metal Insulator - Metal Junction
MIMM........	Management Inventory on Modern Management [*Test*]
MIMM........	Master of Mining and Metallurgy (DD)
MIMM........	Member of the Institute of Mining and Metallurgy [*British*] (EY)
MIMMIS.......	Marine Corps Integrated Manpower Management Information System
MIMMS.......	Marine Corps Integrated Maintenance Management System
MIMO.........	Man In, Machine Out [*Computer science*]
MIMO.........	Modified Input - Modified Output [*Computer science*]
MiMo..........	Monroe County Library System, Monroe, MI [*Library symbol Library of Congress*] (LCLS)
MIMO.........	Multiple-Input/Multiple-Output [*Computer science*]
MiMoHi........	Monroe County Historical Museum, Archives, Monroe, MI [*Library symbol*] [*Library of Congress*] (LCLS)
MIMOLA	Machine Independent Microprogramming Language
MiMor.........	Stair Public Library, Morenci, MI [*Library symbol Library of Congress*] (LCLS)
MiMory........	Morley-Stanwood Community Library, Morley, MI [*Library symbol Library of Congress*] (LCLS)
MIMOSA	Mission Modes and Space Analysis (NASA)
MIMOT........	Master of International Management of Technology (PGP)
MIMP.........	Magazine Industry Market Place [*A publication*]
MIMR.........	Magnetic Ink Mark Recognition
MIMR.........	May Institute of Medical Research
MIMR.........	Minimal Inhibitor Mole Ratio [*Biochemistry*]
MIMS.........	Major Item Management System (AABC)
MIMS.........	Manifest Information Management System (GAAI)
MIMS.........	Master of Integrated Manufacturing Systems (PGP)
MIMS.........	Material Information Management System (MCD)
MIMS.........	Medical Information Management System [*NASA*]
MIMS.........	Medical Information Management System
MIMS.........	Medical Inventory Management System
MIMS.........	Member of the Institute of Management Specialists [*British*] (DBQ)
MIMS.........	Metal Impact Monitoring System [*Nuclear energy*] (NRCH)
MIMS.........	Mineral Insulated, Metal Sheathed [*Cable*]
MIMS.........	Missile Maintenance Squadron [*Air Force*]
MIMS.........	Mitrol Industrial Management System [*Mitrol, Inc.*] [*Information service or system*] (IID)
MIMS.........	Modular Isodrive Memory Series
MIMS.........	Multi-Item Multisource (IEEE)
MIMS.........	Multiple Independently Maneuvering Submunitions (MCD)
MIMSq........	Missile Maintenance Squadron [*Air Force*] (AFM)
MIMT.........	Member of the Institute of Music Teachers (ADA)
MiMtc.........	Mount Clemens Public Library, Mount Clemens, MI [*Library symbol Library of Congress*] (LCLS)
MiMtcM	Macomb County Library, Mount Clemens, MI [*Library symbol Library of Congress*] (LCLS)
MiMtp..........	Mount Pleasant Public Library, Mount Pleasant, MI [*Library symbol Library of Congress*] (LCLS)
MiMtpC........	Chippewa Library League, Mt. Pleasant, MI [*Library symbol Library of Congress*] (LCLS)
MiMtpT........	Central Michigan University, Mount Pleasant, MI [*Library symbol Library of Congress*] (LCLS)
MiMu.........	Hackley Public Library, Muskegon, MI [*Library symbol Library of Congress*] (LCLS)
MiMuB.........	Muskegon Business College, Muskegon, MI [*Library symbol Library of Congress*] (LCLS)

MIMUG .... Meetings Industry Microcomputer Users Group [*Defunct*] (EA)
MiMul .... Mulliken District Library, Mulliken, MI [*Library symbol Library of Congress*] (LCLS)
MiMuM .... Muskegon County Library, Muskegon, MI [*Library symbol Library of Congress*] (LCLS)
MiMun .... Munising Public Library, Munising, MI [*Library symbol Library of Congress*] (LCLS)
MIMunE .... Member of the Institute of Municipal Engineers [*British*] (EY)
MIMUSA .... Matrix Iteration Method of Unfolding Spectra [*Computer science*]
MIMV .... Mirabilis Mosaic Virus [*Plant pathology*]
MIN .... Business European Airways Ltd. [*British*] [*FAA designator*] (FAAC)
MIN .... Marketing Information Network [*Information service or system*] (IID)
MIN .... Master of Insurance
MIN .... Media Industry Newsletter [*A publication*]
MIN .... Meeting Individual Needs [*Educational publishing*]
MIN .... Member Information Network [*for House of Representatives*]
MIN .... Member of the Institute of Navigation [*British*]
MIN .... MFS Intermediate Income SBI [*NYSE symbol*] (SPSG)
MIN .... MFS Intermediate Income Trust [*Associated Press*] (SAG)
MIN .... MFS Interm Incme SBI [*NYSE symbol*] (TTSB)
min .... Microinch (BARN)
Min .... Minaean [*or Minean*] (BJA)
MIN .... Mine [*or Minecraft*] [*Navy*]
MIN .... Mine Identification and Neutralization (PDAA)
MIN .... Mineral [*California*] [*Seismograph station code, US Geological Survey*] (SEIS)
MIN .... Mineral
MIN .... Mineralogy
MIN .... Miniature
MIN .... Minim
MIN .... Minimum (AFM)
min .... Minimum [*A minim measurement*] (DAVI)
Min .... Minimum (DFIT)
MIN .... Mining
min .... Mining (DD)
MIN .... Mining
MIN .... Minion [*Typography*] (DGA)
MIN .... Minister [*or Ministry*]
MIN .... Minister [*or Ministry*] (ODBW)
Min .... Minnesota Reports [*A publication*] (DLA)
MIN .... Minor
MIN .... Minority
Min .... Minor's Alabama Reports [*A publication*] (DLA)
MIN .... Minto Resources [*Vancouver Stock Exchange symbol*]
MIN .... Minute (AFM)
min .... Minute (ODBW)
min .... Minute (IDOE)
min .... Minute
MIN .... Mobile Identification Number (ACRL)
MIN .... Mobilization Identification Number [*Military*]
MIN .... Molasses Information Network (EA)
MIN .... Most in Need Population
MIN .... Movimiento de Integracion Nacional [*National Integration Movement*] [*Venezuela*] [*Political party*] (PPW)
MIN .... Movimiento de Integracion Nacional [*National Integration Movement*] [*Ecuador*] [*Political party*] (PPW)
MIN .... Movimiento de Izquierda Nacional [*National Left-Wing Movement*] [*Bolivia*] [*Political party*] (PPW)
MINA .... Member of the Institution of Naval Architects [*British*]
MINA .... Monoisonitrosoacetone [*Biochemistry*]
MINA .... Multiplexed Input NHRE [*National Hail Research Experiment*] Averager
MINABB .... Minimum Abbreviations [*of MAST*]
MINAC .... Miniature Navigation Airborne Computer
MINAC .... Minuteman Action Committee (SAA)
MINAGE .... Minimum Seed-Bearing Age [*Botany*]
MiNas .... Putnam Public Library, Nashville, MI [*Library symbol Library of Congress*] (LCLS)
MINAT .... Miniature
minat .... Miniature (VRA)
MiNazC .... Nazareth College, Nazareth, MI [*Library symbol Library of Congress*] (LCLS)
MiNb .... New Buffalo Public Library, New Buffalo, MI [*Library symbol Library of Congress*] (LCLS)
MINBATFOR... Minecraft Battle Force, Pacific Fleet
Min B/L .... Minimum Bill of Lading (DS)
M-in-C .... Matron-in-Chief [*Navy British*]
MINC .... Minicomputer
MINCOM ...... Miniaturized Communications [*Navy*] (DNAB)
MINCOMS ..... Multiple Interior Communications System (MCD)
MINCONMAR... Ministerial Conference of West and Central African States on Maritime Transport [*Ivory Coast*] (EAIO)
MIND .... Magnetic Integrator Neuron Duplicator
MIND .... Management Institute for National Development
MIND .... Method in Natural Development [*Mental diet plan*]
MIND .... Methods of Intellectual Development [*National Association of Manufacturers*]
MIND .... Mining Item Name Directory [*A publication*]
MIND .... Mitcham Indus [*NASDAQ symbol*] (TTSB)
MIND .... Mitcham Industries [*NASDAQ symbol*] (SAG)
MIND .... Modular Interactive Network Designer
MIND .... Multidisciplinary Institute for Neuropsychological Development (EA)
MINDAC .... Marine Inertial Navigation Data Assimilation Computer (IEEE)
MIndAdm ...... Master of Industrial Administration (GAGS)

MINDAP .... Microwave-Induced Nitrogen Discharge at Atmospheric Pressure [*Spectrometry*]
MINDAT .... Minerals Data Base [*of the Law of the Sea*] (GNE)
MINDD .... Minimum Due Date per Order
MIndEd .... Master of Industrial Education
MIN-DEF ...... Ministry of Defence [*British*]
Min Dig .... Minot's Digest [*Massachusetts*] [*A publication*] (DLA)
MINDIV .... Mine Division [*Navy*]
MINDO .... Modified Intermediate Neglect of Differential Overlap [*Quantum mechanics*]
MINDS .... Mental Illness Nervous Disorders Society [*Australia*]
MindSpr .... MindSpring Enterprises, Inc. [*Associated Press*] (SAG)
MINE .... Mesna, Ifosfamide, Mitoxantrone, Etoposide [*Antineoplastic drug*] (CDI)
MINE .... Microbial Information Network Europe [*EEC*]
Min E .... Mineral Engineer
Min E .... Mining Engineer
MINE .... Minneapolis Eastern Railway Co. [*AAR code*]
MINE .... Montana Information Network Exchange [*Library network*]
MINE .... Multi-Indenture NORS [*Not Operationally Ready Status*] Evaluator (MCD)
MINEAC .... Miniature Electronic Auto-Collimator
MINEASYFAC.. Mine Assembly Facilities
MINEC .... Military Necessity
MINECTRMEASSTA... Mine Countermeasure Station [*Military*]
MINECTRMEASTA... Mine Countermeasures Station [*Military*] (DNAB)
M In Ed........ Master of Industrial Education (PGP)
MINEDEFLAB... Mine Defense Laboratory [*Navy*]
MiNeg .... Negaunee Public Library, Negaunee, MI [*Library symbol Library of Congress*] (LCLS)
MINELCO ..... Miniature Electronic Component (WDAA)
MINEPACSUPPGRU... Mine Force, Pacific Fleet, Support Group Unit (DNAB)
miner.......... Minerology (DD)
MINERAL .... Mineralogy
MINERALOG... Mineralogical
MINERVA..... Minimization of Earthworks for Vertical Alignment (PDAA)
MineSf........ Mine Safety Appliances Co. [*Associated Press*] (SAG)
MINET......... Medical Information Network [*GTE Telenet Communications Corp.*] [*Reston, VA*] [*Telecommunications*]
MINET......... Metropolitan Information Network
MIN EV .... Minutes of Evidence [*Legal term*] (DLA)
MINEVDET ... Mine Warfare Evaluation Detachment
MiNew .... Newaygo Carnegie Public Library, Newaygo, MI [*Library symbol Library of Congress*] (LCLS)
MiNew-C...... Croton Public Library, Newaygo, MI [*Library symbol Library of Congress*] (LCLS)
MINEX .... Minelaying, Minesweeping, and Mine-Hunting Exercise [*NATO*] (NATG)
MINEX .... Mine Warfare Exercise (NVT)
MINFLOT ..... Mine Flotilla [*Navy*]
MInfoTech .... Master of Information Technology and Communication
MInfSys ...... Master of Information Systems
MING .... Magnetic Induction Nuclear Gyroscope
MIng .... Maitre en Ingenierie [*Master of Engineering*] [*French*]
MIng .... Maitrise en Ingenierie [*Master of Engineering*] (DD)
MING .... Middle Class, Intelligent, Nice Girl [*Lifestyle classification*]
MINGSE .... Minimum Ground Support Equipment Concept (MCD)
MiNhL......... Lenox Township Library, New Haven, MI [*Library symbol Library of Congress*] (LCLS)
MINI.......... Method of Implicit Nonstationary Iteration (PDAA)
MINI.......... Miniature (KSC)
MINI.......... Miniature
MINI.......... Minicomputer Industry National Interchange [*An association*] (EA)
MINI.......... Minimize Individually Negotiated Instruments (AFM)
MINI.......... Minimum (DSUE)
MINI.......... Mobile Mini [*NASDAQ symbol*] (TTSB)
MINI.......... Mobile Mini, Inc. [*NASDAQ symbol*] (SAG)
MiNi.......... Niles Community Library, Niles, MI [*Library symbol Library of Congress*] (LCLS)
MINIA .... Monkey Intranuclear Inclusion Agent (MAE)
MINIACT ...... Minimum Acquisition Tracking System (MUGU)
MINIAPS ..... Miniature Accessory Power Supply
MINICATS .... Miniaturization of Federal Catalog System Publications
MINICOM ..... Minimum Communications
MINI COMP... Miniature Compact (MCD)
MINICS .... Minimal-Input Cataloguing System [*Loughborough University of Technology*]
MINICS/PDS... MINICS Periodicals Data System (NITA)
MINIDOS..... Mini Disk Operating System (IDOE)
MINI-ELS .... Mini-Emitter Location System (MCD)
Miniluv .... Ministry of Love [*From George Orwell's novel, "1984"*]
MiniMd .... MiniMed, Inc. [*Associated Press*] (SAG)
MINI MUX... Miniaturized Multiplexes (MCD)
MiNiN .... National Standard Information Resources, Niles, MI [*Library symbol Library of Congress*] (LCLS)
Mining Chem Engng Rev... Mining and Chemical Engineering Review [*A publication*]
Mining Engng Rev... Mining and Engineering Review [*A publication*]
MiningS....... Mining Services International Corp. [*Associated Press*] (SAG)
Min Inst...... Minor's Institutes of Common and Statute Law [*A publication*] (DLA)
MIN INVEST... Minimum Investment [*Finance*]
Minipax....... Ministry of Peace [*From George Orwell's novel, "1984"*]
Miniplenty ... Ministry of Plenty [*From George Orwell's novel, "1984"*]
MINIRAD..... Minimum Radiation (CAAL)
MINIRAR...... Minimum Radiation Requirements [*Missiles*] (IEEE)

MINISID...... Miniature Seismic Intrusion Detector [*DoD*]
MINISINS..... Miniature Ship Inertial Navigation System (MCD)
MINI-SUBLAB... Miniature Submarine Laboratory
MINIT........ Minimum Interference Threshold [*Telecommunications*] (TEL)
MINITAS ..... Miniature True Airspeed Computer
MINITEX..... Minnesota Interlibrary Telecommunications Exchange [*Library cooperative*] [*Minnesota Higher Education Coordinating Board Minneapolis, MN*]
MINITRACK.. Minimum-Weight Tracking [*System*] (MUGU)
Minitrue..... Ministry of Truth [*From George Orwell's novel, "1984"*]
MINIVAR..... Minimum Variance Orbit Determination (MCD)
MINIW .... Mobile Mini Wrrt [*NASDAQ symbol*] (TTSB)
MINK .... Missouri-Iowa-Nebraska-Kansas League [*Old baseball league*]
MINLANT ...... Mine Warfare Forces, Atlantic [*Navy*]
Minl E......... Mineral Engineer (PGP)
MINLP .... Mixed-Integer Nonlinear Program [*Computer science*]
MINMAC-PC... Mini-Macroeconomic Personal Computer Model [*Department of Energy*] (GFGA)
MIN MC .... Minimum Material Condition [*Computer science*]
MINN .... Minnesota (AFM)
Minn .... Minnesota (ODBW)
Minn .... Minnesota Supreme Court Reports [*A publication*] (DLA)
Minn Admin Reg... Minnesota State Register [*A publication*] (DLA)
MinnBrw....... Minnesota Brewing Co. [*Associated Press*] (SAG)
Minn Code Agency... Minnesota Code of Agency Rules [*A publication*] (DLA)
Minn Code Ann... Minnesota Code, Annotated [*A publication*] (DLA)
Minn Ct Rep... Minnesota Court Reporter [*A publication*] (DLA)
Minn DL & I Comp... Minnesota Department of Labor and Industries. Compilation of Court Decisions [*A publication*] (DLA)
MINN DPW LIB... Minnesota Department of Public Welfare Library Consortium [*Library network*]
MinnEd .... Minnesota Educational Computing Corp. [*Associated Press*] (SAG)
MINNEMAST... Minnesota School Mathematics and Science Teaching Project [*University of Minnesota*] (AEE)
Minn Gen Laws... Minnesota General Laws [*A publication*] (DLA)
Minn (Gil)... Minnesota Reports (Gilfillan Edition) [*A publication*] (DLA)
Minn (Gill)... Minnesota Reports (Gilfillan Edition) [*A publication*] (DLA)
Minn Law J... Minnesota Law Journal [*A publication*] (DLA)
Minn Laws... Laws of Minnesota [*A publication*] (DLA)
Minn LJ........ Minnesota Law Journal [*St. Paul*] [*A publication*] (DLA)
MinnMul ...... Minnesota Municipal Income Trust [*Associated Press*] (SAG)
MinnMuT ..... Minnesota Municipal Term Trust [*Associated Press*] (SAG)
MinnPL........ Minnesota Power & Light Co. [*Associated Press*] (SAG)
Minn R & WCAT Div... Minnesota Railroad and Warehouse Commission. Auto Transportation Co. Division Reports [*A publication*] (DLA)
Minn Reg..... Minnesota Register [*A publication*] (AAGC)
Minn Rep..... Minnesota Reports [*A publication*] (DLA)
Minn Reps.... Minnesota Reports [*A publication*] (DLA)
Minn Sess Law Serv (West)... Minnesota Session Law Service (West) [*A publication*] (DLA)
Minn Stat..... Minnesota Statutes [*A publication*] (AAGC)
Minn Stat Ann... Minnesota Statutes, Annotated [*A publication*] (DLA)
Minn Stat Ann (West)... West's Minnesota Statutes, Annotated [*A publication*] (DLA)
Minntc .... Minntech Corp. [*Associated Press*] (SAG)
MinnTr2 ...... Minnesota Term Trust, Inc. II [*Associated Press*] (SAG)
Minn WCD ... Minnesota Workmen's Compensation Decisions [*A publication*] (DLA)
MiNop.......... Leelanau Township Library, Northport, MI [*Library symbol Library of Congress*] (LCLS)
Minor.......... Minor's Alabama Supreme Court Reports [*1820-26*] [*A publication*] (DLA)
Minor.......... Minor's Institutes [*A publication*] (DLA)
Minor (Ala)... Minor's Alabama Reports [*A publication*] (DLA)
Minor (Ala)... Minor's Institutes [*Alabama*] [*A publication*] (DLA)
Minorc .... Minorco [*Formerly, Minerals & Resources Corp. Ltd.*] [*Associated Press*] (SAG)
Minor Inst.... Minor's Institutes of Common and Statute Law [*A publication*] (DLA)
Minor's Alabama Rep... Minor's Alabama Reports [*A publication*] (DLA)
Minor's Ala R... Minor's Alabama Reports [*A publication*] (DLA)
Minor's Ala Rep... Minor's Alabama Reports [*A publication*] (DLA)
Minor's R .... Minor's Alabama Reports [*A publication*] (DLA)
Minor's Rep... Minor's Alabama Reports [*A publication*] (DLA)
MINOS .... Main Injector Neutrino Oscillation Search [*Particle Physics*]
MINOS .... Manual Intervention and Observation Simulator (AAG)
MINOS .... Mine Operating System (PDAA)
MINOS .... Mixed Integer Operational Scheduling (PDAA)
MINOS .... Modular Input/Output System
Minot St U ... Minot State University (GAGS)
MINOX .... Minimum Oxidizer (KSC)
MinP.......... Minnesota Power & Light Co. [*Associated Press*] (SAG)
MINPAC ...... Mine Warfare Forces, Pacific [*Navy*]
MIN PLEN.... Minister Plenipotentiary (WDAA)
MINPOREN.. National Association of Commercial Broadcasters in Japan (EY)
MINPROC ... Mineral Processing Technology [*Canada Department of Energy, Mines, and Resources*] [*Information service or system*] (CRD)
MINPRT ...... Minimum Processing Time per Operation
MINQU .... Minimum Norm Quadratic Unbiased [*Statistics*]
MINQUE ...... Minimum Norm Quadratic Unbiased Estimation [*Statistics*] (PDAA)
MINR .... Minimum R Factor [*Spectrometry*]
Min R .... Minnesota Reports [*A publication*] (DLA)
MINRA .... Miniature International Racing Association
MINRAD....... Minimum Radiation (MCD)
Min Rep ..... Minnesota Reports [*A publication*] (DLA)
MINRL .... Mineral
MINRON .... Mine Squadron [*Navy*]

MINRTY .... Minority
MINS .... Mare Island Naval Shipyard [*Also, MINSY*] [*Later, MID*]
MINS .... Miniature Inertial Navigation System
MINS .... Minors in Need of Supervision [*Classification for delinquent children*]
MINSAT .... Minimum Safe Air Travel (SAA)
MINSD .... Minimum Planned Start Date per Operation
MINSK .... [*A*] Russian digital computer [*Moscow University*]
MINSOP....... Minimum Slack Time per Operation
MINSQ .... Minimum Squares [*Mathematical statistics*]
MInstAEA ..... Member of the Institute of Automotive Engineer Assessors [*British*] (DBQ)
M Inst AM ... Member of the Institute of Administrative Management [*British*] (DCTA)
MInstBB...... Member of the Institute of British Bakers (DBQ)
MInstBCA ...... Member of the Institute of Burial and Cremation Administration [*British*] (DBQ)
MInstBE ...... Member of the Institution of British Engineers
MInstBRM..... Member of the Institute of Baths and Recreation Management [*British*] (DBQ)
MInstBRMDip... Diploma Member of the Institute of Baths and Recreation Management [*British*] (DBQ)
MInstBTM..... Member of the Institute of Business and Technical Management [*British*] (DBQ)
MInstCE...... Member of the Institution of Civil Engineers [*Later, MICE*] [*British*] (EY)
M Inst CM ... Member of the Institute of Commercial Management [*British*] (DCTA)
MInstD........ Member of the Institute of Directors [*British*] (DI)
MInstE .... Member of the Institute of Energy [*British*] (DBQ)
MInstE .... Member of the Institution of Engineers [*British*] (EY)
MInstF .... Member of the Institute of Fuel [*British*]
MInstFF....... Member of the Institute of Freight Forwarders [*British*] (DBQ)
MInstGasE ... Member of the Institution of Gas Engineers [*British*] (EY)
MInstHE....... Member of the Institution of Highway Engineers [*British*]
M INST J ..... Member of the Institute of Journalists [*British*] (DGA)
M Inst Jour... Member of the Institute of Journalists [*British*] (ROG)
MInstM........ Member of the Institute of Marketing [*British*]
MInstMC...... Member of the Institution of Measurement and Control [*British*] (DBQ)
MInstME ...... Member of the Institution of Mining Engineers [*British*]
MInstMet .... Member of the Institute of Metals [*British*]
MInstMM...... Member of the Institution of Mining and Metallurgy [*British*]
MInstMO...... Member of the Institute of Market Officers [*British*] (DI)
MInstNA...... Member of the Institution of Naval Architects [*British*] (EY)
MInstNDT .... Member of the British Institute of Non-Destructive Testing (DBQ)
MInstP........ Member of the Institute of Physics (ADA)
MInstPE....... Member of the Institute of Petroleum Engineers (ADA)
MInstPet ..... Member of the Institute of Petroleum [*British*] (EY)
MInstPI....... Member of the Institute of Patentees and Inventors [*British*] (EY)
MInstPkg..... Member of the Institute of Packaging [*British*] (DI)
M Inst PS ... Member of the Institute of Purchasing and Supply [*British*] (DCTA)
MInstR........ Member of the Institute of Refrigeration [*British*] (DBQ)
MINSTR .... Minister
MInstRA...... Member of the Institute of Registered Architects [*British*]
MInstSMM ... Member of the Institute of Sales and Marketing Management [*British*] (DBQ)
MInstSP...... Member Institution of Sewage Purification (BABM)
MInstSP...... Member Institution of Sewage Purification [*Ecology*] (DAVI)
MInstStructE... Member of the Institution of Structural Engineers (ADA)
MInstSWM... Member of the Institute of Solid Waste Management [*British*] (DI)
MInstT........ Member of the Institute of Technology [*British*] (EY)
MInstT........ Member of the Institute of Transport [*British*]
M Inst TA ... Member of the Institute of Transport Administration [*British*] (DCTA)
MInstTM..... Member of the Institute of Travel Managers in Industry and Commerce [*British*] (ODBW)
MInstW........ Member of the Institute of Welding [*British*]
MInstWE...... Member of the Institution of Water Engineers [*British*]
MInstWHS... Member of the Institute of Works and Highways Superintendents [*British*] (DI)
MInstWPC... Member of the Institution of Water Pollution Control [*British*] (DI)
MINSY........ Mare Island Naval Shipyard [*Also, MINS*] [*Later, MID*]
MINT.......... Bank of Montreal, Canadian Imperial Bank of Commerce, Bank of Nova Scotia, and Toronto-Dominion Bank
MINT.......... Major International Narcotics Traffickers [*Register*] [*Drug Enforcement Administration*]
MINT.......... Materiel Identification and New Item Control Technique [*AFLC*]
MINT.......... Media Integration [*Computer science*]
MINT.......... Micro-Integration [*NASDAQ symbol*] (TTSB)
MINT.......... Micro-Integration Corp. [*NASDAQ symbol*] (SAG)
MINT.......... Minorities International Network for Trade (EA)
MINT.......... Municipal Insured National Trust
MinTch .... Minerals Technologies, Inc. [*Associated Press*] (SAG)
MINTEC .... Mining Technology Abstracts [*Canada Centre for Mineral and Energy Technology*] [*Information service or system*] (CRD)
MINTECH .... Ministry of Technology [*British*]
MINTEL ...... Market Intelligence Report
MINTER ...... Ministerio do Interior [*Ministry of the Interior*] [*Information service or system*] (IID)
MINTIE .... Minimum Test Instrumentation Equipment
MIntLaw ...... Master of International Law
MIntMed ...... Master of International Medicine (NADA)
MINTR .... Miniature (MSA)
MINTS .... Mutual Institutions National Transfer System, Inc. [*Banking*]
MINTS .... Mutual Insurance National Transfer System, Inc.
MINTWK ...... Minimum Total Work Content
MINU .... Mobile Instrument Investigation Unit
MINucE........ Member of the Institution of Nuclear Engineers [*British*]

MI Nucl E .... Member of the Institution of Nuclear Engineers [*British*]
MINUET .... Minimum Energy Trajectory Model [*Army*] (AABC)
MiNun........... Crockery Township Library, Nunica, MI [*Library symbol Library of Congress*] (LCLS)
MINUS........ Modular Integrated Utility Systems (MCD)
MinutInt........ Minuteman International [*Associated Press*] (SAG)
MINW .... Master Interface Network (MCD)
MINWARTECH... Mine Warfare Technician [*Navy*] (DNAB)
MINWR......... Minimum Weapon Radius (SAA)
MIN WT .... Minimum Weight (WDAA)
MINX .... Multimedia Information Network Exchange [*Computer science*]
MINY .... Mineralogy (ROG)
MINY .... Minority (ROG)
MIO............ Management Improvement and Operating Plan [*Department of Housing and Urban Development*]
MIO............ Management Information Office [*or Officer*] [*Air Force*] (AFM)
MIO............ Management Integration Office [*NASA*] (NASA)
MIO............ Map Information Office [*US Geological Survey*]
MIO............ Marine Inspection Office [*Coast Guard*]
MIO............ Marine Inspection Operations [*USCG*] (TAG)
MIO............ Maritime Interception Operations [*Coast Guard*] (DOMA)
MIO............ Medical Intelligence Office [*Later, MIIA*] [*DoD*]
MIO............ Meteoritic Impact Origin (AAG)
MIO............ Metric Information Office [*National Institute of Standards and Technology*]
MIO............ Miami, OK [*Location identifier FAA*] (FAAL)
MIO............ Midas Commuter Airlines CA [*Venezuela*] [*ICAO designator*] (FAAC)
MIO............ Military Intelligence Officer [*British military*] (DMA)
MIO............ Minimal Identifiable Odor
MIO............ Mobile Ionospheric Observatory [*Boston University*]
MIO............ Mobile Issuing Office [*Navy*]
MIO............ Modular Input/Output [*Telecommunications*]
MIO............ Motility Indol Ornithine [*Medium*] [*Medicine*] (BABM)
MIO............ Motility Indol Ornithine [*Medium*] [*Microbiology*] (DAVI)
MIO............ Movements Identification Officer [*Air Force*]
MIO............ Movements Integration Office
MIO............ Multi-Institutional Organization [*Generic term*] (DHSM)
MIO............ Multiple Input/Output (NITA)
MIO............ Multiple Input/Output Stream [*Computer science*]
MIOA .... Medical Industries of America [*NASDAQ symbol*] (SAG)
MIOAC........ Military Intelligence Officer Advanced Course (DOMA)
MIOB .... Member of the Institute of Building [*British*]
MiOC .... Olivet College, Olivet, MI [*Library symbol Library of Congress*] (LCLS)
MIOD .... Message Input-Output Devices (MCD)
MIOG .... Manual of Investigative and Operational Guidelines [*FBI*]
MIOK .... Magyar Izraelitak Orszagos Kepviselete (BJA)
MiOIA .... Alumni Memorial Library, Orchard Lake, MI [*Library symbol Library of Congress*] (LCLS)
MIONP .... Microwave-Induced Optical Nuclear Polarization [*Physics*]
MiOnt.......... Ontonagon Township Library, Ontonagon, MI [*Library symbol Library of Congress*] (LCLS)
MIOP .... Master Input/Output Processor (NITA)
MIOP .... Member of the Institute of Osteopathy and Physiotherapy [*British*]
MIOP .... Member of the Institute of Printing [*British*] (DBQ)
MIOP .... Multiplexing Input-Output Processor [*Computer science*] (BUR)
MIOS .... Modular Input-Output System [*Telecommunications*] (TEL)
MIOS .... Multi-IMU Operation System [*NASA*] (GFGA)
MIOS .... Multi-IMU [*Internal Measuring Unit*] Operation System [*NASA*]
MIOSH........ Member of the Institution of Occupational Safety and Health [*British*] (DCTA)
MIOT.......... Member of the Institute of Operating Theatre Technicians [*British*]
MIOT.......... Municipal Income Opportunities Trust [*Associated Press*] (SAG)
MiOt............ Otsego District Public Library, Otsego, MI [*Library symbol Library of Congress*] (LCLS)
MIOT2......... Municipal Income Opportunities Trust II [*Associated Press*] (SAG)
MIOT3......... Municipal Income Opportunities Trust III [*Associated Press*] (SAG)
MiOv......... Ovid Public Library, Ovid, MI [*Library symbol Library of Congress*] (LCLS)
MiOw.......... Owosso Public Library, Owosso, MI [*Library symbol Library of Congress*] (LCLS)
MiOwJW ..... John Wesley College, Owosso, MI [*Library symbol Library of Congress*] (LCLS)
MIP............ Machine Independent Package (DGA)
MIP............ Machine Instruction Processor [*Computer science*] (BUR)
MIP............ Macrophage-Induced Protein [*Biochemistry*]
MIP............ Macrophage Inflammatory Protein [*Biochemistry*]
MIP............ Main Instrument Panel (MCD)
MIP............ Maintainer Instructional Package (MCD)
MIP............ Maintenance Implementation Plan [*FAA*] (TAG)
MIP............ Maintenance Improvement Program
MIP............ Maintenance Index Page
MIP............ Major Intrinsic Protein [*Biochemistry*]
MIP............ Malleable Iron Pipe
MIP............ Management Implementation Plan (MCD)
MIP............ Management Improvement Plan
MIP............ Management Improvement Program [*Military*]
MIP............ Management Incentive Program
MIP............ Management Information Protocol [*Telecommunications*] (OSI)
MIP............ Management Intern Program
MIP Nucl E ... Mandatory Inspection Point (KSC)
MIP......... Manual Index Page [*SNMMMS*]
MIP............ Manual Input Processing [*or Program*] [*Computer science*]
MIP .... Manufacturers of Illumination Products (EA)

MIP............ Marche International des Programmes de Television International [*International Marketplace for Buyers and Sellers of Television Programs*] (NTCM)
MIP........... Marine Insurance Policy
MIP........... Master Improvement Program (AFIT)
MIP........... Master Information Paper [*Military*] (CAAL)
MIP........... Master Insurance Program
MIP........... Master of Intellectual Property (PGP)
MIP........... Material Improvement Plan [*or Program*] [*Aviation*]
MIP........... Materiel Improvement Project [*Military*]
MIP........... Matrix Inversion Program [*Computer science*] (BUR)
MIP........... Maximum Inspiratory Pressure [*Medicine*]
MIP........... Mean Indicated Pressure
MIP........... Mean Intravascular Pressure [*Cardiology*] (MAE)
MIP........... Mechanized Infantry Program [*United States Army, Europe*] (MCD)
MIP........... Medicaid Interim Payments
MIP........... Member of the Institute of Plumbing [*British*] (DBQ)
MIP........... Membrane-Intercalated Particles [*Cytology*]
MIP........... Membrane Isolation Process [*Food technology*]
MIP........... Merfin Hygienic [*Vancouver Stock Exchange symbol*]
MIP........... Message Input Processor
MIP........... Methodology Investigation Proposal (MCD)
MIP........... Methods Improvement Program [*IBM Corp.*]
MIP........... Microelectronic Integrated Processing [*Symposium*]
MIP........... Microwave-Induced Plasma [*Spectrometry*]
MIP........... Microwave Interference Protection
MIP........... Middle Interphalangeal Joint [*Anatomy*] (DAVI)
MIP........... Military Improvement Program
MIP........... Military Information Program
MIP........... Military Interdepartmental Purchase
MIP........... Million Instructions per Second
MIP........... Milton, PA [*Location identifier FAA*] (FAAL)
MIP........... Minimum Import Prices [*Economics*]
MIP........... Minimum Impulse Pulse
MIP........... Minimum Impulse Pulse
MIP........... Mint in Package [*Doll collecting*]
MIP........... Missile Impact Predictor [*Air Force*]
MIP........... Missile Instrumentation Package [*Military*] (CAAL)
MIP........... Mission Integration Panel [*NASA*] (SSD)
MIP........... Missouri Institute of Psychiatry Library, St. Louis, MO [*OCLC symbol*] (OCLC)
MIP........... Mixed Integer Programming [*Computer science*]
MIP........... MMU [*Manned Maneuvering Unit*] Integration Plan [*NASA*] (GFGA)
MIP........... Mobilization Improvement Program [*MTMC*] (TAG)
MIP........... Model Implementation Plan
MIP........... Model Improvements Program [*TRADOC*] (MCD)
MIP........... Model Installation Program (AAGC)
MIP........... Modern Irish Printer [*A publication British*] (DGA)
MIP........... Modest Improvement Program [*Military*] (NVT)
MIP........... Modification Instruction Package (KSC)
MIP........... Modulated Interframe Plan
MIP........... Monthly Intelligence Production (MCD)
MIP........... Monthly Investment Plan [*Stock exchange term*] (SPSG)
MIP........... Mortgage Insurance Premium
MIP........... Mortgage Investments Plus, Inc. (MHDW)
MIP........... Most Important Person
MIP........... Motivation Indoctrination Program [*Military*]
MIP........... Mouvement Independent Populaire [*Popular Independent Movement*] [*Luxembourg*] [*Political party*] (PPE)
MIP........... Mouvement Islamique Progressiste [*Islamic Progressive Movement*] [*Tunisia*] [*Political party*] (PD)
MIP........... Movimiento Independiente Peruano [*Peruvian Independent Movement*] [*Political party*]
MIP........... Multipurpose Information Processor [*Computer science*] (MHDB)
MIP........... Mycorrhiza Inoculum Potential [*Soil science*]
MIP........... Myo-inositolphosphate [*Biochemistry*]
MIPA .... Master of International Public Administration (GAGS)
MIPA .... Member of the Institute of Practitioners in Advertising [*British*]
MIPA .... Member of the Institute of Public Administration (ADA)
MIPA .... Methylisopropylaniline [*Organic chemistry*]
MIPA .... Missile Procurement, Army (AABC)
MIPA .... Monoisopropylamine [*Organic chemistry*]
MiPa........... Port Austin Township Library, Port Austin, MI [*Library symbol Library of Congress*] (LCLS)
MIP-AES ..... Microwave-Induced Plasma-Atomic Emission Spectroscopy
MiPal........... Richmond Township Public Library, Palmer, MI [*Library symbol Library of Congress*] (LCLS)
MiPar........... Parchment Community Library, Parchment, MI [*Library symbol Library of Congress*] (LCLS)
MIPAS .... Management Information Planning and Accountancy Service (MHDI)
MiPaw .... Paw Paw Public Library, Paw Paw, MI [*Library symbol Library of Congress*] (LCLS)
MIPB........... Monoisopropylbiphenyl (PDAA)
MIPC........... Manifold Ignition Primary Charge
MIPC........... Member of the Institute of Production Control [*British*] (DBQ)
MIPC........... Metropolitan Information Processing Conference (MCD)
MIPD........... Manpower Intelligence and Planning Division (AIE)
MIPD........... Manufacturing Industry Products Division (MCD)
MIPE........... Magnetic Induction Plasma Engine
MIPE........... Member of the Institution of Production Engineers [*British*] (DAS)
MIPE........... Mobile Intelligence Processing Element (DOMA)
MIPE........... Modular Information Processing Equipment
MiPec........... Elk Township Library, Peck, MI [*Library symbol Library of Congress*] (LCLS)

MiPel	Pellston Public Library, Pellston, MI [*Library symbol Library of Congress*] (LCLS)
MiPen	Pentwater Township Library, Pentwater, MI [*Library symbol Library of Congress*] (LCLS)
MiPet	Petoskey Public Library, Petoskey, MI [*Library symbol Library of Congress*] (LCLS)
MiPetN	North Central Michigan College, Petoskey, MI [*Library symbol Library of Congress*] (LCLS)
MIPEX	Model Improvement Experiment (MCD)
MIPG	Master Index Pulse Generator
MiPh	Saint Clair County Library System, Port Huron, MI [*Library symbol Library of Congress*] (LCLS)
MIPHE	Member of the Institute of Public Health Engineers [*British*] (DBQ)
MiPhM	Saint Clair County Community Mental Health Services, Port Huron, MI [*Library symbol*] [*Library of Congress*] (LCLS)
MiPhS	Saint Clair Community College, Port Huron, MI [*Library symbol Library of Congress*] (LCLS)
MIPI	Medicine in the Public Interest (EA)
MIPI	Member of the Institute of Professional Investigators [*British*] (DBQ)
MiPi	Pigeon District Library, Pigeon, MI [*Library symbol Library of Congress*] (LCLS)
MIPIE	Michigan Products Information Exchange [*Interchange Plus, Inc.*] [*Information service or system*] (IID)
MiPin	Pinckney Community Public Library, Pinckney, MI [*Library symbol Library of Congress*] (LCLS)
MIPIR	Missile Precision Instrumentation RADAR
MIPIR	Multimission Imagery Photographic Interpretation Report (MCD)
MiPit	Pittsford Township Library, Pittsford, MI [*Library symbol Library of Congress*] (LCLS)
MIPK	Methyl Isopropyl Ketone [*Organic chemistry*]
MiPl	Charles A. Ransom Public Library, Plainwell, MI [*Library symbol Library of Congress*] (LCLS)
MIPL	Master Indentured Parts List
MIPL	Monthly Intelligence Production Listing (MCD)
MIPlantE	Member of the Institution of Plant Engineers [*British*]
MIPLOGS	Marine Integrated Personnel and Logistics Subsystem
MiPIS	State Technical Institute and Rehabilitation Center, Plainwell, MI [*Library symbol Library of Congress*] (LCLS)
MiPlySJ	Saint John's Provincial Seminary, Plymouth, MI [*Library symbol Library of Congress*] (LCLS)
MIPM	Member of the Institute of Personnel Management [*British*]
MIP/MA	Missile in Place/Missile Away
MIPMS	Microwave-Induced Plasma Mass Spectrometry
MIPO	Multiple Item Purchase Order (AAG)
MiPon	Pontiac Public Libraries, Pontiac, MI [*Library symbol Library of Congress*] (LCLS)
MiPonO	Oakland County Law Library, Clark J. Adams-Philip Pratt Library, Pontiac, MI [*Library symbol Library of Congress*] (LCLS)
MiPonSJ	Saint Joseph Mercy Hospital, General Medical Library, Pontiac, MI [*Library symbol Library of Congress*] (LCLS)
MiPor	Portage Public Library, Portage, MI [*Library symbol Library of Congress*] (LCLS)
MIPORN	Miami Pornography [*FBI undercover investigation, 1977-80*]
MiPorPS	Portage Public Schools, Portage, MI [*Library symbol Library of Congress*] (LCLS)
MiPorS	Seventh Day Adventists Junior Academy, Portage, MI [*Library symbol*] [*Library of Congress*] (LCLS)
MiPot	Benton Township - Potterville District Library, Potterville, MI [*Library symbol Library of Congress*] (LCLS)
MIPP	Maintainability Index Prediction Procedure
MIPP	Master of International Public Policy (GAGS)
MIPP	Milk Indemnity Payment Program
MiPPT	McMaster Institute for Polymer Production Technology [*McMaster University*] [*Canada*] (IRC)
MIPR	Manhattan Institute for Policy Research (EA)
MIPR	Medical Intelligence Production Requirements (MCD)
MIPR	Member of the Institute of Public Relations [*British*]
MIPR	Military Interdepartmental Procurement [*or Purchase*] Request
MIPR	Military Intergovernmental Purchase Request (NASA)
MIPR	Military Intergovernmental Purchase Request
MIPR	Monthly Interim Progress Report
MIPRCS	Microprocessor (MSA)
MIProdE	Member of the Institution of Production Engineers [*British*] (EY)
MIPS	Management Information Progress Sheets (MCD)
MIPS	Marine Integrated Personnel System (MCD)
MIPS	Martinsried Institute for Protein Sequences [*Database producer*]
MIPS	Member of the Phonographic Society [*British*] (ROG)
MIPS	Membership Information Processing System [*AARP*]
MIPS	Merritt Island Press Site [*NASA*] (NASA)
MIPS	Microprocessor Without Interlocked Pipeline Stages (NITA)
MIPS	Microwave Pulse Storage System [*or Subsystem*] (MCD)
MIPS	Military Information Processing System
mips	Million Instructions Per Second [*Computer science*] (WDMC)
MIPS	Millions of Instructions per Second [*Facetious translations: "Meaningless Indication of Performance"; "Meaningless Instructions per Second"; "Meaningless Indicator of Processor Speed"*] [*Computer science*]
MIPS	Miniature Implantable Power System
MIPS	Missile Impact Prediction System
MIPS	Missile Information Processing System (MCD)
MIPS	Modular Instrumentation Package System (MCD)
MIPS	Modular Integrated Pallet System [*Tank monitoring*] [*Army*] (RDA)
MIPS	Multiple Index Processing System (MCD)
MIPS	Myocardial Isotopic Perfusion Scan [*Cardiology*] (DAVI)

MiPs	Sanilac Township Library, Port Sanilac, MI [*Library symbol Library of Congress*] (LCLS)
MIPsiMed	Member of the Institute of Psionic Medicine [*British*]
MIPSM	Member of the Institute of Purchasing and Supply Management (ADA)
MIPSNY	Metro-International Program Services of New York (EA)
MIPTC	Men's International Professional Tennis Council [*Defunct*] (EA)
MI PTG M	Member of the Institute of Printing Management [*British*] (DGA)
MiPtl	Portland District Library, Portland, MI [*Library symbol Library of Congress*] (LCLS)
MIPTV	Marche International des Programmes de Television [*Cannes Film Festival*] [*France*]
MIPVCE	Multiple-Input Phase-Variable Canonical Form (PDAA)
MIQ	Maiquetia [*Venezuela*] [*Airport symbol*] (AD)
MIQ	Maniwaki [*Quebec*] [*Seismograph station code, US Geological Survey*] (SEIS)
MIQ	Member of the Institute of Quarrying [*British*] (DBQ)
MIQ	Minimum Identifiable Quantity [*Analytical chemistry*]
MIQ	Minnesota Importance Questionnaire [*Vocational test*]
Miq	Miqva'ot [*or Miqwa'ot*] (BJA)
MIQA	Member of the Institute of Quality Assurance [*British*] (DBQ)
MIQPS	Member of the Institute of Qualified Private Secretaries [*British*] (DI)
Mir	Horne's Mirror of Justice [*A publication*] (DLA)
MIR	Magnetic Ink Read
MIR	Main Immunogenic Region [*Immunology*]
MIR	Maintenance Infusion Rate [*Medicine*]
MIR	Maintenance Inspection Report
MIR	Malfunction Investigation Report [*NASA*] (KSC)
MIR	Management Information Report
MIR	Mandatory Inspection Report (MCD)
MIR	Manual Input Room (SAA)
MIR	Master Index of Repairables (MCD)
MIR	Master Inventory Record
MIR	Master of Industrial Relations
MIR	Material Inspection Report [*Navy*]
MIR	Material Investigators Reactor [*NASA*]
MIR	Maverick Interim Report
MIR	Maximum Incremental Reactivity [*Exhaust emissions*] [*Automotive engineering*]
MIR	Maximum Individual Risk [*Environmental science*] (FFDE)
MIR	Medical Incident Report
MIR	Member of the Institute of Population Registration [*British*] (DBQ)
MIR	Memory-Information Register [*Computer science*]
MIR	Memory Input Register [*Computer science*]
MIR	Method Improvement Request (MCD)
MIR	Method of Integral Relations
MIR	Microinstruction Register
MIR	Micropower Impulse RADAR [*For fluid level sensing*]
MIR	Middle Irish [*Language, etc.*]
MIR	Mid-Infrared Spectrum [*Spectroscopy*]
MIR	Military Intelligence, Research [*World War II*]
MIR	Mineta Resources Ltd. [*Vancouver Stock Exchange symbol*]
MIR	Minimum Income Requirements (OICC)
MIR	Minneapolis Industrial Railway Co. [*AAR code*]
MIR	Mirage Resorts [*NYSE symbol*] (SPSG)
MIR	Miramichi Air Services Ltd. [*Canada ICAO designator*] (FAAC)
MIR	MIRLYN [*Michigan Research Library Network*]
MIR	Mirny [*Antarctica*] [*Seismograph station code, US Geological Survey*] (SEIS)
MIR	Mirror (KSC)
MIR	Mirror
MIR	Mirror
MIR	Mishap Investigation Report (MCD)
MIR	Missile Identification Record
MIR	Missile Intelligence Report
MIR	Mission Inherent Reliability
MIR	Mitochondrial Import Receptor [*Biochemistry*]
MIR	Model Incident Report [*Telecommunications*] (TEL)
MIR	Modular Integrated Rack (MCD)
MIR	Monastir [*Tunisia*] [*Airport symbol*] (OAG)
MIR	Monastir [*Tunisia*] [*Airport symbol*] (AD)
MIR	Mouvement International de la Reconciliation [*International Fellowship of Reconciliation*]
MIR	Mouvement pour l'Independance de la Reunion [*Movement for the Independence of Reunion*] [*Political party*] (PD)
MIR	Movimiento de Izquierda Revolucionario [*Movement of the Revolutionary Left*] [*Bolivia*] [*Political party*] (PPW)
MIR	Movimiento de Izquierda Revolucionario [*Movement of the Revolutionary Left*] [*Venezuela Political party*]
MIR	Movimiento de Izquierda Revolucionario [*Movement of the Revolutionary Left*] [*Chile*] [*Political party*]
MIR	Multiband Infrared Radiometer
MIR	Multiple Instrumentation RADAR (MCD)
MIR	Multiple Internal Reflection [*Spectroscopy*]
MIR	Multiple Isomorphous Replacement [*Crystallography*]
MIR	Multiplex Intensity Rules
MIR	Multitarget Instrumentation RADAR [*Military*] (CAAL)
MIR	Music Information Retrieval [*Computer science*]
MIR	Mutual Interference Report (MCD)
MIRA	Merchants Instant Response Authorization (SAA)
MIRA	Miniature Infrared Alarm
MIRA	Monterey Institute for Research in Astronomy
MIRA	Monthly Index of Russian Accessions [*Library of Congress*]
MIRA	Motor Industry Research Association [*British*] (DCTA)

MIRA .... Movimiento de Independencia Revolucionaria en Armas [*Puerto Rican independence group*] [*Political party*]

MIRA .... Movimiento Independentista Armado [*Armed Pro-Independence Movement*] [*Puerto Rico*] [*Political party*] (PD)

MIRA .... Multifunctional Inertial Reference Assembly [*Air Force*] (MCD)

MIRAC .... Management Information Research Assistance Center (AABC)

MIRAC .... Master Index Remote Access Capability (MHDI)

MIRAC .... Microfilmed Reports and Accounts (PDAA)

MIRACL .... Management Information Report Access without Computer Languages [*Computer science*] (IEEE)

MIRACL .... Mid-Infrared Advanced Chemical LASER

MIRACLE ..... Mokum Industrial Research Automatic Calculator for Laboratory and Engineering

MIRACLE ..... Multidisciplinary Integrated Research Activities in Complex Laboratory Environments [*National Science Foundation*]

MIRACODE.. Microfilm Information Retrieval Access Code

MIRAD .... Monostatic Infrared Intrusion Detector (WDAA)

MIRADCOM.. Missile Research and Development Command [*Army*]

MIRADOR .... Minefield Reconnaissance and Detector System [*Army*]

MIRADS .... Management Information and Display System [*NASA*]

MIRADS .... Marshall [*Space Flight Center*] Information Retrieval and Display System [*NASA*] (PDAA)

MIRAGE .... Microelectronic Indicator for RADAR Ground Equipment (MCD)

MIRAGE .... Moessbauer Isotopic Resonant Absorption of Gamma Emission [*Physics*]

MIRAID .... Maintenance Information Retrieval Aid

MIRAID .... Maritime Institute for Research and Industrial Development [*Washington, DC*] (EA)

Miramr .... Miramar Mining Corp. [*Associated Press*] (SAG)

MIRAN .... Miniature Infrared Analyzer [*Spectrometer*]

MIRAN .... Missile Ranging

MIRAS .... Mortgage Interest Relief at Source [*British*] (DCTA)

MIRAS .... Multiple Isomorphous Replacement with Anomalous Scattering [*Crystallography*]

MIRAT .... MILPERCEN Initial Recruiting and Training Plan (MCD)

MIRB .... Mutual Insurance Rating Bureau [*Defunct*] (EA)

MIRBM .... Medium Intermediate-Range Ballistic Missile (MCD)

MIRC .... Market Intelligence Research Co. [*Palo Alto, CA*] (TSSD)

MIRC .... Michael-Initiated Ring Closure [*Organic chemistry*]

MIRC .... Missile-in-Range Computer (MCD)

MiRc .... Reed City Public Library, Reed City, MI [*Library symbol Library of Congress*] (LCLS)

MIRCEN .... Microbiological Resource Center [*UNESCO*]

Mirch D & S.. Mirchall's Doctor and Student [*A publication*] (DLA)

MIRCOM ...... Missile Materiel Readiness Command [*Army*]

MIRCS .... Mechanical Instrument Repair and Calibration Shop (DNAB)

MIRD .... Medical Internal Radiation Dose [*Committee*] [*Society of Nuclear Medicine*]

MIRD .... Medium Internal Radiation Dose (WDAA)

MIRD .... Minor Irregularities and Deficiencies

MiRd .... Seville Township Library, Riverdale, MI [*Library symbol Library of Congress*] (LCLS)

MIRE .... Member of the Institution of Radio Engineers [*British*] (EY)

MiRea .... Reading Community Library, Reading, MI [*Library symbol*] [*Library of Congress*] (LCLS)

MIRECC .... Mental Illness Research, Education, and Clinical Center [*Department of Veterans Affairs*]

MIRED .... Microreciprocal Degrees

Mireh Advow... Mirehouse on Advowsons [*1824*] [*A publication*] (DLA)

Mireh Ti ...... Mirehouse on Tithes [*2nd ed.*] [*1822*] [*A publication*] (DLA)

MiRem .... Wheatland Township Library, Remus, MI [*Library symbol Library of Congress*] (LCLS)

MiRep .... Republic-Michigamme Public Library, Republic, MI [*Library symbol Library of Congress*] (LCLS)

MIREQ .... Minimum Requirements Specified

MiRes .... Reading Community Library, Reading, MI [*Library symbol Library of Congress*] (LCLS)

MIRF .... Major Item Removal Frequency [*Army Aviation Systems Command*]

MIRF .... Multiple Instantaneous Response File

MIRF .... Myopia International Research Foundation (EA)

MIRFAC .... Mathematics in Recognizable Form Automatically Compiled [*Computer science*]

MIRIAM .... Major Incident Room Index and Action Management [*Police computer*] [*British*]

MiRic .... Richmond Public Library, Richmond, MI [*Library symbol Library of Congress*] (LCLS)

MiRicl .... Richland Community Library, Richland, MI [*Library symbol Library of Congress*] (LCLS)

MIRICLE ...... Mirrored Ions Closed-Loop Electrons (MCD)

MIRID .... Miniature RADAR Illumination Detector (MCD)

MIRID .... Monostatic Infrared Intrusion Detector (PDAA)

MIRINZ .... Meat Industry Research Institute of New Zealand

MIR-IR .... Multiple Internal Reflectance Infrared Spectroscopy (MCD)

MIRIS .... Modified Infrared Interferometer Spectrometer

Mir Just ...... Horne's Mirror of Justice [*A publication*] (DLA)

MIRL .... Medium Intensity Runway Edge Lights [*Aviation*] (FAAC)

MIRL .... Medium Intensity Runway Edge Lights [*FAA*] (TAG)

MIRL .... Mineral Industry Research Laboratory

MIRN .... Movimento Independente da Reconstrucao Nacional [*Independent Movement of National Reconstruction*] [*Portugal*] (PPE)

MIRN-PDP ... Movimento Independente de Reconstrucao Nacional - Partido da Derecha Portuguesa [*Independent Movement for National Reconstruction - Party of the Portuguese Right*] [*Political party*] (PPW)

MIRO .... Mineral Industry Research Organisation [*British*] (DBA)

MIRO .... Mining Industry Research Organisation [*British*]

MiRochOU ... Oakland University, Rochester, MI [*Library symbol Library of Congress*] (LCLS)

MiRog........... Presque Isle County Library, Rogers City, MI [*Library symbol Library of Congress*] (LCLS)

MiRom.......... Romeo District Library, Romeo, MI [*Library symbol Library of Congress*] (LCLS)

MIROS .... Modulation Inducing Retrodirective Optical System [*NASA*]

MiRos........... Roseville Public Library, Roseville, MI [*Library symbol Library of Congress*] (LCLS)

MiRosc .... Gerrish-Higgins School District Public Library, Roscommon, MI [*Library symbol Library of Congress*] (LCLS)

MiRoscK ...... Kirtland Community College, Roscommon, MI [*Library symbol Library of Congress*] (LCLS)

MiRoy........... Royal Oak Public Library, Royal Oak, MI [*Library symbol Library of Congress*] (LCLS)

MiRoyWB ..... William Beaumont Hospital, Royal Oak, MI [*Library symbol Library of Congress*] (LCLS)

MIRP .... Manipulated Information Rate Processor

MIRP .... Myocardial Infarction Rehabilitation Program [*Cardiology*] (DAVI)

Mir Parl ...... Mirror of Parliament, London [*A publication*] (DLA)

Mir Pat Off... Mirror of the Patent Office [*Washington, DC*] [*A publication*] (DLA)

MIR-Peru ..... Movimiento de Izquierda Revolucionaria [*Movement of the Revolutionary Left of Peru*] [*Political party*] (PPW)

MIRPF .... Micro Image Relative Position Formula [*Computer science*]

MIRPL .... Major Item Repair Parts List (NATG)

MIRPS .... Multiple Information Retrieval by Parallel Selection

Mirr .... Horne's Mirror of Justice [*A publication*] (DLA)

MIRR .... Material Inspection and Receiving Report [*Military*]

mirr .... Mirror (VRA)

MIRR .... Mitsubishi Research Reactor [*Japan*]

MIRRC .... Motor Insurance Repair Research Centre [*British*] (CB)

MIRRER .... Microwave Identification Railroad Encoding Reflector (DNAB)

MIRROR ...... Management Information Reporting and Review of Operational Resources System

MIRROS....... Modulation Inducing Reactive Retrodirective Optical System [*NASA*]

MirRsrt .... Mirage Resorts [*Associated Press*] (SAG)

MIRS .... Manpower Information Retrieval System (IEEE)

MIRS .... Medical Information Retrieval Service (NITA)

MIRS .... Micro-Interactive Retrieval System (DNAB)

MIRS .... Military Intelligence Research Section [*Navy*]

MIRS .... MOTS [*Module Test Set*] Information Retrieval System

MIRS .... Multiple Internal Reflection Spectroscopy

MIRS .... Multi-purpose Infrared Sight (PDAA)

MiRsc .... Ogemaw District Library, Rose City, MI [*Library symbol Library of Congress*] (LCLS)

MIRSE .... Member of the Institution of Railway Signal Engineers [*British*] (DBQ)

MIRSE .... Multipurpose Imaging Radiometer Spectrometer Equipment

MIRSI .... Monthly Inventory Report of Special Items

MIRSIM .... Mineral Resource Simulation Model (PDAA)

MIRST .... Multiple Infrared Scattered Light Recorder

MIRT .... Molecular Infrared Track (IEEE)

MIRTAK .... Martin Infrared Tracker

MIRTE .... Member of the Institute of Road Transport Engineering [*British*] (DBQ)

MIRTOS .... Minimum Real Time Operating System (NITA)

MIRTRAC ..... Missile Infrared Tracking System (DNAB)

MIRTRAK ..... Martin Infrared Tracker (SAA)

MIRU .... Myocardial Infarction Research Unit [*Cardiology*] (DAVI)

MiRud.......... Rudyard School Public Library, Rudyard, MI [*Library symbol Library of Congress*] (LCLS)

MIRV .... Multiple Independently-Guided Re-entry Vehicle [*NASA*] (PDAA)

MIRV .... Multiple Independently-Targetable Reentry Vehicle [*Military*]

MIS .... Maintenance Indicator System [*TACOM*] [*Army*] (RDA)

MIS .... Managed Internet Service [*Computer science*]

MIS .... Management Information Science

MIS .... Management Information Service

MIS .... Management Information Specialist

MIS .... Management Information Strategy

MIS .... Management Information System [*Generic term*]

MIS .... Management Information Systems [*Corporation for Public Broadcasting*] [*Information service or system*] (IID)

MIS .... Management Integrated System (TEL)

MIS .... Manifold Interest Schedule

MIS .... Man in Space

MIS .... Manpower Information System (MCD)

MIS .... Manson Impact Structure [*Iowa*] [*Geology*]

MIS .... Manufacturing Information System [*Computer science*] (BUR)

MIS .... Marine Information System (NITA)

MIS .... Marine Isotope Stage [*Climatology*]

MIS .... Market Impact Study

MIS .... Marketing Information System

MIS .... Mary Immaculate Seminary [*Pennsylvania*]

MIS .... Master Implementation Schedule [*NATO Air Defense Ground Environment*] (NATG)

MIS .... Master Integrated Schedule (AAG)

MIS .... Master of Individualized Studies (GAGS)

MIS .... Master of Information Science (PGP)

MIS .... Master of Information Services (GAGS)

MIS .... Master of Information Systems (PGP)

MIS .... Master of Interdisciplinary Studies (GAGS)

MIS .... Master of International Service

MIS .... Master of International Studies (PGP)

MIS .... Material Inspection Service [*Navy*]

MIS .... Maturation-Inducing Substance [*Endocrinology*]

MIS.............	Mechanical Impact System [Aerospace]
MIS.............	Mechanical Interruption Summary [FAA]
MIS.............	Mechanically Induced Stress [Agriculture]
MIS.............	Media and Information Services [Queensland, Australia]
MIS.............	Median Iris Society (EA)
MIS.............	Medical Information Science
MIS.............	Member of the Institute of Statisticians [Formerly, AIS] [British]
MIS.............	Member of the Institute of Surveyors (ADA)
MIS.............	Merchandise Information System (PDAA)
MIS.............	Metal Insulated Structure
MIS.............	Metal-Insulator-Semiconductor (MCD)
MIS.............	Meteorological Impact Statement [FAA] (TAG)
MIS.............	Metering Information System [Telecommunications] (OA)
MIS.............	Metrology Information Service [GIDEP]
MIS.............	MICOM [Missile Command] Specification [Army]
MIS.............	MicroServe Information Systems
MIS.............	Midstate Airlines, Inc. [ICAO designator] (FAAC)
MIS.............	Milieu Information Service (EA)
MIS.............	Military Intelligence Section [South Africa]
MIS.............	Military Intelligence Services [Army]
MIS.............	Military Intelligence Summary [Defense Intelligence Agency]
MIS.............	Military Interim Specification [Army] (MCD)
MIS.............	Mine Issuing Ship
MIS.............	Mineral Industry Survey [Department of Commerce] (GFGA)
MIS.............	Mineral Information Section [Natural Environment Research Council] (IID)
MIS.............	Minicube System, Inc., Carlisle PA [STAC]
MIS.............	Minstrel Instruction Service (NADA)
MIS.............	Miscarriage (DSUE)
mis.............	Miscellaneous [MARC language code Library of Congress] (LCCP)
MIS.............	Miscellaneous (NATG)
MIS.............	Miserable (DSUE)
MIS.............	Mishima [Japan] [Seismograph station code, US Geological Survey] (SEIS)
MIS.............	Misima [Papua New Guinea] [Airport symbol] (OAG)
Mis.............	Misopogon [of Julian] [Classical studies] (OCD)
MIS.............	Missile
MIS.............	Missile
MIS.............	Missile Interim Specification [Army]
MIS.............	Missile Specification
MIS.............	Missing (AABC)
MIS.............	Mission College, Santa Clara, CA [OCLC symbol] (OCLC)
MIS.............	Mission Information System [or Subsystem]
Mis.............	Mississippi Reports [A publication] (DLA)
MIS.............	Missouri
Mis.............	Missouri Reports [A publication] (DLA)
MIS.............	Mistico [Ship's rigging] (ROG)
MIS.............	Mobility Information Service [British]
MIS.............	Modified in Situ [Experimental technique for converting shale into oil]
MIS.............	Monte-Carlo Inelastic Scattering [Code] [Computer science] (NRCH)
MIS.............	Month-in-Sample [Bureau of the Census] (GFGA)
MIS.............	Months in Service
MIS.............	Moody Institute of Science (EA)
MIS.............	Moody's Investor Service [A publication] (MHDW)
MIS.............	Motor Inert Storage
MIS.............	Muellerian Inhibiting Substance [Embryology] [Biochemistry]
MIS.............	Multicultural Information Strategy
Mis.............	New York Miscellaneous Reports [A publication] (DLA)
MIS.............	NRA [National Restaurant Association] Management Information Services [Defunct] (EA)
MiS.............	Saginaw Public Libraries, Saginaw, MI [Library symbol Library of Congress] (LCLS)
MISA.............	Maxwell International Subscription Agency
MISA.............	Meat Industry Suppliers Association (EA)
MISA.............	Military-Industrial Supply Agency
MISA.............	Motorists Information Services Association (EA)
MISA.............	Municipal and Industry Strategy for Abatement
MISAA.............	Middle Income Student Assistance Act [1978]
MISAC.............	Member of the Incorporated Society of Advertisement Consultants [British] (DAS)
MiSal.............	Saline Public Library, Saline, MI [Library symbol Library of Congress] (LCLS)
MISAM.............	Multiple Index Sequential Access Method
MiSan.............	Sandusky Public Library, Sandusky, MI [Library symbol Library of Congress] (LCLS)
MISAR.............	Microfilm Information Storage and Retrieval (MCD)
MISAR.............	Microprocessed Sensing and Automatic Regulation [Engine control system] [Automotive industry]
MISAR.............	Miniature Information Storage and Retrieval (PDAA)
MiSaS.............	Spring Arbor College, Spring Arbor, MI [Library symbol Library of Congress] (LCLS)
Mis Astig.............	Mixed Astigmatism [Ophthalmology] (DAVI)
MiSb.............	Bingham Township Library, Suttons Bay, MI [Library symbol Library of Congress] (LCLS)
MiS-B.............	Saginaw Public Libraries, Butman-Fish Library, Saginaw, MI [Library symbol Library of Congress] (LCLS)
MISC.............	Malaysian International Shipping Corp. (DS)
MiSc.............	Mason County Library, Scottville, MI [Library symbol Library of Congress] (LCLS)
MISC.............	Miscarriage [Medicine]
MISC.............	Miscellaneous (AFM)
MISC.............	Miscellaneous
misc.............	Miscellaneous (WDMC)
Misc.............	Miscellaneous (DFIT)
MISC.............	Miscellaneous and Other Operations [USCG] (TAG)

Misc.............	Miscellaneous Reports [New York] [A publication] (DLA)
MISC.............	Movement for an Independent Socialist Canada
MiS-C.............	Saginaw Public Libraries, Claytor Branch Library, Saginaw, MI [Library symbol Library of Congress] (LCLS)
Misc 2d.............	Miscellaneous Reports, Second Series [New York] [A publication] (DLA)
MisCa.............	Mission Capital Ltd. [Associated Press] (SAG)
MISCAP.............	Mission Capability Statement (MCD)
Misc Dec.............	Ohio Miscellaneous Decisions (Gottschall) [1865-73] [A publication] (DLA)
Misc Doc.............	Miscellaneous Document [US. House of Representatives of Senate] (BARN)
Miscel.............	Miscellaneous Reports [New York] [A publication] (DLA)
MISCEND.............	Miscendus [To Be Mixed] [Pharmacy]
MISCEX.............	Miscellaneous Exercise [Military] (NVT)
MISchott.............	Schottenstein [M. I.] Homes, Inc. [Associated Press] (SAG)
MISCL.............	Miscellaneous
Misc New York.............	Miscellaneous New York Reports [A publication] (AAGC)
Misc (NY).............	Miscellaneous Reports [New York] [A publication] (DLA)
MISCO.............	McCall Information Systems Co.
MISCON.............	Misconduct
Misc Rep.............	Miscellaneous Reports [New York] [A publication] (DLA)
Misc Reports.............	New York Miscellaneous Reports [A publication] (DLA)
Misc Repts.............	New York Miscellaneous Reports [A publication] (DLA)
MiScW.............	West Shore Community College, Scottville, MI [Library symbol Library of Congress] (LCLS)
MISD.............	Management Information Systems Directorate [Army Missile Command] [Redstone Arsenal, AL]
MISD.............	Misdemeanor [FBI standardized term]
MISD.............	Multiple Instruction, Single Data [Processor configuration] (IEEE)
MISDAS.............	Mechanical Impact System Design for Advanced Spacecraft (IEEE)
MISDM.............	Misdemeanor [Legal shorthand] (LWAP)
MISDM.............	Misdemeanor and Cure [Legal shorthand] (LWAP)
MISDMR.............	Misdemeanor (ROG)
MISDO.............	Management Information System Development Office (DNAB)
MISE.............	Mechanized Infantry in a Smoke Environment (MCD)
MISE.............	Miniature Sample (AAG)
MiSe.............	Sebewaing Township Library, Sebewaing, MI [Library symbol Library of Congress] (LCLS)
MISEA.............	Management Information Systems Economic Analysis
MISEA.............	Meat Industry Supply and Equipment Association [Later, MISA] (EA)
MISED.............	Machine Independent Systems Effectiveness Data System (MCD)
MISEG.............	Management Information System Executive Group (DNAB)
MISEP.............	Mutual Information System on Employment Policies in Europe (IID)
MISER.............	Management Information System for Expenditure Reporting (PDAA)
MISER.............	Manned Interceptor SAGE Evaluation Routine (MCD)
MISER.............	Mean Integral Square Error (PDAA)
MISER.............	Media Insertion Schedule Evaluation Report [Advertising]
MISER.............	Microwave Space Electronics Relay
MISER.............	Militant Society for the Eradication of Rounds [British] (DI)
MISER.............	Miniature, Indicating and Sampling Electronic Respirometer (PDAA)
MISER.............	Minimum Size Executive Routines
MISES.............	Merchandises (ROG)
MiSf.............	Southfield Public Library, Southfield, MI [Library symbol Library of Congress] (LCLS)
MiSfB.............	Bendix Corp., Engineering Development Center, Bendix Center, Southfield, MI [Library symbol Library of Congress] (LCLS)
MiSfE.............	Eaton Corp. Engineering Research Center, Southfield, MI [Library symbol] [Library of Congress] (LCLS)
MISFET.............	Metal-Insulator-Semiconductor Field-Effect Transistor
MiSfL.............	Lawrence Institute of Technology, Southfield, MI [Library symbol Library of Congress] (LCLS)
MiSfM.............	Midrasha College of Jewish Studies, Southfield, MI [Library symbol Library of Congress] (LCLS)
MiSfP.............	Providence Hospital Library, Southfield, MI [Library symbol] [Library of Congress] (LCLS)
MISFROR.............	Multiple Investment Sinking Fund Rate of Return (ADA)
MISG-C.............	Maintenance Interservice Support Group Center (MCD)
Mish.............	Mishnah [Basis of the Talmud] (BJA)
MiSh.............	Shelby Public Library, Shelby, MI [Library symbol Library of Congress] (LCLS)
MISHAP.............	Missiles High-Speed Assembly Program
MISHAP.............	Much Increased Salary, Hardly Any Pension [Lifestyle classification]
MiShep.............	Coe Township Library, Shepherd, MI [Library symbol Library of Congress] (LCLS)
MiSHS.............	Saginaw Health Sciences Library, Saginaw, MI [Library symbol Library of Congress] (LCLS)
MISI.............	Member of the Iron and Steel Institute [British]
MISI.............	Multipath Intersymbol Interference (PDAA)
MISIAS.............	Management Information Systems Inventory and Analysis System [Navy]
MIS/IL.............	Metal-Insulator-Semiconductor Inversion Layer [Photovoltaic energy systems]
MISIM.............	Metal-Insulator-Semiconductor Insulator Metal (MCD)
MIS(India).............	Member of the Institution of Surveyors of India
MISIP.............	Management Information System Improvement Plan
MISIP.............	Merck Infrared Spectral Interpretation Package [For minicomputers] [Analytical chemistry]
MISIP.............	Minority Institutions Science Improvement Program [National Science Foundation]
MISIS.............	Micro Integrated Storm Information System [Marine science] (OSRA)
MISL.............	Major Indoor Soccer League [Defunct] (EA)
MISL.............	Malfunction Investigation Support Laboratory [NASA] (KSC)
MISL.............	Management Information System Laboratory
MISL.............	Missile

MiSI............ South Lyon Public Library, South Lyon, MI [*Library symbol Library of Congress*] (LCLS)
MIS LABS.... Midwest Integrated Systems Laboratories, Inc. [*Watertown, WI*] (TSSD)
MISLIC........ Mid- and South Staffordshire Libraries in Cooperation (NITA)
MISLPA....... Major Indoor Soccer League Players Association (EA)
MISM......... Member of the Institute of Supervisory Management [*British*] (DBQ)
MISM......... Metal-Insulator-Semiconductor Metal (MCD)
MiSM......... Michigan Lutheran Seminary, Saginaw, MI [*Library symbol Library of Congress*] (LCLS)
MISMA........ Major Item Supply Management Agency
MISMA........ Member of the Incorporated Sales Managers Association [*British*] (DAS)
MISMAC ..... Missile and Munitions Materiel Center (MCD)
MISMD .... Medical Illustration Service for Museum Design [*Armed Forces Institute of Pathology*] (RDA)
MISMDS ..... Multiple Instruction Streams Multiple Data Steams
MISMO .... Maintenance Interservice [*or Intersupport*] Management Office [*DARCOM*] (AFIT)
Mis Mus ...... Mistress of Music
MISN .... Misnumbered (WGA)
MISO .... Maintenance Interservice Office [*Air Force*] (AFIT)
MISO .... Management Information Systems Office (AABC)
MISO .... Military Intelligence Service Organization (NADA)
MISO .... Misonidazole [*Azomycin*] [*Oncology, Radiosensitizer*]
MiSod......... Sodus Township Library, Sodus, MI [*Library symbol Library of Congress*] (LCLS)
Misonix....... Misonix, Inc. [*Associated Press*] (SAG)
Misonx....... Misonix, Inc. [*Associated Press*] (SAG)
MISP......... Management Information System Plan
MISP......... Manned Interceptor Simulation Program
MISP......... Mathematics in Society Project (AIE)
MISP......... Medical Information Systems Program [*Computer science*] (BUR)
MISP......... Member of the Institute of Sales Promotion [*British*] (DI)
MISP......... Microelectronics Industry Support Programme (NITA)
MISP......... Microprocessor Industry Support Programme [*British*] (DCTA)
MISPC........ Mechanized Infantry Squad Proficiency Course [*Army*]
MiSpl......... Warner Baird Library, Spring Lake, MI [*Library symbol Library of Congress*] (LCLS)
MIS-Q .... Maintenance Information System for Quality (MCD)
MISR .... Major Item Status Report
MISR .... Mars In-situ-utilization Sample Return [*Computer science*]
MISR .... Matrix Ion Species Ratio [*Spectroscopy*]
MISR .... Minimum Industrial Sustaining Role (NG)
Mis R .... Missouri Reports [*A publication*] (DLA)
MISR .... Modular Industrial Solar Retrofit Program [*Department of Energy*]
MISR .... Mosler Information Storage and Retrieval System (MCD)
MISR .... Multi-Angle Imaging Spectrometer [*Marine science*] (OSRA)
MISR .... Multi-Angle Imaging Spectrometer (USDC)
MISR .... Multi-Impact Signature Register (PDAA)
MISR .... Multiple Input Signal Register (NITA)
MISRAN...... Missile Range
MISRC .... Management Information Systems Research Center [*University of Minnesota*] [*Research center*] (RCD)
MISRE .... Microwave Space Relay [*Electronics*]
MISREP ...... Misrepresentation [*Legal shorthand*] (LWAP)
MISREP ...... Mission Report [*Air Force*] (AFM)
Mis Rep...... Missouri Reports [*A publication*] (DLA)
MISS.......... Major Item Special Study [*Army Aviation Systems Command*]
MISS.......... Management and Information System Staff [*United Nations Development Program*]
MISS.......... Man in Space Simulator
MISS.......... Man in Space Soonest
MISS.......... Mechanical Interruption Statistical Summary (IEEE)
MISS.......... Medical Information Science Section [*National Institutes of Health*] [*Information service or system*] (IID)
MISS.......... Microwave Imager Sensor Study (MCD)
MISS.......... Mid-Course Surveillance System (MCD)
MISS.......... Miniature SOFAR [*Sound Fixing and Ranging*] System
MISS.......... Minicomputer Interfacing Support System [*Computer science*]
MISS.......... Missile Intercept Simulation System
MISS.......... Mission [*NASA*] (KSC)
MISS.......... Mission
miss.......... Missionary
MISS.......... Mississippi (AFM)
Miss.......... Mississippi (ODBW)
MISS.......... Mississippian [*Period, era, or system*] [*Geology*]
MISS.......... Mississippian [*Railway*] [*AAR code*]
MISS.......... Mississippi Chemical [*NASDAQ symbol*] (TTSB)
MISS.......... Mississippi Chemical Corp. [*NASDAQ symbol*] (SAG)
Miss.......... Mississippi Supreme Court Reports [*A publication*] (DLA)
MISS.......... Mobile Instrumentation Support System
MISS.......... Mobile Integrated Support System (MCD)
MISS.......... Multiband Image Scanning System
MISS.......... Multi-Input-Safety-Shutdown (PDAA)
MISS.......... Multi-Item Single Source (IEEE)
MiS-S .... Saginaw Public Libraries, South Jefferson Branch, Saginaw, MI [*Library symbol Library of Congress*] (LCLS)
MiSs .... Sault Ste. Marie Carnegie Public Library, Sault Ste. Marie, MI [*Library symbol Library of Congress*] (LCLS)
MiSsB .... Baylis Public Library, Sault Ste. Marie, MI [*Library symbol Library of Congress*] (LCLS)
Miss C .... Mississippi College (GAGS)
MissChm ..... Mississippi Chemical Corp. [*Associated Press*] (SAG)
Miss Code Ann... Mississippi Code, Annotated [*A publication*] (DLA)

MISS-D........ Minuteman Integrated Schedules Status and Data Systems [*Missiles*]
Miss Dec .... Mississippi Decisions [*A publication*] (DLA)
MIS-SDS...... Multiple Instruction Streams - Single Data Streams [*Computer science*] (MHDB)
MISSIL........ Management Information System Symbolic Interpretive Language [*Computer science*] (MCD)
MISSILEX .... Missile Firing Exercise (NVT)
MISSIO .... Internationales Katholisches Missionswerk [*Pontifical Mission Society*] [*Aachen, Federal Republic of Germany*] (EAIO)
MISSION...... Manufacturing Information System Support Integrated Online [*Computer science*] (MHDI)
MISSION...... Mission [*Commonly used*] (OPSA)
MISSIS .... Mississippi Student Information System (EDAC)
MiSsL .... Lake Superior State College, Sault Ste. Marie, MI [*Library symbol Library of Congress*] (LCLS)
Miss Law..... Mississippi Lawyer [*A publication*] (DLA)
Miss Law Rev... Mississippi Law Review [*A publication*] (DLA)
Miss Laws ... General Laws of Mississippi [*A publication*] (DLA)
Miss Lawyer... Mississippi Lawyer [*A publication*] (DLA)
Miss L Rev... Mississippi Law Review [*A publication*] (DLA)
MISSN .... Mission [*Commonly used*] (OPSA)
MissnW .... Mission West Properties [*Associated Press*] (SAG)
Misso......... Missouri Reports [*A publication*] (DLA)
MISSOPH..... Man in Space Sophisticated (MUGU)
Misso R....... Missouri Reports [*A publication*] (DLA)
Misso Rep .. Missouri Reports [*A publication*] (DLA)
Missouri ...... Missouri Reports [*A publication*] (DLA)
Missouri R.... Missouri Reports [*A publication*] (DLA)
Missouri Rep... Missouri Reports [*A publication*] (DLA)
Missour Rep... Missouri Reports [*A publication*] (DLA)
MissPw....... Mississippi Power Co. [*Associated Press*] (SAG)
MISSR .... Missioner (ROG)
Miss R .... Mississippi Reports [*A publication*] (DLA)
Miss RC ...... Mississippi Railroad Commission Reports [*A publication*] (DLA)
Miss Reg .... Mississippi Register (AAGC)
Miss Rep .... Mississippi Reports [*A publication*] (DLA)
Miss Serv W.. Missionary Service With
Miss St Ca... Morris' Mississippi State Cases [*1818-72*] [*A publication*] (DLA)
Miss St Cas.. Morris' Mississippi State Cases [*1818-72*] [*A publication*] (DLA)
Miss St U ... Mississippi State University (GAGS)
Miss St U Women... Mississippi State University for Women (GAGS)
MISST .... Missile-Supersonic Transport
MissVly........ Mississippi Valley Bancshares, Inc. [*Associated Press*] (SAG)
MissVw....... Mississippi View Holding Co. [*Associated Press*] (SAG)
MISSY .... Missionary
MIST......... Avalon Capital [*NASDAQ symbol*] (TTSB)
MIST......... Avalon Capital, Inc. [*NASDAQ symbol*] (SAG)
MI St .... Master of Information Studies (PGP)
MIST......... Maximum Isothermal System Temperature [*Nuclear energy*] (NRCH)
MIST......... Medical Information System via Telephone [*University of Alabama*]
MIST......... Member of the Institute of Science Technology [*British*] (DBQ)
MIST......... Metal Insulator Silicon Field-Effect Transistor [*Also, MISFET*] (EECA)
MIST......... Microbursts in Severe Thunderstorms
MIST+......... Microcomputer Information Support Tools [*2B Enterprises*] [*Washington, DC*] (TSSD)
MIST......... Minimum Structure Module
MIST......... Minor Isotopes Safeguards Techniques [*Nuclear energy*]
MIST......... Mistura [*Mixture*] [*Pharmacy*]
MIST......... MIUS [*Modular Integrated Utility Systems*] Integration and Subsystems Test (MCD)
MIST......... Multi-Input Standard Tape
MIST......... Multiloop Integral System Test [*Nuclear energy*] (NRCH)
MIST......... Multipurpose In-Space Throttleable Engine (MCD)
MIST......... Music Information System for Theorists (PDAA)
MISTAF....... Management Information Systems Task Force (SAA)
MiStan....... Stanton Public Library, Stanton, MI [*Library symbol Library of Congress*] (LCLS)
MISTC........ Member of the Institute of Scientific and Technical Communicators [*British*] (DBQ)
MISTC........ Men's International Squash Tournament Council [*Cardiff, Wales*] (EAIO)
MiStc........ Saint Clair Shores Public Library, Saint Clair Shores, MI [*Library symbol Library of Congress*] (LCLS)
MiStch .... Saint Charles Public Library, Saint Charles, MI [*Library symbol Library of Congress*] (LCLS)
MiSte........ Lincoln Township Public Library, Stevensville, MI [*Library symbol Library of Congress*] (LCLS)
MISTE........ Military Intelligence Special Training Element (DOMA)
MiStep........ Menominee County Library, Stephenson, MI [*Library symbol Library of Congress*] (LCLS)
MISTER....... Mobile Integrated System Trainer, Evaluator, and Recorder [*Navy*]
MIST-FOAL.... Multi-Stage Force Allocation (SAA)
MiSth........ Sterling Heights Public Library, Sterling Heights, MI [*Library symbol Library of Congress*] (LCLS)
MiSthe........ Richfield Township Public Library, St. Helen, MI [*Library symbol Library of Congress*] (LCLS)
MISTI........ Multipurpose International Securities Trading Information (MHDW)
MiSti........ St. Ignace Public Library, St. Ignace, MI [*Library symbol Library of Congress*] (LCLS)
MISTIC........ Michigan State Integral Computer
MISTIC........ Missile System Target Illuminator Controlled (MCD)
MISTIC........ Model Interstate Scientific and Technical Information Clearinghouse
MISTIR .... Multifunction Imaging Search/Track Infrared
MiStjo......... Bement Public Library, St. Johns, MI [*Library symbol Library of Congress*] (LCLS)

MiStjW .... Whirlpool Corp., Research Library, St. Joseph, MI [*Library symbol Library of Congress*] (LCLS)

MiStlo.......... Theodore Austin Cutler Memorial Library, St. Louis, MI [*Library symbol Library of Congress*] (LCLS)

MISTM........ Member of the Institute of Sales Technology and Management [*British*] (DBQ)

MISTR .... Management of Items Subject to Repair [*Air Force*] (AFM)

MISTRA .... Minnesota Study of Twins Reared Apart

MISTRAM ..... Missile Trajectory Measurement [*Air Force*]

MISTRANS... Mistranslation (ADA)

MISTRAULANT... Missile Weapons System Training Unit, Atlantic (DNAB)

MISTRAUPAC... Missile Weapons System Training Unit, Pacific (DNAB)

MistrJay ...... Mister Jay Fashions International, Inc. [*Associated Press*] (SAG)

MIStructE..... Member of the Institution of Structural Engineers [*British*] (EY)

MISTT .... Midwest Interstate Sulfur Transformation and Transport [*Meteorology*]

MiStu .... Sturgis Public Library, Sturgis, MI [*Library symbol Library of Congress*] (LCLS)

MistyM .... Misty Mountain Gold Ltd. [*Associated Press*] (SAG)

MiSun.......... Sunfield District Library, Sunfield, MI [*Library symbol Library of Congress*] (LCLS)

MISURA...... Miskito, Sumo, and Rama [*Nicaraguan Indian coalition*]

MISURASATA... Miskito, Sumo, and Rama [*Nicaraguan Indian coalition*]

MiSV.......... United States Veterans Administration Hospital, Saginaw, MI [*Library symbol Library of Congress*] (LCLS)

MISVE........ Management Information Systems for Vocational Education (OICC)

MISW.......... Member of the Institute of Social Welfare [*British*] (DBQ)

MiSW.......... White Pine Library System, Saginaw, MI [*Library symbol Library of Congress*] (LCLS)

MiS-Z......... Saginaw Public Libraries, Zauel Memorial Library, Saginaw, MI [*Library symbol Library of Congress*] (LCLS)

MIT .... Machine Interface Terminal [*Tangram Computer Aided Engineering*] [*Software package*] (NCC)

MIT .... Macrotrends International [*Vancouver Stock Exchange symbol*]

MIT .... Male Impotence Test [*Psychology*]

MIT .... Management Information Tree [*Telecommunications*] (OSI)

MIT .... Mandatory Independent Taxation [*British*] (DI)

MIT .... Manual Inputs-Tracks (SAA)

MIT .... Market if Touched [*Stock exchange term*]

MIT .... Massachusetts Institute of Technology [*Facetious translation: "Made in Taiwan" because of large number of Asian-American students*]

MIT .... Massachusetts Institute of Technology (GAGS)

MIT .... Massachusetts Investors Trust

MIT .... Master Instruction Tape [*Computer science*]

MIT .... Master in Teaching (PGP)

MIT .... Master of Industrial Technology (PGP)

MIT .... Master of Initial Teaching (PGP)

MIT .... Material Improvement Team (MCD)

MIT .... Material in Transit (MCD)

MIT .... Material Introduction Team

MIT .... Medium Intertheater Transport (MCD)

MIT .... Mercury Integrated Test

MIT .... Mercury Ion Thruster

MIT .... Merrill Lynch & Co., Inc. [*NYSE symbol*] (SPSG)

MIT .... Merrill Lynch & Co'MITTS' 2001 [*NASDAQ symbol*] (TTSB)

MIT .... Middle Italian [*Language, etc.*]

MIT .... Miles in Trail [*Aviation*] (FAAC)

MIT .... Miles in-Trail [*FAA*] (TAG)

MIT .... Military Intelligence Translator

MIT .... Milled in Transit [*Commodities*]

MIT .... Miller Air Transporters [*ICAO designator*] (FAAC)

MIT .... Milwaukee Institute of Technology [*Wisconsin*]

MIT .... Minimum Individual Training

MIT .... Ministry of Industry and Trade [*Israel*]

MIT .... Miracidal Immobilization Test [*Parasitology*]

MIT .... Miscellaneous Tool (SAA)

MIT............. Missouri-Illinois Traffic Service, East Saint Louis IL [*STAC*]

Mit............. Mitannian (BJA)

MIT .... Miter

MIT .... Mitigate

MIT............. Mito [*Japan*] [*Seismograph station code, US Geological Survey*] (SEIS)

MIT .... Mitomycin [*Medicine*] (DMAA)

MIT .... Mitsubishi Electric Corporation (NITA)

MIT............. Mitte [*Send*] [*Latin*]

MIT............. Mobile Instructor Team (MCD)

MIT............. Mobile Instructor Training [*Army*]

MIT............. Modern Investment Theory [*Finance*] (MHDB)

MIT............. Modular Industrial Terminal

MIT............. Modular Intelligent Terminal

MIT............. Monoiodotyrosine [*Biochemistry*]

MIT............. Motorist Inclusive Tour [*British*] (DCTA)

MIT............. Movements Identification Technican (SAA)

MIT............. Multiple Incidence Technique [*Structure testing*]

MIT............. Municipal Investment Trust

MIT............. Shafter, CA [*Location identifier FAA*] (FAAL)

MIT............. Society of Management Information Technology [*British*]

MiT............. Traverse City Public Library, Traverse City, MI [*Library symbol Library of Congress*] (LCLS)

MITA .... Member of the Industrial Transport Association [*British*]

MITA .... Microcomputer Industry Trade Association

MITA .... Minority Information Trade Annual [*A publication*]

MITAG .... Minority Affairs Task Group (DNAB)

MITAN .... Microwave Technology as Applied to Air Navigation (ADA)

MITB........... Missile Interface Test Bench

MiTc .... Iosco-Arenac Regional Library, Tawas City, MI [*Library symbol Library of Congress*] (LCLS)

MITC.......... Methylisothiocyanate [*Pesticide*]

MITC.......... Microfilm and Information Technology Center

MiTc-A........ Iosco-Arenac Regional Library, AuGres Branch Library, AuGres, MI [*Library symbol Library of Congress*] (LCLS)

MiTc-E........ Iosco-Arenac Regional Library, East Tawas Branch Library, East Tawas, MI [*Library symbol Library of Congress*] (LCLS)

Mitch .... Mitcham Industries [*Associated Press*] (SAG)

Mitcham ...... Mitcham Industries [*Associated Press*] (SAG)

Mitch B & N... Mitchell on Bills, Notes, Etc. [*1829*] [*A publication*] (DLA)

Mitchell's Mar Reg... Mitchell's Maritime Register [*England*] [*A publication*] (DLA)

Mitch Mod Geog... Mitchell's Modern Geography [*A publication*] (DLA)

Mitch MR.... Mitchell's Maritime Register [*England*] [*A publication*] (DLA)

Mit Ch Pl .... Mitford on Equity Pleading [*A publication*] (DLA)

MiTc-O........ Iosco-Arenac Regional Library, Oscoda Township Branch Library, Oscoda, MI [*Library symbol Library of Congress*] (LCLS)

MiTc-P........ Iosco-Arenac Regional Library, Plainfield Township Branch Library, Hale, MI [*Library symbol Library of Congress*] (LCLS)

MiTc-S........ Iosco-Arenac Regional Library, Standish Branch Library, Standish, MI [*Library symbol Library of Congress*] (LCLS)

MiTc-T........ Iosco-Arenac Regional Library, Tawas City Branch Library, Tawas City, MI [*Library symbol Library of Congress*] (LCLS)

MiTc-W....... Iosco-Arenac Regional Library, Whittemore Branch Library, Whittemore, MI [*Library symbol Library of Congress*] (LCLS)

MITD .... Member of the Institute of Training and Development [*British*] (DBQ)

MITDA .... Maryland Independent Truckers and Drivers Association [*Later, ITDA*] (EA)

Mit Drunk .... Mittermaier's Effect of Drunkenness on Criminal Responsibilty [*A publication*] (DLA)

MITE .... Magnetic Insulation Test Experiment

MITE .... Master Instrumentation Timing Equipment (CET)

MITE .... Meetings and Incentive Travel Exposition [*Trade show*]

MITE .... Microelectronic Integrated Test Equipment

MITE .... Microelectronics Test and Evaluation [*Raytheon Co.*]

MITE .... Microprocessor Industrial Terminal [*Computer science*] (MHDB)

MITE .... Miniaturized Integrated Telephone Equipment

MITE .... Missile Integration Terminal Equipment [*Computer science*]

MITE .... Multiple Input Terminal Equipment

MiTe .... Tecumseh Public Library, Tecumseh, MI [*Library symbol Library of Congress*] (LCLS)

MITECS....... Multi-International Teacher Education Cooperatives (EDAC)

MiTek .... Tekonsha Public Library, Tekonsha, MI [*Library symbol Library of Congress*] (LCLS)

MitekS .... Mitek Systems, Inc. [*Associated Press*] (SAG)

MITEL .... Mike and Terry's Lawnmowers [*Commercial firm*] [*canada*]

Mitel........... Mitel Corp. [*Associated Press*] (SAG)

MITER......... Modular Installation of Telecommunications Equipment Racks (TEL)

MITF .... Municipal Investment Trust Fund

MITF .... Musser International Turfgrass Foundation (EA)

Mitf & Ty Eq Pl... Tyler's Edition of Mitford's Equity Pleading [*A publication*] (DLA)

Mitf Eq Pl .... Mitford on Equity Pleading [*A publication*] (DLA)

MITGS .... Marine Institute of Technology and Graduate Studies [*Baltimore*]

MITH........... Marble-in-the-Hole [*Game used in psychometrics*]

MITH........... Mithracin [*Antineoplastic drug*] (CDI)

Mith............ Mithramycin [*Antineoplastic drug*] (DAVI)

MiTho .... Betsie Valley District Library, Thompsonville, MI [*Library symbol Library of Congress*] (LCLS)

MiThr .... Three Rivers Public Library, Three Rivers, MI [*Library symbol Library of Congress*] (LCLS)

MITI .... Ministry of International Trade and Industry [*Japan*]

MITI............ Moms in Touch International (EA)

MITI............ Myocardial Infarction, Triage, and Intervention Project [*or Trial*] [*Cardiology study*]

MITIC.......... Myanmar International Trust and Investment Co. (ECON)

MITIL.......... Massachusetts Institute of Technology Instrumentation Laboratory (SAA)

MITILAC...... Massachusetts Institute of Technology Information Laboratory Automatic Coding

Mit Insuf...... Mitral Insufficiency [*Cardiology*]

MITJ .... Member of the Institute of Technical Journalists [*British*] (DGA)

MITK.......... Mitek Systems [*NASDAQ symbol*] (TTSB)

MITK.......... Mitek Systems Inc. [*NASDAQ symbol*] (SAG)

MITKA........ Movimiento Indio Tupaj Katari [*Tupaj Katari Indian Movement*] [*Bolivia*] [*Political party*] (PPW)

MITL .... Man-in-the-Loop [*Army*]

MITLA........ Microcircuit Technology in Logistics Applications [*Defense Logistics Agency*]

MIT/LL........ Massachusetts Institute of Technology/Lincoln Laboratory (AAG)

MITLS .... Man-in-the-Loop Simulator [*Military*]

MITM .... Management Inventory on Time Management [*Test*]

MITM .... Military-Industry Technical Manual

MITMA........ Member of the Institute of Trade Mark Agents [*British*]

MITMA........ Military Traffic Management Agency [*Later, DTMS*]

Mit MR .... Mitchell's Maritime Register [*England*] [*A publication*] (ILCA)

MITMS .... Military-Industry Technical Manual Specifications

MiTN........... Northwestern Michigan College, Traverse City, MI [*Library symbol Library of Congress*] (LCLS)

MIT/NSL...... Massachusetts Institute of Technology/Naval Supersonic Laboratory (AAG)

MITO........... Meat Industry Training Organisation (AIE)

MITO........... Member of the Institute of Training Officers [*International Institute of Social Economics*] [*British*] (DI)

MITO........... Minimum Interval Takeoff

Mito............ Mitomycin-C [*Antineoplastic drug*] (DAVI)

MITO-C .... Mitomycin-C [Antineoplastic drug] (DAVI)
MITOC .... Multiple Intercommunications Technical Operations Communications [NASA] (KSC)
MITOCS .... Missile Technical Operations Communications System (MCD)
MITOL.......... Machine-Independent Telemetry-Oriented Language [Computer science] (IEEE)
MiTop .... Topinabee Public Library, Topinabee, MI [Library symbol Library of Congress] (LCLS)
MITP .... Master Intern Training Plan [Military]
MITP........... Measurement and Instrumentation Technology Panel (ACII)
MITP........... Miniature Template [Tool]
MiTP........... Peninsula Community Library, Traverse City, MI [Library symbol Library of Congress] (LCLS)
MITR.......... Massachusetts Institute of Technology Reactor
MITR.......... Mortgage Interest Tax Relief [British]
MiTr........... Troy Public Library, Troy, MI [Library symbol Library of Congress] (LCLS)
MitrArd .... Mitropolia Ardealului [Sibiu, Rumania] (BJA)
MitrBan....... Mitropolia Banatului [Timisoara, Rumania] (BJA)
MITRE.......... Massachusetts Institute of Technology Research Establishment (NATG)
MITRE......... Miniature Individual Transmitter-Receiver Equipment (MCD)
MitrMoldSuc... Mitropolia Moldovei si Sucevei [Jassy, Rumania] (BJA)
MiTrWB .... William Beaumont Hospital, Troy, MI [Library symbol Library of Congress] (LCLS)
MITS .... Management Information and Text System
MITS........... Man-in-the-Sea Program [Navy]
MITS........... Man in the Street [The average man] [Usually "Mr. Mits" See also T C MITS]
MITS........... Master's Intelligent Terminal System [Software package] [Nippon Kokan]
MITS........... Michigan Information Transfer Source [University of Michigan] (IID)
MITS........... Michigan Travel System
MITS........... Microfiche Image Transmission System (MCD)
MITS........... Micro Instrumentation and Telemetry Systems (NITA)
MITS........... Missile Ignition Test Simulator
MITS........... Missile Interface Test Set
MITS........... Missouri-Illinois Traffic Service
MITS......... Mitsui & Co. Ltd. [NASDAQ symbol] (NQ)
MITS........... Mobile Independent Target System (INF)
MITS........... Monthly International Terrorist Summary (MCD)
MITS........... Multiple Inward-Turning Scoop (MCD)
MITS........... Multiplex Information Transfer System (PDAA)
MITSA.......... Member of the Institute of Trading Standards Administration [British] (DBQ)
mit sang...... Mitte Sanguinem [Take Away Blood] [Latin] (MAE)
MitsbBk....... Mitsubishi Bank Ltd. [Associated Press] (SAG)
MITSG .... Massachusetts Institute of Technology Sea Grant Program (NOAA)
MIT/SL......... Massachusetts Institute of Technology/Sloan Laboratory (AAG)
MIT/SmL...... Massachusetts Institute of Technology/Servomechanisms Laboratory (AAG)
MIT/SpL ...... Massachusetts Institute of Technology/Spectroscopy Laboratory (AAG)
Mitsui .... Mitsui & Co. Ltd. [Associated Press] (SAG)
MITSY.......... Mitsui & Co ADR [NASDAQ symbol] (TTSB)
MITT .... Member of the Institute of Travel and Tourism [British] (ODBW)
MITT .... Mitte [Send] [Latin]
MITT .... Mobile Imagery Transmission Terminal (DOMA)
MITT .... Mobile Integrated Tactical Terminal (DOMA)
MITTAT .... Mittatur [Let Be Sent] [Pharmacy] (ROG)
Mitte Sang... Mitte Sanguinem [Bleed] [Pharmacy] (BABM)
mitte sang... Mitte Sanguineum [Bleed] [Latin] (DAVI)
MITTINS ...... Michigan Travel Trade Information Service
MITTS .... Minutes of Telecommunications Traffic [Measure of voice, fax, and data transmission]
MITTS .... Mobile IGOR [Intercept Ground Optical Recorder] Tracking Telescope System [Air Force]
MITT SANG ad UNC SALTEM... Mitte Sanguinem ad Uncias ___ Saltem [Take Away ___ Ounces of Blood at Least] [Pharmacy] (ROG)
MITT TAL ..... Mitte Tales [Send Such] [Pharmacy]
MiTu .... Tustin Public Library, Tustin, MI [Library symbol Library of Congress] (LCLS)
MITY........... Mity Lite, Inc. [NASDAQ symbol] (SAG)
MITY........... Mity-Lite Inc. [NASDAQ symbol] (TTSB)
MityLite ...... Mity Lite, Inc. [Associated Press] (SAG)
MIU .... Machine Interface Unit (HGAA)
MIU .... Maharishi International University [Fairfield, IA]
MIU .... Maharishi International University, Fairfield, IA [OCLC symbol] (OCLC)
MIU .... Maiduguri [Nigeria] [Airport symbol] (OAG)
MIU .... Malfunction Insertion Unit [Aviation]
MIU .... Message Interface Unit (CAAL)
MIU .... Methylisourea [Organic chemistry]
miu .... Michigan [MARC country of publication code Library of Congress] (LCCP)
MIU .... Microalgae International Union (EA)
mIU .... Milli-International Unit
MIU .... Missile Interface Unit
MIU .... Mobile Inspection Unit [Military] (AFM)
MIU .... Model Interface Unit (NITA)
MIU .... Moisture, Insolubles, and Unsaponifiables [Fat analysis]
MIU .... Motor Impeller Unit
MIU .... Multiplex Interface Unit (NASA)
MIU .... Multiplex Interface Unit
MIU........... Multistation Interface Unit [Computer science]

MiU............ University of Michigan, Ann Arbor, MI [Library symbol Library of Congress] (LCLS)
MiU-A......... University of Michigan, Asia Library, Ann Arbor, MI [Library symbol Library of Congress] (LCLS)
MiUb.......... Sleeper Public Library, Ubly, MI [Library symbol Library of Congress] (LCLS)
MiU-BA....... University of Michigan, Graduate School of Business Administration, Ann Arbor, MI [Library symbol Library of Congress] (LCLS)
MiU-C......... University of Michigan, William L. Clements Library, Ann Arbor, MI [Library symbol Library of Congress] (LCLS)
MiUcD .... Delta College, University Center, MI [Library symbol Library of Congress] (LCLS)
MiUcS......... Saginaw Valley College, University Center, MI [Library symbol Library of Congress] (LCLS)
MIU/FCO ...... Mobile Inspection Unit / Functional Checkout (SAA)
MiU-G......... University of Michigan, Bureau of Government Library, Ann Arbor, MI [Library symbol Library of Congress] (LCLS)
MiU-H......... University of Michigan, Michigan Historical Collection, Ann Arbor, MI [Library symbol Library of Congress] (LCLS)
MiU-Ho....... University of Michigan, Avery and Julie Hopwood Room, Ann Arbor, MI [Library symbol Library of Congress] (LCLS)
MiU-L .... University of Michigan, Law Library, Ann Arbor, MI [Library symbol Library of Congress] (LCLS)
MiU-M......... University of Michigan, Medical Center, Ann Arbor, MI [Library symbol Library of Congress] (LCLS)
MiUnv......... Columbia Township Library, Unionville, MI [Library symbol Library of Congress] (LCLS)
MiU-RE....... University of Michigan, Center for Research on Economic Development, Ann Arbor, MI [Library symbol Library of Congress] (LCLS)
MIUS .... Modular Integrated Utility System [HUD]
MIUSA......... Mobility International USA (EA)
MiU-T......... University of Michigan, Transportation Library, Ann Arbor, MI [Library symbol Library of Congress] (LCLS)
MiUt........... Utica Public Library, Utica, MI [Library symbol Library of Congress] (LCLS)
MIUTC .... Military Intelligence Unit Training Center (AABC)
MiUtS......... Shelby Township Library, Utica, MI [Library symbol Library of Congress] (LCLS)
MIUU .... Meteorological Institute of the University of Uppsala [Sweden] (USDC)
MIUU .... Meterorological Institute of the University of Uppsala, Sweden [Marine science] (OSRA)
MIUW .... Mobile Inshore Undersea Warfare [Navy] (NG)
MIUWG .... Mobile Inshore Undersea War Group [Navy] (VNW)
MIUWS .... Mobile Inshore Undersea Warfare Surveillance [Navy] (NVT)
MIUWSU ...... Mobile Inshore Undersea Warfare Surveillance Unit [Navy] (CINC)
MIV .... Main Instrumentation Van [NASA]
MIV .... Mi-Avia [Russian Federation] [ICAO designator] (FAAC)
MIV .... MICC Investments Ltd. [Toronto Stock Exchange symbol]
MIV .... Millville, NJ [Location identifier FAA] (FAAL)
MIV .... Mobile Instrumentation Van (KSC)
MIV .... Moving Ion Voltmeter
MiVa .... Bullard-Sanford Public Library, Vassar, MI [Library symbol Library of Congress] (LCLS)
MIVA-America... Missionary Vehicle Association of America (EA)
MIVAC .... Microwave Vacuum [Dryer] (MCD)
MIVC .... Magnetically Induced Velocity Charge [Southwest Research Institute]
MIVEC......... Mitsubishi Innovative Valve Timing and Lift Electronic Control System [Automotive engineering] (PS)
MiVer.......... Vermontville Public Library, Vermontville, MI [Library symbol Library of Congress] (LCLS)
MiVes .... Vestaburg Public Library, Vestaburg, MI [Library symbol Library of Congress] (LCLS)
MIVI .... Mississippi View Holding [NASDAQ symbol] (TTSB)
MIVI .... Mississippi View Holding Co. [NASDAQ symbol] (SAG)
MiVi .... Vicksburg Community Library, Vicksburg, MI [Library symbol Library of Congress] (LCLS)
MIVPO .... Modified Inside Vapor Phase Oxidation (EECA)
MIW .... Airborne of Sweden AB [ICAO designator] (FAAC)
MIW........... Marshalltown, IA [Location identifier FAA] (FAAL)
MIW........... Microinstruction Word
MIW........... Milk Ingredient Water (OA)
MIW........... Mine Warfare (NVT)
MiWaC......... Wayne County Federated Library System, Wayne, MI [Library symbol Library of Congress] (LCLS)
MiWaC-B...... Wayne County Federated Library System, Department for the Blind and Physically Handicapped, Wayne, MI [Library symbol Library of Congress] (LCLS)
MiWak........ Wakefield Public Library, Wakefield, MI [Library symbol Library of Congress] (LCLS)
MiWal......... Melrose Township Public Library, Walloon Lake, MI [Library symbol Library of Congress] (LCLS)
MiWald....... Waldron District Library, Waldron, MI [Library symbol Library of Congress] (LCLS)
MiWalv....... Walkerville Public Library, Walkerville, MI [Library symbol Library of Congress] (LCLS)
MiWar .... Warren Public Library, Warren, MI [Library symbol Library of Congress] (LCLS)
MiWarBH...... Bi-County Community Hospital, Warren, MI [Library symbol Library of Congress] (LCLS)
MiWarGME.... General Motors Corp., Engineering Library and Information Services, Warren, MI [Library symbol] [Library of Congress] (LCLS)
MiWarGMR... General Motors Corp., Research Laboratories Division, Warren, MI [Library symbol Library of Congress] (LCLS)

MiWarGMR-E... General Motors Corp., Engineering Staff Library, Warren, MI [*Library symbol Library of Congress*] (LCLS)

MiWarM .... Macomb County Community College, Warren, MI [*Library symbol Library of Congress*] (LCLS)

MiWatv........ Watervliet Public Library, Watervliet, MI [*Library symbol Library of Congress*] (LCLS)

MiWbH .... Holocaust Memorial Center, West Bloomfield, MI [*Library symbol Library of Congress*] (LCLS)

MIWE.......... Member of the Institution of Water Engineers [*British*] (EY)

MiWe.......... West Branch Public Library, West Branch, MI [*Library symbol Library of Congress*] (LCLS)

MiWeld........ Gladys MacArthur Memorial Library, Weidman, MI [*Library symbol Library of Congress*] (LCLS)

MIWES........ Member of the Institution of Water Engineers and Scientists [*British*] (DI)

MiWh.......... White Pigeon Township Library, White Pigeon, MI [*Library symbol Library of Congress*] (LCLS)

MiWhc........ E. Jack Sharpe Public Library, White Cloud, MI [*Library symbol Library of Congress*] (LCLS)

MIWHR....... Melpomene Institute for Women's Health Research (EA)

MIWHTE ..... Member of the Institution of Works and Highways Technician Engineers [*British*] (DBQ)

MiWin......... Fremont Township Library, Winn, MI [*Library symbol Library of Congress*] (LCLS)

MIWM........ Member of the Institution of Works Managers [*British*]

MIWMA .... Member of the Institute of Weights and Measures Administration [*British*]

MiWol......... Wolverine Community Library, Wolverine, MI [*Library symbol Library of Congress*] (LCLS)

MiWp.......... Carp Lake Township Library, White Pine, MI [*Library symbol Library of Congress*] (LCLS)

MIWPC .... Member of the Institute of Water Pollution Control [*British*]

MIWS.......... Multipurpose Individual Weapon System (MCD)

MIWSP .... Member of the Institute of Work Study Practitioners [*British*]

MIWT.......... Member of the Institute of Wireless Technology [*British*]

MiWy.......... Bacon Memorial Public Library, Wyandotte, MI [*Library symbol Library of Congress*] (LCLS)

MIX........... Magnetic Ionization Experiment

MIX........... McGraw-Hill Information Exchange for Educators

MIX........... Member Information Exchange [*American Society for Training and Development - ASTD*] [*Alexandria, VA*] [*Information service or system*] (IID)

MIX........... Merrill Lynch & Co. [*NYSE symbol*] (SAG)

MIX........... Merrill Lynch & Co'MITTS' 2001 [*NYSE symbol*] (TTSB)

MIX........... Methylisobutylxanthine [*Also, IBMX*] [*Biochemistry*]

MIX........... Metropolis, IL [*Location identifier FAA*] (FAAL)

MIX........... Mix Canyon Road [*California*] [*Seismograph station code, US Geological Survey*] (SEIS)

MIX........... Mixing

MIX........... Mixture (KSC)

MIX........... Mores Island [*Bahamas*] [*Airport symbol*] (AD)

mix mon ..... Mixed Monitor [*Obstetrics*] (DAVI)

MIXT.......... Mixtura [*Mixture*] [*Pharmacy*]

MIXX.......... Medical Innovations [*NASDAQ symbol*] (TTSB)

MIXX.......... Medical Innovations, Inc. [*NASDAQ symbol*] (NQ)

MIY........... Miyako [*Japan*] [*Seismograph station code, US Geological Survey*] (SEIS)

MIY........... Montgomeryshire Imperial Yeomanry [*British military*] (DMA)

MIY........... MuniYield Michigan Insured Fund [*NYSE symbol*] (SPSG)

MIY........... MuniYield MI Insured Fund [*NYSE symbol*] (TTSB)

MiY........... Ypsilanti Area Public Library, Ypsilanti, MI [*Library symbol Library of Congress*] (LCLS)

MiYCC .... Cleary College, Ypsilanti, MI [*Library symbol Library of Congress*] (LCLS)

MiYEM........ Eastern Michigan University, Ypsilanti, MI [*Library symbol Library of Congress*] (LCLS)

MIZ........... Marginal Ice Zone [*Oceanography*]

MIZ........... Missile Interception Zone [*Military*]

Miz........... Mizrachi [*or Mizrahi*] (BJA)

MIZ........... Mizusawa [*Japan*] [*Seismograph station code, US Geological Survey*] (SEIS)

MiZ........... Zeeland Public Library, Zeeland, MI [*Library symbol Library of Congress*] (LCLS)

Mizar......... Mizar, Inc. [*Associated Press*] (SAG)

MIZEX........ Marginal Ice Zone Experiment [*Oceanography*]

MIZPAC....... Marginal Sea Ice Zone Pacific [*Marine science*] (MSC)

MIZR.......... Mizar, Inc. [*NASDAQ symbol*] (SAG)

MJ .... Lineas Aereas Privadas Argentinas [*ICAO designator*] (AD)

MJ .... Madras Jurist [*India*] [*A publication*] (DLA)

MJ .... Main Jet [*Automotive engineering*]

MJ .... Major Subject Descriptor [*Online database field identifier*]

MJ .... Manufacturers' Junction Railway Co. [*AAR code*]

MJ .... Marijuana

MJ .... Marine Jet

MJ .... Master of Journalism

MJ .... Master of Jurisprudence

MJ .... Mastic Joint [*Technical drawings*]

MJ .... Mead Johnson & Co. [*Research code symbol*]

MJ .... Mechanical Joint (NASA)

MJ .... Megajoule

MJ .... Michael Joseph [*Commercial firm British*]

MJ .... Microturbo [*France ICAO aircraft manufacturer identifier*] (ICAO)

MJ .... Military Judge (AFM)

MJ .... Military Justice Reporter (West) [*A publication*] (DLA)

MJ .... Milwaukee Journal [*A newspaper*]

mj .... Missionaries of St. Joseph (TOCD)

MJ .... Missionaries of St. Joseph (Mexico) (TOCD)

MJ .... Missionary Sisters of Jesus (TOCD)

mj .... Montserrat [*MARC country of publication code Library of Congress*] (LCCP)

MJA .... Manja [*Madagascar*] [*Airport symbol*] (OAG)

MJA .... Master of Justice Administration (PGP)

MJA .... Medical Journalists Association [*British*] (DBA)

MJA .... Merchant Jewellers' Association Ltd. [*British*] (BI)

MJA .... Midstates Jeepster Association (EA)

MJAA .... Messianic Jewish Alliance of America (EA)

MJAJ .... Maanpuolustuksen ja Turvallisuuden Ammattijaerjestoet [*Defence and Security Employees Union*] [*Finalnd*] (EY)

MJAO .... Mediterranean Joint Air Orders

MJB .... Master Jet Base [*Navy*] (NVT)

MJB .... Mejit [*Marshall Islands*] [*Airport symbol*] (OAG)

MJB .... Missile Junction Box

MJB .... Moore Jig Borer

MJC .... Junior College District, Kansas City, MO [*OCLC symbol*] (OCLC)

MJC .... Majestic Contractors Ltd. [*Toronto Stock Exchange symbol*]

MJC .... Man [*Ivory Coast*] [*Airport symbol*] (OAG)

MJC .... Manitoba Journal of Counselling [*A publication*]

MJC .... Marshalltown Junior College [*Iowa*]

MJC .... Medieval Jewish Chronicles [*A publication*] (BJA)

MJC .... Mercy Junior College [*Missouri*] [*Closed, 1971*]

MJC .... Miami-Jacobs College [*Ohio*]

MJC .... Midway Junior College [*Kentucky*]

MJC .... Military Junior College (AABC)

MJC .... Moberly Junior College [*Missouri*]

MJC .... Modesto Junior College [*California*]

MJC .... Montgomery Junior College [*Maryland*]

MJC .... Morse Junior College [*Connecticut*]

MJC .... Morton Junior College [*Later, Morton College*] [*Cicero, IL*]

MJC .... Muscatine Junior College [*Iowa*]

MJCA .... Midbody Jettison Control Assembly (NASA)

MJCA .... Midbody Jettison Control Assembly

MJCC .... Melbourne Junior Chamber of Commerce [*Australia*]

MJCS .... Memorandum for the Joint Chiefs of Staff (MCD)

MJD .... Doctor of Medical Jurisprudence

MJD .... Management Job Description (PDAA)

MJD .... Modified Julian Date [*Astronomy*] (TEL)

MJD .... Mohenjo Daro [*Pakistan*] [*Airport symbol*] (OAG)

MJD .... Mouvement de la Jeunesse Djiboutienne [*Political party*] (EY)

MJDQ .... Minnesota Job Description Questionnaire [*Research test*]

MJ Ed .... Master of Jewish Education (PGP)

MJF .... Greenville, TX [*Location identifier FAA*] (FAAL)

MJF .... Multiple Juxtapositional Fixedness [*Tongue-in-cheek description of unusually strong bonding between metal ions and some ligands*]

MJG .... Mayajigua [*Cuba*] [*Airport symbol*] (AD)

MJG .... Moore Jig Grinder

MJGA .... Manufacturing Jewelers Golf Association (EA)

MJGA .... Midwest Job Galvanizers Association [*Defunct*] (EA)

MJH .... Majma [*Saudi Arabia*] [*Airport symbol*] (AD)

MJI .... Maji [*Ethiopia*] [*Airport symbol*] (AD)

MJI .... Masters and Johnson Institute [*St. Louis, MO*] [*Formerly, Reproductive Biology Research Foundation*] [*Research center*]

MJI .... Member of the Journalists Institute

MJI .... MuniYield New Jersey Insured Fund [*NYSE symbol*] (SPSG)

MJI .... MuniYield NJ Insured Fund [*NYSE symbol*] (TTSB)

MJIE .... Member of the Junior Institute of Engineers [*British*]

MJL .... Medial Joint Line [*Orthopedics*] (DAVI)

MJL .... Meyer, Jr., L. Agnew, Washington DC [*STAC*]

MJL .... Mouila [*Gabon*] [*Airport symbol*] (OAG)

MJL .... Murray's Jat Lancers [*British military*] (DMA)

MJM .... Man-Job Match [*Military*]

MJM .... Mbuji-Mayi [*Zaire*] [*Airport symbol*] (OAG)

MJMA .... Mechanical Jack Manufacturers Association [*Defunct*] (EA)

MJMI .... Messianic Jewish Movement International (EA)

MJMJ .... Missionaries of Jesus, Mary, and Joseph [*Roman Catholic women's religious order*]

MJMT .... Mean Job Mill Time [*Quality control*] (MHDB)

MJN .... Majunga [*Madagascar*] [*Airport symbol*] (OAG)

MJN .... Royal Air Force of Oman (Air Transport) [*ICAO designator*] (FAAC)

MJNMM...... Master of Journalism in New Media Management (GAGS)

MJO .... Mariner Jupiter Orbit [*NASA*]

MJO .... Owens Technical College, Learning Resource Media Center, Toledo, OH [*OCLC symbol*] (OCLC)

MJP .... Jackson Metropolitan Library System, Jackson, MS [*OCLC symbol*] (OCLC)

MJP .... Master of Jewish Pedagogy

MJP .... Mastuj [*Pakistan*] [*Airport symbol*] (AD)

MJP .... Mount John Pukaki [*New Zealand*] [*Seismograph station code, US Geological Survey*] (SEIS)

MJPM .... Master of Justice Policy and Management (PGP)

MJPS .... Mouvement des Jeunesses Progressistes Soudanaises [*Sudanese Progressive Youth Movement*] [*Mali*]

MJQ .... Jackson, MN [*Location identifier FAA*] (FAAL)

MJQ .... Modern Jazz Quartet [*Musical group*]

MJR .... Maintenance Job Request

Mjr .... Major [*Record label*]

MJR .... Major

MJR .... Management Job Review [*LIMRA*]

MJS .... Maintenance Jettison System [*NASA*]

MJS .... Manipulator Jettison System [*or Subsystem*] (MCD)

MJS .... Manipulator Jettison System

MJS .... Mariner Jupiter-Saturn [*NASA*]
MJS .... Master of Japanese Studies (ADA)
MJS .... Master of Judaic Studies (PGP)
MJS .... Master of Juridical Science (DLA)
MJS .... Member of the Japan Society
MJS .... Movimiento Juvenil Salesiano [*Salesian Youth Movement - SYM*] (EAIO)
MJSA .... Manufacturing Jewelers and Silversmiths of America (EA)
MJSA .... Manufacturing Jewelers Sales Association
MJSA .... Mouvement des Jeunesses Socialistes Africaines [*African Socialist Youth Movement*]
MJSD .... March, June, September, and December [*Denotes quarterly payments of interest or dividends in these months*] [*Business term*]
MJSG .... Medem Jewish Socialist Group [*Defunct*] (EA)
MJSTC .... Majestic
MJT .... Majorteck Industries [*Vancouver Stock Exchange symbol*]
MJT .... Materials Joining Tool
MJT .... Mead Johnson Tube [*Medicine*] (DMAA)
MJT .... Multijet Transport
MJT .... Museum of Jurassic Technology
MJT .... Mytilene [*Greece*] [*Airport symbol*] (OAG)
MJU .... Jackson State University, Jackson, MS [*OCLC symbol*] (OCLC)
MJU .... Mamuju [*Indonesia*] [*Airport symbol*] (OAG)
MJU .... Mariner Jupiter-Uranus [*Mission*] [*NASA*]
MJu .... Medica Judaica [*A publication*] (BJA)
MJU .... Multijunction Unit [*Computer science*]
MJUO .... Mount John University Observatory [*New Zealand*]
MJUPG .... Movimiento da Juventude da Uniao Popular da Guine [*Youth Movement of Guinean People's Union*]
MJUPS .... Mouvement des Jeunes de l'Union Progressiste Senegalaise [*Youth Movement of the Senegalese Progressive Movement*]
MJur .... Master of Jurisprudence
MJV .... Murcia [*Spain*] [*Airport symbol*] (OAG)
MJW .... Madison Junction [*Wyoming*] [*Seismograph station code, US Geological Survey Closed*] (SEIS)
MJWG .... MANPRINT [*Manpower and Personnel Integration*] Joint Working Group [*Army*]
MJX .... Masjed Soleyman [*Iran*] [*Airport symbol*] (AD)
MJX .... Toms River, NJ [*Location identifier FAA*] (FAAL)
MJY .... Majesty Resources [*Vancouver Stock Exchange symbol*]
MJZ .... Mahfid [*South Arabia*] [*Airport symbol*] (AD)
MJZ .... Mount John [*New Zealand*] [*Seismograph station code, US Geological Survey*] (SEIS)
MK .... Air Mauritius [*ICAO designator*] (AD)
MK .... Air Mauritius [*Airline flight code*] (ODBW)
MK .... Magic Kingdom [*Walt Disney World*]
MK .... Malawi Kwacha [*Monetary unit*]
MK .... Manual Clock [*Computer science*] (MDG)
MK .... Mark (KSC)
MK .... Mark [*Ammunition*] (NATG)
Mk .... Mark [*New Testament book*]
mk .... Mark (WDMC)
MK .... Markka [*Monetary unit*] [*Finland*] (GPO)
MK .... Marschkolonne [*March Column*] [*German military - World War II*]
MK .... Mask [*Computer science*]
MK .... Master Key [*Locks*] (ADA)
MK .... Mebyon Kernow [*Sons of Cornwall*] [*National liberation party*] [*Political party*]
MK .... Member of Knesset (BJA)
MK .... Menaquinone [*Vitamin K*] [*Also, MQ*] [*Biochemistry*]
MK .... Merck & Co., Inc. [*Research code symbol*]
MK .... Metarrithmistikon Komma [*Reformist Party*] [*Greece*] [*Political party*] (PPE)
MK .... Microphone (MDG)
MK .... Middle Kingdom [*Egyptology*] (ROG)
mK .... Millikelvin
MK .... Milton Keynes [*Russian city*]
MK .... Miscellaneous Kits [*JETDS nomenclature*] [*Military*] (CET)
MK .... Mit Kappe [*With Cap*] [*German military - World War II*]
MK .... Mit Kern [*With Core*] [*German military - World War II*]
MK .... Modification Kit (AAG)
MK .... Mo'ed Katan (BJA)
MK .... Monk
MK .... Monkey Kidney
M-K .... Morgan Keenan [*System for determining the luminosity of stars*]
MK .... Morgan Keenan [*System*] [*Astronomy*]
M-K .... Morrison-Knudsen Co., Inc. [*Boise, ID*] (TSSD)
MK .... Morse Key (DEN)
MK .... Multiple Kill [*Aerospace*]
mk .... Muscat and Oman [*Oman*] [*MARC country of publication code Library of Congress*] (LCCP)
MKA .... Machine Knife Association (EA)
MKA .... Makaopuhi [*Hawaii*] [*Seismograph station code, US Geological Survey*] (SEIS)
MKA .... Marine-Kuestenartillerie [*Naval Coast Artillery*] [*German military - World War II*]
MKA .... Master Kennel Association [*Commercial firm*] (EA)
MKA .... Miller, SD [*Location identifier FAA*] (FAAL)
MKA .... MK Aircargo [*British ICAO designator*] (FAAC)
MKAS .... Meyer-Kendall Assessment Survey [*Interpersonal skills and attitudes test*]
MKAU .... MK Gold [*NASDAQ symbol*] (TTSB)
MKAU .... MK Gold Co. [*NASDAQ symbol*] (SAG)
MKB .... Megakaryoblast [*Hematology*]

MKB .... Mekambo [*Gabon*] [*Airport symbol*] (OAG)
MKBF .... Mean Kilometers between Failures
MKBWU .... Machine Knife and Bayonet Workers' Union [*British*]
MKC .... Kansas City [*Missouri*] [*Airport symbol*] (OAG)
MKC .... Magic Kingdom Club [*Walt Disney Productions*]
MKC .... Mark Resources, Inc. [*Toronto Stock Exchange symbol*]
MKC .... McKeesport Connecting Railroad Co. [*AAR code*]
MKC .... Moncks Corner [*South Carolina*] [*Seismograph station code, US Geological Survey Closed*] (SEIS)
MKC .... University of Health Sciences, Kansas City, MO [*OCLC symbol*] (OCLC)
MKD .... Marked (MSA)
MKDIR .... Make Directory [*Computer science*]
MKE .... General Mitchell International Airport [*FAA*] (TAG)
MKE .... Milwaukee [*Wisconsin*] [*Airport symbol*] (OAG)
MKE .... Molecular Kinetic Energy
MKF .... Mackenzie Financial Corp. [*Toronto Stock Exchange symbol*]
MKFC .... Mackenzie Financial Corp. [*NASDAQ symbol*] (SAG)
MKFCF .... Mackenzie Financial [*NASDAQ symbol*] (TTSB)
MKG .... Magnetocardiogram
MKG .... Making
MKG .... Mallinckrodt Group [*Formerly, IMCERA Group*] [*NYSE symbol*] (SAG)
MKG .... Marking
MKG .... Maurer Kunst Geselle [*Fellowcraft*] [*Freemasonry*] [*German*]
M-KG .... Meteor-Kilogram
M-KG .... Meter-Kilogram (KSC)
MKG .... Munson, K. G., Weyers Cave VA [*STAC*]
MKG .... Muskegon [*Michigan*] [*Airport symbol*] (OAG)
MKG .... Muskegon, MI [*Location identifier FAA*] (FAAL)
MK Gold .... MK Gold Co. [*Associated Press*] (SAG)
MKgP .... Posse School, Inc., Kendal Green, MA [*Library symbol Library of Congress Obsolete*] (LCLS)
MKGPr .... Mallincrodt Group 4% Pfd [*NYSE symbol*] (TTSB)
MKGS .... Markings
MKH .... Mauna Kea [*Hawaii*] [*Seismograph station code, US Geological Survey*] (SEIS)
MKH .... Million of Kilowatt Hours (MCD)
MKH .... Mokhotlong [*Lesotho*] [*Airport symbol*] (OAG)
MKH .... Multiple Key Hashing
MKI .... M-Corp Inc. [*Formerly, Mike's Submarines*] [*Toronto Stock Exchange symbol*]
MKIE .... Mackie Designs [*NASDAQ symbol*] (TTSB)
MKIE .... Mackie Designs, Inc. [*NASDAQ symbol*] (SAG)
M Kin .... Master of Kinesiology (PGP)
MkIS .... Marketing Information System
MKJ .... Makoua [*Congo*] [*Airport symbol*] (OAG)
MKJK .... Kingston [*Jamaica*] [*ICAO location identifier*] (ICLI)
MKJM .... Montego Bay [*Jamaica*] [*ICAO location identifier*] (ICLI)
MKJP .... Kingston/Norman Manley International [*Jamaica*] [*ICAO location identifier*] (ICLI)
MKJS .... Montego Bay/Sangster International [*Jamaica*] [*ICAO location identifier*] (ICLI)
MKK .... Kaunakakai, HI [*Location identifier FAA*] (FAAL)
Mkk .... Markka [*Monetary unit*] [*Finland*]
MKK .... Molokai/Kaunakakai [*Hawaii*] [*Airport symbol*] (OAG)
MkK .... Monkey Kidney [*Medicine*] (DMAA)
MKK .... Morgan, Keenan, Kellman [*System*] [*Astronomy*]
MKL .... Jackson [*Tennessee*] [*Airport symbol*] (OAG)
MKL .... Jackson, TN [*Location identifier FAA*] (FAAL)
MKL .... Lakeland Regional Library, Killarney, Manitoba [*Library symbol National Library of Canada*] (NLC)
MKL .... Maskali [*Djibouti*] [*Seismograph station code, US Geological Survey*] (SEIS)
MKL .... Megakaryocytic Leukemia [*Hematology*]
MKLP .... Mitotic Kinesin-Like Protein [*Biochemistry*]
MKM .... Kansas City, MO [*Location identifier FAA*] (FAAL)
MKM .... Marksman [*Marine Corps*]
MKM .... Mink Minerals Resources, Inc. [*Vancouver Stock Exchange symbol*]
MKM .... Mukah [*Malaysia*] [*Airport symbol*] (OAG)
MKM .... Myopic Keratomileusis [*Ophthalmology*]
MKMA .... Machine Knife Manufacturers Association (EA)
MkmQualBad... Marksman Qualification Badge [*Military decoration*] (AABC)
MKN .... Malekolon [*Papua New Guinea*] [*Airport symbol*] (OAG)
MKN .... Mouvement Cooperatif National [*Haiti*] [*Political party*] (EY)
MKN .... Northeast Missouri State University, Kirksville, MO [*OCLC symbol*] (OCLC)
MKO .... Makung Airlines [*Taiwan*] [*ICAO designator*] (FAAC)
MKO .... Mauna Kea Observatory [*Hawaii*] (BARN)
MKO .... Mikado Resources Ltd. [*Vancouver Stock Exchange symbol*]
MKO .... Modification Kit Order
MKO .... Muskogee, OK [*Location identifier FAA*] (FAAL)
MKP .... Magyar Kommunista Part [*Hungarian Communist Party*] [*Political party*] (PPE)
MKP .... Makemo [*French Polynesia*] [*Airport symbol*] (OAG)
MKP .... McKeesport, PA [*Location identifier FAA*] (FAAL)
MkP .... Mikropress GmbH, Bonn, Germany [*Library symbol Library of Congress*] (LCLS)
MKP .... Myokinetic Psychodiagnosis [*Psychology*] (AEBS)
MKPL .... Computer Marketplace [*NASDAQ symbol*] (TTSB)
MKPL .... Computer Marketplace, Inc. [*NASDAQ symbol*] (SAG)
MKPLW .... Computer Marketplace Wrrt'A' [*NASDAQ symbol*] (TTSB)
MKPLZ .... Computer Marketplace Wrrt'B' [*NASDAQ symbol*] (TTSB)
MKQ .... Merauke [*Indonesia*] [*Airport symbol*] (OAG)
MKQCP .... Member of the King's and Queen's College of Physicians [*Ireland*]

MKR	Glasgow, MT [Location identifier FAA] (FAAL)
MKR	Maker
mkr	Maker (VRA)
MKR	Marker [Beacon]
MKR	Meekatharra [Australia Airport symbol] (OAG)
MK Rail	MK Rail Corp. [Associated Press] (SAG)
mKRB	Modified Krebs-Ringer Bicarbonate [Solution]
MKRL	MK Rail [NASDAQ symbol] (TTSB)
MKRL	MK Rail Corp. [NASDAQ symbol] (SAG)
MKS	Makassar [Celebes] [Seismograph station code, US Geological Survey] (SEIS)
MKS	Marks & Spencer Canada, Inc. [Toronto Stock Exchange symbol]
MKS	Marksman [Marine Corps]
MKS	Mekane [Ethiopia] [Airport symbol] (OAG)
MKS	Meter-Kilogram-Second [System of units]
mks	Meter-Kilogram-Second (IDOE)
MKS	Microwave Keying Switch
MKS	Mikasa, Inc. [NYSE symbol] (SAG)
MKS	Moncks Corner, SC [Location identifier FAA] (FAAL)
MKS	Mortice Kern Systems, Inc. [Waterloo, ON Canada] [Commercial firm] (CDE)
MKSA	Meter-Kilogram-Second-Ampere [System of units]
MKSS	Microwave Keying Switching Station
MKSTNG	Marksmanship Training (NVT)
MKT	Mankato [Minnesota] [Airport symbol] (OAG)
MKT	Mankato, MN [Location identifier FAA] (FAAL)
MKT	Market
MKT	Market
mkt	Market (WDMC)
MKT	Missouri-Kansas-Texas Railroad Co. [AAR code]
MKT	Mobile Kitchen Trailer [Military] (INF)
MKT	Mu Kappa Tau (EA)
MKTA	Makita Corp. [NASDAQ symbol] (SAG)
MKTAY	Makita Corp. [NASDAQ symbol] (TTSB)
MktFct	Market Facts, Inc. [Associated Press] (SAG)
MKTG	Marketing
mktg	Marketing (DD)
MKTG	Marketing
mktg	Marketing (WDMC)
MKTI	Mission Kit Technical Instruction (NASA)
MKTI	Mission Kit Technical Instruction
MKTI	Morrison-Knudsen Technologies, Inc. [Boise, ID] [Telecommunications] (TSSD)
MKTL	MarketLink, Inc. [NASDAQ symbol] (SAG)
MKTLH	Tri-Lake Health Centre, Killarney, Manitoba [Library symbol National Library of Canada] (NLC)
MktLink	MarketLink, Inc. [Associated Press] (SAG)
MKTNG	Marketing
MKTP	Mark Template [Tool]
MKTT	Missouri-Kansas-Texas Railroad Co. (of Texas) [AAR code]
MKTU	Marksmanship Training Unit (AABC)
MkTwain	Mark Twain Bancshares, Inc. [Associated Press] (SAG)
MKU	Makokou [Gabon] [Airport symbol] (OAG)
MKU	Mock-Up
MKUP	Makeup
MKV	Killed-Measles Vaccine [Immunology] (MAE)
MKV	Marksville, LA [Location identifier FAA] (FAAL)
MKV	Miniature Kill Vehicle [Military] (SDI)
MKV	Multiple Kill Vehicle
MKVNV	Muskmelon Vein Necrosis Virus [Plant pathology]
MKW	Magnetokinetic Wave
MKW	Manokwari [Indonesia] [Airport symbol] (OAG)
MKW	Mikawa [Japan] [Seismograph station code, US Geological Survey] (SEIS)
MKW	Military Knight of Windsor [British]
MKW	Munitionskraftwagen [Ammunition Truck] [German military - World War II]
MKX	Mukalla [South Arabia] [Airport symbol] (AD)
MKY	Mackay [Australia Airport symbol] (OAG)
MKY	Makeyevka [Former USSR Seismograph station code, US Geological Survey Closed] (SEIS)
MKY	Marco Island, FL [Location identifier FAA] (FAAL)
MKY	Monky Aerotaxis SA [Mexico ICAO designator] (FAAC)
MKYFC	Mike and Kathy Yager Fan Club [Later, MYFC] (EA)
MKZ	Los Angeles, CA [Location identifier FAA] (FAAL)
MKZ	Malacca [Malaysia] [Airport symbol] (OAG)
ML	Aviation Services [ICAO designator] (AD)
ML	Land Mobile Station [ITU designation] (NATG)
ML	Licentiate in Medicine
ML	Licentiate in Midwifery
ML	Machine Language [Computer science]
ML	Madras Lancers [British military] (DMA)
ML	Magic Lantern Society of the United States and Canada (EA)
ML	Magnetic Latching [Electronics] (OA)
ML	Magnetogasdynamics Laboratory [MIT] (MCD)
ML	Mail
ML	Mainland (MUGU)
ML	Main Line [Business term]
ML	Main Lobe
ML	Maintained Load (WDAA)
ML	Maintenance Laboratory (MUGU)
M/L	Maintenance Loop (MCD)
ML	Major League [Baseball]
ML	Major Lobe (MSA)
ML	Malachi [Old Testament book]
ML	Mali [ANSI two-letter standard code] (CNC)
ml	Mali [MARC country of publication code Library of Congress] (LCCP)
ML	Malignant Lymphoma [Oncology]
M:L	maltase-to-Lactase [Ratio] [Biochemistry] (DAVI)
ML	Management Level
ML	Management List
ML	Mandibular Line [Jaw anatomy]
ML	Manipulation Language (NITA)
ML	Manipulator Language [Computer science]
ML	Mantle Length
ML	Mantle Lip
ML	Manual Loader (AAG)
ML	Manual Local (IAA)
ML	Manufacturing License (NRCH)
ML	Maple Leaf Gardens Ltd. [Toronto Stock Exchange symbol]
ML	March for Life (EA)
ML	Mark-Up Language [Computer science]
Ml	Marl [Quality of the bottom] [Nautical charts]
M-L	Martin-Lewis [Medium] [Microbiology]
M/L	Mass to Luminosity [Ratio] [Astronomy]
ML	Master of Laws
ML	Master of Letters
ML	Master of Librarianship (GAGS)
ML	Master of Literature
ML	Material List (MSA)
ML	Mater Lectionis (BJA)
ML	Maule Aircraft Corp. [ICAO aircraft manufacturer identifier] (ICAO)
ML	Maximum Likelihood [Statistics]
ML	Mean Level
ML	Medial Lemniscus [Neuroanatomy]
ML	Medical Letter (EA)
ML	Medieval Latin [Language, etc.]
ML	Medium Lorry [British]
ML	Megaliter
ML	Member Library [OCLC or RLIN]
ML	Member's Liability [Health insurance] (GHCT)
ML	Memory Location [Computer science]
ML	Mesiolingual [Dentistry]
ML	Metabolic Loss [Physiology]
M-L	Metallic-Longitudinal (IEEE)
ML	Meteorological Devices [JETDS nomenclature] [Military] (CET)
ML	Meteorology Laboratory (GNE)
ML	Methods of Limits (IEEE)
ML	Metromail Corp. [NYSE symbol] (SAG)
ML	Mexican League [Baseball]
ML	Microprogramming Language
ML	Microwave Laboratory [Stanford University] (MCD)
ML	Middeck Left (MCD)
ML	Middle Latin [Language, etc.]
ML	Middle Left (WDAA)
ML	Middle Lobe [Of lung]
ML	Midlife (DAVI)
ML	Midline
ML	Migne Series [Latina] [A publication] (BJA)
ml	Mile (IDOE)
ML	Milieu
ML	Military Law
ML	Military Leave (GFGA)
ML	Military Liaison
ML	Military Payroll Money List
ML	Mill
ML	Mill
mL	Millilambert
mL	Milliliter
ml	Milliliter (IDOE)
ML	Minelayer [or Minelaying]
ML	Mine Layer (WDAA)
ML	Mineral Lease (ADA)
ML	Minerva Library [A publication]
ML	Minilab
ML	Mining and Logging [Tires]
ML	Missile Launcher
ML	Missile Layout
ML	Missile Lethality [Military]
M/L	Missile-Lift [Aerospace] (AAG)
ML	Missile Liner
ML	Mission Life [Aerospace]
ML	Mission Load (AABC)
ML	Mixed Lengths
ML	Mobile Launcher [NASA] (KSC)
ML	Mobile Low-Power [Reactor] (NRCH)
ML	Mode-Locked [Laser technology]
ML	Moderate Load service [Automotive engineering]
ML	Moderately Long [Botany]
ML	Modern Languages (AIE)
ML	Modern Lithographer [A publication] (DGA)
ML	Modified License [FCC] (NTCM)
ML	Molder [Navy rating]
ML	Mold Line [Technical drawings]
ML	Molecular Layer [of the hippocampus] [Neurology]
ML	Monarchist League [Defunct] (EA)
ML	Moneda Legal [Legal Tender] [Spanish Business term]
ML	Money List
M/L	Monocyte-Lymphocyte [Ratio] [Clinical chemistry]
ML	Monolayer [Physical chemistry]

ML.............	Monolithic
ML.............	Morocco Lined [*Covers*] [*Bookbinding*] (ROG)
ML.............	Motherwell [*Postcode*] (ODBW)
ML.............	Motor Launch
ML.............	Mountain Leader [*British military*] (DMA)
ML.............	Mouse Laminin
ML.............	Mouse Lysozyme [*Biochemistry*]
ML.............	Mucolipidosis [*Medicine*]
ML.............	Mucrones Length [*Of Crustacea*]
ML.............	Multilayer [*Pharmacy*]
ML.............	Multiple-Line [*Insurance*]
ML.............	Multiple Location [*Insurance*]
ML.............	Multiple-Locus [*Light flashes*]
ML.............	Munitions List
ML.............	Music Library Records [*Record label*]
ML.............	Muslim League [*Bangladesh*] [*Political party*] (FEA)
ML.............	Mutual Inductance [*Symbol*] (DEN)
ML.............	Muzzle-Loading
ML.............	Myelogenous Leukemia [*Oncology*]
ML.............	Myrialiter [*Unit of measurement*] (ROG)
ML.............	Small Minesweeper [*Navy symbol*]
ML1.............	Molder, First Class [*Navy rating*]
ML2.............	Molder, Second Class [*Navy rating*]
ML3.............	Molder, Third Class [*Navy rating*]
MLA.............	Auxiliary Motor Launches (NATG)
MLA.............	Forty-Mile Air [*ICAO designator*] (FAAC)
MLA.............	Macedonian Literary Association [*Australia*]
MLA.............	Magnetic Lens Assembly
MLA.............	Maine Lobstermen's Association (EA)
mla.............	Malagasy [*MARC language code Library of Congress*] (LCCP)
MLA.............	Malaspina [*Alaska*] [*Seismograph station code, US Geological Survey*] (SEIS)
MLA.............	Malta [*Airport symbol*] (OAG)
MLA.............	Maneuver Limited Altitude (GAVI)
MLA.............	Maneuver Load Alleviation [*Aviation*]
MLA.............	Manpack Loop Antenna
MLA.............	Manufacturing License Agreement
MLA.............	Marine Librarians Association (EA)
MLA.............	Maritime Law Association of the US (EA)
MLA.............	Marlat Resources Ltd. [*Vancouver Stock Exchange symbol*]
MLA.............	Martin Landau Aficionados [*An association*]
MLA.............	Master Locksmiths Association [*British*] (BI)
MLA.............	Master of Landscape Architecture
MLA.............	Master of Liberal Arts (GAGS)
MLA.............	Matching Logic and Adder
MLA.............	MDM [*Manipulator Deployment Mechanism*] Launch Aft [*NASA*]
MLA.............	Mean Line of Advance [*Military*] (NVT)
MLA.............	Mechanical Lubricator Association
MLA.............	Medial Left Abdomen [*Injection site*]
MLA.............	Medical Library Association (EA)
MLA.............	Member of the Legislative Assembly
MLA.............	Member of the Library Association [*British*] (ROG)
MLA.............	Mento-Laeval Anterior [*A fetal position*] [*Obstetrics*]
MLA.............	Merritt Island Tracking Station [*Florida*]
MLA.............	Mesiolabial [*Dentistry*]
MLA.............	Metal Lath Association [*Later, ML/SFA*] (EA)
MLA.............	Metrolina Library Association [*Library network*]
MLA.............	Microprocessor Language Assembler [*Computer science*]
MLA.............	Microwave Linear Accelerator
MLA.............	Midland Co. [*AMEX symbol*] (SPSG)
MLA.............	Military Liaison Assistant (DOMA)
MLA.............	Minimal Lactose-Arabinose [*Culture medium*]
MLA.............	Mining Lease Application
MLA.............	Mistress of Liberal Arts
MLA.............	Mixed Lead Alkyl [*Organic chemistry*]
MLA.............	Modern Language Association (NADA)
MLA.............	Modern Language Association of America (EA)
MLA.............	Monochrome Lens Assembly (MCD)
MLA.............	Monocytic Leukemia, Acute (MAE)
MLA.............	Motor Launch, Auxiliary [*NATO*]
MLA.............	Multi-Housing Laundry Association (EA)
MLA.............	Multilinear Array [*In earth scanning*]
MLA.............	MultiLink Advanced [*Local area network*] [*The Software Link, Inc.*]
MLA.............	Multiple Line Adaptor (NITA)
MLA.............	Multiplex Line Adapter
MLA.............	Multispectral Linear Array (SSD)
MLA.............	Music Library Association (EA)
MLA.............	Muzzle Loaders' Association of Great Britain
MLA.............	Valetta [*Malta*] [*Airport symbol*] (AD)
MLAA.............	Medical Library Assistance Act [*1965*]
MLAB.............	Mesa Laboratories [*NASDAQ symbol*] (TTSB)
MLAB.............	Mesa Laboratories, Inc. [*NASDAQ symbol*] (SAG)
MLAB.............	Modeling Laboratory [*Programming language*] [*1970*] (CSR)
MLAB.............	Multilingual Aphasia Battery [*Medicine*] (DMAA)
M Lab R	Monthly Labor Review [*A publication*] (BRI)
MLAF.............	Missile Loading Alignment Fixture
MLAGB	Muzzle Loaders Association of Great Britain (BI)
MLAi.............	Mesiolabioincisal [*Dentistry*]
M La L........	Master of Latin Letters
MLai.............	Mesiolabioincisal [*Medicine*] (MEDA)
MLAMH.......	Mona Lisas and Mad Hatters [*Defunct*] (EA)
MLANA.......	Melkite Laymen's Association of North America (EA)
MLanc	Lancaster Town Library, Lancaster, MA [*Library symbol Library of Congress*] (LCLS)
MLandArch...	Master of Landscape Architecture [*Canada*] (DD)
M Land Arch...	Master of Landscape Architecture (PGP)
MLandEc......	Master in Land Economy
ML&T..........	Master of Law and Taxation (GAGS)
MLAP..........	Mean Left Atrial Pressure [*Cardiology*]
MLaP..........	Mesiolabiopulpal [*Dentistry*]
MLAP..........	Migrant Legal Action Program (EA)
MLAP..........	Muslim League Assembly Party [*Pakistan*] [*Political party*] (FEA)
MLAPU........	Marxist-Leninist Armed Propaganda Unit [*Turkey*]
MLAR..........	Mill Arbor
MLAR..........	Multilayer Antireflection [*Coating*]
ML Arch......	Master of Landscape Architecture
MLAS..........	Master of Laboratory Animal Science (PGP)
MLASES......	Molasses [*Freight*]
MLA-SMHL...	Medical Library Association, Section on Mental Health Libraries (EA)
MLAT..........	Mean Latitude
MLAT..........	Modern Language Aptitude Test [*Military*] (AFM)
MLAUD........	Master of Landscape Architecture in Urban Development (GAGS)
MLAUK........	Member of the Library Association, United Kingdom (ROG)
M'Laur........	M'Laurin's Scotch Judiciary Cases [*1774*] [*A publication*] (DLA)
MLaw..........	Lawrence Free Public Library, Lawrence, MA [*Library symbol Library of Congress*] (LCLS)
MLB.............	Magnetic Linear Birefringence (MCD)
MLB.............	Major League Baseball
MLB.............	Malabar [*Java*] [*Seismograph station code, US Geological Survey Closed*] (SEIS)
MLB.............	Manufacturing Load Boards (MCD)
MLB.............	Maritime Labor Board [*Terminated, 1942*]
MLB.............	Maritime Law Book Key Number Data Base [*Maritime Law Book Co. Ltd.*] [*Canada Information service or system*] (CRD)
MLB.............	Medallion Books Ltd. [*Vancouver Stock Exchange symbol*]
MLB.............	Melbourne [*Florida*] [*Airport symbol*] (OAG)
MLB.............	Merrill Lynch & Co. [*NYSE symbol*] (SAG)
MLB.............	Metallic Link Belt (AABC)
MLB.............	Metropolitan Toronto Library Board, Systems Unit [*UTLAS symbol*]
MLB.............	Middle Linebacker [*Football*]
MLB.............	Mini Landbridge [*MARAD*] (TAG)
MLB.............	Mobile Logistics Support Base (NVT)
MLB.............	Monaural Loudness Balance [*Audiology*]
MLB.............	Motor Lifeboat
MLB.............	Multilayer Board
MLB.............	Multiple Listing Board (BARN)
MLBC..........	ML Bancorp, Inc. [*NASDAQ symbol*] (SAG)
MLBM..........	Modern Large Ballistic Missile
ML Bncp......	ML Bancorp, Inc. [*Associated Press*] (SAG)
MLBPA........	Mailing List Brokers Professional Association [*Defunct*] (EA)
MLBPA........	Major League Baseball Players Association (EA)
MLBR..........	Medium Low-BIT [*Binary Digit*] Rate [*Computer science*]
MLBU..........	Mobile Laundry and Bath Unit [*Military British*]
MLC.............	Machine Level Control [*Computer science*]
MLC.............	Madras Light Cavalry [*British military*] (DMA)
MLC.............	Magnetic Ledger Card (CMD)
MLC.............	Main Lobe Clutter
MLC.............	Major Landing Craft
MLC.............	Major Legislation of Congress [*Data processing system*] [*Congressional Research Service*]
MLC.............	Major Line Component [*of NOAA*] (NOAA)
MLC.............	Management Level Chart [*Military*] (AFIT)
MLC.............	Management Level Code [*Military*] (AFIT)
ML-C............	Management List - Consolidated
MLC.............	Maneuver Load Control [*Aviation*]
MLC.............	Manhattan National Corp. [*NYSE symbol*] (SPSG)
MLC.............	Manufacturers Life Capital Corp., Inc. [*Toronto Stock Exchange symbol*]
MLC.............	Manzanita Lake [*California*] [*Seismograph station code, US Geological Survey*] (SEIS)
MLC.............	Maple Leaf Club (EA)
MLC.............	Master Labor Contract (AABC)
MLC.............	McAlester [*Oklahoma*] [*Airport symbol*] (OAG)
MLC.............	McAlester, OK [*Location identifier FAA*] (FAAL)
MLC.............	Meat and Livestock Commission [*British*] (ARC)
MLC.............	Medical Liability Commission [*Defunct*] (EA)
MLC.............	Medical Library Center (DIT)
MLC.............	Member of the Legislative Council
MLC.............	Memphis Library Council [*Library network*]
MLC.............	Merrill Lynch & Co., Inc. [*NYSE symbol*] (SAG)
MLC.............	Merrill Lyn GI'MITTS'98 [*NYSE symbol*] (TTSB)
MLC.............	Mesh Level Control
MLC.............	Metropolitan Toronto Library Board, Cataloguing Department [*UTLAS symbol*]
MLC.............	Micellar Liquid Chromatography
MLC.............	Michigan Library Consortium [*Lansing, MI*] [*Library network*]
MLC.............	Microelectric Logic Circuit
MLC.............	Microprogram Location Counter
MLC.............	Midlife Conversion
MLC.............	Miles College, Birmingham, AL [*OCLC symbol*] (OCLC)
MLC.............	Military Landing Craft
MLC.............	Military Liaison Committee [*Energy Research and Development Administration*]
MLC.............	Military Load Class (RDA)
MLC.............	Military Load Classification [*BTS*] (TAG)
MLC.............	Minimum Lethal Concentration
MLC.............	Missile Logistics Center [*Army*]
MLC.............	Mississippi State Library Commission [*Information service or system*] (IID)
MLC.............	Mixed Leukocyte Culture [*Hematology*]

MLC .... Mixed Lymphocyte Culture [*Hematology*]
MLC .... Mobile Launch Center
MLC .... Mobile Launcher Computer [*NASA*] (NASA)
MLC .... Modern Language Caucus [*of New University Conference*]
MLC .... Modern Language Centre [*Ontario Institute for Studies in Education*] [*Canada*] (IRC)
MLC .... Molder, Chief [*Navy rating*]
MLC .... MOL [*Manned Orbiting Laboratory*] Launch Complex (MCD)
MLC .... Monarchist League of Canada (EAIO)
MLC .... Morphine-Like Compound [*Immunology*]
MLC .... Motor Launch, Cabin
MLC .... Motor Load Control
MLC .... Mountain Leadership Certificate [*British*] (DI)
MLC .... Multilamellar Cytosome [*Biochemistry*] (MAE)
MLC .... Multilayer Capacitor [*Electronics*]
MLC .... Multilayer Ceramic [*Materials technology*]
MLC .... Multilayer Ceramic Capacitor (NITA)
MLC .... Multilayer Circuit
MLC .... Multilens Camera
MLC .... Multiline Control (BUR)
MLC .... Multilink Control Field [*Telecommunications*] (ACRL)
MLC .... Multiplanar Link Chain
MLC .... Municipal Leasing Corp.
MLC .... Myelomonocytic Leukemia, Chronic (MAE)
MLC .... Myosin Light Chain [*Muscle biology*]
MLC .... Myth, Legend, Custom in the Old Testament [*A publication*] (BJA)
MLCAEC .... Military Liaison Committee to the Atomic Energy Commission (IEEE)
MLCB .... Missile Launch Control Blockhouse
MLCB .... Moored Limited Capability Buoy [*Marine science*] (MSC)
MLCB .... Multilayer Circuit Board
ML/CB-CC ..... Malignant Lymphoma/Centroblastic-Centrocytic [*Oncology*]
ML/CC .... Malignant Lymphoma/Centrocytic [*Oncology*]
MLCC .... Mined Land Conservation Conference [*Later, BCR*]
MLCC .... Multilayer Ceramic Capacitor [*Electronics*]
MLCG .... Missile Launcher Control Group
MLCH .... Major Logistical Control Headquarters (MCD)
MLCH .... MLC Holdings, Inc. [*NASDAQ symbol*] (SAG)
MLC Hld ...... MLC Holdings, Inc. [*Associated Press*] (SAG)
MLCIM .... Marquette League for Catholic Indian Missions [*Defunct*] (EA)
MLCK .... Myosin Light Chain Kinase [*An enzyme*]
MLCM .... Molder, Master Chief [*Navy rating*]
MLCNY .... Medical Library Center of New York [*Information service or system*] (IID)
MLCO .... Member of the London College of Osteopathy [*British*] (DI)
MLCOM .... Member of the London College of Osteopathic Medicine [*British*] (DBQ)
MLCox99n ... Merrill Lynch & Co. [*Associated Press*] (SAG)
MLCP .... Mobile Land Command Post (AABC)
MLCP .... Multilayer Ceramic Package [*Electronics*]
MLCP .... Multiline Communications Processor
MLCR .... Medical Laboratories Army Chemical Center [*Maryland*]
MLCR .... Medical Laboratory Contract Reports [*Army*] (MCD)
MLCR .... Mixed Lymphocyte Culture Reaction [*Hematology*] (AAMN)
MLCS .... Molder, Senior Chief [*Navy rating*]
MLCS .... Multilayer Ceramic Substrates [*Electronic circuit boards*]
MLCT .... Metal-to-Ligand Charge Transfer [*Physical chemistry*]
MLCU .... Magnetic Ledger Card Unit [*Computer science*] (MHDB)
MLCU .... Mill Cutter [*Tool*]
MLCur .... Merrill Lynch & Co. [*Associated Press*] (SAG)
MLD .... Air Moldova [*ICAO designator*] (FAAC)
MLD .... Legislative Reference Library - Minnesota Document Collection, St. Paul, MN [*OCLC symbol*] (OCLC)
MLD .... Machine Language Debugger [*National Computer Sharing Service*]
MLD .... Main Line of Defense
MLD .... Malad City, ID [*Location identifier FAA*] (FAAL)
MLD .... Malden [*Missouri*] [*Seismograph station code, US Geological Survey Closed*] (SEIS)
MLD .... Marginally Learning Disabled
MLD .... Masking Level Difference [*Hearing*]
MLD .... Master Layout Duplicate (MSA)
MLD .... Master of Landscape Design
MLD .... Maximum Lateral Damage (PDAA)
MLD .... Maximum Likelihood Detection (MCD)
MLD .... Mean Low-Water Datum [*Nuclear energy*] (NRCH)
MLD .... Medial Lethal Dose [*Genetics*] (DOG)
MLD .... Median Lethal Dose [*Also, LD$_{50}$*] [*Lethal for 50%*] [*Medicine*]
MLD .... Metachromatic Leukodystrophy [*Medicine*]
MLD .... Middle Landing
MLD .... Midland [*AAR code*]
MLD .... Mild (WGA)
MLD .... Minimal Lesion Disease
MLD .... Minimum Lethal Dose
MLD .... Minimum Line of Detection [*Air Force*]
MLD .... Missile Launch Detector (MCD)
MLD .... Mixed Layer Depth (MCD)
MLD .... Moderate Learning Difficulties (AIE)
mld .... Mold (VRA)
MLD .... Molded (KSC)
MLD .... Molded
MLD .... Molding [*Technical drawings*]
MLD .... Mouvement pour la Liberation de Djibouti [*Movement for the Liberation of Djibouti*] (PD)
MLDAS .... Meteorological and Lighting Data Acquisition System [*NASA*] (KSC)
MLDB .... Regional Library, Lac Du Bonnet, Manitoba [*Library symbol National Library of Canada*] (NLC)

MLDC .... Miner's Legal Defense Committee [*Defunct*] (EA)
MLDD .... Moderately Lightly Doped Drains (NITA)
MLDD .... Mooring Leg Deployment Device (PDAA)
ML Des .... Master of Landscape Design
MLDG .... Molding (KSC)
MLDG .... Molding
MLDI .... Meter List Display Interval [*FAA*] (TAG)
ML Dig & R... Monthly Law Digest and Reporter [*Canada*] [*A publication*] (DLA)
ML Direct ..... ML Direct, Inc. [*Associated Press*] (SAG)
MLDL .... Mooring Line Data Line [*Environmental buoy cable*]
MLDLP .... Mailing Label and Directory Lookup Package (PDAA)
MLDNG .... Moulding
MLDR .... ML Direct, Inc. [*NASDAQ symbol*] (SAG)
MLDR .... Molder (ADA)
MLDS .... Motor Launch, Double Shelter
MLD/S .... Multi-Legend Display Switch (MCD)
MLDT .... Mean Logistic Delay Time [*Military*] (CAAL)
MLDT .... Mean Logistic Down Time
MLDU .... Marriage Law Defence Union [*British*]
MLE .... Magazine Lee-Enfield [*British military*] (DMA)
MLE .... Male [*Maldives*] [*Airport symbol*] (OAG)
MLE .... Manned Lunar Exploration [*NASA*] (AAG)
MLE .... Mariner-Like Elements [*Genetics*]
MLE .... Martin Lawrence Limited Editions [*NYSE symbol*] (SAG)
MLE .... Martin Lawrence Ltd Editions [*NYSE symbol*] (TTSB)
MLE .... Maryland Law Encyclopedia [*A publication*] (DLA)
MLE .... Master of Applied Linguistics and Exegesis (PGP)
MLE .... Master of Land Economy
MLE .... Maximum Likelihood Estimate [*or Estimator*] [*Statistics*]
MLE .... Maximum Loss Expectancy [*Insurance*]
MLE .... Medium Local Exchange [*Telecommunications*] (TEL)
MLE .... Merrill Lynch Economics (NITA)
MLE .... Microprocessor Language Editor [*Computer science*]
MLE .... Midline Episiotomy [*Obstetrics*] (DAVI)
MLE .... Mile
MLE .... Mileto [*Italy*] [*Seismograph station code, US Geological Survey Closed*] (SEIS)
MLE .... Missile Launch Envelope
MLE .... Mobile Launcher Equipment [*NASA*] (SAA)
MLE .... Module Resources, Inc. [*Vancouver Stock Exchange symbol*]
MLE .... Molecular Layer Epitaxy [*Coating technology*]
MLE .... Muconate Lactonizing Enzyme
MLE .... Myocardial Lactate Extraction [*Clinical chemistry*]
MLE .... Omaha, NE [*Location identifier FAA*] (FAAL)
MLEA .... Multiple-Line Exclusive Agent [*Insurance*]
M'Lean's R... McLean's United States Circuit Court Reports [*A publication*] (DLA)
MLED .... Maximum Likelihood Estimator Deconvolution [*Statistics*]
MLegS .... Master of Legal Studies
MLenB .... Berkshire Christian College, Lenox, MA [*Library symbol Library of Congress*] (LCLS)
ML Eng .... Master of Landscape Engineering
MLeo .... Leominster Public Library, Leominster, MA [*Library symbol Library of Congress*] (LCLS)
MLeoHi .... Leominster Historical Society, Inc., Leominster, MA [*Library symbol*] [*Library of Congress*] (LCLS)
MLEP .... Manned Lunar Exploration Program [*NASA*] (KSC)
MLEP .... Minority Legislative Education Program
MLEP .... Multipurpose Long Endurance Plane
MLES .... Multiple-Line Encryption System (AABC)
MLEV .... Manned Lifting Entry Vehicle (MCD)
MLex .... Cary Memorial Library, Lexington, MA [*Library symbol Library of Congress*] (LCLS)
MLexHi .... Lexington Historical Society, Lexington, MA [*Library symbol Library of Congress*] (LCLS)
MLexK .... Kennecott Copper Corp., Ledgemont Laboratory, Lexington, MA [*Library symbol Library of Congress*] (LCLS)
MLexM .... Museum of Our National Heritage, Lexington, MA [*Library symbol Library of Congress*] (LCLS)
MLexSC .... Scottish Rite of Freemasonry, Northern Jurisdiction USA, Supreme Council Library, Lexington, MA [*Library symbol Library of Congress*] (LCLS)
MLF .... Fast Motor Launches (NATG)
MLF .... Maintenance Level Function
MLF .... Male Liberation Foundation (EA)
MLF .... Malolactic Fermentation
MLF .... Maple Leaf Foods [*Toronto Stock Exchange symbol*] (SPSG)
MLF .... Maximum Load Factor
MLF .... MDM [*Manipulator Deployment Mechanism*] Launch Forward [*NASA*]
MLF .... Media Language and Format (CET)
MLF .... Medial Longitudinal Fasciculus [*Medicine*]
MLF .... Medical Liberation Front (EA)
M/LF .... Medium/Low Frequency (NATG)
MLF .... Milford [*Ohio*] [*Seismograph station code, US Geological Survey*] (SEIS)
MLF .... Milford, UT [*Location identifier FAA*] (FAAL)
MLF .... Mobile Land Force (NATG)
MLF .... Mobile Launcher Facility [*NASA*] (KSC)
MLF .... MOL [*Manned Orbiting Laboratory*] Launch Facilities (MCD)
MLF .... Motor Launch, Fast [*NATO*]
MLF .... Multilateral Force [*NATO*]
MLFA .... Fireman Apprentice, Molder, Striker [*Navy rating*]
MLFA .... Maine Lobster Fishermen's Association (EA)
MLFA .... Merrill Lynch Financial Advantage
MLFAT .... MOL [*Manned Orbiting Laboratory*] Launch Facilities Acceptance Team (MCD)

MLFB.......... MLF Bancorp [*NASDAQ symbol*] (TTSB)
MLFB.......... MLF Bancorp, Inc. [*NASDAQ symbol*] (SAG)
MLF Bc ...... MLF Bancorp, Inc. [*Associated Press*] (SAG)
MLFC.......... Michele Lee Fan Club (EA)
MLFC.......... Michigan Library Film Circuit [*Library network*]
MLFC.......... Mike Lunsford Fan Club (EA)
MLFC.......... Moses Lake Flight Center [*Washington*] (SAA)
MLFN.......... Fireman, Molder, Striker [*Navy rating*]
MLFS.......... Magic Lantern Film Society [*An association*]
MLFX.......... Mill Fixture [*Tool*]
MLG........... Mailing
MLG........... Main Landing Gear
MLG........... Malang [*Indonesia*] [*Airport symbol*] (OAG)
MLG........... Metalgesellschaft Canada Investment [*Toronto Stock Exchange symbol*]
MLG........... Middle Low German [*Language, etc.*]
MLG........... Milling [*Freight*]
MLG........... Mission Liaison Group [*Military*]
MLG........... Mitochondria Lipid Glucogen [*Cytology*] (AAMN)
MLG........... Moulage
MLG........... Multiple Line Group [*Radiation*]
MLG........... Musicland Stores [*NYSE symbol*] (SAG)
MLGCV .... Movement for the Liberation of Portuguese Guinea and the Cape Verde Islands
MLGN .... Minimal Lesion Glomerulonephritis [*Medicine*] (DMAA)
MLGP.......... Movimento de Libertacao da Guine Portuguesa [*Movement for the Liberation of Portuguese Guinea*]
MLGS.......... Microwave Landing Guidance System [*FAA*]
MLGT98....... Merrill Lynch & Co., Inc. [*Associated Press*] (SAG)
MLGW .... Maximum Landing Gross Weight
MLH........... Mauna Loa [*Hawaii*] [*Seismograph station code, US Geological Survey*] (SEIS)
MLH........... Medium Lift Helicopter (MCD)
MLH........... Merlin Resources Ltd. [*Vancouver Stock Exchange symbol*]
MLH........... Minimum List Heading [*Standard Industrial Classification*] (PDAA)
MLH........... Mulhouse/Basel [*France*] [*Airport symbol*] (OAG)
MLHCP .... Mean Lower Hemispherical Candlepower (IAA)
MLHGR .... Maximum Linear Heat Generation Ratio (NRCH)
MLHK .... Merrill Lynch & Co. [*Associated Press*] (SAG)
MLHR .... Master of Labor and Human Resources (PGP)
MLHR .... Miller [*Herman*] [*NASDAQ symbol*] (TTSB)
MLHR .... Miller [*Herman*], Inc. [*NASDAQ symbol*] (NQ)
MLHW .... Mean Lower High Water [*Tides and currents*]
MLI .... Machine Language Instruction
MLI .... Magnetic Level Indicator
MLI .... Maislin Industries Ltd. [*Toronto Stock Exchange symbol*]
MLI .... Malad Range [*Idaho*] [*Seismograph station code, US Geological Survey*] (SEIS)
MLI .... Mali [*ANSI three-letter standard code*] (CNC)
MLI .... Maltese Light Infantry [*British military*] (DMA)
MLI .... Marine Light Infantry [*Navy British*] (ROG)
MLI .... Marker Light Indicator
MLI .... Master Listing Index
MLI .... Master of Literary Interpretation
MLI .... Mean Linear Intercept
MLI .... Mesiolinguoincisal [*Dentistry*]
MLI .... Message Level Interface (NITA)
MLI .... Minimum Line of Interception [*Air Force*]
MLI .... Mixed Lymphocyte Interaction [*Immunology*]
MLI .... Moline [*Illinois*] [*Airport symbol*] (OAG)
MLI .... Moline, IL [*Location identifier FAA*] (FAAL)
MLI .... Mollie Gibson Mines [*Vancouver Stock Exchange symbol*]
MLI .... Mueller Industries [*NYSE symbol*] (SPSG)
MLI .... Muller Industries [*NYSE symbol*] (SAG)
MLI .... Multilayer Insulation
MLI .... Multiple Link Interface [*Computer science*]
MLI .... Munitions List Item (MCD)
MLIA.......... Multiplex Loop Interface Adapter
MLib .... Master of Librarianship
M Libr .... Master of Librarianship (PGP)
M Lib Sc ..... Master of Library Science (BARN)
MLibSci ...... Master of Library Science (NADA)
MLIC.......... Manhattan Life Insurance [*NASDAQ symbol*] (TTSB)
MLIC.......... Manhattan Life Insurance Co. [*NASDAQ symbol*] (SAG)
MLID.......... Multiple Link Interface Drive [*Telecommunications*] (PCM)
MLID.......... Multiple Link Interface Driver [*Telecommunications*] (ACRL)
MLIFC........ Mark Lindsay International Fan Club [*Defunct*] (EA)
MLIFC........ Michelle Lynn International Fan Club (EA)
MLIGL01...... Merrill Lynch & Co. [*Associated Press*] (SAG)
MLIM .... Matrix Log-In Memory
MLIN.......... Micro Linear [*NASDAQ symbol*] (TTSB)
MLIN.......... Micro Linear Corp. [*NASDAQ symbol*] (SAG)
MLing .... Master of Languages [*British*] (DBQ)
MLIP.......... Message Level Interface Port (NITA)
MLIR.......... Master of Labor and Industrial Relations (GAGS)
MLIRB .... Multi-Line Insurance Rating Bureau [*Later, ISO*]
MLIS.......... Master of Library and Information Science
MLIS.......... Measurement Laboratory Information Service [*Battelle Memorial Institute*]
MLIS.......... Metal-Liquid-Insulator Semiconductor [*Electronics*] (PDAA)
MLIS.......... Micropolis Corp. [*NASDAQ symbol*] (NQ)
MLIS.......... Molecular LASER Isotope Separation
MLIS.......... Multiple Level Indexing Scheme [*Computer science*]
MLISP......... Meta LISP [*List Processor*] [*Programming language*] [*Computer science*] (CSR)

M Lit........... Master of Letters
M Lit........... Master of Literature
MLitl.......... Inforonics Inc., Littleton, MA [*Library symbol Library of Congress*] (LCLS)
MLitM .... Master of Liturgical Music (GAGS)
M Lit M ...... Master of Liturgical Music (PGP)
MLitSt........ Master of Literary Studies (ADA)
M Litt.......... Master of Letters
M Litt.......... Master of Literature
ML IV......... Mucolipidosis IV [*A genetic disease*]
MLJ .... Memphis Law Journal [*A publication*] (DLA)
MLJ .... Milledgeville, GA [*Location identifier FAA*] (FAAL)
MLJ .... Modern Language Journal [*A publication*] (BRI)
MLK .... Malta, MT [*Location identifier FAA*] (FAAL)
MLK .... Martin Luther King, Jr.
MLK .... Matlack Systems [*NYSE symbol*] (TTSB)
MLK .... Matlack Systems, Inc. [*NYSE symbol*] (CTT)
MLK .... Milford [*Kansas*] [*Seismograph station code, US Geological Survey*] (SEIS)
MLKCNSC ... Martin Luther King, Jr., Center for Nonviolent Social Change (EA)
MLKCSC .... Martin Luther King, Jr., Center for Social Change [*Later, MLKCNSC*] (EA)
MLKIII........ Martin Luther King III
MLL .... Mandella Resources Ltd. [*Vancouver Stock Exchange symbol*]
MLL .... Manned Lunar Landing [*NASA*]
MLL .... Marshall [*Alaska*] [*Airport symbol*] (OAG)
MLL .... Marshall, AK [*Location identifier FAA*] (FAAL)
MLL .... Master Lines Layout (MSA)
MLL .... Master of Latin Literature
MLL .... Master of Law Librarianship (ILCA)
MLL .... Maynard Listener Library [*Defunct*] (EA)
MLL .... MDM [*Manipulator Deployment Mechanism*] Launch Left [*NASA*]
MLL .... Mean Lesion Length [*Pathology*]
ML/L .... Milliliters per Liter (EG)
MLL .... Mistress of Liberal Learning
MLL .... Music Lovers League (NADA)
MLL .... University of Minnesota, Law Library, Minneapolis, MN [*OCLC symbol*] (OCLC)
MLLAA........ Modern Language Association of America (NADA)
ML/LB .... Malignant Lymphoma/Lymphoblastic [*Oncology*]
MLLE .... Mademoiselle [*Miss*] [*French*] (EY)
MLLE .... Medium Large Local Exchange [*Telecommunications*] (TEL)
Mlles .... Mesdemoiselles [*Misses*] [*French*]
MLLFT........ Modified Lensless Fourier Transform (PDAA)
ML Libr....... Master of Law Librarianship
MLLP......... Manned Lunar Landing Program [*NASA*]
ML/LPC....... Malignant Lymphoma/Lymphoplasmacytoid [*Oncology*]
MLLW .... Mean Lower Low Water [*Tides and currents*]
MLLW .... Medium Level Liquid Waste [*Nuclear energy*] (NUCP)
MLLW .... Mixed Low-Level Waste (GAAI)
MLLWK ...... Millwork
MLLWL....... Mean Lower Low Water Line [*Tides and currents*] (PDAA)
MLLWS ...... Mean Lower Low-Water Springs [*Tides and currents*]
MLM .... Magazine Lee-Metford [*British military*] (DMA)
MLM .... Mailing-List Manager [*Type of database*]
MLM .... Martin Marietta Materials [*NYSE symbol*] (SAG)
MLM .... Massive Liver Metastasis [*Oncology*]
MLM .... Master of Landscape Management
MLM .... Master of Library Media (PGP)
MLM .... Maximum Likelihood Method [*Statistics*]
MLM .... Membrane Light Modulator (PDAA)
MLM .... Mesa Lucera [*New Mexico*] [*Seismograph station code, US Geological Survey*] (SEIS)
MLM .... Metall Mining Corp. [*Toronto Stock Exchange symbol*]
MLM .... Microbial Load Monitor (MCD)
MLM .... Military Liaison Mission [*Germany*]
MLM .... Minesweeper, River [*Navy symbol*] (VNW)
MLM .... Mixed Level Matrix
MLM .... Moody Literature Ministries (EA)
MLM .... Morelia [*Mexico*] [*Airport symbol*] (OAG)
MLM .... Mound Laboratory, Miamisburg [*AEC*] (MCD)
MLM .... Multilayer Metalization (IEEE)
MLM .... Multilevel Marketing
MLM .... Multi-Longitudinal Mode (ACRL)
MLM .... Multipurpose Lightweight Missile
MLM .... Multnomah Literature Ministries [*Publisher*] [*Portland, OR*]
MLMA........ Metal Ladder Manufacturers Association
MLMA........ Metal Lath Manufacturers Association [*Later, ML/SFA*]
MLMA........ Miners' Lamp Manufacturers' Association [*British*] (BI)
MLMA........ Multilevel Multiaccess
MLMGIC98... Merrill Lynch & Co. [*Associated Press*] (SAG)
MLMI......... Microleague Multimedia [*NASDAQ symbol*] (TTSB)
MLMI......... Microleague Multimedia, Inc. [*NASDAQ symbol*] (SAG)
MLMIA....... Multi-Level Marketing International Association [*Irvine, CA*] (EA)
ml/min/m²..... Milliliters per Minute per Square Meter (CPH)
MLMIW....... Microleague Multimedia Wrrt [*NASDAQ symbol*] (TTSB)
MLML........ Moss Landing Marine Laboratories [*San Jose State University*] [*Research center*] (RCD)
MLMS........ Member of the London Mathematical Society
MLMS........ Multipurpose Lightweight Missile System
MLMTT....... Marxism-Leninism-Mao Tse-Tung Thought [*Ideologies guiding the New People's Army, a guerrilla movement in the Philippines*]
MLN.......... Management List - Navy (NVT)
MLN.......... Melilla [*Spain*] [*Airport symbol*] (OAG)
MLN.......... Metropolitan Library Network [*Library network*]

MLN............ Mid-Lateral Nerve
MLN............ Milan Resources & Development [*Vancouver Stock Exchange symbol*]
MLN............ Minuteman Library Network [*Information service or system*] (IT)
MLN............ MLN (Modern Language Notes) [*A publication*] (BRI)
MLN............ Mouvement de Liberation Nationale [*National Liberation Movement*] [*Burkina Faso Banned, 1974*] [*Political party*]
MLN............ Movimiento de Liberacion Nacional [*National Liberation Movement*] [*Guatemala*] [*Political party*] (PPW)
MLN............ Movimiento de Liberacion Nacional [*National Liberation Movement*] [*Uruguay*] [*Political party*]
MLN............ Multiple Length Number
MLN............ Mulungwishi [*Zaire*] [*Seismograph station code, US Geological Survey*] (SEIS)
MLNC.......... Missouri Library Network Corp. [*Information service or system*] (IID)
MInd........... Maximum Landing Weight [*Aviation*] (DA)
MLNG .... Melange
MLNik 97..... Merrill Lynch & Co. [*Associated Press*] (SAG)
MLNIS .... Modified Atlantic Naval Intelligence Summary (MCD)
MLNM......... Millennium Pharmaceuticals [*NASDAQ symbol*] (TTSB)
MLNM......... Millennium Pharmaceuticals, Inc. [*NASDAQ symbol*] (SAG)
MLNR .... Milliner (WGA)
mLNRc........ Mouse Lymph Node Homing Receptor
MLNS.......... Ministry of Labour and National Service [*British World War II*]
MLNS.......... Mucocutaneous Lymph Node Syndrome [*Medicine*]
MLO............ Main Lube Oil [*System*] (NRCH)
MLO............ Manipulative Learning Operation [*in laboratory work*]
MLO............ Manned Lunar Orbiter [*NASA*]
MLO............ Marxisten-Leninisten Oesterreichs [*Marxists-Leninists of Austria*] [*Political party*] (PPE)
MLO............ Master Layout Original (MSA)
MLO............ Mauna Loa Observatory [*Hawaii*] [*National Weather Service*]
MLO............ Mechanized Letter Office (DCTA)
MLO............ Media Liaison Officer
MLO............ Mesiolinguo-Occlusal [*Dentistry*]
MLO............ Military Landing Officer
MLO............ Military Liaison Officer [*British*]
MLO............ Milos [*Greece*] [*Airport symbol*] (OAG)
MLO............ Missile Launch Officer (AAG)
MLO............ Missile Lift-Off (AAG)
MLO............ M. L. Cass Petroleum [*Vancouver Stock Exchange symbol*]
MLO............ Movement Liaison Officer (NATG)
MLO............ Mycoplasma-Like Organisms [*Microbiology*]
MLOG.......... Microlog Corp. [*NASDAQ symbol*] (NQ)
MLOI........... Master List of Outstanding Items [*Military*] (DNAB)
MLon .... Richard Salter Storrs Library, Longmeadow, MA [*Library symbol Library of Congress*] (LCLS)
MLonHi........ Longmeadow Historical Society, Longmeadow, MA [*Library symbol Library of Congress*] (LCLS)
MLOR .... Maintenance/Logistics Observer Report
MLow.......... Lowell City Library, Lowell, MA [*Library symbol Library of Congress*] (LCLS)
MLowT........ Lowell Technological Institute, Lowell, MA [*Library symbol Library of Congress Obsolete*] (LCLS)
MLowTC ...... Lowell State College, Lowell, MA [*Library symbol Library of Congress Obsolete*] (LCLS)
MLowU .... University of Lowell, Lowell, MA [*Library symbol Library of Congress*] (LCLS)
MLowU-N .... University of Lowell - North Campus, Alumni/Lydon Memorial Library, Lowell, MA [*Library symbol Library of Congress*] (LCLS)
MLP............ Machine Language Program [*Computer science*]
MLP............ Major Late Promoter [*Genetics*]
MLP............ Major Late Promotor [*Biochemistry*]
MLP............ Malabang [*Philippines*] [*Airport symbol*] (OAG)
MLP............ Malaspina [*Alaska*] [*Seismograph station code, US Geological Survey*] (SEIS)
MLP............ Malfunction-Linked People
MLP............ Malta Labor Party [*Political party*] (PPW)
MLP............ Master Limited Partnership
MLP............ Master Logistics Plan (AABC)
MLP............ Mauritius Labor Party [*Political party*] (PPW)
MLP............ Maximum Likelihood Program
MLP............ Mentoleva Posterior [*A fetal position*] [*Obstetrics*]
MLP............ Mesiolinguopulpal [*Dentistry*]
MLP............ Metal Lath and Plaster [*Technical drawings*]
MLP............ Michigan Law and Practice [*A publication*] (DLA)
MLP............ Microsomal Lipoprotein [*Immunochemistry*]
MLP............ Millipore Corp., Bedford, MA [*OCLC symbol*] (OCLC)
MLP............ Minimum Latency Programming
MLP............ Mirror Landing Procedures (MCD)
MLP............ Mobile Launcher Platform [*NASA*] (NASA)
MLP............ Modified Longest Path
MLP............ Mortgage Loan Partnership [*Investment term*]
MLP............ Movimiento de Liberacion del Pueblo [*People's Liberation Movement*] [*El Salvador*] [*Political party*] (PD)
MLP............ Movimiento de Liberacion Proletaria [*Proletarian Liberation Movement*] [*Mexico Political party*]
MLP............ Mullan Pass, ID [*Location identifier FAA*] (FAAL)
MLP............ Multi-Layered Packaging (PDAA)
MLP............ Multilevel Precedence
MLP............ Multilevel Procedure (MCD)
MLP............ Multilevel Programmer
MLP............ Multilink Procedure [*Computer science*] (TNIG)
MLP............ Multilink Protocol [*Telecommunications*] (ACRL)
MLP............ Multiple Line Printing (CMD)

MLP............ Multi-Step Products [*Toronto Stock Exchange symbol*]
MLPA.......... Modified Link Pack Area (MCD)
MLPC.......... Management-Labor Policy Committee
MLPC.......... Mouvement de Liberation du Peuple Centrafricain [*Movement for the Liberation of the Central African People*] (PD)
MLPC.......... Multilayer Printed Circuit
MLPCB .... Machine Language Printed Circuit Boards [*Computer science*] (IEEE)
MLPD.......... Maximum Likelihood Predictive Density [*Statistics*]
MLPED........ Mobile Launcher Pedestal [*NASA*] (NASA)
MLPF.......... Miniature Low Pass Filter
MLPFS........ Merrill Lynch, Pierce, Fenner & Smith [*of Merrill Lynch & Co., Inc.*] [*Stockbrokers Wall Street slang name: "Thundering Herd"*]
MLPNPP ...... Mobile Low-Power Nuclear Power Plant
MLPP.......... Multilevel Precedence and Preemption [*Telecommunications*] (TEL)
ML-PPP .... Multilink Point-to-Point Protocol [*Telecommunications*] (ACRL)
MLPS.......... Multilingual Publishing Software
MLPS.......... Myxoid Liposarcoma [*Genetics*]
MLP USA .... Marxist-Leninist Party of the USA (EA)
MLPWB........ Multilayer Printed-Wiring Board (IEEE)
MLQ........... Malabar Law Quarterly [*A publication*] (DLA)
MLQ........... Malalaua [*Papua New Guinea*] [*Airport symbol*] (OAG)
MLR........... Leaf Rapids Public Library, Manitoba [*Library symbol National Library of Canada*] (NLC)
MLR........... Magnetic Latching Relay (MCD)
MLR........... Mailer
MLR........... Main Line of Resistance
M/LR.......... Maintenance Loop Recorder (MCD)
MLR........... Malayan Law Reports [*1950-54*] [*A publication*] (DLA)
MLR........... Manitoba Law Reports [*Canada*] [*A publication*] (DLA)
MLR........... Marginal Lending Rate [*Finance*]
MLR........... Marine Life Resources [*Program*]
MLR........... Maryland Law Record [*A publication*] (DLA)
MLR........... Master-Locating RADAR (AABC)
MLR........... Matched Logistic Regression [*Statistics*]
MLR........... Mauritius Law Reporter [*A publication*] (DLA)
MLR........... MDM [*Manipulator Deployment Mechanism*] Launch Right [*NASA*]
MLR........... Mean Lethal Radius
MLR........... Mechanized Line Records [*Later, LMOS*] [*Bell System*]
MLR........... Medium-Lift Requirement [*Helicopter/VSTOL*] [*Marine Corps*] (DOMA)
MLR........... Memory Lockout Register [*Computer science*]
MLR........... Meston Lake Resources, Inc. [*Toronto Stock Exchange symbol Vancouver Stock Exchange symbol*]
MLR........... Middle Latency Response [*Medicine*]
MLR........... Miller Industries [*NYSE symbol*] (TTSB)
MLR........... Miller Industries [*NYSE symbol*] (SAG)
MLR........... Millersburg, OH [*Location identifier FAA*] (FAAL)
MLR........... Minimum Latency Routine
MLR........... Minimum Lending Rate
MLR........... Minnesota Legislative Reference Library, St. Paul, MN [*OCLC symbol*] (OCLC)
MLR........... Missile Launch Response [*Navy*] (CAAL)
MLR........... Mixed Leukocyte Reaction [*Analytical biochemistry*]
MLR........... Mixed Lymphocyte [*or Leukocyte*] Reaction [*or Response*] [*Immunology*]
MLR........... Modern Language Review [*A publication*] (BRI)
MLR........... Monodisperse Latex Reactor
MLR........... Monotone Likelihood Ratio [*Statistics*]
MLR........... Monthly Letter Report
MLR........... Montreal Law Reports [*A publication*] (DLA)
MLR........... Mortar Locating RADAR (MCD)
MLR........... MPM Launch Right (MCD)
MLR........... Multi-Disperse Latex Reactor
MLR........... Multilayer Resist [*Lithography*]
MLR........... Multilevel Resist [*For microlithography*]
MLR........... Multiple Linear Regression [*Mathematics*]
MLR........... Multiple Location Risk [*Insurance*]
MLR........... Multiply and Round
MLR........... Muntele Rosu [*Romania*] [*Seismograph station code, US Geological Survey*] (SEIS)
MLR........... Muzzle-Loading Rifle
MLRA.......... Major Land Resource Area [*USDA topographic characterization*]
MLRA.......... Marriage Law Reform Association [*British*]
MLRA.......... Multivariate Linear Regression Analysis [*Advertising marketing*]
MLRB.......... Master Logistics Review Board (AAG)
MLRB.......... Mutual Loss Research Bureau [*Later, Property Loss Research Bureau*] (EA)
MLRC.......... Mallon Resources [*NASDAQ symbol*] (TTSB)
MLRC.......... Mallon Resources Corp. [*NASDAQ symbol*] (CTT)
MLRC.......... Master Logistics Review Committee (AAG)
MLRC.......... Minor Language Research Committee (EA)
MLRC.......... Multilevel Rail Car
MLRCA .... Mini Lop Rabbit Club of America (EA)
MLR CS .... Montreal Law Reports, Superior Court [*Canada*] [*A publication*] (DLA)
MLRG .... Marine Life Research Group [*Scripps Institution of Oceanography*]
MLRG .... Muzzle-Loading Rifled Gun
MLRHR........ Master of Labor Relations and Human Resources (PGP)
MLRP.......... Marine Corps Long-Range Plans
MLRP.......... Marine Life Research Program
MLRP.......... Minuteman Long Range Plan [*Telecommunications*] (LAIN)
MLRQB........ Montreal Law Reports, Queen's Bench [*A publication*] (DLA)
MLRS.......... Manual Launch - RADAR Search
MLRS.......... McDonald Laser Ranging System [*For observations*]
MLRS.......... Monodisperse Latex Reactor System
MLRS.......... Multiple Launch Rocket System [*DoD*] (MCD)

MLRSC .... Montreal Law Reports, Superior Court [*Canada*] [*A publication*] (DLA)
MLRS ER ..... Multiple Launch Rocket System Extended Range Rocket [*Military*]
MLRS-PGM... Multiple Launch Rocket System Precision Guided Munitions (RDA)
MLRS-TGW... Multiple Launch Rocket System Terminally Guided Warhead
MLRTP .... Multileaving Remote Terminal Processor [*Computer science*] (MHDI)
MLRus98 ..... Merrill Lynch & Co. [*Associated Press*] (SAG)
MLRV............ Manned Lunar Roving Vehicle [*NASA*] (PDAA)
MLRV........... Myrobalan Latent Ringspot Virus [*Plant pathology*]
MLS .... Machine Literature Searching [*Computer science*] (DIT)
MLS .... Mac Library System [*Computer Advanced Software Products - CASPR*] [*Cupertino, CA*] [*Information service or system*] (IID)
MLS .... Magnetically-Linked Solenoid (MCD)
MLS .... Maintenance Loading Sheet (MCD)
MLS .... Mall Airways, Inc. [*ICAO designator*] (FAAC)
MLS .... Manistique & Lake Superior R. R. [*AAR code*]
MLS .... Manned Lunar Surface [*NASA*]
MLS .... Master Laboratory Station
MLS .... Master of Legal Studies (GAGS)
MLS .... Master of Liberal Studies (GAGS)
MLS .... Master of Librarianship
MLS .... Master of Library Science
MLS .... Master of Library Science (GAGS)
MLS .... Master of Library Services (PGP)
MLS .... Master of Library Studies
MLS .... Master of Life Science (GAGS)
MLS .... Maximized LOD [*Logarithm of the Odds*] Score [*Statistics*]
MLS .... Maximum Life-Span
MLS .... Maxwell Library Systems [*Information service or system*] (IID)
MLS .... Mean Lifespan (AAMN)
MLS .... Mechanical Limit Stop
MLS .... Mechanical Limit Switch
MLS .... Median Life Span [*Oncology*] (DAVI)
MLS .... Median Longitudinal Section
MLS .... Medium Life Span
MLS .... Medium Long Shot [*A photograph or motion picture sequence taken from a relatively great distance*]
MLS .... Metal Slitting
MLS .... Metropolitan Libraries Section [*Public Library Association*]
MLS .... Microwave Landing System [*Aviation*]
MLS .... Microwave Limb Sounder
MLS .... Microwave Line Stretcher
MLS .... Miles City [*Montana*] [*Airport symbol*] (OAG)
MLS .... Miles City, MT [*Location identifier FAA*] (FAAL)
MLS .... Military Labor Service
MLS .... Military Sealift Command
ML/S .... Milliliters per Second
MLS .... Mills (MCD)
MLS .... Mills
MLS .... Mills Corp. [*NYSE symbol*] (SAG)
MLS .... Miniature Linguistic Systems
MLS .... Minimum Launch Speed [*British military*] (DMA)
MLS .... Minimum Legal Size [*Pisciculture*]
MLS .... Minor Lymphocyte Stimulating [*Genetics*]
MLS .... Missile-Launching System (NG)
MLS .... Missile Lift System (AAG)
MLS .... Missile Location System (IEEE)
MLS .... Mississippi County Library System, Blytheville, AR [*Inactive*] [*OCLC symbol*] (OCLC)
MLS .... Mixed Language System (PDAA)
MLS .... Mobile Library Service [*British*]
MLS .... Mobile Logistic Support (CINC)
MLS .... MOL [*Manned Orbiting Laboratory*] Launch Site (MCD)
MLS .... Moulis [*France*] [*Seismograph station code, US Geological Survey*] (SEIS)
MLS .... Movimento per le Liberta Statuarie [*Movement for Statutory Liberty*] [*Sanmarinese*] (PPE)
MLS .... Movimiento de Liberacion Sebta [*Ceuta Liberation Movement*] [*Spain*] (PD)
MLS .... Multifrequency LASER Sounding (MCD)
MLS .... Multilanguage System [*Computer science*] (IEEE)
MLS .... Multilayered Structure [*Botany*]
MLS .... Multi-Layer Steel [*Engine gaskets*] [*Automotive engineering*]
MLS .... Multilevel Security (MCD)
MLS .... Multilevel Security (DOMA)
MLS .... Multiline Selection [*Asahi Glass of Japan*]
MLS .... Multiparameter Light Scattering [*Physics*]
MLS .... Multiple Listing Service [*Real estate*]
MLS .... Music Learning System [*Trademark*]
MLS .... Myelomonocytic Leukemia, Subacute (MAE)
MLSA........... Ministry of Labour Staff Association [*British*]
ML SAI99 ..... Merrill Lynch & Co. [*Associated Press*] (SAG)
MLSB.......... Major League Scouting Bureau [*Baseball*]
MLSB.......... Member of the London School Board
ML Sc .... Master of Library Science
MLSC.......... Member of the London Society of Compositors
MLSC.......... Micronesian Legal Services Corp. (EA)
MLS/CP....... Microwave Landing System / Curved Path [*Aviation*]
MLSE.......... Mechanical Launch Support Equipment [*NASA*] (KSC)
MLSF.......... Mobile Logistic Support Forces (MCD)
ML/SFA....... Metal Lath/Steel Framing Association Division of National Association of Architectural Metal Manufactureres (EA)
MLSG.......... Mobile Logistics Support Group (NVT)
MLSI .... Multilevel Large-Scale Integration
MLSIT........ Master of Library Science and International Technology (PGP)

MLSJ .... Macquarie Law Students Journal [*A publication*]
MLSK........... Master Lock, Skeleton Key
MLSO........... Mode-Locked Surface-Acoustic Wave Oscillator [*Telecommunications*] (TEL)
MLSOP .... Movement for the Liberation of Soa Tome and Principe [*Political party*]
MLSP........... Master of Law and Social Policy (GAGS)
MLSP........... Multiple-Link Satellite Program
MLSP97 ...... Merrill Lynch & Co., Inc. [*Associated Press*] (SAG)
MLSP98 ...... Merrill Lynch & Co., Inc. [*Associated Press*] (SAG)
M-L-S-R....... Missing, Lost, Stolen, or Recovered [*Government property*] (DNAB)
MLSR........... Molder, Ship Repair [*Navy rating*]
MLSRC........ Molder, Ship Repair, Cupola Tender [*Navy rating*]
MLSRF........ Molder, Ship Repair, Foundryman [*Navy rating*]
MLSRM........ Molder, Ship Repair, Molder [*Navy rating*]
MLSS........... Mechanized Letter Sorting System [*Hong Kong Post Office*]
MLSS........... Military and Federal Specifications and Standards [*Information Handling Services*] [*Information service or system*] (CRD)
MLSS........... Mixed-Liquor Suspended Solid [*Water pollution*]
MLST .... Medico-Legal Society of Tasmania [*Australia*]
MLST .... Merrill Language Screening Test [*Educational test*]
MLST .... Milstead [*AAR code*]
MLSTP .... Movimento de Libertacao de Sao Tome e Principe [*Movement for the Liberation of Sao Tome and Principe*] [*Portugal*] (PPW)
ML SYP98 ... Merrill Lynch & Co. [*Associated Press*] (SAG)
MLT .... Madras Law Times [*India*] [*A publication*] (DLA)
MLT .... Magnetic Levitation Transportation
MLT .... Magnetic Local Time
MLT .... Malta [*ANSI three-letter standard code*] (CNC)
mlt .... Maltese [*MARC language code Library of Congress*] (LCCP)
MLT .... Manned Lunar Test [*NASA*] (KSC)
MLT .... Manufacturing Lead Time
MLT .... Mass Loaded Transducer
MLT .... Master Library Tape [*Computer science*]
MLT .... Master of Law and Taxation
MLT .... Maximum Lethal Time [*of radiation exposure*] (DEN)
MLT .... Mean Length per Turn
MLT .... Mean Life Time (NATG)
MLT .... Mean Logistical Time (IEEE)
MLT .... Mean Low Tide [*Tides and currents*]
MLT .... Mechanized Line Testing [*Telecommunications*] (TEL)
MLT .... Mechanized Loop Testing (MCD)
MLT .... Median Lethal Time [*of radiation exposure*]
MLT .... Medical Laboratory Technician [*or Technologist*]
MLT .... Medium Level Tripod [*British military*] (DMA)
MLT .... Melatonin
MLT .... Mentolaeva Transverse [*A fetal position*] [*Obstetrics*] (AAMN)
MLT .... Microlayer Transistor
MLT .... Millinocket, ME [*Location identifier FAA*] (FAAL)
MLT .... Misallat [*Egypt*] [*Geomagnetic observatory code*]
MLT .... Mitel Corp. [*NYSE symbol Toronto Stock Exchange symbol*] (SPSG)
MLT .... Mixing-Length Theory [*Physics of convection*] [*Chemical engineering*]
MLT .... Mobile Laboratory Table
MLT .... Mobile Launch Tower
MLT .... Modulated Lapped Transform [*Telecommunications*]
MLT .... Muexins-Length Theory
MLTA.......... Multiple Line Terminal Adapter [*Computer science*] (BUR)
MLT-AD .... Medical Laboratory Technology-Associate Degree
MLT (AMT)... Medical Laboratory Technician (American Medical Technologists) (DAVI)
MLT(ASCP)... Medical Laboratory Technician (American Society of Clinical Pathologists) (DMAA)
MLTC .... Mixed Lymphocyte-Tumor Culture [*Immunology*]
MltcPrt......... Multicanal Participacoes [*Associated Press*] (SAG)
ML Tech01... Merrill Lynch & Co. [*Associated Press*] (SAG)
MLTF .... Major Late Transcription Factor [*Genetics*]
MLTF .... Military Law Task Force (EA)
MLTG.......... Melting
MLTG.......... Missile Launch Tube Group
MLTI .... Mixed Lymphocyte-Tumor [*Cell*] Interaction [*Immunology*]
ML/TL .... Mucrones Length to Total Body Length Ratio [*Of Crustacea*]
MLTLVL....... Melting Level [*NWS*] (FAAC)
MltmdG........ Multimedia Games, Inc. [*Associated Press*] (SAG)
MLTMS........ Multileg Tanker Mooring System (MCD)
MLTN.......... Molten Metal Technology [*NASDAQ symbol*] (TTSB)
MLTN.......... Molten Metal Technology, Inc. [*NASDAQ symbol*] (SAG)
MLTP .... Ministers Leadership Training Program [*Defunct*] (EA)
MLTPL......... Multiplane
MLTRY......... Military
MLTSL......... Multiple Sail [*Navy*] (NVT)
MLTU.......... Missile Loop Test Unit
MLTY.......... Military (MDG)
MLU .... Major League Umpires Association
MLU .... Malka Resources Ltd. [*Vancouver Stock Exchange symbol*]
MLU .... Mean Length of Utterance [*Linguistics*]
MLU .... Memory Loading Unit [*of FADAC*] [*Military*]
MLU .... Memory Logic Unit [*Computer science*]
MLU .... Mid-Life Update
MLU .... Miscellaneous Live Unit [*Military*] (AFM)
MLU .... Mobile Laundry Unit
MLU .... Mobile Living Unit [*Mobile home*]
MLU .... Monroe [*Louisiana*] [*Airport symbol*] (OAG)
MLU .... Monroe, LA [*Location identifier FAA*] (FAAL)
MLU .... Montlucon Air Service [*France ICAO designator*] (FAAC)
MLU .... Multiple Logical Unit

MLUA.........	Major League Umpires Association (EA)
MLURI........	Macaulay Land Use Research Institute, Aberdeen [*British*] (IRUK)
MLUS.........	Merrill Lynch & Co. [*Associated Press*] (SAG)
ML/USA	Mailing List User and Supplier Association [*Defunct*] (EA)
MLV............	Air Moldova International, SA [*FAA designator*] (FAAC)
MLV............	Magnetic Levitation Vehicle (BARN)
MLV............	Main LOX [*Liquid Oxygen*] Valve [*NASA*] (KSC)
MLV............	Malvaux [*France*] [*Seismograph station code, US Geological Survey*] (SEIS)
MLV............	Matrix Light Valve
MLV............	Maximum Lung Volume [*Physiology*]
MLV............	McDonnell Launch Vehicle [*McDonnell Douglas Corp.*] (MCD)
MLV............	Medium Launch Vehicle
MLV............	Membrane Light Valve [*Optics*]
MLV............	Memory Loader Verifier (DWSG)
MLV............	Mobile Launch Vehicle [*Air Force*]
MLV............	Moloney Leukemia Virus [*Also, MLV(M)*]
MLV............	Mouse Leukemia Virus (MAE)
MLV............	Mulberry Latent Virus [*Plant pathology*]
MLV............	Multilamellar Large Vesicle [*Pharmacy Biochemistry*]
MLV............	Multilaminar Phospholipid Vesicle [*Immunology*]
MLV............	Murine Leukemia Virus [*Also, MuLV*]
MLV(A).......	Murine Leukemia Virus (Abelson)
MLVDP........	Maximum Left Ventricular Developed Pressure [*Cardiology*] (DMAA)
MLV(M).......	Murine Leukemia Virus (Moloney)
MLVP.........	Manned Lunar Vehicle Program [*NASA*] (AAG)
MLVPS........	Manual Low-Voltage Power Supply
MLV(R).......	Murine Leukemia Virus (Rauscher)
MLVS.........	Mill Vise
MLVS.........	Multilevel Voltage Select (MCD)
MLVSS........	Mixed-Liquor Volatile Suspended Solids [*Chemical engineering*]
MLVT.........	Mobile Launch Vehicle Transporter [*Air Force*]
MLW..........	Madras Law Weekly [*India*] [*A publication*] (DLA)
MLW..........	Master Warning Light (IAA)
MLW..........	Maximum Landing Weight [*Aviation*]
MLW..........	Mean Low Water [*Tides and currents*]
MLW..........	Medium-Level Radioactive Waste (NUCP)
MLW..........	Milwaukee [*Wisconsin*] [*Seismograph station code, US Geological Survey Closed*] (SEIS)
MLW..........	Monrovia [*Liberia*] [*Airport symbol*] (OAG)
MLW..........	Multiple Logical Windowing [*Computer science*]
MLWA........	Maximum Landing Weight Authorized [*Aviation*] (DA)
MLWG........	Modern Languages Working Group (AIE)
MLWI.........	Mean Low-Water Lunitidal Interval [*Tides and currents*]
MLWL........	Mail-Well, Inc. [*NASDAQ symbol*] (SAG)
MLWMS.......	Miscellaneous Liquid Waste Management System (NRCH)
MLWN........	Mean Low-Water Neap [*Tides and currents*]
MLWS........	Mean Low-Water Spring [*Tides and currents*]
MLWS........	Miniature LASER Weapon Simulator (MCD)
MLWS........	Minimum Level Water Stand (NATG)
MLX..........	Malatya [*Turkey*] [*Airport symbol*] (OAG)
MLX..........	Mauna Loa 2 [*Hawaii*] [*Seismograph station code, US Geological Survey*] (SEIS)
MLX..........	Merritt Island, Florida [*Spaceflight Tracking and Data Network*] [*NASA*]
MLX..........	MLX Corp. [*Associated Press*] (SAG)
MLX01........	Magnetically-levitated Linear Motor Vehicle
MLXR.........	MLX Corp. [*NASDAQ symbol*] (SAG)
MLy	Lynn Public Library, Lynn, MA [*Library symbol Library of Congress*] (LCLS)
MLY..........	Manley Hot Springs [*Alaska*] [*Airport symbol*] (OAG)
MLY..........	Manley Hot Springs, AK [*Location identifier FAA*] (FAAL)
MLY..........	Moly Mite Resources [*Vancouver Stock Exchange symbol*]
MLY..........	Multiply (MDG)
Mly	National Library of Malaysia, Kuala Lumpur, Malaysia [*Library symbol*] [*Library of Congress*] (LCLS)
MlyKA........	Arkib Negara [*National Archives of Malaysia*], Federal Government Building, Kuala Lumpur, Malaysia [*Library symbol Library of Congress*] (LCLS)
MlyKgM.......	Sarawak Museum, Kuching, Malaysia [*Library symbol*] [*Library of Congress*] (LCLS)
MlyKU........	University of Malaya, Kuala Lumpur, Malaysia [*Library symbol Library of Congress*] (LCLS)
MlyL.........	Lynn Public Library, Lynn, MA [*Library symbol*] [*Library of Congress*] (LCLS)
MlyPS.........	Universiti Sains Malaysia (University of Science, Malaysia), Minden, Penang, Malaysia [*Library symbol Library of Congress*] (LCLS)
MLZ..........	Melo [*Uruguay*] [*Airport symbol*] (OAG)
MM............	Machine Made Paper (DGA)
MM............	Machine-Made Snow [*Skiing*]
MM............	Machinery
MM............	Machinist's Mate [*Navy rating*]
MM............	Made Merchantable
MM............	Maelzel's Metronome [*Music*]
MM............	Magister Melendus [*Flourished, 1188-1209*] [*Authority cited in pre-1607 legal work*] (DSA)
MM............	Main Memory
MM............	Main Module (NASA)
MM............	Maintenance Manual
MM............	Maintenance Monitor
MM............	Majesties
MM............	Major Medical [*Insurance*]
MM............	Major Mode (KSC)
MM............	Malignant Melanoma [*Oncology*]

mm............	Malta [*MARC country of publication code Library of Congress*] (LCCP)
MM............	Management Manual (KSC)
M/M...........	Man/Machine
MM............	Manmade [*Diamonds*]
MM............	Man-Month (AFM)
MM............	Manual Maximal Displacement [*Sports medicine*]
MM............	Manual Morse (MCD)
MM............	Manufacturing Management
MM............	Manufacturing Manual (AAG)
MM............	Marilyn Monroe [*American motion picture star, 1926-1962*]
MM............	Mariner Mars Project [*NASA*]
MM............	Maritime Mobile
MM............	Mark Mason (ROG)
MM............	Mark Master [*Freemasonry*]
MM............	Marshall Manual (SSD)
MM............	Marshall-Marchetti Procedure [*Medicine*] (MAE)
MM............	Martha Movement (EA)
M-M...........	Martin Marietta Corp.
MM............	Martyres [*Martyrs*]
mm............	Maryknoll Fathers, Catholic Foreign Mission Society of America (TOCD)
MM............	Maryknoll Missioners [*Catholic Foreign Mission Society*] [*Roman Catholic religious order*]
MM............	Maryknoll Sisters of St. Dominic (TOCD)
MM............	Mass Memory (NASA)
MM............	Massorah Magna [*or Massora Magna*] (BJA)
MM............	Master Mason [*Freemasonry*]
MM............	Master Mechanic
MM............	Master Monitor
MM............	Master of Management
MM............	Master of Management (GAGS)
MM............	Master of Mathematics (GAGS)
MM............	Master of Medicine
MM............	Master of Ministry (PGP)
MM............	Master of Modern Studies (PGP)
MM............	Master of Music (GAGS)
MM............	Master of Music
MM............	Masters
MM............	Materials Management [*Nuclear energy*]
MM............	Materials Measurement (IEEE)
MM............	Materia Medica (ROG)
MM............	Mathematics Model
MM............	Math Model (KSC)
MM............	Matrimonium [*Matrimony*] [*Latin*]
M/M...........	Maximum and Minimum (KSC)
MM............	Measure for Measure [*Shakespearean work*]
MM............	Mechanical Maintenance
MM............	Medal for Merit [*Military decoration*]
MM............	Medial Malleolus [*Anatomy*] (AAMN)
MM............	Medial Meniscus [*Anatomy*]
MM............	Median Method [*Mathematics*]
MM............	Medical Man (ROG)
mm----........	Mediterranean Sea and Area [*MARC geographic area code Library of Congress*] (LCCP)
MM............	Medium Maintenance
MM............	Med Mera [*And So Forth*] [*Latin*] (ILCA)
MM............	Megamega [*A prefix meaning multiplied by one trillion*] (DEN)
MM............	Megameter
MM............	Melaveh Malka (BJA)
MM............	Melbourne Marathon [*Australia*]
MM............	Membranes [*Leaves of parchment*] (ROG)
MM............	Memory Module (MCD)
MM............	Memory Multiplexer [*Computer science*] (MDG)
MM............	Mercantile Marine
MM............	Merchant Marine
MM............	Mesoscale Model (USDC)
MM............	Mesoscale Model [*Marine science*] (OSRA)
MM............	Messageries Maritimes [*Forwarding agents*] [*French*]
MM............	Messieurs [*Plural of Mister*] [*French*]
MM............	Metal Manufacture [*Department of Employment*] [*British*]
MM............	Metered Market Service [*A. C. Nielsen Co.*] (NTCM)
MM............	Methylmalonyl-CoA Mutase [*An enzyme*]
MM............	Methyl Mercaptan [*Organic chemistry*]
MM............	Methyl Methacrylate [*Also, MMA*] [*Organic chemistry*]
MM............	Metronome Mark (ROG)
MM............	Microfilm
MM............	Micromanipulator [*Instrumentation*]
MM............	Micromodule (AAG)
MM............	Midcourse Mode [*Navy*] (CAAL)
MM............	Middle Manager
MM............	Middle Marker [*in an instrument landing system*]
MM............	Middle Minoan [*Archaeology*] (BJA)
MM............	Military Medal [*World War I nickname: Maconochie Medal*] [*British*]
MM............	Military Medicine
MM............	Milla Wa-Milla (BJA)
mm............	Millimeter [*Metric*]
MM............	Millimeter (DFIT)
mM............	Millimole [*Mass*]
mm............	Million (WDMC)
MM............	Minelayer Fleet [*Navy symbol Obsolete*]
MM............	Minimal Medium [*Microbiology*]
M/M...........	Minimum/Maximum
MM............	Minister of Munitions [*British World War II*]
MM............	Ministry of Mines [*British*] (DAS)

MM	Mint Mark [*Numismatics*]
MM	Minuteman [*Missile*] (AABC)
Mm	Misch Metal [*A commercial mixture of rare earth metals*]
MM	Mismated [*Merchandising slang*]
MM	Missile Master [*Fire direction and coordination system*]
MM	Missile Minder (MCD)
MM	Missile Motion
MM	Mission Manager (NASA)
MM	Mission Manager [*NASA/USAF*]
MM	Mission Module
MM	Mission Monitor (MCD)
M/M	Mister or Mrs. [*In addresses*] [*Correspondence*]
MM	Mistress of Music
MM[2]	Mitochondrial Myopathy [*Medicine*]
mm	Mixed Media (VRA)
MM	Mixed Monitor [*External Tocotransducer and internal scalp exectrode*] [*Neonatology*] [*Obstetrics*] (DAVI)
MM	Moderation Management
MM	Modern Motor [*A publication*]
MM	Modification or Maintenance [*Aircraft*]
MM	Modified Mercalli [*Scale measuring earthquake intensity*] [*Seismology*]
MM	Modigliani-Miller Propositions [*Corporate finance*] (ECON)
MM	Mois Maconnique [*Masonic Month*] [*Freemasonry*] [*French*]
MM	Molecular Mechanics [*Physical chemistry*]
MM	Money Market [*Investment term*]
MM	Monostable Multivibrator [*Electronics*] (OA)
MM	Monthly Meetings [*Quakers*]
MM	Morality in Media (EA)
MM	Moral Majority [*An association*] (EA)
MM	Morbidity and Mortality [*Medicine*] (DMAA)
MM	More Moderate Service [*Automotive engineering*]
MM	Moslem Mosque (EA)
MM	Mothers Matter [*Commercial firm*] (EA)
MM	Motor Magnet
MM	Motor Maintenance [*Army*]
MM	Motor Maintenance Aptitude Area [*Army*]
MM	Motor Meal [*Medicine*] (MEDA)
MM	Motor Mechanic [*British military*] (DMA)
MM	Mould Made Paper (DGA)
MM	Mouse Myoblast [*Cell line*]
MM	Moving Magnet [*Stereo equipment*]
MM	Mozambique Metical [*Monetary unit*] (IMH)
M/M	Mr. & Mrs. (VRA)
MM	Much Married [*Slang*]
MM	Mucous Membrane
MM	Multi-Media (OICC)
MM	Multimeter
MM	Multimode
MM	Multiple Master [*Computer science*] (CDE)
MM	Multiple Myeloma [*Medicine*]
MM	Multipolar Magnetic [*Sun*] (DICI)
MM	Munitions Maintenance (MCD)
mm	Murmur [*Cardiology*] (DAVI)
MM	Muscles [*Medicine*]
MM	Muscularis Mucosa [*Medicine*] (MAE)
MM	Muscularis Mucosa [*Anatomy*] (DAVI)
MM	Museum Media [*A publication*]
MM	Musical Majority [*Defunct*] (EA)
MM	Mutatis Mutandis [*With the Necessary Changes*] [*Latin*]
MM	Mutual Risk Management [*NYSE symbol*] (SPSG)
MM	Myeloid Metaplasia [*Medicine*]
MM	Myelomeningocele [*Medicine*]
MM	Myriameters [*Metric system*] (ROG)
MM	SAM Colombia [*Airline flight code*] (ODBW)
MM	Sociedad Aeronautica Medellin [*ICAO designator*] (AD)
MM	Xaverian Missionary Society of Mary, Inc. [*Roman Catholic women's religious order*]
MM1	Machinist's Mate, First Class [*Navy rating*]
MM2	Machinist's Mate, Second Class [*Navy rating*]
MM[2]	Square Millimeter
MM[3]	Cubic Millimeter
MM3	Machinist's Mate, Third Class [*Navy rating*]
MM4	Mesoscale Meteorological Model-Version 4 (USDC)
MM4	Mesoscale Meteorological Model-Version 4 [*Marine science*] (OSRA)
MM5	Mesoscale Model Version 5 [*Marine science*] [*Pennsylvania State University*] (OSRA)
MMA	Average Male Mass
MMA	MacRobertson Miller Airline Services [*Australia*]
MMA	Magnetotactic Multicellular Aggregate [*Microbiology*]
MMA	Major Machine Accessory (MCD)
MMA	Major Maintenance Availability (MHDB)
MMA	Malmo [*Sweden*] [*Airport symbol*] (OAG)
MMA	Management and Marketing Abstracts [*PIRA*] [*Bibliographic database*] [*British*]
MMA	Maneuver Motor Array (MCD)
MMA	Manual Metal Arc [*Welding*]
MMA	Maria Mitchell Association (EA)
MMA	Marine Mammal Act [*1972*] (MSC)
MMA	Marine Maritime Academy
MMA	Marine Motor Association (ROG)
MMA	Married Man's Allowance [*Taxes*] [*British*]
MMA	Massachusetts Maritime Academy [*Buzzards Bay*]
MMA	Massachusetts Maritime Academy, Captain C. H. Hurley Library, Buzzards Bay, MA [*OCLC symbol*] (OCLC)

MMA	Massachusetts Military Academy
MMA	Master of Management and Administration, Cranfield Institute of Technology [*British*] (DBQ)
MMA	Master of Manpower Administration (GAGS)
MMA	Master of Marine Affairs (GAGS)
MMA	Master of Media Arts (PGP)
MMA	Master of Medical Art (GAGS)
MMA	Master of Municipal Administration
MMA	Master of Musical Art (GAGS)
MMA	Master of Musical Arts
MMA	Masters of Medicine [*A publication*]
MMA	Mastitis-Metritis-Agalactia Syndrome [*Medicine*] (DMAA)
MMA	Material Manufacturing Authorization (AAG)
MMA	Materials Marketing Associates [*Hartford, CT*] (EA)
MMA	Maymac Petroleum Corp. [*Vancouver Stock Exchange symbol*]
MMA	Mazda Motors of America
MMA	Medical Management Analysis System (HCT)
MMA	Medical Materiel Account [*Military*] (AABC)
MMA	Medical Mutual Aid (GNE)
MMA	Memory-to-Memory Adapter [*Computer science*]
MMA	Merchandise Marks Act (ROG)
MMA	Merchants and Manufacturers Association
MMA	Mercy Medical Airlift (EA)
MMA	Merrill's Marauders Association (EA)
MMA	Meter Manufacturers' Association (IAA)
MMA	Methylmalonic Acid [*Organic chemistry*]
MMA	Methylmalonic Acidemia [*Medicine*]
MMA	Methyl Methacrylate [*Also, MM*] [*Organic chemistry*]
MMA	Metro Manila Airways International, Inc. [*Philippines*] [*ICAO designator*] (FAAC)
MMA	Metropolitan Magazine Association [*Later, Magazine Publishers Association*] (EA)
MMA	Metropolitan Museum of Art [*New York*] (BJA)
MMA	Microcomputer Managers Association (HGAA)
MMA	Microminiature Mixer Amplifier
MMA	Microtome Manufacturers Association [*British*] (DBA)
MMA	Middle Meningeal Artery [*Neuroanatomy*]
MMA	Military Medical Academy [*Armed forces medical college*]
MMA	Millimeter Array [*Astronomy*]
MMA	Minelayer Auxiliary Ship [*Navy symbol Obsolete*]
MMA	Mirror Manufacturers Association
MMA	Missile Maintenance Area (AAG)
MMA	Mitomycin A [*Antineoplastic drug*]
MMA	Modified Motorcycle Association
MMA	Monomethylamine [*Organic chemistry*]
MMA	Monomethyl Arsonic Acid [*Organic chemistry*]
MMA	Monorail Manufacturers Association (EA)
MMA	Monovalent Metal Azide [*Inorganic chemistry*]
MMA	Mothers and Midwives Action [*Australia An association*]
MMA	Motoring in Miniature Association (EA)
MMA	Motorsports Marketing Association [*Langhorne, PA*] [*Defunct*] (EA)
MMA	Multifunction Microwave Aperture
MMA	Multiple Module Access
MMA	Multiplexed Matrix Array
MMA	Mummy Mountain [*Arizona*] [*Seismograph station code, US Geological Survey Closed*] (SEIS)
MMA	Municipal Mortgage & Equity LLC [*AMEX symbol*] (SAG)
MMA	Music Masters' Association [*British*]
MMA	Music of Modern Art (NADA)
MMAA	Acapulco/General Juan N. Alvarez Internacional [*Mexico ICAO location identifier*] (ICLI)
MMAA	Man/Machine Assembly Analysis (MCD)
MMAA	Merchandise Mart Apparel Association [*Defunct*]
MMAA	Monomethylarsonic Acid [*Organic chemistry*]
MMAA	Mono-N-methylacetoacetamide [*Organic chemistry*]
MMAC	Material Management Aggregation Code (MCD)
MMAC	Medical Materiel Advice Code [*Military*] (AFM)
MMAC	Multi-Media Access Center [*Cabletron Systems, Inc.*]
MMAC	Multiple Model Adaptive Control [*Flight control*]
MMAC-FNB	Multi-Media Access Center with Flexible Network Bus [*Cabletron Systems, Inc.*]
MMACS	Maintenance Management and Control System (MCD)
MMACS	Medicaid/Medicare Automated Certification System (GFGA)
MMAD	Mass-Median Aerodynamic Diameter [*of particles*]
MM Adm	Master of Municipal Administration
M Ma E	Master of Marine Engineering
MMAE	Master of Mechanical and Aerospace Engineering (PGP)
M Ma Eng	Master of Marine Engineering
MMal	Malden Public Library, Malden, MA [*Library symbol Library of Congress*] (LCLS)
M-MALS	Multimode Aircraft Landing System (MCD)
MMam	Marstons Mills Public Library, Marstons Mills, MA [*Library symbol Library of Congress*] (LCLS)
MMAN	Aeropuerto del Norte [*Mexico ICAO location identifier*] (ICLI)
MMAN	Minuteman International [*NASDAQ symbol*] (SAG)
MMAN	Minuteman Int'l [*NASDAQ symbol*] (TTSB)
MM & F	Merchant Marine and Fisheries Committee [*Congressional committee*] (MSC)
MM & M	Material Manual and Memorandum (AAG)
MM & M	Minerals, Mining, and Metallurgy
MM & M Soc of Am	Member of the Mining and Metallurgical Society of America
MM & SC	Major Mission and Support Category
MM & T	Manufacturing Methods and Technology [*Program*] [*Army Materiel Command*] (RDA)

MManHi......	Manchester Historical Society, Manchester, MA [*Library symbol Library of Congress*] (LCLS)
MMAP.........	Microwave Multi-Application Payload [*NASA*] (PDAA)
MMAR	Main Memory Address Register
MMar..........	Marlborough Public Library, Marlborough, MA [*Library symbol Library of Congress*] (LCLS)
MMAR	Money Management Analytical Research Group
M-MARP.....	Mobilization Manpower Allocations/Requirements Plan [*Military*]
MMarsW.....	Historic Winslow House, Marshfield, MA [*Library symbol Library of Congress*] (LCLS)
MMART.......	Mobile Medical Augmentation Readiness Team (DNAB)
MMAS........	Aguascalientes [*Mexico ICAO location identifier*] (ICLI)
MMAS........	Manufacturing Management Accounting System (PDAA)
MMAS........	Manufacturing Management Accounting Systems (MHDI)
MMAS........	Master of Military Art and Science (MCD)
MMAS........	Material Management Accountability System (NASA)
MMAS........	Material Management and Accounting System (AAGC)
MmAS.........	Minerva Mikrofilm A/S, Hellerup, Denmark [*Library symbol Library of Congress*] (LCLS)
MMAS........	Mini-Manned Aircraft System (PDAA)
MMASC......	Major Mission and Support Category
MMat..........	Free Public Library, Mattapoisett, MA [*Library symbol Library of Congress*] (LCLS)
MMAT........	Mobile Mine Assembly Team (NG)
MMath........	Master of Mathematics
M Math.......	Master of Mathematics (PGP)
MMATP.......	Methadone Maintenance and Aftercare Treatment Program [*Medicine*] (DMAA)
M Mat SE ...	Master of Material Science and Engineering (PGP)
MMAU	Master Multiattribute Utility (IEEE)
MMAU	Millimass Unit (IAA)
MMB	Marine Midland Banks, Inc. [*NYSE symbol*] (SPSG)
MMB	Master Menu Board [*Military*]
MMB	Master of Medical Biochemistry (GAGS)
MMB	Memanbetsu [*Japan*] [*Geomagnetic observatory code*]
MMB	Memanbetsu [*Japan*] [*Airport symbol*] (OAG)
MMB	Membrane [*Medicine*]
MMB	Mercedarian Missionaries of Berriz [*Also, OMerc*] [*Roman Catholic women's religious order*]
MMB	Method of Mass Balance [*Physical chemistry*]
MMB	Methylmercury Bromide [*Organic chemistry*]
MMB	Metropolitan Milk Board [*South Australia*]
MMB	Midwest Motor Carriers Bureau, Inc., Oklahoma City OK [*STAC*]
MMB	Milk Marketing Board (NADA)
MMB	Milk Marketing Board for England and Wales
MMB	Million Barrels
MMB	Minimum Monthly Balance [*Finance*]
MMB	Mixer Manufacturers Bureau [*Defunct*] (EA)
MMB	Multiport Memory Bank [*Computer science*] (MHDB)
MMBAT.......	Main Missile Battery
MMBB.........	Molecular Marine Biology and Biotechnology [*A publication*]
MMB/D	Million Barrels per Day
MMBEMD	Mean Miles between Essential Maintenance Demand [*Quality control*]
MMBF.........	Mean Miles between Failures [*Quality control*]
MMBL.........	MacMillan Bloedel Ltd. [*NASDAQ symbol*] (NQ)
MMBLF.......	MacMillan-Bloedel [*NASDAQ symbol*] (TTSB)
MMBMF	Mean Miles between Mission Failures [*Quality control*] (MCD)
MMBOMF	Mean Miles between Operational Mission Failures [*Quality control*] (MCD)
MMBP.........	Military Medical Benefits Property (AABC)
MMBR	Mean Miles between Removals [*Quality control*] (MCD)
MMBSF.......	Mean Miles between System Failures [*Quality control*] (MCD)
MMBTU......	Million British Thermal Units (MENA)
MMBUMA	Mean Miles between Unscheduled Maintenance Actions [*Quality control*] (MCD)
MMC..........	Ciudad Mante [*Mexico*] [*Airport symbol*] (AD)
MMC..........	Machinist's Mate, Chief [*Navy rating*]
MMC..........	Magnesium Methyl Carbonate [*Organic chemistry*]
MMC..........	Maintenance Management Center
MMC..........	Maintenance Management Course [*Army*]
MMC..........	Man-Machine Communication [*Computer science*]
MMC..........	Man Marketing Council [*New York City*]
MMC..........	Manufacturing Methods Committee
MMC..........	Marine Mammal Commission [*Marine science*] (MSC)
MMC..........	Marsh & McLennan [*NYSE symbol*] (TTSB)
MMC..........	Marsh & McLennan Companies, Inc. [*NYSE symbol*] (SPSG)
MMC..........	Martin Marietta Corp. (KSC)
MMC..........	Martin's Reports of Mining Cases [*Canada*] [*A publication*] (DLA)
MMC..........	Mary Morstan's Companions [*An association*]
MMC..........	Marymount Manhattan College [*New York, NY*]
MMC..........	Massachusetts Microelectronics Center [*Research center*] (RCD)
MMC..........	Master of Mass Communication (GAGS)
MMC..........	Matched Memory Cycle [*Computer science*]
MMC..........	Materiel Management Center [*Military*] (AABC)
MMC..........	Materiel Management Code [*Military*] (AFM)
MMC..........	Maximum Material Condition
MMC..........	Maximum Metal Concept
MMC..........	Maximum Metal Condition (IEEE)
MMC..........	Maximum Miscibility Composition [*Physical chemistry*]
MMC..........	Mazda Motor Corp.
MMC..........	Mean Meridional Circulation [*Climatology*]
MMC..........	Meet Me Conference [*Telecommunications*] (DOM)
MMC..........	Melbourne Magistrates Court [*Australia*]
MMC..........	Memory Management Controller (IEEE)
MMC..........	Merchant Marine Council [*Coast Guard*]
MMC..........	Metabolic Measurement Cart [*Beckman Instruments, Inc.*]
MMC..........	Metal-Matrix Composite
MMC..........	Metropolitan Motor Carriers Conference Inc., Dover NJ [*STAC*]
MMC..........	Microcomputer Marketing Council [*Direct Marketing Association*] (PCM)
MMC..........	Micrometeoroid Capsule (OA)
MMC..........	Micronesian Minerals [*Vancouver Stock Exchange symbol*]
MMC..........	Midcourse Measurement Correction
MMC..........	Middle Cape [*Alaska*] [*Seismograph station code, US Geological Survey*] (SEIS)
MMC..........	Migrating Myoelectric Complexes [*Electrophysiology*]
MMC..........	Millsaps College, Jackson, MS [*OCLC symbol*] (OCLC)
MMC..........	Minelayer, Coastal [*Navy symbol Obsolete*]
MMC..........	Minicar and Microcar Club (EA)
MMC..........	Minimal Medullary Concentration [*Medicine*] (MAE)
MMC..........	Missile Maintenance Crew (AFM)
MMC..........	Missile Measurements Center
MMC..........	Missile Motion Computer
MMC..........	Mission Management Center [*NASA*] (NASA)
MMC..........	Mission Monitoring Center [*Army*]
MMC..........	Mitomycin C [*Mutamycin*] [*Also, Mi, MTC*] [*Antineoplastic drug*]
MMC..........	Mitsubishi Motors Corp.
MMC..........	Money Management Council [*British*]
MMC..........	Money Market Certificate [*Investment term*]
MMC..........	Monopolies and Mergers Commission [*British*]
MMC..........	Mortar Motor Carrier
MMC..........	Mount Marty College [*South Dakota*]
MMC..........	Mount Mary College [*Wisconsin*]
MMC..........	Mount Mercy College [*Iowa; Pennsylvania*]
MMC..........	Mucosal Mast Cell [*Medicine*]
MMC..........	Multimedia Marketing Council (DOM)
MMC..........	Multipart Memory Controller (NITA)
MMC..........	Multiport Memory Controller
MMCA........	Cananea [*Mexico ICAO location identifier*] (ICLI)
MMCA........	Methyl Monochloroacetate [*Organic chemistry*]
MMCA........	Midbody Motor Control Assembly (NASA)
MMCA........	Midbody Motor Control Assembly
MMCA........	Minor Maintenance Construction, Army
M McA........	Montague and McArthur's English Bankruptcy Reports [*A publication*] (DLA)
MM Cas......	Martin's Reports of Mining Cases [*Canada*] [*A publication*] (DLA)
MMCB........	Cuernavaca [*Mexico ICAO location identifier*] (ICLI)
MMCB........	Methods in Molecular and Cellular Biology [*A publication*]
MMCB........	Midwest Motor Carriers Bureau, Inc.
MMCBE......	Machinist's Mate, Construction Battalion, Equipment Operator [*Navy rating*]
MMCC........	Ciudad Acuna [*Mexico ICAO location identifier*] (ICLI)
MMCC........	Manhattan Miniature Camera Club (EA)
MMCC........	Mid-Century Mercury Car Club (EA)
MMCC........	Military Manpower Claimant Code (DNAB)
MMCC........	Multimini Computer Compiler (MHDI)
MMCCS......	MILSTAR [*Military Strategic and Tactical Relay System*] Mobile Consolidation and Control Station (DWSG)
MMCD	Master Monitor Criteria Data File
MMCD	Multimedia CD [*Computer science*]
MMCD	Multimedia Compact Disc
MMCE........	Ciudad Del Carmen [*Mexico ICAO location identifier*] (ICLI)
MMCF........	Million Cubic Feet
MMCFD......	Million Cubic Feet a Day
MMCG	Mid-Murray Citrus Growers [*Australia*]
MMCG	Nuevo Casas Grandes [*Mexico ICAO location identifier*] (ICLI)
MMCH	Chilpancingo [*Mexico ICAO location identifier*] (ICLI)
MMCI..........	Mopar Muscle Club International (EA)
MMCI..........	MultiMedia Concepts International, Inc. [*NASDAQ symbol*] (SAG)
MMCI..........	MultiMedia Concepts Intl. [*NASDAQ symbol*] (TTSB)
MMCIAC	Metal Matrix Composites Information Analysis Center [*DoD Information service or system*] (IID)
MMCIW.......	MultiMeda Concepts Intl-Wrrt [*NASDAQ symbol*] (TTSB)
MMCIW.......	MultiMedia Concepts International, Inc. [*NASDAQ symbol*] (SAG)
MMCL.........	Culiacan [*Mexico ICAO location identifier*] (ICLI)
MMCL.........	Major Missile Component List
MMCL.........	Master Measurement and Control List (MCD)
MMCM........	Chetumal [*Mexico ICAO location identifier*] (ICLI)
MMCM........	Machinist's Mate, Master Chief [*Navy rating*]
MMCM........	Master of Music in Church Music (PGP)
MMCMP......	Mobilization, Military and Civilian Manpower Program (AABC)
MMCN........	Ciudad Obregon [*Mexico ICAO location identifier*] (ICLI)
MMCNA......	Moto Morini Club of North America (EA)
MMCO........	Maintenance Material Control Officer (DNAB)
MMCP........	Campeche [*Mexico ICAO location identifier*] (ICLI)
MMCP........	Micro-Master Control Processor (NITA)
M/MCRP.....	AUTODIN Memory/Memory Control Replacement Program (MCD)
MMCS........	Ciudad Juarez/Abraham Gonzalez Internacional [*Mexico ICAO location identifier*] (ICLI)
MMCS........	Machinist's Mate, Senior Chief [*Navy rating*]
MMCS........	Mass Memory Control Subsystem (TEL)
MMCS........	Minimum Modified Chi-Squared [*Statistics*]
MMCS........	Missile and Munitions Center and School [*Army*] (RDA)
MMCS........	Mitsubishi Multi-Communication System [*Driver information system*]
MMCS........	Modernization Management and Control System [*Social Security Administration*]
MMCS........	Multidimensional-Multiattributional Causality Scale (EDAC)
MMCS........	Multiple-Mission Command System [*NASA*]
MMCSA.......	Microwave Microminiature Communications System for Aircraft (DNAB)

MMCSEER ... Marjorie Mayrock Center for CIS [*Commonwealth of Independent States*] and East European Research [*Israel*] (EAIO)
MMCT.......... Maritime Mobile Coastal Telegraphy
MMCT.......... Metal-to-Metal Charge Transfer [*Physical chemistry*]
MMCT.......... Microcell-Mediated Chromosome Transfer [*Genetics*]
MMCT.......... Mobile Maintenance Contact Team (MCD)
MMCTS....... Material Management Center Theater Supply [*Army*]
MMCU......... Chihuahua/Internacional [*Mexico ICAO location identifier*] (ICLI)
MMCV......... Ciudad Victoria [*Mexico ICAO location identifier*] (ICLI)
MMCY......... Celaya [*Mexico ICAO location identifier*] (ICLI)
MMCZ......... Cozumel/Internacional [*Mexico ICAO location identifier*] (ICLI)
MMD.......... Magnetic Mirror Device
MMD.......... Maintenance Management Division [*Army*] (INF)
MMD.......... Manual of the Medical Department [*Navy*]
MMD.......... Mass Median Diameter
MMD.......... Master Makeup and Display
MMD.......... Master Monitor Display
MMD.......... Material, Maintenance, and Distribution (MCD)
MMD.......... Materiel Management Decision [*Military*]
MMD.......... Materiel Management Division [*Army*]
MMD.......... Maximum Mixing Depths [*Meteorology*]
MMD.......... Mean Mass Density
MMD.......... Mean Mass Diameter
MMD.......... Mean Measure of Divergence [*Statistics*]
MMD.......... Mean Missile [*or Mission*] Duration (KSC)
MMD.......... Merchang Mariner's Document [*Navy*]
MMD.......... Merchant Marine Detail
MMD.......... Microwave Mixer Diode
MMD.......... Middle Management Development
MMD.......... Minami Daito Jima [*Volcano Islands*] [*Airport symbol*] (OAG)
MMD.......... Minelayer, Fast [*Navy symbol*]
MMD.......... Minimal Morbidostatic Dose [*Medicine*] (MAE)
MMD.......... Mini-Module Drive (PDAA)
MMD.......... Missile Miss Distance [*Military*] (CAAL)
MMD.......... Mission Management and Dissemination (MCD)
MMD.......... Mobile Servicing Center, Maintenance Department [*Canada*]
MMD.......... Molecular Mass Distribution [*Organic chemistry*]
MMD.......... Money Market Directories, Inc. [*Also, an information service or system*] (IID)
MMD.......... Moore Medical Corp. [*AMEX symbol*] (SPSG)
MMD.......... Movement for Multi-Party Democracy [*Zambia*] [*Political party*]
MMD.......... Moving Map Display
MMD.......... MSC [*Mobile Servicing Center*] Maintenance Depot (SSD)
MMD.......... MSFC [*Marshall Space Flight Center*] Management Directive [*NASA*]
MMD.......... Multi-Effect Multistage Distillation (PDAA)
MMD.......... Multimode Display
MMD.......... Myotonic Muscular Dystrophy [*Medicine Medicine*] (DMAA)
MMD.......... Servite Missionary Sisters of the Sorrowful Mother (TOCD)
MMDA .... Mass Merchandising Distributors' Association (EA)
MMDA .... (Methoxy)methylenedioxyamphetamine [*A hallucinogen*]
MMDA .... Money Market Deposit Account [*Investment term*]
MMDA .... Myristicin [*or glyceryl trimyristate*] [*Chemical dependency*] (DAVI)
MMDB .... Mass Memory Data Base
MMDB .... Mass Memory Database (NASA)
MMDB .... Master Measurement Database (NASA)
MMDC .... Manual Master Direction Center
MMDC .... Master Message Display Console (MCD)
MMDC .... Mount Misalignment Data Collection Routine
mmddyy....... Month, Day, Year (HGAA)
MMDF.......... Mission Mode Data File
MMDF.......... Mission Model Data File [*NASA*] (NASA)
MMDG......... Mark Morris Dance Group
MMDI.......... Middle Management Development Initiative
MMDL......... Microminiature Delay Line
MMDM........ Ciudad Mante [*Mexico ICAO location identifier*] (ICLI)
MMDM........ Mobile Mixed Deployment Minuteman (SAA)
MMDO......... Durango [*Mexico ICAO location identifier*] (ICLI)
MMDOC....... Merchant Mariners Documentation [*BTS*] (TAG)
MMDP .... Middle Management Development Program
MMDR........ Microcircuit Module, Driver/Receiver
MMDS........ Maintenance Management Data System [*Military*] (CAAL)
MMDS .... Martin Marietta Data Systems
MMDS .... Multichannel Multipoint Distribution Service [*Broadcasting term*]
MMDS .... Multichannel, Multipoint Distribution System [*Telecommunications*] (ACRL)
MME .... Machinist's Mate, Engineman [*Navy rating*]
MME .... Major Machine Equipment (MCD)
MME .... Major Movable Equipment (MEDA)
MME .... Master of Manufacturing Engineering (PGP)
MME .... Master of Material Engineering (GAGS)
MME .... Master of Mathematics for Educators (PGP)
MME .... Master of Mechanical Engineering (GAGS)
MME .... Master of Mechanical Engineering
M Me........... Master of Metaphysics
MME .... Master of Mineral Engineering (GAGS)
MME .... Master of Mining Engineering
MME .... Master of Music Education
MME .... Material Military Establishment [*Formerly, OSRD*] (MCD)
MME .... Maximum Maintenance Effort [*Military*] (AFM)
MMe .... Medford Public Library, Medford, MA [*Library symbol Library of Congress*] (LCLS)
MME .... Mediterranean Medical Entente (EAIO)
MME .... Methylmethacrylate [*Organic chemistry*]
MME .... Micrometeoric Erosion (AAG)
MME .... Mid-Atlantic Medical Services, Inc. [*NYSE symbol*] (SAG)

MME .... Mid Atlantic Medical Svcs [*NYSE symbol*] (TTSB)
MME .... Middlesborough [*England*] [*Airport symbol*] (AD)
MME .... Million Market Edition [*US News and World Report*]
MME .... Minimum Mean Estimate
MME .... Missile Maintenance Equipment (AABC)
MME .... Tees-Side [*England*] [*Airport symbol*] (OAG)
MMEC .... Machinery Maintenance Engineering Center (AFIT)
MMEC .... Machinery-Metals Export Club [*Later, International Industrial Marketing Club*] (EA)
MMEC .... Migrating Myoelectric Complex [*Physiology*]
M Mech E ..... Master of Mechanical Engineering
MMechEng.... Master of Mechanical Engineering (NADA)
MMECT........ Multiple-Monitored Electroconvulsive Therapy [*Schizophrenia*]
MMED......... Mass Median Equivalent Diameter [*of airborne particles*]
M Med......... Master of Medicine
MM Ed .... Master of Music Education
MMed......... Moore Medical Corp. [*Associated Press*] (SAG)
MMED......... Multimedia, Inc. [*NASDAQ symbol*] (SAG)
MMedAnaes... Master of Medicine (Anaesthesia)
MMEDC........ Multimedia, Inc. (MHDW)
MMedCardiol... Master of Medicine (Cardiology)
MMed(CM)... Master of Medicine (Community Medicine)
MMedEd ...... Master of Medical Education
MMedPaed... Master of Medicine (Paediatrics)
MMedPath ... Master of Medicine (Pathology)
MMedRadD.. Master of Medicine (Diagnostic Radiology)
M Med Sc... Master of Medical Science
MMedVen.... Master of Medicine (Venereology)
MMEE .... Medicare, Medicaid, Education and the Environment [*President Clinton political agenda*]
MMEF .... Maximal Midexpiratory Flow [*Also, MMF*] [*Medicine*]
MMEFR........ Maximal Midexpiratory Flow Rate [*Medicine*]
MMEI.......... Military Medicine Education Institute [*DoD*] (DOMA)
MMEL......... Master Minimum Equipment List (DA)
MMel.......... Melrose Public Library, Melrose, MA [*Library symbol Library of Congress*] (LCLS)
MM Eng ...... Master of Mechanical Engineering
MMEP......... Marine Mammal Events Program (EA)
MMEP......... Minuteman Education Program [*Air Force*] (AFM)
MMEP......... Missouri Mathematics Effectiveness Project (EDAC)
MMEP......... Multiple Modality Evoked Potential [*Neurophysiology*]
MMEP......... Tepic [*Mexico ICAO location identifier*] (ICLI)
MMES .... Ensenada [*Mexico ICAO location identifier*] (ICLI)
MMES .... Master Material Erection Schedule [*Shipbuilding*] (NG)
Mmes .... Mesdames [*Ladies*] [*French*]
MMES .... MSFC [*Marshall Space Flight Center*] Mated Element Systems [*NASA*] (NASA)
MMES .... Southwestern Manitoba Regional Library, Melita, Manitoba [*Library symbol National Library of Canada*] (NLC)
MMET......... Maintenance Management Engineering Team [*Military*]
M Met.......... Master of Metallurgy
MMeT.......... Tufts University, Medford, MA [*Library symbol Library of Congress*] (LCLS)
M Met E ..... Master of Metallurgical Engineering
MMetEng..... Master of Metallurgy and Engineering, University of Sheffield [*British*] (DBQ)
MMeT-EP..... Tufts University, Eliot Pearson Department of Child Study, Medford, MA [*Library symbol Library of Congress*] (LCLS)
MMeT-F....... Tufts University, Fletcher School of Law and Diplomacy, Medford, MA [*Library symbol Library of Congress*] (LCLS)
MMeT-Hi...... Tufts University, Universalist Historical Society, Medford, MA [*Library symbol Library of Congress*] (LCLS)
MMeT-M...... Tufts University, Medical and Dental School, Boston, MA [*Library symbol Library of Congress*] (LCLS)
MMEX......... Map Maneuver Exercise (MCD)
MMEX......... Mexico [*Mexico ICAO location identifier*] (ICLI)
MMF .... Fleet Minelayer [*Navy symbol*]
mmf .... Magnetomotive Force
MMF .... Mamfe [*Cameroon*] [*Airport symbol*] (OAG)
MMF .... Maritime Life Assurance Co. [*Toronto Stock Exchange symbol*]
MMF .... Maximum Midexpiratory Flow [*Also, MMEF*] [*Medicine*]
MMF .... Mean Maximum Flow [*Medicine*]
MMF .... Mechanical Machine-Finished Paper (DGA)
MMF .... Member of the Medical Faculty
MMF .... Microelectronics Manufacturing Facility [*Philco-Ford Corp.*] (MCD)
MMF .... Micromation Microfilm
MMF .... Micromembrane Filter
MMF .... Micromicrofarad (MUGU)
mmf .... Micromicrofarad (IDOE)
MMF .... Minelayer, Fleet [*Navy symbol Obsolete*]
MMF .... Mobile Magnetic Field
MMF .... Mobile Missile Facility (MCD)
MMF .... Mobility Maintenance Facility (NVT)
MMF .... Module Maintenance Facility
MMF .... Money Market Fund [*Investment term*]
MMF .... Moravian Music Foundation (EA)
MMF .... Moving Magnetic Feature [*Astronomy*] (OA)
MMF .... Multimode Fiber (ACRL)
MMF .... Mutual Musicians Foundation (EA)
MMF .... National Association of Master Mechanics and Foremen of Naval Shore Establishments
MMFA......... Fireman Apprentice, Machinist's Mate, Striker [*Navy rating*]
MMFC.......... Michael Murphy Fan Club (EA)
MMFCC........ Master of Marriage, Family and Child Counseling (GAGS)
MMFCG........ Maintenance Management Functional Coordinating Group [*Army*]

MMFC-MF....	Marilyn Monroe Fan Club - Marilyn Forever (EA)
MMFCS.......	Multi-Missile Fire Control System [*Military*]
MMFD..........	Micromicrofarad (GPO)
MMFITB......	Man-Made Fibres Producing Industry Training Board [*British*] (BI)
MMFM........	Modified Modified Frequency Modulation (NITA)
MMFN.........	Fireman, Machinist's Mate, Striker [*Navy rating*]
MMFO.........	Maintenance Management Field Office [*Military*] (MCD)
MMFO.........	Material Management Field Office
MMFPA.......	Man-Made Fiber Producers Association [*Later, MMFPAI*] (EA)
MMFPAI......	Man-Made Fiber Producers Association, Inc. (EA)
MMFPB.......	Mill Mutual Fire Prevention Bureau [*Defunct*] (EA)
MMFR.........	Maximal Midflow Rate [*Medicine*] (MAE)
MMFR.........	Maximum Midexpiratory Flow Rate [*Physiology*]
MMFS.........	Manufacturing Message Format Service (NITA)
MMFS.........	Manufacturing Messaging Format Standards [*Automotive engineering*]
MMFT.........	Master of Marriage and Family Therapy (GAGS)
MMFV........	Manned Mars Flyby Vehicle [*Aerospace*]
MMG..........	Machinist's Mate, Industrial Gas Generating Mechanic [*Navy rating*]
MMG..........	MacMillan Gold [*Vancouver Stock Exchange symbol*]
MMG..........	Magdalena Milpas Altas [*Guatemala*] [*Seismograph station code, US Geological Survey*] (SEIS)
MMG..........	Mean Maternal Glucose [*Clinical chemistry*]
MMG..........	Mechanomyography [*Medicine*]
MMG..........	Medium Machine Gun
MMG..........	Metromedia International Group [*AMEX symbol*] (SAG)
MMG..........	Metromedia Intl Grp [*AMEX symbol*] (TTSB)
MMG..........	Motor Machine Gun Corps [*British military*] (DMA)
MMG..........	Motor-Motor Generator [*Nuclear energy*] (NRCH)
MMG..........	Mount Magnet [*Australia Airport symbol*] (OAG)
MMG..........	Movie Makers Guild (EA)
MMG..........	Multimode Guidance (MCD)
MMGA	Mannequin and Models' Guild of Australia
MMGB........	Motor Machine Gun Battalion [*British military*] (DMA)
MMGC........	Mego Mortgage Corp. [*NASDAQ symbol*] (SAG)
MMGI.........	Member of the Mining, Geological, and Metallurgical Institute of India
MMGL.........	Guadalajara/Miguel Hidalgo Y Costilla Internacional [*Mexico ICAO location identifier*] (ICLI)
MMGM.......	Guaymas/General Jose Maria Yanez Internacional [*Mexico ICAO location identifier*] (ICLI)
M Mgmt......	Master of Management (PGP)
MMGS........	Motor Machine Gun Service [*British military*] (DMA)
MMGT........	Guanajuato [*Mexico ICAO location identifier*] (ICLI)
MMgt.........	Master of Management
M Mgt........	Master of Management (PGP)
MMGT........	Medical Management, Inc. [*NASDAQ symbol*] (SAG)
MMgtEng	Master of Management Engineering (NADA)
MMh	Abbot Public Library Marblehead, Ma [*Library symbol*] [*Library of Congress*] (LCLS)
MMH..........	Macromicromodular Hyperplasia [*Medicine*]
MMH..........	Maintenance Man-Hours (NG)
MMH..........	Mammoth Lakes [*California*] [*Airport symbol*] (OAG)
MMH..........	Mammoth Lakes, CA [*Location identifier FAA*] (FAAL)
MMH..........	Maplex Management & Holdings Ltd. [*Toronto Stock Exchange symbol*]
MMH..........	Master of Management in Hospitality (PGP)
MMH..........	Master of Medical Humanities (PGP)
MMH..........	Methylmercuric Hydroxide [*Organic chemistry*]
MMH..........	Mikromatika Air Cargo Ltd. [*Hungary ICAO designator*] (FAAC)
MM/H........	Millimeters per Hour
MMH..........	Monomethylhydrazine [*Organic chemistry*]
MMH..........	Multimode Hydrophone [*Military*] (CAAL)
MMHA	Metropolitan Mutual Housing Association [*Defunct*] (EA)
MMHC	Tehuacan [*Mexico ICAO location identifier*] (ICLI)
MMH/FH	Maintenance Man-Hours per Flight Hours
mmHg........	Millimeters of Mercury [*A measurement of pressure*] (KSC)
MMhHi.......	Marblehead Historical Society, Marblehead, MA [*Library symbol Library of Congress*] (LCLS)
MMHi.........	Milton Historical Society, Milton, MA [*Library symbol Library of Congress*] (LCLS)
MMHIO.......	Midwest Migrant Health Information Office (EA)
MMH/MA	Mean Manhours per Maintenance Action
MMHO	Hermosillo/Internacional [*Mexico ICAO location identifier*] (ICLI)
MMH/OH....	Maintenance Man-Hours per Operating Hours (MCD)
MMHQ	Meta-Methoxyhydroquinone [*Organic chemistry*]
MMHR.......	Maintenance Man-Hours
MMHR/FH...	Maintenance Man-Hours per Flight Hours (MCD)
MMH/S.......	Maintenance Man-Hours per Sortie [*Aerospace*] (MCD)
MMHS.......	Mechanized Materials Handling System [*Air Force*]
MMHSRA.....	Marine Mammal Health and Stranding Response Act
MMI...........	Athens, TN [*Location identifier FAA*] (FAAL)
MMI...........	Macrophage Migration Inhibition [*Cytology*]
MMI...........	Main Memory Interface (NITA)
MMI...........	Major Market Index
MMI...........	Management and Maintenance Inspection (NVT)
MMI...........	Management of Motives Index [*Test*]
MMI...........	Man-Machine Interaction (NITA)
MMI...........	Man-Machine Interface
MMI...........	Manpower Management Information
MMI...........	Manufacturing Message Interface [*Data communications standards*]
MMI...........	Martin Marietta International
MMI...........	Materials Management Institute
MMI...........	Mature Market Institute [*An association Defunct*] (EA)
MMI...........	Mean Motility Index [*For intestine*]
MMI...........	Mechanized Manufacturing Information

MMI	Medicus Mundi Internationalis [*International Organization for Cooperation in Health Care - IOCHC*] [*Nijmegen, Netherlands*] (EAIO)
MMI	Methylmercaptoimidazole [*Also, METHIMAZOLE*] [*Thyroid inhibitor*]
MMI	Michigan Molecular Institute, Inc. [*Formerly, Midland Macromolecular Institute*] [*Research center*] (RCD)
MMI	Micromagnetic Industries
MMI	Middle Management Institute [*Special Libraries Association*]
MMI	Midland Macromolecular Institute [*Midland, MI*]
MMI	Mild [*or Minimal*] Memory Impairment [*Medicine*]
MMI	Minnesota Mining & Manufacturing Co., St. Paul, MN [*OCLC symbol*] (OCLC)
MMI	MMI Companies [*NYSE symbol*] (SPSG)
MMI	Mode-Media Interaction (MCD)
MMI	Modified Mercalli Intensity [*Earthquake magnitude*] [*Seismology*]
MMI	Money Management Institute [*Commercial firm*] (EA)
MMI	Monolithic Memories, Inc. [*Computer science*]
MMI	Montana Myotis Leukoencephalitis [*Virus*]
MMI	MSFC [*Marshall Space Flight Center*] Management Instruction [*NASA*]
MMI	Multi-Message Interface (NITA)
MMI	Multiport Memory Interface [*Computer science*] (MHDB)
MMI	Mutual Mortgage Insurance Fund [*FHA*] (EMRF)
MMIA	Colima [*Mexico ICAO location identifier*] (ICLI)
MMIA	Medical Malpractice Insurance Association
MMIA	Military Mission to the Italian Army [*World War II*]
MMIB	Man-Machine Integration Branch [*Ames Research Center*] [*NASA*]
MMIC	Maintenance Management Information and Control (MCD)
M Mic	Master of Microbiology
MMIC	Millimeter/Microwave Integrated Circuit
MMIC	Miniature Microwave Integrated Circuit
MMIC	Monolithic Microwave Integrated Circuit
MMI CoS	MMI Companies [*Associated Press*] (SAG)
MMICS	Maintenance Management Information and Control System
MMID	Merida [*Mexico ICAO location identifier*] (ICLI)
MMidwif	Master of Midwifery
M Mi E	Master of Mining Engineering
MMiEng	Master of Mining Engineering (NADA)
MMIF	Mutual Mortgage Insurance Fund [*Federal Housing Administration*]
MMIFC	Marilyn Monroe International Fan Club (EA)
MMIHS	Megacystis-Microcolon-Intestinal Hypoperistalsis Syndrome [*Medicine*] (DMAA)
MMII	Mass Marketing Insurance Institute (EA)
MMII	Multimedia Individualized Instruction [*Army*]
MMIIL	Multi-Input Multi-Output Integrated Injection Logic (IAA)
MMIIP	Multimedia Individualized Instructional Package [*Army*]
MMIJ	Mining and Materials Processing Institute of Japan
MMIlt	Milton Public Library, Milton, MA [*Library symbol Library of Congress*] (LCLS)
MMIltC........	Curry College, Milton, MA [*Library symbol Library of Congress*] (LCLS)
MMIM	Isla Mujeres [*Mexico ICAO location identifier*] (ICLI)
M Min	Master of Ministries (PGP)
MMinMgt.....	Master of Mining Management
MMIO	Saltillo [*Mexico ICAO location identifier*] (ICLI)
MMIP	Maintenance Management Improvement Program (MCD)
MMIP	Manual of Meat Inspection Procedures [*of the USDA*]
MMIPS	Man-Machine Interactive Processing System (PDAA)
MMIPS	Multiple Mode Integrated Propulsion System (PDAA)
MMIRC	Mind-Machine Interaction Research Center [*University of Florida*] [*Research center*] (RCD)
MMIS	Maintenance Management Information System [*Military*] (AFM)
MMIS	Master of Management Information Systems (GAGS)
MMIS	Medicaid Management Information System [*HEW*]
MMIS	Multinational Meetings Information Services BV [*Netherlands Information service or system*] (IID)
MMIS	Municipal Management Information System [*Civil Defense*]
M Miss	Master of Missiology (PGP)
MMIT	Iztepec [*Mexico ICAO location identifier*] (ICLI)
MMIT	Man-Machine Interrogation Technique
MMIU	Multi-Part Memory Interface Unit (NITA)
MMIU	Multiport Memory Interface Unit
MMJ	Main Metering Jet [*Automotive engineering*]
MMJ	Matsumoto [*Japan*] [*Airport symbol*] (OAG)
MMJ	Pittsburgh, PA [*Location identifier FAA*] (FAAL)
MMJA	Jalapa [*Mexico ICAO location identifier*] (ICLI)
MMJC	Meridian Municipal Junior College [*Mississippi*]
MMJP	Main Metering Jet-Primary [*Automotive engineering*]
MMJS	Main Metering Jet-Secondary [*Automotive engineering*]
MMK	Loparskaya [*Formerly, Murmansk*] [*Former USSR Geomagnetic observatory code*]
MMK	Maison Master Keyed [*Locks*] (ADA)
MMK	Marshall-Marchetti-Krantz [*Procedure*] [*Medicine*] (MEDA)
MMK	Marshall-Marchetti-Krantz [*Cystourethropexy*] [*Medicine*] (DAVI)
MMK	Material Mark
MMK	Meriden, CT [*Location identifier FAA*] (FAAL)
MMK	Murmansk [*Former USSR Airport symbol*] (OAG)
MMKR	Middle Marker [*in an instrument landing system*]
MML	Maintenance Management Level [*Military*]
MML	Managing the Modern Laboratory [*A publication*]
MML	Man-Machine Language [*Computer science*] (TEL)
MML	Manual of Military Law [*British*]
MML	Marshall [*Minnesota*] [*Airport symbol*] (OAG)
MML	Marshall, MN [*Location identifier FAA*] (FAAL)
MML	Master Measurements List (NASA)

MML............	Master of Modern Languages
MML............	McKinley Memorial Library, Niles, OH [*OCLC symbol*] (OCLC)
MML............	Menika Mining Ltd. [*Vancouver Stock Exchange symbol*]
MML............	Merrill Lyn 6.50%'STRYPES' [*NYSE symbol*] (TTSB)
MML............	Merrill Lynch & Co. [*NYSE symbol*] (SAG)
MML............	Metal-Metal Laminate
MML............	Micromedia Ltd. [*ACCORD*] [*UTLAS symbol*]
mM/L..........	Millimole/Liter [*Chemistry*]
MML............	Mote Marine Laboratory (NOAA)
MML............	Motor Movement Latency
MML............	Multimaterial Laminate
MMLA..........	Midwest Modern Language Association (BARN)
MMLA..........	Military Mission of Liaison Administration [*World War II*]
MMLC..........	Lazaro Cardenas [*Mexico ICAO location identifier*] (ICLI)
MMLD..........	Merchant Mariners Licensing and Documentation [*BTS*] (TAG)
MMLE..........	Modified Maximum Likelihood Estimates [*Statistics*]
MMLEC........	Munitions Management and Labour Efficiency Committee [*British World War II*]
MMLES........	Map-Matching Location - Estimation System [*Aviation*]
MMLL..........	Michigan Regional Libraries Film Program at Cadillac [*Library network*]
MMLM.........	Los Mochis [*Mexico ICAO location identifier*] (ICLI)
MMLME.......	Mediterranean, Mediterranean Littoral, and/or Middle East
MMLO.........	Leon [*Mexico ICAO location identifier*] (ICLI)
MMLP..........	La Paz/General Manuel Marquez de Leon Internacional [*Mexico ICAO location identifier*] (ICLI)
MMLS..........	Military Microwave Landing System (MCD)
M-M-L-S......	Model-Modes-Loads-Stresses (NASA)
MMLS..........	Model-Modes-Loads-Stresses
MMLSA........	Military Microwave Landing System, Avionics (DWSG)
MMLT..........	Loreto [*Mexico ICAO location identifier*] (ICLI)
MMLV..........	Moloney Murine Leukaemia Virus [*Medicine*] (BABM)
M-MLV........	Moloney Murine Leukemia Virus
MMLV..........	Moloney Murine Leukemia Virus [*of mice*] [*Veterinary medicine*] (DAVI)
MMM...........	Aviation Co. Meridian [*Former USSR*] [*FAA designator*] (FAAC)
MMM...........	Maine Maritime Academy, Castine, ME [*OCLC symbol*] (OCLC)
MMM...........	Maintenance and Material Management [*Navy*]
MMM...........	Maintenance Management Manual
MMM...........	Maintenance Man-Minute
MMM...........	Manned Maneuvering Module [*Aerospace*] (IIA)
MMM...........	Manned Mars Mission [*NASA*]
MMM...........	Margaret Morris Movement [*British*] (BI)
MMM...........	Marine & Aviation Management International [*British ICAO designator*] (FAAC)
MMM...........	Marine Multipurpose Missile (DNAB)
MMM...........	Mark Master Mason [*Freemasonry*]
MMM...........	Mars Mission Module
MMM...........	Mass Media Ministries [*An association*]
MMM...........	Master in Media Management
MMM...........	Master of Management in Manufacturing (PGP)
MMM...........	Master of Medical Management (PGP)
MMM...........	Master of Ministry Management (PGP)
MMM...........	Material Maintenance Management (MCD)
MMM...........	McAdam Resources, Inc. [*Toronto Stock Exchange symbol*]
MMM...........	Measuring Monitoring Module (KSC)
MMM...........	Medical Materiel Manager [*Military*] (AABC)
MMM...........	Medical Missionaries of Mary [*Roman Catholic women's religious order*]
MMM...........	Member of the Order of Military Merit
MMM...........	Member of the Order of Military Merit [*Canada*] (DD)
MMM...........	Mesocale and Microscale Meteorology (GNE)
mmm...........	Micromillimeter (WGA)
MMM...........	Middle Management Module
MMM...........	Middlemount [*Australia Airport symbol*] (OAG)
MMM...........	Militia Mea Multiplex [*Pseudonym used by William Tooke*]
mmm...........	Millimicron [*Microscopy*] (CPH)
MMM...........	Minnesota Min'g/Mfg [*NYSE symbol*] (TTSB)
MMM...........	Minnesota Mining & Manufacturing Co. [*Also known as 3M Co.*] [*NYSE symbol*] (SPSG)
MMM...........	Minnesota Mining & Manufacturing Co. [*Also known as 3M Co.*] [*Associated Press*] (SAG)
MMM...........	Modern Music Masters Society
MMM...........	Money Market Monitor [*Financial Products Group*] [*Information service or system*] (IID)
MMM...........	Monomethylmetoxuron [*Organic chemistry*]
MMM...........	Mormon Mesa, NV [*Location identifier FAA*] (FAAL)
MMM...........	Mouvement Militant Mauricien [*Mauritian Militant Movement*] [*Political party*] (PPW)
MMM...........	Mouvement Mondial des Meres [*World Movement of Mothers - WMM*] [*Paris, France*] (EAIO)
MMM...........	Multigrid Modulator Multiplier
MMM...........	Multimission Module [*Aerospace*]
MMM-S........	Multimode Mode Matrix (MCD)
MMM...........	Myelofibrosis and Myeloid Metaplasia [*Hematology*]
MMM...........	Myelosclerosis with Myeloid Metaplasia [*Medicine*] (MAE)
MMMA.........	Matamoros Internacional [*Mexico ICAO location identifier*] (ICLI)
MMMA.........	Metalforming Machinery Makers Association [*British*] (DBA)
MMMA.........	Milking Machine Manufacturers Association [*British*] (DBA)
MMMA.........	Music Masters and Mistresses Association (AIE)
MMMC.........	Medical Materiel Management Center [*Military*] (AABC)
MMMC.........	Milking Machine Manufacturers Council (EA)
MMMC.........	Minimum Monthly Maintenance Charge (MHDW)
MMMD.........	Merida/Lic. Manuel Crecencio Rejon Internacional [*Mexico ICAO location identifier*] (ICLI)

MMME.........	Martin Marietta Missile Electronics Division [*Military*]
MMME.........	Master of Metallurgical and Materials Engineering (PGP)
MMMEP.......	Military Manpower Management Evaluation Project (NG)
MMMF.........	Man-Made Mineral Fiber
MMMF.........	Money Market Mutual Fund [*Investment term*]
MMMF.........	Multinational Mixed Manned Force (NATG)
MMMFS.......	Money Market Mutual Fund Shares [*Investment term*]
MMMI..........	Meat Machinery Manufacturers Institute (EA)
MMMIS........	Maintenance and Material Management Information System
MMML.........	Mexicali/General Rodolfo Sanchez Taboada Internacional [*Mexico ICAO location identifier*] (ICLI)
MMMM........	Man, Material, Machinery, Methods [*Statistical process control*]
MMMM........	Morelia [*Mexico ICAO location identifier*] (ICLI)
MMMN........	[*The*] Memorial of Moses on Mount Nebo [*A publication*] (BJA)
MMMOS.......	Mobile Micrometeorological Observation System
MMMPC.......	Maintenance and Material Management Project Center [*Navy*]
MMMR.........	Medical Material Mission Reserve [*Military*] (AABC)
MMMS.........	Maintenance and Material Management System (KSC)
MMMS.........	Martin Marietta Missile System [*Military*]
MMMS.........	Minerals, Metals, and Materials Society (EA)
MMMS-OL....	Medical Materiel Management System-On Line [*Air Force*] (GFGA)
MMMSP.......	Mouvement Militant Mauricien Socialiste Progressiste [*Mauritius Militant Socialist Progressive Movement*] (PPW)
MMMT.........	Malignant Mixed Muellerian Tumor [*Oncology*]
MMMT.........	Minatitlan [*Mexico ICAO location identifier*] (ICLI)
MMMTF.......	Mobilization Materiel Management Task Force
MMMV.........	Monclova [*Mexico ICAO location identifier*] (ICLI)
MMMX........	Mexico/Lic. Benito Juarez Internacional [*Mexico ICAO location identifier*] (ICLI)
MMMY.........	Monterrey/General Mariano Escobedo Internacional [*Mexico ICAO location identifier*] (ICLI)
MMMZ.........	Mazatlan/General Rafael Buelna [*Mexico ICAO location identifier*] (ICLI)
MMn............	Elizabth Taber Library, Marion, MA [*Library symbol*] [*Library of Congress*] (LCLS)
MMN............	Marathon Minerals [*Vancouver Stock Exchange symbol*]
MMN............	Medial Muscle Motoneuron [*Neuroanatomy*]
MMN............	Miami, FL [*Location identifier FAA*] (FAAL)
MMN............	Mismatch Negativity [*Neurophysiology*]
MMN............	Modified Melin-Norkram's Agar [*Microbiology*]
MMN............	Morbus Maculosus Neonatorum [*Medicine*] (DMAA)
MMNA.........	Moto Morini Club of North America (EA)
MMNAFWB...	Master's Men of the National Association of Free Will Baptists (EA)
MMNG.........	Nogales/Internacional [*Mexico ICAO location identifier*] (ICLI)
MMNIC........	Main Mediterranean Naval Intelligence Center [*Navy*]
MMNL.........	Nuevo Laredo [*Mexico ICAO location identifier*] (ICLI)
MMNOM......	Monmouths Nominal [*Software engineering cost model*]
MM(NSW)....	Milk Marketing (New South Wales) [*Australia*]
MMNU.........	Nautla [*Mexico ICAO location identifier*] (ICLI)
MMO...........	Intel Mobile Module [*Computer science*]
MMO...........	Mach Max Operating (GAVI)
MMO...........	Main Meteorological Office
MMO...........	Maio [*Cape Verde Islands*] [*Airport symbol*] (OAG)
MMO...........	Marseilles, IL [*Location identifier FAA*] (FAAL)
M$_{mo}$......	Maximum Operating Mach Number [*Aviation*] (DA)
MMO...........	Medio Mundo [*Nicaragua*] [*Seismograph station code, US Geological Survey*] (SEIS)
MMO...........	Medium Machine Oil (BARN)
MMO...........	Mercantile Marine Office [*or Officer*] [*British*]
MMO...........	Methane Monooxygenase [*An enzyme*]
MMO...........	Micrographics Management Officer (MCD)
MMO...........	Minuteman Ordnance (SAA)
MMO...........	MIPR [*Military Interdepartmental Purchase Request*] Management Office (AFIT)
MMO...........	MMT Resources [*Vancouver Stock Exchange symbol*]
MMO...........	Mobile Module [*Computer science*]
MMO...........	Monarch Machine Tool Co. [*NYSE symbol*] (SPSG)
MMO...........	Monarch Mach Tool [*NYSE symbol*] (TTSB)
MMO...........	Music Minus One [*Recording label*]
MMOA.........	Maxillary Mandibular Odentectomy Alveolectomy [*Dentistry*] (DAVI)
MMOA.........	Mobile Modular Office Association (EA)
MMOAG......	Research Station, Agriculture Canada [*Station de Recherches, Agriculture Canada*] Morden, Manitoba [*Library symbol National Library of Canada*] (NLC)
MMOB.........	Military Money Order Branch (AFM)
MMOBCD....	Millions of Octane-Barrels per Calendar Day [*Petroleum industry*]
MMOD.........	Micromodule (IEEE)
MMODE.......	Mirror Mode (MCD)
MMODS......	Master Material Ordering and Delivery Schedule (DNAB)
MMOECB....	Maintenance Mode Operational Equipment Checkout Box (MCD)
MMOG........	Merchant Marine Officers Guild [*Defunct*] (EA)
mmol..........	Millimole [*Mass*]
MMoL.........	Myelomonoblastic Leukemia [*Medicine*] (DMAA)
mmol/l........	Millimole per Liter [*Measurement*] (DAVI)
MMONS......	Methyl-methoxy-nitrostilbene [*Organic chemistry*]
MMOS........	Message Multiplexer Operating System
MMOS........	Mobile Micrometeorological Observation System (KSC)
MMOS........	Multicomputing Multitasking Operating System (NITA)
MMOS........	Multimode Optical Sensor (NASA)
MMOU........	Multilateral Memorandum of Understanding
MMOW........	Morden-Winkler Regional Library, Morden, Manitoba [*Library symbol National Library of Canada*] (NLC)
MMOW........	South Central Regional Library, Morden, Manitoba [*Library symbol National Library of Canada*] (NLC)
MMOX.........	Oaxaca [*Mexico ICAO location identifier*] (ICLI)

MMP........... AMP, Inc. [FAA designator] (FAAC)
MMP........... International Organization of Masters, Mates, and Pilots (EA)
MMP........... Machined Metal Part
MMP........... Magnetospheric Multiprobe (SSD)
MMP........... Magnetotactic, Many-Celled Prokaryote [Biology]
MMP........... Magyar Megujulas Partja [Party of Hungarian Renewal] [Political party] (PPE)
MMP........... Maintenance Management Plan
MMP........... Maintenance Message Process [Telecommunications] (TEL)
MMP........... Maintenance Monitor Panel (MCD)
MMP........... M & M Porcupine Gold Mines [Vancouver Stock Exchange symbol]
MMP........... Manufacturing Methods Procedure (MCD)
MMP........... Marian Movement of Priests (EA)
MMP........... Maritime Mobile Phone
MMP........... Mashonaland Mounted Police [British military] (DMA)
MMP........... Master Mobilization Plan [DoD]
MMP........... Master Music Printers and Engravers Association (DGA)
MMP........... Master of Marine Policy (GAGS)
MMP........... Master of Museum Practice (GAGS)
MMP........... Master of Music Performance (PGP)
MMP........... Matabeleland Mounted Police [British military] (DMA)
MMP........... Matrix Metalloproteinase [An enzyme]
MMP........... Maxim Pharmaceuticals, Inc. [AMEX symbol] (SAG)
MMP........... Merchant Marine Personnel Division [Coast Guard]
MMP........... Methadone Maintenance Program
MMP........... Methyl-D-Mannopyranoside [Organic chemistry]
MMP........... Microprogrammable Multiprocessor (MCD)
MMP........... Microsatelite Mutator Phenotype [Oncology]
MMP........... Microsatellite Mutator Phenotype [Cytology]
MMP........... Military Mounted Police
MMP........... Minimum Miscibility Pressure [Physical chemistry]
MMP........... Missile Mode Panel (MCD)
mmp........... Mixed Melting Point [Chemistry]
MMP........... Modernization Management Plan
MMP........... Modes in Math Project [National Science Foundation]
MMP........... Modular Midcourse Package [DoD]
MMP........... Momentum Management Program [NASA] (KSC)
MMP........... Mompos [Colombia] [Airport symbol] (OAG)
MMP........... Money Market Preferred Stock [Investment term]
MMP........... Monitoring/Metering Panel [Telecommunications] (OA)
MMP........... Mortar Master Plan [Military] (INF)
MMP........... Mount Mary [New Zealand] [Seismograph station code, US Geological Survey] (SEIS)
MMP........... Multiplexed Message Processor
MMPA......... Magnetic Materials Producers Association (EA)
MMPA......... Magnetic Materials Products Association (AAGC)
MMPA......... Marine Mammals Protection Act [1972]
MMPA......... Poza Rica [Mexico ICAO location identifier] (ICLI)
MMPAS....... Mobilization Manpower Policy Analysis [Military]
MMPB......... Manpower Management Planning Board
MMPB......... Puebla [Mexico ICAO location identifier] (ICLI)
MMPC......... Maritime Mobile Phone Coastal
MMPC......... Market Milk Producers' Council [Australia]
MMPC......... Mobilization Material Procurement Capability
MMPC......... Pachuca [Mexico ICAO location identifier] (ICLI)
MMPD......... Material Movement Priority Designator (DNAB)
MMPD......... Methoxy-Meta-Phenylenediamine [Organic chemistry]
MMPD......... Money Manager Profile Diskettes [Investment Management Institute] [Information service or system] (IID)
MMPDABC... Medical Materiel Program for Defense Against Biological and Chemical Agents [Army] (AABC)
MMPDC...... Maritime Mobile Phone Distress and Calling
MMPDS....... Methoxy-Meta-Phenylenediamine Sulfate [Organic chemistry]
MMPE......... Punta Penasco [Mexico ICAO location identifier] (ICLI)
MMPF......... Master Military Pay File (AABC)
MMPF......... Microgravity and Materials Processing Facility
MMPG........ Piedras Negras [Mexico ICAO location identifier] (ICLI)
MMPI......... Marquest Medical Products, Inc. [NASDAQ symbol] (NQ)
MMPI......... McGill-Melzack Pain Index [Questionnaire and Home Life Change Index] (DAVI)
MMPI......... Minnesota Multiphasic Personality Inventory [Psychology]
MMPI......... Montgomery Medical and Psychological Institute (EA)
MMPI......... Marquest Medical Products [NASDAQ symbol] (TTSB)
MMPM........ Multimedia Presentation Manager [IBM Corp.] (PCM)
MMPN........ Uruapan [Mexico ICAO location identifier] (ICLI)
MMPNC...... Medical Materiel Program for Nuclear Casualties [Army] (AABC)
MMPP........ Mechanized Market Programming Procedures [Computer science] (TEL)
mmpp......... Millimeters Partial Pressure
MMPPPA.... Medicare and Medicaid Patient and Program Protection Act
MMPR........ Methylmercaptopurine Ribose [Biochemistry]
MMPR........ Missile Manufacturer's Planning Report
MMPR........ Puerto Vallarta/Lic. Gustavo Dias Ordaz Internacional [Mexico ICAO location identifier] (ICLI)
MMPS......... Manufacturing Material Planning System (MHDB)
MMPS......... Manufacturing Message Format System
MMPS......... Medical Media Production Service [Commercial firm] (DAVI)
MMPS......... MEECN Message Processing System [Military]
MMPS......... Puerto Escondido [Mexico ICAO location identifier] (ICLI)
MMPSE....... Multiuse Mission Payload Support Equipment (MCD)
MMPT......... Man-Machine Partnership Translation [Telecommunications] (IEEE)
MMPT......... Monitored and Modulated Periodontal Therapeutics [Dentistry]
mm-PTH...... Mid-Molecule Parathyroid Hormone [Endocrinology] (DAVI)
MMPU........ Memory Manager and Protect Unit (IEEE)
MMPVS....... Modified Military Pay Voucher System (AABC)

MMQ........... Minimum Manufacturing Quality
MMQT......... Queretaro [Mexico ICAO location identifier] (ICLI)
MMR........... Austin, TX [Location identifier FAA] (FAAL)
MMR........... Machinist's Mate, Refrigeration [Navy rating]
MMR........... Mach Meter Reading (MCD)
MMR........... Magnetically-Modulated Microwave Reflection [Spectrometer]
MMR........... Magnetic Memory Record (NITA)
MMR........... Maine State Department of Marine Resources, West Boothbay Harbor, ME [OCLC symbol] (OCLC)
MMR........... Main Memory Register
MMR........... Maintenance Management Review (MCD)
MMR........... Management Milestone Records [Navy] (NG)
MMR........... Mass Miniature Radiography
MMR........... Master Microfiche Record
MMR........... Master of Marketing Research (GAGS)
MMR........... Materiel Management Review [DoD]
MMR........... Maternal Mortality Rate [Gynecology]
MMR........... Mean Motion Resonance [Astrophysics]
MMR........... Measles-Mumps-Rubella [Immunology]
MMR........... Merchant Marine Reserve (DNAB)
MMR........... Method of Mixed Ranges (PDAA)
MMR........... Midline Malignant Reticulosis [Hematology] (DAVI)
MMR........... Military Media Review [A publication] (DNAB)
MMR........... Miniature Micropower Resistor
MMR........... Minimum Marginal Return
MMR........... Minnedosa Regional Library, Minnedosa, Manitoba [Library symbol National Library of Canada] (NLC)
MMR........... Mismatch Repair [Genetics]
MMR........... Missed Message Rate (CAAL)
MMR........... Mitchell's Maritime Register [England] [A publication] (DLA)
MMR........... Mixed Municipal Refuse
MMR........... Mobile Mass X-Ray (MAE)
MMR........... Mobilization Materiel Requirement [Military]
MMR........... Modular Multiband Radiometer
MMR........... Monomethylolrutin [Organic chemistry]
MMR........... Monroe Mendelsohn Research, Inc. [Information service or system] (IID)
MMR........... Monthly Meteorological Records (DNAB)
MMR........... Monumental Maintenance Requirements (MCD)
MMR........... Morris Minor Registry (EA)
MMR........... Motorized Microfilm Reader
MMR........... Multi-Market Radio
MMR........... Multimode RADAR
MMR........... Multimode Radiometer (MCD)
MMR........... Multimode Receiver
MMR........... Multi-Mode Receiver [Navigation systems]
MMR........... Multiple Match Resolver
MMR........... Mumps-Measles-Rubella Vaccine (ECON)
MMR........... Mustang Motorcycle Registry [Defunct] (EA)
MMR........... Myocardial Metabolic Rate [Cardiology] (MAE)
MMRA......... Mobilization Materiel Requirement Adjustment [Military] (NG)
MMR & S ... Military Medical Research and Services Program (CINC)
MMRB .... Maintenance Management Review Board (MCD)
MMRB .... Master Material Review Board (NADA)
MMRB .... Materiel Management Review Board (AFIT)
MMRB .... MOS [Military Occupational Specialty] Medical Retention Board [Army]
MMRBM ..... Mobile Medium-Range Ballistic Missile [Air Force]
MMRC .... Materials and Mechanics Research Center [Army] (MCD)
MMRC .... Mental Retardation Research Center
MMRC .... Mountain Meadow Research Center [Colorado State University] [Research center] (RCD)
M-MRCP ..... Multi-Management Resolution Control Processor
MMRD .... Materials and Molecular Research Division [Lawrence Berkeley Laboratory] [Research center] (RCD)
MMRD .... Miniature Multipurpose RADIAC Device (MCD)
MMRE......... Materials Methods Research and Engineering (MCD)
MMRI......... Macheezmo Mouse Restaurants, Inc. [NASDAQ symbol] (SAG)
MMRI......... Mississippi Mineral Resources Institute [University of Mississippi] [Research center] (RCD)
MMRIM....... Mat Molding Reaction Injection Molding [Plastics technology]
MMRI......... Macheezmo Mouse Restaurants [NASDAQ symbol] (TTSB)
MMRP........ Marine Corps Midrange Objectives Plan (MCD)
MMRP........ Minerals and Materials Research Programs [North Carolina State University] [Research center] (RCD)
MMRP........ Missile Master Replacement Program
MMRR........ Military Manpower Requirements Report (MCD)
MMRRI........ Utah Mining and Minerals Resources Research Institute [University of Utah] [Research center] (RCD)
MMRS........ Manned Military Recovery System (SAA)
MMRX........ Mecdet MPC Corp. [NASDAQ symbol] (SAG)
MMRX........ Mednet MPC [NASDAQ symbol] (TTSB)
MMRX........ Mednet MPC Corp. [NASDAQ symbol] (SAG)
MMRX........ Reynosa/General Lucio Blanco Internacional [Mexico ICAO location identifier] (ICLI)
MMS........... Macbride Museum Society (EA)
MMS........... Machinist's Mate, Shop Mechanic [Navy rating]
MMS........... Macmillan's Manuals for Students [A publication]
MMS........... Magnetic Minesweeping (MSA)
MMS........... Maintenance Management Software
MMS........... Maintenance Management System
MMS........... Man-Machine System (MCD)
MMS........... Manpower Management Staff [NATO] (NATG)
MMS........... Manpower Management System [Marine Corps]

MMS............ Manufacturing Message [*or Messaging*] Specification [*or Standard*] [*Computer science*]
MMS .... Manufacturing Monitoring System [*Computer science*] (IBMDP)
MMS............ Marks, MS [*Location identifier FAA*] (FAAL)
MMS............ Mass Memory Store [*Computer science*] (IEEE)
MMS............ Mass Memory Subsystem [*Aviation*]
MMS............ Master of Management Science (GAGS)
MMS............ Master of Management Studies
MMS............ Master of Marine Science (GAGS)
MMS............ Master of Marketing Science (PGP)
MMS............ Master of Materials Science (GAGS)
MMS............ Master of Mechanical Science
MMS............ Master of Medical Science
MMS............ Master of Modern Studies (PGP)
MMS............ Mast Mounted Sight
MMS............ Mast Mounted Signal (MCD)
MMS............ Matam [*Senegal*] [*Seismograph station code, US Geological Survey Closed*] (SEIS)
MMS............ Maternity and Maternity Services [*British*]
MMS............ Medical Mission Sisters (EA)
MMS............ Member of the Institute of Management Services [*British*] (DBQ)
MMS............ Memory Management System
MMS............ Merchant Management System [*Forman Interactive*] [*Computer science*]
MMS............ Merchant Marine Safety
MMS............ Metabolic Monitoring System
MMS............ Metacaine Methanesulfonate [*Local anesthetic*]
MMS............ Metastable Metal Surface [*Catalyst science*]
MMS............ Meteorological Measuring System
MMS............ Methodist Missionary Society [*British*]
MMS............ Methyl Methanesulfonate [*Experimental mutagen*]
MMS............ Metropolitan Map Series [*Bureau of the Census*] (GFGA)
MMS............ Mexican Meteorological Service
MMS............ Michigan Multispectral Scanner
MMS............ Microfiche Management System
MMS............ Micro Measurement System [*3D Digital Design & Development Ltd.*] [*Software package*] (NCC)
MMS............ Micromembrane Suppressor [*Ion chromatography*]
MMS............ Micro Memory Systems [*NITA*]
MMS............ Middle Meningeal System [*Neuroanatomy*]
MMS............ Military Message Service [*British military*] (DMA)
MM/S........... Millimeters per Second
MMS............ Minerals Management Service [*Department of the Interior Washington, DC*]
MMS............ Mini-Mental State [*Psychometric testing*]
MMS............ Minimum Mean Square (PDAA)
MMS............ Missile Maintenance Squadron (SAA)
MMS............ Missile Mix Study [*NAVAIR*] (NG)
MMS............ Missile Monitor System [*Army*]
MMS............ Mission Modular Spacecraft (MCD)
MMS............ Mississippi County Community College Library, Blytheville, AR [*OCLC symbol*] (OCLC)
MMS............ Mobile Monitoring Station
MMS............ Modular Measuring System
MMS............ Modular Modeling System
MMS............ Modular Multiband Scanner (MCD)
MMS............ Modular Multimission Spacecraft [*NASA*]
MMS............ Modular Multispectral Scanner
MMS............ Mohs' Micrographic Surgery
MMS............ Momentum Management System [*NASA*] (SSD)
MMS............ Money Management System
MMS............ Money Market Services, Inc. [*Belmont, CA*] [*Database producer*]
MMS............ Moravian Missionary Society
MMS............ Motor Minesweeper
MMS............ Multimedia System
MMS............ Multimission Modular Spacecraft [*NASA*] (NASA)
MMS............ Multimission Ship [*DoD*]
MMS............ Multimode Seeker (MCD)
MMS............ Multi-Part Memory System [*Perkin-Elmer*] (NITA)
MMS............ Multiplex Modulation System
MMS............ Municipal Management System (HGAA)
MMS............ Munitions Maintenance and Storage
MMS............ Munitions Maintenance Squadron [*Air Force*]
MMS............ Musical Masterpiece Society [*Record label*] [*USA, Europe*]
MMS............ Myeloma Morphology Score [*Oncology*]
MMSA.......... Man-Machine System Analysis [*Engineering*]
MMSA.......... Manual Molder Shielded Arc
MMSA.......... Master of Midwifery, Society of Apothecaries
MMSA.......... Materials and Methods Standards Association (EA)
MMSA.......... Medical Mycological Society of the Americas (EA)
MMSA.......... Mercantile Marine Service Association [*British*]
MMSA.......... Methods and Materials Standards Association (EA)
MMSA.......... Military Medical Supply Agency [*Later, Defense Medical Supply Center*]
MMSA.......... Mining and Metallurgical Society of America (EA)
MMSA.......... Mitsubishi Motor Sales of America, Inc.
MMSA.......... Multiple-Mission Support Area [*Space Flight Operations Facility, NASA*]
MMSAA........ Metals and Minerals Shippers Association of Australia
MMSB.......... Methyl(methionine)sulfonium Bromide [*Organic chemistry*]
MMSc.......... Master of Management Science (GAGS)
MMSc.......... Master of Marine Science (GAGS)
MM Sc......... Master of Mechanical Science
MM Sc......... Master of Medical Science
MMSc.......... Master of Medical Science (GAGS)

MMSC.......... Mediterranean Marine Sorting Center
MMSC.......... Minnesota Metropolitan State College
MMSC.......... Multimode SONAR Console
MMSCFD ..... Million Standard Cubic Feet per Day
MMSCV........ Manned Military System Capability Vehicle
MMSD .... Mass Memory Storage Device (DWSG)
MMSD .... Mixed Motor and Sensory Deficits [*Neurology*]
MMSD .... Multimode Seeker Deduction (DWSG)
MMSD .... Multiple Minor Symptoms Day [*Environmental medicine*]
MMSD .... San Jose Del Cabo [*Mexico ICAO location identifier*] (ICLI)
MMSE .... Master of Manufacturing Systems Engineering (PGP)
MMSE .... Mini-Mental State Examination [*Psychometrics*]
MMSE .... Minimum Mean Squared Error
MMSE .... Minimum Mean Square Error
MMSE .... Mission Module Simulation Equipment (MCD)
MMSE .... Multiple-Mission Support Equipment [*NASA*]
MMSE .... Multiuse Mission Support Equipment
MMSI .... Merit Medical Systems, Inc. [*NASDAQ symbol*] (SAG)
MMSI .... Multi-Medium Scale Integration (SAA)
MMSIP......... Maintenance Management Systems Improvement Project [*Air Force*] (DOMA)
MMSJ.......... Medical Mobilization for Soviet Jewry (EA)
MMSI .... Merit Medical Systems [*NASDAQ symbol*] (TTSB)
MMSL.......... Microgravity Materials Science Laboratory [*NASA*]
MMSM......... Santa Lucia [*Mexico ICAO location identifier*] (ICLI)
MMSP......... San Luis Potosi [*Mexico ICAO location identifier*] (ICLI)
MMSQ......... Munitions Maintenance Squadron [*Air Force*]
MMSR .... Machinist's Mate, Ship Repair [*Navy rating*]
MMSR .... Master Materiel Support Record
MMSR .... Monthly Materiel Status Report
MMSR .... Multiple-Mission Support Recording [*NASA*]
MMSRC .... Mediterranean Maritime Surveillance and Reconnaissance Center (DNAB)
MMSRE .... Machinist's Mate, Ship Repair, Engine Operator [*Navy rating*]
MMSRI .... Machinist's Mate, Ship Repair, Instrument Maker [*Navy rating*]
MMSRO .... Machinist's Mate, Ship Repair, Outside Machinist [*Navy rating*]
MMSRS .... Machinist's Mate, Ship Repair, Inside Machinist [*Navy rating*]
MMSS .... Manned Maneuverable Space System
MMSS .... Manual Mode Space Simulator
MMSS .... Marine Meteorological Services System [*WMO*] (MSC)
MMSS .... Massachusettssiu Medicinae Societatis Socius [*Fellow of the Massachusetts Medical Society*]
MMSS .... Mast Mounted Sight System (MCD)
M/MSS .... Medicare and Medicaid Statistical Systems (GFGA)
MMSS .... Missile Motion Subsystem
MMSS .... Multimodule Space Station [*NASA*] (KSC)
MM St .... Master of Museum Studies (PGP)
MMST .... Multimode Storage Tube
MM ST .... Muscle Strength (BABM)
mm st .... Muscle Strength [*Neurology*] (DAVI)
MMSTP....... Master Missile System Training Program (SAA)
MMSW........ International Union of Mine, Mill, and Smelter Workers [*Later, USWA*]
MMT .... Alpha-Methyl-m-tyrosine [*Pharmacology*]
MMT .... Columbia, SC [*Location identifier FAA*] (FAAL)
MMT .... Macmillan's Manuals for Teachers [*A publication*]
MMT .... Main Mantle Thrust [*Geology*]
MMT .... Manportable MILSTAR [*Military Strategic and Tactical Relay*] Terminal [*Army*]
MMT .... Manual Muscle Test
MMT .... Manufacturing Methods Technology (AAGC)
MMT .... Marine Minerals Technology [*National Oceanic and Atmospheric Administration*]
MMT .... Maritime Mobile Telegraph
MMT .... Mass Memory Test (NASA)
MMT .... Master of Medical Technology
MMT .... Master of Movement Therapy (GAGS)
MMT .... Master of Music Teaching (GAGS)
MMT .... Math Model Test (MCD)
MMT .... Merchant Marine Technical Division [*Coast Guard*]
MMT .... Metal Mount
MMT .... Methylcyclopentadienyl Manganese Tricarbonyl [*Organic chemistry*]
MMT .... MFS Multimarket Income [*NYSE symbol*] (SPSG)
MMT .... MFS Multimarket Income Trust [*Associated Press*] (SAG)
MMT .... MFS Multimkt Income [*NYSE symbol*] (TTSB)
MMT .... Military Mail Terminal (AFM)
MMT .... Military Maintenance Technician
MMT .... Million Metric Tons (IMH)
MMT .... Miniature Moving Target (MCD)
MMT .... Mini Mobile Target [*Military*] (CAAL)
MMT .... Missile Maintenance Technician (AABC)
MMT .... Missile Mate Test
MMT .... Mobile Maintenance Team (MCD)
MMT .... Modernization Management Team [*Military*] (CAAL)
MMT .... Molten Metal Technology [*Waste management*] (ECON)
MMT .... Monolithic Mirror Telescope
mmt .... Monomethoxytrityl [*As substituent on nucleoside*] [*Biochemistry*]
MMT .... Monthly Mean Temperature [*Meteorology*]
MMT .... Monument Resources [*Vancouver Stock Exchange symbol*]
MMT .... Morse Mission Trainer
mMT .... Mouse Metallothionein [*Biochemistry*]
MMT .... Muenchner Mode-Tage [*Germany*]
MMT .... Multimode Tonotron
MMT .... Multiple-Mirror Telescope [*Mount Hopkins, AZ*] [*Jointly operated by Smithsonian Institution and the University of Arizona Astronomy*]
MMT .... Multiple Mirror Telescope

MMT	Multiple-Mission Telemetry [*NASA*]
MMT	Murine Metallothionein [*Biochemistry*]
MMTA	Mercantile Marine Trawlermen's Association [*A union*] [*British*]
MMTA	Minor Metals Traders' Association [*British*]
MMTA	Tlaxcala [*Mexico ICAO location identifier*] (ICLI)
MMTB	Tuxtla Gutierrez [*Mexico ICAO location identifier*] (ICLI)
MMTC	Marine Minerals Technology Center [*National Oceanic and Atmospheric Administration*]
MMTC	Maritime Mobile Telegraphy Calling
MMTC	Materiel Management Training Center [*Military*]
MMTC	Memtec Ltd. [*NASDAQ symbol*] (SAG)
MMTC	Mouvement Mondial des Travailleurs Chretiens [*World Movement of Christian Workers - WMCW*] [*Brussels, Belgium*] (EAIO)
MMTC	Torreon [*Mexico ICAO location identifier*] (ICLI)
MMTCY	Memtec Ltd ADS [*NASDAQ symbol*] (TTSB)
MMTD	Multimode Tonotron Display
MMTDC	Maritime Mobile Telegraph Distress and Calling
MMTF	Military Manpower Task Force
MMTG	Tuxtla Gutierrez [*Mexico ICAO location identifier*] (ICLI)
MMTJ	Tijuana/General Abelardo L. Rodriguez Internacional [*Mexico ICAO location identifier*] (ICLI)
MMTL	Tulancingo [*Mexico ICAO location identifier*] (ICLI)
M Mtl E	Master of Materials Engineering (PGP)
M Mtl E	Master of Metal Engineering (PGP)
MMTLN	Map Margin Top Line (SAA)
MMT/M	Missile Maintenance Technician/Mechanic (AAG)
MMTM	Multimedia Training Material
MMTM	Tampico/General Francisco Javier Mina Internacional [*Mexico ICAO location identifier*] (ICLI)
MMTN	Tamuin [*Mexico ICAO location identifier*] (ICLI)
MMTO	Missiles Made to Order [*Military*] (RDA)
MMTO	Multiple Mirror Telescope Observatory [*Research center*] (RCD)
MMTO	Toluca [*Mexico ICAO location identifier*] (ICLI)
MMTP	Methadone Maintenance Treatment Program (AAMN)
MMTP	Methyl(methylthio)phenol [*Organic chemistry*]
MMTP	Tapachula [*Mexico ICAO location identifier*] (ICLI)
MMTQ	Tequesquitengo [*Mexico ICAO location identifier*] (ICLI)
MMTR	Mean-Maintenance-Man-Hours to Repair (MCD)
MMTR	Military Manpower Training Report (MCD)
M/MTRG	Main Metering [*Automotive engineering*]
MMTS	Maximum Minimum Temperature System
MMTS	Methyl Methanethiolsulfonate [*Organic chemistry*]
MMTS	Multi-Media Tutorial [*NASDAQ symbol*] (TTSB)
MMTS	Multi-Media Tutorial Services, Inc. [*NASDAQ symbol*] (SAG)
MMTS	Multiple-Mission Telemetry System [*NASA*]
MMTSF	Million Metric Tons of Standard Fuel
MMTSW	Multi-Media Tutorial Wrrt [*NASDAQ symbol*] (TTSB)
MMTT	Mobile Minuteman Train Test (SAA)
MMTT	Multimechanical Thermal Treatment
MMTTU	Modular Magnetic Tape Transport Units (MCD)
MMTV	Mouse Mammary Tumor Virus
MMTX	Tuxpan [*Mexico ICAO location identifier*] (ICLI)
MMTY	Monterrey [*Mexico ICAO location identifier*] (ICLI)
MMU	Main Memory Unit
MMU	Managed Municipal Portfolio [*NYSE symbol*] (SPSG)
MMU	Managed Muni Portfolio [*NYSE symbol*] (TTSB)
MMU	Manchester Metropolitan University [*British*] (AIE)
MMU	Manned Maneuvering Unit [*Aerospace*]
MMU	Mass Memory Unit
M Mu	Master of Music (PGP)
MMu	Master of Music (GAGS)
MMU	Medical Maintenance Unit [*Army World War II*]
MMU	Memory Management Unit [*Computer chip*]
MMU	Memory Mapping Unit (NITA)
MMU	Mercaptomethyl Uracil [*Pharmacology*] (MAE)
MMU	Metered Message Unit [*Telecommunications*] (TEL)
MMU	Midcourse Maneuvering Unit [*Aerospace*] (MCD)
MMU	Midcourse Measurement Unit [*Aerospace*] (KSC)
MMU	Millimass Unit (DEN)
MMU	Million Monetary Units (PDAA)
MMU	Missile Motion Unit
MMU	Mobile Monitoring Unit
MMU	Modular Maneuvering Unit [*Aerospace*]
MMU	Monolithic Memory Unit
MMU	Morristown, NJ [*Location identifier FAA*] (FAAL)
MMU	Multimessage Unit [*Telecommunications*] (TEL)
MMU	University of Missouri, Columbia, Health Sciences Library, Columbia, MO [*OCLC symbol*] (OCLC)
MMUA	Major Mail Users of Australia
MMUC	Mazda Motor Manufacturing USA Corp.
MMUC	Midwest Medical Union Catalog
MMUD	Monolithic Memory Unit Diagnostic
M Mu Ed	Master of Music Education (PGP)
M'Mul Ch SC	M'Mullan's South Carolina Equity Reports [*1840-42*] [*A publication*] (DLA)
M'Mul LSC	M'Mullan's South Carolina Law Reports [*1840-42*] [*A publication*] (DLA)
MMuLV	Moloney Murine Leukemia Virus [*Medicine*] (DMAA)
MMUN	Cancun [*Mexico ICAO location identifier*] (ICLI)
M Mus	Master of Music
MMus	Master of Music (GAGS)
M Mus Ed	Master of Music Education
M Mus (Mus Ed)	Master of Music in Music Education
M Mus (Mus Lit)	Master of Music in Music Literature
M Mus (PSM)	Master of Music in Public School Music

M Mus (RCM)	Master of Music, Royal College of Music
M Mus (W Inst)	Master of Music in Wind Instruments
MMV	Maize Mosaic Virus [*Plant pathology*]
MMV	Mast Mount Visionics (MCD)
MMV	Maubois, Mocquot, and Vassal [*Cheesemaking*]
MMV	McMinnville, OR [*Location identifier FAA*] (FAAL)
MMV	Monostable Multivibrator
mmv	Monostable Multivibrator (IDOE)
MMVA	Villahermosa [*Mexico ICAO location identifier*] (ICLI)
MMVF	Multimedia Video File [*Computer science*]
MMVR	Veracruz/General Heriberto Jara [*Mexico ICAO location identifier*] (ICLI)
MMVS	Mast Mount Visionics System (MCD)
MMW	Main Magnetization Winding [*Telecommunications*] (OA)
MMW	Mean Maximum Weight
MMW	Miami, OK [*Location identifier FAA*] (FAAL)
MMW	Millimeter Wave
MMW	Multimegawatt (SDI)
MMWCS	Multimission Weapons Control System
MMWE	Millimeter Wave Experiment
MMWG	Military Mobilization Working Group
MMX	Mastergroup Multiplex [*AT & T*]
MMX	Matrix Math Extensions (PCM)
MMX	Memory Multiplexer [*Computer science*]
MMX	Micron's Millenia XKU [*Computer science*]
MMX	Miracema do Norte [*Brazil*] [*Airport symbol*] (AD)
MMX	Multimedia Extensions (PCM)
MMY	Many, LA [*Location identifier FAA*] (FAAL)
MMY	Mental Measurements Yearbook [*Psychology A publication*]
MMY	Military Man-Years (AABC)
MMY	Miyakojima [*Japan*] [*Airport symbol*] (OAG)
MMYD	Mental Measurements Yearbook Database [*University of Nebraska, Lincoln*] [*Database*]
MMZ	Maimana [*Afghanistan*] [*Airport symbol Obsolete*] (OAG)
MMZC	Zacatecas [*Mexico ICAO location identifier*] (ICLI)
MMZH	Zihuatanejo [*Mexico ICAO location identifier*] (ICLI)
MMZM	Zamora [*Mexico ICAO location identifier*] (ICLI)
MMZO	Manzanillo [*Mexico ICAO location identifier*] (ICLI)
MMZP	Zapopan [*Mexico ICAO location identifier*] (ICLI)
MMZT	Mazatlan [*Mexico ICAO location identifier*] (ICLI)
MN	Machinery Numeral [*Marine insurance*] (DS)
MN	Madeleine Mines Ltd. [*Toronto Stock Exchange symbol*]
MN	Magnetic North
MN	Main (AAG)
MN	Main
MN	Main Network [*Telecommunications*] (TEL)
MN	Making of the Nations [*A publication*]
MN	Management Network (MCD)
Mn	Manganese [*Chemical element*]
MN	Mantle Nerve
MN	Manual
MN	Manufacturer's Name (NITA)
MN	Manx Airlines Ltd.
MN	Mare Nectaris [*Sea of Nectar*] [*Lunar area*]
MN	Master Navigator [*Air Force*]
MN	Master of Nursing
MN	Material Number
MN	Materiel Needs [*Army*]
MN	Maxim Nordenfelt Gun
Mn	Mean Range [*Difference in height between mean high water and mean low water*] [*Tides and currents*]
MN	Measurement Name (NITA)
MN	Mecanorma [*Graphic artist products*] [*British*]
MN	Medial Interlaminar Nucleus [*Neurology*] (DAVI)
MN	Media Network (EA)
MN	Median Nerve [*Anatomy*]
MN	Meeting Number (NITA)
MN	Meetings Name (NITA)
MN	Meganewton
MN	Meniere's Network [*An association*] (EA)
MN	Meningopneumonitis [*Medicine*]
MN	Merchant Navy
M-N	Merrell-National [*Commercial firm*] (DAVI)
MN	Metanephrine [*Medicine*] (DMAA)
m-N	Meter-Newton
MN	Michigan [*Obsolete*] (ROG)
MN	Micrococcal Nuclease [*Also, MCN*] [*An enzyme*]
M/N	Microcytic/Normochromic [*Anemia*] [*Hematology*] (DAVI)
MN	Microneutralization [*Chemistry*]
MN	Midnight
MN	Migrating Neuron [*Neuroanatomy*]
mN	Millinormal [*One one-thousandth of normal*]
MN	Mineman [*Navy rating*]
MN	Minnesota [*Postal code*]
Mn	Minnesota State Law Library, St. Paul, MN [*Library symbol Library of Congress*] (LCLS)
MN	Minor Subject Descriptor [*Online database field identifier*]
MN	Mission Need
MN	Mnemonic
Mn	Modern [*Linguistics*]
M/N	Moneda Nacional [*National Money*] [*Spanish*]
MN	Mongolia [*ANSI two-letter standard code*] (CNC)
MN	Mononuclear [*Hematology*]
MN	Month Name (BJA)
MN	Moon (ROG)

MN............ Moreh Nebukhim [*Maimonides*] (BJA)
M-N .... Motility Nitrate [*Medium*] [*Medicine*] (BABM)
M-N .... Motility Nitrate [*Medium*] [*Microbiology*] (DAVI)
MN............ Moto Nave [*Motor ship*] [*Latin*] (IIA)
MN............ Motor Neuron [*Anatomy*]
MN............ Mouvement National [*Morocco*] [*Political party*] (EY)
MN............ Movimiento Nacional [*Costa Rica*] [*Political party*] (EY)
MN............ Multinodular [*or Multinodulate*] [*Medicine*]
MN............ Mutato Nomine [*The Name Being Changed*] [*Latin*]
MN............ Myoneural [*Medicine*]
MN1........... Mineman, First Class [*Navy rating*]
MN2........... Mineman, Second Class [*Navy rating*]
MN3........... Mineman, Third Class [*Navy rating*]
MnA........... Aitken Public Library, Aitken, MN [*Library symbol*] [*Library of Congress*] (LCLS)
MNA........... Augsburg College, Minneapolis, MN [*OCLC symbol*] (OCLC)
MNA........... Master Negative Assembly [*Monophoto*] (DGA)
M Na .... Master of Navigation
MNA........... Master of Nonprofit Administration (GAGS)
MNA........... Master of Nurse Anesthesia (PGP)
MNA........... Master of Nursing Administration
MN(A)........ Material Need (Abbreviated) (MCD)
MNA........... Maximum Noise Area
MNA........... Melanguane [*Indonesia*] [*Airport symbol*] (OAG)
MNA........... Melinga Resources Ltd. [*Vancouver Stock Exchange symbol*]
MNA........... Member of the National Assembly [*British*]
MNA........... Member of the National Assembly [*Quebec*] [*Canada*] (BARN)
MNA........... Merpati Nusantara Airlines PT [*Indonesia*] [*ICAO designator*] (FAAC)
MNA........... Meta-Nitroaniline [*Organic chemistry*]
MNA........... Methoxynaphthylamine [*Organic chemistry*]
MNA........... Methylnadic Anhydride [*Organic chemistry*]
MNA........... Methylnitroaniline [*Organic chemistry*]
MNA........... Mina [*Nevada*] [*Seismograph station code, US Geological Survey*] (SEIS)
MNA........... Minnesota Municipal Term Trust [*NYSE symbol*] (SPSG)
MNA........... Minnesota Muni Term Trust [*NYSE symbol*] (TTSB)
MNA........... Missing, Not Enemy Action
MNA........... Mouvement d'Action Politique et Sociale [*Political and Social Action Movement*] [*Switzerland Political party*] (PPW)
MNA........... Mouvement National Algerien [*National Algerian Movement*]
MNA........... Multinetwork Area [*Term used in TV ratings*]
MNA........... Multiple Newsagents Association [*British*] (DBA)
MNA........... Multishare Network Architecture [*Mitsubishi Corp.*] (BUR)
MNA........... Myanmar News Agency (EY)
MNAA .... Molecular Neutron Activation Analysis
MNA,B,C ..... Main Bus A,B, or C (NASA)
MnAbnE ...... Alborn Elementary School, Alborn, MN [*Library symbol*] [*Library of Congress*] (LCLS)
MnAd .... Annandale Public Library, Annandale, MN [*Library symbol*] [*Library of Congress*] (LCLS)
Mn-Ad......... Minnesota State Department of Administration, Budget Library, St. Paul, MN [*Library symbol Library of Congress*] (LCLS)
MnAda .... Ada Public Library, Ada, MN [*Library symbol*] [*Library of Congress*] (LCLS)
MNAdaE...... Ada Elementary School, Ada, MN [*Library symbol*] [*Library of Congress*] (LCLS)
MnAdaH....... Ada High School, Ada, MN [*Library symbol*] [*Library of Congress*] (LCLS)
MnAdBE....... Bendix Elementary School Annandale, MN [*Library symbol*] [*Library of Congress*] (LCLS)
MnAdH........ Annandale High School, Annandale, MN [*Library symbol*] [*Library of Congress*] (LCLS)
MnADM....... Depot Museum, Aitken, MN [*Library symbol*] [*Library of Congress*] (LCLS)
MnAdMS..... Annandale Middle School, Annandale, MN [*Library of Congress*] (LCLS)
MNAEA ...... Member of the National Association of Estate Agents [*British*] (DBQ)
Mn-Ag......... Minnesota Department of Agriculture, St. Paul, MN [*Library symbol Library of Congress*] (LCLS)
MnAJ .... Aitken Jr.-Sr. High School Media Center, Aitken, MN [*Library symbol*] [*Library of Congress*] (LCLS)
MnAkE .... Akeley Elementary School, Akeley, MN [*Library symbol*] [*Library of Congress*] (LCLS)
MnAkH........ Akeley High School, Akeley, MN [*Library symbol*] [*Library of Congress*] (LCLS)
MnAl .... Albany Public Library, Alabany, MN [*Library symbol*] [*Library of Congress*] (LCLS)
MnAlb......... Albert Lea Public Library, Albert Lea, MN [*Library symbol Library of Congress*] (LCLS)
MnAlbeCH ... Chokio-Alberta High School, Alberta, MN [*Library symbol*] [*Library of Congress*] (LCLS)
MnAle .... Alexandria Public Library, Alexandria, MN [*Library symbol*] [*Library of Congress*] (LCLS)
MnAleCJ ..... Central Junior High School, Alexandria, MN [*Library symbol*] [*Library of Congress*] (LCLS)
MnAleDH .... Douglas County Hospital, Health Science Library, Alexandria, MN [*Library symbol*] [*Library of Congress*] (LCLS)
MnAleJH..... Jefferson High School, Alexandria, MN [*Library symbol*] [*Library of Congress*] (LCLS)
MnAleLE ..... Lincoln Elementary School, Alexandria, MN [*Library symbol*] [*Library of Congress*] (LCLS)
MnAleR....... Alexandria Runestone Museum, Alexandria, MN [*Library symbol*] [*Library of Congress*] (LCLS)
MnAleSM .... St. Mary's School, Alexandria, MN [*Library symbol*] [*Library of Congress*] (LCLS)

MnAleTI...... Alexandria Technical Institute, Alexandria, MN [*Library symbol*] [*Library of Congress*] (LCLS)
MnAleWE.... Washington Elementary School, Alexandria, MN [*Library symbol*] [*Library of Congress*] (LCLS)
MnAlFE....... Farming Elementary School, Albany, MN [*Library symbol*] [*Library of Congress*] (LCLS)
MnAlH........ Holy Family School, Albany, MN [*Library symbol*] [*Library of Congress*] (LCLS)
MnAlJ .... Albany Jr. H.S./Elementary Library, Albany, MN [*Library symbol*] [*Library of Congress*] (LCLS)
MnAlmA...... Amador Heritage Center, Almelund, MN [*Library symbol*] [*Library of Congress*] (LCLS)
MnAlS........ Albany Senior High School, Albany, MN [*Library symbol*] [*Library of Congress*] (LCLS)
MnAlSP....... St. Pius V School, Albany, MN [*Library symbol*] [*Library of Congress*] (LCLS)
MnAlvE ...... Albertville Elementary School, Albertville, MN [*Library symbol*] [*Library of Congress*] (LCLS)
MNAM .... Military North African Mission [*World War II*]
MNam........ Nantucket Athenaeum, Nantucket, MA [*Library symbol Library of Congress*] (LCLS)
MnAnA........ Anoka-Ramsey Community College, Anoka, MN [*Library symbol Library of Congress*] (LCLS)
MN & ALOA... Merchant Navy and Air Line Officers' Association [*A union*] [*British*] (DS)
MnAnGS ..... Anoka County Genealogical Society, Anoka, MN [*Library symbol Library of Congress*] (LCLS)
MnAnHi....... Anoka County Historical Society, Anoka, MN [*Library symbol Library of Congress*] (LCLS)
MNanHi ...... Nantucket Historical Association, Nantucket, MA [*Library symbol Library of Congress*] (LCLS)
MNanMM..... Nantucket Maria Mitchell Association, Nantucket, MA [*Library symbol Library of Congress*] (LCLS)
MnAnVT...... Anoka Area Vocational Technical Institute, Anoka, MN [*Library symbol Library of Congress*] (LCLS)
MNanW....... Nantucket Whaling Museum, Nantucket, MA [*Library symbol Library of Congress*] (LCLS)
MNAO .... Mobile Naval Airfield Organization
MNAOA....... Merchant Navy and Air Line Officers' Association [*A union*] [*British*] (DCTA)
MnAp .... Appleton Public Library, Appleton, MN [*Library symbol*] [*Library of Congress*] (LCLS)
MnApH........ Appleton Municipal Hospital, Appleton, MN [*Library symbol*] [*Library of Congress*] (LCLS)
MnApPS...... Appleton Public Schools, Appleton, MN [*Library symbol*] [*Library of Congress*] (LCLS)
MN Arch .... Master of Naval Architecture
MnARE........ Rippleside Elementary School, Rippleside Elementary IMC, Aitken, Mn [*Library symbol*] [*Library of Congress*] (LCLS)
MnArS .... Argyle School, Argyle, MN [*Library symbol*] [*Library of Congress*] (LCLS)
MNAS .... Member of the National Academy of Sciences
MnAsHi...... Pine County Historical Reference Library, Askov, MN [*Library symbol*] [*Library of Congress*] (LCLS)
MnAshS ...... Ashby Public School, Ashby, MN [*Library symbol*] [*Library of Congress*] (LCLS)
MNASSA..... Monthly Notes. Astronomical Society of Southern Africa [*A publication*]
MNASTD ..... Multicultural Network of the American Society for Training and Development (EA)
MnAt.......... Atwater Public Library, Atwater, MN [*Library symbol*] [*Library of Congress*] (LCLS)
MnAtPS....... Atwater-Grove City Public Schools, Atwater, MN [*Library symbol*] [*Library of Congress*] (LCLS)
MNatQ .... United States Quartermaster Research and Development Center, Natick, MA [*Library symbol Library of Congress*] (LCLS)
MNatRes..... Master of Natural Resources (ADA)
MNatSci..... Master of Natural Science (GAGS)
M Nat Sci ... Master of Natural Science (PGP)
MnAtSJS..... St. John's Lutheran School, Atwater, MN [*Library symbol*] [*Library of Congress*] (LCLS)
MnAu .... Austin Public Library, Austin, MN [*Library symbol Library of Congress*] (LCLS)
MNAU .... Mobile Naval Airfield Unit
MnAudS...... Audubon Public School, Audubon, MN [*Library symbol*] [*Library of Congress*] (LCLS)
MnAuH........ Hormel Institute, University of Minnesota, Austin, MN [*Library symbol Library of Congress*] (LCLS)
MnAuPS...... Austin Public Schools Media, Austin, MN [*Library symbol Library of Congress*] (LCLS)
MnAur........ Aurora Public Library, Aurora, MN [*Library symbol*] [*Library of Congress*] (LCLS)
MnAurH...... Mesabi East High School, Aurora,MN [*Library symbol*] [*Library of Congress*] (LCLS)
MnAuS........ Austin State Junior College, Austin, MN [*Library symbol Library of Congress*] (LCLS)
MnAuV........ Austin Vocational Technical Institute, Austin, MN [*Library symbol Library of Congress*] (LCLS)
MnAvoE ...... Avon Elementary School, Avon, MN [*Library symbol*] [*Library of Congress*] (LCLS)
MnAvZ .... Minnesota Zoological Garden, Apple Valley, MN [*Library symbol Library of Congress*] (LCLS)
MnB .... Becker Public Library, Becker Elementary School, Becker, MN [*Library symbol*] [*Library of Congress*] (LCLS)
MNB........... Bemidji State University, Bemidji, MN [*OCLC symbol*] (OCLC)

MNB............ Maldives News Bureau (EY)
MNB............ Maverick Naturalite Beef Corp. [*Vancouver Stock Exchange symbol*]
MNB............ Median Neuroblast [*Cytology*]
MNB............ Minnesota Muni Term Tr-II [*AMEX symbol*] (TTSB)
MNB............ Minnesota Term Trust, Inc. II [*AMEX symbol*] (SAG)
MNB............ Mint No Box [*Doll collecting*]
MNB............ Moanda [*Zaire*] [*Airport symbol*] (OAG)
MNB............ Mobile Naval Base [*British military*] (DMA)
MNB............ Moscow Narodny Bank Ltd. [*Former USSR*]
MNB............ Multinozzle Base
MNB............ Texte de Louvre [*Paris*]: Monuments de Ninive et de Babylone [*A publication*] (BJA)
MnBa .... Balaton Public Library, Balaton, MN [*Library symbol*] [*Library of Congress*] (LCLS)
MNBA .... Minimum Normal Burst Altitude
MNBA .... Mono-normal-butylamine [*Organic chemistry*]
M/NBA .... Multi/National Business Association (EA)
MnBab .... Babbitt Public Library, Babbitt, MN [*Library symbol*] [*Library of Congress*] (LCLS)
MnBabE .... J.F. Kennedy Elementary School, Babbit, MN [*Library symbol*] [*Library of Congress*] (LCLS)
MnBabH .... J.F. Kennedy High School, Babbitt, MN [*Library symbol*] [*Library of Congress*] (LCLS)
MnBacS .... Backus School, Backus, MN [*Library symbol*] [*Library of Congress*] (LCLS)
MnBadS .... Badger School, Badger, MN [*Library symbol*] [*Library of Congress*] (LCLS)
MnBag .... Bagley Public Library, Bagley, MN [*Library symbol*] [*Library of Congress*] (LCLS)
MnBagE .... Bagley Elementary School, Bagley, MN [*Library symbol*] [*Library of Congress*] (LCLS)
MnBaPS .... Balaton Public Schools, Balaton, MN [*Library symbol*] [*Library of Congress*] (LCLS)
MnBar .... Barnesville Public Library, Barnesville, MN [*Library symbol*] [*Library of Congress*] (LCLS)
MnBarFe ...... Florence Atkinson Elementary School, Barnesville, MN [*Library symbol*] [*Library of Congress*] (LCLS)
MnBarH .... Barnesville High School, Barnesville, MN [*Library symbol*] [*Library of Congress*] (LCLS)
MnBaSPL ..... St. Peter's Lutheran School, Balaton, MN [*Library symbol*] [*Library of Congress*] (LCLS)
MnBatS .... Battle Lake Public School, Battle Lake, MN [*Library symbol*] [*Library of Congress*] (LCLS)
MnBau .... Baudette Public Library, Baudette, MN [*Library symbol*] [*Library of Congress*] (LCLS)
MnBauLH ..... Lake of the Woods High School, Baudette, MN [*Library symbol*] [*Library of Congress*] (LCLS)
MnBaxE .... Baxter Elementary School, Baxter, MN [*Library symbol*] [*Library of Congress*] (LCLS)
MNBB .... MNB Bancshares [*NASDAQ symbol*] (SAG)
MNB Bn .... MNB Bancshares [*Associated Press*] (SAG)
MNBDF .... Meta-Nitrobenzenediazonium Tetrafluoroborate [*Organic chemistry*]
MNBDO........ Mobile Naval Base Defence Organization [*British World War II*]
MnBE .... Becker Elementary School, Becker, MN [*Library symbol*] [*Library of Congress*] (LCLS)
MnBeaPS ..... Beardlsey-Brown Valley Public Schools, Beardlsey, MN [*Library symbol*] [*Library of Congress*] (LCLS)
MnBeB .... Bertha-Hweitt School, Bertha, MN [*Library symbol*] [*Library of Congress*] (LCLS)
MNBedf........ New Bedford Free Public Library, New Bedford, MA [*Library symbol Library of Congress*] (LCLS)
MNBedfHi .... Old Dartmouth Historical Society, New Bedford Whaling Museum, New Bedford, MA [*Library symbol Library of Congress*] (LCLS)
MnBelPS ...... Bellingham Public Schools, Bellingham, MN [*Library symbol*] [*Library of Congress*] (LCLS)
MnBem .... Bemidji Public Library, Bemidji, MN [*Library symbol*] [*Library of Congress*] (LCLS)
MnBemCE .... Central Elementary School, Bemidji, MN [*Library symbol*] [*Library of Congress*] (LCLS)
MnBemDE .... Deer Lake Elementary School, Bemidji, MN [*Library symbol*] [*Library of Congress*] (LCLS)
MnBemH...... Bemidji High School, Bemidji, MN [*Library symbol*] [*Library of Congress*] (LCLS)
MnBemHE .... Horace May Elementary School, Bemidji, MN [*Library symbol*] [*Library of Congress*] (LCLS)
MnBemJE .... J.W. Smith Elementary School, Bemidji, MN [*Library symbol*] [*Library of Congress*] (LCLS)
MnBemLE .... Lincoln Elementary School, Bemidji, MN [*Library symbol*] [*Library of Congress*] (LCLS)
MnBemMS... Benidji Middle School, Bemidji, MN [*Library symbol*] [*Library of Congress*] (LCLS)
MnBemNE .... Northern Elementary School, Bemidji, MN [*Library symbol*] [*Library of Congress*] (LCLS)
MnBemOH ... Oak Hills Bible College, Bemidji, MN [*Library symbol*] [*Library of Congress*] (LCLS)
MnBemPE .... Paul Bunyan Elementary School, Bemidji, MN [*Library symbol*] [*Library of Congress*] (LCLS)
MnBemS....... Bemidji State College [*Later, Bemidji State University*], Bemidji, MN [*Library symbol Library of Congress*] (LCLS)
MnBemSE.... Solway Elementary School, Bemidji, MN [*Library symbol*] [*Library of Congress*] (LCLS)
MnBemSP.... St. Philips School, Bemidji, MN [*Library symbol*] [*Library of Congress*] (LCLS)
MnBenPS..... Benson Public Schools, Benson, MN [*Library symbol*] [*Library of Congress*] (LCLS)

MnBenSF .... St. Francis Xavier School, Benson, MN [*Library symbol*] [*Library of Congress*] (LCLS)
MnBevPS .... Belview Public School, Bleview, MN [*Library symbol*] [*Library of Congress*] (LCLS)
MnBf........... Buffalo Public Library, Buffalo, MN [*Library symbol*] [*Library of Congress*] (LCLS)
MnBfaE .... Big Falls Elementary School, Big Falls, MN [*Library symbol*] [*Library of Congress*] (LCLS)
MnBfH .... Buffalo Memorial Hospital, Medical Library, Buffalo, MN [*Library symbol*] [*Library of Congress*] (LCLS)
MnBfHi .... Wright County Historical Society, Buffalo, MN [*Library symbol*] [*Library of Congress*] (LCLS)
MnBfI .... Buffalo Intermediate School, Buffalo, MN [*Library symbol*] [*Library of Congress*] (LCLS)
MnBfJ .... Buffalo Junior High School, Buffalo, MN [*Library symbol*] [*Library of Congress*] (LCLS)
MnBfoS .... Bigfork School, Bigford, MN [*Library symbol*] [*Library of Congress*] (LCLS)
MnBfP .... Buffalo Primary Library, Buffalo, MN [*Library symbol*] [*Library of Congress*] (LCLS)
MnBfS .... Buffalo Senior High School, Buffalo, MN [*Library symbol*] [*Library of Congress*] (LCLS)
MnBfSF .... St. Francis Xavier School, Buffalo, MN [*Library symbol*] [*Library of Congress*] (LCLS)
MnBfW .... Wright Vocational Coop Center, Buffalo, MN [*Library symbol*] [*Library of Congress*] (LCLS)
MnBg.......... Myrtle Mabee Library, Belgrade, MN [*Library symbol*] [*Library of Congress*] (LCLS)
MnBgE .... Belgrade Elementary School, Belgrade, MN [*Library symbol*] [*Library of Congress*] (LCLS)
MnBgH .... Belgrade High School, Media Center, Belgrade, MN [*Library symbol*] [*Library of Congress*] (LCLS)
MnBH.......... Becker High School, Becker, MN [*Library symbol*] [*Library of Congress*] (LCLS)
MnBHi .... Sherbourne County Historical Society, Becker, MN [*Library symbol*] [*Library of Congress*] (LCLS)
MnBhM .... Braham Middle School, Braham, MN [*Library symbol*] [*Library of Congress*] (LCLS)
MnBhSE ...... Southview Elementary School, Braham, MN [*Library symbol*] [*Library of Congress*] (LCLS)
MnBhWH .... Westview High School, Media Center, Braham, MN [*Library symbol*] [*Library of Congress*] (LCLS)
MnBi........... Bird Island Public Library, Bird Island, MN [*Library symbol*] [*Library of Congress*] (LCLS)
MnBirIS .... Indus School, Birchdale, MN [*Library symbol*] [*Library of Congress*] (LCLS)
MnBiSM ...... St. Mary's School, Bird Island, MN [*Library symbol*] [*Library of Congress*] (LCLS)
MnBiwE ...... Bray Elementary School, Biwabik, MN [*Library symbol*] [*Library of Congress*] (LCLS)
MnBiwH ...... V.L. Reishus High School, Biwabik, MN [*Library symbol*] [*Library of Congress*] (LCLS)
MNBK .... Marine National Bank (California) [*NASDAQ symbol*] (SAG)
MNBK .... Marine Nat'l Bank [*NASDAQ symbol*] (TTSB)
MnBkES ...... Blomkest Elementary School, Blomkest, MN [*Library symbol*] [*Library of Congress*] (LCLS)
MNBKW ...... Marine Natl Bk Irvine CA Wrrt [*NASDAQ symbol*] (TTSB)
MnBl........... Big Lake Public Library, Big Lake, MN [*Library symbol*] [*Library of Congress*] (LCLS)
MNBL.......... Bluefields [*Nicaragua*] [*ICAO location identifier*] (ICLI)
MnBla .... Blackduck Public Library, Blackduck, MN [*Library symbol*] [*Library of Congress*] (LCLS)
MnBlaE .... Blackduck Elementary School, Blackduck, MN [*Library symbol*] [*Library of Congress*] (LCLS)
MnBlaH .... Blackduck High School, Blackduck, MN [*Library symbol*] [*Library of Congress*] (LCLS)
MnBlE .... Big Lake Elementary School, Big Lake, MN [*Library symbol*] [*Library of Congress*] (LCLS)
MNBLE........ Modified Nearly Best Linear Estimator [*Statistics*]
MnBlH .... Big Lake High School, Big Lake, MN [*Library symbol*] [*Library of Congress*] (LCLS)
MnBloPS...... Bloomington Public Schools, Bloomington, MN [*Library symbol*] [*Library of Congress*] (LCLS)
MnBmE........ Barnum Elementary School, Barnum, MN [*Library symbol*] [*Library of Congress*] (LCLS)
MnBmH........ Barnum High School, Barnum, MN [*Library symbol*] [*Library of Congress*] (LCLS)
MNBO .... Management Buy-Out
MnBov .... Bovey Public Library, Bovey, MN [*Library symbol*] [*Library of Congress*] (LCLS)
MnBovM ...... Connor-Jasper Middle School, Bovey, MN [*Library symbol*] [*Library of Congress*] (LCLS)
MnBovS ...... Balsam School, Bovey, MN [*Library symbol*] [*Library of Congress*] (LCLS)
MnBr.......... Brainerd Public Library, Brainerd, MN [*Library symbol*] [*Library of Congress*] (LCLS)
MNBR .... Los Brasiles/Carlos Ulloa [*Nicaragua*] [*ICAO location identifier*] (ICLI)
MnBraS........ Brandon Public School, Brandon, MN [*Library symbol*] [*Library of Congress*] (LCLS)
MnBrC .... Brainerd Community College, Brainerd, MN [*Library symbol Library of Congress*] (LCLS)
MnBre......... Breckenridge Public Library, Breckenridge, MN [*Library symbol*] [*Library of Congress*] (LCLS)
MnBreE........ Breckenridge Elementary School, Breckenridge, MN [*Library symbol*] [*Library of Congress*] (LCLS)

MnBreH .... Breckenridge High School, Breckenridge, MN [*Library symbol*] [*Library of Congress*] (LCLS)

MnBrFJ .... Franklin Junior High School, Brainerd, MN [*Library symbol*] [*Library of Congress*] (LCLS)

MnBrGE .... Garfield Elementary School, Brainerd, MN [*Library symbol*] [*Library of Congress*] (LCLS)

MnBrHE .... Harrison Elementary School, Brainerd, MN [*Library symbol*] [*Library of Congress*] (LCLS)

MnBrHS ...... Brainerd High School, Brainerd, MN [*Library symbol*] [*Library of Congress*] (LCLS)

MnBrLE .... Lincoln Elementary School, Brainerd, MN [*Library symbol*] [*Library of Congress*] (LCLS)

MnBrLoE ..... Lowell Elementary School, Brainerd, MN [*Library symbol*] [*Library of Congress*] (LCLS)

MnBro .... Browntown Public Library, Browntown, MN [*Library symbol*] [*Library of Congress*] (LCLS)

MnBroPS ..... Brownton Public Schools, Brownton, MN [*Library symbol*] [*Library of Congress*] (LCLS)

MnBrRE .... Riverside Elementary School, Brainerd, MN [*Library symbol*] [*Library of Congress*] (LCLS)

MnBruE .... Bruno Elementary School, Bruno, MN [*Library symbol*] [*Library of Congress*] (LCLS)

MnBrv .... Carnegie Public Library, Browns Valley, MN [*Library symbol*] [*Library of Congress*] (LCLS)

MnBrvPS ...... Beardsley-Browns Valley Public Schools, Browns Valley, MN [*Library symbol*] [*Library of Congress*] (LCLS)

MnBrWE ...... Whittier Elementary School, Brainerd,MN [*Library symbol*] [*Library of Congress*] (LCLS)

MnBrwES ...... Brewster Elementary School, Brewster, MN [*Library symbol*] [*Library of Congress*] (LCLS)

MnBrWM ..... Washington Middle School, Brainerd, MN [*Library symbol*] [*Library of Congress*] (LCLS)

MnBtH .... Brooten High School, Brooten, MN [*Library symbol*] [*Library of Congress*] (LCLS)

MnBul .... Buhl Public Library, Buhl, MN [*Library symbol*] [*Library of Congress*] (LCLS)

MnBulR .... Range Geneaological Society, Buhl, MN [*Library symbol Library of Congress*] (LCLS)

MnBuS .... St. Michael School, Buckman, MN [*Library symbol*] [*Library of Congress*] (LCLS)

MnBvC .... Christ the King School, Browerville, MN [*Library symbol*] [*Library of Congress*] (LCLS)

MnBvP .... Browerville Public School, Browerville, MN [*Library symbol*] [*Library of Congress*] (LCLS)

MNBZ .... Bonanza [*Nicaragua*] [*ICAO location identifier*] (ICLI)

MNC .... Concordia College, St. Paul, MN [*OCLC symbol*] (OCLC)

MNC .... Magnocellular Neurosecretory Cells

MNC .... Major NATO Command [*or Commander*] (NATG)

MNC .... Mental Nurses' Cooperation (ROG)

MNC .... Microcomputer Numerical Control (MCD)

MNC .... Mineman, Chief [*Navy rating*]

MNC .... Ministerial Nomination Committee [*Australia*]

Mn-C .... Minnesota State Department of Corrections, St. Paul, MN [*Library symbol Library of Congress*] (LCLS)

MNC .... MIT Airlines Ltd. [*ICAO designator*] (FAAC)

MNC .... Moncalieri [*Italy*] [*Seismograph station code, US Geological Survey Closed*] (SEIS)

MNC .... Monica Resources [*Vancouver Stock Exchange symbol*]

MNC .... Mononucleated Cell [*Clinical chemistry*] [*Also, MC*]

MNC .... Mouvement National Congolais [*Congolese National Movement*]

MNC .... Mouvement National du Congo-Lumumba [*Congo National Movement-Lumumba*] [*Zaire*] (PD)

MNC .... Movimiento Nacional Conservador [*National Conservative Movement*] [*Colorado Political party*] (EY)

MNC .... Multinational Company [*Business term*]

MNC .... Multinational Corp.

MNC .... Multiplicative Noise Compensator [*Telecommunications*] (TEL)

MNC .... Nacala [*Mozambique*] [*Airport symbol*] (AD)

MNC .... Shelton, WA [*Location identifier FAA*] (FAAL)

MnCaCC ...... Cambridge Community College, Cambridge, MN [*Library symbol*] [*Library of Congress*] (LCLS)

MnCaE .... East Central Regional Library, Cambridge, MN [*Library symbol Library of Congress*] (LCLS)

MnCaES .... Cambridge Elementary School, Media Center, Cambridge, MN [*Library symbol*] [*Library of Congress*] (LCLS)

MnCaH .... Cambridge Memorial Hospital, Health Sciences Library, Cambridge, MN [*Library symbol*] [*Library of Congress*] (LCLS)

MnCaHi .... Isanti County Historical Society, Cambridge, MN [*Library symbol*] [*Library of Congress*] (LCLS)

MnCaHS ...... Cambridge High School, Media Center, Cambridge, MN [*Library symbol*] [*Library of Congress*] (LCLS)

MnCalE .... Callaway Elementary School, Callaway, MN [*Library symbol*] [*Library of Congress*] (LCLS)

MnCaM .... Cambridge Middle School, Media Center, Cambridge, MN [*Library symbol*] [*Library of Congress*] (LCLS)

MnCamE ...... Campbell-Tintah Elementary School, Campbell, MN [*Library symbol*] [*Library of Congress*] (LCLS)

MnCamH ...... Campbell-Tintah High School, Campbell, MN [*Library symbol*] [*Library of Congress*] (LCLS)

MnCan .... Canby Public Library, Canby, MN [*Library symbol*] [*Library of Congress*] (LCLS)

MnCanH .... Canby Community Hospital, Canby, MN [*Library symbol*] [*Library of Congress*] (LCLS)

MnCanHS .... Canby High School, Canby, MN [*Library symbol*] [*Library of Congress*] (LCLS)

MnCarE .... Carlos Elementary School, Carlos, MN [*Library symbol*] [*Library of Congress*] (LCLS)

MnCas .... Cass Lake Community Library, Lake, MN [*Library symbol*] [*Library of Congress*] (LCLS)

MnCasCB .... Chief Bug-O-Nay-Ge-Shig Library, Cass Lake, MN [*Library symbol*] [*Library of Congress*] (LCLS)

MnCaSD ...... Cambridge Seventh Day Adventist Library, Cambridge, MN [*Library symbol*] [*Library of Congress*] (LCLS)

MnCasE .... Cass Lake Elementary School, Cass Lake, MN [*Library symbol*] [*Library of Congress*] (LCLS)

MnCaSH ...... Cambridge State Hospital, Staff Library, Cambridge, MN [*Library symbol*] [*Library of Congress*] (LCLS)

MnCasHS .... Cass Lake High School, Cass Lake, MN [*Library symbol*] [*Library of Congress*] (LCLS)

MNCC .... Multinational Coordination Center [*NATO*]

MnCcH .... Hazelden Foundation, Staff library, Center City, MN [*Library symbol*] [*Library of Congress*] (LCLS)

MnCgL .... Lakeside Intermediate Media Center, Chisago City, MN [*Library symbol*] [*Library of Congress*] (LCLS)

MnCgP .... Chisago Lakes Primary School, Chisago City, MN [*Library symbol*] [*Library of Congress*] (LCLS)

MnCh .... Carver County Library, Chaska, MN [*Library symbol Library of Congress*] (LCLS)

MNCH .... Chinandega/German Pomares [*Nicaragua*] [*ICAO location identifier*] (ICLI)

MnChaHS .... Chandler-Lake Wilson High School, Chandler, MN [*Library symbol*] [*Library of Congress*] (LCLS)

MnChi .... Chisholm Public Library, Chisholm, MN [*Library symbol*] [*Library of Congress*] (LCLS)

MnChiE .... Vaughan-Steffensrud Elementary School, Chisholm, MN [*Library symbol*] [*Library of Congress*] (LCLS)

MnChiJ .... Chisholm Junior High School, Chisholm, MN [*Library symbol*] [*Library of Congress*] (LCLS)

MnChil .... Iron Range Research Library, Chisholm, MN [*Library symbol Library of Congress*] (LCLS)

MnChiSH .... Chisholm Senior High School, Chisholm, MN [*Library symbol*] [*Library of Congress*] (LCLS)

MnChoE .... Chokio-Alberto Elementary School, Chokio, MN [*Library symbol*] [*Library of Congress*] (LCLS)

MNCI .... Corn Island [*Nicaragua*] [*ICAO location identifier*] (ICLI)

MNCI .... Neepawa Collegiate Institute, Manitoba [*Library symbol National Library of Canada*] (NLC)

MNCIS .... Management Numerical Control Information System (MCD)

MNC-K .... Mouvement National Congolais - Kalonji [*Congolese National Movement*] [*Kalonji Wing*]

MnCl .... Cloquet Public Library, Cloquet, MN [*Library symbol Library of Congress*] (LCLS)

MNCL .... Monoclonal Gammopathy Identified [*Immunology*] (DAVI)

MNC-L .... Mouvement National Congolais - Lumumba [*Congolese National Movement*] [*Lumumba Wing*]

MnClaE .... Clarissa Elementary School, Clarissa, MN [*Library symbol*] [*Library of Congress*] (LCLS)

MnCLaH .... Clarissa High School, Clarissa, MN [*Library symbol*] [*Library of Congress*] (LCLS)

MnClc .... Clara City Public Library, Clara City, MN [*Library symbol*] [*Library of Congress*] (LCLS)

MnClCE .... Churchill Elementary School, Cloquet, MN [*Library symbol*] [*Library of Congress*] (LCLS)

MnClcPS .... Clara City Public Schools, Clara City, MN [*Library symbol*] [*Library of Congress*] (LCLS)

MnCleS .... Clearbrook Public School, Clearbrook, MN [*Library symbol*] [*Library of Congress*] (LCLS)

MnClHi .... Carlton County Historical Society, Cloquet, MN [*Library symbol*] [*Library of Congress*] (LCLS)

MnClim .... Climax Public Library, Climax, MN [*Library symbol*] [*Library of Congress*] (LCLS)

MnClimS .... Climax-Shelly School, Climax, MN [*Library symbol*] [*Library of Congress*] (LCLS)

MnClkE .... Clearview Elementary School, Clear lake, MN [*Library symbol*] [*Library of Congress*] (LCLS)

MnClM .... Cloquet Middle School, Cloquet, MN [*Library symbol*] [*Library of Congress*] (LCLS)

MnClOS .... Fond du Lac Ojibway School, Cloquet, MN [*Library symbol*] [*Library of Congress*] (LCLS)

MnCls .... Cold Spring Community Library, Cold Spring, MN [*Library symbol*] [*Library of Congress*] (LCLS)

MnClsE .... Cold Spring Elementary/Rocori Junior School, Cold Spring, MN [*Library symbol*] [*Library of Congress*] (LCLS)

MnClSH .... Cloquet Senior High School, Cloquet, MN [*Library symbol*] [*Library of Congress*] (LCLS)

MnClsR .... Rocori High School, Cold Spring, MN [*Library symbol*] [*Library of Congress*] (LCLS)

MnClsS .... St. Boniface Elementary School, Cold Spring, MN [*Library symbol*] [*Library of Congress*] (LCLS)

MnClWE .... Washington Elementary School, Cloquet, MN [*Library symbol*] [*Library of Congress*] (LCLS)

MnCm .... Calumet Public Library, Calumet, MN [*Library symbol*] [*Library of Congress*] (LCLS)

MNCM .... Mineman, Master Chief [*Navy rating*]

MNCMPTR ... Minicomputer (MSA)

MnCo .... Cokato Public Library, Cokato, MN [*Library symbol*] [*Library of Congress*] (LCLS)

MnCoD .... Dassel-Cokato Jr./Sr. High School, Cakoto, MN [*Library symbol*] [*Library of Congress*] (LCLS)

MnCoE......... Cokato Elementary School, Media Center, Cokato, MN [*Library symbol*] [*Library of Congress*] (LCLS)

MnCohS...... Cohasset School, Cohasset, MN [*Library symbol*] [*Library of Congress*] (LCLS)

MnCol.......... Coleraine Public Library, Coleraine, MN [*Library symbol*] [*Library of Congress*] (LCLS)

MnColH....... Greenway High School, Coleraine, MN [*Library symbol*] [*Library of Congress*] (LCLS)

MnCoM........ Cokato Museum, Cokato, MN [*Library symbol*] [*Library of Congress*] (LCLS)

MnCoo......... Cook Public Library, Cook, MN [*Library symbol*] [*Library of Congress*] (LCLS)

MnCooS...... Cook Public School, Cook, MN [*Library symbol*] [*Library of Congress*] (LCLS)

MnCosPS..... Cosmos Public School, Cosmos, MN [*Library symbol*] [*Library of Congress*] (LCLS)

MnCotS....... Cotton Public School, Cotton, MN [*Library symbol*] [*Library of Congress*] (LCLS)

MNCP .... Math Network Curriculum Project (EDAC)

MNCPL .... Municipal

MNCPPC ...... Maryland-National Capital Park and Planning Commission

MNCPPLTY... Municipality

MnCr........... Crookston Public Library, Crookston, MN [*Library symbol*] [*Library of Congress*] (LCLS)

MnCr........... Polk County Library, Crookston, MN [*Library symbol Library of Congress*] (LCLS)

MnCrCH....... Central High School, Crookston,MN [*Library symbol*] [*Library of Congress*] (LCLS)

MnCrHE....... Highland Elementary School, Crookston, MN [*Library symbol*] [*Library of Congress*] (LCLS)

MnCrLE....... Lincoln Elementary School, Crookston, MN [*Library symbol*] [*Library of Congress*] (LCLS)

MnCrMS ...... Mount St. Benedict, Crookston, MN [*Library symbol*] [*Library of Congress*] (LCLS)

MnCroE........ Crosby-Ironton Elementary School, Crosby, MN [*Library symbol*] [*Library of Congress*] (LCLS)

MnCroH .... Crosby-Ironton High School, Crosby, MN [*Library symbol*] [*Library of Congress*] (LCLS)

MnCrpM....... Mercy Medical Center, Coon Rapids, MN [*Library symbol Library of Congress*] (LCLS)

MnCrU .... University of Minnesota Technical College, Crookston, MN [*Library symbol Library of Congress*] (LCLS)

MnCrWE ...... Washington Elementary School, Crookston, MN [*Library symbol*] [*Library of Congress*] (LCLS)

MnCrwHS .... Cromwell High School, Cromwell, MN [*Library symbol*] [*Library of Congress*] (LCLS)

MNCS .... Mineman, Senior Chief [*Navy rating*]

MNCS .... Multipoint Network-Control System

MnCS........... St. John's University, Collegeville, MN [*Library symbol Library of Congress*] (LCLS)

MnCt........... Carlton Public Library, Carlton, MN [*Library symbol*] [*Library of Congress*] (LCLS)

MnCtE......... South Terrace Elementary School, Carlton, MN [*Library symbol*] [*Library of Congress*] (LCLS)

MnCtH......... Carlotn High School, Carlton, MN [*Library symbol*] [*Library of Congress*] (LCLS)

MnCtwPS..... Cottonwood Public School, Cottonwood, MN [*Library symbol*] [*Library of Congress*] (LCLS)

MNCV .... Motor Nerve Conduction Velocity [*Medicine*]

MnCyS .... Cyrus Public School, Cyrus, MN [*Library symbol*] [*Library of Congress*] (LCLS)

MND .... Mandalay [*Burma*] [*Seismograph station code, US Geological Survey Closed*] (SEIS)

MND .... Marlin Developments [*Vancouver Stock Exchange symbol*]

MND .... Martin Nuclear Division [*AEC*] (MCD)

MND .... Material Need Document [*DoD*]

MND .... Mean Narrow Dose [*Radiation therapy*] (DAVI)

MND .... Medial Nuclear Division [*Cytology*]

MND .... Mendenhall, AK [*Location identifier FAA*] (FAAL)

MND .... Midsummer Night's Dream [*Shakespearean work*]

MND .... Minimum Necrosing Dose

MND .... Minister of National Defence [*Canada*]

MND .... Ministry of National Defence [*British*] (MCD)

MND .... Minor Neurological Dysfunction

MND .... Mission Need Determination (DOMA)

MND .... Mission Need Document [*DoD*]

MND .... Mission Non-Delivery (MCD)

MND .... Mitchell Energy & Development Corp. [*NYSE symbol*] (SAG)

MND .... Motor Neuron Disease [*Medicine*]

MND .... Mound

MND .... Movimento Nacional Democratico [*National Democratic Movement*] [*Portugal Political party*] (PPE)

MND .... University of Minnesota-Duluth, Duluth, MN [*OCLC symbol*] (OCLC)

MNDA .... Missionary Sisters of Notre Dame des Anges [*Roman Catholic religious order*]

MND A .... Mitchell Energy/Dev'A' [*NYSE symbol*] (TTSB)

MNDA .... Motor Neurone Disease Association [*British*] (DBA)

MnDaw .... Carnegie Library, Dawson, MN [*Library symbol*] [*Library of Congress*] (LCLS)

MNDAWA..... Motor Neurone Disease Association of Western Australia

MnDawJH .... Johnson Memorial Hospital and Nursing School, Dawson, MN [*Library symbol*] [*Library of Congress*] (LCLS)

MnDawPS..... Dawson-Boyd Public Library, Dawson, MN [*Library symbol*] [*Library of Congress*] (LCLS)

MND B .... Mitchell Energy/Dev'B' [*NYSE symbol*] (TTSB)

MNDD......... Mouvement National pour la Democratie et le Developpement [*Benin*] [*Political party*] (EY)

MnDe.......... Delano Public Libbrary, Delano, MN [*Library symbol*] [*Library of Congress*] (LCLS)

MnDeE........ Delano Elementary School, Delano, MN [*Library symbol*] [*Library of Congress*] (LCLS)

MnDeH........ Delano High School, Delano, MN [*Library symbol*] [*Library of Congress*] (LCLS)

MnDeM........ Delano Middle School, Delano, MN [*Library symbol*] [*Library of Congress*] (LCLS)

MnDerE........ King Elementary School, Deer River, MN [*Library symbol*] [*Library of Congress*] (LCLS)

MnDerH .... Deer River High School, Deer River, MN [*Library symbol*] [*Library of Congress*] (LCLS)

MnDES........ Dassel Elementary School, Media Center, Dassel, MN [*Library symbol*] [*Library of Congress*] (LCLS)

MnDeSP ...... St. Peter's School, Delano, MN [*Library symbol*] [*Library of Congress*] (LCLS)

MnDI........... Detroit Lakes Public Library, Detroit Lakes, MN [*Library symbol*] [*Library of Congress*] (LCLS)

MnDIH .... Community High School, Detroit Lakes, MN [*Library symbol*] [*Library of Congress*] (LCLS)

MnDIHi .... Becker County Historical Society, Detroit Lakes, MN [*Library symbol*] [*Library of Congress*] (LCLS)

MnDIJ.......... Community Junior High School, Detroit Lakes, MN [*Library symbol*] [*Library of Congress*] (LCLS)

MnDILe........ Lincoln Elementary School, Detroit Lakes, MN [*Library symbol*] [*Library of Congress*] (LCLS)

MnDIRE .... Rossman Elementary School, Detroit Lakes, MN [*Library symbol*] [*Library of Congress*] (LCLS)

MnDITI........ Detroit Lakes Technical Institute, Detroit Lakes, MN [*Library symbol*] [*Library of Congress*] (LCLS)

MnDIWE....... Washington Elementary School, Detroit Lakes, MN [*Library symbol*] [*Library of Congress*] (LCLS)

MNDO......... Merchant Navy Discipline Organisation [*British*] (DS)

MNDO......... Modified Neglect of Differential Overlap [*Quantum mechanics*]

MNDP .... Bibliotheque Pere Champagne [*Pere Champagne Library*], Notre-Dame-De-Lourdes, Manitoba [*Library symbol National Library of Canada*] (BIB)

MNDP .... Multinational Data Processing (MHDB)

MNDTH .... Minimum Depth (NOAA)

MNDTS .... Member of the Non-Destructive Testing Society of Great Britain

MnDu.......... Duluth Public Library, Duluth, MN [*Library symbol Library of Congress*] (LCLS)

MnDuBE...... Birchwood Elementary School, Duluth, MN [*Library symbol*] [*Library of Congress*] (LCLS)

MnDuBVE..... Bay View Elementary School, Duluth, MN [*Library symbol*] [*Library of Congress*] (LCLS)

MnDuCE...... Cobb Elementary Library, Duluth, MN [*Library symbol*] [*Library of Congress*] (LCLS)

MnDuCH...... Central High School, Duluth, MN [*Library symbol*] [*Library of Congress*] (LCLS)

MnDuCOE..... Congdon Park Elementary School, Duluth, MN [*Library symbol*] [*Library of Congress*] (LCLS)

MnDuCPE..... Chester Park Elementary School, Duluth, MN [*Library symbol*] [*Library of Congress*] (LCLS)

MnDuDH...... Denfeld High School, Duluth, MN [*Library symbol*] [*Library of Congress*] (LCLS)

MnDuEH...... East High School, Duluth, MN [*Library symbol*] [*Library of Congress*] (LCLS)

MnDuEPA .... United States Environmental Protection Agency, National Water Quality Laboratory, Duluth, MN [*Library symbol Library of Congress*] (LCLS)

MnDuGE...... Grant Elementary School, Duluth, MN [*Library symbol*] [*Library of Congress*] (LCLS)

MnDuHE...... Homcroft Elementary School, Duluth, MN [*Library symbol*] [*Library of Congress*] (LCLS)

MnDuHi....... Northeast Minnesota Historical Center Library, Duluth, MN [*Library symbol*] [*Library of Congress*] (LCLS)

MnDuHS...... Hermantown High School, Duluth, MN [*Library symbol*] [*Library of Congress*] (LCLS)

MnDuLE...... Lincoln Elementary School, Duluth, MN [*Library symbol*] [*Library of Congress*] (LCLS)

MnDuLOE..... Lowell Elementary School, Duluth, MN [*Library symbol*] [*Library of Congress*] (LCLS)

MnDuLPE..... Lester Park Elementary School, Duluth, MN [*Library symbol*] [*Library of Congress*] (LCLS)

MnDuLWE.... Lakewood Elementary School, Duluth, MN [*Library symbol*] [*Library of Congress*] (LCLS)

MnDuM........ Miller-Dawn Hospital and Medical Center, Duluth, MN [*Library symbol Library of Congress*] (LCLS)

MnDuME...... Merritt Elementary School, Duluth, MN [*Library symbol*] [*Library of Congress*] (LCLS)

MnDuMPJ..... Morgan Park Junior High School, Duluth, MN [*Library symbol*] [*Library of Congress*] (LCLS)

MnDuMS...... Marshall School, Duluth, MN [*Library symbol*] [*Library of Congress*] (LCLS)

MnDuMWE... MacArthue/West Elementary School, Duluth MN [*Library symbol*] [*Library of Congress*] (LCLS)

MnDuNE ..... Nettleton Elementary School, Duluth, MN [*Library symbol*] [*Library of Congress*] (LCLS)

MnDuNR...... Natural Resources Research Institute, Duluth, MN [*Library symbol*] [*Library of Congress*] (LCLS)

MnDuNSE..... North Shore Elementary School, Duluth, MN [*Library symbol*] [*Library of Congress*] (LCLS)

MnDuOJ...... Ordean Junior High School, Duluth, MN [*Library symbol*] [*Library of Congress*] (LCLS)

MnDuPC...... Duluth Prison Camp, Duluth, MN [*Library symbol*] [*Library of Congress*] (LCLS)

MnDuPE...... Piedmont Elementary School, Duluth, MN [*Library symbol*] [*Library of Congress*] (LCLS)

MnDuSE...... Stowe Elementary School, Duluth, MN [*Library symbol*] [*Library of Congress*] (LCLS)

MnDuSLH ... St. Louis County Helth Dept., Duluth, MN [*Library symbol*] [*Library of Congress*] (LCLS)

MnDuStL ..... Saint Luke's Hospital, Duluth, MN [*Library symbol Library of Congress*] (LCLS)

MnDuStM ... Saint Mary's Hospital, Duluth, MN [*Library symbol Library of Congress*] (LCLS)

MnDuStS ..... College of Saint Scholastica, Duluth, MN [*Library symbol Library of Congress*] (LCLS)

MnDuTI....... Duluth Technical Institute, Duluth, MN [*Library symbol*] [*Library of Congress*] (LCLS)

MnDuTRC .... Teachers' Resource Center, Duluth, MN [*Library symbol*] [*Library of Congress*] (LCLS)

MnDuU .... University of Minnesota, Duluth, MN [*Library symbol Library of Congress*] (LCLS)

MnDuWE..... Washburn Elementary School, Duluth, MN [*Library symbol*] [*Library of Congress*] (LCLS)

MnDuWJ..... Washington Junior High School, Duluth, MN [*Library symbol*] [*Library of Congress*] (LCLS)

MnDuWJH ... Woodland Junior High School, Duluth, MN [*Library symbol*] [*Library of Congress*] (LCLS)

MNDX .... Mobile Non-Director Exchange [*Telecommunications*] (NITA)

MNE .... College of St. Catherine, St. Paul, MN [*OCLC symbol*] (OCLC)

Mne .... Marine [*British military*] (DMA)

MNE........... Master of Naval Engineering

MNE........... Master of Nuclear Engineering

MNE........... Mentone [*France*] [*Airport symbol*] (AD)

MNE........... Merchant Navy Establishment [*British*] (DS)

MNE........... Methylallyl Nitrophenyl Ether [*Organic chemistry*]

MNE........... Methylnorepinephrine [*Also, Normetanephrine*] [*Biochemistry*]

MNE........... Minden, LA [*Location identifier FAA*] (FAAL)

MNE........... Mineo [*Sicily*] [*Seismograph station code, US Geological Survey Closed*] (SEIS)

MNE........... Minimum Number of Elements

Mn-E.......... Minnesota State Department of Education, St. Paul, MN [*Library symbol Library of Congress*] (LCLS)

MNE........... Modern English [*Language, etc.*]

MNE........... Moneygram Payment Systems [*NYSE symbol*] (SAG)

MNE........... Multinational Enterprise

MNe........... Newburyport Public Library, Newburyport, MA [*Library symbol Library of Congress*] (LCLS)

MNEA.......... Merchant Navy Establishment Administration [*British*] (DS)

MnEb .... Eagle Bend Public Library, Eagle Bend, MN [*Library symbol*] [*Library of Congress*] (LCLS)

MnEbS .... Eagle Bend School, Eagle Bend, MN [*Library symbol*] [*Library of Congress*] (LCLS)

MnEcES ...... Echo-Wood Lake Elementary School, Echo, MN [*Library symbol*] [*Library of Congress*] (LCLS)

MNECP........ Mobile National Emergency Command Post [*Air Force*]

MN Ed .... Master of Nursing Education

MN ED .... Material Need Engineering Development (MCD)

MnEdS .... Southdale-Hennepin Area Library, Edina, MN [*Library symbol Library of Congress*] (LCLS)

MNEE.......... Mission Nonessential Equipment [*NASA*] (KSC)

MNeeS........ GTE-Sylvania, Electric Systems Group, Needham, MA [*Library symbol Library of Congress*] (LCLS)

MnEfAE........ Adams Elementary School, Fergus Falls, MN [*Library symbol*] [*Library of Congress*] (LCLS)

MnEfS......... Effie School, Effie, MN [*Library symbol*] [*Library of Congress*] (LCLS)

MnEgfCE...... Crestwood Elementary School, East Grand Forks, MN [*Library symbol*] [*Library of Congress*] (LCLS)

MnEgfH....... East Grand Forks High School, East Grand Forks, MN [*Library symbol*] [*Library of Congress*] (LCLS)

MnEgfJ .... Central Junior High School, Grand Forks, MN [*Library symbol*] [*Library of Congress*] (LCLS)

MnEgfRE...... River Heights Elementary School, East Grand Forks, MN [*Library symbol*] [*Library of Congress*] (LCLS)

MnEgfTI ...... East Grand Forks Technical Institute, East Grand Forks, MN [*Library symbol*] [*Library of Congress*] (LCLS)

MnEgfVE...... Valley Elementary School, East Grand Forks, MN [*Library symbol*] [*Library of Congress*] (LCLS)

MNeHi........ Newburyport Historical Society, Newburyport, MA [*Library symbol Library of Congress*] (LCLS)

MnElb .... Thorsen Memorial Public Library, Elbow Lake, MN [*Library symbol*] [*Library of Congress*] (LCLS)

MnElbE .... West Central Elementary School, Elbow Lake, MN [*Library symbol*] [*Library of Congress*] (LCLS)

MnElbH........ West Central High School, Elbow Lake, MN [*Library symbol*] [*Library of Congress*] (LCLS)

MnEly .... Ely Public Library, Ely, MN [*Library symbol*] [*Library of Congress*] (LCLS)

MnElyJS ...... Memorial Junior/Senior High School, Ely, MN [*Library symbol*] [*Library of Congress*] (LCLS)

MnElyV .... Vermillion Community College, Ely, MN [*Library symbol Library of Congress*] (LCLS)

MnElyWE ..... Washington Elementary School, Ely, MN [*Library symbol*] [*Library of Congress*] (LCLS)

Mnemos ...... Mnemosyne [*A publication*] (OCD)

MN Eng........ Master of Naval Engineering

MnEr.......... Elk River Public Library, Elk River, MN [*Library symbol*] [*Library of Congress*] (LCLS)

MNERAM .... Members of New England Regional Art Museum

MnErHE....... Handke Elementary School, Elk River, MN [*Library symbol*] [*Library of Congress*] (LCLS)

MnErPE....... K.G. Parker Elementary School, Elk River, MN [*Library symbol*] [*Library of Congress*] (LCLS)

MnErS........ Elk River Senior High School, Elk River, MN [*Library symbol*] [*Library of Congress*] (LCLS)

MnErSA....... St. Andrew's School, Elk River, MN [*Library symbol*] [*Library of Congress*] (LCLS)

MnErSJ .... Salk Junior High School, Elk River, MN [*Library symbol*] [*Library of Congress*] (LCLS)

MnErSJL ...... St. John's Lutheran School, Elk River, MN [*Library symbol*] [*Library of Congress*] (LCLS)

MnErsS....... Erksine Public School, Erkskine, MN [*Library symbol*] [*Library of Congress*] (LCLS)

MnErVJ .... Vandenberge Junior High School, Elk River, MN [*Library symbol*] [*Library of Congress*] (LCLS)

MNES.......... Mine Safety Appl [*NASDAQ symbol*] (TTSB)

MNES.......... Mine Safety Appliances Co. [*NASDAQ symbol*] (NQ)

MnEskH ...... Esko High School, Esko, MN [*Library symbol*] [*Library of Congress*] (LCLS)

MnEskWE .... Winterquist Elementary School, Esko, MN [*Library symbol*] [*Library of Congress*] (LCLS)

MNET.......... Mission and Data Operations Directorate Network (MCD)

MNET.......... Multicom Publishing [*NASDAQ symbol*] (SAG)

MNEV.......... Musica Nostra et Vostra, National Corp. of America (EA)

MnEvaE....... Evansville Elementary School, Evansville, MN [*Library symbol*] [*Library of Congress*] (LCLS)

MnEvaH ...... Evansville High School, Evansville, MN [*Library symbol*] [*Library of Congress*] (LCLS)

MnEvH .... Eden Valley-Watkins High School, Eden Valley, MN [*Library symbol*] [*Library of Congress*] (LCLS)

MnEvl .... Eveleth Public Library, Eveleth, MN [*Library symbol*] [*Library of Congress*] (LCLS)

MnEvIFE ..... Franklin Elementary School, Eveleth, MN [*Library symbol*] [*Library of Congress*] (LCLS)

MnEvISH..... Eveleth-Gilbert Senior High School, Eveleth, MN [*Library symbol*] [*Library of Congress*] (LCLS)

MnF .... Buckham Memorial Library, Faribault, MN [*Library symbol Library of Congress*] (LCLS)

MNF........... College of St. Benedict, St. Joseph, MN [*OCLC symbol*] (OCLC)

MNF........... Forbes Library, Northampton, MA [*Library symbol Library of Congress*] (LCLS)

MNF........... Mana [*Fiji*] [*Airport symbol*] (OAG)

MNF........... Manitou Reef Resources [*Vancouver Stock Exchange symbol*]

MNF........... Millers' National Federation (EA)

MNF........... Mizo National Front [*India*] (PD)

MNF........... Morehead & North Fork R. R. [*AAR code*]

MNF........... Mountain View, MO [*Location identifier FAA*] (FAAL)

MNF........... Multilateral Nuclear Force

MNF........... Multinational Force [*Eleven-nation peace-keeping force for the Sinai*]

MNF........... Multisystem Networking Facility

MnFa.......... Martin County Library, Fairmont, MN [*Library symbol Library of Congress*] (LCLS)

MNFD......... Manifold (ECII)

MNFE.......... Missile Not Fully Equipped (AAG)

MnFer......... Fertile Public Library, Fertile, MN [*Library symbol*] [*Library of Congress*] (LCLS)

MnFerS........ Fertile-Betrami School, Fertile, MN [*Library symbol*] [*Library of Congress*] (LCLS)

MnFf .... Fergus Falls Public Library, Fergus Falls, MN [*Library symbol Library of Congress*] (LCLS)

MNFF.......... Magyar Nemzeti Fueggetlensegi Front [*Hungarian National Independence Front*] [*Political party*]

MnFfC......... Fergus Falls Community College, Fergus Falls, MN [*Library symbol Library of Congress*] (LCLS)

MnFfCE....... Cleveland Elementary School, Fergus Falls, MN [*Library symbol*] [*Library of Congress*] (LCLS)

MnFfEC....... West Central Educational Cooperative Service Unit, Fergus Falls, MN [*Library symbol*] [*Library of Congress*] (LCLS)

MnFfH........ Lake Region Hospital, Fergus Falls, MN [*Library symbol Library of Congress*] (LCLS)

MnFfHA....... Hillcrest Academy, Fergus Falls, MN [*Library symbol*] [*Library of Congress*] (LCLS)

MnFfHi........ Otter Tail County Historical Society, Fergus Falls, MN [*Library symbol*] [*Library of Congress*] (LCLS)

MnFfL......... Lutheran Brethren Schools, Fergus Falls, MN [*Library symbol Library of Congress*] (LCLS)

MnFfM........ Fergus Falls Middle School, Fergus Falls, MN [*Library symbol*] [*Library of Congress*] (LCLS)

MnFfME ...... McKinley Elementary School, Fergus Falls, MN [*Library symbol*] [*Library of Congress*] (LCLS)

MnFfO........ Otter Tail Power Co., Fergus Falls, MN [*Library symbol*] [*Library of Congress*] (LCLS)

MnFfRT....... Fergus Falls Regional Treatment Center, Fergus Falls, MN [*Library symbol*] [*Library of Congress*] (LCLS)

MnFfSH....... Fergus Falls Senior High School, Fergus Falls, MN [*Library symbol*] [*Library of Congress*] (LCLS)

MnFfV......... Viking Library System, Fergus Falls, MN [*Library symbol*] [*Library of Congress*] (LCLS)

MNFI........... Michigan Natural Features Inventory [*Michigan State Department of Natural Resources*] [*Information service or system*] (IID)

MnFiE .... Finlayson Elementary School, Finlayson, MN [*Library symbol*] [*Library of Congress*] (LCLS)

MnFiH .... Finlayson High School, Finlayson, MN [*Library symbol*] [*Library of Congress*] (LCLS)

MnFisS .... Fisher Public School, Fisher, MN [*Library symbol*] [*Library of Congress*] (LCLS)

MNFLD .... Manifold (KSC)

MnFILS .... Lincoln School, Floodwood, MN [*Library symbol*] [*Library of Congress*] (LCLS)

MnFo .... Foley Community Library, Foley, MN [*Library symbol*] [*Library of Congress*] (LCLS)

MnFoE .... Foley Elementary School, Foley, MN [*Library symbol*] [*Library of Congress*] (LCLS)

MnFoH .... Foley High School, Foley, MN [*Library symbol*] [*Library of Congress*] (LCLS)

MnFoS .... St. John's School, Foley, MN [*Library symbol*] [*Library of Congress*] (LCLS)

MNFP .... Magyar Nemzeti Fueggetlensegi Part [*Hungarian National Independence Party*] [*Political party*] (PPE)

MNFP .... Multinational Fighter Program [*Air Force*]

MNFP .... Multiple Number of Faults per Pass (PDAA)

MnFpS .... Sacred Heart School, Freeport MN [*Library symbol*] [*Library of Congress*] (LCLS)

MnFraE .... Frazee Elementary School, Frazee, MN [*Library symbol*] [*Library of Congress*] (LCLS)

MnFraHS .... Frazee-Vergas High School, Frazee, MN [*Library symbol*] [*Library of Congress*] (LCLS)

MNFRM .... Main Frame

MnFrnCES .... Cedar Mt. Elementary School, Franklin, MN [*Library symbol*] [*Library of Congress*] (LCLS)

MnFrUH .... Unity Hospital, Fridley, MN [*Library symbol Library of Congress*] (LCLS)

MnFS .... Seabury Divinity School, Faribault, MN [*Library symbol Library of Congress*] (LCLS)

MnFt .... Fosston Public Library, Fosston,MN [*Library symbol*] [*Library of Congress*] (LCLS)

MnFtH .... Fosston High School, Fosston, MN [*Library symbol*] [*Library of Congress*] (LCLS)

MnFtME .... Magelssen Elementary School, Fosston, MN [*Library symbol*] [*Library of Congress*] (LCLS)

MnFu .... Fulda Public Library, Fulda, MN [*Library symbol*] [*Library of Congress*] (LCLS)

MNFU .... Manx National Farmers Union [*British*] (DBA)

MnFuES .... Fulda Elementary School, Fulda, MN [*Library symbol*] [*Library of Congress*] (LCLS)

MnFuJSH ...... Fulda Junior-Senior High School, Fulda, MN [*Library symbol*] [*Library of Congress*] (LCLS)

MnFuStP ...... St. Paul's Lutheran School, Fulda, MN [*Library symbol*] [*Library of Congress*] (LCLS)

MNG .... Gustavus Adolphus College, St. Peter, MN [*OCLC symbol*] (OCLC)

MNG .... Managing (MSA)

MNG .... Mangahao [*New Zealand*] [*Seismograph station code, US Geological Survey*] (SEIS)

MNG .... Maningrida [*Australia Airport symbol Obsolete*] (OAG)

mng .... Meaning

MNG .... Microwave Negative Grid

MNG .... Modulated Noise Generator (PDAA)

MNG .... Mongolia [*ANSI three-letter standard code*] (CNC)

MNG .... Morning

MNG .... Mourning (ROG)

MNG .... Multinodular Goiter [*Endocrinology*] (DAVI)

MnGarE .... Garfield Elementary School, Garfield, MN [*Library symbol*] [*Library of Congress*] (LCLS)

MnGBES ...... Helen Baker Elementary School, Glencoe, MN [*Library symbol*] [*Library of Congress*] (LCLS)

MnGc .... Grove City Public Library, Grove City, MN [*Library symbol*] [*Library of Congress*] (LCLS)

MnGcJH .... Atwater-Grove City Junior High School, Grove City, MN [*Library symbol*] [*Library of Congress*] (LCLS)

MnGeH .... Grey Eagle High School, Grey Eagle, MN [*Library symbol*] [*Library of Congress*] (LCLS)

MnGf .... Granite Falls Public Library, Granite Falls, MN [*Library symbol*] [*Library of Congress*] (LCLS)

MnGfH .... Granite Falls Municipal Hospital, Granite Falls, MN [*Library symbol*] [*Library of Congress*] (LCLS)

MnGfODS ..... Open Door Bible School, Granite Falls, MN [*Library symbol*] [*Library of Congress*] (LCLS)

MnGfPS .... Granite Falls Public School, Granite Falls, MN [*Library symbol*] [*Library of Congress*] (LCLS)

MnGfTC .... Southwest Technical College, Granite Falls, MN [*Library symbol*] [*Library of Congress*] (LCLS)

MnGGH .... Glencoe Hospital, Glencoe, MN [*Library symbol*] [*Library of Congress*] (LCLS)

MnGHS .... Glencoe Public High School, Glencoe, MN [*Library symbol*] [*Library of Congress*] (LCLS)

MnGi .... Gilbert Public Library, Gilbert, MN [*Library symbol*] [*Library of Congress*] (LCLS)

MnGiHi .... Iron Range Historical Society, Gilbert MN [*Library symbol*] [*Library of Congress*] (LCLS)

MnGiJH .... Gilbert-Eveleth Junior High School, Gilbert, MN [*Library symbol*] [*Library of Congress*] (LCLS)

MnGiNSE ..... Nelle Shean Elementary School, Gilbert, MN [*Library symbol*] [*Library of Congress*] (LCLS)

MnGle .... Glenwood Public Library, Glenwood, MN [*Library symbol*] [*Library of Congress*] (LCLS)

MnGLES ...... Lincoln Elementary School, Glencoe, MN [*Library symbol*] [*Library of Congress*] (LCLS)

MnGleSH .... Glenwood Senior High School, Glenwood, MN [*Library symbol*] [*Library of Congress*] (LCLS)

MnGlyE .... Glyndon Elementary School, Glyndon, MN [*Library symbol*] [*Library of Congress*] (LCLS)

MnGlyHS ...... Glyndon-Felton High School, Glyndon, MN [*Library symbol*] [*Library of Congress*] (LCLS)

MnGm .... Grand Marais Public Library, Grand Marais, MN [*Library symbol*] [*Library of Congress*] (LCLS)

MnGmFT ...... United States National Park Service, Grand Portage Northern Minnesota Fur Trade Library, Grand Marais, MN [*Library symbol*] [*Library of Congress*] (LCLS)

MnGmH .... Cook County High School, Grand Marais, MN [*Library symbol*] [*Library of Congress*] (LCLS)

MnGMS .... Glencoe Middle School, Glencoe, MN [*Library symbol*] [*Library of Congress*] (LCLS)

MnGmSE ...... Sawtooth Elementary School, Grand Marais, MN [*Library symbol*] [*Library of Congress*] (LCLS)

MNGMT .... Management (ADA)

MNGNG .... Managing

MnGonS .... Gonvick-Trail Community School, Gonvick, MN [*Library symbol*] [*Library of Congress*] (LCLS)

MnGoos .... Goodridge Public School, Goodridge, MN [*Library symbol*] [*Library of Congress*] (LCLS)

MNGP .... Monticello Nuclear Generating Plant (NRCH)

MnGpE .... Grand Portage Elementary School, Grand Portage, MN [*Library symbol*] [*Library of Congress*] (LCLS)

MnGr .... Grand Rapids Public Library, Grand Rapids, MN [*Library symbol*] [*Library of Congress*] (LCLS)

MNGR .... Manager

MNGR .... Monsignor

MnGra .... Graceville Public Library, Graceville, MN [*Library symbol*] [*Library of Congress*] (LCLS)

MnGraBS .... Big Stone Hutterite Colony School, Graceville, MN [*Library symbol*] [*Library of Congress*] (LCLS)

MnGraCHS ... Clinton-Graceville High School, Graceville, MN [*Library symbol*] [*Library of Congress*] (LCLS)

MnGraH .... Holy Trinity Hospital, Graceville, MN [*Library symbol*] [*Library of Congress*] (LCLS)

MnGre .... Greenbush Public Library, Greenbush, MN [*Library symbol*] [*Library of Congress*] (LCLS)

MnGrEMS ..... Edna I. Murphy School, Grand Rapids, MN [*Library symbol*] [*Library of Congress*] (LCLS)

MnGreS .... Greenbush Public School, Greenbush, MN [*Library symbol*] [*Library of Congress*] (LCLS)

MnGrFLS ...... Forrest Lake School, Grand Rapids, MN [*Library symbol*] [*Library of Congress*] (LCLS)

MnGrFW ...... Forest Wildlife Population and Research Group, Grand Rapids, MN [*Library symbol*] [*Library of Congress*] (LCLS)

MnGrl .... Itasca Community College, Grand Rapids, MN [*Library symbol Library of Congress*] (LCLS)

MnGrM .... Grand Rapids Middle School, Grand Rapids, MN [*Library symbol*] [*Library of Congress*] (LCLS)

MNGRM .... Monogram

MnGrRS .... Riverview School, Grand Rapids, MN [*Library symbol*] [*Library of Congress*] (LCLS)

MnGrSH ...... Grand Rapids Senior HighSchool, Grand Rapids, MN [*Library symbol*] [*Library of Congress*] (LCLS)

MnGrSS ...... Southwest School, Grand Rapids, MN [*Library symbol*] [*Library of Congress*] (LCLS)

MnGryS .... Grygla Public School, Grygla, MN [*Library symbol*] [*Library of Congress*] (LCLS)

Mngt .... Management

MnGvH .... Golden Valley Health Center, Golden Valley, MN [*Library symbol Library of Congress*] (LCLS)

MNH .... Magnum Resources [*Vancouver Stock Exchange symbol*]

MNH .... Makers of National History [*A publication*]

Mn-H .... Minnesota State Department of Health, St. Paul, MN [*Library symbol Library of Congress*] (LCLS)

MNH .... Mint Never Hinged [*Philately*]

MNH .... Monarch Airlines [*ICAO designator*] (FAAC)

MNH .... Munich [*Germany*] [*Seismograph station code, US Geological Survey Closed*] (SEIS)

MNH .... Museum of Natural History [*Smithsonian Institution*]

MNH .... University of Minnesota-Duluth, Health Science Library, Duluth, MN [*OCLC symbol*] (OCLC)

MnHaH .... Norman County West High School, Halstad, MN [*Library symbol*] [*Library of Congress*] (LCLS)

MnHal .... Hallock Public Library, Hallock, MN [*Library symbol*] [*Library of Congress*] (LCLS)

MnHalH .... Hallock High School, Hallock, MN [*Library symbol*] [*Library of Congress*] (LCLS)

MnHan .... Hancock Community Library, Hancock, MN [*Library symbol*] [*Library of Congress*] (LCLS)

MnHanE .... Hancock Elementary School, Hancock, MN [*Library symbol*] [*Library of Congress*] (LCLS)

MnHanH .... Hancock High School, Hancock, MN [*Library symbol*] [*Library of Congress*] (LCLS)

MnHaw .... Hawley Public Library, Hawley, MN [*Library symbol*] [*Library of Congress*] (LCLS)

MnHawE .... Hawley Elementary School, Hawley, MN [*Library symbol*] [*Library of Congress*] (LCLS)

MnHawH ...... Hawley High School, Hawley, MN [*Library symbol*] [*Library of Congress*] (LCLS)

MnHcS......... Hill City School, Hill City, MN [*Library symbol*] [*Library of Congress*] (LCLS)

MnHe........... Hector Public Library, Hector, MN [*Library symbol*] [*Library of Congress*] (LCLS)

MnHE........... Hinckley Elementary School, Hinckley, MN [*Library symbol*] [*Library of Congress*] (LCLS)

MnHel.......... Heron Lake Public Library, Heron Lake, MN [*Library symbol*] [*Library of Congress*] (LCLS)

MnHelES....... Heron Lake Elementary School, Heron Lake, MN [*Library symbol*] [*Library of Congress*] (LCLS)

MnHendH....... Hendricks Community Hospital, Hendricks, MN [*Library symbol*] [*Library of Congress*] (LCLS)

MnHendPS... Hendircks Public School, Hendricks, MN [*Library symbol*] [*Library of Congress*] (LCLS)

MnHenE....... West Elementary School, Hendrum, MN [*Library symbol*] [*Library of Congress*] (LCLS)

MnHennS...... Henning Public School, Henning, MN [*Library symbol*] [*Library of Congress*] (LCLS)

MnHePS...... Hector Public School, Hector, MN [*Library symbol*] [*Library of Congress*] (LCLS)

MnHH.......... Hinckley High School, Hinckley, MN [*Library symbol*] [*Library of Congress*] (LCLS)

MnHi........... Minnesota Historical Society, St. Paul, MN [*Library symbol Library of Congress*] (LCLS)

MnHi-Ar...... minnesota Historical Society, Division of Archives and Manuscripts, St. Paul, MN [*Library symbol*] [*Library of Congress*] (LCLS)

MnHib.......... Hibbing Public Library, Hibbing, MN [*Library symbol Library of Congress*] (LCLS)

MnHibC....... Hibbing Community College, Hibbing, MN [*Library symbol Library of Congress*] (LCLS)

MnHibM....... Central Mesabi Medical Center, Hibbing, MN [*Library symbol*] [*Library of Congress*] (LCLS)

MnHilCS...... Hills Christian School, Hills, MN [*Library symbol*] [*Library of Congress*] (LCLS)

MnHilES..... Hills-Beaver Creek Elementary School, Hills, MN [*Library symbol*] [*Library of Congress*] (LCLS)

MnHilHS..... Hills-Beaver Creek High School, Hills, MN [*Library symbol*] [*Library of Congress*] (LCLS)

MnHitE........ Ulen-Hitterdal Elementary School, Hitterdal, MN [*Library symbol*] [*Library of Congress*] (LCLS)

MnHl........... Howard Lake Public Library, Howard Lake, MN [*Library symbol*] [*Library of Congress*] (LCLS)

MNHLA......... Musicians National Hot Line Association (EA)

MnHldSDS... Seventh Day Adventist School, Holland, MN [*Library symbol*] [*Library of Congress*] (LCLS)

MnHlE.......... Howard Lake-Waverly Elementary School, Howard Lake, MN [*Library symbol*] [*Library of Congress*] (LCLS)

MnHlH.......... Howard Lake-Waverly High School, Howard Lake, MN [*Library symbol*] [*Library of Congress*] (LCLS)

MnHlS......... St. James Lutheran School, Howard Lake, MN [*Library symbol*] [*Library of Congress*] (LCLS)

MnHoE......... Holdingford Elementary School, Holdingford, MN [*Library symbol*] [*Library of Congress*] (LCLS)

MnHofS........ Hoffman Public School, Hoffman, MN [*Library symbol*] [*Library of Congress*] (LCLS)

MnHoH......... Holdingford Jr./Sr. High School, Holdingford, MN [*Library symbol*] [*Library of Congress*] (LCLS)

MnHol.......... Hoyt Lakes Public Library, Hoyt Lakes, MN [*Library symbol*] [*Library of Congress*] (LCLS)

M-NHSS...... Modified New Haven Schizophrenic Scale

MnHu........... Hutchinson Public Library, Hutchinson, MN [*Library symbol*] [*Library of Congress*] (LCLS)

MnHuHMS... Hutchinson Middle School, Hutchinson, MN [*Library symbol*] [*Library of Congress*] (LCLS)

MnHumS...... Humbolt School, Humbolt, MN [*Library symbol*] [*Library of Congress*] (LCLS)

MnHuPES.... Park Elementary School, Hutchinson, MN [*Library symbol*] [*Library of Congress*] (LCLS)

MnHuSH...... Hutchinson Senior High School, Hutchinson, MN [*Library symbol*] [*Library of Congress*] (LCLS)

MnHuStA..... St. Anastasis School, Hutchinson, MN [*Library symbol*] [*Library of Congress*] (LCLS)

Mn-Hw........ Minnesota State Department of Transportation, St. Paul, MN [*Library symbol Library of Congress*] (LCLS)

MNI............. Mach Number Indicated (MCD)

MNI............. Madras Native Infantry [*British*]

MNI............. Maina Air Ltd. [*Nigeria*] [*FAA designator*] (FAAC)

MNI............. Manado [*Celebes*] [*Seismograph station code, US Geological Survey*] (SEIS)

MNI............. Manning, SC [*Location identifier FAA*] (FAAL)

MNI............. McClatchy Newspapers, Inc. [*NYSE symbol*] (SPSG)

MNI............. Member of the Nautical Institute [*British*]

MNI............. Meridian Technologies [*TS, exchange symbol*] (TTSB)

MNI............. Meridian Technologies, Inc. [*Toronto Stock Exchange symbol*]

MnI............. Mille Iacs Lake Community Library, Isle, MN [*Library symbol*] [*Library of Congress*] (LCLS)

MNI............. Minimum Number of Individuals [*Statistics*]

MNI............. Ministry of National Insurance [*British*]

MNI............. Montserrat [*West Indies*] [*Airport symbol*] (OAG)

MNI............. Movimiento Nacionalista de Izquierda [*Bolivia*] (PPW)

MNNI.......... Winona State University, Winona, MN [*OCLC symbol*] (OCLC)

MNIA.......... Member of the National Institute of Accountants [*Australia*]

MnIf............ International Falls Public Library, International Falls, MN [*Library symbol Library of Congress*] (LCLS)

MnIfBC......... Boise Cascade Corp., Research Library, International Falls, MN [*Library symbol Library of Congress*] (LCLS)

MnIfE........... International Falls Elementary School, International Falls, MN [*Library symbol*] [*Library of Congress*] (LCLS)

MnIfH........... International Falls High School, International Falls, MN [*Library symbol*] [*Library of Congress*] (LCLS)

MnIfM........... A.B. Middle School, International Falls, MN [*Library symbol*] [*Library of Congress*] (LCLS)

MnIfRC........ Rainy River Community College, International Falls, MN [*Library symbol Library of Congress*] (LCLS)

MnIgS.......... Inver Hills State Junior College, Inver Grove Heights, MN [*Library symbol Library of Congress*] (LCLS)

MnIH........... Isle High School/Elementary School, Isle, MN [*Library symbol*] [*Library of Congress*] (LCLS)

MNIH.......... Member of the National Institute of Hardware [*British*] (DBQ)

MNIMH........ Member of the National Institute of Medical Herbalists [*British*]

MnIrCS........ Cherry Public School, Iron, MN [*Library symbol*] [*Library of Congress*] (LCLS)

MNIS.......... Manning & Napier Information Services

MnIsE.......... Isanti Elementary School, Isanti, MN [*Library symbol*] [*Library of Congress*] (LCLS)

MnIsM.......... Isnati Middle School, Isanti, MN [*Library symbol*] [*Library of Congress*] (LCLS)

MnIv............ Ivanhoe Public Library, Ivanhoe, MN [*Library symbol*] [*Library of Congress*] (LCLS)

MnIvEHS..... Lincoln Elementary-High School, Ivanhoe, MN [*Library symbol*] [*Library of Congress*] (LCLS)

MnJ............. Jackson County Library System, Jackson, MN [*Library symbol*] [*Library of Congress*] (LCLS)

MNJ............. Mananjary [*Madagascar*] [*Airport symbol*] (OAG)

MNJ............. Microelectronic Noise Jammer

MNJ............. Middletown & New Jersey Railway Co., Inc. [*AAR code*]

MNJ............. Movimiento Nacionalista Justicialista [*Justicialist Nationalist Movement - JNM*] [*Argentina*] (PPW)

MNJ............. Myoneural Junction [*Medicine*]

MNJ............. St. John's University, Collegeville, MN [*OCLC symbol*] (OCLC)

MnJaPS....... Jasper Public Schools, Jasper, MN [*Library symbol*] [*Library of Congress*] (LCLS)

MnJeJSH.... Storden-Jeffers Junior Senior High School, Jeffers, MN [*Library symbol*] [*Library of Congress*] (LCLS)

MnJES......... Jackson Elementary School, Jackson, MN [*Library symbol*] [*Library of Congress*] (LCLS)

MnJoTS....... Trinity Lutheran School, Johnson, MN [*Library symbol*] [*Library of Congress*] (LCLS)

MnJPS......... Jackson Public Schools, Jackson, MN [*Library symbol*] [*Library of Congress*] (LCLS)

MNJTS........ Mouvement National des Jeunes Travailleurs du Senegal [*National Movement of Young Workers of Senegal*]

MNK........... Bethel College, Learning Resources Center, St. Paul, MN [*OCLC symbol*] (OCLC)

MnK............ Kimball Public Library, Kimball, MN [*Library symbol*] [*Library of Congress*] (LCLS)

MNK........... Maiana [*Kiribati*] [*Airport symbol*] (OAG)

MNK........... Mankoya [*Zambia*] [*Airport symbol*] (AD)

MNK........... Pleshenitzi [*Formerly, Minsk*] [*Former USSR Geomagnetic observatory code*]

MNK........... Rochester, MN [*Location identifier FAA*] (FAAL)

MNKA......... Minimum Number of Animals Known Alive [*Ecology*]

MnKaES....... Kandiyohi Elementary School, Kandiyohi, MN [*Library symbol*] [*Library of Congress*] (LCLS)

MnKarE........ Karlstad Elementary School, Karlstad, MN [*Library symbol*] [*Library of Congress*] (LCLS)

MnKarH........ Tri-County High School, Karlstad, MN [*Library symbol*] [*Library of Congress*] (LCLS)

MnKE........... Kimball Elementary School, Kimball, MN [*Library symbol*] [*Library of Congress*] (LCLS)

MnKee......... Keewatin Public Library, Keewatin, MN [*Library symbol*] [*Library of Congress*] (LCLS)

MnKeEs....... Kerkhoven-Murdoch-Sunberg Elementary School, Kerkhoven, MN [*Library symbol*] [*Library of Congress*] (LCLS)

MnKeHS...... Kerkhoven-Murdoch-Sunberg High School, Kerkhoven, MN [*Library symbol*] [*Library of Congress*] (LCLS)

MnKenS....... Kensington Public School, Kensington, MN [*Library symbol*] [*Library of Congress*] (LCLS)

MnKeP......... Kerkoven Public Library, Kerkoven, MN [*Library symbol*] [*Library of Congress*] (LCLS)

MnKH.......... Kimball High School, Kimball, MN [*Library symbol*] [*Library of Congress*] (LCLS)

MnKHC........ Holy Cross School, Kimball, MN [*Library symbol*] [*Library of Congress*] (LCLS)

MnKin.......... Kinney Public Library, City Hall, Kinney, MN [*Library symbol*] [*Library of Congress*] (LCLS)

MNL........... Mangla [*New Mirpur*] [*Pakistan*] [*Seismograph station code, US Geological Survey*] (SEIS)

MNL........... Manila [*Philippines*] [*Airport symbol*] (OAG)

MNL........... Manual (MSA)

MNL........... Marine Navigating Light

MNL........... McClatchy Newspapers 'A' [*NYSE symbol*] (TTSB)

MNL........... McConnell Peel Resources [*Vancouver Stock Exchange symbol*]

MNL........... Medical Nutrition Laboratory [*Army*]

MNL........... Mesenteric Node Lymphocyte

MNL........... Miniliner SRL [*Italy ICAO designator*] (FAAC)

MNL........... Minnesota National Laboratory

MNL........... Molecular Neurobiology Laboratory [*Salk Institute for Biological Studies*]

MNL............ Mononuclear Leukocyte [*Hematology*]
MNL............ Montgomery County-Norristown Public Library, Norristown, PA [*OCLC symbol*] (OCLC)
MNL............ Movement for National Liberation [*Barbados*] [*Political party*] (PPW)
MNL............ Multinomial Logit [*Statistics*]
MNL............ National Liberation Movement [*Guatemala*] [*Political party*] (PD)
MNL............ Valdez, AK [*Location identifier FAA*] (FAAL)
MNLA.......... Mon National Liberation Army [*Myanmar*] [*Political party*] (EY)
MnLaiL........ Lake Itasca Forestry and Biological Station, Lake Itasca, MN [*Library symbol Library of Congress*] (LCLS)
MnLam........ Lamberton Public Library, Lamberton, MN [*Library symbol*] [*Library of Congress*] (LCLS)
MnLamS...... Lamberton School, Lamberton, MN [*Library symbol*] [*Library of Congress*] (LCLS)
MnLanS....... Lancaster Public School, Lancaster, MN [*Library symbol*] [*Library of Congress*] (LCLS)
MnLapS....... Laporte Public School, Laporte, MN [*Library symbol*] [*Library of Congress*] (LCLS)
MnLb.......... Lake Benton Public Library, Lake Benton, MN [*Library symbol*] [*Library of Congress*] (LCLS)
MnLbBa....... Buffalo Ridge Baptist Academy, Lake Benton, MN [*Library symbol*] [*Library of Congress*] (LCLS)
MnLbPS....... Lake Benton Public Schools, Lake Benton, MN [*Library symbol*] [*Library of Congress*] (LCLS)
MNLCA .... Methylnorlaudanosolinecarboxylic Acid [*Biochemistry*]
MNLD .... Mainland (FAAC)
Mn-Leg........ Minnesota State Legislative Library, St. Paul, MN [*Library symbol Library of Congress*] (LCLS)
MnLeoCS..... Leota Christian School, Leota, MN [*Library symbol*] [*Library of Congress*] (LCLS)
MnLepPS..... Lester Prairie Public School, Lester Prairie, MN [*Library symbol*] [*Library of Congress*] (LCLS)
MnLeW........ Washington County Library, Lake Elmo, MN [*Library symbol Library of Congress*] (LCLS)
MnLf.......... Carnegie City Library, Little Falls, MN [*Library symbol*] [*Library of Congress*] (LCLS)
MNLF.......... Malayan National Liberation Front [*Singapore*] [*Political party*] (PD)
MNLF.......... Moro National Liberation Front [*Philippines*] [*Political party*] (PD)
MnLfCL........ Charles Lindbergh Elementary School, Little Falls, MN [*Library symbol*] [*Library of Congress*] (LCLS)
MnLfH......... Little Falls Community High School, Little Falls, MN [*Library symbol*] [*Library of Congress*] (LCLS)
MnLfLE .... Lincoln Elementary School, Little Falls, MN [*Library symbol*] [*Library of Congress*] (LCLS)
MnLfM........ Little Falls Community Middle School, Little Falls, MN [*Library symbol*] [*Library of Congress*] (LCLS)
MnLfMS....... Mid-State Educational Cooperative, Little Falls, MN [*Library symbol*] [*Library of Congress*] (LCLS)
MnLfN......... North Star Christian Academy, Little Falls, MN [*Library symbol*] [*Library of Congress*] (LCLS)
MnLfO......... Our Lady of Lourdes School, Little Falls, MN [*Library symbol*] [*Library of Congress*] (LCLS)
MnLfoE .... Littlefork Elementary School, Littlefork, MN [*Library symbol*] [*Library of Congress*] (LCLS)
MnLfoH .... Littlefork High School, Littlefork, MN [*Library symbol*] [*Library of Congress*] (LCLS)
MnLfS .... St. Francis Convent, Little Falls, MN [*Library symbol*] [*Library of Congress*] (LCLS)
MnLfSG........ St. Gabriel's Hospital, Little Falls, MN [*Library symbol*] [*Library of Congress*] (LCLS)
MnLfSM....... St. Mary's School, Little Falls, MN [*Library symbol*] [*Library of Congress*] (LCLS)
MnLfW........ Weyerhauser Memorial Museum, Little Falls, MN [*Library symbol*] [*Library of Congress*] (LCLS)
MnLi .... Lindstrom Public Library, Lindstrom, MN [*Library symbol*] [*Library of Congress*] (LCLS)
MnLiJ .... Chisago Lakes Area Junior High School, Lindstrom, MN [*Library symbol*] [*Library of Congress*] (LCLS)
MnLiS .... Chisago Lakes Senior High School, Lindstrom, MN [*Library symbol*] [*Library of Congress*] (LCLS)
MnLit .... Litchfield Public Library, Litchfield, MN [*Library symbol*] [*Library of Congress*] (LCLS)
MnLitSH ...... Litchfield Senior High School, Litchfield, MN [*Library symbol*] [*Library of Congress*] (LCLS)
MnLitSP....... St. Philip's School, Litchfield, MN [*Library symbol*] [*Library of Congress*] (LCLS)
MnLitWES.... Wagner Elementary School, Litchfield, MN [*Library symbol*] [*Library of Congress*] (LCLS)
MnLkpE ...... Lake Park Elementary School, Lake Park, MN [*Library symbol*] [*Library of Congress*] (LCLS)
MnLkpH ...... Lake Park High School, Lake Park, MN [*Library symbol*] [*Library of Congress*] (LCLS)
MnLl .... Lake Lillian Public Library, Lake Lillian, MN [*Library symbol*] [*Library of Congress*] (LCLS)
MNLL.......... Malaysian National Liberation League (NADA)
MNLN .... Leon/Fanor Urroz [*Nicaragua*] [*ICAO location identifier*] (ICLI)
MnLon .... Margaret Welch Memorial Library, Longville, MN [*Library symbol*] [*Library of Congress*] (LCLS)
MnLp .... Long Prairie Public Library, Long Prairie, MN [*Library symbol*] [*Library of Congress*] (LCLS)
MnLpCHi...... Christie Home Historical Society, Long Prairie, MN [*Library symbol*] [*Library of Congress*] (LCLS)
MnLpE .... Long Prairie Elementary School, Long Prairie, MN [*Library symbol*] [*Library of Congress*] (LCLS)

MnLpH........ Long Prairie High School, Long Prairie, MN [*Library symbol*] [*Library of Congress*] (LCLS)
MnLpHi....... Todd County Historical Society, Long Prairie, MN [*Library symbol*] [*Library of Congress*] (LCLS)
MnLpM........ Meadowview School, Long Prairie, MN [*Library symbol*] [*Library of Congress*] (LCLS)
MnLpS .... St. Mary of Mt. Carmel, Long Prairie, MN [*Library symbol*] [*Library of Congress*] (LCLS)
MnLpT .... Trinity Lutheran School, Long Prairie, MN [*Library symbol*] [*Library of Congress*] (LCLS)
MNLS.......... Marine Navigating Light System
MNLS.......... Modified New Least Square (PDAA)
MnLS .... St. John Nepomuk School, Lastrup, MN [*Library symbol*] [*Library of Congress*] (LCLS)
MnLsG .... Green Giant Corp., Le Sueur, MN [*Library symbol Library of Congress*] (LCLS)
MnLucOLS... Our Lady of Victory School, Lucan, MN [*Library symbol*] [*Library of Congress*] (LCLS)
MNLY.......... Mainly (FAAC)
MnLyPS....... Lynd Public Library, Lynd, MN [*Library symbol*] [*Library of Congress*] (LCLS)
MNM.......... Mankato State University, Mankato, MN [*OCLC symbol*] (OCLC)
MNM.......... Master of Nonprofit Management (PGP)
MNM.......... Menominee [*Michigan*] [*Airport symbol*] (OAG)
MNM.......... Metal Nonmetal [*Materials science*]
MNM.......... Military Necessity Modification
MNM.......... Minimum
mnm .... Minimum (AD)
MNM.......... Minneapolis [*Minnesota*] [*Seismograph station code, US Geological Survey*] (SEIS)
MnM .... Minneapolis Public Library and Information Center, Minneapolis, MN [*Library symbol Library of Congress*] (LCLS)
mnm .... Mnemonic (AD)
MNM.......... Museum of New Mexico [*Research center*] (RCD)
MnMA......... Augsburg College and Seminary, Minneapolis, MN [*Library symbol Library of Congress*] (LCLS)
MnMAb........ Abbott-Northwestern Hospitals, Inc., Minneapolis, MN [*Library symbol Library of Congress*] (LCLS)
MnMAC....... Anoka County Library, Minneapolis, MN [*Library symbol Library of Congress*] (LCLS)
MnMaE .... Mahnomen Elementary School, Mahnomen, MN [*Library symbol*] [*Library of Congress*] (LCLS)
MnMah .... Mahnomen High School, Mahnomen, MN [*Library symbol*] [*Library of Congress*] (LCLS)
MnMAM....... American Medical Systems, Inc., Minneapolis, MN [*Library symbol Library of Congress*] (LCLS)
MnManBC.... Bethany Lutheran College, Mankato, MN [*Library symbol Library of Congress*] (LCLS)
MnManBS.... Bethany Lutheran Theological Seminary, Mankato, MN [*Library symbol Library of Congress*] (LCLS)
MnManM .... Minnesota Valley Regional Library, Mankato, MN [*Library symbol Library of Congress*] (LCLS)
MnManS ...... Mankato State College [*Later, Mankato State University*], Mankato, MN [*Library symbol Library of Congress*] (LCLS)
MnManTD.... Traverse des Sioux Library System, Mankato, MN [*Library symbol Library of Congress*] (LCLS)
MNMANY..... Men's Neckwear Manufacturers Association of New York [*Defunct*] (EA)
MnMAR....... American Rehabilitation Foundation Minneapolis, MN [*Library symbol Library of Congress*] (LCLS)
MnMar........ Marshall-Lyon County Library, Marshall, MN [*Library symbol Library of Congress*] (LCLS)
MnMarb ...... Marble Public Library, Marble, MN [*Library symbol*] [*Library of Congress*] (LCLS)
MnMarC....... Marshall-Lyon County Library, Marshall, MN [*Library symbol*] [*Library of Congress*] (LCLS)
MnMarH ...... Weiner Memorial Hospital, Marshall, MN [*Library symbol*] [*Library of Congress*] (LCLS)
MnMarLS..... Samuel Lutheran School, Marshall, MN [*Library symbol*] [*Library of Congress*] (LCLS)
MnMarPE..... Parkside Elementary School, Marshall, MN [*Library symbol*] [*Library of Congress*] (LCLS)
MnMarS....... Southwest Minnesota State College, Marshall, MN [*Library symbol Library of Congress*] (LCLS)
MnMarWES... West Side Elementary School, Marshall, MN [*Library symbol*] [*Library of Congress*] (LCLS)
MnMay .... Maynard Public Library, Maynard, MN [*Library symbol*] [*Library of Congress*] (LCLS)
MnMayPS..... Maynard Public Schools, Maynard, MN [*Library symbol*] [*Library of Congress*] (LCLS)
MnMBL....... Bakken Library of Electricity in Life, Minneapolis, MN [*Library symbol Library of Congress*] (LCLS)
MNMC .... Medical Network for Missing Children (EA)
MnMc......... Monticello Public Library, Monticello, MN [*Library symbol*] [*Library of Congress*] (LCLS)
MnMCA....... Minneapolis College of Art and Design, Minneapolis, MN [*Library symbol Library of Congress*] (LCLS)
MnMCC....... Minneapolis Community College, Minneapolis, MN [*Library symbol Library of Congress*] (LCLS)
MnMcgE ..... McGrath Elementary School, McGrath, MN [*Library symbol*] [*Library of Congress*] (LCLS)
MnMcgr....... McGregor Public Library, McGregor, MN [*Library symbol*] [*Library of Congress*] (LCLS)
MnMcgrS ..... McGregor School, McGregor, MN [*Library symbol*] [*Library of Congress*] (LCLS)

MnMcgrSL ... Sandy Lake Visitor Center, McGregor, MN [*Library symbol*] [*Library of Congress*] (LCLS)

MnMcH .... Monticello-Big Lake Community Hospital Library, Monticello, MN [*Library symbol*] [*Library of Congress*] (LCLS)

MnMci .... McInotosh Public Library, McIntosh, MN [*Library symbol*] [*Library of Congress*] (LCLS)

MnMciE ...... McIntosh Elementary School, McIntosh, MN [*Library symbol*] [*Library of Congress*] (LCLS)

MnMciH ...... McIntosh-Winger High School, McIntosh, MN [*Library symbol*] [*Library of Congress*] (LCLS)

MnMcJ .... Monticello Junior High School, Monticello, MN [*Library symbol*] [*Library of Congress*] (LCLS)

MnMck .... McKinley Public Library, McKinley, MN [*Library symbol*] [*Library of Congress*] (LCLS)

MnMcPE ..... Pinewood East Elementary School, Monticello, MN [*Library symbol*] [*Library of Congress*] (LCLS)

MnMcPW .... Pinewood West Elementary School, Monticello, MN [*Library symbol*] [*Library of Congress*] (LCLS)

MnMcR .... Rivercrest Christian School, Monticello, MN [*Library symbol*] [*Library of Congress*] (LCLS)

MnMcS .... Monticello Senior High School, Monticello, MN [*Library symbol*] [*Library of Congress*] (LCLS)

MnMcSR ..... St. Henry Catholic Church, School of Religion Library, Monticello, MN [*Library symbol*] [*Library of Congress*] (LCLS)

MNMD .... MiniMed Inc. [*NASDAQ symbol*] (TTSB)

MNMD .... MiniMed, Inc. [*NASDAQ symbol*] (SAG)

MnMe .... Melrose Public Library, Melrose, MN [*Library symbol*] [*Library of Congress*] (LCLS)

MnMeaS ...... Toivola-Meadowlands School, Meadowlands, MN [*Library symbol*] [*Library of Congress*] (LCLS)

MnMeE .... Melrose, New Munich, Spring Hill Elementary School, Melrose, MN [*Library symbol*] [*Library of Congress*] (LCLS)

MnMeH .... Melrose High School, Melrose, MN [*Library symbol*] [*Library of Congress*] (LCLS)

MnMeJ .... Melrose Junior High School, Melrose, MN [*Library symbol*] [*Library of Congress*] (LCLS)

MnMenE ...... Menahga Elementary School, Menagha, MN [*Library symbol*] [*Library of Congress*] (LCLS)

MnMenH ...... Menagha High School, Menagha, MN [*Library symbol*] [*Library of Congress*] (LCLS)

MnMeS .... St. John-St. Andrew School, Melrose, MN [*Library symbol*] [*Library of Congress*] (LCLS)

MnMeSM ..... St. Mary's Elementary School, Melrose, MN [*Library symbol*] [*Library of Congress*] (LCLS)

MnMF .... Fairview Hospital, Minneapolis, MN [*Library symbol Library of Congress*] (LCLS)

MnMFL .... Association of Free Lutheran Congregation and Seminary Headquarters, Minneapolis, MN [*Library symbol Library of Congress*] (LCLS)

MnMFR .... Federation Reserve Bank of Minneapolis, Minneapolis, MN [*Library symbol*] [*Library of Congress*] (LCLS)

MnMG .... Golden Valley Lutheran College, Minneapolis, MN [*Library symbol Library of Congress*] (LCLS)

MNMG .... Managua/Augusto Cesar Sandino [*Nicaragua*] [*ICAO location identifier*] (ICLI)

MnMGM .... General Mills, Inc., Minneapolis, MN [*Library symbol Library of Congress*] (LCLS)

MnMGS .... Church of Jesus Christ of Latter-Day Saints, Genealogical Society Library, Minneapolis Branch, Minneapolis, MN [*Library symbol Library of Congress*] (LCLS)

MnMH .... Hennepin County Medical Society, Minneapolis, MN [*Library symbol Library of Congress*] (LCLS)

MnMHCL ...... Hennepin County Library, Minneapolis, MN [*Library symbol Library of Congress*] (LCLS)

MnMHen ...... Henkel Corp., Minneapolis, MN [*Library symbol Library of Congress*] (LCLS)

MnMHH .... Hennepin County General Hospital, Minneapolis, MN [*Library symbol Library of Congress*] (LCLS)

MnMHLL ...... Hennepin County Law Library, Minneapolis, MN [*Library symbol Library of Congress*] (LCLS)

MnMI .... Interlutheran Theological Seminary and Bible School, Minneapolis, MN [*Library symbol Library of Congress*] (LCLS)

MNMIA .... Men's Neckwear Manufacturers Institute of America (EA)

MNMIC .... Modernized National Military Intelligence Center

MNMIC .... Modernized NMIC [*National Military Intelligence Center*] (MCD)

MnMiE .... Milaca Elementary School, Milaca, MN [*Library symbol*] [*Library of Congress*] (LCLS)

MnMiH .... Milaca High School, Milaca, MN [*Library symbol*] [*Library of Congress*] (LCLS)

MnMilE .... Miltona Elementary School, Miltona, MN [*Library symbol*] [*Library of Congress*] (LCLS)

MnMiM .... Milaca Middle School, Milaca, MN [*Library symbol*] [*Library of Congress*] (LCLS)

MnMIn .... Interstudy, Minneapolis, MN [*Library symbol Library of Congress*] (LCLS)

MnMinPS ..... Minneota Public Schools, Minneota, MN [*Library symbol*] [*Library of Congress*] (LCLS)

MnMinSE ..... St. Edward School, Minneota, MN [*Library symbol*] [*Library of Congress*] (LCLS)

MnMirS .... Middle River School, Middle River, MN [*Library symbol*] [*Library of Congress*] (LCLS)

MnMK .... Kenny Rehabilitation Institute, Minneapolis, MN [*Library symbol Library of Congress*] (LCLS)

MNMKT .... Money Market (NITA)

MnMLD .... Lutheran Deaconess Hospital, Minneapolis, MN [*Library symbol Library of Congress*] (LCLS)

MNMIE .... Maple Lake Elementary School, Maple Lake, MN [*Library symbol*] [*Library of Congress*] (LCLS)

MnMlH .... Maple Lake High, Maple Lake, MN [*Library symbol*] [*Library of Congress*] (LCLS)

MnMln .... Milan Public Library, Milan, MN [*Library symbol*] [*Library of Congress*] (LCLS)

MnMlnES .... Milan Elementary School, Milan, MN [*Library symbol*] [*Library of Congress*] (LCLS)

MnMlS .... St. Timothy School, Maple Lake, MN [*Library symbol*] [*Library of Congress*] (LCLS)

MnMlyPS .... Milroy Public Schools, Milan, MN [*Library symbol*] [*Library of Congress*] (LCLS)

MnMMC ...... Metropolitan State Community College, Minneapolis, MN [*Library symbol Library of Congress*] (LCLS)

MnMMe .... Medtronic, Inc., Minneapolis, MN [*Library symbol Library of Congress*] (LCLS)

MnMMeH ..... Methodist Hospital, Minneapolis, MN [*Library symbol Library of Congress*] (LCLS)

MnMMet ...... Metropolitan Medical Center, Medical Library, Minneapolis, MN [*Library symbol Library of Congress*] (LCLS)

MnMMet-H... Metropolitan Medical Center, Hospital Services Library, Minneapolis, MN [*Library symbol Library of Congress*] (LCLS)

MnMMetS .... Metropolitan State Junior College, Minneapolis, MN [*Library symbol Library of Congress*] (LCLS)

MnMMH .... Minneapolis-Honeywell Regulator Co., Minneapolis, MN [*Library symbol Library of Congress*] (LCLS)

MnMMSC ..... MTS Systems Corporation, Minneapolis, MN [*Library symbol Library of Congress*] (LCLS)

MnMMSP ..... Minnesota School of Professional Psychology, Minneapolis, MN [*Library symbol*] [*Library of Congress*] (LCLS)

MnMMtS ...... Mount Sinai Hospital, Minneapolis, MN [*Library symbol Library of Congress*] (LCLS)

MnMN .... Normandale Community College, Minneapolis, MN [*Library symbol Library of Congress*] (LCLS)

MnMNC .... North Central Bible College, Minneapolis, MN [*Library symbol Library of Congress*] (LCLS)

MnMnCMS ... Cedar Mountain School, Morgan, MN [*Library symbol*] [*Library of Congress*] (LCLS)

MnMNH .... North Memorial Hospital, Minneapolis, MN [*Library symbol Library of Congress*] (LCLS)

MnMNHe ..... North Hennepin Community College, Minneapolis, MN [*Library symbol Library of Congress*] (LCLS)

MnMnl .... Mountain Lake Public Library, Mountain Lake, MN [*Library symbol*] [*Library of Congress*] (LCLS)

MnMnlCS ..... Mountain Lake Christian School, Mountain Lake, MN [*Library symbol*] [*Library of Congress*] (LCLS)

MnMnlHS ..... Mountain Lake Public High School, Mountain Lake, MN [*Library symbol*] [*Library of Congress*] (LCLS)

MnMnlMB .... Mt. Bethany Christian School, Mountain Lake, MN [*Library symbol*] [*Library of Congress*] (LCLS)

MnMnP .... Morgan Pubic Library, Morgan, MN [*Library symbol*] [*Library of Congress*] (LCLS)

MnMo .... Morris Public Library, Morris, MN [*Library symbol*] [*Library of Congress*] (LCLS)

MnMoE .... Morris Elementary School, Morris, MN [*Library symbol*] [*Library of Congress*] (LCLS)

MnMoh .... Moorhead Public Library, Moorhead, MN [*Library symbol*] [*Library of Congress*] (LCLS)

MnMohC ..... Concordia College, Moorhead, MN [*Library symbol Library of Congress*] (LCLS)

MnMohEE .... Edison Elementary School, Moorhead, MN [*Library symbol*] [*Library of Congress*] (LCLS)

MnMohHi .... Clay County Historical Society, Library and Archives, Moorhead, MN [*Library symbol*] [*Library of Congress*] (LCLS)

MnMohJ ...... Moorhead Junior High School, Moorhead, MN [*Library symbol*] [*Library of Congress*] (LCLS)

MnMohL ...... Lake Agassiz Regional Library, Moorhead, MN [*Library symbol Library of Congress*] (LCLS)

MnMohPS .... Moorhead Public Schools System, Moorhead, MN [*Library symbol Library of Congress*] (LCLS)

MnMohS ...... Moorhead State College, Moorhead, MN [*Library symbol Library of Congress*] (LCLS)

MnMohSA .... St. Ansgar Hospital, Health Science Library, Moorhead, MN [*Library symbol*] [*Library of Congress*] (LCLS)

MnMohSH .... Moorhead Senior High School, Moorhead, MN [*Library symbol*] [*Library of Congress*] (LCLS)

MnMohSJ .... St. Joseph School, Moorhead, MN [*Library symbol*] [*Library of Congress*] (LCLS)

MnMohWE ... Washington Elementary School, Moorhead, MN [*Library symbol*] [*Library of Congress*] (LCLS)

MnMol .... Moose Lake Public Lake, Moose Lake, MN [*Library symbol*] [*Library of Congress*] (LCLS)

MnMolS .... Moose Lake Public School, Moose Lake, MN [*Library symbol*] [*Library of Congress*] (LCLS)

MnMoM .... Morris Middle School, Morris, MN [*Library symbol*] [*Library of Congress*] (LCLS)

MnMoMHS ... Morris High School, Morris, MN [*Library symbol*] [*Library of Congress*] (LCLS)

MnMotS .... Motley School, Motley, MN [*Library symbol*] [*Library of Congress*] (LCLS)

MnMoU .... University of Minnesota, Morris, MN [*Library symbol Library of Congress*] (LCLS)

MnMov .... Chippewa County Library System, Montevideo, MN [*Library symbol Library of Congress*] (LCLS)

MnMovCH .... Chippewa County-Montevideo Hospital, Montevideo, MN [*Library symbol*] [*Library of Congress*] (LCLS)

MnMovMS ... Montevideo Middle School, Montevideo, MN [*Library symbol*] [*Library of Congress*] (LCLS)

MnMovRE .... Ramsey Elementary School, Montevideo, MN [*Library symbol*] [*Library of Congress*] (LCLS)

MnMovSE .... Sanford Elementary School, Montevideo, MN [*Library symbol*] [*Library of Congress*] (LCLS)

MnMovSEC .. Southwest-West Central Educational Cooperative Service Unit, Montevideo, MN [*Library symbol*] [*Library of Congress*] (LCLS)

MnMovSH .... Montevideo Senior High School, Montevideo, MN [*Library symbol*] [*Library of Congress*] (LCLS)

MnMP .... Pillsbury Co., Minneapolis, MN [*Library symbol*] [*Library of Congress*] (LCLS)

MnMrFE .... Fairview Elementary Library, Mora, MN [*Library symbol*] [*Library of Congress*] (LCLS)

MnMrH .... Mora High School, Mora, MN [*Library symbol*] [*Library of Congress*] (LCLS)

MnMrHi .... Kanabec County Historical Society, Mora, MN [*Library symbol*] [*Library of Congress*] (LCLS)

MnMrMS ..... Mora Fairview Central Middle School, Mora, MN [*Library symbol*] [*Library of Congress*] (LCLS)

MnMrR .... Rum River Vocational Center, Mora, MN [*Library symbol*] [*Library of Congress*] (LCLS)

MnMS .... Saint Louis Park Medical Center, Minneapolis, MN [*Library symbol Library of Congress*] (LCLS)

MnMSMC ..... Saint Mary's Junior College, Minneapolis, MN [*Library symbol Library of Congress*] (LCLS)

MnMSMH .... Saint Mary's Hospital, Minneapolis, MN [*Library symbol Library of Congress*] (LCLS)

MNMT......... Monument [*Board on Geographic Names*]

MNMT......... Monument

MnMtE .... Montrose Elementary School, Montrose, MN [*Library symbol*] [*Library of Congress*] (LCLS)

MnMti......... Mountain Iron Public Library, Mt. Iron, MN [*Library symbol*] [*Library of Congress*] (LCLS)

MnMtiE .... Merritt Elementary School, Mt. Iron, MN [*Library symbol*] [*Library of Congress*] (LCLS)

MnMtiHS ..... Mt. Iron High School, Mt. Iron, MN [*Library symbol*] [*Library of Congress*] (LCLS)

MnMuKS ..... Kerkhover-Murdock-Sunberg School, Murdock, MN [*Library symbol*] [*Library of Congress*] (LCLS)

MnMULS..... University of Minnesota Union List of Serials, Minneapolis, MN [*Library symbol Library of Congress*] (LCLS)

MnMVA....... United States Veterans Administration Hospital, Minneapolis, MN [*Library symbol Library of Congress*] (LCLS)

MnMW........ Walker Art Center, Minneapolis, MN [*Library symbol*] [*Library of Congress*] (LCLS)

MNN .... Carleton College, Northfield, MN [*OCLC symbol*] (OCLC)

MNN .... Madness Network News (EA)

MNN .... Marion, OH [*Location identifier FAA*] (FAAL)

MNN .... Minneapolis [*Minnesota*] [*Seismograph station code, US Geological Survey*] (SEIS)

Mn-N .... Minnesota State Department of Natural Resources, St. Paul, MN [*Library symbol Library of Congress*] (LCLS)

MNN .... Monenco Ltd. [*Toronto Stock Exchange symbol*]

MnNaSH ..... Nashwauk-Keewatin Senior High School, Nashwauk, MN [*Library symbol*] [*Library of Congress*] (LCLS)

MnNbU .... United Theological Seminary of the Twin Cities, New Brighton, MN [*Library symbol Library of Congress*] (LCLS)

MnNC......... Carleton College, Northfield, MN [*Library symbol Library of Congress*] (LCLS)

MnNeS........ Nevis Public School, Nevis, MN [*Library symbol*] [*Library of Congress*] (LCLS)

MnNeuL...... Doctor Martin Luther College, New Ulm, MN [*Library symbol Library of Congress*] (LCLS)

MNNG......... Methylnitronitrosoguanidine [*Biochemistry*]

MnNHi .... Norwegian-American Historical Association, Northfield, MN [*Library symbol Library of Congress*] (LCLS)

MnNisE....... Nisswa Elementary School, Nisswa, MN [*Library symbol*] [*Library of Congress*] (LCLS)

MnNl.......... New London Public Library, New London, MN [*Library symbol*] [*Library of Congress*] (LCLS)

MnNIES....... New London Elementary School, New London, MN [*Library symbol*] [*Library of Congress*] (LCLS)

MnNIJSH ..... New London-Spicer Junior Senior High School, New London, MN [*Library symbol*] [*Library of Congress*] (LCLS)

MnNIPES ..... Prairie Woods Elementary School, New London, MN [*Library symbol*] [*Library of Congress*] (LCLS)

MnNmT....... Mankato Area Vocational-Technical Institute, North Mankato, MN [*Library symbol Library of Congress*] (LCLS)

MnNob........ North Branch Area Library, North Branch, MN [*Library symbol*] [*Library of Congress*] (LCLS)

MnNobH ...... North Branch High School, North Branch, MN [*Library symbol*] [*Library of Congress*] (LCLS)

MnNobM...... North Branch Middle School, North Branch, MN [*Library symbol*] [*Library of Congress*] (LCLS)

MnNoS........ Northome School, Northome, MN [*Library symbol*] [*Library of Congress*] (LCLS)

MNNP .... Malawi Nyika National Park (AD)

MnNS......... Saint Olaf College, Northfield, MN [*Library symbol Library of Congress*] (LCLS)

MnNS-K...... Saint Olaf College, Kierkegaard Library, Northfield, MN [*Library symbol*] [*Library of Congress*] (LCLS)

MnNym........ New York Mills Public Library, New York Mills, MN [*Library symbol*] [*Library of Congress*] (LCLS)

MnNymH...... New York Mills High School, New York Mills, MN [*Library symbol*] [*Library of Congress*] (LCLS)

MNO .... Maddona Resources Corp. [*Vancouver Stock Exchange symbol*]

mno .... Manobo [*MARC language code Library of Congress*] (LCCP)

MNO .... Manono [*Zaire*] [*Airport symbol*] (OAG)

MNO .... Master of Nonprofit Organization (PGP)

MnO .... Owatonna Free Public Library, Owatonna, MN [*Library symbol Library of Congress*] (LCLS)

MNO .... Refugio, TX [*Location identifier FAA*] (FAAL)

MNO .... Saint Olaf College, Northfield, MN [*OCLC symbol*] (OCLC)

MNoadT ...... North Adams State College, North Adams, MA [*Library symbol Library of Congress*] (LCLS)

MNoanM...... Merrimack College, North Andover, MA [*Library symbol Library of Congress*] (LCLS)

MNoanMV... Merrimack Valley Textile Museum, North Andover, MA [*Library symbol Library of Congress*] (LCLS)

MNodS........ Southeastern Massachusetts University, North Dartmouth, MA [*Library symbol Library of Congress*] (LCLS)

MNoeS........ Stonehill College, North Easton, MA [*Library symbol Library of Congress*] (LCLS)

MnOgS........ Ogilvie Public School, Ogilvie, MN [*Library symbol*] [*Library of Congress*] (LCLS)

MnOkaHJH... Huron Lake-Okabena-Lakefield Junior High School, Okabena, MN [*Library symbol*] [*Library of Congress*] (LCLS)

MnOkS........ Oklee Public School, Oklee, MN [*Library symbol*] [*Library of Congress*] (LCLS)

MnOl.......... Olivia Public Library, Olivia, MN [*Library symbol*] [*Library of Congress*] (LCLS)

MnOIES....... Olivia Elementary School, Olivia, MN [*Library symbol*] [*Library of Congress*] (LCLS)

MnOIStA ..... St. Aloysious School, Olivia, MN [*Library symbol*] [*Library of Congress*] (LCLS)

MNOMU...... Mobile Nuclear Ordnance Maintenance Unit (MCD)

MnOnC........ Crosier Seminary Library, Onamia, MN [*Library symbol*] [*Library of Congress*] (LCLS)

MnOnE........ Onamia Elementary School, Onamia, MN [*Library symbol*] [*Library of Congress*] (LCLS)

MnOnG .... Galloway Boy's Ranch School, Onamia, MN [*Library symbol*] [*Library of Congress*] (LCLS)

MnOnH .... Onamia High School, Onamia, MN [*Library symbol*] [*Library of Congress*] (LCLS)

MNOPF .... Merchant Navy Officers' Pension Fund [*British*] (DS)

MNOR........ Missile Not Operationally Ready [*Air Force*] (SAA)

MNORM....... Missile Not Operationally Ready - Maintenance [*Air Force*]

MNORP....... Missile Not Operationally Ready - Parts [*Air Force*]

MnOrS .... Orr Public School, Orr, MN [*Library symbol*] [*Library of Congress*] (LCLS)

MnOrv......... Ortonville Public Library, Ortonville, MN [*Library symbol*] [*Library of Congress*] (LCLS)

MnOrvH ...... Ortonville Hospital, Ortonville, MN [*Library symbol*] [*Library of Congress*] (LCLS)

MnOrvPS ..... Ortonville Public School, Ortonville, MN [*Library symbol*] [*Library of Congress*] (LCLS)

mnos .... Metallic Nitrogen-Oxide Semiconductor (AD)

MNOS .... Metal-Nitride-Oxide Silicon [*or Semiconductor*]

MNOSFET .... Metal-Nitride-Oxide-Semiconductor Field-Effect Transistor

MnOsS......... Osakis School, Osakis, MN [*Library symbol*] [*Library of Congress*] (LCLS)

MNOS/SOS... Metal-Nitride Oxide Semiconductor / Silicon-on-Sapphire

MNot........... Cobb Memorial Library, North Truro, MA [*Library symbol*] [*Library of Congress*] (LCLS)

MNoW .... Wheaton College, Norton, MA [*Library symbol Library of Congress*] (LCLS)

MNP............ Malay National Party [*Political party*] (AD)

MNP............ Malay National Party (NADA)

MNP............ Marsabit National Park [*Kenya*] (AD)

MNP............ Maximum Negative Pressure [*Nuclear energy*] (NRCH)

MNP............ Meru National Park [*Equatorial Kenya*] (AD)

MNP............ Meta-Nitrophenol [*Organic chemistry*]

MNP............ Microcom Networking Protocol [*Telecommunications*] (ACRL)

MNP............ Microcomputer Networking Protocol

MNP............ Microcone Networking Protocol

MNP............ Midnapore (1979) Resources, Inc. [*Vancouver Stock Exchange symbol*]

MNP............ Mikumi National Park [*Tanzania*] (AD)

Mn-P........... Minnesota State Department of Planning, St. Paul, MN [*Library symbol Library of Congress*] (LCLS)

MNP............ More Nearly Perfect [*Microsoft Corp.*] [*Computer science*]

MNP............ Mouvement Nationale Patriotique [*Haiti*] [*Political party*] (EY)

MNP............ Movimiento Nacionalista Popular [*Popular Nationalist Movement*] [*Chile*] [*Political party*] (PD)

MNP............ Movimiento Nacional y Popular [*Paraguay*] [*Political party*] (EY)

MNP............ Movimiento No Partidarizado [*Peru*] [*Political party*] (EY)

MNP............ Multinomial Probit [*Statistics*]

MNP............ Municipal Partners Fund [*NYSE symbol*] (SPSG)

MNP............ Mushandike National Park [*Rhodesia*] (AD)

MNP............ Northern Mariana Islands [*ANSI three-letter standard code*] (CNC)

MnP............ Princeton Community Library, Princeton, MN [*Library symbol*] [*Library of Congress*] (LCLS)

MNP............ University of Minnesota, St. Paul, MN [*OCLC symbol*] (OCLC)

MNPA .... Malaysian Newspaper Publishers Association (EAIO)

MNPA .... Mono-normal-propylamine [*Organic chemistry*]
MnPapH....... Parkers Prairie High School, Parkers Prairie, MN [*Library symbol*] [*Library of Congress*] (LCLS)
MnParFE .... Frank White Elementary School, Park Rapids, MN [*Library symbol*] [*Library of Congress*] (LCLS)
MnParH .... Park Rapids Area High School, Park Rapids, MN [*Library symbol*] [*Library of Congress*] (LCLS)
MnParM....... Park Rapids Middle School, Park Rapids, MN [*Library symbol*] [*Library of Congress*] (LCLS)
MnPc .... Pine City Pubic Library, Pine City, MN [*Library symbol*] [*Library of Congress*] (LCLS)
MNPC .... Puerto Cabezas [*Nicaragua*] [*ICAO location identifier*] (ICLI)
MnPcE .... Pine City Elementary School, Pine City, MN [*Library symbol*] [*Library of Congress*] (LCLS)
MnPcH .... Pine City High School, Pine City, MN [*Library symbol*] [*Library of Congress*] (LCLS)
MnPcS .... St. Mary's School, Pine City, MN [*Library symbol*] [*Library of Congress*] (LCLS)
MnPcT .... Pine Technical Institute Learning Resource Center, Pine City, MN [*Library symbol*] [*Library of Congress*] (LCLS)
MNPD .... Missile and Nuclear Programming Data (AABC)
MnPeC .... Pease Community Christian School, Pease, MN [*Library symbol*] [*Library of Congress*] (LCLS)
MnPelE....... Pequot Lakes Elementary School, Pequot Lakes, MN [*Library symbol*] [*Library of Congress*] (LCLS)
MnPelH....... Pequot Lakes High School, Pequot Lakes MN [*Library symbol*] [*Library of Congress*] (LCLS)
MnPerH .... Pelican Rapids High School, Pelican Rapids, MN [*Library symbol*] [*Library of Congress*] (LCLS)
MnPerVE...... Viking Elementary School, Pelican Rapids, MN [*Library symbol*] [*Library of Congress*] (LCLS)
MnPH.......... Princeton High School, Princeton, MN [*Library symbol*] [*Library of Congress*] (LCLS)
MnPhE .... Perham Elementary School, Perham, MN [*Library symbol*] [*Library of Congress*] (LCLS)
MnPhP .... Perham Public Library, Perham, MN [*Library symbol*] [*Library of Congress*] (LCLS)
MNPI .... Microcom, Inc. [*NASDAQ symbol*] (NQ)
MnPi........... Pierz Public Library, Pierz, MN [*Library symbol*] [*Library of Congress*] (LCLS)
MnPiH .... Healy High School, Pierz, MN [*Library symbol*] [*Library of Congress*] (LCLS)
MnPiHE....... Harding Elementary School, Pierz, MN [*Library symbol*] [*Library of Congress*] (LCLS)
MnPilS........ Pillager Public School, Pillager, MN [*Library symbol*] [*Library of Congress*] (LCLS)
MnPiS......... St. Joseph's Elementary School, Pierz, MN [*Library symbol*] [*Library of Congress*] (LCLS)
MnPJ .... Princeton Junior High School, Princeton, MN [*Library symbol*] [*Library of Congress*] (LCLS)
MNPL.......... Machinists Non-Partisan Political League (EA)
MnPluS........ Pershing Public School, Plummer, MN [*Library symbol*] [*Library of Congress*] (LCLS)
MnPNE........ Princeton North Elementary School, Princeton, MN [*Library symbol*] [*Library of Congress*] (LCLS)
mnpo .... Main Port (AD)
MNPO .... Median Preoptic Area [*Brain anatomy*]
MNPO .... Mobile Navy Post Office
MNPP .... Midland Nuclear Power Plant (NRCH)
MnPpBES..... Dr. Brown Elementary School, Pipestone, MN [*Library symbol*] [*Library of Congress*] (LCLS)
MnPpHES .... Hill Elementary School, Pipestone, MN [*Library symbol*] [*Library of Congress*] (LCLS)
MnPpHS ...... Pipestone Cental High School, Pipestone, MN [*Library symbol*] [*Library of Congress*] (LCLS)
MN-PPL .... Machinists Non-Partisan Political League (EA)
MnPpTC....... Southwest Technical College, Pipestone, MN [*Library symbol*] [*Library of Congress*] (LCLS)
MnPr........... Kitchigami Regional Library, Pine River, MN [*Library symbol Library of Congress*] (LCLS)
MnPrbMCS... Central Minnesota Christian School, Prinsburg, MN [*Library symbol*] [*Library of Congress*] (LCLS)
MnPrbPS ..... Prinsburg Public Schools, Prinsburg, MN [*Library symbol*] [*Library of Congress*] (LCLS)
MnPrE......... Pine River Elementary School, Pine River, MN [*Library symbol*] [*Library of Congress*] (LCLS)
MnPrH .... Pine River High School, Pine River, MN [*Library symbol*] [*Library of Congress*] (LCLS)
MnProJ........ Jedlicka Junior High School, Proctor, MN [*Library symbol*] [*Library of Congress*] (LCLS)
MnProSH .... Proctor Senior High School, Proctor, MN [*Library symbol*] [*Library of Congress*] (LCLS)
MnPrP .... Pine River Public Library, Pine River, MN [*Library symbol*] [*Library of Congress*] (LCLS)
MNPS .... Millstone Nuclear Power Station (NRCH)
MNPS .... Minimum Navigation Performance Specification [*Aviation*] (FAAC)
MNPS .... Movimiento Nazionale Pan-Somalo [*Pan-Somali National Movement*] [*Political party*]
MNPSA .... Minimum Navigation Performance Specification Airspace [*Aviation*] (FAAC)
MnPSE .... Princeton South Elementary School, Princeton, MN [*Library symbol*] [*Library of Congress*] (LCLS)
MNPT.......... Meta-Nitro-para-toluidine [*Organic chemistry*]
MnPv .... Paynesville Public Library, Paynesville, MN [*Library symbol*] [*Library of Congress*] (LCLS)

MnPvEM ...... Paynesville Elementary & Middle School, Paynesville, MN [*Library symbol*] [*Library of Congress*] (LCLS)
MnPvH .... Paynesville Hospital, Medical Staff Library, Paynesville, MN [*Library symbol*] [*Library of Congress*] (LCLS)
MnPvHi........ Paynesville Historical Society, Paynesville, MN [*Library symbol*] [*Library of Congress*] (LCLS)
MnPvHS ...... Paynesville, High School, Paynesville, MN [*Library symbol*] [*Library of Congress*] (LCLS)
MNPWR ...... Manpower (AFM)
MNPWR ...... Manpower
MNPZ.......... Mononitrosopiperazine [*Biochemistry*]
mnpz........... Monopolize (AD)
mnpzd .... Monopolized (AD)
mnpzg .... Monopolizing (AD)
mnpzn......... Monopolization (AD)
MNQ .... Manicouagan [*Quebec*] [*Seismograph station code, US Geological Survey*] (SEIS)
MNQ .... Manifest Needs Questionnaire (EDAC)
MNQ .... Methylnaphthoquinone [*Organic chemistry*]
MNQ .... Monto [*Australia Airport symbol*] (OAG)
MNQ .... Montoro Resources [*Vancouver Stock Exchange symbol*]
MNQ .... University of Minnesota, Waseca, Waseca, MN [*OCLC symbol*] (OCLC)
MNR .... James J. Hill Reference Library, St. Paul, MN [*OCLC symbol*] (OCLC)
MNR .... Maintenance/Nonconformance Record (MCD)
MNR .... Manor (MCD)
MNR .... Manor
MNR .... Manor Care [*NYSE symbol*] (TTSB)
MNR .... Manor Care, Inc. [*NYSE symbol*] (SPSG)
MNR .... Marrow Neutrophil Reserve [*Medicine*]
MNR .... Massive Nuclear Retaliation (AAG)
mnr .... Massive Nuclear Retaliation (AD)
MNR .... Maximum Number of Records (MHDB)
MNR .... McMaster Nuclear Reactor [*Canada*]
MNR .... McNellen Resources, Inc. [*Vancouver Stock Exchange symbol Toronto Stock Exchange symbol*]
MNR .... Mean Neap [*Tide*] Rise [*Tides and currents*]
mnr .... Mean Neap Rise (AD)
Mnr .... Mijnherr [*Mr.*] [*Dutch*] (AD)
MNR .... Mines Road [*California*] [*Seismograph station code, US Geological Survey*] (SEIS)
MNR .... Minimum Noise Routes
MNR .... Monair SA [*Switzerland ICAO designator*] (FAAC)
MNR .... Mongu [*Zambia*] [*Airport symbol*] (OAG)
MNR .... Morphine-Naive Rats
MNr .... Morrill Memorial Library, Norwood, MA [*Library symbol Library of Congress*] (LCLS)
MNR .... Mouvement Nationaliste Revolutionnaire [*Revolutionary Nationalist Movement*] [*France Political party*] (PD)
MNR .... Movimiento Nacionalista Revolucionario [*National Revolutionary Movement*] [*Bolivia*] [*Political party*] (PPW)
MNR .... Movimiento Nacional Reformista [*National Reformist Movement*] [*Honduras*] [*Political party*]
MNR .... Movimiento Nacional Revolucionario [*National Revolutionary Movement*] [*El Salvador*] [*Political party*] (PPW)
MNR .... Mozambique National Resistance [*Political party*] (AD)
MNR .... Mozambique National Resistance Movement
MnR .... Rochester Public Library, Rochester, MN [*Library symbol Library of Congress*] (LCLS)
MnRa.......... Raymond Public Library, Raymond, MN [*Library symbol*] [*Library of Congress*] (LCLS)
MnRaKE....... Knight Elementary School, Randall, MN [*Library symbol*] [*Library of Congress*] (LCLS)
MNRC .... Minorco [*Formerly, Minerals & Resources Corp. Ltd.*] [*NASDAQ symbol*] (NQ)
MnRc .... Rush City Public Library, Rush City, MN [*Library symbol*] [*Library of Congress*] (LCLS)
MnRcE......... Rush City Elementary School, Rush City, MN [*Library symbol*] [*Library of Congress*] (LCLS)
MnRcH......... Rush City High School, Rush City, MN [*Library symbol*] [*Library of Congress*] (LCLS)
MNRCS........ Median Normalized RADAR Cross Section
MNRCY........ Minorco ADR [*NASDAQ symbol*] (TTSB)
MnRelE........ Redlake Elementary School, Redlake, MN [*Library symbol*] [*Library of Congress*] (LCLS)
MnRelH........ Redlake High School, Redlake, MN [*Library symbol*] [*Library of Congress*] (LCLS)
MnRemE....... Remer Elementary School, Remer, MN [*Library symbol*] [*Library of Congress*] (LCLS)
MnRemH ..... Northland High School, Remer, MN [*Library symbol*] [*Library of Congress*] (LCLS)
MnRen......... Renville City Library, Renville, MN [*Library symbol*] [*Library of Congress*] (LCLS)
MnRenBPS... Bird Island-Danube-Renville-Sacred Heart (BDRSH) Public Schools, Renville, MN [*Library symbol*] [*Library of Congress*] (LCLS)
MNRF .... Moonroof [*Automotive advertising*]
MnRfE......... Rockford Elementary School, Rockford, MN [*Library symbol*] [*Library of Congress*] (LCLS)
MnRfH .... Rockford High School, Rockford, MN [*Library symbol*] [*Library of Congress*] (LCLS)
MnRfM......... Rockford Middle School, Rockford, MN [*Library symbol*] [*Library of Congress*] (LCLS)
MnRgE......... Rogers Elementary School, Rogers, MN [*Library symbol*] [*Library of Congress*] (LCLS)

MnRgS......... St. Martin's School, Rogers, MN [*Library symbol*] [*Library of Congress*] (LCLS)

MNRH......... Movimiento Nacionalista Revolucionario Historico [*Historic Revolutionary Nationalist Movement*] [*Bolivia*] [*Political party*] (PPW)

MnRiE......... Rice Elementary School, Rice, MN [*Library symbol*] [*Library of Congress*] (LCLS)

MNRJ.......... Museo Nacional de Rio de Janeiro [*National Museum of Rio de Janeiro*] [*Portugal*] (AD)

MNRL .... Mineral (MSA)
MNRL .... Mineral
mnrl .... Mineral (VRA)

MNrL .... Morrill Memorial Library, Norwood, MA [*Library symbol*] [*Library of Congress*] (LCLS)

MnRlF......... Red Lake Falls Public Library, Red Lake Falls, MN [*Library symbol*] [*Library of Congress*] (LCLS)

MnRlfHE ..... J.A. Hughes Elementary School, Red Lake Falls, MN [*Library symbol*] [*Library of Congress*] (LCLS)

MnRlPS .... Sioux Valley-Round Lake-Brewster Public School, Round Lake, MN [*Library symbol*] [*Library of Congress*] (LCLS)

MNRM .... Master of Natural Resource Management (PGP)

MnRM......... Mayo Clinic, Rochester, MN [*Library symbol Library of Congress*] (LCLS)

MnRmE........ Richmond Elementary School, Richmond, MN [*Library symbol*] [*Library of Congress*] (LCLS)

MnRMeH ..... Rochester Methodist Hospital, Rochester, MN [*Library symbol Library of Congress*] (LCLS)

MnRmP........ Richmond Public Library, Richmond, MN [*Library symbol*] [*Library of Congress*] (LCLS)

MnRmS........ Sts. Peter and Paul Elementary School Library, Richmond, MN [*Library symbol*] [*Library of Congress*] (LCLS)

MNRO......... Monroe Muffler Brake [*NASDAQ symbol*] (SPSG)
MNRO......... Monro Muffler Brake, Inc. [*NASDAQ symbol*] (SAG)

MnRoN .... Northwestern College, Roseville, MN [*Library symbol Library of Congress*] (LCLS)

MnRoP........ Minnesota State Pollution Control Agency, Roseville, MN [*Library symbol Library of Congress*] (LCLS)

MnRos......... Roseau Public Library, Roseau, MN [*Library symbol*] [*Library of Congress*] (LCLS)

MnRosE....... Roseau Elementary School, Roseau, MN [*Library symbol*] [*Library of Congress*] (LCLS)

MnRosH....... Roseau High School, Roseau, MN [*Library symbol*] [*Library of Congress*] (LCLS)

MnRosMS.... Malung School, Roseau, MN [*Library symbol*] [*Library of Congress*] (LCLS)

MnRothS...... Rothsay Public School, Rothsay, MN [*Library symbol*] [*Library of Congress*] (LCLS)

MnRoy......... Royalton Public Library, Royalton, MN [*Library symbol*] [*Library of Congress*] (LCLS)

MnRoyS....... Royalton School, Royalton, MN [*Library symbol*] [*Library of Congress*] (LCLS)

MNRP .... Movimiento Nacionalista Revolucionario del Pueblo [*Nationalist Revolutionary People's Movement*] [*Bolivia*] [*Political party*] (PPW)

MNRPM .... Malay Nationalist Revolutionary Party of Malaya [*Partai Kebangsaan Melayu Revolusioner Malaya*] [*Political party*] (PPW)

MnRPS .... Rochester Public Schools, Rochester, MN [*Library symbol Library of Congress*] (LCLS)

MnRR .... Rochester State Junior College, Rochester, MN [*Library symbol Library of Congress*] (LCLS)

MNRS .... Manors
MNRS .... Manors [*Postal Service standard*] (OPSA)
MNRS .... Mobile Neutron Radiographic System
MnRS .... Southeastern Libraries Cooperating [*SELCO*], Rochester Public Library, Rochester, MN [*Library symbol Library of Congress*] (LCLS)

Mnrsm .... Mannerism (VRA)

MnRStM ...... Saint Mary's Hospital, Rochester, MN [*Library symbol Library of Congress*] (LCLS)

mnrt .... Minaret (VRA)

MNRT .... Monmouth Real Estate Investment Trust [*NASDAQ symbol*] (NQ)
MNRTA .... Monmouth R.E. Inv CL'A' [*NASDAQ symbol*] (TTSB)
MNRU .... Medical Neuropsychiatric Research Unit (AD)
MNRU.......... Modulated Noise Reference Unit [*Telecommunications*] (TEL)

MnRuPS ...... Ruthton Public Schools, Ruthton, MN [*Library symbol*] [*Library of Congress*] (LCLS)

MnRusPS..... Russell Public Schools, Russell, MN [*Library symbol*] [*Library of Congress*] (LCLS)

MNRV .... Movimiento Nacionalista Revolucionario - Vanguardia Revolucionaria 9 de Abril [*Bolivia*] [*Political party*] (EY)

MnRvJ .... John Clark Elementary School, Rockville, MN [*Library symbol*] [*Library of Congress*] (LCLS)

MnRw .... Red Wing Public Library, Red Wing, MN [*Library symbol Library of Congress*] (LCLS)

MnRwf......... Redwood Falls Public Library, Redwood Falls, MN [*Library symbol*] [*Library of Congress*] (LCLS)

MnRwfGES... Reede Gray Elementary School, Redwood Falls, MN [*Library symbol*] [*Library of Congress*] (LCLS)

MnRwfH....... Redwood Falls Hospital, Redwood Falls, MN [*Library symbol*] [*Library of Congress*] (LCLS)

MnRwfJSH... Redwood Falls-Morton Junior Senior High School, Redwood Falls, MN [*Library symbol*] [*Library of Congress*] (LCLS)

MnRwfSJL ... St. John's Lutheran School, Redwood Falls, MN [*Library symbol*] [*Library of Congress*] (LCLS)

MNS.......... College of Saint Scholastica Library, Duluth, MN [*OCLC symbol*] (OCLC)

MNS............ MacNeal-Schwendler [*AMEX symbol*] (TTSB)
MNS............ [*The*] MacNeal-Schwendler Corp. [*AMEX symbol*] (SPSG)
MNS............ Management Need Statement (AAGC)
Mns .... Manaus (AD)
MNS............ Mansa [*Zambia*] [*Airport symbol*] (OAG)
MNS............ Martin's Louisiana Reports, New Series [*A publication*] (DLA)
MNS............ Master of Natural Sciences (GAGS)
MNS............ Master of Nuclear Science (GAGS)
MNS............ Master of Nursing Science
MNS............ Master of Nutritional Science
MNS............ Master of Nutritional Sciences (GAGS)
MNS............ Materiel Need Statement [*Army*]
MNS............ Maturity News Service
MNS............ McGuire Nuclear Station (NRCH)
MNS............ Mechanical Neutral Start [*Automotive engineering*]
MNS............ Member of the Numismatical Society [*British*]
mns .... Metal-Nitride-Semiconductor (AD)
MNS............ Meta-Nitride Semiconductor (MCD)
MNS............ Microband National System, Inc. [*New York, NY*] [*Telecommunications*] (TSSD)
MNS............ Microneurography Society (EA)
MNS............ Mine Neutralization System [*Military*] (CAAL)
MNS............ Mines
Mns .... Mines (AD)
MNS............ Ministic Air [*Canada ICAO designator*] (FAAC)
MNS............ Ministry of National Service [*World War I*] [*British*]
MNS............ Minneapolis, Northfield & Southern Railway [*AAR code*]
MNS............ Minutes [*International telex abbreviation*] (WDMC)
MNS............ Mission Needs Statement [*Army*] (RDA)
MNS............ Molded Nylon Screw
MNS............ Movement for a New Society [*Defunct*] (EA)
MNS............ Movimiento Nacional de Salvacion [*National Movement of Salvation*] [*Dominican Republic*] [*Political party*] (PPW)

MNS............ Smith College, Northampton, MA [*Library symbol Library of Congress*] (LCLS)

MnS .... St. Paul Public Library, St. Paul, MN [*Library symbol Library of Congress*] (LCLS)

MnSa .... Sandstone Public Library, Sandstone, MN [*Library symbol*] [*Library of Congress*] (LCLS)

MNSA .... Seaman Apprentice, Mineman, Striker [*Navy rating*]

MnSaE .... Sandstone Elementary School, Sandstone, MN [*Library symbol*] [*Library of Congress*] (LCLS)

MnSaF .... Federal Correctional Institute Library, Sandstone, MN [*Library symbol*] [*Library of Congress*] (LCLS)

MnSAG .... Minnesota Attorney General's Office, St. Paul, MN [*Library symbol Library of Congress*] (LCLS)

MnSagHS .... Albrook High School, Saginaw, MN [*Library symbol*] [*Library of Congress*] (LCLS)

MnSaH......... Sandstone Area Hospital/Nursing Home, Sandstone, MN [*Library symbol*] [*Library of Congress*] (LCLS)

MnSaJS .... Sandstone Junior/Senior High School, Sandstone, MN [*Library symbol*] [*Library of Congress*] (LCLS)

MnSanLS..... Zion Lutheran School, Sanborn, MN [*Library symbol*] [*Library of Congress*] (LCLS)

MnSanPS..... Sanborn Public School, Sanborn, MN [*Library symbol*] [*Library of Congress*] (LCLS)

MnSarH .... Sartell High School, Sartell, MN [*Library symbol*] [*Library of Congress*] (LCLS)

MnSarM....... Sartell Middle School, Sartell, MN [*Library symbol*] [*Library of Congress*] (LCLS)

MnSarS........ St. Francis Xavier School, Sartell, MN [*Library symbol*] [*Library of Congress*] (LCLS)

MNSaS .... Swift River Valley Historical Society, New Salem, MA [*Library symbol Library of Congress*] (LCLS)

MnSB .... Bethel College, St. Paul, MN [*Library symbol Library of Congress*] (LCLS)

MNSBC .... Minnesota North Stars Booster Club (EA)

MnSBH .... Bethesda Lutheran Hospital, St. Paul, MN [*Library symbol Library of Congress*] (LCLS)

MNSC .... Main Network Switching Center [*Telecommunications*] (TEL)
MN Sc .... Master of Nursing Science
MNSC .... San Carlos/San Juan [*Nicaragua*] [*ICAO location identifier*] (ICLI)

MnSc .... Sauk Centre Public Library, Sauk Centre, MN [*Library symbol Library of Congress*] (LCLS)

MnSCC......... Concordia College, St. Paul, MN [*Library symbol Library of Congress*] (LCLS)

MnSCH .... Children's Hospital, St. Paul, MN [*Library symbol Library of Congress*] (LCLS)

MnScHF .... Holy Family School, Sauk Center, MN [*Library symbol*] [*Library of Congress*] (LCLS)

MNSCL .... Miniscule

MnScL .... Sinclair Lewis Foundation, Sauk Centre, MN [*Library symbol Library of Congress*] (LCLS)

MnScM .... Meadow View School, Sauk Centre, MN [*Library symbol*] [*Library of Congress*] (LCLS)

MnScML ...... Mary Lyon School, Minnesota Correctional Facility, Sauk Centre, MN [*Library symbol*] [*Library of Congress*] (LCLS)

MnScP .... Sauk Centre Public Schools, Sauk Centre, MN [*Library symbol*] [*Library of Congress*] (LCLS)

MnScSM ...... St. Michael's Hospital and Convalescent and Nursing Center, Sauk Centre, MN [*Library symbol*] [*Library of Congress*] (LCLS)

MNSD .... Mouvement National pour une Societe de Developpement [*Niger*] [*Political party*] (EY)

MnSEA .... Minnesota Energy Agency, St. Paul, MN [*Library symbol Library of Congress*] (LCLS)

MnSebS ...... Sebeka School, Sebeka, MN [*Library symbol*] [*Library of Congress*] (LCLS)

MNSER .... Mean Normalized Systolic Ejection Rate [*Cardiology*]

MNSF .... Monoclonal-Nonspecific Suppressor Factor [*Immunology*]

MnSG .... Gillette State Hospital for Crippled Children, St. Paul, MN [*Library symbol Library of Congress*] (LCLS)

MnSGC .... Minnesota Governor's Commission on Crime Prevention and Control, St. Paul, MN [*Library symbol of Congress*] (LCLS)

MnSGH .... Group Health, Inc., St. Paul, MN [*Library symbol Library of Congress*] (LCLS)

MnSH .... Hamline University, St. Paul, MN [*Library symbol Library of Congress*] (LCLS)

MnSheS .... Shelly School, Shelly, MN [*Library symbol*] [*Library of Congress*] (LCLS)

MnSH-L ...... Hamline University, School of Law, St. Paul, MN [*Library symbol Library of Congress*] (LCLS)

MnShS .... Scott County Library, Shakopee, MN [*Library symbol Library of Congress*] (LCLS)

MNSI .... Siuna [*Nicaragua*] [*ICAO location identifier*] (ICLI)

MnSib .... Silver Bay Public Library, Silver Bay, MN [*Library symbol*] [*Library of Congress*] (LCLS)

MnSibHS ..... Wm. Kelley High School, Silver Bay, MN [*Library symbol*] [*Library of Congress*] (LCLS)

MnSibME ..... Mary MacDonald Elementary School, Silver Bay, MN [*Library symbol*] [*Library of Congress*] (LCLS)

MnSifE .... Holler Elementary School, South International Falls, MN [*Library symbol*] [*Library of Congress*] (LCLS)

MnSJ .... James J. Hill Reference Library, St. Paul, MN [*Library symbol Library of Congress*] (LCLS)

MnSL .... Luther Theological Seminary, St. Paul, MN [*Library symbol Library of Congress Obsolete*] (LCLS)

MNSL .... Mainsail

MnSLBF ...... Lutheran Brotherhood Foundation Reformation Library, St. Paul, MN [*Library symbol*] [*Library of Congress*] (LCLS)

MnSLN .... Luther-Northwestern Seminary, St. Paul, MN [*Library symbol Library of Congress*] (LCLS)

MnSly .... Slayton Public Library, Slayton, MN [*Library symbol*] [*Library of Congress*] (LCLS)

MnSlyES .... Slayton Elementary School, Slayton, MN [*Library symbol*] [*Library of Congress*] (LCLS)

MnSlyJSH .... Slayton Junior-Senior High School, Slayton, MN [*Library symbol*] [*Library of Congress*] (LCLS)

MnSM .... Macalester College, St. Paul, MN [*Library symbol Library of Congress*] (LCLS)

MnSmH .... St. Michael-Albertville High School, St. Michael, MN [*Library symbol*] [*Library of Congress*] (LCLS)

MnSmM .... St. Michael-Albertville Middle School, St. Michael, MN [*Library symbol*] [*Library of Congress*] (LCLS)

MnSMMfg .... Minnesota Mining & Manufacturing Co., Technical Library, St. Paul, MN [*Library symbol Library of Congress Obsolete*] (LCLS)

MnSMN .... Mounds-Midway School of Nursing, St. Paul, MN [*Library symbol Library of Congress*] (LCLS)

MnSmP .... St. Michael Parish School, St. Michael, MN [*Library symbol*] [*Library of Congress*] (LCLS)

MnSN .... Northwestern Lutheran Theological Seminary, St. Paul, MN [*Library symbol Library of Congress Obsolete*] (LCLS)

MNSN .... Seaman, Mineman, Striker [*Navy rating*]

MnSOD .... Manganese Superoxide Dismutase

MnSOEO ...... Minnesota Office of Economic Opportunity, St. Paul, MN [*Library symbol Library of Congress*] (LCLS)

MnSP .... Saint Paul Public Library, St. Paul, MN [*Library symbol*] [*Library of Congress*] (LCLS)

MnSpES .... Spicer Elementary School, Spicer, MN [*Library symbol*] [*Library of Congress*] (LCLS)

MnSpP .... Spicer Public Library, Spicer, MN [*Library symbol*] [*Library of Congress*] (LCLS)

MNSQ .... Motor Neurone Society of Queensland [*Australia*]

MnSqlS .... Squaw Lake School, Squaw Lake, MN [*Library symbol*] [*Library of Congress*] (LCLS)

MnSrB .... Benton County Historical Museum, Sauk Rapids, MN [*Library symbol*] [*Library of Congress*] (LCLS)

MnSRC .... Ramsey County Public Library, St. Paul, MN [*Library symbol Library of Congress*] (LCLS)

MnSrH .... Sauk Rapids High School, Sauk Rapids, MN [*Library symbol*] [*Library of Congress*] (LCLS)

MnSrHJ .... Hillside Junior High School, Sauk Rapids, MN [*Library symbol*] [*Library of Congress*] (LCLS)

MnSRM .... Ramsey County Medical Society, St. Paul, MN [*Library symbol Library of Congress*] (LCLS)

MnSrPE .... Pleasantview Elementary School, Sauk Rapids, MN [*Library symbol*] [*Library of Congress*] (LCLS)

MnSrS .... Sacred Heart School, Sauk Rapids, MN [*Library symbol*] [*Library of Congress*] (LCLS)

MnSrT .... Trinity Lutheran School, Sauk Rapids, MN [*Library symbol*] [*Library of Congress*] (LCLS)

MNSS .... Modified Need Satisfaction Schedule

MNS-S .... Smith College, Sophia Smith Collection, Northampton, MA [*Library symbol Library of Congress*] (LCLS)

MnSS .... St. Paul Seminary, St. Paul, MN [*Library symbol Library of Congress*] (LCLS)

MNSSA .... Motor Neurone Society of South Australia

MnSSC .... College of St. Catherine, St. Paul, MN [*Library symbol Library of Congress*] (LCLS)

MnSSEP ...... Median Nerve Somatosensory Evoked Potential [*Neurology*] (DAVI)

MnSSJ .... St. John's Hospital, St. Paul, MN [*Library symbol Library of Congress*] (LCLS)

MnSSJos ...... St. Joseph's Hospital, St. Paul, MN [*Library symbol Library of Congress*] (LCLS)

MnSSM .... Science Museum of Minnesota, Louis S. Headley Memorial Library, St. Paul, MN [*Library symbol*] [*Library of Congress*] (LCLS)

MnSSP .... St. Paul Ramsey Hospital, St. Paul, MN [*Library symbol Library of Congress*] (LCLS)

MnSSpU .... Sperry UNIVAC, St. Paul, MN [*Library symbol Library of Congress*] (LCLS)

MnSST .... College of St. Thomas, St. Paul, MN [*Library symbol Library of Congress*] (LCLS)

MNST .... Motor Neurone Society of Tasmania [*Australia*]

MnSt .... Staples Public Library, Staples, MN [*Library symbol*] [*Library of Congress*] (LCLS)

MNSTB .... Monostable (MSA)

MNSTBMV ... Monostable Multivibrator (MSA)

MnStbSP ...... Saint Paul Bible College, Saint Bonifacius, MN [*Library symbol Library of Congress*] (LCLS)

MnStclA .... Appollo High School, St. Cloud, MN [*Library symbol*] [*Library of Congress*] (LCLS)

MnStclBS ..... Benton/Stearns Special Education Professional Library, St. Cloud, MN [*Library symbol*] [*Library of Congress*] (LCLS)

MnStclCF ..... Minnesota Corrections Facility Library, St. Cloud, MN [*Library symbol*] [*Library of Congress*] (LCLS)

MnStclCH ..... St. Cloud Cathedral High School, St. Cloud, MN [*Library symbol*] [*Library of Congress*] (LCLS)

MnStclD .... Diocese of St. Cloud, St. Cloud, MN [*Library symbol*] [*Library of Congress*] (LCLS)

MnStclEC ..... Central Minnesota Educational Cooperative Service Unit, St. Cloud, MN [*Library symbol*] [*Library of Congress*] (LCLS)

MnStclER ..... Central Minnesota Educational Research and Development Council, Film Library, St. Cloud, MN [*Library symbol*] [*Library of Congress*] (LCLS)

MnStclG .... Great River Regional Library, St. Cloud, MN [*Library symbol Library of Congress*] (LCLS)

MnStclGP ..... Green Pastures Christian School, St. Cloud, MN [*Library symbol*] [*Library of Congress*] (LCLS)

MnStclH .... St. Cloud Hospital, Health Sciences Library, St. Cloud, MN [*Library symbol*] [*Library of Congress*] (LCLS)

MnStclHi ...... Stearns County Historical Society, St. Cloud, MN [*Library symbol*] [*Library of Congress*] (LCLS)

MnStclHS ..... Holy Spirit School, St. Cloud, MN [*Library symbol*] [*Library of Congress*] (LCLS)

MnStclJ .... Jefferson Elementary School, St. Cloud, MN [*Library symbol*] [*Library of Congress*] (LCLS)

MnStclL .... Lincoln Elementary School, St. Cloud, MN [*Library symbol*] [*Library of Congress*] (LCLS)

MnStclM .... Madison Elementary School, St. Cloud, MN [*Library symbol*] [*Library of Congress*] (LCLS)

MnStclMc ..... McKinley Elementary School, St. Cloud, MN [*Library symbol*] [*Library of Congress*] (LCLS)

MnStclMS ..... St. Cloud Media Services, St. Cloud, MN [*Library symbol*] [*Library of Congress*] (LCLS)

MnStclN .... St. Cloud School of Nursing Library, St. Cloud, MN [*Library symbol*] [*Library of Congress*] (LCLS)

MnStclP .... Sts. Peter & Paul Primary School, St. Cloud, MN [*Library symbol*] [*Library of Congress*] (LCLS)

MnStclR .... Roosevelt Elementary School, St. Cloud, MN [*Library symbol*] [*Library of Congress*] (LCLS)

MnStclS .... St. Cloud State University, St. Cloud, MN [*Library symbol Library of Congress*] (LCLS)

MnStclSA ..... St. Anthony School, St. Cloud, MN [*Library symbol*] [*Library of Congress*] (LCLS)

MnStclSC ..... Stearns/Benton Counties Law Library, St. Cloud, MN [*Library symbol*] [*Library of Congress*] (LCLS)

MnStclSE ..... St. Cloud South Elementary School, St. Cloud, MN [*Library symbol*] [*Library of Congress*] (LCLS)

MnStclSM ..... St. Mary Help of Christians School, St. Cloud, MN [*Library symbol*] [*Library of Congress*] (LCLS)

MnStclSP ..... Sts. Peter & Paul Middle Schol, St. Cloud, MN [*Library symbol*] [*Library of Congress*] (LCLS)

MnStclSt ...... St. Augustine School, St. Cloud, MN [*Library symbol*] [*Library of Congress*] (LCLS)

MnStclV .... United States Veterans Administration Hospital, St. Cloud, MN [*Library symbol Library of Congress*] (LCLS)

MnStclVT ..... St. Cloud Area Vo-Tech Institute, St. Cloud, MN [*Library symbol*] [*Library of Congress*] (LCLS)

MnStclW ...... Westwood Elementary School, St. Cloud, MN [*Library symbol*] [*Library of Congress*] (LCLS)

MnSteE .... Stephen Elementary School, Stpehen, MN [*Library symbol*] [*Library of Congress*] (LCLS)

MnSteH .... Stephen High School, Stephen, MN [*Library symbol*] [*Library of Congress*] (LCLS)

MnStH .... United District Hospital, Staples, MN [*Library symbol*] [*Library of Congress*] (LCLS)

MnStHS .... Staples High School, Staples, MN [*Library symbol*] [*Library of Congress*] (LCLS)

MnStj .... Watonwan County Library, St. James, MN [*Library symbol Library of Congress*] (LCLS)

MnStjoKE ..... Kennedy Elementary School, St. Joseph, MN [*Library symbol*] [*Library of Congress*] (LCLS)

MnStjoL .... St. Joseph Lab School, St. Joseph, MN [*Library symbol*] [*Library of Congress*] (LCLS)

MnStjoS....... College of St. Benedict, St. Joseph, MN [*Library symbol Library of Congress*] (LCLS)

MnStLE....... Lincoln Model Elementary School, Staples, MN [*Library symbol*] [*Library of Congress*] (LCLS)

MnSTM....... Three M (3M) Co., St. Paul, MN [*Library symbol*] [*Library of Congress*] (LCLS)

MnSTM-A .... Three M (3M) Co., St. Paul, MN [*Library symbol*] [*Library of Congress*] (LCLS)

MnSTM-B .... Three M (3M) Co., Business Information Service, St. Paul, MN [*Library symbol*] [*Library of Congress*] (LCLS)

MnSTM-E .... Three M (3M) Co., Engineering Information Services, St. Paul, MN [*Library symbol Library of Congress*] (LCLS)

MnSTM-G .... Three M (3M) Co., St. Paul, MN [*Library symbol*] [*Library of Congress*] (LCLS)

MnSTM-H .... Three M (3M) Co., Health Care Library, St. Paul, MN [*Library symbol*] [*Library of Congress*] (LCLS)

MnSTM-M .... Three M (3M) Co., St. Paul, MN [*Library symbol*] [*Library of Congress*] (LCLS)

MnSTM-P .... Three M (3M) Co., St. Paul, MN [*Library symbol*] [*Library of Congress*] (LCLS)

MnSTM-T .... Three M (3M) Co., St. Paul, MN [*Library symbol*] [*Library of Congress*] (LCLS)

MnStNE....... North Elementary School, Staples, MN [*Library symbol*] [*Library of Congress*] (LCLS)

MnStoES..... Storden-Jeffers Elementary School, Storden, MN [*Library symbol*] [*Library of Congress*] (LCLS)

MnStpeG...... Gustavus Adolphus College, St. Peter, MN [*Library symbol Library of Congress*] (LCLS)

Mnstr.......... Munster (AD)

MNSTRY..... Ministry

MnStS......... Sacred Heart School, Staples, MN [*Library symbol*] [*Library of Congress*] (LCLS)

MnStT......... Staples Technical Institute, Staples, MN [*Library symbol*] [*Library of Congress*] (LCLS)

MnStwPS.... Stewart Public Schools, Stewart, MN [*Library symbol*] [*Library of Congress*] (LCLS)

MnSU.......... University of Minnesota, St. Paul, MN [*Library symbol Library of Congress*] (LCLS)

MnSU-Bc .... University of Minnesota, Biochemistry Library, St. Paul, MN [*Library symbol Library of Congress*] (LCLS)

MnSuES...... Sunberg Elementary School, Sunberg, MN [*Library symbol*] [*Library of Congress*] (LCLS)

MnSU-Et ..... University of Minnesota, Entomology Library, St. Paul, MN [*Library symbol Library of Congress*] (LCLS)

MnSU-F ...... University of Minnesota, Forestry Library, St. Paul, MN [*Library symbol Library of Congress*] (LCLS)

MnSUH........ United Hospitals, Inc., St. Paul, MN [*Library symbol Library of Congress*] (LCLS)

MnSU-PP .... University of Minnesota, Plant Pathology Library, St. Paul, MN [*Library symbol Library of Congress*] (LCLS)

MnSUSF ...... United States Forest Service, North Central Forest Experiment Station, St. Paul, MN [*Library symbol Library of Congress*] (LCLS)

MnSU-V ...... University of Minnesota, Veterinary Medicine Library, St. Paul, MN [*Library symbol Library of Congress*] (LCLS)

MNSV .... Motor Neurone Society of Victoria [*Australia*]

MnSw .... Swanville Public Library, Swanville, MN [*Library symbol*] [*Library of Congress*] (LCLS)

MnSwE .... Swanville Elementary School, Swanville, MN [*Library symbol*] [*Library of Congress*] (LCLS)

MnSwH .... Swanville High School, Swanville, MN [*Library symbol*] [*Library of Congress*] (LCLS)

MnSWM....... William Mitchell College of Law, St. Paul, MN [*Library symbol Library of Congress*] (LCLS)

MNT............ College of St. Thomas, St. Paul, MN [*OCLC symbol*] (OCLC)

M/N/T.......... Main/Satellite/Tributary Network [*Telecommunications*] (ACRL)

MNT............ Maintained [*Automotive advertising*]

mnt............ Mean Neap Tide (AD)

MNT............ Minnesota and Ontario Paper [*Stock exchange symbol*] (AD)

Mn-T........... Minnesota State Department of Taxation, St. Paul, MN [*Library symbol Library of Congress*] (LCLS)

MNT............ Minto [*Alaska*] [*Airport symbol*] (OAG)

MNT............ Minute [*Angle*]

MNT............ Modern Network Theory [*Electrical engineering computer*]

MNT............ Moffatt New Testament Commentary [*A publication*] (BJA)

MNT............ Monitor

MNT............ Mononitrotoluene [*Organic chemistry*]

MNT............ Montedison SpA [*NYSE symbol*] (SPSG)

MNT............ Montedison S p AADS [*NYSE symbol*] (TTSB)

MNT............ Montoro Gold, Inc. [*Vancouver Stock Exchange symbol*]

MNT............ Montreal [*Quebec*] [*Seismograph station code, US Geological Survey*] (SEIS)

MNT............ Montserrat Airways Ltd. [*Antigua and Barbuda*] [*ICAO designator*] (FAAC)

MNT............ Mount (KSC)

MNT............ Mountain

MNt............ Newton Free Library, Newton, MA [*Library symbol Library of Congress*] (LCLS)

MNTAIN...... Mountain [*Commonly used*] (OPSA)

MnTalE .... North Elementary School, Talmoon, MN [*Library symbol*] [*Library of Congress*] (LCLS)

MntasiaE .... Mountasia Entertainment International, Inc. [*Associated Press*] (SAG)

MNTB.......... Medial Nucleus of Trapezoid Body [*Neuroanatomy*]

MNTB.......... Merchant Navy Training Board [*British*] (DS)

MNTC.......... Mexican National Tourist Council (EA)

MNTC.......... Moffatt New Testament Commentary [*A publication*] (BJA)

MNtcA......... Andover Newton Theological School, Newton Center, MA [*Library symbol Library of Congress*] (LCLS)

MnTcFW ..... United States Fish and Wildlife Service, Science Reference Library, Twin Cities, MN [*Library symbol Library of Congress*] (LCLS)

MnTcM .... United States Bureau of Mines, Twin Cities, MN [*Library symbol Library of Congress*] (LCLS)

MnTEC........ Northwest Education Cooperative Service Unit, Thief River Falls, MN [*Library symbol*] [*Library of Congress*] (LCLS)

MnTf .... Taylor Falls Public Library, Taylor Falls, MN [*Library symbol*] [*Library of Congress*] (LCLS)

MnTFM........ Franklin Middle School, Thief River Falls, MN [*Library symbol*] [*Library of Congress*] (LCLS)

MnTfS......... Taylor Falls School, Taylor Falls, MN [*Library symbol*] [*Library of Congress*] (LCLS)

MNTG......... Mounting

MnTh .... Two Harbors Public Library, Two Harbors, MN [*Library symbol*] [*Library of Congress*] (LCLS)

MnThE .... John A. Johnson Elementary School, Two Harbors, MN [*Library symbol*] [*Library of Congress*] (LCLS)

MnThHS...... Two Harbors High School, Two Harbors, MN [*Library symbol*] [*Library of Congress*] (LCLS)

MNTHLY ..... Monthly

MnThM .... Minnehaha Middle School, Two Harbors, MN [*Library symbol*] [*Library of Congress*] (LCLS)

MNTHZ .... Methylnitrosothiazolidine [*Organic chemistry*]

MNTK......... Mezhotraslevoi Naucho-Tekhni-Cheskii Kompleks [*Interdisciplinary Scientific-Technological Complex*] [*Russian*]

MNTK......... Movimiento Nacional Tupaj Katari [*Bolivia*] [*Political party*] (PPW)

MnTKS........ Knox School, Thief River Falls, MN [*Library symbol*] [*Library of Congress*] (LCLS)

MNTL.......... Mental

MnTLH........ Lincoln High School, Thief River Falls, MN [*Library symbol*] [*Library of Congress*] (LCLS)

MNTMP....... Minimum Temperature (NOAA)

mntmp........ Minimum Temperature (AD)

MnTMT .... Mark Twain School, Thief River Falls, MN [*Library symbol*] [*Library of Congress*] (LCLS)

mntn .... Maintain (AD)

MNTN .... Maintain

MNTN .... Mountain

MnTN.......... Northland State Junior College, Thief River Falls, MN [*Library symbol Library of Congress*] (LCLS)

mntnc .... Maintenance (AD)

MNTNC .... Maintenance

mntnd .... Maintained (AD)

mntng .... Maintaining (AD)

MnTNo........ Northrop Resource Room, Thief River Falls, MN [*Library symbol*] [*Library of Congress*] (LCLS)

MnTNR .... Northwest Regional Library, Thief River Falls, MN [*Library symbol Library of Congress*] (LCLS)

MNTNS .... Mountains [*Commonly used*] (OPSA)

MNTO .... Moroccan National Tourist Office (AD)

MnToS .... Togo School, Togo, MN [*Library symbol*] [*Library of Congress*] (LCLS)

MnTP .... Thief River Falls Public Library, Thief River Falls, MN [*Library symbol*] [*Library of Congress*] (LCLS)

MnTPC........ Pennington County Extension Office, Thief River Falls, MN [*Library symbol*] [*Library of Congress*] (LCLS)

MnTPPS...... Manganese Tetraphenylporphine Sulfonate [*Organic chemistry*]

MNTPr .... Montedison Bearer Svg Pfd ADS [*NYSE symbol*] (TTSB)

MNTR .... Mentor Corp. [*NASDAQ symbol*] (NQ)

MNTR .... Monitor (MDG)

mntr............ Monitor (AD)

mntr............ Monitor (IDOE)

MnTrES........ Tracy Elementary School, Tracy, MN [*Library symbol*] [*Library of Congress*] (LCLS)

MnTrJSH...... Trace Junior-Senior High School, Tracy, MN [*Library symbol*] [*Library of Congress*] (LCLS)

MNTRNG..... Monitoring

MnTrStM...... St. Mary's School, Tracy, MN [*Library symbol*] [*Library of Congress*] (LCLS)

MNTS......... Medial Nucleus Tractus Solitarius [*Neuroanatomy*]

MNTS.......... Methyl(Nitroso) Toluenesulphonamide [*Organic chemistry*]

MNTS......... Mountains

MNtS .... Swedenborg School of Religion, Newton, MA [*Library symbol Library of Congress*] (LCLS)

MnTSB .... St. Bernard's School, Thief River Falls, MN [*Library symbol*] [*Library of Congress*] (LCLS)

MNtSH .... Newton College of the Sacred Heart [*Later, Newton College*], Newton, MA [*Library symbol Library of Congress*] (LCLS)

MNTV .... Mercury Network Test Vehicle (MUGU)

MnTW .... Washington School, Thief River Falls, MN [*Library symbol*] [*Library of Congress*] (LCLS)

MnTwvE ...... Twin Valley Elementary School, Twin Valley, MN [*Library symbol*] [*Library of Congress*] (LCLS)

MnTwvH ...... Twin Valley High School, Twin Valley, MN [*Library symbol*] [*Library of Congress*] (LCLS)

MNTX .... Minntech Corp. [*NASDAQ symbol*] (NQ)

MnTy .... Tyler Public Library, Tyler, MN [*Library symbol*] [*Library of Congress*] (LCLS)

MnTyHS...... Russell-Tyler-Ruthon High School, Tyler, MN [*Library symbol*] [*Library of Congress*] (LCLS)

MNU .... Maniti Sugar [*Stock exchange symbol*] (AD)

MNu.......... Mare Nubium [*Sea of Clouds*] [*Lunar area*]

MNU .... Methylnitrosourea [*Also, NMU*] [*Organic chemistry*]

MNU .... Middle Name Unknown (MCD)

MNU .... Milford North [*Utah*] [*Seismograph station code, US Geological Survey*] (SEIS)

MNU .... Minimum Number of Units [*Chemical engineering*]

mnu .... Minnesota [*MARC country of publication code Library of Congress*] (LCCP)

MNU .... Moulmein [*Myanmar*] [*Airport symbol*] (OAG)

MNU .... Mundee Mines Ltd. [*Vancouver Stock Exchange symbol*]

MnU .... University of Minnesota, Minneapolis, MN [*Library symbol Library of Congress*] (LCLS)

MNU .... University of Minnesota, Minneapolis, MN [*OCLC symbol*] (OCLC)

MnU-Ar .... University of Minnesota, Archives, Minneapolis, MN [*Library symbol Library of Congress*] (LCLS)

MnU-B .... University of Minnesota, Biomedical Library, Minneapolis, MN [*Library symbol Library of Congress*] (LCLS)

MNucSc ...... Master of Nuclear Science (GAGS)

MnU-Fb .... University of Minnesota, Freshwater Biological Institute, Navarre, MN [*Library symbol Library of Congress*] (LCLS)

MnU-IA .... University of Minnesota, Immigration History Research Center, St. Paul, MN [*Library symbol Library of Congress*] (LCLS)

MnU-K .... University of Minnesota, Kerlan Children's Books Collection, Minneapolis, MN [*Library symbol Library of Congress*] (LCLS)

MnU-L .... University of Minnesota, Law Library, Minneapolis, MN [*Library symbol Library of Congress*] (LCLS)

MnUlH .... Ulen-Hitteral High School, Ulen, MN [*Library symbol*] [*Library of Congress*] (LCLS)

MnU-MS ..... University of Minnesota, Manuscript Collection, Minneapolis, MN [*Library symbol Library of Congress*] (LCLS)

MnUnS .... Underwood Public School, Underwood, MN [*Library symbol*] [*Library of Congress*] (LCLS)

MnUpE .... Upsala Elementary School, Upsala, MN [*Library symbol*] [*Library of Congress*] (LCLS)

MnU-Ph .... University of Minnesota, Pharmacy Library, Minneapolis, MN [*Library symbol Library of Congress*] (LCLS)

MnUpH :...... Upsala High School, Upsala, MN [*Library symbol*] [*Library of Congress*] (LCLS)

MNUR .... Mouvement National pour l'Union et la Reconciliation au Zaire [*National Movement for Union and Reconciliation in Zaire*] [*Political party*] (PD)

MnU-Rb .... University of Minnesota, Rare Book Division, Minneapolis, MN [*Library symbol Library of Congress*] (LCLS)

M Nurs .... Master of Nursing (BARN)

MNurs .... Master of Nursing (NADA)

MNursing..... Master of Nursing

MnU-SW ..... University of Minnesota, Social Welfare History Archives Center, St. Paul, MN [*Library symbol Library of Congress*] (LCLS)

MNUT .... Methylnitrosourethane [*Organic chemistry*]

MNutrSc ...... Master of Nutritional Science

MNV........... Madisonville, TN [*Location identifier FAA*] (FAAL)

MNV........... Marginal Net Value

MNV........... Marion Power Shovel [*Stock exchange symbol*] (AD)

MNV........... Mina [*Nevada*] [*Seismograph station code, US Geological Survey*] (SEIS)

MNV........... Mine-Neutralization Vehicle [*Military*] (MCD)

Mn-V.......... Minnesota State Vocational Rehabilitation Library, St. Paul, MN [*Library symbol Library of Congress*] (LCLS)

MNV........... Modular Nuclear Vehicle

MNV........... Southwest State University, Marshall, MN [*OCLC symbol*] (OCLC)

MNV........... United States Veterans Administration Hospital, Northampton, MA [*Library symbol Library of Congress*] (LCLS)

MnV.......... Virginia Public Library, Virginia, MN [*Library symbol Library of Congress*] (LCLS)

MnVA.......... Arrowhead Library System, Virginia, MN [*Library symbol Library of Congress*] (LCLS)

MnVePS ...... Verdi Public School, Verdi, MN [*Library symbol*] [*Library of Congress*] (LCLS)

MnVerS .... Verndale Public School, Verndale, MN [*Library symbol*] [*Library of Congress*] (LCLS)

MnVHS .... Virginia Junior-Senior High School, Virginia, MN [*Library symbol*] [*Library of Congress*] (LCLS)

MnVilS........ Villard Public School, Villard, MN [*Library symbol*] [*Library of Congress*] (LCLS)

MnVM......... Mesabi Community College, Virginia, MN [*Library symbol Library of Congress*] (LCLS)

MNVM........ Million Nighttime Vehicle Mile

MnVME........ James Madison Elementary School, Virginia, MN [*Library symbol*] [*Library of Congress*] (LCLS)

MNVR .... Maneuver

MNVR .... Maneuver (KSC)

MnVRE........ Roosevelt Elementary School, Virginia, MN [*Library symbol*] [*Library of Congress*] (LCLS)

MnVRM........ Virginia Regional Medical Center, Virginia, MN [*Library symbol*] [*Library of Congress*] (LCLS)

Mn-W......... Minnesota State Department of Public Welfare, St. Paul, MN [*Library symbol Library of Congress*] (LCLS)

MNW .... Moneywise Resources [*Vancouver Stock Exchange symbol*]

MNW .... Monowai [*New Zealand*] [*Seismograph station code, US Geological Survey*] (SEIS)

MNW .... Northwest Missouri State University, Maryville, MO [*OCLC symbol*] (OCLC)

MnWa.......... Wabasso Public Library, Wabasso, MN [*Library symbol*] [*Library of Congress*] (LCLS)

MnWad........ Wadena City Library, Wadena, MN [*Library symbol*] [*Library of Congress*] (LCLS)

MnWadE ...... Wadena Elementary School, Wadena, MN [*Library symbol*] [*Library of Congress*] (LCLS)

MnWadH ...... Wadena High School, Wadena, MN [*Library symbol*] [*Library of Congress*] (LCLS)

MnWadJ ...... Wadena Junior High School, Wadena, MN [*Library symbol*] [*Library of Congress*] (LCLS)

MnWaES ...... Wabasso Elementary School, Wabasso, MN [*Library symbol*] [*Library of Congress*] (LCLS)

MnWaHS ...... Wabasso High School, Wabasso, MN [*Library symbol*] [*Library of Congress*] (LCLS)

MnWal........ Walker Public Library, Walker, MN [*Library symbol*] [*Library of Congress*] (LCLS)

MnWalC....... Cass County Extension Office, Walker, MN [*Library symbol*] [*Library of Congress*] (LCLS)

MnWalH ...... Walker-Hackensack High School, Walker, MN [*Library symbol*] [*Library of Congress*] (LCLS)

MnWalHi ..... Cass County Historical Society, Walker, MN [*Library symbol*] [*Library of Congress*] (LCLS)

MnWanS ...... Wannaska School, Wannaska, MN [*Library symbol*] [*Library of Congress*] (LCLS)

MnWar........ Godell Memorial Library, Warren, MN [*Library symbol*] [*Library of Congress*] (LCLS)

MnWarE ...... Warren Elementary School, Warren, MN [*Library symbol*] [*Library of Congress*] (LCLS)

MnWarJS..... Warren Junior/Senior High School, Warren, MN [*Library symbol*] [*Library of Congress*] (LCLS)

MnWarr ...... Warroad Public Library, Warroad, MN [*Library symbol*] [*Library of Congress*] (LCLS)

MnWarrE ..... Warroad Elementary School, Warroad, MN [*Library symbol*] [*Library of Congress*] (LCLS)

MnWarrH ..... Warroad High School, Warroad, MN [*Library symbol*] [*Library of Congress*] (LCLS)

MnWas........ Le Sueur-Waseca Regional Library, Waseca, MN [*Library symbol Library of Congress*] (LCLS)

MnWaStA .... St. Anne School, Wabasso, MN [*Library symbol*] [*Library of Congress*] (LCLS)

MnWasU...... University of Minnesota Technical College, Waseca, MN [*Library symbol Library of Congress*] (LCLS)

MnWatSA .... St. Anthony School, Watkins, MN [*Library symbol*] [*Library of Congress*] (LCLS)

MnWauWE .... Waubon-Ogema-White Earth School, Waubon, MN [*Library symbol*] [*Library of Congress*] (LCLS)

MnWayC ..... Cargill Instructional Center, Wayzata, MN [*Library symbol Library of Congress*] (LCLS)

MnWblL....... Lakewood Community College, White Bear Lake, MN [*Library symbol Library of Congress*] (LCLS)

MnWbS....... Warba School, Warba, MN [*Library symbol*] [*Library of Congress*] (LCLS)

MnWE......... Isle-Wahkon Elementary School, Wahkon, MN [*Library symbol*] [*Library of Congress*] (LCLS)

MNWEB ...... Merseyside and North Wales Electricity Board [*British*] (AD)

MnWeCS...... Westbrook Christian School, Westbrook, MN [*Library symbol*] [*Library of Congress*] (LCLS)

MnWeP........ Westbrook Public Library, Westbrook, MN [*Library symbol*] [*Library of Congress*] (LCLS)

MnWePS...... Westbrook Public School, Westbrook, MN [*Library symbol*] [*Library of Congress*] (LCLS)

MnWgMS..... Westbrook-Walnut Grove Middle School, Walnut Grove, MN [*Library symbol*] [*Library of Congress*] (LCLS)

MNWH .... Mojo Nixon World Headquarters (EA)

MnWhe........ Wheaton Community Library, Wheaton, MN [*Library symbol*] [*Library of Congress*] (LCLS)

MnWheH ...... Wheaton Community Hospital, Wheaton, MN [*Library symbol*] [*Library of Congress*] (LCLS)

MnWheHS ... Wheaton-Dumont High School, Wheaton, MN [*Library symbol*] [*Library of Congress*] (LCLS)

MnWhePE .... J.E. Pearson Elementary School, Wheaton, MN [*Library symbol*] [*Library of Congress*] (LCLS)

MnWil......... Lawson Memorial Library, Willmar, MN [*Library symbol*] [*Library of Congress*] (LCLS)

MnWilCS ..... Christian Community School, Willmar, MN [*Library symbol*] [*Library of Congress*] (LCLS)

MNWiLES .... Lafayette Elementary School, Willmar, MN [*Library symbol*] [*Library of Congress*] (LCLS)

MnWilGES ... Garfield Elementary School, Willmar, MN [*Library symbol*] [*Library of Congress*] (LCLS)

MnWilH .... Rice Memorial Hospital, Willmar, MN [*Library symbol*] [*Library of Congress*] (LCLS)

MnWilIL....... Immanuel Lutheran School, Willmar, MN [*Library symbol*] [*Library of Congress*] (LCLS)

MnWilJES .... Jefferson Elementary School, Willmar, MN [*Library symbol*] [*Library of Congress*] (LCLS)

MnWilJS ...... Willmar Junior High School, Willmar, MN [*Library symbol*] [*Library of Congress*] (LCLS)

MnWilLiS ..... Lincoln Elementary School, Willmar, MN [*Library symbol*] [*Library of Congress*] (LCLS)

MnWilPS ..... Willmar Public Schools, Willmar, MN [*Library symbol*] [*Library of Congress*] (LCLS)

MnWilRC..... Willmar Regional Treatment Center, Staff Library, Willmar, MN [*Library symbol*] [*Library of Congress*] (LCLS)

MnWilRE ..... Roosevelt Elementary School, Willmar, MN [*Library symbol*] [*Library of Congress*] (LCLS)

MnWilRL ..... Crow River Regional Library, Willmar, MN [*Library symbol Library of Congress*] (LCLS)

MnWilS........ Willmar State Junior College, Willmar, MN [*Library symbol Library of Congress*] (LCLS)

MnWilSH .... Willmar Senior High School, Willmar, MN [*Library symbol*] [*Library of Congress*] (LCLS)

MnWilTC...... Willmar Technical Center, Willmar, MN [*Library symbol*] [*Library of Congress*] (LCLS)

MnWilWES... Washington Elementary School, Willmar, MN [*Library symbol*] [*Library of Congress*] (LCLS)

MnWin........ Windom Public Library, Windom, MN [*Library symbol*] [*Library of Congress*] (LCLS)

MnWinH ...... Windom Area Hospital, Windom, MN [*Library symbol*] [*Library of Congress*] (LCLS)

MnWinHS .... Windom Area High School, Windom, MN [*Library symbol*] [*Library of Congress*] (LCLS)

MnWino....... Winona Public Library, Winona, MN [*Library symbol Library of Congress*] (LCLS)

MnWinoCT... College of Saint Teresa, Winona, MN [*Library symbol Library of Congress*] (LCLS)

MnWinoS..... Winona State College [*Later, Winona State University*], Winona, MN [*Library symbol Library of Congress*] (LCLS)

MnWinoSM... Saint Mary's College, Winona, MN [*Library symbol Library of Congress*] (LCLS)

MnWinWES... Winfair Elementary School, Windom, MN [*Library symbol*] [*Library of Congress*] (LCLS)

MnWlHS ...... Echo-Wood Lake High School, Wood Lake, MN [*Library symbol*] [*Library of Congress*] (LCLS)

MnWlSJ....... St. John's School, Wood Lake, MN [*Library symbol*] [*Library of Congress*] (LCLS)

MnWnSJL .... St. John's Lutheran School, Winsted, MN [*Library symbol*] [*Library of Congress*] (LCLS)

MnWoCCS ... Calvary Christian School, Worthington, MN [*Library symbol*] [*Library of Congress*] (LCLS)

MnWoCES.... Central Elementary School, Worthington, MN [*Library symbol*] [*Library of Congress*] (LCLS)

MnWoH........ Worthington Regional Hospital, Worthington, MN [*Library symbol*] [*Library of Congress*] (LCLS)

MnWoJH...... Worthington Junior High, Worthington, MN [*Library symbol*] [*Library of Congress*] (LCLS)

MnWoLS...... Lakeview School, Worthington, MN [*Library symbol*] [*Library of Congress*] (LCLS)

MnWoN........ Nobles County Library, Worthington, MN [*Library symbol Library of Congress*] (LCLS)

MnWoP........ Plum Creek Library System, Worthington, MN [*Library symbol Library of Congress*] (LCLS)

MnWoS........ Worthington State Junior College [*Later, Worthington Community College*], Worthington, MN [*Library symbol Library of Congress*] (LCLS)

MnWoSH ..... Worthington Senior High School, Worthington, MN [*Library symbol*] [*Library of Congress*] (LCLS)

MnWoSMS... St. Mary's School, Worthington, MN [*Library symbol*] [*Library of Congress*] (LCLS)

MnWoWCS... Worthington Christian School, Worthington, MN [*Library symbol*] [*Library of Congress*] (LCLS)

MnWoWES... West Elementary School, Worthington, MN [*Library symbol*] [*Library of Congress*] (LCLS)

MnWp......... Waite Park Public Library, Waite Park, MN [*Library symbol*] [*Library of Congress*] (LCLS)

MnWpS........ St. Joseph's School, Waite Park, MN [*Library symbol*] [*Library of Congress*] (LCLS)

MNWR .... Malheur National Wildlife Refuge [*Oregon*] (AD)

MNWR .... Mattamuskeet National Wildlife Refuge [*North Carolina*] (AD)

MNWR .... Merced National Wildlife Refuge [*California*] (AD)

MNWR .... Mingo National Wildlife Refuge [*Missouri*] (AD)

MNWR .... Minidoka National Wildlife Refuge [*Idaho*] (AD)

MNWR .... Mississiquoi National Wildlife Refuge [*Vermont*] (AD)

MNWR .... Modoc National Wildlife Refuge [*California*] (AD)

MNWR .... Montezuma National Wildlife Refuge [*New York*] (AD)

MNWR .... Moosehorn National Wildlife Refuge [*Maine*] (AD)

MnWrC .... Willow River Camp Library, Willow River, MN [*Library symbol*] [*Library of Congress*] (LCLS)

MnWreS ...... Wrenshall Public School, Wrenshall, MN [*Library symbol*] [*Library of Congress*] (LCLS)

MnWriLE..... Lincoln Elementary School, Wright, MN [*Library symbol*] [*Library of Congress*] (LCLS)

MnWrS .... Willow River School, Willow River, MN [*Library symbol*] [*Library of Congress*] (LCLS)

MnWs .... Winsted Public Library, Winsted, MN [*Library symbol*] [*Library of Congress*] (LCLS)

MnWsHT...... Holy Trinity School, Winsted, MN [*Library symbol*] [*Library of Congress*] (LCLS)

MNWSL .... Merchant Navy War Service League [*Australia*]

MnWspD...... Dakota County Library, West St. Paul, MN [*Library symbol Library of Congress*] (LCLS)

MnWsPS...... Winsted Public School, Winsted, MN [*Library symbol*] [*Library of Congress*] (LCLS)

MNX........... Manx Airlines Ltd. [*British ICAO designator*] (FAAC)

Mnx .... Manx Gaelic (AD)

MNX........... University of Minnesota, Morris, Morris, MN [*OCLC symbol*] (OCLC)

MNY........... Money

MNY........... Mono Island [*Solomon Islands*] [*Airport symbol*] (OAG)

MNY........... Monteynard [*France*] [*Seismograph station code, US Geological Survey*] (SEIS)

MNY........... Saint Mary's College, Winona, MN [*OCLC symbol*] (OCLC)

MNY........... Taurus Municipal New York Holdings [*NYSE symbol*] (SPSG)

MNY........... Taurus MuniNewYork Hldgs [*NYSE symbol*] (TTSB)

MNZ........... College of Saint Teresa, Winona, MN [*OCLC symbol*] (OCLC)

MNZ........... Manassas [*Virginia*] [*Airport symbol*] (OAG)

MNZ........... Manzanillo [*Mexico*] [*Seismograph station code, US Geological Survey*] (SEIS)

MnZE .... Zimmerman Elementary School, Zimmerman, MN [*Library symbol*] [*Library of Congress*] (LCLS)

Mnzlo......... Manzanillo (AD)

MO............. Abbott Laboratories [*Research code symbol*]

MO............. Calm Air International [*ICAO designator*] (AD)

MO............. Macau [*ANSI two-letter standard code*] (CNC)

MO............. Machine Operation (AFM)

Mo............. Maestro GG1MasterGG2 [*Italian*] (AD)

MO............. Magneto-Optic [*Computer science*]

MO............. Magneto-Optical (PCM)

MO............. Magneto-Optical [*Physics*]

MO............. Mail Order [*Business term*]

mo............. Mail Order (AD)

MO............. Maintenance and Operating [*Factor*] (NG)

MO............. Maintenance Officer (MCD)

M/O............ Maintenance/Organization (MCD)

M/O............ Maintenance to Operation [*Ratio*]

m/o............ Maintenance-to-Operation (AD)

MO............. Maize Oil (PDAA)

MO............. Major Objective (KSC)

MO............. Make Offer

MO............. Making Objects [*Research test*] [*Psychology*]

m/O............ Male Oriental (AD)

MO............. Managed Object [*Telecommunications*] (OSI)

MO............. Management Office

MO............. Management Order (NOAA)

M/O............ Manned and Operational (MUGU)

MO............. Manned Orbiter (MCD)

MO............. Manually Operated

mo............. Manual Operation (AD)

MO............. Manual Orientation (MCD)

MO............. Manual Output

MO............. Manufacturer's Output

MO............. Manufacturing Order (NASA)

MO............. Manufacturing Outline

MO............. March Order [*Military*]

MO............. Marketing Organization (AD)

MO............. Mark Off

MO............. Mars Observer Mission (MCD)

MO............. Mars Orbiter [*NASA*] (KSC)

MO............. Masonry Opening [*Technical drawings*]

mo............. Masonry Opening (AD)

mo............. Mass Observation (AD)

MO............. Mass Observation

MO............. Master of Obstetrics

MO............. Master of Oratory

MO............. Master of Osteopathy

MO............. Master Oscillator [*Radio*]

mo............. Master Oscillator (AD)

MO............. Mature Outlook (EA)

MO............. Medial Oblique [*View*] [*Radiology*] (DAVI)

MO............. Medical Officer [*Military*]

MO............. Medium Oocyte

MO............. Member Organisation (ACII)

MO............. Memory Operation

MO............. Memory Output [*Computer science*]

MO............. Mesio-Occlusal [*Dentistry*]

MO............. Mesityl Oxide [*Also, MSO*] [*Organic chemistry*]

MO............. Meteorological Office [*British*]

MO............. Meteorology Officer (MUGU)

MO............. Method of Operation

mo............. Method of Operation (AD)

MO............. Methoxime [*Organic chemistry*]

MO............. Methyl Orange [*Organic chemistry*]

MO............. Micro-Opaque

mo............. Microoperation (MHDB)

MO............. Micro-Osmometer

MO............. Microwave Oven (PDAA)

MO............. Middeck Overhead (MCD)

m0............. Mid-Oxygen [*Beta-alumina crystallography*]

MO............. Military Observer (WDAA)

MO............. Military Operations [*British military*] (DMA)

MO............. Military Orders Issued by the President as Commander in Chief of the Armed Forces [*A publication*] (DLA)

MO............. Military Services [*Diocesan abbreviation*] [*Maryland*] (TOCD)

MO............. Mineral Oil

MO............. Mineral Order [*Defense Minerals Exploration Administration*] [*Department of the Interior A publication*] (DLA)

MO............. Ministerstvo Oborony [*Ministry of Defense*] [*Former USSR*]

MO............. Minute Output [*Of heart*]

m/o............ Mi Orden [*My Order*] [*Spanish*] (AD)

MO............. Miscellaneous Operation (MUGU)

MO............. Missile Officer (AAG)

MO............. Mission Operations [*NASA*]

MO............. Mission Oriented

MO............. Missouri [*Postal code*] (AFM)

Mo............. Missourian (AD)

Mo............. Missouri Reports [*A publication*] (AAGC)

Mo............. Missouri State Library, Jefferson City, MO [*Library symbol Library of Congress*] (LCLS)

MO............. Missouri Supreme Court Reports [*1821-1956*] [*A publication*] (DLA)

MO............	Mitral Valve Opening [*Cardiology*]
MO............	Mixed Oxide (NRCH)
MO............	Mobile Object [*Telecommunications*] (OA)
MO............	Mobile Station [*Air Force*]
Mo	Mode [*Statistics*]
MO............	Moderato [*Moderate Speed*] [*Music*] (ADA)
MO............	Moderator
MO............	Modern Orthodox (BJA)
Mo	Modern Reports [*England*] [*A publication*] (DLA)
MO............	Modification Order (AFIT)
MO............	Modulate Open [*Nuclear energy*] (NRCH)
MO............	Modus Operandi [*Police term for distinctive techniques used by criminals*]
MO............	Mohawk Airlines, Inc. [*Obsolete*]
MO............	Molded [*Construction*]
MO............	Molecular Orbital [*Atomic physics*]
mo............	Molecular Orbital (AD)
Mo	Molybdenum [*Chemical element*]
MO............	Moment (DSUE)
mo............	Moment (AD)
MO............	Monaco [*IYRU nationality code*] (IYR)
Mo	Monaldus [*Flourished, 13th century*] [*Authority cited in pre-1607 legal work*] (DSA)
Mo	Monday (CDAI)
MO............	Money Order
MO............	Monitor Output
MO............	Monooxygenase [*An enzyme*]
MO............	Month (AFM)
mo............	Month (WDMC)
MO............	Monthly Order [*Navy*]
MO............	Months Old (MEDA)
m-o............	Months Old (AD)
MO............	Mooney Aircraft, Inc. [*ICAO aircraft manufacturer identifier*] (ICAO)
Mo	Moore's English Privy Council Reports [*1836-62*] [*A publication*] (DLA)
Mo	Moore's Indian Appeals [*A publication*] (DLA)
MO............	Moral Obligation (MHDW)
MO............	Moravian
MO............	Morning
M-O............	Morris-Oxford (AD)
MO............	Morse Code Light [*or Fog Signal*] [*Navigation signal*]
mo............	Moth Eaten (AD)
MO............	Mother
MO............	Motion for Mandamus Overruled [*Legal term*] (DLA)
MO............	Motor Operated (MSA)
mo............	Motor Operated (AD)
MO............	Moustache (DSUE)
MO............	Mouth
MO............	Move (NASA)
MO............	Move
MO............	Movement Orders
MO............	Move Out (WDMC)
MO............	Multi-Option (MCD)
MO............	Municipal Offices (ROG)
MO............	Murphy Oil Co. Ltd. [*Toronto Stock Exchange symbol*]
MO............	Mustered Out [*of military service*]
mo............	Mustered Out (AD)
MO............	No Evidence of Distal Metastasis [*Oncology*] (DAVI)
MO............	Philip Morris Companies, Inc. [*NYSE symbol*] (SPSG)
MO............	Philip Morris Cos. [*NYSE symbol*] (TTSB)
MO₂............	Mixed Oxides
MO₂............	Myocardial Oxygen Consumption [*Cardiology*] (MAE)
MOA............	Made on Assembly
MOA............	Make on Arrival (NASA)
MOA............	Management Operations Audit [*Navy*] (NG)
MOA............	Manual-Off-Automatic (KSC)
MOA............	Marine Office of America (AD)
MOA............	Marine Officer's Attendant [*British military*] (DMA)
MOA............	Matrix Output Amplifier
MOA............	McDonald's Operators' Association (EA)
MOA............	Mechanism of Action [*Medicine*] (DAVI)
MOA............	Medical Outreach for Armenians (EA)
MOA............	Medium Observation Aircraft
moa............	Medium Observation Aircraft (AD)
M o A	Memorandum of Agreement (AD)
MOA............	Memorandum of Agreement
MOA............	Memorandum of Assistance
MOA............	Method of Accomplishment (AFIT)
MOA............	Method of Adjustment [*Aviation*]
MOA............	Methods of Administration [*Department of Education*] (OICC)
MOA............	Metropolitan Opera Association (AD)
MOA............	Metropolitan Opera Association (NADA)
MOA............	Metropolitan Opera Auditions (AD)
MOA............	Military Assistance Program Order Amendment (AFM)
MOA............	Military Operations Area (AD)
MOA............	Military Operations Area [*FAA*] (TAG)
MoA............	Ministry of Agriculture [*British*] (AD)
MOA............	Ministry of Aviation [*British*]
MOA............	Minnesota Orchestral Association (AD)
moa............	Minute of Angle (AD)
MOAT............	Minute-of-Angle (NASA)
MOA............	Minute of Angle
MOA............	Misr Overseas Airways [*Egypt*]
MOA............	Missile Optical Alignment
moa............	Missile Optical Alignment (AD)

MOA............	Missouri Botanical Garden, St. Louis, MO [*OCLC symbol*] (OCLC)
MOA............	Moa [*Cuba*] [*Airport symbol*] (OAG)
MOA............	Modern Operating Agreement [*Labor negotiations*]
MOA............	Molln [*Austria*] [*Seismograph station code, US Geological Survey*] (SEIS)
MOA............	Mountain Lake Resources, Inc. [*Vancouver Stock Exchange symbol*]
moa	Mud on Airstrip (AD)
MOA............	Municipal Officers' Association (ROG)
MOA............	Music Operators of America [*Later, AMOA*] (EA)
MOAA............	Mail Order Association of America (EA)
MOAA............	Municipal Officers' Association of Australia
MoAB............	Monoclonal Antibody [*Immunochemistry*]
MOABWEPO...	Members of Anything Bill [*Clinton*] Was Ever Part Of [*Pronounced "Mo-ab-wee-po"*]
MOAD	Methotrexate, Oncovin [*Vincristine*] L-asparaginase, Dexamethasone [*Antineoplastic drug regimen*] (DAVI)
MO Admin Code...	Missouri Code of State Regulations [*A publication*] (DLA)
MO Admin Reg...	Missouri Register [*A publication*] (DLA)
MOADS............	Montgomery Air Defense Sector [*of SAGE*] (MUGU)
MOAF............	Meteorological and Oceanographic Analyst/Forecaster [*Course*] (DNAB)
Moak	Moak's English Reports [*A publication*] (DLA)
Moak (Eng)...	Moak's English Reports [*A publication*] (DLA)
Moak Eng Rep...	Moak's English Reports [*A publication*] (DLA)
Moak Und	Moak's Edition of Underhill on Torts [*A publication*] (DLA)
Moak Underh Torts...	Moak's Edition of Underhill on Torts [*A publication*] (DLA)
Moak Van S Pl...	Moak's Edition of Van Santvoord's Equity Pleading [*A publication*] (DLA)
MOAL............	Mail-Order Action Line [*Direct marketing association*] (WDMC)
MOALC............	Mobile Air Logistics Center [*Air Force*]
MOAMA	Mobile Air Materiel Area
MO & DSD...	Mission Operations and Data Systems Directorate (SSD)
MO & G	Master of Obstetrics and Gynaecology
MO & O	Memorandum Opinion and Order (NTCM)
Mo & P.........	Moore and Payne's English Common Pleas Reports [*A publication*] (DLA)
Mo & R.........	Moody and Robinson's English Nisi Prius Reports [*A publication*] (DLA)
Mo & S.........	Moore and Scott's English Common Pleas Reports [*1831-34*] [*A publication*] (DLA)
Mo & Sc	Moore and Scott's English Common Pleas Reports [*1831-34*] [*A publication*] (DLA)
MO Ann Stat (Vernon)...	Vernon's Annotated Missouri Statutes [*A publication*] (DLA)
MO Ap	Missouri Appeal Reports [*A publication*] (DLA)
MO App	Missouri Appeal Reports [*A publication*] (DLA)
MO Appeals...	Missouri Appeal Reports [*A publication*] (DLA)
MO App (KC)...	Missouri Appeal Reports [*Kansas City*] [*A publication*] (DLA)
MO App Rep...	Missouri Appeal Reports [*A publication*] (DLA)
MO Apps......	Missouri Appeal Reports [*A publication*] (DLA)
MO App (St L)...	Missouri Appeal Reports [*St. Louis*] [*A publication*] (DLA)
MO AR.........	Missouri Appellate Reporter [*A publication*] (DLA)
MOARS.........	Mobilization Assignment Reserve Section [*Military*]
moAt.........	Mainstream of American Thought (AD)
MOAT.........	Methods of Appraisal and Test (MHDB)
MOAT.........	Missile on Aircraft Test
moat.........	Missile-on-Aircraft Testing [*Military*] (AD)
MOATL.........	Modal Acoustic Transmission Loss (MCD)
MOB............	Mail Order Buyer (WDMC)
MOB............	Main Olfactory Bulb [*Anatomy*]
MOB............	Main Operating Base
MOB............	Make or Buy [*Economics*]
mob............	Make or Buy (AD)
MOB............	Man-Overboard
MOB............	Master of Organizational Behavior (GAGS)
MOB............	Medical Office Building (DAVI)
MOB............	Medical Office Building (MEDA)
MOB............	Menlo Park [*California*] [*Seismograph station code, US Geological Survey*] (SEIS)
MOB............	Missile Order of Battle (AFM)
MOB............	Mobil Corp. [*NYSE symbol Toronto Stock Exchange symbol*] (SPSG)
MOB............	Mobile [*Alabama*] [*Airport symbol*]
mob............	Mobile (AD)
Mob............	Mobile, Alabama [*Maritime abbreviation*] (AD)
mob............	Mobile Vulgus [*Disorderly Group of People*] [*Latin*] (AD)
MOB............	Mobility [*MTMC*] (TAG)
MOB............	Mobilization [*or Mobilize*] (AFM)
Mob............	Mobley's Contested Election Cases, United States House of Representatives [*1882-89*] [*A publication*] (DLA)
MOB............	Mock-Up Board [*Navy*] (AFIT)
MOB............	Modification of Benefits [*Health insurance*] (GHCT)
MOB............	Money-Order Business
MOB............	Montreux-Oberland-Bernois [*Railway*] [*Canada*] (AD)
MOB............	Municipals over Bonds [*Investment term*]
MOB............	Mustargen [*Nitrogen mustard*], Oncovin , Bleomycin [*Vincristine*] [*Antineoplastic drug regimen*]
MOB............	Southwest Baptist College, Bolivar, MO [*OCLC symbol*] (OCLC)
MOBA............	Military Operations in Built-Up Areas
MOBAC............	Monterey Bay Area Cooperative Library System [*Library network*]
MOBAS	Model Basin
MOBAT.........	Mobile Battalion Antitank Gun [*British military*] (DMA)
Mo' Bay	Mobile Bay, Alabama [*Montego Bay, Jamaica*] (AD)
MOBCOM.........	Mobile Command [*Canada*] (AD)
mobcom	Mobile Communications (AD)
MOBCOM.........	Mobile Communications

MOBCON......	Mobilization Construction Plan [*Military*] (NVT)
MOBCON......	Mobilization Movement Control [*MTMC*] (TAG)
MOBCONBAT...	Mobile Construction Battalion [*Navy*] (DNAB)
MOBCTR......	Mobilization Center (DNAB)
MOBDES......	Mobilization Designation [*or Designee*]
MOBDIC......	Mobile Digital Computer
MOBED.......	Mobile Education Demonstration
MoBeHi........	Scott County Historical Society, Benton, MO [*Library symbol*] [*Library of Congress*] (LCLS)
MOBERS......	Mobilization Equipment Redistribution System
MOBEU	Mobile Emergency Unit (NOAA)
mobeu	Mobile Emergency Unit (AD)
MOBEX	Mobile Excursion (MCD)
MOBEX	Mobile Exploration [*NASA*]
MOBEX	Mobility Test Exercise [*Military*]
MOBIDA	Mobile Data Acquisition System (MCD)
MOBIDAC	Mobile Data Acquisition System
MOBIDACS....	Mobile Data Acquisition System (AD)
mobidic	Mobile Digital Computer (AD)
MOBIDIC......	Mobile Digital Computer [*Sylvania Electric Products Co.*]
MOB-III........	Methotrexate, Oncovin [*Vineristine*], Bleomycin [*Antineoplastic drug regimen*] (DAVI)
MOB-III........	Mitomycin C, Oncovin [*Vincristine*], Bleomycin, Cisplatin [*Antineoplastic drug regimen*]
Mobil	Mobil Corp. [*Associated Press*] (SAG)
MOBIL	Mobility
mobil	Mobility (AD)
Mobilarian...	Mobile Branch Librarian (AD)
mobilary......	Mobile Library (AD)
MOBILESAT...	Mobile Satellite Corp. [*King Of Prussia, PA*] [*Telecommunications*] (TSSD)
MOBIS	Management-Oriented Budget Information System
MOBL...........	Macro-Oriented Business Language [*Computer science*]
mobl	Macro-Oriented Business Language [*Computer science*] (AD)
MOBL...........	Main Operating Base LASER
Mobl	Mobley's Contested Election Cases, United States House of Representatives [*1882-89*] [*A publication*] (DLA)
mobl	Mopliert [*Furnished*] [*German*] (AD)
MoblAm........	Mobile America Corp. [*Associated Press*] (SAG)
moblas	Mobile LASER Satellite Tracking Station (AD)
Mobley	Mobley Environmental Services [*Associated Press*] (SAG)
MoblGs........	Mobile Gas Service Corp. [*Associated Press*] (SAG)
mob lib	Mobile Librarian (AD)
MoblM	Mobile Mini, Inc. [*Associated Press*] (SAG)
MoblMin	Mobile Mini, Inc. [*Associated Press*] (SAG)
mob lt	Man Overboard and Breakdown Light (AD)
MOBMAN	Mobilization Manpower Planning System [*DoD*]
MobMda	MobileMedia Corp. [*Associated Press*] (SAG)
MOBMDR......	Mobilization Master Data Record [*Army*]
MOBOL........	Mohawk Business-Oriented Language [*Mohawk Data Systems*]
MoBolS........	Southwest Baptist College, Bolivar, MO [*Library symbol Library of Congress*] (LCLS)
MOBOT	Mobile Remote-Controlled Robot
mobot..........	Mobile Robot (AD)
MOBOT	Modular Robot
MOBPERSACS...	Mobilization Personnel Structure and Composition System [*DoD*]
MoBr............	Brentwood Public Library, Brentwood, MO [*Library symbol Library of Congress*] (LCLS)
MOBRASOP...	Mobilization Requirements in Support of the Army Strategic Objectives Plan
MOBS	Mobile Hospitals [*Military slang*]
MOBS	Mobile Ocean Basing System (PDAA)
MOBS	Multiple-Orbit Bombardment System
MOBSCOPE...	Mobilization Shipments Configured for Operation Planning and Execution [*MTMC*] (TAG)
MOBSF	Mobility Support Flight [*Military*]
MOBSS	Mobility Support Squadron [*Air Force*]
MOBSS	Mobilization Support System [*MTMC*] (TAG)
MOBSSL-UAF...	Merritt and Miller's Own Block Structured Simulation Language, Unpronounceable Acronym For [*1969*] [*Computer science*] (CSR)
MOBSSq	Mobility Support Squadron [*Air Force*]
MOBSUPPGRU...	Mobile Support Group [*Military*] (DNAB)
MOBTA	Mobilization Table of Distribution and Allowances (AD)
MOBTB	Mobilization Troop Basis [*Army*] (AABC)
MOBTDA	Mobilization Table of Distribution and Allowances [*Military*] (AABC)
MOBTR	Mobile Trainer
MOBU	Mobilization Base Units
MOBULA	Model Building Language [*Programming language*] (IEEE)
mobula	Model-Building Language (AD)
MOBYC	My Own Bloody Yacht Club [*Founded in England; registered with Lloyds of London*]
MOC...........	Magnetic Optic Converter
MOC...........	Maintenance Operational Check
MOC...........	Maintenance Operations Center [*Military*]
MOC...........	Maintenance Operations Control [*Canadian Airlines International*]
MOC...........	Makapuu Oceanic Center [*Hawaii*] (AD)
MOC...........	Management and Operating Contractor (ODBW)
MOC...........	Management of Change
MOC...........	Management-Oriented Computing (MHDB)
MOC...........	Manual Operations Control
moc............	Manufacturing Other Charges (AD)
MOC...........	Manufacturing Outreach Center
MOC...........	Marcos Owners Club [*Formerly, Marcos Club*] (EA)
MOC...........	Marine Operation Center [*NASA*] (NASA)
MOC...........	Marine Operation Center

MOC...........	Marlin Owners' Club (EA)
MOC...........	Master Operational Computer [*or Controller*]
moc............	Master Operation Control (AD)
MOC...........	Master Operations Center
MOC...........	Master Operations Console
MOC...........	Master Operations Control
MOC...........	Master Ordnance Configuration File [*Navy*]
MOC...........	Mathematical Operations Computer
MOC...........	Mauna Olu College [*Maui*] (AD)
MOC...........	Maximum Operational Capacity [*Chemical engineering*]
MOC...........	Maximum Oxygen Consumption
MOC...........	Mechanical Off-Machine Coated Paper (DGA)
MOC...........	Memorandum of Conditions
MOC...........	Memory Operating Characteristic [*Computer science*] (IEEE)
MOC...........	Merland Explorations Ltd. [*Toronto Stock Exchange symbol*]
MOC...........	Messerschmitt Owners Club (EA)
MOC...........	Method of Characteristics [*Equilibrium flow*]
MOC...........	Metropolitan Owners' Club [*Woking, Surrey, England*] (EAIO)
MOC...........	Mid Ocean Limited [*NYSE symbol*] (SAG)
MOC...........	Mid Ocean Ltd [*NYSE symbol*] (TTSB)
MOC...........	Military Occupation Code (MCD)
MOC...........	Military Order of the Carabao (EA)
MOC...........	Minimal Oxygen Consumption
MOC...........	Minimum Obstacle Clearance [*Aviation*] (FAAC)
MOC...........	Minimum Operational Characteristics
MOC...........	Ministry of Communications (CINC)
MOC...........	Missile Operation Center [*Air Force*]
MOC...........	Missionaries of Charity [*Australia*]
MOC...........	Mission Operation Computer
MOC...........	Mission Operations Complex [*NASA*] (KSC)
moc............	Mission Operations Computer (AD)
MOC...........	Mobile Oil Cooler
MOC...........	Mobile Operations Center [*Air Force*] (DOMA)
moc............	Mocassin (AD)
MOC...........	Moccasin
MOC...........	Modern Operating Contract [*Automibile industry labor relations*]
MOC...........	Modular Organization Charting (PDAA)
MOC...........	Montes Claros [*Brazil*] [*Airport symbol*] (OAG)
MOC...........	Morris College, Sumter, SC [*Inactive*] [*OCLC symbol*] (OCLC)
MOC...........	Mother of the Chapel [*Unions*] [*British*] (DI)
MOC...........	Mustang Owners Club (EA)
MOC...........	Supreme Pup Tent, Military Order of the Cootie (EA)
MOCA	Methotrexate, Oncovin [*Vincristine*], Cyclophosphamide, Adriamycin [*Antineoplastic drug regimen*]
MOCA	Methylenebis(ortho-chloroaniline) [*Also, MBOCA*] [*Organic chemistry*]
MOCA	Minimum Obstruction Clearance Altitude [*Aviation*]
moca	Minimum Obstruction Clearance Altitude (AD)
MOCA	Mitsubishi Owner's Club of America
MOCA	Montezuma Castle National Monument
MOCA	Museum of Contemporary Art [*Los Angeles*]
MOCAM	Mobile Checkout and Maintenance (AAG)
mocamp	Motor Camp (AD)
MOCAN	Motor Can
MoCanC.......	Culver-Stockton College, Canton, MO [*Library symbol Library of Congress*] (LCLS)
MOCAS	Mechanization of Contract Administration Service (MCD)
MOCC	Master Operations Control Center (SAA)
MOCC	Metal-Oxygen Cluster Compounds [*Chemistry*]
MOCC	MG Octagon Car Club [*Formerly, Octagon Car Club*] (EA)
MOCC	Mission Operations Control Center (SSD)
MOCC	Mobile Operations Command Center (DOMA)
MOCCA	, Cyclophosphamide, Alkeran [*Lomustine*] [*Melphalan*] [*Antineoplastic drug regimen*]
MOCCC	Massachusetts Organized Crime Control Council (AD)
MOccThy.....	Master of Occupational Therapy (ADA)
MOcE	Master of Oceanographic Engineering (GAGS)
M Oc E	Master of Oceanographic Engineering (PGP)
MOCEM.......	Meteorological and Oceanographic Equipment Maintenance Course (DNAB)
MOCF	Maintenance Operations Control File (MCD)
MOCF	Manchester Open College Federation [*British*] (AIE)
MOCF	Mission Operations Computational Facilities [*NASA*] (NASA)
MoCg	Cape Girardeau Public Library, Cape Girardeau, MO [*Library symbol Library of Congress*] (LCLS)
MoCgS.........	Southeast Missouri State University, Cape Girardeau, MO [*Library symbol Library of Congress*] (LCLS)
MoCheL.......	Logan College of Chiropractic, Chesterfield, MO [*Library symbol*] [*Library of Congress*] (LCLS)
mochwr........	Mochaware (VRA)
MOCI	Ministry of Commerce and Industry [*British*] (AD)
MOCI	Mound City Group National Monument
MOCI	Mustang Owners Club International (EA)
MOCIC	Molecular Orbital Constraint of Interaction Coordinates [*Atomic physics*]
MOCL..........	Metz Owners Club Library (EA)
MoCli..........	Henry County Library, Clinton, MO [*Library symbol*] [*Library of Congress*] (LCLS)
MoCIS.........	Saint Louis Junior College, Clayton, MO [*Library symbol Library of Congress Obsolete*] (LCLS)
MOCM........	Missile Out of Commission for Maintenance (MUGU)
MOCN.........	Mid Ocean Ltd. [*NASDAQ symbol*] (SAG)
MOCN.........	Modern Controls, Inc. [*Associated Press*] (SAG)
MOCNA........	Maserati Owners Club of North America (EAIO)
MOCNA........	Metropolitan Owners Club of North America (EA)

MOCNESS....	Multiple Opening-Closing Net and Environmental Sensing System [*For collecting marine samples*]
MOCNESS....	Multiple Opening-Closing Net Environmental Sampling System (USDC)
MOCO	Machinery Overhaul Co.
MOCO	Missile Operations Control Officer (AAG)
MOCO	Modern Controls [*NASDAQ symbol*] (TTSB)
MOCO	Modern Controls, Inc. [*NASDAQ symbol*] (NQ)
MoCoC........	Christian College, Columbia, MO [*Library symbol Library of Congress*] (LCLS)
Mo Code Regs...	State of Missouri Code of State Regulations Annotated [*A publication*] (AAGC)
MOCODES....	Mobile Coastal Defense System (MCD)
MoCoGS	Church of Jesus Christ of Latter-Day Saints, Genealogical Society Library, Columbia Missouri Branch, Columbia, MO [*Library symbol Library of Congress*] (LCLS)
MoCoJ	Joint Collection, Western Historical Manuscript Collection and State Historical,Columbia, MO [*Library symbol*] [*Library of Congress*] (LCLS)
MoCom........	Mobile Command (AD)
MOCOM......	Mobility Command [*AMC*]
MOCON.......	Mobile Repair Parts Container
MoConA.......	Conception Abbey and Seminary, Conception, MO [*Library symbol Library of Congress*] (LCLS)
MoCoS........	Stephens College, Columbia, MO [*Library symbol Library of Congress*] (LCLS)
MoCoV.........	Harry S Truman Memorial Veterans Hospital, Columbia, MO [*Library symbol Library of Congress*] (LCLS)
MOCP	Missile Out of Commission for Parts (AFM)
mocp	Missile Out of Commission for Parts [*Military*] (AD)
MOCR	Metz Owners Club Register (EA)
mocr	Mission Operation Control Room (AD)
MOCR	Mission Operations Control Room
MOCR	Moores Creek National Military Park
MOCS	Managed Object Conformance Statement [*Telecommunications*] (OSI)
MOCS	Master Operations Control System (KSC)
MOCS	Military Order of Columbia's Shield (EA)
MOCS	Multichannel Ocean Color Sensor [*NASA*]
MOCS	Multiple Output Control System (ECII)
MoCStP.......	Saint Paul's College, Concordia, MO [*Library symbol Library of Congress*] (LCLS)
MOCSW	Monitor and Operations Control Software Subsystem [*Space Flight Operations Facility, NASA*]
MOCT...........	Mean Overhaul Cycle Time [*Quality control*] (MCD)
MOCV	Manual Oxygen Control Valve (NASA)
MOCV	Manual Oxygen Control Valve
MO-CVD......	Metal-Organic Chemical Vapor Deposition [*Also, MO-VPE, OM-CVD, OM-VPE*] [*Semiconductor technology*]
MOD	Drury College, Springfield, MO [*OCLC symbol*] (OCLC)
Mod	Made Over Democrat [*Facetious translation referring to Mods - Moderate Republicans*]
MOD	Magnetic Optical Display
MOD	Magneto-Optical Disc [*Digital audio technology*]
mod	Magneto-Optical Disc (AD)
MOD	Mail-Order Delivery
MOD	Mail Order Department [*Business term*]
MOD	Maintenance of Deception
MOD	Management and Organization Division [*Environmental Protection Agency*] (GFGA)
MOD	Manager on Duty
MOD	Manned Orbital Development Station [*See also MODS, MOSS, MTSS*] [*Air Force/NASA*]
MOD	Manpower and Organization Division [*Air Force*]
MOD	Manual Overdrive [*Automotive engineering*]
MOD	Manufacturers Operations Division [*Environmental Protection Agency*] (GFGA)
MOD	Mapping of Disease
MOD	March on Drugs [*An association*]
MOD	Marine Operations Division [*Environmental Protection Agency*] (GFGA)
Mod	Marxist on Drugs [*Mods - Facetious translation referring to Moderate Republicans*]
MOD	Master of Organizational Development (GAGS)
MOD	Masters of Disaster [*Computer hacker gang*]
MOD	Maturity Onset Diabetes [*Medicine*]
MOD	Medical Officer of the Day [*Military*]
MOD	Medical Officer on Duty (DAVI)
MOD	Medicine, Osteopathy, and Dentistry [*HEW program*]
MOD	Mesial, Occlusal, and Distal [*Describes location of openings in a carious tooth*] [*Dentistry*]
m-o-d..........	Mesial-Occlusal-Distal [*Dentistry*] (AD)
MOD	Message Output Description [*Computer science*]
MOD	Metallo-Organic Deposition [*Materials technology*]
MOD	Method of Delivery
MOD	Microfilm-Output Device
MOD	Microwave Oscillating Diode (MCD)
MOD	Military Obligation Designator
MOD	Military Orbital Development System [*See also MODS, MOSS, MTSS*] [*Air Force/NASA*]
Mod	Mindless Operative of the Devil [*Mods - Facetious translation referring to Moderate Republicans*]
MOD	Ministry of Defence [*British*]
M o D	Ministry of Defence [*British*] (AD)
MOD	Ministry of Overseas Development [*British*] (ILCA)

MOD	Minuteman Operating Directive (SAA)
MOD	Miscellaneous Obligation Document
MOD	Mission Objectives Document (MCD)
MOD	Mission Operations Director [*NASA*] (KSC)
MOD	Mobile Obstacle Detachment (MCD)
MOD	Mobility Opportunity and Development
mod	modality [*Physical therapy*] (DAVI)
MOD	Modal (Verb) [*Linguistics*]
MOD	Modatech Systems, Inc. [*Vancouver Stock Exchange symbol*]
MOD	Model (KSC)
mod	Model (AD)
mod	Moderate (AD)
MOD	Moderate [*or Moderator*] (AABC)
MOD	Moderato [*Moderate Speed*] [*Music*]
MOD	Modern
Mod	Modern (AD)
mod	Modern (AD)
MOD	Modern
Mod	Modern Reports [*England*] [*A publication*] (DLA)
MOD	Modesto [*California*] [*Airport symbol*] (OAG)
MOD	Modification [*or Modify*] (AFM)
mod	Modification (AD)
mod	Modification (IDOE)
MOD	Modifier [*Linguistics*]
MOD	Modiim [*Israel*] [*Later, AMT*] [*Geomagnetic observatory code*]
mod	Modular (AD)
MOD	Modular Observation Device (RDA)
MOD	Modulation [*Telecommunications*] (KSC)
MOD	Modulation
MOD	Modulator (CET)
mod	Modulator (IDOE)
MOD	Modulator-Demodulator [*Telecommunications*] (MCD)
MOD	Module [*or Modular or Modulation*] (KSC)
MOD	Module
mod	Modulo [*Mathematics*] (CDE)
MOD	Modulus
mod	Modulus (IDOE)
MOD	Money-Order Department
MOD	Month of Detachment
MOD	Motor-Operated Disconnect [*Nuclear energy*] (NRCH)
MOD	Moving Domain Memories [*Computer science*] (MDG)
Mod	Style's English King's Bench Reports [*1646-55*] [*A publication*] (DLA)
MOD	Supreme Industries [*AMEX symbol*] (SAG)
MOD10	Modulus 10 Check Digit [*Computer science*]
MODA	Ministry of Defense and Aviation (MCD)
MODA	ModaCad Inc. [*NASDAQ symbol*] (TTSB)
MODA	ModaCad, Inc. [*NASDAQ symbol*] (SAG)
MODA	Motion Detector and Alarm [*Army*]
MODABUND...	Mosquito Data Bank of the University of Notre Dame
MODAC	Mountain System Digital Automatic Computer
MODACS.....	Modular Data Acquisition and Control System [*or Subsystem*] [*Modular Computing Systems, Inc.*]
MOD(AD)	Ministry of Defence (Army Department) [*British*]
Mod Am Law...	Modern American Law [*A publication*] (DLA)
MODAP.......	Modified Apollo [*NASA*] (MCD)
MODAP.......	Multiple Operational Data Acquisition Program [*Computer science*]
MODAPS.....	Maintenance and Operational Data Presentation Study (AAG)
MODAPS.....	Modal Data Acquisition and Processing System
MODAPTS...	Modular Arrangement of Predetermined Time Standards
MODART.....	Methods of Defeating Advanced RADAR Threats (NASA)
MODAS......	Multidirectional Osmotic Drug Absorption System [*Medicine*]
MODASM.....	Modular Air-to-Surface Missile (MCD)
modasm	Modular Air-to-Surface Missile [*Military*] (AD)
MODATS.....	Mohawk Data Transmission System (MCD)
MODAW......	ModaCAD Inc. Wrrt [*NASDAQ symbol*] (TTSB)
m-o-d-b	Mesial-Occlusal-Distal-Buccal [*Dentistry*] (AD)
MODB	Military Occupational Data Bank [*Later, AOSP*] (AABC)
MODCA.......	Mixed Object Document Content Architecture [*Computer science*] (BTTJ)
MO:DCA......	Mixed Object: Document Content Architecure [*Computer science*] (CDE)
MODCAR......	Modified Owners and Drivers Corp. for the Advancement of Racing (EA)
Mod Cas	Modern Cases [*6 Modern Reports*] [*1702-45*] [*A publication*] (DLA)
Mod Cas L & Eq...	Modern Cases at Law and Equity [*8, 9 Modern Reports*] [*1721-55*] [*A publication*] (DLA)
Mod Cas per Far...	Modern Cases Tempore Holt, by Farresley [*7 Modern Reports*] [*A publication*] (DLA)
Mod Cas T Holt...	Modern Cases Tempore Holt, by Farresley [*7 Modern Reports*] [*A publication*] (DLA)
modcom	Modernity Commercialized (AD)
MODCOM.....	Modular Computer System
MODCOMP...	Modular Computer Systems Inc. (NITA)
MODCON.....	Man Machine System for the Optimum Design and Construction of Buildings (PDAA)
MOD CON	Modern Convenience (DSUE)
mod-cons.....	Modern-Construction Houses (AD)
mod cons.....	Modern Conveniences (AD)
MODCPS.....	Multiple Output Direct Current Power Supply
MODD.........	Military Order of Devil Dogs (EA)
Modd.........	Modern Medical Modalities Corp. [*Associated Press*] (SAG)
moddem	Modulator-Demodulator (AD)
mod/demod...	Modulate-Demodulate (AD)
MODDF........	Military Order, Devil Dog Fleas (EA)

MOD DICT ... In the Manner Directed [*Abbreviation from the Latin*] [*Pharmacy*] (ROG)

MODE .... Management of Objectives with Dollars through Employees [*Department of Agriculture*]

MODE .... Merchant Oriented Data Entry

MODE .... Methoxy(O-desmethyl)encainide [*Biochemistry*]

MODE .... Mid-Ocean Dynamics Experiment [*National Science Foundation*]

ModE .... Modern English (AD)

MODE .... Monitor Data Equipment

MODE .... Monitoring Overseas Direct Employment (DNAB)

MODE C ...... Altitude Reporting Mode of Secondary Radar [*FAA*] (TAG)

MO Dec ...... Missouri Decisions [*A publication*] (DLA)

MODEC ...... Motor Optimization Design Evaluation Code (MCD)

Model Bus Corp Act Anno 2d... American Bar Association Model Business Corporation Act, Annotated, Second Series [*A publication*] (DLA)

Model Business Corp Act... American Bar Association Model Business Corporation Act, Annotated [*A publication*] (DLA)

MODELH/PRDH... Mouvement pour la Liberation d'Haiti/Parti Revolutionnaire d'Haiti [*Political party*] (EY)

ModelImp .... Model Imperial, Inc. [*Associated Press*] (SAG)

Model Land Dev Code... American Law Institute Model Land Development Code [*A publication*] (DLA)

Model R ..... Model Railroader [*A publication*]

MODEM .... Modulate/Demodulate [*or Modulation/Demodulation or Modulator-Demodulator*] [*Computer science*]

modem .... Modulating-Demodulating (AD)

modem .... Modulator/Demodulator [*Computer science*] (WDMC)

Mod (Eng) ... English King's Bench Modern Reports [*86-88 English Reprint*] [*A publication*] (DLA)

MOD ENT..... Modern Entries [*Legal term*] (DLA)

Modern Lib... Modern Library (AD)

MODEST ...... Missile Optical Destruction Technique

Modest Pistor... Modestinus Pistoris [*Deceased, 1565*] [*Authority cited in pre-1607 legal work*] (DSA)

MODET .... Mortar Detection

MODEX .... Mobilization Deployment Exercise (MCD)

modf .... Modification (AD)

MODF .... Modify (AAG)

MODFET ..... Modulation-Doped Field-Effect Transistor [*Solid-state physics*]

MODFLIR .... Modular Forward-Looking Infrared Seeker

MODFN .... Modification (AAG)

MODFR .... Modifier (AAG)

Mod'g .... Modifying [*Legal term*] (DLA)

ModGr .... Modern Greek [*Language*]

MODHATR .. Modified Hatrack [*Cyclone forecasting*] [*Navy*]

ModHeb .. Modern Hebrew (AD)

MODI .... Major Oversea Depot and Installation Method [*Army*]

MODI .... Modified Distribution

MODI .... Modine Manufacturing Co. [*NASDAQ symbol*] (NQ)

MODI .... Modine Mfg [*NASDAQ symbol*] (TTSB)

MODI .... Modular Optical Digital Interface

MODIA .... Method of Designing Instructional Alternatives (PDAA)

MODICON .... Modular-Dispersed-Control

MODIF .... Modification (KSC)

MODIG .... Modular Digital Image Generation [*Computer science*]

MODIGSI .... Modular Digital Simulation (MCD)

MODIL .... Manufacturing Operations Development and Integration Laboratory

MODILS ...... Modular Instrument Landing System

MODIM .... MOTS [*Module Test Set*] Design Information Memorandum

Modine .... Modine Manufacturing Co. [*Associated Press*] (SAG)

Mod Int........ Brown's Modus Intrandi [*A publication*] (DLA)

Modio .... MODEM and Radio [*Telecommunications*]

MOD/IRAN... Modification/Inspection and Repair as Necessary

mod/iran..... Modification, Inspection, and Repair as Necessary (AD)

MODIS .... Moderate-Resolution Imaging Spectrometer (MCD)

MODIS .... Mode Shape Display [*Module*]

MODISCO .... Mechanization of Defense Industrial Security Clearance Office [*DoD*]

MODL .... Model Imperial, Inc. [*NASDAQ symbol*] (SAG)

ModL .... Modern Latin [*Language*]

ModLA .... Modern Language Association, New York, NY [*Library symbol Library of Congress*] (LCLS)

Mod L & Soc'y... Modern Law and Society [*A publication*] (DLA)

ModLA-R .... Modern Language Association Research in Progress Program, New York NY [*Library symbol*] [*Library of Congress*] (LCLS)

MOD LITH.... Modern Lithographer [*A publication*] (DGA)

MODLOC...... Modified Location

MODLOG 77... Modernization of Logistics 1977 [*Army*]

MODM .... Magneto-Optical Display Memory

MODM .... Major Oversea Depot Method [*Army*]

MODM .... Manned One-Day Mission [*NASA*]

MODM .... Mature-Onset Diabetes Mellitus (MAE)

MODM .... Modern Medical Modalities Corp. [*NASDAQ symbol*] (SAG)

MODM .... Modern Medl Modalities [*NASDAQ symbol*] (TTSB)

ModMd .... Modern Medical Modalities Corp. [*Associated Press*] (SAG)

ModMed ..... Modern Medical Modalities Corp. [*Associated Press*] (SAG)

Mod Med Aust... Modern Medicine of Australia [*A publication*]

MODMW ...... Modern Med Modalities Wrrr'A' [*NASDAQ symbol*] (TTSB)

MODMZ ...... Modern Med Modalities Wrr'B' [*NASDAQ symbol*] (TTSB)

MOD(N) ...... Ministry of Defence (Navy) [*British*]

MoDNM ...... Morpholinodaunomycin [*Also, MRD*] [*Antineoplastic drug*]

MODO .... Moderato [*Moderate Speed*] [*Music*] (ROG)

modo .... Moderato [*Moderately*] [*Italian*] (AD)

Mod Off Dat Man... Modern Office and Data Management [*A publication*]

Mod Office Data Mgmt... Modern Office and Data Management [*A publication*]

MOD/OP....... Maintenance of Deception/Operation

MODOP........ Mobil Oil Direct Oxidation Process [*Gas desulfurization process*]

MODOR....... Molecularized Doppler RADAR

MODP .... Modern Programming Practice

MODPAC...... Modular Restraint, Recovery, and Survival Package

MOD(PE)...... Ministry of Defence (Procurement Executive) [*British*]

MODPOT...... Model Potential [*Physics*]

Mod Pract Comm... Modern Practice Commentator [*A publication*] (DLA)

mod praes ... Modo Praescripto [*In the manner prescribed*] [*Latin*] [*Pharmacy*] (BARN)

MOD PRAESC... Modo Praescripto [*In the Manner Prescribed*] [*Latin Pharmacy*] (MAH)

MOD PRAESCRIPT... Modo Praescripto [*In the Manner Prescribed*] [*Pharmacy*]

mod pres ..... Modo Prescripto [*In the Manner Prescribed*] [*Latin*] (AD)

MOD PRESCR... Modo Praescripto [*In the Manner Prescribed*] [*Pharmacy*] (ROG)

mod pst ...... Modeling Paste (VRA)

MODR.......... Microwave Optical Double Resonance (PDAA)

modr.......... Moderate Room Rate Desired (AD)

MODR......... Monodetail Drawing (MSA)

MODREFTRA... Modified Refresher Training [*Navy*] (NVT)

Mod Rep...... Modern Reports [*England*] [*A publication*] (DLA)

Mod Rep..... Style's English King's Bench Reports [*1646-55*] [*A publication*] (DLA)

MODS .... Major Operations Data System (NVT)

MODS .... Manned Orbital Development Station [*See also MOD, MOSS, MTSS*] [*Air Force/NASA*]

MODS .... Manpower Operations Data System [*Employment and Training Administration*] [*Department of Labor*]

MODS .... Material Ordering and Delivery Schedule (DNAB)

MODS .... Medically Oriented Data System (MCD)

MODS .... Medium Ocean Data Station

mods .... Mesial-Occlusal-Distal [*Dentistry*] (AD)

MODS .... Military Orbital Development System [*See also MOD, MOSS, MTSS*] [*Air Force/NASA*]

MODS .... Missile Offense/Defense System

MODS .... Mission Operations Design Support

MODS .... Mobility-Planning Data System [*Military*] (GFGA)

MODS .... Models (MCD)

MODS .... Models for Organizational Design and Staffing (DNAB)

Mods .... Moderates [*Reference to political philosophy of some members of the Republican party*]

MODS .... Moderations [*First public Oxford examination*] (ROG)

MODS .... Modifications

MODS .... Modular Oriented Direct Support (MCD)

MODS .... Multiple Organ Dysfunction Syndrome [*Medicine*]

MODSAF...... Modular Semi-Automatic Forces

MODSC .... Magnetooptically Detected Spin Conversion [*Physics*]

MODT .... Mean Operational Delay Time

MODT .... Modtech, Inc. [*NASDAQ symbol*] (SAG)

Modtec .... Modtech, Inc. [*Associated Press*] (SAG)

MODTEPS .... Modular Toxic Environment Protective Suit [*NASA*]

MODTLE ..... Mobilization on Development, Trade, Labor, and Environment [*An association*]

MODTO .... Moderato [*Moderate Speed*] [*Music*]

modto .... Moderato [*Moderately*] [*Italian*] (AD)

MODU .... Mobile Offshore Drilling Unit

MODULA ...... Modular Programming Language (CSR)

MODULAB.... Modular Clinical Laboratory [*Military*] (CAAL)

MOD/UM...... Modulated/Unmodulated (SSD)

Mod Un....... Modern Unionist [*A publication*]

Mod Unionist... Modern Unionist [*A publication*]

MODUS........ Modular One Dynamic User System [*Computer science*] (MHDI)

MODUSSE.... Manufacturers of Domestic Unvented Supply Systems Equipment [*British*] (DBA)

MODWORS... Modification Work Order Report Status

MODY .... Maturity Onset Diabetes of the Young [*Medicine*] (DMAA)

MOE............ Evangel College, Springfield, MO [*OCLC symbol*] (OCLC)

MOE............ MAD Operational Effectiveness (DNAB)

MOE............ Maintenance of Effort [*Medicare Act*]

MOE............ Major Organizational Entity (MCD)

MOE............ Margin of Exposure [*Toxicology*]

MOE............ Mars Orbit Ejection (MCD)

MOE............ Master of Ocean Engineering (GAGS)

MOE............ Master of Oral English

MOE............ Maximum Output Entropy (PDAA)

MOE............ Measure of Effectiveness

moe............ Measure of Effectiveness (AD)

MoE............ Ministry of Education [*British*] (AD)

MOE............ Ministry of Education [*British*] (DAS)

M o E............ Ministry of Energy [*British*] (AD)

MOE............ Ministry of Environment [*Canada*]

MOE............ Mission-Oriented Equipment

MOE............ Model Operational Environment (SAA)

MOE............ Modulus of Elasticity [*Mechanics*]

MOE............ Moli Energy Ltd. [*Toronto Stock Exchange symbol Vancouver Stock Exchange symbol*]

MOE............ Momeik [*Myanmar*] [*Airport symbol*] (OAG)

MOE............ Mythical Operational Environment (SAA)

MOE............ Ontario Ministry of Education, Information Centre, Research Branch [*UTLAS symbol*]

MOE............ Telemetering Mobile Station [*ITU designation*]

MOEA.......... Ministry of Economic Affairs [*British*] (AD)

MOED .... Molecular Orbital Energy Diagram

MOED .... Morristown-Edison National Park Service Group

MOEDA .... Measures of Effectiveness, Development, and Application (MCD)

MOEP .... Meteorological and Oceanographic Equipment Program (NG)

MOER .... MACOM [*Major Command*] Outstanding Excess Report

MOERO........ Medium Orbiting Earth Resources Observatory (IEEE)
MOES.......... Mathematics Olympiads for Elementary Schools (EDAC)
MOETLO...... Meteorological and Oceanographic Equipment Technical Liaison Officer
MoExGS....... Excelsior Springs Genealogical Society, Excelsior Springs, MO [*Library symbol Library of Congress*] (LCLS)
MOF........... Fontbonne College, St. Louis, MO [*OCLC symbol*] (OCLC)
MOF........... Manned Orbital Flight [*NASA*] (NASA)
MOF........... Marine Oxidation/Fermentation
MOF........... Maumere [*Indonesia*] [*Airport symbol*] (OAG)
MOF........... Maximum Observed Frequency [*Radio*]
mof............ Maximum Observed Frequency (AD)
MOF........... Maximum Operating Frequency
MOF........... MeCCNU [*Semustine*], Oncovin , Fluorouracil [*Vincristine*] [*Antineoplastic drug regimen*]
MOF........... Member of the Force (LAIN)
mof............ Member of the Police Force (AD)
mof............ Metal Oxide Film (AD)
MOF........... Metal-Oxide Film
MOF........... Methotrexate, Oncovin [*Vincristine*] 5-Fluorouracil [*Antineoplastic drug regimen*] (DAVI)
MOF........... Methoxyflurane [*Anesthetic*] (AAMN)
MOF........... Methylo-CCNU, Vineristine, Fluorouracil [*Antineoplastic drug regimen*] (DAVI)
MOF........... Michoud Operations Facility [*NASA*] (AAG)
MOF........... Ministry of Finance [*Japan*] (ECON)
MoF........... Ministry of Finance [*British*] (AD)
MOF........... Ministry of Food [*British*]
MOF........... Mission Operations Facility [*NASA*] (KSC)
MOF........... Moffat Communications Ltd. [*Toronto Stock Exchange symbol*]
MOF........... Months of Operational Flying (DNAB)
MOF........... Multi-Option Facility
MOF........... Multioption Fuze (MCD)
MOF........... Multiple Organ Failure [*Medicine*]
MOFA......... Multi-Option Fuze, Artillery
MOFAB....... Mobile Floating Assault Bridge-Ferry [*Military*] (MCD)
MOFACS..... Multiorder Feedback and Compensation Synthesis
MOFAP....... Ministry of Fuel and Power [*British*]
M of Arch.... Master of Architecture
MOFARS..... Maintenance Overload Factor Reporting System
MOFAST..... Mechanization of Freight and Shipping Terminal [*DoD*]
MoFC......... Central Methodist College, Fayette, MO [*Library symbol Library of Congress*] (LCLS)
M of C........ Master of Commerce
MOFC......... Michael O'Leary Fan Club [*Defunct*] (EA)
M of D........ Ministry of Defence [*British*]
M of E........ Ministry of Education [*British*]
M of E........ Minutes of Evidence
MOFERT...... Ministry of Foreign Economic Relations and Trade [*China*]
MOFF......... Multiple Options Funding Facility [*Euronotes*]
M of HA...... Matrons of Hospitals Association (ROG)
M of Hist..... Magazine of History [*A publication*] (BRI)
M of I......... Moment of Inertia
MoFIM........ Mark Twain Shrine, Mark Twain State Park, Florida, MO [*Library symbol Library of Congress*] (LCLS)
MoFloSS...... Saint Stanislaus Seminary, Florissant, MO [*Library symbol Library of Congress*] (LCLS)
M of M....... Maintenance of Membership [*Labor unions*]
MOFN........ MovieFone CI'A' [*NASDAQ symbol*] (TTSB)
MOFN........ MovieFone, Inc. [*NASDAQ symbol*] (SAG)
M of R........ Minister of Reconstruction [*British*] (AD)
MOF-STREP... MeCCNU [*Semustine*], Oncovin , Fluorouracil, Streptozotocin [*Vincristine*] [*Antineoplastic drug regimen*]
MOFTEC...... Ministry of Foreign Trade & Economic Cooperation [*China*]
MOFTU....... MIG Operational Fighter Training Unit [*India*] [*Air Force*]
MoFuWC..... Westminster College, Fulton, MO [*Library symbol Library of Congress*] (LCLS)
M of V........ [*The*] Merchant of Venice [*Shakespearean work*]
M of W....... Maintenance of Way [*Railroading*]
MOFW........ Military Order of Foreign Wars of the United States (EA)
MOG.......... Assemblies of God Graduate School, Springfield, MO [*OCLC symbol*] (OCLC)
MOG.......... Machinery of Government
MOG.......... Mannville Oil & Gas Ltd. [*Toronto Stock Exchange symbol*]
Mog........... Margaret (AD)
MOG.......... Master of Obstetrics and Gynecology (AD)
MOG.......... Material Ordering Guide [*Shipbuilding*]
MOG.......... Material Other than Grape [*Wine making*]
MOG.......... Medical Oncology Group
MOG.......... Metropolitan Opera Guild (EA)
MOG.......... Micro-Optic Gyroscope
MOG.......... Milicias Obreras Guatemaltecas [*Guatemalan Workers' Militia*] (PD)
MOG.......... Mogadishu [*Somalia*] [*Seismograph station code, US Geological Survey Closed*] (SEIS)
MOG.......... Monghsat [*Myanmar*] [*Airport symbol*] (OAG)
MOG.......... Montague, CA [*Location identifier FAA*] (FAAL)
MOG.......... Moog, Inc. [*AMEX symbol*] (SPSG)
MOG.......... Morgan [*Automobile*]
MOG.......... Municipal Officers' Guild (ROG)
MOG.......... Myelin Oligodendrocyte Glycoprotein [*Biochemistry*]
MOGA......... Management of Officer Grade Authorization (MCD)
MOGA......... Microwave and Optical Generation and Amplification (MCD)
MOGA......... Montana Outfitters and Guides Association (EA)
MOGAS....... Motor Gasoline [*Military*]
mogas .... Motor Gasoline (AD)

MOGN.......... MGI PHARMA, Inc. [*NASDAQ symbol*] (NQ)
MOGN.......... Molecular Genetics, Inc. (MHDW)
MOGUNTIA... Model of the Global Universal Tracer Transport in the Atmosphere [*Marine science*] (OSRA)
Moguyde...... Mouvement Guyanais de Decolonisation [*Guiana Decolonization Movement*] [*France Political party*] (PPW)
MoGvS......... Grain Valley Associated School District, Grain Valley, MO [*Library symbol*] [*Library of Congress*] (LCLS)
MoH............ Hannibal Free Public Library, Hannibal, MO [*Library symbol Library of Congress*] (LCLS)
MOH .... Hydrological and Meteorological Mobile Station [*ITU designation*]
MOH .... Master of Occupational Health (PGP)
MOH .... Master of Otter Hounds
moh .... Material Overhead (AD)
moh .... Maximum Operating Hours (AD)
MOH .... Maximum Operating Hours (MCD)
MOH .... Medal of Honor [*Often erroneously called Congressional Medal of Honor*] [*Military decoration*]
MOH .... Medical Officer of Health [*British*]
MOH .... Ministry of Health [*British*]
M o H .... Ministry of Health [*British*] (AD)
MOH .... Moche Resources, Inc. [*Vancouver Stock Exchange symbol*]
moh .... Mohawk [*MARC language code Library of Congress*] (LCCP)
MOH .... Mohawk Airlines, Inc. [*Obsolete*]
MOH .... Museum of Holography [*New York City*]
MOH .... New York, NY [*Location identifier FAA*] (FAAL)
MOH .... St. Louis Priory School, St. Louis, MO [*OCLC symbol*] (OCLC)
MOH .... Tigerfly [*British ICAO designator*] (FAAC)
MoHam....... Hamilton Public Library, Hamilton, MO [*Library symbol*] [*Library of Congress*] (LCLS)
Moham....... Mohammedan (AD)
MOHAM..... Mohammedan (ROG)
MoHarC...... Cass County Public Library, Harrisonville, MO [*Library symbol Library of Congress*] (LCLS)
MOHAT...... Modular Handling and Transport
MOHATS..... Mobile Overland Hauling and Transport System [*Air Force*]
MOHAVE..... Measurement of Haze and Visual Effects [*Study*] [*Marine science*] (OSRA)
MOHAVE..... Measurement of Haze and Visusal Effects [*Study*] (USDC)
Mohawk...... Mohawk Industries, Inc. [*Associated Press*] (SAG)
MOHEC....... Maintenance of Hercules Capability (SAA)
MoHi.......... Missouri State Historical Society, Columbia, MO [*Library symbol Library of Congress*] (LCLS)
MoHig........ Robertson Memorial Library, Higginsville, MO [*Library symbol*] [*Library of Congress*] (LCLS)
MoHigH...... Habilitation Center, Higginsville, MO [*Library symbol*] [*Library of Congress*] (LCLS)
MOHILL...... Machine-Oriented High-Level Language [*Computer science*] (HGAA)
MOHK........ Mohawk Industries [*NASDAQ symbol*] (SAG)
MOHLG....... Ministry of Housing and Local Government [*British*] (AD)
MOH(LHA) ... Medical Officer of Health (Local Health Authority) [*British*]
MoHM........ Mark Twain Museum, Hannibal, MO [*Library symbol Library of Congress*] (LCLS)
MOHMS ...... Milliohms (WDAA)
mohms .... Milliohms (AD)
moho .... Mohorovicic Discontinuity [*Geology*] (AD)
MOHO .... Mohorovicic Discontinuity [*Geology*]
MOHOL....... Machine-Oriented Higher Order Language [*Computer science*] (MHDI)
MOHS .... Master of Occupational Health and Safety
mohs .... Mud, Oil, Hooks, Slings [*Insurance*] (AD)
MOHSLG..... Health Sciences Library [*Library network*]
MoHu......... Huntsville Public Library, Huntsville, MO [*Library symbol Library of Congress*] (LCLS)
MOI............ Main-d'Oeuvre Indigene [*Indigenous Manpower*] [*Congo - Leopoldville*]
MOI............ Maintenance Operating Instruction [*Air Force Logistics Command*]
MOI............ Make on Installation (SAA)
MOI............ Marine Officer Instructor (DOMA)
MOI............ Mars Orbit [*or Orbital*] Insertion [*Aerospace*]
MOI............ Maximum Obtainable Irradiance
moi............ Maximum Obtainable Irradiance (AD)
MOI............ Memorandum of Instruction (INF)
MOI............ Memorandum of Interest (MCD)
MOI............ Message of Operational Intent (NVT)
MOI............ Methods of Instruction
MOI............ Military Occupational Information (AABC)
moi............ Military Occupational Information (AD)
MOI............ Military Operations and Intelligence
MOI............ Minimum Operating Inventory [*Business term*]
MOI............ Ministry of Information [*British World War II*]
Mol............ Ministry of the Interior [*British*] (AD)
MOI............ Mitiaro [*Cook Islands*] [*Airport symbol*] (OAG)
MOI............ Molco Industries [*Vancouver Stock Exchange symbol*]
MOI............ Moment of Inertia
MOI............ Monaco Oceanographic Institute
MOI............ Mouvement Ouvrier International (BJA)
MOI............ Multiplicity of Infection
moi............ Multiplicity of Infection (AD)
MOI............ William Jewell College, Liberty, MO [*OCLC symbol*] (OCLC)
Mo IA .... Moore's Indian Appeals [*A publication*] (DLA)
MOIC .... Medical Officer-in-Charge [*Military*]
MOIC .... Medical Officer in Command (AD)
MOIC .... Military Oceanographic Information Center (NATG)
MOIDE .... Military Occupational Information Data Bank

MOIG .... Master of Occupational Information and Guidance
MOIL .... Marine Operations and Instrumentation Laboratory (USDC)
MOIL .... Marine Operations and Instrumentation Laboratory [*Marine science*] (OSRA)
MOIL .... Maynard Oil [*NASDAQ symbol*] (TTSB)
MOIL .... Maynard Oil Co. [*NASDAQ symbol*] (NQ)
MOIL .... Motor Oil
MoIM .... Mid-Continent Public Library Service, Independence, MO [*Library symbol Library of Congress*] (LCLS)
MoIMC .... Independence Medical Center, Independence, MO [*Library symbol Library of Congress*] (LCLS)
MOIP .... Mandatory Oil Import Program
MOIP .... Missile on Internal Power
moip .... Missile on Internal Power [*Military*] (AD)
MOIPI .... Multi-Purpose Offshore Industrial Port Islands (NOAA)
MoIPS .... Independence Public School District, Independence, MO [*Library symbol*] [*Library of Congress*] (LCLS)
MOIR .... Maximum Ozone Incremental Reactivity [*Environmental science*]
MOIR .... Movimiento Obrero Independiente Revolucionario [*Independent Revolutionary Workers' Movement*] [*Colorado Political party*] (PPW)
MOIR .... Movimiento Obrero Izquierdista Revolucionario [*Colorado Political party*] (PPW)
MOIRA .... Model of International Relations in Agriculture (PDAA)
MoIRC .... Reorganized Church of Jesus Christ of Latter-Day Saints, Independence, MO [*Library symbol Library of Congress*] (LCLS)
Moir Cap Pun... Moir on Capital Punishment [*A publication*] (DLA)
MoIS .... Independence Sanitarium and Hospital, Independence, MO [*Library symbol Library of Congress*] (LCLS)
MOIS .... Maritime Operational Intelligence Summary
MOIS .... Michigan Occupational Information System [*Michigan State Department of Education*] [*Lansing*] [*Information service or system*] (IID)
MOIS .... Minnesota Occupational Information System (AD)
MOIS .... Mission Operations Intercommunication System [*NASA*]
Moish .... Moishe (AD)
MOIST .... Macro Output System [*NASA*] (KSC)
MOISTR .... Moisture
MoIT .... Harry S Truman Library, Independence, MO [*Library symbol Library of Congress*] (LCLS)
MOIV .... Mechanically Operated Inlet Valve (ADA)
moiv .... Mechanically Operated Inlet Valve (AD)
MOJ .... Material on Job Date [*Telecommunications*] (TEL)
MOJ .... Metering over Junction [*Network administration*] [*Telecommunications*] (TEL)
MOJ .... Ministry of Jute [*Bangladesh*]
MOJ .... Muong Sing [*Laos*] [*Airport symbol*] (AD)
MOJA .... Movement for Justice in Africa [*Liberia*] [*Political party*] (PPW)
MOJAC .... Mood, Orientation, Judgment, Affect, Content (AAMN)
MOJA-G .... Movement for Justice in Africa-Gambia [*Political party*]
MoJc .... Thomas Jefferson Library System, Jefferson City, MO [*Library symbol Library of Congress*] (LCLS)
MoJcL .... Lincoln University, Jefferson City, MO [*Library symbol Library of Congress*] (LCLS)
MOJMRP ..... Meteorological Office Joint Meteorological Radio Propagation (IAA)
MoJo .... Joplin Public Library, Joplin, MO [*Library symbol Library of Congress*] (LCLS)
MoJoM .... Missouri Southern State College, Joplin, MO [*Library symbol Library of Congress*] (LCLS)
MOJT .... Managed On-the-Job Training (DNAB)
Mo Jur .... Monthly Jurist [*A publication*] (DLA)
MoK .... Kansas City Public Library, Kansas City, MO [*Library symbol Library of Congress*] (LCLS)
MOK .... Mohawk Carpet Mills [*Stock exchange symbol*] (AD)
MOK .... Mokapu [*Hawaii*] [*Seismograph station code, US Geological Survey*] (SEIS)
Mok .... Mokpo (AD)
MoKA .... American Nurses' Association, Kansas City, MO [*Library symbol Library of Congress*] (LCLS)
MOKA .... Coffee People, Inc. [*NASDAQ symbol*] (SAG)
MoKAI .... Kansas City Arts Institute, Kansas City, MO [*Library symbol Library of Congress*] (LCLS)
MoKAv .... Avila College, Kansas City, MO [*Library symbol Library of Congress*] (LCLS)
MoKB .... Bar Library Association of Kansas City, Kansas City, MO [*Library symbol Library of Congress*] (LCLS)
MoKBa .... Barstow School, Kansas City, MO [*Library symbol Library of Congress*] (LCLS)
MoKBen ...... Bendix Corp., Technical Information Center, Kansas City, MO [*Library symbol Library of Congress*] (LCLS)
MoKBH .... Baptist Memorial Hospital, Kansas City, MO [*Library symbol Library of Congress*] (LCLS)
MoKBM .... Burns and McDonnell Engineering Co., Kansas City, MO [*Library symbol Library of Congress*] (LCLS)
MoKBV .... Black & Veatch Consulting Engineers, Central Library, Kansas City, MO [*Library symbol Library of Congress*] (LCLS)
MoKCH .... Children's Mercy Hospital, Kansas City, MO [*Library symbol Library of Congress*] (LCLS)
MoKChe ...... Chemagro, Kansas City, MO [*Library symbol Library of Congress*] (LCLS)
MoKCO .... Kansas City College of Osteopathic Medicine, Kansas City, MO [*Library symbol Library of Congress*] (LCLS)
MoKCoH ...... Jackson County Public Hospital, Kansas City, MO [*Library symbol Library of Congress*] (LCLS)
MOKE .... Magneto-Optic Kerr Effect

MoKEP .... United States Environmental Protection Agency, Kansas City, MO [*Library symbol Library of Congress*] (LCLS)
MoKF .... Farmland Industries Inc., Communications Services, Kansas City, MO [*Library symbol Library of Congress*] (LCLS)
MoKFR .... Federal Reserve Bank of Kansas City, Kansas City, MO [*Library symbol Library of Congress*] (LCLS)
MoKGH .... Kansas City General Hospital, Kansas City, MO [*Library symbol Library of Congress*] (LCLS)
MoKGS .... Church of Jesus Christ of Latter-Day Saints, Genealogical Society Library, Kansas City Branch, Kansas City, MO [*Library symbol Library of Congress*] (LCLS)
MoKHA .... Kansas City Area Hospital Association, Kansas City, MO [*Library symbol Library of Congress*] (LCLS)
MoKHC .... Hallmark Cards, Inc., Kansas City, MO [*Library symbol*] [*Library of Congress*] (LCLS)
MoKiCO .... Kirksville College of Osteopathy and Surgery, Kirksville, MO [*Library symbol Library of Congress*] (LCLS)
MoKiU .... Northeast Missouri State University, Kirksville, MO [*Library symbol Library of Congress*] (LCLS)
MoKJ .... Jackson County Medical Society, Kansas City, MO [*Library symbol Library of Congress*] (LCLS)
MoKKM .... Martin Luther King Memorial Hospital, Kansas City, MO [*Library symbol Library of Congress*] (LCLS)
MoKL .... Linda Hall Library, Kansas City, MO [*Library symbol Library of Congress*] (LCLS)
MoKLH .... Lakeside Hospital, Kansas City, MO [*Library symbol Library of Congress*] (LCLS)
MoKLo .... Loretto in Kansas City, Kansas City, MO [*Library symbol Library of Congress*] (LCLS)
MoKMB .... Midwestern Baptist Theological Seminary, Kansas City, MO [*Library symbol Library of Congress*] (LCLS)
MoKMC .... Midwest College of Medical Assistants, Kansas City, MO [*Library symbol Library of Congress*] (LCLS)
MoKMI .... Missouri Institute of Technology, Kansas City, MO [*Library symbol Library of Congress*] (LCLS)
MoKML .... Marion Laboratories, Inc., Kansas City, MO [*Library symbol Library of Congress*] (LCLS)
MoKMM ...... Menorah Medical Center, Kansas City, MO [*Library symbol Library of Congress*] (LCLS)
MoKMoC ..... Mobay Chemical Corp., Kansas City, MO [*Library symbol*] [*Library of Congress*] (LCLS)
MoKMR .... Midwest Research Institute, Kansas City, MO [*Library symbol Library of Congress*] (LCLS)
MoKMW ...... Maple Woods Community College, Kansas City, MO [*Library symbol Library of Congress*] (LCLS)
MoKN .... Nazarene Theological Seminary, Kansas City, MO [*Library symbol Library of Congress*] (LCLS)
MoKNA .... Nelson-Atkins Museum of Art, Spencer Art Reference Library, Kansas City, MO [*Library symbol*] [*Library of Congress*] (LCLS)
MoKNE .... Newman Ecumenical Seminary, Kansas City, MO [*Library symbol Library of Congress*] (LCLS)
MoKNG .... Nelson Art Gallery, Art Reference Library, Kansas City, MO [*Library symbol Library of Congress*] (LCLS)
MoKNT .... Saint Paul School of Theology, Kansas City, MO [*Library symbol Library of Congress*] (LCLS)
MoKP .... Penn Valley Junior College, Kansas City, MO [*Library symbol Library of Congress*] (LCLS)
MoKPC .... Pembroke County Day School, Kansas City, MO [*Library symbol Library of Congress*] (LCLS)
MoKPh .... Park Hill North Junior High School, Kansas City, MO [*Library symbol Library of Congress*] (LCLS)
MoKphJH .... Park Hill North Junior High School, Kansas City, MO [*Library symbol*] [*Library of Congress*] (LCLS)
MoKPHS ...... Pembroke Hill School, Kansas City, MO [*Library symbol*] [*Library of Congress*] (LCLS)
MoKPhSD .... Park Hill School District, Kansas City, MO [*Library symbol*] [*Library of Congress*] (LCLS)
MoKPi .... Pioneer Community College Library, Kansas City, MO [*Library symbol*] [*Library of Congress*] (LCLS)
MoKR .... Rockhurst College, Kansas City, MO [*Library symbol Library of Congress*] (LCLS)
MoKRes ...... Research Hospital and Medical Center, Kansas City, MO [*Library symbol Library of Congress*] (LCLS)
MoKRh .... Rockhurst High School, Kansas City, MO [*Library symbol Library of Congress*] (LCLS)
MoKSH .... Sunset Hill School, Kansas City, MO [*Library symbol Library of Congress*] (LCLS)
MoKStJ .... Saint Joseph's Hospital, Kansas City, MO [*Library symbol Library of Congress*] (LCLS)
MoKStL .... Saint Luke's Hospital of Kansas City, Kansas City, MO [*Library symbol Library of Congress*] (LCLS)
MoKStM ...... Saint Mary's Hospital, Kansas City, MO [*Library symbol Library of Congress*] (LCLS)
MoKStP .... Saint Paul Theological Seminary, Kansas City, MO [*Library symbol*] [*Library of Congress*] (LCLS)
MoKStT .... Saint Theresa's Academy, Kansas City, MO [*Library symbol Library of Congress*] (LCLS)
MoKT .... Teachers College of Kansas City, Kansas City, MO [*Library symbol Library of Congress Obsolete*] (LCLS)
MoKTrL .... Trinity Lutheran Hospital, Kansas City, MO [*Library symbol Library of Congress*] (LCLS)
MoKU .... University of Missouri at Kansas City, Kansas City, MO [*Library symbol Library of Congress*] (LCLS)
MoKU-D .... University of Missouri at Kansas City, Dental School, Kansas City, MO [*Library symbol Library of Congress*] (LCLS)

MoKU-I .... University of Missouri at Kansas City, Instructional Materials Center, Kansas City, MO [*Library symbol Library of Congress*] (LCLS)

MoKu-L .... University of Missouri at Kansas City, Law Library, Kansas City, MO [*Library symbol*] [*Library of Congress*] (LCLS)

MoKU-M .... University of Missouri at Kansas City, Medical Library, Kansas City, MO [*Library symbol Library of Congress*] (LCLS)

MoKU-Mus ... University of Missouri at Kansas City, Music Conservatory, Kansas City, MO [*Library symbol Library of Congress*] (LCLS)

MoKVA .... United States Veterans Administration Hospital, Kansas City, MO [*Library symbol Library of Congress*] (LCLS)

MoKW .... Western Missouri Mental Health Center, Kansas City, MO [*Library symbol Library of Congress*] (LCLS)

MOL .... Machine-Oriented Language [*Programming language*]

mol .... Machine-Oriented Language (AD)

MOL .... Manned Orbiting Laboratory [*NASA*]

MOL .... Master of Organizational Leadership (PGP)

MOL .... Master of Oriental Languages

MOL .... Master of Oriental Learning

MOL .... Maximum Operating Level

MOL .... Maximum Order Limitation (AAGC)

mol .... Maximum Output Level (AD)

MOL .... Maximum Output Level

MOL .... Maximum Overall Length (DAC)

MOL .... Metallo-Organic LASER

MOL .... Method of Lines [*Mathematics*]

MOL .... Microtel International, Inc. [*AMEX symbol*] (SAG)

MOL .... Microtel Intl [*AMEX symbol*] (TTSB)

MOL .... Minimum Oxygen Concentration [*at which ignition occurs*]

M o L .... Minister of Labour [*British*] (AD)

MOL .... Ministry of Labour [*Later, DE*] [*British*]

MOL .... Missouri State Library, Jefferson City, MO [*OCLC symbol*] (OCLC)

mol .... Moldavian [*MARC language code Library of Congress*] (LCCP)

MOL .... Molde [*Norway*] [*Airport symbol*] (OAG)

mol .... Mole [*Amount of substance*] [*SI unit*]

mol .... Molecular (AD)

MOL .... Molecular Layer

MOL .... Molecule [*or Molecular*] (AAG)

MOL .... Molecule

MOL .... Molesting [*FBI standardized term*]

MOL .... Moliere [*Pseudonym of French actor and dramatist Jean Baptiste Poquelin, 1622-1673*] (ROG)

Mol .... Mollendo (AD)

mol .... Mollis [*Soft*] [*Latin*] (AD)

Mol .... Molloy's De Jure Maritimo [*A publication*] (DLA)

Mol .... Molloy's Irish Chancery Reports [*1827-31*] [*A publication*] (DLA)

MOL .... Molodezhnaya [*Former USSR Geomagnetic observatory code*]

MOL .... Molson Companies Ltd. [*Toronto Stock Exchange symbol Vancouver Stock Exchange symbol*]

MOL .... Montebello, VA [*Location identifier FAA*] (FAAL)

MOL .... Multiple On-Line Programming [*Computer science*] (EECA)

M-O-L .... My Old Lady [*Wife*] [*Slang*]

MOL .... Universite de Moncton, Law Library [*UTLAS symbol*]

MOLA .... Midwest Open Land Association (EA)

MOLAB .... Mobile Laboratory [*NASA*]

molab .... Mobile Laboratory (AD)

MOLAB .... Mobile Lunar Laboratory (AD)

MOL/ACTS ... Manned Orbiting Laboratory / Altitude Control and Transmission System (DNAB)

MOLARA ...... Motoring Organisations Land Access and Rights Association [*British*] (DBA)

MOLARS ...... Meteorological Office Library Accessions and Retrieval System (NITA)

Mo Law Rep ... Monthly Law Reporter [*A publication*] (DLA)

MO Laws ...... Laws of Missouri [*A publication*] (DLA)

MOLB .... Majestic Circle, Military Order of Lady Bugs of USA (EA)

MolBio .... Molecular Biosystems, Inc. [*Associated Press*] (SAG)

molc .... Molar Concentration [*Chemistry*] (MAE)

MOLC .... Multiple Operational Launch Complex (MUGU)

MOLCAB ...... Mobile Landing Craft Advanced Base

Mol Crys Liq Crys ... Molecular Crystals and Liquid Crystals (AD)

MOLD .... Model of Light Diode

Mol De Jure Mar ... Molloy's De Jure Maritimo et Navali [*A publication*] (DLA)

MOLDS .... Management On-Line Data System [*University of Syracuse*]

MOLDS .... Modernization of Land Data Systems [*North American Institute for the Modernization of Land Data Systems*] [*Falls Church, VA*]

MOLDS .... Multiple Online Debugging System [*Computer science*] (IEEE)

Moldv .... Moldavia (AD)

MOLE .... Market Odd-Lot Execution (PDAA)

MOLE .... Market Odd-Lot Execution System [*Computer science*] (MHDI)

mole .... Molecular (AD)

MOLE .... Molecular Optics LASER Examiner [*Spectrometry*]

MOLEC .... Molecular

MolecDev .... Molecular Devices Corp. [*Associated Press*] (SAG)

MolecDy ...... Molecular Dynamics, Inc. [*Associated Press*] (SAG)

molecom ...... Molecularized Computer (AD)

MOLECOM ... Molecularized Digital Computer

MoLeeH .... Lee's Summit Hospital, Lee's Summit, MO [*Library symbol Library of Congress*] (LCLS)

MoLeeL .... Longview Community College, Lee's Summit, MO [*Library symbol Library of Congress*] (LCLS)

MoLeeS .... Lees Summit Public School District, Lees Summit, MO [*Library symbol*] [*Library of Congress*] (LCLS)

MoLeeU .... Unity School Library, Lee's Summit, MO [*Library symbol Library of Congress*] (LCLS)

Mo Leg Exam ... Monthly Legal Examiner [*New York*] [*A publication*] (DLA)

MO Legis Serv (Vernon) ... Missouri Legislative Service (Vernon) [*A publication*] (DLA)

MOLEM .... Mobile Lunar Excursion Module [*NASA*] (PDAA)

MOLETRONICS ... Molecular Electronics

MOLEVATOR ... Motor Elevator [*Mechanical lifting stand for arc lamps*]

MOLEX .... Molecular Executive [*Graphic substructure chemical search system*]

Molex .... Molex, Inc. [*Associated Press*] (SAG)

molfr .... Mole Fraction [*Chemistry*] (DMAA)

MOLGEN ...... Molecular Genetics [*Program*] [*Computer science*]

MOLIDER ..... Movimiento Liberal Democratico Revolucionario [*Revolutionary Democratic Liberal Movement*] [*Honduras*] [*Political party*]

Molink .... Moscow Link (AD)

MOLINK .... Moscow/Washington Emergency Communications Link (MCD)

MoLiPS .... Liberty Public Schools District, Liberty, MO [*Library symbol*] [*Library of Congress*] (LCLS)

Molirena ...... Movimiento Liberal Republicano Nacionalista [*Nationalist Liberal Republican Movement*] [*Panama*] [*Political party*] (PPW)

MOLISV ...... Movement for Liberation and Development [*Italy Political party*] (EAIO)

MoLiWJ .... William Jewell College, Liberty, MO [*Library symbol Library of Congress*] (LCLS)

Mol JM .... Molloy's De Jure Maritimo et Navali [*A publication*] (DLA)

MOLL .... Metallo-Organic Liquid LASER

moll .... Metallo-Organic Liquid LASER (AD)

mol/l .... Molecules per Liter [*Measurement*] (DAVI)

mol/l .... Molecules per Liter (MAE)

Moll .... Moller Organ Co. [*Record label*]

MOLL .... Mollis [*Soft*] [*Pharmacy*]

Moll .... Molloy's De Jure Maritimo [*A publication*] (DLA)

Moll .... Molloy's Irish Chancery Reports [*1827-31*] [*A publication*] (DLA)

MOLLI .... Micro OnLine Library Information [*Nichols Advanced Technologies, Inc.*]

mollie .... Mollienisia (AD)

MOLLUS .... Military Order of the Loyal Legion of the United States (EA)

Mollus .... Mollusca (AD)

MOLLUSA ..... Military Order of the Loyal Legion of the USA (AD)

MOL/M³ .... Moles per Cubic Meter

Mo L Mag ..... Monthly Law Magazine [*London*] [*A publication*] (DLA)

MOLNS .... Ministry of Labour and National Service [*World War II British*] (DAS)

MOLO .... Mideastern Ohio Library Organization [*Library network*]

MOLOC .... Ministry of Labour Occupational Classification [*Later, CODOT*] [*British*]

MOLP .... Multiple Objective Linear Programming [*Computer science*] (PDAA)

Mol Phys ..... Molecular Physics (AD)

MOLS .... Magnetic-Operated Limit Switch

MOLS .... Mirror Optional Landing System [*Aviation*] (NG)

MOLS .... Mobile Object Location System

MOLS .... Multiple Object Location System [*Army*]

MOLS .... Mutually Orthogonal Latin Square

MOLSINK ..... Molecular Sink of Outer Space [*Vacuum testing chamber for spacecraft systems*]

MOLT .... Manually-Operated Lift Truck (DWSG)

MOLT .... Molten

molt .... Molten (AD)

MoltenM .... Molten Metal Technology, Inc. [*Associated Press*] (SAG)

MOLTOL .... Manned Orbiting Laboratory Test-Oriented Language [*NASA*] (MCD)

MOL WT ...... Molecular Weight [*Also, M, MW*]

mol wt .... Molecular Weight (AD)

MOLX .... Molex, Inc. [*NASDAQ symbol*] (NQ)

MOLXA .... Molex Inc'A' [*NASDAQ symbol*] (TTSB)

MOLY .... Molecular Analysis [*by a computer graphics system*] [*Chemistry*]

moly .... Molybdenum (AD)

Moly .... Molyneaux's Reports. English Courts, Tempore Car. I [*A publication*] (DLA)

MOLY .... Mouse Lymphoma Cells [*Oncology*]

MOM .... Macro Observation Module [*Microscopy*]

MOM .... Maintenance Operations Management (MCD)

MOM .... Management of Migration [*of wastewaters*]

MOM .... Manned Orbiting Mission [*NASA*]

MOM .... Man-on-the-Move [*Military slang*] (DNAB)

MOM .... Mark XII Output and Monitoring System (SAA)

m/ o m/ .... Mas o Menos [*More or Less*] [*Spanish*] (AD)

MOM .... Master of Manufacturing (PGP)

MOM .... Measure of Merit (MCD)

MOM .... Message-Oriented Middleware [*Computer science*]

MOM .... Message Output Module [*Telecommunications*] (TEL)

MOM .... Metal-Oxide Metal (MCD)

MOM .... Methods of Moderation [*An association*] (EA)

MOM .... Methoxymethyl [*Organic chemistry*]

MOM .... Micromation Online Microfilmer

mom .... Micromation Online Microfilmer [*Computer science*] (AD)

MOM .... Microsoft Office Manager [*Microsoft Corp. computer program*] (PCM)

m-o-m .... Middle of Month (AD)

MOM .... Middle of the Month

MOM .... Military Official Mail (AABC)

MOM .... Military Ordinary Mail (AABC)

mom .... Military Ordinary Mail (AD)

MOM .... Military Overseas Mail [*An association*] (EA)

MOM .... Milk of Magnesia

mom .... Milk of Magnesia (AD)

MOM .... Minutes of Meeting

MOM .... Missile Operations Manager (MUGU)

MOM .... Missionary Sisters of Our Lady of Mercy [*Roman Catholic religious order*]

MOM .... Mitochondrial Outer-Membrane [*Biochemistry*]

MOM..........	Modified Operational Missile
MOM..........	Modular Ocean Model [*Marine science*] (OSRA)
MOM..........	Modular Ocean Model (USDC)
MOM..........	Moment
MOM..........	Momentary (MSA)
MOM..........	Momentum
Mom..........	Momma (AD)
MOM..........	Momote [*Admiralty Islands*] [*Seismograph station code, US Geological Survey*] (SEIS)
MOM..........	Mother's Restaurants Ltd. [*Toronto Stock Exchange symbol*]
MOM..........	Musee Oceanographique Monaco [*Monaco Oceanographic Museum*] [*France*] (AD)
M-O-M.......	My Old Man [*Husband*] [*Slang*]
MOMA	Madagasikara Otronin'ny Malagasy [*Formerly, MONIMA*] [*Madagascar Led by Malagasy*]
MOMA	Methoxyhydroxymandelic Acid [*Organic chemistry*]
MOMA	Museum of Modern Art [*New York*]
MoMA	Museum of Modern Art [*New York*] (AD)
MOMAC	Monkey Mountain Advisory Center [*Military*] (CINC)
MOMAG	Mobile Mine Assembly Group [*Military*] (CAAL)
MOMAGDET...	Mobile Mine Assembly Group Detachment (DNAB)
MOMAGU....	Mobile Mine Assembly Group Unit (DNAB)
MoManW	Laura Ingalls Wilder - Rose Wilder Lane Home and Museum, Mansfield, MO [*Library symbol Library of Congress*] (LCLS)
MOMAR	Modern Mobile Army [*Military*]
momar........	Modern Mobile Army (AD)
MoMaryU	Northwest Missouri State University, Maryville, MO [*Library symbol Library of Congress*] (LCLS)
MOMAT.......	Mobile Mine Assembly Team
MOMATLANT...	Mobile Mine Assembly Team, Atlantic (DNAB)
MOMATPAC...	Mobile Mine Assembly Team, Pacific (DNAB)
MOMAU......	Mobile Mine Assembly Unit (NVT)
momau	Mobile Mine Assembly Unit (AD)
MOMAULANT...	Mobile Mine Assembly Unit, Atlantic (DNAB)
MOMAULANTDETKEF...	Mobile Mine Assembly Unit, Atlantic, Keflavik Detachment (DNAB)
MOMAUPAC...	Mobile Mine Assembly Unit, Pacific (DNAB)
MOMB	Mombasa [*Island near Kenya*] (ROG)
MOMBE	Metallo-Organic Molecular Beam Epitaxy [*Solid state physics*]
MOMC	Mount McKinley National Park
MOMCOMS..	Man-on-the-Move Communications
MOMCOMS..	Mobile Mine Countermeasures Command (DNAB)
MoMex	Mexico-Audrain County Library, Mexico, MO [*Library symbol Library of Congress*] (LCLS)
MOMI.........	Museum of the Moving Image [*London*] (ECON)
MOMIMTS ...	Military and Orchestral Musical Instrument Makers' Trade Society [*A union*] [*British*] (DCTA)
m-o-m in am if no bm by pm...	Milk-of-Magnesia in the Morning if No Bowel Movement by Evening [*Medicine*] (AD)
MOMISMAINTU...	Mobile, Missile Maintenance Unit (DNAB)
MOML.........	Moslem Meal [*Airline notation*] (ADA)
Moml.........	Moslem Meal (AD)
MoMLV	Moloney Murine Luekemia Virus [*Used for gene transfer protocols*] (DOG)
MoMM	Missouri Valley College, Marshall, MO [*Library symbol Library of Congress*] (LCLS)
MOMM........	Motor Machinist's Mate [*Navy rating*]
MOMMSR ...	Motor Machinist's Mate, Ship Repair [*Navy rating*]
MOMP	Major Outer Membrane Protein [*Biochemistry*]
MOMP	Michigan Ordnance Missile Plant [*Army*]
MOMP	Mid-Ocean Meeting Place
MOMP	Mustargen [*Nitrogen mustard*], Oncovin , Methotrexate, Prednisone [*Vincristine*] [*Antineoplastic drug regimen*]
MOMR	Mayor's Office of Manpower Resources (AD)
MOMS	Manganese Oxide Mesoporous Structure [*Inorganic Chemistry*]
MOMS	Measure of Mission Success [*Military*] (CAAL)
MOMS	Member of the Organisation and Methods Society [*British*] (DI)
moms	Mervaerdiomsaetningsskat [*Value-Added Tax*] [*Danish*] (AD)
MOMS	Meteorological and Oceanographic Measurements System [*Chevron Oil Co.*]
MOMS	Meteorological Optic Measuring System (MCD)
MOMS	Micro-Opto-Mechanical Systems
MOMS	Missile Operate Mode Simulator
moms	Missile Operate Mode Simulator (AD)
MOMS	Modified Operational Missile System (DNAB)
MOMS	Modular Optoelectronic Multispectral Scanner (MCD)
MOMS	Mothers for Moral Stability [*Group opposing sex education in schools*]
MOMS	Mothers of Men in Service [*World War II*]
MOMS	Multimegabit Operation Multiplexer System
MOMS	Multiple Orbit - Multiple Satellite
MOM's	Multiples over the Median [*Statistics*]
MoMSV.......	Moloney Mouse Sarcoma Virus
MoMuLV......	Moloney Murine Leukemia Virus [*Also, MLV*]
MOM/WOW...	Men Our Masters/Women Our Wonders [*Antifeminist group*] (EA)
MON	Above Mountains [*ICAO*] (FAAC)
mon	Maison [*House*] [*French*] (AD)
MON	Member of the Order of the Niger [*Nigeria*]
MON	Memorandum of Negotiation (MCD)
MON	Missouri Valley College, Marshall, MO [*Inactive*] [*OCLC symbol*] (OCLC)
MON	Mixed Oxides of Nitrogen
MON	Monaco [*Monaco*] [*Seismograph station code, US Geological Survey*] (SEIS)
Mon	Monaco (AD)

MON	Monaghan [*County in Republic of Ireland*] (ROG)
Mon	Monaghan's Unreported Cases (Pennsylvania Superior Court) [*A publication*] (DLA)
Mon	Monarch [*Record label*] [*British*]
MON	Monarch Airlines Ltd. [*British ICAO designator*] (FAAC)
MON	Monarch Investments Ltd. [*Toronto Stock Exchange symbol*]
MON	Monastery
MON	Monday (AFM)
Mon	Monday (ODBW)
Mon	Monday (AD)
Mon	Monegasque (AD)
mon	Monetary (AD)
MON	Monetary (AFM)
mon	Mongol [*MARC language code Library of Congress*] (LCCP)
Mon	Mongol (AD)
Mon	Mongol [*One affected with Down's syndrome*] [*Medicine*] (DAVI)
MON	Mongolian (AABC)
Mon	Moniteur Belge [*A publication*] (ILCA)
MON	Monitor [*Navy ship symbol*]
MON	Monitor (DEN)
mon	Monitor (WDMC)
MON	Monitor
Mon	Monitor (AD)
mon	Monitor/Contractor [*MARC relator code*] [*Library of Congress*] (LCCP)
MON	Monmouthshire [*County in Wales*]
Mon	Monmouthshire (AD)
Mon	Monoceros [*Constellation*]
MON	Monoclinic [*Crystallography*]
Mon	Monoclonal Antibodies, Inc.
MON	Monocyte [*Hematology*]
MON	Monogram [*Numismatics*]
mon	Monograph (BJA)
MON	Monomoy Surfboat [*Coast Guard*] (DNAB)
MON	Monon [*Railroad*] (MHDW)
Mon	Monongahela (AD)
Mon	Monsieur [*Mister*] [*French*]
Mon	Monsignor (WGA)
mon	Monsoon (WG)
Mon	Montag [*Monday*] [*German*] (AD)
MON	Montana
Mon	Montana Reports [*A publication*] (DLA)
Mon	Montana Supreme Court Reports [*A publication*] (DLA)
MON	Month
MON	Monticello, AR [*Location identifier FAA*] (FAAL)
MON	Monument (AAG)
Mon	Monument (AD)
mon	Monument (AD)
MON	Monument Still Exists [*Genealogy*] (ROG)
MON	Motor Octane Number [*Fuel technology*]
mon	Motor Octane Number (AD)
MoN	Mountain Name (BJA)
MON	Mount Cook [*New Zealand*] [*Airport symbol*] (OAG)
MoN	North Kansas City Public Library, North Kansas City, MO [*Library symbol Library of Congress*] (LCLS)
MON	Universite de Moncton, Bibliotheque [*UTLAS symbol*]
Mona	Madonna [*Our Lady*] [*Italian*] (AD)
MONA	Marche des Options Negociables sur Actions [*Options exchange*] [*France*] (EY)
MONA	Modular Navigation [*Aviation*]
Mona	Monaco (VRA)
Mona	Monaghan's Reports [*147-165 Pennsylvania*] [*A publication*] (DLA)
MONA	Monitor Assembly [*Ground Communications Facility, NASA*]
MONAB.......	Mobile Naval Advanced Base [*British military*] (DMA)
MONAB.......	Mobile Noise Analysis Barge
MONAB.......	Mobile Operating Naval Air Base
Monac	Monaco Finance [*Associated Press*] (SAG)
MonacoC	Monaco Coach Corp. [*Associated Press*] (SAG)
MonacoF.....	Monaco Finance [*Associated Press*] (SAG)
Monag	Monaghan (AD)
Monag	Monaghan's Reports [*147-165 Pennsylvania*] [*A publication*] (DLA)
MONAGH	Monaghan [*County in Republic of Ireland*] (ROG)
Monaghan ...	Monaghan's Reports [*147-165 Pennsylvania*] [*A publication*] (DLA)
Monaghan (PA)...	Monaghan's Reports [*147-165 Pennsylvania*] [*A publication*] (DLA)
MONAGN	Monaghan [*County in Republic of Ireland*]
MONAL	Mobile Nondestructive Assay Laboratory [*AEC*]
Mon Anc	Monumentum Ancyranum [*Classical studies*] (OCD)
Mon Angl	Monasticon Anglicanum [*A publication*] (DLA)
Monas	Monastic (AD)
Monash Univ Law Rev...	Monash University. Law Review [*A publication*]
MonAvl	Monarch Avalon, Inc. [*Associated Press*] (SAG)
monbas........	Monobasic (AD)
MONC	Metropolitan Opera National Council
MonCap	Monmouth Capital Corp. [*Associated Press*] (SAG)
MonCasn	Monarch Casino & Resort [*Associated Press*] (SAG)
monch	Monochrome (VRA)
Monc Inn	Moncrieff's Liability of Innkeepers [*1874*] [*A publication*] (DLA)
MOND........	Mondavi [*Robert*] [*NASDAQ symbol*] (SAG)
MOND........	Monday (ROG)
MOND.........	Robert Mondavi 'A' [*NASDAQ symbol*] (TTSB)
Mondavi	Mondavi [*Robert*] [*Associated Press*] (SAG)
MON/DIR	Mission Monitoring Direction
mon/dir........	Monitoring Direction (AD)
MONE	Money Store [*NASDAQ symbol*] (TTSB)

MONE .... [*The*] Money Store, Inc. [*NASDAQ symbol*] (SAG)
MONECA ...... Motor Network Calculator
MONEP .... Marche des Options Negotiables de Paris [*French Traded Options Market*] (ODBW)
MONES .... Molecular Nonthermal Excitation Spectrometry
MONET .... Mobile Networks Integration [*Telecommunications*]
MONET .... Monetary
MONEVAL .... Monthly Evaluation Report [*Military*]
MONEX .... Monsoon Experiment [*Also, MONSOONEX*]
monex .... Monsoon Experiment (AD)
Moneygr ...... Moneygram Payment Systems [*Associated Press*] (SAG)
MoneySt ...... [*The*] Money Store, Inc. [*Associated Press*] (SAG)
MONF .... Monaco Finance [*NASDAQ symbol*] (SAG)
MONFA .... Monaco Finance'A' [*NASDAQ symbol*] (TTSB)
Mong .... Mongol (AD)
MONG .... Mongolian [*Language, etc.*]
mong .... Mongolisch [*Mongolian*] [*German*] (AD)
MONG .... Mongrel (DSUE)
MONG .... Moning [*Tea trade*] (ROG)
Mongo .... Mongolia (VRA)
mon-H .... Monohydrogen (AD)
MoNHI .... Missouri Natural Heritage Inventory [*Missouri State Department of Conservation*] [*Information service or system*] (IID)
MONICA ...... Monitoring of Trends and Determinants in Cardiovascular Disease
monik .... Moniker (AD)
MONIL .... Mobile Non-Destructive Inspection Laboratory (DNAB)
MONIMA ...... Mouvement National pour l'Independance de Madagascar [*National Movement for the Independence of Madagascar*] [*Political party*] (PPW)
Mon Law Mag... Monthly Law Magazine [*London*] [*A publication*] (DLA)
Mon Law Rep... Monthly Law Reporter [*A publication*] (DLA)
Mon Leg R (PA)... Monroe Legal Reporter [*Pennsylvania*] [*A publication*] (DLA)
MONM .... Monmouth Capital [*NASDAQ symbol*] (TTSB)
MONM .... Monmouth Capital Corp. [*NASDAQ symbol*] (SAG)
Mon Meth.... Monahan's Method of the Law [*1878*] [*A publication*] (DLA)
MoNMH .... North Kansas City Memorial Hospital, North Kansas City, MO [*Library symbol Library of Congress*] (LCLS)
Monmouth C... Monmouth College (GAGS)
MONMS .... Monmouthshire [*County in Wales*]
Mon Not Roy Soc Tas... Monthly Notices. Royal Society of Tasmania [*A publication*]
MONO .... Monaural (KSC)
Mono .... Monoceros [*Constellation*]
MONO .... Monochrome (DSUE)
mono .... Monocyte [*Hematology*]
Mono .... Monogram [*Record label*]
MONO .... Mononucleosis [*Medicine*]
mono .... Mononucleosis [*Medicine*] (AD)
mono .... Monophonic (AD)
MONO .... Monophonic
mono .... Monopoly (AD)
mono .... Monopropellant (AD)
mono .... Monorail (AD)
MONO .... Monorail (WDAA)
MONO .... Monotone (DOAD)
MONO .... Monotype (ADA)
mono .... Monotype (AD)
monob .... Mobile Noise Barge (AD)
MONOB .... Mobile Noise Barge
MONOC .... Monocoque (MSA)
MONOCL...... Monoclinic
monocl .... Monoclinic (AD)
monocot ..... Monocotyledon [*Biology*] (BARN)
Monod .... Monon Railroad (AD)
monog .... Monogram (AD)
monog .... Monograph (AD)
MONOG....... Monograph
MONOK....... Monitor Resumed Normal Operation [*Aviation communications*]
MONOP....... Monopoly [*Legal shorthand*] (LWAP)
monos .... Monitor Out of Service (AD)
MONOS .... Monitor Out of Service [*Aviation communications*]
monot .... Monotonous (AD)
monot .... Monotype (AD)
MonP .... Monongahela Power Co. [*Associated Press*] (SAG)
MonP25 ...... Monongahela Power Co. [*Associated Press*] (SAG)
monpl .... Monopoly (AD)
monpr .... Monoprint (VRA)
MonPw .... Montana Power Co. [*Associated Press*] (SAG)
Monrch .... Monarch Machine Tool Co. [*Associated Press*] (SAG)
MoNRDEP.... Ministry of Natural Resources Development and Environmental Protection [*Ethiopia*] (ECON)
MonRE .... Monmouth Real Estate Investment Corp. [*Associated Press*] (SAG)
Mon River ... Monongahela River (AD)
Monro .... Acta Cancellariae [*England*] [*A publication*] (DLA)
Monro AC .... Monro's Acta Cancellariae [*1545-1625*] [*A publication*] (DLA)
Monroc .... Monroc, Inc. [*Associated Press*] (SAG)
Monroe....... Monroe Legal Reporter [*Pennsylvania*] [*A publication*] (DLA)
Monroe LR.... Monroe Legal Reporter [*Pennsylvania*] [*A publication*] (DLA)
MonroM ...... Monro Muffler Brake, Inc. [*Associated Press*] (SAG)
MONS .... Monastery
MONS .... Monmouthshire [*County in Wales*]
MONS .... Monsieur [*In France this form is considered contemptuous*] [*Preferred form is M*]
Mons .... Monsieur [*Mister*] [*French*] (AD)
Monsan........ Monsanto Co. [*Associated Press*] (SAG)

Mons Cur..... Monsoon Current (AD)
MONSEE...... Monitoring of the Sun Earth Environment [*International Council of Scientific Unions*] (MCD)
Monsig .... Monseigneur [*My Lord*] [*French*] (AD)
MONSIG....... Monsignor [*Lord, Sir*] [*French*]
MONSOONEX... Monsoon Experiment [*Also, MONEX*]
MonSt.......... Montgomery Street Income Securities, Inc. [*Associated Press*] (SAG)
monstro ...... Monstrosity (AD)
MONSTRY.... Monastery
Mont .... Montagu's English Bankruptcy Reports [*A publication*] (DLA)
MONT .... Montana (AFM)
Mont .... Montana (ODBW)
Mont .... Montana (AD)
Mont .... Montana Supreme Court Reports [*A publication*] (DLA)
Mont .... Monterrey (AD)
Mont .... Montevideo (AD)
Mont .... Montgomery (AD)
MONT .... Montgomeryshire [*County in Wales*]
Mont .... Montilla [*Record label*] [*USA, Spain, etc.*]
MONT .... Montmorillonite [*Mineralogy*]
Mont .... Montpelier (AD)
Mont .... Montreal (AD)
Mont .... Montriou's Bengal Reports [*A publication*] (DLA)
mont .... Monument (VRA)
Mont Admin R... Administrative Rules of Montana [*A publication*] (DLA)
Mont Admin Reg... Montana Administrative Register [*A publication*] (DLA)
MonTal .... Monumenta Talmudica (BJA)
Mont & A..... Montagu and Ayrton's English Bankruptcy Reports [*1833-38*] [*A publication*] (DLA)
Mont & Ayr... Montagu and Ayrton's English Bankruptcy Reports [*1833-38*] [*A publication*] (DLA)
Mont & Ayr Bankr... Montagu and Ayrton's English Bankruptcy Reports [*1833-38*] [*A publication*] (DLA)
Mont & Ayr Bankr (Eng)... Montagu and Ayrton's English Bankruptcy Reports [*1833-38*] [*A publication*] (DLA)
Mont & Ayr BL... Montagu and Ayrton's Bankrupt Laws [*A publication*] (DLA)
Mont & B..... Montagu and Bligh's English Bankruptcy Reports [*1832-33*] [*A publication*] (DLA)
Mont & B Bankr... Montagu and Bligh's English Bankruptcy Reports [*1832-33*] [*A publication*] (DLA)
Mont & B Bankr (Eng)... Montagu and Bligh's English Bankruptcy Reports [*1832-33*] [*A publication*] (DLA)
Mont & Bl.... Montagu and Bligh's English Bankruptcy Reports [*1832-33*] [*A publication*] (DLA)
Mont & C..... Montagu and Chitty's English Bankruptcy Reports [*1838-40*] [*A publication*] (DLA)
Mont & C Bankr... Montagu and Chitty's English Bankruptcy Reports [*1838-40*] [*A publication*] (DLA)
Mont & C Bankr (Eng)... Montagu and Chitty's English Bankruptcy Reports [*1838-40*] [*A publication*] (DLA)
Mont & Ch... Montagu and Chitty's English Bankruptcy Reports [*1838-40*] [*A publication*] (DLA)
Mont & Chitt... Montagu and Chitty's English Bankruptcy Reports [*1838-40*] [*A publication*] (DLA)
Mont & M..... Montagu and MacArthur's English Bankruptcy Reports [*A publication*] (DLA)
Mont & MacA... Montagu and MacArthur's English Bankruptcy Reports [*A publication*] (DLA)
Mont & M Bankr (Eng)... Mantagu and MacArthur's English Bankruptcy Reports [*1826-30*] [*A publication*] (DLA)
Mon T B ...... T. B. Monroe's Kentucky Reports [*17-23 Kentucky*] [*A publication*] (DLA)
Mont Bankr (Eng)... Montagu's English Bankruptcy Reports [*A publication*] (DLA)
Mont Bank Rep... Montagu's English Bankruptcy Reports [*A publication*] (DLA)
MontBB........ Monterey Bay Bancorp, Inc. [*Associated Press*] (SAG)
Mont BC ...... Montagu's English Bankruptcy Reports [*A publication*] (DLA)
Mont Bk L.... Montagu's Bankrupt Law [*4th ed.*] [*1827*] [*A publication*] (DLA)
Mont Cas.... Montriou's Cases in Hindoo Law [*A publication*] (DLA)
Montclair St C... Montclair State College (GAGS)
Mont CMS&T... Montana College of Mineral Science and Technology (GAGS)
Mont Code Ann... Montana Code, Annotated [*A publication*] (DLA)
Mont Comp... Montagu on Composition [*1823*] [*A publication*] (DLA)
Mont Cond Rep... Montreal Condensed Reports [*A publication*] (DLA)
Mont D & DeG... Montagu, Deacon, and De Gex's English Bankruptcy Reports [*1840-44*] [*A publication*] (DLA)
Mont Dig ..... Montagu's Digest of Pleadings in Equity [*A publication*] (DLA)
Monte .... Montebianco (AD)
Monte .... Monte Carlo (AD)
Monte .... Montefiore (AD)
Monte .... Montevideo (AD)
Monte .... Montgomery (AD)
Monted .... Montedison SpA [*Associated Press*] (SAG)
Monten .... Montenegro
Mont Eq Pl... Montagu's Digest of Pleadings in Equity [*A publication*] (DLA)
Monterey Inst... Monterey Institute of Foreign Studies (GAGS)
montg .... Montage (VRA)
MONTG .... Montgomeryshire [*County in Wales*]
MONTGOM... Montgomeryshire [*County in Wales*]
Montgom..... Montgomeryshire [*England*] (AD)
Month Dig Tax Articles... Monthly Digest of Tax Articles [*A publication*] (DLA)
Month JL ..... Monthly Journal of Law [*A publication*] (DLA)
Month Jur.... Monthly Jurist [*Bloomington, IL*] [*A publication*] (DLA)
Month Law Bul... Monthly Law Bulletin [*New York*] [*A publication*] (DLA)
Month Law Rep... Law Reporter [*Boston*] [*A publication*] (DLA)
Month L Bull (NY)... Monthly Law Bulletin (New York) [*A publication*] (DLA)

Month Leg Ex... Monthly Legal Examiner [New York] [A publication] (DLA)
Month Leg Exam... Monthly Legal Examiner [New York] [A publication] (DLA)
Month Leg Exam (NY)... Monthly Legal Examiner (New York) [A publication] (DLA)
Month LJ.... Monthly Journal of Law [Washington] [A publication] (DLA)
Month LM.... Monthly Law Magazine [London] [A publication] (DLA)
Month L Rep.... Monthly Law Reporter [Boston] [A publication] (DLA)
Month L Rep... Monthly Law Reports [Canada] [A publication] (DLA)
Month L Rev... Monthly Law Review [A publication] (DLA)
Monthly Lab Rev... Monthly Labor Review [A publication] (DLA)
Monthly L Bul... New York Monthly Law Bulletin [A publication] (DLA)
Month West Jur... Monthly Western Jurist [A publication] (DLA)
Mont Ind...... Monthly Index to Reporters [A publication] (DLA)
Mont Inst..... Montriou's Institutes of Jurisprudence [A publication] (DLA)
Mont Law .... Montana Lawyer [A publication] (DLA)
Mont Laws... Laws of Montana [A publication] (DLA)
Mont Leg News... Montreal Legal News [A publication] (DLA)
Mont Liens... Montagu on Liens [A publication] (DLA)
Mont LR ...... Montreal Law Reports, Queen's Bench [A publication] (DLA)
Mont LR ..... Montreal Law Reports, Superior Court [A publication] (DLA)
Mont LRQB... Montreal Law Reports, Queen's Bench [A publication] (DLA)
Mont LRSC... Montreal Law Reports, Superior Court [A publication] (DLA)
Mont Merc Law... Montefiore's Synopsis of Mercantile Law [A publication] (DLA)
montp .... Monotype (VRA)
Montparno .... Montparnasse (AD)
MontPas ..... Monterey Pasta [Associated Press] (SAG)
MONTR .... Montreal [Canada]
Montr.......... Montreal [Canada] (AD)
Montr........... Montriou's Bengal Reports [A publication] (DLA)
Montr........... Montriou's Supplement to Morton's Reports [A publication] (DLA)
Montr Cond Rep... Montreal Condensed Reports [A publication] (DLA)
Montreal LQB (Can)... Montreal Law Reports, Queen's Bench [Canada]
           [A publication] (DLA)
Montreal LRQB... Montreal Law Reports, Queen's Bench [Canada]
           [A publication] (DLA)
Montreal LRSC... Montreal Law Reports, Superior Court [Canada] [A publication]
           (DLA)
Montreal LSC (Can)... Montreal Law Reports, Superior Court [Canada]
           [A publication] (DLA)
Mont Rep..... Montriou's Reports, Supreme Court [1846] [Bengal, India]
           [A publication] (DLA)
Mont Rev Code Ann... Montana Revised Code, Annotated [A publication] (DLA)
MONTRG...... Monitoring (AABC)
montrg.......... Monitoring (AD)
Montr Leg N... Montreal Legal News [A publication] (DLA)
Montr QB .... Montreal Law Reports, Queen's Bench [A publication] (DLA)
Montr Super... Montreal Law Reports, Superior Court [A publication] (DLA)
MontryH........ Monterey Homes Corp. [Associated Press] (SAG)
MontryR........ Monterey Resources, Inc. [Associated Press] (SAG)
Mont S........ Montreal Star [A publication] (AD)
MONTSAME... Mongolyn Tsahilgaan Medeeniy Agentlag [Press agency] [Mongolia]
Mont SO ...... Montagu, Set-Off [2nd ed.] [1828] [A publication] (DLA)
Mont Sp L .... Montesquieu's Spirit of Laws [A publication] (DLA)
Mont St U.... Montana State University (GAGS)
Mont Super... Montreal Law Reports, Superior Court [A publication] (DLA)
MONT TER.... Montana Territory
Monty .... Montgomery (AD)
Monty .... Montmorency (AD)
Mon ULR .... Monash University. Law Review [A publication]
MoNvC......... Cottey College, Nevada, MO [Library symbol Library of Congress]
           (LCLS)
Mon WJ...... Monthly Western Jurist [A publication] (DLA)
Mony .... Monastery (AD)
MONY .... Music Operators of New York (AD)
MONY .... Mutual of New York [Insurance company]
MOO .... Management Operations Officer [Social Security Administration]
MOO .... Milkbottles Only Organization (EA)
MOO .... Missile Operations Officer [NASA] (KSC)
MOO .... Money-Order Office
Moo .... Moody's English Crown Cases [168, 169 English Reprint]
           [A publication] (DLA)
MOO .... Moomba [Australia Airport symbol Obsolete] (OAG)
MOO .... Moongold Resources [Vancouver Stock Exchange symbol]
MOO .... Moorlands [Tasmania] [Seismograph station code, US Geological
           Survey] (SEIS)
MOO .... MUD [Multi-User Dungeon] Object-Oriented [Computer science]
           (DOM)
MOO .... Multiple-User Dimension Object Oriented [Computer technology]
MOO .... School of the Ozarks, Point Lookout, MO [OCLC symbol] (OCLC)
Moo A........ Moore's Reports [Bosanquet and Puller] [England] [A publication]
           (DLA)
Moo & M.... Moody and Malkin's English Nisi Prius Reports [A publication] (DLA)
Moo & Mal... Moody and Malkin's English Nisi Prius Reports [A publication] (DLA)
Moo & P...... Moore and Payne's English Common Pleas Reports [A publication]
           (DLA)
Moo & Pay... Moore and Payne's English Common Pleas Reports [A publication]
           (DLA)
Moo & R...... Moody and Robinson's English Nisi Prius Reports [A publication]
           (DLA)
Moo & Rob... Moody and Robinson's English Nisi Prius Reports [A publication]
           (DLA)
Moo & S...... Moore and Scott's English Common Pleas Reports [1831-34]
           [A publication] (DLA)
Moo & Sc... Moore and Scott's English Common Pleas Reports [1831-34]
           [A publication] (DLA)

Moo CC........ Moody's English Crown Cases Reserved [1824-44] [A publication]
           (DLA)
MOO C of S... Management Office, Office, Chief of Staff
Moo CP....... Moore's English Common Pleas Reports [A publication] (DLA)
Moo Cr C.... Moody's English Crown Cases Reserved [1824-44] [A publication]
           (DLA)
Mood .... Moody's English Crown Cases Reserved [1824-44] [A publication]
           (DLA)
Mood & M... Moody and Malkin's English Nisi Prius Reports [A publication] (DLA)
Mood & Malk... Moody and Malkin's English Nisi Prius Reports [A publication]
           (DLA)
Mood & R.... Moody and Robinson's English Nisi Prius Reports [A publication]
           (DLA)
Mood & Rob.. Moody and Robinson's English Nisi Prius Reports [A publication]
           (DLA)
Mood CC...... Moody's English Crown Cases Reserved [1824-44] [A publication]
           (DLA)
Moody .... Moody's English Crown Cases [168, 169 English Reprint]
           [A publication] (DLA)
Moody & M... Moody and Malkin's English Nisi Prius Reports [A publication] (DLA)
Moody & M (Eng)... Moody and Malkin's English Nisi Prius Reports
           [A publication] (DLA)
Moody & R... Moody and Robinson's English Nisi Prius Reports [A publication]
           (DLA)
Moody & R (Eng)... Moody and Robinson's English Nisi Prius Reports
           [A publication] (DLA)
Moody CC (Eng)... Moody's English Crown Cases [168, 169 English Reprint]
           [A publication] (DLA)
Moody Cr C... Moody's English Crown Cases [168, 169 English Reprint]
           [A publication] (DLA)
Moody Cr Cas... Moody's English Crown Cases [168, 169 English Reprint]
           [A publication] (DLA)
Moog .... Moog, Inc. [Associated Press] (SAG)
Moo GC .... Moore's Gorham Case, English Privy Council [A publication] (DLA)
Moo Ind App... Moore's Reports, Privy Council, Indian Appeals [1836-72]
           [A publication] (DLA)
MOON .... Meeting Our Operational Needs
Moon .... Moon's Reports [133-144 Indiana] [6-14 Indiana Appeals]
           [A publication] (DLA)
moop .... Mechlorethamine, Vincristine, Procarbazine, Prednisone [Medicine]
           (AD)
MOOP .... Ministerstvo Okhrany Obshchestvennogo Poryadka [Ministry for
           Maintenance of Public Order] [Former USSR] (LAIN)
MOOP .... Missile Out of Order for Parts (MCD)
Moo PC....... Moore's English Privy Council Cases, Old and New Series
           [A publication] (DLA)
Moo PCC .... Moore's English Privy Council Cases [A publication] (DLA)
Moo PC Cas NS... Moore's English Privy Council Cases, New Series
           [A publication] (DLA)
Moo PCC NS... Moore's English Privy Council Cases, New Series [A publication]
           (DLA)
Moo PC (NS)... Moore's English Privy Council Cases, New Series [A publication]
           (DLA)
Moor........... Dartmoor Prison [Devon, England] (AD)
Moor........... English King's Bench Reports, by Sir Francis Moore [1512-1621]
           [A publication] (DLA)
Moore .... Moore Corp. Ltd. [Associated Press] (SAG)
Moore .... Moore's English Common Pleas Reports [A publication] (DLA)
Moore .... Moore's English Privy Council Reports [A publication] (DLA)
Moore .... Moore's Reports [Alabama] [A publication] (DLA)
Moore .... Moore's Reports [Arkansas] [A publication] (DLA)
Moore .... Moore's Reports [Texas] [A publication] (DLA)
Moore A ...... Moore's Reports [Bosanquet and Puller] [England] [A publication]
           (DLA)
Moore Abs... Moore's Abstracts of Title [6th ed.] [1925] [A publication] (DLA)
Moore & P... Moore and Payne's English Common Pleas Reports [A publication]
           (DLA)
Moore & P (Eng)... Moore and Payne's English Common Pleas Reports
           [A publication] (DLA)
Moore & S... Moore and Scott's English Common Pleas Reports [1831-34]
           [A publication] (DLA)
Moore & S (Eng)... Moore and Scott's English Common Pleas Reports [1831-34]
           [A publication] (DLA)
Moore & W... Moore and Walker's Reports [22-24 Texas] [A publication] (DLA)
Moore & Walker... Moore and Walker's Reports [22-24 Texas] [A publication] (DLA)
Moore CP .... Moore's English Common Pleas Reports [A publication] (DLA)
Moore Cr Law... Moore's Criminal Law and Procedure [A publication] (DLA)
Moore EI..... Moore's East Indian Appeals [A publication] (DLA)
Moore Fed Practice... Moore's Federal Practice [A publication] (DLA)
Moore GC .... Moore's Gorham Case, English Privy Council [A publication] (DLA)
MooreHd...... Moore-Handley, Inc. [Associated Press] (SAG)
Moore Ind App... Moore's Indian Appeals [A publication] (DLA)
Moore Ind App (Eng)... Moore's Indian Appeals [England] [A publication] (DLA)
Moore Indian App... Moore's Indian Appeals [England] [A publication] (DLA)
Moore Int L... Moore's Digest of International Law [A publication] (DLA)
MooreP........ Moore Products Corp. [Associated Press] (SAG)
Moore PC .... Moore's English Privy Council Reports [A publication] (DLA)
Moore PCC... Moore's English Privy Council Cases [A publication] (DLA)
Moore PCC (Eng)... Moore's English Privy Council Cases [A publication] (DLA)
Moore PCC NS... Moore's English Privy Council Cases, New Series
           [A publication] (DLA)
Moore PCC NS (Eng)... Moore's English Privy Council Cases, New Series
           [A publication] (DLA)

Moore PC NS...	Moore's English Privy Council Reports, New Series [A publication] (DLA)
Moore Presby Dig...	Moore's Presbyterian Digest [A publication] (DLA)
Moore QB....	Moore's English Queen's Bench Reports [A publication] (DLA)
Moore's Adj...	Moore's International Adjudications [Legal term] (AD)
Moore's Arb...	Moore's International Arbitrations [Legal term] (AD)
Moore's Dig...	Moore's Digest [Legal term] (AD)
Moorhead St U...	Moorhead State University (GAGS)
MOORNG.....	Mooring [Freight]
MOOS.........	Modular Ocean Observation System [Marine science] (MSC)
MoOs...........	Saint Clair County Library, Osceola, MO [Library symbol Library of Congress] (LCLS)
MOOSE.......	Man [or Manual] Orbital Operations Safety Equipment [Space life raft] [NASA]
MOOSE.......	Man Out of Space Easiest
MOOSE.......	Move Out of Saigon Expeditiously [or Earliest] [Army project, Vietnam]
MOOSEMUSS...	Maneuver, Objective, Offensive, Surprise, Economy of Force, Mass, Unity of Command, Simplicity, Security [Basic principles of war] [See also MOSS MOUSE]
Moo Sep Rep...	Moore's Separate Report of Westerton Versus Liddell [A publication] (DLA)
MOOSSE......	Manned Orbital Oceanographic Survey System Experiment
moot...........	Moved Out of Town (AD)
MOOT.........	Move Out of Town [Reduction of troop concentrations in cities] [Military]
Moot Ct Bull..	University of Illinois. Moot Court Bulletin [A publication] (DLA)
Moo Tr........	Moore's Divorce Trials [A publication] (DLA)
MOOTW......	Military Operations Other than War (RDA)
MOOV.........	Moovies, Inc. [NASDAQ symbol] (SAG)
Moovie........	Moovies, Inc. [Associated Press] (SAG)
MOOW........	Medical Officer of the Watch
MOP...........	Magnetized Orange Pipe [Minesweeping device] [Navy]
MOP...........	Maintenance of Property
MOP...........	Maintenance Operating Procedure (MCD)
MOP...........	Maintenance Operations Protocol (ACRL)
MOP...........	Maintenance Outline Procedure [Nuclear energy] (NRCH)
MOP...........	Major Overhaul Program [Navy]
MOP...........	Manned Orbital Platform
MOP...........	Manner of Performance [Officer rating]
MOP...........	Manual of Practice (GNE)
MOP...........	Manual Operations Panel
MOP...........	Manual Override Panel (AAG)
MOP...........	Manufacturers Output Policy [Insurance]
MOP...........	Manuscript on Paper
MOP...........	Margin of Profit [Accounting]
MOP...........	Master Operating Panel (CAAL)
MOP...........	Matrix Operations Programming
MOP...........	Measures of Performance (MCD)
MOP...........	Medical Outpatient
mop...........	Medical Outpatient (AD)
M o P.........	Member of Parliament [British] (AD)
MOP...........	Member of Parliament [British]
MOP...........	Memorandum of Policy
MOP...........	Memory Organization Packet [Artificial intelligence]
MOP...........	Message Output Processing
MOP...........	Methallyloxyphenol
MOP...........	Methoxypsoralen [Also, MP] [Pharmacology]
MOP...........	Migrant Opportunity Program [Department of Labor]
MOP...........	Military Operation (GFGA)
MOP...........	Minimum Ordered Partition
MOP...........	Ministerio de Obras Publicas [Ministry of Public Works] [Spanish] (AD)
M o P.........	Minister of Pensions [British] (AD)
M o P.........	Minister of Power [British] (AD)
M o P.........	Minister of Production [British] (AD)
MOP...........	Ministry of Pensions [British]
MOP...........	Ministry of Power [British]
MOP...........	Ministry of Production [British]
MOP...........	Minute of Program [Broadcasting] (NTCM)
MOP...........	Mission Operations Plan (MCD)
MOP...........	Mobility Operating Procedure [Military] (AFM)
MOP...........	Model Office Project
MOP...........	Model Operational Plan
MOP...........	Mode of Operation
MOP...........	Modular Operating Procedure (MUGU)
MOP...........	Modulation on the Pulse (NG)
MOP...........	Monarch Peak [California] [Seismograph station code, US Geological Survey] (SEIS)
MOP...........	Mother-of-Pearl
mop...........	Mother of Pearl (AD)
MOP...........	Mount Pleasant, MI [Location identifier FAA] (FAAL)
MOP...........	Mouvement d'Organisation du Pays [Haiti] [Political party] (EY)
MOP...........	Mouvement Ouvriers-Paysans [Workers' and Peasants' Movement] [Haiti] (PD)
MOP...........	Mouvement pour l'Ordre et la Paix [Movement for Order and Peace] [New Caledonia] [Political party] (PD)
MOP...........	Multiple Online Processing (NITA)
MOP...........	Multiple Online Programming [Computer science] (DIT)
MOP...........	Multiple Output Program (MCD)
MOP...........	Muriate of Potash [Fertilizer]
MOP...........	Mustard, Onions, Pickles [Restaurant slang]
MOP...........	Mustargen [Nitrogen mustard], Oncovin , Prednisone [Vincristine] [Antineoplastic drug regimen]
MOP...........	Mustering-Out Pay [Military]

mop...........	Mustering-Out Pay (AD)
MOP...........	, Procarbazine [Vincristine] [Antineoplastic drug regimen]
MOP...........	St. Louis College of Pharmacy, St. Louis, MO [OCLC symbol] (OCLC)
MOPA.........	Mail Order Publisher Authority (PDAA)
mopa.........	Master Oscilator Power Amplifier (AD)
MOPA.........	Master Oscilator Power Amplifier [Radio]
MOPA.........	Methoxyphenylacetic Acid [Herbicide]
MOPA.........	Methoxypropylamine [Organic chemistry]
MOPA.........	Modus Operandi - Personal Appearance [FBI computer procedure]
MOPA.........	Museum of Photographic Arts [San Diego] (AD)
MOPAC.......	Methoxyphenylacetic Acid [Organic chemistry]
MOPAC.......	Missouri Pacific Railroad Co.
MoPac........	Missouri Pacific - Texas & Pacific (AD)
MOPAC.......	Mixed Oligonucleotide Primed Amplification of cDNA [Biochemistry]
MOPALI......	Movimiento Paraguayo de Liberacion [Political party] (EY)
MOPAR.......	Master Oscillator Power Amplifier RADAR
mopar........	Master Oscillator-Power Amplifier RADAR (AD)
MOPAR.......	Motor Parts [Chrysler Corp.]
MoParkC.....	Park College, Parkville, MO [Library symbol Library of Congress] (LCLS)
MOPB........	Manually Operated Plotting Board
mopb........	Manually Operated Plotting Board (AD)
MOPB........	Metallo-Organic Petroleum-Based Coating [Materials science]
MOP-BAP....	Mustargen [Nitrogen mustard], Oncovin , Procarbazine, Bleomycin, Adriamycin, Prednisone [Vincristine] [Antineoplastic drug regimen]
Mo PC........	Moore's English Privy Council Reports [A publication] (DLA)
MOPC........	Mouse Plasmocytoma [Cell line]
MOPCOM.....	Matrix Operations Programming Combination of Estimates
MOPD........	Maximum Operating Pressure Differential (ECII)
MOPE........	Method of Personnel Evaluation
MOPE........	Multiple Object Parameter Estimation
MOPED......	Ministry of Planning and Economic Development [Ethiopia] (ECON)
MOPED......	Motor/Pedal [Motorized bicycle]
mopeds......	Motorized Pedals (AD)
MOPEG.......	(Methoxyhydroxyphenyl)ethyleneglycol [Also, MHPG] [Organic chemistry]
MoPeS........	Saint Mary's Seminary, Perryville, MO [Library symbol Library of Congress] (LCLS)
MOPET.......	Methoxyhydroxyphenylethanol [Organic chemistry]
MOPF........	Missile Onloading Prism Fixture
mopf........	Missile Onloading Prism Fixture (AD)
MOPF........	Mobile Optical Propagation Facility
MOPH........	Military Order of the Purple Heart of the United States of America (EA)
MOPI.........	Maximum [Rate] Output Initiator
MOPI.........	Maximum Rate Output Initiator (NASA)
MOPIC.......	Motion Picture [Army] (AABC)
mopic........	Motion Picture [Military] (WDMC)
MOPIMS......	Mathematical, Optical, and Philosophical Instrument Makers' Society [A union] [British]
MOPITT......	Measurements of Pollution in the Troposphere
MOPIX........	Motion Pictures
MoPIS........	School of the Ozarks, Point Lookout, MO [Library symbol Library of Congress] (LCLS)
MOPMS......	Modular Pack Mine System (RDA)
MOPN........	Methoxypropionitrile [Organic chemistry]
MoPobT......	Three Rivers Community College, Poplar Bluff, MO [Library symbol Library of Congress] (LCLS)
MoPobV......	United States Veterans Administration Hospital, Medical Library, Poplar Bluff, MO [Library symbol Library of Congress] (LCLS)
MOPOCO.....	Movimiento Popular Colorado [Colorado Popular Movement] [Paraguay] [Political party] (PD)
MOPP........	Mechlorethamine, Oncovin, Procarbazine, Prednisone [Medicine] (MEDA)
MOPP........	Methotrexate, Oncomycin, Prednisone, Procarbazine [Antineoplastic drug regimen] (DAVI)
MOPP........	Military Operational Protective Posture [Chemical warfare] (RDA)
MOPP........	Mission-Oriented Protection Posture [Army] (AABC)
MOPP........	Mission Oriented Protective Posture [Gear] [USA]
MOPP........	Modular Operating Procedure (MUGU)
MOPP........	Mustargen hydrochloride, Oncovin [Vincristine], Procarbazine, Prednisone [Antineoplastic drug regimen]
MOPP........	Mustargen [Nitrogen mustard], Oncovin , Procarbazine, Prednisone [Vincristine] [Antineoplastic drug regimen]
MOPP........	Mustine, Oncovin [Vincristine] Procarbazine, Prednisone [Antineoplastic drug regimen] (DAVI)
MOPP/ABV...	Mustargen [Nitrogen mustard], Oncovin , Procarbazine, Prednisone, Adriamycin, Bleomycin, Vinblastine [Vincristine] [Antineoplastic drug regimen]
MOPP/ABVD...	Mechlorethamine, Oncovin [Vincristine] Procarbazine, Prednisone, Doxo rubicin, Bleomycin, Vinblastine, Dacarbazine [Antineoplastic drug regimen] (DAVI)
MOPP-BLEO...	Mustargen [Nitrogen mustard], Oncovin , Procarbazine, Prednisone, Bleomycin [Vincristine] [Antineoplastic drug regimen]
MOPPCPF...	Mustargen [Nitrogen mustard], Oncovin , Procarbazine, Prednisone (for Patients with Compromised Pulmonary Function) [Vincristine] [Antineoplastic drug regimen]
MOPPE.......	Modified Operational Propulsion Plan Examination [Navy] (NVT)
MOPPHDB ...	Mustargen [Nitrogen mustard], Oncovin , Procarbazine, Prednisone, High-Dose Bleomycin [Vincristine] [Antineoplastic drug regimen]
MOPPLDB...	Mustargen [Nitrogen mustard], Oncovin , Procarbazine, Prednisone, Low-DoseBleomycin [Vincristine] [Antineoplastic drug regimen]

MOPP-LO BLEO... Mechlorethamine [*Vincristine*] Procarbazine, Prednisone, Bleomycin [*Antineoplastic drug regimen*] (DAVI)
mopr............ Manner of Performance Rating (AD)
MOPR.......... Manner of Performing Rating
MOPR.......... Mission Operations Planning Review [*NASA*] (NASA)
MOPR.......... Mission Operations Planning Review
MOPR.......... Mission Operations Planning Room (MCD)
MOPR.......... Mop Rack
mopr............ Mop Rack (AD)
MOPr........... Mustargen [*Nitrogen mustard*], Oncovin , Procarbazine [*Vincristine*] [*Antineoplastic drug regimen*]
MOPr .... , Prednisone [*Vincristine*] [*Antineoplastic drug regimen*]
Mo Prec...... Moile's Precedents [*A publication*] (DLA)
moprl........... Mother-of-Pearl (VRA)
MOPS.......... Mail-Order Protection Scheme [*British*]
MOPS.......... Maneuver Operations Program System [*NASA*]
MOPS.......... Man-Operated Propulsion System
MOPS.......... Marine Oil Pickup Service [*Marine science*] (MSC)
MOPS.......... Maritime Officer Production Study [*Canadian Navy*]
MOPS.......... Mechanization Outside Plant Scheduling System (MHDB)
MOPS.......... Mechanized Outdoor Planning System
MOPS.......... Merchandise Ordering Processing System (AD)
MOPS.......... Microwave Optical-Photoselection Microscopy
MOPS.......... Military Operation Phone System
MOPS.......... Million Operations per Second [*Processing power units*] [*Computer science*]
MOPS.......... Minimum Operational Performance Standard [*Aviation*] (DA)
MOPS.......... Missile Operations
MOPS.......... Missile Operations Paging [*or Phone*] System [*NASA*]
MOPS.......... Missile Operations System (AD)
MOPS.......... Mission Operations Planning System [*NASA*] (KSC)
MOPS.......... Morpholinopropanesulfonic Acid [*A buffer*]
MOPS.......... Mothers of Preschoolers International (PAZ)
MOPS.......... Multispectral Opium Poppy Sensor System
MO PSC...... Missouri Public Service Commission Reports [*A publication*] (DLA)
MO PSC (NS)... Missouri Public Service Commission Reports (New Series) [*A publication*] (DLA)
MO PSCR..... Missouri Public Service Commission Reports [*A publication*] (DLA)
MOPSS........ Management & Operation of Public Services Section [*Reference and User Services Association*] [*American Library Association*]
MOPSS........ Multispectral Opium Poppy Sensor System (AD)
MOPSY........ Multi-Programming Operating System [*Computer science*] (PDAA)
M Opt.......... Master of Optometry
MOpt........... Master of Optometry (GAGS)
MOPT........... Mean One Way Propagation Time [*Telecommunications*] (TEL)
MOPTAR...... Multiobject Phase Tracking and Ranging [*FAA*]
MOPTARS.... Multi-Object Phase-Tracking and Ranging System [*FAA*] (PDAA)
MOPTE........ Measure of Potential Training Effectiveness [*Army*]
MOptom....... Master of Optometry (ADA)
MOPTS .... Mobile Photographic Tracking Station (IEEE)
MO PUR ...... Missouri Public Utility Reports [*A publication*] (DLA)
MOPV .... Monovalent Oral Polio Vaccine [*Immunology*]
MOPW .... Ministry of Population Welfare [*Pakistan*] (ECON)
MOQ .... Fort Stewart (Hinesville), GA [*Location identifier FAA*] (FAAL)
MOQ .... Lindenwood College, St. Charles, MO [*OCLC symbol*] (OCLC)
MOQ .... Married Officer Quarters
MOQ .... Minimum Order Quantity (MCD)
MOQ .... Morocco Explorations [*Vancouver Stock Exchange symbol*]
MOQ .... Morondava [*Madagascar*] [*Airport symbol*] (OAG)
MOR .... AS Morefly [*Norway ICAO designator*] (FAAC)
MOR .... Magneto-Optical Rotation
MOR .... Management Operating Ratios (NG)
MOR .... Mandatory Occurrence Reporting
MOR .... Manufacturing Operation Record (NASA)
MORS .... Manufacturing Operation Record
MOR .... Market Opinion Research, Inc. [*Information service or system*] (IID)
MOR .... Mars Orbital Rendezvous
MOr .... Master of Operations Research (PGP)
M Or .... Master of Oratory
MOR .... Maximum Ozone Reactivity [*Exhaust emissions*] [*Automotive engineering*]
MOR .... Medical Officer Report [*Navy*] (NG)
MOR .... Memory Output Register [*Computer science*]
MOR .... Merchandising and Operating Results
MOR .... Meteorological Optical Range (PDAA)
MOR .... Middle of the Road [*Broadcasting*]
mor............ Middle of the Road (AD)
MOR .... Mid-Oceanic Ridge
MOR .... Military Operations Research
M o R .... Ministry of Reconstruction [*British*] (AD)
MOR .... Missile Operationally Ready [*Air Force*]
MOR .... Mission Operations Room (MCD)
MOR .... Missions Operations Report [*NASA*] (KSC)
MO R .... Missouri Reports [*A publication*] (DLA)
MOR .... Modulus of Rupture [*Mechanics*]
MOR .... Monthly Operating Report (IEEE)
MOR .... Monthly Operating Review (USDC)
MOR .... Monthly Operating Review [*Marine science*] (OSRA)
MOR .... Moral (ROG)
Mor............ Moralia [*of Plutarch*] [*Classical studies*] (OCD)
MOR .... Moravian College, Bethlehem, PA [*OCLC symbol*] (OCLC)
MOR .... Moray [*County in Scotland*] (ROG)
MOR .... Mordenite [*A zeolite*]
Mor............ Morelia (AD)
Mor............ Morelos (AD)

mor............ Morendo [*Dying Away*] [*Italian*] (AD)
MOR .... Morendo [*Gradually Softer*] [*Music*]
MOR .... Morgan Keegan & Co., Inc. [*NYSE symbol*] (SPSG)
MOR .... Morgan Keegan Inc. [*NYSE symbol*] (TTSB)
MOR .... Morgan, M. B., Glen Burnie MD [*STAC*]
MOR .... Morgan Owners Register (EA)
MOR .... Mori [*Japan*] [*Seismograph station code, US Geological Survey Closed*] (SEIS)
Mor......... Morisco (AD)
Mor......... Morison's Dictionary of Decisions, Scotch Court of Session [*1540-1808*] [*A publication*] (DLA)
MOR .... Morning Star Resources [*Vancouver Stock Exchange symbol*]
Mor......... Moroccan (AD)
mor......... Morocco (AD)
MOR .... Morocco
MOR .... Morocco Leather [*Bookbinding*] (ROG)
MOR .... Morphine [*A narcotic*]
MOR .... Morpholine [*Organic chemistry*]
Mor......... Morris' Reports [*Jamaica*] [*A publication*] (ILCA)
MOR .... Morristown, TN [*Location identifier FAA*] (FAAL)
MOR .... Mortality Odds Ratio
MOR .... Mortar
mor......... Mortar (AD)
MOR .... Movimiento Obrero Revolucionario Salvado Cayetano Carpio [*El Salvador*] [*Political party*] (EY)
MOR .... Museum of the Rockies [*Montana, USA*]
MORA .... Mandibular Orthopedic Repositioning Appliance [*Dentistry*]
MORA .... Mimimum Off-Route Altitude [*Aviation*] (DA)
MORA .... Mount Rainier National Park
MORAB....... Morgan and Arabian [*Type of horse developed from these two breeds*] [*Acronym is also said to stand for "Muscular, Outstanding, Refined, Athletic, Beautiful," the horse's distinguishing characteristics*]
MORAL .... Massachusetts Organization for the Repeal of Abortion Laws
Mor & Carl... Moreau-Lislet and Carleton's Laws of Las Siete Partidas in Force in Louisiana [*A publication*] (DLA)
MORASS..... Modern Ramjet System Synthesis (MCD)
Morav .... Moravia (AD)
MORB .... Mid-Ocean Ridge Basalt [*Geology*]
Morb........... Morbihan (AD)
MORBREPT... Morbidity Report
MORBTGREPT... Morbidity Telegraphic Report
MORC .... Medical Officers' Reserve Corps
MORC .... Midget Ocean Racing Class [*or Club*]
Mor Chy Acts... Morgan's Chancery Acts and Orders [*6th ed.*] [*1885*] [*A publication*] (DLA)
Mor Comp ... Morris on Compensations [*A publication*] (DLA)
Mor Corp ..... Morawetz on Private Corporations [*A publication*] (DLA)
MORD........ Magneto-Optic Rotary Dispersion (PDAA)
MORD........ Medical Operations Requirements Document (MCD)
MORD........ Military Operations Research Department
MORD........ Ministry of Revolutionary Development [*Vietnam*]
MORD........ Mission Operations Requirements Document [*NASA*] (NASA)
Mord......... Mordehai (AD)
Mordhy...... Mordehai (AD)
Mor Dic ...... Morison's Dictionary of Decisions, Scotch Court of Session [*1540-1808*] [*A publication*] (DLA)
mor dict....... More Dicto [*As Directed*] [*Latin*] (AD)
Mor Dict ..... Morison's Dictionary of Decisions, Scotch Court of Session [*1540-1808*] [*A publication*] (DLA)
MOR DICT ... Moro Dicto [*As Directed*] [*Pharmacy*]
Mor Dig ..... Morley's Digest of the Indian Reports [*A publication*] (DLA)
Mor Dig ..... Morrison's New Hampshire Digest [*A publication*] (DLA)
Mor Dil....... Morris on Dilapidations [*2nd ed.*] [*1871*] [*A publication*] (DLA)
MORDS...... Manned Orbital Research and Development System
MORDT....... Mobilization Operational Readiness Deployment Test [*DoD*]
Mordy........ Mordechai (AD)
MORE........ Management of Radiographic Environments [*Radiology*] (DAVI)
MORE........ Meal, Ordered Ready-to-Eat [*Army*] (RDA)
MORE........ Microbial Oil Recovery Enhancement [*Petroleum technology*]
MORE .... Midwest Organization for Research in Education (AEBS)
MORE........ Military Officer Record Examination
MORE........ Minority Officer Recruitment Effort
MORE........ Mission for Outreach, Renewal, and Evangelism (AD)
MORE .... Money, Opportunity, Responsibility, and Equality [*Of organization "MORE for Women"*]
MORE........ Multioptical Reconnaissance Equipment [*Military*] (CAAL)
Mor E & RD Law... Morice's English and Roman Dutch Law [*A publication*] (DLA)
Mor Eas...... Morris on the Law of Easements [*A publication*] (DLA)
Moreau & Carleton's Partidas... Moreau-Lislet and Carleton's Laws of Las Siete Partidas in Force in Louisiana [*A publication*] (DLA)
MORE DICT... More Dicto [*As Directed*] [*Pharmacy*] (ROG)
Morehead St U... Morehead State University (GAGS)
Morehouse Sch of Med... Morehouse School of Medicine (GAGS)
MOREL .... Michigan-Ohio Regional Educational Laboratory
More Lect.... More's Lectures on the Law of Scotland [*A publication*] (DLA)
MORENA..... Mouvement de Redressement National [*Gabon*] [*Political party*] (EY)
MORENA..... Movimiento de Renovacion Nacional [*National Renewal Movement*] [*Venezuela Political party*] (PPW)
MORENA..... Movimiento de Restauracion Nacional [*National Restoration Movement*] [*Colorado Political party*] (EY)
MORENET.... Missouri Research and Education Network
MO Rep....... Missouri Reports [*A publication*] (DLA)
MOREP........ Monthly Report
MOREPS...... Monitor Station Reports

moreps .... Monitor Station Reports (AD)
MORES .... Minerals, Oils, and Resources Shares Fund [*British*]
MORE SOL... More Solito [*In the Usual Way*] [*Pharmacy*] (ROG)
MOREST ...... Mobile Arresting Gear [*Navy*]
More St .... More's Notes on Stair's Institutes of Scotland [*A publication*] (DLA)
MORET .... Moreton [*England*]
MO Rev Stat... Missouri Revised Statutes [*A publication*] (DLA)
Morey Out Rom Law... Morey's Outlines of Roman Law [*A publication*] (DLA)
MorF .... Male or Female
MORF .... Male or Female (NHD)
MORF .... Manned Orbital Research Facility [*NASA*] (MCD)
mor fib .... Moral Fiber (AD)
MORG .... Morgan Financial Corp. [*NASDAQ symbol*] (SAG)
MORG .... Morgan Finl (Del) [*NASDAQ symbol*] (TTSB)
Morg .... Morgan's Chancery Acts and Orders [*6th ed.*] [*1885*] [*A publication*] (DLA)
MORG .... Movements Reports Generator (DNAB)
MORG .... Museo Oceanografico de Rio Grande [*Oceanographic Museum of Rio Grande*] [*Brazil*] (AD)
MORGA .... Municipal Organization Act (DICI)
Morgan .... Morgan [*J. P.*] & Co., Inc. [*Associated Press*] (SAG)
Morgan .... Morgan's Digest [*Ceylon*] (DLA)
Morg & Ch Jud Acts... Morgan and Chute on the Judicature Acts [*A publication*] (DLA)
Morg & WLJ... Morgan and Williams' Law Journal [*London*] [*A publication*] (DLA)
Morgan LM... Morgan's Legal Miscellany [*Ceylon*] [*A publication*] (DLA)
Morgan St U... Morgan State University (GAGS)
Morg Ch ..... Morgan's Chancery Acts and Orders [*6th ed.*] [*1885*] [*A publication*] (DLA)
MorgFn .... Morgan Financial Corp. [*Associated Press*] (SAG)
MorgFun ...... Morgan Funshares, Inc. [*Associated Press*] (SAG)
MorgGr .... Morgan Grenfell Smallcap Fund, Inc. [*Associated Press*] (SAG)
MorgK .... Morgan Keegan [*Associated Press*] (SAG)
MorgKeg ...... Morgan Keegan & Co., Inc. [*Associated Press*] (SAG)
Morg Lit ...... Morgan on the Law of Literature [*A publication*] (DLA)
morg mar .... Morganatic Marriage (AD)
Morgn .... Morgan [*J. P.*] & Co., Inc. [*Associated Press*] (SAG)
MorgnF .... Morgan's Foods, Inc. [*Associated Press*] (SAG)
MorgnP .... Morgan Products Ltd. [*Associated Press*] (SAG)
MorgSt .... Morgan Stanley Group, Inc. [*Associated Press*] (SAG)
Morg Tar ..... Morgan on the United States Tariff [*A publication*] (DLA)
Mor Hors ..... Morrell on the Law of Horses [*A publication*] (DLA)
MORI .... Market and Opinion Research International [*Polling organization*]
Mori .... Market and Opinion Research International [*Polling organization*] (ODBW)
Mor IA .... Morris' Iowa Reports [*1839-46*] [*A publication*] (DLA)
MORIF .... Microprogram Optimization Technique Considering Resource Occupancy and Instruction Formats (MHDB)
MoRih.......... Richmond Heights Memorial Library, Richmond Heights, MO [*Library symbol Library of Congress*] (LCLS)
MORITZER ... Mortar Howitzer (NATG)
moritzer....... Mortar Howitzer (AD)
MorKnd........ Morrison-Knudsen Co., Inc. [*Associated Press*] (SAG)
MORL .... Manned Orbital [*or Orbiting*] Research Laboratory [*NASA*]
MORL .... Medium-Sized Orbital Research Laboratory (SAA)
Morl Dig ...... Morley's East Indian Digest [*A publication*] (DLA)
Mor Lib .... Morgan Library (AD)
Mor M .... Master Mortician
MORM .... Mormon (WDAA)
Morm .... Mormon (AD)
MoRM.......... University of Missouri at Rolla, Rolla, MO [*Library symbol Library of Congress*] (LCLS)
Mor Maj ...... Moral Majority (AD)
Mor Min Rep... Morrison's Mining Reports [*A publication*] (DLA)
Mor Miss ..... Morris' Reports [*Mississippi*] [*A publication*] (DLA)
MORN .... Morning
morn........... Morning (AD)
MornGp........ Morningstar Group [*Associated Press*] (SAG)
Morningside C... Morningside College (GAGS)
Moro .... Book of Moroni (AD)
Moro .... Morocco (VRA)
MORO .... Morocco Leather [*Bookbinding*] (ROG)
Moroc .... Moroccan (AD)
MORP .... Medical and Occupational Radiation Program [*HEW*]
MORP .... Meteorite Observation and Recovery Project [*Canada*]
MORP .... Mid-Ocean Ridge Peridotite [*Geology*]
MORP .... Moore Products [*NASDAQ symbol*] (TTSB)
MORP .... Moore Products Co. [*NASDAQ symbol*] (NQ)
MORPH....... Morphine (WDAA)
morph.......... Morphine (AD)
morph .... Morphology (AD)
MORPH....... Morphology
Morphing..... Metamorphosizing [*Video technology*]
MORPHOL ... Morphology
morphophysio... Morphophysiological (AD)
MORPHS...... Minicomputer-Operated Retrieval (Partially Heuristic) System [*Computer science*]
Mor Pr .... Morehead's Practice [*A publication*] (DLA)
Mor Priv Corp... Morawetz on Private Corporations [*A publication*] (DLA)
MORPS .... Maritime Other Ranks Production Study [*Canadian Navy*]
MorR .... Bibliotheque Generale et Archives, Rabat, Morocco [*Library symbol Library of Congress*] (LCLS)
Morr............ Morrell's English Bankruptcy Reports [*A publication*] (DLA)
Morr............ Morris' Iowa Reports [*1839-46*] [*A publication*] (DLA)
Morr............ Morris' Jamaica Reports [*A publication*] (DLA)

Morr............ Morris' Reports [*Oregon*] [*A publication*] (DLA)
Morr............ Morris' Reports [*California*] [*A publication*] (DLA)
Morr............ Morris' Reports [*Bombay, India*] [*A publication*] (DLA)
MORR.......... Morristown National Historical Park
Morr Bankr Cas... Morrell's English Bankruptcy Cases [*A publication*] (DLA)
Morr BC....... Morrell's English Bankruptcy Reports [*A publication*] (DLA)
Morr Bomb... Morris' Reports [*Bombay, India*] [*A publication*] (DLA)
Morr Cal...... Morris' Reports [*California*] [*A publication*] (DLA)
Morr Dict..... Morrison's Dictionary of Decisions, Scotch Court of Session [*A publication*] (DLA)
Morr Dig...... Morrison's Digest of Mining Decisions [*A publication*] (DLA)
Morr Dig...... Morrison's New Hampshire Digest [*A publication*] (DLA)
Morrell Bankr Cas... Morrell's English Bankruptcy Cases [*A publication*] (DLA)
Morrell BC... Morrell's English Bankruptcy Cases [*A publication*] (DLA)
Morrell (Eng)... Morrell's English Bankruptcy Cases [*A publication*] (DLA)
Mor Rep ..... Morris' Law of Replevin [*A publication*] (DLA)
Morris.......... Morris' Iowa Reports [*1839-46*] [*A publication*] (DLA)
Morris.......... Morris' Jamaica Reports [*A publication*] (DLA)
Morris.......... Morris' Reports [*Mississippi*] [*A publication*] (DLA)
Morris.......... Morris' Reports [*Oregon*] [*A publication*] (DLA)
Morris.......... Morris' Reports [*Bombay, India*] [*A publication*] (DLA)
Morris.......... Morris' Reports [*California*] [*A publication*] (DLA)
Morris.......... Morrissett's Reports [*80, 98 Alabama*] [*A publication*] (DLA)
Morris & Har... Morris and Harrington's Reports [*Bombay, India*] [*A publication*] (DLA)
Morris (IA)... Morris' Iowa Reports [*1839-46*] [*A publication*] (DLA)
Morris (Iowa)... Morris' Iowa Reports [*1839-46*] [*A publication*] (DLA)
Morrison...... Morrison Restaurants, Inc. [*Associated Press*] (SAG)
Morrison Min Rep... Morrison's Mining Reports [*United States*] [*A publication*] (DLA)
Morris R ..... Morris' Jamaica Reports [*A publication*] (DLA)
Morris Repl... Morris on Replevin [*A publication*] (DLA)
Morris St Cas... Morris' Mississippi State Cases [*1818-72*] [*A publication*] (DLA)
Morr Jam..... Morris' Jamaica Reports [*A publication*] (DLA)
MorrKn .... Morrison Knudsen Corp. [*Associated Press*] (SAG)
MorrKnud.... Morrison Knudsen Corp. [*Associated Press*] (SAG)
Morr Mines... Morrison's Digest of Mining Decisions [*A publication*] (DLA)
Morr Min R... Morrison's Mining Reports [*United States*] [*A publication*] (DLA)
Morr Min Rep... Morrison's Mining Reports [*A publication*] (DLA)
Morr Miss.... Morris' Reports [*Mississippi*] [*A publication*] (DLA)
Morr MR..... Morrison's Mining Reports [*United States*] [*A publication*] (DLA)
MorrowSn.... Morrow Snowboards, Inc. [*Associated Press*] (SAG)
Morr Repl.... Morris' Law of Replevin [*A publication*] (DLA)
Morr St Cas... Morris' Mississippi State Cases [*1818-72*] [*A publication*] (DLA)
Morr Trans... Morrison's Transcript of United States Supreme Court Decisions [*A publication*] (DLA)
Mor Ry Com... Morris on Railway Compensations [*A publication*] (DLA)
MORS .... Midland Operational Research Society (AD)
MORS .... Military Operations Research Society (EA)
MORS .... Military Operations Research Symposia (MCD)
MORS .... Multi-Outlet Reservoir Study [*Department of the Interior*] (GRD)
mor sal........ More Solito [*In the Usual Manner*] [*Latin*] (AD)
M Or Sc ...... Master of the Science of Oratory
MORSEAFRON... Moroccan Sea Frontier [*Navy World War II*]
Morse Arb ... Morse on the Law of Arbitration and Award [*A publication*] (DLA)
Morse Banks... Morse on the Law of Banks and Banking [*A publication*] (DLA)
Morse Bk.... Morse on the Law of Banks and Banking [*A publication*] (DLA)
Morse Exch Rep... Morse's Exchequer Reports [*Canada*] [*A publication*] (DLA)
MorSEm...... Morgan Stanley Emerging Markets [*Associated Press*] (SAG)
Morse Tr...... Morse's Famous Trials [*A publication*] (DLA)
MORSL .... Mobilization Reserve Stockage List [*Army*] (AABC)
MorsnFr....... Morrison Fresh Cooking, Inc. [*Associated Press*] (SAG)
MorsnHl....... Morrison Health Care, Inc. [*Associated Press*] (SAG)
mor sol........ More Solito [*In the usual manner*] [*Latin*] [*Pharmacy*] (DAVI)
MOR SOL..... More Solito [*In the Usual Way*] [*Pharmacy*]
Mor St Ca.... Morris' Mississippi State Cases [*1818-72*] [*A publication*] (DLA)
Mor St Cas... Morris' Mississippi State Cases [*1818-72*] [*A publication*] (DLA)
Mor Supp..... Morison's Dictionary of Decisions, Scotch Court of Session, Supplement [*1620-1768*] [*A publication*] (DLA)
Mor Syn...... Morison's Synopsis, Scotch Session Cases [*1808-16*] [*A publication*] (DLA)
moRt........... Mainstream of Republican Thought (AD)
MORT .... Management Oversight and Risk Tree
MORT .... Management Oversight and Risk Tree (NASA)
MORT .... Master Operational Recording Tape [*SAGE*]
MORT .... Missile Operation [*or Ordnance*] Readiness Test [*or Testing*]
MORT .... Morse Taper
mor t .... Morse Taper (AD)
mort............ Mortal (AD)
mort............ Mortality
MORT .... Mortar (AABC)
mort............ Mortar (AD)
Mort........... Mortemart (AD)
mort............ Mortgage (AD)
MORT .... Mortgage (ADA)
MORT .... Mortician
mort............ Mortician (AD)
Mort........... Mortimer (AD)
Mort........... Morton (AD)
MORT .... Mortuary (ADA)
MORTAL ..... Mortality (BABM)
mortal.......... Mortality [*Statistics*] (DAVI)
MORTG .... Mortgage
MortnRst...... Mortons Restaurant Group [*Associated Press*] (SAG)

Morton........	Morton's Reports, Calcutta Superior Court [*India*] [*A publication*] (DLA)
Morton Int ..	Morton International, Inc. [*Associated Press*] (SAG)
Mor Tran	Morrison's Transcript of United States Supreme Court Decisions [*A publication*] (DLA)
MORTREP....	Mortar Bombing Report
Mort Vend ..	Morton's Vendors and Purchasers [*1837*] [*A publication*] (DLA)
MORU........	Mount Rushmore National Memorial
MORV........	Mobile Overpass Roadway-Repair Vehicle
Mor Wills ..	Morrell on the Law of Wills [*A publication*] (DLA)
Mos	Book of Mosiah (AD)
Mos	De Vita Mosis [*Philo*] (BJA)
MOS...........	Machinery and Occupational Safety Act [*Environmental science*]
MOS...........	Magneto-Optical System (AD)
MOS...........	Maintenance Operations Section [*Marine Corps*] (DOMA)
MOS...........	Major Operating System [*Army*] (AABC)
MOS...........	Management Operating System
MOS...........	Management Operations Staff [*Environmental Protection Agency*] (GFGA)
MOS...........	Management Orientation School [*LIMRA*]
MOS...........	Manned Orbital Station (AAG)
MOS...........	Man on the Street (WDMC)
MOS...........	Man-on-the-Street Interview [*Journalism*]
MOS...........	Manual Override Switch
MOS...........	Manufacturing Operating System [*IBM Corp.*]
MOS...........	Manufacturing Operations Survey (MCD)
MOS...........	Margin of Safety [*Business term*]
MOS...........	Marine Observation Satellite [*Japan*]
MOS...........	Marine Occupational Standard (DNAB)
MOS...........	Maritime Operational Intelligence Summary (MCD)
MOS...........	Marking of Overseas Shipments
MOS...........	Master Operating System [*Sperry UNIVAC*]
MOS...........	Material Ordering Schedule
MOS...........	Mathematical Off-Print Service [*American Mathematical Society*]
MOS...........	Mean Opinion Score
MOS...........	Measurement of Skill (AEBS)
MOS...........	Measure of Suitability (CAAL)
MOS...........	Mechanical Oblique Sketcher
MOS...........	Memory Operating Software [*Computer science*]
MOS...........	Memory-Oriented System
MOS...........	Mercantile Open Stock
MOS...........	Metal Oxide on a Substrate (MCD)
MOS...........	Metal-Oxide Semiconductor
mos	Metal-Oxide Semiconductor (AD)
mos	Metal-Oxide Silicon (AD)
MOS...........	Metal-Oxide-Silicon [*Integrated circuit*] [*Electronics*]
MOS...........	Microprogram Operating System
MOS...........	Military Occupational Specialty [*Army*]
mos	Military Occupational Specialty (AD)
MOS...........	Military Occupational Specification Serial Number [*British World War II*]
MOS...........	Military Oceanography Subcommittee [*National Security Industrial Association*] (USDC)
MOS...........	Military Oceanography Subcommittee [*Marine science*] (OSRA)
MOS...........	Military Overseas Supply [*British*]
mOs	Milliosmole [*or Milliosmolar*] (AAMN)
MOS...........	Minimum Operating System [*Sperry Univac*] (NITA)
MOS...........	Ministry of State [*British*]
MOS...........	Ministry of Supply [*Also, MS*] [*British*]
MOS...........	Minus Optical Sound [*Film industry*]
MOS...........	MISR Overseas Airways [*Egypt*] [*ICAO designator*] (FAAC)
MOS...........	Missile on Stand
mos	Missile On Stand (AD)
MOS...........	Missile Operations Station
MOS...........	Mission Operations Strategy [*NASA*]
MOS...........	Mission Operations System [*NASA*]
MOS...........	Mit Out Sound [*i.e., "without sound"*] [*Film industry*]
mos	Mit-Out Sound (AD)
MOS...........	Mitral Opening Sound [*Cardiology*]
MOS...........	Model Output Statistics [*Meteorology*]
MOS...........	Modular Operating System (BUR)
MOS...........	Months
mos	Months (WDMC)
mos	Months (AD)
MOS...........	Morton Air Services Ltd.
MOS...........	Mosaic
mos	Mosaic (VRA)
Mos	Mosca [*Moscow*] [*Italian*] (AD)
Mos	Moscou [*Moscow*] [*French*] (AD)
Mos	Moscow (AD)
MOS...........	Moscow [*Russia*] [*Seismograph station code, US Geological Survey*] (SEIS)
Mos	Moscu [*Moscow*] [*Spanish*] (AD)
Mos	Moseley's English Chancery Reports [*25 English Reprint*] [*A publication*] (DLA)
Mos	Mosella [*of Ausonius*] [*Classical studies*] (OCD)
Mos	Moses Point, AK [*Location identifier FAA*] (FAAL)
Mos	Moshe (AD)
Mos	Moskau [*Moscow*] [*German*] (AD)
Mos	Moskou [*Moscow*] [*Dutch*] (AD)
Mos	Moslem (AD)
MOS...........	Mosport Park Corp. [*Vancouver Stock Exchange symbol*]
mos	Mossi [*MARC language code Library of Congress*] (LCCP)
MOS...........	Multiple Object Spectroscopy (PDAA)
MOS...........	Multiprogramming Operating System

MoS	Museum of Sydney [*Australia*]
MOS...........	Springfield-Greene County Library, Springfield, MO [*OCLC symbol*] (OCLC)
MoS	St. Louis Public Library, St. Louis, MO [*Library symbol Library of Congress*] (LCLS)
MOSA	Medical Officers of Schools Associations [*British*]
MOSA	Method of Standard Addition [*Statistics*]
MOSA	Minimum Operational Safe Altitude (DOMA)
MOSA	Ministry of Science and Arts [*US and Israel*]
MoSAB........	Anheuser-Busch, Inc., St. Louis, MO [*Library symbol Library of Congress*] (LCLS)
MOSAIC	Macro Operation Symbolic Assembler and Information Compiler [*Computer science*] (IEEE)
MOSAIC	Metal-Oxide-Semiconductor Advanced Integrated Circuit [*Electronics*] (IEEE)
MOSAIC	Method of Scenic Alternative Impacts by Computer (PDAA)
MOSAIC	Ministry of Supply Automatic Integrator and Computer [*British*] (DEN)
MOSAIC	Mobile System for Accurate ICBM Control (MCD)
MOSAICS	Melcom Optical Software Applications for Integrated Commercial Systems (PDAA)
MOSAR	Modulation Scan Array RADAR [*or Receiver*]
MOSASR......	Metal Oxide Semiconductor Analogue Shift Register [*Electronics*] (PDAA)
MoSavHi	Andrew County Historical Society, Savannah, MO [*Library symbol Library of Congress*] (LCLS)
MOSAW	Medium Operating Speed Automatic Weapon [*Military*]
MOSB	Military Order of the Stars and Bars (EA)
MoSB	Missouri Botanical Garden, St. Louis, MO [*Library symbol Library of Congress*] (LCLS)
Mosbas........	Moscow Basin (AD)
MOSC	Management Orientation Study Course [*LIMRA*]
mosc...........	Manned Orbital Systems Concept (AD)
MOSC	Manned Orbital Systems Concepts [*NASA*]
MOSC	Midland-Odessa Symphony and Chorale (AD)
MOSC	Military Occupational Specialty Code (AABC)
MOSC	Military Oil Subcommittee [*of North African Economic Board*] [*World War II*]
MOSC	Mosaic
MOSCA	McNamara-O'Hara Service Contract Act of 1965 (WYGK)
MOSCAP.....	Modified Service Contract and Procedures [*DoD*]
MoSCC........	St. Louis Community College, Instructional Resource Technical Services, St. Louis, MO [*Library symbol Library of Congress*] (LCLS)
MoSCEx	Christ Seminary-Seminex, St. Louis, MO [*Library symbol Library of Congress*] (LCLS)
MoSCH	Concordia Historical Institute, St. Louis, MO [*Library symbol Library of Congress*] (LCLS)
MOSCH.......	Moschus [*Musk*] [*Pharmacology*] (ROG)
MoSCo........	St. Louis County Library, St. Louis, MO [*Library symbol Library of Congress*] (LCLS)
Moscom.......	Moscom Corp. [*Associated Press*] (SAG)
Mos Cont	Moseley's Contraband of War [*1861*] [*A publication*] (DLA)
MoSCP........	St. Louis College of Pharmacy, St. Louis, MO [*Library symbol Library of Congress*] (LCLS)
MoSCRR......	Center for Reformation Research, St. Louis, MO [*Library symbol Library of Congress*] (LCLS)
MoSCS........	Concordia Seminary, St. Louis, MO [*Library symbol Library of Congress*] (LCLS)
MoSCT	Covenant Theological Seminary, St. Louis, MO [*Library symbol Library of Congress*] (LCLS)
MoSDM.......	United States Air Force, Defense Mapping Agency Aerospace Center, St. Louis, MO [*Library symbol Library of Congress*] (LCLS)
Mose	Moises (AD)
Mose	Moseley (AD)
Mose	Mosen (AD)
Mose	Moses (AD)
MoSe	Sedalia Public Library, Sedalia, MO [*Library symbol Library of Congress*] (LCLS)
MoSE	United States Army, Corps of Engineers, District Library St. Louis, St. Louis, MO [*Library symbol Library of Congress*] (LCLS)
MoSed	Sedalia Public Library, Sedalia, MO [*Library symbol*] [*Library of Congress*] (LCLS)
MOSEL........	Molten-Salt Epithermal Reactor
Moseley.......	Moseley's English Chancery Reports [*25 English Reprint*] [*A publication*] (DLA)
Mos El L	Moseley's Elementary Law [*2nd ed.*] [*1878*] [*A publication*] (DLA)
Mosely (Eng)..	Moseley's English Chancery Reports [*25 English Reprint*] [*A publication*] (DLA)
MOSES	Manned Open Sea Experiment Station (NOAA)
MOSES	Manufacturing Operations Short Event Scheduling
MOSES	Massive Open Systems Environment Standard [*Computer science*]
MOSES	Molecular Orbital Self-Consistent Energy System (PDAA)
MOSES	Motor-Operated Sled Ejection System (MCD)
MOSES	Movable Search System (MCD)
MOSES	Multioccupant Sealed Environment Simulator
MoSF	Fontbonne College, St. Louis, MO [*Library symbol Library of Congress*] (LCLS)
MOSFET......	Metal Oxide Semiconductor Field Effect Transformer (NITA)
mosfet........	Metal-Oxide Semiconductor Field-Effect Transistor (AD)
MOSFET......	Metal-Oxide-Semiconductor [*or Silicon*] Field-Effect Transistor
MOSFET......	Metal-Oxide-Silicon Field-Effect Transistor (IDOE)
MOSFETS ...	Metal Oxide Substrate Field Effect Transistor
MoSFi..........	Eugene Field House, St. Louis, MO [*Library symbol Library of Congress*] (LCLS)

MoSFRR ...... Foundation for Reformation Research, St. Louis, MO [*Library symbol Library of Congress Obsolete*] (LCLS)

MoSGS .... Church of Jesus Christ of Latter-Day Saints, Genealogical Society Library, St. Louis Branch, St. Louis, MO [*Library symbol Library of Congress*] (LCLS)

Mosh .... Moshav [*or Moshava*] (BJA)

MoSHi .... Missouri Historical Society, St. Louis, MO [*Library symbol Library of Congress*] (LCLS)

MoSHS .... Harris-Stowe State College Library, St. Louis, MO [*Library symbol*] [*Library of Congress*] (LCLS)

MoSHT........ Harris Teachers College, St. Louis, MO [*Library symbol Library of Congress*] (LCLS)

MOSI .... Mosinee Paper [*NASDAQ symbol*] (TTSB)

MOSI .... Mosinee Paper Corp. [*NASDAQ symbol*] (NQ)

mosic.......... Metal-Oxide-Semiconductor Integrated Circuit (AD)

MOSID .... Ministry of Supply Inspection Department [*British*] (AD)

MoSIG .... International Graduate School, St. Louis, MO [*Library symbol Library of Congress*] (LCLS)

Mosine .... Mosinee Paper Co. [*Associated Press*] (SAG)

MoSIO .... International Library, Archives, and Museum of Optometry, St. Louis, MO [*Library symbol Library of Congress*] (LCLS)

MoSIP.......... Missouri Institute of Psychiatry, St. Louis, MO [*Library symbol Library of Congress*] (LCLS)

MOSIS .... MOS Implementation Service (NITA)

Mosk.......... Moscovici (AD)

Mosk.......... Moscowitz (AD)

Mosk.......... Moskowitz (AD)

MoSL .... Law Library Association of St. Louis, St. Louis, MO [*Library symbol Library of Congress*] (LCLS)

MOSLS .... Military Occupational Specialty Level System

MOS/LSI ...... Metal Oxide Silicon/Large Scale Integration [*Electronics*]

MOSM .... Metal-Oxide Semimetal (IEEE)

mOsm.......... Milliosmol [*or Milliosmole*] [*Chemistry*]

mosm .... Milliosmol (AD)

MOSM .... Mission Operations System Manager [*NASA*]

MoSM .... St. Louis Mercantile Library Association, St. Louis, MO [*Library symbol Library of Congress*] (LCLS)

MoSMa........ Maryville College, St. Louis, MO [*Library symbol Library of Congress*] (LCLS)

MoSMal ...... Mallinckrodt Chemical Works [*Later, Mallinckrodt, Inc.*], St. Louis, MO [*Library symbol Library of Congress*] (LCLS)

Mos Man ..... Moses on the Law of Mandamus [*A publication*] (DLA)

MoSMc........ McDonnell Douglas Corp., Corporate Library, St. Louis, MO [*Library symbol Library of Congress*] (LCLS)

MoSMcA ...... McDonnell Douglas Automation Co., St. Louis, MO [*Library symbol Library of Congress*] (LCLS)

MoSMed ...... St. Louis Medical Society, St. Louis, MO [*Library symbol Library of Congress*] (LCLS)

mOsmol .... Milliosmole [*Measurement*] (DAVI)

MoSMon ...... Monsanto Chemical Co., St. Louis, MO [*Library symbol Library of Congress*] (LCLS)

MOSNAG...... Mossine Nagant Rifle

MOSOP........ Missouri Sexual Offender Program (AD)

MOSOP........ Movement for the Survival of Ogoni People

MOSOP........ Movement for the Survival of the Ogoni People

MOSP .... Master Ordnance Systems Pattern File [*Navy*]

MOSP .... Medical and Osteopathic Scholarship Program (DNAB)

MoSp .... Public Libraries of Springfield and Greene County, Springfield, MO [*Library symbol Library of Congress*] (LCLS)

MoSpA.......... Assemblies of God Graduate School, Springfield, MO [*Library symbol Library of Congress*] (LCLS)

MoSpBB ...... Baptist Bible College, Springfield, MO [*Library symbol Library of Congress*] (LCLS)

MoSpCB ...... Central Bible College, Springfield, MO [*Library symbol Library of Congress*] (LCLS)

MoSpD .... Drury College, Springfield, MO [*Library symbol Library of Congress*] (LCLS)

MoSPD .... St. Louis Post-Dispatch, St. Louis, MO [*Library symbol Library of Congress*] (LCLS)

MoSpDC ...... Drury College, Springfield, MO [*Library symbol*] [*Library of Congress*] (LCLS)

MoSpE .... Evangel College, Springfield, MO [*Library symbol Library of Congress*] (LCLS)

MoSPI.......... Pet, Inc., St. Louis, MO [*Library symbol*] [*Library of Congress*] (LCLS)

MOSPO........ Mobile Satellite Photometric Observatory [*NASA*] (NASA)

MOS Poland... Ministerstwo Opieki Spotecznes [*Ministry of Social Welfare*] [*Poland*] (AD)

MOSPOR...... Movement for the Struggle for Political Rights [*Uganda*] (PD)

MoSpS.......... Southwest Missouri State College, Springfield, MO [*Library symbol Library of Congress*] (LCLS)

MoSPS.......... St. Louis Priory School, St. Louis, MO [*Library symbol Library of Congress*] (LCLS)

MoSPSc........ Saint Louis Priory School, St. Louis, MO [*Library symbol*] [*Library of Congress*] (LCLS)

MoSR.......... City Art Museum of St. Louis, St. Louis, MO [*Library symbol Library of Congress*] (LCLS)

MoSR.......... Saint Louis Art Museum, Richardson Memorial Library, St. Louis, MO [*Library symbol*] [*Library of Congress*] (LCLS)

MOSRAM...... Metal-Oxide Semiconductor Random-Access Memory (EECA)

MOSRD........ Motor Machinist's Mate, Ship Repair, Diesel Engineering Mechanic [*Navy rating*]

MOSRG........ Motor Machinist's Mate, Ship Repair, Gasoline Engine Mechanic [*Navy rating*]

MOS ROM ... Metal-Oxide Semiconductor Read-Only Memory (MHDB)

MOSROM...... Metal-Oxide-Silicon Read-Only Memory (IDOE)

MOSS .... Maintenance-Operations Support Set (AFM)

moss.......... Maintenance-Operations Support Set (AD)

MOSS ,........ Management and Organisation in Secondary Schools (AIE)

MOSS .... Manned Orbital Space Station [*or System*] [*See also MOD, MODS, MTSS Air Force/NASA*]

MOSS .... Market Opening Sector Specific (AD)

MOSS .... Market-Oriented, Sector-Selective [*or Specific*] [*Trade negotiations between United States and Japan*]

MOSS .... Market Oversight Surveillance System

MOSS .... Middle-Aged, Overstressed, Semiaffluent Suburbanite [*Lifestyle classification*]

MOSS .... Military Orbital Space System [*See also MOD, MODS, MTSS*] [*Air Force/NASA*]

MOSS .... Military Overseas Shelter Survey [*Civil Defense*]

MOSS .... Mobile Submarine Simulator (NVT)

MOSS .... Mobility Support Set [*or System*] [*for aircraft*] (MCD)

MOSS .... Modelling Systems [*Moss Systems Ltd.*] [*Software package*] (NCC)

MOSS .... Monitor Output Signal Strength

MOSS .... Mothers of Sons in Service [*World War II*]

MOSS .... Mutually Owned Society for Songwriters

MOSSA ...... Northern Rhodesia Mine Officials and Salaried Staff Association

Mossies...... Middle-Aged, Overstressed Semiaffluent Suburbanites [*Lifestyle Classification*]

Mossimo...... Mossimo, Inc. [*Associated Press*] (SAG)

MoSSJ .... St. John Cantius Seminary, St. Louis, MO [*Library symbol Library of Congress*] (LCLS)

MOSS MOUSE... Maneuver, Objective, Security, Surprise, Mass, Offensive, Unity of Command, Simplicity, Economy of Force [*Basic principles of war*] [*See also MOOSEMUSS*] (MCD)

MOSSRS ...... Management Order Ship Status Reporting System (MCD)

MOSST ...... Ministry of State for Science and Technology [*Canada*]

MOST.......... Management Operation System Technique

MOST .... Manned Orbital Solar Telescope

MOST .... Mass Optical Storage Technologies [*Computer science*]

MOST .... Metal-Oxide-Semiconductor Transistor

most .... Metal-Oxide Semiconductor Transistor (AD)

MOST .... Metal-Oxide-Silicon Transistor (IDOE)

MOST .... Michigan Opportunities and Skills Training (AD)

MOST .... Mission Oriented System Tape [*Military*] (CAAL)

MOST .... Mobile Optical Surveillance Tracker

MOST .... Mobile Oversnow Transport

MOST .... Mobile SONAR Technology [*Marine science*] (MSC)

MOST .... Modified OECD [*Organization for Economic Cooperation and Development*] Screening Test [*Biodegradability Test*]

MOST .... Molonglo Observatory Synthesis Telescope

MOST .... Mothers of Super Twins [*Military*]

MOST .... Motorcycle Operator Skill Test

MOST .... Multipulse Observation Sizing Technique [*Southwest Research Institute*]

MOSTA ...... Midwest Old Settlers and Threshers Association (EA)

MOSTAB .... Modular Stability [*Derivative program*]

MO St Ann... Missouri Statutes, Annotated [*A publication*] (DLA)

MoStc .... St. Charles City-County Library, St. Charles, MO [*Library symbol Library of Congress*] (LCLS)

MoStcL .... Lindenwood College, St. Charles, MO [*Library symbol Library of Congress*] (LCLS)

Mostell .... Mostellaria [*of Plautus*] [*Classical studies*] (OCD)

MoStgA........ Sainte Genevieve Archives, Sainte Genevieve County Court, Ste. Genevieve, MO [*Library symbol Library of Congress*] (LCLS)

MoStj .... St. Joseph Public Library, St. Joseph, MO [*Library symbol Library of Congress*] (LCLS)

MoStjM........ Methodist Medical Center, St. Joseph, MO [*Library symbol Library of Congress*] (LCLS)

MoStjMW ... Missouri Western State College, St. Joseph, MO [*Library symbol Library of Congress*] (LCLS)

MoStjS.......... St. Joseph State Hospital, St. Joseph, MO [*Library symbol Library of Congress*] (LCLS)

MOSTL........ Metal-Oxide-Semiconductor Transistor Logic (CET)

mostl .... Metal-Oxide Semiconductor Transistor Logic (AD)

MOST/TDIS... Mobile SONAR Technology/Technical Document Information System [*Marine science*] (MSC)

MOSU .... Mobile Ordnance Service Unit

MoSU.......... St. Louis University, St. Louis, MO [*Library symbol Library of Congress*] (LCLS)

MoSU-C ...... St. Louis University, School of Commerce and Finance, St. Louis, MO [*Library symbol Library of Congress*] (LCLS)

MoSU-D ...... St. Louis University, School of Divinity, St. Louis, MO [*Library symbol Library of Congress*] (LCLS)

MoSUE .... Union Electric Co., St. Louis, MO [*Library symbol Library of Congress*] (LCLS)

MoSU-L ...... St. Louis University, School of Law, St. Louis, MO [*Library symbol Library of Congress*] (LCLS)

MoSU-M ...... St. Louis University, School of Medicine, St. Louis, MO [*Library symbol Library of Congress*] (LCLS)

MoSU-P ...... St. Louis University, School of Philosophy, St. Louis, MO [*Library symbol Library of Congress*] (LCLS)

MOSUPPU ... Mobile Support Unit (DNAB)

MoSV.......... Catholic Central Union of America, St. Louis, MO [*Library symbol Library of Congress*] (LCLS)

MoSVA.......... United States Veterans Administration Hospital, St. Louis, MO [*Library symbol Library of Congress*] (LCLS)

MoSW.......... Washington University, St. Louis, MO [*Library symbol Library of Congress*] (LCLS)

MoSW-D	Washington University, School of Dentistry, St. Louis, MO [*Library symbol Library of Congress*] (LCLS)
MoSW-F	Washington University, School of Fine Arts, St. Louis, MO [*Library symbol Library of Congress*] (LCLS)
MoSW-L	Washington University, School of Law, St. Louis, MO [*Library symbol Library of Congress*] (LCLS)
MoSW-M	Washington University, Medical School, St. Louis, MO [*Library symbol Library of Congress*] (LCLS)
MOSZ..........	Massive Offshore Surf Zone
MOT............	Aeromonterrey SA [*Mexico ICAO designator*] (FAAC)
MOT............	Magneto-Optical Trap [*Physics*]
MOT............	Management of Technology
MOT............	Manned Orbital Telescope [*NASA*]
MOT............	Manufacturing Operation and Tooling
MOT............	[*The*] March of Time [*Radio and motion picture series*]
MOT............	Marine Oil Transportation [*AAR code*]
MOT............	Mark on Top (NVT)
MOT............	Master of Occupational Therapy (GAGS)
MOT............	Master Operability Test (CAAL)
MOT............	Maximum Operating Time (NG)
MOT............	McDonald Observatory [*Texas*] [*Seismograph station code, US Geological Survey*] (SEIS)
MOT............	Mean Operating Time
mot............	Mean Operating Time (AD)
MOT............	Means of Testing [*Telecommunications*] (OSI)
MOT............	Mechanical Operability Test
mot............	Mechanical Operability Test (AD)
MOT............	Medial Olfactory Tract [*Anatomy*]
MOT............	Member of Our Tribe [*Jewish slang*]
mot............	Member of Our Tribe (AD)
MOT............	Men of the Trees [*Australia An association*]
MOT............	Method of Testing (MCD)
mot............	Middle of Target (AD)
MOT............	Military Ocean Terminal (AABC)
MOT............	Mineral-Oil Tolerance [*of resin solutions*]
M o T..........	Minister of Transport [*British*] (AD)
MOT............	Ministry of Tourism [*Philippines*] (DS)
MOT............	Ministry of Transport [*British or Canadian*]
MOT............	Minot [*North Dakota*] [*Airport symbol*] (OAG)
MOT............	Missile Operability Test (MCD)
MOT............	Molecular-Orbital Theory [*Physical chemistry*]
MOT............	Monalta Resources, Inc. [*Vancouver Stock Exchange symbol*]
MOT............	Month of Travel [*Military*]
MOT............	Motion
MOT............	Motor (AAG)
mot............	Motor (AD)
MOT............	Motor
MOT............	Motorized
MOT............	Motorola, Inc. [*NYSE symbol*] (SPSG)
MOT............	Motor Operating Time
MOT............	Mouse Operating Table [*Research instrumentation*]
MOT............	Murine Ovarian Teratocarcinoma [*Animal pathology*]
MOT............	Tarkio College, Tarkio, MO [*OCLC symbol*] (OCLC)
MOTA..........	Mail Order Traders Association (MHDB)
MOTA..........	Materials Open-Test Assembly [*Nuclear energy*] (NRCH)
MOTA..........	Michigan Ohio Telecommunications Association (TSSD)
MOTA..........	Mid-Ocean Target Array (AAG)
MOTA..........	Museum of Temporary Art [*Washington, DC*]
MoTaC	Tarkio College, Tarkio, MO [*Library symbol Library of Congress*] (LCLS)
MOTACC	Manufacturers of Telescoping and Articulating Cranes Council (EA)
MOT & E......	Multinational Operational Test and Evaluation
MOTAR	Modular Thermal Analyzer Routine [*Computer science*]
MOTARDES...	Moving Target Detection System (IEEE)
MOTARDIV...	Mobile Target Division [*Mine Force*] [*Navy*]
MOTARDS....	Moving Target Detection System
MOTAS	Member of the Appropriate Sex (NHD)
MOTAT........	Museum of Transport and Technology (AD)
MOTAT........	Museum of Transport and Technology (NADA)
MOTBA	Military Ocean Terminal, Bay Area [*Oakland, CA*] (AABC)
MOTBY	Military Ocean Terminal, Bayonne (AABC)
MOTC..........	Ministry of Transit and Communications [*Philippines*] (AD)
MOTC..........	Montreal Tramways [*AAR code*]
MotClb	Motor Club of America [*Associated Press*] (SAG)
MOTCP	Ministry of Town and Country Planning [*British*] (DAS)
M o TCP	Ministry of Town and Country Planning [*British*] (AD)
MOTE..........	Measure of Training Effectiveness [*Military*]
MOTECS	Mobile Tactical Exercise Control System (DNAB)
MOTEL.........	Motor Hotel
MOTESZ......	Magyar Orvostudomanyi Tarsasagok Szovetsege [*Federation of Hungarian Medical Societies*] (EAIO)
MOTET........	Mother Tongue and English Teaching (AIE)
MOTF..........	Manganese Oxide Thin Film
MOTG	Marine Operations Training Group
MOTG	Morally Obliged to Go [*British Slang*]
moth...........	Mother (AD)
moth-in-law...	Mother-in-Law (AD)
Moth Jones...	Mother Jones [*A publication*] (BRI)
MothrWk......	Mothers Work, Inc. [*Associated Press*] (SAG)
MOTI...........	Message Oriented Text Interchange [*Telecommunications*] (OSI)
MOTIF.........	Maui Optical Tracking and Identification Facility [*Hawaii*] [*Air Force*]
MOTIS	Message Oriented Text Interchange System [*Telecommunications*] (OSI)
MOTIS	Missile on Stand Timing Simulator (MCD)
MOTIS	MOS Timing Simulator Software (NITA)
MOTKI	Military Ocean Terminal, King's Bay (AABC)
MOTN	Motion
MOTNAC	Manual of Tumor Nomenclature [*Medicine*] (DHSM)
MOTNE	Meteorological Operational Telecommunications Network Europe
MOTNEG	Meteorological Operational Telecommunications Network in Europe, Regional Planning Group [*ICAO*] (PDAA)
MOTO	Moto Photo [*NQS*] (TTSB)
MOTO	Moto Photo, Inc. [*NASDAQ symbol*] (NQ)
motoboard ...	Motorized Skateboard (AD)
motocross....	Motorcycle Cross Country Race (AD)
MOTOGAS....	Motor Gasoline [*Military*]
mot op........	Motor Operated (AD)
MotoPh........	Moto Photo, Inc. [*Associated Press*] (SAG)
MOTOR	Mobile Oriented Triangulation of Reentry
MOTOR	Monthly Throughput Observation Report (DNAB)
motorcade....	Motorized-Vehicle Parade (AD)
motorcross...	Motorcycle Cross (AD)
MOTOREDE..	Movement to Restore Decency [*Group opposing sex education in schools*]
Motorola......	Motorola, Inc. [*Associated Press*] (SAG)
MOTORWAY...	Motorway [*Commonly used*] (OPSA)
MOTOS	Member of the Opposite Sex [*Electronic mail language*]
MOTP..........	Manufacturing or Testing Process (KSC)
MOTP..........	Medical Officer Training Plan [*Canada*]
MOTPICT	Motion Picture
MoTr...........	Grundy County-Jewett Norris Library, Trenton, MO [*Library symbol Library of Congress*] (LCLS)
MOTR	Moto Club of Amer [*NASDAQ symbol*] (TTSB)
MOTR	Motor Club of America [*NASDAQ symbol*] (NQ)
MOTR	Multiple Object-Tracking RADAR (MCD)
MotrPrt	Motorcar Parts & Accessories, Inc. [*Associated Press*] (SAG)
MOTS	Mend Our Tongues Society (EA)
MOTS	Metal Oxide Threshold Switches (MCD)
MOTS	Minitrack Optical Tracking Station [*or System*] [*NASA*]
mots	Minitrack Optical Tracking System (AD)
MOTS	Missile Operability Test Station (MCD)
MOTS	Mobile Optical Tracking System
MOTS	Module Test Set
MOTSS	Member of the Same Sex [*Electronic mail language*]
MOTSU	Military Ocean Terminal, Sunny Point (AABC)
MOTT	Mycobacteria Other Than Tubercle Bacilli
MOTU	Mobile Operational Training Unit (MCD)
MOTU	Mobile Optical Tracking Unit (MCD)
MOTU	Mobile Ordnance Technical Unit [*Military*] (CAAL)
MOTU	Mobile Technical Unit (NG)
MOTUDET....	Mobile Ordnance Technical Unit Detachment (DNAB)
MOTV..........	Manned Orbit Transfer Vehicle (MCD)
MOU	Maximum Oxygen Uptake
MOU	Memorandum of Understanding
mou	Memorandum of Understanding (AD)
MoU	Memorandum of Understanding (AD)
mou	Missouri [*MARC country of publication code Library of Congress*] (LCCP)
MOU	Mountain Village [*Alaska*] [*Airport symbol*] (OAG)
Mou	Mouse [*Computer science*] (PCM)
MOU	Southwest Missouri State University, Springfield, MO [*OCLC symbol*] (OCLC)
MoU	University of Missouri, Columbia, MO [*Library symbol Library of Congress*] (LCLS)
MoU-D	University of Missouri, School of Dentistry, Kansas City, MO [*Library symbol Library of Congress*] (LCLS)
MOUG	Map Online Users Group (EA)
MOUG	Maryland Online User Group (NITA)
Moult Ch......	Moulton's New York Chancery Practice [*A publication*] (DLA)
Moult Ch P...	Moulton's New York Chancery Practice [*A publication*] (DLA)
MoU-M	University of Missouri, Medical Library, Kansas City, MO [*Library symbol Library of Congress*] (LCLS)
MOUND........	Mound Plant [*Department of Energy*] [*Miamisburg, OH*] (GAAI)
MOUNT........	Mount [*Commonly used*] (OPSA)
MOUNTAIN...	Mountain [*Commonly used*] (OPSA)
MOUNTAINS...	Mountains [*Commonly used*] (OPSA)
Mountbtn	Mountbatten, Inc. [*Associated Press*] (SAG)
MOUNTIN	Mountain [*Commonly used*] (OPSA)
MountPr.......	Mountain Province Mining, Inc. [*Associated Press*] (SAG)
MOURAD	Mouvement pour la Renovation et l'Action Democratique [*The Comoros*] [*Political party*] (EY)
MOUS	Multiple Occurrences of Unexplained Symptoms [*Medicine*]
MOUSE	Manager Owner User Systems Engineer (OA)
MOUSE	Minimum Orbital Unmanned Satellite (AD)
MOUSE	Minimum Orbital Unmanned Satellite of the Earth
MOUSS	Management and Operation of User Services Section
MoU-St	University of Missouri at St. Louis, St. Louis, MO [*Library symbol Library of Congress*] (LCLS)
MOUT	Military Operations on Urbanized Terrain (MCD)
MOUTH	Modular Output Unit for Talking to Humans
MOUTRE	Mission Oriented Unit Training by Echelon [*Military*] (INF)
MoU-V	University of Missouri, Veterinary Medicine Library, Columbia, MO [*Library symbol Library of Congress*] (LCLS)
mov	Apple QuickTime [*Computer science*]
MOV............	Main Oxidizer Valve (KSC)
MOV............	Manned Orbiting Vehicle [*NASA*]
MOV............	Manuscript on Vellum
MOV............	Mass of Vehicle
MOV............	Materiel Obligation Validation (AFIT)
MOV............	Metal-Oxide Varistor

MOV............ Method of Validation
MOV............ Military-Owned Vehicle
MOV............ Monclova, MX [*Location identifier FAA*] (FAAL)
MOV............ Monument Valley, UT [*Location identifier FAA*] (FAAL)
MOV............ Moranbah [*Australia Airport symbol*] (OAG)
MOV............ Morovis [*Puerto Rico*] [*Seismograph station code, US Geological Survey*] (SEIS)
MOV............ Moshassuck Valley Railroad Co. [*AAR code*]
MOV............ Motor-Operated Valve (NRCH)
MOV............ Movable [*Technical drawings*]
mov .... Movable (AD)
MOV............ Movement (AABC)
MOV............ Movie
mov .... Movimento [*Movement*] [*Italian*] (AD)
mov .... Multiple-Orifice Valve (AD)
MOV............ Stephens College, Columbia, MO [*OCLC symbol*] (OCLC)
MOVA .... Microprocessor Optimized Vehicle Actuation
MOVA .... Movado Group [*NASDAQ symbol*] (TTSB)
MOVA .... Movado Group, Inc. [*NASDAQ symbol*] (SAG)
Movado........ Movado Group, Inc. [*Associated Press*] (SAG)
M-OVAL........ Macrovalocytes [*Microbiology*] (DAVI)
MOVCO .... Movement Control Organisation [*British military*] (DMA)
MOVCORD ... Movement Coordinator
MOVDHHG... Movement of Dependents and Household Goods in Advance of Permanent Change of Station Orders is Authorized [*Army*] (AABC)
MOVE.......... Cinema Ride [*NASDAQ symbol*] (SAG)
MOVE.......... Cinema Ride Inc. [*NASDAQ symbol*] (TTSB)
MOVE.......... Management of Value Engineering
MOVE.......... Manage Old Vehicles Easily [*Performance Data Services, Inc.*] [*Software*]
MOVE.......... Moving
MOVE.......... Multiple Occupancy Vehicles (DICI)
MOVECAP .... Movement Capabilities [*Military*] (CINC)
MOVEM........ Movement Overseas Verification of Enlisted Members [*Army*] (AABC)
movem .... Movement Overseas Verification of Enlisted Members (AD)
moverep ...... Movement Report (AD)
MOVEREP ... Movement Report [*Military*] (NATG)
Move Short Soc... Movement Shorthand Society (AD)
MOVEW .... Cinema Ride Wrrt [*NASDAQ symbol*] (TTSB)
movi .... Movie (AD)
MOVI .... Movie Gallery [*NASDAQ symbol*] (TTSB)
MOVI .... Movie Gallery, Inc. [*NASDAQ symbol*] (SAG)
MovieFn ...... MovieFone, Inc. [*Associated Press*] (SAG)
MovieGal .... Move Gallery, Inc. [*Associated Press*] (SAG)
MovieGal .... Movie Gallery, Inc. [*Associated Press*] (SAG)
MovieStr ..... Movie Star, Inc. [*Associated Press*] (SAG)
MOVIMS ...... Motor Vehicle Information Management System [*Bell System*]
MOVLAS ...... Manually Operated Visual Landing Aid System (NG)
MOVMT........ Movement
MOVORD ..... Movement Order [*Military*] (NVT)
movord .... Movement Order (AD)
MOVP .... Military-Owned Vehicle Plan (AFM)
MO-VPE....... Metal-Organic Vapor Phase Epitaxy [*Also, MO-CVD, OM-CVD, OM-VPE*] [*Semiconductor technology*]
MOVPER...... Supreme Council, Mystic Order Veiled Prophets of Enchanted Realm (EA)
MOVREP...... Movement Report [*Military*] (NVT)
MOVS .... Manual Overseas Visa System
MOVS .... Military-Owned Vehicle Service (AABC)
MOVT.......... Movement [*Music*] (ROG)
MOW .... Catskill Airways, Inc. [*FAA designator*] (FAAC)
MOW .... Meals on Wheels
M o W .... Minister of Works [*British*] (AD)
MOW .... Ministry of Works [*British*] (MCD)
MOW .... Mission Operation Wing [*NASA*] (KSC)
MOW .... Mohawk Airlines [*ICAO designator*] (FAAC)
MOW .... Montana Western Railway [*AAR code*]
MOW .... Moscow [*Former USSR Airport symbol*] (OAG)
MOW .... Movement for the Ordination of Women [*British lobbying group*] (ECON)
MOW .... Movie of the Week [*Television programming*]
MOW .... Westminster College, Fulton, MO [*OCLC symbol*] (OCLC)
MOWA .... Meals-on-Wheels America [*An association*]
MOWAM ...... Mobile Water Mine (MCD)
MoWarbT.... Central Missouri State University, Warrensburg, MO [*Library symbol Library of Congress*] (LCLS)
MoWarbTR... Trails Regional Library, Johnson County-Lafayette County Library, Warrensburg, MO [*Library symbol Library of Congress*] (LCLS)
MOWASP..... Mechanization of Warehousing and Shipment Procedures [*or Processing*] [*Defense Supply Agency*]
mowasp....... Mechanization of Warehousing and Shipment Processing (AD)
MOWB .... Ministry of Works and Buildings [*British*]
MOWBC ...... Winnipeg Bible College, Otterburne, Manitoba [*Library symbol National Library of Canada*] (NLC)
MoWD .... Ministry of Works and Development [*British*] (AD)
MoWgK....... Saint Louis Roman Catholic Theological [*Kenrick*] Seminary, Webster Groves, MO [*Library symbol Library of Congress*] (LCLS)
MoWgT........ Eden Theological Seminary, Webster Groves, MO [*Library symbol Library of Congress*] (LCLS)
MoWgW....... Webster College, Webster Groves, MO [*Library symbol Library of Congress*] (LCLS)
MoWhAF...... United States Air Force, Whiteman Air Force Base Library, Whiteman AFB, MO [*Library symbol*] [*Library of Congress*] (LCLS)

MoWitt......... Mobile Window Thermal Test Facility [*Berkeley, CA*] [*Lawrence Berkeley Laboratory*] [*Department of Energy*] (GRD)
Mo W Jur .... Monthly Western Jurist [*A publication*] (DLA)
MOWOG...... Morris Wolseley Group [*Automobile manufacturing organization*]
MOWOS...... Meteorological Office Weather Observing System (PDAA)
MOWS .... Manned Orbital Weapon Station [*or System*]
Mow St........ Mowbray's Styles of Deeds [*A publication*] (DLA)
M o WT .... Minister of War Transport [*British*] (AD)
MOWT .... Ministry of War Transport [*Terminated, 1956*] [*British*]
MOWW .... Military Order of the World Wars (EA)
MOX........... Manually-Operated Changeover [*Computer science*]
MOX........... Mars Oxident Experiment [*NASA*]
MOX........... Mixed Oxide [*Fuel*]
mox .... Mixed Oxides (AD)
MOX........... Morris, MN [*Location identifier FAA*] (FAAL)
MOX........... Moxa [*German Democratic Republic*] [*Seismograph station code, US Geological Survey*] (SEIS)
MOX........... Moxalactam [*An antibiotic*]
mox .... Oxidized Metal Explosive (AD)
MOXB .... Moxham Bank [*NASDAQ symbol*] (TTSB)
MOXB .... Moxham Bank Corp. [*NASDAQ symbol*] (SAG)
Moxham ...... Moxham Bank Corp. [*Associated Press*] (SAG)
MOXIE .... Men Organized to X-press Indignant Exasperation [*Seattle group opposing below-the-knee fashions introduced in 1970*]
MOXY .... McMoRan Oil & Gas [*NASDAQ symbol*] (TTSB)
MOXY .... McMoRan Oil and Gas Co. [*NASDAQ symbol*] (SAG)
MOXY .... Model X-Y [*AEC computer code*]
MOY........... Mahogany Minerals [*Vancouver Stock Exchange symbol*]
MOY........... Mondy [*Former USSR Seismograph station code, US Geological Survey*] (SEIS)
MOY........... Money
moy .... Money (AD)
MOY........... Monterrey [*Colombia*] [*Airport symbol*] (AD)
MOY........... Salt Lake City, UT [*Location identifier FAA*] (FAAL)
MOYC .... Moyco Technologies [*NASDAQ symbol*] (TTSB)
MOYC .... Moyco Technologies, Inc. [*NASDAQ symbol*] (SAG)
MoycoT....... Moyco Technologies, Inc. [*Associated Press*] (SAG)
Moyle .... Moyle's Criminal Circulars [*India*] [*A publication*] (DLA)
Moyle .... Moyle's Entries [*1658*] [*England*] [*A publication*] (DLA)
MOZ........... Aerocharter GmbH [*Austria ICAO designator*] (FAAC)
MOZ........... Mezhdunarodnaya Organizacia Zhurnalistov [*International Organization of Journalists*] [*Russian*]
MOZ........... Missouri Southern State College, Library, Joplin, MO [*OCLC symbol*] (OCLC)
MOZ........... Moorea Island [*French Polynesia*] [*Airport symbol*] (OAG)
MOZ........... Mozambique [*ANSI three-letter standard code*] (CNC)
Moz........... Mozambique (AD)
Mozam .... Mozambique (AD)
Moz & W..... Mozley and Whiteley's Law Dictionary [*A publication*] (DLA)
Moz Cur...... Mozambique Current (AD)
MOZL......... Military Order of the Zouave Legion of the United States (EA)
Mozley & W... Mozley and Whiteley's Law Dictionary [*A publication*] (DLA)
Mozley & Whiteley... Mozley and Whiteley's Law Dictionary [*A publication*] (DLA)
MOZLUS..... Military Order of the Zouave Legion of the US (EA)
mozza .... Mozzarella (AD)
MP............. All India Reporter, Madhya Pradesh [*A publication*] (DLA)
MP............. Atlantis Airlines [*ICAO designator*] (AD)
Mp............. Import [*Economics*]
MP............. Machine Pistol [*Military*] (IIA)
MP............. Machine Pressed
MP............. Macroprocessor
MP............. Madonna Plan (EA)
MP............. Magnetic Particle
M o WT .... Magnetic Pressure (NVT)
MP............. Magnetopause [*In a magnetic field*]
MP............. Magnifying Power (IIA)
M/P........... Mail Payment [*Banking*]
mp .... Mail Payment (AD)
M/P........... Main Parachute (MCD)
MP............. Main Phase (IEEE)
MP............. Main Propulsion (DNAB)
MP............. Mains Propres [*Personal Delivery*] [*French*]
MP............. Maintainability Plan
MP............. Maintenance Panel (AAG)
mp .... Maintenance Part (AD)
MP............. Maintenance Period
MP............. Maintenance Plan
MP............. Maintenance Point
MP............. Maintenance Prints
MP............. Maintenance Procedure (MCD)
MP............. Maintenance Program
MP............. Major Program (CAAL)
MP............. Mallinckrodt, Inc. [*Research code symbol*]
MP............. Management Package (NASA)
MP............. Management Plan
MP............. Managing Printer [*A publication*] (DGA)
MP............. Manifold Pressure
mp .... Manifold Pressure (AD)
MP............. Manpower
MP............. Manpower and Personnel (MCD)
MP............. Mansfield Park [*Novel by Jane Austen*]
MP............. Manual Proportional [*Attitude control system of Mercury spacecraft*]
MP............. Manual Pulser
MP............. Manufacturing Process
MP............. Manu Propria [*In documents, after king's signature*] [*Italian*]

MP	Marbled Paper (DGA)
MP	Marching Pack (DNAB)
MP	Marginal Physical Product [Economics]
MP	Marginal Product
MP	Marine Police
MP	Marine Pollution
MP	Marine Provost [British military] (DMA)
MP	Maritime Patrol (NATG)
MP	Maritime Polar Air Mass
MP	Maritime Policy [British] (ROG)
MP	Market Price [Business term]
MP	Marshall's Posse (EA)
MP	Maschinenpistole [Submachine Gun] [German] (AD)
MP	Massa Pilularum [A Pill Mass] [Pharmacy] (ROG)
MP	Massorah Parva [or Massora Parva] (BJA)
MP	Mass Properties (MCD)
MP	Master of Painting
MP	Master of Pharmacy (GAGS)
MP	Master of Planning (GAGS)
MP	Master Pointer [Computer science] (BYTE)
MP	Master Printer (DGA)
MP	Master Printers Annual [A publication] (DGA)
MP	Match Problems [Research test] [Psychology]
MP	Material Pass (AAG)
MP	Material Professional [Army]
MP	Mathematical Programming [Computer science]
MP	Matthew Pelosi [Designer's mark when appearing on US coins]
MP	Maturity Phase
MP	Maxillary Process
MP	Maximum Flowering Period [Botany]
M/P	Maximum Performance [Automotive engineering]
MP	Mean Pressure (MAE)
MP	Measurement Pipette
MP	Measurement Pragmatic [Computer science] (OA)
MP	Measuring Point (NASA)
MP	Mechanical Paper
MP	Mechanical Part
MP	Mechanical Printer
MP	Medial Pallium [Neuroanatomy]
MP	Media Processor [Computer science] (BUR)
MP	Media Project (EA)
MP	Medical Payment [Insurance]
MP	Medium Pressure
mp	Medium Pressure (AD)
mp	Meeting Point (AD)
MP	Meeting Point [Military]
MP	Melchor Developments Ltd. [Toronto Stock Exchange symbol]
MP	Melphalan, Prednisone [Antineoplastic drug regimen]
MP	Melphalan, Prednisone [Antineoplastic drug] (CDI)
mp	Melting Point (AD)
MP	Melting Point
MP	Melting Pot
MP	Member of Parliament [British]
MP	Member of Police
MP	Membrane Production (SSD)
M/P	Memorandum of Partnership [Business term]
MP	Menstrual Period [Medicine]
MP	Mental Process [Work-factor system]
MP	Mentum Posterior [In reference to the chin]
MP	Mercaptopurine [Purinethol] [Also, M, P Antineoplastic drug]
MP	Mercator's Projection (BARN)
MP	Meridional Part [Navigation]
MP	Mesiopulpal [Dentistry]
MP	Message Processor
MP	Metacarpophalangeal [Anatomy]
M-P	Metal or Plastic (AAG)
m-p	Metal-Point (AD)
MP	Metal-Powder [Videotape]
MP	Metatarsophalangeal [Anatomy]
MP	Meteorology Panel (MCD)
MP	Methodist Protestant
MP	Methoxypsoralen [Also, MOP] [Pharmacology]
MP	Methyl Palmoxirate [Organic chemistry]
MP	Methyl Parathion [Also, MEP, MPN] [Pesticide]
MP	Methylphenidate [Central Nervous system stimulant]
MP	Methylprednisolone [Endocrinology]
MP	Methylprednisolone Sodium Succinate [Medicine] (DAVI)
MP	Methylpurine [Organic chemistry]
MP	Metra Potential (NITA)
MP	Metropolitan Police
MP	Mexican Peso [Monetary unit]
MP	Mezzo Piano [Moderately Soft] [Music]
mp	Mezzo-Piano [Moderately Soft] [Italian] (AD)
MP	Michoud Plant [NASA] (MCD)
M(P)	Microfilm (Positive)
MP	Micronized Progesterone
MP	Micronized Progesterone [A natural hormone]
MP	Microprint
MP	Microprocessor [Instrumentation]
MP	Microprogram
MP	Middle phalanx [Anatomy] (DAVI)
MP	Middle Point
MP	Midland Plant [Nuclear energy] (NRCH)
MP	Midline Precursor [Cytology]
MP	Mid-Phase
MP	Mile-Post
mp	Milepost (AD)
MP	Military Pay (AFM)
MP	Military Police [Army]
MP	Military Prohibitionist [Slang]
MP	Military Property (MCD)
M/P	Milk/Plasma [Ratio] [Physiology]
m/p	Milk Powder (AD)
mp	Mille Pasuum [Thousand Paces] [Latin] (AD)
MP	Millia Passuum [1,000 Paces; the Roman mile]
MP	Minimum Phase (IEEE)
MP	Minimum Premium [Insurance]
MP	Mining Permit (AD)
MP	[The] Mini Page [A newspaper supplement]
MP	Minister Plenipotentiary
MP	Minister Provincial (AD)
MP	Minuteman Platform
MP	Minutes Played [Hockey]
MP	Miscellaneous Paper [or Publication]
MP	Miscellaneous Proposal (AD)
MP	Missile Platform
MP	Missile Positioning
MP	Missile Possessed (SAA)
MP	Missing Perforation [Philately]
MP	Missing Person
MP	Mission Payload (MCD)
MP	Mission Planner (MCD)
MP	Mission Profile (MCD)
MP	Mississippi Power Co. [NYSE symbol] (SPSG)
MP	Missouri Pacific Railroad Co. [AAR code]
MP	Mistress of Philosophy
MP	Mitsubishi Plastics [Japan] (PDAA)
MP	Mixed Pattern
MP	Mixed Population
MP	Mobilization Plan
MP	Modern Philology [A publication] (BRI)
MP	Modification Package
MP	Modified Construction Permit [FCC] (NTCM)
MP	Modo Praescripto [In the Manner Prescribed] [Pharmacy]
MP	Modus Ponens [Rule of inference] [Logic] [Latin]
MP	Molecular Pair [Physical Chemistry]
MP	Monetary Policy
mp	Mongolia [MARC country of publication code Library of Congress] (LCCP)
MP	Monitor Panel
MP	Monitor Printer (CET)
MP	Monophosphate [Chemistry] (MAE)
MP	[The] Month in Parliament [A publication British]
M/P	Months after Payment [Business term]
MP	Monumentum Posuit [Erected a Monument] [Latin]
MP	Mooring Pipe [or Post] (ADA)
M/P	Morjumiid-Pterocephalid Boundary [Paleogeologic boundary]
MP	Morning Prayer (WGA)
MP	Mortgage-Participation Certificate [Investment term]
MP	Mortgage Payment in Full
MP	Motherland Party [Anatavan Partisi] [Turkey Political party] (PPW)
MP	Motion Picture (NTCM)
mp	Motion Picture (AD)
MP	Motion Picture Production [Navy]
MP	Motor Potential
MP	Mounted Police
MP	Mouth Pressure [Dentistry] (DAVI)
MP	Mouvement Populaire [Popular Movement] [Morocco] [Political party] (PPW)
MP	Mouvement Progressif [Cameroon] [Political party] (EY)
MP	Movement Protein [Cytology]
MP	Mucopeptide [Biochemistry]
MP	Mucopolysaccharide [Also, MPS] [Clinical chemistry]
MP	Mucopurulent [Biochemistry] (DAVI)
MP	Multilink PPP [Point-to-Point Protocol] (PCM)
MP	Multiparous [Obstetrics]
MP	Multiperil [Insurance]
MP	Multiphase [Physics]
MP	Multiple Processor [or Multiprocessing] [Computer science] (BUR)
MP	Multiple Punch (DNAB)
MP	Multiplier Phototube
MP	Multipole
mp	Multipole (AD)
MP	Multiprocessing [Computer science] (CDE)
mp	Multipurpose (AD)
MP	Multipurpose
MP	Municipal Police
M/P	Muscle Plasma [Ratio]
MP	Mycoplasma Pneumonia [Medicine]
MP	Mycoplasma Pulmonis [A bacterium]
mp	Myeloma Protein [Oncology] (DAVI)
MP	My Pal [Slang]
MP	Northern Mariana Islands [ANSI two-letter standard code] (CNC)
MP	Pinawa Public Library, Manitoba [Library symbol National Library of Canada] (NLC)
MP2D	Multipart, Two Dimensional
MPA	Magazine Publisher's Association (NTCM)
MPA	Magazine Publishers of America [New York, NY Database producer] (IID)

MPA.............	Main Political Administration [of the Army and Navy] [Russian] (DOMA)
MPA.............	Main Propulsion Assistant
MPA.............	Main Pulmonary Artery [Anatomy]
MPA.............	Maintenance Planning Analysis (MCD)
MPA.............	Major Projects Association [British] (DBA)
MPA.............	Management Professionals Association [Madras, India] (EA)
MPA.............	Maneuver Propulsion Assembly (MCD)
MPA.............	Manpower and Personnel Administration [Military British]
MPA.............	Man-Powered Aircraft
MPA.............	Marine Physician Assistant (AD)
MPA.............	Marine Preservation Association
MPA.............	Maritime Patrol Aircraft (NATG)
mpa.............	Maritime Patrol Aircraft (AD)
MPA.............	Marketing and Promotion Association [British]
MPA.............	Maryland & Pennsylvania Railroad Co. [AAR code]
mpa.............	Maryland Port Authority (AD)
M Pa.............	Master of Painting
MPA.............	Master of Physician Assistant (PGP)
MPA.............	Master of Professional Accountancy [or Accounting]
MPA.............	Master of Professional Accounting (NADA)
MPA.............	Master of Professional Accounting (GAGS)
MPA.............	Master of Professional Arts
MPA.............	Master of Public Administration
MPA.............	Master of Public Administration (GAGS)
MPA.............	Master of Public Affairs
MPA.............	Master Pastrycooks' Association [Australia]
MPA.............	Master Personnel Administration
MPA.............	Master Photographers Association (AD)
MPA.............	Master Photographers Association of Great Britain (BI)
MPA.............	Master Printers of America (EA)
MPA.............	Master Project Assignment (MCD)
MPA.............	Mechanical Packing Association [Later, Fluid Sealing Association] (EA)
MPA.............	Medical Procurement Agency
MPA.............	Medroxyprogesterone [Medicine] (AD)
MPA.............	Medroxyprogesterone Acetate [Also, MAP] [Endocrinology]
MPa.............	Megapascal
mpa.............	Megapascal (AD)
MPA.............	Mercaptopropionic Acid [Organic chemistry]
MPA.............	Metal Powder Association [Later, MPIF]
MPA.............	Methacrylate Producers Association (EA)
MPA.............	Methoxypropylamine [Organic chemistry]
MPA.............	Methylphosphoric Acid [Organic chemistry]
MPA.............	Methylprednisolone Acetate [A glucocorticoid] (MAE)
MPA.............	Metropolitan Pensions Associations (AD)
MPA.............	Microwave Power Amplifier
MPA.............	Mid Pacific Air Corp. [ICAO designator] (FAAC)
MPA.............	Midwestern Psychological Association (MCD)
MPA.............	Military Pay Account
MPA.............	Military Pay and Allowance
MPA.............	Military Pay Area (AFM)
MPA.............	Military Personnel Appropriation (AFM)
MPA.............	Military Personnel, Army
MPA.............	Military Police Association [Defunct] (EA)
MPA.............	Military Proposal and Analysis
mPa.............	Millipascal [Unit of pressure]
MPA.............	Miniature Pendulum Accelerometer (SAA)
MPA.............	Miniature Photocell Activator
MPA.............	Miniature Piston Actuator (MCD)
MPA.............	Missile Procurement, Army (AABC)
MPA.............	Missionary Pilots Association [Defunct] (EA)
MPA.............	Mission Payload Assessment [Air Force] (DOMA)
MPA.............	Mission Performance Assessment [NASA] (KSC)
mpas.............	Mission Phase Analysis
MPA.............	Mission Profile Analysis
MPA.............	Mixer/Power Amplifier [Telecommunications]
MPA.............	Mobile Press Association (EA)
MPAT.............	Models and Photographers of America (EA)
MPA.............	Modern Poetry Association (EA)
MPA.............	Modification Proposal and Analysis (MCD)
MPA.............	Modulated Pulse Amplifier [Telecommunications] (IAA)
MPA.............	Molybdeophosphoric Acid [Inorganic chemistry]
MPA.............	Monthly Product Announcement [Bureau of the Census] (GFGA)
MPA.............	Moose Pass [Alaska] [Seismograph station code, US Geological Survey] (SEIS)
MPA.............	Mortar Package Assembly
MPA.............	Mortar Producers Association [British] (DBA)
MPA.............	Motion Picture Alliance
MPA.............	Motoring Press Association
MPA.............	Multiplant Action [Nuclear energy] (NRCH)
MPA.............	Multiple Parameter Analysis
MPA.............	Multiple Peptide Analysis [Biochemistry]
MPA.............	Multiple-Period Average (IEEE)
MPA.............	Multiple Peripheral Adapter
MPA.............	Multiple Product Announcement (NTCM)
mpa.............	Multiple Product Announcement (AD)
MPA.............	Multiple Protocol Architecture [Computer science] (PCM)
MPA.............	Multiple-Use Planning Area
MPA.............	Multi-Point Asynchronous (NITA)
MPA.............	Multiprecision Arithmetic
MPA.............	MuniYield Pennsylvania Fund [NYSE symbol] (SPSG)
MPA.............	Museum Publications of America
MPA.............	Music Publishers Association (NADA)
MPA.............	Music Publishers' Association of the United States (EA)
MPA.............	Mycophenolic Acid [Biochemistry]
MPA.............	Nampa, ID [Location identifier FAA] (FAAL)
MPA.............	Premenstrual Asthma [Medicine] (DAVI)
MPAA.............	Motion Picture Association of America (EA)
MPAA.............	Motorcar Parts & Accesories, Inc. [NASDAQ symbol] (SAG)
MPAA.............	Motorcar Parts & Accessories [NASDAQ symbol] (TTSB)
MPAA.............	Musical Performing Arts Association (NTCM)
MPAB.............	Military Petroleum Advisory Board
MPAC.............	Impact Systems [NASDAQ symbol] (TTSB)
MPAC.............	Impact Systems, Inc. [NASDAQ symbol] (NQ)
MPAC.............	Master Plan for Academic Computing (AD)
MPAC.............	Military Pay and Allowance Committee (AFM)
MPAC.............	Multipurpose Application Console (SSD)
MP Acc.............	Master of Professional Accountancy (PGP)
MP Acc.............	Master of Professional Accounting (PGP)
MPAcc.............	Master of Public Accounting (GAGS)
MP Acct.............	Master of Professional Accounting (PGP)
MPACS.............	Management Planning and Control System [IBM Corp.]
MPACT.............	Microprocessor Application to Control-Firmware Translator [Computer science] (MHDI)
MPAD.............	Manpower Personnel Assignment Document (AFM)
MPAD.............	Maximum Permissible Accumulated Dose [of radiation] (ADA)
mpad.............	Maximum Permissible Annual Dose (AD)
MPAD.............	Menlo Park Applications Development [IBM Corp.]
MPAD.............	Mission Planning and Analysis Division [NASA]
MP Adm.............	Master of Public Administration
MPAE.............	Max-Planck-Institut fur Aeronomie [An association]
MPAEA.............	Mountain Plains Adult Education Association (AEBS)
MPaed.............	Master of Paediatrics
MPAFD.............	Multiple Pulse Arm Fire Device (MCD)
MP Aff.............	Master of Public Affairs (PGP)
MPAGB.............	Modern Pentathlon Association of Great Britain (DBA)
mpai.............	Maximum Permissible Annual Intake (AD)
MPAI.............	Maximum Permissible Annual Intake [Radiation] (NRCH)
MPAIAC.............	Movimiento para la Autodeterminacion y Independencia del Archipielago Canario [Movement for the Self-Determination and Independence of the Canary Archipelago] [Canary Islands] [Spanish] (PD)
MPAJA.............	Malayan People's Anti-Japanese Army [World War II]
MPAJU.............	Malayan People's Anti-Japanese Union [World War II]
MPAM.............	Maritime Polar Air Mass (MSA)
mpam.............	Maritime Polar Air Mass (AD)
MPAMA.............	Milk Products Advertising-Merchandising Association (EA)
MP & C.............	Maintenance Planning and Control (MCD)
MP&C.............	Maintenance Planning and Control
MP & CS.............	Management Planning and Control System
MP & IS.............	Material Process and Inspection Specification (AAG)
MP & MAC.............	Marine Petroleum and Minerals Advisory Committee [Terminated, 1976] [National Oceanic and Atmospheric Administration] (NOAA)
mp & rs.............	Motive Power and Rolling Stock (AD)
MP & TF.............	Motion Picture and Television Fund
MPANSW.............	Master Patternmakers' Association of New South Wales [Australia]
MPANSW.............	Master Poulterers' Association of New South Wales [Australia]
MPAP.............	Mean Pulmonary Artery Pressure [Cardiology]
MPAPS.............	Motivation and Potential for Adoptive Parenthood Scale [Psychology]
MPAR.............	Maintenance Program Analysis Report
MPAR.............	Microprogram Address Register
MPAR.............	Multicanal Participacoes [NASDAQ symbol] (SAG)
m part.............	Movable Partition (AD)
MPAS.............	Maritime Patrol Airship Study
MPAS.............	Maryland Parent Attitude Survey [Psychology]
MPAS.............	Master of Physical Activity Studies (PGP)
MPAS.............	Master of Physician Assistant Studies (PGP)
mpas.............	Millipascal Second (AD)
MPASK.............	Multi-Phase and Amplitude-Shift-Keying [Computer science] (PDAA)
MPASS.............	Modular Processing and Support System
MPast.............	Master in Pastoral Studies
MPAT.............	Multipurpose All-Terrain Vehicle
MPATI.............	Midwest Program for Airborne Television Instruction [Defunct]
MPA-URP.............	Master of Public Affairs and Urban and Regional Planning (PGP)
MPAUS.............	Music Publishers' Association of the United States (DGA)
m payl.............	Maximum Payload (AD)
MPB.............	Berkshire Athenaeum, Pittsfield, MA [Library symbol Library of Congress] (LCLS)
MPB.............	Machine-Pressed Bales
MPB.............	Magnetic Particle Brake
MPB.............	Maine Potato Board (EA)
MPB.............	Maintenance Parts Breakdown (KSC)
MPB.............	Male-Pattern Baldness
mpb.............	Male Pattern Baldness (AD)
MPB.............	Master of Physical Biology
MPB.............	Material Performance Branch [Air Force]
MPB.............	Materials Properties Branch [Army] (RDA)
MPB.............	Matrix Program Board
MPB.............	Maximum Participation Base (IIA)
MPB.............	Mechanically Processed Beef [Food technology]
MPB.............	Mephobarbital [Antiepileptic drug]
MPB.............	Merit Promotion Bulletin [Military]
MPB.............	Miami [Florida] Public Seaplane Base [Airport symbol] (OAG)
MPB.............	Miniature Precision Bearing, Inc.
MPB.............	Miniature Precision Bearings (AD)
MPB.............	Missing Persons Bureau
MPB.............	Montpelier & Barre Railroad Co. [Later, MB] [AAR code]
MPB.............	Motorized Pontoon Bridge (MCD)

MPB............. Mouvement Progressiste de Burundi [*Progressive Movement of Burundi*]
MPB............. Multilayer Printed Board
MPB............. Munitions Packaging Branch [*Picatinny Arsenal*] [*Army*] (RDA)
MPB............. Musica Popular Brasileira [*Pop music*]
MPBA.......... Machine Printers' Beneficial Association [*Later, MPEA*]
MPBA.......... Model Power Boat Association [*British*] (DBA)
mpbb........... Maximum Permissible Body Burden [*of Radiation*] (AD)
MPBB.......... Maximum Permissible Body Burden [*Radiation*]
MPBB.......... Methyl(phenyl)(butyl)barbituric (Acid) [*Biochemistry*]
MPBC.......... Berkshire Community College, Pittsfield, MA [*Library symbol Library of Congress*] (LCLS)
MPBC.......... Memphis Power Boat Club [*Tennessee*] (AD)
MPBDS........ Material Properties Bibliographic Data System [*Purdue University*] [*Database*]
MPBE.......... Molten Plutonium Burn-Up Experiment [*Nuclear energy*] (IEEE)
MPBEA........ Mountain Plains Business Education Association (AEBS)
MPBL.......... Berkshire Law Library Association, Pittsfield, MA [*Library symbol Library of Congress*] (LCLS)
MPBME....... Munitions Production Base Modernization, Expansion (RDA)
MPBN .... Military Police Battalion
MPBO.......... Bocas Del Toro [*Panama*] [*ICAO location identifier*] (ICLI)
MPBP.......... Mechanically Processed Beef Product [*Food technology*]
MPBP.......... Metal Polishers, Buffers, Platers, and Allied Workers International Union (EA)
MPBR .... Multipunch Bar
mp br .... Multipunch Bar (AD)
MPBS.......... Medical Pocket-Book Series [*A publication*]
MPBS.......... Multipurpose Bayonet System [*Army*] (INF)
MPBS.......... Mutual Permanent Building Society (AD)
MPBW......... Ministry of Public Building and Works [*Later, DOE*] [*British*]
MPC............. Machine Punch Card
MPC............. Magellan Petroleum [*Exchange Symbol*] (TTSB)
MPC............. Magnetic Particle Clutch
MPC............. Maharashtra Prajatantra Congress [*India*] [*Political party*] (PPW)
MPC............. Maharashtra Progressive Congress [*India*] [*Political party*] (PPW)
MPC............. Maidstone Paper Converters [*Commercial firm British*]
MPC............. Maine Potato Council [*Later, MPB*] (EA)
MPC............. Maintenance Parts Catalog
MPC............. Maintenance Policy Council [*DoD Washington, DC*]
MPC............. Maintenance Priority Code
MPC............. Maintenance Procedure Chart
MPC............. Mandatory Product Control
MPC............. Manpower and Personnel Council [*DoD*]
MPC............. Manpower Planning Council
MPC............. Manpower Priorities Committee
MPC............. Manual Pointing Controller (MCD)
MPC............. Manufacturing Plan Change
MPC............. Manufacturing, Planning, and Control
MPC............. Marco Polo Club (EA)
MPC............. Marginal Producers Cost [*Engineering economics*]
MPC............. Marginal Propensity to Consume [*Economics*]
mpc .... Marginal Propensity to Consume (AD)
MPC............. Marine Policy Center (GNE)
mpc .... Marine Protein Concentrate (AD)
MPC............. Marine Protein Concentrate [*See also FPC*] (MSC)
MPC............. Marker Pulse Conversion [*Telecommunications*] (TEL)
MPC............. Market Performance Committee [*of NYSE*]
MPC............. Master Control Program [*Computer science*] (ECII)
MPC............. Master of Pastoral Counseling (PGP)
MPC............. Master of Personnel Counseling (GAGS)
MPC............. Master of Professional Counseling (PGP)
MPC............. Master of Public Communication (PGP)
MPC............. Master Parts Card
MPC............. Master Phasing Chart (MCD)
MPC............. Master Program Chart (MCD)
MPC............. Materials Preparation Center [*Ames, IA*] [*Ames Laboratory*] [*Department of Energy*] (GRD)
MPC............. Materials Processing Center [*Massachusetts Institute of Technology*] [*Research center*] (RCD)
mpc .... Materials Program Code (AD)
MPC............. Materials Properties Council (EA)
MPC............. Materiel Program Code [*Air Force*] (AFM)
mpc .... Mathematics, Physics, Chemistry (AD)
mpc .... Maximum Permissible Concentration (AD)
MPC............. Maximum Permissible Concentration [*Later, RCG*] [*Radiation*]
MPC............. Mechanical Positioning Control
MPC............. Mechanized Production Control
MPC............. Medium Processing Channel [*Carbon*] (DICI)
MPC............. Megaparsec
MPC............. Member of Parliament of Canada
MPC............. Member Pickwick Club [*From "The Pickwick Papers" by Charles Dickens*]
MPC............. Membrane Protein Complex [*Cytology*]
MPC............. Memory Protection Check (MCD)
MPC............. Meperidine, Promethazine, and Chlorpromazine [*Drug regime*]
MPC............. Merleau-Ponty Circle (EA)
MPC............. Message Processing Center
MPc............. Metallophthalocyanine [*Organic chemistry*]
MPC............. Meteorological Prediction Center (KSC)
MPC............. Metromedia Producers Corp.
MPC............. Metropolitan Police College (AD)
MPC............. Metropolitan Police Commissioner (AD)
MPC............. Microcircuit Power Converter
MPC............. Microparticle Concentration [*Analytical chemistry*]

MPC............. Microprocessor [*Computer science*] [*Unit*] (ECII)
MPC............. Microprogram Control
MPC............. Micropurulent Cervicitis [*Medicine*]
MPC............. Midbody Pyro Controller (NASA)
MPC............. Midwest Parentcraft Center (EA)
MPC............. Military Payment Certificate
mpc............. Military Payment Certificate (AD)
MPC............. Military Personnel Center (AFM)
MPC............. Military Pioneer Corps [*British*]
MPC............. Military Police Corps
MPC............. Military Police Force (AD)
MPC............. Military Postal Clerk (AFM)
MPC............. Military Property Custodian (AFIT)
Mpc............. Million Parsecs [*Interstellar space measure*]
MPC............. Mineral Policy Center (AD)
MPC............. Miniature Protector Connector [*Telecommunications*] (TEL)
MPC............. Minimal Flight Planning Charts [*Air Force*]
MPC............. Minimum Mycoplasmacidal Concentration [*Medicine*] (MAE)
mpc............. Minimum Planning Chart (AD)
MPC............. Minimum Protozoacidal Concentration
MPC............. Minor Planet Center [*Smithsonian Institution*]
MPC............. Mission Planning Center (MCD)
MPC............. Mission Profile Course (MCD)
MPC............. Mississippi Library Commission, Jackson, MS [*OCLC symbol*] (OCLC)
MPC............. Mobile Processing Center (MCD)
MPC............. Mode and Power Control [*Aviation*]
MPC............. Model Penal Code (AD)
MPC............. Model Predictive Control [*Chemical engineering*]
MPC............. Model Procurement Code [*for State and Local Governments*] (AAGC)
MPC............. Modular Peripheral Interface Converter
MPC............. Monagas Pipeline Crude [*Petrochemical engineering*]
MPC............. Monetary Policy Committee [*France*] (ECON)
MPC............. Monitor Proportional Counter (MCD)
MPC............. Monterey Peninsula College [*California*]
MPC............. Montreal Presbyterian College
MPC............. Moore's English Privy Council Cases [*A publication*] (DLA)
MPC............. Morphine Positive Control [*Epidemiology*]
MPC............. Mortgage-Participation Certificate [*Investment term*] (GFGA)
MPC............. Most Probable Cost (AAGC)
MPC............. Mother-of-Pearl Clouds [*Meteorology*] (PDAA)
MPC............. Motion Picture Camera (MCD)
MPC............. Motion Picture Control Panel (MSA)
MPC. .... Mountain Pacific Air Ltd. [*Canada ICAO designator*] (FAAC)
MPC............. Mouse Myeloma Cell [*Cell biology*]
MPC............. Mouvement Patriotique Congolais [*Congo Patriotic Movement*] [*Political party*]
MPC............. Movable Platform Configuration
MPC............. Multicultural Psychiatric Center [*Australia*]
MPC............. Multielectron Photoactive Center [*Physical chemistry*]
MPC............. Multimedia Personal Computer
MPC............. Multi-Party Conference [*Namibia*] [*Political party*] (PPW)
MPC............. Multipath Core
MPC............. Multiple Payload Carrier (SSD)
MPC............. Multiple Process Chart
MPC............. Multiple-Profile Configuration (MCD)
MPC............. Multiple-Purpose Communications (NG)
MPC............. Multiprocessor Computer
MPC............. Multiprogram Control [*Computer science*]
mpc............. Multipurpose Carrier (AD)
MPC............. Multipurpose Center
MPC............. Multipurpose Computer (CMD)
MPC............. Multispectral Photographic Camera (KSC)
MPC............. Myeloblastpromyelocyte Compartment [*Hematology*] (DAVI)
MPC............. Thousand Pieces (EG)
MPCA.......... Magnetic Powder Core Association (EA)
MPCA.......... Marine and Ports Council of Australia (AD)
MPCA.......... Markham Prayer Card Apostolate (EA)
MPCA.......... Master Pastry Cooks Association (AD)
MPCA.......... Melanin-Producing Cell Autoantibody [*Endocrinology*]
MPCA.......... Miniature Pinscher Club of America (EA)
MPCA.......... Multiway Principal Components Analysis [*Mathematics*]
MPCABS ...... Michigan Project for Computer-Assisted Biblical Studies [*University of Michigan*] [*Information service or system*] (IID)
MPCAG .... Military Parts Control Advisory Group [*DoD*]
MPCB.......... Manufacturing Plan Control Board (AD)
MPCB.......... Minuteman Parts Control Board [*Missiles*]
MPCB.......... Multilayer Printed Circuit Board
mpc black.... Medium-Processing Channel Black (AD)
MPCC.......... Manufacturing Planning Change Coordination (MCD)
MPCC.......... Material Purchase Contracts Control
MPCC.......... Microprogrammable Communications Controller [*Computer science*] (MHDI)
MPCC.......... Minnesota Private College Council (AD)
MPCC.......... Multiprocessor Computer Complex
MPCC.......... Multiprotocol Communications Controller
MPCCC....... Metropolitan Post Card Collectors Club (EA)
MPCD .... Manufacturing Process Control Document (KSC)
MPCD .... Minimum Perceptible Color Difference
MPCD. .... Mouvement Populaire Constitutionnel Democratique [*Popular Democratic Constitutional Movement*] [*Morocco*] [*Political party*] (PPW)
MPCD .... Multipurpose Color Display
MPCE......... Music Publishers Contact Employees

MPCF............ Campo De Francia/Enrique A. Jimenez [*Panama*] [*ICAO location identifier*] (ICLI)
MPCF............ Millions of Particles per Cubic Foot (PDAA)
MPCFP.......... Canadian Food Products Development Center, Portage La Prairie, Manitoba [*Library symbol National Library of Canada*] (NLC)
MPCH .... Changuinola/Cap. Manuel Nino [*Panama*] [*ICAO location identifier*] (ICLI)
MPCH .... Methodist Protestant Church
MPCI............ Mandatory Product Control Items (MCD)
MPCI............ Microsoft Press Computer Dictionary
MPCI............ Military Police Criminal Investigation
MPCI............ Multiport Programmable Communications Interface
MPCID........ Military Police Criminal Investigation Detachment
MPCL........... Monolithical Peltier Cooled LASER (MCD)
MPCL........... Mooney Problem Check List [*Psychology*]
MPCL........... Movimiento Patriotico Cuba Libre [*Free Cuba Patriotic Movement*] [*Political party*] (AD)
MPCL(G)....... Maximum Permissible Containment Level (Goal) (GNE)
MPCLP.......... Mental Patient Civil Liberties Project (EA)
MPCM.......... Microprogram Control Memory
MPCM.......... Multi-Purpose Central Mount/Module [*Military*] (LAIN)
MPCO........... Colon [*Panama*] [*ICAO location identifier*] (ICLI)
MPCO........... Military Police Commanding Officer (MCD)
MPCO........... Military Police Company
MPCP........... Mid-Peninsula Conversion Project [*Later, CEC*] (EA)
MP/CP.......... Military Personnel/Civilian Personnel
MPCP........... Missile Power Control Panel (AAG)
mpcp........... Missile Power Control Panel (AD)
MPCPA......... Music Publishers Contact Personnel Association [*British*] (DBA)
MPCR........... Memorandum Program Change Request [*Military*] (CAAL)
MPCR........... Microprogram Count Register [*Computer science*] (MHDB)
MPCRI......... Mercantile Pacific Coastal Routing Instructions
MPCS........... Machinery, Plant Control System [*Navy*]
MPCS........... Manual Propositional Control System (AAG)
MPCS........... Master Plan for Computing Services (AD)
MPCS........... Multiparty Connection Subsystem [*Telecommunications*] (TEL)
MPCS........... Multiprocessing Control System [*Computer science*]
MPCSOT...... Machinery, Plant Control System Operator Trainer [*Navy*]
MPCSW .... Multipurpose Close Support Weapon [*Military*] (AABC)
MPCU .... Marine Pollution Control Unit [*Department of Transportation*]
MPCU .... Maximum Permissible Concentration of Unidentified Radionuclides in Water
mpcur .... Maximum Permissible Concentration of Unidentified Radionuclides (AD)
MPD............. Magnetoplasmadynamic
mpd .... Magnetoplasmadynamics (AD)
MPD............. Magnetospheric Particle Detector (MCD)
MPD............. Main DC [*Direct Current*] Power Distributor Assembly (MCD)
MPD............. Main Pancreatic Duct [*Anatomy*]
MPD............. Maintenance Policy Document [*Deep Space Instrumentation Facility, NASA*]
MPD............. Make per Drawing (SAA)
MPD............. Management Policy and Directives
MPD............. Map Pictorial Display
MPD............. Marlborough Productions Ltd. [*Vancouver Stock Exchange symbol*]
M Pd............ Master of Pedagogy
MPD............. Master of Product Design (GAGS)
MPD............. Material Property Damage (DNAB)
MPD............. Materials Physics Division [*Air Force*]
MPD............. Materials Proximity Detector
MPD............. Maximum Packing Depth (NG)
MPD............. Maximum Permissible Dose [*Radiation*]
mpd .... Maximum Permissible Dose (AD)
MPD............. Mean Phenetic Distance
MPD............. Mean Photon Flux Density
MPD............. Mean Population Doubling [*Cytology*]
MPD............. Medical Pay Date
MPD............. Membrane Polarographic Detector [*Instrumentation*]
MPD............. Membrane Potential Difference [*Medicine*] (DMAA)
MPD............. Meridian Point Realty IV [*AMEX symbol*] (SPSG)
MPD............. Meta-Phenylenediamine [*Organic chemistry*]
MPD............. Methane Phophonyl Dichloride [*Nerve gas intermediate*] [*Organic chemistry*]
MPD............. Methylpentanediol [*Organic chemistry*]
MPD............. Methylphosphonic Diamide [*Flame retardant*] [*Organic chemistry*]
MPD............. Metropolitan Park District (AD)
MPD............. Metropolitan Police Department (AD)
MPD............. Metropolitan Police District [*London*]
MPD............. Microprocessor Developments (NITA)
MPD............. Microwave Plasma Detector [*Instrumentation*]
MPD............. Midwest Presenters Directory [*Information service or system*] (IID)
MPD............. Military Pay Division (AD)
MPD............. Military Pay Division, Finance Center, US Army
MPD............. Military Position Description
MPD............. Military Priority Date
MPD............. Military Prisons Department [*British military*] (DMA)
MPD............. Minimum Permissible Dose
MPD............. Minimum Premarket [*Health and Safety*] Data [*OEEC*]
MPD............. Minnesota Percepto-Diagnostic Test
MPD............. Missile Purchase Description [*Army*]
mpd .... Missile Purchase Description (AD)
MPD............. Missing Pulse Detector (MHDI)
MPD............. Mode-Power Distribution [*Electronics*]
MPD............. Modification Program Directive (AFIT)
MPD............. Movement for Democratic Process [*Zambia*] [*Political party*] (EY)

MPD............. Movement Priority Designator (DNAB)
MPD............. Movimento para Democracia [*Cape Verde*] [*Political party*] (EY)
MPD............. Movimiento Popular Democratico [*Popular Democratic Movement*] [*Ecuador*] [*Political party*] (PPW)
MPD............. Movimiento Popular Dominicano [*Dominican Popular Movement*] [*Dominican Republic*] [*Political party*] (PPW)
MPD............. Mpanda [*Tanzania*] [*Airport symbol*]
MPD............. m-Phenylenediamine [*Also, MPDA*] [*Organic chemistry*]
MPD............. Multiperson Prisoner's Dilemma [*Statistics*]
MPD............. Multiphoton Dissociation [*Physical chemistry*]
MPD............. Multiple Personality Disorder
mpd .... Multiple Personality Disorder (AD)
MPD............. Multipurpose Diffractometer
MPD............. Multipurpose Display (MCD)
MPD............. Myofascial Pain Dysfunction [*Neurology*]
MPDA .... David/Enrique Malek [*Panama*] [*ICAO location identifier*] (ICLI)
MPDA .... Monitor-Printer-Diskette Adapter
MPDA .... Motion Picture Distributors Association (AD)
MPDA .... Motion Picture Distributors Association (NADA)
MPDA .... m-Phenylenediamine [*Also, MPD*] [*Organic chemistry*]
MPDAA .... Motion Picture Distributors' Association of Australia
MPDB .... Main Power Distribution Box (SSD)
MPD-C .... Manpack Personnel Detector-Chemical [*Officially the Olfractronic Personnel Detector*] [*Military*] (VNW)
MPDC .... Mechanical Properties Data Center [*Defense Logistics Agency*] [*Information service or system*]
MPDC .... Missile Prelaunch Data Computer (MCD)
MPDD .... Meteorological Penetration Detection Development
MPDE .... Maximum Permissible Dose Equivalent (ERG)
MPDES .... Microprocessor Data Extraction System [*Military*] (CAAL)
MPDFA .... Master Photo Dealers' and Finishers' Association [*Later, PMA*] (EA)
MPDI .... Marine Products Development Irradiator
MPDI .... Microwave Power Devices [*NASDAQ symbol*] (TTSB)
MPDI .... Microwave Power Devices, Inc. [*NASDAQ symbol*] (SAG)
MPDI .... Multipunch Die
mp di .... Multipunch Die (AD)
MPDL .... Mission Profile Development List
MPDL .... Movimiento Pro-Democracia y Libertad [*Panama*] [*Political party*] (EY)
MPDLRSDB... Commission on the Mentally Disabled [*Formerly, Mental and Physical Disability Legal Research Services and Data Bases*] (EA)
MPDM .... Maintenance Planning Data Manual (MUGU)
MPDP .... Manpower Development Program [*Department of Labor*]
MPDPIS .... Master Plan for Data Processing and Information Systems (AD)
MPDS .... Mechanical Provisioning Data System
MPDS .... Message Processing and Distributing System [*Navy*] (NVT)
MPDS .... Missile Piercing Discarding Sabot (PDAA)
MPDS .... Mission Planning Debriefing Station (MCD)
MPDS .... Multi-Purpose Display System (DA)
MPDS .... Myofascial Pain Dysfunction Syndrome [*Neurology*] (DAVI)
MPDSA .... Master Painters, Decorators, and Signwriters Association (AD)
MPDSANSW... Master Painters, Decorators and Signwriters' Association of New South Wales [*Australia*]
MPDT.......... Magnetoplasmadynamic Thruster [*Electric thruster type*]
MPDT.......... Mean Preventive Downtime [*Computer science*]
MPDT.......... Minnesota Perception Diagnostic Test (AD)
MPDT.......... Minnesota Percepto-Diagnostic Test [*Psychology*]
MPDTL .... Medium-Power Diode-Transistor Logic (ECII)
MPDU .... Message Protocol Data Unit [*Telecommunications*] (OSI)
MPDU .... Mobile Power Distribution Unit (DWSG)
MP-DV .... Multiply-Divide (NITA)
MPE .... Management Program for Executives (ECON)
MPE .... Manual Plot Entry (MCD)
MPE .... Master of Physical Education
MPE .... Mathematical and Physical Sciences and Engineering (IEEE)
MPE .... Maximum Permissible Exposure [*Radiation*]
mpe .... Maximum Permissible Exposure [*to Radiation*] (AD)
MPE .... Maximum Possible Error
MPE .... Max-Planck-Institut fur Extraterrestrische Physik [*Germany*]
MPE .... Meat Promotion Executive [*British*]
MPE .... Mechanized Production of Electronics
MPE .... Meeting Planners Expo (ITD)
MPE .... Memory Parity Error
MPE .... Metaphenoxylene [*Analytical chemistry*]
MPE .... Methidiumpropyl Ethylenediaminetetraacetic Acid [*Analytical biochemistry*]
MPE .... Minimum Perceptible Erythema [*Dermatology*]
MPE .... Minimum Performance Envelope (MCD)
MPE .... Minimum Potential Energy [*Fission*]
MPE .... Missile Positioning Equipment (KSC)
MPE .... Mission and Performance Envelope
MPE .... Mission-Peculiar Equipment
MPE .... Mission to Planet Earth [*Marine science*] (OSRA)
MPE .... Mission to Planet Earth (USDC)
MPE .... Monthly Project Evaluation
MPE .... Moving Paper Electrophoresis
MPE .... Multiphoton Excitation [*Physics*]
MPE .... Multipion Exchange
MPE .... Multiple Phase Ejector
MPE .... Multiple Protective Earthing (IAA)
MPE .... Multiprogramming Executive [*Hewlett-Packard Co.*]
MPEA.......... Machine Printers and Engravers Association of the United States (EA)
MPEA.......... Meat and Poultry Export Association

MPEA .... Motion Picture Exhibitors Association (AD)
MPEA .... Mouvement Populaire d'Evolution Africaine [*African People's Evolution Movement*]
MPEAA .... Motion Picture Export Association of America (EA)
MPeaHi .... Peabody Historical Society, Peabody, MA [*Library symbol Library of Congress*] (LCLS)
MPeal .... Peabody Institute, Peabody, MA [*Library symbol Library of Congress*] (LCLS)
MPEAUS ...... Machine Printers and Engravers Association of the United States (DGA)
MPEAUS ...... Master Printers and Engravers Association of the United States (AD)
MPEC .... Miniature Piano Enthusiast Club (EA)
MPECC .... Multiprocessor Experimental Computer Complex
MPEd .... Master of Physical Education
M Pe E .... Master of Petroleum Engineering
M Pe Eng .... Master of Petroleum Engineering
MPEG .... Methoxypolyethylene Glycol [*Organic chemistry*]
MPEG .... Military Police Escort Guard
mpeg .... Motion Picture Experts Group [*Computer science*]
MPEG .... Motion Picture Experts Group
MPEG .... Moving [*or Motion*] Pictures Experts Group [*Motion video standard*] (PCM)
MPEH. .... Methylphenylethylhydantoin [*Organic chemistry*] (MAE)
MPE/iX .... Multiprogramming Executive / POSIX [*Portable Operating System Interface for Unix*] [*Computer science*] (CDE)
MPEL .... Maximum Permissible Exposure Levels [*Radiation*]
M Pen .... Minister of Pensions [*British*] (AD)
M Pen .... Ministry of Pensions [*British*] (AD)
MPEP .... Manual of Patent Examining Procedures
MPEP .... Metalworking Processes and Equipment Program
MPEP .... Model Performance Evaluation Program [*Centers for Disease Control*]
MPER .... Master of Personnel and Employee Relations (GAGS)
MPER .... Material-in-Process Engineering Request
MP-ER .... Multiple Punch, Error Release (DNAB)
M Perf A ...... Master of Performing Arts (PGP)
MPERR .... Master Personnel Record
MPers .... Middle Persian (AD)
MPES .... Management Planning and Evaluation Staff [*Environmental Protection Agency*] (GFGA)
MPE/S .... Maritime Prepositioned Equipment and Supplies [*Navy*] (ANA)
MPES .... Mass Properties Engineering Section
MPES .... Mathematical, Physical, and Engineering Science (AD)
MPES .... Maximum Performance Ejection Seat [*Navy*]
MPES .... Medical Planning and Execution System [*DOMA*]
MPESS .... Mission Peculiar Experiment Support Structure
MPESS .... Mission-Peculiar Experiment Support Structure (NASA)
MPET .... Magellan Petroleum Corp. [*NASDAQ symbol*] (NQ)
MPetE .... Master of Petroleum Engineering (GAGS)
MP Ex .... Modern Practice of the Exchequer [*A publication*] (DLA)
MPF .... Machine Parts Fabrication
MPF .... Major Project Funding
MPF .... Malaysian Peasants Front [*Political party*] (AD)
MPF .... Mapping Field (ACRL)
MPF .... Maritime Patrol Force (MCD)
MPF .... Maritime Prepositioning Force (DOMA)
MPF .... Master Parts File (MCD)
MPF .... Materials Processing Facility [*NASA*] (KSC)
MPF .... Maturation-Promoting Factor [*Cytology*]
MPF .... Mean Power Frequency [*of myoelectric signals*]
MPF .... Median and Paired Fins [*Ichthyology*]
MPF .... Medical Passport Foundation [*Defunct*] (EA)
MPF .... Meridian Point Realty VI [*AMEX symbol*] (SPSG)
MPF .... Metallurgical Plantmakers Federation (AD)
MPF .... Metal Parts Furnace (MCD)
MPF .... Methodist Peace Fellowship [*Defunct*] (EA)
MPF .... Metropolitan Police Force [*Scotland Yard*] [*London, England*]
MPF .... Mexico Pilgrims Foundation (EA)
MPF .... Micellar Polymer Flooding [*Petroleum technology*]
MPF .... Micro Professor (NITA)
MPF .... Million Pair Feet [*Telecommunications*] (TEL)
MPF .... Missile Pressure Fuel (AAG)
MPF .... Missile Procurement Fund (AAGC)
MPF .... Mission Planning Forecast
MPF .... Mitosis-Promoting Factor [*Cytology*]
MPF .... Mizrachi Palestine Fund (EA)
mpf .... Motion-Picture Film (AD)
MPF .... M-Phase Promoting Factor [*Cytology*]
MPF .... Multiple Primary Feed [*Deep Space Instrumentation Facility, NASA*]
MPF .... Multipurpose Facility (DOMA)
mpf .... Multi-Purpose Food (AD)
MPF .... Multipurpose Food [*Refers to a specific combination of ingredients used in a food relief program*]
MPF .... Multispectral Photographic Facility
MPF .... Murine Pathogen Free [*Rats or mice*]
MPF .... Religious Teachers, Filippini [*Roman Catholic women's religious order*]
MPFASAF .... Military Police Functional Automation System for the Army in the Field (MCD)
MPFC .... Mamas and the Papas Fan Club (EA)
MPFC .... Mobile Petrol Filling Centre [*British military*] (DMA)
MPFC .... Morgan Plus Four Club (EA)
MPFC .... Mountain Parks Financial Corp. [*NASDAQ symbol*] (SAG)
MPFC .... Mountain Parks Fin'l [*NASDAQ symbol*] (TTSB)
MPFC .... Multipurpose Fire Control System

MPFE .... Motion Picture Film Editors [*Defunct*] (EA)
MPFI .... Multi-Point Fuel Injection [*Automotive engineering*]
MPFP .... Melt-Processible Fluoropolymers [*Plastics technology*]
MPFS .... Fuerte Sherman [*Panama*] [*ICAO location identifier*] (ICLI)
MPFS .... MACRIT [*Manpower Authorization Criteria*] Planning Factors Study [*Army*]
MPFS .... Microwave Position-Fixing System (NOAA)
MPFS .... Multiple Primary Feed System [*Deep Space Instrumentation Facility, NASA*]
MPFW .... Multishot Portable Flame Weapon (MCD)
MPG .... General Electric Co., Pittsfield, MA [*Library symbol Library of Congress*] (LCLS)
MPG .... Georgetown University, Medical Library Processing Center, Washington, DC [*OCLC symbol*] (OCLC)
MPG .... Magazine Promotion Group [*Defunct*] (EA)
MPG .... Magnetic Porous Glass [*Materials science*]
MPG .... Magnetopneumogram [*Medicine*]
MPG .... Manhattan Publishing Group (EA)
MPG .... Maritime Patrol Group
MPG .... Matched Power Gain
MPG .... Max-Planck-Gesellschaft [*West German research organization*]
MPG .... McArthur, OH [*Location identifier FAA*] (FAAL)
MPG .... Meridian Point Realty VII [*AMEX symbol*] (SPSG)
MPG .... Micrograms per Gram
MPG .... Microwave Pulse Generator
MPG .... Mid Plate Gyre [*Nuclear energy*] (NUCP)
MPG .... Miles per Gallon
MPG .... Military Products Group
MPG .... Milk Protein Hydrolysate [*Biochemistry*] (DAVI)
MPG .... Miniature Precision Gyrocompass (IEEE)
MPG .... Mobile Protected Gun [*Army*] (RDA)
MPG .... Molecular Presentation Graphics [*Software program*]
MPG .... Monopropylene Glycol [*Chemicals*]
MPG .... MPG Investment Corp. Ltd. [*Toronto Stock Exchange symbol Vancouver Stock Exchange symbol*]
MPG .... Multimedia Publishers Group (EA)
MPG .... Multipoint Grounding (NASA)
MPG .... Patrologia Graeca [*J. P. Migne*] [*Paris*] [*A publication*] (BJA)
MPGA .... Maine Personnel and Guidance Association (AD)
MPGA .... Maryland Personnel and Guidance Association (AD)
MPGA .... Metropolitan Public Gardens Association [*British*] (BI)
MPGA .... Michigan Personnel and Guidance Association (AD)
MPGA .... Minnesota Personnel and Guidance Association (AD)
MPGA .... Missouri Personnel and Guidance Association (AD)
MPGF .... Male Pronucleus Growth Factor [*Biochemistry*]
MPGHM .... Mobile Payload Ground Handling Mechanism (MCD)
MPGI .... Mouvement Populaire pour la Guadeloupe Independante [*Popular Movement for Independent Guadeloupe*] (PD)
MPGM .... Monophosphoglycerate Mutase [*Biochemistry*] (DAVI)
mpgn .... Membrano Proliferative Glomerulonephritis [*Medicine*] (AD)
MPGN .... Membranoproliferative Glomerulonephritis [*Nephrology*]
MPGN .... Mesangioproliferative Glomerulonephritis [*Nephrology*] (DAVI)
MPGR .... Mana Pools Game Reserve [*Rhodesia*]
MPGS .... Microprogram Generating System
MPGS .... Microprogramming Generating System (NITA)
MPGS .... Mobile Protected Gun System [*Army*] (MCD)
MPGS .... Multi-Purpose Graphic System [*Computer science*]
MPH .... Maintenance Parts Handbook
MPH .... Martinair Holland NV [*Netherlands ICAO designator*] (FAAC)
M Ph .... Master of Philosophy
MPH .... Master of Physical Education and Health
MPH .... Master of Public Health
MPH .... McGregor Point, HI [*Location identifier FAA*] (FAAL)
MPH .... Meat Packing House (AD)
MPH .... Melphalan [*Also, A, L-PAM, M, MPL*] [*Antineoplastic drug*]
MPH .... Mentally and Physically Handicapped (OICC)
MPH .... Meridian Point Realty [*AMEX symbol*] (SPSG)
MPH .... Meridian Point Rlty VIII [*AMEX symbol*] (TTSB)
MPH .... Methodist Publishing House (DGA)
MPH .... Methylphenidate [*Pharmacology*] (DAVI)
MPH .... Micro-Phonics Technology International Corp. [*Vancouver Stock Exchange symbol*]
MPH .... Miles per Hour [*Also, M/H*]
mph .... Miles per Hour (IDOE)
MPH .... Milk Protein Hydrolysate (BABM)
MPh .... Missionary Sisters of Our Lady of Perpetual Help (TOCD)
M Ph .... Mistress of Philosophy
MPH .... Multiple Probe Head [*Laboratory technology*]
MPH&TM ...... Master of Public Health and Tropical Medicine (GAGS)
M Phar .... Master of Pharmacy
M Phar C ..... Master of Pharmaceutical Chemistry
M Pharm ..... Master of Pharmacy
M Ph C .... Master of Pharmaceutical Chemistry
MPHC .... Metal-Skinned, Paper-Honeycomb Cored (PDAA)
MPHE .... Master of Public Health Education (PGP)
MPHE .... Master of Public Health Engineering
MPHE .... Material and Personnel Handling Equipment (NASA)
MPHEC .... Maritime Provinces Higher Education Commission (AD)
MPH Ed .... Master of Public Health Education
MPH Eng ..... Master of Public Health Engineering
M Phil .... Master of Philosophy
M Phil F ...... Master of Philosophical Foundations (PGP)
MPHN .... Master of Public Health Nursing
MPHO .... Howard Air Force Base [*Panama*] [*ICAO location identifier*] (ICLI)
M Pho .... Master of Photography

MPHP .... Multiple-Pass Heuristic Procedure (PDAA)
MPHPr .... Meridian Point Rlty VIII Pfd [*AMEX symbol*] (TTSB)
mphps .... Miles Per Hour Per Second (AD)
MPHPS .... Miles per Hour per Second
MPHR .... Maximum Predicted Heart Rate [*Cardiology*]
M Ph S .... Master of Physical Science
M Ph Sc .... Master of Physical Science
MPHTM .... Master of Public Health and Tropical Medicine
MPhty .... Master of Physiotherapy [*British*] (ADA)
M Phy .... Master of Physics
M Phys A ..... Member of the Physiotherapists' Association [*British*]
MPhysics ..... Master of Physics (DD)
MPI .... Magnetic Particle Inspection
mpi .... Magnetic Particle Inspection (AD)
MPI .... Magnetic Peripherals Inc. (NITA)
MPI .... Magnetic Press, Inc. [*Information service or system*] (IID)
MPI .... Malaria Philatelists International (EA)
MPI .... Mamitupo [*Panama*] [*Airport symbol*] (OAG)
MPI .... Management Partnerships International, Inc. (IID)
MPI .... Manitoba Properties, Inc. [*Toronto Stock Exchange symbol Vancouver Stock Exchange symbol*]
MPI .... Mannosephosphate Isomerase [*An enzyme*]
MPI .... Man-Portable Illuminator
MPI .... Manufacturing Process Instructions
MPI .... Marginal Propensity to Invest [*Economics*]
mpi .... Marginal Propensity to Invest (AD)
MPI .... Marine Pollution Incident [*Marine science*] (OSRA)
MPI .... Marriage-Personality Inventory [*Psychology*]
MPI .... Mass Psychogenic Illness
MPI .... Master Patient Index (MEDA)
MPI .... Masterpiece Theatre [*Public television*]
MPI .... Material Process Instruction (AD)
MPI .... Matter of Public Importance (ADA)
MPI .... Maudsley Personality Inventory [*Psychology*]
MPI .... Maximal Permitted Intake [*Medicine*]
MPI .... Maximum Point of Impulse
mpi .... Maximum Point of Impulse (AD)
MPI .... Maximum Precipitation Intensity [*Meteorology*] (PDAA)
MPI .... Max-Planck-Institut
MPI .... Max Planck Institute (AD)
MPI .... Max-Planck Institute for Meteorology [*Marine science*] [*Germany*] (OSRA)
MPI .... Max-Planck-Institut fuer Astronomie [*Max Planck Institute for Astronomy*] [*Germany*]
MPI .... Mean Point of Impact [*Air Force*]
mpi .... Mean Point of Impact (AD)
MPI .... Medicine in the Public Interest (AD)
MPI .... Medi-Physica, Inc. (DAVI)
MPI .... Meeting Planners International (EA)
MPI .... Message Passing Interface [*Software program conducted at Mississippi State University*]
MPI .... Message Pattern Indicator
MPI .... Message Processing Interactive (MCD)
MPI .... Metal Powder Industries Federation
MPI .... Michelson Polarizing Interferometer [*Instrumentation*]
MPI .... Microprocessor Interface
MPI .... Milestone Properties [*NYSE symbol*] (SPSG)
MPI .... Military Police Investigator [*or Investigation*] (AABC)
MPI .... Military Procurement Instruction
MPI .... Miltarpsykologiska Institutet [*Military Psychology Institute*] [*Sweden*] (PDAA)
MPI .... Minneapolis Public Library and Information Center, Minneapolis, MN [*OCLC symbol*] (OCLC)
MPI .... Minnesota Preschool Inventory [*Child development test*]
MPI .... Missile Periodic Inspection (AAG)
MPI .... Missing Persons International (EA)
MPI .... Mission Payload Integration (MCD)
MPI .... Mitsui Petrochemical Industries (AD)
MPI .... Molded Plastic Insulation
MPI .... Molecular Parameter Index
MPI .... Monographs of the Peshitta Institute [*A publication*] (BJA)
MPI .... Monsoon Pollen Index [*Paleoceanography*]
MPI .... Morris Pratt Institute Association (EA)
MPI .... Movimiento Patriotico Institucional [*Panama*] [*Political party*] (EY)
MPI .... Movimiento pro Independencia de Puerto Rico (EA)
MPI .... Multiphase Ionization [*Chemical physics*]
MPI .... Multiphasic Personality Inventory
mpi .... Multiphasic Personality Inventory (AD)
mpi .... Multiphoton Ionization (AD)
MPI .... Multiphoton Ionization [*Spectrometry*]
MPI .... Multiple Power Input (RDA)
MPI .... Multiple Protocol Interface [*Computer science*]
MPI .... Multipoint-Electronic Fuel Injection [*Automotive engineering*]
MPI .... Museum of the Plains Indians (AD)
MPI .... Mutagenic Potency Index [*For toxicology*]
MPI .... Myocardial Perfusion Imaging [*Cardiology*]
MPIA .... Master in Political and Institutional Administration
MPIA .... Master of Pacific International Affairs (GAGS)
MPIA .... Master of Public and International Affairs (GAGS)
MPIA .... Max-Planck-Institut fuer Astronomie [*Max Planck Institute for Astronomy*] [*Germany*]
MPIAD .... MOD [*Maintenance of Deception*] Personnel Interceptor Assembly/ Disassembly
MPIC .... Message Processing Interrupt Count
MPIC .... Mobile Phase Ion Chromatography

MPIC .... Motion Picture Industry Controllers (EA)
MPIC .... Motion Picture Industry Council (EA)
MPIC .... Motion Picture Institute of Canada
MPIF .... Message Passing Interface Forum (USDC)
MPIF .... Message Passing Interface Forum [*Marine science*] (OSRA)
MPIF .... Metal Powder Industries Federation (EA)
MPIIN .... Modification Procurement Instrument Identification Number [*NASA*] (NASA)
M-pill .... Menstruation Pill [*Medicine*] (AD)
MPIM .... Max-Planck-Institute fuer Meteorologie [*Marine science*] [*Germany*] (OSRA)
MPIM .... Max-Planck-Institut fur Meteorologie (USDC)
MPIM .... Multipurpose Individual Munition [*Weapon*]
MPIM/SRAW... Multi-Purpose Individual Munition/Short Range Assault Weapon [*Military*] (RDA)
MPIO .... Mission and Payload Integration Office [*NASA*]
MPIP .... Machine Parts Inspection Plans (MCD)
MPIP .... Maintenance Posture Improvement Program (MCD)
MPIP .... Meat and Poultry Inspection Program [*Department of Agriculture*]
MPIP .... Miniature Precision Inertial Platform (OA)
MPIPrA .... Milestone Properties Cv $0.78Pfd [*NYSE symbol*] (TTSB)
MPIR .... Missile Precision Instrumentation RADAR (MSA)
MPIRO .... Multiple Peril Insurance Rating Organization [*Later, Multiperil Insurance Conference*]
MPIX .... Microelectronic Packaging [*NASDAQ symbol*] (TTSB)
MPIX .... Microelectronic Packaging, Inc. [*NASDAQ symbol*] (SAG)
MPJ .... Member of the Profession of Journalism [*British*] (DGA)
MPJ .... Metacarpophalangeal Joint [*Anatomy*]
MPJ .... Morrilton, AR [*Location identifier FAA*] (FAAL)
MPJ .... Mouvement Panafricain de la Jeunesse [*Pan-African Youth Movement - PYAM*] [*Algeria*]
MPJE .... Jaque [*Panama*] [*ICAO location identifier*] (ICLI)
MP-JFI .... Managerial and Professional Job Functions Inventory [*Test*]
mPK .... Cold Maritime Polar Air Mass [*Meteorology*] (BARN)
mPK .... Maintenance Parts Kit (MSA)
mpk .... Manpack
MPK .... Martis Peak [*California*] [*Seismograph station code, US Geological Survey*] (SEIS)
MPK .... McKinley Park [*Alaska*] [*Airport symbol*] (AD)
MPK .... Microphone Probe Kit
mPk .... Polar Maritime Air Colder than Underlying Surface (AD)
MPKC .... Management Problem-Knowledge Coupler
MPL .... Macro Programming Language [*Computer application*] (PCM)
MPL .... Magnesium Pemoline [*Pharmacology*]
MPL .... Maintenance Parts Lists
MPL .... Mandatory Parts List [*DoD*]
MPL .... Manipulator Positioning Latches (MCD)
MPL .... Man Position Locator
MPL .... Manufacturing Parts List (AAG)
mpl .... Maple (DAC)
MPL .... Maple
MPL .... Maple Technology Ltd. [*Vancouver Stock Exchange symbol*]
MPL .... Marine Physical Laboratory [*Research center*] (RCD)
MPL .... Marine Physics Laboratory [*Scripps*]
MPL .... Mars Probe Lander [*Aerospace*]
MPL .... Master of Patent Law
MPI .... Master of Planning
M PI .... Master of Planning (PGP)
MPL .... Master of Polite Literature
MPL .... Master of Public Law
MPL .... Master Parts List
MPL .... Master Planner, Inc. [*ICAO designator*] (FAAC)
MPL .... Material Processing Laboratory (SSD)
MPL .... Mathematical Programming Language [*Computer science*] (PDAA)
mpl .... Mathematical Programming Language [*Computer science*] (AD)
MPL .... Mavis, Paul A., South Bend IN [*STAC*]
MPL .... Maxillofacial Prosthesis Laboratory [*WRAMC*] (RDA)
mpl .... Maximum Payload (AD)
MPL .... Maximum Penalized-Likelihood [*Statistics*]
mpl .... Maximum Permissible Language (AD)
mpl .... Maximum Permissible Level (AD)
MPL .... Maximum Permissible Level [*Radiation*] (DEN)
MPL .... Maximum Probable Loss [*Insurance*]
MPL .... Maximum Procurement Level (AFIT)
MPL .... Mechanical Parts List (NASA)
MPL .... Mechanical Properties Loop [*Nuclear energy*] (NRCH)
MPL .... Melphalan [*Also, A, L-PAM, M, MPH*] [*Antineoplastic drug*]
MPL .... Memphis Public Library (AD)
MPL .... Mesiopulpolingual [*Dentistry*] (MAE)
MPL .... Message Processing Language [*Burroughs Corp.*]
mpl .... Message Processing Language [*Computer science*] (AD)
MPL .... Metals Processing Laboratory [*MIT*] (MCD)
MPL .... Metering Pumps Limited
MPL .... Metropolitan Police Laboratory (AD)
MPL .... Miami Public Library (AD)
MPL .... Micro Power Light [*Automotive lighting*]
MPL .... Microprocessor [*or Motorola's*] Programming Language [*1975*] [*Computer science*] (CSR)
MPL .... Microprogramming Language (NITA)
MPL .... Milwaukee Public Library (AD)
MPL .... Mine Planter (NATG)
MPL .... Minimum Power Level (KSC)
MPL .... Minnesota Power & Light Co. [*AMEX symbol*] (SAG)
MPL .... Minnesota Power & Light Co. [*NYSE symbol*] (SPSG)
MPL .... Minnesota Pwr & Lt [*NYSE symbol*] (TTSB)

MPL............ Mission Planning Laboratory [NASA] (KSC)
MPL............ Missouri Pacific Lines (AD)
MPL............ Mistress of Polite Literature
MP/L.......... Modified Construction Permit and License [FCC] (NTCM)
MPL............ Monessen Public Library, Monessen, PA [OCLC symbol] (OCLC)
MPL............ Monkey Placental Lactogen
MPL............ Monophosphoryl Lipid [Biochemistry]
MPL............ Montoneros Patria Libre [Guerrila group] [Ecuador] (EY)
MPL............ Montpellier [France] [Airport symbol] (OAG)
MPL............ Montreal Public Library [Canada] (AD)
MPL............ Motion Picture Laboratories [Commercial firm]
MPL............ Motivated Productivity Level [Quality control]
MPL............ Mouvement Politique Lulua [Lulua Political Movement] [Political party]
MPL............ Movimento Politica dei Lavoratori [Workers' Political Movement] [Italy Political party] (PPE)
MPL............ Movimiento Popular de Liberacion "Cinchoneros" ["Cinchoneros" Popular Liberation Movement] [Honduras] [Political party]
MPL............ Multiple Payload Launcher
mpl............ Multiple-Position Lock (AD)
MPL............ Multipurpose Limousine
MPL............ Multischedule Private Line
MPL............ Multi-Services, Inc. [FAA designator] (FAAC)
MPL............ Patrologia Latina [J. P. Migne] [Paris] [A publication] (BJA)
MPI............ Plymouth Public Library, Plymouth, MA [Library symbol Library of Congress] (LCLS)
MPIA.......... Antiquarian House, Plymouth, MA [Library symbol Library of Congress] (LCLS)
MPLA.......... Malayan People's Liberation Army
MPLA.......... Mask Programmable Logic Array (NITA)
MPLa.......... Mesiopulpolabial [Dentistry] (MAE)
MPLA.......... Metropolitan Public Libraries Association [New South Wales, Australia]
MPLA.......... Monophosphoryl Lipid A [Biochemistry]
MPLA.......... Mountain Plains Library Association (AEBS)
MPLA.......... Movimento Popular de Libertacao de Angola [Popular Movement for the Liberation of Angola] [Political party]
MPlan......... Master of Planning
MPlanStud... Master of Planning Studies
MPlanStudies... Master of Planning Studies
MPLA-PT .... Movimento Popular de Libertacao de Angola - Partido do Trabalho [Popular Movement for the Liberation of Angola - Party of Labor] [Political party] (PPW)
MPLAW....... Melamine Paper Laminate (PDAA)
MPLAW....... Modified Programmers Language [Computer science] (PDAA)
MPLAW....... Moving Part Logic (PDAA)
MPLAW....... Multipulse Scaling-Law Code using Data Base Interpolation (PDAA)
MPLB......... Balboa/Albrook [Panama] [ICAO location identifier] (ICLI)
MPLB......... Maximum Permissible Lung Burden [Industrial hygiene]
MPLC......... Medium-Pressure Liquid Chromatography
MPLC......... Mid-Peninsula Library Cooperative [Library network]
MPLC......... Movimento Popular de Libertacao de Cabinda [Popular Movement for the Liberation of Cabinda] [Angola] [Political party] (PD)
MPLC......... Movimiento Popular de Liberacion Cinchonero [Guerrilla forces] [Honduras] (EY)
MPLD......... Mouvement Populaire pour la Liberation de Djibouti [Political party] (EY)
MPLE......... Multipurpose Long Endurance [Aircraft]
MPLG......... Multi-Purpose Lithium Grease
MPLH......... Multipurpose Light Helicopter (DOMA)
MPLI......... Michigan Picture Language Inventory (EDAC)
MPLL......... Malayan People's Liberation League
MPLM........ Mini-Pressurized Logistic Modules [Space technology]
MPLN........ Maintenance Planning [Database] (NASA)
MPLN........ Maintenance Planning [Data base]
MPLO........ Military Postal Liaison Office
MPLP......... La Palma [Panama] [ICAO location identifier] (ICLI)
MPLP......... Marxist Progressive Labor Party [Political party] (AD)
MPLP......... Mental Patients Liberation Projects
MPIP......... Plimoth Plantation, Inc., Plymouth, MA [Library symbol Library of Congress] (LCLS)
MPLP......... Portage Plains Regional Library, Portage La Prairie, Manitoba [Library symbol National Library of Canada] (NLC)
MPLPC....... Multipulse Linear Productive Coding (PDAA)
MPLPDC ..... MDC Library, Manitoba Developmental Centre, Portage La Prairie [Library symbol National Library of Canada] (BIB)
MPLPM...... Manitoba School, Portage La Prairie, Manitoba [Library symbol National Library of Canada] (NLC)
MPLPr....... MP&L Cap I 8.05% 'QUIPS' [NYSE symbol] (TTSB)
MPLPrA...... Minn Pwr & Lt 5% cm Pfd [AMEX symbol] (TTSB)
MPL + PRED... Melphalan and Prednisone [Antineoplastic drug regimen] (DAVI)
MPL + PRED(MP)... Melphalan and Prednisone [Antineoplastic drug regimen] (DAVI)
MPIPS .... Pilgrim Society, Plymouth, MA [Library symbol Library of Congress] (LCLS)
MPLR........ Medium Power Loop Range
MPLS........ Maximal Principle Least Squares
Mpls .... Minneapolis (AD)
MPLSM...... Multiple Position Letter Sorting Machine (PDAA)
MPLSM...... Multiple Position Letter Sort Machine
MPLSS....... Marketing of Public Library Services Section [Public Library Association]
MPLU........ Most Probable Library User
MPLX........ Multiplexer
MPLXR .... Multiplexer

MPM........... Magnetic Phase Modulator
MPM........... Magnum Petroleum [AMEX symbol] (SAG)
MPM........... Main Propulsion Motor
MPM........... Maintenance Planning Manual (NG)
MPM........... Maintenance Program Management [Military] (AABC)
MPM........... Major Program Memorandum [Military]
MPM........... Major Project Manager
MPM........... Malignant Papillary Mesothelioma [Medicine]
MPM........... Manipulator Positioning Mechanism (NASA)
MPM........... Manpower Planning Model
MPM........... Manufacture Procedure Manual (KSC)
MPM........... Maputo [Mozambique] [Airport symbol] (OAG)
MPM........... Marginal Propensity to Import [Economics]
MPM........... Marshall Plan of the Mind [BBC radio program] (ECON)
MPM........... Master of Personnel Management (GAGS)
MPM........... Master of Pest Management (PGP)
MPM........... Master of Pest Management (DD)
MPM........... Master of Professional Management (PGP)
MPM........... Master of Project Management (PGP)
MPM........... Master of Psychological Management
MPM........... Master of Psychological Medicine (ADA)
MPM........... Master of Public Management
MPM........... Master of Public Management (GAGS)
MPM........... Maximum Permitted Mileage [Airlines]
MPM........... Maximum Pionization Method (OA)
MPM........... Medical Planning Module (DOMA)
MPM........... Message Processing Modules (MCD)
MPM........... Metal-Plastic Metal [Automotive engineering]
MPM........... Meters per Minute
mpm........... Meters Per Minute (AD)
MPM........... Metra-Potential Method [Graph theory]
MPM........... Microprogram Memory
MPM........... Microscope-Photometer
MPM........... Microwave Power Meter
MPM........... Mid-Pacific Mountains [Geology]
MPM........... Miles per Minute
MPM........... Milestone Planning Meeting (MCD)
MPM........... Milwaukee Public Museum (AD)
MPM........... Miniaturized Pointing Mount [Spacelab] [NASA]
MPM........... Missile Power Monitor (AAG)
mpm........... Missile Power Monitor (AD)
MPM........... Modest Petrovich Mussorgsky [1839-1881] (AD)
mpm........... Mole-Percent Metal (AD)
MPM........... Monocycle Position Modulation
MPM........... Mortality Probability Models [Medicine]
MPM........... Mouse Peritoneal Macrophages
MPM........... Mouvement Populaire Mahorais [Mayotte People's Movement] [Comoros] [Political party] (PPW)
MPM........... Moving Presentation Mode
MP/M......... Multiprocessing Monitor Control Program [Computer science]
MP/M......... Multiprogramming Control Program for Microcomputers
MP/M......... Multiprogramming Control Program for Microprocessors (NITA)
MPM........... Multiprogramming Monitor
MPM........... Multipurpose Meal
mpm........... Multipurpose Meal (AD)
MPM........... Multipurpose Missile (MCD)
MP-M......... Museum Plantin Moretus [Belgium] (AD)
MPMA........ Master of Public Management and Administration
MPMA........ Metal Packaging Manufacturers Association [British] (DBA)
MPMA........ Methylphorbol Myristate Acetate [Organic chemistry]
MPMA........ Montford Point Marine Association (EA)
MPMA........ Motion Picture Museum Association [British] (BI)
MPM&PH.... Master of Preventive Medicine and Public Health (GAGS)
MPMC........ Microprogram Memory Control (NITA)
MPMC........ Military Personnel, Marine Corps
MPMCANSW... Master Plumbers and Mechanical Contractors Association of New South Wales [Australia]
MPMCAV .... Master Plumbers and Mechanical Contractors' Association of Victoria [Australia]
MPMCAWA... Master Plumbers and Mechanical Contractors' Association of Western Australia
MPMG .... Marine Pollution Management Group [British]
MPMG .... Melt-Powder Melt-Growth [Materials Science]
MPMG .... Multi-Purpose Molybdenum Grease
MPMG .... Panama/Paitilla, Marco A. Gelabert [Panama] [ICAO location identifier] (ICLI)
MPMH .... Mean Preventive Maintenance Hours
MPMI .... Magazine and Paperback Marketing Institute (EA)
MPMIC....... Mechanical Properties of Materials Information Center (MCD)
MPMIS....... Military Police Management Information System
MPML .... Mid-Pacific Marine Laboratory (MSC)
MP/ML....... Modified Construction Permit and Modified License [FCC] (NTCM)
MPML .... MPM Technologies, Inc. [NASDAQ symbol] (SAG)
MPMLE ...... MPM Technologies [NASDAQ symbol] (TTSB)
MPMMG .... Marine Pollution Monitoring Management Group (ASF)
MPMO .... Motion Picture Machine Operator [A union] (NTCM)
MPMP....... Mass Properties Management Plan (NASA)
MPMP....... (Methylpiperidyl)methylphenothiazine [Sedative]
MPMP....... Modification Program Management Plan (MCD)
MPMPR ..... Metropolitan Police Missing Persons Register [British]
MPMPrEC ... Magnum Pete $1.10 Cv'C'Pfd [AMEX symbol] (TTSB)
MPMR .... Movimiento Patriotica Manuel Rodriguez [Manuel Rodriguez Patriotic Movement] [Chile] [Political party] (EY)
MPMRP ...... Master Petroleum Material Requirements Plan (MCD)
MPMS........ Mattress and Palliasse Makers' Society [A union] [British]

MPMS.........	Missile Performance Measuring System (MCD)
MPMS.........	Multiple-Pressure Measuring System
MPMSE.......	Multiuse Payload and Mission Support Equipment (MCD)
MPMT.........	Mean Preventive Maintenance Time (MCD)
MPMT.........	Mellon Participating Mortgage Trust Commercial Properties Series [*NASDAQ symbol*] (NQ)
MPMT.........	Multiple Primary Malignant Tumor [*Oncology*]
MPM Tch....	MPM Technologies, Inc. [*Associated Press*] (SAG)
MPMUL.......	Military Production Master Urgency List
MPMV.........	Mason-Pfizer Monkey Virus
MPN...........	Manpower Personnel, Navy (DOMA)
MPN...........	Manufacturers Part Number (MCD)
MPN...........	Manufacturer's Productivity Network [*Hewlett-Packard Co.*]
MPN...........	Master in Psychiatric Nursing (GAGS)
MPN...........	Master Part Number (MCD)
MPN...........	Mean Probable Number (MCD)
MPN...........	Medial Preoptic Nucleus [*Brain anatomy*]
MPN...........	Methyl Parathion [*Also, MEP, MP*] [*Pesticide*]
MPN...........	Military Pay, Navy [*An appropriation*]
MPN...........	Military Personnel, Navy
MPN...........	Military Procurement, Navy (MCD)
MPN...........	Monongahela Power Co. [*AMEX symbol*] (SPSG)
MPN...........	Most Probable Number
mpn...........	Most Probable Number (AD)
MPNA	Midwest Professional Needlework Association [*Later, APNRA*] (EA)
MPNC.........	Mouvement pour le Progres National Congolais [*Movement for National Congolese Progress*]
MPNDS.......	Material Properties Numerical Data System [*Purdue University*] [*Database*]
MPNE.........	Manpower Needs [*Military*]
MPNF.........	Manpower-Needs Forecasting (MCD)
MPNI	Ministry of Pensions and National Insurance [*Later, MSS*] [*British*]
MPNPrA......	Monogahela Pwr 4.4% Pfd [*AMEX symbol*] (TTSB)
MPNPrC......	Monongah Power 4/50%cm C Pfd [*AMEX symbol*] (TTSB)
MPNST	Malignant Peripheral Nerve Sheath Tumor
MPO...........	Macedonian Patriotic Organization of US and Canada (EA)
MPO...........	Major Program Objective (MCD)
MPO...........	Management and Personnel Office (ODBW)
MPO...........	Management and Personnel Office (AIE)
MPO...........	Managers, Proprietors, and Officials
MPO...........	Manufacturing Production Order (NRCH)
MPO...........	Maputo [*Mozambique*] [*Geomagnetic observatory code*]
MPO...........	Maximum Power Output
MPO...........	Medial Preoptic [*Brain anatomy*]
MPO...........	Member of the Post Office [*British*]
MPO...........	Memorandum Purchase Order (AD)
mpo...........	Memory Printout (AD)
MPO...........	Memory Printout [*Computer science*]
MPO...........	Memory Protect Override
MPO...........	Mercury Project Office [*NASA*] (SAA)
MPO...........	Metropolitan Planning Organization
MPO...........	Metropolitan Planning Organization [*FHWA*] [*MTMC*] (TAG)
MPO...........	Metropolitan Police Office [*Familiarly called "Scotland Yard" from its site at New Scotland Yard*] [*British*]
MPO...........	Miami Philharmonic Orchestra (AD)
MPO...........	Military Pay Order
MPO...........	Military Permit Office [*or Officer*]
MPO...........	Military Personnel Office
MPO...........	Military Planning Office [*SEATO*] (CINC)
MPO...........	Military Post Office
MPO...........	Misconduct Policy Officer [*National Institutes of Health*]
MPO...........	Missile Processing Operation (MCD)
MPO...........	Mobile Post Office
MPO...........	Mobile Printing Office (AD)
MPO...........	Modular Personnel Office (SSD)
MPO...........	Motion Picture Operator
MPO...........	Mount Pocono, PA [*Location identifier FAA*] (FAAL)
MPO...........	Mustering Petty Officer
MPO...........	Myeloperoxidase [*An enzyme*]
MPOA	Medial Preoptic Area [*Medicine*]
MPOA	Puerto Obaldia [*Panama*] [*ICAO location identifier*] (ICLI)
MPOAH.......	Medial Preoptic-Anterior Hypothalamic [*Brain anatomy*]
MPOD.........	Mean Planned Outage Duration [*Electronics*] (IEEE)
MPOI	Master Program of Instruction [*Army*] (AABC)
MPOIS	Military Police Operations and Information System [*Army*] (MCD)
MPol...........	Master of Policy
M Pol.........	Master of Political Science (PGP)
MPolAdmin...	Master of Policy and Administration
MPolEcon	Master of Political Economy [*British*] (ADA)
MPOLL........	Military Post Office Location List (AFM)
MPolLaw.....	Master of Policy and Law
M Pol Sc	Master of Political Science
MPOM	Maintenance Program Operations Management [*Military*] (AABC)
MPOR	Maintenance Plant at Ober Ramstadt [*Army*] (MCD)
MPOS	Manportable Office System [*Army*] (RDA)
MPOS	Military Plans and Operations Staff
MPOS	Mobile Post Office Society (EA)
MPOS	Movie Projector Operator's School (DNAB)
MPOS	Multipurpose Optimization System [*Computer science*]
MPOSC.......	Master of Polar and Ocean Science
MPOT.........	Master in Psychiatric Occupational Therapy (GAGS)
M-POTS	Mobile Psychological Operations Transmitter (DOMA)
MPP...........	Mailer's Postmark Permit
MPP...........	Maintainability Program Plan
MPP...........	Major Program Proposal (AAG)

MPP.............	Manipur People's Party [*India*] [*Political party*] (PPW)
MPP.............	Marginal Physical Product [*Agriculture*]
mpp.............	Marginal Physical Product (AD)
MPP.............	Marine Power Plant (PDAA)
MPP.............	Martens Polarization Photometer [*Physics*]
MPP.............	Massively Parallel Processor [*Image processing*]
MPP.............	Massive Periretinal Proliferation [*Ophthalmology*] (DAVI)
MPP.............	Master in Public Policy [*National University of Singapore*]
MPP.............	Master of Physical Planning (NADA)
MPP.............	Master of Public Policy
MPP.............	Master Patch Panel [*Air Force*] (MCD)
MPP.............	Master Program Plan (NG)
MPP.............	Material Processing Procedure (NASA)
MPP.............	Materials Preparation Program (SAA)
MPP.............	Materiel Performance Package [*Military*] (AFM)
MPP.............	Matrix Processing Peptidase [*An enzyme*]
MPP.............	Maximum Perfusion Pressure [*Cardiology*] (DAVI)
MPP.............	Maximum Positive Pressure [*Nuclear energy*] (NRCH)
MPP.............	Medical Personnel Pool
MPP.............	Melanesian Progressive Parti [*Vanuatu*] [*Political party*] (EY)
MPP.............	Melphalan, Prednisone, Procarbazine [*Antineoplastic drug regimen*]
MPP.............	Member of Provincial Parliament [*British*]
MPP.............	Memory Parity and Protect (NITA)
MPP.............	Mercaptopyrazidopyrimidine [*Antineoplastic drug*] (MAE)
MPP.............	Merit Promotion Plan [*or Program*] [*NASA*] (NASA)
MPP.............	Message Processing Program [*Computer science*]
MPP.............	Meta Postprocessor [*Software program*] [*Symbolic Control, Inc.*]
MPP.............	Methyl(phenyl)pyridine [*Biochemistry*]
MPP.............	Methylpiperazine [*Organic chemistry*]
MPP.............	Microfilm Printer/Plotter
MPP.............	Microprogrammable Processor (MCD)
MPP.............	Miles per Pound [*NASA*] (KSC)
MPP.............	Military Pay Procedures
MPP.............	Minimum Premium Plans [*Insurance*]
MPP.............	Minority Procurement Policy (AAGC)
MPP.............	Miscellaneous Personal Property [*Legal term*] (DLA)
MPP.............	Missile Power Panel (AAG)
MPP.............	Mission-Planning Program [*Gerospace*] (BARN)
MPP.............	Mitochondrial Processing Peptidase [*Biochemistry*]
MPP.............	Modern Programming Practice
MPP.............	Molypermalloy Powder [*Metallurgy*] (EECA)
MPP.............	Mongol People's Party [*Mongolia*] [*Political party*] (FEA)
MPP.............	Monodisperse Polymer Particle
MPP.............	Mono Power Pack (HGAA)
MPP.............	Most Probable Position [*Navigation*]
mpp.............	Most Probable Position (AD)
MPP.............	Mothers in Prison Projects (EA)
MPP.............	Motion Picture Pioneers (EA)
MPP.............	Motion Picture Projector (MSA)
MPP.............	Mount Pasian [*Philippines*] [*Seismograph station code, US Geological Survey*] (SEIS)
MPP.............	Mulatupo [*Panama*] [*Airport symbol*] (OAG)
MPP.............	Multiple Particle Plasma
MPP.............	Multiple Payload Program [*Military*]
MPP.............	Multiple-Product Pricing [*Business term*] (MHDB)
MPP.............	Programme of Mass Privatisation [*Poland*] (ECON)
MPPA...........	Master of Public Policy Administration (GAGS)
MPPA...........	Metal Powder Producers Association (EA)
MPPA...........	Music Publishers' Protective Association [*Later, NMPA*] (EA)
MPPAA........	Multiemployer Pension Plan Amendments Act [*1980*] (GFGA)
MPPAR........	Mouse Peroxisome Proliferator-Activated Receptor [*Biochemistry*]
MPPAV........	Master Poultry Processors' Association of Victoria [*Australia*]
MPPB...........	Methyl(phenyl)(propyl)barbituric (Acid) [*Biochemistry*]
MPPB...........	Mailer's Postmark Permit Club (EA)
MPPC...........	Master Program Phasing Chart (MCD)
MPPC...........	Medical Personnel (Priority) Committee [*World War II*]
MPPC...........	Microsoft Point to Point Compression [*Microsoft Corp.*] [*Computer science*] (PCM)
MPPC...........	Military Pay Procedure Committee
MPPC...........	Multipotent Hematopoietic Progenitor Cell [*Biochemistry*]
MPPC...........	Panama [*Panama*] [*ICAO location identifier*] (ICLI)
MPPCA........	Maryland Probation, Patrol and Corrections Association (AD)
MPPCF........	Million Particles per Cubic Foot [*in air*]
mppcf.........	Millions of Particles per Cubic Foot of Air (AD)
MPPD..........	Maximum Probable Property Damage [*Hazard analysis*]
MPPG..........	Magnesium Pyridoxal Phosphate Glutamate [*Biochemistry*]
MPPH..........	(Methylphenyl)phenylhydantoin [*Organic chemistry*]
MPPH..........	Motion Picture Phonographic Unit
MPPHA.......	Multiparameter Pulse Height Analyzer
MPPhS........	Member of the Royal Pharmaceutical Society [*Canada*] (DD)
MPPL..........	Multipunch Plate
mp pl.........	Multipunch Plate (AD)
MPPL..........	Multipurpose Processing Language [*Computer science*] (IEEE)
MPPL..........	Multipurpose Programming Language
MPPLT........	Military Police Platoon (DNAB)
MPPM.........	Master of Public and Private Management
MPPM.........	Materials-Process-Product Model (PDAA)
MPPM.........	Military Personnel Procurement Manual
MPPM.........	Mission Prediction and Performance Module [*Aerospace*]
MPPN.........	Malignant Persistent Positional Nystagmus [*Medicine*] (DMAA)
MPPO.........	Modified Polyphenylene Oxide [*Plastics technology*]
MPPP.........	Mechanically Processed Pork Product [*Food technology*]
MPPP.........	Methyl(phenyl)(propionoxy)piperidine [*Organic chemistry*]
MPPP.........	Money-Purchase Pension Plan [*Human resources*] (WYGK)
MPPPM.......	Master of Plant Protection and Pest Management (GAGS)

MPPR	Mobilization Production Planning Requirements [*Military*]
MPPR	Modification Program Progress Report (AFIT)
MPPR	Monthly Production Progress Reports (MCD)
MPPrA	Mississippi Pwr 7.25% Dep Pfd [*NYSE symbol*] (TTSB)
MPPRB	Materiel Procurement Priorities Review Board [*Army*] (AABC)
MPPrB	Mississippi Pwr 6.65% Dep Pfd [*NYSE symbol*] (TTSB)
MPPRC	Materiel Procurement Priorities Review Committee [*Army*] (RDA)
MPPrC	Mississippi Pwr 6.32% Dep Pfd [*NYSE symbol*] (TTSB)
MPPRCA	Marine Plastic Pollution Research and Control Act
MPPS	Master Production Planning Schedule [*Air Force*] (AFIT)
MPPS	Master Program Planning Schedule
MPPS	Medicare Prospective Payment System
mpps	Million Pulses per Second (AD)
MPPS	Moroccan Party of Progress and Socialism [*Political party*]
MPPS	Multipurpose (AABC)
MPPSE	Multipurpose Payload Support Equipment (NASA)
MPPSE	Multipurpose Payload Support Equipment
MPPT	Maximum Power Point Tracking [*Power system*]
MPPT	Methylprednisolone Pulse Therapy [*Medicine*]
MPPT	Moller-Plesset Perturbation Theory [*Physical chemistry*]
MPPUP	Master of Public Policy and Urban Planning (PGP)
MPPWCOM ...	Military Police Prisoner of War Command (AABC)
MPQ	Manpower Planning Quota (PDAA)
mpq	Manpower-Planning Quota (AD)
MPQ	McGill Pain Questionnaire [*Dentistry*]
MPQ	Morgan Stanley Group [*AMEX symbol*] (SAG)
MPQ	Multidimensional Personality Questionnaire [*Personality development test*] [*Psychology*]
MPQA	Minuteman Production Quality Assurance (MCD)
MPQ/T	Mean Personnel Quantity per Task (MCD)
MPR	Machined Part Requisition (MCD)
MPR	Madjelis Permusiawaratan Rakat [*People's Deliberative Assembly*] [*Indonesia*] (AD)
MPR	Maintainability Problem Report (NASA)
MPR	Maintainability Program Requirements (AD)
MPR	Maintenance Personnel Roster
MPR	Management Program Review [*NASA*] (NASA)
MPR	Management Program Review
MPR	Mane Primo [*Early in the Morning*] [*Pharmacy*] (ROG)
MPR	Mannose Phosphate Receptor [*Biochemistry*]
MPR	Manpower (AABC)
MPR	Manpower Policy and Requirements Branch [*Department of Defence*] [*Australia*]
MPR	Manufacturing Parts Record (KSC)
MPR	Manufacturing Planning Review (MCD)
MPR	Mariposa Resources, Inc. [*Vancouver Stock Exchange symbol*]
MPR	Maritime Provinces Reports [*Canada*] [*A publication*] (DLA)
MPR	Marrow Production Rate [*Hematology*]
MPR	Master Power Regulator
MPR	Material Purchase Requisition
MPR	Materials and Process Requirement [*Navy*]
MPR	Mauritanian Party for Renewal [*Political party*] (EY)
MPR	Maximum Potential Representation (MUGU)
MPR	Maximum Practical Rate [*Aviation*]
MPR	Mayaguez [*Puerto Rico*] [*Seismograph station code, US Geological Survey*] (SEIS)
MPR	McPherson, KS [*Location identifier FAA*] (FAAL)
MPR	Mechanical Pressure Regulator (NRCH)
MPR	Medium Power RADAR (NATG)
mpr	Medium-Power RADAR (AD)
MPR	Mercaptopurine Ribonucleoside [*Antineoplastic drug*]
MPR	Mercury Plunger Relay
MPR	Message Processing Region [*IBM Corp.*]
MPR	Met-Pro Corp. [*AMEX symbol*] (SPSG)
MPR	Microprogram Register (MHDI)
MPR	Military Pay Record
MPR	Military Personnel Record (AFM)
MPR	Military Photo-Reconnaissance (PDAA)
MPR	Mine Production Report
MPR	Minimum Processing Requirement
MPR	Mock-Up Purchase Request [*NASA*] (NASA)
MPR	Mongolian Peoples Republic
MPR	Monoclonal Antibody Production Rate
MPR	Monopulse RADAR (MSA)
MPR	Monthly Program Review (USDC)
MPR	Monthly Progress Report
MPR	Monthly Project Report
MPR	Mouvement Populaire de la Revolution [*Popular Revolutionary Movement*] [*Zaire*] [*Political party*] (PD)
MPR	Mouvement Populaire Revolutionnaire [*Popular Revolutionary Movement*] [*Tunisia*] [*Political party*] (PD)
MPR	Movimento Popolare Rivoluzionario [*Popular Revolutionary Movement*] [*Italy Political party*] (PD)
MPR	Multiple Provider Router [*Computer science*] (ACRL)
MPR	MultiProtocol Router [*Novell, Inc.*] (PCM)
MPR	Multipurpose Recorder
MPR	Music Power Rating
M Pr A	Master of Professional Accountancy (PGP)
MPRA	Military Police Regimental Association (EA)
MPRC	Maryland Psychiatric Research Center [*University of Maryland*] [*Research center*] (RCD)
MPRC	Medical Program Review Committee [*DoD Washington, DC*] (EGAO)
MPRC	Military Personnel Records Center (MCD)
MPRC	Motion Picture Research Council
MPRC	Multipurpose Range Complex [*Army*] (INF)

MPRC-H......	Multipurpose Range Complex - Heavy [*Army*]
MPRC-L......	Multipurpose Range Complex - Light [*Army*]
MPRE	Medium Power Reactor Experiment
MPRE	Minimum Pure Radium Equivalent (MCD)
MPRESS	Medium Pressure
mpress	Medium Pressure (AD)
mPRF..........	Median Pontine Reticular Formation [*Neurophysiology*]
MPRF..........	Medium Pulse Recurrence Frequency (MCD)
MPRF..........	Motion Picture Relief Fund [*Later, MPTF*] (EA)
M Pr Gph....	Master in Professional Geophysics
MPRH	Rio Hato [*Panama*] [*ICAO location identifier*] (ICLI)
MPRI	Member of the Plastics and Rubber Institute [*British*] (DBQ)
MPRI	Merchant Pacific Routing Instructions [*Shipping*]
MPRI	Mount Prat [*Italy*] [*Seismograph station code, US Geological Survey*] (SEIS)
MPRI	Multiphoton Resonance Ionization [*Spectrometry*]
MPRJ.........	Military Personnel Records Jacket [*Army*] (AABC)
MPRL..........	Manpower and Personnel Research Laboratory [*Army Research Institute for the Behavioral and Social Sciences*] (RDA)
MPRL..........	Master Parts Reference List
MPRL..........	Military Physics Research Laboratory [*University of Texas*] (MCD)
M Pr M	Master of Preventive Medicine
M Pr Met....	Master of Professional Meteorology (PGP)
MPrMet.......	Master of Professional Meteorology (GAGS)
MPRO	Machine Processing Section [*National Security Agency*]
M Prob S	Master of Probability and Statistics (PGP)
MProcEng	Master of Process Engineering, University of Sheffield [*British*] (DBQ)
M Prof Acc...	Master of Professional Accountancy
MProfAcc	Master of Professional Accounting (GAGS)
M Prof Past...	Master of Professional Pastoral (PGP)
MPROM	Mask Programmed Read-Only Memory [*Computer science*]
MPRP	Mercaptopurine Ribonucleotide [*Antineoplastic drug*]
MPRP	Mongolian People's Revolutionary Party [*Mongol Ardyn Khuv'sgalt Nam*] [*Political party*] (PPW)
MPRP	Moslem People's Republican Party [*Iran*] [*Political party*] (PPW)
MPRP	Muslim Peoples Republican Party [*Political party*] (AD)
MPRR	Management Program Review Report [*NASA*] (MCD)
MPRS	Marine Pollution Retrieval System [*BTS*] (TAG)
MPRS	Microform Personnel Records System (NVT)
MPRSA	Marine Protection, Research, and Sanctuaries Act [*1972*]
MPRST	Maximum Probability Ratio Sequential Test (PDAA)
MPRT	Multipurpose Rail Transport (NRCH)
MPRTM........	Master of Park, Recreation, and Tourism Management (GAGS)
MPRT/R	Missile Pneudraulic Repair Technician/Repairman (AAG)
MPS	Magazine Printers Section (EA)
MPS	Magnetic Pole Strength
MPS	Mail Preference Service [*Direct Mail Advertising Association*]
MPS	Main Power Switch
MPS	Main Propulsion System [*or Subsystem*] [*NASA*] (KSC)
MPS	Maintenance Performance System [*DoD*]
MPS	Maintenance Problem Summary
MPS	Management Policy Statement
MPS	Managerial Philosophies Scale [*Test*]
MPS	Manpower System (NRCH)
MPS	Manual Phase Shifter
MPS	Manufacturing Process Specification (AAG)
MPS	Marbled Paper Sides [*Bookbinding*]
mps	Marbled Paper Sides (AD)
MPS	Marginal Propensity to Save [*Economics*]
MPS	Marine Polymetalic Sulfide
MPS	Marine Prepositioned Ships Program
MPS	Maritime Postmark Society [*Later, USCS*] (EA)
MPS	Maritime Prepositioning Ship (MCD)
MPS	Maritime Prepositioning Squadron (DOMA)
MPS	Marriage Prediction Schedule [*Psychology*]
MPS	Master of Pastoral Studies (PGP)
MPS	Master of Personnel Service (GAGS)
MPS	Master of Personnel Services
MPS	Master of Policy Sciences (PGP)
MPS	Master of Political Science (GAGS)
MPS	Master of Professional Studies (PGP)
MPS	Master of Professional Studies in Human Relations
M Ps	Master of Psychology
MPS	Master of Public Service (GAGS)
MPS	Master Performance System
MPS	Master Planning Schedule (MCD)
MPS	Master Production Schedule
MPS	Master Program Schedule (NASA)
MPS	Master Project Summary [*Civil Defense*]
MPS	Material Planning Study
MPS	Material Planning System [*Manufacturing management*]
MPS	Material Processing Specification (NASA)
MPS	Material Processing System
MPS	Material Processing System
MPS	Materials Processing in Space [*NASA*]
MPS	Materials Processing in Space
MPS	Materiel Planning Study [*Army*]
MPS	Mathematical Programming Society [*Voorburg, Netherlands*] (EAIO)
MPS	Mathematical Programming System [*Computer science*]
MPS	Maximum Performance Escape System (MCD)
MPS	Mechanical Phase Shifter
MPS	Mechanical Power Systems
MPS	Median Period of Survival
MPS	Medical Polymers Tech [*VS, exchange symbol*] (TTSB)
MPS	Medical Practice Study

MPS............ Medical Protection Society [*British*] (DBA)
MPS............ Medical Provider Survey [*Department of Health and Human Services*] (GFGA)
MPS............ MegaBITS [*Binary Digits*] per Second [*Transmission rate*] [*Computer science*] (MCD)
mps .... Megacycles per Second (AD)
MPS............ Megacyles [*Also, MCPS*] (WDAA)
MPS............ Meiosis-Preventing Substance [*Cytology*]
MPS............ Member of the Pharmaceutical Society [*British*]
MPS............ Member of the Philological Society [*British*]
MPS............ Member of the Physical Society [*British*]
MPS............ Memory Processor Switch
MPS............ Mercury Procedures Simulator [*NASA*]
MPS............ Merit Pay System (MCD)
MPS............ Mervyn Peake Society (EA)
MPS............ Message Processing System (NVT)
MPS............ Meters per Second
mps .... Meters per Second (IDOE)
mps .... Meters per Second (AD)
MPS............ Methodist Philatelic Society (EA)
MPS............ Methyl Phenyl Sulfide [*Organic chemistry*]
MPS............ Michigan Picture Stories [*Psychology*] (DAVI)
MPS............ Microbial Profile System [*Microbiology*]
MPS............ Microphone Power Supply
MPS............ Microprocessor Series [*or System*] (MDG)
MPS............ Microwave Phase Shifter
MPS............ Microwave Pressure Sounder (MCD)
MPS............ Microwave Pulse Source
MPS............ Miles per Second
mps .... Miles per Second (IDOE)
MPS............ Military Planning Staff (CINC)
MPS............ Military Postal Service (AFM)
MPS............ Military Production Specifications
MPS............ Milwaukee Public Museum (AD)
MPS............ Minimum Performance Specification (DA)
MPS............ Minimum Piecework Standard [*British*]
MPS............ Minimum Property Standards [*FHA*]
MPS............ Minister of Public Security [*British*]
MPS............ Misioneras del Perpetual Socorro (TOCD)
MPS............ Missionary Sisters of Our Lady of Perpetual Help (TOCD)
MPS............ Mission Parcels Society [*British*]
MPS............ Mission Preparation Sheet
MPS............ Mission-Processing Subsystem (MCD)
MPS............ Mission Profile Simulator [*NASA*]
MPS............ Miss Porter's School [*Farmington, CT*]
MPS............ Mixed Potential System (PDAA)
MPS............ Mobile Positioning Ship (DNAB)
MPST.......... Modular Power System (MCD)
MPS............ Modular Processor System [*Computer science*] (PCM)
MPS............ Molecular Photoemission Spectroscopy
MPS............ Mononuclear Phagocyte System [*Hematology*]
MPS............ Mont Pelerin Society (EA)
MPS............ Montreal Platelet Syndrome [*Medicine*] (DMAA)
MPS............ Motion Picture Service [*Department of Agriculture*]
mps .... Motor Parts Stock (AD)
MPS............ Motor Pump System (MCD)
MPS............ Mount Pleasant [*Texas*] [*Airport symbol Obsolete*] (OAG)
MPS............ Mouvement Patriotique du Salut [*Chad*] [*Political party*] (EY)
MPS............ Mouvement Populaire Senegalais [*Senegalese Popular Movement*] [*Political party*]
MPS............ Movement-Produced Stimuli
MPS............ Movimiento de Patria Socialista [*Venezuela Political party*] (EY)
MPS............ MPS [*Mucopolysaccharidoses*] Society (EA)
MPS............ Mucopolysaccharide [*Also, MP*] [*Clinical chemistry*]
MPS............ Mucopolysaccharidosis [*Medicine*]
MPS............ Multi-Format Photointerpretation System (SAA)
MPS............ Multiparticle Spectrometer [*Brookhaven National Laboratory*]
MPS............ Multiphasic Screening [*Medicine*]
MPS............ Multi-Plane Programming System (NITA)
MPS............ Multiple Peptide Synthesis [*Biochemistry*]
MPS............ Multiple Protective Structure [*Missile bases*]
MPS............ Multiple Vertical Protective Shelter [*for missiles*]
MPS............ Multiprocessing System [*Computer science*]
MPS............ Multiprogramming Periodic Tasking System (NITA)
MPS............ Multiprogramming System (AD)
MPS............ Multiprogramming System [*Computer science*]
MPS............ Multipurpose Ship (AABC)
MPS............ Muzzle Position Sensor (MCD)
MPS............ Myeloma Progression Score [*Oncology*]
MPS............ Society for Mucopolysaccharide Diseases (EA)
MPSA.......... Master of Public School Art
MPSA.......... Metropolitan Pharmaceutical Secretaries Association (EA)
MPSA.......... Military Petroleum Supply Agency [*Later, Defense Petroleum Supply Center*]
MPSA.......... Military Postal Service Agency
MPSA.......... Santiago [*Panama*] [*ICAO location identifier*] (ICLI)
MPSC.......... Marianas Political Status Commission
MPSC.......... Material Planning Schedule and Control [*Division of Inspection Offices, Navy*]
MPSC.......... Military Personnel Security Committee
MPSC.......... Military Provost Staff Corps [*British*]
MPSC.......... Movimiento Popular Socialcristiano [*Christian Social Popular Movement*] [*El Salvador*] [*Political party*] (PD)
MPSCL........ Mathematical Programming System Control Language [*1974*] [*Computer science*] (CSR)

MP/SCM ...... Multiport Semiconductor Memory (MHDI)
MPSE.......... Motion Picture Sound Editors (EA)
MPSE.......... Multipurpose Payload Support Equipment (MCD)
MPSF.......... Multi-Purpose Special Fund [*Asian Development Bank*] [*United Nations*] (EY)
MPSG.......... Marketing Programs and Services Group, Inc. [*Gaithersburg, MD*] [*Information service or system Telecommunications*] (TSSD)
MPSG.......... Multi-Band Portable Signal Generator (PDAA)
MPSH.......... Mean Pressure Suction Head (AAG)
mpsh .... Mean Pressure Suction Head (AD)
MPS-HHSA... Master of Professional Studies-Hospital and Health Services Administration
MPSI.......... Message Processing Systems, Inc. [*Charlotte, NC*] [*Telecommunications service*] (TSSD)
MPSI.......... MPSI Systems, Inc. [*NASDAQ symbol*] (SAG)
MPS I .... Mucopolysaccharidoses [*Hurler Syndrome*] [*Also, Scheie Syndrome and Hurler/Scheie Syndrome*] (PAZ)
MPSIG .... Monty Python Special Interest Group (EA)
MPS II .... Mucopolysaccharidoses [*Hunter Syndrome*] (PAZ)
MPS IV .... Mucopolysaccaridoses [*Morquio Syndrome*] (PAZ)
MPSK.......... Multiple Phase Shift Keying [*Computer science*] (TEL)
MPSM.......... Master of Public School Music
MPSM.......... Master Problem Status Manual
MPSM.......... MODEM Pooling Service Module [*Telecommunications*]
MPSM.......... Multipurpose Submunition (RDA)
MPSMT....... Merrill-Palmer Scale of Mental Tests [*Psychology*] (DAVI)
MPSN.......... Microwave Pulse Shaping Network
MPSNY....... Montserrat Progressive Society of New York (EA)
MPsO.......... Master of Psychology Orientation (NADA)
MP SOV GR COM... Most Puissant Sovereign Grand Commander [*United States*] [*Freemasonry*] (ROG)
MPSP.......... Mathematical Problem-Solving Project [*National Science Foundation*]
MP(S)P....... Mechanically Processed (Species) Product (DICI)
MPSP.......... Military Personnel Security Program
MPSR.......... Mission Profile Storage and Retrieval [*NASA*] (NASA)
MPSR.......... Multipurpose Support Room (MCD)
MPSRE........ Master of Professional Studies in Real Estate (PGP)
MPSRON...... Maritime Prepositioning Ship Squadron (DOMA)
MPSRT .... Matched-Pairs Signed-Rank Test [*Statistics*]
MPSS.......... Main Parachute Support Structure (NASA)
MPSS.......... Main Parachute Support Structure
MPSS.......... Maryland Preschool Self-Concept Scale (EDAC)
MPSS.......... Mission Payload System Segment
MPSS.......... Multiple Protective Structure System (AD)
MPSS.......... Multipurpose Sampling System
M Ps Sc....... Master of Physic Sciences
MPsSc......... Master of Psychological Science (GAGS)
MPST.......... Minimum Performance Standard Test [*Military*] (CAAL)
M Ps Th....... Master of Psycho-Therapy
MPSTWG .... Mission Planning System Test Working Group [*Military*] (CAAL)
MPSU.......... Missile Pressure Status Unit (AAG)
MPSV.......... Myeloproliferative Sarcoma Virus
MPSW......... Master of Psychiatric Social Work (NADA)
MP SWAT.... Military Police Special Weapons and Tactics Team (VNW)
MPSX.......... Mathematical Programming System Extended [*IBM Corp.*] [*Computer science*]
MPsych........ Master of Psychology
M Psych ...... Master of Psychology (PGP)
MPsychApp... Master of Applied Psychology (ADA)
MPsych(Clin)... Master of Psychology (Clinical)
MPsych(Ed)... Master of Psychology (Education)
MPsychMed... Master of Psychological Medicine, University of Liverpool [*British*] (DBQ)
MPsychol..... Master of Psychology
MPsychTh.... Master of Psychotherapy
M Psy Med... Master of Psychological Medicine
MPT............ Alpha-Methyl-p-tyrosine [*Also, AMPT*] [*Pharmacology*]
MPT............ Magnetic Particle Testing [*Nuclear energy*] (NRCH)
MPT............ Main Propulsion Test [*NASA*] (NASA)
MPT............ Male Pipe Thread (MSA)
mpt............ Male Pipe Thread (AD)
MPT............ Maneuver Planning Table [*NASA*]
MPT............ Manpower and Training (DOMA)
MPT............ Manpower, Personnel, and Training
MPT............ Marginal Propensity to Tax [*Economics*]
MPT............ Maryland Public Television [*Owings Mills*] [*Information service or system Telecommunications*] (TSSD)
Mpt............ Maryport (AD)
MPT............ Master of Pastoral Theology (PGP)
MPT............ Master of Physical Therapy (GAGS)
MPT............ Matupit Island [*New Britain*] [*Seismograph station code, US Geological Survey*] (SEIS)
MPT............ Maximum Power Transfer (IDOE)
MPT............ Mean Preventive Maintenance Time (MCD)
MPT............ Mean Pulse Time
MPT............ Mechanical Power Transmission
M PT........... Melting Point (ROG)
mpt............ Melting Point (AD)
MPT............ Memory Processing Time
MPT............ Mercury Procedures Trainer
MPT............ Message Processing Task [*Computer science*] (ECII)
MPT............ Metal-Phthalocyanine Tetramine [*Organic chemistry*]
MPT............ Methyl-para-Tyrosine [*Biochemistry*]
MPT............ Michigan Picture Test [*Psychology*]
mpt............ Microprocessing Programmable Terminal [*Computer science*] (AD)

MPT............ Microprogramming Technique
mpt............ Midpoint (AD)
MPT............ Miles per Tankful (AD)
mpt............ Miles per Tankful (AD)
MPT............ Military Potential Test (AABC)
MPT............ Milk Pasteurization Tribunal [*Australia*]
MPT............ Minimum Pressurization Temperature [*Nuclear energy*] (NRCH)
MPT............ Minimum Process Time
MPT............ Ministry of Posts and Telecommunications [*People's Republic of China*] (ECON)
MPT............ Ministry of Posts and Telecommunications
MPT............ Ministry of Posts and Telecommunictions [*China*] (ECON)
MPT............ Missile Preflight Tester
MPT............ Missile Procedure Trainer
MPT............ Mission Planning Table [*NASA*] (KSC)
MPT............ Mission Planning Terminal (MCD)
MPT............ Mixed Parotid Gland Tumor [*Oncology*]
MPT............ Modern Portfolio Theory [*Finance*]
MPT............ Molydopterin [*Biochemistry*]
MPT............ Morphine Provocative Test [*Gastroenterology*] (DAVI)
MPT............ MOS [*Military Occupational Specialty*] Proficiency Training [*DoD*]
MPT............ Motional Pickup Transducer (MCD)
MPT............ Mouvement Populaire Tchadien [*Chadian Popular Movement*] [*Political party*]
MPT............ Mouvement Populaire Togolais [*Togolese Popular Movement*] [*Political party*]
MPT............ Mouvement pour le Progres et la Tolerance [*Burkina Faso*] [*Political party*] (EY)
MPT............ Multilateral Preparatory Talks (NATG)
MPT............ Multiple Pure Tone [*Sound*]
mpt............ Multiple Pure Tone (AD)
MPT............ Multiple-Purpose Telescope
mpt............ Multipower Transmission (AD)
MPT............ Municipal Partners Fund [*NYSE symbol*] (SPSG)
MPT............ Municipal Partners Fund II [*NYSE symbol*] (TTSB)
MPTA.......... Machine Power Transmission Association (AD)
mpta.......... Main Propulsion Test Article (AD)
MPTA.......... Main Propulsion Test Article [*NASA*]
MPTA.......... Manpower, Personnel, and Training Analysis
MPTA.......... Mechanical Power Transmission Association (EA)
MPTA.......... Municipal Passenger Transport Association, Inc. [*British*] (BI)
MPTAO .... Military Personnel and Transportation Assistance Office (MCD)
MPTB.......... Meridian Point Realty Trust [*NASDAQ symbol*] (SAG)
MPTB.......... Monophosphate Tungsten Bronze [*Metallurgy*]
MPTB.......... Multisolid Pneumatic Transport Bed [*Chemical engineering*]
MPTBS........ Meridian Point Rity Tr 83 [*NASDAQ symbol*] (TTSB)
MPTCA........ Motion Picture and Television Credit Association (EA)
MPTCC........ Most Probable Total Contract Cost (AAGC)
MPTCMA..... Motion Picture and Television Credit Managers Association [*Later, MPTCA*] (EA)
MPTDS .... MPTER [*Multiple Point Source Model with Terrain*] Model with Deposition andSettling of Pollutants [*Environmental Protection Agency*] (GFGA)
MPTE.......... Multipurpose Test Equipment
MPTEDA ..... Mechanical Power Transmission Equipment Distributors Association [*Later, Power Transmission Distributors Association*] (EA)
MPTER........ Multiple Point Source Model with Terrain [*Environmental Protection Agency*] (GFGA)
MPTF.......... Main Propulsion Test Facility [*NASA*] (NASA)
MPTF.......... Main Propulsion Test Facility [*NASA*]
MPTF.......... Mission Planning Task Force (KSC)
MPTF.......... Motion Picture and Television Fund (EA)
MPTF.......... Music Performance Trust Funds (EA)
MPTH.......... Methylphenothiazine [*Organic chemistry*]
MPTL.......... Materials Processing Technology Laboratory (SSD)
MPTMH....... Major Peace Treaties of Modern History, 1648-1967 [*A publication*] (DLA)
MPTN.......... Multiprotocol Transport Network [*Telecommunications*] (ACRL)
MPTO.......... Methods and Procedures Technical Orders
MPTO.......... Tocumen/General Omar Torrijos H. [*Panama*] [*ICAO location identifier*] (ICLI)
MPTP.......... Main Propulsion Test Program (MCD)
MPTP.......... Methyl(phenyl)tetrahydropyridine [*Organic chemistry*]
MPTP.......... Music Preference Test of Personality [*Psychology*]
MPTR.......... MedPartners, Inc. [*NASDAQ symbol*] (SAG)
MPTR.......... Mobile Position Tracking RADAR
MPTR.......... Motor, Pain, Touch, Reflex [*Neurology*] (DAVI)
MPTR.......... Multipurpose Training Range [*Army*]
MPTS.......... Manpower, Personnel, and Training Support [*Military*] (CAAL)
MPTS.......... Manpower, Personnel, Training, and Safety [*Army*]
MPTS.......... Metal Parts (AABC)
MPTS.......... Mobile Photographic Tracking Station
MPTS.......... Multi-Protocol Transport Service [*Telecommunications*]
MPTS.......... Multipurpose Test Set (DWSG)
MPTS.......... Multipurpose Tool Set (MCD)
MPT-SD ...... Multipurpose, Tracer, Self-Destruct [*Army*]
MP(TSWG)... Military Police Tripartite Standing Working Group (AABC)
MPTT.......... Maintenance Part Task Trainer [*Army*]
MPTUS .... Marble Polishers' Trade Union Society [*British*]
MPTV.......... MPTV, Inc. [*NASDAQ symbol*] (SAG)
MPTWT....... Medium Power Traveling Wave Tube
MPU............ Magnetic Pickup [*Electronics*]
MPU............ Main Power Unit
MPU............ Main Propulsion Unit
MPU............ Malayan Planning Unit [*World War II*]

MPU............ Manpack Unit (MCD)
MPU............ Mapua [*Papua New Guinea*] [*Airport symbol Obsolete*] (OAG)
MPU............ Medical Practitioners' Union [*Later, Medical Practitioners' Section - MPS*] [*British*] (DCTA)
MPU............ Memory Protection Unit
MPU............ Mental Parents Union (AD)
MPU............ Message Picking-Up
MPU............ Microprocessor Unit [*CPU of microcomputer*] [*Computer science*]
mpu............ Microprocessor Unit (AD)
MPU............ MIDI [*Musical Instrument Digital Interface*] Processing Unit [*Computer technology*]
MPU............ Miniature Portable Unit
MPU............ Minutes per Unit
MPU............ Missile Power Unit (DNAB)
MPU............ Missing Persons Unit (AD)
MPU............ Mixing and Pumping Unit [*Bulk explosives*] (MCD)
MPU............ Mobile Production Unit [*On-site television recording*] (NTCM)
MPU............ Monitor Printing Unit [*Computer science*]
mpu............ Monitor Printing Unit (AD)
MPU............ Motorola Processor Unit
MPU............ Motor Pressurization Unit
M Pub......... Master of Publishing (PGP)
M Pub Adm... Master of Public Administration
MPubAdmin... Master of Public Administration
MPubLaw ... Master of Public Law
MPubPol..... Master of Public Policy
MPUL......... Military Production Urgencies List (NG)
MPUS......... Military Production Urgencies System
MPV............ Magistrae Piae Venerini [*Religious Venerini Sisters*] [*Roman Catholic religious order*]
MPV............ Magnetic Polarization Vector
MPV............ Man-Powered Vehicle
M-P v.......... Mason-Pfizer Virus [*Medicine*] (AD)
MPV............ Mass Mutual Participating Investors [*NYSE symbol*] (CTT)
MPV............ MassMutual Participation Investors [*NYSE symbol*] (SAG)
MPV............ MassMutual Part'n Inv [*NYSE symbol*] (TTSB)
MPV............ Mean Platelet Volume [*Hematology*]
MPV............ Meerwein-Ponndorf-Verley [*Organic chemistry*]
MPV............ Metatarsus Primus Varus [*Orthopedics*] (DAVI)
MPV............ Methane-Powered Vehicle
MPV............ Military Pay Voucher
MPV............ Montpelier [*Vermont*] [*Airport symbol*] (OAG)
MPV............ Mountain Province [*Vancouver Stock Exchange symbol*]
MPV............ Multipurpose Passenger Vehicle
MPV............ Multipurpose Vehicle [*Automotive engineering*]
mpv............ Multipurpose Vehicle (AD)
MPV............ Religious Venerini Sisters (TOCD)
MPVA.......... Main Propellant Valve Actuator (MCD)
MP/VAP....... Maritime Patrol/Reconnaissance Attack Aircraft (NATG)
MPVI.......... Mountain Province Mining, Inc. [*NASDAQ symbol*] (SAG)
MPVIF......... Mountain Province Mining [*NASDAQ symbol*] (TTSB)
MPVM......... Master of Preventive Veterinary Medicine (GAGS)
MPVP.......... Mean Pulmonary Venous Pressure [*Cardiology*]
MPVR .... El Porvenir [*Panama*] [*ICAO location identifier*] (ICLI)
MPVSCS...... Military Pay Voucher Summary and Certification Sheet
MPVT.......... Montpelier [*Vermont*] [*Seismograph station code, US Geological Survey*] (SEIS)
MPW.......... Macintosh Programmer's Workshop [*Computer science*] (BTTJ)
mPw.......... Maritime Polar [*Air Mass*] Warm [*Meteorology*] (BARN)
MPW.......... Master of Public Works (PGP)
MPW.......... Minneapolis-Moline [*Stock exchange symbol*] (AD)
MPW.......... Modified Plane Wave (IEEE)
MPW.......... Whiteshell Nuclear Research Establishment, Atomic Energy of Canada [*Etablissement de Recherche Nucleaire Whiteshell, L'Energie Atomique du Canada*] Pinawa,Manitoba [*Library symbol National Library of Canada*] (NLC)
MPWB......... Multilayer Printed-Wiring Board
MPWBS....... Master Plan Works Breakdown Structure (AD)
MPWC .... Michigan Pure Water Council (EA)
MPWD......... Machine-Prepared Wiring Data [*Telecommunications*] (TEL)
MPWG........ Minuteman Parts Working Group [*Missiles*]
MPWS .... Mobile Protected Weapon System (RDA)
MPWU........ Movement for Political World Union [*Blommenslyst, Fyn, Denmark*] (EA)
MPX............ Aeromexpress, SA de CV [*Mexico*] [*FAA designator*] (FAAC)
MPX............ Magazine Page Exposure [*Publishing*] (WDMC)
MPX............ Mapped Programming Executive [*Systems Engineering Laboratories U.S.*] (NITA)
MPX............ Microprocessor Exchange [*Computer science*]
MPX............ Multiplex [*or Multiplexer*] [*Telecommunications*]
mpx............ Multiplex (AD)
MPX............ Multiprocessor Extension (PCM)
MPX............ Multiprogramming Executive [*Computer science*]
MPXR.......... Multiplexer
mpxr.......... Multiplexor (AD)
Mpy............ Maatschappij [*Company*] [*Dutch*] (AD)
MPY............ Milli-Inches per Year [*Corrosion technology*]
MPY............ Multiple Problem Youth
MPY............ Multiply (MDG)
mpy............ Multiply (AD)
MPZ............ Mid-Continent Petroleum [*Stock exchange symbol*] (AD)
MPZ............ Modified Protamine Zinc [*Insulin*]
MPZ............ Mount Pleasant, IA [*Location identifier FAA*] (FAAL)
MPZL.......... Panama [*Panama*] [*ICAO location identifier*] (ICLI)
MQ............ Magnum Airlines [*ICAO designator*] (AD)

MQ.............	Management Quarterly Magazine [*A publication*] (EAAP)
MQ.............	MARC [*Machine-Readable Cataloging*] Quebecois [*Source file*] [*UTLAS symbol*]
MQ.............	Marketing Quota
mq	Martinique [*MARC country of publication code Library of Congress*] (LCCP)
MQ.............	Martinique [*ANSI two-letter standard code*] (CNC)
MQ.............	Memory Quotient
mq.............	Memory Quotient (AD)
MQ.............	Menaquinone [*Vitamin K*] [*Also, MK*] [*Biochemistry*]
MQ.............	Merit Quotient
MQ.............	Metol-Quinol [*Developer*] [*Photography*] (ROG)
mq.............	Metol-Quinol [*Medicine*] (AD)
MQ.............	Metol-Quinone [*Medicine*] (AD)
mq.............	Metol-Quinone [*Medicine*] (AD)
MQ.............	Mining and Quarrying [*Department of Employment*] [*British*]
MQ.............	Mo'ed Qatan [*or Qattan*] (BJA)
Mq.............	Mosque (AD)
mq.............	Mosque (BARN)
MQ.............	Mothering Quotient
mq.............	Multiple Quotient (AD)
MQ.............	Multiplier Quotient [*Computer science*]
MQ.............	Musical Quarterly [*A publication*] (BRI)
MQ.............	Simmons Airlines [*ICAO designator*] (AD)
MQ.............	Thomas Crane Public Library, Quincy, MA [*Library symbol Library of Congress*] (LCLS)
MQA.............	Adams Mansion, Quincy, MA [*Library symbol Library of Congress*] (LCLS)
MQA.............	Manual of Qualification for Advancement
MQA.............	Manufacturing Quality Assurance
MQA.............	Medical Quality Assurance (AD)
MQA.............	Murrayaquinone-A [*Biochemistry*]
MQAB.........	Medical Quality Assurance Board (AD)
MQAD.........	Materials Quality Assurance Directorate [*Ministry of Defence*] [*British*]
MQB.............	Macomb, IL [*Location identifier FAA*] (FAAL)
MQB.............	Mining Qualifications Board [*British*] (BI)
MQC.............	Macroscopic Quantum Coherence [*Physics*]
MQC.............	Manufacturing Quality Control (MCD)
MQCL.........	Master Quality Characteristic List (MCD)
MQD	Manhattan, KS [*Location identifier FAA*] (FAAL)
MQD	Metallurgical Quenching Dilatometry
MQD	Milner. Questions de Droit [*A publication*] (DLA)
MQD	Monolithic Quad Device
MQE.............	Martinique [*West Indies*] (WDAA)
Mqe.............	Martinique (AD)
MQE.............	Message Queue Element [*Computer science*]
MQEM.........	Michigan Quarterly Economic Model (NITA)
mqf.............	Mobile Quarantine Facility (AD)
MQF.............	Mobile Quarantine Facility [*NASA*]
MQG	General Dynamics, Quincy Shipbuilding Division, Quincy, MA [*Library symbol Library of Congress*] (LCLS)
MQG	Milgarra [*Queensland*] [*Airport symbol*] (AD)
MQHi	Quincy Historical Society, Quincy, MA [*Library symbol Library of Congress*] (LCLS)
MQI.............	Macquarie Island [*Australia Seismograph station code, US Geological Survey Closed*] (SEIS)
MQI.............	Maiquetia [*Venezuelan airport*] (AD)
MQI.............	Manteo, NC [*Location identifier FAA*] (FAAL)
MQIL.............	Miniature Quartz Incandescent Lamp
mqil.............	Miniature Quartz Incandescent Lamp (AD)
MQJ.............	Indianapolis, IN [*Location identifier FAA*] (FAAL)
MQK.............	Youngstown, OH [*Location identifier FAA*] (FAAL)
MQL.............	Mildura [*Australia Airport symbol*] (OAG)
MQL.............	Miniature Quartz Lamp
mql.............	Miniature Quartz Lamp (AD)
MQM.............	Master of Quality Management (PGP)
MQM.............	Master of the Queen's Music [*British*] (AD)
MQM.............	Message Queue Manager [*Computer science*] (MCD)
MQM.............	Monida, MT [*Location identifier FAA*] (FAAL)
MQM.............	Muhajir Qaumi Movement [*Pakistan*] [*Political party*] (ECON)
MQM.............	University of New Mexico, Medical Center Library, Albuquerque, NM [*OCLC symbol*] (OCLC)
MQN	Magnetic Quantum Number [*Atomic physics*]
MQO	Marksmanship Qualification Order [*Marine Corps*]
MQO	Mosquito Creek Gold Mining [*Vancouver Stock Exchange symbol*]
MQP.............	Military Qualification Program (NG)
MQP.............	Mineral Wells, TX [*Location identifier FAA*] (FAAL)
MQP.............	Motor Qualification Program (NG)
MQQ	Moundou [*Chad*] [*Airport symbol*] (AD)
MQR.............	Michigan Quarterly Review [*A publication*] (BRI)
MQR.............	Miscellaneous Quote Request (MCD)
MQR.............	Multiplier Quotient Register [*Computer science*]
MQRNS.......	Modified Quadratic Residue Number System (MCD)
MQS.............	Coatesville, PA [*Location identifier FAA*] (FAAL)
MQS.............	Maintenance Quality Specialist (MCD)
MQS.............	Master of Quantitative Systems
MQS.............	Military Qualification Standard
MQS.............	Mobile Quality Services (AD)
MQS.............	Motion to Quash Subpoena (NRCH)
MQS.............	Multiprogrammed Queued Tasking System (NITA)
MQS.............	Mustique [*Windward Islands*] [*Airport symbol*] (OAG)
MQSS.........	Mary Queen of Scots Society (EAIO)
MQT.............	Macquest Resources Ltd. [*Toronto Stock Exchange symbol*]
MQT.............	Macroscopic Quantum Tunneling [*Quantum mechanics*]

MQT.............	Marquette [*Michigan*] [*Airport symbol*] (OAG)
MQT.............	Military Qualification Test (NG)
MQT.............	Mission Qualification Training
MQT.............	Model Qualification Test
MQT.............	Motor Qualification Test (NG)
MQT.............	MuniYield Quality Fund II [*NYSE symbol*] (SPSG)
MQU.............	Beckley, WV [*Location identifier FAA*] (FAAL)
MQU.............	Makus Resources, Inc. [*Vancouver Stock Exchange symbol*]
MQU.............	Mariquita [*Colombia*] [*Airport symbol*] (OAG)
MQU.............	Media Quality Unit [*Communications*]
MQU.............	Multiplier Quotient Unit [*Computer science*]
MQV.............	Ministere de la Qualite de la Vie [*Ministry of the Quality of Life*] [*France*] (AD)
MQW	McRae, GA [*Location identifier FAA*] (FAAL)
MQW	Multiple Quantum Well [*Switch for an optical computer*]
MQW	Multiquantum Well (NITA)
MQWL	Multiquantum Well Lasers (NITA)
MQX.............	Makale [*Ethiopia*] [*Airport symbol*] (OAG)
MQY.............	MuniYield Quality Fund [*NYSE symbol*] (SPSG)
MQY.............	Smyrna, TN [*Location identifier FAA*] (FAAL)
mqyco.........	Minimum Quantity Yards per Color (AD)
mqyds.........	Minimum Quantity Yards per Design (AD)
MR.............	Air Mauritanie [*Mauritania*] [*ICAO designator*] (ICDA)
MR.............	Application for Writ of Mandamus Refused [*Legal term*] (DLA)
M/R.............	Machine Receipt
mr.............	Machine Record (AD)
MR.............	Machine Records
MR.............	Machine Rifle
mr.............	Machine Rifle (AD)
MR.............	Machinery Repairman [*Navy rating*]
MR.............	Macrophage Rich
MR.............	Magister [*Master*] [*Latin*] (ROG)
MR.............	Magnetic Recorder (DEN)
MR.............	Magnetic Resonance
MR.............	Magnetic Resonating (AD)
MR.............	Magnetoresistive
MR.............	Magnitude of Rotation
MR.............	Maintainability Report
M+R.............	Maintenance and Refurbishment
M+R.............	Maintenance and Repair
MR.............	Maintenance Ratio (MCD)
MR.............	Maintenance Review
MR.............	Management Requirements (MCD)
MR.............	Management Reserve (MCD)
MR.............	Mandelate Racemase [*An enzyme*]
MR.............	Manitoba Law Reports [*Canada*] [*A publication*] (DLA)
MR.............	Mannose Resistant [*Biochemistry*]
MR.............	Manpower Requirements
MR.............	Manual Removal [*Medicine*]
MR.............	Manufacturer's Representative
MR.............	Manufacturing Requisition
MR.............	Map Reading
M/R.............	Map Reading (AD)
m/r.............	Map Reading (AD)
mr.............	Map Reference (AD)
MR.............	Map Reference
MR.............	Marble (AAG)
MR.............	Marca Registrada [*Registered Trademark*] [*Spanish*]
MR.............	March
MR.............	Marginal Return [*Army*] (AABC)
MR.............	Marginal Revenue [*Economics*]
mr.............	Marginal Revenue (AD)
MR.............	Marianist Sisters (TOCD)
MR.............	Maritime Reconnaissance (NATG)
MR.............	Maritime Regiment
MR.............	Marketing Research Division [*of AMS, Department of Agriculture*]
MR.............	Mark Russell (AD)
MR.............	Mask Register
MR.............	Master [*British military*] (DMA)
Mr.............	Master (AD)
MR.............	Master of the Rolls
MR.............	Master Relay [*Electrical*] (DICI)
MR.............	Master Reset (MCD)
MR.............	Master Routing (SAA)
MR.............	Material Request [*or Requisition*] (MCD)
MR.............	Material Review [*Aviation*] (AAG)
MR.............	Materiel Readiness [*Army*]
MR.............	Mate's Receipt
M/R.............	Mates Receipt (AD)
MR.............	Mauritania [*ANSI two-letter standard code*] (CNC)
MR.............	Mauritius Decisions [*A publication*] (DLA)
MR.............	Mauritius Reports [*A publication*] (DLA)
MR.............	Maximal Response
MR.............	Maximum Range (IAA)
MR.............	May Repeat [*Medicine*]
MR.............	McCloud River [*Railroad*] (MHDW)
MR.............	Mean Radius (MCD)
MR.............	Measles, Rubella [*Immunology*]
MR.............	Measured Rating [*IOR*] [*Yacht racing*]
MR.............	Mechanical Restraint [*for mental patients*] [*British*]
MR.............	Medial Rectus [*Eye anatomy*]
MR.............	[*The*] Media Report [*A publication*] (NTCM)
MR.............	Medical Record
MR.............	Medical Rectus [*Muscle*] [*Anatomy*]
MR.............	Medical Report

MR	Medium Range
mr	Medium Range (AD)
MR	Medium-Range Planes [Navy]
MR	Medium Reduction (NITA)
MR	Medium Resolution
MR	Medullary Ray [Botany] (BARN)
mr	Meester [Master] [Dutch] (AD)
MR	Megarayleigh [Optics]
MR	Memorandum for Record [Military] (AFM)
MR	Memorandum Receipt [Military] (MUGU)
MR	Memorandum Report
MR	Memory Read [Computer science]
MR	Memory Recall [Computer science] (PCM)
MR	Memory Reclaimer
MR	Memory Register [Computer science]
mr	Mentally Retarded (AD)
MR	Mental Retardation
MR	Mercury-Redstone [NASA]
MR	Message Register (AAG)
MR	Message Repeat
MR	Metabolic Rate
mr	Metabolic Rate (AD)
MR	Meter
MR	Methacholine Response [Medicine]
MR	Methyl Red [A dye]
mr	Methyl Red (AD)
MR	Methyl Reductase [An enzyme]
MR	Metropolitan Railway [British]
MR	Michael Resources Ltd. [Vancouver Stock Exchange symbol]
MR	Michigan Reformatory (AD)
MR	Microminiature Relay
MR	Microplate Reader [Computer science]
MR	Middle Repetitive [Genetics]
m/r	Middle Right (AD)
MR	[The] Middlesex Regiment [British]
MR	Mid-Engine, Rear-Drive [Automotive engineering]
MR	Midland Railway [British]
MR	Midrib [Botany]
MR	Migration Ratio (DNAB)
MR	Military Railroad (AD)
MR	Military Readiness
MR	Military Region [Viet Cong term]
MR	Military Regulation
MR	Military Representative (NATG)
MR	Military Requirement
M/R	Military Reserve (CINC)
MR	Military Review (MCD)
MR	Militia Reserve [British military] (DMA)
MR	Milk-Ring [Test] [Medicine] (MEDA)
MR	Milliradian (DEN)
MR	Millirem (DEN)
mr	Milliroentgen
mR	Milliroentgen (AD)
mr	Mill Run (AD)
MR	Mill Run [Unselected lot of a manufactured product]
MR	Milrinone [Biochemistry]
MR	Mine Rake (DWSG)
MR	Mineralo-Corticoid Receptor [Endocrinology]
MR	Mineral Range Railroad (IIA)
MR	Mineral Rubber
mr	Mineral Rubber (AD)
mr	Mine Run (AD)
mr	Mine-Run
MR	Minimum Required
MR	Mining Reports, Edited by R. S. Morrison [Chicago] [A publication] (DLA)
MR	Mining Review [A publication]
MR	Mini Registry (EA)
MR	Minister-Residentiary [Diplomacy]
MR	Ministry of Reconstruction [World War I] [British]
MR	Minnesota Review [A publication] (BRI)
MR	Minor Repair (MCD)
MR	Mi Remesa [My Remittance] [Spanish Business term]
MR	Miscellaneous Report
MR	Missed Recognition (SAA)
MR	Missile RADAR [Military] (CAAL)
MR	Missile Receiver
MR	Missile Reference
MR	Missile Rounds (MCD)
M/R	Missiles and Rockets [A publication]
MR	Missionarius Rector [Missionary Rector] [Latin]
MR	Mission Radius (MCD)
MR	Mission Ready [Aircraft]
MR	Mission Reliability
MR	Mission Report [NASA]
MR	Mister
MR	Mister
MR	Mistura [Mixture] [Pharmacy] (ROG)
MR	Mitochondriarich [Cytology]
MR	Mitral Reflux [Cardiology] (MAE)
MR	Mitral Regurgitation [Cardiology]
MR	Mittleres Reich in Aegypten [A publication] (BJA)
MR	Mixture Ratio (KSC)
M/R	Mixture Ratio [Fuel to oxidizer]
Mr	Mobile Revertant [Bacteriology]
MR	Mobility Required [Civil Service]
MR	Mobilizacion Republicana [Republican Mobilization] [Nicaragua] [Political party] (AD)
MR	Mobilization Regulation [Army]
MR	MODEM Ready [Computer science]
MR	Moderately Resistant [Plant pathology]
MR	[The] Modern Reader's Bible (1907) [A publication] (BJA)
M-R	Modification and Restriction [of DNA] [Biochemistry, genetics]
MR	Modification Request [or Requirement]
MR	Modular Redundancy
MR	Modulation Response
MR	Moisture Resistant (IEEE)
MR	Molar Refraction
MR	Molecular Replacement [Crystallography]
MR	Moment of Resistance
MR	Mondcivitan Republic [Defunct] (EAIO)
MR	Monitor Recorder
MR	Monon Railroad (AD)
MR	Monthly Report
MR	Monthly Review
MR	Moon Rise (DNAB)
MR	Morgan's Food [AMEX symbol] (TTSB)
MR	Morgan's Foods, Inc. [AMEX symbol] (SPSG)
MR	Morning Report [Army]
mr	Morocco [MARC country of publication code Library of Congress] (LCCP)
MR	Morris Register [An association] (EAIO)
MR	Mortality Rates
MR	Mortality Ratio (MAE)
Mr	Mother (AD)
mr	Motivational Research (AD)
mr	Motivational Research [Psychology] (WDMC)
MR	Motivation Research
MR	Motormannes Riksforbund [Motorists' Association] [Swedish] (AD)
MR	Motor Reduction
MR	Multifamily Residential Zone (AD)
MR	Multi-Mirror Reflector [Lamp]
MR	Multiple Requesting [IBM Corp.]
MR	Multiplier Register
MR	Multi-Reflecton [Lighting]
MR	Municipal Reform [or Reformer]
MR	Muscle Receptor [Medicine] (DMAA)
MR	Muscle Relaxant [Medicine] (DMAA)
MR	Music Records [Record label]
MR	Muster Report
MR	Mutual Recognition
MR	Mutual Responsibility [Movement within Anglican Communion to make its mission more efficacious]
MR	Mycorrhizal Roots [Botany]
MR	Radiolocation Mobile Station [ITU designation]
MR	Reading Public Library, Reading, MA [Library symbol Library of Congress] (LCLS)
mr----	Red Sea and Area [MARC geographic area code Library of Congress] (LCCP)
Mr	Relative Molecular Mass (DOG)
MR1	Machinery Repairman, First Class [Navy rating]
MR2	Machinery Repairman, Second Class [Navy rating]
MR3	Machinery Repairman, Third Class [Navy rating]
MR-13 Movement of 13 NoGuatemala...	Movimiento Revolucionario de 13 de Noviembre [Revolutionary Movement of 13 November] [Guatemala] [Political party] (AD)
MRA	Golden Myra Resources, Inc. [Toronto Stock Exchange symbol]
MRA	Machine Readable Archives Division [Public Archives of Canada] [Information service or system] (IID)
MRA	Machine Records Activity
MRA	Magnetic Reaction Analyzer (PDAA)
MRA	Maneuver Right Area [Army]
MRA	Manufacturers Representatives of America (EA)
MRA	Maritime Royal Artillery [British military] (DMA)
MRA	Marketing Research Association [Chicago, IL] (EA)
MRA	Martinaire [ICAO designator] (FAAC)
MRA	Masonic Relief Association of USA and Canada (EA)
MRA	Master of Recreation Administration (GAGS)
MRA	Master of Rehabilitation Administration (GAGS)
MRA	Master of Resource Administration (GAGS)
MRA	Master Retailers Association (AD)
MRA	Masters Retailers Association (NADA)
MRA	Material Review Activity
MRA	Materials Requirement Analysis (PDAA)
MRA	Materials Review Area (AAG)
MRA	Matrix Reducibility Algorithm (PDAA)
MRA	Maximum Rendezvous Altitude
MRA	Mazda Research & Development of North America
MRA	Mean Reference Axis (MCD)
MRA	Mean Right Atrial [Cardiology]
MRA	Mechanical Readiness Assessment (NASA)
MRA	Mechanical Readiness Assessment
MRA	Medial Right Abdomen [Injection site]
MRA	Medical Record Administrator
MRA	Medical Record Analyst (HCT)
MRA	Medical Resource Co. of America [AMEX symbol] (SPSG)
mra	Medium-Powered Radio Range (AD)
MRA	Medium-Powered Radio Range (Adcock)
MRA	Men's Rights Association (EA)
MRA	Menswear Retailers of America (EA)

MRA............ Messtechnik, Regelungstechnik, Automatik [*Hoppenstedt Wirtschaftsdatenbank GmbH*] [*Germany Information service or system*] (CRD)
MRA............ Metro Rating Area [*Arbitron television ratings*] (NTCM)
mra............ Metro Rating Area (AD)
MRA............ Microgravity Research Associates
MRA............ Midwest Resources Association [*Defunct*]
MRA............ Minimum Reception Altitude [*Aviation*]
mra............ Minimum Reception Altitude (AD)
MRA............ Minimum Reserve Authorization
MRA............ Minimum Resolvable Angle
MRA............ Minimum Retirement Age (GFGA)
MRA............ Missile RADAR Altimeter (MCD)
MRA............ Misurata [*Libya*] [*Airport symbol*] (OAG)
MRA............ Mixed Refrigerant Autocascade [*Cryogenic system*]
MRA............ Model Reporting Area [*for Blindness Statistics*] [*HEW*]
MRA............ Module Rack Assembly
MRA............ Moral Re-Armament (EA)
MRA............ Motorcycle Retailers of America [*Later, NMRA*] (EA)
MRA............ Mountain Rescue Association (EA)
MRA............ Multiple Recording Accelerometer
MRA............ Multiple Resource Area Nomination [*National Register of Historic Places*]
MRA............ Mycelium Radius Atrovirens [*A fungus*]
MRA............ Rapid City Regional Library, Manitoba [*Library symbol National Library of Canada*] (NLC)
MRAA .... Marine Retailers Association of America (EA)
MRAA .... Mental Retardation Association of America (EA)
MRAALS ..... Marine Corps Remote Area Approach and Landing System (MCD)
MRAAM ...... Medium-Range Air-to-Air Missile (MCD)
mraam .... Medium-Range Air-to-Air Missile [*Military*] (AD)
MRA & L ..... Manpower, Reserve Affairs and Logistics (MCD)
MRAC .... Manifold-Regulator Accumulator Charging [*Formerly, NCP*] (AAG)
mrac .... Manifold-Regulator Accumulator Charging (AD)
MRAC .... Member of the Royal Agricultural College [*British*]
MRAC .... Meter-Reading Access Circuit [*Bell Laboratories*]
MRACGP..... Member of the Royal Australasian College of General Practice (BABM)
MRACO....... Member of the Royal Australasian College of Ophthalmologists [*British*] (BABM)
MRACP .... Member of Royal Australasian College of Physicians
MRACR .... Member of the Royal Australasian College of Radiologists [*British*] (BABM)
MRAD .... Mass Random Access Disk [*Computer science*]
M Rad .... Master of Radiology
mrad........... Megarad (AD)
mrad........... Millirad (AD)
mrad........... Milliradian (IDOE)
MRAD .... Milliradians (KSC)
MRAD .... Minor Restricted Activity Day [*Environmental medicine*]
MRadA........ Multiple Range Alignment Device [*Army*] (INF)
MRadA........ Member of the Radionic Association [*British*]
M Rad (D) ... Master of Radiology (Radiodiagnosis)
MRAD/IN..... Milliradians per Inch
MRADS........ Mass Random Access Data Storage [*Computer science*]
M Rad (T).... Master of Radiology (Radiotherapy)
M Ra E .... Master of Radio Engineering
M Ra Eng ... Master of Radio Engineering
MRAeS .... Member of the Royal Aeronautical Society [*British*] (ADA)
MRAF.......... Marshal of the Royal Air Force [*British*]
MRAF.......... Missile Round Assembly Facility
M-RAG........ Moderately Repressive Authoritarian Government
MRAIC .... Member of the Royal Architectural Institute of Canada
MRAJ.......... Aranjuez [*Costa Rica*] [*ICAO location identifier*] (ICLI)
MRaK.......... Myth, Ritual, and Kingship. Essays on the Theory and Practice of Kingship in theAncient Near East and in Israel [*A publication*] (BJA)
MRAL.......... Alajuela [*Costa Rica*] [*ICAO location identifier*] (ICLI)
MRAL.......... Mandatory Retirement Age Law of 1978 (WYGK)
MRAL.......... Materiel Readiness Authorization List [*Military*]
MRAM .... Amubri [*Costa Rica*] [*ICAO location identifier*] (ICLI)
MRAM .... Magnetic Random-Access Memory [*Computer science*] (PS)
MRAM .... Member of the Royal Academy of Music [*British*]
MRAM .... Multi-Mission Redeye Air-Launched Missile [*Military*] (PDAA)
MRAN .... Medical Resident Admitting Note (MEDA)
MRAn.......... Medical Resident Admitting Note (DAVI)
MR & A ...... Market Research and Analysis
MR & D ...... Material Redistribution and Disposal
MR & DA .... Material Redistribution and Disposal Administration
MR & DC .... Medical Research and Development Command [*Army*] (AD)
MR&DF....... Malleable Research and Development Foundation (AD)
MR & S ...... Materials Research and Standards (AD)
MR & T....... Mississippi River and Tributaries [*Flood-control project*]
MRANZCP ... Member of the Royal Australian and New Zealand College of Psychiatrists [*British*] (BABM)
MRAO .... Mobilization Reserve Acquisition Objective [*Military*]
MRAO .... Mullard Radio Astronomy Observatory (USDC)
MRAO .... Mullard Radio Astronomy Observatory [*Marine science*] (OSRA)
MRAP .... Management Review and Analysis Program (AD)
MRAP .... Marginal Revenue/Average Physical Product [*Economics*]
MRAP .... Mean Right Atrial Pressure [*Cardiology*]
MRAP .... Mortgage and Rental Assistance Program [*Australia*]
MRAP .... Mouvement Contre le Racisme et pour l'Amitie Entre les Peuples [*Movement Against Racism and for Friendship between People*] (EAIO)

MRAP .... Movimiento de Resistencia Armada Puertorriquena [*Puerto Rican Armed Resistance Movement*] [*Political party*] (PD)
MRAPCON ... Mobile RADAR Approach Control (AFM)
MRAPM ...... Materials Research and Protection Methods (SAA)
MRAR .... Atirro [*Costa Rica*] [*ICAO location identifier*] (ICLI)
MRAR .... Manpower Requirements Analysis Report [*Military*]
MRAS .... Main Renal Artery Stenosis [*Medicine*] (DMAA)
MRAS .... Management Resources Accounting System
MRAS .... Manpower Resources Accounting System [*Air Force*]
MRAS .... Member of the Royal Academy of Science [*British*]
MRAS .... Member of the Royal Asiatic Society [*British*]
MRAS .... Member of the Royal Astronomical Society [*British*] (DI)
MRAS .... Model Reference Adaptive System (PDAA)
MRASB .... Member of the Royal Asiatic Society of Bengal
MRASE .... Member of the Royal Agricultural Society of England
MRASM ...... Medium-Range Air-to-Surface Missile (MCD)
mrasm .... Medium-Range Air-to-Surface Missile [*Military*] (AD)
MRASTU ..... Marine Reserve Aviation Supply Training Unit (DNAB)
MRAT .... Altamira De San Carlos [*Costa Rica*] [*ICAO location identifier*] (ICLI)
mrat........... Medium-Range Applied Technology (AD)
MRAT .... Mobile Radiation Tester (IAA)
MRATE .... Money Market Rates [*I. P. Sharp Associates*] [*Canada Information service or system*] (CRD)
MR ATOMIC... Multiple Rapid Automatic Test of Monolithic Integrated Circuits (PDAA)
MRAUSCAN... Masonic Relief Association of the United States and Canada (AD)
MRB............ Magnetic Recording Boresight [*or Borescope*]
MRB............ Magnetospheric Radio Burst
MRB............ Maintenance Review Board (MCD)
MRB............ Malaysian Rubber Bureau (EA)
MRB............ Marble [*Technical drawings*]
MRB............ Marble Base (AAG)
mrb............ Marble Base (AD)
MRB............ Martinsburg, WV [*Location identifier FAA*] (FAAL)
MRB............ Master Reference Buoy [*Navy*] (NVT)
MRB............ Material Review Board [*Aviation*] (MCD)
MRB............ Metals Reserve Board [*of the Reconstruction Finance Corp.*]
MRB............ Microcircuit Reliability Bibliography (NITA)
MRB............ Mileage Rationing Board [*World War II*]
MRB............ Mission Review Board [*NASA*]
MRB............ Mister Build Industry, Inc. [*Vancouver Stock Exchange symbol*]
MRB............ Mobile Riverine Base [*Navy*]
MRB............ Modification Requirements Board [*NASA*] (KSC)
MRB............ Modification Review Board (AFM)
MRB............ Mortgage Revenue Bond
MRB............ Motorized Rifle Battalion [*Former USSR*]
MRB............ Motor Rescue Boat
MRB............ Motor Surfboat [*Coast Guard*] (DNAB)
MRB............ Motor Truck Rate Bureau Inc., Columbia SC [*STAC*]
MRB............ Multi-Role Bomber [*Program*] [*DoD*]
MRB............ Mutual Reinsurance Bureau (EA)
MRBA .... Buenos Aires [*Costa Rica*] [*ICAO location identifier*] (ICLI)
MRBA .... Mississippi River Bridge Authority (AD)
MRBB .... Babilonia [*Costa Rica*] [*ICAO location identifier*] (ICLI)
MRBC .... Barra Del Colorado [*Costa Rica*] [*ICAO location identifier*] (ICLI)
MRBC .... Missouri River Basin Commission
MRBC .... Molded Rubber Blended Cover
MRBC .... Monkey Red Blood Cells
MRBC .... Mouse Red Blood Cell [*Medicine*] (DMAA)
MRBCMA .... Mean Rounds between Corrective Maintenance Actions [*Quality control*] (MCD)
MR-BD .... Mercury-Redstone Booster Development [*Spacecraft*] [*NASA*]
MRBF.......... Mean Renal Blood Flow [*Nephrology*]
MRBF.......... Mean Rounds between Failures [*Military*] (CAAL)
MRBIR .... Municipal Registered Bond Interest Record [*Standard & Poor's Corp.*] [*Information service or system*] (CRD)
MRBK .... Mercantile Bankshares [*NASDAQ symbol*] (TTSB)
MRBK .... Mercantile Bankshares Corp. [*NASDAQ symbol*] (NQ)
MRBL.......... Marble
MRBL.......... Marble Financial Corp. [*NASDAQ symbol*] (NQ)
MRBM .... Bremen [*Costa Rica*] [*ICAO location identifier*] (ICLI)
MRBM .... Medium [*or Mid*]-Range Ballistic Missile
mrbm.......... Medium-Range Ballistic Missile [*Military*] (AD)
MRBN .... Bataan [*Costa Rica*] [*ICAO location identifier*] (ICLI)
MRBNA .... Member of the Royal British Nursing Association (ROG)
MRBO .... Boca Naranjo [*Costa Rica*] [*ICAO location identifier*] (ICLI)
MRBOMF .... Mean Rounds between Operational Mission Failures [*Quality control*] (MCD)
MRBP .... Barra De Parismina [*Costa Rica*] [*ICAO location identifier*] (ICLI)
MRBP .... Missouri River Basin Project
MRBS .... Mean Rounds between Stoppages [*Quality control*] (MCD)
MRBS .... Modified Road Brigade Slice (MCD)
MRBT.......... Barra De Tortuguero [*Costa Rica*] [*ICAO location identifier*] (ICLI)
MRBT.......... Multirod Burst Test [*Nuclear energy*] (NRCH)
MRC............ Columbia/Mt. Pleasant, TN [*Location identifier FAA*] (FAAL)
MRC............ Graduate Center for Materials Research [*University of Missouri - Rolla*] [*Research center*] (RCD)
MRC............ Interdepartmental Committee on Manpower Requirements [*British World War II*]
MRC............ Machine-Readable Code
MRC............ Machinery Repairman, Chief [*Navy rating*]
MRC............ Magnetic Rectifier Control
mrc............ Magnetic Rectifier Control (AD)
MRC............ Magnetic Research Corp. (MCD)
MRC............ Maintenance and Repair Craft [*Military*]

MRC	Maintenance and Repair Cycle
MRC	Maintenance Requirement Card
MRC	Major Readiness Command (MCD)
MRC	Major Regional Contingency (DOMA)
MRC	Major Retail Center
MRC	Malaria Research Centre [India]
MRC	Management Research Center [University of Wisconsin - Milwaukee] [Research center] (RCD)
MRC	Management Research Corp. [Shelbyville, IN] [Information service or system] (IID)
MRC	Manitoba Research Council [Research center] (RCD)
MRC	Manpower Requirements Change [Military] (GFGA)
MRC	Manufacturing Resource Control [Kongsberg Vaapenfabrikk] [Software package] (NCC)
MRC	Marietta College, Marietta, OH [OCLC symbol] (OCLC)
MRC	Marine Research Committee
MRC	Marine Research Corp. [Marine science] (OSRA)
MRC	Marine Research Corporation (USDC)
MRCH	Marine Resources Council
MRC	Market Research Council
MRC	Marlin-Rockwell Corp. (AD)
MRC	Master of Rehabilitation Counseling
MRCHN	Master Requirements Code
MRC	Master Routing Control (SAA)
MRC	Material Redistribution Center
MRC	Materials Research Center [Northwestern University] (RCD)
MRC	Materials Research Center [Lehigh University] (RCD)
MRC	Materials Research Corp.
MRC	Materials Review Crib (AAG)
MRC	Materiel Readiness Command [Military] (MCD)
MRC	Materiel Release Confirmation [Army] (AABC)
MRC	Mathematics Research Center (MCD)
Mrc	Mauricio [Mauritius] [Spanish] (AD)
MRCN	Maximum Reverse Current
MRC	Measurement Requirements Committee [NASA] (NASA)
MRC	Measurement Research Center [University of Iowa]
MRC	Media Resource Center [Adelaide, Australia]
MRC	Medical Registration Council [British] (DAVI)
MRC	Medical Research Committee
MRC	Medical Research Council [Research center British] (IRC)
MRCOA	Medical Reserve Corps
MRC	Mekong River Commission [Thailand]
MRC	Memorial Research Center [University of Tennessee] [Research center] (RCD)
MRC	Memory Request Controller
MRC	Men's Republican Club [Political party] (AD)
MRC	Men's Republican Club (NADA)
MRC	Men's Resource Center (EA)
MRC	Men's Resource Connection [An association] (EA)
MRC	Metals Reserve Co. [World War II]
MRC	Meteorological Research Committee [British]
MRC	Methods Research Corp. (AD)
MRC	Methylrosaniline Chloride [Also, GV] [A dye]
MRC	Metrics Research Corp. [Information service or system] (IID)
MRC	Mid-Roll Interchange [Advanced photo system]
MRC	Midwestern Relay Co. [Milwaukee, WI] [Telecommunications] (TSSD)
MRC	Military Reform Caucus (EA)
MRC	Military Region Command (MCD)
MRC	Military Representatives Committee [NATO] (NATG)
MRC	Military Reunions Council (EA)
MRC	Military Revolutionary Council (CINC)
MRC	Minnesota Restitution Center (AD)
MRC	Minorco Canada Ltd. [Toronto Stock Exchange symbol]
MRC	Missile Research Corp.
MRC	Mission Requirements Change [NASA] (KSC)
MRC	Mission Resources Center [Sydney, Australia]
MRC	Mississippi River Commission [Vicksburg, MS] [Army]
MRC	Mobile Radio Communications
MRC	Model Railway Club [British]
MRC	Modern Railroad Club
MRC	Monterey Resources, Inc. [NYSE symbol] (SAG)
MRC	Montrose [Colorado] [Seismograph station code, US Geological Survey Closed] (SEIS)
MRC	Moon's RADAR Coordinates
MRC	Morning Readiness Check
MRC	Motorized Rifle Co. (INF)
MRC	Motor Racing Club (NADA)
MRC	Motor Racing Club (AD)
MRC	Mouvement des Renovateurs Communistes [France Political party] (EY)
MRC	Movement Report Center [Military]
MRC	Multiple Register Counter (IEEE)
MRC	Multiple Regression/Correlation [Statistical analysis]
MRCA	Canas [Costa Rica] [ICAO location identifier] (ICLI)
MRCA	Market Research Corp. of America (AD)
MRCA	Market Research Corp. of America (NADA)
MRCA	Most Recent Common Ancestor
MRCA	Multirole Combat Aircraft
mrca	Multirole Combat Aircraft (AD)
MRCAS	Monetary Ration Credit Allowance System [Military] (AFM)
MRCAT	Miniature Radio-Controlled Aerial Target (MCD)
MrcBnc	Merchants Bancshares [Associated Press] (SAG)
MRCC	Coto 47 [Costa Rica] [ICAO location identifier] (ICLI)
MRCC	Maritime Rescue Coordination Center [Australia]
MRCC	Material Review Central Control [Aviation] (MCD)

MRCC	Medical Research Council of Canada (BARN)
MRCC	Member of the Royal College of Chemistry [British]
MRCC	Mercury Recovery Control Center
MRCC	Molded Rubber Coupling Cushion
MRCC	Movement Report Control Center [Military]
MRCCC	Medical Research Council, Collaborative Centre [British] (CB)
MRCD	Caledonia [Costa Rica] [ICAO location identifier] (ICLI)
MRCD	Memory Raster Colour Display (PDAA)
MRCE	Carate [Costa Rica] [ICAO location identifier] (ICLI)
MRCE	Marginal Relative Certainty Effect [Statistics]
MRCF	Martin Color-Fi, Inc. [NASDAQ symbol] (SAG)
MRCF	Martin Color-FI [NASDAQ symbol] (TTSB)
MRCF	Mayo Biotechnology Research Computer Facility [Mayo Clinic] [Research center] (RCD)
MRCF	Microsoft Real-Time Compression Format [Microsoft Corp.] (PCM)
MRCF	Missile Recycle Facility (SAA)
MRCF	Module Repair Calibration Facility
MRCGP	Member of the Royal College of General Practitioners [British]
MRCH	Chacarita [Costa Rica] [ICAO location identifier] (ICLI)
MrchBcp	Merchants Bcp. [Associated Press] (SAG)
MrchBnc	Merchants Bancshares, Inc. [Associated Press] (SAG)
MrchGp	Merchants Group, Inc. [Associated Press] (SAG)
MRCHNT	Merchant
MRCI	Ciruelas [Costa Rica] [ICAO location identifier] (ICLI)
MRCI	Medical Registration Council of Ireland (AD)
MRCi	Medical Registration Council of Ireland (DAVI)
MRCI	Medical Research Council of Ireland (SLS)
MRCI	Microsoft Real-Time Compression Interface [Microsoft Corp.] (PCM)
MRCI	Mine Readiness/Certification Inspection (MCD)
MRCI	Multireference Configuration Interaction [Quantum chemistry] (MCD)
MRCL	Master Cross-Reference List
MRCL	Mercurial
MRCM	Machinery Repairman, Master Chief [Navy rating]
MRCN	Minuteman Requirement Control Number (SAA)
MRCo.	Malaysian Refrigerator Co. (AD)
MRCO	Manufacturing Research Corp. of Ontario [Research center Canada] (RCD)
MRCO	Member of the Royal College of Organists [British]
MRCO	Meridan Natl [NASDAQ symbol] (TTSB)
MRCO	Meridian National Corp. [NASDAQ symbol] (NQ)
MRCOA	Medical Research Council Trial in Older Adults
MRCOG	Member of the Royal College of Obstetricians and Gynaecologists [British]
MRCOL	Meridan Natl Wrrt'A' [NASDAQ symbol] (TTSB)
MRCOP	Meridan Natl $3.75 Cv'B'Pfd [NASDAQ symbol] (TTSB)
MRCOZ	Meridian Natl Wrrt [NASDAQ symbol] (TTSB)
MRCP	Maoist Revolutionary Communist Party [Political party] (AD)
MRCP	Maoist Revolutionary Communist Party (NADA)
MRCP	Master of Regional and City Planning (PGP)
MRCP	Master of Regional and Community Planning (GAGS)
MRCP	Member of the Royal College of Physicians [British]
MRCP	Member of the Royal College of Preceptors [British]
MRCP	Microfilm Research Centers Project [Defunct] (EA)
MRCP	Mobile RADAR Control Post
MRCPA	Mobilization Reserve Components Program of the Army (AABC)
MRC Path	Member of the Royal College of Pathologists [British]
MRCPE	Member of the Royal College of Physicians, Edinburgh
MRCPEd	Member of the Royal College of Physicians of Edinburgh
MRCP Edin	Member of the Royal College of Physicians of Edinburgh
MRCPGlas	Member of the Royal College of Physicians of Glasgow
MRCP (Glasg)	Member of the Royal College of Physicians and Surgeons of Glasgow (AAMN)
MRCP Glasg	Member of the Royal College of Physicians of Glasgow
MRCPI	Member of the Royal College of Physicians of Ireland
MRCP Irel	Member of the Royal College of Physicians of Ireland
MRC Psych	Member of the Royal College of Psychiatrists [British]
MRCPUK	Member of the Royal College of Physicians of the United Kingdom [British] (AD)
MRCP UK	Member of the Royal Colleges of Physicians of the United Kingdom
MRCR	Carrillo [Costa Rica] [ICAO location identifier] (ICLI)
MRCR	Measurement Requirement Change Request [NASA] (KSC)
MRCRR	Machine-Readable Collections Reading Room [Library of Congress] (IT)
MRCS	Machinery Repairman, Senior Chief [Navy rating]
MRCS	Mechanoreceptor Cueing Subsystem (MCD)
MRCS	Medium Resolution Camera System (MCD)
MRCS	Member of the Royal College of Surgeons [British]
MRCS	Missile Range Calibration Satellite
MRCS	Multiple Report Creation System
MRCS	Multiple RPV [Remotely Piloted Vehicle] Control System (PDAA)
MRCSA	Migrant Resource Center of South Australia
MRCSE	Member of the Royal College of Surgeons, Edinburgh
MRCSI	Member of the Royal College of Surgeons, Ireland (ROG)
MRCTS	Missile Round Cable Test System
MRCU	Mini-Remote Control Unit (MHDI)
MRCV	Cabo Velas [Costa Rica] [ICAO location identifier] (ICLI)
MRCV	Mixture Ratio Control Valve (KSC)
MRCVS	Member of the Royal College of Veterinary Surgeons [British] (EY)
MRCWA	Midland Railway Company of Western Australia (AD)
MRCY	Mercury General [NASDAQ symbol] (TTSB)
MRCY	Mercury General Corp. [NASDAQ symbol] (NQ)
MRCZ	Carrizal [Costa Rica] [ICAO location identifier] (ICLI)
MRD	Mandatory Retirement Date [Army] (AABC)
MRD	Manual Ringdown [Telecommunications] (TEL)
MRD	Maritime Research Department [An association Inactive] (EA)

MRD	Marketing Requirement Document
MRD	Master Requirements Directory [*Military*] (AFM)
MRD	Material Required Date
MRD	Material Requirements Deck (AAG)
MRD	Material Requirements Drawing (MCD)
MRD	Material Review Disposition [*Aviation*]
MRD	Materiel Redistribution Division [*Army*] (AFIT)
MRD	Materiel Release Denial [*Military*] (AABC)
MRD	Materiel Requirements Document [*Army*]
MRD	Medical Records Department (DAVI)
MRD	Medical Reference Department (AD)
MRD	Medical Research Division
MRD	Melcor Developments Ltd. [*Toronto Stock Exchange symbol*]
MRD	Memorandum for Regional Directors (AAGC)
MRD	Memory Raster Display [*Computer science*]
MRD	Memory Read [*Computer science*] (MHDI)
MRD	Merida [*Venezuela*] [*Airport symbol*] (OAG)
MRD	Meridian Air Cargo, Inc. [*ICAO designator*] (FAAC)
MRD	Mesoscale Research Division [*Marine science*] (OSRA)
MRD	Mesoscale Research Division [*National Severe Storms Laboratory*] (USDC)
mrd	Metal Rolling Door (AD)
MRD	Metal Rolling Door [*Technical drawings*]
MRD	Metal Roof Deck [*Technical drawings*]
mrd	Metal Roof Deck (AD)
MRD	Microbiological Research Department (AD)
MRD	Milestone Review Documentation [*Army*]
MRD	Military Reference Data
MRD	Military Requirements Determination
mrd	Millirutherford
MRD	Minimal Residual Disease [*Medicine*]
MRD	Minimum Reacting Dose
mrd	Minimum Reacting Dose (AD)
MRD	Mission Requirements Document [*NASA*] (KSC)
MRD	Mississippi River Division [*Army Corps of Engineers*]
MRD	Missouri River Division [*Army Corps of Engineers*]
MRD	Mobil Research & Development Corp., Engineering Information Center, Princeton, NJ [*OCLC symbol*] (OCLC)
MRD	Monostable Relay Driver
MRD	Morpholinodaunorubicin [*Also, MoDNM*] [*Antineoplastic drug*]
MRD	Mortality Rate to Double
MRD	Motorized Rifle Division [*Former USSR*] (NATG)
MRD	Motorized Rifle Division [*Military*] (AD)
MRD	Motor Racing Developments
MRD	Motor Receiving Dolly
MRD	Movement for the Restoration of Democracy [*Nepal*] [*Political party*]
MRD	Movement for the Restoration of Democracy [*Pakistan*] [*Political party*] (PD)
MRD	Multireference Double Excitation [*Physics*]
MRD	Russell and District Regional Library, Russell, Manitoba [*Library symbol National Library of Canada*] (NLC)
MRDA	Maintenance Requirement Development Activity [*Military*] (CAAL)
MRDA	Media Research Directors Association (EA)
MRDAC	Manpower Research and Data Analysis Center [*DoD*] (DNAB)
MRDB	Mission Requirements Data Base [*NASA*] (SSD)
MRDC	Medical Research and Development Command [*Frederick, MD*] [*Army*]
MRDC	Military Requirement and Development Committee (NATG)
MRDC	Military Research and Development Center [*US-Thailand*]
MRDC	Missile Research and Development Command [*Army*] (MCD)
MRDC	Module RADAR Display Console
MRDCC	Metropolitan Refuse Disposal Consultative Committee [*Melbourne, Australia*]
MRDD	Don Diego [*Costa Rica*] [*ICAO location identifier*] (ICLI)
MR/DD	Mentally Retarded and Developmentally Disabled
MRDD	Mental Retardation and Developmental Disabilities [*National Institutes of Health*]
MRDE	Mining Research and Development Establishment [*National Coal Board*] [*British*]
MRDEC	Missile Research Development and Engineering Center [*Formerly, Army Missile Laboratory*] (RDA)
MRDF	Machine-Readable Data Files
mrdf	Machine-Readable Data Files [*Computer science*] (AD)
MRDF	Marine Resources Development Foundation
MRDF	Maritime Radio Direction Finding
MRDF	Metals Research and Development Foundation [*Defunct*] (EA)
MRDFS	Man-Portable Radio Direction-Finding System
MRDG	Manufacturing Research and Design Group [*McMaster University*] [*Canada Research center*] (RCD)
mrdhd	Maximum Recommended Daily Human Dose (AD)
MRDIS	Message Reproduction and Distribution System [*Military*] (CAAL)
MRDL	Mean Reciprocal Detection Latency
MRDL	Mineral Respurces Development Laboratory [*Australia*]
MRDL	Missouri River Division Laboratory [*Army Corps of Engineers*]
MRDN	Material Receipt Discrepancy Notice (AD)
MRDN	Meridian Bancorp, Inc. [*NASDAQ symbol*] (NQ)
MrdN	Meridian National Corp. [*Associated Press*] (SAG)
MRDN	Mouvement Revolutionnaire pour la Democratie Nouvelle [*Revolutionary Movement for New Democracy*] [*Senegal*] (PD)
MrdN 99	Meridian National Corp. [*Associated Press*] (SAG)
MrdnBc	Meridian Bancorp, Inc. [*Associated Press*] (SAG)
MRDNL	Meridional
MRDO	Dieciocho [*Costa Rica*] [*ICAO location identifier*] (ICLI)
MRDOS	Mapped Real-Time Disk Operating System [*Computer science*] (MDG)

MRDR	Material Receipt Discrepancy Record
MRDR	Material Review Disposition Record (NASA)
MRDS	Malfunction Rate Detection System (DNAB)
MRDS	MARC [*Machine-Readable Cataloging*] Records Distribution Service [*National Library of Canada*] (IID)
MRDS	Member of the Royal Drawing Society [*British*] (ROG)
MRDS	Message Reproduction and Distribution System [*Military*] (MCD)
MRDS	Mineral Resources Data System [*US Geological Survey*] [*Information service or system*] (IID)
MRDS	Mission Recorder Display Set (MCD)
MRDS	Modular Responsive Defense System
MRDS	Molded Rubber Duct System
MRDT	Mortality Rate Doubling Time
MRDTI	Metal Roof Deck Technical Institute [*Later, Steel Deck Institute*] (EA)
MRDV	Maize Rough Dwarf Virus [*Plant pathology*]
MRDY	Message Ready [*Computer science*] (MHDI)
MRE	Major Research Equipment
MRE	Manicore [*Brazil*] [*Airport symbol*] (AD)
MRE	Mara Lodges [*Kenya*] [*Airport symbol*] (OAG)
MRE	Maritime Radio Executive [*British*]
M Re	Master of Religion
MRE	Master of Religious Education
MRE	Materiel Readiness Expediter [*Army*]
MRE	Matter (ROG)
MRE	Maximal Relative Error [*Mathematical statistics*]
MRE	Mazda Research of Europe [*Automobile manufacturer operations*]
MRE	Meal, Ready-to-Eat [*Army rations designation, replaces C-rations*]
mre	Meal Ready to Eat (AD)
MRE	Meals Rejected by Everyone
mre	Mean Radial Error (AD)
MRE	Mean Radial Error
MRE	Medco Research [*AMEX symbol*] (TTSB)
MRE	Medco Research, Inc. [*AMEX symbol*] (SAG)
MRE	Melissa Resources, Inc. [*Vancouver Stock Exchange symbol*]
MRE	Memory Register Exponent [*Computer science*] (MHDI)
MRE	Metal Regulatory Element [*Genetics*]
MRE	Metal-Responsive Element [*Genetics*]
MR-E	Methemoglobin Reductase [*An enzyme*] (MAE)
MRE	Microbiological Research Establishment [*British*]
MRE	Microrocket Engine
MRE	Mid-Range Estimate
MRE	Militia Royal Engineers [*British military*] (DMA)
MRE	Missile Recertification Equipment
MRE	Missile Recycle Equipment (SAA)
MRE	Mobil Research & Development Corp., Paulsboro, NJ [*OCLC symbol*] (OCLC)
MRE	Modern Ramjet Engine (MCD)
MRE	Morally Repugnant Elite [*Lifestyle classification*] (ECON)
MRE	Movimiento Revolucionario Espartaco [*Bolivia*] [*Political party*] (PPW)
MRE	Movimiento Revolucionario Estudantil [*Colorado Political party*] (EY)
MRE	Multiple-Response Enable (IEEE)
MREA	Estero Azul [*Costa Rica*] [*ICAO location identifier*] (ICLI)
MREAC	Mon Repos Est au Ciel [*My Rest Is in Heaven*] [*Motto of Ludwig Philipp, Count of the Palatinate of Simmern (1602-1654)*] [*French*]
MREC	El Carmen [*Costa Rica*] [*ICAO location identifier*] (ICLI)
MREC	Medical Research Ethics Committee
MRECM	Master of Real Estate and Construction Management (GAGS)
MRED	Master of Real Estate Development (GAGS)
MREd	Master of Recreation Education (GAGS)
MR Ed	Master of Religious Education
MREDA	Marine Resources and Engineering Development Act [*1966*] (MSC)
M Re E	Master of Refrigeration Engineering
M Re Eng	Master of Refrigeration Engineering
MREF	Medical Research Endowment Fund
MRefEng	Master of Refrigeration Engineering (NADA)
MREGAD	Multiplexer Regenerator Address [*Computer science*] (MHDI)
MRegSc	Master of Regional Science (ADA)
MReh	Blanding Free Public Library, Rehoboth, MA [*Library symbol Library of Congress*] (LCLS)
MREHIS	Member of the Royal Environmental Health Institute of Scotland (DBQ)
MREI	Marriage Role Expectation Inventory [*Psychology*]
M-REIT	Mutual Real Estate Investment Trust
M Rel	Master of Religion (PGP)
MRELB	Malaysian Rubber Exchange and Licensing Board (AD)
M Rel Ed	Master of Religious Education (PGP)
MRelEd	Master of Religious Education (GAGS)
mrem	Millirem
MREM	Milliroentgen Equivalent Man [*Radiation measurement*]
mrem	Milliroentgen Equivalent Man (AD)
mrem/h	Millirem per Hour (DS)
MREmpS	Member of the Royal Empire Society [*British*]
MREP	Maneuvering Room Equipment Panel (DNAB)
MREP	Medical Remedial Enlistment Program (DNAB)
mrep	Milliroentgen Equivalent Physical (MAE)
MRER	El Ron Ron [*Costa Rica*] [*ICAO location identifier*] (ICLI)
MRERF	Manufacturers Representatives Educational Research Foundation [*Rolling Meadows, IL*] (EA)
MRES	Material Requirements Estimation System [*Navy*]
MRES	Member of the Royal Entomological Society [*British*] (ROG)
MRES	Military Requirements Estimation System
MResEnvS	Master of Resource and Environmental Studies
MResEnvSt	Master of Resource and Environmental Studies

MRESS .... Marine Recreational Fishing Statistics Survey [*Marine science*] (OSRA)
MResSc ...... Master of Resource Science
MRET .... Esterillos [*Costa Rica*] [*ICAO location identifier*] (ICLI)
M Ret .... Master of Retailing
MRET .... Merit Holding [*NASDAQ symbol*] (TTSB)
MRET .... Merit Holding Corp. [*NASDAQ symbol*] (SAG)
M REV .... Most Reverend
MRev .... Revere Public Library, Revere, MA [*Library symbol Library of Congress*] (LCLS)
MRF .... Magnetorheological Finishing [*Optics manufacturing*] (RDA)
MRF .... Maintenance and Refurbishment Facility [*NASA*] (KSC)
MRF .... Maintenance Repair Facility
MRF .... Maintenance Repair Frequency
MRF .... Maintenance Replacement Factor (NG)
mrf .... Maintenance Replacement Factor (AD)
mrf .... Maintenance Responsibility File (MCD)
MRF .... Mankind Research Foundation (EA)
MRF .... Marble Floor (AAG)
mrf .... Marble Floor (AD)
MRF .... Marfa, TX [*Location identifier FAA*] (FAAL)
MRF .... MariFarms, Inc. [*Later, Marine Harvest International*] [*AMEX symbol*] (SPSG)
MRF .... Marine Recreational Fishing [*Marine science*] (MSC)
MRF .... Markov Random Field [*Mathematics*]
MRF .... Materials Recovery Facility [*for recycling of glass, plastics, etc.*]
MRF .... Maternal Resistance Factor (BARN)
MRF .... Maximum Retarding Force (NASA)
MRF .... Mayo Research Foundation (AD)
MRF .... Mayo Research Foundation (NADA)
MRF .... Measurements/Stimuli Request Form [*NASA*] (NASA)
MRF .... Medium-Range Forecast [*Model*] [*Marine science*] (OSRA)
MRF .... Medium-Range Forecast [*Model*] (USDC)
MRF .... Megawatt Receiver Filter
MRF .... Melanocyte-Stimulating Hormone Releasing Factor [*Endocrinology*]
MRF .... Melanotropin Releasing Factor [*Biochemistry*]
MRF .... Mental Retardation Facility
MRF .... Mentor Income Fund [*Formerly, RAC Income Fund*] [*NYSE symbol*] (SPSG)
MRF .... Mentor Income Fund [*NYSE symbol*] (TTSB)
MRF .... Merfin Resources Ltd. [*Vancouver Stock Exchange symbol*]
MRF .... Mesencephalic [*or Midbrain*] Reticular Formation [*Anatomy*]
MRF .... Message Refusal [*Telecommunications*] (TEL)
MRF .... Metal Regulatory Factor [*Genetics*]
MRF .... Meteorological Rocket Facility
MRF .... Metering Research Facility [*Research center*] (RCD)
MRF .... Methodist Relief Fund [*British*]
MRF .... Midbrain Reticular Formation [*Medicine*] (DMAA)
MRF .... Midbrain Reticular Formation [*Brain anatomy*]
MRF .... Milestone Reference File [*Military*] (CAAL)
MRF .... Military Reconnaissance Force [*British military*] (DMA)
MRF .... Miraflores [*Peru*] [*Seismograph station code, US Geological Survey*] (SEIS)
MRF .... Missile Reconstitution Force [*Air Force*] (DOMA)
MRF .... Mission Readiness Flying
MRF .... Mission Reliability Factor [*Military*] (AABC)
MRF .... Mitral Regurgitant Flow [*Medicine*]
MRF .... Mobile Riverine Force [*Navy*] (NVT)
MRF .... Modular Rigid Frame (PDAA)
MRF .... Module Repair Facility (DNAB)
MRF .... Movement for Rights and Freedoms [*Bulgaria*] [*Political party*]
MRF .... MSH [*Melanophore-Stimulating Hormone*] Releasing Factor [*Medicine*] (DAVI)
MRF .... Muellerian Regression Factor [*Embryology*] (DAVI)
MRev .... Muellerian Repressor Factor [*Embryology*]
MRF .... Multipath Reduction Factor [*Electronics*]
MRF .... Multirole Fighter [*Replacement for the F-16*] [*Air Force*] (DOMA)
MRF .... Muscle Regulatory Factor [*Physiology*]
MRF .... Music Research Foundation
MRF .... Myopia Research Foundation [*Later, MIRF*]
MRFA .... Fireman Apprentice, Machinery Repairman, Striker [*Navy rating*]
MRFAC .... Manufacturers Radio Frequency Advisory Committee (EA)
MRFB .... Malayan Rubber Fund Board (AD)
MRFC .... Malawi Rural Finance Co. Ltd.
MRFCA .... Mental Residual Functional Capacity Assessment [*Social Security Administration*]
MRFD .... Finca Delicias [*Costa Rica*] [*ICAO location identifier*] (ICLI)
MRFDK .... Mechanical Remote Fuze Disassembly Kit [*Military*] (CAAL)
MRFI .... Finca 10 (Nuevo Palmar Sur) [*Costa Rica*] [*ICAO location identifier*] (ICLI)
MRFI .... Mutually Responsible Facilitation Inventory [*Personality development test*] [*Psychology*]
MRFIT .... Multiple Risk Factor Intervention Trial [*Cardiology*]
MRFL .... Flamengo [*Costa Rica*] [*ICAO location identifier*] (ICLI)
MRFL .... Master Radio Frequency List (NATG)
mr flight ...... Meteorological Research Flight (AD)
MRFN .... Fireman, Machinery Repairman, Striker [*Navy rating*]
MRFP .... Finca La Promesa [*Costa Rica*] [*ICAO location identifier*] (ICLI)
MRFR .... Mobilization Reserve for Retention [*Military*]
MRFS .... Finca 63 [*Costa Rica*] [*ICAO location identifier*] (ICLI)
MRFS .... Mid-Range Force Study [*DoD*]
MRFSS .... Marine Recreational Fishing Statistics Survey (USDC)
MRFT .... Missile Ready for Test (MCD)
MRFT .... Modified Rapid Fermentation Test
MRFU .... Multiple Rocket Firing Unit

MRFV .... Maize Rayado Fino Virus [*Plant pathology*]
MRG .... Magnetic Radiation Generator
mrg .... Magnetic Radiation Generator (AD)
MRG .... Magnetic Resonance Gyro (MCD)
MRG .... Main Repair Group [*British military*] (DMA)
MRG .... Maintainability Requirements Group (AD)
MRG .... Maintenance Requirements General (MCD)
MRG .... Management Research Groups [*British*]
MRG .... Mandatory Resource Group (MCD)
MRG .... Manridge Explorations Ltd. [*Toronto Stock Exchange symbol*]
mrg .... Margin (AD)
mrg .... Marginalia (AD)
MRG .... Master of Religious Guidance
MRG .... Master Reference Gyro (PDAA)
MRG .... Material Review Group [*Aviation*]
MRG .... Medium Range
MRG .... Merge [*Computer science*]
MRG .... Mesters Vig [*Greenland*] [*Airport symbol*] (AD)
mrg .... Methane-Rich Gas (AD)
MRG .... Methane Rich Gas
MRG .... Minorities Research Group (AD)
MRG .... Minority Rights Group (EAIO)
MRG .... Mission Rules Guidelines [*NASA*] (KSC)
MRG .... Mobile River Group [*Navy*] (VNW)
MRG .... Modelling Research Group [*University of Southern California*] [*Research center*] (RCD)
MRG .... Modern Rythmic Gynmastics (EDAC)
MRG .... Mooring (MSA)
MRG .... Morgantown [*West Virginia*] [*Seismograph station code, US Geological Survey*] (SEIS)
MRG .... Mortons Restaurant Group [*NYSE symbol*] (SAG)
MRG .... Morton's Restaurant Group [*NYSE symbol*] (TTSB)
MRG .... Mouvement des Radicaux de Gauche [*Left Radical Movement*] [*Wallis and Futuna Islands*] [*Political party*] (EY)
MRG .... Mouvement des Radicaux de Gauche [*Left Radical Movement*] [*France Political party*] (PPE)
MRG .... Movement Requirements Generator
MRG .... Municipal Reform Group [*Tasmania, Australia*]
MRG .... Murmurs, Rubs, and Gallops [*Cardiology*] (DAVI)
MRGA .... Garza [*Costa Rica*] [*ICAO location identifier*] (ICLI)
MRGA .... Manhattan Ryegrass Growers Association (EA)
MRGF .... Golfito [*Costa Rica*] [*ICAO location identifier*] (ICLI)
MRGI .... Minority Rights Group International [*British*] (EAIO)
MRGITF .... Machine-Readable Government Information Task Force [*Government Documents Round Table*] [*American Library Association*]
MRGO .... Margo Nursery Farms [*NASDAQ symbol*] (TTSB)
MRGO .... Margo Nursery Farms, Inc. [*NASDAQ symbol*] (NQ)
MRGO .... Mississippi River Gulf Outflow (AD)
MR-GO .... Mississippi River-Gulf Outlet
MRGP .... Guapiles [*Costa Rica*] [*ICAO location identifier*] (ICLI)
MRGR .... Mean Relative Growth Rate [*Physiology*]
MRGS .... Member of the Royal Geographical Society [*British*]
MrgS .... Morgan Stanley Group, Inc. [*Associated Press*] (SAG)
MrgSHY .... MorgaN Stanley High Yield Fund [*Associated Press*] (SAG)
MRGT .... Guatuso [*Costa Rica*] [*ICAO location identifier*] (ICLI)
MRGU .... Guanacaste [*Costa Rica*] [*ICAO location identifier*] (ICLI)
MRGV .... Marine Research Group of Victoria [*Australia*]
MRH .... Beaufort, NC [*Location identifier FAA*] (FAAL)
MRH .... Hinds Junior College, Raymond, MS [*OCLC symbol*] (OCLC)
MRH .... Magnetic Recording Head
MRH .... Mango Resources [*Vancouver Stock Exchange symbol*]
MRH .... Master of Russian History
MRH .... Mechanical Recording Head
MRH .... Melanocyte-Releasing Hormone [*Endocrinology*]
MRH .... Member of the Royal Household [*British*] (AD)
MRH .... Mild Resid Hydrocracking [*M. W. Kellogg Co. process*]
mr/h .... Milliroentgens per Hour (DS)
MRH .... Mission-Related Hardware
MRH .... Mobile Remote Handler
MRH .... MSH [*Melanophore-Stimulating Hormone*] Releasing Hormone [*Laboratory Science*] (DAVI)
MRH .... Rossburn District Hospital, Rossburn, Manitoba [*Library symbol National Library of Canada*] (NLC)
MRHA .... Mannose-Resistant Hemagglutination
MRHD .... Mounted Ration Heating Device [*Army*] (INF)
MRHG .... Hacienda Rancho Grande [*Costa Rica*] [*ICAO location identifier*] (ICLI)
MRHIB .... Multiantimicrobial Resistant Hemophilus Influenza B
MRHJ .... Hacienda Jaco (Harbor Land) [*Costa Rica*] [*ICAO location identifier*] (ICLI)
mrhm .... Milliroentgens per Hour at One Meter
MRHMC .... Michael Reese Hospital and Medical Center (AD)
MRHO .... Hacienda Rio Cuarto [*Costa Rica*] [*ICAO location identifier*] (ICLI)
MRHP .... Hacienda Platanar [*Costa Rica*] [*ICAO location identifier*] (ICLI)
mr/hr .... Milliroentgens per Hour
MRHS .... Hacienda La Suerte [*Costa Rica*] [*ICAO location identifier*] (ICLI)
MRHS .... Materiel Request History and Status
MRHS .... Member of the Royal Historical Society [*British*] (ROG)
MRHS .... Midwest Railway Historical Society (EA)
MRHSF .... Materiel Request History and Storage File
MRI .... Anchorage, AK [*Location identifier FAA*] (FAAL)
MRI .... Information Dynamics Corp., Reading, MA [*Library symbol Library of Congress*] (LCLS)
MRI .... Machine Records Installation [*Military*]
MRI .... Magazine Research, Inc. (AD)

mri	Magnetic-Resonance Imager (AD)
MRI	Magnetic Resonance Imaging [Medical]
MRI	Magnetic Resonance Imaging [Medicine]
mri	Magnetic Rubber Inspection (AD)
MRI	Malt Research Institute [Later, NMRI]
MRI	Management Recruiters International (HGAA)
MRI	Manufacturing Run-In
MRI	Marine Research Institute
MRI	Marital Roles Inventory [Psychology]
MRI	Mass Retailing Institute [Formerly, Mass Merchandising Research Institute] [Later, NMRI]
MRI	Material Receiving Instruction [Bechtel] [Nuclear energy] (NRCH)
MRI	Material Review Item [Aviation]
MRI	Mauritius Island [Mascarene Islands] [Seismograph station code, US Geological Survey Closed] (SEIS)
MRI	McRae Industries, Inc. [AMEX symbol] (SPSG)
MRI	Mean Rise Interval [Tides and currents]
mri	Mean Rise Interval (AD)
MRI	Measurement Requirements and Interface (MCD)
MRIC	Meat Research Institute [British]
MRI	Mediamark Research, Inc. [Database producer and database] [Information service or system] (IID)
MRI	Mediator Release Inhibitor [Biochemistry]
MRJ	Medical Records Index (AD)
MRI	Medical Research Institute [Florida Institute of Technology] [Research center] (RCD)
MRI	Medium-Range Interceptor
mri	Medium-Range Interceptor (AD)
MRI	Member of the Royal Institution [British]
MRI	Memory Reference Instruction
MRI	Mental Research Institute (EA)
MRI	Meteorological Research Institute (AD)
MRI	Microwave Research Institute [Polytechnic Institute of Brooklyn] (MCD)
MRI	Midwest Research Institute
MRI	Military Reform Institute (AD)
mri	Milstrip Routing Identifier (AD)
MRI	MILSTRIP [Military Standard Requisitioning and Issue Procedure] Routing Identifier (AFM)
MRI	Mineral Resources Institute [University of Alabama] [Research center] (RCD)
MRI	Mineral Resources International Ltd. [Toronto Stock Exchange symbol]
MRI	Minimum Release Interval (DNAB)
MRI	Minority Research Institution [Program] [National Science Foundation]
MRI	Miscellaneous RADAR Input
MRI	Missile Range Index
MRI	Moderate Renal Insufficiency [Medicine]
MRI	Monopulse Resolution Improvement
mri	Monopulse Resolution Improvement (AD)
MRI	Motor Repair Insurance (AD)
MRI	Multiple RADAR Interrogator (MUGU)
MRIA	Magnetic Recording Industry Association [Later, Electronic Industries Association] (EA)
MRI.A	McRae Indus'A' [AMEX symbol] (TTSB)
MRIA	Member of the Royal Irish Academy (EY)
MRIA	Model Railroad Industry Association (EA)
MRIAI	Member of the Royal Institute of the Architects of Ireland
MRI.B	McRae Indus Cv 'B' [AMEX symbol] (TTSB)
MRIBA	Member of the Royal Institute of British Architects (ROG)
MRIC	Mandatory Recovery Items Code (MCD)
M-RIC	Manpower Resource Identification Code [Military]
MRIC	Member of the Royal Institute of Chemistry [British]
MRIC	Morning Report Indicator Code [Army] (AABC)
MRIC	Revolutionary Movement of the Christian Left [Ecuador] [Political party] (PPW)
MRICC	Missile and Rockets Inventory Control Center [Army]
MRICD	Medical Research Institute of Chemical Defense (RDA)
MRICS	Member of the Royal Institution of Chartered Surveyors [British]
MRIF	Maintenance Ratio Intermediate Forward
MRIF	Melanocyte-Stimulating-Hormone Release Inhibiting Factor [Also, MIF] [Endocrinology]
MRIF	MSH [Melanophore-Stimulating Hormone] Release Inhibiting Factor [Laboratory science] (DAVI)
MRIH	Melanocyte-Stimulating Hormone-Release-Inhibiting Hormone [Endocrinology] (MAE)
MRII	Medical Resources [NASDAQ symbol] (TTSB)
MRII	Medical Resources, Inc. [NASDAQ symbol] (SAG)
MRIID	Medical Research Institute of Infectious Diseases [Army] (RDA)
MRIL	Mandatory Recovery Items List (MCD)
MRIL	Master Repairable Item List
MRIN	Member of the Royal Institute of Navigation [British] (DBQ)
MRINA	Member of the Royal Institution of Naval Architects [British]
MR INC	Men's Rights, Inc. (EA)
MRINDO	Modified Rydberg Intermediate Neglect of Differential Overlap [Physics]
MRINZ	Meat Research Institute of New Zealand (AD)
MRIO	Multiregional Input-Output
MRIP	Imperio [Costa Rica] [ICAO location identifier] (ICLI)
MRIP	Management Review and Improvement Program [Department of Labor]
MRIP	Prairie Crocus Regional Library, Rivers, Manitoba [Library symbol National Library of Canada] (NLC)
MRIPA	Member of the Royal Institute of Public Administration (ADA)

MRIPHH	Member of the Royal Institute of Public Health and Hygiene [British]
MRIPWC	Member of the Royal Institute of Painters in Water Colours [British] (ROG)
mrir	Medium Resolution Infrared (AD)
MRIR	Medium-Resolution Infrared Radiometer [NASA]
MRIRBM	Medium-Range and Intermediate-Range Ballistic Missile (MCD)
MRIS	Maritime Research Information Service [National Academy of Sciences]
MRIS	Market Research Information System [Bell System]
MRIS	Marshall & Ilsley [NASDAQ symbol] (TTSB)
MRIS	Marshall & Isley Corp. [NASDAQ symbol] (NQ)
MRIS	Material Readiness Index System [Military]
MRIS	Medical Research Information System [Veterans Administration]
MRIS	Mobile Range Instrumentation System
MRIS	Modernization Resource Information Submission [Army] (RDA)
MRISAN	Maintenance Requirement Interim Support Asset Notice (MCD)
MRIT	Marine RADAR Interrogator-Transponder (PDAA)
MRIT	Mean Re-Initialization Time
MRIT	Merit Software, Inc. [NASDAQ symbol] (SAG)
MRITC	Methylrhodamine Isothiocyanate [Organic chemistry]
MRIU	Missile Round Interface Unit
MRIX	Midland Resources [NASDAQ symbol] (SPSG)
MRIXZ	Midland Res Inc. Wrrt [NASDAQ symbol] (TTSB)
MRJ	Microwave Rotary Joint
MRJ	Mineral Point, WI [Location identifier FAA] (FAAL)
MRJ	Miniature Revolving Joint
MRJE	Multileaving Remote Job Entry [IBM Corp.]
MRJE	Multiple Remote Job Entry (NITA)
MRJY	Mister Jay Fashions International, Inc. [NASDAQ symbol] (SAG)
MRJY	Mr Jay Fashions Intl [NASDAQ symbol] (TTSB)
MRK	Marco Island [Florida] [Airport symbol] (OAG)
MRK	Mark
mrk	Mark (VRA)
MRK	Markair, Inc. [ICAO designator] (FAAC)
MRK	Merck & Co. [NYSE symbol] (TTSB)
MRK	Merck & Co., Inc. [NYSE symbol] (SPSG)
MRK	Merrimack College, McQuade Library, North Andover, MA [OCLC symbol] (OCLC)
MRK	Millrock Development Corp. [Vancouver Stock Exchange symbol]
MRK	Modified Redlich-Kwong [Chemical equation]
MRK	Morioka [Japan] [Seismograph station code, US Geological Survey] (SEIS)
MRK	Myth, Ritual, and Kingship [A publication] (BJA)
MRK	Rayville, LA [Location identifier FAA] (FAAL)
MRKD	Marked [Computer science] (MDG)
mrkd	Marked (AD)
mrkg	Marking (AD)
mrkr	Marker (AD)
MRKR	Marker (WGA)
MRKR	Marker International [NASDAQ symbol] (SAG)
MRKR	Marker Intl. [NASDAQ symbol] (TTSB)
MRKTPLC	Marketplace
MRKTR	Marketer
Mrkts	Markets (AD)
MRL	Aeromorelos SA de CV [Mexico ICAO designator] (FAAC)
MRL	Machine Representation Language
MRL	Main Rail Launcher (DWSG)
MRL	Maintenance Repair Level (MCD)
MRL	Maintenance Requirements List (MCD)
MRL	Manipulator Retention Latch [or Lock] (NASA)
MRL	Manufacturing Reference Line
MRL	Manufacturing Research Laboratory
MRL	Maritime Rear Link (MCD)
MRL	Marketing Research Library
MRL	Martel Oil & Gas [Vancouver Stock Exchange symbol]
MRL	Master Repair List (AFIT)
MRL	Master Report List
MRL	Material Requirements Lists
MRL	Materials Research Laboratories [National Science Foundation] [Research center]
MRL	Materiel Requirements List [Military]
MRL	Maximized Relative Likelihood (PDAA)
MRL	Maximum Recording Level
MRL	Maximum Residue Limit (PDAA)
MRL	Meaning-Representation Language [Computer science]
MRL	Medical Record Librarian
MRL	Medical Records Library (AD)
MRL	Medical Research Laboratory [Navy and Air Force] (MCD)
MRL	Medium-Powered Radio Range [Loop radiators]
mrl	Medium-Powered Radio Range (AD)
MRL	Merrell-National Laboratories [Research code symbol]
MRL	Minerals Research Laboratory (MCD)
MRL	Minimal Response Level [Audiometry]
MRL	Minimum Response Level
MRL	Missionary Research Library (EA)
MRL	Mobile Replenishment List (AFIT)
MRL	Motor Refrigeration Lighter (ADA)
mrl	Motor Refrigerator Lighter (AD)
mrl	Multiple Rocket Launcher (AD)
MRL	Multiple Rocket Launcher
MRL	Multiple Ruby LASER
MRL	Multipoint Recorder/Logger
MRLA	La Paquita [Costa Rica] [ICAO location identifier] (ICLI)
MRLA	Malayan Races Liberation Army

MRLB........... Liberia/Tomas Guardia Internacional [*Costa Rica*] [*ICAO location identifier*] (ICLI)
MRLC........... Los Chiles [*Costa Rica*] [*ICAO location identifier*] (ICLI)
MRLE........... Laurel [*Costa Rica*] [*ICAO location identifier*] (ICLI)
MRLF........... La Flor [*Costa Rica*] [*ICAO location identifier*] (ICLI)
MRLF........... Monthly Report on the Labor Force (OICC)
MRLG .... La Garroba [*Costa Rica*] [*ICAO location identifier*] (ICLI)
MRLI........... La Ligia [*Costa Rica*] [*ICAO location identifier*] (ICLI)
MRLL........... Las Lomas [*Costa Rica*] [*ICAO location identifier*] (ICLI)
MRLL........... Merrill Corp. [*NASDAQ symbol*] (NQ)
MRLL........... Merrill Corp. [*NASDAQ symbol*] (TTSB)
MRLM........... Limon/Limon Internacional [*Costa Rica*] [*ICAO location identifier*] (ICLI)
MRLOGAEUR... Minimum Required Logistics Augmentation Europe (MCD)
MRLPC .... Mouvement de Regroupement et de Liberation du Peuple Congolais [*Movement for the Regroupment and Liberation of the Congolese People*]
MRLR .... La Roca [*Costa Rica*] [*ICAO location identifier*] (ICLI)
MRLT........... Las Trancas [*Costa Rica*] [*ICAO location identifier*] (ICLI)
MRLU........... La Maruca [*Costa Rica*] [*ICAO location identifier*] (ICLI)
MRLV........... La Cueva [*Costa Rica*] [*ICAO location identifier*] (ICLI)
MRLY........... La Yolanda [*Costa Rica*] [*ICAO location identifier*] (ICLI)
MRM........... Aerocharter, Inc. [*Canada ICAO designator*] (FAAC)
MRM........... Mail Readership Measurement
mrm........... Mail Readership Measurement (AD)
MRM........... Maintenance, Reporting, and Management [*Military*] (MCD)
MRM........... Management Responsibility Matrix
MRM........... Management Review Meeting (AFIT)
MRM........... Manari [*Papua New Guinea*] [*Airport symbol*] (OAG)
MRM........... Master of Resource Management (GAGS)
mrm........... Mechanically Recovered Meat (AD)
MRM........... Mechanically Removed Meat
MRM........... Medical Record Manager
MRM........... Medical Repair Technician [*Navy*]
MRM........... Medium-Range Missile (MCD)
MRM........... Merrimac Industries [*AMEX symbol*] (TTSB)
MRM........... Merrimac Industries, Inc. [*AMEX symbol*] (SPSG)
MRM........... Metabolic Rate Monitor [*Trademark*]
MRM........... Metastable Reaction Monitoring [*Analytical chemistry*]
MRM........... Michelson Rotating Mirror
MRM........... Miles of Relative Movement [*Navigation*]
mrm........... Miles of Relative Movement (AD)
MRM........... Miscellaneous Radioactive Material (GAAI)
MRM........... Most Recently Used Master [*Computer science*]
MRM........... Movement for the Redemption of Liberian Muslims [*Political party*] (EY)
MRM........... Movimento da Resistencia de Mozambique [*Mozambique Resistance Movement*]
MRM........... Multiple Reaction Monitoring [*Chemistry*]
MRM........... Music for the Rights of Man (EA)
MRMA........... Montealto [*Costa Rica*] [*ICAO location identifier*] (ICLI)
MRMC .... Medical Research Modernization Committee (EA)
MRMC .... Murcielago [*Costa Rica*] [*ICAO location identifier*] (ICLI)
MRMJ........... Mojica [*Costa Rica*] [*ICAO location identifier*] (ICLI)
MRML........... Medium-Range Missile Launcher
MRML........... Montelimar O Los Sitios [*Costa Rica*] [*ICAO location identifier*] (ICLI)
MRMO........... Mobilization Reserve Materiel Objective [*Army*]
MRMO-A..... Mobilization Reserve Materiel Objective - Acquisition [*Army*] (AFIT)
MRMP........... Marginal Revenue/Marginal Physical Product [*Economics*]
MRMPO........ Mobilization Reserve Materiel Procurement Objective [*Army*]
MRMR........... Mining Rock-Mass Rating [*Mining technology*]
MRMR........... Mobilization Reserve Materiel Requirement [*Army*]
MRMS........... MARC [*Machine-Readable Cataloging*] Record Management System
MRMS........... Metabolic Rate Measuring System
MRMS........... Mobile Remote Manipulator System (MCD)
MRMS........... Mobile/Tracked Remote Manipulator System (SSD)
MRMS........... Monetary Ration Management System [*Military*] (AFM)
MRMS........... Mount Rushmore Memorial Society (EA)
MRMU........... Mobile Radiological Measuring Unit
MRMU........... Mobile Remote Manipulating Unit [*Air Force*]
MRMVA........ Master Retail Milk Vendors Association (AD)
MRMW .... Memory Write [*Computer science*] (MHDI)
MRN .... Marion [*South Africa*] [*Geomagnetic observatory code*]
MRN .... Maritime Radionavigation
MRN .... Material Recorder Notice (AD)
MRN .... Median Raphe Nucleus [*Medicine*]
MRN .... Medium-Round Nose [*Diamond drilling*]
MRN .... Meteorological Rocket Network [*NASA*]
MRN .... Minimum Rejection Number
MRN .... Missions Gouvernementales Francaises [*France ICAO designator*] (FAAC)
MRN .... Modified Random Network [*Crystallography*]
MRN .... Moran Resources Corp. [*Vancouver Stock Exchange symbol*]
MRN .... Morganton, NC [*Location identifier FAA*] (FAAL)
MRN .... Morning (ROG)
MRN .... Morrison Knudsen [*NYSE symbol*] (TTSB)
MRN .... Morrison-Knudsen Co., Inc. [*NYSE symbol*] (SPSG)
MRN .... Motor Racing Network
MRN .... Mouvement pour la Reconstruction Nationale [*Haiti*] [*Political party*] (EY)
MRN .... Movimiento de Renovacion Nacional [*Movement for National Renovation*] [*Colorado Political party*] (PPW)
MRNA .... Marina
mRNA .... Ribonucleic Acid, Messenger [*Biochemistry, genetics*]
MRNC .... Marine Ltd. Partnership [*NASDAQ symbol*] (SAG)

MRNC .... Meteorological Rocket Network Committee [*NASA*] (SAA)
MRNC .... Nicoya [*Costa Rica*] [*ICAO location identifier*] (ICLI)
MRNCZ .... Marina Ltd Partnership [*NASDAQ symbol*] (TTSB)
MRND .... Maintenance Required Not Developed (MSA)
MRND .... Mouvement Revolutionnaire National pour le Developpement [*National Revolutionary Movement for Development*] [*Rwanda*] [*Political party*] (PPW)
MRNE .... Marine
MRNet .... [*The*] Minnesota Regional Network [*Computer science*] (TNIG)
mrng .... Mooring (AD)
mrng .... Morning (AD)
MRNG .... Morning
MRNJ .... Naranjo (Seevers) [*Costa Rica*] [*ICAO location identifier*] (ICLI)
MRNL .... Medical Research and Nutrition Laboratory [*Army*] (MCD)
MRNP .... Mount Rainier National Park [*Washington*] (AD)
MRNP .... Mount Revelstoke National Park [*British Columbia*] (AD)
mRNP .... Ribonucleoprotein, Messenger [*Biochemistry*]
MRNPF .... Member, Royal Nurses Pension Fund [*British*] (ROG)
MRNR .... Mariner Health Group [*NASDAQ symbol*] (TTSB)
MRNR .... Mariner Health Group, Inc. [*NASDAQ symbol*] (SAG)
MRNS .... Modular Reusable Nuclear Shuttle
MRNS .... Nosara [*Costa Rica*] [*ICAO location identifier*] (ICLI)
Mro .... Maestro (AD)
mro .... Maintenance, Repair, and Operating (AD)
MRO .... Maintenance, Repair, and Operating Supplies (AAGC)
MRO .... Maintenance, Repair, and Operation
MRO .... Maintenance, Repair, and Overhaul
MRO .... Maintenance Report Order (SAA)
MRO .... Management Review Officer
MRO .... Manufacturing Rework Order
MRO .... Masterton [*New Zealand*] [*Airport symbol*] (OAG)
MRO .... Materiel Readiness Officer (MCD)
MRO .... Materiel Release Order [*Air Force*]
MRO .... Mechanized RADAR Observer
MRO .... Media Resources Officer (AIE)
MRO .... Medical Regulating Office [*or Officer*] [*Army*] (AABC)
MRO .... Medical Research Organization [*Generic term*]
MRO .... Medical Review Officer (GFGA)
MRO .... Member of the Register of Osteopaths [*British*]
MRO .... Meridor Resources Ltd. [*Vancouver Stock Exchange symbol*]
MRO .... Message Releasing Officer
MRO .... Message Review Officer (MCD)
MRO .... Mid-Range Objectives
MRO .... Military Release Orders
MRO .... Mine Radiographic Outfit [*Military*] (PDAA)
MRO .... Minimal Recognizable Odor [*Medicine*] (DMAA)
MRO .... Minority Recruiting Officer (DNAB)
MRO .... Morrison Flying Service, Inc. [*ICAO designator*] (FAAC)
MRO .... Motor Routing Order
MRO .... Movement Report Office [*Military*]
MRO .... Multi-Region Option (HGAA)
MRO .... Muscle Receptor Organ [*Neurophysiology*]
MRO .... Rossburn Regional Library, Manitoba [*Library symbol National Library of Canada*] (NLC)
MRO .... USX-Marathon Group [*NYSE symbol*] (SPSG)
MRO .... USX-Marathon Grp [*NYSE symbol*] (TTSB)
MROA .... Magnetic Raman Optical Activity [*Spectrometry*]
MROAR........ Modification and Repair Order and Acceptance Record (AD)
MROC .... Mobile Range Operation Center (NVT)
MROC .... Monroc, Inc. [*NASDAQ symbol*] (SAG)
MROC .... San Jose/Juan Santamaria Internacional [*Costa Rica*] [*ICAO location identifier*] (ICLI)
MROD .... Medical Research and Operations Directorate [*NASA*] (KSC)
MROF .... Maintenance, Repair, and Operation of Facility (KSC)
MROL .... Minimum Resolvable Object Length
MROM .... Macro Read-Only Memory [*Computer science*]
MROM .... Masked Read-Only Memory [*Computer science*]
mrov .... Moreover (AD)
MRoxH......... Hebrew Teachers College, Roxbury, MA [*Library symbol Library of Congress*] (LCLS)
MRP .... Application for Writ of Mandamus Refused in Part [*Legal term*] (DLA)
MRp .... Carnegie Library, Rockport, MA [*Library symbol Library of Congress*] (LCLS)
MRP .... Machine-Readable Passport (DA)
mrp .... Machine-Readable Passport (AD)
MRP .... Magnum Rifle Powder (DICI)
MRP .... Maintenance Rally Point [*Military*] (INF)
MRP .... Maintenance Real Property (NVT)
MRP .... Malfunction Reporting Program [*Navy*]
MRP .... Manned Reusable Payload
mrp .... Manned Reusable Payload (AD)
mrp .... Manned Reusable Product (AD)
MRP .... Manned Rotating Platform
MRP .... Manual Reporting Post (NATG)
MRP .... Manufacturer's Recommended Price (ODBW)
MRP .... Manufacturing Requirements Planning [*Purchasing computer program*] (PCM)
MRP .... Manufacturing Resource Planning [*Computer science*]
MRP .... Marginal Revenue Product [*Economics*]
mrp .... Marginal Revenue Product (AD)
MRP .... Markov Renewal Program
MRP .... Marla [*Australia Airport symbol*] (OAG)
MRP .... Mass Resolving Power [*Physics*]
MRP .... Master in Regional Planning (DD)
MRP .... Master of Regional Planning

MRP............ Master Restationing Plan [*DoD*]
MRP............ Material Reliability Program [*Military*] (AFIT)
MRP............ Material Requirements Planning [*Pronounced "merp"*]
MRP............ Material Reserve Planning
MRP............ Material Resource Planning (ACII)
MRP............ Materiel Returns Program [*Military*] (AFIT)
MRP............ Mathematics Resources Project [*National Science Foundation*]
MRP............ Maximum Rated Power
MRP............ Maximum Resolving Power
mrp............ Maximum Resolving Power (AD)
mrp............ Maximum Retail Price (AD)
MRP............ Maximum Retail Price [*British*]
MRP............ Medical Record Practitioner [*Medicare*] (DHSM)
MRP............ Medical Reimbursement Plan
MRP............ Members Retirement Plan [*of the American Medical Association*]
                 (DAVI)
MRP............ Merapi [*Java*] [*Seismograph station code, US Geological Survey
                 Closed*] (SEIS)
MRP............ Message Routing Process [*Telecommunications*] (TEL)
MRP............ Mid-Range Plan [*1969-70*] [*Military*]
MRP............ Militarism Resource Project (EA)
MRP............ Military Rated Power (NG)
MRP............ Military Representatives of Associated Pacific Powers [*World War II*]
MRP............ Military Requirements Plan (NATG)
MRP............ Minimum Reaction Posture (NVT)
MRP............ Miscellaneous Relay Panel (MCD)
MRP............ Mississippi River Plume [*Marine science*] (OSRA)
MRP............ Mississippi River Plume (USDC)
MRP............ Mitochondrial RNA [*Ribonucleic Acid*] Processing [*Cytology*]
MRP............ Mobile RADAR Post
MRP............ Mobile Repair Party (MCD)
MRP............ Modern Religious Problems [*A publication*]
MRP............ Molybdate-Reactive Phosphorus [*Analytical chemistry*]
MRP............ Monthly Report of Progress
MRP............ Morley Library, Painesville, OH [*OCLC symbol*] (OCLC)
MRP............ Morrison Petroleums Ltd. [*Toronto Stock Exchange symbol*]
MRP............ Motor Racing Publications [*Publisher*] [*British*]
MRP............ Mouvement Republicain Populaire [*Popular Republican Movement*]
                 [*France Political party*] (PPE)
MRP............ Mouvement Revolutionnaire du Peuple [*Chad*] [*Political party*] (EY)
MRP............ Movimiento Republicano Progresista [*Progressive Republican
                 Movement*] [*Venezuela Political party*]
MRP............ Movimiento Revolucionario del Pueblo - Ixim [*People's Revolutionary
                 Movement - Ixim*] [*Guatemala*] [*Political party*] (PD)
MRP............ Movimiento Revolucionario Popular [*Venezuela Political party*] (EY)
MRP............ Multiplex Recording Photography
MRP............ Multi-Racial Party [*Zambia*] [*Political party*] (EY)
MRP............ Reston and District Regional Library, Reston, Manitoba [*Library
                 symbol National Library of Canada*] (NLC)
MR/PA....... Make Ready / Put Away (DNAB)
MRPA....... Master of Recreation and Parks Administration (GAGS)
MRPA....... Metropolitan Region Planning Authority (AD)
MRPA....... Modified Random Phase Approximation
MRPA....... Punta Burica [*Costa Rica*] [*ICAO location identifier*] (ICLI)
MRPARABAD... Master Parachutist Badge [*Military decoration*]
MRPB....... Playa Blanca [*Costa Rica*] [*ICAO location identifier*] (ICLI)
MRPC....... Mercury Rankine Power Conversion [*Nuclear energy*]
MRPC....... Mouvement de Regroupement des Populations Congolaises
                 [*Movement for the Regroupment of the Congolese People*]
                 [*Political party*]
MRPC....... Paso Canoas [*Costa Rica*] [*ICAO location identifier*] (ICLI)
MRPD....... Pandora [*Costa Rica*] [*ICAO location identifier*] (ICLI)
MRPE....... Palo Verde [*Costa Rica*] [*ICAO location identifier*] (ICLI)
MRPF....... Maintenance of Real Property Facilities (AABC)
MRPG....... Potrero Grande [*Costa Rica*] [*ICAO location identifier*] (ICLI)
MRPhS...... Member of the Royal Pharmaceutical Society [*Canada*] (DD)
MRPI....... Paissa [*Costa Rica*] [*ICAO location identifier*] (ICLI)
MRPJ....... Puerto Jimenez [*Costa Rica*] [*ICAO location identifier*] (ICLI)
MRPL....... Material Requirements Planning List [*Navy*]
MRPL....... Portalon [*Costa Rica*] [*ICAO location identifier*] (ICLI)
MRPM....... Material Research and Production Methods (MCD)
MRPM....... Palmar Sur [*Costa Rica*] [*ICAO location identifier*] (ICLI)
MRPN....... Pelon Nuevo [*Costa Rica*] [*ICAO location identifier*] (ICLI)
MRPP....... Maoist Reorganization Movement of the Party of the Proletariat
                 [*Political party*] (AD)
MRPP....... Mortgage Rate Protection Program [*Canada*]
MRPR....... Parrita [*Costa Rica*] [*ICAO location identifier*] (ICLI)
MRPRA...... Malaysian Rubber Producers' Research Association [*Research center
                 British*] (IRC)
MRPS....... Manufacturing and Resource Planning System [*Cincom Systems
                 Ltd.*] [*Software package*] (NCC)
MRPS....... Marine Petrol Tr [*NASDAQ symbol*] (TTSB)
MRPS....... Materials Requirement Planning System (HGAA)
M rps........ Maurituis Rupee [*Monetary unit*] (AD)
MRPS....... Paissa [*Costa Rica*] [*ICAO location identifier*] (ICLI)
MRPV....... Mini-Remotely Piloted Vehicle (PDAA)
MRPV....... San Jose/Tobias Bolanos Internacional [*Costa Rica*] [*ICAO location
                 identifier*] (ICLI)
MRQ.......... Marinduque [*Philippines*] [*Airport symbol*] (OAG)
MRQ.......... Marquardt Corp. [*Stock exchange symbol*] (AD)
MRQ.......... Maximum Release Quantity [*DoD*]
MRQE....... Marquee Group, Inc. (The) [*NASDAQ symbol*] (SAG)
MRQP....... Quepos (La Managua) [*Costa Rica*] [*ICAO location identifier*] (ICLI)
MRR.......... Macara [*Ecuador*] [*Airport symbol*] (OAG)
MRR.......... Machine-Readable Record (MCD)

MRR............ [*The*] Magistrates of the Roman Republic [*A publication*] (OCD)
MRR............ Maintenance, Repairs, and Replacements [*Military*]
MRR............ Maintenance, Replacement, Removal (AFIT)
MRR............ Mandatory Removal Roster [*Army*]
MRR............ Manistee Railroad
MRR............ Marrow Release Rate [*Hematology*]
MRR............ Master Record Repository (MCD)
MRR............ Material Readiness Report (MCD)
MRR............ Material Receiving [*Inspection*] Report [*Nuclear energy*] (NRCH)
MRR............ Material Rejection Report
MRR............ Material Reliability Report (MCD)
MRR............ Material Removal Rate (MCD)
MRR............ Material Review Record [*or Reports*] [*Aviation*] (MCD)
MRR............ Material Review Request
MRR............ Materiel Readiness Report [*Army*] (AABC)
MRR............ Maximal Relaxation Rate [*Medicine*]
MRR............ Maximum Rate of Rise [*Biometrics*]
MRR............ Mechanical Reliability Report [*FAA*]
MRR............ Mechanical Research Report
MRR............ Medical Research Reactor
mrr............ Medical Research Reactor (AD)
MRR............ Medium-Range RADAR (NG)
MRR............ Medium-Range Recovery
MRR............ Metal Removal Rate
MRR............ Microelectronic Radio Receiver
MRR............ Microfilm Reader Recorder
MRR............ Mid-Atlantic Realty Trust [*AMEX symbol*] (SPSG)
MRR............ Milestone Readiness Review [*NASA*] (KSC)
MRR............ Military Renegotiation Regulation
MRR............ Miniature Reed Relay
MRR............ Minimum Rediscount Rate
MRR............ Minimum Reporting Requirement [*NASA*] (KSC)
MRR............ Minimum Risk Route (MCD)
MRR............ Missile Restraint Release
MRR............ Mission Reconfiguration Request (MCD)
MRR............ Molecular Rotational Resonance
MRR............ Monomer Reactivity Ratio (PDAA)
MRR............ Monthly Review Report
MRR............ Motorized Rifle Regiment [*Former USSR*]
MRR............ Multiple Response Resolver
MRR............ Multirole RADAR
MRR............ Muroran [*Japan*] [*Seismograph station code, US Geological
                 Survey*] (SEIS)
MRRA........ Master of Recreation Resources (F6) Administration (PGP)
MRRA........ Military Retirement Reform Act
MRRAS...... Murder Release Risk Assessment Scale (AD)
MRRB........ Maintenance Requirements Review Board [*Military*] (AFIT)
MRRB........ Materiel Release Review Board [*Military*]
MRRB........ Materiel Requirements Review Board [*Military*] (AFIT)
MRRC........ Materiel Requirements Review Committee [*Military*]
MRRC........ Mechanical Reliability Research Center
MRRC........ Mental Retardation Research Center [*University of California, Los
                 Angeles*] [*Research center*] (RCD)
MRRC........ Ralph L. Smith Mental Retardation Research Center [*University of
                 Kansas*] [*Research center*] (RCD)
MRRD........ Marine Resources Research Division [*Now Ocean Environment
                 Research Division*] (USDC)
MRRD........ Marine Resources Research Division [*Marine science*] (OSRA)
MRRDB...... Malaysian Rubber Research and Development Board (AD)
MRRF........ Monitor Research and Recovery Foundation
MRRF........ Rio Frio O Progreso [*Costa Rica*] [*ICAO location identifier*] (ICLI)
MRRI........ Marine Resources Research Institute [*South Carolina Wildlife and
                 Marine Resources Department*] [*Research center*] (RCD)
MRRL........ Materiel Repair Requirement List [*Military*] (AFIT)
MRRL........ Metabolism and Radiation Research Laboratory [*North Dakota State
                 University*] [*Research center*] (RCD)
MRRM........ Rancho Del Mar [*Costa Rica*] [*ICAO location identifier*] (ICLI)
MRRN........ Rancho Nuevo [*Costa Rica*] [*ICAO location identifier*] (ICLI)
MRRP........ Maintenance and Repair of Real Property [*Military*]
MRRP........ Motorways, Roads, and Road Programmes [*British*]
MRRS........ Magnetic Reed Rotary Switch
MRRS........ Materiel Readiness Reporting System [*Army*]
MRRS........ Mobile Rail Repair Shop (MCD)
MRRS........ Multiple Railroad System
MRRS........ Multi-Rail Rocket System (PDAA)
MRRT........ Maintenance Requirements Review Team (MUGU)
MRRW....... Morrow Snowboards [*NASDAQ symbol*] (TTSB)
MRRW....... Morrow Snowboards, Inc. [*NASDAQ symbol*] (SAG)
MRRX....... Roxana Farms [*Costa Rica*] [*ICAO location identifier*] (ICLI)
MRS.......... Airline of the Marshall Islands [*ICAO designator*] (FAAC)
MRS.......... Maars [*Alaska*] [*Seismograph station code, US Geological Survey*]
                 (SEIS)
MRS.......... Mado Robin Society [*Defunct*] (EA)
MRS.......... Magnetic Reed Switch
MRS.......... Magnetic-Resonance Spectroscopy [*Biochemistry*] (ECON)
MRS.......... Magnetic-Resonance Spectrum
MRS.......... Maintenance, Repair, and Service
MRS.......... Maintenance Reporting System [*Army*]
MRS.......... Maintenance Requirement Substantiated (MSA)
MRS.......... Malfunction Reporting System [*Boeing*]
MRS.......... Management Relations Survey [*Test*]
MRS.......... Management Reporting System
MRS.......... Management Review System (NASA)
MRS.......... Manipulator Repair Shop (NRCH)
MRS.......... Manned Reconnaissance Satellite [*Air Force*]

MRS............	Manned Repeater Station [Telecommunications] (OA)
MRS............	Manufacturers Railway Co. [AAR code]
MRS............	Marches (ROG)
MRS............	Marginal Rate of Substitution [Economics]
mrs............	Marginal Rate of Substitution (AD)
MRS............	Mariah Resources Ltd. [Vancouver Stock Exchange symbol]
MRS............	Market Research Society [British]
MRS............	Marseille [France] [Airport symbol] (OAG)
MRS............	Master Repair Schedule [Air Force]
MRS............	Material Request [or Requirement] Summary
MRS............	Material Returned to Store [NASA] (KSC)
MRS............	Material Routing Slip
MRS............	Materials Research Society (EA)
MRS............	Materiel Repair System [Air Force] (AFM)
MRS............	Media Recognition System [Computer science] (PCM)
MRS............	Media Report Service (NITA)
MRS............	Media Resource Service [Scientists' Institute for Public Information] [Information service or system] (IID)
MRS............	Medical Receiving Station
MRS............	Medical Reception Station [Military]
MRS............	Medical Research Society [British]
MRS............	Medium Range Search
MRS............	Medium-Range SONAR (NVT)
MRS............	Melkersson-Rosenthal Syndrome [Medicine] (DMAA)
MRS............	Memo Routing Slip
MRS............	Metals Removal System [Petroleum refining]
MRS............	Methicillin-Resistant Staphylococcus [Qureus] [Medicine] (DAVI)
MRS............	Methicillin-Resistant Staphylococcus Aureus [Antimicrobial therapy] (MEDA)
MrS............	Microfilm Records System, Inc., Mamaroneck, NY [Library symbol] [Library of Congress] (LCLS)
MRS............	Microfilm Replacement System [Computer science]
MRS............	Micro Reflective Structure [Computer science]
MRS............	Midcoast Energy Resources, Inc. [AMEX symbol] (SAG)
MRS............	Migration and Refugee Services (EA)
MRS............	Military Railway Service [Army]
MRS............	Military Requirements Study (AAGC)
MRS............	Military Retirement System
MRS............	Minimum Radial Separation [Manufacturing term]
MRS............	Minimum Reporting Standard [Broadcasting] (NTCM)
MRS............	Mini-Reconstruction System (MCD)
MRS............	Ministry of Recreation and Sport [British] (AD)
MRS............	Missile Reentry Systems (AFIT)
MRS............	Missile Round Simulator
MRS............	Mission de Ras Shamra [A publication] (BJA)
MRS............	Mission-Related Software
Mrs............	Missus (AD)
Mrs............	Mistress (AD)
MRS............	Mistress (DAVI)
MRS............	Mixed Reproductive Strategy [Avian biology]
MRS............	Mobile Radio Service (DA)
MRS............	Mobile Remote Servicer (SSD)
MRS............	Mobility Requirements Study [DoD]
MRS............	Mobilization Requirement Study
MRS............	Mobilization Reserve Stocks [Army]
MRS............	Modification Record Sheet [NASA] (KSC)
MRS............	Monitored Retrievable Storage [of nuclear waste]
MRS............	Monorail System
MRS............	Moore-Rott-Sears [Theory]
MRS............	Mortgage-Related Security (EMRF)
MRS............	Mothers Return to School
MRS............	Motor Rotation Stand
MRS............	Mountain Rescue Service (AD)
MRS............	Mouvement Republicain Senegalais [Senegalese Republican Movement] [Political party] (PPW)
MRS............	Movement and Reinforcement Study (MCD)
MRS............	Movement Report Sheet [Military]
MRS............	Movement Report System [Military]
MRS............	Multilateral RADAR Strike System [Air Force] (MCD)
MRS............	Multilateral RADAR Surveillance System [Air Force] (MCD)
MRS............	Multiple Representative Sections [Pathology] (DAVI)
MRS............	Multipurpose Research System
MRS............	Multipurpose Reusable Spacecraft (IIA)
MRS............	Music Reading Software (PCM)
MRS............	Muzzle Reference System (MCD)
MRS3............	Multilateral RADAR Surveillance/Strike System [Air Force]
MRSA.........	Machinery Repairman, Seaman Apprentice [Navy rating]
MRSA.........	Maine Revised Statutes, Annotated [A publication] (DLA)
MRSA.........	Mandatory RADAR Service Area
MRSA.........	Marisa Christina [NASDAQ symbol] (TTSB)
MRSA.........	Marisa Christina, Inc. [NASDAQ symbol] (SAG)
MRSA.........	Materiel Readiness Support Activity [Army] (RDA)
MRSA.........	Materiel Readiness Support Agency [Navy]
MRSA.........	Medium Range Surveillance Aircraft [Military] (PDAA)
mrsa.........	Medium-Range Surveillance Aircraft (AD)
MRSA.........	Member of the Royal Society of Arts [British]
MRSA.........	Methicillin-Resistant Staphylococcus Aureus [Antimicrobial therapy]
MRSA.........	Microwave Radiometer, Scatterometer, and Altimeter (MCD)
MRSA.........	Military RADAR Service Area [Aviation] (AIA)
MRSA.........	San Alberto [Costa Rica] [ICAO location identifier] (ICLI)
MR San A....	Member of the Royal Sanitary Association of Scotland
MR San Asn...	Member of the Royal Sanitary Association [British] (AD)
MRSB.........	Material Requirements for Stock Balance
MRSB.........	San Cristobal [Costa Rica] [ICAO location identifier] (ICLI)
Mr SBA........	Maryland State Bar Association, Report [A publication] (DLA)

MRSC.........	Maritime Rescue Sub-Center [Canada]
MRSc.........	Master of Rural Science [British] (ADA)
MRSC.........	Member of the Royal Society of Canada
MRSC.........	Member of the Royal Society of Chemistry [British] (DBQ)
MRSC.........	Mississippi Remote Sensing Center [Mississippi State University] [Research center] (RCD)
MRSC.........	Santa Cruz [Costa Rica] [ICAO location identifier] (ICLI)
MRSD.........	Maximum Rated Standard Deviation [Statistics]
MRSD.........	Mission Requirements on System Design [NASA]
MRSG.........	Santa Clara De Guapiles [Costa Rica] [ICAO location identifier] (ICLI)
MRSH.........	Marsh (ADA)
MRSH.........	Member of the Royal Society of Health [British]
MRSH.........	Shiroles [Costa Rica] [ICAO location identifier] (ICLI)
MRSHLL.....	Marshall
MrshllInd.....	Marshall Industries [Associated Press] (SAG)
MrshMc.......	Marsh & McLennan Companies, Inc. [Associated Press] (SAG)
MrshS.........	Marsh Supermarkets, Inc. [Associated Press] (SAG)
MrshSu.......	Marsh Supermarkets, Inc. [Associated Press] (SAG)
MRSI.........	Maintenance and Repair Support Items
MRSI.........	Maintenance Repair Spares Instruction (MCD)
MRSI.........	Medium-Range SOF [Special Operations Forces] Insertion (DOMA)
MRSI.........	Member of the Royal Sanitary Institute [British] (ROG)
MRSI.........	Mobilization Requirements, Secondary Items
MRSI.........	MRS Technology [NASDAQ symbol] (TTSB)
MRSI.........	MRS Technology, Inc. [NASDAQ symbol] (SAG)
MRSI.........	San Isidro De El General [Costa Rica] [ICAO location identifier] (ICLI)
MRSJ.........	San Jose [Costa Rica] [ICAO location identifier] (ICLI)
MRSJ.........	United Church of Christ Ministers for Racial and Social Justice (EA)
MRSL.........	Member of the Royal Society of Literature [British]
MRSM.........	Maintenance and Reliability Simulation Model (PDAA)
MRSM.........	Member of the Royal Society of Medicine [British] (DI)
MRSM.........	Member of the Royal Society of Musicians [British] (DI)
MRSM.........	Mississippi River Suspended Matter
MRSM.........	Santa Marta [Costa Rica] [ICAO location identifier] (ICLI)
MRSMA.......	Member of the Royal Society of Marine Artists [British] (DI)
MRSMGB.....	Member of the Royal Society of Musicians of Great Britian (AD)
MRSMP.......	Member of the Royal Society of Miniature Painters [British] (DI)
MRSN.........	Machinery Repairman, Seaman [Navy rating]
MRSN.........	Sirena [Costa Rica] [ICAO location identifier] (ICLI)
MRSO.........	Mobilization Reserve Stockage Objective [Army]
MRSO.........	Santa Maria De Guacimo [Costa Rica] [ICAO location identifier] (ICLI)
MRSP.........	Multifunction RADAR Signal Processor (MCD)
MRSP.........	Myakka River State Park [Florida] (AD)
MRSP.........	San Pedro [Costa Rica] [ICAO location identifier] (ICLI)
MRSPE.......	Member of the Royal Society of Painters and Etchers [British] (DI)
MRSPWC.....	Member of the Royal Society of Painters in Water Colours [British]
MR-SR.........	Material Review - Ships Record (MCD)
MRSR.........	Multi-Role Survivable Radar [Army] (DOMA)
MRSR.........	Samara [Costa Rica] [ICAO location identifier] (ICLI)
MRSS.........	Main and Reheat Steam System [Nuclear energy] (NRCH)
MRSS.........	Manned Rovolving Simulated Space Station (SAA)
MRSS.........	Master Remote Slave Station (MCD)
MRSS.........	Missile Response Simulation Software
MRSS.........	San Joaquin de Abangares [Costa Rica] [ICAO location identifier] (ICLI)
mrsss.........	Manned Revolving Space Systems Simulator (AD)
MRST.........	Member of the Royal Society of Teachers [British]
MRST.........	Minimum Remaining Slack Time (PDAA)
MRST.........	San Agustin [Costa Rica] [ICAO location identifier] (ICLI)
MRS Tch.....	MRS Technology, Inc. [Associated Press] (SAG)
MRSV.........	Maneuverable Recoverable Space Vehicle
MRSV.........	Military Railway Service Veterans (EA)
MRSV.........	San Vito De Jaba [Costa Rica] [ICAO location identifier] (ICLI)
MRSW.........	Member of the Royal Society of Scottish Painters and Watercolours [British] (DAS)
MRSX.........	Sixaola [Costa Rica] [ICAO location identifier] (ICLI)
MRT............	Air Mauritanie [Mauritania] [ICAO designator] (FAAC)
Mrt............	Maart [March] [Dutch] (AD)
MRT............	Machine-Readable Tapes [Computer science]
MRT............	Maintainability Review Team [Navy] (NG)
MRT............	Maintenance Readiness Training (DNAB)
MRT............	Major Role Therapy [Schizophrenia]
MRT............	Marble Threshold (AAG)
MRT............	Marietta Resources [Vancouver Stock Exchange symbol]
Mrt............	Martinique (AD)
MRT............	Marysville, OH [Location identifier FAA] (FAAL)
MRT............	Mass Rapid Transit (AD)
MRT............	Mass Rapid Transport [British]
MRT............	Material Review Tag [Aviation] (MCD)
MRT............	Mauritania [ANSI three-letter standard code] (CNC)
MRT............	Maximum Rated Thrust (MCD)
MRT............	Maximum Repair Time (PDAA)
MRT............	Maze-Running Time [Psychology]
MRT............	MBB [Messerschmidt, Boelkow, Blohm] Raytheon-Thompson
MRT............	Mean Radiant Temperature
mrt............	Mean Radiant Temperature (AD)
MRT............	Mean Radiative-Transfer [Meteorology]
MRT............	Mean Ready Time (MCD)
MRT............	Mean Repair Time
MRT............	Mean Residence Time [Kinetics]
MRT............	Mean Retention Time [Physiology]
MRT............	Measured Rate of Time (PDAA)

MRT............	Median Recognition Threshold (MAE)
MRT............	Medical Records Technician (DAVI)
MRT............	Medical Record Technician (HCT)
MRT............	Medium Range Truck [Military]
MRT............	Medium-Range Typhon [Missile] (NG)
MRT............	Meridional Ray Trace
Mrt.............	Merit [Record label]
MRT............	Metropolitan Readiness Test
mrt.............	Mid-Range Trajectory (AD)
mrt.............	Mildew-Resistant Thread (AD)
MRT............	Mildew-Resistant Thread
MRT............	Milestones Reporting Techniques
MRT............	Military Rated Thrust (NG)
mrt.............	Military-Rated Thrust (AD)
MRT............	Military Reserve Technician (GFGA)
MRT............	Military Review Team (AD)
MRT............	Milk Ring Test (PDAA)
MRT............	Miniature Receiver Terminal
MRT............	Minimum Resolvable Temperature (MCD)
MRT............	Ministere de la Recherche et de la Technologie (USDC)
MRT............	Missile Round Trainer (MCD)
MRT............	Missile Round Transporter (MCD)
mrt.............	Mission Readiness Tester (AD)
MRT............	Mobile RADAR Target
MRT............	Modified Rhyme Test
MRT............	Modulus of Rupture Test (AD)
MRT............	Movimento Revolucionario Tiradentes [Revolutionary Tiradentes Movement] [Brazil Political party] (PD)
MRT............	Multiple Requests Terminal [Computer science] (HGAA)
MRT............	Murotomisaki [Japan] [Seismograph station code, US Geological Survey] (SEIS)
MRT............	Muscle Response Test
MRT............	Reformed Theological Seminary, Jackson, MS [OCLC symbol] (OCLC)
MRTA..........	Maintenance Requirements Task Analysis (AD)
MRTA..........	Marietta Corp. [NASDAQ symbol] (NQ)
MRTA..........	Marketing Research Trade Association [Later, MRA] (EA)
MRTA..........	Mechanical Response Tissue Analyzer [For measuring bone strength]
MRTA..........	Movimiento Revolucionario Tupac Amaru [Peru] [Political party] (EY)
MRTA..........	Tamarindo de Bagaces [Costa Rica] [ICAO location identifier] (ICLI)
MRTB..........	Ticaban [Costa Rica] [ICAO location identifier] (ICLI)
MRTC..........	Marine Corps Reserve Training Center
MRTC..........	Military Real-Time Computer (AAG)
MRTC..........	Multiple Real-Time Commands (NASA)
MRTC..........	Multiple Real-Time Commands
MRTD	Minimum Resolvable Temperature Difference (PDAA)
MRTE..........	Master of Radio and Television Engineering
MRTE..........	Missile Round Test Equipment
MRT Eng......	Master of Radio and Television Engineering
MRTFB........	Major Range and Test Facility Base [Military] (CAAL)
MRTFM.......	Mean Rounds to First Maintenance [Army]
MRTG.........	Mortgage
MRTG	Taboga [Costa Rica] [ICAO location identifier] (ICLI)
MRTHN.......	Marathon
MRTI..........	Multirole Thermal Imager [Defense electronics]
MRTK..........	Movimiento Revolucionario Tupaj Katari [Tupaj Katari Revolutionary Movement] [Bolivia] [Political party] (PPW)
MRTM.........	Maritime
mrtm..........	Maritime (AD)
MRTM.........	Tamarindo de Santa Cruz [Costa Rica] [ICAO location identifier] (ICLI)
MRTN	Marten Transport [NASDAQ symbol] (TTSB)
MRTN	Marten Transport Ltd. [NASDAQ symbol] (NQ)
Mrtnz.........	Martinez (AD)
mrto...........	Miscellaneous Reference Tool (AD)
MRTP..........	Master of Regional and Town Planning
MRTP..........	Master of Rural and Town Planning (GAGS)
MRTP..........	Military Reliable Tube Program
MRTPI........	Member of the Royal Town Planning Institute [British]
MRTR.........	Mortar [Technical drawings] (DAC)
MRTR	Tambor [Costa Rica] [ICAO location identifier] (ICLI)
MRTRY.......	Mortuary
MRTS..........	Marginal Rate of Technical Substitution [Ecology]
mrts...........	Marginal Rate of Technical Substitution (AD)
MRTS..........	Mass Rapid Transit System (AD)
MRTS..........	Master RADAR Tracking Station
Mrts...........	Mauritius (AD)
MRTS..........	Meteorological Real-Time System [Computer science] (KSC)
MRTS..........	Microwave Repeater Test Set (DA)
MRTS..........	Missile Round Test Set
MRTS..........	Multi-Media Remote Teaching System [AT & T Co., Illinois Institute of Technology]
MRTT..........	Modular Record Traffic Terminal [Formerly, COED] [Army] (MCD)
MRTU	Multiplex Remote Terminal Unit (MCD)
MRU............	Machine Records Unit [Computer science]
MRU............	Main Resource Unit
MRU............	Maintenance Replaceable Unit (MCD)
MRU............	Mano River Union [See also UFM] (EAIO)
MRU............	Maritime Reconnaissance Unit [British military] (DMA)
MRU............	Mass Radiography Unit
mru............	Mass Radiography Unit (AD)
MRU............	Material Recovery Unit
MRU............	Mauritius [Airport symbol] (OAG)
MRU............	Medical Rehabilitation Unit (AD)

MRU	Message Retransmission Unit
MRU	Microfilm Recording Unit
MRU	Microwave Relay Unit
MRU	Military RADAR Unit [Aviation] (FAAC)
mru	Minimal Reproductive Unit (AD)
MRU	Minimal Reproductive Units [Bacteriology]
MRU	Minimum Replacement Unit
MRU	Mobile Radio Unit [Air Force]
mru	Mobile Radio Unit (AD)
MRU	Mobile Refrigeration Unit (KSC)
MRU	Mobile Remote Unit [From computer game "Hacker II"]
MRU	Most Recently Used [Computer science]
MRU	Most Recently Used Data [Computer science] (PCM)
MRU	Motion Reference Unit (MCD)
MRU	Movement Release Unit [MTMC] (TAG)
MRU	Much Regret, I Am Unable
MRU	Multifunction Reference Unit (MCD)
MRUA	Mobile Radio Users' Association (IAA)
MRUASTAS...	Medium-Range Unmanned Aerial Surveillance and Target Acquisition System (NATG)
M Ru E	Master of Rural Engineering
M Ru Eng	Master of Rural Engineering
MRUP	Upala [Costa Rica] [ICAO location identifier] (ICLI)
MRurSc.......	Master of Rural Science [British] (ADA)
MRUSI........	Member of the Royal United Service Institution [British]
MRV...........	Maneuvering Reentry Vehicle
MRV...........	Mark V Petroleums & Mines [Vancouver Stock Exchange symbol]
MRV...........	Mars Roving Vehicle [NASA] (PDAA)
MRV...........	Marvel Entertainment Group [NYSE symbol] (SPSG)
MRV...........	Marvel Entertainment Grp [NYS] (TTSB)
mrv...........	Material Receipt Voucher (AD)
MRV...........	Middlesex Rifle Volunteers [Military British] (ROG)
MRV...........	Mineral Nyye Vody [Former USSR Airport symbol] (OAG)
MRV...........	Mini-Rotary Viscometer [Mechanical engineering]
MRV...........	Minute Respiratory Volume
MRV...........	Miravia Ltd. [Romania] [FAA designator] (FAAC)
MRV...........	Missile Recovery Vessel (AD)
mrv...........	Missile Re-Entry Vehicle (AD)
mrv...........	Mixed Respiratory Vaccine [Medicine] (AD)
MRV...........	Mixed Respiratory Vaccine
MRV...........	Mouvement de Regroupement Voltaique [Upper Volta Regroupment Movement] [Political party]
MRV...........	Mulberry Ringspot Virus [Plant pathology]
MRV...........	Multiple Reentry Vehicle [Military]
MRVA	Member of the Rating and Valuation Association [British] (DI)
MRVC	Member of the Royal Veterinary College [British]
MRVC	MRV Communications, Inc. [NASDAQ symbol] (SAG)
MRVC	MRV Communicatons [NASDAQ symbol] (TTSB)
MRV Cm	MRV Communications, Inc. [Associated Press] (SAG)
MRVI..........	Monte Reale Valcellina [Italy] [Seismograph station code, US Geological Survey] (SEIS)
MRVLP	Maneuvering Reentry Vehicle for Low-Level Penetration (MCD)
MRVP	Mean Right Ventricular Pressure [Cardiology]
MRVP	Methyl-Red, Voges-Proskauer [Medium] [Bacteriology]
mrV-P.........	Methyl Red Voges-Proskauer [Bacteriology] (AD)
MRVT.........	Miravant [NASDAQ symbol]
MRVT.........	Miravant Medical Technologies
MRVT.........	Multiple Rate Voice Terminal [Telecommunications] (LAIN)
MRVTB	Maximally Restrictive Verifiable Test Ban [For nuclear bombs]
MRW..........	Morale, Recreation, and Welfare [Military] (AFM)
mrw	Morale, Recreation, and Welfare (AD)
MRW..........	Morioka [Japan] [Airport symbol] (OAG)
mr/w..........	Multiple Read/Write (AD)
MRWA........	Midland Railway of Western Australia (AD)
mrwc..........	Multiple Reading, Writing, Compiling (AD)
MRWC........	Multiple Read-Write Compute
MRWS	Mobile RADAR Weather System (DNAB)
MRX...........	Hermens/Markair Express [ICAO designator] (FAAC)
MRX...........	Magnetoresistive Extended [Computer science]
MRX...........	Memorex (NITA)
MRX...........	Memorex Corp. (IAA)
MRX...........	Mineiros [Brazil] [Airport symbol] (AD)
MRX...........	Mobil Oil Corp., Toxicology Division, Information Center, Princeton, NJ [OCLC symbol] (OCLC)
MRX...........	Movement Research Exchange
MRX...........	Riverside, CA [Location identifier FAA] (FAAL)
MRY...........	Marilyn Resources [Vancouver Stock Exchange symbol]
MRY...........	Mary [Former USSR Seismograph station code, US Geological Survey Closed] (SEIS)
MRY...........	Merry Land & Invest [NYSE symbol] (TTSB)
MRY...........	Merry Land & Investment [NYSE symbol] (SAG)
MRY...........	Monterey [California] [Airport symbol] (OAG)
MRYPr........	Merry Land & Inv Sr'A'Cv Pfd [NYSE symbol] (TTSB)
MRYPrC......	Merry Land & Inv Sr'C'Cv Pfd [NYSE symbol] (TTSB)
mrytm.........	Must Have Reply Here by Tomorrow Morning (AD)
mrz............	Marzo [March] [Spanish] (AD)
MRZ...........	Moree [Australia Airport symbol] (OAG)
MRZ...........	Syracuse, NY [Location identifier FAA] (FAAL)
MRZP.........	Zapotal De Guanacaste [Costa Rica] [ICAO location identifier] (ICLI)
MS..............	Egyptair [ICAO designator] (AD)
MS..............	IEEE Magnetics Society (EA)
MS..............	Ma'aser Sheni (BJA)
MS..............	Machinery Survey [Shipping]
MS..............	Machine Screw
ms..............	Machine Screw (AD)

MS .... Machine Selection (IEEE)
MS .... Machine Steel
ms .... Machine Steel (AD)
MS .... Machining System (IAA)
MS .... Macromodular System [*Computer science*] (IEEE)
MS .... Macro Society (EA)
MS .... Magnetic South
MS .... Magnetic Stirrer [*Biotechnology*]
MS .... Magnetic Storage [*Computer science*]
MS .... Magnetic Strip (IAA)
MS .... Magnetic Synchron (IAA)
MS .... Magnetostatic [*Telecommunications*] (IAA)
MS .... Magnetostriction
MS .... Mail Steamer
M/S .... Mail Stop
MS .... Main Sequence [*Astronomy*]
M/S .... Mainstage [*NASA*] (KSC)
MS .... Main Stage (IAA)
MS .... Main Steam (NRCH)
MS .... Main Storage
MS .... Main Switch
ms .... Main Switch (AD)
ms .... Maintenance and Service (AD)
MS .... Maintenance and Service
MS .... Maintenance Schedule (DA)
MS .... Maintenance Squadron
MS .... Maintenance Standard
MS .... Maintenance Superintendent [*Military*] (AFIT)
MS + ... Maintenance Support Positive
MS .... Maintenance System (ACII)
MS .... Majority Stockholder
MS .... Major Subject [*Military*]
ms .... Major Subject (AD)
MS .... Maladjustment Score [*Psychology*]
MS .... Male Servant
MS .... Malone Society (EA)
MS .... Mammal Society (EAIO)
MS .... Management Science [*Computer science*] (BUR)
MS .... Management Services (KSC)
MS .... Management Staff [*Environmental Protection Agency*] (GFGA)
MS .... Management System (OICC)
MS .... Manned Station (IAA)
M/S .... Mannlicher-Schoenauer (AD)
MS .... Mannose Sensitive [*Biochemistry*]
MS .... Mano Sinistra [*With the Left Hand*] [*Music*]
M/S .... Manslaughter
MS .... Man Station [*Military*]
MS .... Manual Sequential (NRCH)
MS .... Manual Supplement
MS .... Manual System (DCTA)
MS .... Manufacturing in Space
MS .... Manufacturing Specification (AAG)
MS .... Manufacturing Standard
MS .... Manufacturing Status (AAG)
MS .... Manufacturing Support
MS .... Manuscript (WDAA)
ms .... Manuscript (WDMC)
ms .... Manuscript (VRA)
MS .... Manuscript Reports [*A publication*] (DLA)
MS .... Manuscript Society (EA)
MS .... Manuscriptum [*Manuscript*] [*Latin*]
MS .... Mare Serenitatis [*Sea of Serenity*] [*Lunar area*]
MS .... Margin of Safety [*Engineering*]
ms .... Margin of Safety (AD)
MS .... Marian Sisters of the Diocese of Lincoln (TOCD)
MS .... Marijuana Smoke
Ms .... Mariners [*Seattle Baseball Team*] (AD)
MS .... Marital Status
MS .... Marker Switch (IAA)
m/s .... Marking and Stenciling (AD)
MS .... Mark Sense (NITA)
MS .... Mark Sensing (MSA)
MS .... Marquandia Society (EA)
MS .... Marshall Steel Ltd. [*Toronto Stock Exchange symbol*]
MS .... Mass Spectrography
ms .... Mass Spectrometric (AD)
MS .... Mass Spectrometry
MS .... Mass Storage [*Computer science*]
MS .... Master of Science [*Facetious translation "More of the Same"*]
MS .... Master of Science (GAGS)
MS .... Master of Sociology
MS .... Master of Surgery
MS .... Master Scene [*Major script sequence*] (NTCM)
MS .... Master Scheduler (CMD)
MS .... Master Sequencer (AAG)
MS .... Master Sergeant
M-S .... Master-Servant [*Legal shorthand*] (LWAP)
MS .... Master Shot [*Film production*] (NTCM)
MS .... Master-Slave [*Computer science*] (MHDI)
MS .... Master Switch
ms .... Master Switch (AD)
MS .... Master Synchronizer (CET)
MS .... Mast Section (IAA)
MS .... Matched Set [*Philately*]
ms .... Matched Set (AD)

MS .... Material Specifications
MS .... Materials Science
MS .... Material Standard (AD)
MS .... Material Support
MS .... Mathis Society [*Defunct*] (EA)
MS .... Mating Sequence and Control (NASA)
MS .... Matrix Spike
Ms .... Mature Motion Pictures (AD)
MS .... Mauritius
MS .... Maximum Stress
ms .... Maximum Stress (AD)
ms .... Mean Square (AD)
MS .... Mean Square
MS .... Measured Service Pricing [*Telecommunications*] (TEL)
M/S .... Measurement Stimuli (NASA)
MS .... Measuring Set
MS .... Measuring System
MS .... Mechanical Seal
MS .... Mechanized Scheduling [*Telecommunications*] (TEL)
MS .... Meckel Syndrome [*Medicine*] (DMAA)
MS .... Medial Septum [*Anatomy*]
MS .... Media-Service GmbH [*Database producer*] (IID)
MS .... Media Society [*British*] (DBA)
MS .... Medical Science (DAVI)
MS .... Medical Services [*Navy British*]
MS .... Medical Staff [*British military*] (DMA)
MS .... Medical Student (DAVI)
MS .... Medical Supplies [*Military*]
MS .... Medical Survey [*Navy*]
MS .... Medicine and Surgery [*Navy*] (IEEE)
MS .... Medium-Scale (IAA)
MS .... Medium Setting [*Asphalt grade*]
MS .... Medium Shot [*Refers to distance from which a photograph or motion picture sequence is taken*]
ms .... Medium Shot (AD)
MS .... Medium Soft (IAA)
MS .... Medium-Speed (IAA)
MS .... Medium Steel
ms .... Medium Steel (AD)
MS .... Meeting of Signatories [*INTELSAT*]
MS .... Meeting Series [*Online database field identifier*]
MS .... Megasecond (IAA)
MS .... Mega Society (EA)
MS .... Megasporocyte [*Botany*]
MS .... Melville Society (EA)
M/S .... Member State (DCTA)
M/S .... Memorandum Slip [*for informal interoffice communications*]
MS .... Memoriae Sacrum [*Sacred to the Memory Of*] [*Latin*]
MS .... Memory Store [*Computer science*] (PCM)
MS .... Memory System
MS .... Mencken Society (EA)
Ms .... Mendes (AD)
MS .... Men of the Stones (EA)
MS .... Mental Status [*Psychology*]
MS .... Merchant Shipping
MS .... Mercury-Scout [*Spacecraft*] [*NASA*]
MS .... Merit System (OICC)
MS .... Mesa [*Type of transistor*] (MDG)
ms .... Mesothorium (AD)
MS .... Message Store [*Telecommunications*] (OSI)
MS .... Message Switching [*Telecommunications*] (IAA)
MS .... Mestome Sheath [*Botany*]
Ms .... Mesyl [*Organic chemistry*]
MS .... [*The*] Metallurgical Society [*Later, TMS*]
MS .... Metallurgical Society (NADA)
m/s .... Metal Shank (AD)
MS .... Metals Society [*Later, IOM*] (EAIO)
MS .... Metal Stamping
MS .... Meteoritical Society (EA)
MS .... Meteoroid Shield (KSC)
MS .... Meteor Scatter (PDAA)
M/S .... Meters per Second
ms .... Meters per Second (AD)
MS .... Methionine Synthase [*An enzyme*]
MS .... Method of Sale
MS .... Methyl Salicylate [*Organic chemistry*]
MS .... Metric Size (IAA)
MS .... Metric System
ms .... Metric System (AD)
MS .... Mezzo Soprano [*Music*] (ROG)
MS .... Michigan State University of Agriculture and Applied Sciences (AD)
MS .... Microcirculatory Society (EA)
MS .... Microprogram Storage [*Computer science*] (MDG)
MS .... Microscope Slide (DMAA)
MS .... Microscopic System
ms .... Microseismic (AD)
MS .... Microsoft [*Software manufacturer*]
MS .... Microsoft Corporation (WDMC)
MS .... Microsphere
MS .... Microwave Scanner [*Marine science*] (OSRA)
MS .... Microwave Spectrum
MS .... Mid-Shot
MS .... Mild Steel
ms .... Mild Steel (AD)
m/s .... Milestone (AD)

MS............	Milestone (KSC)
MS............	Military Science (AABC)
MS............	Military Secretary [British]
MS............	Military Service
MS............	Military Service Act [British]
MS............	Military Specification (AAG)
MS............	Military Staff [British military] (DMA)
MS............	Military Standard
MS............	Military Standard [Parts designation]
MS............	Military Survivors (EA)
MS............	Millennium Society (EA)
ms............	Millisecond
mS............	Millisiemens
MS............	Minesweeper [or Minesweeping]
MS............	Miniature Screw [Lamp base] (NTCM)
m/s............	Miniature Sheet of Stamps (AD)
MS............	Minimal Support (DAVI)
ms............	Minimum Stress (AD)
MS............	Minister of State [British]
MS............	Ministry of Shipping [British]
MS............	Ministry of Supply [Also, MOS] [British]
MS............	Minority Stockholder
M/S............	Minor Support (KSC)
MS............	Mint State
ms............	Mint State (AD)
MS............	Minus
MS............	Minutes (AAG)
MS............	Miscellaneous
MS............	Miscellaneous Services [Department of Employment] [British]
MS-3............	Missile Station (AAG)
MS............	Missile System
ms............	[The] Missionaries of Our Lady La Salette (TOCD)
MS............	Missionaries of Our Lady of LaSalette [Roman Catholic religious order]
MS............	Missionary Sisters of Our Lady of Africa [White Sisters] [Roman Catholic religious order]
MS............	Missionary Society [British]
MS............	Mission Sequencer (SAA)
MS............	Mission Simulator
MS............	Mission Specialist (MCD)
MS............	Mission Station (MCD)
MS............	Missions to Seamen (EA)
MS............	Mission Support
MS............	Mississippi [Postal code]
Ms............	Mississippi State Library, Jackson, MS [Library symbol Library of Congress] (LCLS)
MS............	Miss or Mrs. [Pronounced "Miz"]
MS............	Mistress (DAVI)
ms............	Mitral Stenosis (AD)
MS............	Mitral Stenosis [Cardiology]
MS............	Mittelsatz [Middle Movement] [Music]
M-S............	Mitte-Seite [Stereo] (IEEE)
MS............	Mobile Searchlight [British]
MS............	Mobile Service [Telecommunications] (TEL)
MS............	Mobile Surgery [British]
MS............	Mobilization Station [DoD]
MS............	Modal Sensation [Psychology]
MS............	Modal Sensitivity [Medicine]
MS............	Model Station
MS............	Moderately Susceptible [Plant pathology]
MS............	Modern Science [A publication]
MS............	Modulation Sensitivity
MS............	Moessbauer Spectroscopy
MS............	Molar Degree of Substitution [Organic chemistry]
MS............	Molar Solution [Dentistry]
MS............	Molecular Sieve (MCD)
MS............	Molecular Staffing [Optics] (EECA)
M-S............	Monday through Saturday (AD)
MS............	Money Supply
MS............	Mongolian Spot [Medicine]
MS............	Monitor Station
MS............	Monorail Society (EA)
m/s............	Month after Sight (AD)
ms............	Months after Sight (AD)
MS............	Months after Sight [or Month's Sight] [Business term]
MS............	Montserrat [ANSI two-letter standard code] (CNC)
MS............	More Significant [Statistics]
MS............	Morgan Stanley Group [NYSE symbol] (TTSB)
MS............	Morgan Stanley Group, Inc. [NYSE symbol] (SPSG)
MS............	Morphine Sulfate [Narcotic]
MS............	Morse Tape (IAA)
MS............	Most Severe [Automotive engineering]
MS............	Most Significant
MS............	Motile Sperm
MS............	Motion Sensitivity (KSC)
MS............	Motor Ship
m/s............	Motorskib [Motorship] [Norwegian] (AD)
MS............	Motor Starting (IAA)
MS............	Motor Supports
MS............	Mucosubstance (MAE)
MS............	Multilateral Staff [Environmental Protection Agency] (GFGA)
MS............	Multiple Sclerosis [Medicine]
ms............	Multiple Sclerosis (AD)
MS............	Multiple Section (MSA)
ms............	Multiple Starters (AD)
MS............	Multiplexer Storage (IAA)
MS............	Multistart [Optimization method]
MS............	Multistring (NASA)
MS............	Multistring
MS............	Murashige-Skoog [Medium] [Botany]
Ms............	Murmurs [Medicine] (DMAA)
MS............	Muscle Shortening [Medicine]
MS............	Muscle Strength
ms............	Muscle Strength (AD)
MS............	Musculactive Substance [Medicine]
MS............	Musculoskeletal [Medicine]
Ms............	Mussels [Quality of the bottom] [Nautical charts]
MS............	Mustard Seed (EA)
MS............	Mycoplasma Synoviae [A pathogen]
MS............	Mythopoeic Society (EA)
MS............	Ship Station [ITU designation] (CET)
MS............	Somerset Library [Bibliotheque Somerset], Manitoba [Library symbol National Library of Canada] (BIB)
MS............	Springfield City Library, Springfield, MA [Library symbol Library of Congress] (LCLS)
MS1............	Mess Management Specialist, First Class [Navy rating] (DNAB)
MS-2............	Mare Serenitatis [Sea of Serenity] [Lunar area]
MS2............	Mess Management Specialist, Second Class [Navy rating] (DNAB)
M/S²............	Meters per Second Squared
MS2............	Micro-Set System 2 (NITA)
MS3............	Mess Management Specialist, Third Class [Navy rating] (DNAB)
MS-3............	Military Staffing Standards System
MS3............	Munitions Support Structure Study [Army]
MS3............	Munitions System Support Structure
MS3-X............	Munitions System Support Structure - Extended [Army]
mS-222............	Tricaine Methane Sulphonate [Chemistry] (DAVI)
MSA............	Magazine Shippers Association
MSA............	Mahri, Suqutri, and Shahri (BJA)
MSA............	Main Store Allocator
MSA............	Maintenance Support Activity
MSA............	Malaysia-Singapore Airlines
MSA............	Male Specific Antigen (PDAA)
MSA............	Management Science Associates, Inc. [Information service or system] (IID)
MSA............	Management Science of America (HGAA)
MSA............	Management System Analysis
MSA............	Mandusa Resources Ltd. [Vancouver Stock Exchange symbol]
MSA............	Manitoba Society of Artists [1925] [Canada] (NGC)
MSA............	Mannitol Salt Agar (MAE)
MSA............	Marigold Society of America (EA)
MSA............	Marine Safety Agency (NADA)
MSA............	Marine Science Activities [Program] [Coast Guard]
MSA............	Marine Stewards' Association [Australia]
MSA............	Mariological Society of America (EA)
MSA............	Maritime Safety Agency (NADA)
MSA............	Marker Signal Attenuation
MSA............	Market Science Associates, Inc. [Information service or system] (IID)
MSA............	Marlowe Society of America (EA)
MSA............	Marquetry Society of America (EA)
MSA............	Marshal Sprayable Ablative [NASA]
MSA............	Masonic Service Association of the United States (EA)
MSA............	Massachusetts School of Art
MSA............	Mass-Separating Agent [Chemical engineering]
MSA............	Mass Storage Adapter
MSA............	Master of School Administration (PGP)
MSA............	Master of Science Administration (PGP)
MSA............	Master of Science and Arts
MSA............	Master of Science in Accountancy
MSA............	Master of Science in Accounting (GAGS)
MSA............	Master of Science in Administration (GAGS)
MSA............	Master of Science in Agriculture
MSA............	Master of Science in Anesthesia (PGP)
MSA............	Master of Science in Anthropology (PGP)
MSA............	Master of Scientific Agriculture
MSA............	Master of Sport Administration (GAGS)
MSA............	Material Service Area
MSA............	Material Service Area (NASA)
MSA............	Material Stores Area (KSC)
MSA............	Material Surveillance Assembly [Nuclear energy] (NRCH)
MSA............	Matrix Scheme for Algorithms (PDAA)
MSA............	Mature Students' Association [British] (BI)
MSA............	Mean Spherical Approximation [Physical chemistry]
MSA............	Measure of Sampling Adequacy Index (EDAC)
MSA............	Mechanical Signature Analysis
MSA............	Media Studies Association [British]
MSA............	Medical Savings Account
MSA............	Medical Savings Account
MSA............	Medical Savings Account
MSA............	Medical Scientists' Association [Australia]
MSA............	Medical Service Agency (WYGK)
MSA............	Medical Services Account
MSA............	Medical Services Administration [HEW]
MSA............	Medusa Corp. [NYSE symbol] (CTT)
MSA............	Member of the Society of Apothecaries [British]
MSA............	Member of the Society of Architects [British] (DAS)
MSA............	Member of the Society of Arts [British]
MSA............	Membrane-Stabilizing Activity [Cardiology]
MSA............	Membrane Surface Area [Cytology]
MSA............	Merchant Shipping Act
MSA............	Mercury Singapore Airlines

MSA............	Mermaid Series [A publication]
MSA............	Mesa Public Library, Mesa, AZ [OCLC symbol] (OCLC)
MSA............	Metaphysical Society of America (EA)
MSA............	Meteorological Satellite Activity (IAA)
MSA............	Meteorological Support Activity [Army Electronics Command]
MSA............	Methacrylate Structural Adhesive
MSA............	Methanesulfonic Acid [Organic chemistry]
MSA............	Method of Standard Additions
MSA............	Methyltrimethylsilylacetamide [Organic chemistry]
MSA............	Metropolitan Service Area [Telecommunications] (TSSD)
MSA............	Metropolitan Statistical Area [Census Bureau]
MSA............	Michigan Statutes Annotated [A publication] (AAGC)
MSA............	Microcomputer Software Association (EA)
MSA............	Microgravity Science and Applications
MSA............	Microsomal Antibody
MSA............	Middle States Association (NADA)
MSA............	Middle States Association of Colleges and Schools (EA)
MSA............	Middle Stone Age [Anthropology]
MSA............	Military Service Act [British] (DMA)
MSA............	Military Subsistence Agency [Merged with Defense Supply Agency]
MSA............	Milton Society of America (EA)
MSA............	Mineralogical Society of America (EA)
MSA............	Mine Safety Appliance
MSA............	Minesweeper, Auxiliary [Navy symbol Obsolete]
MSA............	Minimum Safe Altitude [Aviation]
MSACE..........	Minimum Surface Area (KSC)
MSA............	Minnesota Statutes, Annotated [A publication] (DLA)
MSA............	Misce Secundum Artem [Mix Pharmaceutically] [Latin]
MSA............	Missile Support Activity (MCD)
MSA............	Missile System Analyst (SAA)
MSA............	Missile System Availability (MCD)
MSA............	Missionary Sisters of the Assumption [Roman Catholic religious order]
MSA............	Mission Services Association (EA)
MSA............	Mission Support Area [NASA]
MSA............	Mistral Air SRL [Italy ICAO designator] (FAAC)
MSA............	Mobile Subscriber Access (MCD)
MSA............	Modern Studies Association [British] (DBA)
MSA............	Monitor and Switching Assembly
MSA............	Morale Support Activities [Military] (AABC)
MSA............	Most Seriously Affected [Food-deficient nations]
MSA............	Motor Schools' Association of Great Britain (BI)
MSA............	Mount Pleasant, TX [Location identifier FAA] (FAAL)
MSA............	Mount San Antonio [New Mexico] [Seismograph station code, US Geological Survey] (SEIS)
MSA............	Mouse Serum Albumin [Clinical chemistry]
MSA............	Mouvement Socialiste Africain [African Socialist Movement] [Political party]
MSA............	Mouvement Souverainete Association [Canada] (PPW)
MSA............	Multichannel Signal Averager [Computer science]
MSA............	Multiple System Atrophy [Medicine]
MSA............	Multiplication Stimulating Activity [Cytochemistry]
MSA............	Multisubsystem Adapter [Sperry UNIVAC]
MSA............	Multivariate Survival Analysis [Statistics]
MSA............	Municipal Saleyards Association [Victoria, Australia]
MSA............	Muscle Sympathetic Activity [Medicine] (DMAA)
MSA............	Museum Store Association (EA)
MSA............	Muslim Students' Association of the US and Canada (EA)
MSA............	Mutual Security Act [1954]
MSA............	Mutual Security Agency [Functions transferred to Foreign Operations Administration, 1953]
MSA............	Mutual Society of Arts (NADA)
MSA............	Mycological Society of America (EA)
MSa............	Salem Public Library, Salem, MA [Library symbol Library of Congress] (LCLS)
MSAA............	Master of Science in Astronautics and Aeronautics (PGP)
MSAA............	Membrane Structures Association of Australasia
MSAA............	Microsoft Active Accessibility [Computer science]
MSAA............	Moderately Severe Aplastic Anemia [Hematology]
MSAA............	Multiple-Sclerosis-Associated Agent [A virus]
MSAA............	Multiple Sclerosis Association of America
MSAA............	Multiple Sclerosis Association of America
MSAAB	Military Services Ammunition Allocation Board (AABC)
MSAAC.........	Mower Specialists' Association of Australia Cooperative
MSAAE.........	Master of Science in Aeronautical and Astronautical Engineering (GAGS)
MSAAP.........	Mississippi Army Ammunition Plant (AABC)
MSAAT.........	Member of the Society of Architectural and Allied Technicians [British] (DI)
MsAb	Evans Memorial Library, Aberdeen, MS [Library symbol Library of Congress] (LCLS)
MS/AB	Massenet Society/American Branch (EA)
MSAc...........	Master of Science in Accounting
MSAC...........	Missile System Analyst Console (AAG)
MSAC...........	Moore School of Automatic Computers [University of Pennsylvania]
MSAC...........	Mount Saint Agnes College [Maryland] [Merged with Loyola College]
MSAC...........	Murray State Agricultural College [Oklahoma]
MSAC...........	Sonsonate/Acajutla [El Salvador] [ICAO location identifier] (ICLI)
MSACC.........	Master of Science in Accounting (PGP)
MS Acct.......	Master of Science in Accounting (PGP)
MS/Accy	Master of Science in Accountancy
MSACHA	Mid-South Automated Clearing House Association
MSACM.........	Master of Science in Acquisition and Contract Management (PGP)
MSAD	Materials Summary Acceptance Document (MCD)
MSAD	Motor Safe and Arm Device
MSAD	Multisatellite Attitude Determination [NASA]
MS Admin ...	Master of Science in Administration (PGP)
MSADY	Mid-States plc ADS [NASDAQ symbol] (TTSB)
MSaE..........	Essex Institute, Salem, MA [Library symbol Library of Congress] (LCLS)
MSAE..........	Master of Science in Aeronautical Engineering
MSAE..........	Master of Science in Aerospace Engineering (GAGS)
MSAE..........	Master of Science in Agricultural Engineering (PGP)
MSAE..........	Master of Science in Architectural Engineering (PGP)
MSAE..........	Master of Science in Art Education (PGP)
MSAE..........	Member of the Society of Automotive Engineers
MSAER	Master of Science in Aerospace Engineering (PGP)
MSAF..........	Meconium Stained Amniotic Fluid [Neonatology] (DAVI)
MSafetySc ...	Master of Safety Science
MSAFP.........	Maternal Serum Alpha Fetoprotein [Clinical chemistry]
MSAfrica......	Morgan Stanley Africa Investment Fund [Associated Press] (SAG)
MSafSc........	Master of Safety Science
MS (Ag)......	Master of Science in Agriculture
MSAg..........	Master of Science in Agriculture (GAGS)
MS (Ag E)....	Master of Science in Agricultural Engineering
MS Agr	Master of Science in Agriculture
MSAgrEng.....	Master of Science in Agricultural Engineering (NADA)
MSAI..........	American International College, Springfield, MA [Library symbol Library of Congress] (LCLS)
MSAI..........	Master of Science in Artificial Intelligence (GAGS)
MSAICE........	Member of the South African Institution of Civil Engineers
MSAInstMM...	Member of the South African Institute of Mining and Metallurgy
MsAM..........	Alcorn Agricultural and Mechanical College, Lorman, MS [Library symbol Library of Congress] (LCLS)
MSAM..........	Master of Science in Applied Mechanics
M-SAM	Medium Surface-to-Air Missile [Army]
MSAM..........	Mobile Surface-to-Air Missile
MSAM..........	Morgan Stanley Asset Management [Commercial firm]
MSAM..........	Morpholinomethyl Salicyclamide [Analgesic compound]
MSAM..........	Multi-Indexed Sequential Access Method [Computer science]
MSAM..........	Multiple Sequential Access Method (NITA)
MSAMP.........	Master Ship Acquisition Milestone Plan
MSAMS.........	Mobile Surface-to-Air Missile System (MCD)
M San..........	Master of Sanitation
MS & C.......	Marley, Scrooge, and Cratchit [Accounting agency]
MS & E.......	Materials Science and Engineering
MS & FR.....	Missile Stability and Frequency Response
MS & LR	Manchester, Sheffield & Lincolnshire Railway [Later, Great Central] [British] (ROG)
MS & NI.....	Michigan Southern & Northern Indiana Railroad
MS & P.......	Materials Synthesis and Processing [National Science Foundation]
MS & R	Merchant Shipbuilding and Repairs
MS & W	Maintenance Shop and Warehouse (NRCH)
MSanHi........	Sandwich Historical Society, Sandwich, MA [Library symbol Library of Congress] (LCLS)
MSANS.........	Multiple Small-Angle Neutron Scattering [Surface analysis]
M San Sc......	Master of Sanitary Science
MSanSc&PH...	Master of Sanitary Science and Public Health (GAGS)
MSAO..........	Medical Services Accountable Officer
MSAO..........	Morale Support Activities Office
MSAP..........	Master of Science in Applied Physics (PGP)
MSAP..........	Master of Science in Applied Psychology (PGP)
MSAP..........	Master Space Allocation Plan (MCD)
MSAP..........	Mean Systemic Arterial Pressure [Cardiology]
MSAP..........	Military Security Assistance Projection [Military]
MSAP..........	Multisatellite Attitude Prediction [NASA]
MSaP..........	Peabody Museum of Salem, Salem, MA [Library symbol Library of Congress] (LCLS)
MSApSc.......	Master of Science in Applied Science (GAGS)
MSAR	Mines Safety Appliance Research (IEEE)
Ms-Ar..........	Mississippi Department of Archives and History, Jackson, MS [Library symbol Library of Congress] (LCLS)
MSARC	Marine Systems Acquisition Review Council (MCD)
MS Arch	Master of Science in Architecture
MS Arch St...	Master of Architectural Studies (PGP)
MSAS..........	Malaysia Singapore Australia Society
MSAS..........	Mandel Social Adjustment Scale [Psychology]
MSAS..........	Marine Sciences Affairs Staff [A publication]
MSAS..........	Master of Science in Architectural Studies (GAGS)
MSa/s..........	MegaSamples per Second (CDE)
MSAS..........	Microwave Signature Acquisition System (MCD)
MSAS..........	Minnesota School Attitude Survey [Educational test]
MSAS..........	Modal Suppression Augmentation System [Aerospace]
M Sa Sc	Master of Sacred Sciences
MSAsia........	Morgan Stanley Asia Pacific Fund [Associated Press] (SAG)
MSAT..........	Master of Science in Advanced Technology (PGP)
MSAT..........	Minnesota Scholastic Aptitude Test
MSAT..........	Missile System Analyst Technician (SAA)
MSaT..........	Salem State College, Salem, MA [Library symbol Library of Congress] (LCLS)
MSATA.........	Motorcycle, Scooter, and Allied Trades Association [Later, MIC]
MSAT-A.......	Multisensor Aided Targeting-Air [Army] (DOMA)
MSATF.........	Missile Site Activation Task Force (SAA)
MSATT.........	Martian Surface and Atmosphere through Time [NASA]
MSAT-X	Mobile Satellite Experiment (MCD)
MSAU..........	Multistation Access Unit [Telecommunications] (TSSD)
MSAUSC......	Muslim Students' Association of the United States and Canada (EA)
MSAutE.......	Member of the Society of Automobile Engineers [British]
MSAV..........	Medical Scientists' Association of Victoria [Australia]
MSAV..........	Microsoft Anti-Virus [Microsoft Corp.] [Computer science] (PCM)

MSAW .... Minimum Safe Altitude Warning [Aviation]
MSAWA .... Migrant and Seasonal Agricultural Worker Act of 1983 (WYGK)
MSAWS ...... Mobile Surface-to-Air Weapon System (MCD)
MsB .... Biloxi Public Library, Biloxi, MS [Library symbol Library of Congress] (LCLS)
MSB .... Iola, KS [Location identifier FAA] (FAAL)
MSB .... Magnetic Susceptibility Bridge
MSB .... Main Steamline Break [Nuclear energy] (NRCH)
MSB .... Main Support Base [Air Force] (AFM)
MSB .... Main Support Battalion [Army] (INF)
MSB .... Main Support Battalion [Army] (DOMA)
MSB .... Main Switchboard
MSB .... Maintenance Standard Book
MSB .... Maintenance Support Base [Military]
MSB .... Male Sexual Biomass [Botany]
MSB .... Manpower Services Branch [Military] (MCD)
MSB .... Maritime Subsidy Board [Maritime Administration] [Department of Commerce]
MSB .... Martin's Scarlet Blue [Histologic stain]
MSB .... Mass Spectrometry Bulletin [Mass Spectrometry Data Centre] [Bibliographic database] [British]
Ms B .... Master of Bacteriology
MSB .... Master of Science in Business
MSB .... Material Support Branch [NASA] (KSC)
MSB .... Mediterranean Shipping Board [World War II]
MSB .... Member of the School Board [British] (ROG)
MSB .... Memory Storage Buffer [Computer science] (CAAL)
MSB .... Mesabi Tr Ctfs SBI [NYSE symbol] (TTSB)
MSB .... Mesabi Trust [NYSE symbol] (SAG)
MSB .... Methylstyrylbenzene [Fluorescent compound]
MSB .... Metropolitan Separate School Board [UTLAS symbol]
MSB .... Michael Stanley Band [Musical group]
MSB .... Mid-Small Bowel [Gastroenterology] (DAVI)
MSB .... Military Security Board
MSB .... Military Service Branch [World War I] [Canada]
MSB .... Mine Subsidence Board [New South Wales, Australia]
MSB .... Minesweeping Boat [Navy symbol]
MSB .... Minority Small Business (BARN)
MSB .... Missile Storage Building (NATG)
MSB .... Missile Support Base (SAA)
MSB .... Mission Simulator Building (MCD)
MSB .... Mobile Support Base (DNAB)
MSB .... Montadale Sheep Breeders Association (EA)
MSB .... Most Significant BIT [Binary Digit] [Computer science]
MSB .... Motor Surfboat
MSB .... Multi-Step Industries [Vancouver Stock Exchange symbol]
MSB .... Multnomah School of the Bible [Oregon]
MSB .... Municipal Securities Board [Approved by Congress May 22, 1975] [Securities and Exchange Commission]
MSB .... Museum of Southwestern Biology [University of New Mexico] [Research center] (RCD)
MSB .... Music Sound Books [Record label]
MSB .... Mutual Savings Bank
MSBA .... Malaysia, Singapore, and Brunei Association [British] (DBA)
MSBA .... Master of Science in Business Administration
MSBA .... Military School Band Association (EA)
MSBAE .... Master of Science in Biological and Agricultural Engineering (PGP)
MSBAE .... Master of Science in Biosystems and Agricultural Engineering (PGP)
MsBB .... Beauvoir, the Jefferson Davis Shrine, Biloxi, MS [Library symbol Library of Congress] (LCLS)
MSBB .... MSB Bancorp [NASDAQ symbol] (TTSB)
MSBB .... MSB Bancorp, Inc. [NASDAQ symbol] (SAG)
MSB Bcp ...... MSB Bancorp, Inc. [Associated Press] (SAG)
MSBC .... MainStreet BankGroup [NASDAQ symbol] (TTSB)
MSBC .... MainStreet BankGroup, Inc. [NASDAQ symbol] (SAG)
MSBC .... Master of Science in Building Construction
MSBC .... Steinbach Bible College, Manitoba [Library symbol National Library of Canada] (BIB)
MSBCA .... Maryland State Board of Contract Appeals (AAGC)
MSB-COD .... Minority Small Business-Capital Ownership Development Program [Small Business Administration]
MSBE .... Master of Science in Biomedical Engineering (GAGS)
MSBE .... Master of Science in Business Education (PGP)
MSBE .... Molten-Salt Breeder Experiment [Nuclear energy]
MsBel .... Humphreys County Library, Belzoni, MS [Library symbol Library of Congress] (LCLS)
MSBENG ...... Master of Science in Bioengineering (PGP)
MSBF .... Mean Sorties between Flights (MCD)
MSBF .... MSB Financial [NASDAQ symbol] (TTSB)
MSBF .... MSB Financial, Inc. [NASDAQ symbol] (SAG)
MSB Fn .... MSB Financial, Inc. [Associated Press] (SAG)
MSBIC .... Minority Small Business Investment Company (AAGC)
MSBK .... Mutual Savings Bank [NASDAQ symbol] (TTSB)
MSBK .... Mutual Savings Bank FSB [NASDAQ symbol] (SAG)
MSBL .... Member of the School Board, London [Defunct British] (ROG)
MSBLA .... Mouse Specific B Lymphocyte Antigen [Immunology]
MSBLK .... Mild Steel, Black Finish (IAA)
MSBLMS ...... Multi Station Boundary Layer Model System (PDAA)
MSBLS .... Microwave Scanning Beam Landing Station [or System] [NASA] (NASA)
MSBLS .... Microwave Scanning Beam Land Station [NASA]
MSBLS-GS ... Microwave Scanning Beam Landing System Ground Station [NASA]
MSBLS-GS ... Microwave Scanning Beam Landing System Ground Station [NASA] (NASA)

MsBm .... Blue Mountain College, Blue Mountain, MS [Library symbol Library of Congress] (LCLS)
MSBM .... Master of Science in Business Management (PGP)
MSBME .... Master of Science in Biomedical Engineering (PGP)
MSBMS .... Master of Science in Basic Medical Science (PGP)
MSBNSW ..... Maritime Services Board of New South Wales [Australia]
MSBO .... Mooring and Salvage Officer [Navy British]
MSBP .... Munchausen Syndrome by Proxy [Medicine]
Ms-BPH ...... Mississippi Library Commission, Services for the Handicapped, Jackson, MS [Library symbol Library of Congress] (LCLS)
MsBr .... Lincoln-Lawrence-Franklin Regional Library, Brookhaven, MS [Library symbol Library of Congress] (LCLS)
MSBR .... Maximum Storage Bus Rate
MSBR .... Military Strength Balance Report (AFM)
MSBR .... Molten-Salt Breeder Reactor
MSbrA .... American Optical Corp., Southbridge, MA [Library symbol Library of Congress] (LCLS)
MSBRT .... Mild Steel, Bright Finish (IAA)
MsBs .... City-County Memorial Library, Bay St. Louis, MS [Library symbol Library of Congress] (LCLS)
MSBS .... Minimum Social Behavior Scale [Psychology]
MsBsNA .... National Aeronautics and Space Administration, NASA/NSTL Research Library, NSTL Station, Bay St. Louis, MS [Library symbol Library of Congress] (LCLS)
MsBsNO .... United States Naval Oceanographic Office NSTL Station, Bay St. Louis, MS [Library symbol] [Library of Congress] (LCLS)
MsBsS .... Divine Word Seminary, Bay St. Louis, MS [Library symbol Library of Congress] (LCLS)
MSBT .... Missionary Servants of the Most Blessed Trinity [Roman Catholic women's religious order]
MSBTh .... Member of the Society of Health and Beauty Therapists [British] (DBQ)
MSBu .... Thousand Standard Bushels (EG)
MS Bus .... Master of Science in Business
MSBV .... Mooring Salvage and Boom Vessel (PDAA)
MSBVW .... Magnetostatic Backward Volume Wave [Telecommunications] (TEL)
MSBY .... Most Significant Byte [Computer science]
MSC .... Chief Mess Management Specialist [Formerly, CSC, CST, SDC] [Navy rating]
MSC .... College de St.-Boniface, Manitoba [Library symbol National Library of Canada] (NLC)
MSC .... Congregation of the Marianites of the Holy Cross (TOCD)
MSC .... Congregation of the Sisters Marianites of Holy Cross [Roman Catholic religious order]
MSC .... [The] MacNeal-Schwendler Corp.
MSC .... Macro Selection Compiler [Computer science] (BUR)
MSC .... Madras Staff Corps [British]
MSC .... Magnetically Settable Counter
MSC .... Magnetic Surface Current
MSC .... Magnitude Square of the Complex Coherence (PDAA)
MSC .... Maharashtra Socialist Congress [India] [Political party] (PPW)
MSC .... Mailstop Code
MSC .... Maine Sardine Council (EA)
MSC .... Main Storage Control [Computer science] (BUR)
MSC .... Main Switching Centre [Telecommunications] (NITA)
MSC .... Maintenance Support Center (MCD)
MSc .... Maisach [Federal Republic of Germany] [Geomagnetic observatory code]
MSC .... Major Subcontract (MCD)
MSC .... Major Subordinate Command [Military]
MSC .... Malaysian Multimedia Super Corridor
MSC .... Management Service Center (USDC)
MSC .... Management Service Center [Marine science] (OSRA)
MSC .... Management Services Contractor [INTELSAT]
MSC .... Manchester Ship Canal
MSC .... Mandatum sine Clausula [Authority without Restriction] [Latin]
MSC .... Mankato State College [Later, Mankato State University] [Minnesota]
MSC .... Manned Spacecraft Center [Later, Johnson Space Center] [NASA]
MSC .... Manpower Services Commission [British]
MSC .... Maple Syrup Council (EA)
MSC .... Marine Safety Council [Coast Guard]
MSC .... Marine Science Center [Oregon State University] [Research center] (RCD)
MSC .... Marine Science Council [Marine science] (MSC)
MSC .... Marital Status Code [IRS]
MSC .... Maritime Safety Committee [Advisory Committee on Pollution of the Sea]
MSC .... Maritime Service Committee [New York, NY] (EA)
MSC .... Marketing Services Conference [LIMRA]
MSC .... Marquise [Marchioness] [French] (ROG)
MSC .... Marrow Stromal Cell [Biochemistry]
MSC .... Maryland State College [Merged with University of Maryland]
MSC .... Mass Storage Control [Computer science] (BUR)
MSC .... Mass Storage Controller (NITA)
MSc .... Master of Science [Academic degree] (AIE)
M Sc .... Master of Science
MSC .... Master of Science in Commerce (DD)
MSC .... Master of Science in Commerce (PGP)
MSC .... Master of Science in Communication (PGP)
MSC .... Master of Science in Counseling (GAGS)
MSC .... Master of Speech Communication (GAGS)
MSC .... Master Sequence Controller (NASA)
MSC .... Master Status Chart
MSC .... Material Sciences [NYSE symbol] (TTSB)
MSC .... Material Sciences Corp. [NYSE symbol] (SPSG)

MSC............	Material Source Code
MSC............	Materials Science Center [Cornell University]
MSC............	Materials Service Center [NASA] (NASA)
MSC............	Materiel Screening Code [DoD] (AFIT)
MSC............	Materiel Status Committee [Military] (AABC)
MSC............	Materiel Support Center (MCD)
MSC............	Materiel Support Command (MCD)
MSC............	Mathematics/Science/Computer
MSC............	Mean Spherical Candlepower [Computer science] (IAA)
MSC............	Mechanical Super-Calendered Paper (DGA)
MSC............	Medical Service Commission [Canada]
MSC............	Medical Service Corps [Military]
MSC............	Medical Social Coordinator
MSC............	Medical Specialist Corps [Military]
MSC............	Medical Staff Corps [British]
MSC............	Mediterranean Society of Chemotherapy (EAIO)
MSC............	Mediterranean Sub-Commission [Silva Mediterranea] [FAO]
MSC............	Medium-Scale Computer (IAA)
MSC............	Memory Storage Control [Computer science]
MSC............	Memphis Service Center [IRS]
MSC............	Mesa [Arizona] [Airport symbol Obsolete] (OAG)
MSC............	Mesitylenesulfonyl Chloride [Biochemistry]
MSC............	Message Sequence Chart [Telecommunications] (TEL)
MSC............	Message Switching Center [Telecommunications]
MSC............	Message Switching Computer [Telecommunications] (TEL)
MSC............	Message Switching Concentration
MSC............	Metal Shielded Cabinet
MSC............	Meteorological Satellite Center [Aerospace] (IAA)
MSC............	Methane Sulfonyl Chloride [Organic chemistry]
MSC............	Metric System - Conversion (NATG)
MSC............	Metropolitan State College [Denver, CO]
MSC............	Micronesia Support Committee [Later, MC] (EA)
MSC............	Microscale Cloud [Module] [Air Force]
MSC............	Microsystems Centre (NITA)
MSC............	Microwave Stripline-Circuit (PDAA)
MSC............	Midwestern Simulation Council
MSC............	Migent Software [Vancouver Stock Exchange symbol]
MSC............	Mile of Standard Cable
MSC............	Milestone Schedule Charts (MCD)
MSC............	Military Scout Car [British]
MSC............	Military Sealift Command [Formerly, MSTS, NTS] [Navy] (NOAA)
MSC............	Military Staff Committee [United Nations] (DLA)
MSC............	Military Studies Center (EA)
msc............	Millisecond (WGA)
MSC............	Milliwatts per Square Centimeter
MSC............	Minesweeper, Coastal [Nonmagnetic] [Navy symbol]
MSC............	Minor Suma Corp. [Kansas City, MO] (TSSD)
MSC............	Mirror Sign Convention
MSC............	Mirror Streak Camera
MSC............	Miscellaneous (ADA)
MSC............	Missile and Space Council [Defunct] (AAG)
MSC............	Missile Sequence Charts (AAG)
MSC............	Missile Support Co. [Army]
MSC............	Missile System Checkout (AAG)
msc............	Missionaries of the Sacred Heart (TOCD)
MSC............	Missionaries of the Sacred Heart (TOCD)
MSC............	Missionarii Sacratissimi Cordis [Missionaries of the Most Sacred Heart] [Roman Catholic men's religious order]
MSC............	Missionarii Sancti Caroli [Missionaries of St. Charles] [Roman Catholic men's religious order]
msc............	Missionary Servants of Christ (TOCD)
MSC............	Missionary Sisters of the Most Sacred Heart of Jesus [Roman Catholic religious order]
MSC............	Missionary Sisters of the Most Sacred Heart of Jesus of Hiltrup (TOCD)
MSC............	Missionary Sisters of the Sacred Heart [Cabrini Sisters] [Roman Catholic religious order]
MSC............	Mississippi Central R. R. [AAR code]
Ms-C............	Mississippi Library Commission, Jackson, MS [Library symbol Library of Congress] (LCLS)
MSC............	Mississippi Southern College
MSC............	Mixing Smoke Chamber (MCD)
MSC............	Mobile Servicing Center [Canada]
MSC............	Mobile Switching Center (ACRL)
MSC............	Mode Selector Controller (MCD)
MSC............	Moding Sequencing and Control (MCD)
MSC............	Mono-Stereo Compatible (PDAA)
MSC............	Montana State College (MCD)
MSC............	Moorhead State College [Minnesota]
MSC............	Morgan State College [Later, Morgan State University] [Baltimore, MD]
MSC............	Moscow Airways [Russian Federation] [ICAO designator] (FAAC)
MSC............	Most Significant Character [Computer science] (MDG)
MSC............	Motor Speed Changer (IAA)
MSC............	Motor Speed Control
MSC............	Motor Starting Contractor
MSC............	Motor Submersible Canoe [British Marines' Special Forces] [World War II]
MSC............	Moved, Seconded, and Carried
MSC............	Multimedia Super Corridor [Proposed, Malaysia]
MSC............	Multiple Scan Correlator
MSC............	Multiple Spindle Chucker
MSC............	Multiple Systems Coupling [Computer science]
MSC............	Multipotential Stem Cells [Hematology]
MSC............	Multisensor Correlator (CAAL)

MSC............	Multiservice Center
MSC............	Multistrip Coupler [Telecommunications] (TEL)
MSC............	Multisystem Coupling [Computer science]
MSC............	Murray State College [Later, MSU] [Kentucky]
MSC............	Museum Support Center [Smithsonian Institution]
MSC............	Muskingum College, New Concord, OH [OCLC symbol] (OCLC)
Msc............	New York Miscellaneous Reports [A publication] (DLA)
MSC............	Springfield College, Springfield, MA [Library symbol Library of Congress] (LCLS)
Msc 2d	New York Miscellaneous Reports. Second Series [A publication] (DLA)
MsCa	Canton Public Library, Canton, MS [Library symbol Library of Congress] (LCLS)
MScA	Maitre es Sciences Appliquees [Master of Applied Science] [French]
MSCA	Make or Subcontract Authorization (AAG)
MScA	Master of Applied Science (DD)
M Sc A	Master of Science (Applied) (PGP)
MScA	Master of Social Administration (GAGS)
MSCA	McCarthy Scales of Children's Abilities [Education]
MSCA	Microwave Switch Control Assembly
MSCA	Military Support to Civil Authorities (AABC)
MSCA	Missile Site Construction Agency [Army]
msca	Missing Cargo (DS)
MSCA	Mixed Spectrum Critical Assembly [Nuclear energy]
MSCA	M.S Carriers [NASDAQ symbol] (TTSB)
MSCA	MS Carriers, Inc. [NASDAQ symbol] (NQ)
MSc(Acoustics)...	Master of Science (Acoustics) (ADA)
MSc(AeroMed)...	Master of Science (Aeromedicine)
MSc(Ag)	Master of Science (Agriculture)
MScAgri	Master of Science in Agriculture
MSc(Agric)	Master of Science in Agriculture
MSc(AgricE)...	Master of Science (Agricultural Economics) (ADA)
MSc(AgricEc)...	Master of Science (Agricultural Economics) (ADA)
MSCAJC	Martin Steinberg Center of the American Jewish Congress (EA)
MsCaM	Madison County Library, Canton, MS [Library symbol Library of Congress] (LCLS)
MSc(Appl)	Master of Science (Applied) (ADA)
MsCar..........	Leake County Library, Carthage, MS [Library symbol Library of Congress] (LCLS)
MSc(Arch) ...	Master of Science (Architecture)
MSc(Arch)(Cons)...	Master of Science (Architectural) (Conservation)
M Sc (Architecture)...	Master of Science in Architecture
MS Carr.......	MS Carriers, Inc. [Associated Press] (SAG)
MSCAT........	Minesweeper Catamaran [Military]
MSCB	Missile Site Control Building (AABC)
MsCba	Shelby Memorial Library, Columbia, MS [Library symbol Library of Congress] (LCLS)
MSc(Biochem)...	Master of Science (Biochemistry)
MSc(Biotech)...	Master of Science (Biotechnology) (ADA)
M Sc BMC ...	Master of Science in Biomedical Communications (PGP)
MSc(BuildServ)...	Master of Science (Building Services) (ADA)
MSCC..........	Major Subcontract Change Coordination (MCD)
MSCC..........	Manned Space Flight Control Center [Air Force]
MSCC..........	Master of Science in Christian Counseling (PGP)
MScC..........	Master of Science in Commerce (DD)
MSCC..........	Master Simulator Control Console (MCD)
MSCC..........	Microsemi Corp. [NASDAQ symbol] (NQ)
MSCC..........	Midstream Clean Catch [Urine Sample] (DAVI)
MSCC..........	Military Space Surveillance Control Center (IAA)
MSCC..........	Missile Site Control Center (MCD)
MSCC..........	Morgan Sports Car Club (EA)
MSCCC	Minimum Shuffle Control Cell Core [Nuclear energy] (NUCP)
M Sc CE	Master of Science in Chromo-Electronic Science
MScCE	Master of Science in Civil Engineering [British] (ADA)
MSc(Cer)	Master of Science in Ceramics (ADA)
MScChemTech...	Master of Science in Chemical Technology [British] (ADA)
MScCom	Master in Commercial Sciences
MScComm ...	Master in Commercial Science (DD)
MSc(CommMed)...	Master of Science (Community Medicine)
M Sc CS	Master of Science in Computer Science (PGP)
MScD.........	Doctor of Medical Science (DAVI)
M Sc D	Doctor of Medical Science
MScD.........	Doctor of Science in Medicine (DAVI)
M Sc D	Doctor of the Science of Medicine
MScD.........	Magister Scientia Dentalis [Master of Dental Science] [British]
MScD.........	Master of Dental Science
MScD.........	Master of Dental Science (DAVI)
MSCD.........	Master of Science in Communication Disorders (PGP)
MScD.........	Master of Science in Dentistry (GAGS)
MSCD.........	Military Support of Civil Defense (AABC)
MSCD.........	Mobile Source Control Division
MSCDC	Missouri State Census Data Center [Information service or system] (IID)
MSc(Dent)	Master of Science in Dentistry
MSCDEX	Microsoft Compact Disc Extension [Computer science] (DOM)
MSCDEX	MS-DOS, CD-ROM Extension [Computer science]
MSCDIS	Master of Science in Communication Disorders (PGP)
MSCDR	Mohawk Synchronous Communication Data Recorder [Military] (PDAA)
MSCE..........	Main Storage Control Element [Computer science] (IEEE)
MSCE..........	Master of Science in Civil Engineering
MSCE..........	Master of Science in Clinical Engineering (PGP)
MSCE..........	Master of Science in Clinical Epidemiology (PGP)
MSCE..........	Master of Science in Computer Engineering (GAGS)
M Sc E	Master of Science in Engineering (PGP)

MScE .... Master of Science in Engineering (DD)
MScEcon...... Master of Science in Economics (DD)
M Sc (Econ)... Master of Science in Economics
MSCEd........ Master of Science in Continuing Education (GAGS)
M Sc Ed...... Master of Science in Education
MSCEE........ Master of Science in Civil and Environmental Engineering (PGP)
M Sc EE...... Master of Science in Electrical Engineering
MSc(Elec)..... Master of Science in Electronics [British] (ADA)
M Sc (Elec Eng)... Master of Science in Electrical Engineering
MSCELM...... Military Sealift Command, Eastern Atlantic and Mediterranean (DNAB)
MSCEM........ Master of Science in Civil Engineering Management (PGP)
M Sc (Eng)... Master of Science (Engineering)
MSc(Engg)... Master of Science (Engineering)
M Sc Engr .. Master of Science in Engineering (PGP)
MSc(Epid)... Master of Science (Epidemiology)
MS (Cer E)... Master of Science in Ceramic Engineering
MSCF .... Master of Science in Computational Finance (PGP)
M Sc F ...... Master of Science in Forestry (PGP)
MScF .... Master of the Science of Forestry [or Master of Science in Forestry]
MSCF .... Millions of Standard Cubic Feet (AAG)
MSCF.......... Multisource Correlation Facility (MCD)
MSCFAM...... Royal Canadian Army Museum, Canadian Forces Base, Shilo, Manitoba [Library symbol National Library of Canada] (NLC)
M Sc FE...... Master of Science in Forest Engineering (PGP)
MSCFE........ Military Sealift Command, Far East (DNAB)
M Sc (For)... Master of Science in Forestry
MSCGpe ..... Missionaries of the Sacred Heart of Jesus and of Our Lady of Guadalupe (TOCD)
msch.......... Microscheduler (MHDI)
MSCH .... Mode Switch Chassis
MsCh .... Tallahatchie County Library, Charleston, MS [Library symbol Library of Congress] (LCLS)
MSchE........ Master of Science in Chemical Engineering
MS Ch E ..... Master of Science in Chemical Engineering (PGP)
MSChE........ Master of Science in Chemical Engineering (GAGS)
M Sch Mus... Master of School Music
MSc(HomeScience)... Master of Science (Home Science)
MSc(Hort)... Master of Science in Horticulture [British] (ADA)
MSCI.......... Madrid Stock-Exchange Index [Spain] (ECON)
MSCI.......... Master Ships Configuration Index (MCD)
MSCI.......... Mediterranean Secret Convoy Instructions [World War II]
MSCI.......... Missile Status Control Indicator [Military] (CAAL)
M/SCI.......... Mission/Safety Critical Item [NASA] (NASA)
MSCI.......... Molten Steel Coolant Interaction (NRCH)
MSCI.......... Morgan Stanley Capital International
MSCI-EAFE... Morgan-Stanley Capital International - Europe, Australia, Far East [Free] [Index - Financial]
M Sci Mil .... Master of Military Science
M Sc in Agr Eng... Master of Science in Agricultural Engineering
M Sc in Agr Ex... Master of Science in Agricultural Extension
MSC(IndDes)... Master of Science (Industrial Design) (ADA)
M Sc in ME... Master of Science in Mechanical Engineering
MSCIS .... Master of Science in Computer Information Science (PGP)
MSCIS .... Master of Science in Computer Information Systems
MScitHi....... Scituate Historical Society, Scituate, MA [Library symbol Library of Congress] (LCLS)
MSCJ.......... Master of Science in Criminal Justice (WGA)
MSCJA........ Master of Science in Criminal Justice Administration (PGP)
MSCJA-AJC... Martin Steinberg Center for Jewish Artists - American Jewish Congress [Defunct] (EA)
MSCK.......... Missionary Sisters of Christ the King (TOCD)
MSCKC........ Measurement of Self Concept in Kindergarten Children [Psychology]
M Sc L ...... Master of the Science of Law
MSCL.......... Master Ships Configuration List (MCD)
MSCL.......... Mississippi State Chemical Laboratory [Mississippi State University] [Research center] (RCD)
MSCL.......... Springfied City Library, Springfield, MA [Library symbol] [Library of Congress] (LCLS)
MSCLANT .... Military Sealift Command, Atlantic (DNAB)
MSCLANTDET... Military Sealift Command, Atlantic Detachment (DNAB)
MsCld .... Carnegie Public Library, Clarksdale, MS [Library symbol Library of Congress] (LCLS)
MsCle .... Bolivar County Library, Cleveland, MS [Library symbol Library of Congress] (LCLS)
MSCLE........ Maximum Space Charge Limited Emission (IAA)
MsCleD........ Delta State College, Cleveland, MS [Library symbol Library of Congress] (LCLS)
MsCleP........ Presbyterian Church Library, Cleveland, MS [Library symbol Library of Congress] (LCLS)
MsCliBHi ..... Mississippi Baptist Historical Society, Clinton, MS [Library symbol Library of Congress] (LCLS)
MsCliM........ Mississippi College, Clinton, MS [Library symbol Library of Congress] (LCLS)
MSC LNO..... Major Subordinate Command Liaison Officer
M Sc (Lond)... Master of Science, London
MSCLS........ Master of Science in Clinical Laboratory Science (PGP)
MSCLS........ Master of Science in Clinical Laboratory Studies (PGP)
MSCM........ Master Chief Mess Management Specialist [Formerly, SDCM] [Navy rating]
M Sc M ...... Master of the Science of Medicine
MSCM........ Mobile Surface Contamination Monitor
MSCM......... MOSCOM Corp. [NASDAQ symbol] (NQ)
M Sc (Mech Eng)... Master of Science in Mechanical Engineering
M Sc Med.... Master of Medical Science

MScMed ..... Master of Science in Medicine [British] (ADA)
MSc(Med).... Master of Science (Medical)
M Sc Met..... Master of Science in Metallurgy
MSc(Min).... Master of Science in Mining [British] (ADA)
MScN......... Master of Science in Nursing
M Sc N ...... Master of Science in Nursing (PGP)
MSc(NatResMgt)... Master of Science in Natural Resources Management
MSc(NeuChem)... Master of Science (Neurochemistry)
MSCNU....... Master of Science in Clinical Nutrition (PGP)
MSc(Nut).... Master of Science (Nutrition)
MSc(Nutr).... Master of Science in Nutrition [British] (ADA)
MSCNY....... Marine Society of the City of New York (EA)
MSCO .... Manned Spacecraft Operations [NASA] (KSC)
MSCO .... Manual Sustainer Cutoff [NASA] (KSC)
M Sc O ...... Master of the Science of Oratory
MSC(O)....... Minesweeper, Coastal (Old) [Navy symbol]
MSc(OccMed)... Master of Science (Occupational Medicine)
MsCol......... Lowndes County Library System, Columbus, MS [Library symbol Library of Congress] (LCLS)
MsColS........ Mississippi State College for Women, Columbus, MS [Library symbol Library of Congress] (LCLS)
MS Cons...... Master of Science in Conservation
MSCOP .... Missile Systems Checkout Program [Aerospace] (IAA)
MSc(Ophth)... Master of Science (Ophthalmology)
MScOptom... Master of Science in Optometry (ADA)
MsCor......... Northeast Regional Library, Corinth, MS [Library symbol Library of Congress] (LCLS)
M Sc (Ost)... Master of Science in Osteopathy
MSCOTSG.... Medical Service Corps, Office of the Surgeon General
MS Coun..... Master of Science in Counseling (PGP)
MSCP......... Mass Storage Control Protocol (NITA)
MSCP......... Master of Science in Community Planning
MSCP......... Master of Science in Counseling Psychology (PGP)
M Sc P ...... Master of Science in Planning (PGP)
MSCP......... Mean Spherical Candlepower
MSCP......... Member of the Society of Certified Professionals [British] (DBQ)
MSCP......... Missile Systems Checkout Programmer [Aerospace] (IAA)
MSCP......... Motor Short-Circuit Protector (IAA)
MSCPAC...... Military Sealift Command, Pacific (DNAB)
MS Cp E ..... Master of Science in Computer Engineering (PGP)
MScPhm...... Master of Science in Pharmacy (ADA)
M Sc Pl ...... Master of Science in Planning (PGP)
M/S/CPO..... Master/Senior/Chief Petty Officer of the Command (DNAB)
MSCPR .... Mixed-Suspension, Classified-Product Removal [Crystallizer] [Chemical engineering]
M Sc PT ..... Master of Science in Physical Therapy (PGP)
MSCR .... Machine Screw
MSCR .... Measurement/Stimuli Change Request (MCD)
MSCR .... Multilayer Side-Cladded Ridge Waveguide (PDAA)
MSCR/A...... Major Subcontract Change Request/Approval (MCD)
MSc(Rehab)... Master of Science (Rehabilitation Medicine)
MSCREP ...... Military Sealift Command Representative (DNAB)
MSCRP .... Master of Science in City and Regional Planning (PGP)
MSCRP .... Master of Science in Community and Regional Planning (PGP)
MsCs .... Crystal Springs Library, Crystal Springs, MS [Library symbol Library of Congress] (LCLS)
MSCS .... Management Scheduling and Control System [Telecommunications] (TEL)
MSCS .... Manual SHORAD [Short Range Air Defense] Control System (RDA)
MSCS .... Mass Storage Control System [Computer science] (IAA)
MSCS .... Master of Science in Computer Science
MSCS .... Merchant Ship Control Service [Navy]
MSCS .... Microsoft Clustering Server [Computer science]
MSCS .... Miner Sentence Completion Scale [Psychology]
MSCS .... Multiservice Communications Systems (RDA)
MSCS .... Senior Chief Mess Management Specialist [Formerly, CSCS, SDCS] [Navy rating]
MS CSCO .... Morgan Stanley Group, Inc. [Associated Press] (SAG)
MSCSD .... Master of Science in Communication Sciences and Disorders (PGP)
MSCSE .... Master of Science in Computer and Systems Engineering (PGP)
MSCSE .... Master of Science in Computer Science and Engineering (PGP)
M Sc (Social Sciences)... Master of Science in the Social Sciences
M Sc (Soc Sci)... Master of Science (Social Science)
MSCSO-M & R... Military Sealift Command Service Office - Maintenance and Repair (DNAB)
MSCSO-OCPO... Military Sealift Command Service Office - Operations Cargo Passenger Office (DNAB)
MSCSO-SA... Military Sealift Command Service Office - Supply Assistant (DNAB)
MScSt......... Master of Scientific Studies (ADA)
MSCT.......... Malignant Small Cell Tumor [Oncology]
M Sc T........ Master of Science in Teaching (PGP)
MScT......... Master of Science in Teaching (GAGS)
MScT......... Master of Science Teaching (GAGS)
MSCT.......... Member of the Society of Cardiological Technicians [British]
MSCT.......... Miniature Synaptic Calcium Transient [Neurophysiology]
MSCTC........ Mass Storage Control Table Create [Computer science] (MHDI)
M Sc Tech... Master of Science in Technology
M Sc Tech... Master of Technical Science
MSCTRANSU... Military Sealift Command Transportation Unit (DNAB)
MSCU .... Military Sealift Command Unit (DNAB)
MSCU .... Modular Store Control Unit
MSCU .... Multistation Control Unit [Telecommunications] (IAA)
MSC(UN) ..... Military Staff Committee of the United Nations
MSCV.......... Connecticut Valley Historical Museum, Springfield, MA [Library symbol Library of Congress] (LCLS)

MSCVAN......	[An] MSC [Military Sealift Command] Leased/Controlled Seavan or Milvan
MSCW.........	Marked Stack Control Word
MSCW.........	Mississippi State College for Women [Columbus]
MSD...........	Doctor of Medical Science
Ms D...........	Doctor of Metaphysics
MsD............	Holmes County Library, Durant, MS [Library symbol Library of Congress] (LCLS)
MSD...........	Magnetic Storage Drum [Computer science]
MSD...........	Major Seismic Disturbance
MSD...........	Management Services Department [British] (DCTA)
MSD...........	Management Services Division (NITA)
MSD...........	Management Systems Division [Environmental Protection Agency] (EPA)
MSD...........	Mansfield, LA [Location identifier FAA] (FAAL)
MSD...........	Manual SHORAD [Short Range Air Defense] Control System [Army]
MsD............	Manuscript Decisions [Comptroller General] [United States] [A publication] (DLA)
MSD...........	Marine Sanitation Device
MSD...........	Marine Sciences Directorate [Canada] (MSC)
MSD...........	Marine Signal Detachment (SAA)
MSD...........	Maritime-Self-Defense
MSD...........	MARS [Modular Airborne Recorder System] Supplemental Data (GFGA)
MSD...........	Mass Selector Detector [Gas chromatography]
MSD...........	Mass Sensor Demonstration
MSD...........	Mass Storage Device [Computer science]
MSD...........	Master of Dietetics (GAGS)
MSD...........	Master of Science in Dentistry
MSD...........	Master of Science in Design (PGP)
MSD...........	Master of Science in Dietetics (PGP)
MSD...........	Master of Scientific Didactics
MSD...........	Master Resources & Developments Ltd. [Vancouver Stock Exchange symbol]
MSD...........	Master Standard Data
MSD...........	Master Surgeon Dentist
MSD...........	Material Safety Data
MSD...........	Materials and Structures Division [NASA]
MSD...........	Material Support Data (MCD)
MSD...........	Material Support Date (DOMA)
MSD...........	Matrix Spike Duplicate
MSD...........	McNaney Spectroelectric Device
MSD...........	Mean Solar Day
MSD...........	Mean Squared Distance [Data analysis]
MSD...........	Mean Square Deviation [or Difference]
MSD...........	Mean-Square Displacement [Statistical graphing]
MSD...........	Mechanical Setting Device
MSD...........	Merck, Sharp & Dohme [Later, Merck & Co., Inc.]
MSD...........	Merck, Sharp & Dohme [Later, Merck & Co., Inc.] Research Laboratory, West Point, PA [OCLC symbol] (OCLC)
MSD...........	Metal Sensor Detection
MSD...........	Metering Suction Differential (NG)
MSD...........	Method of Steepest Descent
MSD...........	Metropolitan Sewer District (GNE)
MSD...........	Microdata Software Development (MCD)
MSD...........	Microsoft Diagnostics [Microsoft Corp.] [Computer science] (PCM)
MSD...........	Mild Sickle Cell Disease (AAMN)
MSD...........	Military Sales Department
MSD...........	Military Store Department [British military] (DMA)
MSD...........	Military Support Division [of Materiel Testing Directorate] (RDA)
MSD...........	Minesweeper, Drone [Navy symbol]
MSD...........	Minimal Steric Difference [Organic chemistry]
MSD...........	Minimum Safe Distance (AABC)
MSD...........	Misce, Signa, Da [Mix, Write (the Directions), and Give (to the Patient)] [Pharmacy] (ROG)
MSD...........	Missiles and Space Division [NASA] (KSC)
MSD...........	Missile Support Days (AAG)
MSD...........	Missile Systems Development (AAG)
MSD...........	Mission Systems Data (SAA)
MSD...........	MODEM Sharing Device
MSD...........	Molecular Size Distribution [Chemistry]
MSD...........	Molecular Structures and Dimensions [A publication]
MSD...........	Molten Salt Destruction [Incineration process]
MSD...........	Monorail and Suspension Device [British]
MSD...........	Morale Support Detachment [Army]
MSD...........	Morgan Stanley Emerging Markets Debt Fund, Inc. [NYSE symbol] (SAG)
MSD...........	Morgan Stanley Emer'g Mkt Debt [NYSE symbol] (TTSB)
MSD...........	Mossoro [Brazil] [Airport symbol] (AD)
MSD...........	Most Significant Decade (IAA)
MSD...........	Most Significant Digit [Computer science]
MSD...........	Motor Storage Dolly
MSD...........	Mount Pleasant [Utah] [Airport symbol] (OAG)
MSD...........	Movimento Social Democrata [Social Democrat Movement] [Portugal Political party] (PPE)
MSD...........	Moving Scene Display
MSD...........	Multifrequency Signal Detector [Telecommunications]
MSD...........	Multiple Spark Discharge [Autotronic Controls Corp.] [Automotive engineering]
MSD...........	Multiple Sulfatase Deficiency [Medicine] (AAMN)
MSD...........	Multisatellite Dispenser (MCD)
MSD...........	Multisensor Display
MSD...........	Multisensory Disorder
MSDA.........	Masada Security Holdings, Inc. [NASDAQ symbol] (SAG)
MSDAC.......	Minnesota State Drafting Advisory Committee (EDAC)
MSDB.........	Main Storage Database
MSDBP.......	Mean Squared Distance Between Pairs [Statistics] (PDAA)
MSDC.........	Maintenance Signal Data Cassette (MCD)
MSDC.........	Maintenance Signal Data Converter (MCD)
MSDC.........	Manual Slave Direction Center [RADAR site]
MSDC.........	Mass Spectrometry Data Centre [Royal Society of Chemistry] (IID)
MSDC.........	Microwave Spectra Data Center [National Institute of Standards and Technology]
MSDC.........	Molten Salts Data Center [Rensselaer Polytechnic Institute] [National Institute of Standards and Technology Research center] (IID)
MSDD.........	Master of Science in Design and Development (PGP)
MSDD.........	Milli-Second Delay Detonator [Military] (PDAA)
MSde.........	Tilton Library, South Deerfield, MA [Library symbol Library of Congress] (LCLS)
MSDEF.......	Missile System Development and Evaluation Facility (MCD)
MS Dent.....	Master of Science in Dentistry
MSDEQ.......	Mothers' Sensory Developmental Expectation Questionnaire [Occupational therapy]
MSDerm......	Master of Science in Dermatology (NADA)
MS Des.......	Master of Science in Design
MSDF.........	Maritime Self-Defense Force [Japan]
MSDF.........	Maritime Staff Defense Force (CINC)
MSDFF.......	Master Slave D Flip Flop (NITA)
MSDG.........	Multiple Sensor Display Group (MCD)
MSDI.........	Mainstream Data, Inc. [NASDAQ symbol] (SAG)
MS Di.........	Master of Scientific Didactics
MSDI.........	Mayonnaise and Salad Dressings Institute [Later, Association for Dressings and Sauces] (EA)
MSDIG........	McGuire Safe Driver Interview Guide (AEBS)
MSDL.........	Magnetostrictive Delay Line
MSDM........	Medium-Speed DynaBIT [Binary Digit] Memory [Computer science]
MSDM........	Morgan Stanley Group, Inc. [Associated Press] (SAG)
MSDN........	Microbial Strain Data Network [Information service or system] (IID)
MSDN........	Microsoft Developer Network [Computer software] (PCM)
MSDN........	Microsoft Developer Network [Computer science]
MSDN........	Microsoft Developer's Network [Computer science] (PCM)
MSDNA.......	Multicopy Single-Stranded Deoxyribonucleic Acid [Biochemistry, genetics]
MSDO.........	Management Systems Development Office
MS-DOS......	Microsoft Disk Operating System [IBM Corp.] [Computer science]
MSDP.........	Missile Site Data Processor (AABC)
MSDPS.......	Missile Site Data Processing System (AABC)
MSDPSS.....	Missile Site Data Processing Subsystem (AABC)
MSDR.........	Main Storage Data Register [Computer science] (IAA)
MSDR.........	Maintenance Signal Data Recorder (MCD)
MSDR.........	Master Sensor Data Record [For spacecraft]
MSDR........	Materials Science Double Rack
MSDR.........	Multiplexer Storage Data Register [Computer science] (IAA)
MSDRS.......	Maintenance Signal Data Recording Set [or System] (MCD)
MSDS.........	Magnetic Storage Drum System [Computer science]
MSDS.........	Maintenance Safety Data Sheets (MCD)
MSDS.........	Master Simulation Data System (Model) [Army]
MSDS.........	Material Safety Data Sheet (GNE)
MSDS.........	Material Safety Data Sheets [Occupational Health Services, Inc.] [Information service or system]
MSDS	McGuire Safe Driver Scale (AEBS)
MSDS.........	Message Switching Data Service
MSDS.........	Missile Static Development Site (AAG)
MSDS.........	Missile System Development Stand (AAG)
MSDS.........	Multisolvent Delivery System
MSDS.........	Multispectral Scanner and Data System
MSDS.........	Multispectral Scanner and Data System
MSDT.........	Maintenance Strategy Diagraming Technique (IEEE)
MSDT.........	Mean Supply Downtime (CAAL)
MSDT.........	Meshless Storage Display Tube
MSDX.........	Mason-Dixon Bancshares [NASDAQ symbol] (TTSB)
MSDX	Mason-Dixon Bancshares, Inc. [NASDAQ symbol] (SAG)
MSE...........	Magnetic Strain Energy
MSE...........	Maintenance Support Equipment [Deep Space Instrumentation Facility, NASA]
MSE...........	Major Source of Employment
MSE...........	Major Support Element (DOMA)
MSE...........	Manned Spacecraft Engineer (MCD)
MSE...........	Manston [England] [Airport symbol] (AD)
MSE...........	Manufacturing Systems Engineering
MSE...........	Marshall Energy Ltd. [Vancouver Stock Exchange symbol]
MSE...........	Mask Superposition Error [Computer science] (IAA)
MSE...........	Mass Storage Editor [Computer science] (MCD)
MSE...........	Master of Sanitary Engineering
MSE...........	Master of Science in Chemical Engineering
MSE...........	Master of Science in Education
MSE...........	Master of Science in Education (GAGS)
MSE...........	Master of Science in Engineering
MSE...........	Master of Software Engineering (GAGS)
MSE...........	Master of Systems Engineering
MSE...........	Materiel Status Evaluation [Army] (AABC)
MSE...........	Mean Square Error [Statistics]
MSE...........	Measuring and Stimuli Equipment (NASA)
MSE...........	Measuring and Stimuli Equipment
MSE...........	Mechanical Support Equipment (KSC)
MSE...........	Medical Support Equipment (NASA)
MSE...........	Member of the Society of Engineers [British]
MSE...........	Mental Status Examination [Neurology] (DAVI)
MSE...........	Merck, Sharp & Dohme [Later, Merck & Co., Inc.] Research Laboratory, Rahway , NJ [OCLC symbol] (OCLC)

MSE............	Merit Students Encyclopedia [*A publication*]
MSE............	Metaphloem Sieve Element [*Botany*]
MSE............	Mexican Stock Exchange (MHDW)
MSE............	Mid-Song Element [*Ornithology*]
MSE............	Midwest Stock Exchange [*Chicago, IL*] (EA)
MSE............	Military Specification Exception (RDA)
MSE............	Military Standard Engines
MSE............	Milk-Sensitive Enteropathy [*Medicine*]
MSE............	Milwaukee School of Engineering [*Wisconsin*]
MSE............	Minus Sense (SAA)
MSE............	Missile Support Element (AABC)
MSE............	Missile Support Equipment
MSE............	Mission Staff Engineer (MCD)
MSE............	Mission Support Element (MCD)
MSE............	Mississippi Export Railroad Co. [*AAR code*]
MSE............	Mobile Subscriber Equipment [*Military*]
MSE............	Mobile Subscriber Equipment [*Army*] (DOMA)
MSE............	Modern Ship Equivalent
MSE............	Montreal Stock Exchange (CDAI)
MSE............	Moose
MSE............	Morgan Stan Fin 8.40% Cp Uts [*NYSE symbol*] (TTSB)
MSE............	Morgan Stanley Finance PLC Capital Unit [*NYSE symbol*] (SAG)
MSE............	Motorsteuerelectronik
MSE............	Multiple Simultaneous Engagement (MCD)
MSE............	Multi-Position Small Engine [*Automotive engineering*]
MSE............	Muscle-Specific Enhancer [*Genetics*]
MSEA.........	M & S [*Modeling and Simulation*] Executive Agent [*Army*]
M Se A.......	Master of Secretarial Arts
MSEA.........	Medical Society Executives Association [*Later, AAMSE*] (EA)
MSEA.........	Metropolitan Bancorp [*NASDAQ symbol*] (TTSB)
MSEA.........	Metropolitan Bancorp Seattle [*NASDAQ symbol*] (SAG)
MSEC.........	Maintenance Support Equipment Center
MSEC.........	Master of Science in the Economic Aspects of Chemistry
MSEC.........	Master Separation Events Controller (MCD)
MSEC.........	Materials Science and Engineering Commission [*British*]
msec.........	Millisecond
MSECE........	Master of Science in Electrical and Computer Engineering (PGP)
MS Eco.......	Master of Science in Economics (PGP)
MS Econ......	Master of Science in Economics (PGP)
MSecSchSci...	Master of Secondary School Science (GAGS)
MS Ed.........	Master of Sanitary Education
MSEd..........	Master of Science Education (GAGS)
MS Ed.........	Master of Science in Education
MSED.........	Minimum Signal Element Duration [*Telecommunications*] (TEL)
MSED........	Ministry of State for Economic Development [*Canada*]
MSED........	Mobile Source Enforcement Division [*Environmental Protection Agency*]
MS EdU.......	Master of Science in Education (PGP)
MSEE..........	Major Source Enforcement Effort [*Environmental Protection Agency*] (GFGA)
MSEE..........	Master of Science in Electrical Engineering
MSEE..........	Master of Science in Electrical Engineering (GAGS)
MSEE..........	Master of Science in Environmental Engineering (GAGS)
MSEE..........	Mean Square Error Efficiency [*Statistics*]
MSE (Elec)...	Master of Science in Engineering - Electrical
MSEF.........	Missile System Evaluation Flight (MUGU)
MSEG.........	Medical Service Group [*Military*]
MSEG..........	Memory-Segment [*Computer science*]
MSEG..........	Missile Systems Evaluation Group (CINC)
MSEH.........	Master of Science in Environmental Health (PGP)
MSEI..........	Mean Square Error Inefficiency [*Statistics*]
MSEL..........	Lord Selkirk Regional School, Selkirk, Manitoba [*Library symbol National Library of Canada*] (NLC)
MSEL.........	Master of Science and English Literature
MSEL.........	Master of Science in Environmental Law (PGP)
MSEL.........	Master Scenario Events List (MCD)
MSEL.........	Merisel, Inc. [*NASDAQ symbol*] (SPSG)
MSEL..........	Mullen Scales of Early Learning [*Child development test*] [*Psychology*]
MSEL..........	Selkirk Community Library, Manitoba [*Library symbol National Library of Canada*] (NLC)
MS Elect E...	Master of Science in Electrical Engineering
MSEM........	Mainstreamed Special Educator Model (EDAC)
MSEM........	Master of Science in Engineering and Mining (GAGS)
MSEM.........	Master of Science in Engineering Management (PGP)
MSEM.........	Master of Science in Engineering Mechanics
MSEM.........	Master of Science in Engineering of Mines (PGP)
MSEM.........	Master of Science in Environmental Management (PGP)
MSEM.........	Mission Status and Evaluation Module
MS EMD......	Morgan Stanley Emerging Markets Debt Fund, Inc. [*Associated Press*] (SAG)
MSEMech	Master of Science in Engineering Mechanics (GAGS)
MSEMgt.....	Master of Science in Engineering Management (GAGS)
MSE Mgt......	Master of Science in Engineering Management (PGP)
MSEMH........	Selkirk Mental Health Centre, Manitoba [*Library symbol National Library of Canada*] (NLC)
MS/EMI.......	Mission Sequence/Electromagnetic Interference
MSEMPR	Missile Support Equipment Manufacturers Planning Reports (MCD)
MS En E	Master of Science in Environmental Engineering (PGP)
MS Eng........	Master of Sanitary Engineering
MS Eng........	Master of Science in Engineering
MS Engr	Master of Science in Engineering (PGP)
MS Engr Sci...	Master of Science in Engineering Science (PGP)
MS Ent.........	Master of Science in Entomology
MS Env E	Master of Science in Environmental Engineering (PGP)

MSEnvrE......	Master of Science in Environmental Engineering (GAGS)
MSEO.........	Marine Services Engineer Officer [*Navy British*]
MSEP.........	Maintenance Standardization Evaluation Program [*Air Force*] (AFM)
MSEP.........	Mean Square Error of Prediction [*Statistics*] (PDAA)
MSEP.........	Mercury Scientific Experiment Panel
MSEP.........	Military Standard Evaluation Program
MSEPN.......	School of Psychiatric Nursing, Selkirk, Manitoba [*Library symbol National Library of Canada*] (NLC)
MSEPS........	Modular Space Electrical Power Station
M/SEQ.......	Master Sequencer
MSER.........	Management System Evaluation Review (NG)
MSER.........	Master of Science in Energy Resources (GAGS)
MSER.........	Mean Systolic Ejection Rate [*Cardiology*]
MSER.........	Multiple Stores Ejection Rack [*For munitions*] (MCD)
MSERD	Ministry of State for Economic and Regional Development [*Canada*]
MSERT........	Member of the Society of Electronic and Radio Technicians [*British*] (DBQ)
MSES.........	Marine Scientific Equipment Service [*British*]
MSES.........	Master of Science in Engineering Science (PGP)
MSES.........	Master of Science in Environmental Studies (PGP)
MSES.........	Medical School Environmental Stress
MSES.........	Medical Service Squadron [*Military*]
MSES.........	Mobile Status Entry System
M Se Sc	Master of Secretarial Science
MSESM.......	Master of Science in Engineering Science and Mechanics (PGP)
MSESS........	Master of Science in Exercise and Sport Studies (GAGS)
M Se St	Master of Secretarial Studies
MSET.........	Maintenance Standardization and Evaluation Team (MCD)
MSET.........	Multistage Exercise Test [*Medicine*] (CPH)
MSETM.......	Master of Science in Environmental Technology Management (PGP)
MSE TPN	Mobile Subscriber Equipment Tactical Packet Network [*Computer science Military*] (RDA)
MSEUE........	Mouvement Socialiste pour les Etats Unis d'Europe
MSEuro........	Morgan Stanley European Emerging Markets Ltd. [*Associated Press*] (SAG)
MSEVM.......	Master of Science in Environmental Management (PGP)
MSEW........	Medical Service Wing [*Military*]
MSEX.........	Middlesex Water [*NASDAQ symbol*] (TTSB)
MSEX.........	Middlesex Water Co. [*NASDAQ symbol*] (NQ)
MS Exp Surg...	Master of Science in Experimental Surgery (PGP)
MSF............	Congregatio Missionariorum a Sancta Familia [*Congregation of the Missionaries of the Holy Family*] [*Roman Catholic men's religious order*]
msf	Congregation of the Missionaries of the Holy Family (TOCD)
MSF...........	Congregation of the Missionaries of the Holy Family (TOCD)
MSF...........	Macrophage Spreading Factor [*Hematology*]
MSF...........	Magnetic Silencing Facility [*Kingsburg, GA*] (DWSG)
MSF...........	Maintenance Source File (MCD)
MSF...........	Manned Space Flight [*NASA*] (KSC)
MSF...........	Manufacturing Science Finance [*A union*] [*British*]
MSF...........	Mark Sense Form (MCD)
MSF...........	Mass Storage Facility [*Computer science*] (IBMDP)
MSF...........	Master of Finance
MSF...........	Master of the Science of Forestry
MSF...........	Master Source File [*Computer science*] (BUR)
MSF...........	Matched Spatial Filter [*Optics*]
MSF...........	Maximum Shear Force
MSF...........	Max Sea Food SA de CV [*El Salvador*] [*ICAO designator*] (FAAC)
MSF...........	Medecins sans Frontieres [*Doctors without Borders - DWB*] [*France*] (EAIO)
MSF...........	Medium Standard Frequency (DEN)
MSF...........	Member of the Society of Floristry [*British*] (DI)
MSF...........	Merit Shop Foundation [*Washington, DC*] (EA)
MSF...........	Metal Space-Frame (MCD)
MSF...........	MetaScience Foundation (EA)
MSF...........	Metastasis-Stimulating Factor [*Immunosuppressant*]
MSF...........	Methanesulfonyl Fluoride [*Organic chemistry*]
MSF...........	Migration Stimulating Factor [*Cytology*]
MSF...........	Military Support Fund (MCD)
MSF...........	Mind Science Foundation (EA)
MSF...........	Minesweeper, Fleet [*Steel hull*] [*Navy symbol*]
MSF...........	Minimum Sustaining Field [*Atomic reactor*]
MSF...........	Missionary Sisters of the Holy Family (TOCD)
MSF...........	Mission Simulator Facility
MSF...........	Mobile Striking Force [*Military*]
MSF...........	Mobility Support Forces [*Military*]
MSF...........	Moisture Seekers Foundation [*Later, Sjogren's Syndrome Foundation - SSF*] (EA)
MSF...........	Monoecious Sex Form
MSF...........	Month-Second-Foot [*Measurement*]
MSF...........	Morale Support Funds (MCD)
MSF...........	Morgan Stanley Emerging Market [*NYSE symbol*] (SPSG)
MSF...........	Morgan Stanley Emerging Mkt [*NYSE symbol*] (TTSB)
MSF...........	Moroccan Sea Frontier [*Navy World War II*]
MSF...........	Motorcycle Safety Foundation (EA)
MSF...........	Mott Scattering Formula [*Physics*]
MSF...........	Multiaxial Stress Field
MSF...........	Multistage Flash [*Desalination method*]
MSF...........	Muscle Shock Factor
MsFa.........	Jefferson County Library, Fayette, MS [*Library symbol Library of Congress*] (LCLS)
MSFAM......	Master of Science in Family Studies (PGP)
MSFB.........	Multi-Solids Fluidized Bed [*Chemical engineering*]
MSFC.........	Mark Slade Fan Club (EA)
MSFC.........	Marshall Space Flight Center [*Also known as GCMSC*] [*NASA*]

MSFC...........	McCarver Sisters Fan Club (EA)
MSFC...........	Medical Students for Choice
MSFC...........	Mobile Strike Force Command [Military] (VNW)
MSFC...........	Morale Support Fund Council [Military] (AABC)
MSFC...........	Mutual Society of the French Community (EA)
MSFCV.........	Main Stream Flow Control Valve [Nuclear energy] (NUCP)
MSFD...........	Millimeter Wave Seeker Feasibility Demonstration
MSFDC.........	Microsoft and First Data Corp.
MSFDPS.......	Manned Space Flight Data Processing System [NASA]
MSFEB.........	Manned Space Flight Experiments Board [NASA] (KSC)
MSFET.........	Metal-on-Silicon Field-Effect Transistor [Electronics] (IAA)
MSFET.........	Metal Schottky Gate Field Effect Transistor [Electronics] (IAA)
MSFF...........	Master Slave Flipflop [Nuclear energy] (IAA)
MSFH...........	Manned Space Flight Headquarters [NASA]
MSFI...........	MS Financial [NASDAQ symbol] (TTSB)
MSFI...........	MS Financial Corp. [NASDAQ symbol] (SAG)
MS Fin.........	Morgan Stanley Finance PLC Capital Unit [Associated Press] (SAG)
MSFL...........	Manned Space Flight Laboratory [NASA] (IAA)
MSFLV.........	Manned Space Flight and Launch Vehicles [Panel]
MSFM..........	Master of Financial Management (PGP)
MSFM..........	Master of Science in Forest Management
MSFN..........	Manned Space Flight Network [NASA]
MSFN..........	Morgan Stanley Finance PLC Capital Unit [Associated Press] (SAG)
MS Fncl........	MS Financial, Inc. [Associated Press] (SAG)
MSFNOC.......	Manned Space Flight Network Operations Center [NASA] (KSC)
MSFO...........	Manned Space Flight Operations [NASA] (KSC)
MS For.........	Master of Science in Forestry
MSFOR.........	Master of Science in Forestry (PGP)
MSFP...........	Manned Space Flight Program [NASA] (KSC)
MSFP...........	Migrant and Seasonal Farmworkers Program [Title III] (OICC)
MSFRSP.......	Male Sterile-Facilitated Recurrent Selection Population [Plant breeding]
MSFS...........	Main Steam and Feed Water System (IEEE)
MSFS...........	Manned Space Flight Subcommittee [NASA] (AAG)
MSFS...........	Manned Space Flight System [NASA] (IAA)
MSFS...........	Master of Science in Family Studies (PGP)
MSFS...........	Master of Science in Financial Services (PGP)
MSFS...........	Master of Science in Foreign Service (GAGS)
MSFS...........	Master of Science in Forensic Science (GAGS)
MSFS...........	Missionaries of St. Francis of Sales [Roman Catholic religious order]
MSFSG.........	Manned Space Flight Support Group (MCD)
MSFSRD.......	Manned Space Flight Support Requirements Documentation [NASA]
MSFT...........	Microsoft Corp. [NASDAQ symbol] (NQ)
MSFU..........	Merchant Service Fighter Unit [Air Force British]
MSFVW........	Magnetostatic Forward Volume Wave [Telecommunications] (TEL)
MSFW..........	Migrant and Seasonal Farmworkers
MSFX..........	Master Fixture
MSG............	[The] Imperial Merchant Service Guild [British]
MSG............	Madison Square Garden [New York, NY] (NADA)
MSG............	Madison Square Garden Network [Cable-television system]
MSG............	Maintenance Steering Group (MCD)
MSG............	Manufacturers Standard Gauge
MSG............	Mapper Sweep Generator
MSG............	Mapping Supervisor Gap Filler (SAA)
MSG............	Marine Security Guard
MSG............	Maritime Studies Group [Military] (VNW)
MSG............	Mascot Gold Mines Ltd. [Toronto Stock Exchange symbol Vancouver Stock Exchange symbol]
MSG............	Massage (DAVI)
MSG............	Master of Science in Gerontology (GAGS)
MSG............	Master Sergeant [Army] (AABC)
MSG............	Maximum Stable Gain (IAA)
MSG............	Mechanical Subsystem Group [NASA] (NASA)
MSG............	Message (AFM)
msg............	Message (IDOE)
MSG............	Methysergide [A serotonin antagonist] [Pharmacology] (DAVI)
MSG............	Microcomputer Support Group
MSG............	Microwave Signal Generator
MSG............	Ministry of Solicitor General [Canada]
MSG............	Ministry of the Solicitor General Library [UTLAS symbol]
MSG............	Miscellaneous Simulation Generator
MSG............	Missile Systems Group [of General Motors Corp.]
MSG............	Missing [Military]
MSG............	Mission Support Groups (MCD)
MSG............	Mobile Support Group [Military] (NVT)
MSG............	Modular Steam Generator (NRCH)
MSG............	Modulation Signal Generator (NITA)
MSG............	Moessingen [Federal Republic of Germany] [Seismograph station code, US Geological Survey] (SEIS)
MSG............	Monosodium Glutamate [Food additive] [Pharmacology]
MSG............	Multiplicand Select Gate (IAA)
MsG............	William Alexander Percy Memorial Library, Greenville, MS [Library symbol Library of Congress] (LCLS)
MSGA..........	Master Gauge
MSGA..........	Merchant Service Guild of Australia
MSGB..........	Manorial Society of Great Britain (EAIO)
MSGB..........	Muslim Society in Great Britain
MSGBI.........	Mineralogical Society of Great Britain and Ireland (EAIO)
MSGC..........	Master of Science in Genetic Counseling (PGP)
MSGC..........	Multinucleated Stromal Giant Cell
MSGCEN.......	Message Center
MSGCTR.......	Message Center [Aviation] (FAAC)
MSGDPU.......	Message-Drop and Pick-Up [Military] (IAA)
MSGE..........	Master of Science in Geological Engineering (NADA)
MS Geo E	Master of Science in Geological Engineering (PGP)

MSGFLG	Message Flag [Computer science] (MHDI)
MSGFM........	Message Form (MUGU)
MS-GFW	Memory for Sequence Subtest of the Goldman-Fristoe-Woodcock Auditory Skills TestBattery (EDAC)
MSGG	Message Generator (MSA)
MSGI	Marketing Services Group
MSGID	Message Identifier
MSGL..........	Multishot Grenade Launcher (RDA)
MSGlobl	Morgan Stanley Global Opportunities Bond Fund, Inc. [Associated Press] (SAG)
MSGM	Master of Science in Government Management
MSG Mgt	Master of Science in Game Management
MSGO	Mediterranean Secret General Orders
MsGoH........	Holmes Junior College, Goodman, MS [Library symbol Library of Congress] (LCLS)
MSGP	Mobile Support Group [Military]
MSGR	Messenger (AFM)
MSGR	Mobile Support Group [Military]
MSGR	Monseigneur
MSGR	Monsignor
MsGren........	Grenada County Library, Grenada, MS [Library symbol Library of Congress] (LCLS)
MSGT..........	Master Sergeant
MsGu..........	Gulfport-Carnegie-Harrison County Library, Gulfport, MS [Library symbol Library of Congress] (LCLS)
MSGV	Mouse Salivary Gland Virus [Medicine] (DMAA)
MsGW.........	Washington County Library System, Greenville, MS [Library symbol Library of Congress] (LCLS)
MSGWA	Military and Sporting Gun Workers' Association [A union] [British]
MsGwL........	Greenwood-Leflore Public Library, Greenwood, MS [Library symbol Library of Congress] (LCLS)
MSG/WTG	Message Waiting (MDG)
MSh...........	Ma'aser Sheni (BJA)
MSH...........	Magnetoelastic Static Hysteresis (MCD)
MSH...........	Mashhad [Iran] [Seismograph station code, US Geological Survey Closed] (SEIS)
MSH...........	Master of Science in Horticulture (NADA)
MSH...........	Master of Science in Hospice (PGP)
MSH...........	Master of Science in Hygiene (NADA)
MSH...........	Master of Staghounds
MSH...........	Mauler Seeker Head
MSH...........	Medical Self-Help [Defunct]
MSH...........	Melanocyte-Stimulating Hormone [Also, MH] [Endocrinology]
MSH...........	Melanophore-Stimulating Hormone [Endocrinology] (AAMN)
MSH...........	Men of the Sacred Hearts (EA)
MSH...........	Metastable Helium (MCD)
MSH...........	Metropolitan Cooperative Library System, Pasadena, CA [OCLC symbol] (OCLC)
MSH...........	Minesweeper Hunter Vessel
MSH...........	Mishibishu Resources [Vancouver Stock Exchange symbol]
MSH...........	Missionaries of the Sacred Heart [Roman Catholic men's religious order]
Ms-H..........	Mississippi State Board of Health, Jackson, MS [Library symbol Library of Congress] (LCLS)
MSH...........	Mount St. Helens [Washington] [Geology]
MSH...........	US Marshal Service [Department of Justice] [ICAO designator] (FAAC)
MsHa..........	Hattiesburg Public Library, Hattiesburg, MS [Library symbol Library of Congress] (LCLS)
MSHA	Master of Science in Health Administration (PGP)
MSHA	Master of Science in Hospital Administration
MSHA	Mine Safety and Health Administration [Department of Labor]
MSha..........	Sharon Public Library, Sharon, MA [Library symbol Library of Congress] (LCLS)
MSHAA.......	Member of the Society of Hearing Aid Audiologists [British] (DBQ)
MSHAA.......	Morocco Spotted Horse Association of America [Defunct] (EA)
MShaK........	Kendall Whaling Museum, Sharon, MA [Library symbol Library of Congress] (LCLS)
MSH & Ph Ed...	Master of Science in Health and Physical Education
MsHaP........	The Library-Hattiesburg, Petal Forrest County, Hattiesburg, MS [Library symbol] [Library of Congress] (LCLS)
MsHaU........	University of Southern Mississippi, Hattiesburg, MS [Library symbol Library of Congress] (LCLS)
MsHaW.......	William Carey College, Hattiesburg, MS [Library symbol Library of Congress] (LCLS)
MSHB	Minimum Safe Height of Burst [Military]
MSHCS	Master of Science in Human and Consumer Science (PGP)
MsHe..........	First Regional Library, Hernando, MS [Library symbol Library of Congress] (LCLS)
MSHE	Master of Science in Home Economics
MSHE	Master of Science in Hydraulic Engineering
MSH Ec.......	Master of Science in Home Economics
MSH Ed	Master of Science in Health Education (PGP)
MSHES	Master of Science in Human Environmental Sciences (PGP)
MSHG	Meshing
MSHI	Medium Scale Hybrid Integration [Computer science] (IAA)
MSH-IF.......	Melanocyte-Stimulating Hormone-Inhibiting Factor [Endocrinology] (MAE)
MSH-IF.......	Melanophore-Stimulating Hormone [Intermedin] Inhibiting Factor [Laboratory science] (DAVI)
MSHK........	Megadata Corp. (MHDW)
MSHK........	Morgan Stanley Group, Inc. [Associated Press] (SAG)
MshI..........	Marshal (BARN)
MShM.........	Mount Holyoke College, South Hadley, MA [Library symbol Library of Congress] (LCLS)

MS Hort.......	Master of Science in Horticulture
MsHos.........	Marshall County Library, Holly Springs, MS [*Library symbol Library of Congress*] (LCLS)
MsHosR.........	Rust College, Holly Springs, MS [*Library symbol Library of Congress*] (LCLS)
MsHou.........	Houston Carnegie Public Library, Houston, MS [*Library symbol Library of Congress*] (LCLS)
Mshp..........	Machine Shop (MHDB)
MSHP..........	Maintain System History Program [*IBM Corp.*]
MSHP..........	Master of Science in Health Professions (PGP)
MSHP..........	Missionary Sisters of the Holy Family (Poland) (TOCD)
MSHR..........	Master of Science in Human Resources (PGP)
MSHR..........	Missionary Sisters of Our Lady of the Holy Rosary [*Blackrock, County Dublin, Republic of Ireland*] (EAIO)
MSHRM.......	Master of Science in Human Resources Management (PGP)
MSHS.........	Master of Science in Health and Safety (GAGS)
MSHS.........	Master of Science in Health Science (PGP)
MSHS.........	Master of Science in Health Systems (GAGS)
MSHS.........	Medical Sciences History Society [*British*] (DBA)
MSHSA........	Master of Science in Human Service Administration (PGP)
MSHSE........	Master of Science in Health Science Education (PGP)
MSHy..........	Master of Science in Hygiene (DAVI)
MS Hyg.......	Master of Science in Hygiene
MsHz..........	Copiah-Jefferson Regional Library, Hazelhurst, MS [*Library symbol Library of Congress*] (LCLS)
MSI...........	Maintenance Significant Items (NASA)
MSI...........	Maintenance Supply Item
MSI...........	Maintenance Support Index
MSI...........	Manned Satellite Inspector
MSI...........	Man System Integration (IAA)
MSI...........	Marine Science Institute [*University of California, Santa Barbara*] [*Research center*] (RCD)
MSI...........	Marine Science Institute [*Philippines*]
MSI...........	Marital Satisfaction Inventory [*Psychology*]
MSI...........	Marketing Science Institute [*Cambridge, MA*] (EA)
MSI...........	Master of Science in Instruction (PGP)
MSI...........	Master of Science in Insurance
MSI...........	Mathematical Sciences Institute [*Cornell University*] [*Research center*] (RCD)
MSI...........	Maximum Speed Indicator
MSI...........	Maxwell Scientific International [*Inc.*]
MSI...........	Mean Spleen Index
MSI...........	Medical Seminars International (EA)
MSI...........	Medium-Scale Integration [*Circuit packaging*]
MSI...........	Megapounds per Square Inch
MSI...........	Member of the Sanitary Institute [*British*] (ROG)
MSI...........	Member of the Surveyors' Institution [*British*] (ROG)
MSI...........	Messina ING [*Istituto Nazionale Geodetico*] [*Sicily*] [*Seismograph station code, US Geological Survey*] (SEIS)
MSI...........	Metal Support Interaction [*Catalysis*]
MSI...........	Microwave Services International, Inc. [*Denville, NJ*] [*Telecommunications*] (TSSD)
MSI...........	Middle-Scale Integration [*Computer science*] (IAA)
MSI...........	Military Service Indicator (MCD)
MSI...........	Military Standard Item (MCD)
MSI...........	Military Static Inverter
MSI...........	Minesweeper, Inshore [*Navy symbol*]
MSI...........	Missile Status Indicator
MSI...........	Missile Subsystem Integration (SAA)
MSI...........	Mission Success Indicator (MCD)
MSI...........	Moderate Scale Integration [*Electronics*]
MSI...........	Molecular Sciences Institute
MSI...........	Molecular Surface Ionization
MSI...........	Moon Sphere of Influence (KSC)
MSI...........	Moshi [*Tanzania*] [*Airport symbol*] (AD)
MSI...........	Mother Symptom Inventory [*Psychology*]
MSI...........	Motor Sich [*Ukraine*] [*FAA designator*] (FAAC)
MSI...........	Motor Skills Inventory [*Sensorimotor skills test*]
MSI...........	Movie Star, Inc. (SPSG)
MSI...........	Movimento Sociale Italiano [*Italian Social Movement*] [*Political party*] (PPE)
MSI...........	Multicomm Sciences International, Inc. [*Denville, NJ*] (TSSD)
MSI...........	Multiple Spark Igniter
MSI...........	Multiple Subcutaneous Insulin [*Medicine*]
MSI...........	Multisensor Imagery
MSI...........	Multispectral Imagery (DOMA)
MSI...........	Multisystem Involvement [*Medicine*]
MSI...........	Museum of Science and Industry [*Chicago, IL*]
MSI...........	Museum Services Institute [*Department of Education*] (OICC)
MSI...........	Mustang Software International [*California*] [*Bulletin board system*]
MSI...........	Second Independence Movement [*Ecuador*] [*Political party*] (PPW)
MSIA..........	Church of the Movement for Spiritual Inner Awareness (ECON)
MSIA..........	Mass Spectrometric Immunoassay
MSIA..........	Master of Institutional Administration (GAGS)
MSIA..........	Master of Science in Industrial Administration
MSIA..........	Master of Science in International Administration (PGP)
MSIA..........	Master of Science in International Affairs (GAGS)
MSIA..........	Member of the Society of Industrial Artists [*British*]
MSIA..........	Multispectral Image Analyzer (MCD)
MSIAD.........	Member of the Society of Industrial Artists and Designers [*British*] (DBQ)
MSIB..........	Master of Science in International Business (PGP)
MSIB..........	Modular Systems Interface Bus (NITA)
MSIBK.........	Master of Science in International Banking (PGP)

MsIbM.........	Mississippi Valley State College, Itta Bena, MS [*Library symbol Library of Congress*] (LCLS)
MSIC..........	Missile and Space Intelligence Center [*DoD*]
MSIC..........	Mixed-Signal Integrated Circuit [*Electronics*]
M-SID.........	Magnetic Sensing Intrusion Device [*Remote sensor*] [*Also, MAGNA-SID*] [*Military*] (VNW)
MSID.........	Mass Spectrometric Isotope Dilution
MSID.........	Measurement Stimulation Identification (MCD)
MSID.........	Medium-Scale Integration Device [*Circuit packaging*]
MSI-DN.......	Movimento Sociale Italiano-Destra Nazionale [*Italian Social Movement-National Right*] [*Political party*] (EY)
MSIE.........	Master of Science in Industrial Engineering
MSIE.........	Master of Science in Industrial Engineering (GAGS)
MSIE.........	Master of Science in International Economics (PGP)
MSIEOR.......	Master of Science in Industrial Engineering and Operations Research (GAGS)
MSIF.........	Multi-Systems Integration Facility (SSD)
MSIG.........	Most Significant (IAA)
MSIGM........	Macintosh Special Interest Group of Mensa (EA)
MS IGT.......	Morgan Stanley Group, Inc. [*Associated Press*] (SAG)
MSIIP........	Missile System Installation Interrupted for Parts (NVT)
MSIL.........	Master of Science in International Logistics (PGP)
MSIM.........	Master of Science in Industrial Management
MSIM.........	Master of Science in Information Management (GAGS)
MSIMC........	Master of Science in Information Management and Communication (PGP)
MSIMD........	Multiple Single Instruction, Multiple Data (MCD)
MsIn..........	Henry M. Seymour Library, Indianola, MS [*Library symbol Library of Congress*] (LCLS)
MS in Aero E...	Master of Science in Aeronautical Engineering
MS in Ag....	Master of Science in Agriculture
MS in Ag E...	Master of Science in Agricultural Education
MS in Ag Ec...	Master of Science in Agricultural Economics
MS in Agr....	Master of Science in Agriculture
MS in Agr Ed...	Master of Science in Agricultural Education
MS in AN....	Master of Science in Agricultural Engineering
MS in Aud & Sp...	Master of Science in Audiology and Speech
MS in BA....	Master of Science in Business Administration
MS in Bl Sc...	Master of Science in Biological Sciences
MS in C......	Master of Science in Commerce
MS in C & BA...	Master of Science in Commercial and Business Administration
MS in CE....	Master of Science in Civil Engineering
MS in Cer....	Master of Science in Ceramics
MS in Cer E...	Master of Science in Ceramic Engineering
MS in Cer Tech...	Master of Science in Ceramic Technology
MS in Ch....	Master of Science in Chemistry
MS in Ch E...	Master of Science in Chemical Engineering
MS in Ch Eng...	Master of Science in Chemical Engineering
MS in Con...	Master of Science in Conservation
MS in CRP...	Master of Science in City and Regional Planning
MS Ind E....	Master of Science in Industrial Engineering
MSIndEng....	Master of Science in Industrial Engineering (NADA)
MS in Derm...	Master of Science in Dermatology
MS India......	Morgan Stanley India Investment Fund [*Associated Press*] (SAG)
MS in Dt....	Master of Science in Dietetics
MS in E......	Master of Science in Education
MS in E......	Master of Science in Engineering
MS in Ed....	Master of Science in Education
MS in EE....	Master of Science in Electrical Engineering
MS in EM....	Master of Science in Engineering Mechanics
MS in EM....	Master of Science in Engineering of Mines
MS in E Mgt...	Master of Science in Engineering Management
MS in EP.....	Master of Science in Engineering Physics
MS in ES....	Master of Science in Engineering Science [*or Sciences*]
MS in For....	Master of Science in Forestry
MS in GE....	Master of Science in General Engineering
MS in Gp Engr...	Master of Science in Geophysical Engineering
MS in GSM...	Master of Science in General Science and Mathematics
MS in HE....	Master of Science in Home Economics
MS in H Ec...	Master of Science in Home Economics
MS in HR....	Master of Science in Human Relations
MS in ID.....	Master of Science in Industrial Design
MS in IE....	Master of Science in Industrial Engineering
MS in IM....	Master of Science in Industrial Management
MS in Ind Ed...	Master of Science in Industrial Education
MS in LS.....	Master of Science in Library Science
MS in ME....	Master of Science in Mechanical Engineering
MS in Mech...	Master of Science in Engineering Mechanics
MS in Med...	Master of Science in Medicine
MS in Met...	Master of Science in Metallurgy
MS in Met E...	Master of Science in Metallurgical Engineering
MS in Mus...	Master of Science in Music
MS in Mus Ed...	Master of Science in Music Education
MS in N.....	Master of Science in Nursing
MS in NE....	Master of Science in Nursing Education
MS in N Ed...	Master of Science in Nursing Education
MS in Nr Ed...	Master of Science in Nursing Education
MS in NT.....	Master of Science in Nuclear Technology
MS in Nucl E...	Master of Science in Nuclear Engineering
MS in PA.....	Master of Science in Public Administration
MS in PE....	Master of Science in Petroleum Engineering
MS in PE....	Master of Science in Physical Education
MS in P Ed...	Master of Science in Physical Education
MS in Pet E...	Master of Science in Petroleum Engineering
MS in PH.....	Master of Science in Public Health

MS in Phar... Master of Science in Pharmacy
MS in Phy ... Master of Science in Physics
MS in PRE... Master of Science in Petroleum Refining Engineering
MS in PSM... Master of Science in Public School Music
MS in Py Sc... Master of Science in Poultry Science
MS in Rad... Master of Science in Radiology
MS in Rec ... Master of Science in Recreation
MS in Ret... Master of Science in Retailing
MS in Sp ... Master of Science in Speech
MS in SS ... Master of Science in Sanitary Science
MS in SS ... Master of Science in Social Service
MS in SW ... Master of Science in Social Work
MS in T & I... Master of Science in Trade and Industrial Education
MS in Trans E... Master of Science in Transportation Engineering
MSINZ .... Member of the Surveyors' Institute of New Zealand
MSIO .... Mass Storage Input-Output [Computer science] (IEEE)
MSIO .... Medical Systems Integration Office [Army] (RDA)
MSIP .... Mechanical Stress Improvement Process [Nuclear energy] (NUCP)
MSIP .... Minority Science Improvement Program [Department of Education] (GFGA)
MSIP .... Modeling and Simulation Investment Plan [Army]
MSIP .... Multinational Staged Improvement Program (MCD)
MSIP .... Multistage Improvement Program (DOMA)
MSIPC .... Master of Science in Information Processing and Communications (PGP)
MSIR .... Machine Survey and Installation Report
MSIR .... Master of Science in Industrial Relations (GAGS)
MSIR .... Master of Social and Industrial Relations
MSIR .... Master Stock Item Record
MSIS .... Main Steam Isolation Signal [Nuclear energy] (NRCH)
MSIS .... Manned Satellite Inspection System
MSIS .... Man-Systems Integration Standard (SSD)
MSIS .... Marine Safety Information System [Coast Guard] (MSC)
MSIS .... Mask Shop Information System [Bell Laboratories]
MSIS .... Mass Spectral Information System
MSIS .... Master of Science in Computer-Based Information Systems
MSIS .... Master of Science in Information Science (GAGS)
MSIS .... Master of Science in Information Systems (PGP)
MSIS .... Master of Science in Interdisciplinary Studies (PGP)
MSIS .... Model State Information System [Environmental Protection Agency] (GFGA)
MSIS .... Multisensor Stabilized Integrated System
MSIS .... Multistate Information System [Patient records]
MSISL.......... Moore School Information Systems Laboratory
Ms IT .... Manuscript, Inner Temple [A publication] (DLA)
MSIT .... Master of Science in Industrial Technology (PGP)
MSIT .... Member of the Society of Instrument Technology [British]
MSIV.......... Main Steam Isolation Valve [Nuclear energy] (NRCH)
MSIVLCS ..... Main Steam Isolation Valve Leakage Control System [Nuclear energy] (NRCH)
MS/IWS ...... Master of Science/Industry Work Study
MSIX .... Mining Services International Corp. [NASDAQ symbol] (NQ)
MSIX .... Mining Svcs Intl [NASDAQ symbol] (TTSB)
MsJ .... Jackson Municipal Library, Jackson, MS [Library symbol Library of Congress] (LCLS)
MSJ .... Machine Screw Jack
MSJ .... Master of Science in Journalism
MSJ .... Medical Sisters of St. Joseph (TOCD)
MSJ .... Misawa [Japan] [Airport symbol] (OAG)
MSJ .... Mission San Jose [California] [Seismograph station code, US Geological Survey] (SEIS)
MSJ .... Multiple Subsonic Jet
MSJ96 .... Morgan Stanley Group, Inc. [Associated Press] (SAG)
MSJA .... Master of Science in Judicial Administration (GAGS)
MsJB .... Belhaven College, Jackson, MS [Library symbol Library of Congress] (LCLS)
MSJBS .... Master of Science in Japanese Business Studies (PGP)
MsJG .... Mississippi Bureau of Geology, Jackson, MS [Library symbol] [Library of Congress] (LCLS)
MsJMC .... Millsaps College, Jackson, MS [Library symbol Library of Congress] (LCLS)
MsJPED .... Episcopal Diocese of Mississippi, Jackson, MS [Library symbol Library of Congress] (LCLS)
MSJPS........ Master of Science in Justice and Public Safety (PGP)
MSJPS........ Master of Science in Justice and Public Service (GAGS)
MsJRD .... Research and Development Center Library, Jackson, MS [Library symbol Library of Congress] (LCLS)
MsJRT .... Reformed Theological Seminary, Jackson, MS [Library symbol Library of Congress] (LCLS)
MsJS .... Jackson State College [Later, Jackson State University], Jackson, MS [Library symbol Library of Congress] (LCLS)
MSJS .... Master of Science in Jewish Studies (PGP)
MsJV .... United States Veterans Administration Hospital, Jackson, MS [Library symbol Library of Congress] (LCLS)
MsJW .... Wesley Biblical Seminary, Jackson, MS [Library symbol Library of Congress] (LCLS)
MSK.......... Grupo Indl Maseca ADS [NYSE symbol] (TTSB)
MSK.......... Grupo Industrial Maseca SA de CV [NYSE symbol] (SAG)
MSK.......... Magyar Statisztikai Kozlemenyek [Hungary]
MSK.......... Major Subcontractor
MSK.......... Manual Select Keyboard [Computer science] (KSC)
MSK.......... Mask [Computer science] (IAA)
MSK.......... Master of Science in Kinesiology (GAGS)
MSK.......... Mastic Point [Andros Islands, Bahamas] [Airport symbol] (AD)
MSK.......... Medullary Sponge Kidney [Anatomy] (MAE)

MSK............ Medvedev, Sponheuer, Karnick [Earthquake intensity scale]
MsK............ Mid-Mississippi Regional Library, Kosciusko, MS [Library symbol Library of Congress] (LCLS)
MSK.......... Minimal Shift Keying (NITA)
MSK.......... Minimum Shift Keying
MSK.......... Misaki [Japan] [Seismograph station code, US Geological Survey Closed] (SEIS)
MSK.......... Mission Support Kit
MSK.......... Mobility Support Kit
MSK.......... Mostek Corporation (NITA)
MSK.......... Musculoskeletal [Orthopedics] (DAVI)
MSKB.......... Microsoft Knowledge Base [Computer science] (PCM)
MSKC.......... Memorial Sloan-Kettering Cancer Center [Research center] (RCD)
MSKCC .... Memorial Sloan-Kettering Cancer Center [New York]
MSKCP .... Missionary Sisters of Christ the King of Polonia (TOCD)
MSKM.......... Minimum Shift Keyed Modulation (NITA)
MSKP.......... Management Skills - Knowledge Profile [Business term]
MSKP.......... Medical Sciences Knowledge Profile (DAVI)
MsL .... Laurel Library Association, Laurel, MS [Library symbol Library of Congress] (LCLS)
MSL .... Machine Specification Language
MSL .... Magnetic Surfaces Laboratory
MSL .... Main Sea Level (AAG)
MSL .... Main Steam Line [Nuclear energy] (NRCH)
MSL .... Maintenance Supply Liaison [Air Force] (AFM)
MSL .... Major Soccer League (BARN)
MSL .... Management Selection Ltd.
MSL .... Management Systems Laboratories [Virginia Polytechnic Institute and State University] [Research center] (RCD)
MSL .... Manned Space Laboratory [NASA] (IAA)
MSL .... Manpower Source Listing (MCD)
MSL .... Marine Systems Laboratory [Smithsonian Institution]
MSL .... Master of Sacred Literature
MSL .... Master of Science in Language
MSL .... Master of Science in Librarianship (PGP)
MSL .... Master of Science in Limnology (PGP)
MSL .... Master of Science in Linguistics
MSL .... Master of Studies in Law (PGP)
MSL .... Master Save List [Military] (AFIT)
MSL .... Master Scheduling Letter
MSL .... Masterseal [Record label]
MSL .... Master Support List (MCD)
MSL .... Materialien zum Sumerischen Lexikon. B. Landsberger. Patrologiae Cursus Completus. Series Latina [A publication] (BJA)
MSL .... Materials and Structures Laboratory [Texas A & M University] [Research center] (RCD)
MSL .... Maximum Service Life [or Limit] (AAG)
MSL .... Maximum Stillwater Level [Nuclear energy] (NRCH)
MSL .... Mean Sea Level
MSL .... Mean Sea Level
MSL .... Measurement Standards Laboratory
MSL .... Measurement System Laboratory (MCD)
MSL .... Mechanical Systems Laboratory [NASA] (NASA)
MSL .... Message Switched Line (MCD)
MSL .... Meteorological Satellite Laboratory
MSL .... Methuen's Standard Library [A publication]
MSL .... Microcomputer Sales and Leasing, Inc.
MSL .... Microgravity Science Laboratory [NASA]
MSL .... Microstar Software Ltd. [Nepean, ON] [Telecommunications] (TSSD)
MSL .... MidSouth Bancorp [AMEX symbol] (TTSB)
MSL .... Midsouth Bancorp, Inc. [AMEX symbol] (SAG)
MSL .... Midsternal Line
MSL .... Military Shipping Label
MSL .... Military Side Loader [Air transport] [British]
MSL .... Military Support List (MCD)
MSL .... Minesweeping Launch [Navy ship symbol]
MSL .... Minimum Size Limit [Pisciculture]
MSL .... Minneapolis & St. Louis [Railroad] (MHDB)
MSL .... Minnesota State Law Library, St. Paul, MN [OCLC symbol] (OCLC)
MSL .... Missile (AFM)
MSL .... Missile Sea Level
MSL .... Missile Site Load (MCD)
MSL .... Molecular Spectroscopy Laboratory [Fisk University] [Research center] (RCD)
MSL .... Mouvement des Sociaux-Liberaux [Movement of Social Liberals] [France Political party] (PPW)
MSL .... Multiple Stinger Launcher
MSL .... Municipal Savings & Loan Corp. [Toronto Stock Exchange symbol]
MSL .... Muscle Shoals [Alabama] [Airport symbol] (OAG)
MSL .... Snow Lake Community Library, Manitoba [Library symbol National Library of Canada] (NLC)
MSIA.......... Atlantic Union College, South Lancaster, MA [Library symbol Library of Congress] (LCLS)
MSIA.......... Atlantic Union College, South Lancaster, MA [Library symbol] [Library of Congress] (LCLS)
MSLA.......... Main Steam Line Accident [Nuclear energy] (NRCH)
MSLA.......... Master of Science in Legal Administration (PGP)
MSLA.......... Missionary Sisters of Our Lady of the Angels [Lennoxville, PQ] (EAIO)
MSLA.......... Mouse Specific Lymphocyte Antigen [Immunology]
MSLA.......... Multisample Luer Adapter [Medicine] (MEDA)
MSLAET....... Member of the Society of Licensed Aircraft Engineers and Technologists [British] (DBQ)
MsLb .... Long Beach Public Library, Long Beach, MS [Library symbol Library of Congress] (LCLS)

MSLB.......... Main Steam Line Break [*Nuclear energy*] (NRCH)
MsLbU........ University of Southern Mississippi, Gulf Park, Richard G. Cox Library, Long Beach, MS [*Library symbol Library of Congress*] (LCLS)
MSLC.......... Minnesota Short Lines Co. [*AAR code*]
MSLC.......... Missile Sites Labor Commission [*A federal government body*] [*Abolished 1967; functions transferred to Federal Mediation and Conciliation Service*]
MSLCOMD.. Missile Command [*Army*]
MSLD.......... Masland Corp. [*NASDAQ symbol*] (SAG)
MSLD.......... Mass Spectrometer Leak Detector (NRCH)
MSLD.......... Mass Spectrometer Leak Detector
MsLE .... Lauren Rogers Library and Museum of Art, Laurel, MS [*Library symbol Library of Congress*] (LCLS)
MSLEX........ Missile Exercise (DOMA)
MSLF.......... Mountain States Legal Foundation (EA)
MSLFM........ Massenet Society and Lovers of French Music [*Later, MSAB*] (EA)
MSLG.......... Maintenance Support Logistics Group [*Military*] (CAAL)
Ms LI .... Manuscript, Lincoln's Inn [*A publication*] (DLA)
MsLi .... Microfilm Services Ltd., Auckland, New Zealand [*Library symbol Library of Congress*] (LCLS)
MSLIR .... Master of Science in Labor and Industrial Relations
MS Litt .... Master of Sacred Letters
MSLIVSS ..... Main Steam Line Isolation Valve Sealings System [*Nuclear energy*] (NRCH)
MSLM.......... Microchannel Spatial Light Modulator [*Electronics*]
MSLMAINTSq.. Missile Maintenance Squadron [*Air Force*]
MSLN.......... Mari Sandoz Library Network [*Library network*]
MSLO.......... Master Layout
MSLO.......... Medical Service Liaison Officer [*Air Force*]
MSLOUG...... Medium-Sized Libraries/OCLC [*Online Computer Library Center*] Users Group
MSLP.......... Malawi Socialist Labour Party [*Political party*] (EY)
MSLP.......... Master of Speech-Language Pathology (PGP)
MSLP.......... San Salvador/El Salvador Internacional [*El Salvador*] [*ICAO location identifier*] (ICLI)
MSLPr .... MidSouth Bancorp Sr'A'Cv Pfd [*AMEX symbol*] (TTSB)
MSLR.......... Mixed Skin Cell-Leukocyte Reaction [*Medicine*] (DMAA)
MSLS.......... Maneuverable Satellite Landing System (MUGU)
MSLS.......... Master of Science in Law and Society (DLA)
MSLS.......... Master of Science in Library Science
MSLS.......... Master of Science in Logistics Systems (PGP)
MSLS.......... Missile Site Location System (MCD)
MSLSc........ Master of Science in Library Science
MSLT.......... Military Solid Logic Technology (IAA)
MSLT.......... Multiple Sleep Latency Test
MSLWARNINGSq... Missile Warning Squadron [*Air Force*]
MSLY.......... Mostly (MSA)
MSM.......... Maastricht School of Management [*Netherlands*]
MSM.......... Major System Mode (CAAL)
MSM.......... Manhattan School of Music
MSM.......... Manned Support Module [*NASA*] (NASA)
MSM.......... Manufacturing Shop Manual (SAA)
MSM.......... Manufacturing Standards Manual
MSM.......... Marine Safety Manual [*Coast Guard*] [*A publication*] (DLA)
MSM.......... Mars Surface Module (MCD)
MSMA.......... Mass Scatterable Mine (RDA)
MSM.......... Master of Medical Science
MSM.......... Master of Sacred Ministry (PGP)
MSM.......... Master of Sacred Music
MSM.......... Master of Science in Management
MSM.......... Master of Science in Music
MSM.......... Master of Service Management (PGP)
MSM.......... Master Scheduling Manager
MSM.......... Master Slave Manipulator [*Nuclear energy*]
MSM.......... Mauritian Socialist Movement [*Political party*]
MSM.......... Meal Semiconductor Metal (IAA)
MSM.......... Mechanically Separated Meat [*Food technology*]
MSM.......... Medium Minesweeper (NATG)
MSM.......... Memory Storage Module
MSM.......... Men Who Have Sex with Men [*Australia An association*]
MSM.......... Mercury Specialist Management [*Commercial firm British*]
MsM.......... Meridian Public Library, Meridian, MS [*Library symbol Library of Congress*] (LCLS)
MSM.......... Meritorious Service Medal [*Military decoration*]
MSM.......... Messman
MSM.......... Metal-Semiconductor-Metal (IEEE)
MSM.......... Methyl Sulfonylmethane [*Biochemistry*]
MSM.......... Micro Surface Mapping [*Software package*] (NCC)
MSM.......... Microwave Switch Matrix (LAIN)
MSM.......... Millimeter and Submillimeter Conference (MCD)
MSM.......... Mineral Salts Medium [*Medicine*] (DMAA)
MSM.......... Minesweeper, River [*Navy symbol Obsolete*]
MSM.......... Missile Standards Manual [*Military*] (IAA)
MSM.......... Mission Simulation Model
MSM.......... Missouri School of Mines
MSM.......... Modified Source Multiplication (NRCH)
MSM.......... Montana School of Mines
MSM.......... Morehouse School of Medicine [*Atlanta, GA*]
MSM.......... Motorized Switching Matrix
MSM.......... Motorsteuermonolith
MSM.......... Mount St. Mary's College, Emmitsburg, MD [*OCLC symbol*] (OCLC)
MSM.......... Mouvement Social Mohutu [*Mohutu Social Movement*]
MSM.......... Mouvement Solidaire Muluba [*Muluba Solidarity Movement*] [*Political party*]
MSM.......... MSC Industrial Direct'A' [*NYSE symbol*] (TTSB)

MSM.......... Mystic Seaport Museum (EA)
MSM.......... Thousand Feet Surface Measure [*Lumber*]
MSMA.......... Mail Systems Management Association [*New York, NY*] (EA)
MSMA.......... Major Symphony Managers Association (EA)
MSMA.......... Margarine and Shortening Manufacturers Association (EAIO)
MSMA.......... Master Sign Makers' Association (NADA)
MSMA.......... Medical-Surgical Manufacturers Association [*Later, HIMA*]
MSMA.......... Metal Sink Manufacturers Association [*British*] (DBA)
MSMA.......... Meteorological Services to Marine Activities [*WMO*] (MSC)
MSMA.......... Metropolitan Symphony Managers Association (EA)
MSMA.......... Monosodium Methyl Arsonate [*Herbicide*]
MSMA.......... Monosodium Salt of Methylarsonic Acid [*Agriculture*]
MsMac........ Noxubee County Library, Macon, MS [*Library symbol Library of Congress*] (LCLS)
MSMAE........ Master of Science in Materials Engineering (PGP)
MSMAN........ Master Sign Makers' Association [*British*] (BI)
MsMar........ Quitman County Library, Marks, MS [*Library symbol Library of Congress*] (LCLS)
MSMAS........ Master of Science in Media Arts and Sciences (PGP)
MS Mat........ Master of Science in Materials Engineering (PGP)
MS Mat E ... Master of Science in Materials Engineering (PGP)
MS Mat SE... Master of Science in Material Science and Engineering (PGP)
MSMatSE... Master of Science in Materials Science Engineering (GAGS)
MSMAV........ Master Stone Masons' Association of Victoria [*Australia*]
MSMB........ Mortgage Secondary Market Board [*Australia*]
MSMC.......... Master of Science in Marketing Communication (GAGS)
MSMC.......... Master of Science in Mass Communication (GAGS)
MSMC.......... Master Schedule and Milestone Chart (MCD)
MSMC.......... Member of the Spectacle Makers Co. [*British*] (ROG)
MSMC.......... Migrant Studies and Media Center [*Australia*]
MSMC.......... Military Subsistence Market Center (MUGU)
MsMc.......... Pike-Amite Library System, McComb, MS [*Library symbol Library of Congress*] (LCLS)
MSMCS........ Master of Science in Management and Computer Science (PGP)
MSMD.......... Madras Subordinate Medical Department [*British military*] (DMA)
MSMDA ...... Mutual Sewing Machine Dealers Association (EA)
MSME.......... Master of Science in Mathematics Education (PGP)
MSME.......... Master of Science in Mechanical Engineering
MSMEA........ Multiwall Sack Manufacturers Employers Association [*British*] (DBA)
MS Mech E... Master of Science in Mechanical Engineering
MSMed........ Master of Medical Science (NADA)
MS Met E .... Master of Science in Metallurgical Engineering
MS Metr ..... Master of Science in Meteorology (PGP)
MSMF.......... Maintenance Support Management File (MCD)
MSMFE........ Master of Science in Manufacturing Engineering (PGP)
MS Mfg E .... Master of Science in Manufacturing Engineering (PGP)
MsMFM ...... Masonic Library, Meridian, MS [*Library symbol Library of Congress*] (LCLS)
MS Mf SE ... Master of Science in Manufacturing Systems Engineering (PGP)
MSMG.......... Missionary Sisters of the Mother of God [*Roman Catholic religious order*]
MS Mgt........ Master of Science in Management (PGP)
MSMgt........ Master of Science in Management (GAGS)
MS Mgt E .... Master of Science in Management Engineering
MSMI.......... Master of Science in Medical Illustration (GAGS)
MSMIA........ Medical and Sports Music Institute of America (EA)
MS Min........ Master of Science in Mining (PGP)
MS Min E .... Master of Science in Mining Engineering (PGP)
MSMIS........ Master of Science in Management Information Systems (PGP)
MS/MIS....... Master of Science/Management Information Systems
MSML.......... Minesweeping Motorlaunch [*Navy*]
MSMLCS..... Mass Service Mainline Cable Systems
MSMM.......... Master of Science in Manufacturing Management (PGP)
MsMM .... Meridian Junior College, Meridian, MS [*Library symbol Library of Congress*] (LCLS)
MsMo .... Lawrence County Public Library, Monticello, MS [*Library symbol Library of Congress*] (LCLS)
MS Mot........ Master of Science in Management of Technology (PGP)
MSMOT........ Master of Science in Management of Technology (PGP)
MSMP.......... Master Sensitized Material Print (MSA)
MSMP.......... Modeling and Simulation Master Plan [*Army*]
MSMP.......... Multispectral Measurements Program (MCD)
MSMPR ...... Mixed-Suspension, Mixed-Product Removal [*Crystallizer*] [*Chemical engineering*]
MSMR.......... Missouri School of Mines Reactor
MSMS.......... Machine Strap Makers' Society [*A union*] [*British*]
MSMS.......... Marine Safety Management System [*BTS*] (TAG)
MS/MS....... Mass Spectrometry/Mass Spectrometry
MSMS.......... Master of Science in Management Science (PGP)
MSMS.......... Master of Science in Medical Sciences (PGP)
MS/MS....... Materials Science and Manufacturing in Space [*Program*] [*NASA*]
MSMS.......... Max Steiner Memorial Society (EA)
MSMS.......... Membership Section for Multihospital Systems [*Later, HCS*] (EA)
MSMS.......... Meteorological Systems Management Section
MSMS.......... Mutual Security Military Sales
MS-MS....... Tandem Mass Spectroscopy
MSMSA........ Master of Science in Management Systems Analysis (PGP)
MSMSE........ Master of Science in Manufacturing Systems Engineering (PGP)
MSMSE........ Master of Science in Material Science Engineering (PGP)
MSMSEd...... Master of Science in Mathematics and Science Education (GAGS)
MSMSP........ Project Manager, Surface Missile Systems [*Navy*]
MsMStA ...... Saint Aloysius Academy, Meridian, MS [*Library symbol Library of Congress*] (LCLS)
MS MT........ Manuscript, Middle Temple [*A publication*] (DLA)
MSMT.......... Master of Science in Medical Technology (GAGS)

MSMT.........	Measurement (KSC)
MS Mt E......	Master of Science in Materials Engineering (PGP)
MSMTH.......	Metalsmith [Navy]
MsMU........	Mississippi State University, Meridian Branch, Meridian, MS [Library symbol Library of Congress] (LCLS)
MSMU	Mobile Spectrum Monitoring Unit
MSMus	Master of Science in Music (NADA)
MSMusEd	Master of Science in Music Education (NADA)
MSMV........	Monk Seal Morbillivirus
MSMV........	Monostable Multivibrator
MSMW.......	Magnetically Suspended Momentum Wheel
MSN.........	Dane County Regional-Truax Field [FAA] (TAG)
MSN.........	Emerson Radio [AMEX symbol] (TTSB)
MSN.........	Emerson Radio Corp. [AMEX symbol] (SAG)
MSN.........	Madison [Wisconsin] [Airport symbol] (OAG)
MSN.........	Main-Stem Node [Botany]
MSN.........	Maintenance and Support Network
MSN.........	Manned Space Network [NASA] (MCD)
MSN.........	Mason
MSN.........	Master of Science in Nursing
MSN.........	Master of Science in Nursing (GAGS)
MSN.........	Master Serial Number (AAG)
MSN.........	Material Supply Notice (AAG)
MSN.........	Median Sample Number (PDAA)
MSN.........	Message Sequence Number (CAAL)
MSN.........	Microsoft Network [Online information service launched in 1995] (WDMC)
MSN.........	Microsoft Network [Microsoft Corp.]
MSN.........	Mildly Subnormal [Medicine] (MAE)
MSN.........	Military Serial Number
MSN.........	Military Service Number
MSN.........	Mission (AFM)
MSN.........	Mission
MSN.........	Mobil Showcase Network [Television]
MSN.........	Modern Satellite Network [Cable-television system]
MSN.........	Morrison Minerals Ltd. [Toronto Stock Exchange symbol]
MSN.........	Movimiento de Salvacion Nacional [National Salvation Movement] [Colorado Political party] (EY)
MSN.........	Mozambique Support Network (EA)
MSN.........	Multiple Subscriber Number [Telecommunications] (DOM)
MSN.........	Music, Sport, News [Radio broadcasting format]
MsN.........	Public Library of Natchez and Adams County, Natchez, MS [Library symbol Library of Congress] (LCLS)
MsNa.........	Jennie Belle Stephens Smith Library, New Albany, MS [Library symbol Library of Congress] (LCLS)
MSNA........	Master of Science in Nurse Anesthesia (GAGS)
MSNA........	Master of Science in Nursing Administration (GAGS)
MSNA........	Mission Accomplished [Military] (AABC)
MSNAP......	Merchant Ship Naval Augmentation Program [Navy]
MSNAP......	Microwave Steerable Null Antenna Processor (MCD)
MSNBC......	Microsoft Corp. National Broadcasting Co. [Cable news channel]
MSNC........	Masonic
MSNCDRFAIRECONRON...	Mission Commander, Fleet Air Reconnaissance Squadron (DNAB)
MSND........	Mercury Substitution and Nucleonic Detection (PDAA)
MSND........	Mouvement Social pour la Nouvelle Democratie [Cameroon] [Political party] (EY)
MSNE........	Master of Science in Nuclear Engineering (GAGS)
MsNe.........	Newton Public Library, Newton, MS [Library symbol Library of Congress] (LCLS)
MsNeC.......	Clarke Memorial College, Newton, MS [Library symbol Library of Congress] (LCLS)
MSNEd.......	Master of Science in Nursing Education (NADA)
MS-Net......	Microsoft Network [Computer science] [Also, MSN] (CDE)
MSNET......	Microsoft Network [Computer science] (HGAA)
MSNF........	Milk Solids - Not Fat [Food industry]
MSNF........	Multisystem Networking Facility [Computer science]
MSNGR......	Messenger (ADA)
MSNHP......	Mississippi Natural Heritage Program [Mississippi State Department of Wildlife Conservation] [Jackson, MS] [Information service or system] (IID)
MSNI........	(Mesitylenesulfonyl)nitroimidazole [Organic chemistry]
MSNik 97....	Morgan Stanley Group, Inc. [Associated Press] (SAG)
MSN(R)......	Master of Science in Nursing (Research) (PGP)
MSNRY......	Masonry (MSA)
MSNS........	Master of Science in Natural Science (PGP)
MSNS........	MediSense, Inc. [NASDAQ symbol] (SAG)
MSN/SSN....	Military Service Number / Social Security Number (DNAB)
MS Nsurg ...	Master of Science in Neurosurgery (PGP)
MSNT........	(Mesitylenesulfonyl)nitrotriazolide [Biochemistry]
MSNuclEng...	Master of Science in Nuclear Engineering (NADA)
MSNY........	Massena [New York] [Seismograph station code, US Geological Survey] (SEIS)
MSNY........	Mattachine Society of New York [Defunct] (EA)
MSO.........	Main Signal Office [British]
MSO.........	Maintenance Standard Order
MSO.........	Maintenance Support Office [Navy]
MSO.........	Malaysian Students' Organization [Australia]
MSO.........	Managed Service Organization [Health Insurance]
MSO.........	Management Science Office
MSO.........	Management Service Organization
MSO.........	Management Systems Office [NASA]
MSO.........	Mandatory Second Surgical Opinion [Health insurance] (GHCT)
MSO.........	Manned Solar Observatory (MCD)
MSO.........	Manned Spacecraft Operations [NASA] (KSC)

MSO.........	Manufacturer's Statement of Origin
MSO.........	Manufacturer's Statement of Origin [Automobile sales]
MSO.........	Manufacturing Sequence Outline (MCD)
MSO.........	Marine Safety Office (MCD)
MSO.........	Marine Staff Officers (EA)
MSO.........	Marketing Services Officer [Insurance]
MSO.........	Mars Surface Operation
MSO.........	Mass Spectrometer Outgasing (KSC)
MSO.........	Master of Science in Orthodontics (GAGS)
M So.........	Master of Sociology
MSO.........	Master of the Science of Oratory
MSO.........	Material Sales Order
MSO.........	Materiel Status Office (MCD)
MSO.........	Medial Superior Olive [Brain anatomy]
MSO.........	Medical Staff Organization (HCT)
MSO.........	Medisave-cum-Subsidized Outpatient Scheme [Medical benefit program] [Singapore]
MSO.........	Member of the Society of Osteopaths [British]
MSO.........	Mesityl Oxide [Also, MO] [Organic chemistry]
MSO.........	Methionine Sulfoxime [Biochemistry]
MSO.........	Military Satellite Organization
MSO.........	Military Service Obligation (AFM)
MSO.........	Military Supply Officer (AFM)
MSO.........	Minesweeper, Ocean [Nonmagnetic] [Navy symbol]
MSO.........	Missabe Southern Railroad
MSO.........	Missile Safety Officer (AFM)
MSO.........	Missoula [Montana] [Airport symbol] (OAG)
MSO.........	Missoula [Montana] [Seismograph station code, US Geological Survey] (SEIS)
MSO.........	Mixed Services Organisation [British Armed Services]
MSO.........	Mobile Switching Office [Bell System]
MSO.........	Model for Spare Optimization (MCD)
MSO.........	Morale Support Officer [Military] (AABC)
MSO.........	Moss Resources Ltd. [Vancouver Stock Exchange symbol]
MSO.........	Mouvement Socialiste Occitan [Occitanian Socialist Movement] [France Political party] (PPE)
MSO.........	Mozambique Solidarity Office (EA)
MSO.........	Multiple System Operator [Cable television]
MSO.........	Multiple System Operator (WDMC)
MSO.........	Multiple Systems Operator (ACRL)
MSO.........	Multistage Operation (MHDI)
MSo.........	Public Library of the City of Somerville, Somerville, MA [Library symbol Library of Congress] (LCLS)
MSOA	Military Studies and Operational Analysis (ADA)
MSOB	Manned Spacecraft Operations Building [NASA] (KSC)
MSOB	Manned Spacecraft Operations Building
MSOB	Master of Science in Organizational Behavior
MSobPR......	New England Regional Primate Research Center, Harvard University, Southborough, MA [Library symbol] [Library of Congress] (LCLS)
MSOC	MANPRINT [Manpower and Personnel Integration] Staff Officer Course [Military] (RDA)
MSOC	Marine Systems Operational Compiler
MSOC	Maritime Sector Operations Center [NATO] (NATG)
MSoc	Master of Sociology (ADA)
M Soc	Master of Sociology (PGP)
MSocAdmin...	Master of Social Administration
MSOCC	Multisatellite Operations Control Center [NASA]
M Soc E	Member of the Society of Engineers [British]
MSocPol......	Master of Social Policy
M Soc Sc.....	Master of Social Science (PGP)
MSocSc	Master of Social Sciences
MSocSci	Master of Social Sciences
MSocSt	Master of Social Studies
MSocStud....	Master of Social Studies (ADA)
MSocWk	Master of Social Work
MSOD	Master of Science in Organizational Development (GAGS)
MSOD	Military Service Obligation Date (AFM)
MSOD	Mobile Source Operations Division
MSOE.........	Master of Science in Ocean Engineering (PGP)
MSOE.........	Milwaukee School of Engineering [Wisconsin]
MSOE.........	Multiband Spectral Observation Equipment
MSOF.........	Multisystem Organ Failure [Medicine] (CPH)
MSOG	Glenwood and Souris Regional Library, Souris, Manitoba [Library symbol National Library of Canada] (NLC)
MSOG.........	Molecular Sieve Oxygen Generating (PDAA)
MSohG.......	Gordon-Conwell Theological Seminary Library, South Hamilton, MA [Library symbol Library of Congress] (LCLS)
MSOIN.......	Minor Subcontractor or IDWA [Interdivisional Work Authorization] Notification [NASA] (NASA)
MSOIN.......	Minor Subcontractor Or Iowa [Interdivisional Work Authorization] Notification
MSOINST....	Maintenance Support Office Instructions [Navy]
MSOL........	Manned Scientific Orbital Laboratory [NASA] (IAA)
MSOLA	Missionary Sisters of Our Lady of Africa (TOCD)
MSOM	Master of Science in Organization and Management (PGP)
MSOM	Modernized Systems Operations Manual [Computer science]
MSom........	Somerset Public Library, Somerset, MA [Library symbol] [Library of Congress] (LCLS)
MSON........	Misonix, Inc. [NASDAQ symbol] (SAG)
MSonHi.......	South Natick Historical, Natural History, and Library Society, South Natick, MA [Library symbol Library of Congress] (LCLS)
MSONW......	Misonix Inc. Wrrt [NASDAQ symbol] (TTSB)
MSOP........	Measurement System Operating Procedure (NG)
MSOP........	Mezzo Soprano [Music]
MSOP........	Mutual Security Objectives Plan (CINC)

MSOphthal...	Master of Ophthalmological Surgery (NADA)
M Sopr	Mezzo Soprano [*Music*]
MSOR..........	Master of Science in Operations Research (GAGS)
MSOR..........	Maximum System Operational Range
MSOR..........	Missile Systems Operational Report [*Military*] (IAA)
MS Orn Hort...	Master of Science in Ornamental Horticulture
MSORS........	Mechanized Sales Office Record System [*Telecommunications*] (TEL)
MS(Orth)......	Master of Surgery (Orthopedic)
MSOS	Mass Storage Operating System [*Control Data Corp.*] [*Computer science*] (NVT)
M So Sc	Master of Social Science
M So Se	Master of Social Service
MSOT..........	Master of Science in Occupational Technology (PGP)
MSOT..........	Master of Science in Occupational Therapy (GAGS)
MS Otol	Master of Science in Otolaryngology (PGP)
M So W	Master of Social Work
MSOW	Modular Standoff Weapon [*Ballistic missile*]
MsP	Jackson County - Pascagoula City Library, Pascagoula, MS [*Library symbol Library of Congress*] (LCLS)
MSP...........	Macrophage Stimulating Protein [*Biochemistry*]
MSP...........	Magnetic Scalar Potential
MSP...........	Maintenance Service Plan
MSP...........	Maintenance Support Plan [*or Program*] [*Army*]
MSP...........	Maintenance Surveillance Procedure (IEEE)
MSP...........	Management System Programmers Ltd. (NITA)
MSP...........	Manager Software Products Ltd. (NITA)
MSP...........	Manager Support Programs (MCD)
MSP...........	Manual Switching Position (IAA)
MSP...........	Marine Security Program [*FHWA*] (TAG)
MSP...........	Maritime Shore Patrol
MSP...........	Market Stabilization Price [*Department of Agriculture*]
MSP...........	Mass Storage Processor [*Honeywell, Inc.*]
MSP...........	Master of School Psychology (PGP)
MSP...........	Master of Science in Pharmacy
MSP...........	Master of Science in Planning (PGP)
MSP...........	Master of Social Psychology (PGP)
M Sp	Master of Speech
MSP...........	Master of Speech Pathology (PGP)
MSP...........	Master Shuttle Verification Plan (MCD)
MSP...........	Master Simulator Program (NVT)
MSP...........	Matched Sale-Purchase Agreement [*Business term*]
MSP...........	Material Support Plan [*or Program*]
MSP...........	Maximum Silo Price [*Farming terminology*]
MSP...........	Maximum Sound Pressure
MSP...........	Measurement Sensitive Products (DICI)
MSP...........	Mededelingen Spinozahuis [*A publication*] (BJA)
MSP...........	Media Suite Pro [*Computer software*] (CDE)
MSP...........	Medical Specialist
MSP...........	Medium Side Prong [*Lamp base type*] (NTCM)
MSP...........	Medium-Speed Printer (AABC)
MSP...........	Medium Stressed Platform
MSP...........	Merozoite Surface Protein [*Of protozoa*]
MSP...........	Metal Splash Pan (AAG)
MSP...........	Microsoft Paint [*Computer science*] (CDE)
MSP...........	Microsoft Solution Provider [*Computer science*] (CDE)
MSP...........	Microspectrophotometry
MSP...........	Microsuspension Seeded Polymerization (DICI)
MSP...........	Military Space Program (AAG)
MSP...........	Millisecond Pulsar [*Astronomy*]
MSP...........	Minesweeper, Patrol [*Navy*] (DNAB)
MSP...........	Miniature Series of Painters [*A publication*]
MSP...........	Minimum Sustaining Power
MSP...........	Minneapolis-St. Paul [*Minnesota*] [*Airport symbol*]
MSP...........	Miscellaneous Small Parts
MSP...........	Missile Setting Panel [*Military*] (CAAL)
MSP...........	Missile Simulator Plug
MSP...........	Missile Support Plan
MSP...........	Missionaries of St. Paul (TOCD)
msp...........	Missionaries of St. Paul (TOCD)
MSP...........	Mission Scientifique en Perse (BJA)
MSP...........	Mission Support Plan (MCD)
MSP...........	Mobile Support Package (MCD)
MSP...........	Moderata Samlingspartiet [*Moderate Unity Party*] [*Sweden Political party*] (PPE)
MSP...........	Mode Select Panel (IAA)
MSP...........	Modular System Programs [*IBM Corp.*]
MSP...........	Monosodium Orthophosphate [*Inorganic chemistry*]
MSP...........	Morgan Stan Fin 8.20% Cp Uts [*NYSE symbol*] (TTSB)
MSP...........	Morgan Stanley Finance PLC Capital Unit [*NYSE symbol*] (SAG)
msp...........	Mortuus sine Prole [*Dead without Issue*] [*Latin*] (WGA)
MSP...........	Mosaic Sensor Program (MCD)
MSP...........	Most Significant Position (CMD)
MSP...........	Motorized Set Point (IAA)
MSP...........	Mount St. Thomas [*Philippines*] [*Seismograph station code, US Geological Survey*] (SEIS)
MSP...........	Mouse Serum Protein [*Biochemistry*] (DAVI)
MSP...........	Movimento Socialista Popular [*Popular Socialist Movement*] [*Portugal Political party*] (PPE)
MSP...........	Multiprocessing Server Pack [*Computer science*] (CDE)
MSP...........	Multipurpose Semi-Submersible Platform (DNAB)
MSP...........	Multisensor Processor (CAAL)
MSP...........	Multi-Tech Supervisory Protocol [*Telecommunications*] (PCM)
MSP...........	Mutual Security Program
MSP...........	Mutual Support Program
MSP...........	Servicio de Vigilancia Aerea del Ministerio de Seguridad Publica [*Costa Rica*] [*ICAO designator*] (FAAC)
MSPA..........	Maine Sardine Packers Association (EA)
MSPA..........	Marin Self-Publishers Association (EA)
MSPA..........	Master of Science in Professional Accountancy (PGP)
MSPA..........	Master of Science in Public Administration (GAGS)
MSPA..........	Master of Speech Pathology and Audiology (PGP)
MSPA..........	Member, Society of Pension Actuaries [*American Society of Pension Actuari es*] [*Designation awarded by*]
MSPA..........	Modified Sodium Polyacrylate [*Organic chemistry*]
MSP & SSM...	Minneapolis, St. Paul & Sault Ste. Marie Railway Co. (IIA)
MSPAW........	Miedzynarodowe Stowarzyszenie Przyjaciele Angkor Wat [*International Association of Friends of Angkor Wat*] [*Multinational association based in Poland*] (EAIO)
MSPB..........	Medical Specialist Preference Blank
MSPB..........	Merit Systems Protection Board [*Formerly, Civil Service Commission*]
MSPC..........	Manufacturer Standard Paint Color [*Motor vehicle specification*]
MSPC..........	Medical Specialist Corps [*Military*]
MSPC..........	MOPAR Scat Pack Club (EA)
MSPC..........	Multivariate Statistical Process Control
MSPCL.........	Lower Fort Garry National Historic Park, Parks Canada [*Parc Historique National Lower Fort Garry, Parcs Canada*] Selkirk, Manitoba [*Library symbol National Library of Canada*] (NLC)
MSPCP........	Mobile Source Pollution Control Program [*Environmental Protection Agency*]
MSPD.........	Master of Social Planning and Development (ADA)
MSPD	Matrix Solid-Phase Dispersion [*Analytical chemistry*]
MSPD.........	Maximum Speed
MSPD.........	Mulheres Portuguesas Social-Domocratas [*An association*] (EAIO)
MSPE.........	Maintenance Safety and Protection Equipment (AFIT)
MSPE.........	Master of Science in Petroleum Engineering (PGP)
MSPE.........	Master of Science in Physical Education
MSPE.........	Master Plate [*Tool*] (AAG)
MSpecEd	Master of Special Education
MSpEd	Master of Special Education
M Sp Ed	Master of Special Education (PGP)
MsPeM.......	Mississippi Gulf Coast Junior College, Perkinston, MS [*Library symbol Library of Congress*] (LCLS)
MSPEQ	Morgan Stanley Group [*Associated Press*] (SAG)
MSpeSJ.......	Saint Joseph's Abbey, Spencer, MA [*Library symbol Library of Congress*] (LCLS)
MS Pet E	Master of Science in Petroleum Engineering (PGP)
MSPetE.......	Master of Science in Petroleum Engineering (GAGS)
MSPetEng...	Master of Science in Petroleum Engineering (NADA)
MSP Ex.......	Master of Science in Exercise Physiology (PGP)
MSPEx.......	Master of Science in Physiology of Exercise (GAGS)
MSPF.........	Multispectral Photographic Facility
MSPFW.......	Multishot Portable Flame Weapon (DNAB)
MSPG	Magnetic Shock Pulse Generator (IAA)
MSPG	Master of Science in Psychology (PGP)
MSPG	Materiel Support Planning Guidance [*Military*] (AABC)
MSPG	Measure Specific Performance Guarantee [*Calculation*] (AAGC)
MSPG	MindSpring Enterprises [*NASDAQ symbol*] (TTSB)
MSPG	MindSpring Enterprises, Inc. [*NASDAQ symbol*] (SAG)
MSPGN.......	Mesangial Proliferative Glomerulonephritis [*Nephrology*]
MSPH	Master of Science in Poultry Husbandry
MSPH	Master of Science in Public Health
MsPh	Neshoba County Library, Philadelphia, MS [*Library symbol Library of Congress*] (LCLS)
MSPharm	Master of Science in Pharmacy (NADA)
MSPHE	Master of Science in Public Health Engineering
MSPH Ed	Master of Science in Public Health Education
MSPHR........	Master of Science in Pharmacy (PGP)
MS Phr	Master of Science in Pharmacy (PGP)
MS Phys Op...	Master of Science in Physiological Optics (PGP)
MsPi.........	Crosby Memorial Library, Picayune, MS [*Library symbol Library of Congress*] (LCLS)
MSPI..........	Modified Ship Plan Index
MSPIR	Master of Science in Personnel and Industrial Relations
MSPLT........	Master Source Program Library Tape [*Computer science*] (BUR)
MsPMF.......	United States Department of Commerce, National Marine Fisheries Service, Pascagoula, MS [*Library symbol Library of Congress*] (LCLS)
MSPM Rehab...	Master of Science in Physical Medicine and Rehabilitation (PGP)
MSPNGE......	Master of Science in Petroleum and Natural Gas Engineering (PGP)
MSPO........	Mercury Support Planning Office (MUGU)
MSPO........	Meridian Sports [*NASDAQ symbol*] (TTSB)
MSPO........	Meridian Sports, Inc. [*NASDAQ symbol*] (SAG)
MSPO........	Military Support Planning Officer [*Civil Defense*]
MSPO........	Mission System Project Office [*Military*] (CAAL)
MsPog	Harriette Person Memorial Library, Port Gibson, MS [*Library symbol Library of Congress*] (LCLS)
MSPoly.......	Master of Science in Polymers (GAGS)
MsPon	Dixie Regional Library, Pontotoc, MS [*Library symbol Library of Congress*] (LCLS)
MsPop	Poplarville Public Library, Poplarville, MS [*Library symbol Library of Congress*] (LCLS)
MSPP.........	Merit System Protection Plan
MSPP.........	Michigan Screening Profile of Parenting [*Psychology*]
MsPr.........	Jefferson Davis County Library, Prentiss, MS [*Library symbol Library of Congress*] (LCLS)
MSPR	Master Spares Positioning Resolver [*Data processing*]
MSPR	Medical System Program Review [*Army*] (RDA)
MSPR	Model State Packaging Regulation [*National Institute of Standards and Technology*]

MSPr	Morgan Stanley 9.36% Pfd [*NYSE symbol*] (TTSB)
MSPRB	Meteorological Satellite Program Review Board [*NOAA and NASA*]
MSPrB	Morgan Stanley 8.88% Dep Pfd [*NYSE symbol*] (TTSB)
MSPrC	Morgan Stanley 8.75% Dep Pfd [*NYSE symbol*] (TTSB)
MSPrD	Morgan Stanly 7.375% Dep Pfd [*NYSE symbol*] (TTSB)
MSPRS	Multispectral Photographic Reconnaissance (MCD)
MSPS	Maneuvering Satellite Propulsion System (MCD)
MSPS	Master of Science in Planning Studies (PGP)
MSPS	Master of Science in Psychological Services (GAGS)
MSPS	Megasample per Second (IAA)
MSPS	Mega Symbols per Second (MCD)
MSpS	Misioneros del Espiritu Santo [*Missionaries of the Holy Spirit*] [*Mexico*] (EAIO)
msps	Missionaries of the Holy Spirit (TOCD)
MSpS	Missionaries of the Holy Spirit (TOCD)
MSPS	Mobilization Station Planning System [*MTMC*] (TAG)
MSPS	Modular Space Power Station
MSPS	Multisource Processing System (MCD)
MSPS	Myocardial Stress Perfusion Scintigram [*Medicine*]
MSPT	Master of Science in Physical Therapy (GAGS)
MSpThy	Master of Speech Therapy (ADA)
MS Pw	Mississippi Power Co. [*Associated Press*] (SAG)
Msq	Masque [*Record label*]
MSQ	Minnesota Satisfaction Questionnaire
MSQ	Minsk [*Former USSR Airport symbol*] (OAG)
MSQ	Mosquito Construction Gold [*Vancouver Stock Exchange symbol*]
MSQT	Missile Ship Qualification Test [*Navy*] (NVT)
MSQT	Modified Ship Qualification Test
MsR	Capital Area Regional Library, Raymond, MS [*Library symbol Library of Congress*] (LCLS)
MSR	Egypt Air [*ICAO designator*] (FAAC)
MSR	Machine Status Register [*Computer science*] (OA)
MSR	Machine Stress Rated
MSR	Macrophage Scavenger Receptor [*Immunology*]
MSR	Magnetic Shift Register
MSR	Magnetic Silencing Range [*Navy*] (DOMA)
MSR	Magnetic Silencing Ranger (DWSG)
MSR	Magnetic Storage Ring [*Computer science*]
MSR	Magnetic Stripe Reader (IAA)
MSR	Magnetic Superresolution
MSR	Main Supply Road [*or Route*]
MSR	Makassar [*Sulawesi, Indonesia*] [*Airport symbol*] (AD)
MSR	Male Seniors [*International Bowhunting Organization*] [*Class equipment*]
MSR	Mammalian Selectivity Ratio (FFDE)
MSR	Management Systems Representative (MCD)
MSR	Manual Sliding Roof [*Automotive accessory*]
MSR	Manufacturing Service Request (MCD)
MSR	Manufacturing Specification Request (AAG)
MSR	Marketing Service Representative
MSR	Marketing Support Representative
MSR	Market Share Reporter [*A publication*]
MSR	Mark Sense Reading
MSR	Mark Sheet Reader [*Computer science*] (BUR)
MSR	Mass Storage Resident [*Computer science*] (IEEE)
MS (R)	Master of Science in Research
MSR	Master Stock Record (DNAB)
MSR	Material Status Report [*AEC*]
MSR	Maximum Steam Rate [*Nuclear energy*] (NRCH)
MSR	McDonnell Simulator Recorder [*McDonnell Douglas Corp.*] (MCD)
MSR	Mean Spring Rise [*Tides and currents*]
MSR	Mean Square Root (IAA)
MSR	Mechanized Storage and Retrieval [*Computer science*]
MSR	Medium Stocking Rate [*Agriculture*] (OA)
MSR	Member of the Society of Radiographers [*British*]
MSR	Membrane-Spanning Region [*Cytology*]
MSR	Memory Select Register (NITA)
MSR	Merchant Ship Reactor [*Navy*]
MSR	Message Has Been Misrouted [*Communications*]
MSR	Metal Seal Ring
MSR	Metalsmith, Ship Repair [*Navy*]
MSR	Meteorological Sounding Rocket
MSR	Micro Support Resource Corp. [*Atlanta, GA*]
MSR	Midwest Sunbeam Registry (EA)
MSR	Milestone Status Report [*Military*] (AFIT)
MSR	Mineral-Surface Roof [*Technical drawings*]
MSR	Mine Smelter and Refinery Databank [*Commodities Research Unit Ltd.*] [*Information service or system*] (CRD)
MSR	Minesweeper, Patrol [*Navy symbol Obsolete*]
MSR	Minesweeper River [*Navy symbol*] (VNW)
MSR	Minimum Sales Responsibility [*Automotive sales quotas*]
MSR	Minimum Security Requirement
MSR	Minimum Sustaining Rate (MCD)
MSR	Missile Scoring Reliability (MCD)
MSR	Missile Site RADAR [*Army*] (MCD)
MSR	Missile Site Range
MSR	Missile Surface RADAR (MCD)
MSR	Mission Success Ratio [*Military*] (CAAL)
MSR	Mission Support Recording [*Deep Space Instrumentation Facility, NASA*]
MSR	Mission Support Room [*NASA*] (KSC)
MSr	Mobile Sea Range (NVT)
MSR	Mode Status Register (IAA)
MSR	Modification Status Report (KSC)
MSR	Module Support Rack (NASA)
MSR	Module Support Rack
MSR	Moisture Separator Reheater (NRCH)
MSR	Molten-Salt Reactor
MSR	Monthly Status Report [*Navy*]
MSR	Montserrat [*ANSI three-letter standard code*] (CNC)
MSR	Movimiento Socialista Revolucionario [*Revolutionary Socialist Movement*] [*Panama*] [*Political party*] (PPW)
MSR	MSR Exploration [*AMEX symbol*] (TTSB)
MSR	MSR Exploration Ltd. [*AMEX symbol Toronto Stock Exchange symbol*] (SPSG)
MSR	MSR Exploration Ltd. [*Associated Press*] (SAG)
MSR	Multi-Carrier Station Radio [*or Remote*] Control Equipment (PDAA)
MSR	Multicomet Sample Return [*Space science*]
MSR	Multijunction Semiconductor Rectifier
MSR	Multispeed Repeater
MSR	Munster [*Germany Airport symbol*] (OAG)
MSR	Muscle Stretch Reflexes [*Medicine*] (DAVI)
MSR	Musicians for Social Responsibility (EA)
MSR	St. Louis Art Museum, St. Louis, MO [*OCLC symbol*] (OCLC)
MSRA	Master of Science in Recreation Administration (PGP)
MSRA	Middle States Regatta Association (EA)
MSRA	Midwest Ski Representatives Association (EA)
MSRA	Multiple Shoe Retailers' Association [*British*] (BI)
MSRadSc	Master of Science in Radiation Science (GAGS)
MSR/ASR	Main Supply Route/Alternative Supply Route (MCD)
MSRB	Margaret Sanger Research Bureau [*Defunct*] (EA)
MSRB	Metalsmith, Ship Repair, Blacksmith [*Navy*]
MSRB	Metrology Standards Requirements Board (ACII)
MSRB	Municipal Securities Rulemaking Board [*Securities and Exchange Commission*]
MSRC	Marine Sciences Research Center [*State University of New York at Stony Brook*] [*Research center*] (RCD)
MSRC	Marine Spill Response Corp. [*An association*]
MSRC	Master of Science in Resource Conservation (PGP)
MSRC	Materiel Studies Review Committee [*Army*]
MSRC	Medical and Surgical Relief Committee [*Defunct*] (EA)
MSRC	Metalsmith, Ship Repair, Coppersmith [*Navy*]
MSRD	Marine Services Research Division [*Now Coastal and Arctic Research Division*] (USDC)
MSRD	Marine Services Research Division [*Marine science*] (OSRA)
MSRD	Mean Square Relative Displacement [*Spectra*]
MSRD	Mobile Servicing and Repair Detachment [*Military British*]
MSRE	Master of Science in Real Estate and Urban Affairs
MSRE	Master of Science in Religious Education (PGP)
MSRE	Molten Salt Reactor Experiment
MSRec	Moon Signal Rejection Equipment (AFM)
MSRec	Master of Science in Recreation (NADA)
MSRet	Master of Science in Retailing (NADA)
MSRF	Metalsmith, Ship Repair, Forger-Anglesmith [*Navy*]
MSRF	Microwave Space Research Facility
MSRFT	Minesweeper Refresher Training [*Navy*] (NVT)
MSRG	Medieval Settlement Research Group [*British*] (DBA)
MSRG	Member of the Society of Remedial Gymnasts [*British*]
MSRG	Moated Sites Research Group (EA)
MSRG	Modular Shift Register Generator
MsRH	Hinds Junior College, Raymond, MS [*Library symbol Library of Congress*] (LCLS)
MSRI	Mathematical Sciences Research Institute [*University of California, Berkeley*] (PDAA)
MSRI	Mathematical Sciences Research Institute [*University of Minnesota*] (PDAA)
MsRi	Pine Forest Regional Library, Richton, MS [*Library symbol Library of Congress*] (LCLS)
MSRIS	Molten-Salt Reactor Information System
MSRK	Mathias-Soave-Redlich-Kwong [*Equation of state*]
MSRL	Marine Sciences Research Laboratory [*Canada*] (MSC)
MSRL	Mobile Secondary Reference Laboratory
MSRM	Main Steam Radiation Monitor (IEEE)
MSRMNT	Measurement
MSRMP	Master of Science in Radiological Medical Physics (PGP)
MSRNW	North-West Regional Library, Swan River, Manitoba [*Library symbol National Library of Canada*] (NLC)
MSRO	Missile System Requirements Outline (MCD)
MSRP	Management Sciences Research Project [*University of California*] (MCD)
MSRP	Manufacturer's Suggested Retail Price
MSRP	Massive Selective Retaliatory Power (NATG)
MSRP	Meteorological Sounding Rocket Program [*NASA*]
MSRP	Missile, Space and Range Pioneers (EA)
MSRP	Mission Support Real Property [*NASA*] (KSC)
MSRPP	Multidimensional Scale for Rating Psychiatric Patients
MS(R)PT	Master of Science (Research) in Physical Therapy (PGP)
MSR (R)	Member of the Society of Radiographers (Radiography) [*British*]
MSRR	Mission and System Requirements Review [*NASA*]
MSRS	Main Steam Radiation System (IEEE)
MSRS	Master of Science in Recreational Studies (PGP)
MSRS	Materiel System Requirements Specification [*Military*]
MSRS	Metalsmith, Ship Repair, Sheet Metal Worker [*Navy*]
MSRS	Meteoroid Shield Release System (MCD)
MSRS	Military Spending Research Services, Inc. [*Information service or system*] (IID)
MSRS	Missile Strike Reporting System
MSRS	Multiple Stylus Recording System (OA)
MSRSIM	Missile Site RADAR Simulation [*Missile system evaluation*] (RDA)
MSRT	Mean Supply Response Time

MSR (T) Member of the Society of Radiographers (Radiotherapy) [*British*]
MSRT Missile System Readiness Test (IEEE)
MSRT Mobile Subscriber Radio Terminal [*Army*]
MSRTE Misroute
MS-RTP Micelle-Stabilized Room-Temperature Phosphorescence
MSRTS Migrant Student Records Transfer System (GFGA)
MS Russ Morgan Stanley Russia & New Europe Fund, Inc. [*Associated Press*] (SAG)
MSRV Main Steam Relief Valve [*Nuclear energy*] (NRCH)
MSRY Masonry
mss Illuminated Manuscript (VRA)
MSS Magnetic Spark Spectrometer (PDAA)
MSS Magnetic Stereotaxis System [*Surgery*]
MSS Magnetic Storm Satellite [*Air Force/NASA*]
MSS Main Steam System [*Nuclear energy*] (NRCH)
MSS Main Support Structure (NRCH)
MSS Maintenance Standards Study (MCD)
MSS Maintenance Status System (MCD)
MSS Maintenance Support Schedule [*Air Force*] (AFM)
MSS Major Stationary Source [*Environmental Protection Agency*]
MSS Make Suitable Substitution
MSS Management Science Systems (IEEE)
MSS Management Statistics Subsystem (TEL)
MSS Management Summary Sheets (MCD)
MSS Management Supplier Selection (AAG)
MSS Management Support Staff [*Social Security Administration*]
MSS Management Support System (USDC)
MSS Management Support System [*Marine science*] (OSRA)
MSS Management Systems Study (MCD)
MSS Manned Space Station [*NASA*]
MSS Manual Safety Switch
MSS Manufacturers Standardization Society (AAGC)
MSS Manufacturers Standardization Society of the Valve and Fittings Industry (EA)
MSS Manuscripta [*Manuscripts*] [*Latin*]
MSS Manuscript, Signed
MSS MAP [*Manufacturing Automation Protocol*]/One System Software [*Industrial Networking, Inc.*]
MSS Marine Safety Services [*British*] (DCTA)
MSS Marital Satisfaction Scale [*Psychology*] (DAVI)
MSS Maritime Support Service
MSS Mary Stuart Society of America (EA)
MSS Massage
MSS Massena [*New York*] [*Airport symbol*] (OAG)
MSS Mass Storage Service [*Computer science*]
MSS Mass Storage System [*Computer science*]
MSS Mastergroup Surveillance System [*AT & T*]
MSS Master of Sanitary Science
MSS Master of Science in Safety (GAGS)
MSS Master of Selected Studies (PGP)
MSS Master of Social Science
MSS Master of Social Service
MSS Master of Social Service (GAGS)
MSS Master of Social Studies
MSS Master of Sport Science (GAGS)
MSS Master Station Subsystem
MSS Master Surveillance Station [*Air Force*]
MSS Master Switching Station (MCD)
MSS Master System Schedule (MCD)
MSS Mayo Smith Society (EA)
MSS Mean Solar Second (IAA)
MSS Measurement Specialities, Inc. [*AMEX symbol*] (SAG)
MSS Measurement Specialties [*AMEX symbol*] (TTSB)
MSS Measurement Standard Sensitivity (DICI)
MSS Mechanical and Structural Subsystems (MCD)
MSS Mechanically Separated Spleen [*Food technology*]
MSS Mechanical Speed Switch
MSS Mechanical Support System (MCD)
MSS Medical Service School [*Air Force*] (AFM)
MSS Medical Social Services
MSS Medical Superintendents' Society (DAVI)
MSS Medium Survey Ship [*Marine science*] (MSC)
MSS Megasample per Second (IAA)
MSS Member of the Statistical Society [*British*] (ROG)
MSS Memory System Security [*Computer science*] (ECII)
MSS Men's Social Services [*Salvation Army*]
MSS Mental Status Schedule [*Psychology*]
MSS Message Support Subsystem (MCD)
MSS Message Switching Station [*Telecommunications*] (CET)
MSS Message Switching System
MSS Messtetten [*Federal Republic of Germany*] [*Seismograph station code, US Geological Survey*] (SEIS)
MSS Metal Spring Seal
MSS Metastable State (IAA)
MSS Meteorological Satellite Section
MSS Meter Stamp Society (EA)
MSS Methylprednisolone Sodium Succinate [*Antirheumatoid compound*]
MSS Metropolitan Speleological Society [*Australia*]
MSS Mexican-Spanish Speaking (OICC)
MSS Microwave Switching Station
MSS Midcourse Surveillance System (MCD)
MSS Midwest Sociological Society (AEBS)
MSS Military Security Service [*RVNAF*]
MSS Military Supply Standards [*DoD*] (MCD)
MSS Mine Search System [*Navy*] (DOMA)

MSS Minesweeper, Special [*Device*] [*Navy symbol*]
MSS Miniature Signaling System [*Railway term*] (DCTA)
MSS Miniature Stepping Switch
MSS Ministry of Social Security [*British*]
MSS Minnesota Satisfactoriness Scale [*Job performance test*]
MSS Minor Surgery Suite [*Medicine*] (DAVI)
MSS Missile Safety Set (IAA)
MSS Missile Security Squadron
MSS Missile Select Switch
MSS Missile Sight System [*Army*]
MSS Missile Stabilization System
MSS Missile Station Select
MSS Missile Subsystem
MSS Missile Support Stand (MCD)
MSS Mission Simulator System
MSS Mission Specialist Station [*NASA*] (NASA)
MSS Mission Status Summary (MCD)
MSS Mission Support Site [*Army*]
MSS Mission System Simulator (MCD)
MSS Mississauga Public Library [*UTLAS symbol*]
MSS Mixed Spectrum Superheater [*Nuclear energy*]
MSS Mobile Satellite Service
MSS Mobile Satellite System (DA)
MSS Mobile Service Structure (KSC)
MSS Mobile Servicing System [*For space station*]
MSS Mobility Subsystem (KSC)
MSS Modelling and Simulation Studies [*Marine science*] (MSC)
MSS Model Skin Surface [*Artificial skin*]
MSS Modern Satellite Systems, Inc. [*Whitehouse Station, NJ*] [*Telecommunications*] (TSSD)
MSS Mode Selection Switch (KSC)
MSS Mode Sickness Susceptibility (KSC)
MSS Modified Scram System [*Nuclear energy*] (NRCH)
MSS Modular Space Station
MSS Moored Sonobuoy System (MCD)
MSS Moored Surveillance System [*To detect and destroy enemy submarines*] [*Navy*]
MSS Morris Air Service [*ICAO designator*] (FAAC)
MSS Motion Sickness Susceptibility (MCD)
MSS Motor Surveillance Service [*MTMC*] (TAG)
MSS Movement Shorthand Society [*Later, Center for Sutton Movement Writing*] (EA)
MSS Mucus-Stimulating Substance
MSS Multibeam Steering System
MSS Multi-LAN Storage System [*Computer science*] (HGAA)
MSS Multiple Sclerosis Society [*British*]
MSS Multiple Selling Service (OA)
MSS Multiple Steady States [*Chemical engineering*]
MSS Multispectral Scanner [*or Sensor*]
MSS Multispectral Scanner System
MSS Multitask Single Stream System (NITA)
MSS Muscular Subaortic Stenosis [*Cardiology*]
MSS Music Story Series [*A publication*]
MSS Special Minesweeper [*Navy symbol*]
MSs Swansea Free Public Library, Swansea, MA [*Library symbol*] [*Library of Congress*] (LCLS)
MSSA Maintenance Supply Services Agency (NATG)
MSSA Manchester Scales of Social Adaptation [*Psychology*]
MSSA Master of Science in Social Administration (GAGS)
MSSA Master Safeguards and Security Agreements (DOMA)
MSSA Midland Steel Stockholders Association [*British*] (DBA)
MSSA Military Selective Service Act (OICC)
MSSA Military Subsistence Supply Agency [*Later, Defense Subsistence Supply Center*]
MSsA Missionaries of the Holy Apostles [*Roman Catholic men's religious order*]
mssa Missionaries of the Holy Apostles (TOCD)
MSSA Missionary Servants of St. Anthony [*Roman Catholic women's religious order*]
MSSA Modification of Special Service Authorization [*FCC*] (NTCM)
MSS & H Master of Science in Speech and Hearing
MSSanE Master of Science in Sanitary Engineering
MSS AS Multistatic Sonar System Acoustic Source (DOMA)
MSSB Missile Servicing and Storage Building [*Military*] (IAA)
MSSC Main Storage Stock Control [*Computer science*] (IAA)
MSSC Management System for Support Contracts [*Social Security Administration*]
MSSC Mass Storage System Communications (NITA)
MSSC Mass Storage System Communicator [*Computer science*] (IBMDP)
MSSC Mass Storage System Control [*Computer science*] (BUR)
MS Sc Master of Sanitary Science
MS Sc Master of Social Science
MSSc Master of Surgical Science, University of Dundee [*British*] (DBQ)
MSSc Medium SEAL [*Sea, Air, and Land*] Support Craft [*Navy symbol*]
MSSC Metropolitan School Study Council [*Columbia University*] (AEE)
MSSC Military Standard and Specification Committee
MSSC Military Store Staff Corps [*British military*] (DMA)
MSSC Missile System Software Center
MSSC Missionary Society of St. Columban (EAIO)
MSSC Mobile Service Switching Center
MSSCB Missionary Sisters of St. Charles Borromeo (TOCD)
MSSCC Military Space Surveillance Control Center (MUGU)
msscc Missionaries of the Sacred Hearts of Jesus and Mary (TOCD)
MSSCC Missionaries of the Sacred Hearts of Jesus and Mary (TOCD)

MSSCC .... Missionarii a Sacris Cordibus Jesus et Mariae [*Missionaries of the Sacred Hearts of Jesus and Mary*] [*Roman Catholic men's religious order*]
MSSCC .... Multicolor Spin-Scan Cloudcover Camera
MSSCE .... Mixed Spectrum Superheater Critical Experiment [*Nuclear energy*]
MSSCS .... Manned Space Station Communications System [*NASA*]
MSSD .... Model Secondary School for the Deaf (EA)
MSSE .... Master of Science in Sanitary Engineering
MSSE .... Master of Science in Secondary Education of Students (who are Deaf or Hard of Hearing)
MSSE .... Missile System Support Equipment
MSS/EC ...... Missile System Supervisor/Engagement Controller [*Military*] (CAAL)
MSSEng ...... Master of Science in Sanitary Engineering (NADA)
MSSG .... Marine Expeditionary Unit Service Support Group (DOMA)
MSSG .... Message
MSSH .... Master of Science in Speech and Hearing (PGP)
MSSH .... Springfield Hospital, Medical Center Library, Springfield, MA [*Library symbol Library of Congress*] (LCLS)
MSSI .... Master of Science in Strategic Intelligence (PGP)
MSSJ .... Missionary Servants of St. Joseph [*Roman Catholic women's religious order*]
MSSJ .... Multiple Subsonic Jet
MSSL .... Management Systems Summary List
MSSL .... Master of Science in Speech and Language (PGP)
MSSL .... Missile System Stockage List (AFIT)
MSSL .... Mullard Space Science Laboratory [*University of London*] (PDAA)
MSSM .... Mars Spinning Support Module [*NASA*] (KSC)
MSSM .... Master of Science in Science Management (PGP)
MSSM .... Master of Science in Systems Management (PGP)
MSSM .... Missionary Sisters of the Society of Mary [*Italy*] (EAIO)
MsSM .... Mississippi State University, State College, MS [*Library symbol Library of Congress*] (LCLS)
MSSM .... Mount Sinai School of Medicine [*New York*] (PDAA)
MSSM .... Multiple-Sine-Slit Microdensitometer (PDAA)
MSSMS .... Munitions Section of Strategic Missile Squadron (AAG)
MSSN .... Mean Square Signal-to-Noise (IAA)
MSSN .... Mission
MSSN .... Mission
MSSNRY ..... Missionary
MSSNSW ..... Multiple Sclerosis Society of New South Wales [*Australia*]
MSSP .... International Association of Marble, Slate and Stone Polishers, Rubbers and Sawyers, Tile and Marble Setters' Helpers, and Marble Mosaic and Terrazzo Workers' Helpers [*Later, Tile, Marble, Terrazzo Finishers, Shopworkers, and Granite Cutters International Union*] (EA)
MSSP .... Miscellaneous Small Special Projects (AAG)
MSSP .... Missionary Society of Saint Paul [*Australia*]
MSSp .... Mission Sisters of the Holy Spirit [*Roman Catholic religious order*]
MSSP .... Model Seafood Surveillance Project [*National Marine Fisheries Service*]
MSSPA .... Master of Speech Pathology and Audiology (GAGS)
MSSPA .... Missionary Society of St. Paul the Apostle (EA)
MSSPC .... Missionary Sisters of St. Peter Claver (EA)
MS Sp Ed ... Master of Science in Special Education (PGP)
MS-SPRING... Multiplex-Section, Shared-Protection Rings
MSSQ .... Mission Support Squadron
MSSQ .... Multiple Sclerosis Society of Queensland [*Australia*]
MSSR .... Mars Soil [*or Surface*] Sample Return
MSSR .... Medical Society for the Study of Radiesthesia (EA)
MSSR .... Mixed Spectrum Superheat Reactor
MSSR .... Mobility, Survivability, Sizing Recommendations (MCD)
MSSR .... Monopulse Secondary Surveillance RADAR (DA)
MSSS .... Main Steam Supply System [*Nuclear energy*] (NRCH)
MSSS .... Maintenance and Service Subsystem (IAA)
MSSS .... Maintenance Supply Services System (NATG)
MSSS .... Manned Space Station Simulator [*NASA*] (MUGU)
MSSS .... Manned Static Space Simulator
MSSS .... Manuscripts, Signed
MSSS .... Mass Spectral Search System [*National Bureau of Standards, Environmental Protection Agency, and National Institutes of Health*] [*Database*]
MSSS .... Master of Science in Social Science
MSSS .... Missionary Sisters of the Most Blessed Sacrament [*Roman Catholic religious order*]
MSSS .... Missionary Sisters of the Most Blessed Sacrament (TOCD)
MSSS .... Mobile Spectrum Search System
MSSS .... Mobile Submarine Simulator System (DWSG)
MSSS .... Multiple-Start Systematic Sampling [*Statistics*]
MSSS .... San Salvador/Ilopango Internacional [*El Salvador*] [*ICAO location identifier*] (ICLI)
MSSSM-MMS... Missionary Sisters of the Society of Saint Mary - Marist Missionary Sisters (EA)
MSSST .... Meeting Street School Screening Test [*Used to detect learning disabilities*]
MSSSW .... Mass Spectral Search System-Wiley [*Cornell University*] [*Database*]
MSST .... Manufacturing Standards and Specifications for Textbooks
MSST .... Master of Science in Science Teaching
MSST .... Master of Science in Science Teaching (GAGS)
MSST .... Mean Sea Surface Temperature
MSST .... Meldesammelstelle [*Message Center*] [*German military - World War II*]
MSST .... Member of the Society of Surveying Technicians [*British*] (DBQ)
MSST .... Ministry of State for Science and Technology [*Canada*]
MSST .... Missionary Servants of the Most Holy Trinity [*Roman Catholic men's religious order*]

MSST .... Multiple Sclerosis Society of Tasmania [*Australia*]
MsSt .... Oktibbeha County Library System, Starkville, MS [*Library symbol Library of Congress*] (LCLS)
MSST .... Springfield Technical Community College, Springfield, MA [*Library symbol Library of Congress*] (LCLS)
MSStat.......... Master of Science in Statistics (GAGS)
MS Stat ...... Master of Science in Statistics (PGP)
MSSTC........ Mobile Service Structure Test Conductor (KSC)
MSStEng...... Master of Science in Structural Engineering (NADA)
MsStL .... Oktibbeha County Library System, Starkville, MS [*Library symbol*] [*Library of Congress*] (LCLS)
MSSTM........ Military Space Systems Technology Model (MCD)
MSSU .... Meteorology on Stamps Study Unit [*American Topical Association*] (EA)
MSSU .... Midstream Specimen of Urine [*Medicine*]
MSSU .... Mississippi State University (PDAA)
MsSu .... Sunflower County Library, Sunflower, MS [*Library symbol Library of Congress*] (LCLS)
MS Surg ..... Master of Science in Surgery (PGP)
MSSV.......... Maize Sterile Stunt Virus [*Plant pathology*]
MSSV.......... Maximum Safe Sampling Volume [*Analytical chemistry*]
MSSV.......... Multiple Sclerosis Society of Victoria [*Australia*]
MSSVD .... Medical Society for the Study of Venereal Diseases [*Leeds, England*] (EAIO)
MSSVFI....... Manufacturers Standardization Society of the Valve and Fittings Industry (EA)
MSSW .... Magnetostatic Surface Wave [*Telecommunications*] (TEL)
MSSW .... Master of Science in Social Work
MSSWA ..... Multiple Sclerosis Society of Western Australia
MS Sy Sc... Master of Science in Systems Science (PGP)
MST .... Aeroamistad SA de CV [*Mexico ICAO designator*] (FAAC)
MST .... Association of Maximum Service Telecasters (EA)
MsT .... Lee-Itawamba Regional Library, Tupelo, MS [*Library symbol Library of Congress*] (LCLS)
MST .... Maastricht [*Netherlands*] [*Airport symbol*] (OAG)
MST .... Machinery Safety Tag
MST .... Machine Shock Test
MST .... Machine Steel
MST .... Magnetostrictive Transducer
MST .... Maintenance Standard Tests [*Military*]
MST .... Maintenance Support Team (MCD)
MST .... Management Survey Team (AAG)
MST .... Manifold Surface Temperature [*Automotive engineering*]
MST .... Marconi Self-Tuning (IAA)
MST .... Mass Spectrometer Tube
MST .... Mass Storage Task [*Computer science*] (NOAA)
MST .... Master (MCD)
MST .... Master of Sacred Theology
MST .... Master of Sacred Theology (GAGS)
MST .... Master of Science in Taxation (GAGS)
MST .... Master of Science in Taxation
MST .... Master of Science in Teaching
MST .... Master of Science in Tourism (GAGS)
MST .... Master of Science Teaching (GAGS)
MST .... Master of Science Technology (PGP)
MST .... Master of Secondary Teaching (GAGS)
MST .... Master of Speech Therapy (GAGS)
M St. .... Master of Statistics
MSt .... Master of Studies, University of Oxford [*British*] (DBQ)
MST .... Master of Systems Technology (PGP)
MST .... Master of Teaching
MST .... Maximum Service Telecasters
MST .... Maximum Summer Temperature [*Climatology*]
MST .... Mean Selected Temperature
MST .... Mean Solar Time
MST .... Mean Survival Time
MST .... Mean Swell Time [*Botulism test*] [*Food analysis*]
MST .... Measurement
MST .... Measurement Status Table (NASA)
MST .... Mechanics Support Team [*Military*] (GFGA)
MST .... Medial Superior Temporal [*Brain Anatomy*]
MST .... Median Survival Time
MST .... Media Systems Technology (HGAA)
MST .... Medium-Scale Technology
MST .... Medium STOL [*Short Takeoff and Landing*] Transport [*Aircraft*]
MST .... Memotron Storage Tube
MST .... Mercantile Stores [*NYSE symbol*] (TTSB)
MST .... Mercantile Stores Co., Inc. [*NYSE symbol*] (SPSG)
MST .... Mercury System Test [*NASA*]
MST .... Mesosphere-Stratosphere-Troposhere (USDC)
MST .... Mesosphere-Stratosphere-Troposphere [*Marine science*] (OSRA)
MST .... Message Status Table (MCD)
MST .... Microsecond Trip
MST .... Microwave Satellite Technologies, Inc. [*Wellington, NJ*] (TSSD)
MST .... Midsummer Time
MST .... Military Science Training
MST .... Military Shipping Tag
MST .... Miniature Situations Test (EDAC)
MST .... Minimal Spanning Tree [*Computer science*]
MST .... Minimum Spawning Time [*Pisciculture*]
MST .... Ministry, Society, and Theology [*A publication*] (APTA)
MST .... Missile Surveillance Technology (MCD)
MST .... Missile System Test
MST .... Mission Simulator Test (MCD)
MST .... Mission Support Team (MCD)

MST	Mistral Resources Ltd. [*Vancouver Stock Exchange symbol*]
MST	Mobile Service Tower [*Aerospace*]
MST	Mobile Strike Team
MST	Mobile Support Team (NVT)
MST	Modal Survey Test (MCD)
MST	Module Service Tool (NASA)
MST	Module Service Tool
MST	Moisture-Proof Heat-Sealing Transparent [*Flexography*] (DGA)
MST	Monolithic Systems Technology
M St	More's Notes on Stair's Institutes of Scotland [*A publication*] (ILCA)
MST	Mostar [*Yugoslavia*] [*Seismograph station code, US Geological Survey Closed*] (SEIS)
MST	Mountain Standard Time
MST	Movimento Sem Terra [*Political party*] [*Brazil*]
MST	Multimode Storage Tube
MST	Multisystem Test [*Military*]
MST	Mutual Security Treaty (MCD)
MST	St. Cloud State University, St. Cloud, MN [*OCLC symbol*] (OCLC)
MST3K	Mystery Science Theater 3000 [*Cable television program*]
MSTA	Manufacturers Surgical Trade Association [*Later, HIMA*] (EA)
MSTA	Master of Science in Statistics (PGP)
MSTA	Master Tape (AAG)
MSTA	Member of the Swimming Teachers' Association [*British*] (DBQ)
MSTA	Mumps Skin Test Antigen [*Clinical chemistry*]
MSTACCMB	Master Aircraft Crewman Badge [*Military decoration*] (GFGA)
MSTAN	Modal Stamen Number per Flower [*Botany*]
MST & E	Multiservice Test and Evaluation [*Military*]
MSTAR	MLRS [*Multiple Launch Rocket System*] Smart Tactical Rocket [*USA*]
MSTARAVB	Master Army Aviator Badge [*Military decoration*] (GFGA)
MSTAT	Marine Safety Training and Assistance Team [*RSPA*] (TAG)
M Stat	Master of Statistics (PGP)
MStat	Master of Statistics
mstb	Mastaba (VRA)
MSTB	Mission Simulator and Training Building
MS TBR	Morgan Stanley Group [*Associated Press*] (SAG)
MSTC	Management Systems Training Council [*British*]
MSTC	Manned Spacecraft Test Center [*NASA*] (KSC)
MSTC	Manufacturing Systems and Technology Center [*Baltimore, MD*] [*Westinghouse Electric Corp.*]
MSTC	Maryland State Teachers College
MSTC	Massachusetts State Teachers College
MSTC	Master of Science in Telecommunications (PGP)
MSTC	Mastic
MSTC	Microwave Sensitivity Time Control [*Circuit*]
MSTC	Midwest Securities Trust Co.
MSTCS(GB)	Member of the Society of Thoracic and Cardiovascular Surgeons (Great Britain)
MSTD	Master Steward [*Marine Corps*]
MSTD	Member of the Society of Typographic Designers (DGA)
MSTDIVB	Master Diver Badge [*Military decoration*] (GFGA)
MSTE	Master of Science in Technical Education (GAGS)
MSTE	Master of Science in Transportation Engineering (GAGS)
M St E	Master of Structural Engineering
MSTE	Steinbach Public Library, Manitoba [*Library symbol National Library of Canada*] (NLC)
MS (T Ed)	Master of Science in Teacher Education
MSTEd	Master of Science in Technical Education (GAGS)
MST Ed	Master of Science in Technical Education (PGP)
MSTEL	Member of the Society of Telegraph Engineers, London [*British*] (ROG)
M St Eng	Master of Structural Engineering
MSTEODBAD	Master Explosive Ordnance Disposal Badge [*Military decoration*] (GFGA)
M-STEP	Multi-State Teacher Education Project
MS Text	Master of Science in Textiles (PGP)
MSText	Master of Science in Textiles (GAGS)
MS Text Chem	Master of Science in Textile Chemistry (PGP)
MSTFA	(Methyl)trimethylsilyltrifluoroacetamide [*Organic chemistry*]
MSTFLSB	Master Flight Surgeon Badge [*Military decoration*] (GFGA)
MSTG	Mass Storage Task Group [*CODASYL*]
MstG	Master Glaziers Karate International [*Associated Press*] (SAG)
MSTG	Material Safety Task Group [*Air Force*] (AFM)
MSTG	Melbourne Screen and Theatre Guild [*Australia*]
MSTG	Mustang Software [*NASDAQ symbol*] (TTSB)
MSTG	Mustang Software, Inc. [*NASDAQ symbol*] (SAG)
MSTGA	Library Allard, St. Georges, Manitoba [*Library symbol National Library of Canada*] (BIB)
MstGlaz	Master Glaziers Karate International [*Associated Press*] (SAG)
MSTGP	Material Safety Task Group [*Air Force*]
MSTh	Mesothorium [*Radioelement*]
MsTI	Itawamba Junior College, Tupelo Campus, Tupelo, MS [*Library symbol Library of Congress*] (LCLS)
MSTI	Miniature Sensor Technology Integration [*Orbital satellites*]
M ST J	Ordinary Member of the Order of the Order of St. John of Jerusalem
MSTJ	Public Library, St. James-Assiniboia, Manitoba [*Library symbol National Library of Canada*] (NLC)
MSTL	Military Subvention Type Lorry [*British*]
MSTL	Minneapolis & St. Louis Railway Co. [*Later, MSL Industries, Inc.*] [*AAR code*]
MSTLAB	Materials and Science Toxicology Laboratory [*University of Tennessee*] [*Research center*] (RCD)
MSTLY	Mostly [*NWS*] (FAAC)
MSTM	Master of Science in Teaching Mathematics (PGP)
MSTM	Master of Science in Technology Management (GAGS)
MSTM	Master of Science in Tropical Medicine (GAGS)

MSTM	Mennonite Village Museum, Steinbach, Manitoba [*Library symbol National Library of Canada*] (NLC)
MSTM	Missile Service Test Model [*Military*] (IAA)
MS TMX	Morgan Stanley Group, Inc. [*Associated Press*] (SAG)
MSTO	Main-Sequence Turnoff [*Stellar physics*]
MSTO	Military System Training Organization (SAA)
MStoc	Stockbridge Library Association, Stockbridge, MA [*Library symbol Library of Congress*] (LCLS)
MStocA	Austen Riggs Center, Inc., Stockbridge, MA [*Library symbol Library of Congress*] (LCLS)
MSTOL	Medium-Slow Takeoff and Landing
MSTOS	South Interlake Regional Library, Stonewall, Manitoba [*Library symbol National Library of Canada*] (NLC)
MsToT	Tougaloo College, Tougaloo, MS [*Library symbol Library of Congress*] (LCLS)
MSTP	Maintenance Support Test Package [*Military*]
MStp	Maize Stripe [*Plant pathology*]
MSTP	Manual System Training Program (SAA)
MSTP	Master Template
MSTP	Medical Scientist Training Program [*National Institutes of Health*]
MStP & A	Minneapolis, St. Paul & Ashland Railway
MSTP & SSM	Minneapolis, St. Paul & Sault Ste. Marie Railway Co.
MSTPHC	Multistop Time-to-Pulse Height Converter [*NASA*]
MSTPJ	Jolys Regional Library, St. Pierre, Manitoba [*Library symbol National Library of Canada*] (NLC)
MSTPRCHT	Master Parachutist Badge [*Military decoration*] (GFGA)
MStpV	Maize Stripe Virus [*Plant pathology*]
MSTR	[*The*] Massena Terminal Railroad Co. [*AAR code*]
MSTR	Master
MSTR	Master
MSTR	Master
mstr	Master (VRA)
MSTR	Moisture [*NWS*] (FAAC)
MSTR	Morningstar Group [*NASDAQ symbol*] (SAG)
MSTR	Multivariable Self-Tuning Regulator [*Control technology*]
MSTR	Ste-Rose Regional Library, Manitoba [*Library symbol National Library of Canada*] (NLC)
MSTrans	Master of Science in Transportation (NADA)
MSTransE	Master of Science in Transportation Engineering (NADA)
MSTRE	Moisture (MSA)
MSTS	Manifold Surface Temperature Sensor [*Automotive engineering*]
MSTS	McDonnell Scrap Tool System [*McDonnell Douglas Corp.*] (MCD)
MSTS	Mean Standard Toxicity Score (MCD)
MSTS	Microprocessor Spark Timing System
MSTS	Military Sea Transportation Service [*Later, MSC*] [*Navy*]
MSTS	Missile Simulator Test Set (MCD)
MSTS	Missile Static Test Site [*Air Force*]
MSTS	Missile Station Test Set (MCD)
MSTS	Missile Subsystem Test Set [*Military*] (CAAL)
MSTS	Multisubscriber Time-Sharing Systems [*Computer system*]
MSTS	Multisystem Training System
MSTSFE	Military Sea Transport Service, Far East
MSTSL	Master of Science in Teaching a Second Language (GAGS)
MSTSO	Military Sea Transportation Service Office [*Obsolete*]
MSTU	Military Sea Transport Union
MStuO	Old Sturbridge Village Library, Sturbridge, MA [*Library symbol Library of Congress*] (LCLS)
MSTV	Maize Stripe Virus [*Plant pathology*]
MSTV	Manned Supersonic Test Vehicle (MCD)
MSTV	Master-Scale Television
MsTy	Walthall County Library, Tylertown, MS [*Library symbol Library of Congress*] (LCLS)
MSu	Goodnow Library, Sudbury, MA [*Library symbol Library of Congress*] (LCLS)
MSU	Main Storage Unit [*Computer science*]
MSU	Main Switching Unit [*Telecommunications*] (NITA)
MSU	Maintenance and Status Unit [*Telecommunications*] (TEL)
MSU	Maintenance Service Unit (IAA)
MSU	Maintenance Signal Unit [*Telecommunications*] (TEL)
MSU	Malaria Survey Unit [*Army World War II*]
MSU	Management Signal Unit [*Telecommunications*] (TEL)
MSU	Management Support Unit
MSU	Management Systems Unit
MSU	Maple Sugar [*or Syrup*] Urine [*Medicine*] (DMAA)
MSU	Marysvale [*Utah*] [*Seismograph station code, US Geological Survey*] (SEIS)
MSU	Maseru [*Lesotho*] [*Airport symbol*] (OAG)
MSU	Masonic Study Unit [*American Topical Association*] (EA)
MSU	Mass Storage Unit [*Computer science*] (NASA)
MSU	Material Salvage Unit
MSU	Mathematical Study Unit [*American Topical Association*] (EA)
MSU	Measuring Stimuli Units (NASA)
MSU	Medical Service Unit [*Air Force*] (AFM)
MSU	Medical Studies Unit (DAVI)
MSU	Medical Subjects Unit [*American Topical Association*] (EA)
MSU	Memory Service Unit [*Computer science*]
MSU	Memphis State University [*Tennessee*]
MSU	Message Switching Unit
MSU	Meteorology on Stamps Study Unit [*American Topical Association*] (EA)
MSU	Michigan State University [*East Lansing*]
MSU	Microelectronics Support Unit [*Department of Education and Science*] (NITA)
MSU	Microwave Sounding Unit [*Telecommunications*] (TEL)
MSU	Midstream Specimen of Urine [*Medicine*]

MSU............	Mill Sawyers' Union [*British*]
msu	Mississippi [*MARC country of publication code Library of Congress*] (LCCP)
MSU............	Mobile Signals Unit [*British military*] (DMA)
MSU............	MODEM-Sharing Unit [*Telecommunications*] (TSSD)
MSU............	Modern Sharing Unit [*Computer science*] (OA)
MSU............	Mode Selector Unit
MSU............	Monosodium Urate [*Organic chemistry*]
MSU............	Montana State University [*Bozeman*]
MSU............	Morgan Stan Fin 7.82% Cp Uts [*NYSE symbol*] (TTSB)
MSU............	Morgan Stanley Financial [*NYSE symbol*] (SPSG)
MSU............	Morgan State University, Baltimore, MD [*OCLC symbol*] (OCLC)
MSU............	Motor-Switching Unit (MCD)
MSU............	Multiblock Synchronization Signal Unit [*Telecommunications*] (TEL)
MSU............	Multiple Signal Unit [*Telecommunications*] (TEL)
MSU............	Murray State University [*Kentucky*]
MsU............	University of Mississippi, University, MS [*Library symbol Library of Congress*] (LCLS)
MSUAG........	Michigan State University Advisory Group [*Contracted with the Government of South Vietnam to provide-civilian training*] (VNW)
MSU Business Topics...	Michigan State University Business Topics [*A publication*] (DLA)
MSUCLE	Missouri State University Continuing Legal Education (DLA)
MSUD	Maple Sugar [*or Syrup*] Urine Disease [*Medicine*]
MSUD	Master of Science in Urban Design (GAGS)
MSUDC.......	Michigan State University Discrete Computer
MSUDFSG...	MSUD [*Maple Syrup Urine Disease*] Family Support Group (EA)
MSUESM	Master of Science in Urban Environmental Systems Management (PGP)
MSuL..........	Goodnow Library, Sudbury, MA [*Library symbol*] [*Library of Congress*] (LCLS)
MSUL..........	Medical Schools of the University of London (DAS)
MsU-L.........	University of Mississippi, Law School, University, MS [*Library symbol Library of Congress*] (LCLS)
MSUM	Mission Society for United Methodists (EA)
MSUM	Monosodium Urate Monohydrate [*Organic chemistry*]
MsU-M........	University of Mississippi, Medical Center, Jackson, MS [*Library symbol Library of Congress*] (LCLS)
MSUP	Mouvement pour la Solidarite, l'Union et le Progres [*Benin*] [*Political party*] (EY)
MsU-P	University of Mississippi, School of Pharmacy, University, MS [*Library symbol Library of Congress*] (LCLS)
M Sur	Master of Surgery
MSurg.........	Master of Surgery (BABM)
MSurg.........	Master of Surgery (DAVI)
MSurgery.....	Master of Surgery (NADA)
MSurv	Master of Surveying
MSurvMap ...	Master of Surveying and Mapping
MSurvSc......	Master of Surveying Science
MSUS	Mouvement Socialiste d'Union Senegalaise [*Senegalese Socialist Movement*] [*Political party*]
MSUSM	Medical Society of the United States and Mexico (EA)
MSUS/PALS...	Minnesota State Universities System Project for Automated Library Systems [*Mankato State University Library*] [*Mankato, MN*] [*Information service or system*]
MSuSR	Sperry Rand Research Center, Sudbury, MA [*Library symbol Library of Congress*] (LCLS)
MSV............	Catskills/Sullivan County [*New York*] [*Airport symbol Obsolete*] (OAG)
MSV............	Magnetically Supported Vehicle
MSV............	Maintenance Support Vessel
MSV............	Maize Streak Virus [*Plant pathology*]
MSV............	Manned Space Vehicle [*NASA*] (AAG)
MSV............	Martian Surface Vehicle
MSV............	Mass Stimulated Vehicles (MCD)
MSV............	Mass Storage Volume
MSV............	Maximal Sustained Level of Ventilation [*Medicine*]
MSV............	Mean Square Velocity
MSV............	Mean Square Voltage (NRCH)
MSV............	Meteor Simulation Vehicle (SAA)
mSv............	Millisievert [*Radiation dose*]
MSV............	Miniature Solenoid Valve
MSV............	Missionary Sisters of Verona [*Roman Catholic religious order*]
MSV............	Mississippi & Skuna Valley Railroad Co. [*AAR code*]
MSV............	Mobile Surface Vehicle (AAG)
MSV............	Molecular Solution Volume
MSV............	Molinia Streak Virus
MSV............	Moloney Sarcoma Virus (AAMN)
MSV............	Monitored Sine Vibration [*Test*] (MCD)
MSV............	Monticello, NY [*Location identifier FAA*] (FAAL)
MSV............	Morgan Stan Fin 9% Cp Uts [*NYSE symbol*] (TTSB)
MSV............	Morgan Stanley Finance Markets Ltd. Capital Units [*NYSE symbol*] (SAG)
MSV............	Mouse Sarcoma Virus
MSV............	Multifunctional Service Vessel [*Off-shore drilling technology*]
MSV............	Multipurpose Support Vessel [*Offshore drilling*]
MSV............	Murine Sarcoma Virus
MSV............	Musica sul Velluto (EAIO)
MsV............	Vicksburg Public Library, Vicksburg, MS [*Library symbol Library of Congress*] (LCLS)
MSVA..........	Magnetic Speed Variable Assist [*General Motors*] [*Power steering*]
MSVC..........	Mass Storage Volume Control [*Computer science*] (BUR)
MSVC..........	Master of Vocational Counseling (GAGS)
MSVC..........	Mount St. Vincent College [*New York*]
MSVCS	Missile Sight Video Camera Systems (MCD)

MSVD	Missile and Space Vehicle Department [*NASA*] (KSC)
MsVE	United States Army, Corps of Engineers, Waterways Experiment Station, Vicksburg, MS [*Library symbol Library of Congress*] (LCLS)
MSVI..........	Mass Storage Volume Inventory [*Computer science*] (IAA)
MSV(M).......	Murine Sarcoma Virus (Moloney)
MSVO	Missile and Space Vehicle Office [*NASA*] (IAA)
MsVO	Old Court House Museum Library, Vicksburg, MS [*Library symbol Library of Congress*] (LCLS)
MSVP	Master Shuttle Verification Plan (MCD)
MSVR	Mandatory Securities Valuation Reserve [*National Association of Insurance Commissioners*]
MSW	Machine Status Word [*Computer science*]
MSW	Macht Sich Wichtig (BJA)
MSW	Magnetostatic Waves [*Telecommunications*] (TEL)
MSW	Massawa [*Ethiopia*] [*Airport symbol*] (OAG)
MSW	Master of Social Welfare
MSW	Master of Social Work
MSW	Master Switch
MSW	Maximum Shipping Weight [*MTMC*] (TAG)
MSW	Mean Sea Water
MSW	Mean Shallow Water
MSW	Medical Social Worker [*British*]
MSW	Meters of Seawater [*Deep-sea diving*]
MSW	Metres of Salt Water
MSW	Microswitch
MSW	Microswitch (KSC)
MSW	Microwave Spectrometer (TEL)
MSW	Mikheyev-Smirnov-Wolfenstein Theory [*Oscillation effect*] [*Particle physics*]
MSW	MI Software Co. [*Vancouver Stock Exchange symbol*]
MSW	Mission West Prop [*AMEX symbol*] (TTSB)
MSW	Mission West Properties [*AMEX symbol*] (SPSG)
MSW	Multiple Shrapnel Wounds
MSW	Multiple Stab Wounds [*Emergency medicine*] (DAVI)
MSW	Municipal Solid Waste
MSW	Western Massachusetts Regional Public Library System, Springfield, MA [*Library symbol Library of Congress*] (LCLS)
MSWAP	Master of Social Welfare and Administration Planning
MSWD	Mean Square Weighted Deviation [*Statistics*]
MSWD	Multisystem Weapon Delivery [*Air Force*]
M Sw En	Master of Software Engineering (PGP)
MSWG	Manpower Systems Work Group
MSWG	Modeling and Simulation Working Group
MsWJ	Jefferson College, Washington, MS [*Library symbol Library of Congress Obsolete*] (LCLS)
MSWJ.........	Midland and South Western Junction Railway [*British*]
MSWL.........	Municipal Solid Waste Landfill
MSWLF.......	Municipal Solid Waste Landfill
MSWM........	Men Who Have Sex With Men [*AIDS transmission group*]
MsWov	Wilkinson County Library System, Woodville, MS [*Library symbol Library of Congress*] (LCLS)
MsWp	Tombigbee Regional Library, West Point, MS [*Library symbol Library of Congress*] (LCLS)
MsWpCt.......	Court House Library, West Point, MS [*Library symbol Library of Congress*] (LCLS)
MsWpMH....	Mary Holmes College, West Point, MS [*Library symbol Library of Congress*] (LCLS)
MSWREE	Master of Science in Water Resources and Environmental Engineering (PGP)
MSWT.........	Minimum-Speed Wind Tunnel (MCD)
MsWv	Water Valley Public Library, Water Valley, MS [*Library symbol Library of Congress*] (LCLS)
MSWYE.......	Modified Seawater Yeast Extract [*Agar*] [*Microbiology*] (DAVI)
MSX............	Mascota [*Mexico*] [*Airport symbol*] (AD)
MSX............	MascoTech, Inc. [*NYSE symbol*] (SPSG)
MSX............	Microsoft Extended Basic (NITA)
MSX............	Midcourse Space Experiment (MCD)
MSX............	Minesweeper, Experimental [*Navy symbol*]
MSX............	Mossendjo [*Congo*] [*Airport symbol*] (OAG)
MSX............	Multinucleate Nature, Spherical Shape, Unknown History
MSXPr	Masco Tech Inc. Cv Pfd [*NYSE symbol*] (TTSB)
MSY............	Massey University School of Aviation [*New Zealand*] [*ICAO designator*] (FAAC)
MSY............	Maximum Sustainable Yield
MSY............	Minimum Sustainable Yield [*Pisciculture*]
MSY............	Morgan Stanley High Yield Fund [*NYSE symbol*] (SPSG)
MSY............	Morgan Stanley Hi Yld Fd [*NYSE symbol*] (TTSB)
MSY............	New Orleans [*Louisiana*] [*Airport symbol*]
MsY............	Yazoo-Sharkey Library System, Yazoo City, MS [*Library symbol Library of Congress*] (LCLS)
MSYNC	Master Synchronization [*Telecommunications*] (TEL)
MSYNC	Master Synchronizer (MSA)
MSYS..........	Medical Technology Systems, Inc. [*NASDAQ symbol*] (NQ)
M-SysFD......	M-Systems Flash Disk Pioneers Ltd. [*Associated Press*] (SAG)
M Sy Th.......	Master of Systematic Theology
MSZ............	Massive Surf Zone
MSZ............	Milford Sound [*New Zealand*] [*Seismograph station code, US Geological Survey*] (SEIS)
MSZ............	Moga Stan Fin 7.80% Cp Uts [*NYSE symbol*] (TTSB)
MSZ............	Morgan Stanley Finance Markets Ltd. Capital Unit [*NYSE symbol*] (SAG)
MSZ............	Mossamedes [*Angola*] [*Airport symbol*] (OAG)
MSZDP	Magyar Szocial Demokrata Part [*Hungarian Social Democratic Party*] [*Political party*] (PPE)

MSZMP .... Magyar Szocialista Munkaspart [*Hungarian Socialist Workers' Party*] [*Political party*] (PPE)

MSzP .... Magyar Szocialista Part [*Hungarian Socialist Party*] [*Political party*] (EY)

MT .... Core Melt Through [*Nuclear energy*] (IEEE)

MT .... Empty [*Slang*]

MT .... Flame Tight

MT .... Internacia Asocio Monda Turismo [*International Association for World Tourism*] (EAIO)

MT .... Internal Revenue Bureau Miscellaneous Tax Ruling [*United States*] [*A publication*] (DLA)

MT .... Machine Tool

MT .... Machine Tool Technology Program [*Association of Independent Colleges and Schools specialization code*]

MT .... Machine Translation [*Computer science*]

MT .... Mac Knight Airlines [*ICAO designator*] (AD)

M-T .... Macroglobulin-Trypsin [*Complex*] (DAVI)

M-T .... Macroglobulin-Trypsin Complex [*Medicine*] (BABM)

MT .... Magic Tee (IAA)

MT .... Magnetic

MT .... Magnetic Particle Testing [*Nuclear energy*] (IEEE)

MT .... Magnetic Tape

MT .... Magnetic Tube

mt .... Magnetite [*CIPW classification*] [*Geology*]

MT .... Magnetotelluric [*Geological surveying*]

MT .... Mail Transfer

MT .... Mail Tray (AAG)

MT .... Main Telescope

MT .... Maintenance Technician (MUGU)

MT .... Maintenance Time

MT .... Maintenance Trailer

MT .... Maintenance Trainer (MCD)

MT .... Malaria Therapy [*British*]

MT .... Malignant Teratoma [*Oncology*]

MT .... Malta [*IYRU nationality code*] [*ANSI two-letter standard code*] (CNC)

MT .... Mammary Tumor [*Medicine*]

MT .... Mammilothalamic Tract [*Anatomy*]

MT .... Management Team

MT .... Mandated Territory

MT .... Mannesman Tally (NITA)

MT .... Mantle Tentacle

MT .... Manual Test

M/T .... Manual Transmission [*Automotive engineering*]

MT .... Manufacturing Technology (RDA)

MT .... Mare Tranquillitatis [*Sea of Tranquility*] [*Lunar area*]

MT .... Maritime Tropical Air Mass

MT .... Market Town [*Geographical division*] [*British*]

MT .... Mark Trunk (IAA)

MT .... Masking Template (MCD)

MT .... Masoretic Text [*of the Bible*] [*Hebrew tradition*]

M/T .... Masses or Tumors [*Medicine*] (CPH)

MT .... Mast (IAA)

MT .... Master of Taxation (GAGS)

MT .... Master of Teaching (GAGS)

MT .... Master of Teaching

MT .... Master of Technology (GAGS)

MT .... Master of Textiles (PGP)

MT .... Master Teacher (ADA)

MT .... Master Timer

MT .... Master Tool (NASA)

MT .... Mat

MT .... Materials Test (IEEE)

MT .... Material Test (IAA)

MT .... Material Transfer (NRCH)

Mt .... Matthew [*New Testament book*]

MT .... Maximal Therapy [*Medicine*]

MT .... Maximum Torque

MT .... Mean Tide [*Tides and currents*]

MT .... Mean Time

MT .... Measured Time

MT .... Measurement (IAA)

MT .... Measurement Ton (MUGU)

MT .... Measuring Transformer (IAA)

MT .... Mechanical Technician (KSC)

MT .... Mechanical Test (MCD)

MT .... Mechanical Time [*Fuse*] (AABC)

MT .... Mechanical Traction [*British military*] (DMA)

MT .... Mechanical Translation [*Computer science*]

MT .... Mechanical Transport

MT .... Mediaeval Towns [*A publication*]

MT .... Medial Triceps Brachii [*Medicine*]

MT .... MediaTel [*Database*] [*British*]

MT .... Medical Technician [*British military*] (DMA)

MT .... Medical Technologist

MT .... Medical Transcriptionist (DAVI)

MT .... Meditrust SBI [*NYSE symbol*] (SPSG)

MT .... Medium Truck [*British*]

MT .... Megaton [*Nuclear equivalent of one million tons of high explosive*] (AFM)

MT .... Megatron (CET)

Mt .... Meitnerium [*Proposed name and symbol for recently-discovered element*]

MT .... Melt Through [*Nuclear energy*] (NRCH)

MSzP .... Membrana Tympani [*Anatomy*]

MT .... Mesenteric Traction [*Medicine*]

MT .... Mesotocin [*Endocrinology*]

MT .... Message Table [*Computer science*] (OA)

MT .... Metallothionein [*Biochemistry*]

MT .... Metal Threshold (AAG)

MT .... Metatarsal [*Anatomy*]

MT .... Meteor Construzioni Aeronautiche & Elettroniche SpA [*Italy ICAO aircraft manufacturer identifier*] (ICAO)

MT .... Meter (MCD)

MT .... Methoxytryptamine [*Biochemistry*]

MT .... Methoxytyramine [*Biochemistry*]

MT .... methoxytyramine [*Chemistry*] (DAVI)

MT .... Methyltryptophan [*Biochemistry*]

MT .... Methyltyrosine [*Biochemistry*]

Mt .... Metical (ODBW)

MT .... Metric Ton [*1,000 kilograms*]

MT .... Michaelmas Term [*British Legal term*] (ROG)

MT .... Microptic Theodolite

MT .... Microsyn Torquer (SAA)

MT .... Microthrombus [*Hematology*]

MT .... Microtome [*Instrumentation*]

MT .... Microtubule [*Cytology*]

MT .... Microwave Thermograph [*Medical instrumentation*]

MT .... Middle Temple [*London*] [*One of the Inns of Court*]

MT .... Middle Temporal [*Anatomy*]

MT .... Middle Temporal Lobe [*of the brain*]

MT .... Middle Turbinate [*Otorhinolaryngology*] (DAVI)

MT .... Midland Terminal Railroad (IIA)

MT .... Midrash Tanna'im (BJA)

MT .... Midship Deep Tank

MT .... Might

MT .... Migratory Trout

MT .... Military Tanker [*British*]

MT .... Military Technician

MT .... Military Tractor [*British*]

MT .... Military Train [*British military*] (DMA)

MT .... Military Training

MT .... Military Transport

mT .... Millitesla

MT .... Miniature Tube (NTCM)

MT .... Minimum Temperature (DS)

MT .... Minimum Transfer (DCTA)

MT .... Ministry of Transport [*Later, DOE*] [*British*]

MT .... Mishneh Torah [*Maimonides*] (BJA)

MT .... Missile Technician [*Navy rating*]

MT .... Missile Test

MT .... Missile Tilt

MT .... Mission Time (MCD)

MT .... Mission Trajectory (MCD)

MT .... Mitomycin [*Also, M, MC*] [*Antineoplastic drug*]

MT .... Mitral [*Valve*] [*Cardiology*]

MT .... Mobile Team

MT .... Mobile Terminal (DA)

MT .... Mobile Traveler [*Recreational vehicle*]

MT .... Mode Transducer

MT .... Modified Tape Armor [*Telecommunications*] (TEL)

MT .... Modus Tolens [*Rule of inference*] [*Logic*] [*Latin*]

MT .... Monroe Tidal Drainage [*Medicine*] (DMAA)

MT .... Montana [*Postal code*]

MT .... Montana Reports [*A publication*] (DLA)

Mt .... Montana State Library, Helena, MT [*Library symbol Library of Congress*] (LCLS)

MT .... More Than

MT .... Morse Taper (IAA)

MT .... Most (WGA)

MT .... Motilin [*Biochemistry*]

MT .... Mo Time [*An association*] (EA)

MT .... Motor Driver [*British military*] (DMA)

MT .... Motor Tanker

MT .... Motor Terminal (IAA)

MT .... Motor Threshold [*Medicine*]

MT .... Motor Transport [*Military*]

MT .... Motor Trend Magazine [*A publication*]

MT .... Mount [*Maps and charts*] (KSC)

Mt .... Mount (ODBW)

MT .... Mount

MT .... Mountain [*Board on Geographic Names*]

mt .... Mountain (VRA)

MT .... Mountain Time

MT .... Mounted [*Technical drawings*]

MT .... Mountings [*JETDS nomenclature*] [*Military*] (CET)

MT .... Mounting Tray

MT .... Movement Time [*Physical education*]

MT .... MTC Electronic [*Vancouver Stock Exchange symbol*]

MT .... Muertos Trough [*Geology*]

MT .... Multiple Transfer

MT .... Multiple Twin (IAA)

MT .... Multitasking

MT .... Muscle and Tendon [*Medicine*] (MAE)

MT .... Music Therapist [*or Therapy*]

MT .... MUX [*Multiplex*] Terminal (MCD)

MT .... Mycobacterium Tuberculosis [*Bacteriology*]

MT .... Myelotomography [*Medicine*]

MT .... Transcona Public Library, Manitoba [*Library symbol National Library of Canada*] (NLC)

MT1 .... Missile Technician, First Class [*Navy rating*]

MT2 .... Missile Technician, Second Class [*Navy rating*]
MT3 .... Missile Technician, Third Class [*Navy rating*]
MT6 .... Mercaptomerin [*Pharmacology*] (DAVI)
MTA .... MAC [*Military Airlift Command*] Transportation Authorization (AFM)
MTA .... Magnetic Tape Accessory [*General Electric Co.*]
MTA .... Maintenance Task Analysis
MTA .... Maintenance Task Analysis
MTA .... Major Test Article (NASA)
MTA .... Major Training Area [*Army*]
MTA .... Malignant Teratoma, Anaplastic [*Medicine*] (DMAA)
MTA .... Mammary Tumor Agent (DOG)
MTA .... Managed Thermactor Air [*Automotive engineering*]
MTA .... Management by Talking Around [*Business term*]
MTA .... Management Transactions Audit [*Test*]
MTA .... Manpower Training Association (AEBS)
MTA .... Man-Tended Approach (SSD)
MTA .... Manual Target Acquisition (MCD)
MTA .... Marine Trades Association [*British*] (DBA)
MTA .... Maritime Training Association (EA)
MTA .... Market Technicians Association (NADA)
MTA .... Mark Twain Association (EA)
MTA .... Mass Thermal Analysis (MCD)
MTA .... Master of Tax Accounting (GAGS)
MTA .... Master of Teaching Arts (GAGS)
MTA .... Master of Theater Arts (GAGS)
MTA .... Master Timer Assembly
MTA .... Materials Testing Activity (MCD)
MTA .... Materiel Transfer Agreement [*DoD*]
MTA .... Mean Tryptic Activity (PDAA)
MTA .... Media Technology Associates Ltd. [*Bethesda, MD*] [*Telecommunications service*] (TSSD)
MTA .... Medical and Technical Assistant
MTA .... Melamine Tableware Association (EA)
MTA .... Message Terminal Area (MCD)
MTA .... Message Transfer Agent [*Telecommunications*] (PCM)
MTA .... Message Transport Agent [*Telecommunications*] (PCM)
MTA .... Meta Communications Group, Inc. [*Toronto Stock Exchange symbol*]
MTA .... Metatarsus Adductus [*Anatomy*] (DAVI)
MTA .... MetaTechnologies Associates [*Oakland, CA*] [*Telecommunications service*] (TSSD)
MTA .... Methods-Time Analysis [*Industrial engineering*]
MTA .... Methylthionadenosine [*Biochemistry*]
MTA .... Metric Tons per Annum
MTA .... Metropolitan Transit Authority [*Later, MBTA*] [*Initialism also title of folk song about Boston's transit system*]
MTA .... Metropolitan Transportation Authority [*Greater New York City*]
MTA .... Metropolitan Travel Agents [*Inactive*] (EA)
MTA .... Midterm Availability
MTA .... Mid-West Truckers Association (EA)
MTA .... Military Technical Advisor (DNAB)
MTA .... Military Testing Association (MCD)
MTA .... Military Training Airspace (NATG)
MTA .... Military Training Area (DA)
MTA .... Military Transportation Authorization [*Air Force*]
MTA .... Miniature Truck Association [*Defunct*] (EA)
MTA .... Minimum Terms Agreement
MTA .... Minimum Terrain-Clearance Altitude [*Aviation*]
MTA .... Minor Task Authorization [*Navy*]
MTA .... Missile Transfer Area (IAA)
MTA .... Missile Tube Air
MTA .... Mississippi Test Area [*Aerospace*] (AAG)
MTA .... Mitchell Aero, Inc. [*ICAO designator*] (FAAC)
MTA .... Mobile Training Assistance (CINC)
MTA .... Mobility Test Article [*Lunar-surface rover*] [*NASA*]
MTA .... Modified Tape Armor [*Telecommunications*] (IAA)
MTA .... Monopulse Tracking Antenna
MTA .... Motion-Time Analysis
MTA .... Motorhome Travelers Association [*Defunct*] (EA)
MTA .... Motor Trade Association (NADA)
MTA .... Mount Allison University Library [*UTLAS symbol*]
MTA .... Mount Auburn Hospital, Cambridge, MA [*OCLC symbol*] (OCLC)
MTA .... Movimiento Teresiano de Apostolado [*Teresian Apostolic Movement - TAM*] [*Italy*] (EAIO)
MTA .... Multilateral Trade Agreement (AAGC)
MTA .... Multiple Tailors Association [*British*] (BI)
MTA .... Multiple-Terminal Access [*Computer science*] (IBMDP)
MTA .... Multiterminal Adapter (IEEE)
MTA .... Multitumor Antibody [*Clinical chemistry*]
MTA .... Municipal Treasurers Association of the United States and Canada
MTA .... Museum Trustee Association (EA)
MTA .... Musical Theatres Association
MTA .... Music Teachers' Association [*British*] (BI)
MTA .... Music Trades' Association [*British*] (BI)
MTA .... Muslim Teachers' Association (AIE)
MTA .... Myoclonic Twitch Activity [*Neurology*] (DAVI)
MTA .... Reference My Talk Address [*Military*] (IAA)
MTa .... Taunton Public Library, Taunton, MA [*Library symbol Library of Congress*] (LCLS)
MTA 4 .... Medical Technician, Acting, 4th Class [*British military*] (DMA)
MTAA .... Mopar Trans-Am Association [*Commercial firm*] (EA)
MTaB .... Bristol County Law Library, Taunton, MA [*Library symbol Library of Congress*] (LCLS)
MTAB .... Marginal Terrain Assault Bridge [*Military*] (RDA)
MTAB .... Military Technical Acceptance Board (MCD)
MTAC .... Mailers Technical Advisory Committee (EA)

MTAC .... Mathematical Tables and Other Aids to Computation
MTAC .... Mid-Atlantic Technology Applications Center [*University of Pittsburgh*] [*Research center*] (RCD)
MTAC .... Multiple Acceptance Test Criteria [*Lubricant testing*]
MTAC .... Multiple Test Acceptance Code [*Lubricants testing*] [*Automotive engineering*]
MTAC .... Multiple Test Acceptance Criteria
MTAC .... Multiple Time Around Clutter
MTACCS .... Marine Tactical Command and Control System (MCD)
MTACLS .... Marine Tactical Air Control and Landing System
MTAD .... N-methyl-triazolinedione
MTADS .... Marine Corps Tactical Data System (AFIT)
MTAE .... Message Transfer Agent Entity [*Telecommunications*] (OSI)
MTAF .... Mediterranean Tactical Air Force Headquarters
MTAG .... Manufacturing Technology Advisory Group [*DoD*] (RDA)
MTaHi .... Old Colony Historical Society, Taunton, MA [*Library symbol Library of Congress*] (LCLS)
MtAHS .... Alberton High School, Alberton, MT [*Library symbol*] [*Library of Congress*] (LCLS)
MTAI .... Meal Tickets Authorized and Issued [*Army*] (AABC)
MTAI .... Member of the Institute of Travel Agents [*British*]
MTAI .... Minnesota Teacher Attitude Inventory
MTAIF .... Member of the Australasian Institute for Fundraising (NFD)
MTAK .... Magyar Tudomanyos Akademia Konyvtara [*Hungarian Academy of Sciences Library*] (IID)
mTAL .... Medullary Thick Ascending Limb [*Anatomy*]
MTAM .... Maritime Tropical Air Mass (MSA)
MT(AMT) ..... Medical Technologist (American Medical Technologists) (DAVI)
MT & AETF.. Missile Tilt and Azimuth Error Test Fixture
MT & CE..... Missile Test and Checkout Equipment
MT&RC .... Marine Training and Replacement Command (SAA)
MT & SE..... Maintenance Test and Support Equipment
MTANSW ...... Motor Trades Association of New South Wales [*Australia*]
MTANSW ...... Music Teachers' Association of South Australia
MTAP .... Management Technical Applications Plan (MCD)
MTAP .... Methylthioadenosine Phosphorylase [*An enzyme*]
MTAR .... Manual Terrain Avoidance RADAR
MTAR .... Moving Target Acquisition RADAR (MCD)
MTAS .... Multisensor Target Acquisition System [*Military*] (RDA)
MTASA .... Motor Trade Association of South Australia
MT(ASCP).... Registered Medical Technologist (American Society of Clinical Pathologists)
MT(ASCP)SBB... Medical Technologist (American Society of Clinical Pathologists) Specialist in Blood Bank [*Technology*] (DAVI)
MTase .... Methyltransferase [*An enzyme*]
MTA/SME .... Machining Technology Association of the Society of Manufacturing Engineers (EA)
MTAT .... Mean Turn-Around Time [*Quality control*]
MTA US & C.. Municipal Treasurers Association of the US and Canada (EA)
MTAWA....... Motor Trade Association of Western Australia
M Tax .... Master of Taxation (PGP)
MtB .... Bozeman Pubic Library, Bozeman, MT [*Library symbol*] [*Library of Congress*] (LCLS)
MTB .... Maintenance of True Bearing
MTB .... Maintenance Time Budget
MTB .... Main Terminal Board
MTB .... Main Time Base [*Electronics*]
MTB .... Malaysian Tin Bureau [*Defunct*] (EA)
MTB .... Marcaptan Terminated Polybutadiene (PDAA)
MTB .... Marine Test Boat
MTB .... Mark Twain Bancshares, Inc. [*NYSE symbol*] (SAG)
MTB .... Materials Testing Branch [*NASA*]
MTB .... Materials Testing Branch [*Kennedy Space Center*]
MTB .... Materials Transportation Bureau [*Department of Transportation*]
MTB .... Maximum Theoretical Bandwidth (MHDI)
MTB .... Mechanical Time Base
MTB .... Medium Tank Battalion
MTB .... Message to Base
MTB .... Methantheline [*or Methanthine*] Bromide [*Pharmacology*]
MTB .... Methoxy(trifluoromethyl)butyrophenone [*Biochemistry*]
MTB .... Methylthymol Blue [*An indicator*] [*Chemistry*]
MTB .... Modified Tyrode's Buffer [*Clinical chemistry*]
MTB .... Module Test Bed [*Military*] (CAAL)
MTB .... Monte Libano [*Colombia*] [*Airport symbol*] (OAG)
MTB .... Monterey, CA [*Location identifier FAA*] (FAAL)
MTB .... (Morpholinylthio)benzothiazole [*Organic chemistry*]
MTB .... Motor Tariff Bureau, Charleston WV [*STAC*]
MTB .... Motor Torpedo Boat
MTB .... Multichannel Triple Bridge
MTB .... Seaplane Bomber [*Russian symbol*]
MTBA .... Machine Tool Builders' Association
MTBA .... Melbourne Tenpin Bowling Association [*Australia*]
MTBA .... Methyl-tert-butylaniline [*Organic chemistry*]
MTBA .... Multi-Threat Body Armor [*Army*]
MtBaF .... Fallon County Library, Baker MT [*Library symbol*] [*Library of Congress*] (LCLS)
MtBaHS ...... Baker High School, Baker, MT [*Library symbol*] [*Library of Congress*] (LCLS)
MTBAMA..... Mean Time between Any Maintenance Actions [*Quality control*] (MCD)
MTBASIC ... Multitasking BASIC [*Computer science*]
MtBC.......... Montana State University at Bozeman, Bozeman, MT [*Library symbol Library of Congress*] (LCLS)
MTBCA........ Mean Time between Corrective Action (MCD)
MTBCD .... Mean Time Between Confirmed Defects [*Quality control*] (MHDI)

MTBCF.......... Mean Time between Confirmed Failures [*Quality control*]
MTBCF.......... Mission Time between Critical Failures
MTBCME...... Mean Time between Corrective Maintenance Events [*Quality control*] (CAAL)
MTBCMI....... Mean Time between Corrective Maintenance Interrupts [*Quality control*] (CAAL)
MTBD.......... Mean Time between Defects [*Quality control*] (PDAA)
MTBD.......... Mean Time between Degradations [*Quality control*] [*Telecommunications*] (TEL)
MTBD.......... Mean Time between Demands [*Quality control*] (MCD)
MTBD.......... Mean Time between Discrepancies [*Quality control*]
MTBD.......... Methyl(triazabicyclo)decene [*Organic chemistry*]
MTBDE........ Mean Time between Downing Events [*Quality control*]
MTBDR....... Mean Time between Depot Repair [*Quality control*] (PDAA)
MTBE......... Mean Time between Errors [*Quality control*]
MTBE......... Mean Time between Events [*Quality control*]
MTBE......... Methyl Tertiary Butyl Ether [*Fuel additive*]
MtBeHS ...... Rocky Boy Tribal High School, Box Elder, MT [*Library symbol*] [*Library of Congress*] (LCLS)
MTBEMA..... Mean Time between Essential Maintenance Actions [*Quality control*]
MTBER........ Mean Time between Engine Removal [*Quality control*] (DNAB)
MTBERA ..... Mean Time between Essential Replacement Actions [*Quality control*]
MtBeS......... Stone Child Community College, Box Elder, MT [*Library symbol*] [*Library of Congress*] (LCLS)
MTBETF ...... Methyl Tertiary Butyl Ether Task Force (EA)
MTBF......... Mean Time between [*or before*] Failures [*Quality control*]
MTBFA....... Mean Time between False Alarms [*Quality control*] (AABC)
MTBFC....... Mean Time between Failures, Critical [*Military*]
MTBFC....... Mean Time between Flight Cancellations [*Quality control*]
MTBFEC...... Motor Truck, Bus, and Fire Engine Club [*Defunct*] (EA)
MTBFL....... Mean Time between Function Loss [*Quality control*]
MTBFRO...... Mean Time between Failures Requiring Overhaul [*Quality control*]
MTBHA ...... Mark Twain Boyhood Home Associates (EA)
MTBHMF...... Maintenance between Hardware Mission Failures [*Quality control*]
MTBHQ....... Mono-Tertiarybutylhydroquinone [*Also, TBHQ*] [*Organic chemistry*]
MTBI.......... Mean Time between Interrupts [*Quality control*]
MtBil.......... Billings Public Library, Billings, MT [*Library symbol Library of Congress*] (LCLS)
MtBilB .... Bureau of Land Management, Billings, MT [*Library symbol Library of Congress*] (LCLS)
MtBilBH ...... Big Sky Hospice, Billings, MT [*Library symbol*] [*Library of Congress*] (LCLS)
MtBilC .... Billings Clinic, Billings, MT [*Library symbol*] [*Library of Congress*] (LCLS)
MtBilD .... Deaconess Medical Center, Billings, MT [*Library symbol*] [*Library of Congress*] (LCLS)
MtBilE.......... Eastern Montana College, Billings, MT [*Library symbol Library of Congress*] (LCLS)
MtBilFW ...... United States Fish and Wildlife, Billings, MT [*Library symbol Library of Congress*] (LCLS)
MtBilGS .... Church of Jesus Christ of Latter-Day Saints, Genealogical Society Library, Billings Branch, Billings, MT [*Library symbol Library of Congress*] (LCLS)
MtBilMH ...... Billings Mental Health Center, Billings, MT [*Library symbol*] [*Library of Congress*] (LCLS)
MtBilNC .... Northern Rockies Cancer Center, Billings, MT [*Library symbol*] [*Library of Congress*] (LCLS)
MtBilPP .... Planned Parenthood of Billings, Billings, MT [*Library symbol*] [*Library of Congress*] (LCLS)
MtBilR .... Rocky Mountain College, Billings, MT [*Library symbol Library of Congress*] (LCLS)
MtBilRF .... Rimrock Foundation Library, Billings, MT [*Library symbol*] [*Library of Congress*] (LCLS)
MtBils.......... Billings Public Schools, Billings, MT [*Library symbol*] [*Library of Congress*] (LCLS)
MtBilSV .... Saint Vincents Hospital, Billings, MT [*Library symbol Library of Congress*] (LCLS)
MtBilY .... Yellowstone Treatment Center, Billings, MT [*Library symbol*] [*Library of Congress*] (LCLS)
MtBilYH .... Yellowstone City-County Helth Department, Billings, MT [*Library symbol*] [*Library of Congress*] (LCLS)
MTBM.......... Mean Time between Maintenance [*Quality control*] (AFM)
MTBM.......... Mean Time between Malfunctions [*Quality control*]
MTBM.......... Microtunneling Boring Machine (RDA)
MTBMA....... Mean Time between Maintenance Actions [*Quality control*]
MTBMAF...... Mean Time between Mission Affecting Failures [*Quality control*]
MTBMCF...... Mean Time between Mission Critical Failure [*Quality control*]
MTBME....... Mean Time between Malfunction Events [*Quality control*] (CAAL)
MTBN.......... Motor Transportation Battalion [*Military*]
MTBN.......... Mountbatten, Inc. [*NASDAQ symbol*] (SAG)
MTBO.......... Mean Time Before Obsolescence [*Navy*] (DOMA)
MTBO.......... Mean Time between Outages [*Quality control*] [*Telecommunications*] (TEL)
MTBO.......... Mean Time between Overhauls [*Quality control*] (MCD)
MTBO.......... Minimum Time before Overhaul [*Quality control*]
MTBOF........ Mean Time between Operational Failures [*Quality control*]
MTBOMF...... Mean Time between Operational Mission Failures [*Quality control*] (MCD)
MTBPER ...... Mean Time between Permanent Engine Removal [*Quality control*] (DNAB)
MTBPM....... Mean Time Between Planned Maintenance [*Engineering*]
MtBr........... Broadus Public Library, Broadus, MT [*Library symbol*] [*Library of Congress*] (LCLS)
MTBR.......... Mean Time between Removal [*or Repair or Replacement*] [*Quality control*]

MTBR.......... Mean Time Between Replacement
MTBRDR...... Mean Time between Removal for Depot Repair [*Quality control*] (MCD)
MTBRON...... Motor Torpedo Boat Squadron [*Navy*]
MTBS......... Mean Time between Service [*Quality control*] (MCD)
MTBS......... Mean Time Between Stops [*Quality control*] (IAA)
MTBS......... Methuen's Text-Books of Science [*A publication*]
MTBSD....... Mean Time between Supply Demands [*Quality control*] (MCD)
MTBSE....... Mean Time Between Software Errors [*Quality control*] (MHDI)
MTBSF....... Mean Time between Software Failures [*Quality control*] (CAAL)
MTBSF....... Mean Time between System Failures [*Quality control*]
MTBSHF...... Mean Time between System Hardware Failures [*Quality control*] (MCD)
MTBSOF ..... Mean Time between System Operational Failures [*Quality control*] (MCD)
MTBSP....... Mobilization Troop Basic Stationing Plan (MCD)
MTBSTC...... Motor Torpedo Boat Squadrons Training Center [*Melville, RI*] [*Navy*]
MTBT......... Miniature Thermal Bar Torch [*Army*] (RDA)
MTBTF....... Mean Time between Testable Failures [*Quality control*]
MtBu......... Butte Free Public Library, Butte, MT [*Library symbol Library of Congress*] (LCLS)
MtBuE........ Montana Energy Research and Development Institute, Butte, MT [*Library symbol Library of Congress*] (LCLS)
MTBUF........ Mean Time Between Undetected Failures [*Quality control*] (IAA)
MtBULM ..... Union List of Montana Serials, Bozeman, MT [*Library symbol Library of Congress*] (LCLS)
MTBUM ...... Mean Time Between Unscheduled Maintenance [*Quality control*] (MHDI)
MtBuM........ Montana College of Mineral Science and Technology, Butte, MT [*Library symbol Library of Congress*] (LCLS)
MTBUMA .... Mean Time between Unscheduled Maintenance Actions [*Quality control*]
MTBUR ...... Mean Time between Unscheduled Removals [*or Replacements*] [*Quality control*]
MtBwB........ Blackfeet Community College Library, Browning, MT [*Library symbol*] [*Library of Congress*] (LCLS)
MTC.......... Carroll College, Library, Helena, MT [*OCLC symbol*] (OCLC)
MTC.......... Machine Tool Control
MTC.......... Machine Trim Compensator (AAG)
MTC.......... Magnetic Tape Cassette [*Computer science*]
MTC.......... Magnetic Tape Channel [*Computer science*]
MTC.......... Magnetic Tape Command [*Computer science*] (IAA)
MTC.......... Magnetic Tape Control [*Computer science*]
MTC.......... Magnetic Tape Controller (NITA)
MTC.......... Magnetization Transfer Contrast [*Imaging technique*]
MTC.......... Maintenance Task Cycle
MTC.......... Maintenance Time Constraint (IEEE)
MTC.......... Main Trunk Circuit [*World Meteorological Organization*] [*Telecommunications*] (TEL)
MTC.......... Majestic Resources [*Vancouver Stock Exchange symbol*]
MTC.......... Make Today Count (EA)
MTC.......... Maneuver Training Command [*Army*] (AABC)
MTC.......... Manhattan Theater Club
MTC.......... Man-Tended Capability (SSD)
MTC.......... Man-Tended Committee (SSD)
MTC.......... Manual Traffic Control (MCD)
MTC.......... Manufacturing Technology Center
MTC.......... Manufacturing Technology Centre of New Brunswick [*Research center*] (RCD)
MTC.......... Marcus Tullius Cicero [*Roman orator and author, 106-43 BC*]
MTC.......... Maritime Transport Committee [*OECD*] (DS)
MTC.......... Mass Transfer Coefficient
MTC.......... Master of Textile Chemistry
MTC.......... Master Table of Contents (IAA)
MTC.......... Master Tape Control
MTC.......... Master Thrust Control [*or Controller*] [*NASA*] (NASA)
MTC.......... Master Training Concept [*Problem solving*]
MTC.......... Material Testing Center
MTC.......... Materiel Testing Command [*Merged with Weapons and Mobility Command*] [*Army*]
MTC.......... Maximum Tolerable Concentration [*Toxicology*]
MTC.......... Maximum Toxic Concentration [*Medicine*]
MTC.......... Maximum Track Capacity
MTC.......... Mechanical Torpedo Countermeasure [*Military*] (CAAL)
MTC.......... Mechanical Transport Corps
MTC.......... Medical Test Cabinet
MTC.......... Medical Training Center [*Later, Academy of Health Sciences*] [*Army*]
MTC.......... Medium Terminal Complexes (MCD)
MTC.......... Medullary Thyroid Carcinoma [*Medicine*]
MTC.......... Meet the Composer (EA)
MTC.......... Member of Technical College [*British*] (DI)
MTC.......... Memory Test Computer [*SAGE*]
MTC.......... Message Table of Contents (MCD)
MTC.......... Message Transmission Controller
MTC.......... Meteorological Training Center
Mtc .... Methylthiocarbamoyl [*Biochemistry*]
MTC.......... Metocurine [*A muscle relaxant*]
MTC.......... MIDI [*Musical Instrument Digital Interface*] Time Code
MTC.......... Military Tactical Computer (MCD)
MTC.......... Military Training Cadets [*A boys' World War II organization*]
MTC.......... Military Transportation Command
MTC.......... Military Transportation Committee [*NATO*] (NATG)
MTC.......... Missile Technician, Chief [*Navy rating*]
MTC.......... Missile Test Center
MTC.......... Missile Transfer Car

MTC .... Missile Tube Control
MTC .... Mission and Test Computer
MTC .... Mission and Traffic Control
MTC .... Mitomycin C [*Mutamycin*] [*Also, Mi, MMC*] [*Antineoplastic drug*]
MTC .... Mitsui Toatsu Chemicals, Inc. [*Japan*]
MTC .... Mobile Tactical Computer (PDAA)
MTC .... Mobile Target Carrier
MTC .... Moderator Temperature Coefficient (NRCH)
MTC .... Modulation Transfer Curve (OA)
MTC .... Monsanto Co. [*NYSE symbol*] (SPSG)
MTC .... Morgan Territory [*California*] [*Seismograph station code, US Geological Survey*] (SEIS)
MTC .... Morse Telegraph Club (EA)
MTC .... Motor Transport Corps [*Military*]
MTC .... Mount Clemens, MI [*Location identifier FAA*] (FAAL)
MTC .... MOUT [*Military Operations on Urbanized Terrain*] Training Complex [*Army*] (INF)
MTC .... Mouvement Traditionaliste Congolais [*Congolese Traditionalist Movement*]
MTC .... Moving Target Carrier (MCD)
MTC .... Multicomm Telecommunications Corp. [*Formerly, Mutual Satellite Services*]
MTC .... Multiple Tube Counts
MTC .... Multistate Tax Commission (EA)
MTC .... Music Teacher's Certificate [*British*] (DI)
MTC .... Mutating Transformation Converter (IAA)
MTC .... Mystic Terminal Co. [*AAR code*]
MTC .... Ontario Ministry of Transportation and Communications [*Canada*] (TSSD)
MTCA .... Cayes [*Haiti*] [*ICAO location identifier*] (ICLI)
MTCA .... Methyltetrahydrocarbolinecarboxylic Acid [*Organic chemistry*]
MTCA .... Methylthiazolidinecarboxylic Acid [*Organic chemistry*]
MTCA .... Military Terminal Control Area
MTCA .... Minimum Terrain-Clearance Altitude [*Aviation*]
MTCA .... Ministry of Transport and Civil Aviation [*Later, MT*] [*British*] (MCD)
MTCA .... Monitor and Test Control Area [*NASA*] (NASA)
MTCA .... Multiple-Terminal Communication Adapter [*Computer science*]
MtCaC .... Little Big Horn College, Crow Agency, MT [*Library symbol*] [*Library of Congress*] (LCLS)
MTCACS ..... Marine Corps Tactical Command and Control System (MCD)
MTCB .... Metropolitan Taxicab Board (NADA)
MTCC .... Magnetics Technology [*NASDAQ symbol*] (SAG)
MTCC .... Magnetic Technologies [*NASDAQ symbol*] (TTSB)
MTCC .... Master Timing and Control Circuit
MTCC .... Military Air Transport Service [*later, Military Airlift Command*] TransportControl Center
MTCC .... Modular Tactical Communications Center
MTCD .... Microvolume Thermal Conductivity Detector [*Instrumentation*]
MTCE .... Maintenance [*Telecommunications*] (TEL)
MTCE .... Million Tons of Coal Equivalent [*A comparative unit of energy content widely used in the oil industry*]
MTCF .... Mean Time to Catastrophic Failure [*Quality control*]
MTCF .... Missile Tube Comparator Fixture
MtCG .... Glacier County Library, Cut Bank, MT [*Library symbol Library of Congress*] (LCLS)
MtCG .... Glacier County Library, Cut Bank, MT [*Library symbol*] [*Library of Congress*] (LCLS)
MtCh .... Blaine County library, Chinook, MT [*Library symbol*] [*Library of Congress*] (LCLS)
MTCH .... Cap Haitien Internacional [*Haiti*] [*ICAO location identifier*] (ICLI)
MTCH .... Magnetic Tape Channel (NITA)
MT Ch .... Master of Textile Chemistry
MTCH .... Mining Technology Clearing House [*British Information service or system*] (IID)
MtchBnc ..... Mitchell Bancorp, Inc. [*Associated Press*] (SAG)
MtChe .... Liberty County Library, Chester, MT [*Library symbol*] [*Library of Congress*] (LCLS)
MtchlE .... Mitchell Energy & Development Corp. [*Associated Press*] (SAG)
MtCi .... George McCone Memorial County Library, Circle, MT [*Library symbol*] [*Library of Congress*] (LCLS)
MTCI .... Magnetic Tape Control Interface (MCD)
MTCI .... Management Technologies [*NASDAQ symbol*] (TTSB)
MTCI .... Management Technologies, Inc. [*NASDAQ symbol*] (NQ)
MTCI .... Member of the Trust Companies Institute (DD)
MTCL .... Motorcycle
MTCM .... Master of Traditional Chinese Medicine (PGP)
MTCM .... Missile Technician, Master Chief [*Navy rating*]
MTCNOLD ... Minimum Tax Credit Net Operating Loss Deduction [*Business term*]
MTCO .... Macon Terminal Co. [*AAR code*]
MTCOECD ... Maritime Transport Committee of the Organization for Economic Cooperation and Development [*France*] (EAIO)
MtCoHS .... Columbus High School, Columbus, MT [*Library symbol*] [*Library of Congress*] (LCLS)
MtCol .... Colstrip Bicentennial Library, Colstrip, MT [*Library symbol*] [*Library of Congress*] (LCLS)
MtCon .... Conrad Public Library, Conrad, MT [*Library symbol*] [*Library of Congress*] (LCLS)
MTCON .... Microwave Aerospace Terminal Control [*Air Force*] (IAA)
MTCP .... Master of Town and Country Planning (ADA)
MTCP .... Ministry of Town and Country Planning [*British*]
MTCR .... Missile Technology Control Regime [*US, Canada, Britain, France, West Germany, Japan*]
MTCS .... Madelian Thomas Completion Stories [*Psychology*] (DAVI)
MTCS .... Melbourne Theatre Cooperative Society [*Australia*]
MTCS .... Meteor Trail Communications System

MTCS .... Minimal Terminal Communications System (NVT)
MTCS .... Minimum Teleprocessing Commmunications System
MTCS .... Missile Technician, Senior Chief [*Navy rating*]
MTCT .... Manipulator/Teleoperator Control Technology (SSD)
MTCU .... Magnetic Tape Control Unit [*Computer science*]
MTCV .... Main Turbine Control Valve (IEEE)
MTCW .... Major 20th-Century Writers [*A publication*]
MTD .... Macknight Airlines [*Australia ICAO designator*] (FAAC)
MTD .... Magnetic Tape Disk (MCD)
MTD .... Main Technical Directorate (RDA)
MTD .... Maintenance Task Demand File (MCD)
MTD .... Maintenance Tasks Distribution
MTD .... Maintenance Technical Directive (SAA)
MTD .... Maintenance Technology Development
MTD .... Maintenance Training Department
MTD .... Manager, Traffic Department
MTD .... Manager, Transportation Department
MTD .... Manufacturing Technology Development (RDA)
MTD .... Manufacturing Technology Directorate [*Army*] (RDA)
MTD .... Manufacturing Technology Division [*Air Force*]
MTD .... Marine Technology Directorate [*British*]
MTD .... Maritime Trades Department, AFL-CIO [*American Federation of Labor and Congress of Industrial Organizations*] (EA)
MTD .... Mass Tape Duplicator/Verifier [*Computer science*] (MCD)
MTD .... Master of Textile Dyeing
MTD .... Master of Textile Design
MTD .... Master Tape Data
MTD .... Master Time Display
MTD .... Master Tracking Data [*NASA*]
MTD .... Materiel Testing Directorate [*Army*] (RDA)
MTD .... Maximum Tolerated Dose [*Medicine*]
MTD .... Mean Temperature Difference
MTD .... Mean Therapeutic Dose [*Medicine*]
MTD .... Mean Tolerated Dose [*Medicine*]
MTD .... Mean Total Dose [*Medicine*] (DMAA)
MTD .... Mean Tubular Diameter
MTD .... Mechanical Road Transport Driver [*British military*] (DMA)
MTD .... Metacarpal Total Density [*Anatomy*]
MTD .... Metal Trades Department, AFL-CIO [*American Federation of Labor and Congress of Industrial Organizations*] (EA)
MTD .... Metastatic Trophoblastic Disease [*Medicine*] (AAMN)
MTD .... Meta-Toluenediamine [*Organic chemistry*]
MTD .... Methyltriazolinedione [*Organic chemistry*]
MTD .... Microwave Target Designator
MTD .... Midwife Teacher's Diploma [*British*]
MTD .... Military Test Directorate [*Program*] [*Army*] (RDA)
MTD .... Minimal Toxic Dose (IEEE)
MTD .... Mintel International Development Corp. [*Vancouver Stock Exchange symbol*]
MTD .... Mitte Tales Doses [*Send Such Doses*] [*Pharmacy*]
MTD .... Mobile Target Division [*Mine Force*] [*Navy*]
MTD .... Mobile Training Detachment
MTD .... Mobilization Table of Distribution [*Military*]
MTD .... Monroe Tidal Drainage [*Urology*] (DAVI)
MTD .... Mount Darwin [*Zimbabwe*] [*Seismograph station code, US Geological Survey*] (SEIS)
MTD .... Mounted
MTD .... Mounted
mtd .... Mounted (VRA)
MTD .... Moving Target Detector [*RADAR*]
MTD .... Multiple Target Deception (MCD)
MTD .... Multiple Target Discrimination (MCD)
MTD .... Multiple Tile Duct [*Telecommunications*] (TEL)
MTDA .... Marine Tactical Data (IAA)
MTDA .... Methyl Trimethylsilyl Dimethylketene Acetal [*Organic chemistry*]
MTDA .... Modification Table of Distribution and Allowances [*Army*] (AABC)
MTDB .... Metropolitan Transit Development Board (NADA)
MTDC .... Modified Total Direct Costs [*Economics*]
MTDDA .... Minnesota Test for Differential Diagnosis of Aphasia [*Psychology*]
MTDDIS .... Mesoscale Transport Diffusion and Deposition Model for Industrial Sources [*Environmental Protection Agency*] (GFGA)
MTDE .... Maritime Tactical Data Exchange (NATG)
MTDE .... Modern Technology Demonstration Engine
MT Des .... Master of Textile Design
MtDeSP .... Montana State Prison, Conley Lake, Deer Lodge, MT [*Library symbol*] [*Library of Congress*] (LCLS)
MTDF .... Master Tracking Data File [*NASA*]
MTDF .... Mobile Tank Depermer Facility (DWSG)
MtDi .... Dillon City Library, Dillon, MT [*Library symbol*] [*Library of Congress*] (LCLS)
MtDiGS .... Church of Jesus Christ of Latter-Day Saints, Genealogical Society Library, ButteStake Branch, Dillon Chapel, Dillon, MT [*Library symbol Library of Congress*] (LCLS)
MtDiW .... Western Montana College, Dillon, MT [*Library symbol Library of Congress*] (LCLS)
MTDL .... Multiple Tap Delay Line
mtDNA .... Deoxyribonucleic Acid, Mitochondrial [*Biochemistry, genetics*]
mtDNA .... Mitochondrial DNA [*Deoxyribonucleic acid*] (USDC)
MTDP .... Medium Term Defense Plan (NATG)
MTDP .... Medium Term Development Plan [*Economics*] (FEA)
MTDS .... Manufacturing Test Data System (IEEE)
MTDS .... Marine Tactical Data System
MTDS .... Marine Toebreak Data System (NG)
MTDS .... Metallurgical and Thermochemical Data Service [*Department of Trade and Industry*] [*Information service or system*] (IID)

MTDS............ Missile Trajectory Data System (MUGU)
MTDSK........ Magnetic Tape Disk [*Computer science*] (NASA)
MTDSK........ Magnetic Tape Disk
MTDT............ Modified Tone Decay Test (MAE)
MTE............ AirTran Airways, Inc. [*FAA designator*] (FAAC)
MtE............ Ekalaka Public Library, Ekalaka, MT [*Library symbol*] [*Library of Congress*] (LCLS)
MTE............ Magnetic Tape Encoder [*Computer science*] (IAA)
MTE............ Magnetosphere-Thermosphere Explorer [*NASA*]
MTE............ Maintenance Test Equipment (MCD)
MTE............ Maintenance Training Equipment (MCD)
MTE............ Manteigas [*Portugal*] [*Seismograph station code, US Geological Survey*] (SEIS)
MTE............ Master of Teacher Education (PGP)
MTE............ Master of Textile Engineering
MTE............ Maximum Temperature Engine
MTE............ Maximum Tracking Error
MTE............ Member of the Telegraph Engineers [*British*] (ROG)
MTE............ Merit Technologies Ltd. [*Vancouver Stock Exchange symbol*]
mte............ Metal-Engraver [*MARC relator code*] [*Library of Congress*] (LCCP)
MtE............ Metropolitan Edison Co. [*Associated Press*] (SAG)
MTE............ Microwave Test Equipment
MTE............ Missile Test Engineer (MUGU)
MTE............ Mitre Corp., Bedford Operations Library, Bedford, MA [*OCLC symbol*] (OCLC)
MTE............ Mobile Telephone Exchange [*Nordic Mobile Telephone*]
MTE............ Modern Technology Engine
MTE............ Modular Threat Emitter (DWSG)
MTE............ Module Table Entry [*Computer science*] (BYTE)
MTE............ Monte Alegre [*Brazil*] [*Airport symbol*] (AD)
MTE............ Multiple Terminal Emulator
MTE............ Multiple Terminator Emulator (NITA)
MTE............ Multipurpose Test Equipment
MTE............ Multisystem Test Equipment [*Military*]
MTE............ Multithreshold Element (IAA)
MTE-5.......... Multielectrolyte Concentrate [*Pharmacology*] (DAVI)
MTEA............ Maintenance Training Effectiveness Analysis [*Army*]
MTEA............ Metal Trades Employers Association (NADA)
MTEA............ Minimum Target Elevation Angle (MCD)
MTEAA.......... (Methylthio)ethyl Acetoacetate [*Organic chemistry*]
MTEC............ Maintenance Test Equipment Catalog (MCD)
MTec............ Metric Tons Energy Consumption
MTEC............ Microtec Research, Inc. [*NASDAQ symbol*] (SAG)
MTEC............ Monash Timber Engineering Center [*Australia*]
M Tech.......... Master of Technology
MTECP.......... Maintenance Test Equipment Certification Procedure (SAA)
MTECR.......... Maintenance Test Equipment Certification Requirement (SAA)
MTEE............ Electrical Maintenance Test Equipment
MTEE............ Maintenance Test Equipment, Electrical (NASA)
MTEE............ Mean Transverse Emmission Energy (PDAA)
MTEE............ Mission Time Extreme Environment [*NASA*] (KSC)
MTEEC.......... Maintenance Test Equipment, Electronic (NASA)
MTEF............ Maintenance Test Equipment, Fluid (NASA)
MTEG............ Mickey Thompson Entertainment Group [*Auto racing*]
MTEG............ Port-Au-Prince [*Haiti*] [*ICAO location identifier*] (ICLI)
MTEL............ Manning Table and Equipment List
MTEL............ Maximum Tolerable Exposure Level [*Toxicology*]
MTEL............ Methyltriethyllead [*Organic chemistry*]
MTEL............ Mobile Telecommunications & Technology Corp. [*NASDAQ symbol*] (SAG)
MTEL............ Mobile Telecommun Tech [*NASDAQ symbol*] (TTSB)
MTelEng........ Master of Telecommunications Engineering (NADA)
MtELH.......... Lincoln County Senior High School, Eureka, MT [*Library symbol*] [*Library of Congress*] (LCLS)
MTEM............ Maintenance Test Equipment Module (MCD)
MTEM............ Mechanical Maintenance Test Equipment (NASA)
MT Eng........ Master of Textile Engineering
MTEO............ Maintenance Test Equipment, Optical (NASA)
M'TER.......... Manchester [*City in England*] (ROG)
MTER............ Multitest Evaluation Report [*Nuclear energy*] (NRCH)
MTES............ Metastable Transfer Emission Spectroscopy
MTES............ Methyltriethoxysilane [*Organic chemistry*]
MTESL.......... Master in Teaching English as a Second Language (PGP)
MTET............ Maximal Treadmill Exercise Test
Mtewan.......... Matewan BancShares [*Associated Press*] (SAG)
MTEWS/AD... Mobile Tactical Early Warning System for Air Defense [*NATO*]
MTEX............ Mission Template Expert (SSD)
MText............ Master of Textiles (NADA)
MTF............ Fairbanks, AK [*Location identifier FAA*] (FAAL)
MTF............ Machine Tool Forum
MTF............ Maintenance Test Flight (MCD)
MTF............ Maintenance Training Flight [*Military*]
MTF............ Manufacturing Technology Facility [*US Army Communications-Electronics Command*] [*Fort Monmouth, NJ*] (RDA)
MTF............ Matrix Test Facility (MCD)
MTF............ Maximum Terminal Flow (MAE)
MTF............ Mean Time to Failure [*Quality control*]
MTF............ Mechanical Time Fuze
MTF............ Medical Treatment Facility (AABC)
MTF............ Medical Treatment Faculty (DAVI)
MTF............ Megawatt Transmitter Filter
MTF............ Men's Tie Foundation [*Later, NAA*] (EA)
MTF............ Message Text Formatting
MTF............ Message Transfer Facility [*Telecommunications*] (OSI)
MTF............ Metal Trades Federation (NADA)

MTF............ Metastable Time of Flight
MTF............ Meteorological Task Force (MCD)
MTF............ Microsoft Tape Format [*Computer science*]
MTF............ Microsoft Tape Format [*Microsoft Corp.*] [*Computer science*] (PCM)
MTF............ Microwave Test Facility
MTF............ Military Treatment Facility [*DoD*]
MTF............ Mississippi Test Facility [*Later, NSTL*] [*NASA*]
MTF............ Mizan Teferi [*Ethiopia*] [*Airport symbol Obsolete*] (OAG)
MTF............ Mock-Up Test Facility (MCD)
MTF............ Modulation Transfer Function [*Resolution measure*]
mtf............ More to Follow [*Copyediting*] (WDMC)
MTF............ Motif
MTF............ Moulded Fiber Technology
MTF............ Multiple Tube Fermentation
MTF............ Multitarget Frequency
MTFA............ Medium-Term Financial Assistance
MTFA............ Modulation Transfer Function Analyzer
MtFb............ Chouteau County Free Library, Fort Benton, MT [*Library symbol*] [*Library of Congress*] (LCLS)
MTFC............ Masters Track and Field Committee (EA)
MTFCA.......... Model "T" Ford Club of America (EA)
MTFCI.......... Model T Ford Club International (EA)
MTFD............ Minimum Tracking Flux Density
MTFE............ Mercury Thin Film Electrode [*Electrochemistry*]
MTFEX.......... Mountain Field Exercise [*Military*] (NVT)
MTFF............ Man-Tended Free Flyer (MCD)
MTFF............ Mean Time to First Failure [*Quality control*] (AAG)
MtFhV.......... United States Veterans Administration Center, Fort Harrison, MT [*Library symbol Library of Congress*] (LCLS)
MTFL............ Mean Time to Fault Locate [*Quality control*] (CAAL)
MTFMPP........ Meta-Trifluoromethylphenylpiperazine [*Biochemistry*]
MTFO............ Modular Training Field Option (NASA)
MTFP............ Marema Tlou Freedom Party [*Lesotho*]
MTFR............ Mean Time for Repair [*Quality control*] (IAA)
MTFR............ Message Text Formatting Reporting
MTFR............ Metal Furring [*Technical drawings*]
MTFR............ [*The*] Minnesota Transfer Railway Co. [*AAR code*]
MtFR............ Rosebud County Library, Forsyth, MT [*Library symbol*] [*Library of Congress*] (LCLS)
MtFrHS........ Frenchtown High School, Frenchtown, MT [*Library symbol*] [*Library of Congress*] (LCLS)
MTFS............ Marine Terminal Fuel Separator (MCD)
MTFS............ Medium-Term Financial Strategy
MTFSC.......... Ministerial Task Force on Soil Conservation [*Australia*]
MTFTS.......... Marine Terminal Fuel Tankage System (MCD)
MTG............ Aviation Co. Mostransgas [*Former USSR*] [*FAA designator*] (FAAC)
MtG............ Glendive Public Library, Glendive, MT [*Library symbol Library of Congress*] (LCLS)
MTG............ Main Tank Gun [*Army*]
MTG............ Main Traffic Group [*Telecommunications*] (TEL)
MTG............ Main Turbogenerator
MTG............ Media Task Group [*Environmental Protection Agency*] (GFGA)
MTG............ Meeting (AFM)
MTG............ Meeting
MTG............ Melt-Textured Growth [*Chemistry*]
MTG............ Methanol-to-Gasoline [*Process*] [*Mobil Oil Corp.*]
MTG............ Methoxytriglycol [*Organic chemistry*]
MTG............ Methyl Tetradecylglycidate [*Biochemistry*]
MTG............ (Methyl)thiogalactoside [*Biochemistry*]
MTG............ MGIC Investment [*NYSE symbol*] (TTSB)
MTG............ MGIC Investment Co. [*NYSE symbol*] (SPSG)
MTG............ Microsyn Torque Generator (SAA)
MTG............ Montague Island [*Alaska*] [*Seismograph station code, US Geological Survey*] (SEIS)
MTG............ Mortgage [*Finance*] (SPSG)
MTG............ Motorsports Technology Group [*General Motors Corp.*]
MTG............ Motor-Torque Generator
MTG............ Mounting
MTG............ Mounting
MTG............ Multiple-Trigger Generator
MTG............ Multipurpose Target Generator
MTGAS.......... Mechanical Transport Gasoline [*Military British*]
MTGBKT........ Mounting Bracket (IAA)
MTGC............ Mounting Center (MSA)
MTGCF.......... Mobile Transportation Ground Command Facility (MCD)
MtGD............ Dawson College, Glendive, MT [*Library symbol Library of Congress*] (LCLS)
MTGD............ Mortgaged (ROG)
MtGDH.......... Dawson County High School, Glendive, MT [*Library symbol*] [*Library of Congress*] (LCLS)
MTGE............ Mortgage
mtge............ Mortgage (DD)
MTGEE.......... Mortgagee
MTGF............ Mouse Transforming Growth Factor [*Biochemistry*]
MTGHS.......... Magnetic, True, and Grid Heading Select (MCD)
MtGl............ Glasgow City-County Library, Glasgow, MT [*Library symbol Library of Congress*] (LCLS)
MTGOR.......... Mortgagor
MTGP.......... Monitor Table Generator Program (MCD)
MtGr............ Great Falls Public Library, Great Falls, MT [*Library symbol Library of Congress*] (LCLS)
MtGrCE........ College of Great Falls, Great Falls, MT [*Library symbol Library of Congress*] (LCLS)
MtGrCH........ Columbus Hospital, Health Sciences Library, Great Falls, MT [*Library symbol Library of Congress*] (LCLS)

MtGrGS........ Church of Jesus Christ of Latter-Day Saints, Genealogical Society Library, GreatFalls Branch, Great Falls, MT [*Library symbol Library of Congress*] (LCLS)

MtGrPS........ Great Falls Public Schools, Great Falls, MT [*Library symbol*] [*Library of Congress*] (LCLS)

MTGS.......... Metal-to-Glass Seal

MTGS.......... Midcourse and Terminal Guidance System [*NASA*]

MTGU .... Australian Master Tax Guide Updater [*A publication*]

MTGU .... Main Turbine / Gearing Unit (PDAA)

MTGW .... Maximum Total Gross Weight (MCD)

MTG/WESS... Main Tank Gunfire/Weapon Effects Signature Simulator (MCD)

MtH............. Helena Public Library, Helena, MT [*Library symbol Library of Congress*] (LCLS)

MTH............ Magnetic Tape Handler [*Computer science*]

MTH............ Marathon [*Florida*] [*Airport symbol*] (OAG)

MTH............ Massachusetts Institute of Technology [*ICAO designator*] (FAAC)

M Th............ Master of Theology

MTH............ Master of Tropical Health

MTH............ Meath [*County in Ireland*] (ROG)

MTH............ Metharbital [*An anticonvulsant*] [*Pharmacology*] (DAVI)

MTH............ Methylthiohydantoin [*Organic chemistry*]

MTH............ Microptic Theodolite

MTH............ Mithramycin (Aureolic acid, mithracin) [*Antineoplastic drug*]

MTH............ Monterey Homes Corp. [*NYSE symbol*] (SAG)

MTH............ Month

MTH............ Mount Holyoke College, South Hadley, MA [*OCLC symbol*] (OCLC)

MTH............ Mount Hood Railway Co. [*Later, MH*] [*AAR code*]

Mth............. Mouth [*Maps and charts*]

MTH............ Thompson Public Library, Manitoba [*Library symbol National Library of Canada*] (NLC)

MtHa........... Havre Hill County Library, Havre, MT [*Library symbol*] [*Library of Congress*] (LCLS)

MThA.......... Master of Theatre Arts

MtHam........ Bitter Root Public Library, Hamilton, MT [*Library symbol*] [*Library of Congress*] (LCLS)

MtHamRL .... United States National Institute of Health, Rocky Mountain Laboratory Library, Hamilton, MT [*Library symbol Library of Congress*] (LCLS)

MtHaN .... Northern Montana College, Havre, MT [*Library symbol*] [*Library of Congress*] (LCLS)

MtHar .... Big Horn County Public Library, Hardin, MT [*Library symbol Library of Congress*] (LCLS)

MtHarC .... Fort Belknap College, Harlem, MT [*Library symbol*] [*Library of Congress*] (LCLS)

MtHarlF .... Fort Belknap Community College, Harlem, MT [*Library symbol*] [*Library of Congress*] (LCLS)

MTHB.......... Mark Twain Home Board (EA)

MTHBD........ Motherboard (MSA)

MtHC .... Carroll College, Helena, MT [*Library symbol Library of Congress*] (LCLS)

MtHCE .... Montana Census and Economic Information Center, Helena, MT [*Library symbol*] [*Library of Congress*] (LCLS)

MTHD .... Method (MSA)

MtHe........... Laurie Hill Library, Heron, MT [*Library symbol*] [*Library of Congress*] (LCLS)

M Theol...... Master of Theology

MTHF.......... Methyltetrahydrofolate [*or Methyltetrahydrofolic*] [*Biochemistry*]

MTHF.......... Methyltetrahydrofuran [*Organic chemistry*]

MtHG .... United States Geological Survey, Water Resources Division, Helena, MT [*Library symbol*] [*Library of Congress*] (LCLS)

MThGH .... Metallothionein-Human Growth Hormone [*Endocrinology*]

MtHGS........ Church of Jesus Christ of Latter-Day Saints, Genealogical Society Library, Helena Branch, Helena, MT [*Library symbol Library of Congress*] (LCLS)

MTHHF .... Methyltetrahydrohomofolate [*Biochemistry*]

MtHHS .... Helena High School, Helena, MT [*Library symbol*] [*Library of Congress*] (LCLS)

MtHi........... Montana Historical Society, Helena, MT [*Library symbol Library of Congress*] (LCLS)

Mthly.......... Monthly (DLA)

MTHM......... Metric Ton of Heavy Metal (NUCP)

MTHM......... Million Tons Heavy Metal

MtHMv......... Mountain View School, Helena, MT [*Library symbol*] [*Library of Congress*] (LCLS)

Mt Holyoke C... Mount Holyoke College (GAGS)

MTHPA .... Methyltetrahydrophthalic Anhydride [*Organic chemistry*]

MThPast ..... Maitre en Theologie Pastorale [*Master in Pastoral Theology*] [*French*]

M Th Past.... Master of Pastoral Theology (PGP)

MtHPI .... Montana Office of Public Instruction, Resource Center, Helena, MT [*Library symbol*] [*Library of Congress*] (LCLS)

MTHR .... Merthyr [*Cardiff*] [*Welsh depot code*]

MTHR .... Mother

MTHR .... Mother

MTHRD........ Male Threaded

MtHs........... Hot Springs Public Library, Hot Springs, MT [*Library symbol*] [*Library of Congress*] (LCLS)

MtHS .... Shodair Children's Hospital, Helena, MT [*Library symbol Library of Congress*] (LCLS)

MtHSH .... Shodair Hospital, Helena, MT [*Library symbol*] [*Library of Congress*] (LCLS)

MtHsHS .... Hot Springs High School, Hot Springs, MT [*Library symbol*] [*Library of Congress*] (LCLS)

MtHSP .... Saint Peter's Community Hospital, Helena, MT [*Library symbol Library of Congress*] (LCLS)

MTHWL........ Motherwell [*Scotland*]

---

mthy .... Monthly [*Publishing*] (WDMC)

MTI .... Arturo Rodriguez Martinez [*Mexico*] [*FAA designator*] (FAAC)

MTI .... Machine Tools Industry (MCD)

MTI .... Maeventec Travel Information [*Maeventec*] [*Information service or system*] (CRD)

MTI .... Magyar Tavviati Iroda [*Hungarian News Agency*] (BARN)

MTI .... Main Tank Injection

MTI .... Malignant Teratoma Intermediate [*Oncology*] (MAE)

MTI .... Manitoba Technical Institute [*Canada*]

MTI .... Manpower Training Institute

MTI .... Marked Temperature Inversion [*Aviation*] (DA)

MTI .... Marketing and Training Institute (EA)

MTI .... Materials Technology Institute of the Chemical Process Industries (EA)

MTI .... Material Thickness Indicator

MTI .... Mechanical Technology, Inc.

MTI .... Mechanical Tolerance Index [*Food technology*]

MTI .... Media Technology International [*British*]

MTI .... Member of the Trust Institute (DD)

MTI .... Metal Treating Institute (EA)

MTI .... Methylthioinosine [*Biochemistry*]

MTI .... Methyltransferase I [*An enzyme*]

MTI .... Military Training Instructor (AFM)

MTI .... Minimum Time Interval [*Medicine*]

MTI .... Ministry of Trade and Industry [*Canada*]

MTI .... Missile Training Installation (NATG)

MTI .... Mobile Training Institute [*Klamath Falls, OR*] [*Telecommunications service*] (TSSD)

MTI .... Modern Telecommunications, Inc. [*New York, NY*] (TSSD)

MTI .... Mosteiros [*Cape Verde Islands*] [*Airport symbol*] (OAG)

MTI .... Mouvement de la Tendance Islamique [*Islamic Trend Movement*] [*Tunisia*] (PD)

MTI .... Moving Target Indicator

MTI .... Multi-Spectral Thermal Imager Spacecraft [*Department of Energy*]

MTI .... MuniYield Insured Fund II [*NYSE symbol*] (SPSG)

MTIA .... Metal Trades Industry Association (NADA)

MTIAA......... Metal Trades Industry Association of Australia

MTIAC......... Manufacturing Technology Information Analysis Center [*DoD Information service or system*] (IID)

MTIC .... Malaysia Tourist Information Center (EA)

MTIC .... Moving Target Indicator Coherent (IEEE)

MTICFAR ..... Moving Target Indicator Constant False Alarm Rate (CET)

MTID .... Master of Technology for International Development (PGP)

MTIE .... Microthrust Ion Engine

MTIF .... Maritime Technical Information Facility [*Maritime Administration*] [*Database producer*] (IID)

MTIF .... Master Tailored Interest File [*Navy*] (NG)

MTIG .... MTI Technology [*NASDAQ symbol*] (TTSB)

MTIHM......... Metric Tons Initial Heavy Metal (GAAI)

MTIK.......... Miller Building Sys [*NASDAQ symbol*] (TTSB)

MTIK.......... Miller Building Systems, Inc. [*NASDAQ symbol*] (NQ)

MTIK.......... Missile Test Installation Kit

MTIK.......... Moving Target Indicator Kit

MTIL .... Maximum Tolerable Insecurity Level (OA)

MTIM .... Manual Trim in Motion [*Aviation*]

MTIN .... Martin Industries [*NASDAQ symbol*] (TTSB)

MTIN .... Martin Industries, Inc. [*NASDAQ symbol*] (SAG)

MTIN .... Mountain [*Commonly used*] (OPSA)

MTIRA .... Machine Tool Industry Research Association [*Research center British*]

MTIRI.......... Multispectral Thermal Infrared Imager (SSD)

MTIS........... Maintenance Task Information System (NG)

MTIS........... Material Turned into Stores

MTIS........... Mean Time in Shop [*Quality control*] (MCD)

MTIS........... Multimodal Traveler Information Systems [*FTA*] (TAG)

MTIS........... Multiplex Transmitter Input Signals (PDAA)

MTI Tch ...... MTI Technology Corp. [*Associated Press*] (SAG)

MTJ .... Mesifta Tifereth Jerusalem (BJA)

MTJ .... Midtarsal Joint [*Anatomy*] (DAVI)

MTJ .... Missile Track Jamming [*Military*] (CAAL)

MTJ .... Montrose [*Colorado*] [*Airport symbol*] (OAG)

MTJ .... Mount Tsukuba [*Japan*] [*Seismograph station code, US Geological Survey*] (SEIS)

MTJA .... Jacmel [*Haiti*] [*ICAO location identifier*] (ICLI)

MTJE .... Jeremie [*Haiti*] [*ICAO location identifier*] (ICLI)

MtJG .... Garfield County Library, Jordan, MT [*Library symbol*] [*Library of Congress*] (LCLS)

MTK .... Camp Ripley/Little Falls, MN [*Location identifier FAA*] (FAAL)

MtK .... Flathead County Free Library, Kalispell, MT [*Library symbol Library of Congress*] (LCLS)

MTK .... Makin [*Kiribati*] [*Airport symbol*] (OAG)

MTK .... Mechanical Time Keeping (NASA)

MTK .... Medium Tank

MTK .... Mintek Resources [*Vancouver Stock Exchange symbol*]

MTK .... Mitaka [*Japan*] [*Seismograph station code, US Geological Survey Closed*] (SEIS)

mtk .... Tropical Maritime Cold Air Mass [*Meteorology*] (BARN)

MtKF .... Flathead Valley Community College, Kalispell, MT [*Library symbol Library of Congress*] (LCLS)

MtKFH .... Flathead Senior High School, Kalispell, MT [*Library symbol*] [*Library of Congress*] (LCLS)

MtKGS........ Church of Jesus Christ of Latter-Day Saints, Genealogical Society Library, Kalispell Branch, Kalispell, MT [*Library symbol Library of Congress*] (LCLS)

MtKH .... Kalispell Regional Hospital, Kalispell, MT [*Library symbol Library of Congress*] (LCLS)
MTL .... Magnetic Tape Loader
MTL .... Main Transfer Line (MCD)
MTL .... Maitland [*Australia Airport symbol*] (OAG)
MTL .... Manufacturing and Technology Laboratory
MTL .... Mass-Transport-Limited [*Chemical engineering*]
MTL .... Master Tape Loading
MTL .... Matched Transmission Line
MTL .... Material (KSC)
MTL .... Material
MTL .... Materials Technology Laboratory [*Watertown, MA*] [*Army*] (RDA)
MTL .... Materials Test Loop [*Nuclear energy*] (NRCH)
MTL .... Mean Tide Level [*Tides and currents*]
MTL .... Mean Time Level
MTL .... Medial Temporal Lobe [*Brain anatomy*]
MTL .... Median Tolerance Limit [*Toxicity*]
MTL .... Medium Term Loan (DCTA)
MTL .... Mercantile Bancorp [*NYSE symbol*] (TTSB)
MTL .... Mercantile Bancorp, Inc. [*NYSE symbol*] (SPSG)
MTL .... Merged-Transistor Logic
MTL .... Message Transfer Layer [*Telecommunications*] (OSI)
MTL .... Metal (AAG)
MTL .... Microelectronic Test Laboratory (IAA)
MTL .... Minimum Time Limit
MTL .... Minimum Triggering Level [*Aviation*] (DA)
MTL .... Mobilization Training Loss [*Military*]
MTL .... Mobiltherm Light (NRCH)
Mt-L .... Montana State Law Library, Helena, MT [*Library symbol Library of Congress*] (LCLS)
MTL .... Motel
MTL .... Motivation and Training Laboratory [*Army*] (RDA)
MTL .... Mount Taylor [*New Mexico*] [*Seismograph station code, US Geological Survey*] (SEIS)
MTL .... Multiple Conductor Transmission Line (PDAA)
MTL .... Raf-Avia [*Latvia*] [*ICAO designator*] (FAAC)
MTLA .... Micropublishers' Trade List Annual [*A publication*]
MTLC .... Mass Transfer Limiting Current (PDAA)
MTLC .... Metalclad Corp. [*NASDAQ symbol*] (SAG)
MTLC .... Metallic (MSA)
MTLD .... Mouvement pour le Triomphe des Libertes Democratiques [*Movement for the Triumph of Democratic Liberties*] [*Algeria*]
MtLdD .... Dull Knife Memorial College Library, Lame Deer, MT [*Library symbol*] [*Library of Congress*] (LCLS)
MtLe .... Lewistown City Library, Lewistown, MT [*Library symbol Library of Congress*] (LCLS)
MTLG .... Metrologic Instruments [*NASDAQ symbol*] (TTSB)
MTLG .... Metrologic Instruments, Inc. [*NASDAQ symbol*] (SAG)
Mtlg .... Mitteilung [*Report*] [*German*] (BJA)
MTLGY .... Metallurgy
MTLI .... MTL, Inc. [*NASDAQ symbol*] (SAG)
MtLib .... Lincoln County Free Library, Libby, MT [*Library symbol*] [*Library of Congress*] (LCLS)
MtLibH .... Libby High School, Libby, MT [*Library symbol*] [*Library of Congress*] (LCLS)
MtLibJ .... Libby Junior High School, Libby, MT [*Library symbol*] [*Library of Congress*] (LCLS)
MTL Inc .... MTL, Inc. [*Associated Press*] (SAG)
MTLM .... Metal Management [*NASDAQ symbol*] (TTSB)
MTLNG .... Metallizing
MTLP .... Master Tape Loading Program
MTLP .... Metabolic Toxemia of Late Pregnancy [*Medicine*]
MTLP .... Monitor Table Listing Program (NASA)
MTLR .... Moving Target Locating RADAR (AABC)
MTLS .... Mesial Temporal Lobe Seizure [*Medicine*]
MTLS .... MetaTools Inc. [*NASDAQ symbol*] (TTSB)
MTLS .... Munitions Transfer [*or Transporter*] and Loading System (MCD)
MtLv .... Livingston Public Library, Livingston, MT [*Library symbol*] [*Library of Congress*] (LCLS)
MtLvHS .... Park High School, Livingston, MT [*Library symbol*] [*Library of Congress*] (LCLS)
MtLvMS .... Livingston Middle School, Livingston, MT [*Library symbol*] [*Library of Congress*] (LCLS)
MtLvSD .... Livingston Elementary Schools, Livingston, MT [*Library symbol*] [*Library of Congress*] (LCLS)
M-TLX .... Mitsubishi Transfer-Line Heat Exchanger
MTLZ .... Metallize (MSA)
MTM .... Magnetic Tape Message
MTM .... Maintenance Task Monitor (MCD)
MTM .... Maintenance Test Module
MTM .... Manpower Tradeoff Methodology [*Military*]
MTM .... Mark-to-Market [*Securities*]
MTM .... Mark Twain Memorial (EA)
MTM .... Marlborough Technical Management [*British*]
MTM .... Mary Tyler Moore [*Actress after whom film studio MTM Enterprises is named*]
MTM .... Masked Terrain Map [*Military*]
MTM .... Master in the Teaching of Mathematics (PGP)
MTM .... Master of Theology and Ministry (PGP)
MTM .... Master of Transport Management
MTM .... Master of Tropical Medicine
MTM .... Matsumoto [*Japan*] [*Seismograph station code, US Geological Survey*] (SEIS)
MTM .... Mean Time Measurement
MTM .... Mechanical Road Transport Mechanic [*British military*] (DMA)

MTM .... Mechanical Test Model
MTM .... Methods-Time Measurement [*Industrial engineering*]
MTM .... Method-Times Measurement (DICI)
MTM .... Methylthiomethyl [*Organic chemistry*]
MTM .... Metlakatla [*Alaska*] [*Airport symbol*] (OAG)
MTM .... Metlakatla, AK [*Location identifier FAA*] (FAAL)
MTM .... Michelin Tire Monitor [*System*] [*Automotive engineering*]
MTM .... Million Ton Miles
MTM .... Million Train Miles
MTM .... Mission Test Module (IAA)
MTM .... Mobile Transfer Method (AAG)
MTM .... Modified Thayer-Martin [*Medium*] [*Microbiology*]
MTM .... Modular Torque Motor
MTM .... Moving Terrain Model
MTM .... Mt. Grant Mines Ltd. [*Vancouver Stock Exchange symbol*]
MTM .... MTM [*Methods-Time Measurement*] Association for Standards and Research (EA)
MTM .... MTM Productions, Inc. [*Named for actress Mary Tyler Moore*]
MTM .... Multiple Terminal Manager (NITA)
MTM .... Multiple Threat Modulation [*Military*] (CAAL)
MTM .... Multi-Taper Method [*Spectroscopy*]
MTM .... Multi-Tasking Monitor (NITA)
MTM .... Multi-Terminal Monitor (NITA)
MTMA .... Methods Time-Measurement Association (IAA)
MTMA .... Military Terminal Major Aerodromes (NATG)
MTMA .... Military Traffic Management Agency [*Later, DTMS*]
MtMa .... Phillips County Library, Malta, MT [*Library symbol*] [*Library of Congress*] (LCLS)
MTMAINTCO... Motor Maintenance Company (DNAB)
MTMASR .... MTM [*Methods-Time Measurement*] Association for Standards and Research [*Later, MTM*] (EA)
MTMB .... Military Traffic Management Bulletin (SAA)
MTMC .... (Methylthio)-meta-Cresol [*Organic chemistry*]
MTMC .... Micros-To Mainframe, Inc. [*NASDAQ symbol*] (SAG)
MTMC .... Micros To Mainframes [*NASDAQ symbol*] (TTSB)
MtMc .... Miles City Public Library, Miles City, MT [*Library symbol Library of Congress*] (LCLS)
MTMC .... Military Traffic Management Command [*DoD*]
MtMcC .... Miles Community College, Miles City, MT [*Library symbol Library of Congress*] (LCLS)
MTMCEA .... Military Traffic Management Command, Eastern Area [*Bayonne, NJ*]
MTMC-OA .... Military Traffic Management Command Operations Analysis Division [*Newport News, VA*]
MtMcPh .... Pine Hill School, Miles City, MT [*Library symbol*] [*Library of Congress*] (LCLS)
MTMCTEA... Military Traffic Management Command Transportation Engineering Agency (AABC)
MTMCTTC... Military Traffic Management Command Transportation Terminal Command, Europe [*MTMC*] (TAG)
MTMCTTU... Military Traffic Management Command Transportation Terminal Unit (AABC)
MTMCWA .... Military Traffic Management Command, Western Area [*Oakland, CA*]
MTM/D .... Million Ton Miles/Day (MCD)
MT/MF .... Magnetic Tape to Microfilm
MTMF .... Multiple Task Management Feature (NITA)
MTM-GPD .... Methods Time Measurement and General Purpose Data (PDAA)
MTMH .... Master of Tropical Medicine and Hygiene (GAGS)
MTMI .... Microtek Medical [*NASDAQ symbol*] (TTSB)
MTMI .... Microtek Medical, Inc. [*NASDAQ symbol*] (SAG)
MtMis .... Missoula Public and Missoula County Free Library, Missoula, MT [*Library symbol Library of Congress*] (LCLS)
MtMisGS...... Church of Jesus Christ of Latter-Day Saints, Genealogical Society Library, Missoula Branch, Missoula, MT [*Library symbol Library of Congress*] (LCLS)
MtMisSP...... Saint Patrick Hospital, Missoula, MT [*Library symbol Library of Congress*] (LCLS)
MtMisW....... Western Montana Clinic, Missoula, MT [*Library symbol Library of Congress*] (LCLS)
MTMOD .... Magnetic Tape Module (IAA)
MTMP .... MACOM [*Major Command*] Telephone Modernizations Program
MTMR .... Military Traffic Management Regulation
mt mRNA .... Mitochondrial Messenger RNA[*Ribonucleic Acid*] [*Genetics*] (DOG)
MTM's .... Magnetic Tape Transmissions (CET)
MTMS .... Memorex Tape Management System [*Computer science*] (IAA)
MTMS .... Metal-to-Metal Seal
MTMS .... Methyltrimethoxysilane [*Organic chemistry*]
MTMS .... Military Traffic Management Service (MCD)
MTMS .... Mobilization Training Management System [*DoD*]
MTMS .... Multi-Terminal Modular System (DGA)
MTMTS .... Military Traffic Management and Terminal Service [*Later, MTMC*] [*Army*]
MTMTS-TSP... Military Traffic Management and Terminal Service Transportation Strike Plan (DNAB)
MTN .... Baltimore, MD [*Location identifier FAA*] (FAAL)
MTN .... Main Telecommunication Network [*United Nations*] (EY)
MTN .... Manton [*Australia Seismograph station code, US Geological Survey*] (SEIS)
MTN .... Medical Television Network (BARN)
MTN .... Medium-Term Note [*Finance*]
MTN .... Metatolylnitrile [*Organic chemistry*]
MTN .... Mirtone International, Inc. [*Toronto Stock Exchange symbol*]
MTN .... Mizlou Television Network
MTN .... Mobil Producing TX & NM, Inc., Houston, TX [*OCLC symbol*] (OCLC)
MTN .... Motion (MSA)
MTN .... Mountain

MTN............	Mountain
MTN............	Mountain Air Cargo, Inc. [ICAO designator] (FAAC)
MTN............	Multilateral Trade Negotiations
MTN............	Multinational Trade Negotiations (IAA)
MTNA............	Music Teachers National Association (EA)
MTND.........	Mercury Tube Nutation Damper
MTNFC.........	Mel Tillis National Fan Club (EA)
MTNHP.........	Montana Natural Heritage Program [Helena, MT] [Information service or system] (IID)
MtnPkFn........	Mountain Parks Financial Corp. [Associated Press] (SAG)
MTNS...........	Metal-Thick Nitride Semiconductor (IAA)
MTNS...........	Metal-Thick Nitride-Silicon (IAA)
MTNS...........	Metal-Thick Oxide-Nitride-Silicon
MTNS...........	Mountains [Postal Service standard] (OPSA)
MTNT...........	Metro Networks, Inc. [NASDAQ symbol] (SAG)
MtNxPS........	Noxon Public School, Noxon, MT [Library symbol] [Library of Congress] (LCLS)
MTO............	Made to Order (ODBW)
MTO............	Magnetic Tape Operator (MCD)
MTO............	Maintenance Technology Office [Air Force Logistics Command]
MTO............	Manitoulin Air Services Ltd. [Canada ICAO designator] (FAAC)
MTO............	Man-Tended Operation (SSD)
MTO............	Manufacturing Technical Order (SAA)
MTO............	Master Terminal Operator (IAA)
MTO............	Master Timing Oscillator (MCD)
MTO............	Mattoon [Illinois] [Airport symbol] (OAG)
MTO............	Maximum Time Out (MCD)
MTO............	Medical Transport Officer [Navy]
MTO............	Mediterranean Theater of Operations, United States Army [Shortened form of MTOUSA] [World War II]
MTO............	Message Terminal Operation [Military] (CAAL)
MTO............	Methanol-to-Olefin [Process]
MTO............	Missile Test Operator (SAA)
MTO............	Mission, Task, Objective
MTO............	Mission Type Order (DOMA)
MTO............	Mississippi Test Operations [NASA]
MTO............	Modification Task Outline (KSC)
MTO............	Motor Transport Officer [Military]
MTO............	Mouvement Togolais pour la Democratie [Togolese Movement for Democracy] [Political party] (PD)
MTO............	Movement Transfer Order (MCD)
MTO............	Muffin-Tin Orbital [Physics]
MTO............	Multilateral Trading Organization (ECON)
MTO............	Multimodal Transport Operator
MTOAL.........	Mobilization Table of Allowance Listing [Military] (DNAB)
MTOB..........	Manned Test Operations Board [NASA]
MTOC..........	Microtubular Organizing Complex [Physiology]
MTOC..........	Microtubule Organizing Center [Cytology]
MTOC..........	Mitotic Organizing Center [Cytology]
MTOC..........	Monitoring Transport of Ocean Currents [Project] [Marine science] (OSRA)
MTOCs.........	Microtubule Organizing Centers (DOG)
MTOE..........	Million Tons of Oil Equivalent
MTOE..........	Modification Table of Organization and Equipment [Army] (AABC)
MTOGW.......	Maximum Takeoff Gross Weight [Aviation] (MCD)
MTOM..........	Master of Traditional Oriental Medicine (PGP)
MTON.........	Measurement Ton
MTON.........	Metro One Telecommunications, Inc. [NASDAQ symbol] (SAG)
MTONS........	Metal-Thick Oxide-Nitride-Silicon (MSA)
MTOP..........	Molecular Total Overlap Population (IEEE)
MTOPS........	Million Theoretical Operations per Second [Computer science]
MTORQ........	Maximum Torque
MTOS..........	Magnetic Tape Operating System (NITA)
MTOS..........	Magnetic Tape Operations System [Computer science] (NRCH)
MTOS..........	Major Trauma Outcome Study [American College of Surgeons Committee on Trauma]
MTOS..........	Metal-Thick Oxide Semiconductor (IAA)
MTOS..........	Metal-Thick Oxide-Silicon
MTOS..........	Multi-Tasking Operating System (NITA)
MTOSFET.....	Metal-Thick Oxide Semiconductor Field Effect Transistor (IAA)
MTOUSA......	Mediterranean Theater of Operations, United States Army [Sometimes shortened to MTO] [World War II]
MTOW	Maximum Takeoff Weight [Aviation] (MCD)
MTox	Master of Toxicology (GAGS)
M Tox	Master of Toxicology (PGP)
MTP	Island Helicopters, Inc. [ICAO designator] (FAAC)
MTP	Magnetic Tape Processor (NITA)
MTP	Maintenance Test Package (MCD)
MTP	Manual Troubleshooting Procedures [Army]
MTP	Manufacturing Technical Procedure [NASA] (NASA)
MTP	Manufacturing Technology Program [Aviation Systems Command] (RDA)
MTP	Manufacturing Technology Projects [Manufacturing Technology Information Analysis Center] [Information service or system] (CRD)
MTP	Manufacturing Test Procedure
MTP	Master of Town and Country Planning
MTP	Master of Town Planning
MTP	Master of Transpersonal Psychology (PGP)
MTP	Master Test Plan (KSC)
MTP	Master Training Plan [Navy] (ANA)
MTP	Master Transportation Plan (AAG)
MTP	Master Typography Program (DNAB)
MTP	Materiel Test Procedure [Army]
MTP	Materiel Transfer Plan [Army]

MTP	Maximum Tire Pressure (ADA)
MTP	Maximum Total Trihalomethane Potential (EG)
MTP	Mechanical Thermal Pulse (IEEE)
MTP	Message Transfer Protocol [Telecommunications] (OSI)
MTP	Message Transmission Part [Telecommunications] (TEL)
MTP	Metatarsophalangeal [Anatomy]
MTP	Methods Test Panel [Bureau of the Census] (GFGA)
MTP	(Methylthio)phenol [Organic chemistry]
MTP	Microsomal Triglyceride Transfer Protein [Biochemistry]
MTP	Microtubule Protein [Cytology]
MTP	Military Type Property
MTP	Miniature Trimmer Potentiometer
MTP	Minimum Time Path (OA)
MTP	Missile Transfer Panel (AAG)
MTP	Missile Tube Pressurization
MTP	Mission Tailored Product
MTP	Mission Test Plan (KSC)
MTP	Mission Training Plan [Military] (INF)
MTP	Mobilization Training Program [Military]
MTP	Mobilization Troop Program [Army]
MTP	Modular Terminal Processor (NITA)
MTP	Montana Power [NYSE symbol] (TTSB)
MTP	Montana Power Co. [NYSE symbol] (SPSG)
MTP	Montauk Point [New York] [Airport symbol Obsolete] (OAG)
MTP	Monte Pirata [Puerto Rico] [Seismograph station code, US Geological Survey] (SEIS)
MTP	MOS [Military Occupation Specialty] Training Plan
MTP	Mother Tongue Project (AIE)
MTP	Movimiento Todos par la Patria [Argentina Political party] (EY)
MTP	Multiple-Task Performance
MTP	Multiply Twinned Particles (DICI)
MTP	Multipoint (DNAB)
MtP	Plains Public Library, Plains, MT [Library symbol] [Library of Congress] (LCLS)
MTP	The Pas Public Library, Manitoba [Library symbol National Library of Canada] (NLC)
MTPA	Master Textile Printers Association (EA)
MTPA	(Methoxy)trifluoromethylphenylacetic Acid [Organic chemistry]
MTPA	Mobile Transponder Performance Analyzer [Aviation] (DA)
MtPaS...........	Salish Kootenai College Library, Pablo, MT [Library symbol] [Library of Congress] (LCLS)
MtPaTS........	Two Eagle School, Pablo, MT [Library symbol] [Library of Congress] (LCLS)
MTPC...........	Metal Tube Packaging Council of North America [Later, TCNA] (EA)
MTPC...........	Minimal Total Processing Time (NITA)
MTPCNA	Metal Tube Packaging Council of North America [Later, TCNA]
MTPE...........	Mission to Planet Earth [Proposed NASA satellite]
MTPF	Maximum Total Peaking Factor [Nuclear energy] (NRCH)
MTP FET.....	Metal/Tunnelling-Nitride Polysilicon Gate FET (NITA)
MTPH..........	Maximum Temperature of Previous Heating [Archaeology]
MTPI...........	Member of the Town Planning Institute [British]
MTPK..........	Keewatin Community College, The Pas, Manitoba [Library symbol National Library of Canada] (NLC)
MTPM..........	Mean Time to Provide Manpower (DNAB)
MtPoF..........	Fort Peck Community College, Poplar, MT [Library symbol] [Library of Congress] (LCLS)
MtPol...........	Polson City Library, Polson, MT [Library symbol] [Library of Congress] (LCLS)
MTPP..........	Material Test Procedure Pamphlet
MTPP..........	Missile-to-Target Patch Panel
MTPP..........	Port-Au-Prince/Internacional [Haiti] [ICAO location identifier] (ICLI)
MTP-PE........	Muramyl Tripeptide Phosphatidylethanolamine [Antineoplastic drug] (CDI)
MtPPS	Plains Public School Library, Plains, MT [Library symbol] [Library of Congress] (LCLS)
MTPR..........	Miniature Temperature Pressure Recorder (USDC)
MTPR..........	Miniature Temperature Pressure Recorder [Marine science] (OSRA)
MTPS..........	Magnetic Tape Programming System [Computer science] (IEEE)
MTPS..........	Modern Talking Picture Service, Inc. [Funded by U.S. Department of Education] (PAZ)
MTPT..........	Minimal Total Processing Time (IEEE)
MTPU..........	Missile Tank Pressurization Unit (AAG)
MTPUG	Pascal/MT Users Group [Defunct] (EA)
MTPW..........	Master of Technical and Professional Writing (GAGS)
MtPw	Sheridan County Free Library, Plentywood, MT [Library symbol] [Library of Congress] (LCLS)
MTPX..........	Port-De-Paix [Haiti] [ICAO location identifier] (ICLI)
MTPY..........	Millions of Tons per Year [of solids, e.g., coal]
MTQ............	CAAA Air Martinique [France ICAO designator] (FAAC)
MTQ............	Greenville, MS [Location identifier FAA] (FAAL)
MTQ............	Martinique [ANSI three-letter standard code] (CNC)
MTQ............	Methaqualone [or Methyltolylquinazolone, or Metolquizolone] [Sedative]
MTQ............	Mitchell [Australia Airport symbol] (OAG)
MTQ............	Mount Allard Resources [Vancouver Stock Exchange symbol]
MTQAS	Methadone Treatment Quality Assurance System [National Institute on Drug Abuse]
MTQM..........	Master of Total Quality Management (PGP)
MTR............	Magic-Tone Records [Record label]
MTR............	Magnetic Core Transistor Relay (IAA)
MTR............	Magnetic Tape Reader (NITA)
MTR............	Magnetic Tape Recorder
MTR............	Main Timing Register
MTR............	Major Trouble Report (MCD)

MTR............	Mass, Tenderness, Rebound [*On abdominal examination*] [*Gastroenterology*] (DAVI)
MTR............	Mass-Transfer Rate [*Chemical engineering*]
MTR............	Mass Transit Railway (DS)
MTR............	Master Tool Record (SAA)
MTR............	Materials Testing Reactor
MTR............	Materials Testing Report
MTR............	Material Transfer Recorder [*LASER*] [*Army*]
MTR............	Maximum Tracking Range
MTR............	Mean Time to Removal [*Quality control*]
MTR............	Mean Time to Restore [*Quality control*] (IAA)
MTR............	Measa Royalty Trust [*NYSE symbol*] (SAG)
MTR............	Meinicke Turbidity Reaction [*Obsolete test for syphilis*]
MTR............	Mental Treatment Rules [*British*]
MTR............	Mesa Royaty Tr UBI [*NYSE symbol*] (TTSB)
MTR............	Meter [*or Metering*] (AAG)
mtr............	Meter (IDOE)
MTR............	Methylthioribose [*Biochemistry*]
MTR............	Metroflight, Inc. [*ICAO designator*] (FAAC)
Mtr............	Metronome [*Record label*] [*Scandinavia, Germany, etc.*]
MTR............	Mid-Term Review
MTR............	Migration Traffic Rate (OA)
MTR............	Military Technical Revolution (DOMA)
MTR............	Military Temperature Range
MTR............	Military Training Route [*Aviation*] (FAAC)
MTR............	Military Training Routes [*FAA*] (TAG)
MTR............	Milliammeter (IAA)
MTR............	Miniature Temperature Recorder (USDC)
MTR............	Minimum Technological Requirement
MTR............	Minimum Time Rate
MTR............	Miscellaneous Tax Ruling [*IRS*] (AAGC)
MTR............	Missile Track [*or Tracking*] RADAR [*Air Force*]
MTR............	MITRE Corp., Library Department, McLean, VA [*OCLC symbol*] (OCLC)
MTR............	Mobile Tracking Range [*Military*] (CAAL)
MTR............	Modification Traceability Record (MCD)
MTR............	Modular Tree Representation (MHDI)
MTR............	Monitor [*Computer science*] (BUR)
MTR............	Monopulse Tracking Receiver
MTR............	Monteria [*Colombia*] [*Airport symbol*] (OAG)
MTR............	Monterrey [*California*] [*Seismograph station code, US Geological Survey*] (SEIS)
MTR............	Montour Railroad Co. [*AAR code*]
MTR............	Motor (AABC)
MTR............	Motor
MTR............	Motor
MTR............	Moving Target Reactor
MTR............	Moving Target Resolver (MCD)
MTR............	Multiple Thermocouple Reference
MTR............	Multiple Token Ring [*Telecommunications*] (OSI)
MTR............	Multiple Tracking Range
MTR............	Multiple Track RADAR
MTR............	Museum of Television and Radio [*New York*]
MTR............	Mutual Resources [*Vancouver Stock Exchange symbol*]
MTR............	Universite de Montreal, Bibliotheque [*UTLAS symbol*]
MTRA..........	Meta Biosystems [*NASDAQ symbol*] (SAG)
MTRA..........	Metra Biosystems [*NASDAQ symbol*] (SAG)
M/TRANS.....	Manual Transmission [*Automotive engineering*]
MTransEc....	Master of Transport Economics
MTRB..........	Man-Tended Review Board (SSD)
MTRB..........	Maritime Transportation Research Board [*National Research Council*]
MTRB..........	Motor Truck Rate Bureau
MTRC..........	Man-Tended Reference Configuration (SSD)
MTRC..........	Metric
MTRCL........	Motorcycle (AABC)
Mtrclt........	Motorcyclist [*Army*]
MTRCYL	Motorcycle
MtRd..........	Community Library, Roundup, MT [*Library symbol*] [*Library of Congress*] (LCLS)
MtRd-E	Roundup Central Elementary School Library, Roundup, MT [*Library symbol*] [*Library of Congress*] (LCLS)
MTRDN.......	Motor-Driven
MTRE..........	Magnetic Tape Recorder End
MTRE..........	Missile Test and Readiness Equipment
MTRE..........	Missile Test and Readiness Evaluation [*Military*] (IAA)
MT REVD....	Most Reverend (ROG)
MTRF..........	Mark Twain Research Foundation (EA)
MTRF..........	Master Training File [*Computer science*]
MTRG	Metering (MSA)
MTRI..........	Missile Test Range Instrumentation
MTRK..........	Minitrack (KSC)
MTRL..........	Material
MTRL..........	Material (FAAC)
MTRM.........	Modulated Throat-Rocket Motor (MCD)
MTRN.........	Metrotrans Corp. [*NASDAQ symbol*] (SAG)
mtRNA........	Ribonucleic Acid, Mitochondrial [*Biochemistry, genetics*]
MTRNTY	Maternity
MTRO	Metro-Tel Corp. [*NASDAQ symbol*] (NQ)
MTRO	Metro Tel Corp. [*NASDAQ symbol*] (TTSB)
MtRo..........	Ronan City Library, Ronan, MT [*Library symbol*] [*Library of Congress*] (LCLS)
MtroOne	Metro One Telecommunications, Inc. [*Associated Press*] (SAG)
MTR OP......	Motor Operated [*Freight*]
MTRP..........	Machine Tool Retrofit Program
MTRP..........	Master of Town and Regional Planning [*British*] (ADA)
mtrRNA......	Mitochondrial Ribosomal RNA[*Ribonucleic Acid*] [*Genetics*] (DOG)
MTRS..........	Magnetic Tape Recorder Set
MTRS..........	Magnetic Tape Recorder Start
MTRS..........	Magnetic Tape Reformatting System [*Hewlett-Packard Co.*]
MTRS..........	Mattress (MSA)
MTRS..........	Metris Companies, Inc. [*NASDAQ symbol*] (SAG)
MT Rulings...	Miscellaneous Tax Rulings [*Australia A publication*]
MTRUW.......	Mixed Transuranic Waste (GAAI)
MtrVac........	MotorVac Technologies, Inc. [*Associated Press*] (SAG)
MTRX..........	Matrix Service [*NASDAQ symbol*] (TTSB)
MTRX..........	Matrix Service Corp. [*NASDAQ symbol*] (NQ)
MTRY..........	Momentary (FAAC)
MTS............	Machine-Tractor Stations
MTS............	Magnetic Tape Station [*Computer science*] (CET)
MTS............	Magnetic Tape Storage [*Computer science*] (IAA)
MTS............	Magnetic Tape System [*Computer science*]
MTS............	Magnetic Type System [*Computer science*] (IAA)
MTS............	Mainsborne Telecontrol System (NITA)
MTS............	Maintenance Training Set (MCD)
MTS............	Maintenance Transmittal Sheet
MTS............	Main Trunk System [*Telecommunications*] (TEL)
MTS............	Management Tracking System [*Environmental Protection Agency*] (EPA)
MTS............	Manitoba Telephone System [*Telecommunications service*] (TSSD)
MTS............	Manned Teller System
MTS............	Manpower Training Services
MTS............	Mantrust Asahi Airways PT [*Indonesia*] [*ICAO designator*] (FAAC)
MTS............	Manual Testing System [*Sports medicine*]
MTS............	Manufacturing Technology Section [*Navy*]
MTS............	Manzini [*Swaziland*] [*Airport symbol*] (OAG)
MTS............	Mardan Test Set
MTS............	Marine Technology Society (EA)
MTS............	Maritime Tactical Schools (MCD)
MTS............	Marketing and Transportation Situation [*Series*] [*A publication*]
MTS............	Marketing Technical Services
MTS............	Mark Twain Society [*Defunct*] (EA)
MTS............	MARS [*Military Affiliate Radio System*] Technical Service (CET)
MTS............	Mass Target Sensor
MTS............	Mass Termination System [*Computer science*] (IEEE)
MTS............	Master of Teaching of Science (GAGS)
MTS............	Master of Theological Studies (WGA)
MTS............	Master Test Station
MTS............	Master Timing Schedule
MTS............	Master Timing System
MTS............	Material Test Specification (MSA)
MTS............	Matsue [*Japan*] [*Seismograph station code, US Geological Survey*] (SEIS)
MTS............	Medical Testing Systems [*Commercial firm*]
MTS............	Member of the Technical Staff [*A generic term*]
MTS............	Memory Test System
MTS............	Meridian Telecommunication Services [*Indianapolis, IN*] (TSSD)
MTS............	Message Telecommunications Service
MTS............	Message Telephone Service (NITA)
MTS............	Message Toll Service [*Communications*]
MTS............	Message Traffic Study
MTS............	Message Transfer Service
MTS............	Message Transfer System [*Telecommunications*] (OSI)
MTS............	Message Transfer Subsystem [*Telecommunications*] (TEL)
MTS............	Meteoroid Technology Satellite [*NASA*]
MTS............	Methods-Time Study [*Industrial engineering*]
MTS............	Methyltrichlorosilane [*Organic chemistry*]
MTS............	Metric Time System (NASA)
MTS............	Metric Time System
MTS............	Michigan Terminal System [*Computer science*]
MTS............	Microprocessor Training System [*Integrated Computer Systems*] (NITA)
MTS............	Microsoft Transaction Server [*Computer science*]
MTS............	Microtubule-Stabilizing Solution [*Cytology*]
MTS............	Microwave Test Set (MCD)
MTS............	Military Test Satellite
MTS............	Military Training Standard (AFM)
MTS............	Million (10^6) Transitions Per Second [*Of magnetic storage*] (NITA)
MTS............	Missile Test Set
MTS............	Missile Test Stand
MTS............	Missile Test Station
MTS............	Missile Tracking Station [*DoD*]
MTS............	Missile Tracking System (IEEE)
MTS............	Missile Training Squadron
MTS............	Missile Tube Supply
MTS............	Missions to Seamen [*British*]
MTS............	Mississippi Test Site [*Aerospace*] (AAG)
MTS............	Mobile Telephone Service
MTS............	Mobile Terminal System [*IBM Corp.*]
MTS............	Mobile Tracking Station [*NASA*]
MTS............	Mobile Training Set (AFM)
MTS............	Mobil-Trac System [*MTMC*] (TAG)
MTS............	Modem Test Set (NITA)
MTS............	Moderate Tactile Stimulus [*Neurology*] (DAVI)
MTS............	Modernization through Spares [*Army program*]
MTS............	Modernization through Spares
MTS............	Modular Television System [*Telecommunications*] (CDE)
MTS............	Modular Terminal System (NITA)
MTS............	Module Test Set (MCD)
MTS............	Module Test System (IAA)
MTS............	Module Tracking System (NRCH)

MTS	Money Transfer System (IAA)
MTS	Monosyllable, Trochee, Spondee Test [Of speech discrimination] (DAVI)
MTS	Montgomery St Inc. Sec [NYSE symbol] (TTSB)
MTS	Montgomery Street Income Securities, Inc. [NYSE symbol] (SPSG)
MTS	Monthly Treasury Statement [Government] (AFM)
MTS	Morale Tendency Score (AEE)
MTS	Motion-Time Standards [Industrial engineering]
MTS	Motor-Operated Transfer Switch
MTS	Motor Tariff Service
MTS	Motor Turbine Ship (IIA)
MTS	Mountains [Board on Geographic Names]
MTS	Moving Target Screen (MCD)
MTS	Moving Target Simulator (RDA)
MTS	Moving Time Series
MTS	MTS Systems Corp. [Associated Press] (SAG)
MTS	Multichannel Television Sound [or Stereo]
MTS	Multichannel TV Sound (WDMC)
MTS	Multichannel TV Stereo (WDMC)
MTS	Multiple Target Screen
MTS	Multiple Terminal System (NITA)
MTS	Multiple Time Scale
MTS	Multiple Tumor Suppressor [Oncology]
MTS	Muscle Testing System [Myology]
MTS	State Law Library of Montana, Helena, MT [OCLC symbol] (OCLC)
MTS1	Multiple Tumour Suppressor 1 [Genetics] (ECON)
MTSA	Seaman Apprentice, Missile Technician, Striker [Navy rating]
MTSAT	Multi-functional Transport Satellite
MtSc	Daniels County Free Library, Scobey, MT [Library symbol] [Library of Congress] (LCLS)
MTSC	Magnetic Tape Selectric Composer [IBM Corp.]
MTSC	Master of Teaching Speech Communication (GAGS)
MTSC	Master of Technical and Scientific Communication (GAGS)
MTSC	Master of Theological Studies Counseling (PGP)
MTSC	MTS Systems [NASDAQ symbol] (TTSB)
MTSC	MTS Systems Corp. [NASDAQ symbol] (NQ)
MTSD	Military Transmission Systems Department [NORAD]
MTSE	Magnetic Trap Stability Experiment (IEEE)
MTSF	Mean Time to System Failure [Quality control] (PDAA)
MTS/GMS	Module Test Set / Guided Missile System (DWSG)
MTSGT	Master Technical Sergeant [Marine Corps]
MTSGT(C)	Master Technical Sergeant (Commissary) [Marine Corps]
MtSh	Toole County Free Library, Shelby, MT [Library symbol] [Library of Congress] (LCLS)
MTSI	Micro Touch Systems [NASDAQ symbol] (TTSB)
MTSI	Microtouch Systems, Inc. [NASDAQ symbol] (SAG)
MtSid	Sidney Public Library, Sidney, MT [Library symbol] [Library of Congress] (LCLS)
Mt Sinai Sch Med	Mount Sinai School of Medicine of The City University of New York (GAGS)
MTSL	Message Transfer Sublayer [Telecommunications] (OSI)
MTSL	Monitoring and Technical Support Laboratory [Environmental Protection Agency] [GFGA]
MTSN	Mattson Technology [NASDAQ symbol] (TTSB)
MTSN	Mattson Technology, Inc. [NASDAQ symbol] (SAG)
MTSN	Seaman, Missile Technician, Striker [Navy rating]
MTSO	Mobile Telephone Switching Office [Telecommunications]
MTSP	Maintenance Test Support Package [Army]
MTSPS	Multiple Transducer Seismic Profiling System
MTSQ	Mechanical Time, Superquick [Fuse] [Weaponry]
MTSQF	Mechanical Time, Superquick Fuze [Weaponry] (MCD)
MTSR	Maximal Temperature of the Synthesis Reaction [Chemical engineering]
MTSR	Mean Time to Service Restoral [Quality control] [Telecommunications] (TEL)
MTSR	Mid-Term Status Reports
MTSS	Magnetic Tape Storage System
MTSS	Manned Test Space System [See also MOD, MODS, MOSS] [Air Force/NASA]
MTSS	Military Test Space Station [See also MOD, MODS, MOSS] [Air Force/NASA]
MTSSL	Methanethiosulphonate Spin Label [Analytical chemistry]
MTST	Magnetic Tape Selectric Typewriter [IBM Corp.]
MT/ST	Magnetic Tape Selectric Typewriter [NITA]
MTST	Microtest, Inc. [NASDAQ symbol] (SAG)
Mt St Mary's C	Mount St. Mary's College (GAGS)
MtStrS	St. Regis School, St. Regis, MT [Library symbol] [Library of Congress] (LCLS)
MTSU	Magnetic Tape Search Unit [Computer science]
MTSU	Middle Tennessee State University
MtSu	Mineral County Public Library, Superior, MT [Library symbol] [Library of Congress] (LCLS)
MTS/VO	Motor Transportation Supervisor/Vehicle Operator (AAG)
MTT	Magnetic Tape Terminal [Computer science]
MTT	Magnetic Tape Transport [Computer science] (IEEE)
MTT	Maintenance Training Team (MCD)
MTT	Malignant Trophoblastic Teratoma [Oncology] (MAE)
MTT	Mammillothalamic Tract [Neuroanatomy]
MTT	Maritime Telegraph & Telephone Co. Ltd. [Toronto Stock Exchange symbol]
MTT	Masked Terrain Trainer [Military]
MTT	Master of Textile Technology
MTT	Material Testing Technology (MCD)
MTT	Maximal Treadmill Test (CPH)
MTT	Maximum Touch Temperature (MCD)

MTT	Mean Transit Time
MTT	Mediterranean Tours and Travel [Egypt]
MTT	Medium Tactical Transport [Army]
MTT	Medium Tactical Truck [Army] (RDA)
MTT	Message Transfer Time (NITA)
MTT	Methyl(thio)tetrazole [Biochemistry]
MTT	Metropolitan Edison Co. [NYSE symbol] (SPSG)
MTT	Microwave Theory and Technique (MCD)
MTT	Military Training Team (MCD)
MTT	Minatitlan [Mexico] [Airport symbol] (OAG)
MTT	Missionary Tech Team (EA)
MTT	Mi-Tsiyon Tetse Torah [Tel Aviv] (BJA)
MTT	Mobile Training Team
MTT	Mobile Travel Team (MCD)
MTT	Monetta Fire Tower [South Carolina] [Seismograph station code, US Geological Survey] (SEIS)
MTT	Monotetrazolium [Medicine] (MAE)
MTT	Multiple Target Tracker
MTT	Munitions Transfer Truck (MCD)
MTT	Orion SpA [Italy ICAO designator] (FAAC)
MtT	Prairie County Library, Terry, MT [Library symbol] [Library of Congress] (LCLS)
MTTA	Machine Tool Technologies Association [British] (EAIO)
MTTA	Machine Tool Trades Association (ACII)
MTTA	Machine Tool Trades' Association (NADA)
MTTA	Mean Time to Accomplish [Quality control] (NASA)
MTTA	Multi-Tenant Telecommunications Association (EA)
MTTB	Mean Time to Bench [Repair] [Quality control]
MTTc	Mean Time to Change Parts [Quality control] (MCD)
MTTC	Mechanised Transport Training Corps [British military] (DMA)
MtTcES	Trout Creek Elementary School, Trout Creek, MT [Library symbol] [Library of Congress] (LCLS)
MTTD	Mean Time to Detect [Quality control] (MCD)
MTTD	Mean Time to Diagnosis [Quality control] (BUR)
MTTE	Magnetic Tape Terminal Equipment [Computer science] (CET)
MTTE	Mean Time to Exchange [Quality control] (MCD)
MTTEA	Marine Towing and Transportation Employers Association [Defunct] (EA)
MTTF	Mean Time to Failure [Quality control]
MtTf	Thompson Falls Public Library, Thompson Falls, MT [Library symbol] [Library of Congress] (LCLS)
MTTFF	Mean Time to First Failure [Quality control]
MtTfS	Thompson Falls Schools, Thompson Falls, MT [Library symbol] [Library of Congress] (LCLS)
MTTFSF	Mean Time to First System Failure [Quality control] (PDAA)
MTTFSR	Mean Time to First System Repair [Quality control] (PDAA)
MTTHS	Modern Transport Technical and Historical Society [Later, SFCH] (EA)
MTTI	Magnetic Tape Transport Interface [Computer science] (MCD)
MTTI	Mean Time to Inspect [Quality control] (CAAL)
MTTI	Modified Tension Time Index [Cardiology]
MTTL	Motorola Transistor-Transistor Logic (IAA)
MTTM	Magnetic Tape and Telemetry (MCD)
MTTM	Mean Time to Maintain [Quality control] (CMD)
MTTN	Multi-Tranche Tap Note [Finance] [British]
MTTO	Minuetto [Slow Air] [Music] (ROG)
MTTOP	Machine Tool Trigger Order Program (MHDB)
MTTP	Materials Testing and Technology Program
MTTP	Maximum Total Trihalomethane Potential (FFDE)
MTTPO	Mean Time to Planned Outage (IEEE)
MTTPrC	Metropol Ed 3.90% cm Pfd [NYSE symbol] (TTSB)
MTTPrZ	Met-Ed Capital L.P.'MIPS' [NYSE symbol] (TTSB)
MTTR	Magnetic Tape Transport Replacement (DWSG)
MTTR	Maximum Time to Repair (MCD)
MTTR	Maximum Time to Replace [Navy] (IAA)
MTTR	Mean Time to Removal [Quality control]
MTTR	Mean Time to Repair [Quality control] (CAAL)
MTTR	Mean Time to Replacement [Quality control]
MTTR	Mean Time to Restore [Quality control] (IEEE)
MTTR	Missile Target Tracking RADAR (MCD)
MTTRF	Mission Time to Restore Function
mttRNA	Mitochondrial Transfer RNA[Ribonucleic Acid] [Genetics] (DOG)
MTTRS	Mean Time to Restore Software [Quality control] (CAAL)
MTTRS	Mean Time to Restore System [Quality control]
MTTS	IEEE Microwave Theory and Techniques Society (EA)
MTTS	Marine Terminal Tankage System (MCD)
MTTS	Mean Time to Service [Quality control]
MTTS	Mobile Target Tracking System
MTTS	Multiple Target Tracking System
MTTS	Multitask Terminal System
MTTSF	Mean Time to System Failure [Quality control] (PDAA)
MTTT	Mean Time to Test (MCD)
MTTU	Modular Timing Terminal Unit
MTTUO	Mean Time to Unplanned Outage (IEEE)
MTTV	Maneuvering Target Test Vechicle
MTTW	Mean Time to Wait for Parts [Quality control] (MCD)
MtTyrSH	Troy Senior High School, Troy, MT [Library symbol] [Library of Congress] (LCLS)
MTU	Magnetic Tape Unit [Computer science]
MTU	Maintenance Training Unit
MTU	malignant Teratoma Undifferentiated [Oncology] (DAVI)
MTU	Managed Municipal Portfolio II [NYSE symbol] (SPSG)
MTU	Managed Muni Portfolio II [NYSE symbol] (TTSB)
MTU	Manchester Terminal Unit (NITA)
MTU	Master Terminal Unit [Instrumentation]

MTU .... Master Time Unit
MTU .... Master Trigger Unit (IAA)
MTU .... Memory Transfer Unit (NITA)
MTU .... Methylthiouracil [*Pharmacology*]
MTU .... Metric Tons of Uranium
MTU .... Metric Ton Unit
MTU .... Metric Units (DFIT)
MTU .... Michigan Technological University [*Houghton*]
MTU .... MIRA [*Multifunctional Inertial Reference Assembly*] Transport Unit
            [*Air Force*] (MCD)
MTU .... Missile Tracking Unit (MCD)
MTU .... Missile Training Unit [*Air Force*]
MTU .... Mist Therapy Unit [*Medicine*]
MTU .... Mobile Technical Unit (MCD)
MTU .... Mobile Test Unit [*Army*] (RDA)
MTU .... Mobile Training Unit
MTU .... Mobile Treatment Unit [*Environmental Protection Agency*] (GFGA)
MTU .... Module Test Unit [*Nuclear energy*] (NRCH)
mtu .... Montana [*MARC country of publication code Library of Congress*]
            (LCCP)
MTU .... Montreal Trustco, Inc. [*Toronto Stock Exchange symbol*]
MTU .... Mosquito Training Unit [*British military*] (DMA)
MTU .... Motorinen Turbo-Union [*Germany*]
MTU .... Multiplexer and Terminal Unit
MTU .... Multiterminal Unit (TEL)
MTU .... Myton, UT [*Location identifier FAA*] (FAAL)
MtU .... University of Montana at Missoula, Missoula, MT [*Library symbol
            Library of Congress*] (LCLS)
M TUBERC... Mycobacterium Tuberculosis [*Bacteriology*] (CPH)
MtU-L .... University of Montana at Missoula, Law School, Missoula, MT
            [*Library symbol Library of Congress*] (LCLS)
MTUMR .... MIRA [*Multifunctional Inertial Reference Assembly*] Transport Unit
            MountingRack [*Air Force*] (MCD)
MTUOP .... Mobile Training Units Out for Parts
MTUR .... Mean Time between Unscheduled Removals [*or Replacements*]
            [*Quality control*] (IIA)
MTUR .... Mean Time to Unscheduled Replacement [*Quality control*] (PDAA)
MTV .... Conference des Ministres Europeens du Travail [*Conference of
            European Ministers of Labour*] (EAIO)
MTV .... Mammary Tumor Virus
MTV .... Management Television [*Air Force*] (AFM)
MTV .... Maneuvering Technology Vehicle
MTV .... Marginal Terrain Vehicle
MTV .... Martinsville, VA [*Location identifier FAA*] (FAAL)
M TV .... Master of Television
MTV .... Mean Transformed Value
MTV .... Media Transforming Virus [*Alleged virus causing immunodeficiency
            disease*]
MTV .... Medium Tactical Vehicle [*Army*] (RDA)
MTV .... Medium Tactical Vehicle
MTV .... Metatarsus Varus [*Anatomy*] (DAVI)
MTV .... Missile Test Vehicle
MTV .... Missile Training Vehicle
MTV .... Modulated Throttle Valve [*Automotive engineering*]
MTV .... Mota Lava [*Vanuatu*] [*Airport symbol*] (OAG)
MTV .... Motor Test Vehicle (IAA)
MTV .... Motor Torpedo Vessel [*British*]
MTV .... Motor Transport Volunteers [*Military unit*] [*British*]
MTV .... Mountain Valley Air Service, Inc. [*ICAO designator*] (FAAC)
MTV .... Mount Tassie [*Australia Seismograph station code, US Geological
            Survey Closed*] (SEIS)
MTV .... Multicultural Television (ADA)
MTV .... Munitions Tow Vehicle (MCD)
MTV .... Munition Test Vehicle
MTV .... Music Television [*Warner Amex Satellite Entertainment Co.*]
            [*Cable-television system*]
MTV .... Mutatur Terminatio Versiculi [*The Termination of the Little Verse Is
            Changed*]
MTVAL .... Master Tape Validation
MTVC .... Manned [*or Manual*] Thrust Vector Control (MCD)
MTVP .... Moving Target Video Processor
MTVS .... Mission Test and Video System
MTVU .... Module Thruster Valve Unit
MTW .... Machine Tool Wire
MTW .... Main Trawl Winch
MTW .... Manitowoc [*Wisconsin*] [*Airport symbol*] (OAG)
MTW .... Manitowoc Co. [*NYSE symbol*] (SPSG)
MTW .... Marinette, Tomahawk & Western Railroad Co. [*AAR code*]
MTW .... Maximum Taxi Weight [*Aviation*]
MTW .... Military Transport Wagon [*British*]
MTW .... Mission to the World (EA)
MTW .... Mobile Training Wing [*Air Force*]
MTW .... Music Treasures of the World [*Record label*]
mtw .... Tropical Maritime Warm Air Mass [*Meteorology*] (BARN)
MtW .... Wibaux Public Library, Wibaux, MT [*Library symbol*] [*Library of
            Congress*] (LCLS)
MTWA .... Maximum Total Weight Authorized [*Aviation*] (AIA)
MTWC .... Morgan Three-Wheeler Club (EA)
MTWF .... Metal Thru-Wall Flashing [*Technical drawings*]
MtWfSH .... Whitefish Senior High School, Whitefish, MT [*Library symbol*] [*Library
            of Congress*] (LCLS)
MTWN .... Mark Twain Bancshares, Inc. [*NASDAQ symbol*] (NQ)
MTWN .... Mark Twain Bancshrs [*NASDAQ symbol*] (TTSB)
MTWO .... Material Test Work Order (SAA)
MTWO .... Melamine Chemicals [*NASDAQ symbol*] (TTSB)

MTWO .... Melamine Chemicals, Inc. [*NASDAQ symbol*] (NQ)
MTWP .... Multiplier Traveling Wave Phototube (IAA)
MtWp .... Roosevelt County Library, Wolf Point, MT [*Library symbol*] [*Library of
            Congress*] (LCLS)
MTWS .... MAGTF [*Marine Air-Ground Task Force*] Tactical Warfare Simulation
            [*DoD*]
MTWS .... Manual Track While Scan
MtWs .... Montana State Hospital, Patient Library, Warm Springs, MT [*Library
            symbol*] [*Library of Congress*] (LCLS)
MTWX .... Mechanized Teletypewriter Exchange (TEL)
MTWY .... Motorway
MTWY .... Motorway [*Postal Service standard*] (OPSA)
MTX .... Fairbanks [*Alaska*] Metro Field [*Airport symbol Obsolete*] (OAG)
MTX .... Manual Transaxle
MTX .... Master of Taxation
MTX .... Matrix (IAA)
MTX .... Methotrexate [*Antineoplastic drug*]
MTX .... Microwave TOKAMAK [*Toroidal Kamera Magnetic*] Experiment
            [*Plasma physics*]
MTX .... Military Traffic Expediting Service (AABC)
MTX .... Minerals Technologies [*NYSE symbol*] (SPSG)
MTX .... Morrell Tank Line [*AAR code*]
MTXC .... Matrix Capital Corp. [*NASDAQ symbol*] (SAG)
MTX-CF ...... Methotrexate with Citrovorum Factor Rescue [*Antineoplastic drug
            regimen*]
MTX + MP ... Methotrexate and Mercaptopurine [*Antineoplastic drug regimen*]
            (DAVI)
MTX + MP + CTX... Methotrexate, Mercaptopurine, and Cytoxan
            [*Cyclophosphamide*] [*Antineoplastic drug regimen*] (DAVI)
MTY .... Empty
MTY .... Marlton Technologies [*AMEX symbol*] (TTSB)
MTY .... Marlton Technologies, Inc. [*AMEX symbol*] (SPSG)
MTY .... Matsuyama [*Japan*] [*Seismograph station code, US Geological
            Survey*] (SEIS)
MTY .... Maturity [*Business term*]
MTY .... Mekhon ha-Tekanim ha-Yisre'eli (BJA)
MTY .... Million Tons per Year
MTY .... Monterrey [*Mexico*] [*Airport symbol*] (OAG)
mtydm .... Martyrdom (VRA)
MTZ .... Mass Transfer Zone [*Chemical engineering*]
MTZ .... Montezuma [*Chile*] [*Seismograph station code, US Geological Survey
            Closed*] (SEIS)
MTZ .... Motorized (AAG)
MTZ .... Tuskegee, AL [*Location identifier FAA*] (FAAL)
MU .... Akaflieg Muenchen Mitsubishi Heavy Industries [*Germany Japan
            ICAO aircraft manufacturer identifier*] (ICAO)
MU .... China Eastern Airlines [*ICAO designator*] (AD)
Mu .... Mache Unit [*Measure of radium emanation from solutions*] (AAMN)
MU .... Machine Unit
MU .... Mail Unit (KSC)
MU .... Maintenance Unit [*Military*]
MU .... Makeup (NRCH)
MU .... Management Unit [*Aviation*]
MU .... Maneuvering Unit (KSC)
mu .... Map Unit (DOG)
MU .... Marginal Utility [*Economics*]
MU .... Markup
MU .... Mass Units
MU .... Master Unit (NASA)
mu .... Mauritania [*MARC country of publication code Library of Congress*]
            (LCCP)
MU .... Mauritius [*ANSI two-letter standard code*] (CNC)
MU .... Measurement Unit
MU .... Memory Unit [*Computer science*] (MCD)
MU .... Mental Units of Growth [*Psychology*]
MU .... Message Unit [*Telecommunications*]
MU .... Methylene Unit
MU .... Methylumbelliferone [*Biochemistry*]
MU .... Methylurea [*Organic chemistry*]
MU .... Micro [*One millionth*] (WDAA)
mu .... Micron [*Micrometer*] (AAMN)
MU .... Micron Technology [*NYSE symbol*] (TTSB)
MU .... Micron Technology, Inc. [*NYSE symbol*] (SPSG)
mu .... Millimicro- [*Now nano*] (IDOE)
mu .... Millimicron [*Nanometer*] (IDOE)
Mu .... Millimicron (AAG)
MU .... Million Units
mU .... Milliunit (AAMN)
MU .... Misrair [*ICAO designator*] (AD)
MU .... Mobile Unit
MU .... Mock-Up (AAG)
M/U .... Mockup
MU .... Modular Unit (IAA)
MU .... Monetary Unit (ADA)
M/U .... Monitor Unit [*Telecommunications*] (TEL)
MU .... Montevideo Units [*Of uterine activity*]
MU .... Mothers' Union [*Episcopalian*]
MU .... Motor Union
MU .... Motor Unit
MU .... Mouse Unit [*Medicine*] (DMAA)
MU .... Mueller Cell [*Eye anatomy*]
MU .... Multidestination [*Carrier*]
MU .... Multiple Unit
MU .... Multiple Use (IAA)
MU .... Multiplexing Unit

MU............ Munitions Command [Later, Armaments Command] [Army] (MCD)
Mu............ Muscle [Anatomy] (DAVI)
MU............ Musical Union [Oberlin College] [Ohio]
MU............ Musician [Navy rating]
MU............ Musicians' Union [British] (DCTA)
MU............ Music Program [Association of Independent Colleges and Schools specialization code]
MU............ Muster [Business term] (DCTA)
Mu............ Mutator [A bacteriophage]
MU............ University of Massachusetts, Amherst, MA [Library symbol Library of Congress] (LCLS)
MU1.......... Musician, First Class [Navy rating]
MU2.......... Musician, Second Class [Navy rating]
MU3.......... Musician, Third Class [Navy rating]
MUA.......... Machinery Users' Association [British] (BI)
MUA.......... Mail Users' Association [British]
MUA.......... Manned Undersea [or Underwater] Activity [Marine science]
MUA.......... Maritime Union of Australia
MUA.......... Master of Urban Affairs (GAGS)
MUA.......... Master of Urban Architecture (GAGS)
MUA.......... Materials Usage Agreement (NASA)
MUA.......... Maximum Usable Altitude [Aviation]
MUA.......... Memorandum of Understanding and Agreement
MUA.......... Metallurgistes Unis d'Amerique [United Steelworkers of America - USWA]
MU A......... Microampere (WDAA)
MUA.......... Ministry of State for Urban Affairs [Canada]
MUA.......... Mixed Underachievers [Education]
MUA.......... Monotype Users' Association (NADA)
MUA.......... Mothers' Union in Australia
MUA.......... Multiple Unit Activity [Neurophysiology]
MUA.......... Munda [Solomon Islands] [Airport symbol] (OAG)
MUAS......... Muniassets Fund [NYSE symbol] (SPSG)
MUA.......... Murray Aviation, Inc. [ICAO designator] (FAAC)
MUAA........ Major Unit Assembly Area (MCD)
MUAC........ Mid Upper Arm Circumference [Anatomy]
MUACS....... Manpower Utilization and Control System
MUADEE..... [The] Mars Upper Atmosphere Dynamics, Energetics and Evolution Spacecraft [NASA] (ECON)
MUAG......... Central Agramonte [Cuba ICAO location identifier] (ICLI)
MU/AG....... Mid-Upper [Turret] Air Gunner [British military] (DMA)
MU & P...... Makeup and Purification [Nuclear energy] (NRCH)
MUAP........ Motor Unit Action Potential [Physiology]
MUARC....... Monash University Accident Research Center [Australia]
MUART....... Microprocessor Universal Asynchronous Receiver Transmitter (IAA)
MUAT......... Antilla [Cuba ICAO location identifier] (ICLI)
MUAT......... Mobile Underwater Acoustic Unit (NATG)
MUB.......... Maun [Botswana] [Airport symbol] (OAG)
MUB.......... University of Maryland, Baltimore County Campus, Catonsville, MD [OCLC symbol] (OCLC)
MUBA........ Baracoa/Oriente [Cuba ICAO location identifier] (ICLI)
MU BAR...... Microbar (WDAA)
MUBE........ El Caribe [Cuba ICAO location identifier] (ICLI)
MUBI......... Cayo Mambi [Cuba ICAO location identifier] (ICLI)
MUBIS....... Multiple Beam Interval Scanner
MUBO........ Batabano [Cuba ICAO location identifier] (ICLI)
MUBR........ Mean Units between Replacement [Quality control]
MUBY........ Bayamo [Cuba ICAO location identifier] (ICLI)
MUC.......... Maximum Urinary Concentration [Medicine]
MUC.......... Meritorious Unit Citation [Military decoration]
MUC.......... Meritorious Unit Commendation [Military decoration] (AFM)
MUC.......... Missionary Union of the Clergy [British] (BI)
MUC.......... Mount Union College [Alliance, OH]
MUC.......... Mucilaginous (ROG)
MUC.......... Mucosal Ulcerative Colitis [Medicine]
MUC.......... Multicoupler
MUC.......... Multiple Use Counter (IAA)
MUC.......... Munich [Germany Airport symbol] (OAG)
MUC.......... Musician, Chief [Navy rating]
MUCA........ Ciego De Avila [Cuba ICAO location identifier] (ICLI)
MuCA2....... Muniyield California Insured Fund II [Associated Press] (SAG)
MuCAIns..... MuniYield California Insured Fund [Associated Press] (SAG)
MUCB........ Caibarien [Cuba ICAO location identifier] (ICLI)
MUCC........ Cunagua [Cuba ICAO location identifier] (ICLI)
MUCC........ Michigan United Conservation Clubs
MUCF........ Cienfuegos [Cuba ICAO location identifier] (ICLI)
MUCG........ Macquarie University Caving Group [Australia]
MUCG........ Management/Union Consultative Group [Australia]
Much D & S... Muchall's Doctor and Student [A publication] (DLA)
MUCHFET.... Multichannel Field Effect Transistor (IAA)
MUCIA....... Midwest Universities Consortium for International Activities [University of Indiana]
MUCILAG..... Mucilaginous (ROG)
MUCL........ Cayo Largo Del Sur [Cuba ICAO location identifier] (ICLI)
MUCM........ Camaguey/Ignacio Agramonte [Cuba ICAO location identifier] (ICLI)
MUCM........ Musician, Master Chief [Navy rating]
MUCN........ Ciego De Avila Norte [Cuba ICAO location identifier] (ICLI)
MUCO........ Colon [Cuba ICAO location identifier] (ICLI)
MUCO........ Materiel Utilization Control Office (AFIT)
MUCOM...... Munitions Command [Later, Armaments Command] [Army]
Mu Corp Ca... Municipal Corporation Cases [United States] [A publication] (DLA)
Mu Corp Cir... Municipal Corporation Circular [England] [A publication] (DLA)
MUCROMAF.. Multiple Critical Root Maximally Flat (PDAA)
MUCS........ Central Noel Fernandez [Cuba ICAO location identifier] (ICLI)
MUCS........ Musician, Senior Chief [Navy rating]

MUCU........ Santiago De Cuba/Antonio Maceo [Cuba ICAO location identifier] (ICLI)
MUCUSA..... Missionary Union of the Clergy in the United States of America [Later, PMUPR] (EA)
MUCV........ Las Clavellinas [Cuba ICAO location identifier] (ICLI)
MUCY........ Cayajabo [Cuba ICAO location identifier] (ICLI)
MUD.......... Macromind Utility Disk
MUD.......... Master of Urban Design (GAGS)
MUD.......... Master User Directory (MHDI)
MUD.......... Memory Unit Drum [Computer science]
MUD.......... Mercaptoundecanol [Organic chemistry]
MUD.......... Mercaptoundecanol [Organic chemistry]
MUD.......... Middle, Up, Down [in game of bridge]
MUD.......... Mouvement pour l'Unite et la Democratie [Djibouti] [Political party] (EY)
MUD.......... Mouvement Union Democratique [Democratic Union Movement] [Monaco] [Political party] (PPE)
MUD.......... Multiple User Dimension [Computer science]
MUD.......... Multi-User Domain [Computer science]
MUD.......... Multi-User Dungeon [Computer game]
MUD.......... Municipal Utility District [Investment term] (DFIT)
MUD.......... Murchison Falls [Uganda] [Airport symbol] (AD)
MUDAID...... Multivariate, Univariate, and Discriminant Analysis of Irregular Data [Statistics] (IAA)
MUDAR....... Mulheres por um Desenvolvimento Alternativo [Development Alternatives with women for a New Era - DAWN] [Brazil] (EAIO)
MUDD........ Multisource Unified Data Distribution (PDAA)
MUDDC...... Multiunit Direct Digital Control (IAA)
MUDET....... Militarized Universal Digital Element Tester (MCD)
MUDL........ Microwave Ultrasonic Delay Line
MUDPIE...... Museum and University Data Processing Information Exchange (IAA)
MUDR........ Multidetail Drawing (MSA)
MUDS........ Multiple Usage Data Sheet (MCD)
Mudst........ Mudstone Soil [Agronomy]
MUDWNT.... Makeup Demineralizer Waste Neutralizer Tank (IEEE)
MUE.......... Kamuela [Hawaii] [Airport symbol] (OAG)
MUE.......... Meritorious Unit Emblem [Military decoration]
MUE.......... Microcomputer Users in Education (AIE)
MUEI......... Micron Electronics, Inc. [NASDAQ symbol] (SAG)
MUEI......... Micron Electronics [NASDAQ symbol] (TTSB)
MUEL........ Mueller [Paul] Co. [NASDAQ symbol] (NQ)
Mueller...... Mueller Industries [Associated Press] (SAG)
MuellerInd... Muller Industries [Associated Press] (SAG)
MuellerP..... Mueller [Paul] Co. [Associated Press] (SAG)
MUERI....... Murdoch University Energy Research Institute [Australia]
MUF.......... Makeup Feed [Boiler]
MUF.......... Material Unaccounted For [Nuclear energy]
MUF.......... Maximum Usable Frequency [Signal transmission]
MU F......... Microfarad (WDAA)
MUF.......... Muffler
MUF.......... Muting [Indonesia] [Airport symbol] (OAG)
MUFC........ Central Amancio Rodriguez [Cuba ICAO location identifier] (ICLI)
MUFD........ Makeup Feed [Boiler]
MUFFIN...... Multi-Use Interagency News [FSS database] (AAGC)
MUFL........ Florida [Cuba ICAO location identifier] (ICLI)
MuFLIn...... MuniYield Florida Insured Fund [Associated Press] (SAG)
MUFLNG..... Mouvement pour l'Unification des Forces de Liberation de la Guadeloupe [Movement for the Unification of National Liberation Forces of Guadeloupe] [Political party] (PD)
MUFLR....... Muffler
MUFM........ Mouvement Universel pour une Federation Mondiale [World Association of World Federalists - WAWF] [Netherlands]
MUFON...... Mutual UFO [Unidentified Flying Object] Network (EA)
MUFT........ Multigroup Fourier Transform [Code] [Nuclear energy] (NRCH)
MUFTI....... Minimum Use of Force Tactical Intervention [British police]
MUG.......... Macintosh User Group [Computer science] (WDMC)
MUG.......... Macintosh User Group [Computer science] (CDE)
MUG.......... Make-Up Gas [Chemical engineering]
MUG.......... Manning Unit Group [Air Force] (AFM)
MUG.......... Marcive Users Group [Library network]
MUG.......... MARC Users Group (NITA)
MUG.......... Maximum Unilateral Gain (IAA)
MUG.......... Maximum Usable Gain [Bell System]
MUG.......... Methylumbelliferylglucuronide [Biochemistry]
MU G......... Microgram (WDAA)
MUG.......... Ministry of Useless Gestures [Organization to increase number of voters] [British]
MUG.......... Mitosis with Unreplicated Genome [Cytology]
MUG.......... Mulege [Mexico] [Airport symbol Obsolete] (OAG)
MUG.......... Multiset Users Group (EA)
MUG.......... MUMPS [Massachusetts General Hospital Utility Multiprogramming System] Users' Group (EA)
MUG.......... Murgor Resources, Inc. [Vancouver Stock Exchange symbol]
MUGA........ Multigated Angiogram [Cardiology] (DAVI)
MUGA........ Multiple Gate Acquisition Analysis [Scan] (DAVI)
MUGA........ Multiple-Gated Acquisition [Nuclear medicine]
MU-GAL...... Methylumbelliferyl-B-Galactosidase [Biochemistry] (MAE)
MUGB........ Methylumbelliferyl Guanidinobenzoate [Biochemistry]
MUGEx....... Multigated Blood Pool Image during Exercise [Hematology] (DMAA)
MUGM....... Guantanamo, US Naval Air Base [Cuba ICAO location identifier] (ICLI)
MUGN........ Giron [Cuba ICAO location identifier] (ICLI)
MUGR........ Multigated Blood Pool Image at Rest [Medicine] (DMAA)
MUGSE....... Multimission-Unique Ground Support Equipment (MCD)
MUGT........ Guantanamo [Cuba ICAO location identifier] (ICLI)

MUGX.........	Multiple Gated Acquisition Exercise [Scan] [Cardiology] (DAVI)
MUH	Memorial University of Newfoundland, Health Sciences Library [UTLAS symbol]
MUH	Mersa Matruh [Egypt] [Airport symbol] (AD)
MU H	Microhenry (WDAA)
MUHA	Habana/Jose Marti [Cuba ICAO location identifier] (ICLI)
MUHG	Holguin [Cuba ICAO location identifier] (ICLI)
MUI	Fort Indiantown Gap (Annville), PA [Location identifier FAA] (FAAL)
MUI.............	Machine Utilization Index [Computer science]
MUI.............	Mashhad University [Iran] [Seismograph station code, US Geological Survey] (SEIS)
MUI.............	Mass Unbalance Input [Computer science]
MUI.............	Mode-Independent Unnumbered Information
MUI.............	Monsoonal Upwelling Index [Paleoceanography]
MUI.............	Movement for the Unity of the Left [Ecuador] [Political party] (PPW)
MUIG	Minicomputer Users Interest Group [Later, Mini/Micro Special Interest Group] (EA)
MU IN	Microinch (WDAA)
MuInII........	Muniyield Insured Fund [Associated Press] (SAG)
MUIR	Microinstruction Register (MHDI)
Muir Gai	Muirhea's Institutes of Gaius [A publication] (DLA)
MUIS	Isabella [Cuba ICAO location identifier] (ICLI)
MuIT	Municipal Income Trust [Associated Press] (SAG)
MuIT2	Municipal Income Trust II [Associated Press] (SAG)
MuIT3	Municipal Income Trust III [Associated Press] (SAG)
MUJ	Mui [Ethiopia] [Airport symbol] (OAG)
MUJA	Majana [Cuba ICAO location identifier] (ICLI)
MUK	Alamogordo, NM [Location identifier FAA] (FAAL)
MUK	Mauke [Cook Islands] [Airport symbol] (OAG)
MUK	MEPC International Capital LP [NYSE symbol] (SAG)
MUK	Muk Air Taxi [Denmark ICAO designator] (FAAC)
MUK............	Mukerian [India] [Seismograph station code, US Geological Survey Closed] (SEIS)
MUKPrA	MEPC Intl Cap 9.125%'QUIPS' [NYSE symbol] (TTSB)
MUL............	Manned Underwater Laboratories [Marine science] (MSC)
MUL............	Manufacturing under Licence [British] (DS)
MUL............	Master Urgency List [Navy]
MUL............	Mobile-Moored Undersea Laboratory
MUL............	Moultrie, GA [Location identifier FAA] (FAAL)
MUL............	Mullan [Idaho] [Seismograph station code, US Geological Survey] (SEIS)
MUL............	MULS [Minnesota Union List of Serials], Minneapolis, MN [OCLC symbol] (OCLC)
MUL............	Multicae Companies [NYSE symbol] (SAG)
MUL............	Multicare Cos. [NYSE symbol] (TTSB)
mul.............	Multilingual [MARC language code Library of Congress] (LCCP)
MUL............	Multiplexer
MUL............	Multiply (MDG)
MULASSS	Multiple LASER Source Signature Simulator (MCD)
MULB..........	Habana [Cuba ICAO location identifier] (ICLI)
MULDEM	Multiplexer/Demultiplexer [Bell Laboratories]
MULDEX	Multiplexer/Demultiplexer
MULDEX	Multipoint Cross-Reference Index
MULE..........	Manned-Unmanned Lunar Explorer
MULE..........	Modular Universal LASER Equipment (MCD)
MULE..........	Multiple-Use Linear Engergizer [Automotive engineering]
MULH..........	Habana [Cuba ICAO location identifier] (ICLI)
Mu LJ	Municipal Law Journal [A publication] (DLA)
MULL...........	Modern Uses of Logic in Law
MULL...........	Mullion [Technical drawings]
MULM..........	La Coloma [Cuba ICAO location identifier] (ICLI)
MuIMR........	Multi-Market Radio, Inc. [Associated Press] (SAG)
MuIMRad.....	Multi-Market Radio, Inc. [Associated Press] (SAG)
MULO..........	Multipurpose Lightweight Overboot [Army]
MULQUAL....	Multiple Goal Water Quality Model (PDAA)
MULR..........	Malayan Union Law Reports [1946-47] [A publication] (ILCA)
MULR..........	Muller
MULS..........	Mobile Unit Launch Site (IAA)
MULS..........	Signed Multiplication [Computer science]
MULSF........	Macquarie University Law School Foundation [Australia]
MULSP........	Missouri Union List of Serial Publications [St. Louis Public Library] [Missouri] [Information service or system] (IID)
MULT..........	Multiple
MULT..........	Multiply (NASA)
MULTA........	Multiple-Use Land Alliance (EA)
MultClr	Multi-Color Corp. [Associated Press] (SAG)
MULTEWS ...	Multiple Electronics Warfare Surveillance [DoD]
MULTEWS ...	Multitarget Electronic Warfare System
MULTH	Multilith
multi...........	Multicolored [Philately]
MULTI.........	Multiple (DAVI)
MULTI.........	Multiplexer
Multicne	Multicare Companies [Associated Press] (SAG)
MULTICOR...	Multinational Finance Corp. [Indonesia] (EY)
MultiCp.......	Multi-Corp, Inc. [Associated Press] (SAG)
Multicre.......	Multicare Companies [Associated Press] (SAG)
MULTICS	Multiplexed Information and Computing Service [Honeywell, Inc.]
MultiCul R ...	MultiCultural Review [A publication] (BRI)
Multilink PPP...	Multichannel Connection Protocol Based on the Point-to-Point Protocol [Computer science]
MultiMC......	MultiMedia Concepts International, Inc. [Associated Press] (SAG)
MultiMed.....	MultiMedia Concepts International, Inc. [Associated Press] (SAG)
multip.........	Multiparous [Obstetrics]
MULTIPAC ...	Multiple Pool Processor and Computer (PDAA)
MULTIPLE....	Multipurpose Program that Learns [Computer science] (PDAA)

MULTIV.......	Multivibrator (IAA)
multivits......	Multivitamins [Pharmacy]
MultM.........	Multi-Market Radio, Inc. [Associated Press] (SAG)
MultMC.......	MultiMedia Concepts International, Inc. [Associated Press] (SAG)
Multmd.......	Multimedia Concepts International, Inc. [Associated Press] (SAG)
MultMT	Multi-Media Tutorial Services, Inc. [Associated Press] (SAG)
MULTOTS	Multiple Units Link 11 Test and Operational Training System [Navy] (NVT)
MULTP........	Multiplier (NITA)
MultPb........	Multicom Publishing [Associated Press] (SAG)
MULTR	Multimeter (AAG)
MULTR	Multiplier
MultZns	Multiple Zones International, Inc. [Associated Press] (SAG)
MULU	Unsigned Multiplication [Computer science]
MuLV	Murine Leukemia Virus [Also, MLV]
Mum App.....	Chrysanthemum [Horticulture]
MUM	Maximum Useful Magnification (MCD)
MUM	Method of Unweighted Means [Statistics]
MUM	Methodology for Unmanned Manufacture [Robotics project] [Japan]
MUM	Multiple Unit Message [Telecommunications] (IEEE)
MUM	Multiuse Manuscript
MUM	Multiuse Mnemonics (IAA)
MUM	Multi-User Message (NITA)
MUM	Multiuser Monitor
MUM	Mumias [Kenya] [Airport symbol Obsolete] (OAG)
MUM	University of Mississippi, University, MS [OCLC symbol] (OCLC)
MU M²	Square Micrometer (WDAA)
MU M³	Cubic Micrometer (WDAA)
MUMA	Punta De Maisi [Cuba ICAO location identifier] (ICLI)
MUMAD	Museum Angkatan Darat [Indonesia]
Mumf	Mumford's Jamaica Reports [A publication] (DLA)
MUMG	Managua [Cuba ICAO location identifier] (ICLI)
MUMH	Matahambre [Cuba ICAO location identifier] (ICLI)
MUMI	Manzanillo [Cuba ICAO location identifier] (ICLI)
MUMJ	Mayajigua [Cuba ICAO location identifier] (ICLI)
Mum Jam	Mumford's Jamaica Reports [A publication] (DLA)
MUMMERS...	Manned-Unmanned Environmental Research Station (MSC)
MUMMS	Marine Corps Unified Materiel Management System
Mummy	Mature Upwardly Mobile Mommy [Lifestyle classification]
MUMO	Moa [Cuba ICAO location identifier] (ICLI)
MUMP	Marshall - University of Michigan Probe [Rocket flight]
MUMPS	Massachusetts General Hospital Utility Multiprogramming System [Programming language]
MUMPS	Multiple-Unit, Moving-Projectile System (MCD)
MUMS	Mobile Utility Module System (IEEE)
MUMS	Mothers United for Moral Support
MUMS	Multiple Unguided Mine System (MCD)
MUMS	Multiple-Use MARC [Machine-Readable Cataloging] System [Online retrieval system] [Information service or system Library of Congress]
MUMSU	Monash University Malaysian Students' Union [Australia]
MUMT	Matanzas [Cuba ICAO location identifier] (ICLI)
MuMTV	Murine Mammary Tumor Virus
MUMZ	Manzanillo [Cuba ICAO location identifier] (ICLI)
MUN	Aeromundo Ejecutivo, SA de CV [Mexico] [FAA designator] (FAAC)
MUN	Maturin [Venezuela] [Airport symbol] (OAG)
MUN	Memorial University of Newfoundland [Marine science] (MSC)
MUN	Memorial University of Newfoundland Library [UTLAS symbol]
MUN	Mundaring [Australia Seismograph station code, US Geological Survey] (SEIS)
Mun	Munford's Reports [15-20 Virginia] [A publication] (DLA)
MUN	Municipal
Mun	Municipal Law Reporter [A publication] (DLA)
MUN	Munitions (AFM)
Mun	Munitions Appeals Reports [England] [A publication] (DLA)
MUN	Munsingwear [NYSE symbol] (SPSG)
MUNA	La Cubana [Cuba ICAO location identifier] (ICLI)
MUNA	United Nations Association of Mauritius (EAIO)
MunAdv	Municipal Advantage Fund [Associated Press] (SAG)
MUNAF	Movimento de Unidade Nacional Antifacista [National United Antifascist Movement] [Portugal Political party] (PPE)
Mun & El Cas...	Municipal and Election Cases [India] [A publication] (DLA)
Mun App.....	Munitions Appeals Reports [England] [A publication] (DLA)
Mun App Rep...	Munitions Appeals Reports [England] [A publication] (DLA)
Mun App Sc...	Munitions of War Acts, Appeal Reports [1916-20] [Scotland] [A publication] (DLA)
MUNB	San Nicolas De Bari [Cuba ICAO location identifier] (ICLI)
MUNBG	Munitions Building [Washington, DC] [Obsolete]
MUNBLDG ...	Munitions Building [Obsolete Washington, DC] (DNAB)
MUNC	Munitions Command [Later, Armaments Command] [Army]
MUNC	Nicaro [Cuba ICAO location identifier] (ICLI)
MunCA	MuniYield California Fund [Associated Press] (SAG)
Mun Corp Cas...	Municipal Corporation Cases [A publication] (DLA)
Mun Ct........	Municipal Court (DLA)
Mun Ct App Dist Col...	Municipal Court of Appeals for the District of Columbia (DLA)
Mund	De Mundo [of Aristotle] [Classical studies] (OCD)
MUND	Model Urban Neighborhood Demonstration
Mundy	Abstracts of Star Chamber Proceedings [1550-58] [A publication] (DLA)
MUNE	Multiple Negative [Circuit] (AAG)
Munf	Munford's Reports [15-20 Virginia] [A publication] (DLA)
MunFL	MuniYield Florida Fund [Associated Press] (SAG)
MUNFLA	Memorial University of Newfoundland Folklore and Language Archive [Research center Canada] (RCD)

Munf (VA)..... Munford's Reports [15-20 Virginia] [A publication] (DLA)
MUNG......... Mush until No Good [Describes destruction of computer software]
MUNG......... Nueva Gerona [Cuba ICAO location identifier] (ICLI)
MUNGE....... Movimiento para la Unificacion Nacional de Guinea Ecuatorial [Movement for National Unification of Equatorial Guinea] [Political party] (EY)
Mung Pay.... Munger on Application of Payments [A publication] (DLA)
MunHi......... Municipal High Income Fund, Inc. [Associated Press] (SAG)
MUNI......... Municipal (AFM)
Muniast....... Muniassets Fund, Inc. [Associated Press] (SAG)
MUNIC........ Municipal
Munic & PL.. Municipal and Parish Law Cases [England] [A publication] (DLA)
Munic LR (PA)... Municipal Law Reporter [Pennsylvania] [A publication] (DLA)
MUNIDB...... Municipal Bonds Databank (NITA)
MuniFd........ MuniEnhanced Fund [Associated Press] (SAG)
MuniIn........ Muni Insured Fund, Inc. [Associated Press] (SAG)
MUNIMT ..... Muniment (ROG)
MuniMtg...... Municipal Mortgage & Equity LLC [Associated Press] (SAG)
MunIns........ MuniYield Insured Fund [Associated Press] (SAG)
MUNIREP..... Munitions Report [Worldwide report of location and status of air munitions] [Military]
MUniv......... Master of the University
Muniv2........ Munivest Fund II [Associated Press] (SAG)
MuniYld....... MuniYield Fund, Inc. [Associated Press] (SAG)
MuNJIn........ MuniYield New Jersey Insured Fund [Associated Press] (SAG)
Munk Emp Liab... Munkman's Employer's Liability at Common Law [8th ed.] [1975] [A publication] (DLA)
Mun LJ .... Municipal Law Journal [A publication] (DLA)
Mun LR....... Municipal Law Reporter [Pennsylvania] [A publication] (DLA)
Mun LR....... Municipal Law Reports [1903-13] [Scotland] [A publication] (DLA)
Mun L Rep.... Chrostwaite's Pennsylvania Municipal Law Reporter [A publication] (DLA)
MunMI........ MuniYield Michigan Fund [Associated Press] (SAG)
MunMIIn...... MuniYield Michigan Insured Fund [Associated Press] (SAG)
MunNJ........ MuniYield New Jersey Fund [Associated Press] (SAG)
MunNY....... MuniYield New York Insured Fund [Associated Press] (SAG)
MunPA........ MuniYield Pennsylvania Fund [Associated Press] (SAG)
MunPrt........ Municipal Partners Fund [Associated Press] (SAG)
MunPrt2...... Municipal Partners Fund 2 [Associated Press] (SAG)
MunQ12...... MuniYield Quality Fund, Inc. [Associated Press] (SAG)
MunQIty...... MuniYield Quality Fund, Inc. [Associated Press] (SAG)
Mun Rep..... Municipal Reports [Canada] [A publication] (DLA)
Munsng....... Munsingwear, Inc. [Associated Press] (SAG)
MUNSS ...... Munition Support Squadron
Mun Tort Lib... Municipal, School, and State Tort Liability [A publication] (DLA)
MUNU .... Central Brasil [Cuba ICAO location identifier] (ICLI)
Munvst........ MuniVest Fund, Inc. [Associated Press] (SAG)
MuNY2........ Muniyield New York Insured Fund II [Associated Press] (SAG)
MuNY3........ Muniyield New York Insured Fund III [Associated Press] (SAG)
MunyAZ ...... Muniyield Arizona Fund II [Associated Press] (SAG)
MunylAZ ..... Muniyield Arizona Fund [Associated Press] (SAG)
MUO .... Maximum Undistorted Output
MUO .... Mountain Home, ID [Location identifier FAA] (FAAL)
MUO .... Municipal University of Omaha [Later, University of Nebraska at Omaha]
MUO .... Myocardiopathy of Unknown Origin [Cardiology]
MUO .... Pioneer Interest Shares [Formerly, Mutual of Omaha Interest Shares, Inc.] [NYSE symbol] (SPSG)
MUO .... Pioneer Interest Shs [NYSE symbol] (TTSB)
MUOD .... Mean Unplanned Outage Duration (IEEE)
MUON .... Mu-Meson [An elementary particle]
MUP.......... Make-Up Pay (MHDB)
MUP.......... Manchester University Press [Manchester, England]
MUP.......... Master of Urban Planning
MUP.......... Metalworking under Pressure (PDAA)
MUP.......... Molded Urea Plastics
MUP.......... Motor Unit Potential
MUP.......... Mouse Urine Protein [Biochemistry] (DAVI)
MUP.......... Mouvement de l'Unite Populaire [Popular Unity Movement] [Tunisia] [Political party] (PD)
MUP.......... Movimiento da Unidade Progressiva [Brazil Political party] (EY)
MUP.......... Multiple Utility Peripheral (NITA)
MUPA .... Punta Alegre [Cuba ICAO location identifier] (ICLI)
MuPAIns ..... MuniVest Pennsylvania Insured Fund [Associated Press] (SAG)
MUPB .... Baracoa Playa/Habana [Cuba ICAO location identifier] (ICLI)
MUPDD...... Master of Urban Planning, Design, and Development (PGP)
MUPEJARS... Multiple Peanut-Butter Jars [Unconventional musical instrument used in performance by the "Music for Homemade Instruments" ensemble]
MUPF......... Modified Ultrapherical Polynominal Filter (IAA)
MUPID........ Multiple Universally Programmable Intelligent Decoder [Telecommunications] (TSSD)
MUPID........ Multi-Purpose Universal Programmable Intelligent Decoder (NITA)
MuPIT........ Municipal Premier Income Trust [Associated Press] (SAG)
MUPL......... Military Urgency Planning List (NG)
MUPL......... Mock-Up Planning
MUPL......... Pilon [Cuba ICAO location identifier] (ICLI)
MUPO........ Maximum Undistorted Power Output
MUPO........ Multiple Positive [Circuit] (AAG)
MUPP .... Master of Urban Planning and Policy (GAGS)
MUPPATS.... Multiparticle Position- and Time- Sensitive Detector
MUPPET ..... Marionette and Puppet
Muppie .... Mennonite Urban Professional [Lifestyle classification]
Muppie .... Middle-Aged Urban Pinhead [Lifestyle classification]
Muppie .... Middle-Aged Urban Professional [Lifestyle classification]

Muppy........ Male Urban Professional [Lifestyle classification]
MUPR........ Pinar Del Rio [Cuba ICAO location identifier] (ICLI)
MUPROF..... Multiple Projected Fibonacci [Microwave circuit]
MUPS .... Central Guatemala [Cuba ICAO location identifier] (ICLI)
MUPS .... Manpower Utilisation and Payment Structure [Imperial Chemical Industries] [British]
MUPS .... Mechanized Unit Property System [Telecommunications] (TEL)
MUPS .... Minimum Universal Pension System [Proposed to reform pension coverage]
MUPS .... Multiple Utility Peripheral System [Computer science]
MUPT........ Patria [Cuba ICAO location identifier] (ICLI)
MuPV........ Murine Polyomavirus [Medicine]
MUR .... Aerolinea Muri [Mexico ICAO designator] (FAAC)
MUR .... Management Update and Retrieval System (NRCH)
MUR .... Manpower Utilization Report (MCD)
MUR .... Marudi [Malaysia] [Airport symbol] (OAG)
MUR .... Mock-Up Reactor [NASA]
MUR .... Montana Utilities Reports [A publication] (DLA)
MUR .... Movimiento de Unidad Revolucionaria [Guerrilla forces] [Honduras] (EY)
mur .... Mural (VRA)
Mur.......... Muramic Acid [Also, MurA] [Biochemistry]
MUR .... Murder [FBI standardized term]
MUR .... Murgab [Former USSR Seismograph station code, US Geological Survey Closed] (SEIS)
Mur.......... Murlyn [Record label]
Mur.......... Murphey's Reports [5-7 North Carolina] [A publication] (DLA)
MUR .... Murphy Oil [NYSE symbol] (TTSB)
MUR .... Murphy Oil Corp. [NYSE symbol] (SPSG)
Mur.......... Murray's Ceylon Reports [A publication] (DLA)
Mur.......... Murray's Jury Court Cases [1815-30] [Scotland] [A publication] (DLA)
MUR .... Mustang Resources, Inc. [Vancouver Stock Exchange symbol]
Mur.......... Pro Murena [of Cicero] [Classical studies] (OCD)
MUR .... Radio Relay Message Unit [Telecommunications] (TEL)
MURA .... Midwestern Universities Research Association
MurA.......... Muramic Acid [Also, Mur] [Biochemistry]
Mur & H ..... Murphy and Hurlstone's English Exchequer Reports [1836-37] [A publication] (DLA)
Mur & Hurl... Murphy and Hurlstone's English Exchequer Reports [1836-37] [A publication] (DLA)
Murat Antiq Med Aevi... Muratori's Antiquitates Medii Aevi [A publication] (DLA)
MURATREC.. Multi-RADAR Track Reconstitution [Aviation] (DA)
MURB .... Multiple Unit Residential Building [Canada]
MUrbDes(Arch)... Master of Urban Design
MUrbRegPlg... Master of Urban and Regional Planning
MURC .... Measurable Undesirable Respiratory Contaminants [Pollution index] [Superseded by PSI]
MURC .... Murdock Communications Corp. [NASDAQ symbol] (SAG)
MURD .... Murder (ROG)
Murdck ...... Murdock Communications Corp. [Associated Press] (SAG)
Murd Epit.... Murdoch's Epitome Canada [A publication] (DLA)
Murdock ..... Murdock Communications Corp. [Associated Press] (SAG)
MURF .... Material Utilization Reference File [Military]
MURFAAM ... Mutual Reduction of Forces and Armaments and Associated Measures
MURFAAMCE... Mutual Reduction of Forces and Armaments and Associated Measures in Central Europe
Murfree Off Bonds... Murfree on Official Bonds [A publication] (DLA)
MURG .... Machine Utilization Report Generator
MURI .... Mild Upper Respiratory Illness [Virus] [Obsolete usage]
MURL .... Major Urban Resource Library [Department of Education] (GFGA)
MURL .... Mock-Up Release
MurNAc...... N-Acetylmuramate [Laboratory science] (DAVI)
MURP .... Manned Upperstage Reusable Payload
MURP .... Master of Urban and Regional Planning
MURP .... Master of Urban and Rural Planning (GAGS)
Murp & H .... Murphy and Hurlstone's English Exchequer Reports [1836-37] [A publication] (ILCA)
Murph .... Murphey's Reports [5-7 North Carolina] [A publication] (DLA)
Murph & H... Murphy and Hurlstone's English Exchequer Reports [1836-37] [A publication] (DLA)
Murph (NC)... Murphey's Reports [5-7 North Carolina] [A publication] (DLA)
MURPL .... Master of Urban and Regional Planning (PGP)
MurpO .... Murphy Oil Corp. [Associated Press] (SAG)
Murr.......... Murray's Ceylon Reports [A publication] (DLA)
Murr.......... Murray's Jury Court Cases [1815-30] [Scotland] [A publication] (DLA)
Murr.......... Murray's Laws and Acts of Parliament [Scotland] [A publication] (DLA)
MURR .... University of Missouri Research Reactor
Murray........ Murray's Scotch Jury Court Reports [A publication] (DLA)
Murray (Ceylon)... Murray's Ceylon Reports [A publication] (DLA)
Murray (Scot)... Murray's Scotch Jury Trials [A publication] (DLA)
Murray's Eng Dict... Murray's English Dictionary [A publication] (DLA)
Murray St U... Murray State University (GAGS)
Murr Over Cas... Murray's Overruled Cases [A publication] (DLA)
MURS .... Machine Utilization Reporting System (PDAA)
MURS .... Machine Utilization Report System [Computer science] (IAA)
MURS .... Minority Undergraduate Research Support
MURS .... Mouvement Universel de la Responsabilite Scientifique [Universal Movement for Scientific Responsibility - UMSR] (EAIO)
MURS .... Mursley [England]
Mur Tab Cas... Murray's Table of United States Cases [A publication] (DLA)
MURTF .... Nur Advanced Technologies [NASDAQ symbol] (TTSB)

MURTS .... Multiple User Remote Terminal Supervisor (MHDI)
Mur Us .... Murray's History of Usury [*A publication*] (DLA)
Mur US Ct ... Murray's Proceedings in the United States Courts [*A publication*] (DLA)
MURXF .... International Murex Technologies [*NASDAQ symbol*] (SAG)
MURXF .... Intl Murex Technologies [*NASDAQ symbol*] (TTSB)
MUS............ Magnetic Unloading System
MUS............ Maintenance Utilization Sheet
MUS............ Manned Underwater Station
MUS............ Manual Update Service (NITA)
MUS............ Mass Unbalance Spin
MUS............ Master of Urban Studies (ADA)
MUS............ Mauritius [*ANSI three-letter standard code*] (CNC)
MUS............ Methylumbelliferone Sulfate [*Biochemistry*]
MU S .... Microsecond (WDAA)
MUS............ Monetary Unit Sampling (ADA)
MUS............ Multiprogramming Utility System [*Regnecentralen*] [*Denmark*]
MUS............ Multiutility System (MCD)
Mus .... Musca [*Constellation*]
MUS............ Muschocho Explorations Ltd. [*Toronto Stock Exchange symbol*]
MUS............ Muscimol [*Biochemistry*]
mus .... Musee (VRA)
mus .... Museen (VRA)
mus .... Museo (VRA)
mus .... Museum (VRA)
MUS............ Museum
MUS............ Museum
MUS............ Music
MUS............ Muskinabad [*Former USSR Seismograph station code, US Geological Survey Closed*] (SEIS)
mus .... Muskogee [*MARC language code Library of Congress*] (LCCP)
Mus .... Muslim
MUS............ University of Southern Mississippi, Hattiesburg, MS [*OCLC symbol*] (OCLC)
MUSA .... Manufacturing USA [*A publication*]
MUSA .... Multiple Unit Steerable Antenna [*Electronics*]
MUSA .... Multiple Unit Steerable Array (NITA)
MUSA .... San Antonio De Los Banos [*Cuba ICAO location identifier*] (ICLI)
MUSA .... Seaman Apprentice, Musician, Striker [*Navy rating*]
Mus AD... Doctor of Musical Arts
MUS & T ... Manned Undersea Science and Technology [*Marine science*] (MSC)
MUSAP .... Multisatellite Augmentation Program [*NASA*]
MUSARC..... Major United States Army Reserve Command (AABC)
MUSAT .... Multiple Station Analytical Triangulation (PDAA)
MUSAT .... Multipurpose UHF [*Ultra High Frequency*] Satellite (IAA)
MUSB .... Mobile Unit Support Base (AAG)
Mus B .... Musicae Baccalaureus [*Bachelor of Music*] [*Latin*]
Mus Bac ...... Musicae Baccalaureus [*Bachelor of Music*] [*Latin*]
Mus Bach ... Musicae Baccalaureus [*Bachelor of Music*] [*Latin*]
Mus Belge... Musee Belge [*A publication*] (OCD)
MUSC .... Medical University of South Carolina
MUSC .... Memphis Union Station Co. [*AAR code*]
MUSC .... Multiunit Supervisory Control (IAA)
Musc............ Musca [*Constellation*]
MUSC .... Muscarine [*Alkaloid*]
MUSC .... Muscles [*or Muscular*]
MUSC .... Music
MUSC .... Santa Clara [*Cuba ICAO location identifier*] (ICLI)
MUSCL .... Musical
MUSCLE ...... Millions of Unusual Small Creatures Lurking Everywhere [*Toy by Mattel, Inc.*]
MUSCM .... Missile Unit Simulated Combat Mission (SAA)
Mus D.......... Musicae Doctor [*Doctor of Music*] [*Latin*]
Mus Doc ...... Musicae Doctor [*Doctor of Music*] [*Latin*]
MUSE........... Mace Utilities Sector Editor [*Computer science*]
MUSE........... Machine User Symbiotic Environment (PDAA)
MUSE........... Machine User Symbolic Environment (IAA)
MUSE........... Medical Urethral System for Erection
MUSE........... Medical Use of Simulation Electronics
MUSE........... Microcomputer Users in Education
MUSE........... MIDI [*Musical Instrument Digital Interface*] Users Sequencer/Editor [*Roland International Corp.*]
MUSE........... Mobile Utilities Support Equipment [*Navy*] (NG)
MUSE........... Model to Understand Simple English (PDAA)
MUSE........... Modular Utilities for Systems Education (IAA)
MUSE........... Monitor of Ultraviolet Solar Energy
MUSE........... Multimedia User Environment [*Computer science*]
MUSE........... Multiple Sub-Nyquist Subsampling Encoding [*Digital recording system introduced 1984*]
MUSE........... Multi-User-Simulated Environment (PS)
MUSE........... Musicians United for Safe Energy (EA)
MUSE........... Musicians United to Stop Exclusion [*Defunct*] (EA)
Mus Ed B... Bachelor of Music Education
Mus Ed D... Doctor of Music Education
MUSEDET ... Mobile Utilities Support Equipment Detachment [*Navy*] (DNAB)
Mus Ed M... Master of Music Education
MUSF........... Habana/Santa Fe [*Cuba ICAO location identifier*] (ICLI)
MUSG........... Sagua La Grande [*Cuba ICAO location identifier*] (ICLI)
Mus G Paed... Musicae Graduatus Paedogogus [*Graduate Teacher in Music*]
MusH........... Music Hall [*Record label*] [*Argentina*]
MUSI .... Mexico-United States Institute (EA)
musi .... Musical (VRA)
MUSIC .... Machine Utilization Statistical Information Collection (IAA)
MUSIC .... Mass Unity Sounding in Concert [*Duke Ellington definition of music*]
MUSIC .... McGill University System for Interactive Computing

MUSIC .... Multiple System Intelligent Controller [*Computer science*]
MUSIC .... Multisensor Intelligence Correlator (IAA)
MUSICAM .... Masking Pattern Universal Sub-Band Integrated Coding and Multiplexing [*Broadcasting*]
MusicLd....... Musicland Stores [*Associated Press*] (SAG)
MUSICOL..... Musical Instruction Composition Oriented Language (NITA)
MUSICOMP... Music Composition
MUSIL .... Multiprogramming Utility System Interpretive Language [*Regnecentralen*] [*Denmark*]
MUSJ........... San Julian (Escuela de Aviacion) [*Cuba ICAO location identifier*] (ICLI)
MUSL........... Marconi Underwater Systems Ltd. [*British*]
MUSL........... Multiple Stinger Launcher
MUSL........... Musician's Library [*A publication*]
MUSL........... Muslin (ROG)
musl .... Muslin (VRA)
MUSL........... Santa Lucia [*Cuba ICAO location identifier*] (ICLI)
MUSLE......... Modified Universal Soil Loss Equation [*Agricultural Research Service*]
MUSLO......... Morocco-United States Liaison Office (AFM)
Mus M .... Musicae Magister [*Master of Music*] [*Latin*]
MusMComp... Master of Music Composition, University of Manchester [*British*] (DBQ)
MusMPerf.... Master of Music Performance, University of Manchester [*British*] (DBQ)
Musn .... Musician [*British military*] (DMA)
MUSN .... Seaman, Musician, Striker [*Navy rating*]
MUSN .... Siguanea, Isla De La Juventud [*Cuba ICAO location identifier*] (ICLI)
MUSR .... Simon Reyes [*Cuba ICAO location identifier*] (ICLI)
MUSRP......... McGill University Savanna Research Project (MCD)
MUSS .... Manchester University Software System (NITA)
MUSS .... Missile Unit Support System
MUSS .... Mobile Unit Support System (IAA)
MUSS .... Module Utility Support Structure (NASA)
MUSS .... Musical Series [*A publication*]
MUSS .... Sancti Spiritus [*Cuba ICAO location identifier*] (ICLI)
MUST .... Machine Utilization Report Generator (DNAB)
MUST .... Malaysian University of Science and Technology
MUST .... Manned Undersea Science and Technology [*Marine science*] (OSRA)
MUST .... Manned Undersea Science and Technology (USDC)
MUST .... Manned Undersea Station
MUST .... Manpower Utilization System and Techniques [*Department of State*]
MUST .... Maximum Utilization of Skills and Training [*Civil Service Commission*]
MUST .... Medical Unit Self-Contained Transportable [*Field hospital*] [*Army*]
MUST .... Meeting Updates in Skill Training [*International Labor Organization*] [*Information service or system United Nations*] (DUND)
MUST .... Message User Service Transcriber (IAA)
MUST .... Mobile Underwater Surveillance Team (MCD)
MUST .... Mobile Unit Sanitation Trailer
MUST .... Multi-Mission UHF [*Ultra High Frequency*] SATCOM [*Satellite Command*] Terminal
MUST .... Multiple Source Technique
MUST .... Multipurpose User-Oriented Software Technology (MHDI)
MUSTA .... Mock-Up Spallation Target Assembly (PDAA)
MUSTARD.... Multi-Racial Union of Squatters to Alleviate Racial Discrimination [*British*] (DI)
MUSTARD.... Multiunit Space Transport and Recovery Device (MCD)
MUSTARD.... Museum and University Storage and Retrieval of Data (NITA)
MUSTPAC-1... Medical Ultrasound, Three-Dimensional and Portabel with Advanced Communications [*An imaging device*] (INF)
MUSTRAC.... Multiple-Simultaneous-Target Steerable Telemetry Tracking System [*Navy*]
MUSTRAN.... Music Translation (NITA)
MustSft....... Mustang Software, Inc. [*Associated Press*] (SAG)
MUSYA........ Multiple-Use Sustained-Yield Act of 1960
MU Sys E.... Master of Urban Systems Engineering (PGP)
Mut.............. De Mutatione Nominum [*Philo*] (BJA)
MUT............. Makeup Tank [*Nuclear energy*] (NRCH)
MUT............. Mean Up Time [*NASA*] (KSC)
MUT............. Mercury Unit Test
MUT............. Mock-Up Template
MUT............. Modular Universal Terminal (IAA)
MUT............. Module under Test
MUT............. Multinational Resources [*Vancouver Stock Exchange symbol*]
MUT............. Multiservicios Aeronauticos SA de CV [*Mexico ICAO designator*] (FAAC)
MUT............. Muntinlupa [*Philippines*] [*Geomagnetic observatory code*]
MUT............. Muscatine, IA [*Location identifier FAA*] (FAAL)
MUT............. Mutilated
MUT............. Mutual (ADA)
Mut.............. Mutukisna's Ceylon Reports [*A publication*] (DLA)
MUTA........... Made-Up Textiles Association [*British*] (DBA)
MUTA........... Military Upper Traffic Control Area (DA)
MUTA........... Multiple Unit Training Assembly [*Army*] (AABC)
MUTACI .... Mutuelle des Autochtones de la Cote d'Ivoire [*Mutual Association of the Natives of the Ivory Coast*]
MUTCD .... Manual on Uniform Traffic Control Devices [*Highway engineering*] [*A publication*]
MUTCD .... Manual on Uniform Traffic Control Traffic Control Devices [*Federal Housing Adminstration*]
MUTD........... Trinidad [*Cuba ICAO location identifier*] (ICLI)
MUTE........... Mobile Universal Test Equipment (PDAA)
MUTE........... Multiple Unit for Transmission Elimination [*Military*] (CAAL)
MUTES......... Multiple Threat Emitter System [*Air Force*]
MUTEX......... Multiuser Terminal Executive (MHDI)
MUTEX......... Multi-User Transaction Executive (NITA)

MUTI	Manati [Cuba ICAO location identifier] (ICLI)
MUTL	Mutual (ROG)
MUTL	Mutual
MUTR	Makai Undersea Test Range (DNAB)
MutRisk	Mutual Risk Management Ltd. [Associated Press] (SAG)
MUTS	Manual Unit Test Set
MUTS	Multiple Target Simulation (MCD)
MutSvg	Mutual Savings Bank FSB [Associated Press] (SAG)
MUTT	Military Utility Tactical Transport
MUTT	Military Utility Tactical Truck
MUTT	Mobile Utility Transfer Tank [To collect used oils]
MUTT	Multiuse Terminal Translator (MHDI)
mutt	Mutton [An em space] [Typesetting] (WDMC)
MUTTS	Multiple Unit Terminal Test Set (MCD)
MutualB	Mutual Bancompany, Inc. [Associated Press] (SAG)
Mutukisna	Mutukisna's Ceylon Reports [A publication] (DLA)
MUU	Mount Union, PA [Location identifier FAA] (FAAL)
MUU	Mouse Uterine Unit [Gynecology] (MAE)
MUU	University of Missouri, Columbia, Columbia, MO [OCLC symbol] (OCLC)
MUV	Marine Unit Vietnam (VNW)
MUV	Mechanized Utility Vehicle (MCD)
MU V	Microvolt (WDAA)
MUV	Middle Ultraviolet
MUV	Mobile Underwater Vehicle
MUV	Philadelphia, PA [Location identifier FAA] (FAAL)
MUVA	Central Primero De Enero [Cuba ICAO location identifier] (ICLI)
MuvCAIn	Munivest California Insured Fund [Associated Press] (SAG)
MuvMIIn	MuniVest Michigan Insured Fund [Associated Press] (SAG)
MuvNJFd	MuniVest New Jersey Fund [Associated Press] (SAG)
MuvNYIn	MuniVest New York Insured Fund [Associated Press] (SAG)
MUVR	Varadero [Cuba ICAO location identifier] (ICLI)
MUVT	Las Tunas [Cuba ICAO location identifier] (ICLI)
MUW	Mascara [Algeria] [Airport symbol] (OAG)
MU W	Microwatt (WDAA)
MUW	Music Wire
MUW	Mutarara [Mozambique] [Airport symbol] (AD)
MUW	University of Mississippi, School of Law Library, University, MS [OCLC symbol] (OCLC)
MUWO	Muir Woods National Monument
MUWS	Manned Underwater Station
MUWU	Mouse Uterine Weight Unit [Gynecology]
MUX	Multan [Pakistan] [Airport symbol] (OAG)
MUX	Multiplex [or Multiplexer] [Telecommunications]
MUX	Musto Explorations Ltd. [Toronto Stock Exchange symbol]
MUXARC	Multiplexing Automatic Error Correction (IAA)
MUXART	Multiplexed Asynchronous Receiver/Transmitter (MCD)
MUX/DEMUX	Multiplexer and Demultiplexer
MUXER	Multiplexer
MUXES	Multiplexes [or Multiplexers] [Telecommunications]
MUXIC	Multiplex/Multiple Voice Interior Communications (DNAB)
MUXMOD	Multiplex Modulation
MUX/PRI/SEC	Multiplexer/Priority/Second
MUY	Lehman Br Micron"YEELD"97 [AMEX symbol] (TTSB)
MUY	Lehman Brothers, Inc. [AMEX symbol] (SAG)
MUY	Toolik, AK [Location identifier FAA] (FAAL)
MUZ	Musoma [Tanzania] [Airport symbol] (OAG)
Muza	Muza and Other Labels [Record label] [Poland]
MUZAK	Music and Kodak [Terms combined to coin brand name for canned music]
MUZG	Zaragoza [Cuba ICAO location identifier] (ICLI)
MUZH	Muzzle Hatch
MUZM	Makerere-University Zoology Museum [Uganda]
MV	Airlines of Western Australia [Australia ICAO designator] (ICDA)
MV	MacRobertson-Miller Airline Service [ICAO designator] (AD)
M/V	Magnetic Variation (MCD)
MV	Mahzor Vitry [A publication] (BJA)
MV	Maintenance Version (IAA)
MV	Main Verb [Linguistics]
MV	Majority-Vote Technique [Parapsychology]
MV	Maldives [ANSI two-letter standard code] (CNC)
MV	Manifold Vacuum [Automotive engineering]
MV	Manned Vehicle
MV	Manpower Voucher [Army] (AABC)
MV	Mantle Vessel
MV	Manual Valve (MCD)
MV	Manufacturing Verification (NASA)
MV	Mare Vaporum [Sea of Vapor] [Lunar area]
MV	Mariner Venus Project [NASA]
MV	Market Value
MV	Mauve [Philately] (ROG)
MV	Mean Value
MV	Mean Variation
MV	Mean Voltage (IAA)
MV	Measles Virus
MV	Measured Value
MV	Mechanical Ventilation [Medicine]
MV	Medial Vestibular Nucleus [Neuroanatomy]
MV	Medicus Veterinarius [Veterinary Physician]
MV	Medium Voltage
MV	Medium Volume
MV	Megavolt
Mv	Mendelevium [Symbol is Md] [Chemical element]
MV	Mentor Exploration & Development Co. Ltd. [Toronto Stock Exchange symbol]
MV	Merchant Vessel
MV	Mercury Vapor
MV	Methyl Violet [A dye]
MV	Methyl Viologen [Organic chemistry]
MV	Mezza Voce [Half the Power of the Voice] [Music]
MV	Microvilli [Cytology]
MV	Microwave [Physics] (DAVI)
MV	Midland Valley R. R. [AAR code]
MV	Military Vehicle
MV	Military Vigilance (NATG)
MV	Million Volts
mV	Millivolt
MV	Miniature Vehicle (MCD)
MV	Minimal Variant (IAA)
MV	Minimum Viscosity
MV	Minute Ventilation [Medicine]
MV	Minute Volume [Medicine]
MV	Mitoxantrone, VePesid [Antineoplastic drug] (CDI)
MV	Mitral Valve [Cardiology]
MV	Mixed Venous [Blood]
MV	Modern Varieties [Agriculture]
MV	Modus Vivendi [Way of Living] [Latin]
MV	Molar Volume [Chemistry]
MV	Money Velocity [Economics]
MV	Monochromatic Vision (WDAA)
MV	Montevideo [City in Uruguay] (ROG)
MV	Mostly Verbatim [FAR clauses] (AAGC)
MV	Motorized Valve (KSC)
MV	Motor Vehicle (CDAI)
MV	Motor Vehicle Mishap (DNAB)
MV	Motor Vessel
mv	Motor Vessel (ODBW)
MV	Motor Volunteers [British military] (DMA)
MV	Move [Telecommunications] (TEL)
MV	Multiconverter Vector [Computer science] (IAA)
MV	Multivibrator
MV	Multivitamins [Nutrition]
MV	Musica Viva (ADA)
MV	Muzzle Velocity [Ballistics]
MV	Mycoplasmatales Virus
MVA	Machine Vision Association [Later, MVA/SME] (EA)
MVA	Machinists Vise Association [Later, HTI] (EA)
MVA	Main Valve Actuator (NASA)
MVA	Main Valve Actuator
MVA	Malignant Ventricular Arrhythmias [Cardiology] (DAVI)
MVA	Manufacturing Value Added
MVA	Marginal Value Analysis (MCD)
MVA	Market-Value Accounting [Banking] (ECON)
MVA	Market Value Added
MVA	Market Value Appraiser (DD)
MVA	Master of Visual Arts (GAGS)
MVA	Mean Vertical Acceleration
MVA	Megavolt-Ampere
MVA	Mercury Volatilizing Activity
MVA	Merrimack Valley College Library, Manchester, NH [OCLC symbol] (OCLC)
MVA	Mevalonic Acid [Organic chemistry]
MVA	Million Volt Amperes
MVA	Millivolt Ampere [Nuclear energy] (IAA)
MVA	Mina, NV [Location identifier FAA] (FAAL)
MVA	Minimum Vectoring Altitude [FAA] (TAG)
MVA	Minnova, Inc. [Toronto Stock Exchange symbol] (SPSG)
MVA	Mississippi Valley Airlines, Inc. [ICAO designator] (FAAC)
MVA	Missouri Valley Authority
MVA	Mitral Valve Area [Cardiology]
MVA	Modern Volunteer Army
MVA	Monovinylacetylene [Organic chemistry]
MVA	Motor Vehicle Accident [Medicine] (AFM)
MVA	Motor Vehicle Allowance
MVA	Motor Vehicle Assembly [Military World War II]
MVA	Multivariate Analysis (GFGA)
MVA	Music Video Association (EA)
MVA	Myvatn [Iceland] [Airport symbol Obsolete] (OAG)
M-VAC	Methotrexate, Vinblastine, Adriamiacin [Doxorubicin] Cisplatin [Antineoplastic drug regimen] (DAVI)
MVAC	Methotrexate, Vinblastine, Adriamycin, Cisplatin [Antineoplastic drug] (CDI)
MVAC	MotorVac Technologies [NASDAQ symbol] (TTSB)
MVAC	MotorVac Technologies, Inc. [NASDAQ symbol] (SAG)
MVACS	Mars Volatiles and Climate Survey [NASA]
MVal	Market Value [Insurance]
MV & P	Morton's Vendors and Purchasers [1837] [A publication] (DLA)
MVAP	Modern Volunteer Army Program (AABC)
MVAPCA	Motor Vehicle Air Pollution Control Act (GFGA)
MVAR	Megavar
MVAR	Megavolt-Ampere Reactive [Nuclear energy] (IAA)
MVARH	Megavar-Hour
MVAS	Multipurpose Ventricular Actuating System (NASA)
MVAS	Murray Valley Air Service [Australia]
MVA/SME	Machine Vision Association [Society of Manufacturing Engineers] (EA)
MVAT	MediVators, Inc. [NASDAQ symbol] (SAG)
MVAT	Metacyclic Variant Antigen Type [Immunology]
MVAU	Maximum Volt-Ampere Utilization [Electronics]
MVB	Martin Van Buren [US president, 1782-1862]

MVB............ Mechanical Vacuum Booster
MVB............ Mississippi Valley Motor Freight Bureau, Saint Louis MO [*STAC*]
MVB............ Mixed Venous Blood [*Medicine*] (DAVI)
MVB............ Motor V-Belt
MVB............ Motor Vessel Boat
MVB............ Multivesicular Body
MVB............ Multivibrator
MVB............ Mvengue [*Gabon*] [*Airport symbol*] (OAG)
MVBD......... Multiple V-Belt Drive
MVBF......... Motor Vehicle Brake Fluid [*Automotive engineering*]
MVBFC....... Martin Van Buren Fan Club (EA)
MVBI.......... Mississippi Valley Bancshares [*NASDAQ symbol*] (TTSB)
MVBI.......... Mississippi Valley Bancshares, Inc. [*NASDAQ symbol*] (SAG)
MVBL......... Movable (MSA)
MVBR......... Multivibrator
MVC........... Management Verification Consortium (AIE)
MVC........... Manual Volume Control
MVC........... Maryville College, St. Louis, MO [*OCLC symbol*] (OCLC)
MVC........... Master Vellum Center [*Jet Propulsion Laboratory, NASA*]
MVC........... Master Volume Control (NASA)
MVC........... Maui Volcanic Complex [*Geology*]
MVC........... Maximal Voluntary Contraction
MVC........... Maximum Vital Capacity [*Medicine*] (DAVI)
MVC........... Mechanical Vapor Compressor [*Engineering*]
MVC........... Micro Ventures Ltd. [*Vancouver Stock Exchange symbol*]
MVC........... Mississippi Vocational College
MVC........... Missouri Valley College
MVC........... Missouri Valley Conference [*Sports*]
MVC........... Model-View-Controller [*Computer science*]
MVC........... Monroeville, AL [*Location identifier FAA*] (FAAL)
MVC........... Motor Volunteer Corps [*British military*] (DMA)
MVC........... Multiple Variate Counter (IEEE)
MVC........... MuniVest CA Insured Fund [*NYSE symbol*] (TTSB)
MVC........... MuniVest California Insured Fund [*NYSE symbol*] (SPSG)
MVC........... Myocardial Vascular Capacity [*Cardiology*] (MAE)
MVCC......... Military Vehicle Collectors Club [*Later, MVPA*] (EA)
MVCM......... Millivolt per Centimeter [*Nuclear energy*] (IAA)
MVCMB...... Murray Valley Citrus Marketing Board [*Australia*]
MVCO........ Meadow Valley [*NASDAQ symbol*] (TTSB)
MVCO........ Meadow Valley Corp. [*NASDAQ symbol*] (SAG)
MVCOW...... Meadow Valley Wrrt [*NASDAQ symbol*] (TTSB)
MVCS......... Marine Vapor Control System
MVCS......... Motor Vehicle Certification System
MVCU......... Multivariable Control Unit [*Computer science*]
MVD........... Doctor of Veterinary Medicine
MVD........... Map and Visual Display
MVD........... Mineralny Vody Department of Cibil Aviation [*Former USSR*] [*FAA designator*] (FAAC)
MVD........... Minimum-Variance Deconvolution (MCD)
MVD........... Mission Variation Drawing (MCD)
MVD........... Mitral Valve Disease [*Cardiology*]
MVD........... Montevideo [*Uruguay*] [*Airport symbol*] (OAG)
MVD........... Motor Vehicle Department (DLA)
MVD........... Motor Vehicle Distributing [*Military*]
MVD........... Motor Vehicle Driver Selection Battery [*Army*]
MVD........... Motor Voltage Drop (IAA)
MVDA......... Motor Vehicle Dealers Act
MVDA......... Motor Vehicles Dismantlers Association [*British*] (BI)
MVDA......... Multivariate Variance and Discriminant Analysis [*Mathematics*]
MVDC......... Megavolt Direct Current [*Nuclear energy*] (IAA)
MVDC......... Millivolt Direct Current [*Nuclear energy*] (IAA)
MVDF......... Medium- and Very-High-Frequency Direction-Finding Station
MVDFC....... Mamie Van Doren Fan Club (EA)
MVDI.......... Microfield Virtual Device Interface [*Computer science*] (HGAA)
MVDLB....... Motor Vehicle Dealers' Licensing Board [*Western Australia*]
MVDM......... Multiple Virtual DOS [*Disk Operating System*] Machine [*Computer science*] (PCM)
MVD-MGB.... Ministerstvo Vnutrennikh Del-Ministerstvo Gosudarstvennoe Bezopasnosti [*Later, KGB*]
MVDr.......... Medicus Veterinarius Doctor [*Doctor of Veterinary Medicine*]
MVDS......... Modular Vault Dry Store [*Nuclear energy*] (NUCP)
MVDS......... Modular Video Data System [*Sperry UNIVAC*]
MVE........... Maple Valley Explorations Ltd. [*Vancouver Stock Exchange symbol*]
MVE........... Master of Vocational Education (NADA)
MVE........... Mauve [*Philately*] (ROG)
MVE........... Methyl Vinyl Ether [*Organic chemistry*]
MVE........... Mitral Valve Echogram [*Cardiology*]
MVE........... Mobile Vocational Evaluation [*Vocational guidance test*]
MVE........... Montevideo, MN [*Location identifier FAA*] (FAAL)
MVE........... Multivariate Exponential Distribution [*Statistics*]
MVE........... Murray Valley Encephalitis [*Virus*]
MVE........... Virden-Elkhorn Regional Library, Virden, Manitoba [*Library symbol National Library of Canada*] (NLC)
MV Ed........ Master of Vocational Education
MVEE......... Military Vehicles and Engineering Establishment [*Research center British*]
MVEL......... Motor Vehicle Emission Laboratory [*Environmental Protection Agency*]
MVEMJSUNP... My Very Excellent Mother Just Served Us Nine Pies [*Mnemonic guide to the nine planets: Mercury, Venus, Earth, Mars, Jupiter, Saturn, Uranus, Neptune, Pluto*]
MVetClinStud... Master of Veterinary Clinical Studies
MVetMed..... Master of Veterinary Medicine (NADA)
M Vet Sc ... Master of Veterinary Science (PGP)
MVetSc........ Master of Veterinary Science [*British*] (ADA)

MVetSci....... Master of Veterinary Science (NADA)
MVetSt........ Master of Veterinary Studies
MVF............ Manned Vertical Flight (MCD)
MVF............ Missile Verification Firing
MVF............ Moisture Volume Fraction (PDAA)
MVF............ MuniVest Fund [*AMEX symbol*] (TTSB)
MVF............ MuniVest Fund, Inc. [*AMEX symbol*] (SPSG)
MVFC.......... Mack Vickery Fan Club (EA)
MVFC.......... Mr. V Fan Club [*Defunct*] (EA)
MVFC.......... Municipal Valuation Fees Committee [*Victoria, Australia*]
MVFV.......... Manned Venus Flyby Vehicle
MVG........... Mengenverbrauchsguttern [*Mass Consumption Goods*] [*German*]
MVG........... Minven Gold Corp. [*Toronto Stock Exchange symbol*]
MVG........... Minven Gold Corp. [*Vancouver Stock Exchange symbol*]
MVG........... Most Valuable Girl
MVG........... Moving
MVG........... Mycoplasmatales Virus [*from*] Goat
MVGA .... Monochrome Video Graphics Array [*Computer science*] (CDE)
MVGF.......... Myxoma Virus Growth Factor [*Biochemistry*]
MV Grad ..... Mitral Valve Gradient [*Cardiology*] (MAE)
MVGVT .... Mated Vertical Ground Vibration Test [*NASA*] (NASA)
MVH........... Methotrexate, VP-16 Hyxamethylmelamine [*Antineoplastic drug regimen*] (DAVI)
MVH........... Mohave Gold, Inc. [*Vancouver Stock Exchange symbol*]
MVH........... Mountain View [*Hawaii*] [*Seismograph station code, US Geological Survey*] (SEIS)
MVh........... Vineyard Haven Public Library, Vineyard Haven, MA [*Library symbol Library of Congress*] (LCLS)
MVHD .... Hospital District Number 10, Virden, Manitoba [*Library symbol National Library of Canada*] (NLC)
MVI........... Macrotrends Ventures, Inc. [*Vancouver Stock Exchange symbol*]
MvI........... Marcive, Inc., San Antonio, TX [*Library symbol*] [*Library of Congress*] (LCLS)
MVI........... Maximum Visual Impact (DNAB)
MVI........... Medium Value Item (NATG)
MVI........... Medium Viscosity Index (PDAA)
MVI........... Melt Volume Index [*Materials science*]
MVI........... Merchant Vessel Inspection Division [*Coast Guard*]
MVI........... Mercury Vapor Isolator
MVI........... Metal Ventilator Institute (EA)
MV/I........... Millivolt to Current [*Converter*] [*Nuclear energy*] (NRCH)
MVI........... Minami Daito Jima [*Volcano Islands*] [*Seismograph station code, US Geological Survey*] (SEIS)
MVI........... Miniature Variable Inductor
MVI........... Motor Vehicle Inspection
MVI........... Multiple Vitamin Infusion [*Pharmacology*] (DAVI)
MVI........... Multivitamins Intravenously [*Pharmacology*] (DAVI)
MVIC.......... Mitsubishi Variable Intake System [*Automotive engine design*]
MVICSA ...... Motor Vehicle Information and Cost Saving Act
MVICSA ...... Motor Vehicle Information and Cost Savings Act (EG)
MVII........... Mark VII [*NASDAQ symbol*] (TTSB)
MVII........... Mark VII, Inc. [*NASDAQ symbol*] (SAG)
MVII........... Minnesota Vocational Interest Inventory
MVIJC........ Motor Vehicle Industry Joint Council [*British*] (DCTA)
MVI/M......... Motor Vehicle Inspection/Maintenance (GFGA)
MVIN.......... Medium Viscosity Index-Naphthenic (PDAA)
MVIP.......... Medium Viscosity Index-Paraffinic (PDAA)
MVIP.......... Multi-Vendor Integration Protocol [*Computer science*]
MVIS.......... Maximum Voluntary Isometric Strength
MVIS.......... Microvision, Inc. [*NASDAQ symbol*] (SAG)
MVIS.......... Murrumbidgee Irrigation Area Vine Improvement Society [*Australia*]
MVJ........... Mandeville [*Jamaica*] [*Airport symbol Obsolete*] (OAG)
MVJ........... MuniVest New Jersey Fund [*NYSE symbol*] (SPSG)
MVJ........... MuniVest NJ Fund [*NYSE symbol*] (TTSB)
MVJC.......... Mount Vernon Junior College [*Washington, DC*]
MVK........... Methyl Vinyl Ketone [*Organic chemistry*]
MVK........... Mulka [*Australia Airport symbol Obsolete*] (OAG)
MVL........... Magadan Airlines [*Russian Federation*] [*ICAO designator*] (FAAC)
MVL........... Man-Vehicle Laboratory [*Massachusetts Institute of Technology*] [*Research center*] (RCD)
MVL........... Manville Corp. [*NYSE symbol*] (CTT)
MVL........... Marley Vehicle Leasing [*Commercial firm British*]
MVL........... Mercury Vapor Lamp
MVL........... Metal Vapor LASER
MVL........... Morrisville, VT [*Location identifier FAA*] (FAAL)
MVL........... Mountain Valley Library System, Sacramento, CA [*OCLC symbol*] (OCLC)
MVL........... Multiple-Valued Logic [*Computer science*]
MVL........... Murray Valley League [*Australia*]
MVL........... Mycoplasmatales Virus [*from*] Acholeplasma laidlawii
MVL........... Mylan Ventures Ltd. [*Vancouver Stock Exchange symbol*]
MVL........... Naval
MVLA.......... Mount Vernon Ladies' Association of the Union (EA)
MVLDC....... Murray Valley League for Development and Conservation [*Australia*]
MVLS......... Magic Valley Regional Library System [*Library network*]
MVLS......... Mandibular Vestibulolingual Sulcoplasty [*Surgery*]
MVLS......... Meecham Verbal Language Scale (DAVI)
MVLU......... Minimum Variance Linear Unbiased [*Statistics*]
MVLUE....... Minimum Variance Linear Unbiased Estimator [*Statistics*] (OA)
MVM........... Air Cargo America, Inc. [*ICAO designator*] (FAAC)
MVM........... Mariner Venus-Mercury Project [*NASA*]
MVM........... Massachusetts Volunteer Militia (HGAA)
MVM........... Master of Veterinary Medicine
MVM........... Medium-Voltage Mode
MVM........... Microvillous Membrane [*Cytology*] (MAE)

MVM............ Million Vehicle Miles
mV/m.......... Millivolts per Meter (DEN)
MVM............ Minimum Virtual Memory
MVM............ Minute Virus of Mice
MVM............ Multivolume Monographs
MVM............ MuniVest Michigan Insured Fund [NYSE symbol] (SPSG)
MVMA.......... Motor Vehicle Manufacturers Association (NADA)
MVMA.......... Motor Vehicle Manufacturers Association of the United States (EA)
MVMC.......... Motor Vehicle Maintenance Course
MVMF.......... Ministerstvo Voenno-Morskogo Flota [Ministry of the Navy] [1950-53; merged into the MO] [Former USSR]
MVMFB....... Mississippi Valley Motor Freight Bureau
MVMNT....... Movement
MVMT......... Movement (AFM)
MVN............ Magna Ventures Ltd. [Vancouver Stock Exchange symbol]
MVN............ Marvin Ltd. [British ICAO designator] (FAAC)
MVN............ Median Ventricular Nerve [Medicine]
MVN............ Mount Vernon [Illinois] [Airport symbol] (OAG)
MVO............ Maximum Venous Outflow [Medicine]
MVO............ Member of the Royal Victorian Order [British]
MVO............ Military Vehicles Operation [of General Motors Corp.]
MVO............ MMC Video One Canada Ltd. [Toronto Stock Exchange symbol Vancouver Stock Exchange symbol]
MVO............ Money Value Only (AFIT)
MVO............ Mongo [Chad] [Airport symbol] (AD)
MVO₂.......... Myocardial Oxygen Consumption [Cardiology] (DAVI)
MVo₂.......... Myocardial Oxygen Ventilation Rate [Cardiology] (MAE)
MVOA.......... Mitral Valve Orifice Area [Cardiology] (DMAA)
MVP............ Magnetic Vector Potential
MVP............ Maintenance Verification Plan
MVP............ Manpower Validation Program
MVP............ Marginal Value of Product [Agriculture]
MVP............ Master Verification Plan (MCD)
MVP............ Mechanical Vacuum Pump
MVP............ Methylvinylpyridine [Organic chemistry]
MVP............ Methyl-Violet Paper (MSA)
MVP............ Millivolt Potentiometer (IDOE)
MVP............ Minimum Viable Population [Demographics]
MVP............ Minority Vendors Program
MVP............ Mitral Valve Prolapse [Cardiology]
MVP............ Mitu [Colombia] [Airport symbol] (OAG)
MVP............ Most Valuable Player [Athletics] [Facetious translation: "Most Volatile Player"]
MVP............ Most Valuable Princess [Princess Diana] [British Slang]
MVP............ Most Valuable Product (PCM)
MVP............ Mountain View Public Library, Mountain View, CA [OCLC symbol] (OCLC)
MVP............ Multimedia Video Processor [Texas Instruments] (PS)
MVP............ Multiple Virtual Processing (NITA)
MVP............ Multivalue Program [Computer science]
MVP............ Multivariable Program [Computer science] (IAA)
MVP............ MuniVest Pennsylvania Insured Fund [NYSE symbol] (SPSG)
MVP............ MVP Capital Corp. [Toronto Stock Exchange symbol]
MVPA.......... Military Vehicle Preservation Association (EA)
MVPA.......... Motor Vehicle Plan Administration
MVPCB........ Motor Vehicle Pollution Control Board (NADA)
MVPCCS...... Motor Vehicle Post Crash Communications System (PDAA)
MVPD-26 .... metrotrexate, Citrovorum Factor, VM-26, Procarbazine, Dexamethasone [Antineoplastic drug regimen] (DAVI)
MVPP.......... Mustargen [Nitrogen mustard], Vinblastine, Procarbazine, Prednisone [Antineoplastic drug regimen]
MVPp.......... Mustine, Vinblastine, Procarbazine, prednisone [Antineoplastic drug regimen] (DAVI)
MVPR.......... Master Verification Process Requirement (SSD)
MVPS.......... Manually Variable Phase Shifter
MVPS.......... Mechanical Vacuum Pump System
MVPS.......... Medicare Volume Performance Standard
MVPS.......... Medium-Voltage Power Supply (IAA)
MVPS.......... Mitral Valve Prolapse Syndrome [Cardiology]
MVPS.......... Multiple Vertical Protective Shelter [for missiles] (MCD)
MVPT.......... Motor-Free Visual Perception Test
MVPTG .... Medial Vascularized Patellar Tendon Graft [Sports medicine]
MVQ............ Malvern, AR [Location identifier FAA] (FAAL)
MVR............ Malabar Volunteer Rifles [British military] (DMA)
MVR............ Maneuver (AABC)
MVR............ Maroua [Cameroon] [Airport symbol] (OAG)
MVR............ Massive Vitreous Retraction (MAE)
MVR............ Massive Vitreous Retractor [Blade] [Ophthalmology] (DAVI)
MVR............ Master Verification Requirement (SSD)
MVR............ Maximum Ventilation Rate [Medicine] (DAVI)
MVR............ Mean Value Reference [Mathematics]
MVR............ Mechanical Vapor Recompression [For evaporators]
MVR............ Minisatellite Variant Repeat [Genetics]
MVR............ Missing Volume Report
MVR............ Mitral Valve Regurgitation [Cardiology] (DAVI)
MVR............ Mitral Valve Replacement [Cardiology]
mvr............ Moldavian Soviet Socialist Republic [MARC country of publication code Library of Congress] (LCCP)
MVR............ Mondavi Resources Ltd. [Vancouver Stock Exchange symbol]
MVR............ Motor Vehicle Report
MVR............ Mover
MVR............ Mussoorie Volunteer Rifles [British military] (DMA)
MVRA.......... Metropolitan Visiting and Relief Association [British]
MVRDC........ Motor Vehicle Repair Disputes Committee [New South Wales, Australia]

MVRG.......... Medieval Village Research Group (EA)
MVRI.......... Mixed Vaccine, Respiratory Infection [Medicine]
MVRIAG...... Murray Valley Rural Industry Assistance Group [Australia]
MVRIC........ Motor Vehicle Repair Industry Council [New South Wales, Australia]
MVRO.......... Minimum-Variance Reduced-Order [Statistics] (PDAA)
MVRS.......... Marine Vapor Recovery System (GNE)
MVRS.......... Mechanical Vapor Recovery System [Engineering]
MVRS.......... Mystic Valley Railway Society (EA)
MVS............ Magnetic Voltage Stabilizer
MVS............ Manifold Vacuum Sensor [Automotive engineering]
MVS............ Master of Valuation Sciences (GAGS)
MVS............ Master of Veterinary Studies
MVS............ Master of Veterinary Surgery
MVS............ Mechanical Vibration System
MVS............ Megastar Ventures [Vancouver Stock Exchange symbol]
MVS............ Mennonite Voluntary Service
MVS............ Metal Vapour Synthesis [Chemistry]
MVS............ Metering Valve Sensor [Automotive engineering]
MVS............ Middle Valve Select (MCD)
MVS............ Millersville State College, Millersville, PA [OCLC symbol] (OCLC)
MVS............ Mine Ventilation System [Engineering]
MVS............ Minimum Visual Signal
MVS............ Ministerstvo Vooruzhennykh Sil [Ministry of the Armed Forces] [1946-50; superseded by VM, MVMF] [Former USSR]
MVS............ Missile Velocity Servo
MVS............ Mission Video System [NASA]
MVS............ Mitral Valve Stenosis [Cardiology] (DAVI)
MVS............ Mobile Video Services Ltd. [Washington, DC] [Telecommunications] (TSSD)
MVS............ Modular 8mm Video System [Eastman Kodak Co.]
MVS............ Modularized Vehicle Stimulation [Program]
MVS............ Most Valued Supplier [Mazda Motor Corp.]
MVS............ Multiple Vibration System
MVS............ Multiple Virtual Storage [IBM Corp.] [Computer science]
MVS............ Multiple Virtual System [Computer science]
MVS............ Multiprogramming with Virtual Storage [Computer science] (ECII)
MVS............ Multivariable Storage [Computer science]
MVS............ MuniVest Florida Fund [NYSE symbol] (SPSG)
MVSB.......... Motor Vehicle Storage Building
MV Sc......... Master of Veterinary Science
MVSI.......... MVSI, Inc. [NASDAQ symbol] (SAG)
MVSL.......... Mouse Visible Specific Locus [Test for mutagenesis]
MVSMA....... Mechanical Vibrating Screen Manufacturers Association [Later, Vibrating Screen Manufacturers Association] (EA)
MVSP.......... Maintain Visual Separation [Aviation]
MVSR.......... Monthly Vital Statistics Report [A publication] (DHSM)
MVSS.......... Motor Vehicle Safety Standard
MVSS.......... Motor Vehicle Storage Shed [Army] (AABC)
MVSSE........ Multiple Virtual Storage System Extension
MVS/SE....... MVS/System Extension (NITA)
MVS/SP....... MVS/System Product (NITA)
MVSt.......... Master of Veterinary Studies (ADA)
MVS/XA....... MVS/Extended Architecture (NITA)
MVSZGA ..... Mein Vertrauen Steht zu Gott Allein [My Trust Is in God Alone] [Motto of Johann Adolf II, Duke of Saxony-Weissenfels (1649-97)] [German]
MVT............ Malfunction Verification Test (MCD)
MVT............ Marginal Value Theorem [Mathematical model developed by Dr. Eric Charnov]
MVT............ Market-Value Transmission [Pricing concept]
MVT............ Mataiva [French Polynesia] [Airport symbol] (OAG)
MVT............ Maximal Ventilation Time [Medicine] (DAVI)
MVT............ Miscellaneous Vector Table
MVT............ Mission Verification Test [NASA] (NASA)
MVT............ Mission Verification Test
MVT............ Mississippi Valley Type [Ore deposits] [Geology]
MVT............ Moisture Vapor Transmission Rate
MVT............ Monte Vettore [Italy] [Seismograph station code, US Geological Survey] (SEIS)
MVT............ Motor Vehicle Title
MVT............ Mount Vernon Terminal [AAR code]
MVT............ Movement (MSA)
MVT............ Multinational Volunteer Teams
MVT............ Multiprogramming with a Variable Number of Tasks [IBM Corp.] [Control program] [Computer science]
MVT............ Multivariable Task (MCD)
MVT............ Munivest Fund II [NYSE symbol] (SAG)
MVT............ MuniVest Fund II [NYSE symbol] (TTSB)
MVT............ MuniVest Fund, Inc. [NYSE symbol] (SPSG)
MVTE.......... Master of Vocational Technical Education (GAGS)
MVT Ed....... Master of Vocational and Technical Education (PGP)
MVTL.......... Modified Variable-Threshold Logic [Computer science]
MVTLEA...... Motor Vehicle Theft Law Enforcement Act [1984]
MVTR.......... Moisture Vapor Transmission Rate
MVT/TSO..... MVT/Time Sharing Option (NITA)
MVTV.......... MetroVision of North America, Inc. [NASDAQ symbol] (SAG)
MVU............ Minimum Variance Unbiased [Statistics]
MVU............ Mulege [Mexico] [Airport symbol] (AD)
MVU............ Musgrave [Australia Airport symbol Obsolete] (OAG)
MVUE.......... Man/Vehicular User Equipment
MVUE.......... Minimum Variance Unbiased Estimate [Statistics]
MVULE........ Minimum Variance Unbiased Linear Estimator [Statistics]
MVV............ Mannheimer Versorgungs und Verkehrsgesellschaft [Germany]
MVV............ Maximum Voluntary Ventilation
MVV............ Maximum Voluntary Volume [Medicine] (DAVI)

MVV............	Mean Vertical Velocity
MVV............	Mitsubishi Vertical Vortex [*Automotive engineering*]
MVV............	Mixed Vespid Venom [*Pharmacology*] (DAVI)
MVV₁	Maximal Ventilatory Volume (MAE)
MVVPP	Mustargen [*Nitrogen mustard*], Vincristine, Vinblastine, Procarbazine, Prednisone [*Antineoplastic drug regimen*]
MVW............	Missile Viewing Window
MVW............	Mount Vernon [*Washington*] [*Airport symbol*] (OAG)
MVW............	Mud Volcano [*Wyoming*] [*Seismograph station code, US Geological Survey*] (SEIS)
MVWDU......	Missile Viewing Window Deicing Unit
MVWGS......	Multi-Vintage Wine Growers Society [*British*] (DBA)
MVX............	Media Videotex [*Vancouver Stock Exchange symbol*]
MVX............	Minvoul [*Gabon*] [*Airport symbol*] (OAG)
MVX............	Multiplex
MVY............	Martha's Vineyard [*Massachusetts*] [*Airport symbol*] (OAG)
MVY............	MuniVest New York Insured Fund [*NYSE symbol*] (SPSG)
MVY............	MuniVest NY Insured Fund [*NYSE symbol*] (TTSB)
MVZ............	Museum of Vertebrate Zoology [*University of California, Berkeley*]
MVZG..........	Mein Verlangen zu Gott [*My Desires (I Give) to God*] [*Motto of Anna Marie, Margravine of Brandenburg (1609-80)*] [*German*]
MVZS..........	Manifold Vacuum Zone Switch [*Automotive engineering*]
MW.............	Machine Word (IAA)
MW.............	Magnesiowustite [*Mineralogy*]
mw.............	Malawi [*MARC country of publication code Library of Congress*] (LCCP)
MW.............	Malawi [*ANSI two-letter standard code*] (CNC)
M-W............	Mallory-Weiss Syndrome [*Medicine*] (MEDA)
MW.............	Management World [*Administrative Management Society*] [*A publication*]
MW.............	Manual Word
MW.............	Manufacturing Week (MCD)
MW.............	Man Watchers (EA)
MW.............	Man-Week (NASA)
MW.............	Man Week
MW.............	Marginal Wage [*Economics*]
MW.............	Marginal Wings [*Botany*]
MW.............	Master of Wine [*Bestowed by the Worshipful Company of Vintners, one of the ancient guilds in the City of London*]
M/W............	Mate With (MCD)
MW.............	Maya Airways [*ICAO designator*] (AD)
MW.............	Media Watch [*An association*] (EA)
MW.............	Medium Wall
MW.............	Medium Wave Band
MW.............	Meetings Word (NITA)
MW.............	Megawatt [*Also, MEGW*]
MW.............	Memory Write [*Computer science*]
M-W............	Merriam-Webster [*Publisher*]
MW.............	Message Waiting
MW.............	Metachrondral Wave [*Physiology*]
MW.............	Metalworker [*British military*] (DMA)
M/W............	Methanol/Water
MW.............	Microwave
MW.............	Middle Welsh [*Language, etc.*]
MW.............	Midwing [*Aviation*] (AIA)
MW.............	Migratory Worker (OICC)
MW.............	Million (10⁶) Words (NITA)
mW.............	Milliwatt
mW.............	Milliwatt
MW.............	Mine Warfare
MW.............	Mine Warning (NATG)
MW.............	Ministry of Works [*British*]
MW.............	Minnesota Western Railroad (IIA)
MW.............	Mixed Widths
MW.............	Mobile Workshop [*British*]
MW.............	Modulated Wave (IAA)
MW.............	Moewe Flugzeugbau, Heini Dittmar [*Germany ICAO aircraft manufacturer identifier*] (ICAO)
MW.............	Molecular Weight [*Also, M, MOL WT*]
MW.............	Money Wages [*Economics*]
MW.............	Monier-Williams Method (RDA)
MW.............	Montana Western Railway (IIA)
MW.............	Most Worshipful [*Freemasonry*]
MW.............	Most Worthy
MW.............	Motor Wagon [*British*]
MW.............	Mud Weight [*Well drilling technology*]
MW.............	Multiple Wounds
MW.............	Multipurpose Weapon (MCD)
MW.............	Multiwire (IAA)
MW.............	Music of the World [*American Forces Radio and Television Service*] (DNAB)
MW.............	Music Wire
Mw.............	Weighted Mean [*Psychology*]
MW.............	Winnipeg Centennial Library, Manitoba [*Library symbol National Library of Canada*] (NLC)
MW.............	Worcester Public Library and Central Massachusetts Regional Library System Headquarters, Worcester, MA [*Library symbol Library of Congress*] (LCLS)
MWA............	American Antiquarian Society, Worcester, MA [*Library symbol Library of Congress*] (LCLS)
MWA............	Major World Authors [*A publication*]
MWA............	Management by Walking Around
MWA............	Manitoba Department of Agriculture, Winnipeg, Manitoba [*Library symbol National Library of Canada*] (NLC)
MWA............	Manufacturing Work Authority

MWA............	Marion [*Illinois*] [*Airport symbol*] (OAG)
MWA............	Married Women's Association [*British*] (DBA)
MWA............	Mayflower Warehousemen's Association (EA)
MWA............	Media Women's Association
MWA............	Meteorological Watch Advisory
MWA............	Mineral Workings Act [*Town planning*] [*British*]
MWA............	Modern Woodmen of America (EA)
MWA............	Momentum-Wheel Assembly
MWA............	Movers' & Warehousemen's Association of America Inc., Washington DC [*STAC*]
MWA............	Munitions of War Act [*British*]
MWA............	Mystery Writers of America (NADA)
MW/AA........	Missile Warning/Attack Assessment (MCD)
MWAA..........	Movers' and Warehousemen's Association of America [*Defunct*] (EA)
MWAC	Air Command Headquarters, Canadian Forces Base, Westwin, Manitoba [*Library symbol National Library of Canada*] (NLC)
MWAC	Assumption College, Worcester, MA [*Library symbol Library of Congress*] (LCLS)
MWAC	Midwest Archeological Center [*National Park Service*] (GRD)
MWAD	Alcohol and Drug Education Service, Winnipeg, Manitoba [*Library symbol National Library of Canada*] (NLC)
MWAE..........	Minimum-Weighted-Absolute Error [*Statistics*] (PDAA)
MWAF..........	Alcoholism Foundation of Manitoba, Winnipeg, Manitoba [*Library symbol National Library of Canada*] (NLC)
MWAG	Research Station, Agriculture Canada [*Station de Recherches, Agriculture Canada*] Winnipeg, Manitoba [*Library symbol National Library of Canada*] (NLC)
MWAI..........	Mystery Writers of America Inc. (NADA)
MWaI..........	Waltham Public Library, Waltham MA [*Library symbol Library of Congress*] (LCLS)
MWaIA........	American Jewish Historical Society, Waltham, MA [*Library symbol Library of Congress*] (LCLS)
MWaIAF......	African Studies Association, Brandeis University, Waltham, MA [*Library symbol Library of Congress*] (LCLS)
MWaIB........	Brandeis University, Waltham, MA [*Library symbol Library of Congress*] (LCLS)
MWaIBe......	Bentley College, Waltham, MA [*Library symbol Library of Congress*] (LCLS)
MWaIFAR ...	Federal Archives and Records Center, General Services Administration, Waltham, MA [*Library symbol Library of Congress*] (LCLS)
MWaIG	General Telephone & Electronics Laboratories, Inc., Waltham Research Center Library, Waltham, MA [*Library symbol Library of Congress*] (LCLS)
MWaIK........	John F. Kennedy Library, Waltham, MA [*Library symbol Library of Congress*] (LCLS)
MWaIMT......	Mobil Tyco Solar Energy Corp., Waltham, MA [*Library symbol Library of Congress*] (LCLS)
MWAMA	Administration Branch, Manitoba Department of Municipal Affairs, Winnipeg, Manitoba [*Library symbol National Library of Canada*] (NLC)
MWAMT........	Aikins, MacAulay, and Thorvaldson Law Firm, Winnipeg, Manitoba [*Library symbol National Library of Canada*] (NLC)
MWAR	Microware Systems Corp. [*NASDAQ symbol*] (SAG)
MWAR	Microwave Systems [*NASDAQ symbol*] (TTSB)
MWar..........	Wareham Free Library, Wareham, MA [*Library symbol*] [*Library of Congress*] (LCLS)
MWARA........	Major World Air Route Area
MWARN........	Manitoba Association of Registered Nurses, Winnipeg, Manitoba [*Library symbol National Library of Canada*] (NLC)
MWARS........	Major Command Worldwide Ammunition Reporting System [*Army*]
MWARS	Synod Office, Diocese of Rupert's Land, Anglican Church of Canada, Winnipeg, Manitoba [*Library symbol National Library of Canada*] (NLC)
MWAS	Arthritis Society, Winnipeg, Manitoba [*Library symbol National Library of Canada*] (NLC)
MWASD	Assiniboine South School Division No. 3, Winnipeg, Manitoba [*Library symbol National Library of Canada*] (NLC)
MWat..........	Watertown Free Public Library, Watertown, MA [*Library symbol Library of Congress*] (LCLS)
MWatM........	Massachusetts Bay Community College, Watertown, MA [*Library symbol Library of Congress*] (LCLS)
MWatP........	Perkins School for the Blind, Watertown, MA [*Library symbol Library of Congress*] (LCLS)
MWatP-BP ...	Massachusetts Regional Library for the Blind and Physically Handicapped, PerkinsSchool for the Blind, Watertown, MA [*Library symbol*] [*Library of Congress*] (LCLS)
MWatP-BPH...	Regional Library for the Blind and Physically Handicapped, Perkins School for the Blind, Watertown, MA [*Library symbol Library of Congress*] (LCLS)
MWAV	M-Wave, Inc. [*NASDAQ symbol*] (SAG)
MWAV	M-Wave Inc. [*NASDAQ symbol*] (TTSB)
MWAVE........	Microwave
M-Wave......	M-Wave, Inc. [*Associated Press*] (SAG)
MWAX........	Mountain West Airline [*Air carrier designation symbol*]
M-Way........	Motorway [*British*]
M (Way)......	Motorway [*British*]
MWayR........	Raytheon Co., Wayland, MA [*Library symbol Library of Congress*] (LCLS)
MWB............	Master Work Book (NASA)
MWB............	Maxwell-Wien Bridge [*Electronics*]
MWB............	Metropolitan Water Board [*British*]
MWB............	Middlewest Motor Freight Bureau, Kansas City MO [*STAC*]
MWB............	Ministry of Works and Buildings [*British*]
MWB............	Motor Whale Boat

MWB............ Multilayer Wiring Board
MWBA .... Bristol Aerospace Ltd., Winnipeg, Manitoba [*Library symbol National Library of Canada*] (NLC)
MWBAS .... Mail Will Be Addressed to Show
MWBC .... Technical Library, Boeing of Canada Ltd., Winnipeg, Manitoba [*Library symbol National Library of Canada*] (NLC)
MWBe.......... Becker Junior College, Worcester, MA [*Library symbol Library of Congress*] (LCLS)
MWBH .... Bethel Hospital, Winkler, Manitoba [*Library symbol National Library of Canada*] (NLC)
MWBI........... Midwest Bacshares Del [*NASDAQ symbol*] (TTSB)
MWBI........... Midwest Bancshares [*NASDAQ symbol*] (SAG)
MWBL.......... Mounted Warfighting Battlespace Laborarory [*Army*] (RDA)
MWBM......... Bethania Mennonite Personal Care Home, Winnipeg, Manitoba [*Library symbol National Library of Canada*] (NLC)
MWBP.......... Missile Warning Bypass (DWSG)
MWbriM ...... Massasoit Community College, West Bridgewater, MA [*Library symbol Library of Congress*] (LCLS)
MWC........... Clark University, Worcester, MA [*Library symbol Library of Congress*] (LCLS)
MWC........... Mad World Campaign [*An association Defunct*] (EA)
MWC........... Magnetoionic Wave Component
MWC........... Major Wingfield Club (EA)
MWC........... Mary Washington College [*University of Virginia*]
MWC........... Maxwell Communication Corp. [*Toronto Stock Exchange symbol*]
MWC........... Medium Weight Coated Paper (DGA)
MWC........... Melbourne Walking Club [*Australia*]
MWC........... Miltonvale Wesleyan College [*Kansas*]
MWC........... Milwaukee, WI [*Location identifier FAA*] (FAAL)
MWC........... Minister for [*or Ministry of*] War Communications [*British World War II*]
MWC........... Missile Weapons Control (MCD)
MWC........... Monod-Wyman-Changeux [*Model*] [*Enzymology*]
MWC........... Mount Wilson [*California*] [*Seismograph station code, US Geological Survey*] (SEIS)
MWC........... Moving-Withdrawal Chromatography
MWC........... Multiple Water Connector (KSC)
MWC........... Municipal Waste Combustor (GFGA)
MWC........... Music and Record Library, Canadian Broadcasting Corp. [*Musicotheque et Discotheque, Societe Radio-Canada*] Winnipeg, Manitoba [*Library symbol National Library of Canada*] (NLC)
MWCA .... Monetary Working Capital Adjustment [*British*]
MWCA .... Monterey Wine Country Association (EA)
MWCB .... Cayman Brac/Gerrard Smith [*Cayman Islands*] [*ICAO location identifier*] (ICLI)
MWCB .... Manufacturer's Working Cell Bank [*Cell line*]
MWCC .... Mineral Water Co. of Canada (ECON)
MWCCA ...... Manitoba Department of Consumer and Corporate Affairs, Winnipeg, Manitoba [*Library symbol Obsolete National Library of Canada*] (NLC)
MWCCI .... Manitoba Consumer's Bureau, Winnipeg, Manitoba [*Library symbol National Library of Canada*] (NLC)
MWCCIR ...... Central Region Information Resources Center, Canada Department of Communications[*Centre de Documentation Region du Centre, Ministere des Communications*] Winnipeg, Manitoba [*Library symbol National Library of Canada*] (NLC)
MWC/CS ...... Mechanized Wire Centering/Cross Section [*AT & T*] [*Telecommunications*] (TEL)
MWCE.......... Controlled Environments Ltd., Winnipeg, Manitoba [*Library symbol National Library of Canada*] (NLC)
MWCE.......... Millimeter Wave Communications Experiment
MWCF.......... Canadian Forces Aerospace and Navigation School, Canadian Forces Base Winnipeg, Westwin, Manitoba [*Library symbol National Library of Canada*] (NLC)
MWCG .... Grand Cayman [*Cayman Islands*] [*ICAO location identifier*] (ICLI)
MWCH .... Concordia Hospital, Winnipeg, Manitoba [*Library symbol National Library of Canada*] (NLC)
MWCHA .... Charles Howard & Associates, Winnipeg, Manitoba [*Library symbol National Library of Canada*] (NLC)
MWCHD .... Charleswood Public Library, Winnipeg, Manitoba [*Library symbol National Library of Canada*] (NLC)
MWCI........... Canertech, Inc., Winnipeg, Manitoba [*Library symbol National Library of Canada*] (NLC)
MWCL.......... Little Cayman/Boddenfield [*Cayman Islands*] [*ICAO location identifier*] (ICLI)
MWCL.......... Worcester County Law Library Association, Worcester, MA [*Library symbol Library of Congress*] (LCLS)
MWCM......... Canadian Mennonite Bible College, Winnipeg, Manitoba [*Library symbol National Library of Canada*] (NLC)
MWCM......... Milliwatt per Square Centimeter (IAA)
MWCMS ...... Centre for Mennonite Brethren Studies in Canada, Winnipeg, Manitoba [*Library symbol National Library of Canada*] (NLC)
MWCO .... Medium Weight Coated Offset Paper (DGA)
MWCO .... Molecular Weight Cutoff [*Chemistry*]
MWCR .... Georgetown/Owen Roberts International [*Cayman Islands*] [*ICAO location identifier*] (ICLI)
MWCR .... Mercury-Wetted Contact Relay
MWCS .... Marine Wing Communication Squadron
MWCS .... Mental Welfare Commission for Scotland
MWCS .... Midwest Cable & Satellite, Inc. [*Minneapolis, MN*] [*Telecommunications*] (TSSD)
MWCS .... Millimeter Wave Contrast Seeker (MCD)
MWCS .... Missile Weapons Control System (MCD)
MWCS .... Mobile Weapons Control System
MWCSCC ...... Midwest Council of Sports Car Clubs

MWCSJ........ Minimum Wage Coalition to Save Jobs [*Defunct*] (EA)
MWCT.......... Manitoba Cancer Treatment and Research Foundation, Winnipeg, Manitoba [*Library symbol National Library of Canada*] (NLC)
MWCU .... Credit Union Central of Manitoba, Winnipeg, Manitoba [*Library symbol National Library of Canada*] (NLC)
MWCU .... Molecular Weight Cut-Off [*Metallurgy*]
MWCWB ...... Canadian Wheat Board [*Commission Canadienne du Ble*] Winnipeg, Manitoba [*Library symbol National Library of Canada*] (NLC)
MWD .... Measurement-While Drilling [*Drilling technology*]
MWD .... Measurement while Drilling
MWD .... Megawatt-Day
MWD .... Megaword
MWD .... Metering Water Dispenser [*Apollo*] [*NASA*]
MWD .... Meters Water Depth
MWD .... Metropolitan Water District
MWD .... Microwave Diathermy [*Physical therapy*] (DAVI)
MWD .... Military Working Dog (DOMA)
MWD .... Millimeter Wave Device
MWD .... Molecular Weight Distribution
MWD .... Moving Window Display (MCD)
MWD .... Rochester, NY [*Location identifier FAA*] (FAAL)
MWDAC .... Mountain West Desegregation Assistance Centers (EDAC)
MWDCA .... Midwest Decoy Collectors Association (EA)
MWDDEA ..... Mutual Weapons Development Data Exchange Agreement [*NATO*]
MWDDEP ..... Mutual Weapons Development Data Exchange Procedures [*NATO*]
MWDI .... Master Water Data Index [*US Geological Survey*] [*Information service or system*] (CRD)
MWDL .... Deer Lodge Hospital, Winnipeg, Manitoba [*Library symbol National Library of Canada*] (NLC)
MWD/MTU ... Megawatt-Days per Metric Ton of Uranium
MWDP .... Mutual Weapons Development Program [*NATO*]
MWDRR .... Manitoba Department of Renewable Resources, Winnipeg, Manitoba [*Library symbol National Library of Canada*] (NLC)
MWDS .... Med Waste [*NASDAQ symbol*] (SAG)
MWDS .... Med/Waste Inc. [*NASDAQ symbol*] (TTSB)
MWDS .... Missile Warning and Display System [*or Subsystem*] (MCD)
MWDSW ...... Med/Waste Inc. Wrrt'A' [*NASDAQ symbol*] (TTSB)
MWD/T .... Megawatt-Days per Ton
MWDT .... Mutual Weapons Development Team [*Military*]
MWDU .... Ducks Unlimited, Winnipeg, Manitoba [*Library symbol National Library of Canada*] (NLC)
MWE .... Manitoba Department of Education, Winnipeg, Manitoba [*Library symbol National Library of Canada*] (NLC)
MWE .... Manufacturer's Weight Empty (DA)
MWE .... Megawatt Electric (IAA)
MWe .... Megawatts of Electric Power
MWE .... Merowe [*Sudan*] [*Airport symbol*] (OAG)
MWE .... Meters of Water Equivalent
MWE .... Millimeter Wave Experiment
MWeA .... Westfield Athenaeum, Westfield, MA [*Library symbol Library of Congress*] (LCLS)
MWEAE........ Central Region Headquarters, Atmospheric Environment Service, Environment Canada[*Quartier-General de la Region Centrale, Service de l'Environnement Atmosphe rique, Environnement Canada*] Winnipeg, Manitoba [*Library symbol National Library of Canada*] (NLC)
MWeba .... Whelden Memorial Library, West Barnstable, MA [*Library symbol*] [*Library of Congress*] (LCLS)
MWebaC ...... Cape Cod Community College, West Barnstable, MA [*Library symbol Library of Congress*] (LCLS)
MWECW ...... Canadian Wildlife Service, Environment Canada [*Service Canadien de la Faune, Environnement Canada*] Winnipeg, Manitoba [*Library symbol National Library of Canada*] (NLC)
MWEE .... Mechanised Warfare Experimental Establishment [*British military*] (DMA)
MWEEP........ Environmental Protection Service, Environment Canada [*Service de la Protection de l'Environnement, Environnement Canada*] Winnipeg, Manitoba [*Library symbol National Library of Canada*] (NLC)
MWEIA .... Montessori World Educational Institute Australia
MWeIC .... Wellesley College, Wellesley, MA [*Library symbol Library of Congress*] (LCLS)
MWeID .... Dana Hall School Library, Wellesley, MA [*Library symbol Library of Congress*] (LCLS)
MWeldI .... Member of the Welding Institute [*British*] (DBQ)
MWEM .... Manitoba Environmental Management Division, Winnipeg, Manitoba [*Library symbol National Library of Canada*] (NLC)
MWEM .... Mine Warfare Evaluation Model
MWEMM ...... Manitoba Energy and Mines, Winnipeg, Manitoba [*Library symbol National Library of Canada*] (NLC)
MWenhG...... Gordon College, Wenham, MA [*Library symbol Library of Congress*] (LCLS)
MWenhHi .... Wenham Historical Society and Museum, Wenham, MA [*Library symbol Library of Congress*] (LCLS)
MWES .... Member of the Women's Engineering Society [*British*] (DBQ)
MWESM........ Special Materials Services, Manitoba Department of Education, Winnipeg, Manitoba [*Library symbol National Library of Canada*] (NLC)
MWesR........ Regis College, Weston, MA [*Library symbol*] [*Library of Congress*] (LCLS)
MWestonGS... Church of Jesus Christ of Latter-Day Saints, Genealogical Society Library, Weston Branch, Weston, MA [*Library symbol Library of Congress*] (LCLS)
MWestonR... Regis College, Weston, MA [*Library symbol Library of Congress*] (LCLS)

MWeT .... Westfield State College, Westfield, MA [*Library symbol Library of Congress*] (LCLS)

MWEWSH .... Manitoba Department of Environment, Workplace Safety and Health, Winnipeg, Manitoba [*Library symbol National Library of Canada*] (NLC)

MWeyAA ...... Abigail Adams Historical Society, Weymouth, MA [*Library symbol Library of Congress*] (LCLS)

MWF .... Make-a-Wish Foundation [*Later, MWFA*] (EA)

MWF .... Marine General Workers' Federation

MWF .... Medical Women's Federation [*British*] (DAS)

MWF .... Medical Working File (DOMA)

MWF .... Monday, Wednesday, Friday (BARN)

MWFA .... Make-a-Wish Foundation of America (EA)

MWFC .... Mary Wilson Fan Club (EA)

MWFCA .... Motor Wheel and Flyer Club of America [*Defunct*] (EA)

MWFCS .... Multiweapons Fire Control System (DNAB)

MWFD .... Fred Douglas Lodge Nursing Home, Winnipeg, Manitoba [*Library symbol National Library of Canada*] (NLC)

MWFD .... Midwest Federal Financial [*NASDAQ symbol*] (SAG)

MWFD .... Midwest Fed Finl [*NASDAQ symbol*] (TTSB)

MWFG .... Fort Garry Public Library, Winnipeg, Manitoba [*Library symbol National Library of Canada*] (NLC)

MWFI .... Manitoba Department of Finance, Winnipeg, Manitoba [*Library symbol National Library of Canada*] (NLC)

MWFM .... Microwave Window Failure Mechanism

MWfo .... J. V. Fletcher Library, Westford, MA [*Library symbol Library of Congress*] (LCLS)

MWFOPS ..... Mine Warfare Operations (NVT)

MWFP .... Winnipeg Free Press Co. Ltd., Manitoba [*Library symbol National Library of Canada*] (NLC)

MWFRS .... Manitoba Department of Fitness, Recreation and Sport, Winnipeg, Manitoba [*Library symbol National Library of Canada*] (NLC)

MWFS .... Marine Wing Facilities Squadron

MWFS .... Maritime Warfare School [*Canadian Navy*]

MWFSD .... Frontier School Division, Winnipeg, Manitoba [*Library symbol National Library of Canada*] (NLC)

MWFW .... Freshwater Institute, Fisheries and Oceans Canada [*Institut des Eaux Douces, Peches et Oceans Canada*] Winnipeg, Manitoba [*Library symbol National Library of Canada*] (NLC)

MWG .... Maintenance Analyzer Working Group (MCD)

MWG .... Management Working Group [*Army*] (RDA)

MWG .... Meteorological Working Group

MWG .... Missile-Warning Group [*Military*]

MWG .... Model Work Group [*Environmental Protection Agency*] (GFGA)

MWG .... Muenster-Westfalen [*Federal Republic of Germany*] [*Seismograph station code, US Geological Survey*] (SEIS)

MWG .... Music Wire Gauge

MWGBP .... Guertin Brothers Paint Library, Winnipeg, Manitoba [*Library symbol National Library of Canada*] (NLC)

MWGC .... Midwestern Governors Conference

MWGCP .... Most Worthy Grand Chief Patriarch

MWGH .... Grace Hospital, Winnipeg, Manitoba [*Library symbol National Library of Canada*] (NLC)

MWGHA .... Gunn Hoffer & Associates Law Firm, Winnipeg, Manitoba [*Library symbol National Library of Canada*] (NLC)

MWGM .... Most Worshipful [*or Worthy*] Grand Master [*Freemasonry*]

MWGP .... Midwest Grain Products [*NASDAQ symbol*] (TTSB)

MWGP .... Midwest Grain Products, Inc. [*NASDAQ symbol*] (CTT)

MWGR .... Canadian Grain Commission, Agriculture Canada [*Commission Canadienne des Grains, Agriculture Canada*] Winnipeg, Manitoba [*Library symbol National Library of Canada*] (NLC)

MWGW .... Great West Life Assurance Co., Winnipeg, Manitoba [*Library symbol National Library of Canada*] (NLC)

MWH .... College of the Holy Cross, Worcester, MA [*Library symbol Library of Congress*] (LCLS)

MWH .... Manitoba Hydro, Winnipeg, Manitoba [*Library symbol National Library of Canada*] (NLC)

MWh .... Megawatt-Hour (MCD)

Mwh .... Megawatt Hour

MW(H) .... Megawatts (Heat) (IEEE)

MWH .... Milliwatt Hour

MWH .... Model Wave Height

MWH .... Mokuaweoweo [*Hawaii*] [*Seismograph station code, US Geological Survey*] (SEIS)

MWH .... Moses Lake [*Washington*] [*Airport symbol*] (OAG)

MWHB .... Hudson's Bay House, Winnipeg, Manitoba [*Library symbol National Library of Canada*] (NLC)

MWhB .... Marine Biological Laboratory, Woods Hole, MA [*Library symbol Library of Congress*] (LCLS)

MWHF .... Michigan Wildlife Habitat Foundation

MWHG .... Marine Wing Headquarters Group

MWHGL .... Multiple Wheel Heavy Gear Loading [*Aviation*]

MWHi .... Worcester Historical Society, Worcester, MA [*Library symbol Library of Congress*] (LCLS)

MWhN .... United States National Marine Fisheries Service, Northeast Fisheries Center, Woods Hole, MA [*Library symbol Library of Congress*] (LCLS)

MWHO .... Manitoba Health Organizations, Winnipeg, Manitoba [*Library symbol National Library of Canada*] (NLC)

MWHP .... Information Resources Center, Manitoba Health, Winnipeg, Manitoba [*Library symbol National Library of Canada*] (NLC)

MWHR .... Henderson Regional Library, Winnipeg, Manitoba [*Library symbol National Library of Canada*] (NLC)

MWHS .... Library Services, Health Sciences Centre, Winnipeg, Manitoba [*Library symbol National Library of Canada*] (NLC)

MWHS .... Marine Wing Headquarters Squadron (NVT)

MWHS .... Micro Warehouse [*NASDAQ symbol*] (TTSB)

MWHS .... Micro Warehouse, Inc. [*NASDAQ symbol*] (SAG)

MWHS .... Modified Warhead Section (MCD)

MWHSC .... Manitoba Health Services Commission, Winnipeg, Manitoba [*Library symbol National Library of Canada*] (NLC)

MWHSDET ... Marine Wing Headquarters Squadron Detachment (DNAB)

MWHT .... Miscellaneous Waste Holdup Tank [*Nuclear energy*] (NRCH)

MWHX .... MarkWest Hydrocarbon, Inc. [*NASDAQ symbol*] (SAG)

MWI .... Insurance Institute of Winnipeg, Manitoba [*Library symbol National Library of Canada*] (NLC)

MWI .... Malawi [*ANSI three-letter standard code*] (CNC)

MWI .... Mantle Width Index

MWI .... Many Worlds Interpretation [*Term coined by authors John Barrow and Frank Tipler in their book, "The Anthropic Cosmological Principle"*]

MWI .... Master Weavers Institute (EA)

MWI .... Measured Workload Index [*Aviation*]

MWI .... Message-Waiting Indicator

MWI .... Missionary Women International (EA)

MWI .... Montserrat [*West Indies*] [*Seismograph station code, US Geological Survey*] (SEIS)

MWI .... Motor-Ways Inc., Des Moines IA [*STAC*]

MWIA .... Medical Women's International Association [*See also AIFM*] [*Cologne, Federal Republic of Germany*] (EAIO)

MWIAP .... Prairie Regional Office, Parks Canada [*Bureau Regional des Pres, Parcs Canada*] Winnipeg, Manitoba [*Library symbol National Library of Canada*] (NLC)

MWIC .... Manitoba Department of Economic Development, Winnipeg, Manitoba [*Library symbol National Library of Canada*] (NLC)

MWiCA .... Sterling and Francine Clark Art Institute, Williamstown, MA [*Library symbol Library of Congress*] (LCLS)

MWIDE .... IDE Engineering Co., Winnipeg, Manitoba [*Library symbol National Library of Canada*] (NLC)

MWIE .... Indus Electronic, Winnipeg, Manitoba [*Library symbol National Library of Canada*] (NLC)

MWIF .... Ivan Franko Museum & Library, Winnipeg, Manitoba [*Library symbol National Library of Canada*] (NLC)

MWIN .... Indian and Northern Affairs Canada [*Affaires Indiennes et du Nord Canada*],Winnipeg, Manitoba [*Library symbol National Library of Canada*] (BIB)

MWIP .... Mixed Waste Integrated Program [*Department of Energy*]

MWIP .... Mixed Waste Integrated Program (DOGT)

MWIR .... Medium-Wavelength Infrared

MWIR .... Midwave Infrared Sensor (MCD)

MWIR .... Mixed Waste Inventory Report [*Department of Energy*]

MWIR .... Mixed Waste Inventory Report (DOGT)

MWIR .... Mixed Waste Inventory Report [*Department of Energy*] (GAAI)

MWIS .... National Network of Minority Women in Science (EA)

MWIV .... Mean Wildlife Index Value [*Statistics*] (PDAA)

MWiW .... Williams College, Williamstown, MA [*Library symbol Library of Congress*] (LCLS)

MWiW-C ..... Williams College, Chapin Library, Williamstown, MA [*Library symbol Library of Congress*] (LCLS)

MWJ .... Canada Department of Justice [*Ministere de la Justice*] Winnipeg, Manitoba [*Library symbol National Library of Canada*] (NLC)

MWJ .... Matthews Ridge [*Guyana*] [*Airport symbol*] (OAG)

MWJC .... Marjorie Webster Junior College [*Washington, DC*]

MWJHS .... Jewish Historical Society of Western Canada, Winnipeg, Manitoba [*Library symbol National Library of Canada*] (NLC)

MWJP .... Jewish Public Library, Winnipeg, Manitoba [*Library symbol National Library of Canada*] (NLC)

MWK .... Kelvin High School, Winnipeg, Manitoba [*Library symbol National Library of Canada*] (NLC)

MWK .... Mill Work [*Technical drawings*]

MWK .... Milwaukee Land [*AMEX symbol*] (TTSB)

MWK .... Milwaukee Land Co. [*AMEX symbol*] (SPSG)

MWK .... Mount Airy, NC [*Location identifier FAA*] (FAAL)

MWL .... Law Society of Manitoba, Winnipeg, Manitoba [*Library symbol National Library of Canada*] (NLC)

MWL .... Malawi Women's League

MWL .... Mean Water Level

MWL .... Meteoric Water Line [*Geology*]

MWL .... Milled-Wood Lignin

mWL .... Milliwatt Logic

MWL .... Mineral Wells [*Texas*] [*Airport symbol*] (AD)

MWL .... Mineral Wells, TX [*Location identifier FAA*] (FAAL)

MWL .... Minimum Wage Laws (OICC)

MWL .... Motor Water Lighter (ADA)

MWL .... Municipal Waste Leachate (GNE)

MWL .... Muslim World League (BJA)

MWL .... Mutual Welfare League (NADA)

MWLAE .... Millimeter Wave Large Antenna Experiment [*NASA*] (PDAA)

MWLCC .... Lutheran Council in Canada, Winnipeg, Manitoba [*Library symbol National Library of Canada*] (NLC)

MWLD .... Man Worn LASER Detector [*Assembly*] (MCD)

MWLD .... Man-Worn LASER Device [*Army*]

MWLDA .... Maine Wholesale Lobster Dealers Association [*Defunct*] (EA)

MWLG .... Midwest Women's Legal Group (EA)

MWLMV .... Maize White Line Mosaic Virus [*Plant pathology*]

MWLR .... Labour Research Library, Manitoba Department of Labour and Manpower, Winnipeg, Manitoba [*Library symbol National Library of Canada*] (NLC)

MWLS .... Faculty of Law, University of Manitoba, Winnipeg, Manitoba [*Library symbol National Library of Canada*] (NLC)

MWM .... Maxwell-Wagner Mechanism [Physics]
MWM .... Medical Library, University of Manitoba, Winnipeg, Manitoba [Library symbol National Library of Canada] (NLC)
MWM .... Millimeter Wave Mixer
MWM .... Minskoff, Wiseman, Minskoff [Program for the development of language abilities]
MWM .... Mode-Woche-Muenchen [Munich Fashion Week - International Fashion Fair] [Germany] (TSPED)
MWM .... Moments with Meredith - Meredith Baxter-Birney Fan Club [Defunct] (EA)
MWM .... Morfee Wheel Manufacturing [Vancouver Stock Exchange symbol]
MWM .... Windom, MN [Location identifier FAA] (FAAL)
MWM .... Worcester Art Museum, Worcester, MA [Library symbol Library of Congress] (LCLS)
MWMA .... Manitoba Department of Municipal Affairs, Winnipeg, Manitoba [Library symbol National Library of Canada] (NLC)
MWMA .... Multiple Wine Merchants Association [British] (BI)
MWM & R .... Metal-Working Machine and Robot
MWMBC ...... Mennonite Brethren Bible College, Winnipeg, Manitoba [Library symbol National Library of Canada] (NLC)
MWMC .... Metropolitan Waste Management Council [Melbourne, Australia]
MWMC .... Midwest Microfilm Service, Co., Springfield, IL [Library symbol] [Library of Congress] (LCLS)
MWMCA ...... Michigan Women for Medical Control of Abortion (EA)
MWME .... Maclaren Engineering, Winnipeg, Manitoba [Library symbol National Library of Canada] (NLC)
MWMFB .... Middlewest Motor Freight Bureau
MWMG .... Misericordia General Hospital, Winnipeg, Manitoba [Library symbol National Library of Canada] (NLC)
MWMH .... Winnipeg Municipal Hospital, Manitoba [Library symbol National Library of Canada] (NLC)
MWMHC ...... Mennonite Heritage Centre, Winnipeg, Manitoba [Library symbol National Library of Canada] (NLC)
MWMM .... Manitoba Museum of Man & Nature, Winnipeg, Manitoba [Library symbol National Library of Canada] (NLC)
MWMMP ...... Meadowood Manor Personal Care Home, Winnipeg, Manitoba [Library symbol National Library of Canada] (NLC)
MWMP .... City of Winnipeg Metro Planning Division, Manitoba [Library symbol National Library of Canada] (NLC)
MWMPE .... Manitoba Pool Elevators Library, Winnipeg, Manitoba [Library symbol National Library of Canada] (NLC)
MWMRC ...... Manitoba Research Council, Winnipeg, Manitoba [Library symbol National Library of Canada] (NLC)
MWMRTL .... Milliwatt Motorola Resistor Transistor Logic (IAA)
MWMSE .... Minimum-Weighted Mean Square Error (IAA)
MWMT .... Metal-Working Machine Tool
MWMTC .... Manitoba Theater Center, Winnipeg, Manitoba [Library symbol National Library of Canada] (NLC)
MWMTS ...... Manitoba Teachers Socity, Winnipeg, Manitoba [Library symbol National Library of Canada] (NLC)
MWMU .... University of Massachusetts, Medical Center, Worcester, MA [Library symbol Library of Congress] (LCLS)
MWn .... GAR Memorial Library, West Newbury, MA [Library symbol Library of Congress] (LCLS)
MWN .... Gordon College, Wenham, MA [Inactive] [OCLC symbol] (OCLC)
MWN .... Madras Weekly Notes [India] [A publication] (DLA)
MWN .... Mount Washington, NH [Location identifier FAA] (FAAL)
MWNCC .... Madras Weekly Notes, Criminal Cases [India] [A publication] (DLA)
MWNT .... Multiwalled Nanotube [Materials science]
MWNT .... Multiwall Nanotube [Materials science]
MWO .... Maintenance Work Order
MWO .... Manufacturing Work Order
MWO .... Master Warrant Officer [Canadian Forces, since 1964]
MWO .... Master Work Order (AAG)
MWO .... Mental Welfare Officer [British]
MWO .... Middletown, OH [Location identifier FAA] (FAAL)
MWO .... Millimeter Wavelength Oscillator
MWO .... Millimeter Wave Observatory [University of Texas at Austin] [Research center] (RCD)
MWO .... Modification Work Order
MWO .... Mount Wilson Observatory (NADA)
MWO .... Rev. Peres Oblats, Winnipeg, Manitoba [Library symbol National Library of Canada] (NLC)
MWo .... Woburn Public Library, Woburn, MA [Library symbol Library of Congress] (LCLS)
MWOA .... Mizrachi Women's Organization of America [Later, AMW] (EA)
MWOC .... Mothers without Custody (EA)
MWOFP .... Modification Work Order Fielding Plan
MWolIE........ Eastern Nazarene College, Wollaston, MA [Library symbol Library of Congress] (LCLS)
MWOP .... Mixed Waste Office Paper [Pulp and paper technology]
MWOT .... Master Warrant Officer Training [DoD]
MWP .... Legislative Library of Manitoba, Winnipeg, Manitoba [Library symbol National Library of Canada] (NLC)
MWP .... Malta Workers Party [Political party] (PPE)
MWP .... Maneuvering Work Platform [NASA]
MWP .... Mangla [Pakistan] [Airport symbol] (AD)
MWP .... Master of Welfare Policy
MWP .... Maximum Working Pressure
MWP .... Mechanical Wood Pulp [Paper]
MWP .... Medieval Warm Period [Geoscience]
MWP .... Membrane Waterproofing
MWP .... Metabolic Waste Production
MWP .... Meteorological Weather Processor (GAVI)
MWP .... Meteorologist Weather Processor [FAA] (TAG)

MWP .... Mexican Water Plan [Land use]
MWP .... Millimeter Wave Propagation
MWP .... Ministry of Works and Planning [British]
MWP .... Missile Warning Position (MCD)
MWP .... Most Worthy Patriarch
MWP .... Worcester Polytechnic Institute, Worcester, MA [Library symbol Library of Congress] (LCLS)
MWPA .... Married Women's Property Act [1882] [British] (AIA)
MWPA .... Provincial Archives of Manitoba, Winnipeg, Manitoba [Library symbol National Library of Canada] (NLC)
MWPC .... Moorepark Whey Protein Concentrate (OA)
MWPC .... Multiple Wire Proportional Counter
MWPC .... Multiwire Proportional Chamber (IAA)
MWPCPA ..... Archaeology Subsection Office, Prairie Region Library, Parks Canada [Recherches Archeologiques, Bibliotheque de la Region des Pres, Parcs Canada] Winnipeg, Manitoba [Library symbol National Library of Canada] (NLC)
MWPCPH .... Historic Resources Conservation Subsection Office, Prairie Region Library, ParksCanada [Ressources et Conservation Historiques, Bibliotheque de la Region de s Pres, Parcs Canada] Winnipeg, Manitoba [Library symbol National Library of Canada] (NLC)
MWPCR .... Riding Mountain National Park, Parks Canada [Parc National Riding Mountain, Parcs Canada] Wasagaming, Manitoba [Library symbol National Library of Canada] (NLC)
MWPF .... Marine Wildlife Preservation Fund
MWPI.......... Munson-Williams-Proctor Institute [Utica, NY]
MWPL......... Public Library Services, Manitoba Department of Culture, Heritage and Recreation, Winnipeg, Manitoba [Library symbol National Library of Canada] (NLC)
MWPNR .... Park Management Library, Manitoba Department of Natural Resources, Winnipeg, Manitoba [Library symbol National Library of Canada] (NLC)
MWPO .... Mine Warfare Project Office [Naval Material Command]
MWpP......... Westport Free Public Library, Westport, MA [Library symbol] [Library of Congress] (LCLS)
MWPPH ...... Provincial Public Health Nursing Services, Winnipeg, Manitoba [Library symbol National Library of Canada] (NLC)
MWPR .... Monthly Work Package Report [NASA] (NASA)
MWPS .... Manitoba Probation Services, Winnipeg, Manitoba [Library symbol National Library of Canada] (NLC)
MWPS .... Master of Wood and Paper Science (GAGS)
MWPS .... Multimeter Wave Power Source
MWQ .... Magwe [Myanmar] [Airport symbol] (OAG)
MWQ .... Quinsigamond Community College, Worcester, MA [Library symbol Library of Congress] (LCLS)
MWQCG ...... Media and Information Services, Quadraplegic Communications Group, Inc., Winnipeg, Manitoba [Library symbol National Library of Canada] (NLC)
MWR .... Maintenance Work Request [or Requirement]
MWR .... Man-Worn Receiver (MCD)
mwr .... Marwari [MARC language code Library of Congress] (LCCP)
MWR .... Mean Width Ratio
MWR .... Metal Whisker Reinforcement
MWR .... Method of Weighted Residual
MWR .... Millimeter-Wave Radar (DOMA)
MWR .... Mine Watching RADAR (NATG)
MWR .... Mini Web Reel (DGA)
MWR .... Missile-Warning Receiver (MCD)
MWR .... Morale, Welfare, and Recreation [DoD]
MWR .... Mountain-West Resources [Vancouver Stock Exchange symbol]
MWR .... Mower
MWR .... Muncie & Western Railroad Co. [AAR code]
MWR .... Royal Winnipeg Ballet, Manitoba [Library symbol National Library of Canada] (NLC)
MWRA .... Master of Water Resources Administration (PGP)
MWRA .... Morale, Welfare, and Recreation Activity [DoD] (AFIT)
MWRAILS .... Microwave Remote Area Instrument Landing System (IAA)
MWRC .... Maintain Well to Right of Course [Aviation] (FAAC)
MWRC .... Melbourne Western Region Commission [Australia]
MWRC .... Mount Washington Railway Co. [AAR code]
MWRC .... RCMP [Royal Canadian Mounted Police] Crime Laboratory, Winnipeg, Manitoba [Library symbol National Library of Canada] (NLC)
MWRCC ...... Roman Catholic Chancery Office, Winnipeg, Manitoba [Library symbol National Library of Canada] (NLC)
MWRK .... Mothers Work [NASDAQ symbol] (TTSB)
MWRK .... Mothers Work, Inc. [NASDAQ symbol] (SAG)
MWroxV....... United States Veterans Administration Hospital, West Roxbury, MA [Library symbol Library of Congress] (LCLS)
MWRR .... Learning Resources Centre, Red River Community College, Winnipeg, Manitoba [Library symbol National Library of Canada] (NLC)
MWRRC ...... Montana Water Resources Research Center [Montana State University, University ofMontana, and Montana College of Mineral Science and Technology] [Research center] (RCD)
MWRRL ...... Library Technician Program, Red River Community College, Winnipeg, Manitoba, LS [National Library of Canada] (NLC)
MWRS .... Millimeter Wave Radio System (MCD)
MWRS .... Richardson Securities of Canada, Winnipeg, Manitoba [Library symbol National Library of Canada] (NLC)
MWRT .... Mobile Wing Reconnaissance Technical [Squadron]
mWRTL....... Milliwatt Resistor-Transistor Logic (IDOE)
MWS........... Major Weapon System [Manager] (MCD)
MWS........... Management Work Station (BUR)
MWS........... Marden-Walker Syndrome [Medicine] (DMAA)

MWS............ Marine Weather Service (NOAA)
MWS............ Master of Women's Studies (PGP)
MWS............ Mawashi [Ryukyu Islands] [Seismograph station code, US Geological Survey Closed] (SEIS)
MWS............ Maximum Wind Speed
MWS............ Medium Wide Shot [Photography]
MWS............ Megawatt Waveguide Switch
MWS............ Member of the Wernerian Society [British] (ROG)
MWS............ Microwave Scatterometer [Telecommunications] (TEL)
MWS............ Microwave Station
MWS............ Microwave Wind Spectrometer
MWS............ Mikity-Wilson Syndrome [Neonatology] (DAVI)
MWS............ Mini Workstation (SSD)
MWS............ Missile Warning Squadron
MWS............ Missile Weapon System [Military] (CAAL)
MWS............ Missouri Western State College, St. Joseph, MO [OCLC symbol] (OCLC)
MWS............ Mobile Weapon System
MWS............ Modular Weapons System (MCD)
MWS............ Moersch-Woltman Syndrome [Medicine] (DMAA)
MWS............ Most Wise Sovereign [Freemasonry]
MWS............ Most Worshipful Scribe [Freemasonry] (ROG)
MWS............ Mount Wilson, CA [Location identifier FAA] (FAAL)
MWS............ Multiwork Station
MWSA .... St. Andrew's College, Winnipeg, Manitoba [Library symbol National Library of Canada] (NLC)
MWSAC .... St. Amant Center, Winnipeg, Manitoba [Library symbol National Library of Canada] (NLC)
MWSACB .... Salvation Army Catherine Booth Bible College, Winnipeg, Manitoba [Library symbol National Library of Canada] (BIB)
MWSB .... Saint Boniface Public Library, Winnipeg, Manitoba [Library symbol National Library of Canada] (NLC)
MWSBM ...... Saint Boniface General Hospital Medical Library, Winnipeg, Manitoba [Library symbol National Library of Canada] (NLC)
MWSBN ...... Saint Boniface General Hospital School of Nursing Library, Winnipeg, Manitoba [Library symbol National Library of Canada] (NLC)
MWSC .... American Men and Women of Science [Database] [R. R. Bowker Co.] [Information service or system] (CRD)
MWSC .... Midwestern Simulation Council
MWSC .... Society for Manitobans with Disabilities, Inc., Winnipeg, Manitoba [Library symbol National Library of Canada] (NLC)
MWSCS ...... Midwestern Signal Corps School
MWSD .... Missile and Weapons Systems Division [Military] (IAA)
MWSD .... Teachers' Library and Resource Centre, Winnipeg School Division No. 1, Manitoba [Library symbol National Library of Canada] (NLC)
MWSE......... Midwest Stock Exchange, Inc. (HGAA)
MWSG .... Marine Wing Support Group (NVT)
MWSGDET... Marine Wing Support Group Detachment (DNAB)
MWSGR ...... Marine Wing Staff Ground (MCD)
MWSH .... Worcester State Hospital, Worcester, MA [Library symbol Library of Congress] (LCLS)
MWSJ......... St. John's College, Winnipeg, Manitoba [Library symbol National Library of Canada] (NLC)
MWSM........ Stony Mountain Institution Library, Winnipeg, Manitoba [Library symbol National Library of Canada] (NLC)
MWSOGH .... Educational Services, Seven Oaks General Hospital, Winnipeg, Manitoba [Library symbol National Library of Canada] (NLC)
MWSP .... St. Paul's College, Winnipeg, Manitoba [Library symbol National Library of Canada] (NLC)
MWSPA ...... Spiece Associates, Winnipeg, Manitoba [Library symbol National Library of Canada] (NLC)
MWSPC ...... Social Planning Council of Winnipeg, Manitoba [Library symbol National Library of Canada] (NLC)
MW Sprg ..... Mid-West Spring Manufacturing Co. [Associated Press] (SAG)
MWSR .... Magnetic Wire Shift Register
MWSR .... Microwave Water Substance Radiometer [Marine science] (OSRA)
MWSR .... Microwave Water Substance Radiometer (USDC)
MWSS .... Manitoba Regional Library, Secretary of State Canada [Bibliotheque Regionale du Manitoba, Secretariat d'Etat], Winnipeg, Manitoba [Library symbol National Library of Canada] (NLC)
MWSS .... Marine Wing Support Squadron [Navy] (ANA)
MWSS .... Metropolitan Waterworks and Sewerage System [Philippines]
MWSS .... Metwork Six [NASDAQ symbol] (TTSB)
MWSS .... Mid-West Spring Manufacturing Co. [NASDAQ symbol] (SAG)
MWSSE........ Mid-West Spring Mfg [NASDAQ symbol] (TTSB)
MWST......... Mean Weighted Skin Temperature
MWST......... Miscellaneous Waste Storage Tank [Nuclear energy] (NRCH)
MWST......... Missile Warning System Test (MCD)
MWSV .... St. Vital Public Library, Winnipeg, Manitoba [Library symbol National Library of Canada] (NLC)
MWT........... Makeup Water Treatment (IEEE)
MWT........... Marconi Wireless Telegraph [Telecommunications] (IAA)
MWT........... Master of Wood Technology
MWT........... McWhorter Technologies, Inc. [NYSE symbol] (SAG)
MWT........... Mean Water Temperature
MWT........... Megawatt Thermal [Nuclear energy] (NRCH)
MWT........... Midwest Aviation [Southwest Aviation, Inc.] [ICAO designator] (FAAC)
MWT........... Millimeter Wave Tube
MWT........... Ministry of War Transport [Terminated, 1956] [British]
MWT........... M McWhorter Technologies [NYSE symbol] (TTSB)
MWt........... Molecular Weight [Also, M, MOL WT, MW] (AAMN)
MWT........... Moolawatana [Australia Airport symbol Obsolete] (OAG)
MWT........... Mountain War Time

Mwt .... Thermal Megawatt [Also, TMW]
MWT........... Winnipeg Tribune, Manitoba [Library symbol National Library of Canada] (NLC)
MWTA......... Airworthiness Library, Central Region, Transport Canada [Bibliotheque de la Navigabilite Aerienne, Region Centrale, Transports Canada], Winnipeg, Manitoba [Library symbol National Library of Canada] (NLC)
MWTA......... Medical Waste Tracking Act [1988] (FFDE)
MWTA......... Medical Waste Treatment Act
MWTC......... Ministry of War Time Communications [British World War II]
MWTC......... Teshmount Consultants, Winnipeg, Manitoba [Library symbol National Library of Canada] (NLC)
MWTCR ...... Central Regional Library, Transport Canada [Bibliotheque Regionale du Centre, Transports Canada], Winnipeg, Manitoba [Library symbol National Library of Canada] (NLC)
MWTCS....... Modernized Weather Teletypewriter Communications System (FAAC)
MWTE......... Interdisciplinary Engineering, Winnipeg, Manitoba [Library symbol National Library of Canada] (NLC)
MWTE......... Modern Weapons Training Exercises (MCD)
MW(th)....... Megawatts (Thermal)
MWTHA....... Michigan Wild Turkey Hunters Association
MWTP......... Mixed Waste Treatment Project
MWTR......... Mean Waiting Time for Supply Replacement (DNAB)
MWTR......... Monthly Wholesale Trade Report [A publication]
MWTS......... Manitoba Telephone System, Winnipeg, Manitoba [Library symbol National Library of Canada] (NLC)
MWTU......... Marble Workers' Trade Union [British]
MWU.......... Maccabi World Union [Ramat Gan, Israel] (EAIO)
MWU.......... Mercer University, Southern School of Pharmacy, Atlanta, GA [OCLC symbol] (OCLC)
MWU.......... Mine Workers Union [South Africa] (IMH)
MWU.......... Modified Wohlgemuth Unit [Of hydrolytic enzyme activity]
MWU.......... Mussau [Papua New Guinea] [Airport symbol] (OAG)
MWU.......... University of Manitoba, Winnipeg, Manitoba [Library symbol National Library of Canada] (NLC)
MWUA........ Ukrainian Academy of Arts and Science, Winnipeg, Manitoba [Library symbol National Library of Canada] (NLC)
MWUAF ...... Architecture and Fine Arts Library, University of Manitoba, Winnipeg, Manitoba [Library symbol National Library of Canada] (NLC)
MWUC........ University of Winnipeg, Manitoba [Library symbol National Library of Canada] (NLC)
MWUCE ...... Ukrainian Cultural and Educational Centre, Winnipeg, Manitoba [Library symbol National Library of Canada] (NLC)
MWUD........ Dental Library, University of Manitoba, Winnipeg, Manitoba [Library symbol National Library of Canada] (NLC)
MWUG........ Department of Geography, University of Manitoba, Winnipeg, Manitoba [Library symbol National Library of Canada] (NLC)
MWUGG...... United Grain Growers, Winnipeg, Manitoba [Library symbol National Library of Canada] (NLC)
MWUM........ Map and Atlas Collection, University of Manitoba, Winnipeg, Manitoba [Library symbol National Library of Canada] (NLC)
MWUML...... Underwood McLellan Ltd., Winnipeg, Manitoba [Library symbol National Library of Canada] (NLC)
MWUSA ...... Minute Women of the United States of America (EA)
MWV.......... Maximum Working Voltage [Electronics]
MWV.......... Mexican War Veteran
MWV.......... Milkweed Virus
MWV.......... Modulated Wavy Vortex [Fluid mechanics]
MWV.......... Motor Tariff Bureau of West Virginia, Charleston WV [STAC]
MWVGH ...... Victoria General Hospital, Winnipeg, Manitoba [Library symbol National Library of Canada] (NLC)
MWVS .... Branch Library, Manitoba Veterinarian Services, Winnipeg, Manitoba [Library symbol National Library of Canada] (NLC)
MWW......... Majestic Wine Warehouses [Commercial firm] [British]
MWW......... Manual Wire Wrap
MWW......... Mark's Work Wearhouse Ltd. [Toronto Stock Exchange symbol]
MWW......... Marquis Who's Who [Marquis Who's Who, Inc.] [Information service or system A publication]
MWW......... [The] Merry Wives of Windsor [Shakespearean work] (BARN)
MWW......... Municipal Wastewater
MWW......... William Ave. Branch, Winnipeg Public Library, Manitoba [Library symbol National Library of Canada] (NLC)
MWW......... Worcester State College, Worcester, MA [Library symbol Library of Congress] (LCLS)
MWWA........ Winnipeg Art Gallery, Manitoba [Library symbol National Library of Canada] (NLC)
MWWC........ Military Weather Warning Center (NOAA)
MWWC........ Winnipeg Clinic, Manitoba [Library symbol National Library of Canada] (NLC)
MWWF........ Manual Wire Wrap Fixture
MWWII........ Mothers of World War II
MWWK........ West Kildonan Public Library, Winnipeg, Manitoba [Library symbol National Library of Canada] (NLC)
MWWLW ..... W. L. Wardrop & Associates, Winnipeg, Manitoba [Library symbol National Library of Canada] (NLC)
MWWR........ Water Resources Division, Manitoba Department of Natural Resources, Winnipeg, Manitoba [Library symbol National Library of Canada] (NLC)
MWWSH...... Manitoba Workplace Safety and Health Division, Winnipeg, Manitoba [Library symbol National Library of Canada] (NLC)
MWWU........ Marine Wing Weapon Unit
MWWV........ Movement of Working Women and Volunteers [Tel Aviv, Israel] (EAIO)
MWX........... Montpelier, VT [Location identifier FAA] (FAAL)
MWY........... Midway Games, Inc. [NYSE symbol] (SAG)

MWY	Miranda Downs [*Australia Airport symbol Obsolete*] (OAG)
MWYE	Megawatt Year of Electricity (IAA)
MWZ	Mwanza [*Tanzania*] [*Airport symbol*] (OAG)
MX	Compania Mexicana de Aviacion [*ICAO designator*] (OAG)
MX	Mail Exchange [*Computer science*]
mx	Management (DAVI)
MX	Master Agility Excellent
MX	Matrix (BUR)
Mx	Maxwell [*Unit of magnetic flux*] [*Also, abWb*]
MX	Measurex Corp. [*NYSE symbol*] (SPSG)
MX	Metaxylene
MX	Mexicana [*Airline*] (DS)
MX	Mexicana de Aviacion [*ICAO designator*] (AD)
MX	Mexican L & P Co. Ltd. [*Toronto Stock Exchange symbol*]
MX	Mexico [*ANSI two-letter standard code*] (CNC)
mx	Mexico [*IYRU nationality code*] [*MARC country of publication code Library of Congress*] (LCCP)
MX	Middlesex [*Region of London*]
MX	Missile, Experimental
MX	Mix
MX	Motocross (WGA)
MX	Multiple Address
MX	Multiplex [*or Multiplexer*]
MX	Multiplex
MX	Murexide [*An indicator*] [*Chemistry*]
MXA	Compania Mexicana de Aviacion SA [*Mexico ICAO designator*] (FAAC)
MXA	Manila, AR [*Location identifier FAA*] (FAAL)
MXA	Minnesota Municipal Income Portfolio [*AMEX symbol*] (SPSG)
MXA	Minnesota Muni Inc. Portfolio [*AMEX symbol*] (TTSB)
MXA	Mobile Exercise Area [*Military*] (NVT)
MXAL	Mercury Xenon Arc Lamp
MXB	Masamba [*Indonesia*] [*Airport symbol*] (OAG)
MXC	MATEC Corp. [*AMEX symbol*] (SPSG)
MXC	Maxon Computer Systems, Inc. [*Toronto Stock Exchange symbol*]
MXC	Mexair SA [*Switzerland ICAO designator*] (FAAC)
MXC	Monticello [*Utah*] [*Airport symbol*] (OAG)
MXC	Multiplexer Channel [*Computer science*]
MXC	University of Cincinnati, Medical Center, Cincinnati, OH [*OCLC symbol*] (OCLC)
MxChGS	Church of Jesus Christ of Latter-Day Saints, Genealogical Society Library, Colonia Juarez Branch, Chihuahua, Mexico [*Library symbol Library of Congress*] (LCLS)
MXD	Marion Downs [*Queensland*] [*Airport symbol*] (AD)
MXD	Mixed
MXD	Mixed
MXD	Mixed Artillery [*Military*] (VNW)
MXD	Multiple Transmitter Duplicator
MXDA	Meta-Xylenediamine [*Organic chemistry*]
MXD CL	Mixed Carload [*Freight*]
MXDCR	Mode Transducer (MSA)
MXDTH	Maximum Depth (NOAA)
MXE	Manx Airlines (Europe) Ltd. [*British ICAO designator*] (FAAC)
MXE	Mexico Eqty & Income Fd [*NYSE symbol*] (TTSB)
MXE	Mexico Equity & Income Fund [*NYSE symbol*] (SPSG)
MXE	Modena, PA [*Location identifier FAA*] (FAAL)
MXF	Mexico Fund [*NYSE symbol*] (TTSB)
MXF	[*The*] Mexico Fund, Inc. [*NYSE symbol*] (SPSG)
MXF	Montgomery, AL [*Location identifier FAA*] (FAAL)
MXFL	Mixed Flow
MXG	Mixing (MSA)
MxGuBF	Biblioteca Benjamin Franklin, Guadalajara, Mexico [*Library symbol Library of Congress*] (LCLS)
MXIC	MX Information Center [*Defunct*] (EA)
MXICY	Macronix Intl ADR [*NASDAQ symbol*] (TTSB)
MXIM	Maxim Integrated Prod [*NASDAQ symbol*] (TTSB)
MXIM	Maxim Integrated Products, Inc. [*NASDAQ symbol*] (NQ)
MXIS	Maxis, Inc. [*NASDAQ symbol*] (SAG)
MXK	Camp Springs, MD [*Location identifier FAA*] (FAAL)
MXK	Metekel [*Ethiopia*] [*Airport symbol*] (AD)
MXK	Multiple-Frequency X- and K-Band
MXL	Mexicali [*Mexico*] [*Airport symbol*] (OAG)
MXL	Mixed Workload [*Computer science*] (PCM)
MXLU	Malcolm X Liberation University
MXM	Matrix Memory (MHDI)
MXM	Maximum (ADA)
MXM	MAXXAM, Inc. [*AMEX symbol*] (SPSG)
MXM	Morombe [*Madagascar*] [*Airport symbol*] (OAG)
MxMBF	Biblioteca Benjamin Franklin, Mexico City, Mexico [*Library symbol Library of Congress*] (LCLS)
MxMBN	Biblioteca Nacional de Mexico, Mexico City, Mexico [*Library symbol Library of Congress*] (LCLS)
MxMC	Centro de Investigacion y de Estudios Avanzados, Instituto Politecnico Nacional,Mexico City, Mexico [*Library symbol Library of Congress*] (LCLS)
MxMCM	Colegio de Mexico, Mexico, Mexico City, Mexico [*Library symbol Library of Congress*] (LCLS)
MxMGS	Church of Jesus Christ of Latter-Day Saints, Genealogical Society Library, Mexico City Branch, Mexico City, Mexico [*Library symbol Library of Congress*] (LCLS)
MxMI	Universidad Iberoamericana, Mexico [*Library symbol Library of Congress*] (LCLS)
MX/MM	Missile X/Minuteman Missile
MxMoT	Instituto Tecnologico y de Estudios Superiores de Monterrey, Monterrey, Mexico [*Library symbol Library of Congress*] (LCLS)
MX/MPS	Missile X [*Deploy In*] Multiple Protective Shelters
MxN	Maxillary Nerve [*Neuroanatomy*]
MXN	Morlaix [*France*] [*Airport symbol*] (OAG)
MX-NM	Matrix - National Module
MXO	Monticello, IA [*Location identifier FAA*] (FAAL)
MXP	May Air Xpress, Inc. [*ICAO designator*] (FAAC)
MXP	Mesa, Inc. [*NYSE symbol*] (SAG)
MXP	Milan [*Italy*] Malpensa Airport [*Airport symbol*] (OAG)
MXPST	Maximum Possible Storm (NOAA)
MXQ	Modular X-Ray Quantometer
MXQ	Wilmington, OH [*Location identifier FAA*] (FAAL)
MXR	Mask Index Register
MXR	Mass X-Ray
MXR	Merrix Air Ltd. [*British ICAO designator*] (FAAC)
MXR	Mixer (MSA)
MXR	Moussoro [*Chad*] [*Airport symbol*] (AD)
MXR	Raton, NM [*Location identifier FAA*] (FAAL)
MXRAN	Maximum Rainfall (NOAA)
M-X/RES	M-X [*Missile*] Renewable Energy System
MXRV	Middlesex Rifle Volunteers [*Military British*] (DMA)
MXS	Max Minerals, Inc. [*Vancouver Stock Exchange symbol*]
MXS	Maxus Energy Corp. [*NYSE symbol*] (SPSG)
MXSBP	Maxus Energy [*NASDAQ symbol*] (SAG)
MXSBP	Maxus Energy $4 Cv Pfd [*NASDAQ symbol*] (TTSB)
MXSPrA	Maxus Energy $2.50 Pfd [*NYSE symbol*] (TTSB)
MXSV	Maxserv, Inc. [*NASDAQ symbol*] (SAG)
MXT	Chicago, IL [*Location identifier FAA*] (FAAL)
MXT	Maintirano [*Madagascar*] [*Airport symbol*] (OAG)
MXT	Message Exchange Terminal
MXT	Mixture
MXT	Morgan StanGp 6.00% Tele'PERQS' [*AMEX symbol*] (TTSB)
MXT	Morgan Stanley Group, Inc. [*AMEX symbol*] (SAG)
MXTMP	Maximum Temperature (NOAA)
MXTR	Maxtor Corp. [*NASDAQ symbol*] (NQ)
MXU	Mobile Exhibition Unit (NITA)
MXU	Mullewa [*Australia Airport symbol Obsolete*] (OAG)
MXU	Multiplexer Unit [*Telecommunications*]
MxU	Universidad Nacional Autonoma de Mexico, Mexico City, Mexico [*Library symbol Library of Congress*] (LCLS)
MXVRC	Middlesex Volunteer Rifle Corps [*British military*] (DMA)
MXW	Maxwell, CA [*Location identifier FAA*] (FAAL)
MXWL	Maxwell Laboratories, Inc. [*NASDAQ symbol*] (NQ)
MXWL	Maxwell Labs [*NASDAQ symbol*] (TTSB)
MXWL	Maxwell Technologies, Inc. [*NASDAQ symbol*] (SAG)
MXWND	Maximum Wind (NOAA)
MXX	Merchant Express Aviation [*Nigeria*] [*ICAO designator*] (FAAC)
MXX	Mora [*Sweden*] [*Airport symbol*] (OAG)
MXY	McCarthy [*Alaska*] [*Airport symbol*] (OAG)
MXY	McCarthy, AK [*Location identifier FAA*] (FAAL)
MXY	[*The*] Yarumal Foreign Mission Institute (Colombia) (TOCD)
MY	Air Mali [*ICAO designator*] (AD)
My	All India Reporter, Mysore Series [*A publication*] (ILCA)
MY	Machine Yield [*Agriculture*] (OA)
MY	Mahzor Yanai (BJA)
MY	Malaysia [*IYRU nationality code*] [*ANSI two-letter standard code*] (CNC)
my	Malaysia [*MARC country of publication code Library of Congress*] (LCCP)
MY	Man-Year (AFM)
MY	Man Year
M/Y	Marshaling Yards [*Military*]
MY	May
my	Mayer [*A unit of heat capacity*]
MY	Mean Year (IAA)
MY	Mean Yield [*Agriculture*]
MY	Miller-Yoder Language Comprehension Test
MY	Million Years
MY	Model Year [*Automotive industry*]
MY	Montgomeryshire Yeomanry [*British military*] (DMA)
MY	Motor Yacht
MY	Muddy [*Track condition*] [*Thoroughbred racing*]
MY	Myopia
MY	Myria [*A prefix meaning multiplied by 10^4*]
MY	Myxedematous [*Endocrinology*] (DAVI)
MYA	Million Years Ago
MYA	Model Yachting Association [*British*] (DBA)
MYA	Moruya [*Australia Airport symbol*] (OAG)
MYA	Myasishchev [*Aircraft*] [*Commonwealth of Independent States*]
MYA	Myflug HF [*Iceland*] [*ICAO designator*] (FAAC)
mya	Myiare (BARN)
MYAB	Clarence Bain, Andros Island [*Bahamas*] [*ICAO location identifier*] (ICLI)
MYAF	Andros Town, Andros Island [*Bahamas*] [*ICAO location identifier*] (ICLI)
MYAG	Gorda Cay, Abaco Island [*Bahamas*] [*ICAO location identifier*] (ICLI)
MYAK	Congo Town, Andros Island [*Bahamas*] [*ICAO location identifier*] (ICLI)
MYAM	Marsh Harbour, Abaco Island [*Bahamas*] [*ICAO location identifier*] (ICLI)
MYAN	San Andros, Andros Island [*Bahamas*] [*ICAO location identifier*] (ICLI)
My & C	Mylne and Craig's English Chancery Reports [*A publication*] (DLA)
My & Cr	Mylne and Craig's English Chancery Reports [*A publication*] (DLA)
My & K	Mylne and Keen's English Chancery Reports [*A publication*] (DLA)

MYAO .... Moores Island, Abaco Island [*Bahamas*] [*ICAO location identifier*] (ICLI)
MYAP .... Spring Point [*Bahamas*] [*ICAO location identifier*] (ICLI)
MYAPP .... Main Yankee Atomic Power Plant (NRCH)
MYAS .... Sandy Point, Abaco Island [*Bahamas*] [*ICAO location identifier*] (ICLI)
MYAT .... Treasure Cay, Abaco Island [*Bahamas*] [*ICAO location identifier*] (ICLI)
MYAW .... Walker Cay, Abaco Island [*Bahamas*] [*ICAO location identifier*] (ICLI)
MYB .... Aerolineas Del Mayab, SA de CV [*Mexico*] [*FAA designator*] (FAAC)
MYB .... Mayoumba [*Gabon*] [*Airport symbol*] (OAG)
MYBC .... Chub Cay, Berry Island [*Bahamas*] [*ICAO location identifier*] (ICLI)
MYBG .... Bullocks Harbour/Great Harbour Cay, Berry Island [*Bahamas*] [*ICAO location identifier*] (ICLI)
MYBO .... Ocean Cay, Bimini Island [*Bahamas*] [*ICAO location identifier*] (ICLI)
MYBP .... Million Years before Present [*Geology*]
MYBS .... Alice Town/South Bimini, Bimini Island [*Bahamas*] [*ICAO location identifier*] (ICLI)
MYBT .... Cistern Cay, Berry Island [*Bahamas*] [*ICAO location identifier*] (ICLI)
MYBW .... Big Whale Cay, Berry Island [*Bahamas*] [*ICAO location identifier*] (ICLI)
MYBX .... Little Whale Cay, Berry Island [*Bahamas*] [*ICAO location identifier*] (ICLI)
MYC .... Malartic Hygrade Gold Mines Ltd. [*Vancouver Stock Exchange symbol*]
MYC .... Maracay [*Venezuela*] [*Airport symbol*] (OAG)
MYC .... Massenya [*Chad*] [*Airport symbol*] (AD)
MYC .... Middlesex Yeomanry Cavalry [*British military*] (DMA)
MYC .... Montgomeryshire Yeomanry Cavalry [*British military*] (DMA)
MYC .... Multiyear Contract
MYC .... MuniYield California Fund [*NYSE symbol*] (SPSG)
MYC .... Mycology (WGA)
MYCA .... Arthur's Town, Eleuthera Island [*Bahamas*] [*ICAO location identifier*] (ICLI)
MYCB .... New Bight, Cat Island [*Bahamas*] [*ICAO location identifier*] (ICLI)
MYCH .... Hawks Nest Creek/Hawks Nest, Cat Island [*Bahamas*] [*ICAO location identifier*] (ICLI)
MYCI .... Colonel Hill, Crooked Island [*Bahamas*] [*ICAO location identifier*] (ICLI)
MYCI .... Mirrer Yeshiva Central Institute (EA)
MYCO .... Mycobacterium
MYCO .... Mycogen Corp. [*NASDAQ symbol*] (NQ)
Myco .... Mycoplasma [*A bacterium*] (DAVI)
Mycogn .... Mycogen Corp. [*Associated Press*] (SAG)
MYCOL .... Mycology
MYCOS .... My Compact Operating System [*Toshiba*]
MYCOS/SS ... MYCOS Support System (NITA)
MYCP .... Pittsdown, Crooked Island [*Bahamas*] [*ICAO location identifier*] (ICLI)
MYCS .... Cay Sal [*Bahamas*] [*ICAO location identifier*] (ICLI)
MYCX .... Cutlass Bay, Cat Island [*Bahamas*] [*ICAO location identifier*] (ICLI)
MYD .... Malindi [*Kenya*] [*Airport symbol*] (OAG)
MYD .... Miyadu [*Japan*] [*Seismograph station code, US Geological Survey Closed*] (SEIS)
MYD .... MuniYield Fund [*NYSE symbol*] (SPSG)
MYDP .... Multi-Year Development Plan [*Environmental Protection Agency*] (ERG)
MYDW .... Multiple Yield Defense Weapon
MYE .... Mary Ellen Resources Ltd. [*Vancouver Stock Exchange symbol*]
MYE .... Miyake Jima [*Japan*] [*Airport symbol*] (OAG)
MYE .... Myers Indus [*AMEX symbol*] (TTSB)
MYE .... Myers Industries, Inc. [*AMEX symbol*] (SPSG)
MYEC .... Cape Eleuthera, Eleuthera Island [*Bahamas*] [*ICAO location identifier*] (ICLI)
MYEG .... George Town, Exuma Island [*Bahamas*] [*ICAO location identifier*] (ICLI)
MYEH .... North Eleuthera, Eleuthera Island [*Bahamas*] [*ICAO location identifier*] (ICLI)
MYEL .... Mulitple Myeloma [*Hematology*] (DAVI)
MYEL .... Myelin [*or Myelinated*] [*Medicine*]
MYEL .... Myelocyte [*Hematology*]
MYEL .... Myelogram [*Medicine*] (AAMN)
MYEL .... Staniel Cay, Exuma Island [*Bahamas*] [*ICAO location identifier*] (ICLI)
myelo .... Myelocyte [*Hematology*]
MYEM .... Governor's Harbour, Eleuthera Island [*Bahamas*] [*ICAO location identifier*] (ICLI)
MYEN .... Norman's Cay, Exuma Island [*Bahamas*] [*ICAO location identifier*] (ICLI)
MYER .... Rock Sound/International, Eleuthera Island [*Bahamas*] [*ICAO location identifier*] (ICLI)
Myer Dig ..... Myer's Texas Digest [*A publication*] (DLA)
Myer Fed Dec... Myer's Federal Decisions [*A publication*] (DLA)
MyerL .... [*The*] Myers [*L. E.*] Co. Group [*Associated Press*] (SAG)
Myer's Fed Dec... Myer's Federal Decisions [*United States*] [*A publication*] (DLA)
MyersInd ..... Myers Industries, Inc. [*Associated Press*] (SAG)
MYES .... Lee Stocking Island, Exuma Island [*Bahamas*] [*ICAO location identifier*] (ICLI)
MYEY .... Hog Cay, Exuma Island [*Bahamas*] [*ICAO location identifier*] (ICLI)
MYF .... Methodist Youth Fellowship
MYF .... MuniYield Florida Fund [*NYSE symbol*] (SPSG)
MYF .... San Diego [*California*] Montgomery Field [*Airport symbol Obsolete*] (OAG)
MYFV .... Melandrium Yellow Fleck Virus [*Plant pathology*]
MYG .... Massachusetts Institute of Technology, Cambridge, MA [*OCLC symbol*] (OCLC)

MYG .... Matka [*Yugoslavia*] [*Seismograph station code, US Geological Survey*] (SEIS)
MYG .... Mayaguana [*Bahamas*] [*Airport symbol*] (OAG)
MYG .... Maytag [*NYSE symbol*] (SAG)
MYG .... Maytag Corp. [*NYSE symbol*] (TTSB)
MYG .... Myasthenia Gravis [*Medicine*]
MYG .... Myriagram [*Ten Thousand Grams*]
MYGD .... Deep Water Cay, Grand Bahama Island [*Bahamas*] [*ICAO location identifier*] (ICLI)
MYGF .... Freeport/International, Grand Bahama Island [*Bahamas*] [*ICAO location identifier*] (ICLI)
MYGM .... Grand Bahama Auxiliary Air Force Base, Grand Bahama Island [*Bahamas*] [*ICAO location identifier*] (ICLI)
MYGN .... Myriad Genetics [*NASDAQ symbol*] (TTSB)
MYGN .... Myriad Genetics, Inc. [*NASDAQ symbol*] (SAG)
MYGW .... West End, Grand Bahama Island [*Bahamas*] [*ICAO location identifier*] (ICLI)
MYH .... Rosh-Pina [*Israel*] [*Airport symbol*] (AD)
MYHEC .... Michigan Youth Hunter Education Challenge
MY I .... First Multiyear Contract [*Military*] (RDA)
MYI .... Magical Youths International (EA)
MYI .... Metallic Yarns Institute [*Defunct*]
MYI .... MuniYield Insured Fund [*NYSE symbol*] (SPSG)
MYIG .... Matthew Town, Great Inagua Island [*Bahamas*] [*ICAO location identifier*] (ICLI)
MY II .... Second Multiyear Contract [*Military*] (RDA)
MYIM .... Mylar Insulation Material
MYJ .... Matsuyama [*Japan*] [*Airport symbol*] (OAG)
MYJ .... MuniYield New Jersey Fund [*NYSE symbol*] (SPSG)
MYK .... May Creek [*Alaska*] [*Airport symbol*] (OAG)
MYK .... May Creek, AK [*Location identifier FAA*] (FAAL)
MYK .... Miyakojima [*Ryukyu Islands*] [*Seismograph station code, US Geological Survey*] (SEIS)
MYL .... Aeromyl SA de CV [*Mexico ICAO designator*] (FAAC)
MYL .... McCall, ID [*Location identifier FAA*] (FAAL)
MYL .... Mylan Laboratories, Inc. [*NYSE symbol*] (SPSG)
MYL .... Mylan Labs [*NYSE symbol*] (TTSB)
MYL .... Myrialiter [*Unit of measurement*]
Mylan .... Mylan Laboratories, Inc. [*Associated Press*] (SAG)
Myl & C ...... Mylne and Craig's English Chancery Reports [*A publication*] (DLA)
Myl & C (Eng)... Mylne and Craig's English Chancery Reports [*A publication*] (DLA)
Myl & Cr ..... Mylne and Craig's English Chancery Reports [*A publication*] (DLA)
Myl & K ...... Mylne and Keen's English Chancery Reports [*A publication*] (DLA)
Myl & K (Eng)... Mylne and Keen's English Chancery Reports [*A publication*] (DLA)
MYLD .... Deadman's Cay, Long Island [*Bahamas*] [*ICAO location identifier*] (ICLI)
Mylex .... Mylex Corp. [*Associated Press*] (SAG)
My LJ .... Mysore Law Journal [*India*] [*A publication*] (DLA)
Mylne & K .... Mylne and Keen's English Chancery Reports [*A publication*] (DLA)
MYLR .... Diamond Roads, Long Island [*Bahamas*] [*ICAO location identifier*] (ICLI)
MYLS .... Mid-York Library System [*Library network*]
MYLS .... Stella Maris, Long Island [*Bahamas*] [*ICAO location identifier*] (ICLI)
MYLX .... Mylex Corp. [*NASDAQ symbol*] (NQ)
MYM .... Managing Your Money [*MECA Software, Inc.*] (PCM)
MYM .... Marley Mines Ltd. [*Vancouver Stock Exchange symbol*]
MYM .... Monkey Mountain [*Guyana*] [*Airport symbol*] (OAG)
MYM .... Muniyield Michigan Fund [*NYSE symbol*] (SAG)
MYM .... Myriameter
MyMD .... Myotonic Muscular Dystrophy [*See also MD*] [*Medicine*]
MYMM .... Mayaguana Auxiliary Air Force Base, Mayaguana Island [*Bahamas*] [*ICAO location identifier*] (ICLI)
MYMS .... Mothers of Young Mongoloids [*Later, PODSC*] (EA)
MYMV .... Mungbean Yellow Mosaic Virus [*Plant pathology*]
MYN .... Mareb [*Yemen*] [*Airport symbol Obsolete*] (OAG)
myn .... Mayan [*MARC language code Library of Congress*] (LCCP)
MYN .... Mayan Energy, Inc. [*Vancouver Stock Exchange symbol*]
MYN .... MuniYield New York Insured Fund [*NYSE symbol*] (SPSG)
MYN .... MuniYield NY Insured Fund [*NYSE symbol*] (TTSB)
MYNA .... Nassau [*Bahamas*] [*ICAO location identifier*] (ICLI)
MYNN .... Nassau/International, New Providence Island [*Bahamas*] [*ICAO location identifier*] (ICLI)
MYO .... Myocardial [*or Myocardium*] [*Cardiology*] (AAMN)
MYOB .... Mind Your Own Business [*Slang*]
MYOBB .... Mind Your Own Business, Buster [*Slang*]
MYOC-A ...... Myocarditis, Pericarditis [*Cardiology*] (DAVI)
MYOGLB ...... Myoglobin [*hematology*] (DAVI)
MYOP .... Multiyear Operational Plan [*Long-range forecast produced by the Canadian government*]
myop .... Myopia [*Ophthalmology*] (DAVI)
MYP .... Mannito-Egg Yolk Polymyxin (OA)
MY/P .... Mean Yield/Plants [*Agriculture*]
MYP .... Montgomery [*Pakistan*] [*Airport symbol*] (AD)
MYP .... Multiyear Procurement [*DoD*]
MYPO .... Multiyear Procurement Objective [*DoD*]
MYQ .... Windsor Locks, CT [*Location identifier FAA*] (FAAL)
MYR .... Maximum Yield Research [*Agricultural technology*]
m/yr .... Milli-Inches per Year [*Corrosion technology*]
MYR .... Million Years [*Also, MY*]
MYR .... Miriadair [*France ICAO designator*] (FAAC)
MYR .... [*The*] Myers [*L. E.*] Co. Group [*NYSE symbol*] (SPSG)
MYR .... MYR Group [*NYSE symbol*] (TTSB)

Myr	Myrick's California Probate Court Reports [*1872-79*] [*A publication*] (DLA)
myr	Myrtle [*Philately*]
MYR	Myrtle Beach [*South Carolina*] Myrtle Air Force Base [*Airport symbol*] (OAG)
MYRA	Multiyear Rescheduling Agreement [*Banking*]
MYRAA	Model Yacht Racing Association of America (EA)
Myr Cal Prob	Myrick's California Probate Court Reports [*1872-79*] [*A publication*] (DLA)
MYRD	Duncan Town, Exuma Island [*Bahamas*] [*ICAO location identifier*] (ICLI)
Myriad	Myriad Genetics, Inc. [*Associated Press*] (SAG)
Myrick (Cal)	Myrick's California Probate Court Reports [*1872-79*] [*A publication*] (DLA)
Myrick Prob (Cal)	Myrick's California Probate Court Reports [*1872-79*] [*A publication*] (DLA)
Myrick's Prob Rep	Myrick's California Probate Court Reports [*1872-79*] [*A publication*] (DLA)
MYRP	Port Nelson, Exuma Island [*Bahamas*] [*ICAO location identifier*] (ICLI)
Myr Prob	Myrick's California Probate Court Reports [*1872-79*] [*A publication*] (DLA)
Myr Prob Rep	Myrick's California Probate Court Reports [*1872-79*] [*A publication*] (DLA)
Mys	All India Reporter, Mysore [*A publication*] (DLA)
MYS	Maderas y Sinteticos [*NYSE symbol*] (SPSG)
MYS	Maderas y Sinteticos ADS [*NYSE symbol*] (TTSB)
MYS	Malaysia [*ANSI three-letter standard code*] (CNC)
MYS	Man-Year-Space [*Army*] (AABC)
MYS	Myasthenic Syndrome [*Neurology*]
MYS	Mystery Mountain Minerals [*Vancouver Stock Exchange symbol*]
MYS	Mystic, KY [*Location identifier FAA*] (FAAL)
MYS	Mystic Marinelife Aquarium, New London, CT [*OCLC symbol*] (OCLC)
Mys Ch Ct	Mysore Chief Court Reports [*India*] [*A publication*] (DLA)
Mys HCR	Mysore High Court Reports [*India*] [*A publication*] (DLA)
Mys LJ	Mysore Law Journal [*India*] [*A publication*] (DLA)
Mys LR	Mysore Law Reports [*India*] [*A publication*] (DLA)
MYSM	Cockburn Town, San Salvador Island [*Bahamas*] [*ICAO location identifier*] (ICLI)
MySoft	My Software Co. [*Associated Press*] (SAG)
MySoft	MySoftware Co. [*Associated Press*] (SAG)
MYSOLN	Mysoline [*An anticonvulsant*] [*Wyeth-Ayerst Laboratorie*] (DAVI)
Mysore	Mysore Law Reports [*India*] [*A publication*] (DLA)
Mysore LJ	Mysore Law Journal [*India*] [*A publication*] (DLA)
Mys R (R)	Mysore Reports (Reprint) [*1878-1923*] [*India*] [*A publication*] (DLA)
MYST	Mystery
MYSTIC	Mystic
MYSW	MySoftware Co. [*NASDAQ symbol*] (SAG)
Mys WN	Mysore Weekly Notes [*1891-92*] [*India*] [*A publication*] (DLA)
MYT	MuniYield New York Insured Fund II [*NYSE symbol*] (SPSG)
MYT	MuniYield NY Insured Fund II [*NYSE symbol*] (TTSB)
MYT	Myitkyina [*Myanmar*] [*Airport symbol*] (OAG)
MYT	Mytec Technology, Inc. [*Vancouver Stock Exchange symbol*]
MYT	Mythology
MYTA	Maintainability Task Analyses (NASA)
MYTA	Maintainability Task Analyses
MYTAB	Myristyltrimethylammonium Bromide [*Organic chemistry*]
MYTD	Model Year to Date
MYTGC	Miller-Yoder Test of Grammatical Comprehension [*Speech and lanaguage therapy*] (DAVI)
MYTH	Mythology
MYTHOL	Mythology (WGA)
Myth Vat	Mythographi Vaticani [*A publication*] (OCD)
MYU	Mekoryuk [*Alaska*] [*Airport symbol*] (OAG)
MYV	Malva Yellows Virus [*Plant pathology*]
MYV	Marysville [*California*] [*Airport symbol*] (AD)
MYV	Marysville, CA [*Location identifier FAA*] (FAAL)
MYVAL	Maintainability Evaluation (NASA)
MYVAL	Maintainability Evaluation
MYW	Mtwara [*Tanzania*] [*Airport symbol*] (OAG)
MYW	Multiple Yield Weapon
MYWF	Masonic Youth Welfare Fund [*Australia*]
MYX	Marion, VA [*Location identifier FAA*] (FAAL)
MYX	Menyamya [*Papua New Guinea*] [*Airport symbol*] (OAG)
MYX	Methotrexate [*Antineoplastic drug*] (CDI)
MYXO	Myxomatosis (DSUE)
MYY	Miri [*Malaysia*] [*Airport symbol*] (OAG)
MYY	MuniYield MY Insured Fund III [*NYSE symbol*] (TTSB)
MYY	MuniYield New York Insured Fund III [*NYSE symbol*] (SPSG)
MYY	Philadelphia, PA [*Location identifier FAA*] (FAAL)
MYZ	Marysville, KS [*Location identifier FAA*] (FAAL)
MYZ	Mayoko [*Gabon*] [*Airport symbol*] (AD)
MYZ	Miyazaki [*Japan*] [*Seismograph station code, US Geological Survey*] (SEIS)
MZ	Mantle Zone
MZ	Marginal Zone [*Neurology*]
m-z	Mass to Charge Ratio
MZ	Merpati Nusatnara Airlines [*ICAO designator*] (AD)
Mz	Methoxyphenylazobenzyloxycarbonyl [*Biochemistry*]
MZ	Mezzo [*Moderate*] [*Music*] (ROG)
MZ	Midzone Phenomenon [*Immunology*]
MZ	Miesiecznik Zydowski (BJA)
MZ	Minus Zero (IAA)
MZ	Monozygotic [*Genetics*]
mz	Mozambique [*MARC country of publication code Library of Congress*] (LCCP)
MZ	Mozambique [*ANSI two-letter standard code*] (CNC)
MZ	Museum of Zoology (NADA)
MZA	Air Zory [*Bulgaria*] [*FAA designator*] (FAAC)
MZA	Mariazell [*Austria*] [*Seismograph station code, US Geological Survey*] (SEIS)
MZA	Monozygotic Twins Reared Apart [*Genetics*]
MZA	MuniYield Arizona Fund [*AMEX symbol*] (TTSB)
MZA	MuniYield Arizona Fund, Inc. [*AMEX symbol*] (SPSG)
MZAD	Mains Army Depot [*Germany*]
MZB	Mocimboa da Praia [*Mozambique*] [*Airport symbol*] (AD)
MZB	San Diego, CA [*Location identifier FAA*] (FAAL)
MZBZ	Belize/International [*Belize*] [*ICAO location identifier*] (ICLI)
MZC	Mitzic [*Gabon*] [*Airport symbol*] (OAG)
MZCP	Mean Zonal Candlepower (IAA)
MZF	Manganese Zinc Ferrite
MZF	Mazirat [*France*] [*Seismograph station code, US Geological Survey*] (SEIS)
MZFR	Mehrzweck Forschungs [*Reactor*] [*Germany*] (NRCH)
MZFW	Maximum Zero Fuel Weight [*Aviation*] (MCD)
MZG	Makung [*Taiwan*] [*Airport symbol*] (OAG)
MZI	Mopti [*Mali*] [*Airport symbol*] (OAG)
MZJ	Marana, AZ [*Location identifier FAA*] (FAAL)
MZK	Marakei [*Kiribati*] [*Airport symbol*] (OAG)
MZL	Aerovias Montes Azules, SA de CV [*Mexico*] [*FAA designator*] (FAAC)
MZL	Manizales [*Colombia*] [*Airport symbol*] (OAG)
MZL	Muzzle (MSA)
MZM	Metz [*France*] [*Airport symbol*] (OAG)
MZN	Maruzen Co. Ltd. [*UTLAS symbol*]
MZN	Minj [*New Guinea*] [*Airport symbol*] (AD)
MZN	Mount Vernon Nazarene College, Mount Vernon, OH [*OCLC symbol*] (OCLC)
MZO	Manzanillo [*Cuba*] [*Airport symbol*] (OAG)
MZO	Mazie Landing [*Oklahoma*] [*Seismograph station code, US Geological Survey*] (SEIS)
MZOA	Masada of the Zionist Organization of America (EA)
MZON	Multiple Zones International, Inc. [*NASDAQ symbol*] (SAG)
M-ZONE	Manufacturing Zone (MHDB)
MZP	Meta-Azidopyrimethamine [*Biochemistry*]
MZP	Modulated Zone Plate (PDAA)
MZPI	Microwave Zone Position Indicator (IAA)
MZQ	Mozambique [*Mozambique*] [*Airport symbol*] (AD)
MZR	Mazar-I-Sharif [*Afghanistan*] [*Airport symbol*] (OAG)
MZR	Monroe, LA [*Location identifier FAA*] (FAAL)
MZS	Mahfooz Aviation [*Gambia*] [*FAA designator*] (FAAC)
MZS	Master of Zoology Science (GAGS)
MZS	Spokane, WA [*Location identifier FAA*] (FAAL)
MZ Sc	Master of Zoological Science
MZSCS	Martinek-Zaichkowsky Self-Concept Scale for Children [*Child development test*]
MZSH	Missionary Zelatrices of the Sacred Heart [*Roman Catholic women's religious order*]
MZsL	Magyar Zsido Lexikon [*A publication*] (BJA)
MZT	Mazatlan [*Mexico*] [*Airport symbol*] (AD)
MZT	Monozygotic Twins Reared Together [*Genetics*]
MZU	Muzaffarpur [*India*] [*Airport symbol*] (AD)
MZV	Magyar Zsidok Vilagszovetsege [*World Federation of Hungarian Jews*] (EAIO)
MZV	Moline, IL [*Location identifier FAA*] (FAAL)
MZX	Augusta, GA [*Location identifier FAA*] (FAAL)
MZX	Massio [*Ethiopia*] [*Airport symbol*] (AD)
MZY	Mzimba [*Malawi*] [*Airport symbol*] (AD)
MZZ	Marion [*Indiana*] [*Airport symbol*] (AD)
MZZ	Marion, IN [*Location identifier FAA*] (FAAL)

N
By Acronym

N	All India Reporter, Nagpur Series [*A publication*] (ILCA)
n	Amino [*As substituent on nucleoside*] [*Biochemistry*]
n	Amount of Substance [*Molecular quantity*] [*Symbol IUPAC*]
N	Asparagine [*Biochemistry*] (DAVI)
N	Avogadro Number [*Number of molecules in one gram-molecular weight of a substance*]
N	Carbon Star [*Astronomy*] (BARN)
N	Cementex [*Research code symbol*]
N	Digestum Novum [*A publication Authority cited in pre-1607 legal work*] (DSA)
N	Dr. Karl Thomae GmbH [*Germany*] [*Research code symbol*]
N	Dumb [*Auxiliary craft suffix*] [*British Navy*]
N	Educational Premises [*Public-performance tariff class*] [*British*]
N	Efficiency [*Physics*] (BARN)
N	Electron N-Type Semiconductor Material
N	Employment [*Economics*]
N	En [*Typography*] (WDAA)
n	En [*Printing measurement*] (WDMC)
N	Flying Boat [*Russian aircraft symbol*]
n	Footnote (DLA)
N	Haploid Chromosome Number (DOG)
N	Haploid Number [*Genetics*]
N	H. Lundbeck [*Denmark*] [*Research code symbol*]
N	INCO Ltd. [*Formerly, International Nickel Co. of Canada Ltd.*] [*NYSE symbol Toronto Stock Exchange symbol*] (SPSG)
n	[*An*] Indefinite Quantity [*Mathematics*] (ROG)
N	Knight [*Chess*]
N	Magnetic Flux [*Symbol*] (ROG)
N	Nail
N	Name
N	Nan [*Phonetic alphabet*] [*World War II*] (DSUE)
n	Nano [*A prefix meaning divided by one billion*] [*SI symbol*]
N	Naringenin [*Organic chemistry*]
N	Naris [*Nostril*] [*Pharmacy*]
N	Narrow
N	Nasal
N	National [*Screw threads*]
N	Nationalist (ROG)
N	Nationalist Party [*British Political party*]
N	National League [*Baseball*]
N	Native [*Ecology*]
N	Natural Division [*Geography*]
N	Naturalization (DNAB)
N	Natural Number (IDOE)
N	Natus [*Birth*] [*Latin*]
N	Nautical
N	Naval [*British military*] (DMA)
N	Navigation
N	Navigational Aids [*JETDS nomenclature*]
N	Navy
N	Nay [*Vote*]
N	Near [*Optics*] (WDAA)
N	Near the Nut (or Heel) of the Bow [*Music*] (ROG)
N	Necrotic
n	Need [*Psychology*]
N	Negative [*Crystal*]
N	Negro
N	Neisseria [*Medicine*]
N	Nematic Phase [*Physical chemistry*]
N	Nematocyst [*Zoology*]
N	Neper [*A unit on a natural logarithmic scale*] (DEN)
N	Nephew
N	Nepos [*Grandson*] [*Latin*]
N	Nervus [*Nerve*] [*Anatomy*]
N	Nested [*Freight*]
N	Nesting [*Ornithology*]
N	Net
N	Network [*FCC program source designation*] (NTCM)
n	Network (WDMC)
N	Neuraminidase [*An enzyme*]
N	Neurogenic Element
N	Neurology
N	Neuropathy [*Medicine*] (DAVI)
N	Neuter
N	Neutral
n	Neutron [*A nuclear particle*]
N	Neutron Number [*Physics*] (DAVI)
N	Neutrophil [*Hematology*]
N	New [*Stock exchange term*] (SPSG)
N	New Issue [*Investment term*] (DFIT)
N	New Persian
N	News
n	News (WDMC)
N	Newspaper
N	News Program (NTCM)
N	Newton [*Symbol*] [*SI unit of force*]
N	New York State Library, Albany, NY [*Library symbol Library of Congress*] (LCLS)
N	New York Stock Exchange [*New York, NY*]
n	Next [*Computer science*] [*Telecommunications*]
N	Ngultrum [*Monetary unit*] [*Bhutan*] (BARN)
N	Nichrome (IAA)
N	Nicolaus Furiosus [*Flourished, 12th century*] [*Authority cited in pre-1607 legal work*] (DSA)
N	Nicotinamide [*Also, NAA*] [*Vitamin*]
N	Niece (ADA)
N	Nifedipine [*Pharmacology*]
N	Night [*Approach and landing charts*] [*Aviation*]
N	Night [*Broadcasting term*]
n	Night (WDMC)
N	Night Fighter [*When suffix to plane designation*] [*Navy*]
N	Night Game [*Baseball*]
N	Nighttime (NTCM)
N	Nitrogen [*Chemical element*]
N	No
N	Nocardia [*Genus of bacteria*] (MAE)
N	Nocte [*At Night*] [*Pharmacy*]
N	Nodal [*Oncology*]
N	Node [*Lymphatic*] [*Anatomy*]
N	Noise [*Broadcasting*]
N	Nomen [*Name*] [*Latin*]
N	Nominal [*Stock exchange term*] (SPSG)
N	Nominally Labeled [*Compound, with radioisotope*]
N	Nominative
N	None
N	Nonmalignant [*Of tumors*] [*Medicine*]
N	Nonne [*Globulin test*]
N	Nontactical [*Military*]
N	Noon
n	Noon (WDMC)
N	Norein [*Geology*]
N	Norland Potato
N	Norm (WDAA)
N	Normal
N	Normal [*Solute concentration*] [*Chemistry*]
n	Normal [*Molecular structure*] [*Chemistry*]
N	Normal Depth [*Earthquakes*]
N	Normal Horsepower
N	Normal Solution (DOG)
N	Norse [*Language, etc.*]
N	Norske Veritas [*Norwegian ship classification society*] (ROG)
N	North [*or Northern*]
n-----	North America [*MARC geographic area code Library of Congress*] (LCCP)
N	Northeastern Reporter [*Commonly cited NE*] [*A publication*] (DLA)
N	Northern Ireland Law Reports [*A publication*] (DLA)
N	Northgate Exploration Ltd. [*Gold producer*] [*Canada*]
N	North London [*Postcode*] (ODBW)
N	Northwestern Reporter [*Commonly cited NW*] [*A publication*] (DLA)
N	Norway [*IYRU nationality code*]
N	Noster [*Our*] [*Latin*]
N	Nostril (AAMN)
N	Not (DAVI)
N	Notative Speed (WDAA)
N	Note
n	Note (WDMC)
n	Noun (WDMC)
N	Noun
N	No Uniform [*For schoolgirls*] [*British*]
N	Novellae [*Novels*] [*New Constitutions of Justinian*] [*A publication*] (DLA)
N	Novelty [*Insulation*]

N................. November [*Phonetic alphabet*] [*International*] (DSUE)
N................. Novice Slope [*Skiing*]
N................. Nu [*Thirteenth letter of the Greek alphabet*] (DAVI)
N................. Nuclear
N................. Nuclear Propelled [*When following vessel classification, as CAG(N)*] [*Navy*]
N................. [*A*] Nucleoside [*One-letter symbol; see Nuc*]
n................. Nucleus [*Psychology*]
N................. Nucleus [*of a cell*] [*Biology*]
N................. Nucleus (of Syllable) [*Linguistics*]
N................. Nullity [*Divorce cases*] [*British*] (ROG)
N................. Number
N................. Number (IDOE)
n................. Number [*Usually integer*] (IDOE)
N................. Number (of Bits) [*Computer science*] (ECII)
N................. Number of Molecules [*Symbol*] [*IUPAC*]
n................. Number of Observations [*Statistics*] (DAVI)
N................. Number (of Turns) [*Electronics*] (ECII)
N................. Numeric
N................. Nun [*Buoy*]
N................. Nunnery
N................. Nupta [*Married*] [*Latin*]
N................. Nurse (ADA)
N................. Nuts [*Phonetic alphabet*] [*Royal Navy World War I Pre-World War II*] (DSUE)
N................. Nylon (AAG)
N................. Nymph [*Entomology*]
N................. Nystatin [*Antifungal antibiotic*]
N................. Population Size [*Symbol*] (MAE)
N................. Population size [*Statistics*] (DAVI)
n................. Principal Quantum Number [*Atomic physics*] (DEN)
N................. Probe [*Missile vehicle type symbol*]
n................. Refractive Index [*Symbol*] [*Physics*]
N................. Rockwell International Corp. [*ICAO aircraft manufacturer identifier*] (ICAO)
N................. Size of Sample [*Statistics*] (DAVI)
N................. Sound in Air [*JETDS nomenclature*]
N................. South African Law Reports, Natal Province Division [*1910-46*] [*A publication*] (DLA)
N................. Special Test, Permanent [*Aircraft classification letter*]
N................. Stauffer Chemical Co. [*Research code symbol*]
N................. Tilt Correction
N1E............. Nosed One Edge [*Lumber*] (DAC)
N₂ .... Molecular Nitrogen [*Chemistry*] (DAVI)
N2............. Nitrogen
N2E............. Nosed Two Edges [*Lumber*] (DAC)
N2N .... Project Neighbor to Neighbor (EA)
N₂0............. Nitrous Oxide [*An Anesthetic*] (DAVI)
N₂0:0₂.......... Nitrous Oxide to Oxygen Ratio [*Anesthesiology*] (DAVI)
N3............. Cyclophosphamide, Vincristine, Triflurothymidine, Papaverine [*Antineoplastic drug regimen*] (DAVI)
N3F............. National Fantasy Fan Federation (EA)
N4A............. National Association of Academic Advisors for Athletics (EA)
N4A............. National Association of Area Agencies on Aging [*Also, NAAAA*] (EA)
N4-HC......... National 4-H Council (EA)
N4WDA........ National 4 Wheel Drive Association (EA)
N/30............ Net in Thirty Days
NA................. Academician of the National Academy of Design, New York [*1825*] (NGC)
Na................. Avogadro's Number [*Chemistry*] (DAVI)
NA................. De Natura Animalium [*of Aelianus*] [*Classical studies*] (OCD)
Na................. Exchangeable Body Sodium (AD)
NA................. Nabisco Holdings 'A' [*NYSE symbol*] (TTSB)
NA................. Nabisco Holdings Corp. [*NYSE symbol*] (SAG)
NA................. Nachrichtenabteilung [*Signal battalion*] [*German military - World War II*]
NA................. Nachrichten-Aufklaerung [*Signal intelligence*] [*German military - World War II*]
NA................. Nadir (WGA)
Na................. Nahum [*Old Testament book*]
NA................. Nailable [*Technical drawings*]
Na................. Naira [*Monetary unit*] [*Nigeria*]
N/A................. Name and Address
NA................. Namibia [*ANSI two-letter standard code*] (CNC)
nA................. Nanoampere [*One billionth of an ampere*]
NA................. Naphthalene Dicarboxylic Acid
NA................. Naphthylacetamide [*Organic chemistry*]
NA................. Naphthylamine [*Organic chemistry*]
NA................. Napoleonic Association [*Enfield, Middlesex, England*] (EAIO)
NA................. Narcolepsy Association [*British*] (DBA)
NA................. Narcotics Anonymous (EA)
NA................. Narrow Angle
NA................. Nash Papyrus (BJA)
NA................. National Academician
NA................. National Academy (ROG)
NA................. National Acme [*Thread*]
NA................. National Action [*Australia*]
NA................. National Aerospace Standards Committee (AAGC)
NA................. National Airlines, Inc. [*ICAO designator*]
NA................. National Airport [*Under control of BAA*] [*British*]
NA................. National Alliance (EA)
NA................. National Ambucs (EA)
NA................. [*The*] National Archives [*of the United States*]
NA................. National Army
NA................. National Assistance [*British*]

NA................. National Association [*National Bank*]
NA................. National Bank of Canada [*Toronto Stock Exchange symbol Vancouver Stock Exchange symbol*]
NA................. Nationale Aktion fuer Volk und Heimat [*National Action for People and Homeland*] [*Switzerland Political party*] (PPE)
NA................. Natl Bk of Canada [*MS, exchange symbol*] (TTSB)
Na................. Natrium [*Sodium*] [*Chemical element*]
NA................. Natural Axis
NA................. Naturally Aspirated [*Diesel engines*]
NA................. Nautical Almanac
NA................. Nautical Archaeology [*Oceanography*]
NA................. Naval Academy
NA................. Naval Accounts [*British*]
NA................. Naval Aircraft
NA................. Naval Airman [*Navy rating British*]
NA................. Naval Air Systems Command Manual
NA................. Naval Architect
NA................. Naval Assistant [*Navy rating British*]
NA................. Naval Attache [*Diplomacy*]
NA................. Naval Auxiliary
NA................. Naval Aviator
NA................. Navigation Aid (IAA)
NA................. Navion Aircraft Co. [*ICAO aircraft manufacturer identifier*] (ICAO)
NA................. Navy Aircraft (IAA)
NA................. Needle Aspiration [*Surgery*]
NA................. Needs Assessment (OICC)
NA................. Nelson Associates [*Also, an information service or system*] (IID)
NA................. Neo-Assyrian [*or New Assyrian*] [*Language, etc.*] (BJA)
NA................. Net Assessment Organization [*Navy*]
NA................. Net Assets [*Banking*]
na .... Netherlands Antilles [*MARC country of publication code Library of Congress*] (LCCP)
NA................. Network Adapter (MCD)
NA................. Neuraminidase Activity [*An enzyme*]
NA................. Neuropathology [*Medicine*] (DHSM)
NA................. Neurotics Anonymous (NADA)
NA................. Neutral Axis
NA................. Neutralizing Antibody [*Immunochemistry*]
NA................. Neutrophil Antibody [*Immunology*] (DAVI)
NA................. New Account
NA................. New Age [*Later, LR*] [*An association*] (EA)
NA................. New Alternative Party [*Venezuela Political party*]
NA................. New Associations [*Later, NAP*] [*A publication*]
NA................. Newsletter Association (EA)
NA................. Newton Abbot [*British depot code*]
NA................. Next Action (NASA)
NA................. Next Assembly
N/A................. Next Assembly
NA................. Ney-Allen [*Astronomy*]
NA................. Nicotinic Acid [*Biochemistry*]
NA................. Night Alarm [*Telecommunications*] (TEL)
NA................. Night Answer (WDMC)
NA................. Nitrobenzene Association [*Defunct*] (EA)
NA................. Nizamut Adalat Reports [*India*] [*A publication*] (DLA)
NA................. No Abnormality [*Medicine*] (MAE)
NA................. No Access [*Telecommunications*] (TEL)
NA................. No Account [*Banking*]
N/A................. No Action
N/A................. No Advice [*Business term*]
N/A................. No Alternative (DAVI)
NA................. No Answer (WDMC)
NA................. No Approval Required (MHDW)
NA................. No Assets (AFIT)
NA................. Noctes Atticae [*of Gellius*] [*Classical studies*] (OCD)
NA................. Nomina Anatomica [*System of anatomical terminology*]
N/A................. Nonacceptance [*Business term*]
NA................. Nonacquiescence [*Legal term*] (DLA)
NA................. Nonactivated
NA................. Nonalcoholic
NA................. Non Allocatur [*Legal*] [*Latin*] (ROG)
NA................. Non-Attached [*European political movement*] (ECON)
NA................. Nonattendance
NA................. Nora Alice [*DoD satellite*]
NA................. Noradrenaline [*Also known as NE: Norepinephrine*] [*Biochemistry*]
NA................. Normal Adult
NA................. Normal Alarm (SAA)
NA................. Normally Aspirated [*Automotive engineering*]
NA................. North Africa
NA................. North America
NA................. Northanger Abbey [*Novel by Jane Austen*]
NA................. North Atlantic Industries
NA................. Northern Alberta Railways Co. (IIA)
NA................. Nostra Aetate [*Declaration on the Relationship of the Church to the Non-Christian Religions*] [*Vatican II document*]
NA................. Nostro Account [*Our Account*] [*An account maintained by a bank with a bank in a foreign country*]
N/A................. Not Above
NA................. Not Admitted [*Medicine*] (MAE)
N/A................. Not Affected (AAG)
NA................. Not Allowed
NA................. Not And [*Logical operator*] [*Computer science*]
NA................. Not Applicable
NA................. Not Appropriated
NA................. Not Assigned
NA................. Not Authorized

NA............ Not Available
NA............ Noticias Argentinas SA [*News agency*] [*Argentina*] (EY)
NA............ Novice Agility
NA............ Nozzle Assembly
NA............ Nucleic Acid [*Biochemistry*]
NA............ Nucleus Accumbens [*Neuroanatomy*]
NA............ Nucleus Ambiguus [*Neuroanatomy*]
NA............ Nueva Alternativa [*Venezuela Political party*] (EY)
NA............ Number of Aimpoints [*Military*]
NA............ Numerical Analysis [*Computer science*] (BUR)
NA............ Numerical Aperture [*Microscopy*]
NA............ Nurse Anesthetist (AAMN)
NA............ Nurse's Aide
NA............ Nurses Almanac
NA............ Nursing Assistant
NA............ Nursing Auxiliary [*British*]
NA............ Nurturant-Authoritative [*Psychotherapy*]
NA............ Nutrient Agar [*Microbiology*]
NA............ Organon, Inc. [*Research code symbol*]
Na............ Sodium [*Chemical element*] (AAMN)
nA............ Transitional Antarctic Coastal Air Mass [*Meteorology*] (BARN)
NA 1SL....... Naval Assistant to the First Sea Lord [*British military*] (DMA)
NAA .... Naalehu [*Hawaii*] [*Seismograph station code, US Geological Survey Closed*] (SEIS)
NAA .... Nanny Academy of America [*Defunct*] (EA)
NAA .... Naphthaleneacetic Acid [*Biochemistry*] (DAVI)
NAA .... Naphthylacetic [*or Napthaleneacetic*] Acid [*Organic chemistry*]
NAA .... Narrabri [*Australia Airport symbol*] (OAG)
NAA .... Narrow-Angle Acquisition
NAA .... National Academy of Arbitrators (EA)
NAA .... National Academy of Astrology [*Defunct*] (EA)
NAA .... National Aeronautic Association (NADA)
NAA .... National Aeronautic Association of the USA (EA)
NAA .... National Aeronautics and Space Administration, Washington, DC [*OCLC symbol*] (OCLC)
NAA .... National Aerosol Association (EA)
NAA .... National Aftermarket Audit Co.
NAA .... National Airspace Analysis [*FAA*] (TAG)
NAA .... National Alumni Association (EA)
NAA .... National Apartment Association (EA)
NAA .... National Arborist Association (EA)
NAA .... National Archery Association of the United States (EA)
NAA .... National Ash Association (EA)
NAA .... National Association of Accountants [*Montvale, NJ*] (EA)
NAA .... National Auctioneers Association (EA)
NAA .... National Automobile Association (NADA)
NAA .... National Oceanic and Atmospheric Administration [*Department of Commerce ICAO designator*] (FAAC)
NAA .... Natural Areas Association (EA)
NAA .... Naval Air Arm [*British*]
NAA .... Naval Airship Association (EA)
NAA .... Naval Attache for Air
NAA .... Neckwear Association of America (EA)
NAA .... Network Analysis Area [*Space Flight Operations Facility, NASA*]
NAA .... Neuron Activation Analysis [*Neurology*] (DAVI)
NAA .... Neutral Amino Acid [*Biochemistry*]
NAA .... Neutron Activation Analysis
NAA .... New Art Association (EA)
NAA .... Newsletter Association of America (EA)
NAA .... Newspaper Association of America [*Reston, VA*] (WDMC)
NAA .... Nicotinic Acid Amide [*Also, N*]
NAA .... Nigerian-American Alliance (EA)
NAA .... Nitroanthranilic Acid [*Organic chemistry*]
NAA .... No Apparent Abnormalities [*Medicine*]
NAA .... Nocturnal Acid Accumulation [*Botany*]
NAA .... Nonattainment Area [*Environmental Protection Agency*] (EPA)
NAA .... Nord Africa Aviazione
NAA .... North American Aviation, Inc. [*Later, Rockwell International Corp.*]
NAA .... North Atlantic Alliance
NAA .... North Atlantic Assembly
NAA .... Northern Attack Area
NAA .... Norway-America Association (EA)
NAA .... Notable Asian Americans [*A publication*]
NAA .... Not Always Afloat [*Shipping*]
naa .... Not Always Afloat [*Shipping*] (ODBW)
NAA .... Nuclear Activation Analysis (PDAA)
NAAA .... National Agricultural Aviation Association (EA)
NAAA .... National Alarm Association of America (EA)
NAAA .... National Alliance of Athletic Associations [*Defunct*] (EA)
NAAA .... National Association of American Academicians (NADA)
NAAA .... National Association of Arab Americans (EA)
NAAA .... National Auto Auction Association [*Lincoln, NE*] (EA)
NAAAA .... National Association for the Advancement of Aardvarks in America [*Defunct*] (EA)
NAAAA .... National Association of Area Agencies on Aging [*Also, N4A*] (EA)
NAAACC...... National Association of Antique Automobile Clubs of Canada
NAAACPA.... National Association of Asian American Certified Public Accountants (EA)
NAAAID...... National Association of Americans of Asian Indian Descent (EA)
NAAAP .... National Association of Asian-American Professionals (EA)
NAAAP .... North American Association of Alcoholism Programs [*Later, ADPA*] (EA)
NAAAS .... National Association for Applied Arts and Sciences (EA)
NAAASL ..... National Association of African American Students of Law (EA)
NAAB .... National Architectural Accrediting Board (EA)

NAAB .... National Archival Appraisal Board [*Canada*]
NAAB .... National Association of Animal Breeders (EA)
NAABA .... National Association for the Advancement of the Black Aged (EA)
NAABAVE .... National Association for the Advancement of Black Americans in Vocational Education (EA)
NAABC .... National Association American Business Clubs [*High Point, NC*]
NAABCV ..... National Association American Balloon Corps Veterans (EA)
NAABI .... National Association of Alcoholic Beverage Importers [*Later, NABI*] (EA)
NAABSA...... Not Always Afloat but Safe Aground [*Shipping*]
NAAC .... National Adoption Assistance Center (EA)
NAAC .... National Agricultural Advisory Commission (NADA)
NAAC .... National Association for Ambulatory Care (EA)
NAAC .... National Association of Agricultural Contractors [*British*] (BI)
NAAC .... National Association of Avon Collectors (EA)
NAAC .... Navy Aeroballistics Advisory Committee (MCD)
NAAC .... North American Adoption Congress (EA)
NAACC ...... National Association for American Composers and Conductors (EA)
NAACC ...... National Association of Angling and Casting Clubs [*Later, ACA*]
NAACE ...... National Association of Advisers in Computer Education (AIE)
NAACLS ..... National Accrediting Agency for Clinical Laboratory Sciences (EA)
NAACO....... National Association of American Community Organizations (EA)
NAACOG .... NAACOG: the Organization for Obstetric, Gynecologic, and Neonatal Nurses [*Formerly, Nurses Association of the American College of Obstetricians and Gynecologists*] (EA)
NAACP ...... National Association for the Advancement of Colored People (EA)
NAACP ...... Neoplasia, Allergy, Addison's Disease, Collagen Disease, and Parasites [*Medicine*]
NAACPA...... National Association of Asian American Certified Public Accountants (MHDB)
NAACS ...... National Association of Accredited Cosmetology Schools (EA)
NAACS ...... National Association of Adult College Students (EA)
NAACS ...... National Association of Aircraft and Communications Suppliers [*Defunct*] (EA)
NAACSS...... National Association for the Accreditation of Colleges and Secondary Schools (EA)
NAACSW..... North American Association of Christians in Social Work [*Later, NACSW*] (EA)
NAACT .... National Association of Assessors and Collectors of Taxes [*A union*] [*British*]
NAAD .... National Association of Aluminum Distributors (EA)
NAAD .... Navajo Army Depot [*Arizona*] (AABC)
NAAD .... Nicotinic Acid Adenine Dinucleotide [*Biochemistry*]
NAAD .... North American Association for the Diaconate (EA)
NAADAA...... National Antique and Art Dealers Association of America (EA)
NAADAC..... National Association of Alcoholism and Drug Abuse Counselors (EA)
NAADC....... National Association of Art and Design Companies (EA)
NAADC....... North American Air Defense Command (AAG)
NAADD....... National Association of Athletic Development Directors
NAADI....... National Association of Approved Driving Instructors [*British*] (DBA)
NAADS ...... New Army Authorization Documents System (AABC)
NAADS ...... New Army Automatic Data System
NAAE .... National Association of Aeronautical Examiners (EA)
NAAE .... National Association of Afro-American Educators
NAAE .... National Association of Agriculture Employees (EA)
NAAE .... Nordic Association for Adult Education (EAIO)
NAAE .... North American Academy of Ecumenists (EA)
NAAEE ...... North American Association of Environmental Educators
NAAF .... National Alopecia Areata Foundation (EA)
NAAF .... Naval Auxiliary Air Facility
NAAF .... New Amino Acid Formula [*Nutrition*]
NAAF .... North African Air Force [*World War II*]
NAAFA ...... National Association to Advance Fat Acceptance (EA)
NAAFI .... Navy, Army, and Air Force Institutes [*Responsible for clubs, canteens, and provision of some items for messing of British armed forces*]
NAAFW ...... National Association of Air Forces Women
NAAG .... N-Acetylaspartylglutamic Acid [*Biochemistry*]
NAAG .... National Association of Attorneys General (EA)
NAAG .... NATO Army Advisory Group (NATG)
NAAG .... NATO Army Armaments Group (AABC)
NAAG .... Nordic Association of Applied Geophysics (EA)
NAAG .... North African Adjutant General [*World War II*]
NAAGA........ North African Adjutant General, Analysis and Control Division [*World War II*]
NAAGC....... North African Adjutant General, Casualty Branch [*World War II*]
NAAGE ...... North African Adjutant General, Personnel Division [*World War II*]
NAAGG....... North African Adjutant General, Executive Division [*World War II*]
NAAGO....... North African Adjutant General, Operations Division [*World War II*]
NAAGP....... North African Adjutant General, Postal Division [*World War II*]
NAAGS....... North African Adjutant General, Statistical Division [*World War II*]
NAAHE ...... National Association for the Advancement of Humane Education [*LA NAHEE*] (EA)
NAAHP ...... National Association of Advisors for the Health Professions (EA)
NAAHSC...... North American Association of Hunter Safety Coordinators
NAAI .... National Alliance of Arts and Industry
NAAI .... National Association of Accountants in Insolvencies (EA)
NAA-ICIF..... North American Association of the ICIF [*International Cooperative Insurance Federation*] [*Detroit, MI*]
NAAIS .... National Aircraft Accident Investigation School [*FAA*]
NAAIS .... North American Association of Inventory Services [*Greensboro, NC*] (EA)
NAAJHHA.... North American Association of Jewish Homes and Housing for the Aging (EA)
NAAJS .... National Academy for Adult Jewish Studies (EA)

NAAK .... Nerve Agent Antidote Kit [*Military*] (RDA)
NAAL .... National Alliance for Animal Legislation [*Defunct*] (EA)
NAAL .... North American Academy of Liturgy (EA)
NAAL .... North American Aerodynamic Laboratory [*Wind tunnel*] (NASA)
NAALBWV ... National Association for the Advancement of Leboyer's Birth Without Violence (EA)
NAALC .... National Afro-American Labor Council [*Later, NALC*]
NAALS .... Navigational Aids and Landing Systems (MCD)
NAAM .... National Association of Anvil Makers [*A union*] [*British*]
NAAM .... National Association of Architectural Metal Manufacturers (IAA)
NAAM .... North American Aliyah Movement (EA)
NAAMA .... National Agricultural Advertising and Marketing Association [*Later, NAMA*]
NAAMACC ... National Association for the Accreditation of Martial Arts Colleges and Curriculum (EA)
NAAMIC .... National Association of Automotive Mutual Insurance Companies [*Later, American Insurers Highway Safety Alliance*] (EA)
NAAMM .... National Association of Architectural Metal Manufacturers (EA)
NAAMM .... North American Academy of Musculoskeletal Medicine (EA)
NAAN .... National Advertising Agency Network [*New York, NY*] (EA)
NAAN .... Nuclear Arms Alert Network [*Defunct*] (EA)
NAANACM.... National Association for the Advancement of Native American Composers and Musicians
NAANBW ...... National Amalgamated Association of Nut and Bolt Workers [*A union*] [*British*]
NAAND .... North American Association for the Diaconate (EA)
NA & D C & O... Selection of Cases Decided in the Native Appeal and Divorce Court, Cape and Orange Free State [*A publication*] (DLA)
NA & DT & N... Transvaal and Natal Native Appeal and Divorce Court Decisions [*A publication*] (DLA)
NA & G .... Norgulf Lines (North Atlantic & Gulf) (AD)
NA & G .... North Atlantic & Gulf Steamship Co. (MHDW)
Na & K .... Sodium and Potassium [*Urine test*] [*Biochemistry*] (DAVI)
Na & KSP .... Sodium and Potassium Spot [*Urine Test*] (DAVI)
NAANGHT .... National Association of Air National Guard Health Technicians (EA)
NAANP .... National Alliance for the Advancement of Nodnarbian Philosophy (EA)
NAAO .... National Association of Amateur Oarsmen [*Later, USRA*] (EA)
NAAO .... National Association of Artists' Organizations (EA)
NAAO .... National Association of Assessing Officers [*Later, IAAO*]
NAAO .... Navy Area Audit Office [*London*]
NAAO .... North American Automotive Operations [*Ford Motor Co.*]
NAAOJ .... National Association for the Advancement of Orthodox Judaism (EA)
NAAOP .... National Association for the Advancement of Older People (EA)
NAAOSE .... National Association of Advisory Officers Special Education [*British*] (DBA)
NAAP .... N-Acetylaminophenazone [*Organic chemistry*]
NAAP .... National Association for Accreditation in Psychoanalysis (EA)
NAAP .... National Association of Activity Professionals (EA)
NAAP .... National Association of Advertising Publishers [*Later, AFCP*] (EA)
NAAP .... National Association of Apnea Professionals (EA)
NAAP .... Newport Army Ammunition Plant (AABC)
NAAPABAC... National Association for the Advancement of Psychoanalysis and the American Boards for Accreditation and Certification (EA)
NAAPAE ...... National Association for Asian and Pacific American Education (EA)
NAAPHE ...... National Association for the Advancement of Private Higher Education [*Later, United Student Association*] (EA)
NAAPI .... National Association of Accountants for the Public Interest [*Later, API*] (EA)
NAAPM .... National Association for the Advancement of Perry Mason (EA)
NAAPPB .... National Association of Amusement Parks, Pools, and Beaches [*Later, IAAPA*]
NAAPS .... Nozzle Actuator Auxiliary Power Supply (SAA)
NAAQS .... National Ambient Air Quality Standards [*Environmental Protection Agency*]
NAAR .... National Association of Advertising Representatives (DGA)
NAARD .... North American Aviation Rocketdyne Division (SAA)
Naar Elec ... Naar on Suffrage and Elections [*A publication*] (DLA)
NAARFC ...... National Association of Auto Racing Fan Clubs
NAARMC ...... National Association of Auto Racing Memorabilia Collectors (EA)
NAARPR ...... National Alliance Against Racist and Political Repression (EA)
NAARS .... National Automated Accounting Research System [*American Institute of Certified Public Accountants*] [*Database*] [*Information service or system*] (IID)
NAAS .... National Academy of American Scholars (EA)
NAAS .... National Agricultural Advisory Service [*Later, ADAS*] [*British*]
NAAS .... National Air Audit System [*Environmental Protection Agency*] (GFGA)
NAAS .... National Anorexic Aid Society (EA)
NAAS .... National Association of Academies of Science (EA)
NAAS .... National Association of Art Services [*Later, NAADC*] (EA)
NAAS .... National Aviation Assistance
NAAS .... Naval Area Audit Service
NAAS .... Naval Auxiliary Air Station
NAAS .... Navy Aircraft Accounting System
NAAS .... Navy Area Audit Service (DNAB)
NAAS .... NORAD Attack Alert System (MCD)
NAAS .... Nordic Association for American Studies (EAIO)
NAAS .... North American Apiotherapy Society (EA)
NAASC .... North American Aviation Science Center (SAA)
NAASC .... Northwest African Air Service Command [*World War II*]
NAASD .... North American Aviation Space Division (SAA)
NAASER .... National Association of American School Employees and Retirees (EA)
NAASERLDC... National Association of American School Employees and Retirees Legal Defense Counsel (EA)

NAASFEP .... National Association of Administrators of State and Federal Education Programs (EA)
NAASL .... North American Academy of the Spanish Language (EA)
NAASLANT... Navy Auxiliary Air Stations, Atlantic
NAASLN ...... National Association for Adults with Special Learning Needs (EA)
NAASMWB... National Amalgamated Association of Sheet Metal Workers and Blaziers [*A union*] [*British*]
NAASPAC.... Navy Auxiliary Air Stations, Pacific
NAASPL ...... North American Association of State and Provincial Lotteries (EA)
NAASR .... National Association for Armenian Studies and Research (EA)
NAASR .... North American Association for the Study of Jean-Jacques Rousseau (EA)
NAASS .... North American Association of Summer Sessions (EA)
NAASW .... Nonacoustic Antisubmarine Warfare [*Military*]
NAAT .... National Association of Agricultural Teachers [*Australia*]
NAAT .... Naval Air Advance Training (SAA)
NAATA .... National Asian American Telecommunications Association (EA)
NAATC .... Naval Air Advanced Training Command
NAATP .... National Association of Alcoholism Treatment Programs (EA)
NAATPWB.... National Amalgamated Association of Tin Plate Workers and Blaziers [*A union*] [*British*]
NAATS .... National Association of Air Traffic Specialists (EA)
NAATS .... National Association of Auto Trim Shops (EA)
NAATTFO ..... National Association of Alcohol and Tobacco Tax Field Officers
NAAUS .... National Archery Association of the United States (NADA)
NAAUTC .... National Amateur Athletic Union Taekwondo Committee [*Later, NAAUTUUSA*] (EA)
NAAUTUUSA... National AAU [*Amateur Athletic Union*] Taekwondo Union of the United States of America [*Formerly, NAAUTC*] (EA)
NAAV .... National Alliance Against Violence (EA)
NAAV .... National Association of Atomic Veterans (EA)
NAAV .... North American Association of Ventriloquists (EA)
NAAW .... National Association of Accordion Wholesalers [*Defunct*] (EA)
NAAWER ...... National Association of Arc Welding Equipment Repairers [*British*] (DBA)
NAAWFS ...... Naval Air All Weather Flight Squadron
NAAWP .... National Association for the Advancement of White People [*Defunct*] (EA)
NAAWS .... NATO Anti-Air Warfare System (DOMA)
NAAWS .... NORAD Automatic Attack Warning System (TEL)
NAAWS .... North American Association of Wardens and Superintendents (EAIO)
NAAWUL ...... National Agricultural and Allied Workers' Union of Liberia (IMH)
NAB .... Mina Airline Company [*Egypt*] [*FAA designator*] (FAAC)
Nab .... Nabatean (BJA)
NAB .... National Acoustics Board (MUGU)
NAB .... National Advisory Board (ACII)
NAB .... National Advisory Body [*British*]
NAB .... National Aircraft Beacon
NAB .... National Alliance of Business [*Washington, DC*] (EA)
NAB .... National Alliance of Businessmen (NADA)
NAB .... National Associated Businessmen [*Defunct*] (EA)
NAB .... National Association of Bioengineers [*Defunct*] (EA)
NAB .... National Association of Boards of Examiners for Nursing Home Administrators (EA)
NAB .... National Association of Bookmakers Ltd. [*British*] (BI)
NAB .... National Association of Broadcasters (EA)
NAB .... National Audience Board [*An association*] (NTCM)
NAB .... National Australia Bank ADS [*NYSE symbol*] (SPSG)
NAB .... Natl Australia Bk ADR [*NYSE symbol*] (TTSB)
NAB .... Naval Advanced Base
NAB .... Naval Air Base
NAB .... Naval Amphibious Base
NAB .... Navigational Aid to Bombing [*Air Force*]
NAB .... Needle Aspiration Biopsy [*Surgery*]
NAB .... Net Asset Backing
NAB .... New American Bible
NAB .... News Agency of Burma
NAB .... Newspaper Advertising Bureau [*New York, NY*] (EA)
NAB .... Nickel Alkaline Battery
NAB .... Nigeria-Arab Bank Ltd.
NAB .... Nitrosoanabasine [*Organic chemistry*]
NAB .... Non-A, Non-B [*Hepatitis*] [*Infectious diseases*] (DAVI)
NAB .... None of the Above
NAB .... North American Biologicals, Inc.
NAB .... Not Above [*Aviation*]
NAB .... Nuclear Air Burst
NAB .... Nuclear Assembly Building
NAB .... Nut and Bolt
NAB$2CC .... National Association of Bicentennial $2 Cancellation Collectors (EA)
NAB A .... NAB Asset Corp. [*Associated Press*] (SAG)
NABA .... National Alliance of Black Americans
NABA .... National Amateur Basketball Association (EA)
NABA .... National Association of Black Accountants [*Washington, DC*] (EA)
NABA .... National Association of Breweriana Advertising (EA)
NABA .... Naval Amphibious Base Annex
NABA .... Nitro-(amino)butyric Acid
NABA .... North American Ballet Association [*Defunct*] (EA)
NABA .... North American Benefit Association [*Port Huron, MI*] (EA)
NABA .... North American Bungee Association (EA)
NABA .... North American Butterfly Association
NABAC .... National Association for Bank Auditors and Comptrollers [*Later, BAI*] (EA)
NABAS .... National Association of Balloon Artists and Suppliers [*Great Britain*]
NABATRA ..... Naval Air Basic Training Center
NABB .... National Association for Better Broadcasting (EA)

NABB National Association of Barber Boards (EA)

NABB National Association of Business Brokers (EA)

NABBA National Amateur Body Building Association [*British*] (BI)

NABBA North American Brass Band Association (EA)

NABBEA National Association of Boards of Barbers Examiners of America [*Later, NABB*] (EA)

NABBS National Association of Bench and Bar Spouses (EA)

NABC NAB Asset Corp. [*NASDAQ symbol*] (SAG)

NABC National Association of Basketball Coaches of the United States (EA)

NABC National Association of Bingo Clubs [*British*] (BI)

NABC National Association of Boys' Clubs [*British*]

NABC North American Blueberry Council (EA)

NABCA National Alcoholic Beverage Control Association (EA)

NABCA National Association for Bank Cost Analysis (EA)

NABCA National Association for Bank Cost and Management Accounting (EA)

NABCA National Association of Black Catholic Administrators (EA)

NABCE National Association of Black Consulting Engineers (EA)

NABCJ National Association of Blacks in Criminal Justice (EA)

NABCM National Association of Baby Carriage Manufacturers (EA)

NABCM National Association of Brattice Cloth Manufacturers (EA)

NABCO National Alliance of Breast Cancer Organizations (EA)

NABCO National Association of Black County Officials (EA)

NABCO Nippon Air Brake Co. Ltd. [*Tokyo, Japan*]

NABD National Association of Bank Directors [*Later, ASBD*] (EA)

NABD National Association of Brick Distributors (EA)

NABD Naval Advanced Base Depot

NABDC National Association of Blueprint and Diazotype Coaters [*Later, ARMM*]

NABDCC North American Band Directors Coordinating Committee (EA)

NABE National Association for Bilingual Education (EA)

NABE National Association of Bar Executives (EA)

NABE National Association of Biological Engineering

NABE National Association of Boards of Education (EA)

NABE National Association of Book Editors [*Defunct*] (EA)

NABE National Association of Business Economists (EA)

NABE National Association of Business Education (IAA)

NABE Nuclear Air Burst Effect

NABEA North American Bicycle Exhibitor Association [*Defunct*] (EA)

NABER National Association of Business and Educational Radio (EA)

NABESS National Association of Business Education State Supervisors [*Stillwater, OK*] (EA)

NABET National Association Broadcast Employees and Technicians (EA)

NABF National Alliance of Black Feminists (EA)

NABF National Amateur Baseball Federation (EA)

NABF North American Baptist Fellowship (EA)

NABF North American Boxing Federation (EA)

NABG National Association of Blacks within Government (EA)

NABGG National Association of Black Geologists and Geophysicists (EA)

NABHP National Association of Black Hospitality Professionals (EA)

NABI NABI Inc. [*NASDAQ symbol*] (TTSB)

NABI NABI, Inc. [*NASDAQ symbol*] (SAG)

NABI NABI, Inc. [*Associated Press*] (SAG)

NABI National Association of Beverage Importers (EA)

NABI National Association of Biblical Instructors [*Later, American Academy of Religion*] (EA)

NABI National Association of Bunco Investigators

NABIM National Association of Band Instrument Manufacturers (EA)

NABIM National Association of British and Irish Millers [*Incorporated*] (DBA)

NABio North American Biologicals, Inc. [*Associated Press*] (SAG)

NABIR Natural and Accelerated Bioremediation Research [*Department of Energy*]

NABIS National Association of Business and Industrial Saleswomen [*Denver, CO*] (EA)

NABIS National Biological Survey

NABISCO National Biscuit Co. [*Acronym now used as company name*]

NabisH Nabisco Holdings Corp. [*Associated Press*] (SAG)

NABJ National Association of Black Journalists (EA)

NAB-JOBS National Alliance of Business - Job Opportunities in the Business Sector (OICC)

NABL National Association of Bond Lawyers (EA)

NABL National Association of Builders' Labourers [*A union*] [*British*]

NABLOC Brussels Tariff Nomenclature for the Latin American Free Trade Association (BARN)

NABLT National Association of Business Law Teachers [*Later, NBLC*] (EA)

NABM National Association of Bedding Manufacturers [*Later, ISPA*] (EA)

NABM National Association of Black Manufacturers (EA)

NABM National Association of Blouse Manufacturers (EA)

NABM National Association of Boating Magazines [*Defunct*] (EA)

NABM National Association of Boat Manufacturers (EA)

NABM National Association of Book Manufacturers [*Defunct*] (EA)

NABM National Association of British Manufacturers

NABM National Association of Building Manufacturers [*Later, HMC*] (EA)

NABMA National Association of British Market Authorities

NABMCC National Association of Black and Minority Chambers of Commerce [*Later, NBCC*] (EA)

NABMO NATO Bullpup Management Office [*Missiles*] (NATG)

NABMP National Association of Black Media Producers

NABO National Alliance of Black Organizations (EA)

NABO North Atlantic Biocultural Organization [*A research cooperative*]

NABOB National Association of Black Owned Broadcasters (EA)

NABOM National Association of Building Owners and Managers [*Later, BOMA*] (EA)

NABOR National Association of Bank Club Organization

Nabors Nabors Industries, Inc. [*Associated Press*] (SAG)

NABP National Association of Black Professors (EA)

NABP National Association of Boards of Pharmacy (EA)

NABP National Association of Book Publishers (NADA)

NABPAC National Association of Business Political Action Committees (EA)

NABPARS Navy Automatic Broadcasting, Processing, and Routing System (NG)

NABPLEX National Association of Boards of Pharmacy Licensure Examination

NABPO NATO Bullpup Production Organization [*Missiles*] (NATG)

NABPR National Association of Baptist Professors of Religion (EA)

NABR National Association for BioMedical Research (EA)

NABR National Association of Baby Sitter Registries [*Later, NASR*] (EA)

NABR National Association of Basketball Referees (EA)

NABR Natural Bridges National Monument

NaBr Sodium Bromide [*Pharmacology*] (DAVI)

NABREP National Association of Black Real Estate Professionals (EA)

NABRT National Association for Better Radio and Television (NADA)

NABRTI National Association of Bar-Related Title Insurers [*San Diego, CA*] (EA)

NABS National Advertising Benevolent Society [*British*]

NABS National AIDS Behavioral Survey

NABS National Alliance of Blind Students (EA)

NABS National Association of Bank Servicers (EA)

NABS National Association of Barber Schools [*Later, NABSS*] (EA)

NABS National Association of Black Students (EA)

NABS National Association of Breeders Services (DBA)

NABS National Association of Business Services [*Baldwin, NY*] (EA)

NABS National Association of Buying Services (EA)

NABS NATO Airborne SATCOM (MCD)

NABS Normal Abdominal Bowel Sound [*Medicine*] (CPH)

NABS Normoactive Bowel Sounds [*Gastroenterology*] (DAVI)

NABS North American Benthological Society (EA)

NABS North American Blue-Bird Society (EA)

NABS Nuclear-Armed Bombardment Satellite [*Study*] [*Air Force*] (AAG)

NABSC National Association of Building Service Contractors [*Later, BSCA*]

NABSCAN National Advertised Brands Scanning Reports [*Research project*]

NABSE National Alliance of Black School Educators (EA)

NABS/GMF NATO Airbase Satellite/Ground Mobile Force (MCD)

NABSP National Association of Blue Shield Plans [*Later, BCBSA*] (EA)

NABSS National Alliance of Black School Superintendents (AEE)

NABSS National Association of Barber Styling Schools (EA)

NABST National Advisory Board on Science and Technology [*Canada*]

NABSTP Navy Adult Basic Skills Training Program (NVT)

NABSW National Association of Black Social Workers (EA)

NABT National Association of Bankruptcy Trustees (EA)

NABT National Association of Biology Teachers (EA)

NABT National Association of Blind Teachers (EA)

NABTA National Association of Business Travel Agents (EA)

NABTC National Associated Building Trades Council [*A union*] [*British*]

NABTC Naval Air Base Training Command

NABTE National Association for Business Teacher Education [*Reston, VA*] (EA)

NABTFP National Association of Black Television and Film Producers (NTCM)

NABTRACOM Naval Air Basic Training Command (DNAB)

NABTS National Alliance Building Trades Society [*A union*] [*British*]

NABTS National Association of Broadcast Transmission Standards (PCM)

NABTS North American Basic Teletext Specification (WDMC)

NABTS North American Braodcast Teletext Standard (OSI)

NABTS North American Broadcast Teletext Standard (NTCM)

NABTTI National Association of Business Teacher-Training Institutions

NABU Naval Advanced Base Unit

NABU Nonadjusting Ball-Up [*A hopeless state of confusion*] [*Military slang*]

NABUG National Association of Broadcast Unions and Guilds (EA)

NABV National Association for Black Veterans (EA)

NABVICU National Association of Blind and Visually Impaired Computer Users [*Defunct*] (EA)

NABW National Association of Bank Women [*Chicago, IL*] (EA)

NABWA National Association of Black Women Attorneys (EA)

NABWE National Association of Black Women Entrepreneurs [*Detroit, MI*] (EA)

NABWMT National Association of Black and White Men Together: A Gay Multiracial Organiz ation for All People (EA)

NABWS National Amalgamated Brass Workers' Society [*A union*] [*British*]

NAC Association of Chiropodists (NADA)

NAC Nacelle

NAC Nacelle [*Aviation*]

NAC N-Acetyl-L-Cysteine [*Biochemistry*]

NAC Naples Alcofuel Club [*Defunct*] (EA)

NAC National Abortion Campaign [*British*] (DBA)

NAC National Academy of Conciliators (EA)

NAC National Accelerator Center [*South Africa*] [*Research center*]

NAC National Access Center [*Defunct*] (EA)

NAC National Accreditation Council for Agencies Serving the Blind and Visually Handicapped (EA)

NAC National Achievement Clubs (EA)

NAC National Action Committee on the Status of Women [*Canada*] (CROSS)

NAC National Adoption Center [*Information service or system*] (IID)

NAC National Advertising Campaign [*Army*]

NAC National Advisory Committee

NAC National Advisory Council

NAC National Aero Club (EA)

NAC National Aeronautical Corp.

NAC National Agency Check [*Security clearance*]

NAC National Agricultural Centre [*British*] (CB)

NAC National Air Carrier Association (MCD)

NAC National Air Communications [*British*]

NAC .... National Alumni Council of the United Negro College Fund (EA)
NAC .... National Anglers' Council [British]
NAC .... National Anxiety Center (EA)
NAC .... National Aquaculture Council (EA)
NAC .... National Arts Centre [Canada]
NAC .... National Arts Club (EA)
NAC .... National Asbestos Council (EA)
NAC .... National Association for the Childless [British] (DBA)
NAC .... National Association of Cemeteries [Later, ACA] (EA)
NAC .... National Association of Choirs [British] (BI)
NAC .... National Association of Composers, USA (EA)
NAC .... National Association of Concessionaires (EA)
NAC .... National Association of Conveyancers [British] (DBA)
NAC .... National Association of Coopers [A union] [British]
NAC .... National Association of Coroners (EA)
NAC .... National Association of Counselors (EA)
NAC .... National Association of Counties
NAC .... National Asthma Center [Later, NJCIRM]
NAC .... National Audience Composition [Nielsen Television Index] (NTCM)
NAC .... National Audiovisual Center [General Services Administration]
NAC .... National Automotive Center [Army] (RDA)
NAC .... National Aviation Club (EA)
NAC .... National Aviation Corp.
NAC .... Native American Church (ECON)
NAC .... Native Appeal Courts [South Africa] [A publication] (DLA)
NAC .... Natural Area Council (EA)
NAC .... Naval Academy
NAC .... Naval Air Center
NAC .... Naval Air Command [British]
NAC .... Naval Aircraftman [British]
NAC .... Naval Amyloid Component [Medicine]
NAC .... Naval Avionics Center (MCD)
NAC .... Navy Acquisition Circular (AAGC)
NAC .... Navy Activity Control (DNAB)
NAC .... Navy Advanced Concept (CAAL)
NAC .... Nebraska Administrative (Code) Rules and Regulations
         [A publication] (AAGC)
NAC .... Negative Air Cushion [Aviation Air Force]
NAC .... Neighbourhood Advice Council
NAC .... Neo-American Church (EA)
NAC .... Net Advertising Circulation (DOAD)
NAC .... Network Access Center [Telecommunications]
NAC .... Network Access Controller
NAC .... Network Advisory Committee [to Library of Congress and Council on
         Library Resources]
NAC .... Network Analysis Center [Contel, Inc.] [Telecommunications
         service] (TSSD)
NAC .... Network Appliance Corp. [Commercial firm]
NAC .... New American Community (MHDB)
NAC .... New Apostolic Church
NAC .... Nielson Audience Composition
NAC .... Nipple Areolar Complex [Oncology]
NAC .... Nitric Acid Concentrator (MCD)
NAC .... Nitrogen Mustard [Mustargen], Adriamycin, CCNU [Lomustine]
         [Antineoplastic drug regimen]
NAC .... NMCS [Nuclear Material Control System] Automatic Control
NAC .... No Additional Charge
NAC .... No Apparent Change (MCD)
NAC .... Noise Advisory Council [British]
NAC .... Nonairline Carrier [Aerospace]
NAC .... Nordic Academic Council [Defunct] (EA)
NAC .... Nordic Actors' Council (EAIO)
NAC .... Nordic Association for Campanology (EA)
NAC .... Normal Approach Course [Navy] (NVT)
NAC .... North America Mtge [NYSE symbol] (TTSB)
NAC .... North American Collectors (EA)
NAC .... North American Mortgage Co. [NYSE symbol] (SPSG)
NAC .... North Atlantic Coast
NAC .... North Atlantic Council
NAC .... North Atlantic Current [Oceanography]
NAC .... North Atlantic Shipping Conference (DS)
NAC .... Northeast Air Command
NAC .... Northern Air Cargo, Inc. [ICAO designator] (FAAC)
NAC .... Nozzle Area Control
NAC .... Nursing Audit Committee (MEDA)
NAC .... US Catholic Bishops' National Advisory Council (EA)
NACA .... National Academy of Code Administration (EA)
NACA .... National Acoustical Contractors Association [Later, CISCA] (EA)
NACA .... National Advisory Committee for Aeronautics [Functions transferred
         to NASA, 1958]
NACA .... National Advisory Committee on Aeronautics [OST] (TAG)
NACA .... National Agricultural Chemicals Association (EA)
NACA .... National Air Carrier Association (EA)
NACA .... National Animal Control Association (EA)
NACA .... National Armored Car Association (EA)
NACA .... National Association for Campus Activities (EA)
NACA .... National Association for Court Administration (EA)
NACA .... National Association of Catastrophe Adjusters [Comfort, TX] (EA)
NACA .... National Association of Cellular Agents (EA)
NACA .... National Association of Childbirth Assistants (EA)
NACA .... National Association of Christians in the Arts (EA)
NACA .... National Association of Cost Accountants [Later, NAA]
NACA .... National Association of County Administrators (EA)
NACA .... National Association of Cuban Architects (in Exile) [Defunct] (EA)
NACA .... National Athletic and Cultural Association [Ireland] (EAIO)

NACA .... National Autosound Challenge Association [Later, IASCA] (EA)
NACA .... Naval Aviation Cadet Act of 1942
NACA .... Netherlands-America Community Association (EA)
NACA .... North American Center on Adoption [Defunct] (EA)
NACA .... North American College of Acupuncture
NACA .... North American Corriente Association (EA)
NACA .... North American Currach Association (EA)
NACA .... North Australian Canine Association
NACAA .... National Assembly of Community Arts Agencies (EA)
NACAA .... National Association of Community Action Agencies (EA)
NACAA .... National Association of Computer-Assisted Analysis (IAA)
NACAA .... National Association of Consumer Agency Administrators (EA)
NACAA .... National Association of County Agricultural Agents (EA)
NACAB .... National Accreditation Council for Agencies Serving the Blind and
         Visually Handicapped [New York, NY]
NACAB .... National Association of Citizens Advice Bureaus [British] (DBA)
NACA BCA ... Nationalo Advisory Commission for Aeronautics Board of Contract
         Appeals (AAGC)
NACAC .... National Association of Catholic Alumni Clubs [Later, CACI] (EA)
NACAC .... National Association of College Admission Counselors (EA)
NACAC .... North African Antiaircraft Section [World War II]
NACAC .... North American Council on Adoptable Children (EA)
NACACP ...... National Cash Register Applied COBOL [Common Business-Oriented
         Language] Package (IAA)
NACADA ...... National Academic Advising Association (EA)
NACAE .... National Advisory Council on Adult Education [Washington, DC]
NACAF .... Northwest African Coastal Air Force [World War II]
NACAL .... Navy Air Cooperation and Liaison Committee
NAC & O ...... Cape and Orange Free State Native Appeal Court, Selected
         Decisions [A publication] (DLA)
NACAP .... National Association of Claims Assistance Professionals (EA)
NACAP .... National Association of Co-Op Advertising Professionals [Defunct]
         (EA)
NACARM ...... Northwest America Civil Air Routes Manual
NACAS .... National Association of College Auxiliary Services (EA)
NACAT .... National Association of College Automotive Teachers (EA)
NACATS .... North American Clear Air Turbulence Tracking System [Aviation]
NACAWM-USA... National Association of Cuban Women and Men of the United
         States (EA)
NACAW-USA... National Association of Cuban-American Women of the USA (EA)
NACB .... National Association of Catering Butchers [British] (DBA)
NACB .... National Association of College Broadcasters (EA)
NACB .... National Association of Convention Bureaus (NADA)
NACB .... Native American Community Board (EA)
NACB .... Navy and Army Canteen Board [British military] (DMA)
NACBA .... National Association of Church Business Administration (EA)
NACBFAA ..... National Association of Customs Brokers and Forwarders Association
         of America
NACBO .... National Association of Cosmetic Boutique Owners (EA)
NACBP .... No-Adjust Car Building Process [Ford Motor Co.] [Automotive
         engineering]
NACBS .... National Affiliation of Concerned Business Students [Defunct] (EA)
NACBS .... National Association and Council of Business Schools
NACBS .... North American Conference on British Studies (EA)
NACC .... National Advisory Cancer Council
NACC .... National Agency Check Center (AFM)
NACC .... National Air Conservation Commission (EA)
NACC .... National Alliance of Czech Catholics (EA)
NACC .... National Association for Core Curriculum (EA)
NACC .... National Association of Catholic Chaplains (EA)
NACC .... National Association of Childbearing Centers (EA)
NACC .... National Association of Collegiate Commissioners [Later, CCA] (EA)
NACC .... National Association of Counsel for Children (EA)
NACC .... National Automatic Controls Conference
NACC .... Naval Academy Computer Center
NACC .... North American-Chilean Chamber of Commerce (EA)
NACC .... North Atlantic Cooperation Council
NACC .... Norwegian American Chamber of Commerce
NACC .... Novel Architectures Computing Committee [British]
NAC (C) ...... Selected Decisions of the Native Appeal Court (Central Division)
         [1948-51] [South Africa] [A publication] (DLA)
NACCA .... National Association for Creative Children and Adults (EA)
NACCA .... National Association of Claimants' Counsel of America [Also known
         as NACCA Bar Association] [Later, ATLA]
NACCA .... National Association of Consumer Credit Administrators (EA)
NACCA .... National Association of County 4-H Club Agents [Later, NAE4-HA]
         (EA)
NACCA .... National Association of County Civil Attorneys (EA)
NACCALJ ...... National Association of Claimants' Compensation Attorneys. Law
         Journal [A publication] (DLA)
NACCAM ...... National Coordinating Committee for Aviation Meteorology
NAC (C & O)... Reports of the Decisions of the Native Appeal Courts, Cape
         Province and the Orange Free State [South Africa]
         [A publication] (ILCA)
NACCAS .... National Accrediting Commission of Cosmetology Arts and
         Sciences (EA)
NACCB .... National Accreditation Council for Certification Bodies (AIE)
NACCB .... National Association of Computer Consultant Businesses (EA)
NACCC .... National Association of Citizens Crime Commissions (EA)
NACCC .... National Association of Congregational Christian Churches [Later,
         CCCNA] (EA)
NACCCA .... National Association of Civilian Conservation Corps Alumni (EA)
NACCCAN ..... National Centre for Christian Communities and Networks [Westhill
         College] [British] (CB)
NACCD .... National Advisory Commission on Civil Disorders (NADA)

NACCDD ...... National Association of County Community Development Directors (EA)
NACCE .... National Advisory Council on Continuing Education (OICC)
NACCE ...... North American Conference on Christianity and Ecology (EA)
NACCES ...... Naval Air Crew Combat Ejection Seat (DWSG)
NACCG .... National Association of Crankshaft and Cylinder Grinders [British] (BI)
NACCHO ...... National Aboriginal Community-Controlled Health Organization [Australia]
NACCM .... National Association for Child Care Management [Defunct] (EA)
NACCO .... NACCO Industries, Inc. [Associated Press] (SAG)
NACCRRA ... National Association of Child Care Resource and Referral Agencies (EA)
NACCRT ...... North America Coordinating Center for Responsible Tourism (EA)
NACCSMA .... NATO Command and Control Systems Management Agency (PDAA)
NACCSS ...... National Association of Commodity Cargo Superintendents and Suveyors [British] (DBA)
NACCW .... National Advisory Centre on Careers for Women [British] (CB)
NACD .... National Alliance of Cleaning Distributors [Commercial firm] (EA)
NACD .... National Association for Cave Diving [Inactive]
NACD .... National Association for Community Development [Defunct] (EA)
NACD .... National Association of Chemical Distributors (EA)
NACD .... National Association of Conservation Districts
NACD .... National Association of Container Distributors (EA)
NACD .... National Association of Corporate Directors [Washington, DC] (EA)
NACD .... Not Acidified [Biochemistry] (DAVI)
NACDA .... National Archive for Computerized Data on Aging [Department of Health and Human Services] (GFGA)
NACDA .... National Arts and Cultural Development Act of 1964
NACDA .... National Association of Collegiate Directors of Athletics (EA)
NACDAC ...... National Association for City Drug and Alcohol Coordination [Defunct] (EA)
NACDAP ...... National Advisory Council for Drug Abuse Prevention [Terminated, 1975] (EGAO)
NACDC .... National Association of Career Development Consultants (EA)
NACDD .... National Advisory Council on Services and Facilities for the Developmentally Disabled [Terminated, 1978] [HEW] (EGAO)
NACDE .... National Association for Child Development and Education [Later, NACCM] (EA)
NACDFB ...... National Association of Canada Dry Franchise Bottlers (EA)
NACDFLM ... National Association of Catholic Diocesan Family Life Ministers [Later, NACFLM] (EA)
NACDL .... National Association of Criminal Defense Lawyers (EA)
NACDLF ...... National Association of Community Development Loan Funds (EA)
NACDPA ...... National Association of County Data Processing Administrators (EA)
NACDR .... National Association of College Deans and Registrars [Later, NACDRAO] (EA)
NACDRAO ... National Association of College Deans, Registrars, and Admissions Officers (EA)
NACDS .... National Association of Chain Drug Stores (EA)
NACDS .... North American Clinical Dermatologic Society (EA)
NACE .... National Advisory Committee for Electronics
NACE .... National Association for Career Education (EA)
NACE .... National Association for Curriculum Enrichment and Extension [British] (EAIO)
NACE .... National Association of Catering Executives (EA)
NACE .... National Association of Childbirth Education [Defunct] (EA)
NACE .... National Association of Corrosion Engineers (EA)
NACE .... National Association of Counsellors in Education (AIE)
NACE .... National Association of County Engineers (EA)
NACE .... National Autobody Congress and Exposition [Precision Planning and Sales, Inc.] (TSPED)
NACE .... Native Americans for a Clean Environment (EA)
NACE .... Neutral Atmospheric Composition Experiment [Geophysics]
NACE .... NMCSSC [National Military Command System Support Center] Automated ControlExecutive
NACE .... North American Commission on the Environment
NACE .... North American Cycle Exhibitor Association (EA)
NACEBE ...... National Association of Classroom Educators in Business Education [Cambridge City, IN] (EA)
NACEC .... National Association of Charitable Estate Counselors (EA)
NACEC .... North American Committee of Enamel Creators (EA)
NACECE ...... National Advisory Council on Extension and Continuing Education
NACED .... National Advisory Committee on the Education of the Deaf [Terminated, 1973] [HEW] (EGAO)
NACED .... National Advisory Council on the Employment of the Disabled [British]
NACEDC ...... National Advisory Council on Education of Disadvantaged Children (OICC)
NAC/EDP ..... National Advisory Council on Education Professions Development [HEW] (EGAO)
NAC-EDTA .... N-Acetyl-L-Cysteine Ethylenediaminetetra-Acetic Acid [Biochemistry] (MAE)
NACEEO ...... National Advisory Council on Equality of Educational Opportunity [Termina ted, 1979] [HEW] (EGAO)
NACEHC ...... National Accreditation Council for Environmental Health Curricula (EA)
NACEIC .... National Advisory Council on Education for Industry and Commerce (MCD)
NACEL .... Navy Air Crew Equipment Laboratory [Philadelphia, PA]
NACEO .... National Advisory Council on Economic Opportunity (EA)
NACEPD ...... National Advisory Council on Education Professions Development [Terminate d, 1976] [HEW] (OICC)
NACEPT ...... National Advisory Committee for Environmental Policy and Technology [Environmental Protection Agency]

NACERI .... National Advisory Council for Educational Research and Improvement [Washington, DC Department of Education] (GRD)
NACES .... National Association of Credential Evaluation Services (EA)
NACES .... Navy Aircrew Common Ejection Seat [British]
NACESW ...... National Association of Chief Education Social Workers (AIE)
NACETA ...... National Association of County Employment and Training Administrators [Later, NACTEP] (EA)
NACF .... National Art-Collectors' Fund [British]
NACF .... National Association of Church Furnishers [British] (BI)
NACF .... Navy Air Combat Fighter (MCD)
NACFA .... North American Clun Forest Association (EA)
NACFE .... National Association of Certified Fraud Examiners (EA)
NACFFA ...... National Advisory Committee for the Flammable Fabrics Act
NACFL .... National Advisory Committee on Farm Labor [Defunct] (EA)
NACFLM ...... National Association of Catholic Family Life Ministers (EA)
NACFR .... National Association of Casual Furniture Retailers (EA)
NACFT .... National Academy of Counselors and Family Therapists (EA)
NACG .... National Association of Conservative Graduates (AIE)
NACG .... National Association of County Governments (OICC)
NACG .... North African Commanding General [World War II]
NACGC .... National Association of Collegiate Gymnastics Coaches (Men) (EA)
NACGC .... National Association of Colored Girls Clubs [Later, NAGC] (EA)
NACGG .... North American Commercial Gladiolus Growers [Later, CGD-NAGC] (EA)
NACGM .... National Association of Chewing Gum Manufacturers (EA)
NACGT .... National Association of Careers and Guidance Teachers [British] (DBA)
NACH .... National Academy of Clinicians and Holistic Health (EA)
NACH .... National Advisory Committee on the Handicapped
NACH .... National Advisory Council for the Handicapped (NADA)
NACH .... National Association for the Craniofacially Handicapped (EA)
NACH .... National Association of Clergy Hypnotherapists (EA)
NACH .... National Association of Coal Haulers [Defunct] (EA)
nAch .... Need for Achievement
NACHA .... National Automated Clearing House Association [Washington, DC] (EA)
NACHC .... National Advisory Committee on Handicapped Children [Terminated, 1973] [HEW] (EGAO)
NACHC .... National Association of Community Health Centers (EA)
NACHES ...... Association of Jewish Family, Children's Agency Professionals (EA)
NACHFA ...... National Association of County Health Facility Administrators (EA)
NACHM .... Nachmittags [Afternoon] [German]
NACHO .... National Association of County Health Officials (EA)
NACHP .... North African Chaplain's Section [World War II]
NAChR .... Nicotinic Acetylcholine Receptor [Immunology]
NACHRI .... National Association of Children's Hospitals and Related Institutions (EA)
NACHRK ...... North American Coalition for Human Rights in Korea (EA)
NACHSA ...... National Association of County Human Services Administrators (EA)
NACHVRO .... National Air Conditioning, Heating, Ventilating, and Refrigeration Officials (EA)
NACI .... Naphthenic Acid Corrosion Index
NACI .... National Agency Check and Written Inquiries
NACI .... National Association for the Cottage Industry (EA)
NACIA .... National Association of Crop Insurance Agents [Anoka, MN] (EA)
NACIE .... National Advisory Council on Indian Education (OICC)
NACIFO ...... National Association of Church and Institutional Financing Organizations [Atlanta, GA] (EA)
NACIME ...... North American Committee for IME [Institut Medical Evangelique] [Defunct] (EA)
NACIO .... National Association of County Information Officers (EA)
NACIO .... Naval Air Combat Information Office [or Officer]
NACIP .... Navy Assessment and Control of Installation Pollutants
NACIS .... National Credit Information Service [TRW, Inc.] [Long Beach, CA Credit-information databank] (IID)
NACIS .... Naval Air Combat Information School
NACIS .... Navy Air Control and Identification System
NACIS .... Networking Analytical and Computing Information Systems [National Aeronautics and Space Administration]
NACIS .... North American Cartographic Information Society (EA)
NACISA ...... North Atlantic Communications and Information Systems Agency [NATO]
NACISO ...... NATO Communications and Information Systems Organization (EAIO)
NACJ .... National Association of Costume Jewelers [Defunct] (EA)
NACJP .... National Association of Criminal Justice Planners [Defunct] (EA)
NACK .... Negative Acknowledgment [Telecommunications]
NACK .... Nonacknowledgment Character [Computer science]
NACL .... National Advisory Commission on Libraries
NACL .... National Association for Community Leadership (EA)
NACL .... Navy/ARPA [Advanced Research Projects Agency] Chemical LASER (MCD)
NACL .... Nippon Aviatronics Corp. Ltd. [Japan]
NaCl .... Sodium Chloride [Salt] [Chemistry] (DAVI)
NACLA .... North American Congress on Latin America (EA)
NACLC .... National Association of Community Legal Centers [Australia]
NACLE .... National Association of Chimney Lining Engineers [British] (DBA)
NACLEO ...... National Association of Coin Laundry Equipment Operators (EA)
NACLIS .... National Commission on Libraries and Information Science [Washington, DC]
NACLM .... North African Claims Section [World War II]
NACLO .... National Association of Canoe Liveries and Outfitters (EA)
NACLO .... National Association of Community Leadership Organizations [Later, National Association for Community Leadership] (EA)
NACLS .... National Association of Commission Lumber Salesmen

NACLS .... North Alabama Cooperative Library System [Library network]
NACLSO .... National Assembly of Chief Livestock Sanitary Officials [Later, United States Animal Health Association] (EA)
NACM .... National Association for Court Management (EA)
NACM .... National Association of Chain Manufacturers (EA)
NACM .... National Association of Charcoal Manufacturers [British] (DBA)
NACM .... National Association of Cider Makers [British] (BI)
NACM .... National Association of Colliery Managers [British] (DBA)
NACM .... National Association of Credit Management
NACM .... National Association of Credit Management [New York, NY] (EA)
NACMA .... National Armored Cable Manufacturers Association (EA)
NACMA .... National Association of Collegiate Marketing Administrators
NACMB .... National Association of Certified Mortgage Bankers [Later, NSREF] (EA)
NACMC .... National Association for Church Management Consultants (EA)
NACMC .... National Association of Christian Marriage Counselors [Defunct] (EA)
NACMCF ..... National Advisory Committee on Microbiological Criteria for Foods
NACME .... National Action Council for Minorities in Engineering (EA)
NACMEMS ... National Association of Continuing Medical Education Meetings and Seminars [Defunct] (EA)
NACMIS ...... Navy Automated Civilian Management Information System
NACMO .... National Association of Cigarette Machine Operators [British] (DBA)
NACMO .... National Association of Competitive Mounted Orienteering (EA)
NACMW .... North American Council for Muslim Women (EA)
NACN .... Newspaper Advertising Co-Op Network (EA)
NAC (N & T)... Decisions of the Native Appeal and Divorce Court (Transvaal and Natal) [South Africa] [A publication] (ILCA)
NAC (NE) ..... Decisions of the Native Appeal Court (North Eastern Division) [South Africa] [A publication] (ILCA)
NACNE .... National Advisory Council on Nutrition Education [British]
NACO .... Name Authority Co-Operative (NITA)
NACO .... National Advisory Committee on Oceanography [Marine science] (MSC)
NACO .... National Association of Charterboat Operators (EA)
NACO .... National Association of Condominium Owners
NACO .... National Association of Consumer Organizations
NACO .... National Association of Cooperative Officials [A union] [British] (DCTA)
NACo .... National Association of Counties (EA)
NACO .... National Coordinated Cataloging Operations [Library science]
NACO .... Navy Acquisition-Contracting Officer (MCD)
NACO .... Navy Coolant [Gunpowder]
NACO .... Night Alarm Cutoff (AAG)
NACOA .... If Not Available Your Command, Obtain Accounting Data from Administrative Command [Army] (AABC)
NACOA .... National Advisory Committee on Oceans and Atmosphere [Marine science] (MSC)
NACOA .... National Association for Children of Alcoholism and Other Addictions (EA)
NACODS ..... National Association of Colliery Overmen, Deputies, and Shotfirers [A union] [British] (DCTA)
NACOEJ ...... North American Conference on Ethiopian Jewry (EAIO)
NACOI .... National Association of Canadians of Origins in India
NACOL .... National Advisory Commission on Libraries
NACOM .... National Communications [System]
NACOM .... Northern Area Command
NACOMEX ... National Computer Exchange
NACON .... Newspaper Advertising Co-Op Network (EA)
NACOPRW ... National Conference of Puerto Rican Women (EA)
NACOR .... National Advisory Committee on Radiation
NaCOR .... National Center on Occupational Readjustment [Defunct] (EA)
NACORE ...... National Association of Corporate Real Estate Executives (EA)
NACORF ...... National Association of Counties Research Foundation
NACOS .... National Communications Schedule
NACOS .... NATO Courier Service (NATG)
NACOS .... North African Chief of Staff [World War II]
NACOSH ..... National Advisory Committee on Occupational Safety and Health
NACOSH ..... National Advisory Committee on Scouting for the Handicapped (EA)
NACP .... National Academy of Cable Programming (NTCM)
NACP .... National Accounts Capability Programme [United Nations] (EY)
NACP .... National Association of Chiefs of Police (AD)
NACP .... National Association of County Planners (EA)
NACP .... Navy Acoustical Communication Program (MCD)
NACP .... NORAD/CONAD Airborne Command Post
NACP .... North Atlantic Consultive Process (OSI)
NACPA .... National Association of Church Personnel Administrators (EA)
NACPA .... National Association of County and Prosecuting Attorneys [Later, NDAA]
NACPC .... North American Christian Peace Conference (EA)
NACPD .... National Association of County Planning Directors [Later, NACP] (EA)
NACPDCG .... National Association of Catholic Publishers and Dealers in Church Goods (EA)
NACPR .... National Association of Corporate and Professional Recruiters (EA)
NACPRO ...... National Association of County Park and Recreation Officials (EA)
NACPU .... National Amalgamated Coal Porters' Union [British]
NACPUISCW... National Amalgamated Coal Porters' Union of Inland and Seaborne Coal Workers [British]
NACR .... National Advisory Committee on Radiation
NACRC .... National Association of County Recorders and Clerks (EA)
NACRCD ...... National Advisory Council on Rural Civil Defense
NAC Re .... NAC RE Corp. [Associated Press] (SAG)
NACRE .... North American Coalition on Religion and Ecology (EA)
NACRF .... National Association of Counties Research Foundation (OICC)
NACRMR...... National Advisory Committee on Rhesus Monkey Requirements

NACRO .... National Association for the Care and Resettlement of Offenders [British]
nacro .... Night-Alarm Cutoff (AD)
NACRS .... North African Censorship Section, US [World War II]
NACR (SR) .... Native Appeal Court Reports (Southern Rhodesia) [A publication] (ILCA)
NACRT .... National Association of Canadian Race Tracks
NACRU .... North American Committee for Reconciliation in Ulster (EA)
NACS .... National Advisory Committee on Semiconductors
NACS .... National Association for Check Safekeeping [Washington, DC] (EA)
NACS .... National Association for Chicano Studies (EA)
NACS .... National Association of Carpet Specialists [Defunct]
NACS .... National Association of Chimney Sweeps [British] (DBA)
NACS .... National Association of Christian Schools [Defunct] (EA)
NACS .... National Association of Christian Singles (EA)
NACS .... National Association of Civic Secretaries (EA)
NACS .... National Association of College Stores (EA)
NACS .... National Association of Computer Stores [Later, IVCI] [Defunct] (EA)
NACS .... National Association of Concession Services (EA)
NACS .... National Association of Convenience Stores (EA)
NACS .... National Association of Cosmetology Schools (EA)
NACS .... Natural Areas of Canadian Significance [NPPAC]
NACS .... NetWare Asynchronous Communication Service [Novell, Inc.]
NACS .... Neurologic and Adaptive Capacity Scoring [System]
NACS .... North Atlantic Current System [Oceanography]
NACS .... Northern Area Communications System (MCD)
NACS .... Nucleic Acid Chromatography System
NAC (S) .... Selected Decisions of the Native Appeal Court (Southern Division) [South Africa] [A publication] (ILCA)
NACSA .... National Advisory Committee on Safety in Agriculture
NACSA .... National Association for Corporate Speaker Activities (EA)
NACSA .... National Association of Casualty and Surety Agents [Bethesda, MD] (EA)
NACSA .... North American Computer Service Association (EA)
NACSAA ...... National Advisory Council for South Asian Affairs (EA)
NACSAP....... National Alliance Concerned with School-Age Parents [Defunct] (EA)
NACSARS ... National Association of Companion Sitter Agencies and Referral Services [Later, PCA] (EA)
NACSB .... Naval Aviation Cadet Selection Board
NACSC......... National Association of Cold Storage Contractors (EA)
NACSCAOM... National Accreditation Commission for Schools and Colleges of Acupuncture and Oriental Medicine (EA)
NACSCC....... National Association of Community Schools, Colleges, and Centres [British] (DBA)
NACSCS ...... National Advisory Council on Supplementary Centers and Services
NACSDA....... National Association of Commissioners, Secretaries, and Directors of Agriculture[Later, NASDA] (EA)
NACSDC....... North American Conference of Separated and Divorced Catholics (EA)
NACSE .... National Association of Casualty and Surety Executives [New York, NY] (EA)
NACSE .... National Association of Civil Service Employees (EA)
NACSE .... Non-Avionics Common Support Equipment (MCD)
NACSIC........ National Association of Cold Storage Insulation Contractors (EA)
NACSIM ...... NATO Communications Security Information (NATG)
NACSIS .... [The] National Center for Science Information Systems [Computer science] (TNIG)
NACSIS........ National Center for Science Information Systems [Japan]
NACSM........ National Association of Catalog Showroom Merchandisers (EA)
NACSPMR.... National Association of Coordinators of State Programs for the Mentally Retarded[Later, National Association of State Mental Retardation Program Directors] (EA)
NACST .... National Association of Catholic School Teachers (EA)
NACSW........ National Action Committee on the Status of Women [Canada] (AD)
NACSW........ North American Association of Christians in Social Work (EA)
NACT .... NASA Activities [A publication]
NACT .... National Alliance of Cardiovascular Technologists (EA)
NACT .... National Association of Careers Teachers (AD)
NACT .... National Association of Chapter 13 Trustees (MHDB)
NACT .... National Association of Clinical Tutors [British] (DBA)
NACT .... National Association of Consumers and Travelers (EA)
NACT .... National Association of Corporate Treasurers [Washington, DC] (EA)
NACT .... National Association of Craftsman Tailors [British] (BI)
NACT .... National Association of Cycle Traders [British] (BI)
NACT .... National Association of Cycle Trades (AD)
NACT .... National Automatic Controller for Testing (MUGU)
NACTA .... National Association of Colleges and Teachers of Agriculture (EA)
NACTAC ...... Navy Antenna Computer Tracking and Command
NAC (T & N)... Reports of the Decisions of the Native Appeal Courts (Transvaal and Natal) [South Africa] [A publication] (ILCA)
NACTEFL ..... National Advisory Council on the Teaching of English as a Foreign Language (EA)
NACTEP .... National Association of County Training and Employment Professionals [Washington, DC] (EA)
NACTFO .... National Association of County Treasurers and Finance Officers (EA)
NACTP .... National Association of Computerized Tax Processors (EA)
NACTST ...... National Advisory Council on the Training and Supply of Teachers (AD)
NACTU .... Night Attack Combat Training Unit [Navy]
NACU .... National Association of Colleges and Universities
NACUA........ National Association of College and University Administrators [Superseded by NEA Higher Education Council]
NACUA........ National Association of College and University Attorneys (EA)
NACUBO ...... National Association of College and University Business Office Associations (AD)

NACUBO	National Association of College and University Business Officers [*Washington, DC*] (EA)
NACUC.........	National Association of College and University Chaplains and Directors of Religious Life (EA)
NACUFS	National Association of College and University Food Services (EA)
NACUP.........	National Association of Credit Union Presidents (EA)
NACUSA......	National Association of Composers, USA (EA)
NACUSS......	National Association of College and University Summer Sessions [*Later, NAASS*]
NACUTCD	National Advisory Committee on Uniform Traffic Control Devices [*Terminated, 1979*] [*Department of Transportation*] (EGAO)
NACUTSO	National Association of College and University Traffic and Security Officers (EA)
NACV	National Association of Concerned Veterans (EA)
NACVCB	National Association of Crime Victim Compensation Boards (EA)
NACVE	National Advisory Council on Vocational Education
NA-CVR.......	National Association for Crime Victims Rights (EA)
NACW	National Advisory Committee on Women (AD)
NACW	National Advisory Committee on Women (NADA)
NACW	National Association of College Women [*Later, NAUW*] (EA)
NACW	National Association of Commissions for Women (EA)
NACWC........	National Association of Colored Women's Clubs (EA)
NACWD........	National Association of County Welfare Directors [*Later, NACHSA*] (EA)
NACWEP	National Advisory Council on Women's Educational Programs (OICC)
NACWIS........	Navy Controlled Waste Information System
NACWPI.......	National Association of College Wind and Percussion Instructors (EA)
NACWPI.......	National Association of College Wind and Percussion Instruments (AD)
NACWRR	National Advisory Committee on Water Resources Research [*Canada*]
NACWS........	North African Chemical Warfare Section [*World War II*]
NACX	Northern Air Cargo, Inc. [*Air carrier designation symbol*]
NACYS	National Advisory Council for Youth Services (AIE)
NAd..............	Addison Public Library, Addison, NY [*Library symbol Library of Congress*] (LCLS)
NAD	Nadir (WDAA)
nad	Nadir (AD)
NAD	Naphthaleneacetamide [*Herbicide*]
NAD	National Academy of Design (EA)
NAD	National Advertising Division [*of the Council of Better Business Bureaus*]
NAD	National Alliance for Democracy [*Political party*] (AD)
NAD	National Armaments Director (NATG)
NAD	National Association of the Deaf (EA)
NAD	National Audience Demographics Report [*Nielsen Television Index*] (NTCM)
NAD	NATO Air Doctrine (NATG)
NAd..............	Naval Adviser [*British*]
NAD	Naval Air Defense (NATG)
NAD	Naval Air Depot
NAD	Naval Air Detachment (MCD)
NAD	Naval Air Detail
NAD	Naval Air Development Center
NAD	Naval Air Development Center, Warminster, PA [*OCLC symbol*] (OCLC)
NAD	Naval Air Division [*British*]
NAD	Naval Ammunition Depot [*Charleston, SC*]
NAD	Naval Armament Depot [*British*]
NAD	Naval Aviation Depot (AAGC)
Nad..............	Nedezhda (AD)
NAD	Network Access Device
nad	Networking Addressing Device [*Computer science*] (AD)
NAD	New Antigenic Determinant [*Immunochemistry*]
NAD	Nicotinamide-Adenine Dinucleotide [*Preferred form, but also see ARPPRN, DPN, NADH*] [*Biochemistry*]
NAD	Nicotinic Acid Dehydrogenase [*An enzyme*] (AAMN)
NAD	Nielson Audience Demographic Report [*A publication*] (DOAD)
NAD	Night Air Defence [*British World War II*]
NAD	Nitric Acid Dihydrate [*Inorganic chemistry*]
Nad..............	Nitrosamide [*Biochemistry*]
NAD	No Abnormality Detected [*Medicine*]
NAD	No-Acid Descaling (IEEE)
NAD	No Active Disease (DAVI)
NAD	No Acute Distress [*Medicine*]
NAD	No Apparent Defect [*Shipping*]
nad	No Apparent Defect (AD)
NAD	No Apparent Distress [*Medicine*]
nad	No Appreciable Difference (AD)
nad	No Appreciable Disease (AD)
NAD	No Appreciable Disease [*Medicine*]
NAD	Nobelair [*Turkey*] [*ICAO designator*] (FAAC)
NAD	Node Administration (NITA)
NAD	Noise Amplitude Distribution
NAD	Nordiska Namden for Alkohol- och Drogforskning [*Nordic Council for Alcohol and Drug Research - NCADR*] (EAIO)
NAD	Normal Axis Deviation [*Medicine*]
NAD	North American Aero Dynasty [*Vancouver Stock Exchange symbol*]
NAD	North American Datum
NAD	North Atlantic Division [*Army Engineers*]
NAD	Nothing Abnormal Detected [*or Discovered*] [*Medicine*]
nad	Nothing Abnormal Detected (AD)
nad	Not on Active Duty [*Military*] (AD)
NAD	Not on Active Duty
NAD	Nuclear Accident Dosimetry
NAD83	North American Datum of 1983 (USDC)
NAD83	North American Datum of 1983 [*Marine science*] (OSRA)
NADA..........	N-Acetyldopamine [*Biochemistry*]
NADA..........	National Art Dealers Association [*Later, ADA*] (EA)
NADA..........	National Association for Disabled Athletes (EA)
NADA..........	National Association of Dealers in Antiques (EA)
NADA..........	National Association of Dental Assistants (EA)
NADA..........	National Association of Drama Advisers [*British*]
NADA..........	National Association of Drug Addiction (AD)
NADA..........	National Association of Drug Addiction (NADA)
NADA..........	National Automobile Dealers Association [*McLean, VA*] (EA)
NADA..........	National Democratic Alliance [*Zambia*] [*Political party*] (EY)
NADA..........	Navajo Army Depot Activity [*Arizona*] [*Army*]
NADA..........	New Animal Drug Application [*Food and Drug Administration*]
NADABB.......	National Alzheimer's Disease Autopsy and Brain Bank (AD)
NADAC.......	National Air Duct Cleaners Association
NADAC.......	National Anti-Drug Abuse Campaign (AD)
NADAC.......	National Damage Assessment Center
NADAC.......	Naval ASW [*Antisubmarine Warfare*] Data Center (NVT)
NADAC.......	Navigation Data Assimilation Computer (IAA)
NADAC.......	Pacific Command, North Vietnam Air Defense Analysis and Coordinating Group (CINC)
NADAF.......	National Association of Decorative Architectural Finishes (EA)
NADAG.......	National Association of Diocesan Altar Guilds of the Protestant Episcopal Church (EA)
NADAP.......	National Association on Drug Abuse Problems (EA)
NADAPI.......	National Alcoholism and Drug Abuse Program Inventory [*Department of Health and Human Services*] (GFGA)
NADAR.......	No After Duty Action Required [*Military*]
NADAR.......	North American Data Airborne Recorder
NADase.......	Nicotinamide-Adenine Dinucleotide Glycohydrolase [*Also, DPNase*] [*An enzyme*]
NADASO	National Association Drug and Allied Sales Organizations [*Wyncote, PA*] (EA)
NADASO	National Association of Design and Art Service Organizations (EA)
NADB	National Aerometric Data Bank (AD)
NADB	National Air Data Branch [*Environmental Protection Agency Information service or system*] (IID)
NADB	National Atmospheric Data Bank (GNE)
NADB	National Audience Data Bank [*Newspaper Marketing Bureau*] [*Information service or system*] (CRD)
NADBR.......	National Association for the Deaf, Blind, and Rubella [*British*]
NADC..........	National Advisory Drug Committee [*HEW*]
NADC..........	National Animal Disease Center [*Ames, IA*] [*Department of Agriculture*] [*Research center*] (GRD)
NADC..........	National Anti-Drug Coalition [*Defunct*] (EA)
NADC..........	National Anti-Dumping Committee (EA)
NADC..........	National Association of Demolition Contractors (EA)
NADC..........	National Association of Dredging Contractors (EA)
NADC..........	NATO Air Defense Committee
NADC..........	NATO Defense College [*Also, NADEFCOL, NDC*]
NADC..........	Naval Aide-de-Camp [*British military*] (DMA)
NADC..........	Naval Air Development Center [*Also, NADEVCEN, NAVAIRDEVCEN*] [*Warminster, PA*]
NADC..........	Naval Air Development Center [*Marine science*] (OSRA)
NADC..........	Naval Ammunition Depot, Concord [*California*]
NADC..........	Northern Agricultural Development Corp. (AD)
NADCA........	National Animal Damage Control Association (EA)
NADCA........	North American Draft Cross Association (EA)
NADC-AC	Naval Air Development Center - Aerospace Crew Equipment Department
NADC-ACL ...	Naval Air Development Center - Aeronautical Computer Laboratory (DNAB)
NADC-AE......	Naval Air Development Center - Aero-Electronic Technology Department
NADC-AI	Naval Air Development Center - Aeronautical Instruments Laboratory
NADC-AM.....	Naval Air Development Center - Aero-Mechanics Department
NADC-AML...	Naval Air Development Center - Aeronautical Materials Laboratory (DNAB)
NADCAP.......	National Aerospace and Defense Contractors Accreditation Program [*DoD*]
NADC-AP	Naval Air Development Center - Aeronautical Photographic Experimental Laboratory
NADC-AR	Naval Air Development Center - Aviation Armament Laboratory
NADC-ASL ...	Naval Air Development Center - Aeronautical Structures Laboratory (DNAB)
NADC-ASW...	Naval Air Development Center - Antisubmarine Warfare Laboratory
NADC-AW	Naval Air Development Center - Air Warfare Research Department
NADC-AWG...	Naval Air Development Center - Acoustical Working Group
NADC-CS	Naval Air Development Center - Crew Systems Department
NADC-ED	Naval Air Development Center - Engineering Development Laboratory
NADC-EL......	Naval Air Development Center - Aeronautical Electronic and Electrical Laboratory
NADC-LS	Naval Air Development Center - Life Sciences and Bio-Equipment Group
NADC-ML.....	Naval Air Development Center - Aviation Medical Acceleration Laboratory
NADC-MR	Naval Air Development Center - Aerospace Medical Research Department
NADCO........	National Association of Development Companies (EA)
NAD-CO	Naval Ammunition Depot, Concord [*California*]
NAD-CR	Naval Ammunition Depot, Crane [*Indiana*]

NADC-SD	Naval Air Development Center - Systems Analysis and Engineering Department
NADC-ST	Naval Air Development Center - Aero Structures Department
NADC-SY	Naval Air Development Center - Systems Project Department
NADC-WR	Naval Air Development Center - Air Warfare Research Department
NADD	National Association for the Dually Diagnosed (PAZ)
NADD	National Association of Deputising Doctors [*British*] (DBA)
NADD	National Association of Diemakers and Diecutters [*Formerly, DDA*] (EA)
NADD	National Association of Disco Disc Jockeys [*Defunct*] (EA)
NADD	National Association of Distributors and Dealers of Structural Clay Products [*Later, NABD*] (EA)
NADDC	National Association of Developmental Disabilities Councils (EA)
NADDIS	Narcotics and Dangerous Drugs Intelligence File (AD)
NADDM	National Association of Daytime Dress Manufacturers [*Defunct*]
NADDRG	North American Deep Drawing Research Group [*Automotive metal stampings*]
NADE	National Association for Design Education [*British*]
NADE	National Association for Developmental Education (EA)
NADE	National Association for Drama in Education [*Australia*]
NADE	National Association of Disability Examiners (EA)
NADE	National Association of Document Examiners (EA)
NADEC	National Association of Development Education Centres [*British*] (DBA)
NADEC	Navy Decision Center
NADEC	Navy Development Center (CAAL)
NADEE	National Association of Divisional Executives for Education [*British*]
NADEEC	NATO Air Defense Electronic Environment Committee
NaDefCo	NATO [*North Atlantic Treaty Organization*] Defense College (AD)
NADEFCOL	NATO Defense College [*Also, NADC, NDC*] [*Rome, Italy*]
NADEM	National Association of Dairy Equipment Manufacturers [*Later, DFISA*] (EA)
NADEO	National Association of Diocesan Ecumenical Officers (EA)
NADEP	National Association of Disability Evaluating Professionals [*Later, IHC*] (EA)
NADEP	Naval Aviation Depot (MCD)
NADEPA	National Democratic Party [*Solomon Islands*] [*Political party*] (PPW)
NADET	National Association of Distributive Education Teachers
NADE(V)	National Association for Drama in Education (Victoria) [*Australia*]
NADEVCEN	Naval Air Development Center [*Also, NADC, NAVAIRDEVCEN*]
NaDevCen	Naval Air Development Center (AD)
NADEX	NATO Data Exchange (NATG)
NADF	National Addison's Disease Foundation (EA)
NADF	National Alzheimer's Disease Foundation (AD)
NADF	National Alzheimer's Disease Foundation (NADA)
NADF	National Arbor Day Foundation (EA)
NADF	North American Directory Forum
NADFA	North American Deer Farmers Association (EA)
NADFAS	[*The*] National Association of Decorative and Fine Arts Societies [*British*]
NADFAS	National Association of Design and Fine Art Societies (AD)
NADFD	National Association of Decorative Fabric Distributors (EA)
NADFPM	National Association of Domestic and Farm Pump Manufacturers [*Later, WSC*]
NADFS	National Association of Drop Forgers and Stampers (AD)
NADG	Nicotinamide Adenine Dinucleotide Glycohydrolase [*An enzyme*] (DMAA)
NADGE	NATO Air Defense Ground Environment
NADGE	NATO Air Defense Ground Equipment
NADGECO	NATO Air Defense Ground Environment Consortium
NADGEMO	NADGE [*NATO Air Defense Ground Environment*] Management Office [*Belgium*]
NADGEMO	NATO Air Defense Ground Environment Management Organization (NATG)
NADH	Dihydronicotinamide Adenine Dinucleotide (AD)
NADH	Naval Ammunition Depot, Hawaii
NADH	Nicotinamide-Adenine Dinucleotide (Reduced) [*See also NAD*] [*Biochemistry*]
NADHCI	North American District Heating and Cooling Institute [*Defunct*] (EA)
NADHPRS	Naval Ammunition Depot Hawthorne Police Records System (DNAB)
NADI	National Association of Display Industries [*New York, NY*] (EA)
NADI	Naval Ammunition Depot, Indiana
NADIB	North American Defense Industrial Base
NADIBO	North American Defense Industrial Base Organization
NADIN	National Airspace Data Interchange Network [*FAA*] (TAG)
NADIN II	National Airspace Data Interchange Network II [*National digital message switching network for aeronautical data*] (GAVI)
NADIP	Navy Display Improvement Program
NADIS	National Aerometric Data Information System [*Environmental Protection Agency*]
NADL	National Animal Disease Laboratory [*Iowa*]
NADL	National Association of Dental Laboratories (EA)
NADL	Navy Authorized Data List (NG)
NADLCC	National Association of Defense Lawyers in Criminal Cases [*Later, NACDL*] (EA)
NAD-LLL	Naval Ammunition Depot - Lwlualei [*Hawaii*] (DNAB)
NADM	National Association of Discount Merchants [*Defunct*] (EA)
NADM	National Association of Doll Manufacturers [*Later, NADSTM*] (EA)
NADM	Naval Administration
NADMC	Naval Air Development and Material Center
NADME	Noise Amplitude Distribution Measuring Equipment (PDAA)
NADMR	National Association of Diversified Manufacturers Representatives [*Later, NAGMR*] (EA)
NADMW	National Association of Direct Mail Writers
NAD/NADH	Nicotinamide Adenine Dinucleotide (AD)

NADO	National Association of Development Organizations (EA)
NADO	Navy Accounts Disbursing Office
NADOA	National Association of Division Order Analysts (EA)
NADOC	Naval Aviation Depot Operations Center (DOMA)
NADOI	National Association of Dog Obedience Instructors (EA)
NADONA/LTC	National Association of Directors of Nursing Administration in Long Term Care (EA)
NADOP	North American Defense Operation Plan [*NORAD*]
NADORF	National Association of Development Organization Research Fund
NADOT	North Atlantic Deepwater Oil Terminal (PDAA)
NADOW	National Association for Training the Disabled in Office Work (AD)
NADP	National Acid Deposition Program [*Air pollution*]
NADP	National Association of Desktop Publishers (EA)
NADP	National Association of Doctors in Practice [*British*] (DI)
NADP	National Atmospheric Deposition Program [*Department of Agriculture*]
NADP	National Atmospheric Deposition Program [*Marine science*] (OSRA)
NADP	NAVAIR Advanced Development Plan (MCD)
NADP	Nicotinamide-Adenine Dinucleotide Phosphate [*Preferred form, but see also TPN*] [*Biochemistry*]
nadp	Nicotinamide Adenine Dinucleotide Phosphate (AD)
NADPAS	National Association of Discharged Prisoners' Aid Societies [*British*] (DI)
NADPB	North Atlantic Defense Production Board (NATG)
nadph	Dihydronicotinamide Adenine Dinucleotide Phosphate (AD)
NADPH	Dihydronicotinamide Adenine Dinucleotide Phosphate (AD)
NADPH	Nicotinamide-Adenine Dinucleotide Phosphate (Reduced) [*Preferred form, but see also TPNH*] [*Biochemistry*]
NADREG	National Alliance for Democratic Restoration in Equatorial Guinea [*Switzerland*] (EAIO)
NADREPS	National Armaments Directors Representatives
NADS	National Advanced Driver Simulator [*NHTSA*] (TAG)
NADS	National Armament Directors [*NATO*]
NADS	National Association Diaper Services (EA)
NADS	National Association for Down Syndrome (EA)
NADS	Naval Air Development Station
NADS	North American Dostoevsky Society (EA)
NADS	North Atlantic Defense System
NADSA	National Association of Dramatic and Speech Arts (EA)
NADSC	National Association of Direct Selling Companies [*Later, DSA*] (EA)
NADSP	National Association of Dental Service Plans [*Insurance*] (DHSM)
NADSTM	National Association for Doll and Stuffed Toy Manufacturers (EA)
NADT	National Association for Drama Therapy (EA)
NADU	Naval Aircraft Delivery Unit
NADU	Naval Air Development Unit (MUGU)
NADUG	North American Datamanager Users Group (EA)
NADUS	National Association of Doctors in the United States (EA)
NADUSM	National Association of Deputy United States Marshals (EA)
NADW	North Atlantic Deep Water [*Oceanography*]
NADWAGNS	National Association of Deans of Women and Advisors to Girls in Negro Schools [*Defunct*]
NADWARN	National Disaster Warning System (AD)
NADWARN	Natural Disaster Warning
NADWARN	Natural Disaster Warning System (IAA)
NADWAS	Natural Disaster Warning Survey (NOAA)
NADWAS	North American Dr. Who Appreciation Society (EA)
NADX	National Dentex Corp. [*NASDAQ symbol*] (SAG)
NADX	Natl Dentex [*NASDAQ symbol*] (TTSB)
Nae	Exchangeable Body Sodium (MAE)
NAE	N-Acylethanolamine [*Organic chemistry*]
NAE	Nake [*Tuamotu Archipelago*] [*Seismograph station code, US Geological Survey*] (SEIS)
NAE	National Academy of Education
NAE	National Academy of Engineering [*Washington, DC*] (GRD)
NAE	National Administrative Expenses (NATG)
nae	National Administrative Expenses (AD)
NAE	National Adoption Exchange (EA)
NAE	National Aeronautical Establishment [*Research center Canada*] (IRC)
NAE	National Association of Entrepreneurs
NAE	National Association of Evangelicals (EA)
NAE	Naval Aeronautical Establishment [*Canada*] (AD)
NAE	Naval Aircraft Establishment (AD)
NAE	Navy Acquisition Executive (MCD)
NAE	Netware Application Engine [*Networth, Inc.*]
NAE	New Age Encyclopedia [*A publication*]
NAE	No American Equivalent [*Language*]
nAe	No American Equivalent (AD)
NAE	Noise Acoustic Emitter [*Military*] (CAAL)
NAE	Noram Energy Corp. [*Formerly, Arkla, Inc.*] [*NYSE symbol*] (SAG)
NAE	Noram Financing I [*NYSE symbol*] (SAG)
nae	Not Always Excused (AD)
NAE	Nursery Association Executives [*Later, NAENA*] (EA)
NAE4-HA	National Association of Extension 4-H Agents (EA)
NAEA	National Aerospace Education Association [*Formerly, NAEC*] [*Defunct*]
NAEA	National Art Education Archive (AIE)
NAEA	National Art Education Association (EA)
NAEA	National Artists Equity Association (EA)
NAEA	National Association of Enrolled Agents (EA)
NAEA	National Association of Estate Agents [*British*] (EAIO)
NAEA	National Association of Extension 4-H Agents (EA)
NAEA	Newspaper Advertising Executives Association [*Later, INAME*] (EA)
NAEA	Newspaper Advertising Executives' Associaton (DOAD)
NAE-ASEB	National Academy of Engineering Aeronautics and Space Engineering Board

NAEB .... National Association of Educational Broadcasters [*Formerly, Association of Collegeand University Broadcasting Stations (1934)*] (EA)
NAEB .... National Association of Educational Buyers [*Woodbury, NY*] (EA)
NAEB .... Naval Aviation Evaluation Board
NAEB .... North African Economic Board [*World War II*]
NAEBM .... National Association of Engine and Boat Manufacturers [*Later, NMMA*] (EA)
NAEC .... National Advisory Eye Council
NAEC .... National Aerospace Education Council [*Later, NAEA*] (EA)
NAEC .... National Association Executives Club
NAEC .... National Association for Educational Computing (EA)
NAEC .... National Association of Electric Companies [*Later, EEI*] (EA)
NAEC .... National Association of Elevator Contractors (EA)
NAEC .... National Association of Engineering Companies (EA)
NAEC .... National Association of Exhibition Contractors [*British*] (BI)
NAEC .... National Aviation Education Council [*Later, National Aerospace Education Council*] (AEBS)
NAEC .... Naval Air Engineering Center [*Closed*]
NAEC .... Northern Agricultural Energy Center
NAECA .... National Appliance Energy Conservation Act [*1987*]
NAEC-ACEL... Naval Air Engineering Center Aerospace Crew Equipment Laboratory [*Lakehurst, NJ*]
NAEC-AEL ... Naval Air Engineering Center Aeronautical Engine Laboratory [*Lakehurst, NJ*]
NAEC-AML ... Naval Air Engineering Center Aeronautical Materials Laboratory [*Lakehurst, NJ*]
NAEC-ASL ... Naval Air Engineering Center Aeronautical Structures Laboratory [*Lakehurst, NJ*]
NAEC-ENG ... Naval Air Engineering Center Engineering Department [*Lakehurst, NJ*]
NAECFO .... Naval Air Engineering Center Field Office (DNAB)
NAEC-GSED... Naval Air Engineering Center Ground Support Equipment Department [*Lakehurst, NJ*]
NAECOE .... National Academy of Engineering Committee on Ocean Engineering
NAECON....... National Aerospace Electronics Conference [*IEEE*] (MCD)
NAEd .... National Academy of Education (EA)
NAED .... National Association of Electrical Distributors (EA)
NAEDA .... National American Eskimo Dog Association (EA)
NAEDA .... North American Equipment Dealers Association (EA)
NAEDS .... National Association of Educational Data Systems (IAA)
NAEDS .... National Association of Engravers and Die-Stampers [*British*] (BI)
NAEE .... National Association of Environmental Education [*British*] (DBA)
NAEE .... North American Association for Environmental Education (EA)
NAEEO .... National Association for Equal Educational Opportunities (EA)
NAEF .... Naval Air Engineering Facility (MCD)
NAEFA .... North American Economics and Finance Association (EA)
NAEF-ENG ... Naval Air Engineering Facility Ship Installations Engineering Department [*Philadelphia, PA*]
NAEFR .... North American English Ford Registry (EA)
NAEFTA....... National Association of Enrolled Federal Tax Accountants (EA)
NAEGA .... North American Export Grain Association (EA)
NAEGS .... National Association of Educational Guidance Services for Adults [*British*] (DBA)
NAEH .... National Alliance to End Homelessness (EA)
NAEHCA .... National Association of Employers on Health Care Action
NAEHCA .... National Association of Employers on Health Care Alternatives (EA)
NAEHE .... National Association of Extension Home Economists (EA)
NAEHMO..... National Association of Employers on Health Maintenance Organizations [*Later, NAEHCA*] (EA)
NAEIAC .... National Association of Educational Inspectors, Advisers, and Consultants (AIE)
NAEIC .... Nevada Applied Ecology Information Center [*Department of Energy*] (IID)
NAEIR .... National Association for the Exchange of Industrial Resources (EA)
NAEKM .... National Association of Electronic Keyboard Manufacturers (EA)
NAEL.......... Naval Air Engineering Laboratory (MCD)
NAELA .... National Academy of Elder Law Attorneys (EA)
NAELC .... National Architect-Engineer Liaison Commission [*Defunct*] (EA)
NAEL-ENG.... Naval Air Engineering Laboratory Ship Installations Engineering Department [*Philadelphia, PA*]
NAELSI .... Naval Air Electronics Shipboard Installation
NAEM.......... National Association for Environmental Management
NAEM.......... National Association of Exposition Managers (EA)
NAEM.......... Naval Air Effect Model (PDAA)
NAEMB .... National Academy of Engineering Marine Board
NAEMSP ...... National Association of Emergency Medical Service Physicians (EA)
NAEMT....... National Association of Emergency Medical Technicians (EA)
NAEN .... National Association of Educational Negotiators (EA)
NAENA .... Nursery Association Executives of North America (EA)
NAE-NEPP.... National Academy of Engineering Navy Environmental Protection Program Study Group
NAENG .... North African Engineer Section [*World War II*]
NAEO .... National Activity Education Organization (EA)
NAEO .... National Association of Extradition Officials (EA)
NAEOM .... National Association of Electronic Organ Manufacturers
NAEOP .... National Association of Educational Office Personnel (EA)
NAEP .... National Assessment of Educational Progress (AD)
NAEP .... National Assessment of Educational Progress, The Nation's Report Card (EA)
NAEP .... National Association of Educational Programs [*Carnegie Foundation*] (AD)
NAEP .... National Association of Environmental Professionals (EA)
NAEPC .... National Association of Estate Planning Councils (EA)

NAEPIRS...... National Assessment of Educational Progress Information Retrieval System [*National Institute of Education*] [*Database*]
NAEPIS .... North America Engineering Parts Inquiry System
NAEPrA........ Noram Energy $3 Cv Ex A Pfd [*NYSE symbol*] (TTSB)
NAEPS .... National Academy of Economics and Political Science (EA)
NAER .... National Association of Executive Recruiters (EA)
NAERC .... North American Electric Reliability Council (EA)
NAES .... National Association for Ethnic Studies (EA)
NAES .... National Association of Ecumenical Staff (EA)
NAES .... National Association of Educational Secretaries [*Later, NAEOP*] (EA)
NAES .... National Association of Episcopal Schools (EA)
NAES .... National Association of Executive Secretaries (EA)
NAES .... Native American Educational Service [*Later, NAESC*] (EA)
NAES .... Naval Air Experimental Station
NAES .... Nevada Agricultural Experiment Station [*University of Nevada - Reno*] [*Research center*] (RCD)
NAES .... North African Army Exchange Service [*World War II*]
NAESA .... National Association of Elevator Safety Authorities (EA)
NAESA .... North American Economic Studies Association (EA)
NAESC .... National Association of Energy Service Companies (EA)
NAESC .... Native American Educational Services College (EA)
NAESCO ...... National Association of Energy Service Companies (EA)
NAESP .... National Association of Elementary School Principals (EA)
NAEST .... National Archives for Electrical Science and Technology (PDAA)
NAESU .... Naval Aviation Electronic Service Unit (MCD)
NAESU .... Naval Aviation Engineering Service Unit [*Philadelphia, PA*]
NAESUDET... Naval Aviation Engineering Service Unit Detachment (DNAB)
NAET .... National Association for Educational Television (NTCM)
NAET .... National Association of Educational Technicians [*British*]
NAETS .... Naval Air Emission-Tracking System
NAETV .... National Association for Educational Television [*Defunct*]
NAEW .... NATO Airborne Early Warning
NAEWS .... NATO Airborne Early Warning System
NAEWTF .... NATO Aircrew Electronic Warfare Tactics Facility (NATG)
NAEYC .... National Association for the Education of Young Children (EA)
NAF............. Guilder [*Florin*] [*Monetary unit Netherlands Antilles*]
NAF............. Nafimidone [*Biochemistry*]
NAF............. Name and Address File [*IRS*]
NAF............. National Abortion Federation (EA)
NAF............. National Abortion Foundation (AD)
NAF............. National Aging Foundation (EA)
NAF............. National Amputation Foundation (EA)
NAF............. National Analytical Facility [*National Oceanic and Atmospheric Administration*]
NAF............. National Angling Federation [*British*]
NAF............. National Arts Foundation (EA)
NAF............. National Ataxia Foundation (EA)
NAF............. National Aviation Forum
NAF............. Naval Aircraft Factory
NAF............. Naval Air Facility
NAF............. Naval Air Force
NAF............. Naval Avionics Facility [*Later, NAC*] [*Indianapolis, IN*]
NAF............. Nernst Approximation Formula [*Physics*]
NAF............. Net Acid Flux [*Medicine*] (DMAA)
NAF............. Netherland-America Foundation [*Later, Netherlands-America Community Association*] (EA)
NAF............. Network Access Facility
NAF............. New Age Federation (EA)
NAF............. New Age Media Fund [*NYSE symbol*] (SPSG)
NAF............. No Abnormal Findings [*Medicine*]
NAF............. Nonappropriated Fund [*or Funds*]
naf............. Nonappropriated Funds (AD)
NAF............. Non-urea Adducting Fatty Acid [*Food science*]
NAF............. Nordisk Anaestesiologisk Forening [*Scandinavian Society of Anaesthesiologists - SSA*] (EA)
NAF............. Norges Automobil Fornund [*Norway Automobile Association*] (AD)
NAF............. North American Federation of Third Order Franciscans (EA)
NAF............. North American Fire [*Vancouver Stock Exchange symbol*]
NAF............. Northern Attack Force [*Navy*]
NAF............. North West Atlantic Fisheries, Memorial University [*UTLAS symbol*]
NAF............. Notice of Adverse Finding [*Food and Drug Administration*]
NAF............. Nouvelle Action Francaise [*New French Action*] [*Political party*] (PPE)
NAF............. Numbered Air Force (AFM)
NAF............. Royal Netherlands Air Force [*ICAO designator*] (FAAC)
NaF............. Sodium Fluoride [*Chemistry*] (DAVI)
NAFA .... National Academy of Foreign Affairs (AD)
NAFA .... National Aerobic Fitness Award (AD)
NAFA .... National Aircraft Finance Association (EA)
NAFA .... National Air Filtration Association (EA)
NAFA .... National American Farmers Association [*Defunct*] (EA)
NAFA .... National Association of Fine Arts [*Defunct*] (EA)
NAFA .... National Association of Fleet Administrators [*Iselin, NJ*] (EA)
NAFA .... National Association of Furniture Agents [*Australia*]
NAFA .... National Association to Aid Fat Americans [*Bellrose, NY*]
NAFA .... Net Acquisition of Financial Assets (ADA)
NAFA .... Nonappropriated Fund Activity (CINC)
NAFA .... North American Falconers Association (EA)
NAFA .... North American Farm Alliance (EA)
NAFA .... Northwest Atlantic Fisheries Act of 1950
NAFAC .... National Association for Ambulatory Care [*Formerly, NAFEC*] (EA)
NAFAD .... National Association of Fashion and Accessory Designers (EA)
NAFAG .... NATO Air Force Advisory Group (NATG)
NAFAG .... NATO Air Force Armaments Group
NAFAPAC..... National Association for Association Political Action Committees (EA)

NAFARE....... National Association for Families and Addiction Research and Education (PAZ)
NAFAS......... National Association of Flower Arrangement Societies (AD)
NAFAS......... National Association of Flower Arrangement Societies of Great Britain (BI)
NAFAS......... Nonappropriated Fund Accounting System [*Military*] (DNAB)
NAFAX......... National Facsimile Network [*National Weather Service*]
NAFB........... National Association of Farm Broadcasters (EA)
NAFB........... National Association of Franchised Businessmen [*Defunct*] (EA)
NAFB........... Norton Air Force Base [*California*]
NAFB & AE... National Association of Farriers, Blacksmiths, and Agricultural Engineers [*British*] (DBA)
NAFBO......... National Association for Business Organizations [*Baltimore, MD*] (EA)
NAFBRAT..... National Association for Better Radio and Television [*Later, NABB*] (EA)
NAFC........... Nash-Finch Co. [*NASDAQ symbol*] (NQ)
NAFC........... Nash Finch Co. [*NASDAQ symbol*] (TTSB)
NAFC........... Nash Finch Co. [*NASDAQ symbol*] (SAG)
NAFC........... National Accounting and Finance Council [*Alexandria, VA*] (EA)
NAFC........... National Anthropological Film Center [*Smithsonian Institution*] (GRD)
NAFC........... National Anti-Fluoridation Campaign [*British*] (DBA)
NAFC........... National Association of Fan Clubs (EA)
NAFC........... National Association of Financial Consultants (EA)
NAFC........... National Association of Food Chains [*Later, FMI*] (EA)
NAFC........... National Association of Food Chains (NADA)
NAFC........... National Association of Formwork Contractors [*British*] (DBA)
NAFC........... National Association of Friendship Centres [*Canada*]
NAFC........... National Average Fuel Consumption
NAFC........... Naval Air Ferry Command [*World War II*]
NAFC........... Navy Accounting and Finance Center
NAFC........... North American Fishing Club (EA)
NAFC........... North American Forestry Commission [*UN Food and Agriculture Organization*]
NAFC........... North American Forum on the Catechumenate (EA)
NAFC........... Northern Attack Force Commander [*Navy*]
NAFCA......... North American Family Campers Association (EA)
NAFCD......... National Association of Floor Covering Distributors (EA)
NAFCE......... National Association of Federal Career Employees [*Defunct*] (EA)
NAFCI.......... National Association of Floor Covering Installers [*Later, AIDS International*] (EA)
NAFCO......... National Association of Franchise Companies (EA)
NAFCO......... National Floor Products Co., Inc.
NAFCR......... National Association of Foster Care Reviewers (EA)
NAFCU......... National Association of Federal Credit Unions (EA)
NAFD........... National Air Forwarding Division [*Institute of Freight Forwarders*] (AD)
NAFD........... National Association of Farm Directors (NTCM)
NAFD........... National Association of Flour Distributors (EA)
NAFD........... National Association of Funeral Directors [*British*] (BI)
NAFDC......... National Association for Family Day Care (EA)
NAFDI.......... National Foundation for Depressive Illness (EA)
NAFE........... National Association for Female Executives [*New York, NY*] (EA)
NAFE........... National Association for Film in Education [*British*]
NAFE........... National Association for Free Enterprise [*Defunct*] (EA)
NAFE........... National Association of Forensic Economists (EA)
NAFE........... Non-Advanced Further Education [*British*]
NAFEC......... National Association of Farmer Elected Committeemen (EA)
NAFEC......... National Association of Freestanding Emergency Centers [*Later, NAAC*] (EA)
NAFEC......... National Aviation Facilities Experimental Center [*of FAA*] [*Atlantic City, NJ*]
NAFED......... National Association of Fire Equipment Distributors (EA)
NAFEM......... National Association of Food Equipment Manufacturers (EA)
NAFEMS...... National Agency for Finite Element Methods and Standards [*British*] (IRUK)
NAFEO......... National Association for Equal Opportunity in Higher Education (EA)
NAFEX......... North American Fruit Explorers (EA)
NAFF........... National Association for Freedom [*British*]
nAff............ Need for Affection
NAFF........... Need for Affiliation (MHDB)
naff............ Need for Affiliation (AD)
NAFFP......... National Association of Frozen Food Packers [*Later, AFFI*] (EA)
NAFFP......... National Association of Frozen Food Producers (AD)
NAFFS......... National Association of Fruits, Flavors, and Syrups (EA)
NAFFW......... National Association of Full Figured Women (EA)
NAFGDA....... National Auto and Flat Glass Dealers Association [*Later, NGA*]
NAFGPD....... National Association of Foster Grandparent Program Directors (EA)
NAFI............ National Association of Fire Investigators (EA)
NAFI............ National Association of Flight Instructors (EA)
NAFI............ Naval Air Fighting Instructions
NAFI............ Naval Avionics Facility (AD)
NAFI............ Naval Avionics Facility, Indianapolis [*Later, NAC*]
NAFI............ Nonappropriated Fund Instrumentalities [*DoD*] (MCD)
NAFIC.......... National Association of Fraternal Insurance Counsellors [*Sheboygan, WI*] (EA)
NAFIN.......... North African Finance Section [*World War II*]
NAFINSA...... Nacional Financiera [*National Finance Coro.*] [*Spanish*] (AD)
NAFIP.......... National Foreign Intelligence Program [*DoD*] (MCD)
NAFIPS........ North American Fuzzy Information Processing Society (EA)
NAFIS.......... National Association of Federally Impacted Schools (EA)
NAFIS.......... Naval Forces Intelligence Study (MCD)
NAFIS.......... Navigational Aid Flight Inspection System (AFM)
NAFISS........ Nonappropriated Funds Information Standard System [*Army*]
NAFL............ National Alliance for Family Life [*Later, NACFT*] (EA)
NAFLAC....... Navy Department Fuel and Lubricants Advisory Committee [*Ministry of Defense*] [*British*] (PDAA)
NAFLANT..... Naval Air Facilities, Atlantic
NAFLFD....... National Association of Federally Licensed Firearms Dealers (EA)
NAFLI.......... Natural Flight Indication (MCD)
NAFLI.......... Natural Flight Instrument System
NAFM.......... National Armed Forces Museum (AD)
NAFM.......... National Association of Fan Manufacturers [*Later, AMCA*]
NAFM.......... National Association of Flag Manufacturers
NAFM.......... National Association of Furniture Manufacturers [*Later, AFMA*] (EA)
NAFMA........ NATO European Fighter Management Agency
NAFMAB..... National Armed Forces Museum Advisory Board [*Smithsonian Institution*]
NAFMB........ National Association of FM [*Frequency Modulation*] Broadcasters [*Later, NRBA*] (EA)
NAFMC........ Nonappropriated Funds, Marine Corps (DNAB)
NAFMG........ National Association of Foreign Medical Graduates [*Later, ACIP*]
NAFMIS....... Nonappropriated Funds Management Information System
NAFMOW..... National Action Forum for Midlife and Older Women (EA)
NAFMW....... National Action for Former Military Wives (EA)
NAFN.......... Norton Administrator for Networks [*Symantec Corp.*] [*Telecommunications*] (PCM)
NAFO.......... National Association of Farmworker Organizations [*Defunct*] (EA)
NAFO.......... National Association of Fire Officers [*British*] (DI)
NAFO.......... Northwest Atlantic Fisheries Organization (EA)
NAFOW........ National Action Forum for Older Women [*Later, NAFMOW*] (EA)
NAFP.......... National Association of Food Processors (ECON)
NAFP.......... Naval Air Force, Pacific Fleet (DNAB)
NAFP.......... New Armed Forces of the Philippines (AD)
NAFPA........ National Alcohol Fuels Producers Association [*Defunct*] (EA)
NAFPA........ National Association of Federal Education Program Administrators (EA)
NAFPAC...... Naval Air Facilities, Pacific
NAFPB........ National Association of Freight Payment Banks [*Pittsburgh, PA*] (EA)
NAFPC........ National Academy for Fire Prevention and Control [*of FEMA*]
NAFPD........ National Association of Family Planning Doctors [*British*] (DBA)
NAFPP........ National Accelerated Food Production Project [*Agency for International Development*]
NAFPP........ National Association of Fresh Produce Processors (EA)
NAFPU........ North American Friends of Palestinian Universities [*Defunct*] (EA)
N Afr.......... North Africa
NAFRC........ National Association of Fiscally Responsible Cities [*Defunct*] (EA)
NAFRC........ North Atlantic Fisheries Research Center (PDAA)
NAFRD........ National Association of Fleet Resale Dealers [*Los Angeles, CA*] (EA)
NAFRF........ Navy Alternate Fuel Reference File [*Battelle Memorial Institute*] [*Information service or system Defunct*] (IID)
NAFRLG...... National Alliance of Financially-Responsible Local Governments (AD)
NAFRTM...... National Association of Farm and Ranch Trailer Manufacturers [*Defunct*] (EA)
NAFS.......... National Association of Fastener Stockholders [*British*] (DBA)
NAFS.......... National Association of Foot Specialists (AD)
NAFS.......... National Association of Forensic Sciences (AD)
NAFS.......... Naval Air Fighter School
NA/FS........ Naval Aviator/Flight Surgeon (MCD)
NAFS.......... Newark Air Force Station [*Ohio*]
NAFSA........ National Association for Foreign Student Affairs (EA)
NAFSA........ National Association of Fire Science and Administration [*Defunct*] (EA)
NAFSA........ National Association of Foreign Student Advisors (AD)
NAFSA........ No American Flag Shipping Available
NAFSLAC..... National Association of Federations of Syrian and Lebanese American Clubs (EA)
NAFSO........ National Association of Field Studies Officers [*British*] (DBA)
NAFSONW... Nonappropriated Fund Statement of Operations and Net Worth
NAFSWMA... National Association of Flood and Storm Water Management Agencies (EA)
NAFT.......... National Alternative Fuel Test (AD)
NAFT.......... Natural Adjuvant Factor Toxoid [*Medicine*]
NAFT.......... Network for Analysis of Fireball Trajectories (EA)
NAFTA........ National Amalgamated Furnishing Trades Association [*A union*] [*British*]
NAFTA........ National Association of Futures Trading Advisors [*Defunct*] (EA)
NAFTA........ National Association of Future Teachers of America [*Later, Student National Education Association*] (AEBS)
NAFTA........ New Zealand-Australia Free Trade Agreement (AD)
NAFTA........ North American Free Trade Agreement [*Passed in 1993*]
NAFTA........ North American Free-Trade Area (ECON)
NAFTA........ North Atlantic Free Trade Area
NAFTAT...... National Association for the Advancement of Time (EA)
NAFTC........ National Association of Freight Transportation Consultants (EA)
NAFTF........ National Association of Finishers of Textile Fabrics [*Later, ATMI*] (EA)
NAFTOC...... NORAD Automated Forward Tell Output to Canada (MCD)
NAFTRAC.... National Foreign Trade Council (EA)
NAFTZ........ National Association of Foreign-Trade Zones [*Washington, DC*] (EA)
NAFV.......... National Association of Federal Veterinarians (EA)
NAFW.......... National Association of Future Women [*Later, NAFWIC*] (EA)
NAFWA........ North American Flowerbulb Wholesalers Association (EA)
NAFWIC...... National Association for Women in Careers (EA)
NAFWR........ National Association of Furniture Warehousemen and Removers (AD)
Nag............ All India Reporter, Nagpur [*A publication*] (DLA)
NAG............ Goddard Space Flight Center, Greenbelt, MD [*OCLC symbol*] (OCLC)
Nag............ Indian Law Reports, Nagpur Series [*A publication*] (DLA)

Nag............	Indian Rulings, Nagpur Series [*A publication*] (DLA)
NAG............	N-Acetylglucosamine [*Biochemistry*]
NAG	N-Acetylglucosaminidase [*An enzyme*]
NAG	Nachrichten der Akademie der Wissenschaften in Goettingen. Philologisch-Historische Klasse [*A publication*] (BJA)
Nag.............	Nagasaki [*Japan*] (AD)
Nag.............	Nagoya [*Japan*] (AD)
NAG	Nagoya [*Japan*] [*Seismograph station code, US Geological Survey*] (SEIS)
NAG	Nagpur [*India*] [*Airport symbol*] (OAG)
NAG	Narrow Angle Glaucoma [*Medicine*]
NAG	National Academy of Geosciences (EA)
NAG	National Acquisitions Group [*Libraries*] [*British*]
NAG	National Action Group [*Antibusing organization*]
NAG	National Advisory Group, Convenience Stores/Petroleum Companies (EA)
NAG	National Air-Racing Group (EA)
NAG	National Association of Gagwriters (EA)
NAG	National Association of Gardeners [*Later, PGMS*] (EA)
NAG	National Association of Goldsmiths [*British*]
NAG	National Association of Grooms [*British*] (DI)
NAG	National Association of Groundsmen [*British*] (DI)
NAG	Naval Advisory Group
NAG	Naval Analysis Group (MCD)
NAG	Naval Applications Group
NAG	Navy Astronautics Group (MUGU)
NAG	Negro Actors Guild (NADA)
NAG	Negro Actors Guild of America (EA)
NAG	Neighborhood Action Group (AD)
NAG	NERVA [*Nuclear Engine for Rocket Vehicle Application*] Advisory Group [*NASA*] (KSC)
NAG	Net Annual Gain [*Business term*] (PDAA)
nag	Net Annual Gain (AD)
NAG	Networking Advisory Group [*Library of Congress*]
N-Ag	Neutralization Antigenic Site [*Immunogenetics*]
Nag.............	No-Acronym Sort of Guy [*Term coined by William F. Doescher, publisher of "D & B Reports"*] [*Lifestyle classification*]
NAG	Nonagglutinable [*or Nonagglutinating*] [*Immunochemistry*]
NAG	Nor-Acme Gold Mines Ltd. [*Toronto Stock Exchange symbol*]
NAG	Northern Army Group (NATG)
NAG	Nova Scotia Agricultural College Library [*UTLAS symbol*]
NAG	Numerical [*formerly, Nottingham*] Algorithms Group
NAG	Nystagmus Action Group [*British*] (DBA)
NAGA	National Advertising Golf Association (EA)
NAGA	National Amputee Golf Association (EA)
NAGA	North American Gamebird Association (EA)
NAGA	North American Ginseng Association [*Defunct*] (EA)
NAGAP........	National Association of Gay Alcoholism Professionals [*Later, NALGAP*] (EA)
NAGARA	National Association of Government Archives and Records Administrators (EA)
NAGARD	NATO Advisory Group for Aeronautical Research and Development
Nagas.........	Nagasaki [*Japan*] (AD)
NAGB & SPA...	North American Game Breeders and Shooting Preserve Association [*Later, NAGA*] (EA)
NAGBM........	National Association of Golf Ball Manufacturers (EA)
NAGC..........	National Association for Gifted Children (EA)
NAGC..........	National Association of Girls Clubs (EA)
NAGC..........	National Association of Government Communicators (EA)
NAGC..........	National Gaming Corp. [*NASDAQ symbol*] (SAG)
NAGC..........	Naval Armed Guard Center
NAGC..........	Navy Astronautics Group Conference [*Navy*]
NAGC..........	North American Gladiolus Council (EA)
NAGCD........	National Association of Glass Container Distributors [*Later, NACD*] (EA)
NAGCM........	National Association of Golf Club Manufacturers (EA)
NAGCO........	Naval Air Ground Center
NAGCP........	National Association of Greeting Card Publishers [*Later, GCA*] (EA)
NAGCR........	North American Guild of Change Ringers (EA)
NAGDCA	National Association of Government Deferred Compensation Administrators (EA)
NAGDM.......	National Association of Garage Door Manufacturers (EA)
NAGE	National Association of Government Employees (EA)
NAGE	NATO Air Defense Group Environment (AABC)
N-age..........	Nuclear Age (AD)
NagHammSt...	Nag Hammadi Studies [*A publication*] (BJA)
NAGHSR	National Association of Governors' Highway Safety Representatives (EA)
NAGI	National Association of Government Inspectors [*Later, National Association of Government Inspectors and Quality Assurance Personnel*] (EA)
NAGIM........	North American Gunnery Instruction Monitor
NAGI/QAP	National Association of Government Inspectors and Quality Assurance Personnel (EA)
NAGIS.........	National Airport Grant Information System [*FAA*] (TAG)
Nag LJ........	Nagpur Law Journal [*India*] [*A publication*] (DLA)
Nag LN........	Nagpur Law Notes [*India*] [*A publication*] (DLA)
NAGLO........	National Association of Governmental Labor Officials (EA)
Nag LR........	Nagpur Law Reports [*India*] [*A publication*] (DLA)
NAGM..........	National Association of Glove Manufacturers (EA)
NAGM..........	National Association of Glue Manufacturers [*Defunct*] (EA)
NAGM..........	National Association of Governors and Managers [*British*] (DBA)
NAGMR........	National Association of General Merchandise Representatives [*Chicago, IL*] (EA)
Nagp..........	Nagpur, India (AD)

NAGPM........	National Association of Grained Plate Makers (AD)
NAGP/NCP ...	North American Great Plains/North China Plain Project [*Agriculture*]
NAGPRA	Native American Graves Protection and Repatriation Act [*Enacted 1990*]
NAGPTDU	National Action Group for the Prevention and Treatment of Decubitus Ulcers (EA)
NAGRA........	National Association of Gambling Regulatory Agencies (EA)
NAGRA........	Nationalen Genossenschaft fuer die Lagerung Radioaktiver Abfaelle [*National Cooperative Society for the Storage of Radioactive Wastes*] [*Germany*] (AD)
NAGS	National Allotments and Gardens Society Ltd. [*British*] (BI)
NAGS	National Association of Government Secretaries [*Defunct*]
NAGS	Naval Air Gunners School
NAGSC........	National Association of Government Service Contractors [*Defunct*] (EA)
NAGSCT.......	National Association of Guidance Supervisors and Counselor Trainers
NAGT	National Association of Geology Teachers (EA)
NAGTC........	North American Gasoline Tax Conference (EA)
Nag UCL Mag...	Nagpur University. College of Law. Magazine [*1933-34*] [*India*] [*A publication*] (DLA)
NAGVG........	National Association Greenhouse Vegetable Growers (EA)
NAGWS........	National Association for Girls and Women in Sport (EA)
NAH	Naha [*Ryukyu Islands*] [*Seismograph station code, US Geological Survey*] (SEIS)
NAH	Naha [*Ryukyu Islands*] [*Airport symbol*] (OAG)
NAH	Nahanni Air Services Ltd. [*Canada ICAO designator*] (FAAC)
nah	Nahuatlan [*MARC language code Library of Congress*] (LCCP)
Nah...........	Nahum [*Old Testament book*]
Nah...........	[*The Book of*] Nahum (AD)
NAH	National Association of Homebuilders (AD)
NAH	National Autism Hotline (EA)
NAH	Night Adoration in the Home (EA)
NAH	No-Antihalation Film
NAH	Nordic Association for Hydrology (EA)
NAH	Nordic Association for the Handicapped (EA)
NAH	Nordic Association of Hairdressers [*Sweden*] (EAIO)
NAH	Not at Home
NAHA	National Association of Handwriting Analysts
NAHA	National Association of Health Authorities [*British*] (EAIO)
NAHA	National Association of Health Authorities in England and Wales (AIE)
NAHA	National Association of Hotel Accountants [*Later, International Association of Hospitality Accountants*] (EA)
NAHA	North American Highway Association
NAHA	Norwegian-American Historical Association (EA)
NAHAD........	National Association of Hose and Accessories Distributors (EA)
Nahal........	Na'or Halutsi Lohem [*Fighting Pioneer Youth*] [*Israel*] (AD)
NAHAL........	Noar Halutzi Lohem [*Pioneering Fighting Youth*] [*Israel*]
NAHAM........	National Association of Hospital Admitting Managers (EA)
NAHAT........	National Association of Health Authorities and Trusts [*British*] (EAIO)
NAHAWA......	North American Heating and Airconditioning Wholesalers Association
NAHB..........	National Alliance of Homebased Businesswomen [*Defunct*] (EA)
NAHB..........	National Association of Home Builders (NADA)
NAHB..........	National Association of Home Builders of the United States (EA)
NAHB..........	National Association of Homes for Boys [*Later, NFCCE*]
NAHBB........	National Association of Home Based Businesses [*Baltimore, MD*] (EA)
NAHBE........	Naval Academy Heat Balanced Engine [*Pronounced "knobby"*]
NAHBO........	National Association of Hospital Broadcasting Organizations [*British*] (DBA)
NAHB/RC	NAHB Remodelers Council (EA)
NAHC	National Advisory Health Council
NAHC	National Anti-Hunger Coalition (EA)
NAHC	National Association for Home Care (EA)
NAHC	National Association of Holiday Centres [*British*] (DBA)
NAHC	National Association of Homes for Children (EA)
NAHC	National Association of Housing Cooperatives (EA)
NAHC	North American Hunting Club (EA)
NAHC	North American Hunting Club
NAHCAC......	National Ad Hoc Committee Against Censorship (AD)
NAHCR........	National Association of Healthcare Recruitment (EA)
NAHCS........	National Association of Health Career Schools (EA)
NAHCSP.......	National Association of Hospital Central Service Personnel [*Later, IAHCSM*] (EA)
NAHD..........	National Association for Hospital Development (EA)
NAHD..........	National Association for Human Development (EA)
NAHD..........	National Association of Hillel Directors [*Later, IAHD*] (EA)
NAHDDM	National Association of House and Daytime Dress Manufacturers (EA)
NAHDO........	National Association of Health Data Organizations (EA)
NAHDSA	National Association of Hebrew Day School Administrators (EA)
NAHE	National Alliance for Hydroelectric Energy (EA)
NAHE	National Association for Holocaust Education (EA)
NAHE	National Association for Humanities Education (EA)
NAHEE	National Association for Humane and Environmental Education (EA)
NAHEM........	National Association of Health Estates Managers [*British*] (DBA)
NAHES	National Association of Home Economics Supervisors [*Later, NASSVHE*] (EA)
NAHFAGIF...	National Archives and Historical Foundation of the American GI Forum (EA)
NAHFE........	National Association of Hispanic Federal Executives (EA)
NAHFO........	National Association of Hospital Fire Officers [*British*] (DBA)
NAHG..........	National Association of Homoeopathic Groups [*British*] (DBA)
NAHG..........	National Association of Humanistic Gerontology (EA)

NAHGT.......... National Aboriginal Health Goals and Targets [*Australia*]
NAHHA......... National Association of Home Health Agencies [*Later, NAHC*] (EA)
NAHHH......... National Association of Hospital Hospitality Houses (EA)
NAHHIC........ National Association of House to House Installment Companies [*Later, NAIC*] (EA)
NAHI............ National Athletic Health Institute (EA)
NAHICUS ..... Nuclear Attack Hazards in the Continental United States
NAHIS.......... National Arts and Handicapped Information Service (EA)
NAHJ............ National Association of Hispanic Journalists (EA)
NAHL............ North American Hockey League
NAHM........... National Association of Home Manufacturers [*Later, HMC*] (EA)
NAHM........... National Association of Hosiery Manufacturers (EA)
NAHMA......... National Association of Hotel and Motel Accountants [*Later, International Association of Hospitality Accountants*]
NAHMOR ..... National Association of HMO [*Health Maintenance Organization*] Regulators
NAHN........... National Association of Hispanic Nurses (EA)
NAHNS......... National Association of the Holy Name Society (EA)
NAHO........... National Association of Homeowners [*British*] (DBA)
NAHP........... National Association of Hispanic Publications (EA)
NAHP........... National Association of Horseradish Packers [*Defunct*] (EA)
NAHP........... National Association of Hypnotists and Psychotherapists [*British*] (DBA)
NAHPA......... National Association of Hospital Purchasing Agents [*Later, NAHPMM*] (EA)
NAHPM........ National Association of Hospital Purchasing Management [*Later, NAHP MM*] (EA)
NAHPMM..... National Association of Hospital Purchasing Materials Management (EA)
NAHPS......... North American Habitat Preservation Society (EA)
NAHRMP...... National Association of Hotel and Restaurant Meat Purveyors [*Later, NAMP*] (EA)
NAHRO......... National Association of Housing and Redevelopment Officials (EA)
NAHRW........ National Association of Human Rights Workers (EA)
NAHS .... National Aboriginal Health Strategy [*Australia*]
NAHS .... National Association of Health Stores [*British*] (DBA)
NAHS .... National Association of Horological Schools (EA)
NAHS .... North American Heather Society (EA)
NAHSA......... National Association for Hearing and Speech Action (EA)
NAHSA......... National Association of Hearing and Speech Agencies (AEBS)
NAHSA......... North American Horticultural Supply Association (EA)
NAHSC........ National Automated Highway System Consortium
NAHSC........ National Automated Highway System Consortium
NAHSE........ National Association of Health Services Executives (EA)
NAHSO........ National Association of Hospital Supplies Officers [*British*] (BI)
NAHSPO ...... National Association of Health Service Personnel Officers [*British*] (DBA)
NAHSSO ...... National Association of Health Service Security Officers [*British*] (DBA)
NAHST......... National Association of Human Services Technologies [*Defunct*] (EA)
NAHSTA....... National Hiking and Ski Touring Association (AD)
NAHSWP...... National Aboriginal Health Strategy Working Party [*Australia*]
NAHT .... National Association of Head Teachers [*British*]
NAHU........... NAHU, an Association of Bull Users [*Formerly, North American Honeywell Users Association*] (EA)
NAHU........... National Association of Health Underwriters [*Washington, DC*] (EA)
NAHUC........ National Association of Health Unit Clerks-Coordinators (EA)
NAHW.......... National Association of Hardwood Wholesalers [*Defunct*]
NAHWMUMC... National Association of Health and Welfare Ministries of the United Methodist Church [*Later, United Methodist Association of Health and Welfare Ministries - UMA*] (EA)
NAHWW....... National Association of Home and Workshop Writers (EA)
NAI............. Annai [*Guyana*] [*Airport symbol*] (OAG)
NAI............. N-Acetylimidazole [*Organic chemistry*]
NAI............. Nairobi [*Kenya*] [*Seismograph station code, US Geological Survey*] (SEIS)
NAI............. Named Areas of Interest [*Army intelligence matrix*] (INF)
NAI............. National Agricultural Institute [*Later, ACA*] (EA)
NAI............. National Apple Institute [*Later, IAI*] (EA)
NAI............. National Association of Interpretation (EA)
NAI............. Natural Alternatives International [*AMEX symbol*] (SPSG)
NAI............. Natural Alternatives Intl [*AMEX symbol*] (TTSB)
NAI............. Negro Airmen International (EA)
NAI............. Net Annual Inflow [*Pensions*]
NAI............. Netherlands Arbitration Institute (ILCA)
NAI............. New Acronyms and Initialisms [*Later, NAIA*] [*A publication*]
NAI............. New Alchemy Institute [*Defunct*] (EA)
NAI............. No Action Indicated
nai .... No Action Indicated (AD)
nai .... No Address Instruction (AD)
NAI............. No-Address Instruction (AAG)
NAI............. No Airborne Intercept [*Fighter aircraft lacking airborne intercept RADAR*]
NAI............. Nonaccidental Injury
nai .... North American Indian [*MARC language code Library of Congress*] (LCCP)
NAI............. North American Internet Co.
NAI............. Northern Alberta Institute of Technology [*UTLAS symbol*]
NAI............. Northrop Aeronautical Institute [*Later, Northrop University*]
NAI............. Northrop Aircraft, Inc. (MCD)
NAI............. N'shei Agudath Israel (BJA)
NAIA .... National Agricultural and Industrial Association [*Australia*]
NAIA .... National Association of Industrial Artists [*Later, IG*]
NAIA .... National Association of Insurance Agents [*Later, IIAA*] (EA)
NAIA .... National Association of Intercollegiate Athletics (EA)

NAIA .... New Acronyms, Initialisms, and Abbreviations [*Formerly, NAI*] [*A publication*]
NAIA .... North American Indian Association (EA)
NAIAD .... Nerve Agent Immobilised Enzyme Alarm and Detector (PDAA)
NAIB .... National Association of Independent Business [*Defunct*]
NAIB .... National Association of Insurance Brokers [*Washington, DC*] (EA)
NAIBD .... National Association of Industries for the Blind and Disabled [*British*] (DBA)
NAIC .... National Adoption Information Clearinghouse (EA)
NAIC .... National Advice and Information Centre for Outdoor Education [*Doncaster Metropolitan Institute of Higher Education*] [*British*] (CB)
NAIC .... National AIDS [*Acquired Immune Deficiency Syndrome*] Information Clearinghouse [*Information service or system*] (IID)
NAIC .... National Art Industry Council [*Australia*]
NAIC .... National Association of Installment Companies [*New York, NY*] (EA)
NAIC .... National Association of Insurance Commissioners [*Kansas City, MO*] (EA)
NAIC .... National Association of Intercollegiate Commissioners (EA)
NAIC .... National Association of Investment Clubs [*British*] (DBA)
NAIC .... National Association of Investment Companies
NAIC .... National Association of Investment Companies (EA)
NAIC .... National Association of Investors Corp. (EA)
NAIC .... National Astronomy and Ionosphere Center [*Ithaca, NY*] [*National Science Foundation*]
NAIC .... Naval Aircraft Investigation Center (AD)
NAIC .... Nuclear Accident and Incident Control [*Army*] (AABC)
NAICA .... National American Indian Cattlemen's Association (EA)
NAICC .... National Alliance of Independent Crop Consultants (EA)
NAICC .... National Association of Independent Computer Companies
NAICC .... Nuclear Accident and Incident Control Center [*Army*] (AABC)
NAICCA....... National American Indian Court Clerks Association (EA)
NAICJA .... National American Indian Court Judges Association (EA)
NAICO .... Nuclear Accident and Incident Control Officer [*Army*] (AABC)
NAICOM/MIS... Navy Integrated Command Management Information System
NAICP .... Nuclear Accident and Incident Control Plan [*Army*]
NAICPS .... National Association of Independent Colleges and Private Schools (EA)
NAICS .... North American Industry Classification System [*BTS*] (TAG)
NAICS .... North American Industry Classification System (AAGC)
NAICU .... National Association of Independent Colleges and Universities (EA)
NAICV .... National Association of Ice Cream Vendors [*Defunct*] (EA)
NAID .... National Associates for Informed Depressives [*Defunct*] (EA)
NAID .... National Association of Industrial Distributors [*British*] (DBA)
NAID .... National Association of Installation Developers (EA)
NAID .... National Association of Interior Designers [*Defunct*] (EA)
NAIDA .... National Agricultural and Industrial Development Association [*Republic of Ireland*] (BI)
NAIDS .... North Atlantic Institute for Defense Studies [*NATO*] (AD)
NAIDST .... National AIDS Trust [*British*]
NAIEA .... National Association of Inspectors and Educational Advisers [*British*]
NAIEC .... National Association for Industry-Education Cooperation [*Buffalo, NY*] (EA)
NAIEHS .... National Association of Importers and Exporters of Hides and Skins [*Later, USHSLA*] (EA)
NAIEM .... National Association of Insect Electrocutor Manufacturers (EA)
NAIEO .... National Association of Inspectors of Schools and Educational Organisers [*British*] (BI)
NAIES .... National Adoption Information Exchange System [*Formerly, ARENA*] (EA)
NAIES .... National Association of Interdisciplinary Ethnic Studies (EA)
NAIF .... National Association for Irish Freedom (EA)
NAIF .... Nordiska Akademiska Idrottsforbund [*Scandinavian Federation for University Sport*] (EA)
NAIFA .... National Association of Independent Fee Appraisers (EA)
NAIFR .... National Association of Independent Food Retailers [*Defunct*] (EA)
NAIG .... National Insurance Group [*NASDAQ symbol*] (NQ)
NAIG .... Natl Insurance Group [*NASDAQ symbol*] (TTSB)
NAIG .... Nippon Atomic Industry Group [*Japan*]
NAIHC .... National American Indian Housing Council (EA)
NAII .... National Association of Ice Industries [*Later, PIA*]
NAII .... National Association of Independent Insurers [*Des Plaines, IL*] (EA)
NAII .... Natural Alternatives International [*NASDAQ symbol*] (SAG)
NAIIA .... National Association of Independent Insurance Adjusters [*Chicago, IL*] (EA)
NAIIU .... Not Authorized If Issued Under [*Army*]
NAIJ .... National Association for Irish Justice [*Superseded by National Association for Irish Freedom*] (EA)
NAIL .... National Association for Independent Living (EA)
NAIL .... National Association of Independent Lubes (EA)
NAIL .... National Association of Independent Lumbermen [*Defunct*] (EA)
NAIL .... Naval Aircraft Inventory Log (AD)
NAIL .... Neurotics Anonymous International Liaison (EA)
NAIL .... North American Indian Landmarks [*A publication*]
NAILBA .... National Association of Independent Life Brokerage Agencies [*Washington, DC*] (EA)
NAILD .... National Association of Independent Lighting Distributors (EA)
NAILG .... National Awards for Innovation in Local Government [*Australia*]
NAILM .... National Association of Institutional Laundry Managers [*Later, National Association of Institutional Linen Management*] (EA)
NAILM .... National Association of Institutional Linen Management (EA)
NAILS .... National Airspace Integrated Logistics Support [*FAA*] (TAG)
NAILS .... National Automated Immigration Lookout System [*Immigration and Naturalization Service*]
NAILS .... Naval Aviation Integrated Logistic Support Task Force (NG)

NAILSC	Naval Aviation Integrated Logistic Support Center (MCD)
NAILTE.........	National Association of Instructional Leaders in Technical Education (EA)
NAIM	NAIM [*North American Indian Mission*] Ministries (EA)
NAIM	Number Allocation and Inspection Module (PDAA)
NAIMA	North American Indian Museums Association (EA)
NAIMD	National Association of Independent Music Dealers [*Defunct*] (EA)
NAIME	National Association of Independent Maritime Educators (EA)
NAIMIS	NAVAIRSYSCOM [*Naval Air Systems Command*] Integrated Management InformationSystem (DNAB)
NAIMS	National Airspace Information System [*BTS*] (TAG)
NAIMSAL	National Anti-Imperialist Movement in Solidarity with African Liberation (EA)
NAION..........	Nonarteritic Anterior Ischemic Optic Neuropathy
NAION..........	Nonarteritic Anterior Ischemic Optic Neuropathy
NAIOP..........	National Association of Industrial and Office Parks (EA)
NAIOP..........	Navigational Aid Inoperative for Parts
naiop	Navigational Aids Inoperative for Parts (AD)
NAIP	National Assault on Illiteracy Program (EA)
NAIP	National Association of Independent Publishers (EA)
NAIP	National Association of Industrial Parks [*Later, NAIOP*]
NAIP	National Association of Insured Persons [*Defunct*] (EA)
NAIP	Neuronal Apoptosis Inhibitory Protein [*Genetics*]
NAIP	Neuronal Apoptpsos Inhibitory Protein [*Cytology*]
NAIPFA	National Association of Independent Public Finance Advisors
NAIPRC	Netherlands Automated Information Processing Research Centre (NITA)
NAIPTS	National Amalgamated Iron Plate Trade Society [*A union*] [*British*]
NAIR	Narrow Absorption Infrared
NAIR	National Arrangements for Incidents Involving Radioactivity [*Nuclear energy*] (NUCP)
NAIR	National Association of Independent Resurfacers (EA)
NAIR	Network Action Item Report (MCD)
NAIRD.........	National Association of Independent Record Distributors and Manufacturers (EA)
NAIRDM.......	National Association of Independent Record Distributors and Manufacturers (EA)
NAIRE	National Association of Internal Revenue Employees [*Later, NTEU*] (EA)
NAIREC.......	Nimbus Arctic Ice Reconnaissance [*Canadian project*]
Nairns..........	Nairnshire, Scotland (AD)
NAIRO	National Association of Intergroup Relations Officials [*Later, NAHRW*] (EA)
NAIRS..........	National Athletic Injury/Illness Reporting System [*Pennsylvania State University*] [*Defunct*]
NAIRS..........	Navy Aircraft and Readiness System
NAIRU.........	Naval Air Intelligence Reserve Units
NAIRU.........	Non-Accelerating-Inflation Rate of Unemployment
NAIS	National Administrative Information System [*Computer science*] (IID)
NAIS	National Aquaculture Information System (NOAA)
NAIS	National Assistance for Information Services (EA)
NAIS	National Association of Independent Schools (EA)
NAIS	National Association of Investigative Specialists (EA)
NAIS	Navy Attitudinal Information System (NVT)
NAIS	Night Attack Interdiction System
NAISC	National American Indian Safety Council (EA)
NAISEO........	National Association of Inspectors of Schools and Educational Organisers [*British*]
NAISS	National Association of Iron and Steel Stockholders (AD)
NAIT...........	National Alliance for Infusion Therapy [*An association*]
NAIT...........	National Association of Industrial Technology (EA)
NAIT...........	Naval Air Intermediate Training
NAIT...........	North American Islamic Trust (EA)
NAIT...........	Northern Alberta Institute of Technology [*Edmonton, AB*]
NAI Tc	NAI Technologies [*Associated Press*] (SAG)
NAIT(C)........	Naval Air Intermediate Training (Command)
NAITE.........	National Association of Industrial Teacher Educators [*Later, NAITTE*] (EA)
NAI Tech......	NAI Technologies [*Associated Press*] (SAG)
NAITF.........	Naval Air Intercept Training Facility (MUGU)
NAITP	National Association of Income Tax Preparers [*Defunct*] (EA)
NAITPD........	National Association of Independent Television Producers and Distributors [*Defunct*] (EA)
NAITTE........	National Association of Industrial and Technical Teacher Educators (EA)
NAIW	National Association of Insurance Women (International) [*Tulsa, OK*] (EA)
NAIWA	North American Indian Women's Association (EA)
NAIWC........	National Association of Inland Water Carriers [*British*] (BI)
NAIWC........	National Association of Inland Waterway Carriers [*British*] (DBA)
NAJ............	Napierville Junction Railway Co. [*Later, NJ*] [*AAR code*]
NAJ............	National Academy of Jazz (EA)
NAJ............	National Aeronautics and Space Administration, Johnson Space Center, Houston, TX [*OCLC symbol*] (OCLC)
NAJ............	National Association for Justice
NAJA..........	National Association of Jewelry Appraisers (EA)
NAJA..........	National Association of Junior Auxiliaries (EA)
NAJA..........	North American Judges Association [*Later, AJA*]
NAJAFRA	National Jazz Fraternity
NAJAG	North African Judge Advocate General's Section [*World War II*]
NAJC..........	National Assessment of Juvenile Correction [*University of Michigan*] (AD)
NAJC..........	Northern Australia Jockey Club (AD)
NAJC..........	Northwest Alabama Junior College (AD)
NAJCA	National Association of Juvenile Correctional Agencies (EA)

NAJCW	National Association of Jewish Center Workers [*Later, AJCW*] (EA)
NAJD	National Association of Journalism Directors [*Later, JEA*] (EA)
NAJD/MBAP...	National Association of JD/MBA [*Juris Doctor/Master of Business Administration*] Professionals [*Defunct*] (EA)
NAJE	National Association of Jazz Education (AD)
NAJE	National Association of Jazz Educators [*Later, IAJE*] (EA)
NAJEM........	North African Joint Economic Mission [*World War II*]
NAJF	National Association of Jai Alai Frontons (EA)
NAJFCHP	National Association of Jewish Family, Children's, and Health Professionals (EA)
NAJHA	National Association of Jewish Homes for the Aged [*Later, NAAJHHA*] (EA)
NAJLA.........	North American Junior Limousin Association (EA)
NAJRC	North African Joint Rearmament Committee [*World War II*]
NAJSA	North American Jewish Students Appeal (EA)
NAJSN	North American Jewish Students' Network (EA)
NAJU	Nordic Association of Journalists' Unions (EA)
NAJVS	National Association of Jewish Vocational Services (EA)
NAJYC	North American Jewish Youth Council [*Defunct*] (EA)
NAK	Nakhichevan [*Former USSR Seismograph station code, US Geological Survey Closed*] (SEIS)
NAK	National Auto Credit, Inc. [*NYSE symbol*] (SAG)
NAK	Natl Auto Credit [*NYSE symbol*] (TTSB)
NAK	Negative Acknowledge [*or Acknowledgment*] [*Data communication*]
NAK	Negative Acknowledge Character (ECII)
nak...........	Negative Acknowledge Character [*Computer science*] (AD)
NAK	Negative Acknowledgment (DOM)
nak...........	Negative Knowledge (AD)
NAK	Network Acknowledgment
NAK	Nothing Adverse Known (ADA)
nak...........	Nothing Adverse Known (AD)
Na K-ATPase...	Adenosine Triphosphatase (Na, K-Activated) [*An enzyme*]
NAKBA	National Association to Keep and Bear Arms (EA)
nakl	Naklad [*Edition*] [*Polish*] (AD)
nakl	Nakladatel [*Edition*] [*Czech*] (AD)
NAKN	National Anti-Klan Network (EA)
NAKOSTA......	Natural Convection in the Stationary Condition [*Computer program*]
NAKS	North American Kant Society (EA)
NAl............	Albany Public Library, Albany, NY [*Library symbol Library of Congress*] (LCLS)
NAL...........	N-Acetyllactopamine [*Biochemistry*]
NAL...........	Naloxone [*A drug*]
NAL...........	Name, Address, and Legal File [*Real estate*]
NAL...........	National Accelerator Laboratory [*AEC*]
NAL...........	National Acoustics Laboratory [*Australia*] (ECON)
NAL...........	National Aeronautical Laboratory (MCD)
NAL...........	National Aerospace Laboratory (AD)
NAL...........	National Agricultural Library [*Department of Agriculture*] [*Beltsville, MD*]
NAL...........	National Airlines (AD)
NAL...........	National Assistance League (EA)
NAL...........	National Association of Laity (EA)
NAL...........	National Association of Landowners (EA)
NAL...........	National Astronomical League
NAL...........	Naval Aeronautical Laboratory
NAL...........	New Aalesund [*Norway*] [*Geomagnetic observatory code*]
NAL...........	Newalta Corp. [*Toronto Stock Exchange symbol*]
NAL...........	New American Library [*Publisher*]
NAL...........	New Assembly Language
NAL...........	Nigeria America Line (AD)
NAL...........	Niue Airways Ltd. (EY)
NAL...........	No Activity Log (MCD)
NAL...........	North American Lighting [*Automotive industry supplier*]
NAL...........	Northway Aviation Ltd. [*Canada ICAO designator*] (FAAC)
NAL...........	Norwegian America Line
NAL...........	Novell Application Launcher [*Computer science*]
NAL...........	Novell Application Launcher [*Computer science*]
NAL...........	Numerical Analysis Laboratory (MCD)
nal	Sodium Iodide [*Pharmacology*] (DAVI)
NAIA	Albany Medical College, Albany, NY [*Library symbol Library of Congress*] (LCLS)
NALA	National Academy of Literary Arts (EA)
NALA	National Affiliation for Literacy Advance (EA)
NALA	National Agricultural Limestone Association [*Later, National Limestone Institute*]
NALA	National Association of Language Advisers [*British*]
NALA	National Association of Legal Assistants (EA)
NALAA	National Assembly of Local Arts Agencies (EA)
NALAM	National Association of Livestock Auction Markets
NAIb...........	Shelter Rock Public Library, Albertson, NY [*Library symbol Library of Congress*] (LCLS)
NALBA	North American Log Builders Association (EA)
NAIBC........	Albany Business College, Albany, NY [*Library symbol Library of Congress*] (LCLS)
NAIbH........	Human Resources Center, Albertson, NY [*Library symbol Library of Congress*] (LCLS)
NAIbHM.......	Herricks Middle School, Albertson, NY [*Library symbol*] [*Library of Congress*] (LCLS)
NAIbi	Swan Library, Albion, NY [*Library symbol Library of Congress*] (LCLS)
NAIbiH.........	Arnold Gregory Memorial Hospital, Albion, NY [*Library symbol Library of Congress*] (LCLS)
NAIbME.......	Meadow Drive Elementary School, Albertson, NY [*Library symbol*] [*Library of Congress*] (LCLS)
NALBOH.......	National Association of Local Boards of Health

NAIbSE	Searington Elementary School, Albertson, NY [*Library symbol*] [*Library of Congress*] (LCLS)
NALC	National Afro-American Labor Council (EA)
NALC	National Association of Ladies Circles [*British*] (DBA)
NALC	National Association of Laryngectomee Clubs [*British*] (DBA)
NALC	National Association of Letter Carriers (NADA)
NALC	National Association of Letter Carriers of the USA (EA)
NALC	National Association of Life Companies [*Washington, DC*] (EA)
NALC	National Association of Litho Clubs (EA)
NALC	National Association of Local Councils [*British*]
NALC	National Association of Louisiana Catahoulas (EA)
NALC	Natl Lodging [*NASDAQ symbol*] (TTSB)
NALC	Naval Aviation Logistics Center (NVT)
NALC	Navy Ammunition Logistics Code
NALC	New Age Learning Center [*Defunct*] (EA)
NALCC	National Automatic Laundry and Cleaning Council (EA)
NALCDVE	National Association of Large City Directors of Vocational Education (EA)
NAICI	Center for International Studies, Albany, NY [*Library symbol Library of Congress*] (LCLS)
NAICJ	New York State Division of Criminal Justice Services, Albany, NY [*Library symbol*] [*Library of Congress*] (LCLS)
NALCM	National Association of Lace Curtain Manufacturers [*Defunct*]
Nalco	Nalco Chemical Co. [*Associated Press*] (SAG)
NALCO	Naval Air Logistics Control Office
NALCO	Newfoundland & Labrador Corp.
NALCOEASTPAC	Naval Air Logistics Control Office Eastern Pacific (DNAB)
NALCOEURREP	Naval Air Logistics Control Office European Representative
NALCOLANT	Naval Air Logistics Control Office Atlantic
NALCOMIS	Naval Aviation Logistics Command Management Information System (MCD)
NALCOMIS-OS	Naval Air Logistics Command Management Information System for Operating and Support (DNAB)
NALCON	Navy Laboratory Computer Network
NALCOPAC	Naval Air Logistics Control Office Pacific
NALCOPACREP	Naval Air Logistics Control Office Pacific Representative
NALCOREP	Naval Air Logistics Control Office Representative
NALCOWESTPAC	Naval Air Logistics Control Office Western Pacific (DNAB)
NALCOWESTPACREP	Naval Air Logistics Control Office Western Pacific Representative (DNAB)
NAICSR	College of Saint Rose, Albany, NY [*Library symbol Library of Congress*] (LCLS)
NAID	Dudley Observatory, Albany, NY [*Library symbol Library of Congress*] (LCLS)
NALD	National Association of Limbless and Disabled [*British*] (DBA)
NALDA	Naval Aviation Logistics Data Analysis (NVT)
NaLDAP	National Learning Disabilities Assistance Project
NALDEF	Native American Legal Defense and Education Foundation (EA)
NAIDH	New York State Department of Health, Division of Laboratories and Research, Albany, NY [*Library symbol Library of Congress*] (LCLS)
NAIDS	New York State Department of State, Community Affairs Library, Albany, NY [*Library symbol Library of Congress*] (LCLS)
NALEAO	National Association of Latino Elected and Appointed Officials (AD)
NALECOM	National Law Enforcement Telecommunications System
NALED	National Association of Limited Edition Dealers (EA)
NAIeNH	E. J. Noble Hospital, Medical Library, Alexandria Bay, NY [*Library symbol Library of Congress*] (LCLS)
NALEO	National Association of Latino Elected and Appointed Officials (EA)
NAIf	Alfred University, Alfred, NY [*Library symbol Library of Congress*] (LCLS)
NALF	NAL Financial Group [*NASDAQ symbol*] (TTSB)
NALF	NAL Financial Group, Inc. [*NASDAQ symbol*] (SAG)
NALF	National Agricultural Legal Fund [*Defunct*] (EA)
NALF	Naval Auxiliary Landing Field (NG)
NALF	North American Limousin Foundation (EA)
NALF	North American Loon Fund (EA)
NAIfC	State University of New York, College of Ceramics at Alfred University, Alfred, NY [*Library symbol Library of Congress*] (LCLS)
NALFMA	National Association of Law Firm Marketing Administrators (EA)
NAL Fn	NAL Financial Group, Inc. [*Associated Press*] (SAG)
NAIf-ST	Alfred University, School of Theology, Alfred, NY [*Library symbol Library of Congress Obsolete*] (LCLS)
NAIfUA	State University of New York, Agricultural and Technical College at Alfred, Alfred, NY [*Library symbol Library of Congress*] (LCLS)
NALG	National Association for Loss and Grief [*Australia*]
NALG	National Association of Left-Handed Golfers (EA)
NALGAP	National Association of Lesbian/Gay Alcoholism Professionals (EA)
NALGG	National Association for Lesbian and Gay Gerontology (AD)
NALGHW	National Association of Local Governments on Hazardous Wastes (EA)
NALGM	National Association of Lawn and Garden Manufacturers [*Defunct*] (EA)
NALGM	National Association of Leather Glove Manufacturers [*Later, NAGM*]
NALGO	National and Local Government Officers' Association [*British*]
NALGO	National Association of Local Government Officers (AIE)
NAIGS	United States Geological Survey, Water Resources Services, New York District, Albany, NY [*Library symbol Library of Congress*] (LCLS)
NAIH	Hospital Educational and Research Fund, Inc., Albany, NY [*Library symbol Library of Congress*] (LCLS)
NALHC	National Acoustic Laboratories Hearing Center [*Australia*]
NALHC	North American Log Homes Council (EA)
NALHF	National Association of Leagues of Hospital Friends [*British*] (DI)
NALHI	National Authority for the Ladies Handbag Industry (EA)
NALHM	National Association of Licensed House Managers [*Pronounced "nalem"*] [*A union*] [*British*] (DCTA)
NAII	Albany Institute of History of Art, Albany, NY [*Library symbol Library of Congress*] (LCLS)
NALI	National Agricultural Limestone Institute [*Later, National Limestone Institute*]
NALI	National Association of Legal Investigators (EA)
NALI	National Association of the Launderette Industry [*British*] (DBA)
NALI	North Atlantic Lobster Institute (EA)
NALIC	National Association of Loft Insulation Contractors [*British*] (DI)
NAIJ	Junior College of Albany, Albany, NY [*Library symbol Library of Congress*] (LCLS)
NALJS	Nordic Atomic Libraries Joint Secretariat [*Information service or system*] (IID)
NALLA	National Long-Lines Agency (NATG)
NALLD	National Association of Learning Laboratory Directors [*Later, IALL*]
NAILL	New York State Department of Law Library, Albany, NY [*Library symbol*] [*Library of Congress*] (LCLS)
NALLO	National Association of License Law Officials [*Later, NARELLO*] (EA)
NAILS	Albany Law School, Albany, NY [*Library symbol Library of Congress*] (LCLS)
NALLS	National Aboriginal Literacy and Language Strategy [*Australia*]
NAIM	Maria College, Albany, NY [*Library symbol Library of Congress*] (LCLS)
NALM	National Association for Lay Ministry (EA)
NALM	National Association of Lift Makers [*British*] (BI)
NALMA	North American Land Mammal Age [*Geological epoch*]
NALMC	National Association of Labor-Management Committees (EA)
NALMCO	International Association of Lighting Management Companies (EA)
NALMCO	National Association of Lighting Maintenance Contractors (EA)
NAIMem	Memorial Hospital, Medical Library, Albany, NY [*Library symbol Library of Congress*] (LCLS)
NAIMH	New York State Department of Mental Hygiene, Mental Hygiene Research Library, Albany, NY [*Library symbol Library of Congress*] (LCLS)
NALMS	North American Lake Management Society (EA)
NAIMV	New York State Department of Motor Vehicles, Research Library, Albany, NY [*Library symbol Library of Congress*] (LCLS)
NALN	National Agricultural Libraries Network [*National Agricultural Library*]
NALN	Native Authority Legal Notice [*Northern Nigeria*] [*A publication*] (DLA)
NALN	North African Liaison Section [*World War II*]
NALNET	NASA Library Network [*NASA Washington, DC Library network*] (MCD)
NALO	National Association of Launderette Owners Ltd. [*British*] (BI)
NALO	Naval Air Liaison Officer
NALO	Naval Air Logistics Office (DOMA)
NALOG	Natural Logarithm (IAA)
NALOH	National Association Legions of Honor (EA)
NALOP	NATO Letter of Promulgation
NALOXONE	N-Allylnoroxymorphone [*Narcotic antagonist*]
NAIP	Albany College of Pharmacy, Albany, NY [*Library symbol Library of Congress*] (LCLS)
NALP	National Association for Law Placement (EA)
NALPA	National American Legion Press Association (EA)
NALPM	National Association of Lithographic Plate Manufacturers [*Defunct*] (EA)
NALPN	National Association of Licensed Practical Nurses (EA)
NALR	National Acid Lakes Registry [*Environmental Protection Agency*]
NALR	National Association of Lighting Representatives (EA)
NALS	National Advisory Logistics Staff (NATG)
NALS	National Association of Laboratory Suppliers [*Defunct*] (EA)
NALS	National Association of Labor Students [*British*] (DI)
NALS	National Association of Legal Secretaries (International) [*Tulsa, OK*] (EA)
NALS	National Association of Lumber Salesmen (EA)
NALS	North American Lily Society (EA)
NAIS	Saint Peter's Hospital, Albany, NY [*Library symbol Library of Congress*] (LCLS)
NALSA	Native American Law Students Association (EA)
NALSA	North American Land Sailing Association (AD)
NALSAS	National Association for Legal Support of Alternative Schools (EA)
NALSAT	National Association of Land Settlement Association Tenants (AD)
NALSF	National ALS [*Amyotrophic Lateral Sclerosis*] Foundation (EA)
NALSI	National Association of Life Science Industries [*Defunct*] (EA)
NALSO	National Association of Labour Student Organisations [*British*] (BI)
NAISS	New York State Department of Social Sciences, Social Services and Statistics Library, Albany, NY [*Library symbol Library of Congress*] (LCLS)
Nal St P	Nalton's Collection of State Papers [*A publication*] (DLA)
NAISU	State University of New York, Union List of Serials, Albany, NY [*Library symbol Library of Congress*] (LCLS)
NALSVHE	National Association of Local Supervisors of Vocational Home Economics (EA)
NALT	Naltrexone [*A drug*]
NALT	National Association of the Legitimate Theatre [*Defunct*] (EA)
NaI (TI)	Thallium-Activated Sodium Iodide [*Scintillation detector*] [*Medicine*] (MEDA)
NAItL	La Salette Seminary, Altamont, NY [*Library symbol Library of Congress*] (LCLS)
NALTOACS	Navy Laboratory Technical Office for ADP and Communication Systems (GFGA)
NALTS	National Advertising Lead Tracking System [*Navy*] (NVT)
NALU	National Association of Life Underwriters [*Washington, DC*] (EA)

NAIU	State University of New York at Albany, Albany, NY [*Library symbol Library of Congress*] (LCLS)
NALUAS	North American Life Union Assurance Society (EA)
NAIU-F	State University of New York at Albany, Filmdex, Albany, NY [*Library symbol Library of Congress*] (LCLS)
NAIUHL	Upper Hudson Library Federation, Albany, NY [*Library symbol Library of Congress*] (LCLS)
NAIU-L	State University of New York at Albany Library School, Albany, NY [*Library symbol Library of Congress*] (LCLS)
NAIULS	New York State Union List of Serials, Albany, NY [*Library symbol Library of Congress*] (LCLS)
NAIU-PA	State University of New York at Albany, Graduate School of Public Affairs, Albany, NY [*Library symbol Library of Congress*] (LCLS)
NALUS	National Association of Leagues, Umpires, and Scorers (EA)
NAIVA	United States Veterans Administration Hospital, Albany, NY [*Library symbol Library of Congress*] (LCLS)
NALW	Not an A-List Writer [*Screenwriter's lexicon*]
NAM	N-Acetylmethionine [*Organic chemistry*]
NAM	N-(Acridinyl)maleimide [*Organic chemistry*]
NAM	Namangan [*Former USSR Seismograph station code, US Geological Survey Closed*] (SEIS)
NAM	NAM Corp. [*Associated Press*] (SAG)
NAM	Named
NAM	Namibia [*ANSI three-letter standard code*] (CNC)
NAM	Namlea [*Indonesia*] [*Airport symbol*] (OAG)
NAM	National Account Management [*Bell System*]
NAM	National Aero Manufacturing (AD)
NAM	National Air Museum [*of the Smithsonian Institution*] [*Later, NASM*]
NAM	National Apple Month (EA)
NAM	National Army Museum [*British military*] (DMA)
NAM	National Association of Manufacturers (NTCM)
NAM	Natural Actomyosins [*Biochemistry*]
NAM	Nautical Air Miles
NAM	Naval Aircraft Modification
NAM	Naval Air Material (SAA)
NAM	Naval Air Mechanic [*British military*] (DMA)
NAM	Naval Aviation Museum [*Pensacola, FL*]
NAM	Navy Achievement Medal [*Military decoration*]
NAM	Nederlandsche Aluminium Maatschappij [*Netherlands Aluminum Co.*] (AD)
nam	Network Access Machine [*Computer science*] (AD)
NAM	Network Access Machine [*National Institute of Standards and Technology Computer science*]
NAM	Network Access Method [*Control Data Corp.*] [*Telecommunications*] (TEL)
NAM	Network Analysis Model
NAM	New America Movement (EA)
NAM	New American Man [*Lifestyle classification coined by Robert Bly*] (ECON)
NAM	New Architectural Movement [*British*] (DI)
NAM	Newspaper Association Managers (EA)
NAM	NOAA [*National Oceanic and Atmospheric Administration*] Accounting Manual (NOAA)
NAM	Nonadditive Mixing (DICI)
NAM	Nonaligned Movement
nam	Non-Aligned Movement (AD)
N Am	North America (AD)
NAM	North America
N Am	North America (ODBW)
NAM	North American Metals Corp. [*Vancouver Stock Exchange symbol*]
NAM	North American Movement (AD)
NAM	North American Region [*USTTA*] (TAG)
NAM	Nortland Air Manitoba [*Canada ICAO designator*] (FAAC)
NAM	Norwegian American Museum Corp. (EA)
NAM	Numerical Assignment Number [*Computer science*]
NAM	Nurses Against Misrepresentation (EA)
NAM	State University of New York at Albany, Albany, NY [*OCLC symbol*] (OCLC)
Nam	Vietnam
NAma	Amagansett Free Library, Amagansett, NY [*Library symbol Library of Congress*] (LCLS)
NAMA	National Account Marketing Association (EA)
NAMA	National Agenda for a Multicultural Australia
NAMA	National Agri-Marketing Association (EA)
NAMA	National Air-Monitoring Audit [*Environmental Protection Agency*] (GFGA)
NAMA	National Assistance Management Association [*Washington, DC*] (EA)
NAMA	National Association of Master Appraisers (EA)
NAMA	National Association of Mathematics Advisers [*British*] (DBA)
NAMA	National Automatic Merchandising Association [*Chicago, IL*] (EA)
NAMA	National Automotive Muffler Association [*Defunct*] (EA)
NAMA	Naval Aeronautical Material Area (NG)
NAMA	New Amsterdam Musical Association (AD)
NAMA	North American Manx Association (EA)
NAMA	North American Maritime Agencies (AD)
NAMA	North American Mycological Association (EA)
NAMAB	National Air Museum Advisory Board (MUGU)
NAMAC	National Alliance of Media Arts Centers (EA)
NAMAC	National Amateur Missile Analysis Center
NAMAC	National Association of Men's Apparel Clubs [*Later, NAMBAC, Bureau of WholesaleSales Representatives*]
NAMAC	National Association of Merger and Acquisition Consultants (EA)
NAMAD	National Association of Minority Automobile Dealers [*Detroit, MI*] (EA)
NAMAE	Northern Air Materiel Area, Europe [*Army*]

NAmaHi	Amagansett Historical Association, Amagansett, NY [*Library symbol Library of Congress*] (LCLS)
NAMAINTRADET	Naval Air Maintenance Training Detachment (DNAB)
NAMAINTRAGRU	Naval Air Maintenance Training Group (DNAB)
NAMAP	Northern Air Materiel Area, Pacific [*Army*]
NAMAPUS	Naval Assistant to the Military Aide to the President of the United States
NAMAR	North American Mustang Association and Registry (EA)
NAMARA	Navy and Marine Corps Appellate Review Activity (DNAB)
NAMAS	National Measurement Accreditation Service [*Research center British*] (IRC)
NAMAST	System of National Accounts and System of Material Product Balances [*United Nations Statistical Office*] [*Information service or system*] (CRD)
NAMATCEN	Naval Air Material Center [*Also, NAMC, NAVAIRMATCEN*]
NAMATE	Naval Air Material Command
NAMB	National Association of Master Bakers [*British*] (DI)
NAMB	National Association of Master Bakers, Confectioners, and Caterers [*British*] (DBA)
NAMB	National Association of Media Brokers (EA)
NAMB	National Association of Minority Businesses (AAGC)
NAMB	National Association of Mortgage Brokers [*Washington, DC*] (EA)
NAMB	Naval Academy Midshipmen Branch
NAMB	Naval Amphibious Base
NAMBAC	National Association of Men's and Boys' Apparel Clubs [*Later, Bureau of Wholesale Sales Representatives*] (EA)
NAMBC	National Association of Milk Bottle Collectors (EA)
NAMBLA	North American Man-Boy Love Association
NAMBO	National Association of Motor Bus Operators (AD)
NAMBO	National Association of Motor Bus Owners [*Later, ABA*] (EA)
NAMC	NAM Corp. [*NASDAQ symbol*] (SAG)
NAMC	National Air Material Center (KSC)
NAMC	National Association of Management Consultants (EA)
NAMC	National Association of Minority Contractors (EA)
NAMC	National Association of Mothers' Centers (EA)
NAMC	Naval Aerospace Medical Center
NAMC	Naval Air Material Center [*Also, NAMATCEN, NAVAIRMATCEN*]
NAMC	Naval Air Materiel Command
NAMC	Nihon Aeroplane Manufacturing Co. (AD)
NAMC	North Atlantic Military Committee
NAMCA	National Association for Middle Class Americans (EA)
NAMC-AEL	Naval Air Material Center - Aeronautical Engine Laboratory
NAMC-AIL	Naval Air Material Center - Aeronautical Instruments Laboratory [*Philadelphia, PA*]
NAMC-AML	Naval Air Material Center - Aeronautical Materials Laboratory
NAMC-APEL	Naval Air Material Center - Aeronautical Photographic Experimental Laboratory
NAMCAR	North America/Caribbean
NAMC-ARRL	Naval Air Material Center - Aeronautical Radio and RADAR Laboratory
NAMC-ASL	Naval Air Material Center - Aeronautical Structures Laboratory
NAMCC	National Association of Mutual Casualty Companies (EA)
NAM-CDH	Non Absorbing Mirror Constricted Double Heterostructure (NITA)
NAMCF	National Association of Minority CPA [*Certified Public Accounting*] Firms
NAMCO	Air-Cushion Vehicle built by Nakamura Seisakusho [*Usually used in com bination with numerals*] [*Japan*]
NAMCO	Naval and Mechanical Co. (AD)
NAM Cp	NAM Corp. [*Associated Press*] (SAG)
NAMCP	National Association of Managed Care Physicians (EA)
NAMCPAF	National Association of Minority Certified Public Accounting Firms (EA)
NAMCS	National Ambulatory Medical Care Survey [*National Center for Health Statistics*]
NAMCU	National Association of Minority Consultants and Urbanologists [*Defunct*] (EA)
NAMCW	National Association of Maternal and Child Welfare [*British*]
NAMD	National Association of Marble Dealers [*Later, MIA*] (EA)
NAMD	National Association of Marine Dealers
NAMD	National Association of Market Developers [*New York, NY*] (EA)
NAMD	National Association of Membership Directors of Chambers of Commerce [*Defunct*] (EA)
NAMD	Naval Ammunition Depot [*Charleston, SC*]
NAMD	Newsletter of the Army Medical Department
NAMDA	North American Medical/Dental Association (EA)
NAMDAR	North American Data Airborne Recorder (IAA)
NAMDB	National Association of Medical-Dental Bureaus [*Later, MDHBA*]
NAMDDU	Naval Air Mine Defense Development Unit (MUGU)
NAMDEX	Name Index
NAMDI	National Marine Data Inventory
NAMDRA	National American Motors Drivers and Racers Association (EA)
NAMDRP	Naval Aviation Maintenance Discrepancy Reporting Program (DNAB)
NAMDT	National Association of Milliners, Dressmakers, and Tailors (EA)
NAME	National Anti-Racist Movement in Education [*British*] (DBA)
NAME	National Association for Mediation in Education (EA)
NAME	National Association for Minority Education
NAME	National Association for Multiracial Education [*British*]
NAME	National Association of Management/Marketing Educators [*Defunct*] (EA)
NAME	National Association of Marine Enginebuilders [*British*] (BI)
NAME	National Association of Marine Engineers (AD)
NAME	National Association of Marine Engineers (NADA)
NAME	National Association of Media Educators (EA)
NAME	National Association of Medical Examiners (EA)
NAME	National Association of Metal Name Plate Manufacturers (AD)

NAME.......... National Association of Miniature Enthusiasts (EA)
NAME.......... National Association of Minority Entrepreneurs (EA)
NAME.......... National Association of Modeling and Entertainment (EA)
NAME.......... Nitroarginine Methyl Ester [Organic chemistry]
NAME.......... North American Monogrammers and Embroiderers [Defunct] (EA)
NAMEB........ National Association of Marine Engine Builders (AD)
NAMEC........ National Association of Marine Engineers of Canada
NAMED........ North African Medical Section [World War II]
NAMEDCEN... Naval Aviation Medical Center (DNAB)
NAMEPA....... National Association of Minority Engineering Program
     Administrators (EA)
NAMES........ National Association of Medical Equipment Suppliers (EA)
NAMES........ NAVDAC [Naval Data Automation Command] Assembly, Monitor,
     Executive System (PDAA)
NAMESAKES... Naval Aviators Must Energetically Sell Aviation to Keep Effective
     Strength
NAMESU....... National Association of Music Executives in State Universities (EA)
NAMET........ Naval Mathematics and English Test [British military] (DMA)
NAMF.......... National Association of Metal Finishers (EA)
NAMF.......... Naval Aviation Museum Foundation (DNAB)
NAMFAX...... National and Aviation Meteorological Facsimile Network [National
     Weather Service]
NAMFC........ North Atlantic Mediterranean Freight Conference (EA)
NAMFI......... NATO Missile Firing Installation
NAMFREL .... National Citizens' Movement for Free Elections [Philippines] [Political
     party]
NAMFSM ..... National Association of Meat and Food Seasoning Manufacturers
     [Later, NSMA] (EA)
NAMG .... Narrow-Angle Mars Gate [NASA]
NAMG .... National Association of Mining Groups (EA)
NAMG .... National Association of Multiple Grocers [British] (BI)
NAMGAR...... North American MGA [Morris Garage Automobile] Register (EA)
NAMH .... National Association for Mental Health (EA)
NAMHA .... North American Morab Horse Association (EA)
NAMHH....... National Association of Methodist Hospitals and Homes
NAMHI........ National Association for the Mentally Handicapped of Ireland (EAIO)
NAMHO....... National Association of Mining History Organizations [British] (DBA)
NAmi .... Amityville Public Library, Amityville, NY [Library symbol Library of
     Congress] (LCLS)
NAMI .... National Alliance for the Mentally Ill (EA)
NAMI .... National Association of Malleable Ironfounders [British] (BI)
NAMI .... Naval Aerospace Medical Institute
NAMIA .... National Association of Mutual Insurance Agents [Later, PIA] (EA)
Namib......... Namibia (AD)
NAMIC .... National Association of Mutual Insurance Companies [Indianapolis,
     IN] (EA)
NAMID .... National Moving Image Database [American Film Institute]
     [Information service or system] (IID)
NAmiGH....... Brunswick General Hospital, Amityville, NY [Library symbol Library of
     Congress] (LCLS)
NAmiHS....... Amityville Memorial High School, Amityville, NY [Library symbol]
     [Library of Congress] (LCLS)
NAmiJH .... Amityville Junior High School, Amityville, NY [Library symbol] [Library
     of Congress] (LCLS)
NAMIlCom ... North Atlantic Military Committee (AD)
NAMILCOM... North Atlantic Military Committee
NAMILPO.... NATO Military Posture (AABC)
NAMIM .... National Association of Musical Instrument Mechanics (EA)
NAMIS .... Nitride-Barrier Avalanche Injection Missile (MCD)
NAmiSH....... South Oaks Hospital, Amityville, NY [Library symbol Library of
     Congress] (LCLS)
NAMISTESTCEN... Naval Air Missile Test Center
naml .... Namligen [Namely] [Swedish] (AD)
NAML.......... National Applied Mathematics Laboratory [National Institute of
     Standards and Technology] (MCD)
NAML.......... Naval Aircraft Materials Laboratory (MCD)
NAML Dig.... National Association of Manufacturers Law Digest [A publication]
     (DLA)
NAMLM....... National Association for Multi-Level Marketing (EA)
NAMLNC..... National Association of Medical Legal Nurse Consultants (EA)
NAMM .... National Association of Margarine Manufacturers (EA)
NAMM .... National Association of Mass Merchandisers (EA)
NAMM .... National Association of Master Masons [British] (DBA)
NAMM .... National Association of Mirror Manufacturers (EA)
NAMM .... National Association of Music Merchandisers (AD)
NAMM .... National Association of Music Merchants (EA)
NAMM .... North African Military Mission [World War II]
NAMMA ...... NATO Multi-Role Combat Aircraft Development and Production
     Management Agency
NAMMC ...... Natural Asphalt Mineowners' and Manufacturers' Council (AD)
NAMMD ...... National Association of Marinas and Marine Dealers (EA)
NAMME....... National Association of Medical Minority Educators (EA)
NAMMIS ..... Navy Aviation Maintenance and Material Support System (NG)
NAMMM ..... National Association of Musical Merchandise Manufacturers [Later,
     GAMA] (EA)
NAMMO ...... NATO Multi-Role Combat Aircraft Management Organization (PDAA)
NAMMO ...... North Atlantic Treaty Organization [NATO] Multi-Role Combat Aircraft
     Development and Production Management Organization (AAGC)
NAMMO Development a... NATO [North Atlantic Treaty Organization] Multi-Role
     Combat Aircraft Development a (AD)
NAMMOS...... Navy Manpower Mobilization System
NAMMR .... National Association for Milk Marketing Reform [Later, NIDA] (EA)
NAMMR .... North American Mini Moke Registry (EA)
NAMMS .... Navy Aviation Maintenance and Material Support System

NAMMW ...... National Association of Musical Merchandise Wholesalers [Later,
     MDA] (EA)
NAMNPM ..... National Association of Metal Name Plate Manufacturers
NAMO......... National Agricultural Marketing Officials [Richmond, VA] (EA)
NAMO......... National Association of Manufacturing Opticians (EA)
NAMO......... National Association of Multifamily Owners
NAMO......... Naval Aircraft Maintenance Orders
NAMOA....... National Association of Miscellaneous Ornamental and Architectural
     Products Contractors (EA)
NAMORB...... North Atlantic Mid-Ocean-Ridge Basalt [Geology]
NAMOS....... National Art Museum of Sport (EA)
NAMP .... National Alliance of Mental Patients [Later, NAPS] (EA)
NAMP .... National Antibiotic Minimization Program [Australia]
NAMP .... National Association of Magazine Publishers [Later, Magazine
     Publishers Association]
NAMP .... National Association of Marble Producers (EA)
NAMP .... National Association of Married Priests (AD)
NAMP .... National Association of Mature People (EA)
NAMP .... National Association of Meal Programs (EA)
NAMP .... National Association of Meat Purveyors (EA)
NAMP .... National Association of Midwifery Practitioners [Defunct] (EA)
NAMP .... NATO Annual Manpower Plan (NATG)
NAMP .... Naval Aviation Maintenance Program (MCD)
NAMP .... Nonaccounting Majors Program
NAMPA....... NATO Maritime Patrol Aircraft Agency (NATG)
NAMPBG...... National Association of Manufacturers of Pressed and Blown
     Glassware [Defunct] (EA)
nampg .... Nautical Air Miles per Gallon (AD)
NAMPI .... National Association of Missing Persons Investigators [Defunct] (EA)
NAMPMW ..... Vietnam Prisoners of War [An association] (AD)
namppf .... Nautical Air Miles per Pound of Fuel (AD)
NAMPPF ...... Nautical Air Miles per Pound of Fuel (AAG)
NAMPS .... National Association of Marine Products and Services (EA)
NAMPS .... Navy Manpower Planning System (NVT)
NAMPW ...... National Association of Meat Processors and Wholesalers (EA)
NAMPW ...... National Association of Minority Political Women (EA)
NAMRA .... North American Mini-Champ Racing Association (EA)
NAMRAD ..... Non-Atomic Military Research and Development [Subcommittee]
NAMRC....... North American Marten Rabbit Club (EA)
NAMRI .... Naval Aerospace Medical Research Institute (DNAB)
NAMRI/SME... North American Manufacturing Research Institution of SME [Society
     of Manufacturing Engineers] (EA)
NAMRL .... Naval Aerospace Medical Research Laboratory
NAMRP .... National Apostolate with Mentally Retarded Persons (EA)
NAMRU .... Navy Medical Research Unit [World War II]
NAMRU .... Navy Medical Reserve Unit (DAVI)
NAms .... Amsterdam Free Library, Amsterdam, NY [Library symbol Library of
     Congress] (LCLS)
NAMS .... National Air Monitoring [Environmental Protection Agency] (GNE)
NAMS .... National Air Monitoring Station [Environmental Protection Agency]
     (ERG)
NAMS .... National Ambient Air Monitoring Station [or System] [Environmental
     Protection Agency]
NAMS .... National Association of Marine Services (EA)
NAMS .... National Association of Marine Surveyors (EA)
NAMS .... National Association of Military Spouses (EA)
NAMS .... National Association of Municipal Securities Dealers
NAMS .... North American Membrane Society (EA)
NAMS .... North American Menopause Society (EA)
NAMS .... Nurses and Army Medical Specialists
NAMSA .... NATO Maintenance and Supply Agency
NAMSA .... North American Multihull Sailing Association (EA)
NAMSB .... National Association of Men's Sportswear Buyers (EA)
NAMSB .... National Association of Mutual Savings Banks (EA)
NAMSC .... North American Maple Syrup Council (EA)
NAMSCO...... National Association of MDS [Multipoint Distribution System] Service
     Companies [Later, MDSIA] (EA)
NAMSDIC.... National Arthritis and Musculoskeletal and Skin Diseases Information
     Clearinghouse [Later, NAMSIC] (EA)
NAMSE .... National Association of Minority Students and Educators in Higher
     Education (EA)
NAMSIC .... National Arthritis and Musculoskeletal and Skin Diseases Information
     Clearinghouse (EA)
NAmsM .... Mohasco Corp., Corporate Planning Library, Amsterdam, NY [Library
     symbol Library of Congress] (LCLS)
NAMSO .... NATO Maintenance and Supply Organization [Formerly, NATO
     Maintenance Supply Service Agency] [Luxembourg]
NAMSO .... Navy Maintenance Support Office
NAMSOINST... Navy Maintenance Support Office Instruction (MCD)
NAMSP .... National Association of Mail Service Pharmacies [Later, AMCPA]
     (EA)
NAMSR .... National Association of Multiple Shoe Repairers [British] (DBA)
NAMSRC.... National AM Stereophonic Radio Committee
NAMSS .... National Association Medical Staff Services (EA)
NAmSv........ North American Savings Bank [Associated Press] (SAG)
NAMT.......... National Association for Music Therapy (EA)
NAMT.......... Naval Aircraft Mobile Trainer
NAMT.......... Naval Air Maintenance Trainer (MUGU)
NAMTA .... National Art Materials Trade Association (EA)
NAMTAC ..... National Association of Management and Technical Assistance
     Centers [Washington, DC] (EA)
NamTai....... Nam Tai Electronics, Inc. [Associated Press] (SAG)
NAMTC .... Naval Air Missile Test Center
NAmTch....... North American Technologies Corp. [Associated Press] (SAG)
NAMTD .... Naval Air Maintenance Training Detachment

NAMTD	Naval Air Maintenance Training Devices
NAMTG	Naval Air Maintenance Training Group (MCD)
NAMTGD	Naval Air Maintenance Training Group Detachment (DNAB)
NAMtge	North American Mortgage Co. [*Associated Press*] (SAG)
NAMTM	Naval Air Mobile Training Maintenance
NAMTRA	Naval Air Maintenance Training
NAMTRADET	Naval Air Maintenance Training Detachment (MCD)
NAMTRAGRU	Naval Air Maintenance Training Group (MCD)
NAMTRAGRUDET	Naval Air Maintenance Training Group Detachment (DNAB)
NAMTRAGRUP	Naval Air Maintenance Training Group (SAA)
NAMTRATCLOFLT	Naval Air Maintenance Training Type Commander Liaison Office, Fleet (DNAB)
NAMTRATCLOLANT	Naval Air Maintenance Training Type Commander Liaison Officer, Atlantic (DNAB)
NAMTRATCLOPAC	Naval Air Maintenance Training Type Commander Liaison Office, Pacific (DNAB)
NAMU	Naval Aircraft Material Utility
NAMU	Naval Aircraft Modification Unit
NAMV	Narcissus Mosaic Virus [*Plant pathology*]
NAMW	National Association of Media Women (EA)
NAMW	National Association of Military Widows (EA)
NAMW	National Association of Ministers' Wives [*Later, NAMWMW*] (EA)
NAMWB	National Association of Minority Women in Business [*Kansas City, MO*] (EA)
NAMWMW	National Association of Ministers' Wives and Ministers' Widows (EA)
NAMZ	Neue Allgemeine Missions-Zeitschrift [*A publication*] (BJA)
NAN	N-Acetylneuraminic Acid [*Also, AcNeu, NANA*] [*Biochemistry*]
NAN	Nadi [*Fiji*] [*Airport symbol*] (OAG)
Nan	Nancy (AD)
Nan	Nanette (AD)
Nan	Nanking [*China*] (AD)
NAN	Nanking [*Republic of China*] [*Seismograph station code, US Geological Survey*] (SEIS)
NAN	Nantucket Indus [*AMEX symbol*] (TTSB)
NAN	Nantucket Industries, Inc. [*AMEX symbol*] (SPSG)
NAN	National Academy of Needlearts (EA)
NAN	National Academy of Neuropsychology (EA)
NAN	National AIDS [*Acquired Immune Deficiency Syndrome*] Network [*Defunct*] (EA)
NAN	National Airlines, Inc. [*ICAO designator*] (FAAC)
NAN	National Association of Neighborhoods (EA)
NAN	Network Application Node
NAN	News Agency of Nigeria (EY)
NAN	Nisi Aliter Notetur [*Unless Otherwise Noted*] [*Latin*]
nan	Nisi Aliter Notetur [*Unless It is Otherwise Noted*] [*Latin*] (AD)
Nan	Nitrosamine [*Biochemistry*]
NAN	No Action Necessary [*Military*] (CINC)
NAN	Non-Ammonia-Nitrogen (PDAA)
NAN	North American Nippon Technologies Corp. [*Vancouver Stock Exchange symbol*]
NAN	North Atlantic Network (EA)
NAN	Norton Administrator for Networks [*Computer software*] [*Symantec Corp.*] (PCM)
NaN	Not a Number [*Computer programming*] (BYTE)
NANA	N-Acetylneuraminic Acid [*Also, AcNeu, NAN*] [*Biochemistry*]
nana	N-Acetylneuraminic Acid (AD)
NANA	National Advertising News Association (AD)
NANA	National Advertising Newspaper Association [*Later, SNA*] (EA)
NANA	National Association of Nail Artists [*Later, NANAA*] (EA)
NANA	Newsagents' Association of New South Wales and the Australian Capital Territory,Inc.
NANA	North American Newspaper Alliance
NANA	North American Normande Association (EA)
NANA	Northwest Alaska Native Association [*Later, MA*]
NANAA	National Aesthetician and Nail Artist Association [*Formerly, NANA*] [*WINBA*] [*Absorbed by*] (EA)
NANAC	National Aircraft Noise Abatement Council [*Defunct*] (EA)
NANAC	National Aviation Noise Abatement Council (AD)
NANACA	National Association for Native American Children of Alcoholics (EA)
NANAI	Dutch Actiongroup for Indians of North America
NANASP	National Association of Nutrition and Aging Services Programs (EA)
NAnB	Bard College, Annandale-On-Hudson, NY [*Library symbol Library of Congress*] (LCLS)
NANB	Non-A, Non-B [*Virology*]
NANB	Non-A, Non-B [*Hepatitis*] [*Medicine*] (DAVI)
NANBA	North American National Broadcasters Association (EA)
NANBH	Non-A, Non-B Hepatitis [*Medicine*]
NANBPWC	National Association of Negro Business and Professional Women's Clubs [*Washington, DC*] (EA)
NANBV	Non-A, Non-B Hepatic Virus
NANC	National Association of New Careerists (EA)
NANC	Non-Adrenergic, Non-Cholinergic [*Neurology*]
NANCA	North American Natural Casing Association (EA)
NANCB	National Association of Negotiated Commissioned Brokers [*Defunct*] (EA)
NANCF	North Atlantic Naval Coastal Frontier
NANCI	New Aeronautical and Nautical Chart Investigations (NOAA)
NANCO	National Association of Noise Control Officials (EA)
NANCRFUG	North American NCR [*National Cash Register Co.*] Financial Users Group (EA)
NAND	Naval Ammunition and Net Depot
NAND	Not And [*Logical operator*] [*Computer science*]
NAND	'Not' and 'And' (NITA)
N & A	Nautical & Aviation Publishing Co.
NANDA	North American Nursing Diagnosis Association (EA)

N&CR	[*The*] Nash and Cibinic Report [*A publication*] (AAGC)
N & D	Nodular and Diffuse Lymphoma [*Oncology*]
N & G	Navigation and Guidance [*G & N is preferred*] [*NASA*] (KSC)
N&G	Navigation and Guidance
N & GS	Navigation and Guidance Subsystem [*NASA*] (KSC)
N & H	Nott and Hopkins' Reports [*United States Court of Claims*] [*A publication*] (DLA)
N & H	Nott and Huntington's Reports [*1-7 United States Court of Claims*] [*A publication*] (DLA)
N & Hop	Nott and Hopkins' Reports [*United States Court of Claims*] [*A publication*] (DLA)
N & Hunt	Nott and Huntington's Reports [*1-7 United States Court of Claims*] [*A publication*] (DLA)
N & M	Nevile and Manning's English King's Bench Reports [*A publication*] (DLA)
N & M	November and May [*Denotes semiannual payments of interest or dividends in these months*] [*Business term*]
N & Macn	Neville and Macnamara's Railway and Canal Cases [*1855-1950*] [*A publication*] (DLA)
N & MC	Navy and Marine Corps [*Medal*]
N & Mc	Nott and McCord's South Carolina Reports [*A publication*] (DLA)
N & McC	Nott and McCord's South Carolina Reports [*A publication*] (DLA)
N & MCM	Navy and Marine Corps Medal [*Military decoration*]
N & McN	Neville and Macnamara's Railway and Canal Cases [*1855-1950*] [*A publication*] (DLA)
N & M Mag	Nevile and Manning's English Magistrates' Cases [*A publication*] (DLA)
N & MMC	Nevile and Manning's English Magistrates' Cases [*A publication*] (DLA)
N & P	Nevile and Perry's English King's Bench Reports [*1836-38*] [*A publication*] (DLA)
N & P Mag	Nevile and Perry's English Magistrates' Cases [*1836-37*] [*A publication*] (DLA)
N & PMC	Nevile and Perry's English Magistrates' Cases [*1836-37*] [*A publication*] (DLA)
N & S	Nicholls and Stops' Reports [*1897-1904*] [*Tasmania*] [*A publication*] (DLA)
N & SDCP	Neurological and Sensory Disease Control Program
N & SE	Nacogdoches & Southeastern Railroad (IIA)
N & T	Navigation and Timing
N & T	Nose and Throat [*Medicine*]
N & V	Nausea and Vomiting
N & W	Norfolk & Western Railway Co.
NANE	National Association for Nursery Education [*Later, NAEYC*] (EA)
NANEAP	North Africa, Near East, Asia, and Pacific Region [*Program of ACTION, an independent government agency*]
NANEP	Navy Air Navigation Electronic Project
NANEWS	Naval Aviation News
NANFA	North American Native Fishes Association (EA)
NANFAC	Naval Air Navigation Facility Advisory Committee
NANFORMS	Naval Aviator/Naval Flight Officer Reporting Management System (DNAB)
NAng	Angelica Free Library, Angelica, NY [*Library symbol Library of Congress*] (LCLS)
NANHC	National Association of Neighborhood Health Centers [*Later, NACHC*] (EA)
NANHPH	National Association of Nursing Homes and Private Hospitals [*Australia*]
NANI	National Academy of Nannies, Inc. (EA)
NA/NLP	National Association of Neuro-Linguistic Programming (EA)
NANM	N-Allylnormetazocine [*Biochemistry*]
NANM	N-Allylnormorphine [*Narcotic antagonist*]
NANM	National Association of Negro Musicians (EA)
NANMT	National Association of Nurse Massage Therapists
NANMV	Nandina Mosaic Virus [*Plant pathology*]
NANN	National Association of Neonatal Nurses (EA)
NANNP	Nordic Association of Non-Commercial Phonogram Producers (EA)
nano-	Billionth (IDOE)
NANO	Nanometrics, Inc. [*NASDAQ symbol*] (NQ)
nano	One billionth [*From the Latin nanus*] (WDMC)
NanomtR	Nanometrics, Inc. [*Associated Press*] (SAG)
NANOVA	Nonorthogonal Analysis of Variance (ADA)
nanova	Non-Orthogonal Analysis of Variance (AD)
NANP	National Alliance of Nurse Practitioners (EA)
NANP	National Association of Naturopathic Physicians [*Defunct*] (EA)
NANPA	North American Nature Photography Association
NANPE	National Association of Newspaper Purchasing Executives [*Later, NPMA*] (EA)
NANPMA	North American Nutrition and Preventive Medicine Association (EA)
NANPRH	National Association of Nurse Practitioners in Reproductive Health (EA)
NANR	National Association of Nurse Recruiters [*Later, NAHCR*] (EA)
NANS	National Association for Neighborhood Schools (EA)
NANS	National Association of Non-Smokers (EA)
NANS	National Catholic News Service (EA)
NANS	Naval Air Navigation School
NANS	North American Nietzsche Society (EA)
NANS	North Atlantic and Neighboring Seas
NANT	National Association of Nephrology Technologists (EA)
Nantck	Nantucket Industries, Inc. [*Associated Press*] (SAG)
NANTDDDC	National Association of Negro Tailors, Designers, Dressmakers, and Dry Cleaners (EA)
NANTIS	Nottingham and Nottinghamshire Technical Information Service [*British*] (AD)
NANTS	National Association of Naval Technical Supervisors (EA)

NANU.......... National Association of NIDS [*National Investor Data Service*] Users (EA)

NANVH&SWO... National Assembly of National Voluntary Health and Social Welfare Organizations (AD)

NANWEP...... Navy Numerical Weather Prediction [*Computer system*] [*Control Data Corp.*]

NANWEP...... Navy Numerical Weather Problems [*Group*]

NANWR........ North American Network of Women Runners (EA)

NAO .... Charleston, SC [*Location identifier FAA*] (FAAL)

NAO .... Her Majesty's Nautical Almanac Office [*British*] (PDAA)

NAO .... National Academy of Opticianry (EA)

NAO .... National Accordion Organization [*British*] (DBA)

NAO .... National Association of Outfitters (AD)

NAO .... National Astronomical Observatory [*Japan*]

NAO .... National Audit Office [*British*] (ECON)

NAO .... Naval Audit Office (DNAB)

NAO .... Naval Aviation Observer [*Obsolete*]

NAO .... NOAA [*National Oceanic and Atmospheric Administration*] Administrative Order (USDC)

NAO .... NOAA [*National Oceanic and Atmospheric Administration*] Administrative Order [*Marine science*] (OSRA)

NAO .... Noise Abatement Office (AD)

NAO .... Non-Asbestos Organic [*Friction materials*]

NAO .... Norsar Array Site 01A00 [*Norway*] [*Seismograph station code, US Geological Survey*] (SEIS)

NAO .... North American Airlines, Inc. [*ICAO designator*] (FAAC)

NAO .... North Atlantic Oscillation [*Climatology*]

NAO .... Nurse Aide/Orderly (OICC)

NAOA......... National Apartment Owners Association [*Later, NAA*] (EA)

NAOA......... National Association of Older Americans [*Later, Heartline/National Association of Older Americans*] (EA)

NAOA......... Naval Aviation Observer Aerology (SAA)

NAOA......... Navy Officers Accounts Office (AD)

NAOB......... Naval Aviation Observer Bombardier (MUGU)

NAOBMISB... National Association of Operative Boiler Makers and Iron Ship Builders [*A union*] [*British*]

NAOC .... National Antique Oldsmobile Club (EA)

NAOC .... Naval Aviation Observer Controller (MUGU)

NAOC .... Naval Aviation Officer Candidate

NAOC .... Nigerian Agip Oil Co. (AD)

NAOCJ .... National Association of Operative Carpenters and Joiners [*A union*] [*British*]

NAOCP........ Novice Amateur Operator's Certificate of Proficiency [*Radio*]

NAOE .... National Association for Outdoor Education [*British*]

NAOEJ .... National Association of Oil Equipment Jobbers [*Later, PEI*] (EA)

NAOGE........ National Association of Government Engineers [*Defunct*] (EA)

NAOGTC...... North American Opel GT [*Gran Turismo*] Club (EA)

NaOH .... Sodium Hydroxide

NaOH .... Sodium Hydroxide (AD)

NAOHSM..... National Association of Oil Heating Service Managers (EA)

NAOI .... Naval Aviation Observer Intercept (MUGU)

NAOIG........ North African Inspector General's Section [*World War II*]

NAOJ .... National Astronomical Observatory of Japan

NAOL .... National Association of Orchestra Leaders (EA)

NAOMI........ National Association of Ovulation Method Instructors [*British*] (DBA)

NAON .... National Association of Orthopaedic Nurses (EA)

NAON .... Naval Aviation Observer Navigator (MUGU)

NAOO .... National Association of Optometrists and Opticians (EA)

NAOODA ...... North American Offshore One-Design Association (EA)

NAOP .... National Alliance for Optional Parenthood [*Formerly, NON*]

NAOP .... National Alliance for Optional Parenthood (DAVI)

NAOP .... National Association for Olmsted Parks (EA)

NAOP .... National Association of Operative Plasterers

NAOP .... National Association of Operative Plumbers [*A union*] [*British*]

NAOP .... Nonadditive Operational Project [*Military*]

NAOPL .... National Association of Operative Plasterers' Labourers [*A union*] [*British*]

NAOR......... Naval Aviation Observer RADAR (MUGU)

NAORD....... North African Ordnance Section [*World War II*]

NAORPB ..... North Atlantic Ocean Regional Planning Board [*NATO*]

NAORPG ..... North Atlantic Ocean Regional Planning Group [*NATO*] (NATG)

NAORTS...... Naval Aviation Ordnance Test Station

NAOS .... NASA Aircrew Oxygen System

NAOS .... North Atlantic Ocean Station [*WMO*]

NAOSMM..... National Association of Scientific Material Managers (EA)

NAOSOF...... National Association of Soap Opera Fans

NAOSP .... North Atlantic Ocean Stations Program (MUGU)

NAOSW....... National Association of Oncology Social Workers (EA)

NAOT .... National Association of Organ Teachers [*Later, IAOT*]

NAOT .... National Association of Orthopaedic Technologists (EA)

NAOT .... Naval Air Operational Training

NAOT .... Naval Aviation Observer Tactical (SAA)

NAOTB .... National Association of Off-Track Betting (EA)

NAOTC .... National Association of OTC [*Over-the-Counter*] Companies [*Later, APTC*] (EA)

NAOTC .... National Association of Timetable Collectors (EA)

NAOTC .... Naval Air Operational Training Command

NAOTS .... Naval Aviation Ordnance Test Station

NAOWES..... National Association of Older Worker Employment Services [*Washington, DC*] (EA)

NAP .... Armed Proletarian Nuclei [*Italy*]

NAP .... Bangladesh National Awami Party [*Political party*] (PPW)

nap .... Knapsack (AD)

nap .... Napalm (AD)

NAP .... Napa Resources, Inc. [*Vancouver Stock Exchange symbol*]

NAP .... Napay [*Former USSR Seismograph station code, US Geological Survey Closed*] (SEIS)

nap .... Naphtha (AD)

NAP .... Napier Air Service, Inc. [*ICAO designator*] (FAAC)

NAP .... Naples [*Italy*] [*Airport symbol*] (OAG)

Nap .... Naples (OAG)

Nap .... Napoleon (AD)

NAP .... Napoleon [*or Napoleonic*]

NAP .... Napoleonic Age Philatelists (EA)

NAP .... [*The*] Narragansett Pier Railroad Co., Inc. [*AAR code*]

NAP .... Nasion Pogonion [*Anatomy*] (MAE)

NAP .... National Action Party [*Sierra Leone*] [*Political party*] (EY)

NAP .... National Action Party [*Turkey Political party*] (PD)

NAP .... National Advertising Program

NAP .... National Aerospace Plane (AD)

NAP .... National Apprenticeship Program [*Bureau of Apprenticeship and Training*] [*Department of Labor*]

NAP .... National Archives Publication

NAP .... National Association for the Paralysed (AD)

NAP .... National Association of Parliamentarians (EA)

NAP .... National Association of Planners [*Defunct*] (EA)

NAP .... National Association of Postmasters (NADA)

NAP .... National Association of Postmasters of the United States

NAP .... National Association of Publishers [*Defunct*] (EA)

NAP .... National Association of the Professions (EA)

NAP .... National Audit Plan

NAP .... National Awami Party [*Pakistan*] [*Political party*] (PD)

NAP .... National Awami Party-Bashani [*Bangladesh*] [*Political party*] (FEA)

NAP .... National Processing, Inc. [*NYSE symbol*] (SAG)

NAP .... Native American Program (OICC)

NAP .... Native Americans in Philanthropy

NAP .... Naval Academy Prepatory Student (DNAB)

NAP .... Naval Air Plan (CAAL)

NAP .... Naval Airplane Pusher [*Slang*] (DNAB)

NAP .... Naval Air Priorities

NAP .... Naval Auxiliary Patrol [*British military*] (DMA)

NAP .... Naval Aviation Pilot

nap .... Naval Aviation Pilot (AD)

NAP .... Naval Aviation Plan (NVT)

NAP .... Navigation Analysis Program [*NASA*] (NASA)

NAP .... Neighborhood Action Program [*New York City*] (EA)

NAP .... Neighborhood Awareness Program (AD)

NAP .... Network Access Point [*Telecommunications*]

NAP .... Network Access Pricing [*Telecommunications*] (TEL)

NAP .... Network Access Protocol

NAP .... Neutrophil Activating Protein

NAP .... Neutrophil Alkaline Phosphatase [*An enzyme*]

NAP .... New Age Patriot [*An association*] (EA)

NAP .... New Aspiration Party [*Thailand*]

NAP .... New Associations and Projects [*Formerly, NA*] [*A publication*]

NAP .... Night Attack Program [*Military*]

NAP .... Nitroaminophenol [*Organic chemistry*]

NAP .... Noise Abatement Procedure (AAG)

NAP .... Noise Analysis Program

NAP .... Nomina Anatomica Parisiensia [*Medicine*]

NAP .... Nonacquisition Project [*Military*] (CAAL)

NAP .... Nonadvertising Promotion [*Public relations*] (WDMC)

NAP .... Nonagency Purchase

nap .... Non-Agency Purchase (AD)

NAP .... Nonaggression Pact

NAP .... Nonnuclear Armament Plan (MCD)

NAP .... Normal Administrative Practice

NAP .... Normalized Abundance Pattern [*Geochemistry*]

NAP .... North American Philips Corp. (IAA)

NAP .... North Australia Program

NAP .... Not a Priori

NAP .... Not at Present

nap .... Not at Present (AD)

NAP .... Nuclear-Active Particles [*Astrophysics*]

NAP .... Nuclear Auxiliary Power

NAP .... Nuclei Armati Proletari [*Armed Proletarian Nuclei*] [*Italian*] (PD)

NAP .... Nucleic Acid Phosphorus [*Biochemistry*]

NAP .... Nucleoacidic Protein [*Cytochemistry*]

NAPA .... N-Acetyl-p-aminophenol [*Organic chemistry*]

NAPA .... N-Acetylprocainamide [*Cardiac depressant*]

NAPA .... National Academy of Public Administration (EA)

NAPA .... National Academy of Public Administration

NAPA .... National Agricultural Plastics Association [*Later, ASP*] (EA)

NAPA .... National Agricultural Press Association (EA)

NAPA .... National Amateur Press Association (EA)

NAPA .... National Asphalt Pavement Association (EA)

NAPA .... National Association for Photographic Art [*Canada*] (EAIO)

NAPA .... National Association for the Practice of Anthropology (EA)

NAPA .... National Association of Park Administrators [*British*] (BI)

NAPA .... National Association of Performing Artists

NAPA .... National Association of Polish Americans

NAPA .... National Association of Pro America (EA)

NAPA .... National Association of Purchasing Agents [*Later, NAPM*] (EA)

NAPA .... National Association of the Partners of the Alliance [*Later, Partners of the Americas*] (EA)

NAPA .... National Automotive Parts Association (EA)

NAPA .... National Police Officers Association of America

NAPA .... Native American Press Association (EA)

NAPA .... Network Against Psychiatric Assault (EA)

NAPA .... North American Photonics Association [*Defunct*] (EA)

NAPA .... North American Pizza Association [*Defunct*]
NAPA .... North Atlantic Ports Association (EA)
NAPAAW ...... National Association of Professional Asian-American Women (EA)
NAPAC .... National Arson Prevention and Action Coalition (EA)
NAPAC .... National Association for Professional Associations and Corporations (EA)
NAPAC .... National Association of Paper and Advertising Collectors (EA)
NAPAC .... National Program for Acquisitions and Cataloging [*Library of Congress*]
NAPAEO ...... National Association of Principal Agricultural Education Officers [*British*]
NAPAF .... National Association of Private Art Foundations [*Defunct*] (EA)
NAPAG .... National Academies Policy Advisory Group
NAPall .... North American Palladium [*Associated Press*] (SAG)
napalm .... Naphthene Palmitate (AD)
NAPALM ...... Naphthenic and Palmitic Acids [*Major constituents of flame thrower*]
NAPALM ...... National ADP [*Automatic Data Processing*] Program for AMC Logistics Management [*Army Materiel Command*]
NAPALM ...... National Automatic Data Processing Program for Army Material Command Logistics Management (IAA)
NAPALSA .... National Asian Pacific American Law Student Association (EA)
NAPAMA ..... National Association of Performing Arts Managers and Agents (EA)
NAPAMS ...... Navy Automated Pilot Aptitude Measurement System
NAPAN .... National Association for the Prevention of Addiction to Narcotics [*Later, NADAP*]
NAPAP .... National Acid Precipitation Assessment Program [*Council on Environmental Quality*] [*Washington, DC*]
NAPAP .... Noyaux Armes pour l'Autonomie Populaire [*Armed Cells for Popular Autonomy*] [*France*] (PD)
NAPARE ...... National Association for Perinatal Addiction Research and Education (EA)
NAPAS .... National Association of Protection and Advocacy Systems (EA)
NAPATMO .... NATO Patriot Management Office
NAPAVHEE... National Association of Postsecondary and Adult Vocational Home Economics Educators (EA)
NAPB .... National Association for the Preservation of Baseball (EA)
NAPB .... National Association of Professional Bureaucrats [*Later, INATAPROBU*]
NAPBC .... National Action Plan on Breast Cancer
NAPBC .... Native American Public Broadcasting Consortium (EA)
NAPBFC ...... National Association of Pat Boone Fan Clubs (EA)
NAPBIRT ...... National Association of Professional Band Instrument Repair Technicians (EA)
NAPBL .... National Association of Professional Baseball Leagues (EA)
NAPBN .... National Air Pollution Background Network [*Environmental Protection Agency*] (GFGA)
NAPBTA ...... National American Pit Bull Terrier Association (EA)
NAPC .... National Air Pollution Control (KSC)
NAPC .... National Alliance of Preservation Commissions (EA)
NAPC .... National Assault Prevention Center (EA)
NAPC .... National Association of Parish Councils [*British*] (BI)
NAPC .... National Association of Pastoral Counselors [*Defunct*] (EA)
NAPC .... National Association of Personnel Consultants [*Defunct*] (EA)
NAPC .... National Association of Pet Cemeteries [*Later, IAPC*]
NAPC .... National Association of Plumbing Contractors [*Later, NAPHCC*]
NAPC .... National Association of Precancel Collectors (EA)
NAPC .... Naval Air Photographic Center (DNAB)
NAPC .... Naval Air Priorities Center (DNAB)
NAPC .... Naval Air Propulsion Center [*Trenton, NJ*]
NAPC .... Non-Adherent Peritoneal Cell (PDAA)
napc .... Non-Adherent Peritoneal Cells (AD)
NAPC .... North American Paleontological Convention
NAPCA .... National Air Pollution Control Administration (AAGC)
NAPCA .... National Air Pollution Control Administration [*Obsolete*]
NAPCA .... National Association of Pension Consultants and Administrators [*Atlanta, GA*] (EA)
NAPCA .... National Association of Pipe Coating Applicators (EA)
NAPCA .... National Association of Professional Contracts Administrators [*Later, NCMA*] (EA)
NAPCA .... National Association of Professional Contracts Administrators (AAGC)
NAPCA .... National Automatic Pistol Collectors Association (EA)
NAPCA .... North American Poultry Cooperative Association [*Defunct*] (EA)
NAPCAE ...... National Association for Public Continuing and Adult Education (EA)
NAPCE .... National Association of Pastoral Care in Education [*British*] (DBA)
NAPCE .... National Association of Professors of Christian Education (EA)
NAPCMM-ELCA... Native American Program Commission for Multicultural Ministries of ELCA [*Evangelical Lutheran Church in America*] (EA)
NAPC/MS .... Naval Air Propulsion Center Measurement and Information Systems Department [*Trenton, NJ*]
Napco .... Napco Security Systems, Inc. [*Associated Press*] (SAG)
NAPCOR ...... National Association for Plastic Container Recovery (EA)
NAPC-PE ...... Naval Air Propulsion Center Propulsion Engineering Department [*Trenton, NJ*]
NAPCR .... National Association for Puerto Rican Civil Rights
NAPCRG ...... North American Primary Care Research Group (EA)
NAPCRO ...... National Association of Police Community Relations Officers (EA)
NAPCS .... National Association of Postpartum Care Services (PAZ)
NAPCTAC .... National Air Pollution Control Techniques Advisory Committee [*Environmental Protection Agency*] (GFGA)
NAPCU .... Northwest Association of Private Colleges and Universities [*Library network*] (EA)
NAPCWA ..... National Association of Public Child Welfare Administrators (EA)
NAPD .... National Association of Pharmaceutical Distributors [*British*] (BI)
NAPD .... National Association of Plastics Distributors (EA)
NAPD .... National Association of Police Driving (AD)

NAPD .... National Association of Precollege Directors (EA)
NAPDA .... North American Professional Driver's Association [*Defunct*] (EA)
NAPDD......... Non-Acquisition Program Definition Document [*Navy*] (DOMA)
NAPDEA ...... North American Professional Driver Education Association (EA)
NAPE .... Naphthenic-Palmitic Acid [*Mixture used in flame-throwing weapons and bombs*] [*Also, NAPALM*] (VNW)
NAPE .... National Alliance of Postal Employees [*Later, NAPFE*]
NAPE .... National Association of Partners in Education
NAPE .... National Association of Partners in Education
NAPE .... National Association of Port Employers [*British*]
NAPE .... National Association of Power Engineers (EA)
NAPE .... National Association of Primary Education [*British*] (DBA)
NAPE .... National Association of Private Enterprise [*Fort Worth, TX*] (EA)
NAPE .... National Association of Professional Educators (EA)
NAPE .... National Association of Professional Engravers (EA)
NAPE .... Nuclear Attack Preparedness Evaluation
NAPEC .... Naval Ammunition Production Engineering Center
NAPECW ..... National Association for Physical Education of College Women [*Later, NAPEHE*] (EA)
NAPEDNC ... National Association of Political Ex-Deportees of the Nazi Camps [*Italy Political party*] (EAIO)
NAPEGG....... Association of Professional Engineers, Geologists & Geophysicists of the Northwest Territories (AC)
NAPEHE ...... National Association for Physical Education in Higher Education (EA)
NAPEM .... National Association of Public Exposition Managers [*Later, HGSEI*] (EA)
NAPENA ...... National Association of Public Employer Negotiators and Administrators [*Later, NAPPENA*] (EA)
Na Pent ...... Sodium Pentothal [*Thiopental Sodium*] [*A brand name*] [*Pharmacology*] (DAVI)
NAPEP .... National Association of Planners, Estimators, and Progressmen (EA)
NAPET .... National Association of Photo Equipment Technicians (EA)
NAPEX .... National Philatelic Exhibition
NAPF .... National Association of Pension Funds [*British*] (DI)
NAPF .... National Association of Petroleum Funds [*British*]
NAPF .... National Association of Plastic Fabricators (EA)
NAPF .... Naval Aviation Publication Facility
NAPF .... Nonappropriated Funds (DNAB)
NAPF .... Nuclear Age Peace Foundation (EA)
NAPFA .... National Association of Personal Financial Advisors (EA)
NAPFE .... National Alliance of Postal and Federal Employees (EA)
NAPFM .... National Association of Packaged Fuel Manufacturers [*Defunct*] (EA)
NAPFR .... National Association of Professional Fund Raisers (EA)
NAPG .... National Association of Professional Gardeners [*Later, PGMS*]
NAP(G) .... Naval Aviation Pilot (Glider)
NaPG .... Sodium Pregnanediol Glucuronide [*Medicine*] (DMAA)
NAPGC .... National Association of Public Golf Courses [*British*] (BI)
NAPGCM ...... National Association of Private Geriatric Care Managers (EA)
NAPGCW ...... National Association of Plasters, Granolithic, and Cement Workers [*A union*] [*British*]
NAPH .... Naphtha (ADA)
naph .... Naphtha (AD)
naph .... Naphthyl (AD)
NAPH .... Naphthyl [*Organic chemistry*] (MAE)
NAPH .... National Association of Professors of Hebrew (EA)
NAPH .... National Association of Public Hospitals (EA)
NAPH .... National Association of the Physically Handicapped (EA)
NAPH .... Nicotinamide Adenine Dinucleotide Phosphate [*An enzyme*] (DMAA)
NAPHA .... National Amusement Park Historical Association (EA)
NAPhA .... North American Photonics Association (EA)
NAPH & MSC... National Association of Plumbing, Heating, and Mechanical Service Contractors [*British*] (DBA)
NAPHC .... National Association of Plumbing/Heating/Cooling Contractors (AD)
NAPHCC ...... National Association of Plumbing-Heating-Cooling Contractors [*Formerly, NAPC*] (EA)
NAPHT .... National Association of Patients on Hemodialysis and Transplantation [*Later, AAKP*] (EA)
NAPI .... National Appaloosa Pony (EA)
NAPI .... National Association of the Pet Industry [*Defunct*] (EA)
NAPI .... Naval Aeronautical Publications Index (DNAB)
NAPIA .... National Affiliate of Printing Industries of America (AD)
NAPIA .... National Association of Public Insurance Adjusters [*Baltimore, MD*] (EA)
NAPIAP .... National Agricultural Pesticide Impact Assessment Program [*Department of Agriculture*]
NAPIC .... National Association of Private Industry Councils [*Washington, DC*] (EA)
NAPIL .... National Association for Public Interest Law (EA)
NAPIM .... National Association of Printing Ink Manufacturers (EA)
NAPJPO .... National Aerospace Plane Joint Programs Office
NAPL .... National Air Photo Library [*Canada*] (PDAA)
NAPL .... National Association of Photolithographers (IAA)
NAPL .... National Association of Police Laboratories (EA)
NAPL .... National Association of Printers and Lithographers (EA)
NAPL .... Nonaqueous Phase Liquid [*Chemistry*]
NAPL .... Nonaqueous-Phase Liquid [*Environmental Science*]
NAPLIB .... National Association Aerial of Photographic Libraries [*British*] (DBA)
NAPLO .... National Association of Power Loom Overlookers [*British*] (DBA)
NAPLP .... National Association of Para-Legal Personnel (AD)
NAP-LP .... National Association of Para-Legals Personnel (EA)
NAPLPS .... North American Presentation Level Protocol Standard (DOM)
NAPLPS .... North American Presentation Level Protocol Syntax [*Computer display system*] [*Pronounced "naplips"*]
NAPM .... National Association of Paper Merchants [*British*]
NAPM .... National Association of Pattern Manufacturers [*LA PPTBA*] (EA)

NAPM	National Association of Perry Makers [*British*] (DBA)
NAPM	National Association of Pharmaceutical Manufacturers (EA)
NAPM	National Association of Photographic Manufacturers (EA)
NAPM	National Association of Punch Manufacturers (EA)
NAPM	National Association of Purchasing Management (EA)
NAP-M	National Awami Party-Muzaffar [*Bangladesh*] [*Political party*] (FEA)
NAPMA	NATO AEWC [*Airborne Early Warning and Control*] Program Management Agency
NAPMDAC...	National Air Pollution Manpower Development Advisory Committee [*Terminate d, 1976*] [*HEW*] (EGAO)
NAPMG	North African Provost Marshal General [*World War II*]
NAPMM	National Association of Produce Market Managers [*Hartford, CT*] (EA)
NAPMO	NATO Airborne Early Warning and Control Programme Management Organization [*Brunssum, Netherlands*]
NAPMW	National Association of Professional Mortgage Women
NAPN	National Association of Physician Nurses (EA)
NAPN	Native American Policy Network (EA)
NAPN	Native Authority Public Notice [*Nigeria*] [*A publication*] (ILCA)
NAPN	North American Poetry Network (EA)
NAPNAP.......	National Association of Pediatric Nurse Associates and Practitioners (EA)
NAPNE	National Association for Practical Nurse Education (DAVI)
NAPNES	National Association for Practical Nurse Education and Service (EA)
NAPNM	National Association of Pipe Nipple Manufacturers [*Defunct*] (EA)
NAPNOC	Neighborhood Arts Program National Organizing Committee (EA)
NAPNSC.......	National Association of Private, Nontraditional Schools and Colleges (EA)
NAPNW........	Nurses Alliance for the Prevention of Nuclear War [*Defunct*] (EA)
NAPO	NASA Pasadena Office
NAPO	National Association of Performing Artists (AD)
NAPO	National Association of Pizza Operators [*Commercial firm*] (EA)
NAPO	National Association of Police Organizations (EA)
NAPO	National Association of Pool Owners
NAPO	National Association of Prison Officers [*British*] (DI)
NAPO	National Association of Probation Officers [*British*] (DI)
NAPO	National Association of Professional Organizers (EA)
NAPO	National Association of Property Owners (EA)
NAPO	National Association of Purchasing Agents (AD)
NAPO	NATO Airborne Early Warning Program Office (NATG)
NAPO	Naval Air Priorities Office
NAPO	New Afrikan People's Organization (EA)
NAPO	United National Association of Post Office Craftsmen [*Later, APWU*]
NAPOG........	Naval Airborne Project Press Operations Group [*Hickam AFB, HI*]
NAPOLI........	National Politics [*Behavioral science game*]
NAPOMHWMGL...	National Association of Post Office Mail Handlers, Watchmen, Messengers, and Group Leaders [*Later, NPOMHWMGL*] (EA)
NAPOTS.......	National Aboriginal Project Officer Training Scheme [*Australia*]
NAPP	National Association of Patient Participation [*British*] (DBA)
NAPP	National Association of Play Publishers
NAPP	National Association of Poultry Packers Ltd. [*British*] (BI)
NAPP	National Association of Priest Pilots (EA)
NAPP	National Association of Printing Purchasers [*Defunct*] (EA)
NAPP	National Association of Private Process Servers (EA)
NAPP	Native American Publishing Program [*of Harper & Row, Publishers, Inc.*]
NAPP	Naval Aviation Preparatory Program
NAPP	Neighborhood Adult Participation Project
NAPP	Net Aerial Primary Productivity [*Forestry*]
NAPP	Nonattainment Plan Provision [*Environmental Protection Agency*]
NAPPA	National Association of Physical Plant Administrators of Universities and Colleges [*Later, Association of Physical Plant Administrators of Universities and Colleges*] (EA)
NAPPA	National Association of Pupil Personnel Administrators [*Later, NAPSA*] (EA)
NAPPB	National Association of Professional Print Buyers (EA)
NAPPC	National Association of Party Plan Companies [*Defunct*] (EA)
NAPPENA....	National Association of Public and Private Employer Negotiators and Administrators (EA)
NAPPH	National Association of Private Psychiatric Hospitals (EA)
Nappie	Neuilly, Auteil, and Passy [*Elegant Paris neighborhoods; the term, Nappie, is used as a nickname for French Yuppies*]
Nappies	New Age Professional People in Esoteric Studies [*Lifestyle classification*]
NAPPO	National Association of Plant Patent Owners (EA)
Nap Pres	Napier. Prescription [*A publication*] (ILCA)
NAPPS	National Association for the Preservation and Perpetuation of Storytelling (EA)
NAPPS	National Association of Private Placement Syndicators [*Later, California Investment Real Estate Forum*] (EA)
NAPPS	National Association of Professional Process Servers (EA)
NAPPS	North American Pediatric Pseudo-Obstruction Society (EA)
na pr	Na Priklad [*For Example*] [*Czech*] (AD)
NAPR	NASA Procurement Regulation
NAPR	National Association for Pastoral Renewal [*Defunct*] (EA)
NAPR	National Association of Park Rangers (EA)
NAPR	National Association of Physician Recruiters (EA)
NAPR	National Association of Publishers' Representatives (EA)
NAPR	NATO Armaments Planning Review (NATG)
NAPRA	National Association of Progressive Radio Announcers (EA)
NAPRA	New Age Publishing and Retailing Alliance (EA)
NAPRALERT...	Natural Products Alert [*University of Illinois at Chicago*] [*Information service or system*] (IID)
NAPRC	National Association for the Prevention of Rape by Castration (AD)
NAPRCR	National Association for Puerto Rican Civil Rights (EA)
NAPRE	National Association Practical Refrigerating Engineers [*Later, RETA*] (EA)
NAPRFMR...	National Association of Private Residential Facilities for the Mentally Retarded (EA)
NaPro	NaPro BioTherapeutics, Inc. [*Associated Press*] (SAG)
NaProBio	NaPro BioTherapeutics, Inc. [*Associated Press*] (SAG)
NAPRS	National Airspace Performance Reporting System [*Aviation*] (FAAC)
NAPRW.........	Northwest African Photographic Reconnaissance Wing [*World War II*]
NAPS	National Alliance of Postal Supervisors (AD)
NAPS	National Association for Professional Saleswomen (EA)
NAPS	National Association of Pet Sitters (EA)
NAPS	National Association of Postal Supervisors (EA)
NAPS	National Association of Premenstrual Syndrome [*British*] (DBA)
NAPS	National Association of Presbyterian Scouters (EA)
NAPS	National Association of Private Secretaries [*British*] (BI)
NAPS	National Association of Psychiatric Survivors (EA)
NAPS	National Auxiliary Publications Service [*American Society for Information Science*]
NAPS	Nationwide Association of Preserving Specialists [*British*] (DBA)
NAPS	Naval Academy Preparatory School
NAPS	Navy Acquisition Procedures Supplement [*A publication*] (AAGC)
NAPS	Nerve Agent Pre-Treatment Set [*A cholinergic drug*] [*Used for protective immunization by the military*]
NAPS	Night Aerial Photographic System
NAPS	Nimbus Automatic Programming System (IEEE)
NAPS	Nissan Air Pollution System (AD)
NAPS	Nonspecific Air Pollution Syndrome
NAPS	North American Patristic Society (EA)
NAPS	North American Precis Syndicate
NAPS	North American Pro Series [*Auto racing*]
NAPS	North Anna Power Station [*Virginia*] [*Nuclear energy*] (NRCH)
NAPSA	National Appliance Parts Suppliers Association (EA)
NAPSA	National Association of Pretrial Service Agencies (AD)
NAPSA	National Association of Public Service Advertisers [*British*] (DBA)
NAPSA	National Association of Pupil Services Administrators (EA)
NAPSAA	National Association of Public School Adult Administrators [*Later, NAPSAE*]
NAPSAC	International Association of Parents and Professionals for Safe Alternatives in Childbirth [*Association retains acronym of its former name*] (EA)
NAPSAC	Naval Atomic Planning, Support, and Capabilities Report (NG)
NAPSAE.......	National Association for Public School Adult Educators [*Later, NAPCAE*] (EA)
NAPSAP......	Naval Airship Program for Sizing and Performance (MCD)
Nap's bones...	Napier's Bones [*First slide rule*] (AD)
NAPSEC	National Association of Private Schools for Exceptional Children (EA)
NAPSEO	National Association of Public Sector Equal Opportunity Officers
NAPSG	National Association of Principals of Schools for Girls (EA)
NAPSIC	North American Power Systems Interconnection Committee [*US and Canada*] [*Electric power*]
NAPSIS	Navy Air Pollution Source Information System
NAPSLO	National Association of Professional Surplus Lines Offices (EA)
NAPSOE	National Association of Public Service Organization Executives (EA)
NAPSS	National Association of Professional Secretarial Services [*Later, PASS*] (EA)
NAPSS	Numerical Analysis Problem Solving System
NAPSV	National Association of Private Security Vaults (EA)
Napt	Napton's Reports [*4 Missouri*] [*A publication*] (DLA)
NAPT	National Association for Poetry Therapy (EA)
NAPT	National Association for Pupil Transportation (EA)
NAPT	National Association for the Prevention of Tuberculosis [*British*] (DI)
NAPT	National Association of Physical Therapists (EA)
NAPT	Naval Air Primary Training
NAPT	Nordic Association of Plumbers and Tinsmiths (EAIO)
NAPTC	Naval Air Primary Training Command
NAPTC	Naval Air Propulsion Test Center [*Later, NAPC*]
NAPTCA	National Alliance for the Prevention and Treatment of Child Abuse (EA)
NAPTC-AED...	Naval Air Propulsion Test Center - Aeronautical Engine Department
NAPTC-ATD...	Naval Air Propulsion Test Center - Aeronautical Turbine Department
NAPTCC	National Association of Psychiatric Treatment Centers for Children (EA)
NAPTC-OP ...	Naval Air Propulsion Test Center - Operations and Plant Engineering Department
NAPTC-PE...	Naval Air Propulsion Test Center - Propulsion Technology and Project EngineeringDepartment
NAPTCRO.....	Naval Air Primary Training Command Regional Office
NAPTDC......	National Association of Professional Truck Driving Champions (EA)
NAPTE	National Association of Part-Time and Temporary Employees
NaPTEC.......	National Primary Teacher Education Conference (AIE)
NAPTIC	National Air Pollution Technical Information Center [*of National Air Pollution Control Administration*] [*Also, APTIC*] (DIT)
Napton	Napton's Reports [*4 Missouri*] [*A publication*] (DLA)
NAPTR	National Association of Property Tax Representatives [*Defunct*] (EA)
NAPTS	National Association of Public Television Stations [*Later, APB*] (EA)
NAPU	National Association of Professional Upholsterers [*Defunct*] (EA)
NAPU	Nuclear Auxiliary Power Unit
NAPUBFAC...	Naval Air Publication Facility (MCD)
NAPUS	National Association of Postmasters of the United States (EA)
NAPUS	Nuclear Auxiliary Power Unit System
NAPV	National Association of Prison Visitors [*British*] (BI)
NAPVD..........	National Association for the Prevention of Venereal Disease (AD)
NAPVI..........	National Association for Parents of the Visually Impaired (EA)
NAPVO..........	National Association of Passenger Vessel Owners (EA)
NAPW..........	National Association of Personnel Workers (EA)

NAPWA........	National Association of People with AIDS (EA)
NAPWDA.....	North American Police Work Dog Association (EA)
NAPWPT......	National Association of Professional Word Processing Technicians [*Philadelphia, PA*] (EA)
NAQ	Narssarssuaq [*Denmark*] [*Geomagnetic observatory code*]
NAQAP........	National Association of Quality Assurance Professionals (EA)
NAQDC........	National Air Quality Data Center [*Australia*]
NAQF	North Atlantic Quality Figure
NAQI	National Air Quality Index (AD)
NAQMC.......	North African Quartermaster Section [*World War II*]
NAQP	National Association of Quick Printers (EA)
NAQUADAT...	National Water Quality Data Bank [*Environment Canada*] [*Information service or system*] (IID)
NAR	Air Continental, Inc. [*ICAO designator*] (FAAC)
NAR	Nagase Analbuminemia Rat
NAR	Nara [*Japan*] [*Seismograph station code, US Geological Survey*] (SEIS)
NAR	Narcotic (ROG)
NAR	Nare [*Colombia*] [*Airport symbol*] (OAG)
Nar	Narragansett (AD)
NAR	Narration [*Films, television, etc.*]
NAR	Narrow (AAG)
nar	Narrow (AD)
NAR	Nasal Airway Resistance [*Medicine*]
NAR	National Archives and Records Service, Washington, DC [*OCLC symbol*] (OCLC)
NAR	National Asbestos Registry [*Environmental Protection Agency*] (GFGA)
NAR	National Association of Realtors (EA)
NAR	National Association of Rocketry (EA)
NAR	Naval Air Reserve
NAR	Naval Auxiliary Reserve
NAR	Naval Research and Development
NAR	Navy Ammunition Reclassification
NAR	Nelson Aldrich Rockefeller (AD)
NAR	Neo Aristero Revma [*Greece*] [*Political party*] (ECED)
NAR	Net Advertising Revenue [*Television*] [*British*]
NAR	Net Assimilation Rate [*Botany*]
nar	Net Assimilation Rate (AD)
NAR	No Action [*or Answer*] Required (NVT)
nar	No Apparent Rate (AD)
NAR	Noise-Adding Radiometer
NAR	Nordic Association for Rehabilitation [*Denmark*] (EAIO)
NAR	Nordiska Akademiker Radet [*Nordic Academic Council - NAC*] [*Defunct*] (EA)
NAR	North American Review [*A publication*] (BRI)
NAR	North American Rockwell Corp. [*Later, Rockwell International Corp.*] (MCD)
NAR	North American Route [*Aviation*]
NAR	North American Royalties (AD)
NAR	North Australia Railway
NAR	Northern Alberta Railways Co. [*AAR code*]
NAR	Nose Alone Reference [*Aviation*] (MCD)
NAR	Not According to Routine
NAR	Notice of Ammunition Reclassification [*Navy*] (NG)
NAR	Nuclear Acoustic Resonance
NAR	Nuclear Androgen Receptor [*Endocrinology*]
NAR	Nuclear Assessment Routine (MCD)
NAR	Nuclei Armati Rivoluzionari [*Armed Revolutionary Nuclei*] [*Italian*] (PD)
NAR	Nucleic Acids Research [*A publication*]
NAR	Numerical Analysis Research (MCD)
NARA	Narcotics Addict Rehabilitation Act [*1966*]
NARA	National Air Resources Act (GFGA)
NARA	National Alliance for Rural Action (EA)
NARA	National Aquatic Resources Agency [*Sri Lanka*] [*Marine science*] (OSRA)
NARA	National Archives and Records Administration [*Independent government agency*] [*Formerly, NARS*]
NARA	National Association for the Rescue of Animals [*British*] (DI)
NARA	National Association of Recovered Alcoholics [*Defunct*] (EA)
NARA	National Association of Rehabilitation Agencies (EA)
NARA	National Association of Republican Attorneys (EA)
NARA	National Association of Review Appraisers (EA)
NARA	Naval Aircraft Restorers Association (EA)
NARA	Nippon Australian Relations Agreement (AD)
NARA	North American Radio Archives (EA)
NARA	North American Radon Association [*Defunct*] (EA)
NARA	North American Regional Alliance of IATA [*International Amateur Theatre Association*] (EA)
NARA	Northern Auto Racing Association [*Sanctioning organization*]
NARAA........	National Association of Recruitment Advertising Agencies [*Defunct*] (EA)
NARACC......	National Association for Research and Action in Community Care [*British*] (DI)
NARACS......	National Radio Communications System [*FAA*] (TAG)
NARAD........	Naval Air Research and Development (MUGU)
NARAD........	Navy Research and Development (AD)
NARADCOM...	Natick Research and Development Command [*Army*]
NARAG........	National Association of Ratepayers' Action Groups [*British*] (DI)
NARAL........	National Abortion Rights Action League (EA)
NARAL........	National Association for the Repeal of Abortion Laws
NARAL........	Net Advertising Revenue after Levy [*Television*] [*British*]
NARA/MU	National Association of Review Appraisers and Mortgage Underwriters (EA)

NARANEXOS...	Name, Rate, Service Number, and Expiration of Obligated Service [*Navy*]
NARANO	Name, Rate, and Service Number [*Navy*]
NARAS........	National Academy of Recording Arts and Sciences (EA)
NARASO	Nevada Association Race and Sports Book Operators (EA)
NARASPO	Navy Regional Airspace Officer (MUGU)
NARAT	NATO Request for Air Transport Support [*Military*]
NARATE	Navy Automatic RADAR Test Equipment (KSC)
NARATE	Northrop Automatic RADAR Test System (SAA)
NARAVA.......	National Archives and Records Administration Volunteer Association (EA)
NARB	Narcotic Addict Rehabilitation Branch [*National Institute of Mental Health*]
NARB	National Advertising Review Board [*New York, NY*] (EA)
NARB	National Assembly of Religious Brothers (EA)
NARB	National Assocation of Radio Broadcasters (NTCM)
NARB	National Association for Regional Ballet [*Later, RDA*]
NARB	National Association of Referees in Bankruptcy [*Later, National Conference of Bankruptcy Judges*] (EA)
NARB	National Association of Retired Bankers [*Later, RBA*] (EA)
NARB	Navy Art Review Board (DNAB)
NARB	Nonazeotropic Refrigerant Blend
NARBA	North American Regional Broadcasting Agreement [*To minimize interference between AM stations*]
NARBC........	National Angora Rabbit Breeders Club (EA)
NARBL........	Net Advertising Revenue before Levy [*Television*] [*British*]
NARBW.......	National Association of Railway Business Women (EA)
narc	Narcotic (AD)
NARC	Narcotics [*FBI standardized term*]
narc	Narcotics Agent (AD)
NARC	Narcotism [*Chemical dependency*] (DAVI)
NARC	National Agricultural Research Center
NARC	National Amateur Retriever Club (EA)
NARC	National Archives and Records Service (AD)
NARC	National Army Revolutionary Committee [*or Council*] [*Laos*]
NARC	National Association for Retarded Children (AEBS)
NARC	National Association for Retarded Citizens [*Later, ARC*] (EA)
NARC	National Association of Regional Councils (AD)
NARC	National Association of Retired Catholics (AD)
NARC	Naval Air Research Center (DNAB)
NARC	Naval Air Reserve Center (DNAB)
NARC	Naval Alcohol Rehabilitation Center (DNAB)
NARC	Nonautomatic Relay Center (AABC)
NARC	North American Riders Club (EA)
NARC	North American Rockwell Corp. [*Later, Rockwell International Corp.*] (MCD)
NARC	Northern Automobile Racing Club [*Sanctioning organization*]
NARC	Nuclear Age Resource Center (EA)
NARCA........	National Antidrug Reorganization and Coordination Act
NARCE	National Association of Retired Civil Employees [*Later, NARFE*] (EA)
NARCF........	National Association of Retail Clothiers and Furnishers [*Later, MRA*] (EA)
NARCINT.....	Narcotics Intelligence [*Military*] (ADDR)
NARCL........	Nuclear Accident Response Capability Listing (MCD)
narco	Narcolepsy [*Neurology*] (DAVI)
narco	Narcotic (AD)
NARCO........	Narcotics Commission [*United Nations*] (AD)
NARCO........	Narcotics Commission [*United Nations*]
narco	Narcotics Hospital (DAVI)
narco	Narcotics Officer (AD)
narco	Narcotics Treatment Center (DAVI)
NARCO........	National Aeronautical Corp. (MCD)
narcocard.....	Narcotic-Addict Registration Card (AD)
narcodollars...	Narcotic Traffic Dollars (AD)
NARCOG......	Narcotics Coordination Group [*CIA*]
NARCOM......	Narration, Commentary [*Motion pictures*]
NARCOM......	North Atlantic Relay Communication Satellite
Narconon.....	Narcotics Anonymous [*An association*] (AD)
Nar Conv	Nares' Penal Convictions [*1815*] [*A publication*] (DLA)
NAR CORP...	North American Rockwell Corp. [*Later, Rockwell International Corp.*]
narcos	Narcotics (AD)
narcos	Narcotics Police Officers (AD)
narcot	Narcotic (AD)
narcotest	Narcotics Test (AD)
Narcotics L Bull...	Narcotics Law Bulletin [*A publication*] (DLA)
narco-traf.....	Narcotics Traffick (AD)
narcs	Narcotics (AD)
narcs	Narcotics Agents (AD)
narcs	Narcotics Hospital (AD)
narcs	Narcotics Officers (AD)
narcs	Narcotics Treatment Centers (AD)
NARCU........	National Association of Railroad and Utility Commissioners (NTCM)
NARCUP	National Association for Retired Credit Union People (EA)
NArd	Ardsley Public Library, Ardsley, NY [*Library symbol Library of Congress*] (LCLS)
NARD	National Association of Regimental Drummers (AD)
NARD	National Association of Retail Druggists (EA)
NARD	National Association of Rudimental Drummers [*Defunct*]
NARD	Navy Alcohol Rehabilitation Drydock (DNAB)
nard	Spikenard (AD)
NARDA	National Appliance and Radio TV Dealers Association (IAA)
NARDA	National Association of Retail Dealers of America (EA)
NARDA/MU	Naval Air Research and Development Activities (SAA)
NARDAC	Navy Regional Data Automation Center

NARDACWASHDC... Navy Regional Data Automation Center, Washington, DC (DNAB)
NArdCG........ CIBA-GEIGY Corp., Corporate Library, Ardsley, NY [Library symbol] [Library of Congress] (LCLS)
NARDELOG...... Navy Rapid Delivery Logistics (AFIT)
NARDET....... Naval Air Reserve Detachment (DNAB)
NARDIC........ Navy Research and Development Information Center
NARDIS........ Navy Automated Research and Development Information System [Later, NAVWUIS]
Nar Div........ Narodni Divadlo [National Theater] [Czechoslavakia] (AD)
NARDIV........ Naval Air Reserve Divisions
NARDIV(FA)... Naval Air Reserve Division (Fleet Air) (DNAB)
NARDV........ National Association Rainbow Division Veterans (EA)
NARE.......... National Association for Remedial Education [British]
NARE.......... North Atlantic Regional Experiment [Ozone measurement]
NAREA........ National Association of Real Estate Appraisers (EA)
Na_reab........ Sodium Reabsorption Rate [Biochemistry] (DAVI)
NAREB........ National Association of Real Estate Boards [Later, National Association of Realtors] (EA)
NAREB........ National Association of Real Estate Brokers
NAREBB...... National Association of Real Estate Buyer Brokers (EA)
NAREC........ National Association of Real Estate Companies (EA)
NAREC........ Naval Research Electronic Computer
narec.......... Naval Research Electronic Computer (AD)
NAREE........ National Association of Real Estate Editors (EA)
NAREIF........ National Association of Real Estate Investment Funds [Later, NAREIT] (EA)
NAREIT........ National Association of Real Estate Investment Trusts (EA)
NARELLO...... National Association of Real Estate License Law Officials (EA)
NAREMCO...... National Records Management Council (EA)
NARESU........ Naval Air Reserve Unit (DNAB)
NARETPA...... National Agricultural Research, Extension, and Teaching Policy Act of 1977
NARETU........ Naval Air Reserve Electronics Training Unit (DNAB)
NARF.......... National Association of Rehabilitation Facilities (EA)
NARF.......... National Association of Retail Furnishers (AD)
NARF.......... Native American Rights Fund (EA)
NARF.......... Natural Axial Resonant Frequency (PDAA)
narf.......... Natural Axial-Resonant Frequency (AD)
NARF.......... Naval Aerospace Research Facility
NARF.......... Naval Air Reservé Force
NARF.......... Naval Air Rework Facility
NARF.......... Navy Arctic Research Facility
NARF.......... Nuclear Aerospace Research Facility (IEEE)
NARF.......... Nuclear Aircraft Research Facility (AD)
NARFE........ National Association of Retired Federal Employees (EA)
NARFFO...... Naval Air Rework Facility Field Office (DNAB)
NARFS........ Naval Air Reserve Force Squadron (DNAB)
NARGA........ National Association of Retail Grocers of Australia (AD)
NARGOM..... North American Research Group on Management (PDAA)
NARGUS..... National Association of Retail Grocers of the United States [Later, NGA] (EA)
NARHA........ North American Riding for the Handicapped Association (EA)
NARHC........ National Association of River and Harbor Contractors [Later, NADC] (EA)
NARHS........ National Auto Racing Historical Society (EA)
NARI.......... National Agriculture Research Institute (WDAA)
NARI.......... National AIDS Research Institute [India]
NARI.......... National Alliance for Reduction of Imprisonment [Defunct] (EA)
NARI.......... National Association of Recycling Industries [Later, ISRI] (EA)
NARI.......... National Association of Rehabilitation Instructors (EA)
NARI.......... National Association of Residents and Interns (EA)
NARI.......... National Association of the Remodeling Industry (EA)
NARI.......... National Atmospheric Research Institute (AD)
NARI.......... Native American Research Institute (AD)
NARI.......... Nuclear Aerospace Research Institute [Air Force]
NARIC........ National Academic Recognition Information Centre (AIE)
NARIC........ National Rehabilitation Information Center (EA)
NARICM...... National Association of Retail Ice Cream Manufacturers [Later, NICYRA] (EA)
Nar Inv........ Narcotics Investigation (AD)
NARISCO...... North American Rockwell Information Systems Co.
NARIST....... Naristillae [Nasal Drops] [Pharmacy]
narist.......... Naristillae [Nasal Drops] [Latin] (AD)
NARK.......... Nikolai Andreyvich Rimsky-Korsakov (AD)
Narkomvneshtorg... Narodny Komissariat Vneshney Torgovli [People's Commissariat of Foreign Trade] [Russian] (AD)
NARKOMVNUDEL... Narodnyi Komissariat Vnutrennikh Del [People's Commissariat of Internal Affairs (1917-1946)] [Also known as NKVD Soviet secret police organization]
NARL.......... National Aero Research Laboratory [Canada] (PDAA)
NARL.......... Naval Arctic Research Laboratory
NARL.......... No Adverse Response Level [Medicine] (HCT)
NARM.......... National Association of Recording Merchandisers (EA)
NARM.......... National Association of Relay Manufacturers (EA)
NARM.......... National Association of Restaurant Managers [Scottsdale, AZ] (EA)
NARM.......... National Association of Retail Merchants (AD)
NARM.......... National Association of Retail Merchants (NADA)
NARM.......... Naturally Occurring or Accelerator-Produced Radioactive Material
NARM.......... Naval Resource Model (MCD)
N-arm.......... Nuclear Armament (AD)
NARMC........ National Association of Regional Media Centers (EA)
NARMC........ Naval Aerospace and Regional Medical Center [Bureau of Medicine]
NARMCO...... National Research and Manufacturing Co. (AD)
N-armed...... Nuclear-Armed (AD)

NARMFD...... National Association of Retail Meat and Food Dealers
NARMH........ National Association for Rural Mental Health (EA)
NARMIC...... National Action/Research on the Military Industrial Complex (EA)
NArmN........ North Castle Library, Armonk, NY [Library symbol Library of Congress] (LCLS)
NARMP........ National Antibacterial Residue Minimization Program [Australia]
NARMPU...... Naval Air Reserve Mobile Photographic Unit (DNAB)
NARMU........ Naval Air Reserve Maintenance Units
NARN.......... National Association of Registered Nurses (EA)
NARND........ National Association of Radio News Directors (IAA)
NARO.......... National Agricultural Research Organization [Netherlands] (ECON)
NARO.......... National Association of Reimbursement Officers [Washington, DC] (EA)
NARO.......... National Association of Royalty Owners (EA)
NARO.......... North American Regional Office (EA)
NAROCTESTSTA... Naval Air Rocket Test Station
NARP.......... National Administrative Rehabilitation Programme [United Nations program]
NARP.......... National Association for Registered Plans (EA)
NARP.......... National Association of Railroad Passengers (EA)
NARP.......... Neurogenic Muscle Weakness, Ataxia, and Retinitis Pigmentosa [Medicine]
NARP.......... New Australian Republican Party [Political party]
NARP.......... Nonaqueous Reversed Phase [Chromatography]
NARP.......... Nuclear Weapons Accident Report Procedures (AD)
NARPA........ National Air Rifle and Pistol Association [British]
NARPA........ National Association for Rights Protection and Advocacy (EA)
NARPD........ National Association for the Relief of Paget's Disease [British]
NARPO........ National Association of Retired Police Officers [British] (DBA)
NARPPS...... National Association of Rehabilitation Professionals in the Private Sector (EA)
NARPV........ National Association for Remotely Piloted Vehicles (MCD)
NARR.......... Narrator [or Narration]
NARRD........ National Association of Record Retailer Dealers [Defunct] (EA)
Nar Rep Bul... Narodna Republika Bulgaria [Bulgarian People's Republic] [Political party] (AD)
Narr Mod..... Narrationes Modernae [Style's English King's Bench Reports] [1646-55] [A publication] (DLA)
NARS.......... Narrative Accomplishment Reporting System [Department of Agriculture] [Information service or system] (IID)
NARS.......... National Acupuncture Research Society (EA)
NARS.......... National Agricultural Research Systems (ECON)
NARS.......... National Annual Report Service [NYSE]
NARS.......... National Archives and Records Service [of GSA] [Washington, DC Later, NARA]
NARS.......... National Association of Radiation Survivors (EA)
NARS.......... National Association of Radiator Specialists [British] (DBA)
NARS.......... National Association of Radiotelephone Systems [Later, Telocator Network of America] (EA)
NARS.......... National Association of Rail Shippers (EA)
NARS.......... National Association of Refunders and Shoppers [Defunct] (EA)
NARS.......... National Association of Rehabilitation Secretaries (EA)
NARS.......... Naval Air Rescue Service (MUGU)
NARS.......... New Atlantean Research Society [Defunct] (EA)
NARS.......... Nonaffiliated Reserve Section
NARS.......... Northampton Activity Rating Scale [Psychology]
NARS.......... North Atlantic Radio System
NARSA........ National Automotive Radiator Service Association (EA)
NARS-A1...... National Archive and Record Service-Automation 1 (NITA)
NARSAB...... National Association of Rail Shippers Advisory Boards (EA)
NARSAD...... National Alliance for Research on Schizophrenia and the Depressions (EA)
NARSC........ National Association of Reinforcing Steel Contractors (EA)
NARSIS........ National Association for Road Safety Instruction in Schools (AD)
NARSLL...... National Association to Reform State Liquor Laws [Later, National Association to Reform State Drinking Ages] [Defunct] (EA)
NARST........ National Association for Research in Science Teaching (EA)
NARSTC...... Naval Air Rescue Training Command
NARSUP...... Navy Acquisition Regulations Supplement
NARSVA...... National Archives and Record Service Volunteer Association [Later, NARAVA] (EA)
NARSVPD...... National Association of Retired Senior Volunteer Program Directors (EA)
NART.......... National Association for Remedial Teaching (AEBS)
NART.......... National Association of Recreation Therapists [Later, NTRS] (EA)
NART.......... New Adult Reading Test
NART.......... North American Racing Team [Auto racing]
NARTA........ North American Restaurant and Tavern Alliance (EA)
NARTB........ National Association of Radio and Television Broadcasters [Later, NAB] (EA)
NARTC........ National Association of Railroad Trial Counsel (EA)
NARTC........ Naval Air Research Training Command
NARTC........ Naval Air Rocket Test Center (MUGU)
NARTC........ North America Regional Test Center (NATG)
NARTCE...... National Association for Released Time Christian Education (EA)
NARTE........ National Association of Radio and Telecommunications Engineers (EA)
NARTEL...... North Atlantic Radio Telephone Committee
NARTM........ National Association of Rope and Twine Merchants (AD)
NARTRANS... North American Rockwell Training and Services [Obsolete]
NARTS........ National Association of Radio Telephone Systems [Later, Telocator Network of America] (IAA)
NARTS........ National Association of Reporter Training Schools [Defunct] (EA)
NARTS........ National Association of Resale and Thrift Shops (EA)
NARTS........ Naval Aeronautics Test Station

NARTS.........	Naval Air Rocket Test Station
NARTU.........	Naval Air Reserve Training Unit
NARU...........	Natural Rate of Unemployment [*Economics*]
NARU...........	Naval Air Reserve Unit (NVT)
NARU...........	North Australian Research Unit (AD)
NARUC.........	National Association of Regulatory Utility Commissioners (EA)
NARUCE.......	National Association of Regulatory Utility Commission Engineers (IAA)
NARUS.........	Navy Aircraft Resources Utilization Study
NARVRE.......	National Association of Retired and Veteran Railroad Employees (EA)
NARW..........	National Assembly of Religious Women (EA)
NARW..........	National Association of Refrigerated Warehouses [*Later, IARW*] (EA)
NARWA........	Nordic Agricultural Research Workers Association (EA)
NARWACL....	North American Regional World Anti-Communist League (AD)
NAS.............	N-Acetylserotonin [*Biochemistry*]
NAS.............	Narrow-Angle Sensor
NAS.............	Nasal
nas.............	Nasal (AD)
NAS.............	Nasangga [*Fiji*] [*Seismograph station code, US Geological Survey*] (SEIS)
NAS	Nassau [*Bahamas*] [*Airport symbol*] (OAG)
NAS	National Academy of Sciences [*Washington, DC*]
NAS	National Academy of Songwriters
NAS	National Academy of Sports (EA)
NAS	National Adoption Society (WDAA)
NAS	National Advanced Systems (HGAA)
NAS	National Advocates Society (EA)
NAS	National Aerospace Standards (MCD)
NAS	National Aerospace Standards Industrial Association (AAGC)
NAS	National Agricultural Society (NADA)
NAS	National Agricultural Society (AD)
NAS	National Aircraft Standards
NAS	National Airspace System [*NASA*]
NAS	National Alliance for Salvation [*Sudan*] [*Political party*] (MENA)
NAS	National Aquarium Society (EA)
NAS	National Aquatic School [*Red Cross*]
NAS	National Association of Sanitarians [*Later, NEHA*] (EA)
NAS	National Association of Scholars (EA)
NAS	National Association of Schoolmasters [*British*]
NAS	National Association of Shopfitters [*British*] (BI)
NAS	National Association of Shopkeepers [*British*] (DBA)
NAS	National Association of Specialized Carriers, Marietta GA [*STAC*]
NAS	National Association of Stevedores (EA)
NAS	National Association of Supervisors [*Later, Federal Managers Association*] (EA)
NAS	National Astrological Society [*Defunct*] (EA)
NAS	National Audubon Society (EA)
NAS	National Autistic Society [*British*]
NAS	National Aviation System [*FAA*]
NAS	National Avionics Society (EA)
NAS	National Seastar [*Vancouver Stock Exchange symbol*]
NAS	Native American Studies (AD)
NAS	Naval Air Service
NAS	Naval Air Station
NAS	Naval Air Systems Command, Washington, DC [*OCLC symbol*] (OCLC)
NAS	Naval Audit Service (DOMA)
NAS	Navigation Avoidance System (KSC)
NAS	Navy Advisory Section [*Vietnam*] (VNW)
NAS	Neonatal Abstinence Syndrome (DAVI)
NAS	NetWare Access Server [*Computer science*]
NAS	Network Access Switch [*Telecommunications*] (MCD)
NAS	Network Application Support [*Computer science*] (BTTJ)
NAS	Neuroallergic Syndrome [*Medicine*] (DMAA)
NAS	Newsreel Access Systems, Inc. [*Also, an information service or system*] (IID)
NAS	No Added Salt [*Medicine*]
n-a-s.............	No Added Salt (AD)
NAS	Nocturnal Adoration Society (EA)
NAS	Noise Abatement Society [*British*]
N A S	Noise Abatement Society (AD)
NAS	Non-Assessable Stock [*Investment term*] (MHDW)
NAS	Nonavailability Statement [*Military*]
NAS	Non-Indigenous Aquatic Species [*Marine science*] (OSRA)
NAS	Non-indigenous Aquatic Species (USDC)
NAS	Nonlinear Antenna System
NAS	NORAD Alert System (MCD)
NAS	Nord Amerikanischer Sangerbund (EA)
NAS	Normalized Alignment Score
NAS	North American Shale [*Geology*]
NAS	North American Supply [*World War II*]
NAS	Northeast Aviation Services Ltd. [*British ICAO designator*] (FAAC)
NAS	Nozzle Actuating System [*Aerospace*] (MCD)
NAS	Numerical Aerodynamic Simulation [*NASA supercomputer system*]
NAS	Numerical Analysis Subroutines [*Computer science*] (BUR)
NAS	Numerical and Atmospheric Sciences Network [*NASA*]
NAS	Nursery Association Secretaries [*Later, Nursery Association Executives*] (EA)
NAS	Nursing Auxiliary Service [*British*]
NASA	National Acoustical Suppliers Association [*Defunct*] (EA)
NASA	National Advertising Sales Association (EA)
NASA	National Aeronautics and Space Act of 1958
NASA	National Aeronautics and Space Administration [*Washington, DC*]
NASA	National Aerospace Services Association [*Defunct*] (MCD)

NASA	National Appliance Service Association (EA)
NASA	National Association of School Affiliates (EA)
NASA	National Association of Schools of Art (EA)
NASA	National Association of Securities Administrators
NASA	National Association of Shippers' Agents [*Washington, DC*] (EA)
NASA	National Association of State Archeologists (EA)
NASA	National Association of Synagogue Administrators (EA)
NASA	National Automobile Salesmen's Association
NASA	Naval Aircraft Safety Activity (SAA)
NASA	Newspaper Advertising Sales Association (EA)
NASA	North American Sailing Association (AD)
NASA	North American Sailing Association (NADA)
NASA	North American Saxophone Alliance (EA)
NASA	North American Securities Administrators Association [*Also, NASAA*] (EA)
NASA	North American Shippers Association (EA)
NASA	North American Singers Association (EA)
NASA	North American Swiss Alliance (EA)
NASA	North Atlantic Seafood Association [*Defunct*] (EA)
NASA	North Atlantic Shippers Association (DS)
NASAA	National Aeronautics and Space Administration Act (AD)
NASAA	National Assembly of State Arts Agencies (EA)
NASAA	National Association of State Approval Agencies (EA)
NASAA	National Association of Student Activity Advisers (EA)
NASAA	North American Securities Administrators Association [*Topeka, KS*] (EA)
NASAA	North American Securities Administrators Association
NASA-AEC...	National Aeronautics and Space Administration and Atomic Energy Commission (SAA)
NASAB	National Association of Shippers Advisory Boards (EA)
NASABCA....	National Aeronautics and Space Administration Board of Contract Appeals
NASA-CF Florida...	National Aeronautics and Space Administration - Cocoa Beach, Florida (AD)
NASA-CO	National Aeronautics and Space Administration - Cleveland, Ohio (AD)
NASACRE....	National Association for Standing Advisory Councils for Religious Education (AIE)
NASACT.......	National Association of State Auditors, Comptrollers, and Treasurers (EA)
NASACU.......	National Association of State Approved Colleges and Universities (EA)
NASAD.........	National Association of Schools of Art and Design (EA)
NASAD	National Association of Sport Aircraft Designers (EA)
NASADAD ...	National Association of State Alcohol and Drug Abuse Directors (EA)
NASAE.........	National Association of Supervisors of Agricultural Education (EA)
NASA-EC California...	National Aeronautics and Space Administration - Edwards, California (AD)
NASAEN.......	National Association for State-Enrolled Assistant Nurses (AD)
NASAERC.....	NASA Electronic Research Center (IAA)
NASAF	Northwest African Strategic Air Force [*British military*] (DMA)
NASA FAR Supp...	National Aeronautics and Space Administration FAR Supplement [*A publication*] (AAGC)
NASAGA.......	North American Simulation and Gaming Association (EA)
NASA-GM Maryland...	National Aeronautics and Space Administration - Greenbelt, Maryland (AD)
NASA-HA Alabama...	National Aeronautics and Space Administration - Huntsville, Alabama (AD)
NASAHOE	National Association of Supervisors and Administrators of Health Occupations Education (EA)
NASA-HT......	National Aeronautics and Space Administration - Houston, Texas (AD)
NASAKOM....	Nasional, Agama, Kommunist [*Indonesian President Sukarno's policy of unity among National, Religious, and Communist forces*]
Nasakom	Nationalist-Communist (AD)
NASA-KSC ...	National Aeronautics and Space Administration - Kennedy Space Center
NASAL	National Association of Single Adult Leaders (EA)
NASA LST Telescope...	National Aeronautics and Space Administration Large Space Telescope (AD)
NASA-LV Virginia...	National Aeronautics and Space Administration - Langley Field, Virginia (AD)
NASA-MC California...	National Aeronautics and Space Administration - Moffett Field, California (AD)
NASAMECU...	Natura Sanat, Medicus Curat [*Nature Heals, the Doctor Cures*] [*Title of collected talks by Dr. Georg Groddeck, published in 1913*]
NASA-MSC...	National Aeronautics and Space Administration - Manned Spacecraft Center
NAS & FCA...	National Automatic Sprinkler and Fire Control Association (AD)
NASANX.......	Naval Air Station Annex (DNAB)
NASAO.........	National Association of State Aviation Officials (EA)
NASAOCARE...	National Association of State Aviation Officials Center for Aviation Research and Education (EA)
NASAP.........	Navy Alcohol Safety Action Program (DNAB)
NASAP.........	Network Analysis for Systems Applications Program [*Computer program*] [*NASA*]
NASAP.........	Nonproliferation Alternative Systems Assessment Program [*Nuclear energy*] (NRCH)
NASAP.........	North American Society of Adlerian Psychology (EA)
NASAP.........	Nuclear Alternative System Assessment Program
NASAPOFF...	Navy Alcohol Safety Action Program Office (DNAB)
NASAPR.......	National Aeronautics and Space Administration Procurement Regulations
NASAPRD	National Aeronautics and Space Administration Procurement Regulations Directive

NASAR......... National Association for Search and Rescue (EA)
NASA/RECON... National Aeronautics and Space Administration Remote Console
NASARR ...... North American Search and Range RADAR [Military]
NASA-SC California... National Aeronautics and Space Administration - Santa Monica, California (AD)
NASASP......... National Association State Agencies for Surplus Property (EA)
NASASPS.... National Association of State Administrators and Supervisors of Private Schools (EA)
NASA-STAR... NASA Scientific and Technical Reports (NITA)
NASA/STIF... National Aeronautics and Space Administration/Scientific and Technical Information Facility
NASATE .... National Association of Substance Abuse Trainers and Educators (EA)
NASA-TR...... NASA Tank Reactor
NASB .... Nancy Ann Story Book [Doll collecting]
NASB .... National Association of School Boards (OICC)
NASB .... National Association of Spanish Broadcasters (EA)
NASB .... National Association of State Boards of Accountancy (AAGC)
NASB .... Navigational Aid Support Base
NASB .... New American Standard Bible [A publication] (BJA)
NASB .... North American Savings Bank FSB [NASDAQ symbol] (SAG)
NASB .... North Amer Svgs Bk [NASDAQ symbol] (TTSB)
NASBA .... National Association of State Boards of Accountancy [New York, NY] (EA)
NASBA .... National Automobile Safety Belt Association [British]
NASBA .... Nucleic Acid Sequence-Based Amplification [Biochemistry]
NASBCO....... National Association of School Bus Contract Operators [Later, NSTA] (EA)
NASBE .... National Association of State Boards of Education (EA)
NASBE .... National Association of Supervisors of Business Education [Fort Lauderdale, FL] (EA)
NASBERM.... Naval Air Station, Bermuda
NASBIC........ National Association of Small Business Investment Companies [Washington, DC] (EA)
NASBLA .... National Association of State Boating Law Administrators (EA)
NASBO......... National Association of State Budget Officers (EA)
NASBO......... North African Shipping Board [World War II]
NASBOE....... National Association of Supervisors of Business and Office Education [Later, NASBE]
NASBOSA .... National Academy of Sciences Board on Ocean Science Affairs (PDAA)
NASBP .... National Association of Surety Bond Producers [Bethesda, MD] (EA)
NASC .... National Aeronautics and Space Council [Terminated, 1973]
NASC .... National Aircraft Standards Committee
NASC .... National Alliance for Safer Cities (EA)
NASC .... National Alliance of Senior Citizens (EA)
NASC .... National Aloe Science Council [Later, IASC] (EA)
NASC .... National Amalgamated Society of Coopers [A union] [British]
NASC .... National Aquatic Sports Camps (EA)
NASC .... National Association of Scaffolding Contractors [British] (DBA)
NASC .... National Association of School Counselors [Defunct] (EA)
NASC .... National Association of Service Contractors [Defunct] (EA)
NASC .... National Association of Solar Contractors (EA)
NASC .... National Association of Specialized Carriers [Defunct] (EA)
NASC .... National Association of Student Councils (EA)
NASC .... National Athletic Steering Committee (EA)
NASC .... NATO Supply Center
NASC .... Naval Aircraft Standards Committee (AFIT)
NASC .... Naval Air Systems Command
NASC .... Navy Aviation Safety Center (MUGU)
NASC .... North American Shale Composite [Geology]
NASC .... North American Sporting Clays [An association]
NASC .... North America Supply Council
NASC .... North Atlantic Salmon Convention [Marine science] (OSRA)
NASC .... North Atlantic Salmon Convention (USDC)
NASC .... Northwest Association of Schools and Colleges (EA)
NASCA .... National Association for Corporate Speaker Activities [Reston, VA] (WDMC)
NASCA .... National Association of State Cable Agencies (EA)
NASCA .... National Association of State Conservation Agencies [Washington, DC]
NASCA .... North American Swing Club Association (EA)
NASCAP....... NASA Charging Analyzer Program (MCD)
NASCAR...... National Association for Stock Car Advancement and Research (AD)
NASCAR...... National Association for Stock Car Auto Racing (EA)
NASCAR...... National Association of Sports Car Racing (AD)
NASCAS....... National Academy of Sciences Committee on Atmospheric Science
NASCAT....... National Association of Securities and Commercial Law Attorneys (EA)
NASCC .... National Association of Service and Conservation Corps (EA)
NASCCD....... National Association of State Catholic Conference Directors (EA)
NASCCEN..... Naval Air Systems Command Representative, Central
NAS-CD........ National Academy of Sciences - Chemistry Division
NASCD .... National Association for Sickle Cell Disease (EA)
NASCD......... National Association of Soil Conservation Districts [Later, National Association of Conservation Districts]
NASCDC....... National Association for Sick Child Daycare Centers (PAZ)
NASCDD ...... National Association of State Civil Defense Directors [Later, NEMA] (EA)
NASCH .... National Association of Swimming Clubs for the Handicapped [British] (DBA)
NASCIS........ National Acute Spinal Cord Injury Study
NASCL .... North American Student Cooperative League
NASCLANT... Naval Air Systems Command Representative, Atlantic

NASCMVE.... National Academy of Sciences Committee on Motor Vehicle Emissions (PDAA)
NASCO......... National Academy of Sciences Committee on Oceanography
NASCO......... National Association of Smaller Communities (EA)
NASCO......... National Association of State Charity Officials (EA)
NASCO......... National Automotive Service Co. (AD)
NASCO......... National Scientific Committee on Oceanography [Marine science] (MSC)
NASCO......... North American Students of Cooperation (EA)
NASCO......... North Atlantic Salmon Conservation Organization [Edinburgh, Scotland] (EAIO)
NASCOE....... National Association of ASCS [Agricultural Stabilization and Conservation Service] County Office Employees (EA)
Nascom .... NASA Communications
NASCOM...... NASA Communications Network
NASCOM...... NASA Worldwide Communications Network (MCD)
NASCOM...... National Aeronautics and Space Administration Tracking Network (AD)
NASCOM...... National Airspace Communications System
NASCOM...... Naval Air Systems Command (MCD)
NASCom ..... Naval Air Systems Command (AD)
NASCOMIS... Naval Air Station/Command Management Information System (MCD)
NASCOP....... NASA Communications Operating Procedures (MCD)
NAS/COW .... National Academy of Sciences/Committee on Water [Marine science] (MSC)
NASCP .... National Association of Sports for Cerebral Palsy [Later, USCPAA] (EA)
NASCP .... North American Society for Corporate Planning [Later, PF] (EA)
NASCPA....... North American Study Center for Polish Affairs (EA)
NASCPAC..... Naval Air Systems Command Representative, Pacific
NASCPD....... National Association of Senior Companion Project Directors (EA)
NASCPNCLA... Naval Air Systems Command Representative, Naval Air Training Command, Pensacola [Florida]
NASCRIST.... Naval Air Station Corpus Christi
NASCRL....... Naval Air Systems Command Representative, Atlantic
NASCRP....... Naval Air Systems Command Representative-Pacific (MCD)
NASCS .... National Association of Shoe Chain Stores [Later, FDRA] (EA)
NASCSP .... National Association for State Community Service Programs (EA)
NASCUMC.... National Association of Schools and Colleges of the United Methodist Church (EA)
NASCUS....... National Association of State Credit Union Supervisors (EA)
NASD .... National Amalgamated Stevedores and Dockers (AD)
NASD .... National Association of Schools of Dance (EA)
NASD .... National Association of Schools of Design [Later, NASA]
NASD .... National Association of Securities Dealers [Washington, DC] (EA)
NASD .... National Association of Selective Distributors [Defunct] (EA)
NASD .... National Association of Service Dealers (EA)
NASD .... Naval Air [or Aviation] Supply Depot
NASD .... Naval Aviation Supply Depot (AD)
NASD .... Nippon Advanced Ship Design (AD)
NASDA .... National Association of Sign and Display Advertisers [Defunct]
NASDA .... National Association of State Departments of Agriculture (EA)
NASDA .... National Association of State Development Agencies (EA)
NASDA .... National Space Development Agency [Japan]
NASDA .... North American South Devon Association (EA)
NASDAC .... National Aviation Safety Data Analysis Center [FAA] (TAG)
NASDAD ...... National Association of Seventh-Day Adventist Dentists (EA)
NASDAGS .... National Association of State Directors of Administration and General Service (EA)
NASDAPC .... National Association of State Drug Abuse Program Coordinators [Later, NASADAD] (EA)
NASDAQ ...... National Association of Securities Dealers Automated Quotations [Over-the-counter stock quotations] [Bunker Ramo Corp. Trumbell, CT] [Information service or system]
Nasdaq .... National Association of Securities Dealers Automated Quotations [The full name is the Nasdaq Stock Market] [Washington, DC] (WDMC)
NASDAQS .... National Association of Security Dealers Automated Quotation System (AD)
NASDCD .... National Association of State Directors of Child Development
NASDDP .... National Association of State Directors for Disaster Preparedness [Later, NEMA] (EA)
NASDI.......... National Association of Selective Distributors (EA)
NASDIEGO ... Naval Air Station San Diego
NASDIM....... National Association of Securities Dealers and Investment Managers [Securities and Investment Board] [British]
NASDLET .... National Association of State Directors of Law Enforcement Training
NASDM .... National Association of Special Delivery Messengers [Later, APWU] [AFL-CIO] (EA)
NASDME ...... National Association of State Directors of Migrant Education (EA)
NASDS......... National Amalgamated Stevedores' and Dockers' Society [A union] [British]
NASDS......... National Association of Scuba Diving Schools [Later, CA] [Commercial firm] (EA)
NASDS......... Naval Aviation Supply Distribution System (AFIT)
NASDS......... North American Sheep Dog Society (EA)
NASDSE....... National Association of State Directors of Special Education [Database producer] (EA)
NASDSSE..... National Association of State Directors and Supervisors of Secondary Education [Later, NASSDSE] (EA)
NASDT......... Naval Aviators' Speech Discrimination Test
NASDT......... North American Society for Dialysis and Transplantation (EA)
NASDTEC..... National Association of State Directors of Teacher Education and Certification (EA)
NASDU......... National Amalgamated Stevedores and Dockers Union [British] (BI)

NASDVA...... National Association of State Directors of Veterans Affairs (EA)
NASDVE...... National Association of State Directors of Vocational Education (EA)
NASE .... National Academy of School Executives [*of American Association of School Administrators*]
NASE .... National Academy of Stationary Engineers [*British*] (DAS)
NASE .... National Association for the Self-Employed [*Fort Worth, TX*] (EA)
NASE .... National Association for the Self-Employed
NASE .... National Association for the Study of Epilepsy (DAVI)
NASE .... National Association of Stationary Engineers (AD)
NASE .... National Association of Steel Exporters [*Defunct*] (EA)
nase........... Neutral Atom Space Engine (AD)
NASE .... Nonacoustic Submarine Effects (NVT)
NASEA .... National Association of Student Employment Administrators (EA)
NASEA .... Native American Science Education Association [*Defunct*] (EA)
NASEAB ...... Naval Air Systems Effectiveness Advisory Board
NASEAN ...... National Association for State Enrolled Assistant Nurses
NASECODE... Numerical Analysis of Semiconductor Devices and Integrated Circuits [*Computer science*]
NASEDIO..... National Association of State Education Department Information Officers (EA)
NASEES .... National Association for Soviet and East European Studies [*British*]
NASEM .... National Association of Satellite Equipment Manufacturers [*Defunct*] (EA)
NASEMP ..... National Association of State Educational Media Professionals (EA)
NASEMSD... National Association of State EMS Directors (EA)
NASEN .... National Association for Special Educational Needs (AIE)
NASEN .... National Association of State Enrolled Nurses [*British*] (BI)
NASEPA ...... National Association of State Environmental Programs Agencies [*Marine science*] (MSC)
NAS/ESB ..... National Academy of Sciences/Environmental Studies Board [*Marine science*] (MSC)
NASF .... National Aboriginal Sports Foundation (AD)
NASF .... National American Studies Faculty [*Defunct*] (EA)
NASF .... National Arts Stabilization Fund [*Defunct*] (EA)
NASF .... National Association of State Foresters (EA)
NASF .... Native American Scholarship Fund [*An association*] (EA)
NASF .... NIC [*Naval Intelligence Center*] Analyst Support Facility
NASF .... North American Soccer Foundation [*Defunct*] (EA)
NASF .... Numerical Aerodynamic Simulation Facility
NASFA .... National Association of State Facilities Administrators (EA)
NASFAA ...... National Association of Student Financial Aid Administrators (EA)
NASFCA ...... National Automatic Sprinkler and Fire Control Association (EA)
NASFCB ...... National Association of Specialty Food and Confection Brokers (EA)
NASFM .... National Association of Store Fixture Manufacturers (EA)
NASFO .... National Asset Seizure and Forfeiture Office (AD)
NASFT .... National Association for the Specialty Food Trade (EA)
NASFW .... National Association of Solid Fuel Wholesalers [*British*] (DBA)
NASG .... National Alliance for Spiritual Growth (EA)
NASGA .... North American Strawberry Growers Association (EA)
NAS-GB........ Noise Abatement Society of Great Britain (AD)
NASGC .... National Association of Small Government Contractors (EA)
NAS/GRB ..... National Academy of Sciences/Geophysical Research Board [*Marine science*] (MSC)
NASGS........ North African Secretary General Staff [*World War II*]
NASGTMO.... Naval Air Station Guantanamo
NASGW .... National Association of Sporting Goods Wholesalers (EA)
NASH.......... Nahariya to Ashkelon [*Proposed name for possible "super-city" formed by the urban sprawl between these two*] [*Israel*]
Nash .... Nashville [*Tennessee*] (AD)
NASH .... National Association of Safety at Home [*British*] (DBA)
NASH .... National Association for Specimen Hunters (AD)
NASHA........ National Association for Speech and Hearing Action (EA)
NASHA........ North American Survival and Homesteading Association (AD)
NASHAC....... National Association for Safety and Health in the Arts and Crafts (EA)
NASHAW...... National Association for Statewide Health and Welfare (EA)
NASHC........ National All States Hobby Club [*Defunct*] (EA)
NashCtr........ Nashville Country Club [*Associated Press*] (SAG)
NashF......... Nash Finch Co. [*Associated Press*] (SAG)
NASHOC ...... North American Student Humanist Organizing Committee [*Defunct*] (EA)
Nash Pl........ Nash's Ohio Pleading and Practice [*A publication*] (DLA)
NASHRD ...... National Association of State Human Resource Directors (EA)
Nashua........ Nashua Corp. [*Associated Press*] (SAG)
NASI .... National Association of Systems Integrators (CDE)
NASI .... NetWare Asynchronous Services Interface [*Computer science*] (PCM)
NASI .... Nigerian Army School of Infantry
NASI .... Novell Asynchronous Services Interface
NASIB .... Naval Air Station, Imperial Beach (DNAB)
NASIC .... Northeast Academic Science Information Center
NASID .... National Association of the Sixth Infantry Division (EA)
NASIG .... North African Signal Section [*World War II*]
NASIG .... North American Serials Group (EA)
NASILP .... National Association of Self-Instructional Language Programs (EA)
NASIMD....... National Association of the Sixth Infantry/Motorized Division [*Later, NASID*] (EA)
Nas Inst....... Nasmith's Institutes of English Private Law [*1873*] [*A publication*] (DLA)
Nas Inst Priv... Nasmith's Institutes of English Private Law [*1873*] [*A publication*] (DLA)
Nas Inst Pub.. Nasmith's Institutes of English Public Law [*1873*] [*A publication*] (DLA)
NASIP .... National Aviation Safety Inspection Program [*RSPA*] (TAG)
NASIR......... Nuclear Amplification by Stimulated Isomer Radiation (SAA)

NASIRC........ NASA Automated Systems Incident Response Capability
NASIRE........ National Association of State Information Resource Executives (AAGC)
NASIS .... NASA Aerospace Safety Information System
NASIS .... National Association for State Information Systems (EA)
NASIS .... NATO Subject Indicator System (NATG)
NASISS .... National Association of Sailing Instructors and Sailing Schools (EA)
NASJA .... North American Ski Journalists Association (EA)
NASJAX .... Naval Air Station Jacksonville
NASL .... Nasal (DAVI)
NASL .... National Association of State Lotteries (EA)
NASL .... Naval Applied Science Laboratory
NASL .... North American Soccer League [*Defunct*] (EA)
NASLAKE .... Naval Air Station Lakehurst
NASLI .... National Association for Senior Living Industries (EA)
NASLPA .... North American Soccer League Players Association [*Defunct*] (EA)
NASLR .... National Association of State Land Reclamationists (EA)
NASLS .... National Association of Small Loan Supervisors (EA)
NASM .... National Air and Space [*Warfare*] Model [*Air Force*]
NASM .... National Air and Space Museum [*Smithsonian Institution*] [*Formerly, NAM*]
NASM .... National Association for School Magazines [*British*] (BI)
NASM .... National Association of Sandwich Manufacturers [*Defunct*] (EA)
NASM .... National Association of Schools of Music (EA)
NASM .... National Association of Service Managers (EA)
NASM .... National Association of Service Merchandising (EA)
NASM .... National Association of State Militia (EA)
NASM .... National Association of Surrogate Mothers (EA)
NASM .... Naval Aviation School of Medicine
NASMA .... Parti Nasionalis Malaysia [*Political party*] (FEA)
NASMAC....... Naval Air Software Management Advisory Committee (MCD)
NASMAP...... NAS Management Automation Program [*FAA*] (TAG)
NASMAR...... National Association of Sack Merchants and Reclaimers [*British*] (BI)
NASMBCM... National Association of Sanitary Milk Bottle Closure Manufacturers [*Defunct*] (EA)
NASMD....... National Association of School Music Dealers (EA)
NASMD....... National Association of Sewing Machine Dealers [*Defunct*] (EA)
NASMD....... National Association of Sewing Machine Distributors [*Defunct*] (EA)
NASMD....... National Association of Sheet Music Dealers [*Later, NAMM*] (EA)
NASMD....... Northamerican Association of Sheet Metal Distributors [*Later, division of NHAW*] (EA)
NASMHPD ... National Association of State Mental Health Program Directors (EA)
NASMI .... National Association of Secondary Material Industries [*Later, NARI*] (EA)
NAS(MISC)... North American Supply Committee, Miscellaneous [*World War II*]
NASML........ National Air and Space Museum Library [*Smithsonian Institute*] (AD)
NASMO .... National Association of School Meals Organisers [*British*] (DBA)
NASMO .... NATO Starfighter Management Office
NASMP .... National Association of Sales and Marketing Professionals [*Defunct*] (EA)
NASMV .... National Association on Standard Medical Vocabulary (EA)
NASN .... National Air Sampling Network [*Public Health Service*]
NASN .... National Air Surveillance Network [*Environmental Protection Agency*]
NASN .... National Association of School Nurses (EA)
NAS/NAE...... National Academy of Sciences/National Academy of Engineering [*Marine science*] (MSC)
NAS/NAE-SECAN... NAS/NAE [*National Academy of Sciences/National Academy of Engineering*] Science and Engineering Committee Advisory to NOAA [*National Oceanic and Atmospheric Administration*] [*Defunct*] (USDC)
NAS/NAE-SECAN... National Academy of Sciences/National Academy of Sciences Engineering Science and Engineering Committee Advisory to NOAA[*National Oceanic and Atmospheric Administration*] [*Marine science*] (OSRA)
NASNI .... Naval Air Station North Island
NAS-NRC...... National Academy of Sciences - National Research Council (EA)
NASNSA....... National Association of Special Needs State Administrators (EA)
NASO.......... Natchez & Southern Railway Co. [*AAR code Terminated*]
NASO.......... National Adult School Organisation [*British*]
NASO.......... National Association of Sports Officials (EA)
NASO.......... National Astrological Society [*Defunct*] (EA)
NASO.......... National Astronomical Space Observatory
NASO.......... Naval Aviation Supply Office
NASO.......... Nonacoustic Sensor Operator [*Military*] (CAAL)
NAS/OAB...... National Academy of Sciences/Ocean Affairs Board [*Marine science*] (MSC)
NASOC........ North American Singer Owners Club (EA)
NASOH........ North American Society for Oceanic History (EA)
NASOPT....... Network Analysis System with Optimization Facility [*NASA*] (IAA)
NA So Rhod... Southern Rhodesia Native Appeal Court Reports [*A publication*] (DLA)
NASORLO .... National Association of State Outdoor Recreation Liaison Officers (EA)
NAS/OSB...... National Academy of Sciences/Ocean Sciences Board [*Marine science*] (MSC)
NASP .... National Achievement Scholarship Program [*National Merit Scholarship Corp.*] (AEBS)
NASP .... National Aero-Space Plane (AD)
NASP .... National Aerospace Plane (AAGC)
NASP .... National Aerospace Plane Program [*NASA, DoD*]
NASP .... National Airport System Plans [*Department of Transportation*]
NASP .... National Airspace System Plan [*FAA*] (TAG)
NASP .... National Alternative Schools Program
NASP .... National Association for the Southern Poor (EA)
NASP .... National Association of School Psychologists (EA)

NASP .... National Association of Schools and Publishers (EA)
NASP .... National Association of Securities Professionals (EA)
NASP .... National Association of Single Persons (EA)
NASP .... National Atmospheric Sciences Program
NASP .... National Aviation System Plan [*A publication*]
NASP .... Naval Air Survivability Program (MCD)
NASP .... Navy Advanced SATCOM [*Satellite Communications*] Program (ANA)
NASP .... Negro, Anglo-Saxon Protestant
NASPA .... National Association for Public Accountants (HGAA)
NASPA .... National Association of Student Personnel Administrators (EA)
NASPA .... National Society of Public Accountants (MCD)
NaSPA .... National Systems Programmers Association (EA)
NASPA .... North American Soccer Players Association [*Later, NASLPA*] (EA)
NASPAA .... National Association of Schools of Public Affairs and Administration (EA)
NASPAC .... National Airspace System Performance Analysis Capability [*FAA*] (TAG)
NASPALS ..... Nas Precision Approach and Landing System [*FAA*] (TAG)
Nas Par ...... Nasionale Party [*National Party*] [*Political party*] (AD)
NASPD .... National Association of State Park Directors (EA)
NASPD .... National Association of Steel Pipe Distributors (EA)
NASPE .... National Association for Sport and Physical Education (EA)
NASPE .... National Association of State Personnel Executives (EA)
NASPE .... North American Society of Pacing and Electrophysiology (EA)
NASPENSA ... Naval Air Station Pensacola
Nas Pers ..... Nasionale Pers [*National Press*] [*South Africa*] (AD)
NASPG .... North American Society for Pediatric Gastroenterology [*Later, NASPGN*] (EA)
NASPGN ...... North American Society for Pediatric Gastroenterology and Nutrition (EA)
NASPHV ...... National Association of State Public Health Veterinarians (EA)
NASPM .... National Association of Seed Potato Merchants [*British*] (BI)
NASPM .... National Association of Slipper and Playshoe Manufacturers (EA)
NASPO .... National Airspace System Program Office [*FAA*] (MCD)
NASPO .... National Alliance of Statewide Preservation Organizations (EA)
NASPO .... National Association of State Purchasing Officials (EA)
NASPO .... NATO Starfighter Production Organization
NASPR .... NASA Procurement Regulation (KSC)
NASPRFMR... National Association of Superintendents of Public Residential Facilities for theMentally Retarded
NASPSM ...... National Association of Shirt, Pajama, and Sportswear Manufacturers [*Later, AAMA*]
NASPSPA ..... North American Society for the Psychology of Sport and Physical Activity (EA)
Na-Spt .... Sodium Spot [*Urine Test*] [*Biochemistry*] (DAVI)
NASQAN ...... National Stream Quality Accounting Network [*Department of the Interior*]
NASQUON .... Naval Air Station Quonset Point
NASR .... National Annual Symposium on Reliability [*IEEE*] (MCD)
NASR .... National Association of Sitter Registries [*Defunct*] (EA)
NASR .... National Association of Solvent Recyclers (EA)
NASR .... National Association of Swine Records (EA)
NASRA .... National Association of State Retirement Administrators (EA)
NASRC .... National Association of State Racing Commissioners [*Later, ARCI*] (EA)
NASRC .... North American Salmon Research Center [*Later, Atlantic Salmon Research Institute*] [*Canada Research center*] (RCD)
NASRC .... North Atlantic Salmon Research Center [*Marine science*] (MSC)
NASRN .... National Association of State Radio Networks (EA)
NASRO .... National Association of Shooting Range Owners (EA)
NASRP .... National Association of Special and Reserve Police [*Defunct*]
NASRP .... National Association of State Recreation Planners (EA)
NASRPM ...... National Association of State River Program Managers (EA)
NASRR .... North American Search and Range RADAR [*Military*]
NASRS .... Not Available Status Report System [*DoD*]
NASRU .... Naval Air Systems Command Reserve Unit (MCD)
NASRWCBL... National Amalgamated Society of Railway Wagon and Carriage Builders and Lifters [*A union*] [*British*]
NASS .... Narrow Angle Sun Sensor (SAA)
NASS .... Nassau (ROG)
Nass .... Nassau, Bahamas (AD)
NASS .... National Accident Sampling System [*National Highway Traffic Safety Administration*] [*Washington, DC*]
NASS .... National Agricultural Statistics Service [*Department of Agriculture*] [*Information service or system*] (IID)
NASS .... National Aids Support System [*Military*] (SAA)
NASS .... National Alliance for Safe Schools (EA)
NASS .... National Alliance of Supermarket Shoppers (EA)
NASS .... National Ankylosing Spondylitis Society [*British*] (DBA)
NASS .... National Association for Small Schools [*British*] (DI)
NASS .... National Association of Saw Shops (EA)
NASS .... National Association of School Superintendents (AD)
NASS .... National Association of School Superintendents (NADA)
NASS .... National Association of Secretarial Services [*St. Petersburg, FL*] (EA)
NASS .... National Association of Secretaries of State
NASS .... National Association of Specialized Schools [*Defunct*] (EA)
NASS .... National Association of Steel Stockholders (MHDB)
NASS .... National Association of Suggestion Systems (EA)
NASS .... National Association of Summer Sessions [*Later, NAASS*]
NASS .... Naval Air Signal School
NASS .... Naval Armaments Stores System (PDAA)
NASS .... Navigation Satellite System (PDAA)
NASS .... Navy Advent Ship Station (SAA)
NASS .... Network Access Switching Subsystem [*Telecommunications*] (MCD)
NASS .... North African Special Service Section [*World War II*]

NASS .... North American Shagya-Arabian Society (EA)
NASS .... North American Spine Society (EA)
NASS .... North American Super Sports [*Defunct*] (EA)
NAS(S) .... North American Supply Committee, Scientific Subcommittee [*World War II*]
NASSA .... National Aerospace Services Association [*Defunct*] (EA)
NASSA .... National Art School Students' Association [*Australia*]
NASSAM ...... National Association for the Self-Supporting Active Ministry (EA)
NASS & LS... National Association of State Savings and Loan Supervisors [*Later, ACSSS*] (EA)
NASSB .... National Association of Supervisors of State Banks [*Later, CSBS*] (EA)
NASSC .... National Alliance on Shaping Safer Cities [*Later, NASC*] (EA)
NASSCO ...... National Association of Sewer Service Companies (EA)
NASSCO ...... National Steel & Shipbuilding Co.
NASSCOM... National Association of Software and Service Companies
NASSD .... National Association of School Security Directors (EA)
NASSDC ...... National Social Science Documentation Centre [*Information service or system*] (IID)
NASSDE ...... National Association of State Supervisors of Distributive Education (EA)
NASSDOC ... National Social Science Documentation Centre [*Information service or system*] (IID)
NASSDSE .... National Association of State Supervisors and Directors of Secondary Education (EA)
NAS/SEC ..... National Academy of Sciences' Site Evaluation Committee
NASSH .... North American Society for Sport History (EA)
NASSHE ...... National Association of State Supervisors of Home Economics [*Later, NASSVHE*]
NASSL .... National Association of Spanish Speaking Librarians (EA)
NASSM .... National Association of Scissors and Shears Manufacturers (EA)
NASSM .... National Association of State Supervisors of Music (EA)
NASSM .... North American Society for Sport Management (EA)
NASSO .... National Association of Socialist Students' Organizations [*Political party*] (AD)
NASSP .... National Association of Secondary School Principals (EA)
NASSP .... North American Society for Social Philosophy (EA)
NASSP-B ..... National Association of Secondary School Principals. Bulletin [*A publication*] (BRI)
NASSPE ...... National Alliance of Spanish-Speaking People for Equality (EA)
NASSR .... Nahichevan Autonomous Soviet Socialist Republic (AD)
NASSS .... National Association of Support for Small Schools [*British*] (DBA)
NASSS .... North American Society for the Sociology of Sport (EA)
NASSSA ...... National Association of State Social Security Administrators [*Later, NCSSSA*] (EA)
NASSTA ...... National Association of Secretaries of State Teachers Associations [*Later, NCSEA*] (EA)
NASSTIE ...... National Association of State Supervisors of Trade and Industrial Education (EA)
NASSTRAC... National Small Shipments Traffic Conference [*Acronym now used as official name of association*] (EA)
NASSTRAC... National Small Shipments Traffic Council
NASSVHE .... National Association of State Supervisors of Vocational Home Economics (EA)
NAST .... National Association of Schools of Theatre (EA)
NAST .... National Association of State Treasurers (EA)
NAST .... Navigation/Attack Systems Trainer (PDAA)
NAST .... Navy Advent Ship Terminal (SAA)
NAST .... Nuclear Accident Support Team [*Canada*]
NASTA .... National Association of State Text Book Administrators (EA)
NASTAD ...... Naval Acoustic Sensor Training Aids Department (DNAB)
NASTAR ...... National Standard Race [*Skiing*]
NASTAT ...... North American Society of Teachers of the Alexander Technique (EA)
NASTBD ...... National Association of State Text Book Directors [*Later, NASTA*] (EA)
Nastc .... Nastech Pharmaceutical Co., Inc. [*Associated Press*] (SAG)
NASTC .... Naval Air Station Twin Cities (DNAB)
NASTD .... National Association of State and Territorial Apprenticeship Directors [*Bureau of Apprenticeship and Training*] [*Department of Labor*]
NASTD .... National Association of State Telecommunications Directors (EA)
Nastech ...... Nastech Pharmaceutical Co., Inc. [*Associated Press*] (SAG)
NASTEMP ... National Association of State Educational Media Professionals (EA)
NASTI .... Naval Air Station, Terminal Island (AD)
NASTI .... Next Assembly Support Table Index [*Aerospace*] (MCD)
NASTL .... National Anti-Steel-Trap League (AD)
NASTL .... National Anti-Steel-Trap League (NADA)
NASTOCK.... North American Stock Market [*I. P. Sharp Associates*] [*Canada Information service or system*]
NASTPHV.... National Association of State and Territorial Public Health Veterinarians [*Later, NASPHV*] (EA)
NASTRAN ... NASA Structural Analysis [*Computer program*]
NAS/TRB...... National Academy of Sciences/Transportation Board [*Marine science*] (MSC)
NASTS .... National Association for Science, Technology, and Society (EA)
NASTT .... North American Society for Trenchless Technology (EA)
NASU .... National Adult School Union [*British*] (DAS)
NASU .... National Association of State Universities [*Later, NASULGC*]
NASU .... National Association of System 3 Users (IAA)
NASU .... Navy Air Support Unit
NASU .... Navy Underwater Sound Laboratory (MUGU)
NASU .... North American Singers Union (EA)
NASUA .... National Association of State Units on Aging (EA)
NASUCA....... National Association of State Utility Consumer Advocates (EA)

NASULGC	National Association of State Universities and Land-Grant Colleges (EA)
NASUP........	National Association on Service to Unmarried Parents (EA)
NAS-UWT	National Association of Schoolmasters - Union of Women Teachers [British]
NASV	International Academy of Sports Vision [Formerly, National Academy of Sports Vision] (EAIO)
NASV	National Academy of Sports Vision (EA)
NASVG........	Nordic Association for Study and Vocational Guidance [See also NRSY] (EAIO)
NASVH........	National Association of State Veterans Homes (EA)
NASW	National Association of Science Writers (EA)
NASW	National Association of Social Workers (EA)
NASW	North American Slope Water [Oceanography] (MSC)
NASWA	North American Shortwave Association (EA)
NASWF	Naval Air Special Weapons Facility
NASWHP......	National Association of Sheltered Workshops and Homebound Programs [Later, NARF]
NASWM	National Association of Scottish Woollen Manufacturers [British] (BI)
NASWS	National Aeronautics and Space Administration White Sands [Proving ground]
NASWSO......	National Association of Soft Water Service Operators [Later, WQA]
NAT.............	Information Content Natural Unit [Information theory]
NAT.............	N-Acetyltransferase [An enzyme]
NAT.............	N-Acetyltryptophan [Biochemistry]
NAT.............	NASA Apollo Trajectory (KSC)
NAT.............	NASA STI [Scientific and Technical Information] Facility, BWI Airport, MD [Baltimore-Washington International] [OCLC symbol] (OCLC)
NAT.............	Natal [Brazil] [Seismograph station code, US Geological Survey] (SEIS)
NAT.............	Natal [Brazil] [Airport symbol] (OAG)
NAT.............	Natal [Neonatology] (DAVI)
Nat.............	Natalia (AD)
Nat.............	Natalie (AD)
Nat.............	Natasha (AD)
Nat.............	Nathalie (AD)
Nat.............	Nathan (AD)
Nat.............	Nathaniel (AD)
nat.............	Nation (AD)
Nat.............	Nation [A publication] (BRI)
NAT.............	Nation
Nat.............	National (ODBW)
NAT.............	National
Nat.............	National (AD)
nat.............	National (AD)
NAT.............	National Academy of Teaching (EA)
NAT.............	National Agency for Tourism
NAT.............	National Air Transport (SAA)
NAT.............	National Arbitration Tribunal [British]
NAT.............	National Association of Toolmakers [A union] [British]
NATaT........	National Drug Co. [Research code symbol]
NAT.............	Nationalist (WDAA)
Nat.............	Nationalist (ODBW)
NAT.............	Nationality (AAG)
Nat.............	National Party [Australia Political party]
NAT.............	National Transport, Inc.
NAT.............	Native (AAG)
nat.............	Native (AD)
NAT.............	Nativity [Church calendars] (ROG)
NAT.............	Natrolite [A zeolite]
NAT.............	Natural (AAG)
Nat.............	Natural (ODBW)
nat.............	Natural (AD)
nat.............	Naturalist (AD)
nat.............	Naturalization (AD)
Nat.............	Naturalized [Botany]
NAT.............	Natural Unit (IAA)
Nat.............	Nature [or Naturalist]
nat.............	Nature (AD)
NAT.............	Naturist (WDAA)
NAT.............	Natus [Birth] [Latin]
nat.............	Natuurkunde [Natural Science] [Dutch] (AD)
NAT.............	Naval Air Technical Services Facility (MUGU)
NAT.............	Naval Air Terminal
NAT.............	Naval Air Training
NAT.............	Naval Anthropomorphic Teleoperater (DNAB)
NAT.............	Navigational Aids Technician (DNAB)
NAT.............	Nearly Airborne Truck (PDAA)
NAT.............	Network Address Translation [Computer science]
NAT.............	Network Address Translation [Computer science]
NAT.............	Network Address Translation [Computer science]
NAT.............	Network Address Translation [Computer science]
NAT.............	Network Analysis Team
NAT.............	Network Analysis Technique (IAA)
NAT.............	New Age Thinking
NAT.............	New Attainment Target (AIE)
NAT.............	Nitric Acid Trihydrate [Inorganic chemistry]
NAT.............	Nitrosoanatabine [Also, NAtB] [Organic chemistry]
NAT.............	No Action Taken
NAT.............	Non-Verbal Ability Tests [Intelligence test]
NAT.............	Nordic American Tanker Shipping Ltd. [AMEX symbol] (SAG)
NAT.............	Normal Allowed Time (IEEE)
nat.............	Normal Allowed Time (AD)
NAT.............	North African Theater [World War II]
NAT.............	North Atlantic Air, Inc. [ICAO designator] (FAAC)
NAT.............	North Atlantic Region [USTTA] (TAG)
NAT.............	North Atlantic Regional Area [Aviation]
NAT.............	North Atlantic Treaty
NAT.............	Not Attending Training
NATA	N-Acetyl-Tryptophan-Amide [Organic chemistry]
NATA	N-Acetyltyramine [Biochemistry]
NATA	Narcotic Addict Treatment Act of 1974
NATA	National Airfreight Trucking Alliance (EA)
NATA	National Air Transportation Association (EA)
NATA	National Association of Tax Accountants [Defunct] (EA)
NATA	National Association of Tax Administrators (EA)
NATA	National Association of Teachers' Agencies (EA)
NATA	National Association of Teachers of Agriculture [Australia]
NATA	National Association of Temple Administrators (EA)
NATA	National Association of Testing Authorities (IAA)
NATA	National Association of Transportation Advertising [Later, Transit Advertising Association]
NATA	National Athletic Trainers Association (EA)
NATA	National Automated Transportation Association (AD)
NATA	National Automobile Transporters Association [Detroit, MI] (EA)
NATA	National Automotive Trade Association
NATA	National Aviation Trades Association
NATA	North American Tasar Association (EA)
NATA	North American Telecommunications Association (EA)
NATA	North American Telephone Association (EA)
NATA	North American Trakehner Association (EA)
NATA	North American Travel Association [Defunct] (EA)
NATA	North Atlantic Treaty Alliance
Nat Absten...	National Abstentionalist (AD)
NATAD	National Association of Textile and Apparel Distributors [Defunct] (EA)
NATAF	Northwest African Tactical Air Force [World War II]
Natal LJ......	Natal Law Journal [South Africa] [A publication] (DLA)
Natal LM.....	Natal Law Magazine [South Africa] [A publication] (DLA)
Natal LQ	Natal Law Quarterly [South Africa] [A publication] (DLA)
Natal LR	Natal Law Reports [South Africa] [A publication] (DLA)
NatAlt.........	Natural Alternatives International [Associated Press] (SAG)
NA T & N....	Selected Decisions of the Native Appeal Court, Transvaal and Natal [A publication] (DLA)
NATAPROBU...	National Association of Professional Bureaucrats [Later, INATAPROBU]
Nat Arc	National Archives (AD)
NATARI........	National Association of Traffic Accident Reconstructionists and Investigators (EA)
NATAS	National Academy of Television Arts and Sciences (EA)
NATAS	National Appropriate Technology Assistance Service [Butte, MT] [Department of Energy] (GRD)
NATAS	North American Thermal Analysis Society (EA)
Nat Assn	National Association (AD)
natat...........	Natation (AD)
NATaT.........	National Association of Towns and Townships (EA)
NatAutoC	National Auto Credit, Inc. Holding [Associated Press] (SAG)
NATAW	National Association of Textile and Apparel Wholesalers [Later, NATAD] (EA)
NATB	National Automobile Theft Bureau (EA)
NATB	Naval Air Training Base
NATB	Naval Training Bulletin
NAtB	Nitrosoanatabine [Organic chemistry]
NATB	Nonreading Aptitude Test Battery [US Employment Service] [Department of Labor]
Nat Bank Reg...	National Bankruptcy Register Reports [United States] [A publication] (DLA)
Nat Bankr Law...	National Bankruptcy Law [A publication] (DLA)
Nat Bankr N & R...	National Bankruptcy News and Reports [A publication] (DLA)
Nat Bankr R...	National Bankruptcy Register [United States] [A publication] (DLA)
Nat Bankr Reg...	National Bankruptcy Register [United States] [A publication] (DLA)
Nat Bankr Rep...	National Bankruptcy Register Reports [United States] [A publication] (DLA)
Nat Bar J	National Bar Journal [A publication] (DLA)
NATBASES...	Naval Air Training Bases
Nat BC	National Bank Cases [United States] [A publication] (DLA)
NatBev........	National Beverage Corp. [Associated Press] (SAG)
NATBF	Northwest African Tactical Bomber Force [World War II]
Nat BJ	National Bar Journal [A publication] (DLA)
Nat BR	National Bankruptcy Register [United States] [A publication] (DLA)
Nat Brev	Fitzherbert's Natura Brevium [A publication] (DLA)
NAT BUR ECON RES...	National Bureau of Economic Research (WDAA)
Nat Bur Econ Res...	National Bureau of Economic Research (AD)
Nat Bur Stand Circ...	National Bureau of Standards Circular [A publication] (AD)
NAtC	Columbia-Greene Community College, Athens, NY [Library symbol Library of Congress] (LCLS)
NATC	National Air Taxi Conference (SAA)
NATC	National Air Traffic Controllers (AD)
NATC	National Air Transportation Conferences [Later, NATA]
NATC	National Alcohol Tax Coalition (EA)
NATC	National Association of Taurine Clubs
NATC	National Association of Tax Consultants (EA)
NATC	National Association of Telemarketing Consultants [Defunct] (EA)
NATC	Naval Air Test Center
NATC	Naval Air Training Center
NATc	Naval Air Training Command (CAAL)
NATC	Nordic Amateur Theatre Council (EAIO)
NATC	Nordic Automobile Technical Committee [Defunct Denmark] (EAIO)
NATC	North Atlantic Treaty Council (NATG)

NATC .... Northwest African Training Command [*World War II*]
NATC .... Noval Air Test Center (IAA)
NATCA .... National Air Traffic Controllers Association (EA)
NATCA .... National Association of Trial Court Administrators (EA)
NATCA .... North American Trap Collector Association (EA)
NATCC .... Northwest African Troop Carrier Command [*World War II*]
NATCD .... National Association of Tobacco & Confectionery Distributors (AC)
NATCEM .... National Cemetery
NATCENTATHLIT... National Centre for Athletic Literature (NITA)
NATCG .... National Association of Training Corps for Girls [*British*] (BI)
Natch .... Natchez (AD)
natch .... Naturally (AD)
NATCO .... National Association of Transit Consumer Organizations (EA)
NATCO .... National Automatic Tool Co.
NATCO .... National Coordinator [*Marine science*] (MSC)
NATCO .... National Tank Co. (AD)
NATCO .... Navy Air Traffic Coordinating Officer
NATCO .... North American Transplant Coordinators Organization (EA)
NATCO .... Northern Advanced Technologies Corp. [*Research center*] (RCD)
NATCO .... Nuclear Auditing and Testing Co.
natcol .... Natural Color (AD)
NATCOL .... Natural Food Colours Association [*Basel, Switzerland*] (EAIO)
natcom .... National Communications (AD)
NATCOM .... National Communications Symposium [*IEEE*]
NATCOM .... National Conference on Communications (MCD)
NATCOM .... NATO Communication (NATG)
Nat Con .... Nature Conservancy (BARN)
NatConv .... National Convenience Stores [*Associated Press*] (SAG)
NATCS .... National Air Traffic Control Service (IEEE)
NATCS .... National Air Traffic Control System (NATG)
Nat D .... De Natura Deorum [*of Cicero*] [*Classical studies*] (OCD)
NATD .... National Association of Teachers of Dancing [*British*] (DBA)
NATD .... National Association of Telecommunications Dealers (EA)
NATD .... National Association of Test Directors (EA)
NATD .... National Association of Tobacco Distributors (EA)
NATD .... National Association of Tool Dealers [*British*] (BI)
NATD .... National Diagnostics, Inc. [*NASDAQ symbol*] (SAG)
NATD .... Natl Diagnostics [*NASDAQ symbol*] (TTSB)
NATDEC .... Naval Air Training Division Engineering Command (DNAB)
NATDEFSM... National Defense Service Medal [*Military decoration*]
Nat Dem ...... National Democrats [*Political party*] (AD)
NatDiag .... National Diagnostics, Inc. [*Associated Press*] (SAG)
NATDP .... National Agricultural Text-Digitizing Project [*National Agricultural Library*]
NATDS .... National Association of Truck Driving Schools (EA)
NATDS .... Naval Air Tactical Data System (MCD)
NATDS .... Navy Automated Transportation Data System (DNAB)
NATDW .... National Diagnostics Wrrt [*NASDAQ symbol*] (TTSB)
NATE .... National Association for Teachers of Electronics [*Defunct*] (EA)
NATE .... National Association for the Teaching of English (AD)
NATE .... National Association of Teachers of English
NATE .... National Association of Temple Educators (EA)
NATE .... Native American Teacher Education (AD)
NATE .... Neutral Atmosphere Temperature Experiment
NATEBE .... National Association of Teacher Educators for Business Education [*DeKalb, IL*] (EA)
NATEBOE ..... National Association of Teacher Educators for Business and Office Education [*Later, NATEBE*] (EA)
NATEC .... Naval Air Technical Evaluation Center (IAA)
NATEC .... Naval Air Training and Experimental Command
NATECHTRA... Naval Air Technical Training (DNAB)
NATECHTRACEN... Naval Air Technical Training Center
NATECHTRAU... Naval Air Technical Training Unit
NATECOM .... Naval Airship Training and Experimentation Command
NatEdu .... National Education Corp. [*Associated Press*] (SAG)
NATEF .... National Automotive Technicians Education Foundation (EA)
NATEL .... Nortronics Automatic Test Equipment Language [*Computer science*]
NATELCA ..... National Association for Teaching English and other Community Languages to Adults [*Formerly, NATELSA*] (AIE)
NatEng .... National Energy Group [*Associated Press*] (SAG)
NATES .... National Analysis of Trends in Emergency Systems [*Canada*] (MSC)
NATESA .... National Alliance of Television and Electronics Services Associations (IAA)
NATESA .... National Association of Television and Electronic Servicers of America [*N ESSDA*] [*Absorbed by*] (EA)
NATESLA ..... National Association for Teaching English as a Secondary Language to Adults [*British*] (DI)
NATESTCEN... Naval Air Test Center
NATEVHE ..... National Association of Teacher Educators for Vocational Home Economics (EA)
NATEX .... National Stock Exchange [*Dissolved, 1975*]
NATF .... National Automobile Theft Bureau
NATF .... Naval Air Test Facility
NATF .... Navy Advanced Tactical Fighter (MCD)
NATF .... New Arrivals Task Force (MCD)
NATFB .... National Archives Trust Fund Board
NATFC .... North American Toyah Fan Club (EA)
Nat Fed .... National Federation (AD)
NatFGs .... National Fuel Gas Co. [*Associated Press*] (SAG)
NATFHE .... National Association of Teachers in Further and Higher Education [*British*]
Nat For .... National Forum [*A publication*] (BRI)
NATFREQU... Natural Frequency (IAA)
NATF-SI .... Naval Air Test Facility - Ship Installations
NATG .... National Association of Training Groups [*British*] (DBA)
NATGA .... National Amateur Tobacco Growers' Association [*British*] (BI)
NAT GAL ...... National Gallery [*London*] (WDAA)
Nat Gal .... National Gallery (AD)
NatGam .... National Gaming Corp. [*Associated Press*] (SAG)
Nat Geog Mag... National Geographic Magazine [*A publication*] (AD)
NatGolf .... National Golf Properties [*Associated Press*] (SAG)
NatGsO .... National Gas & Oil Co. [*Associated Press*] (SAG)
NATH .... Nathan's Famous [*NASDAQ symbol*] (TTSB)
NATH .... Nathan's Famous, Inc. [*NASDAQ symbol*] (NQ)
Nathan .... Nathan's Common Law of South Africa [*A publication*] (DLA)
Nathans .... Nathan's Famous, Inc. [*Associated Press*] (SAG)
Nath B .... Nathaniel Bowditch (AD)
NATHE .... National Associations of Teachers of Home Economics [*British*]
NATHHAN .... National Challenged Homeschoolers Associated Network (PAZ)
nat hist .... Natural History (AD)
Nathl .... Nathaniel (AD)
NatHlth .... Natural Health Trends Corp. [*Associated Press*] (SAG)
NatHme .... National Home Centers [*Commercial firm Associated Press*] (SAG)
NatHP .... Nationwide Health Properties, Inc. [*Associated Press*] (SAG)
NATI .... National Instrument Corp. [*NASDAQ symbol*] (SAG)
NATICH .... National Air Toxics Information Clearinghouse [*Environmental Protection Agency*] (GFGA)
NATIDC .... Netherlands-Australia Trade and Industrial Development Council (AD)
NATIE .... National Association for Trade and Industrial Education (EA)
NATII .... National Association of Trade and Industrial Instructors (EA)
NATINADS ... NATO Integrated Air Defense System (NATG)
Nat Inc Tax Mag... National Income Tax Magazine [*A publication*] (DLA)
NatInst .... National Instrument Corp. [*Associated Press*] (SAG)
nation .... Nationality (AD)
National PTA... National Congress of Parents and Teachers (PAZ)
NATIP .... Navy Technical Information Program
NATIS .... National Information Systems [*Later, GIP*] [*UNESCO*]
NATIS .... Naval Air Training Information System
NATIS .... North Atlantic Treaty Information Service (NATG)
NATIV .... Nativity
Nativ .... Nativity (AD)
NATIV .... North American Test Instrument Vehicle [*Air Force test rocket*]
NATIVE .... North American Test Instrument Vehicle [*Air force test rocket*] (IAA)
Nat J Leg Ed... National Journal of Legal Education [*A publication*] (DLA)
NATK .... North American Technologies Corp. [*NASDAQ symbol*] (SAG)
NATK .... North Amer Technologies Group [*NASDAQ symbol*] (TTSB)
NATKE .... National Association of Theatrical and Kine Employees (AD)
NATKE .... National Association of Theatrical and Kinema Employees [*British*] (DI)
NATL .... NAI Technologies [*NASDAQ symbol*] (SAG)
NATL .... National (AAG)
natl .... National (WDMC)
natl .... National (AD)
NATL .... National
NATL .... National Agricultural Transportation League [*Defunct*] (EA)
NATL .... Natl Instruments [*NASDAQ symbol*] (TTSB)
NATL .... Naval Aeronautical Turbine Laboratory
N Atl .... North Atlantic (AD)
N Atlantic Reg Bus L Rev... North Atlantic Regional Business Law Review [*A publication*] (DLA)
NATLAS .... National Testing Laboratory Accreditation Scheme [*Military British*]
Nat Law Guild Q... National Lawyers Guild Quarterly [*A publication*] (DLA)
NatlBev .... National Beverage Corp. [*Associated Press*] (SAG)
NatlCity .... National City Corp. [*Associated Press*] (SAG)
Natl Civ Rev... National Civic Review [*A publication*] (ILCA)
N Atl Cur ..... North Atlantic Current (AD)
Nat L Guild Q... National Lawyers Guild Quarterly [*A publication*] (DLA)
Nat Lib .... National Liberal (AD)
NatLib .... National Liberal Party [*Australia Political party*]
Nat Lib .... National Library of Canada (AD)
NATLIBCAN... National Library of Canada (AD)
NATLIBNZ .... National Library of New Zealand (AD)
Nat'l Income Tax Mag... National Income Tax Magazine [*A publication*] (DLA)
Nat LJ .... Natal Law Journal [*South Africa*] [*A publication*] (DLA)
Nat'l Legal Mag... National Legal Magazine [*A publication*] (DLA)
Nat LM .... Natal Law Magazine [*South Africa*] [*A publication*] (DLA)
Natlm .... Naturalism (VRA)
Nat Louis U... National-Louis University (GAGS)
Nat'l Pub Empl Rep... National Public Employment Reporter [*A publication*] (DLA)
Nat LQ .... Natal Law Quarterly [*South Africa*] [*A publication*] (DLA)
Nat LR .... Natal Law Reports [*South Africa*] [*A publication*] (ILCA)
Nat L Rec .... National Law Record [*A publication*] (DLA)
NatlReg .... National Registry [*Associated Press*] (SAG)
Nat L Rep .... National Law Reporter [*A publication*] (DLA)
Natl Rep Sys... National Reporter System (DLA)
Nat L Rev .... National Law Review [*A publication*] (DLA)
NatlRV .... National R.V. Holdings, Inc. [*Associated Press*] (SAG)
Nat'l School L Rptr... National School Law Reporter [*A publication*] (DLA)
NATLSEMICON... National Semiconductor Corp. (IAA)
NatlStl .... National Steel Corp. [*Associated Press*] (SAG)
NATM .... New Austrian Tunnel Method [*Civil engineering*]
NATMA .... National Award and Trophy Manufacturers Association (EA)
NATMAC ...... National Air Traffic Management Advisory Committee [*British*]
NATMAP ...... National Mapping (AD)
NATMATMUS... National Automotive and Truck Model and Toy Museum of the United States
NATMC .... National Advanced Technology Management Conference
NatMFS .... National Medical Financial Services Corp. [*Associated Press*] (SAG)

NATMH....... National Association of Teachers of the Mentally Handicapped [*British*]
NatMicr....... Natural Microsystems Corp. [*Associated Press*] (SAG)
NATMILCOMSYS... National Military Command System
NAT MON..... National Monument (WDAA)
Nat Mon ..... National Monument (AD)
NATMSACT... Naval Air Training Support Facility (AAGC)
Nat Mus...... Natal Museum (AD)
NATMUS...... National Automobile and Truck Museum of the United States
NATMUS...... National Automotive and Truck Museum of United States (EA)
Nat Mus...... National Museum (AD)
NATN .... National Association of Theatre Nurses [*British*] (BI)
NATN .... National Association of Traveling Nurses
NATNAV...... North Atlantic Navigation
NATNAVDENCEN... National Naval Dental Center (DNAB)
NATNAVMEDCEN... National Naval Medical Center [*Bethesda, MD*]
NATNAVRESMASTCONRADSTA... National Naval Reserve Master Control Radio Station (DNAB)
Natn Bank Mon Sum... National Bank. Monthly Summary [*A publication*]
Natn Bank Mon Sum Aust Cond... National Bank of Australasia. Monthly Summary of Australian Conditions [*A publication*]
Natnet.......... National Network [*Telecommunications British*]
Natn Farmer... National Farmer [*A publication*]
NatnGv03.... Nations Government Income Term 2003 [*Associated Press*] (SAG)
NatnGv04.... Nations Government Income Term 2004 [*Associated Press*] (SAG)
Natn Hosp ... National Hospital [*A publication*]
Natn Parks J... National Parks Journal [*A publication*]
Natn Rehab Digest... National Rehabilitation Digest [*A publication*]
NatnsBal...... Nations Balanced Target Maturity Fund [*Associated Press*] (SAG)
NatnsBk ...... NationsBank Corp. [*Associated Press*] (SAG)
Natn Times Mag... National Times Magazine [*A publication*]
NATO .... Narrow-Angle Target of Opportunity [*Photography*] [*NASA*]
NATO .... National Association of Taxicab Owners [*Later, ITA*] (EA)
NATO .... National Association of Telephone Operators [*A union*] [*British*]
NATO .... National Association of Theatre Owners (EA)
NATO .... National Association of Trailer Owners (EA)
NATO .... National Association of Travel Organizations [*Later, TIA*] (EA)
NATO .... No Action, Talk Only (DICI)
NATO .... North African Theater of Operations [*World War II*]
NATO .... North American Treat Organization [*AIA*] (TAG)
NATO .... North Atlantic Treaty Organization [*Facetious translation: "No Action, Talk Only"*] [*Brussels, Belgium*]
NATOA........ National Association of Telecommunications Officers and Advisors (EA)
NATO AEW... North Atlantic Treaty Organization Airborne Early Warning Program
NATO-AGARD... North Atlantic Treaty Organization - Advisory Group for Aeronautical Research and Development
Nat Obs ...... National Observer [*A publication*] (AD)
NATODC...... North Atlantic Treaty Organization Defense College (DNAB)
NATODEFCOL... North Atlantic Treaty Organization Defense College (DNAB)
NATOELLA ... North Atlantic Treaty Organization - European Long Lines Agency
NatOilwll .... National Oilwell, Inc. [*Associated Press*] (SAG)
NAT-OJT ..... National On-the-Job Training Program [*Department of Labor*]
NATO-LRSS... North Atlantic Treaty Organization - Long-Range Scientific Studies
NATO MC..... North Atlantic Treaty Organization Military Committee
NATOMILOCGRP... North Atlantic Treaty Organization - Military Oceanography Group (NATG)
NATOPS...... Naval Air Training and Operating Procedures Standardization (MCD)
Nat Ord .... Natural Order [*Botany*] (BARN)
NATO-RDPP... North Atlantic Treaty Organization - Multilateral Research and Development Production Program
NATOSAT.... North Atlantic Treaty Organization Satellite
NATO-SC..... North Atlantic Treaty Organization - Science Committee
NATOUSA .... North African Theater of Operations, United States Army [*World War II*]
NATP .... National Association of Tax Practitioners (EA)
NATP .... Natl Power plc [*LO, exchange symbol*] (TTSB)
NATPA .... North America Taiwanese Professors' Association (EA)
NAT PAC .... National PAC [*Political Action Committee*] (EA)
NATPE .... National Association of Television Program Executives (NTCM)
NATPE .... NATPE [*National Association of Television Program Executives*] International (EA)
Nat Peop .... Native Peoples [*A publication*] (BRI)
nat phil....... Natural Philosophy (AD)
Nat Phil ...... Natural Philosophy (BARN)
Nat Pk .... National Park (BARN)
NATPN....... North African Transportation Section [*World War II*]
NatProc...... National Processing, Inc. [*Associated Press*] (SAG)
NatProp ...... National Propane Partners LP [*Associated Press*] (SAG)
NATPS .... National Association of Trade Protection Societies [*British*] (DBA)
NATR .... Natchez Trace Parkway [*National Park Service designation*]
NATR .... National Association of Tenants and Residents [*British*] (BI)
NATR .... National Association of Toy Retailers [*British*] (BI)
NATR .... National Representative [*Red Cross*]
Nat R .... National Review [*A publication*] (BRI)
natr........... Natrium [*Sodium*] [*Latin*] (AD)
NATR .... Natrium [*Sodium*] [*Pharmacy*]
NATR .... Natural Resources
NATR .... Nature's Sunshine Prod [*NASDAQ symbol*] (TTSB)
NATR .... Nature's Sunshine Products, Inc. [*NASDAQ symbol*] (NQ)
NATR .... No Additional Traffic Reported [*Aviation*]
NATR .... Nordischer Amator Theater Rat [*Nordic Amateur Theatre Council - NATC*] (EAIO)
NATRA........ National Association of Television and Radio Announcers (NTCM)
NATRA........ National Association of Television and Radio Artists [*Inactive*]

NATRA .... Naval Air Training Command (AFIT)
NATRACOM... Naval Air Training Command (DNAB)
NATRADIVENGCOM... Naval Air Training Division Engineering Command (DNAB)
NATRAP...... Narrow-Band Transmission of RADAR Pictures (MCD)
NATRC .... North American Trail Ride Conference (EA)
NatRe .... National Re Corp. [*Associated Press*] (SAG)
NatRecd ..... National Record Mart, Inc. [*Associated Press*] (SAG)
Nat Reg ..... National Register, Edited by Mead [*1816*] [*A publication*] (DLA)
Nat Rept Syst... National Reporter System (DLA)
NATRFD ..... National Association of Television-Radio Farm Directors [*Later, NAFB*] (EA)
NATRI .... National Association of Treasurers of Religious Institutes (EA)
NATRI .... Navy Training Requirements Information
NatrlHlth...... Natural Health Trends Corp. [*Associated Press*] (SAG)
NATRON ..... National Cash Register Electronic Data Processing System (MCD)
NAT-RPG .... North Atlantic Treaty Regional Planning Group (NATG)
NatrSun ..... Natures Sunshine Products [*Associated Press*] (SAG)
NATS .... National Activity to Test Software
NATS .... National Air Toxics Strategy [*Environmental Protection Agency*] (GFGA)
NATS .... National Air Traffic Services [*British*]
NATS .... National Association of Teachers of Singing (EA)
NATS .... National Association of Temporary Services [*Alexandria, VA*] (EA)
NATS .... National Association of Textile Supervisors (EA)
Nats .... Nationalists (AD)
NATS .... National Secs [*NASDAQ symbol*] (TTSB)
NATS .... National Securities Corp. [*NASDAQ symbol*] (NQ)
Nats .... Natsionalnyii [*National*] [*Russian*] (AD)
NATS .... Naval Air Test Station (AD)
NATS .... Naval Air Transport Service
NATS .... Needlework and Accessories Trade Show (ITD)
NATS .... Negative Authorization Terminal System [*Computer science*] (MHDB)
NATS .... New Aircraft Tool System [*Army*]
NATS .... Noise Abatement Test System (FAAC)
NATS .... Nordisk Avisteknisk Samarbetsnamnd [*Nordic Joint Technical Press Board*] [*Sweden*] (EAIO)
NATS .... North American Truffling Society (EA)
NATSA .... National Associated Truck Stops and Associates (EA)
NATSAA ...... NATO Air Traffic Service Advisory Agency (NATG)
NATSC .... National Association of Training School Chaplains (EA)
NATSC .... National Association of Trap and Skeet Clubs (EA)
NAT SC ...... Natural Sciences (WDAA)
NAT SC D .... Doctor of Natural Science (WDAA)
Nat ScD ..... Doctor of Natural Science (AD)
Nat Sci Fdn.. National Science Foundation (AD)
NATSECM ... National Security Medal
Nat Sec Soc... National Secular Society (AD)
Nat Semi .... National Semiconductor Corp.
NATSEMI .... National Semiconductor Inc. (AD)
NATSF .... Naval Air Technical Services Facility (MCD)
NATSFERRY... Naval Air Transport Service, Ferry Command [*World War II*]
NATSFQADIVLANT... Naval Air Technical Services Facility, Quality Assurance Division, Atlantic (DNAB)
NATSFQADIVPAC... Naval Air Technical Services Facility, Quality Assurance Division, Pacific (DNAB)
NATSIEP ..... National Aboriginal and Torres Strait Islander Education Policy [*Australia*]
NATSJA....... National Association of Training School and Juvenile Agencies [*Later, NAJCA*] (EA)
NATSLANT... Naval Air Transport Service, Atlantic Wing [*World War II*]
NATSO........ National Association of Truck Stop Operators (EA)
NATSOPA.... National Society of Operative Printers and Assistants [*British*]
NAT sound... Natural Sound [*Broadcasting*] (WDMC)
NATSPAC.... Naval Air Transport Service, Pacific Wing [*World War II*]
NATSPG...... North Atlantic Systems Planning Group [*Military*] (WDAA)
NAT-STD .... NATO STANAG International Standards
NATSU .... Naval Air Technical Services Unit (NVT)
NATSU .... Nominated Air Traffic Service Unit (DA)
Nat Sup ..... National Superannuation (AD)
NatSurg...... National Surgery Centers, Inc. [*Associated Press*] (SAG)
NATSYN..... Natural and Synthetic [*Type of long-wearing rubber, which is actually wholly synthetic*]
NATT........... National Association of Teachers of Travellers [*British*] (DBA)
NATT........... National Association of Towns and Township Officials (EA)
NATT........... Naval Air Technical Training
N ATT .... Naval Attache (WDAA)
N Att .... Naval Attache (AD)
NAtt .... Stevens Memorial Library, Attica, NY [*Library symbol Library of Congress*] (LCLS)
NATTA .... Network of Alternative Technology and Technology Assessment (EAIO)
NATTA .... North American Trackless Trolley Association (EA)
N-attack....... Nuclear Attack (AD)
Nat Tax Mag.. National Tax Magazine [*A publication*] (DLA)
NATTC .... National Tank Truck Carriers (AD)
NATTC .... Naval Air Technical Training Center
NATTCDET ... Naval Air Technical Training Center Detachment (DNAB)
NATTCL....... Naval Air Technical Training Center, Lakehurst (DNAB)
NATTFU ...... National Transsexual-Transvestite Feminization Union (EA)
NATTKE....... National Association of Theatrical, Television, and Kine Employees [*A union*] [*British*] (DCTA)
NATTS .... National Association of Trade and Technical Schools (EA)
NATTS .... Naval Air Turbine Test Station
NATTS .... North American Transvestite/Transsexual Society [*Defunct*] (EA)
NATTS-ATL... Naval Air Turbine Test Station - Aeronautical Turbine Laboratory

NATTU	Naval Air Technical Training Unit
Nat U	Nations Unies [*United Nations*] [*French*] (AD)
NATU	Naval Aircraft Torpedo Unit
Nat UL Rev...	National University. Law Review [*1921-31*] [*A publication*] (DLA)
Nat Uni	National University (AD)
natur	Naturalist (AD)
NATUR	Naturalist (WDAA)
NATURBTESTSTA...	Naval Air Turbine Test Station
NaturlAlt	Natural Alternatives International [*Associated Press*] (SAG)
NATUS	Naturalized United States Citizen
NATUSA......	North African Theater of Operations (AD)
NATUSA......	North African Theater, United States Army [*World War II*]
NATVA	National All Terrain Vehicle Association (EA)
NATVAS	National Academy of Television Arts and Sciences (EA)
NatVisn	National Vision Associates [*Associated Press*] (SAG)
NATW	National Association of Texaco Wholesalers (EA)
NATW	National Association of Town Watch (EA)
NATW	Natural Wonders [*NASDAQ symbol*] (TTSB)
NATW	Natural Wonders, Inc. [*NASDAQ symbol*] (SAG)
NATWA	National Auto and Truck Wreckers Association [*Later, ADRA*] (EA)
NATwA........	North American Tiddlywinks Association (EA)
NATWARCOL...	National War College [*Later, UND*] [*DoD*] (DNAB)
NATWC.......	National War College [*Later, UND*] [*DoD*]
NatWest......	National Westminster [*Bank*]
NATWF	North American Tug of War Federation (EA)
NATWJ	National Alliance of Third World Journalists (EA)
NatWndr......	Natural Wonders, Inc. [*Associated Press*] (SAG)
NATWP	Naval Air Transport Wing, Pacific
NAT WS......	Nordic Amer Tanker Ship Wrrt [*AMEX symbol*] (TTSB)
naty	Naturally (AD)
NaTY	Sodium Hydrogen Phosphate-Tryptone-Yeast Extract [*Growth medium*] [*Microbiology*]
Natzd	Naturalized [*Biology*] (BARN)
NAU	Confederation Nordique des Cadres, Techniciens, et Autres Responsables [*Nordic Confederation of Supervisors, Technicians, and Other Managers*] (EAIO)
NAU	Nalcus Resources [*Vancouver Stock Exchange symbol*]
NAU	Napuka [*Marquesas Islands*] [*Airport symbol*] (OAG)
NAU	Narcotics Assistance Unit [*Department of State*]
Nau	Nauruan (AD)
Nau	Nauru Island (AD)
nau	Nautica [*Nautical*] [*Spanish*] (AD)
NAU	Naval Administrative Unit
NAU	Network Access Unit [*Telecommunications*]
NAU	Network Addressable Unit (NITA)
NAU	Network Address [*or Addressable*] Unit [*Computer science*] (BUR)
NAU	Network Administration Utilities [*Honeywell*] (NITA)
NAU	Noise Augmentation Unit [*Military*] (CAAL)
NAU	Nordic Confederation of Supervisors, Technicians, and Other Managers [*Formerly, Nordic Union of Foremen*] (EA)
NAU	North Arizona University (AD)
NAu	Seymour Library, Auburn, NY [*Library symbol Library of Congress*] (LCLS)
NAUA	National Aircraft Underwriters' Association (AD)
NAUA	National Automobile Underwriters Association [*Later, ISO*] (EA)
NAUB	National Association of Urban Bankers (EA)
NAuC	Cayuga County Community College, Auburn, NY [*Library symbol Library of Congress*] (LCLS)
NAUE	New and Unused Equipment (MCD)
NAUF	Name and Address Update File [*IRS*]
NAUFMA......	National Association of Urban Flood Management Agencies [*Later, NAFSWMA*] (EA)
NAUFOF.......	North American UFO Federation [*Defunct*] (EA)
NAUG..........	National AppleWorks Users Group (EA)
nauga	Naugahide (AD)
NAUHF........	Northern Area Ultrahigh Frequency Radio System [*Green Pine*] (MCD)
NAuHi	Cayuga County Historical Society, Auburn, NY [*Library symbol Library of Congress*] (LCLS)
NAUI	National Association of Underwater Instructors (EA)
NAUL	Netherland-America University League [*Defunct*] (EA)
NAULAS......	North American Union Life Assurance Society [*Chicago, IL*] (EA)
NAUM	National Association of Uniform Manufacturers [*Later, NAUMD*] (EA)
NAUMD	National Association of Uniform Manufacturers and Distributors (EA)
NAuMH	Auburn Memorial Hospital, Learning Resources Center, Auburn, NY [*Library symbol Library of Congress*] (LCLS)
NAUN..........	Nearest Active Upstream Neighbor [*Computer science*]
NAU-OLC.....	North American Union of Sisters of Our Lady of Charity (TOCD)
NAUP.........	National Association of Unemployed Persons [*Defunct*] (EA)
NAUPA........	National Amalgamated Union of Shop Assistants [*A union*] [*British*]
NAUPA........	National Association of Unclaimed Property Administrators (EA)
NAURI.........	Nonaccelerating-Unemployment Rate of Inflation [*Economics*]
NAurW	Wells College, Aurora, NY [*Library symbol Library of Congress*] (LCLS)
NAUS	National Aerospace Utilization System (NOAA)
NAUS	National Association for Uniformed Services (EA)
NAuS	Seward House, Auburn, NY [*Library symbol Library of Congress*] (LCLS)
NAUSAWC ...	National Amalgamated Union of Shop Assistants, Warehousemen, and Clerks [*A union*] [*British*]
NAuT..........	Auburn Theological Seminary, Auburn, NY [*Library symbol Library of Congress Obsolete*] (LCLS)
NAUT	Nautica Enterprises [*NASDAQ symbol*] (TTSB)
NAUT	Nautica Enterprises, Inc. [*NASDAQ symbol*] (SAG)
NAUT	Nautical (AAG)

naut	Nautical (AD)
NAUTIC........	Naval Autonomous Intelligent Console (PDAA)
Nautica........	Nautica Enterprises, Inc. [*Associated Press*] (SAG)
NAUTIS-F.....	Naval Autonomous Information System-Frigate (DOMA)
NAUTO	Nautophone
NAUTS........	Nautical Miles (ROG)
NAUTT	National Association of Unions in the Textile Trade [*British*] (DCTA)
NAUW.........	National Association of University Women (EA)
NAUWS	Naval Advanced Undersea Weapons School
n aux b........	New Auxiliary Boiler (AD)
NAV	Narrows [*Virginia*] [*Seismograph station code, US Geological Survey*] (SEIS)
NAV	National American Veterans
NAV	National Association of Videographers [*Defunct*] (EA)
NAV	Natividade [*Brazil*] [*Airport symbol*] (AD)
Nav	Navaho (AD)
nav	Navajo [*MARC language code Library of Congress*] (LCCP)
NAV	Naval (MSA)
Nav	Naval (AD)
nav.	Naval (AD)
NAV	Naval Artillery Volunteers [*British*] (ROG)
Nav	Navarra (AD)
Nav	Navarre (AD)
Nav	Navassa Island (AD)
nav.	Navigable (AD)
NAV	Navigate (AAG)
nav.	Navigation (AD)
NAV	Navigation (GAVI)
NAV	Navigator (DSUE)
Nav	Navistar International Corp. [*Associated Press*] (SAG)
NAV	Navistar International Corp. [*NYSE symbol*] (SPSG)
NAV	Navistar Intl [*NYSE symbol*] (TTSB)
NAV	Navy (AAG)
NAV	Net Annual Value [*Business term*] (ADA)
NAV	Net Asset Value
n/a/v	Net Asset Value
NAV	Next Generation Advanced Vehicle [*Nippon Steel Corp.*]
NAV	Nonalcoholic Volunteers
NAV	North American Ventures, Inc. [*Vancouver Stock Exchange symbol*]
NAV	Visual Navigation (MCD)
NAVA	National Association for Variable Annuities
NAVA	National Association for Veterinary Acupuncture (EA)
NAVA	National Association of Veterinary Assistants [*Defunct*] (EA)
NAVA	National Audio-Visual Association [*Later, ICIA*] (EA)
NAVA	Navajo National Monument
NAVA	Net Asset Value (AD)
NAVA	North American Vexillological Association (EA)
NAVABSCOLLU...	Navy Absentee Collection Unit (DNAB)
NAVAC	National Audiovisual Aids Centre [*British*]
NAVACAD	Naval Academy
NA Vacc.......	North American Vaccine, Inc. [*Associated Press*] (SAG)
NAVACCTGFINCEN...	Navy Accounting and Finance Center (DNAB)
NAVACD.......	Naval Academy (DNAB)
navaco........	Navigation Action Cutout (AD)
NAVACO.......	Navigation Action Cutout Switchboard
NAVACT.......	All Navy Activities [*A dispatch to all activities in an area*]
NAVACTDET...	Naval Activities Detachment (DNAB)
NAVAD........	Naval Administrator At [*Place*]
NAVADCOM...	Naval Administrative Command
NAVADGP ...	Naval Advisory Group
NAVADGRU...	Naval Advisory Group (CINC)
NAVADGRU...	Navy Advisory Group
NAV-ADMIN...	Navigation-Administration [*Inquiry program*] (AFIT)
NAVADMINCOM...	Naval Administrative Command (DNAB)
NAVADMINO...	Navy Administrative Office [*or Officer*]
NAVADMINU...	Naval Administration Unit (MUGU)
NAVADMINUANX...	Naval Administrative Unit Annex (DNAB)
NAVADS.......	Navy Automated Transport Documentation System (DNAB)
NAVADUNIT...	Naval Administrative Unit
NAVADUNSEAWPNSCOL...	Naval Advanced Undersea Weapons School (DNAB)
NAVADVUSEAWPNSCOL...	Naval Advanced Undersea Weapons School (MUGU)
NAVAE........	National Association for Vietnamese American Education (EA)
NAVAER.......	Navy Aeronautics
NAVAERAUDOFC...	Navy Area Audit Office [*London*] (DNAB)
NAVAEROMEDCEN...	Naval Aeronautical Medical Center
NAVAERORECOV...	Naval Aerospace Recovery Facility
NAVAERORECOVF...	Naval Aerospace Recovery Facility (AD)
NAVAERORECOVFAC...	Naval Aerospace Recovery Facility
NAVAEROSPMEDINST...	Naval Aerospace Medical Institute
NAVAEROSPMEDRSCHINST...	Naval Aerospace Medical Research Institute (DNAB)
NAVAERO(SP)OMEDRSCHLAB...	Naval Aerospace Medical Research Laboratory (DNAB)
NAVAERO(SP)RECFAC...	Naval Aerospace Recovery Facility (DNAB)
NAVAERO(SP)REGMEDCEN...	Naval Aerospace Medical Center (DNAB)
NAVAGLOBE...	Long-Distance Navigation System, Global [*Air Force*]
NAVAID........	Navigation Aid
NAVAID........	Navigational Aid (DNAB)
NAVAIDE.......	Naval Aide
NAVAIDSUPPUNIT...	Navigational Aids Support Unit (DNAB)
NAVAIR........	Naval Air Systems Command
NAVAIR........	Naval Air Systems Command Headquarters (USDC)
NAVAIRANDACT...	Naval Air Research and Development Activities (MUGU)
NAVAIRDEVCEN...	Naval Air Development Center [*Also, NADC, NADEVCEN*] (MUGU)
NAVAIRDEVU...	Naval Air Development Unit (MUGU)

NAVAIRECONTECHSUPCEN... Naval Air Reconnaissance Technical Support Center
NAVAIRENGCEN... Naval Air Engineering Center [Closed]
NAVAIRENGCENFO... Naval Air Engineering Center Field Office (DNAB)
NAVAIRENGLAB... Naval Air Engineering Laboratory (DNAB)
NAVAIRENGRCEN... Naval Air Engineering Center [Closed]
NAVAIRENGRFAC... Naval Air Engineering Facility (MUGU)
NAVAIRESCEN... Naval Air Reserve Center (DNAB)
NAVAIRESFORRON... Naval Air Reserve Force Squadron (DNAB)
NAVAIRESMOPIXU... Naval Air Reserve Mobile Photographic Unit (DNAB)
NAVAIRESU... Naval Air Reserve Unit (DNAB)
NAVAIREWORKF... Naval Air Rework Facility
NAVAIREWORKFAC... Naval Air Rework Facility
NAVAIRFAC... Naval Air Facility
NAVAIRINST... Naval Air Systems Command Instruction
NavAirInstr... Naval Air Command Instruction (AAGC)
NAVAIRINTO... Naval Air Intelligence Office (MUGU)
NAVAIRLANT... Naval Air Force, Atlantic Fleet
NAVAIRLOGOFF... Naval Air Logistics Office (DNAB)
NAVAIRLOGTASKFORREP... Naval Air Logistics Task Force Representative (DNAB)
NAVAIRMAINTRAGRU... Naval Air Maintenance Training Group (DNAB)
NAVAIRMATCEN... Naval Air Material Center [Also, NAMATCEN, NAMC] (MUGU)
NAVAIRMINDEFDEVU... Naval Air Mine Defense Development Unit (MUGU)
NAVAIRNEWS... Naval Aviation News [A publication] (DNAB)
NAVAIRPAC... Naval Air Force, Pacific Fleet
NAVAIRPROPCEN... Naval Air Propulsion Center (GRD)
NAVAIRPROPTESTCEN... Naval Air Propeller Test Center
NAVAIRRES... Naval Air Reserve
NAVAIRREWORKF... Naval Air Rework Facility (AD)
NAVAIRSTA... Naval Air Station (DNAB)
NAVAIRSUPPU... Naval Air Support Unit
NAVAIRSYSCO... Naval Air Systems Command (MCD)
NAVAIR SYSCOM... Naval Air System Command (DOMA)
NAVAIRSYSCOM... Naval Air Systems Command
NAVAIRSYSCOMFLEREADREP... Naval Air Systems Command Fleet Readiness Representative (DNAB)
NAVAIRSYSCOMFLESUPREPCEN... Naval Air Systems Command Fleet Supply Representative Center (DNAB)
NAVAIRSYSCOMHQ... Naval Air Systems Command Headquarters
NAVAIRSYSCOMMETSYSDIV... Naval Air Systems Command, Meteorological Systems Division (DNAB)
NAVAIRSYSCOMREP... Naval Air Systems Command Representative
NAVAIRSYSCOMREPAC... Naval Air Systems Command Representative, Pacific
NAVAIRSYSCOMREPCENT... Naval Air Systems Command Representative, Central
NAVAIRSYSCOMREPLANT... Naval Air Systems Command Representative, Atlantic
NAVAIRSYSCOMREP PNCLA... Naval Air Systems Command Representative, Naval Air Training Command, Pensacola [Florida]
NAVAIRSYSCOMTARANDSYSDIV... Naval Air Systems Command Target and Range Systems Command (DNAB)
NAVAIRTECHREP... Naval Air Systems Command Technical Representative (DNAB)
NAVAIRTECHSERVFAC... Naval Air Technical Services Facility (MUGU)
NAVAIRTERM... Naval Air Terminal (DNAB)
NAVAIRTESTCEN... Naval Air Test Center (MUGU)
NAVAIRTESTCENT... Naval Air Test Center (GRD)
NAVAIRTESTFAC... Naval Air Test Facility (MUGU)
NAVAIRTESTFACSHIPINSTAL... Naval Air Test Facility - Ship Installations (DNAB)
NAVAIRTORPU... Naval Aircraft Torpedo Unit (MUGU)
NAVAIRTRACEN... Naval Air Training Center
NAVAIRTU... Naval Air Training Unit (DNAB)
NAVAIRTURBTESTSTA... Naval Air Turbine Test Station (MUGU)
NAVAL... National Audio Visual Aids Library (AIE)
Naval E... Naval Engineer (PGP)
NAVALOT... Allotment Division [Navy]
NAVALREHCEN... Naval Alcohol Rehabilitation Center (DNAB)
NAVALREHDRYDOCK... Navy Alcohol Rehabilitation Drydock (DNAB)
NAVALT... Navy Alterations
NAVAMDEP... Naval Ammunition Depot [Charleston, SC]
NAVAMPROENGCEN... Naval Ammunition Production Engineering Center (DNAB)
NAVANTRA... Naval Air Advanced Training Center
NAVANTRACOM... Naval Air Advanced Training Command
NAVAP... National Association of VA [Veterans Administration] Physicians (EA)
NAVAPI... North American Voltage and Phase Indicator (IEEE)
NAVAPSCIENCLAB... Naval Applied Science Laboratory (DNAB)
NAVAR... Navigation Air RADAR (IAA)
NAVAR... Navigation and Ranging (IAA)
NAVAR... Navigation RADAR
NAVARA... Navy Appellate Review Activity
Nav Arch... Naval Architect [Academic degree]
NAVAREAAUDSVC... Naval Area Audit Service
NAVARHO... Navigation and Radio Homing [Aviation]
NAVARMDEP... Naval Armament Depot
Navarre... Navarre Corp. [Associated Press] (SAG)
NAVASCOPE... Navigation Airborne RADAR Scope [Air Force]
NAVASCREEN... Navigation RADAR Screen [Air Force]
NAVASTROGRU... Navy Astronautics Group (MUGU)
NAVASTROGRUHQTRINJFAC... Navy Astronautics Group Headquarters, Tracking and Injection Facility (DNAB)
NAVASTROGRUP... Navy Astronautics Group (SAA)
NAVASWDATACEN... Navy Antisubmarine Warfare Data Center
NAVASWDATCEN... Navy Antisubmarine Warfare Data Center (DNAB)
NAVATR... Naval Air Systems [Command Headquarters] [Marine science] (OSRA)
NAVAUD... Navy Auditor
NAVAUDO... Navy Audit Office (DNAB)
NAVAUDSVC... Director, Naval Audit Service
NAVAUDSVCAP... Naval Audit Service, Capital Area (DNAB)

NAVAUDSVCHQ... Naval Audit Service Headquarters (DNAB)
NAVAUDSVCNE... Naval Audit Service, Northeast Area (DNAB)
NAVAUDSVCSE... Naval Audit Service, Southeast Area (DNAB)
NAVAUDSVCWEST... Naval Audit Service, Western Area (DNAB)
NavAus... Navigation in Australian Waters (AD)
NAVAUTH... Naval Authority
NAVAUTODINSCEN... Navy Automatic Digital Network Switching Center (DNAB)
NAVAVCEN... Naval Audio-Visual Center (DNAB)
NAVAVENGSERVU... Naval Aviation Engineering Services Unit [Philadelphia, PA] (DNAB)
NAVAVENGSERVUDET... Naval Aviation Engineering Service Unit Detachment (DNAB)
NAVAVIONICFAC... Naval Avionics Facility [Later, NAC] (MUGU)
NAVAVIONICSCEN... Naval Avionics Center (DNAB)
NAVAVMEDCEN... Naval Aviation Medical Center (DNAB)
NAVAVMUSEUM... Naval Aviation Museum [Pensacola, FL] (DNAB)
NAVAVNENGRSERVU... Naval Aviation Engineering Service Unit [Philadelphia, PA] (DNAB)
NAVAVNLOGCEN... Naval Aviation Logistics Center (NVT)
NAVAVNLOGCENDET... Naval Aviation Logistics Center Detachment (DNAB)
NAVAVNLOGCENFSO... Naval Aviation Logistics Center Field Service Office (DNAB)
NAVAVNLOGCENMETALABOPS... Naval Aviation Logistics Center Meteorology Calibration Laboratory Operations (DNAB)
NAVAVNMEDCEN... Naval Aviation Medical Center (DNAB)
NAVAVNSAFECEN... Naval Aviation Safety Center
NAVAVNSCOLCOM... Naval Aviation School Command
NAVAVNWEPSFAC... Naval Aviation Weapons Facilities
NAVAVNWPNSFAC... Naval Aviation Weapons Facilities (DNAB)
NAVAVNWPNSFACDET... Naval Aviation Weapons Facility Detachment (DNAB)
NAVB... National Association of Volunteer Bureaux [British] (EAIO)
NAVBALTAP... Allied Naval Forces, Baltic Approaches [NATO] (NATG)
NAVBALTAP... Naval Forces Baltic Approaches [NATO] (AD)
NAVBASE... Naval Base
NAVBASELANT... Naval Bases Atlantic
NAVBASEPAC... Naval Bases Pacific
NAVBCHGRU... Naval Beach Group (DNAB)
NAVBCHPHIBREFTRAGRU... Navy Beach Amphibious Refresher Training Group (DNAB)
NAVBCSTSVCDET... Navy Broadcasting Service Detachment (DNAB)
NAVBCSTSVCDETTASA... Navy Broadcasting Service Detachment Television Audio Support Activity (DNAB)
NAVBCSTSVCWASHDC... Navy Broadcasting Service, Washington, DC (DNAB)
NAVBE... National Association for Vocational Business Education (AEBS)
NAVBEACHGRU... Naval Beach Group (CINC)
NAVBIODYNLAB... Naval Biodynamics Laboratory (DNAB)
NAVBIOLAB... Naval Biological Laboratory (MUGU)
NAVBIOSCILAB... Naval Biosciences Research Laboratory (DNAB)
NAVBIT... Naval Basic Instrument Trainer (PDAA)
navbm... Naval Ballistic Missile (AD)
NAVBM... Navy Ballistic Missile
NAVBMC... Navy Ballistic Missile Committee
NAVBOILAB... Navy Boiler Laboratory
nav brz... Naval Bronze (AD)
Nav Bs... Naval Base (AD)
NAVC... Naval Aviation Cadet
NAVC... North American Voyageur Council (EA)
NAVCAD... Naval Aviation Cadet
NavCad... Naval Cadet (AD)
NAVCALAB... Navy Calibration Laboratory (DNAB)
NAVCALABANX... Navy Calibration Laboratory Annex (DNAB)
NAVCALABMSG... Navy Calibration Laboratory Meteorology Support Group (DNAB)
NAVCALABOPS... Navy Calibration Laboratory Operations (DNAB)
NAVCALS... Naval Communication Area Local Station (NVT)
NAVCAMS... Naval Communication Area Master Station (NVT)
NAVCAMSEASTPAC... Naval Communication Area Master Station, Eastern Pacific (DNAB)
NAVCAMSLANT... Naval Communication Area Master Station, Atlantic (DNAB)
NAVCAMSMED... Naval Communication Area Master Station, Mediterranean (DNAB)
NAVCAMSOAM... Naval Communication Area Master Station, South America (DNAB)
NAVCAMSSPECCOMDIVLANT... Naval Communication Area Master Station, Special Communications Division, Atlantic (DNAB)
NAVCARGOHANBN... Naval Cargo Handling Battalion
NAVCAT... Naval Career Appraisal Team (MUGU)
NAVCAT... Naval Construction Action Team [Vietnam] (VNW)
NAVCBCEN... Naval Construction Battalion Center
NAVCC... Naval Communications Center (MCD)
NAVCENFRACO... Navy Central Freight Control Office
NAVCENT... Allied Naval Forces, Central Europe [NATO]
NAVCENT... Naval Forces [US] Central [Command] (DOMA)
NAVCG... Coast Guard Publication [Formerly, NCG]
NAVCHAPGRU... Navy Cargo Handling and Port Group (NVT)
NAVCHAPGRUDET... Navy Cargo Handling and Port Group Detachment (DNAB)
NAVCINSUPPACT... Navy Counterintelligence Support Activity (DNAB)
NAVCINTSUPPCEN... Navy Counterintelligence Support Center (DNAB)
NAVCINTSUPPGRU... Navy Counterintelligence Support Unit (DNAB)
NAVCIVENGLAB... Navy Civil Engineering Laboratory (DNAB)
NAVCIVENGRLAB... Naval Civil Engineering Laboratory
NAVCJ... National Association on Volunteers in Criminal Justice [Later, IAJV] (EA)
NAVCLODEP... Naval Clothing Depot
NAVCLOTEXTOFC... Navy Clothing and Textile Office (DNAB)
NAVCLOTEXTRSCHFAC... Navy Clothing and Textile Research Facility [Natick, MA] (DNAB)

NAVCLOTEXTRSCHU...   Navy Clothing and Textile Research Unit
NAVCLOTHTEXOFC...   Navy Clothing and Textile Office   (DNAB)
NAVCM ....   Navigation Countermeasure   (IAA)
NAVCM ....   Navigation Countermeasures and Deception
NavCm ....   Navigation Countermeasures and Deception   (AD)
NAVCMD ......   Navigation Command   (MCD)
NAVCOASTSYSCEN...   Naval Coastal Systems Center [*Panama City, FL*]   (DNAB)
NAVCOM ......   Naval Communications [*System*]
navcom ....   Navigation Communication   (AD)
NAVCOMCOM...   Naval Communications Command
NAVCOMM .....   Naval Communications [*System*]
NAVCOMMAREA...   Naval Communications Area   (NVT)
NAVCOMMCOM...   Naval Communications Command
NAVCOMMDET...   Naval Communication Station Detachment   (DNAB)
NAVCOMMDETSPECCOMMDIV...   Naval Communication Station Detachment, Special Communications Division   (DNAB)
NAVCOMMFAC...   Naval Communications Facility   (NVT)
NAVCOMMHQ...   Naval Communications Headquarters   (DNAB)
NAVCOMMIS...   Naval Communications Command Management Information System   (MCD)
NAVCOMMOPNET...   Naval Communications Operation Network   (DNAB)
NAVCOMMSTA...   Naval Communication Station
NAVCOMMSTASPECCOMMDIV...   Naval Communication Station, Special Communications Division   (DNAB)
NAVCOMMSYS...   Naval Communication System   (MUGU)
NAVCOMMSYSSUPPACT...   Naval Communications System Support Activity   (DNAB)
NAVCOMMTRACEN...   Naval Communications Training Center   (MUGU)
NAVCOMMU...   Naval Communication Unit
NAVCOMMUNR...   Naval Communications Unit, Naval Reserve   (IAA)
NAVCOMPARS...   Naval Communications Processing and Routing System   (MCD)
NAVCOMPT...   Office of the Comptroller of the Navy
NAVCOMPTINST...   Office of the Comptroller of the Navy Instruction
NAVCOMPTMAN...   Naval Comptroller Manual
NAVCOMSYSSUPPACT...   Naval Command Systems Support Activity   (DNAB)
NAVCOMSYSSUPPCEN...   Naval Command Systems Support Center   (DNAB)
NAVCOMSYSTO...   Navy Commissary Store   (DNAB)
NAVCOMSYSTORE...   Navy Commissary Store
NAVCOMU...   Naval Communications Unit
NAVCON ......   Naval Countermeasures   (CINC)
NAVCON ......   Navigation Control Systems   (RDA)
Nav Const....   Naval Constructor [*Academic degree*]
NAVCONSTRACEN...   Naval Construction Training Center   (DNAB)
NAVCONSTRAU...   Naval Construction Training Unit   (DNAB)
NAVCONSTREGT...   Naval Construction Regiment   (DNAB)
NAVCONTDEP...   Navy Contracting Department   (DNAB)
NAVCONTRACEN...   Naval Construction Training Center
NAVCONVHOSP...   Naval Convalescent Hospital
NAVCORCOURSECEN...   Naval Correspondence Course Center   (DNAB)
NAVCORRCUSUNIT...   Navy Correctional Custody Unit   (DNAB)
NAVCOSSACT...   Naval Command Systems Support Activity
NAVCOSSCEN...   Naval Command Systems Support Center   (DNAB)
NAVCRUITAREA...   Navy Recruiting Area
NAVCRUITBRSTA...   Navy Recruiting Branch Station   (DNAB)
NAVCRUITCOM...   Navy Recruiting Command   (DNAB)
NAVCRUITCOMORIENTUNIT...   Navy Recruiting Command Orientation Unit   (DNAB)
NAVCRUITCOMSAT...   Navy Recruiting Command Standardization and Audit Team   (DNAB)
NAVCRUITCOMYPFLDREP...   Navy Recruiting Command Youth Programs Field Representative   (DNAB)
NAVCRUITDIST...   Navy Recruiting District   (DNAB)
NAVCRUITEXHIBCEN...   Navy Recruiting Exhibit Center   (DNAB)
NAVCRUITEXHIBCENCAT...   Navy Recruiting Exhibit Center Catalog   (DNAB)
NAVCRUITRACOM...   Navy Recruit Training Command   (DNAB)
NAVCRUITSTA...   Navy Recruiting Station
NAVCSG ....   National Archives Volunteers Constitution Study Group [*Defunct*]   (EA)
NAVCURRSUPPGRULANTFLT...   Naval Current Support Group, Atlantic Fleet   (DNAB)
NAVCURRSUPPGRUNAVEUR...   Naval Current Support Group, Naval Forces, Europe   (DNAB)
NAVCURRSUPPGRUPACFLT...   Naval Current Support Group, Pacific Fleet   (DNAB)
NAVCURSERV...   Naval Courier Service
NAVCURSERVDET...   Naval Courier Service Detachment   (DNAB)
NAVCURSERVHQ...   Naval Courier Service Headquarters
NAVD ....   National Association of Video Distributors   (EA)
NAVD ....   North American Vertical Datum [*National Oceanic and Atmospheric Administration*]
NAVD88 ......   North American Vertical Datum of 1988 [*Marine science*]   (OSRA)
NAVD88 ......   North American Vertical Datum of 1988   (USDC)
NAVDAB.......   Navy Ocean Experimental Acoustic Data Bank   (MSC)
NAVDAC......   Naval Data Automation Command   (MCD)
NAVDAC......   Navigation Data Assimilation Center   (AD)
navdac........   Navigation Data Assimilation Computer   (AD)
NAVDAC......   Navigation Data Assimilation Computer
NAVDAD ......   Navigationally-Derived Air Data   (MCD)
NAVDAF ......   Navy Data Automation Center   (DNAB)
NAVDAMCONTRACEN...   Navy Damage Control Training Center
NAVDAR ......   Naval Defense Acquisition Regulations   (MCD)
NAVDATACEN...   Naval Data Center   (DNAB)
NAVDEFEASTPAC...   Naval Defense Forces, Eastern Pacific   (DNAB)
NAVDEGSTA...   Navy Degaussing Station   (DNAB)
NAVDEGSTALANT/PAC...   Naval Degaussing Station, Atlantic/Pacific
NAVDENCEN...   Naval Dental Center
NAVDENCLINIC...   Naval Dental Clinic
NAVDENSCOL...   Naval Dental School

NAVDENTECHSCOL...   Naval Dental Technicians School
NAVDEP.......   Naval Deputy [*NATO*]   (NATG)
Nav Dep ......   Naval Deputy [*NATO*]   (AD)
NAVDEPCENT...   Naval Deputy to Commander-in-Chief, Allied Forces, Central Europe [*NATO*]   (NATG)
NAVDEPNOAA...   Naval Deputy National Oceanic and Atmospheric Administration   (DNAB)
NAVDEPT.....   Navy Department
NAVDES......   Navy Design Selection List
NAVDESCOL...   Naval Destroyer School   (NVT)
NAVDESSCOL...   Naval Destroyer School
NAVDET......   Naval Detachment
NAVDEVTRACEN...   Navy Development Training Center
NAVDI........   National Association for Ventilator Dependent Individuals   (EA)
NAVDIS.......   Naval District
NAVDISBAR...   Navy Disciplinary Barracks   (DNAB)
NAVDISCBAR...   Naval Disciplinary Barracks
NAVDISCOM...   Navy Disciplinary Command
NAVDISEAVECTORCONCEN...   Navy Disease Vector Control Center
NAVDISP.....   Naval Dispensary
NAVDIST......   Naval District
NAVDISVECTTECOLCONCEN...   Navy Disease Vector Ecology and Control Center   (DNAB)
NAVDIVSALVTRACEN...   Naval Diving and Salvage Training Center   (DNAB)
NAVDOC ......   Navy Department Orientation Course   (NG)
NAVDOCKS...   Bureau of Yards and Docks Publications [*Obsolete Navy*]
NAVDOCSP...   Bureau of Yards and Docks Publications [*Obsolete Navy*]
NAVDRUGREHCEN...   Naval Drug Rehabilitation Center   (DNAB)
NAVE ....   National Assessment of Vocational Education [*Department of Education*]   (GFGA)
Nav E ....   Naval Engineer [*Academic degree*]
NAVEA ....   National Adult Vocational Education Association   (EA)
NAVEAMS ....   Navigational Warning East Atlantic and Mediterranean [*Navy*]   (PDAA)
NavEams ....   Navigation in the Eastern Atlantic and the Mediterranean   (AD)
NAVEARB ....   Navy Employee Appeals Review Board   (DNAB)
NavEast ......   Navigation along the East Coast of Asia   (AD)
NAVEASTOCEANCEN...   Naval Eastern Oceanography Center   (DNAB)
NAVED ....   National Association of Visual Education Dealers [*Later, National Audio-Visual Association*]   (AEBS)
NAVEDTRA...   Naval Education and Training Command   (MCD)
NAVEDTRA...   Naval Education and Training Program Development Center [*Pensacola, FL*]
NAVEDTRACOM...   Naval Education and Training Center [*or Command*]   (DNAB)
NAVEDTRAPRODEVCEN...   Naval Education and Training Program Development Center [*Pensacola, FL*]   (DNAB)
NAVEDTRAPRODEVCENCODIV...   Naval Education and Training Program Development Center Coordination Division   (DNAB)
NAVEDTRAPRODEVCENDET...   Naval Education and Training Program Development Center Detachment   (DNAB)
NAVEDTRASUPPCEN...   Naval Education and Training Support Center   (DNAB)
NAVEDTRASUPPCENLANT...   Naval Education and Training Support Center, Atlantic   (DNAB)
NAVEDTRASUPPCENPAC...   Naval Education and Training Support Center, Pacific   (DNAB)
NAVEDTRASUPPCENPACNCFA...   Naval Education and Training Support Center, Pacific, Navy Campus for Achievement   (DNAB)
NAVELEC .....   Naval Electronics System Command   (IAA)
NAVELECS ...   Naval Electronic Systems Command   (SAA)
NAVELECSYSCOM...   Naval Electronics Systems Command
NAVELECSYSCOMCENLANTDIV...   Naval Electronics Systems Command, Central Atlantic Division
NAVELECSYSCOMHQ...   Naval Electronics Systems Command Headquarters
NAVELECSYSCOMNEDIV...   Naval Electronics Systems Command, Northeast Division
NAVELECSYSCOMSEDIV...   Naval Electronics Systems Command, Southeast Division
NAVELECSYSCOMWESTDIV...   Naval Electronics Systems Command, Western Division
NAVELEM ....   Navy Element   (DNAB)
NAVELEX .....   Naval Electronics Systems Command
NAVELEX .....   Naval Electronic Systems Command Headquarters   (USDC)
NAVELEXACTS...   Naval Electronic Systems Command Activities   (DNAB)
NAVELEXDET...   Naval Electronic Systems Command Detachment   (DNAB)
NAVELEXENGOFF...   Naval Electronics Engineering Office   (DNAB)
NAVELEXINST...   Naval Electronics Systems Command Instruction
NAVELEXSITEREP...   Naval Electronic Systems Command, Site Representative   (DNAB)
NAVELEXSYSCOMCENDET...   Naval Electronic Systems Command Center Detachment   (DNAB)
NAVELEXSYSCOMDIV...   Naval Electronic Systems Command Division   (DNAB)
NAVELEXSYSCOMMIDWESTDIV...   Naval Electronic Systems Command, Midwest Division   (DNAB)
NAVELEXSYSCOMSEDIV...   Naval Electronic Systems Command, Southeast Division   (DNAB)
NAVELEXSYSTRAPUBMO...   Naval Electronic Systems Command Training and Publications Management Office   (DNAB)
NAVELEXTECHREP...   Naval Electronic Systems Command Technical Representative   (DNAB)
NAVELXSYSCOMTECHLREP...   Naval Electronic Systems Command Technician Liaison Representative   (DNAB)
NAVEMSCEN...   Navy Electromagnetic Spectrum Center   (DNAB)
NAVENENVSA...   Navy Energy and Environmental Support Activity   (DNAB)
NAVENGRXSTA...   Naval Engineering Experiment Station
NAVENPVNTMEDU...   Navy Environmental and Preventive Medicine Unit   (DNAB)
NAVENVPREDRSCHFAC...   Naval Environmental Prediction Research Facility   (MCD)

NAVENVRHLTHCEN... Navy Environmental Health Center (DNAB)
NAVENVSUPPCEN... Navy Environmental Support Center (DNAB)
NAVENVSUPPO... Navy Environmental Support Office [*Obsolete*] (DNAB)
NAVEODFAC... Naval Explosive Ordnance Disposal Facility
NAVEODTECHCE... Naval Explosive Ordnance Disposal Technology Center [*Indian Head, MD*]
NAVEODTECHCEN... Naval Explosive Ordnance Disposal Technology Center [*Indian Head, MD*] (DNAB)
NAVESNP..... National Association of Vocational Education Special Needs Personnel (EA)
NAVETC .... Navy Educational Tape Catalog (DNAB)
NAVEURWWMCCS DP... Naval Forces, Europe, Worldwide Military Command Control System, Data Processing (DNAB)
NAVEURWWMCCS EMSKD... Naval Forces, Europe, Worldwide Military Command Control System, Employment Schedule (DNAB)
NAVEURWWMCCS MOVREP... Naval Forces, Europe, Worldwide Military Command Control System, Movement Reports (DNAB)
NAVEURWWMCCS NAVFORSTA... Naval Forces, Europe, Worldwide Military Command Control System, Naval Forces Status (DNAB)
NAVEX .... Navigation Exercise [*Navy*] (NVT)
navex.......... Navigation Exercise (AD)
NAVEXAM .... Naval Examining Board
NAVEXAMBD... Naval Examining Board (DNAB)
NAVEXAMCEN... Navy Examination Center
NAVEXAMCENADVAUTHLIST... Naval Examining Center Advancement Authorization List (DNAB)
NAVEXENGLANDCOM... Navy Exchange, England Complex (DNAB)
NAVEXHIBCEN... Naval Exhibit Center
NAVEXOS..... Executive Office of the Secretary [*Navy*]
NAVF .... Naval Avionics Facility [*Later, NAC*] (AFIT)
NAVF .... Norges Allmennvitenskapelige Forskningsrad [*Norwegian Research Council for Science and the Humanities*] [*Information service or system*] (IID)
NAVFAC .... Naval Facilities Engineering Command [*Formerly, Bureau of Yards and Docks*]
NAVFAC .... Naval Facilities Engineering Command Headquarters (USDC)
NAVFAC .... Naval Facility
NAVFAC .... Navy Faces (NITA)
NAVFACCHESDIV... Naval Facilities Engineering Command, Chesapeake Division (DNAB)
NAVFACDM... Naval Facilities Engineering Command Design Manuals
NAVFACENG... Naval Facilities Engineering Command (CAAL)
NAVFACENGCOM... Naval Facilities Engineering Command [*Formerly, Bureau of Yards and Docks*]
NAVFACENGCOMCHESDIV... Naval Facilities Engineering Command, Chesapeake Division (DNAB)
NAVFACENGCOMCONTR... Naval Facilities Engineering Command Contractor (DNAB)
NAVFACENGCOMHQ... Naval Facilities Engineering Command Headquarters (DNAB)
NAVFACENGCOMLANTDIV... Naval Facilities Engineering Command, Atlantic Division (DNAB)
NAVFACENGCOMNORDIV... Naval Facilities Engineering Command, Northern Division (DNAB)
NAVFACENGCOMPACDIV... Naval Facilities Engineering Command, Pacific Division (DNAB)
NAVFACENGCOMSODIV... Naval Facilities Engineering Command, Southern Division (DNAB)
NAVFACENGCOMWESDIV... Naval Facilities Engineering Command, Western Division (DNAB)
NAVFACENSYSCOM... Naval Facilities Engineering Systems Command
NAVFACINST... Naval Facilities Engineering Command Instructions
NAVFACLANTDIV... Naval Facilities Engineering Command, Atlantic Division (DNAB)
NAVFACLANT/PAC... Naval Facilities Atlantic/Pacific
NAVFACNORDIV... Naval Facilities Engineering Command, Northern Division (DNAB)
NAVFACOC... Naval Facility Operational Center (DNAB)
NAVFACP..... Naval Facilities Engineering Command Publications
NAVFAC P-68... Naval Facilities Engineering Command Contracting Manual [*A publication*] (AAGC)
NAVFACSODIV... Naval Facilities Engineering Comamnd, Southern Division (DNAB)
NAVFAC-TP-AD... Naval Facilities Engineering Command Technical Publications - Administration
NAVFAC-TP-MO... Naval Facilities Engineering Command Technical Publications - Maintenance Operation
NAVFAC-TP-PL... Naval Facilities Engineering Command Technical Publications - Planning
NAVFAC-TP-PU... Naval Facilities Engineering Command Technical Publications - Public Utilities
NAVFACWESDIV... Naval Facilities Engineering Command, Western Division (DNAB)
NAVFAMALWACT... Navy Family Allowance Activity
NAVFE .... Naval Forces Far East (AD)
NAVFEC ..... Naval Facilites (AD)
NAVFEC ..... Naval Facilities Engineering Command [*Formerly, Bureau of Yards and Docks*]
NAVFECENGCOM... Naval Facilities Engineering Command (AD)
NAVFECO ..... Naval Facilities Engineering Command (PDAA)
NAVFINCEN... Navy Finance Center
NAVFINCEN-CLEVE... Navy Finance Center - Cleveland [*Ohio*] (DNAB)
NAVFINCEN-WASH... Navy Finance Center - Washington, DC (DNAB)
NAVFINOFF..... Navy Finance Office
NAVFITWEPSCOL... Navy Fighter Weapons School (DNAB)
NAVFLDINTO... Navy Field Intelligence Office (DNAB)
NAVFLDOPINTO... Naval Field Operational Intelligence Office

NAVFLDOPSUPPGRU... Naval Field Operations Support Group
NAVFLIGHTPREPSCOL... Naval Flight Preparatory School
NAVFLITHTDEMORON... Navy Flight Demonstration Squadron (DNAB)
NAVFOODMGTM... Navy Food Management Team (DNAB)
NAVFOR..... Naval Forces (AD)
NAVFORJAP... Naval Air Forces, Japan (AD)
NAVFORKOR... Naval Air Forces, Korea (AD)
NAVFORSTAT... Naval Force Status Report (NVT)
NAVFRCOORD... Navy Frequency Coordinator (DNAB)
NAVFROF..... Navy Freight Office
NAVFSSO..... Navy Food Services Office (DNAB)
NAVFSSO..... Navy Food Service Systems Office
NAVFUELDEP... Naval Fuel Depot
NAVFUELSUPO... Naval Fuel Supply Office
NAVFW .... Norton AntiVirus for Firewalls [*Symantec*] [*Computer science*]
NAVG .... Navigators Group [*NASDAQ symbol*] (TTSB)
NAVG .... [*The*] Navigators Group, Inc. [*NASDAQ symbol*] (NQ)
NAVGDENSCOL... Naval Graduate Dental School (DNAB)
NAVGEN ..... Navy General Publications
NavgGp..... [*The*] Navigators Group, Inc. [*Associated Press*] (SAG)
NAVGMSCHOL... Navy Guided Missile School
NAVGMU..... Navy Guided Missile Unit
NAVGP .... Naval Advisory Group
NAVGRU..... Naval Group
NAVGSUP ... Navigational Guidance Support (NVT)
NAVGUN ..... Naval Gun Factory [*Later, NWF*]
NAVH .... National Aid to Visually Handicapped (AD)
NAVH .... National Association for Visually Handicapped (EA)
NAVH .... National Association of Voluntary Hostels [*British*] (DBA)
NAVHARS ..... Navigation Heading and Altitude Reference System [*Aviation*] (PDAA)
NAVHET ..... National Association of Vocational Home Economics Teachers (EA)
NAVHISTCEN... Naval History Center (DNAB)
NAVHISTDISPLAYCEN... Navy Historical Display Center
NAVHLTHRSCHC... Naval Health Research Center
NAVHLTHRSCHCEN... Naval Health Research Center (DNAB)
NAVHO......... National Association of Voluntary Help Organisers [*British*] (DBA)
NAVHOME... Naval Home [*Philadelphia, PA*]
NAVHOMERESINFOSYS... Naval Home Resident Information System (DNAB)
NAVHOSINGACT... Naval Housing Activity (DNAB)
NAVHOSP ... Naval Hospital
NAVHOSPCORPSCOL... Naval Hospital Corps School
NAVHOUSINGACT... Naval Housing Activity
NAVHT .... National Association of Vocational Homemakers Teachers [*Later, National Association of Vocational Home Economics Teachers*] (EA)
Nav I............ Navassa Island (AD)
NAVIC .... Navy Information Center (MCD)
navicert .... Naval Inspection Certificate (AD)
NAVICERT .... Navigation Certificate [*Paper issued by British government to merchant vessel, certifying that cargo was non-contraband, that is, not consigned to Germany*] [*World War II*]
NAVID .... Navigation Aid (NASA)
NAVIG .... Navigation
NAVIGA....... Welt Organisation fur Schiffsmodellbau und Schiffsmodellsport [*World Organization for Modelship Building and Modelship Sport*] [*Austria*] (EAIO)
NAVILCO...... Navy International Logistics Control Office (MCD)
NAVIMAC ..... Naval Immediate Area Coordinator (DNAB)
NavInd .... Navigation in the Indian Ocean (AD)
NAVINFO...... Navy Information Office (DNAB)
NAVINRELACT... Navy Internal Relations Activity (DNAB)
NAVINSGEN... Naval Inspector General
NAVINTCOM... Naval Intelligence Command
NAVINTCOMINST... Naval Intelligence Command Instructions
NAVINTCOMM... Naval Intelligence Command
NAVINTEL ..... Naval Intelligence
NAVINTSUPPCEN... Naval Intelligence Support Center (DNAB)
NAVINVSERV... Naval Investigative Service (DNAB)
NAVINVSERVHQ... Naval Investigative Service Headquarters (NVT)
NAVINVSERVO... Naval Investigative Service Office
NAVINVSERVOREP... Naval Investigative Service Office Representative (DNAB)
NAVINVSERVRA... Naval Investigative Service Resident Agent (DNAB)
NAVION....... North American Aviation, Inc. [*Later, Rockwell International Corp.*] [*Acronym also used to refer to light aircraft of World War II*]
NAVISLO...... Naval Interservice Liaison Office (DNAB)
Navistar...... Navistar International Corp. [*Associated Press*] (SAG)
NAVJAC ...... North American Vane Jump Angle Computer
NAVJAG ...... Judge Advocate General's Office Publications [*Navy*]
NAVJIT........ Naval Jet Instrument Trainer
NAVJNTSERVACT... Naval Joint Services Activity (DNAB)
NAVJUSTSCOL... Naval Justice School
NAVL .... National Anti-Vaccination League [*British*] (BI)
NAVL .... Navigation Light (IAA)
NAVLEGSERVOFF... Naval Legal Service Office (DNAB)
NAVLEGSERVOFFDET... Naval Legal Service Office Detachment (DNAB)
NAVLIAGRU... Naval Liaison Group (DNAB)
NAVLINKSTA... Naval Link Station (DNAB)
NAVLIS .... Navy Logistics Information System
NAVLO .... Naval Liaison Officer
NAVLOGENGRU... Naval Logistics Engineering Group (DNAB)
NAVLOGSIP... Navy Logistic Support Improvement Plan (NG)
NAVLOS...... Navy Liaison Officer for Scouting (DNAB)
NAVMAA...... Naval Mutual Aid Association (DNAB)
NAVMAC ..... Navy Manpower and Material Analysis Center (DNAB)
NAVMACPAC... Navy Manpower and Material Analysis Center, Pacific (DNAB)

NAVMACS.... Naval Modular Automated Communications System (NVT)

NAVMAIRCOMCON... Naval and Maritime Air Communications-Electronics Conference [*NATO*]

NAVMAP...... Navy Missile Analysis Program (MCD)

NAVMAR...... Naval Forces, Marianas (AD)

NAVMARCORESTRACEN... Navy and Marine Corps Reserve Training Center

NAVMAREXHIBCEN... Navy-Marine Corps Exhibit Center (DNAB)

NAVMARJUDACT... Navy-Marine Corps Judiciary Activity

NAVMARTRIJUDCIR... Navy-Marine Corps Trial Judiciary Court (DNAB)

NAVMARTRIJUDCIRBROFF... Navy-Marine Corps Trial Judiciary Court Branch Office (DNAB)

NAVMARTRIJUDIC... Navy-Marine Corps Trial Judiciary (DNAB)

NAVMASSO... Navy Maintenance and Supply Systems Office (DNAB)

NAVMASSO... Navy Management Systems Support Office (AAGC)

NAVMASSODET... Navy Maintenance and Supply Systems Office Detachment (DNAB)

NAVMASSODETPAC... Navy Maintenance and Supply Systems Office Detachment, Pacific (DNAB)

NAVMAT ...... Naval Material Command [*Formerly, NMSE*] (MCD)

NAVMATCOM... Naval Material Command [*Formerly, NMSE*]

NAVMATCOMSUPPACT... Naval Material Command Support Activity

NAVMAT COOPLAN... Naval Material Command Contingency/Emergency Planning (DNAB)

NAVMATDATASYSGRU... Naval Material Data Systems Group (DNAB)

NAVMATDET... Naval Material Command Detachment (DNAB)

NAVMATEVALU... Naval Material Evaluation Unit (DNAB)

NAVMATINST... Naval Material Command Instruction

NAVMATMOCON... Navy Material Movement Control Plan

NAVMATRANSOFC... Naval Material Transportation Office (DNAB)

NAVMC...... Navy-Marine Corps

NAVMEC...... Naval Manpower Engineering Center (MCD)

NAVMED...... Naval Aerospace Medical Institute (MCD)

NAVMED...... Navy Medicine

NAVMEDADMINU... Navy Medical Administrative Unit (DNAB)

NAVMEDATASERVCEN... Naval Medical Data Service Center

NAVMEDCEN... Navy Medical Center (DNAB)

NAVMEDCOM... Naval Medical Command (ANA)

NAVMEDFLDRSCHLAB... Navy Medical Field Research Laboratory (DNAB)

NAVMEDIS... Navy Medical Information System

NAVMEDLAB... Naval Medical Laboratory (DNAB)

NAVMEDLABDET... Naval Medical Laboratory Detachment (DNAB)

NAVMEDMATSUPPCOM... Naval Medical Materiel Support Command (DNAB)

NAVMEDNPRSCHU... Navy Medical Neuropsychiatric Research Unit (DNAB)

NAVMEDRSCHDEVCOM... Naval Medical Research and Development Command (DNAB)

NAVMEDRSCHINST... Naval Medical Research Institute

NAVMEDRSCHINSTDET... Navy Medical Research Institute Detachment (DNAB)

NAVMEDRSCHU... Naval Medical Research Unit

NAVMEDRSCHUDET... Naval Medical Research Unit Detachment (DNAB)

NAVMEDRSHCHLAB... Navy Medical Research Laboratory (DNAB)

NAVMEDSCOL... Naval Medical School

NAVMEDSUPPU... Navy Medical Support Unit (DNAB)

NAVMGTSYSCEN... Naval Management Systems Center (MCD)

NAVMIC...... Naval Maritime Intelligence Center [*Formerly, NISC and then NTIC*] (DOMA)

NAVMILPERSCOM... Naval Military Personnel Command (MCD)

NAVMINCOMEASTA... Navy Mine Countermeasures Station

NAVMINDEFLAB... Navy Mine Defense Laboratory [*Later, NCSC*] (DNAB)

NAVMINDEP... Naval Mine Depot

NAVMINENGRFAC... Naval Mine Engineering Facility

NAVMINWARTRACEN... Naval Mine Warfare Training Center

NAVMIRO .... Naval Material Industrial Resources Office

NAVMIS... Naval Mission

NAVMIS...... Navy Management Information System (MCD)

NAVMISCEN... Naval Missile Center [*Point Mugu, CA*] (MCD)

NavMisCen... Naval Missile Center (AD)

NAVMISFAC... Naval Missile Facility [*Also, NMF*] (MUGU)

NAVMMAC... Navy Manpower and Material Analysis Center (NVT)

NAVMMACLANT... Navy Manpower and Material Analysis Center, Atlantic

NAVMMACPAC... Navy Manpower and Material Analysis Center, Pacific

NAVMOBCONSTBN... Navy Mobile Construction Battalion

NAVMORTOFF... Naval Mortuary Office (DNAB)

NAVMTO...... Navy Material Transportation Office

NAVMTO...... Navy Material Transportation Office [*MTMC*] (TAG)

NAVMTO...... Navy Movement and Transportation Office

NAVMTONORVA... Naval Military Transportation Office, Norfolk, Virginia (DNAB)

NAVMTOREP... Naval Military Transportation Office Representative (DNAB)

NAVMUTAID... Navy Mutual Aid

NAVN.......... Naval Aviation News

NAVNET...... Navigation Network (NVT)

NAVNET...... Navy Network (DOMA)

NAVNETDEP... Naval Net Depot

NAVNON...... Allied Naval Forces, North Norway [*NATO*] (NATG)

NAVNON...... Naval Forces, Northern Norway [*NATO*] (AD)

NavNoPac... Navigation in the North Pacific (AD)

NavNorlant... Navigation in the North Atlantic (AD)

NAVNORTH... Allied Naval Forces, Northern Europe [*NATO*]

NAVNUPWRSCOL... Navy Nuclear Power School (DNAB)

NAVNUPWRTRAU... Naval Nuclear Power Training Unit (MCD)

NAVNUPWRU... Naval Nuclear Power Unit

NAVO.......... National Association of Volvo Owners [*Defunct*] (EA)

NAVO.......... Naval Oceanographic Office [*Marine science*] (OSRA)

NAVO.......... Naval Oceanographic Office (USDC)

NAVOBS...... Naval Observatory (MUGU)

NAVOBSY .... Naval Observatory [*Navy*]

NAVOBSYFLAGSTAFFSTA... Naval Observatory Flagstaff [*Arizona*] Station

NAVOBSYSTA... Naval Observatory Station (DNAB)

NAVOCEANCOM... Naval Oceanography Command Support System (GFGA)

NAVOCEANCOMCEN... Naval Oceanography Command Center (DNAB)

NAVOCEANCOMDET... Naval Oceanography Command Detachment (MCD)

NAVOCEANCOMFAC... Naval Oceanography Command Facility (DNAB)

NAVOCEANCOMMDET... Naval Oceanography Communications Detachment (DNAB)

NAVOCEANDISTO... Naval Oceanographic District Office

NAVOCEANO... Naval Oceanographic Office [*Also known as NOO; formerly, HO, NHO, USNHO*] [*Bay St. Louis, MS*]

NavOceanO... Naval Oceanographic Officer (AD)

NAVOCEANOAIRSUPPGRU... Naval Oceanographic Office Aircraft Support Squadron (DNAB)

NAVOCEANODET... Naval Oceanographic Office Detachment (DNAB)

NAVOCEANOFC... Naval Oceanographic Office (DNAB)

NAVOCEANPROFAC... Naval Ocean Processing Facility (DNAB)

NAVOCEANSURVINFOCEN... Naval Ocean Surveillance Information Center (DNAB)

NAVOCEANSYSCEN... Naval Ocean Systems Center [*Formerly, NELC*] (DNAB)

NAVOCEANSYSCENLAB... Naval Ocean Systems Center Laboratory (DNAB)

NAVOCEANSYSCENLABDET... Naval Ocean Systems Center Laboratory Detachment (DNAB)

NAVOCFORMED... Naval On-Call Force, Mediterranean [*NATO*] (NATG)

NAVOCS...... Naval Officer Candidate School

NAVOLF ...... Navy Outlying Landing Field (DNAB)

NAVOPFAC... Naval Operating Facility

NAVOPHTHALSUPPTRACT... Naval Ophthalmic Support and Training Activity (DNAB)

NAVOPNET... Naval Operations Network (CINC)

NAVOPSUPPGRU... Naval Operations Support Group (DNAB)

NAVOPSUPPGRULANT... Naval Operations Support Group, Atlantic

NAVOPSUPPGRUPAC... Naval Operations Support Group, Pacific

NAVORD ...... Naval Ordnance (MUGU)

NAVORD ...... Naval Ordnance Systems Command [*Later, Naval Sea Systems Command*]

NAVORD ...... Naval Ordnance Systems Command Headquarters (USDC)

NAVORDCH... Naval Ordnance Chart (MCD)

NAVORDENGFAC... Naval Ordnance Engineering Facility (DNAB)

NAVORDFAC... Naval Ordnance Facility

NAVORD ILS/MIS... Naval Ordnance Systems Command, Integrated Logistics Support / Management Information System (DNAB)

NAVORDINST... Naval Ordnance Systems Command Instruction

NAVORDLABFIELDIV... Naval Ordnance Laboratory Field Division (DNAB)

NAVORDLIST... Navy Ordnance List (DNAB)

NAVORDMISTESTFAC... Naval Ordnance Missile Test Facility

NAVORDSTA... Naval Ordnance Station

NAVORDSTADET... Naval Ordnance Station Detachment (DNAB)

NAVORD-SWOP... Naval Ordnance Systems Command, Special Weapons Ordnance Publication

NAVORDSYSCO... Naval Ordnance Systems Command [*Later, Naval Sea Systems Command*] (MCD)

NAVORDSYSCOM... Naval Ordnance Systems Command [*Later, Naval Sea Systems Command*]

NAVORDSYSCOMHQ... Naval Ordnance Systems Command Headquarters

NAVORDSYSSUPPO... Naval Ordnance Systems Support Office

NAVORDSYSSUPPO... Naval Ordnance Systems Support Office (DNAB)

NAVORDSYSSUPPOLANT... Naval Ordnance Systems Support Office, Atlantic (DNAB)

NAVORDSYSSUPPOPAC... Naval Ordnance Systems Support Office, Pacific (DNAB)

NAVORDTECHREP... Naval Ordnance Technical Representative (MCD)

NAVORDTESTU... Naval Ordnance Test Unit

NAVORDU... Naval Ordnance Unit

NAVORECSUPPACT... Naval Officer Record Support Activity (DNAB)

NAVOROUS... Naval Order of the United States [*Later, NOUS*] [*An association*] (EA)

NAVOSH ...... Navy Occupational Safety and Health (MCD)

NAVOSH DAP/MIS... Navy Occupational Safety and Deficiency Abatement/ Management Information System

NAVOSTAT... Navigation by Visual Observation of Satellites (DNAB)

NAVP.......... National Association of Vision Professionals (EA)

NAVPA.......... National Association of Veterans Program Administrators (EA)

NAVPAC...... Navigation Package (DNAB)

NAVPACEN... Navy Public Affairs Center (DNAB)

NAVPAOEASCO... Naval Public Affairs Office, East Coast

NAVPAOMWEST... Naval Public Affairs Office, Midwest

NAVPAOWESCO... Naval Public Affairs Office, West Coast

NAVPBRO ...... Naval Plant Branch Representative Officer (DNAB)

NAVPC ...... National Association of Vision Program Consultants [*Later, NAVP*] (EA)

NAVPECO...... Naval Production Equipment Control Office

NAVPECOS... Navy Pentagon Computer Services Division (DNAB)

NAVPEP...... Navy Program Evaluation Procedures

NAVPERS...... Bureau of Naval Personnel [*Also, BNP, BUPERS*]

NAVPERS...... Naval Personnel (AD)

NAVPERSCEN... Naval Personnel Center

NAVPERSINST... Bureau of Naval Personnel Instruction

NAVPERS-PRD... Bureau of Naval Personnel - Personnel Research Division

NAVPERSPROGSUPPACT... Naval Personnel Program Support Activity

NAVPERSRANDCEN... Naval Personnel Research and Development Center

NAVPERSRANDCENWB... Naval Personnel Research and Development Center, Washington [*DC*] Branch (DNAB)

NAVPERSRANDLAB... Navy Personnel Research and Development Laboratory

NAVPERSREACT... Naval Personnel Research Activity

NAVPERSRSCHACT... Naval Personnel Research Activity

NAVPETOFF... Navy Petroleum Office

NAVPETRAU... Naval Petroleum Training Unit (DNAB)
NAVPETRES... Naval Petroleum Reserves
NAVPETRESO... Naval Petroleum Reserves Office
NAVPGCOL... Navy Postgraduate College
NAVPGSCOL... Naval Postgraduate School
NAVPHIBASE... Naval Amphibious Base (MUGU)
NAVPHIBASELANT... Naval Amphibious Base Atlantic
NAVPHIBSCOL... Naval Amphibious School (NVT)
NAVPHIL... Naval Forces - Philippines
NAVPHOTOCEN... Naval Photographic Center
NAVPLANTDEVU... Naval Plant Development Unit (DNAB)
NAVPLANTREP... Naval Plant Representative Office [or Officer] (MCD)
NAVPLANTREPO... Naval Plant Representative Office [or Officer]
NAVPLANTTECHREP... Naval Plant Technical Representative (DNAB)
NAVPO......... National Association of Van Pool Operators [Later, Association of Commuter Transportation] (EA)
NAVPOLAROCEANCEN... Naval Polar Oceanography Center (DNAB)
NAVPOOL... Navigation Parameter Common Pool (NASA)
NAVPOOL .... Navigation [Parameter Common] Pool
NAVPORCO... Naval Port Control Office [or Officer]
NAVPORCOF... Naval Port Control Office [or Officer]
NAVPORTCO... Naval Port Control Office [Or officer] (DNAB)
NAVPOSTGRADSCOL... Naval Postgraduate School
NAVPOWFAC... Naval Powder Factory
NAVPrD... Navistar Intl Cv Jr D Pref [NYSE symbol] (TTSB)
NAVPREFLIGHTSCOL... Naval Preflight School
NAVPrG... Navistar Intl $6 cm Cv Pfd [NYSE symbol] (TTSB)
NAVPRIMSTDEPT... Navy Primary Standards Department (DNAB)
NAVPRIS...... Naval Prison
NAVPRO ...... Naval Plant Representative Office [or Officer]
NAVPROPLT... Naval Propellant Plant (DNAB)
NAVPROV .... Naval Proving Ground [Dahlgren, VA]
NAVPTO....... Navy Passenger Transportation Office (DNAB)
NAVPUB...... Naval Publications (AD)
NAVPUB...... Navy Publications and Printing Service
NAVPUBFORMCEN... Naval Publications and Forms Center (MCD)
NAVPUBINST... Navy Publications and Printing Service Instruction
NAVPUBPRINTO... Navy Publications and Printing Office
NAVPUBPRINTSERV... Naval Publications and Printing Service (DNAB)
NAVPUBPRINTSERVO... Navy Publications and Printing Service Office
NAVPUBSCONBD... Navy Department Publications Control Board
NAVPUBWKSCEN... Navy Public Works Center
NAVPUBWKSDEPT... Navy Public Works Department (DNAB)
NAVPUR ...... Navy Purchasing Office
NAVPURDEP... Navy Purchasing Department (DNAB)
NAVPURO... Navy Purchasing Office
NAVPVNTMEDU... Navy Preventive Medicine Unit
NAVR.......... Navarre Corp. [NASDAQ symbol] (SAG)
NAVR.......... Navigator (WGA)
NAVRA.......... National Association of Volunteer Referral Agencies [Australia]
NAVRADCO... Naval Regional Active Duty Cryptologic Officer (DNAB)
NAVRADCON... Naval Radiological Control
NAVRADLDEFLAB... Navy Radiological Defense Laboratory
NAVRADRECFAC... Naval Radio Receiving Facility (DNAB)
NAVRADSTA... Naval Radio Station
NAVRADTRANSFAC... Naval Radio Transmitting Facility (DNAB)
NAVRDSATCOMMGRU... Naval Research and Development Satellite Communications Group (MUGU)
NAVRECCEN... Naval Recreation Center (DNAB)
NAVRECONTACSUPPCENLANT... Naval Reconnaissance and Tactical Support Center, Atlantic (DNAB)
NAVRECONTECHSUPPCEN... Naval Reconnaissance and Technical Support Center
NAVRECONTECHSUPPCENLANT... Naval Reconnaissance and Technical Support Center, Atlantic (DNAB)
NAVRECONTECHSUPPCENPAC... Naval Reconnaissance and Technical Support Center, Pacific (DNAB)
NAVRECSTA... Naval Receiving Station (NVT)
NAVREGAIRCARCONO... Navy Regional Air Cargo Central [or Control] Office (DNAB)
NAVREGCONTO... Navy Regional Contracting Office (DNAB)
NAVREGCONTODET... Navy Regional Contracting Office Detachment (DNAB)
NAVREGDENCEN... Navy Regional Dental Center (DNAB)
NAVREGDENCENBRFAC... Navy Regional Dental Center Branch Facility (DNAB)
NAVREGDENCLIN... Navy Regional Dental Clinic (DNAB)
NAVREGFINCEN... Navy Regional Finance Center
NAVREGFINCENBRKLN... Navy Regional Finance Center, Brooklyn [New York]
NAVREGFINCENGLAKES... Navy Regional Finance Center, Great Lakes (DNAB)
NAVREGFINCENNORVA... Navy Regional Finance Center, Norfolk, Virginia (DNAB)
NAVREGFINCENPEARL... Navy Regional Finance Center, Pearl Harbor [Hawaii] (DNAB)
NAVREGFINCENSDIEGO... Navy Regional Finance Center, San Diego [California]
NAVREGFINCENSFRAN... Navy Regional Finance Center, San Francisco [California] (DNAB)
NAVREGFINOFC... Navy Regional Finance Office (DNAB)
NAVREGMEDCEN... Naval Regional Medical Center (DNAB)
NAVREGMEDCENBRCLINIC... Naval Regional Medical Center Branch Clinic (DNAB)
NAVREGMEDCENBRHOSP... Naval Regional Medical Center Branch Hospital
NAVREGMEDCENCLINIC... Naval Regional Medical Center Clinic (DNAB)
NAVREGMEDCENDET... Naval Regional Medical Center Detachment (DNAB)
NAVREGPEO... Naval Regional Plant Equipment Office [or Officer] (DNAB)
NAVREGPROCO... Navy Regional Procurement Office (DNAB)
NAVREGS .... Navy Regulations

NAVREL....... Navy Relief Society
NAVREPFAC... Naval Repair Facility (MCD)
NAVRES....... Naval Reserve
NAVRESCEN... Naval Research Center (DNAB)
NAVRESCEN... Naval Reserve Center (DNAB)
NAVRESCOMICEDEFOR... Naval Reserve Commander, Iceland Defense Force (DNAB)
NAVRESFOR... Naval Reserve Force (DNAB)
NAVRESLAB... Naval Research Laboratory [ONR]
NAVRESMANPOWERCEN... Naval Reserve Manpower Center
NAVRESMANPWRCEN... Naval Reserve Manpower Center (DNAB)
NAVRESMIDSCOL... Naval Reserve Midshipmen's School
NAVRESO ... Navy Resale System Office (PDAA)
NAVRESO .... Navy Resale Systems Office
NAVRESOFSO... Navy Resale Systems Field Support Office (DNAB)
NAVRESOREACT... Naval Reserve Officer Recording Activity (DNAB)
NAVRESOREP... Navy Resale Systems Office Representative (DNAB)
NAVRESREDCOM... Naval Reserve Readiness Command (DNAB)
NAVRESREDCOMREG... Naval Reserve Readiness Command Region (DNAB)
NAVRESSECGRP... Naval Reserve Security Group (DNAB)
NAVRESSO... Navy Resale and Services Support Office
NAVRESSOFO... Navy Resale and Services Support Office, Field Office (DNAB)
NAVRESTRA... Naval Reserve Training (DNAB)
NAVRESTRACEN... Naval Reserve Training Center
NAVRESTRACOM... Naval Reserve Training Command
NAVRESTRAFAC... Naval Reserve Training Facility
NAVRESUBDET... Naval Reserve Submarine Detachment (DNAB)
NAVRESUPPOFC... Naval Reserve Support Office (DNAB)
NAVRESUPPOFCDET... Naval Reserve Support Office Detachment (DNAB)
NAVRETRAINCOM... Naval Retraining Command
NAVROM... Romanian Merchant Marine (AD)
NAVROUTE... Navy Routing Office
NAVRSCHLAB... Naval Research Laboratory [ONR]
NAVS .... National Anti-Vivisection Society (EA)
NAVS .... National Association of Variety Stores [Defunct] (EA)
NAVS .... Navigation System
NAVS .... North American Vegetarian Society (EA)
NAVSAFECEN... Naval Safety Center
NAVSANDA... Bureau of Supplies and Accounts [Later, NSUPSC] [Navy]
NAVSAT....... Navigational Satellite [NASA]
navsat......... Navigational Satellite (AD)
NavSat......... Navigation in the South Atlantic (AD)
NAVSATCOMMDET... Navy Satellite Communications Detachment (DNAB)
NAVSATCOMMFAC... Navy Satellite Communications Facility (DNAB)
NAVSATCOMMNET... Navy Satellite Communications Network (DNAB)
NAVSCAP... Allied Naval Forces, Scandinavian Approaches [NATO] (NATG)
NAVSCAP..... Naval Forces, Scandinavian Approaches [NATO] (AD)
NAVSCIADV... Naval Science Advisor (DNAB)
NAVSCIENTECHINTCEN... Naval Scientific and Technical Intelligence Center
NAVSCITECHGRUFE... Naval Scientific and Technical Group, Far East (DNAB)
NAVSCOLCEOFF... Naval Civil Engineer Corps Officers School (DNAB)
NAVSCOLCOM... Naval Schools Command
NAVSCOLCOM NORVA... Naval Schools Command, Norfolk, Virginia
NAVSCOLCONST... Naval Schools Construction
NAVSCOLCRYPTOREP... Naval School of Cryptographic Repair (DNAB)
NAVSCOLCRYOGENICS... Naval School of Cryogenics (DNAB)
NAVSCOLDEEPSEADIVER... Navy School for Deep Sea Divers (DNAB)
NAVSCOLEOD... Naval School of Explosive Ordnance Disposal (DNAB)
NAVSCOLHOSPADMIN... Naval School of Hospital Administration (DNAB)
NAVSCOLMINWAR... Naval School of Mine War (DNAB)
NAVSCOLMINWARFARE... Naval Mine Warfare School
NAVSCOLPHYDISTMGT... Naval School of Physical Distribution Management (DNAB)
NAVSCOLTRANSMGT... Naval School of Transportation Management (DNAB)
NAVSCSCOL... Naval Supply Corps School
NAVSCSCOLDET... Naval Supply Corps School Detachment (DNAB)
NAVSEA ...... Naval Avionics Support Equipment Appraisal (NG)
NAVSEA ...... Naval Sea [formerly, Ship] Systems Command (MCD)
NAVSEAADSO... Naval Sea Systems Command Automated Data Systems Office (DNAB)
NAVSEAADSODET... Naval Sea Systems Command Automated Data Systems Office Detachment (DNAB)
NAVSEACARCOORD... Naval Sea Cargo Coordinator (DNAB)
NAVSEACARCOR... Naval Sea Cargo Coordinator (NVT)
NAVSEACEN... Naval Sea Support Center (DNAB)
NAVSEACENFSO... Naval Sea Support Center, Fleet Support Office (DNAB)
NAVSEACENHAWLAB... Naval Sea Support Center, Hawaii Laboratory (DNAB)
NAVSEACENLANT... Naval Sea Support Center, Atlantic (MCD)
NAVSEACENLANTDET... Naval Sea Support Center, Atlantic Detachment (DNAB)
NAVSEACENPACDET... Naval Sea Support Center, Pacific Detachment (DNAB)
NAVSEACENREP... Naval Sea Support Center Representative (DNAB)
NAVSEACENTLANT... Naval Sea Support Center - Atlantic (AD)
NAVSEACENTPAC... Naval Sea Support Center - Pacific (AD)
NAVSEACOHREP... Naval Sea Systems Command Complex Overhaul Representative (DNAB)
NAVSEADET... Naval Sea Systems Command Detachment (DNAB)
NAVSEAMATREP... Naval Sea Systems Command Material Representative (DNAB)
NAVSEAMQAO... Naval Sea Systems Command Material Quality Assessment Office (DNAB)
NAVSEASYSCOM... Naval Sea [Formerly, Ship] Systems Command (DNAB)
NAVSEASYSCOMGTOWESTPAC... Naval Sea Systems Command Management Office, Western Pacific (DNAB)
NAVSEASYSCOMHQ... Naval Sea Systems Command Headquarters (DNAB)
NAVSEATECHREP... Naval Sea Systems Command Technical Representative (DNAB)

NAVSEC....... Naval Ship Engineering Center
NAVSECENGRFAC... Naval Security Engineering Facility
NAVSECGRU... Naval Security Group
NAVSECGRUACT... Navy Security Group Activity
NAVSECGRUACTFO... Naval Security Group Activity Field Office (DNAB)
NAVSECGRUACTSPECOMMDIV... Naval Security Group Activity, Special Communications Division (DNAB)
NAVSECGRUCOM... Naval Security Group Command (MCD)
NAVSECGRUDET... Naval Security Group Detachment
NAVSECGRUHQ... Navy Security Group Headquarters
NAVSECGRUMGDAT... Naval Security Group Command Management Data (DNAB)
NAVSECGRU MIS... Naval Security Group Management Information System (DNAB)
NAVSECINST... Naval Ship Engineering Center Instruction
NAVSECMECHSDIV... Naval Ship Engineering Center, Mechanicsburg [Pennsylvania] Division (DNAB)
NAVSECNORDIV... Naval Ship Engineering Center, Norfolk Division
NAVSECPHILA... Naval Ship Engineering Center, Philadelphia Division
NAVSECPHILAD... Naval Ship Engineering Center Philadelphia Division
NAVSECPHILADIV... Naval Ship Engineering Center, Philadelphia Division
NAVSECSDIEGODIV... Naval Ship Engineering Center, San Diego [California] Division (DNAB)
NAVSECSTA... Naval Security Station
NAVSEEACT... Naval Shore Electronics Engineering Activity
NAVSEEC..... Naval Electronics Systems Command Headquarters
NAVSEG..... Navigation Satellite Executive Steering Group
NAVSERVSCOLCOM... Naval Service School Command
NAVSEX....... Naval Standing Exercises (NATG)
NAVSHIP...... Naval Ship Systems Command [Later, NAVSEA, NSSC]
NAVSHIPCOM... Naval Ship Systems Command (AD)
NAVSHIPENGCEN... Naval Ship Engineering Center
NAVSHIPENGSUPPACT... Naval Ship Engineering Support Activity
NAVSHIPLO... Navy Shipbuilding Office
NAVSHIPMISENGSYS... Naval Ships Missile Systems Engineering System (DNAB)
NAVSHIPMISYSENGSTA... Naval Ship Missile System Engineering Station
NAVSHIPREPFAC... Naval Ship Repair Facility
NAVSHIPREPO... Naval Ship Repair Officer (DNAB)
NAVSHIPRSCHDEVCEN... Naval Ship Research and Development Center [Also, DTNSRDC] (DNAB)
NAVSHIPRSCHDEVCENANNA... Naval Ship Research and Development Center, Annapolis [Maryland] Division (DNAB)
NAVSHIPS ... Naval Ship Systems Command [Later, NAVSEA, NSSC]
NAVSHIPS ... Naval Ship Systems Command Headquarters [Formerly, BuShips] (USDC)
NAVSHIPSA... Navy Shipbuilding Scheduling Activity
NAVSHIPSINST... Naval Ship Systems Command Instruction
NAVSHIPSO... Navy Shipbuilding Scheduling Office
NAVSHIPSTO... Navy Ships' Store Office (DNAB)
NAVSHIPSYSCOM... Naval Ship Systems Command [Later, NAVSEA, NSSC]
NAVSHIPSYSCOMHQ... Naval Ship Systems Command Headquarters
NAVSHIPTECHSMAN... Navy Ship Technical Manual (DNAB)
NAVSHIPWPNSYSENGSTA... Naval Ship Weapon Systems Engineering Station [Port Hueneme, CA] (DNAB)
NAVSHIPWPNSYSENGSTADET... Naval Ship Weapon Systems Engineering Station Detachment (DNAB)
NAVSHIPWPNSYSENGSTAREP... Naval Ship Weapon Sytems Engineering Station Representative (DNAB)
NAVSHIPY... Naval Shipyard (SAA)
NAVSHIPYD... Naval Shipyard
NavShipyd ... Naval Shipyard (AD)
NAVSIT .... Navy Scholarship Information Team (DNAB)
NAVSMO...... Navigation Satellite Management Office
NAVSO...... Naval Supply Office
NAVSO......... Navy, Secretary's Office
NAVSO......... Navy Staff Offices
NavSoPac... Navigation of the South Pacific (AD)
NAVSOUTH... Allied Naval Forces, Southern Europe [NATO] (NATG)
NAVSOUTH... Naval Forces, Southern Europe (AD)
NAVSPACCOM... Naval Space Command (DOMA)
NAVSPASUR... Naval Space Surveillance [Center or System]
NAVSPASYSAC... Naval Space Systems Activity (DNAB)
NAVSPEC..... Navy Specification (AAGC)
NAVSPECWARGP... Naval Special Warfare Group (AABC)
NAVSPECWARGRAUDET... Naval Special Warfare Group Detachment (DNAB)
NAVSPECWARGRU... Naval Special Warfare Group (NVT)
NAVSPECWARU... Naval Special Warfare Unit (DNAB)
NAVSPECWARUDET... Naval Special Warfare Unit Detachment (DNAB)
NAVSSES...... Naval Ship Systems Engineering Station
NAVSSESDET... Naval Ship Systems Engineering Station Detachment (DNAB)
NAVSTA....... Naval Station
NAVSTAG...... Naval Standardization Agreement [NATO]
NAVSTALANT... Naval Stations Atlantic
NAVSTAPAC... Naval Stations Pacific
NAVSTAR..... Navigation Satellite Tracking and Ranging [Later, GPS] [Air Force]
NAVSTAR..... Navigation System Using Time and Ranging (AD)
NAVSTAR..... Navy Study of Transport Aircraft Requirements
NAVSTAR-GPS... Navigation Satellite Tracking and Ranging Global Positioning System [Air Force] (MCD)
NAVSTD....... Navy Standard (AAGC)
NAVSTIC ...... Naval Scientific and Technical Intelligence Center
NAVSTKWARCEN... Naval Strike Warfare Center (DOMA)
NAVSTRIP... Navy Standard Requisitioning and Issuing Procedure
NAVSUBBASE... Naval Submarine Base
NAVSUBINSURV... Naval Sub-Board of Inspection and Survey (DNAB)
NAVSUBMEDCEN... Naval Submarine Medical Center

NAVSUBMEDRSCHLAB... Naval Submarine Medical Research Laboratory (DNAB)
NAVSUBSCOL... Naval Submarine School
NAVSUBSUPPBASE... Naval Submarine Support Base (DNAB)
NAVSUBSUPPBASEDET... Naval Submarine Support Base Detachment (DNAB)
NAVSUBSUPPFAC... Navy Submarine Support Facility (DNAB)
NAVSUBTRACENPAC... Naval Submarine Training Center, Pacific (DNAB)
NAVSUP....... Naval Supplies
NAVSUP....... Naval Supply Systems Command [Formerly, Bureau of Supplies and Accounts] (MCD)
NAVSUPACT... Naval Support Activity (NVT)
NAVSUPCEN... Naval Supply Center
NAVSUPDEP... Naval Supply Depot (DNAB)
NAVSUPDEPT... Naval Supply Department (DNAB)
NAVSUPFORANT... Naval Support Forces, Antarctica
NAVSUPGRU... Naval Support Group (NVT)
NAVSUPINST... Naval Supply Systems Command Instruction
NAVSUPMIS... Navy Supply Management Information System
NAVSUPO .... Navy Supply Office (DNAB)
NAVSUPOANX... Navy Supply Office Annex (DNAB)
NAVSUPORANT... Naval Support Forces, Antarctica (AD)
NAVSUPPACT... Naval Supply [or Support] Activity
NAVSUPPACTDET... Naval Support Activity Detachment (DNAB)
NAVSUPPFOR... Naval Support Force
NAVSUPPFORANTARCTIC... Naval Support Forces, Antarctic
NAVSUPRANDDFAC... Navy Supply Research and Development Facility (DNAB)
NAVSUPRANDFA... Naval Supply Research and Development Facility
NAVSUPSYSCOM... Naval Supply Systems Command [Formerly, Bureau of Supplies and Accounts]
NAVSUPSYSCOMHQ... Naval Supply System Command Headquarters
NAVSURFAC... Naval Surface Force, Pacific
NAVSURFLANT... Naval Surface Force, Atlantic (DNAB)
NAVSURFLANTREADSUPPGRU... Naval Surface Force, Atlantic Readiness Support Group (DNAB)
NAVSURFPACDAT... Naval Surface Force, Pacific Dependents' Assistance Team (DNAB)
NAVSURFWPNCEN... Naval Surface Weapons Center (PDAA)
NAVSURMISYS... Naval Surface Missile Systems (MCD)
NAVSWC... Naval Surface Warfare Center [Silver Spring, MD]
NAVSWC...... Naval Surface Weapons Center [Later, NSWC] (CAAL)
NAVSWCFAC... Naval Surface Weapons Center Facility (DNAB)
NAVSWCREP... Naval Surface Weapons Center Representative (DNAB)
NAVSWOP... Naval Special Weapons Ordnance Publication
NAVSYD...... Naval Shipyard
NAVTA .... National Automatic Vendors' Trade Association (EA)
navtac.......... Navigation Tactical (AD)
NAVTAC...... Navigation Tactical (AD)
NAVTAC ...... Tactical Navigation System
NAVTACDATASYSDEVSITE... Naval Tactical Data Systems Development and Evaluation Site (DNAB)
NAVTACDOCACT... Navy Tactical Doctrine Activity
NAVTACDOCDEVPRODACT... Navy Tactical Doctrine Development and Production Activity (DNAB)
NAVTACINTEROPSUPPACT... Navy Tactical Interoperability Support Activity (DNAB)
NAVTACINTEROPSUPPACTDET... Navy Tactical Interoperability Support Activity Detachment (DNAB)
NAVTACSAT... Naval Tactical Satellite (DNAB)
NAVTACSTANS... Naval Tactical Standards (MCD)
NAVTACSUPPACT... Navy Tactical Support Activity (NVT)
NAVTAG...... Naval Tactical Game
NAVTAG...... Navy Tactical Action Game
NAVTASC..... Naval Telecommunications Automation Support Center (DNAB)
NAVTASCDETLANT... Naval Telecommunications Automation Support Center, Atlantic (DNAB)
NAVTASCDETPAC... Naval Telecommunications Automation Support Center, Pacific (DNAB)
NAVTEC...... National Association of Vocational-Technical Education Communicators (EA)
NAVTECHJAP... Naval Technical Mission to Japan
NAVTECHMISJAP... Naval Technical Mission to Japan (DNAB)
NAVTECHREP... Naval Technical Representative
NAVTECHTRACEN... Naval Air Technical Training Center
NAVTECHTRACENDET... Naval Technical Training Center Detachment (DNAB)
NAVTECMISEU... Naval Technical Mission in Europe
NAVTELCOM... Naval Telecommunications Command
NAVTELSYSIC... Naval Telecommunications System Integration Center (DNAB)
NAVTIS .... National Vessel Traffic Information System (AD)
NAVTIS .... Naval Training Information System (MCD)
NAVTIS ADS... Naval Training Information System with Automated Data Systems (DNAB)
NAVTNG...... Navigator Training [Air Force]
NAVTNGSq... Navigator Training Squadron [Air Force]
NAVTORPSTA... Naval Torpedo Station
NAVTP .... National Association of Vertical Transportation Professionals
NAVTRA...... Naval Training Command
NAVTRACEN... Naval Training Center (DNAB)
NAVTRACOM... Naval Training Command
NAVTRADEV... Naval Training Device Center
NAVTRADEVCEN... Naval Training Device Center
NAVTRADEVSUPCEN... Naval Training Devices Supply Center (DNAB)
NAVTRADISTCEN... Naval Training and Distribution Center
NAVTRAEQUIPCEN... Naval Training Equipment Center
NAVTRAEQUIPCEN... Naval Training Equipment Center
NAVTRAEQUIPCENFEO... Naval Training Equipment Center Field Office (DNAB)
NAVTRAEQUIPCENREPCEN... Naval Training Equipment Center, Representative for the Center (DNAB)

NAVTRAEQUIPCENREPLANT... Naval Training Equipment Center Representative, Atlantic (DNAB)
NAVTRAEQUIPCENREPPAC... Naval Training Equipment Center Representative, Pacific (DNAB)
NAVTRAFSAT... Navigational/Traffic-Control Satellite (MCD)
NAVTRAIDSCEN... Naval Training Aids Center
NAVTRAINST... Naval Training Support Command Instruction (MCD)
NAVTRANSCO... Naval Transportation Coordinating Office
NAVTRAPUBCEN... Naval Training Publications Center (MCD)
NAVTRASAT... Navigation/Traffic Control Satellite (MCD)
NAVTRASCOL... Naval Training School
NAVTRASTA... Naval Training Station
NAVTRASYSCEN... Naval Training Systems Center [*Orlando, FL*]
NAVUSEARANDCEN... Naval Undersea Research and Development Center (MCD)
NAVUSEARESDEVCEN... Naval Undersea Research and Development Center
NAVUSEAWARCEN... Naval Undersea Warfare Center
NAVUWSEC... Naval Underwater Weapons Systems Engineering Center (AD)
NAVUWSES... Naval Underwater Systems Engineering Center
NAVUWSOUNDLAB... Naval Underwater Sound Laboratory [*Later, NUSC*]
NAVWAG... Naval Warfare Analysis Group
NAVWARCOL... Naval War College
Nav War C Rev... Naval War College. Review [*A publication*] (DLA)
NAVWASS... Navigation and Weapon-Aiming Subsystem (MCD)
NAVWEARSCHFA... Navy Weather Research Facility
NAVWEASERV... Naval Weather Service Command
NAVWEPEVALFAC... Naval Weapons Evaluation Facility [*Kirtland Air Force Base, NM*] (DNAB)
NAVWEPS... Bureau of Naval Weapons [*Obsolete*]
NAVWESA... Naval Weapons Engineering Support Activity
NAVWESS... National Aviation Weather System Study (NOAA)
NAVWESTOCEANCEN... Naval Western Oceanographic Center (DNAB)
NAVWPNCEN... Naval Weapons Center (MCD)
NAVWPNENGSUPPACT... Naval Weapons Engineering Support Activity (DNAB)
NAVWPNEVALFAC... Naval Weapons Evaluation Facility [*Kirtland Air Force Base, NM*]
NAVWPNLAB... Naval Weapons Laboratory [*Later, NSWC*]
NAVWPNQAO... Naval Weapons Quality Assurance Office [*Washington, DC*]
NAVWPNQUALASSURO... Naval Weapons Quality Assurance Office [*Washington, DC*]
NAVWPNSCEN... Naval Weapons Center
NAVWPNSERVO... Naval Weapons Services Office [*Also, NWSO, WEPSO*]
NAVWPNSTA... Naval Weapons Station (MCD)
NAVWPNSTRACEN... Naval Weapons Training Center (DNAB)
NAVWPNSUPPACT... Naval Weapons Support Activity (DNAB)
NAVWPNSUPPCEN... Naval Weapons Support Center (DNAB)
NAVWPNSYSANALO... Naval Weapons Systems Analysis Office
NAVWUIS.... Navy Work Unit Information Service (IID)
NAVXDIVINGU... Navy Experimental Diving Unit
NAVYCAB... Navy Contract Adjustment Board (AAGC)
NAVYEO....... Navigator's Yeoman [*British military*] (DMA)
NAW .... Narathiwat [*Thailand*] [*Airport symbol*] (OAG)
NAW .... National Agricultural Workers Union
NAW .... National Association for Women (NADA)
NAW .... National Association of Wholesaler-Distributors [*Washington, DC*] (EA)
NAW .... National Association of Wholesalers (NADA)
NAW .... National Association of Widows [*British*] (DI)
NAW .... Negative Afterwave [*Microelectrode recording*]
NAW .... Newair [*Denmark ICAO designator*] (FAAC)
N/AW .... Night/Adverse Weather Evaluator (IEEE)
NAW .... Non-All-Weather (CINC)
NAW .... North African Waters
NAW .... Northwest African Waters
NAWA .... National Academy of Western Art (EA)
NAWA .... National Apple Week Association [*Later, NAM*] (EA)
NAWA .... National Association of Women Artists (EA)
NAWA .... North American Warmblood Association (EA)
NAWAC....... National Aviation Weather Advisory Committee (USDC)
NAWAC....... National Aviation Weather Advisory Committee [*Marine science*] (OSRA)
NAWAC....... National Weather Analysis Center [*Air Force, Navy*]
NAWAF....... Navy with Air Force
NAWAPA...... North American Water and Power Alliance
NAWAR....... Navy with Army
NAWARCOL... Naval War College (MUGU)
NAWAS....... National Attack Warning System [*Military*] (IAA)
NAWAS....... National Warning System [*Civil Defense*]
NAWatch..... North American Watch Corp. [*Associated Press*] (SAG)
NAWAU....... National Aviation Weather Advisory Unit [*Marine science*] (OSRA)
NAWAU....... National Aviation Weather Advisory Unit [*Federal Aviation Administration*] (USDC)
NAWB .... National Association of Wine and Beer Makers [*British*] (DBA)
NAWB .... National Association of Wine Bottlers [*Later, NWA*] (EA)
NAWBM....... National Association of Window Blind Manufacturers [*British*] (BI)
NAWBO....... National Association of Women Business Owners [*Chicago, IL*] (EA)
NAWC....... National Art Workers Community [*Later, FCA*] (EA)
NAWC....... National Association for Women in Careers [*Later, NAFWIC*] (EA)
NAWC....... National Association of Water Companies (EA)
NAWC....... National Association of Women's Centers [*Defunct*] (EA)
NAWC....... National Association of Women's Clubs [*British*] (DBA)
NAWC....... Naval Air Warfare Center (DOMA)
NAWC....... Naval War College
NAWC....... North American Watch Corp. [*NASDAQ symbol*] (SAG)
NAWCAS...... National Association of Women's and Children's Apparel Salesmen [*Later, Bureau of Wholesale Sales Representatives*] (EA)

NAWCC....... National Association of Watch and Clock Collectors (EA)
NAWCC....... National Association of Women in Chambers of Commerce (EA)
NAWCH....... National Association for the Welfare of Children in Hospital [*British*]
NAWCJ....... National Association of Women in Criminal Justice (EA)
NAWCM....... National Association of Wiping Cloth Manufacturers [*Later, IAWCM*] (EA)
NAWCWPNS... Naval Air Warfare Center Weapons Division
NAWD........ Notice of Award
NAWD........ Notice of Award (AAGC)
NAWDA....... North American Working Dog Association (EA)
NAWDAC...... National Association for Women Deans, Administrators, and Counselors (EA)
NAWDC....... National Association of Waste Disposal Contractors [*British*] (DCTA)
NAWDC....... National Association of Women Deans and Counselors [*Later, NAWDAC*] (EA)
NAWDEX...... National Water Data Exchange [*United States Geological Survey*] [*Reston, VA*] [*Information service or system*]
NAWESA...... Naval Weapons Engineering Support Activity (PDAA)
NAWF .... National Aborigine Welfare Fund [*Australia*] (NADA)
NAWF .... Nodes Above White Flower [*Botany*]
NAWF .... North American Waterfowl Federation
NAWF .... North American Wildlife Foundation (EA)
NAWF .... North American Wolf Society (EA)
NAWFA....... North Atlantic Westbound Freight Association (DS)
NAWFC....... National Association of Wholesale Fur Cleaners
NAWFC....... National Association of Women Federal Contractors [*Later, NAWGC*] (EA)
NAWG .... National Association of Wheat Growers (EA)
NAWGA....... National-American Wholesale Grocers' Association (EA)
NAWGC....... National Association of Women Government Contractors [*Defunct*] (EA)
NAWGF....... National Association of Wheat Growers Foundation (EA)
NAWGP....... National Agenda for Women's Grants Program [*Australia*]
NAWH........ National Association of Women in Horticulture [*Defunct*] (EA)
NAWH........ Norwegian-American Historical Museum (AD)
NAWHSL...... National Association of Women Highway Safety Leaders (EA)
NAWiC....... National Association for Women in Careers [*Later, NAFWIC*] (EA)
NAWIC....... National Association of Women in Construction (EA)
NAWID....... National Association of Water Institute Directors (EA)
NAWID....... National Association of Writing Instrument Distributors (EA)
NAWJ........ National Association of Women Judges (EA)
NAWK........ National Association of Warehouse Keepers [*British*] (DBA)
NAWL........ National Association of Women Lawyers (EA)
NAWL........ North American Iterative Weighted Least Squares (SAA)
NAWLA....... North American Wholesale Lumber Association (EA)
NAWM........ National Association of Wool Manufacturers [*Later, American Textile Manufacturers Institute*] (EA)
NAWM........ Naval Air Weapons Meet (MUGU)
NAWMD...... National Association of Waste Material Dealers [*Later, NARI*]
NAWME...... National Average Weekly Male Earning
NAWMP...... National Association of Waste Material Producers [*Defunct*] (EA)
NAWMP...... Naval Aviation Weapons Maintenance Program (MCD)
NAWND...... National Association of Wholesale Newspaper Distributors (DGA)
NAWP........ National Anti-Waste Programme [*British*] (DCTA)
NAWP........ National Association for Widowed People [*Later, IAWP*] (EA)
NAWP........ National Association of Women Pharmacists [*British*] (DBA)
NAWPA....... North American Water and Power Alliance
NAWPB....... National Association of Wholesale Pie Bakers (EA)
NAWPB....... National Association of Wine Producers and Bottlers [*Later, NWA*] (EA)
NAWPC....... National Aircraft War Production Council [*World War II*]
NAWPF....... National Aviation Weather Processing Facility [*FAA*] (TAG)
NAWPF....... North American Wildlife Park Foundation (EA)
NAWPM...... National Association of Wholesale Paint Merchants [*British*] (BI)
NAWPS....... National Association of Word Processing Specialists [*Later, WPS*] (EA)
NAWPU....... National Association of Water Power Users [*British*] (DBA)
NAWR........ National Assembly of Women Religious (EA)
NAWRSRF... New Age World Religious and Scientific Research Foundation (EA)
NAWS........ National Agricultural Workers Survey
NAWS........ National Aviation Weather System
NAWS........ Naval Air Weapons Station
NAWS........ NORAD Attack Warning System (MCD)
NAWS........ North African War Shipping [*World War II*]
NAWS........ North American Wolf Society (EA)
NAWSS....... North American Wilderness Survival School
NAWTPD...... Naval All Weather Testing Program Detachment
NAWTS....... National Association of World Trade Secretaries [*Later, AWTCE*] (EA)
NAWU........ National Agricultural Workers Union (EA)
NAWU........ National Asphalt Workers' Union [*A union*] [*British*]
NAWW....... National Association of Wheat Weavers (EA)
NAWWO...... National Association of Woolen and Worsted Overseers [*Later, NATS*] (EA)
NAX .... Ewa, HI [*Location identifier FAA*] (FAAL)
NAX .... New Arcadia Explorations [*Vancouver Stock Exchange symbol*]
NAX .... Norwegian Air Shuttle, AS [*FAA designator*] (FAAC)
NAXSTA....... Naval Air Experimental Station
NAY .... Navegacion y Servicios Aereos Canarios SA [*Spain ICAO designator*] (FAAC)
NAY .... New Alster Energy [*Vancouver Stock Exchange symbol*]
NAYA .... North American Yngling Association (EA)
NAYC .... National Association of Youth Clubs [*British*] (DI)
NAYCEO....... National Association of Youth and Community Education Officers [*British*] (DI)

NAYGTA.......	North American Youth Glider Training Association
NAYO..........	National Association of Youth Orchestras (EAIO)
NAYPCAS....	National Association of Young People's Counselling and Advisory Services [British] (DI)
NAYPIC.......	National Association of Young People in Care [British]
NAYRE........	National Association for Year-Round Education (EA)
NAYRU........	North American Yacht Racing Union (EA)
NAYSI.........	North American Youth Sport Institute (EA)
NAYT..........	National Association of Youth Theatres [British] (DBA)
NAYTA........	National Association of Youth Training Agencies (AIE)
NAYW..........	National Association for Young Writers [Defunct] (EA)
NAZ............	Nazarene
Naz.............	Nazir (BJA)
NAZ............	Normal Analytical Zone [Chemistry]
NAZ............	Nuveen Arizona Premium Income [NYSE symbol] (SAG)
NAZ............	Nuveen AZ Prem Inc. Muni Fd [NYSE symbol] (TTSB)
NAZ............	Servicios Aereos del Nazas SA de CV [Mexico ICAO designator] (FAAC)
NAZI...........	Nationalsozialistische Deutsche Arbeiterpartei [National Socialist German Workers' Party, 1919-45] [Political party]
NB..............	Brooklyn Public Library, Brooklyn, NY [Library symbol Library of Congress] (LCLS)
NB..............	Nabonidus and Belshazzar (BJA)
NB..............	Nanobarn [Unit of Measure]
NB..............	Narrowband
n/b	Narrowband (IDOE)
nb	Narrowband (IDOE)
N/B............	Narrow Band
NB..............	Narrow Beam (NATG)
NB..............	National Battlefield (BARN)
NB..............	National Board
NB..............	NationsBank Corp. [NYSE symbol] (SPSG)
NB..............	Naval Base
NB..............	Navigation Base (NASA)
NB..............	Navy Band
NB..............	Neath and Brecon Railway [Wales]
NB..............	Nebraska (IAA)
Nb..............	Nebraska State Library, Lincoln, NE [Library symbol Library of Congress] (LCLS)
NB..............	Needle Biopsy [Surgical procedure] (DAVI)
NB..............	Negative Binomial Distribution [Statistics]
NB..............	Negri Body (AAMN)
NB..............	Nemzeti Bank [National Bank] [Hungarian]
NB..............	Neo-Babylonian [or New Babylonian] (BJA)
NB..............	Network Booter [Computer science] (BYTE)
NB..............	Neuroblast [Cytology]
NB..............	Neurometric Test Battery [Neurometrics]
NB..............	Neutral Buoyancy [Navy] (SSD)
NB..............	New Benloe's Reports, English King's Bench [1531-1628] [A publication] (DLA)
NB..............	New Boiler
NB..............	Newborn
NB..............	New Bottom [On ships]
NB..............	New Brunswick [Canadian province] [Postal code]
NB..............	New Brunswick Reports [A publication] (DLA)
NB..............	New Business
NB..............	New Haven Airways [ICAO designator] (AD)
NB..............	Next Brochure
NB..............	Nimbus [Cloud] [Meteorology]
Nb..............	Niobium [See Cb] [Chemical element]
NB..............	Nitrobenzene [Organic chemistry]
NB..............	Nitrogen Base (NASA)
NB..............	Nitrous Oxide-Barbiturate [Organic chemistry] (MAE)
NB..............	No Ball [Cricket]
NB..............	No Bias [Relay] [Electronics]
NB..............	No Bias [Relay]
NB..............	No Bid [or Bidders]
NB..............	No Bowel Movement [Gastroenterology] (DAVI)
NB..............	Noise Blanker
N/B............	Noise Power/Bandwidth
NB..............	Nomenclature Board [Tasmania, Australia]
NB..............	Nominal Bore [Tubing]
NB..............	Nonbattle [Army] (AABC)
NB..............	Nonbusiness [IRS]
NB..............	Nordiska Batradet [Nordic Boat Council] [Sweden] (EAIO)
NB..............	Nordlands Bank [Norway]
NB..............	Normal Bowel Movement [Gastroenterology] (DAVI)
NB..............	Normoblast [Hematology] (AAMN)
NB..............	Northampton & Bath Railroad Co. [AAR code]
NB..............	Northbound
NB..............	North Britain [i.e., Scotland]
NB..............	Not a Bean [Penniless] [Facetious translation of NB, Nota Bene (Note Well)] (DSUE)
NB..............	Nota Bene [Note Well] [Latin]
nb..............	Nota Bene [Note Well] [Latin] (WDMC)
NB..............	Not Bent [Freight]
NB..............	Not Blind [Experimental conditions]
NB..............	Notch-Bend (PDAA)
NB..............	Nuclear Blank (NRCH)
NB..............	Nuclear Boiler (NRCH)
NB..............	Nucleus Basalis [Brain anatomy]
NB..............	Nulla Bona [No Goods] [Latin Legal term] (DLA)
Nb..............	Numbers [Old Testament book] (BJA)
NB2..........	Norsar Array Site 02B00 [Norway] [Seismograph station code, US Geological Survey] (SEIS)

NB 2d	New Brunswick Reports, Second Series [A publication] (DLA)
NB3............	Norsar Array Site 03B00 [Norway] [Seismograph station code, US Geological Survey] (SEIS)
NB4............	Norsar Array Site 04B00 [Norway] [Seismograph station code, US Geological Survey] (SEIS)
NB5............	Norsar Array Site 05B00 [Norway] [Seismograph station code, US Geological Survey] (SEIS)
NBA...........	Amateur Astronomers Association, Brooklyn, NY [Library symbol Library of Congress] (LCLS)
NBa............	Davenport Library, Bath, NY [Library symbol Library of Congress] (LCLS)
NBA	Narrowband Allocation
NBA	Narrowband Analyzer
NBA	Narrow-Beam Adapter
NBA	National Ballet of America
NBA	National Band Association (EA)
NBA	National Bank Act of 1863
NBA	National Bankers Association [Washington, DC] (EA)
NBA	National Bankruptcy Act [1898]
NBA	National Bar Association (EA)
NBA	National Basketball Association (EA)
NBA	National Beefmaster Association (EA)
NBA	National Benevolent Association of the Christian Church [Disciples of Christ] (EA)
NBA	National Benzole and Allied Products Association [British] (BI)
NBA	National Biographical Association (EA)
NBA	National Boat Association (EA)
NBA	National Book Awards [Discontinued]
NBA	National Bowling Association (EA)
NBA	National Boxing Association (NADA)
NBA	National Boxing Association of America [Later, WBA]
NBA	National Braille Association (EA)
NBA	National Brassfoundry Association [British] (BI)
NBA	National Broadcasting Authority [Bangladesh] (EY)
NBA	National Broiler Association [Later, NBC]
NBA	National Buffalo Association (EA)
NBA	National Building Agency [British]
NBA	National Business Association (EA)
NBA	National Butterfly Association (EA)
NBA	National Button Association
NBA	N-Bromoacetamide [Organic chemistry]
NBA	N-Butylamine [Organic chemistry]
NBA	Net Book Agreement [British]
NBA	Net Building Area (ADA)
NBA	New Brunswick Area (SAA)
NBA	Nickel-Base Alloy
NBA	Non-Weight-Bearing Ambulation [Orthopedics] (DAVI)
NBA	North British Academy
NBA	North East Bolivian Airways [ICAO designator] (FAAC)
NBAA	Amateur Astronomers Association, Brooklyn, NY [Library symbol] [Library of Congress] (LCLS)
NBAA	National Business Aircraft Association (EA)
NBab..........	Babylon Public Library, Babylon, NY [Library symbol Library of Congress] (LCLS)
NBAB	Biological Station, Fisheries and Oceans Canada [Station de Biologie, Peches et Oceans Canada] St. Andrews, New Brunswick [Library symbol National Library of Canada] (NLC)
NBab..........	Neo-Babylonian [or New Babylonian] (BJA)
NBAC	National Biotechnology Advisory Committee [Canada]
NBAC	National Black Alcoholism Council (EA)
NBACCH......	Charlotte County Historical Society, Inc., St. Andrews, New Brunswick [Library symbol National Library of Canada] (NLC)
NBAD	National Bank of Abu Dhabi
NBAD	Naval Bases Air Defense
NBAD	N-beta-Alanyldopamine [Biochemistry]
NBADA	National Barrel and Drum Association [Later, NABADA - The Association of Container Reconditioners] (EA)
NBAF	National Blonde d'Aquitaine Foundation (EA)
NBAGLE.......	National Black Alliance for Graduate Level Education [Defunct] (EA)
NBAJ	National Buffalo Association Juniors [Defunct] (EA)
NBAK	National Bancorp of Alaska, Inc. [NASDAQ symbol] (NQ)
NBAK	Natl Bancorp(AK) [NASDAQ symbol] (TTSB)
NBald.........	Baldwin Public Library, Baldwin, NY [Library symbol Library of Congress] (LCLS)
NBaldBE	Brookside Elementary School, Baldwin, NY [Library symbol Library of Congress] (LCLS)
NBaldCE	Collidge Elementary School, Baldwin, NY [Library symbol Library of Congress] (LCLS)
NBaldGE	Grand Avenue Elementary School, Baldwin, NY [Library symbol] [Library of Congress] (LCLS)
NBaldHE	Harbor Elementary School, Baldwin, NY [Library symbol Library of Congress] (LCLS)
NBaldHJ	Harbor Junior High School, Baldwin, NY [Library symbol Library of Congress] (LCLS)
NBaldLE......	Lenox Elementary School, Baldwin, NY [Library symbol Library of Congress] (LCLS)
NBaldME	Meadow Elementary School, Baldwin, NY [Library symbol Library of Congress] (LCLS)
NBaldMiE ...	Milburn Elementary School, Baldwin, NY [Library symbol Library of Congress] (LCLS)
NbaldPE.......	Plaza Elementary School, Baldwin, NY [Library symbol Library of Congress] (LCLS)
NBaldPrE	Prospect Elementary School, Baldwin, NY [Library symbol Library of Congress] (LCLS)

NBaldSE	Shubert Elementary School, Baldwin, NY [*Library symbol Library of Congress*] (LCLS)
NBaldSH	Baldwin Senior High School, Baldwin, NY [*Library symbol Library of Congress*] (LCLS)
NBaldStE	Steele Elementary School, Baldwin, NY [*Library symbol Library of Congress*] (LCLS)
NB Alsk	National Bancorp of Alaska, Inc. [*Associated Press*] (SAG)
NB & BA	National Bed-and-Breakfast Association (EA)
NB & C	Norfolk, Baltimore & Carolina Line [*Steamship*] (MHDB)
NBAO	New Brunswick Area Office [*Later, NBL*] [*AEC*]
NBar	Barker Free Library, Barker, NY [*Library symbol Library of Congress*] (LCLS)
nbar	Nanobar [*One billionth of a bar*]
NBAR	Nonbinding Preliminary Allocation of Responsibility [*Environmental Protection Agency*] (FFDE)
NBaryU	Unified Theological Seminary, Barrytown, NY [*Library symbol*] [*Library of Congress*] (LCLS)
NBAS	Neonatal Behavioural Assessment Scale [*Developed by Brazelton*]
NBAS-K	Neonatal Behavioral Assessment Scale-Kansas Revision (EDAC)
NBASLH	National Black Association for Speech, Language and Hearing (EA)
NBat	Richmond Memorial Library, Batavia, NY [*Library symbol Library of Congress*] (LCLS)
NBatC	Genesee Community College, Batavia, NY [*Library symbol Library of Congress*] (LCLS)
NBatGB	Genesee-Wyoming Board of Cooperative Education Services, Batavia, NY [*Library symbol*] [*Library of Congress*] (LCLS)
NBatGH	Genesee Memorial Hospital, Batavia, NY [*Library symbol Library of Congress*] (LCLS)
NBatHHi	Holland Purchase Historical Society, Batavia, NY [*Library symbol Library of Congress*] (LCLS)
NBatStJ	Saint Jerome Hospital, Medical Library, Batavia, NY [*Library symbol Library of Congress*] (LCLS)
NBatV	United States Veterans Administration Hospital, Library Service, Batavia, NY [*Library symbol Library of Congress*] (LCLS)
NBAU	No Business as Usual (EA)
NBaVA	United States Veterans Administration Hospital, Bath, NY [*Library symbol Library of Congress*] (LCLS)
NBAW	Notable Black American Women [*A publication*]
NBAWADU	National Black Anti-War Anti-Draft Union (EA)
NBayv	Bayville Free Library, Bayville, NY [*Library symbol Library of Congress*] (LCLS)
NBayvE	Bayville Elementary School, Bayville, NY [*Library symbol*] [*Library of Congress*] (LCLS)
NBayvI	Bayville Intermediate School, Bayville, NY [*Library symbol*] [*Library of Congress*] (LCLS)
NBayvP	Bayville Primary School, Bayville, NY [*Library symbol*] [*Library of Congress*] (LCLS)
NbB	Beatrice Public Library, Beatrice, NE [*Library symbol Library of Congress*] (LCLS)
NBB	Brooklyn Museum, Brooklyn, NY [*Library symbol Library of Congress*] (LCLS)
NBB	Narrowband Beam [*Physics*]
NBB	National Bank of Bahrain (EY)
NBB	National Bank of Brunei
NBBA	National Beep Baseball Association (EA)
NBBA	National Black Business Alliance (EA)
NBB & L	National Bath, Bed, and Linen Show (ITD)
NBBB	National Better Business Bureau [*Later, CBBB*] (EA)
NBBB	National Better Business Bureau (NADA)
NBBC	Bibliotheque Medicale, Hopital Regional Chaleur [*Medical Library, Chaleur Regional Hospital*] Bathurst, New Brunswick [*Library symbol National Library of Canada*] (NLC)
NBBC	National Black Business Council
NBBCC	College Communautaire du New Brunswick, Bathurst, New Brunswick [*Library symbol National Library of Canada*] (NLC)
NBBDA	National Burlap Bag Dealers Association [*Later, Textile Bag and Packaging Association*] (EA)
NbBe	Bellevue Public Library, Bellevue, NE [*Library symbol Library of Congress*] (LCLS)
NBB-E	Brooklyn Museum, Wilbour Library of Egyptology, Brooklyn, NY [*Library symbol Library of Congress*] (LCLS)
NBBE	National Board for Bakery Education [*British*] (BI)
NbBea	Beatrice Public Library, Beatrice, NE [*Library symbol*] [*Library of Congress*] (LCLS)
NbBeL	Bellevue Public Library, Bellevue, NE [*Library symbol*] [*Library of Congress*] (LCLS)
NBBI	National Blue Books, Inc. [*Canoga Park, CA*] [*Publisher*]
NBBI	Nederlands Bureau voor Bibliotheekwezen en Informatieverzorging [*Netherlands Organization for Libraries and Information Services*] [*Information service or system*] (IID)
NBBL	National Bath, Bed, and Linen Association (EA)
NbBla	Blair Public Library, Blair, NE [*Library symbol Library of Congress*] (LCLS)
NBBLA	National Bath, Bed, and Linen Association [*Later, NBBL*] (EA)
NbBlaD	Dana College, Blair, NE [*Library symbol Library of Congress*] (LCLS)
NBBLC	National Black on Black Love Campaign (EA)
NBBMA	National Beauty and Barber Manufacturers Association [*Later, ABA*] (EA)
NBBMK	Mussee de Kent, Bouctouche, New Brunswick [*Library symbol National Library of Canada*] (NLC)
NBBN	Nepisiguit Centennial Public Library, Bathurst, New Brunswick [*Library symbol National Library of Canada*] (NLC)
Nb-BPH	Nebraska Library Commission, Library for Blind and Physically Handicapped, Lincoln, NE [*Library symbol Library of Congress*] (LCLS)
NBBPVI	National Board of Boiler and Pressure Vessel Inspectors (EA)
NBBQA	National Barbecue Association
NbBro	Broken Bow Carnegie Library, Broken Bow, NE [*Library symbol Library of Congress*] (LCLS)
NBBS	New British Broadcasting Station (NADA)
NBBWM	Central New Brunswick Woodmen's Museum, Boiestown, New Brunswick [*Library symbol National Library of Canada*] (NLC)
NBC	Beaufort, SC [*Location identifier FAA*] (FAAL)
NBC	Brooklyn College, Brooklyn, NY [*Library symbol Library of Congress*] (LCLS)
NBC	Concordia College, Seward, NE [*OCLC symbol*] (OCLC)
NBC	Cook [*N. B.*] Corp. Ltd. [*Toronto Stock Exchange symbol Vancouver Stock Exchange symbol*]
NBC	Narrowband Conducted (IEEE)
NBC	National Baseball Congress (EA)
NBC	National Basketball Congress (NADA)
NBC	National Battlefields Commission [*See also CCBN*]
NBC	National Beagle Club (EA)
NBC	National Beef Congress
NBC	National Bibliographic Control
NBC	National Board for Certification in Dental Laboratory Technology (EA)
NBC	National Book Committee [*Defunct*]
NBC	National Book Council [*Later, NBL*] [*United Kingdom*]
NBC	National Bowling Council (EA)
NBC	National Boxing Council [*British*]
NBC	National Boys' Club (WDAA)
NBC	National Braille Club [*Later, NBA*] (EA)
NBC	National Broadcasters' Club (NTCM)
NBC	National Broadcasting Co., Inc. [*New York, NY*]
NBC	National Broadcasting Commission (NADA)
NBC	National Broiler Council (EA)
NBC	National Broom Council [*Later, NBMC*] (EA)
NBC	National Building Code
NBC	National Building Code of Canada (HGAA)
NBC	National Bus Co. [*British*]
NBC	Natural Background Clutter
NBC	Natural Birth Control
NBC	Navy Beach Commando
NBC	Neumann Boundary Conditions
NBC	Newfoundland Base Command [*Army World War II*]
NBC	Nies Babylonian Collection [*Yale University*] (BJA)
NBC	Nigerian Broadcasting Corp.
NBC	Noise Balancing Circuit (DEN)
NBC	Noise Balancing Control (IAA)
NBC	Nonbattle Casualty (NVT)
NBC	Nordic Boat Council (EA)
NBC	Nostalgia Book Club
NBC	Nuclear, Biological, and Chemical [*Warfare*]
NBC	Number Base Conversion
NBCA	Campbellton Centennial Public Library, New Brunswick [*Library symbol National Library of Canada*] (NLC)
NBCA	National Band Council of Australia
NBCA	National Baseball Congress of America (NADA)
NBCA	National Beagle Club of America (EA)
NBCA	National Bituminous Concrete Association [*Later, NAPA*] (EA)
NBCA	National Business Circulation Association (EA)
NBCA	Navy Department Board of Contract Appeals [*1944-50*] (AAGC)
NBCAC	Chaleur Library Region, Campbellton, New Brunswick [*Library symbol National Library of Canada*] (NLC)
NBCAM	Campobello Public Library, New Brunswick [*Library symbol National Library of Canada*] (BIB)
NBCAP	National Becaon Code Allocation Plan (FAAC)
NBCBP	Bibliotheque Publique Mgr. Paquet, Caraquet, New Brunswick [*Library symbol National Library of Canada*] (NLC)
NBCC	National Baby Care Council [*Defunct*] (EA)
NBCC	National Beauty Career Center (EA)
NBCC	National Bidders Control Center
NBCC	National Bituminous Coal Commission [*Functions transferred to Department of the Interior, 1939*]
NBCC	National Black Chamber of Commerce (EA)
NBCC	National Board for Certified Counselors (EA)
NBCC	National Book Critics Circle (EA)
NBCC	National Breast Cancer Coalition
NBCC	National Budget and Consultation Committee [*Defunct*] (EA)
NBCC	National Building Code of Canada
NBCC	National Bureau for Co-Operation in Child Care [*British*]
NBCC	National Business Career Center (EA)
NBCC	Netherlands British Chamber of Commerce (DS)
NBCC	Nevoid Basal-Cell Carcinoma [*Oncology*]
NBCC	Nigerian British Chamber of Commerce [*London*] (DCTA)
NBCC	Nuclear, Biological, and Chemical Contamination (DOMA)
NBCC	Nuclear, Biological, Chemical, Conventional [*Warfare*]
NBCCA	National Business Council for Consumer Affairs [*Terminated, 1974*] [*Department of Commerce*] (EGAO)
NBCCC	Miramichi Campus, New Brunswick Community College [*Campus Miramichi, College Communautaire du Nouveau-Brunswick*], Chatham, New Brunswick [*Library symbol National Library of Canada*] (NLC)
NBCCC	National Black Catholic Clergy Caucus (EA)
NBCCC	National Bureau for Co-Operation in Child Care [*British*] (BI)
NBC-CDTP	National Board for Certification - Certified Dental Technician Program (EA)
NBCCS	Nevoid Basal Cell Carcinoma Syndrome [*Oncology*] (DMAA)
NBCD	Natural Binary-Coded Decimal
NBCD	Negate BCD [*Binary-Coded Decimal*] Number [*Computer science*]

NBCD .... Nuclear, Biological, and Chemical Defense (NATG)
NBCDCE ...... Nuclear, Biological, and Chemical Defense Control Element [Military]
NBCDI .... National Black Child Development Institute (EA)
NBCDL .... National Board for Certification of Dental Laboratories [Later, CDL] (EA)
NBCDX .... Nuclear, Biological, and Chemical Defense Exercise [NATO] (NATG)
NBCE .... Nuclear, Biological, and Chemical Element
NbCen .... Hards Memorial Library, Central City, NE [Library symbol Library of Congress] (LCLS)
NbCenC .... Nebraska Central College, Central City, NE [Library symbol Library of Congress Obsolete] (LCLS)
NBCFAE .... National Black Coalition of Federal Aviation Employees (EA)
NBCFD .... Naval Base Consolidated Fire Department (DNAB)
NBCG .... National Bulk Commodities Group [Australia]
NBCGT .... National Business Consortium for the Gifted and Talented [Defunct] (EA)
NbCh .... Chadron Public Library, Chadron, NE [Library symbol Library of Congress] (LCLS)
NBCH .... Historical Society Nicolas Denys, Societe Historique Nicolas Denys, Caraquet, New Brunswick [Library symbol National Library of Canada] (NLC)
NBCHD .... Health Sciences Library, Hotel-Dieu Hospital, Chatham, New Brunswick [Library symbol National Library of Canada] (BIB)
NBCHR .... Bibliotheque de la Sante, Centre Hospitalier Restigouche, Campbellton, New Brunswick [Library symbol National Library of Canada] (BIB)
NbChS .... Chadron State College, Chadron, NE [Library symbol Library of Congress] (LCLS)
NBCI .... Nigerian Bank for Commerce and Industry
NBCIA .... National Blue Crab Industry Association (EA)
NBCL .... National Beauty Culturists' League (EA)
NBCL .... National Birth Control League
NBC/LEO ...... National Black Caucus of Local Elected Officials (EA)
NBCM .... Miramichi Natural History Society, Chatham, New Brunswick [Library symbol National Library of Canada] (NLC)
NBCMA .... Mussee Acadien, Caraquet, New Brunswick [Library symbol National Library of Canada] (NLC)
NBCMu .... Brooklyn Children's Museum, Brooklyn, NY [Library symbol Library of Congress] (LCLS)
NbCo .... Columbus Public Library, Columbus, NE [Library symbol Library of Congress] (LCLS)
NbCoC .... Platte Technical Community College, Columbus, NE [Library symbol Library of Congress] (LCLS)
NBCOT .... National Board for Certification of Orthopaedic Technologists (EA)
NBCP .... Brooklyn College of Pharmacy, Brooklyn, NY [Library symbol Library of Congress] (LCLS)
NBCP .... National Bladder Cancer Project [National Cancer Institute]
NBCPC .... National Board for Cardiovascular and Pulmonary Credentialing [Later, Cardiovascular Credentialing International - CCI] (EA)
NbCr .... Crete Public Library, Crete, NE [Library symbol Library of Congress] (LCLS)
NbCrD .... Doane College, Crete, NE [Library symbol Library of Congress] (LCLS)
NBCRS .... Nuclear-Biological-Chemical Reconnaissance System [Military]
NBCS .... National Black Communicators Society (EA)
NBCS .... St. Thomas University, Fredericton, New Brunswick [Library symbol National Library of Canada] (NLC)
NBCSA .... National Black Catholic Seminarians Association (EA)
NBCSDA ...... National Broom Corn and Supply Dealers Association (EA)
NBCSH .... La Societe Historique de Clair, Inc., New Brunswick [Library symbol National Library of Canada] (NLC)
NBCSI .... National Board of the Coat and Suit Industry [Defunct] (EA)
NBCSL .... National Black Caucus of State Legislators (EA)
NBcs TX ...... National Bancshares Corp. of Texas [Associated Press] (SAG)
NBCU .... National Bureau of Casualty Underwriters [Later, ISO] (EA)
NBC USA ..... National Baptist Convention, USA (EA)
NBCV .... Narrowband Coherent Video (IEEE)
NBCVHA .... Le Village Historique Acadien, Caraquet, New Brunswick [Library symbol National Library of Canada] (NLC)
NBCW .... National Bird Cage Week
NBCW .... National Board of Catholic Women [British]
NBCWRS ...... Nuclear, Biological, and Chemical Warning and Reporting System
NBD .... Doane College, Crete, NE [OCLC symbol] (OCLC)
NBD .... Narrowband Detector
NBD .... National Bank of Dubai
NBD .... NBD Bancorp, Inc. [NYSE symbol] (SPSG)
NBD .... Negative Binomial Distribution [Statistics]
NBD .... Neurogenic Bladder Dysfunction [Medicine]
NBD .... Neutral Beam Divider
NBD .... Nitrobenzoxadiazole [Organic chemistry]
nbd .... No Big Deal [Internet language] [Computer science]
NBD .... Nondirectional Beacon
NBD .... Norbornadiene [Organic chemistry]
NBD .... Nucleotide Binding Domain [Biochemistry]
NBDA .... National Barrel and Drum Association
NBDA .... National Bicycle Dealers Association (EA)
NBDC .... National Blood Data Center [American Blood Commission] [Information service or system] (IID)
NBDC .... National Bomb Data Center
NBDCA .... National Baptist Deacons Convention of America (EA)
NBDE .... National Bureau of Document Examiners (EA)
NBDEA .... National Beverage Dispensing Equipment Association (EA)
NBDF .... Narrow Band Device - Fix
NBDF .... Narrowband Dicke-Fix [Electronics] (CET)
NBDFB .... Nitrobenzenediazonium Tetrafluoroborate [Organic chemistry]

NBDFX .... Narrowband Dicke-Fix [Electronics] (MSA)
NBDKH .... Keillor House Museum, Dorchester, New Brunswick [Library symbol National Library of Canada] (NLC)
NBDL .... Narrowband Data Line
NBDL .... Narrowband Data Link (IAA)
NBDL .... Naval Biodynamics Laboratory (GRD)
NBDM .... Miramichi Salmon Museum, Inc., Doaktown, New Brunswick [Library symbol National Library of Canada] (NLC)
NBDMO .... N-Bromo(dimethyl)oxazolidinone [Organic chemistry]
NBD-PS .... Nitrobenzoxadiazole Phosphatidylserine [Biochemistry]
NBDRRM ...... Restigouche Regional Museum, Dalhousie, New Brunswick [Library symbol National Library of Canada] (NLC)
NBDS .... Nuclear Burst Detection Systems (MCD)
NBDVS .... Narrow Band Digital Voice System [Telecommunications] (LAIN)
NBE .... Dallas, TX [Location identifier FAA] (FAAL)
NbE .... Exeter Public Library, Exeter, NE [Library symbol Library of Congress] (LCLS)
NBE .... Neutron Binding Energy
NBE .... Newburyport Birders' Exchange (EA)
NBE .... Nominal Band Edge
NBE .... Normal Binocular Experience [Ophthalmology]
NbE .... North by East
NBE .... Nova Beaucage Mines Ltd. [Toronto Stock Exchange symbol]
NBE .... Nuclear Binding Energy
NBEA .... National Ballroom and Entertainment Association (EA)
NBEA .... National Black Evangelical Association (EA)
NBEA .... National Broadcast Editorial Association (EA)
NBEA .... National Business Education Association [Reston, VA] (EA)
NBEBR .... Bibliotheque Regionale du Haut Saint-Jean, Edmundston, New Brunswick [Library symbol National Library of Canada] (NLC)
NBEC .... National Business and Education Council (OICC)
NBECC .... New Brunswick Community College, Edmundston, New Brunswick [Library symbol National Library of Canada] (NLC)
NBECS .... Nonresidential Building Energy Comsumption Survey [Department of Energy] (GFGA)
NBed .... Bedford Free Library, Bedford, NY [Library symbol Library of Congress] (LCLS)
NBEDC .... National Black Economic Development Conference
NBedh .... Bedford Hills Free Library, Bedford Hills, NY [Library symbol Library of Congress] (LCLS)
NBEF .... National Bowhunter Education Foundation (EA)
NBel .... Bellport Memorial Library, Bellport, NY [Library symbol Library of Congress] (LCLS)
NBelf .... Belfast Public Library, Belfast, NY [Library symbol Library of Congress] (LCLS)
NBelL .... Long Island Library Resources Council, Inc., Bellport, NY [Library symbol Library of Congress] (LCLS)
NBellm .... Bellmore Memorial Library, Bellmore, NY [Library symbol Library of Congress] (LCLS)
NBellmCM .... Wellington C. Mepham High School, Bellmore, NY [Library symbol] [Library of Congress] (LCLS)
NBellmGJ .... Grand Avenue Junior High School, Bellmore, NY [Library symbol] [Library of Congress] (LCLS)
NBellmKH ..... John F. Kennedy High School, Bellmore, NY [Library symbol] [Library of Congress] (LCLS)
NBellmR .... C.H. Reinhard School, Bellmore, NY [Library symbol] [Library of Congress] (LCLS)
NBellmSE .... Shore Road Elementary School, Bellmore, NY [Library symbol] [Library of Congress] (LCLS)
NBellmWE .... Winthrop Avenue Elementary School, Bellmore, NY [Library symbol] [Library of Congress] (LCLS)
NBelS .... Suffolk Cooperative Library System, Bellport, NY [Library symbol Library of Congress] (LCLS)
NBEMM .... Musee de Madawaska, Edmundston, New Brunswick [Library symbol National Library of Canada] (NLC)
N Ben .... New Benloe's Reports, English King's Bench [1531-1628] [A publication] (DLA)
N Benl .... New Benloe's Reports, English King's Bench [1531-1628] [A publication] (DLA)
NBEO .... National Board of Examiners in Optometry (EA)
NBEOPS ...... National Board of Examiners for Osteopathic Physicians and Surgeons [Later, NBOME] (EA)
NB Eq .... New Brunswick Equity Reports [A publication] (DLA)
NB Eq Ca .... New Brunswick Equity Cases [A publication] (DLA)
NB Eq R ...... New Brunswick Equity Reports [A publication] (DLA)
NB Eq Rep .. New Brunswick Equity Reports [A publication] (DLA)
NBER .... National Bureau of Economic Research (EA)
NBER .... National Bureau of Engineering Registration
NBERA .... National Bicentennial Ethnic-Racial Alliance
NBerG .... Gillam-Grant Community Center Library, Bergen, NY [Library symbol Library of Congress] (LCLS)
NBernN .... Bernardsville News, Bernardsville, NJ [Library symbol Library of Congress] (LCLS)
NBerR .... Bergen Reading Center, Bergen, NY [Library symbol Library of Congress] (LCLS)
NBES .... National Business Equipment Survey [British]
NBESLM ...... Centre Universitaire Saint-Louis Maillet, Edmundston, New Brunswick [Library symbol National Library of Canada] (NLC)
NBet .... Bethpage Public Library, Bethpage, NY [Library symbol Library of Congress] (LCLS)
NBET .... National Business Entrance Test [Education] (AEBS)
NBetCaE ...... Campagne Elementary School, Bethpage, NY [Library symbol Library of Congress] (LCLS)
NBetCE .... Central Elementary School, Bethpage, NY [Library symbol Library of Congress] (LCLS)

NBETF.......... Neutral-Beam Engineering Test Facility [*Lawrence Berkeley Laboratory*] [*Terminated Department of Energy*] (GRD)

NBetG........... Grumman Aerospace Corp., Bethpage, NY [*Library symbol Library of Congress*] (LCLS)

NBetH........... Mid-Island Hospital, Bethpage, NY [*Library symbol Library of Congress*] (LCLS)

NBethKJ........ John F. Kennedy Junior High School, Bethpage, NY [*Library symbol Library of Congress*] (LCLS)

NBethSH........ Bethpage Senior High School, Bethpage, NY [*Library symbol Library of Congress*] (LCLS)

NBetKE.......... Kramer Elementary School, Bethpage, NY [*Library symbol Library of Congress*] (LCLS)

NBetKJ........... John F. Kennedy Junior High School, Bethpage, NY [*Library symbol*] [*Library of Congress*] (LCLS)

NBetSH.......... Bethpage Senior High School, Bethpage, NY [*Library symbol*] [*Library of Congress*] (LCLS)

NBetWE........ John H. West Elementary School, Bethpage, NY [*Library symbol*] [*Library of Congress*] (LCLS)

NBF.............. Brooklyn Friends School, New York, NY [*Library symbol Library of Congress*] (LCLS)

NBF.............. Narrowband Filter

NBF.............. National Bed Federation [*British*] (DBA)

NBF.............. National Birman Fanciers (EA)

NBF.............. National Boating Federation (EA)

NBF.............. National Burn Federation (EA)

NBF.............. Neutral Buoyancy Facility [*Navy*] (MCD)

NBF.............. New Biotechnology Firm

NBF.............. New Business Funds (MCD)

NBF.............. Nordisk Barnkirurgisk Forening [*Scandinavian Association of Paediatric Surgeons - SAPS*] [*Denmark*] (EAIO)

NBF.............. Northbay Financial Corp. [*AMEX symbol*] (SPSG)

NBF.............. North Bergen Federation of Public Libraries [*Library network*]

NBF.............. Northwest AHEC [*Area Health Education Center*] - Bowman Gray School of Medicine, Taylorsville, NC [*OCLC symbol*] (OCLC)

NBF.............. Nucleotide Binding Fold [*Genetics*]

NBFA........... National Baseball Fan Association (EA)

NBFA........... National Business Forms Association [*Alexandria, VA*] (EA)

NBFA........... New Business Fund Authorization (MCD)

NBFA........... Provincial Archives of New-Brunswick [*Archives Provinciales du Nouveau-Brunswick*] Fredericton, New Brunswick [*Library symbol National Library of Canada*] (NLC)

NBFAA........ National Burglar and Fire Alarm Association (EA)

NBFAFA....... Archives, Diocese of Fredericton, Anglican Church of Canada, New Brunswick [*Library symbol National Library of Canada*] (NLC)

NBFAG........ Research Station, Agriculture Canada [*Station de Recherches, Agriculture Canada*] Fredericton, New Brunswick [*Library symbol National Library of Canada*] (NLC)

NBFB........... Beaverbrook Collection, New Brunswick Archives, Fredericton, New Brunswick [*Library symbol National Library of Canada*] (NLC)

NbFb............ Fairbury Public Library, Fairbury, NE [*Library symbol Library of Congress*] (LCLS)

NbFbC.......... Southeast Community College, Fairbury, NE [*Library symbol Library of Congress*] (LCLS)

NBFBS........ New Brunswick Barristers Society, Fredericton, New Brunswick [*Library symbol National Library of Canada*] (NLC)

NbFC........... Central Lutheran Theological Seminary, Fremont, NE [*Library symbol Library of Congress*] (LCLS)

NBFC........... New Brunswick Library Service, Fredericton, New Brunswick [*Library symbol National Library of Canada*] (NLC)

NbFc............ Woods Memorial Library, Falls City, NE [*Library symbol Library of Congress*] (LCLS)

NbFcP........... Woods Memorial Library, Falls City, NE [*Library symbol*] [*Library of Congress*] (LCLS)

NBFDEC....... Dr. Everett Chalmers Hospital, Fredericton, New Brunswick [*Library symbol National Library of Canada*] (NLC)

NBFE........... Maritimes Forest Research Centre, Environment Canada [*Centre de Recherches Forestieres des Maritimes, Environnement Canada*] Fredericton, New Brunswick [*Library symbol National Library of Canada*] (NLC)

NBFED......... New Brunswick Department of Education, Fredericton, New Brunswick [*Library symbol National Library of Canada*] (NLC)

NBFFO......... National Board of Fur Farm Organizations (EA)

NBFHR........ New Brunswick Department of Historical Resources, Fredericton, New Brunswick [*Library symbol National Library of Canada*] (NLC)

NBFI............ Non-Bank Financial Institutions [*Ghana*]

NBFI............ Non-Bank Financial Intermediary (ADA)

NBFJS.......... Sunbury West Historical Society, Fredericton Junction, New Brunswick [*Library symbol National Library of Canada*] (NLC)

NBFJWO...... National Bureau of Federated Jewish Women's Organizations (EA)

NBFKL........ Kings Landing Historical Settlement, Fredericton, New Brunswick [*Library symbol National Library of Canada*] (NLC)

NBFL........... Legislative Library [*Bibliotheque Legislative*] Fredericton, New Brunswick [*Library symbol National Library of Canada*] (NLC)

NBFLM........ Photogrammetry Branch, New Brunswick Department of Lands and Mines, Fredericton,New Brunswick [*Library symbol National Library of Canada*] (NLC)

NBFM.......... Narrowband Frequency Modulation [*Radio*]

NBFMM....... Medley Memorial Library, Christ Church Cathedral, Fredericton, New Brunswick [*Library symbol National Library of Canada*] (NLC)

NBFNR......... New Brunswick Department of Natural Resources and Energy, Fredericton, New Brunswick [*Library symbol National Library of Canada*] (NLC)

NBFO........... National Black Feminist Organization

NBFP........... New Brunswick Power, Fredericton, New Brunswick [*Library symbol National Library of Canada*] (NLC)

NBFPO......... Premier's Office, Province of New Brunswick, Fredericton, New Brunswick [*Library symbol National Library of Canada*] (NLC)

NbFr............ Fremont Public Library, Fremont, NE [*Library symbol Library of Congress*] (LCLS)

NBFR........... Not Before [*ICAO designator*] (FAAC)

NbFrM.......... Midland Lutheran College, Fremont, NE [*Library symbol Library of Congress*] (LCLS)

NBFRP......... New Brunswick Research and Productivity Council, Fredericton, New Brunswick [*Library symbol National Library of Canada*] (NLC)

NBFS........... National Bird-Feeding Society (EA)

NBFS........... New Balanced File Organization Scheme (MHDB)

NBFS........... Societe d'Histoire de la Riviere Saint Jean, Fredericton, New Brunswick [*Library symbol National Library of Canada*] (BIB)

NBFSS......... New Brunswick Department of Social Services, Fredericton, New Brunswick [*Library symbol National Library of Canada*] (NLC)

NBFT............ Bureau de Traduction, Gouvernement du Nouveau-Brunswick [*Translation Bureau, Governement of New Brunswick*] Fredericton, New Brunswick [*Library symbol National Library of Canada*] (NLC)

NBFTR......... New Brunswick Department of Transportation, Fredericton, New Brunswick [*Library symbol National Library of Canada*] (NLC)

NBFU........... National Board of Fire Underwriters [*Later, AIA*] (EA)

NBFU........... University of New Brunswick, Fredericton, New Brunswick [*Library symbol National Library of Canada*] (NLC)

NBFUA......... Archives and Special Collections Department, University of New Brunswick, Fredericton, New Brunswick [*Library symbol National Library of Canada*] (NLC)

NBFUE......... Engineering Library, University of New Brunswick, Fredericton [*Library symbol National Library of Canada*] (BIB)

NBFUL......... Law Library, University of New Brunswick, Fredericton, New Brunswick [*Library symbol National Library of Canada*] (NLC)

NBFUM........ Map Room, Government Documents Department, University of New Brunswick, Fredericton, New Brunswick [*Library symbol National Library of Canada*] (NLC)

NBFY........... York-Sunbury Historical Society, Fredericton, New Brunswick [*Library symbol National Library of Canada*] (NLC)

NBFYR......... York Regional Library, Fredericton, New Brunswick [*Library symbol National Library of Canada*] (NLC)

NBFYRC....... New Brunswick Department of Youth, Recreation and Cultural Resources, Fredericton, New Brunswick [*Library symbol National Library of Canada*] (NLC)

NBG............ Bowman Gray School of Medicine, Winston-Salem, NC [*OCLC symbol*] (OCLC)

NBG............ Brooklyn Botanic Garden, Brooklyn, NY [*Library symbol Library of Congress*] (LCLS)

NbG............ Grand Island Public Library, Grand Island, NE [*Library symbol Library of Congress*] (LCLS)

NBG............ National Bank of Greece

NBG............ Naval Beach Group (NVT)

NBG............ New Orleans, LA [*Location identifier FAA*] (FAAL)

NBG............ Nieuwe Vertaling Nederlands Bijbelgenootschap [*A publication*] (BJA)

NBG............ No Blasted Good [*Slang*]

NBG............ No Bloody Good [*British slang*]

NBG............ Nuclear Beta Gauge

NBGA.......... National Bingo Game Association [*British*] (DBA)

NBGACF....... Canadian Forces Base, Gagetown, New Brunswick [*Library symbol National Library of Canada*] (NLC)

NBGFCC....... New Brunswick Community College, Grand Falls, New Brunswick [*Library symbol National Library of Canada*] (NLC)

NBGFH......... Grand Falls Historical Society, New Brunswick [*Library symbol National Library of Canada*] (NLC)

NBGG.......... Grand Manan Historical Society, Grand Harbour, Grand Manan Island, New Brunswick [*Library symbol National Library of Canada*] (NLC)

NbGi............ Grand Island Public Library, Grand Island, NE [*Library symbol*] [*Library of Congress*] (LCLS)

NBGMM....... Grand Manan Museum, Grand Harbour, Grand Manan Island, New Brunswick, [*Library symbol National Library of Canada*] (NLC)

NBGQA......... National Building Granite Quarries Association (EA)

NBGRN........ Narrow Band Gaussian Random Noise (PDAA)

NBGS.......... New Bedford Glass Society [*Defunct*] (EA)

NBH............ Hastings College, Hastings, NE [*OCLC symbol*] (OCLC)

NbH............ Hastings Public Library, Hastings, NE [*Library symbol Library of Congress*] (LCLS)

NBH............ National Bank of Hungary

NBH............ National Bellas Hess [*Inc.*] [*Commercial firm*]

NBH............ Network Busy Hour [*Telecommunications*] (TEL)

NBH............ North Bay [*Hawaii*] [*Seismograph station code, US Geological Survey Closed*] (SEIS)

NBHA.......... National Bicentennial Hospitality Alliance [*American Revolution Bicentennial Administration*]

NBHA.......... National Builders' Hardware Association [*Later, DHI*] (EA)

NbHC........... Hastings College, Hastings, NE [*Library symbol Library of Congress*] (LCLS)

NBHCA......... Albert County Historical Society, Inc., Hopewell Cape, New Brunswick [*Library symbol National Library of Canada*] (NLC)

NBHCA......... National Belgian Hare Club of America [*Defunct*] (EA)

NbHCC......... Central Technical Community College, Hastings, NE [*Library symbol Library of Congress*] (LCLS)

NbHCro......... Crosier Fathers' Library, Hastings, NE [*Library symbol Library of Congress*] (LCLS)

NbHi............ Nebraska State Historical Society, Lincoln, NE [*Library symbol Library of Congress*] (LCLS)

NbHo .... Holdrege-Phelps County Library, Holdrege, NE [*Library symbol Library of Congress*] (LCLS)

NBHPA .... National Black Health Planners Association (EA)

NBHS .... National Bureau for Handicapped Students [*British*] (CB)

NBi .... Binghamton Public Library, Binghamton, NY [*Library symbol Library of Congress*] (LCLS)

NBI .... Nabisco Brands, Inc. [*Toronto Stock Exchange symbol*]

NBI .... Nathaniel Branden Institute

NBI .... National BankAmericard, Inc. [*Later, Visa USA, Inc.*]

NBI .... National Bridge Inventory [*FHWA*] (TAG)

NBI .... Neutral Beam Injection (MCD)

NBI .... Nielsen Broadcast Index [*A. C. Nielsen Co.*] (NTCM)

NBI .... No Bone Injury [*Medicine*]

NBI .... Nonbattle Injuries

NBI .... Northern Business Information, Inc. [*New York, NY*] [*Information service or system*] (TSSD)

NBI .... Nothing but Initials [*Initialism is name of commercial word processor firm*]

NBI .... Nuclear Burst Indicator (NATG)

NBIA .... National Business Incubation Association [*Carlisle, PA*] (EA)

NBIA .... National Business Incubation Association

NBIAP .... National Biological Impact Assessment Program [*Computer science*] (IID)

NBiBT .... Broome Technical Community College, Binghamton, NY [*Library symbol Library of Congress*] (LCLS)

NBIC .... National Business Information Center [*Dun & Bradstreet*]

NBIE .... National Burn Information Exchange [*Information service or system*] (CRD)

NBiF .... Four County Library System, Binghamton, NY [*Library symbol Library of Congress*] (LCLS)

NBiL .... Our Lady of Lourdes Hospital, Binghamton, NY [*Library symbol Library of Congress*] (LCLS)

NBIO .... North American Biologicals, Inc. [*NASDAQ symbol*] (NQ)

NBIP .... National Biomonitoring Inventory Program [*Department of Energy*] (MSC)

NBIRF .... National Brain Injury Research Foundation (EA)

NBiRM .... Roberson Museum and Science Center, Binghamton, NY [*Library symbol*] [*Library of Congress*] (LCLS)

NBIS .... National Bridge Inspection Standards [*FHWA*] (TAG)

NBiSC .... New York State Supreme Court Law Library, Binghamton, NY [*Library symbol Library of Congress*] (LCLS)

NBiSEG .... New York State Electric & Gas Corp., Binghamton, NY [*Library symbol Library of Congress*] (LCLS)

NBiSL .... Singer Co., Link Division, Binghamton, NY [*Library symbol Library of Congress*] (LCLS)

NBiSU .... State University of New York at Binghamton, Binghamton, NY [*Library symbol Library of Congress*] (LCLS)

NBIT .... New Bedford Institute of Technology [*Massachusetts*]

NBIX .... Neurocrine Biosciences [*NASDAQ symbol*] (TTSB)

NBIX .... Neurocrine Biosciences, Inc. [*NASDAQ symbol*] (SAG)

NBJ .... Kingsbrook Jewish Medical Center, Brooklyn, NY [*Library symbol Library of Congress*] (LCLS)

NBJ .... National Bar Journal [*A publication*] (DLA)

NbK .... Kearney Public Library, Kearney, NE [*Library symbol Library of Congress*] (LCLS)

NBK .... Kingsborough Community College of the City University of New York, Brooklyn, NY [*Library symbol Library of Congress*] (LCLS)

NBK .... Nabu Network Corp. [*Toronto Stock Exchange symbol*]

NBK .... National Bank of Kuwait

NBK .... Natural Born Killers [*Movie title*]

NBK .... Nebelkerze [*Smoke-Candle*] [*German military - World War II*]

NBK .... Nordisk Bilteknisk Kommitte [*Nordic Automobile Technical Committee - NATC*] [*Defunct Denmark*] (EAIO)

NBKC .... Kingsborough Community College of the City University of New York, Brooklyn, NY [*Library symbol*] [*Library of Congress*] (LCLS)

NBkCmce ..... Northern Bank of Commerce [*Associated Press*] (SAG)

NBkCmce ..... Northwest Bank of Commerce [*Oregon*] [*Associated Press*] (SAG)

NbKi .... Kimball Public Library, Kimball, NE [*Library symbol Library of Congress*] (LCLS)

N Bkpt R ...... National Bankruptcy Register Reports [*United States*] [*A publication*] (DLA)

N Bkpt Reg... National Bankruptcy Register Reports [*United States*] [*A publication*] (DLA)

N Bk R .... National Bankruptcy Register Reports [*United States*] [*A publication*] (DLA)

NbKS .... Kearney State College, Kearney, NE [*Library symbol Library of Congress*] (LCLS)

NBL .... Brooklyn Law School, Brooklyn, NY [*Library symbol Library of Congress*] (LCLS)

NbL .... Lincoln City Libraries, Lincoln, NE [*Library symbol Library of Congress*] (LCLS)

NBL .... National Basketball League (NADA)

NBL .... National Bicycle League (EA)

NBL .... National Book League [*Formerly, NBC*]

NBL .... National Business League [*Washington, DC*] (EA)

NBL .... Naval Biosciences Laboratory [*Research center*]

NBL .... Navy Basic Logistic [*Plan*]

NBL .... Nebraska Library Commission, Lincoln, NE [*OCLC symbol*] (OCLC)

NBL .... New Brunswick Laboratory [*Formerly, NBAO*] [*Argonne, IL*] [*Department of Energy*]

NBL .... Night Bombardment - Long Distance [*Air Force*]

NBL .... No Berth List [*Shipping*] (DS)

NBL .... Noble Affiliates [*NYSE symbol*] (TTSB)

NBL .... Noble Affiliates, Inc. [*NYSE symbol*] (SPSG)

NBL .... Norbaska Mines Ltd. [*Toronto Stock Exchange symbol*]

nbl .... Normoblast [*Hematology*]

NBL .... Not Bloody Likely [*British slang*]

NBL .... Nuclear Bomb Line (CINC)

NBia .... Blauvelt Free Library, Blauvelt, NY [*Library symbol Library of Congress*] (LCLS)

NBLA .... National Businesswomen's Leadership Association [*Defunct*] (EA)

NBIaD .... Dominican College, Blauvelt, NY [*Library symbol Library of Congress*] (LCLS)

NBLB .... Nebraska Law Bulletin [*A publication*] (DLA)

NBLC .... National Business Law Council [*Formerly, NABLT*] (EA)

Nb-LC .... Nebraska Public Library Commission, Lincoln, NE [*Library symbol Library of Congress*] (LCLS)

NBLCC .... National Black Lay Catholic Caucus (EA)

NBLD .... Narrowband Linear Detector (MCD)

NbID .... Noble Drilling Corp. [*Associated Press*] (SAG)

NBLE .... Nearly Best Linear Estimator [*Statistics*]

NbleDr .... Noble Drilling Corp. [*Associated Press*] (SAG)

NBLiCH .... Long Island College Hospital, Brooklyn, NY [*Library symbol Library of Congress*] (LCLS)

NBLiHi .... Long Island Historical Society, Brooklyn, NY [*Library symbol Library of Congress*] (LCLS)

NBLiU .... Long Island University, Brooklyn, NY [*Library symbol Library of Congress*] (LCLS)

NbLL .... Lincoln City Libraries, Lincoln, NE [*Library symbol*] [*Library of Congress*] (LCLS)

NbLNP .... United States Department of the Interior, National Park Service, Midwest Archaeological Center, Lincoln, NE [*Library symbol Library of Congress*] (LCLS)

NbLo .... Loup City Township Library, Loup City, NE [*Library symbol Library of Congress*] (LCLS)

NBLP .... National Bureau for Lathing and Plastering [*Later, International Institute for Lath and Plaster*] (EA)

NBLR .... National Black Leadership Roundtable (EA)

Nb-LR .... Nebraska Legislative Council, Reference Library, Lincoln, NE [*Library symbol Library of Congress*] (LCLS)

NBLR .... North Borneo Law Reports [*A publication*] (DLA)

NBLSA .... National/Black Law Student Association (EA)

NbLSc .... Southeast Community College, Lincoln, NE [*Library symbol Library of Congress*] (LCLS)

NbLU .... Union College, Lincoln, NE [*Library symbol Library of Congress*] (LCLS)

NbLVA .... United States Veterans Administration Hospital, Lincoln, NE [*Library symbol Library of Congress*] (LCLS)

NbLW .... Nebraska Wesleyan University, Lincoln, NE [*Library symbol Library of Congress*] (LCLS)

NBm .... Briarcliff Manor Public Library, Briarcliff Manor, NY [*Library symbol Library of Congress*] (LCLS)

NbM .... McCook Public Library, McCook, NE [*Library symbol Library of Congress*] (LCLS)

NBM .... Medical Research Library of Brooklyn, Brooklyn, NY [*Library symbol Library of Congress*] (LCLS)

NBM .... National Building Museum (EA)

NBM .... National Bureau of Metrology

NBM .... Nation's Balanced Target Maturity Fund [*NYSE symbol*] (SAG)

NBM .... Nations Bal Target Mat Fd [*NYSE symbol*] (TTSB)

NBM .... Navy Basic Modernization [*Plan*]

NBM .... Nitro-Form Bind Medium [*Analytical biochemistry*]

NBM .... No Bowel Movement [*Medicine*] (DMAA)

NBM .... Nonbook Materials (ADA)

NBM .... Normal Bone Marrow [*Medicine*] (DMAA)

NBM .... Normal Bowel Movement [*Medicine*] (DMAA)

NBM .... Nothing by Mouth

NBM .... Nuclear Ballistic Missile

NBM .... Nucleus Basalis Magnocellularis [*Cytology*]

nbM .... Nucleus Basalis of Meynert [*Brain anatomy*]

NBMAIA .... National Broom Manufacturers and Allied Industries Association [*Later, NBMC*] (EA)

NBmB .... Briarcliff College, Briarcliff Manor, NY [*Library symbol Library of Congress*] (LCLS)

NBMB .... National Bus Military Bureau (EA)

NBMB .... N Binary Digits-M Binary Digits (NITA)

NBMBAA ..... National Black MBA [*Master of Business Administration*] Association [*Chicago, IL*] (EA)

NbMC .... McCook Community College, McCook, NE [*Library symbol Library of Congress*] (LCLS)

NBMC .... National Bar Mitzvah Club [*Later, AZYF*] (EA)

NBMC .... National Black Media Coalition (EA)

NBMC .... National Black Music Caucus - of the Music Educators National Conference (EA)

NBMC .... National Broom and Mop Council [*Defunct*]

NBMC .... National Businessmen's Council [*Defunct*] (EA)

NBMCM .... Minto Coal Museum, New Brunswick [*Library symbol National Library of Canada*] (NLC)

NBMCR .... Non-Book Materials Cataloguing Rules (NITA)

NBMDA .... National Building Material Distributors Association (EA)

NBMDR .... National Bone Marrow Donor Registry (EA)

NBME .... Medgar Evers College of the City University of New York, Brooklyn, NY [*Library symbol Library of Congress*] (LCLS)

NBME .... National Board of Medical Examiners (EA)

NBMG .... Navigational Bombing and Missile Guidance (MCD)

NBMGS .... Navigational Bombing and Missile Guidance System (AAG)

NBMHD........ Hopital Docteur Georges - L. Dumont [*Docteur Georges - L. Dumont Hospital*]Moncton, New Brunswick [*Library symbol National Library of Canada*] (NLC)

NbMi............ Milford Public Library, Milford, NE [*Library symbol Library of Congress*] (LCLS)

NbMiS .... Southeast Community College, Milford, NE [*Library symbol Library of Congress*] (LCLS)

NBmK .... King's College, Briarcliff Manor, NY [*Library symbol Library of Congress*] (LCLS)

NBML............ McCook Public Library, McCook, NE [*Library symbol*] [*Library of Congress*] (LCLS)

NBmIA .... Adirondack Historical Association Museum Library, Blue Mountain Lake, NY [*Library symbol Library of Congress*] (LCLS)

NBMMH....... Health Sciences Library, The Moncton Hospital, New Brunswick [*Library symbol National Library of Canada*] (NLC)

NBMO.......... Nonbonding Molecular Orbital [*Physical chemistry*]

NBMOA........ National Black McDonald's Operators Association (EA)

NBMOAL...... Atlantic Lottery Corp. [*Societe des Loteries de l'Atlantique*], Moncton, New Brunswick [*Library symbol National Library of Canada*] (NLC)

NBMOCC...... New Brunswick Community College, Moncton, New Brunswick [*Library symbol National Library of Canada*] (NLC)

NBMOF .... Fisheries and Oceans Canada [*Peches et Oceans Canada*] Moncton, New Brunswick [*Library symbol National Library of Canada*] (NLC)

NBMOLM..... Lutz Mountain Heritage Foundation, Inc., Moncton, New Brunswick [*Library symbol National Library of Canada*] (NLC)

NBMOM....... Moncton Museum, New Brunswick [*Library symbol National Library of Canada*] (NLC)

NBMORE...... Canada Department of Regional Industrial Expansion [*Ministere de l'Expansion Industrielle Regionale*] Moncton, New Brunswick [*Library symbol National Library of Canada*] (NLC)

NBMOTA...... Airworthiness Library, Atlantic Region, Transport Canada [*Bibliotheque de la Navigabilite Aerienne, Region de l'Atlantique, Transports Canada*], Moncton, New Brunswick [*Library symbol National Library of Canada*] (NLC)

NBMOTAR.... Atlantic Regional Library, Transport Canada [*Bibliotheque Regionale de l'Atlantique, Transports Canada*], Moncton, New Brunswick [*Library symbol National Library of Canada*] (NLC)

NBMOU........ Universite de Moncton, New Brunswick [*Library symbol National Library of Canada*] (NLC)

NBMOUA...... Archives Acadiennes, Universite de Moncton, New Brunswick [*Library symbol National Library of Canada*] (NLC)

NBMOUD ..... Bibliotheque de Droit, Universite de Moncton, New Brunswick [*Library symbol National Library of Canada*] (NLC)

NBMOW....... Albert-Westmorland-Kent Regional Library, Moncton, New Brunswick [*Library symbol National Library of Canada*] (NLC)

NBMR .... NATO Basic Military Requirements (AABC)

NBMR .... Northern Bengal Mounted Rifles [*British military*] (DMA)

NBMS .... National Bulk Mail System [*Postal Service*]

NBMT........... NATO Basic Military Techniques (NATG)

NBmtT .... Bear Mountain Trailside Museum, Bear Mountain, NY [*Library symbol*] [*Library of Congress*] (LCLS)

Nbn .... Nabonidus (BJA)

NBN .... Narrow Band Nerve [*Neurology*] (DAVI)

NBN .... Narrowband Network

NBN .... Narrowband Noise

NBN .... National Bank of Nigeria Ltd.

NBN .... National Bibliography Number

NBN .... National Black Network [*A radio network*]

NBN .... National Book Number [*British*]

NBN .... Nationality Broadcasting Network [*Cable-television system*]

NBN .... Network for Better Nutrition (EA)

NBN .... Neubabylonisches Namenbuch zu den Geschaeftsurkunden [*A publication*] (BJA)

NBN .... Newborn Nursery [*Medicine*]

NBN .... Newcastle Broadcasting Network [*Australian company broadcasting in Papua New Guinea*] (FEA)

NBN .... Nixdorf Broadband Network [*Communications*] [*British*]

NBN .... North British Airlines Ltd. [*ICAO designator*] (FAAC)

NBN .... Old Manse Library, Newcastle, New Brunswick [*Library symbol National Library of Canada*] (NLC)

NBNA .... National Bank of North America [*New York*]

NBNA .... National Black Nurses Association (EA)

NBNAM........ Archives of the Miramichi Historical Society, Newcastle, New Brunswick [*Library symbol National Library of Canada*] (NLC)

NbNb .... Neubabylonisches Namenbuch zu den Geschaeftsurkunden [*A publication*] (BJA)

NbNc........... Nebraska City Public Library, Nebraska City, NE [*Library symbol Library of Congress*] (LCLS)

NBNC .... New York City Community College of the City University of New York, Brooklyn, NY [*Library symbol Library of Congress*] (LCLS)

NBNC .... Noted but Not Corrected (MCD)

NbNcM........ Morton-James Public Library, Nebraska City, NE [*Library symbol*] [*Library of Congress*] (LCLS)

NBNDH .... New Denmark Historical Museum, New Brunswick [*Library symbol National Library of Canada*] (NLC)

NbNf .... Norfolk Public Library, Norfolk, NE [*Library symbol Library of Congress*] (LCLS)

NbNfN .... Northeast Technical Community College, Norfork, NE [*Library symbol Library of Congress*] (LCLS)

NBNM .... Health Sciences Library, Miramichi Hospital, Newcastle, New Brunswick [*Library symbol National Library of Canada*] (NLC)

NbNp .... North Platte Public Library, North Platte, NE [*Library symbol Library of Congress*] (LCLS)

NbNpM .... Mid-Plains Community College, North Platte, NE [*Library symbol Library of Congress*] (LCLS)

NBNR.......... National Bankruptcy News and Reports [*A publication*] (DLA)

NBN Rep...... National Bankruptcy News and Reports [*A publication*] (DLA)

NBo............. Bolivar Free Library, Bolivar, NY [*Library symbol Library of Congress*] (LCLS)

NBO .... Nairobi [*Kenya*] [*Airport symbol*] (OAG)

NBO .... National Bank of Oman Ltd. SAO (EY)

NBO .... Navy Bureau of Ordnance [*Obsolete*]

NBO .... Nebo Air Co. Ltd. [*Former USSR*] [*FAA designator*] (FAAC)

NBO .... Network Buildout (IEEE)

NBO .... Nonbed Occupancy (AAMN)

NBO .... Nonbridging Oxygen [*Materials science*]

NBO .... Nordiska Kooperativa och Allmannyttiga Bostadsforetags Organisation [*Organization of Cooperative and Non-Profit Making Housing Enterprises in the Nordic Countries*] (EAIO)

NBO .... Normal-Branch Oscillation [*Astronomy*]

NBO .... Norsar Array Site 01B00 [*Norway*] [*Seismograph station code, US Geological Survey*] (SEIS)

NbO .... Omaha Public Library, Omaha, NE [*Library symbol Library of Congress*] (LCLS)

NBO .... Omaha Public Library, Omaha, NE [*OCLC symbol*] (OCLC)

NBO .... Oromocto Public Library, New Brunswick [*Library symbol National Library of Canada*] (NLC)

NBOA........... National Ballroom Operators Association [*Later, National Ballroom and Entertainment Association*]

NBOA........... National Business Owners Association (EA)

NbOB .... Boys Town Center for the Study of Youth Development, Omaha, NE [*Library symbol Library of Congress*] (LCLS)

NbOC .... Creighton University, Omaha, NE [*Library symbol Library of Congress*] (LCLS)

NBOC .... Network Building Out Capacitor [*Telecommunications*] (TEL)

NBOC .... Northern Bank of Commerce [*NASDAQ symbol*] (SAG)

NBOC .... Northern Bk Comm Ore [*NASDAQ symbol*] (TTSB)

NBOC .... Northwest Bank of Commerce [*Oregon*] [*NASDAQ symbol*] (SAG)

NbOC-A........ Creighton University, Alumni Library, Omaha, NE [*Library symbol Library of Congress*] (LCLS)

NbOC-D........ Creighton University, School of Dentistry, Omaha, NE [*Library symbol Library of Congress*] (LCLS)

NbOC-H........ Creighton University, Health Sciences Library, Omaha, NE [*Library symbol Library of Congress*] (LCLS)

NbOC-L........ Creighton University, School of Law, Omaha, NE [*Library symbol Library of Congress*] (LCLS)

NbOC-M....... Creighton University, School of Medicine and School of Pharmacy, Omaha, NE [*Library symbol Library of Congress*] (LCLS)

NbOD .... Duchesne College, Omaha, NE [*Library symbol Library of Congress*] (LCLS)

NbOg .... Goodall City Library, Ogallala, NE [*Library symbol Library of Congress*] (LCLS)

NbOGS........ Church of Jesus Christ of Latter-Day Saints, Genealogical Society Library, OmahaBranch, Omaha, NE [*Library symbol Library of Congress*] (LCLS)

NBoh.......... Connetquot Public Library, Bohemia, NY [*Library symbol Library of Congress*] (LCLS)

NBohCH....... Connetquot High School, Bohemia, NY [*Library symbol Library of Congress*] (LCLS)

NbOJ........... Joslyn Art Museum, Omaha, NE [*Library symbol Library of Congress*] (LCLS)

NBoL........... Bolivar Free Library, Bolivar, NY [*Library symbol*] [*Library of Congress*] (LCLS)

NBoIS .... Marcella Sembrich Memorial Studio, Bolton Landing, NY [*Library symbol*] [*Library of Congress*] (LCLS)

N (Bomb)..... Neutron Bomb

NbOMC........ Metropolitan Technical Community College, Omaha, NE [*Library symbol Library of Congress*] (LCLS)

NBOME........ National Board of Osteopathic Medical Examiners (EA)

NbONPS....... United States National Park Service, Midwest Regional Office, Omaha, NE [*Library symbol Library of Congress*] (LCLS)

NbOP .... Presbyterian Theological Seminary, Omaha, NE [*Library symbol Library of Congress*] (LCLS)

NBOR........... Network Building Out Resistor [*Telecommunications*] (TEL)

NBOR........... Nucleus of Basal Optic Root [*Neuroanatomy*]

NbOsc......... Osceola Public Library, Osceola, NE [*Library symbol Library of Congress*] (LCLS)

NBOT .... National Board of Orthopaedic Technologists [*British*] (DAVI)

NbOU .... University of Nebraska at Omaha, Omaha, NE [*Library symbol Library of Congress*] (LCLS)

NbOV .... United States Veterans Administration Hospital, Omaha, NE [*Library symbol Library of Congress*] (LCLS)

NbOW .... Westside Community Schools, Omaha, NE [*Library symbol*] [*Library of Congress*] (LCLS)

NBp............. Bayport-Blue Point Public Library, Blue Point, NY [*Library symbol Library of Congress*] (LCLS)

NBP .... Name Binding Protocol [*Computer science*]

NBP .... National Battlefield Park (BARN)

NBP .... National Booster Program (AAG)

NBP .... National Braille Press (EA)

NBP .... National Business Publications [*Later, ABP*] (EA)

NBP .... Needs-Based Payment [*Job Training and Partnership Act*] (OICC)

NBP .... Neutral Bitter Principle [*Pharmacy*]

NBP .... New Birth Party [*Cyprus*] [*Political party*]

NBP .... (Nitrobenzyl)pyridine [*Organic chemistry*]

NBP .... NonBacterial Prostatis [*Medicine*]

NBP .... Normal Boiling Point

NBP .... Northern Border Partners Ltd. [*NYSE symbol*] (SPSG)

NBP .... Northern Border Ptnrs L.P. [*NYSE symbol*] (TTSB)

NBP .... Nucleic Acid Binding Protein [*Biochemistry*]

NBP .... Peru State College Library, Peru, NE [*OCLC symbol*] (OCLC)

NBP	Pratt Institute, Brooklyn, NY [*Library symbol Library of Congress*] (LCLS)
NBPA	National Back Pain Association (EAIO)
NBPA	National Bark Producers Association (EA)
NBPA	National Basketball Players Association (EA)
NBPA	National Beverage Packaging Association (EA)
NBPA	National Black People's Assembly (EA)
NBPA	National Black Police Association (EA)
NBPA	National Building Products Association [*Defunct*] (EA)
NBPA	Navy Board for Production Awards
NBPASV	Southern Victoria Historical Society, Perth-Andover, New Brunswick [*Library symbol National Library of Canada*] (NLC)
NBPB	National Biotechnology Policy Board
NBPC	National Black Political Convention [*1972*]
NBPC	National Black Programming Consortium (EA)
NBPC	National Border Patrol Council (EA)
NBPDW	National Brotherhood of Packinghouse and Dairy Workers [*Formerly, NBPW*] (EA)
NBPE	National Board of Podiatry Examiners
NBPE	National Board of Polygraph Examiners [*Later, APA*] (EA)
NbPerS	Peru State College, Peru, NE [*Library symbol Library of Congress*] (LCLS)
NBPHA	N-Benzoyl(phenyl)hydroxylamine [*Organic chemistry*]
NBPI	National Board for Prices and Incomes [*British*]
NBPI	Newspaper Benevolent and Provident Institution [*British*] (DGA)
NBPIW	National Brotherhood of Packinghouse and Industrial Workers (EA)
NbPl...........	Plattsmouth Public Library, Plattsmouth, NE [*Library symbol Library of Congress*] (LCLS)
NBPM	Narrowband Phase Modulation (MCD)
NBPM	Network-Based Project Management (PDAA)
NBPME	National Board of Podiatric Medical Examiners (EA)
NBPNPA	National Board of Pediatric Nurse Practitioners and Associates [*Later, NCBPNP/N*] (EA)
NBPO	NATO Bullpup Production Organization [*Missiles*] (NATG)
NBPol	Polytechnic Institute of New York, Brooklyn, NY [*Library symbol Library of Congress*] (LCLS)
NBPol-G.......	Polytechnic Institute of New York, Long Island Graduate Center, Farmingdale, NY [*Library symbol Library of Congress*] (LCLS)
NBpP	Bayport-Blue Point Public Library, Blue Point, NY [*Library symbol*] [*Library of Congress*] (LCLS)
NBPP	National Black Political Party
NBPRP	National Board for the Promotion of Rifle Practice (EA)
NBPS	National Backgammon Players Society [*British*] (DBA)
NBPTE	National Board of Physical Therapy Examiners
NBPTS	National Board for Professional Teaching Standards (EA)
NBPu	Brooklyn Public Library, Brooklyn, NY [*Library symbol*] [*Library of Congress*] (LCLS)
NBPW	National Brotherhood of Packinghouse Workers [*Later, NBPDW*]
NBQ	Nitro(benzothiazolo)quinolinium Perchlorate [*Antineoplastic drug*]
NBR	Nabors Industries [*AMEX symbol*] (TTSB)
NBR	Nabors Industries, Inc. [*AMEX symbol*] (SPSG)
NBR	Narrowband Radiated (IEEE)
NBR	National Bankruptcy Register Reports [*United States*] [*A publication*] (DLA)
NBR	National Board of Review of Motion Pictures
NBR	National Buildings Record [*British*]
NBR	Neighborhood Business Revitalization [*Program*]
NBR	Net Borrowing Requirement [*Banking*] (MHDW)
NBR	New Beginnings Resources [*Vancouver Stock Exchange symbol*]
NBR	New Brunswick Reports [*Maritime Law Book Co. Ltd.*] [*Canada Information service or system A publication*] (CRD)
NBR	[*The*] Nightly Business Reports [*Television program*]
NBR	Nitrile-Butadiene Rubber
NBR	Nonborrowed Reserve [*Banking*]
NBR	Nonbreathing
NBR	North British Railway
NBR	Nuclear Boiler Rated (NRCH)
NBR	Null Balance Recorder
NBR	Number (KSC)
NBR	Number of Bids Received [*DoD*]
NBR	Nursing Boards Review [*Course*] [*American Journal of Nursing*]
NBR 2d	New Brunswick Reports, Second Series [*A publication*] (DLA)
NBRA	National Brain Research Association (EA)
NbRal	Ralston Public Library, Ralston, NE [*Library symbol Library of Congress*] (LCLS)
NBR All.......	Allen's New Brunswick Reports [*Canada A publication*] (DLA)
NBR Ber	Berton's New Brunswick Reports [*A publication*] (DLA)
NBRC	National Black Republican Council (EA)
NBRC..........	National Board for Respiratory Care (EA)
NBRCA........	Atlantic Institution, Correctional Service Canada [*Etablissement Atlantique, Service Correctionnel Canada*], Renous, New Brunswick [*Library symbol National Library of Canada*] (BIB)
NBR Carl	Carleton's New Brunswick Reports [*A publication*] (DLA)
NBR Chip.....	Chipman's New Brunswick Reports [*1825-35*] [*A publication*] (DLA)
NbRcW........	Willa Cather Pioneer Memorial, Red Cloud, NE [*Library symbol Library of Congress*] (LCLS)
NBre	Brewster Public Library, Brewster, NY [*Library symbol Library of Congress*] (LCLS)
NBREH........	L'Eglise Historique St-Henri-De-Barachois, Robichaud, New Brunswick [*Library symbol National Library of Canada*] (NLC)
NBren	Brentwood Public Library, Brentwood, NY [*Library symbol Library of Congress*] (LCLS)
NBrenEJ......	East Junior High School, Brentwood, NY [*Library symbol*] [*Library of Congress*] (LCLS)
NBrenIMC	District Instructional Media Center, Brentwood, NY [*Library symbol Library of Congress*] (LCLS)
NBrenSJ	Saint Joseph's College, Brentwood, NY [*Library symbol Library of Congress*] (LCLS)
NB Rep.......	New Brunswick Reports [*A publication*] (DLA)
NB Rev Stat..	New Brunswick Revised Statutes [*Canada*] [*A publication*] (DLA)
NBRF	National Biomedical Research Foundation [*Georgetown University*] [*Research center*]
NBRG	National Basic Reference Graphic (MCD)
NBR Han......	Hannay's New Brunswick Reports [*12, 13 New Brunswick*] [*A publication*] (DLA)
NBri	Bay Shore-Brightwaters Public Library, Brightwaters, NY [*Library symbol Library of Congress*] (LCLS)
NBrih	Hampton Library, Bridgehampton, NY [*Library symbol Library of Congress*] (LCLS)
NBR Kerr	Kerr's New Brunswick Reports [*A publication*] (DLA)
NBRL	Naval Biomedical Research Laboratory
NBRL	Naval Blood Research Laboratory [*Bureau of Medicine*]
NBRMP	National Board of Review of Motion Pictures (EA)
NBRN	Nestart Library, Richibucto, New Brunswick [*Library symbol National Library of Canada*] (NLC)
NBrockU	State University of New York, College at Brockport, Brockport, NY [*Library symbol Library of Congress*] (LCLS)
NBron	Bronxville Public Library, Bronxville, NY [*Library symbol Library of Congress*] (LCLS)
NBronC	Concordia College, Bronxville, NY [*Library symbol Library of Congress*] (LCLS)
NBronSL	Sarah Lawrence College, Bronxville, NY [*Library symbol Library of Congress*] (LCLS)
NBroo	Brookhaven Free Library, Brookhaven, NY [*Library symbol Library of Congress*] (LCLS)
NBrooHS......	Bellport Senior High School, Brookhaven, NY [*Library symbol Library of Congress*] (LCLS)
NBRP & B....	Pugsley and Burbridge's New Brunswick Reports [*A publication*] (DLA)
NBRP & T....	Pugsley and Trueman's New Brunswick Reports [*A publication*] (DLA)
NBRPC........	New Brunswick Research and Productivity Council
NBR Pug......	Pugsley's New Brunswick Reports [*A publication*] (DLA)
NBR Pugs....	Pugsley's New Brunswick Reports [*1876-93*] [*Canada*] [*A publication*] (DLA)
NBRSA........	National Bench Rest Shooters Association (EA)
NBRT	National Board for Respiratory Therapy [*Formerly, ARIT*] [*Later, NBRC*] (EA)
NBR Tru	Trueman's New Brunswick Reports [*A publication*] (DLA)
N Bruns	New Brunswick Reports [*A publication*] (DLA)
NBrunS	New Brunswick Scientific Co., Inc. [*Associated Press*] (SAG)
NbRVt	Neubabylonische Rechts- und Verwaltungstexte [*A publication*] (BJA)
NbRVu	Neubabylonische Rechts- und Verwaltungsurkunden Uebersetzt und Erlaeutert [*A publication*] (BJA)
NBS	Bureau of Ships Publications [*Obsolete Navy*]
NBS	Kekaha, Kauai, HI [*Location identifier FAA*] (FAAL)
NBS	Narrowband Search (MCD)
NBS	National Australia Bank. Monthly Summary [*A publication*] (ADA)
NBS	National Bakery School [*British*] (BI)
NBS	National Battlefield Site (BARN)
NBS	National Biological Survey [*Department of the Interior*]
NBS	National Bookkeepers' Society (EA)
NBS	National Book Sale [*British*]
NBS	National Bridal Service (EA)
NBS	National Broadcasting Service [*Trinidad and Tobago*] (EY)
NBS	National Broadcasting Service [*New Zealand*]
NBS	National Broadcasting System
NBS	National Brotherhood of Skiers (EA)
NBS	National Bureau of Standards [*Department of Commerce*] [*Later, NIST*]
NBS	National Bureau of Standards, Gaithersburg, MD [*OCLC symbol*] (OCLC)
NBS	National Business Systems, Inc. [*Toronto Stock Exchange symbol*]
NBS	National Button Society (EA)
NBS	Natural Black Slate (MSA)
NBS	Navigational Bombing System [*British military*] (DMA)
NBS	N-Bromosuccinimide [*Organic chemistry*]
NBS	Needs-Based Staffing (ADA)
NBS	Neighborhood Bible Studies (EA)
NBS	Netherland Benevolent Society of New York [*Later, Netherlands-America Community Association*] (EA)
NBS	Neurobehavioral Scale
NBS	Neutral Buoyancy Simulator [*Navy*] (MCD)
NBS	Nevoid Basal Cell Carcinoma Syndrome [*Oncology*] (DMAA)
NBS	New British Standard [*Imperial wire gauge*]
NBS	New Brunswick Scientific Co., Inc.
NBS	Newcastle Business School [*British*] (ODBW)
NBS	Night Bombardment - Short Distance [*Air Force*]
NBS	Nijmegen Breakage Syndrome [*Medicine*] (DMAA)
NBS	Nimbus Aviation [*British ICAO designator*] (FAAC)
NBS	No Bacteria Seen [*Clinical microbiology*]
NBS	Nonbaseline Software Library (MCD)
NBS	Nordiska Byggforskningsorgans Samarbetsgrupp [*Nordic Building Research Cooperation Group*] [*Iceland*] (EAIO)
NBS	Normal Blood Serum (MAE)
NBS	Normal Bowel Sounds [*Gastroenterology*] (DAVI)
NBS	Normal Burro Serum [*Biochemistry*] (DAVI)
NBS	Normandy Base Section [*World War II*]
NBS	Nothing Before Something [*Library cataloguing*] (DGA)

NBS .... Nucleotide Binding Site [*Genetics*]
NBS .... Numeric Backspace Character [*Computer science*]
NBS .... Numismatic Bibliomania Society (EA)
NBS .... Saint John Regional Library, New Brunswick [*Library symbol National Library of Canada*] (NLC)
NbS .... Scottsbluff Public Library, Scottsbluff, NE [*Library symbol Library of Congress*] (LCLS)
NBSA .... National Bakery Suppliers Association (EA)
NBS-A .... National Bureau of Standards - Atomic (SAA)
NBSA .... Nurses' Board of South Australia
NBSAB .... Fort Beausejour Museum, Sackville, New Brunswick [*Library symbol National Library of Canada*] (NLC)
NBSAC .... National Boating Safety Advisory Council [*Department of Transportation*] [*Washington, DC*] (EGAO)
NBSACW ...... Canadian Wildlife Service, Environment Canada [*Service Canadien de la Faune, Environnement Canada*] Sackville, New Brunswick [*Library symbol National Library of Canada*] (NLC)
NBSAE .... Norwegian-British-Swedish Antarctic Expedition [*1949-52*]
NBSAM .... Mount Allison University, Sackville, New Brunswick [*Library symbol National Library of Canada*] (NLC)
NBSARM .... Ross Memorial Library, St. Andrews, New Brunswick [*Library symbol National Library of Canada*] (BIB)
NBSBL .... National Bureau of Standards Boulder Laboratories
NBSC .... Health Sciences Library, Centracare Saint John, Inc., New Brunswick [*Library symbol National Library of Canada*] (NLC)
NBSC .... National Black Sisters' Conference (EA)
NBSC .... New Brunswick Scient [*NASDAQ symbol*] (TTSB)
NBSC .... New Brunswick Scientific Co., Inc. [*NASDAQ symbol*] (NQ)
NBSC .... Nitrobenzenesulfenyl Chloride [*Organic chemistry*]
NBSCA .... National Beauty Salon Chain Association [*Later, ICSA*] (EA)
NBSCCST ..... National Bureau of Standards Center for Computer Sciences and Technology (DIT)
NBSCM .... Centre Marin, Shippagan, New Brunswick [*Library symbol National Library of Canada*] (NLC)
NBSCU .... Centre Universitaire de Shippagan, New Brunswick [*Library symbol National Library of Canada*] (NLC)
NBSD .... Night Bombardment - Short Distance [*Air Force*] (IEEE)
NBSDI .... National Brands Soft Drinks Institute (EA)
NBsdQ .... Queensborough Community College of the City University of New York, Bayside, NY [*Library symbol Library of Congress*] (LCLS)
NbSe .... Seward Public Library, Seward, NE [*Library symbol Library of Congress*] (LCLS)
NbSeT .... Concordia Teachers College, Seward, NE [*Library symbol Library of Congress*] (LCLS)
NBSF .... Nitrobenzenesulfonyl Fluoride [*Organic chemistry*]
NBSFS .... National Bureau of Standards Frequency Standard (IEEE)
NBSG .... National Biotherapy Study Group (EA)
NbSHS .... Hiram Scott College, Scottsbluff, NE [*Library symbol Library of Congress Obsolete*] (LCLS)
NBSI .... North Bancshares [*NASDAQ symbol*] (TTSB)
NBSI .... North Bancshares, Inc. [*NASDAQ symbol*] (SAG)
NbSi .... Sidney Public Library, Sidney, NE [*Library symbol Library of Congress*] (LCLS)
NBSIR .... National Bureau of Standards Interagency Reports
NBSL .... New York City School Library System, Brooklyn, NY [*Library symbol*] [*Library of Congress*] (LCLS)
NBSLD .... National Bureau of Standards Load Determination [*Computer program*]
NBSM .... New Brunswick Museum, Saint John, New Brunswick [*Library symbol National Library of Canada*] (NLC)
NBSMA .... National Boot and Shoe Manufacturers' Association [*Later, FIA*]
NbSN .... Nebraska Western College, Scottsbluff, NE [*Library symbol Library of Congress*] (LCLS)
NBSQH .... Quaco Historical and Library Society, St. Martins, New Brunswick [*Library symbol National Library of Canada*] (NLC)
NBSR .... National Bureau of Standards Reactor
NBSRH .... Health Sciences Library, Saint John Regional Hospital [*Bibliotheque des Sciences de la Sante, Hopital Regional de Saint-Jean*], New Brunswick [*Library symbol National Library of Canada*] (NLC)
NBSS .... National Bank Surveillance System
NBSS .... National British Softbill Society (BI)
NBSS .... Naval Beach Signal Section
NBsSH .... Southside Hospital, Bay Shore, NY [*Library symbol Library of Congress*] (LCLS)
NBS-SIS ...... NBS-Standard Information Services (NITA)
NBSSSC .... St. Croix Public Library, St. Stephen, New Brunswick [*Library symbol National Library of Canada*] (NLC)
NBST .... Narrowband Subscriber Terminal (CET)
NBST .... National Board for Science and Technology [*Ireland*] (PDAA)
NBST .... [*The*] New Braunfels & Servtex Railroad, Inc. [*AAR code*]
NBSt .... Nimbostratus [*Cloud*] [*Meteorology*] (AIA)
NBSTAC .... St. Andrews Campus, New Brunswick Community College [*Library symbol National Library of Canada*] (BIB)
NBS/TAD ...... National Bureau of Standards/Technical Analysis Division (NOAA)
NB Stat ...... New Brunswick Statutes [*Canada*] [*A publication*] (DLA)
NBStF .... Saint Francis College, Brooklyn, NY [*Library symbol Library of Congress*] (LCLS)
NBSTIM .... Le Musee de St-Isidore, Inc., New Brunswick [*Library symbol National Library of Canada*] (NLC)
NBStJC .... Saint Joseph's College, Brooklyn, NY [*Library symbol Library of Congress*] (LCLS)
NbSu .... Superior Carnegie Library, Superior, NE [*Library symbol Library of Congress*] (LCLS)
NBSU .... University of New Brunswick, Saint John, New Brunswick [*Library symbol National Library of Canada*] (NLC)

NBSUH .... Kings County Historical Society, Sussex, New Brunswick [*Library symbol National Library of Canada*] (NLC)
NBSU-M .... State University of New York at Brooklyn, Medical Research Library, Brooklyn, NY [*Library symbol*] [*Library of Congress*] (LCLS)
NBSUS .... Sussex Public Library, New Brunswick [*Library symbol National Library of Canada*] (NLC)
NBSV .... Narrowband Secure Voice System [*Army*] (CAAL)
NBSVS .... Narrowband Secure Voice System [*Army*] (MCD)
NBSVS .... Saint John Vocational School, New Brunswick [*Library symbol National Library of Canada*] (NLC)
NBT .... Brunswick, ME [*Location identifier FAA*] (FAAL)
NBT .... Nagoya Bumpy Torus [*Military*]
NBT .... Narrow-Beam Transducer [*National Ocean Survey*]
NBT .... National Bancshares Corp. of Texas [*AMEX symbol*] (SAG)
NBT .... Natl Bacshares Texas [*AMEX symbol*] (TTSB)
NBT .... Navigator Bombardier Training [*Air Force*] (AFM)
NBT .... Negative Balance Test (IAA)
NBT .... Netherlands Board of Tourism (EA)
NBT .... Networks for Biotechnology
NBT .... Neurobiotin [*Biochemical labelling compound*]
NBT .... Neutral Buoyancy Trainer [*Navy*] (MCD)
NBT .... New Brunswick Telephone Co. Ltd. [*Toronto Stock Exchange symbol*]
NBT .... Nimbus Beacon Transmitter
NBT .... Nitroblue Tetrazolium [*A stain*] [*Hematology*]
NBT .... Northern Ballet Theatre [*England*]
NBT .... Null-Balance Transmissometer (IEEE)
NBTA .... National Basketball Trainers Association (EA)
NBTA .... National Baton Twirling Association (EA)
NBTA .... National Board of Trial Advocacy (EA)
NBTA .... National Business Teachers Association (NADA)
NBTA .... National Business Travel Association (EA)
NBTA .... National Bus Traffic Association (EA)
NBTB .... NBT Bancorp. [*NASDAQ symbol*] (SAG)
NBT Bcp ...... NBT Bancorp [*Associated Press*] (SAG)
NBTC .... New Brands and Their Companies [*Formerly, NTN*] [*A publication*]
NBTC .... New Brunswick Teachers College
NBT-DF .... Nitroblue Tetrazolium Diformazan [*A stain*] [*Hematology*]
NBTDR .... Narrowband Time Domain Reflectometry (MCD)
NBTE .... Nonbacterial Thrombotic Endocarditis [*Cardiology*]
NbTe .... Tekamah Carnegie Public Library, Tekamah, NE [*Library symbol Library of Congress*] (LCLS)
NBTF .... National Building Trades Federation [*A union*] [*British*]
NBTH .... Bibliotheque Medicale, Hotel-Dieu Saint-Joseph-De-Tracadie, New Brunswick [*Library symbol National Library of Canada*] (BIB)
NBTI .... Nitrobenzylthioinosine [*Organic chemistry*]
NBTL .... National Battery Test Laboratory [*Department of Energy*]
NBTL .... Naval Boiler and Turbine Laboratory
NBTM .... Le Musee Historique de Tracadie, New Brunswick [*Library symbol National Library of Canada*] (NLC)
NBTNF .... Newborn, Term, Normal, Female [*Obstetrics*]
NBTNM .... Newborn, Term, Normal, Male [*Obstetrics*]
NBTPI .... National Book Trade Provident Institution [*British*] (DGA)
NBTPS .... National Book Trade Provident Society [*British*] (DI)
NBTR .... Narrowband Tape Recorder
NBTS .... National Blood Transfusion Service
NBTS .... New Boston Tracking Station (SAA)
NBTS .... New Brunswick Theological Seminary [*New Jersey*]
NBTS .... Northern Baptist Theological Seminary [*Lombard, IL*]
NBTT .... Net Barter Terms of Trade
NBTY .... NBTY, Inc. [*NASDAQ symbol*] (SAG)
NBu .... Buffalo and Erie County Public Library, Buffalo, NY [*Library symbol Library of Congress*] (LCLS)
NBU .... Glenview, IL [*Location identifier FAA*] (FAAL)
NBU .... NBU Mines Ltd. [*Toronto Stock Exchange symbol*]
nbu .... Nebraska [*MARC country of publication code Library of Congress*] (LCCP)
NBU .... New Better than Used [*Statistics*]
NBU .... Nordiska Bankmannaunionen [*Confederation of Nordic Bank Employees' Unions*] (EA)
NBU .... University of Nebraska at Omaha, Omaha, NE [*OCLC symbol*] (OCLC)
NbU .... University of Nebraska, Lincoln, NE [*Library symbol Library of Congress*] (LCLS)
NBuA .... Allied Corp., Specialty Chemicals Division, Buffalo, NY [*Library symbol Library of Congress*] (LCLS)
NbU-A .... University of Nebraska, Agriculture Library, Lincoln, NE [*Library symbol Library of Congress*] (LCLS)
NBuAA .... Acres American, Inc., Buffalo, NY [*Library symbol Library of Congress*] (LCLS)
NBuACE .... United States Army, Corps of Engineers, Buffalo, NY [*Library symbol*] [*Library of Congress*] (LCLS)
NBuAK .... Albright-Knox Art Gallery Library, Buffalo Fine Arts Academy, Buffalo, NY [*Library symbol Library of Congress*] (LCLS)
NBuAn .... Andco, Inc., Buffalo, NY [*Library symbol Library of Congress*] (LCLS)
NBuB .... Buffalo Society of Natural Sciences, Buffalo Museum of Science, Buffalo, NY [*Library symbol Library of Congress*] (LCLS)
NBuBA .... Bell Aerosystems Co., Buffalo, NY [*Library symbol Library of Congress*] (LCLS)
NBuBE .... Buffalo and Erie County Public Library, Buffalo, NY [*Library symbol*] [*Library of Congress*] (LCLS)
NBuBLH .... Bry-Lin Hospital, Buffalo, NY [*Library symbol Library of Congress*] (LCLS)
NBuBM .... Brystol-Myers Pharmaceuticals R & D, Buffalo, NY [*Library symbol*] [*Library of Congress*] (LCLS)

NBuBO .... Buffalo Organization for Social and Technological Innovation, Inc. (BOSTI), Buffalo, NY [*Library symbol Library of Congress*] (LCLS)

NBuBR .... Biblial Research Institute, Inc., Buffalo, NY [*Library symbol*] [*Library of Congress*] (LCLS)

NBuC .... State University of New York, College at Buffalo, Buffalo, NY [*Library symbol Library of Congress*] (LCLS)

NBuCA .... Cornell Aeronautical Laboratory, Buffalo, NY [*Library symbol Library of Congress*] (LCLS)

NBuCBL .... Christel, Bean & Linihan, Buffalo, NY [*Library symbol*] [*Library of Congress*] (LCLS)

NBuCC .... Canisius College, Buffalo, NY [*Library symbol Library of Congress*] (LCLS)

NBuCEC .... CECOS International, Buffalo, NY [*Library symbol Library of Congress*] (LCLS)

NBuCH .... Children's Hospital, Buffalo, NY [*Library symbol Library of Congress*] (LCLS)

NBuCo .... Buffalo Color Corp., Buffalo, NY [*Library symbol Library of Congress*] (LCLS)

NBuCoH .... Buffalo Columbus Hospital, Buffalo, NY [*Library symbol*] [*Library of Congress*] (LCLS)

NBuD .... D'Youville College, Buffalo, NY [*Library symbol Library of Congress*] (LCLS)

NBuDa .... Daemen College, Buffalo, NY [*Library symbol Library of Congress*] (LCLS)

NBuDD .... DeLancey Divinity School, Buffalo, NY [*Library symbol Library of Congress Obsolete*] (LCLS)

NBuDY .... E. I. Du Pont de Nemours & Co., Yerkes Research Laboratory, Buffalo, NY [*Library symbol Library of Congress*] (LCLS)

NBUE .... New Better than Used in Expectation [*Statistics*]

NBuEC .... Erie Community College-North, Buffalo, NY [*Library symbol Library of Congress*] (LCLS)

NBuEC-C ...... Erie Community College-North, City Campus, Buffalo, NY [*Library symbol Library of Congress*] (LCLS)

NBuEC-U ...... Erie Community College-North, Urban Center, Buffalo, NY [*Library symbol Library of Congress*] (LCLS)

NBuEE .... Ecology and Environment, Inc., Buffalo, NY [*Library symbol Library of Congress*] (LCLS)

NBuEMH .... Edward J. Meyer Memorial Hospital Medical Library, Buffalo, NY [*Library symbol Library of Congress*] (LCLS)

NBuF .... Falcon Research & Development, Inc., Buffalo, NY [*Library symbol Library of Congress*] (LCLS)

NBUF .... National Black United Front (EA)

NBUF .... National Black United Fund (EA)

NBuG .... Grosvenor Reference Division, Buffalo and Erie County Public Library, Buffalo, NY [*Library symbol Library of Congress*] (LCLS)

NBuGC .... Graphic Controls Corp., Buffalo, NY [*Library symbol Library of Congress*] (LCLS)

NBuGD .... Goldome FSB, Bufflo, NY [*Library symbol*] [*Library of Congress*] (LCLS)

NBuGH .... Buffalo General Hospital, Buffalo, NY [*Library symbol Library of Congress*] (LCLS)

NBuGH-N ..... Buffalo General Hospital, School of Nursing, Buffalo, NY [*Library symbol Library of Congress*] (LCLS)

NBuHi .... Buffalo and Erie County Historical Society, Buffalo, NY [*Library symbol Library of Congress*] (LCLS)

NBuHSA .... Health Systems Agency of Western New York, Inc., Buffalo, NY [*Library symbol Library of Congress*] (LCLS)

NBuKMH ..... Kenmore Mercy Hospital, Medical Library, Buffalo, NY [*Library symbol*] [*Library of Congress*] (LCLS)

NbU-L .... University of Nebraska, College of Law, Lincoln, NE [*Library symbol Library of Congress*] (LCLS)

NBuLH .... Lafayette General Hospital, Buffalo, NY [*Library symbol Library of Congress*] (LCLS)

NBuLTV .... LTV Aerospace & Defense Co., Buffalo, NY [*Library symbol*] [*Library of Congress*] (LCLS)

NBuM .... Medaille College, Buffalo, NY [*Library symbol Library of Congress*] (LCLS)

NbU-M .... University of Nebraska, College of Medicine, Omaha, NE [*Library symbol Library of Congress*] (LCLS)

NBuMM .... Marine Midland Services Corp., Technical Information Center, Buffalo, NY [*Library symbol Library of Congress*] (LCLS)

NBuNCE ...... National Center for Earthquake Engineering, Research Information Services, State, Buffalo, NY [*Library symbol*] [*Library of Congress*] (LCLS)

NBuPC .... Buffalo Psychiatric Center, Buffalo, NY [*Library symbol Library of Congress*] (LCLS)

NBuPL .... Pennwalt Corp., Lucidol Division, Buffalo, NY [*Library symbol Library of Congress*] (LCLS)

NBuRH .... Rosary Hill College, Buffalo, NY [*Library symbol Library of Congress Obsolete*] (LCLS)

NBuRSI .... Reichert Scientific Instruments, Buffalo, NY [*Library symbol*] [*Library of Congress*] (LCLS)

NBUSA .... United States Army, Fort Hamilton Post Library, Fort Hamilton, Brooklyn, NY [*Library symbol Library of Congress*] (LCLS)

NBuSCA .... SCA Chemical Services, Inc., Buffalo, NY [*Library symbol Library of Congress*] (LCLS)

NBuSCH .... Sisters of Charity Hospital, Buffalo, NY [*Library symbol Library of Congress*] (LCLS)

NBuSD .... Buffalo City School District, Buffalo, NY [*Library symbol*] [*Library of Congress*] (LCLS)

NBuSFH .... St. Francis Hospital of Buffalo, Buffalo, NY [*Library symbol*] [*Library of Congress*] (LCLS)

NBuSK .... Spencer Kellogg Division, Textron, Inc., Buffalo, NY [*Library symbol Library of Congress*] (LCLS)

NBuSMH ...... Sheehan Memorial Emergency Hospital, Buffalo, NY [*Library symbol Library of Congress*] (LCLS)

NBuSR .... Sierra Research Corp., Buffalo, NY [*Library symbol Library of Congress*] (LCLS)

NBuStM .... Saint Mary's School for the Deaf, Buffalo, NY [*Library symbol Library of Congress*] (LCLS)

NBuTC .... Trocaire College, Buffalo, NY [*Library symbol Library of Congress*] (LCLS)

NBuU .... State University of New York at Buffalo, Buffalo, NY [*Library symbol Library of Congress*] (LCLS)

NBuU-A .... State University of New York at Buffalo, Art Library, Buffalo, NY [*Library symbol Library of Congress*] (LCLS)

NBuU-AR ...... State University of New York at Buffalo, Archives, Buffalo, NY [*Library symbol Library of Congress*] (LCLS)

NBuU-BA ...... State University of New York at Buffalo, Bell Annex, Buffalo, NY [*Library symbol Library of Congress*] (LCLS)

NBuU-BS ...... State University of New York at Buffalo, Bell Science Library, Buffalo, NY [*Library symbol Library of Congress*] (LCLS)

NBuU-C .... State University of New York at Buffalo, Chemistry Library, Buffalo, NY [*Library symbol Library of Congress*] (LCLS)

NBuU-CT ...... University of Buffalo Foundation, Inc., Center for Tomorrow, State University of New York at Buffalo, Amherst, NY [*Library symbol*] [*Library of Congress*] (LCLS)

NBuU-D .... State University of New York at Buffalo, Documents Library, Buffalo, NY [*Library symbol Library of Congress*] (LCLS)

NBuU-E .... State University of New York at Buffalo, Educational Opportunity Center, Buffalo, NY [*Library symbol Library of Congress*] (LCLS)

NBuU-H .... State University of New York at Buffalo, Health Sciences Library, Buffalo, NY [*Library symbol Library of Congress*] (LCLS)

NBuU-HA ..... State University of New York at Buffalo, Harriman Library, Buffalo, NY [*Library symbol Library of Congress*] (LCLS)

NBuU-L .... State University of New York at Buffalo, Law Library, Buffalo, NY [*Library symbol Library of Congress*] (LCLS)

NBuU-LL ...... State University of New York at Buffalo, Library Literature Library, Buffalo, NY [*Library symbol Library of Congress*] (LCLS)

NBuU-LS ...... State University of New York at Buffalo, Library Science Library, Buffalo, NY [*Library symbol Library of Congress*] (LCLS)

NBuU-Mu ..... State University of New York at Buffalo, Music Library, Buffalo, NY [*Library symbol Library of Congress*] (LCLS)

NBuU-P .... State University of New York at Buffalo, Physics Library, Buffalo, NY [*Library symbol Library of Congress*] (LCLS)

NBuU-PO ...... State University of New York at Buffalo, Poetry Library, Buffalo, NY [*Library symbol Library of Congress*] (LCLS)

NBuU-R .... State University of New York at Buffalo, Reference, Buffalo, NY [*Library symbol Library of Congress*] (LCLS)

NBuU-RL ...... State University of New York at Buffalo, Ridge Lea, Buffalo, NY [*Library symbol Library of Congress*] (LCLS)

NBuU-RP ...... State University of New York at Buffalo, Roswell Park Memorial Institute, Buffalo, NY [*Library symbol Library of Congress*] (LCLS)

NBuU-SE ...... State University of New York at Buffalo, Science and Engineering Library, Buffalo, NY [*Library symbol Library of Congress*] (LCLS)

NBuVA .... United States Veterans Administration Hospital, Buffalo, NY [*Library symbol Library of Congress*] (LCLS)

NBuVM .... Villa Maria College of Buffalo, Buffalo, NY [*Library symbol Library of Congress*] (LCLS)

NBuVNA .... Visiting Nursing Association of Buffalo, Buffalo, NY [*Library symbol Library of Congress*] (LCLS)

NBuW .... Worthington Compressor & Engine International, Buffalo, NY [*Library symbol Library of Congress*] (LCLS)

NBuWeP ...... Westwood Pharmaceuticals, Inc., Buffalo, NY [*Library symbol Library of Congress*] (LCLS)

NBUWH .... Carleton County Historical Society, Upper Woodstock, New Brunswick [*Library symbol National Library of Canada*] (NLC)

NBuWNED .... WNED-TV, Buffalo, NY [*Library symbol Library of Congress*] (LCLS)

NBuX .... XACO, Inc., Buffalo, NY [*Library symbol*] [*Library of Congress*] (LCLS)

NBV .... Net Book Value (TEL)

NbV .... Valentine Public Library, Valentine, NE [*Library symbol Library of Congress*] (LCLS)

NBVA .... National Bulk Vendors Association (EA)

NBVA .... United States Veterans Administration Hospital, Brooklyn, NY [*Library symbol Library of Congress*] (LCLS)

NBV Ad .... New Brunswick Vice Admiralty Reports [*A publication*] (DLA)

NBVA-O .... United States Veterans Administration Hospital, Outpatient Clinic, Brooklyn, NY [*Library symbol Library of Congress*] (LCLS)

NBVCXO ...... Narrowband Voltage-Controlled Crystal Oscillator

NBVF .... National Burn Victim Foundation (EA)

NBVM .... Narrow-Band Voice Modulation (PDAA)

NBVO .... National Black Veterans Organization [*Defunct*] (EA)

NBW .... L. P. Fisher Public Library, Woodstock, New Brunswick [*Library symbol National Library of Canada*] (NLC)

NBW .... National Barristers' Wives [*Later, NABBS*] (EA)

NBW .... National Book Week (NTCM)

NBW .... Natural Bandwidths [*Spectroscopy*]

NBW .... Nebraska Wesleyan University, Lincoln, NE [*OCLC symbol*] (OCLC)

NBW .... Noise Bandwidth

nbw .... Noise Bandwidth (IDOE)

NBW .... Normal Birth Weight

NbW .... North by West

NBWA .... National Beer Wholesalers' Association (EA)

NBWA .... National Blacksmiths and Welders Association (EA)

NBWA .... National Buddhist Women's Associations (EA)

NbWayS .... Wayne State College, Wayne, NE [*Library symbol Library of Congress*] (LCLS)

NBWH.......... Carleton Memorial Hospital, Woodstock, New Brunswick [*Library symbol National Library of Canada*] (BIB)
NBWHP........ National Black Women's Health Project (EA)
NbWi .... Dvoracek Memorial Library, Wilber, NE [*Library symbol Library of Congress*] (LCLS)
NBWPLC ...... National Black Women's Political Leadership Caucus (EA)
NBWROP ..... Naval Bureau of Weapons Reserve Ordnance Plant
NBWTAU...... National British Women's Total Abstinence Union (EAIO)
NBWV .... Victoria-Carleton Courthouse, Woodstock, New Brunswick [*Library symbol National Library of Canada*] (NLC)
NBWY .... York Regional Library, Headquarters No. 2, Woodstock, New Brunswick [*Library symbol National Library of Canada*] (NLC)
NBX .... Jeffersn-Pilot 7.25% 'ACES' [*NYSE symbol*] (TTSB)
NBX .... Jefferson Pilot [*NYSE symbol*] (SAG)
NBX .... Nabire [*Indonesia*] [*Airport symbol*] (OAG)
NBY .... Nearest Besselian Year
NBY .... Nutrient Broth Yeast [*Microbiology*]
NbY .... York Public Library, York, NE [*Library symbol Library of Congress*] (LCLS)
NbYC .... York College, York, NE [*Library symbol Library of Congress*] (LCLS)
NBYLC .... National Black Youth Leadership Council (EA)
NBysSH........ Bay Shore Senior High School, Bay Shore, NY [*Library symbol Library of Congress*] (LCLS)
nc---- .... Central America [*MARC geographic area code Library of Congress*] (LCCP)
NC................ Chloropicrin Stannic Chloride [*Inorganic chemistry*]
NC................ La Nouvelle Clio [*Brussels*] [*A publication*] (BJA)
NC................ NACCO Indus Inc. Cl'A' [*NYSE symbol*] (TTSB)
NC................ Name Control [*IRS*]
nc................ Nanocurie [*Pne billionth of a curie*]
NC................ Narrowband Communicative Services [*Telecommunications*]
NC................ Narrow Coverage
NC................ Nasal Cannula [*Medicine*] (MEDA)
NC................ Nasal Cannula [*Medicine*] (DAVI)
NC................ Nashville, Chattanooga & St. Louis [*Louisville & Nashville Railroad Co.*] [*AAR code*]
NC................ Natal Carabiniers [*British military*] (DMA)
NC................ National Catholic News Service
NC................ National Cemetery (IIA)
NC................ National Center (IAA)
NC................ National Certificate (WDAA)
NC................ National Churches [*A publication*]
NC................ National Coarse [*Thread*]
NC................ National Colonialist Party [*Australia Political party*]
NC................ National Cooperatives [*Later, UNICO*] [*An association*]
NC................ National Curriculum [*Education*] (AIE)
NC................ Native Cavalry [*British military*] (DMA)
NC................ NATO Center (NATG)
NC................ NATO Confidential (NATG)
NC................ Natural Cytotoxic [*Cells*] [*Immunochemistry*]
NC................ Nature Conservancy [*NERC*] [*British*]
NC................ Naval Cadet [*British*] (ROG)
NC................ Naval Correspondence
NC................ Navigation Computer
NC................ Navigation Console
NC................ Navy Component
NC................ Navy Cross
NC................ Neanderthal Conservative [*Slang*]
NC................ Nearly Commensurate Model [*Physics*]
NC................ Necrosis
Nc................ Negative Wave in Children [*Neurophysiology*]
NC................ Neighborhood Coalition (EA)
NC................ Nerve Center [*An association*] (EA)
NC................ Nerve Conduction
NC................ Net Capital [*Business term*]
NC................ Net Charter [*Business term*] (DS)
NC................ Net Control (MCD)
NC................ Net Cost
NC................ Netilmicin-Clindamycin [*Antibiotic combination*]
NC................ Network Card [*British Rail*]
NC................ Network Channel [*Broadcasting*] (NTCM)
NC................ Network Computer (PCM)
NC................ Network Computer [*Computer science*]
NC................ Network Computer (PCM)
NC................ Network Computing
NC................ Network Congestion [*Telecommunications*] (TEL)
NC................ Network Connect
NC................ Network Control (IAA)
NC................ Network Controller
NC................ Network Countdown
NC................ Neural Crest [*Anatomy*]
NC................ Neurocirculatory [*Medicine*] (DAVI)
NC................ Neurologic Check [*Medicine*]
NC................ Neutral Current [*Physics*]
NC................ Neutralization Capacitor (IAA)
NC................ Neutralizing Capacitance [*or Coil*] (DEN)
NC................ Neutron Controller [*Nuclear energy*] (NRCH)
N/C.............. New Account (ROG)
NC................ Newair [*ICAO designator*] (AD)
NC................ New Caledonia [*ANSI two-letter standard code*] (CNC)
NC................ New Canada Press
NC................ New Cases (Bingham's New Cases) in Common Pleas [*1834-40*] [*A publication*] (DLA)
NC................ New Cavendish Books [*Publisher*] [*British*]
N/C.............. New Charter [*Navigation*]

NC................ New Church (ROG)
NC................ New Construction [*Navy*]
NC................ New Consultants [*A publication*]
NC................ New Crop
NC................ Neylan Conference (EA)
NC................ Nickel Cadmium (IAA)
NC................ Nickel Clad
NC................ Night Coach [*Airline designation*]
N-C.............. Nightingale-Conant [*Audio publisher*]
NC................ Nippon Club (EA)
NC................ Nitrocellulose [*Organic chemistry*]
NC................ Nixdorf Computer (IAA)
NC................ NOAA [*National Oceanic and Atmospheric Administration*] Corps (USDC)
NC................ NOAA [*National Oceanic and Atmospheric Administration*] Corps [*Marine science*] (OSRA)
NC................ No Casualty (MAE)
NC................ No Change
N/C.............. No Change (AAGC)
NC................ No Charge
NC................ No Circuits
NC................ No Coil (MSA)
NC................ No Collaterals [*Medicine*]
NC................ No Comment (NASA)
N/C.............. No Complaints [*Medicine*]
NC................ No Connection [*Valve pins*] [*Radio*] [*Technical drawings*]
nc................ No Connection (IDOE)
NC................ No Contact
NC................ No Contest [*Sports*]
NC................ No Cost (AAG)
NC................ No Credit (WGA)
NC................ Noise Correlation (MSA)
NC................ Noise Criterion
NC................ Noiseless Camera (NTCM)
NC................ Nominal Correction
NC................ Nominating Committee [*American Occupational Therapy Association*]
NC................ Noncallable Bond [*Investment term*]
NC................ Noncoin (IAA)
NC................ Noncollectable
NC................ Non-Color Sensitized Emulsion [*Also called color-blind emulsion*] (WDMC)
NC................ Noncommercial [*Rate*] [*Value of the English pound*]
NC................ Noncommissioned
NC................ Noncomplex (MCD)
NC................ Noncompliance [*Noncompliant*] (DAVI)
NC................ Nonconforming
NC................ Nonconformist [*Indicating religious preference*] [*Military British*]
NC................ Non-Continuous Liner [*Shipping*] (DS)
NC................ Noncontributory [*Medicine*]
NC................ Noncontributory (DAVI)
NC................ Nonconversational (IAA)
NC................ Non-Crystalline (OA)
NC................ Non-Curling [*Photographic film*] (ROG)
NC................ Nonlinear Capacitance
NC................ Nonrecurring Costs (AAGC)
NC................ Nordic Council
NC................ NORDLEK Council (EAIO)
NC................ Normal Children
NC................ Normal Control
NC................ Normal Copy [*Oncology*]
NC................ Normally Closed [*Switch*]
N/C.............. Normally Closed
NC................ Norman Conquest [*of England, 1066*]
NC................ Normocephalic [*On physical examination*] [*Medicine*] (DAVI)
NC................ North Carolina [*Postal code*]
NC................ North Carolina Railroad
NC................ North Carolina Reports [*A publication*] (DLA)
NC................ North Carolina Reports [*A publication*] (AAGC)
Nc................ North Carolina State Library, Raleigh, NC [*Library symbol Library of Congress*] (LCLS)
NC................ North Carolina Supreme Court Reports [*A publication*] (DLA)
NC................ North Central Airlines, Inc. [*ICAO designator*] (OAG)
NC................ North Coast (ADA)
NC................ Northcor Resources Ltd. [*Vancouver Stock Exchange symbol*]
NC................ North Country (ROG)
NC................ Northern Command
NC................ Northern Consolidated Airlines, Inc.
NC................ Northrop Corp. (KSC)
NC................ Norwegian Club (EA)
NC................ Nose Cone [*Aviation*] (AFM)
NC................ Not Carried
NC................ Not Coded (MCD)
NC................ Not Competitive [*Rejected research proposals*] [*National Institutes of Health*]
NC................ Not Completed [*Medicine*] (DMAA)
NC................ Not Connected [*Electronics*] (DEN)
NC................ Not Controlled [*Experimental conditions*]
N/C.............. Not Critical (NASA)
N/C.............. Not Critical
NC................ Not Cultured (MAE)
NC................ Notes of Cases at Madras (Strange) [*A publication*] (DLA)
NC................ Notes of Cases, English Ecclesiastical and Maritime Courts [*1841-50*] [*A publication*] (DLA)
NC................ Novo Cruzado [*Brazilian currency*]
NC................ Nuclear Capability

NC.............	Nuclear Congress
NC.............	Nuclear-Cytoplasmic [*Ratio*] [*Cytology*] (MAE)
NC.............	Nucleus of Ciliated Cell
NC.............	Nuestra Cuenta [*Our Account*] [*Business term Spanish*]
NC.............	"Nuff Ced" [*Enough Said*] [*Slang*]
NC.............	Numbering Counter [*Computer science*] (OA)
NC.............	Numerical Control [*Computer science*]
N/C............	Numerical Control [IDOE]
NC.............	Nurse Corps [*Military*]
NC.............	Sagrada Biblia [*1944*] [*Eloino Nacar Fuster and Alberto Colunga*] (BJA)
NC.............	Sandoz Pharmaceuticals [*Research code symbol*]
nc.............	Sodium Carbonate [*CIPW classification*] [*Geology*]
NC.............	Warner-Lambert Pharmaceutical Co. [*Research code symbol*]
NC1...........	Navy Counselor First Class (DNAB)
NC3...........	Norsar Array Site 03C00 [*Norway*] [*Seismograph station code, US Geological Survey*] (SEIS)
NC³D........	National Coordinating Center for Curriculum Development
NC5...........	Norsar Array Site 05C00 [*Norway*] [*Seismograph station code, US Geological Survey*] (SEIS)
NC-17	No Children under 17 Admitted [*Movie rating*]
NCa...........	Canton Free Library, Canton, NY [*Library symbol Library of Congress*] (LCLS)
NCA	College of New Caledonia Library [*UTLAS symbol*]
NCA	Jacksonville, NC [*Location identifier FAA*] (FAAL)
NCA	National Campaign for the Arts [*British*] (DBA)
NCA	National Camping Association (EA)
NCA	National Candle Association (EA)
NCA	National Canners Association [*Later, NFPA*] (EA)
NCA	National Capital Award
NCA	National Carousel Association (EA)
NCA	National Cashmere Association [*Defunct*] (EA)
NCA	National Caterers Association [*Later, ICA*] (EA)
NCA	National Cathedral Association (EA)
NCA	National Cattlemens Association (EA)
NCA	National Caves Association (EA)
NCA	National Caving Association [*British*] (DBA)
NCA	National Ceramic Association [*Later, ICA*] (EA)
NCA	National Certificate of Agriculture [*British*]
NCA	National Certification Agency for Medical Laboratory Personnel (EA)
NCA	National Chaplain's Association (EA)
NCA	National Charcoal Association
NCA	National Chastity Association (EA)
NCA	National Cheerleaders Association (EA)
NCA	National Childminding Association [*British*] (EAIO)
NCA	National Chiropractic Association [*Universal Chiropratic Association and American Chiropratic Association*] [*Later, American Chiropractic Association*] [*Formed by a merger of*]
NCA	National Christian Association (EA)
NCA	National Civic Association
NCA	National Club Association (EA)
NCA	National Coal Association (EA)
NCA	National Coal Authority [*Australia*]
NCA	National Coffee Association of the United States of America (EA)
NCA	National Color-Bred Association (EA)
NCA	National Command Authorities
NCA	National Commission on Accrediting [*Later, COPA*] (EA)
NCA	National Communication Agencies (NATG)
NCA	National Communications Association (EA)
NCA	National Composition Association [*Later, NCPA*] (EA)
NCA	National Computer Association (EA)
NCA	National Concilio of America (EA)
NCA	National Confectioners Association of the United States (EA)
NCA	National Conference of Artists (EA)
NCA	National Congressional Analysis Corp. (IID)
NCA	National Constables Association (EA)
NCA	National Constructors Association (EA)
NCA	National Contesters Association (EA)
NCA	National Contingency Account (OICC)
NCA	National Cosmetology Association (EA)
NCA	National Costumers Association (EA)
NCA3.........	National Council for Aviculture [*British*] (DBA)
NCA	National Council on Alcoholism [*Later, NCADD*] (EA)
NCA	National Council on the Aging [*Washington, DC*]
NCA	National Council on the Arts [*of NFAH*]
NCA5.........	National Coursing Association [*Later, NGA*] (EA)
NCA	National Cranberry Association
NCA	National Creameries Association [*Later, NMPF*] (EA)
NCa...........	National Credit Association (NADA)
NCA	National Cricket Association [*British*]
NCA	National Crop Acreage Program [*Department of Agriculture*]
NCA	Naval Center for Cost Analysis
NCA	Naval Command Assistant
NCA	Naval Communications Annex
NCA	Navy Contract Administrator
NCA	NCA Minerals [*Vancouver Stock Exchange symbol*]
NCA	N-Carboxy Anhydride [*Organic chemistry*]
NCA	N-Chloroacetamide [*Organic chemistry*]
NCA	N-Chloroethylnorapomorphine [*Organic chemistry, biochemistry*]
NCA	Network Career Advancement Institute [*Telecommunications service*] (TSSD)
NCA	Network Computing Architecture [*Computer science*] (TNIG)
NCA	Network for Community Activities
NCA	Neurocirculatory Asthenia [*Medicine*]
NCA	Neutrophil Chemotactic Activity [*Clinical chemistry*]
NCA	New Communities Administration [*HUD*]
NCA	Newfoundland Club of America (EA)
NCA	Nickel-Copper Alloy (MSA)
NCA	Nippon Cargo Airlines [*Japan*]
NCA	Nippon Cargo Airlines Co. Ltd. [*Japan ICAO designator*] (FAAC)
NCA	No Copies Available (ADA)
NCA	No Coupons Attached (DLA)
NCA	Nodulocystic Acne [*Medicine*] (DMAA)
NCA	Noise Control Act (EG)
NCA	Noise Control Association (EA)
NCA	Noncombat Aircraft [*Military*] (MCD)
NCA	Noncontractual Authorization
NCA	Nonorganic Ceramic Adhesive
NCA	Nonspecific Cross-Reacting Antigen [*Immunology*]
NCA	Normal Coordinate Analysis
NCA	North Caicos [*British West Indies*] [*Airport symbol*] (OAG)
NCA	North Carolina Court of Appeals Reports [*A publication*] (DLA)
NCA	North Central Association of Colleges and Secondary Schools [*Later, NCACS*]
NCA	North Central Bible College, Minneapolis, MN [*OCLC symbol*] (OCLC)
NCA	North Coast Airlines [*Australia*]
NCA	Northern Communications Area [*Military*]
NCA	Northern Consolidated Airlines, Inc.
NCA	Northwest Computing Association
NCA	Nuclear and Chemical Agency [*Army*]
NCA	Nurse Consultants Association (EA)
NCA	Nuveen California Municipal Fund [*NYSE symbol*] (SPSG)
NCA	Nuveen CA Muni Val Fd [*NYSE symbol*] (TTSB)
NcA...........	Pack Memorial Public Library, Asheville, NC [*Library symbol Library of Congress*] (LCLS)
NCAA	National Center for Audio Tapes Archive (EA)
NCAA	National Center on Arts and the Aging (EA)
NCAA	National Change of Address Association [*Commercial firm New York, NY*] (EA)
NCAA	National Collegiate Athletic Association (EA)
NCAA	National Command Authority Aircraft-747 [*MTMC*] (TAG)
NCAA	National Credit Adjustment Association [*New York, NY*] (EA)
NCAA	NATO Civil Air Augmentation (DOMA)
NCAA	Naval Civilian Administrators Association [*Later, NCMA*] (EA)
NCAA	Nonnuclear Consumable Annual Analysis (MCD)
NCAAA	National Center of Afro-American Artists
NCAAA	National Council of Affiliated Advertising Agencies [*Later, First Network of Affiliated Advertising Agencies*] (EA)
NcAAB	Asheville-Buncombe Technical Institute, Asheville, NC [*Library symbol Library of Congress*] (LCLS)
NCAADA......	National Community Action Agency Directors Association [*Formerly, NCAAEDA*] [*Later, NACAA*] (EA)
NCAADACCB...	National Commission on Accreditation of Alcoholism and Drug Abuse Counselor Credentialing Bodies (EA)
NCAAE	National Council of Administrators of Adult Education (EA)
NCAAEDA....	National Community Action Agency Executive Directors Association (EA)
NcAAH	Appalachian Hall Medical Library, Asheville, NC [*Library symbol*] [*Library of Congress*] (LCLS)
NcAAP	Amcel Propulsion Co., Asheville, NC [*Library symbol Library of Congress*] (LCLS)
NCAAP........	National Coalition for Adequate Alcoholism Programs [*Defunct*] (EA)
NCAB	National Association of Citizen Advice Bureaux [*British*]
NCAB	National Cancer Advisory Board
NCAB	National Collegiate Athletic Bureau [*Later, NCSS*] (EA)
NCAB	National Committee for Amateur Baseball [*Later, USBF*]
NCAB	Navy Contract Adjustment Board
NCABC.......	National Citizens' Advice Bureaux Committee [*British*] (BI)
NcAbd.........	Page Memorial Library, Aberdeen, NC [*Library symbol*] [*Library of Congress*] (LCLS)
NCABHP.....	National Center for the Advancement of Blacks in the Health Professions (EA)
NcAbMR	North Carolina Marine Resources Center, Bogue Banks Library, Atlantic Beach, NC [*Library symbol Library of Congress*] (LCLS)
NcAC.........	Cecils Junior College, Asheville, NC [*Library symbol*] [*Library of Congress*] (LCLS)
NCAC	National Cancer Advisory Committee [*Australia*]
NCAC	National Catholic Action Coalition [*Defunct*] (EA)
NCAC	National Christian Action Coalition [*Defunct*] (EA)
NCAC	National Civil Aviation Council [*British*] (BI)
NCAC	National Clean Air Coalition [*Defunct*] (EA)
NCAC	National Coalition Against Censorship (EA)
NCAC	National Consumer Advisory Council
NCAC	National Copyright Advisory Committee (NADA)
NCAC	National Council Against Conscription [*World War I*] [*British*]
NCAC	National Council of Acoustical Consultants (EA)
NCAC	Navy Combat Art Collection (DNAB)
NCAC	Nordic Customs Administrative Council (EA)
NCAC	North Carolina Administrative Code [*A publication*] (AAGC)
NCAC	Northern Combat Area Command [*Myanmar*]
NCACC.......	National Conference of Appellate Court Clerks (EA)
NCACE	National Capital Association for Cooperative Education (MCD)
NCACME.....	National Center for Adult, Continuing, and Manpower Education [*Office of Education*]
NCACP........	National Campaign for the Abolition of Capital Punishment [*Founded in 1955*] [*British*]
NCACPS.......	National Coalition to Abolish Corporal Punishment in Schools (EA)
NCACS........	National Coalition of Alternative Community Schools (EA)
NCACS........	North Central Association of Colleges and Schools (EA)

NCAD .... New Cumberland Army Depot [*Pennsylvania*] (AABC)
NCAD .... Notice of Cancellation at Anniversary Date [*Insurance*] (DCTA)
NCADD .... National Commission Against Drunk Driving (EA)
NCADD .... National Council on Alcoholism and Drug Dependence (EA)
NCADH .... National Committee Against Discrimination in Housing [*Defunct*] (EA)
NCADI .... National Clearinghouse for Alcohol and Drug Abuse Information (PAZ)
NCADI .... National Clearinghouse for Alcohol and Drug Information [*US Public Health Service*] [*Information service or system*] (IID)
NC Admin Code... North Carolina Administrative Code [*A publication*] (DLA)
NCADP .... National Coalition Against the Death Penalty (EA)
NCADV .... National Coalition Against Domestic Violence (EA)
NC Adv Legis Serv... North Carolina Advance Legislative Service (Michie) [*A publication*] (DLA)
NCAE .... National Center for Alcohol Education [*National Institutes of Health*]
NCAE .... National Center for Audio Experimentation [*Defunct*] (EA)
NCAE .... National College of Agricultural Engineering [*British*] (ARC)
NCAE .... National Conference on Airborne Electronics (MCD)
NCAE .... National Council of Agricultural Employers (EA)
NCAEE .... National Committee on Art Education for the Elderly [*Defunct*] (EA)
NCAEF .... National Ceramic Association Educational Foundation (EA)
NCAEG .... National Confederation of American Ethnic Groups (EA)
NCAEI .... National Conference on the Application of Electrical Insulation
NCAES .... Northern New England Association of Energy Systems (HGAA)
NCAF .... National Clean Air Fund (GFGA)
NCAF .... National Committee Against Fluoridation [*National Health Federation - NHF*] [*Absorbed by*] (EA)
NCAF .... National Community Action Foundation (EA)
NCAFB .... Normal Crop Acreage Farm Base
NCAFP .... National Committee on American Foreign Policy (EA)
NCAG .... National Council on the Arts and Government (EA)
NcAh .... Ahoskie Public Library, Ahoskie, NC [*Library symbol Library of Congress*] (LCLS)
NCAH .... National Committee, Arts for the Handicapped [*Later, VSA*] (EA)
NCAHCP .... National Council on Alternative Health Care Policy (EA)
NcAHE .... Mountain Area Health Education Center, Health Sciences Library, Asheville, NC [*Library symbol Library of Congress*] (LCLS)
NCAHE .... National Commission on Allied Health Education [*American Occupational Therapy Association*]
NCAHF .... National Council Against Health Fraud (EA)
NcAHH .... Highland Hospital, Medical Library, Asheville, NC [*Library symbol Library of Congress*] (LCLS)
NcAhRC .... Roanoke-Chowan Technical Institute, Ahoskie, NC [*Library symbol Library of Congress*] (LCLS)
NCAHRN ..... National Central American Health Rights Network (EA)
NCAHUAC .... National Committee to Abolish the House Un-American Activities Committee [*Later, NCARL*] (EA)
NCAI .... Aitutaki [*Cook Islands*] [*ICAO location identifier*] (ICLI)
NCAI .... National Clearinghouse for Alcohol Information [*Rockville, MD*] [*National Institutes of Health*]
NCAI .... National Coalition for Adult Immunization
NCAI .... National Congress of American Indians (EA)
NCAI .... National Council of American Importers [*Later, AAEI*] (EA)
NCAI .... National Council on Alcoholism, Inc. (NADA)
NCAIAE .... National Center for American Indian Alternative Education (EA)
NCAIANMHR... National Center for American Indian and Alaska Native Mental Health Research (EA)
NCAIC .... Nuclear Chemical Accident Incident Control (MCD)
NCAIE .... National Center for American Indian Education [*Later, NCAIAE*] (EA)
NCAIE .... National Council of the Arts in Education [*Later, ACAE*] (EA)
NCAIL .... National Council Against Illegal Liquor [*Defunct*] (EA)
NCAIP .... National Consumer Affairs Internship Program [*Defunct*] (EA)
NCAIR .... National Center for Automated Information Retrieval (IID)
NCAIR .... North Carolina Association for Institutional Research (EDAC)
NCAJ .... National Center for Administrative Justice [*Formerly, CAJ*] (EA)
NCA/JCS ...... National Command Authorities and Joint Chiefs of Staff
NCAJL .... National Council on Art in Jewish Life (EA)
NCaL .... Canton Free Library, Canton, NY [*Library symbol*] [*Library of Congress*] (LCLS)
NCAL .... National Centre for Athletics Literature (AIE)
NCAL .... National Committee for Adult Literacy [*British*] (DI)
N Cal .... New Caledonia
NcAlb .... Albemarle-Stanly County Public Library, Albemarle, NC [*Library symbol Library of Congress*] (LCLS)
NcAlbS .... Stanly Technical Institute, Albemarle, NC [*Library symbol Library of Congress*] (LCLS)
NCALHBCU... National Consortium of Arts and Letters for Historically Black Colleges and Universities
NCALI .... National Clearinghouse for Alcohol Information [*National Institutes of Health*] (IID)
NCALL .... National Council on Agricultural Life and Labor Research Fund (EA)
NcAlP .... Pamlico Technical Institute, Alliance, NC [*Library symbol Library of Congress*] (LCLS)
NcAlv .... Baiting Hollow Free Library, Calverton, NY [*Library symbol Library of Congress*] (LCLS)
NCAM .... National Center for Advanced Materials [*Later, Berkeley Center for Advanced Materials*]
NCAM .... Network Communication Access Method
N-CAM .... Neural Cell Adhesion Molecule [*Biochemistry*]
NCAM .... Neural Cell Adhesion Molecule [*Medical*]
NCAMI .... National Committee Against Mental Illness [*Defunct*] (EA)
NCAMLP ...... National Certification Agency for Medical Laboratory Personnel (MAE)
NCAMP .... National Coalition Against the Misuses of Pesticides (EA)
NCAMR .... Nordic Council for Arctic Medical Research (EA)

NCAN .... Incan Superior Ltd. [*AAR code*]
NCAN .... National Catholic AIDS Network (EA)
NCAN .... National Citizens Action Network (EA)
NCAN .... National Coalition of American Nuns (EA)
NCAN .... National Committee for Amnesty Now (EA)
NCaN .... North Country Reference and Research Resources Council, Canton, NY [*Library symbol Library of Congress*] (LCLS)
NCAnA .... Anson Technical Institute, Ansonville, NC [*Library symbol Library of Congress*] (LCLS)
NCanC .... Community College of the Finger Lakes, Canandaigua, NY [*Library symbol Library of Congress*] (LCLS)
NcANCC .... United States National Oceanic and Atmospheric Administration, National ClimaticCenter, Ashville, NC [*Library symbol Library of Congress*] (LCLS)
NcAnd .... Andrews Carnegie Library, Andrews, NC [*Library symbol Library of Congress*] (LCLS)
NC & B .... Naval Courts and Boards
NC & CS .... Navigation Command and Control System
NC & SL .... Nashville, Chattanooga & St. Louis Railway (IIA)
NC & ST L .... Nashville, Chattanooga & St. Louis Railway
NCANH .... National Council for the Accreditation of Nursing Homes (NADA)
NCanHi .... Ontario County Historical Society, Canandaigua, NY [*Library symbol Library of Congress*] (LCLS)
NCaNNH ...... Northern New York Health Information Cooperative, Canton, NY [*Library symbol Library of Congress*] (LCLS)
NCanV .... United States Veterans Administration Hospital, Canandaigua, NY [*Library symbol Library of Congress*] (LCLS)
NCAO .... National Commission on Air Quality [*Environmental Protection Agency*] (ERG)
NCAO .... Naval Civil Affairs Officer [*World War II*]
N-CAP .... National Coalition Against Pornography (EA)
NCAp .... Naval Combat Air Patrol (DNAB)
NCAP .... Neighborhood Community Action Program
NCAP .... Nematic Curvilinear Aligned Phase [*Emulsion film used in windows*] [*Taliq Corp.*]
NCAP .... New Car Assessment Program [*Automobile testing*]
NCAP .... Night Combat Air Patrol [*Military*]
NCAP .... Nonlinear Circuit Analysis Program (MCD)
NCAP .... Nordic Council for Animal Protection (EA)
NCAP .... Northwest Coalition for Alternatives to Pesticides [*An association*]
NCAP .... Northwest Coalition for Alternatives to Pesticides (GNE)
NCAP .... Nucleotide Column Affinity for Purification [*Biochemical analysis*]
N-CAP .... Nurses Coalition for Action in Politics
NCAPC .... National Center for Air Pollution Control [*Public Health Service*] [*Obsolete*]
NCAPI .... Nuveen California Premium Income Municipal Fund [*Associated Press*] (SAG)
NCAPO .... National Council of Adoptive Parents Organizations [*NACAC*] [*Absorbed by*]
NC App .... North Carolina Appellate Reports [*A publication*] (AAGC)
NC App .... North Carolina Court of Appeals Reports [*A publication*] (DLA)
NCAPS .... Naval Control and Protection of Shipping (NVT)
NCapV .... United States Veterans Administration Hospital, Medical Library, Castle Point, NY [*Library symbol*] [*Library of Congress*] (LCLS)
NCAQ .... National Commission on Air Quality (GNE)
NCAR .... National Center for Association Resources (EA)
NCAR .... National Center for Atmospheric Research [*Boulder, CO*] [*National Science Foundation*] (GRD)
NCAR .... National Conference on the Advancement of Research (EA)
NCAR .... Navy Center for Acquisition Research [*Monterey, CA*]
NCAR .... Nonconformance and Corrective Action Reporting System [*NASA*] (KSC)
N Car .... North Carolina (DLA)
N Car .... North Carolina Reports [*A publication*] (DLA)
Nc-Ar .... North Carolina State Department of Archives and History, Raleigh, NC [*Library symbol Library of Congress*] (LCLS)
NcAr .... Sallie H. Jenkins Memorial Public Library, Aulander, NC [*Library symbol*] [*Library of Congress*] (LCLS)
NCARAI........ Navy Center for Applied Research in Artificial Intelligence [*Washington, DC*] (GRD)
NCARB .... National Council of Architectural Registration Boards (EA)
NCaRC .... North Country Reference and Research Resources Council, Canton, NY [*Library symbol Library of Congress Obsolete*] (LCLS)
NCARF .... National Committee for Amish Religious Freedom (EA)
NCARL .... National Committee Against Repressive Legislation (EA)
N Car Law Rep... Carolina Law Repository (Reprint) [*North Carolina*] [*A publication*] (DLA)
NCARMD...... National Commission on Arthritis and Related Musculoskeletal Disease
NCarNG....... North Carolina Natural Gas Corp. [*Associated Press*] (SAG)
N Carolina Cases... North Carolina Reports [*A publication*] (DLA)
NCARP......... Collegiate Association for Research of Principle (EA)
N Car Rep .... North Carolina Reports [*A publication*] (DLA)
NCAS .... National Coalition Against Surrogacy (EA)
NCAS .... National Coalition of Advocates for Students (EA)
NCAS .... National Collegiate Association for Secretaries [*Defunct*] (EA)
NCAS .... Neocarzinostatin [*Zinostatin*] [*Antineoplastic drug*]
NcA-S .... Pack Memorial Public Library, Sondley Reference Library, Asheville, NC [*Library symbol Library of Congress*] (LCLS)
NCaS .... Saint Lawrence University, Canton, NY [*Library symbol Library of Congress*] (LCLS)
NCASA......... National Campaign Against Solvent Abuse [*British*] (DBA)
NCASA......... National Coalition Against Sexual Assault (EA)
NCASA......... Naval Civil Affairs Staging Area
NCASAA....... National Court Appointed Special Advocates Association (EA)

NcAsbC........ Randolph Public Library, Asheboro, NC [*Library symbol Library of Congress*] (LCLS)
NcAsbH........ Randolph Hospital, Inc., Asheboro, NC [*Library symbol*] [*Library of Congress*] (LCLS)
NcAsbR........ Randolph Technical Institute, Asheboro, NC [*Library symbol Library of Congress*] (LCLS)
NCASC........ National Capital Administrative Support Center (USDC)
NCASC........ National Capital Administrative Support Center [*Marine science*] (OSRA)
NCASC........ National Council of Acupuncture Schools and Colleges (EA)
NCASC........ Nordic Council for Adult Studies in Church [*See also NKS*] (EAIO)
NCASEPS.... North Central Alaskan Seasonal Earned Premium Scale [*Aviation*] (AIA)
NCASF........ National Council of American-Soviet Friendship (EA)
NCASI........ National Council of the Paper Industry for Air and Stream Improvement (EA)
NCAT.......... Atiu [*Cook Islands*] [*ICAO location identifier*] (ICLI)
NCAT........ National Center for Advanced Technology [*Vienna, VA*]
NCAT........ National Center for Appropriate Technology (EA)
NCAT........ National Center for Audiotape [*Later, NCATA*] (EA)
NCAT........ National Centre for Alternative Technology [*British*]
NCAT........ National Program for Clear Air Turbulence [*Air Force*]
NCAT........ Naval College Aptitude Test (NVT)
NC/AT........ Normal Cephalic Atraumatic [*Medicine*] (DMAA)
NCATA........ National Cable Antenna Television Association of Canada (NTCM)
NCATA........ National Center for Audiotape Archive [*Defunct*] (EA)
NCATA........ National Coalition of Arts Therapy Associations (EA)
NCATB........ National Congress of Animal Trainers and Breeders (EA)
NCATE........ National Council for Accreditation of Teacher Education (EA)
NCATH........ National Campaign Against Toxic Hazards (EA)
NcATH........ Thoms Rehabilitation Hospital, Medical Library, Asheville, NC [*Library symbol*] [*Library of Congress*] (LCLS)
NcAu.......... Sallie H. Jenkins Memorial Public Library, Aulander, NC [*Library symbol Library of Congress*] (LCLS)
NcAU.......... University of North Carolina at Asheville, Asheville, NC [*Library symbol Library of Congress*] (LCLS)
NCaUA........ State University of New York, Agricultural and Technical College, Canton, NY [*Library symbol Library of Congress*] (LCLS)
NCAV.......... National Coursing Association of Victoria [*Australia*]
NcAV.......... United States Veterans Administration, Hospital Library Service, Asheville, NC [*Library symbol Library of Congress*] (LCLS)
NCAVAE...... National Committee for Audio-Visual Aids in Education [*British*]
NCAVC........ National Center for the Analysis of Violent Crime [*Quantico, VA*] [*Department of Justice*] (GRD)
NCAW........ National Council for Animal Welfare (NADA)
NCAWA........ National Coinamatic Auto Wash Association [*Later, ICA/NCC*]
NCAWE........ National Council of Administrative Women in Education (EA)
NCAWP........ National Council for Alternative Work Patterns (EA)
NCAWRR...... National Committee Against War, Racism, and Repression
NCAYR........ National Chaplains Association for Youth Rehabilitation [*Defunct*]
NCazC.......... Cazenovia College, Cazenovia, NY [*Library symbol Library of Congress*] (LCLS)
NCB.......... Barber-Scotia College, Concord, NC [*OCLC symbol*] (OCLC)
NCB.......... Nanyang Commercial Bank [*China*]
NCB.......... National Cargo Bureau (EA)
NCB.......... National Central Bureau [*INTERPOL term*]
NCB.......... National Children's Bureau [*British*]
NCB.......... National Classification Board [*American Trucking Association*]
NCB.......... National Coal Board [*British*]
NCB.......... National Codification Bureau [*NATO*] (NATG)
NCB.......... National Collection of Industrial Bacteria [*British*]
NCB.......... National College of Business (IAA)
NCB.......... National Commercial Bank [*Saudi Arabia*]
NCB.......... National Commercial Bank [*Jamaica*]
NCB.......... National Compliance Board [*New Deal*]
NCB.......... National Conservation Bureau [*Defunct*]
NCB.......... National Cooperative Bank (USGC)
NCB.......... Naval Communications Board
NCB.......... Naval Construction Battalion
NCB.......... Navy Comptroller Budget (NG)
NCB.......... Nederlandse Creditbank NV [*Financial institution*] [*Netherlands*] (EY)
NCB.......... NetBIOS [*Network Basic Input/Output System*] Control Block [*Computer science*]
NCB.......... Net Clearing Balance [*Finance*]
NCB.......... Netherlands Convention Bureau (EA)
NCB.......... Network Control Block
NCB.......... New Century Bible [*A publication*] (BJA)
NCB.......... New Crime Buffer
NCB.......... Nickel-Cadmium Battery
NCB.......... Nippon Credit Bank [*Japan*]
NCB.......... No Claim Bonus [*Insurance*] (ADA)
NCB.......... No Code Blue [*For terminal cases*] [*Medicine*] (DAVI)
NCB.......... Noncallable Bond [*Investment term*]
NCB.......... North Caribou Flying Service Ltd. [*Canada ICAO designator*] (FAAC)
NCB.......... Northwest Cherry Briners Association (EA)
NcBa.......... Mitchell County Library, Bakersville, NC [*Library symbol Library of Congress*] (LCLS)
NCBA.......... National Candy Brokers Association (EA)
NCBA.......... National Catholic Bandmasters' Association (EA)
NCBA.......... National Cattle Breeders Association [*British*] (DBA)
NCBAC.......... National Caucus and Center on Black Aged (EA)
NCBA.......... National Chinchilla Breeders of America [*Later, ECBC*] (EA)
NCBA.......... National Color-Bred Association (EA)
NCBA.......... National Commodity and Barter Association (EA)

NCBA.......... National Cooperative Business Association (EA)
NCBA.......... National Council on Black Aging (EA)
NCBAE.......... No-Claim Bonus as Earned [*Insurance*] (ODBW)
NcBaneL...... Lees-McRae College, Banner Elk, NC [*Library symbol Library of Congress*] (LCLS)
NCBBC........ National Council of Bible Believing Churches [*Later, CBBC*] (EA)
NcBc.......... Marianna Black Library, Bryson City, NC [*Library symbol Library of Congress*] (LCLS)
NCBC.......... National Commerce Bancorp [*NASDAQ symbol*] (NQ)
NCBC.......... National Committee for the Berne Convention [*Defunct*] (EA)
NCBC.......... Natl Commerce Bancorp [*NASDAQ symbol*] (TTSB)
NCBC.......... Naval Construction Battalion Center
NCBC.......... New Century Bible Commentary [*A publication*]
NCBC.......... North Carolina Biotechnology Center [*Research center*] (RCD)
NcBcF.......... Fontana Regional Library, Bryson City, NC [*Library symbol Library of Congress*] (LCLS)
NCBCS........ National Conference of States on Building Codes and Standards (OICC)
NcBe.......... Belmont Abbey College, Belmont, NC [*Library symbol Library of Congress*] (LCLS)
NCBE.......... National City Bancshares [*NASDAQ symbol*] (SAG)
NCBE.......... National Clearinghouse for Bilingual Education [*Wheaton, MD*]
NCBE.......... National Conference of Bar Examiners (EA)
NCBE.......... National Conference of Bar Executives [*Later, NABE*] (EA)
NCBE.......... National Council for Better Education (EA)
NCBE.......... Natl City Bancshares [*NASDAQ symbol*] (TTSB)
NcBea.......... Cateret County Public Library, Beaufort, NC [*Library symbol Library of Congress*] (LCLS)
NCBEA.......... National Catholic Business Education Association [*Emporia, KS*] (EA)
NCBEA.......... North Central Business Education Association (AEBS)
NcBeaAE...... United States Marine Fisheries Service, Southeast Fisheries Center, Beaufort Laboratory, Beaufort, NC [*Library symbol Library of Congress*] (LCLS)
NCBEC.......... National Center for Business and Economic Communication [*American University*] [*Research center*] (RCD)
NCBEE.......... National Council of State Boards of Engineering Examiners [*Later, NCEE*] (IAA)
NCBEL.......... [*The*] New Cambridge Bibliography of English Literature [*A publication*]
NcBeSH........ Sacred Heart College, McCarthy Library, Belmont, NC [*Library symbol Library of Congress*] (LCLS)
NcBesL........ Lithium Corp. of America, Ellestad Research Library, Bessemer City, NC [*Library symbol Library of Congress*] (LCLS)
NCBF.......... National Conference of Bar Foundations (EA)
NCBF.......... Non-Conventional Brake Fluid [*Automotive engineering*]
NCBFAA........ National Customs Brokers and Forwarders Association of America [*New York, NY*] (EA)
NCBFE.......... National Center for a Barrier Free Environment (EA)
NCBG.......... National Coalition of Black Gays (EA)
ncbh--.......... British Honduras [*MARC geographic area code Library of Congress*] (LCCP)
NCBH.......... National Coalition to Ban Handguns [*Later, CSGV*] (EA)
NCBHC........ National Committee on Black and Hispanic Concerns (EA)
NCBI.......... National Center for Biotechnology Information (IID)
NCBI.......... National Cotton Batting Institute (EA)
NCBIAE........ National Council of BIA [*Bureau of Indian Affairs*] Educators (EA)
NCBJ.......... National Conference of Bankruptcy Judges (EA)
NCBJS.......... National Council of Beth Jacob Schools [*Later, FCBJS*] (EA)
NcBl.......... Bridger Memorial Public Library, Bladenboro, NC [*Library symbol Library of Congress*] (LCLS)
NCBL.......... National Conference of Black Lawyers (EA)
NCBL.......... Natural Convection Boiling Loops
NCBLG.......... National Coalition of Black Lesbians and Gays (EA)
NcBlm.......... Black Mountain Public Library, Black Mountain, NC [*Library symbol Library of Congress*] (LCLS)
NCBLRDC.... National Coalition of Black Lung and Respiratory Disease Clinics (EA)
NcBlv.......... Phillip Leff Memorial Library, Beulaville, NC [*Library symbol Library of Congress*] (LCLS)
NCBM.......... National City Bancorp [*NASDAQ symbol*] (NQ)
NCBM.......... National Conference of Black Mayors (EA)
NCBM.......... National Council on Business Mail (EA)
NCBM.......... Natl City Bancorp'n [*NASDAQ symbol*] (TTSB)
NCBMP........ National Coalition of Black Meeting Planners (EA)
NCBMP........ National Council of Building Material Producers [*A union*] [*British*]
NcBo.......... Watauga County Library, Boone, NC [*Library symbol Library of Congress*] (LCLS)
NcBoA.......... Appalachian State University, Boone, NC [*Library symbol Library of Congress*] (LCLS)
NcBoHE........ Northwest Area Health Education Center, Boone, NC [*Library symbol*] [*Library of Congress*] (LCLS)
NcBoNM...... New River Area Mental Health, Boone, NC [*Library symbol*] [*Library of Congress*] (LCLS)
NCBOR.......... No Claim Bonus on Renewal [*Insurance*] (AIA)
NCBP.......... National Conference of Bar Presidents (EA)
NCBPD.......... National Consortium for Black Professional Development (EA)
Nc-BPH........ North Carolina Library for the Blind and Physically Handicapped, Raleigh, NC [*Library symbol Library of Congress*] (LCLS)
NCBPNP/N... National Certification Board of Pediatric Nurse Practitioners and Nurses (EA)
NCBR.......... National Center for Bilingual Research [*National Institute of Education*] [*Research center*] (RCD)
NCBR.......... Near Commercial Breeder Reactor [*Also, PLBR*]

NcBre........... Transylvania County Library, Brevard, NC [*Library symbol Library of Congress*] (LCLS)

NcBreC........ Brevard College, Brevard, NC [*Library symbol Library of Congress*] (LCLS)

NCBS .... National Cage Bird Show (EA)

NCBS .... National Council for Black Studies (EA)

NCBSA........ National Candy Brokers and Salesmen's Association [*Later, NCBA*] (EA)

NcBsG......... Gardner-Webb College, Boiling Springs, NC [*Library symbol Library of Congress*] (LCLS)

NcBuC......... Campbell College, Buies Creek, NC [*Library symbol Library of Congress*] (LCLS)

NcBuC-L ...... Campbell University, Law Library, Buies Creek, NC [*Library symbol*] [*Library of Congress*] (LCLS)

NcBur.......... Central North Carolina Regional Library, Burlington, NC [*Library symbol Library of Congress*] (LCLS)

NcBurAT ...... AT&T Technologies Inc., Technical Library, Burlington, NC [*Library symbol*] [*Library of Congress*] (LCLS)

NcBurgP ..... Pender County Library, Burgaw, NC [*Library symbol Library of Congress*] (LCLS)

NcBurgP-H... Pender County Library, Hampstead Branch Library, Hampstead, NC [*Library symbol*] [*Library of Congress*] (LCLS)

NcBurT........ Technical Institute of Alamance, Burlington, NC [*Library symbol Library of Congress*] (LCLS)

NcBurWE .... Western Electric Co., Technical Library, Burlington, NC [*Library symbol Library of Congress*] (LCLS)

NcButM........ Murdoch Center, School Library, Butner, NC [*Library symbol Library of Congress*] (LCLS)

NcBv .... Yancey County Public Library, Burnsville, NC [*Library symbol Library of Congress*] (LCLS)

NCBVA........ National Concrete Burial Vault Association (EA)

NCBVP .... National Coalition on Black Voter Participation (EA)

NCBW .... National Cage Bird Week Association [*Defunct*] (EA)

NCBWA....... National Collegiate Baseball Writers Association (EA)

NcBy .... Palmico County Library, Bayboro, NC [*Library symbol Library of Congress*] (LCLS)

NCC .... Chadron State College, Chadron, NE [*OCLC symbol*] (OCLC)

NCC .... NAACOG [*Nurses Association of the American College of Obstetricians and Gynecologists*] Certification Corp. (EA)

NCC .... NASA Class Code (NASA)

NCC .... National Cadet Corps (NADA)

NCC .... National Cambridge Collectors (EA)

NCC .... National Cancer Center (EA)

NCC .... National Capital Commission [*Canada*]

NCC .... National Capon Council [*Defunct*] (EA)

NCC .... National Caravan Council Ltd. [*British*] (BI)

NCC .... National Carbon Co. (MCD)

NCC .... National Career Center (EA)

NCC .... National Carwash Council [*Later, ICA*] (EA)

NCC .... National Castings Council [*Defunct*] (EA)

NCC .... National Chile Center [*Formerly, NCCSC*] (EA)

NCC .... National Citizens Coalition [*Canada*]

NCC .... National Citizens Committee. Bulletin [*A publication*]

NCC .... National City Corp. [*NYSE symbol*] (CTT)

NCC .... National Clearing Corp. [*National Association of Securities Dealers*]

NCC .... National Clients Council (EA)

NCC .... National Climatic Center [*National Oceanic and Atmospheric Administration*]

NCC .... National Coaches Council [*Later, ANCC*] (EA)

NCC .... National Coal Council [*Department of Energy*] [*Arlington, VA*] (EGAO)

NCC .... National Communications Club (EA)

NCC .... National Communications Command [*Army*] (RDA)

NCC .... National Communications Commission [*Uganda*] (ECON)

NCC .... National Company of Crossbowmen [*Defunct*] (EA)

NCC .... National Computer Center [*IRS*]

NCC .... National Computer Conference

NCC .... National Computer Council (NADA)

NCC .... National Computing Centre [*Manchester, England*]

NCC .... National Conference on Citizenship (EA)

NCC .... National Congressional Club (EA)

NCC .... National Consumer Council [*British*] (ILCA)

NCC .... National Consumers Congress [*Later, NCL*]

NCC .... National Container Committee [*Later, Uniform Classification Committee*] (EA)

NCC .... National Coordinating Committee (USGC)

NCC .... National Coordinating Committee for the Promotion of History (EA)

NCC .... National Coordinating Committee to End the War [*Organization formed in 1965*] (VNW)

NCC .... National Coordinating Council on Drug Abuse Education and Information [*Later, NCCDE*] (EA)

NCC .... National Coordination Committee [*Responsible for administering the Work Incentive Program*]

NCC .... National Cotton Council of America (EA)

NCC .... National Council Against Conscription [*World War I*] [*British*]

NCC .... National Council of Churches of Christ in the USA (EA)

NCC .... National Counselor Certification [*Psychology*]

NCC .... National Crime Commission

NCC .... National Cryptologic Command [*National Security Agency*]

NCC .... National Cultural Center [*Later, John F. Kennedy Center for the Performing Art s*]

NCC .... National Curriculum Council [*British*] (ECON)

NCC .... Native Council of Canada

NCC .... Natl City Corp. [*NYSE symbol*] (TTSB)

NCC .... Natural Circulation Cooldown [*Nuclear energy*] (NUCP)

NCC .... Naturally Commutated Cycloconverter [*Electronics*] (EECA)

NCC .... Nature Conservancy Council [*British*]

NCC .... Navajo Community College [*Chinle, AZ*]

NCC .... Naval Command College (DOMA)

NCC .... Naval Component Command (CINC)

NCC .... Navigation Computer Control

NCC .... Navigation Control Console

NCC .... Navy Command Center (MCD)

NCC .... Navy Cost Center

NCC .... NetWare Console Commander [*Frye Computer Systems*] [*Telecommunications*] (PCM)

NCC .... NetWare Control Center [*Novell, Inc.*] [*Computer science*] (PCM)

NCC .... Network Communications Corp.

NCC .... Network Computer Center (OA)

NCC .... Network Control Center [*Telecommunications*]

NCC .... Network Control Computer (HGAA)

NCC .... Network Coordination Center [*NASA*]

NCC .... Network of Concerned Correspondents (EA)

NCC .... Neural Crest Cell [*Cytology*]

NCC .... Neuronal Correlate of Consciousness

NCC .... New Chancery Cases (Younge and Collyer) [*1841-43*] [*England*] [*A publication*] (DLA)

NCC .... New Chemical Compound [*Food science*]

NCC .... New Common Carriers

NCC .... New Computer Center [*Social Security Administration*]

NCC .... New Construction and Conversion [*Navy*] (AFIT)

NCC .... New Consultants and Consulting Organizations Directory [*A publication*]

NCC .... Newfoundland Capital Corp. Ltd. [*Toronto Stock Exchange symbol*]

NCC .... Newspaper Comics Council [*Later, NFC*] (EA)

NCC .... Niagara County Community College [*UTLAS symbol*]

NCC .... Nitrogen Charging Console

NCC .... Noise Control Committee

NCC .... Nominal Corrective Combination (MCD)

NCC .... Noncancelable Commitment (SDI)

NCC .... Noncarbohydrate Craver [*Nutrition*]

NCC .... Noncombatant Corps [*British*]

NCC .... NORAD Control Center [*Military*]

NCC .... Nordic Choral Committee (EAIO)

NCC .... Normal-Control Children [*Psychology*]

NCC .... Normally Closed Contact [*Switch*] (IAA)

NCC .... North Calotte Committee [*See also NKK*] [*Nordic Council of Ministers*] [*Finland*] (EAIO)

NCC .... North Central College [*Naperville, IL*]

NCC .... North Coast Air Services Ltd. [*Canada ICAO designator*] (FAAC)

NCC .... Northwest Christian College [*Oregon*]

NCC .... Notre Cause Commune [*Benin*] [*Political party*] (EY)

NCC .... Numerical Control Code

NCC .... Nursing Clerical Coordinator

NcC .... Public Library of Charlotte and Mecklenburg County, Charlotte, NC [*Library symbol Library of Congress*] (LCLS)

NcCA........... Arthur Andersen & Co., Carolinas Central Library, Charlotte, NC [*Library symbol*] [*Library of Congress*] (LCLS)

NCCA .... Nash Car Club of America (EA)

NCCA .... National Carpet Cleaners Association [*British*] (EAIO)

NCCA .... National Catholic Camping Association [*Defunct*] (EA)

NCCA .... National Cedar Chest Association [*Defunct*] (EA)

NCCA .... National Center for Child Advocacy

NCCA .... National Center for Community Action (EA)

NCCA .... National Chemical Credit Association (EA)

NCCA .... National Clergy Council on Alcoholism and Related Drug Problems (EA)

NCCA .... National Club Cricket Association [*British*] (BI)

NCCA .... National Coil Coaters Association (EA)

NCCA .... National Collegiate Conference Association (EA)

NCCA .... National Columbia Challenger Association (EA)

NCCA .... National Commission for the Certification of Acupuncture (EA)

NCCA .... National Committee on Central America (EA)

NCCA .... National Concrete Contractors Association [*Later, ASCC*] (EA)

NCCA .... National Cotton Council of America [*Memphis, TN*]

NCCA .... National Council for Critical Analysis [*Defunct*] (EA)

NCCA .... National Council for Culture and Art (EA)

NCCA .... National Court Clubs Association [*Later, IRSA*] (EA)

NCCA .... Negligence and Compensation Cases, Annotated [*A publication*] (DLA)

NCCA .... Nordic Committee for Central Africa [*Defunct*] (EA)

NCCA 3d...... Negligence and Compensation Cases, Annotated, Third Series [*A publication*] (DLA)

NCCAA........ National Christian College Athletic Association (EA)

NCCAC........ National Catholic Conference of Airport Chaplains (EA)

NCCACS...... National Council of Columbia Associations in Civil Service (EA)

NCCAE........ National Conference of Catholic Art Educators (AEBS)

NCCAE........ National Council of County Association Executives (EA)

NCCAFV...... National Council on Child Abuse and Family Violence (EA)

NcCaLM....... United States Naval Medical Field Research Laboratory, Camp Lejeune, NC [*Library symbol Library of Congress*] (LCLS)

NcCaLMC.... United States Marine Corps, Marine Corps Base General Library, Camp Lejeune, NC [*Library symbol Library of Congress*] (LCLS)

NcCaLNM .... United States Navy, Naval Regional Medical Center, Library, Camp Lejeune, NC [*Library symbol Library of Congress*] (LCLS)

NCCAN........ National Center on Child Abuse and Neglect [*Department of Health and Human Services*] [*Washington, DC*]

NCCAN........ National Clearinghouse on Child Abuse and Neglect Information (PAZ)

NCCA NS ..... Negligence and Compensation Cases, Annotated, New Series [*A publication*] (DLA)

NcCar........... Moore County Library, Carthage, NC [*Library symbol Library of Congress*] (LCLS)

NCCAS .... National Center of Communication Arts and Sciences (EA)

NCCAS .... National Council for Clean Air and Streams

NCCAT .... National Committee for Clear Air Turbulence (KSC)

NCCB .... National Carpenters Craft Board [*Defunct*] (EA)

NCCB .... National Citizens Committee for Broadcasting (EA)

NCCB .... National Conference of Catholic Bishops (EA)

NCCB .... National Consumer Cooperative Bank

NCCB .... National Council to Combat Blindness [*Also known as Fight for Sight - FS*] (EA)

NCCBA .... National Caucus and Center on Black Aged (EA)

NCCBI .... National Coordinating Committee of the Beverage Industry

NCCBMI ...... National Consortium for Computer Based Music Instruction [*University of Delaware*] [*Research clearinghouse*] (EA)

NCCBN .... National Council of Churches Broadcasting Network (NTCM)

NCCC .... National Cambodia Crisis Committee [*Defunct*] (EA)

NCCC .... National Cancer Cytology Center [*Later, NCC*] (EA)

NCCC .... National Catholic Cemetery Conference (EA)

NCCC .... National Civilian Community Corps

NCCC .... National Conference of Catholic Charities (EA)

NCCC .... National Conservative Congressional Committee (EA)

NCCC .... National Consumer Credit Consultants

NCCC .... National Council of Churches of Christ in the USA [*Later, NCC*] (EA)

NCCC .... National Council of Community Churches [*Later, ICCC*] (EA)

NCCC .... National Council of Corvette Clubs (EA)

NCCC .... Norris Cotton Cancer Center [*Dartmouth-Hitchcock Medical Center*] [*Research center*] (RCD)

NCCCC .... National Coalition for Campus Child Care (EA)

NCCCC .... Naval Command, Control Communications Center (IAA)

NCCCCA ...... National Collegiate Cross Country Coaches Association [*Later, USCCCA*] (EA)

NCCCD .... National Center Confraternity of Christian Doctrine (EA)

NCCCD .... National Center for Computer Crime Data (EA)

NcCCed........ Cedalion Systems, Inc., Information Resources, Charlotte, NC [*Library symbol*] [*Library of Congress*] (LCLS)

NcCCel......... Celanese Fibers Co., Technical Information Center, Charlotte, NC [*Library symbol Library of Congress*] (LCLS)

NCCCHE ...... National Certification Commission in Chemistry and Chemical Engineering (IAA)

NCCCLC ...... Naval Command Control Communications Laboratory Center

NcCCP .... Central Piedmont Community College, Charlotte, NC [*Library symbol Library of Congress*] (LCLS)

NCCCP .... National Center for Community Crime Prevention (EA)

NCCCR .... National Citizens Committee for Community Relations [*Defunct*]

NCCCWA...... National Cotton Compress and Cotton Warehouse Association [*Later, CWAA*] (EA)

NcCD .... Duke Power Co., Information Systems Library, Charlotte, NC [*Library symbol*] [*Library of Congress*] (LCLS)

NCCD .... National Center for Chronic Disease Control [*Public Health Service*]

NCCD .... National College for Criminal Defense (EA)

NCCD .... National Council for Community Development (EA)

NCCD .... National Council for Criminal Defense (EA)

NCCD .... National Council on Crime and Delinquency (EA)

NCCDC .... National Center for Chronic Disease Control (DAVI)

NcCDD .... Duke Power Co., David Nabow Library, Charlotte, NC [*Library symbol*] [*Library of Congress*] (LCLS)

NCCDE .... National Coordinating Council on Drug Education [*Formerly, NCC*]

NCCDL .... National College of Criminal Defense Lawyers and Public Defenders (DLA)

NCCDN........ National Consortium of Chemical Dependency Nurses (EA)

NCCDPC...... NATO Command, Control, and Information Systems and Automatic Data Processing Committee (NATG)

NCCD-R & I... National Council on Crime and Delinquency, Research and Information Division [*Research center*] (RCD)

NCCDS........ National Cooperative Crohn's Disease Study

NCCDS........ Network Control Center Data System (SSD)

NCCE .... National Center for Community Education (EA)

NCCE .... National Coalition for Consumer Education (EA)

NCCE .... National Commission for Cooperative Education (EA)

NCCE .... National Committee for Citizens in Education (EA)

NCCE .... Nordic Committee for Commercial Education [*See also NKH*] [*Odense, Denmark*] (EAIO)

NCCEA .... Neurosensory Center Comprehensive Examination for Aphasia (DAVI)

NCCED .... National Congress for Community Economic Development (EA)

NCCEM .... National Coordinating Council on Emergency Management (EA)

NCCEM .... National Council of Catholic Employers and Managers (EA)

NCCEWV...... National Coordinating Committee to End the War in Vietnam [*Defunct*]

NCCF .... National Cancer Care Foundation (EA)

NCCF .... National Commission on Consumer Finance [*Terminated*]

NCCF .... National Council on Community Foundations [*Later, CF*] (EA)

NCCF .... Network Communications Control Facility [*IBM program product*]

NCCFL .... National Catholic Conference on Family Life (EA)

NCCG .... National Council on Compulsive Gambling [*Later, NAPG*] (EA)

NCCG .... Navy Central Clearance Group (DNAB)

NCCGDP ...... National Council of Chairmen of Graduate Departments of Psychology

NcCGS .... Church of Jesus Christ of Latter-Day Saints, Genealogical Society Library, Charlotte North Carolina Branch, Charlotte, NC [*Library symbol Library of Congress*] (LCLS)

NcCh........... Chapel Hill Public Library, Chapel Hill, NC [*Library symbol Library of Congress*] (LCLS)

NCCH .... National Council of Community Hospitals (EA)

NCCH .... National Council to Control Handguns [*Later, HCI*] (EA)

NCCH .... Nurses' Central Clearing House (AIE)

NCCHB .... National Committee on Concerns of Hispanics and Blacks [*Defunct*] (EA)

NCCHC .... National Commission on Correctional Health Care (EA)

NCCHE .... National Chicano Council for Higher Education [*Defunct*] (EA)

NCCHI .... National Cap and Cloth Hat Institute (EA)

NcCHM .... Helms, Mullis & Johnston Law Library, Charlotte, NC [*Library symbol*] [*Library of Congress*] (LCLS)

NCCHR .... National Commission on Confidentiality of Health Records [*Defunct*] (EA)

NCCHS........ National Commission on Community Public Health Services

NcCI .... IBM Corp., Library/15C, Charlotte, NC [*Library symbol Library of Congress*] (LCLS)

NCCI .... Nashville Country Club [*NASDAQ symbol*] (SAG)

NCCI .... National Commission on Coping with Interdependence (EA)

NCCI .... National Council on Compensation Insurance [*New York, NY*] (EA)

NCCI .... North Central Computer Institute [*Research center*] (RCD)

NCC/IBL ...... Nederlandse Centrale Catalogus/Interbibliothecair Leenverkeer System [*Netherlands Central Catalogue/Interlibrary Loan System*] [*Consortium of the Royal Library and University Libraries*] [*Information service or system*] (IID)

NCCIJ.......... National Catholic Conference for Interracial Justice (EA)

NCCIP.......... National Center for Clinical Infant Programs (EA)

NCCIP.......... Nordic Cooperation Committee for International Politics, Including Conflict and Peace Research (EA)

NCCIR......... National Catholic Commission for Industrial Relations [*Australia*]

NCCIS .... NATO Command, Control, and Information System (NATG)

NCCIW .... Nashville Country Club Wrrt [*NASDAQ symbol*] (TTSB)

NcCJ .... Johnson C. Smith University, Charlotte, NC [*Library symbol Library of Congress*] (LCLS)

NCCJ........... National Conference of Christians and Jews (EA)

NCCJP & A... National Clearinghouse for Criminal Justice Planning and Architecture [*Defunct*] (EA)

NCCK .... Noncoherent Carrier Keying (IAA)

NCCL .... National Citizen Communication Lobby (EA)

NCCL .... National Council for Civil Liberties [*British*]

NCCL .... National Council of Canadian Labour

NCCL .... National Council of Catholic Laity [*Defunct*] (EA)

NCCL .... National Council of Coal Lessors (EA)

NcCla........... Hocutt-Ellington Memorial Library, Clayton, NC [*Library symbol Library of Congress*] (LCLS)

NCC-LAW..... North Carolina Center for Laws Affecting Women, Inc. [*Research center*] (RCD)

NcCIH .... Haywood Technical Institute, Clyde, NC [*Library symbol Library of Congress*] (LCLS)

NcCli .... Sampson-Clinton Public Library, Clinton, NC [*Library symbol Library of Congress*] (LCLS)

NcCliS .... Sampson Technical Institute, Clinton, NC [*Library symbol Library of Congress*] (LCLS)

NCCLS .... National Committee for Clinical Laboratory Standards (EA)

NCCLS .... National Consumer Center for Legal Services [*Later, NRCCLS*] (EA)

NCCLVP....... National Coordinating Committee on Large Volume Parenterals (BABM)

NCCLVP....... National Coordinating Committee on Large Volume Parenterals (DAVI)

NCCM .... Master Chief Navy Counselor [*Navy rating*] (DNAB)

NcCM .... Mecklenburg County Medical Society, Charlotte, NC [*Library symbol Library of Congress*] (LCLS)

NCCM .... National Council of Catholic Men (EA)

NCCMA .... National Corporate Cash Management Association (EA)

NCCMCU ..... National Committee to Commemorate the Millenium of Christianity in the Ukraine (EA)

NCCMGI ...... National Clearinghouse for Corporate Matching Gift Information (EA)

NCCMHC ..... National Council of Community Mental Health Centers (EA)

NCCMHS..... National Consortium for Child Mental Health Services (EA)

NCCMIRS..... Navy Civilian Career Management Inventory and Referral System (DNAB)

NcCML........ Medical Library of Mecklenburg County, Inc., Charlotte, NC [*Library symbol Library of Congress*] (LCLS)

NCCML .... National Committee for Careers in the Medical Laboratory [*Defunct*] (EA)

NCCMP .... National Coordinating Committee for Multiemployer Plans (EA)

NCCMP .... Navy Civilian Career Management Program (DNAB)

NCCMT .... National Committee for Careers in Medical Technology [*Later, NCCML*] (EA)

NCCN .... National Comprehensive Cancer Network [*Medical*]

NCCN .... National Council of Catholic Nurses [*Defunct*] (EA)

NCCN .... New Century Cyclopedia of Names [*A publication*]

NCCNA........ National Clearinghouse on Child Neglect and Abuse [*HEW*]

NCCNHR ...... National Citizens Coalition for Nursing Home Reform (EA)

NcCo .... Concord Public Library, Concord, NC [*Library symbol Library of Congress*] (LCLS)

NCCO .... Neodymium, Cerium, Copper, Oxide [*Inorganic chemistry*]

NcCoB .... Barber-Scotia College, Concord, NC [*Library symbol Library of Congress*] (LCLS)

NcCoC......... Cabarrus County Library, Concord, NC [*Library symbol*] [*Library of Congress*] (LCLS)

NcCoCH ...... Cabarrus County Health Department, Concord, NC [*Library symbol Library of Congress*] (LCLS)

NcCoi........... Currituck County Public Library, Coinjock, NC [*Library symbol Library of Congress*] (LCLS)

NcCol............ Polk County Public Library, Columbus, NC [*Library symbol Library of Congress*] (LCLS)

NcCola........... Tyrrell County Public Library, Columbia, NC [*Library symbol Library of Congress*] (LCLS)

NcConC........ Concordia College, Conover, NC [*Library symbol Library of Congress Obsolete*] (LCLS)

NC Conf........ North Carolina Conference Reports [*A publication*] (DLA)

NC Conf Rep... North Carolina Conference Reports [*A publication*] (DLA)

NCCOP.......... National Corporation for the Care of Old People [*British*] (BI)

NcCorD......... Duke Power Co., Information Resource Center, Cornelius, NC [*Library symbol Library of Congress*] (LCLS)

NCCOS.......... National Committee for Certificates in Office Studies [*British*]

NCCOSC........ Naval Command, Control, and Ocean Surveillance Center [*Formerly, NOSC and other activities*] (DOMA)

NCCP............ National Chinese Curriculum Project [*Australia*]

NCCP............ National Clearinghouse for Commuter Programs (EA)

NCCP............ National Coordinated Cataloging Program [*Library science*]

NCCP............ National Council on City Planning

NCCP............ NATO Commanders Communications Publication (NATG)

NCCP............ Navigation Control Console Panel

NCCP............ Northern California Cancer Program [*Research center*] (RCD)

NCCPA.......... National Cinder Concrete Products Association (EA)

NCCPA.......... National Commission on Certification of Physician's Assistants (EA)

NCCPA.......... National Council of College Publications Advisers (EA)

NCCPAP........ National Conference of CPA [*Certified Public Accountant*] Practitioners [*New York, NY*] (EA)

NCCPB.......... National Council of Commercial Plant Breeders (EA)

NCCPC.......... NATO Civil Communications Planning Committee (NATG)

NCCPG.......... National Council for the Conservation of Plants and Gardens (PDAA)

NCCPL.......... National Community Crime Prevention League (EA)

NcCpM.......... United States Marine Corps, Air Station, Cherry Point, NC [*Library symbol Library of Congress*] (LCLS)

NCCPS.......... National Citizens Commission for the Public Schools (AEBS)

NCCPT.......... National Congress of Colored Parents and Teachers (AEBS)

NCCPV.......... National Commission on the Causes and Prevention of Violence (EA)

NcCQ............ Queens College, Charlotte, NC [*Library symbol Library of Congress*] (LCLS)

nccr--........... Costa Rica [*MARC geographic area code Library of Congress*] (LCCP)

NCCR............ National Coalition for Cancer Research (EA)

NCCR............ National Committee for Cultural Resources

NCCR............ National Council for Children's Rights (EA)

NCCR............ National Council for Community Relations [*Later, NCMPR*] (EA)

NCCR............ Network Control Center Representative (SSD)

NCCR............ New Construction/Conversion Requirements System [*Navy*]

NCCRE.......... National Consumers Committee for Research and Education [*Later, NCL*] (EA)

NCCRI.......... National Catholic Coalition for Responsible Investment (EA)

NcCS............ Charlotte-Mecklenburg Schools, Staff Development Center, Charlotte, NC [*Library symbol Library of Congress*] (LCLS)

NCCS............ National Carriers Contract Services [*National Freight Consortium*] [*British*]

NCCS............ National Catholic Committee on Scouting (EA)

NCCS............ National Catholic Community Service [*Defunct*] (EA)

NCCS............ National Catholic Conference for Seafarers (EA)

NCCS............ National Center for Charitable Statistics (EA)

NCCS............ National Center for Constitutional Studies (EA)

NCCS............ National Christ Child Society (EA)

NCCS............ National Climbing Classification System

NCCS............ National Coalition for Cancer Survivorship (EA)

NCCS............ National Command and Control System

NCCS............ National Council for Community Services to International Visitors [*Later, NCIV*]

NCCS............ Navy Camera Control System

NCCS............ Navy Command and Control System (NVT)

NCCS............ Navy Command and Control System (DOMA)

NCCS............ Nordic Church Council for Seamen [*Denmark*] (EAIO)

NCCS............ Nordic Council for Church Studies (EA)

NCCSA.......... National Council for the Church and Social Action (EA)

NCCSA.......... Nature Conservation Council of South Australia

NCCSC.......... National Coordinating Center in Solidarity with Chile [*Later, NCC*] (EA)

NcCSC.......... Sandoz Chemical, Charlotte, NC [*Library symbol*] [*Library of Congress*] (LCLS)

NCCSCE........ National Council on Community Services and Continuing Education (EA)

NcCSH.......... Sun-Health, Inc., Charlotte, NC [*Library symbol*] [*Library of Congress*] (LCLS)

NcCSI........... SIM International Resource Center, Charlotte, NC [*Library symbol*] [*Library of Congress*] (LCLS)

NCCSL.......... National Center for Cross-Cultural Studies in Law [*Monash University*] [*Australia*]

NCCSS.......... North Central Conference on Summer Schools (EA)

NCCT............ National Council for Civic Theatres Ltd. [*British*] (BI)

NCCTA.......... National Council of Chemical Technician Affiliates

NCCTS.......... National Catholic Conference for Total Stewardship (EA)

NCCU............ National Conference of Canadian Universities

NCCU............ Newborn Convalescent Care Unit [*Medicine*]

NCCU............ North Carolina Central University [*Durham*]

NcCU............ University of North Carolina at Charlotte, Charlotte, NC [*Library symbol Library of Congress*] (LCLS)

NCC/USA...... National Council of Churches of Christ in the USA (NTCM)

NCCUSL........ National Commission for Creation of Uniform State Laws

NCCUSL........ National Conference of Commissioners on Uniform State Laws (EA)

NcCuW.......... Western Carolina University, Cullowhee, NC [*Library symbol Library of Congress*] (LCLS)

NCCV............ National Center for Church Vocations [*Later, NCVC*] (EA)

NCCV............ New Construction and Conversion [*Navy*]

NCCW............ National Chamber of Commerce for Women [*New York, NY*] (EA)

NCCW............ National Council of Career Women (EA)

NCCW............ National Council of Catholic Women (EA)

NCCWAO...... National Council of Community World Affairs Organizations (EA)

NCCWHO ..... National Citizens Committee for the World Health Organization [*Later, AAWH*] (EA)

NCCY............ National Committee for Children and Youth [*Later, NCOCY*] (EA)

NCCY............ National Council of Catholic Youth [*Defunct*] (EA)

NcCyL.......... Lord Corp. Research and Development Library, Cary, NC [*Library symbol*] [*Library of Congress*] (LCLS)

NcCyS.......... SAS Institute, Inc., Cary, NC [*Library symbol*] [*Library of Congress*] (LCLS)

NCCYSA........ National Conference of Catholics in Youth Serving Agencies [*Defunct*] (EA)

nccz--.......... Canal Zone [*MARC geographic area code Library of Congress*] (LCCP)

NcD.............. Duke University, Durham, NC [*Library symbol Library of Congress*] (LCLS)

NCD.............. National Center for the Diaconate [*Later, NAAND*] (EA)

NCD.............. National Commission for Democracy [*Ghana*] [*Political party*]

NCD.............. National Commission on Diabetes

NCD.............. National Control Data

NCD.............. National Council on Drugs [*Defunct*] (EA)

NCD.............. Navy Cargo Document (DNAB)

NCD.............. Navy Contracting Directives (MCD)

NCD.............. Negotiable Certificate of Deposit (ADA)

NCD.............. Negotiated Critical Dates [*Telecommunications*] (TEL)

NCD.............. Nemine Contradicente [*No One Contradicting*] [*Latin Legal term*] (DLA)

NCD.............. Network Cryptographic Device

NCD.............. Neurocirculatory Dystonia [*Medicine*] (DMAA)

NCD.............. New Component Design (IAA)

NCD.............. Nicotinamide Cytosine Dinucleotide [*Biochemistry*]

NCD.............. No Can Do [*From pidgin English*]

NCD.............. No Claim Discount [*Insurance*] (AIA)

NCD.............. Noncallable Deposit [*Investment term*]

NCD.............. Non-Communicable Disease

NCD.............. Non-Cumulative Dividend [*Business term*] (MHDW)

NCD.............. Nonlinear Control Design [*Computer science*]

NCD.............. Nordic Committee on Disability (EAIO)

NCD.............. Nordic Council for the Deaf [*See also DNR*] (EAIO)

NCD.............. Normal Childhood Diseases (DAVI)

NCD.............. Normal Childhood Disorders [*Medicine*]

NCD.............. Normalized Cumulative Deviation

NCD.............. North Central Dairy Forwarders Tariff Bureau, Minneapolis MN [*STAC*]

NCD.............. North Central Division [*Army Engineers*]

NCD.............. Norton Change Directory [*Computer science*]

NCD.............. Not Considered Disabling [*Medicine*] (MAE)

NCD.............. Not Considered Disqualifying

NCD.............. Notice of Credit Due

NCD.............. Nova Scotia College of Art and Design Library [*UTLAS symbol*]

NCD.............. Nuclear Commission Date (DNAB)

NCD.............. Numerically Controlled Drafting (MCD)

NCDA............ National Career Development Association (EA)

NCDA............ National Center for Drug Analysis [*St. Louis*] [*FDA*]

NCDA............ National Ceramic Dealers Association (EA)

NCDA............ National College of District Attorneys (EA)

NCDA............ National Community Development Association (EA)

NCDA............ National Council on Drug Abuse [*Defunct*] (EA)

NCDAC.......... National Civil Defense Advisory Council (EA)

NcDaD.......... Davidson College, Davidson, NC [*Library symbol Library of Congress*] (LCLS)

NCDAD.......... National Council for Diplomats in Art and Design [*British*] (BI)

NCDAI.......... National Clearinghouse for Drug Abuse Information [*Public Health Service*] [*Rockville, MD*]

NcDalG......... Gaston College, Dallas, NC [*Library symbol Library of Congress*] (LCLS)

NcDan........... Stokes County Public Library, Danbury, NC [*Library symbol Library of Congress*] (LCLS)

NCDAPA........ National Curtain, Drapery, and Allied Products Association [*Later, HFPA*]

NcD-B........... Duke University, Fuqua School of Business, Durham, NC [*Library symbol Library of Congress*] (LCLS)

NCDB............ National Center for Drugs and Biologics [*FDA*]

NCDB............ National Commercial and Development Bank [*Dominica*]

NCDBC.......... National Center for the Development of Bilingual Curriculum (EA)

NCDC............ National Catholic Development Conference (EA)

NCDC............ National Center for Disease Control [*Public Health Service*]

NCDC............ National Centers for Disease Control (NADA)

NCDC............ National Climatic Data Center [*National Oceanic and Atmospheric Administration Information service or system*] (IID)

NCDC............ National Coalition for a Democratic Constitution [*Political group*] [*South Korea*]

NCDC............ National Committee for the Day Care of Children [*Later, DCCA*]

NCDC............ National Communicable Disease Center (MCD)

NCDC............ National Criminal Defense College (EA)

NCDC............ Naval Contract Distribution Center

NCDC............ New Community Development Corp. [*HUD*]

NCDC............ Nitro(carboxyphenyl)diphenylcarbamate [*Biochemistry*]

NCDC............ Norchenodeoxycholic Acid [*Biochemistry*]

NCDCA......... National Child Day Care Association (EA)

NCDCF......... National Civil Defense Computer Facility

NCDCV......... Neonatal Calf Diarrhea Coronavirus

NcD-D.......... Duke University, Divinity School, Durham, NC [*Library symbol Library of Congress*] (LCLS)

NCDD........... No Change in the Due Date (AFM)

NCDDRE-CCD... National Conference of Diocesan Directors of Religious Education - CCD [*Continuing Christian Development*] (EA)

NcDe............ Denton Public Library, Denton, NC [*Library symbol Library of Congress*] (LCLS)

NCDE.......... National Coalition for Democracy in Education [*Defunct*] (EA)

NCDF.......... National Computer Dealer Forum (EA)

NCDH.......... National Committee Against Discrimination in Housing (EA)

NCDHM......... National Children's Dental Health Month [*American Dental Association*]

NCDI........... Network Computing Devices, Inc. [*NASDAQ symbol*] (SAG)

NCDIE.......... Network Computing Devices [*NASDAQ symbol*] (TTSB)

NcD-L.......... Duke University, School of Law, Durham, NC [*Library symbol Library of Congress*] (LCLS)

NCDL.......... National Canine Defence League [*British*] (DI)

NCDM.......... Numerically Controlled Drafting Machine (MCD)

NcD-MC....... Duke University, Medical Center, Durham, NC [*Library symbol Library of Congress*] (LCLS)

NCDO.......... Navy Central Disbursing Office

NcDo........... Surry County-Dobson Library, Dobson, NC [*Library symbol Library of Congress*] (LCLS)

NcDoS........ Surry Community College, Dobson, NC [*Library symbol Library of Congress*] (LCLS)

NCDP.......... Namibie Christelike Demokratiese Party [*Namibian Christian Democratic Party*] [*Political party*] (PPW)

NCDP.......... Navigation Control/Display Panel (MCD)

NCDPEH....... National Coalition for Disease Prevention and Environmental Health

NCDRC......... National Catholic Disaster Relief Committee (EA)

NCDS.......... National Center for Dispute Settlement [*American Arbitration Association*] [*Later, CDS*]

NCDS.......... National Child Development Study [*British*]

NCDS.......... National Council for the Divorced and Separated [*British*] (DBA)

NCDS.......... Naval Combat Data System

NCDS.......... Navy Combat Direction System (MCD)

NCDS.......... Numerical Control Distribution System [*Computer science*] (MHDI)

NCDT.......... National Council for Drama Training [*British*]

NCDT.......... Noble-Collip Drum Trauma [*Physiology*]

NCDT.......... Non-Chargeable Downtime

NCDT.......... North Carolina Dance Theater

NCDT & E..... Naval Combat Demolition Training and Experimental Base [*Maui, HI*] (KSC)

NCDT & EBASE... Naval Combat Demolition Training and Experimental Base [*Maui, HI*]

NCDTO......... National Council of Dance Teacher Organizations [*Later, NDCA*] (EA)

NcDu........... Dunn Public Library, Dunn, NC [*Library symbol Library of Congress*] (LCLS)

NCDU.......... Naval Combat Demolition Unit

NCDU.......... Navigation Control and Display Unit

NcDubB........ Bladen Technical College, Dublin, NC [*Library symbol Library of Congress*] (LCLS)

NcDur.......... Durham City-County Public Library, Durham, NC [*Library symbol Library of Congress*] (LCLS)

NcDurBC....... Blue Cross & Blue Shield of North Carolina, Durham, NC [*Library symbol Library of Congress*] (LCLS)

NcDurBD...... Becton, Dickinson & Co., Research Center Library, Research Triangle Park, Durham, NC [*Library symbol Library of Congress*] (LCLS)

NcDurC........ North Carolina Central University, Durham, NC [*Library symbol Library of Congress*] (LCLS)

NcDurCG....... Ciba-Geigy Corp., Biotechnology Library, Durham, NC [*Library symbol*] [*Library of Congress*] (LCLS)

NcDurCL...... North Carolina Central University, School of Library Science, Durham, NC [*Library symbol Library of Congress*] (LCLS)

NcDurCR...... Chemstrand Research Center, Inc., Durham, NC [*Library symbol Library of Congress*] (LCLS)

NcDurEP...... United States Environmental Protection Agency, Office of Administration, LibraryServices Branch, Park, Durham, NC [*Library symbol Library of Congress*] (LCLS)

NcDurF........ Forest History Society, Inc., Durham, NC [*Library symbol*] [*Library of Congress*] (LCLS)

NcDurG........ Glaxo, Inc., Durham, NC [*Library symbol*] [*Library of Congress*] (LCLS)

NcDurGH...... Durham County General Hospital, Medical Library, Durham, NC [*Library symbol Library of Congress*] (LCLS)

NcDurHS...... United States National Environmental Health Sciences Center, Durham, NC [*Library symbol Library of Congress*] (LCLS)

NcDurIBM.... International Business Machines Corp., IBM CPD Library, Durham, NC [*Library symbol Library of Congress*] (LCLS)

NcDurIF....... International Fertility Research Program, Durham, NC [*Library symbol Library of Congress*] (LCLS)

NcDurIT....... Chemical Industry institute of Toxicology, Durham, NC [*Library symbol*] [*Library of Congress*] (LCLS)

NcDurL........ Liggett & Myers, Inc. [*Later, Liggett Group, Inc.*], Durham, NC [*Library symbol Library of Congress*] (LCLS)

NcDurM....... Monsanto Triangle Park Development Center, Durham, NC [*Library symbol Library of Congress*] (LCLS)

NcDurMi...... Microelectronics Center Library, Durham, NC [*Library symbol*] [*Library of Congress*] (LCLS)

NcDurNH...... National Humanities Center, Durham, NC [*Library symbol Library of Congress*] (LCLS)

NcDurRa...... Radian Corp. Library, Durham, NC [*Library symbol*] [*Library of Congress*] (LCLS)

NcDurRT...... Research Triangle Institute, Technical Library, Durham, NC [*Library symbol Library of Congress*] (LCLS)

NcDurSci..... North Carolina School of Science and Mathematics, Durham, NC [*Library symbol Library of Congress*] (LCLS)

NcDurST...... North Carolina Science and Technology Research Center, Durham, NC [*Library symbol Library of Congress*] (LCLS)

NcDurT........ Durham Technical Institute, Durham, NC [*Library symbol Library of Congress*] (LCLS)

NcDurUC...... Union Carbide Agricultural Products Co., Inc., Research Triangle Park, Durham, NC [*Library symbol Library of Congress*] (LCLS)

NcDurV........ United States Veterans Administration Hospital, Durham, NC [*Library symbol Library of Congress*] (LCLS)

NcDurW....... Wellcome Research Laboratories, Durham, NC [*Library symbol Library of Congress*] (LCLS)

NcDurW-Gv... Burroughs Wellcome & Co., Greenville, NC [*Library symbol Library of Congress*] (LCLS)

NCDV.......... Nebraska Calf Diarrhea Virus

NCDVD......... National Conference of Diocesan Vocation Directors (EA)

NcD-W......... Duke University, Woman's College, Durham, NC [*Library symbol Library of Congress*] (LCLS)

NcE............ Bladen County Public Library, Elizabethtown, NC [*Library symbol Library of Congress*] (LCLS)

NCe............ Middle Country Public Library, Centereach, NY [*Library symbol Library of Congress*] (LCLS)

NCE............ Nasa Cotopaxi [*Ecuador*] [*Seismograph station code, US Geological Survey*] (SEIS)

NCE............ National College of Education [*Illinois*]

NCE............ National Commission for Education (AIE)

NCE............ National Committee on the Emeriti (EA)

NCE............ National Council of Exchangors (EA)

NCE............ Navy Calibration Equipment List

NCE............ Navy Civil Engineer [*A publication*]

NCE............ Network Connection Element

NCE............ Network Control Elements (MCD)

NCE............ Network Control Engine [*Synoptics Communications, Inc.*]

NCE............ Neuritis of the Cauda Equina [*Medicine*]

NCE............ Newark College of Engineering [*New Jersey*]

NCE............ New Catholic Edition [*Bible*]

NCE............ New Catholic Encyclopedia [*A publication*]

NCE............ New Chemical Entity

NCE............ Nice [*France*] [*Airport symbol*] (OAG)

NCE............ No Change in Estimates

NCE............ Nomadic Computing Environment

NCE............ Noncommercial Education [*FCC*] (NTCM)

NCE............ Nonconvulsive Epilepsy [*Medicine*]

NCE............ Normal Calomel Electrode [*Electrochemistry*]

NCE............ Normal Chick Embryo

NCE............ Normal Curve Equivalent [*Testing*] (EDAC)

NCE............ Northcoast Executive Airlines [*ICAO designator*] (FAAC)

NCE............ NTID [*National Technical Institute for the Deaf*] Center on Employment (PAZ)

NCE............ Nuclear Capability Evaluation

NCE............ Nuclear Capability Exercise [*Army*] (AABC)

NCE............ Nuclear/Chemical Environment [*Battlefield condition*] (RDA)

NCEA.......... National Catholic Educational Association (EA)

NCEA.......... National Center for Economic Alternatives (EA)

NCEA.......... National Christian Education Association (EA)

NCEA.......... National College Education and Admissions Foundation (EA)

NCEA.......... National Community Education Association (EA)

NCEA.......... National Consortium for Education Access (EA)

NCEA.......... National Council for Educational Awards [*Ireland*]

NCEA.......... N-(Carboxyethyl)alanine [*Biochemistry*]

NcEB........... Bladen Technical Institute, Elizabethtown, NC [*Library symbol Library of Congress*] (LCLS)

NcEb........... East Bend Public Library, East Bend, NC [*Library symbol*] [*Library of Congress*] (LCLS)

NCEB.......... National Center for Educational Brokering [*Defunct*] (EA)

NCEB.......... National Council for Environmental Balance (EA)

NCEB.......... NATO Communications Electronics Board

NCEB.......... North Coast Energy [*NASDAQ symbol*] (TTSB)

NCEB.......... North Coast Energy [*NASDAQ symbol*] (SAG)

NCEBP......... North Coast Energy Cv'B'Pfd [*NASDAQ symbol*] (TTSB)

NCEBVS........ National Chronic Epstein-Barr Virus Syndrome Association (EA)

NCEBW........ North Coast Energy Wrrt [*NASDAQ symbol*] (TTSB)

NCEC.......... National Center for Educational Communication [*Office of Education*]

NCEC.......... National Chemical Emergency Centre [*Atomic Energy Authority*] [*Didcot, Oxon., England*]

NCEC.......... National Christian Education Council [*Church of England*]

NCEC.......... National Commission for Electrologist Certification (EA)

NCEC.......... National Committee for an Effective Congress (EA)

NCEC.......... National Construction Employers Council [*Defunct*] (EA)

NCEC.......... North Coast Export Co. [*An association Defunct*] (EA)

NCECA........ National Council on Education for the Ceramic Arts (EA)

NC Ecc........ Notes of Cases, English Ecclesiastical and Maritime Courts [*1841-50*] [*A publication*] (DLA)

NCECD........ National Commission for Economic Conversion and Disarmament (EA)

NCECE......... National Council of Elected County Executives (EA)

NCECF......... National Children's Eye Care Foundation (EA)

NCECG......... National Coalition to Expand Charitable Giving [*Defunct*] (EA)

NCECS......... North Carolina Educational Computing Services (NITA)

NcEd .... Eden Public Library, Eden, NC [Library symbol] [Library of Congress] (LCLS)
NCED .... National Center on Employment of the Deaf (EA)
NCEDC .... Northern California Earthquake Data Center
NCedHS .... Lawrence High School, Cedarhurst, NY [Library symbol] [Library of Congress] (LCLS)
NCEDL .... National Committee for Effective Design Legislation (EA)
NcEdR .... Rockingham County Public Library, Eden, NC [Library symbol] [Library of Congress] (LCLS)
NcEdR-M ..... Mayodan Public Library, Mayodan, NC [Library symbol] [Library of Congress] (LCLS)
NcEdR-R ...... Rockingham County Public Library, Reidsville Branch Library, Reidsville, NC [Library symbol Library of Congress] (LCLS)
NcEdR-S ...... Stoneville Public Library, Stoneville, NC [Library symbol] [Library of Congress] (LCLS)
NcEdt .... Shepard-Pruden Memorial Library, Edenton, NC [Library symbol Library of Congress] (LCLS)
NCEE.......... National Catholic Educational Exhibitors (EA)
NCEE.......... National Center on Education and Employment [New York, NY Department of Education] (GRD)
NCEE.......... National Congress for Educational Excellence (EA)
NCEE.......... National Council of Engineering Examiners (EA)
NCEEC .... Nested Cone Extendable Exit Cone (MCD)
NCEEF .... National Committee for Electrical Engineering Films
NCEER .... National Center for Earthquake Engineering Research [Buffalo, NY] (GRD)
NCEF.......... National Calling and Emergency Frequencies (CET)
NCEF.......... National Commission on Electronic Funds Transfers (MHDW)
NCEF.......... Nomads' Charitable and Educational Foundation [Australia]
NCEF.......... Non-Circumcision Educational Foundation (EA)
NCEFF .... National Committee for Education in Family Finance (EA)
NCEFR .... National Council of Erectors, Fabricators, and Riggers (EA)
NCEFT .... National Commission on Electronic Fund Transfers
NCEHAI .... National Committee on Ethics of the Hearing Aid Industry [Defunct] (EA)
NCEHELP .... National Conference of Executives of Higher Education Loan Plans [Later, NCHELP] (EA)
NCEHP .... National Center for the Exploration of Human Potential (EA)
NCEHPHP .... National Council on the Education of Health Professionals in Health Promotion (DAVI)
NCEHS .... National Center for Environmental Health Strategies (EA)
NcEl .... Kemp Memorial Library, Ellerbe, NC [Library symbol Library of Congress] (LCLS)
NCEL .... Naval Civil Engineering Laboratory
NCEL .... Navy Contractor Experience List
NCEL .... Nuclear Certified Equipment List (DNAB)
NcElc .... East Albemarle Regional Library, Elizabeth City, NC [Library symbol Library of Congress] (LCLS)
NcElcA .... College of the Albemarle, Elizabeth City, NC [Library symbol Library of Congress] (LCLS)
NcElcE .... Elizabeth City State University, Elizabeth City, NC [Library symbol Library of Congress] (LCLS)
NcElcP .... Pasquotank-Camden Library, Elizabeth City, NC [Library symbol Library of Congress] (LCLS)
NcElcR .... Roanoke Bible College, Mary E. Griffith Memorial Library, Elizabeth City, NC [Library symbol Library of Congress] (LCLS)
NcElk .... Elkin Public Library, Elkin, NC [Library symbol Library of Congress] (LCLS)
NcElon .... Elon College, Elon College, NC [Library symbol Library of Congress] (LCLS)
NcElonCH .... Historical Society of the Southern Convention, Congregation of Christian Churches, Elon College, NC [Library symbol Library of Congress] (LCLS)
NcElonP ...... Primitive Baptist Library, Elon College, NC [Library symbol Library of Congress] (LCLS)
NCEM.......... National Center for Electron Microscopy [Berkeley, CA] [Lawrence Berkeley Laboratory] [Department of Energy]
NCEMC .... National Committee on the Education of Migrant Children [of the National Child Labor Committee] (EA)
NCEMCH ...... National Center for Education in Maternal and Child Health (EA)
NCEMMH .... National Center, Educational Media and Materials for the Handicapped [Defunct] (EA)
NCEMP .... National Center for Energy Management and Power
NCEMT .... National Center for Excellence in Metalworking Technology [Navy]
NcEn .... Lilly Pike Sullivan Municipal Library, Enfield, NC [Library symbol Library of Congress] (LCLS)
NCEN .... National Commission on Egg Nutrition
NCEN .... North Central
NcEnk .... American Enka Corp., Enka, NC [Library symbol Library of Congress] (LCLS)
NCentBsh..... North Central Bancshares, Inc. [Associated Press] (SAG)
N Cent School L Rev... North Central School Law Review [A publication] (DLA)
NCEO .... National Center for Employee Ownership (EA)
NCEO .... National Center for Exploitation of the Oceans
NCEOA .... National Council of Educational Opportunity Associations (EA)
NCEP .... National Center for Education in Politics [Defunct] (EA)
NCEP .... National Centers for Environmental Prediction [Marine science] (OSRA)
NCEP .... National Cholesterol Education Program Coordinating Committee [National Institutes of Health] (EGAO)
NCEP .... National Council for the Encouragement of Patriotism (EA)
NCEP .... National Council on Employment Policy (EA)
NcEr.......... Erwin Public Library, Erwin, NC [Library symbol Library of Congress] (LCLS)
NCER .... National Center for Earthquake Research [US Geological Survey]

NCER .... National Conference on Electromagnetic Relays
NCER .... National Council on Educational Research [Later, NCERI] [Department of Education Washington, DC]
NCERACCS... National Coalition to End Racism in America's Child Care System (EA)
NCERD .... National Center for Educational Research and Development [HEW]
NCERT .... National Council for Educational Research and Training (WDAA)
nces-- .... El Salvador [MARC geographic area code Library of Congress] (LCCP)
NCES .... National Center for Education Statistics [Office of Education] [Later, CES]
NCES .... National Council for Educational Standards (AIE)
NCES .... New Careers in Employment Security (OICC)
NCES .... Normal Curve Equivalent Scores [Testing] (EDAC)
NCES .... North Central Experiment Station [University of Minnesota] [Research center] (RCD)
NCES .... North Country Educational Services [Library network]
NCESA .... National Class E Scow Association (EA)
NCESGR....... National Committee for Employer Support of the Guard and Reserve (EA)
NCESGR....... National Committee for Employer Support of the Guard and Reserve
NCET.......... National Center for Educational Technology [Office of Education]
NCET.......... National Coastal Ecosystems Team [Office of Biological Services, United States Fish and Wildlife Service] (MSC)
NCET.......... National Conference of English Teachers (BARN)
NCET.......... National Council for Educational Technology [British]
NCETA .... National Center for Education and Training in Addictions [Australia]
NCEUS .... National Commission on Employment and Unemployment Statistics [Bureau of Labor Statistics] (GFGA)
NCEW .... National Conference of Editorial Writers (EA)
NCEY .... National Committee on Employment of Youth [National Child Labor Committee] (EA)
NCEZ.......... National Coalition for Enterprise Zones [San Diego, CA] (EA)
NCF........... Narramore Christian Foundation (EA)
NCF........... National Cancer Foundation
NCF........... National Chamber Foundation (EA)
NCF........... National Civics Federation
NCF........... National Clayware Federation [British] (DBA)
NCF........... National Commission on a Free and Responsible Media (EA)
NCF........... National Communications Forum [National Engineering Consortium, Inc.] [Chicago, IL] [Telecommunications] (TSSD)
NCF........... National Conservative Foundation (EA)
NCF........... National Consumer Federation (NADA)
NCF........... National Control Facility [FAA] (TAG)
NCF........... National Craniofacial Foundation [Later, ICF] (EA)
NCF........... National Cristina Foundation (EA)
NCF........... NATO Composite Force
NCF........... Naval Communications Facility (MUGU)
NCF........... Naval Construction Force (NVT)
NCF........... Nerve Cell Food
NCF........... Net Cash Flow
NCF........... NetWare Configuration File [Computer science]
NCF........... Neutrophil Chemotactic Factor [Hematology]
NCF........... Neutrophil Cytosol Factor [Cytology]
NCF........... Newton-Cotes Formula [Mathematics]
NCF........... No Clean Flux Process [Computer manufacturing] (PCM)
NCF........... No Conscription Fellowship [England, World War I]
NCF........... Nominal Characteristics File (IEEE)
NCF........... Noncold Front [Meteorology]
NCF........... Nonflammable Cellulosic Foam
NCF........... Nuclear Capable Forces (MCD)
NCF........... Nucleonics Calibration Facility (RDA)
NCF........... Nugget Coombs Foundation for Indigenous Studies [Australia]
NCF........... Nurses Christian Fellowship (EA)
NCFA .... Narcolepsy and Cataplexy Foundation of America (EA)
NCFA .... National Cat Fanciers' Association [Defunct] (EA)
NCFA .... National Collection of Fine Arts [Later, National Museum of American Art]
NCFA .... National Collegiate Football Association (EA)
NCFA .... National Commercial Finance Association (EA)
NCFA .... National Commission of Fine Arts (NADA)
NCFA .... National Committee for Adoption (EA)
NCFA .... National Consumer Finance Association (EA)
NCFA .... National Council for Adoption [Formerly National Committee for Adoption] (PAZ)
NCFA .... Naval Campus for Achievement (NVT)
NCFA .... North Central Field Area
NCFA .... Nurses' Christian Fellowship of Australia
NCFAE .... National Council of Forestry Association Executives (EA)
NCFAP .... Naval Campus for Achievement Program (MCD)
NcFayC .... Cumberland County Public Library, Fayetteville, NC [Library symbol Library of Congress] (LCLS)
NcFayC-F .... Cumberland County Public Library, North Carolina Foreign Language Center, Fayetteville, NC [Library symbol Library of Congress] (LCLS)
NcFayCFH.... Cape Fear Valley Hospital, Medical Library, Fayetteville, NC [Library symbol Library of Congress] (LCLS)
NcFayH .... Fayetteville Area Health Education Foundation, Inc., Fayetteville, NC [Library symbol Library of Congress] (LCLS)
NcFayM .... Methodist College, Fayetteville, NC [Library symbol Library of Congress] (LCLS)
NcFayR .... Rutledge College, Fayetteville, NC [Library symbol Library of Congress] (LCLS)
NcFayS .... Fayetteville State University, Fayetteville, NC [Library symbol Library of Congress] (LCLS)

NcFayT	Fayetteville Technical Institute, Fayetteville, NC [*Library symbol Library of Congress*] (LCLS)
NcFayV	United States Veterans Administration Medical Center, Fayetteville, NC [*Library symbol Library of Congress*] (LCLS)
NcFb	United States Army, Special Services Library System, Fort Bragg, NC [*Library symbol Library of Congress*] (LCLS)
NcFbH	United States Army, Womack Army Hospital, Fort Bragg, NC [*Library symbol Library of Congress*] (LCLS)
NcFbIM	United States Army, Institute for Military Assistance, Marquat Memorial Library, Fort Bragg, NC [*Library symbol Library of Congress*] (LCLS)
NcFc	Mooneyham Public Library, Forest City, NC [*Library symbol Library of Congress*] (LCLS)
NCFC	National Coalition for a Free Cuba (EA)
NCFC	National Commercial Finance Conference [*Later, NCFA*] (EA)
NCFC	National Congress for Men and Children [*An association*] (PAZ)
NCFC	National Council of Farmer Cooperatives (EA)
NCFCA	National Congress of Floor Covering Associations [*Defunct*] (EA)
NCFD	National Corporate Fund for Dance (EA)
NCFD	New Computer Family D (SAA)
NCFDA	National Council on Federal Disaster Assistance
NCFDAL	National Committee for Fair Divorce and Alimony Laws (EA)
NCFDITFS	National Committee for the Full Development of Instructional Television Fixed Services [*ITFS regulation*] (NTCM)
NCFE	National Campaign for Freedom of Expression
NCFE	National Center for Financial Education (EA)
NCFE	National Committee for Full Employment [*Defunct*] (EA)
NCFE	National Commodity Futures Examination
NCFEAD	National Council for Foundation Education in Art and Design (AIE)
NCFEPS	National Commission for Full Employment Policy Studies (OICC)
NCFES	North Central Forest Experiment Station [*St. Paul, MN*] [*Department of Agriculture*] (GRD)
NCFFR	National Commission on Fraudulent Financial Reporting [*Defunct*] (EA)
NCFI	National Cold Fusion Institute [*Closed June 30, 1991*]
NCFIS	National Center for Freedom of Information Studies (EA)
NCFJE	National Committee for the Furtherance of Jewish Education (EA)
NCFL	National Catholic Forensic League (EA)
NCFL	National Center for Family Literacy (PAZ)
NCFLIS	National Council on Foreign Language and International Studies (EA)
NCFM	National Coalition of Free Men (EA)
NCFM	National Commission on Food Marketing
NCFMF	National Committee for Fluid Mechanics Films
NCFMS	Naval Comptroller Financial Management Service
NCFNP	National Committee for a Freedom Now Party [*Defunct*] (EA)
NCFP	National Conference on Fluid Power (EA)
NCFPC	National Center for Fish Protein Concentrate [*Fish and Wildlife Service*]
NCFPC	National Commission on Fire Prevention and Control
NCFPI	National Clearinghouse for Family Planning Information [*Database*]
NCFPS	National Center for Family Planning Services [*Health Services and Mental Health Administration, HEW*]
NcFr	Macon County Public Library, Franklin, NC [*Library symbol Library of Congress*] (LCLS)
NCFR	National Campaign for Firework Reform [*British*] (DBA)
NCFR	National Council for Family Reconciliation (EA)
NCFR	National Council on Family Relations (EA)
NCFRF	National Cystic Fibrosis Research Foundation [*Later, Cystic Fibrosis Foundation*] (EA)
NcFrt	Franklinton Public Library, Franklinton, NC [*Library symbol Library of Congress*] (LCLS)
NCFS	National College of Foot Surgeons (EA)
NCFS	National Committee on Films for Safety [*Defunct*] (EA)
NCFS	National Conference of Friendly Societies [*British*] (DBA)
NCFS	Near Constant Force Suspension
NCFS	Noncontingent Footshock
NCFSA	National Chronic Fatigue Syndrome Association (EA)
NCFSD	NORAD Cost Factors and System Data [*Military*] (MCD)
NCFSK	Noncoherent Frequency Shift Keying
NCFSU	Naval Construction Force Support Unit (NVT)
NCFT	National Council for Families and Television (EA)
NCFTF	National Consumer Fraud Task Force (EA)
NCFTJ	National Conference on Federal Trial Judges (EA)
NcFv	Farmville Public Library, Farmville, NC [*Library symbol Library of Congress*] (LCLS)
NCFVP	National Center for Film and Video Preservation (EA)
NCFVSI	National Council for Fishing Vessel Safety and Insurance (EA)
NCG	Coast Guard Publication [*Later, NAVCG*]
NcG	Greensboro Public Library, Greensboro, NC [*Library symbol Library of Congress*] (LCLS)
NCG	Nanochannel Glass
NCG	National Contractors Group [*British*] (DBA)
NCG	National Council for the Gifted (EA)
NCG	Network Control Group [*Manned Space Flight Network*]
NCG	New College Graduate (BARN)
NCG	Nickel-Coated Graphite [*Materials technology*]
NCG	Nicotine Chewing Gum (PDAA)
NCG	Noncondensible Gases
NCG	North Carolina Nat Gas [*NYSE symbol*] (TTSB)
NCG	Nova-Cogesco Resources, Inc. [*Toronto Stock Exchange symbol*]
NCG	Nuclear Cratering Group [*Later, EERA*] [*Army*]
NCG	Nueva Casas Grandes [*Mexico*] [*Airport symbol*] (AD)
NCG	Null Command Generator
NCG	Numerical Control Graphics (MCD)
NcGa	Gaston-Lincoln Regional Library, Gastonia, NC [*Library symbol Library of Congress*] (LCLS)
NCGA	National Church Goods Association (EA)
NCGA	National Computer Graphics Association (EA)
NCGA	National Corn Growers Association (EA)
NCGA	National Cotton Ginners' Association (EA)
NCGA	National Council on Governmental Accounting (EA)
NcGA	North Carolina Agricultural and Technical State University, Greensboro, NC [*Library symbol Library of Congress*] (LCLS)
NcGaH	Gaston Memorial Hospital, Inc., Medical Library, Gastonia, NC [*Library symbol Library of Congress*] (LCLS)
NcGaL	Gaston-Lincoln Regional Library, Gastonia, NC [*Library symbol*] [*Library of Congress*] (LCLS)
NcGAT	AT&T Technologies Inc., Legal Library, Greensboro, NC [*Library symbol*] [*Library of Congress*] (LCLS)
NcGav	Gates County Library, Gatesville, NC [*Library symbol Library of Congress*] (LCLS)
NcGB	Bennett College, Greensboro, NC [*Library symbol Library of Congress*] (LCLS)
NcGBI	Burlington Industries, Inc., Information Services Library, Greensboro, NC [*Library symbol Library of Congress*] (LCLS)
NcGBur	Burlington Industries, Inc., Information Services Library, Greensboro, NC [*Library symbol Library of Congress*] (LCLS)
NcGC	Greensboro College, Greensboro, NC [*Library symbol Library of Congress*] (LCLS)
NCGC	National Catholic Guidance Conference [*Later, ARVIC*] (EA)
NCGCC	National Convention of Gospel Choirs and Choruses (EA)
NcGCG	Ciba-Geigy Corp., Technical Information Service, Greensboro, NC [*Library symbol Library of Congress*] (LCLS)
NcGCH	Wesley Long Community Hospital, Inc., Greensboro, NC [*Library symbol Library of Congress*] (LCLS)
NcGCL	Center for Creative Leadership, Greensboro, NC [*Library symbol Library of Congress*] (LCLS)
NcGCM	Cone Mills Corp., Greensboro, NC [*Library symbol Library of Congress*] (LCLS)
NCGE	National Council for Geographic Education (EA)
NC Gen Stat	General Statutes of North Carolina [*A publication*] (DLA)
NCGEP	National Council on Graduate Education in Psychology
NcGf	Granite Falls Public Library, Granite Falls, NC [*Library symbol Library of Congress*] (LCLS)
NcGG	Guilford College, Greensboro, NC [*Library symbol Library of Congress*] (LCLS)
NCGG	National Committee for Geodesy and Geophysics (MCD)
NcGGil	Gilbarco Corp. Library, Greensboro, NC [*Library symbol Library of Congress*] (LCLS)
NcGGT	Guilford Technical Community College, Learning Resource Center, Greensboro, NC [*Library symbol Library of Congress*] (LCLS)
NcGH	Moses H. Cone Memorial Hospital, Medical Library, Greensboro, NC [*Library symbol Library of Congress*] (LCLS)
NCGIC	National Cartographic and Geographic Information Center [*Geological Survey*] [*Reston, VA Database*]
NCGIF	National Cherry Growers and Industries Foundation (EA)
NCGIS	National Council of Guilds for Infant Survival (EA)
NcGL	Lorillard Research Center, Greensboro, NC [*Library symbol Library of Congress*] (LCLS)
NCGLC	National Caucus of Gay and Lesbian Counselors (EA)
NCGMCTC	National Chevy/GMC Truckin' Club [*Defunct*] (EA)
NcGo	Wayne County Public Library, Goldsboro, NC [*Library symbol Library of Congress*] (LCLS)
NcGoCH	Cherry Hospital, Learning Resource Center, Goldsboro, NC [*Library symbol Library of Congress*] (LCLS)
NcGoO	O'Berry Center, Professional Library, Goldsboro, NC [*Library symbol Library of Congress*] (LCLS)
NcGoW	Wayne Community College, Goldsboro, NC [*Library symbol Library of Congress*] (LCLS)
NcGPS	Greensboro Public Schools, Greensboro, NC [*Library symbol Library of Congress*] (LCLS)
NCGR	National Center for Genome Resources
NCGR	National Clonal Germplasm Repository [*Corvallis, OR*] [*Agricultural Research Service*] [*Department of Agriculture*] (GRD)
NCGR	National Council for GeoCosmic Research (EA)
NCGR	National Council on Gene Resources (EA)
NcGrE	East Carolina University, Greenville, NC [*Library symbol Library of Congress*] (LCLS)
NcGrE-H	East Carolina University, Health Sciences Library, Greenville, NC [*Library symbol Library of Congress*] (LCLS)
NcGrP	Pitt Technical Institute, Greenville, NC [*Library symbol Library of Congress*] (LCLS)
NcGrS	Sheppard Memorial Library, Greenville, NC [*Library symbol Library of Congress*] (LCLS)
NCGS	National Cooperative Gallstone Study
NCGS	New Century Gilders Society [*A union*] [*British*]
NCGS	Nuclear Criteria Group Secretariat [*Air Force Weapons Laboratory*] [*Kirtland Air Force Base, NM*]
NCGSTDS	National Coalition of Gay Sexually Transmitted Disease Services [*Defunct*] (EA)
ncgt--	Guatemala [*MARC geographic area code Library of Congress*] (LCCP)
NcGU	University of North Carolina at Greensboro, Greensboro, NC [*Library symbol Library of Congress*] (LCLS)
NcGWE	Western Electric Co., Legal Library, Greensboro, NC [*Library symbol Library of Congress*] (LCLS)
NCGWR	National Center for Ground Water Research [*Stillwater, OK*] [*Environmental Protection Agency*] (GRD)

NCH .... Hamilton & Kirkland Colleges, Clinton, NY [*Library symbol Library of Congress*] (LCLS)
NCH .... Nachingwea [*Tanzania*] [*Airport symbol*] (OAG)
NCH .... National Center for Homeopathy (EA)
NCH .... National Center on Educational Media and Materials for the Handicapped, Columbus, OH [*Inactive*] [*OCLC symbol*] (OCLC)
NCH .... National Children's Home [*British*]
NCH .... National Clearinghouse [*Public Health Service*]
NCH .... National Coalition for the Homeless (EA)
NCH .... National Cocaine Hotline
NCH .... National Committee on Housing
NCH .... National Council on the Humanities [*Washington, DC*]
NCH .... NCH Corp. [*Formerly, National Chemsearch Corp.*] [*NYSE symbol*] (SPSG)
NCH .... Negative Channel [*Computer science*] (IAA)
NCH .... Network Connection Handler
NCH .... Nielson Clearing House [*A.C. Nielson Co.*] (DOAD)
NCH .... Notched
NCH .... Number [*or Name*] Changed [*Telephone Listing*] (BARN)
NCha .... Chatham Public Library, Chatham, NY [*Library symbol Library of Congress*] (LCLS)
NcHa .... Hamlet Public Library, Hamlet, NC [*Library symbol Library of Congress*] (LCLS)
NCHA .... National Campers and Hikers Association (EA)
NCHA .... National Capital Housing Authority
NCHA .... National Crossbow Hunters Association (EA)
NCHA .... National Cutting Horse Association (EA)
NCHAA .... National Cutting Horse Association of Australia
NChaL .... Chatham Public Library, Chatman, NY [*Library symbol*] [*Library of Congress*] (LCLS)
NcHal .... Halifax County Library, Halifax, NC [*Library symbol Library of Congress*] (LCLS)
NChap .... Chappaqua Library, Chappaqua, NY [*Library symbol Library of Congress*] (LCLS)
NcHaR .... Richmond Technical Institute, Hamlet, NC [*Library symbol Library of Congress*] (LCLS)
NcHav .... Havelock-Craven County Public Library, Havelock, NC [*Library symbol Library of Congress*] (LCLS)
NcHavCr ...... Craven Community College, Havelock Learning Center, Havelock, NC [*Library symbol*] [*Library of Congress*] (LCLS)
NcHay .... Moss Memorial Library, Hayesville, NC [*Library symbol Library of Congress*] (LCLS)
NCHC .... National Clogging and Hoedown Council (EA)
NCHC .... National Collegiate Honors Council (EA)
NCHC .... National Council of Health Centers [*Formerly, NCHCS*] [*Later, AHCA*] (EA)
NCHCA .... National Commission for Health Certifying Agencies (EA)
NCHCS .... National Council of Health Care Services (EA)
NCHCT .... National Center for Health Care Technology [*US Congress agency*]
NCHDI .... National Center for Hearing Dog Information [*Later, HDRC*] (EA)
NcHe .... H. Leslie Perry Memorial Library, Henderson, NC [*Library symbol Library of Congress*] (LCLS)
NCHE .... National Center for Health Education (EA)
NCHE .... National Committee on Household Employment
NCHE .... National Council for History Education (EA)
NCheH .... Saint Joseph Intercommunity Hospital, Cheektowaga, NY [*Library symbol Library of Congress*] (LCLS)
NCHELP ...... National Council of Higher Education Loan Programs (EA)
NCHEML ...... National Chemical Laboratory (MCD)
NCHEMS ...... National Center for Higher Education Management Systems (EA)
NCHER .... National Center for Homecare Education and Research [*Defunct*] (EA)
NCHES .... National Child Health and Education Study [*University of Bristol*] [*British*]
NcHeV .... Vance County Technical Institute, Henderson, NC [*Library symbol Library of Congress*] (LCLS)
NcHf .... Perquimans County Library, Hertford, NC [*Library symbol Library of Congress*] (LCLS)
NCHFCI ...... National Committee to Honor the Fourteenth Centennial of Islam (EA)
N CHG .... Normal Charge (MHDB)
NCHGD ...... National Clearinghouse for Human Genetic Diseases [*Later, NCEMCH*] [*Public Health Service*] [*Information service or system*] (IID)
NCHGR ...... National Center for Human Genome Research
NCHGR ...... National Center for Human Genome Research [*Renamed*]
NCHHA ...... National Council of Homemakers and Home Health Aides
NCHHHSO ... National Coalition of Hispanic Health and Human Services Organizations (EA)
NCHI .... National Council of the Housing Industry (EA)
NcHil .... Confederate Memorial Library, Hillsboro, NC [*Library symbol Library of Congress*] (LCLS)
NCHLA .... National Committee for a Human Life Amendment (EA)
NCHLRR ...... National Commission on Human Life, Reproduction, and Rhythm (EA)
NCHLS .... National Council on Health Laboratory Services (EA)
NCHM .... National Center for Housing Management (EA)
NCHMHHSO... National Coalition of Hispanic Mental Health and Human Services Organizations [*Later, NCHHHSO*]
NCHMI .... National Centers for Health and Medical Informations, Inc. [*Research center*] (RCD)
NCHMOS ...... Negative Channel Metal-Oxide Semiconductor (IAA)
NCHMT ...... National Capital Historical Museum of Transportation (EA)
ncho-- .... Honduras [*MARC geographic area code Library of Congress*] (LCCP)
NCHO .... National Chicano Health Organization (EA)

NcHp .... High Point Public Library, High Point, NC [*Library symbol Library of Congress*] (LCLS)
NCHP .... National Corp. for Housing Partnerships
NCHP .... Nickel-Chromium Honeycomb Panel
NCHPA .... National Center for Health Promotion and Aging (EA)
NcHpC .... High Point College, High Point, NC [*Library symbol Library of Congress*] (LCLS)
NCHPD ...... National Council on Health Planning and Development
NcHpH ...... High Point Regional Hospital Medical Library, High Point, NC [*Library symbol*] [*Library of Congress*] (LCLS)
NCHR .... National Coalition for Haitian Refugees (EA)
N Ch R .... Nelson's English Chancery Reports [*A publication*] (DLA)
NCHRP .... National Cooperative Highway Research Program
NCHRTM...... National Clearing House of Rehabilitation Training Materials [*Oklahoma State University*] [*Information service or system*] (IID)
NcHs .... Hudson Library, Highlands, NC [*Library symbol Library of Congress*] (LCLS)
NCHS .... National Center for Health Statistics [*Public Health Service*] [*Hyattsville, MD Originator and database*]
NCHa .... National Committee on Homemaker Service [*Superseded by NHC*] (EA)
NCHSR .... National Center for Health Services Research
NCHSR .... National Center for Health Services Research and Health Care Technology Assessment [*Rockville, MD*] [*Public Health Service*] (GRD)
NCHSR & D... National Center for Health Services Research and Development [*Later, NCHSR*] [*HEW*]
NCHSRD ...... National Center for Health Services Research and Development [*Later, NCHSR*] [*HEW*]
NcHu .... Hudson Public Library, Hudson, NC [*Library symbol Library of Congress*] (LCLS)
NcHv .... Henderson County Public Library, Hendersonville, NC [*Library symbol Library of Congress*] (LCLS)
NcHvH .... Blue Ridge Technical Institute, Hendersonville, NC [*Library symbol Library of Congress*] (LCLS)
NcHvME...... Mother Earth News, Hendersonville, NC [*Library symbol Library of Congress*] (LCLS)
NCHVR .... National Center for HIV [*Human Immunodeficiency Virus*] Virology Research [*Australia*]
NCHVRFE...... National College for Heating, Ventilating, Refrigeration, and Fan Engineering (MCD)
NCHW .... National Council of Hispanic Women (EA)
NCHWPPTA... National Conference of Health, Welfare, and Pension Plans, Trustees and Administrators [*Later, International Foundation of Employee Benefit Plans*] (EA)
NcHy .... Elbert Ivey Memorial Library, Hickory, NC [*Library symbol Library of Congress*] (LCLS)
NcHyC .... Catawba Valley Technical Institute, Hickory, NC [*Library symbol Library of Congress*] (LCLS)
NcHyCH ...... Catawba Memorial Hospital, Northwest AHEC Library at Hickory, Hickory, NC [*Library symbol*] [*Library of Congress*] (LCLS)
NcHyCM...... Catawba Area Mental Health Center, Hickory, NC [*Library symbol*] [*Library of Congress*] (LCLS)
NcHyFH...... Glenn R. Frye Memorial Hospital, Hickory, NC [*Library symbol*] [*Library of Congress*] (LCLS)
NcHyL .... Lenoir Rhyne College, Hickory, NC [*Library symbol Library of Congress*] (LCLS)
NcHyMH ...... Hickory Memorial Hospital Library, Hickory, NC [*Library symbol*] [*Library of Congress*] (LCLS)
NcHyS .... Siecor Corp., Technical Information Center, Hickory, NC [*Library symbol Library of Congress*] (LCLS)
NCi .... Central Islip Public Library, Central Islip, NY [*Library symbol Library of Congress*] (LCLS)
nCi .... Nanocurie [*One billionth of a curie*]
NCI .... Naphthalene Creosote, Iodoform [*Powder for lice*]
NCI .... National Cancer Institute [*Database producer*] [*Bethesda, MD*] [*National Institutes of Health*] [*Department of Health and Human Services*]
NCI .... National Captioning Institute (EA)
NCI .... National Cheese Institute (EA)
NCI .... National Computer Index [*National Computing Centre Ltd.*] [*British Information service or system*] (CRD)
NCI .... National Computer Institute (MCD)
NCI .... National Computing Industries (NITA)
NCI .... National Council for Inordinacy (EA)
NCI .... National Critics Institute (EA)
NCI .... Natural Casing Institute [*Later, International Natural Sausage Casing Institute*] (EA)
NCI .... Naval Cost Inspector
NCI .... Navigation Control Indicator (MCD)
NCI .... Necocli [*Colombia*] [*Airport symbol*] (OAG)
NCI .... Negative Chemical Ionization [*Spectrometry*]
NCI .... Network Communications International [*Telecommunications service*] (TSSD)
NCI .... Network Computer, Inc.
NCI .... Neutral Countries Intelligence [*of Ministry of Economic Warfare*] [*British World War II*]
NCI .... New Community Instrument [*European Community*] (MHDB)
NCI .... New Creation Institute (EA)
NCI .... No Common Interest
NCI .... No-Cost Item (AAG)
NCI .... Nomenclature Control Index (MCD)
NCI .... Nominal Correction I [*Phasing maneuver*] (MCD)
NCI .... Noncoded Information [*Computer science*] (IBMDP)
NCI .... Noncoherent Integration

NCI.............. North Conway Institute (EA)
NCI.............. Northeast Computer Institute (HGAA)
NCI.............. Notice of Change Inception (MCD)
NCI.............. Notice of Change Incorporation (MCD)
NCI.............. Nuclear Capability Inspection (CINC)
NCI.............. Nuclear Contour Index [Cytology]
NCI.............. Nuclear Control Institute (EA)
NCI.............. Nurse Competency Inventory
NCI.............. Nursing Care Integration [Medicine] (DMAA)
NCI.............. Nursing Citation Index
NCI.............. Office of New Concepts and Initiatives [Air Force] (TEL)
NCI.............. Southwest New Jersey Consortium for Health Information Service,
          Voorhees, NJ [OCLC symbol] (OCLC)
NCIA .... National Cavity Installation Association [British]
NCIA .... National Center on Institutions and Alternatives (EA)
NCIA .... National Crop Insurance Association [Shawnee Mission, KS] (EA)
NCIAC .... National Construction Industry Arbitration Committee (EA)
NCIAED .... National Center for Information and Advice on Educational
          Disadvantage
NCIB .... National Charities Information Bureau (EA)
NCIB .... National Collection of Industrial Bacteria [British]
NCI Bldg...... NCI Building Systems [Associated Press] (SAG)
NCIBRD....... National Center for Integrated Bioremediation Research &
          Development [Initiated in Michigan with government funding,
          1994]
NCIC .... National Cancer Institute of Canada
NCIC .... National Career Information Center [Defunct] (EA)
NCIC .... National Cartographic Information Center [United States Geological
          Survey] [Reston, VA]
NCIC .... National Commission on the Indian Canadian
NCIC .... National Congress of Italian Canadians
NCIC .... National Construction Industry Council (EA)
NCIC .... National Crime Information Center [FBI] [Washington, DC]
NCIC .... National Crop Insurance Council [Inactive] (EA)
NCIC .... Network Communications Interface, Common (MCD)
NCIC .... Non-Circumcision Information Center (EA)
NCIC .... Northwest Coastal Information Center [Marine science] (MSC)
NCICA .... National Counter Intelligence Corps Association (EA)
NCIC Ops..... North Carolina Industrial Commission Advance Sheets
          [A publication] (DLA)
NCICU......... National Council of Independent Colleges and Universities [Later,
          NAICU]
NCID .... National Council for Industrial Defense (EA)
NCIDQ........ National Council for Interior Design Qualification (EA)
NCIES .... National Center for the Improvement of Educational Systems [Office
          of Education]
NCIES .... National Committee for International Education through Satellites
          (EA)
NCIESD .... National Conference on International Economic and Social
          Development [Later, IDC]
NCIH .... National Conference on Industrial Hydraulics
NCIH .... National Council for International Health (EA)
NCIHC......... National Council for Interior Horticultural Certification (EA)
NCII .... National Council for Industrial Innovation (EA)
NCII .... National Council of Individual Investors
NCIJC......... National Council of Independent Junior Colleges [Defunct]
NCIL .... National Council on Independent Living (EA)
NCILT......... National Centre for Industrial Language Training [British] (DI)
NCIMA .... National Cellulose Insulation Manufacturers Association
NCIMC .... National Council of Industrial Management Clubs [Later, IMC] (EA)
NCIMS .... National Conference on Interstate Milk Shipments
NCIMS .... Negative Chemical Ionization Mass Spectra
NCIMS .... Numerical Control Information Management System (MCD)
NCIN .... National Credit Information Network
NCIN .... North Carolina Information Network [Library network]
NCINAS....... National Council of Industrial Naval Air Stations (EA)
NCINASEO ... National Council of Industrial Naval Air Stations Employee
          Organizations [Formerly, NCNASEO] (EA)
NCIO .... National Congress of Inventors Organizations (EA)
NCIO .... National Council on Indian Opportunity (EA)
NCIP .... National Council for Industrial Peace [Defunct] (EA)
NCIP .... No Change in Price (MCD)
NCIP .... Non-Contributory Invalid Pension [British] (DI)
NCIP .... North American Collections Inventory Project [Established 1982]
          [Library science]
NCIPA......... National Committee for Independent Political Action (EA)
NCIPLA....... National Council of Intellectual Property Law Associations (EA)
NCIR .... National Center for Immigrants' Rights [Later, NILC] (EA)
NCIR .... National Center for Initiative Review (EA)
NCIR .... National Conference on Industrial Research
NCIRF......... National Center for Initiative Review Foundation [Defunct] (EA)
NCIRLS........ North Central Regional Library System [Library network]
NCIS .... Nadir Climate Interferometer Spectrometer (MCD)
NCIS .... National Chemical Information System (DIT)
NCIS .... National Coalition of Independent Scholars
NCIS .... National Council of Independent Schools [Later, National Association
          of Independent Schools] (AEBS)
NCIS .... National Credit Information Service [TRW, Inc.] [Long Beach, CA
          Credit-information databank]
NCIS .... National Crop Insurance Services (EA)
NCIS .... Navy Cost Information System
NCIS .... Nuclear Criticality Information System [Lawrence Livermore National
          Laboratory] [Information service or system] (IID)
NCISC......... Naval Counterintelligence Support Center
NCISD......... National Coalition on Immune System Disorders (EA)

NCISE .... National Center for Improving Science Education (EA)
NCiSH........ Central Islip State Hospital, Central Islip, NY [Library symbol Library
          of Congress] (LCLS)
NCISS......... National Council of Investigation and Security Services (EA)
NCIT.,........ National Committee for Insurance Taxation (EA)
NCIT........... National Council of Independent Truckers [Defunct] (EA)
NCIT........... National Council of Inland Transport [British] (DBA)
NCIT........... Numerical Control Inspection Tape (MCD)
NCITC .... National Clothing Industry Training Committee [Australia]
NCITD .... National Committee on International Trade Documentation
          [MARAD] (TAG)
NCITD .... National Council on International Trade Documentation [In
          association name: NCITD - The International Trade Facilitation
          Council] (EA)
NCITR .... National Center for Intermedia Transport Research [Los Angeles,
          CA] (GRD)
NCITT.......... National Committee for the In-Service Training of Teachers
          [Scotland] (AIE)
NCIU .... Network Common Interface Unit
NCIU .... Network Common Interference Unit (MCD)
NCIU .... Network Communications Interface, Unique
NCIV .... National Council for International Visitors (EA)
NcJ .... Jamestown Public Library, Jamestown, NC [Library symbol] [Library
          of Congress] (LCLS)
NCJ............ Johnson C. Smith University, James B. Duke Memorial Library,
          Charlotte, NC [OCLC symbol] (OCLC)
NCJ............ Needle Catheter Jejunostomy [Medicine] (DMAA)
NCJA .... National Criminal Justice Association (EA)
NcJa .... Onslow County Public Library, Jacksonville, NC [Library symbol
          Library of Congress] (LCLS)
NcJaC .... Coastal Carolina Community College, Jacksonville, NC [Library
          symbol Library of Congress] (LCLS)
NcJac......... Northampton County Memorial Library, Jackson, NC [Library symbol
          Library of Congress] (LCLS)
NcJacL........ Northampton County Memorial Library, Jackson, NC [Library symbol]
          [Library of Congress] (LCLS)
NcJaMC ...... United States Marine Corps, Marine Corps Air Station, Special
          Services for Station Library, New River Base, Jacksonville, NC
          [Library symbol Library of Congress] (LCLS)
NCJAR .... National Council for Japanese American Redress [Defunct] (EA)
NCJAVM ...... National Council on Jewish Audio-Visual Materials (EA)
NCJC.......... National Conference of Judicial Councils [Defunct] (EA)
NCJCC .... National Council of Jewish Correctional Chaplains [Later, AJCCA]
          (EA)
NCJCJ......... National Council of Juvenile Court Judges [Later, NCJFCJ] (EA)
NCJCS .... National Conference of Jewish Communal Service [Later, CJCS]
          (EA)
NCJD .... National Coalition for a Just Draft (EA)
NCJD .... National Congress of Jewish Deaf (EA)
NCJE .... National Council for Jewish Education [Later, CJE] (EA)
NCJF.......... National Center for Jewish Film (EA)
NCJFCJ........ National Council of Juvenile and Family Court Judges (EA)
NcJG .... Guilford Technical Institute, Jamestown, NC [Library symbol Library
          of Congress] (LCLS)
NCJISN .... National Council of Jewish Invalids Survivors of Nazism [Later,
          CHSD] (EA)
NCJISS .... National Criminal Justice Information and Statistics Service
NCJJ .... National Center for Jobs and Justice (EA)
NCJJ .... National Center for Juvenile Justice (EA)
NCJMS .... National Center for Job Market Studies [Commercial firm
          Washington, DC] (EA)
NcJo .... Jonesville-Arlington Public Library, Jonesville, NC [Library symbol
          Library of Congress] (LCLS)
NCJO .... National Council of Junior Outdoorsmen (EA)
NCJ of L ...... North Carolina Journal of Law [A publication] (DLA)
NCJPS .... National Center for Jewish Policy Studies
NCJR .... National Coalition for Jail Reform [Defunct] (EA)
NCJRS .... National Criminal Justice Reference Service [Department of Justice]
          [Information service or system]
NcJRS......... Ragsdale Senior High School, Jamestown, NC [Library symbol]
          [Library of Congress] (LCLS)
NCJSB .... National Commission on Jobs and Small Business [Defunct] (EA)
NCJSC .... National Criminal Justice Statistics Center
NCJT.......... Nordic Committee of Journalism Teachers (EA)
NCJW......... National Council of Jewish Women (EA)
NCJWA .... National Council of Jewish Women of Australia
NCK........... Camden County College, Voorhees, NJ [OCLC symbol] (OCLC)
NcK........... Kinston-Lenoir County Public Library, Kinston, NC [Library symbol
          Library of Congress] (LCLS)
NCK .... Nagycenk [Hungary] [Geomagnetic observatory code]
NCK .... Neck
NCK .... Neck
NCK .... Nickelodeon Industries Corp. [Vancouver Stock Exchange symbol]
NCK .... Norman, Craig & Kummel [Advertising agency]
NcKa .... Cannon Memorial YMCA Public Library, Kannapolis, NC [Library
          symbol Library of Congress] (LCLS)
NCKA .... National Catholic Kindergarten Association (AEBS)
NcKbMR ..... North Carolina Marine Resources Center, Fort Fisher, Kure Beach,
          NC [Library symbol Library of Congress] (LCLS)
NcKC......... Kinston-Lenoir County Public Library, Caswell Center Library,
          Kinston, NC [Library symbol Library of Congress] (LCLS)
NcKeD .... Duplin County, Dorothy Wightman Library, Kenansville, NC [Library
          symbol Library of Congress] (LCLS)
NcKeS.......... James Sprunt Technical Institute, Kenansville, NC [Library symbol
          Library of Congress] (LCLS)

NcKg............ King Public Library, King, NC [*Library symbol Library of Congress*] (LCLS)

NcKiK.......... Kittrell College, Kittrell, NC [*Library symbol Library of Congress*] (LCLS)

NcKL........... Lenoir Community College, Kinston, NC [*Library symbol Library of Congress*] (LCLS)

NCKL........... North Central Kansas Libraries System [*Library network*]

NcKm.......... Jacob S. Mauney Memorial Library, Kings Mountain, NC [*Library symbol Library of Congress*] (LCLS)

NcKn........... Kenly Public Library, Kenly, NC [*Library symbol*] [*Library of Congress*] (LCLS)

NCKWM...... National Committee for the Korean War Memorial [*Later, KWVM*] (EA)

NCKWR....... Neckwear

NCL............ Camden County Library, Voorhees, NJ [*OCLC symbol*] (OCLC)

NCL............ Financial

NCL............ National Carriers Ltd. [*British*] (DCTA)

NCL............ National Central Library [*United Kingdom*]

NCL............ National Character Laboratory (EA)

NCL............ National Chemical Laboratory

NCL............ National Civic League (EA)

NCL............ National Coalition for Literacy (EA)

NCL............ National Commuter Airways [*British ICAO designator*] (FAAC)

NCL............ National Consumers League (EA)

NCL............ National Council of Labour [*British*] (DCTA)

NCL............ National Cycle League (EA)

NCL............ Navy Calibration Laboratory

NCL............ Navy Code Logistic [*Plan*]

NCL............ Network Control Language

NCL............ Neuronal Ceroid Lipofuscinosis [*Medicine*]

NCL............ New Caledonia [*ANSI three-letter standard code*] (CNC)

NCL............ Newcastle [*England*] [*Airport symbol*] (OAG)

NCL............ Node Compatibility List [*Telecommunications*] (TEL)

NCL............ Noise Control Laboratory [*Pennsylvania State University*] [*Research center*] (RCD)

NCL............ Norfolk, VA [*Location identifier FAA*] (FAAL)

NCL............ Norwegian Caribbean Lines

NCL............ Numerically Controlled Lathe

NCL............ NuVeen Ins CA Prem Inc Muni 2 [*NYSE symbol*] (TTSB)

NCL............ Nuveen Insured California Premium Income Municipal II [*NYSE symbol*] (SPSG)

NcL............. Scotland County Memorial Library, Laurinburg, NC [*Library symbol Library of Congress*] (LCLS)

NCLA .... National C-Lark Association (EA)

NCLA .... National Council of Local Administrators of Vocational Education and Practical Arts (EA)

NCLAN .... National Crop Loss Assessment Network

NCL & SW ... National Conference of Lawyers and Social Workers

NC Law Repos... North Carolina Law Repository [*A publication*] (DLA)

NC Law Repository... North Carolina Law Repository (Reprint) [*A publication*] (DLA)

NCLC .... National Catholic Liturgical Conference (EA)

NCLC .... National Caucus of Labor Committees

NCLC .... National Chamber Litigation Center (EA)

NCLC .... National Child Labor Committee (EA)

NCLC .... National Consumer Law Center (EA)

NCLC .... National Council of Labour Colleges

NCLC .... National Council on Legal Clinics [*Later, CLEPR*]

NCLC .... Nineteenth Century Literary Criticism [*A publication*]

NCLC .... Noncombatant Labour Corps [*British*]

NCLCH........ National Civil Liberties Clearing House [*Defunct*] (EA)

NCLCI .... National Christian Leadership Conference for Israel (EA)

NCLD .... National Center for Law and the Deaf (EA)

NCLD .... National Center for Learning Disabilities (EA)

NCLD .... Williamsport District Library Center [*Library network*]

NCLE .... National Contact Lens Examiners (EA)

NcLeC........ Caldwell County Public Library, Lenoir, NC [*Library symbol Library of Congress*] (LCLS)

NcLeCT....... Caldwell Community College and Technical Institute, Lenoir, NC [*Library symbol Library of Congress*] (LCLS)

NCLEHA....... National Conference of Local Environmental Health Administrators (EA)

NCLER .... National Clearinghouse on Licensure, Enforcement, and Regulation (EA)

NCLEX .... National Council Licensure Examination

NCLEX-RN .. National Council Licensure Examination for Registered Nurses

NCLF .... National Coalition to Legalize Freedom (EA)

NCLG.......... National Committee for Latin and Greek (EA)

NCLG.......... National Conference of Lieutenant Governors (EA)

NCLH .... National Center for Law and the Handicapped [*Defunct*] (EA)

NCLHA .... National Conference of Law Historians of America (EA)

NCLI .... National Committee for Labor Israel [*Later, NCLIIHC*] (EA)

NCLIIHC...... National Committee for Labor Israel-Israel Histadrut Campaign (EA)

NcLil........... Harnett County Public Library, Lillington, NC [*Library symbol Library of Congress*] (LCLS)

NcLiL.......... Lincoln County Memorial Library, Lincolnton, NC [*Library symbol Library of Congress*] (LCLS)

NClinc......... Clinton Corners Reading Center, Clinton Corners, NY [*Library symbol Library of Congress*] (LCLS)

NCLIP .... North Coast Life Ins Cv'A'Pfd [*NASDAQ symbol*] (TTSB)

NCLIP .... North Coast Life Insurance Co. [*NASDAQ symbol*] (SAG)

NCLIS .... National Commission on Libraries and Information Science [*Washington, DC*]

NCLIS .... National Council for Languages and International Studies (EA)

NcLit............ Littleton Public Library, Littleton, NC [*Library symbol Library of Congress*] (LCLS)

NCLJ........... North Carolina Law Journal [*A publication*] (DLA)

NcLjUM........ United Methodist Church, Commission on Archives and History, Lake Junaluska, NC [*Library symbol Library of Congress*] (LCLS)

NcLk .... Rockingham County Library, Leakesville, NC [*Library symbol Library of Congress*] (LCLS)

NCLLF......... National Civil Liberties Legal Foundation [*Inactive*] (EA)

NcLo .... Franklin County Library, Louisburg, NC [*Library symbol Library of Congress*] (LCLS)

NCLO .... Naval Communication Liaison Officer (IAA)

NcLo-B........ Franklin County Library, Bunn Branch Library, Bunn, NC [*Library symbol*] [*Library of Congress*] (LCLS)

NcLoC......... Louisburg College, Louisburg, NC [*Library symbol Library of Congress*] (LCLS)

NCLP .... National Conference on Law and Poverty

NCLP .... Numerically Controlled Line Plotter

NCLPWA ..... National Council of Local Public Welfare Administrators (EA)

NCLR .... National Center for Legislative Research [*Defunct*] (EA)

NCLR .... National Coalition for Land Reform (EA)

NCLR .... National Council for Labor Reform (EA)

NCLR .... National Council of La Raza (EA)

NCL Rep .... North Carolina Law Repository [*A publication*] (DLA)

NCL Reps ... North Carolina Law Repository (Reprint) [*A publication*] (DLA)

NCLS .... National Clearinghouse for Legal Services [*Legal Services Corp.*] [*Information service or system*] (IID)

NCLS .... National Committee for Liberation of Slovakia (EA)

NCLS .... National Conference of Lawyers and Scientists [*Joint project of the American Association for the Advancement of Science and the American Bar Association*]

NCLS .... National Conference of State Legislatures [*Australia*]

NCLS .... North Country Library System [*Library network*]

NcLS .... Saint Andrews Presbyterian College, Laurinburg, NC [*Library symbol Library of Congress*] (LCLS)

NCLT........... Night Carrier Landing Trainer [*Navy*]

NCLTA .... National Cigar Leaf Tobacco Association [*Defunct*] (EA)

NcLu .... Robeson County Public Library, Lumberton, NC [*Library symbol Library of Congress*] (LCLS)

NcLuH......... Southeastern General Hospital, Medical Library, Lumberton, NC [*Library symbol Library of Congress*] (LCLS)

NcLuR......... Robeson Technical Institute, Lumbarton, NC [*Library symbol Library of Congress*] (LCLS)

NcLxD......... Davidson County Public Library, Lexington, NC [*Library symbol Library of Congress*] (LCLS)

NcLxDC....... Davidson County Community College, Lexington, NC [*Library symbol Library of Congress*] (LCLS)

NCm........... Center Moriches Free Public Library, Center Moriches, NY [*Library symbol Library of Congress*] (LCLS)

NCM........... Court Martial Reports, Navy Cases [*A publication*] (DLA)

NCM........... Mars Hill College, Mars Hill, NC [*OCLC symbol*] (OCLC)

NCM........... Nailfold Capillary Microscope (DAVI)

NCM........... National Center for Men (EA)

NCM........... National Coal Model [*Department of Energy*] (GFGA)

NCM........... National Coastal Monitoring (USDC)

NCM........... National Coastal Monitoring [*Marine science*] (OSRA)

NCM........... National College of Music [*British*] (DI)

NCM........... National Congress for Men (EA)

NCM........... National Corvette Museum

NCM........... National Cursillo Movement (EA)

NCM........... Natural Clay Mosaic (DICI)

NCM........... Navy Commendation Medal

NCM........... Navy Correspondence Manual

NCM........... Net Control Master (MCD)

NCM........... Network Control Module

NCM........... Newcastle Conservatorium of Music [*Australia*]

NCM........... New Moon [*Queensland*] [*Airport symbol*] (AD)

NCM........... Nicaraguan Campaign Medal

NCM........... Nippon Calculating Machine Co. [*Japan*] (PDAA)

NCM........... Nitrocellulose Membrane

NCM........... No Compromise Majority [*An association*] (EA)

NCM........... Noise Canceling Microphone

NCM........... Non Compos Mentis [*Not of Sound Mind*] [*Latin*] (LWAP)

NCM........... Noncorrosive Metal

NCM........... Noncrew Member

NCM........... Nordic Council of Ministers (EAIO)

NCM........... Nordic Council on Medicines [*See also NLN*] (EAIO)

NCM........... Normal Human Colon Mucosal [*Cells*]

NCM........... North Carolina Motor Carriers Association [*STAC*]

NCM........... Northern Conservatory of Music [*Maine*]

NCM........... Northern Cruise Master (SAA)

NCM........... Notice of Commencement of Manufacture [*Toxic Substances Control Act*] [*Environmental Protection Agency*] (EPA)

NCM........... Numerical Controlled Machine

NCM........... Nuveen California Municipal Income [*NYSE symbol*] (SPSG)

NCMA .... National Campus Ministry Association (EA)

NCMA .... National Catalog Managers Association (EA)

NCMA .... National Ceramic Manufacturers Association

NCMA .... National Childminding Association [*British*] (DBA)

NCMA .... National Concrete Masonry Association (EA)

NCMA .... National Contract Management Association (EA)

NCMA .... National Corporate Medical Associates [*An association*]

NCMA .... National Council of Millinery Associations (EA)

NCMA .... National Council of Moving Associations (EA)

NCMA .... Naval Civilian Manager's Association (EA)

NCMA .... Newspaper Credit Managers' Association (EA)

NcMad .... Madison Public Library, Madison, NC [*Library symbol Library of Congress*] (LCLS)

NCMAF .... National Conference on Ministry to the Armed Forces (EA)

NcMaM .... McDowell Technical Institute, Marion, NC [*Library symbol Library of Congress*] (LCLS)

NcMaMC..... McDowell County Public Library, Marion, NC [*Library symbol Library of Congress*] (LCLS)

NcMan .... Dare County Library, Manteo, NC [*Library symbol Library of Congress*] (LCLS)

NcManA ...... College of the Albemarle, Dare County Center Library, Manteo, NC [*Library symbol*] [*Library of Congress*] (LCLS)

NcManMR.... North Carolina Marine Resources Center, Roanoke Island Resource Library, Manteo,NC [*Library symbol Library of Congress*] (LCLS)

NcMarM....... Madison County Public Library, Marshall, NC [*Library symbol Library of Congress*] (LCLS)

NcMauDC .... North Carolina Department of Corrections, Eastern Correctional Center Library, Maury, NC [*Library symbol*] [*Library of Congress*] (LCLS)

NcMax .... Gilbert Patterson Memorial Public Library, Maxton, NC [*Library symbol Library of Congress*] (LCLS)

NCMC .... National Capital Management Corp. [*NASDAQ symbol*] (NQ)

NCMC .... National Center on Missing Children (NADA)

NCMC .... National Coalition for Marine Conservation (EA)

NCMC .... Natl Capital Mgmt [*NASDAQ symbol*] (TTSB)

NCMC .... Natural Cell-Mediated Cytotoxicity [*Immunochemistry*]

NCMC .... N-Carboxymethylchitosan [*Biochemistry*]

NCMC .... NORAD Cheyenne Mountain Complex [*Military*] (AABC)

NCMC .... Nordic Council for Music Conservatories (EA)

NCMC .... Numerically-Controlled Machine Center (IAA)

NcMcC .... Carteret Technical Institute, Morehead City, NC [*Library symbol Library of Congress*] (LCLS)

NcMccH ...... McCain Hospital, Medical Library, McCain, NC [*Library symbol Library of Congress*] (LCLS)

NcMccS ...... Sandhills Youth Center, McCain, NC [*Library symbol Library of Congress*] (LCLS)

NCMCE .... National Council of Minority Consulting Engineers (IAA)

NCMCG....... National Construction Machinery Credit Group [*Park Ridge, IL*] (EA)

NCMD .... National Center for Municipal Development (EA)

NCMDA....... National Coin Machine Distributors Association (EA)

NCMDA....... National Commission on Marijuana and Drug Abuse [*Presidential advisory committee, terminated 1973*]

NCMDLRJO... National Council of Marriage and Divorce Law Reform and Justice Organizations (EA)

NCME.......... National Center for Mediation Education (EA)

NCME.......... National Council on Measurement in Education (EA)

NCME.......... Network for Continuing Medical Education (EA)

NCME.......... Northern Counties Motor & Engineering Co. Ltd. [*British*] (DCTA)

NCME.......... Numerically Controlled Machine Equipment

NCMEA .... National Catholic Music Educators Association [*Later, NPM*] (EA)

NCMEC .... National Center for Missing and Exploited Children (EA)

NCMEC .... National Center for Missing and Exploited Children

NCMES .... Numerically-Controlled Measuring and Evaluating System (IAA)

NCMESD ..... National Coalition for More Effective School Discipline (EA)

NCMET....... Nonclosed Shell Many Electron Theory [*Physics*]

NcMf.......... Murfreesboro Public Library, Murfreesboro, NC [*Library symbol Library of Congress*] (LCLS)

NCMF......... National Carvers Museum Foundation [*Defunct*] (EA)

NCMF......... National Church Music Fellowship [*Defunct*]

NcMfC........ Chowan College, Murfreesboro, NC [*Library symbol Library of Congress*] (LCLS)

NCMFST ..... National Committee for Motor Fleet Supervisor Training (EA)

NcMG.......... Graham Evangelistic Association, Montreat, NC [*Library symbol Library of Congress*] (LCLS)

NCMG .... Mangaia [*Cook Islands*] [*ICAO location identifier*] (ICLI)

NCMH .... National Clearinghouse for Mental Health Information (NITA)

NCMH .... National Committee for Mental Health (DAVI)

NCMH .... National Committee for Mental Hygiene (DAVI)

NCMH .... National Committee on Maternal Health (EA)

NCMH .... National Council for Monday Holidays

NcMhC........ Mars Hill College, Mars Hill, NC [*Library symbol Library of Congress*] (LCLS)

NcMHi .... Historical Foundation of the Presbyterian and Reformed Churches, Montreat, NC [*Library symbol Library of Congress*] (LCLS)

NCMHI .... National Clearinghouse for Mental Health Information [*Public Health Service*] [*Rockville, MD Database*] [*HEW*]

NCMHS .... National Conference on Mental Health Statistics [*Department of Health and Human Services*] (GFGA)

NCMI .... National Coin Machine Institute (EA)

NCMI .... National Committee Against Mental Illness (EA)

NCMI .... National Council of Music Importers [*Later, NCMIE*]

NCMI .... National Country Maintenance Index (IAA)

NCMIE .... National Council of Music Importers and Exporters (EA)

NcMiP........ Pfeiffer College, Misenheimer, NC [*Library symbol Library of Congress*] (LCLS)

NCMJ.......... National Contract Management Journal [*A publication*] (AAGC)

NCMK .... Mauke [*Cook Islands*] [*ICAO location identifier*] (ICLI)

NCMLB .... National Council of Mailing List Brokers [*Later, MLBPA*] (EA)

NcMM......... Montreat-Anderson College, Montreat, NC [*Library symbol Library of Congress*] (LCLS)

NCmM .... Museum Manor of Saint George, Center Moriches, NY [*Library symbol Library of Congress*] (LCLS)

NCMM .... Nuveen California Municipal Market Opportunity Fund [*Associated Press*] (SAG)

NCmMM ...... Museum Manor of Saint George, Center Moriches, NY [*Library symbol*] [*Library of Congress*] (LCLS)

NCMN .... Manuae [*Cook Islands*] [*ICAO location identifier*] (ICLI)

NCMO .... Navigational Aids/Communications Management Office [*Air Force*] (CET)

NcMoBH ...... Broughton Hospital, Staff Library, Morganton, NC [*Library symbol Library of Congress*] (LCLS)

NcMoc .... Davie County Public Library, Mocksville, NC [*Library symbol Library of Congress*] (LCLS)

NcMoFM ...... Foothills Area Mental Health, North Carolina School for the Deaf, Morganton, NC [*Library symbol*] [*Library of Congress*] (LCLS)

NcMoGH ...... Grace Hospital, Medical Library, Morganton, NC [*Library symbol*] [*Library of Congress*] (LCLS)

NcMoM .... Morganton-Burke Library, Inc., Morganton, NC [*Library symbol Library of Congress*] (LCLS)

NcMon .... Union County Public Library, Monroe, NC [*Library symbol Library of Congress*] (LCLS)

NcMorB .... Bell Northern Research, Inc., Learning Resources Center, Morrisville, NC [*Library symbol*] [*Library of Congress*] (LCLS)

NcMoW .... Western Piedmont Community College, Morganton, NC [*Library symbol Library of Congress*] (LCLS)

NcMoWC..... Western Carolina Center, Staff Library, Morganton, NC [*Library symbol Library of Congress*] (LCLS)

NcMoWCC ... Western Correctional Center, Morganton, NC [*Library symbol*] [*Library of Congress*] (LCLS)

NCMP .... National Commission for Manpower Policy [*Department of Labor*]

NCMP .... National Commission on Materials Policy

NCMP .... Navy Capabilities and Mobilization Plan (DOMA)

NCMPA .... National Corrugated Metal Pipe Association [*Later, NCSPA*] (EA)

NCMPR .... National Council for Marketing and Public Relations (EA)

NCMR .... Matiaro [*Cook Islands*] [*ICAO location identifier*] (ICLI)

NCMR .... National Committee for Monetary Reform (EA)

NCMR .... Nonconforming Material Report

NCMR .... North Canterbury Mounted Rifles [*British military*] (DMA)

NCMRED..... National Council on Marine Resources and Engineering Development [*Later, ICMSE*]

NCMS .... National Center for Manufacturing Sciences [*Research center*]

NCMS .... National Classification Management Society (EA)

NCMS .... National Council of Marine Sciences

NCMS .... Numerically-Controlled Machine System (IAA)

NCMS .... Numerically-Controlled Manufacture System (IAA)

NCMT.......... Numerically Controlled Machine Tool

NcMta .... Mount Airy Public Library, Mount Airy, NC [*Library symbol Library of Congress*] (LCLS)

NCMTA .... National Council of Marine Trade Associations

NcMtaC....... Crossroads Center, Mount Airy, NC [*Library symbol*] [*Library of Congress*] (LCLS)

NcMtC........ Mount Olive College, Mount Olive, NC [*Library symbol Library of Congress*] (LCLS)

NCMTE........ National Council on Medical Technology Education [*Defunct*]

NCMTI .... Noncoherent Moving Target Indicator (MCD)

NCMTT .... National Council for Mother Tongue Teaching (AIE)

NcMu .... Murphy Public Library, Murphy, NC [*Library symbol Library of Congress*] (LCLS)

NCMUE .... National Council on Measurements Used in Education [*Later, National Council on Measurement in Education*] (AEBS)

NcMuN........ Nantahala Regional Library, Murphy, NC [*Library symbol Library of Congress*] (LCLS)

NcMuT........ Tri-County Technical Institute, Murphy, NC [*Library symbol Library of Congress*] (LCLS)

NcMv .... Mooresville Public Library, Mooresville, NC [*Library symbol Library of Congress*] (LCLS)

NCMV .... Northern Cereal Mosaic Virus [*Plant pathology*]

n-cn--.......... Canada [*MARC geographic area code Library of Congress*] (LCCP)

NCN .... National Airlines (Chile), SA [*FAA designator*] (FAAC)

NCN .... National Cardiovascular Network

NCN .... National Christian Network [*Cable-television system*]

NCN .... National Computer Network Corp. [*Information service or system*] (IID)

NCN .... National Council of Nurses [*British*] (DI)

NCN .... Navy Control Number (MCD)

NCN .... Network Control Node

NCN .... Nixdorf Communications Network [*Nixdorf*] [*Germany*]

NCN .... Non-Casein Nitrogen (OA)

NCNA .... National Council of Nonprofit Associations

NCNA .... National Council on Noise Abatement (EA)

NCNA .... New China News Agency

n-cn-ab .... Alberta [*MARC geographic area code Library of Congress*] (LCCP)

NCNASEO ... National Council of Naval Air Stations Employee Organizations [*Later, NCINASEO*]

NCNB .... National Center for Nonprofit Boards (EA)

n-cn-bc .... British Columbia [*MARC geographic area code Library of Congress*] (LCCP)

NcNbC .... Craven Technical Institute, New Bern, NC [*Library symbol Library of Congress*] (LCLS)

NcNbCP ...... Craven-Pamlico-Carteret Regional Library, New Bern, NC [*Library symbol Library of Congress*] (LCLS)

NCNC .... National Captive Nations Committee (EA)

NCNC .... National Council of Nigeria and the Cameroons [*Political party*]

NCNC .... Normochromic Normocytic [*Medicine*] (MEDA)

NCNC .... Normochromic, Normocytic Anemia [*Hematology*] (DAVI)

NCNCA........ Normochromic, Normocytic Anemia [*Hematology*] (DAVI)

NCND.......... Neither Confirm nor Deny

NCNE .... National Campaign for Nursery Education [*British*]

NCNE .... National Center for Neighborhood Enterprise (EA)

NcNep.......... Newport Public Library, Newport, NC [*Library symbol*] [*Library of Congress*] (LCLS)

NCNEVAW.... National Communications Network for the Elimination of Violence Against Women [*NCADV*] [*Absorbed by*] (EA)

NcNew........ Avery-Morrison Public Library, Newland, NC [*Library symbol Library of Congress*] (LCLS)

NCNGD...... Not Crushed or Not Ground

n-cnh-...... Hudson Bay [*MARC geographic area code Library of Congress*] (LCCP)

n-cnm-...... Maritime Provinces [*MARC geographic area code Library of Congress*] (LCCP)

n-cn-mb...... Manitoba [*MARC geographic area code Library of Congress*] (LCCP)

n-cn-nf...... Newfoundland [*MARC geographic area code Library of Congress*] (LCCP)

n-cn-nk...... New Brunswick [*MARC geographic area code Library of Congress*] (LCCP)

n-cn-ns...... Nova Scotia [*MARC geographic area code Library of Congress*] (LCCP)

n-cn-nt...... Northwest Territories [*MARC geographic area code Library of Congress*] (LCCP)

N/CNO...... Navy/Chief of Naval Operations (AAG)

n-cn-on...... Ontario [*MARC geographic area code Library of Congress*] (LCCP)

NCNP........ National Child Nutrition Project (EA)

NCNP........ National Conference for New Politics [*Organization formed in 1966 to support peace candidates*] (VNW)

n-cnp-...... Prairie Provinces [*MARC geographic area code Library of Congress*] (LCCP)

n-cn-pi...... Prince Edward Island [*Canada*] [*MARC geographic area code Library of Congress*] (LCCP)

NCNPSA...... National Conference of Non-Profit Shipping Associations (EA)

ncnq--...... Nicaragua [*MARC geographic area code Library of Congress*] (LCCP)

n-cn-qu...... Quebec [*MARC geographic area code Library of Congress*] (LCCP)

NCNR........ National Center for Nursing Research [*Bethesda, MD*] [*Department of Health and Human Services*] (GRD)

NCNS........ Nassau [*Cook Islands*] [*ICAO location identifier*] (ICLI)

NCNS........ National Catholic News Service (EA)

NCNS........ North Central Name Society (EA)

n-cn-sn...... Saskatchewan [*MARC geographic area code Library of Congress*] (LCCP)

NcNt.......... Catawba County Library, Newton, NC [*Library symbol Library of Congress*] (LCLS)

NCNTUCW ... National Commission on New Technological Uses of Copyrighted Works [*Terminated, 1978*] [*Library of Congress*]

NcNv.......... Harold D. Cooley Library, Nashville, NC [*Library symbol*] [*Library of Congress*] (LCLS)

NCNW........ National Congress of Neighborhood Women (EA)

NCNW........ National Council of Negro Women (EA)

NCNW........ Nearly Certain New Work (MCD)

NcNw........ Wilkes County Public Library, North Wilkesboro, NC [*Library symbol Library of Congress*] (LCLS)

NcNwA........ Appalachian Regional Library, North Wilkesboro, NC [*Library symbol Library of Congress*] (LCLS)

NCNY.......... Netherland Club of New York (EA)

NCNY.......... Newswomen's Club of New York (EA)

n-cn-yk...... Yukon Territory [*MARC geographic area code Library of Congress*] (LCCP)

NCo.......... Commack Public Library, Commack, NY [*Library symbol Library of Congress*] (LCLS)

NCO.......... National Commission for Information and Conscientization on Development Cooperation [*Netherlands*]

NCO.......... National Council of Obesity (EA)

NCO.......... Nationalist Chams Organization (EA)

NCO.......... Negotiated Consent Order [*Environmental Protection Agency*] (ERG)

NCO.......... Net Control (CAAL)

NCO.......... Net Control Outstation [*Military*] (DOMA)

NCO.......... Network Control Office [*Telecommunications*] (TEL)

NCO.......... New Consultants [*A publication*]

NCO.......... Noncombatant Evacuation Order [*Navy*] (CINC)

NCO.......... Noncombat Operations [*Military*] (CAAL)

NCO.......... Noncommissioned Officer [*Military*]

NCO.......... Non Compliance Order [*Environmental Protection Agency*]

NCO.......... Norsar Array Site 01C00 [*Norway*] [*Seismograph station code, US Geological Survey*] (SEIS)

NCO.......... North Canadian Oils Ltd. [*Toronto Stock Exchange symbol*]

NCO.......... North Carolina Department of Transportation, Raleigh, NC [*OCLC symbol*] (OCLC)

NCO.......... Number-Controlled Oscillator

NCO.......... Nuveen California Municipal Market Opportunities [*NYSE symbol*] (SPSG)

NCO.......... Nuveen CA Muni Mkt Oppt [*NYSE symbol*] (TTSB)

NCOA........ National Campground Owners Association (EA)

NCOA........ National Change of Address Service [*US Postal Service*]

NCOA........ National Chevelle Owners Association (EA)

NCOA........ National Condominium Owners Association [*Defunct*]

NCOA--...... National Corvette Owners' Association (EA)

NCOA........ National Council on the Aging (EA)

NCOA........ Noncommissioned Officer Academy [*Military*] (AABC)

NCOA........ Non-Commissioned Officers Association of the United States of America (EA)

NCoBJ........ Burr Junior High School, Commack, NY [*Library symbol*] [*Library of Congress*] (LCLS)

NCOBPS...... National Conference of Black Political Scientists (EA)

NCOBQ...... Noncommissioned Officer Bachelor Quarters [*Military*] (AFM)

N'COBRA ...... National Coalition of Blacks for Reparations in America (ECON)

NCobUA........ State University of New York, Agricultural and Technical College at Cobleskill, Cobleskill, NY [*Library symbol Library of Congress*] (LCLS)

NCOC.......... National Commission on Organized Crime (NADA)

NCOC.......... National Council on Organized Crime (EA)

NCOC.......... Noncommissioned Officer Course (VNW)

NCoCE........ Cedar Road Elementary School, Commack, NY [*Library symbol*] [*Library of Congress*] (LCLS)

NCOCY........ National Council of Organizations for Children and Youth (EA)

NCOD.......... National Catholic Office for the Deaf (EA)

NCOD.......... National Coming Out Day Campaign (EA)

NCOD.......... National Commission on Orphan Diseases [*Department of Health and Human Services*] (GFGA)

NCODE........ National Clearinghouse on Development Education [*Information service or system*] (IID)

NCODP........ Noncommissioned Officer Development Program [*Army*] (INF)

NCO-ER...... Noncommissioned Officer Evaluation Reporting [*Army*] (INF)

NCOES........ Noncommissioned Officer Education System [*Military*] (AABC)

NC of A...... Newfoundland Club of America (EA)

NCOG.......... NCO Group, Inc. [*NASDAQ symbol*] (SAG)

NcOG.......... Richard H. Thornton Memorial Library, Oxford, NC [*Library symbol Library of Congress*] (LCLS)

NCOGD........ National Council for the Observance of Grandparent's Day (EA)

NCO Grp...... NCO Group, Inc. [*Associated Press*] (SAG)

NCOHC........ Northern California Occupational Health Center [*University of California*] [*Research center*] (RCD)

NCO/HPCC ... National Coordination Office for High Performance Computing and Communications

NCoHS-N...... North High School, Commack, NY [*Library symbol*] [*Library of Congress*] (LCLS)

NCoHS-S...... South High School, Commack, NY [*Library symbol*] [*Library of Congress*] (LCLS)

NCOI.......... National Council for the Omnibus Industry [*British*]

NCOIC........ Noncommissioned Officer-in-Charge [*Military*]

NCoIE........ Indian Hollow Elementary School, Commack, NY [*Library symbol*] [*Library of Congress*] (LCLS)

NCOIL........ National Conference of Insurance Legislators (EA)

NCOL.......... National Council on Occupational Licensing [*Formerly, COL*] [*Defunct*] (EA)

NCOLANT...... Net Control Officer, Atlantic [*Navy*] (DNAB)

NCOLG........ National Coordinating Office for Latin and Greek [*Later, NCLG*] (EA)

NCoInA........ Albany Area Board of Cooperative Education Services, Colonie, NY [*Library symbol*] [*Library of Congress*] (LCLS)

NCOLP........ Noncommissioned Officer Logistics Program [*Army*] (AABC)

NCOLS........ Noncommissioned Officers' Leadership School [*Air Force*] (AFM)

NCOLUG...... North Carolina Online User Group (NITA)

NCOM.......... NEC Computerised Operation and Maintenance System (NITA)

NCOM.......... News Communications [*NASDAQ symbol*] (TTSB)

NCOM.......... News Communications, Inc. [*NASDAQ symbol*] (SAG)

NCOMBL...... Noncombustible (MSA)

NCOMD........ National Committee on the Observance of Mothers' Day [*Later, MDC*] (EA)

NCOMDR...... National Clearinghouse on Marital and Date Rape (EA)

NCOMED...... Net Control Officer, Mediterranean [*Navy*] (DNAB)

NCOMM...... Naval Communications Command

NCOMP...... National Catholic Office for Motion Pictures [*Later, Office for Film and Broadcasting*]

NCOMR........ National Clearinghouse on Marital Rape [*Later, NCOMDR*] (EA)

NCON.......... Encon Systems [*NASDAQ symbol*] (SAG)

NCoNE........ North Ridge Elementary School, Commack, NY [*Library symbol*] [*Library of Congress*] (LCLS)

NCoOE........ Old Farms Elementary School, Commack, NY [*Library symbol*] [*Library of Congress*] (LCLS)

NCooHi........ New York State Historical Association, Cooperstown, NY [*Library symbol Library of Congress*] (LCLS)

NCOOM........ Noncommissioned Officers' Open Mess [*Military*] (AFM)

NCop.......... Copiague Memorial Public Library, Copiague, NY [*Library symbol Library of Congress*] (LCLS)

NCOP.......... National Council on Philanthropy [*Later, IS*] (EA)

NCOP.......... New Choreographers On Point

NCOPA........ National Conference of Police Associations (EA)

NCOPAC...... Net Control Officer, Pacific [*Navy*] (DNAB)

NCOPD........ National Catholic Office for Persons with Disabilities (EA)

NCOPDP...... Noncommissioned Officer Professional Development Program [*Army*] (INF)

NCOPDR...... NCO [*Noncommissioned Officer*] Professional Development Ribbon [*Military decoration*] (GFGA)

NCOPE........ National Council of Preservation Executives (EA)

NCOPF........ National Council for One Parent Families [*British*]

NCopH........ Lakeside Hospital, Copiague, NY [*Library symbol Library of Congress*] (LCLS)

NCopHS...... Copiague High School, Copiague, NY [*Library symbol*] [*Library of Congress*] (LCLS)

NCoRE........ Rolling Hills Elementary School, Commack, NY [*Library symbol*] [*Library of Congress*] (LCLS)

NCorf.......... Corfu Free Library, Corfu, NY [*Library symbol Library of Congress*] (LCLS)

NCorn.......... Cornwall Public Library, Cornwall, NY [*Library symbol Library of Congress*] (LCLS)

NCornB........ Harvard Black Rock Forest, Cornwall, NY [*Library symbol Library of Congress*] (LCLS)

NCorni........ Corning Public Library, Corning, NY [*Library symbol Library of Congress*] (LCLS)

NCorniC........ Corning Glass Works, Corning, NY [*Library symbol Library of Congress*] (LCLS)

NCorniCC ..... Corning Community College, Corning, NY [*Library symbol Library of Congress*] (LCLS)

NCorniFL ..... College Center of the Finger Lakes, Corning, NY [*Library symbol Library of Congress*] (LCLS)

NCorniM .... Corning Museum of Glass, Corning, NY [*Library symbol Library of Congress*] (LCLS)

NCorniS .... Southern Tier Library System, Corning, NY [*Library symbol Library of Congress*] (LCLS)

NCort .... Cortland Free Library, Cortland, NY [*Library symbol Library of Congress*] (LCLS)

NCORT .... National Catholic Office for Radio and Television [*Later, Office for Film and Broadcasting*]

NCortHi .... Cortland County Historical Society, Cortland, NY [*Library symbol Library of Congress*] (LCLS)

NCortSC .... Smith-Corona Laboratory, Cortland, NY [*Library symbol Library of Congress*] (LCLS)

NCortU .... State University of New York, College at Cortland, Cortland, NY [*Library symbol Library of Congress*] (LCLS)

NCOS .... Comite de Liaison des Organisations Non-Gouvernmentales de Developpement aupres des Communautes Europeennes [*Liaison Committee of Development Non-Governmental Organizations to the European Communities*] (EAIO)

NCOS .... National Centre for Orchestral Studies [*Goldsmiths' College*] [*British*] (CB)

NCOS .... National Commission on Space [*Terminated, 1986*] (EGAO)

NCOS .... National Commission on Superconductivity [*Presidential advisory commission*] (EGAO)

NCOS .... National Council on Stuttering (EA)

NCOS .... Non-Concurrent Operating System [*Sperry UNIVAC*]

NCOSCC ...... National Central Office for the Suppression of Counterfeit Currency [*British*]

NCoSJ .... Saw Mill Junior High School, Commack, NY [*Library symbol*] [*Library of Congress*] (LCLS)

NCOSTA ...... National Council of Officers of State Teachers Associations (EA)

NcOtV .... United States Veterans Administration Hospital, Oteen, NC [*Library symbol Library of Congress*] (LCLS)

NCoWE .... Wood Park Elementary School, Commack, NY [*Library symbol*] [*Library of Congress*] (LCLS)

NCOWFL ...... National Center on Women and Family Law (EA)

NCoxHi .... Greene County Historical Society, Inc., Coxsakie, NY [*Library symbol Library of Congress*] (LCLS)

NcP .... Given Memorial Library, Pinehurst, NC [*Library symbol Library of Congress*] (LCLS)

NCP .... National Cancer Program [*National Institutes of Health*]

NCP .... National Caries Program [*Public Health Service*] (GRD)

NCP .... National Car Parks [*British*]

NCP .... National Choreography Project

NCP .... National Circus Project (EA)

NCP .... National Climate Program [*Rockville, MD*] [*National Oceanic and Atmospheric Administration*]

NCP .... National Collegiate Players (EA)

NCP .... National Commission on Productivity [*Later, National Productivity Council*]

NCP .... National Commodity-Processing Program [*Department of Agriculture*] (GFGA)

NCP .... National Contingency Plan [*Hazardous wastes*] [*Environmental Protection Agency*]

NCP .... National Convention Party [*Gambia*] [*Political party*] (PPW)

NCP .... National Council of Psychotherapists and Hypnotherapy Register [*British*] (DBA)

NCP .... National Council on Philanthropy [*Later, IS*]

NCP .... National Curriculum Project

NCP .... National Cycling Proficiency (BARN)

NCP .... Natural Clay Pavers (DICI)

NCP .... Naval Capabilities Plan

NCP .... N-Chlorothiophosphoramide [*Organic chemistry*]

NCP .... N-Cholorpiperidine [*Organic chemistry*]

NCP .... Nepali Congress Party [*Political party*] (EY)

NCP .... Net Combat Power

NCP .... Net Community Productivity (FFDE)

NCP .... Net Control Procedure

NCP .... Netherlands and Colonial Philately

NCP .... NetWare Core Protocol [*Computer science*]

NCP .... Network Control Point [*Telecommunications*]

NCP .... Network Control Processor [*Telecommunications*] (TSSD)

NCP .... Network Control Program [*IBM Corp.*] [*Telecommunications*] (BUR)

NCP .... Network Control Protocol [*Telecommunications*]

NCP .... New Call to Peacemaking (EA)

NCP .... New Communities Program [*Defunct*] (EA)

NCP .... New Community Projects [*A publication*]

NCP .... Nickel-Chromium Panel

NCP .... Nitrogen Charge Panel [*Later, MRAC*] (AAG)

NCP .... No Caffeine [*or*] Pepper (DAVI)

NCP .... No-Copy Paper

NCP .... Noctilucent Cloud Particles

NCP .... Noncarbon Paper (IAA)

NCP .... Noncollagen Protein

NCP .... Noncompliance Penalty [*Environmental Protection Agency*] (EPA)

NCP .... Non-Conformance Penalties [*Automotive emissions standards*]

NCP .... Non-Custodial Parent

NCP .... Non-United States Coalition Partner (DOMA)

NCP .... Normal Circular Pitch (MSA)

NCP .... North Celestial Pole [*Astronomy*]

NCP ...niFL ..... Nuclear Contingency Plan (MCD)

NCP .... Numerically-Controlled Peripheral (IAA)

NCP .... Nursing Care Plan

NCP .... Nuveen California Performance Plus Municipal [*NYSE symbol*] (SPSG)

NCP .... Nuveen CA Perf Plus Muni [*NYSE symbol*] (TTSB)

NCPA .... National Center for Policy Alternatives [*Later, CPA*] (EA)

NCPA .... National Coalition of Patriotic Americans

NCPA .... National Committee for the Prevention of Alcoholism and Drug Dependency [*Later, NCPADD*] (EA)

NCPA .... National Composition and Prepress Association (EA)

NCPA .... National Conservation Policy Act [*1979*]

NCPA .... National Cottonseed Products Association (EA)

NCPA .... National Crime Prevention Association [*Defunct*] (EA)

NCPAC .... National Conservative Political Action Committee (EA)

NCPAD .... National Council on Psychological Aspects of Disability (EA)

NCPADD .... National Committee for the Prevention of Alcoholism and Drug Dependency (EA)

NCPAG .... National CPA [*Certified Public Accountant*] Group [*Later, BKR International*] (EA)

NCPAMA ...... Noise Control Product and Materials Association [*Later, NCA*] (IAA)

NCPAMT ...... National Coalition of Psychiatrists Against Motorcoach Therapy (EA)

N-CPAP .... Nasal Continuous Positive Airway Pressure [*Medicine*] (DMAA)

NCPAS .... National Computer Program Abstract Service, Inc. (IID)

NC/PAT .... National Council for the Public Assessment of Technology [*Defunct*]

NCPB .... National Cancer Policy Board

NcPb .... Pinebluff Public Library, Pinebluff, NC [*Library symbol Library of Congress*] (LCLS)

NCPC .... National Cancer Pain Coalition

NCPC .... National Capital Planning Commission [*Formerly, NCPPC*]

NCPC .... National Chrysler Products Club (EA)

NCPC .... National Citizens Participation Council (EA)

NCPC .... National Coal Policy Conference [*Defunct*] (EA)

NCPC .... National Collegiate Poultry Club

NCPC .... National Crime Prevention Council (EA)

NCPC .... Nose Cone Protective Covering [*Aviation*]

NCPCA .... National Center for the Prosecution of Child Abuse (EA)

NCPCA .... National Committee for Peace in Central America [*Defunct*] (EA)

NCPCA .... National Committee for Prevention of Child Abuse (EA)

NCPCC .... National Clearinghouse for Poison Control Centers (EA)

NCpCE .... Cherry Lane Elementary School, Carle Place, NY [*Library symbol*] [*Library of Congress*] (LCLS)

NCPCINST .... Naval Civilian Personnel Command Instructions (MCD)

NCPCO .... National Climate Program Coordinating Office

NCPCR .... National Center for Prevention and Control of Rape [*National Institutes of Health*]

NCPD .... Navy Current Procurement Directive

NCPDM .... National Council of Physical Distribution Management

NCPDP .... National Council for Prescription Drug Programs (EA)

NCPDS .... Navy Civilian Personnel Data System

NCPE .... National Committee on Pay Equity (EA)

NCPE .... National Council for Preservation Education

NCPE .... Noncardiac Pulmonary Edema [*Medicine*]

NCPEA .... National College Physical Education Association [*Later, NCPEAM*] (EA)

NCPEA .... National Conference of Professors of Educational Administration [*Later, NAPEHE*] (EA)

NCPEAM ...... National College Physical Education Association for Men [*Later, NAPEHE*]

NCPEARL ...... National Coalition for Public Education and Religious Liberty (EA)

NCPEG .... Navy Contractor Performance Evaluation Group

NCPEP .... New Century Policies Educational Programs (EA)

NCPERL .... National Coalition for Public Education and Religious Liberty (EA)

NCPERS .... National Conference on Public Employee Retirement Systems (EA)

NcPeS .... Pembroke State University, Pembroke, NC [*Library symbol Library of Congress*] (LCLS)

NCPF .... National Council on Private Forests (EA)

NcPfO .... Olin Corp., Ecusta-Film Technical Library, Pisgah Forest, NC [*Library symbol Library of Congress*] (LCLS)

NCPG .... National Catholic Pharmacists Guild of the United States (EA)

NCPG .... National Committee on Planned Giving (NFD)

NCPG .... National Council on Problem Gambling (EA)

NCPG .... Nozzleless Center-Perforated Grain (MCD)

NCPGG .... National Center for Petroleum Geology and Geophysics [*Australia*]

NCPH .... National Council on Public History [*Database producer*] (EA)

NCpHS .... Carle Place High School, Carle Place, NY [*Library symbol*] [*Library of Congress*] (LCLS)

NCPI .... National Clay Pipe Institute (EA)

NCPI .... National Committee on Property Insurance [*Boston, MA*] (EA)

NCPI .... National Computer Program Index (IAA)

NCPI .... National Conference on Parent Involvement (EA)

NCPI .... National Crime Prevention Institute (EA)

NCPI .... Navy Civilian Personnel Instructions

NCPIE .... National Coalition for Parent Involvement in Education

NCPIE .... National Conference on Prescription Medicine Information and Education

NCPIE .... National Council of Patient Information and Education (EA)

NCPIM .... National Commission to Prevent Infant Mortality

NCPL .... Kirkland Town Library, Clinton, NY [*Library symbol*] [*Library of Congress*] (LCLS)

NCPL .... National Center for Preservation Law (EA)

NCPL .... National Collegiate Parachuting League (EA)

NCPLA .... National Council of Patent Law Associations [*Later, NCIPLA*] (EA)

NCPLD .... Noncoupled

NcPly .... Washington County Library, Plymouth, NC [*Library symbol Library of Congress*] (LCLS)

NcPlyP......... Pettigrew Regional Library, Plymouth, NC [*Library symbol Library of Congress*] (LCLS)

NcPm............ Charles H. Stone Memorial Library, Pilot Mountain, NC [*Library symbol Library of Congress*] (LCLS)

NCPM .... National Clay Pot Manufacturers (EA)

NCPM .... National Conference of Personal Managers (EA)

NCPM .... Noncritical Phase Matching (IAA)

NCPMA .... Noise Control Products and Materials Association [*Later, NCA*] (EA)

ncpn--.......... Panama [*MARC geographic area code Library of Congress*] (LCCP)

NCPNFUNW... National Coalition for a Policy of No-First-Use of Nuclear Weapons (EA)

NCPO .... National Chronic Pain Outreach Association (EA)

NCPO .... National Climate Program Office [*National Oceanic and Atmospheric Administration*]

NCPO .... Nordic Council for Physical Oceanography (EA)

NcPo............ United States Air Force, Pope Air Force Base, Base Library, Pope AFB, NC [*Library symbol Library of Congress*] (LCLS)

NCPOA......... National Chronic Pain Outreach Association, Inc. (PAZ)

NcPolA......... Anson Technical College, Learning Resources Center, Polk Campus, Polkton, NC [*Library symbol Library of Congress*] (LCLS)

NCPP .... National Coal Policy Project

NCPP .... National Council on Public Policy (EA)

NCPP .... National Council on Public Polls (EA)

NCPPC .... National Capital Park and Planning Commission [*Later, NCPC*]

NCPPR .... National Center for Public Policy Research (EA)

NCPQWL...... National Center for Productivity and Quality of Working Life [*Later, National Productivity Council*]

NCPR .... National Championship Poker Run [*American Motorcyclists Association*]

NCPR .... National Congress of Petroleum Retailers [*Later, SSDA*] (EA)

NCPR .... No Cardiopulmonary Resuscitation [*For terminal patients*] (DAVI)

NCpRE .... Rushmore Elementary School, Carle Place, NY [*Library symbol*] [*Library of Congress*] (LCLS)

NCPRP .... National Coastal Pollution Research Program [*Environmental Protection Agency*] (MSC)

NCPRR .... National Congress for Puerto Rican Rights (EA)

NCPRV .... National Congress of Puerto Rican Veterans (EA)

NCPRV .... National Council of Puerto Rican Volunteers [*Defunct*] (EA)

NCPS .... National Cat Protection Society (EA)

NCPS .... National Circus Preservation Society (EA)

NCPS .... National Coalition to Prevent Shoplifting (EA)

NCPS .... National Commission on Product Safety

NCPS .... National Commission on the Public Service [*Defunct*] (EA)

NCPS .... Non-Contributory Pension Scheme (DLA)

NCPS .... Nuclear Contingency Planning System (MCD)

NCPSA .... National Child Passenger Safety Association [*Later, NPSA*] (EA)

NCPSC .... National Committee on Paper Stock Conservation

NCPSF .... National Council of Professional Services Firms [*Later, PSC*] (EA)

NCPSIDS...... National Center for the Prevention of Sudden Infant Death Syndrome (EA)

NCPSSM ...... National Committee to Preserve Social Security and Medicare (EA)

NCPT .... National Conference on Power Transmission (EA)

NCPT .... National Congress of Parents and Teachers [*Later, National PTA*] (EA)

NCPT .... Nationally-Certified Psychiatric Technician

NCPT .... Navy Central Planning Team [*NATO*] (NATG)

NCPTA .... National Confederation of Parent Teacher Associations [*British*]

NCPTCAN.... National Center for the Prevention and Treatment of Child Abuse and Neglect (EA)

NCPTF .... National Campaign for a Peace Tax Fund (EA)

NCPTO .... National China Painting Teachers Organization [*Later, IPAT*] (EA)

NCPTWA ...... National Clearinghouse for Periodical Title Word Abbreviations [*ANSI*]

NCPUA .... National Committee on Pesticide Use in Agriculture [*Canada*]

NCP/VS .... NCP Virtual Storage (NITA)

NCPVS .... Network Control Program Virtual Storage [*Telecommunications*] (IAA)

NCPW .... National Country Party of Western Australia [*Political party*]

NCPWB .... National Certified Pipe Welding Bureau (EA)

NCPWSF ...... National Congenital Port Wine Stain Foundation (EA)

NCPY .... Penrhyn [*Cook Islands*] [*ICAO location identifier*] (ICLI)

NCPYA .... National Conference of Public Youth Agencies [*Defunct*] (EA)

NCQ .... Marietta, GA [*Location identifier FAA*] (FAAL)

NCQA .... National Committee for Quality Assurance (EA)

NCQHC........ National Committee for Quality Health Care (EA)

NCQIE .... National Coalition for Quality Integrated Education (EA)

NCQR .... National Council for Quality and Reliabiltiy [*British*] (BI)

NCR .... Air Sur [*Spain ICAO designator*] (FAAC)

NCR .... National Capital Region

NCR .... National Cash Register [*Computer science*] (NADA)

NCR .... National Cash Register Co. [*Later, NCR Corp.*] [*Computer manufacturer*]

NCR .... National Civic Review [*A publication*] (BRI)

NCR .... National Coalition for Research in Neurological and Communicative Disorders (EA)

NCR .... National Council of Resistance for Liberty and Independence [*Iran*] (PD)

NCR .... Naval Construction Regiment (NVT)

NCR .... Navy Code Room

NCR .... Network Change Request [*NASA*] (KSC)

NCR .... Network Control Room [*Television*]

NCR .... Neutrophil Complement Rosettes [*Hematology*]

NCRP .... New Cinema Review [*A publication*]

N Cr .... New York Criminal Reports [*A publication*] (DLA)

NCR .... Nickerson, C. R., San Francisco CA [*STAC*]

NCR .... Nicorandil [*Biochemistry*]

NCR .... Nitrile-Chloroprene Rubber

NCR .... No Calibration Required (MCD)

NCR .... No Canadian Rights

NCR .... No Carbon Required (NG)

NCR .... Noncoding Region [*Genetics*]

NCR .... Non-Combat Ready [*Military*] (SAA)

NCR .... Noncompliance Report [*Environmental Protection Agency*] (EPA)

NCR .... Nonconformance Record [*NASA*] (KSC)

NCR .... Nonconformance Report [*Nuclear energy*] (NRCH)

NCR .... Nonconserved Region [*Genetics*]

NCR .... Non-Selective Catalyst Reduction [*Diesel engine emissions*]

NCR .... North Carolina Register [*A publication*] (AAGC)

NCR .... Northern Central Railway [*British*] (ROG)

NCR .... Notification of Change Report (NRCH)

NCR .... Nucal Resources Ltd. [*Vancouver Stock Exchange symbol*]

NCR .... Nuclear (AAG)

NCR .... Nuclear Cytoplasmic Ratio [*Cytology*]

NCR .... Ontario Library Service - Voyageur [*UTLAS symbol*]

NcR............. Wake County Public Libraries, Raleigh, NC [*Library symbol Library of Congress*] (LCLS)

NcRa............ Hoke County Public Library, Raeford, NC [*Library symbol Library of Congress*] (LCLS)

NCRA .... National Cellular Resellers' Association (EA)

NCRA .... National Center on Rural Aging (EA)

NCRA .... National Championship Racing Association [*Auto racing*]

NCRA .... National Coalition of Redevelopment Agencies (EA)

NCRA .... National Cooperative Refinery Association [*Commercial firm*] (EA)

NCRA .... National Cooperative Research Act [*1984*]

NCRA .... National Correctional Recreational Association (EA)

NCRA .... National Council of Research Administrators

NCRAC .... National Community Relations Advisory Council [*Later, NJCRAC*] (EA)

NCRC .... National Catholic Resettlement Council (EA)

NCRC .... National Cave Rescue Commission

NCRC .... National Committee for a Representative Congress (EA)

NCRC .... National Community Reinvestment Coalition

NCRC .... Nickel-Cadmium Rechargeable Cell

NcR-C .... Wake County Public Libraries, Cameron Village Regional Library, Raleigh, NC [*Library symbol*] [*Library of Congress*] (LCLS)

NCRC/AODA... National Certification Reciprocity Consortium/Alcoholism and Other Drug Abuse (EA)

NCRCH........ Nordic Committee of the Research Councils for the Humanities (EA)

NcRCPL ...... Carolina Power & Light Co., Technical Library, Raleigh, NC [*Library symbol Library of Congress*] (LCLS)

NCRCRD ...... North Central Regional Center for Rural Development [*Iowa State University*] [*Research center*] (RCD)

NCRD.......... National Council on Resource Development (EA)

NCRD.......... National Council to Repeal the Draft [*Defunct*] (EA)

NCRDA........ National Center for Research into Drug Abuse [*Australia*]

NCRDC........ National Capital Region, District of Columbia (MCD)

NcRDC .... North Carolina Department of Corrections, Central Prison School, Raleigh, NC [*Library symbol Library of Congress*] (LCLS)

NCRDC........ Northern Colorado Research-Demonstration Center [*Colorado State University*] [*Research center*] (RCD)

NcRDD........ North Carolina Department of Human Resources, Dorothea Dix Hospital, F. T. Fuller Staff Library, Raleigh, NC [*Library symbol Library of Congress*] (LCLS)

NCRDL........ Nautical Charting Research and Development Laboratory [*National Oceanic and Atmospheric Administration*]

NCRDS........ National Coal Resources Data System [*Geological Survey*] [*Databank*] [*Information service or system*] (IID)

NCRDTA....... National Council of Refuse Disposal Trade Associations

NCRE .... National Conference on Research in English (EA)

NCRE .... National Council on Rehabilitation Education (EA)

NCRE .... Naval Construction Research Establishment [*British*] (AAG)

NC Reg........ North Carolina Register [*A publication*] (AAGC)

NcReH .... Annie Penn Hospital, Medical Library, Reidsville, NC [*Library symbol Library of Congress*] (LCLS)

NCREIF .... National Council of Real Estate Investment Fiduciaries (EA)

NCREL .... North Central Regional Educational Laboratory [*Elmhurst, IL*] [*Department of Education*] (GRD)

NC Rep........ North Carolina Reports [*A publication*] (DLA)

NC Rep Appendix... North Carolina Reports, Appendix [*A publication*] (DLA)

NC Reports... North Carolina Reports [*A publication*] (DLA)

NcRf............ Eden Public Library, Eden, NC [*Library symbol Library of Congress*] (LCLS)

NcR-F .... Wake County Public Libraries, Fuquay-Varina Public Library, Fuquay-Varina, NC [*Library symbol*] [*Library of Congress*] (LCLS)

NCRFCL....... National Commission on Reform of Federal Criminal Laws

NCRFP .... National Council for a Responsible Firearms Policy [*Defunct*] (EA)

NCRFRA....... National Committee to Repeal the Federal Reserve Act (EA)

NCRFSCU ... National Commission on the Role and Future of State Colleges and Universities [*Defunct*] (EA)

NCRG .... Avarua/Rarotonga International [*Cook Islands*] [*ICAO location identifier*] (ICLI)

NcRGM........ North Carolina Department of Human Resources, The Governor Morehead School, Raleigh, NC [*Library symbol Library of Congress*] (LCLS)

NcRGP .... State of North Carolina, Governor's Press Office State Capital Building, Raleigh, NC [*Library symbol*] [*Library of Congress*] (LCLS)

NcRGS .... Church of Jesus Christ of Latter-Day Saints, Genealogical Society Library, Raleigh Branch, Raleigh, NC [*Library symbol Library of Congress*] (LCLS)

NCRH.......... National Center for Radiological Health [*Public Health Service*]

NCRH........... North Coast Railroad Historical Society (EA)
NcRH........... W. W. Holding Technical Institute, Raleigh, NC [*Library symbol Library of Congress*] (LCLS)
NcRHR....... North Carolina Department of Human Resources, Public Health Library, Raleigh, NC [*Library symbol Library of Congress*] (LCLS)
NCRI........... National Center for Resource Innovations
NCRI........... National Coastal Resources Research and Development Institute [*Newport, OR*] [*Department of Commerce*] (GRD)
NCRI........... National Consumer Research Institute
NCRIB........ Naval Communications Improvement Review Board (DNAB)
NCRIC......... National Chemical Response and Information Center [*Established by the Chemical Manufacturers Association to provide information and advice during emergencies*]
NCRIPTAL.... National Center for Research to Improve Postsecondary Teaching and Learning [*Ann Arbor, MI*] [*Department of Education*] (GRD)
NCRIS......... National Committee to Restore Internal Security (EA)
NcRJP......... Jaakko Poyry, Inc., Raleigh, NC [*Library symbol*] [*Library of Congress*] (LCLS)
NCRK......... Rakahanga [*Cook Islands*] [*ICAO location identifier*] (ICLI)
NCRL........... National Canners Association Research Laboratory
NCRL........... National Citizens Radio League (IAA)
NCRLC........ National Catholic Rural Life Conference (EA)
NCRLC........ National Committee on Regional Library Cooperation
NCRLS........ National Committee for Russian Language Study [*American Association for the Advancement of Slavic Studies*] (EDAC)
NCRLS........ National Committee of Religious Leaders of Safety (EA)
NcRM.......... Meredith College, Raleigh, NC [*Library symbol Library of Congress*] (LCLS)
NCRM........ National Conference on Radiation Measurements
NCRM........ Nordic Council for Railway Music (EA)
NcRm.......... Thomas Hackney Braswell Memorial Library, Rocky Mount, NC [*Library symbol Library of Congress*] (LCLS)
NcRMA........ North Carolina Museum of Art in Raleigh, Raleigh, NC [*Library symbol Library of Congress*] (LCLS)
NcRMC........ Meredith College, Raleigh, NC [*Library symbol*] [*Library of Congress*] (LCLS)
NCRMD........ National Capital Region, Maryland (MCD)
NcRmE........ Edgecombe Technical College, Learning Resources Center, Rocky Mount, NC [*Library symbol Library of Congress*] (LCLS)
NcRMG .... Measurements Group, Inc., Raleigh, NC [*Library symbol Library of Congress*] (LCLS)
NcRmHE ...... Area L AHEC Library, Rocky Mount, NC [*Library symbol*] [*Library of Congress*] (LCLS)
NcRmN .... Nash Technical Institute, Rocky Mount, NC [*Library symbol Library of Congress*] (LCLS)
NcRMNH...... North Carolina State Museum of Natural History, Raleigh, NC [*Library symbol Library of Congress*] (LCLS)
NcRMNH-B... North Carolina State Museum of Natural History, H. H. Brimley Memorial Library, Raleigh, NC [*Library symbol Library of Congress*] (LCLS)
NcRmW .... North Carolina Wesleyan College, Rocky Mount, NC [*Library symbol*] [*Library of Congress*] (LCLS)
NCRND .... National Committee for Research in Neurological Disorders [*Later, NCR*] (EA)
NcRNO......... News and Observer Publishing Co., Raleigh, NC [*Library symbol*] [*Library of Congress*] (LCLS)
NcRNR......... North Carolina Department of Natural Resources and Community Development, Raleigh, NC [*Library symbol*] [*Library of Congress*] (LCLS)
NCRNT........ National Committee for Rescue from NAZI Terror [*British*]
NcRo........... Rockingham-Richmond County Library, Rockingham, NC [*Library symbol Library of Congress*] (LCLS)
NcRob.......... Bemis Memorial Library, Robbinsville, NC [*Library symbol Library of Congress*] (LCLS)
NcRobS........ Snowbird Community Library, Robbinsville, NC [*Library symbol Library of Congress*] (LCLS)
NCroh .... Croton Free Library, Croton-On-Hudson, NY [*Library symbol Library of Congress*] (LCLS)
NCrohH........ Hudson Institute, Croton-On-Hudson, NY [*Library symbol Library of Congress*] (LCLS)
NcRop.......... Roper Community Library and Resource Center, Inc., Roper, NC [*Library symbol*] [*Library of Congress*] (LCLS)
NCROPA ...... National Campaign for the Reform of the Obscene Publications Acts [*British*] (DBA)
NcRoS .... Sandhills Regional Library, Rockingham, NC [*Library symbol Library of Congress*] (LCLS)
NcRov.......... Robersonville Public Library, Robersonville, NC [*Library symbol Library of Congress*] (LCLS)
NcRox.......... Person County Public Library, Roxboro, NC [*Library symbol Library of Congress*] (LCLS)
NcRoxP........ Person Technical Institute, Roxboro, NC [*Library symbol Library of Congress*] (LCLS)
NCRP........... National Climatic Research Program
NCRP........... National Commission on Radiological Protection
NCRP........... National Committee for Responsible Patriotism (EA)
NCRP........... National Committee for Responsive Philanthropy (EA)
NCRP........... National Council for Research and Planning (EA)
NCRP........... National Council on Radiation Protection and Measurements [*Later, NCRPM*]
NcRP .... Peace College, Raleigh, NC [*Library symbol Library of Congress*] (LCLS)
NCRPC........ National Capital Regional Planning Council [*Terminated, 1966*]
NCRPCV....... National Council of Returned Peace Corps Volunteers (EA)
NCRPE......... National Council on Religion and Public Education (EA)

NcRPI .... North Carolina Department of Public Instruction, Education Information Services, Raleigh, NC [*Library symbol*] [*Library of Congress*] (LCLS)
NCRPM .... National Council on Radiation Protection and Measurements (EA)
NcRPS .... Pointer & Spruill Library, Raleigh, NC [*Library symbol*] [*Library of Congress*] (LCLS)
NCRR.......... National Center for Research Resources [*National Institutes of Health*]
NCRR.......... National Center for Resource Recovery [*Defunct*]
NCRR.......... National Credit Union Administration Rules and Regulations
NCRR.......... Nordic Council of Reindeer Research (EAIO)
NcRr .... Roanoke Rapids Public Library, Roanoke Rapids, NC [*Library symbol Library of Congress*] (LCLS)
NCRRC........ National Committee to Reopen the Rosenberg Case (EA)
NCRRF........ Norris Communications Corp. [*NASDAQ symbol*] (SAG)
NcRRH......... Rex Hospital Library, Raleigh, NC [*Library symbol*] [*Library of Congress*] (LCLS)
NCRRHA ..... National Confederation of Registered Rest Home Associations [*British*] (DBA)
NCRRRC...... North Country Reference and Research Resources Council [*Information service or system*] (IID)
NCRS.......... National Clearinghouse on Revenue Sharing [*Defunct*]
NCRS.......... National Committee for Rural Schools [*Defunct*] (EA)
NCRS.......... National Corvette Restorers Society (EA)
NcRS .... North Carolina State University at Raleigh, Raleigh, NC [*Library symbol Library of Congress*] (LCLS)
NCRSA........ National Commercial Refrigeration Sales Association (EA)
NcRSA .... Saint Augustine's College, Raleigh, NC [*Library symbol Library of Congress*] (LCLS)
NcRSh .... Shaw University, Raleigh, NC [*Library symbol Library of Congress*] (LCLS)
NcRSM .... Saint Mary's Junior College, Raleigh, NC [*Library symbol Library of Congress*] (LCLS)
NcRS-P....... North Carolina State University at Raleigh, Photocopy Services, Raleigh, NC [*Library symbol*] [*Library of Congress*] (LCLS)
NCRSR........ National Congenital Rubella Syndrome Registry [*Centers for Disease Control*]
NcRS-V....... North Carolina State University, School of Veterinary Medicine, Raleigh, NC [*Library symbol Library of Congress*] (LCLS)
NCRT.......... National College of Rubber Technology (PDAA)
NCRTE .... National Center for Research on Teacher Education [*East Lansing, MI*] [*Department of Education*] (GRD)
NCR/TSI...... NCR Telecommunication Services, Inc. (TSSD)
NcRu.......... Norris Public Library, Rutherfordton, NC [*Library symbol Library of Congress*] (LCLS)
NCRUCE...... National Conference of Regulatory Utility Commission Engineers (EA)
NcRuR......... Rutherford County Library, Inc., Rutherfordton, NC [*Library symbol Library of Congress*] (LCLS)
NCRV.......... National Committee for Radiation Victims (EA)
NCRVA........ National Capital Region, Virginia (MCD)
NCRVD........ National Conference of Religious Vocation Directors [*Later, NRVC*] (EA)
NCRVDM..... National Conference of Religious Vocation Directors of Men [*Later, NCRVD*]
NCRVE........ National Center for Research in Vocational Education (EA)
NCRW......... National Council for Research on Women (EA)
NcRWCM..... Wake County Hospital System, Wake County Medical Center, Raleigh, NC [*Library symbol Library of Congress*] (LCLS)
NcRWHD..... Wake County Health Department, Raleigh, NC [*Library symbol*] [*Library of Congress*] (LCLS)
NCRWS........ National Campaign for Radioactive Waste Safety (EA)
NCRY.......... National Commission on Resources for Youth
NCS .... National Cartoonists Society (EA)
NCS .... National Cemetery System
NCS .... National Center for Stuttering (EA)
NCS .... National Chrysanthemum Society (EA)
NCS .... National Commemorative Society [*Defunct*]
NCS .... National Committee on Safety
NCS .... National Communications System [*DoD*]
NCS .... National Compliance Strategy (GNE)
NCS .... National Computer Systems, Inc.
NCS .... National Conference on Solicitations (EA)
NCS .... National Consensus Standards (MCD)
NCS .... National Conservation Strategy (GNE)
NCS .... National Convenience Stores, Inc. [*NYSE symbol*] (SPSG)
NCS .... National Corrosion Service [*British*] (IRUK)
NCS .... National Council of Stutterers [*Later, NCOS*] (EA)
NCS .... National Crime Stoppers [*Later, ACF*] (EA)
NCS .... National Crime Survey [*University of Michigan*] [*Database*]
NCS .... National Cryptologic School [*National Security Agency*]
NCS .... Naval Canteen Service [*British military*] (DMA)
NCS .... Naval Communications Station [*or System*]
NCS .... Naval Compass Stabilizer (PDAA)
NCS .... Naval Control of Shipping [*NATO*] (NATG)
NCS .... Navigational Computer Set (MCD)
NCS .... Navigation Control Simulator
NCS .... N-Chlorosuccinimide [*Organic chemistry*]
NCS .... NCR [*NCR Corp.*] Century Software
NCS .... Nearest Cross Street (ADA)
NCS .... Needlework and Craft Showcase (ITD)
NCS .... Neocarzinostatin [*Zinostatin*] [*Antineoplastic drug*]
NCS .... Nerve Conduction Studies [*Neurology*] (DAVI)
NCS .... Net Control Station [*Communications*] [*Amateur radio*]
NCS .... Network Communications Server [*J & L Information Systems*]

NCS .... Network Communication System (IAA)
NCS .... Network Control Station (IAA)
NCS .... Network Control System
NCS .... Network Coordination Station
NCS .... Network Co-ordination System (NITA)
NCS .... Newborn Calf Serum [Immunology]
NCS .... Newcastle [South Africa] [Airport symbol] (OAG)
NCS .... Nielsen Coverage Service [A.C. Nielson Co.] (DOAD)
NCS .... Nineteenth Century Series [A publication]
NCS .... NMIC [National Military Intelligence Center] Control Subsystem
NCS .... No Checking Signal [Telecommunications] (TEL)
NCS .... No Concentrated Sweets [Medicine] (DMAA)
NCS .... Noncallable Security [Investment term]
NCS .... Noncircumferential Stenosis [Medicine] (DMAA)
NCS .... Non-Collimated Source (PDAA)
NCS .... Non-Conventional System [Post coordinate indexing] (NITA)
NCS .... Noncoronary Sinus [Cardiology] (AAMN)
NCS .... Noncritical Sensitive [DoD]
NCS .... Noncrystalline Solid [Physics]
NCS .... Noncrystallographic Symmetry [Chemistry]
NCS .... Nonwater Cooling System
NCS .... North Carolina State Library, Raleigh, NC [OCLC symbol] (OCLC)
NCS .... Northern Cross Society (EA)
NCS .... Nuclear-Chicago Solubilizer
NCS .... Nuclear Components Spare (IAA)
NCS .... Nuclear Criticality Safety (NRCH)
NCS .... Nuclear-Powered Container Ship (PDAA)
NCS .... Nucleolar Channel System
NCS .... Nucleus Support Crew [Navy] (DNAB)
NCS .... Nueva Concepcion [El Salvador] [Seismograph station code, US Geological Survey Closed] (SEIS)
NCS .... Numerical Category Scaling
NCS .... Numerical Control Society [Later, NCS/AIMTECH] (EA)
NCS .... Numerical Control System (IAA)
NCS .... Nutation Control System (MCD)
NCS .... Simpson Air Ltd. [Canada ICAO designator] (FAAC)
NCSA .... National Capital Speakers Association (EA)
NCSA .... National Carl Schurz Association [Defunct] (EA)
NCSA .... National Center for Statistics and Analysis [National Highway Traffic Safety Administration] [Washington, DC] (GRD)
NCSA .... National Center for Supercomputer Applications (NITA)
NCSA .... National Center for Supercomputing Applications [University of Illinois] [National Science Foundation] [Research center] (RCD)
NCSA .... National Church Secretaries Association [Defunct] (EA)
NCSA .... National Club Sports Association (EA)
NCSA .... National Coffee Service Association [Vienna, VA] (EA)
NCSA .... National Collegiate Ski Association (EA)
NCSA .... National Computer Security Association [Computer science] (PCM)
NCSA .... National Confectionery Salesmen's Association of America (EA)
NCSA .... National Construction Software Association (EA)
NCSA .... National Contract Sweepers Association [Later, NCSI] (EA)
NCSA .... National Council of Seamen's Agencies [Later, ICOSA] (EA)
NCSA .... National Crushed Stone Association [Later, NSA] (EA)
NCSA .... National Cued Speech Association (EA)
NCSA .... National Customs Service Association [Later, NTEU] (EA)
NCSA .... Newsagency Council of South Australia
NCSA .... Newspaper Collectors Society of America (EA)
NCSA .... No Charge Storage Agreement (AAGC)
NCSA .... Non-Chemical Shift Anisotropy [Physical chemistry]
NCSA .... Noncommercial Spot Announcement [Public service announcement] (NTCM)
NCSAB ...... National Council of State Agencies for the Blind (EA)
NCSABMT ... National Campaign to Save the ABM [Antiballistic missile] Treaty [Defunct] (EA)
NcSaC........ Central Carolina Technical Institute, Sanford, NC [Library symbol Library of Congress] (LCLS)
NCSAC ...... National Catholic Social Action Conference [Defunct] (EA)
NCSAC ...... National Child Support Advocacy Coalition (EA)
NCSAC ...... Nuclear Cross Sections Advisory Committee
NcSaCi....... Cilco, Sanford, NC [Library symbol] [Library of Congress] (LCLS)
NCSAG........ Nuclear Cross Section Advisory Group (NRCH)
NCS/AIMTECH... Numerical Control Society/AIMTECH [Association for Integrated Manufacturing Technology] (EA)
NcSaL........ Lee County Library, Sanford, NC [Library symbol Library of Congress] (LCLS)
NcSal......... Rowan Public Library, Salisbury, NC [Library symbol Library of Congress] (LCLS)
NcSalC....... Catawba College, Salisbury, NC [Library symbol Library of Congress] (LCLS)
NcSaLCL..... Lee County Library, Sanford, NC [Library symbol] [Library of Congress] (LCLS)
NcSal-E...... Rowan Public Library East Branch, Rockwell, NC [Library symbol] [Library of Congress] (LCLS)
NcSalL....... Livingstone College, Salisbury, NC [Library symbol Library of Congress] (LCLS)
NcSalR ...... Rowan Technical Institute, Salisbury, NC [Library symbol Library of Congress] (LCLS)
NcSalRH..... Rowan Memorial Hospital Area, Health Education Center, Salisbury, NC [Library symbol Library of Congress] (LCLS)
NcSal-S...... Rowan Public Library, South Rowan Branch, Landis, NC [Library symbol Library of Congress] (LCLS)
NcSalTM..... Tri-County Mental Health Center, Salisbury, NC [Library symbol] [Library of Congress] (LCLS)
NcSalVA ...... United States Veterans Administration Center, Medical Library, Salisbury, NC [Library symbol Library of Congress] (LCLS)

NCSAnet ...... [The] National Center for Supercomputing Applications Network [Computer science] (TNIG)
NCSASR...... National Center for Small-Angle Scattering Research [Oak Ridge, TN] [Department of Energy] (GRD)
NCSAW ...... National Catholic Society for Animal Welfare [Later, ISAR] (EA)
NCSB .... National Centre for School Biotechnology (AIE)
NCSBCS ...... National Conference of States on Building Codes and Standards (EA)
NCSBEE ...... National Council of State Boards of Engineering Examiners [Later, NCEE] (EA)
NCSBI .... National Council for Small Business Innovation
NcSbJ .... North Carolina Justice Academy, Salemburg, NC [Library symbol Library of Congress] (LCLS)
NCSBMD..... National Council for Small Business Management Development [Later, ICSB] (EA)
NCSBN .... National Council of State Boards of Nursing (EA)
NcSbP .... Southwood College, Salemburg, NC [Library symbol Library of Congress] (LCLS)
NCSC .... National Catholic Stewardship Council (EA)
NCSC .... National Center for State Courts (EA)
NCSC .... National Child Safety Council (EA)
NCSC .... National Communication System Circulars
NCSC .... National Computer Security Council
NCSC .... National Council of Senior Citizens (EA)
NCSC .... National Council on Schoolhouse Construction [Later, CEFP] (EA)
NCSC .... Naval Coastal Systems Center [Panama City, FL]
NCSC .... Navy Command Support Center (MCD)
NCSC .... North Carolina State College
Nc-SC .... North Carolina State Supreme Court, Raleigh, NC [Library symbol Library of Congress] (LCLS)
NCSCBHEP... National Center for the Study of Collective Bargaining in Higher Education and the Professions (EA)
NCSCC........ National Championship Stock Car Racing [Later, NASCAR]
NCSCCY...... National Council of State Committees for Children and Youth (EA)
NCSCEE ...... National Council of State Consultants in Elementary Education [Defunct] (EA)
NCSCI .... National Center for Standards and Certification Information [Gaithersburg, MD] [Database] [National Institute of Standards and Technology]
NCSCJ .... National Conference of Special Court Judges (EA)
NCSCJPA ...... National Conference of State Criminal Justice Planning Administrators [Later, NCJA] (EA)
NCSCL .... National Committee for Sexual Civil Liberties (EA)
NcScn .... Scotland Neck Memorial Library, Scotland Neck, NC [Library symbol Library of Congress] (LCLS)
NCSCPAS ...... National Center for the Study of Corporal Punishment and Alternatives in the Schools (EA)
NCSCR .... North Carolina State College Reactor
NCSCT .... National Center for School and College Television
NCSD .... National Child Safety Development [British]
NCSD .... National Council on Student Development (EA)
NCSE .... National Center for Science Education (EA)
NCSE .... National Commission on Safety Education [Defunct] (EA)
NCSE .... National Committee on Secondary Education [of NASSP]
NCSE .... National Council for Special Education [British]
NcSe .... Selma Public Library, Selma, NC [Library symbol] [Library of Congress] (LCLS)
NCSEA .... National Child Support Enforcement Association (EA)
NCSEA .... National Community School Education Association [Later, NCEA] (EA)
NCSEA .... National Council of State Education Associations (EA)
NCSEE .... National Coalition for Sex Equity in Education (EA)
NCSEER ...... National Council for Soviet and East European Research (EA)
NCSEES ...... Nordic Committee for Soviet and East European Studies (EA)
NCSEMSTC... National Council of State Emergency Medical Services Training Coordinators (EA)
NC Sess Laws... Session Laws of North Carolina [A publication] (DLA)
NCSEX .... Naval Control of Shipping Exercises
NCSF .... National Catholic Society of Foresters (EA)
NCSF .... National Cold Storage Federation [British] (DBA)
NCSF .... National College Student Foundation [Defunct] (EA)
NCSFA .... National Conference of State Fleet Administrators (EA)
NCSFI .... National Coalition to Stop Food Irradiation (EA)
NCSFP .... National Council on Synthetic Fuels Production [Later, CSF] (EA)
NCSFWI ...... National Coalition to Stop Food and Water Irradiation (EA)
NCSG .... National Chimney Sweep Guild (EA)
NCSGC .... National Council of State Garden Clubs (EA)
NCSGSO ...... National Conference of State General Service Officers [Later, NASDAGS] (EA)
NcSh .... Cleveland County Memorial Library, Shelby, NC [Library symbol Library of Congress] (LCLS)
NCsh .... Cold Spring Harbor Public Library, Cold Spring Harbor, NY [Library symbol Library of Congress] (LCLS)
NCSH .... National Clearinghouse for Smoking and Health [Public Health Service]
NCSH .... Newton College of the Sacred Heart [Later, Newton College] [Massachusetts]
NCSHA .... Naval Communications System Headquarters Activity (SAA)
NCshB......... Cold Spring Harbor Biological Laboratory, Cold Spring Harbor, NY [Library symbol Library of Congress] (LCLS)
NcShC........ Cleveland County Technical Institute, Shelby, NC [Library symbol Library of Congress] (LCLS)
NCshL......... Cold Spring Harbor Public Library, Cold Spring Harbor, NY [Library symbol] [Library of Congress] (LCLS)
NCS Hlt........ NCS Healthcare, Inc. [Associated Press] (SAG)

NCSHPO	National Conference of State Historic Preservation Officers (EA)
NCSHSA	National Council of State Human Service Administrators (EA)
NCshWM	Whaling Museum Society, Inc., Cold Spring Harbor, NY [*Library symbol Library of Congress*] (LCLS)
NCSI	National Communication System Instructions
NCSI	National Contract Sweepers Institute (EA)
NCSI	National Convenience Stores, Inc. [*NASDAQ symbol*] (SAG)
NCSI	National Council for Stream Improvement (EA)
NCSI	National Council of Savings Institutions (EMRF)
NCSI	National Council of Self-Insurers [*Chicago, IL*] (EA)
NCSI	National Curriculum Study Institute [*Associaton for Supervision and Curriculum Development*] (EDAC)
NCSI	Network Communications Services Interface [*Computer science*] (PCM)
NCSIT	National Coalition to Support Indian Treaties (EA)
NCSITSG	National Community Services Industry Training Steering Group [*Australia*]
NCSJ	National College of the State Judiciary (DLA)
NCSJ	National Conference on Soviet Jewry (EA)
NCSJ	Naval Communication Station, Japan
NcSj	United States Air Force, Seymour Johnson Air Force Base, Base Library, Seymour Johnson AFB, NC [*Library symbol Library of Congress*] (LCLS)
NCSL	National Center for Service-Learning [*Defunct*] (EA)
NCSL	National Civil Service League [*Defunct*] (EA)
NCSL	National Conference of Standards Laboratories (EA)
NCSL	National Conference of State Legislatures (EA)
NCSL	Naval Coastal Systems Laboratory [*Later, NCSC*]
NCSL	Naval Code and Signal Laboratory
NCSL	Near-Coincident Site Lattice [*Crystallography*]
NCSLA	National Conference of State Liquor Administrators (EA)
NCSLL	National Conference of State Legislative Leaders [*Later, NCSL*] (EA)
NCSLO	Naval Control of Shipping Liaison Officer
NCSM	National Communication System Memoranda
NCSM	National Council of Supervisors of Mathematics (EA)
NCSMHC	National Council for the Single Mother and Her Child [*Australia*]
NcSmJ	Johnston County Technical Institute, Smithfield, NC [*Library symbol Library of Congress*] (LCLS)
NCSMX	National Campaign to Stop the MX [*Defunct*] (EA)
NcSn	Greene County Public Library, Snow Hill, NC [*Library symbol Library of Congress*] (LCLS)
NCSN	National Computer Service Network (EA)
NCSN	National Council for School Nurses [*of AAHPER*]
NCSNE	Naval Control of Shipping in Northern European Command Area [*NATO*] (NATG)
NCSO	National Council of Salesmen's Organizations [*New York, NY*] (EA)
NCSO	Naval Control of Shipping Officer
NCSO	Naval Control of Shipping Operations
NCSO	Naval Control Service Office [*World War II British Routing Service*]
NCSOICC	North Carolina State Occupational Information Coordinating Committee (EDAC)
NcSopS-L	Southport-Brunswick County Library, Leland Branch Library, Leland, NC [*Library symbol Library of Congress*] (LCLS)
NcSopS-W ...	Southport-Brunswick County Library, West Brunswick Branch Library, Shallotte, NC [*Library symbol Library of Congress*] (LCLS)
NCSORG	Naval Control of Shipping Organization
NCSP	National Center for Surrogate Parenting [*Later, IAI*] [*Commercial firm*] (EA)
NCSP	National Conference on State Parks [*Later, NRPA*] (EA)
NCSP	National Crime Stop Program (EA)
NCSP	Naval Communication Station, Philippines (DNAB)
NCSP	Nordic Committee on Salaries and Personnel [*Nordic Council of Ministers*] [*Copenhagen, Denmark*] (EAIO)
NcSp	Southern Pines Public Library, Southern Pines, NC [*Library symbol Library of Congress*] (LCLS)
NcSpa	Alleghany County Public Library, Sparta, NC [*Library symbol Library of Congress*] (LCLS)
NCSPA	National Corrugated Steel Pipe Association (EA)
NCSPAA	National Council of School Press and Advisers Association
NCSPAE	National Council of State Pharmaceutical Association Executives (EA)
NCSPAS	National Conference of State Pharmaceutical Association Secretaries [*Later, NCSPAE*]
NcSph	Spring Hope Public Library, Spring Hope, NC [*Library symbol Library of Congress*] (LCLS)
NcSpi	Spindale Public Library, Spindale, NC [*Library symbol Library of Congress*] (LCLS)
NcSpiI	Isothermal Community College, Spindale, NC [*Library symbol Library of Congress*] (LCLS)
NcSpiR	Rutherford County Library, Inc., Spindale, NC [*Library symbol*] [*Library of Congress*] (LCLS)
NCSPP	National Center for Social Policy and Practice (EA)
NcSppA	Avery-Mitchell-Yancey Regional Library, Spruce Pine, NC [*Library symbol Library of Congress*] (LCLS)
NcSppM	Mayland Technical Institute, Spruce Pine, NC [*Library symbol Library of Congress*] (LCLS)
NcSpr	Spray Public Library, Spray, NC [*Library symbol*] [*Library of Congress*] (LCLS)
NCSPS	National Committee for Support of the Public Schools [*Later, NCCE*] (EA)
NcSpS	Sandhills Community College, Southern Pines, NC [*Library symbol Library of Congress*] (LCLS)
NCSPWA	National Council of State Public Welfare Administrators [*Later, NCSHSA*] (EA)
NCSR	National Centre for Systems Reliability [*Research center British*] (CB)

NCSRA	National Conference of State Retail Associations (EA)
NCSS	National Cactus and Succulent Society [*British*] (BI)
NCSS	National Center for Social Statistics [*HEW*]
NCSS	National Collegiate Sports Services (EA)
NCSS	National Commission on Supplies and Shortages [*Terminated, 1977*]
NCSS	National Conference of Shomrim Societies (EA)
NCSS	National Conference of State Societies (EA)
NCSS	National Conference on Student Services (EA)
NCSS	National Conversational Software Systems, Inc.
NCSS	National Cooperative Soil Survey
NCSS	National Council for the Social Studies (EA)
NCSS	National Council of Social Service [*British*]
NCSS	National Crash Severity Study [*National Highway Traffic Safety Administration*]
NCSS	Navy Command Support System (MCD)
NCSS	NCS HealthCare 'A' [*NASDAQ symbol*] (TTSB)
NCSS	NCS Healthcare, Inc. [*NASDAQ symbol*] (SAG)
NCSS	Nordic Council of Ski Schools (EAIO)
NCSS	Number Cruncher Statistical System [*Computer software*] (PCM)
NCSSA	Naval Command Systems Support Activity
NCSSAD	National Council of Secondary School Athletic Directors (EA)
NCSSB	National Coalition for Seat Belts on School Buses (EA)
NCSSC	Naval Command Systems Support Center
NCSSE	National Coalition to Support Sexuality Education [*Fact sheet published by the Sexuality Information and Education Coalition of the United States (SIECUS)*] (PAZ)
NCSSFL	National Council of State Supervisors of Foreign Languages (EA)
NCSSIA	National Council of State Self-Insurers Associations [*Later, NCSI*] (EA)
NCSSM	National Council of State Supervisors of Music (EA)
NCSSM	North Carolina School of Science and Mathematics [*Free, residential public high school for gifted students*]
NCSSMA	National Council of Social Security Management Associations (EA)
NCSSSA	National Conference of State Social Security Administrators (EA)
NCSSW	Nordic Committee of Schools of Social Work (EAIO)
NcSt	Iredell Public Library, Statesville, NC [*Library symbol Library of Congress*] (LCLS)
NCST	National Certification Skills Test [*Psychiatry*]
NCST	National Coalition for Science and Technology [*Defunct*] (EA)
NCSTAR	National Committee of Shatnez Testers and Researchers (EA)
NCSTAS	National Council of Scientific and Technical Art Societies [*Later, IG*] (EA)
NCSTD	National Council of State Travel Directors (EA)
NcStH	Iredell Memorial Hospital, Statesville, NC [*Library symbol*] [*Library of Congress*] (LCLS)
NCstLf	North Coast Life Insurance Co. [*Associated Press*] (SAG)
NcStMC	Mitchell College, Statesville, NC [*Library symbol Library of Congress*] (LCLS)
NcStpR	Robeson Technical Institute, St. Pauls, NC [*Library symbol Library of Congress Obsolete*] (LCLS)
NCSTR	NATO Communication System Technical Recommendation (NATG)
NC Str	Strange's Notes of Cases, Madras [*1798-1816*] [*A publication*] (DLA)
NC/STRC	North Carolina Science and Technology Research Center [*North Carolina Department of Commerce*] [*Research center*] (RCD)
NCSTS	National Conference of State Transportation Specialists (EA)
NCSTSR	National Conference of Superintendents of Training Schools and Reformatories [*Later, International Conference of Administrators Residential Centers for Youth -ICA*] (EA)
NCSU	Network Channel Service Unit [*Computer science*] (TNIG)
NCSU	North Carolina State University [*Raleigh*]
NcSupB	Brunswick Technical College, Supply, NC [*Library symbol Library of Congress*] (LCLS)
NCSW	National Conference of Social Workers
NCSW	National Conference on Social Welfare [*Defunct*] (EA)
NCSW	National Council for the Single Woman and Her Dependants Ltd. [*British*] (BI)
NcSw	Swannanoa Public Library, Swannanoa, NC [*Library symbol Library of Congress*] (LCLS)
NcSwC	Chemtronics, Inc., Swannanoa, NC [*Library symbol*] [*Library of Congress*] (LCLS)
NCSWCL	National [*Presidential*] Commission on State Workmen's Compensation Laws
NCSWD	National Center for Solid Waste Disposal [*Later, National Center for Resource Recovery*] (EA)
NCSWD	National Council for the Single Woman and Her Dependants (EA)
NCSWDI	National Combination Storm Window and Door Institute [*Defunct*] (EA)
NcSwW	Warren Wilson College, Swannanoa, NC [*Library symbol Library of Congress*] (LCLS)
NCSX	Shipping Control Exercise [*NATO exercises*] (NATG)
NcSy	Jackson County Public Library, Sylva, NC [*Library symbol Library of Congress*] (LCLS)
NCSY	National Conference of Synagogue Youth (EA)
NcSyS	Southwestern Technical Institute, Sylva, NC [*Library symbol Library of Congress*] (LCLS)
NCT	Name Changed To
NCT	National Centre of Tribology [*Risley Nuclear Laboratories*] [*British*] (CB)
NCT	National Chamber of Trade [*British*] (BI)
NCT	National Childbirth Trust [*British*]
NCT	National College Television [*Cable-television system*] (WDMC)
N Ct	Native Court [*Ghana*] [*A publication*] (DLA)
NCT	NATO Comparative Testing (RDA)
NCT	Neoclassical Radiation Theory
NCT	Nerve Conduction Tests [*Neurology*] (DAVI)

NCT.............. Nerve Conduction Time [neurology] (DAVI)
NCT.............. Net Cost of Transport
NCT.............. Network Control Terminal (MCD)
NCT.............. Neural Crest Tumor [Oncology]
NCT.............. Neutral Contour Technology [Automotive engineering]
NCT.............. New Curing Technology
NCT.............. Nicoya [Costa Rica] [Airport symbol] (AD)
NCT.............. Night Closing Trunks [Telecommunications] (TEL)
NCT.............. Noise Cancellation Technology (PS)
NCT.............. Non-Chargeable Time (DGA)
NCT.............. Non-Competitive Tenders [Business term] (MHDW)
NCT.............. Non-Contact Time (AIE)
NCT.............. Nordic Cooperation on Telecommunications (EAIO)
NCT.............. North Coast Industries Ltd. [Vancouver Stock Exchange symbol]
NCT.............. Northern Cultural Trust [South Australia]
NCT.............. Number Connection Test
NcTA............. Edgecombe County Memorial Library, Tarboro, NC [Library symbol Library of Congress] (LCLS)
NCTA .... National Cable Television Association (EA)
NCTA .... National Capital Transportation Agency [Functions transferred to Washington Metropolitan Area Transit Authority]
NCTA .... National Cattle Theft Act
NCTA .... National Ceramic Teachers Association (EA)
NCTA .... National Christmas Tree Association (EA)
NCTA .... National Council for Technological Awards [British]
NCTA .... National Council for the Traditional Arts (EA)
NCTA .... Navajo Code Talkers Association (EA)
NCTA .... North Country Trail Association (EA)
NcTaE........... Edgecombe County Technical Institute, Tarboro, NC [Library symbol Library of Congress] (LCLS)
NcTaH.......... Edgecomb General Hospital Library, Tarboro, NC [Library symbol] [Library of Congress] (LCLS)
NCTAM .... National Committee for Theoretical and Applied Mechanics [British]
NCTAMS ..... Naval Computer and Telecommunications Area Master Station (DOMA)
NcTa-P........ Edgecombe County Memorial Library, Pinetops Branch, Pinetops, NC [Library symbol Library of Congress] (LCLS)
NcTayA .... Alexander County Public Library, Taylorsville, NC [Library symbol Library of Congress] (LCLS)
NCTC .... National Cancer Institute Tissue Culture [Medium]
NCTC .... National Catholic Theatre Conference (EA)
NCTC .... National Collection of Type Cultures [British]
NCTC .... Naval Communications Training Center
NCTC .... Naval Communications and Telecommunications Command (DOMA)
NCTC .... Naval Construction Training Center
NCTCA .... National Collegiate Track Coaches Association (EA)
NCTCA .... National Council of Teachers for Critical Analysis (AEBS)
NCTCP .... National Coalition of Title I/Chapter I Parents (EA)
NCTD .... National College of Teachers of the Deaf [British]
NCTE............. National Council for Textile Education (EA)
NCTE............. National Council for Torah Education (EA)
NCTE............. National Council of Teachers of English (EA)
NCTE............. Network Channel Terminating Equipment [Telecommunications]
NCTE............. No-Cost Time Extension (MCD)
NCTE............. North Central Turfgrass Exposition [Illinois Turfgrass Foundation] (TSPED)
NCTEPS .... National Commission on Teacher Education and Professional Standards [Defunct] (EA)
NC Term R... North Carolina Term Reports [A publication] (DLA)
NC Term Rep... North Carolina Term Reports [A publication] (DLA)
NCTF............ National Check Traders Federation [British] (BI)
NCTF............ National Corporate Theatre Fund (EA)
NCTFC .... North Central Texas Film Cooperative [Library network]
NCTGA .... National Christmas Tree Growers Association [Later, National Christmas Tree Association] (EA)
NcTh .... Thomasville Public Library, Thomasville, NC [Library symbol Library of Congress] (LCLS)
NcThCH...... Community General Hospital Library, Thomasville, NC [Library symbol] [Library of Congress] (LCLS)
NcThDM...... Davidson Area Mental Health Center, Thomasville, NC [Library symbol] [Library of Congress] (LCLS)
NCTI............. National Cable Television Institute (EA)
NCTI............. National Consumer Testing Institute (BARN)
NCTI............. Noise Cancellation Tech [NASDAQ symbol] (TTSB)
NCTI............. Noise Cancellation Technologies, Inc. [NASDAQ symbol] (SAG)
NCTIP .... National Coalition of ESEA [Elementary and Secondary Education Act] Title I Parents (EA)
NCTIP .... National Committee on the Treatment of Intractable Pain (EA)
NCTJ............ National Council for the Training of Journalists [British]
NCTL............ National Commercial Temperance League [British] (BI)
NCTM........... National Council of Teachers of Mathematics (EA)
NCTO .... Naval Central Torpedo Office
NCTO .... Navy Clothing and Textile Supply Office
NCTP .... National Cryptologic Training Plan (MCD)
NCTPD .... National Council for Teacher-Centred Professional Development [British] (DBA)
NCTPI .... Nuveen Connecticut Premium Income Municipal Fund [Associated Press] (SAG)
NcTr............. Montgomery County Public Library, Troy, NC [Library symbol Library of Congress] (LCLS)
NCTR .... National Center for Telephone Research [Louis Harris and Associates] [Commercial firm] (EA)
NCTR .... National Center for Therapeutic Riding (EA)
NCTR .... National Center for Toxicological Research [Department of Health and Human Services] [Jefferson, AR]

NCTR .... National Council on Teacher Retirement (EA)
NCTR .... Naval Commercial Traffic Regulations
NCTR .... Noncooperative Target Recognition (MCD)
NCTR .... Nordic Council for Tax Research (EA)
NCTR .... Taylor's North Carolina Term Reports [A publication] (DLA)
NCTRC......... National Council for Therapeutic Recreation Certification (EA)
NcTrDC........ North Carolina Department of Corrections, Troy, NC [Library symbol] [Library of Congress] (LCLS)
NCT Rep ..... North Carolina Term Reports [A publication] (DLA)
NCTRF......... Navy Clothing and Textile Research Facility [Natick, MA]
NCTRH........ National Council for Therapy and Rehabilitation through Horticulture (EA)
NcTrM......... Montgomery Technical Institute, Troy, NC [Library symbol Library of Congress] (LCLS)
NCTRP........ National Cooperative Transit Research and Development Program [TRB] (TAG)
NCTRU........ Navy Clothing and Textile Research Unit (MCD)
NCTS .... National Center for Tourism Studies [Australia]
NCTS .... National Council of Technical Schools (EA)
NCTS .... Navy Civilian Technical Specialist (MCD)
NCTS .... Northeast Corridor Transportation System [Boston to Washington high-speed transportation]
NCTSI .... National Council of Technical Service Industries [Later, Contract Services Association of America - CSA]
NCTT .... National Committee on Tunneling Technology
NCTT .... Nuclear Certification Test Team (MCD)
NCTTA .... National Competitiveness Technology Transfer Act [1989] [Department of Energy]
NCTTF......... Northern Counties Textile Trades' Federation [British] (DCTA)
NCTU .... Northern Carpet Trades Union [British] (DCTA)
NCTV .... National Coalition on Television Violence (EA)
NCTV .... National College Television [Cable-television system]
NCTW .... National Conference of Tuberculosis Workers [Later, CLAS] (EA)
NCTWU....... National Cigar and Tobacco Workers' Union [British]
NcTy .... Lanier Library Association, Inc., Tryon, NC [Library symbol Library of Congress] (LCLS)
NCtyB.......... National City Bancorp [Associated Press] (SAG)
NCtyBn........ National City Bancshares [Associated Press] (SAG)
NcTyI .... Isothermal Community College, Polk Campus, Tryon, NC [Library symbol Library of Congress] (LCLS)
NCTYL .... National College for the Training of Youth Leaders [British] (BI)
NCu............. Cuba Library, Cuba, NY [Library symbol Library of Congress] (LCLS)
NCU .... National Communications Union [British]
NCU .... National Conference for Unification [South Korea Political party] (PPW)
NCU .... National Cutlery Union [British]
NCU .... National Cyclists' Union [British]
NCU .... Naval Communications Unit (IAA)
NCU .... Navigation Computer Unit
NCU .... Navigation Control and Display Unit (MCD)
NCU .... Network Configuration Utility [Telecommunications]
NCU .... Network Control Unit [Computer science]
NCU .... New Cinch Uranium [Vancouver Stock Exchange symbol]
NCU .... Nitrogen Control Unit (AAG)
NCU .... Nonconforming Use (ADA)
ncu.............. North Carolina [MARC country of publication code Library of Congress] (LCCP)
NCU .... Nozzle Control Unit [NASA]
NCU .... Number Crunching Unit (MHDB)
NCU .... Nuveen California Premium Income Municipal (SPSG)
NCU .... Nuveen California Premium Income Municipal Fund [AMEX symbol] (SAG)
NCU .... Nuveen CA Prem Inc. Muni [AMEX symbol] (TTSB)
NCU .... Union College, Lincoln, NE [OCLC symbol] (OCLC)
NcU............. University of North Carolina, Chapel Hill, NC [Library symbol Library of Congress] (LCLS)
NCUA .... National Credit Union Administration
NCUA .... National Credit Union Association (NADA)
NCUAAE ..... National Council of Urban Administrators of Adult Education (OICC)
NcU-BPR..... University of North Carolina, Bureau of Public Records, Collection and Research,Chapel Hill, NC [Library symbol Library of Congress] (LCLS)
NCUC.......... National Commission on Unemployment Compensation (NADA)
NCUC.......... North Carolina Utilities Commission Reports [A publication] (DLA)
NCUC.......... Nuclear Chemistry Users Committee
NCU(E)........ National Communications Union, Engineering Group [British]
NCUEA........ National Center for Urban Ethnic Affairs (EA)
NCUEA........ National Council of Urban Education Associations (EA)
NCUES .... National Center for Urban Environmental Studies [Defunct] (EA)
NCUF .... National Computer Users Forum [National Computing Center] (PDAA)
NCUG.......... Nevada COBOL [Common Business-Oriented Language] Users Group [Defunct] (EA)
NCUGAE...... National Computer User Group in Agricultural Education (NITA)
NcU-H......... University of North Carolina, Division of Health Affairs, Chapel Hill, NC [Library symbol Library of Congress] (LCLS)
NCUI .... National Center for Urban and Industrial Health [Public Health Service]
NcU-IG........ University of North Carolina, Institute of Government Library, Chapel Hill, NC [Library symbol Library of Congress] (LCLS)
NCuL........... Cuba Library, Cuba, NY [Library symbol] [Library of Congress] (LCLS)
NcU-L .... University of North Carolina, Law Library, Chapel Hill, NC [Library symbol Library of Congress] (LCLS)

NcU-LS .... University of North Carolina at Chapel Hill, Library School, Chapel Hill, NC [*Library symbol Library of Congress*] (LCLS)

NCUMA .... National Credit Union Management Association (EA)

NCUMC .... National Council for the Unmarried Mother and Her Child [*British*] (ILCA)

NcU-MS .... University of North Carolina, Institute of Marine Sciences, Morehead City, NC [*Library symbol Library of Congress*] (LCLS)

NCUP .... National Conference of University Professors (AIE)

NCUP .... No Commission until Paid

NCUPI .... National Coalition for Universities in the Public Interest [*Defunct*] (EA)

NCUPM .... National Council of United Presbyterian Men (EA)

NcU-Pop ...... University of North Carolina, Carolina Population Center, Technical Information Service, Chapel Hill, NC [*Library symbol Library of Congress*] (LCLS)

NCUPRSE .... National Consortium of Universities Preparing Rural Special Educators [*Defunct*] (EA)

NCUR .... National Committee for Utilities Radio (MCD)

NCUR .... National Conferences on Undergraduate Research [*An association*]

NCURA .... National Council of University Research Administrators (EA)

NCUSA .... Navy Club of the United States of America (EA)

NCUSAA ...... Navy Club of the United States of America Auxiliary (EA)

NCUSAR ...... National Council on US-Arab Relations (EA)

NCUSCR ...... National Committee on United States-China Relations (EA)

NCUSCT ...... National Council for US-China Trade [*Later, USCBC*] (EA)

NCUSIF .... National Credit Union Share Insurance Fund

NCUSIOGT ... National Council of the United States, International Organization of Good Templars (EA)

NCUTLO .... National Committee on Uniform Traffic Laws and Ordinances (EA)

NCUUA .... National Council for Universal and Unconditional Amnesty [*For Vietnam-War resisters*] [*Defunct*] (EA)

NCV .... Navigation Computer Unit

NCV .... Nerve Conduction Velocity [*Electrophysiology*]

NCV .... Net Calorific Value (PDAA)

NCV .... No Commercial Value [*Business term*]

NCV .... No Core Value [*Business term*]

NCV .... No Customs Value (DS)

NCV .... Non-Cholera Vibrios [*Microbiology*]

NCV .... Normalized Critical View

NCVA .... National Center for Voluntary Action [*Later, NVC*]

NcVal .... Valdese Public Library, Valdese, NC [*Library symbol Library of Congress*] (LCLS)

NcValH .... Valdese General Hospital, Valdese, NC [*Library symbol*] [*Library of Congress*] (LCLS)

NCVC .... National Catholic Vocation Council [*Defunct*] (EA)

NCVC .... National Congress on Volunteerism and Citizenship [*Bicentennial event, 1976*]

NCVE .... National Council on Vocational Education [*Department of Education Washington, DC*] (EGAO)

NCVECS ...... National Center for Vehicle Emissions Control and Safety [*Colorado State University*]

NCVHS .... National Committee on Vital and Health Statistics [*Department of Health and Human Services*] (GFGA)

NCVO .... National Council for Voluntary Organisations [*British*] (ILCA)

NCVOTE .... National Center for Vocational, Occupational, and Technical Education [*Office of Education*]

NCVP .... Natural Circulation Verification Program [*Nuclear energy*] (NRCH)

NCVP .... Noncapsid Viral Protein [*Biochemistry*]

NCVQ .... National Council for Vocational Qualifications [*British*]

NCVR .... National Conference of Vicars for Religious (EA)

NCVS .... National Credential Verification Service (MCD)

NCVS .... National Crime Victimization Survey [*Department of Justice*] (ECON)

NCVS .... Nerve Conduction Velocity Studies [*Medicine*] (MEDA)

NCW .... National Council of Women of Great Britain (BI)

NCW .... National Council of Women of the United States (EA)

NCW .... Newberry College, Newberry, SC [*OCLC symbol*] (OCLC)

NCW .... Nose Cone Warhead [*Aviation*] (NATG)

NCW .... Not Complied With [*Military*]

NcW .... Wilmington Public Library, Wilmington, NC [*Library symbol Library of Congress*] (LCLS)

NcWa .... George H. and Laura E. Brown Library, Washington, NC [*Library symbol Library of Congress*] (LCLS)

NCWA .... National Candy Wholesalers Association (EA)

NCWA .... National Children's Wear Association [*British*] (EAIO)

NCWA .... NATO Civil Wartime Agency (NATG)

NCWA .... Newsagency Council of Western Australia

NcWaB .... Beaufort County Technical Institute, Washington, NC [*Library symbol Library of Congress*] (LCLS)

NcWaBHM ... Beaufort, Hyde, Martin Regional Library, Washington, NC [*Library symbol Library of Congress*] (LCLS)

NcWad .... Anson County Library, Wadesboro, NC [*Library symbol Library of Congress*] (LCLS)

NcWadAS ..... Anson County Senior High School, Medial Center, Wadesboro, NC [*Library symbol*] [*Library of Congress*] (LCLS)

NcWal .... Thelma Dingus Bryant Library, Wallace, NC [*Library symbol Library of Congress*] (LCLS)

NCWAO .... National Council of World Affairs Organizations (EA)

NcWarW ...... Warren County Memorial Library, Warrenton, NC [*Library symbol Library of Congress*] (LCLS)

NCWAS .... National Coal Workers Autopsy Study

NcWaw .... Warsaw Public Library, Warsaw, NC [*Library symbol Library of Congress*] (LCLS)

NcWayH .... Haywood County Public Library, Waynesville, NC [*Library symbol Library of Congress*] (LCLS)

NcWayH-C ... Haywood County Public Library, Canton Branch, Canton, NC [*Library symbol Library of Congress*] (LCLS)

NCWBA .... National Conference of Women's Bar Associations (EA)

NCWC .... National Carwash Council

NCWC .... National Catholic Welfare Conference [*Later, USCC*] (EA)

NCWC .... National Catholic Welfare Conference News Service (NTCM)

NCWC .... National Council of Women Chiropractors (EA)

NCWC .... National Council of Women of Canada

NcWc .... Walnut Cove Public Library, Walnut Cove, NC [*Library symbol Library of Congress*] (LCLS)

NcW-C .... Wilmington Public Library, College Square Branch, Wilmington, NC [*Library symbol Library of Congress*] (LCLS)

NcWC .... Wilmington Public Library, College Square Branch, Wilmington, NC [*Library symbol*] [*Library of Congress*] (LCLS)

NcWCF .... Cape Fear Technical Institute, Wilmington, NC [*Library symbol Library of Congress*] (LCLS)

NcWcL .... Walnut Cove Public Library, Walnut Cove, NC [*Library symbol*] [*Library of Congress*] (LCLS)

NCWD .... National Coalition for Women in Defense (EA)

NcWea .... Bess Tilson Sprinkle Memorial Library, Weaverville, NC [*Library symbol Library of Congress*] (LCLS)

NcWel .... Weldon Memorial Library, Weldon, NC [*Library symbol Library of Congress*] (LCLS)

NcWelc .... North Davidson Public Library, Welcome, NC [*Library symbol Library of Congress*] (LCLS)

NcWelH .... Halifax County Technical Institute, Weldon, NC [*Library symbol Library of Congress*] (LCLS)

NcWeR .... Rockingham Community College, Wentworth, NC [*Library symbol Library of Congress*] (LCLS)

NCWFC .... National Council of Women of Free Czechoslovakia (EA)

NCWFD .... National Committee for World Food Day [*Later, USNCWFD*] (EA)

NcWfSB .... Southeastern Baptist Theological Seminary, Wake Forest, NC [*Library symbol Library of Congress*] (LCLS)

NCWGA .... Natural Colored Wool Growers Association (EA)

NCWGB .... National Council of Women of Great Britain (DI)

NcWGE .... General Electric Co., WMD Technical Library, Wilmington, NC [*Library symbol Library of Congress*] (LCLS)

NCWGE .... National Coalition for Women and Girls in Education (EA)

NcWhC .... Columbus County Public Library, Whiteville, NC [*Library symbol Library of Congress*] (LCLS)

NcWHE .... Wilmington Area Health Education Center Medical Library, Wilmington, NC [*Library symbol*] [*Library of Congress*] (LCLS)

NcWhS .... Southeastern Community College, Whiteville, NC [*Library symbol Library of Congress*] (LCLS)

NcWil .... Wilson County Public Library, Wilson, NC [*Library symbol Library of Congress*] (LCLS)

NcWilA .... Atlantic Christian College, Wilson, NC [*Library symbol Library of Congress*] (LCLS)

NcWilB .... Beddingfield High School Library, Wilson, NC [*Library symbol*] [*Library of Congress*] (LCLS)

NcWilC .... Carolina Discipliana Library, Wilson, NC [*Library symbol Library of Congress*] (LCLS)

NcWilE .... North Carolina Department of Human Resources, Eastern North Carolina School for the Deaf, Wilson, NC [*Library symbol Library of Congress*] (LCLS)

NcWilF .... Fike High School Library, Wilson, NC [*Library symbol*] [*Library of Congress*] (LCLS)

NcWilH .... Wilson Memorial Hospital, Wilson, NC [*Library symbol*] [*Library of Congress*] (LCLS)

NcWilHS .... Hunt High School Library, Wilson, NC [*Library symbol*] [*Library of Congress*] (LCLS)

NcWill .... Martin Memorial Library, Williamston, NC [*Library symbol Library of Congress*] (LCLS)

NcWilM .... Martin Technical Institute, Williamston, NC [*Library symbol Library of Congress*] (LCLS)

NcWilW .... Wilson County Technical Institute, Wilson, NC [*Library symbol Library of Congress*] (LCLS)

NcWin .... Wingate College, Wingate, NC [*Library symbol Library of Congress*] (LCLS)

NcWind .... Lawrence Memorial Library, Windsor, NC [*Library symbol Library of Congress*] (LCLS)

NcWintA ..... Albermarle Regional Library, Winton, NC [*Library symbol Library of Congress*] (LCLS)

NCWIS .... New Computerized World Information Service [*Information service or system*] (IID)

NcWiW .... Wilkes Community College, Wilkesboro, NC [*Library symbol Library of Congress*] (LCLS)

NcWj .... Ashe County Public Library, West Jefferson, NC [*Library symbol Library of Congress*] (LCLS)

NCWM .... National Conference on Weights and Measures (EA)

NCWM .... National Congress of Women in Music (EA)

NcWMM .... Miller-Motte Business College, Wilmington, NC [*Library symbol*] [*Library of Congress*] (LCLS)

NcWN .... New Hanover County Public Library, Wilmington, NC [*Library symbol Library of Congress*] (LCLS)

NcWN-C .... New Hanover County Public Library, Carolina Beach Branch Library, Carolina Beach, NC [*Library symbol Library of Congress*] (LCLS)

NcWNC .... New Hanover County Public Library, Carolina Beach Branch Library, Carolina Beach, NC [*Library symbol*] [*Library of Congress*] (LCLS)

NCWNSW ... National Council of Women of New South Wales [*Australia*]

NCWP .... National Communications Working Party [*Australia Political party*]

NCWPA .... National Committee for Women in Public Administration (EA)

NCWPA .... National Council for the Welfare of Prisoners Abroad [*British*] (DI)

NCWPTF ...... National Council for a World Peace Tax Fund (EA)

NCWQ.......... National Commission on Water Quality [*National Academy of Sciences*]
NCWQ.......... National Council of Women of Queensland [*Australia*]
NCWR.......... Nordic Council for Wildlife Research (EAIO)
NCWRU....... North Central Watershed Research Unit [*Department of Agriculture*] (GRD)
NcWs.......... Forsyth County Public Library System, Winston-Salem, NC [*Library symbol Library of Congress*] (LCLS)
NCWS.......... Non-Community Water System [*Environmental Protection Agency*]
NCWSA....... National Collegiate Water Ski Association (EA)
NcWsA....... North-West AHEC Library at Winston-Salem, Bowman-Gray School of Medicine, Winston-Salem, NC [*Library symbol*] [*Library of Congress*] (LCLS)
NcWsAT....... AT & Technologies, Inc., Winston-Salem, NC [*Library symbol*] [*Library of Congress*] (LCLS)
NcWsAT-R ... AT & T Technologies, Inc., Winston-Salem, NC [*Library symbol*] [*Library of Congress*] (LCLS)
NCWSBA....... National Council of Wool Selling Brokers of Australia
NcWs-C....... Forsyth County Public Library, Clemmons Branch Library, Clemmons, NC [*Library symbol Library of Congress*] (LCLS)
NcWs-E....... Forsyth County Public Library, East Winston Branch, Winston-Salem, NC [*Library symbol Library of Congress*] (LCLS)
NcWsF....... Forsyth Technical Institute, Winston-Salem, NC [*Library symbol Library of Congress*] (LCLS)
NcWsFM....... Forsyth-Stokes Area Mental Health Center, Winston-Salem, NC [*Library symbol*] [*Library of Congress*] (LCLS)
NcWs-K....... Forsyth County Public Library, Kernersville Branch Library, Kernersville, NC [*Library symbol Library of Congress*] (LCLS)
NcWsM....... Moravian Archives, Winston-Salem, NC [*Library symbol Library of Congress*] (LCLS)
NcWsMES.... Museum of Early Southern Decorative Arts, MESDA Library, Winston-Salem, NC [*Library symbol Library of Congress*] (LCLS)
NcWsMM....... Moravian Music Foundation, Winston-Salem, NC [*Library symbol Library of Congress*] (LCLS)
NcWsN....... North Carolina School of the Arts, Winston-Salem, NC [*Library symbol Library of Congress*] (LCLS)
NcWs-R .... Forsyth County Public Library, Reynolda Manor Branch, Winston-Salem, NC [*Library symbol Library of Congress*] (LCLS)
NcWsR....... Reynolds Tobacco Co., Winston-Salem, NC [*Library symbol*] [*Library of Congress*] (LCLS)
NcWsRI....... Reynolds Industries, Corporate Library, Winston-Salem, NC [*Library symbol Library of Congress*] (LCLS)
NcWsR-M .... Reynolds Tobacco Co., Marketing Development Intelligence Center, Winston-Salem, NC [*Library symbol Library of Congress*] (LCLS)
NcWsR-R .... Reynolds Tobacco Co., Research and Development Technical Information Services, Winston-Salem, NC [*Library symbol Library of Congress*] (LCLS)
NcWs-RS .... Forsyth County Public Library, Rural Hall/Stanleyville Branch Library, Rural Hall, NC [*Library symbol Library of Congress*] (LCLS)
NcWs-S....... Forsyth County Public Library, Southside Branch, Winston-Salem, NC [*Library symbol Library of Congress*] (LCLS)
NcWsS....... Salem College, Winston-Salem, NC [*Library symbol Library of Congress*] (LCLS)
NcWs-T....... Forsyth County Public Library, Thruway Branch, Winston-Salem, NC [*Library symbol*] [*Library of Congress*] (LCLS)
NcWsU....... Winston-Salem State University, Winston-Salem, NC [*Library symbol Library of Congress*] (LCLS)
NcWsW....... Wake Forest University, Winston-Salem, NC [*Library symbol Library of Congress*] (LCLS)
NcWsW-B .... Wake Forest University, Babcock Graduate School of Management, Winston-Salem, NC [*Library symbol Library of Congress*] (LCLS)
NcWsWE....... Western Electric Co., Lexington Road Technical Library, Winston-Salem, NC [*Library symbol Library of Congress*] (LCLS)
NcWsWE-R... Western Electric Co., Reynolda Road Technical Library, Winston-Salem, NC [*Library symbol Library of Congress*] (LCLS)
NcWsW-L..... Wake Forest University, Law Library, Winston-Salem, NC [*Library symbol Library of Congress*] (LCLS)
NcWsW-M ... Wake Forest University, Bowman Gray School of Medicine, Wake Forest, NC [*Library symbol Library of Congress*] (LCLS)
NCWT.......... National Council of Women of Tasmania [*Australia*]
NCWTF........ Naval Commander Western Task Force
NCWTM....... National Council on Wholistic Therapeutics and Medicine [*Defunct*] (EA)
NCWU.......... National Catholic Women's Union (EA)
NcWU.......... University of North Carolina at Wilmington, Wilmington, NC [*Library symbol Library of Congress*] (LCLS)
NCWUS....... National Council of Women of the United States (WDAA)
NCWUSA...... National Council of Women of the United States of America (DI)
NCWV.......... National Council of Women of Victoria [*Australia*]
NCWW.......... National Commission on Working Women (EA)
NCWWA....... National Council of Women of Western Australia
NCX.......... Corpus Christi, TX [*Location identifier FAA*] (FAAL)
NCX.......... NCN Exploration & Development [*Vancouver Stock Exchange symbol*]
NCX.......... North Carolina Central University, Durham, NC [*OCLC symbol*] (OCLC)
NCY.......... Annecy [*France*] [*Airport symbol*] (OAG)
NcY.......... Hyconeechee Regional Library, Yanceyville, NC [*Library symbol Library of Congress*] (LCLS)
NCY.......... Nancy Aviation [*France ICAO designator*] (FAAC)
NCY.......... National Collaboration for Youth (EA)
N-CY.......... Natural-Colored Yellow [*Diamonds*]
NCY.......... New Century Resources [*Vancouver Stock Exchange symbol*]
NCY.......... North Central Yiddish (BJA)
NCY.......... Yorktown, VA [*Location identifier FAA*] (FAAL)

NCYA.......... National Catholic Youth Association [*British*] (BI)
NcYad.......... Yadkin County Public Library, Yadkinville, NC [*Library symbol Library of Congress*] (LCLS)
NCYC.......... National Catholic Youth Council
NCYC.......... National Collection of Yeast Cultures [*AFRC Institute of Food Research*] [*British Information service or system*] (IID)
NCYC.......... National Council of Yacht Clubs (EA)
N CYC BN.... Northern Cyclist Battalion [*British military*] (DMA)
NCYC CAT.... National Collection of Yeast Cultures Catalogue [*Norwich Laboratory*] [*Norfolk, England*] [*Information service or system*] [*A publication*]
NCYD.......... National Center for Youth with Disabilities (EA)
NCYF.......... National Crusaders Youth Federation (EA)
NCYFS......... National Children and Youth Fitness Study [*HHS*]
NcYG.......... Gunn Memorial Public Library, Yanceyville, NC [*Library symbol Library of Congress*] (LCLS)
NCYI.......... National Council of Young Israel (EA)
NCYL.......... National Center for Youth Law (EA)
NcYo.......... Youngsville Public Library, Youngsville, NC [*Library symbol Library of Congress*] (LCLS)
NCYOF........ National CYO [*Catholic Youth Organizations*] Federation (EA)
NCYP.......... National Conference of Yeshiva Principals (EA)
NCYRE........ National Council for Year-Round Education [*Later, NAYRE*] (EA)
NCYSI........ National Clearinghouse for Youth Sports Information [*Operated by the National Alliance for Youth Sports*] (PAZ)
NCYSP........ National Committee on Youth Suicide Prevention (EA)
NCYWA....... Nordic Child and Youth Welfare Alliance (EA)
NCz.......... New Cruzado [*Monetary unit*] [*Brazil*] (BARN)
NcZG.......... Glaxo, Inc., Zebulon, NC [*Library symbol*] [*Library of Congress*] (LCLS)
ND.......... Aerospatiale [*Societe Nationale Industrielle Aerospatiale*] [*France ICAO aircraft manufacturer identifier*] (ICAO)
ND.......... Diploma in Naturopathy [*British*]
ND.......... Doctor of Naturopathic Medicine (PGP)
ND.......... Doctor of Naturopathy
ND.......... Doctor of Nursing (PGP)
ND.......... Named (ROG)
ND.......... Narrowband Distributive Services [*Telecommunications*]
ND.......... NASA Document (KSC)
ND.......... NASA [*National Aeronautics and Space Administration*] Document
ND.......... Nasal Deformity (DAVI)
ND.......... National Debt
ND.......... National Diploma [*Academic degree*] (AIE)
ND.......... Natural Death [*Medicine*]
ND.......... Natural Draught
ND.......... Naval Dispensary
ND.......... Naval Distillate Fuel (NVT)
ND.......... Naval District
ND.......... Naval Draftsman (ROG)
ND.......... Navigation Display (MCD)
ND.......... Navy Department
N-D.......... N-Dimensional (MCD)
ND.......... Nea Demokratia [*New Democracy*] [*Greece*] [*Political party*] (PPE)
N/D.......... Need Date (MCD)
ND.......... Negative Declaration (NRCH)
ND.......... Negatives and Deposition (DGA)
Nd.......... Neodymium [*Chemical element*]
Nd.......... Neodymium
ND.......... Neonatal Death [*Medicine*] (MAE)
ND.......... Neoplastic Disease [*Medicine*]
ND.......... Nervous Debility [*Medicine*]
ND.......... Net Debt
ND.......... Network Directorate (SSD)
ND.......... Neurologic Deficit [*Medicine*]
ND.......... Neuropathic Doctor (BARN)
ND.......... Neurotic Depression [*Psychiatry*]
ND.......... Neutral Density [*Photography*]
ND.......... Neutral Density Filter (WDMC)
ND.......... Neutral-Drive [*Automotive engineering*]
ND.......... Neutron Diffraction (MCD)
ND.......... Newcastle Disease [*Virus*] [*Also, NDV*]
ND.......... New Dawn [*An association*] (EA)
ND.......... New Deal (DAS)
ND.......... New Deck [*On ships*]
ND.......... New Democracy [*European political movement*] (ECON)
ND.......... New Developments Research Branch [*Bureau of Naval Personnel*] [*Washington, DC*]
ND.......... New Directions [*Later, Democratic Alternatives - DA*] (EA)
ND.......... New Dramatists (EA)
ND.......... New Drug
ND.......... New Drugs [*A publication*]
Nd.......... Newfoundland Reports [*A publication*] (DLA)
ND.......... News Director (NTCM)
ND.......... News Director (WDMC)
ND.......... Newsletters Directory [*Later, NIP*] [*A publication*]
ND.......... Next Day [*Stock exchange term*] (SPSG)
ND.......... Next Day's Delivery
ND.......... Nickajack Dam [*TVA*]
ND.......... Nippondenso Co. [*Toyota Motor Corp.*]
ND.......... No Data
ND.......... No Date [*of publication*]
nd.......... No Date (WDMC)
nd.......... No Date (VRA)
ND.......... No Decision [*Sports*]
ND.......... Node Dissection [*Medicine*]

N/D	No Defects
ND	No Detect
ND	No Discount [Business term] (DS)
ND	No Disease [Medicine]
ND	No Drawing [Engineering]
ND	Nondelay [Military]
ND	Nondelivery [Shipping]
ND	Non-Denominational
ND	Non-Descript (WDMC)
N/D	Nondestructive
ND	Nondeterministic (IAA)
ND	Nondiabetic [Medicine]
ND	Nondirectional (IAA)
ND	Nondirectional Antenna
ND	Nondirectional Microphone (WDMC)
ND	Nondirector (IAA)
ND	Nondisabling [Medicine]
ND	Non Disponible [Not Available] [French]
N/D	Non-Drinker [Medicine]
ND	Nonduty [Military]
ND	Nordair [ICAO designator] (AD)
ND	Nordair Ltd. [Canada ICAO designator] (OAG)
ND	Normal Delivery [Obstetrics]
ND	Normal Development [Pediatrics] (DAVI)
ND	North Dakota [Postal code]
Nd	North Dakota State Library, Bismarck, ND [Library symbol Library of Congress] (LCLS)
ND	North Dakota Supreme Court Reports [1890-1953] [A publication] (DLA)
ND	Northern District (DLA)
ND	Nose Down [Aviation]
ND	Nose Drops [Pharmacy] (DAVI)
ND	Nostra Domina [Our Lady] [Latin]
ND	Not Dated [Banking, bibliography]
N/D	Not Detected [or Detectable] [Medicine]
ND	Not Determined [Medicine]
ND	Not Diagnosed [Medicine]
ND	Not Directly (DGA)
ND	Not Done
ND	Nothing Doing [Amateur radio slang]
ND	Notre Dame Sisters (TOCD)
ND	Nuclear Device (AAG)
Nd	Number of Dissimilar Matches
ND	Number of Document [Online database field identifier]
ND	Nursing Doctorate
ND	Ny Demokrati [New Democracy] [Sweden Political party] (EY)
ND	Romania [License plate code assigned to foreign diplomats in the US]
ND	University of Notre Dame [Indiana]
nd	Updated (VRA)
Nd2	Nord-Aviation 262 [Airplane code]
NDA	Bandanaira [Indonesia] [Airport symbol] (OAG)
NDA	Naphthalenedicarboxaldehyde [Organic chemistry]
NDA	National Dairy Association (NADA)
NDA	National Dairymen's Association, Inc. [British] (BI)
NDA	National Dance Association (EA)
NDA	National Defense Act
NDA	National Defense Area (AABC)
NDA	National Democratic Alliance [Sierra Leone] [Political party] (EY)
NDA	National Dental Association (EA)
NDA	National Denturist Association (EA)
NDA	National Diploma in Agriculture [British]
NDA	National Dome Association [Later, NDC] (EA)
NDA	National Door Association [Defunct]
NDA	NAUI [National Association of Underwater Instructors] Diving Association (EA)
NDA	Naval Discipline Act [British military] (DMA)
NDA	Neutral Detector Assembly
NDA	Nevada (ROG)
NDA	New Desk Accessories [Utility program] [Apple Computers, Inc.] [Computer science]
NDA	New Drug Application [FDA]
NDA	Newspaper Design Award (DGA)
NDA	Ninos de las Americas [Children of the Americas] (EAIO)
NDA	No Data Available [Computer science]
NDA	No Demonstrable Antibody [Medicine] (MAE)
NDA	No Detectable Activity
NDA	No Diagnosis of Anything
NDA	Nonadecanoic Acid [Organic chemistry]
NDA	Nondestructive Assay
NDA	Nondimensional Analysis
NDA	Non-Disclosure Agreement (WDMC)
NDA	Nonresonant Deflection Amplifier
NDA	Nordair Ltd. [Toronto Stock Exchange symbol]
NDA	Northern Airways, Inc. [ICAO designator] (FAAC)
NDA	Nuclear Device Association (AAG)
NDA	[The] Nuzi Dialect of Akkadian [A publication] (BJA)
NDAA	National Dental Assistants Association (EA)
NDAA	National District Attorneys Association (EA)
NDAAC	Navy Drug and Alcohol Advisory Council (DNAB)
NDA & LB	Naval District Affairs and Logistics Branch
NDAB	Numerical Data Advisory Board [National Academy of Sciences] [Information service or system] (IID)
NDAC	National Defense Advisory Commission [World War II]
NDAC	National Defense Advisory Committee (NADA)

NDAC	NATO Data-Buoy System [National Oceanic and Atmospheric Administration]
NDAC	No Data Accepted [Computer science] (IAA)
NDAC	North Dakota Administrative Code [A publication] (AAGC)
NDAC	North Dakota Agricultural College
NDAC	Nuclear Defense Affairs Committee [NATO]
NDACP	Navy Drug Abuse Control Program (DNAB)
NDACS	Navy Drug Abuse Counselor School (DNAB)
NDACS	Network Diagnostic and Control Systems (ADA)
NDACSS	Navy Department Advisory Committee on Structural Steel
ND Admin Code	North Dakota Administrative Code [A publication] (DLA)
NDAFA	National Directory of Accounting Firms and Accountants [A publication]
ND Agr E	National Diploma in Agricultural Engineering [British]
N DAK	North Dakota (AAG)
N Dak	North Dakota Reports [A publication] (DLA)
ND Ala	United States District Court for the Northern District of Alabama (DLA)
NDAM	New Disk Access Method [Computer science] (MHDI)
NDAP	Nationalsozialistische Deutsche Arbeiterpartei [National Socialist German Workers' Party, 1919-45] [Political party] (PPW)
NDAPTA	National Drivers Association for the Prevention of Traffic Accidents [Defunct] (EA)
NDARC	National Drug and Alcohol Research Center [University of New South Wales] [Australia]
NDAT	Nondestructible Aiming Target
NDAT	Non-Destructive Assay Technique [Military] (PDAA)
NData	National Data Corp. [Associated Press] (SAG)
NDATUS	National Drug and Alcohol Treatment Utilization Survey [Department of Health and Human Services] (GFGA)
NDB	Nautical Directional Beacon (IAA)
NDB	Naval Disciplinary Barracks
NDB	Navy Department Bulletin [A publication]
NDB	Net Debit Balance
NDB	Net Decision Benefit (NUCP)
NDB	Nondirectional Beacon (AFM)
NDB	Nouadhibou [Mauritania] [Airport symbol] (OAG)
NDB	Nuclear Depth Bomb (NVT)
NDB	Numeric Data Base [INPADOC] [Computer science]
NDBA	National Data Base on Aging (EDAC)
NDBA	National Deaf Bowling Association (EA)
NDBA	New Directions in Biblical Archaeology [A publication] (BJA)
NDBA	Nitrosodibutylamine [Organic chemistry]
NDBB	North Dakota Bar Brief [A publication] (DLA)
NdBC	Bismarck Junior College, Bismarck, ND [Library symbol Library of Congress] (LCLS)
NDBC	National Data Buoy Center [National Oceanic and Atmospheric Administration Also, an information service or system] (IID)
NDBC	National Day of Bread Committee [Defunct] (EA)
NDBC	National Dry Bean Council (EA)
NDBC	National Duckpin Bowling Congress (EA)
NDBCA	Navy Department Board of Contract Appeals
NDBDM	Navy Department Board of Decorations and Medals (DNAB)
NDBDP	National Data Buoy Development Project [Later, NDBO] [Coast Guard] (MSC)
NdBH	Bismarck Hospital, School of Nursing Library, Bismarck, ND [Library symbol Library of Congress] (LCLS)
NdBHD	North Dakota State Health Department, Bismarck, ND [Library symbol Library of Congress] (LCLS)
NdBHwy	North Dakota State Highway Department, Bismarck, ND [Library symbol Library of Congress] (LCLS)
NDBI	National Dairymen's Benevolent Institution, Inc. [British] (BI)
NDBL	National Deaf-Blind League [British] (EAIO)
NDBLO	Not to Descend Below [Aviation] (FAAC)
NdBM	Mary College, Bismarck, ND [Library symbol Library of Congress] (LCLS)
NDBMS	Network Database Management System
NDBO	National Data Buoy Office (USDC)
NDBO	National Data Buoy Office [Marine science] (OSRA)
NDBO	NOAA [National Oceanic and Atmospheric Administration] Data Buoy Office [or Operation] (IID)
NdBoU	North Dakota State University, Bottineau Branch, Bottineau, ND [Library symbol Library of Congress] (LCLS)
NDBP	National Data Buoy Program [National Oceanic and Atmospheric Administration] (GFGA)
NdBPI	North Dakota State Department of Public Instruction, Bismarck, ND [Library symbol Library of Congress] (LCLS)
NDBPSA	Non-Denominational Bible Prophecy Study Association (EA)
NdBPW	North Dakota State Public Welfare Board, Bismarck, ND [Library symbol Library of Congress] (LCLS)
NdBQ	Quain and Ramstad Clinic, Bismarck, ND [Library symbol Library of Congress] (LCLS)
NDBS	National Data Buoy System
NDBS	Naval Despatch Boat Service
NDBULCUMED	Navy Department Bulletins, Cumulative Editions [A publication]
NdBV	Bismarck [Veterans Memorial] Public Library, Bismarck, ND [Library symbol Library of Congress] (LCLS)
NDC	Air Nordic SWE Aviation, AB [Sweden] [FAA designator] (FAAC)
NDC	Naphthalene Dicarboxylate [Organic chemistry]
NDC	Natick Development Center [Massachusetts] [Army]
NDC	National Dairy Council (EA)
NDC	National Data Communication
NDC	National Data Corp. [NYSE symbol] (SPSG)
NDC	National Debt Commission [Australia]
NDC	National Defence College [British]

NDC	National Defence Committee [*Ghana*] [*Political party*] (PPW)
NDC	National Defence Company [*British military*] (DMA)
NDC	National Defence Contribution [*British*]
NDC	National Defence Corps [*British*]
NDC	National Defense College [*Australia*]
NDC	National Defense Corps (NADA)
NDC	National Defense Council (KSC)
NDC	National Democratic Club (EA)
NDC	National Democratic Congress [*Ghana*] [*Political party*] (ECON)
NDC	National Democratic Congress [*Grenada*] [*Political party*] (EY)
NDC	National Design Council [*Canada*]
NDC	National DeSoto Club (EA)
NDC	National Development Corp. [*Dominica*] (EY)
NDC	National Development Council (EA)
NDC	National Directory of Churches, Synagogues, and Other Houses of Worship [*A publication*]
NDC	National Diving Council
NDC	National Dome Council (EA)
NDC	National Drug Code [*FDA*]
NDC	National Duckling Council [*Defunct*] (EA)
NDC	Natl Data [*NYSE symbol*] (TTSB)
NDC	NATO Defense College [*Also, NADC, NADEFCOL*] (NATG)
NDC	Natural Distribution Certificate (WDAA)
NDC	Naval Data Center
NDC	Naval Dental Clinic
NDC	Navigation Display and Computer (MCD)
NDC	Negative Differential Conductivity (OA)
NDC	Network Data Control (MCD)
NDC	Network Diagnostic Control
NDC	Neurologic Disease Control
NDC	New Democratic Coalition
NDC	New Die Cast [*Honda Motor Co. Ltd.*]
NDC	New Directions in Creativity Program (EDAC)
NDC	New Dramatists Committee [*Later, ND*] (EA)
NDC	Nippon Decimal Classification [*Library science*]
NDC	No Date Club [*Brooklyn girls - no dates for the duration*] [*World War II*]
NDC	No Direct Charge
NDC	Noise Dose Count (IAA)
NDC	Nondifferentiated Cell [*Medicine*] (DMAA)
NDC	Non-Double-Couple [*Seismology*]
NDC	NORAD Direction Center [*Military*]
NDC	Normalized Device Coordinates [*Computer science*]
NDC	Northern Development Co. [*British*] (ECON)
NDC	Northwest Drama Conference (EA)
NDC	Notice of Drawing Change [*Navy*] (DNAB)
NDC	Notre Dame College [*Missouri, New Hampshire, Ohio*]
NDC	Notre Dame College, Manchester, NH [*Inactive*] [*OCLC symbol*] (OCLC)
NDC	Noyes Data Corp.
NDC	Nuclear Data Committee (NRCH)
NDC	Nuclear Design and Construction [*British*]
NDC	Nuclear Design Calculations [*Program*]
NDCA	Naphthalenedicarboxylic Acid [*Organic chemistry*]
NDCA	National Dance Council of America (EA)
NDCA	National Deaf Children's Association [*British*]
NDCA	National Drilling Contractors Association (EA)
NDCA	Nuclear Development Corp. of America
ND Cal	United States District Court for the Northern District of California (DLA)
NdCan	Cando Public Library, Cando, ND [*Library symbol Library of Congress*] (LCLS)
NDCC	National Defense Cadet Corps
NDCC	Navy Department Corrosion Committee
NDCC	Nondirectional Cross-Country (MCD)
NDCC	North Dakota Century Code [*A publication*]
NDCCC	National Defense Communications Control Center (MCD)
NDCD	National Drug Code Directory [*FDA*] [*A publication*]
NDCDAR	National Defense Committee of the Daughters of the American Revolution (EA)
NDCEE	National Defense Center for Environmental Excellence [*DoD*] (RDA)
ND Cent Code	North Dakota Century Code [*A publication*] (DLA)
NDCF	National Defense Council Foundation (EA)
NdCo	Cooperstown Public Library, Cooperstown, ND [*Library symbol Library of Congress*] (LCLS)
NDColl	National Defence College [*British*]
NDCP	Navy Decision Coordinating Paper
NDCP	Navy Development Concept Paper (CAAL)
NDC-PS	No Drawing Change Project Slip
NdCr	Divide County Library, Crosby, ND [*Library symbol Library of Congress*] (LCLS)
NDCS	National Deaf Children's Society [*British*] (BI)
NDCT	Natural Draft Cooling Tower [*Nuclear energy*] (NRCH)
NDCT	Non-Secure Data Communication Terminal (DWSG)
NDD	Duke University Library, Durham, NC [*OCLC symbol*] (OCLC)
NDd	Dundee Library, Dundee, NY [*Library symbol Library of Congress*] (LCLS)
NDD	National Diploma in Dairying [*British*]
NDD	National Diploma in Design [*British*]
NDD	Navigation and Direction Division [*British military*] (DMA)
NDD	Negotiation Decision Document [*Environmental Protection Agency*] (EPA)
NDD	Net Defence Department [*Navy British*]
NDD	New Democratic Dimensions (EA)
NDD	Nitro(dimethyl)dihydrobenzofuran [*Organic chemistry*]

NDD	No Dialysis Days [*Nephrology*] (DAVI)
NDD	Nondeferred Development (MCD)
NDD	Norton Disk Doctor [*Computer science*]
NDD	Novo Redondo [*Angola*] [*Airport symbol*] (AD)
NDD	Nuclear Detection Device (MCD)
NDD	Sumbe [*Angola*] [*Airport symbol*] (OAG)
NDd	Woman's Study Club & Library, Dundee, NY [*Library symbol*] [*Library of Congress*] (LCLS)
NDD & RF	Naval Dry Dock and Repair Facility
NDDC	National Defeat Dukakis Campaign (EA)
NDDC	Navy Department Duty Chaplain (DNAB)
NDDC	NORAD Division Direction Center [*Military*] (AABC)
NdDe	Devils Lake Carnegie Library, Devils Lake, ND [*Library symbol Library of Congress*] (LCLS)
NdDeH	Mercy Hospital, Devils Lake, ND [*Library symbol Library of Congress*] (LCLS)
NDDEIC	National Digestive Diseases Education and Information Clearinghouse [*Public Health Service*] [*Later, NDDIC*] (IID)
NdDeL	Lake Region Junior College, Devils Lake, ND [*Library symbol Library of Congress*] (LCLS)
NDDG	National Diabetes Data Group [*British*]
NdDi	Dickinson Public Library, Dickinson, ND [*Library symbol Library of Congress*] (LCLS)
NDDIC	National Digestive Diseases Information Clearinghouse (EA)
NdDiS	Dickinson State College, Dickinson, ND [*Library symbol Library of Congress*] (LCLS)
NdDiStJ	Saint Joseph Hospital, Dickinson, ND [*Library symbol Library of Congress*] (LCLS)
NDDN	National Dry Deposition Network (GNE)
NDDO	Neglect of Diatomic Differential Overlap [*Quantum mechanics*]
NDDP	NATO Defense Data Program (AABC)
NDDS	National Disability Data System [*Social Security Administration*] (GFGA)
NDDS	Nuclear Detonation Detection System (DOMA)
NDE	Mandera [*Kenya*] [*Airport symbol*] (OAG)
NDE	National Defense Education
NDE	National Defense Emergency [*Headquarters*] (MCD)
NDE	National Dinghy Exhibition [*British*]
NDE	Navy Department Establishments [*British*]
NDE	N-Demethylencainide [*Organic chemistry*]
NDE	Near-Death Experience
NDE	Nevada Desert Experience (EA)
NDE	No Date Established
NDE	No Delay Expected
NDE	Nondestructive Evaluation
NDE	Nondestructive Examination [*Nuclear energy*] (NRCH)
NDE	Nonlinear Differential Equations
NDE	Notodden [*Norway*] [*Airport symbol*] (AD)
NDEA	National Defense Education Act [*1958*]
NDEA	National Defense Emergency Authorization
NDEA	National Display Equipment Association [*British*] (BI)
NDEA	Nitrosodiethylamine [*Organic chemistry*]
nDEA	No Deviation of Electrical Axis [*On electrocardiogram*] [*Cardiology*] (DAVI)
N de Aqi	Nicholas de Aquila [*Flourished, 1197-1217*] [*Authority cited in pre-1607 legal work*] (DSA)
NDEC	NDE Environmental Corp. [*NASDAQ symbol*] (NQ)
NDEI	National Defense Education Institute
NDEITA	National Dance-Exercise Instructor's Training Association (EA)
NDEL	Non-Destructive Evaluation Laboratory [*NASA*]
NDELA	Nitrosodiethanolamine [*Also, NDEOL*] [*Organic chemistry*]
NdEIN	State Normal and Industrial School, Ellendale, ND [*Library symbol Library of Congress Obsolete*] (LCLS)
NdEIT	Trinity Bible Institute, Ellendale, ND [*Library symbol Library of Congress*] (LCLS)
NDemP	National Democratic Party [*British*]
NDEOL	Nitrosodiethanolamine [*Also, NDELA*] [*Organic chemistry*]
NDEP	Nevada Division of Environmental Protection
NDEP	Nevada Division of Environmental Protection (DOGT)
NDER	National Defense Executive Reserve
NDERR	National Defense Executive Reserve Roster [*of the CSC*]
NDERWF	Navy Department Employees Recreation and Welfare Fund (MCD)
NDES	Normal Digital Echo Suppressor [*Telecommunications*] (TEL)
NDETP	National Drug Education Training Program [*HEW*]
NDeUA	State University of New York, Agricultural and Technical College at Delhi, Delhi, NY [*Library symbol Library of Congress*] (LCLS)
NDEW	Nuclear Directed-Energy Weapon
NDEW	Nuclear-Driven Directed-Energy Weapon
NDex	Dexter Free Library, Dexter, NY [*Library symbol Library of Congress*] (LCLS)
NDEX	Newspaper Index [*Bell & Howell Co.*] [*Database*]
NDf	Dobbs Ferry Public Library, Dobbs Ferry, NY [*Library symbol Library of Congress*] (LCLS)
NdF	Fargo Public Library, Fargo, ND [*Library symbol Library of Congress*] (LCLS)
NDF	Nacelle Drag Efficiency [*Factor*] [*Aerospace*]
NDF	Nandi [*Fiji*] [*Seismograph station code, US Geological Survey*] (SEIS)
NDF	National Democratic Front [*Pakistan*] [*Political party*] (FEA)
NDF	National Democratic Front [*Philippines*] [*Political party*] (FEA)
NDF	National Democratic Front [*Myanmar*] [*Political party*] (FEA)
NDF	National Democratic Front [*Iran*] [*Political party*] (PD)
NDF	National Democratic Front [*Guyana*] [*Political party*] (EY)
NDF	National Democratic Front [*Yemen*] [*Political party*] (PD)
NDF	National Diploma in Forestry [*British*]

NDF .... National Dividend Foundation (EA)
NDF .... National Drilling Federation [*Later, IDF*] (EA)
NDF .... Naval Dairy Farm
NDF .... Naval Defence Force [*British military*] (DMA)
NDF .... Navy Distillate Fuel (DNAB)
NDF .... Neutral Density Filter
NDF .... Neutral Detergent Fiber [*Food analysis*]
NDF .... New Democratic Forum (EA)
NDF .... New Dimensions Foundation (EA)
NDF .... New Dosage Form [*Medicine*] (MAE)
NDF .... Night Defense Fire (DNAB)
NDF .... No Defect Found
NDF .... No Disease Found (DAVI)
NDF .... Nondipole Field [*Electromagnetism*]
NDF .... Nonlinear Distortion Factor [*Telecommunications*] (OA)
NDF .... Nonrecursive Digital Filter [*Navy*] (IAA)
NDFA .... National Dietary Foods Association [*Later, NNFA*] (EA)
NDFA .... National Drama Festivals Association [*British*] (BI)
NdFA........... North Dakota State University, Fargo, ND [*Library symbol Library of Congress*] (LCLS)
NdFC........... Cass County Court House, Fargo, ND [*Library symbol Library of Congress*] (LCLS)
NDFC .... National Days Fan Club (EA)
NdFD .... Dakota Clinic, Fargo, ND [*Library symbol Library of Congress*] (LCLS)
NDFEA .... Northwest Dried Fruit Export Association [*Defunct*] (EA)
nd filter ...... Neutral-Density Filter [*Photography*] (WDMC)
NDfL .... Dobbs Ferry Public Library, Dobbs Ferry, NY [*Library symbol Library of Congress*] (LCLS)
NDFL .... National Defense Foreign Language [*Fellowship*]
ND Fla .... United States District Court for the Northern District of Florida (DLA)
NdFM.......... Masonic Grand Lodge Library, Fargo, ND [*Library symbol Library of Congress*] (LCLS)
NDfM .... Mercy College, Dobbs Ferry, NY [*Library symbol Library of Congress*] (LCLS)
NdFMG .... Masonic Grand Lodge, Fargo, ND [*Library symbol*] [*Library of Congress*] (LCLS)
NdFN .... Neuropsychiatric Hospital, Fargo, ND [*Library symbol Library of Congress*] (LCLS)
NDFS .... Non-Dwelling Floor Space (SAA)
NDfS .... Stauffer Chemical Co., Eastern Research Center, Dobbs Ferry, NY [*Library symbol Library of Congress*] (LCLS)
NdFStJ .... Saint John's Hospital, Fargo, ND [*Library symbol Library of Congress*] (LCLS)
NdFStL .... Saint Luke's Hospital, Fargo, ND [*Library symbol Library of Congress*] (LCLS)
NdFStLN ...... Saint Luke's School of Nursing, Fargo, ND [*Library symbol Library of Congress*] (LCLS)
NDFTA .... National Dried Fruit Trade Association [*British*] (DBA)
NdFVA .... United States Veterans Administration Hospital, Fargo, ND [*Library symbol Library of Congress*] (LCLS)
NDFYP .... Navy Department Five Year Plan
NdG .... Grand Forks Public Library, Grand Forks, ND [*Library symbol Library of Congress*] (LCLS)
NDG .... National Dance Guild [*Later, ADG*]
NDG .... National Distribution Guide [*Mailing technique*]
NDG .... No Date Given (AFM)
NDGA .... National Depression Glass Association (EA)
NDGA .... National Dog Groomers Association (EA)
NDGA .... Nordihydroguaiaretic Acid [*Antioxidant, food additive*]
ND GA .... United States District Court for the Northern District of Georgia (DLA)
NDGAA .... National Dog Groomers Association of America (EA)
NDGE .... NATO Air Defense Ground Environment
NdGIT .... United States Air Force Institute of Technology, Grand Forks AFB, ND [*Library symbol Library of Congress*] (LCLS)
NDGL .... Neodymium-Doped Glass LASER
NDGO.......... Navy Department General Order
NdGrC......... Carnegie Bookmobile Library, Grafton, ND [*Library symbol Library of Congress*] (LCLS)
NDGS.......... National Defense General Staff (NATG)
NDGS.......... National Duncan Glass Society (EA)
NdGUH........ Grand Forks United Hospital, Grand Forks, ND [*Library symbol Library of Congress*] (LCLS)
NDGW......... Native Daughters of the Golden West (EA)
NDH .... Delhi [*India*] [*Airport symbol*] (AD)
NDH .... National Defense Headquarters [*Canada*]
NDH .... National Diploma in Horticulture [*British*]
NDH .... Natural Disaster Hospitals [*Public Health Service*]
NDH .... New Departure Hyatt Division [*General Motors Corp.*]
NDH .... Royal North Devonshire Yeomanry Hussars [*British military*] (DMA)
NdHa .... Harvey Public Library, Harvey, ND [*Library symbol Library of Congress*] (LCLS)
NDHA.......... National Dental Hygienists' Association (EA)
NDHA.......... National District Heating Association [*Later, IDHCA*] (EA)
NDHFP........ New Developments Human Factors Program [*Navy*]
NdHi .... State Historical Society of North Dakota, Bismarck, ND [*Library symbol Library of Congress*] (LCLS)
NDHQ.......... National Defence Headquarters [*Canada*]
NDHS.......... Nimbus Data Handling System
NDHX.......... Natural Draft Heat Exchanger [*Nuclear energy*] (NRCH)
NDI .... Dickinson State College, Dickinson, ND [*OCLC symbol*] (OCLC)
NDI .... KS Nordic Air, Denmark [*ICAO designator*] (FAAC)
NDI .... Namudi [*Papua New Guinea*] [*Airport symbol*] (OAG)
NDI .... National Dance Institute (EA)

NDI .... National Death Index [*Department of Health and Human Services*] (GFGA)
NDI .... National Design, Inc. (PCM)
NDI .... Nephrogenic Diabetes Insipidus [*Endocrinology*]
NDI .... Network Development and Implementation Group [*National Research Council of Canada*]
NDI .... New Delhi [*India*] [*Seismograph station code, US Geological Survey*] (SEIS)
NDI .... Nielsen Drug Index [*Marketing*] (DOAD)
NDI .... Nissan Design International
NDI .... No-Dig International [*A publication*]
NDI .... Noise Depreciation Index
NDI .... Non-Combat Development Item
NDI .... Nondestructive Inspection (AFM)
NDI .... Non-Developmental Item [*Military*] (INF)
NDI .... Non-Development [*or Developmental*] Issue [*or Item*]
NDI .... Nondevelopment Item (MCD)
NDI .... Numerical Designation Index (IEEE)
NDiag .... National Diagnostics, Inc. [*Associated Press*] (SAG)
NDIC .... National Diabetes Information Clearinghouse [*Public Health Service*] (IID)
NDIC .... NATO Defense Information Complex (NATG)
NDIC .... Nuclear Data Information Center [*ORNL*]
NDIC .... Nuclear Desalination Information Center
NDICE .... Non-Developmental Items Candidate Evaluation
NDIIA .... National Democratic Institute for International Affairs (EA)
ND III .... United States District Court for the Northern District of Illinois (DLA)
NDIMC .... NATO Defense Information Management Committee (NATG)
ND Ind .... United States District Court for the Northern District of Indiana (DLA)
ND Iowa ...... United States District Court for the Northern District of Iowa (DLA)
NDIR .... Nondispersive Infrared [*Analyzer*]
NDIS .... National Document and Information Service [*Australia*]
NDIS .... Network Driver Interface Specification [*Computer science*] (PCM)
NDIS .... Nissan Direct Ignition System [*Automotive engineering*]
NDIS .... North Dakota State Industrial School
NDIU .... National Drugs Intelligence Unit [*Metropolitan Police*] [*British*]
NDIY .... North Devon Imperial Yeomanry [*British military*] (DMA)
NdJ .... Alfred Dickey Free Library, Jamestown, ND [*Library symbol Library of Congress*] (LCLS)
NDJ .... Jamestown College, Jamestown, ND [*OCLC symbol*] (OCLC)
NDJ .... N'Djamena [*Chad*] [*Airport symbol*] (OAG)
NdJC........... Jamestown College, Jamestown, ND [*Library symbol Library of Congress*] (LCLS)
NdJF .... North Dakota Farmers Union Resource Library, Jamestown, ND [*Library symbol Library of Congress*] (LCLS)
NdJN........... Northern Prairie Wildlife Research Center, Jamestown, ND [*Library symbol Library of Congress*] (LCLS)
NdJSH .... State Hospital, Jamestown, ND [*Library symbol Library of Congress*] (LCLS)
NDK .... Namorik [*Marshall Islands*] [*Airport symbol*] (OAG)
NDK .... Nucleoside Diphosphate Kinase [*An enzyme*]
NDK .... South Weymouth, MA [*Location identifier FAA*] (FAAL)
NDL .... Duke University, Law Library, Durham, NC [*OCLC symbol*] (OCLC)
NDL .... National Defence Headquarters Library [*UTLAS symbol*]
NDL .... National Democratic League [*Early British political party*]
NDL .... National Demographics & Lifestyles, Inc.
NDL .... National Diet Library [*Japan*]
NDL .... Natural Daylight
NDL .... Needle (MSA)
NDL .... Neon Discharge Lighting [*Automotive lighting*]
NDL .... Network Database Language [*Telecommunications*] (OSI)
NDL .... Network Definition Language [*Burroughs Corp.*]
NDL .... Ni-Cal Developments Ltd. [*Vancouver Stock Exchange symbol*]
NDL .... No Decompression Limit
NDL .... Norddeutscher Lloyd [*German steamship company*]
Nd-L........... North Dakota State Law Library, Bismarck, ND [*Library symbol Library of Congress*] (LCLS)
NDL .... Nuclear Data Link System [*Nuclear Regulatory Commission*]
NDL .... Nuclear Defense Laboratory [*Army*]
NDL .... Numerical Drawing List
NDLB .... National Dock Labour Board [*British*]
NDLC .... Network Data Link Control
NdLibC........ North Dakota State Library Commission, Bismarck, ND [*Library symbol Library of Congress*] (LCLS)
NDLOA........ National Disabled Law Officers Association (EA)
NDLT .... N-Channel Depletion-Load Triode Inverter
ndlwk.......... Needlework (VRA)
NDM .... Ferrocarriles Nacionales de Mexico [*AAR code*]
NDM .... Mary College, Library, Bismarck, ND [*OCLC symbol*] (OCLC)
NDM .... Nadym Airlines [*Russian Federation*] [*ICAO designator*] (FAAC)
NDM .... National Dried (Milk) [*Brand name for the British government's dried milk for babies - manufacturer undisclosed*]
NDM .... N-Desmethyl-Methsuximide [*Biochemistry*] (AAMN)
NDM .... Negative Differential Mobility (IEEE)
NDM .... Neutron Dose Monitor
NDM .... New Democratic Movement (EA)
NDM .... New Dimensions in Medicine
NDM .... Newspaper Designated Market (WDMC)
NDM .... NOAA [*National Oceanic and Atmospheric Administration*] Directives Manual (NOAA)
NDM .... Nomad Energy & Resources [*Vancouver Stock Exchange symbol*]
NDM .... North Durham Militia [*British military*] (DMA)
NDMA .... National Dimension Manufacturers Association (EA)
NDMA .... National Door Manufacturers Association [*Later, NWWDA*]
NDMA .... National Dress Manufacturers Association [*Later, AMA*] (EA)

NDMA .... Nitrosodimethylaniline [*Chemistry*] (DAVI)
NDMA .... N-Nitrosodimethylamine [*Also, DMN, DMNA*] [*Organic chemistry*]
NDMA .... Nonprescription Drug Manufacturers Association (EA)
NdMan .... Mandan Public Library, Mandan, ND [*Library symbol Library of Congress*] (LCLS)
NdManMH ... North Dakota Memorial Mental Health and Retardation Center, Mandan, ND [*Library symbol Library of Congress*] (LCLS)
NdManN ...... North Dakota Industrial School, Mandan, ND [*Library symbol Library of Congress*] (LCLS)
NdManNG .... United States Northern Great Plains Research Center, Mandan, ND [*Library symbol Library of Congress*] (LCLS)
NdMayS .... Mayville State College, Mayville, ND [*Library symbol Library of Congress*] (LCLS)
NDMB .... National Defense Mediation Board [*World War II*]
NDMC .... NATO Defense Manpower Committee (NATG)
NDMC .... N-Desmethylclobazam [*Biochemistry*]
NDMDA .... National Depressive and Manic Depressive Association (EA)
NdMin .... Minot Public Library, Minot, ND [*Library symbol Library of Congress*] (LCLS)
NdMinAF .... United States Air Force, Base Library, Minot AFB, ND [*Library symbol Library of Congress*] (LCLS)
NdMinIT .... United States Air Force Institute of Technology, Minot AFB, ND [*Library symbol Library of Congress*] (LCLS)
NdMinN .... Northwest Bible College, Minot, ND [*Library symbol Library of Congress*] (LCLS)
NdMinS .... Minot State College, Minot, ND [*Library symbol Library of Congress*] (LCLS)
NdMinT-M ... Trinity Medical Center, August Cameron Medical Library, Minot, ND [*Library symbol Library of Congress*] (LCLS)
NdMinT-N .... Trinity Medical Center, School of Nursing, Minot, ND [*Library symbol Library of Congress*] (LCLS)
ND Miss ...... United States District Court for the Northern District of Mississippi (DLA)
NDML .... Neutral Data Manipulation Language [*Computer science*]
NdMo .... Mott Public Library, Mott, ND [*Library symbol Library of Congress*] (LCLS)
NDMPI .... Nitrosodimethylpiperazinium Iodide [*Organic chemistry*]
NDMS .... National Debt Management System [*Social Security Administration*] (GFGA)
NDMS .... National Disaster Medical System
NDMS .... Netware Distributed Management Services [*Novell, Inc.*] (PCM)
NDMS .... Network Design and Management System
NDMS .... Noise Deficiency Management System
NDMS .... Non-Directional Mud-and-Snow (PDAA)
NDMSP .... Navy Department Mobilization Security Plan (NG)
NDMTB .... Nondeployment Mobilization Troop Basis (AABC)
NDMTP .... National Defense Manufacturing Technology Plan
NDMWC .... National Domestic Meatworks Wholesalers Council [*Australia*]
NDN .... National Diffusion Network [*Department of Education*] [*Information service or system*] (IID)
NDN .... National Directory of Newsletters and Reporting Services [*A publication*]
NDN .... New Data Network (IAA)
NDN .... Ninety-Nine Cent Only Stores [*NYSE symbol*] (SAG)
NDN .... Nonsynaptic Diffusion Neurotransmission [*Neurology*]
NDN .... Nu-Dawn Resources, Inc. [*Vancouver Stock Exchange symbol*]
nDNA .... Deoxyribonucleic Acid, Nuclear [*Biochemistry, genetics*]
NDNHI .... North Dakota Natural Heritage Inventory [*North Dakota State Department of Natural Resources*] [*Bismarck*] [*Information service or system*] (IID)
NDNO .... National Directory of Nonprofit Organizations [*A publication*]
NDNT .... Not Dressed nor Tanned
NDNY .... United States District Court for the Northern District of New York (DLA)
NDO .... National Debt Office [*British*]
NDO .... Navy Disbursing Office
NDO .... Negotiate Downward Only (MCD)
NDO .... Network Development Office [*Library of Congress*]
NDOA .... National Dog Owners' Association [*British*] (BI)
NDOC .... Neurological Dysfunctions of Children [*Test*]
ND Ohio .... United States District Court for the Northern District of Ohio (DLA)
ND Okla .... United States District Court for the Northern District of Oklahoma (DLA)
NDOP .... Navy Designated Overhaul Point (CAAL)
NDOS .... National Defense Operations Section [*FCC*]
NDOS .... New Disc Operating System (NITA)
NDp .... Deer Park Public Library, Deer Park, NY [*Library symbol Library of Congress*] (LCLS)
NDP .... National Democracy Party [*Thailand*] [*Political party*] (PPW)
NDP .... National Democratic Party [*Rhodesia and Nyasaland*] [*Political party*]
NDP .... National Democratic Party [*Sierra Leone*] [*Political party*] (EY)
NDP .... National Democratic Party [*Grenada*] [*Political party*] (PPW)
NDP .... National Democratic Party [*India*] [*Political party*] (PPW)
NDP .... National Democratic Party [*Morocco*] [*Political party*] (PPW)
NDP .... National Democratic Party [*Iraq*] [*Political party*] (BJA)
NDP .... National Democratic Party [*Namibia*] [*Political party*] (PPW)
NDP .... National Democratic Party [*Egypt*] [*Political party*] (PPW)
NDP .... National Democratic Party [*Pakistan*] [*Political party*] (PD)
NDP .... National Democratic Party [*Solomon Islands*] [*Political party*] (PPW)
NDP .... Nationaldemokratische Partei [*National Democratic Party*] [*Austria Political party*] (PPW)
NDP .... National Determination Party (EA)
NDP .... National Development Party [*Montserrat*] [*Political party*] (EY)
NDP .... National Diocesan Press [*Later, Episcopal Communicators*] (EA)
NDP .... National Diploma in Poultry Husbandry [*British*]
NDP .... National Disclosure Policy [*Military*] (MCD)
NDP .... Nationalist Democracy Party [*Turkey Political party*] (PPW)
NDP .... Nationwide Demonstration Program
NDP .... Naval Doctrine Publication (DOMA)
NDP .... Navy Department Personnel
NDP .... Neighborhood Development Program [*Urban renewal*]
NDP .... Net Dietary Protein (MAE)
NDP .... Net Domestic Product [*Business term*] (PDAA)
NDP .... Neurological Disorders Program [*National Institute of Neurological and Communicative Disorders and Stroke*]
NDP .... Neutron Depth Profiling [*Analytical chemistry*]
NDP .... New Democratic Party [*Facetious translations: "Never Dies Politically," "No Dreams of Prosperity"*] [*Canada Political party*] (PPW)
NDP .... New Democratic Party [*South Korea Political party*] (PPW)
NDP .... New Democratic Party [*St. Vincent*] [*Political party*] (PPW)
NDP .... New Democratic Party [*Seychelles*] [*Political party*] (EY)
NDP .... Night Defensive Position [*Military*]
NDP .... Normal Diametral Pitch (MSA)
NDP .... Nuclear Desalination Plant
NDP .... Nuclear Disarmament Party [*Australia Political party*]
NDP .... Nucleoside Diphosphate [*Biochemistry*]
NDP .... Numeric Data Processor
NDP .... Pensacola, FL [*Location identifier FAA*] (FAAL)
NDPA .... National Decorated Packaging Association
NDPA .... National Decorating Products Association (EA)
NDPA .... Nitrosodipropylamine [*Also, DPN, DPNA*] [*Organic chemistry*]
NDPB .... National Drug Policy Board [*Department of Justice*] (GFGA)
NDPB .... Non-Departmental Public Body [*British*]
NDPBC .... National Duck Pin Bowling Congress [*Later, NDBC*] (EA)
NDPC .... National Democratic Policy Committee (EA)
NDPC .... National [*Military Information*] Disclosure Policy Committee
NDPC .... National Dropout Prevention Center (EA)
NDPC .... National Drowning Prevention Coalition (EA)
NDPD .... National Data Processing Division [*Environmental Protection Agency*] (GFGA)
NDPD .... Nationaldemokratische Partei Deutschlands [*German National Democratic Party*] [*Political party*]
NDPF .... NASA Data Processing Facility (MCD)
NDPhA .... N-Nitrosodiphenylamine [*Organic chemistry*]
NDpHS .... Deer Park High School, Deer Park, NY [*Library symbol*] [*Library of Congress*] (LCLS)
NDPIC .... Navy Department Program Information Center
NDPK .... Nucleoside Diphosphokinase [*An enzyme*]
NDPK .... Nucleotide Diphosphate Kinase [*An enzyme*]
NDPL .... National Democratic Party of Liberia [*Political party*] (EY)
NDPN .... National Dropout Prevention Network (EA)
NDPP .... (Nitrobenzyl)(Diethylaminophenylazo)-pyridinium Bromide [*Reagent*]
NDPR .... NATO Defense Planning Review (NATG)
NDPR .... Nuclear Duty Position Roster (MCD)
NDPRP .... National Defense Project Rating Plan
NDPS .... National Data Processing Service [*British*] (DCTA)
NDPS .... Novell Distributed Print Services [*Computer science*]
NDPS .... Novell Distributed Print Services [*Computer science*]
NDQ .... NASA Delta Quotation (MCD)
ND(Q) .... Nominal Defendant (Queensland) [*Australia*]
NDR .... Andrea Airlines SA [*Peru*] [*ICAO designator*] (FAAC)
NDR .... Nador [*Morocco*] [*Airport symbol*] (AD)
NDR .... National Derby Rallies (EA)
NDR .... National Dog Registry (EA)
NDR .... National Driver Register
NDR .... National Drug Co. [*Research code symbol*]
NDR .... Negative Differential Resistance [*Electronics*]
NDR .... Net Difference Report (IAA)
NDR .... Network Data Reduction
NDR .... Network Data Representation [*Computer science*]
NDR .... Neutral Detergent Residue [*Food analysis*]
NDR .... New Dimensions Radio (EA)
NDR .... Nondestructive Read [*Computer science*]
NDR .... Norddeutscher Rundfunk [*Radio network*] [*Germany*]
NDR .... Normal Daily Requirement [*Military*]
NDR .... Normotensive Donor Rat
NDR .... Nuclear Double Resonance [*Analytical chemistry*]
NDRA .... Nostalgia Drag Race Association (EA)
NDRB .... New Developments Research Branch [*Navy*] (MCD)
NDRC .... National Defense Research Committee [*of Office of Scientific Research and Development*] [*World War II*]
NDRE .... Norwegian Defense Research Establishment
ND Res Found Bull... North Dakota Research Foundation Bulletin [*A publication*]
NDRF .... National Debt Repayment Foundation (EA)
NDRF .... National Defense Reserve Fleet [*Maritime Administration, Department of Commerce*]
NDRG .... NATO Defense Research Group (NATG)
NDRI .... National Diabetes Research Interchange [*Research center*] (RCD)
NDRI .... Naval Dental Research Institute
NDRL .... Notre Dame Radiation Laboratory [*University of Notre Dame*] [*Research center*] (RCD)
NDRM .... Neesby Delayed Release Mechanism [*Medicine*]
NDRO .... Nondestructive Read Only [*Computer science*] (IAA)
NDRO .... Nondestructive Readout [*Computer science*]
NDRP .... New Democratic Republican Party [*South Korea Political party*] (EY)
NDRS .... National Driver Register Service [*Department of Transportation*]
NDRS .... Nuclear Definition and Reporting System (AAG)
NDRSWG ..... NATO Data Requirements and Standards Working Group (NATG)
NDRT .... Nelson-Denny Reading Test (EDAC)

NDRW..........	Nondestructive Read/Write [Computer science]
NDryT	Tompkins-Cortland Community College, Division of Instructional and Learning Resources, Dryden, NY [Library symbol Library of Congress] (LCLS)
NDS	Congregation of Notre Dame de Sion [Roman Catholic women's religious order]
NDS	National Dahlia Society [British] (DBA)
NDS	National Decision Systems [Information service or system] (IID)
NDS	National Defense Stockpile [Collection of materials essential to the defense industry]
NDS	National Dioxin Study [Environmental Protection Agency] (GFGA)
NDS	National Disposal Site [Environmental Protection Agency] (GFGA)
NDS	Naval Dental School
NDS	Navigation Development Satellite (MCD)
NDS	Navigation Display System
NDS	Navy Data System
NDS	Navy Directive System (NVT)
NDS	Navy Display System
NDS	Needs [Automotive advertising]
NDS	NetWare Directory Services [Novell, Inc.] [Computer science] (PCM)
NDS	Network Data Series (MHDI)
NDS	Network Development System (IAA)
NDS	Neurologic Disability Score
NDS	Neutral-Drive Switch [Automotive engineering]
NDS	Neutron Doped Silicon (IAA)
NDS	Nicholas Data [Vancouver Stock Exchange symbol]
NDS	Nominal Detectable Signal (IAA)
NDS	Noncommunications Detection System (MCD)
NDS	Non-Developmental Software
NDS	Nonparametric Detection Scheme [Communication signal]
NDS	Nordic Demographic Society (EA)
NDS	Nordstress (Australia) Pt Ltd. [FAA designator] (FAAC)
NDS	Normal Dog Serum [Medicine] (DMAA)
NDS	North Dakota State Library Commission, Bismarck, ND [OCLC symbol] (OCLC)
NDS	Novell Directory Service [Computer Networking] (PCM)
NDS	NPIC [National Photographic Interpretation Center] Data System (MCD)
NDS ;...........	Nuclear Data Sheets [National Academy of Sciences]
NDS ;...........	Nuclear Detection Satellite
NDS ;...........	Nuclear Detection System (MCD)
NDS	Nuclear Detonation Detection System
NDSA	National Disposal Services Association (EA)
NDSB..........	Narcotic Drugs Supervisory Body [UN]
NDSB..........	Navy Dependents School Branch
ND/SB	Nuclear Depth/Strike Bomb (DOMA)
NDSC..........	National Down Syndrome Congress (EA)
NDSC..........	Network for the Detection of Stratospheric Change [New Zealand] (USDC)
NDSC..........	Network for the Detection of Stratospheric Change [New Zealand] [Marine science] (OSRA)
NDSE	Nondeliverable Support Equipment
NDSEG	National Defense Science and Engineering Graduate
ND Sess Laws...	Laws of North Dakota [A publication] (DLA)
NDSF	National Defense Sealift Fund (DOMA)
NDSF	North Dakota School of Forestry
NDSL	National Direct [formerly, Defense] Student Loan [later, Perkins Loan] [Department of Education]
NDSL	Non Domestic Substances List [Canada]
NDSM	National Defense Service Medal [Military decoration]
NDSN..........	National Drug Strategy Network (EA)
NDSN..........	Nobody Don't Say Nothing
NDSN..........	Nordson Corp. [NASDAQ symbol] (NQ)
NDSOS.........	Navy Deep Sea Oceanographic System
NDSS	National Down Syndrome Society (EA)
NDSS	National DS Society
NDSTC	Naval Diving and Salvage Training Center (DNAB)
NDSU	North Dakota State University
NDT	Ferrocarril Nacional de Tehuantepec [AAR code]
NDT	National Diploma in the Science and Practice of Turfculture and Sports Ground Management [British]
NDT	Net Data Throughout
NDT	Network Description Table (MHDI)
NDT	Neuro-Developmental Treatment [Physical therapy]
NDT	Nevada Dance Theatre
NDT	New Dictionary of Thoughts [A publication]
NDT	New Dimensions [Vancouver Stock Exchange symbol]
NDT	Nil-Ductility Temperature [Metallurgy]
NDT	Nil-Ductility Transition [Metallurgy] (IEEE)
NDT	No Dial Tone [Of a telephone] (WDMC)
NDT	Nondestructive Testing
NDT	Non-Lethal Disabling Technology
NDT	Nuclear Detection Test (IAA)
NDTA	National Defense Transportation Association (EA)
NDTA	National Dental Technicians Association [Defunct] (EA)
NDTA	Neurodevelopmental Treatment Association (EA)
NDTA	Non-Destructive Testing Association of Australia
NDT & E	Nondestructive Testing and Evaluation Programs [Pennsylvania State University] [Research center] (RCD)
NDTC	National Drug Trade Conference (EA)
NDTC	Naval Device Training Center
NDTC	Nondestructive Testing Center (IEEE)
NDTE	North Dakota Tracer Experiment (USDC)
ND Tex	United States District Court for the Northern District of Texas (DLA)
NDTF	Nondestructive Test Facility (MCD)

Ndthl...........	Neanderthal (VRA)
NDTI	Nondestructive Testing and Inspection
NDTIAC	Non-Destructive Testing Information Center [Army Materials and Mechanics Research Center] (PDAA)
NDTIB	Nondestructive Testing and Inspection Building
NDTL	Nondestructive Test Laboratory (MCD)
NDTMA	National Drain Tile Manufacturers Association [Defunct] (EA)
NDTP	Nuclear Data Tape Program
NDTRAN	Notre Dame Translator [Programming language] [1977] [Computer science] (CSR)
NDTT	Nil-Ductility Transition Temperature [Metallurgy]
NDU............	National Defense University [DoD]
NDU............	National Defense University, Washington, DC [OCLC symbol] (OCLC)
NDU	National Democratic Union [Zimbabwe] [Political party] (PPW)
NDU	Navigation Display Unit [Military]
NDU	NDU Resources [Vancouver Stock Exchange symbol]
NDU	Nederlandse Dagbladunie
N/D/U...........	None Done Up [Bookselling]
ndu	North Dakota [MARC country of publication code Library of Congress] (LCCP)
NDU	Nuclear Data Unit [International Atomic Energy Agency] (DIT)
NDU	Rundu [Namibia] [Airport symbol] (OAG)
NdU	University of North Dakota, Grand Forks, ND [Library symbol Library of Congress] (LCLS)
NDUC..........	Nimbus Data Utilization Center
NdU-El........	University of North Dakota, Ellendale Branch, Ellendale, ND [Library symbol Library of Congress Obsolete] (LCLS)
NDUF	National Democratic United Front [Later, FNDF] [Myanmar] [Political party] (PD)
NdU-L	University of North Dakota, Law Library, Grand Forks, ND [Library symbol Library of Congress] (LCLS)
NdU-M	University of North Dakota, Medical Library, Grand Forks, ND [Library symbol Library of Congress] (LCLS)
NDunBH......	Brooks Memorial Hospital Medical Center, Dunkirk, NY [Library symbol Library of Congress] (LCLS)
NDUP..........	Nonduplicate
NDUSTA......	New Duty Station [Navy]
NDUV..........	Nondispersive Ultraviolet
NDV	Newcastle Disease Virus [Also, ND]
NDV	Not to Delay Delivery
NDV	Not to Delay Vessel
NDV	Nuclear Delivery Vehicle
NDV	Valley City State College, Valley City, ND [OCLC symbol] (OCLC)
NDV	Washington, DC [Location identifier FAA] (FAAL)
NdVc..........	Valley City Public Library, Valley City, ND [Library symbol Library of Congress] (LCLS)
NdVcT........	Valley City State College, Valley City, ND [Library symbol Library of Congress] (LCLS)
NDVI	Normalized Difference Vegetation Index [Plant biota]
NDW	Naval District Washington
NDW	North Dakota State School of Science, Mildred Johnson Library, Wahpeton, ND [OCLC symbol] (OCLC)
NDW	Norton Desktop for Windows [Symantec Corp.] [Computer science] (PCM)
NDWAC.......	National Drinking Water Advisory Council [Environmental Protection Agency]
NdWah........	Leach Public Library, Wahpeton, ND [Library symbol Library of Congress] (LCLS)
NdWahS	North Dakota State School of Science, Wahpeton, ND [Library symbol Library of Congress] (LCLS)
NDWBA.......	National Deaf Women's Bowling Association (EA)
NdWi	James Memorial Library, Williston, ND [Library symbol Library of Congress] (LCLS)
NdWiU	University of North Dakota, Williston Branch, Williston, ND [Library symbol Library of Congress] (LCLS)
NdWiW	West Plains Rural Library, Williston, ND [Library symbol Library of Congress] (LCLS)
NDWP..........	National Demonstration Water Project (EA)
NDWRRI.......	North Dakota Water Resources Research Institute [Fargo, ND] [Department of the Interior] (GRD)
NDWU..........	National Domestic Workers Union (EA)
NDX	Northern Dynasty Explorations Ltd. [Toronto Stock Exchange symbol Vancouver Stock Exchange symbol]
NDxhBJ........	Burr's Lane Junior High School, Dix Hills, NY [Library symbol Library of Congress] (LCLS)
NDxhFE........	Forest Park Elementary School, Dix Hills, NY [Library symbol] [Library of Congress] (LCLS)
NDxhH	Half Hollow Hills Community Public Library, Dix Hills, NY [Library symbol] [Library of Congress] (LCLS)
NDxhHH-E....	Half Hollow Hills High School East, Dix Hills, NY [Library symbol Library of Congress] (LCLS)
NDxhHH-W...	Half Hollow Hills High School West, Dix Hills, NY [Library symbol Library of Congress] (LCLS)
NDxhHT	Half Hollow Hills District Teacher's Center, Dix Hills, NY [Library symbol Library of Congress] (LCLS)
NDY	Dahlgren, VA [Location identifier FAA] (FAAL)
NDY	Neodymium-Doped Yttralox [Ceramic]
NDY	Nonresonant Deflection Yoke
NDY	Sanday [Scotland] [Airport symbol] (OAG)
Nd:YAG	Neodymium-Doped: Yttrium Aluminum Garnet [LASER technology]
NDYL	Neodymium-Doped YAG [Yttrium Aluminum Garnet] LASER
NDZ	Milton, FL [Location identifier FAA] (FAAL)
NE...............	Air New England [ICAO designator] (AD)

Ne	Algemeen Rijksarchief te s'Gravenhage (Central State Archives), The Hague, Netherlands [*Library symbol Library of Congress*] (LCLS)
NE	Left Nationalists [*Spain Political party*] (PPW)
NE	Narcotics Education [*An association*] (EA)
NE	National Emergency
NE	National Estate
NE	National Exchequer [*British*]
NE	National Executive (ADA)
NE	National Exhibition [*British*]
NE	Naval Engineer [*Academic degree*]
NE	Navy Evaluation
NE	Near East (BJA)
NE	Nebraska [*Postal code*]
NE	Negative Expectancy [*Psychometrics*]
NE	Negatives and Etching (DGA)
NE	Negotiated Exit [*Telecommunications*] (OSI)
Ne	Nehemiah [*Old Testament book*] (BJA)
NE	Neiva [*Sociedade Construtora Aeronautica Neiva Ltda.*] [*Brazil ICAO aircraft manufacturer identifier*] (ICAO)
NE	Neomycin [*Antibacterial compound*]
NE	Neon [*Chemical element*]
ne	Neon (IDOE)
Ne	Neon [*Chemical element*] (ODBW)
ne	Neon (VRA)
Ne	Neon [*Chemical element*] (DOG)
ne	Nephelite [*CIPW classification*] [*Geology*]
NE	Nephropathia Epidemica [*Medicine*]
NE	Nerve Ending (MAE)
NE	Nerve Excitability [*Test*]
NE	Net Earnings
ne	Netherlands [*MARC country of publication code Library of Congress*] (LCCP)
NE	Netherlands
NE	Neumann-Electroporation [*Gene technology*]
NE	Neural Excitation [*neurology*] (DAVI)
NE	Neurologic Examination [*Medicine*]
NE	Neutral Endopeptidase [*An enzyme*]
NE	Neutral Excitation
NE	New Edition
NE	New Editions [*Record label*]
NE	New Engine [*On ships*]
NE	New England
NE	[*The*] New English Bible [*1961*] [*A publication*] (BJA)
NE	New Executable [*Computer science*] (PCM)
NE	News Editor (ADA)
NE	Niacin Equivalent
NE	Nickel Equivalent [*Coinage*]
NE	Niger [*ANSI two-letter standard code*] (CNC)
NE	Night Experimental [*British military*] (DMA)
NE	Nodal Exchange (MCD)
NE	No Earthly Chance (DSUE)
NE	No Ectopy [*Medicine*] (MEDA)
NE	No Effects
NE	Noise-Equivalent (IAA)
NE	Nonelastic [*Medicine*] (MAE)
NE	Non-English Speaker [*Airline notation*]
NE	Nonessential
NE	Norepinephrine [*Also known as NA: Noradrenaline*] [*Biochemistry*]
NE	Normal Excitability [*Medicine*]
NE	Normally Energized (NRCH)
NE	Northeast
NE	Northeast Airlines, Inc. [*Obsolete*]
NE	North Eastern Reporter [*A publication*] (DLA)
NE	Not Elevated [*Laboratory science*] (DAVI)
NE	Not Employed
NE	Not Engaged
NE	Not Enlarged [*Medicine*]
NE	Not Entitled [*British military*] (DMA)
NE	Not Equal [*Relational operator*]
NE	Not Equal To (NITA)
NE	Not Evaluated (INF)
NE	Not Examined [*Medicine*]
N/E	Not Exceeding
NE	Not Explosive
NE	Notice of Exception (MCD)
NE	Nuclear Engineer
NE	Nuclear Envelope [*Cytology*]
NE	Nuclear Explosive
NE	Nuclear Extract [*Cytology*]
NE	Nursing Educator (AAMN)
NE 2d	Northeastern Reporter, Second Series [*A publication*] (DLA)
NE 2d	North Eastern Reporter, Second Series [*West*] [*A publication*] (AAGC)
NEa	Eastchester Public Library, Eastchester, NY [*Library symbol Library of Congress*] (LCLS)
NEA	Nashville Entertainment Association (EA)
NEA	National Economic Association (EA)
NEA	National Editorial Association [*Later, NNA*] (EA)
NEA	National Education Association (EA)
NEA	National Electronic Associations [*Later, NESSDA*]
NEA	National Employment Association [*Later, NAPC*] (EA)
NEA	National Endowment for the Arts
NEA	National Energy Accounts [*Department of Commerce*] [*Information service or system*] (IID)
NEA	National Energy Act (GFGA)
NEA	National Erectors Association (EA)
NEA	Natural Energy Association [*British*]
NEA	Nearctic Resources, Inc. [*Toronto Stock Exchange symbol*]
NEA	Near-Earth Asteroid [*Astronomy*]
NEA	Near Eastern Affairs [*Department of State*]
NEA	Neath [*Welsh depot code*]
NEA	Negative Electron Affinity [*Photocathode*]
NEA	Nelson & Albemarle Railway [*AAR code*]
NEA	Nenana [*Alaska*] [*Seismograph station code, US Geological Survey*] (SEIS)
NEA	Network Equivalent Analysis
NEA	New England Airlines, Inc. [*ICAO designator*] (FAAC)
NEA	New Entitlement Authority
NEA	Newsletter Editors' Association [*Australia*]
NEA	Newspaper Enterprise Association [*A syndicate*]
NEA	Noise-Equivalent Angle (MCD)
NEA	Northeast Airlines, Inc. [*Obsolete*]
NEA	Northeast Asia (CINC)
NEA	Northern Examining Association [*British*]
NEA	Nuclear Energy Agency [*See also AEN*] [*Organization for Economic Cooperation and Development*] (EAIO)
NEA	Null Error Amplifier
NEA	Nutrition Education Association (EA)
NeAA	Gemeente Archief van Amsterdam, Amsterdam, Netherlands [*Library symbol Library of Congress*] (LCLS)
NEAA	National Employment Assistance Act (OICC)
NEAA	Norwegian Elkhound Association of America (EA)
NEAAN	Non-Essential Amino Acid N [*Biochemistry*] (PDAA)
NEAATS	Northeast Asia Association of Theological Schools
NEAB	Northern Examinations and Assessment Board (AIE)
NEABFGP	New England Advisory Board for Fish and Game Problems [*Defunct*] (EA)
NEabG	Genesee County Landmark Society, East Bethany, NY [*Library symbol Library of Congress*] (LCLS)
NEAC	New English Art Club [*British*]
NEAC	Nippon Electric Automatic Computer (IEEE)
NEAC	Northeast Air Command
NEACDS	Naval Emergency Air Cargo Delivery System (CAAL)
NEACH	New England Automated Clearing House Association
NEACP	National Emergency Airborne Command Post [*Pronounced "kneecap"*] [*Modified Boeing 747 jet to be used as a military control center by the President or Vice President during a nuclear war or other crisis*]
NEACRP	Nuclear Energy Agency Committee on Reactor Physics [*OECD*] (EY)
NEACSS	New England Association of Colleges and Secondary Schools [*Later, NEASC*] (EA)
NEA-DB	NEA [*Nuclear Energy Agency*] Data Bank [*OECD*] [*Information service or system*] (IID)
NEADS	National Education for Assistance Dog Services [*Formerly, New England Assistance Dog Service*] (PAZ)
NEADS	Near East and African Development Service
NEADS	Network Engineering Administrative Data System [*AT & T*]
NEADS	Northeast Atlantic Dynamics Studies [*Marine science*] (MSC)
NEADW	Northeast Atlantic Deep Water [*Oceanography*]
NEAF	Near East Air Force [*British*]
NEAFC	North-East Atlantic Fisheries Commission [*British*] (EAIO)
NEAGC	National Early American Glass Club (EA)
NEAHI	Near East Animal Health Institute
NEAM	Nonvolatile Electrically Alterable Memory
NEAN	National Execution Alert Network (EA)
NEANDC	Nuclear Energy Agency Nuclear Data Committee [*OECD*] (EY)
NEANMCC	Navy Element Alternate National Military Command Center (MCD)
NEanpHE	Harley Avenue Elementary School, East Northport, NY [*Library symbol Library of Congress*] (LCLS)
NeAO	Rijksinstituut voor Orlogsdocumentatie, Amsterdam, Netherlands [*Library symbol Library of Congress*] (LCLS)
NEAP	National Energy Audit Program [*Canada*]
NEAPD	Northeastern Air Procurement District
NEAQ	Northern Electricity Authority of Queensland [*Australia*]
NEAR	National Emergency Alarm Repeater [*Civil defense warning system for homes*]
NEAR	Nationwide/Worldwide Emergency Ambulance Return
NEAR	Near-Earth Asteroid Rendezvous (MCD)
NEAR	New England Action Research Project
NEAR	Nielsen Engineering & Research, Inc.
NEARA	New England Antiquities Research Association (EA)
NEARELF	Near East Land Forces [*British military*] (DMA)
NEARNAVDIST	Nearest Naval District
NEARnet	[*The*] New England Academic and Research Network [*Computer science*] (TNIG)
NEARO	New England Albanian Relief Organization
NEARP	New England Appalachian Research Project [*University of Maine at Orono*] [*Research center*] (RCD)
NEARS	Navy Evaluation of Advanced Reconnaissance Systems
NEARS	Near Earth Asteroid Returned Samples [*NASA, proposed*]
NEARTIP	Near-Term Improvement Program [*For torpedos*] (MCD)
NEARYP	National Employers Association of Rayon Yarn Producers [*British*] (BI)
NEAS	National Engineering Aptitude Search
NEAS	National European American Society (EA)
NEAS	Near East Archaeological Society
NEAS	Newsletter of Engineering Analysis Software [*A publication*] (MCD)
NEASA	Near Eastern, African, and South Asian Affairs [*Department of State*]
NEASC	New England Association of Schools and Colleges (EA)
NEASCUS	New England Association of School, College, and University Staffing

NEASIM	Network Analytical Simulator (PDAA)
NEASP	Navy Enlisted Advanced School Program
NEaspHS	Eastport High School, Eastport, NY [*Library symbol Library of Congress*] (LCLS)
NeAT	Koninklijk Instituut voor de Tropen, Amsterdam, Netherlands [*Library symbol Library of Congress*] (LCLS)
NEAT	National Cash Register Electronic Autocoding Technique [*Computer science*] (IAA)
NEAT	National Electronic Autocoding Technique (MHDB)
NEAT	Navy Electronics Application Trainer
NEAT	Navy Embarked Advisory Team
NEAT	NCR [*NCR Corp.*] Electronic Autocoding Technique [*Computer science*]
NEAT	Near-Earth Asteroid Tracking
NEAT	New Enhanced Technology
NEATE	New England Association of Teachers of English (AEBS)
NEATICC	Northeast Asia Tactical Information Communications Center (DNAB)
NEATO	North East Asian Treaty Organization (NATG)
NeAU	University of Amsterdam, Amsterdam, Netherlands [*Library symbol Library of Congress*] (LCLS)
NEAuC	Christ the King Seminary, East Aurora, NY [*Library symbol Library of Congress*] (LCLS)
NEAuF	Fisher-Price Toys, East Aurora, NY [*Library symbol Library of Congress*] (LCLS)
NEAuH	Elbert Hubbard Library Museum, East Aurora, NY [*Library symbol Library of Congress*] (LCLS)
NEAuS	Saint John Vianney Seminary, East Aurora, NY [*Library symbol Library of Congress*] (LCLS)
NEawNE	North Side Elementary School, East Williston, NY [*Library symbol Library of Congress*] (LCLS)
NEB	National Energy Board [*Canada*]
NEB	National Enterprise Board [*Later, BTG*] [*British*]
NEB	Nebelwerfer [*German six-barrelled mortar*] (DSUE)
NEB	Nebraska
Neb	Nebraska (ODBW)
Neb	Nebraska Supreme Court Reports [*A publication*] (DLA)
NEB	Nebula [*Spray*] [*Pharmacy*]
NEB	Neuroepithelial Bodies [*Anatomy*]
NEB	New England Business Services [*NYSE symbol*] (SAG)
NEB	New England Bus Svc [*NYSE symbol*] (TTSB)
NEB	New England Motor Rate Bureau Inc., Burlington MA [*STAC*]
NEB	[*The*] New English Bible [*1961*] [*A publication*]
NEB	Nissim Ezra Benjamin [*Shanghai*] (BJA)
NEB	Noise-Equivalent Bandwidth
NEB	Nonenzymatic Maillard Browning [*Food technology*]
NEB	North-Eastbound [*Aviation*] (FAAC)
NEB	North Equatorial Belt [*Planet Jupiter*]
NEB	Nuclear Energy Board [*Republic of Ireland*] (NUCP)
NEB	Nuclear Envelope Breakdown [*Also, NEBD*] [*Cytology*]
Neb	United States District Court for the District of Nebraska (DLA)
NEBA	North East Bolivian Airways [*ICAO designator*] (FAAC)
Neb Admin R	Nebraska Administrative Rules and Regulations [*A publication*] (DLA)
NEBB	National Environmental Balancing Bureau (EA)
NEBBA	Northeastern Bird-Banding Association [*Later, AFO*] (EA)
NEBBS	Naval Environmental Bulletin Board System
Nebby	Negative-Equity Baby Boomer [*Lifestyle classification*]
NEBD	Nuclear Envelope Breakdown [*Also, NEB*] [*Cytology*]
NEbE	Northeast by East
NEBHE	New England Board of Higher Education [*Information service or system*]
NEBI	National Employee Benefits Institute [*Washington, DC*] (EA)
NEBIC	New England Bibliographic Instruction Collection
NEBIS	North of England Biotechnology Information Service [*University of Newcastle-Upon-Tyne Medical School*] [*England*] [*Information service or system*] (IID)
NEBIT	New and Expanding Business and Industry Training (OICC)
NEBK	National Enterprise Bank [*Washington, DC*] (NQ)
Neb LB	Nebraska Law Bulletin [*A publication*] (DLA)
Neb Leg N	Nebraska Legal News [*A publication*] (DLA)
NEBM	No Eating between Meals
NEBMA	Neben-Munitionsanstalt [*Branch ammunition depot*] [*German military - World War II*]
NEbN	Northeast by North
NEBOSH	National Examination Board in Occupational Safety and Health (PDAA)
NEBR	Nebraska (AAG)
Nebr	Nebraska (ODBW)
Nebr	Nebraska Reports [*A publication*] (DLA)
Neb RC	Nebraska Railway Commission Reports [*A publication*] (DLA)
Neb Rev Stat	Revised Statutes of Nebraska [*A publication*] (DLA)
Nebr LB	Nebraska Law Bulletin [*A publication*] (DLA)
NEBS	New England Business Service, Inc. [*NASDAQ symbol*] (NQ)
NEBSS	National Examinations Board in Supervisory Studies [*British*]
Neb Sup Ct J	Nebraska Supreme Court Journal [*A publication*] (DLA)
NEBUL	Nebula [*Spray*] [*Pharmacy*]
NEBULA	Natural Electronic Business User's Language [*International Computers Ltd.*]
Neb (Unof)	Nebraska Unofficial Reports [*A publication*] (DLA)
Neb Unoff	Nebraska Unofficial Reports [*A publication*] (DLA)
NE Bus	New England Business Services [*Associated Press*] (SAG)
NEBW	Nonvacuum Electron Beam Welding
Neb WCC	Nebraska Workmen's Compensation Court. Bulletin [*A publication*] (DLA)
NEC	National Economic Council [*Defunct*] (EA)
NEC	National Economists Club (EA)
NEC	National Ecumenical Coalition (EA)
NEC	National Education Center for Paraprofessionals in Mental Health (EA)
NEC	National Education Corp. [*NYSE symbol*] (SPSG)
NEC	National Egg Council [*Later, PEIA*] (EA)
NEC	National Electoral Commission [*Nigeria*] (ECON)
NEC	National Electrical Code
NEC	National Electronics Conference (AEBS)
NEC	National Electronics Council [*British*] (NUCP)
NEC	National Electronics Council (NITA)
NEC	National Emblem Club (EA)
NEC	National Emergency Council [*Abolished, 1939*]
NEC	National Employers' Committee
NEC	National Empowerment Consortium [*Investment group*] [*South Africa*]
NEC	National Engineering Consortium (EA)
NEC	National Entertainment Conference [*Later, NECAA*] (EA)
NEC	National Exchange Club (EA)
NEC	National Executive Committee [*British*] (DCTA)
NEC	National Exhibition Centre [*British*]
NEC	National Extension College [*England*]
NEC	Natl Education [*NYSE symbol*] (TTSB)
NEC	Naval Examining Center
NEC	Naval Exercise Coordinator (CINC)
NEC	Naval Exhibit Center
NEC	Navy Enlisted Classification (NG)
NEC	Navy Enlisted Code
NEC	Nebraska State Railway Commission [*STAC*]
NEC	NEC Corp. [*Associated Press*] (SAG)
NEC	Necessary (AABC)
NEC	Necessity
NEC	Necochea [*Argentina*] [*Airport symbol*] (OAG)
NEC	Necrotizing Enterocolitis [*Medicine*]
NEC	Negro Ensemble Company [*A theatre group*]
NEC	Netherlands Electrotechnical Committee
NEC	Neuroendocrine Cell [*Cytology*]
NEC	New England College, Henniker, NH [*OCLC symbol*] (OCLC)
NEC	New England Conservatory of Music (BARN)
NEC	New England Council (EA)
NEC	Newspaper Editor's Course [*Defense Information School*] (DNAB)
NEC	Nippon Electric Co. [*Japan*]
NEC	No-Error Check (IAA)
NEC	No Eye Contact [*Psychology*]
NEC	Noise-Equivalent Charge (PDAA)
NEC	Nonengineering Change (DNAB)
NEC	Northeast Conference on the Teaching of Foreign Languages (EA)
NEC	North East Corner [*Freemasonry*]
NEC	Northeast Corridor [*Railroad line*] (EGAO)
NEC	North Equatorial Current [*Oceanography*] (MSC)
NEC	Northern European Command [*NATO*] (NATG)
NEC	Northern European Countries
NEC	Northern Europe Committee [*NATO*] (NATG)
NEC	Not Elsewhere Classified
nec	Not Elsewhere Classified (ODBW)
NEC	Notes of English Ecclesiastical Cases [*A publication*] (DLA)
NEC	Nuclear Energy Center (NRCH)
NEC	Nuclear Energy Commission (USDC)
NEC	Nuclear Energy Commission [*Marine science*] (OSRA)
NEC	Nucleus of Epidermal Cell
NECA	National Electrical Contractors Association (EA)
NECA	National Employment Counselors Association (EA)
NECA	National Episcopal Coalition on Alcohol [*Later, NECAD*] (EA)
NECA	National Exchange Carrier Association (EA)
NECA	National Explorers and Collectors Association (EA)
NECA	Near East College Association (EA)
NECA	N-Ethylcarboxamide Adenosine [*Biochemistry*]
NECA	Numismatic Error Collectors of America (EA)
NECAA	National Entertainment and Campus Activities Association [*Formerly, NEC*] (EA)
NECAD	National Episcopal Coalition on Alcohol and Drugs (EA)
NECAF	National Electromagnetic Compatibility Analysis Facility [*Department of Commerce*] (PDAA)
NECAP	NASA Energy-Cost Analysis Program
NECAP	Navigation Equipment Capability Analysis (KSC)
NECAP	Nutmeg Electric Companies Atomic Project
NECAR	National Engineers Commission on Air Resources (PDAA)
NECAR	New Electric Car [*Daimler-Benz AG*] (PS)
NECB	New England Comm Bancorp'A' [*NASDAQ symbol*] (TTSB)
NECB	New England Community Bancorp, Inc. [*NASDAQ symbol*] (SAG)
NE CBcp	New England Community Bancorp, Inc. [*Associated Press*] (SAG)
NECC	National Education Computer Center
NECC	National Emergency Coordination Center (BARN)
NECC	New England Congressional Caucus [*Defunct*] (EA)
NECC	Northeast Computer Center [*Military*] (AABC)
NECC	North Equatorial Countercurrent [*Oceanography*]
NECC	Northern Essex Community College [*Haverhill, MA*]
NECCB	National Education Council of the Christian Brothers [*Later, RECCB*] (EA)
NECCO	New England Confectionery Co.
NECCO	Northern Essex Community College [*Haverhill, MA*]
NECCTA	National Educational Closed-Circuit Television Association [*British*]
NECDC	New England Consumer Development Council
NECEA	National Engineering Construction Employers Association [*British*] (DBA)
NECEC	New England Catholic Education Center (AEBS)

NECF.......... National Exchange Club Foundation for the Prevention of Child Abuse (EA)
NECG .... National Engineering Council for Guidance (EA)
NECH .... National Employment Clearing House [*American Chemical Society*]
NECH .... National Event Clearinghouse Database [*National Event Clearinghouse, Inc.*] [*Information service or system*] (CRD)
NECHE........ Northeastern Colorado Hail Experiment
NECHI.......... Northeastern Consortium for Health Information [*Library network*]
NECI............ Noise Exposure Computer Integrator (PDAA)
NECIES .... North East Coast Institution of Engineers and Shipbuilders (EAIO)
NECIP .... Northeast Corridor Improvement Project [*Department of Transportation*]
NECIS .... Naval Environmental Compliance Information System
NECIS .... NEC Information Systems, Inc. [*Boxborough, MA*]
NECK .... Neck [*Commonly used*] (OPSA)
NECLC .... National Emergency Civil Liberties Committee (EA)
NECM.......... New England Conference Management [*Australia*]
NECM.......... New England Conservatory of Music [*Boston, MA*]
NECMA........ New England County Metropolitan Areas
NECMD .... Newark Contract Management District (SAA)
NECNVA...... New England Committee for Nonviolent Action [*Later, CNVA*] (EA)
NECO .... Nippon Electric Co. (IAA)
NECO .... Nuclear Engineering Co., Inc.
NECOE .... New England Center for Organizational Effectiveness (EA)
NECOP........ Nutrient-Enhanced Coastal Ocean Productivity [*Program*] (USDC)
NECOP........ Nutrient-Enhanced Coastal Ocean Productivity [*Marine science*] (OSRA)
NECOS........ Communication Net Control Station [*Navy*] (NVT)
NECOS........ Northern European Chiefs of Staff [*NATO*] (NATG)
NECP .... National Eye Care Project [*Foundation of the American Academy of Ophthalmology*] (EA)
NECP .... New England College of Pharmacy
NECP .... Nonengineering Change Proposal
NECPA........ National Emergency Command Post Afloat
NECPA........ National Energy Conservation Policy Act [*1978*]
NECPL .... NATO Exploratory Conference on Production Logistics (NATG)
NECPR .... New External Cardiopulmonary Resuscitation
NECPWA...... Northeast Club for Pre-War Austins [*British*] (EAIO)
NECRMP........ Northeast Corridor Regional Modeling Project [*Environmental Protection Agency*] (GFGA)
Necro.......... Necrofile [*A publication*]
NECROL........ Necrology (WDAA)
necrp .... Necropolis (VRA)
NECS .... National Electrical Code Standards
NECS .... National Elephant Collectors Society (EA)
NECS .... Nationwide Educational Computer Service (IEEE)
NECSS .... Nuclear Energy Center Site Survey (NRCH)
NECTA .... National Electric Comfort Trade Association [*Defunct*] (EA)
NECTAR ...... Network of European CNS [*Central Nervous System*] Transplantation and Restoration
NECTP .... Northeast Corridor Transportation Project
NECY .... Necessary
NECY .... Necessity (WDAA)
NED .... Naphthylethylenediamine Dihydrochloride [*Organic chemistry*]
NED .... National Endowment for Democracy
NED .... Naval Equipment Department [*British military*] (DMA)
NED .... Navigation Error Data (MUGU)
Ned .... Nedarim (BJA)
NED .... NeverEnding Disk [*Computer software*] [*Sytron Corp.*] (PCM)
NED .... Newark [*Delaware*] [*Seismograph station code, US Geological Survey*] (SEIS)
NED .... New Editor [*Computer program*] [*Air Force*] (MCD)
NED .... New England Division [*Army Engineers*]
NED .... New English Dictionary [*i.e., the Oxford English Dictionary*]
NED .... No Evidence of Disease
NED .... No Expiration Date
NED .... Nonenzymatic Glycosylation [*Biochemistry*] (DAVI)
NED .... Normal Equivalent Deviation
NED .... North, East, and Down
NED .... Northeastern University, Boston, MA [*OCLC symbol*] (OCLC)
NED .... Nuclear Energy Division [*General Electric Co.*]
NED .... Nuclear Engineering Directorate [*Army*]
NEDA .... National Economic Development Association
NEDA .... National Electronic Distributors Association (EA)
NEDA .... National Emergency Defense Airlift
NEDA .... National Environmental Development Association (EA)
NEDA .... National Equipment Distributors Association [*Defunct*] (EA)
NEDA .... National Exhaust Distributors Association [*Later, NEDA/USA*] (EA)
Neda .... Nedarim (BJA)
NEDA/CAAP... National Environmental Development Association/Clean Air Act Project [*Defunct*] (EA)
NEDA/GRND... National Environmental Development Association/Ground Water Project (EA)
NEDA/USA ... National Exhaust Distributors Association/Undercar Specialists Association [*Defunct*] (EA)
NEDC .... National Economic Development Council [*Nickname: Neddie*] [*British*]
NeDC .... New England Document Conservation Center, Andover, MA [*Library symbol Library of Congress*] (LCLS)
NEDCC .... New England Document Conservation Center [*Information service or system*] (IID)
NEDCC........ Northeast Document Conservation Center
NEDCO........ Non-Electronic Part Data Collection (PDAA)
NEDCO........ Northeast Dairy Cooperative Federation [*Defunct*] (EA)
NEDECO...... Netherlands Engineering Consultants
NEDED .... Naval Explosive Development Engineering Department (DNAB)

NEDEL .... No Epidemiologically Detectable Exposure Level [*Medicine*] (HCT)
NEDELA ...... Network Definition Language [*Computer science*] (PDAA)
NEDEP .... Navy Enlisted Dietetic Education Program
NEDEPA...... Nea Demokratiki Parataxi [*Cyprus*] [*Political party*] (PPE)
NeDF .... New England Data Film, Inc., Milford, CT [*Library symbol Library of Congress*] (LCLS)
NEDI .... Nobel Education Dynamics, Inc. [*NASDAQ symbol*] (SAG)
NEDIPA........ Nea Demokratiki Parataxi [*Cyprus*] [*Political party*] (PPW)
NEDIPS........ NEC Dataflow Image Processing System (NITA)
NEDIS .... National Environmental Data and Information Service [*Marine science*] (MSC)
NEDL .... New England Deposit Library
NEDI .... Nobel Ed Dynamics [*NASDAQ symbol*] (TTSB)
NEDLC .... National Economic Development and Law Center [*Berkeley, CA*] [*Research center*] (EA)
NEDN .... Naval Environmental Data Network
NEDN .... Naval Worldwide Environmental Data Network (MCD)
NEDO .... National Economic Development Office [*British*]
NEDRES........ National Environmental Data Referral Service [*Online database*] [*National Oceanic and Atmospheric Administration Washington, DC*]
NEDS .... National Emissions Data System [*Environmental Protection Agency Information service or system*]
NEDS .... Naval Environmental Data System (CAAL)
NEDS .... Naval Environmental Display Station (CAAL)
NEDS .... New Enlisted Distribution System (NVT)
NEDS .... Nonviolent Explosive Destructive System (MCD)
NEDSA........ Nonerasing Deterministic Stack Automation [*Computer science*] (IAA)
NEDT .... National Educational Development Test
NEDT .... Noise-Equivalent Differential Temperature
NeDTH .... Technische Hogeschool Delft, Delft, Netherlands [*Library symbol Library of Congress*] (LCLS)
NEDTRA ...... Naval Education and Training Command (MCD)
NEDU .... Navy Experimental Diving Unit [*Panama City, FL*]
NEE .... National Electrical Effect
NEE .... National Electrology Educators (EA)
NEE .... Net Ecosystem Exchange [*Biology*]
NEE .... New England Express [*Steamship*] (MHDW)
NEE .... Noise-Equivalent Energy (MCD)
NEE .... Noise Equivalent Exposure [*Photonics*]
NEE .... Norethindrone/Ethinyl Estradiol [*Oral contraceptive*]
NEE .... Northeast Express Regional Airlines, Inc. [*ICAO designator*] (FAAC)
NEEB .... North Eastern Electricity Board [*British*]
NEEC .... National Environmental Enforcement Council [*National Association of Attorneys General*] (EPA)
NEEC .... National Export Expansion Council [*Terminated, 1973*] [*Department of Commerce*]
NEEC .... Not Entailing Excessive Cost [*Environmental technology*]
NEEC .... Nuclear Explosion Effects Center
NEED .... National Energy Education Development Project (EA)
NEED .... National Environmental Education Development [*Program of National Park Service*] [*Defunct*]
NEED .... Native Employment and Educational Development [*Canada*]
NEED .... Near East Emergency Donations
Need .... Needham's Annual Summary of Tax Cases [*England*] [*A publication*] (DLA)
NEED .... Negro Education Emergency Drive
NEED .... New Employment Expansion and Development [*Canada*]
NEEDHA...... National Electrical Engineering Department Heads Association (EA)
NEEDIS .... National Enterprise Education Development and Information Service (AIE)
NEEDS .... NASA End-to-End Data Systems
NEEDS .... National Emergency Equipment Data System (NITA)
NEEDS .... Navy Education and Employment Development System (MCD)
NEEDS .... Neighborhood Environmental Evaluation and Decision System [*Health Services and Mental Health Administration*]
NEEDS .... New England Educational Data Systems
NEEDS-IR ... NIKKEI Economic Electronic Databank Service - Information Retrieval [*Information service or system Japan*] (IID)
NEEDS-TS ... NIKKEI Economic Electronic Databank Service - Time Sharing [*Information service or system Japan*] (IID)
NEEE .... Near East Equine Encephalomyelitis [*Medicine*] (DMAA)
NeEinP.......... Philips Research Laboratories, Eindhoven, Netherlands [*Library symbol Library of Congress*] (LCLS)
NeEinT........ Technische Hogeschool te Eindhoven, Eindhoven, Netherlands, [*Library symbol Library of Congress*] (LCLS)
NEEITC........ National Electrical and Electronic Industry Training Committee [*Australia*]
NEEJ .... National Environmental Enforcement Journal [*National Association of Attorneys General*] [*A publication*] (EPA)
NEEL.......... National Environmental Education Landmarks [*Department of the Interior*]
NEELS.......... National Emergency Equipment Locator System [*Environment Canada*] [*Information service or system*] (CRD)
NEEMIS........ New England Energy Management Information System
NEEP.......... Negative End Expiratory Pressure [*Medicine*]
NEEP.......... New England Economic Project (NITA)
NEEP.......... Nuclear Electronics Effects Program
NE'ER.......... Never (ROG)
NEERI.......... National Environmental Engineering Research Institute
NEERS.......... National Earthquake Early Reporting System (NOAA)
NEES.......... Naval Engineering Experiment Station
NEES.......... New England Electric System
NEESA.......... Naval Energy and Environmental Support Activity

NEESAB .... National Energy Extension Service Advisory Board [*Department of Energy Washington, DC*] (EGAO)

NEET .... Navy Extended Electrode Technique (PDAA)

NEETF .... National Environmental Education and Training Foundation [*An association*] (PS)

NEETS .... Naval Electronics Environmental Training System (MCD)

NEETU .... National Engineering and Electrical Trade Union [*Republic of Ireland*] (BI)

NEEWSSOP... NATO Europe Early Warning System Standard Operating Procedures (NATG)

NEF .... National Educators Fellowship [*Later, CEAI*]

NEF .... National Energy Foundation (EA)

NEF .... National Extra Fine [*Thread*]

NEF .... Naval Emergency Fund [*A budget category*]

NEF .... Near East Foundation (EA)

NEF .... Negative-Regulatory Factor [*Genetics*]

NeF .... Nephritic Factor [*Clinical medicine*]

NEF .... New Education Fellowship [*Later, WEF*]

NEF .... No Further Clearance Required [*Aviation*] (FAAC)

NEF .... Noise-Equivalent Flux

NEF .... Noise Exposure Forecast [*Aircraft*]

NEF .... Nordiska Ekonomiska Forskningsradet [*Nordic Economic Research Council - NERC*] (EAIO)

NEF .... Nurses Educational Funds (EA)

NEF .... Scudder New Europe Fund [*NYSE symbol*] (SPSG)

NEFA .... Narcotic Educational Foundation of America (EA)

NEFA .... New European Fighter Aircraft (PS)

NEFA .... Nonesterified Fatty Acid [*Biochemistry*]

NEFARS ...... Nuclear Effects from Analysis of Residual Signatures

NEFBRACS... Nearfield Bearing and Range Accuracy Calibration System (PDAA)

NEFC .... Near East Forestry Commission

NEFC .... Northeast Fisheries Center [*Department of Commerce*] [*Woods Hole, MA*]

NEFCO .... New England Fish Co.

NEFD .... Noise-Equivalent Flux Density

NEFDA .... New England Fisheries Development Association (EA)

NEFDF .... New England Fisheries Development Foundation [*Later, NEFDA*] (EA)

NEFE .... New England Fish Exchange (EA)

NEFEC .... Northeast Fisheries Center [*National Marine Fisheries Service*] (USDC)

NEFES .... Northeastern Forest Experiment Station [*Department of Agriculture*] [*Broomall, PA*] (GRD)

NEFI .... New England Fuel Institute

NEFMC .... New England Fisheries Management Council

NEFMO .... NATO European Fighter Management Organization (MCD)

NEFO .... National Electronics Facilities Organization

NEFOS .... New Emerging Forces

NEFP .... New England Free Press [*Publisher*]

NEFPS .... National Enginemen and Firemen's Protection Society [*A union*] [*British*]

NEFSA .... National Education Field Service Association [*Defunct*] (EA)

Neg .... Nega'im (BJA)

NEG .... Negate a Binary Number [*Computer science*]

NEG .... Negation (WDAA)

NEG .... Negative (AAG)

neg .... Negative (VRA)

NEG .... Neglect [*FBI standardized term*]

NEG .... Negligible (AAG)

NEG .... Negotiable (ADA)

NEG .... Negril [*Jamaica*] [*Airport symbol*] (OAG)

NEG .... Negro

NEG .... Numerical Experimentation Group [*Marine science*] (OSRA)

NEGA .... National Ex-Offender Grant Alliance [*Defunct*] (EA)

Negb .... Negotiable

Neg C .... Negligence Cases [*Commerce Clearing House*] [*A publication*] (DLA)

Neg Cas ...... Bloomfield's Manumission (or Negro) Cases [*New Jersey*] [*A publication*] (DLA)

NEGD .... Negotiated (ROG)

NEGDEF .... Navy Enlisted Ground Defense Emergency Force

NEGI .... National Federation of Engineering and General Ironfounders [*British*] (BI)

Neg Inst ...... Negotiable Instrument [*Legal term*] (DLA)

NEGISTOR ... Negative Resistor (PDAA)

NEGIT .... Negative Impedance Transistor [*Electronics*] (IAA)

Negl .... Negligence

Negl & Comp Cas Ann ... Negligence and Compensation Cases, Annotated [*A publication*] (DLA)

Negl & Comp Cas Ann 3d ... Negligence and Compensation Cases, Annotated, Third Series [*A publication*] (DLA)

Negl & Comp Cas Ann (NS) ... Negligence and Compensation Cases, Annotated, New Series [*A publication*] (DLA)

Negl Cas ...... Negligence Cases [*Commerce Clearing House*] [*A publication*] (DLA)

Negl Cas 2d ... Negligence Cases, Second Series [*Commerce Clearing House*] [*A publication*] (DLA)

NEGN .... Negotiation (ROG)

NEGOA .... Northeast Gulf of Alaska [*Marine science*] (MSC)

NEGOT .... Negotiable [*Legal shorthand*] (LWAP)

NEGPED .... Negotiator's Planned Execution Date (MCD)

NEGPR .... Negative Print

NEGPT .... Negative Print (VRA)

NEGRO .... National Economic Growth and Reconstruction Organization [*Black entrepreneurial organization*]

NEGRO .... New England Grass Roots Organization

Negro Cas ... Bloomfield's Manumission (or Negro) Cases [*New Jersey*] [*A publication*] (DLA)

NEGRS .... Negative Report Submitted [*Army*] (AABC)

NEGRSBM .... Negative Report Submitted [*Army*] (AABC)

negs .... Negatives [*Film*] (WDMC)

NEGTAX .... Negative Tax (MHDW)

NEGX .... National Energy Group [*NASDAQ symbol*] (SAG)

NEGX .... Natl Energy Group'A' [*NASDAQ symbol*] (TTSB)

NEGX .... Negate a Binary Number with Extend [*Computer science*]

NEGY .... Neutral-Equivalent Gasoline Yield [*Petroleum chemistry*]

NEH .... East Carolina University, Health Sciences Library, Greenville, NC [*OCLC symbol*] (OCLC)

NEh .... East Hampton Free Library, East Hampton, NY [*Library symbol Library of Congress*] (LCLS)

NEH .... National Endowment for the Humanities

Neh .... Nehemiah [*Old Testament book*]

NEH .... Nuclear Effects Handbook

NEHA .... National Environmental Health Association (EA)

NEHA .... National Executive Housekeepers Association (EA)

NeHB .... Bureau voor de Industriele Eigendom, Bibliotheek Octrooiraad, The Hague, Netherlands [*Library symbol Library of Congress*] (LCLS)

NEHC .... National Extension Homemakers Council (EA)

NEHE .... Nurses for Environmental Health Education (DAVI)

NEHEP .... National Eye Health Education Program [*Information service or system*] (IID)

NEHF .... National Eye and Health Foundation (EA)

NEHGS .... New England Historic Genealogical Society (EA)

NEHI .... Northwest Educators of the Hearing Impaired (EDAC)

NeHKB .... Koninklijke Bibliotheek [*Royal Library*], The Hague, Netherlands [*Library symbol Library of Congress*] (LCLS)

NEHRC .... New England History Resources Center [*University of New England*] [*Australia*]

NEHRP .... National Earthquake Hazards Reduction Program [*Federal Emergency Management Agency*] [*Washington, DC*] (EGAO)

NeHSU .... Staatsuitgeverij Christoffel Plantijnstaat (State Printing Office), The Hague, Netherlands [*Library symbol Library of Congress*] (LCLS)

NEi .... East Islip Public Library, East Islip, NY [*Library symbol Library of Congress*] (LCLS)

NEI .... Narcotics Education, Inc. (EA)

NEI .... National Estuarine Inventory

NEI .... National Eye Institute [*Formerly, NINDB*] [*Department of Health and Human Services Bethesda, MD*] [*National Institutes of Health*]

NEI .... Nature Expeditions International (GNE)

NEI .... Neipperg [*Federal Republic of Germany*] [*Seismograph station code, US Geological Survey*] (SEIS)

NEI .... Netherlands East Indies

NEI .... New Enterprise Institute [*University of Southern Maine*] [*Research center*] (RCD)

NEI .... New Equipment Introduction [*Army*] (AABC)

NEI .... Noise-Equivalent Input

NEI .... Noise-Equivalent Intensity

NEI .... Non Est Inventus [*It Has Not Been Found or Discovered*] [*Latin*]

NEI .... Nordic Energy Index [*Database*] [*Nordic Atomic Libraries Joint Secretariat*] [*Denmark*] [*Information service or system*] (IID)

NEI .... Northern Electric Industries [*British*]

NEI .... Northern Engineering Industries [*Commercial firm British*]

NEI .... Not Elsewhere Indicated

NEI .... Nouvelles Equipes Internationales [*Later, European Christian Democratic Union*]

NEIAL .... North East Iowa Academic Libraries [*Library network*]

NEIB .... Northeast Indiana Banc [*NASDAQ symbol*] (TTSB)

NEIB .... Northeast Indiana Bancorp, Inc. [*NASDAQ symbol*] (SAG)

NEIC .... National Earthquake Information Center [*US Geological Survey*]

NEIC .... National Electronic Information Corp. [*Information service or system*] (IID)

NEIC .... National Energy Information Center [*Department of Energy*] [*Washington, DC*]

NEIC .... National Enforcement Investigations Center [*Environmental Protection Agency*] (EG)

NEIC .... National Equivalence Information Centre (AIE)

NEIC .... NATO Equipment Interpretation Course (MCD)

NEIC .... New England Information Center [*Information service or system*]

NEIC .... North East Insurance [*NASDAQ symbol*] (TTSB)

NEIC .... North East Insurance Co. [*NASDAQ symbol*] (NQ)

NEICA .... National Energy Information Center Affiliate [*University of New Mexico*] (IID)

NEICE .... North of England Institute for Christian Education

NEIDA .... Network of Educational Innovation for Development in Africa (EAIO)

NEIED .... National Educational Institute for Economic Development (EA)

NEIETC .... New England Interstate Environmental Training Center

NEIF .... Near-Earth Instrumentation Facility [*NASA*] (KSC)

NEII .... National Elevator Industry, Inc. (EA)

NEIL .... Neon Indicating Light

NEIL .... Nordic Energy Index, Literature [*Database*] [*Nordic Atomic Libraries Joint Secretariat*] [*Information service or system*] (CRD)

NeimM .... Neiman-Marcus Group [*Associated Press*] (SAG)

NeINBc .... Northeast Indiana Bancorp, Inc. [*Associated Press*] (SAG)

NE Ins .... North East Insurance Co. [*Associated Press*] (SAG)

NEIPG .... National Electronic Industries Procurement Group

NEIR .... Narrative End Item Report [*NASA*] (KSC)

NEIR .... Neither (ROG)

NEIRLS .... Northeast Regional Library System [*Library network*]

NEIS .... National Earthquake Information Service [*United States Geological Survey*] (IID)

NEIS............ National Emissions Inventory System [*Database*] [*Environment Canada*] [*Information service or system*] (CRD)
NEIS............ National Engineering Information System (BUR)
NEIS............ National Environmental Information Symposium
NEIS............ Nuclear Energy Information Service [*An association*] (EA)
NEISA .... New England Intercollegiate Sailing Association
NEISS .... National Electronic Injury Surveillance System [*Consumer Product Safety Commission*] [*Washington, DC Databank*]
NEIT............ New Equipment Introductory Team [*Army*] (AABC)
NEITA.......... National Excellence in Teaching Award [*Australia*]
NEIULS........ Northeast Iowa Union List of Serials
NEIWPCC..... New England Interstate Water Pollution Control Commission
NEIX............ Nordic Energy Index [*Database*] [*Nordic Atomic Libraries Joint Secretariat*] [*Information service or system*] (CRD)
NEJ.............. Seattle, WA [*Location identifier FAA*] (FAAL)
NEJA........... National Entertainment Journalists Association [*Defunct*] (EA)
NEJS........... Near Eastern and Judaistic Studies (BJA)
NEK............. Naval Equerry to the King
NEKASA ...... New England Knitwear and Sportswear Association (EA)
NEKDA .... New England Kiln Drying Association (EA)
NEKL........... Northeast Kansas Library System [*Library network*]
NEKOA .... New England Knitted Outerwear Association [*Later, NEKASA*] (EA)
NEL............. East Carolina University, Department of Library Science, Greenville, NC [*OCLC symbol*] (OCLC)
NEI.............. Greenburgh Public Library, Elmsford, NY [*Library symbol Library of Congress*] (LCLS)
NEL............. Lakehurst, NJ [*Location identifier FAA*] (FAAL)
NEL............. National Electronics Laboratory (IDOE)
NEL............. National Emancipation League [*Nigeria*]
NEL............. National Engineering Laboratory [*Superseded IAT*] [*Gaithersburg, MD*] [*National Institute of Standards and Technology*]
NEL............. National Engineering Laboratory [*Scotland*]
NEL............. National Epilepsy League [*Later, EFA*] (EA)
NEL............. Naval Command Control Communications Laboratory Center
NEL............. Naval Electronics Laboratory
NEL............. Naval Explosive Laboratory
NEL............. Navy Electronics Laboratory [*San Diego, CA*]
NEL............. Nelson [*Nevada*] [*Seismograph station code, US Geological Survey*] (SEIS)
Nel.............. Nelson's English Chancery Reports [*A publication*] (DLA)
NEL............. Neon Light (IAA)
NEL............. New English Library [*Publishers*] [*British*]
NEL............. NewTel Enterprises Ltd. [*Toronto Stock Exchange symbol*]
NEL............. No Effect Level (ADA)
NEL............. Non-English Language
NEL............. Nonspecific Excitability Level [*Animal behavior*]
NEL............. Northern Extratropical Land [*Geography*]
NEL............. Nuclear Energy Laboratory [*Research center*] (RCD)
NEL............. Nuclear Engineering Laboratory [*University of Utah*] [*Research center*] (RCD)
NELA........... National Electric Light Association
NELA........... National Employment Lawyers Association (EA)
NELA........... National Employment Lawyers Association
NELA........... New England Library Association
NELA........... Northeastern Loggers Association (EA)
NELAC .... National Environment Laboratory Accreditation Conference [*Environmental Protection Agency*]
NELAT......... Navy Electronics Laboratory Assembly Tester
NELATS....... Naval Electronics Laboratory Automatic Tester System (DNAB)
NELB........... New England Library Board [*Library network*]
NELC........... Naval Electronics Laboratory Center [*Later, NOSC*]
NELCON NZ. National Electronics Conference, New Zealand [*IEEE*]
Nel CR .... Nelson's English Chancery Reports [*A publication*] (DLA)
NEld............ Sunshine Hall Free Library, Eldred, NY [*Library symbol Library of Congress*] (LCLS)
NELEC........ Nonelectric
NELEX........ Naval Electronics Systems Command Headquarters
NELIA......... Nuclear Energy Liability Insurance Association [*Later, ANI*] (EA)
NELIAC .... Naval Electronics Laboratory International ALGOL Compilers
NELINET ..... New England Library Information Network
NELIS......... Noncommunications Emitter Location and Identification System (MCD)
NELIS-A ...... Noncommunications Emitter Location and Identification System - Airborne
NELL........... Nellcor, Inc. [*NASDAQ symbol*] (NQ)
NELL........... Nellcor Puritan Bennett [*NASDAQ symbol*] (TTSB)
Nell............. Nell's Reports [*1845-55*] [*Ceylon*] [*A publication*] (DLA)
NELLCO ...... New England Law Library Consortium, Inc. [*Harvard Law School*] [*Information service or system*] (IID)
Nellcor......... Nellcor, Inc. [*Associated Press*] (SAG)
NElle........... Ellenville Public Library, Ellenville, NY [*Library symbol Library of Congress*] (LCLS)
NElm........... Steele Memorial Library of Elmira and Chemung County, Elmira, NY [*Library symbol Library of Congress*] (LCLS)
NELMA........ Northeastern Lumber Manufacturers Association (EA)
NElmC .... Elmira College, Elmira, NY [*Library symbol Library of Congress*] (LCLS)
NElmhC .... City Hospital at Elmhurst, Elmhurst, NY [*Library symbol Library of Congress*] (LCLS)
NElmHi........ Chemung County Historical Society, Elmira, NY [*Library symbol Library of Congress*] (LCLS)
NElmM......... Mount Saviour Monastery, Elmira, NY [*Library symbol Library of Congress*] (LCLS)
NElmo.......... Elmont Public Library, Elmont, NY [*Library symbol Library of Congress*] (LCLS)

NElmoAE..... Alden Terrace Elementary School, Elmont, NY [*Library symbol*] [*Library of Congress*] (LCLS)
NElmoCCE ... Clara H. Carlson Elementary School, Elmont, NY [*Library symbol*] [*Library of Congress*] (LCLS)
NElmoCE..... Covert Elementary School, Elmont, NY [*Library symbol Library of Congress*] (LCLS)
NElmoDE..... Dutch Broadway Elementary School, Elmont, NY [*Library symbol*] [*Library of Congress*] (LCLS)
NElmoGE..... Gotham Avenue Elementary School, Elmont, NY [*Library symbol*] [*Library of Congress*] (LCLS)
NElmoMH.... Elmont Memeorial High School, Elmont, NY [*Library symbol*] [*Library of Congress*] (LCLS)
NElmoSE..... Stewart Elementary School, Elmont, NY [*Library symbol Library of Congress*] (LCLS)
NElmP .... Elmira Psychiatric Center, Elmira, NY [*Library symbol Library of Congress*] (LCLS)
NElmsAr ...... Weschester County Archives, Elmsford, NY [*Library symbol*] [*Library of Congress*] (LCLS)
NElmSC ...... Supreme Court Law Library-Elmira, Elmira, NY [*Library symbol*] [*Library of Congress*] (LCLS)
NElmsSW ... Southern Westchester BOCES School, Elmsford, NY [*Library symbol*] [*Library of Congress*] (LCLS)
NELOS .... Navy Electronics Laboratory Operating System
NELP.......... National Employment Law Project [*New York, NY*] (EA)
NELP.......... North East London Polytechnic [*School*] [*England*]
NELPAC ...... National Engineering Laboratory's Thermophysical Properties Package [*British Information service or system*] (IID)
NELPIA .... Nuclear Energy Liability Property Insurance Association [*Later, ANI*]
NeLR .... Rijksuniversiteit Leiden, Leiden, Netherlands [*Library symbol Library of Congress*] (LCLS)
NELRC .... National Epilepsy Library and Resource Center [*Epilepsy Foundation of America*] [*Information service or system*] (IID)
NELS .... National Educational Longitudinal Survey
NELS........... National Environmental Laboratories [*Proposed*]
Nels .... Nelson's English Chancery Reports [*A publication*] (DLA)
Nels 8vo ..... Nelson's English Chancery Reports [*A publication*] (DLA)
NELS:88..... National Education Longitudinal Study of 1988 [*Department of Education*] (GFGA)
NELSA .... Northeast Library Service Area [*Library network*]
Nels Abr ..... Nelson's Abridgment of the Common Law [*A publication*] (DLA)
Nels Cler .... Nelson's Rights of the Clergy [*A publication*] (DLA)
Nels F......... Finch's English Chancery Reports, by Nelson [*1673-81*] [*A publication*] (DLA)
Nels Fol...... Finch's English Chancery Reports, by Nelson [*1673-81*] [*A publication*] (DLA)
Nels Lex Man... Nelson's Lex Maneriorum [*A publication*] (DLA)
NelsnB........ Nelson [*Thomas*], Inc. [*Associated Press*] (SAG)
NelsnT........ Nelson [*Thomas*], Inc. [*Associated Press*] (SAG)
NELSON...... News Editing and Layout System of Newspapers (DGA)
Nelson (Eng).. Nelson's English Chancery Reports [*A publication*] (DLA)
Nelson's Rep... Nelson Tempore Finch [*1673-81*] [*A publication*] (DLA)
NELTS......... Number of Elements Loaded [*Army*]
NeLV........... Koninklijk Instituut voor Taal-, Land-, en Volkenkunde, Leiden, Netherlands [*Library symbol Library of Congress*] (LCLS)
NELV.......... Nerine Latent Virus [*Plant pathology*]
NELWA .... New England Lumber Women's Association [*Defunct*] (EA)
NEm............ East Meadow Public Library, East Meadow, NY [*Library symbol Library of Congress*] (LCLS)
NEM............ Metropolitan Technical Community College, Omaha, NE [*OCLC symbol*] (OCLC)
nem............ Nahrungs Einheit Milch [*Nahrungsteinheit Milch*] [*Nutritional milk unit*] [*Dietetics*] (DAVI)
Nem............ Nemean [*of Pindar*] [*Classical studies*] (OCD)
NEM............ Nemuro [*Japan*] [*Seismograph station code, US Geological Survey*] (SEIS)
NEM............ N-Ethylmaleimide [*Also, NEMI*] [*Organic chemistry*]
NEM............ N-Ethylmorpholine [*Organic chemistry*]
nEM............ NetworkMCI Enterprise Management
NEM............ New Electronic Media (NTCM)
NeM............ New England Micrographics, Inc., Waltham, MA [*Library symbol Library of Congress*] (LCLS)
NEM............ Newmont Mining [*NYSE symbol*] (TTSB)
NEM............ Newmont Mining Corp. [*NYSE symbol*] (SPSG)
NEM............ Nickel Electroformed Mold
NEM............ Nonelectronic Maintenance
NEM............ Noram Environment [*Vancouver Stock Exchange symbol*]
NEM............ Not Elsewhere Mentioned
NEMA.......... National Early Music Association [*British*] (DBA)
NEMA.......... National Eclectic Medical Association [*Defunct*] (EA)
NEMA.......... National Educational Management Association (EA)
NEMA.......... National Electrical Manufacturers Association (EA)
NEMA.......... National Electricity Manufacturers' Association (NITA)
NEMA.......... National Emergency Management Association (EA)
NEMA.......... National Emergency Medicine Association (EA)
NEMA.......... Nematode [*Threadworm*]
NEMA.......... Nematron Corp. [*NASDAQ symbol*] (SAG)
NEMAC .... National Energy Management Advisory Committee [*British*]
NEMAC .... Normal Error Model Analysis Chart
NEMAG .... Negative Effective Mass Amplifiers and Generators
NEMAS .... New England Marine Advisory Service
NEMAS .... Nursing Education Module Authoring System
NEMATOL .... Nematology
NEmBGE..... Bowling Green Elementary School, East Meadow, NY [*Library symbol Library of Congress*] (LCLS)

NEmBWE	Barnum Woods Elementary School, East Meadow, NY [*Library symbol Library of Congress*] (LCLS)
NEMC............	National Export Meatworks Council [*Australia*]
NEMC............	New England Medical Center [*Boston, MA*]
NEMCA	NATO Electromagnetic Compatibility Agency (NATG)
NEMCA	Non-Faradaic Electrochemical Modification of Catalytic Activity [*Chemistry*]
NEMCC	Nonessential Motor Control Center (AAG)
NEMCH	New England Medical Center Hospitals
NEmCJS.......	W. T. Clarke Junior-Senior High School, East Meadow, NY [*Library symbol Library of Congress*] (LCLS)
NEM CON.....	Nemine Contradicente [*No One Contradicting*] [*Latin Legal term*]
NEMD	Nonequilibrium Molecular Dynamics [*Chemical property simulation technique*]
NEMD	Nonspecific Esophageal Motility Disorder [*Gastroenterology*] (DAVI)
NEMD	Nonspecific Esophageal Motor Dysfunction [*Medicine*]
NEMDA	Northeastern Minnesota Development Association
NEM DISS....	Nemine Dissentiente [*No One Dissenting*] [*Latin*]
NEMEA.........	New England Media Evaluators Association
NEMEDRI.......	North European and Mediterranean Routing Information [*Naval Oceanographic Office*]
NEMEX........	National Energy Management Exhibition and Conference (ITD)
NEMG T RL...	New England MG "T" Register Ltd. (EA)
NEmH	Meadowbrook Hospital, East Meadow, NY [*Library symbol Library of Congress*] (LCLS)
NEMI............	National Elevator Manufacturing Industry [*Later, NEII*] (EA)
NEMI............	N-Ethylmaleimide [*Also, NEM*] [*Organic chemistry*]
NEMIC..........	New England Materials-Instruction Center
NEMISYS......	New Mexico Information System [*Library network*]
NEmL............	East Meadow Public Library, East Meadow, NY [*Library symbol*] [*Library of Congress*] (LCLS)
NEMLA.........	New England Modern Language Association (AEBS)
NEmMC........	Nassau County Medical Center, East Meadow, NY [*Library symbol Library of Congress*] (LCLS)
NEmMcE.......	McVey Elementary School, East Meadow, NY [*Library symbol Library of Congress*] (LCLS)
NEMMCO	National Electricity Market Management Company, Ltd. [*Australia*] [*Commercial firm*]
NEmME........	Meadowbrook Elementary School, East Meadow, NY [*Library symbol Library of Congress*] (LCLS)
NEmMH	East Meadow High School, East Meadow, NY [*Library symbol*] [*Library of Congress*] (LCLS)
NEmNHi.......	Nassau County Historical Museum, East Meadow, NY [*Library symbol Library of Congress*] (LCLS)
NEMO	Naval Experimental Manned Observatory
NEMO	Never Ever Mention Outside [*Secret computer toy project of Axlon, Inc.*]
NEMO	Nonempirical Molecular Orbitals [*Atomic physics*]
NEMO	Not Emanating Main Office [*Remote broadcast*] (NTCM)
NEMO	Nuclear Exchange Model
NEMP..........	Nuclear Electromagnetic Propagation
NEMP..........	Nuclear Electromagnetic Pulse (AABC)
NEmPE........	Parkway Elementary School, East Meadow, NY [*Library symbol Library of Congress*] (LCLS)
NEMPS	National Environmental Monitoring and Prediction System (MCD)
NEMQO........	Non Est Mortale Quod Opto [*It Is No Mortal Thing I Desire*] [*Motto of Friedrich III, Duke of Schleswig-Holstein-Gottorp (1597-1659)*] [*Latin*]
NEMR	National E [*Electronic*]-Mail Registry [*Information service or system*] (TSSD)
NEMRA	National Electrical Manufacturers Representatives Association (EA)
NEMRB	New England Motor Rate Bureau
NEMRIP	New England Marine Resources Information Program [*University of Rhode Island*] [*Later, NEMAS*]
NEMS............	National Aeronautics and Space Administration [*NASA*] Equipment Management System (AAGC)
NEMS............	National Exchange Market System
NEMS............	Near-Earth Magnetospheric Satellite
NEMS...........	Nimbus E Microwave Spectrometer [*Meteorology*]
NEMSPA	National EMS [*Emergency Medical Service*] Pilots Association (EA)
NEMT..........	Naval Emergency Monitoring Teams (PDAA)
NEMVAC	Noncombatant Emergency and Evacuation Plan (NVT)
NEmWJ........	Woodland Junior High School, East Meadow, NY [*Library symbol*] [*Library of Congress*] (LCLS)
NEN	New Eyes for the Needy (EA)
NEN	North-East Airlines Ltd. [*Nigeria*] [*FAA designator*] (FAAC)
NEN	Northstar Energy Corp. [*Toronto Stock Exchange symbol*]
NEN	Whitehouse, FL [*Location identifier FAA*] (FAAL)
NENCL	Nonenclosure
NE/ND.........	New Edition / No Date [*of Publication*] (DGA)
NENEP........	Navy Enlisted Nursing Education Program
NENG	New England
NEngEl........	New England Electric System [*Associated Press*] (SAG)
NEngInv	New England Investment Companies Ltd. [*Associated Press*] (SAG)
N Eng J Prison L...	New England Journal on Prison Law [*A publication*] (DLA)
N Eng Rep ...	New England Reporter [*A publication*] (DLA)
NEnI............	International Business Machines Corp., Systems Development Library, Endicott, NY [*Library symbol Library of Congress*] (LCLS)
N ENMLD	Not Enameled [*Freight*]
NEnoVM.......	James Vernon Middle School, East Norwich, NY [*Library symbol*] [*Library of Congress*] (LCLS)
NEO	National Electrolysis Organization [*Later, SCME*] (EA)
NEO	National Energy Office [*Executive Office of the President*]
NEO	Near-Earth Object [*Astronomy*]
NEO	Near-Earth Orbit

NEO	Neoarsphenamine [*or Neosalvarsan*] [*Medicine*]
NEO	Neocomian [*Paleontology*]
NEO	Neomycin [*Antibiotic compound*]
NEO	Neonatal [*Medicine*]
NEO	Neopharm, Inc. [*AMEX symbol*] (SAG)
NEO	Noncombatant Evacuation Operation [*Army*] (INF)
NEO	Noncombatant Evacuation Order [*Army*] (AABC)
NEO	Northeastern Operations Office [*NASA*]
NEO	Northeast Oklahoma R. R. [*AAR code*]
NEO	Pensacola, FL [*Location identifier FAA*] (FAAL)
NEOB	New Executive Office Building [*Washington, DC*]
NEOC	National Earth Observations Center [*National Oceanic and Atmospheric Administration*]
NEOCOMP.....	New Computational Formulas
NEOCON	National Exposition of Contract Interior Furnishings
NEOCON	Neoconservative
NEOCON	Neomycin, Colistin, Nystatin [*Antineoplastic drug regimen*]
NEOCS.........	Navy Enlisted Occupational Classification System (NVT)
NEODA.........	National Edible Oil Distributors Association [*British*] (DBA)
NEODA.........	Naval Explosive Ordnance Disposal Association
NEODF.........	Naval Explosive Ordnance Disposal Facility
NEO-DHC	Neohesperidin Dihydrochalcone [*Also, NHDC*] [*Sweetening agent*]
NEODTC.......	Naval Explosive Ordnance Disposal Technology Center [*Indian Head, MD*] (DNAB)
NEOF	No Evidence of Failure (MCD)
NEOF	Nordic Engineer Officers' Federation (EA)
NEOG	Neogen Corp. [*NASDAQ symbol*] (NQ)
Neogen........	Neogen Corp. [*Associated Press*] (SAG)
NEOL	Neolens, Inc. [*NASDAQ symbol*] (NQ)
Neol............	Neolithic (VRA)
NEOL	Neologism
NEOM	NeoMedia Technologies, Inc. [*NASDAQ symbol*] (SAG)
NEOMAL	Northeastern Ohio Major Academic Libraries [*The College of Wooster*] [*Wooster, OH Later, NEOMARL*] [*Library network*]
NEOMARL....	Northeast Ohio Major Academic and Research Libraries [*Library network Information service or system*] (IID)
NeoMd.........	NeoMedia Technologies, Inc. [*Associated Press*] (SAG)
NeoMdia......	NeoMedia Technologies, Inc. [*Associated Press*] (SAG)
NEOME	New Electroactive Organic Materials for Electronics [*Esprit*]
NEOP	Neoprobe Corp. [*NASDAQ symbol*] (SAG)
NEOP	New England Order of Protection [*Later, Woodmen of the World Life Insurance Society*] (EA)
NeoPath.......	NeoPath, Inc. [*Associated Press*] (SAG)
Neophrm......	Neopharm, Inc. [*Associated Press*] (SAG)
NEO-PI........	NEO [*Neuroticism, Extraversion, Openness to Experience*] Personality Inven tory [*Personality development test*] [*Psychology*]
Neopr..........	Neoprobe Corp. [*Associated Press*] (SAG)
Neoprobe.....	Neoprobe Corp. [*Associated Press*] (SAG)
NEOPW.......	Neoprobe Corp. Wrrt'E' [*NASDAQ symbol*] (TTSB)
NeoRx.........	NeoRx Corp. [*Associated Press*] (SAG)
NEOS	NeoStar Retail Group [*NASDAQ symbol*] (SAG)
NeoStar	NeoStar Retail Group [*Associated Press*] (SAG)
NEOT	NeoTherapeutics, Inc. [*NASDAQ symbol*] (SAG)
NeoTher.......	NeoTherapeutics, Inc. [*Associated Press*] (SAG)
NeoThr.........	NeoTherapeutics, Inc. [*Associated Press*] (SAG)
NEOU	Navigators' and Engineering Officers' Union [*British*]
Neoz	Neozyme Corp. [*Associated Press*] (SAG)
N/EP...........	Name on End-Paper [*Antiquarian book trade*]
NEP............	National Education Program (EA)
NEP............	National Emphasis Program [*Occupational Safety and Health Administration*]
NEP............	National Energy Program [*or Plan*] [*Canada*]
NEP............	National Estuary Program [*Federal government*]
NEP............	Natural Effects Processor
NEP............	Near-Earth Phase [*NASA*]
NEP............	Nearest Equivalent Product
NEP............	Needle Exchange Program
NEP............	Negative Equally Probable
NEP............	Negative Expiratory Pressure [*Medicine*]
NEP............	Nemzeti Egyseg Partja [*Party of National Unity*] [*Hungary Political party*] (PPE)
Nep.............	Nepal (VRA)
nep.............	Nepali [*MARC language code Library of Congress*] (LCCP)
NEP............	Nepean Public Library [*UTLAS symbol*]
NEP............	Nephrology [*Medical specialty*] (DHSM)
Nep.............	Nepos [*First century BC*] [*Classical studies*] (OCD)
NEP............	Neptune (ROG)
NEP............	Nerve-Ending Particle (OA)
NEP............	Net Ecosystem Production [*Biology*]
NEP............	N-Ethylpyrrolidinone [*Organic chemistry*]
NEP............	Network Entry Point (AAGC)
NEP............	Neutral Endopeptidase [*An enzyme*]
N-Ep...........	Neutralizing Epitope [*Immunogenetics*]
NEP............	Neverending Program (IAA)
NEP............	New Economic Policy [*Program of former USSR, 1921-28; also US wage/price freeze and controls of Nixon Administration, 1971*]
NEP............	New Edition Pending [*Publishing*]
NEP............	New England Plant (NRCH)
NEP............	New Equipment Practice
NEP............	Newton Extrapolation Ploynominal (IAA)
NEP............	Noise-Equivalent Power
NEP............	Nonelectronic Part
NEP............	Nonelutable Polar Compounds [*Analytical chemistry*]
NEP............	Non-English-Proficient

NEP	Normal Entry Point (MCD)
NEP	Nuclear Electric Propulsion [System]
NEP	Nu Pacific Resources Ltd. [Vancouver Stock Exchange symbol]
NEPA	National Enginemen's Protection Association [A union] [British]
NEPA	National Environmental Policy Act (EG)
NEPA	National Environmental Policy Act (DOGT)
NEPA	National Environmental Policy Act of 1969
NEPA	National Environmental Protection Agency [China]
NEPA	National Euchre Players Association (EA)
NEPA	Northeast Pacific Area
NEPA	Nuclear Energy for Propulsion of Aircraft
NEPAL	National Egg Packers' Association Ltd. [British] (BI)
NEP & P	New England Printer and Publisher [A publication] (DGA)
NEPB	National Energy Protection Board
NEPBC	Northeastern Pennsylvania Bibliographic Center [King's College] [Wilkes-Barre, PA] [Library network]
NEPC	New England Power Co.
NEPCC	North East Pacific Culture Collection [of marine organisms] [University of British Columbia]
NEPCO	New England Provision Co.
NEPCON	National Electronic Packaging and Production Conference
NEPD	No Evidence of Pulmonary Disease (DAVI)
NEPD	Noise-Equivalent Power Density
NEPDB	Navy Environmental Protection Data Base [Obsolete]
NEPE	National Emergency Planning Establishment [Canada]
NEPE	Nez Perce National Historical Park
NEPE	Nitrate Ester Plasticized Polyethylene (PDAA)
NEPEA	New England Project on Education of the Aging [Defunct] (EA)
NEPEC	National Earthquake Prediction Evaluation Council [US Geological Survey]
NEPEX	New England Power Exchange
neph	Nephrite (VRA)
NEPH	Nephrology (DAVI)
NEPH	Nephrology
NEPHAT	Northeastern Pacific Hurricane Analog Tracker
NEPHGE	Nonequilibrium pH Gradient Gel Electrophoresis
NEPHIS	Nested Phrase Indexing System [Automated indexing system] [University of Western Ontario]
NEPI	National Environmental Policy Institute [Washington, D.C.]
NEPIA	Nuclear Energy Property Insurance Association [Later, ANI] (EA)
NEPIS	N-Ethyl(phenylisoxazolium)sulfonate [Organic chemistry]
NEPL	National Endowment for the Preservation of Liberty [Foundation created by Carl Channell to collect funds for Nicaraguan CONTRAs]
NEPMA	National Engine Parts Manufacturers Association (EA)
NEPMU	Navy Environmental and Preventive Medicine Unit (NVT)
NEPN	Near-Earth Phase Network [NASA] (KSC)
NEPO	NATO Equipment Policy Objective (NATG)
NEPOOL	New England Power Pool
NEPP	National Energy Policy Plan
NEPPCO	Northeastern Poultry Producers Council [Later, PEIA] (EA)
NEPR	NATO Electronic Parts Recommendations (AABC)
NEPr	Noble Drilling $1.50 Cv Pfd [NYSE symbol] (TTSB)
NEPR	Nuclear Explosion Pulse Reaction (AAG)
NEPRAC	National Electron Probe Resource for Analysis of Cells [Harvard University] [Research center] (RCD)
NEPRF	Naval Environmental Prediction Research Facility
NEPRS	New Equipment Personnel Requirements Summary [Army]
NEPS	National Economic Projections Series [NPA Data Services, Inc.] [Information service or system] (CRD)
NEPS	National Estuarine Pollution Study [Federal Water Quality Administration] (MSC)
NEPSS	Navy Environmental Protection Support Service
NEPSWL	New England Plant, Soil, and Water Laboratory [Department of Agriculture] [Research center] (RCD)
NEPT.	Neptune (WDAA)
NEPT.	No Evidence of Pulmonary Tuberculosis [Medicine]
NEPTUNE	North-Eastern Electronic Peak Tracing Unit and Numerical Evaluator (IEEE)
NEPU	Northern Elements Progression Union [Nigeria] [Political party]
NEQ	New England Quarterly [A publication] (BRI)
NEQ	Not Equal (EECA)
NER	Air Newark, Inc. [ICAO designator] (FAAC)
NEr	East Rockaway Public Library, East Rockaway, NY [Library symbol Library of Congress] (LCLS)
NER	National Educational Radio
NER	National Emissions Report [Environmental Protection Agency] (GFGA)
NER	National Engineers Register (IAA)
NER	Near East Report [A publication] (BJA)
Ner.	Neriglissar (BJA)
Ner.	Nero [of Suetonius] [Classical studies] (OCD)
NER	Nervine [Medicine] (ROG)
NER	Network for Economic Rights [Defunct] (EA)
NER	Neutral External Rotation [Sports medicine]
NER	Never-Exceed Redline [Aerospace] (AAG)
NER	New England Reporter [A publication] (DLA)
NER	Niger [ANSI three-letter standard code] (CNC)
NER	No Evidence of Recurrence [Medicine] (MAE)
NER	Noise-Equivalent Radiance
NER	Nonconformance Event Record [NASA] (KSC)
NER	Nonionizing Electromagnetic Radiation
NER	North Eastern Railway [British]
NER	Northeastern Regional Library, Cimarron, NM [OCLC symbol] (OCLC)
NER	North Eastern Reporter [Commonly cited NE] [A publication] (DLA)
NER	Not Economically Repairable
NER	Nuclear Electric Resonance (PDAA)
NER	Nucleotide-Excision Repair
NERA	National Economic Research Associates
NERA	National Emergency Relief Administration
NERA	Naval Enlisted Reserve Association (EA)
Nera	Nera & Musica [Record label] [Norway]
NERA	New England Reading Association (AEBS)
NeraAS	Nera AS [Associated Press] (SAG)
NERAC	New England Research Application Center [University of Connecticut]
NERAIC	North European Region Air Information Center (NATG)
NERAM	Network Reliability Assessment Model (PDAA)
NERAy	Nera-AS [NASDAQ symbol] (SAG)
NERAY	Nera AS ADS [NASDAQ symbol] (TTSB)
NERBC	New England River Basin Commission
NERBS	National Electric Rate Book by States [A publication]
NERC	National Electronic Reliability Council (NTCM)
NERC	National Electronics Research Council
NERC	National English Rabbit Club [British] (BI)
NERC	National Environmental Research Center [Later, CERL] [Environmental Protection Agency]
NERC	National Environmental Research Council (NITA)
NERC	National Environment Resource Council [British] (NRCH)
NERC	National Equal Rights Council (EA)
NERC	Natural Environment Research Council [Research center British] (IRC)
NERC	New England Regional Commission [Terminated, 1981] [Department of Commerce]
NERC	Newton-Evans Research Co., Inc. [Ellicott City, MD] [Information service or system] (TSSD)
NERC	Nordic Economic Research Council (EA)
NERC	North American Electric Reliability Council (EA)
NERC	Nuclear Energy Research Center [Also, CEEN, SCK] [Belgium]
NERC	Regional Conference for the Near East [UN Food and Agriculture Organization]
NErCE	Centre Elementary School, East Rockaway, NY [Library symbol Library of Congress] (LCLS)
NERCIC	Northeast Regional Coastal Information Center [Marine science] (MSC)
NERCOE	New England Resource Center for Occupational Education
NERCOM	New England Regional Commission [Department of Commerce] [Terminated, 1981] (EGAO)
NERCOMM	New England Regional Commission [Terminated, 1981] [Department of Commerce] (NOAA)
NERComP	New England Regional Computing Program, Inc. [Boston, MA]
NERCP	Naval European Research Contract Program (NG)
NERD	Newman's Electronic Rhyming Dictionary [Computer software] (PCM)
NERD	No Evidence of Recurrent Disease [Medicine] (MAE)
NERDA	New England Rural Development Association
NERDAS	NASA Earth Resources Data Annotation System (MCD)
NERDC	Northeast Regional Data Center [University of Florida] [Research center] (RCD)
NEREM	Northeast Electronics Research and Engineering Meeting
NE Rep	New England Reporter [A publication] (DLA)
NE Rep	North Eastern Reporter [Commonly cited NE] [A publication] (DLA)
NE Reporter	North Eastern Reporter [Commonly cited NE] [A publication] (DLA)
NE Repr	North Eastern Reporter [Commonly cited NE] [A publication] (DLA)
NERF	National Eye Research Foundation [Later, NEHF] (EA)
NERHL	Northeastern Radiological Health Laboratory [Massachusetts]
NErHS	East Rockaway High School, East Rockaway, NY [Library symbol] [Library of Congress] (LCLS)
NERI	National Electronics Research Initiative [British]
NERIS	National Educational Resources Information Service [British]
NERIS	National Energy Referal Information System
NERIT	Northeast Regional Implementation Team [Army Corps of Engineers]
NERL	National Ecological Research Laboratory [Environmental Protection Agency]
NE Rlty	New England Realty Associates Ltd. [Associated Press] (SAG)
NERMLS	New England Regional Medical Library Service (EA)
NERN	National Educational Radio Network [Defunct] (NTCM)
NERO	National Energy Resources Organization (EA)
NERO	Near-Earth Rescue and Operations [NASA]
NERO	Nuclear Effects Rocket Operations
NERO	Sodium [Na] Experimental Reactor of Zero Power [British] (DEN)
NEROC	Northeast Radio Observatory Corp.
NEROS	Northeast Regional Oxidant Study [Environmental Protection Agency] (GFGA)
NERP	National Environmental Research Park [Marine science] (MSC)
NERP	Nicaraguan Exile Relocation Program [CIA]
NERPG	Northern European Regional Planning Group [NATO] (NATG)
NERPRC	New England Regional Primate Research Center [Harvard University] [Research center] (RCD)
NERRA	New Equipment Resources Requirements Analysis [Army] (AABC)
NErRE	Rhame Elementary School, East Rockaway, NY [Library symbol Library of Congress] (LCLS)
NERRS	National Estuarine Research Reserve System (USDC)
NERSA	Centrale Nucleaire Europeenne a Neutrons Rapides SA [France] (PDAA)
NERSA	Northeast Rail Service Act [1981] [Also, NRSA]
NERSE	Nutrition, Exercise, Relaxation, Sleep, and Enjoyment
NERSICA	National Established Repair, Service, and Improvement Contractors Association [Later, National Remodelers Association]
NERSP	Navy Environmental Remote Sensing Program

NERU .... Nursing Education Research Unit
NERV .... Nervous [Medicine]
NERV .... Nuclear Emergency Recovery Vehicle (NUCP)
NERV .... Nuclear Emulsion Recovery Vehicle (MUGU)
NERV .... Nuclear Energy Research Vehicle
NERVA .... Nuclear Engine for Rocket Vehicle Application [NASA]
NErWE .... Waverly Park Elementary School, East Rockaway, NY [Library symbol] [Library of Congress] (LCLS)
NERX .... NeoRx Corp. [NASDAQ symbol] (NQ)
NERXP .... NeoRx $2.4375 Cv Exch Pfd [NASDAQ symbol] (TTSB)
NERXW .... Neorx Corp. Wrrt [NASDAQ symbol] (TTSB)
NES .... National Eczema Society [British]
NES .... National Election Studies [Conducts national surveys of the American electorate]
NES .... National Energy Software [Department of Energy Information service or system] (CRD)
NES .... National Energy Strategy [Department of Energy] (ECON)
NES .... National Estimating Society [Later, SCEA] (EA)
NES .... National Eutrophication Survey [Environmental Protection Agency]
NES .... Naval Examination Service [British military] (DMA)
NES .... Naval Experimenting Station
NES .... Near Eastern Society (EA)
NES .... Near Eastern Studies [A publication] (BJA)
NES .... Near-End Suppressor (IAA)
NES .... Nesmont Industry [Vancouver Stock Exchange symbol]
NES .... Netherlands' Ecological Society [Multinational association] (EAIO)
NES .... N-Ethylsuccinimide [Organic chemistry]
NES .... Neurobehavioral Evaluation System
NES .... New Earnings Survey [British]
NES .... New England Electric System [NYSE symbol] (SPSG)
NES .... New England El Sys [NYSE symbol] (TTSB)
NES .... New Enlisted System [Navy] (DNAB)
NES .... News Election Service [Vote-counting consortium of the major TV networks and two wire services]
NES .... Nintendo Entertainment System [Video game]
NES .... Noise-Equivalent Signal [IEEE]
NES .... Non-English-Speaking (ADA)
NES .... Nonerasable Storage [Computer science]
NES .... Nordeste, Linhas Aereas Regionais SA [Brazil] [ICAO designator] (FAAC)
NES .... Nordic Ergonomic Society (EAIO)
NES .... Nordiska Ergonomisallskapet [Nordic Ergonomic Society] (EAIO)
NES .... Not Elsewhere Specified
NES .... Nuclear Export Signal [Biochemistry]
NES .... Nuclear Export Signal [Immunochemistry]
NES .... Numerical Engineering Society [British] (DBA)
NESA .... John H. Nelson Environmental Study Area [University of Kansas] [Research center] (RCD)
NESA .... National Eagle Scout Association (EA)
NESA .... National Electric Sign Association (EA)
NESA .... National Emission Standards Act [1967]
NESA .... National Employment Service Act [1933]
NESA .... National Energy Specialist Association (EA)
NESA .... National Environmental Specialist Association (EA)
NESA .... National Environmental Study Areas Program [National Park Service] [Defunct]
NESA .... Near East and South Asia [Department of State]
NE/SA .... Near East/South Asia Council of Overseas Schools (EA)
NESA .... New England School of Art
NESAC .... National Environmental Services Administration Committee [Marine science] (MSC)
NESB .... National Environmental Specimen Bank [Energy Research and Development Administration]
NESB .... Non-English-Speaking Background (ADA)
NESB .... Number of Equally Strong Beams [Military] (CAAL)
NESB1 .... First Generation Non-English-Speaking Background
NESB2 .... Second Generation Non-English-Speaking Background
NESBA .... National Earth Shelter Builders Association [Defunct] (EA)
NESBA .... National Executive of Small Business Agencies [Australia]
NESC .... National Electrical Safety Code [Also, NEC] (NTCM)
NESC .... National Electric Safety Code (SAA)
NESC .... National Energy Software Center [Department of Energy] [Information service or system] (IID)
NESC .... National Enquiry into Scholarly Communication
NESC .... National Environmental Satellite Center [Formerly, National Weather Satellite Center] [Later, National Environmental Satellite Service]
NESC .... National Environmental Svc. [NASDAQ symbol] (TTSB)
NESC .... National Executive Service Corps [New York, NY] (EA)
NESC .... Naval Electronics Systems Command
NESC .... Navy Electromagnetic Spectrum Center (DNAB)
NESC .... Neuroepithelial Stem Cells [Medicine]
NESC .... Non-English-Speaking Country
NESC .... Nuclear Engineering and Scientific Congress (MCD)
NESCA .... National Environmental Systems Contractors Association [Later, ACCA] (EA)
NESCAC ...... New England Small College Athletic Conference
NESCAUM .... North East States for Coordinated Air Use Management
NESCNSC .... Net Evaluation Subcommittee, National Security Council (AABC)
NESCO .... National Energy Supply Corp. [Proposed]
NESCO .... National Engineering Science Co.
NESCO .... Naval Environmental Support Office [Marine science] (MSC)
NESCO .... Nigerian Electricity Supply Corp. African Workers' Union
NESCTM ...... National Environmental Satellite Center Technical Memoranda (NOAA)

NESCWS ...... Nonessential Services Chilled Water System [Nuclear energy] (NRCH)
NESDA .... National Electronic Service Dealers Association [Later, NESSDA] (EA)
NESDA .... National Equipment Servicing Dealers Association (EA)
NESDEC ...... New England School Development Council (EA)
NESDIS .... National Environmental Satellite, Data, and Information Service [Washington, DC National Oceanic and Atmospheric Administration] (GRD)
NESDRES .... National Environmental Data Referral Service (USDC)
NESDRES .... National Environmental Data Referral Service [Marine science] (OSRA)
NESE .... Neue Ephemeris fuer Semitische Epigraphik [Wiesbaden] [A publication] (BJA)
NESEA .... Naval Electronic Systems Engineering Activity
NESEC .... Naval Electronics Systems Engineering Center (MCD)
NESEP .... Navy Enlisted Scientific Education Program
NESF .... Normal Engineered Safety Features [Nuclear energy] (NRCH)
NESHAP ...... National Emission Standards for Hazardous Air Pollutants [Environmental Protection Agency]
NESIP .... Naval Explosive Safety Improvement Program
NESIP/POA & M... Naval Explosive Safety Improvement Program / Plan of Action and Milestones (DNAB)
NESL .... Northeast Shipbuilders Ltd. [Commercial firm British]
NESLA .... New England Shoe and Leather Association (EA)
NEsM .... Mount Saint Alphonsus Seminary, Esopus, NY [Library symbol Library of Congress] (LCLS)
NESMRA ...... New England Super-Modified Racing Association
NESN .... NATO English-Speaking Nations
NESN .... New England Sports Network [Cable-television system]
NESO .... Naval Air Engineering Support Office [Norfolk, VA]
NESO .... Naval Electronic Sensor Operator [Canadian Navy]
NESO .... Naval Engineering Service Office (MCD)
NESO .... Navy Environmental Support Office [Obsolete]
NESOSC ...... New England Society of Open Salts Collectors (EA)
NESP .... National Environmental Studies Project [Defunct] (EA)
NESP .... Navy EHF [Extremely High Frequency] Satellite Program (DOMA)
NESP .... Nurse Education Support Program
NESR .... Natural Environment Support Room (MCD)
NESR .... Noise-Equivalent Spectral Radiance [Physics]
NESRA .... National Employee Services and Recreation Association (EA)
NESS .... NASA Expert Simulation System (NITA)
NESS .... National Easter Seal Society (EA)
NESS .... National Emergency Steel Specification [World War II]
NESS .... National Environmental Satellite Service [National Oceanic and Atmospheric Administration Telecommunications] (TEL)
NESS .... Network and Evaluation Simulation System (NITA)
NESS .... Northeast Satellite Systems [Avoca, PA] [Telecommunications] (TSSD)
NESS .... Nuclear Effects Simulation Study
NESSDA ...... National Electronic Sales and Service Dealers Association (EA)
NEssDS ...... Dunlap Society, Essex, NY [Library symbol Library of Congress] (LCLS)
NESSEC ...... Naval Electronics Systems Security Engineering Center (MCD)
NEST .... National Emergency Survivable Troop System (AABC)
NEST .... Naval Experimental Satellite Terminal (IEEE)
NEST .... New and Emerging Sciences and Technologies
NEST .... New El Salvador Today (EA)
NEST .... New Expanding Shelter Technology [Residential construction]
NEST .... Nonelectric Stimulus Transfer
NEST .... Novell Embedded Systems Technology [Novell, Inc.] [Computer science]
NEST .... Nuclear Effects Support Team
NEST .... Nuclear Emergency Search Team [Department of Energy]
NEST .... Nuclear Explosive Simulation Technique
NESTA .... National Earth Science Teachers Association (EA)
NESTED ...... Naval Electronic Systems Test and Evaluation Detachment
NESTEF ...... Naval Electronic Systems Test and Evaluation Facility
NESTEV ...... Naval Electronics Systems Test and Evaluation (IAA)
NESTOR ...... Neutron Source Thermal Reactor [British] (DEN)
NESTS .... Nonelectric Stimulus Transfer System
NestU .... Northeast Utilities [Associated Press] (SAG)
NESW .... Nonessential Service Water Relay Pump [Nuclear energy] (IAA)
NET .... Centre for Agricultural Publications and Documents, Wageningen, Netherlands [OCLC symbol] (OCLC)
NET .... Nasoendotracheal Tube [Medicine]
NET .... National Educational Television [Later, EBC]
NET .... National Empowerment Television
NET .... National Estate Tasmania [Australia]
NET .... National Evangelization Teams (EA)
NET .... Negative Entropy Trap
NET .... Net Energy Thrust
NET .... Net Equivalent Temperature
NET .... Net Explosive Weight (MSA)
NET .... NETI Technologies, Inc. [Vancouver Stock Exchange symbol]
NET .... Netto [Lowest]
NET .... Network [Telecommunications] (AAG)
net .... Network (WDMC)
NET .... Network Aviation Services (NIG) Ltd. [FAA designator] (FAAC)
NET .... Neuroelectric Therapy [Substance detoxification]
NET .... New Equipment Training [Army] (AABC)
NET .... New Era Technologies, Inc. [Washington, DC] [Telecommunications] (TSSD)
NET .... Newton Emission Theory [Physics]
NET .... Next European Torus [Formerly, Joint European Torus (JET)]

NET............ Nimbus Experiment Team [*NASA*]
NET............ Nitrigin Eireann Teoranta [*Nationalized industry*] [*Ireland*] (EY)
NET............ No Evidence of Tumor [*Medicine*]
NET............ Noise-Equivalent Temperature
NET............ Noise Evaluation Test (IAA)
NET............ Nonlethal Entanglement Technology
NET............ Nonradiative Energy Transfer [*Physics*]
NET............ Norethisterone [*Oral contraceptive ingredient*]
NET............ Norme Europeene de Telecommunications [*Telecommunications*] (OSI)
NET............ North European Oil Royalty Trust [*NYSE symbol*] (SPSG)
NET............ North Europn Oil Rty Tr [*NYSE symbol*] (TTSB)
NET............ Not Earlier Than
NET............ Nuclear Effects Test
NET............ Nuclear Emergency Teams [*DASA*]
NET............ Nuclear Energy Team
NET............ Nuclear Engineer Trainee
NET............ Number of Element Types
NETA.......... International Electrical Testing Association (EA)
NETA.......... National Employment and Training Association [*Upland, CA*] (EA)
NETA.......... National Environmental Training Association (EA)
NETA.......... Northeast Test Area [*Military*] (MCD)
NETAC........ Nuclear Energy Trade Associations' Conference
NETANAL..... Network Analysis (PDAA)
NETAPPS..... Net Ad-Produced Purchases [*Advertising*]
NetBEUI....... NetBIOS [*Network Basic Input/Output System*] Extended User Interface [*Microsoft Corp.*] (PCM)
NETBIOS..... Network Basic Input/Output System [*Computer software*]
NetBIOS...... Network Basic Input/Output System [*Computer science*] (DOM)
NETC.......... National Emergency Training Center
NETC.......... National Emergency Transportation Center
NETC.......... Naval Education and Training Center [*or Command*] (NVT)
NETC.......... NETCM On-Line Comm Svcs [*NASDAQ symbol*] (TTSB)
NETC.......... Netcom On-Line Communications Services, Inc. [*NASDAQ symbol*] (SAG)
NETC.......... New England Theatre Conference (EA)
NETC.......... New England Trail Conference (EA)
NETC.......... No Explosion of the Total Contents [*Business term*] (DCTA)
NETC.......... Northeast Transportation Coalition
NET CDF...... Network Common Data Format [*Computer science*]
NETCHE...... Nebraska Educational Television Council for Higher Education, Inc. [*Library network*]
NETCO........ North Western Employes Transportation Corp. [*Successor to Chicago & North Western Railway*]
Netcom....... Netcom On-Line Communictions Services, Inc. [*Associated Press*] (SAG)
NETCOM...... Network Communications
NETCOM...... Network Control Communications [*Deep Space Instrumentation Facility, NASA*]
NETCON...... Network Control [*Computer science*] (MHDB)
NETD.......... Noise-Equivalent Temperature Difference [*Thermography*]
NETDC........ New England Trophoblastic Disease Center
NETDS........ Near-Earth Tracking and Data System
NETE.......... Naval Engineering Test Establishment [*Canadian Armed Forces*] (PDAA)
NETE.......... Network of European Teacher Education (AIE)
NETF.......... Netframe Systems [*NASDAQ symbol*] (SAG)
NETF.......... Nuclear Energy Test Facility (AFM)
NETF.......... Nuclear Engineering Test Facility (AAG)
NETFIPCBR... Naval Education and Training Financial Information Processing Branch (DNAB)
NETFMS...... Naval Education and Training Financial Management System (DNAB)
Netframe..... Netframe Systems [*Associated Press*] (SAG)
NETFS........ National Educational Television/Film Service (WGA)
NETG.......... Network General [*NASDAQ symbol*] (TTSB)
NETG.......... Network General Corp. [*NASDAQ symbol*] (CTT)
NetGALA..... Network of Gay and Lesbian Alumni Associations (EA)
NETGEN...... Network Generation [*Computer science*] (MHDB)
NETH.......... National Employ the Handicapped Week
NETH.......... Netherlands
Neth........... Netherlands (ODBW)
Neth Ant..... Netherlands Antilles
Netherl Intl L Rev... Netherlands Yearbook of International Law [*The Hague, Netherlands*] [*A publication*] (DLA)
Neth Int'l L Rev... Netherlands International Law Review [*A publication*] (DLA)
Nethl.......... Netherlands (VRA)
Neth P........ Netherlands Pharmacopoeia [*A publication*]
NETHW....... National Employ the Handicapped Week (OICC)
Neth YB Int'l Law... Netherlands Yearbook of International Law [*A publication*] (DLA)
NETI........... Network Technologies International, Inc. [*Ann Arbor, MI*] [*Telecommunications*] (TSSD)
Netiquette.... Internet Etiquette [*Computer science*]
NETISA....... Naval Education and Training Information Systems Activity (DNAB)
NETK.......... Network Express [*NASDAQ symbol*] (TTSB)
NETK.......... Network Express, Inc. [*NASDAQ symbol*] (SAG)
NETL.......... National Export Traffic League [*New York, NY*] (EA)
NETL.......... NetLive Communications, Inc. [*NASDAQ symbol*] (SAG)
NETL.......... Nuclear Engineering Teaching Laboratory [*University of Texas at Austin*] [*Research center*] (RCD)
NetLive....... NetLive Communications, Inc. [*Associated Press*] (SAG)
NETLS........ Northeast Texas Library System [*Library network*]
NETLS/DPL... Northeast Texas Library System/Dallas Public Library Film Service [*Library network*]
NET Ltd....... Nigerian External Telecommunications Ltd. [*Lagos*]

NETM......... NetManage, Inc. [*NASDAQ symbol*] (SAG)
N et M........ Nocte et Mane [*Night and Morning*] [*Pharmacy*]
n et m......... Nocte et Mane [*Night and Morning*] [*Latin*] [*Pharmacy*] (DAVI)
NETMA....... Nobody Ever Tells Me Anything [*Executive complaint*]
Netmed....... Netmed, Inc. [*Associated Press*] (SAG)
NETMIS....... Naval Education and Training Management Information System (MCD)
Netmng...... NetManage, Inc. [*Associated Press*] (SAG)
NETMUX..... Network Multiplexer (NITA)
NET/NLT..... No Earlier Than/No Later Than (MCD)
NETOP....... Network Operator Process [*Computer science*] (MHDB)
NETOPS...... Nuclear Emergency Team Operations (AFM)
NETP.......... New Equipment Training Program [*Army*] (AABC)
NETPDC..... Naval Education and Training Program Development Center [*Pensacola, FL*] (DNAB)
NETR .... NATO Electronic Technical Recommendation (PDAA)
NETR .... No Essential Traffic Reported [*Aviation*]
NETR .... Nuclear Engineering Test Reactor [*Air Force*]
NETRA........ New England Trail Rider Association (EA)
NETRB........ New England Territory Railroad Bureau
NETRC........ National Educational Television and Radio Center [*Later, EBC*] (EA)
NETREM ...... Net Requirementes Estimation Model (PDAA)
NETR-FTC... New England Territory Railroads Freight Traffic Committee
Netrix........ Netrix Corp. [*Associated Press*] (SAG)
NETRJE....... Network Remote Job Entry [*Telecommunications*] (OSI)
NE TR S NUM... Ne Tradas sine Nummo [*Cash on Delivery*] [*Latin*]
NETS.......... National Electronics Teachers' Service [*Defunct*]
NETS.......... Nationwide Emergency Telecommunications System [*DoD*]
NETS.......... Navy Engineering Technical Services (NG)
NETS.......... Nebraska Electronic Transfer System
NETS.......... Network Electrical Technique System (IAA)
NETS.......... Network Event Theater [*NASDAQ symbol*] (TTSB)
NETS.......... Network Event Theatre, Inc. [*NASDAQ symbol*] (SAG)
NETS.......... Network for Electronic Transfers System
NETS.......... Network of Employees for Traffic Safety [*NHTSA*] (TAG)
NETS.......... Network Techniques
NETS.......... Network Testing Section [*Social Security Administration*]
NETS.......... Neurodysfunction Eye Test System [*Medical*]
NETS.......... New Examiner Training School [*Federal Home Loan Bank Board*]
NETSC........ Naval Education and Training Support Center (DNAB)
NETSCL...... Naval Education and Training Support Center, Atlantic (DNAB)
NETSCP...... Naval Education and Training Support Center, Pacific (DNAB)
Netscpe...... Netscape Communications Corp. [*Associated Press*] (SAG)
NETSET...... Network Synthesis and Evaluation Technique [*Computer science*]
NETSET...... Network Systems and Evaluation Technique (NITA)
NETSIM...... [*Traffic*] Network Simulation [*TXDOT*] (TAG)
NETSL........ New England Technical Services Librarians
Netsmrt...... Netsmart Technologies, Inc. [*Associated Press*] (SAG)
NETSO........ Northern European Transhipment Organization [*NATO*] (NATG)
NETSP........ New Equipment Training Support Package
NetSrce...... NetSource Communications, Inc. [*Associated Press*] (SAG)
NETSS........ National Electronic Telecommunications System for Surveillance [*Center for Disease Control*]
NetStar....... NetStar, Inc. [*Associated Press*] (SAG)
NETSW....... Network Event Theater Wrrt [*NASDAQ symbol*] (TTSB)
NETT.......... Netter Digital Entertainment [*NASDAQ symbol*] (TTSB)
NETT.......... Netter Digital Entertainment, Inc. [*NASDAQ symbol*] (SAG)
NETT.......... Net Tons [*Shipping*]
NETT.......... Network Environmental Technology Transfer [*Europe*] [*An association*]
NETT.......... New Employment, Transition, and Training [*Department of Labor*] (OICC)
NETT.......... New Equipment Training Team [*Army*]
NETTEL....... Network Telecommunications, Inc. [*Denver, CO*] [*Telecommunications*] (TSSD)
Netter........ Netter Digital Entertainment, Inc. [*Associated Press*] (SAG)
NetterD...... Netter Digital Entertainment, Inc. [*Associated Press*] (SAG)
NETTSP...... New Equipment Training Test Support Package (MCD)
NETTW....... Netter Digital Entm't Wrrt [*NASDAQ symbol*] (TTSB)
NETV.......... Nebraska ETV [*Educational Television*] Network [*Lincoln, NE*] [*Telecommunications*] (TSSD)
NetV.......... NetVantage, Inc. [*Associated Press*] (SAG)
NETVA........ NetVantage, Inc. [*NASDAQ symbol*] (SAG)
NETVA........ NetVantage Inc.'A' [*NASDAQ symbol*] (TTSB)
NetVant...... NetVantage, Inc. [*Associated Press*] (SAG)
NETVU........ NetVantage Inc. Unit [*NASDAQ symbol*] (TTSB)
NETVW....... NetVantage Inc. Wrrt'A' [*NASDAQ symbol*] (TTSB)
NETVZ........ NetVantage Inc. Wrrt'B' [*NASDAQ symbol*] (TTSB)
NetwkAp..... Network Appliance Corp. [*Associated Press*] (SAG)
NetwkE....... Network Event Theatre, Inc. [*Associated Press*] (SAG)
Networth..... Networth, Inc. [*Associated Press*] (SAG)
netwrkg..... Networking (BARN)
NETX.......... Network Equipment Technologies, Inc. (MHDW)
NEU .... (Naphthyl)ethyl Urea [*Organic chemistry*]
NEU .... Neuchatel [*Switzerland*] [*Seismograph station code, US Geological Survey Closed*] (SEIS)
Neu........... Neuraminic Acid [*Biochemistry*]
neu........... Neurilemma [*Neurology*] (DAVI)
NEU .... Transportes Aereos Neuquinos Sociedad de Estado [*Argentina ICAO designator*] (FAAC)
NEUC......... National Engine Use Council [*Defunct*] (EA)
NEUCC....... Northern European Universities Computer Centre [*Denmark*] (PDAA)
Neucrine..... Neurocrine Biosciences, Inc. [*Associated Press*] (SAG)
NEUDATA..... Neutron Data Under Direct Access (NITA)
NEUFCH...... Neufchatel [*Imprint*] (ROG)

NEUG	National Epson Users Group (EA)
NEUM	Non-European Unity Movement [*South Africa*] (PD)
Neumed	Neuromedical Systems, Inc. [*Associated Press*] (SAG)
neur...........	Neurology [*Medicine*] (MAE)
NeUR	Rijksuniversiteit te Utrecht, Utrecht, Netherlands [*Library symbol Library of Congress*]
NEUR-A.......	Neurogenic Battery Acute (DAVI)
Neurex........	Neurex Corp. [*Associated Press*] (SAG)
Neurgn........	Neurogen Corp. [*Associated Press*] (SAG)
NEURO........	Neurology [*or Neurological*]
NEurO	North European Oil Royalty Trust [*Associated Press*] (SAG)
NEUROBIOL...	Neurobiology
NEUROL.......	Neurology
NEUROLGST...	Neurobiologist
Neuropath....	Neuropathology [*or Neuropathologist*] (DAVI)
Neuro-Surg..	Neurosurgeon (BABM)
Neuro-Surg..	Neurosurgery [*or Neurosurgeon*] (DAVI)
NeuroTc......	Neurobiological Technologies, Inc. [*Associated Press*] (SAG)
NEURS........	Navy Energy Usage Reporting System (DNAB)
NEUS	New Extensions for Utilizing Scientists, Inc.
NEUS	Northeastern United States
NEUS	Nuclear-Electric Unmanned Spacecraft
NEUSSN......	Northeastern United States Seismic Network (NRCH)
NEUT	Neuter
NEUT	Neutral (AAG)
neut...........	Neutrophil [*Hematology*]
neut equiv ..	Neutralization Equivalent [*Chemistry*]
NEUTN	Neutralization [*Electronics*] (ECII)
NEV...........	Nederlandse Ecologen Vereniging [*Netherlands Ecological Society*] [*Multinational association*] (EAIO)
NEV...........	Negative Expected Value
NEV...........	Neighborhood Electric Vehicle
NEV...........	Net Economic Value
NEV...........	Neutral-to-Earth Voltage [*Electrical power transmission*]
NEV...........	Nevada (AAG)
Nev...........	Nevada (ODBW)
Nev...........	Nevada Supreme Court Reports [*A publication*] (DLA)
NEV...........	Nevis [*Leeward Islands*] [*Airport symbol*] (OAG)
NEV...........	Nieghborhood Electric Vehicle
NEV...........	Nuevo Energy [*NYSE symbol*] (TTSB)
NEV...........	Nuevo Energy Co. [*NYSE symbol*] (SPSG)
NEV...........	Nuevo Financing I [*NYSE symbol*] (SAG)
NEVA	North Eastern Vecturists Association
Nevada Rep...	Nevada Reports [*A publication*] (DLA)
Nevada Repts...	Nevada Reports [*A publication*] (DLA)
Nev Admin Code...	Nevada Administrative Code [*A publication*] (DLA)
Nev & M......	Nevile and Manning's English King's Bench Reports [*A publication*] (ILCA)
Nev & Mac...	Neville and Macnamara's Railway Cases [*1855-1950*] [*A publication*] (DLA)
Nev & MacN...	Neville and Macnamara's Railway and Canal Cases [*1855-1950*] [*A publication*] (DLA)
Nev & Man...	Nevile and Manning's English King's Bench Reports [*A publication*] (DLA)
Nev & Man Mag Cas...	Nevile and Manning's English Magistrates' Cases [*A publication*] (DLA)
Nev & Mcn...	Neville and Macnamara's Railway Cases [*England*] [*A publication*] (DLA)
Nev & M (Eng)...	Nevile and Manning's English King's Bench Reports [*A publication*] (DLA)
Nev & MKB...	Nevile and Manning's English King's Bench Reports [*A publication*] (DLA)
Nev & MMC...	Nevile and Manning's English Magistrates' Cases [*A publication*] (DLA)
Nev & P......	Nevile and Perry's English King's Bench Reports [*1836-38*] [*A publication*] (DLA)
Nev & P......	Nevile and Perry's English Magistrates' Cases [*1836-37*] [*A publication*] (DLA)
Nev & PKB...	Nevile and Perry's English King's Bench Reports [*1836-38*] [*A publication*] (DLA)
Nev & P Mag Cas...	Nevile and Perry's English Magistrates' Cases [*1836-37*] [*A publication*] (DLA)
Nev & PMC...	Nevile and Perry's English Magistrates' Cases [*1836-37*] [*A publication*] (DLA)
NEVATV	Nebraska VA Television Network [*Telecommunications service*] (TSSD)
NEVE..........	Nonempirical Valence-Electron [*Physics*]
NevEngy......	Nevada Energy Co., Inc. [*Associated Press*] (SAG)
NEVLESS	Nevertheless (ROG)
Nev PSC Op...	Nevada Public Service Commission Opinions [*A publication*] (DLA)
NevPw........	Nevada Power Co. [*Associated Press*] (SAG)
Nev Rev Stat...	Nevada Revised Statutes [*A publication*] (DLA)
Nev SBJ......	Nevada State Bar Journal [*A publication*] (DLA)
Nev Stats.....	Statutes of Nevada [*A publication*] (DLA)
Nev St Bar J...	Nevada State Bar Journal [*A publication*] (DLA)
NEVX.........	Nerine Virus X [*Plant pathology*]
NEW...........	Hawarden BAE [*British ICAO designator*] (FAAC)
NEW...........	National Electronics Week
NEW...........	National Energy Watch [*Edison Electric Institute*]
NEW...........	Native Egg White
NEW...........	Navy Early Warning
NEW...........	Net Economic Welfare [*Economic indicator*]
NEW...........	Net Explosive Weight (AFM)
new...........	Newari [*MARC language code Library of Congress*] (LCCP)
NEW...........	Newark [*Diocesan abbreviation*] [*New Jersey*] (TOCD)
NEW...........	New College of California, San Francisco, CA [*OCLC symbol*] (OCLC)
New...........	Newell's Illinois Appeal Reports [*A publication*] (DLA)
NEW...........	New England Air Express, Inc. [*ICAO designator*] (FAAC)
NEW...........	New England Inv Cos. L.P. [*NYSE symbol*] (TTSB)
NEW...........	New England Investment Companies [*Formerly, Reich & Tang Ltd.*] [*NYSE symbol*] (SPSG)
NEW...........	New Orleans, LA [*Location identifier FAA*] (FAAL)
NEW...........	Newport [*Quebec*] [*Geomagnetic observatory code*]
NEW...........	Newport [*Washington*] [*Seismograph station code, US Geological Survey*] (SEIS)
NEW...........	Newtec Industries Ltd. [*Vancouver Stock Exchange symbol*]
NEW...........	Newton
NEW...........	Non-Traditional Employment for Women
NEW...........	Nuclear Energy Women [*Defunct*] (EA)
NEW...........	Nursery Education Week (AEBS)
NEw...........	Thomas E. Ryan Public Library, East Williston, NY [*Library symbol Library of Congress*] (LCLS)
NEWA	National Electrical Wholesalers Association
NEWA	Nuclear Energy Writers Association [*Defunct*]
NEWAC.......	NATO Electronic Warfare Advisory Committee (NATG)
New Ad.......	New Advocate [*A publication*] (BRI)
NewAD........	Newspaper Archive Developments Ltd., New Haven, CT [*Library symbol Library of Congress*] (LCLS)
New Age......	New Age Journal [*A publication*] (BRI)
NewAge.......	New Age Media Fund [*Associated Press*] (SAG)
NewAm.......	New America High Income Fund [*Associated Press*] (SAG)
New Am Cyc...	New American Cyclopaedia [*A publication*] (ROG)
New Ann Reg...	New Annual Register [*London*] [*A publication*] (DLA)
Newark L Rev...	University of Newark. Law Review [*A publication*] (DLA)
NEWB........	Newberry Bancorp [*NASDAQ symbol*] (TTSB)
NEWB........	Newberry Bancorp, Inc. [*NASDAQ symbol*] (SAG)
Newb.........	Newberry's United States District Court, Admiralty Reports [*A publication*] (DLA)
NEWB........	Newbury [*Municipal borough in England*]
Newb Adm...	Newberry's United States District Court, Admiralty Reports [*A publication*] (DLA)
New Benl.....	New Benloe's Reports, English King's Bench [*1531-1628*] [*A publication*] (DLA)
New B Eq Ca...	New Brunswick Equity Cases [*A publication*] (DLA)
New B Eq Rep...	New Brunswick Equity Reports [*A publication*] (DLA)
Newberry.....	Newberry's United States District Court, Admiralty Reports [*A publication*] (DLA)
Newberry Adm (F)...	Newberry's United States District Court, Admiralty Reports [*A publication*] (DLA)
Newberry's Ad Rep...	Newberry's United States District Court, Admiralty Reports [*A publication*] (DLA)
NewbNk......	Newbridge Networks, Inc. [*Associated Press*] (SAG)
Newbon	Newbon's Private Bills Reports [*1895-99*] [*England*] [*A publication*] (DLA)
New Br	New Brunswick Reports [*A publication*] (DLA)
New Br Eq (Can)...	New Brunswick Equity Reports [*Canada*] [*A publication*] (DLA)
New Br Eq Cas (Can)...	New Brunswick Equity Cases [*Canada*] [*A publication*] (DLA)
New Br R.....	New Brunswick Reports [*A publication*] (DLA)
Newbyth	Newbyth's Manuscript Decisions, Scotch Session Cases [*A publication*] (DLA)
NEWC	Newcastle [*Name of two cities in England*]
NEWC	Newcor, Inc. [*NASDAQ symbol*] (SAG)
NewCare.....	New Care Health Corp. [*Associated Press*] (SAG)
New Cas......	New Cases (Bingham's New Cases) [*A publication*] (DLA)
New Cas Eq...	New Cases in Equity [*8, 9 Modern Reports*] [*1721-55*] [*A publication*] (DLA)
NEWCC	Northeastern Weed Control Conference [*Later, NEWSS*] (EA)
NEWC L.......	Newcastle-Under-Lyme [*City in England*] (ROG)
NEWCN.......	New Construction [*Navy*]
Newcor.......	Newcor, Inc. [*Associated Press*] (SAG)
NewDay......	New Day Beverage, Inc. [*Associated Press*] (SAG)
Newell........	Newell Co. [*Associated Press*] (SAG)
Newell........	Newell's Appeals Reports [*48-90 Illinois*] [*A publication*] (DLA)
Newell Defam...	Newell on Defamation, Slander, and Libel [*A publication*] (DLA)
Newell Eject...	Newell's Treatise on the Action of Ejectment [*A publication*] (DLA)
Newell Mal Pros...	Newell's Treatise on Malicious Prosecution [*A publication*] (DLA)
Newell Sland & L...	Newell on Slander and Libel [*A publication*] (DLA)
New Eng......	New England Reporter [*A publication*] (DLA)
New Eng Cons Music...	New England Conservatory of Music (GAGS)
NEWENGGRU...	New England Group (DNAB)
New Engl Univ Bull...	New England University. Bulletin [*A publication*]
New Eng R...	New England Reporter [*A publication*] (DLA)
New Eng Rep...	New England Reporter [*A publication*] (DLA)
New Eng Sch Law...	New England School of Law (GAGS)
New ER.......	New England Review [*A publication*] (BRI)
NEWF.........	Newfoundland [*with Labrador, a Canadian province*]
NewfEx.......	Newfield Exploration [*Associated Press*] (SAG)
NEWFLD	Newfoundland [*with Labrador, a Canadian province*]
Newfld LR ...	Newfoundland Law Reports [*A publication*] (DLA)
Newf LR	Newfoundland Law Reports [*A publication*] (DLA)
NEWFO	Newfoundland [*with Labrador, a Canadian province*]
Newfoundl LR...	Newfoundland Law Reports [*A publication*] (DLA)
Newfoundl R...	Newfoundland Reports [*A publication*] (DLA)
Newfoundl Sel Cas...	Newfoundland Select Cases [*A publication*] (DLA)
NEWFS	New England Wild Flower Society (EA)
Newf S Ct....	Newfoundland Supreme Court Decisions [*A publication*] (DLA)
Newf Sel Cas...	Newfoundland Select Cases [*A publication*] (DLA)

NEWH .... New Horizons Worldwide, Inc. [*NASDAQ symbol*] (SAG)
Newhal .... Newhall Land & Farming Co. [*Associated Press*] (SAG)
New Hamp... New Hampshire Reports [*A publication*] (DLA)
New Hamp R.. New Hampshire Reports [*A publication*] (DLA)
New Hamp Rep... New Hampshire Reports [*A publication*] (DLA)
New Hampshire Rep... New Hampshire Reports [*A publication*] (DLA)
NewHrz........ New Horizons Savings & Loan Association [*Associated Press*] (SAG)
NEWI .... New West Eyeworks [*NASDAQ symbol*] (TTSB)
NEWI .... New West Eyeworks, Inc. [*NASDAQ symbol*] (SAG)
NEWIL .... Northeast Wisconsin Intertype Libraries [*Library network*]
New Ir Jur... New Irish Jurist and Local Government Review [*1900-05*] [*A publication*] (DLA)
NEWISA ...... New England Women's Intercollegiate Sailing Association
New Jersey... New Jersey Law Reports [*A publication*] (DLA)
New Jersey Eq... New Jersey Equity Reports [*A publication*] (DLA)
New Jersey Equity... New Jersey Equity Reports [*A publication*] (DLA)
New Jersey Leg Rec... New Jersey Legal Record [*A publication*] (DLA)
New Jersey L Rev... New Jersey Law Review [*A publication*] (DLA)
New Jersey SBA Qu... New Jersey State Bar Association. Quarterly [*A publication*] (DLA)
New Journ... New Journalist [*A publication*]
NEWLC .... NATO Electronic Warfare Liaison Committee
Newl Ch PR... Newland's Chancery Practice [*A publication*] (DLA)
Newl Ch Prac... Newland's Chancery Practice [*A publication*] (DLA)
Newl Cont... Newland on Contracts [*1806*] [*A publication*] (DLA)
NEWLON...... New London, Connecticut [*Navy*]
NEWM .... New England and World Missions (EA)
NEW M .... New Mexico (ROG)
New Mag Cas... New Magistrates' Cases (Bittleston, Wise, and Parnell) [*1844-51*] [*A publication*] (DLA)
Newm Conv... Newman on Conveyancing [*A publication*] (DLA)
New Mex BA... New Mexico State Bar Association, Minutes [*A publication*] (DLA)
New Mex SBA... New Mexico State Bar Association, Report of Proceedings [*A publication*] (DLA)
NEWMOA...... Northeast Waste Management Officials Association
NEW MOONS... NASA Evaluation with Models of Optimized Nuclear Spacecraft
NewmtM...... Newmont Mining [*Associated Press*] (SAG)
New Nat Brev... New Natura Brevium [*A publication*] (DLA)
New NB ...... New Natura Brevium [*A publication*] (DSA)
NEwNE........ North Side Elementary School, East Williston, NY [*Library symbol*] [*Library of Congress*] (LCLS)
NEWOT .... Naval Electronic Warfare Operator Trainer (MCD)
NewOv .... Newscorp Overseas Ltd. [*Associated Press*] (SAG)
NEWP .... Newport [*England*]
NEWP .... Newport Corp. [*NASDAQ symbol*] (NQ)
NEWPEX ...... Northeast Wood Products Expo [*In company name, NEWPEX, Inc.*] (TSPED)
NEWPIL .... NADGE [*NATO Air Defense Ground Environment*] Early Warning Program Information Leaflet (NATG)
NEWPIN...... New Parent-Infant Network (AIE)
NEWPOSITREP... New [*Corrected*] Position Report (NVT)
New Pract Case... New Practice Cases [*1844-48*] [*A publication*] (DLA)
New Pr Cases... New Practice Cases [*1844-48*] [*A publication*] (DLA)
Newpt .... Newport Corp. [*Associated Press*] (SAG)
NEWQ .... Newquay [*Urban district in England*]
NEWR .... New England Realty Associates Ltd. [*NASDAQ symbol*] (NQ)
New R .... New Republic [*A publication*] (BRI)
NEWRADS ... Nuclear Explosion Warning and Radiological Data System
New Rep...... Bosanquet and Puller's New Reports, English Common Pleas [*1804-07*] [*A publication*] (DLA)
New Rep...... New Reports [*1862-65*] [*England*] [*A publication*] (DLA)
NEWRIT .... Northeast Water Resources Information Terminal (IID)
NEWRZ........ New Englad Rlty Assoc L.P. [*NASDAQ symbol*] (TTSB)
NEWS .... Naval Electronic Warfare Simulator
NEWS .... Neighborhood Environmental Workshops (EA)
NEWS .... NetWare Early-Warning System [*Frye Computer Systems, Inc.*] [*Computer science*] (PCM)
NEWS .... Network Extensible Window System [*Computer science*]
NEWS .... New England Wild Flower Society (EA)
NEWS .... New European Wide Warranty System [*General Motors Corp.*]
NEWS .... New Product Early Warning System
NewSAfr ...... New South Africa Fund [*Associated Press*] (SAG)
NEWSAR...... Nuclear Energy Waste Space Transportation and Removal (GFGA)
New Sci ...... New Scientist [*A publication*] (BRI)
NewsCm...... News Communications, Inc. [*Associated Press*] (SAG)
NEWSCOMP... Newspaper Composition (PDAA)
NewsCorp .... News Corp Ltd. [*Associated Press*] (SAG)
NewsCp .... [*The*] News Corp. Ltd. [*Associated Press*] (SAG)
New Series... Martin's Louisiana Reports, New Series [*A publication*] (DLA)
New Sess Cas... New Session Cases (Carrow, Hamerton, and Allen) [*1844-51*] [*A publication*] (DLA)
NEWSL .... Newsletter
Newsl Aust Coll Ed Qd... Australian College of Education. Queensland Chapter. Newsletter [*A publication*]
Newsl Aust Natn Ass Ment Hlth... Australian National Association for Mental Health. Newsletter [*A publication*]
Newsl Leg Act... Newsletter on Legislative Activities [*Council of Europe*] [*A publication*] (DLA)
Newsl Statist Soc Aust... Statistical Society of Australia. Newsletter [*A publication*]
NEWSLTR ..... Newsletter
NEWSS .... Northeastern Weed Science Society [*Formerly, NEWCC*] (EA)
NewSvg .... Newnan Savings Bank [*Associated Press*] (SAG)
NEW T .... Newcastle-Upon-Tyne [*City in England*] (ROG)
NEWT.......... Newton [*England*]
New TB....... New Technical Books [*A publication*] (BRI)

New Term Rep... Dowling and Ryland's English King's Bench Reports [*A publication*] (DLA)
New Term Rep... New Term Reports [*A publication*] (DLA)
NEWTS .... Naval Electronic Warfare Training System
NewWrld..... New World Communictions Corp. [*Associated Press*] (SAG)
New York..... New York Magazine [*A publication*] (BRI)
New York Att'y Gen Annual Rep... New York Attorney General Reports [*A publication*] (DLA)
New York City BA Bul... Bulletin. Association of the Bar of the City of New York [*A publication*] (DLA)
New York R... New York Court of Appeals Reports [*A publication*] (DLA)
New York Rep... New York Court of Appeals Reports [*A publication*] (DLA)
New York Supp... New York Supplement [*A publication*] (DLA)
New Yugo L... New Yugoslav Law [*A publication*] (DLA)
NEWZAD ...... New Zealand Army Detachment (CINC)
New Zeal Jur R... New Zealand Jurist Reports [*A publication*] (DLA)
New Zeal L... New Zealand Law Reports [*A publication*] (DLA)
New Zeal LR... New Zealand Law Reports [*A publication*] (DLA)
NEX............. National Exchange, Inc. [*McLean, VA*] [*Telecommunications*] (TSSD)
NEX............. Nonepoxide Xanthophyll [*Organic chemistry*]
NEX............. Northern Executive Aviation Ltd. [*British ICAO designator*] (FAAC)
NEX............. Nose to Ear to Xiphoid [*Medicine*]
N EX .... Not Exceeding [*Freight*]
NEXAFS ...... Near-Edge X-Ray Absorption Fine Structure [*For study of surfaces*]
NEXAIR .... Next Generation Upper Air System [*National Weather Service*]
NEXCO .... National Association of Export Companies [*New York, NY*] (EA)
NEXCOM ...... Navy Exchange Service Command
NexGen....... NexGen, Inc. [*Associated Press*] (SAG)
NEXRAD...... Next Generation Weather RADAR [*National Weather Service*]
Nexstar........ NeXstar Pharmaceuticals [*Associated Press*] (SAG)
NEXT........... Nationwide Evaluation of X-Ray Trends
NEXT........... NATO Experimental Tactics (NATG)
NEXT........... Near-End Crosstalk [*Bell System*]
NExt........... New Experiences in Teaching [*Mathematics*]
NEXT........... New/Experimental Techniques (MCD)
NEXT........... NextHealth, Inc. [*NASDAQ symbol*] (SAG)
NexT........... Nexus Telecommunication Systems Ltd. [*Associated Press*] (SAG)
NextelCm..... Nextel Communications [*Commercial firm Associated Press*] (SAG)
NextHlth...... NextHealth, Inc. [*Associated Press*] (SAG)
NEXUS .... Nature and Earth United with Science [*Brand of hair products*]
NEXUS .... Nucleus Expert User System (NITA)
NEXUS .... Numerical Examination of Urban Smog (IAA)
NexusTel...... Nexus Telecommunication Systems Ltd. [*Associated Press*] (SAG)
NEY............ Neomycin Egg Yolk [*Agar*] [*Microbiology*]
NEY............ Neyland [*British depot code*]
NEY............ Northeastern Yiddish [*Language, etc.*] (BJA)
NEYO .... New York City National Park Service Group
NEZP.......... Net Euphotic Zone Production [*Oceanography*]
NEZP.......... Nezperce Railroad Co. [*AAR code*]
NF.............. Air Vanuatu [*Airline code*] [*Australia*]
NF.............. Eaton Laboratories, Inc. [*Research code symbol*]
NF.............. EJA/Newport [*ICAO designator*] (AD)
NF.............. Fujisawa Pharmaceutical Co. [*Japan*] [*Research code symbol*]
NF.............. Nafcillin [*An antibiotic*]
nF.............. Nanofarad [*One billionth of a farad*]
NF.............. Nanofiltration
NF.............. Narodni Fronta [*National Front*] [*Former Czechoslovakia*] [*Political party*] (PPE)
NF.............. National Fine [*Thread*]
NF.............. National Forest (IIA)
NF.............. National Formulary [*A publication listing standard drugs*]
NF.............. National Foundation
NF.............. National Front [*British Political party*] (CDAI)
NF.............. Natural Flood (MCD)
NF.............. Natural Flood
NF.............. Natural Food (MCD)
NF.............. Near Face [*Technical drawings*]
NF.............. Nebramycin Factor [*An antibacterial compound*]
NF.............. Negro Female
NF.............. Neighborhood Final Fade
NF.............. Nephritic Factor [*Clinical medicine*]
NF.............. Nested or Flat [*Freight*]
NF.............. Neue Folge [*New Series*] [*Bibliography*] [*German*]
NF.............. Neurofibromatosis [*Medicine*]
NF.............. Neurofibromatosis, Inc. [*An association*] (EA)
NF.............. Neurofilament [*Neurophysiology*]
NF.............. Neutral Fraction
NF.............. Neutron Flux [*Nuclear energy*] (NRCH)
N/F............. Neutrons per Fission
NF.............. Newfoundland [*with Labrador, a Canadian province*] [*Postal code*]
NF.............. Newfoundland Reports [*A publication*] (DLA)
NF.............. New French [*Language, etc.*] (ROG)
NF.............. Newspaper Fund (EA)
NF.............. Nichibei Fujinkai [*An association*] (EA)
NF.............. Nickel Faced (DGA)
NF.............. Niederfrequenz [*Audio Frequency*] [*German military - World War II*]
NF.............. Nieman Foundation (EA)
NF.............. Nieuw Front [*New Front*] [*Suriname*] [*Political party*] (EY)
NF.............. Night Fighter Aircraft
NF.............. Night Frequency [*Aviation*] (IAA)
NF.............. Nitrofluoranthene [*Organic chemistry*]
NF.............. Nobel Foundation (EA)
NF.............. No Flash [*Phototypesetting*] (DGA)
NF.............. No Fly [*Shrewd tradesman*] [*Slang British*] (DSUE)
NF.............. No Fool

NF	No Form (AAG)
NF	No Funds [*Banking*]
n/f	No Funds (WDMC)
NF	Noise Factor
NF	Noise Figure
NF	Noise Frequency (MSA)
NF	Noise Fuse (MCD)
NF	None Found [*Medicine*]
NF	Nonferrous
NF	Nonfiction (NTCM)
NF	Nonfiler [*IRS*]
NF	Nonfiltered
NF	Non-Fragments (NITA)
NF	Nonfunction (AAMN)
NF	Nonfundable
NF	Nonwhite Female
NF	Noranda Forest, Inc. [*Toronto Stock Exchange symbol Vancouver Stock Exchange symbol*]
NF	Nordiska Fabriksarbetarefederationen [*Nordic Federation of Factory Workers Unions - NFFWU*] (EAIO)
NF	Nordmanns-Forbunder [*Norsemen's Federation*] (EA)
NF	Norfolk [*Virginia*] [*Navy Yard*]
NF	Norfolk Island [*ANSI two-letter standard code*] (CNC)
NF	Normal Flow [*Medicine*]
NF	Normal Form [*Database design rule*] [*Computer science*] (PCM)
NF	Normal Formula
NF	Normal Frequency [*Telecommunications*] (NTCM)
NF	Norman French [*Language, etc.*]
NF	Norsk Front [*Norwegian Front*] (PD)
NF	Northern Foundation [*Canada*] (EAIO)
NF	Northern French [*Language, etc.*] (ROG)
NF	North Following [*Astronomy*]
NF	Northumberland Fusiliers [*British military*] (DMA)
NF	Nose Fairing [*Missiles*]
NF	Nose Fuse [*Aviation*]
NF	Not Fertilized
NF	Not Fordable [*Maps and charts*]
NF	Not Found [*Telephone listing*] [*Telecommunications*] (TEL)
NF	Nouveau Franc [*New Franc*] [*Monetary unit Introduced in 1960*] [*France*]
NF	Nuclear Factor [*Cytology*]
NF	Nuclear Red Fast [*A dye*]
NF	Nutrition Foundation [*Later, ILSI-NF*]
NF	Royal Northumberland Fusiliers [*Military unit*] [*British*]
NF1	Neurofibromatosis Type 1 [*Medicine*]
NFA	Cast Metals Association (EA)
NFA	Naga Federal Army [*India*]
NFA	Natal Field Artillery [*British military*] (DMA)
NFA	National Faculty Association (NADA)
NFA	National Faculty Association of Community and Junior Colleges [*Later, NEA Higher Education Council*]
NFA	National Families in Action (EA)
NFA	National Farmers' Association [*Republic of Ireland*] (BI)
NFA	National Federation of Anglers [*British*] (BI)
NFA	National Film Archive [*British Film Institute*]
NFA	National Film, Television, and Sound Archives [*Ottawa*] [*UTLAS symbol*]
NFA	National Fire Academy
NFA	National Firearms Act
NFA	National Firearms Association [*Canada*]
NFA	National Fishermen's Association [*Australia*]
NFA	National Fitness Association [*Later, NHCA*] (EA)
NFA	National Florist Association (EA)
NFA	National Flute Association (EA)
NFA	National Food Administration
NFA	National Foremen's Association [*A union*] [*British*]
NFA	National Forensic Association (EA)
NFA	National Foundation for Asthma (EA)
NFA	National Foundry Association (EA)
NFA	National Franchisee Association (EA)
NFA	National Freedom Academy (EA)
NFA	National Front of Ahvaz [*Iran*]
NFA	National Frumps of America (EA)
NFA	National Futures Association (EA)
NFA	Natural Food Associates (EA)
NFA	Naval Fuel Annex
NFA	Net Financial Assets (BARN)
NFA	New Farmers of America [*Later, FFA*] (EA)
NFA	New Fighter Aircraft (MCD)
NFA	News and Feature Assistant (WDMC)
nfa	News and Feature Assistant [*An employee of a TV network*] (WDMC)
NFA	Night Fighter Association
NFA	Nitrogen Filling Assembly
NFA	Nixon Family Association (EA)
NFA	No Fire Area [*Military*] (INF)
NFA	No Fixed Abode
NFA	No Further Action
NFA	Nondeterministic Finite Automaton
NFA	Non-Financial Agreement
NFA	Non-Food Agricultural [*Commodity Price Index*] (ECON)
NFA	Nonhydroxylated Fatty Acid [*Organic chemistry*]
NFA	North Flying AS [*Denmark ICAO designator*] (FAAC)
NFA	Northwest Festivals Association (EA)
NFA	Northwest Fisheries Association (EA)
NFA	Northwest Forestry Association (EA)

NFA	Not for Attribution [*Military*]
NFA	Not Forgotten Association [*British*] (DBA)
NFA	Nuclear Free America (EA)
NFA	Nutritional Foods Association [*Australia*]
NFAA	National Federation of Advertising Agencies [*Later, IFAA*] (EA)
NFAA	National Field Archery Association (EA)
NFAA	National Forum for the Advancement of Aquatics (EA)
NFAA	National Foundation for Advancement in the Arts (EA)
NFAA	Neuro-Fibromatosis Association of Australia
NFAA	Nordic Forwarding Agents Association [*Defunct*] (EA)
NFAA	Northern Federation of Advertisers Associations [*Stockholm, Sweden*] (EAIO)
NFAA	Nuclear Fuel Assurance Act
NFAAUM	National Federation of Asian American United Methodists (EA)
NFAC	Arnolds Cove Public Library, Newfoundland [*Library symbol National Library of Canada*] (NLC)
NFAC	National Food and Agricultural Council (NADA)
NFAC	National Foreign Assessment Center [*CIA*]
NFAC	National Foundation for Asthmatic Children at Tucson [*Later, NFA*] (EA)
NFAC	National Franchise Association Coalition (EA)
NFAC	National Full-Scale Aerodynamics Complex [*Ames Research Center, CA*] [*NASA*]
NFAC	Naval Facilities Engineering Command Headquarters
NFACJC	National Faculty Association of Community and Junior Colleges [*Later, NEA Higher Education Council*]
NFADB	National Family Association for Deaf-Blind [*Sponsored by the Helen Keller National Center for Deaf-Blind Youths and Adults (HKNC)*] (PAZ)
NFAF	Naval Fleet Auxiliary Force
NFAH	National Federation of American Hungarians (EA)
NFAH	National Foundation on the Arts and Humanities
NFAHA	National Foundation on the Arts and Humanities Act [*1965*]
NFAHS	National Foundation for Affordable Housing Solutions (EA)
NFaiB	Board of Cooperative Educational Services - Monroe I, Fairport, NY [*Library symbol Library of Congress*] (LCLS)
NFAIO	National Federation of Asian Indian Organizations in America [*Later, NFIAA*] (EA)
NFAIS	National Federation of Abstracting and Indexing Services (NITA)
NFAIS	National Federation of Abstracting and Information Services (EA)
NFAIS	National Federation of American Information Services [*International Council of Scientific Unions*]
NFAL	National Foundation of Arts and Letters (WDAA)
NFAM	National Foundation for the Australian Musical
NFAM	Network File Access Method
NFAN	National Filter Analysis Network [*Environmental Protection Agency*] (GFGA)
NFANA	Norwegian Fjord Association of North America (EA)
NF & F	Natural Food and Farming [*A publication*]
NFAP	Nerve Fiber Action Potentials [*Neurophysiology*]
NFAP	Network File Access Protocol
NFAP	Nuclear Free Australia Party [*Political party*]
NFAPC	National Fisheries Adjustment Program Committee [*Australia*]
NFar	Farmingdale Public Library, Farmingdale, NY [*Library symbol Library of Congress*] (LCLS)
NFAR	No Further Action Required (DAVI)
NFarB	BioResearch, Inc., Farmingdale, NY [*Library symbol Library of Congress*] (LCLS)
NFarEE	East Memorial Elementary School, Farmingdale, NY [*Library symbol Library of Congress*] (LCLS)
NFarF	Fairchild-Hiller Corp. [*Later, Fairchild Industries, Inc.*], Republic Aviation Division, Farmingdale, NY [*Library symbol Library of Congress*] (LCLS)
NFarHS	Howitt School, Farmingdale, NY [*Library symbol*] [*Library of Congress*] (LCLS)
NFarNE	Northside Elementary School, Farmingdale, NY [*Library symbol*] [*Library of Congress*] (LCLS)
NFARS	NORAD Forward Automated Reporting System (MCD)
NFarSH	Farmingdale Senior High School, Farmingdale, NY [*Library symbol*] [*Library of Congress*] (LCLS)
NFarUA	State University of New York, Agricultural and Technical College at Farmingdale, Farmingdale, NY [*Library symbol Library of Congress*] (LCLS)
NFarWP	Woodward Parkway School, Farmingdale, NY [*Library symbol*] [*Library of Congress*] (LCLS)
NFAS	National Field Archery Society [*British*] (DBA)
NFASG	National Fashion Accessories Salesmen's Guild (EA)
NFAT	Nuclear Factor of Activated T-Cells [*Genetics*]
NFay	Fayetteville Free Library, Fayetteville, NY [*Library symbol Library of Congress*] (LCLS)
NFB	Booth Memorial Hospital, Flushing, NY [*Library symbol Library of Congress*] (LCLS)
NFB	Mount Clemens, MI [*Location identifier FAA*] (FAAL)
NFB	National Federation of the Blind (EA)
NFB	National Film Board [*Canada*] (WDMC)
NFB	National Film Board of Canada [*UTLAS symbol*]
NFB	Naval Frontier Base
NFB	Negative Feedback (DEN)
NFB	New Fibers International [*Vancouver Stock Exchange symbol*]
NFB	Niagara Frontier Tariff Bureau, Inc., Buffalo NY [*STAC*]
NFB	Node of First-Fruiting Branch [*Botany*] (OA)
NFB	No Feed Back (AEBS)
NFB	Nonfermenting Bacteria
NFB	North Fork Bancorp [*NYSE symbol*] (SPSG)
NFBA	National Family Business Association [*Tarzana, CA*] (EA)

NFBA	National Farm Borrowers Association (EA)
NFBA	National Food Brokers Association (EA)
NFBA	National Frame Builders Association (EA)
NFBC	National Family Business Council [*Northbrook, IL*] (EA)
NFBC	National Film Board of Canada
NFBC	Newfoundland Base Command [*Army World War II*]
NFBC	North Fork Bancorp (MHDW)
NFBCA	National Federation of Blind Citizens of Australia
NFBF	Bishops Falls Public Library, Newfoundland [*Library symbol National Library of Canada*] (NLC)
NFBF	National Farm Bureau Federation
NFBG	National Federation of Badger Groups [*British*] (DBA)
NFBI	Bell Island Public Library, Newfoundland [*Library symbol National Library of Canada*] (NLC)
NFBI	Netherlands Flower-Bulb Institute [*Defunct*] (EA)
NFBI	Nonresidential Fixed Business Investment (MCD)
NFBN	National Food Bank Network (EA)
NFBO	Bonavista Public Library, Newfoundland [*Library symbol National Library of Canada*] (NLC)
NFBOT	Botwood Public Library, Newfoundland [*Library symbol National Library of Canada*] (NLC)
NFBPA	National Forum for Black Public Administrators (EA)
NFBPM	National Federation of Builders' and Plumbers' Merchants [*British*] (BI)
NFBPT	National Federation for Biblio/Poetry Therapy (EA)
NFBPW	National Federation of Business and Professional Women's Clubs (WGA)
NFBPWC	National Federation of Business and Professional Women's Clubs (EA)
NFBQ	Rural District Memorial Library, Badgers Quay, Newfoundland [*Library symbol National Library of Canada*] (NLC)
NFBR	Bay Roberts Public Library, Newfoundland [*Library symbol National Library of Canada*] (NLC)
NFBR	National Foundation for Biomedical Research [*An association*]
NFBR	National Foundation for Brain Research (EA)
NFBRI	Brigus Public Library, Newfoundland [*Library symbol National Library of Canada*] (NLC)
NFBS	National Freehold Building Society [*British*]
NFBSS	National Federation of Bakery Students' Societies [*British*] (BI)
NFBTE	National Federation of Building Trades Employers [*British*] (DCTA)
NFBTO	National Federation of Building Trades Operatives [*British*]
NFBU	Buchans Public Library, Newfoundland [*Library symbol National Library of Canada*] (NLC)
NFBU	National Federation of Bus Users [*British*]
NFBU	National Fire Brigades Union (ROG)
NFBUK	National Federation for the Blind [*British*] (DBA)
NFBUR	Burgeo Public Library, Newfoundland [*Library symbol National Library of Canada*] (NLC)
NFBURI	Burin Public Library, Newfoundland [*Library symbol National Library of Canada*] (NLC)
NFBV	Baie Verte Public Library, Newfoundland [*Library symbol National Library of Canada*] (NLC)
NFBWA	National Federation of Buddhist Women's Associations [*Later, BCAFBWA*] (EA)
NFBWW	Nordic Federation of Building and Wood Workers (EA)
NFC	Carbonear Public Library, Newfoundland [*Library symbol National Library of Canada*] (NLC)
NFC	Name Formula Card
NFC	National Farm Coalition [*Defunct*] (EA)
NFC	National Federated Craft (EA)
NFC	National Fenestration Council [*Later, PGMC*] (EA)
NFC	National Fertility Center (DAVI)
NFC	National Film Carriers (EA)
NFC	National Finance Center (USDC)
NFC	National Firebird Club (EA)
NFC	National Fire Code
NFC	National Food Conference Association (EA)
NFC	National Football Conference [*of NFL*]
NFC	National Forensic Center (EA)
NFC	National Fraternal Congress [*Later, NFCA*]
NFC	National Freight Consortium (ODBW)
NFC	National Freight Corp. [*British*]
NFC	National Fructose Center (EA)
NFC	National Fund Chairman [*or Co-chairman*] [*Red Cross*]
NFC	Native Forest Council (EA)
NFC	Navy Federal Credit Union
NFC	Navy Finance Center
NFC	Negative Factor Counting
NFC	Negative Feedback Circuit
nfc	Newfoundland [*MARC country of publication code Library of Congress*] (LCCP)
NFC	News for Farmer Cooperatives [*A publication*]
NFC	Newsline Fan Club (EA)
NFC	Newspaper Features Council (EA)
NFC	NFC Ltd. [*Associated Press*] (SAG)
NFC	NFC PLC [*AMEX symbol*] (SPSG)
NFC	NFC plc ADS [*AMEX symbol*] (TTSB)
NFC	Nighttime Fatal Crash
NFC	No Further Clearance Required (KSC)
NFC	No Further Consequences (NRCH)
NFC	Nonfavorably Considered (DAVI)
NFC	Nordisk Forening for Cellforskning [*Nordic Society for Cell Biology - NSCB*] (EAIO)
NFC	Nose Fairing Container [*Missiles*]
NFC	Not Favorably Considered

NFC	Nuclear Fuel Cycle (NUCP)
NFC	Numbered Fleet Commander (DOMA)
NFCA	Carmanville Public Library, Newfoundland [*Library symbol National Library of Canada*] (NLC)
NFCA	National Federation of Community Associations [*British*] (DI)
NFCA	National Floor Covering Association [*Canada*] (EAIO)
NFCA	National Foster Care Association [*British*] (EAIO)
NFCA	National Fraternal Congress of America [*Naperville, IL*] (EA)
NFCA	National Fuel Credit Association [*Defunct*]
NFCA	Near-Field Calibration Array (PDAA)
NFCA	Nonfuel Core Array [*Nuclear energy*] (NRCH)
NFCAA	National Fencing Coaches Association of America (EA)
NFCADA	National Family Council Against Drug Abuse [*Formerly, NFCDA*] (EA)
NFC(ALLOT)..	Navy Finance Center (Allotments Division) (DNAB)
NFCARW	National Federation of Cuban-American Republican Women (EA)
NFCAT	Joseph E. Clouter Memorial Library, Catalina, Newfoundland [*Library symbol National Library of Canada*] (NLC)
NFCB	Corner Brook City Public Library, Newfoundland [*Library symbol National Library of Canada*] (NLC)
NFCB	National Federation of Community Broadcasters (EA)
NFCBF	Newfoundland Department of Forest Resources and Lands, Corner Brook, New Foundland [*Library symbol National Library of Canada*] (NLC)
NFCBFT	Fisher Institute of Applied Arts and Technology, Corner Brook, Newfoundland [*Library symbol National Library of Canada*] (NLC)
NFCBM	Sir Wilfred Grenfell College, Memorial University, Corner Brook, Newfoundland [*Library symbol National Library of Canada*] (NLC)
NFCBR	Regional Library, Corner Brook, Newfoundland [*Library symbol National Library of Canada*] (NLC)
NFCBRO	National Federation of Citizen Band Radio Operators (EA)
NFCBW	Western Memorial Hospital, Corner Brook, Newfoundland [*Library symbol National Library of Canada*] (NLC)
NFCC	National Family Conciliation Council [*British*] (DI)
NFCC	National Farm-City Council (EA)
NFCC	National Foundation for Consumer Credit [*Silver Spring, MD*] (EA)
NFCC	National Free Clinic Council [*Superseded by NCAHCP*]
NFCC	Neighborhood Family-Care Center (MEDA)
NFC(CAD)	Navy Finance Center (Central Accounts Division) (DNAB)
NFCCE	National Fellowship of Child Care Executives (EA)
NFC-CLEVE...	Navy Finance Center - Cleveland [*Ohio*] (DNAB)
NFCCS	National Federation of Catholic College Students [*Defunct*] (EA)
NFCDA	National Family Council on Drug Addiction [*Later, NFCADA*] (EA)
NFCDCU	National Federation of Community Development Credit Unions [*New York, NY*] (EA)
NFCDS	National Federation of Clubs for Divorced and Separated [*British*] (BI)
NFCE	Centreville Public Library, Newfoundland [*Library symbol National Library of Canada*] (NLC)
NFCEO	National Foundation for Conservation and Environmental Officers [*Defunct*] (EA)
NFCF	Churchill Falls Public Library, Newfoundland [*Library symbol National Library of Canada*] (NLC)
NFCF	National Federation of City Farms [*British*] (EAIO)
NFCG	National Federation of Consumer Groups [*British*] (ILCA)
NFCGA	National Federation of Constructional Glass Associations [*British*] (BI)
NFCGC	National Federation of Coffee Growers of Colombia [*See also FNCC*] (EA)
NFCGH	Carbonear General Hospital, Newfoundland [*Library symbol National Library of Canada*] (NLC)
NFCH	Cow Head Public Library, Newfoundland [*Library symbol National Library of Canada*] (NLC)
NFCH	National Foundation for the Chemically Hypersensitive (EA)
NFCI	Change Islands Public Library, Newfoundland [*Library symbol National Library of Canada*] (NLC)
NFCI	National Federation of Clay Industries [*British*] (BI)
NFCIS	Nuclear Fuel Cycle Information System [*Database*] [*International Atomic Energy Agency*] [*United Nations*] (DUND)
NFCJ	National Forum on Criminal Justice [*Formerly, NICD*] [*Inactive*] (EA)
NFCL	Clarenville Public Library, Newfoundland [*Library symbol National Library of Canada*] (NLC)
NFC-L	National Fisheries Center - Leetown [*Department of the Interior*] (GRD)
NFCM	National Front Constitutional Movement [*British*]
NFCO	Cormack Public Library, Newfoundland [*Library symbol National Library of Canada*] (NLC)
NFCO	National Federation of Community Organizations [*British*] (EAIO)
NFCP	Channel/Port Aux Basques Public Library, Newfoundland [*Library symbol National Library of Canada*] (NLC)
NFCPG	National Federation of Catholic Physicians' Guilds (EA)
NFCPO	National Forum of Catholic Parent Organizations [*Defunct*] (EA)
NFCR	National Foundation for Cancer Research (EA)
NFCRC	National Fisheries Contaminant Research Center (EA)
NFCS	National Federation of Catholic Seminarians [*Defunct*] (EA)
NFCS	National Federation of Construction Supervisors [*British*] (BI)
NFCS	Naval Field Contracting System (AAGC)
NFCS	Night-Fire [*Rifle*] Control Sight [*Army*]
NFCS	Nuclear Forces Communications Satellite
NFCSG	Cape St. George Public Library, Newfoundland [*Library symbol National Library of Canada*] (NLC)
NFCSIT	National Federation of Cold Storage and Ice Trades [*British*] (BI)
NFCT	National Federation of Class Teachers (AIE)
NFCT	Nonfederal Control Tower [*For chart use only*]
NFCTA	National Federation of Continuative Teachers' Associations [*British*]

NFCTA .... National Federation of Corn Trade Associations [*British*] (BI)
NFCTA .... National Fibre Can and Tube Association [*Later, CCTI*] (EA)
NFCU .... Navy Federal Credit Union
NFCUS .... National Federation of Canadian University Students
NFCW .... Cartwright Public Library, Newfoundland [*Library symbol National Library of Canada*] (BIB)
NFC-WASH.... Navy Finance Center - Washington, DC (DNAB)
NFCYM .... National Federation for Catholic Youth Ministry (EA)
NFD .... Dover Public Library, Newfoundland [*Library symbol National Library of Canada*] (BIB)
NFD .... Eurowings (NFD & RFG Luftverhehrs AG) [*Germany ICAO designator*] (FAAC)
NFD .... National Faculty Directory [*A publication*]
NFD .... National Fax Directory [*A publication*]
NFD .... National Federation for Decency (EA)
NFD .... National Federation of Drapers and Allied Traders Ltd. [*Republic of Ireland*] (BI)
NFD .... Naval Fuel Depot
NFD .... Neurofibrillary Degeneration [*Medicine*]
NFD .... Neutron Flux Density [*Nuclear energy*]
NFD .... Newfoundland [*with Labrador, a Canadian province*]
NFD .... Newfoundland Tracking Station
NFD .... No Fixed Date
NFD .... No Foreign Dissemination [*Intelligence classification*] (MCD)
NFD .... Norfolk, Franklin & Danville Railway Co. [*AAR code*]
NFD .... Northern Frontier District [*Kenya*]
NFD .... Nueva Fuerza Democratica [*New Democratic Force*] [*Colorado Political party*] (EY)
NFDA .... National Fastener Distributors Association (EA)
NFDA .... National Food Distributors Association (EA)
NFDA .... National Funeral Directors Association (EA)
NFDC .... Dark Cove Public Library, Newfoundland [*Library symbol National Library of Canada*] (NLC)
NFDC .... National Father's Day Committee (EA)
NFDC .... National Federation of Demolition Contractors [*British*] (EAIO)
NFDC .... National Fertilizer Development Center [*Tennessee Valley Authority*] [*Muscle Shoals, AL*]
NFDC .... National Flight Data Center [*FAA*]
NFDCAMD.... National Food, Drug, and Cosmetic Association of Manufacturers and Distributors [*Defunct*] (EA)
NFDD .... National Flight Data Digest [*FAA*] (TAG)
NFDF .... National Flag Day Foundation (EA)
NFDH .... Daniels Harbour Public Library, Newfoundland [*Library symbol National Library of Canada*] (NLC)
NFDH .... National Foundation of Dentistry for the Handicapped (EA)
NFDL .... Deer Lake Public Library, Newfoundland [*Library symbol National Library of Canada*] (NLC)
NFDM .... Nonfat Dry Milk
NFDMA .... National Funeral Directors and Morticians Association (EA)
NFDPM .... National Federation of Data Processing Manufacturing (NITA)
NFDPS .... National Flight Data Processing System [*ICAO*] (DA)
NFDR .... Neurofacial-Digitorenal Syndrome [*Medicine*] (DMAA)
NFDRS .... National Fire Danger Rating System [*US Forest Service*]
NFDW .... National Federation of Democratic Women (EA)
NFE............. Fentress, VA [*Location identifier FAA*] (FAAL)
NFE............. National Faculty Exchange (EA)
NFE............. Naval Facilities Engineering Command, Alexandria, VA [*OCLC symbol*] (OCLC)
NFE............. Nearly Free Electron [*Physics*] (OA)
NFE............. Network Front End
NFE............. Nitride Forming Element [*Metal treating*]
NFE............. Nitrogen-Free Extract [*Analytical chemistry*]
NFE............. Nonformal Education
NFE............. Nose Fairing Exit [*Missiles*]
NFE............. Not Fully Equipped [*of aircraft*] [*Air Force*]
NFEA .... National Federated Electrical Association (MHDB)
NFEA .... National Federation of Export Associations [*New York, NY*] (EA)
NFEA .... Newspaper Farm Editors of America (EA)
NFEA .... Non-Fleet Experienced Aviator (NVT)
NFEAC .... National Foundation for Education in American Citizenship (EA)
NFEC .... National Food and Energy Council (EA)
NFEC .... National Foundation for Environmental Control (EA)
NFEC .... Naval Facilities Engineering Command [*Formerly, Bureau of Yards and Docks*] (IEEE)
NFEC .... Newspaper Food Editors Conference (EA)
NFECC .... National Fusion Energy Computer Center [*Lawrence Livermore National Laboratory*] (MCD)
NFED .... National Foundation for Ectodermal Dysplasias (EA)
NFEF .... National Free Enterprise Foundation [*Australia*]
NFER .... National Foundation for Educational Research in England and Wales (IID)
NFER .... National Foundation for Eye Research (EA)
NFER .... Nonferrous
NFERF .... National Fisheries Education and Research Foundation (EA)
NFET .... N-Channel Junction Field-Effect Transistor (IDOE)
NFETA .... National Foundry and Engineering Training Association [*British*]
NFETM .... National Federation of Engineers' Tools Manufacturers (MHDB)
NFEW .... National Forum for Executive Women [*Washington, DC*] (EA)
NFEWA .... Newspaper Food Editors and Writers Association (EA)
NFF............. Fogo Public Library, Newfoundland [*Library symbol National Library of Canada*] (NLC)
NFF............. Jacksonville, FL [*Location identifier FAA*] (FAAL)
NFF............. Natal Field Force [*British military*] (DMA)
NFF............. National Fatherland Front [*Afghanistan*] [*Political party*] (FEA)
NFF............. National Federation of Fishermen [*Inactive*] (EA)

NFF............. National Federation of Fishmongers [*British*] (DBA)
NFF............. National Fitness Foundation (EA)
NFF............. National Flag Foundation (EA)
NFF............. National Flood Frequency Program [*Computer science*]
NFF............. National Football Foundation and Hall of Fame (EA)
NFF............. National Forum Foundation (EA)
NFF............. National Froebel Foundation [*British*] (BI)
NFF............. Naval Fuel Facility
NFF............. Nemzeti Fueggetlensegi Front [*National Independence Front*] [*Hungary Political party*] (PPE)
NFF............. New Forests Fund (EA)
NFF............. No Fault Found (MCD)
NFF............. No Frills Fund
Nff............. Nordisk Forening for Folkendansforskning [*Nordic Association for Folk Dance Research*] [*Sweden*] (EAIO)
NFF............. Nuclear Freeze Foundation [*Defunct*] (EA)
NFF............. Numbered Fleet Flagship [*Navy*]
NFFA........... Ba [*Fiji*] [*ICAO location identifier*] (ICLI)
NFFA........... National Flying Farmers Association [*Later, International Flying Farmers*]
NFFA........... National Folk Festival Association [*Later, National Council for the TraditionalArts*]
NFFA........... National Frozen Food Association (EA)
NFFAO .... National FFA [*Future Farmers of America*] Organization (EA)
NFFC........... Nancy Fisher Fan Club (EA)
NFFC........... National Family Farm Coalition (EA)
NFFC........... National Fantasy Fan Club for Disneyana Enthusiasts
NFFC........... National Film Finance Corp. [*British*] (BI)
NFFDA .... National Frozen Food Distributors Association [*Later, NFFA*]
NFFDF .... National Fraternal Flag Day Foundation [*Defunct*] (EA)
NFFE........... National Federation of Federal Employees (EA)
NFFF........... Nandi [*Fiji*] [*ICAO location identifier*] (ICLI)
NFFF........... National Fantasy Fan Federation
NFFF........... National Federation of Fish Friers [*British*] (BI)
NFFGB .... National Federation of Flemish Giant Breeders [*Later, NFFGRB*]
NFFGRB ...... National Federation of Flemish Giant Rabbit Breeders (EA)
NFFH .... Fox Harbour Public Library, Newfoundland [*Library symbol National Library of Canada*] (NLC)
NFFI........... Not Fit for Issue [*Navy*]
NFFL........... Northern Forest Fire Laboratory [*Later, Intermountain Fire Sciences Laboratory*] [*Research center*] (RCD)
NFFN........... Nandi/International [*Fiji*] [*ICAO location identifier*] (ICLI)
NFFO .... Fortune Public Library, Newfoundland [*Library symbol National Library of Canada*] (NLC)
NFFO .... Malolo Lailai [*Fiji*] [*ICAO location identifier*] (ICLI)
NFFO .... National Federation of Fishermen's Organisations (EAIO)
NFFO .... Non-Fossil Fuel Obligation [*Pronounced "Noffo"*] [*Nuclear power*]
NFFPT .... National Federation of Fruit and Potato Trades [*British*] (BI)
NFFQO .... National Federation of Freestone Quarry Owners [*British*] (BI)
NFFR .... Freshwater Public Library, Newfoundland [*Library symbol National Library of Canada*] (NLC)
NFFR .... National Foundation for Facial Reconstruction (EA)
NFFR .... Rabi [*Fiji*] [*ICAO location identifier*] (ICLI)
NFFS........... National Foundation of Funeral Service (EA)
NFFS........... Non-Ferrous Founders Society (EA)
NFFTU .... National Federation of Furniture Trade Unions [*British*] (BI)
NFFWU .... Nordic Federation of Factory Workers Unions (EA)
NFG............. Gander Public Library, Newfoundland [*Library symbol National Library of Canada*] (NLC)
NFG............. Nagaland Federal Government [*India*]
NFG............. National Freight Group
NFG............. National Fuel Gas Co. [*NYSE symbol*] (SPSG)
NFG............. Natl Fuel Gas [*NYSE symbol*] (TTSB)
NFG............. Northwest Fruit Growers (EA)
NFG............. Oceanside, CA [*Location identifier FAA*] (FAAL)
NFGA.......... Garnish Public Library, Newfoundland [*Library symbol National Library of Canada*] (NLC)
NFGAU........ Gaultois Public Library, Newfoundland [*Library symbol National Library of Canada*] (BIB)
NFGB.......... Grand Bank Public Library, Newfoundland [*Library symbol National Library of Canada*] (NLC)
NFGBM .... Medical Library, Melville Hospital, Goose-Bay, Newfoundland [*Library symbol National Library of Canada*] (BIB)
NFGBM .... National Fellowship of Grace Brethren Ministers (EA)
NFGC.......... National Federation of Grain Cooperatives [*Later, NCFC*] (EA)
NFGCA .... National Federation of Grandmother Clubs of America (EA)
NFGF .... Regional Library, Grand Falls, Newfoundland [*Library symbol National Library of Canada*] (NLC)
NFGFC .... Central Region Libraries, Grand Falls, Newfoundland [*Library symbol National Library of Canada*] (NLC)
NFGFH........ Central Newfoundland Hospital, Grand Falls, Newfoundland [*Library symbol National Library of Canada*] (NLC)
NFGFHA...... Harmsworth Public Library, Grand Falls, Newfoundland [*Library symbol National Library of Canada*] (NLC)
NFGJPH...... James Paton Memorial Hospital, Gander, Newfoundland [*Library symbol National Library of Canada*] (NLC)
NFGL .... Glenwood Public Library, Newfoundland [*Library symbol National Library of Canada*] (NLC)
NFGLO........ Glovertown Public Library, Newfoundland [*Library symbol National Library of Canada*] (NLC)
NFGMIC ...... National Federation of Grange Mutual Insurance Companies [*Glastonbury, CT*] (EA)
NFGND........ National Foundation for Genetics and Neuromuscular Disease [*Later, NGF*]
NFGNE......... National Fund for Graduate Nursing Education [*Defunct*]

NFGO .... Goulds Public Library, Newfoundland [*Library symbol National Library of Canada*] (BIB)
NFGOCM ...... National Forum of Greek Orthodox Church Musicians (EA)
NFGOPC ...... National Federation of the Grand Order of Pachyderm Clubs (EA)
NFGR .... Greenspond Public Library, Newfoundland [*Library symbol National Library of Canada*] (NLC)
NFGS .... National Federation of Gramophone Societies (EAIO)
NFGS .... National Fenton Glass Society (EA)
NFH .... Holyrood Public Library, Newfoundland [*Library symbol National Library of Canada*] (BIB)
NFH .... National Fish Hatchery
NFH .... Native Field Hospital [*British military*] (DMA)
NFH .... Nonfamilial Hematuria [*Medicine*] (DMAA)
NFHA .... National Federation of Housing Associations [*British*] (DBA)
NFHA .... National Fox Hunters Association (EA)
NFHANA ...... Norwegian Fjord Horse Association of North America [*Later, NFANA*] (EA)
NFHAS .... National Faculty of Humanities, Arts, and Sciences (EA)
NFHB .... Harbour Breton Public Library, Newfoundland [*Library symbol National Library of Canada*] (NLC)
NFHBA .... Hare Bay Public Library, Newfoundland [*Library symbol National Library of Canada*] (NLC)
NFHC .... National Federation of Hispanics in Communication (EA)
NFHC .... National Federation of Housing Coops [*British*] (DBA)
NFHC .... National Federation of Housing Counselors (EA)
NFHC .... National Foot Health Council [*Defunct*] (EA)
NFHC .... National Foundation for History of Chemistry (EA)
NFHCF ...... National Flotation Health Care Foundation (EA)
NFHD .... National Foundation for the Handicapped and Disabled [*Defunct*] (EA)
NFHE .... Hermitage Public Library, Newfoundland [*Library symbol National Library of Canada*] (NLC)
NFHE .... Non-Irradiated Fuel Handling Equipment [*Nuclear energy*] (NRCH)
NFHEA .... National Farm Home Editors Association [*Defunct*] (EA)
NFHG .... Harbour Grace Public Library, Newfoundland [*Library symbol National Library of Canada*] (NLC)
NFHH .... Harrys Harbour Public Library, Newfoundland [*Library symbol National Library of Canada*] (NLC)
NFhM .... Medical Society of the County of Queens, Forest Hills, NY [*Library symbol Library of Congress*] (LCLS)
NFHO .... Caaf Ho Nandi [*Fiji*] [*ICAO location identifier*] (ICLI)
NFHO .... National Federation of Housestaff Organizations (EA)
NFHPER ...... National Foundation for Health, Physical Education, and Recreation [*Defunct*]
NFHRL .... National Fish Health Research Laboratory [*Department of the Interior*] [*Kearneysville, WV*] (GRD)
NFHTP .... National Federation of Hebrew Teachers and Principals [*Defunct*] (EA)
NFHV .... Happy Valley Public Library, Newfoundland [*Library symbol National Library of Canada*] (NLC)
NFI .... Narrow Fabrics Institute (EA)
NFI .... National Fisheries Center (USDC)
NFI .... National Fisheries Center [*Marine science*] (OSRA)
NFI .... National Fisheries Institute (EA)
NFI .... Natural Food Institute [*Defunct*] (EA)
NFI .... Naturfreunde-Internationale [*International Friends of Nature - IFN*] (EAIO)
NFI .... Net Fundable Issues (DNAB)
NFI .... News Features of India [*Press agency*]
NFI .... New Signet Resources [*Vancouver Stock Exchange symbol*]
NFI .... Nielsen Food Index [*Marketing*] (DOAD)
NFI .... No Further Service (Inspections)
NFI .... Noise Figure Indicator
NFI .... Not Further Identified (MCD)
NFIA .... National Feed Ingredients Association (EA)
NFIA .... National Flood Insurers Association [*Defunct*] (EA)
NFIA .... National Forest Industries Association [*Australia*]
NFIA .... Nonappropriated Fund Instrumentalities Act
NFIAA .... National Federation of Indian American Associations (EA)
NFIB .... National Federation of Independent Business [*San Mateo, CA*] (EA)
NFIB .... National Foreign Intelligence Board [*Formerly, USIB*] [*Military*]
NFIC .... National Foundation for Ileitis and Colitis (EA)
NFIC .... National Fraud Information Center
NFICA .... National Federation Interscholastic Coaches Association (EA)
NFICA .... National Forest Industries Campaign Association [*Australia*]
NFICSC ...... National Foundation for Ileitis and Colitis Sports Council (EA)
NFID .... National Foundation for Infectious Diseases (EA)
NFIE .... National Foundation for the Improvement of Education (EA)
NFIL .... Nuclear Factor Interleukin [*Genetics*]
NFIMA .... National Federation Interscholastic Music Association (EA)
NFIOA .... National Federation Interscholastic Officials Association (EA)
NFIP .... National Flood Insurance Program [*Federal Emergency Management Agency*]
NFIP .... National Foreign Intelligence Program [*DoD*]
NFIP .... National Foundation for Infantile Paralysis [*Later, MDBDF*]
NFIPS .... National Flood Insurance Program System [*Federal Emergency Management Agency*] (GFGA)
NFIR .... National Federation of Indian Railwaymen
NFIRF .... Nature Farming International Research Foundation (EAIO)
NFIRS .... National Fire Incident Reporting System [*Federal Emergency Management Agency*] (GFGA)
NFIS .... Naval Fighting Instruction School
NFISDA ...... National Federation Interscholastic Speech and Debate Association (EA)

NFisi .... Fishers Island Library Association, Fishers Island, NY [*Library symbol Library of Congress*] (LCLS)
NFisk .... Blodgett Memorial Library, Fishkill, NY [*Library symbol Library of Congress*] (LCLS)
NFISM .... National Federation of Iron and Steel Merchants [*British*] (BI)
NFISYD ...... National Federation of Independent Scrap Yard Dealers (EA)
NFITC .... National Forest Industries Training Council [*Australia*]
NFIU .... National Federation of Independent Unions (EA)
NFJ .... Milton, FL [*Location identifier FAA*] (FAAL)
NFJC .... National Foundation for Jewish Culture (EA)
NFJGD ...... National Foundation for Jewish Genetic Diseases (EA)
NFJM .... National Foundation for Junior Museums [*Later, NSYF*]
NFJMC ...... National Federation of Jewish Men's Clubs (EA)
NFK .... Norfolk Island [*ANSI three-letter standard code*] (CNC)
NFKK .... Nordisk Forening for Klinisk Kemi [*Scandinavian Society for Clinical Chemistry - SSCC*] [*Finland*] (EAIO)
NFKP .... Kings Point Public Library, Newfoundland [*Library symbol National Library of Canada*] (NLC)
NFKPA ...... National Federation of Kidney Patients Association [*British*] (DI)
NFL .... Fallon, NV [*Location identifier FAA*] (FAAL)
NFL .... Labrador City Public Library, Newfoundland [*Library symbol National Library of Canada*] (NLC)
NFL .... National Federation of Laymen (EA)
NFL .... National Film Library (NADA)
NFL .... National Football League (EA)
NFL .... National Forensic League (EA)
NFL .... National Foresters League (NADA)
NFL .... National Fund Leadership [*Group*] [*Red Cross*]
NFL .... Naval Standard Flange (MSA)
NFL .... Nerve Fiber Layer [*Neurology*] (DAVI)
NFL .... Newfoundland and Prince Edward Island Reports [*Maritime Law Book Co. Ltd.*] [*Canada Information service or system*] (CRD)
NFL .... Newfoundland Light & Power Co. Ltd. [*Toronto Stock Exchange symbol*]
NFL .... Newlands Field Laboratory [*University of Nevada - Reno*] [*Research center*] (RCD)
NFL .... No Field Lubrication (PDAA)
NFL .... No Fire Line [*Military*]
NFL .... No Phone Listed [*Cablegram marking*] [*British*]
NFL .... Normal Female Liver [*Hepatology*]
NFL .... Northaire Freight Lines Ltd. [*ICAO designator*] (FAAC)
NFL .... Nurses for Laughter
NFL .... Nuveen Ins FL Prem Inc. Muni [*NYSE symbol*] (TTSB)
NFL .... Nuveen Insured Florida Premium Income Municipal [*NYSE symbol*] (SPSG)
NFLA .... L'Anse Au Loup Public Library, Newfoundland [*Library symbol National Library of Canada*] (NLC)
NFLA .... National Football League Alumni (EA)
NFLA .... National Front for the Liberation of Angola (EA)
NFLC .... National Federation of Land Councils [*Australia*]
NFLCC ...... National Fishing Lure Collectors Club (EA)
NFLCP ...... National Federation of Local Cable Programmers (EA)
NFLD .... Nerve Fiber Layer Defect [*Medicine*] (DMAA)
NFLD .... Newfoundland [*with Labrador, a Canadian province*]
Nfld .... Newfoundland [*Canada*] (DD)
Nfld .... Newfoundland Supreme Court Decisions [*Canada*] [*A publication*] (DLA)
NFLD .... Northfield Laboratories [*NASDAQ symbol*] (TTSB)
NFLD .... Northfield Laboratories, Inc. [*NASDAQ symbol*] (SAG)
Nfld LR ...... Newfoundland Law Reports [*A publication*] (DLA)
Nfld R ...... Newfoundland Reports [*A publication*] (DLA)
Nfld Rev Stat... Newfoundland Revised Statutes [*Canada*] [*A publication*] (DLA)
NFLDS .... National Fire Loss Data System [*Military*] (PDAA)
Nfld Sel Cas... Newfoundland Select Cases [*A publication*] (DLA)
Nfld Stat .... Newfoundland Statutes [*Canada*] [*A publication*] (DLA)
NFLE .... Lewisporte Public Library, Newfoundland [*Library symbol National Library of Canada*] (NLC)
NFLF .... National Family Life Foundation (EA)
NFLF .... Nylon Full-Line Filter
NFLHB .... Blow Me Down School/Public Library, Lark Harbour, Newfoundland [*Library symbol National Library of Canada*] (NLC)
NFLI .... Northern Fraternal Life Insurance (EA)
NFLI .... Nutrition For Life International, Inc. [*NASDAQ symbol*] (SAG)
NFLI .... Nutrition For Life Intl. [*NASDAQ symbol*] (TTSB)
NFLIO .... Training Department, Iron Ore Co. of Canada, Labrador City, Newfoundland [*Library symbol National Library of Canada*] (NLC)
NFLIW ...... Nutrition For Life Intl. Wrrt [*NASDAQ symbol*] (TTSB)
NflkSo .... Norfolk Southern Corp. [*Associated Press*] (SAG)
NFLO .... Lourdes Public Library, Newfoundland [*Library symbol National Library of Canada*] (NLC)
NFlp .... Floral Park Public Library, Floral Park, NY [*Library symbol Library of Congress*] (LCLS)
NFLPA .... National Football League Players Association (EA)
NFLPA .... National Free Lance Photographers Association (EA)
NFlpBE ...... Floral Park-Bellerose Elementary School, Floral Park, NY [*Library symbol*] [*Library of Congress*] (LCLS)
NFlpCE ...... John Lewis Childs Elementary School, Floral Park, NY [*Library symbol*] [*Library of Congress*] (LCLS)
NFlpMH ...... Floral Park Memorial High School, Floral Park, NY [*Library symbol*] [*Library of Congress*] (LCLS)
NFLPN .... National Federation of Licensed Practical Nurses (EA)
NFlpSH ...... Sewanhaka High School, Floral Park, NY [*Library symbol*] [*Library of Congress*] (LCLS)
NFLQI .... Nuveen Florida Quality Income Municipal Fund [*Associated Press*] (SAG)

NFLS............ La Scie Public Library, Newfoundland [*Library symbol National Library of Canada*] (NLC)
NFLS............ Nicolet Federated Library System [*Library network*]
NFLSV .... National Front for the Liberation of South Vietnam
NFLTHC .... National Foundation for Long Term Health Care [*Defunct*] (EA)
NFLU .... Lumsden Public Library, Newfoundland [*Library symbol National Library of Canada*] (NLC)
NFM............ Conception Bay South Public Library, Manuels, Newfoundland [*Library symbol National Library of Canada*] (NLC)
NFM............ Midland Lutheran College, Fremont, NE [*OCLC symbol*] (OCLC)
NFM............ Narrowband Frequency Modulation [*Radio*]
NFM............ Next Full Moon [*Freemasonry*] (ROG)
NFM............ Noise Figure Meter
NFM............ Nonfat Milk (OA)
NFM............ Nonferrous Metal
NFM............ Northern Fowl Mite [*Immunology*]
NFM............ North-Finding Module (RDA)
NFMA.......... Marystown Public Library, Newfoundland [*Library symbol National Library of Canada*] (NLC)
NFMA.......... National Fireplace Makers Association [*British*] (BI)
NFMA.......... National Footwear Manufacturers Association [*Later, FIA*]
NFMA.......... National Forest Management Act (GFGA)
NFMA.......... Needleroom Felt Manufacturers Association [*British*] (DBA)
NFMA.......... Northwest Farm Managers Association (EA)
NFMA.......... November, February, May, and August [*Denotes quarterly payments of interest or dividends in these months*] [*Business term*]
NFMAA .... National Federation Music Adjudicator Association (EA)
NFMC.......... National Federation of Music Clubs (EA)
NFMC.......... National Film Music Council [*Defunct*]
NFMD .... National Foundation for Muscular Dystrophy
NFMD .... National Foundation for the March of Dimes (NADA)
NFME .... National Fund for Medical Education (EA)
NFME .... Nordic Federation for Medical Education [*Denmark*] (EAIO)
NFMHA .... National Federation of Milk Hauler Associations (EA)
NFMHJ......... John B. Wheeler Memorial Library, Musgrave Harbour, Newfoundland [*Library symbol National Library of Canada*] (NLC)
NFMHO .... National Foundation Manufactured Home Owners (EA)
NFMLTA....... National Federation of Modern Language Teachers Associations (EA)
NFMM .... National Fellowship of Methodist Musicians (EA)
NFMN .... National Fallout Monitoring Network
NFMOA .... National Fish Meal and Oil Association (EA)
NFMP.......... Mount Pearl Public Library, Newfoundland [*Library symbol National Library of Canada*] (NLC)
NFMP.......... National Federation of Master Painters and Decorators of England and Wales (BI)
NFMP.......... Nonferrous Metal Powder
NFMPC .... Non-Ferrous Metals Producers Committee (EA)
NFMR .... National Foundation for Metabolic Research [*Defunct*] (EA)
NFMR .... Non-Linear Ferromagnetic Resonance (PDAA)
NFMR .... Nordisk Forening for Medisinsk Radiologi [*Scandinavian Radiological Society - SRS*] (EAIO)
NFMRAD ...... Null Filter Mobile RADAR (PDAA)
NFMS.......... National Federation of Music Societies [*British*]
NFMS.......... National Fetal Mortality Survey [*Department of Health and Human Services*] (GFGA)
NFMS.......... Navy Fleet Material Support (MCD)
NFMS.......... Nitrogen Flow Measuring System
NFMS.......... Noise Figure Meter System
NFMS.......... Nonfat Milk Solids (OA)
NFMSAEG ..... Naval Fleet Missile System Analysis and Evaluation Group
NFMSAEGA... Naval Fleet Missile System Analysis and Evaluation Group Annex (MCD)
NFMSO .... Navy Fleet Material Support Office (DNAB)
NFMT .... National Federation of Meat Traders [*British*] (BI)
NFMT .... Navy Food Management Team (DNAB)
NFMWC .... National Federation of Master Window Cleaners [*British*] (DBA)
NFMY.......... National Festival of Music for Youth (AIE)
NFN .... National Fathers' Network [*An association*] (PAZ)
NFN .... Newly Founded Nest [*Ornithology*]
NFN .... No Form Necessary
NFN .... No Further Need (MUGU)
NFN .... Nouvelle Front NAZI [*New NAZI Front*] [*French*] (PD)
NFNA .... National Flight Nurses Association (EA)
NFNA .... Nausori/International [*Fiji*] [*ICAO location identifier*] (ICLI)
NFNA .... Norris Arm Public Library, Newfoundland [*Library symbol National Library of Canada*] (NLC)
NFNB .... Bureta [*Fiji*] [*ICAO location identifier*] (ICLI)
NFND .... Deumba [*Fiji*] [*ICAO location identifier*] (ICLI)
NFND .... National Foundation for Neuromuscular Diseases [*Later, NGF*] (EA)
NFNG .... Ngau [*Fiji*] [*ICAO location identifier*] (ICLI)
NFNH .... Lauthala Islands [*Fiji*] [*ICAO location identifier*] (ICLI)
NFNID .... National Foundation for Non-Invasive Diagnostics (EA)
NFNK .... Lakemba [*Fiji*] [*ICAO location identifier*] (ICLI)
NFNL .... Lambasa [*Fiji*] [*ICAO location identifier*] (ICLI)
NFNLI .... Labrador Inuit Association, Nain, Newfoundland [*Library symbol National Library of Canada*] (NLC)
NFNLI .... Labrador Unit Association, Nain, Newfoundland [*Library symbol National Library of Canada*] (NLC)
NFNM .... Matei [*Fiji*] [*ICAO location identifier*] (ICLI)
NFNN .... Vanuabalavu [*Fiji*] [*ICAO location identifier*] (ICLI)
NFNO .... Koro [*Fiji*] [*ICAO location identifier*] (ICLI)
NFNP .... National Food and Nutrition Policy [*Australia*]
NFNP .... Norris Point Public Library, Newfoundland [*Library symbol National Library of Canada*] (NLC)

NFNR .... Rotuma [*Fiji*] [*ICAO location identifier*] (ICLI)
NFNS .... Savusavu [*Fiji*] [*ICAO location identifier*] (ICLI)
N FNSHD .... Not Finished [*Freight*]
NFNTU .... National Federation of Furniture Trade Union [*British*]
NFNU .... Bua [*Fiji*] [*ICAO location identifier*] (ICLI)
NFNU .... National Federation of Nurses' Unions [*See also FNSII*]
NFNV .... Vatukoula [*Fiji*] [*ICAO location identifier*] (ICLI)
NFNW .... Wakaya [*Fiji*] [*ICAO location identifier*] (ICLI)
NFNWF .... Navy Fleet Numerical Weather Facility [*Marine science*] (MSC)
NFO .... National Family Opinion
NFO .... National Farmers Organization (EA)
NFO .... Naval Flight Officer
NFO .... Navy Finance Office
NFO .... News from the Ukraine [*A publication*]
NFO .... Normal Fuel Oil (DNAB)
NFO .... Norvell Family Organization (EA)
NFO .... Not Fully Open (MCD)
NFOAPA ...... National Federation of Old Age Pensioners' Associations [*British*] (BI)
NFO(B)........ Naval Flight Officer (Bombardier) (DNAB)
NFOBA .... National Fats and Oils Brokers Association [*Defunct*] (EA)
NFOC .... Naval Facility Operational Center (DNAB)
NFOC .... Naval Flight Officer Candidate (DNAB)
NFO(C)........ Naval Flight Officer (Controller) (DNAB)
NFOF .... Fiji [*Fiji*] [*ICAO location identifier*] (ICLI)
NFOHA .... National Federation of Off-Licence Holders Associations of England and Wales (BI)
NFO(I)......... Naval Flight Officer (RADAR Intercept) (DNAB)
NFOIO .... Naval Field Operational Intelligence Office (NVT)
NFOIODET... Naval Field Operational Intelligence Office Detachment (DNAB)
NFO(N) .... Naval Flight Officer (Navigator) (DNAB)
NFOO .... Naval Forward Observing Officer [*British military*] (DMA)
NFOP .... Old Perlican Public Library, Newfoundland [*Library symbol National Library of Canada*] (NLC)
NFoPA .... National Forest Products Association [*Washington, DC*]
NFOR .... NFO Research [*NASDAQ symbol*] (TTSB)
NFOR .... NFO Research, Inc. [*NASDAQ symbol*] (SAG)
NFO Rs .... NFO Research, Inc. [*Associated Press*] (SAG)
NFOSG .... Naval Field Operations Support Group
NFOV .... Narrow Field of View
NFP............ Marietta, GA [*Location identifier FAA*] (FAAL)
NFP............ Nandrolone Furylpropionate [*Pharmacology*]
NFP............ National Federation of Parents for Drug-Free Youth (EA)
NFP............ National Federation Party [*Fiji*] [*Political party*] (PPW)
NFP............ National Fire Academy Library, Emmitsburg, MD [*OCLC symbol*] (OCLC)
NFP............ National Focal Points (DCTA)
NFP............ Nationalist Front for Progress [*Solomon Islands*] [*Political party*] (FEA)
NFP............ Natural Family Planning
NFP............ Neighborhood Facilities Program (OICC)
NFP............ Network for Fitness Professionals [*Australia*]
NFP............ Neurofilament Protein [*Neurophysiology*]
NFP............ New Federalist Party (EA)
NFP............ New Forests Project (EA)
NFP............ New Frontier Party [*Japan*] [*Political party*]
NFP............ N-Formylmethionylphenylalanine [*Biochemistry*]
NFP............ Nonflare Proton
NFP............ Norfolk Petroleum Ltd. [*Vancouver Stock Exchange symbol*]
NFP............ Normal Failure Period
NFP............ Northern Frontier Province [*Kenya*]
NFP............ Not for Profit (ADA)
NFP............ Not for Publication (ADA)
NFP............ Placentia Public Library, Newfoundland [*Library symbol National Library of Canada*] (NLC)
NFPA .... National Federation of Paralegal Associations (EA)
NFPA .... National Fire Protection Association (EA)
NFPA .... National Flaxseed Processors Association (EA)
NFPA .... National Flexible Packaging Association [*Later, FPA*] (EA)
NFPA .... National Flight Paramedics Association (EA)
NFPA .... National Fluid Power Association (EA)
NFPA .... National Food Processors Association (EA)
NFPA .... National Forest Products Association (EA)
NFPA .... National Foster Parent Association (EA)
NFPA .... Natural Family Planning Association of Connecticut (EA)
NFPA .... Pasadena Public Library, Newfoundland [*Library symbol National Library of Canada*] (NLC)
NFPB .... National Friends of Public Broadcasting (EA)
NFPC .... National Federation of Plastering Contractors [*British*] (BI)
NFPC .... National Federation of Priests' Councils (EA)
NFPC .... Pouch Cove Public Library, Newfoundland [*Library symbol National Library of Canada*] (NLC)
NFPCA .... National Fire Prevention and Control Administration [*Later, United States Fire Administration*] [*Department of Commerce*]
NFPDC .... National Federation of Painting and Decorating Contractors [*British*] (DBA)
NFPDHE....... National Federation of Plumbers and Domestic Heating Engineers [*British*] (BI)
NFPE.......... NATO Force Planning Exercise (NATG)
NFPE.......... Non-Financial Public Enterprise [*British*]
NFPEC .... Curran Memorial Library, Port Au Port East, Newfoundland [*Library symbol National Library of Canada*] (NLC)
NFPEDA....... National Farm and Power Equipment Dealers Association [*Later, NAEDA*] (EA)
NF/PFOG....... National Federation of Parents and Friends of Gays (EA)

NFPHC	National Federation of Permanent Holiday Camps Ltd. [*British*] (BI)
NFPI	National Frozen Pizza Institute (EA)
NFPL	Point Leamington Public Library, Newfoundland [*Library symbol National Library of Canada*] (NLC)
NFPLA	National Foundation for Professional Legal Assistants (EA)
NFPM	Nuclear Flight Propulsion Module (KSC)
NFPMA	National Feeder Pig Marketing Association (EA)
NFPMA	National Foundation for Peroneal Muscular Atrophy (EA)
NFPMC	National Farm Products Marketing Council [*Canada*]
NFPNS	Natural Family Planning National Secretariat [*Australia*]
NFPO	National Federation of Professional Organizations (EA)
NFPO	National Federation of Property Owners [*British*] (BI)
NFPOC	National Federation of Post Office Clerks [*Later, APWU*]
NFPOD	National Foundation for the Prevention of Oral Disease [*Defunct*] (EA)
NFPR	National Fund for Research into Poliomyelitis and Other Crippling Diseases [*British*] (BI)
NFPRHA	National Family Planning and Reproductive Health Association (EA)
NFPS	Naval Flight Preparatory School
NFPS	Naval Future Policy Staff [*British*]
NFPS	Navy Field Purchase Systems (NG)
NFPS	Nuclear Flight Propulsion System (AAG)
NFPS	Port Saunders Public Library, Newfoundland [*Library symbol National Library of Canada*] (NLC)
NFPTC	National Federation of Postal and Telegraph Clerks [*A union*] [*British*]
NFPW	National Federation of Press Women (EA)
NFPW	National Federation of Professional Workers [*British*] (DI)
NFPW	Port Au Port West School/Public Library, Newfoundland [*Library symbol National Library of Canada*] (NLC)
NFQ	Night Frequency (FAAC)
NFQC	Queens College, Flushing, NY [*Library symbol Library of Congress*] (LCLS)
NFR	National Field Research [*British*]
NFR	National Film Board Reference Library [*UTLAS symbol*]
NFR	Naturvetenskapliga forskingsradet [*Swedish Natural Science Research Council*]
NFR	Near-Field Recording [*Computer science*] (PCM)
NFR	Negative Flux Rate (IEEE)
NFR	Nephron Filtration Rate [*Physiology*]
NFR	Net Financing Requirement
NFR	Net Flux Radiometer [*Instrumentation*]
NFR	New Frontier Petroleum Corp. [*Vancouver Stock Exchange symbol*]
NFR	No Further Requirement
NFR	Nordisk Forening for Rehabilitering [*Nordic Association for Rehabilitation*] (EAIO)
N FR	Northern French [*Language, etc.*] (ROG)
NFR	Not for Resuscitation [*Hospital patient classification*]
NFR	Nuclear Fission Reactor
NFR	Nursing Field Representative [*Red Cross*]
NFR-90	NATO Frigate for the 1990s
NFRA	National Forest Recreation Association (EA)
NFRA	Robert's Arm Public Library, Newfoundland [*Library symbol National Library of Canada*] (BIB)
NFRC	National Federation of Roofing Contractors [*British*] (EAIO)
NFRC	National Fenestration Rating Council (EA)
NFRC	National Finals Rodeo Committee (EA)
NFRC	National Forest Reservation Commission [*Terminated, 1976; functions transferred to Department of Agriculture*]
NFRCD	National Fund for Research into Crippling Diseases [*British*] (DI)
NFred	Darwin R. Barker Library Association, Fredonia, NY [*Library symbol Library of Congress*] (LCLS)
NFredCB	Chautauqua County Board of Cooperative Educational Services, Fredonia, NY [*Library symbol*] [*Library of Congress*] (LCLS)
NFredU	State University of New York, College at Fredonia, Fredonia, NY [*Library symbol Library of Congress*] (LCLS)
NFree	Freeport Memorial Library, Freeport, NY [*Library symbol Library of Congress*] (LCLS)
NFreeAE	Archer Elementary School, Freeport, NY [*Library symbol Library of Congress*] (LCLS)
NFreeAtE	Caroline G. Atkinson Elementary School, Freeport, NY [*Library symbol*] [*Library of Congress*] (LCLS)
NFreeBE	Bayview Avenue Elementary School, Freeport, NY [*Library symbol*] [*Library of Congress*] (LCLS)
NFreeCE	Columbus Elementary School, Freeport, NY [*Library symbol Library of Congress*] (LCLS)
NFreeDH	Doctors Hospital, Freeport, NY [*Library symbol Library of Congress*] (LCLS)
NFreeDJ	Dodd Junior High School, Freeport, NY [*Library symbol Library of Congress*] (LCLS)
NFreeEC	Early Childhood Center, Freeport, NY [*Library symbol*] [*Library of Congress*] (LCLS)
NFreeGE	Leo F. Giblyn Elementary School, Freeport, NY [*Library symbol*] [*Library of Congress*] (LCLS)
NFreeH	Freeport Hospital, Freeport, NY [*Library symbol Library of Congress*] (LCLS)
NFreeHS	Freeport High School, Freeport, NY [*Library symbol Library of Congress*] (LCLS)
NFRH	Rocky Harbour Public School, Newfoundland [*Library symbol National Library of Canada*] (NLC)
NFRM	National Foundation for Research in Medicine (EA)
NFRMC	National Foundation for Rural Medical Care [*Defunct*] (EA)
NFRN	National Federation of Retail Newsagents [*British*]
NFRP	Marie S. Penney Memorial Library, Ramea, Newfoundland [*Library symbol National Library of Canada*] (NLC)
NFRRC	Nuclear Fuel Recovery and Receiving Center (NRCH)
NFRS	National Fancy Rat Society [*British*]
NFRS	National Fancy Rat Society [*British*] (DBA)
NFRW	National Federation of Republican Women (EA)
NFS	Fayetteville State University, Fayetteville, NC [*OCLC symbol*] (OCLC)
NFs	Franklin Square Public Library, Franklin Square, NY [*Library symbol Library of Congress*] (LCLS)
NFS	National Aeronautics and Space Administration FAR Supplement [*A publication*] (AAGC)
NFS	National Federation of Settlements [*Later, UNCA*]
NFS	National Fertility Study
NFS	National Field Service Corp. [*Suffern, NY*] [*Telecommunications*] (TSSD)
NFS	National Film Society [*Defunct*] (EA)
NFS	National Fire Service [*British*]
NFS	National Flying Service [*British*]
NFS	National Food Situation [*Series*] [*A publication*]
NFS	National Food Survey [*British*]
NFS	National Forest System (GNE)
NFS	National Fuchsia Society (EA)
NFS	Naval Flying Station [*British*]
NFS	Navy Facilities System
NFS	Navy Field Service
NFS	Network File System [*Facetious translation: Nightmare File Systems*] [*Sun Microsystems, Inc.*]
NFS	Network File System
NFS	Neutron Flux Spectra [*Nuclear energy*]
NFS	Nitrofuraldehyde Semicarbazone [*Germicide*]
NFS	Nitrogen Flow System
NFS	Noise Frequency Spectrum
NFS	Nonfriendly Submarines (MCD)
NFS	Nordiska Forbundet for Statskunskap [*Nordic Political Science Association - NPSA*] [*Norway*] (EAIO)
NFS	Not for Sale
NFS	Not on Flying Status
NFS	Nozzle Flow Sensor (MCD)
NFS	Nuclear Fuel Services Fuel Fabrication Plant
NFS	Nuclear Fuel Services Plant (NRCH)
NFS	NWFS Capital Financing Trust [*NYSE symbol*] (SAG)
NFSA	National Federation of Sea Anglers [*British*]
NFSA	National Fertilizer Solutions Association (EA)
NFSA	National Fire Sprinkler Association (EA)
NFSA	National Food Service Association (EA)
NFSA	National Food Standards Agreement [*Australia*]
NFSA	Navy Field Safety Association (EA)
NFSA	New Fuel Storage Area (NRCH)
NFSA	News from Saudi Arabia [*A publication*] (BJA)
NFSA	Provincial Archives of Newfoundland and Labrador, St. John's, Newfoundland [*Library symbol National Library of Canada*] (NLC)
NFSAG	Research Station, Agriculture Canada [*Station de Recherches, Agriculture Canada*] St. John's, Newfoundland [*Library symbol National Library of Canada*] (NLC)
NFSAIC	Charles Curtis Memorial Hospital, International Grenfell Association, St. Anthony, Newfoundland [*Library symbol National Library of Canada*] (NLC)
NFSAIS	National Federation of Science Abstracting and Indexing Services [*Later, NFAIS*] (EA)
NFSAL	St. Alban's Public Library, Newfoundland [*Library symbol National Library of Canada*] (NLC)
NFSAN	St. Anthony Public Library, Newfoundland [*Library symbol National Library of Canada*] (NLC)
NFS & NC	National Federation of Settlements and Neighborhood Centers [*Later, UNCA*] (EA)
NFSANS	Naskapi School/Public Library, Sops Arm, Newfoundland [*Library symbol National Library of Canada*] (NLC)
NFSB	Spaniards Bay Public Library, Newfoundland [*Library symbol National Library of Canada*] (NLC)
NFSBC	Boys' Club, St. John's, Newfoundland [*Library symbol National Library of Canada*] (NLC)
NFSBCS	Cape Shore Public Library, St. Brides, Newfoundland [*Library symbol National Library of Canada*] (NLC)
NFSBS	Bay St. George Community College, Stephenville, Newfoundland [*Library symbol National Library of Canada*] (NLC)
NFSC	National Federation of Stamp Clubs (EA)
NFSC	Seal Cove Public Library, Newfoundland [*Library symbol National Library of Canada*] (NLC)
NFSCA	Children's and Adults' Library, St. John's, Newfoundland [*Library symbol National Library of Canada*] (NLC)
NFSCAEE	Environment Division, Newfoundland Department of Consumer Affairs and Environment, St. John's, Newfoundland [*Library symbol National Library of Canada*] (NLC)
NFSCCU	National Federation of Savings and Cooperative Credit Unions [*British*] (DBA)
NFSCF	Newfoundland and Labrador Institute of Fisheries and Marine Technology (Marine Institute), St. John's, New Foundland [*Library symbol National Library of Canada*] (NLC)
NFsCH	H. Frank Carey High School, Franklin Square, NY [*Library symbol*] [*Library of Congress*] (LCLS)
NFSCJ	Dr. Charles A. Janeway Child Health Centre, St. John's, Newfoundland [*Library symbol National Library of Canada*] (NLC)
NFSCR	Children's Rehabilitation Centre, St. John's, Newfoundland [*Library symbol National Library of Canada*] (NLC)
NFSCSW	National Federation of Societies for Clinical Social Work (EA)
NFSCT	Cabot Institute of Applied Arts and Technology, St. John's, Newfoundland [*Library symbol National Library of Canada*] (NLC)

NFSCTM ...... Topsail Campus Resource Centre, Cabot Institute of Applied Arts and Technology, St. John's, Newfoundland [*Library symbol National Library of Canada*] (NLC)

NFSD .... National Aeronautics and Space Administration FAR Supplement Directive (AAGC)

NFSD .... National Federation of Spiritual Directors (EA)

NFSD .... National Fraternal Society of the Deaf [*Mount Prospect, IL*] (EA)

NFSD .... Nonfused (MSA)

NFSE .... National Federation for the Self-Employed and Small Businesses [*British*] (DBA)

NFSE .... National Federation of Sales Executives [*Later, Sales and Marketing Executives International*]

NFSE .... National Federation of Self Employed [*British*]

NFSEC .... Newfoundland Forest Research Centre, Environment Canada [*Centre de RecherchesForestieres de Terre-Neuve, Environnement Canada*] St. John's, Newfoundland [*Library symbol National Library of Canada*] (NLC)

NFSEEP .... National Foundation for the Study of Equal Employment [*Washington, DC*] (EA)

NFSF .... National Freedom Shrine Foundation (EA)

NFSF .... NFS Financial Corp. [*NASDAQ symbol*] (NQ)

NFSF .... North-West Atlantic Fisheries Centre, Fisheries and Oceans Canada [*Centre de Pecheries de l'Atlantique du Nord-Ouest, Peches et Oceans Canada*] St. John's,Newfoundland [*Library symbol National Library of Canada*] (NLC)

NFSFJG .... St. Judes Central High School Public Library/Bay St. George South Public LibraryLibrary, St. Fintans, Newfoundland [*Library symbol National Library of Canada*] (NLC)

NFSFS .... Newfoundland Forest Service, St. John's, Newfoundland [*Library symbol National Library of Canada*] (NLC)

NFSG .... National Federation of Students of German (EA)

NFSG .... Newfoundland Public Library Services, St. John's, Newfoundland [*Library symbol National Library of Canada*] (NLC)

NFSG .... Provinical Reference and Resource Library, Newfoundland Public Library Services,St. John's, New Foundland [*Library symbol National Library of Canada*] (NLC)

NFSGE .... St. Georges Public Library, Newfoundland [*Library symbol National Library of Canada*] (NLC)

NFSGGH ...... C. A Pippy Jr. Medical Library, Grace General Hospital, St. John's, Newfoundland [*Library symbol National Library of Canada*] (NLC)

NFSGGHN .... School of Nursing, Grace General Hospital, St. John's, Newfoundland [*Library symbol National Library of Canada*] (NLC)

NFSGH .... General Hospital Corp., St. John's, Newfoundland [*Library symbol National Library of Canada*] (NLC)

NFSGHN ...... Nursing Education, General Hospital Corp., St. John's, Newfoundland [*Library symbol National Library of Canada*] (NLC)

NFSGO .... Gosling Library, St. John's, Newfoundland [*Library symbol National Library of Canada*] (NLC)

NFSH .... National Federation of Spiritual Healers (EA)

NFSH .... Southern Harbour Public Library, Newfoundland [*Library symbol National Library of Canada*] (NLC)

NFSHC .... National Federation of State Humanities Councils (EA)

NFSHE .... Health Education Division, Newfoundland Department of Health, St. John's, Newfoundland [*Library symbol National Library of Canada*] (NLC)

NFSHPH .... Public Health Nursing Division, Newfoundland Department of Health, St. John's, Newfoundland [*Library symbol National Library of Canada*] (NLC)

NFSHSA .... National Federation of State High School Associations (EA)

NFSHSAA .... National Federation of State High School Athletic Associations [*Later, NFSHSA*] (EA)

NFSICA .... Institute of Chartered Accountants of Newfoundland, St. John's, Newfoundland [*Library symbol National Library of Canada*] (NLC)

NFsJE .... John Street Elementary School, Franklin Square, NY [*Library symbol Library of Congress*] (LCLS)

NFSJL .... Law Library, Newfoundland Department of Justice, St. John's, Newfoundland [*Library symbol National Library of Canada*] (NLC)

NFSK .... Kindale Public Library, Stephenville, Newfoundland [*Library symbol National Library of Canada*] (NLC)

NFSK .... Narrowband Frequency Shift Keying (MCD)

NFSL .... Legislative Library, St. John's, Newfoundland [*Library symbol National Library of Canada*] (NLC)

NFSL .... Newnan Savings Bank [*NASDAQ symbol*] (NQ)

NFSL .... Newnan Svgs Bank FSB [*NASDAQ symbol*] (TTSB)

NFSL .... No Fighter Suitably Located (SAA)

NFSL .... Nucleus Fleet Sealift

NFSLA .... St. Lawrence Public Library, Newfoundland [*Library symbol National Library of Canada*] (NLC)

NFSLG .... St. Lunaire-Griquet Public Library, St. Lunaire, Newfoundland [*Library symbol National Library of Canada*] (NLC)

NFSLP .... Central Records Library, Newfoundland Light and Power Co. Ltd., St. John's, Newfoundland [*Library symbol National Library of Canada*] (NLC)

NFSLS .... Law Society of Newfoundland, St. John's, Newfoundland [*Library symbol National Library of Canada*] (NLC)

NFSM .... Memorial University, St. John's, Newfoundland [*Library symbol National Library of Canada*] (NLC)

NFSM .... National Fraternity of Student Musicians (EA)

NFSM .... Queen Elizabeth II Library, Memorial University of Newfoundland, St. John's, Newfoundland [*Library symbol National Library of Canada*] (NLC)

NFSMA .... National Fruit and Syrup Manufacturers Association (EA)

NFSMA .... Provincial Planning Office, Newfoundland Department of Municipal Affairs, St. John's, Newfoundland [*Library symbol National Library of Canada*] (NLC)

NFSME .... Newfoundland Department of Mines and Energy, St. John's, Newfoundland [*Library symbol National Library of Canada*] (NLC)

NFSMEC ...... Curriculum Materials Centre, Education Library, Memorial University, St. John's,Newfoundland [*Library symbol National Library of Canada*] (NLC)

NFSMED ...... Education Library, Memorial University, St. John's, Newfoundland [*Library symbol National Library of Canada*] (NLC)

NFSMEM ...... Publications and Information Section, Mineral Development Division Library, Newfoundland Department of Mines and Energy, St. John's, Newfoundland [*Library symbol National Library of Canada*] (NLC)

NFSMG .... Department of Geography, Memorial University, St. John's, Newfoundland [*Library symbol National Library of Canada*] (NLC)

NFSMLS ..... Library Studies Program, Memorial University of Newfoundland, St. John's, Newfoundland [*Library symbol National Library of Canada*] (BIB)

NFSMM .... Health Sciences Library, Memorial University, St. John's, Newfoundland [*Library symbol National Library of Canada*] (NLC)

NFSMMH ..... Maritime History Archive, Memorial University, St. John's, Newfoundland [*Library symbol National Library of Canada*] (BIB)

NFSMO .... Ocean Engineering Centre, Memorial University, St. John's, Newfoundland [*Library symbol National Library of Canada*] (NLC)

NFSN .... NATO French-Speaking Nations

NFsNH .... North Junior-Senior High School, Franklin Square, NY [*Library symbol*] [*Library of Congress*] (LCLS)

NFSNI .... National Research Council IRAP [*Industrial Research Assistance Program*], St. John's, Newfoundland [*Library symbol National Library of Canada*] (NLC)

NFSNL .... Newfoundland and Labrador Hydro, St. John's, Newfoundland [*Library symbol National Library of Canada*] (NLC)

NFSNLD .... Newfoundland and Labrador Development Corp., St. John's, Newfoundland [*Library symbol National Library of Canada*] (NLC)

NFSNM .... Marine Dynamics Branch, Canada Institute for Scientific and Technical Information, National Research Council [*Direction de la Dynamique Marine Institut Canadien de l'Information Scientifique et Technique, Conseil National de Recherches*], St. John's, Newfoundland [*Library symbol National Library of Canada*] (NLC)

NFSNO .... National Federation for Specialty Nursing Organizations (EA)

NFSO .... Navy Fuel Supply Office

NFSP .... National Federation of Sub-Postmasters [*British*] (DBA)

NFSP .... Nonflight Switch Panel (NASA)

NFSP .... Non-Flight Switch Panel

NFSP .... Springdale Public Library, Newfoundland [*Library symbol National Library of Canada*] (NLC)

NFsPE .... Polk Street Elementary School, Franklin Square, NY [*Library symbol*] [*Library of Congress*] (LCLS)

NFSPR .... Provincial Reference Library, St. John's, Newfoundland [*Library symbol National Library of Canada*] (NLC)

NFSPS .... National Federation of State Poetry Societies (EA)

NFSQ .... Queen's College, St. John's, Newfoundland [*Library symbol National Library of Canada*] (NLC)

NFSRA .... National Fitness Southern Recreation Association [*Australia*]

NFSRD .... Newfoundland Department of Rural Development, St. John's, Newfoundland [*Library symbol National Library of Canada*] (NLC)

NFSREX .... Canada Department of Regional Industrial Expansion [*Ministere de l'Expansion Industrielle Regionale*] St. John's, Newfoundland [*Library symbol National Library of Canada*] (NLC)

NFSS .... National Fallout Shelter Survey [*Civil Defense*]

NFSS .... National Federation of Sailing Schools [*British*]

NFSS .... National Finch and Softbill Society (EA)

NFSS .... Nucleus Fleet Scientific Support

NFSSC .... St. Clare's Mercy Hospital, St. John's, Newfoundland [*Library symbol National Library of Canada*] (NLC)

NFSSCN ...... School of Nursing, St. Clare's Mercy Hospital, St. John's, Newfoundland [*Library symbol National Library of Canada*] (NLC)

NFSSW .... Newfoundland Status of Women Council, St. John's, Newfoundland [*Library symbol National Library of Canada*] (NLC)

NFST .... Newfoundland Department of Tourism, St. John's, Newfoundland [*Library symbol National Library of Canada*] (NLC)

NFSTA .... Newfoundland Teachers' Association, St. John's, Newfoundland [*Library symbol National Library of Canada*] (NLC)

NFSTC .... Stephenville Crossing Public Library, Newfoundland [*Library symbol National Library of Canada*] (NLC)

NFSTCG ...... Canadian Coast Guard [*Garde Cotiere Canadienne*] St. John's, Newfoundland [*Library symbol Obsolete National Library of Canada*] (NLC)

NFSTPG .... National Foundation for the Study and Treatment of Pathological Gambling [*Defunct*] (EA)

NFSTR .... Medical Library, Sir Thomas Roddick Hospital, Stephenville, Newfoundland [*Library symbol National Library of Canada*] (NLC)

NFSU .... Nonflying Support Unit

NFSU .... Summerford Public Library, Newfoundland [*Library symbol National Library of Canada*] (NLC)

NFSU .... Suva/Nausori [*Fiji*] [*ICAO location identifier*] (ICLI)

NFSVP .... National Forest Service Volunteers Program (EA)

NFsWE .... Washington Street Elementary School, Franklin Square, NY [*Library symbol*] [*Library of Congress*] (LCLS)

NFSWH .... Health Services, Waterford Hospital, St. John's, Newfoundland [*Library symbol National Library of Canada*] (NLC)

NFSWMM ..... National Federation of Scale and Weighing Machine Manufacturers [*British*] (DBA)

NFsWS .... Willow Road School, Franklin Square, NY [*Library symbol*] [*Library of Congress*] (LCLS)

NFT .... National Film and Television Sound Archives [*National Film Board of Canada*] [*UTLAS symbol*]

NFT............	National Film Theatre [*British*]
NFT............	Navigation Flight Test [*Aviation*] (DA)
NFT............	Navy Flight Test (MCD)
NFT............	Nefteyugansk Aviation Division [*Russian Federation*] [*ICAO designator*] (FAAC)
NFT............	Networks File Transfer
NFT............	Neurofibrillary Tangle [*Brain anatomy*]
NFT............	Newfoundland Telephone Co. Ltd. [*Toronto Stock Exchange symbol*]
NFT............	New Frontiers in Theology [*A publication*] (BJA)
NFT............	N-Formimidoylthienamycin [*Biochemistry*]
NFT............	No Filing Time [*Aviation*]
NFT............	Non-Firing Test [*Military*]
NFT............	Non-Functional Test (SAA)
NFT............	Normal Fuel-Oil Tank (MSA)
NFT............	Nutrient Film Technique
NFTA..........	National Federation of Taxicab Associations [*British*] (DBA)
NFTA..........	National Feminist Therapist Association (EA)
NFTA..........	National Fillings Trades Association [*British*] (DBA)
NFTA..........	National Freight Transportation Association [*Rocky River, OH*] (EA)
NFTA..........	New Feminist Talent Associates (EA)
NFTA..........	Night-Fire [*Rifle*] Training Aid [*Army*] (INF)
NFTA..........	Nitrogen Fixing Tree Association [*University of Hawaii*] [*Research center*] (RCD)
NFTB..........	National Federation of Temple Brotherhoods (EA)
NFTB..........	Naval Fleet Training Base
NFTB..........	Niagara Frontier Tariff Bureau
NFTB..........	Nuclear Flight Test Base
NFTC..........	National Foreign Trade Council [*New York, NY*] (EA)
NFTC..........	National Furniture Traffic Conference (EA)
NFTD..........	Normal, Full Term Delivery [*Obstetrics*]
NFTE..........	Eua [*Tonga*] [*ICAO location identifier*] (ICLI)
NFTF..........	Night Fighting Training Facility [*Army*] (INF)
NFTF..........	Tongatapu/Fua'Amotu International [*Tonga*] [*ICAO location identifier*] (ICLI)
NFTL..........	Ha'Apai Lifuka [*Tonga*] [*ICAO location identifier*] (ICLI)
NFTMS........	National Federation of Terrazzo-Mosaic Specialists [*British*] (BI)
NFTN..........	Nuku'Alofa [*Tonga*] [*ICAO location identifier*] (ICLI)
NFTO..........	Niuafo'Ou [*Tonga*] [*ICAO location identifier*] (ICLI)
NFTO..........	Torbay Public Library, Newfoundland [*Library symbol National Library of Canada*] (NLC)
NFTP..........	Niuatoputapu [*Tonga*] [*ICAO location identifier*] (ICLI)
NFTR..........	Trepassey Public Library, Newfoundland [*Library symbol National Library of Canada*] (NLC)
NFTS..........	National Federation of Temple Sisterhoods (EA)
NFTS..........	National Film and Television School [*British*]
NFTS..........	Naval Flight Training School
NFTSA........	National Film, Television, and Sound Archives [*Canada*]
NFTSD........	Normal Full-Term Spontaneous Delivery [*Obstetrics*] (DAVI)
NFtT...........	Fort Ticonderoga Association Museum and Library, Fort Ticonderoga, NY [*Library symbol Library of Congress*] (LCLS)
NFTT..........	Nonorganic Failure to Thrive [*Neonatology*] [*Pediatrics*] (DAVI)
NFTV..........	Vava'u [*Tonga*] [*ICAO location identifier*] (ICLI)
NFTW..........	National Federation of Telephone Workers [*Later, CWA*]
NFTW..........	National Federation of Tobacco Workers [*A union*] [*British*]
NFTW..........	Twillingate Public Library, Newfoundland [*Library symbol National Library of Canada*] (NLC)
NFTY..........	North American Federation of Temple Youth (EA)
NFTZ..........	Non Free Trade Zone (DS)
NFU............	National Farmers' Union [*British*]
NFU............	National Film Unit (BARN)
NFU............	Niho Fukushi University [*UTLAS symbol*]
NFU............	Not for Us [*Communications*]
NFUCWC.....	National Foundation for Unemployment Compensation and Workers Compensation (EA)
NFUF..........	Codroy Valley Public Library, Upper Ferry, Newfoundland [*Library symbol National Library of Canada*] (NLC)
NFUI..........	Upper Island Cove Public Library, Newfoundland [*Library symbol National Library of Canada*] (NLC)
NFV............	National Field Volunteer [*Red Cross*]
NFV............	Naval Forces Vietnam (VNW)
NFV............	No Further Visits [*Medicine*]
NFV............	Nordischer Friseurverband [*Nordic Association of Hairdressers*] [*Sweden*] (EAIO)
NFV............	Point Barrow, AK [*Location identifier FAA*] (FAAL)
NFV............	Victoria Public Library, Newfoundland [*Library symbol National Library of Canada*] (NLC)
NFVA..........	Net Free Vent Area [*Roofing*]
NFVC..........	National Frozen Vegetable Council [*Later, FVC*] (EA)
NFVLS........	National Federation of Voluntary Literacy Schemes [*British*]
NFVOA........	Northern Fishing Vessel Owners Association [*Defunct*] (EA)
NFVP..........	National Film and Video Productions [*Australia*]
NFVT..........	National Federation of Vehicle Trades [*British*] (BI)
NFW............	Lakehurst, NJ [*Location identifier FAA*] (FAAL)
NFW............	Non-Fuel-Wasting (MCD)
NFW............	Nursed Fairly Well [*Medicine*] (DMAA)
NFWA..........	National Farm Workers of America
NFWA..........	National Furniture Warehousemen's Association [*Later, NMSA*] (EA)
NFWA..........	Neuromuscular Foundation of Western Australia
NFWA..........	Wabush Public Library, Newfoundland [*Library symbol National Library of Canada*] (NLC)
NFWBO........	National Foundation for Women Business Owners
NFWC..........	National Fire Waste Council
NFWD..........	New Field Wildcat Drilling [*Petroleum technology*]
NFWE..........	Edgar L. M. Roberts Memorial Library, Woodypoint, Newfoundland [*Library symbol National Library of Canada*] (NLC)

NFWE..........	National Federation of Woman's Exchanges (EA)
NFWF..........	National Fish and Wildlife Foundation (EPA)
NFWG..........	National Federation of Wholesale Grocers and Provision Merchants [*British*] (BI)
NFWH	National Foundation for Wholistic Medicine [*Defunct*] (EA)
NFWH	Whitbourne Public Library, Newfoundland [*Library symbol National Library of Canada*] (NLC)
NFWHF........	National Fresh Water Fishing Hall of Fame
NFWI..........	National Federation of Women's Institutes [*British*]
NFWI..........	Windsor Memorial Public Library, Newfoundland [*Library symbol National Library of Canada*] (NLC)
NFWIN........	Winterton Public Library, Newfoundland [*Library symbol National Library of Canada*] (NLC)
NFWM..........	National Farm Worker Ministry (EA)
NFWPM	National Federation of Wholesalers and Poultry Merchants [*British*] (DBA)
NFWS..........	Navy Fighter Weapons School (DNAB)
NFWT..........	National Foundation of Wheelchair Tennis (EA)
NFWV..........	Wesleyville Public Library, Newfoundland [*Library symbol National Library of Canada*] (NLC)
NFWW..........	National Federation of Women Workers [*British*]
NFX............	Newfield Exploration [*NYSE symbol*] (TTSB)
NFX............	Newfield Exploration Co. [*NYSE symbol*] (SPSG)
NFXD..........	National Fax Directory [*A publication*]
NFXF..........	National Fragile X Foundation (EA)
NFY............	Notify [*Telecommunications*] (TEL)
NFYD..........	Notified [*Telecommunications*] (TEL)
NFYFC........	National Federation of Young Farmers' Clubs (EAIO)
NFZ............	National Front of Zimbabwe (PPW)
NFZ............	(Nitro)furfuralsemicarbazone [*Organic chemistry*]
NFZ............	No Fire Zone [*Military*]
NFZ............	Nuclear Free Zone (AFM)
NFZR	Nuclear Free Zone Registry [*Defunct*] (EA)
NG............	Green Hills Aviation [*ICAO designator*] (AD)
ng	Nanogram [*One billionth of a gram*]
NG	Narrow Gauge
NG	Nasogastric [*Medicine*]
NG	National Gallery [*London*]
NG	National Gathering [*Jordan*] [*A publication*] (BJA)
NG	National Grange (EA)
NG	National Grid [*British Ordnance Survey maps*]
NG	National Guard [*or Guardsman*]
NG	Natural Gas
NG	Natural Gas Shutoff [*NFPA pre-fire planning symbol*] (NFPA)
NG	Natural, Grazed [*Agriculture*]
NG	Naval Gunfire (SAA)
NG	Navy General [*MCD files*]
NG	NAZI Government (BJA)
NG	Negative Glow (IDOE)
NG	Neopentyl Glycol [*Organic chemistry*]
NG	Nephridial Gland
NG	New Genus
NG	New Gnostics Special Interest Group (EA)
NG	New Granada
NG	New Group
NG	New Growth [*Medicine*]
NG	New Guinea
NG	Newly Generated
ng	Niger [*MARC country of publication code Library of Congress*] (LCCP)
NG	Nigeria [*ANSI two-letter standard code*] (CNC)
NG	Nitrogen Gauge (MCD)
NG	Nitroglycerin [*Also, GTN, NTG*] [*Explosive, vasodilator*]
NG	Nitroguanidine [*Organic chemistry*]
NG	Noble Gases [*Nuclear energy*] (NRCH)
NG	Noble Grand
NG	Noble Guard [*Freemasonry*] (ROG)
NG	No Go [*i.e., an unacceptable arrangement*]
NG	No Good [*Similar to IC - Inspected and Condemned*]
NG	No Gum [*Philately*]
NG	Nongraduate
NG	Normal Graduate
NG	Normotensive Group [*Cardiology*]
NG	Norwegian
NG	Norwegium [*Chemistry*] (ROG)
NG	Nose Gear [*Aviation*] (MCD)
NG	Not Given (ADA)
NG	Not Good
NG	Not Guilty
NG	Nottingham [*Postcode*] (ODBW)
NG	Nuclear Galaxy (BARN)
NG	Royal North Gloucestershire Militia [*British military*] (DMA)
NGA	National Gallery of Art [*Washington, DC*]
NGA	National Gallery of Art, Washington, DC [*OCLC symbol*] (OCLC)
NGA	National Gallery of Australia
NGA	National Gallery of Canada Library [*UTLAS symbol*]
NGA	National Gardening Association (EA)
NGA	National Glass Association (EA)
NGA	National Gliding Association [*Later, SSA*]
NGA	National Governors' Association (EA)
NGA	National Grant Agency
NGA	National Graphical Association [*British printers' union*]
NGA	National Greyhound Association (EA)
NGA	National Grocers Association (EA)
NGA	NATO Guidelines Area (NATG)

NGA .... Natural Gas Association (EPA)
NGA .... Naval Gunfire Assistant
NGA .... Needlework Guild of America [Later, NGAI] (EA)
NGA .... Nigeria [ANSI three-letter standard code] (CNC)
NGA .... Nutrient Gelatin Agar [Microbiology]
NGA .... WAAC (Nigeria) Ltd. Nigeria Airways [ICAO designator] (FAAC)
NGA .... Young [Australia Airport symbol] (OAG)
NGAA .... National Girls Athletic Association [Defunct]
NGAA .... Natural Gasoline Association of America [Later, GPA]
NGAB .... Abaiang [Kiribati] [ICAO location identifier] (ICLI)
NGaC .... Capuchin Theological Seminary, Garrison, NY [Library symbol Library of Congress] (LCLS)
NGAC .... National Greenhouse Advisory Committee [Australia]
NGAC .... National Guard Air Corps (WDAA)
NGAD .... Nobody Gives a Damn
NGADA......... National Graphic Arts Dealers Association (EA)
NGAI .... NGA [Needlework Guild of America], Inc. (EA)
NGAL .... Chestatee Regional Library [Library network]
NGAM .... Noble Gas Activity Monitor (IEEE)
NG & A .... National Gift and Art Association (EA)
NGAO .... New Governmental Advisory Organizations [A publication]
NGAPI .... Nuveen Georgia Premium Income Municipal Fund [Associated Press] (SAG)
NGARP......... National Guard and Army Reserve Policy
NGAS .... Naval Gunfire Air Spotting
NGAS .... Needs-Based Goal Attainment Scale (EDAC)
NGATM .... New Generation Air Traffic Manager (GAVI)
NGAUS......... National Guard Association of the United States (EA)
NGAYA .... National Gay Alliance for Young Adults (EA)
NGAZ .... NATO Gazetteer (MCD)
NGB .... National Garden Bureau (EA)
NGB .... National Governing Body [United States Olympic Committee]
NGB .... National Guard Bureau [Army]
ngb .... Natural Gum Blend [Philately]
NGB .... Neues Goettinger Bibelwerk [A publication] (BJA)
NGBR.......... Beru [Kiribati] [ICAO location identifier] (ICLI)
NGBRI .... Not Guilty by Reason of Insanity
NGc .... Garden City Public Library, Garden City, NY [Library symbol Library of Congress] (LCLS)
NGC .... Gloucester County College, Voorhees, NJ [OCLC symbol] (OCLC)
NGC .... National Gallery of Canada
NGC .... National Gambling Commission (NADA)
NGC .... National Gasohol Commission [Defunct] (EA)
NGC .... National Giro Centre [British] (DCTA)
NGC .... National Glass Clubs (EA)
NGC .... National Gloster Club (EA)
NGC .... National Governors Conference [Later, NGA]
NGC .... National Guild of Churchmen (EA)
NGC .... National Guinea Club
NGC .... National Gypsy Council [British] (DBA)
NGC .... Natural Gas Clearinghouse
ngc .... Natural Gum Crease [Philately]
NGC .... Near Galactic Catalog
NGC .... New General Catalogue [Astronomy]
NGC .... Newmont Gold [NYSE symbol] (TTSB)
NGC .... Newmont Gold Co. [NYSE symbol] (SPSG)
NGC .... Noise Generator Card
NGC .... Nordic Geodetic Commission (EA)
NGC .... North Georgia College [Dahlonega]
NGC .... Nozzle Gap Control [Aerospace] (AAG)
NGC .... Nucleus Reticularis Gigantocellularis [Brain anatomy]
NGcA .... Adelphi University, Garden City, NY [Library symbol Library of Congress] (LCLS)
NGCAA......... National Golf Clubs Advisory Association [British] (DBA)
Ng-CAM ...... Neuralglial Cell Adhesion Molecule [Biochemistry]
NGCC .... National Guard Computer Center
NGCC .... North German Coal Control [Post-World War II]
NGcCC .... Nassau Community College, Garden City, NY [Library symbol Library of Congress] (LCLS)
NGC Cp .... NGC Corp. [Associated Press] (SAG)
NGCDO .... North German Coal Distribution Organization [Post-World War II]
NGcE .... Endo Laboratories, Inc., Garden City, NY [Library symbol Library of Congress] (LCLS)
NGcG .... George Mercer, Jr., School of Theology, Garden City, NY [Library symbol Library of Congress] (LCLS)
NGcHE .... Homestead Elementary School, Garden City, NY [Library symbol] [Library of Congress] (LCLS)
NGCIC .... Natural Gas Consumers Information Center (EA)
NGcJ .... Garden City Junior High School, Garden City, NY [Library symbol] [Library of Congress] (LCLS)
NGcLE .... Locust Elementary School, Garden City, NY [Library symbol] [Library of Congress] (LCLS)
NGCM .... Navy Good Conduct Medal
NGcMH .... Mineola High School, Garden City Park, NY [Library symbol Library of Congress] (LCLS)
NGCMS .... National Guild of Community Music Schools [Later, NGCSA] (EA)
NGcN .... Nassau Academy of Medicine, Garden City, NY [Library symbol Library of Congress] (LCLS)
NGcNe .... Newsday, Garden City, NY [Library symbol Library of Congress] (LCLS)
NGcNLS .... Nassau Library System, Garden City, NY [Library symbol Library of Congress] (LCLS)
NGCOW........ National Gypsum Wrrt [NASDAQ symbol] (TTSB)
NGCP .... National Guild of Catholic Psychiatrists (EA)

NGcpMH ...... Mineola High School, Garden City Park, NY [Library symbol] [Library of Congress] (LCLS)
NGcR .... Nassau County Research Library, Garden City, NY [Library symbol Library of Congress] (LCLS)
NGCR .... Next Generation Computer Resources (DWSG)
NGCSA .... National Guild of Community Schools of the Arts (EA)
NGcSAE .... Stratford Avenue Elementary School, Garden City, NY [Library symbol] [Library of Congress] (LCLS)
NGcSE .... Stewart Avenue Elementary School, Garden City, NY [Library symbol] [Library of Congress] (LCLS)
NGcSH .... Garden City Senior High School, Garden City, NY [Library symbol] [Library of Congress] (LCLS)
NGcSS .... Scully, Scott, Murphy, and Presser, Garden City, NY [Library symbol Library of Congress] (LCLS)
NGcStP .... Saint Paul's School, Garden City, NY [Library symbol] [Library of Congress] (LCLS)
NGCT .... Navy General Classification Test (DNAB)
NGD .... National Grassland Demonstration [British]
NGD .... National Guild of Decoupeurs (EA)
NGD .... New Golden Sceptre Minerals Ltd. [Toronto Stock Exchange symbol Vancouver Stock Exchange symbol]
Ngd .... Nitrosoguanidine [Biochemistry]
NGDA .... National Glass Dealers Association [Later, NGA] (EA)
NGDB .... National Geochemical Data Bank [Natural Environment Research Council] [Information service or system] (IID)
NGDBFC....... Nitty Gritty Dirt Band Fan Club (EA)
NGDC .... National Geophysical Data Center [Later, NGSDC] [Boulder, CO] [National Oceanic and Atmospheric Administration] (MCD)
NGDF .... National Grave's Disease Foundation (EA)
NGDS .... Naval Graduate Dental School
NGE .... National Grain Exchange [Australia]
NGE .... Navigation Guidance Equipment (MCD)
NGE .... New York State E&G [NYSE symbol] (TTSB)
NGE .... New York State Electric & Gas Corp. [NYSE symbol] (SPSG)
NGE .... N'Gaoundere [Cameroon] [Airport symbol] (OAG)
NGEC .... National Gypsy Education Council [British]
n gen .... New Genus [Biology] (BARN)
NGEN .... Noise Generator (MSA)
NGeno .... Wadsworth Library, Geneseo, NY [Library symbol] [Library of Congress] (LCLS)
NGenoA .... Livingston County Archives, Geneseo, NY [Library symbol Library of Congress] (LCLS)
NGenoLS ..... Livingston-Steuben-Wyoming Educational Communication Center (BOCES), Geneseo, NY [Library symbol Library of Congress] (LCLS)
NGenoU .... State University of New York, College at Geneseo, Geneseo, NY [Library symbol Library of Congress] (LCLS)
NGEPr .... N.Y. State E&G, 3.75% Pfd [NYSE symbol] (TTSB)
NGEPrD .... N.Y. State E&G Adj Rt B Pfd [NYSE symbol] (TTSB)
NGEPrE .... N.Y. State E&G 7.40% Pfd [NYSE symbol] (TTSB)
NGEPSSC.... Navy Graduate Education Program Select Study Committee [Terminated, 1975] (EGAO)
NGF .... Kaneohe, HI [Location identifier FAA] (FAAL)
NGF .... National Gaucher Foundation (EA)
NGF .... National Genetics Foundation [Defunct] (EA)
NGF .... National Golf Foundation (EA)
NGF .... Nations Government Income Term Trust 2004 [NYSE symbol] (SAG)
NGF .... Nations Gvt Inc. Term Tr 2004 [NYSE symbol] (TTSB)
NGF .... Natural Guard Fund [Defunct] (EA)
NGF .... Naval Gun Factory [Later, NWF]
NGF .... Naval Gunfire
NGF .... Nerve Growth Factor [A protein] [Biochemistry]
NGF .... Nevada Goldfields Corp. [Toronto Stock Exchange symbol]
NGF .... New Games Foundation [Defunct] (EA)
NGF .... New Guinea Force [Army World War II]
NGF .... Northern Group of Forces [Commonwealth of Independent States] (NATG)
NGFA .... National Grain and Feed Association (EA)
NGFCF .... Nevada Goldfields Corp. (MHDW)
NGFEX .... Naval Gunfire Exercise (NVT)
NGFF .... Funafuti [Tuvalu] [ICAO location identifier] (ICLI)
NGFLO .... Naval Gunfire Liaison Officer
NGFLT .... Naval Gunfire Liaison Team
NGFO .... Nanumea [Tuvalu] [ICAO location identifier] (ICLI)
NGFO .... Naval Gunfire Officer
NGFP .... National Graduate Fellowship Program [Department of Education] (GFGA)
NGFR .... Nerve Growth Factor Receptor [Neurobiology]
NGFS .... Naval Gunfire Support (NVT)
NGFT .... National Guard on Field Training Exercises
NGFT .... Naval Gunfire Liaison Team (MUGU)
NGFU .... Funafuti/International [Tuvalu] [ICAO location identifier] (ICLI)
NGG .... Air Trans NG Group Moldova [FAA designator] (FAAC)
NGG .... Negative Grid Generator
NGGA .... National Greentown Glass Association (EA)
NGH .... Hobart and William Smith Colleges, Geneva, NY [Library symbol Library of Congress] (LCLS)
NGH .... NASA Grant Handbook
NGH .... National Guard [Hawaii] [Seismograph station code, US Geological Survey] (SEIS)
NGH .... National Guild of Hypnotists (EA)
NGHBRHD... Neighborhood
NGHEF .... National Gay Health Education Foundation (EA)
NGI .... National Garden Institute
NGI .... Nations Government Income Term Trust [NYSE symbol] (SPSG)

NGI	Nations Gvt Inc. Term Tr 2003 [NYSE symbol] (TTSB)
NGI	Natural Gas Industry [Australia]
NGI	Next Generation Internet [Computer science]
NGI	Next Generation Internet [A governmental research initiative]
NGI	Next-Generation Internet [Proposed]
NGI	Ngau [Fiji] [Airport symbol] (OAG)
NGI	Not Guilty by Reason of Insanity
NGI	N-W Group, Inc. [Toronto Stock Exchange symbol]
NGIB	National Geodetic Information Branch [National Oceanic and Atmospheric Administration]
NGIC	National Geodetic Information Center [National Oceanic and Atmospheric Administration] (IID)
NGIC	National Guard Intelligence Center [USA]
NGiG	Gibco/Invenex, Grand Island, NY [Library symbol Library of Congress] (LCLS)
NGiHC	Hooker Chemicals & Plastics Corp., Corporate Technical and Services Center Research Library, Grand Island, NY [Library symbol Library of Congress] (LCLS)
NGIPSCA	National GI Pipe Smokers Club of America (EA)
NgIU	University of Ibadan, Ibadan, Nigeria [Library symbol Library of Congress] (LCLS)
n giv	Not Given (DAVI)
NGJ	Beaufort, SC [Location identifier FAA] (FAAL)
NGJ	Nigerian Geographical Journal [A publication]
NGJA	National Gymnastics Judges Association (EA)
NGJC	North Greenville Junior College [South Carolina]
NGK	New Greek [Language, etc.]
NGK	Niemegk [German Democratic Republic] [Geomagnetic observatory code]
n-gl--	Greenland [MARC geographic area code Library of Congress] (LCCP)
NGl	Harborfields Public Library, Greenlawn, NY [Library symbol Library of Congress] (LCLS)
NGl	Harborfields Public Library, Greenlawn, NY [Library symbol] [Library of Congress] (LCLS)
NGL	Natural Gas Liquids
NGL	Natural Ground Level
NGL	Neodymium Glass LASER
NGL	Neon Glow Lamp
NGL	NGC Corp. [NYSE symbol] (TTSB)
NGL	No Gimbal Lock
NGL	No Greater Love (EA)
NGL	Normalair-Garrett Ltd. [British] (IRUK)
NGL	North Gasline [Alaska] [Seismograph station code, US Geological Survey] (SEIS)
NGL	Nose Gear Launch (MCD)
NGL	Trident NGL Holdings, Inc. [NYSE symbol] (SPSG)
NGIc	Glen Cove Public Library, Glen Cove, NY [Library symbol Library of Congress] (LCLS)
NGIcC	Community Hospital at Glen Cove, Glen Cove, NY [Library symbol Library of Congress] (LCLS)
NGIcCE	Coles Elementary School, Glen Cove, NY [Library symbol] [Library of Congress] (LCLS)
NGIcCoE	Connolly Elementary School, Glen Cove, NY [Library symbol] [Library of Congress] (LCLS)
NGIcDE	Deasy Elementary School, Glen Cove, NY [Library symbol] [Library of Congress] (LCLS)
NGIcF-L	Friends Academy, Lower School, Glen Cove, NY [Library symbol] [Library of Congress] (LCLS)
NGIcF-U	Friends Academy, Upper School, Glen Cove, NY [Library symbol] [Library of Congress] (LCLS)
NGIcGE	Gribbin Elementary School, Glen Cove, NY [Library symbol] [Library of Congress] (LCLS)
NGIcHS	Glen Cove High School, Glen Cove, NY [Library symbol] [Library of Congress] (LCLS)
NGIcLE	Landing Elementary School, Glen Cove, NY [Library symbol] [Library of Congress] (LCLS)
NGIcM	Garvie's Point Museum, Glen Cove, NY [Library symbol Library of Congress] (LCLS)
NGIcMS	Glen Cove Middle School, Glen Cove, NY [Library symbol Library of Congress] (LCLS)
NGIcP	Pall Corp., Glen Cove, NY [Library symbol Library of Congress] (LCLS)
NGIcW	Webb Institute of Naval Architecture, Glen Cove, NY [Library symbol Library of Congress] (LCLS)
NGlf	Crandall Library, Glens Falls, NY [Library symbol Library of Congress] (LCLS)
NGIfAC	Adirondack Community College, Glens Falls, NY [Library symbol Library of Congress] (LCLS)
NGIH	Hazeltine Corp., Greenlawn, NY [Library symbol Library of Congress] (LCLS)
NGIH	Hazeltine Corp., Greenlawn, NY [Library symbol] [Library of Congress] (LCLS)
NGIhC	New York Chiropractic College, Glen Head, NY [Library symbol Library of Congress] (LCLS)
NGIhES	Glen Head Elementary School, Glen Head, NY [Library symbol Library of Congress] (LCLS)
NGIhGE	Glenwood Landing Elementary School, Glen Head, NY [Library symbol] [Library of Congress] (LCLS)
NGIhNH	North Shore High School, Glen Head, NY [Library symbol] [Library of Congress] (LCLS)
NGIhNJ	North Shore Junior High School, Glen Head, NY [Library symbol Library of Congress] (LCLS)
NGIHS	Harborfields High School, Greenlawn, NY [Library symbol] [Library of Congress] (LCLS)
NGLIOGT	National Grand Lodge, International Order of Good Templars [Later, NCUSIOGT] (EA)
NGlo	Gloversville Free Library, Gloversville, NY [Library symbol] [Library of Congress] (LCLS)
NGLO	Naval Gunfire Liaison Officer
NGLR	Neodymium Glass LASER Rod
NGLS	Non-Governmental Liaison Service [World Resources Institute]
NGLTF	National Gay and Lesbian Task Force (EA)
NGIwES	Glenwood Landing Elementary School, Glenwood Landing, NY [Library symbol Library of Congress] (LCLS)
N GLZD	Not Glazed [Freight]
NGM	Agana Naval Air Station [FAA] (TAG)
ngm	Nanogram [Measurement] (DAVI)
NGM	Nested Grid Model [Marine science] (OSRA)
NGM	Nested Grid Model [National Marine Center] (USDC)
NGM	NetWare Global Messaging [Computer science] (CDE)
NGM	Neutron-Gamma Monte Carlo [Computer science]
NGM	New Ridge Resources [Vancouver Stock Exchange symbol]
NGM	Nitrogen Generation Module (NASA)
NGM	Nitrogen Generation Module
NGM	Noise Generation Mechanism
NGMA	Maiana [Kiribati] [ICAO location identifier] (ICLI)
NGMA	National Gadget Manufacturers Association
NGMA	National Gas Measurement Association (EA)
NGMA	National Geoscience Mapping Accord [Australia]
NGMA	National Gospel Music Association (EA)
NGMA	National Grants Management Association (AAGC)
NGMA	National Greenhouse Manufacturers Association (EA)
NGMK	Marakei [Kiribati] [ICAO location identifier] (ICLI)
ng/ml	Nanograms [One billionth of a gram] per Milliliter
NGMN	Makin [Kiribati] [ICAO location identifier] (ICLI)
NGN	Nagano [Japan] [Seismograph station code, US Geological Survey] (SEIS)
NGN	Nargana [Panama] [Airport symbol] (OAG)
NGN	National Geographic Names Data Base [Geological Survey] [Database]
NGN	News Group Newspapers [British]
NGN	NRG Resources Ltd. [Vancouver Stock Exchange symbol]
NGNC	Non-Government Non-Catholic [School]
NGNF	National Guard Not in Federal Service
NG/NS	Next Generation/Notional System [Army]
NGNU	Nikunau [Kiribati] [ICAO location identifier] (ICLI)
NGO	Nago [Ryukyu Islands] [Seismograph station code, US Geological Survey] (SEIS)
NGO	Nagoya [Japan] [Airport symbol] (OAG)
NGO	National Gas Outlet [Thread]
NGO	Naval Gunfire Officer
NGO	Navy Guidance Official [British]
NGO	Neuro-Genetic Optimizer (PCM)
NGO	Nitroglycerin Ointment [Pharmacy] (CPH)
NGO	Nongovernmental Observer
NGO	Nongovernmental Organization [Generic term]
NGOC	Naval Gunfire Operations Center
NGOC	North German Oil Control [Post-World War II]
NGOCD	Non-Governmental Organization Committee on Disarmament (EA)
NGOCS	National Guard Officer Candidate School
NGoH	Hillside Hospital, Glen Oaks, NY [Library symbol Library of Congress] (LCLS)
NGON	Onotoa [Kiribati] [ICAO location identifier] (ICLI)
NGos	Goshen Library and Historical Society, Goshen, NY [Library symbol Library of Congress] (LCLS)
NGosA	Arden Hill Hospital Medical Library, Goshen, NY [Library symbol Library of Congress] (LCLS)
NGou	Reading Room Association Library, Gouveneur, NY [Library symbol Library of Congress] (LCLS)
NGowH	Tri-County Memorial Hospital, Gowanda, NY [Library symbol Library of Congress] (LCLS)
NGP	Corpus Christi, TX [Location identifier FAA] (FAAL)
NGP	Greensboro Public Library, Greensboro, NC [OCLC symbol] (OCLC)
NGP	Nano Glass Pellet
NGP	Natural Gas Pressure
NGP	Nearest Grid Point (PDAA)
NGP	Network Graphics Protocol
NGP	Neue Grosse Partei [New Great Party] [Germany Political party] (PPW)
NGP	New Gatineau Pulp [Pulp and paper technology]
NGP	N-Glycidylpyrrolidone [Organic chemistry]
Ngp	Nominal Group [Linguistics]
NGP	Northern Galactic Pole
NGP	North Galactic Pole
NGPA	National Gas Policy Act (GFGA)
NGPA	National Guard Personnel, Army
NGPA	Natural Gas Policy Act [1978]
NGPA	Natural Gas Processors Association [Later, GPA] (EA)
NGPEC	National Guard Professional Education Center [North Little Rock, AR]
NGPL	Natural Gas Plant Liquids [DOE] (TAG)
NGPP	National Guild of Professional Paperhangers (EA)
NGPRP	Northern Great Plains Resource Program [Dept. of the Interior, Dept. of Agriculture and Environmental Protection Agency] (PDAA)
NGPRS	Northern Great Plains Research Center [Department of Agriculture] [Research center] (RCD)
NGPSA	Natural Gas Pipeline Safety Act [1968]
NGPSA	Natural Gas Processors Suppliers Association [Later, GPSA] (EA)
NGPT	National Guild of Piano Teachers (EA)
NGQ	Nongovernment Quarters (AFM)

NGR .... Narrow Gauge Railways Ltd. [*Wales*]
NGR .... Narrow Gauze Roll [*Medicine*]
NGR .... Nasogastric Replacement [*Medicine*] (DMAA)
NGR .... National Guard Register
NGR .... National Guard Regulations
N GR .... New Greek [*Language, etc.*] (ROG)
N-GR .... New York State Library, General Reference Library, Albany, NY
                   [*Library symbol Library of Congress*] (LCLS)
NGR .... Nigerum [*Papua New Guinea*] [*Airport symbol*] (OAG)
NGR .... Non-Grain-Raising [*Coating technology*]
NGR .... Norgold Resources [*Vancouver Stock Exchange symbol*]
NGRA .... National Gay Rights Advocates [*Defunct*] (EA)
NGRC .... National Government of the Republic of China
NGRC .... National Greyhound Racing Club [*British*] (DI)
NGRE .... Negative Glucocorticoid Response Element [*Biochemistry*]
NGRF .... National Ghost Ranch Foundation (EA)
NGRI .... Not Guilty by Reason of Insanity
NGrl .... Greenwood Lake Public Library, Greenwood, NY [*Library symbol
                   Library of Congress*] (LCLS)
NGrlHS .... Harborfields High School, Greenlawn, NY [*Library symbol Library of
                   Congress*] (LCLS)
NGrn .... Great Neck Library, Great Neck, NY [*Library symbol Library of
                   Congress*] (LCLS)
NGrnBE ...... Baker Elementary School, Great Neck, NY [*Library symbol Library of
                   Congress*] (LCLS)
NGrnKE ...... Kennedy Elementary School, Great Neck, NY [*Library symbol Library
                   of Congress*] (LCLS)
NGrnKJE ..... Kensington-Johnson Elementary School, Great Neck, NY [*Library
                   symbol Library of Congress*] (LCLS)
NGrnLE .... Lakeville Elementary School, Great Neck, NY [*Library symbol Library
                   of Congress*] (LCLS)
NGrnMiS ...... John L. Miller-Great Neck North High School, Great Neck, NY
                   [*Library symbol*] [*Library of Congress*] (LCLS)
NGrnMS ...... Great Neck South Middle School, Great Neck, NY [*Library symbol
                   Library of Congress*] (LCLS)
NGrnNA .... Network Analysis Corp., Great Neck, NY [*Library symbol Library of
                   Congress*] (LCLS)
NGrnNM ...... Great Neck North Middle School, Great Neck, NY [*Library symbol*]
                   [*Library of Congress*] (LCLS)
NGrnPE .... Parkville Elementary School, Great Neck, NY [*Library symbol Library
                   of Congress*] (LCLS)
NGrnS .... Sperry Rand Corp., Sperry Gyroscope Division, Great Neck, NY
                   [*Library symbol Library of Congress*] (LCLS)
NGrnSH .... Great Neck South Senior High School, Great Neck, NY [*Library
                   symbol Library of Congress*] (LCLS)
NGrnSRE ..... Saddle Rock Elementary School, Great Neck, NY [*Library symbol
                   Library of Congress*] (LCLS)
NGroT .... Tompkins-Cortland Community College, Groton, NY [*Library symbol
                   Library of Congress Obsolete*] (LCLS)
NGrpAg .... United States Department of Agriculture, Plum Island Animal Disease
                   Laboratory Library, Greenport, NY [*Library symbol Library of
                   Congress*] (LCLS)
NGrpEH .... Eastern Long Island Hospital, Greenport, NY [*Library symbol Library
                   of Congress*] (LCLS)
NGRS .... Narrow Gauge Railway Society [*British*]
NGRS .... National Geodetic Reference System [*National Oceanic and
                   Atmospheric Administration*]
NGRS .... National Goals Research Staff
NGS .... General Air Services Ltd. [*Nigeria*] [*ICAO designator*] (FAAC)
NGS .... Nagasaki [*Japan*] [*Seismograph station code, US Geological
                   Survey*] (SEIS)
NGS .... Nagasaki [*Japan*] [*Airport symbol*] (OAG)
NGS .... National Gardens Scheme Charitable Trust (EAIO)
NGS .... National Gas Straight [*Thread*]
NGS .... National Genealogical Society (EA)
NGS .... National Geodetic Survey [*National Oceanic and Atmospheric
                   Administration*]
NGS .... National Geographic Service
NGS .... National Geographic Society (EA)
NGS .... National Geriatrics Society (EA)
NGS .... National Gladiolus Society (EA)
NGS .... National Goldfish Society
NGS .... National Graniteware Society (EA)
NGS .... Natural Ground Surface
NGS .... Naval Gunfire Support
NGS .... Neutral Gear Switch [*Automotive engineering*]
NGS .... Neutral Grain Spirits
NGS .... No Gallstones [*Medicine*]
NGS .... Nominal Guidance Scheme (OA)
NGS .... Non-Immune [*or Normal*] Goat Serum
NGS .... Nuclear Generating Station (BARN)
NGS .... Nucleonic Gauging System
NGSA .... National Golf Salesmen Association [*Defunct*] (EA)
NGSA .... Natural Gas Supply Association
NGSA .... Nerve Growth Stimulating Activity [*Biochemistry*]
NGSC .... National Gay Student Center [*Defunct*] (EA)
NGSC .... National Gender Selection Center (EA)
NGSCO .... National Geodetic Survey Operations Center [*National Oceanic and
                   Atmospheric Administration*]
NGSDC .... National Geophysical and Solar-Terrestrial Data Center [*National
                   Oceanic and Atmospheric Administration*] (IID)
NGSEF .... National Geographic Society Education Foundation (EA)
NGSF .... Noble Gas Storage Facility (NRCH)
NGSFO .... Naval Gunfire Support Forward Observer [*British*]

NGSIC .... National Geodetic Survey Information Center [*National Oceanic and
                   Atmospheric Administration*] (IID)
NGSLO .... Naval Gunfire Support Liaison Officer
NGSM .... National Gold Star Mothers [*Defunct*] (EA)
NGSMA .... Natural Gasoline Supply Men's Association [*Later, GPSA*]
NGSNY .... National Guard State of New York (HGAA)
NGSP .... National Geodetic Satellite Program [*NASA*]
NGSP .... National Guilds of St. Paul (EA)
NGSP .... Nonglycosylated Serum Protein
NGSQ .... National Genealogical Society Quarterly [*A publication*] (BRI)
NGSS .... Non-Government Schools' Secretariat [*South Australia*]
NGSSO .... Naval Gunfire Support Staff Officer
NGST .... Next Generation Space Telescope [*Proposed, 1996*] [*NASA*]
NGST .... Next Generation Space Telescope [*NASA*]
NGSTDC ...... National Geophysical and Solar-Terrestrial Data Center [*National
                   Oceanic and Atmospheric Administration*]
NGT .... Berclair, TX [*Location identifier FAA*] (FAAL)
NGT .... Eastern American Natural Gas Trust [*NYSE symbol*] (SAG)
NGT .... Eastern AmerNatlGasTr'SPERs' [*NYSE symbol*] (TTSB)
NGT .... Nagatsuro [*Irozaki*] [*Japan*] [*Seismograph station code, US
                   Geological Survey*] (SEIS)
NGT .... NASA Ground Terminal (MCD)
NGT .... Nasogastric Tube [*Medicine*] (CPH)
NGT .... National Gas Taper [*Thread*]
NGT .... National Guard Technician (MCD)
NGT .... National Guild of Telephonists [*British*] (BI)
NGT .... Natural Gas Temperature
NGT .... Neon Globe Tube
NGT .... New Generation Truck [*Concept vehicle*]
NGT .... Next Generation Trainer [*Air Force*]
NGT .... Night
NGT .... Noise Generator Tube
NGT .... Nominal Grouping Technique
NGT .... Nonsymmetric Gravitational Theory
NGT .... Northern General Transport Co. [*British*] (DCTA)
NGT .... Not Greater Than
NGTA .... Next Generation Trainer Aircraft (MCD)
NGTA .... Nonguaranteed Trade Arrears (IMH)
NGTA .... Tarawa/Bonriki International [*Kiribati*] [*ICAO location identifier*] (ICLI)
NGTB .... Abemama [*Kiribati*] [*ICAO location identifier*] (ICLI)
NGTC .... National Grain Trade Council (EA)
NGTE .... National Gas Turbine Establishment [*British*]
NGTE .... Tabiteuea (North) [*Kiribati*] [*ICAO location identifier*] (ICLI)
NGTF .... National Gay Task Force [*Later, NGLTF*] (EA)
NGTG .... NCAR [*National Center for Atmospheric Research*] GARP Task
                   Group [*Global Atmospheric Research Program*]
NGTM .... Tamana [*Kiribati*] [*ICAO location identifier*] (ICLI)
NGTO .... Nonouti [*Kiribati*] [*ICAO location identifier*] (ICLI)
NGTP .... Natural Gas Tank Pressure
NGTR .... Arorae [*Kiribati*] [*ICAO location identifier*] (ICLI)
NGTS .... Tabiteuea (South) [*Kiribati*] [*ICAO location identifier*] (ICLI)
NGTT .... Natural Gas Tank Temperature
NGTT .... Tarawa/Betio [*Kiribati*] [*ICAO location identifier*] (ICLI)
NGTU .... Butaritari [*Kiribati*] [*ICAO location identifier*] (ICLI)
NGU .... Nachalnik Glavnoyo Upravlenia [*Chief of Main Directorate*] [*Soviet
                   military rank*]
nGU .... Nano-Goldblatt Units [*Clinical chemistry*]
NGU .... Nongonococcal Urethritis [*Medicine*]
NGU .... Norfolk, VA [*Location identifier FAA*] (FAAL)
NGU .... University of North Carolina, Greensboro, Greensboro, NC [*OCLC
                   symbol*] (OCLC)
N GUI .... New Guinea Territory (WDAA)
N Guin .... New Guinea
NGUK .... Aranuka [*Kiribati*] [*ICAO location identifier*] (ICLI)
NGuNA .... New York State Nurses Association, Guilderland, NY [*Library symbol
                   Library of Congress*] (LCLS)
NGUS .... National Guard of the United States
NGUT .... National Group of Unit Trusts [*British*] (DI)
NGV .... Angoavia Angola [*FAA designator*] (FAAC)
NGV .... Natural Gas for Vehicles
NGV .... Natural Gas Vehicle
NGV .... New Goldcore Ventures [*Vancouver Stock Exchange symbol*]
NGV .... Nozzle Guide Vanes [*Aviation*] (AIA)
NGVC .... National Guard Volunteer Corps [*British military*] (DMA)
NGVC .... Natural Gas Vehicle Coalition [*VDOT*] (TAG)
NGVD .... National Geodetic Vertical Datum [*National Oceanic and Atmospheric
                   Administration*]
NGvHI .... Harbor Hill Intermediate School, Greenvale, NY [*Library symbol*]
                   [*Library of Congress*] (LCLS)
NGvP .... Long Island University, C. W. Post Center, Greenvale, NY [*Library
                   symbol Library of Congress*] (LCLS)
NGVP .... Natural Gas Vehicle Partnership
NGVR .... New Guinea Volunteer Reserve
NGW .... Corpus Christi, TX [*Location identifier FAA*] (FAAL)
NGW .... Gardner-Webb College, Boiling Springs, NC [*OCLC symbol*] (OCLC)
NGW .... National Gallery of Art, Washington, DC
NGW .... No Gift Wrap [*Mail-order catalogs*]
NGWIC .... National Ground Water Information Center [*National Water Well
                   Association*] [*Information service or system*] (IID)
NGX .... Northgate Explor [*NYSE symbol*] (TTSB)
NGX .... Northgate Exploration Ltd. [*NYSE symbol Toronto Stock Exchange
                   symbol*] (SPSG)
NGYN .... National Gay Youth Network (EA)
NGZ .... Alameda, CA [*Location identifier FAA*] (FAAL)
NH .... All Nippon [*ICAO designator*] (AD)

NH .... Editions Nouveaux Horizons [US government imprint]
NH .... Hamilton Public Library, Hamilton, NY [Library symbol Library of Congress] (LCLS)
NH .... Nahum [Bible]
nH .... Nanohenry [One billionth of a henry] (IEEE)
NH .... Nash-Healey [Model of automobile, now out of production]
NH .... National Heritage [British] [An association] (DBA)
NH .... National Highway
NH .... National Hunt [British]
NH .... NATO Helicopter [NH-90] (DOMA)
NH .... Natural History [A publication] (BRI)
NH .... Naval Home [Philadelphia, PA]
NH .... Naval Hospital
NH .... Neo-Hebrew (BJA)
NH .... Neonatal Hypothyroidism [Cretinism] [Medicine]
NH .... Never Hinged [Philately]
NH .... New Hampshire [Postal code]
Nh .... New Hampshire State Library, Concord, NH [Library symbol Library of Congress] (LCLS)
NH .... New Hampshire Supreme Court Reports [A publication] (DLA)
NH .... New Haven [Connecticut]
NH .... New Head [Also, NL] [News stories] (NTCM)
NH .... New High [Investment term]
NH .... New York, New Haven & Hartford R. R. [AAR code]
N/H .... Next Higher Assembly [Engineering]
NH .... Nike Hercules [Surface-to-air missile system] (MCD)
NH .... Nodal-His [Medicine] (MEDA)
NH .... Nodular Histiocytic [Lymphoma] [Oncology] (DAVI)
NH .... Nominal Height (MCD)
NH .... Nonhandicapped
NH .... Nonhuman (MAE)
NH .... Nonhygroscopic
NH .... Norfolk Howard [Refers to a bed-bug] [Slang] (DSUE)
NH .... Northern Canada Mines Ltd. [Toronto Stock Exchange symbol]
NH .... Northern Hemisphere
Nh .... Northern Hogsucker [Ichthyology]
NH .... Northumberland Hussars [British military] (DMA)
NH .... Not Held
NH .... Nursing Home
NH₃ .... Ammonia (GNE)
NHA .... American Foundation for Management Research, Hamilton, NY [Library symbol Library of Congress] (LCLS)
NHA .... Nahanni Mines Ltd. [Toronto Stock Exchange symbol]
NHA .... National Fashion Accessories Association (EA)
NHA .... National Hairdressers' Association [British] (BI)
NHA .... National Handbag Association (EA)
NHA .... National Hay Association (EA)
NHA .... Notable Health Agencies (EA)
NHA .... National Health Association
NHA .... National Hearing Association (EA)
NHA .... National Hemophilia Association (DAVI)
NHA .... National Heritage Act [Protects national treasures from sale out of the country] [British]
NHA .... National Hide Association [Later, USHSLA] (EA)
NHA .... National Hobo Association (EA)
NHA .... National Hockey Association [to 1917]
NHA .... National Holiness Association [Later, CHA] (EA)
NHA .... National Homeowners Association (EA)
NHA .... National Homeschool Association (EA)
NHA .... National Housewives Association [British] (DBA)
NHA .... National Housing Act [1934, 1954]
NHA .... National Housing Administration
NHA .... National Housing Agency [Superseded by HHFA, 1947; then by HUD, 1965]
NHA .... National Humanities Alliance (EA)
NHA .... National Hunters Association (EA)
NHA .... National Hydropower Association (EA)
NHA .... National Hypertension Association (EA)
NHA .... National Hypoglycemia Association (EA)
NHA .... Nationwide Hotel Association
NHA .... New Homemakers of America [Later, FHA] (EA)
NHA .... New Humanity Alliance (EA)
NHA .... Next Higher Assembly [Engineering]
NHA .... Next Higher Authority (MUGU)
NHA .... Nhatrang [Vietnam] [Seismograph station code, US Geological Survey Closed] (SEIS)
NHA .... Nitrohippuric Acid [Organic chemistry]
NHA .... Nonhydrogen Atom [Chemistry]
NHA .... Nonspecific Hepatocellular Abnormality [Medicine] (MAE)
NHA .... Northwest Hardwood Association [Later, WHA] (EA)
NHA .... Nutritional Health Alliance
NHAAP .... National Heart Attack Alert Program
NHAC .... National Health Awareness Center [Later, NHSAC] (EA)
NHACE .... National Hispanic Association of Construction Enterprises (EA)
NHACES .... New Hampshire Association for Computer Education Statewide (EDAC)
NHACFC ...... National Health Agencies for the Combined Federal Campaign [Formerly, FSCNHA] [Later, NVHA] (EA)
NH Act .... National Housing Act [1934, 1954] (DLA)
NH Admin Code... New Hampshire Code of Administrative Rules [A publication] (DLA)
NH Admin Rules Ann... New Hampshire Code of Administrative Rules Annotated [A publication] (AAGC)
NHAES .... New Hampshire Agricultural Experiment Station [University of New Hampshire] [Research center] (RCD)

NHaHS .... Harborfields High School, Harborfields, NY [Library symbol] [Library of Congress] (LCLS)
NHAIAC .... National Highway Accident and Injury Analysis Center
NHAM .... National Hose Assemblies Manufacturers Association [Defunct]
NHamB .... Hampton Bays Public Library, Hampton Bays, NY [Library symbol Library of Congress Obsolete] (LCLS)
NHamH .... Hilbert College, Hamburg, NY [Library symbol Library of Congress] (LCLS)
N Hamp .... New Hampshire Reports [A publication] (DLA)
NHampB .... Hampton Bays Public Library, Hampton Bays, NY [Library symbol Library of Congress] (LCLS)
N Hamp Rep... New Hampshire Reports [A publication] (DLA)
N Hampshire Rep... New Hampshire Reports [A publication] (DLA)
NH & C .... Railway and Canal Cases [1835-55] [England] [A publication] (DLA)
NH & S .... Needham, Harper & Steers [Advertising agency]
NH & S .... Nuclear Hardening and Survivability
NHANES .... National Health and Nutritional Examination Survey
NHaOM .... Oldfield Middle School, Harborfield, NY [Library symbol] [Library of Congress] (LCLS)
NHapS .... Suffolk County Department of Health Service, Hauppauge, NY [Library symbol] [Library of Congress] (LCLS)
NHapSA .... Suffolk Academy of Medicine, Hauppauge, NY [Library symbol Library of Congress] (LCLS)
Nh-Ar .... New Hampshire Department of Administration and Control, Division of Archives andRecords Management, Concord, NH [Library symbol Library of Congress] (LCLS)
NHAR .... Next Higher Assembly Removal Frequency [Engineering] (MCD)
NHarC .... Harriman College, Harriman, NY [Library symbol Library of Congress] (LCLS)
NHARC .... Nursing Home Advisory and Research Council (EA)
NHarn .... Harrison Public Library, Harrison, NY [Library symbol Library of Congress] (LCLS)
NHarnC .... Westchester County Courthouse, Harrison, NY [Library symbol] [Library of Congress] (LCLS)
NHas .... Hastings-On-Hudson Public Library, Hastings-On-Hudson, NY [Library symbol Library of Congress] (LCLS)
NHAS .... National Healthcare Antifraud Association [Address unknown] (EA)
NHAS .... National Hearing Aid Society (EA)
NHASA .... National Handbag and Accessories Salesmen's Association (EA)
NHasI .... Institute of Society, Ethics, and Life Sciences, The Hastings Center, Hastings-On-Hudson, NY [Library symbol Library of Congress] (LCLS)
NHAT .... Neutron Hardness Assurance Test
NHauS .... Suffolk County Department of Health Service, Hauppauge, NY [Library symbol Library of Congress] (LCLS)
NHAW .... Northamerican Heating and Airconditioning Wholesalers Association (EA)
NHAW .... Notable Hispanic American Women [A publication]
NHB .... Kodiak [Alaska] [Airport symbol] (AD)
NHB .... NASA Handbook (KSC)
NHB .... National Harbours Board [Canada]
NHB .... National Health Board
NHB .... National Naval Medical Center [Maryland] [Seismograph station code, US Geological Survey Closed] (SEIS)
NHB .... New Hibernian [Vancouver Stock Exchange symbol]
NHB .... Nitro(hydroxy)benzoic Acid [Organic chemistry]
NHBC .... National House Building Council [British]
NHBE .... Normal Human Bronchial Epithelial [Cells]
NHBPCC ...... National High Blood Pressure Coordinating Committee
NHBPEP ...... National High Blood Pressure Education Program
NHBPM .... National Housebuilders' and Plumbers' Merchants [British] (DI)
NHBRA .... National Housebuilders' Registration Association [British] (DI)
NHBRC .... National House-Builders Registration Council [British] (ILCA)
NHBS .... Navy Headquarters Budgeting System (GFGA)
NHBS/NHPS... Navy Headquarters Budgeting System/Navy Headquarters Programming System (GFGA)
NHBW .... National Hook-Up of Black Women (EA)
NHC .... Colgate University, Hamilton, NY [Library symbol Library of Congress] (LCLS)
NHC .... National Havurah Committee (EA)
NHC .... National Healthcare Ltd. [AMEX symbol] (SPSG)
NHC .... National Health Council (EA)
NHC .... National Homecaring Council [Later, FHH] (EA)
NHC .... National Horse Carriers Association, Inc., Frankfort KY [STAC]
NHC .... National Housing Center
NHC .... National Housing Conference (EA)
NHC .... National Housing Council [of the HHFA] [Abolished, 1965]
NHC .... National Humanities Center (EA)
NHC .... National Hunt Committee [British] (DI)
NHC .... National Hunt Cup [British] (ROG)
NHC .... National Hurricane Center [National Weather Service]
NHC .... Native High Court Reports [South Africa] [A publication] (DLA)
NHC .... Natl Healthcare L.P. [AMEX symbol] (TTSB)
NHC .... Natural Hydrocarbon [Organic chemistry]
NHC .... Navy Department Library, Naval Historical Center, Washington, DC [OCLC symbol] (OCLC)
NHC .... Neighborhood Health Center [Generic term] (DHSM)
NHC .... Neohemocyte [An artificial red blood cell]
NHC .... New Haven [Connecticut] [Seismograph station code, US Geological Survey Closed] (SEIS)
NHC .... N-Hexylcarborane [Rocket fuel] (RDA)
NHC .... Nicaraguan Humanitarian Coalition (EA)
NHC .... Nonhistone Chromosomal Protein [Genetics] (MAE)
NHC .... Normal-Hexylcarbane (MCD)
NHC .... Northwest Horticultural Council (EA)

NHCA .... National Hairdressers and Cosmetologists Association (EA)
NHCA .... National Health Club Association (EA)
NHCA .... National Hearing Conservation Association (EA)
NHCA .... National Hispanic Congress on Alcoholism [Defunct] (EA)
NHCA .... National Hispanic Council on Aging (EA)
NHCAP .... Native Hawaiian Culture and Arts Program [An association] (EA)
NHCC .... NASA Headquarters Computer Center
N-HCC .... Nash-Healey Car Club (EA)
NHCC .... National Havurah Coordinating Committee (EA)
NHCC .... National Health Care Campaign [Defunct] (EA)
NHCC .... National Hebrew Culture Council (EA)
NHCC .... National Hispanic Corporate Council (EA)
NHCE .... Non-Highly Compensated Employee
NHCES .... National Health Care Expenditures Study (DHSM)
NHCFD .... National Health Care Foundation for the Deaf [Later, Deaf-REACH] (EA)
NHCI .... National Home Centers [NASDAQ symbol] (SAG)
NhCla .... Fiske Free Library, Claremont, NH [Library symbol Library of Congress] (LCLS)
NHCP .... National HUMINT Collection Plan (MCD)
NHCP .... Nonhistone Chromosomal Protein [Genetics]
NHCS .... National Health Care Survey [Department of Health and Human Services] (GFGA)
NHCS .... National Home Center Show (ITD)
NHCSA .... National Historic Communal Societies Association [Later, CSA] (EA)
NhCSp .... Saint Paul's School, Concord, NH [Library symbol Library of Congress] (LCLS)
NhCT .... New Hampshire Technical Institute, Concord, NH [Library symbol Library of Congress] (LCLS)
NHCU .... Nursing Home Care Unit [Veterans Administration]
NHCUC .... New Hampshire College and University Council, Library Policy Committee [Library network]
NhD .... Dartmouth College, Hanover, NH [Library symbol Library of Congress] (LCLS)
NHD .... Doctor of Natural History (WDAA)
NHD .... National History Day (EA)
NHD .... New Harding Group, Inc. [Toronto Stock Exchange symbol]
NHD .... Normal Hair Distribution [Medicine] (DAVI)
NHD .... Not Heard [Communications]
NHDA .... National Huntington's Disease Association [Later, HDSA] (EA)
NHDAA .... National Home Demonstration Agents' Association [Later, NAEHE] (EA)
NhD-BE .... Dartmouth College, Business Administration and Engineering Library, Hanover, NH [Library symbol Library of Congress] (LCLS)
NHDC .... National Home Demonstration Council [Later, NEHC] (EA)
NHDC .... NATO HAWK Documentation Center [Missiles] (NATG)
NHDC .... Naval Historical Display Center
NHDC .... Neohesperidin Dihydrochalcone [Also, NEO-DHC] [Sweetening agent]
NhD-D .... Dartmouth College, Dana Biomedical Library, Hanover, NH [Library symbol Library of Congress] (LCLS)
NHDF .... Normal Human Diploid Fibroblast [Medicine] (DMAA)
NhD-H .... Dartmouth College, Hood Museum, Hanover, NH [Library symbol] [Library of Congress] (LCLS)
NHDI .... Notch Die [Tool] (AAG)
NhD-K .... Dartmouth College, Kresge Physical Sciences Library, Hanover, NH [Library symbol Library of Congress] (LCLS)
NHDL .... Nonhigh Density Lipoprotein [Medicine] (DMAA)
NHDNA .... Nucleohistone Deoxyribonucleic Acid
NhDo .... Dover Public Library, Dover, NH [Library symbol Library of Congress] (LCLS)
NhD-P .... Dartmouth College, Paddock Music Library, Hanover, NH [Library symbol] [Library of Congress] (LCLS)
NHDS .... National Hospital Discharge Survey
NHDS .... Nonhazardous Dry Solid [Shipping classification]
NHDSC .... National Hot Dog and Sausage Council (EA)
NHE .... National Housing Endowment (EA)
NHE .... Nitrogen Heat Exchange
NHE .... Normal Hydrogen Electrode
NHE .... North Hennepin Community College Library, Brooklyn Park, MN [OCLC symbol] (OCLC)
NHE .... Nuclease-Hypersensitive Element [Biochemistry]
NHEA .... National Higher Education Association (EA)
NHEB .... National Home Enlargement Bureau [British] (DI)
N HEB .... New Hebrew [Language, etc.] (ROG)
N HEB .... New Hebrides (ROG)
NHEDLP .... National Housing and Economic Development Law Project
NHEF .... National Health Education Foundation
NHEFS .... NHANES [National Health and Nutritional Examination Survey] Epidemiologic Follow-Up Study [Department of Health and Human Services] (GFGA)
NHEK .... Normal Human Epidermal Keratinocyte
NHeLP .... National Health Law Program (EA)
NHELP .... New Hitachi Effective Library for Programming (NITA)
NHem .... Hempstead Public Library, Hempstead, NY [Library symbol Library of Congress] (LCLS)
NHEM .... Normal Human Epidermal Melanocyte [Cytology]
NHemB .... Burns & Roe, Inc., Branch Library, Hempstead, NY [Library symbol Library of Congress] (LCLS)
NHemCE .... William S. Covert School, Hempstead, NY [Library symbol] [Library of Congress] (LCLS)
NHemFE ...... Franklin School, Hempstead, NY [Library symbol] [Library of Congress] (LCLS)
NHemFuE .... Fulton School, Hempstead, NY [Library symbol] [Library of Congress] (LCLS)

NHemGH ...... Hempstead General Hospital, Medical Center, Hempstead, NY [Library symbol Library of Congress] (LCLS)
NHemH .... Hofstra University, Hempstead, NY [Library symbol Library of Congress] (LCLS)
NHemJE .... Jackson Elementary School, Hempstead, NY [Library symbol] [Library of Congress] (LCLS)
NHEML .... National Hurricane and Experimental Meteorology Laboratory [Marine science] (MSC)
NHemLE .... Ludlum School, Hempstead, NY [Library symbol] [Library of Congress] (LCLS)
NHemLJ .... Lawrence Road Junior High School, Hempstead, NY [Library symbol] [Library of Congress] (LCLS)
NHemME ...... Marshall School, Hempstead, NY [Library symbol] [Library of Congress] (LCLS)
NHemMS .... Hempstead Middle School, Hempstead, NY [Library symbol] [Library of Congress] (LCLS)
NHemNH ...... Nassau County Department of Health, Hempstead, NY [Library symbol Library of Congress] (LCLS)
NHemNHR ... Nassau County Department of Health, Division of Laboratories and Research, Hempstead, NY [Library symbol Library of Congress] (LCLS)
NHemPE ...... Prospect School, Hempstead, NY [Library symbol] [Library of Congress] (LCLS)
NHemSH ...... Hempstead Senior High School, Hempstead, NY [Library symbol] [Library of Congress] (LCLS)
NHemWE .... Washington School, Hempstead, NY [Library symbol] [Library of Congress] (LCLS)
NHen .... Henderson Free Library, Henderson, NY [Library symbol Library of Congress] (LCLS)
NHEN .... National Holistic Education Network (EA)
NHENMA ...... National Hand Embroidery and Novelty Manufacturers Association [Defunct] (EA)
NHEP .... Nicaragua-Honduras Education Project (EA)
NHERI .... National Home Education Research Institute (EA)
NHerkCHi .... Herkimer County Historical Society, Herkimer, NY [Library symbol Library of Congress] (LCLS)
NHerrSH ..... Herricks Senior High School, Herricks, NY [Library symbol] [Library of Congress] (LCLS)
NHES .... National Health Enhancement Systems, Inc. [NASDAQ symbol] (NQ)
NHES .... National Health Examination Survey [Department of Health and Human Services] (GFGA)
NHES .... Natl Health Enhacement Sys [NASDAQ symbol] (TTSB)
NHESA .... National Higher Education Staff Association [Defunct] (EA)
NHESP .... Natural Heritage and Endangered Species Program [Massachusetts State Division of Fisheries and Wildlife] [Also, an information service or system] (IID)
NHew .... Hewlett-Woodmere Public Library, Hewlett, NY [Library symbol Library of Congress] (LCLS)
NHewE .... Hewlett Elementary School, Hewlett, NY [Library symbol Library of Congress] (LCLS)
NHewFC ...... Franlin Early Childhood Center, Hewlett, NY [Library symbol] [Library of Congress] (LCLS)
NHewFE ...... Franklin Elementary School, Hewlett, NY [Library symbol Library of Congress] (LCLS)
NHewLD ..... Lawrence Country Day School, Hewlett, NY [Library symbol] [Library of Congress] (LCLS)
NHewOE ...... Ogden Elementary School, Hewlett, NY [Library symbol Library of Congress] (LCLS)
NHewSH ..... G. W. Hewlett Senior High School, Hewlett, NY [Library symbol] [Library of Congress] (LCLS)
NHewWM ... Woodmere Middle School, Hewlett, NY [Library symbol] [Library of Congress] (LCLS)
NhExP .... Phillips Exeter Academy, Exeter, NH [Library symbol Library of Congress] (LCLS)
NHF .... National Hairdressers' Federation [British] (BI)
NHF .... National Handicapped Foundation (EA)
NHF .... National Headache Foundation (EA)
NHF .... National Health Federation (EA)
NHF .... National Health Foundation (NADA)
NHF .... National Heart Foundation (NADA)
NHF .... National Hemophilia Foundation (EA)
NHF .... National Humanities Faculty [Later, NFHAS] (EA)
NHF .... National Hunting and Fishing [In "NHF" Day] [National Rifle Association]
NHF .... National Hydrocephalus Foundation (EA)
NHF .... Nausori Highlands [Fiji] [Seismograph station code, US Geological Survey] (SEIS)
NHF .... Naval Historical Foundation (EA)
NHF .... New Halfa [Sudan] [Airport symbol] (OAG)
NHF .... Nordiska Handikappforbundet [Nordic Association for the Handicapped - NAH] (EAIO)
NHF .... Nordisk Herpetologisk Forening [Scandinavian Herpetological Society - SHS] (EAIO)
NHF .... Nordisk Hydrologisk Forening [Nordic Association for Hydrology - NAH] [Denmark] (EAIO)
NHFA .... National Home Furnishings Association (EA)
NHFF .... National Historical Fire Foundation (EA)
NHFL .... National Home Fashions League (EA)
NHFP .... New Hebrides Federal Party [Political party] (PPW)
NhFr .... Franklin Public Library, Franklin, NH [Library symbol Library of Congress] (LCLS)
NHFRA .... National Hay Fever Relief Association [Defunct] (EA)
NHG .... Newhawk Gold Mines Ltd. [Toronto Stock Exchange symbol Vancouver Stock Exchange symbol]
NHG .... New High German [Language, etc.]

NHG .... Normal Human Globulin [*or anticancer substance derived from NHG*] [*Biochemistry*]

NHG .... Northern Hemisphere Glaciation

NHGJ .... Normal Human Gastric Juice [*Medicine*] (DMAA)

NHH .... Neither Help nor Hinder

NhHaCR .... United States Army, Cold Regions Research and Engineering Laboratory, Hanover, NH [*Library symbol Library of Congress*] (LCLS)

NHHC .... National Home Health Care Corp. [*NASDAQ symbol*] (SPSG)

NHHC .... Natl Home Health Care [*NASDAQ symbol*] (TTSB)

NhHen .... Tucker Free Library, Henniker, NH [*Library symbol Library of Congress*] (LCLS)

NhHenN .... New England College, Henniker, NH [*Library symbol Library of Congress*] (LCLS)

NhHi .... New Hampshire Historical Society, Concord, NH [*Library symbol Library of Congress*] (LCLS)

NhHopA .... New Hampshire Antiquarian Society, Hopkinton, NH [*Library symbol Library of Congress*] (LCLS)

NHHRA .... National Hereford Hog Record Association (EA)

NH-HY .... Harvard University, Harvard-Yenching Institute [*Chinese-Japanese Library*],Cambridge, MA [*Library symbol Library of Congress*] (LCLS)

NHI .... Jacksonville, FL [*Location identifier FAA*] (FAAL)

NHI .... Naphtali Herz Imber (BJA)

NHI .... Nathan Hale Institute (EA)

NHI .... National Health Insurance [*British*]

NHI .... National Health Investors [*NYSE symbol*] (SPSG)

NHI .... National Heart Institute [*Later, NHLI, NHLBI*] [*National Institutes of Health*]

NHI .... National Highway Institute

NHI .... National Hobby Institute [*Defunct*]

NHI .... National Humanities Institute (EA)

NHI .... Nelson Holdings International Ltd. [*Toronto Stock Exchange symbol Vancouver Stock Exchange symbol*]

NHi .... New York Historical Society, New York, NY [*Library symbol Library of Congress*] (LCLS)

NHI .... Nielsen Home Video Index [*A. C. Nielsen Co.*] (NTCM)

NHIA .... National Holography and Imaging Association (EA)

NHIC .... NASA Hazards Identification Committee (KSC)

NHIC .... National Health Information Clearinghouse [*Public Health Service*] [*Later, ODPHP Health Information Center*] (IID)

NHIC .... National Home Improvement Council [*Later, NARI*] (EA)

NHick .... Hicksville Free Public Library, Hicksville, NY [*Library symbol Library of Congress*] (LCLS)

NHickAd .... Hicksville Administration, Hicksville, NY [*Library symbol Library of Congress*] (LCLS)

NHickBE .... Burns Elementary School, Hicksville, NY [*Library symbol Library of Congress*] (LCLS)

NHickCE .... Old Country Elementary School, Hicksville, NY [*Library symbol Library of Congress*] (LCLS)

NHickDLE ..... Dutch Lane Elementary School, Hicksville, NY [*Library symbol Library of Congress*] (LCLS)

NHickEE .... East Elementary School, Hicksville, NY [*Library symbol Library of Congress*] (LCLS)

NHickFE .... Fork Elementary School, Hicksville, NY [*Library symbol Library of Congress*] (LCLS)

NHickHT .... Holy Trinity Diocesan High School, Hicksville, NY [*Library symbol*] [*Library of Congress*] (LCLS)

NHickL .... Long Island Lighting Co., Hicksville, NY [*Library symbol*] [*Library of Congress*] (LCLS)

NHickLE .... Lee Elementary School, Hicksville, NY [*Library symbol Library of Congress*] (LCLS)

NHickOL .... Our Lady of Mercy School, Hicksville, NY [*Library symbol*] [*Library of Congress*] (LCLS)

NHickSH .... Hicksville Senior High School, Hicksville, NY [*Library symbol Library of Congress*] (LCLS)

NHickWE .... Willet Elementary School, Hicksville, NY [*Library symbol Library of Congress*] (LCLS)

NHickWoE ..... Woodland Avenue Elementary School, Hicksville, NY [*Library symbol*] [*Library of Congress*] (LCLS)

NHIF .... National Head Injury Foundation (EA)

NHig .... Highland Free Library, Highland, NY [*Library symbol Library of Congress*] (LCLS)

NHigfL .... Ladycliff College, Highland Falls, NY [*Library symbol Library of Congress*] (LCLS)

NHigm .... Rushmore Memorial Library, Highland Mills, NY [*Library symbol Library of Congress*] (LCLS)

NHIP .... Natl Hlth Inv 8.50%Cv Pfd [*NYSE symbol*] (TTSB)

NHIP .... Nursing Home Improvement Program [*National Institute of Mental Health*]

NHIR .... Natural History Information Retrieval System [*Smithsonian Institution*]

NHIR .... New Hope & Ivyland Railroad Co. [*AAR code*]

NHIS .... National Health Interview Survey [*Department of Health and Human Services*] (GFGA)

NHIS .... Navy Hazardous Materials Information System (DNAB)

NHIS .... New Hampshire International Speedway [*Loudon*]

NHIS .... Nuclear Hardening Interceptor Structure

NHIS .... Nursing Home Information Service (EA)

NHISCH .... National Health Interview Survey of Child Health [*Department of Health and Human Services*]

NHIY .... Northumberland Hussars Imperial Yeomanry [*British military*] (DMA)

NHJA .... National Hunter and Jumper Association (EA)

NHjl .... International Business Machines Corp., Components Division Library, Hopewell Junction, NY [*Library symbol Library of Congress*] (LCLS)

NHK .... Nippon Hoso Kyokai [*Japanese national broadcasting system*] (NTCM)

NHK .... Patuxent River, MD [*Location identifier FAA*] (FAAL)

NhKe .... Keene Public Library, Keene, NH [*Library symbol Library of Congress*] (LCLS)

NhKeHi .... Historical Society of Cheshire County, Keene, NH [*Library symbol Library of Congress*] (LCLS)

NhKeK .... Keene State College, Keene, NH [*Library symbol Library of Congress*] (LCLS)

NHKidQ .... New Horizon Kids Quest, Inc. [*Associated Press*] (SAG)

NHKYA .... National Hand Knitting Yarn Association [*Later, NHKYC*] (EA)

NHKYC .... National Hand Knitting Yarn Committee [*Defunct*] (EA)

NHL .... Hamilton Public Library, Hamilton, NY [*Library symbol*] [*Library of Congress*] (LCLS)

NHL .... National Historic Landmark

NHL .... National Hockey League (EA)

NHL .... Negro Heritage Library

NHL .... Newhall Land & Farming Co. [*NYSE symbol*] (SPSG)

NHL .... Newhall Land/Farming [*NYSE symbol*] (TTSB)

NHL .... Nodular Histiocytic Lymphoma [*Oncology*]

NHL .... Non-Hodgkin's Lymphoma [*Oncology*]

NHL .... Nordic Federation of Heart and Lung Associations (EA)

NHL .... Normal Human Lymphocyte

NHL .... Northcal Resources [*Vancouver Stock Exchange symbol*]

NHL .... Notes from Hume's Lectures [*A publication*] (DLA)

NHLA .... National Hardwood Lumber Association (EA)

NHLA .... National Health Lawyers Association (EA)

NHLA .... National Hispanic Leadership Agenda (EA)

NHLA .... National Housewives' League of America (EA)

NHLBAC .... National Heart, Lung, and Blood Advisory Council [*National Institutes of Health*]

NHLBCA .... National Hockey League Booster Clubs Association (EA)

NHLBI .... National Heart, Lung, and Blood Institute [*Bethesda, MD*] [*National Institutes of Health*]

NHLBIC .... National Heart, Lung, and Blood Information Center (PAZ)

NHLC .... National Hispanic Leadership Conference (EA)

NHLC .... National Home Loans Corp. [*British*]

NhLe .... Lebanon Public Library, Lebanon, NH [*Library symbol Library of Congress*] (LCLS)

NhLeHi .... Lebanon Historical Society, Lebanon, NH [*Library symbol Library of Congress*] (LCLS)

NHLI .... National Heart and Lung Institute [*Later, NHLBI*] [*National Institutes of Health*]

NHLP .... National Housing Law Project (EA)

NHLPA .... National Hockey League Player's Association (EA)

NHL Rep ...... New Hampshire Law Reporter [*A publication*] (DLA)

NHltCre .... National Healthcare Ltd. [*Associated Press*] (SAG)

NhM .... Manchester City Library, Manchester, NH [*Library symbol Library of Congress*] (LCLS)

NHM .... Natural History Museum [*British*]

NHM .... Niihama [*Japan*] [*Seismograph station code, US Geological Survey Closed*] (SEIS)

NHM .... Nitrosohexamethyleneimine [*Organic chemistry*]

NHM .... No Hot Metal [*Photocomposition*]

NHM .... Nonhostile Missing [*Military*] (CINC)

NHM .... Normal Human Milk

NHM .... Nozzle Hinge Moment

NHM .... Nuclear Hyperfine Magnetic [*Rare-earth alloy*]

NHM .... University of New Hampshire, Durham, NH [*OCLC symbol*] (OCLC)

NHMA .... National Handle Manufacturers Association [*Defunct*] (EA)

NHMA .... National Housewares Manufacturers Association (EA)

NHMC .... National Hispanic Media Coalition (EA)

NHMC .... National Hispanic Media Conference (EA)

NHMC .... Normal Human Mammary Cell

NHMEL .... National High Magnetic Field Laboratory

NHMF .... National Heritage Memorial Fund (AIE)

NHMFL .... National High Magnetic Field Laboratory [*Florida State University*]

NHMILCOM... NATO HAWK Military Committee [*Missiles*] (AABC)

NHML .... Non-Hodgkin's Malignant Lymphoma [*Oncology*] (DMAA)

NhMND .... Notre Dame College, Manchester, NH [*Library symbol Library of Congress*] (LCLS)

NHMO .... NATO HAWK Management Office [*Missiles*] (NATG)

NHmpTh .... New Hampshire Thrift Bancshares, Inc. [*Associated Press*] (SAG)

NHMRC .... National Health and Medical Research Council (DAVI)

NHMRC .... National Hotel & Motel Reservations Corp.

NhMSA .... Saint Anselm's College, Manchester, NH [*Library symbol Library of Congress*] (LCLS)

NhMV .... United States Veterans Administration Hospital, Manchester, NH [*Library symbol Library of Congress*] (LCLS)

NHN .... National Homes Network [*British*] (DI)

NHN .... Nebraska HealthNetwork [*Information service or system*] (IID)

NHN .... Northern Horizon [*Vancouver Stock Exchange symbol*]

NhNa .... Nashua Public Library, Nashua, NH [*Library symbol Library of Congress*] (LCLS)

NhNaR .... Rivier College, Nashua, NH [*Library symbol Library of Congress*] (LCLS)

NhNaS .... Sanders Associates, Inc., Technical Library, Nashua, NH [*Library symbol Library of Congress*] (LCLS)

NhNelC .... Colby Junior College for Women [*Later, CSC*], New London, NH [*Library symbol Library of Congress*] (LCLS)

NHNP .... New Hebrides National Party [*Political party*] (FEA)

NHNR .... National Highway Needs Report [*Department of Transportation*]

NHO .... M/I Schottenstein Homes [*NYSE symbol*] (TTSB)

NHO .... National Hospice Organization (EA)

NHO .... Navy Hydrographic Office [*Later, NOO*]

NHO .... Northern Hemisphere Observatory [*Canary Islands*] (PDAA)
NHOA .... National Hemi Owners Association (EA)
NHolb .... Sachem Public Library, Holbrook, NY [*Library symbol Library of Congress*] (LCLS)
NHolbHS ...... Sachem High School North, Holbrook, NY [*Library symbol Library of Congress*] (LCLS)
NHolbSJ ...... Seneca Junior High School, Holbrook, NY [*Library symbol Library of Congress*] (LCLS)
NHoll .... Community Free Library, Holley, NY [*Library symbol Library of Congress*] (LCLS)
NHOP .... National Hurricane Operations Plan (DNAB)
NHorizn .... New Horizon Kids Quest, Inc. [*Associated Press*] (SAG)
NHorW .... Westinghouse Electric Corp., Engineering Library, Horseheads, NY [*Library symbol Library of Congress*] (LCLS)
NHOS .... Naval Hospital
NHP .... National Hamiltonian Party (EA)
NHP .... National Historic Park (BARN)
NHP .... National Housing Partnership [*HUD*]
NHP .... National Humanitarian Party [*Political party Australia*]
NHP .... Nationwide Health Prop [*NYSE symbol*] (TTSB)
NHP .... Nationwide Health Properties, Inc. [*NYSE symbol*] (SPSG)
NHP .... Natural History Press (DGA)
NHP .... Neighborhood Health Program [*Generic term*]
NHP .... Net Horsepower [*Engineering*]
NHP .... Network Host Protocol
NHP .... New Haven Free Public Library, New Haven, CT [*OCLC symbol*] (OCLC)
NHP .... New Health Practitioners [*Nurse practitioners and physician assistants*]
NHP .... NHP, Inc. [*Associated Press*] (SAG)
NHP .... Nitrogen High Pressure
NHP .... Nominal Horsepower
NHP .... Nonhuman Primate
NHP .... Noninverted Hand Position [*Neuropsychology*]
NHP .... Normal Hearing Peer [*of the hearing-impaired*]
NHP .... Normal Human-Pooled Plasma
NHP .... Nuclear Heart Pacer
NHP .... Nursing Home Placement (DAVI)
NHPA .... National Hispanic Psychological Association [*Defunct*] (EA)
NHPA .... National Historic Preservation Act (GNE)
NHPA .... National Historic Preservation Act
NHPA .... National Historic Preservation Act of 1966
NHPA .... National Horseshoe Pitchers Association of America (EA)
NHPA .... Nurse Healers - Professional Association (EA)
NHPAA .... National Horseshoe Pitchers Association of America (EA)
NHPC .... National Historical Publications Commission [*Later, NHPRC*]
NHPDA .... National Honey Packers and Dealers Association (EA)
NHPF .... National Health Policy Forum
NhPHi .... Peterborough Historical Society, Peterborough, NH [*Library symbol Library of Congress*] (LCLS)
NHPI .... NHP, Inc. [*NASDAQ symbol*] (SAG)
NHPIC .... National Health Planning Information Center [*Public Health Service*] [*Database*] (IID)
NHpJR .... James Roosevelt Library, Hyde Park, NY [*Library symbol Library of Congress Obsolete*] (LCLS)
NHPLO .... NATO HAWK Production and Logistics Organization [*France*] (NATG)
NhPIS .... Plymouth State College of the University of New Hampshire, Plymouth, NH [*Library symbol Library of Congress*] (LCLS)
NHPMA .... Northern Hardwood and Pine Manufacturers Association [*Defunct*] (EA)
NHPN .... National Highway Planning Network [*FHWA*] (TAG)
NHPO .... NATO HAWK Production Organization [*Missiles*]
NhPoA .... Portsmouth Athenaeum, Portsmouth, NH [*Library symbol Library of Congress*] (LCLS)
NhPoS .... Strawbery Banke, Portsmouth, NH [*Library symbol Library of Congress*] (LCLS)
NHPP .... National Health Professions Placement Network
NHPP .... National Hormone and Pituitary Program (EA)
NHpR .... Franklin D. Roosevelt Library, Hyde Park, NY [*Library symbol Library of Congress Obsolete*] (LCLS)
NHPRC .... National Historical Publications and Records Commission [*Formerly, NHPC*] [*Washington, DC*]
NHPRO .... National Historical Publications and Records Commission
NHPRO .... Nitrosohydroxyproline [*Organic chemistry*]
NHPSCR ...... New Hampshire Public Service Commission Reports [*A publication*] (DLA)
NHPYR .... Nitrosohydroxypyrrolidine [*Organic chemistry*]
NHQ .... NASA Headquarters
NHQ .... National Headquarters
NHQ .... Nuclear Hyperfine Quadrupolar [*Rare-earth alloy*]
NHQC .... National Hispanic Quincentennial Commission (EA)
NHQRA .... Nursing Home Quality Reform Act
NHR .... National Housewives Register [*British*]
NHR .... National Hunt Rules [*British*]
NHR .... Net Histocompatibility Ratio
NHR .... New Hampshire Reports [*A publication*] (DLA)
NHR .... North Hart Resources [*Vancouver Stock Exchange symbol*]
NHR .... Nova/Husky Research Corp. Ltd. [*UTLAS symbol*]
NHRA .... National Hot Rod Association (EA)
NHRA .... National Housing and Rehabilitation Association (EA)
NHRA .... Next Higher Repairable Assembly (MCD)
NHRAC .... National Health Resources Advisory Committee [*Terminated, 1978*] [*General Services Administration*] (EGAO)
NHRAIC .... Natural Hazards Research and Applications Information Center [*University of Colorado - Boulder*] [*Research center*] (RCD)

NHRB .... National Health Review Board [*Proposed medical-care price regulator*] (ECON)
NHRC .... National Health Research Center (DAVI)
NHRC .... National Human Rights Committee (EA)
NHRC .... National Human Rights Congress [*Australia*]
NHRC .... Naval Health Research Center (GRD)
NHRCPPUS... National Human Rights Campaign for Political Prisoners in the US (EA)
NHRD .... National Health Planning and Resource Development Act [*1974*] (DHSM)
NHRDP .... National Health Research and Development Program [*Canada*]
NHRE .... National Hail Research Experiment
NH Rep .... New Hampshire Reports [*A publication*] (DLA)
NH Rev Stat... New Hampshire Revised Statutes [*A publication*] (AAGC)
NH Rev Stat Ann... New Hampshire Revised Statutes, Annotated [*A publication*] (DLA)
NHRI .... National Health Research Institutes [*Taiwan*]
NHRI .... National Hydrology Research Institute [*Canada*]
NHRL .... National Hurricane Research Laboratory [*Later, AOML*]
NHRL .... Northern Hemisphere Reference Line [*Geology*]
NHRP .... National Heart Research Project
NHRP .... National Hurricane Research Project
NHRP .... Next Hop Resolution Protocol [*Computer science*]
NHRR .... New Haven Railroad
NHRRC .... National Hybrid Rice Research Center [*China*]
NHRS .... New Hampshire Revised Statutes [*A publication*] (DLA)
NHrzWrld ..... New Horizons Worldwide, Inc. [*Associated Press*] (SAG)
NHS .... Das Nordhebraeische Sagenbuch [*A publication*] (BJA)
NhS .... Kelley Memorial Library, Salem, NH [*Library symbol Library of Congress*] (LCLS)
NHS .... Nag Hammadi Studies [*A publication*] (BJA)
NHS .... Nathaniel Hawthorne Society (EA)
NHS .... National Handcraft Society [*Commercial firm*] (EA)
NHS .... National Handicapped Sports (EA)
NHS .... National Health Service [*British*]
NHS .... National Health Survey
NHS .... National Highway System [*Federal transportation planning*]
NHS .... National Highway System
NHS .... National Historical Society [*Commercial firm*] (EA)
NHS .... National Historic Site (BARN)
NHS .... National Honor Society (EA)
NHS .... National Huguenot Society (EA)
NHS .... Native Human Serum Pooled [*Hematology*] (DAVI)
NHS .... Natural Human Serum
NHS .... Naval Honor Schools (AFIT)
NHS .... Neighborhood Housing Services [*Generic term*]
NHS .... New Hampshire State Library, Concord, NH [*OCLC symbol*] (OCLC)
NHS .... New Hampshire Tracking Station
NHS .... N-Hydroxysuccinimide [*Organic chemistry*]
NHS .... Nikon Historical Society (EA)
NHS .... Normal Horse Serum
NHS .... Normal Human Serum
NHS .... North Hampton [*South Carolina*] [*Seismograph station code, US Geological Survey Closed*] (SEIS)
NHSA .... National Handicapped Skiers Association [*British*] (DBA)
NHSA .... National Head Start Association (EA)
NHSA .... National Heart Savers Association (EA)
NHSA .... National Highway Safety Administration [*Formerly, NHSB; later, NHTSA*] [*Department of Transportation*]
NHSA .... National Home Service Association [*Defunct*] (EA)
NHSA .... National Horse Show Association of America (EA)
NHSA .... Natural Health Society of Australia
NHSA .... Naval Historical Society of Australia
NHSA .... Negro Historical Society of America
NHSA .... Neighborhood Housing Services of America (EA)
NHSAA .... National Horse Show Association of America (EA)
NHSAC .... National Health and Safety Awareness Center [*Defunct*] (EA)
NHSAC .... National Highway Safety Advisory Committee
NHSACA ...... National High School Athletic Coaches Association (EA)
NHSAS .... National Health Service Audit Staff [*Department of Health and Social Security*] [*British*]
NHSB .... National High School Band Institute (EA)
NHSB .... National Highway Safety Bureau [*Later, NHSA, NHTSA*] [*Department of Transportation*]
NHsBE .... Birchwood Elementary School, Huntington Station, NY [*Library symbol*] [*Library of Congress*] (LCLS)
NHSBVA ...... National High School Boys Volleyball Association (EA)
NHSC .... National Health Service Corps [*Department of Health and Human Services*]
NHSC .... National Highway Safety Council (NADA)
NHSC .... National Home Study Council (EA)
NHSC .... National Horse Show Commission (EA)
NHsCE .... Countrywood Elementary School, Huntington Station, NY [*Library symbol*] [*Library of Congress*] (LCLS)
NHSCP .... National Household Survey Capability Program [*United Nations*]
NHSCVO ...... National Health Screening Council for Volunteer Organizations (EA)
NHSD .... National Health Survey Division [*of OSG*]
NHSD .... NATO HAWK Support Department [*Missiles*] (NATG)
NHSF .... National Hispanic Scholarship Fund (EA)
NHSF .... National Horse Show Foundation (EA)
NHsH .... Half Hollow Hills Community Public Library, Huntington Station, NY [*Library symbol Library of Congress*] (LCLS)
NHsK .... KLD Associates, Inc., Huntington Station, NY [*Library symbol*] [*Library of Congress*] (LCLS)

NHSL .... New Horizons Savings & Loan Association [*NASDAQ symbol*] (SPSG)

NHSL .... NHS Financial [*NASDAQ symbol*] (TTSB)

NHSM .... No Hepatosplenomegaly [*On physical examination*] [*Gastroenterology*] (DAVI)

NHsME .... Maplewood Elementary School, Huntington Station, NY [*Library symbol*] [*Library of Congress*] (LCLS)

NHsMJ .... Memorial Junior High School, Huntington Station, NY [*Library symbol*] [*Library of Congress*] (LCLS)

NHsOE .... Oakwood Elementary School, Huntington Station, NY [*Library symbol*] [*Library of Congress*] (LCLS)

NHSP .... N-Hydroxysuccinimidyl Palmitate [*Organic chemistry*]

NHSR .... National Hospital Service Reserve [*British*]

NHSRA .... National Handicapped Sports and Recreation Association [*Later, NHS*] (EA)

NHSRA .... National High School Rodeo Association (EA)

NHSS .... National Herb Study Society (EA)

NHsS .... South Huntington Public Library, Huntington Station, NY [*Library symbol Library of Congress*] (LCLS)

NHsSAHS .... Saint Anthony's High School, Huntington Station, NY [*Library symbol*] [*Library of Congress*] (LCLS)

NHsSE .... Silaswood Elementary School, Huntington Station, NY [*Library symbol*] [*Library of Congress*] (LCLS)

NHsSJH .... Henry L. Stinson Junior High School, Huntington Station, NY [*Library symbol*] [*Library of Congress*] (LCLS)

NHSV .... Normal Hourly Space Velocity [*Emission control*]

NHsW .... Walt Whitman Birthplace Association, Huntington Station, NY [*Library symbol Library of Congress*] (LCLS)

NHsWH .... Walt Whitman High School, Huntington Station, NY [*Library symbol*] [*Library of Congress*] (LCLS)

NHT .... Corpus Christi, TX [*Location identifier FAA*] (FAAL)

NHT .... Nationwide Housing Trust [*British*]

NHT .... Nernst Heat Theorem [*Physics*]

NHT .... Nursing Home Type (ADA)

NHTB .... New Hampshire Thrift [*NASDAQ symbol*] (TTSB)

NHTB .... New Hampshire Thrift Bancshares, Inc. [*NASDAQ symbol*] (NQ)

NHTC .... Natural Health Trends Corp. [*NASDAQ symbol*] (SAG)

NHTCW .... Natural Health Trends Wrrt'A' [*NASDAQ symbol*] (TTSB)

NHTCZ .... Natural Health Trends Wrrt'B' [*NASDAQ symbol*] (TTSB)

NHTD .... NASA Headquarters Telephone Directory

NHTP .... Nursing Home-Type Patient

NHTPC .... National Housing and Town Planning Council [*British*]

NHTS .... New Hampshire Tracking Station (SAA)

NHTSA .... National Highway Traffic Safety Administration [*Formerly, NHSB, NHSA*] [*Department of Transportation*]

NHTU .... Naval Hovercraft Trials Unit

NHu .... Huntington Public Library, Huntington, NY [*Library symbol Library of Congress*] (LCLS)

nhu .... New Hampshire [*MARC country of publication code Library of Congress*] (LCCP)

NhU .... University of New Hampshire, Durham, NH [*Library symbol Library of Congress*] (LCLS)

NHUBW .... National Hook-Up of Black Women (EA)

NHUC .... National Highway Users Conference [*Later, HUF*]

NHuCE .... Cuba Hill Elementary School, Huntington, NY [*Library symbol Library of Congress*] (LCLS)

NHudC .... Columbia-Greene Community College, Hudson, NY [*Library symbol Library of Congress*] (LCLS)

NHudDAR .... Daughters of the American Revolution, Hendrick Hudson Chapter, Hudson, NY [*Library symbol Library of Congress*] (LCLS)

NHudHi .... Columbia County, New York Official Historian, Hudson, NY [*Library symbol Library of Congress*] (LCLS)

NhudO .... Olana State Historic Site, Hudson, NY [*Library symbol*] [*Library of Congress*] (LCLS)

NHuEJ .... Elwood Junior High School, Huntington, NY [*Library symbol Library of Congress*] (LCLS)

NHuFE .... Flower Hill Elementary School, Huntington, NY [*Library symbol*] [*Library of Congress*] (LCLS)

NHuFJ .... Finley Junior High School, Huntington, NY [*Library symbol Library of Congress*] (LCLS)

NHuGH .... John H. Glenn High School, Huntington, NY [*Library symbol*] [*Library of Congress*] (LCLS)

NHuH .... Huntington Hospital, Huntington, NY [*Library symbol Library of Congress*] (LCLS)

NHuHAE .... Harley Avenue Elementary School, Huntington, NY [*Library symbol*] [*Library of Congress*] (LCLS)

NHuHE .... Huntington Elementary School, Huntington, NY [*Library symbol*] [*Library of Congress*] (LCLS)

NHuHi .... Huntington Historical Society, Huntington, NY [*Library symbol Library of Congress*] (LCLS)

NHuHS .... Huntington High School, Huntington, NY [*Library symbol Library of Congress*] (LCLS)

NHuI .... Immaculate Conception Seminary, Huntington, NY [*Library symbol Library of Congress*] (LCLS)

NHuJE .... Jefferson Elementary School, Huntington, NY [*Library symbol*] [*Library of Congress*] (LCLS)

NHuL .... Huntington Public Library, Huntington, NY [*Library symbol*] [*Library of Congress*] (LCLS)

NHuMHS .... Madonna Heights High School, Huntington, NY [*Library symbol*] [*Library of Congress*] (LCLS)

NhuSE .... Southdown Elementary School, Huntington, NY [*Library symbol*] [*Library of Congress*] (LCLS)

NHusk .... KLD Associates, Inc., Huntington Station, NY [*Library symbol Library of Congress*] (LCLS)

NHusMJ .... Memorial Junior High School, Huntington Station, NY [*Library symbol Library of Congress*] (LCLS)

NHusWH .... Walt Whitman High School, Huntington Station, NY [*Library symbol Library of Congress*] (LCLS)

NHuTJ .... R. K. Toaz Junior High School, Huntington, NY [*Library symbol Library of Congress*] (LCLS)

NHV .... Nuku Hiva [*French Polynesia*] [*Airport symbol*] (OAG)

NHvL .... Long Island Lighting Co., Hicksville, NY [*Library symbol Library of Congress*] (LCLS)

NHW .... National Health and Welfare Mutual Life Insurance Association [*Formerly, NHWRA*] (EA)

NHW .... Neuhebraeisches Woerterbuch [*A publication*] (BJA)

NHW .... New Hospital for Women [*1904*] [*British*] (ROG)

NHW .... Night Hawk Resources Ltd. [*Vancouver Stock Exchange symbol*]

NhWalHi .... Walpole Historical Society, Walpole, NH [*Library symbol Library of Congress*] (LCLS)

NHWK .... Harris Computer Systems [*NASDAQ symbol*] (TTSB)

NHWK .... Harris Computer Systems Corp. [*NASDAQ symbol*] (SAG)

NHWP .... Northeast Hazardous Waste Project [*Environmental Protection Agency*] (GFGA)

NHWRA .... National Health and Welfare Retirement Association [*Later, NHW*] (EA)

NHWS .... National Hurricane Warning Service [*National Weather Service*]

NHWU .... Non-Heatset Web Unit (EA)

NHWZSP .... National Highway Work Zone Safety Program

nhx .... Albany, GA [*Location identifier FAA*] (FAAL)

nhx .... Narthex (VRA)

NHY .... NIPSCO Industries [*NYSE symbol*] (TTSB)

NHY .... Norsk Hydro AS [*NYSE symbol*] (SPSG)

NHY .... Northumberland Hussars Yeomanry [*British military*] (DMA)

NHyF .... General Services Administration, National Archives and Record Service, Franklin D. Roosevelt Library, Hyde Park, NY [*Library symbol Library of Congress*] (LCLS)

NHZ .... Brunswick, ME [*Location identifier FAA*] (FAAL)

NI .... [*First*] Cranial Nerve [*Second cranial nerve is NII, etc., through NVIII*] [*Medicine*] (DAVI)

NI .... Das Neue Israel [*A publication*] (BJA)

NI .... NAMBA [*North American Model Boating Association*] International (EA)

NI .... National Income

NI .... National Insurance [*British*]

NI .... National Interest

NI .... National Intervenors [*Defunct*] (EA)

NI .... Nation Institute (EA)

NI .... Nation of Ishmael [*An association*] (EA)

NI .... Native Infantry [*Indian Armed Forces regiment*]

NI .... Nautical Institute [*British*] (EAIO)

NI .... Naval Instructor [*British*]

NI .... Naval Intelligence

NI .... Need International [*An association*] (EA)

NI .... Negotiable Instrument

NI .... Netherlands Indies [*Later, Republic of Indonesia*]

NI .... Net Income

NI .... Net Interest

NI .... Network Identification [*Broadcasting*] (NTCM)

NI .... Network International (EA)

NI .... Neuraminidase Inhibition [*Medicine*] (DMAA)

NI .... Neurointermediate Lobe [*Of the pituitary*]

NI .... Neurological Impairment

NI .... Neurological Institute

NI .... Neurologically Intact [*Medicine*]

NI .... Neutralization Index [*Medicine*] (DMAA)

NI .... Neutraminidase Inhibition (PDAA)

NI .... New Impression [*Publishing*]

NI .... New Internationalist [*Australia A publication*]

NI .... New Ireland

NI .... New Issue [*Publishing*]

NI .... News International [*An association*] (EA)

NI .... Niagara Institute (EA)

NI .... Nicaragua [*ANSI two-letter standard code*] (CNC)

NI .... Nickel [*Chemical element*]

ni .... Nickel (VRA)

NI .... Nicolaus de Tudeschis [*Deceased, 1445*] [*Authority cited in pre-1607 legal work*] (DSA)

NI .... Nicolaus Furiosus [*Flourished, 12th century*] [*Authority cited in pre-1607 legal work*] (DSA)

NI .... Night (AABC)

NI .... NIPSCO Industries [*NYSE symbol*] (SPSG)

NI .... Nitrogen [*Chemical element*]

NI .... No Imprint (ADA)

NI .... No Information

NI .... No Interaction [*Medicine*]

NI .... Noise Index

N/I .... Noise to Interference Ratio [*Telecommunications*] (TEL)

NI .... No Issue

NI .... Non-Aligned [*Political group*] [*EC*] (ECED)

NI .... Noninductive (DEN)

NI .... Non-Inhibitable Interrupt (MHDB)

NI .... Non-Interlaced (CDE)

NI .... Nonintervention

NI .... Noninvasive Index [*Medicine*]

NI .... Normal Impurity [*Metals*]

NI .... Normal Inferior

NI .... Northern Indiana Public Service Co. [*NYSE symbol*] (SAG)

NI .... Northern Indiana Railway

NI............ Northern Ireland
NI............ Northern Ireland Law Reports [*A publication*] (DLA)
NI............ North Indiana Public Service Co. [*AMEX symbol*] (SAG)
NI............ North Island [*New Zealand*] (BARN)
NI............ Notice of Information [*Computer science*]
NI............ Not Identified
NI............ Not Illustrated [*Publishing*]
NI............ Not In
NI............ Not Indicated [*Laboratory science*] (DAVI)
NI............ Not Informed
NI............ Not Inoculated
NI............ Not Interested
NI............ Not Isolated
NI............ Not Issued (AAG)
NI............ Nuclear Instrumentation (NRCH)
NI............ Nuclear Island (NRCH)
NI............ Numerical Index (BUR)
NI............ Numismatics International (EA)
NI............ Tompkins County Public Library, Ithaca, NY [*Library symbol Library of Congress*] (LCLS)
NIA........... National Ice Association [*Later, PIA*] (EA)
NIA........... National Iceboat Authority
NIA........... National Impala Association (EA)
NIA........... National Income Accounts
NIA........... National Inholders Association [*Database producer*] (EA)
NIA........... National Institute on Aging [*Bethesda, MD*] [*National Institutes of Health*]
NIA........... National Insulator Association (EA)
NIA........... National Insurance Association [*Chicago, IL*] (EA)
NIA........... National Intelligence Authority [*1946-1947*]
NIA........... National International Academy
NIA........... National Involvement Association (EA)
NIA........... National Irrigation Administration (NADA)
NIA........... Naval Intelligence Activity (DOMA)
NIA........... Navy Industrial Association [*Later, NSIA*]
NIA........... Neighborhood Improvement Association (BARN)
NIAT.......... Neighborhoods-in-Action [*An association*] (EA)
NIA........... Nephelometric Immunoassay [*Analytical chemistry*]
NIA........... Nephelometric Inhibition Assay [*Analytical chemistry*] (MAE)
NIA........... Net Internal Area
NIA........... Newspaper Institute of America (EA)
NIA........... Nickel-Iron Alloy
NIA........... Nitroisatoic Anhydride [*Organic chemistry*]
NIA........... No Information Available
NIA........... No Input Acknowledge [*Computer science*]
NIA........... Norfolk Island [*Australia Seismograph station code, US Geological Survey Closed*] (SEIS)
NIA........... Norfolk Island Airlines [*Australia ICAO designator*] (FAAC)
NIA........... Nutrition Institute of America [*Inactive*] (EA)
NIAA......... National Independent Agents' Association [*Australia*]
NIAA......... National Indian Athletic Association (EA)
NIAA......... National Industrial Advertisers Association [*Later, B/PAA*]
NIAA......... National Institute of Animal Agriculture [*Defunct*] (EA)
NIAAA....... National Institute on Alcohol Abuse and Alcoholism [*Rockville, MD*] [*Public Health Service*] [*Department of Health and Human Services*]
NIAAA....... National Interscholastic Athletic Administrators Association (EA)
NIAA-DTF.... National Industry Associations Anti-Dumping Task Force [*Australia*]
NIAB......... National Institute of Agricultural Botany [*Research center British*] (IRC)
NIAB......... Naval Intelligence Advisory Board (DNAB)
NIABS....... National Institute for Applied Behavioral Science
NIAC........ NASA Industrial Application Center [*University of Southern California*] [*Los Angeles*] [*Information service or system*] (IID)
NIAC........ NASA Industrial Applications Center [*University of Pittsburgh*] [*Pittsburgh, PA*]
NIAC........ National Industry Advisory Committee [*Terminated, 1986*] [*FCC*]
NIAC........ National Information and Analysis Center
NIAC........ National Insulation and Abatement Contractors Association (EA)
NIAC........ National Insurance Advisory Committee [*British*] (DCTA)
NIAC........ Northern Ireland Automation Centre [*Queen's University of Belfast*] (CB)
NIAC........ Nuclear Insurance Association of Canada
NIAC........ Nutritional Information and Analysis Center [*Illinois Institute of Technology and Institute of Food Technologists*] (IID)
NIACA....... National Indirect Air Carrier Association [*Defunct*] (EA)
NIACE....... National Institute for the Advancement of Career Education [*Defunct*] (EA)
NIACE....... National Institute of Adult Continuing Education [*British*]
NIACRO..... Northern Ireland Association for the Care and Resettlement of Offenders (DI)
NIACT....... Night Action [*American diplomat's jargon*]
NIAD........ National Institute on Adult Daycare (EA)
NIADA....... National Independent Automobile Dealers Association (EA)
NIADA....... National Institute of American Doll Artists (EA)
NIADDK..... National Institute of Arthritis, Diabetes, and Digestive and Kidney Diseases [*National Institutes of Health*] (EA)
NIAE........ National Institute for Architectural Education (EA)
NIAE........ National Institute of Agricultural Engineering [*Research center British*] (IRC)
NIAF........ National Italian American Foundation (EA)
NIAG........ NATO Industrial Advisory Group (MCD)
NIAG........ Niagara (ROG)
NIAG........ Niagara Corp. [*NASDAQ symbol*] (TTSB)
NIAG........ Niagara Corp. [*NASDAQ symbol*] (SAG)

Niag.......... Niagara Corp. [*Associated Press*] (SAG)
Niagara U.... Niagara University (GAGS)
NiagCp....... Niagara Corp. [*Associated Press*] (SAG)
NIAGW....... Niagar Corp. Wrrt [*NASDAQ symbol*] (TTSB)
NIAID........ National Institute of Allergy and Infectious Diseases [*of National Institutes of Health*] [*Department of Health and Human Services Bethesda, MD*]
NIAJ......... Niagara Junction Railway Co. [*Absorbed into Consolidated Rail Corp.*] [*AAR code*]
NIAL......... National Institute of Arts and Letters [*Later, AAIAL*] (EA)
NIAL......... Network for Informal Adult Learning (AIE)
NIAL......... Not In Active Labor [*Obstetrics*] (DAVI)
NIALSA...... Northwest Indiana Area Library Services Authority [*Library network*]
NIAM........ National Institute of Advertising Management
NiaM........ Niagara Mohawk Power Corp. [*Associated Press*] (SAG)
NIAMDD..... National Institute of Arthritis, Metabolism, and Digestive Diseases [*Formerly, NIAMD*] [*Later, NIADDK*] [*National Institutes of Health*]
NiaMP....... Niagara Mohawk Power Corp. [*Associated Press*] (SAG)
NIAMS....... National Institute of Arthritis and Musculoskeletal and Skin Diseases [*Bethesda, MD*] [*Department of Health and Human Services*] (GRD)
NIAMSD..... National Institute of Arthritis and Musculoskeletal and Skin Diseases [*Department of Health and Human Services*] (GFGA)
NI & C...... Nippon Information and Communication [*Joint venture of IBM Corp. Japan and Nippon Telegraph and Telephone*]
NI & RT..... Numerical Index and Requirement Table (MCD)
NIANSW..... Nursery Industry Association of New South Wales [*Australia*]
NIAP........ National Income and Products [*Economics*]
NIAP........ Noninverting Amplifier Pair
NIAR........ National Institute of Atmospheric Research
NIAR........ Neutron-Induced Autoradiography
NIAS........ National Institute for Advanced Studies (EA)
NIAS........ National Institute of Aeronautical Sciences
NIAS........ National Institute of Airworthiness Surveyors [*Australia*]
NIASA....... National Insurance Actuarial and Statistical Association [*Later, ISO*]
NIASE....... National Institute for Automotive Service Excellence
NIAT........ Non-Indexable Address Tag (SAA)
NIAT........ Nursery Industry Association of Tasmania [*Australia*]
NIAWA...... Nursery Industry Association of Western Australia [*Australia*]
NIAWR...... National Institute on Aging, Work, and Retirement [*Washington, DC*] (EA)
NIB......... National Identification Bureau [*British*]
NIB......... National Industries for the Blind (EA)
NIB......... National Information Bureau [*Information service or system*] (EA)
NIB......... National Institute for the Blind (EA)
NIB......... National Investment Bank [*Ghana*] (EY)
NIB......... Navigation Information Bulletin
NIB......... Negative Impedance Booster [*Electronics*]
NIB......... Negative Ion Beam
NIB......... Negative Ion Blemish
NIB......... Network Interface Board
NIB......... New Iberia Bancorp [*AMEX symbol*] (TTSB)
NIB......... New Iberia Bancorp, Inc. [*AMEX symbol*] (SAG)
NIB......... Nigeria International Bank Ltd.
NIB......... Node Initialization Block [*Computer science*] (IBMDP)
NIB......... Noninterference Basis
NIB......... Nordic Investment Bank (GNE)
NIB......... Not to Interface Base
NIBA........ National Industrial Belting Association (EA)
NIBA........ National Insurance Buyers Association
NIBAA....... National Insurance Brokers' Association of Australia
NIBC........ Northern Ireland Base Command [*World War II*]
NIBCA....... National Intercollegiate Boxing Coaches Association (EA)
NIberia...... New Iberia Bancorp, Inc. [*Associated Press*] (SAG)
NIberiaB.... New Iberia Bancorp [*Associated Press*] (SAG)
NIBESA...... National Independent Bank Equipment and Systems Association [*Park Ridge, IL*] (EA)
NIBGE....... National Institute of Biotechnology and Genetic Engineering [*Pakistan*]
NIBID....... National Investment Bank for Industrial Development [*Greece*]
NIBJL....... National Information Bureau for Jewish Life (EA)
NIBL........ National Industrial Basic Language (MHDB)
NIBL........ National Industrial Basketball League (EA)
NIBM........ National Institute for Burn Medicine (EA)
NIBMAR...... No Independence before Majority African Rule [*British policy in regard to Rhodesia*]
NIBOR....... New York Interbank Official Rate
NIBRA....... National Independent Bicycle Rep Association [*Defunct*] (EA)
NIBS........ National Institute of Building Sciences (EA)
NIBS........ National Interim Bankruptcy System (AAGC)
NIBS........ Neural, Informational, and Behavioral Science
NIBS........ Neutral Industry Booking System (AAGC)
NIBS........ Nippon Institute of Biological Sciences (DAVI)
NIBSC....... National Institute for Biological Standards and Control [*British*]
NIBTN....... Nitroisobutametriol Trinitrate [*An explosive*]
NIC......... Cornell University, Ithaca, NY [*Library symbol Library of Congress*] (LCLS)
NIC......... Naphthylisocyanate [*Organic chemistry*]
NIC......... National Impeachment Coalition [*Defunct*] (EA)
NIC......... National Incomes Commission [*Nickname: Nicky*] [*British*]
NIC......... National Indications Center [*Disbanded*] [*DoD*]
NIC......... National Industrial Council (EA)
NIC......... National Informatics Center [*India*] [*Information service or system*]
NIC......... National Information Clearinghouse [*for Infants with Disabilities and Life-Threatening Conditions*] (PAZ)

NIC National Information Clearinghouse for Infants with Disabilities and Life-Threatening Conditions
NIC National Institute of Corrections [*Department of Justice*]
NIC National Institute of Creativity [*Defunct*] (EA)
NIC National Institute of Credit [*New York, NY*] (EA)
NIC National Insurance Certificate [*British*]
NIC National Insurance Contribution [*British*] (ECON)
NIC National Insurance Contributions [*British*]
NIC National Intelligence Committee
NIC National Interagency Council on Smoking and Health [*New York, NY*]
NIC National Interfraternity Conference (EA)
NIC National Interrogation Center [*Military*]
NIC National Interstate Council of State Boards of Cosmetology (EA)
NIC National Inventors Council [*Terminated, 1974*] [*National Institute of Standards and Technology*]
NIC Natural Image Computer (PDAA)
NIC Nauru Island Council [*Australia*]
NIC Naval Intelligence Code [*World War II British*]
NIC Naval Intelligence Command
NIC Navigation Information Center
NIC Navy Information Center
NIC Nearly Instantaneous Compounding (MCD)
NIC Neck Injury Criteria [*Automotive safety testing*]
NIC Negative Immittance Converter [*Electronics*]
NIC Negative Impedance Converter [*Electronics*]
NIC Negative Ion Chamber
NIC Neighborhood Info Centers Project (EA)
NIC Neonatal Intensive Care
NIC Netherlands Information Combine [*Delft*] [*Information service or system*] (IID)
NIC Net Interest Cost [*Investment term*]
NIC Network Information Center [*Advanced Research Projects Agency*] [*DoD*]
NIC Network Interface Card [*Computer science*]
NIC Network Interface Card [*Computer science*]
NIC Network Interface Control
NIC Neurogenic Intermittent Claudication [*Medicine*] (DMAA)
NIC New Initial Commissions [*Business term*]
NIC New International Commentary on the New Testament [*A publication*] (BJA)
NIC Newly Industrializing Country (ECON)
NIC Newspaper Indexing Center [*Flint, MI*]
NIC Newsprint Information Committee [*Defunct*] (EA)
Nic Nicander [*Second century BC*] [*Classical studies*] (OCD)
NIC Nicaragua [*ANSI three-letter standard code*] (CNC)
Nic Nicaragua (VRA)
NIC Nicaraguan Information Center (EA)
NIC Nickling Resources, Inc. [*Vancouver Stock Exchange symbol*]
Nic Nicolaus de Tudeschis [*Deceased, 1445*] [*Authority cited in pre-1607 legal work*] (DSA)
NIC Nicosia [*Cyprus*] [*Airport symbol*] (AD)
NIC Nicotinyl Alcohol [*Biochemistry*] (MAE)
nic Niger-Congo [*MARC language code Library of Congress*] (LCCP)
NIC Nineteen-Hundred Indexing and Cataloging (DIT)
NIC NIPSCO Capital Markets [*NYSE symbol*] (SAG)
NIC NIPSCO Cap Mkt 7.75% Debt Sec [*NYSE symbol*] (TTSB)
NIC Noise Isolation Class (PDAA)
NIC Non-Intel [*Corp.*]-Compatible Chips [*Computer science*]
NIC Non-Intervention in Chile [*An association*] (EA)
NIC Noninvasive Carotid [*Study*] [*Cardiology*] (DAVI)
NIC Northern Illinois Commuter [*ICAO designator*] (FAAC)
NIC Not in Contact [*Electronics*] (DEN)
NIC Not in Contract [*Technical drawings*]
NIC Nudist Information Center [*Defunct*] (EA)
NICA National Ice Carving Association (EA)
NICA National Indian Counselors Association (EA)
NICA National Institute of Conveyancing Agents [*British*] (DBA)
NICA National Insulation Contractors Association [*Later, NIAC*] (EA)
NICA National Interfaith Coalition on Aging (EA)
NICA Netherlands Indies Civil Affairs Organization [*World War II*]
NICA Nicaragua Interfaith Committee for Action (EA)
NICA Nicaraguense de Aviacion SA [*Nicaragua*] [*ICAO designator*] (FAAC)
NICAD Nickel Cadmium (NG)
Nic Adult Bast Nicolas' Adulterine Bastardy [*1836*] [*A publication*] (DLA)
Nic & Fl Reg Nicoll and Flaxman on Registration [*A publication*] (DLA)
NICAP National Investigations Committee on Aerial Phenomena [*Defunct*] (EA)
NICAP National Investigations Committee on Aerial Phenomena
NICAP Nuveen Insured California Premium Income Municipal [*Associated Press*] (SAG)
NICAP2 Nuveen Insured California Premium Income Municipal Fund 2 [*Associated Press*] (SAG)
NICAR Nicaragua
NICARD Navy/Industry Cooperative Research and Development Program (MCD)
NICAS Nuveen Insured California Select Tax Free [*Associated Press*] (SAG)
NICATELSAT Nicaraguan Telecommunication by Satellite [*Commercial firm*]
NICB National Industrial Conference Board [*Later, TCB*] (EA)
Nic Bel Nicolaus Bellonus [*Flourished, 1542-47*] [*Authority cited in pre-1607 legal work*] (DSA)
Nic Boe Nicolaus Boerius [*Authority cited in pre-1607 legal work*] (DSA)
NICC National Industrial Conservation Conference
NICC National Inventory Control Center (MCD)
NICC Nationalized Industries Computer Committee (NITA)
NICC Neonatal Intensive Care Center (DAVI)
NICC Nevis Island Cultural Center of the US (EA)
NICCYH National Information Center for Children and Youth with Handicaps (EA)
NICD National Information Center on Deafness (EA)
NICD National Institute on Crime and Delinquency [*Later, NFCJ*] (EA)
NICD Nickel Cadmium (MCD)
Ni-Cd Nickel-Cadmium
NICDA National Imported Car Dealers Association (EA)
NICE National Information Conference and Exposition [*Associated Information Managers*]
NICE National Institute for Computers in Engineering [*Defunct*] (EA)
NICE National Institute for Consumer Education
NICE National Institute of Ceramic Engineers (EA)
NICE Nationally-Integrated Caring Employees [*Union*] [*British*] (DI)
NICE National Society of Fund Raisers Institute of Continuing Education [*Former name of the National Society of Fund Raising Executives Foundation*] (NFD)
NICE Noninvasive Carotid Examination [*Cardiology*] (DAVI)
NICE Noninvasive Cerebrovascular Examination [*Cardiology*] (DAVI)
NICE Nonlinear, Iterative Constrained Estimator (MCD)
NICE Nonprofit International Consortium for Eiffel (EA)
NICE Normal Input-Output Control Executive [*Computer science*]
NICE Northern Indiana Consortium for Education [*Library network*]
NICE^3 National Industrial Competitiveness through Efficiency: Energy, Environment, andEconomics [*Environmental Protection Agency*]
NICEC National Institute for Careers Education and Counselling [*Research center British*] (IRC)
NICEDD National Institute for Continuing Education in Developmental Disabilities (EA)
NICEIC National Inspection Council for Electrical Installation Contracting [*British*]
NICEL National Institute for Citizen Education in the Law (EA)
Nic Elec Nicolson's Elections in Scotland [*A publication*] (DLA)
NICEM National Information Center for Educational Materials (NITA)
NICEM National Information Center for Educational Media [*Later, AV Online*] (EA)
NICER Northern Ireland Council for Educational Research (AIE)
NICET National Institute for Certification in Engineering Technologies (EA)
NICEY NICE-Systems ADR [*NASDAQ symbol*] (TTSB)
NICF National Institute of Carpet Fitters [*British*] (DBA)
NICG National Interagency Coordination Group [*National Atmospheric Electricity Hazards Program*] (MCD)
NICH National Information Center for the Handicapped (EA)
NICH Nitches Inc. [*NASDAQ symbol*] (TTSB)
NICH Nitches, Inc. [*NASDAQ symbol*] (SAG)
NICH Non-Intervention in Chile [*An association*] (EA)
Nic Ha C Nicholl, Hare, and Carrow's Railway and Canal Cases [*1835-55*] [*A publication*] (DLA)
Nich Adult Bast Nicholas on Adulterine Bastardy [*A publication*] (DLA)
Nic H & C Nicholl, Hare, and Carrow's Railway and Canal Cases [*1835-55*] [*A publication*] (ILCA)
NICHCY National Information Center for Children and Youth with Disabilities (PAZ)
NICHD National Institute of Child Health and Human Development [*Bethesda, MD*] [*National Institutes of Health*] (GRD)
Nich H & C Nicholl, Hare, and Carrow's Railway and Canal Cases [*1835-55*] [*A publication*] (DLA)
NICHHD National Institute of Child Health and Human Development [*National Institutes of Health*]
Nicholl H & C Nicholl, Hare, and Carrow [*1835-55*] [*A publication*] (DLA)
Nichols-Cahill Nichols-Cahill's Annotated New York Civil Practice Acts [*A publication*] (DLA)
Nicholson Nicholson's Manuscript Decisions, Scotch Session Cases [*A publication*] (DLA)
NICHROME Nickel Chromium [*Alloy*] [*Trade name*]
NichRs Nichols Research Corp. [*Associated Press*] (SAG)
NICI National Insulation Certification Institute (EA)
NICI National Interagency Counterdrug Institute [*Camp San Luis Obispo, CA*] (DOMA)
NICI Negative Ion Chemical Ionization [*Spectrometry*]
NICIMS Negative Ion Chemical Ionization Mass Spectroscopy
NICIS Nikon Intracellular Calcium Ion System
NICJ National Institute for Consumer Justice
NICK Name Information Correlation Key
NICK Nature's Initial Cosmic Kickstart
NICK Nickelodeon [*Cable television channel*]
nick Nickname
NICLC National Institute on Community-Based Long-Term Care (EA)
NICLF Ni-Cal Developments Ltd. (MHDW)
NICLOG National Information Center for Local Government Records [*Canada*]
NICM National Institute for Campus Ministries (EA)
NICM National Institute of Comparative Medicine (DAVI)
NICMA National Ice Cream Mix Association (EA)
NICMA National Industrial Cafeteria Managers Association [*Later, SFM*] (EA)
NICMOS Near-Infrared Camera and Multiobject Spectrograph [*Astronomy*]
NICN Navy Item Control Number (MCD)
NICNT New International Commentary on the New Testament [*A publication*] (BJA)
NICO National Insurance Consumer Organization (EA)
NICO Navy Indochina Clearing Office (DNAB)
NICO Navy Inventory Control Office
Nico Nicolaus de Tudeschis [*Deceased, 1445*] [*Authority cited in pre-1607 legal work*] (DSA)
NICOA National Independent Coal Operators Association [*Defunct*] (EA)
NICOA National Indian Council on Aging (EA)

Nico Alex.....	Nicolaus de Alexandria [*Authority cited in pre-1607 legal work*] (DSA)
NICOL..........	National Insurance Corp. of Liberia (EY)
NICOL..........	New Integrated Computer Language
NICOL..........	Nineteen-Hundred Commercial Language
Nicolas........	Proceedings and Ordinances of the Privy Council, Edited by Sir Harry Nicolas [*A publication*] (DLA)
Nicollet.......	Nicollet Process Engineering, Inc. [*Associated Press*] (SAG)
NICOP..........	Navy Industry Cooperation Plan
NICOP..........	Nickel Copper
NICOR..........	NICOR, Inc. [*Formerly, Northern Illinois Gas Co.*] [*Associated Press*] (SAG)
NICORD.......	Navy/Industry Cooperative Research and Development Program
NICOS..........	Newfoundland Institute for Cold Ocean Science [*Memorial University of Newfoundland*] [*Canada Research center*] (RCD)
NICOV..........	National Information Center on Volunteerism [*Later, NVC*] (EA)
NICP...........	National Inventory Control Point [*Military*]
NICP...........	NOAA [*National Oceanic and Atmospheric Administration*] Interoceanic Canal Project (NOAA)
NICP...........	Nuclear Incident Control Plan
Nic R..........	Nicolaus Rufulus [*Flourished, 13th century*] [*Authority cited in pre-1607 legal work*] (DSA)
NICRA.........	National Ice Cream Retailers Association [*Later, NICYRA*] (EA)
NICRA.........	Northern Ireland Civil Rights Association
NICRAD.......	Navy/Industry Cooperative Research and Development
NICRISP......	Navy Integrated Comprehensible Repairable Item Scheduling Program
NICRO.........	National Institute for Crime Prevention and Rehabilitation of Offenders
NICS	NAS Interfacility Communications System [*FAA*] (TAG)
NICS	National Airspace System Interfacility Communications System (FAAC)
NICS	National Institute for Chemical Studies (EA)
NICS	National Insurance Contributions System [*Department of Health and Social Security*] [*British*]
NICS	NATO Integrated Communications System (NATG)
NICS	Network Integrity Control System
NICS	Newly Industrialized Countries (DFIT)
NICS	Nissan's Induction Control System [*Automotive engineering*]
NICSE	National Institute for Child Support Enforcement [*Commercial firm*] (EA)
NICSEM	National Information Center for Special Education Materials [*University of Southern California*] [*Los Angeles, CA*]
NICSEM/NIMIS...	National Information Center for Special Education Material/ National Instructional Material Information System (EDAC)
NICSH.........	National Interagency Council on Smoking and Health [*Defunct*] (EA)
Nic Sic Do...	Nicolaus (Siculus Doctor) de Tudeschis [*Deceased, 1445*] [*Authority cited in pre-1607 legal work*] (DSA)
NICSMA.......	NATO Integrated Communications System Management Agency (NATG)
NICSO.........	NATO Integrated Communications System Organization [*Brussels, Belgium*] (NATG)
NIC-TRANS...	Naval Intelligence Command - Translation Division
NICU	Neonatal [*or Newborn*] Intensive Care Unit
NICU	Neurological Intensive Care Unit [*Medicine*]
NICUFO........	National Investigations Committee on Unidentified Flying Objects (EA)
NICWM	National Information Center on Women and the Military [*Later, WMP*] (EA)
NICYRA.......	National Ice Cream and Yogurt Retailers Association (EA)
NID	Inyokern, CA [*Location identifier FAA*] (FAAL)
NID	National Institute for the Deaf (WDAA)
NID	National Institute of Drycleaning [*Later, IFI*] (EA)
NID	National Institute of Dyslexia [*Defunct*] (EA)
NID	Naval Intelligence Database (DOMA)
NID	Naval Intelligence Division [*British*]
NID	Network In-Dial [*Automatic Voice Network*] (CET)
NID	Network Interface Device [*Telecommunications*]
NID	New Interactive Display [*NEC*] [*Computer science*] (PCM)
NID	New International Dictionary [*Webster's*] [*A publication*]
Nid...........	Niddah (BJA)
NID	Nonequilibrium Ionospheric Disturbance [*Geophysics*]
NID	Nonillusion Direction [*Ophthalmology*]
NID	Noninsulin-Dependent [*Diabetes*] [*Endocrinology*] (DAVI)
NID	Non-Internal Development [*DoD*]
NID	Northern Ireland District
NID	Nuclear Instruments and Detectors [*IEEE*] (MCD)
NIDA	National Independent Dairy-Food Association (EA)
NIDA	National Industrial Distributors Association [*Philadelphia, PA*] (EA)
NIDA	National Institute on Drug Abuse [*Department of Health and Human Services*] [*Rockville, MD*]
NIDA	National Insurance Development Act of 1975
NIDA	Northeastern Industrial Developers Association
NIDA	Numerically Integrated Differential Analyzer [*Computer science*]
NIDC	National Insurance Development Corp. [*Government-sponsored organization*]
NIDC	Newly Industrialized Developing Country
NIDCC.........	National Internal Defense Coordination Center [*Army*] (AABC)
NIDCD........	National Institute on Deafness and Other Communication Disorders [*National Institutes of Health*] (EGAO)
NIDD	Non-Insulin-Dependent Diabetes [*Medicine*]
NIDDK........	National Institute of Diabetes and Digestive and Kidney Diseases [*Public Health Service*] [*Also, an information service or system*] (IID)
NIDDKD	National Institute of Diabetes and Digestive and Kidney Diseases [*Department of Health and Human Services*] (GFGA)

NIDDM.........	Non-Insulin-Dependent Diabetes Mellitus [*Medicine*]
NiDI...........	Nickel Development Institute (EAIO)
NIDL..........	Network Interface Definition Language [*Computer science*]
NIDLR.........	Office of the Director of Law Reform, Northern Ireland (DLA)
NIDM..........	National Institute for Disaster Mobilization (EA)
NIDM..........	Noninsulin-Dependent Diabetes Mellitus [*Endocrinology*] (DAVI)
NIDN..........	Navy Intelligence Data Network (MCD)
NIDOC.........	National Information and Documentation Center
NIDOCD	National Institute on Deafness and Other Communication Disorders [*NIH*]
NIDR..........	National Institute for Dispute Resolution (EA)
NIDR..........	National Institute of Dental Research [*Public Health Service*] [*Bethesda, MD*]
NIDRR........	National Institute on Disability and Rehabilitation Research [*Washington, DC Department of Education*] (GRD)
NIDS..........	National Institute of Diaper Services [*Defunct*] (EA)
NIDS..........	National Inventory of Documentary Sources [*British*]
NIDS..........	National Investor Data Service (EA)
NIDS..........	Navigation Instrument Development Unit
NIDS..........	Network Interface Data System (MCD)
NIDS..........	Network Interface Data System [*NASA*]
NIDS..........	Nuclear Integrated Data System
NIE...........	NASA Interface Equipment (MCD)
NIE...........	National Index of Ecosystems [*Australia*]
NIE...........	National Institute for the Environment [*Proposed government agency*]
NIE...........	National Institute of Education [*Department of Education*] [*Washington, DC*]
NIE...........	National Institute of Education, Washington, DC [*OCLC symbol*] (OCLC)
NIE...........	National Intelligence Estimate
NIE...........	Negative Ion Erosion
NIE...........	Netherlands Institute of Ecology
NIE...........	Neutron Ionization Effect
NIE...........	Newly-Industrialized Economy
NIE...........	Newspaper in Education Program
NIE...........	Niedzica [*Poland*] [*Seismograph station code, US Geological Survey*] (SEIS)
NIE...........	Not Included Elsewhere
NIEA..........	National Indian Education Association (EA)
NIEAC	National Indian Education Advisory Committee [*Terminated, 1974*] [*Department of the Interior*] (EGAO)
NIECC........	National Industrial Energy Conservation Council (MCD)
NIEF..........	National Ironfounding Employers Association [*British*] (BI)
NIEHS........	National Institute of Environmental Health Sciences [*Research Triangle Pa rk, NC*] [*National Institutes of Health*]
NIEHS........	National Institute of Environmental Health Service [*Marine science*] (OSRA)
NIEI..........	National Indoor Environmental Institute (EPA)
NIEI..........	National Institute of Electromedical Information (EA)
niel..........	Niello (VRA)
NIEM..........	National Industrial Engineering Mission (AABC)
Nient Cul	Nient Culpable [*Not Guilty*] [*Latin Legal term*] (DLA)
NIEO..........	New International Economic Order
NIER..........	National Industrial Equipment Reserve [*of DMS*]
NIER..........	National Institute for Educational Research (NITA)
NIERC........	Northern Ireland Economic Research Centre
NIES..........	National Intelligence Estimates [*Summaries of foreign policy information and advice prepared for the president*] [*Known informally as "knees"*]
NIESR........	National Institute of Economic and Social Research [*British*]
NIETB........	National Imagery Exploitation Target Base (MCD)
NIETS........	National Imagery Exploitation Tasking Study
NIETU........	National Independent Enginemen's Trade Union [*British*]
NIEU..........	Negro Industrial and Economic Union
NIF...........	National Ichthyosis Foundation (EA)
NIF...........	National Ignition Facility [*Lawrence Livermore National Laboratory*] [*Department of Energy*] (PS)
NIF...........	National Ignition Facility [*For nuclear fusion research*]
NIF...........	National Income Forecasting (ADA)
NIF...........	National Innovation Fund [*South Africa*]
NIF...........	National Institute for the Family (EA)
NIF...........	National Interfraternity Foundation (EA)
NIF...........	National Inventors Foundation (EA)
NIF...........	National Investment Fund [*Poland*] [*Finance*]
NIF...........	National Iranian Front [*Political party*]
NIF...........	National Islamic Front [*Sudan*] [*Political party*]
NIF...........	National Issues Forums (EA)
NIF...........	Navy Industrial Fund
NIF...........	Negative Inspiratory Force [*Medicine*]
NIF...........	Network Information Files [*Burroughs Corp.*]
NIF...........	Neutrophil Migration Inhibition Factor
NIF...........	New Israel Fund (EA)
NIF...........	Nickel-Iron Film
NIF...........	Nifedipine [*Pharmacology*]
nif...........	Nitrogen-Fixing [*Biology*] (BARN)
NIF...........	Noise Improvement Factor (IEEE)
NIF...........	Note-Issuance Facility [*Banking*]
NIF...........	Not Industrially Funded [*Military*]
NIF...........	Not in File
NIF...........	Nuclear Information File (AFM)
NIF...........	Nuveen Prem Insured Muni Inc. [*NYSE symbol*] (TTSB)
NIF...........	Nuveen Premium Insured Municipal Income [*NYSE symbol*] (SPSG)
NIFA..........	National Intercollegiate Flying Association (EA)
NIFAC	Night Forward Air Controller [*Aircraft*]
NIFADCS......	National Institute of Furnace and Air Duct Cleaning Specialists (EA)

NIFAST	National Industrial Fire and Safety Centre (ACII)
NIFB	National Institute of Farm Brokers [Later, NIFLB] (EA)
NIFC	National Interagency Firefighting Center
NIFDA	National Institutional Food Distributor Associates (EA)
NIFE	Nomenclature-in-Federal Employment
NIFEGS	Northern Ireland Further Education Guidance Service (AIE)
NIFER	National Institute for Full Employment Research [Department of Labor] (OICC)
NIFES	National Industrial Fuel Efficiency Service [British]
NIFF	Nordiska Ickekommersielles Fonogramproducenters Forening [Nordic Association of Non-Commercial Phonogram Producers - NANPP] (EAIO)
NIFFTE	Noncooperative Identification Friend or Foe Technology Evaluation (RDA)
NIFI	National Institute for the Foodservice Industry (EA)
NIFL	Finger Lakes Library System, Ithaca, NY [Library symbol Library of Congress] (LCLS)
NIFLB	National Institute of Farm and Land Brokers [Later, FLI] (EA)
NIFLP	Nuveen Insured Florida Premium Income Municipal Fund [Associated Press] (SAG)
NIFMS	NAVAIR [Naval Air Systems Command] Industrial Finance Management System (MCD)
NIFO	Next In, First Out [Queuing technique]
NIFOB	Non-Injurious Free-on-Board
NIFP	National Institute for Federal Procurement (AAGC)
NIFP	National Institute of Fresh Produce [British] (DBA)
NIFRS	Navy Industrial Fund-Reporting System (MCD)
NIFS	National Institute for Farm Safety (EA)
NIFS	NT [New Technology] File System [Microsoft Corp.]
NIFTE	Neon Indicator Functional Test Equipment
NIFTI	Near-Isotropic Flux Turbulence Instrument [Oceanography]
NIFTP	Network Independent File Transfer Program (HGAA)
NIFTP	Network Independent File Transfer Protocol (PDAA)
NIFTS	Naval Integrated Flight Training System (MCD)
NI/FWM	New, Incorporated/Fourth World Movement (EA)
NIG	Aero Contractors Company of Nigeria Ltd. [ICAO designator] (FAAC)
NIG	Nationwide Investigations Group [British]
NIG	Naval Inspector General
NIG	Negative Ion Generator (ADA)
NIG	Niger [Black] [Pharmacy]
NIG	Nigeria
NIG	Nikunau [Kiribati] [Airport symbol] (OAG)
NIG	Nude Ionization Gauge
NIGA	Neutron-Induced Gamma Activity (AABC)
NIGA	Nuclear-Induced Ground Radioactivity (NATG)
NIG&P	Nanjing Institute of Geology and Paleontology [China]
Nig Ann Int'l L	Nigerian Annual of International Law [A publication] (DLA)
Nig Bar J	Nigerian Bar Journal [A publication] (DLA)
Nig BJ	Nigerian Bar Journal [A publication] (DLA)
NIGCS	National Imperial Glass Collectors Society (EA)
NIGDA	National Industrial Glove Distributors Association (EA)
NIGEC	National Institute for Global Environmental Change [University of Southern California and Department of Energy]
Nigeria Bar J	Nigerian Bar Journal. Annual Journal of the Nigeria Bar Association [Lagos, Nigeria] [A publication] (DLA)
Nigeria LR	Nigeria Law Reports [A publication] (DLA)
Nigerian Ann Int'l L	Nigerian Annual of International Law [A publication] (DLA)
Nigerian LJ	Nigerian Law Journal [A publication] (DLA)
NIGHTCAP	Night Combat Air Patrol [Military] (NVT)
Nig Lawy Q	Nigeria Lawyer's Quarterly [A publication] (DLA)
Nig LJ	Nigerian Law Journal [A publication] (DLA)
Nig LQ	Nigeria Lawyer's Quarterly [A publication] (ILCA)
Nig LQR	Nigerian Law Quarterly Review [A publication] (DLA)
Nig LR	Nigeria Law Reports [A publication] (DLA)
NIGMS	National Institute of General Medical Sciences [National Institutes of Health] [Bethesda, MD]
NIGP	National Institute of Governmental Purchasing (EA)
Nigr	Nigeria (VRA)
Nigr	Nigrinus [of Lucian] [Classical studies] (OCD)
NIGS	Non-Inertial Guidance Set (SAA)
NIH	Hoffmann-La Roche, Inc. [Research code symbol]
NIH	National Institute for the Humanities [Yale University] [National Endowment for the Humanities]
NIH	National Institute of Hardware [British] (BI)
NIH	National Institute of Housecraft [British] (BI)
NIH	National Institute on the Holocaust [Later, AFIP] (EA)
NIH	National Institutes of Health [Public Health Service] [Bethesda, MD]
NIH	New Inn Hall [British] (ROG)
NIH	Nonimmune Hydrops [Medicine]
NIH	North Irish Horse [Military unit] [British]
NIH	Not Invented Here (NITA)
NIH	Not Invented Here Syndrome [Business Management]
NIHB	National Indian Health Board (EA)
NIHC	Northern Ireland House of Commons
NIHCA	Northern Ireland Hotels and Caterers Association (ODBW)
NIHD	Noise-Induced Hearing Damage [Medicine] (MEDA)
NIHE	National Institute for Higher Education [Defunct] (ACII)
NIHERST	National Institute of Higher Education (Research, Science, and Technology) [Spain]
NIHF	Nonimmune Hydrops Fetalis [Medicine]
NIHGR	National Institute for Human Genome Research [National Institutes of Health] (BARN)
NIHHD	National Institute of Health and Human Development
NIHi	DeWitt Historical Society of Tompkins County, Ithaca, NY [Library symbol Library of Congress] (LCLS)

NIHL	Noise-Induced Hearing Loss
NIHOE	Nitrogen, Helium, and Oxygen Experiment (DNAB)
NIHR	National Institute of Handicapped Research [Department of Health and Human Services] [Later, NIDRR] [Washington, DC]
NIHS	National Institute of Hypertension Studies - Institute of Hypertension School ofResearch (EA)
NIHS	NAVEUR Intelligence Highlights Summary (MCD)
NIHTA	Northern Ireland Head Teachers' Association
NIHYSOB	Now I Have You, Son of a Bitch [Term coined by Kenneth Blanchard, author of "The One-Minute Manager"]
NII	National Information Infrastructure [Proposed 1992] [Telecommunications]
NII	NATO Item Identification (NATG)
NII	Negative Immittance Inverter (PDAA)
NII	Net Interest Income (TDOB)
NII	Niigata [Japan] [Seismograph station code, US Geological Survey] (SEIS)
NII	Nuclear Installations Inspectorate [British]
NIIA	Nonisotropic Immunoassay
NIIC	Ithaca College, Ithaca, NY [Library symbol Library of Congress] (LCLS)
NIIC	National Injury Information Clearinghouse [Consumer Product Safety Commission]
NIIC	NORAD Intelligence Indications Center (MCD)
NIICP	No Increase in Contract Price
NIICU	National Institute of Independent Colleges and Universities (EA)
NIIG	NATO Item Identification Guide (NATG)
NIIN	National Item Identification Number (MCD)
NII Nor	NII Norsat International, Inc. [Associated Press] (SAG)
NIIO	New International Information Order (NITA)
NIIP	National Institute of Industrial Psychology (PDAA)
NIIP	Net International Investment Position
NIIRS	National Imagery Interpretation Rating Scale (MCD)
NIIS	National Institute of Infant Services [Later, NADS]
NIIS	New Image Industries [NASDAQ symbol] (TTSB)
NIIS	New Image Industries, Inc. [NASDAQ symbol] (NQ)
NIIS	New Item Introductory Schedule (AAGC)
NIIS	Niagara Institute for International Studies [Canada]
NIIS	Nuclear Issues Information Service (IID)
NIIT	National Information Infrastructure Testbed [Telecommunications] (PCM)
NIIU	Neozyme Corp. [NASDAQ symbol] (SAG)
NIJ	National Institute of Justice [Department of Justice] [Washington, DC]
NIJ	National Institute of Justice
NIJ	National Institute of Justice (USGC)
NIJ	New Irish Jurist [A publication] (DLA)
NIJD	National Institute of Judicial Dynamics [Defunct] (EA)
NIJH	National Institute for Jewish Hospice (EA)
NIJJDP	National Institute for Juvenile Justice and Delinquency Prevention
NIJR	New Irish Jurist [A publication] (DLA)
NIK	Boston, MA [Location identifier FAA] (FAAL)
NIK	Nickel [Watchmaking] (ROG)
NIK	Nickel Rim Mines Ltd. [Toronto Stock Exchange symbol]
NIK	Nikolski [Alaska] [Seismograph station code, US Geological Survey Closed] (SEIS)
nik	Northern Ireland [MARC country of publication code Library of Congress] (LCCP)
NIK	Novye Inostrannyye Knigi [New Foreign Books] [A publication]
NIKA	Northern Ireland Korfball Association (EAIO)
NikeB	Nike, Inc. [Associated Press] (SAG)
NIKKEI	Nihon Keizai Shimbun, Inc. [Tokyo, Japan] (IID)
NIL	Negotiable Instruments Law (DLA)
NIL	Neurointermediate Lobe [Neuroanatomy]
NIL	Nilore [Pakistan] [Seismograph station code, US Geological Survey] (SEIS)
NIL	Nitrogen Inerting Line (IEEE)
NIL	No Limit (NASA)
NIL	Nothing in Light Disease [Nephrotic Syndrome] (DAVI)
NIL	Not in Labor [Medicine]
NIL	Nuclear-Induced Lightning
NILA	National Industrial Leather Association [Later, NIBA] (EA)
NILab	Northern Ireland Labour Party [Political party Defunct]
NILB	National Indian Lutheran Board (EA)
NILC	National Immigration Law Center (EA)
NILE	National Institute of Labor Education [Defunct] (EA)
NILE	Naval Inflatable Life-Saving Equipment [British military] (DMA)
NILE	Number of Inverters Along Any Loop is Even (MHDI)
NILE & CJ	National Institute of Law Enforcement and Criminal Justice [Law Enforcement Assistance Administration]
NILECJ	National Institute of Law Enforcement and Criminal Justice [Law Enforcement Assistance Administration]
Niles Reg	Niles' Weekly Register [A publication] (DLA)
NILF	Not in Labor Force (GFGA)
NILFP	National Institute of Locker and Freezer Provisioners [Later, AAMP] (EA)
NILGOSC	Northern Ireland Local Government Officers Superannuation Committee
NIIH	Herkimer County Community College, Ilion, NY [Library symbol Library of Congress] (LCLS)
NILI	Netsah Israel Lo Yeshakker (BJA)
NILI	Newark Island Layered Intrusion [Geology] [Canada]
NILKY	No Income, Lots of Kids [Lifestyle classification]
NILN	Nylon Insert Lock Nut
NILO	Naval Intelligence Liaison Officer (NVT)

NILP............ Northern Ireland Labour Party [*Political party Defunct*] (PPW)
NILPT.......... National Institute for Low Power Television [*Defunct*] (EA)
NILR .... Northern Ireland Law Reports [*A publication*] (DLA)
NILRC.......... Northern Illinois Learning Resources Cooperative [*Library network*]
Nil Reg........ Niles' Weekly Register [*A publication*] (DLA)
NILS............ Naval Intelligence Locating Summary (MCD)
NILS............ Newsletter of International Labour Studies [*Netherlands*]
NILS............ Northern Illinois Library System [*Library network*]
NILS............ Nuclear Instrument Landing System
NILT............ National Institute for Lay Training [*Defunct*] (EA)
NILTC.......... National Industrial Language Training Centre (AIE)
NILUG.......... National Independent Lynx User Group (NITA)
NIM............. National Impact Model [*Environmental Protection Agency*] (ERG)
NIM............. Naval Inspector of Machinery
NIM............. Net Interest Margin [*Banking*]
NIM............. Networked Interactive Multimedia
NIM............. Network Injection Molding
NIM............. Network Interface Machine [*Datapac*]
NIM............. Network Interface Module [*Telecommunications*] (TSSD)
NIM............. Network Interface Monitor
NIM............. Neurological Impress Method (EDAC)
NIM............. Newspapers in Microform (NITA)
NIM............. Niamey [*Niger*] [*Airport symbol*] (OAG)
NIM............. Night Intruder Mission [*Air Force*]
NIM............. No Immediate Miracles [*Acronym and facetious translation derived from turning President Gerald Ford's anti-inflation WIN buttons upside down*] [*See WIN entry*]
NIM............. Noninterrupt Mode
NIM............. NORAD Intelligence Memorandum (MCD)
NIM............. Normal Integration Mode
NIM............. North Irish Militia [*Military unit*] [*British*]
NIM............. Nothing in Mind [*Acronym and facetious translation derived from turning President Gerald Ford's anti-inflation WIN buttons upside down*] [*See WIN entry*]
NIM............. Nuclear Instrumentation Module
NIM............. Nuveen Select Maturities Muni [*NYSE symbol*] (TTSB)
NIM............. Nuveen Select Maturities Municipal [*NYSE symbol*] (SPSG)
NIM............. Nylon Insulation Material
NIM............. University of North Carolina at Asheville, Asheville, NC [*OCLC symbol*] (OCLC)
NIMA .... National Insulation Manufacturers Association [*Later, Thermal Insulation Manufacturers Association*] (EA)
NIMA .... Noninherited Maternal Antigen [*Genetics*] [*Immunology*]
NIMAB .... National Indian Manpower Advisory Board
NIMAC .... National Interscholastic Music Activities Commission [*Defunct*] (EA)
NIMBAS ...... The Netherlands Insitute for MBA Studies
NIMBIN .... Nuclear Instrumentation Modular Bin
NIMBUS...... Network Information Management Client-Based User Service (USDC)
NIMBUS...... Network Information Management Client-Based User Service [*Marine science*] (OSRA)
Nimbus........ Nimbus CD International, Inc. [*Associated Press*] (SAG)
NIMBUS-7.... NOAA [*National Oceanic and Atmospheric Administration*] Satellite (USDC)
NIMBY .... Not in My Back Yard [*i.e., garbage incinerators, prisons, roads, etc.*]
NIMC .... National Institute of Management Counsellors (EA)
NIMC .... National Institute of Municipal Clerks [*Later, IIMC*]
NIMC .... Nodding Image Motion Compensation [*Instrumentation*]
NIMCGA ...... Northern Indiana Muck Crop Growers Association [*Defunct*] (EA)
NIMCP .... NATO Information Management Control Point (NATG)
NIME .... National Institute for Multicultural Education [*Defunct*] (EA)
NIMEX .... Nomenclature for Imports and Exports [*European Community*] (PDAA)
NIMEY .... Not in My Election Year [*Slang*]
NIMFR .... National Institutes of Marriage and Family Relations (EA)
NIMFY .... Not in My Front Yard [*i.e., Garbage incinerators, landfills, etc.*]
NIMH .... National Institute of Medical Herbalists [*British*]
NIMH .... National Institute of Mental Health [*Rockville, MD*] [*Department of Health and Human Services*]
NiMH .... Nickel-Metal Hydride [*Organic chemistry*] (PS)
NIMIC .... NATO [*North Atlantic Treaty Organization*] Insensitive Munitions Information Center
NIMIC .... Not in My Insurance Company [*Insurance slang*]
NIMIS .... National Instructional Materials Information System
NIMIT.......... Nimbus Integration and Test [*NASA*] (KSC)
NIMJ........... Near Infrared Miniaturized Jammer
NIML .... National Independence Movement of Latvia [*Political party*]
NIMLO .... National Institute of Municipal Law Officers (EA)
NIMLO Mun L Rev... National Institute of Municipal Law Officers. Municipal Law Review [*A publication*] (DLA)
NIMMA .... Northern Ireland Mixed Marriage Association
NIMMP .... National Institute of Marine Medicine and Pharmacology [*Proposed*] [*National Institutes of Health*]
NIMMS .... Nineteen-Hundred Integrated Modular Management System
NIMP .... National Intern Matching Program [*Later, NRMP*] (EA)
NIMP .... New and Improved Materials and Processes (PDAA)
N IMP .... New Impression [*Publishing*] (DGA)
NIMPA .... National Independent Meat Packers Association [*Later, NMA*] (EA)
NIMPH .... Network Interface Message Processing Host [*NERComP*]
NIMPHE ...... Nuclear Isotope Monopropellant Hydrazine Engine
NIMR .... National Institute for Medical Research [*British*]
NIMR .... Navy Industrial Management Reviews (NG)
NIMROD ...... National Institute for Medical Research Online Database (PDAA)
NIMROD ...... Nineteen-Hundred [*Computer*] Management and Recovery of Documentation (PDAA)

NIMROD ...... Northern Illinois Meteorological Research on Downbursts [*National Center for Atmospheric Research*]
NIMRS .... Navy Integrated Message Reporting System (MCD)
NIMS .... National Infant Mortality Survey [*Department of Health and Human Services*] (GFGA)
NIMS .... National Information Management System
NIMS .... National Ingredient Marketing Specialists (EA)
NIMS .... Nationwide Improved Mail Service [*Postal Service*]
NIMS .... Near Infrared Mapping Spectrometer [*Instrument on Galileo spacecraft*] [*NASA*]
NIMS .... Nuclear Instrumentation Modular System (MCD)
NIMSC .... Nonconsumable Item Materiel Support Code [*Military*] (AFIT)
NIMSCO ...... NODC [*National Oceanographic Data Center*] Index to Instrument Measures Subsurface Current Observations [*Marine science*] (MSC)
NIMSDP...... Non-Innovator Multiple Source Drug Product
NIMSR........ Nonconsumable Item Materiel Support Request [*Military*] (AFIT)
NIMT........... National Institute for Music Theater [*Defunct*] (EA)
NIMTECH .... New and Improved Technology [*British*]
NIMTOF ...... Not in My Term of Office [*Government slang*]
NIN .... National Information Network [*ASTIA*]
NIN .... National Inservice Network
NIN .... Neighbors in Need [*An association*]
NIN .... Nine Inch Nails [*Rock music group*]
NIN .... Nine West Group [*NYSE symbol*] (TTSB)
NIN .... Nine West Group, Inc. [*NYSE symbol*] (SPSG)
NIN .... Ninhydrine [*Chemical agent used in espionage*]
NIN .... Ninilchik [*Alaska*] [*Seismograph station code, US Geological Survey Closed*] (SEIS)
NIN .... Ninilchik, AK [*Location identifier FAA*] (FAAL)
NIN .... Norsat International, Inc. [*Vancouver Stock Exchange symbol*]
NINA .... National Institute Northern Accelerator (PDAA)
NINA .... Neutron Instruments for Nuclear Analysis (PDAA)
NINA .... No Irish Need Apply [*Classified advertising*]
NINB .... National Institute of Neurology and Blindness (WDAA)
NINCDS....... National Institute of Neurological and Communicative Disorders and Stroke [*Formerly, NINDS*] [*Public Health Service Bethesda, MD*]
NINDB .... National Institute of Neurological Diseases and Blindness [*Later, NEI, NINDS*] [*National Institutes of Health*]
NInDE .... Elementary School No. 2, Inwood, NY [*Library symbol*] [*Library of Congress*] (LCLS)
NINDS......... National Institute of Neurological Diseases and Stroke [*Formerly, NINDB*] [*Later, NINCDS*] [*National Institutes of Health*]
NINDS......... National Institute of Neurological Disorders and Stroke
NIndTP........ National Independent Teenage Party [*British*]
NINE .... National Infertility Network Exchange [*An association*] (EA)
NINE .... Ninth-Plate (VRA)
NINE .... Number Nine Visual Tech [*NASDAQ symbol*] (TTSB)
NINE .... Number Nine Visual Technology, Inc. [*NASDAQ symbol*] (SAG)
Nine-C Lit.... Nineteenth-Century Literature [*A publication*] (BRI)
NINES .... Norfolk Information Exchange Scheme (NITA)
NineWest..... Nine West Group, Inc. [*Associated Press*] (SAG)
NINFRA....... National Independent Nursery Furniture Retailers Association (EA)
NINIA .... Nephelometric Inhibition Immunoassay [*Analytical chemistry*]
Nink............ No Income, No Kids [*Lifestyle classification*]
NINO .... No Inspector, No Operator (ODBW)
NINOW........ Non-Interest-Bearing Negotiable Order of Withdrawal [*Banking*]
NINR .... National Institute for Nursing Research
NINS .... Northern Ireland News Service [*Information service or system*] (IID)
NINST .... Non-Instrument Runway [*Aviation*] (DA)
NINST .... Nose Instantaneous [*Aerospace*]
NINVS........ Noninvasive Neurovascular Study [*Medicine*] (DAVI)
NInWE .... Elementary School No. 4, Inwood, NY [*Library symbol*] [*Library of Congress*] (LCLS)
NINYP .... Nuveen Insured New York Premium Income Municipal [*Associated Press*] (SAG)
NINYS........ Nuveen Insured New York Select Tax Free Income [*Associated Press*] (SAG)
NIO .... National Institute of Oceanography [*British*] (IID)
NIO .... National Intelligence Officer (MCD)
NIO .... Naval Inspector of Ordnance
NIO .... Navigational Information Office
NIO .... Navy Institute of Oceanography
NIO .... Nieuwe Internationale Orde [*Netherlands*]
NIO .... Niobium [*See Cb*] [*Chemical element*] (ROG)
NIO .... Nioki [*Zaire*] [*Airport symbol*] (OAG)
NIO .... Northern Ireland Office
NIO .... Nuveen Ins Muni Oppt Fd [*NYSE symbol*] (TTSB)
NIO .... Nuveen Insured Municipal Opportunity Fund [*NYSE symbol*] (SPSG)
NIOBE .... Numerical Integration of the Boltzmann Transport Equation
NIOD.......... Network In-Out Dial [*Automatic Voice Network*] (CET)
NIOF.......... National Institute of Oceanography and Fisheries [*Egypt*] [*Marine science*] (OSRA)
NIOG.......... Nationalized Industries Overseas Group [*British*] (DCTA)
NIOK.......... National Institute for Overseas Koreans (EA)
NIOK.......... Nederlands Instituut voor Onderzoek in de Katalyse [*Netherlands Institute for Catalysis Research*]
NIOP.......... National Institute of Oilseed Products (EA)
NIOPSWL.... New Input/Output Program Status Word Location [*Computer science*] (MHDI)
NIOS .... Nixdorf Integrated Office System (HGAA)
NIOS .... Northern Ireland Orchid Society (EAIO)
NIOSH......... National Institute for Occupational Safety and Health [*Public Health Service*] [*Cincinnati, OH Database producer*]

NIOSHTIC .... National Institute for Occupational Safety and Health Technical Information Center [*Database*] [*NIOSH*] [*Information service or system*] (CRD)

NIOSHTIC .... NIOSH Technical Information Center (NITA)

NIOTC .... Naval Inshore Operations Training Center (NVT)

NIOZ .... Netherlands Institute for Sea Research [*Marine science*] (OSRA)

NIp .... Island Park Public Library, Island Park, NY [*Library symbol Library of Congress*] (LCLS)

NIP .... Jacksonville, FL [*Location identifier FAA*] (FAAL)

NIP .... Mononitroiodophenyl [*Organic chemistry*] (DAVI)

NIP .... NADGE [*NATO Air Defense Ground Environment*] Improvement Plan (NATG)

NIP .... Namibia Independence Party [*Political party*] (PPW)

NIP .... National Identification Program for the Advancement of Women in Higher EducationAdministration (EA)

NIP .... National Impatient Profile (MEDA)

NIP .... National Independence Party [*Namibia*] [*Political party*] (PPW)

NIP .... National Industrial Partner

NIP .... National Inspection Plan [*RSPA*] (TAG)

NIP .... National Institute of Polarology [*Research center British*] (IRUK)

NIP .... National Integration Party [*Liberia*] [*Political party*] (EY)

NIP .... National Intelligence Priorities (MCD)

NIP .... National Inventory Programme [*National Museums of Canada*] [*Later, CHIN*]

NIP .... Naval Institute Press [*Publisher*]

NIP .... Naval Intelligence Professionals (EA)

NIP .... Navy Interceptor Program

NIP .... Negative Inspiratory Pressure [*Medicine*] (DAVI)

NIP .... Neighbourhood Improvement Program [*Canada*]

NIP .... Network Input Processor [*Computer science*] (MCD)

NIP .... Network Interface Processor (MCD)

NIP .... New Impact Resources, Inc. [*Vancouver Stock Exchange symbol*]

NIP .... New Incentive Package (ADA)

NIP .... Newsletters in Print [*Formerly, ND*] [*A publication*]

NIP .... Nipple (AAG)

NIP .... Nipple

NIP .... Nipponese

NIP .... Nonimpact Printer

NIP .... Normal Impact Point

NIP .... Normal Incidence Pyrheliometer (PDAA)

NIP .... Normal Investment Practice

NIP .... Notice of Intelligence Potential [*Military*] (AFM)

NIP .... Notice of Intent to Purchase [*DoD*]

NIP .... Nucleus Initialization Program [*Computer science*]

NIP .... Numeric Indicator Performance

NIP .... Numero d'Identification Personnel [*Personal Identification Number - PIN*]

NIPA .... National Income and Product Accounts [*The WEFA Group*] [*Information service*] [*Information service or system*] (CRD)

NIPA .... National Institute of Pension Administrators [*Santa Ana, CA*] (EA)

NIPA .... National Institute of Public Affairs

NIPA .... N-Isopropylacrylamide [*Organic chemistry*]

NIPA .... Noninherited Paternal Antigen [*Genetics*] [*Immunology*]

NIPA .... Noninterference Performance Assessment

NIPA .... Nordens Institut pa Aland [*Nordic Institute in Aland - NIA*] [*Finland*] (EAIO)

NIPA .... Northern Ireland Ploughing Association (EAIO)

NIPA .... Northern Ireland Police Authority

NIPA .... Notice of Initiation of Procurement Action (NRCH)

NIPAGRAM... National Income and Product Account Data by Mailgram [*NTIS*]

NIPALS ...... Noniterative Partial Least Squares [*Algorithm*]

NIP & TB .... Northern Ireland Postal and Telecommunications Board

NIPC .... N-Isopropylcarbazole [*Organic chemistry*]

NIPCC .... National Industrial Pollution Control Council [*Terminated, 1973*] [*Department of Commerce*]

NIPD .... Not in the Public Domain

NIPDWR ...... National Interim Primary Drinking Water Regulations [*Environmental Protection Agency*]

NIPDWS ...... National Interim Primary Drinking Water Standards [*Environmental Protection Agency*]

NIPE .... Noninvasive Peripheral Vascular Examination [*or Evaluation*] (DAVI)

NIPER .... National Institute for Petroleum and Energy Research [*Formerly, BETC*] [*Department of Energy Bartlesville, OK*]

NIPERA .... Nickel Producers Environmental Research Association

NIPF .... Northern Ireland Peace Forum

NIPFDA .... National Independent Poultry and Food Distributors Association (EA)

NIPGM .... National Institute on Park and Grounds Management (EA)

NIPH .... National Institute of Poultry Husbandry [*British*] (BI)

NIPH .... National Institute of Public Health

NIpHE .... Francis X. Hegarty Elementary School, Island Park, NY [*Library symbol*] [*Library of Congress*] (LCLS)

NIPHL .... Noise-Induced Permanent Hearing Loss (PDAA)

NIPHLE .... National Institute of Packaging, Handling, and Logistic Engineers (EA)

NIPILS .... New Irish Professionals in London [*Lifestyle classification*]

NIPIM2 .... Nuveen Insured Premium Income Municipal Fund 2 [*Associated Press*] (SAG)

NIPIMn .... Nuveen Insured Premium Income Municipal Fund [*Associated Press*] (SAG)

NIPIMS .... NAVMAT Instructional Procurement Inventory Monitoring System (MCD)

NIPIR .... Nuclear Immediate Photo Interpretation Report (MCD)

NIpL .... Lincoln Orens School, Island Park, NY [*Library symbol*] [*Library of Congress*] (LCLS)

NIPM .... National Institute of Public Management (EA)

NIPN .... NEC Corp. [*NASDAQ symbol*] (SAG)

NIP/NLG ...... National Immigration Project of the National Lawyers Guild (EA)

NIPNY .... NEC Corp. ADR [*NASDAQ symbol*] (TTSB)

NIPO .... Negative Input, Positive Output

NIPOLOS ..... Nonimpact Off-Line Operating System [*Computer science*]

NIPP .... National Institute for Public Policy (EA)

NIPP .... National Intelligence Projection for Planning (AFM)

NIPP .... Net Income per Partner [*Business term*]

NIPP .... Nonimpact Printing Process (MCD)

NIPPE .... National Income per Person Employed

NIPPING ...... Nonimpact Printing (DGA)

NippnTT ...... Nippon Telegraph & Telephone Co. [*Associated Press*] (SAG)

NIPR .... National Industrial Plant Reserve

NIPR .... Naval Intelligence Publication Register (NVT)

ni pr .... Nisi Prius [*Unless Before*] [*Legal term Latin*] (WGA)

NIPr .... North'n Ind Pub Sv.4 1/4%cmPfd [*AMEX symbol*] (TTSB)

NIPrA .... North'n Ind Pub Sv Adj RtA Pfd [*NYSE symbol*] (TTSB)

NI PRI .... Nisi Prius [*Unless Before*] [*Legal term Latin*]

NIPS .... National Information Processing System [*Military*]

NIPS .... National Institute for Public Services

NIPS .... National Inventory of Pollution Sources [*Database*] [*Environment Canada*] [*Information service or system*] (CRD)

NIPS .... Nationwide Integrated Postal Service [*Postal Service*]

NIPS .... Naval Intelligence Processing System

NIPS .... Navy Information Policy Summaries (NG)

NIPS .... New Inventory Pricing Systems (MCD)

NIPS .... Nippon Information Processing System [*Nippon Shuppan Hanbai, Inc.*] [*Database*]

NIPS .... NIPSCO Capital Markets [*Associated Press*] (SAG)

NIPS .... NMCS Information Processing System (NITA)

NIPS .... Northern Indiana Public Service Co. [*Associated Press*] (SAG)

NIPSA .... Northern Ireland Public Service Alliance (EAIO)

NIPSCO .... NIPSCO Industries [*Associated Press*] (SAG)

NIPSSA .... Naval Intelligence Processing System Support Activity

NIPT .... New Information Processing Technology Project [*Japan*] (ECON)

NIPTS .... Noise-Induced Permanent Threshold Shift [*Hearing*]

NIR .... Beeville, TX [*Location identifier FAA*] (FAAL)

NIr .... Irvington Public Library, Irvington, NY [*Library symbol Library of Congress*] (LCLS)

NIR .... National Inventory Record [*DoD*]

NIR .... Near Infrared (ECII)

NIR .... Near Infrared Region

NIR .... Nerve Impulse Recorder

NIR .... Network Information Retrieval

NIR .... New Ireland Review [*A publication*] (ROG)

NIR .... Next Inferior Rank

NIR .... Next Instruction Register (NITA)

NIR .... Nitrite Reductase [*An enzyme*]

NIR .... No Individual Requirement (MSA)

NIR .... Noninductive Resistor

NIR .... Non-Insulin-Requiring [*Medicine*]

NIR .... Norskair [*Norway ICAO designator*] (FAAC)

N Ir .... Northern Ireland Law Reports [*A publication*] (DLA)

NIR .... Northern Ireland Railways Co. Ltd.

NIR .... Nose Impact Rocket (NATG)

NIRA .... National Industrial Recovery Act [*1933*]

NIRA .... National Industrial Recovery Administration (WDAA)

NIRA .... National Industrial Recreation Association [*Later, NESRA*] (EA)

NIRA .... National Industrial Reserve Act of 1948

NIRA .... National Intercollegiate Rodeo Association (EA)

NIRA .... Navy Industrial Relations Activity (DNAB)

NIRA .... Navy Internal Relations Activity (DNAB)

NIRA .... Near Infrared Reflectance Analysis

NIRAP .... Naval Industrial Reserve Aircraft Plant (MUGU)

NIRAS .... National Institute of Research and Advanced Studies [*Proposed*]

NIRB .... National Industrial Recovery Board [*Terminated, 1935*]

NIRB .... Nuclear Insurance Rating Bureau

NIRC .... National Industrial Relations Court [*British*]

NIRC .... National Information Retrieval Colloquium [*Later, Benjamin Franklin Colloquium on Information Science*]

NIRC .... National Institute of Rug Cleaning [*Superseded by AIDS International*] (EA)

NIRC .... Negative Ion Recombination Chamber

NIRCF .... National Immigration, Refugee and Citizenship Forum (EA)

NIRD .... National Institute for Research in Dairying [*British*]

NIRD .... Nonimmune Renal Disease [*Medicine*] (DMAA)

NIRDR .... Nonintegrated RADAR (MCD)

NIRE .... National Institute for Rehabilitation Engineering

N IRE .... Northern Ireland

NIREB .... National Institute of Real Estate Brokers [*Later, Realtors National Marketing Institute*] (EA)

NIREX .... Nuclear Industry Radioactive Waste Executive [*British*] (ECON)

NIRI .... National Information Research Institute

NIRI .... National Investor Relations Institute [*Washington, DC*] (EA)

NIRL .... Negligible Individual Risk Level (GNE)

N Ir LR .... Northern Ireland Law Reports [*A publication*] (DLA)

NIRM .... Network for Information Retrieval in Mammology

NIRMA .... Nuclear Information and Records Management Association (EA)

NIRMP .... National Intern and Resident Matching Program [*Later, NRMP*] (EA)

NIRMP .... National Intern and Resident Matching Program (DAVI)

NIRNS .... National Institute for Research in Nuclear Science [*British*]

NIRO .... Nike-Iroquois [*Rockets*]

NIROC .... National Institute of Red Orange Canaries and All Other Cage Birds (EA)

NIROP .... Naval Industrial Reserve Ordnance Plant (MCD)

NIROS.......... Near Infrared Oxygen Sufficiency Scope [*Monitors oxygen delivery to brain during surgery*] (DAVI)
NIROS.......... Nixdorf Real-Time Operating System (NITA)
NIRPL.......... Navy Industrial Readiness Planning List (NG)
N Ir Pub Gen Acts... Northern Ireland Public General Acts [*A publication*] (DLA)
NIRS .... National Inorganic and Radionuclides Survey [*Environmental Protection Agency*]
NIRS .... National Institute for Radiological Science [*Japan*]
NIRS .... Near Infrared Reflectance Spectroscopy [*Britton Chance*]
NIRS .... Nuclear Information and Resource Service (EA)
NIRSA.......... National Intramural-Recreational Sports Association (EA)
N Ir Stat ...... Northern Ireland Statutes [*A publication*] (DLA)
NIRTS .... National Income Realty Trust [*NASDAQ symbol*] (NQ)
NIRTS .... Natl Inc. Rlty Tr SBI [*NASDAQ symbol*] (TTSB)
NIRTS .... New Integrated Range Timing System
NIrvH .... Lake Shore Hospital, Irving, NY [*Library symbol Library of Congress*] (LCLS)
NIs.............. Islip Public Library, Islip, NY [*Library symbol Library of Congress*] (LCLS)
NIS.............. NASA Interface System (MCD)
NIS.............. National Income Statistics [*British*]
NIS.............. National Information Systems [*Later, GIP*] [*UNESCO*] (BUR)
NIS.............. National Information Systems, Inc. [*Information service or system*] (IID)
NIS.............. National Institute of Science (EA)
NIS.............. National Insurance Surcharge [*A separately accounted tax on employment*] [*British*]
NIS.............. National Intelligence Service (NADA)
NIS.............. National Intelligence Summary (MCD)
NIS.............. National Intelligence Survey
NIS.............. National Interdepartmental Seminar [*Military*]
NIS.............. National Inventory System [*Department of Agriculture*] (GFGA)
NIS.............. NATO Identification System
NIS.............. Naval Intelligence School
NIS.............. Naval Investigative Service
NIS.............. Navy Inspection Service
NIS.............. Negative Ion Source
NIS.............. Negotiation Information System
NIS.............. Neighborhood Information Service
NIS.............. Network Information Service
NIS.............. Network Information Services (NITA)
NIS.............. Network Information System [*AT & T*]
NIS.............. Network Interface System
NIS.............. Neutron Inelastic Scattering
NIS.............. Neutron Instrumentation System (IEEE)
NIS.............. Newly-Independent States [*Of former Soviet Union*]
NIS.............. News and Information Service [*National Broadcasting Co.*]
NISM.......... Nicaraguense de Aviacion SA [*Nicaragua*] [*ICAO designator*] (FAAC)
NIS.............. Nickel-Iron System
NIS.............. Night Illumination System
NIS.............. N-Iodosuccinimide [*Organic chemistry*]
NIS.............. No Intermediate Storage [*Industrial engineering*]
NIS.............. Noise Information System [*Environmental Protection Agency*] (IID)
NIS.............. Nonconsumable Item Subgroup [*Military*] (AFIT)
NIS.............. Normal Incidence Spectrometer (PDAA)
NIS.............. Not in Stock
NIS.............. NOVA Corp. [*NYSE symbol*] (TTSB)
NIS.............. Nova Corp. (Georgia) [*NYSE symbol*] (SAG)
NIS.............. Nuclear Instrumentation System (NRCH)
NIS.............. Shekel (ODBW)
NISA .... National Inconvenienced Sportsmen's Association [*Later, NHSRA*] (EA)
NISA .... National Industrial Sand Association (EA)
NISA .... National Industrial Service Association [*Later, EASA*]
NISA .... National Industrial Stores Association (EA)
NISA .... National Institute of Supply Associations
NISA .... Numerically Integrated Elements for System Analysis (MCD)
NISARC.......... National Information Storage and Retrieval Center
NISBCO.......... National Interreligious Service Board for Conscientious Objectors (EA)
Nisbet.......... Nisbet of Dirleton's Scotch Session Cases [*1665-77*] [*A publication*] (DLA)
NISBS .... National Institute of Social and Behavioral Science (EA)
NISC .... National Independent Study Center [*Civil Service Commission*]
NISC .... National Industrial Space Committee
NISC .... National Industry Safety Committee (NADA)
NISC .... National Information Services Corp. (IID)
NISC .... National Institute of Senior Centers (EA)
NISC .... National Intelligence Study Center (EA)
NISC .... Nonlinear Inter Seminary Council
NISC .... National Intramural Sports Council
NISC .... Naval Intelligence Support Center
NISCA.......... National Interscholastic Swimming Coaches Association of America (EA)
NISCO.......... Nuclear Installation Services Co. (NRCH)
NISCON.......... National Industrial Safety Conference (PDAA)
NISCR.......... South Central Research Library Council, Ithaca, NY [*Library symbol Library of Congress*] (LCLS)
NISC-TRANS... Naval Intelligence Support Center Translation Division
NISCUE.......... National Institute for State Credit Union Examination [*McLean, VA*] (EA)
NISD .... National Institute of Steel Detailing (EA)
N-ISDN .... National ISDN [*Integrated Services Digital Network*] [*Telecommunications*]
NISE.......... Neighborhood Information Sharing Exchange [*Defunct*] (EA)

NISE.......... Normalized Integral Squared Error
NISEC .... National Institute for the Study of Educational Change
NISEC .... Northern Ireland Schools Examination Council (AIE)
NISEE.......... National Information Service for Earthquake Engineering (EA)
NISG .... National Institute of Student Governments [*Defunct*] (EA)
NISG .... Navy Installation Survey Group
NISGAZ.......... National Intelligence Survey Gazetteer
NISGUA.......... Network in Solidarity with the People of Guatemala (EA)
NISH .... National Industries for the Severely Handicapped (EA)
NISH .... National Information Sources on the Handicapped [*Clearinghouse on the Handicapped*] [*Database*]
NISH .... National Institute of Senior Housing (EA)
NISH .... Nonisotopic In Situ Hybridization [*Analytical biochemistry*]
NISHQ.......... Naval Investigative Service Headquarters
NI-SIL .... Nickel-Silver
Nisi Prius & Gen T Rep... Nisi Prius and General Term Reports [*Ohio*] [*A publication*] (DLA)
Nisi Prius Rep... Ohio Nisi Prius Reports [*A publication*] (DLA)
NISL.......... National Indoor Soccer League [*Australia*]
NISLAPP .... National Institute for Science, Law, and Public Policy (EA)
NISM .... Non-Deterministic Incomplete Sequential Machine (PDAA)
NISMART .... National Incidence Studies of Missing, Abducted, Runnaway, and Thrownaway Children
NISMF .... Naval Inactive Ship Maintenance Facility
NISMO.......... Nissan Motorsports
NISO .... National Information Standards Organization - Z39 (EA)
NISO .... Naval Investigative Service Office (NVT)
NISOA .... National Intercollegiate Soccer Officials Association (EA)
NISOD .... National Institute for Staff and Organizational Development (OICC)
NISOR.......... Naval Investigative Service Office Representative (DNAB)
NISP .... National Industrial Security Program [*A publication*] (AAGC)
NISP .... National Information System for Psychology
NISP .... Navy Integrated Space Program (NG)
NISP .... NUWEP [*Nuclear Weapon*] Intelligence Support Plan [*Military*]
NISPA .... National Information System for Physics and Astronomy (NITA)
NISPOM.......... National Industrial Security Program Manual [*A publication*] (AAGC)
NISR .... National Intelligence Situation Report (MCD)
NISR .... Navy Initial Support Requirement (AFIT)
NISRA .... National Industrial Salvage and Recovery Association [*British*] (BI)
NISRA .... National Intercollegiate Squash Racquets Association (EA)
NISRA .... Naval Investigative Service Resident Agent (NVT)
NISREGFORENSICLAB... Naval Investigative Service Regional Forensic Laboratory (DNAB)
NISS .... National Information of Software and Services (AIE)
NISS .... National Institute of Social Sciences (EA)
NISS .... New Information Systems and Services [*A publication*]
Nissan .... Nissan Motor Co. Ltd. [*Associated Press*] (SAG)
NISSM .... Navy Interim Surface Ship Model (CAAL)
NISSOL .... NAVAIR [*Naval Air Systems Command*] Initial Supply Support Outfitting List (MCD)
NISSPO.......... NATO Identification System Special Project Office
NISSU .... Naval Investigative Service Satellite Unit (DNAB)
NIST .... National Information System for Science and Technology (NITA)
NIST .... National Institute of Science and Technology
NIST .... National Institute of Science and Technology (NADA)
NIST .... National Institute of Standards and Technology [*Formerly, NBS*] [*Gaithersburg, MD*] [*Department of Commerce*]
NISTA .... Northern Independent Steel Training Association (AIE)
NISTARS .... Naval Integrated Storage Tracking and Retrieval System
NIST-EEEL .... National Institute of Standards & Technology - Electronics and EE Lab
NISTF.......... National Information Systems Task Force [*Society of American Archivists*] [*Information service or system*] (IID)
NISU .... National Injury Surveillance Unit [*Australia*]
NISUS .... Neutron Intermediate Standard Uranium Source (PDAA)
NISW .... National Institute of Social Work [*British*]
NISW .... Naval In-Shore Warfare (PDAA)
NISWA.......... National Indian Social Workers Association (EA)
NIT............ Midwest Aviation Corp. [*ICAO designator*] (FAAC)
NIT............ National Institute of Technology
NIT............ National Instructional Television [*Superseded by AIT*] (EA)
NIT............ National Intelligence Test [*Psychology*]
NIT............ National Intelligence Topic (MCD)
NIT............ National Invitation Tournament [*Basketball*]
NIT............ Negative Income Tax
NIT............ New Information Technology
NIT............ Nitrum [*Chemistry*] (ROG)
NIT............ None in Town [*Bookselling*]
NIT............ Non-Intelligent Terminal (NITA)
NIT............ Nonlinear Inertialess Three-Pole [*Telecommunications*] (OA)
NIT............ Normal Incidence Technique [*Structural testing*]
NIT............ Nuclear Irradiation Test
NIT............ Nurses in Transition (EA)
NITA.......... National Indoor Tennis Association [*Formerly, ITA*] [*Later, NTA*] (EA)
NITA.......... National Industrial Television Association [*Later, ITVA*] (EA)
NITA.......... National Institute for Trial Advocacy (EA)
NITA.......... National Instructional Television Association (NTCM)
NITA.......... National Intravenous Therapy Association [*Later, INS*] (EA)
NITB.......... Northern Ireland Tourist Board
NITB.......... Tompkins-Seneca-Tioga Board of Cooperative Educational Services, Ithaca, NY [*Library symbol*] [*Library of Congress*] (LCLS)
NITC.......... National Information Transfer Centre (NITA)
NITC.......... National Instructional Television Center (NTCM)
NITC.......... National Intelligence Tasking Center [*CIA*]
NITCCU.......... Northern Information Technology Centre Consultancy Unit (NITA)

Nitches .... Nitches, Inc. [Associated Press] (SAG)
NITE .... Navy Integrated Terminal Evaluation
NITE .... Night Imaging Thermal Equipment [Army] (INF)
NITEC .... National Information Technology in Education Centre (ACII)
NITEDEVRON... Night Development Squadron
NITEOP .... Night Imaging Through Electro-Optic Package [Military British]
NITEP .... National Incinerator Testing and Evaluation Program [Environmental
                 Protection Agency] (GFGA)
NITEWOG ..... Naval Integrated Test and Evaluation Working Group (MCD)
NITF .... National Imagery Transmission Format (DOMA)
NITFSJ .... National Interreligious Task Force on Soviet Jewry (EA)
NITINOL .... Nickel Titanium Naval Ordnance Laboratory [An alloy named by
                 William Buehler of the NOL] (KSC)
Nitinol .... Nitinol Medical Technologies, Inc. [Associated Press] (SAG)
NITL .... National Industrial Traffic League (EA)
NITL .... National Industrial Transportation League (EA)
NITM .... National Income Tax Magazine [A publication] (DLA)
NITMDA .... National Indoor Track Meet Directors Association (EA)
NIT OX .... Nitrous Oxide [Laughing gas] (AAMN)
NITP .... National Industrial Training Program [Canada]
NITP .... National Institutional Training Program [Canada]
NITP .... Nibbling Template
NITPA .... National Institutional Teacher Placement Association [Later, ASCUS]
NITPICKERS... National Institute of Technical Processors, Information Consultants,
                 Keyword Experts, and Retrieval Specialists [Fictitious
                 organization]
NITRAS .... Navy Integrated Training Resources and Administration System
                 (NVT)
NITRC .... National Indian Training and Research Center (EA)
NITRO .... Nitrocellulose (WDAA)
NITRO .... Nitrogen [Chemical element]
nitro .... Nitroglycerin [Pharmacy]
NITRO .... Sodium Nitroprusside [Pharmacology] (DAVI)
NITROS .... Nitrostarch (AAG)
NITSTL .... Nitride Steel
NITU .... Notice of Interim Trail Use [Interstate Commerce Commission]
NITUC .... National Independent Truckers Unity Council [Defunct] (EA)
NITV .... National Iranian Television (NADA)
NIU .... NATO Interface Unit (MCD)
NIU .... Naval Intelligence Unit
NIU .... Navigation Interface Unit [Navy] (CAAL)
NIU .... Network Interface Unit [Computer science]
NIU .... Niue [ANSI three-letter standard code] (CNC)
NIU .... Niumate [Tonga] [Seismograph station code, US Geological Survey
                 Closed] (SEIS)
NIU .... Northern Illinois University [Dekalb, IL]
NIU .... University of Northern Iowa, Cedar Falls, IA [OCLC symbol] (OCLC)
NIUC .... National Independent Union Council [Later, NFIU]
NIUE .... Alofi/Niue International [Niue Island] [ICAO location identifier] (ICLI)
NIUF .... National Inshore Union of Fishermen [British]
NIULPE .... National Institute for Uniform Licensing of Power Engineers'
NIUW .... National Institute for Urban Wildlife (EA)
NIV .... National Institute of Victimology (EA)
NIV .... Negative Ion Vacancy
NIV .... Neutron-Induced Voltagwe (NUCP)
NIV .... Newbury International Ventures, Inc. [Vancouver Stock Exchange
                 symbol]
NIV .... New International Version [of the Bible] [A publication]
NIV .... Nivalenol [A mycotoxin]
NIV .... Nodule-Inducing Virus
NIVA .... National Independent Vendors Association [Defunct] (EA)
NIVC .... National Interactive Video Centre [British]
NIVEA .... Night Vision Equipment for Armor
NIVR .... Netherlands Agency for Aerospace Programs
NIW .... National Industrial Workers Union
NIW .... Naval Inshore Warfare Project
NIW .... Nonlethal Incapacitating Weapon
NIWC .... National Institute for Women of Color (EA)
NIWC .... Naval Inshore Warfare Command (NVT)
NIWFA .... National Intercollegiate Women's Fencing Association (EA)
NIWG .... National Institute for the Word of God (EA)
NIWKC .... National Institute of Wood Kitchen Cabinets [Later, KCMA]
NIWL .... National Institute for Work and Learning (EA)
NIWS .... National Institute on Workshop Standards [Defunct] (EA)
NIWS .... National Integrated Wage Structure (ADA)
NIWS .... News Information Weekly Service
NIWTU .... Naval Inshore Warfare Task Unit (MCD)
NIWU .... National Industrial Workers Union (EA)
NIX .... Nioro [Mali] [Airport symbol] (OAG)
Nix .... Nixa [Record label] [Great Britain, etc.; including Vanguard label
                 re-issues]
NIX .... Nix-O-Tine Pharmaceuticals Ltd. [Vancouver Stock Exchange
                 symbol]
NIX .... Pacific Beach, WA [Location identifier FAA] (FAAL)
Nix Dig .... Nixon's Digest of Laws [New Jersey] [A publication] (DLA)
Nix F .... Nixon's Forms [A publication] (DLA)
NIXT .... Normal Incidence X-Ray Telescope
NIY .... Norfolk, VA [Location identifier FAA] (FAAL)
NIY .... Northamptonshire Imperial Yeomanry [British military] (DMA)
NIY .... Northumberland Imperial Yeomanry [British military] (DMA)
NIYC .... National Indian Youth Council (EA)
NIZ .... Nizhne-Angarsk [Former USSR Seismograph station code, US
                 Geological Survey] (SEIS)
NIZC .... National Industrial Zoning Committee (EA)
NJ .... Namakwaland Lugdiens [ICAO designator] (AD)

NJ .... Namakwaland Lugdiens Bpk [South Africa] [ICAO designator] (ICDA)
nJ .... Nanojoule [One billionth of a joule]
NJ .... Napierville Junction Railway Co. [AAR code]
NJ .... Nasojejunal [Medicine]
NJ .... Network Junction [Telecommunications] (OA)
NJ .... Neue Justiz. Zeitschrift fuer Recht und Rechtswissenschaft [Berlin,
                 German Democratic Republic] [A publication] (DLA)
NJ .... New Jaguar [Jaguar PLC]
NJ .... New Japan Aircraft Maintenance Co. Ltd. [Japan ICAO aircraft
                 manufacturer identifier] (ICAO)
NJ .... New Jason [Charter-party clause] [Business term] (DS)
NJ .... New Jersey [Postal code]
Nj .... New Jersey State Library, Trenton, NJ [Library symbol Library of
                 Congress] (LCLS)
NJ .... New Jersey Supreme Court Reports [A publication] (DLA)
NJ .... New Journalism [Refers to specific style, as that of writer Tom Wolfe]
NJ .... Non Justifying [Typography] (DGA)
NJ .... Notice of Judgment (Official) [Legal term] (DLA)
NJ .... Nylon Jacket
NJA .... National Jail Association [Later, AJA] (EA)
NJA .... National Jewellers' Association [British] (BI)
NJA .... National Jogging Association [Later, ARFA] (EA)
NJA .... National Jousting Association (EA)
NJA .... National Judges Association (EA)
NJA .... New Jewish Agenda (EA)
NJA .... Nozzle Jetevator Assembly
NJA .... Sky Air Cargo Services (UK) Ltd. [British ICAO designator] (FAAC)
NJAA .... National Junior Angus Association
NjAc .... Atlantic City Free Public Library, Atlantic City, NJ [Library symbol
                 Library of Congress] (LCLS)
NJAC .... National Joint Advisory Council [on labor-management relations]
                 [British]
NJAC .... New Jersey Administrative Code [A publication]
NjAcCoC ..... Atlantic County Clerk, Atlantic City, NJ [Library symbol Library of
                 Congress] (LCLS)
NjAcFA .... United States Federal Aviation Administration, National Aviation
                 Facilities Experimental Center, Atlantic City, NJ [Library symbol
                 Library of Congress] (LCLS)
NjAcJ .... Jewish Record, Atlantic City, NJ [Library symbol Library of
                 Congress] (LCLS)
NjAcP .... Press Publishing Co., Atlantic City, NJ [Library symbol Library of
                 Congress] (LCLS)
NjAcPI .... Popolo Italiano, Atlantic City, NJ [Library symbol Library of
                 Congress] (LCLS)
NjAcR .... Atlantic City Reporter, Atlantic City, NJ [Library symbol Library of
                 Congress] (LCLS)
NJ Admin Code... New Jersey Administrative Code [A publication] (DLA)
NJAG .... National Jewish Artisans Guild [Defunct] (EA)
NJAIC .... New Jersey Asparagus Industry Council (EA)
NjAl .... Allentown Public Library, Allentown, NJ [Library symbol Library of
                 Congress] (LCLS)
NjAIA .... Allentown Printing Service, Allentown, NJ [Library symbol Library of
                 Congress] (LCLS)
NjAIB .... Allentown Borough Hall, Allentown, NJ [Library symbol Library of
                 Congress] (LCLS)
NjAIHi .... Allentown Historical Society, Allentown, NJ [Library symbol Library of
                 Congress] (LCLS)
NJam .... James Prendergast Free Library, Jamestown, NY [Library symbol
                 Library of Congress] (LCLS)
NJamC .... Chautauqua-Cattaraugus Library System, Jamestown, NY [Library
                 symbol Library of Congress] (LCLS)
NJamCC ...... Jamestown Community College, Jamestown, NY [Library symbol
                 Library of Congress] (LCLS)
NJamH .... Jamestown General Hospital, Jamestown, NY [Library symbol Library
                 of Congress] (LCLS)
NJamW .... Woman's Christian Association Hospital, Jamestown, NY [Library
                 symbol Library of Congress] (LCLS)
NJAR .... New Jersey Administrative Reports [A publication]
NjAs .... Asbury Park Free Public Library, Asbury Park, NJ [Library symbol
                 Library of Congress] (LCLS)
NjAsP .... Asbury Park Press, Asbury Park, NJ [Library symbol Library of
                 Congress] (LCLS)
NjAsS .... Spotlight Magazine, Asbury Park, NJ [Library symbol Library of
                 Congress] (LCLS)
NjAt .... Atlantic Highlands Public Library Association, Atlantic Highlands, NJ
                 [Library symbol Library of Congress] (LCLS)
NjAuV .... Weekly Visitor, Audubon, NJ [Library symbol Library of Congress]
                 (LCLS)
NjAveT .... Tabloid Lithographers, Inc., Avenel, NJ [Library symbol Library of
                 Congress] (LCLS)
NjAvH .... Herald, Avalon, NJ [Library symbol Library of Congress] (LCLS)
NJB .... Appalachian State University, Boone, NC [OCLC symbol] (OCLC)
NjB .... Bridgeton Free Public Library, Bridgeton, NJ [Library symbol Library
                 of Congress] (LCLS)
NjBa .... Bayonne Free Public Library, Bayonne, NJ [Library symbol Library of
                 Congress] (LCLS)
NjBaF .... Facts of Bayonne Publishing Co., Bayonne, NJ [Library symbol
                 Library of Congress] (LCLS)
NjBaFAR ...... Federal Archives and Records Center, General Services
                 Administration, Bayonne, NJ [Library symbol Library of
                 Congress] (LCLS)
NjBaNSRF.... United States Naval Supply Research and Development Facility,
                 Bayonne, NJ [Library symbol Library of Congress] (LCLS)
NjBAP .... Cumberland County Advertiser-Press, Inc., Bridgeton, NJ [Library
                 symbol Library of Congress] (LCLS)

NjBarHi........ Barrington Historical Society, Barrington, NJ [*Library symbol Library of Congress*] (LCLS)

NjBas........... Bernards Township Library, Inc., Basking Ridge, NJ [*Library symbol Library of Congress*] (LCLS)

NjBb............ Bound Brook Memorial Library, Bound Brook, NJ [*Library symbol Library of Congress*] (LCLS)

NjBbA .... American Cyanamid Co., Organic Chemicals Division, Bound Brook, NJ [*Library symbol Library of Congress*] (LCLS)

NjBbC .... Bound Brook Chronicle, Bound Brook, NJ [*Library symbol Library of Congress*] (LCLS)

NJBBF......... National Judo Black Belt Federation of the USA (EA)

NjBbU .... Union Carbide Plastics Co., Bound Brook, NJ [*Library symbol Library of Congress*] (LCLS)

NjBCoC .. Cumberland County Clerk, Bridgeton, NJ [*Library symbol Library of Congress*] (LCLS)

NjBe............ Belleville Free Public Library, Belleville, NJ [*Library symbol Library of Congress*] (LCLS)

NjBeA .... Ad-Print, Belleville, NJ [*Library symbol Library of Congress*] (LCLS)

NjBeacO ..... Daily Observer, Beachwood, NJ [*Library symbol Library of Congress*] (LCLS)

NjBel .... Belmar Public Library, Belmar, NJ [*Library symbol Library of Congress*] (LCLS)

NjBelvCoC .. Warren County Clerk, Belvidere, NJ [*Library symbol Library of Congress*] (LCLS)

NjBelvW ...... Warren County Library, Belvidere, NJ [*Library symbol Library of Congress*] (LCLS)

NjBer .... Bergenfield Free Public Library, Bergenfield, NJ [*Library symbol Library of Congress*] (LCLS)

NjBerl .... Marie Fleche Memorial Library, Berlin, NJ [*Library symbol Library of Congress*] (LCLS)

NjBern .... Bernardsville Library Association, Bernardsville, NJ [*Library symbol Library of Congress*] (LCLS)

NjBernN....... Bernardsville News, Bernardsville, NJ [*Library symbol Library of Congress*] (LCLS)

NjBeT.......... Belleville Telegram, Belleville, NJ [*Library symbol Library of Congress*] (LCLS)

NjBh........... Berkley Heights Public Library, Berkley Heights, NJ [*Library symbol Library of Congress*] (LCLS)

NjBl .... Bloomfield Public Library, Bloomfield, NJ [*Library symbol Library of Congress*] (LCLS)

NjBla .... Gloucester Township [*Blackwood*] Library, Blackwood, NJ [*Library symbol Library of Congress*] (LCLS)

NjBlaC .... Camden County College, Blackwood, NJ [*Library symbol Library of Congress*] (LCLS)

NjBlaCG....... Camden-Gloucester Newspapers, Blackwood, NJ [*Library symbol Library of Congress*] (LCLS)

NjBlaiP .... Blairstown Press, Blairstown, NJ [*Library symbol Library of Congress*] (LCLS)

NjBlC .... Bloomfield College, Bloomfield, NJ [*Library symbol Library of Congress*] (LCLS)

NjBlHi......... Historical Society of Bloomfield, Bloomfield, NJ [*Library symbol Library of Congress*] (LCLS)

NjBll .... Independent Press, Bloomfield, NJ [*Library symbol Library of Congress*] (LCLS)

NjBlM .... Academy of Medicine of New Jersey, Bloomfield, NJ [*Library symbol Library of Congress*] (LCLS)

NjBlS .... Shering Corp., Bloomfield, NJ [*Library symbol Library of Congress*] (LCLS)

NjBlW .... Westinghouse Electric Corp., Lamp Division, Bloomfield, NJ [*Library symbol Library of Congress*] (LCLS)

NjBN .... Bridgeton Evening News, Bridgeton, NJ [*Library symbol Library of Congress*] (LCLS)

NjBo............ Bogota Public Library, Bogota, NJ [*Library symbol Library of Congress*] (LCLS)

NjBoo.......... Holmes Library, Boonton, NJ [*Library symbol Library of Congress*] (LCLS)

NjBooT........ Times-Bulletin, Boonton, NJ [*Library symbol Library of Congress*] (LCLS)

NjBorHi....... Bordentown Historical Society, Bordentown, NJ [*Library symbol Library of Congress*] (LCLS)

NjBorL .... Lorraine Publishing, Inc., Bordentown, NJ [*Library symbol Library of Congress*] (LCLS)

NjBriCN....... Plainfield Courier-News, Bridgewater, NJ [*Library symbol Library of Congress*] (LCLS)

NjBrigT .... Brigantine Times, Brigantine, NJ [*Library symbol Library of Congress*] (LCLS)

NjBro .... Mendham Township Library, Brookside, NJ [*Library symbol Library of Congress*] (LCLS)

NjBrS .... Seacoast Newspapers, Brick Town, NJ [*Library symbol Library of Congress*] (LCLS)

NjBu............ Library Co. of Burlington, Burlington, NJ [*Library symbol Library of Congress*] (LCLS)

NjBuHi........ Burlington County Historical Society, Burlington, NJ [*Library symbol Library of Congress*] (LCLS)

NjButA .... Argus Printing & Publishing Co., Butler, NJ [*Library symbol Library of Congress*] (LCLS)

NjC............. Chatham Public Library, Chatham, NJ [*Library symbol Library of Congress*] (LCLS)

NJC............. Natchez Junior College [*Mississippi*]

NJC............. National Jewish Center [*Australia*]

NJC............. National Jewish Coalition (EA)

NJC............. National Joint Council (AIE)

NJC............. National Judicial College (EA)

NJC............. Navarro Junior College [*Texas*]

NJC............. Navy Job Classification Manual

NJC............ New Jersey Central Railroad

NJC............. Newton Junior College [*Massachusetts*]

NJC............. Norfolk Junior College [*Nebraska*]

NjCa............ Camden Free Public Library, Camden, NJ [*Library symbol Library of Congress*] (LCLS)

NJCAA .... National Job Corps Alumni Association [*Washington, DC*] (EA)

NJCAA .... National Junior College Athletic Association (EA)

NjCaC .... Cooper Medical Center, Camden, NJ [*Library symbol Library of Congress*] (LCLS)

NjCaHi........ Camden County Historical Society, Camden, NJ [*Library symbol Library of Congress*] (LCLS)

NjCal .... Caldwell Free Public Library, Caldwell, NJ [*Library symbol Library of Congress*] (LCLS)

NjCalC .... Caldwell College, Caldwell, NJ [*Library symbol Library of Congress*] (LCLS)

NjCalP .... Caldwell Progress, Caldwell, NJ [*Library symbol Library of Congress*] (LCLS)

NjCaN .... Camden News, Camden, NJ [*Library symbol Library of Congress*] (LCLS)

NjCapS .... Star and Wave, Cape May, NJ [*Library symbol Library of Congress*] (LCLS)

NJCAPT & C... National Joint Council for Administrative, Professional, Technical, and ClericalStaff [*British*]

NjCaRD .... Radio Corp. of America, Communications Systems Division, Camden, NJ [*Library symbol Library of Congress*] (LCLS)

NjCarpD ...... E. I. Du Pont de Nemours & Co., Carney's Point Development Laboratory, Carney's Point, NJ [*Library symbol Library of Congress*] (LCLS)

NjCaSH .... Catholic Star Herald, Camden, NJ [*Library symbol Library of Congress*] (LCLS)

NjCaUR....... Union Reporter, Camden, NJ [*Library symbol Library of Congress*] (LCLS)

NJCBI......... National Joint Council for the Building Industry [*British*] (DCTA)

NJCBSPT .... New Jersey College Basic Skills Placement Test (EDAC)

NjCC .... Chatham Courier, Chatham, NJ [*Library symbol Library of Congress*] (LCLS)

NJCC.......... National Joint Computer Committee [*of ACM, AIEE, IRE*] [*Superseded by AFIPS*]

NJCC.......... Northeastern Junior College of Colorado [*Sterling*]

NJCCA .... National Japanese Canadian Citizens' Association

NJCCOE ...... Nordic Joint Committee of Commercial and Office Executives (EA)

NJCDE .... Nordic Joint Committee for Domestic Education (EA)

NjCE........... Chatham Township Echoes, Chatham, NJ [*Library symbol Library of Congress*] (LCLS)

NJCEC........ NATO Joint Communications-Electronics Committee (NATG)

NJCF.......... National Juvenile Court Foundation (EA)

NjCg............ Cedar Grove Public Library, Cedar Grove, NJ [*Library symbol Library of Congress*] (LCLS)

NjCh............ Cherry Hill Free Public Library, Cherry Hill, NJ [*Library symbol Library of Congress*] (LCLS)

NJ Ch.......... New Jersey Equity Reports [*A publication*] (DLA)

NJCHC .... National Joint Council for Handicapped Children [*British*]

NjChCP .... Courier Post, Cherry Hill, NJ [*Library symbol Library of Congress*] (LCLS)

NjChe.......... Chester Free Public Library, Chester, NJ [*Library symbol Library of Congress*] (LCLS)

NjChJ.......... Jewish Federation of Camden County, Cherry Hill, NJ [*Library symbol Library of Congress*] (LCLS)

NjChM .... Cherry Hill Medical Center, Cherry Hill, NJ [*Library symbol Library of Congress*] (LCLS)

NjChSG .... Shoppers Guide, Cherry Hill, NJ [*Library symbol Library of Congress*] (LCLS)

NjChSN....... Suburban Newspaper Group, Cherry Hill, NJ [*Library symbol Library of Congress*] (LCLS)

NjCiL .... Cinnaminson Little Paper, Cinnaminson, NJ [*Library symbol Library of Congress*] (LCLS)

NjCl .... Clark Free Public Library, Clark, NJ [*Library symbol Library of Congress*] (LCLS)

NJCL.......... Network Job Control Language [*Computer science*]

NJCLAFB...... National Joint Council for Local Authority Fire Brigades [*British*]

NJCLD .... National Joint Committee for Learning Disabilities

NJCLE......... Institute for Continuing Legal Education, New Jersey (DLA)

NjClif .... Clifton Public Library, Clifton, NJ [*Library symbol Library of Congress*] (LCLS)

NjClifB......... New Jersey Business Review, Clifton, NJ [*Library symbol Library of Congress*] (LCLS)

NjClifl .... Clifton Independent Prospector, Clifton, NJ [*Library symbol Library of Congress*] (LCLS)

NjClifL .... Clifton Leader, Clifton, NJ [*Library symbol Library of Congress*] (LCLS)

NjClifP .... Clifton Publishing Co., Clifton, NJ [*Library symbol Library of Congress*] (LCLS)

NjClifPE ...... Post Eagle Publishing Co., Clifton, NJ [*Library symbol Library of Congress*] (LCLS)

NjClifW........ Woodward-Clyde Consultants, Clifton, NJ [*Library symbol Library of Congress*] (LCLS)

NjClinH........ Hunterdon Review, Clinton, NJ [*Library symbol Library of Congress*] (LCLS)

NjClp .... Cliffside Park Public Library, Cliffside Park, NJ [*Library symbol Library of Congress*] (LCLS)

NjClpP .... Palisades Printing Corp., Cliffside Park, NJ [*Library symbol Library of Congress*] (LCLS)

NjCmCo .... Cape May County Library, Cape May Court House, NJ [*Library symbol Library of Congress*] (LCLS)

NjCmCoC ..... Cape May County Clerk, Cape May Court House, NJ [*Library symbol Library of Congress*] (LCLS)

NjCmG .... Cape May County Gazette, Cape May Court House, NJ [*Library symbol Library of Congress*] (LCLS)

NjCo .... Collingswood Free Public Library, Collingswood, NJ [*Library symbol Library of Congress*] (LCLS)

NjCoB .... Christian Beacon, Collingswood, NJ [*Library symbol Library of Congress*] (LCLS)

NjCoC .... Collingswood Publishing Co., Collingswood, NJ [*Library symbol Library of Congress*] (LCLS)

NjColS .... South Jersey Ad-Visor, Cologne, NJ [*Library symbol Library of Congress*] (LCLS)

NjConC .... College of Saint Elizabeth, Convent Station, NJ [*Library symbol Library of Congress*] (LCLS)

NjCoT .... Camden County Times, Collingswood, NJ [*Library symbol Library of Congress*] (LCLS)

NjCr .... Cranford Public Library, Cranford, NJ [*Library symbol Library of Congress*] (LCLS)

NJCRAC ...... National Jewish Community Relations Advisory Council (EA)

NjCrbP .... Cranbury Press, Cranbury, NJ [*Library symbol Library of Congress*] (LCLS)

NjCrC .... Cranford Citizen & Chronicle, Cranford, NJ [*Library symbol Library of Congress*] (LCLS)

NjCrHi .... Cranford Historical Society, Cranford, NJ [*Library symbol Library of Congress*] (LCLS)

NjCrU .... Union College, Cranford, NJ [*Library symbol Library of Congress*] (LCLS)

NJCS .... National Jewish Committee on Scouting (EA)

NJCSA .... National Juvenile Court Services Association (EA)

NJCSE .... National Jewish Civil Service Employees (EA)

NjD .... Dover Public Library, Dover, NJ [*Library symbol Library of Congress*] (LCLS)

NjDA .... Daily Advance, Dover, NJ [*Library symbol Library of Congress*] (LCLS)

NJDA .... National Juvenile Detention Association (EA)

NjDC .... County College of Morris, Dover, NJ [*Library symbol*] [*Library of Congress*] (LCLS)

NJDDC .... New Jersey Development Disabilities Council (EDAC)

NjDe .... Denville Free Public Library, Denville, NJ [*Library symbol Library of Congress*] (LCLS)

NjDeC .... Citizen of Morris County, Denville, NJ [*Library symbol Library of Congress*] (LCLS)

NJDEP .... New Jersey Department of Environmental Protection

NJDEP .... New Jersey Department of Environmental Protection (DOGT)

NJDFC .... New Jersey Devils Fan Club (EA)

NjDPA .... United States Army, Armament Research and Development Command, Science and Technical Library, Dover Site, Dover, NJ [*Library symbol Library of Congress*] (LCLS)

NJE .... Network Job Entry

NJE .... New Jersey Equity Reports [*A publication*] (DLA)

Nj-E .... New Jersey State Library, Department of Education, Trenton, NJ [*Library symbol Library of Congress*] (LCLS)

NJE .... Office of Cancer and Toxic Substances Research, Trenton, NJ [*OCLC symbol*] (OCLC)

NjEa .... Eatontown Public Library, Eatontown, NJ [*Library symbol Library of Congress*] (LCLS)

NjEb .... East Brunswick Public Library, East Brunswick, NJ [*Library symbol Library of Congress*] (LCLS)

NjEbGS .... Church of Jesus Christ of Latter-Day Saints, Genealogical Society Library, East Brunswick Stake Branch, East Brunswick, NJ [*Library symbol Library of Congress*] (LCLS)

NjEbS .... Sentinel Publishing Co., East Brunswick, NJ [*Library symbol Library of Congress*] (LCLS)

NjEdE .... Engelhard Minerals & Chemicals Corp. [*Later, Engelhard Corp.*], Research Library, Edison, NJ [*Library symbol Library of Congress*] (LCLS)

NjEdM .... Middlesex County College, Edison, NJ [*Library symbol Library of Congress*] (LCLS)

NjEgN .... Egg Harbor News, Egg Harbor City, NJ [*Library symbol Library of Congress*] (LCLS)

NjEh .... East Hanover Public Library, East Hanover, NJ [*Library symbol Library of Congress*] (LCLS)

NjEli .... Elizabeth Free Public Library, Elizabeth, NJ [*Library symbol Library of Congress*] (LCLS)

NjEliCoC ...... Union County Clerk, Elizabeth, NJ [*Library symbol Library of Congress*] (LCLS)

NjEliJ .... Daily Journal, Elizabeth, NJ [*Library symbol Library of Congress*] (LCLS)

NjEIT .... Elmer Times, Elmer, NJ [*Library symbol Library of Congress*] (LCLS)

NjEn .... Englewood Library, Englewood, NJ [*Library symbol Library of Congress*] (LCLS)

NjEncL .... Thomas J. Lipton, Inc., Englewood Cliffs, NJ [*Library symbol Library of Congress*] (LCLS)

NjEncStP ...... Saint Peter's College, Englewood Cliffs, NJ [*Library symbol Library of Congress*] (LCLS)

NJE/NJI .... Network Job Entry, Including Network Job Interface

NjEnP .... Englewood Press, Englewood, NJ [*Library symbol Library of Congress*] (LCLS)

NjEnPa .... Palisades Newspapers, Englewood, NJ [*Library symbol Library of Congress*] (LCLS)

NjEnS .... North Jersey Suburbanite, Englewood, NJ [*Library symbol Library of Congress*] (LCLS)

NjEo .... East Orange Free Public Library, East Orange, NJ [*Library symbol Library of Congress*] (LCLS)

NjEoA .... Advocate, East Orange, NJ [*Library symbol Library of Congress*] (LCLS)

NjEoS .... Sokol USA, East Orange, NJ [*Library symbol Library of Congress*] (LCLS)

NjEoU .... Upsala College, East Orange, NJ [*Library symbol Library of Congress*] (LCLS)

NjEoV .... United States Veterans Administration Hospital, East Orange, NJ [*Library symbol Library of Congress*] (LCLS)

NJ Eq .... New Jersey Equity Reports [*A publication*] (DLA)

NJ Eq R .... New Jersey Equity Reports [*A publication*] (DLA)

NJ Equity ..... New Jersey Equity Reports [*A publication*] (DLA)

NJer .... Jericho Public Library, Jericho, NY [*Library symbol Library of Congress*] (LCLS)

NJerC .... Long Island Association of Commerce and Industry, Jericho, NY [*Library symbol Library of Congress*] (LCLS)

NJerCE .... Cantiague Elementary School, Jericho, NY [*Library symbol*] [*Library of Congress*] (LCLS)

NJerHS .... Jericho Senior High School, Jericho, NY [*Library symbol Library of Congress*] (LCLS)

NJerJE .... George Jackson Elementary School, Jericho, NY [*Library symbol Library of Congress*] (LCLS)

NJerS .... Staff Supermarket Associates, Inc., Jericho, NY [*Library symbol Library of Congress*] (LCLS)

N Jersey R ... New Jersey Law Reports [*A publication*] (DLA)

NJESS .... Nigerian Journal of Economic and Social Studies [*A publication*]

NjEwB .... Bergen Citizen, Edgewater, NJ [*Library symbol Library of Congress*] (LCLS)

NjEwJJ .... Johnson & Johnson Dental Product Co., East Windsor, NJ [*Library symbol Library of Congress*] (LCLS)

NJF .... Cherry Point, NC [*Location identifier FAA*] (FAAL)

NjF .... Fair Lawn Free Public Library, Fair Lawn, NJ [*Library symbol Library of Congress*] (LCLS)

NJF .... Nordiska Journalistforbundet [*Nordic Association of Journalists Unions - NAJU*] (EAIO)

NJF .... Nordiske Jordbrugsforskeres Forening [*Nordic Agricultural Research Workers Association - NARWA*] (EAIO)

NJF .... Scandinavian Agricultural Research Workers' Association

NJFA .... National Justice Foundation of America (EA)

NJFAA .... Federal Aviation Administration, Eastern Region Library, Jamaica, NY [*Library symbol Library of Congress*] (LCLS)

NJFC .... Norma Jean Fan Club (EA)

NJFD .... Notices of Judgment, United States Food and Drug Administration [*A publication*] (DLA)

NjFdA .... United States Army, Special Services Post Library, Fort Dix, NJ [*Library symbol Library of Congress*] (LCLS)

NjFf .... Fairfield Free Public Library, Fairfield, NJ [*Library symbol Library of Congress*] (LCLS)

NjFhUGA ..... United States Golf Association, Far Hills, NJ [*Library symbol Library of Congress*] (LCLS)

NjFlCoC .... Hunterdon County Clerk, Flemington, NJ [*Library symbol Library of Congress*] (LCLS)

NjFlD .... Hunterdon County Democrat, Flemington, NJ [*Library symbol Library of Congress*] (LCLS)

NjFlH .... Hunterdon County Library, Flemington, NJ [*Library symbol Library of Congress*] (LCLS)

NjFlHi .... Hunterdon County Historical Society, Flemington, NJ [*Library symbol Library of Congress*] (LCLS)

NjFlM .... Hunterdon Medical Center, Flemington, NJ [*Library symbol Library of Congress*] (LCLS)

NjFmE-TD .... United States Army, Electronics Command, Technical Documents Branch, Fort Monmouth, NJ [*Library symbol Library of Congress*] (LCLS)

NjFmS .... United States Army, Signal School, Fort Monmouth, NJ [*Library symbol Library of Congress*] (LCLS)

NjFNB .... Shopper-News Beacon, Fair Lawn, NJ [*Library symbol Library of Congress*] (LCLS)

NjFp .... Florham Park Public Library, Florham Park, NJ [*Library symbol Library of Congress*] (LCLS)

NjFpEx .... Exxon Research & Engineering Co., Engineering Information Center, Florham Park, NJ [*Library symbol Library of Congress*] (LCLS)

NjFpN .... Florham Park Community News, Florham Park, NJ [*Library symbol Library of Congress*] (LCLS)

NjFr .... Freehold Public Library, Freehold, NJ [*Library symbol Library of Congress*] (LCLS)

NJFR .... National Joint Fiction Reserve

NjFraS .... Suburban News, Franklin Lakes, NJ [*Library symbol Library of Congress*] (LCLS)

NjFrCoC .... Clerk of Monmouth County, Freehold, NJ [*Library symbol Library of Congress*] (LCLS)

NjFrHi .... Monmouth County Historical Association, Freehold, NJ [*Library symbol Library of Congress*] (LCLS)

NjFrM .... Monmouth County Library, Freehold, NJ [*Library symbol Library of Congress*] (LCLS)

NjFrS .... Schreiber Publishing Co., Freehold, NJ [*Library symbol Library of Congress*] (LCLS)

NjFrtD .... Delaware Valley News, Frenchtown, NJ [*Library symbol Library of Congress*] (LCLS)

NjFrvA .... Advertiser, Franklinville, NJ [*Library symbol Library of Congress*] (LCLS)

NjFvW .... West New Yorker, Inc., Fairview, NJ [*Library symbol Library of Congress*] (LCLS)

NJG .... Glassboro State College, Glassboro, NJ [*OCLC symbol*] (OCLC)

NJG .... Nachtjagdgeschwader [*Night Fighter*] [*German*]

NJG .... Nice Jewish Girl [*Slang*]

NjGaB .... Bergen Gazette, Inc., Garfield, NJ [*Library symbol Library of Congress*] (LCLS)

NjGaG .... Garfield Guardian, Garfield, NJ [*Library symbol Library of Congress*] (LCLS)

NjGb .... Glassboro Public Library, Glassboro, NJ [*Library symbol Library of Congress*] (LCLS)

NjGbS .... Glassboro State College, Glassboro, NJ [*Library symbol Library of Congress*] (LCLS)

NJGFE .... Nordic Joint Group for Forest Entomology (EA)

NjGiD .... E. I. Du Pont de Nemours & Co., Eastern Laboratory Library, Gibbstown, NJ [*Library symbol Library of Congress*] (LCLS)

NjGl .... Gloucester City Library, Gloucester City, NJ [*Library symbol Library of Congress*] (LCLS)

NjGlN .... Gloucester City News, Gloucester City, NJ [*Library symbol Library of Congress*] (LCLS)

NjGlri .... Glen Ridge Free Public Library, Glen Ridge, NJ [*Library symbol Library of Congress*] (LCLS)

NjGlriA .... Associated Technical Services, Inc., Glen Ridge, NJ [*Library symbol Library of Congress*] (LCLS)

NjGrbR .... Raritan Valley Hospital, Greenbrook, NJ [*Library symbol Library of Congress*] (LCLS)

NjGrHi .... Cumberland County Historical Society, Greenwich, NJ [*Library symbol Library of Congress*] (LCLS)

NJGSC .... National Jewish Girl Scout Committee (EA)

NjH .... Haddonfield Public Library, Haddonfield, NJ [*Library symbol Library of Congress*] (LCLS)

NJHA .... National Junior Horticultural Association (EA)

NjHaC .... Centenary College for Women, Hackettstown, NJ [*Library symbol Library of Congress*] (LCLS)

NjHack .... Johnson Free Public Library, Hackensack, NJ [*Library symbol Library of Congress*] (LCLS)

NjHackR ...... Bergen Record, Hackensack, NJ [*Library symbol Library of Congress*] (LCLS)

NjHam .... Hammonton Public Library, Hammonton, NJ [*Library symbol Library of Congress*] (LCLS)

NjHamN .... News Publishing Co., Hammonton, NJ [*Library symbol Library of Congress*] (LCLS)

NjHanS .... Sandoz, Inc., Hanover, NJ [*Library symbol Library of Congress*] (LCLS)

NjHarN .... Diamond Shamrock Corp., Harrison, NJ [*Library symbol Library of Congress*] (LCLS)

NjHarR .... Radio Corp. of America, Electronics Division, Harrison, NJ [*Library symbol Library of Congress*] (LCLS)

NjHas .... Hasbrouck Heights Free Public Library, Hasbrouck Heights, NJ [*Library symbol Library of Congress*] (LCLS)

NjHaS .... Star Gazette, Hackettstown, NJ [*Library symbol Library of Congress*] (LCLS)

NjHaSG .... Star Gazette, Hackettstown, NJ [*Library symbol*] [*Library of Congress*] (LCLS)

NjHasO .... Observer, Hasbrouck Heights, NJ [*Library symbol Library of Congress*] (LCLS)

NjHawD .... Dodds Publishing Co., Hawthorne, NJ [*Library symbol Library of Congress*] (LCLS)

NjHawP .... Hawthorne Press, Inc., Hawthorne, NJ [*Library symbol Library of Congress*] (LCLS)

NjHb .... Hillsborough Public Library, Hillsborough, NJ [*Library symbol Library of Congress*] (LCLS)

NJHC .... National Jewish Hospitality Committee (EA)

NjHh .... Haddon Heights Public Library, Haddon Heights, NJ [*Library symbol Library of Congress*] (LCLS)

NJHHCC .... National Joint Heavy and Highway Construction Committee (EA)

NjHHi .... Historical Society of Haddonfield, Haddonfield, NJ [*Library symbol Library of Congress*] (LCLS)

NjHi .... New Jersey Historical Society, Newark, NJ [*Library symbol Library of Congress*] (LCLS)

NjHibP .... High Bridge Painting Co., High Bridge, NJ [*Library symbol Library of Congress*] (LCLS)

NjHig .... Hightstown Memorial Library, Hightstown, NJ [*Library symbol Library of Congress*] (LCLS)

NjHigG .... Hightstown Gazette, Hightstown, NJ [*Library symbol Library of Congress*] (LCLS)

NjHigN .... NL Industries, Inc., Hightstown, NJ [*Library symbol Library of Congress*] (LCLS)

NjHigP .... Peddie School, Hightstown, NJ [*Library symbol Library of Congress*] (LCLS)

NjHil .... Hillside Free Public Library, Hillside, NJ [*Library symbol Library of Congress*] (LCLS)

NjHilT .... Hillside Times, Hillside, NJ [*Library symbol Library of Congress*] (LCLS)

NJH/NAC .... National Jewish Hospital/National Asthma Center [*Later, National Jewish Center for Immunology and Respiratory Medicine*] (EA)

NjHo .... Hoboken Free Public Library, Hoboken, NJ [*Library symbol Library of Congress*] (LCLS)

NjHoGF .... General Foods Corp., Hoboken, NJ [*Library symbol Library of Congress*] (LCLS)

NjHolB .... Bell Telephone Laboratories, Inc., Technical Information Library, Holmdel, NJ [*Library symbol Library of Congress*] (LCLS)

NjHop .... Hopewell Public Library, Hopewell, NJ [*Library symbol Library of Congress*] (LCLS)

NjHopM .... Hopewell Museum, Hopewell, NJ [*Library symbol Library of Congress*] (LCLS)

NjHopN .... Hopewell Valley News, Hopewell, NJ [*Library symbol Library of Congress*] (LCLS)

NjHoS .... Stevens Institute of Technology, Hoboken, NJ [*Library symbol Library of Congress*] (LCLS)

NjHowB .... Booster Press, Howell, NJ [*Library symbol Library of Congress*] (LCLS)

NJHS .... National Junior Honor Society (EA)

NjI .... Free Public Library of Irvington, Irvington, NJ [*Library symbol Library of Congress*] (LCLS)

NJI .... Network Job Interface

NJI .... New Jersey Institute of Technology, Newark, NJ [*OCLC symbol*] (OCLC)

NJIC .... National Joint Industrial Council [*Pharmacology British*]

NJIFR .... Notices of Judgment, Federal Insecticide, Fungicide, and Rodenticide Act [*A publication*] (DLA)

NJII .... New Jersey, Indiana & Illinois Railroad Co. [*AAR code*]

NJIS .... National Jewish Information Service (for the Propagation of Judaism) [*Defunct*] (EA)

NJIT .... New Jersey Institute of Technology [*Newark*]

NJIT .... New Jersey Institute of Technology (GAGS)

NjJ .... Jersey City Free Public Library, Jersey City, NJ [*Library symbol Library of Congress*] (LCLS)

NJJ .... Jersey City State College, Jersey City, NJ [*OCLC symbol*] (OCLC)

NJJ .... Niijima [*Japan*] [*Seismograph station code, US Geological Survey Closed*] (SEIS)

NjJa .... Library at Jamesburg, Jamesburg, NJ [*Library symbol Library of Congress*] (LCLS)

NjJacN .... Jackson News, Jackson, NJ [*Library symbol Library of Congress*] (LCLS)

NjJacP .... Jackson Township Publishing Co., Jackson, NJ [*Library symbol Library of Congress*] (LCLS)

NjJJ .... Jewish Standard, Jersey City, NJ [*Library symbol Library of Congress*] (LCLS)

NjJJJ .... Jersey Journal, Jersey City, NJ [*Library symbol Library of Congress*] (LCLS)

NjJS .... Jersey City State College, Jersey City, NJ [*Library symbol Library of Congress*] (LCLS)

NjJStP .... Saint Peter's College, Jersey City, NJ [*Library symbol Library of Congress*] (LCLS)

NjJUB .... Urner-Barry Publications, Jersey City, NJ [*Library symbol Library of Congress*] (LCLS)

NJK .... El Centro, CA [*Location identifier FAA*] (FAAL)

NJK .... Kean College of New Jersey, Union, NJ [*OCLC symbol*] (OCLC)

NjK .... Kearny Public Library, Kearny, NJ [*Library symbol Library of Congress*] (LCLS)

NjKeHS .... Keansburg High School, Keansburg, NJ [*Library symbol*] [*Library of Congress*] (LCLS)

NjKey .... Keyport Free Public Library, Keyport, NJ [*Library symbol Library of Congress*] (LCLS)

NjKO .... Kearny Observer, Kearny, NJ [*Library symbol Library of Congress*] (LCLS)

NjKWT .... Western Electric Co., Kearny, NJ [*Library symbol Library of Congress*] (LCLS)

NjL .... Lodi Memorial Library, Lodi, NJ [*Library symbol Library of Congress*] (LCLS)

NJL .... New Jersey Law Reports [*A publication*] (DLA)

NJL .... New Jersey State Library, Trenton, NJ [*OCLC symbol*] (OCLC)

NjLaHi .... Lake Hopatcong Historical Society, Lake Hopatcong, NJ [*Library symbol Library of Congress*] (LCLS)

NjLak .... Lakewood Public Library, Lakewood, NJ [*Library symbol Library of Congress*] (LCLS)

NjLakC .... Ocean County Citizen, Lakewood, NJ [*Library symbol Library of Congress*] (LCLS)

NjLakG .... Georgian Court College, Lakewood, NJ [*Library symbol Library of Congress*] (LCLS)

NjLakhM ...... Manchester Publishing Co., Lakehurst, NJ [*Library symbol Library of Congress*] (LCLS)

NjLakT .... Ocean County Daily Times, Lakewood, NJ [*Library symbol Library of Congress*] (LCLS)

NjLamB .... Lambertville Beacon, Lambertville, NJ [*Library symbol Library of Congress*] (LCLS)

NJ Law .... New Jersey Law Reports [*A publication*] (DLA)

NJ Law N ..... New Jersey Law News [*A publication*] (DLA)

NjLawR .... Rider College, Lawrenceville, NJ [*Library symbol Library of Congress*] (LCLS)

NJ Law Rep ... New Jersey Law Reports [*A publication*] (DLA)

NJLC .... National Juvenile Law Center [*Later, NCYL*] (EA)

NjLe .... Leonia Public Library, Leonia, NJ [*Library symbol Library of Congress*] (LCLS)

NjLedW .... West Morris Star Journal, Ledgewood, NJ [*Library symbol Library of Congress*] (LCLS)

NJ Leg Rec ... New Jersey Legal Record [*A publication*] (DLA)

NjLF .... Felician College, Lodi, NJ [*Library symbol Library of Congress*] (LCLS)

NjLf .... Little Falls Free Public Library, Little Falls, NJ [*Library symbol Library of Congress*] (LCLS)

NJLFC .... New Jersey Film Circuit [*Library network*]

NjLh .... Lake Hiawatha Public Library, Lake Hiawatha, NJ [*Library symbol Library of Congress*] (LCLS)

NjLhP .... Pennysaver Publishing Co., Lake Hiawatha, NJ [*Library symbol Library of Congress*] (LCLS)

NjLi .... Free Public Library of Livingston, Livingston, NJ [*Library symbol Library of Congress*] (LCLS)

NjLin .... Linden Free Public Library, Linden, NJ [*Library symbol Library of Congress*] (LCLS)

NjLincB .... Brookdale Community College, Lincroft, NJ [*Library symbol Library of Congress*] (LCLS)

NjLinEx....... Exxon Research & Engineering Co., Company and Literature Information Center Library, Linden, NJ [*Library symbol Library of Congress*] (LCLS)

NjLinEx-M.... Exxon Research & Engineering Co., Medical Research Library, Linden, NJ [*Library symbol Library of Congress*] (LCLS)

NjLivStB ...... Saint Barnabas Medical Center, Staff Library, Livingston, NJ [*Library symbol Library of Congress*] (LCLS)

NjLiW .... West Essex Tribune, Livingston, NJ [*Library symbol Library of Congress*] (LCLS)

NjLob........... Long Branch Public Library, Long Branch, NJ [*Library symbol Library of Congress*] (LCLS)

NjLp............. Lincoln Park Public Library, Lincoln Park, NJ [*Library symbol Library of Congress*] (LCLS)

NjLP............. Paci Press, Lodi, NJ [*Library symbol Library of Congress*] (LCLS)

NjLpBHi....... Beavertown Historical Society, Lincoln Park, NJ [*Library symbol Library of Congress*] (LCLS)

NjLpH.......... Lincoln Herald, Lincoln Park, NJ [*Library symbol Library of Congress*] (LCLS)

NjLPP .... Paci Press, Lodi, NJ [*Library symbol*] [*Library of Congress*] (LCLS)

NJL Rep ...... New Jersey Law Reports [*A publication*] (DLA)

NJL Rev....... New Jersey Law Review [*A publication*] (DLA)

NjLwR.......... Record Breeze, Lindenwold, NJ [*Library symbol Library of Congress*] (LCLS)

NjLy.............. Lyndhurst Public Library, Lyndhurst, NJ [*Library symbol Library of Congress*] (LCLS)

NjLyL .... Leader Publications, Lyndhurst, NJ [*Library symbol Library of Congress*] (LCLS)

NjLyoV......... United States Veterans Administration Hospital, Lyons, NJ [*Library symbol Library of Congress*] (LCLS)

NjM.............. Free Public Library of the Borough of Madison, Madison, NJ [*Library symbol Library of Congress*] (LCLS)

NJM .... Montclair State College, Upper Montclair, NJ [*OCLC symbol*] (OCLC)

NJM .... New Jersey Miscellaneous Reports [*A publication*] (DLA)

NJM .... Swansboro, NC [*Location identifier FAA*] (FAAL)

NJMA........... National Jail Managers Association [*Later, AJA*] (EA)

NjMah.......... Free Public Library of the Township of Mahwah, Mahwah, NJ [*Library symbol Library of Congress*] (LCLS)

NjMahR .... Ramapo College of New Jersey, Mahwah, NJ [*Library symbol Library of Congress*] (LCLS)

NjMal........... Franklin Township Public Library, Malaga, NJ [*Library symbol Library of Congress*] (LCLS)

NjMan.......... Manasquan Public Library, Manasquan, NJ [*Library symbol Library of Congress*] (LCLS)

NjManhT...... Times Beacon Co., Manahawkin, NJ [*Library symbol Library of Congress*] (LCLS)

NjManS........ Coast Star, Manasquan, NJ [*Library symbol Library of Congress*] (LCLS)

NjMap.......... Maplewood Memorial Library, Maplewood, NJ [*Library symbol Library of Congress*] (LCLS)

NjMapW ...... Worrall Publishing Co., Maplewood, NJ [*Library symbol Library of Congress*] (LCLS)

NjMat........... Matawan Joint Free Public Library, Matawan, NJ [*Library symbol Library of Congress*] (LCLS)

NjMatB .... Bayshore Independent, Matawan, NJ [*Library symbol Library of Congress*] (LCLS)

NjMatHi ...... Madison Township Historical Society, Matawan, NJ [*Library symbol Library of Congress*] (LCLS)

NjMayO .... Our Town, Maywood, NJ [*Library symbol Library of Congress*] (LCLS)

NJMC........... National Jewish Music Council [*Later, Jewish Welfare Board Jewish Music Council*] (EA)

NjMcUSAF ... United States Air Force, Base Library, McGuire Air Force Base, NJ [*Library symbol Library of Congress*] (LCLS)

NJMD .... Drew University, Madison, NJ [*Library symbol Library of Congress*] (LCLS)

NJMDC .... NORAD Joint Manual Direction Center [*Military*]

NjMD-T....... Drew University, Theological School, Madison, NJ [*Library symbol Library of Congress*] (LCLS)

NjMe............ Free Public Library, Metuchen, NJ [*Library symbol Library of Congress*] (LCLS)

NjME............ Madison Eagle, Madison, NJ [*Library symbol Library of Congress*] (LCLS)

NjMedR .... Central Record, Medford, NJ [*Library symbol Library of Congress*] (LCLS)

NjMen.......... Mendham Public Library, Mendham, NJ [*Library symbol Library of Congress*] (LCLS)

NjMenO .... Observer-Tribune, Mendham, NJ [*Library symbol Library of Congress*] (LCLS)

NjMF............ Fairleigh Dickinson University, Madison, NJ [*Library symbol Library of Congress*] (LCLS)

NjMhB .... Burlington County Area Reference Library, Mount Holly, NJ [*Library symbol Library of Congress*] (LCLS)

NjMhCoC ..... Burlington County Clerk, Mount Holly, NJ [*Library symbol Library of Congress*] (LCLS)

NjMhH .... Burlington County Herald, Mount Holly, NJ [*Library symbol Library of Congress*] (LCLS)

NjMHi .... Madison Historical Society, Madison, NJ [*Library symbol Library of Congress*] (LCLS)

NjMhL.......... Burlington County Lyceum [*Mount Holly Publich Library*], Mount Holly, NJ [*Library symbol Library of Congress*] (LCLS)

NjMhPM....... Burlington County Prison Museum, Mount Holly, NJ [*Library symbol Library of Congress*] (LCLS)

NJMI............ Catholic Medical Center of Brooklyn & Queens, Inc., Jamaica, NY [*Library symbol*] [*Library of Congress*] (LCLS)

NJMI............ Mary Immaculate Hospital, School of Nursing, Jamaica, NY [*Library symbol Library of Congress*] (LCLS)

NjMi............. Middletown Township Free Public Library, Middletown, NJ [*Library symbol Library of Congress*] (LCLS)

NJMI .... New Junior Maudsley Inventory [*Psychology*]

NjMiA........... Advisor, Middletown, NJ [*Library symbol Library of Congress*] (LCLS)

NjMiC .... Courier, Middletown, NJ [*Library symbol Library of Congress*] (LCLS)

NjMid........... Middlesex Public Library, Middlesex, NJ [*Library symbol Library of Congress*] (LCLS)

NjMil............ Millburn Free Public Library, Millburn, NJ [*Library symbol Library of Congress*] (LCLS)

NjMilt .... Milltown Public Library, Milltown, NJ [*Library symbol Library of Congress*] (LCLS)

NjMilv........... Millville Public Library, Millville, NJ [*Library symbol Library of Congress*] (LCLS)

NjMilvHi .... Wheaton Historical Association, Millville, NJ [*Library symbol Library of Congress*] (LCLS)

NjMilvM........ Millville Daily, Millville, NJ [*Library symbol Library of Congress*] (LCLS)

NjMiP........... Middletown Township Public Library, Middletown, NJ [*Library symbol*] [*Library of Congress*] (LCLS)

NJ Mis......... New Jersey Miscellaneous Reports [*A publication*] (DLA)

NJ Misc........ New Jersey Miscellaneous Reports [*A publication*] (DLA)

NJ Mis R ...... New Jersey Miscellaneous Reports [*A publication*] (DLA)

NjMj............. South Brunswick Free Public Library, Monmouth Junction, NJ [*Library symbol Library of Congress*] (LCLS)

NjMIA .... Atlantic County Library, Mays Landing, NJ [*Library symbol Library of Congress*] (LCLS)

NjMIAC .... Atlantic Community College, Mays Landing, NJ [*Library symbol Library of Congress*] (LCLS)

NjMICoC ...... Atlantic County Clerk, Mays Landing, NJ [*Library symbol Library of Congress*] (LCLS)

NjMIR .... Atlantic County Record, Mays Landing, NJ [*Library symbol Library of Congress*] (LCLS)

NjMo............ Joint Free Public Library of Morristown and Morris Township, Morristown, NJ [*Library symbol Library of Congress*] (LCLS)

NjMoAT........ American Telephone & Telegraph Co., Morristown Corporate Marketing Library, Morristown, NJ [*Library symbol Library of Congress*] (LCLS)

NjMoCoC ..... Morris County Clerk, Morristown, NJ [*Library symbol Library of Congress*] (LCLS)

NjMoH .... Morristown Memorial Hospital, Morristown, NJ [*Library symbol Library of Congress*] (LCLS)

NjMoHP .... Morristown National Historical Park, Morristown, NJ [*Library symbol Library of Congress*] (LCLS)

NjMon.......... Montclair Free Public Library, Montclair, NJ [*Library symbol Library of Congress*] (LCLS)

NjMonM........ Montclair Times, Montclair, NJ [*Library symbol Library of Congress*] (LCLS)

NjMor........... Moorestown Free Library, Moorestown, NJ [*Library symbol Library of Congress*] (LCLS)

NjMorR......... Radio Corp. of America, Missile and Surface Radar Division, Moorestown, NJ [*Library symbol Library of Congress*] (LCLS)

NjMou.......... Mountain Lakes Public Library, Mountain Lakes, NJ [*Library symbol Library of Congress*] (LCLS)

NjMouHi ...... Mountain Lakes Historical Society, Mountain Lakes, NJ [*Library symbol Library of Congress*] (LCLS)

NjMov........... Montvale Free Public Library, Montvale, NJ [*Library symbol Library of Congress*] (LCLS)

NjMovL .... Lehn & Fink Products Co., Montvale, NJ [*Library symbol Library of Congress*] (LCLS)

NjMp............ Morris Plains Public Library, Morris Plains, NJ [*Library symbol Library of Congress*] (LCLS)

NJMP........... New Jewish Media Project [*JMS*] [*Absorbed by*] (EA)

NjMpN.......... Morris News-Bee, Morris Plains, NJ [*Library symbol Library of Congress*] (LCLS)

NjMpW .... Warner-Lambert Research Institute, Morris Plains, NJ [*Library symbol Library of Congress*] (LCLS)

NJMR........... Nordisk Verbane Musik Rad [*Nordic Council for Railway Music - NCRM*] (EAIO)

NjMs............ Maple Shade Public Library, Maple Shade, NJ [*Library symbol Library of Congress*] (LCLS)

NJMS........... New Jersey Medical School [*Newark*]

NjMsP.......... Maple Shade Progress Press, Maple Shade, NJ [*Library symbol Library of Congress*] (LCLS)

NjMuA.......... Air Reduction Co., Inc., Central Research Department Library, Murray Hill, NJ [*Library symbol Library of Congress*] (LCLS)

NjMuB .... Bell Telephone Laboratories, Inc., Murray Hill, NJ [*Library symbol Library of Congress*] (LCLS)

NjMuhHi ...... Harrison Township Historical Society, Mullica Hill, NJ [*Library symbol Library of Congress*] (LCLS)

NJN............. College of Medicine and Dentistry of New Jersey, Newark, NJ [*OCLC symbol*] (OCLC)

NjN.............. Newark Public Library, Newark, NJ [*Library symbol Library of Congress*] (LCLS)

NJN.............. New Jersey Network [*Trenton*] [*Telecommunications service*] (TSSD)

NjNA............ United States Attorney's Office, Law Library, Newark, NJ [*Library symbol Library of Congress*] (LCLS)

NjNAA.......... New Jersey Afro-American, Newark, NJ [*Library symbol Library of Congress*] (LCLS)

NjNb............ New Brunswick Free Public Library, New Brunswick, NJ [*Library symbol Library of Congress*] (LCLS)

NjNbH.......... Home News, New Brunswick, NJ [*Library symbol Library of Congress*] (LCLS)

NjNbJJ......... Johnson & Johnson, Research Center, New Brunswick, NJ [*Library symbol Library of Congress*] (LCLS)

NjNbM .... Middlesex General Hospital, New Brunswick, NJ [*Library symbol Library of Congress*] (LCLS)

NjNbS .... New Brunswick Theological Seminary, New Brunswick, NJ [*Library symbol Library of Congress*] (LCLS)

NjNbSI......... Squibb-Beechnut, Inc., New Brunswick, NJ [*Library symbol Library of Congress*] (LCLS)

NjNbSp .... New Brunswick Spokesman, New Brunswick, NJ [*Library symbol Library of Congress*] (LCLS)

NjNbStP........ Saint Peter's Medical Center, New Brunswick, NJ [*Library symbol Library of Congress*] (LCLS)

NjNC .... New Jersey Institute of Technology, Newark, NJ [*Library symbol Library of Congress*] (LCLS)

NjNCM .... New Jersey College of Medicine and Dentistry, Newark, NJ [*Library symbol Library of Congress*] (LCLS)

NjNE .... Essex County College, Newark, NJ [*Library symbol Library of Congress*] (LCLS)

NjNeP .... New Egypt Press, New Egypt, NJ [*Library symbol Library of Congress*] (LCLS)

NjNet .... Dennis Memorial Library, Newton, NJ [*Library symbol Library of Congress*] (LCLS)

NjNetcN .... News Leader, Netcong, NJ [*Library symbol Library of Congress*] (LCLS)

NjNetCoC..... Sussex County Clerk, Newton, NJ [*Library symbol Library of Congress*] (LCLS)

NjNetDB....... Don Bosco College, Newton, NJ [*Library symbol Library of Congress*] (LCLS)

NjNetH......... New Jersey Herald, Newton, NJ [*Library symbol Library of Congress*] (LCLS)

NjNetS .... Sussex County Library, Newton, NJ [*Library symbol Library of Congress*] (LCLS)

NjNetSHi...... Sussex County Historical Society, Newton, NJ [*Library symbol Library of Congress*] (LCLS)

NjNhBHi....... Bergen County Historical Society, North Hackensack, NJ [*Library symbol Library of Congress*] (LCLS)

NjNI .... Ironbound Crier, Newark, NJ [*Library symbol Library of Congress*] (LCLS)

NjNIJS .... Institute of Jazz Studies, Rutgers, the State University, Newark, NJ [*Library symbol*] [*Library of Congress*] (LCLS)

NjNIM .... International Musician, Newark, NJ [*Library symbol Library of Congress*] (LCLS)

NjNIT .... Italian Tribune, Newark, NJ [*Library symbol Library of Congress*] (LCLS)

NjNJL........... Jewish Ledger, Newark, NJ [*Library symbol Library of Congress*] (LCLS)

NjNJN .... Jewish News, Newark, NJ [*Library symbol Library of Congress*] (LCLS)

NjNL .... Luso-Americano, Newark, NJ [*Library symbol Library of Congress*] (LCLS)

NjNLH.......... New Jersey Labor Herald, Newark, NJ [*Library symbol Library of Congress*] (LCLS)

NjNN............ Nite-Lite, Newark, NJ [*Library symbol Library of Congress*] (LCLS)

NjNoA .... Atlantic County Advertiser, Northfield, NJ [*Library symbol Library of Congress*] (LCLS)

NjNoa .... North Arlington Free Public Library, North Arlington, NJ [*Library symbol Library of Congress*] (LCLS)

NjNoaP .... North Arlington Free Public Library, North Arlington, NJ [*Library symbol*] [*Library of Congress*] (LCLS)

NjNor .... Norwood Public Library, Norwood, NJ [*Library symbol Library of Congress*] (LCLS)

NjNp .... New Providence Memorial Library, New Providence, NJ [*Library symbol Library of Congress*] (LCLS)

NjNpD .... Dispatch, New Providence, NJ [*Library symbol Library of Congress*] (LCLS)

NjNpHi .... New Providence Historical Society, New Providence, NJ [*Library symbol Library of Congress*] (LCLS)

NjNpl .... Independent Press, New Providence, NJ [*Library symbol Library of Congress*] (LCLS)

NjNPSE........ Public Service Electric & Gas Co., Newark, NJ [*Library symbol*] [*Library of Congress*] (LCLS)

NjNT .... Tribuna di North Jersey, Newark, NJ [*Library symbol Library of Congress*] (LCLS)

NjNu .... Nutley Free Public Library, Nutley, NJ [*Library symbol Library of Congress*] (LCLS)

NjNuH.......... Hoffmann-La Roche, Inc., Scientific Library, Nutley, NJ [*Library symbol Library of Congress*] (LCLS)

NjNuHi......... Nutley Historical Society, Nutley, NJ [*Library symbol Library of Congress*] (LCLS)

NjNuS .... Sun-Bank Newspapers, Nutley, NJ [*Library symbol Library of Congress*] (LCLS)

NJNY .... New Jersey & New York R. R. [*AAR code*]

NjO .... Free Public Library of the City of Orange, Orange, NJ [*Library symbol Library of Congress*] (LCLS)

NjOak.......... Oakland Public Library, Oakland, NJ [*Library symbol Library of Congress*] (LCLS)

NjOaS .... Shore Publishers, Inc., Oakhurst, NJ [*Library symbol Library of Congress*] (LCLS)

NjOcM .... Ocean City Historical Museum, Ocean City, NJ [*Library symbol Library of Congress*] (LCLS)

NjOcS .... Sentinel Ledger, Ocean City, NJ [*Library symbol Library of Congress*] (LCLS)

NjOgT .... Ocean Grove Times, Ocean Grove, NJ [*Library symbol Library of Congress*] (LCLS)

NjOrd........... Oradell Public Library, Oradell, NJ [*Library symbol Library of Congress*] (LCLS)

NjOrdB......... Burns & Roe, Inc., Oradell, NJ [*Library symbol Library of Congress*] (LCLS)

NJosnU......... United Health Services, Wilson Hospital, Johnson City, NY [*Library symbol Library of Congress*] (LCLS)

NJostF .... Fulton-Montgomery Community College, Johnstown, NY [*Library symbol Library of Congress*] (LCLS)

NjOtR........... Fleming H. Revell Co., Old Tappan, NJ [*Library symbol Library of Congress*] (LCLS)

NjOW .... Worrall Publications, Inc., Orange, NJ [*Library symbol Library of Congress*] (LCLS)

NJP............. National Jury Project (EA)

NJP............. Network Job Processing

NJP............. Nonjudicial Punishment [*Military*]

NjP............. Princeton University, Princeton, NJ [*Library symbol Library of Congress*] (LCLS)

NJP............. Warminster, PA [*Location identifier FAA*] (FAAL)

NJP............. William Patterson College of New Jersey, Wayne, NJ [*OCLC symbol*] (OCLC)

NjPA .... American Cyanamid Co., Agricultural Division, Princeton, NJ [*Library symbol Library of Congress*] (LCLS)

NjP-A........... Art Museum of Princeton University, Princeton, NJ [*Library symbol*] [*Library of Congress*] (LCLS)

NJPA .... National Juice Products Association (EA)

NjPalN .... Bergen News, Palisades Park, NJ [*Library symbol Library of Congress*] (LCLS)

NjPar .... Paramus Public Library, Paramus, NJ [*Library symbol Library of Congress*] (LCLS)

NjParB .... Bergen Community College, Paramus, NJ [*Library symbol Library of Congress*] (LCLS)

NjParkHi .... Pascack Historical Society and Museum, Park Ridge, NJ [*Library symbol Library of Congress*] (LCLS)

NjParkP .... Pascack Publications Corp., Park Ridge, NJ [*Library symbol Library of Congress*] (LCLS)

NjParR......... Ridgewood Newspapers, Paramus, NJ [*Library symbol Library of Congress*] (LCLS)

NjParT .... Town News, Paramus, NJ [*Library symbol Library of Congress*] (LCLS)

NjPas........... Passaic Public Library, Passaic, NJ [*Library symbol Library of Congress*] (LCLS)

NjPasC......... Passaic Citizen, Passaic, NJ [*Library symbol Library of Congress*] (LCLS)

NjPasCS ...... Catholic Sokol Printing Co., Passaic, NJ [*Library symbol Library of Congress*] (LCLS)

NjPasE......... Eastern Catholic Life, Passaic, NJ [*Library symbol Library of Congress*] (LCLS)

NjPasH .... Herald News, Passaic, NJ [*Library symbol Library of Congress*] (LCLS)

NjPat .... Paterson Free Public Library, Paterson, NJ [*Library symbol Library of Congress*] (LCLS)

NjPatCoC ..... Passaic County Clerk, Paterson, NJ [*Library symbol Library of Congress*] (LCLS)

NjPatNe .... News, Paterson, NJ [*Library symbol Library of Congress*] (LCLS)

NjPatPHi ...... Passaic County Historical Society, Paterson, NJ [*Library symbol Library of Congress*] (LCLS)

NjPatSA........ Saint Anthony's Guild, Franciscan Monastery, Paterson, NJ [*Library symbol Library of Congress*] (LCLS)

NjPatV .... Voce Italiana, Paterson, NJ [*Library symbol Library of Congress*] (LCLS)

NjPauR .... Record, Paulsboro, NJ [*Library symbol Library of Congress*] (LCLS)

NjPauS .... Mobil Research & Development Corp., Paulsboro, NJ [*Library symbol Library of Congress*] (LCLS)

NjPD .... Daily Princetonian, Princeton, NJ [*Library symbol Library of Congress*] (LCLS)

NJPDDATC... National Joint Painting, Decorating, and Drywall Apprenticeship and Training Committee (EA)

NjPE............ Educational Testing Service, Princeton, NJ [*Library symbol Library of Congress*] (LCLS)

NjPeB .... Burlington County College, Pemberton, NJ [*Library symbol Library of Congress*] (LCLS)

NjPegR .... Penns Grove Record, Penns Grove, NJ [*Library symbol Library of Congress*] (LCLS)

NjPenP .... Pennsauken Resume, Pennsauken, NJ [*Library symbol Library of Congress*] (LCLS)

NjPeqB .... Beacon, Pequannock, NJ [*Library symbol Library of Congress*] (LCLS)

NjPera .... Perth Amboy Free Public Library, Perth Amboy, NJ [*Library symbol Library of Congress*] (LCLS)

NjPeraSo ..... Universum Sokol Publishers, Perth Amboy, NJ [*Library symbol Library of Congress*] (LCLS)

NjPeraSt....... Saint John's Church, Perth Amboy, NJ [*Library symbol Library of Congress*] (LCLS)

NjPERS........ E. R. Squibb & Sons, Princeton, NJ [*Library symbol Library of Congress*] (LCLS)

NjPeT.......... Times Advertising Printing Co., Pemberton, NJ [*Library symbol Library of Congress*] (LCLS)

NjPF............ FMC Corp., Princeton, NJ [*Library symbol Library of Congress*] (LCLS)

NjP-G.......... Princeton University, Gest Library, Princeton, NJ [*Library symbol Library of Congress*] (LCLS)

NjPh............ Phillipsburg Free Public Library, Phillipsburg, NJ [*Library symbol Library of Congress*] (LCLS)

NJPHA .... National Junior Polled Hereford Association (EA)

NJPHC .... National Junior Polled Hereford Council [*Later, NJPHA*] (EA)

NjPHi .... Historical Society of Princeton, Princeton, NJ [*Library symbol Library of Congress*] (LCLS)

NjPhP .... Free Press, Phillipsburg, NJ [*Library symbol Library of Congress*] (LCLS)

NjPI .... Institute for Advanced Study, Princeton, NJ [*Library symbol Library of Congress*] (LCLS)

NjPi .... McCowan Memorial Library, Pitman, NJ [*Library symbol Library of Congress*] (LCLS)

NjPiM .... McCowan Memorial Library, Pitman, NJ [*Library symbol*] [*Library of Congress*] (LCLS)

NjPJ............ Robert Wood Johnson Foundation Library, Princeton, NJ [*Library symbol Library of Congress*] (LCLS)

NjPl .... Emanuel Einstein Free Public Library, Pompton Lakes, NJ [*Library symbol Library of Congress*] (LCLS)

NjPla .... Plainfield Public Library, Plainfield, NJ [*Library symbol Library of Congress*] (LCLS)

NjPlaM .... Muhlenberg Hospital, Plainfield, NJ [*Library symbol Library of Congress*] (LCLS)

NjPlaSDB.... Seventh Day Baptist Historical Society, Plainfield, NJ [*Library symbol Library of Congress*] (LCLS)

NjPlaT .... Plainfield Times, Plainfield, NJ [*Library symbol Library of Congress*] (LCLS)

NjPlaV .... Voice, Plainfield, NJ [*Library symbol Library of Congress*] (LCLS)

NjPleM .... Mainland Journal, Pleasantville, NJ [*Library symbol Library of Congress*] (LCLS)

NjPM .... Mobil Research & Development Corp., Central Research Division Library, Princeton, NJ [*Library symbol Library of Congress*] (LCLS)

NJPMB........ Navy Jet-Propelled-Missile Board

NjPMC .... Medical Center at Princeton, Princeton, NJ [*Library symbol Library of Congress*] (LCLS)

NjPoiO .... Ocean County Leader, Point Pleasant Beach, NJ [*Library symbol Library of Congress*] (LCLS)

NjPoR .... Richard Stockton State College, Pomona, NJ [*Library symbol Library of Congress*] (LCLS)

NjPP .... Princeton Packet, Inc., Princeton, NJ [*Library symbol Library of Congress*] (LCLS)

NjPpE.......... Eastern Historical Commission, Prospect Park, NJ [*Library symbol Library of Congress*] (LCLS)

NjP-Pop .... Princeton University, Office of Population Research, Princeton, NJ [*Library symbol Library of Congress*] (LCLS)

NjPPP .... Princeton Public Library, Princeton, NJ [*Library symbol Library of Congress*] (LCLS)

NjPRCA....... Radio Corp. of America, Laboratories Division, Princeton, NJ [*Library symbol Library of Congress*] (LCLS)

NjPS .... Princeton Shopping News, Princeton, NJ [*Library symbol Library of Congress*] (LCLS)

NjP-SC........ Princeton University, Princeton Special Collection, Princeton, NJ [*Library symbol*] [*Library of Congress*] (LCLS)

NjPStJ .... Saint Joseph's College, Princeton, NJ [*Library symbol Library of Congress*] (LCLS)

NjPT............ Princeton Theological Seminary, Princeton, NJ [*Library symbol Library of Congress*] (LCLS)

NjPTe.......... Textile Research Institute, Princeton, NJ [*Library symbol Library of Congress*] (LCLS)

NjPTT.......... Town Topics, Inc., Princeton, NJ [*Library symbol Library of Congress*] (LCLS)

NjPW .... Western Electric Co., Inc., Engineering Research Center, Princeton, NJ [*Library symbol Library of Congress*] (LCLS)

NjPwAT....... American Telephone & Telegraph Co. Resource Center, Piscataway, NJ [*Library symbol Library of Congress*] (LCLS)

NjPwC......... Colgate-Palmolive Co., Technical Information Center, Piscataway, NJ [*Library symbol Library of Congress*] (LCLS)

NjPwIE........ Institute of Electrical and Electronics Engineers, Piscataway, NJ [*Library symbol Library of Congress*] (LCLS)

NJQ............. Queens Borough Public Library, Jamaica, NY [*Library symbol Library of Congress*] (LCLS)

NJQH .... Queens Hospital Center, Jamaica, NY [*Library symbol Library of Congress*] (LCLS)

NJR............. New Jersey Register [*A publication*] (DLA)

NJR............. New Jersey Resources [*NYSE symbol*] (TTSB)

NJR............. New Jersey Resources Corp. [*NYSE symbol*] (SPSG)

NJR............. New JEWEL Regime [*Grenada*]

NJR............. Nonjob Routed [*Military*] (AFIT)

NjR .... Rutgers-[*The*] State University, New Brunswick, NJ [*Library symbol Library of Congress*] (LCLS)

NJRA .... National Juvenile Restitution Association [*Later, ARA*] (EA)

NjRah .... Rahway Public Library, Rahway, NJ [*Library symbol Library of Congress*] (LCLS)

NjRahB .... Bauer Publishing & Printing Ltd., Rahway, NJ [*Library symbol Library of Congress*] (LCLS)

NjRahM ...... Merck, Sharp & Dohme [*Later, Merck & Co., Inc.*] Research Laboratory, Research Library, Rahway, NJ [*Library symbol Library of Congress*] (LCLS)

NjRam .... Ramsey Free Public Library, Ramsey, NJ [*Library symbol Library of Congress*] (LCLS)

NjRamH....... Home and Store News, Ramsey, NJ [*Library symbol Library of Congress*] (LCLS)

NjRamI .... Immaculate Conception Theological Seminary, Ramsey, NJ [*Library symbol Library of Congress*] (LCLS)

NjRarO......... Ortho Pharmaceutical Corp., Raritan, NJ [*Library symbol Library of Congress*] (LCLS)

NjRarOD ...... Ortho Diagnostics, Raritan, NJ [*Library symbol Library of Congress*] (LCLS)

NjRb .... Red Bank Public Library, Red Bank, NJ [*Library symbol Library of Congress*] (LCLS)

NjRbR .... Daily Register, Red Bank, NJ [*Library symbol Library of Congress*] (LCLS)

NJRC .... National Jewish Resource Center (EA)

NJRC .... New Jersey Board of Railroad Commissioners Annual Reports [*A publication*] (DLA)

NjRdR .... Riverdale Publishing Co., Riverdale, NJ [*Library symbol Library of Congress*] (LCLS)

NJ Rep .... New Jersey Law Reports [*A publication*] (DLA)

NJ Re Tit N... New Jersey Realty Title News [*A publication*] (DLA)

NJ Rev Stat.. New Jersey Revised Statutes [*A publication*] (DLA)

NjRf .... Ridgefield Public Library, Ridgefield, NJ [*Library symbol Library of Congress*] (LCLS)

NjRh .... Rocky Hill Public Library, Rocky Hill, NJ [*Library symbol Library of Congress*] (LCLS)

NjRiv .... Riverside Public Library, Riverside, NJ [*Library symbol Library of Congress*] (LCLS)

NjRive .... River Edge Free Public Library, River Edge, NJ [*Library symbol Library of Congress*] (LCLS)

NjR-L .... Rutgers-[*The*] State University, Rutgers-Camden School of Law, Camden, NJ [*Library symbol Library of Congress*] (LCLS)

NjR-NL........ Rutgers, The State University, Law School Library-Newark, Newark, NJ [*Library symbol*] [*Library of Congress*] (LCLS)

NjRo .... Roseland Public Library, Roseland, NJ [*Library symbol Library of Congress*] (LCLS)

NjRocM....... Morris County News, Rockaway, NJ [*Library symbol Library of Congress*] (LCLS)

NjRos.......... Roselle Free Public Library, Roselle, NJ [*Library symbol Library of Congress*] (LCLS)

NJROTC ...... Naval Junior Reserve Officer Training Corps

NjRp .... Ridgefield Park Free Public Library, Ridgefield Park, NJ [*Library symbol Library of Congress*] (LCLS)

NjRpS .... Sun Bulletin, Ridgefield Park, NJ [*Library symbol Library of Congress*] (LCLS)

NjR-S .... Rutgers-[*The*] State University, College of South Jersey, Camden, NJ [*Library symbol Library of Congress*] (LCLS)

NJRsc .... New Jersey Resources [*Associated Press*] (SAG)

NjRu .... Rutherford Free Public Library, Rutherford, NJ [*Library symbol Library of Congress*] (LCLS)

NjRuB .... Becton, Dickinson & Co., Rutherford, NJ [*Library symbol Library of Congress*] (LCLS)

NjRuF .... Fairleigh Dickinson University, Rutherford, NJ [*Library symbol Library of Congress*] (LCLS)

NjRw........... Ridgewood Library, Ridgewood, NJ [*Library symbol Library of Congress*] (LCLS)

NjRwN .... Ridgewood News, Ridgewood, NJ [*Library symbol Library of Congress*] (LCLS)

NjRwPHi...... Paramus Historical and Preservation Society, Ridgewood, NJ [*Library symbol Library of Congress*] (LCLS)

NJS............. New Jersey Superior Court Reports [*A publication*] (DLA)

NJS............. Noise Jammer Simulator [*Telecommunications*] (TEL)

NJSTe.......... Stockton State College, Pomona, NJ [*OCLC symbol*] (OCLC)

NjS............. Summit Free Public Library, Summit, NJ [*Library symbol Library of Congress*] (LCLS)

NJSA .... New Jersey Statutes, Annotated [*A publication*]

NjSabN .... News Dispatch, Saddle Brook, NJ [*Library symbol Library of Congress*] (LCLS)

NjSalCoC .... Salem County Clerk, Salem, NJ [*Library symbol Library of Congress*] (LCLS)

NjSalHi........ Salem County Historical Society, Salem, NJ [*Library symbol Library of Congress*] (LCLS)

NjSalS .... Sunbeam Publishing Co., Salem, NJ [*Library symbol Library of Congress*] (LCLS)

NJSBAQ .... New Jersey State Bar Association. Quarterly [*A publication*] (DLA)

NjSbB .... Beachcomber, Ship Bottom, NJ [*Library symbol Library of Congress*] (LCLS)

NjSbbU .... Saint Sophia Ukrainian Orthodox Seminary, South Bound Brook, NJ [*Library symbol Library of Congress*] (LCLS)

NJSBJ .... New Jersey State Bar Journal [*A publication*] (DLA)

NJSBTA Ops... New Jersey State Board of Tax Appeals, Opinions [*A publication*] (DLA)

NjSC .... Ciba Pharmaceutical Co., Research Library, Summit, NJ [*Library symbol Library of Congress*] (LCLS)

NjSCC .... Summit City Clerk, Summit, NJ [*Library symbol Library of Congress*] (LCLS)

NjScp.......... Scotch Plains Public Library, Scotch Plains, NJ [*Library symbol Library of Congress*] (LCLS)

NjScpT......... Times, Scotch Plains, NJ [*Library symbol Library of Congress*] (LCLS)

NJSD .... National Joint Service Delegations (NATG)

NJSDC .... New Jersey State Data Center [*New Jersey State Department of Labor*] [*Trenton*] [*Information service or system*] (IID)

NjSe............. Secaucus Free Public Library, Secaucus, NJ [*Library symbol Library of Congress*] (LCLS)

NjSeH .... Secaucus Home News, Secaucus, NJ [*Library symbol Library of Congress*] (LCLS)

NJ Sess Law Serv... New Jersey Session Law Service [*A publication*] (DLA)

NjSewG........ Gloucester County College, Sewell, NJ [*Library symbol Library of Congress*] (LCLS)

NjSewHi ...... Washington Township Historical Society, Sewell, NJ [*Library symbol Library of Congress*] (LCLS)

NJSGA .... National Junior Santa Gertrudis Association (EA)

NjSGS.......... Church of Jesus Christ of Latter-Day Saints, Genealogical Society Library, Caldwell Branch, Summit, NJ [*Library symbol Library of Congress*] (LCLS)

NjSH............ Summit Herald, Summit, NJ [*Library symbol Library of Congress*] (LCLS)

NjShO.......... Ocean County Review, Seaside Heights, NJ [*Library symbol Library of Congress*] (LCLS)

NJSHS........ National Junior Science and Humanities Symposium

NjSicTR....... Cape May County Times and Seven Mile Beach Reporter, Sea Isle City, NJ [*Library symbol Library of Congress*] (LCLS)

NJSN.......... National Job Sharing Network (EA)

NJSO.......... National Jazz Service Organization (EA)

NjSo............ Somerville Free Public Library, Somerville, NJ [*Library symbol Library of Congress*] (LCLS)

NjSoa.......... South Amboy Public Library, South Amboy, NJ [*Library symbol Library of Congress*] (LCLS)

NjSoaP....... South Amboy Publishing Co., South Amboy, NJ [*Library symbol Library of Congress*] (LCLS)

NjSobC....... Central Post, South Brunswick, NJ [*Library symbol Library of Congress*] (LCLS)

NjSoCo....... Somerset County Library, Somerville, NJ [*Library symbol Library of Congress*] (LCLS)

NjSoCoC...... Somerset County Clerk, Somerville, NJ [*Library symbol Library of Congress*] (LCLS)

NjSoE.......... Ethicon, Inc., Somerville, NJ [*Library symbol Library of Congress*] (LCLS)

NjSoH.......... Somerset Hospital, Somerville, NJ [*Library symbol Library of Congress*] (LCLS)

NjSoHR....... Hoechst-Roussel Pharmaceuticals, Inc., Somerville, NJ [*Library symbol Library of Congress*] (LCLS)

NjSoM......... Somerset Messenger-Gazette, Somerville, NJ [*Library symbol Library of Congress*] (LCLS)

NjSomHi...... Atlantic County Historical Society, Somers Point, NJ [*Library symbol Library of Congress*] (LCLS)

NjSoo.......... South Orange Public Library, South Orange, NJ [*Library symbol Library of Congress*] (LCLS)

NjSooS........ Seton Hall University, South Orange, NJ [*Library symbol Library of Congress*] (LCLS)

NjSooS-L..... Seton Hall University, Law Library, Newark, NJ [*Library symbol Library of Congress*] (LCLS)

NjSop.......... South Plainfield Free Public Library, South Plainfield, NJ [*Library symbol Library of Congress*] (LCLS)

NjSopA........ American Smelting & Refining Co., Research Department Library, South Plainfield,NJ [*Library symbol Library of Congress*] (LCLS)

NjSopP....... PAMCAM, Inc., South Plainfield, NJ [*Library symbol Library of Congress*] (LCLS)

NjSoS.......... Somerset County College, Somerville, NJ [*Library symbol Library of Congress*] (LCLS)

NjSosS........ Somerset Spectator, Somerset, NJ [*Library symbol Library of Congress*] (LCLS)

NjSoVA........ United States Veterans Administration Supply Depot, Somerville, NJ [*Library symbol Library of Congress*] (LCLS)

NjSp........... Springfield Free Public Library, Springfield, NJ [*Library symbol Library of Congress*] (LCLS)

NjSpl.......... Spring Lake Public Library, Spring Lake, NJ [*Library symbol Library of Congress*] (LCLS)

NjSpW........ Western Electric Co., Springfield, NJ [*Library symbol Library of Congress*] (LCLS)

NJST.......... New Jersey Steel [*NASDAQ symbol*] (TTSB)

NJST.......... New Jersey Steel Corp. [*NASDAQ symbol*] (NQ)

NjSt........... Passaic Township Public Library, Stirling, NJ [*Library symbol Library of Congress*] (LCLS)

NJ Stat Ann (West)... New Jersey Statutes, Annotated (West) [*A publication*] (DLA)

NJ St BJ..... New Jersey State Bar Journal [*A publication*] (DLA)

NJ Stl.......... New Jersey Steel Corp. [*Associated Press*] (SAG)

NjStR.......... Recorder Publishing Co., Stirling, NJ [*Library symbol Library of Congress*] (LCLS)

NjStrK........ John F. Kennedy Memorial Hospital, Stratford, NJ [*Library symbol Library of Congress*] (LCLS)

NjSu........... Roxbury Public Library, Succasunna, NJ [*Library symbol Library of Congress*] (LCLS)

NJ Sup........ New Jersey Superior Court Reports [*A publication*] (DLA)

NJ Super..... New Jersey Superior Court Reports [*A publication*] (DLA)

NjSw.......... Swedesboro Free Public Library, Swedesboro, NJ [*Library symbol Library of Congress*] (LCLS)

NjSwN........ Swedesboro News, Swedesboro, NJ [*Library symbol Library of Congress*] (LCLS)

NJT............ National Jewish Television [*Cable-television system*]

NJT............ Societe Novajet [*France ICAO designator*] (FAAC)

NjT............. Trenton Free Public Library, Trenton, NJ [*Library symbol Library of Congress*] (LCLS)

NJT............ Trenton State College, Trenton, NJ [*OCLC symbol*] (OCLC)

NjTCP......... Commercial Printing Co., Trenton, NJ [*Library symbol Library of Congress*] (LCLS)

NjTea.......... Teaneck Public Library, Teaneck, NJ [*Library symbol Library of Congress*] (LCLS)

NjTeaF........ Fairleigh Dickinson University, Teaneck, NJ [*Library symbol Library of Congress*] (LCLS)

NjTeaL........ Luther College, Teaneck, NJ [*Library symbol Library of Congress*] (LCLS)

NjTen.......... Tenafly Public Library, Tenafly, NJ [*Library symbol Library of Congress*] (LCLS)

NJTL.......... National Junior Tennis League (EA)

NjTM.......... Monitor, Trenton, NJ [*Library symbol Library of Congress*] (LCLS)

NjTMC......... Mercer County Community College, Trenton, NJ [*Library symbol Library of Congress*] (LCLS)

NjTPP......... Planned Parenthood of Mercer Area, Trenton, NJ [*Library symbol Library of Congress*] (LCLS)

NjTR........... Rider College, Trenton, NJ [*Library symbol Library of Congress*] (LCLS)

NjTrCo........ Ocean County Public Library, Toms River, NJ [*Library symbol Library of Congress*] (LCLS)

NjTrCoC...... Ocean County Clerk, Toms River, NJ [*Library symbol Library of Congress*] (LCLS)

NjTrO......... Ocean County College, Toms River, NJ [*Library symbol Library of Congress*] (LCLS)

NjTrR......... Reporter, Toms River, NJ [*Library symbol Library of Congress*] (LCLS)

NjTS.......... Trenton State College, Trenton, NJ [*Library symbol Library of Congress*] (LCLS)

NjTSch........ Schweats, Inc., Trenton, NJ [*Library symbol Library of Congress*] (LCLS)

NjTStF........ Saint Francis Medical Center, Health Science Library, Trenton, NJ [*Library symbol Library of Congress*] (LCLS)

NjTTr.......... Trentonian, Trenton, NJ [*Library symbol Library of Congress*] (LCLS)

NjTTT......... Trenton Times Newspapers, Trenton, NJ [*Library symbol Library of Congress*] (LCLS)

nju............. New Jersey [*MARC country of publication code Library of Congress*] (LCCP)

NJU........... Nordic Judo Union (EAIO)

NJU........... Northern Jiaotong Univeristy [*China*]

NjU........... Union Township Public Library, Union, NJ [*Library symbol Library of Congress*] (LCLS)

NjUbl.......... International Flavors & Fragrances, Inc., Union Beach, NJ [*Library symbol Library of Congress*] (LCLS)

NjUc........... Union City Free Public Library, Union City, NJ [*Library symbol Library of Congress*] (LCLS)

NjUcD......... Dispatch, Union City, NJ [*Library symbol Library of Congress*] (LCLS)

NjUcS......... Shield, Union City, NJ [*Library symbol Library of Congress*] (LCLS)

NjUcSM....... Saint Michael's Passionist Monastery, Union City, NJ [*Library symbol Library of Congress*] (LCLS)

NjUJ.......... Jewish Community News, Union, NJ [*Library symbol Library of Congress*] (LCLS)

NjUN.......... Kean College of New Jersey, Union, NJ [*Library symbol Library of Congress*] (LCLS)

NjUpM......... Montclair State College, Upper Montclair, NJ [*Library symbol Library of Congress*] (LCLS)

NjUpM-C...... China Institute of New Jersey, Montclair State College, Upper Montclair, NJ [*Library symbol Library of Congress*] (LCLS)

NJUS.......... Netherlands Jurisprudence (NITA)

NjUS.......... Suburban Publishing Co., Union, NJ [*Library symbol Library of Congress*] (LCLS)

NjUsrHi........ Upper Saddle River Historical Committee, Upper Saddle River, NJ [*Library symbol Library of Congress*] (LCLS)

NJV............ Nederlandse Juristenvereniging [*Netherlands Lawyers Association*] (ILCA)

NjV............ Vineland Free Public Library, Vineland, NJ [*Library symbol Library of Congress*] (LCLS)

NjVC........... Cumberland County College, Vineland, NJ [*Library symbol Library of Congress*] (LCLS)

NjVcP......... Ventnor City Public Library, Ventnor City, NJ [*Library symbol*] [*Library of Congress*] (LCLS)

NJVGA........ National Junior Vegetable Growers Association [*Later, NJHA*] (EA)

NjVHi.......... Vineland Historical and Antiquarian Society, Vineland, NJ [*Library symbol Library of Congress*] (LCLS)

NjVT.......... Times Journal, Vineland, NJ [*Library symbol Library of Congress*] (LCLS)

NJW........... Norris Junction [*Wyoming*] [*Seismograph station code, US Geological Survey*] (SEIS)

NjW........... Wayne Public Library, Wayne, NJ [*Library symbol Library of Congress*] (LCLS)

NjWa.......... Warren Township Public Library, Warren, NJ [*Library symbol Library of Congress*] (LCLS)

NjWas......... Washington Free Public Library, Washington, NJ [*Library symbol Library of Congress*] (LCLS)

NjWasW...... Washington Star, Washington, NJ [*Library symbol Library of Congress*] (LCLS)

NJWB......... National Jewish Welfare Board [*Later, JWB*]

NjWdHi........ Gloucester County Historical Society, Woodbury, NJ [*Library symbol Library of Congress*] (LCLS)

NjWdT........ Woodbury Daily Times, Woodbury, NJ [*Library symbol Library of Congress*] (LCLS)

NjWef......... Westfield Memorial Library, Westfield, NJ [*Library symbol Library of Congress*] (LCLS)

NjWefW....... Wyckoff Printing Co., Westfield, NJ [*Library symbol Library of Congress*] (LCLS)

NjWem........ Haddon Township Free Library, Westmont, NJ [*Library symbol Library of Congress*] (LCLS)

NjWemT...... Camden County Times, Westmont, NJ [*Library symbol Library of Congress*] (LCLS)

NjWesny...... West New York Public Library, West New York, NJ [*Library symbol Library of Congress*] (LCLS)

NjWew........ Westwood Free Public Library, Westwood, NJ [*Library symbol Library of Congress*] (LCLS)

NjWewP....... Pascack Valley Community Life, Westwood, NJ [*Library symbol Library of Congress*] (LCLS)

NjWewW...... Westwood Publications, Westwood, NJ [*Library symbol Library of Congress*] (LCLS)

NjWF .... Fairleigh Dickinson University, Wayne, NJ [*Library symbol Library of Congress*] (LCLS)

NjWhi .... Whippanong Public Library, Whippany, NJ [*Library symbol Library of Congress*] (LCLS)

NjWhiB .... Bell Telephone Laboratories, Inc., Technical Information Library, Whippany, NJ [*Library symbol Library of Congress*] (LCLS)

NjWhiM ...... Morris County Free Library, Whippany, NJ [*Library symbol Library of Congress*] (LCLS)

NjWhiR .... Regional Weekly News, Whippany, NJ [*Library symbol Library of Congress*] (LCLS)

NjWhsH ...... Hunterdon Review, Whitehouse Station, NJ [*Library symbol Library of Congress*] (LCLS)

NjWi .... Willingboro Public Library, Willingboro, NJ [*Library symbol Library of Congress*] (LCLS)

NjWilH .... Williamstown High School, Williamstown, NJ [*Library symbol Library of Congress*] (LCLS)

NjWiT .... Burlington County Times, Willingboro, NJ [*Library symbol Library of Congress*] (LCLS)

NjWIM .... Monmouth College, West Long Beach, NJ [*Library symbol Library of Congress*] (LCLS)

NjWMN .... Matzner Suburban Newspapers, Wayne, NJ [*Library symbol Library of Congress*] (LCLS)

NjWo .... West Orange Free Public Library, West Orange, NJ [*Library symbol Library of Congress*] (LCLS)

NjWoE .... Edison National Historic Site, West Orange, NJ [*Library symbol Library of Congress*] (LCLS)

NjWolA .... Alphonsus College, Woodcliff Lake, NJ [*Library symbol Library of Congress*] (LCLS)

NjWoo .... Free Public Library of Woodbridge, Woodbridge, NJ [*Library symbol Library of Congress*] (LCLS)

NjWooN ...... News-Tribune, Woodbridge, NJ [*Library symbol Library of Congress*] (LCLS)

NjWor .... Wood Ridge Memorial Library, Wood Ridge, NJ [*Library symbol Library of Congress*] (LCLS)

NjWP .... William Paterson College of New Jersey, Wayne, NJ [*Library symbol Library of Congress*] (LCLS)

NJWPC .... National Jobs with Peace Campaign (EA)

NjWw .... Wildwood Crest Public Library, Wildwood, NJ [*Library symbol*] [*Library of Congress*] (LCLS)

NjWwHi ...... Wildwood Historical Commission, Wildwood, NJ [*Library symbol Library of Congress*] (LCLS)

NjWwL .... Wildwood Leader, Wildwood, NJ [*Library symbol Library of Congress*] (LCLS)

NjWwP .... National Association of Precancel Collectors, Wildwood, NJ [*Library symbol Library of Congress*] (LCLS)

NjWy .... Wyckoff Free Public Library, Wyckoff, NJ [*Library symbol Library of Congress*] (LCLS)

NjWyN .... Wyckoff News, Wyckoff, NJ [*Library symbol Library of Congress*] (LCLS)

NJY .... Newjay Resources Ltd. [*Vancouver Stock Exchange symbol*]

NJY .... York College of the City University of New York, Jamaica, NY [*Library symbol Library of Congress*] (LCLS)

NjZaA .... Alma White College, Zarephath, NJ [*Library symbol Library of Congress*] (LCLS)

Nk .... Naik [*British military*] (DMA)

NK .... Natural Killer [*Cell*] [*Immunochemistry*]

NK .... Neck (AAG)

NK .... Neon Komma [*New Party*] [*Greek Political party*] (PPE)

NK .... Neurokinin [*Biochemistry*]

NK .... New Kingdom [*Egyptology*] (ROG)

NK .... Next of Kin

NK .... Nielsen-Kellerman

NK .... Nippon Kaiji Kyokai [*Japanese ship classification society*] (DS)

NK .... No Ketones [*Organic chemistry*] (DAVI)

NK .... No Kidding [*An association Canada*] (EAIO)

NK .... Nomemklatur Kommission [*Commission on Nomenclature*] [*Germany*] (DAVI)

NK .... Nordiska Kemistradet [*Chemical Societies of the Nordic Countries*] (EAIO)

NK .... North Korean

NK .... Not Known

NK .... Nuclear Kill

NKa .... Katonah Village Library, Katonah, NY [*Library symbol Library of Congress*] (LCLS)

NKA .... National Kindergarten Association [*Defunct*] (EA)

NKA .... Neurokinin A [*Biochemistry*]

NKA .... Nikiskha [*Alaska*] [*Seismograph station code, US Geological Survey*] (SEIS)

NKA .... No Known Allergies [*Medicine*]

NKA .... Norcanair [*Canada ICAO designator*] (FAAC)

NKA .... Nordisk Kontaktorgan for Atomenergisporgsmal [*Nordic Liaison Committee for Atomic Energy*] (EAIO)

NKA .... North Korean Army

NKA .... Now Known As (DLA)

NKABEA ...... National Korean American Bilingual Educators Association [*Defunct*] (EA)

NKAF .... Natural Killer-Cell Activating Factor [*Immunology*]

NKAF .... North Korean Air Force

NKAO .... Nagorno-Karabakh Autonomous Oblast

NKB .... Bear Stearns Companies, Inc. [*AMEX symbol*] (SAG)

NKB .... Neurokinin B [*Biochemistry*]

NKB .... Nordiska Kommitten for Byggbestammelser [*Nordic Committee on Building Regulations - NCBR*] [*Finland*] (EAIO)

NKB .... Norges Kommunalbank [*Bank*] [*Norway*]

NKBA .... National Kitchen and Bath Association (EA)

NKC .... Merrill Lynch & Co. [*AMEX symbol*] (SAG)

NKC .... National Kidney Centre [*British*] (CB)

NKC .... Natural Killer Cells [*Microbiology*] (DAVI)

nkc............. New Brunswick [*MARC country of publication code Library of Congress*] (LCCP)

NKC .... Nouakchott [*Mauritania*] [*Airport symbol*] (OAG)

NKCA .... National Kitchen Cabinet Association [*Later, KCMA*] (EA)

NKCA .... National Knife Collectors Association (EA)

NKCF .... Natural Killer (Cell) Cytotoxic Factor [*Immunochemistry*]

NKCP .... North Kalimantan Communist Party [*Malaysia*] [*Political party*] (PD)

NKDA .... No Known Drug Allergies [*Medicine*]

NKDC .... Nonketotic Diabetic Coma [*Medicine*] (CPH)

NKDF .... National Kidney Disease Foundation [*Later, NKF*] (EA)

NKDS .... Navy Key Distribution System (CAAL)

NKE .... Nake [*Ryukyu Islands*] [*Seismograph station code, US Geological Survey Closed*] (SEIS)

NKE .... Nike, Inc. Class B [*NYSE symbol*] (SPSG)

NKE .... NIKE, Inc. Cl'B' [*NYSE symbol*] (TTSB)

NKE .... Nortek Capital Corp. [*Formerly, Nortek Energy Corp.*] [*Vancouver Stock Exchange symbol*]

NKendOHi ... Orleans County Historical Society, Kendall, NY [*Library symbol Library of Congress*] (LCLS)

NKEWA .... New Kuban Education and Welfare Association (EA)

NKF .... National Kidney Foundation (EA)

NKF .... Nordiske Kvinners Fredsnettverk [*Nordic Women's Peace Network*] [*Denmark, Finland, Norway, and Sweden*] (EAIO)

NKF .... Nordisk Konstforbund [*Nordic Art Association*] [*Norway*] (EAIO)

NKFO .... Nordisk Kollegium for Fysisk Oceanografi [*Nordic Council for Physical Oceanography - NCPO*] (EAIO)

NKFTA .... National Kosher Food Trade Association [*Defunct*] (EA)

NKG .... Nanjing [*China*] [*Airport symbol*] (OAG)

NkG .... Newton K. Gregg, Novato, CA [*Library symbol Library of Congress*] (LCLS)

NKGB-NKVD... Narodnyi Komissariat Gosudarstvennoe Bezopasnosti-Narodnyi Komissariat Vnutrennikh Del [*Later, KGB*]

NKH .... Kaneohe Bay, HI [*Location identifier FAA*] (FAAL)

NKH .... Nonketotic Hyperglycemia [*Endocrinology*] (DAVI)

NKH .... Nonketotic Hyperosmotic [*Medicine*] (MAE)

NKH .... Nordisk Komite for Handelsundervisning [*Nordic Committee for Commercial Education - NCCE*] [*Odense, Denmark*] (EAIO)

NKHA .... National Kerosene Heater Association (EA)

NKHA .... Nonketotic Hyperosmolar Acidosis [*Medicine*]

NKHHC........ Nonketotic Hyperosmolar Hyperglycemis Coma [*Also, HHNK*] [*Medicine*]

NKHS .... Nonketotic Hyperosmolar Syndrome [*Biochemistry*] (DAVI)

NKI .... Nash-Kelvinator International [*Automobile manufacturer, now out of production*]

NKI .... Nikolski [*Alaska*] [*Seismograph station code, US Geological Survey*] (SEIS)

NKiB .... Benedictine Hospital, Medical Library, Kingston, NY [*Library symbol Library of Congress*] (LCLS)

NKiC .... Children's Home of Kingston, Kingston, NY [*Library symbol Library of Congress*] (LCLS)

NKID .... Narodnyi Komissariat Inostrannykh Del [*People's Commissariat of Foreign Affairs*] [*Former USSR*] (LAIN)

NKID .... Noodle Kidoodle [*NASDAQ symbol*] (TTSB)

NKID .... Noodle Kidoodle, Inc. [*NASDAQ symbol*] (SAG)

NKiHL .... Kingston Hospital Libraries, Kingston, NY [*Library symbol Library of Congress*] (LCLS)

NKil .... International Business Machines Corp., Kingston, NY [*Library symbol Library of Congress*] (LCLS)

NKipM .... United States Merchant Marine Academy, Kings Point, NY [*Library symbol Library of Congress*] (LCLS)

NKJV .... New King James Version of the Bible [*A publication*]

NKK .... Nordkalottkommitten [*North Calotte Committee - NCC*] [*Finland*] (EAIO)

NKK .... Novo-Kazalinsk [*Former USSR Geomagnetic observatory code*]

NKL .... Nemeth-Kellner Leukemia

NKL .... New Keel [*On ships*]

NKL .... New Kelore Mines Ltd. [*Toronto Stock Exchange symbol*]

NKL .... Nickel

NKL .... Nkolo [*Zaire*] [*Airport symbol*] (AD)

NKL C .... Nickel Copper [*Freight*]

NKL FCD...... Nickel Faced (DGA)

NKM .... Nakhla [*Morocco*] [*Seismograph station code, US Geological Survey*] (SEIS)

NKM .... University of North Carolina at Charlotte, Charlotte, NC [*OCLC symbol*] (OCLC)

NKMA .... National Knitwear Manufacturers Association (EA)

NKMA .... No Known Medication Allergies (DAVI)

NKMB .... Nordisk Kollegium for Marinbiologi [*Nordic Council for Marine Biology - NCMB*] (EAIO)

NKMU .... National Kangaroo Monitoring Unit [*Australia*]

NKN .... North Korean Navy

NKO .... Narodnyi Komissariat Oborony [*People's Commissariat of Defense*] [*Existed until 1946*] [*Former USSR*]

NKO .... Need to Know Only [*Espionage*]

NKOA .... National Knitted Outerwear Association [*Later, NKSA*] (EA)

NKOT .... Nu-kote Holding 'A' [*NASDAQ symbol*] (TTSB)

NKOT .... Nu-Kote Holding, Inc. [*NASDAQ symbol*] (SAG)

NKOTB........ New Kids on the Block [*Music group*]

NKP .... Nakorn Phanom [*Air base northeast of Bangkok*]

NKP .... Nasionale Konserwatiewe Party [*National Conservative Party*] [*South Africa*] [*Political party*] (PPW)

NKP .... New Kensington [*Pennsylvania*] [*Seismograph station code, US Geological Survey Closed*] (SEIS)
NKP .... Norges Kommunistiske Parti [*Norwegian Communist Party*] [*Political party*] (PPE)
NKPA .... National Kraut Packers Association (EA)
NKPA .... North Korean People's Army
NKpaH .... Kings Park State Hospital, Kings Park, NY [*Library symbol Library of Congress*] (LCLS)
NKpK .... Keuka College, Keuka Park, NY [*Library symbol Library of Congress*] (LCLS)
NKPR .... Innkeepers USA Trust [*NASDAQ symbol*] (SAG)
NKP RTAB ... Nakhon Phanom Royal Thai Air Base [*Leased by USAF during the Vietnam War*] (VNW)
NKR .... Nakanohara [*Japan*] [*Seismograph station code, US Geological Survey*] (SEIS)
NKR .... New Kenrell Resources [*Vancouver Stock Exchange symbol*]
NKR .... Nordisk Konservatorierad [*Nordic Council for Music Conservatories - NCMC*] (EAIO)
N KR .... Norwegian Krone [*Monetary unit*]
NKRC .... No Known Relatives or Concerned
NKS .... Network of Kindred Spirits (EA)
NKS .... Nordisk Kirkelig Studierad [*Nordic Council for Adult Studies in Chruch - NCASC*] (EAIO)
NKSA .... National Knitwear and Sportswear Association (EA)
NKSC .... National Korean Studies Center [*Australia*]
NKSF .... Natural Killer-Cell Stimulatory Factor [*Immunology*]
NKT .... Cherry Point, NC [*Location identifier FAA*] (FAAL)
NKT .... Nankipoo [*Tennessee*] [*Seismograph station code, US Geological Survey*] (SEIS)
NKT .... None Kept in Town
NKU .... Nakusp Resources Ltd. [*Vancouver Stock Exchange symbol*]
NKU .... Nkaus [*Lesotho*] [*Airport symbol*] (OAG)
NKUDIC .... National Kidney and Urologic Diseases Information Clearinghouse (EA)
NKUSA .... Neturei Karta of USA (EA)
NKVD .... Narodnyi Kommissariat Vnutrennikh Del [*People's Commissariat for Internal Affairs*] [*Former USSR*] (NADA)
NKVMF .... Narodnyy Komissariat Voyenno-Morskogo Flota [*People's Commissariat of the Navy*] [*Former USSR*] (LAIN)
NKX .... San Diego, CA [*Location identifier FAA*] (FAAL)
N Ky St LF ... Northern Kentucky State Law Forum [*A publication*] (DLA)
NKYu .... Narodnyy Komissariat Yustitsii [*People's Commissariat of Justice*] [*Former USSR*] (LAIN)
NKz .... Kwanza (ODBW)
NKZ .... Nuclear Killing Zone [*Military British*]
NL .... Air Liberia [*ICAO designator*] (AD)
nl---- .... Great Lakes [*MARC geographic area code Library of Congress*] (LCCP)
NL .... Lima Public Library, Lima, NY [*Library symbol Library of Congress*] (LCLS)
NL .... Nailable [*Technical drawings*]
nl .... Nanoliter [*One billionth of a liter*] (MAE)
NL .... Nasolacrimal [*Medicine*] (DAVI)
NL .... Natick Laboratories [*Army*] (MCD)
NL .... National Lakeshore (BARN)
NL .... National League of Professional Baseball Clubs (EA)
NL .... National Liberal [*British politics*]
NL .... National Library [*Canada*]
NL .... Native Language (BARN)
NL .... Naturalist's Library [*A publication*]
NL .... Natural Language [*Computer software*]
NL .... Natural Log [*or Logarithm*] (WDAA)
NL .... Naval Lighter
NL .... Navigating Lieutenant [*Navy British*] (ROG)
N/L .... Navigation/Localizer (IEEE)
NL .... Navy League of the United States
NL .... Navy Library (WDAA)
NL .... Navy List [*British military*] (DMA)
NL .... Nebenlager [*Branch Camp*] [*German military - World War II*]
NL .... Nelson's Lutwyche, English Common Pleas Reports [*A publication*] (DLA)
NL .... Neon Lamp (KSC)
NL .... Netherlands [*ANSI two-letter standard code*] (CNC)
NL .... Net Loss
NL .... Neurilemmona [*Oncology*]
nl .... New Caledonia [*MARC country of publication code Library of Congress*] (LCCP)
NL .... New Latin [*Language, etc.*]
NL .... New Lead [*Also, NH*] [*News stories*] (NTCM)
NL .... New Leader [*A publication*] (BRI)
NL .... New Line [*Computer science*]
nl .... New Line (WDMC)
NL .... New London, Connecticut [*Navy*]
NL .... Newsletter (WDMC)
N-L .... New York State Library, Law Library, Albany, NY [*Library symbol Library of Congress*] (LCLS)
NL .... Night Letter
NL .... NL Industries, Inc. [*Formerly, National Lead Co.*] [*NYSE symbol*] (SPSG)
NL .... Nodular Lymphoma [*Oncology*] (DAVI)
N/L .... No Ledger (SAA)
NL .... No Liability (ADA)
NL .... No License [*Traffic offense charge*]
NL .... No Limit (NASA)
NL .... No Liner (DS)

NL .... No Load
NL .... Non-Labeled [*Tape*] [*Computer science*]
NL .... Non Licet [*It Is Not Permitted*] [*Latin*]
NL .... Nonlinear
NL .... Non Liquet [*It Is Not Clear*] [*Latin*]
NL .... Non-Loaded (NITA)
NL .... Nonlocking
NL .... Non Longe [*Not Far*] [*Latin*]
NL .... Nonprogrammer Language [*Computer science*] (PDAA)
NL .... Normal (DAVI)
n/l .... Normal Limits
NL .... Normal Lungs
NL .... North Latitude
NL .... Nose Left [*Aviation*] (MCD)
NL .... Not Listed (AFM)
NL .... Not Located
NL .... Nulead [*Journalism*] [*Slang*] (WDMC)
NL .... Nurses for Laughter [*Defunct*] (EA)
NLA .... National Landscape Association (EA)
NLA .... National Leather Association (EA)
NLA .... National Leukemia Association (EA)
NLA .... National Liberation Army [*Bolivia*]
NLA .... National Librarians Association (EA)
NLA .... National Libraries Authority
NLA .... National Library Act
NLA .... National Library of Australia (NITA)
NLA .... National Library of Canada, Cataloguing Branch [*UTLAS symbol*]
NLA .... National Lime Association (EA)
NLA .... National Limousine Association (EA)
NLA .... National Locksmiths Association (EA)
NLA .... NATO Lot Acceptance (MCD)
NLA .... Navy League of Australia
NLA .... Ndola [*Zambia*] [*Airport symbol*] (OAG)
NLA .... Neiltown Air Ltd. [*Canada ICAO designator*] (FAAC)
NLA .... Net Lettable Area
NLA .... Neuroleptanalgesia [*Altered state of awareness*] [*Medicine*] (AAMN)
NLA .... Neuroleptic Anesthesia
NLA .... New Large Airplane
NLA .... New Libertarian Alliance (EA)
NLA .... Next Lower Assembly (MCD)
NLA .... Nine Lives Associates (EA)
NLA .... Nonlinear Amplifier
NLA .... Nonuniform Linear Array
NLA .... Normalized Load Access (NITA)
NLA .... Normal Lactase Activity [*Medicine*] (DMAA)
NLA .... Norris-LaGuardia Act (MHDB)
NLA .... Northwestern Lumbermen's Association (EA)
NLAA .... National Legal Aid Association
NLAAM .... N-Desmethyl-levo-alpha-Acetylmethadol [*Opiate*]
NLABS .... Natick Laboratories [*Army*] (AABC)
NLAC .... National Listen America Club (EA)
NLacOH ...... Our Lady of Victory Hospital, Lackawanna, NY [*Library symbol Library of Congress*] (LCLS)
NLADA .... National Legal Aid and Defender Association (EA)
NLADA Brief... National Legal Aid and Defender Association Briefcase [*A publication*] (DLA)
NLakrHS ..... Sachem High School South, Lake Ronkonkoma, NY [*Library symbol Library of Congress*] (LCLS)
NLanEB .... Erie No. 1 Board of Coopertive Educational Services, Lancaster, NY [*Library symbol*] [*Library of Congress*] (LCLS)
NLanS .... Scott Aviation, Lancaster, NY [*Library symbol*] [*Library of Congress*] (LCLS)
NLAPW .... National League of American Pen Women (EA)
NLar .... Larchmont Public Library, Larchmont, NY [*Library symbol Library of Congress*] (LCLS)
NLAS .... National Lum and Abner Society (EA)
NLaw .... Peninsula Public Library, Lawrence, NY [*Library symbol Library of Congress*] (LCLS)
NLawBS ...... Brandeis School, Lawrence, NY [*Library symbol*] [*Library of Congress*] (LCLS)
NLawCE ...... Central Elementary School, Lawrence, NY [*Library symbol Library of Congress*] (LCLS)
NLawChE ..... Cedarhurst Elementary School, Lawrence, NY [*Library symbol Library of Congress*] (LCLS)
NLawDE ...... Donahue Elementary School, Lawrence, NY [*Library symbol Library of Congress*] (LCLS)
NLawJH ...... Lawrence Junior High School, Lawrence, NY [*Library symbol Library of Congress*] (LCLS)
NLawPE ...... Peninsula Elementary School, Lawrence, NY [*Library symbol Library of Congress*] (LCLS)
NLawSH ...... Lawrence Senior High School, Lawrence, NY [*Library symbol*] [*Library of Congress*] (LCLS)
NLawWE ..... Wansee Elementary School, Lawrence, NY [*Library symbol Library of Congress*] (LCLS)
NLB .... National Labor Board (WDAA)
NLB .... National Library for the Blind
NLB .... National Library of Canada, Locations Division [*UTLAS symbol*]
NLB .... National Lighting Bureau (EA)
NLB .... Needle Liver Biopsy [*Medicine*] (DMAA)
NLB .... No Lunch Break
NLB .... Nuclear Light Bulb
NLBA .... National Lead Burning Association (EA)
NLBA .... National Licensed Beverage Association (EA)
NLB & D ...... National League for the Blind and Disabled [*British*] (DBA)

NLBC .... National Livestock Brand Conference [Later, International Livestock Brand Conference]
NLBD .... National League of the Blind and Disabled [A union] [British] (DCTA)
NLBI .... National League of the Blind of Ireland (EAIO)
NLBMDA ...... National Lumber and Building Material Dealers Association (EA)
NLBRA .... National Little Britches Rodeo Association (EA)
NLC............. Lemoore, CA [Location identifier FAA] (FAAL)
NLC............. NADGE [NATO Air Defense Ground Environment] Logistics Committee (NATG)
NLC............. Nalco Chemical [NYSE symbol] (TTSB)
NLC............. Nalco Chemical Co. [NYSE symbol] (SPSG)
NLC............. National Laboratory Center [Bureau of Alcohol, Tobacco, and Firearms] [Rockville, MD] (GRD)
NLC............. National Labour Congress [Nigeria] (ECON)
NLC............. National Lawyers Club (EA)
NLC............. National Leadership Committee [Military]
NLC............. National Leadership Council [Defunct] (EA)
NLC............. National League of Cities (EA)
NLC............. National Legislative Conference [Later, NCSL] (EA)
NLC............. National Legislative Council [Later, NCSL]
NLC............. National Liberal Club [British]
NLC............. National Liberation Committee [South Africa]
NLC............. National Liberty Committee (EA)
NLC............. National Library of Canada
NLC............. National Library of Canada, Ottawa, ON, Canada [OCLC symbol] (OCLC)
NLC............. National Library of China
NLC............. National Lifeguard Championships (EA)
NLC............. National Liturgical Commission [Catholic Church] [Australia]
NLC............. National Location Code [Civil Defense]
NLC............. National Logistical Command (MCD)
NLC............. National Lutheran Council [Later, LC/USA] (EA)
NLC............. Navy Law Center (DNAB)
NLC............. Negro Labor Committee [Defunct] (EA)
NLC............. Nematic Liquid Crystal [Physical chemistry]
NLC............. Network Language Center (MHDB)
NLC............. New Liberal Club [Shin Jiyu Club] [Japan] (PPW)
NLC............. New Line Character [Keyboard] [Computer science] (MDG)
NLC............. New Location Code [Military]
NLC............. New Orleans & Lower Coast Railroad Co. [AAR code]
NLC............. News and Letters Committee (EA)
NLC............. Next Linear Collider [Proposed]
NLC............. Noctilucent Clouds
NLC............. Node Location Code (PDAA)
NLC............. Noise-Level Cable
NLC............. Nordic Literature Committee [Copenhagen, Denmark] (EAIO)
NLC............. Northern Libraries Colloquy (EA)
NLC............. Northland Library System [Library network]
NLCA .... Norlaudanosolinecarboxylic Acid [Biochemistry]
NLCA .... Norlithocholic Acid [Biochemistry]
NLCA .... Norwegian Lutheran Church of America (IIA)
NLCAA .... National Little College Athletic Association [Later, NSCAA] (EA)
NLCAB .... National Library of Canada Advisory Board
NLCACBC .... National League of Cuban American Community-Based Centers (EA)
NLCC .... Navy League Cadet Corps
NLCD .... National Liberation Council Decree [1966-69] [Ghana] [A publication] (DLA)
NLCEA .... Naval Laboratory Centers' Employee Association (DNAB)
NLCH .... National Legislative Council for the Handicapped (EA)
NLCIF.......... National Light Castings Ironfounders' Federation [British] (BI)
NLCM.......... National Lutheran Campus Ministry (EA)
NLCMDD ..... National Legal Center for the Medically Dependent and Disabled (EA)
NLCOA .... National Leadership Coalition on AIDS [Acquired Immune Deficiency Syndrome] (EA)
NLCP .... Navy Logistics Capabilities Plan
NLCP-FY ..... Navy Logistics Capabilities Plan - Fiscal Year (DNAB)
NLCPI .... National Legal Center for the Public Interest (EA)
NLCS .... National Computer Systems, Inc. [NASDAQ symbol] (NQ)
NLCS .... National League Championship Series [Baseball]
NLCS .... National Lutheran Commission on Scouting [Defunct] (EA)
NLCS .... Natl Computer Sys [NASDAQ symbol] (TTSB)
NLCS .... Nordic Leather Chemists Society [Formerly, IVLIC Scandinavian Section] (EA)
NLCSDHRES... National Labor Committee in Support of Democracy and Human Rights in El Salvador (EA)
NLCSE .... Non-Linear Charge Storage Element (PDAA)
NLCSJ .... National Lawyers Committee for Soviet Jewry (EA)
NLCWC .... National Lincoln-Civil War Council (EA)
NLD .... Namakwaland Lugdiens (EDMS) BPK [South Africa ICAO designator] (FAAC)
NLD .... NASA Launch Director
NLD .... Nasolacrimal Duct [Medicine] (DAVI)
NLD .... National League for Democracy [Political party] [Myanmar]
NLD .... National League for Democracy [Myanmar] [Political party] (EY)
NLD .... National Legal Databases (IID)
NLD .... National Legion of Decency [Later, National Catholic Office for Motion Pictures] (EA)
NLD .... Naval Electrical Department [British military] (DMA)
NLD .... Naval Lighter [Pontoon] Dock
NLD .... Necrobiosis Lipoidica Diabeticorum [Medicine]
NLD .... Netherlands [ANSI three-letter standard code] (CNC)
NLD .... No Load (MSA)
NLD .... Northland Bank [Toronto Stock Exchange symbol Vancouver Stock Exchange symbol]

NLD .... Not in Line of Duty [as of an injury] [Military]
NLD .... Nuevo Laredo [Mexico] [Airport symbol] (OAG)
NLDA .... National Livestock Dealers Association [Later, Livestock Marketing Association] (EA)
NLDA .... National Luggage Dealers Association (EA)
NLDB .... Natural Language Data Base
NLDC .... National Legal Data Center [Defunct] (EA)
NLDF .... Naval Local Defense Forces
NLDM .... Network Logical Data Manager (NITA)
NLDN .... National Lightning Detection Network
NLDV .... National League of Disabled Voters (EA)
NLE .... National Livestock Exchange [Defunct] (EA)
NLE .... Nonlinear Element
Nle .... Norleucine [A nonessential amino acid] [Biochemistry]
NLE .... Northern Commuter Airlines [New Zealand] [ICAO designator] (FAAC)
NLEA .... National Lumber Exporters Association [Later, AHEC] (EA)
NLEA .... Nutrition Labeling and Education Act [1990] [Food and Drug Administration]
NLEACH ...... Northleach [England]
NLEC .... National Law Enforcement Council (EA)
NLEC .... National Lutheran Educational Conference [Later, LECNA] (EA)
NLEEF .... National Law Enforcement Emergency Frequency (LAIN)
NLEF .... National Legislative Education Foundation (EA)
NLEF .... National Lupus Erythematosus Foundation [Defunct] (EA)
NLEMA .... National Lutheran Editors and Managers Association [Defunct] (EA)
NLEOMF ...... National Law Enforcement Officers Memorial Fund (EA)
NLer........... Woodward Memorial Library, LeRoy, NY [Library symbol Library of Congress] (LCLS)
NLerHi .... LeRoy Historical Society, LeRoy, NY [Library symbol Library of Congress] (LCLS)
NLETS......... National Law Enforcement Telecommunications System
NLev .... Levittown Public Library, Levittown, NY [Library symbol Library of Congress] (LCLS)
NLEV .... National Low-Emission Vehicles
NLevAE .... Abbey Lane Elementary School, Levittown, NY [Library symbol] [Library of Congress] (LCLS)
NLevDH .... Division Avenue High School, Levittown, NY [Library symbol] [Library of Congress] (LCLS)
NLevEC .... Levittown Memorial Education Center, Levittown, NY [Library symbol] [Library of Congress] (LCLS)
NLevGE .... Gardiners Avenue Elementary School, Levittown, NY [Library symbol] [Library of Congress] (LCLS)
NLevGGE ..... Geneva N. Gallow Elementary School, Levittown, NY [Library symbol] [Library of Congress] (LCLS)
NLevI .... Island Trees Public Library, Levittown, NY [Library symbol Library of Congress] (LCLS)
NLevIH .... Island Trees High School, Levittown, NY [Library symbol Library of Congress] (LCLS)
NLevIJ .... Island Trees Memorial Junior High School, Levittown, NY [Library symbol Library of Congress] (LCLS)
NLevJSE ..... J. Fred Sparke Elementary School, Levittown, NY [Library symbol] [Library of Congress] (LCLS)
NLevLE .... Lee Road Elementary School, Levittown, NY [Library symbol] [Library of Congress] (LCLS)
NLevMH...... General Douglas McArthur High School, Levittown, NY [Library symbol] [Library of Congress] (LCLS)
NLevMSE ..... Michael F. Stokes Elementary School, Levittown, NY [Library symbol] [Library of Congress] (LCLS)
NLevNE .... Northside Elementary School, Levittown, NY [Library symbol] [Library of Congress] (LCLS)
NLevSJ .... Jonas E. Salk Junior High School, Levittown, NY [Library symbol] [Library of Congress] (LCLS)
NLevSLE ..... Summit Lane Elementary School, Levittown, NY [Library symbol] [Library of Congress] (LCLS)
NLevSNE ..... Seaman Neck Elementary School, Levittown, NY [Library symbol] [Library of Congress] (LCLS)
NLevWM..... Wisdom Middle School, Levittown, NY [Library symbol] [Library of Congress] (LCLS)
NLew .... Lewiston Public Library, Lewiston, NY [Library symbol Library of Congress] (LCLS)
NLewStM ..... Mount Saint Mary's Hospital, Lewiston, NY [Library symbol Library of Congress] (LCLS)
NLf .... Little Falls Public Library, Little Falls, NY [Library symbol Library of Congress] (LCLS)
NLF............. Nasolabial Fold [Medicine] (DAVI)
NLF............. National Fuelcorp Ltd. [Vancouver Stock Exchange symbol]
NLF............. National League of Families of Prisoners and Missing in Southeast Asia
NLF............. National Legal Foundation (EA)
NLF............. National Liberal Federation [British]
NLF............. National Liberation Front [Vietnam] [Political party]
NLF............. National Liberation Front [Myanmar] [Political party] (PD)
NLF............. National Liberation Front [Aden] [Political party]
NLF............. National Liberation Front [South Africa] [Political party] (PD)
NLF............. Navigation Light Flasher
NLF............. Nearest Landing Field
NLF............. Neonatal Lung Fibroblast [Medicine] (DMAA)
NLF............. Neutral Lipid Fraction [Biochemistry]
NLF............. New Leadership Fund (EA)
NLF............. No-Load Funds
NLF............. North Luzon Force [Army World War II]
NLF............. Westair Aviation, Inc. [Canada ICAO designator] (FAAC)
NLFA........... National Lamb Feeders Association (EA)
NLFA........... National Livestock Feeders Association [Later, NCA] (EA)

NLFED .... Naval Landing Force Equipment Depot
NLFM .... Noise-Level Frequency Monitor
NLFMA .... National Law Firm Marketing Association (EA)
NLFPA .... National Liberation Front Party Apparatus [Algeria]
NLFS .... Nucleus Landing Force Staff (DNAB)
NLFSV .... National Liberation Front of South Vietnam [Political party]
NLFT .... No-Load Frame Time
NLG .... National Gas & Oil Corp. [AMEX symbol] (SPSG)
NLG .... National Lawyers Guild (EA)
NLG .... Natl Gas & Oil [AMEX symbol] (TTSB)
NLG .... Nelson Lagoon [Alaska] [Airport symbol] (OAG)
NLG .... North Louisiana & Gulf Railroad Co. [AAR code]
NLG .... Nose Landing Gear [Aviation]
NLG .... Null Line Gap
NLG .... Numismatic Literary Guild (EA)
NLGA .... National Lumber Grading Agency [Canada]
NLGAWVA.... National Legion of Greek-American War Veterans in America (EA)
NLGC .... Nauru Local Government Council [Australia]
NLGC .... Noise-Level Gain Control (MCD)
NLGDA .... National Lawn and Garden Distributors Association (EA)
NLGHF .... National Lesbian and Gay Health Foundation (EA)
NLGI .... National Lubricating Grease Institute (EA)
NLGPDC...... National Lawyer's Guild Peace and Disarmament Committee [Later, NLGPDS] (EA)
NLGPDS....... National Lawyer's Guild Peace and Disarmament Subcommittee (EA)
NLGQ .... National Lawyers Guild Quarterly [A publication] (DLA)
NLH .... New Lao Hak [Lao Patriotic Front] [Vietnam] [Political party]
NLH .... New Life Hamlet [See also NLHS, NLHZ] [Vietnam] [Military]
NLH .... Non-Locating Head [Engineering] (OA)
NLHA .... National Leased Housing Association [Washington, DC] (EA)
NLHO .... National Latina Health Organization (EAIO)
NLHRSA....... National Left-Handers Racquet Sports Association (EA)
NLHS .... New Lao Hak Sat [New Life Hamlet] [See also NLH Vietnam] [Military]
NLHZ .... New Lao Hak Zat [New Life Hamlet] [See also NLH, NLHS Vietnam] [Military]
NLI .... National Landscape Institute
NLI .... National Language Interface (NITA)
NLI .... National Leadership Institute [Defunct] (EA)
NLI .... National Library of Ireland (AIE)
NLI .... National Limestone Institute [Later, NSA] (EA)
NLI .... Neodymium LASER Illuminator
NLI .... New Learning Initiative (AIE)
NLI .... Noise Limit Indicator
NLI .... Nonlinear Interpolating (IEEE)
NLI .... Northern Lights College Library [UTLAS symbol]
NLIA .... National Languages Institute of Australia
NLib .... Liberty Public Library, Liberty, NY [Library symbol Library of Congress] (LCLS)
NLIC............ National Landslide Information Center [US Geological Survey]
NLicL........... LaGuardia Community College of the City University of New York, Long Island Cit y, NY [Library symbol Library of Congress] (LCLS)
NLicP........... PepsiCo, Inc., Research Library, Long Island, NY [Library symbol Library of Congress] (LCLS)
NLIF .... Nonlinear Interference Filter [Electronics]
NLIHC .... National Low Income Housing Coalition (EA)
NLin .... Lindenhurst Memorial Library, Lindenhurst, NY [Library symbol Library of Congress] (LCLS)
NLIN .... NOAA [National Oceanic and Atmospheric Administration] Library and Information Network (USDC)
NLIN .... NOAA [National Oceanic and Atmospheric Administration] Library and Information Network [Marine science] (OSRA)
NLin............ Nonlinear
NL Ind .... NL Industries, Inc. [Formerly, National Lead Co.] [Associated Press] (SAG)
NLinHS .... Lindenhurst High School, Lindenhurst, NY [Library symbol] [Library of Congress] (LCLS)
NLinJS........ Lindenhurst Junior High School, Lindenhurst, NY [Library symbol] [Library of Congress] (LCLS)
NLIS............ National Lesbian Information Service
NLIS............ Navy Logistics Information System
NLISA .... National League of Insured Savings Associations [Later, NSLL] (EA)
NLJ .... Nagpur Law Journal [India] [A publication] (DLA)
NLJ .... New Law Journal [A publication] (ILCA)
NLK .... Neuroleukin [Biochemistry]
NLK .... Norfolk Island [Airport symbol] (OAG)
NLK .... Norlink Air Ltd. [British ICAO designator] (FAAC)
NLKF........... Nonlinear Kalman Filter
NLL .... National Aeronautical Research Institute [Netherlands] (SAA)
NLL .... National Lacrosse League [Disbanded]
NLL .... National Lending Library for Science and Technology [Later, BLLD] [British Library]
NLL .... National Liberal League [Later, NLSCS] (EA)
NLL .... Negative Logic Level
NLL .... New England School of Law Library, Boston, MA [OCLC symbol] (OCLC)
NLL .... New Library of Law [Harrisburg, PA] [A publication] (DLA)
NLL .... New Library of Law and Equity [England] [A publication] (DLA)
NLL .... New Life League (EA)
NLL .... New London [Connecticut] Laboratory [Navy] (DNAB)
NLL .... Normal Liquid Level [Engineering]
NLL .... Northern Limit Line [Korea]
NLL .... Nullagine [Australia Airport symbol] (OAG)
NLLC........... National Labor Law Center (EA)

NLLC........... National Languages and Literacy Council [Australia]
NLLS........... Nonlinear Least Square [Mathematics]
NLLSQ........ Nonlinear Least Squares [Computer program]
NLLST........ National Lending Library for Science and Technology [Later, BLL] [British]
NL LT.......... Net Laying Light (SAA)
NLM .... National Language Mediator
NLM .... National Library of Medicine [Public Health Service] [Bethesda, MD Database producer]
NLM .... National Library of Medicine, Bethesda, MD [OCLC symbol] (OCLC)
NLM .... Natural Language Mode [Computer science]
NLM .... Naval Ordnance Lab [Maryland] [Seismograph station code, US Geological Survey Closed] (SEIS)
NLM .... Nederlands Luchtvaart Maatschappij [Airline] [Netherlands]
NLM .... NetWare Loadable Module [Computer science] (PCM)
NLM .... Network Loadable Module (GAVI)
NLM .... New Library of Music [A publication]
NLM .... Noise-Level Monitor [SONAR]
NLM .... Nonlinear Mapping (MCD)
NLM .... Nuclear Level Mixing [Physics]
NLMA .... National Lumber Manufacturers Association [Later, NFPA] (EA)
NLMA .... Northeastern Lumber Manufacturers Association
NLMC.......... National Latino Media Coalition [Citizen's group] (NTCM)
NLMC.......... National League of Masonic Clubs (EA)
NLMC.......... Nordic Labour Market Committee (EAIO)
NLMC.......... North Lilly Mining Co. [NASDAQ symbol] (NQ)
NLMC.......... North Lily Mining [NASDAQ symbol] (TTSB)
NLME .... Non-Linear Material Effect (PDAA)
NLMF .... National Labor-Management Foundation (EA)
NLMF .... Nucleus of Longitudinal Muscle Fiber
NLMFA .... No-Load Mutual Fund Association (EA)
NLMS .... Navigational Lane Marking System [Navy] (DOMA)
NLMS .... Navy Logistics Management School
NLMS .... Numerical Largeness of More Significant [Statistics]
NLMWT........ National Liberation Movement of Western Togoland
NLN .... National League for Nursing (EA)
NLN .... National Library Network
NLN .... New Lintex Minerals [Vancouver Stock Exchange symbol]
NLN .... No Longer Needed (AABC)
NLN .... Nordiska Lakemedelsnamnden [Nordic Council on Medicines - NCM] (EAIO)
NLN .... Northwest Missouri Library Network [Library network]
NLNA .... National Landscape Nurserymen's Association [Later, NLA] (EA)
NLNE .... National League for Nursing Education (DAVI)
NLnet .... [The] Newfoundland and Labrador Network [Canada] [Computer science] (TNIG)
NLNGNE...... National League of Nursing Graduate Nursing Examination (GAGS)
NLNR .... Nonlinear (MSA)
NLNS .... New Lightweight Night Sight (INF)
NLO .... Nasolacrimal Occlusion [Medicine]
NLO .... Naval Liaison Officer
NLO .... No-Limit Order
NLO .... Nonlinear Optics (IEEE)
NLob .... Long Beach Public Library, Long Beach, NY [Library symbol Library of Congress] (LCLS)
NLobBK....... Blackhealth Kindergarten School, Long Beach, NY [Library symbol] [Library of Congress] (LCLS)
NLobES....... East School, Long Beach, NY [Library symbol Library of Congress] (LCLS)
NLobH .... Long Beach Memorial Hospital, Long Beach, NY [Library symbol Library of Congress] (LCLS)
NLobJH....... Long Beach Junior High School, Long Beach, NY [Library symbol Library of Congress] (LCLS)
NLobLE .... Lido Elementary School, Long Beach, NY [Library symbol Library of Congress] (LCLS)
NLobLS........ Lindell Boulevard School, Long Beach, NY [Library symbol Library of Congress] (LCLS)
NLobM .... Long Beach Middle School, Long Beach, NY [Library symbol] [Library of Congress] (LCLS)
NLobMS....... Magnolia School, Long Beach, NY [Library symbol Library of Congress] (LCLS)
NLobSH ...... Long Beach Senior High School, Long Beach, NY [Library symbol Library of Congress] (LCLS)
NLobWE...... West Elementary School, Long Beach, NY [Library symbol Library of Congress] (LCLS)
NLock .... Lockport Public Library, Lockport, NY [Library symbol Library of Congress] (LCLS)
NLockH .... Lockport Memorial Hospital, Doctor's Library, Lockport, NY [Library symbol Library of Congress] (LCLS)
NLockMt...... Mount View Health Facility, Lockport, NY [Library symbol Library of Congress] (LCLS)
NLockNHi..... Niagara County Historical Society, Lockport, NY [Library symbol Library of Congress] (LCLS)
NLOGM........ Navy Liaison Office for Guided Missiles (MCD)
NLOMA .... National Lutheran Outdoors Ministry Association (EA)
NLONTEVDET... New London Test and Evaluation Detachment [Navy]
NLOP .... Nonlinear Optical Polymer
NLOrLanyard... Netherlands Orange Lanyard [Military decoration]
NLOS .... Natural Language Operating System
NLOS .... Nonline of Sight
NLOS-AT/AD... Nonline-of-Sight Antitank/Air Defense Vehicle [Army]
NLOS-CA...... Non-Line-of-Sight-Combined Arms System (INF)
NLOS/IOE..... Nonline-of-Sight / Internal Operator Equipment (DWSG)
NLOS-R........ Non-Line-of-Sight-Rear [Army] (DOMA)

NLouvGS...... Church of Jesus Christ of Latter-Day Saints, Genealogical Society Library, Albany New York Stake Branch, Loudonville, NY [*Library symbol Library of Congress*] (LCLS)
NLouvS........ Siena College, Loudonville, NY [*Library symbol Library of Congress*] (LCLS)
NLowLH....... Lewis County General Hospital, Medical Library, Lowville, NY [*Library symbol Library of Congress*] (LCLS)
NLp............. Lake Placid Public Library, Lake Placid, NY [*Library symbol Library of Congress*] (LCLS)
NLP............. Narodnoliberalna Partiia [*National Liberal Party*] [*Bulgaria*] [*Political party*] (PPE)
NLP............. National Labour Party [*Sierra Leone*] [*Political party*] (EY)
NLP............. National Land for People [*An association*] (EA)
NLP............. National League of Postmasters of the United States
NLP............. National Liberal Party [*Bermuda*] [*Political party*] (EY)
NLP............. National Liberation Party [*Gambia*] [*Political party*] (PPW)
NLP............. National Realty Ltd. [*AMEX symbol*] (SPSG)
NLP............. Natl Realty L.P. [*AMEX symbol*] (TTSB)
NLP............. Natural Language Processing [*Computer science*]
NLP............. Natural Law Party [*Australia Political party*]
NLP............. Neglected Language Program
NLP............. Neighborhood Loan Program
NLP............. Nelspruit [*South Africa*] [*Airport symbol*] (OAG)
NLP............. Net Level Premium [*Insurance*]
NLP............. Neurolinguistic Programming
NLP............. New Left Party [*Political party Australia*]
NLP............. Nodular Liquifying Panniculitis [*Dermatology*] (DAVI)
NLP............. No Light Perception [*Ophthalmology*]
NLP............. Nonlinear Programming [*Algorithm*]
NLP............. Normal Light Perception [*Physiology*] (MAH)
NLPC .... n-Laurylpyridinium Chloride [*Detergent*]
NLPGA........ National LP-Gas Association (EA)
NLPM.......... National League of Postmasters of the United States (EA)
NLPM.......... Newspaper Lines per Minute (DGA)
NLPNEF...... National Licensed Practical Nurses Educational Foundation [*Defunct*] (EA)
NLPQ .... Natural Language Processing System for Queuing Problems [*Computer science*] (PDAA)
NLPR .... National Laboratory of Psychical Research [*British*]
NLPS .... Natural Language Processing Segment [*Computer science*]
NLpSA .... Lake Placid School of Art, Fine Arts Library, Lake Placid, NY [*Library symbol Library of Congress*] (LCLS)
NLpT........... Tissue Culture Association, Lake Placid, NY [*Library symbol Library of Congress*] (LCLS)
NLPTL......... National Lutheran Parent-Teacher League (EA)
NLQ .... Natural Language Query [*Software*] [*Battelle Software Products Center*]
NLQ .... Near Letter Quality [*Computer printer*]
NLQ .... Nigeria Lawyer's Quarterly [*A publication*] (DLA)
NLQ .... Nonlinear Quantization [*Telecommunications*] (NTCM)
NLQ .... Not Letter Quality (NITA)
NLQR .... Nigeria Law Quarterly Review [*A publication*] (DLA)
NLR .... Nagpur Law Reports [*India*] [*A publication*] (DLA)
NLR .... Natal Law Reports [*India*] [*A publication*] (DLA)
NLR .... National Liquid Reserves Money Market Fund
NLR .... National Research Laboratory [*Netherlands*] (GAVI)
NLR .... NATO Liaison Representative (MCD)
NLR .... Neodymium LASER Range-Finder
NLR .... Net Liquidity Ratio (PDAA)
NLR .... Newfoundland Law Reports [*A publication*] (DLA)
NLR .... New Law Reports [*Ceylon*] [*A publication*] (DLA)
N-LR .... New York State Library, Legislative Reference Library, Albany, NY [*Library symbol Library of Congress*] (LCLS)
NLR .... Nigeria Law Reports [*A publication*] (DLA)
NLR .... Noise Load Ratio
NLR .... Nolan Resources Ltd. [*Vancouver Stock Exchange symbol*]
NLR .... Nonlinear Regression [*Mathematics*]
NLR .... Nonlinear Resistance (IDOE)
NLR .... Nonlinear Resistive
NLR .... Nonlinear Resistor [*Electronics*] (ECII)
NLR .... North London Railway [*British*]
NLR .... Nyasaland Law Reports [*A publication*] (DLA)
NLR .... South African Law Reports, Natal Province Division [*1910-46*] [*A publication*] (DLA)
NLRA .... National Labor Relations Act [*1935*]
NLRA .... National Lakes and Rivers Association [*Defunct*] (EA)
NLRB .... National Labor Relations Board [*Department of Labor*] [*Washington, DC*]
NLRB .... National Labor Relations Board Decisions and Orders [*A publication*] (DLA)
NLRB Ann Rep... National Labor Relations Board Annual Report [*A publication*] (DLA)
NLRB Dec.... National Labor Relations Board Decisions [*A publication*] (DLA)
NLRBP........ National Labor Relations Board Professional Association
NLRBPA...... National Labor Relations Board Professional Association (EA)
NLRBU........ National Labor Relations Board Union (EA)
NLRCA .... National Lilac Rabbit Club of America (EA)
NLRCCAP..... National Legal Resource Center for Child Advocacy and Protection [*Later, ABACCL*] (EA)
NL Rev .... Northeastern Law Review [*A publication*] (DLA)
NLRG .... Narrow-Line Radio Galaxy
NLRG.......... Navy Long-Range Guidance
NLROG........ Navy Long-Range Objectives Group (DNAB)
NLR (OS).... Natal Law Reports, Old Series [*1867-72*] [*South Africa*] [*A publication*] (DLA)

NLRSS .... Navy Long-Range Strategic Study
NLRU .... Nordens Liberale og Radikale Ungdom [*Nordic Liberal and Radical Youth*] (EAIO)
NLS............. Nassau Library System [*Library network*]
NLS............. National Language Support [*Computer science*] (PCM)
NLS............. National Launch System (ECON)
NLS............. National Library of Scotland (NITA)
NLS............. National Library Service for the Blind and Physically Handicapped [*Also, NLS /BPH*] [*Library of Congress*]
NLS............. National Longitudinal Survey [*Statistics*]
NLS............. National Longitudinal Surveys of Labor Market Experience [*Ohio State University*] [*Columbus*] [*Information service or system*] (IID)
NLS............. Natural Law Society (EA)
NLS............. Navigating Light System
NLS............. Negative Lens Systems
NLS............. Neodymium LASER System
NLS............. Network Library System
NLS............. New Least Square (PDAA)
NLS............. No-Load Speed
NLS............. No-Load Start
NLS............. Non-Linear Least Squares [*Statistics*]
NLS............. Nonlinear Smoothing
NLS............. Nonlinear Systems
NLS............. Nordic Language Secretariat [*See also SLN*] [*Norway*] (EAIO)
NLS............. Nordiske Laererorganisationers Samrad [*Council of Nordic Teachers' Association*] [*Sweden*] (EAIO)
NLS............. North Carolina Central University, School of Library Science, Durham, NC [*OCLC symbol*] (OCLC)
NLS............. Nuclear Localization Signal [*Biochemistry*]
NLS............. Nuclear Location Sequence [*Cytology*]
NLS............. On-Line System [*Stanford Research Institute*] [*Computer science*]
NLSA .... National Liquor Stores Association (EA)
NLSA .... National Lithuanian Society of America (EA)
NLSA .... National Locksmith Suppliers Association (EA)
NLSBA .... National Lincoln Sheep Breeders' Association (EA)
NLS/BPH .... National Library Service for the Blind and Physically Handicapped [*Also, NLS*] [*Library of Congress Computer science*] (IID)
NLSC .... National Logistics Supply Center [*Marine science*] (OSRA)
NLSC .... Navy Lockheed Service Center
NLSC .... Northeastern Louisiana State College
NLSCS .... National League for Separation of Church and State (EA)
NLSF .... National Life Share Foundation (EA)
NLSF .... Navy Logistics Support Force (DOMA)
NLsH .... Frederic R. Harris, Inc., Lake Success, NY [*Library symbol Library of Congress*] (LCLS)
NLSI........... National Library of Science and Invention [*British*] (DIT)
NLSLS .... National Library of Scotland Lending Services (NITA)
NLsM .... Medical Society of the State of New York, Lake Success, NY [*Library symbol Library of Congress*] (LCLS)
NLSMA .... National Lamp and Shade Manufacturers' Association (IAA)
NLSMA .... National Longitudinal Study of Mathematical Abilities
NLSMB .... National Live Stock and Meat Board (EA)
NLSP .... Neighborhood Legal Services Program
NLSP .... NetWare Link Services Protocol [*Novell, Inc.*] (PCM)
NLSPA .... National Live Stock Producers Association (EA)
NLSPN .... National List of Scientific Plant Names [*Department of Agriculture*] (IID)
NLSS .... Navy Logistics Systems School
NLSS .... New London Submarine School [*Navy*] (MCD)
NLSST .... Nonlinear Sea Surface Temperature (USDC)
NLST .... Nonlisted Name [*Telecommunications*] (TEL)
NLSU .... National League for Social Understanding (EA)
NLSY .... National Longitudinal Study of Youth
NLT ,........... Negative Line Transmission [*Noise limiter*] (IAA)
NLT............. Net Long Ton
NLT............. Newfoundland Labrador Air Transport Ltd. [*Canada ICAO designator*] (FAAC)
NLT............. New London Training Unit [*Navy*]
NLT............. Night Letter [*Telegraphic communications*]
NLT............. Noise Limiter (IAA)
NLT............. Normal Lube-Oil Tank (MSA)
NLT............. Normal Lymphocyte Transfer [*Immunochemistry*]
NLT............. Not Later Than
NLT............. Not Less Than
NLTA .... National Lawn Tennis Association (WDAA)
NLTA .... National League of Teachers' Associations [*Defunct*] (EA)
NLTC .... National Livestock Tax Committee [*Later, NCA*] (EA)
NLTCDP .... National Long-Term Care Channeling Demonstration Program [*Department of Health and Human Services*] (GFGA)
NLTE .... Nonlocal Thermodynamic Equilibrium
NLTF .... National Leather Trades Federation [*A union*] [*British*]
NLTNIF .... National Low-Temperature Neutron Irradiation Facility [*Oak Ridge, TN*] [*Department of Energy*] (GRD)
NLTRA .... National Land Title Reclamation Association (EA)
NLTS........... Near Launch Tracking System
NLU .... Naval Field Liaison Unit (DNAB)
NLUC .... National Land Use Classification (PDAA)
NLUF .... National LASER Users Facility [*Rochester, NY*] [*Department of Energy*] (GRD)
NLUS .... Navy League of the United States (EA)
NLUTS .... National Labourers' Union Trade Society [*British*]
NLv............. Locust Valley Public Library, Locust Valley, NY [*Library symbol Library of Congress*] (LCLS)
NLV............. Narcissus Latent Virus

NLVA............ National Licensed Victuallers Association [*British*] (DBA)
NLvBI............ Bayville Intermediate School, Locust Valley, NY [*Library symbol Library of Congress*] (LCLS)
NLvHS......... Locust Valley High School, Locust Valley, NY [*Library symbol Library of Congress*] (LCLS)
NLvI............ Locust Valley Intermediate School, Locust Valley, NY [*Library symbol Library of Congress*] (LCLS)
NLvMP......... A.M. MacArthur Primary School, Locust Valley, NY [*Library symbol*] [*Library of Congress*] (LCLS)
NLVP .... NASA Launch Vehicle Planning Project (MCD)
NLVR .... Nonlinear Vacuum Regulator Valve [*Automotive engineering*]
NLW............ National Lawyers Wives (EA)
NLW............ National Library Week
NLW............ Nominal Line Width
NLWF.......... Futuna/Pointe Vele [*Wallis and Futuna Islands*] [*ICAO location identifier*] (ICLI)
NLWW .... Wallis/Hihifo [*Wallis and Futuna Islands*] [*ICAO location identifier*] (ICLI)
NLX............ NLX Resources, Inc. [*Toronto Stock Exchange symbol*]
NLY............ Northerly
NLynAE....... Atlantic Avenue School, Lynbrook, NY [*Library symbol*] [*Library of Congress*] (LCLS)
NLynd .... Yates Community Library, Lyndonville, NY [*Library symbol Library of Congress*] (LCLS)
NLynDE....... Davidson Avenue Elementary School, Lynbrook, NY [*Library symbol*] [*Library of Congress*] (LCLS)
NLyndHi....... Lyndonville Historical Society, Lyndonville, NY [*Library symbol Library of Congress*] (LCLS)
NLynHS....... Lynbrook High School, Lynbrook NY [*Library symbol*] [*Library of Congress*] (LCLS)
NLynME .... Marion Street Elementary School, Lynbrook, NY [*Library symbol*] [*Library of Congress*] (LCLS)
NLynNM....... North Middle School, Lynbrook, NY [*Library symbol*] [*Library of Congress*] (LCLS)
NLynSM....... Lynbrook South Middle School, Lynbrook, NY [*Library symbol*] [*Library of Congress*] (LCLS)
NLynWPE.... Waverly Park Elementary School, Lynbrook, NY [*Library symbol Library of Congress*] (LCLS)
nm----.......... Gulf of Mexico [*MARC geographic area code Library of Congress*] (LCCP)
NM............. Mt. Cook Airlines [*ICAO designator*] (AD)
NM............. Nachmittag [*Afternoon*] [*German*]
NM............. Nanomemory (IAA)
nm............. Nanometer [*One billionth of a meter*]
nM............. Nanomole [*One billionth of a mole*]
NM............. Narrow Market [*Investment term*]
NM............. Nationalist Movement (EA)
NM............. National Magazine Co. Ltd. [*Publisher*] [*British*]
NM............. National Match
NM............. National Media Corp. [*NYSE symbol*] (SPSG)
NM............. National Monument (GNE)
NM............. National Motor Volunteers [*British military*] (DMA)
NM............. Nations Ministries (EA)
NM............. Natl Media Corp. [*NYSE symbol*] (TTSB)
NM............. Natriuretic Material [*Physiology*]
NM............. Naturally Occurring Mutants
NM............. Nautical Mile [*6,080 feet*]
NM............. Naval Mission (AFIT)
NM............. Navigation Multiplexer [*Navy*] (CAAL)
NM............. Navy Mines (MCD)
NM............. Near Match (MCD)
nm............. Near-Metacentric [*Botany*]
NM............. Near Mint [*Condition*] [*Numismatics, deltiology, etc.*]
NM............. Negro Male
NM............. Neiman-Marcus
NM............. Netherlands Museum [*Later, HHT*] (EA)
NM............. Net Imports [*Economics*]
NM............. Network Manager (MCD)
NM............. Neuromotor [*Neurology*] (DAVI)
NM............. Neuromuscular
NM............. Newly Molded
NM............. New Material [*FAR clauses*] (AAGC)
NM............. New Measurement
NM............. New Mexico [*Postal code*]
Nm............. New Mexico State Library, Santa Fe, NM [*Library symbol Library of Congress*] (LCLS)
NM............. New Mexico Supreme Court Reports [*A publication*] (DLA)
NM............. New Mexico Territorial Court (DLA)
NM............. New Moon [*Moon phase*]
N/m............. Newton per Meter
N-M .... New York State Library, Medical Library, Albany, NY [*Library symbol Library of Congress*] (LCLS)
Nm............. Nicotiana mesophilia [*Tobacco*]
NM............. Nictitating Membrane [*Animal anatomy*]
NM............. Night and morning (DAVI)
NM............. Night Message
NM............. Nitrogen Mustard [*Also, HN, M, MBA*] [*Antineoplastic drug, war-gas base*]
NM............. Nitromethane [*Organic chemistry*]
NM............. Nocte et Mane [*Night and Morning*] [*Pharmacy*]
NM............. Nodular Melanoma [*Oncology*]
NMA........... Nodular Mixed Lymphoma [*Onocology*] (DAVI)
NM............. Noise Meter (MSA)
NM............. No Mark
NM............. Nomen Masculinam [*Masculine Name*] [*Latin*] (ROG)

NM............. No Message
NM............. Nonmagnetic (IAA)
NM............. Nonmetallic
NM............. Nonmotile [*Microbiology*]
NM............. Nonwhite Male
NM............. Nordiska Metallarbetaresekretariatet [*Nordic Metalworkers Secretariat - NMS*] (EAIO)
NM............. Normetadrenaline [*Biochemistry*] (DAVI)
NM............. Notice to Mariner
N/M............. Not Marked [*Business term*]
NM............. Not Married
NM............. Not Measurable [*or Measured*]
n/m............. Not Mentioned [*Medicine*]
NM............. Noun Modifier [*Linguistics*]
NM............. Nuclear Magnetic
NM............. Nuclear Magnetron (MSA)
NM............. Nuclear Measurement (IAA)
NM............. Nuclear Medicine
Nm............. Numbers [*Old Testament book*]
NM............. Nutmeg (ADA)
NM............. Nux Moschata [*Nutmeg*] [*Pharmacology*] (ROG)
N/m^2............. Newtons per Square Meter [*Pascals*] (IDOE)
NmA........... Albuquerque Public Library, Albuquerque, NM [*Library symbol Library of Congress*] (LCLS)
NMA........... Miami, FL [*Location identifier FAA*] (FAAL)
NMA........... Minute Men of America (NADA)
NMA........... Naphthalenemethylamine [*Reagent*] [*Organic chemistry*]
NMA........... Nashville Music Association [*Later, NEA*] (EA)
NMA........... National Malaria Association (DAVI)
NMA........... National Management Association [*Dayton, OH*] (EA)
NMA........... National Management Award [*GAMC*]
NMA........... National Marina Association [*Defunct*] (EA)
NMA........... National Maritime Authority [*Australia*]
NMA........... National Meat Association [*Formerly, NIMPA*] (EA)
NMA........... National Medical Association (EA)
NMA........... National Microfilm Association [*Later, National Micrographics Association, now AIIM*] [*Trade association*]
NMA........... National Microform Association (NITA)
NMA........... National Micrographics Association [*Later, AIIM*] [*Trade association*] (EA)
NMA........... National Midwives Association (EA)
NMA........... National Military Authority (NATG)
NMA........... National Mime Association [*Later, NMTA*] (EA)
NMA........... National Motorists Association (EA)
NMA........... National Museum of Antiquities in Scotland
NMA........... National Music Academy [*Australia*]
NMA........... National Mustang Association (EA)
NMA........... NATO Military Authorities (NATG)
NMA........... Natural Marketing Association [*Woodland Hills, CA*] (EA)
NMA........... Navy Mutual Aid Association (EA)
NMA........... Needle Makers Association [*British*] (BI)
NMA........... Negligee Manufacturers Association [*Later, IAMA*]
NMA........... Netherlands Military Administration [*World War II*]
NMA........... Neue Mozart-Ausgabe [*A publication*]
NMA........... Neurogenic Muscular Atrophy [*Medicine*]
NMA........... New Music Articles [*A publication*]
NMA........... Nicaragua Medical Aid (EA)
NMA........... N-Methylaspartate [*Organic chemistry*]
NMA........... N-Methylaspartic Acid [*An amino acid*]
NMA........... N-Methylolacrylamide [*Organic chemistry*]
NMA........... Noma Industries Ltd. [*Toronto Stock Exchange symbol*]
NMA........... Non-Marine Association [*Lloyd's Underwriters*] (AIA)
NMA........... Nonmass Analyzed [*Photovoltaic energy systems*]
NMA........... Nonmedical Attendant (AABC)
NMA........... Nonprofit Management Association (EA)
NMA........... Nonresonant Magnetic Amplifier
NMA........... Normal Method of Acquisition (MCD)
NMA........... Northwest Mining Association (EA)
NMA........... Nuveen Muni Advantage Fd [*NYSE symbol*] (TTSB)
NMA........... Nuveen Municipal Advantage Fund [*NYSE symbol*] (SPSG)
NMA........... University of Albuquerque, Albuquerque, NM [*OCLC symbol*] (OCLC)
NMa............ Wead Library, Malone, NY [*Library symbol Library of Congress*] (LCLS)
NMAA .... National Machine Accountants Association [*Later, DPMA*]
NMAA .... National Metal Awning Association [*Defunct*] (EA)
NMAA .... National Mobilization Against AIDS [*Acquired Immune Deficiency Syndrome*] (EA)
NMAA .... National Museum of African Art [*Smithsonian Institution*]
NMAA .... Navy Mutual Aid Association
NMAA .... Nursing Mothers' Association of Australia
NmAAc........ Albuquerque Academy, Albuquerque, NM [*Library symbol*] [*Library of Congress*] (LCLS)
NmAACF ..... ACF Industries, Inc., Albuquerque, NM [*Library symbol Library of Congress*] (LCLS)
NmAAF .... United States Air Force, Weapons Laboratory, Kirtland Air Force Base, Albuquerque, NM [*Library symbol Library of Congress*] (LCLS)
NmAAM ...... United States Army, Medical Library, Sandia Base, Albuquerque, NM [*Library symbol Library of Congress*] (LCLS)
NMAB .... National Market Advisory Board [*SEC*]
NMAB .... National Materials Advisory Board (EA)
N-MAb .... Neutralizing Monoclonal Antibody [*Immunology*]
NMAB .... N-Monochloro(amino)butyric Acid [*Organic chemistry*]
NmABD .... BDM Corp., Albuquerque, NM [*Library symbol*] [*Library of Congress*] (LCLS)

NMAC .... National Medical Audiovisual Center [*of the National Library of Medicine*] [*LHNCBC*] [*Absorbed by*] (EA)

NMAC .... National Minority AIDS [*Acquired Immune Deficiency Syndrome*] Council (EA)

NMAC .... Naval Missile and Astronautics Center

NMAC .... Near Midair Collision

NMAC .... Nissan Motor Acceptance Corp.

NMAC .... Nuclear Materials Accounting and Control

NMACT .... Nuclear Materials Accounting Control Team [*British*] (NUCP)

NmADAS ...... United States Defense Atomic Support Agency, Sandia Base, Albuquerque, NM [*Library symbol Library of Congress*] (LCLS)

NmA-EP .... Albuquerque Public Library, Ernie Pyle Memorial Branch, Albuquerque, NM [*Library symbol Library of Congress*] (LCLS)

NMAF .... National Medical Association Foundation [*Defunct*] (EA)

NMAFA .... National Museum of African Art [*Smithsonian Institution*] (GFGA)

NMAG .... Nonmagnetic (MSA)

N Mag Ca .... New Magistrates' Cases [*England*] [*A publication*] (DLA)

NmAGen ...... New Mexico Genealogical Society, Inc., Albuquerque, NM [*Library symbol Library of Congress*] (LCLS)

NmAGS .... Church of Jesus Christ of Latter-Day Saints, Genealogical Society Library, Albuquerque Branch, Albuquerque, NM [*Library symbol Library of Congress*] (LCLS)

NMah .... Mahopac Library Association, Mahopac, NY [*Library symbol Library of Congress*] (LCLS)

NmAHS .... Honeywell Sperry Inc., Defense System Division, Albuquerque, NM [*Library symbol*] [*Library of Congress*] (LCLS)

NMAHSTC .... National Museum of American History, Science, Technology, and Culture [*Smithsonian Institution*]

NmAl .... Alamogordo Public Library, Alamogordo, NM [*Library symbol Library of Congress*] (LCLS)

NmAL .... Lovelace Foundation for Medical Education and Research, Albuquerque, NM [*Library symbol Library of Congress*] (LCLS)

NmA-LG .... Albuquerque Public Library, Los Griegos Branch, Albuquerque, NM [*Library symbol Library of Congress*] (LCLS)

NMalv .... Malverne Public Library, Malverne, NY [*Library symbol Library of Congress*] (LCLS)

NMalvDE ...... Davison Elementary School, Malverne, NY [*Library symbol Library of Congress*] (LCLS)

NMalvHM ...... Howard T. Herber Middle School, Malverne, NY [*Library symbol*] [*Library of Congress*] (LCLS)

NMalvLE .... Lindner Elementary School, Malverne, NY [*Library symbol Library of Congress*] (LCLS)

NMalvSH ..... Malverne Senior High School, Malverne, NY [*Library symbol*] [*Library of Congress*] (LCLS)

NMam .... Mamaroneck Free Library, Mamaroneck, NY [*Library symbol Library of Congress*] (LCLS)

NmAM .... Montessori School, Albuquerque, NM [*Library symbol Library of Congress*] (LCLS)

NMamL .... Mamaroneck Free Library, Mamaroneck, NY [*Library symbol*] [*Library of Congress*] (LCLS)

NM & S .... Bureau of Medicine and Surgery Publications [*Navy*]

NM&SA .... National Moving & Storage Association [*MTMC*] (TAG)

NManh .... Manhasset Public Library, Manhasset, NY [*Library symbol Library of Congress*] (LCLS)

NManhH ...... North Shore Hospital, Manhasset, NY [*Library symbol Library of Congress*] (LCLS)

NManhJH ..... Manhasset Junior High School, Manhasset, NY [*Library symbol*] [*Library of Congress*] (LCLS)

NManhJSH ... Manhasset Junior-Senior High School, Manhasset, NY [*Library symbol Library of Congress*] (LCLS)

NManhM ...... Manhasset Medical Center Hospital, Manhasset, NY [*Library symbol Library of Congress*] (LCLS)

NManhME ..... Munsey Park Elementary School, Manhasset, NY [*Library symbol*] [*Library of Congress*] (LCLS)

NManhSE ..... Shelter Rock Elementary School, Manhasset, NY [*Library symbol*] [*Library of Congress*] (LCLS)

NManhSH .... Manhasset Senior High School, Manhasset, NY [*Library symbol*] [*Library of Congress*] (LCLS)

NManhSM .... Saint Mary's Boys High School, Manhasset, NY [*Library symbol*] [*Library of Congress*] (LCLS)

NMAP .... Navy Military Assistance Programs

NmA-PP .... Albuquerque Public Library, Prospect Park Branch, Albuquerque, NM [*Library symbol Library of Congress*] (LCLS)

NM App ...... New Mexico Court of Appeals (DLA)

NmAr .... Artesia Public Library, Artesia, NM [*Library symbol Library of Congress*] (LCLS)

NMar .... Marcellus Free Library, Marcellus, NY [*Library symbol Library of Congress*] (LCLS)

Nm-Ar .... New Mexico State Records Center and Archives, Santa Fe, NM [*Library symbol Library of Congress*] (LCLS)

NMARC .... Navy and Marine Corps Acquisition Review Committee [*Terminated, 1975*] (MCD)

NMarcP .... Marcy Psychiatric Center, Marcy, NY [*Library symbol Library of Congress*] (LCLS)

NmArP .... Artesia Public Library, Artesia, NM [*Library symbol*] [*Library of Congress*] (LCLS)

NMas .... Henry H. Warren Memorial Library, Massena, NY [*Library symbol Library of Congress*] (LCLS)

NMAS .... National Map Accuracy Standards (PDAA)

NMAS .... National Marine Advisory Service [*National Oceanic and Atmospheric Administration*] (MSC)

NmAS .... Sandia Corp., Albuquerque, NM [*Library symbol Library of Congress*] (LCLS)

NMasL .... Massena Public Library, Massena, NY [*Library symbol*] [*Library of Congress*] (LCLS)

NMasMH ...... Massena Memorial Hospital, Massena, NY [*Library symbol*] [*Library of Congress*] (LCLS)

NMass .... Massapequa Public Library, Massapequa, NY [*Library symbol Library of Congress*] (LCLS)

NMassAJ ..... J. Lewis Ames Junior High School, Massapequa, NY [*Library symbol*] [*Library of Congress*] (LCLS)

NMassBE ..... Birch Elementary School, Massapequa, NY [*Library symbol Library of Congress*] (LCLS)

NMassBH ..... Berner High School, Massapequa, NY [*Library symbol Library of Congress*] (LCLS)

NMassELE .... East Lake Elementary School, Massapequa, NY [*Library symbol Library of Congress*] (LCLS)

NMassFE ..... Fairfield Elementary School, Massapequa, NY [*Library symbol Library of Congress*] (LCLS)

NMassHE ..... Hawthorn Elementary School, Massapequa, NY [*Library symbol Library of Congress*] (LCLS)

NMassHS ..... Masspequa High School, Massapequa, NY [*Library symbol*] [*Library of Congress*] (LCLS)

NMassLE ..... Lockhart Elementary School, Massapequa, NY [*Library symbol Library of Congress*] (LCLS)

NmassMJ ..... J.P. McKenna Junior High School, Massapequa, NY [*Library symbol*] [*Library of Congress*] (LCLS)

NMassSE ..... Charles E. Schwarting Elementary School, Massapequa, NY [*Library symbol*] [*Library of Congress*] (LCLS)

NMassUE ..... Unqua Elementary School, Massapequa, NY [*Library symbol Library of Congress*] (LCLS)

NMat .... Mattituck Free Library, Mattituck, NY [*Library symbol Library of Congress*] (LCLS)

NMAT .... Night-Time Marine Air Temperature

NMATP .... Navy Military Assistance Training Program (NG)

Nmatrn .... Nematron Corp. [*Associated Press*] (SAG)

NMAU .... Naval Medical Administration Unit (DNAB)

NmAU .... University of Albuquerque, Albuquerque, NM [*Library symbol Library of Congress*] (LCLS)

NmAVA .... United States Veterans Administration Hospital, Albuquerque, NM [*Library symbol Library of Congress*] (LCLS)

NMAX .... Nonwireline Multiple-Access Communications Exchange System (PDAA)

NMb .... Mastics-Moriches-Shirley Community Library, Mastic Beach, NY [*Library symbol Library of Congress*] (LCLS)

NMB .... Namib Air (Pty) Ltd. [*Namibia*] [*ICAO designator*] (FAAC)

NMB .... National Marine Board [*British World War II*]

NMB .... National Maritime Board

NMB .... National Meat Brokers [*Australia*]

NMB .... National Mediation Board [*Department of Labor*]

NMB .... National Metric Board

NMB .... National Motel Brokers (EA)

NMB .... National Mutual Benefit [*Madison, WI*] (EA)

NMB .... Naval Meteorological Branch [*British*]

NMB .... Naval Minecraft Base

NMB .... Naval Model Basin

NMB .... Neuromuscular Blockade [*Medicine*]

NMB .... New Methylene Blue [*Organic chemistry*]

NMB .... Noise, Measurement Buoy

NMB .... No Military Branch

NMB .... Not Member of a Branch

NMBA .... National Marine Bankers Association [*Chicago, IL*] (EA)

NMBA .... Neuromuscular Blocking Agent

NMBA .... (Nitrosomethylamino) Butyric Acid [*Organic chemistry*]

NMBC .... National Minority Business Campaign [*Later, NMBD*] (EA)

NMBC .... National Minority Business Council [*New York, NY*] (EA)

NMbCH .... Bayview Community Hospital, Mastic Beach, NY [*Library symbol Library of Congress*] (LCLS)

NMBD .... National Minority Business Directories [*Minneapolis, MN*] (EA)

NmBeN .... Northwestern Regional Library, Belen, NM [*Library symbol Library of Congress*] (LCLS)

NMBF .... National Manufacturers of Beverage Flavors [*Defunct*] (EA)

NMBHF .... Naismith Memorial Basketball Hall of Fame (EA)

NMBMMR ..... New Mexico Bureau of Mines and Mineral Resources [*New Mexico Institute of Mining and Technology*] [*Research center*] (RCD)

NMbr .... Millbrook Library, Millbrook, NY [*Library symbol*] [*Library of Congress*] (LCLS)

NMBR .... NATO Military Basic Requirement (MCD)

NMbrB .... Bennett College, Millbrook, NY [*Library symbol Library of Congress*] (LCLS)

NMBS .... Nationale Maatschappij der Belgische Spoorwegen [*Railway*] [*Belgium*] (EY)

NMBS .... Nimbus CD International, Inc. [*NASDAQ symbol*] (SAG)

NMBS .... Nimbus CD Intl. [*NASDAQ symbol*] (TTSB)

NMBT .... New Main Battle Tank [*Military*] (RDA)

NMBT .... New Milford Bank & Trust Co. [*NASDAQ symbol*] (CTT)

NMBT .... New Milford BK & Tr Conn [*NASDAQ symbol*] (TTSB)

NmC .... Carlsbad Public Library, Carlsbad, NM [*Library symbol Library of Congress*] (LCLS)

NMC .... Marine Corps Publications [*Later, NAVMC*]

NMC .... Meredith College, Raleigh, NC [*OCLC symbol*] (OCLC)

NMC .... Nail Manufacturers Council (EA)

NMC .... Natal Medical Corps [*British military*] (DMA)

NMC .... National Magazine Co.

NMC .... National Mail Centers, Inc. [*Telecommunications service*] (TSSD)

NMC .... National Manpower Council

NMC .... National Marine Center (USDC)

NMC .... National Marine Center [*Marine science*] (OSRA)

NMC .... National Maritime Council [*Defunct*] (EA)

NMC .... National Mastitis Council (EA)

NMC	National Medical Care
NMC	National Memorials Committee [*Australia*]
NMC	National Message Center [*Overland Park, KS*] (TSSD)
NMC	National Meteorological Center [*National Oceanic and Atmospheric Administration Information service or system*] (IID)
NMC	National Migrant Clearinghouse (OICC)
NMC	National Military Council [*Surinam*] (PD)
NMC	National Missionary Council [*Australia*]
NMC	National Motorsports Committee (EA)
NMC	National Mouse Club [*British*] (BI)
NMC	National Museum of Canada
NMC	National Music Camp [*Interlochen, MI*]
NMC	National Music Council (EA)
NMC	NATO Manual on Codification (NATG)
NMC	Naval Material Command [*Formerly, NMSE*]
NMC	Naval Medical Center [*Bethesda, MD*]
NMC	Naval Memorandum Correction (NVT)
NMC	Naval Missile Center [*Point Mugu, CA*]
NMC	Naval Mission Center (KSC)
NMC	NAVA [*National Audio-Visual Association*] Materials Council (EA)
NMC	Navigation Map Computer
NMC	Navy Mail Clerk
NMC	Navy Memorandum Correction
NMC	Nebraska Motor Carriers Association, Petroleum Carriers' Conference, Inc., OmahaNE [*STAC*]
NMC	Net Matchable Cost
NMC	Network Management Center [*Computer science*]
NMC	Network Management Console [*Industrial Networking, Inc.*]
NMC	Network Measurement Center
NMC	Neuromuscular Control [*Medicine*] (DMAA)
NMC	Nine Mile Canyon [*California*] [*Seismograph station code, US Geological Survey*] (SEIS)
NMC	Noble Metal Catalyst [*Automotive engineering*]
NMC	No More Credit [*Business term*] (ADA)
NMC	Non-Metropolitan Counties [*British*]
NMC	Non-Mission Capable [*Military*] (INF)
NMC	Northern Montana College [*Havre*]
NMC	Northwestern Michigan College [*Traverse City*]
NMC	Not Mission Capable (MCD)
NMC	Nuclear Metal Conference
NMC	Numac Energy [*AMEX symbol*] (SPSG)
NMC	Nurse Managed Center (MEDA)
NMC	Nursery Marketing Council (EA)
NMC	Public Archives of Canada, National Map Collection [*UTLAS symbol*]
NMC	San Francisco, CA [*Location identifier FAA*] (FAAL)
NMCA	National Marble Club of America (EA)
NMCA	National Meat Canners Association (EA)
NMCA	National Military Command Authority (NVT)
NMCA	National Mossberg Collectors Association (EA)
NMCA	National Motorcycle Commuter Association [*Defunct*] (EA)
NMCA	National Musclecar Association (EA)
NMCA	Navy Mothers' Clubs of America (EA)
N-McAb	Neutralizing Monoclonal Antibody [*Immunology*]
NMCAC	National Motor Carrier Advisory Committee [*MTMC*] (TAG)
NMCB	National Metric Conversion Board (NADA)
NMCB	National Munitions Control Board [*World War II*]
NMCB	National Museum of Canada Bulletin [*A publication*]
NMCB	Navy Mobile Construction Battalion (CINC)
NMCC	National Management Career Curriculum [*Office of Personnel Management*] (GFGA)
NMCC	National Manpower Coordinating Committee [*Department of Labor*]
NMCC	National Military Command Center [*DoD*]
NMCC	Navy-Marine Corps Council [*Defunct*] (EA)
NMCC	Network Management Control Center [*Telecommunications*]
NMCC	Northeast-Midwest Congressional Coalition (EA)
NMCCDDA	National Model Cities Community Development Directors Association [*Later, NCDA*] (EA)
NMCCIS	NATO Military Command and Control and Information System (NATG)
NMCDA	National Model Cities Directors Association [*Later, NCDA*] (EA)
NMCEC	Navy-Marine Corps Exhibit Center
NMCES	National Medical Care Expenditures Survey [*Department of Health and Human Services*] (GFGA)
NMCGB	National Music Council of Great Britain (EAIO)
NMCGRF	Navy-Marine Corps-Coast Guard Residence Foundation
NMCHC	National Maternal and Child Health Clearinghouse (EA)
NmCiN	Northeastern Regional Library, Cimarron, NM [*Library symbol Library of Congress*] (LCLS)
NmCiN	Northeastern Regional Library, Cimarron, NM [*Library symbol*] [*Library of Congress*] (LCLS)
NMCIRD	Naval Material Command Industrial Resources Detachment (DNAB)
NMCJS	Naval Member, Canadian Joint Staff
NmCl	Clovis-Carver Public Library, Clovis, NM [*Library symbol Library of Congress*] (LCLS)
NMCL	Navy Missile Center Laboratory (KSC)
NmCla	Albert W. Thompson Memorial Library, Clayton, NM [*Library symbol Library of Congress*] (LCLS)
NMCLA	Bethesda Military Librarians Group [*Library network*]
NmCIA	United States Air Force, Cannon Air Force Base, Clovis, NM [*Library symbol Library of Congress*] (LCLS)
NmClaP	Albert W. Thompson Memorial Library, Clayton, NM [*Library symbol*] [*Library of Congress*] (LCLS)
NMCLK	Navy Mail Clerk
NMCM	Navy and Marine Corps Medal [*Military decoration*]
NMCM	Not Mission Capable, Maintenance (NVT)

NMCO	Navy Material Cataloging Office
NMCOM	Naval Material Command [*Formerly, NMSE*] (MCD)
NmCP	United States Potash Co., Carlsbad, NM [*Library symbol Library of Congress*] (LCLS)
NMCRB	Navy Military Construction Review Board
NMCRC	Navy-Marine Corps Reserve Center (NVT)
NMCRTC	Navy and Marine Corps Reserve Training Center
NMCS	National Medic-Card [*Commercial firm*] (EA)
NMCS	National Medicinal Chemistry Symposium
NMCS	National Military Command System
NMCS	Navy Mine Countermeasures Station (MUGU)
NMCS	Not Mission Capable, Supply (MCD)
NMCS	Nuclear Materials Control System (IEEE)
NMCSA	Navy Material Command Support Activity
NMCSHA	National Morgan Cutting and Stock Horse Association (EA)
NMCSS	National Military Command System Standards (AFM)
NMCSSC	National Military Command System Support Center (AABC)
NMCUES	National Medical Care Utilization and Expenditure Survey [*Department of Health and Human Services A publication*] (DHSM)
NmD	Deming Public Library, Deming, NM [*Library symbol Library of Congress*] (LCLS)
NMD	NASA Management Delegations (MCD)
NMD	National Missile Defense [*DoD*]
NMD	Naval Mine Depot
NMD	Navy Marine Diesel Fuel
NMD	Netmed, Inc. [*AMEX symbol*] (SAG)
NMD	Nonmonetary Determination [*Unemployment insurance*] (OICC)
NMD	Normal Muscle Development (DAVI)
NMD	Nu-Media Industry International [*Vancouver Stock Exchange symbol*]
NMD	Nutrition Monitoring Division [*Department of Agriculture*] (GFGA)
NMDA	National Marine Distributors Association (EA)
NMDA	National Medical and Dental Association (EA)
NMDA	National Metal Decorators Association (EA)
NMDA	National Midas Dealers Association (EA)
NMDA	National Motorcycle Dealers Association [*Later, NMRA*] (EA)
NMDA	National Motorcycle Dismantelers Association (EA)
NMDA	National Motor Drivers' Association [*A union*] [*British*]
NMDA	N-Methyl-D-Aspartic Acid [*An amino acid*]
NMDA	Nonresonant Magnetic Deflection Amplifier
NMDAR	N-Methyl-D-Aspartic Acid Receptor [*Neurochemistry*]
NMDC	Nonmagnetic Drill Collar [*Well drilling technology*]
NMDCEF	National Medico-Dental Conference for the Evaluation of Fluoridation [*Later, Medical-Dental Committee on Evaluation of Fluoridation*] (EA)
NMDF	Navy Management Data File (DNAB)
NMDG	N-Methyl-D-Glucamine [*Biochemistry*]
NMD/GBR	National Missile Defense-Ground Based RADAR [*Army*] (RDA)
NMDIS	National Marine Data and Information Service [*China*] [*Marine science*] (OSRA)
NMDIS	National Music and Disability Information Service [*British*]
NMDL	Naval Mine Defense Laboratory [*Naval Facilities Engineering Command*] [*Panama City, FL*]
NMDL	Navy Management Data List (NG)
NMDL	Navy Material Data List
NMDP	National Marrow Donor Program [*Department of Health and Human Services*]
NMDP	Neomenthyldiphenylphosphine [*Organic chemistry*]
NMDPI	Nuveen Maryland Premium Income Municipal Fund [*Associated Press*] (SAG)
NMDR	Nuclear Magnetic Double Resonance
NMDRP	National Military Discharge Review Project (EA)
NMDS	Naval Mine Disposal School
NMDS	Network Management Directory Services (NITA)
NMDS	New Music Distribution Service (EA)
NMDS	Nonmetric Multidimensional Scaling [*Statistics*]
NMDSC	Naval Medical Data Service Center (DNAB)
NMDSG	Naval Material Data Systems Group (DNAB)
NMDU	Newspaper and Mail Deliverers Union of New York and Vicinity (EA)
NMDY	Nonresonant Magnetic Deflection Yoke
NMDZ	NATO Maritime Defense Zone (NATG)
NmE	Espanola Public Library, Espanola, NM [*Library symbol Library of Congress*] (LCLS)
NME	National Marriage Encounter (EA)
NME	National Military Establishment [*Designated Department of Defense, 1949*]
NME	Naval Material Establishment (DOMA)
NME	Necrolytic Migratory Erythema [*Dermatology*]
NME	Newly Maturing Economy [*Business term*]
NME	New Molecular Entity [*Chemistry*]
NME	Nightmute [*Alaska*] [*Airport symbol*] (OAG)
NME	Nissan Motorsports Europe
NME	Noise-Measuring Equipment
NME	Nonsupervisory Manufacturing Engineer
NMEA	National Marine Educators Association (EA)
NMEA	National Marine Electronics Association (EA)
NMEBA	National Marine Engineers' Beneficial Association (EA)
NMEC	National Metric Education Center [*Western Michigan University*]
NMEC	Nuclear Material Control Center (NUCP)
NMed	Lee-Whedon Memorial Library, Medina, NY [*Library symbol Library of Congress*] (LCLS)
NMED	New Mexico Environmental Department
NMED	New Mexico Environmental Department (DOGT)
NMedH	Medina Memorial Hospital, Medina, NY [*Library symbol Library of Congress*] (LCLS)

NMedia........ National Media Corp. [*Associated Press*] (SAG)
NMEF.......... Naval Mine Engineering Facility
NMEFC........ National Marine Environmental Forecasting Center [*China*] [*Marine science*] (OSRA)
NMEG .... Nisei Mass Evacuation Group
NMEIA .... National Machine Embroidery Instructors Association (EA)
NMEIAA .... National Machine Embroidery Instructors Association of America (EA)
NMEL .... Navy Marine Engineering Laboratory [*Later, David W. Taylor Naval Ship Research and Development Center*] (KSC)
NMeIA .... Airborne Institute Laboratories, Melville, NY [*Library symbol Library of Congress*] (LCLS)
NMeIH .... Holzmacher, McLendon & Murrell, Inc., Melville, NY [*Library symbol Library of Congress*] (LCLS)
NMeIL.......... Litcom Library, Melville, NY [*Library symbol Library of Congress*] (LCLS)
NMeIS .... Suffolk State School, Melville, NY [*Library symbol Library of Congress*] (LCLS)
NMeISC .... Sagamore Children's Center, Melville, NY [*Library symbol Library of Congress*] (LCLS)
NmEN .... Northern Regional Library, Espanola, NM [*Library symbol Library of Congress*] (LCLS)
NMERI .... New Mexico Engineering Research Institute [*University of New Mexico*] [*Research center*] (RCD)
NMerk.......... Merrick Public Library, Merrick, NY [*Library symbol Library of Congress*] (LCLS)
NMerkBE..... Birch Elementary School, Merrick, NY [*Library symbol*] [*Library of Congress*] (LCLS)
NMerk CE .... Chatterton Elementary School, Merrick, NY [*Library symbol*] [*Library of Congress*] (LCLS)
NMerkCH..... Sanford H. Calhoun High School, Merrick, NY [*Library symbol*] [*Library of Congress*] (LCLS)
NMerkF........ Five Towns College, Merrick, NY [*Library symbol Library of Congress*] (LCLS)
NMerkLE..... Lakeside Elementary School, Merrick, NY [*Library symbol*] [*Library of Congress*] (LCLS)
NMerkMJ..... Merrick Avenue Junior High School, Merrick, NY [*Library symbol*] [*Library of Congress*] (LCLS)
NMES.......... National Medical Expenditure Survey [*Department of Health and Human Services*] (GFGA)
NMES.......... Naval Marine Engineering Station
NMEU .... Naval Material Evaluation Unit (DNAB)
NMEX.......... New Mexico
N Mex Highlands U... New Mexico Highlands University (GAGS)
N Mex Inst M&T... New Mexico Institute of Mining and Technology (GAGS)
N Mex St U .. New Mexico State University (GAGS)
NMF.............. Boston, MA [*Location identifier FAA*] (FAAL)
NmF............. Farmington Public Library, Farmington, NM [*Library symbol Library of Congress*] (LCLS)
NMF.............. National Marfan Foundation (EA)
NMF.............. National Medical Fellowships (EA)
NMF.............. National Migraine Foundation [*Later, National Headache Foundation - NHF*] (EA)
NMF.............. National Motor Freight Traffic Association Inc., Agent, Washington DC [*STAC*]
NMF.............. National Myoclonus Foundation [*Defunct*] (EA)
NMF.............. Naval Missile Facility [*Also, NAVMISFAC*]
NMF.............. Navy Management Fund
NMF.............. New Master File
NMF.............. N-Methylformamide [*Antineoplastic compound*]
NMF.............. N-Methyl Fucosamine [*Organic chemistry*]
NMF.............. Nonmaster File [*Computer science*]
NMF.............. Nonmember Firm [*of NYSE*]
NMF.............. Nonmigrating Fraction [*of spermatozoa*] [*Medicine*]
NMF.............. Nonprofit Mailers Federation (EA)
NMF.............. Nonuniform Magnetic Field
NMF.............. Nordiska Maskinbefalsfederationen [*Nordic Engineer Officers' Federation - NEOF*] (EAIO)
NMFA.......... National Military Family Association (EA)
NMFC.......... National Motor Freight Classification
NMFCR .... National Motor Freight Classification Rules
NMFEC........ National Medical Foundation for Eye Care [*Later, AAO*] (EA)
NMFECC ..... National Magnetic Fusion Energy Computer Center [*Department of Energy*] (MCD)
NmFGS .... Church of Jesus Christ of Latter-Day Saints, Genealogical Society Library, Farmington Branch, Farmington, NM [*Library symbol Library of Congress*]
NMFHAWAREA... Naval Missile Facility, Hawaiian Area (MUGU)
NMFHG........ National Master Farm Homemakers Guild (EA)
NMFI............ National Master Facility Inventory [*Department of Health and Human Services*] (GFGA)
NmfL........... National Microfilms Ltd., Dublin, Ireland [*Library symbol*] [*Library of Congress*] (LCLS)
NMFMA........ National Mutual Fund Managers Association [*Defunct*] (EA)
NMFPA .... Naval Missile Facility, Point Arguello
NMFPM....... Naval Missile Facility, Point Mugu [*California*] (SAA)
NMFR .... NAPALM [*National ADP Program for AMC Logistics Management*] Master File Record
NMFRL .... Naval Medical Field Research Laboratory [*Camp Lejeune, NC*]
NmFs.......... Fort Sumner Public Library, Fort Sumner, NM [*Library symbol Library of Congress*] (LCLS)
NMFS.......... National Marine Fisheries Service [*Formerly, Bureau of Commercial Fisheries*] [*National Oceanic and Atmospheric Administration Washington, DC*]
NMFS.......... National Medical Financial Services Corp. [*NASDAQ symbol*] (SAG)

NMFS.......... National Mortality Followback Survey [*National Center for Health Statistics*]
NMFS.......... Natl Medical Finl Svcs [*NASDAQ symbol*] (TTSB)
NMFS.......... Night Missile Flash Simulator (MCD)
NMFT .... New Material Flight Tests
NMFTA .... National Motor Freight Traffic Association [*Alexandria, VA*] (EA)
NMFWA ...... National Military Fish and Wildlife Association (EA)
NMFWA ...... Neuromuscular Foundation of Western Australia
NmG .... Gallup Public Library, Gallup, NM [*Library symbol Library of Congress*] (LCLS)
NMG .... Navy Metrication Group (DNAB)
NMG .... Navy Military Government
NMG .... Neiman-Marcus Group [*NYSE symbol*] (SPSG)
NMG .... Neiman-Marcus Group [*NYSE symbol*] (TTSB)
NM (G) .... New Mexico Reports (Gildersleeve) [*1852-89*] [*A publication*] (DLA)
NMG .... New Orleans, LA [*Location identifier FAA*] (FAAL)
NMG .... Numerical Master Geometry [*System*]
NMG .... San Miguel [*Panama*] [*Airport symbol*] (OAG)
NMGA .... National Military Guidance Association (EA)
NMGC .... National Marriage Guidance Council [*British*] (ILCA)
NMGCS .... National Milk Glass Collectors Society
NmGr .... Mother Whiteside Memorial Library, Grants, NM [*Library symbol Library of Congress*] (LCLS)
NMGRA .... National Museum and Gallery Registration Association (EA)
NMh............ Library of Poultney Bigelow, Malden-On-Hudson, NY [*Library symbol*] [*Library of Congress*] (LCLS)
NMH .... Nautical Miles per Hour
NMH .... New Mexico Highlands [*New Mexico*] [*Seismograph station code, US Geological Survey*] (SEIS)
NMH .... New Mexico Highlands University, Las Vegas, NM [*OCLC symbol*] (OCLC)
NMH .... N-Methylhydroxylamine [*Organic chemistry*]
NmHa .... Hatch Public Library, Hatch, NM [*Library symbol Library of Congress*] (LCLS)
NMHA .... National Mental Health Association (EA)
NMHA .... National Minority Health Association (EA)
NMHA .... National Mobile Home Association (EA)
NmHARL...... Aeromedical Library, 6571st Aeromedical Research Laboratory, Holloman AFB, NM [*Library symbol Library of Congress*] (LCLS)
NMHC.......... National Materials Handling Centre [*Cranfield Institute of Technology*] [*British*] (CB)
NMHC.......... National Multi Housing Council (EA)
NMHC.......... Nonmethane Hydrocarbons [*Organic chemistry*]
NMHCA........ National Mental Health Consumers' Association (EA)
NMHCSHC ... National Mental Health Consumer Self-Help Clearinghouse (EA)
NMHF .... National Manufactured Housing Federation (EA)
NMHFA .... National Manufactured Housing Finance Association [*Defunct*] (EA)
NmHi........... Historical Society of New Mexico, Santa Fe, NM [*Library symbol Library of Congress*] (LCLS)
NmHo .... Hobbs Public Library, Hobbs, NM [*Library symbol Library of Congress*] (LCLS)
NmHoC .... New Mexico Junior College, Hobbs, NM [*Library symbol Library of Congress*] (LCLS)
NmHORA ..... United States Air Force, Office of Research Analyses, Technical Library, Holloman AFB, Albuquerque, NM [*Library symbol Library of Congress*] (LCLS)
NmHoSW..... College of the Southwest, Hobbs, NM [*Library symbol Library of Congress*] (LCLS)
NM/HR......... Nautical Mile/Hour (MCD)
NMHS .... National Maritime Historical Society (EA)
NMHSPE...... New Mexico High School Proficiency Examination (EDAC)
NMHT .... National Museum of History and Technology [*Later, National Museum of American History*] (GRD)
NMHU .... New Mexico Highlands University [*Las Vegas, NM*]
NMI.............. Minot State College, Minot, ND [*OCLC symbol*] (OCLC)
NMI.............. NASA Management Instruction (KSC)
NMI.............. NASA Management Issuance (MCD)
NMI.............. National Macaroni Institute (EA)
NMI.............. National Maglev Initiative [*Department of Transportation*]
NMI.............. National Maintenance Index (IAA)
NMI.............. National Manpower Institute [*Later, NIWL*] (EA)
NMI.............. National Maritime Institute [*British*]
NMI.............. Nautical Mile
NMI.............. New Material Introductory [*Team*] [*Military*]
NMI.............. Nissan Motorsports International [*Automotive competition*]
NMI.............. No Middle Initial
NMI.............. Nonmajor Item (MCD)
NMI.............. Nonmasking [*or Nonmaskable*] Interrupt
NMI.............. Northeast-Midwest Institute (EA)
NMI.............. Northwest Microfilm, Inc. [*Information service or system*] (IID)
NMI.............. Nuclear Magnetic Imaging
NMI.............. Nuclear Metals, Inc.
NMI.............. Nuveen Municipal Income Fund [*NYSE symbol*] (SPSG)
NMi............. Thrall Library, Middletown, NY [*Library symbol Library of Congress*] (LCLS)
NMIA .... National Military Intelligence Association (EA)
NMIAPO....... New Montreal International Airport Project [*Canada*]
NMIB .... New Material Introductory Briefing [*Military*] (MCD)
NMIBT .... New Material Introductory Briefing Team [*Military*] (MCD)
NMIC .... National Maritime Intelligence Center [*Created in 1992 from intelligence activities in the Washington, D.C., area*] [*Navy*] (DOMA)
NMIC .... National Meat Industry Council (EA)
NMIC .... National Military Information Center
NMIC .... National Missile Industry Conference (AAG)

NMIC .... Not Made in Canada [Business term]
NMICSS ...... NMIC [National Military Information Center] Support System (MCD)
NMIDA .... N-Methyliminodiacetic Acid [Organic chemistry]
NMidp .... Middleport Free Library, Middleport, NY [Library symbol Library of Congress] (LCLS)
NMidpF .... FMC Corp., Niagara Chemical Division, R and D Library, Middleport, NY [Library symbol Library of Congress] (LCLS)
NMIHS .... National Maternal and Infant Health Survey [Department of Health and Human Services] (GFGA)
NMil .... Millerton Free Library, Millerton, NY [Library symbol Library of Congress] (LCLS)
NMIL .... New Materiel Introductory Letter [Army] (AABC)
NMILA .... NASA Merritt Island Launch Area (SAA)
NMilBc .... New Milford Savings Bank [Associated Press] (SAG)
NMilt .... Sarah Hull Hallock Free Library, Milton, NY [Library symbol Library of Congress] (LCLS)
NMIMT .... New Mexico Institute of Mining and Technology [Socorro]
NMin .... Mineola Memorial Library, Mineola, NY [Library symbol Library of Congress] (LCLS)
NMinH .... Nassau Hospital, Mineola, NY [Library symbol Library of Congress] (LCLS)
NMinHe .... Hampton Elementary School, Mineola, NY [Library symbol Library of Congress] (LCLS)
NMinJE .... Jackson Avenue Elementary School, Mineola, NY [Library symbol Library of Congress] (LCLS)
NMinME .... Meadow Elementary School, Mineola, NY [Library symbol Library of Congress] (LCLS)
NMinMJ .... Mineola Junior High School, Mineola, NY [Library symbol Library of Congress] (LCLS)
NMinMS ...... Mineola Middle School, Mineola, NY [Library symbol] [Library of Congress] (LCLS)
NMinNCL ..... Nassau County Law Library, Mineola, NY [Library symbol Library of Congress] (LCLS)
NMiOC .... Orange County Community College, Middletown, NY [Library symbol Library of Congress] (LCLS)
NMIP .... New Major Investment Program [Australia]
NMIQI .... Nuveen Michigan Quality Income Municipal Fund [Associated Press] (SAG)
NMiR .... Ramapo Catskill Library System, Middletown, NY [Library symbol Library of Congress] (LCLS)
NMIRO .... Naval Material Industrial Resources Office
NMIS .... National Military Indications System (MCD)
NMIS .... Naval Manpower Information System
NMIS .... Newspapers Mutual Insurance Society Ltd. [British] (BI)
NMIS .... Nuclear Materials Information System
NMIS .... Nuclear Materials Inventory System (NRCH)
NMISMAN .... Navy Manpower Information System Manual (DNAB)
NMIST .... National Military Intelligence Support Team [Defense Intelligence Agency] (DOMA)
NMIT .... New Materiel Introductory Team [Army] (AABC)
NMITC .... Navy and Marine Corps Intelligence Training Center (DOMA)
NMIU .... Nordic Meat Industry Union (EA)
NMIW .... Northwest Marine Iron Works (AAGC)
NmJ .... Jal Public Library, Jal, NM [Library symbol Library of Congress] (LCLS)
NMJ .... Neuromuscular Junction [Anatomy]
NM (J) .... New Mexico Reports (Johnson) [A publication] (DLA)
NMJC .... National Men's Judo Championships [British]
NMJC .... Northeastern Mississippi Junior College [Senatobia]
NMJC .... Northwest Mississippi Junior College
NMJL .... National Mah Jongg League (EA)
NMK .... Cape May, NJ [Location identifier FAA] (FAAL)
NMK .... Niagara Mohawk Power Corp. [NYSE symbol] (SPSG)
NMK .... Niagara Mohawk Pwr [NYSE symbol] (TTSB)
NMKL .... Nordisk Metodikkommitte for Livsmedel [Nordic Committee on Food Analysis] (EAIO)
NMKPr .... Niagara Moh Pwr Adj Rt A Pfd [NYSE symbol] (TTSB)
NMKPrA .... Niag Moh Pwr 3.40% Pfd [NYSE symbol] (TTSB)
NMKPrB .... Niag Moh Pwr 3.60% Pfd [NYSE symbol] (TTSB)
NMKPrC .... Niag Moh Pwr 3.90% Pfd [NYSE symbol] (TTSB)
NMKPrD .... Niag Moh Pwr 4.10% Pfd [NYSE symbol] (TTSB)
NMKPrE .... Niag Moh Pwr 4.85% Pfd [NYSE symbol] (TTSB)
NMKPrG .... Niag Moh Pwr 5.25% Pfd [NYSE symbol] (TTSB)
NMKPrI .... Niag Moh Pwr 7.72% Pfd [NYSE symbol] (TTSB)
NMKPrK .... Niagara Mohawk Pwr Adj C Pfd [NYSE symbol] (TTSB)
NMKPrM ...... Niag Moh Pwr 9.50% Pfd [NYSE symbol] (TTSB)
NML .... Narragansett Marine Laboratory [University of Rhode Island]
NML .... National Magnet Laboratory
NML .... National Measurement Laboratory [Gaithersburg, MD] [National Institute of Standards and Technology] (GRD)
NML .... National Medical Library (DAVI)
NML .... National Metrology Laboratory (ACII)
NML .... National Municipal League (EA)
NML .... National Music League (EA)
NML .... Native Machine Language [Computer science]
NML .... Nautical Mile
NML .... Naval Materials Management (SAA)
NML .... Navy Management List (AFIT)
NML .... New Mathematical Library [School Mathematics Study Group]
Nm-L .... New Mexico Supreme Court Law Library, Santa Fe, NM [Library symbol Library of Congress] (LCLS)
NML .... Nodular Mixed Lymphoma [Oncology] (DAVI)
NML .... No Man's Land [Medical slang, cardiology]
NML .... Normal
NML .... Nuclear Magnetic Logging (IAA)

NML .... Nuclear Magnetism Log (PDAA)
NML .... University of New Mexico, School of Law, Albuquerque, NM [OCLC symbol] (OCLC)
NmLa .... Mesa Public Library, Los Alamos, NM [Library symbol Library of Congress] (LCLS)
NmLaS .... Los Alamos Scientific Laboratory, Los Alamos, NM [Library symbol Library of Congress] (LCLS)
NmLaS-M .... Los Alamos Scientific Laboratory, Medical Library, Los Alamos, NM [Library symbol Library of Congress] (LCLS)
NmLaU .... University of New Mexico, Los Alamos, NM [Library symbol Library of Congress] (LCLS)
NMLC .... Normalized Mass Loss Coefficient [Nuclear energy] (NUCP)
NmLc .... Thomas Branigan Memorial Library, Las Cruces, NM [Library symbol Library of Congress] (LCLS)
NmLcU .... New Mexico State University, Las Cruces, NM [Library symbol Library of Congress] (LCLS)
NMLO .... National Media Liaison Officer
NmLor .... Lordsburg-Hidalgo Public Library, Lordsburg, NM [Library symbol Library of Congress] (LCLS)
NmLov .... Lovington Public Library, Lovington, NM [Library symbol Library of Congress] (LCLS)
NmLovS .... Southeastern Regional Library Center, Lovington, NM [Library symbol Library of Congress] (LCLS)
NMLR .... Nigerian Monthly Law Reports [1964-65] [A publication] (DLA)
NMLRA .... National Muzzle Loading Rifle Association (EA)
NMLS .... National Microwave Landing System (MCD)
NMLT .... New Material Laboratory Tests
NmLv .... Las Vegas Carnegie Library, Las Vegas, NM [Library symbol Library of Congress] (LCLS)
NmLvH .... New Mexico Highlands University, Las Vegas, NM [Library symbol Library of Congress] (LCLS)
NmLvSH ...... New Mexico State Hospital, Las Vegas, NM [Library symbol Library of Congress] (LCLS)
NMM .... Meridian, MS [Location identifier FAA] (FAAL)
NMM .... NASA Management Manual
NMM .... National Maritime Museum [British]
NMM .... Network Measurement Machine [Computer Network] (IAA)
NMM .... Neutron Magnetic Moment
NMM .... New Madrid [Missouri] [Seismograph station code, US Geological Survey Closed] (SEIS)
NMM .... New Mexico Military Institute, Roswell, NM [OCLC symbol] (OCLC)
NMM .... N-Methylmorpholine [Organic chemistry]
NMM .... Norsemont Mining [Vancouver Stock Exchange symbol]
NMM .... Nuclear Materials Management
NMMA .... National Macaroni Manufacturers Association [Later, NPA] (EA)
NMMA .... National Maintenance Management Association [Defunct] (EA)
NMMA .... National Marine Manufacturers Association (EA)
NMMC .... National Adult Education Clearinghouse (NAEC)/National Multimedia Center for Adult Education [Information service or system Defunct] (IID)
NMMC .... National Marina Manufacturers Consortium [Defunct] (EA)
NmMeB .... Bent-Mescalero School Library, Mescalero, NM [Library symbol Library of Congress] (LCLS)
NMMFO .... Navy Maintenance Management Field Office
NMMFO(W)... Navy Maintenance Management Field Office (West) (DNAB)
NMMHMO.... Network and Mixed Model Health Maintenance Organization [Insurance] (WYGK)
NMMHOF..... National Mobile/Manufactured Home Owners Foundation [Later, NFMHO] (EA)
NMMI .... New Mexico Military Institute [Roswell] (MCD)
NMML .... National Marine Mammal Laboratory [National Marine Fisheries Service]
NMMLC .... New Moon Matchbox and Label Club (EA)
NMMM .... Navy Maintenance and Material Management System [Also known as MMM, NMMMS, 3M]
NMMMS ...... Navy Maintenance and Material Management System [Also known as MMM, NMMM, 3M]
NmMS .... Montezuma Seminary, Montezuma, NM [Library symbol Library of Congress] (LCLS)
NMMSB .... Non-Nuclear Munitions Safety Board
NMMSN .... National Marine Mammal Stranding Network (EA)
NMMSS .... Nuclear Materials Management and Safeguards System (NRCH)
NMMW .... Near Millimeter Wave System [Telecommunications] (TEL)
NMN .... Nicotinamide-Mononucleotide [Biochemistry]
NMN .... No Middle Name
NMN .... Normetanephrine [Also, Methylnorepinephrine] [Biochemistry]
NMN .... Normetanephrine [Biochemistry] (DAVI)
NMN .... NRD Mining Ltd. [Vancouver Stock Exchange symbol]
NMNA .... National Male Nurse Association [Later, AAMN] (EA)
NMNase ...... Nicotinamidenucleotide Phosphoribohydrolase [An enzyme]
NMND .... Naval Magazine and Net Depot
NMNFO .... Navy Maintenance Field Office (NVT)
NMNH .... National Museum of National History
NMNH .... National Museum of Natural History [Smithsonian Institution]
NMNRU .... Naval Medical Neuropsychiatric Research Unit
NMNS .... National Museum of Natural Sciences [National Museums of Canada] [Research center] (RCD)
NMO .... Long Beach, CA [Location identifier FAA] (FAAL)
NMO .... National Medical Organisation (ACII)
NMO .... National Mobility Office [British]
NMO .... Navy Management Office
NMO .... N-Methylmorpholine N-Oxide [Organic chemistry]
NMO .... Noble Mines & Oils Ltd. [Toronto Stock Exchange symbol]
NMO .... Normal Manual Operation (KSC)
NMO .... Normal Manual Operation

NMO	Normal Mode Operation
NMO	Norman [*Oklahoma*] [*Seismograph station code, US Geological Survey Closed*] (SEIS)
NMO	Number of Critical Micro-Operations [*Computer science*] (MHDI)
NMO	Nuveen Municipal Market Opportunities [*NYSE symbol*] (SPSG)
NMO	Nuveen Muni Mkt Oppt [*NYSE symbol*] (TTSB)
NMOA	National Mail Order Association [*Los Angeles, CA*] (EA)
NMOC	Non-Methane Organic Compound [*Environmental chemistry*]
NMOCOD	[*The*] Nonmateriel Objectives Coordinating Document [*Army*] (RDA)
NMOG	Non-Methane Organic Gas [*Organic chemistry*]
nmol	Nanomole [*One billionth of a mole*] (MAE)
NMoN	New York Ocean Science Laboratory, Montauk, NY [*Library symbol Library of Congress*] (LCLS)
NMONA.......	National Mail Order Nurserymen's Association [*Later, MAN*] (EA)
NMontr	Hendrick Hudson Free Library, Montrose, NY [*Library symbol Library of Congress*] (LCLS)
NMontrVA...	United States Veterans Administration Hospital, Montrose, NY [*Library symbol Library of Congress*] (LCLS)
NMOP	National Mission Operating Procedures (AAG)
NMOPI.........	Nuveen Missouri Premium Income Municipal Fund [*Associated Press*] (SAG)
NMOR	Nitrosomorpholine [*Also, NNM*] [*Organic chemistry*]
NMOS	Negative Channel Metal-Oxide Semiconductor
NMOS	Network Mission and Operations Support
NMOS	Nonvolatile Metal-Oxide Semiconductor (MCD)
NMOSAW.....	Naval and Military Order of the Spanish-American War (EA)
NMP	National Maintenance Point [*Military*] (AABC)
NMP	National Meter Programming (NRCH)
NMP	National Municipal Policy [*Environmental Protection Agency*] (EPA)
NMP	Naval Management Program
NMP	Naval Medical Publication
NMP	Naval Message Processing (MCD)
NMP	Navigational Microfilm Projector
NMP	Navy Manning Plan (NVT)
NMP	Nederlands Middenstands Partij [*Netherlands Middle Class Party*] [*Political party*] (PPE)
NMP	Net Material Product [*Economics*]
NMP	Network Management Protocol [*Computer science*] (TNIG)
NM/P	New Material/Process (MCD)
NMP	N-Methylphenazium [*Organic chemistry*]
NMP	N-Methylphthalimide [*Organic chemistry*]
NMP	N-Methylpyrrolidone [*Organic chemistry*]
NMP	Normal Menstrual Period [*Gynecology*] (MAE)
NMP	Not Machine Pressed
NMP	Nucleoside Monophosphate [*Biochemistry*]
NMP	Nuveen Michigan Premium Income Municipal [*NYSE symbol*] (SPSG)
NMP	Nuveen MI Prem Inc. Muni [*NYSE symbol*] (TTSB)
NmP	Portales Public Library, Portales, NM [*Library symbol Library of Congress*] (LCLS)
NMPA	National Motorsports Press Association (EA)
NMPA	National Music Publishers' Association (EA)
NMPA	NATO Maritime Patrol Aircraft (NATG)
NMPA	New Mexico Philatelic Association (EA)
NMPA	(Nitrosomethylamino) Propionic Acid [*Organic chemistry*]
NMPA	Nitrosomethylpropylamine [*Organic chemistry*]
NMPASC	NATO Maritime Patrol Aircraft Steering Committee (NATG)
NMPATA	National Music Printers and Allied Trades Association (EA)
NMPB	National Millinery Planning Board [*Defunct*] (EA)
NMPC	National Maintenance Publications Center [*Army*] (AABC)
NMPC	National Milk Publicity Council [*British*] (BI)
NMPC	National Minority Purchasing Council [*Later, NMSDC*] (EA)
NMPC	National Moratorium on Prison Construction [*Defunct*] (EA)
NMPC	Naval Military Personnel Command (ANA)
NMPC	NutraMax Products, Inc. [*NASDAQ symbol*] (SAG)
NMPCRECSREDIVREGOFF...	Naval Military Personnel Command, Recreational Services Division, Regional Office (DNAB)
NMPD	Nitromethylpropanediol [*Organic chemistry*]
NMPDN.......	National Materials Property Data Network (EA)
NmPE..........	Eastern New Mexico University, Portales, NM [*Library symbol Library of Congress*] (LCLS)
NMPF..........	National Milk Producers Federation (EA)
NMPF..........	Normal Magnitude Probability Function
NMPG.........	New Mexico Proving Ground [*Army*]
NMPIS	National Marine Pollution Information System [*Marine science*] (OSRA)
NMPIS	National Marine Pollution Information Systems (USDC)
NMPL.........	New Material Planning Letter (MCD)
NMPNC.......	Naval Medical Program for Nuclear Casualties
NMPNS.......	Nine Mile Point Nuclear Station (NRCH)
NMPO	Navy Motion Picture Office
NMPO	Nordic Master Painters' Organization (EA)
NMPP	Nautical Miles per Pound (MCD)
NMPP	Nouvelles Messageries de la Presse Parisienne [*Paris press distribution agency*]
NMPPO	National Marine Pollution Program Office (USDC)
NMPPO	National Marine Pollution Program Office [*Marine science*] (OSRA)
NMPS	Matritech, Inc. [*NASDAQ symbol*] (SAG)
NMPS	Nautical Miles per Second
NMPS..........	Navy Motion Picture Service
NMPSMOPIXDISTOFF...	Navy Motion Picture Service, Motion Picture Distribution Office (DNAB)
NMPTP	N-Methyl(phenyl)tetrahydropyridine [*Biochemistry*]
NMPX	Navy Motion Picture Exchange
NMQR	New Music Quarterly Review [*Record label*]
NMQUE........	Nocte Maneque [*Night and Morning*] [*Pharmacy*]
NMR	Centre for Nuclear Magnetic Resonance [*University of Warwick*] [*British*] (CB)
NMR	Nappamerrie [*Queensland*] [*Airport symbol*] (AD)
NMR	Natal Mounted Rifles [*British military*] (DMA)
NMR	National Military Representatives with SHAPE [*NATO*]
NMR	National Milk Record [*British*] (BI)
NMR	National Missile Range (KSC)
NMR	National Museum of Racing (EA)
NMR	Natural Magnetic Remanence [*Geophysics*]
NMR	Naval Medical Research Institute, Washington, DC [*OCLC symbol*] (OCLC)
NMR	Naval Missile Range
NMR	Navy Management Review [*A publication*]
NMR	Neomar Resources Ltd. [*Toronto Stock Exchange symbol*]
NMR	Neonatal Mortality Risk [*Medicine*]
NMR	New Material Release (MCD)
NMR	Nictitating Membrane Response [*Neurophysiology*]
NMR	N. M. De Rothschild & Co. [*Merchant bank*] [*British*]
NMR	NMR of America, Inc. [*Associated Press*] (SAG)
NMR	No Maintenance Requirement (NVT)
NMR	No Master Record [*Military*] (AFIT)
NMR	Nonconforming Material Report (MCD)
NMR	Normal Mode Rejection
NMR	Nuclear Magnetic Relaxation
NMR	Nuclear Magnetic Resonance [*Also, NUMAR*] [*Atomic physics*]
NmR	Roswell Carnegie Library, Roswell, NM [*Library symbol Library of Congress*] (LCLS)
NMR	San Juan, PR [*Location identifier FAA*] (FAAL)
NmRa	Arthur Johnson Memorial Library, Raton, NM [*Library symbol Library of Congress*] (LCLS)
NMRA	National Marine Representatives Association (EA)
NMRA	National Mine Rescue Association
NMRA	National Mobile Radio Association [*Defunct*] (EA)
NMRA	National Model Railroad Association (EA)
NMRA	National Motorcycle Racing Association (EA)
NMRA	National Motorcycle Retailers Association [*Defunct*] (EA)
NMRA	National Mud Racing Association
NMR & DA...	Navy Material Redistribution and Disposition Administration
NMR & DO...	Navy Material Redistribution and Disposal Office [*or Officer*]
NMRAS	Nuclear Material Report and Analysis System [*Energy Research and Development Administration*]
NMRB	National Mutual Royal Bank [*Australia*] (ADA)
NMRC	National Maritime Research Center [*Maritime Administration*] [*Also, an information service or system*] (IID)
NMRC	National Meat Retail Council [*Australia*]
NMRC	National Microelectronics Research Centre (NITA)
NMRC	Navy Material Redistribution Center
NMRC	Neuromuscular Research Center [*Boston University*]
NMRD	Nuclear Magnetic Relaxation Dispension [*Physics*]
NMRDC.......	Naval Medical Research and Development Command (MCD)
NmRE	Eastern New Mexico University, Roswell Campus, Roswell, NM [*Library symbol Library of Congress*] (LCLS)
NMREC	National Maritime Resource Center [*MARAD*] (TAG)
NM Reg	New Mexico Register [*A publication*] (AAGC)
NMRF	Navy-Marine Corps Residence Foundation (DNAB)
NMRG	Navy Mid-Range Guidance
NMRI	National Mass Retailing Institute [*New York, NY*] (EA)
NMRI	National Medical Research Institute (MAE)
NMRI	Naval Medical Research Institute
NMRI	Nuclear Magnetic Resonance Imaging
NMRL	Naval Medical Research Laboratory
NMRLIT	Nuclear Magnetic Resonance Literature System [*Chemical Information Systems, Inc.*] [*Information service or system*]
NmRM	New Mexico Military Institute, Roswell, NM [*Library symbol Library of Congress*] (LCLS)
NMRN	National Meteorological Rocket Network
NMRO	Navy Mid-Range Objectives
NMRP	National Migrant Resource Program (EA)
NMRP	Nuclear Magnetic Resonance Program
NMRR	NMR of America [*NASDAQ symbol*] (TTSB)
NMRR	NMR of America, Inc. [*NASDAQ symbol*] (NQ)
NMRR	Normal-Mode Rejection Ratio [*Electronics*] (BARN)
NMRS	National Mobile Radio System [*Later, Telocator Network of America*] (EA)
NMRS	Navy Manpower Requirements System (NVT)
NMRS	Numerous (FAAC)
NMRT	New Members Round Table [*American Library Association*]
NMRT	Nimbus Meteorological Radiation Tape [*NASA*]
NMRTC	Navy and Marine Corps Reserve Training Center
NMRU	Naval Medical Research Unit
NmRu	Ruidoso Public Library, Ruidoso, NM [*Library symbol Library of Congress*] (LCLS)
NMRX	Numerex Corp. [*NASDAQ symbol*] (SAG)
NMS............	Ancient Egyptian Arabic Order Nobles of the Mystic Shrine (EA)
NMS............	Namsang [*Myanmar*] [*Airport symbol*] (OAG)
NMS............	National Management Systems [*Information service or system*] (IID)
NMS............	National Maritime System [*MARAD*] (TAG)
NMS............	National Market System
NMS............	National Master Specification [*Construction Specifications Canada*] [*Information service or system*] (IID)
NMS............	National Measurement System [*National Institute of Standards and Technology*]
NMS............	National Medicine Society [*British*]
NMS............	National Military Strategy (DOMA)
NMS............	National Mobility Scheme [*British*]

NMS............. Natural Mortality Schedule [*Biology*]
NMS............. Naval Medical School (MCD)
NMS............. Naval Meteorological Service
NMS............. Navigation Management System (PDAA)
NMS............. Navy Mid-Range Study
NMS............. NetWare Management System [*Novell, Inc.*] (PCM)
NMS............. Network Management Services [*Ohio Bell Communications, Inc.*] [*Cleveland, OH*] [*Telecommunications*] (TSSD)
NMS............. Network Management Signal [*Telecommunications*] (TEL)
NMS............. Network Management System (DA)
NMS............. Network Measurement System [*Computer network*]
NMS............. Neuroleptic Malignant Syndrome
NMS............. Neuromuscular Stimulator [*Neurology*] (DAVI)
NMS............. Neuro-Musculo-Skeletal [*Medicine*]
NMS............. Neutral Mass Spectrometer [*Instrumentation*]
NMS............. Neutron Monitoring System [*Nuclear energy*] (NRCH)
NMS............. New Manning System [*Army*] (MCD)
NMS............. New Mexico State Library, Santa Fe, NM [*OCLC symbol*] (OCLC)
NMS............. New Mexico Statutes [*A publication*] (DLA)
NMS............. New Music Seminar
NMS............. New Music Society [*Australia*]
NMS............. Nitrogen Measuring System
NMS............. Noise Measuring Set [*Telecommunications*] (TEL)
NMS............. Nonmajor System (MCD)
NMS............. Nonmedical Science Category (DAVI)
NMS............. Non-Metric Multidimensional Scaling (PDAA)
NMS............. Nonprofit Management Strategies [*A publication*]
NMS............. Nordic Metalworkers Secretariat (EA)
NMS............. Normal Market Size Transaction
NMS............. Normal Mouse Serum
NMST............ Nuclear Materials Safeguards
NMS............. Nuclear-Powered Merchant Ship (PDAA)
NmS............. Santa Fe City and County Public Library, Santa Fe, NM [*Library symbol Library of Congress*] (LCLS)
NMSA .... National Metal Spinners Association (EA)
NMSA .... National Middle School Association (EA)
NMSA .... National Moving and Storage Association (EA)
NMSA .... New Mexico Statutes Annotated [*A publication*] (AAGC)
NMSA .... Nonnuclear Munitions Storage Area [*Air Force*] (DOMA)
NMSA .... Nonstandard Metropolitan Statistical Area
NMSA .... North Atlantic Treaty Organization [*NATO*] Mutual Support Act (AAGC)
NMSB .... Navy Manpower Survey Board
NMSB .... NewMil Bancorp [*NASDAQ symbol*] (TTSB)
NMSB .... New Milford Savings Bank [*NASDAQ symbol*] (NQ)
NmSC .... College of Santa Fe, Santa Fe, NM [*Library symbol Library of Congress*] (LCLS)
NMSC .... National Main Street Center (EA)
NMSC .... National Maple Syrup Council [*Later, NAMSC*]
NMSC .... National Merit Scholarship Corp. (EA)
NMSC .... Naval Medical Supply Unit (DNAB)
NMSC .... Navy Management Systems Center (PDAA)
NMSC .... Nerve and Muscle Stimulating Current
NMSC .... Nonmelanoma Skin Cancer [*Medicine*]
NMSC .... Non-Melanoma Skin Cancer
NMSC .... Non-Military Supplies Committee [*Combined Production and Resources Board*] [*British World War II*]
NMSC .... Northeast-Midwest Senate Coalition (EA)
NMSC .... Northwest Missouri State College [*Later, Northwest Missouri State University*]
NMSC .... Nutrition Management [*NASDAQ symbol*] (SAG)
NmSc........... Silver City Public Library, Silver City, NM [*Library symbol Library of Congress*] (LCLS)
NMSCA .... Navy Material Command Support Activity (PDAA)
NMSCA .... Nutrition Mgmt Svcs'A' [*NASDAQ symbol*] (TTSB)
NmSCS .... College of Santa Fe, Santa Fe, NM [*Library symbol*] [*Library of Congress*] (LCLS)
NmScSW ..... Southwestern Regional Library, Silver City, NM [*Library symbol Library of Congress*] (LCLS)
NMSCW ...... Nutrition Mgmt Svcs Wrrt [*NASDAQ symbol*] (TTSB)
NmScW........ Western New Mexico University, Silver City, NM [*Library symbol Library of Congress*] (LCLS)
NMSD .... National Match Support Detachment [*Ammunition supplier*]
NMSD .... National Military Strategy Document (DOMA)
NMSD .... Naval Medical Supply Depot
NMSD .... Next Most Significant Digit [*Computer science*]
NMSDC....... National Minority Supplier Development Council (EA)
NMSE........... Naval Material Support Establishment [*After 1966, NAVMAT, NMCOM, NMC*]
NMSHC .... Bureau of Medicine and Surgery Hospital Corps Publication [*Later, NAVMED*] [*Navy*]
NMSI .... National Mini-Storage Institute [*Defunct*] (EA)
NMSK .... Namesake (ABBR)
NMSL .... National Maximum Speed Limit [*NHTSA*] (TAG)
NmSM .... Museum of New Mexico, Santa Fe, NM [*Library symbol Library of Congress*] (LCLS)
NMSM .... New Mexico School of Mines (AAG)
NmSM-A...... Museum of New Mexico, Laboratory of Anthropology, Santa Fe, NM [*Library symbol Library of Congress*] (LCLS)
NMSMK ...... Numismatic (ABBR)
NMSMTST ... Numismaticist (ABBR)
NMSO .... NATO Maintenance and Support Operation (AFM)
NMSO .... Naval Manpower Survey Office (NVT)
NMSO .... N-Methylnitroanisole [*Organic chemistry*]
NMSO .... Nuclear Missile Safety Office [*or Officer*] (AFM)

NmSo........... Socorro Public Library, Socorro, NM [*Library symbol Library of Congress*] (LCLS)
NmSoI .... New Mexico Institute of Mining and Technology, Socorro, NM [*Library symbol Library of Congress*] (LCLS)
NmSP .... New Mexico State Penitentiary Library, Santa Fe, NM [*Library symbol Library of Congress*] (LCLS)
NMSP .... New Mon State Party [*Myanmar*] [*Political party*]
NMSP .... N-Methylspiperone [*Biochemistry*]
NmSp........... Springer Public Library, Springer, NM [*Library symbol Library of Congress*] (LCLS)
NmSpP .... Springer Public Library, Springer, NM [*Library symbol*] [*Library of Congress*] (LCLS)
NMSQT .... National Merit Scholarship Qualifying Test
NmSr .... Moise Memorial Library, Santa Rosa, NM [*Library symbol Library of Congress*] (LCLS)
NMSRA .... National Master Shoe Rebuilders Association (EA)
NMSRC .... National Middle School Resource Center (EA)
NMSS .... NASCOM [*Naval Air Systems Command*] Manual Scheduling System
NMSS .... National Meteorological Satellite System (IAA)
NMSS .... National Multiple Sclerosis Society (EA)
NMSS .... National Multipurpose Space Station
NMSS .... Natural Microsystems [*NASDAQ symbol*] (TTSB)
NMSS .... Natural Microsystems Corp. [*NASDAQ symbol*] (SAG)
NMSS .... Nemesis (ABBR)
NMSS .... Office of Nuclear Materials Safety and Safeguards [*Nuclear Regulatory Commission*]
NMSSA .... National Multiple Sclerosis Society of Australia
NMSSA .... NATO Maintenance Supply Service Agency [*Later, NAMSO*]
NMSSO .... Navy Maintenance and Supply Systems Office (DNAB)
NMSSS .... NATO Maintenance Supply Service System
NMSST .... Naval Manpower Shore Survey Team (NVT)
NmSStJ....... Saint John's College in Santa Fe, Santa Fe, NM [*Library symbol Library of Congress*] (LCLS)
NMST .... New Materials System Test [*Obsolete Nuclear energy*]
NM Stat Ann... New Mexico Statutes, Annotated [*A publication*] (DLA)
NMSU .... Naval Motion Study Unit [*British*]
NMSU .... New Mexico State University
NmSuAF...... United States Air Force, Sacramento Peak Observatory, Sunspot, NM [*Library symbol Library of Congress*] (LCLS)
NMSVA .... Navy Mail Service Veterans Association (EA)
NMSZ........... New Madrid Seismic Zone [*Geology*]
NMT............. Barrow, AK [*Location identifier FAA*] (FAAL)
NMT............. National Museum of Transport [*Later, TMA*] (EA)
NMT............. Neuromuscular Tension [*Medicine*]
NMT............. Neuromuscular Transmission [*Physiology*]
NMT............. New Mexico Institute of Mining and Technology, Socorro, NM [*OCLC symbol*] (OCLC)
NMT............. N-Monomethyltryptamine [*Organic chemistry*]
NMT............. N-Myristoyl Acyltransferase [*An enzyme*]
NMT............. Noble-Metal-Coated Titanium [*Anode*]
NMT............. No More Than [*Pharmacy*] (DAVI)
NMT............. No More Trouble [*Coates' brand of cotton thread*] (ROG)
NMT............. Nonmetalic [*Technical drawings*]
NMT............. Nordic Mobile Telephone [*Radio-telephone system for car users*] [*Denmark, Finland, Norway, Sweden*]
NMT............. Nordic Mobile Telephone Network (NITA)
NMT............. Northwest Marine Trade Association (EA)
NMT............. Norwegian Method of Tunnelling [*Civil engineering*]
NMT............. Notification of Master Tool (NASA)
NMT............. Not More Than
NMT............. Nuclear Medicine Technology
NMT............. Number of Module Types
NMT............. Nuveen MA Prem Inc. Muni Fd [*NYSE symbol*] (TTSB)
NMT............. Nuveen Massachusetts Premium Income Municipal Fund [*NYSE symbol*] (SPSG)
NMTA........... National Manpower Training Association [*Later, NETA*] (EA)
NMTA........... National Metal Trades Association [*Later, AAIM*] (EA)
NMTA........... National Movement Theatre Association (EA)
NMTBA .... National Machine Tool Builders' Association [*Later, AMT*] (EA)
NMTBD .... No More to Be Done [*Medicine*]
NMTC........... Naval Mine Testing Center (MCD)
NMTC........... Naval Missile Testing Center
NMTC........... North Metropolitan Tramways Co. [*British*] (ROG)
NMTC........... Nucleon-Meson Transport Code
NMTCB .... Nuclear Medicine Technology Certification Board (EA)
NMTD........... Nonmetastatic Trophoblastic Disease [*Medicine*] (DMAA)
NMTD........... Nuclear Materials Transfer Document
NMTF........... National Market Traders Federation [*British*] (DBA)
NMTF........... National Metal Traders Federation [*British*] (DBA)
NMTF........... Naval Mine Test Facility
NMTFA......... National Master Tile Fixers Association [*British*] (DBA)
NMTHC .... Nonmethane Total Hydrocarbons [*Organic chemistry*]
NmTHF........ Harwood Foundation, Taos, NM [*Library symbol Library of Congress*] (LCLS)
NMTI........... Nitinol Medical Technologies, Inc. [*NASDAQ symbol*] (SAG)
NMtK .... Mount Kisco Public Library, Mount Kisco, NY [*Library symbol Library of Congress*] (LCLS)
NmTKC........ Kit Carson Memorial Foundation, Inc., Taos, NM [*Library symbol Library of Congress*] (LCLS)
NMTLK .... Nonmetallic (ABBR)
NMTN .... National Music Theater Network (EA)
NMTO .... Navy Material Transportation Office
NMTP........... National Means Test Proposal
NMTR .... Nuclear Materials Transfer Report

NmTr	Truth Or Consequences Public Library, Truth Or Consequences, NM [*Library symbol Library of Congress*] (LCLS)
NMTS..........	National Milk Testing Service
NMTS..........	Navy Military Technical Specialist (MCD)
NMTS..........	Noise Measurement Test Set
NmTu..........	Tucumcari Public Library, Tucumcari, NM [*Library symbol Library of Congress*] (LCLS)
NmTuE........	Eastern Plains Regional Library, Tucumcari, NM [*Library symbol Library of Congress*] (LCLS)
NMtv	Mount Vernon Public Library, Mount Vernon, NY [*Library symbol Library of Congress*] (LCLS)
NMTX..........	Novametrics Medical Systems [*NASDAQ symbol*] (SAG)
NMTX..........	Novametrix Medical Systems, Inc. [*NASDAQ symbol*] (NQ)
NMTX..........	Novametrix Med Sys [*NASDAQ symbol*] (TTSB)
NMTXW	Novametrix Med Sys Wrt'A' [*NASDAQ symbol*] (TTSB)
NMTXZ.......	Novametrix Med Sys Wrrt'B' [*NASDAQ symbol*] (TTSB)
NMU	Brunswick, ME [*Location identifier FAA*] (FAAL)
NMU	National Maritime Union (USDC)
NMU	National Maritime Union of America (EA)
NMU	National Museums of Canada Library [*UTLAS symbol*]
NMU	Network Monitor Unit [*Telecommunications*] (TSSD)
NMU	Neuromuscular Unit [*Medicine*]
nmu	New Mexico [*MARC country of publication code Library of Congress*] (LCCP)
NMU	Nitrosomethylurea [*Also, MNU*] [*Organic chemistry*]
NMU	Nordic Musicians' Union (EA)
NMU	Northern Michigan University [*Marquette*]
NmU	University of New Mexico, Albuquerque, NM [*Library symbol Library of Congress*] (LCLS)
NMUC	National Medical Utilization Committee [*HEW*]
NmU-L	University of New Mexico, Law Library, Albuquerque, NM [*Library symbol Library of Congress*] (LCLS)
NmU-M	University of New Mexico, Library of the Medical Sciences, School of Medicine and Bernalillo County Medical Society, Albuquerque, NM [*Library symbol Library of Congress*] (LCLS)
NMuP..........	Muttontown Preserve, Muttontown, NY [*Library symbol Library of Congress*] (LCLS)
NMV	Nitrogen Manual Valve (MCD)
NMVCA	National Military Vehicle Collectors Association [*Defunct*]
NMVO	Navy Manpower Validation Office (DNAB)
NMVOC.......	Nonmethane Volatile Organic Carbon [*Environmental chemistry*]
NMVOLANT...	Navy Manpower Validation Office, Atlantic (DNAB)
NMVOPAC...	Navy Manpower Validation Office, Pacific (DNAB)
NMVP	Navy Manpower Validation Program (NG)
NMVSA	Navy Manpower Validation Support Activity
NMVSAC....	National Motor Vehicle Safety Advisory Council (EA)
NMVTA	National Motor Vehicle Theft Act
NMvUA	State University of New York, Agricultural and Technical College at Morrisville, Morrisville, NY [*Library symbol Library of Congress*] (LCLS)
NMW	Astoria, OR [*Location identifier FAA*] (FAAL)
NMW	Naval Mine Warfare (DOMA)
NMW	Normal Molecular Weight
NMW	Western Carolina University, Cullowhee, NC [*OCLC symbol*] (OCLC)
NMWA	National Military Wives Association [*Later, NMFA*] (EA)
NMWA	National Mineral Wool Association [*Later, MIMA*]
NMWC	National Migrant Workers Council [*Farmington Hills, MI*] (EA)
NMWC	Nelson, Marlborough, and West Coast Regiment [*British military*] (DMA)
NMWC	New Mexico Western College
NMWIA	National Mineral Wool Insulation Association [*Formerly, NMWA*] [*Later, MIMA*] (EA)
NMWL	Normal Molecular Weight, Low in Extractables
NmWM	White Sands Missile Range Library, White Sands Missile Range, NM [*Library symbol Library of Congress*] (LCLS)
NMWP	National Migrant Worker Program [*Department of Labor*]
NMWQL.......	National Marine Water Quality Laboratory [*Environmental Protection Agency*] (MSC)
NMWS	Naval Mine Warfare School
NMWTC	Naval Mine Warfare Training Center
NMWTS	Naval Mine Warfare Test Station
NMWTS	Naval Mine Warfare Training School
n-mx--	Mexico [*MARC geographic area code Library of Congress*] (LCCP)
NMxAr	New Mexico & Arizona Land Co. [*Associated Press*] (SAG)
NMxB..........	Board of Cooperative Educational Services, Regional Resource Center, Mexico, NY [*Library symbol Library of Congress*] (LCLS)
NMY...........	Mayville State College, Mayville, ND [*OCLC symbol*] (OCLC)
NMY...........	Nonresonant Magnetic Yoke
NMY...........	Nuveen Maryland Premium Income Municipal Fund [*NYSE symbol*] (SPSG)
NMY...........	Nuveen MD Prem Inc. Muni Fd [*NYSE symbol*] (TTSB)
NMyM..........	Maryknoll Fathers Seminary, Maryknoll, NY [*Library symbol Library of Congress*] (LCLS)
NMZ...........	Norman Resources Ltd. [*Vancouver Stock Exchange symbol*]
NMZ...........	Willow Grove, PA [*Location identifier FAA*] (FAAL)
NN	Air Trails [*ICAO designator*] (AD)
N:N	Azo Group [*Chemical group with two nitrogen atoms*] (MEDA)
nn	Footnotes (DLA)
NN	Names (ABBR)
NN	NASA Notice
NN	National Neighbors (EA)
NN	Natural, Nongrazed [*Agriculture*]
NN	Nearest Neighbor [*Mathematics*] [*Computer search term*]
NN	Necessary Nuisance [*i.e., a husband*] [*Slang*]
NN	Neonatal (DAVI)

NN	Nerves
nn	Nervi Nerves [*Neurology*] [*Latin*] (DAVI)
NN	Neurotics Nomine [*British*]
NN	Neutral and Nonaligned [*Nations*]
NN	Nevada Northern Railway Co. [*AAR code*]
NN	Newbridge Networks [*NYSE symbol*] (TTSB)
NN	Newbridge Networks, Inc. [*NYSE symbol*] (SAG)
nn	New Hebrides [*MARC country of publication code Library of Congress*] (LCCP)
NN	New Nationals [*Political party Australia*]
NN	Newspaper News [*A publication*]
NN	New York Public Library, New York, NY [*Library symbol Library of Congress*] (LCLS)
NN	Nicaragua Network (EA)
NN	Nigerian Navy
nn	Nomen Nescio [*Unknown*] [*Latin*] (GPO)
nn	Nomen Novum [*New Name*] [*Latin*] (DAVI)
NN	Nomina [*Names*] [*Latin*]
NN	No Name
NN	Non-Nuclear Lance (MCD)
NN	Noon
NN	Normalnull [*Mean Sea Level*] [*German*]
N/N	Normocytic/Normochromic Anemia (DAVI)
NN	Northampton [*Postcode*] (ODBW)
NN	Notes [*Finance*]
NN	Not Nested [*Freight*]
NN	Not Normal
N/N	Not North Of
N/N	Not to Be Noted [*Business term*]
NN	Nouns
NN	Nuclear Network (EA)
NN	Nucleon-Nucleon
N/N	Nurses' Notes (MAE)
NN	Nurturing Network [*An association*] (EA)
NNA	American Geographical Society, New York, NY [*Library symbol Library of Congress*] (LCLS)
NNA	Nana [*Peru*] [*Seismograph station code, US Geological Survey*] (SEIS)
NNA	National Neckwear Association (EA)
NNA	National Needlework Association (EA)
NNA	National Newman Apostolate
NNA	National News Agency [*Lebanon*]
NNA	National Newspaper Association (EA)
NNA	National Notary Association (EA)
NNA	National Notion Association [*Later, AHSA*] (EA)
NNA	National Numismatic Association (EA)
NNA	Neutral/Nonaligned [*Countries*]
NNA	New Nadina Explorations [*Vancouver Stock Exchange symbol*]
NNA	New Network Architecture
NNA	N-Nitrosamine [*Organic chemistry*]
NNA	Nonhistone Nucleoprotein Antibodies [*Immunochemistry*]
NNA	Normochromic, Normocytic Anemia (DAVI)
NNAA	Augusta Warshaw Advertising Library, New York, NY [*Library symbol Library of Congress*] (LCLS)
NNAA	National Newman Alumni Association [*Defunct*] (EA)
NNAA	Native North American Almanac [*A publication*]
NNAAI	American Alpine Club, New York, NY [*Library symbol Library of Congress*] (LCLS)
NNAAr.........	American Arbitration Association, New York, NY [*Library symbol Library of Congress*] (LCLS)
NNAB	American Bible Society, New York, NY [*Library symbol Library of Congress*] (LCLS)
NNABA........	American Bankers Association, New York, NY [*Library symbol Library of Congress*] (LCLS)
NNAC	National Native American Cooperative (EA)
NNAC	National Noise Abatement Council [*Defunct*]
NNACC........	National Native American Chamber of Commerce [*Defunct*] (EA)
NNACS........	American Cancer Society, New York, NY [*Library symbol Library of Congress*] (LCLS)
NNAD	Anti-Defamation League of B'nai B'rith, New York, NY [*Library symbol Library of Congress*] (LCLS)
NNADAP ...	National Native Alcohol and Drug Abuse Program [*Canada*]
NNAdv	American Association of Advertising Agencies, New York, NY [*Library symbol Library of Congress*] (LCLS)
NNAF	American Foundation for the Blind, New York, NY [*Library symbol Library of Congress*] (LCLS)
NNAFS	National Newman Association of Faculty and Staff [*Defunct*] (EA)
NNAG	American Gas Association, New York, NY [*Library symbol Library of Congress*] (LCLS)
NNAG	NATO Naval Advisory Group (NATG)
NNAG	NATO Naval Armaments Group (NATG)
NNAI	American Irish Historical Society, New York, NY [*Library symbol Library of Congress*] (LCLS)
NNAIA	American Institute of Certified Public Accountants, New York, NY [*Library symbol Library of Congress*] (LCLS)
NNAIAA.......	American Institute of Aeronautics and Astronautics, Technical Information Service, New York, NY [*Library symbol*] [*Library of Congress*] (LCLS)
NNAIL........	Austrain Institute Library, New York, NY [*Library symbol*] [*Library of Congress*] (LCLS)
NNAIP	American Institute of Physics, New York, NY [*Library symbol Library of Congress*] (LCLS)
NNAJ	American Jewish Committee, New York, NY [*Library symbol Library of Congress*] (LCLS)

NNAJN .... American Journal of Nursing Co., New York, NY [*Library symbol Library of Congress*] (LCLS)

NNAKC .... American Kennel Club, New York, NY [*Library symbol Library of Congress*] (LCLS)

NNAL .... American Academy of Arts and Letters, New York, NY [*Library symbol Library of Congress*] (LCLS)

NNAMA .... American Management Associations, New York, NY [*Library symbol Library of Congress*] (LCLS)

NNAMM .... American Merchant Marine Library Association, New York, NY [*Library symbol Library of Congress*] (LCLS)

NNAN .... American Numismatic Society, New York, NY [*Library symbol Library of Congress*] (LCLS)

NNAn .... Anthology Film Archives, New York, NY [*Library symbol Library of Congress*] (LCLS)

NNan .... Nanuet Public Library, Nanuet, NY [*Library symbol Library of Congress*] (LCLS)

NNAnF .... Anthology Film Archives, New York, NY [*Library symbol*] [*Library of Congress*] (LCLS)

NNanL .... Nanuet Public Library, Nanuet, NY [*Library symbol*] [*Library of Congress*] (LCLS)

NNAP .... NAVAIR [*Naval Air Systems Command*] Naval Aviation Plan (MCD)

NNAPS .... Night Navigation and Pilotage System

NNAPW .... National Network of Asian and Pacific Women (EA)

NNAS .... Neonatal Narcotic Abstinence Syndrome [*Medicine*] (DMAA)

NNASA .... American National Standards Institute, New York, NY [*Library symbol Library of Congress*] (LCLS)

NNASF .... American-Scandinavian Foundation, New York, NY [*Library symbol Library of Congress*] (LCLS)

NNASovM ..... American-Soviet Medical Society, New York, NY [*Library symbol Library of Congress Obsolete*] (LCLS)

NNASP .... American Society for Psychical Research, New York, NY [*Library symbol Library of Congress*] (LCLS)

NNAT .... American Telephone & Telegraph Co., Corporate Research Library, New York, NY [*Library symbol Library of Congress*] (LCLS)

NNAUR .... Australian Consulate-General, Australian Reference Library, New York, NY [*Library symbol*] [*Library of Congress*] (LCLS)

NNAuS .... National Audubon Society, New York, NY [*Library symbol Library of Congress*] (LCLS)

N/NAVEXOS... Navy/Executive Offices (AAG)

NNAVS .... Association for Voluntary Sterilization, Inc., International Project, New York, NY [*Library symbol Library of Congress*] (LCLS)

NNAW .... Native North American Writers [*A publication*]

NNAy .... American Home Products Corp., Ayerst Medical Library, New York, NY [*Library symbol Library of Congress*] (LCLS)

NNB .... Association of the Bar of the City of New York, New York, NY [*Library symbol Library of Congress*] (LCLS)

NNB .... National Needlecraft Bureau (EA)

NNB .... National News Bureau [*Commercial firm*] (EA)

NNB .... New Natura Brevium [*A publication*] (DSA)

NN-B .... New York Public Library, Albert A. and Henry W. Berg Collection, New York, NY [*Library symbol Library of Congress*] (LCLS)

NNb .... North Babylon Public Library, North Babylon, NY [*Library symbol Library of Congress*] (LCLS)

NNB .... Northumberland and Newcastle Board of Education [*UTLAS symbol*]

NNBa .... Barnard College, Columbia University, New York, NY [*Library symbol Library of Congress*] (LCLS)

NNBA .... National Nurses in Business Association (EA)

NN Ball .... NN Ball & Roller, Inc. [*Associated Press*] (SAG)

NNBBC .... Bernard M. Baruch College of the City University of New York, New York, NY [*Library symbol Library of Congress*] (LCLS)

NNbBE .... Belmont Elementary School, North Babylon, NY [*Library symbol*] [*Library of Congress*] (LCLS)

NNBC .... Bronx Community College, New York, NY [*Library symbol Library of Congress*] (LCLS)

NNBC .... National Network of Bilingual Centers (EA)

NNBCLA .... Negative Negabinary Carry-Look-Ahead Adder [*Computer science*] (MHDI)

NNbe .... North Bellmore Public Library, North Bellmore, NY [*Library symbol Library of Congress*] (LCLS)

NNbeDE .... Dinkelmeyer Elementary School, North Bellmore, NY [*Library symbol Library of Congress*] (LCLS)

NNbeGE .... Gunther Elementary School, North Bellmore, NY [*Library symbol Library of Congress*] (LCLS)

NNbeJJ .... Jerusalem Avenue Junior High School, North Bellmore, NY [*Library symbol*] [*Library of Congress*] (LCLS)

NNbeNE .... Newbridge Road Elementary School, North Bellmore, NY [*Library symbol*] [*Library of Congress*] (LCLS)

NNbePE .... Park Elementary School, North Bellmore, NY [*Library symbol Library of Congress*] (LCLS)

NNBeS .... Bentley School, New York, NY [*Library symbol Library of Congress*] (LCLS)

NNbeSME .... Saw Mill Elementary School, North Bellmore, NY [*Library symbol Library of Congress*] (LCLS)

NNBG .... New York Botanical Garden, Bronx, NY [*Library symbol Library of Congress*] (LCLS)

NNbHS .... North Babylon High School, North Babylon, NY [*Library symbol*] [*Library of Congress*] (LCLS)

NNBI .... Beth Israel Medical Center, New York, NY [*Library symbol Library of Congress*] (LCLS)

NNBIS .... National Narcotics Border Interdiction System

NNBL .... National Negro Business League [*Later, National Business League*]

NNbL .... North Babylon Public Library, North Babylon, NY [*Library symbol*] [*Library of Congress*] (LCLS)

NNbLE .... William E. De Luca Jr. Elementary School, North Babylon, NY [*Library symbol*] [*Library of Congress*] (LCLS)

NNBLI .... British Information Services, New York, NY [*Library symbol Library of Congress*] (LCLS)

NNBMC .... Borough of Manhattan Community College, New York, NY [*Library symbol Library of Congress*] (LCLS)

NNbMJ .... Robert Moses Junior High School, North Babylon, NY [*Library symbol*] [*Library of Congress*] (LCLS)

NNbPE .... Parliment Place Elementary School, North Babylon, NY [*Library symbol*] [*Library of Congress*] (LCLS)

NN-Br .... New York Public Library, Branch Library System, New York, NY [*Library symbol Library of Congress*] (LCLS)

NNBR .... NN Ball & Roller [*NASDAQ symbol*] (TTSB)

NNBR .... NN Ball & Roller, Inc. [*NASDAQ symbol*] (SAG)

NNBS .... Biblical Seminary in New York, New York, NY [*Library symbol Library of Congress*] (LCLS)

NNBSC .... Bank Street College of Education, New York, NY [*Library symbol Library of Congress*] (LCLS)

NNbWE .... Woods Road Elementary School, North Babylon, NY [*Library symbol*] [*Library of Congress*] (LCLS)

NNC .... Columbia University, New York, NY [*Library symbol Library of Congress*] (LCLS)

NNC .... Naga National Council [*India*] (PD)

NNC .... Natal Native Contingent [*British military*] (DMA)

NNC .... National Namibia Concerns (EA)

NNC .... National Neighborhood Coalition (EA)

NNC .... National Network Congestion Signal (NITA)

NNC .... National News Council (EA)

NNC .... National Nomad Club [*Defunct*] (EA)

NNC .... National Nuclear Corp. [*British*]

NNC .... National Nudist Council [*Defunct*] (EA)

NNC .... National Nutrition Consortium [*Defunct*] (EA)

NNC .... Navy Nurse Corps

NNC .... Neutral Nations Committee [*CINCPAC*] (CINC)

NN/C .... Night Noise Group C [*Aircraft*]

NNC .... Nolan, Norton & Co., Inc., Lexington, MA [*OCLC symbol*] (OCLC)

NNC .... Non-Noise Certificated Aircraft (DA)

NNC .... Northern Navigation Co. Ltd. [*AAR code*]

NNC .... Northwest Nazarene College [*Nampa, ID*]

NNC .... Notice of Noncompliance (EPA)

NNC .... Nuance (ABBR)

NNC .... Nudist National Committee (EA)

NNC .... Nuveen NC Prem Inc. Muni [*NYSE symbol*] (TTSB)

NNC .... Nuveen North Carolina Premium Income Municipal Fund [*NYSE symbol*] (SPSG)

NNC-A .... Columbia University, Avery Library of Architecture, New York, NY [*Library symbol Library of Congress*] (LCLS)

NNCA .... National Newman Chaplains Association [*Later, CCMA*] (EA)

NNCAA .... National Negro County Agents Association (EA)

NNCAM .... Cravath, Swaine & Moore, New York, NY [*Library symbol*] [*Library of Congress*] (LCLS)

NNCar .... Carnegie Corp. of New York, New York, NY [*Library symbol Library of Congress*] (LCLS)

NNCB .... [*The*] College Board, New York, NY [*Library symbol*] [*Library of Congress*] (LCLS)

NNC-B .... Columbia University, Biological Sciences Library, New York, NY [*Library symbol Library of Congress*] (LCLS)

NNC-BE .... Columbia University, Business-Economic Library, New York, NY [*Library symbol*] [*Library of Congress*] (LCLS)

NNCBN .... City Bank, North America, New York, NY [*Library symbol*] [*Library of Congress*] (LCLS)

NNCBS .... Columbia Broadcasting System, Inc., New York, NY [*Library symbol Library of Congress*] (LCLS)

NNCC .... Chemists' Club, New York, NY [*Library symbol Library of Congress*] (LCLS)

NNCC .... National Network Control Centre [*Communications*] [*British*]

NNCC .... National Nursing Consultative Committee [*Australia*]

NNCC .... Navy Nurse Corps Candidate (DNAB)

NNCCA .... Canadian Centre for Architecture, New York, NY [*Library symbol*] [*Library of Congress*] (LCLS)

NNCCG .... Canadian Consulate General Library, New York, NY [*Library symbol*] [*Library of Congress*] (LCLS)

NNCCVTE .... National Network for Curriculum Coordination in Vocational and Technical Education (OICC)

NNCE .... Carnegie Endowment for International Peace, New York, NY [*Library symbol Library of Congress*] (LCLS)

NNC-EA .... Columbia University, East Asiatic Library, New York, NY [*Library symbol Library of Congress*] (LCLS)

NNCEF .... Child Education Foundation, New York, NY [*Library symbol Library of Congress Obsolete*] (LCLS)

NNCenC .... Century Association, New York, NY [*Library symbol Library of Congress*] (LCLS)

NNCEP .... Centro de Estudios Puertorriquenos, New York, NY [*Library symbol Library of Congress*] (LCLS)

NNCF .... Commonwealth Fund, New York, NY [*Library symbol Library of Congress*] (LCLS)

NNCF .... National Newman Club Federation [*Defunct*] (EA)

NNCFo .... Council on Foundations, New York, NY [*Library symbol Library of Congress*] (LCLS)

NNCFR .... Council on Foreign Relations, New York, NY [*Library symbol Library of Congress*] (LCLS)

NNC-G .... Columbia University, Lamont-Doherty Geological Observatory, Palisades, NY [*Library symbol Library of Congress*] (LCLS)

NNCG .... Norwegian Consulate General, New York, NY [*Library symbol*] [*Library of Congress*] (LCLS)

NNCh .... Chadbourne & Parke, New York, NY [*Library symbol*] [*Library of Congress*] (LCLS)

NNCl	College of Insurance, New York, NY [*Library symbol Library of Congress*] (LCLS)
NNCit	Cities Service Co., Corporate Library, New York, NY [*Library symbol Library of Congress*] (LCLS)
NNC-L	Columbia University, Law Library, New York, NY [*Library symbol Library of Congress*] (LCLS)
NNC-M	Columbia University, Medical Library, New York, NY [*Library symbol Library of Congress*] (LCLS)
NNCN	Northern Nigeria Case Notes [*A publication*] (DLA)
NNCo	Collectors Club, New York, NY [*Library symbol Library of Congress*] (LCLS)
NNcoM	Moore-Cottrell Subscription Agencies, Inc., North Cohocton, NY [*Library symbol Library of Congress*] (LCLS)
NNConE	Consolidated Edison Co., Inc., New York, NY [*Library symbol Library of Congress*] (LCLS)
NNCoo	Cooper Union for the Advancement of Science and Art, New York, NY [*Library symbol Library of Congress*] (LCLS)
NNCorI	Cornell University, New York State School of Industrial and Labor Relations, Sanford V. Lenz Library, New York, NY [*Library symbol*] [*Library of Congress*] (LCLS)
NNCorM	Cornell University, Medical College, New York, NY [*Library symbol Library of Congress*] (LCLS)
NNCorM-A	New York Hospital-Cornell Medical Center Archives, New York, NY [*Library symbol*] [*Library of Congress*] (LCLS)
NNCorM-D	Cornell University, Medical College, Oskar Diethelm Historical Library, New York, NY [*Library symbol*] [*Library of Congress*] (LCLS)
NNCorM-D	Cornell University, Medical College, Oskar Diethelm Historical Library, New York, NY [*Library symbol Library of Congress*] (LCLS)
NNC-P	Columbia University, College of Pharmacy, New York, NY [*Library symbol Library of Congress*] (LCLS)
NNCP	Pfizer, Inc., New York, NY [*Library symbol Library of Congress*] (LCLS)
NNCPI	Nuveen North Carolina Premium Income Municipal Fund [*Associated Press*] (SAG)
NNCPL	College of Police Science, New York, NY [*Library symbol Library of Congress*] (LCLS)
NNCPM	New York College of Podiatric Medicine, New York, NY [*Library symbol Library of Congress*] (LCLS)
NNC-Pop	Columbia University, International Institute for the Study of Human Reproduction, Center for Population and Family Health, New York, NY [*Library symbol Library of Congress*] (LCLS)
NNC-Ps	Columbia University, Psychology Library, New York, NY [*Library symbol Library of Congress*] (LCLS)
NNcR	Roberts Wesleyan College, North Chili, NY [*Library symbol Library of Congress*] (LCLS)
NNCre	Creedmore Psychiatric Center, Queens Village, New York, NY [*Library symbol Library of Congress*] (LCLS)
NNCS	Child Study Association of America, New York, NY [*Library symbol Library of Congress*] (LCLS)
NNCSC	National Neutron Cross Section Center [*AEC*] (MCD)
NNC-T	Columbia University, Teachers College, New York, NY [*Library symbol Library of Congress*] (LCLS)
NNC-Typ	Columbia University, American Typefounders' Library, New York, NY [*Library symbol Library of Congress*] (LCLS)
NNCU-C	City University of New York, Central Office, New York, NY [*Library symbol*] [*Library of Congress*] (LCLS)
NNCU-G	City University of New York, Graduate Center, New York, NY [*Library symbol Library of Congress*] (LCLS)
NNCU-L	City University of New York, Law School, Flushing, NY [*Library symbol Library of Congress*] (LCLS)
NNCU-T	City University of New York, Division of Teacher Education, New York, NY [*Library symbol Library of Congress*] (LCLS)
NND	Dover Publications, New York, NY [*Library symbol Library of Congress*] (LCLS)
NND	National Network Dialing [*Telecommunications*] (TEL)
NND	National Number Dialing [*Telecommunications*] (DCTA)
NND	Naval Net Depot
NND	Neo-Natal Death [*Medicine*]
NND	New and Nonofficial Drugs [*AMA*]
NNDC	National Naval Dental Center
NNDC	National New Democratic Coalition (EA)
NNDC	National Nuclear Data Center [*Department of Energy*] [*Database producer*] (IID)
NNDCG	Danish Consulate General, Reference Library, New York, NY [*Library symbol*] [*Library of Congress*] (LCLS)
NNDE	Nearest-Neighbor Distance Error [*Algorithm*]
NNDP	Debevoise & Plimpton, New York, NY [*Library symbol*] [*Library of Congress*] (LCLS)
NNDP	Naga National Democratic Party [*India*] [*Political party*] (PPW)
NNDPA	N-Nitrosodiphenylamine [*Organic chemistry*]
NNDPW	Davis, Polk & Wardwell, Law Library, New York, NY [*Library symbol Library of Congress*] (LCLS)
NNDR	National Non-Domestic Rate [*British*]
NNDSS	National Notification Disease Surveillance System [*Centers for Disease Control*]
NNDTC	National Nondestructive Testing Centre [*Atomic Energy Authority*] [*Information service or system*] (IID)
NNE	Engineering Societies Library, New York, NY [*Library symbol Library of Congress*] (LCLS)
NNE	Neonatal Necrotizing Enterocolitis [*Medicine*] (AAMN)
NNE	Noise and Number Exposure (PDAA)
NNE	Nonneuron-Specific Enolase [*An enzyme*]
NNE	Nonstandard Negro English

NNE	North-Northeast
NNEA	National Negro Evangelical Association [*Later, NBEA*]
NNEB	National Nursery Examination Board
NNebg	Newburgh Free Library, Newburgh, NY [*Library symbol Library of Congress*] (LCLS)
NNebgE	Epiphany Apostolic College, Newburgh, NY [*Library symbol Library of Congress*] (LCLS)
NNebgL	Ninth Judicial District Law Library, Newburgh, NY [*Library symbol Library of Congress*] (LCLS)
NNebgM	Mount Saint Mary College, Newburgh, NY [*Library symbol*] [*Library of Congress*] (LCLS)
NNebgWM	Washington's Headquarters Museum, Newburgh, NY [*Library symbol*] [*Library of Congress*] (LCLS)
NNEC	Explorers Club, New York, NY [*Library symbol Library of Congress*] (LCLS)
NNec	New City Free Library, New City, NY [*Library symbol Library of Congress*] (LCLS)
NNECA	National Network of Episcopal Clergy Associations (EA)
NNECH	National Nutrition Education Clearing House [*Society for Nutrition Education*] (IID)
NnecL	New City Free Library, New City, NY [*Library symbol*] [*Library of Congress*] (LCLS)
NNEF	Educational Film Library Association, New York, NY [*Library symbol Library of Congress*] (LCLS)
NNef	Newfane Public Library, Newfane, NY [*Library symbol Library of Congress*] (LCLS)
NNefH	Inter-Community Memorial Hospital, Newfane, NY [*Library symbol Library of Congress*] (LCLS)
NNefL	Newfane Free Library, Newfane, NY [*Library symbol*] [*Library of Congress*] (LCLS)
NNegbM	Mount St. Mary College, Newburgh, NY [*Library symbol Library of Congress*] (LCLS)
NNegbWM	Washington's Headquarters Museum, Newburgh, NY [*Library symbol Library of Congress*] (LCLS)
NNehpHH	Herricks High School, New Hyde Park, NY [*Library symbol Library of Congress*] (LCLS)
NNEL	Equitable Life Assurance Society of the United States, Medical Library, New York, NY [*Library symbol Library of Congress*] (LCLS)
NNEL-M	Equitable Life Assurance Society of the United States, Medical Library, New York, NY [*Library symbol Library of Congress*] (LCLS)
NNepa	Elting Memorial Library, New Paltz, NY [*Library symbol Library of Congress*] (LCLS)
NNepaSU	State University of New York, College at New Paltz, New Paltz, NY [*Library symbol Library of Congress*] (LCLS)
NNer	New Rochelle Public Library, New Rochelle, NY [*Library symbol Library of Congress*] (LCLS)
NNerAIS	United States Army, Information School, Fort Slocum, New Rochelle, NY [*Library symbol Library of Congress*] (LCLS)
NNerC	College of New Rochelle, New Rochelle, NY [*Library symbol Library of Congress*] (LCLS)
NNerI	Iona College, New Rochelle, NY [*Library symbol Library of Congress*] (LCLS)
NNES	National Nuclear Energy Series [*of AEC-sponsored books*]
NNEU	Naval Nuclear Evaluation Unit
NNEW	Ernst & Whinney, Audit Management Services, New York, NY [*Library symbol Library of Congress*] (LCLS)
NNEWD	North-Northeastward (FAAC)
NNEXF	Newscope Resources Ltd. [*NASDAQ symbol*] (SAG)
NNF	Fordham University, New York, NY [*Library symbol Library of Congress*] (LCLS)
NNF	Namibia National Front [*Political party*] (PPW)
NNF	National Nephrosis Foundation [*Later, NKF*]
NNF	National Neurofibromatosis Foundation (PAZ)
NNF	National Newman Foundation [*Defunct*] (EA)
NNF	National Newspaper Foundation (EA)
NNF	National Nothing Foundation [*Defunct*] (EA)
NNF	Nordisk Neurokirurgisk Forening [*Scandinavian Neurosurgical Society - SNS*] (EAIO)
NNF	Nordisk Neurologisk Forening [*Scandinavian Neurological Association - SNA*] (EAIO)
NNF	Northern Nurses Federation [*Norway*]
NNF	Nuveen Ins. NY Prem Inc. Muni [*NYSE symbol*] (TTSB)
NNF	Nuveen Insured New York Premium Income Municipal [*NYSE symbol*] (SPSG)
NNFA	National Nutritional Foods Association (EA)
NNFB	Ford, Bacon & Davis, Inc., New York, NY [*Library symbol Library of Congress*] (LCLS)
NNFBC	First Boston Corporation, New York, NY [*Library symbol Library of Congress*] (LCLS)
NNFC	Finch College, New York, NY [*Library symbol Library of Congress*] (LCLS)
NNFE	Free Europe Committee, New York, NY [*Library symbol Library of Congress*] (LCLS)
NNFF	Ford Foundation, New York, NY [*Library symbol Library of Congress*] (LCLS)
NNFF	National Neurofibromatosis Foundation (EA)
NNFF	Not Nested or Folded Flat [*Freight*]
NNFF-FL	Ford Foundation, Ford Foundation Library, New York, NY [*Library symbol Library of Congress*] (LCLS)
NNFFu	Franklin Furnance Archives, New York, NY [*Library symbol*] [*Library of Congress*] (LCLS)
NNFI	French Institute/Alliance Francaise, New York, NY [*Library symbol Library of Congress*] (LCLS)

NNFIT .... Fashion Institute of Technology, New York, NY [*Library symbol Library of Congress*] (LCLS)

NNF-L .... Fordham University, Law Library, New York, NY [*Library symbol Library of Congress*] (LCLS)

NNFL .... Religious Society of Friends [*Quakers*], New York, NY [*Library symbol Library of Congress*] (LCLS)

NNF-LC .... Fordham University, Library at Lincoln Center, New York, NY [*Library symbol Library of Congress*] (LCLS)

NNFM .... Grand Lodge of New York, F & AM Library and Museum, New York, NY [*Library symbol Library of Congress*] (LCLS)

NNFoC .... Foundation Center Library, New York, NY [*Library symbol Library of Congress*] (LCLS)

NNFoM .... Forbes Magazine, Inc., New York, NY [*Library symbol Library of Congress*] (LCLS)

NNFP .... Nuclear Nitrogen Fixation Plant

NNFr .... Frick Art Reference Library, New York, NY [*Library symbol Library of Congress*] (LCLS)

NNF-RS .... Fordham University, Institute of Contemporary Russian Studies, New York, NY [*Library symbol Library of Congress*] (LCLS)

NNFS .... Nordic Narrow/16mm Film Society (EA)

NNFT .... National Federation of Textiles, New York, NY [*Library symbol Library of Congress*] (LCLS)

NNFU .... Nuclear Nonfirst Use

NNG .... General Theological Seminary of the Protestant Episcopal Church, New York, NY [*Library symbol Library of Congress*] (LCLS)

NNG .... Nanning [*China*] [*Airport symbol*] (OAG)

NNG .... National Network of Grantmakers (EA)

NNG .... National Number Group (NITA)

NNGA .... Northern Nut Growers Association (EA)

NNGBSW ..... National Network of Graduate Business School Women [*Knoxville, TN*] (EA)

NNGI .... National Aeronautics and Space Administration, Goddard Institute for Space Studies, New York, NY [*Library symbol*] [*Library of Congress*] (LCLS)

NNGoe .... Goethe House, German Cultural Institute, New York, NY [*Library symbol Library of Congress*] (LCLS)

NNGr .... Grolier Club, New York, NY [*Library symbol Library of Congress*] (LCLS)

NNGS .... Church of Jesus Christ of Latter-Day Saints, Genealogical Society Library, New York Branch, New York, NY [*Library symbol Library of Congress*] (LCLS)

NNGu .... Solomon R. Guggenheim Museum, New York, NY [*Library symbol Library of Congress*] (LCLS)

NNH .... Hispanic Society of America, New York, NY [*Library symbol Library of Congress*] (LCLS)

NNH .... Natal Native Horse [*British military*] (DMA)

NNH .... National Humanities Center, Research Triangle Park, NC [*OCLC symbol*] (OCLC)

NNH .... Nordiska Namnden for Handikappfragor [*Nordic Committee on Disability - NCD*] [*Sweden*] (EAIO)

NNHA .... National Novice Hockey Association [*Later, HNA*] (EA)

NNHC .... Hostos Community College, New York, NY [*Library symbol Library of Congress*] (LCLS)

NNHC .... Natal Native High Court Reports [*1899-1915*] [*South Africa*] [*A publication*] (DLA)

NNHCF-C ..... Holy Cross Friary, Juniper Carol Library, New York, NY [*Library symbol Library of Congress*] (LCLS)

NNHE .... New York City Board of Higher Education, New York, NY [*Library symbol Library of Congress*] (LCLS)

NNHeb .... Hebrew Union College - Jewish Institute of Religion, New York, NY [*Library symbol Library of Congress*] (LCLS)

NNHH .... Harlem Hospital Center, Medical Library, New York, NY [*Library symbol Library of Congress*] (LCLS)

NNHHR .... Hughes, Hubbard & Reed, New York, NY [*Library symbol*] [*Library of Congress*] (LCLS)

NNHL .... National Novice Hockey League [*Later, NNHA*] (EA)

NNHol .... Holland Society of New York, New York, NY [*Library symbol Library of Congress*] (LCLS)

NNHor .... Horticultural Society of New York, Inc., New York, NY [*Library symbol Library of Congress*] (LCLS)

NNhp .... New Hyde Park Public Library, New Hyde Park, NY [*Library symbol Library of Congress*] (LCLS)

NNhpDE .... Denton Avenue Elementary School, New Hyde Park, NY [*Library symbol*] [*Library of Congress*] (LCLS)

NNhpGE .... Garden City Park School, New Hyde Park, NY [*Library symbol*] [*Library of Congress*] (LCLS)

NNhpH .... Hillside Public Library, New Hyde Park, NY [*Library symbol Library of Congress*] (LCLS)

NNhpHE .... Hillside Grade School, New Hyde Park, NY [*Library symbol*] [*Library of Congress*] (LCLS)

NNhpHH .... Herricks High School, New Hyde Park, NY [*Library symbol*] [*Library of Congress*] (LCLS)

NNhpJ .... Long Island Jewish Hospital, New Hyde Park, NY [*Library symbol Library of Congress*] (LCLS)

NNhpME .... Manor-Oaks-William R. Bowie School, New Hyde Park, NY [*Library symbol*] [*Library of Congress*] (LCLS)

NNhpMH ...... New Hyde Park Memorial High School, New Hyde Park, NY [*Library symbol*] [*Library of Congress*] (LCLS)

NNhpNE .... New Hyde Park Road School, New Hyde Park, NY [*Library symbol*] [*Library of Congress*] (LCLS)

NNHR .... New York City Human Resources Administration, New York, NY [*Library symbol Library of Congress*] (LCLS)

NNHS .... Hospital for Special Surgery, New York, NY [*Library symbol Library of Congress*] (LCLS)

NNHS .... National Nursing Home Survey [*Department of Health and Human Services*] (GFGA)

NNhS .... Special Metals Corp., New Hartford, NY [*Library symbol Library of Congress*] (LCLS)

NNHuC .... Hunter College of the City University of New York, New York, NY [*Library symbol Library of Congress*] (LCLS)

NNHWW ...... H.W. Wilson Co., Bronx, NY [*Library symbol*] [*Library of Congress*] (LCLS)

NNI .... National Newspaper Index [*Information Access Co.*] [*Bibliographic database*] [*Information service or system*] (IID)

NNI .... Net National Income [*Economics*]

NNI .... Net-Net Income [*Business term*]

NNI .... Network Node Interface [*Computer science*]

NNI .... New Nickerie [*Surinam*] [*Airport symbol*] (AD)

NNI .... Noise and Number Index

NNI .... Noise Nuisance Index (PDAA)

NNI .... Nonnuclear Instrumentation (NRCH)

NNI .... Nucleon-Nucleon Interaction

NNI .... Office of Naval Intelligence Publications

NNIA .... American Institute of Aeronautics and Astronautics, New York, NY [*Library symbol Library of Congress*] (LCLS)

NNia .... Niagara Falls Public Library, Niagara Falls, NY [*Library symbol Library of Congress*] (LCLS)

NNiaA .... Airco Speer Research & Development Laboratories, Niagara Falls, NY [*Library symbol Library of Congress*] (LCLS)

NNiaB .... Bell Aerospace Textron, Technical Library, Niagara Falls, NY [*Library symbol Library of Congress*] (LCLS)

NNiaC .... Niagara County Community College, Niagara Falls, NY [*Library symbol Library of Congress*] (LCLS)

NNiaCa .... Carborundum Co., Niagara Falls, NY [*Library symbol Library of Congress*] (LCLS)

NNiaD .... E. I. Du Pont de Nemours & Co., Electrochemical Department, Niagara Falls, NY [*Library symbol Library of Congress*] (LCLS)

NNiaEM .... Elkem Metals Co., Niagara Falls, NY [*Library symbol Library of Congress*] (LCLS)

NNiaH .... Hooker Chemical Corp. [*Later, Hooker Chemicals & Plastics Corp.*], Niagara Falls, NY [*Library symbol Library of Congress*] (LCLS)

NNiaHC .... Hooker Chemicals & Plastics Corp., Business Library, Niagara Falls, NY [*Library symbol Library of Congress*] (LCLS)

NNiaM .... Moore Business Forms, Niagara Falls, NY [*Library symbol Library of Congress*] (LCLS)

NNiaMed ..... Niagara Falls Memorial Medical Center, Medical Library, Niagara Falls, NY [*Library symbol Library of Congress*] (LCLS)

NNiaN .... National Lead Co., Research Library, Niagara Falls, NY [*Library symbol Library of Congress*] (LCLS)

NNiaNC .... NIACET Corporation, Niagara Falls, NY [*Library symbol Library of Congress*] (LCLS)

NNiaNL .... Nioga Library System, Niagara Falls, NY [*Library symbol Library of Congress*] (LCLS)

NNiaO .... Occidental Chemical Corp., Technical Information Center, Niagara Falls, NY [*Library symbol*] [*Library of Congress*] (LCLS)

NNiaSE .... Sohio Engineered Materials Co., Research and Development Library, Niagara Falls, NY [*Library symbol*] [*Library of Congress*] (LCLS)

NNiaTC .... TAM Ceramics, Inc., Niagara Falls, NY [*Library symbol Library of Congress*] (LCLS)

NNiaTV .... Trott Vocational High School, Niagara Falls, NY [*Library symbol Library of Congress*] (LCLS)

NNiaU .... Niagara University, Niagara University, NY [*Library symbol Library of Congress*] (LCLS)

NNiaUC .... Union Carbide Corp., Niagara Falls, NY [*Library symbol Library of Congress*] (LCLS)

NNICC .... National Narcotics Intelligence Consumers Committee [*Drug Enforcement Administration*] [*Washington, DC*] (EGAO)

NNIIC .... Istituto Italiano Di Cultura Biblioteca, New York, NY [*Library symbol*] [*Library of Congress*] (LCLS)

NNIIE .... Institute of International Education, New York, NY [*Library symbol Library of Congress*] (LCLS)

NNIMD .... Institute for Muscle Disease, New York, NY [*Library symbol Library of Congress Obsolete*] (LCLS)

NNIND .... International Nickel Co., Technical Library, New York, NY [*Library symbol Library of Congress*] (LCLS)

NNInS .... Insurance Society of New York, New York, NY [*Library symbol Library of Congress*] (LCLS)

NNIP .... Institute of Public Administration, New York, NY [*Library symbol Library of Congress*] (LCLS)

NNIPF .... International Planned Parenthood Federation, Documentation and Publications Center, New York, NY [*Library symbol Library of Congress*] (LCLS)

NNIR .... Industrial Relations Counselors, New York, NY [*Library symbol Library of Congress*] (LCLS)

NNIRR .... National Network for Immigrant and Refugee Rights (EA)

NNIS .... Library for Intercultural Studies, Inc., New York, NY [*Library symbol Library of Congress*] (LCLS)

NNIS .... National Nosocomial Infections Surveillance [*Medicine*]

NNIS .... Nonnuclear Instrumentation System (NRCH)

NNISS .... Nosocomial Infections Surveillance System [*Center for Disease Control*]

NNJ .... Jewish Theological Seminary of America, New York, NY [*Library symbol Library of Congress*] (LCLS)

NNJ .... Nakano [*Japan*] [*Seismograph station code, US Geological Survey*] (SEIS)

NNJ .... Nuveen New Jersey Premium Income Municipal [*NYSE symbol*] (SPSG)

NNJ .... Nuveen NJ Prem Inc. Muni [*NYSE symbol*] (TTSB)

NNJef.......... Jefferson School of Social Science, New York, NY [*Library symbol Library of Congress Obsolete*] (LCLS)

NNJH .... Joint Health Library, New York, NY [*Library symbol Library of Congress Obsolete*] (LCLS)

NNJHK .... Jenny Hunter's Kindergarten and Primary Training School, New York, NY [*Library symbol Library of Congress Obsolete*] (LCLS)

NNJJ .... John Jay College of Criminal Justice, New York, NY [*Library symbol Library of Congress*] (LCLS)

NNJS .... Japan Society Library, New York, NY [*Library symbol*] [*Library of Congress*] (LCLS)

NNJu............ Juilliard School of Music, New York, NY [*Library symbol Library of Congress*] (LCLS)

NNK .... Naknek [*Alaska*] [*Airport symbol*] (OAG)

NNK .... Nic-Nik Resources [*Vancouver Stock Exchange symbol*]

NNK .... Nonnuclear Kill

NNKRAS ..... Non-Nuclear Kill Requirements and Applications Study [*Military*]

NNL .... Beeville, TX [*Location identifier FAA*] (FAAL)

NNL .... Herbert H. Lehman College of the City University of New York, New York, NY [*Library symbol Library of Congress*] (LCLS)

NN-L .... New York Public Library, Research Library for the Performing Arts at Lincoln Center, New York, NY [*Library symbol Library of Congress*] (LCLS)

NNL .... Ninilchik [*Alaska*] [*Seismograph station code, US Geological Survey*] (SEIS)

NNL .... Nondalton [*Alaska*] [*Airport symbol*] (OAG)

NNL .... No Net Loss

NNL .... Non-Nuclear Lance Missile (PDAA)

NNLBI .... Leo Baeck Institute, New York, NY [*Library symbol Library of Congress*] (LCLS)

NNLC .... Lutheran Council in the USA, New York, NY [*Library symbol Library of Congress*] (LCLS)

NNLC .... Ngwane National Liberatory Congress [*Swaziland*]

NNLDA .... National Network of Learning Disabled Adults (EA)

NNLehman... Lehman Corp., New York, NY [*Library symbol Library of Congress*] (LCLS)

NNLH .... Lenox Hill Hospital, Medical Library, New York, NY [*Library symbol Library of Congress*] (LCLS)

NNLI .... New York Law Institute, New York, NY [*Library symbol Library of Congress*] (LCLS)

NNLM .... National Network of Libraries of Medicine

NNLN .... Northern Nigeria Legal Notes [*A publication*] (DLA)

NNLR .... Law Reprints, New York, NY [*Library symbol*] [*Library of Congress*] (LCLS)

NNLR .... Northern Nigeria Law Reports [*A publication*] (DLA)

NNLS .... New York Law School Library, New York, NY [*Library symbol Library of Congress*] (LCLS)

NNM .... American Museum of Natural History, New York, NY [*Library symbol Library of Congress*] (LCLS)

NNM .... Davidson College, Davidson, NC [*OCLC symbol*] (OCLC)

NN-M .... New York Public Library, Municipal Reference Library, New York, NY [*Library symbol Library of Congress*] (LCLS)

NNM .... Next (or Nearest) New Moon [*Freemasonry*] (ROG)

NNM .... Nicolle-Novy-MacNeal [*Medium*] [*Microbiology*] (DAVI)

NNM .... N-Nitrosomorpholine [*Also, NMOR*] [*Organic chemistry*]

NNM .... No Neutral Mode

NNm .... North Merrick Public Library, North Merrick, NY [*Library symbol Library of Congress*] (LCLS)

NNM .... Nuveen New York Municipal Income [*AMEX symbol*] (SPSG)

NNMa .... Marymount Manhattan College, New York, NY [*Library symbol Library of Congress*] (LCLS)

NNMAI .... Museum of the American Indian, New York, NY [*Library symbol Library of Congress*] (LCLS)

NNMan .... Manhattan College, New York, NY [*Library symbol Library of Congress*] (LCLS)

NNMB .... Methodist Board of Missions, New York, NY [*Library symbol Library of Congress*] (LCLS)

NNmBJ .... Brookside Junior High School, North Merrick, NY [*Library symbol*] [*Library of Congress*] (LCLS)

NNMC .... Mannes College of Music, New York, NY [*Library symbol Library of Congress*] (LCLS)

NNMC .... National Naval Medical Center [*Bethesda, MD*]

NNmCE .... Camp Avenue Elementary School, North Merrick, NY [*Library symbol*] [*Library of Congress*] (LCLS)

NNMcGraw... McGraw-Hill, Inc., New York, NY [*Library symbol Library of Congress*] (LCLS)

NNME .... Mid-European Studies Center, New York, NY [*Library symbol Library of Congress*] (LCLS)

NNMec......... General Society of Mechanics and Tradesmen, New York, NY [*Library symbol Library of Congress*] (LCLS)

NNMel .... Andrew W. Mellon Foundation, New York, NY [*Library symbol Library of Congress*] (LCLS)

NN-Mel........ New York Public Library, Mellon Microfilm Collection, New York, NY [*Library symbol Library of Congress*] (LCLS)

NNMer......... Mercantile Library Association, New York, NY [*Library symbol Library of Congress*] (LCLS)

NNMF .... Markle Foundation, New York, NY [*Library symbol Library of Congress*] (LCLS)

NNmFE .... Harold D. Fayette Elementary School, North Merrick, NY [*Library symbol*] [*Library of Congress*] (LCLS)

NNMH.......... Montefiore Hospital, New York, NY [*Library symbol Library of Congress*] (LCLS)

NNMi .... Millenium Film Workshop, New York, NY [*Library symbol Library of Congress*] (LCLS)

NNML .... Metropolitan Life Insurance Co., New York, NY [*Library symbol Library of Congress*] (LCLS)

NNMLC .... Medical Library Center of New York, New York, NY [*Library symbol Library of Congress*] (LCLS)

NNMM .... Metropolitan Museum of Art, New York, NY [*Library symbol Library of Congress*] (LCLS)

NNMMA ...... Museum of Modern Art, New York, NY [*Library symbol Library of Congress*] (LCLS)

NNMMA-F... Museum of Modern Art, Film Study Center, New York, NY [*Library symbol Library of Congress*] (LCLS)

NNMMA-U ... Metropolitian Museum of Art, Uris Library and Resources Center, New York, NY [*Library symbol*] [*Library of Congress*] (LCLS)

NNMM-C.... Metropolitan Museum of Art, The Cloisters Library, New York, NY [*Library symbol*] [*Library of Congress*] (LCLS)

NNMM-CI.... Metropolitan Museum of Art, Costume Institute, New York, NY [*Library symbol Library of Congress*] (LCLS)

NNmN.......... North Merrick Public Library, North Merrick, NY [*Library symbol*] [*Library of Congress*] (LCLS)

NNMO .... Mobil Oil Corp., Secretariat Library, New York, NY [*Library symbol*] [*Library of Congress*] (LCLS)

NnmOE .... Old Mill Road Elementary School, North Merrick, NY [*Library symbol*] [*Library of Congress*] (LCLS)

NNMoMA .... Museum of Modern Art, New York, NY [*Library symbol Library of Congress*] (LCLS)

NNMP .... Motion Picture Association of America, Inc., Research Department Library, New York, NY [*Library symbol Library of Congress*] (LCLS)

NNMPA........ Museum of Primitive Art, New York, NY [*Library symbol Library of Congress*] (LCLS)

NNmPE .... Park Avenue Elementary School, North Merrick, NY [*Library symbol*] [*Library of Congress*] (LCLS)

NN-MPH ..... New York Public Library, Public Health Division, New York, NY [*Library symbol Library of Congress*] (LCLS)

NNMR.......... Missionary Research Library, New York, NY [*Library symbol Library of Congress*] (LCLS)

NNMRR .... New York Metropolitan Reference and Research Library Agency, Inc., New York, NY [*Library symbol Library of Congress*] (LCLS)

NNMS .... Manhattan State Hospital, New York, NY [*Library symbol Library of Congress*] (LCLS)

NNMS .... National Nutrition-Monitoring System [*Department of Agriculture*] (GFGA)

NNMSB .... Nazareth National Motor Speedway [*Pennsylvania*]

NNMSB .... Nonnuclear Munitions Safety Board [*Military*]

NNMSCP...... Nonnuclear Munitions Safety Control Program [*Military*]

NNMSG .... Nonnuclear Munitions Safety Group [*Air Force*] (AFM)

NNMSGP...... Nonnuclear Munitions Safety Group [*Air Force*]

NNMSK .... Memorial Sloan-Kettering Cancer Center, New York, NY [*Library symbol Library of Congress*] (LCLS)

NNMSM ...... Manhattan School of Music, New York, NY [*Library symbol Library of Congress*] (LCLS)

NNMtS .... Mount Sinai Hospital, New York, NY [*Library symbol Library of Congress*] (LCLS)

NNMtSM ..... Mount Sinai School of Medicine of the City University of New York, New York, NY [*Library symbol Library of Congress*] (LCLS)

NNMtSV ...... College of Mount Saint Vincent, New York, NY [*Library symbol Library of Congress*] (LCLS)

NNMus......... Museum of the City of New York, New York, NY [*Library symbol Library of Congress*] (LCLS)

NNN .... Commercial Net Lease Realty, Inc. [*NYSE symbol*] (SAG)

NNN .... Commercial Net Lease Rlty [*NYSE symbol*] (TTSB)

NNN .... Nannies Need Nannies Association [*British*] (DBA)

NNN .... National Navy Notice

NNN .... National Nostalgic Nova (EA)

NNN .... Next Nearest Neighbor [*Chemical physics*]

NNN .... Nicolle-Novy-MacNeal [*Medium*] [*Medicine*] (MEDA)

NNN .... Nitrosonornicotine [*Organic chemistry*]

NNN .... N-Nitrosonornicotine [*Organic chemistry*]

NNN .... No National Name

NNN .... No No Nanette [*Broadway musical*]

NNN .... Noramco Mining Corp. [*Toronto Stock Exchange symbol Vancouver Stock Exchange symbol*]

NNN .... Novy, MacNeal, and Nicolle's Medium [*Medicine*] (MAE)

NNNA .... No Name, No Address

NNNAM .... New York Academy of Medicine, New York, NY [*Library symbol Library of Congress*] (LCLS)

NNNASA ...... National Aeronautical and Space Administration, Institute for Space Studies, NewYork, NY [*Library symbol Library of Congress*] (LCLS)

NNNBC......... National Broadcasting Co., Inc., General Library, New York, NY [*Library symbol Library of Congress*] (LCLS)

NNNBC-I ...... National Broadcasting Co., Inc., Information Unit, Research Department, New York, NY [*Library symbol Library of Congress*] (LCLS)

NNNC.......... New York Chamber of Commerce, New York, NY [*Library symbol Library of Congress*] (LCLS)

NNNCC-Ar.... New York County Clerk Archives, Division of Old Records, New York, NY [*Library symbol*] [*Library of Congress*] (LCLS)

NNNCL......... New York County Lawyers Association, New York, NY [*Library symbol Library of Congress*] (LCLS)

NNNCR .... National Council for Resources on Women, New York, NY [*Library symbol*] [*Library of Congress*] (LCLS)

NNNDO .... Neglect of Non-Neighbor Differential Overlap [*Physics*]

NNNDR .... Narcotic and Drug Research, Inc., New York, NY [*Library symbol*] [*Library of Congress*] (LCLS)

NNNel.......... Netherlands Information Service, New York, NY [*Library symbol Library of Congress*] (LCLS)

NNNGB .... New York Genealogical and Biographical Society, New York, NY [*Library symbol Library of Congress*] (LCLS)

NNNH .... National Health Agencies Library, New York, NY [*Library symbol Library of Congress Obsolete*] (LCLS)

NNNHi .... Naval History Society, New York, NY [*Library symbol Library of Congress Obsolete*] (LCLS)

NNNM .... New York Medical College, Flower and Fifth Avenue Hospitals, New York, NY [*Library symbol Library of Congress*] (LCLS)

NNNMCA ...... New Museum of Contemporary Art, New York, NY [*Library symbol*] [*Library of Congress*] (LCLS)

NNNPsan ..... New York Psychoanalytic Institute, New York, NY [*Library symbol Library of Congress*] (LCLS)

NNNPSC .... National No-Nukes Prison Support Collective (EA)

NNNPsI .... New York State Department of Mental Hygiene, Psychiatric Institute, New York, NY [*Library symbol Library of Congress*] (LCLS)

NNNS .... New School for Social Research, New York, NY [*Library symbol Library of Congress*] (LCLS)

NNNSB .... National Society for the Prevention of Blindness, New York, NY [*Library symbol Library of Congress*] (LCLS)

NNNT .... New York Theological Seminary, New York, NY [*Library symbol Library of Congress*] (LCLS)

NNNTSH ...... Naukove Tovarystvo Imeni Shevchenka (Shevchenko Scientific Society, Inc.), New York, NY [*Library symbol Library of Congress*] (LCLS)

NNNWA .... N. W. Ayer & Son, New York, NY [*Library symbol Library of Congress*] (LCLS)

NNO .... Naga Nationalist Organization [*India*]

NNO .... No New Orders [*Medical Records*] (DAVI)

NNO .... Nord-Nord-Ouest [*North-Northwest*] [*French*]

NNO .... Northern Orion Explorations [*Vancouver Stock Exchange symbol*]

NNOA .... National Naval Officers Association (EA)

NNOC .... National Network Operations Center [*Ottawa, ON*] [*Telecommunications*] (TSSD)

NNomAE ...... Albany Avenue Elementary School, North Massapequa, NY [*Library symbol*] [*Library of Congress*] (LCLS)

NNomEE ...... Eastplain Elementary School, North Massapequa, NY [*Library symbol*] [*Library of Congress*] (LCLS)

NNomPH ...... Plainedge High School, North Massapequa, NY [*Library symbol*] [*Library of Congress*] (LCLS)

NNomPJ ...... Sylvia Packard Junior High School, North Massapequa, NY [*Library symbol*] [*Library of Congress*] (LCLS)

NNOPE .... Naturists and Nudists Opposing Pornographic Exploitation (EA)

NNopo .... Northport Public Library, Northport, NY [*Library symbol Library of Congress*] (LCLS)

NNopo-E ...... Northport Public Library, East Northport Branch, East Northport, NY [*Library symbol Library of Congress*] (LCLS)

NNopoHS ..... Northport High School, Northport, NY [*Library symbol*] [*Library of Congress*] (LCLS)

NNopoJH ..... Northport Junior High School, Northport, NY [*Library symbol*] [*Library of Congress*] (LCLS)

NNopoVA ..... United States Veterans Administration Hospital, Northport, NY [*Library symbol Library of Congress*] (LCLS)

NNOR .... Nonnuclear Ordnance Requirement (MCD)

NNorP .... Norwich Pharmacal Co., Norwich, NY [*Library symbol Library of Congress*] (LCLS)

nNOS .... Neuronal Nitric Oxide Synthase [*An enzyme*]

NNosCE .... Sea Cliff Elementary School, North Shore, NY [*Library symbol*] [*Library of Congress*] (LCLS)

NnosJH .... North Shore Junior High School, North Shore, NY [*Library symbol*] [*Library of Congress*] (LCLS)

NNosSH .... North Shore Senior High School, North Shore, NY [*Library symbol*] [*Library of Congress*] (LCLS)

NNOt .... New York Orthopaedic Hospital, New York, NY [*Library symbol Library of Congress*] (LCLS)

NNot .... North Tonawanda Public Library, North Tonawanda, NY [*Library symbol Library of Congress*] (LCLS)

NNotD .... DeGraff Memorial Hospital, North Tonawanda, NY [*Library symbol Library of Congress*] (LCLS)

NNotHC .... Hooker Chemicals & Plastics Corp., Durez Division Library, North Tonawanda, NY [*Library symbol Library of Congress*] (LCLS)

NNotL .... Lawless Container Corp., North Tonawanda, NY [*Library symbol Library of Congress*] (LCLS)

NNotP .... North Tonawanda Public Library, North Tonawanda, NY [*Library symbol*] [*Library of Congress*] (LCLS)

n nov .... Nomen Novum [*New Name*] [*Latin*] [*Pharmacy*] (DAVI)

N NOV .... Nomen Novum [*New Name*] [*Latin*] (BABM)

NNP .... Needle-Nosed Probe

NNP .... Negative Node Point

NNP .... Neonatal Nurse Practitioner (DAVI)

NNP .... Nerve Net Pulse [*Neurobiology*]

NNP .... Net National Product [*Economics*]

NNP .... Nuveen New York Performance Plus Municipal [*NYSE symbol*] (SPSG)

NNP .... Nuveen NY Perform Plus Muni [*NYSE symbol*] (TTSB)

NNPA .... National Negro Press Association [*Defunct*] (EA)

NNPA .... National Newspaper Promotion Association [*Later, INPA*] (EA)

NNPA .... National Newspaper Publishers Association (EA)

NNPA .... Nuclear Nonproliferation Act [*1975*]

NNPA .... Port Authority of New York and New Jersey, New York, NY [*Library symbol Library of Congress*] (LCLS)

NNParS .... Parsons School of Design, New York, NY [*Library symbol Library of Congress*] (LCLS)

NNPaul .... Paul, Weiss, Rifkind, Wharton & Garrison, Law Library, New York, NY [*Library symbol Library of Congress*] (LCLS)

NNPaW .... Payne Whitney Clinic, New York, NY [*Library symbol Library of Congress*] (LCLS)

NNPC .... Nigerian National Petroleum Corp. (ECON)

NNPC .... Pace College, New York, NY [*Library symbol Library of Congress*] (LCLS)

NNPC-L .... Pace University, Law Library, White Plains, NY [*Library symbol Library of Congress*] (LCLS)

NNPE-NC ...... National Council of the Protestant Episcopal Church, New York, NY [*Library symbol Library of Congress*] (LCLS)

NNPennie .... Pennie, Edmonds, Morton, Taylor & Adams, New York, NY [*Library symbol Library of Congress*] (LCLS)

NNPf .... Carl H. Pforzheimer Library, New York, NY [*Library symbol Library of Congress*] (LCLS)

NNPH-O .... Institute of Ophthalmology, Presbyterian Hospital, New York, NY [*Library symbol Library of Congress*] (LCLS)

NNPHR .... New York City Public Health Research Laboratory, New York, NY [*Library symbol Library of Congress*] (LCLS)

NNPHW .... National New Professional Health Workers [*Later, NPSAPHA*] (EA)

NNPI .... Naval Nuclear Propulsion Information (MCD)

NNPIA .... Polish Institute of Art and Sciences in America, Inc., Research Library, New York, NY [*Library symbol*] [*Library of Congress*] (LCLS)

NNPlan .... Planning Assistance, Inc., New York, NY [*Library symbol Library of Congress*] (LCLS)

NNPM .... Pierpont Morgan Library, New York, NY [*Library symbol Library of Congress*] (LCLS)

NNPopC .... Population Council, New York, NY [*Library symbol Library of Congress*] (LCLS)

NNPPFA .... Planned Parenthood Federation of America, Inc., Katharine Dexter McCormick Library, New York, NY [*Library symbol Library of Congress*] (LCLS)

NNPPNYC .... Planned Parenthood of New York City, Inc., Abraham Stone Memorial Library, Margaret Sanger Center, New York, NY [*Library symbol Library of Congress*] (LCLS)

NNPRM .... United Presbyterian Mission Library of the United Presbyterian Church in the USA, New York, NY [*Library symbol Library of Congress*] (LCLS)

NNPS .... Navy Nuclear Power School (DNAB)

NNPS .... Norco Nuclear Power Station (NRCH)

NNPSPP .... National Non-Point Source Pollution Program (GNE)

NNPTU .... Naval Nuclear Power Training Unit (DNAB)

NNPU .... Naval Nuclear Power Unit [*Obsolete*]

NNR .... City College of City University of New York, New York, NY [*Library symbol Library of Congress*] (LCLS)

NNR .... National Nature Reserve [*British*]

NNR .... National Number Routed [*Telecommunications*] (TEL)

NNR .... Nearest-Neighbor Rule [*Mathematics*]

NNR .... Nevada North Resources [*Vancouver Stock Exchange symbol*]

NNR .... New and Nonofficial Remedies [*A publication*]

NNR .... Nordiska Nykterhetsradet [*Nordic Temperance Council - NTC*] (EAIO)

NNR .... Northern NORAD [*North American Air Defense*] Region (SAA)

NNRA .... National Negro Republican Assembly [*Defunct*]

NNRB .... National Neurological Research Bank [*Veterans Administration Medical Center*] [*Research center*] (RCD)

NNRB .... Recording for the Blind, Inc., New York, NY [*Library symbol Library of Congress*] (LCLS)

NNRDC .... National Nuclear Rocket Development Center [*Also known as NRDS*]

NNRDF .... National Nuclear Rocket Development Facility (AAG)

NNRecA .... National Recreation Association [*Later, NRPA*], New York, NY [*Library symbol Library of Congress*] (LCLS)

NNreP .... Regional Plan Association, Inc., Library, New York, NY [*Library symbol Library of Congress*] (LCLS)

NNRF .... National Neurological Research Foundation (EA)

NNRG .... Nevada Energy Co., Inc. [*NASDAQ symbol*] (SAG)

NNRGA .... Nevada Energy [*NASDAQ symbol*] (TTSB)

NNRH .... Roosevelt Hospital, Medical Library, New York, NY [*Library symbol Library of Congress*] (LCLS)

NNRIS .... Nebraska Natural Resources Information System [*Nebraska State Natural Resources Commission*] [*Lincoln*] [*Information service or system*] (IID)

NNRo .... Theodore Roosevelt Association, New York, NY [*Library symbol Library of Congress*] (LCLS)

NNRocF .... Rockefeller Foundation, New York, NY [*Library symbol Library of Congress*] (LCLS)

NNRocFA ..... Rockefeller Family & Associates, Inc., Office Library, New York, NY [*Library symbol Library of Congress*] (LCLS)

NNRoI .... Rochdale Institute, New York, NY [*Library symbol Library of Congress*] (LCLS)

NNRom .... Romanian Library, New York, NY [*Library symbol Library of Congress*] (LCLS)

NNRRB .... R. R. Bowker Co., New York, NY [*Library symbol Library of Congress*] (LCLS)

NNRT .... Non-Nucleoside Reverse Transcriptase [*Biochemistry*]

NNRT .... Racquet and Tennis Club, New York, NY [*Library symbol Library of Congress*] (LCLS)

NNRTI .... Non-Nucleoside Reverse Transcriptase Inhibitor [*Biochemistry*]

NNRU .... Rockefeller University, New York, NY [*Library symbol Library of Congress*] (LCLS)

NNRU-P .... Rockefeller University, Population Council, Bio-Medical Library, New York, NY [*Library symbol Library of Congress*] (LCLS)

NNRY .... Nunnery (ABBR)

NNRYS .... National Network of Runaway and Youth Services (EA)

NNS .... National Narrowcast Service [*Public Broadcasting Service*] [*Arlington, VA*] [*Telecommunications service*] (TSSD)

NNS .... National Natality Survey

NNS	National Network Services (NITA)
NNS	National Newspaper Syndicate
NNS	Navy Navigation Satellite
NNS	Navy News Service (DOMA)
NNS	Neonatal Society [*British*] (DBA)
NNS	Neural Network Simulator
NNS	Newhouse News Service (WDMC)
NNS	Newport News Shipbuilding (DOMA)
NNS	New York Society Library, New York, NY [*Library symbol Library of Congress*] (LCLS)
NNS	Non-Native Speakers (EDAC)
NNS	Nonnuclear Safety (NRCH)
NNS	Nonnutritive Sweetener
NNS	Norfolk Naval Shipyard [*Portsmouth, VA*] (MCD)
NNs	North Salem Free Library, North Salem, NY [*Library symbol Library of Congress*] (LCLS)
NNS	Nucleon-Nucleon Scattering
NNSA	National Nurses Society on Addictions (EA)
NNSaB	Salomon Brothers, New York, NY [*Library symbol Library of Congress*] (LCLS)
NNSAE	Society of Automotive Engineers, New York, NY [*Library symbol Library of Congress*] (LCLS)
NNSAR	Sons of the American Revolution, Empire State Society Library, New York, NY [*Library symbol Library of Congress*] (LCLS)
NNSAS	Skadden, Arps, Slate, Meagher & Flom, New York, NY [*Library symbol Library of Congress*] (LCLS)
NNSB	Simmons-Boardman Publishing Corp., New York, NY [*Library symbol Library of Congress Obsolete*] (LCLS)
NNSB & DDCO	Newport News Shipbuilding & Dry Dock Co. (DNAB)
NNSC	Neutral Nations Supervisory Commission
NN-Sc	New York Public Library, Schomburg Collection, New York, NY [*Library symbol Library of Congress*] (LCLS)
NNSC	NSF [*National Science*] Network Service Center [*Internet*] (TNIG)
NNSC	Smithsonian Institution, Cooper-Hewitt Museum of Decorative Arts and Design, NewYork, NY [*Library symbol*] [*Library of Congress*] (LCLS)
NNSeag	Joseph E. Seagram & Sons, Inc., New York, NY [*Library symbol Library of Congress*] (LCLS)
NNSG	NASCOM [*NASA Communications Network*] Network Scheduling Group
NNShA	Shubert Archive, New York, NY [*Library symbol*] [*Library of Congress*] (LCLS)
NNSIHi	Staten Island Historical Society, New York, NY [*Library symbol Library of Congress*] (LCLS)
NNSII	Staten Island Institute of Arts and Sciences, New York, NY [*Library symbol Library of Congress*] (LCLS)
NNSIS	Swedish Information Service, New York, NY [*Library symbol*] [*Library of Congress*] (LCLS)
NNSJD	Cathedral of Saint John the Divine, New York, NY [*Library symbol Library of Congress*] (LCLS)
NNSN	No National Stock Number (AABC)
NNSNP	National Network in Solidarity with the Nicaraguan People (EA)
NNSPG	National Network in Solidarity with the People of Guatemala (EA)
NNSPo	Standard & Poor's Corp., New York, NY [*Library symbol Library of Congress*] (LCLS)
NNSR	Sons of the Revolution in the State of New York, New York, NY [*Library symbol Library of Congress*] (LCLS)
NNSS	Navy Navigational Satellite System
NNSS	Shearman & Sterling Library, New York, NY [*Library symbol*] [*Library of Congress*] (LCLS)
NNSSS	South Street Seaport Museum, New York, NY [*Library symbol*] [*Library of Congress*] (LCLS)
NNSTB	Simpson, Thacher & Bartlett, Law Library, New York, NY [*Library symbol*] [*Library of Congress*] (LCLS)
NNStJ	St. John's University, Jamaica, NY [*Library symbol Library of Congress*] (LCLS)
NNStL	Saint Luke's Hospital, Richard Walker Bolling Memorial Medical Library, New York, NY [*Library symbol Library of Congress*] (LCLS)
NNStOD	Standard Oil Co. (New Jersey), New York, NY [*Library symbol Library of Congress*] (LCLS)
NNSTWG	Nonnuclear Survivability Technology Working Group (AFIT)
NNSU-MC	State University of New York, Maritime College, Fort Schuyler, Bronx, NY [*Library symbol Library of Congress*] (LCLS)
NNSU-Op	State University of New York, College of Optometry, New York, NY [*Library symbol Library of Congress*] (LCLS)
NNSW	Nonnuclear Strategic Warfare
NNSWM	National Network for Social Work Managers (EA)
NNSY	Norfolk Naval Shipyard [*Portsmouth, VA*]
NNT	Nan [*Thailand*] [*Airport symbol*] (OAG)
NNT	Nanotec Canada, Inc. [*Vancouver Stock Exchange symbol*]
NNT	Nearest Neighbor Tool [*Mathematical technique*] (USDC)
NNT	Nearest Neighbor Tool [*Mathematical method*] [*Marine science*] (OSRA)
NNT	New York Times, New York, NY [*Library symbol Library of Congress*] (LCLS)
NNT	Notice Number Tracking (MCD)
NNT	Number Needed to Treat
NNTAICH	Technical Assistance Information Clearing House, New York, NY [*Library symbol Library of Congress*] (LCLS)
NNTax	Tax Foundation, Inc., New York, NY [*Library symbol Library of Congress*] (LCLS)
NNTC	National Nondestructive Testing Centre [*Atomic Energy Authority*] [*Information service or system*] (IID)
NNTC	Norwich and Norfolk Terrier Club (EA)

NNTC	Teachers College, New York, NY [*Library symbol Library of Congress*] (LCLS)
NNTEP	Northern Nigeria Teacher Education Project [*University of Wisconsin*] (AEBS)
NNTF	Traphagen School of Fashion, New York, NY [*Library symbol Library of Congress*] (LCLS)
NNTIA	Teachers Insurance and Annuity Association of America, New York, NY [*Library symbol*] [*Library of Congress*] (LCLS)
NNTM	Tobacco Merchants Association of the United States, New York, NY [*Library symbol Library of Congress*] (LCLS)
NNTN	Not Necessarily the News [*Cable television comedy program*]
NNTP	National Nuclear Test Plan [*Later, NNTRP*]
NNTP	Network News Transport Protocol [*Telecommunications*]
NNTRP	National Nuclear Test Readiness Program [*Formerly, NNTP*]
NNTT	National New Technology Telescope [*Proposed*] [*National Science Foundation*]
NNttR	Rockefeller Archive Center, Rockefeller University, North Tarrytown, NY [*Library symbol*] [*Library of Congress*] (LCLS)
NNU	Nanuque [*Brazil*] [*Airport symbol*] (AD)
NNU	Net Nitrogen Utilization [*Medicine*] (DAVI)
NNU	New York University, New York, NY [*Library symbol Library of Congress*] (LCLS)
NNU	Nordic Numismatic Union (EAIO)
NNU-B	New York University, Graduate School of Business Administration, New York, NY [*Library symbol Library of Congress*] (LCLS)
NNU-C	New York University, School of Commerce, New York, NY [*Library symbol Library of Congress*] (LCLS)
NNU-D	New York University, College of Dentistry, New York, NY [*Library symbol Library of Congress*] (LCLS)
NNU-ES	New York University, Engineering and Science Library, New York, NY [*Library symbol Library of Congress*] (LCLS)
NNU-F	New York University, Fales Collection, New York, NY [*Library symbol Library of Congress*] (LCLS)
NNU-FA	New York University, Institute of Fine Arts, New York, NY [*Library symbol Library of Congress*] (LCLS)
NNU-G	New York University, Wall Street Library, New York, NY [*Library symbol Library of Congress*] (LCLS)
NNU-H	New York University, University Heights Library, Bronn, NY [*Library symbol Library of Congress*] (LCLS)
NNUH	United Hospital Fund of New York, New York, NY [*Library symbol Library of Congress*] (LCLS)
NNU-IEM	New York University, Institute of Environmental Medicine, Tuxedo Park, NY [*Library symbol Library of Congress*] (LCLS)
NNU-L	New York University, School of Law, New York, NY [*Library symbol Library of Congress*] (LCLS)
NNU-LA	New York University, Fobert F. Wagner Labor Archives, New York Labor Records Survey, New York,NY [*Library symbol*] [*Library of Congress*] (LCLS)
NNU-M	New York University, Medical Center, New York, NY [*Library symbol Library of Congress*] (LCLS)
NNUN	United Nations Library, New York, NY [*Library symbol Library of Congress*] (LCLS)
NNUnC	University Club, New York, NY [*Library symbol Library of Congress*] (LCLS)
NNUN-CF	United Nations Childrens Fund, New York, NY [*Library symbol Library of Congress*] (LCLS)
NNUni	Unipub, Inc., New York, NY [*Library symbol Library of Congress*] (LCLS)
NNUnionC	Union Club, New York, NY [*Library symbol Library of Congress*] (LCLS)
NNUnionL	Union League Club, New York, NY [*Library symbol Library of Congress*] (LCLS)
NNUN-PA	United Nations Fund for Population Activities, New York, NY [*Library symbol Library of Congress*] (LCLS)
NNUN-W	United Nations, Woodrow Wilson Memorial Library, New York, NY [*Library symbol Library of Congress*] (LCLS)
NNU-T	New York University, Tamiment Library, New York, NY [*Library symbol Library of Congress*] (LCLS)
NNUT	Union Theological Seminary, New York, NY [*Library symbol Library of Congress*] (LCLS)
NNUT-Mc	Union Theological Seminary, McAlpin Collection, New York, NY [*Library symbol Library of Congress*] (LCLS)
NNUVAN	Ukrainian Academy of Arts and Sciences in the United States, New York, NY [*Library symbol Library of Congress*] (LCLS)
NNUVE	Nonnegative Unbiased Variance Estimator [*Statistics*]
NNU-W	New York University, Washington Square Library, New York, NY [*Library symbol Library of Congress*] (LCLS)
NNU-We	New York University, Joe Weinstein Residence Halls Library, New York, NY [*Library symbol Library of Congress*] (LCLS)
NNV	National Naval Volunteers
NNVAB	United States Veterans Administration Hospital, Bronx, NY [*Library symbol Library of Congress*] (LCLS)
NNVAM	United States Veterans Administration Hospital (Manhattan), New York, NY [*Library symbol Library of Congress*] (LCLS)
NNW	North-Northwest
NNWB	Navy Nuclear Weapons Bulletin [*A publication*]
NNWB	Net National Well Being
NNWC	Nonnuclear Weapons Country
NNWF	National Network of Women's Funds (EA)
NNWFG	Wilkie, Farr & Gallagher, New York, NY [*Library symbol Library of Congress*] (LCLS)
NNWG	Wenner-Gren Foundation for Anthropological Research, New York, NY [*Library symbol Library of Congress*] (LCLS)
NNWH	Nonnormal Working Hours

NNWH.......... Walter Hampden Memorial Library, New York, NY [*Library symbol Library of Congress*] (LCLS)
NNWhit........ Whitney Museum of American Art, New York, NY [*Library symbol Library of Congress*] (LCLS)
NNWI........... Neonatal Narcotic Withdrawal Index [*Medicine*] (DMAA)
NNWM......... William Douglas McAdams, Inc., Medical Library, New York, NY [*Library symbol Library of Congress*] (LCLS)
NNWML...... Wagner College, Staten Island, NY [*Library symbol Library of Congress*] (LCLS)
NNWO.......... Navy Nuclear Weapons Officer (DNAB)
NNWP.......... National Network of Women Philanthropists (NFD)
NNWRN...... North-Norwestern (FAAC)
NNWS.......... National Network of Women in Sales [*Defunct*] (EA)
NNWS.......... Nonnuclear Weapons State
NNWSI........ Nevada Nuclear Waste Storage Investigations
NNWWD...... North-Westward (FAAC)
NNY............. Nanyang [*China*] [*Airport symbol*] (OAG)
NNY............. Nuveen New York Municipal Fund [*NYSE symbol*] (SPSG)
NNY............. Nuveen NY Muni Val Fd [*NYSE symbol*] (TTSB)
NNy............. Nyack Library, Nyack, NY [*Library symbol Library of Congress*] (LCLS)
NNYAB........ National Network of Youth Advisory Boards (EA)
NNYC.......... Yale Club, New York, NY [*Library symbol Library of Congress*] (LCLS)
NNYD.......... Norfolk Navy Yard [*Virginia*] [*Later, Norfolk Naval Shipyard*]
NNYI........... YIVO Institute for Jewish Research, New York, NY [*Library symbol Library of Congress*] (LCLS)
NNYIQ......... Nuveen New York Investment Quality Municipal Fund [*Associated Press*] (SAG)
NNyM.......... Nyack Missionary College, Nyack, NY [*Library symbol Library of Congress*] (LCLS)
NNYMCA..... Young Men's Christian Association, National Council Historical Library, New York, NY [*Library symbol*] [*Library of Congress*] (LCLS)
NNYMCA-GC... Young Men's Christian Association, Grand Central Branch Library, New York, NY [*Library symbol Library of Congress*] (LCLS)
NNYMCA-NC... Young Men's Christian Association, National Council Historical Library, New York, NY [*Library symbol Library of Congress*] (LCLS)
NNYMI........ Nuveen New York Municipal Income Fund [*Associated Press*] (SAG)
NNYMV...... Nuveen New York Municipal Value Fund [*Associated Press*] (SAG)
NNYSQ........ Nuveen New York Select Quality Municipal Fund [*Associated Press*] (SAG)
NNYU.......... Yeshiva University, New York, NY [*Library symbol Library of Congress*] (LCLS)
NNYU-HJ..... Yeshiva University, Mendel Gottesman Library of Hebraica Judaica, New York, NY [*Library symbol Library of Congress*] (LCLS)
NNYU-M...... Yeshiva University, Albert Einstein College of Medicine, Bronx, NY [*Library symbol Library of Congress*] (LCLS)
NNYU-S...... Yeshiva University, Stern College, New York, NY [*Library symbol Library of Congress*] (LCLS)
NNZ............. New York Zoological Society, New York, NY [*Library symbol Library of Congress*] (LCLS)
NNZ............. Point Sur, CA [*Location identifier FAA*] (FAAL)
NNZCG........ New Zealand Consulate General, Library, New York, NY [*Library symbol*] [*Library of Congress*] (LCLS)
NNZi........... Zionist Archives and Library, New York, NY [*Library symbol Library of Congress*] (LCLS)
NO............. Air North [*ICAO designator*] (AD)
NO............. Lifts Not Operating [*Skiing*]
NO............. Nachalnik Otdelenia [*Chief of Department*] [*Soviet military rank*]
NO............. Narcotics Officer
NO............. National Office
NO............. National Office, Office of Federal Contract Compliance Programs (AAGC)
NO............. National Outlook: an Australian Christian Monthly [*A publication*] (APTA)
NO............. Native Officer [*British military*] (DMA)
NO............. Natural Orbital [*Physical chemistry*]
NO............. Natural Order [*Botany*]
NO............. Naval Observatory [*Navy*]
NO............. Naval Officer
NO............. Navigation Officer
NO............. Negative [*British naval signaling*]
NO............. New Options (EA)
NO............. New Order [*Defunct*] (EA)
NO............. New Orleans [*Louisiana*]
NO............. Nitric Oxide (GNE)
NO............. Nitric Oxide
NO............. Nitrogen Oxide [*Emission control*] [*Automotive engineering*]
NOEL.......... Noah (ABBR)
No.............. Nobelium [*Chemical element*]
No.............. Nocturia [*Urology*] (DAVI)
n/o............. None Obtained [*Medicine*]
NO............. Nonofficial
NO............. Nonoriginal
N/O............. No Orders [*Business term*]
NO............. No Palpable Nodes [*Oncology*]
NO............. Nord-Ouest [*Northwest*] [*French*]
NO............. Normally Open [*Switch*]
N/O............. Normally Open
NO............. North
NO............. North Central Airlines, Inc.
NO............. Northern (ABBR)
N/O............. North Of [*In outdoor advertising*] (WDMC)

NO............. Norway [*ANSI two-letter standard code*] (CNC)
no............. Norway [*MARC country of publication code Library of Congress*] (LCCP)
NO............. Nose [*Horse racing*]
NO............. Notes [*Online database field identifier*]
NO............. Not Or [*Logical operator*] [*Computer science*]
N/O............. Not Otherwise
NO............. Not Our Publication
N/O............. Not Out [*Bookselling*]
NO............. November (ADA)
NO............. Nuestra Orden [*Our Order*] [*Spanish Business term*]
NO............. Number (EY)
No.............. Number (IDOE)
no............. Number (WDMC)
NO............. Numero [*In Number*] [*Pharmacy*] (ROG)
NO............. Nursing Officer [*British*]
NO............. Oneida Library, Oneida, NY [*Library symbol Library of Congress*] (LCLS)
NO2............. Nitrogen Dioxide
NO₃............. Nitrate (GNE)
No9Vis........ Number Nine Visual Technology, Inc. [*Associated Press*] (SAG)
NOA............. National Oceanographic Association
NOA............. National Officers Association (EA)
NOA............. National Onion Association (EA)
NOA............. National Opera Association (EA)
NOA............. National Optical Association [*Later, NAOO*]
NOA............. National Optometric Association (EA)
NOA............. National Orchestral Association (EA)
NOA............. National Outboard Association [*Defunct*] (EA)
NOA............. National Outdoorsmen's Association [*Defunct*] (EA)
NOA............. NATO Oil Authority (NATG)
NOA............. Natural Orange Aroma
NOA............. Nature of Action [*Military*] (AFM)
NOA............. Network-Oriented Analysis and Transformation Unit [*Computer science*] (MHDB)
NOA............. New London, CT [*Location identifier FAA*] (FAAL)
NOA............. New Obligational Authority
NOA............. Norontair [*Canada ICAO designator*] (FAAC)
NOA............. Northwest Orient Airlines, Inc.
NOA............. Notice of Availability (MCD)
NOA............. Not Operationally Assigned
N-O-A............. Not-Or-And [*Computer science*]
NOA............. Not Otherwise Authorized
NOA............. Nueva Organizacion Antiterrorista [*New Anti-Terrorist Organization*] [*Guatemala*] (PD)
NOA............. University of North Carolina, Chapel Hill Library School, Chapel Hill, NC [*OCLC symbol*] (OCLC)
NOAA.......... National Oceanic and Atmospheric Administration [*Rockville, MD*] [*Pronounced "Noah"*]
NOAA.......... Nonoperating Aircraft Authorization
NOAADN...... National Organization for Advancement of Associate Degree Nursing (EA)
NOAA-FSL... NOAA [*National Oceanic and Atmospheric Administration*]-Forecast Systems Lab
NOAA-JTRE... National Oceanic and Atmospheric Administration Joint Tsunami Research Effort
NOAA-NOS... National Oceanic and Atmospheric Administration - National Ocean Service (DNAB)
NOAA-NWS... National Oceanic and Atmospheric Administration - National Weather Service (DNAB)
NOAA-PMEL... National Oceanic and Atmospheric Administration Pacific Marine Environmental Laboratory
NOAA-TR-NMFS-Circ... National Oceanic and Atmospheric Administration Technical Report-National MarineFisheries Service-Circular [*A publication*] (PDAA)
NOAA-TR-NMFS-SSRF... National Oceanic and Atmospheric Administration-Technical Report-National MarineFisheries Service-Special Scientific Report Fisheries (PDAA)
NOAB.......... National Outdoor Advertising Bureau [*Defunct*] (EA)
NOAC.......... National Operations and Automation Conference (HGAA)
NOAC.......... Nuclear Operations Analysis Center [*Department of Energy*] [*Information service or system*] (IID)
NOACT........ Naval Overseas Air Cargo Terminal
NOACT........ No Action (MUGU)
NOACTLANT... Naval Ordnance Activities, Atlantic
NOACTPAC... Naval Ordnance Activities, Pacific
NOaD.......... Dowling College, Oakdale, NY [*Library symbol Library of Congress*] (LCLS)
No Adams St C... North Adams State College (GAGS)
NOADN....... National Oceanic and Atmospheric Data Network
NOAEL........ No Observed Adverse Effect Level [*Toxicology*] (EG)
NOaf.......... Oakfield Public Library (Haxton Memorial), Oakfield, NY [*Library symbol Library of Congress*] (LCLS)
NOAFIRM.... Affirmative Replies Neither Required nor Desired (MUGU)
NOAG.......... Naval Objectives Analysis Group
NOAH.......... Narrow-Band Optimiziation of the Alignment of Highways (PDAA)
NOAH.......... National Ocean Agency Headquarters
NOAH.......... National Organization for Albinism and Hypopigmentation (EA)
NOAH.......... Norwegian Adapted HAWK [*Hughes Aircraft Co.*]
NOAHS........ New Opportunities in Animal Health Sciences
NOaJH......... Oakdale-Bohemia Junior High School, Oakdale, NY [*Library symbol Library of Congress*] (LCLS)
NOALA........ Noise-Operated Automatic Level Adjustment
NOAM.......... Noan Mizrachi [*American Zionist organization*]
NOAM.......... Nuclear Ordnance Air Force Materiel [*Military*] (AFIT)

NOAMTRAC... North America Trail Complex (EA)
NO & LC...... New Orleans & Lower Coast Railroad Co. (IIA)
NOAO......... National Optical Astronomy Observatories [Tucson, AZ] [National Science Foundation]
NOAO......... Navy Officers, Accounts Office (MUGU)
NOAP......... National Ocean Access Project (EA)
NOAP......... Naval Overseas Air Cargo Terminal, Pearl (MUGU)
NOAP......... Navy Oil Analysis Program (NG)
NOAPP........ National Organization of Adolescent Pregnancy and Parenting (EA)
NOAPP........ National Organization on Adolescent Pregnancy, Parenting, and Prevention (PAZ)
NOAPS........ National Oil and Acrylic Painters Society
NOAR......... National Organization for an American Revolution (EA)
NOARB........ New Orleans Army Base (SAA)
No Ariz U... Northern Arizona University (GAGS)
NOARL........ National Oceanographic and Atmospheric Research Laboratory (USDC)
NOARL........ Naval Ocean and Atmosphere Research Laboratory [USA] [Marine science] (OSRA)
NOART........ New Orleans Army Terminal
NOB.......... National Oil Board (NATG)
NOB.......... Naval Operating Base
NOB.......... Naval Order of Battle
NOB.......... Naval Ordnance Bulletin [A publication]
NOB.......... Nobeoka [Japan] [Seismograph station code, US Geological Survey] (SEIS)
NOB.......... Nobile [Nobly] [Music] (ROG)
NOB.......... Nobility (ABBR)
NOB.......... Nobis [With Us] [Latin] (ROG)
NOB.......... Noble (ABBR)
NOB.......... Nonobese [A diabetic mouse strain]
NOB.......... North Bay Cooperative Library System, Santa Rosa, CA [OCLC symbol] (OCLC)
NOB.......... Norwest Corp. [NYSE symbol] (SPSG)
NOB.......... Not on Bonus
NOB.......... Nuclear Order of Battle (AFM)
NOB.......... Number of Bursts
NOB.......... San Francisco, CA [Location identifier FAA] (FAAL)
NOBA......... Nitrosobenzamide [Organic chemistry]
NOBAR........ National Organization for Birthfathers and Adoption Reform (EA)
NOBC......... National Office for Black Catholics (EA)
NOBC......... National Order of Battlefield Commissions (EA)
NOBC......... National Organization of Bar Counsel (EA)
NOBC......... Naval Officer Billet Classifications [or Code]
NOBCA........ National Organization of Black College Alumni (EA)
NOBCCE...... National Organization of Black Chemists and Chemical Engineers [Later, NOPABCCE] (EA)
NOBCChE.... National Organization for Professional Advancement of Black Chemists and Chemical Engineers
NOBCO........ National Organization of Black County Officials (EA)
NOBDUCHAR... Naval Operating Base, Dutch Harbor, Aleutians
NOBE......... Nordstrom, Inc. [NASDAQ symbol] (NQ)
NoBeFi........ Fiskeridirektoratet [Directorate of Fisheries], Bergen-Nordens, Norway [Library symbol Library of Congress] (LCLS)
Nobel......... Nobel Insurance Ltd. [Associated Press] (SAG)
NobelEd....... Nobel Education Dynamics, Inc. [Associated Press] (SAG)
NOBELS....... New Office and Business Education Learning System
NoBeU........ Universitetet i Bergen [University of Bergen], Bergen, Norway [Library symbol Library of Congress] (LCLS)
NOBFRAN... Naval Operating Base, San Francisco, California
NOBH......... Nobility Homes [NASDAQ symbol] (TTSB)
NOBH......... Nobility Homes, Inc. [NASDAQ symbol] (NQ)
NobiltyH...... Nobility Homes, Inc. [Associated Press] (SAG)
NOBIN........ Stichting Nederlands Orgaan voor de Bevordering van de Informatieverzorging [Netherlands Organization for Information Policy] [Information service or system Defunct] (IID)
NOBL......... Nobel Insurance Ltd. [NASDAQ symbol] (NQ)
NoblAf........ Noble Affiliates, Inc. [Associated Press] (SAG)
NOBLE........ National Organization of Black Law Enforcement Executives (EA)
Noble......... Noble's Current Court Decisions [New York] [A publication] (DLA)
NobleR........ Noble Roman's, Inc. [Associated Press] (SAG)
NOBLF........ Nobel Insurance [NASDAQ symbol] (TTSB)
NobltyH....... Nobility Homes [Associated Press] (SAG)
NOBMN....... Nobleman (ABBR)
NoBncshs.... North Bancshares, Inc. [Associated Press] (SAG)
NOBNEWT.... Naval Operating Base, Newport, Rhode Island
NoBordr...... Northern Border Partners Ltd. [Associated Press] (SAG)
NOBP......... Nitrosobenzopyrone [Organic chemistry]
NOBR......... Nobler (ABBR)
NOBS......... Naval Observatory [Navy]
NOBS......... Naval Operating Base Supplies (DNAB)
N Obs........ Nihil Obstat [Official Approval] [Latin]
NOBS......... Nonanoyloxybenzene Sulfonate [Laundry bleach activator]
NOBSOLO.... Naval Operating Base, Coco Solo, Canal Zone
NOBST........ Noblest (ABBR)
NOBSY........ Naval Observatory [Navy]
NOBT......... New Orleans Board of Trade (EA)
NOBT......... Nobility (ABBR)
NOBTRIN..... Naval Operating Base, Trinidad
NOBTS........ Naval Order of Battle Textual Summary (MCD)
NOBWN....... Noblewomen (ABBR)
NOBY......... Nobly (ABBR)
NOC.......... Ascor Flyservice AS [Norway ICAO designator] (FAAC)
NOC.......... National Oceanographic Center [Marine science] (MSC)
NOC.......... National Oceanographic Council (NADA)

NOC.......... National Offshore Council (EA)
NOC.......... National Olympic Committee (NADA)
NOC.......... National Olympic Committees
NOC.......... National Online Circuit [Defunct] (EA)
NOC.......... National Opportunity Camps for the Pre-Teen Child (EA)
NOC.......... Natural Organic Carbon
NOC.......... Naval Operations Center (NVT)
NOC.......... Navy Officer's Classification
NOC.......... Network Operations Center [Bell System]
NOC.......... Network Operations Control [NASA] (KSC)
NOC.......... New Orleans Consortium [Library network]
noc.......... Noctis [Night] [Medicine]
NOC.......... Nominal Operating Cell [Photovoltaic energy systems]
NOC.......... Nonionic Organic Compound [Organic chemistry]
NOC.......... Nonionic Organic Contaminant [Environmental chemistry]
NOC.......... Non-Ionic Organic Contaminant [Environmental chemistry]
NOC.......... Normally Open Contact [Switch] (IAA)
NOC.......... Norris Communications Corp. [Vancouver Stock Exchange symbol]
NOC.......... Northrop Corp. [NYSE symbol] (SPSG)
NOC.......... Northrop Grumman [NYSE symbol] (TTSB)
NOC.......... Northrop Grumman Corp. [NYSE symbol] (SAG)
NOC.......... Northwest Ohio Consortium [Library network]
NOC.......... Norwegian Government Office of Culture [Record label]
NOC.......... Notation of Content [Aerospace]
NOC.......... Notation of Content
NOC.......... Notice of Cancellation (AAGC)
NOC.......... Notice of Change (MCD)
NOC.......... Notice of Commencement (EPA)
NOC.......... Notice of Contents [Indexing]
NOC.......... Not Otherwise Classified
NOC.......... Not Otherwise Coded (GFGA)
NOC.......... Nuclear Operations Center (MCD)
NOC.......... Nuclear Ordnance Commission [Military] (AFIT)
NOC.......... Numerical Optimisation Centre [British]
NOC.......... Nuttall Ornithological Club (EA)
NOc.......... Oceanside Free Library, Oceanside, NY [Library symbol Library of Congress] (LCLS)
NOC.......... University of North Carolina, Chapel Hill, Chapel Hill, NC [OCLC symbol] (OCLC)
NOCA......... Nitrosooxazolidinecarboxylic Acid [Organic chemistry]
NOCA......... North Cascades National Park
No Ca Ecc & Mar... Notes of Cases, English Ecclesiastical and Maritime Courts [1841-50] [A publication] (DLA)
No Car Ag & Tech... North Carolina Agricultural & Technical State University (GAGS)
No Car Cent U... North Carolina Central University (GAGS)
No Car St U (Raleigh)... North Carolina State University (Raleigh) (GAGS)
NOcaS........ Shaker Museum Foundation, Inc., Old Catham, NY [Library symbol Library of Congress] (LCLS)
No Cas LJ... Notes of Cases, Law Journal [A publication] (DLA)
NOCB......... New Orleans City Ballet
NocBE........ Walter S. Boardman Elementary School, Oceanside, NY [Library symbol] [Library of Congress] (LCLS)
NOCC......... NATO Oil Crisis Contingent (NATG)
NOCC......... Navigation Operational Checkout Computer
NOCC......... Navigation Operator's Control Console
NOCC......... Network Operations Control Center [Manned Space Flight Network, NASA]
NOCCC........ No Control Circuit Contacts (MSA)
NOCC/JTWC... Naval Oceanography Command Center/Joint Typhoon Warning Center
NOCD......... Not Our Class, Dear [Slang]
NOCE......... New Orleans Commodity Exchange (EA)
NOCERCC .... National Organization for Continuing Education of Roman Catholic Clergy (EA)
NOCF......... National Office Computer Facility [IRS]
NOCF......... Naval Oceanography Command Facility (DNAB)
NocFE........ Elementary School #3, Oceanside, NY [Library symbol] [Library of Congress] (LCLS)
NOcH......... South Nassau Communities Hospital, Oceanside, NY [Library symbol Library of Congress] (LCLS)
NOCHA........ National Off-Campus Housing Association [Defunct] (EA)
NOCI......... Nederlandse Organisatie voor Chemische Informatie (NITA)
NOCIG........ Night Only Calligraphic Image Generator
NOC II........ Nuclear Operations Concept II [Military]
NO-CIRC...... National Organization of Circumcision Information Resource Centers (EA)
NOCIRC....... National Organization of Circumcision Information Resource Centers (PAZ)
NOCM......... National Organization for Changing Men (EA)
NOCM......... Nuclear Ordnance Commodity Manager (AFM)
NocME........ Elementary School #8, Oceanside, NY [Library symbol] [Library of Congress] (LCLS)
NocMS........ Oceanside Middle School, Oceanside, NY [Library symbol] [Library of Congress] (LCLS)
NOCN......... National Ocean Communications Network (USDC)
NOCN......... National Open College Network (AIE)
NocNE........ Elementary School #5, Oceanside, NY [Library symbol] [Library of Congress] (LCLS)
NOCO......... Noise Correlation
NOCO......... Nuclear Ordnance Cataloging Officer [Military]
NOCO......... Nuclear Ordnance Catalog Office [DoD]
NOCONIT..... No Continuing Interest (NG)
NOCONTRACT... Not Releasable to Contractors (MCD)
NOCOPS...... NORAD Combat Operations System (MCD)

NOCOR .... Neglect of Core Orbitals [*Physical chemistry*]
NOCP .... Network Operator Control Program
NOCSA .... National Olympic Committee of South Africa (ECON)
NOCSAE....... National Operating Committee on Standards for Athletic Equipment (EA)
NOcSE .... Florence A. Smith School, Oceanside, NY [*Library symbol*] [*Library of Congress*] (LCLS)
NocSH .... Oceanside Senior High School, Oceanside, NY [*Library symbol*] [*Library of Congress*] (LCLS)
NOCT .... Navy Overseas Cargo Terminals
NOCT .... Nocte [*At Night*] [*Pharmacy*] (ROG)
noct .... Nocturnal (CPH)
NOCT .... Nominal [*or Normal*] Operating Cell Temperature [*Photovoltaic energy systems*]
NOCT MANEQ... Nocte Maneque [*Night and Morning*] [*Pharmacy*]
NOD .... National Organization on Disability (EA)
NOD .... National Organization on Disability
NOD .... Naval Ordnance Department [*British*]
NOD .... Naval Ordnance Depot
NOD .... Navy Operational Deception (MCD)
NOD .... Network Operations Directive [*NASA*] (KSC)
NOD .... Network Out-Dial [*Automatic Voice Network*] (CET)
NOD .... New Offshore Dischargement (NATG)
NOD .... Night Observation Device
NOD .... Noise Output Device
NOD .... Nondefinitive Pattern [*Laboratory science*] (DAVI)
NOD .... Nonobese Diabetic [*Mouse strain*]
NOD .... Norris Dam [*TVA*]
NOD .... Notice of Deficiency (EPA)
NOD .... Notify of Death (DAVI)
NODA .... National Operatic and Dramatic Association (EAIO)
NODA .... National Orientation Directors Association (EA)
NODA .... National Outdoor Drama Association [*Defunct*] (EA)
NODA .... Normal-Octyl & -Deyl Adipate [*Organic chemistry*]
NODAC .... Naval Ordnance Data Automation Center
NODAC......... Navy Occupational Development and Analysis Center (DNAB)
No Dak St U... North Dakota State University (GAGS)
NODAL......... Network-Oriented Data Acquisition Language
NODAN......... Noise-Operated Device for Antinoise [*Telecommunications*] (TEL)
NODAP......... Nonlinear Distortion Analysis Program [*Bell System*]
NODAS......... Network-Oriented Data Acquisition System (MHDI)
NODC........... National Oceanographic Data Center [*Databank originator*] [*Washington, DC*] [*National Oceanic and Atmospheric Administration*]
NODC........... Naval Oceanographic Distribution Center
NODC........... Naval Operating Development Center
NODC........... Non-OPEC Developing Country (NUCP)
NODCAB ...... National Oceanographic Data Center Advisory Board [*National Oceanic and Atmospheric Administration*] (NOAA)
NODCC .... Noble Order, Descendants of the Conqueror and His Companions (EA)
NODDS .... Naval Oceanographic Data Distribution System
NODE .... National Organization of Downsized Employees
NODE .... Noise Diode [*Electronics*] (IAA)
NODEL......... Not to Delay
NODESTA..... Will Not Depart This Station [*Army*] (AABC)
NODEX .... New Offshore Dischargement Exercise (NATG)
NODI........... Notice of Delayed [*or Delinquent*] Item
NODIS .... No Distribution [*Military security classification*] (AFM)
NODIS.......... Northern Ohio Data and Information Service [*Cleveland State University*] [*Information service or system*] (IID)
NODL........... National Office for Decent Literature [*Defunct*]
NODL........... Not on Drawing List (MCD)
NODLR......... Night Observation Device, Long-Range [*Army*] (RDA)
NODM.......... Ferrocarril Nor-Oeste de Mexico [*Mexico North Western Railroad*] [*AAR code*]
NODM.......... National Organization of Dance and Mime [*British*] (DBA)
NODMR........ Night Observation Device, Medium-Range [*Army*]
NODRA .... National One Design Racing Association (EA)
NODS........... Navy Overseas Dependents School
NODS........... Near-Object Detection Sensor [*Automotive electronics*]
NODS........... Near Obstacle Detection System [*General Motors-Delco Co.*]
NOE .... Nap of the Earth [*Night helicopter flight*] [*Army*]
NOE .... No Ophthalmologic Examination [*Medicine*]
NOE .... No Other Entry (ADA)
NOE .... NORAD Operational Evaluation (MCD)
NOE .... Norden-Norddeich [*Germany*] [*Airport symbol*]
NOE .... Notice of Exception
NOE .... Notice of Execution
NOE .... Not Otherwise Enumerated
NOE .... Nuclear Overhauser Effect
NOEA .... National Outdoor Events Association [*British*] (DBA)
No East Rep... Northeastern Reporter [*Commonly cited NE*] [*A publication*] (DLA)
NOEB .... NATO Oil Executive Board (NATG)
NOEB-E .... NATO Oil Executive Board - East
NOEB-W....... NATO Oil Executive Board - West
NOEC .... No Effects Concentration [*British environmental standard*]
NOEC .... No Observed Effect Concentration [*Toxicology*]
NOECOMM... Nap-of-the-Earth Communications [*Night helicopter flight*]
NOED .... New Oxford English Dictionary [*Proposed*]
NOEDS......... Nuclear Overhauser Enhancement Difference Spectrometry
NOEF .... Naval Ordnance Engineering Facility (DNAB)
NOEHI......... No One Else Has It [*Lexicography*]
No E III U .... Northeastern Illinois University (GAGS)
NOEL .... National Organization of Episcopalians for Life (EA)

NOEL .... National Ornament and Electric Lights Christmas Association (EA)
NOEL .... Naval Ordnance Electronics Laboratory
NOEL .... Noel Group [*NASDAQ symbol*] (TTSB)
NOEL .... Noel Group, Inc. [*NASDAQ symbol*] (SAG)
NOEL .... No Observed Effect Level [*Toxicology*]
No E La U ..... Northeast Louisiana University (GAGS)
NoelGp .... Noel Group, Inc. [*Associated Press*] (SAG)
NOELS .... New Office Education Learning System
No E Mo St U... Northeast Missouri State University (GAGS)
No E Ohio U... Northeastern Ohio University (GAGS)
NOEP .... Neue Oekonomische Politik [*New Economic Policy*] [*Germany*]
NOES .... National Operational Environmental Satellite Service (MCD)
NOESS .... National Operational Environmental Satellite System
No E St U ..... Northeastern State University (GAGS)
NoestUt........ Northeast Utilities [*Associated Press*] (SAG)
NOESY .... Nuclear Overhauser Effect Spectroscopy
No et Vet Test... Novi et Veteris Testamenti (DSA)
NOEU .... Naval Ordnance Experimental Unit
No E U .... Northeastern University (GAGS)
NOEV .... NORAD Operational Evaluation (IAA)
NOF .... Fonnafly AS [*Norway ICAO designator*] (FAAC)
NOF .... National Oceanographic Facility (USDC)
NOF .... National Oceanographic Facility [*Marine science*] (OSRA)
NOF .... National Optical Font [*Typography*]
NOF .... National Osteopathic Foundation (EA)
NOF .... National Osteoporosis Foundation (EA)
NOF .... Naval Operating Facility
NOF .... Naval Ordnance Facility
NOF .... NCR [*NCR Corp.*] Optical Font (MCD)
NOF .... Network Operations and Facilities
NOF .... Network Operations Forum [*Exchange Carriers Standards Association*] [*Telecommunications*]
NOF .... Neurite Outgrowth Factor [*Biochemistry*]
NOF .... Nickel Offsets Ltd. [*Toronto Stock Exchange symbol*]
NOF .... Nitrosyl Fluoride (SAA)
NOF .... NOTAM Office
NOF .... St. Petersburg, FL [*Location identifier FAA*] (FAAL)
NOFA .... National Office Furniture Association [*Later, NOPA*] (EA)
NOFA .... Natural Organic Farmers Association (EA)
NOFA .... Notice of Funding Availability [*Department of Housing and Urban Development*] (GFGA)
NOFAD......... Naval Ocean Floor Analysis Division (DNAB)
N of Cas ..... Notes of Cases at Madras (Strange) [*A publication*] (DLA)
N of Cas ..... Notes of Cases, English Ecclesiastical and Maritime Courts [*1841-50*] [*A publication*] (DLA)
NOFI........... National Oil Fuel Institute [*Later, NOJC*] (EA)
NOFIN......... No Further Information
NoFkBc........ North Fork Bancorp [*Associated Press*] (SAG)
NOFMA .... National Oak Flooring Manufacturers Association (EA)
NOFOA........ Naval Office for Occupied Areas [*World War II*]
NOFODIS ..... No Foreign Dissemination [*Intelligence classification*]
NOFORN ...... Not Releasable to Foreign Nationals [*Military security classification*]
NOFRC......... Northern Forest Research Centre [*Canadian Forestry Service of Agriculture Canada*] [*Research center*] (RCD)
NOFS .... National Option and Futures Society [*Defunct*] (EA)
NOFT .... Naval Overseas Freight Terminal
NOFT .... Nonorganic Failure-to-Thrive [*Medicine*] (DMAA)
NOFT .... Notification of Foreign Travel (AFM)
NOFTT .... Nonorganic Failure-to-Thrive [*Medicine*] (MEDA)
NOG .... Arizona-Nogales [*Mexico*] [*Airport symbol*] (AD)
NOG .... North Carolina Natural Gas [*NYSE symbol*] (SAG)
NOG .... NSAPAC Operations Group
NOG .... Nuclear Ordnance Group [*Air Force*] (MCD)
NOG .... Numbering
NOg .... Ogdensburg Public Library, Ogdensburg, NY [*Library symbol Library of Congress*] (LCLS)
NOGA .... National Osteopathic Guild Association (EA)
NOGAD .... Noise-Operated Gain-Adjusting Device
NOGAPS ...... Navy Operational Global Atmospheric Prediction System
NOGGA .... National Ornamental Goldfish Growers Association (EA)
NOgH .... A. Barton Hepburn Hospital, Ogdensburg, NY [*Library symbol Library of Congress*] (LCLS)
NOGL .... Naval Ordnance Gauge Laboratory
NOGL .... Nizam's Own Golgonda Lancers [*British military*] (DMA)
NOGLSTP..... National Organization of Gay and Lesbian Scientists and Technical Professionals (EA)
NOgM .... Mater Dei College, Ogdensburg, NY [*Library symbol Library of Congress*] (LCLS)
NOGM .... No Gammopathy Detected [*Biochemistry*] (DAVI)
NOgRM........ Remington Art Memorial Museum, Ogdensburg, NY [*Library symbol*] [*Library of Congress*] (LCLS)
NOGS .... Night Observation Gunship (MCD)
NOgSH......... Saint Lawrence State Hospital, Ogdensburg, NY [*Library symbol Library of Congress*] (LCLS)
NOgW .... Wadhams Hall Seminary College, Ogdensburg, NY [*Library symbol Library of Congress*] (LCLS)
NOH............ Chicago, IL [*Location identifier FAA*] (FAAL)
NOH............ Night Observation Helicopter (MCD)
NOH............ University of North Carolina, Health Science Library, Chapel Hill, NC [*OCLC symbol*] (OCLC)
NOHA .... Nutrition for Optimal Health Association (EA)
NOHARMM... National Organization to Halt the Abuse and Routine Mutilation of Males (EA)
NOHIC......... National Oral Health Information Clearinghouse (PAZ)
NOHIMS....... Navy Occupational Health Information Management System

NoHo	North of Houston Street [*Artists' colony in New York City*] [*See also SoHo, SoSo, TriBeCa*]
NOHOL	Not Holding [*a given course or altitude*] [*Aviation*]
NOHP	Not Otherwise Herein Provided
NOHQI	Nuveen Ohio Quality Income Municipal Fund [*Associated Press*] (SAG)
NOHS	National Oceanographic Hazard Survey (NITA)
NOHS	National Organization of Human Services [*Defunct*] (EA)
NOHSCP	National Oil and Hazardous Substances Contingency Plan [*Environmental Protection Agency*] (ERG)
NOHSE	National Organization of Human Service Education (EA)
NOHSM	National Occupational Health Survey of Mining [*Department of Health and Human Services*] (GFGA)
NOHSN	National Organization of Hospital Schools of Nursing [*Defunct*] (EA)
NOI	Detroit, MI [*Location identifier FAA*] (FAAL)
NOI	National Oilwell, Inc. [*NYSE symbol*] (SAG)
NOI	National Opera Institute (EA)
NOI	Nation of Islam [*Religion*]
NOI	NAVWEPS ORDALT Instruction (MCD)
NOI	Netherlands Offset Industry
NOI	Net Operating Income
NOI	Node Operator Interface (NITA)
NOI	Noise Com, Inc. (SPSG)
NOI	Nonoperational Intelligence
NOI	Notice of Inquiry (IEEE)
NOI	Notice of Intent (MCD)
NOI	Notice of Intention
NOI	Not Otherwise Identified (NG)
NOI	Not Otherwise Indexed
NOIA	National Ocean Industries Association (EA)
NOIAW	National Organization of Italian-American Women (EA)
NOIBN	Not Otherwise Identified [*or Indicated*] by Name [*Military*] (AABC)
NOIBN	Not Otherwise Indexed by Name [*Tariffs*]
NOIC	National Oceanographic Instrumentation Center [*National Oceanic and Atmospheric Administration*]
NOIC	National Osteopathic Interfraternity Council (EA)
NOIC	Naval Ocean Intelligence Center (DOMA)
NOIC	Naval Officer-in-Charge
NOIC	Navy Operational Intelligence Center [*Now Naval Maritime Intelligence Center (NAVMIC)*] (DOMA)
NOICC	National Occupational Information Coordinating Committee [*Washington, DC*]
NOIE	Naval Ordnance Inspection Establishment [*Ministry of Defence*] [*British*] (PDAA)
NOII	Non-Occlusive Intestinal Ischemia [*Medicine*] (DMAA)
No III U	Northern Illinois University (GAGS)
NOIO	Naval Ordnance Inspecting Officer
NOIS	National Occupational Information Service
NOISE	National Organisation of Initiatives for Social Education [*British*] (DBA)
NOISE	National Organization for Improving School Environments [*Defunct*] (EA)
NOISE	National Organization to Insure a Sound-Controlled Environment (EA)
NOISE	National Organization to Insure Survival Economics (EA)
NOISE	Noise Information Service
NoiseCT	Noise Cancellation Technologies, Inc. [*Associated Press*] (SAG)
Noise Reg Rep	Noise Regulation Reporter [*Bureau of National Affairs*] [*A publication*] (DLA)
NOITU	National Organization of Industrial Trade Unions (EA)
NOIWON	National Operations and Intelligence Watch Officers Network (MCD)
NOIZ	Micronetics, Inc. [*NASDAQ symbol*] (NQ)
NOIZ	Micronetics Wireless [*NASDAQ symbol*] (TTSB)
NOJ	Kodiak, AK [*Location identifier FAA*] (FAAL)
NOJC	National Oil Jobbers Council [*Later, PMAA*] (EA)
NOJC	New Orleans Jazz Club (EA)
NOJC	Northern Oklahoma Junior College
NOJSM	National Office of Jesuit Social Ministries (EA)
NOK	Next of Kin
NOK	Nokia Corp. [*NYSE symbol*] (SAG)
NOK	Noril'sk [*Former USSR Geomagnetic observatory code*]
NOKD	Not Our Kind, Dear [*Slang*]
No Kent U	Northern Kentucky University (GAGS)
Nokia	Nokia Corp. [*Associated Press*] (SAG)
NOKL	Northwestern Oklahoma Railroad Co. [*AAR code*]
Nok Mort	Nokes' Mortgages and Receiverships [*3rd ed.*] [*1951*] [*A publication*] (DLA)
NOKW	NAZI Oberkommando der Wehrmacht [*NAZI Armed Forces High Command*] [*World War II German*] (BJA)
NOL	National Old Lacers [*Later, IOL*] (EA)
NOL	National Ordnance Laboratory
NOL	National Overseas Airline Co. [*Egypt*] [*ICAO designator*] (FAAC)
NOL	Naval Ordnance Laboratory [*Later, NSWC*]
NOL	Net Operating Loss
NOL	New Orleans - Loyola [*Louisiana*] [*Seismograph station code, US Geological Survey*] (SEIS)
Nol	Nolan's English Magistrates' Cases [*A publication*] (DLA)
Nol	Nolan's English Settlement Cases [*A publication*] (DLA)
NOL	Normal Operational Loss [*Nuclear energy*]
NOL	Normal Overload
NOL	Norse Oriental Lines (MHDW)
NOL	Northland Oils Ltd. [*Toronto Stock Exchange symbol*]
NOI	Olean Public Library, Olean, NY [*Library symbol Library of Congress*] (LCLS)
NOLA	National Association for Outlaw and Lawman History (EA)

NOLA	Northeastern Ohio Library Association [*Library network*]
NOLAC	National Organization of Liaison for Allocation of Circuit (NATG)
Nolan	Nolan on the Poor Laws [*A publication*] (DLA)
Nolan	Nolan's English Magistrates' Cases [*A publication*] (DLA)
Noland	Noland Co. [*Associated Press*] (SAG)
NOLAP	Non-Linear Analysis Program (PDAA)
NOLC	National Obscenity Law Center (IID)
NOLC	National One-Liners Club (EA)
NOLC	Naval Ordnance Laboratory Corona
nol con	Nolo Contendere [*I Do Not Wish to Contend*] [*Legal term*] [*Latin*] (BARN)
NOID	Dresser Industries, Inc., Dresser Clark Division, Olean, NY [*Library symbol Library of Congress*] (LCLS)
NOLD	Noland Co. [*NASDAQ symbol*] (NQ)
NOLDAR	Noludar [*A hypnotic*] [*Roche laboratories*] (DAVI)
NOLDC	Non-Oil Less-Developed Country
NOLEO	Notice to Law Enforcement Officials
NOIH	Olean General Hospital, Olean, NY [*Library symbol Library of Congress*] (LCLS)
NOLHGA	National Organization of Life and Health Guaranty Associations [*An association*]
NOLM	Nonlinear Optical Loop Mirror [*Optical computing*]
Nol Mag	Nolan's English Magistrates' Cases [*A publication*] (DLA)
NOL-MDI	Naval Ordnance Laboratory Miss Distance Indicator
NOLO	No Live Operator (NG)
NOLOC	No Location (AABC)
NOLPE	National Organization on Legal Problems of Education (EA)
NOLPE Sch LJ	NOLPE [*National Organization on Legal Problems of Education*] School Law Journal [*A publication*] (DLA)
NOLPE School LJ	NOLPE [*National Organization on Legal Problems of Education*] School Law Journal [*A publication*] (DLA)
NOLPE School L Rep	NOLPE [*National Organization on Legal Problems of Education*] School Law Reporter [*A publication*] (DLA)
Nol PL	Nolan on the Poor Laws [*A publication*] (DLA)
NOL PROS	Nolle Prosequi [*Unwilling to Prosecute*] [*Legal term Latin*]
NOLS	National Oceanographic Laboratory System
NOLS	National Organization for Legal Services (EA)
NOLS	National Outdoor Leadership School
NOISFH	Saint Francis Hospital, Olean, NY [*Library symbol Library of Congress*] (LCLS)
NoISL	Cattaraugus-Allegany School Library System, Olean, NY [*Library symbol*] [*Library of Congress*] (LCLS)
NOLTESTFAC	Naval Ordnance Laboratory Test Facility (SAA)
NOLTF	Naval Ordnance Laboratory Test Facility
NOL/WO	Naval Ordnance Laboratory, White Oak [*Maryland*]
NOM	National Online Meeting [*Conference*] (IT)
NOM	National Organization for Men (EA)
NOM	National Organization for Men Legal Defense and Education Fund
NOM	Natural Organic Matter
NOM	Network Operations Manager [*Manned Space Flight Network, NASA*]
NOM	Network Output Multiplexer [*Telecommunications*] (MCD)
NOM	Newspapers on Microfilm
NOM	Nomad River [*Papua New Guinea*] [*Airport symbol*] (OAG)
NOM	Nome [*Alaska*] [*Seismograph station code, US Geological Survey Closed*] (SEIS)
NOM	Nomenclature (AAG)
NOM	Nominal (AAG)
NOM	Nominate (AFM)
NOM	Nominative
NOM	Norbeau Mines, Inc. [*Toronto Stock Exchange symbol*]
NOM	Normal Extraocular Movements [*Ophthalmology*] (DAVI)
NOM	Number of Open Microphones
NOM	Nuveen Missouri Premium Income Municipal Fund [*AMEX symbol*] (SPSG)
NOM	Nuveen MO Prem, Inc. Muni [*AMEX symbol*] (TTSB)
NOM	Opa Locka, FL [*Location identifier FAA*] (FAAL)
NOMA	National Office Management Association [*Later, AMS*]
NOMA	National Oil Marketers Association [*Defunct*] (EA)
NOMA	National Organization of Minority Architects (EA)
NOMAD	National Organisational Management Database
NOMAD	National Organization of Miniaturists and Dollers (EA)
NOMAD	Navy Oceanographic Meteorological Association (USDC)
NOMAD	Navy Oceanographic Meteorological Association [*Marine science*] (OSRA)
NOMAD	Navy Oceanographic Meteorological Automatic Device
NOMAD	Navy Operation and Maintenance Aviation Deck (MCD)
NOMAD	Nozzle Materials Application and Design (MCD)
NOMAG	Nonmagnetic (IAA)
NOMb	Nitric Oxide Myoglobin [*Food technology*]
NOMBOS	Nonmine Bottom Objects [*Navy*] (NVT)
NOMC	National Organization for Migrant Children [*Later, NCEMC*] (EA)
nom cons	Nomen Conservandum [*Retained Name*] [*Latin*]
NOMD	Nominated (ABBR)
NOMDA	National Office Machine Dealers Association (EA)
nom dub	Nomen Dubium [*Doubtful Name*] [*Latin*]
NOME	National Origin Minority Education [*New Hampshire Department of Education*] (EDAC)
NOMEE	Nominee (ABBR)
NOMEE	Nominee [*Legal shorthand*] (LWAP)
NOMEN	Nomenclature (AFM)
NOMES	New England Offshore Mining Experiment Study (NOAA)
NOMG	Nominating (ABBR)
NOMI	Nonocclusive Mesenteric Infarction [*Medicine*] (AAMN)
NOMI	Nonocclusive Mesenteric Ischemia [*Medicine*]
No Mich U	Northern Michigan University (GAGS)

nom illeg.....	Nomen Illegitimum [*Illegitimate Name*] [*Latin*]
NOMIN........	Nominative (WDAA)
nom inval ...	Nomen Invalidum [*Name Not Valid*] [*Latin*]
NOMIS........	National Online Manpower Information System [*Manpower Services Commission*] [*Information service or system*] (IID)
NOMIS........	Naval Ordnance Management Information System
NOMIS........	Nuclear Operations and Maintenance Information Service (IID)
NOML........	Nominal (ROG)
NOMLM.......	Nominalism (ABBR)
NOMLT.......	Nominalist (ABBR)
NOMLY.......	Nominally (ABBR)
NOMMA......	National Ornamental and Miscellaneous Metals Association (EA)
NOM MUD ...	Nomen Nudum [*A Name without Designation*] [*Latin*] (BABM)
NOMN........	Nomination
nom nov	Nomen Novum [*New Name*] [*Latin*]
nom nud	Nomen Nudum [*Invalid Name*] [*Biology, taxonomy*] [*Latin*]
NOMOP.......	No Record of Mustering-Out Payment (DNAB)
NOMOTC.....	National Organization of Mothers of Twins Clubs (EA)
nom prov.....	Nomen Provisiorum [*Provisional Name*] [*Latin*]
NOMR........	Nominator (ABBR)
nom rej.......	Nomen Rejiciendum [*Rejected Name*] [*Latin*]
NOMRP.......	Normal Return Point (MCD)
NOMS........	Network Operations Management System [*Computer science*]
NOMS........	Nuclear Operations Monitoring System (MCD)
NOMSA.......	National Office Machine Service Association [*Paramount, CA*] (EA)
NOMSS.......	National Operational Meteorological Satellite System
NOMSS.......	Navy Oceanographic and Meteorological Support System (MCD)
nom superfl...	Nomen Superfluum [*Superfluous Name*] [*Latin*]
NOMTF	Naval Ordnance Missile Test Facility
NOMTS	Naval Ordnanace Missile Test Station [*White Sands Missile Range, NM*] (GRD)
NOMUS.......	Nordisk Musikkomite [*Nordic Music Committee*] (EAIO)
NOMV........	Nominative (ABBR)
NOMW........	National Organizational of Mall Walkers
NOMW........	National Organization of Mall Walkers (EA)
NON............	National Organization for Non-Parents [*Later, NAOP*]
NON............	Nonouti [*Kiribati*] [*Airport symbol*] (OAG)
NON............	Normine Resources Ltd. [*Vancouver Stock Exchange symbol*]
NON............	North Norway (NATG)
NON N.........	Notice of Noncompliance (EPA)
No N...........	Novae Narrationes [*New Counts*] [*1516*] [*A publication*] (DLA)
NONA.........	Notice of Nonavailability
Nonacq	Nonacquiescence by Commissioner in a Tax Court or Board of Tax Appeals Decision [*United States*] [*Legal term*] (DLA)
NONADD.....	Nonadditivity [*Statistics*]
NON AL OCC...	Non Alibi Occurrit [*It Occurs in No Other Place*] [*Latin*] (ROG)
NON-BUS.....	Nonbusiness [*IRS*]
NONCAN......	Noncancellable [*Insurance*]
NONCIT.......	Noncitizen (AABC)
NON-CM......	Noncumulative (ABBR)
NONCNST	Nonconsent
NONCOHO....	Noncoherent Oscillator (MCD)
noncoll.......	Noncollinear (MHDI)
NONCOM.....	Noncommissioned Officer [*Military*]
NON COM	Non Compos Mentis [*Not in Sound Mind*] [*Latin*] (ROG)
NONCOMECM...	Noncommunications Electronics Countermeasures [*Military*] (AABC)
NONCOMJAM...	Noncommunications Jamming [*Military*] (AABC)
NONCON......	Nonconformist
NON CUL	Non Culpabilis [*Not Guilty*] [*Latin*] (ROG)
NON-CUM....	Non-Cumulative [*Business term*]
NOND........	Non Detected [*Laboratory science*] (DAVI)
NONE........	New Orleans & Northeastern R. R. [*AAR code*]
NONEG.......	Negative Replies Neither Required nor Desired
NOneoC	Hartwick College, Oneonta, NY [*Library symbol Library of Congress*] (LCLS)
NOneoU.......	State University of New York, College at Oneonta, Oneonta, NY [*Library symbol Library of Congress*] (LCLS)
NONF........	Nonfasting [*Laboratory science*] (DAVI)
NONFLMB....	Nonflammable
NON-FRAG....	Non-Fragmentation [*Bomb*]
NONGAP	Nonlinear Grain Analysis Program (MCD)
N/ONI..........	Navy/Office of Naval Intelligence (AAG)
NONLIN.......	Nonlinear (IAA)
NONMAGCI...	Nonmagnetic Cast Iron (IAA)
NON-MSA	Non-Standard Metropolitan Statistical Area (OICC)
NON/NOV.....	Notices of Noncompliance/Notices of Violation [*Navy*]
NON-NSN....	Not Assigned a National Stock Number
NON OBS	Non Obstante [*Notwithstanding*] [*Latin*]
NON OBST...	Non Obstante [*Notwithstanding*] [*Latin*] (ROG)
NONP.........	Nonpackaged
NONP.........	Nonpareil (ADA)
NONP.........	Non-Precision Approach Runway [*Aviation*] (DA)
NONPAR	Nonparticipating [*Insurance*]
Non-Par	Non-Participating Provider
NONPAYT ...	Nonpayment (ROG)
NONPERF	Nonperforated (ABBR)
nonpoly.......	Nonpolychrome (VRA)
NONPROF	Nonprofessional
NON PROS...	Non Prosequitur [*Does Not Prosecute*] [*Latin*]
N/ONR........	Navy/Office of Naval Research (AAG)
Non-REM	Nonrapid Eye Movement [*Type of sleep*] (MAE)
NON REP	Non Repetatur [*Do Not Repeat*] [*Pharmacy*]
Non Repetat...	Non Repetatur [*Do Not Repeat*] [*Pharmacy*]
NON RES	Nonresident (WDAA)

NONRSNT	Nonresonant (IAA)
NONS........	Nonspecific [*Laboratory science*] (DAVI)
NONSAP	Nonlinear Structural Analysis Program [*Computer science*]
non segs......	Nonsegmented Neutrophils [*Medicine*] (CPH)
NON SEQ	Non Sequitur [*It Does Not Follow*] [*Latin*]
NONSKED ...	Nonscheduled (ABBR)
NON-SLIP ...	Non-Speech Language Initiation Program
NONSTAND...	Nonstandard (WDAA)
NONSTD	Nonstandard
NONStY.......	Non-Standard Yiddish (BJA)
NONSUB	Nonsubmarine [*Navy*] (NVT)
NONSYN	Nonsynchronous
NONTSDSL..	Not Included in Technical Service Demand Stockage Lists [*Army*] (AABC)
NONTT	Nonentity (ABBR)
NONUM......	Notional Number (NVT)
non-vis........	Nonvisualization (DAVI)
NON-VON....	Non-Von Neumann [*Experimental computer, not based on the principles of Von Neumann computer design, under construction at Columbia University*]
NON-VTG	Non-Voting [*Business term*]
NOO..........	Naoro [*Papua New Guinea*] [*Airport symbol*] (OAG)
NOO..........	National Organization Order (USDC)
NOO..........	Naval Oceanographic Office [*Also known as NAVOCEANO; formerly, HO, NHO, USNHO*]
NOO..........	Naval Oceanographic Office, Washington, DC [*Inactive*] [*OCLC symbol*] (OCLC)
NOO..........	Nevada Operations Office [*Department of Energy*]
NOO..........	Notice of Obligation [*Military*] (AFM)
NOOB........	Not Out of Bed [*Medicine*] (DAVI)
NOOD........	Nitric Oxide Optical Detector
NoodKid.......	Noodle Kidoodle, Inc. [*Associated Press*] (SAG)
No of Cas Madras...	Notes of Cases at Madras (Strange) [*A publication*] (DLA)
NOOIAC......	National Offshore Operations Industry Advisory Committee [*Coast Guard*]
Nooney.......	Nooney Realty Trust, Inc. [*Associated Press*] (SAG)
NOOOA.......	NORAD Office of Operational Analysis (IAA)
NO-OP........	Flight Not Operating [*Travel industry*]
NOOP.........	No Operation [*Computer science*]
no-op.........	No Operator [*Telemarketing*] (WDMC)
NOOS........	Nuclear Orbit-to-Orbit Shuttle [*NASA*]
NOO-SP......	Naval Oceanographic Office Special Publication
NOOU........	Not One of Us [*Slang*]
NoOU.........	Universitetet i Oslo [*University of Oslo*], Oslo, Norway [*Library symbol Library of Congress*] (LCLS)
NoOU-M.......	Universitetet i Oslo, Matematisk-Naturvitenskapelige Fakultet [*University of Oslo, Department of Mathematics and Natural Sciences*], Oslo, Norway [*Library symbol Library of Congress*] (LCLS)
NOP...........	Brooklyn, NY [*Location identifier FAA*] (FAAL)
NOP...........	National Onderzoek Persmedia [*Database*] [*Stichting Nationaal Onderzoek Persmedia*] [*Netherlands*] [*Information service or system*] (CRD)
NOP...........	National Opinion Poll
NOP...........	National Oracy Project (AIE)
NOP...........	National Outpatient Profile [*Medicine*] (MEDA)
NOP...........	Naval Oceanographic Publication
NOP...........	Naval Officer Procurement
NOP...........	Naval Ordnance Plant
NOP...........	Navigation Operating Procedure
NOP...........	Navy Objectives Plan
NOP...........	Near Object Probe (SAA)
NOP...........	Net Orders Processed [*Business term*] (DOAD)
NOP...........	Network Operations Procedure [*Manned Space Flight Network, NASA*]
NOP...........	Newscorp Overseas Ltd. [*NYSE symbol*] (SPSG)
NOP...........	Noncoherent Optical Processor
NOP...........	Nonoperating (KSC)
NOP...........	No Operation [*Computer science*]
NOP...........	Normal Operating Procedure (NRCH)
NOP...........	North Oscura Peak [*White Sands Missile Range*] [*Army*]
NOP...........	Notice of Procurement [*Navy*] (NG)
NOP...........	Not Otherwise Provided
NOP...........	Not Our Publication
NOP...........	Novair-Aviacao Geral SA [*Portugal ICAO designator*] (FAAC)
NOP...........	Nuclear Operations Plan (MCD)
NOP...........	Nuclear Ordnance Platoon [*Marine Corps*] (NVT)
NOP...........	Null Operation [*Computer science*]
NOP...........	Number of Openings [*Technical drawings*]
NOP...........	Number of Passes (MSA)
NOP...........	Numerical Oceanographic Prediction (PDAA)
NOPA.........	National Office Products Association (EA)
NOPA.........	National Oilseed Processors Association (EA)
NOPA.........	Network Operations Performance Analysis [*Manned Space Flight Network, NASA*]
NOPAA.......	National Office Products Association of Australia
NOPABCCE..	National Organization for Professional Advancement of Black Chemists and Chemical Engineers (EA)
NOPAC.......	North Pacific [*Aviation*] (FAAC)
NOPAR.......	Do Not Pass to Air Defense RADAR [*Air Traffic Control*] (FAAC)
NOPAT.......	Net Operating Profit after Tax
NOPB........	New Orleans Public Belt Railroad [*AAR code*]
NOPC........	Naval Oceanographic Processing Center (DOMA)
NOPCL.......	Naval Officer Personnel Circular Letter
NOPCO.......	National Oil Products Co. [*Later, NOPCO Chemical Co.*]

NOPD	New Orleans Police Department [*Initialism also used as title of TV series*]
NOPE	National Organization of Poll-Ettes (EA)
NOPE	Naturists and Nudists Opposing Pornographic Exploitation (EA)
NOPE	New Orleans Port of Embarkation
NOPE	No Promotion [*Refers to lack of publicity in the record business*]
NOPE	Not on Planet Earth [*Waste management slang*]
NOPEC	Non-OPEC [*Oil producing countries which are not members of OPEC*]
NOPEOL	National Organization to Promote English as the Official Language (EA)
NOPES	Non-Occupational Pesticide Exposure Study [*Environmental Protection Agency*] (GFGA)
NOPF	National Oceanographic Processing Facility (DOMA)
NOPF	Naval Oceanographic Processing Facility (ANA)
NOPF	Naval Ordnance Plant, Forest Park [*Illinois*]
NOPHN	National Organization for Public Health Nursing (HGAA)
NOPHYSRET...	Not Required to Take New Physical Provided No Material Change since Recent Retirement Physical [*Military*]
NOPI	Naval Ordnance Plant Institute (MCD)
NOPL	Naval Ordnance Plant, Louisville [*Kentucky*]
NOPMS	Network-Oriented Project Management System (PDAA)
NOP-N	Nordiska Publiceringsnamnden for Naturvetenskap [*Nordic Publishing Board in Science*] (EAIO)
NOPN	Normally Open [*Switch*]
NOPOL	No Pollution
NOPPA	National Ocean Pollution Planning Act of 1978
NOPPA	Nitroso(oxopropyl)propylamine [*Organic chemistry*]
NOPPO	National Ocean Pollution Program Office (GNE)
NOPPrA	Newscp Pverseas Ltd Pref [*NYSE symbol*] (TTSB)
NOPPrB	Newscp Overseas Ltd Adj Pref [*NYSE symbol*] (TTSB)
NOPR	Notice of Proposed Rule Making [*Federal agencies*]
NOPRI	National Orthotic and Prosthetic Research Institute (EA)
NOPROCAN...	If Not Already Processed, Orders Cancelled [*Military*]
NOPS	National Ocean Policy Study [*US Senate*]
NOPS	Nike Operator Proficiency Scale [*Army*]
NOPS	Noncoherent Optical Processing System
NOPT	No Procedure Turn Required [*Aviation*]
NOPUS	National Occupant Protection Use Survey [*NHTSA*] (TAG)
NoPVDM	N'Oubliez Pas Vos Decorations Maconniques [*Do Not Forget Your Masonic Regalia*] [*Freemasonry*] [*French*]
NOPWC	National Old People's Welfare Council (NADA)
NO-PYR	N-Nitrosopyrrolidine [*Also, NYPR*] [*Biochemistry, organic chemistry*]
NOQUIS	Nucleonic Oil Quantity Indication System [*Air Force*]
NOR	AS Norving [*Norway ICAO designator*] (FAAC)
NOR	National Organization for Rehabilitation [*British*]
nor	Nitrogen ohne Radikal [*Chemical prefix*]
NOR	Nitrogen Oxide Reduction [*Research in automotive air pollution*]
NOR	Nonoperational Ready (NVT)
NOR	Non-Ordinary Resident [*British*]
NOR	Noradrenaline [*or Norepinephrine*] [*Endocrinology*] (DAVI)
NOR	Noranda, Inc. [*Toronto Stock Exchange symbol Vancouver Stock Exchange symbol*]
NOR	Norbornadiene [*Also, NBD*] [*Organic chemistry*]
NOR	Nord [*Greenland*] [*Seismograph station code, US Geological Survey Closed*] (SEIS)
NOR	Nordfjordur [*Iceland*] [*Airport symbol*] (OAG)
NOR	Nordisk Organ for Reinforskning [*Nordic Council of Reindeer Research*] [*Norway*] (EAIO)
Nor.	Norma [*Constellation*]
NOR	Normal (KSC)
NOR	Normal
NOR	Norman
NOR	Normandale Community College, Bloomington, MN [*OCLC symbol*] (OCLC)
NOR	North
NOR	North Central Airlines, Inc.
NOR	Norway [*ANSI three-letter standard code*] (CNC)
Nor.	Norway (VRA)
nor	Norwegian [*MARC language code Library of Congress*] (LCCP)
NOR	Norwich [*City in England*] (ROG)
NOR	Norwich [*Diocesan abbreviation*] [*Connecticut*] (TOCD)
NOR	Notice of Readiness [*Shipping*]
NOR	Notice of Revision
NOR	Not Operationally Ready [*Military*] (AFM)
NOR	Not Or [*Logical operator*] [*Computer science*]
NOR	Nucleolar Organizer Region [*in chromosomes*]
NOR	Nucleolus Organizer Region [*Genetics*] (DOG)
NOR	Number of Rounds [*Military*] (CINC)
NOR	San Diego, CA [*Location identifier FAA*] (FAAL)
NORA	National Oil Recyclers Association (GNE)
NORA	National Online Regulatory Access [*Data Development, Inc.*] [*Information service or system*] (CRD)
NORA	Norwegian Zero Power Reactor Assembly
NORAC	No Radio Contact [*Aviation*]
NORAD	North American Aerospace Defense Command [*FAA*] (TAG)
NORAD	North American Air Defense [*Integrated United States-Canada command*]
NORAD	North American Air Defense Command (AAGC)
NORAD	Norwegian Agency for International Development
NORADCOC	North American Air Defense Combat Operations Center [*Military*] (AFM)
NORAD CPX...	North American Air Defense Command Post Exercise (SAA)
NORADCRU...	North American Air Defense Orientation Cruise (NVT)
NORADEX	North American Air Defense Exercise (NVT)

Noradr	Noradrenaline [*Norepinephrine*] [*Endocrinology*] (DAVI)
NorAE	Norwegian Antarctic Expedition [*1956-*]
NORAID	Irish Northern Aid Committee (EA)
NORAID	Norwegian Agency for International Development
NORAIL	Northrop Overhead Rail Assembly and Installation Line (SAA)
NORAIM	Not Operationally Ready, Aircraft Intermediate Maintenance [*Military*] (DNAB)
Noram	Noram Energy Corp. [*Associated Press*] (SAG)
Noram	Noram Financing I [*Associated Press*] (SAG)
NoramE	Noram Energy Corp. [*Formerly, Arkla, Inc.*] [*Associated Press*] (SAG)
Norand	Norand Corp. [*Associated Press*] (SAG)
NORAP	Northwestern Alumni Players
NORAPS	Navy Operational Regional Atmospheric Prediction System (MCD)
NORASDEFLANT...	North American Antisubmarine Defense Force, Atlantic (NATG)
NORATS	Navy Operational Radio and Telephone Switchboard (NVT)
NOrb	Orangeburg Public Library, Orangeburg, NY [*Library symbol Library of Congress*] (LCLS)
NORBA	National Off-Road Bicycle Association [*Later, USCF*] (EA)
NOrbR	Rockland State Hospital, Medical Library, Orangeburg, NY [*Library symbol Library of Congress*] (LCLS)
NORBS	Northern Base Section [*Corsica*]
NORC	National Oceanographic Records Center
NORC	National Opinion Research Center [*University of Chicago*]
NORC	National Opinion Research Center [*The University of Chicago (IL)*] [*Later, NORC: A Social Science Research Center*] (WDMC)
NORC	Naturally Occurring Retirement Community
NORC	Naval Ordnance Research Calculator [*or Computer*] [*Naval Ordnance Proving Ground*]
Norc	Norcross' Reports [*23-24 Nevada*] [*A publication*] (DLA)
NORC	Normal Curve [*Laboratory science*] (DAVI)
Norc	Normally Occurring Retirement Community
NORC	Nuclear Ordnance Record Card (NVT)
NOrc	Orchard Park Public Library, Orchard Park, NY [*Library symbol Library of Congress*] (LCLS)
NORCALSEC...	Northern California Section, Western Sea Frontier
NORCANUKUS...	Norway, Canada, United Kingdom, United States (DOMA)
NORCAP	National Organisation of Counselling Adoptees and Their Parents [*British*] (DBA)
NOrcE	Erie Community College-South, Orchard Park, NY [*Library symbol Library of Congress*] (LCLS)
NorcEB	Erie-Cattaraugus Board of Cooperative Educational Services, Orchard Park, NY [*Library symbol*] [*Library of Congress*] (LCLS)
NORCO	National Oil Recovery Corp.
NorCran	Northland Cranberries [*Associated Press*] (SAG)
NORCUS	Northwest College and University Association for Science [*Richland, WA*] [*Department of Energy*] (GRD)
NORD	Bureau of Ordnance Publication [*Later, NAVORD*] [*Navy*]
NORD	National Organization for Rare Disorders (EA)
NORD	Naval Ordnance
NORD	Norsk Data (NITA)
NORD	Not Ordered, This Part of Package (DAVI)
NORDA	Naval Oceanographic Research and Development Administration [*USA*] [*Marine science*] (OSRA)
NORDA	Naval Ocean Research and Development Activity [*Bay St. Louis, MS*]
NORDEK	Norway, Denmark, Finland, Sweden [*Nordic Economic Community*] [*Trade bloc*]
NORDEL	Organization for Nordic Electrical Cooperation (EA)
NORDIATRANS...	Association for Nordic Transplant and Dialysis Personnel (EAIO)
Nordic	Nordic American Tanker Shipping Ltd. [*Associated Press*] (SAG)
NORDICOM...	Nordic Documentation Center for Mass Communication Research [*Database ori ginator*] [*Finland Information service or system*] (IID)
NORDINFO...	Nordiska Samarbetsorganet for Vetenskaplig Information [*Nordic Council for Scientific Information and Research Libraries*] [*Finland*] (EAIO)
NORDITA	Nordic Institute for Theoretic Atomic Physics [*Later, NIIP*] (EY)
NORDO	No Radio
Nord P	Nordic Pharmacopoeia [*A publication*]
NordPac	Nord Pacific Ltd. [*Associated Press*] (SAG)
NordPc	Nord Pacific Ltd. [*Associated Press*] (SAG)
NordRs	Nord Resources Corp. [*Associated Press*] (SAG)
NORDSAT	Scandinavian Countries Broadcast Satellite (MCD)
Nordser	Nordisk Samkatalog foer Seriella Medicinska Publikationer [*Karolinska Institutets Bibliotek och Informationscentral*] [*Sweden Information service or system*] (CRD)
Nordsn	Nordson Corp. [*Associated Press*] (SAG)
Nordst	Nordstrom, Inc. [*Associated Press*] (SAG)
NORDTEL	Nordiskt Samarbete Inom Telekommunikation [*Nordic Cooperation on Telecommunications*] [*Finland*] (EAIO)
NORDUnet	[*The*] Nordic University Network (TNIG)
NORE	Northeast
NOREASTNAVFACENGCOM...	Northeast Division Naval Facilities Engineering Command
NOREC	No Record
NOREC	Northern Environmental Council [*Defunct*] (EA)
NORECHAN...	Northeast Subarea Channel (NATG)
NOREF	No Reference
NOREP	No Reply Received
NOREP	Not Reportable
NORESS	Norwegian Regional Seismic Array
Norex	Norex America, Inc. [*Associated Press*] (SAG)
NOREX	Nuclear Operational Readiness Exercise (NVT)
NORF	Norfolk [*County in England*]
Norf	Norfolk [*County in England*] (ODBW)

NORFISH ..... North Pacific Fisheries Project (NOAA)
NORFLK....... Norfolk [County in England]
NORFORM ... Not Releasable to Foreign Nationals
Nor Fr......... Norman French [Language, etc.] (DLA)
NORGD .... National Organization for the Rights of Guide Dogs (EA)
NORGLAC .... Northern Great Lakes Area Council
NORGRAPH... Northeast Graphics Conference and Printing Show [Printing Industry Association of Connecticut and Western Massachusetts] (TSPED)
NORI........... National Office for the Rights of the Indigent [Later, LDF]
NORIANE ..... Normes et Reglements Informations Automatisees Accessibles en Ligne [Automated Standards and Regulations Information Online] [Database French Association for Standardization] [Information service or system] (IID)
NORIF.......... Natural Oocyte Retrieval Intravaginal Fertilization [Alternative to traditional in-vitro fertilization (IVF)] (PAZ)
NORIMB........ Norimberge [Nuremberg] [Imprint] (ROG)
NORIP.......... NORAD Intelligence Plan [Military] (AABC)
NORIS.......... North Island (MUGU)
NORIV.......... No Arrival Report [Aviation] (FAAC)
NORK.......... [The] New Orleans Rhythm Kings [Jazz band]
NORKZ......... Norsk-Data AS (MHDW)
Norland....... Norland Medical Systems, Inc. [Associated Press] (SAG)
NORLANT...... North Atlantic Area (MUGU)
NORLANTAACS... North Atlantic Airways and Air Communications Service (SAA)
NORLANTEX... North Atlantic - Training Exercise (MCD)
NorldCr........ Northland Cranberries, Inc. [Associated Press] (SAG)
NORLEU....... Norleucine [A nonessential amino acid] [Biochemistry]
norleu......... Norleucine [Biochemistry] (DAVI)
NORM.......... National Office Resources Management [IRS]
NORM.......... National Organization for Raw Materials (EA)
NORM.......... Naturally Occurring Radioactive Material (FFDE)
Norm .... Norma [Constellation]
NORM.......... Normal [or Normalize] (AAG)
NORM.......... Normal
NORM.......... Norman [or Normandy]
NORM.......... Normative Operating Reporting Method
NORM.......... Normetal [AAR code]
NORM.......... Not Operationally Ready Maintenance [Military] (NG)
NORM.......... Not Operational Ready Materiel [Military] (AFIT)
NORM.......... Nuclear Operational Readiness Maneuver (NVT)
NORM.......... Nuclear Ordnance Readiness Manpower
NORMARC .... Norwegian MARC (NITA)
NORMATERM... Normalisation, Automatisation de la Terminologie [Standardization and Automation of Terminology] [Databank] [France] [Information service or system] (IID)
NORMCLSD... Normally Closed [Switch] [Electronics] (IAA)
NORMET ...... Normetanephrine [Also, Methylnorepinephrine] [Biochemistry] (AAMN)
NORM(F)...... Not Operationally Ready Maintenance - Flyable [Military] (MCD)
NORM(G)..... Not Operationally Ready Maintenance - Grounded [Military] (MCD)
NORML........ National Organization for the Reform of Marijuana Laws (EA)
NORML........ National Organization for the Reinforcement of Marijuana Laws (NADA)
NORML........ National Organization for the Repeal of Marijuana Laws (NADA)
NORML........ Normal (DAVI)
NORMOPN... Normally Open [Switch] [Electronics] (IAA)
NORMSHOR... Normal Tour of Shore Duty
NORO.......... Not Operationally Ready Other [Military] (AFM)
NOROEC ...... NORAD Operational Employment Concept [Military] (AABC)
NORP.......... New Oil Reference Price
NORP.......... Nord Pacific Ltd. [NASDAQ symbol] (SAG)
NORPAC...... Naval Overhaul and Repair Pacific (MUGU)
NORPAC...... Northern Pacific Railway Co.
NORPAC...... North Pacific [Military]
Nor Pat....... Norman. Letters Patent [1853] [A publication] (DLA)
NORPAX...... North Pacific Experiment [National Science Foundation]
NORPI......... No Pilot Balloon Observation Will Be Filed Next Collection Unless Weather Changes Siginificantly [NWS] (FAAC)
NOrpOHi ...... Oyster Pond Historical Society, Orient Point, NY [Library symbol Library of Congress] (LCLS)
Nor Pro Pr... North's Probate Practice [Illinois] [A publication] (DLA)
NORPY........ Nord Pacific Ltd ADR [NASDAQ symbol] (TTSB)
NORQR .... NORAD Qualitative Requirement [Military] (AABC)
NORR.......... No Reply Received (FAAC)
Norr .... Norris' Reports [82-96 Pennsylvania] [A publication] (DLA)
NORRA .... National Off-Road Racing Association
NORRD .... No Reply Received (NOAA)
Norrell........ Norrell Corp. [Associated Press] (SAG)
NORRF........ Norris Communications [NASDAQ symbol] (TTSB)
Norris .... Norris' Reports [82-96 Pennsylvania] [A publication] (DLA)
Norris & L Perpetuities... Norris and Leach on Rule Against Perpetuities [A publication] (DLA)
NorrisC .... Norris Communications Corp. [Associated Press] (SAG)
Norris Seamen... Norris' Law of Seamen [A publication] (DLA)
Norr Peake... Norris' Edition of Peake's Law of Evidence [A publication] (DLA)
NORRS .... Naval Operational Readiness Reporting Systems
NORS.......... National Organization for River Sports (EA)
NORS.......... New Old Replacement Stock [Automotive parts]
NORS.......... Not Operationally Ready for Service [Military] (VNW)
NORS.......... Not Operationally Ready Supply [Military]
NORS.......... Not Operationally Ready System [Military]
NORSAIR ..... Not Operationally Ready Supply Aviation Items Report [Military]
NORSAR ...... Norwegian Seismic Array [Royal Norwegian Council for Scientific and Industrial Research]
NORSAT....... Norwegian Satellite System

NORSEACENT... North Sea Subarea (NATG)
NORSEC....... Northern Security Exhibition [British] (ITD)
NORSEX...... Norwegian Remote Sensing Experiment [in marginal ice zone]
NORSF........ Not Operationally Ready Supply Flyable [Military] (MCD)
NORS-G....... Not Operationally Ready for Service - Grounded (VNW)
NORSG .... Not Operationally Ready Supply Grounded [Military] (NG)
NORSIB....... NORAD Space Intelligence Bulletin [DoD]
Norsk......... Norsk Hydro [Associated Press] (SAG)
NORSN....... Not Operationally Ready Supply Nongrounded [Military] (NG)
NORSNET .... National Oceanographic Reference Station Network (NOAA)
NORSOLS .... Northern Solomons Area
NORST........ No Restrictions (FAAC)
Norstan....... Norstan, Inc. [Associated Press] (SAG)
NORSTAR .... Norden Search Terrain Avoidance RADAR (SAA)
NorSys........ Nortech Systems, Inc. [Associated Press] (SAG)
NORT .... Nuclear Ordnance Readiness Test (NVT)
NORTAM...... Northrop Terminal Attrition Model (SAA)
NORTEB...... Norwegian Telecommunications Users Group
Nortek......... Nortek, Inc. [Associated Press] (SAG)
Nortel .... Northern Telecom [Canada]
NorTel .... Northern Telecom Ltd. [Associated Press] (SAG)
Nortel100 .... Nortel Inversora SA [Associated Press] (SAG)
North .... Northampton County Reporter [Pennsylvania] [A publication] (DLA)
NORTH........ Northerly (ABBR)
NORTH........ Northern (ABBR)
NORTH........ Northern Operations of Rail Transportation and Highways [Alaska]
North .... Reports Tempore Northington [Eden. English Chancery Reports] [1757-67] [A publication] (DLA)
NORTHAG .... North [European] Army Group [NATO]
Northam ...... Northampton Law Reporter [Pennsylvania] [A publication] (DLA)
Northam Law Rep... Northampton County Law Reporter [Pennsylvania] [A publication] (DLA)
Northam L Rep... Northampton Law Reporter [Pennsylvania] [A publication] (DLA)
Northamp Co Repr... Northampton County Reporter [Pennsylvania] [A publication] (DLA)
Northampton Co Rep... Northampton County Reporter [Pennsylvania] [A publication] (DLA)
North & G.... North and Guthrie's Appeals Reports [68-80 Missouri] [A publication] (DLA)
NORTHANTS... Northamptonshire [County in England]
Northbay...... Northbay Financial Corp. [Associated Press] (SAG)
North Car J Int'l L & Comm... North Carolina Journal of International Law and Commercial Regulation [A publication] (DLA)
North Carolina College LJ... North Carolina College Law Journal [A publication] (DLA)
North Co...... Northampton County Reporter [Pennsylvania] [A publication] (DLA)
North Co Rep... Northampton County Reporter [Pennsylvania] [A publication] (DLA)
North Co R (PA)... Northampton County Reporter [Pennsylvania] [A publication] (DLA)
NORTHD ...... Northumberland [County in England] (ROG)
North Ken'y SL Rev... Northern Kentucky State Law Review [A publication] (DLA)
NORTHM...... Northumberland (ABBR)
NORTH'N ..... Northampton [City in England] (ROG)
Northop U..... Northop University (GAGS)
North Pr...... North's Probate Practice [Illinois] [A publication] (DLA)
Northrim...... Northrim Bank [Associated Press] (SAG)
Northrop ULJ... Northrop University. Law Journal of Aerospace, Energy, and the Environment [A publication] (DLA)
North St L.... North. Study of the Laws [1824] [A publication] (DLA)
NORTHUM ... Northumberland [County in England]
Northum ...... Northumberland County Legal News [Pennsylvania] [A publication] (DLA)
NORTHUMB... Northumberland [County in England] (ROG)
Northumb .... Northumberland [County in England] (ODBW)
Northumb Co... Northumberland County Legal News [Pennsylvania] [A publication] (DLA)
Northumberland Co Leg Jour... Northumberland Legal Journal [Pennsylvania] [A publication] (DLA)
Northumberland LJ... Northumberland Legal Journal [Pennsylvania] [A publication] (DLA)
Northumb Legal J... Northumberland Legal Journal [Pennsylvania] [A publication] (DLA)
Northumb LJ... Northumberland Legal Journal News [Pennsylvania] [A publication] (DLA)
Northumb LN... Northumberland Legal Journal [Pennsylvania] [A publication] (DLA)
Northum Co Leg N... Northumberland County Legal News [Pennsylvania] [A publication] (ILCA)
Northum Leg J... Northumberland Legal Journal [Pennsylvania] [A publication] (DLA)
Northum Leg J (PA)... Northumberland Legal Journal [Pennsylvania] [A publication] (DLA)
Northum Leg N (PA)... Northumberland County Legal News [Pennsylvania] [A publication] (DLA)
Northwestern U... Northwestern University (GAGS)
North WLJ... Northwestern Law Journal [A publication] (DLA)
Northw Rep... Northwestern Reporter [Commonly cited NW] [A publication] (DLA)
NORTIC........ NORAD [North American Aerospace Defense Command] Technical Intelligence Center (DOMA)
NORTLANT... North Atlantic
Nort LC....... Norton's Leading Cases on Inheritance [India] [A publication] (DLA)
NortMc....... Norton McNaughton, Inc. [Associated Press] (SAG)
Norton .... Norton's Cases on Hindu Law of Inheritance [1870-71] [India] [A publication] (DLA)
NORTR......... Nortronics Corp.

NortrpG......... Northrop Grumman Corp. [Formerly, Northrup Corp.] [Associated Press] (SAG)
NorTrst .... Northern Trust Corp. [Associated Press] (SAG)
NorTst........ Northern Trust Corp. [Associated Press] (SAG)
NORVA........ Norfolk, Virginia [Navy]
NORVAGRP... Norfolk, Virginia Group [Navy]
NORVAL....... Norvaline [Biochemistry]
NORVIC....... Norvicensis [Norwich] [Imprint] (ROG)
NORVIPS .... Northrup Voice Interruption Priority System (MUGU)
NORW........ Norway [or Norwegian]
NORW........ Norwich [City in England] (ROG)
NORWEB...... Northwestern Electricity Board (NADA)
Norweb....... NORWEB PLC [Associated Press] (SAG)
NORWELD ... Northwest Library District [Library network]
NORWESSEAFRON... Northwestern Sea Frontier
NORWESSEC... Northwestern Sector, Western Sea Frontier
Norwest....... Norwest Corp. [Associated Press] (SAG)
NORWESTLANT... Northwest Atlantic [Military]
NORWESTNAVFACENGCOM... Northwest Division Naval Facilities Engineering Command
NorwFn........ Norwich Financial Corp. [Associated Press] (SAG)
NORWICH ... Knickers Off Ready When I Come Home [Correspondence] (DSUE)
NorwlkSv .... Norwalk Savings Society [Associated Press] (SAG)
Norwood..... Norwood Promotional Products [Associated Press] (SAG)
Norwt........ Norwest Corp. [Associated Press] (SAG)
NORWY........ NORWEB PLC [NASDAQ symbol] (SAG)
NOS .... National Ocean Service [Formerly, Coast and Geodetic Survey] [Washington, DC National Oceanic and Atmospheric Administration]
NOS .... National Ocean Survey (NOAA)
NOS .... National Office Staff [American Occupational Therapy Association]
NOS .... National Operational Satellite
NOS .... National Oratorio Society [Defunct] (EA)
NOS .... National Osteoporosis Society [British]
NOS .... NATO Office of Security (NATG)
NOS .... Naval Ordnance Station
NOS .... Nederlandse Omroep Stichting [Radio and television network] [Netherlands]
NOS .... Network Operating System
NOS .... New Old Stock [Automotive parts]
NOS .... Night Observation Sight [Air Force]
NOS .... Night Observation System [Navy] (CAAL)
NOS .... Night Operation System [Aviation]
NOS .... Nimbus Operational System
NOS .... Nitric Oxide Synthase [An enzyme]
NOS .... Non-Ocular Source [Physiology]
NOS .... Nonoriented Satellite
NOS .... Nopaline Synthase [An enzyme]
NOS .... Northern State College Library, Aberdeen, SD [OCLC symbol] (OCLC)
NOS .... Northstar Resources Ltd. [Toronto Stock Exchange symbol]
NOS .... Norway Airlines [ICAO designator] (FAAC)
NOS .... Nosing (ABBR)
NOS .... Nossi-Be [Madagascar] [Airport symbol] (OAG)
NOS .... Nostalgia [A radio station format] (WDMC)
NOS .... Not on Shelf (ADA)
NOS .... Not Otherwise Specified (AFM)
NOS .... Not Otherwise Stated
NOS .... Nouvel Ordre Social [New Social Order] [Switzerland] (PD)
NOS .... Number of Stops (IAA)
NOS .... Numbers (AAG)
nos............. Numbers (WDMC)
NOs............. Oswego City Library, Oswego, NY [Library symbol Library of Congress] (LCLS)
NOSA.......... National Occupational Safety Association (NADA)
NOSA.......... National Outerwear and Sportswear Association (EA)
NOSAC........ National Offshore Safety Advisory Committee [Coast Guard]
NOSAD........ National Organization for Seasonal Affective Disorder (EA)
NOSALF....... Nordiska Samfundet for Latinamerika Forskning [Nordic Association for Research on Latin America] [Sweden] (EAIO)
NOSAP........ National Ocean Survey Analytical Plotter [NOAA] (PDAA)
NOSB........ National Organic Standards Board
NOSBE........ Network Operating System/Batch Environment
NOSC........ Naval Ocean Systems Center [Formerly, NELC]
NOSC........ Naval Ordnance Systems Command [Later, Naval Sea Systems Command]
NOSC........ Nonoscillating
NOsC........ Oswego County Library System, Oswego, NY [Library symbol] [Library of Congress] (LCLS)
NOSCL........ Naval Ocean Systems Center Laboratory (DNAB)
NOSCP........ National Ocean Sediment Coring Program (NOAA)
NOSD........ Nosed (ABBR)
NoSdeSv..... North Side Savings Bank [Associated Press] (SAG)
NOSE........ National Odd Shoe Exchange (EA)
NOSE........ Neighbors Opposing Smelly Emissions [Student legal action organization]
NOSE........ Neotronics Olfactory Sensing Equipment [Neotronics Scientific] (PS)
NOSG........ Nosing (ABBR)
NOSGLANT... Naval Operations Support Group, Atlantic
NOSGPAC .... Naval Operations Support Group, Pacific
NOSH........ Hain Food Group [NASDAQ symbol] (TTSB)
NOSH........ Hain Food Group, Inc. [NASDAQ symbol] (SAG)
NOS-H .... Nordiska Samarbetsnamnden for Humanistisk Forskning [Nordic Committee of the Research Councils for the Humanities - NCRCH] (EA)

NOsH .... Oswego Hospital, Oswego, NY [Library symbol] [Library of Congress] (LCLS)
NOsHi......... Oswego County Historical Society, Oswego, NY [Library symbol Library of Congress] (LCLS)
NOsI............ International Business Machines Corp., Oswego, NY [Library symbol Library of Congress] (LCLS)
NOSIC .... Naval Ocean Surveillance Information Center
NOSIC .... Naval Operations Support Center [Navy]
NOSIE .... Nurses Observation Scale for Inpatient Evaluation [Psychiatry]
NOSIG .... No Significant Change [Used to qualify weather phenomena]
NOSIH .... Naval Ordnance Station, Indian Head (MCD)
NOSINS .... Nosiness (ABBR)
NOSL .... Naval Ordnance Station, Louisville [Kentucky]
NOSL .... Night-Day Optical Survey of Lightning [NASA]
NOSLA .... National Oil Scouts and Landmen's Association [Later, IOSA]
NOSL-QA ..... Naval Ordnance Station, Louisville Quality Assurance Department [Kentucky]
NOS-LSCR ... National Ocean Survey Lake Survey Center [National Oceanic and Atmospheric Administration]
NOSM .... Navy Occupation Service Medal
NOSM .... Noise Diotic, Signal Monaural (PDAA)
NOSMO .... Norden Optics Setting, Mechanized Operation [Air Force bombsight]
NOS-N .... Samarbetsnamnden for de Nordiska Naturvetenskapliga Forskningraden [Joint Committee of the Nordic Natural Science Research Councils - JCNNSRC] (EA)
NOSO .... Naval Ordnance Supply Office (MUGU)
NOSP .... National Ophthalmic Speakers Programme [Canada]
NOSP .... Naval Ordnance Special Projects
NOSP .... Network Operations Support Plan [NASA] (KSC)
NOSP .... Network Operation Support Program [Computer science]
NOSPL .... No Special Observation Taken [NWS] (FAAC)
NOSR .... National Office for Social Responsibility (EA)
NOSS .... National Oceanic Satellite System (MCD)
NOSS .... National Ocean Survey System [Cooperative program of governmental agencies]
NOSS .... National Office Support System (NITA)
NOSS .... National Orbiting Space Station
NOSS .... Navy Ocean Surveillance System
NOSS .... Nimbus Operational Satellite System [GSFC/USWB]
NOss........... Ossining Public Library, Ossining, NY [Library symbol Library of Congress] (LCLS)
NOSSA .... New Orleans Steamship Association (EA)
NOSSCR ...... National Organization of Social Security Claimants' Representatives (EA)
NOSSO .... Naval Ordnance Systems Support Office (MCD)
NOSSOLANT... Naval Ordnance Systems Support Office, Atlantic
NOSSOPAC... Naval Ordnance Systems Support Office, Pacific
NOSSOREP... Naval Ordnance Systems Support Office Representative (DNAB)
NOST .... Knights of the Square Table (EA)
NOST .... Nuclear Operational Systems Test
NOSTA .... National Ocean Science and Technology Agency
NOSTA .... Naval Ophthalmic Support and Training Activity
No St C .... Northern State College (South Dakota) (GAGS)
NoStPw........ Northern States Power Co. [Associated Press] (SAG)
NOSTS .... National Ocean Survey Tide Station [Marine science] (MSC)
NOsU .... State University of New York, College at Oswego, Oswego, NY [Library symbol Library of Congress] (LCLS)
NOS/VE .... Network Operating System / Virtual Environment (HGAA)
NOT .... New Organization Training
NOT .... New Orleans Terminal [AAR code]
NOT .... Nordic Optical Telescope
NOT .... Noront Resources Ltd. [Vancouver Stock Exchange symbol]
NOT .... Notary (WDAA)
NOT .... Notation (ROG)
NOT .... Noted
NOT .... Notice (ROG)
NOT .... Notion
NOT .... Not Our Title [Publishing] (WDMC)
NOT .... Nucleus of the Optic Tract [Eye anatomy]
NOT .... Number of Turns (IAA)
NOTA .... National Organ Transplant Act [1984]
NOTA .... None of the Above [Politics]
NOTACGENSEA... Nontactical Generator, Southeast Asia
NOTACK....... No Attack Area [Military] (NVT)
NOTAD........ Notice to Airmen Address
NOTAEI........ National Old Timers' Association of the Energy Industry (EA)
NOTAL .... Not at All
NOTAL .... Not to, nor Needed by, All
NOTAM........ Notice to Airmen
NOTAM........ Notice to Mariners (DOMA)
NOTAP........ Navy Occupational Task Analysis Program (NVT)
NOTAR......... No-Tail Rotor [Helicopters]
NOTARC....... National Old Timers Auto Racing Club (EA)
NOTAS .... Notice to Airmen Summary
NOTB .... National Ophthalmic Treatment Board [British]
NOTBA .... National Ophthalmic Treatment Board Association [British]
NOTC .... Naval Ordnance Test Center (KSC)
NOTC .... NOAA [National Oceanic and Atmospheric Administration] Operational Telecommunications Coordinator (NOAA)
Not Cas....... Notes of Cases at Madras (Strange) [A publication] (DLA)
Not Cas....... Notes of Cases, English Ecclesiastical and Maritime Courts [1841-50] [A publication] (DLA)
Not Cas Ecc & M... Notes of Cases, English Ecclesiastical and Maritime Courts [1841-50] [A publication] (DLA)
Not Cas Madras... Notes of Cases at Madras (Strange) [A publication] (DLA)

NOTCOMM... Not Commissioned [*Military*]
Notc on Fac... Notcutt on Factories and Workshops [*2nd ed.*] [*1879*] [*A publication*] (DLA)
Not Dec .... Notes of Decisions [*Martin's North Carolina Reports*] [*A publication*] (DLA)
Not Dig .... Boddam and Greenwood's Notanda Digest [*A publication*] (DLA)
Not Dign ...... Notitia Dignitatum [*Classical studies*] (OCD)
note .... Footnote in Cross-Reference (DLA)
NOTEF .... National Organ Transplant Education Foundation (EA)
NOTEMPS .... Nontemporary Storage System (MCD)
NOTES .... National Organization of Telecommunications Engineers and Scientists [*Washington, DC Telecommunications*] (TSSD)
Notes .... Notes (Music Library Association) [*A publication*] (BRI)
Notes Higher Ed... Notes on Higher Education [*A publication*]
Notes of Ca... Notes of Cases [*England*] [*A publication*] (DLA)
Notes of Cas... Notes of Cases, English Ecclesiastical and Maritime Courts [*1841-50*] [*A publication*] (DLA)
Notes of Cases... Notes of Cases, English Ecclesiastical and Maritime Courts [*1841-50*] [*A publication*] (DLA)
Notes on US... Notes on United States Reports [*A publication*] (DLA)
No Test........ Novum Testamentum (DSA)
NO-TFA........ National Old-Time Fiddlers' Association (EA)
NOTIF .... Notification
NOTIN .... Notification (ROG)
NOTIP .... Night Observation Television in a Pod
NOTIP .... Northern-Tier Integration Project [*Military*] (DNAB)
NOTIS .... Network Operations Trouble Information System [*Telecommunications*] (TEL)
NOTIS .... Northwestern Online Total Integrated System [*Northwestern University Library*] [*Library automation project*] [*Information service or system*] (IID)
Not J............ Notaries Journal [*A publication*] (DLA)
N-O-T-L........ Niagara-On-The-Lake [*Ontario*]
NOTL .... Notarial (ROG)
NOTM .... National Organization of Tutoring and Mentoring Centers (EA)
NOTM .... New Orleans, Texas & Mexico [*AAR code*]
NOTMAR...... Notice to Mariner (NVT)
NoTN .... Norges Tekniske Vitenskapsakademi [*Norwegian Academy for Technical Sciences*], Trondheim, Norway [*Library symbol Library of Congress*] (LCLS)
NOTN .... Notion (ABBR)
NoTNG .... Norges Geologiske Undersoeklse Biblioteket [*Geological Survey of Norway*], Trondheim, Norway [*Library symbol*] [*Library of Congress*] (LCLS)
NOTNO........ Notional Number (NVT)
NOTO .... Non-Official Trade Organisation [*British*]
NOTO .... Numbering Tool (AAG)
NOTOF........ Notice to Airmen Office
Not Op .... Wilmot's Notes of Opinions and Judgments [*A publication*] (DLA)
NOTOX....... No Toxic Incinerator Group [*Political party*]
NOTOX........ Not to Exceed (NOAA)
NOTR .... National Order of Trench Rats (EA)
Notrad .... No Traditions [*Internet*]
Notre Dame Est Plan Inst... Notre Dame Estate Planning Institute. Proceedings [*A publication*] (DLA)
Notre Dame J Leg... Notre Dame Journal of Legislation [*A publication*] (DLA)
NOTRTR....... National Organization of Test, Research, and Training Reactors [*Later, TRTR*] (EA)
NOTS .... Naval Ocean Transport Service [*Changed to MSTS in 1949 now MSC*] (DOMA)
NOTS .... Naval Ordnance Test Station
NOTS .... Naval Overseas Transport Service
NOTS .... NOAA [*National Oceanic and Atmospheric Administration*] Operational Telecommunications System (NOAA)
NOTS .... Nuclear Orbit Transfer Stage (PDAA)
NOT SAFE... National Organization Taunting Safety and Fairness Everywhere (EA)
Nott & Hop... Nott and Hopkins' Reports [*United States Court of Claims*] [*A publication*] (DLA)
Nott & Hunt... Nott and Huntington's Reports [*1-7 United States Court of Claims*] [*A publication*] (DLA)
Nott & McC... Nott and McCord's South Carolina Reports [*A publication*] (DLA)
Nott & M'C (SC)... Nott and M'Cord's South Carolina Reports [*A publication*] (DLA)
NOTTM .... Nottingham [*County in England*]
Nott Mech L.. Nott on the Mechanics' Lien Law [*A publication*] (DLA)
NOTTS .... Nottinghamshire [*County in England*]
Notts .... Nottinghamshire [*County in England*] (ODBW)
NOTU .... Naval Operational Training Unit
NOTU .... Naval Ordnance Test Unit
NoTU .... Universitetet i Trondheim [*University of Trondheim*], Trondheim, Norway [*Library symbol Library of Congress*] (LCLS)
NOTUN........ Notice of Unreliability
NoTU-T .... Universitetet i Trondheim, Norges Tekniske Hogskole [*University of Trondheim, Norwegian Institute of Technology*], Trondheim-NTH, Norway [*Library symbol Library of Congress*] (LCLS)
NoTU-V........ Universitetet i Trondheim, Kongelige Norske Videnskabers Selskabs [*University of Trondheim, Royal Norwegian Society of Sciences and Letters*], Trondheim, N orway [*Library symbol Library of Congress*] (LCLS)
NOTWG....... Notwithstanding
NOTWSTG... Notwithstanding
NOTWT .... Do Not Transmit by Radio (NATG)
NOTY .... Notary (ROG)
NOU .... Naval Ordnance Unit
NOU .... Noumea [*New Caledonia*] [*Airport symbol*] (OAG)

NOU............ Noumea [*New Caledonia*] [*Seismograph station code, US Geological Survey*] (SEIS)
NOU .... Nouvelles (NITA)
NOU .... Sitka, AK [*Location identifier FAA*] (FAAL)
NOUR.......... Nourish (ABBR)
NOURD .... Nourished (ABBR)
NOURG .... Nourishing (ABBR)
NOURT........ Nourishment (ABBR)
NOUS.......... Naval Order of the United States (EA)
Nouv Rev.... Nouvelle Revue de Droit Francais [*Paris*] [*A publication*] (DLA)
NOV .... Avianova SpA [*Italy ICAO designator*] (FAAC)
NOV .... Huambo [*Angola*] [*Airport symbol*] (OAG)
NOV .... Nodamura Virus
NOV .... Non Obstante Veredicto [*Judgment Notwithstanding*] [*Latin Legal term*] (DLA)
NOV .... Nonoccluded Virus
NOV .... Notice of Violation [*Nuclear energy*] (NRCH)
NOV .... NovaCare [*NYSE symbol*] (SPSG)
NOV .... Nova Lisboa [*Angola*] [*Airport symbol*] (AD)
NOV .... Novamin, Inc. [*Toronto Stock Exchange symbol*]
NOV .... Novara [*Sicily*] [*Seismograph station code, US Geological Survey*] (SEIS)
NOV .... Novation [*Legal term*] (DLA)
NOV .... Novel (ROG)
NOV .... Novelist (ABBR)
Nov .... Novellae [*Classical studies*] (OCD)
NOV .... November (AAG)
Nov .... November (ODBW)
NOV .... Novitiate (ROG)
nov............. Novum [*New*] [*Latin*] (MAE)
NOVA .... National Organization for Victim Assistance (EA)
NOVA .... National Outdoor Volleyball Association [*Defunct*] (EA)
NOVA .... National Overhead Evaluation Assessment [*Term for the restructuring process begun at E. F. Hutton after the October 1987 stock market collapse*]
NOVA .... Network Organization via Advanced Architecture [*Marubeni Corp.*]
NOVA .... Northern Valley Private Industry Council [*Sunnyvale, CA*] (ECON)
Nova .... Nova Corp. [*Associated Press*] (SAG)
NOVA .... Nova Omega Ventura Apollo [*General Motors automobiles*]
NOVA .... Nurses Organization of Veterans Affairs (EA)
NOVA .... Nutritional Oncology Vascular Access
NovaCre..... NovaCare [*Associated Press*] (SAG)
Novadig ...... Novadigm, Inc. [*Associated Press*] (SAG)
Novatk .... Novatek International, Inc. [*Associated Press*] (SAG)
NOVATOR ... Novye Torit [*Newly Flattened*] [*KGB term for newly recruited agent abroad*]
Nova U .... Nova University (GAGS)
Novavx........ Novavax, Inc. [*Associated Press*] (SAG)
NOVC.......... Novice (ABBR)
NOVCAM...... Nonvolatile Charge-Addressed Memory [*Computer science*] (PDAA)
NOV/CD....... Notice of Violation / Compliance Demand (EPA)
Nov Com Fragm... Novae Comoediae Fragmenta in Papyris Reperta Exceptis Menandreis [*A publication*] (OCD)
NOVE .... NOMOS Verlagskatalog [*NOMOS Datapool*] [*Information service or system*] (IID)
NOVEL .... Narrative Output Vocabulary Editing Language [*Psychiatric test*]
Novell......... Novell, Inc. [*Associated Press*] (SAG)
Noven .... Noven Pharmaceuticals, Inc. [*Associated Press*] (SAG)
NOVI........... Novitron International, Inc. [*NASDAQ symbol*] (NQ)
NOVICE .... Night Operational Vision and the Individual Combat Engineer (MCD)
Novitrn........ Novitron International, Inc. [*Associated Press*] (SAG)
NOVL .... Novell, Inc. [*NASDAQ symbol*] (NQ)
NOVL .... Novell Inc. [*NASDAQ symbol*] (TTSB)
NOVLT .... Novelty
Novlus .... Novellus Systems, Inc. [*Associated Press*] (SAG)
NOVM.......... No Obvious Value Mail [*Postal service*]
Novmtx........ Novametrics Medical Systems [*Associated Press*] (SAG)
Novmtx .... Novametrix Medical Systems, Inc. [*Associated Press*] (SAG)
NOVN.......... Noven Pharmaceuticals [*NASDAQ symbol*] (TTSB)
NOVN.......... Noven Pharmaceuticals, Inc. [*NASDAQ symbol*] (NQ)
NOV N .... Novum Nomen [*New Name*] [*Latin*] (BABM)
nov n .... Novum Nomen [*New Name*] [*Latin*] (DAVI)
NovoNdk..... Novo Nordisk AS [*Associated Press*] (SAG)
Novoste....... Novoste Corp. [*Associated Press*] (SAG)
NOVP.......... Novantrone, Oncovin, Vinblastine, Prednisone [*Antineoplastic drug*] (CDI)
NOVRAM..... Non-Volatile Random Access Memory [*Computer science*]
NOVRAM..... Nonvolotile Static RAM (NITA)
NOVS.......... National Office of Vital Statistics [*Public Health Service*] [*Obsolete*]
Nov Sc Dec.. Nova Scotia Decisions [*A publication*] (DLA)
Nov Sc LR ... Nova Scotia Law Reports [*A publication*] (DLA)
NOV SP....... Novum Species [*New Species*] [*Latin*] (BABM)
nov sp .... Novum Species [*New species*] [*Latin*] (DAVI)
NOVST........ Novelist
NOVT .... Novelty (ABBR)
NOVT .... Novoste Corp [*NASDAQ symbol*] (TTSB)
NOVT .... Novoste Corp. [*NASDAQ symbol*] (SAG)
NOW .... MAI Systems [*AMEX symbol*] (TTSB)
NOW .... MAI Systems Corp. [*AMEX symbol*] (SAG)
NOW .... National Organization for Women (EA)
NOW .... National Organizations of the World [*A publication*]
NOW .... National Overhaul Warranty [*Automotive engineering*]
NOW .... Negotiable Order of Withdrawal [*Banking*]
NOW .... Neighbors of Woodcraft [*Portland, OR*] (EA)
NOW .... Network Order Wire [*Military*] (CAAL)

NOW	News of the World [*A publication*] (DGA)
NOW	Nonhazardous Oil Field Waste [*Environmental Protection Agency*] (FFDE)
NOW	Northway Explorations Ltd. [*Toronto Stock Exchange symbol*]
NOW	Nurture-Outreach-Witness [*Religion*]
NOW	Port Angeles, WA [*Location identifier FAA*] (FAAL)
NOW	Royal Norwegian Air Force [*ICAO designator*] (FAAC)
NOWAI	Neshei Ubenos Agudath Israel [*Antwerp*] (BJA)
NOWAPA	North American Water and Power Alliance (NADA)
NOWD	Northward (ABBR)
No West Rep...	Northwestern Reporter [*Commonly cited NW*] [*A publication*] (DLA)
NOweWJ	Wheatley Junior-Senior High School, Old Westbury, NY [*Library symbol Library of Congress*] (LCLS)
NOwHC-U	Old Westbury School of the Holy Child, Upper School, Old Westbury, NY [*Library symbol*] [*Library of Congress*] (LCLS)
NOWIS	National Older Workers Information System [*American Association of Retired Persons*] [*Information service or system Defunct*] (IID)
NOWL	National Order of Women Legislators (EA)
NOW LDEF...	NOW [*National Organization for Women*] Legal Defense and Education Fund (EA)
NOWME	National Organisation for Women's Management Education [*British*] (DI)
No W Mo St U...	Nortwest Missouri State University (GAGS)
NOwNC	New York College of Osteopathic Medicine, Old Westbury, NY [*Library symbol Library of Congress*] (LCLS)
NOwNI	New York Institute of Technology, Old Westbury, NY [*Library symbol Library of Congress*] (LCLS)
NOwNI-C......	New York Institute of Technology, Commack Center Library, Commack, NY [*Library symbol Library of Congress*] (LCLS)
NOwNI-CI.....	New York Institute of Technical, Central Islip, NY [*Library symbol*] [*Library of Congress*] (LCLS)
NOwNI-N......	New York Institute of Technology, New York, NY [*Library symbol Library of Congress*] (LCLS)
No W Okla St U...	Northwestern Oklahoma State University (GAGS)
NOWPA........	National Osteopathic Women Physician's Association (EA)
NOWP-OM ...	National Older Workers Programs - Operation Mainstream [*Department of Labor*]
NOWR.........	Nuclear Ordnance War Reserve [*Military*] (AFIT)
NOWSA........	National One-Write Systems Association (EA)
Nowsc.........	Nowsco Well Services Ltd. [*Associated Press*] (SAG)
No W St U La...	Northwestern State University of Louisiana (GAGS)
NOwU	State University of New York, College at Old Westbury, Oyster Bay, NY [*Library symbol Library of Congress*] (LCLS)
NOWUS........	Normal Operation with Unscram [*Nuclear energy*] (NRCH)
NOwWJ.......	Wheatley Junior-Senior High School, Old Westbury, NY [*Library symbol*] [*Library of Congress*] (LCLS)
NOWWN	National Organization of World War Nurses (EA)
NOX	Air Nordic in Vasteras AB [*Sweden ICAO designator*] (FAAC)
NOX	Nitrous Oxide [*Laughing gas*]
NOX	Novavax Inc. [*AMEX symbol*] (TTSB)
NOX	Novavax, Inc. [*AMEX symbol*] (SAG)
NOX	Noxious (ABBR)
NOx............	Oxford Memorial Library, Oxford, NY [*Library symbol Library of Congress*] (LCLS)
NOXA	Naphthoxyacetic Acid [*Organic chemistry*]
NOXO	Noxso Corp. [*NASDAQ symbol*] (NQ)
Noxso	Noxso Corp. [*Associated Press*] (SAG)
NOXY	Noxiously (ABBR)
NOXZEMA	Knocks Eczema [*Acronym, brand name for skin cream, said to be taken from this phrase*]
NOY	Not Out Yet
Noy	Noy's English King's Bench Reports [*1559-1649*] [*A publication*] (DLA)
NOy.............	Oyster Bay-East Norwich Public Library, Oyster Bay, NY [*Library symbol Library of Congress*] (LCLS)
Noy Ch U	Noyes on Charitable Uses [*A publication*] (DLA)
Noye	Grounds and Maxims of English Law, by William Noye [*A publication*] (DLA)
Noy (Eng)	Noy's English King's Bench Reports [*1559-1649*] [*A publication*] (DLA)
Noye's Max...	Maxims of the Laws of England, by William Noye [*A publication*] (DLA)
NOyHS	Oyster Bay High School, Oyster Bay, NY [*Library symbol Library of Congress*] (LCLS)
Noy Max......	Noy's Maxims [*A publication*] (DLA)
NOyRE	Theodore Roosevelt Elementary School, Oyster Bay, NY [*Library symbol*] [*Library of Congress*] (LCLS)
NOYS	National Organization for Youth Safety [*NHTSA*] (TAG)
NOyStD	Saint Dominic High School, Oyster Bay, NY [*Library symbol*] [*Library of Congress*] (LCLS)
NOZ	Elizabeth City, NC [*Location identifier FAA*] (FAAL)
NOZ	No Operating Zone (DA)
NOZ	Nozzle (AAG)
NOZ	Nozzle
NOZE	US National Ozone Expedition [*1986*] [*McMurdo Station, Antarctica*]
NP	Adriance Memorial Library, Poughkeepsie, NY [*Library symbol Library of Congress*] (LCLS)
NP	Desert Pacific [*ICAO designator*] (AD)
np----	Great Plains [*MARC geographic area code Library of Congress*] (LCCP)
NP...............	Nacionalista Party [*Philippines*]
NP...............	Name of Publisher (NITA)
NP...............	Nameplate
NP...............	NAPALM [*Naphthenic and Palmitic Acids*] (NATG)
NP...............	[*The*] Narragansett Pier Railroad Co. Inc. (IIA)

NP	Nasal Prongs [*For administration of oxygen*] (DAVI)
NP	Nasionale Party van Suid-Afrika [*National Party of South Africa*] [*Political party*] (PPW)
NP	Nasionale Party van Suidwesafrika [*National Party of South West Africa*] [*Namibia*] [*Political party*] (PPW)
NP	Nasopharyngeal [*or Nasopharynx*] [*Medicine*]
NP	Nationalist Parnellite [*British*] (ROG)
NP	Nationalist Party [*Malta*] [*Political party*] (PPE)
NP	Nationalist Party [*Philippines*] [*Political party*] (PPW)
NP	National Parks [*A publication*] (BRI)
NP	National Party [*Papua New Guinea*] [*Political party*] (PPW)
NP	National Pipe [*Thread*]
NP	National Police (CINC)
NP	National Porkettes (EA)
NP	National Power PLC [*NYSE symbol*] (SAG)
NP	National Publishing Co. [*Philadelphia*]
NP	Nation Party [*Turkey*] [*Political party*] (PPW)
NP	Natural Passivation [*Metallurgy*]
NP	Naval Party [*British military*] (DMA)
NP	Naval Patrol [*British military*] (DMA)
NP	Naval Pattern [*British military*] (DMA)
NP	Naval Pension [*British*] (ROG)
NP	Naval Police [*British*] (ROG)
NP	Naval Prison
NP	Naval Publication (IEEE)
NP	Neap Tide
NP	Near Point
NP	Needle Position [*on dial*]
NP	Negative Prescreening [*Marketing*]
NP	Negative Pressure (NRCH)
NP	Neo-Punic (BJA)
np	Nepal [*MARC country of publication code Library of Congress*] (LCCP)
NP	Nepal [*ANSI two-letter standard code*] (CNC)
Np	Neper [*A unit on a natural logarithmic scale*]
Np	Neptunium [*Chemical element*]
NP	Net Position [*Business term*]
NP	Net Price [*Business term*] (MHDW)
NP	Net Proceeds
NP	Net Profit
NP	Network Planning [*Computer science*]
NP	Network Program (NASA)
NP	Network Project [*An association*] (EA)
NP	Neuritic Plaque [*Pathology*]
NP	Neuropathology [*Medicine*]
NP	Neurophysin [*Biochemistry*]
NP	Neurophysiological
NP	Neuropsychiatric
N/P	Neuro-Psychiatry [*Medical Officer designation*] [*British*]
NP	Newly Presented (DMAA)
NP	New Paragraph
np	New Paragraph (WDMC)
NP	New Party (EA)
NP	New Patient
NP	New Pattern [*British military*] (DMA)
np	New Pence [*Monetary unit in Great Britain since 1971*]
NP	New Permutations
NP	New Point [*Used in correcting manuscripts, etc.*]
NP	Newport [*Rhode Island*]
NP	New Position
NP	New Providence
N/P	Newspaper
NP	Nickel Plated [*Guns*]
NP	Nippon Investment Corp. [*Vancouver Stock Exchange symbol*]
NP	Nisi Prius [*Unless Before*] [*Legal term Latin*]
NP	Nitrogen-Phosphorus [*Chemistry*] (MAE)
NP	Nitrophenide [*Pharmacology*]
NP	Nitrophenoacetylamino Caproate
NP	Nitropropane [*Organic chemistry*]
NP	Nitro Proved [*Rifle mark*] (DICI)
NP	Nitroprusside [*A vasodilator*]
NP	Nitropyrene [*Organic chemistry*]
NP	Nitrosopiperidine [*Organic chemistry*]
NP	Nobel Prize
NP	Nomen Proprium [*Proper Name*] [*Latin*]
NP	Nominal Horsepower (IAA)
NP	Nondeterministic Polynomial [*Mathematics*]
NP	Nonpapillate [*Type of seed*] [*Botany*]
NP	Nonparticipating [*Insurance or finance*]
NP	Non-Patents (NITA)
N/P	Nonpayment (ROG)
NP	Nonperson
NP	Nonpolarized [*Computer science*]
NP	Nonpolice (BARN)
NP	Nonpractising Member [*Chiropody*] [*British*]
NP	Nonprint [*Computer science*] (IAA)
NP	Nonprocurable
NP	Nonprofit (BARN)
NP	Nonpropelled (AAG)
NP	Nonylphenol [*Organic chemistry*]
NP	No Paging
NP	No Parity
NP	No Party with the Name of the Recipient of the Message [*International telex abbreviation*] (WDMC)
NP	No Pin [*Electronics*] (OA)

NP	No Place [of publication] [Bibliography]
np	No Place (WDMC)
NP	No Predators [Ecology]
NP	No Print [Telecommunications] (TEL)
NP	No Printer Listed (NTCM)
NP	No Prospect [In sports]
NP	No Protest [Banking]
NP	No Publisher Listed (NTCM)
NP	Normal Phase [Chromatography]
NP	Normal Pitch (ADA)
NP	Normal Plasma [Medicine] (MAE)
NP	Normal Pregnancy [Medicine]
NP	Normal Pressure
NP	Normal Profit [Business term] (MHDW)
NP	Northern Pacific Railway Co. (MHDW)
NP	Northern Pine [Utility pole] [Telecommunications] (TEL)
NP	North Pole [Also, PN]
NP	Notary Public
N/P	Notes Payable
N/P	Notes Payable [Finance] (DFIT)
NP	Not Perceptible [Medicine]
NP	Not Performed
NP	Not Planned
NP	Not Practiced [Medicine]
NP	Not Preferred
NP	Not Present (DAVI)
NP	Not Pressed or Glazed [Paper] (DGA)
NP	Not Printed (ILCA)
N/P	Not Provided (KSC)
N/P	Not Provided
NP	Noun Phrase [Linguistics]
NP	Nucleoplasmic [Index] [Cytology]
NP	Nucleoprotein [Biochemistry]
NP	Nucleoside Phosphorylase [An enzyme]
np	Nucleotide Pair [Genetics] (DOG)
NP	Nucleus Pulposus [Medicine] (DAVI)
NP	Number of Primary Turns (IAA)
N_p	Number of Primary Turns (IDOE)
NP	Number of Steps, Polynomial Time [Mathematics]
NP	Nursed Poorly [Medicine] (DMAA)
NP	Nurse Practitioner
NP	Nursing Procedure
NP	Ohio Nisi Prius Reports [A publication] (DLA)
NP0	Negative-Positive-Zero
NPA	Committee for a National Peace Academy [Later, N-PAC] (EA)
NPA	Napan [West Irian, Indonesia] [Airport symbol] (AD)
NPA	Naphthylphthalamic Acid [Organic chemistry]
NPA	National Paddleball Association (EA)
NPA	National Panel of Arbitrators
NPA	National Paperboard Association [Later, API]
NPA	National Paralegal Association (EA)
NPA	National Parenthood Association (NADA)
NPA	National Parents Association
NPA	National Parking Association (EA)
NPA	National Parks and Access to the Countryside Act [Town planning] [British]
NPA	National Parks Association [Later, NPCA] (EA)
NPA	National Particleboard Association (EA)
NPA	National Pasta Association (EA)
NPA	National Patrolmen's Association
NPA	National Pawnbrokers Association (EA)
NPA	National Payphone Association (EA)
NPA	National Peace Academy
NPA	National Pediculosis Association (EA)
NPA	National People's Action (EA)
NPA	National Perinatal Association (EA)
NPA	National Peripheral Association (EA)
NPA	National Personnel Associates
NPA	National Pet Association [Defunct] (EA)
NPA	National Petroleum Association [Later, NPRA]
NPA	National Pharmaceutical Association [Washington, DC]
NPA	National Phlebotomy Association (EA)
NPA	National Pigeon Association [Defunct] (EA)
NPA	National Pilots Association [Defunct] (EA)
NPA	National Pistol Association [British] (DI)
NPA	National Pituitary Agency [Later, NHPP]
NPA	National Planning Association (EA)
NPA	National Plastercraft Association (EA)
NPA	National Playbus Association [British] (DBA)
NPA	National Podiatry Association [Later, NPMA] (EA)
NPA	National Poker Association (EA)
NPA	National Portage Association [British] (DBA)
NPA	National Ports Authority [British]
NPA	National Postmasters Auxiliary (EA)
NPA	National Poultry Association [Australia]
NPA	National Prescription Audit
NPA	National Preservers Association [Later, International Jelly and Preserve Association] (EA)
NPA	National Priority Area [Military]
NPA	National Proctologic Association (EA)
NPA	National Production Authority [Functions merged into BDSA, 1953]
NPA	National Productivity Authority (MHDB)
NPA	National Prohibition Act
NPA	National Psychological Association [Defunct] (EA)
NPA	Naval Procurement Account

NPA	Navy Postal Affairs Section Publication
NPA	Navy Purchasing Activity (AFIT)
NPA	Near Point Accommodation [Ophthalmology]
NPA	Neighborhood Publication Area Report [Bureau of the Census] (GFGA)
NPA	Network Program Analysis by ADI [Area of Dominant Influence] [Arbitron Ratings Co.] [Information service or system] (CRD)
NPA	Neutrons per Absorption (DEN)
NPA	New People's Army [Philippines] (PD)
NPA	New Populist Action [Defunct] (EA)
NPA	New Product Announcements [Predicasts, Inc.] [Cleveland, OH] [Information service or system] (IID)
NPA	Newspaper Publishers' Association [British] (DCTA)
NPA	Nine Pin Association [Schauenburg, Federal Republic of Germany] (EAIO)
NPA	Nonbuffered Pyrophosphatase Activity
NPA	Non-Par Approved
NPA	Non-Principal Axis
NPA	No Previous Admission [Medicine] (MEDA)
NPA	No Price Available [Business term] (ADA)
NPA	Normal Pressure Angle
NPA	Northern Pipeline Agency [Ottawa, ON]
NPA	Notice of Proposed Amendment (DA)
NPA	Novel Plasminogen Activator [Anticlotting agent]
NPA	N-Propylamine [Organic chemistry]
NPA	Nuclear Plant Analyzer (NRCH)
NPA	Numbering Plan Area [Bell System] [Telecommunications]
NPA	Numerical Production Analysis (IEEE)
NPA	Pensacola, FL [Location identifier FAA] (FAAL)
NPA	PTS [Predicasts, Inc.] New Product Announcements/Plus [Information service or system] (IID)
NPAA	National Park Academy of the Arts (EA)
NPAA	National Photographic Art Archive [Victoria and Albert Museum] [British]
NPAA	National Postal Arts Association (EA)
NPAA	Noise Pollution and Abatement Act (GFGA)
NPAACT	National Parks Association of the Australian Capital Territory
NPAB	Navy Price Adjustment Board
NPAB	Nuclear Power Advisory Board (PDAA)
NPABC	National Public Affairs Center for Television (NADA)
NPAC	National Parks Advisory Council [Australia]
N-PAC	National Peace Academy Campaign [Formerly, NPA] (EA)
NPAC	National Peace Action Coalition
NPAC	National Plantation Advisory Committee
NPAC	National Political Action Committee (EA)
NPAC	National Program for Acquisitions and Cataloging [Library of Congress]
NPAC	National Project in Agricutural Communication (PDAA)
NPAC	Navy Procurement Assignment Committee
NPAC	Northeast Parallel Architectures Center [Syracuse University] [Research center] (RCD)
NPAC	Northern Pipeline Agency Canada [See also APNC]
NPACI	National Production Advisory Council on Industry [British]
NPACOE	National Panhellenic Association of Central Office Executives (EA)
NPACSE	National Political Action Committee for Scientists and Engineers
NPACT	National Public Affairs Center for Television [Defunct]
NPAED	National Progress Association for Economic Development (EA)
NPAF	National Peace Academy Foundation (EA)
NPAF	National Picture & Frame Co. [NASDAQ symbol] (SAG)
NPAF	National Pledge of Allegiance Foundation (EA)
NPA(G)R	National Parks and Access to the Countryside (Grants) Regulations [Town planning] [British]
NPAH	Nitrated Polycyclic Aromatic Hydrocarbons [Automotive emissions] [Organic chemistry]
NPAI	Network Protocol Addressing Information [Telecommunications] (OSI)
NPAI	Nevada Public Affairs Institute [University of Nevada - Reno] [Research center] (RCD)
NPals	Palisades Free Library, Palisades, NY [Library symbol Library of Congress] (LCLS)
NPAM	Navy Priorities and Allocations Manual (DNAB)
NPAM	Nonpermanent Active Militia
NPAN	National Plan for Australian Newspapers
NP & GT Rep	Nisi Prius and General Term Reports [Ohio] [A publication] (DLA)
NP & OSR	Naval Petroleum and Oil Shale Reserve
NP & PA	National Paperbox and Packaging Association (EA)
NPANX	Naval Potomac Annex
NPAP	National Psychological Association for Psychoanalysis (EA)
NPAP	Navy Public Affairs Plan (DNAB)
NPAP	Niue People's Action Party [Political party] (EY)
NPAR	Negative-Positive Acknowledgment and Retransmission [Telecommunications] (IAA)
NPAR	Nonstandard Part Approval Request (MCD)
NP/ARCA	National Pacific/Asian Resource Center on Aging (EA)
NPAS	National Policy Assistance Standards (AAGC)
NPAS	Normalized Photoacoustic Signal [Instrumentation]
NPASO	National Postsecondary Agriculture Student Organization (EA)
NPAT	National Political Awareness Test [Sent to all candidates in presidential, congressional, gubernatorial, and most state legislative races]
NPat	Patchogue Library, Patchogue, NY [Library symbol Library of Congress] (LCLS)
NPatB	Brookhaven Town Hall, Historical Collection, Patchogue, NY [Library symbol Library of Congress] (LCLS)
NPatBH	Brookhaven Memorial Hospital, Patchogue, NY [Library symbol Library of Congress] (LCLS)

NPatSJ......... Saint Joseph's College, Patchogue, NY [*Library symbol Library of Congress*] (LCLS)
NPAV......... National Parks Association of Victoria [*Australia*]
NPAWT......... National Plan of Action for Women in TAFE [*Technical and Further Education*] [*Australia*]
NPB......... NADGE [*NATO Air Defense Ground Environment*] Policy Board (NATG)
NPB......... National Park Board (NADA)
NPB......... National Parole Board [*Canada*]
NPB......... National Planning Board [*Terminated, 1944; superseded by National Resources Board*]
NPB......... National Plant Board (EA)
NPB......... National Prayer Breakfast (EA)
NPB......... National Productivity Board (NADA)
NPB......... Neutral Particle Beam (MCD)
NPB......... Newspaper Bag (ROG)
NPB......... Nodal Premature Beat [*Cardiology*]
NPB......... Nonplasminogen Binding [*Hematology*]
NPB......... Nonprimate Biosatellite
NPB......... Non-Protein Bound [*Medicine*] (DMAA)
NPB......... Norfolk & Portsmouth Belt Line Railroad Co. [*AAR code*]
NPBA......... National Palomino Breeders Association [*Inactive*]
NPBA......... National Paper Box Association [*Formerly, NPBMA; later NP & PA*] (EA)
NPBA......... National Perinatal Bereavement Association [*Defunct*] (EA)
NPBA......... National Pig Breeders' Association [*British*] (BI)
NPBA......... National Pocket Billiards Association (EA)
NPBA......... National Police Bloodhound Association (EA)
NPBA......... National Poro Beautician Association [*Defunct*] (EA)
NPBA......... Natural Product Broker Association [*St. Augustine, FL*] (EA)
NPBC......... National Penn Bancshares, Inc. [*NASDAQ symbol*] (NQ)
NPBC......... National Progressive Broadcast Coalition [*Defunct*] (EA)
NPBC......... Natl Penn Bancshares [*NASDAQ symbol*] (TTSB)
NPBE......... National Political Button Exchange [*An association Defunct*] (EA)
NPBE......... Nitrophenyl Butyl Ether [*Organic chemistry*]
NPBE......... Nonlinear Poisson-Boltzmann Equation [*Physical chemistry*]
NPBEA......... National Poultry, Butter, and Egg Association [*Defunct*] (EA)
NPBI......... National Pretzel Bakers Institute [*Defunct*] (EA)
NPBMA......... National Paper Box Manufacturers Association (EA)
NPBOA......... National Party Boat Owners Alliance (EA)
NPBRO......... Naval Plant Branch Representative Office
NPBS......... Navy Personnel Billeting System (DNAB)
NPBSA......... National Paper Box Supplies Association [*Defunct*] (EA)
NPC......... NASA Procurement Circular
NPC......... NASA Publication Control (KSC)
NPC......... Nasopharyngeal Carcinoma [*Medicine*]
NPC......... National Packaging Confederation [*British*] (DBA)
NPC......... National Panhellenic Conference (EA)
NPC......... National Patent Council (EA)
NPC......... National Peace Council [*British*]
NPC......... National Peach Council (EA)
NPC......... National Peanut Council (EA)
NPC......... National People's Congress [*Nigeria*] [*Political party*]
NPC......... National People's Congress [*China*] [*Political party*] (PPW)
NPC......... National Periodicals Center
NPC......... National Personnel Consultants [*Later, NAPC*] [*Defunct*] (EA)
NPC......... National Petroleum Council [*Department of Energy*] (EA)
NPC......... National Petroleum Council [*Marine science*] (OSRA)
NPC......... National Pharmaceutical Council (EA)
NPC......... National Philatelic Center [*Australia*]
NPC......... National Philatelic Collections [*Smithsonian Institution*]
NPC......... National Playwrights Conference (EA)
NPC......... National Plumbing Code
NPC......... National Poetry Circle [*Cambridge*] [*British*]
NPC......... National Ports Council [*British*]
NPC......... National Potato Council (EA)
NPC......... National Press Club (EA)
NPC......... National Prime Contractor (NATG)
NPC......... National Processing Centre [*Marine science*] (MSC)
NPC......... National Productivity Council [*Inactive*]
NPC......... National Publicity Council for Health and Welfare Services [*Later, NPRC*]
NPC......... Native Preacher Co. [*An association*] (EA)
NPC......... NATO Parliamentarians' Conference
NPC......... NATO Pipeline Committee
NPC......... NATO Programming Center (NATG)
NPC......... Nauru Phosphate Commission [*Australia*]
NPC......... Naval Personnel Committee [*British military*] (DMA)
NPC......... Naval Photographic Center
NPC......... Navy Policy Council
NPC......... Navy Procurement Circular
NPC......... Near Point of Convergence [*Ophthalmology*]
NPC......... Needle Punch Card
NPC......... Neplanocin A [*Biochemistry*]
NPC......... Neuropsychiatry Clerical Procedure [*Navy*]
NPC......... Neuropsychiatry Clerical Technician [*Navy*]
NPC......... New Practice Cases [*Legal*] [*British*]
NPC......... New Practice Cases. Bail Court [*1844-48*] [*A publication*] (DLA)
NP-C......... Niemann-Pick Type C [*Disease*] [*Medicine*]
NPC......... Ninety Pound Charge
NPC......... Nisi Prius Cases [*England*] [*A publication*] (DLA)
NPC......... Nitrogen Purge Control (NASA)
NPC......... Nitrogen Purge Control
NPC......... Nodal Premature Contraction [*Cardiology*] (MAE)
NPC......... Nominal Protection Coefficient [*Business term*]
NPC......... Nonphased Color [*Television signals*] (NTCM)
NPC......... Nonplayer Characters [*Computer science*]
NPC......... Nonprinting Character [*Computer science*]
NPC......... Nonproductive Cough [*Medicine*] (MEDA)
NPC......... Nonproductive Cough [*Medicine*] (DAVI)
NPC......... No Previous Carrier [*Insurance*]
NPC......... No Previous Complaint [*Medicine*] (DAVI)
NPC......... Normal Phase Chromatography
NPC......... North Pacific Coast Freight Bureau, Seattle WA [*STAC*]
NPC......... North Pacific Industry [*Vancouver Stock Exchange symbol*]
NPC......... North Polar Cap [*A filamentary mark on Mars*]
NPC......... NPC International, Inc. [*Associated Press*] (SAG)
NPC......... Nuclear Pore Complex [*Protein*]
NPC......... Nuclear Power Co. (NRCH)
NPC......... Nursing and Personal Care
NPC......... Nuveen Ins CA Prem Inc. Muni [*NYSE symbol*] (TTSB)
NPC......... Nuveen Insured California Premium Income Municipal [*NYSE symbol*] (SPSG)
NPC......... Public Library of Charlotte and Mecklenburg County, Charlotte, NC [*OCLC symbol*] (OCLC)
NPCa......... Nasopharyngeal Carcinoma [*Medicine*] (MAE)
NPCA......... National Paint and Coatings Association (EA)
NPCA......... National Parks and Conservation Association (EA)
NPCA......... National Pest Control Association (EA)
NPCA......... National Pig Carvers Association (EA)
NPCA......... National Plastercraft Association (EA)
NPCA......... National Precast Concrete Association (EA)
NPCA......... National Progressive Consumers Alliance (EA)
NPCBW......... National Political Congress of Black Women (EA)
NPCC......... National Poison Control Center (DAVI)
NPCC......... National Pop Can Collectors (EA)
NPCC......... Northeast Power Coordinating Council [*Regional power council*]
NPCC......... North Peralta Community College [*California*]
NPC/COES......... National Panhellenic Conference of Central Office Executives (EA)
NPCD......... National Association of Parish Coordinators/Directors of Religious Education (EA)
NPCDN......... National Private Circuit Digital Network (PDAA)
NPCF......... National Pollution Control Foundation
NPCFB......... North Pacific Coast Freight Bureau
NPCI......... National Potato Chip Institute [*Later, SFA*]
NPCI......... NPC International, Inc. [*NASDAQ symbol*] (SAG)
NPCI......... NPC Intl. [*NASDAQ symbol*] (TTSB)
NPCIL......... Nuclear Power Corp. of India Ltd.
NPC Intl......... NPC International, Inc. [*Associated Press*] (SAG)
NPCL......... North Pacific Coast Line (MHDB)
N-PCL......... Not-for-Profit Corp. Law [*New York, NY A publication*]
NP-CLT......... Neuropsychiatry Clerical Procedure Technician [*Navy*]
NPCMW......... North Pacific Central Mode Water [*Marine science*] (OSRA)
NPCN......... National Poison Center Network (EA)
NPCNU......... Neopentyl(chloroethyl)nitrosourea [*Biochemistry*]
N-P, Complete... Nondeterministic Polynomial Complete Problem [*Mathematics*]
NPCP......... Nairobi Peoples' Convention Party
NPCP......... National Prostatic Cancer Project
NPCR......... No Periodic Calibration Required (MCD)
NPCR......... No Programmed Calibration Required (MCD)
NPCS......... National Population Control Secretariat [*Australia*]
NP-CT......... Naval Personnel Conversion Tables
NP Cult......... Nasopharyngeal Culture [*Bacteriology*] (CPH)
NPCW......... National Pork Council Women (EA)
NPD......... Napped (ABBR)
NPD......... Narcissistic Personality Disorder [*Medicine*] (DMAA)
NPD......... NASA Policy Directive
NPD......... NASA Program Director (SSD)
NPD......... Nationaldemokratische Partei Deutschlands [*National Democratic Party of Germany*] [*Germany Political party*] (PPE)
NPD......... National Paint Distributors (EA)
NPD......... National Party for Democracy [*Zambia*] [*Political party*] (EY)
NPD......... National Patent Development Corp. [*AMEX symbol*] (SPSG)
NPD......... National Philanthropy Day (NFD)
NPD......... National Policy Debate [*Nuclear energy*] (NRCH)
NPD......... National Power Demonstration (IEEE)
NPD......... National Program Director
NPD......... National Program for Dermatology
NPD......... Natl Patent Devel [*AMEX symbol*] (TTSB)
NPD......... Natriuretic Plasma Dialysate [*Medicine*] (MAE)
NPD......... Navy Procurement Directives
NPD......... Nees Politikes Dynameis [*New Political Forces*] [*Greek Political party*] (PPE)
NPD......... Neimann-Pick Disease (CPH)
NPD......... Network Protection Device [*Telecommunications*] (TEL)
NPD......... Network Protective Device (NITA)
NPD......... New Product Development [*Business term*]
NPD......... New Providence Development Co. Ltd. [*Toronto Stock Exchange symbol*]
NPD......... Newspaper Press Directory [*A publication*] (DGA)
NPD......... Niemann-Pick Disease [*Medicine*]
NPD......... Night Perimeter Defense
NPD......... Nitrogen-Phosphorus Detector [*Analytical instrumentation*]
NPD......... Nitrogen, Phosphorus Gas Chromatographic Detector [*Spectroscopy*]
NPD......... Nominal Percent Defective
NPD......... Nonparental Ditype [*Genetics*]
NPD'......... No Pathologic Diagnosis [*Medicine*] (BARN)
NPD......... No Pay Due [*Military*] (ADDR)
NPD......... No Payroll Division
NPD......... North Pacific Division [*Army World War II*]

NPD .... North Pacific Drift [*Oceanography*]
NPD .... North Polar Distance
NPD .... Nouveau Parti Democratique [*New Democratic Party*] [*Canada Political party*] (EAIO)
NPD .... N-Player Prisoneris Dilemma
NPD .... Nuclear Power Demonstration [*of a reactor*]
NPD .... Nuclear Power Division (SAA)
NPD .... South African Law Reports, Natal Province Division [*A publication*] (DLA)
NPDA .... National Pharmaceutical Distributors' Association [*Australia*]
NPDA .... National Plywood Distributors Association (EA)
NPDA .... National Privy Diggers Association (EA)
NPDA .... National Pyrotechnic Distributors Association [*APA*] [*Absorbed by*] (EA)
NPDA .... Network Problem Determination Aid (NITA)
NPDA .... Network Problem Determination Application [*Computer science*]
NPDAA .... National Pharmaceutical Direct Advertising Association [*Defunct*] (EA)
NPDB .... National Practitioner Data Bank [*Information service or system*] (IID)
NPDB .... Nuclear Plant Databank (NRCH)
NPDBA .... National Pet Dealers and Breeders Association [*Defunct*] (EA)
NPDC .... Dutchess Community College, Poughkeepsie, NY [*Library symbol Library of Congress*] (LCLS)
NPDC .... National Patent Development Corp.
NPDC .... National Peace Day Celebration (EA)
NPDC .... National Planning Data Corp. [*Information service or system*] (IID)
NPDC .... National Poetry Day Committee (EA)
NPDCM .... Dutchess County Mental Health Center, Poughkeepsie, NY [*Library symbol Library of Congress*] (LCLS)
NPDDE .... Nitrophenyl Dodecyl Ether [*Organic chemistry*]
NPDE .... Nonlinear Partial Differential Equation
NPDEA .... National Professional Driver Education Association (AEBS)
NPDES .... National Pollutant Discharge Elimination System [*Environmental Protection Agency*]
NPDF .... Normal Probability Distribution Function
NPDI .... Nonperformance of Duty because Imprisoned [*Navy*]
NPDL .... Nodular Poorly Differentiated Lymphocyte
NPDM .... Navy Program Decision Meeting (DOMA)
NPDN .... Nordic Public Data Network [*Denmark, Finland, Iceland, Norway and Sweden*] (PDAA)
NPDNA .... Nucleoprotamine Deoxyribonucleic Acid
NPDO .... Nacelle Product Development Organization (MCD)
NPDO .... Non-Profit Distributing Organization (PDAA)
NPDR .... NCO Professional Development Ribbon [*Military decoration*]
NPDR .... Nonproliferative Diabetic Retinopathy [*Medicine*] (MAE)
NPDS .... National Pollutant Discharge Elimination System [*Environmental Protection Agency*] (ERG)
NPDS .... Nuclear Particle Detection System (KSC)
NPDSA .... National Public Domain Software Archive (AIE)
NPDU .... Naval Plant Development Unit (DNAB)
NPDU .... Network Protocol Data Unit [*Telecommunications*] (OSI)
NPDW .... North Pacific Deep Water [*Oceanography*]
NPDWG .... Networking Project for Disabled Women and Girls (EA)
NPDWR .... National Primary Drinking Water Regulations [*Environmental Protection Agency*]
NPE .... Elizabeth City State University, Elizabeth City, NC [*OCLC symbol*] (OCLC)
NPE .... Napier [*New Zealand*] [*Airport symbol*] (OAG)
NPE .... Nasal Physical Examination
NPE .... National Plastic Exposition
NPE .... National Population Enquiry
NPE .... Natural Parity Exchange [*Physics*] (OA)
NPE .... Naval Pilot Evaluation (MUGU)
NPE .... Navy Preliminary Evaluation
NPE .... Network Processing Element (NITA)
NPE .... New Preliminary Evaluation (MCD)
NPE .... Nonpolluting Engine [*Rocketdyne/Commonwealth Edison Co.*]
NPE .... Nonpotential Energy [*of molecules*]
NPE .... Nonylphenol Ethoxylate [*Organic chemistry*]
NPE .... Nuclear Photographic Emulsion
NPE .... Nuclear Planning and Execution System (MCD)
NPE .... Nuclear Power Engineering (IAA)
NPE .... Nuveen Ins Prem Inc. Muni [*NYSE symbol*] (TTSB)
NPE .... Nuveen Insured Premium Income Municipal [*NYSE symbol*] (SPSG)
NPEA .... National Patio Enclosure Association (EA)
NPEA .... National Printing Equipment Association [*Later, NPES*] (EA)
NPEB .... Nonparametric Empirical Bayes [*Statistics*]
NPEC .... National Panhellenic Editors Conference (EA)
NPEC .... Native Plants Extracts Cooperative [*Australia*]
NPEC .... Nuclear Power Engineering Committee [*Nuclear Regulatory Commission*] (NRCH)
NPECCD .... National Public Education Campaign on Clinical Depression
NPED .... Nuclear-Powered Energy Depot
NPee .... Field Library, Inc., Peekskill, NY [*Library symbol Library of Congress*] (LCLS)
NPEF .... New Product Evaluation Form
NPel .... Pelham Public Library, Pelham, NY [*Library symbol Library of Congress*] (LCLS)
NPELRA .... National Public Employer Labor Relations Association (EA)
NPEO .... Nonylphenol Polyethoxylate [*Organic chemistry*]
NPER .... National Public Employment Reporter Database [*Information service or system*] (IID)
NPerbA .... J. N. Adam Developmental Center, Perrysburg, NY [*Library symbol Library of Congress*] (LCLS)
NPES .... National Printing Equipment and Supply Association (EA)

NPES .... National Printing Equipment Show
NPE(S) .... Nuclear Planning and Execution (Service) (DOMA)
NPESO .... NAVSHIPS [*Naval Ship Systems Command*] Plant Equipment Support Office
NPET .... Nicollet Process Engineering, Inc. [*NASDAQ symbol*] (SAG)
NPET .... Nicollet Process Engr [*NASDAQ symbol*] (TTSB)
NPET .... Nonpetroleum
NPEV .... Nonpolio Enterovirus [*Infectious Diseases*] (DAVI)
NPEX .... Normal Priority Exit (IAA)
NPF .... Names Project Foundation (EA)
NPF .... National Paraplegia Foundation (EA)
NPF .... National Park Foundation (EA)
NPF .... National Parkinson Foundation (EA)
NPF .... National Pharmaceutical Foundation (EA)
NPF .... National Piano Foundation (EA)
NPF .... National Pig Fair [*British*] (ITD)
NPF .... National Poetry Foundation (EA)
NPF .... National Police Force [*South Vietnam*] (VNW)
NPF .... National Policy Forum
NPF .... National Press Foundation (EA)
NPF .... National Progressive Front [*Iraq*] [*Political party*] (PPW)
NPF .... National Psoriasis Foundation (EA)
NPF .... Naval Parachute Facility (MCD)
NPF .... Naval Powder Factory
NPF .... Naval Procurement Fund [*Budget appropriation title*]
NPF .... NAVSTAR [*Navigation Satellite Tracking and Ranging*] Processing Facility (MCD)
NPF .... Net Propulsion Force (MCD)
NPF .... Network Pulse Forming
NPF .... Neutrons per Fission (DEN)
NPF .... Newspaper Press Fund (DGA)
NPF .... Newtonian Potential Function [*Mathematics*]
NPF .... Nicaragua Peace Fleet [*Defunct*] (EA)
NPF .... Nonpublic Funds [*Canadian Forces*]
NPF .... Nordisk Plastikkirurgisk Forening [*Scandinavian Association of Plastic Surgeons - SAPS*] (EAIO)
NPF .... North Pyrenean Fault [*Geology*]
NPF .... Not Provided For
npf .... Not Provided For (ODBW)
NPF .... Nuclear Power Facility (NRCH)
NPF .... Nuveen Premium Municipal Income [*NYSE symbol*] (SPSG)
NPF .... Nuveen Prem Muni Income [*NYSE symbol*] (TTSB)
NPFA .... National Peanut Festival Association (EA)
NPFA .... National Playing Fields Association [*British*]
NPF & PP ..... Naval Prison Farms and Prison Personnel [*Budget appropriation title*]
NPFC .... National Pro-Family Coalition (EA)
NPFC .... Naval Publications and Forms Center
NPFC .... North Pacific Fisheries Commission (NOAA)
NPFC .... North Pacific Fur Seal Commission [*Defunct*]
NPFF .... National Police Field Force [*Military*]
NPFF .... Normal Probability Frequency Function
NPFFA .... National Prepared Frozen Food Association (EA)
NPFFG .... National Plant, Flower, and Fruit Guild (EA)
NPFFPA .... National Prepared Frozen Food Processors Association [*Later, NPFFA*] (EA)
NPFI .... National Plant Food Institute [*Later, TFI*] (EA)
NPFID .... Nitrogen-Phosphorus-Flame Ionization Detector [*Instrumentation*]
NPFL .... National Patriotic Front of Liberia [*Political party*] (EY)
NPFM .... Neural Pulse Frequency Modulation (PDAA)
NPFMC .... Northern Prawn Fishery Management Committee [*Australia*]
NPFMC .... North Pacific Fishery Management Council [*National Oceanic and Atmospheric Administration*] (GFGA)
NPFO .... Nuclear Power Field Office (IEEE)
NPFR .... Normalized Peak Filling Rate [*Cardiology*]
NPFRC .... North Pacific Fisheries Research Center [*National Oceanic and Atmospheric Administration*]
NPFS .... Naval Preflight School
NPFS .... No Prior or Current Federal Service (AABC)
NPFSC .... North Pacific Fur Seal Commission [*Defunct*]
NPFT .... Neurotic Personality Factor Test [*Psychology*]
NPFTA .... National Personal Fitness Trainers Association (EA)
NPFZ .... North Pyrenean Fault Zone [*Geology*]
NPG .... Napping (ABBR)
NPG .... National Peace Garden (EA)
NPG .... National Portrait Gallery [*Smithsonian Institution*]
NPG .... NATO Planning Group (NATG)
NPG .... Naval Proving Ground [*Dahlgren, VA*]
NPG .... Negative Population Growth (EA)
NPG .... Neopentylglycol [*Organic chemistry*]
NPG .... Nevada Proving Ground (BARN)
NPG .... New Performance Gallery [*San Francisco*]
NPG .... Nonprocessor Grant (IAA)
NPG .... Nonunit Personnel Generator (DOMA)
NPG .... Normalized Electron-Peak to Gamma-Peak [*Electronics*] (OA)
NPG .... Normalized Programming Generator (IAA)
NPG .... Not Paged [*Publishing*]
NPG .... N-Phenylglycine [*Organic chemistry*]
NPG .... Nuclear Planning Group [*NATO*]
NPG .... Nuclear Power Group [*British Defunct*] (NUCP)
NPG .... Nuveen GA Prem Inc. Muni [*AMEX symbol*] (TTSB)
NPG .... Nuveen Georgia Premium Income Municipal Fund [*AMEX symbol*] (SPSG)
NPG .... Ontario Library Service Nipigon/Thunder Bay Public Library [*UTLAS symbol*]
NPGA .... National Propane Gas Association

NPGA .... National Pygmy Goat Association (EA)
NPGB .... (Nitrophenyl)guanidinobenzoate [Organic chemistry]
NPGC .... National Pell Grant Coalition (EA)
NPG-GMA .... N-Phenylglycine Glycidyl Methacrylate [Organic chemistry]
NPGLINAC ... Naval Postgraduate School Linear Accelerator
NPGPA .... Non-Powder Gun Products Association (EA)
NPGS .... National Plant Germplasm System [Department of Agriculture]
NPGS .... Naval Postgraduate School
NPGS .... Nuclear Power Generating Station (NRCH)
NPGTC .... National Prairie Grouse Technical Council (EA)
NPH .... Association of Nordic Paper Historians [See also FNPH] [Sweden]
                    (EAIO)
NPH .... Nalcap Holdings, Inc. [Vancouver Stock Exchange symbol]
NPH .... Natural Period in Heave
NPH .... Natural Protamine Hagadorn [Insulin]
NPH .... Nephi [Utah] [Airport symbol] (OAG)
NPH .... Neurophysin [Biochemistry]
NPH .... Neutral Protamine Hagedorn [Insulin suspension]
NPH .... No Previous History [Medicine] (DAVI)
NPH .... No Profit Here [Business term]
NPH .... Normal Paraffin Hydrocarbon
NPH .... Normal Pressure Hydrocephalus [Medicine]
NPh .... Northern Phoenician (BJA)
NPH .... North Pit [Hawaii] [Seismograph station code, US Geological
                    Survey] (SEIS)
NPHA .... Nanga Parbat/Haramosh Axis [Himalayan geology]
NPHA .... National Peer Helpers Association (EA)
NPhA .... National Pharmaceutical Association (EA)
NPHA .... National Plott Hound Association (EA)
NPHB .... Nonphotochemical Hole Burning [Spectrometry]
NPhD .... Doctor of Natural Philosophy
NPHE .... Nitrophenyl Hexyl Ether [Organic chemistry]
NPHOE .... Nitrophenyl Hydroxyoctyl Ether [Organic chemistry]
NPHPRS ..... National Public Health Program Reporting System [Department of
                    Health and Human Services]
NPHR .... National Foreign Intelligence Plan for Human Resources (MCD)
NPhR .... Neue Philologische Rundschau [A publication] (BJA)
NPHRC .... National Pediatric HIV Resource Center (PAZ)
NPHS .... Northwick Park Heart Study (DAVI)
NPHWA .... National Presbyterian Health and Welfare Association [Later,
                    PHEWA]
NPhx .... Nasopharynx [Anatomy] (DAVI)
NPI .... International Business Machines Corp., Systems Development
                    Division, Poughkeepsie, NY [Library symbol Library of
                    Congress] (LCLS)
NPI .... Narcissistic Personality Inventory [Psychology] (EDAC)
NPI .... National Paralegal Institute (EA)
NPI .... National Parkinson Institute
NPI .... National Pollutant Inventory
NPI .... National Provident Institution [Wales]
NPI .... National Purchasing Institute (EA)
NPI .... Net Premium Income [Insurance] (AIA)
NPI .... NeuroPsychiatric Institute [UCLA]
NPI .... NEXRAD [Next Generation Weather Radar] Product Interface
                    (USDC)
NPI .... NEXRAD [Next Generation Weather Radar] Product Interface
                    [Marine science] (OSRA)
NPI .... Nonprocedural Interface [Computer science]
NPI .... No Present Illness
NPI .... No Previous Information [to tip off a US Customs Service seizure]
NPI .... Normick Perron, Inc. [Toronto Stock Exchange symbol]
NPI .... North Pocatello Valley [Idaho] [Seismograph station code, US
                    Geological Survey] (SEIS)
NPI .... Numbering Plan Indicator [Computer science] (TNIG)
NPI .... Nuveen Prem Income Muni [NYSE symbol] (TTSB)
NPI .... Nuveen Premium Income Municipal Fund, Inc. [NYSE symbol]
                    (SPSG)
NPIA .... Nanny Pop-Ins Association [Defunct] (EA)
NPIA .... National Photography Instructors Association (EA)
NPIAS .... National Plan of Integrated Airport Systems [BTS] [FAA] (TAG)
NPIC .... National Pesticide Information Clearinghouse [Later, NPTN] (EA)
NPIC .... National Pharmacy Insurance Council [Defunct] (EA)
NPIC .... National Photographic Interpretation Center [CIA]
NPIC .... Naval Photographic Interpretation Center
NPIC .... Neurogenic Peripheral Intermittent Claudication [Medicine] (DMAA)
NPIC .... Nitrosopipecolic Acid [Organic chemistry]
NPie .... Piermont Public Library, Piermont, NY [Library symbol Library of
                    Congress] (LCLS)
NPIF .... National Peace Institute Foundation (EA)
NPIG .... Nuclear Power Information Group [British] (NUCP)
NPIN .... National Parent Information Network
NPIN .... Negative-Positive-Intrinsic-Negative [Electron device] (MSA)
NPIP .... National Poultry Improvement Plan (EA)
NPIP .... Nitrosopiperidine [Also, NP] [Organic chemistry]
NPIPF .... Newspaper and Printing Industries Pension Fund [British] (BI)
NPiPNA .... N-Paraffins, iso-Paraffins, Naphthenes and Aromatics [Gasoline
                    analysis]
NPIR .... No Periodic Inspection Required [Military] (AFIT)
NPIRG .... National Public Interest Research Group (EA)
NPIRI .... National Printing Ink Research Institute (EA)
NPIRS .... National Pesticide Information Retrieval System [Purdue University]
                    [West Lafayette, IN Database]
NPIS .... National Physics Information System [American Institute of Physics]
                    [New York, NY] (DIT)
NP/IS .... National Premium Incentive Show (ITD)

NPIS .... New Product Information Service [Department of Commerce]
NPIS .... Nuclear Plant Island Structure (NRCH)
NPITI .... National Project for the Improvement of Televised Instruction
                    [National Association of Educational Broadcasters]
NPIU .... Network Processing and Interface Unit (NITA)
NPIU .... Numerical Processing and Interface Unit [Computer science] (MHDB)
NPIW .... North Pacific Intermediate Water [Marine science] (OSRA)
NPIX .... Network Peripherals [NASDAQ symbol] (TTSB)
NPIX .... Network Peripherals, Inc. [NASDAQ symbol] (SAG)
NPJ .... Corpus Christi, TX [Location identifier FAA] (FAAL)
NPj .... Port Jefferson Free Library, Port Jefferson, NY [Library symbol
                    Library of Congress] (LCLS)
NPjES .... Port Jefferson Elementary School, Port Jefferson, NY [Library symbol
                    Library of Congress] (LCLS)
NPjMH .... John T. Mather Memorial Hospital, Port Jefferson, NY [Library symbol
                    Library of Congress] (LCLS)
NPJPA .... National Prune Juice Packers Association (EA)
NPjs .... Port Jefferson Station-Terryville Public Library, Port Jefferson Station,
                    NY [Library symbol Library of Congress] (LCLS)
NPjSCH .... Saint Charles Hospital, Port Jefferson, NY [Library symbol Library of
                    Congress] (LCLS)
NPJT .... Nonparoxysmal Atrioventricular Junction Tachycardia [Cardiology]
NPjVH .... Earl L. Vandermeulen High School, Port Jefferson, NY [Library
                    symbol Library of Congress] (LCLS)
NPK .... Nationale Partij Kombinatie [National Party Alliance] [Surinam]
                    [Political party] (PPW)
NPK .... National Presto Industries, Inc. [NYSE symbol] (SPSG)
NPK .... Natl Presto Indus [NYSE symbol] (TTSB)
NPK .... Nitrogen, Phosphorus, Potassium [Fertilizer components]
NPK .... Noble Peak Resources Ltd. [Vancouver Stock Exchange symbol]
NPK .... Nodal Point Keying
NPKA .... National Paving and Kerb Association [British] (DBA)
NPL .... Free Public Library of Newark, Newark, NJ [OCLC symbol] (OCLC)
NPL .... Nameplate (MSA)
NPL .... Naples [Italy] [Seismograph station code, US Geological Survey
                    Closed] (SEIS)
NPL .... National Physical Laboratory [Research center British] (IRC)
NPL .... National Physics Laboratory (KSC)
NPL .... National Priorities List [Hazardous wastes] [Environmental Protection
                    Agency]
NPL .... National Propane Partners LP [NYSE symbol] (SAG)
NPL .... National Puzzlers' League (EA)
NPL .... Natural Processing Language [Computer science] (HGAA)
NPL .... Neon Pilot Light
NPL .... Neoproteolipid [Hematology]
NPL .... Nepal [ANSI three-letter standard code] (CNC)
NPL .... Nepheline Resources Ltd. [Vancouver Stock Exchange symbol]
NPL .... Newfoundland Public Library Services [UTLAS symbol]
NPL .... New Plymouth [New Zealand] [Airport symbol] (OAG)
NPL .... New Process Line (IAA)
NPL .... New Product Line
NPL .... New Programming Language [1974] [Later, PL/1] [Computer
                    science]
NPL .... Nodular Poorly Differentiated Lymphoma [Oncology] (DAVI)
NPL .... Noise Pollution Level
NPL .... Nonparametric Multipoint Linkage [Mathematics]
NPL .... Nonpartisan League [Political party in North Dakota opposed by the
                    IVA]
NPL .... Nonpersonal Liability
NPL .... Nonprogramming Language (IAA)
NPL .... Nonstandard Parts List (MCD)
NPL .... No Perception of Light [Ophthalmology] (CPH)
NPL .... Normal Power Level (KSC)
npl .... Noun, Plural [Grammar] (CDAI)
NPL .... Numerical Parts List (MCD)
NPL .... Numerical Preference List [Military] (AFIT)
NPI .... Plainview-Old Bethpage Public Library, Plainview, NY [Library symbol
                    Library of Congress] (LCLS)
NPIa .... Plattsburgh Public Library, Plattsburgh, NY [Library symbol Library of
                    Congress] (LCLS)
NPIaB .... Bellarmine College, Plattsburgh, NY [Library symbol Library of
                    Congress] (LCLS)
NPIaC .... Champlain College, Plattsburgh, NY [Library symbol Library of
                    Congress Obsolete] (LCLS)
NPLAC .... National People Living with AIDS [Acquired Immune Deficiency
                    Syndrome] Coalition [Australia]
NPIaCC .... Clinton Community College, Plattsburgh, NY [Library symbol Library
                    of Congress] (LCLS)
NPIaCEF ...... Clinton-Essex-Franklin Library System, Plattsburgh, NY [Library
                    symbol Library of Congress] (LCLS)
NPIaCN .... Champlain Valley School of Nursing, Plattsburgh, NY [Library symbol
                    Library of Congress] (LCLS)
NPL-AERO ... National Physical Laboratory, Aerodynamics Division [British]
NPLAN .... National Plan for Australian Newspapers
NPIaP .... Champlain Valley Physicians Hospital, Plattsburgh, NY [Library
                    symbol Library of Congress] (LCLS)
NPIaU .... State University of New York, College at Plattsburgh, Plattsburgh, NY
                    [Library symbol Library of Congress] (LCLS)
NPIBE .... Old Bethpage Elementary School, Plainview, NY [Library symbol
                    Library of Congress] (LCLS)
NPIBM .... Plainview-Old Bethpage Middle School, Plainview, NY [Library
                    symbol] [Library of Congress] (LCLS)
NPLC .... National Pedigree Livestock Council (EA)
NPLC .... National Product Liability Council (EA)
NPLC .... Normal Phase Liquid Chromatography

NPICH.......... Central General Hospital, Plainview, NY [*Library symbol Library of Congress*] (LCLS)
NPLD .... National Pro-Life Democrats (EA)
NPIe............ Mount Pleasant Public Library, Pleasantville, NY [*Library symbol Library of Congress*] (LCLS)
NPLEI.......... National Police Law Enforcement Institute (EA)
NPIeP .... Pace University Westchester, Pleasantville, NY [*Library symbol Library of Congress*] (LCLS)
NPLF........... National Preservation Loan Fund [*National Trust for Historic Preservation*]
NPLG .... Navy Program Language Group
NPLG .... Night Plane Guard Station (NVT)
NPLG .... Night Plane Landing Guard (NVT)
NPIGS......... Church of Jesus Christ of Latter-Day Saints, Genealogical Society Library, Plainview Branch, Plainview, NY [*Library symbol Library of Congress*] (LCLS)
NPIJE.......... Jamaica Elementary School, Plainview, NY [*Library symbol Library of Congress*] (LCLS)
NPIKH......... John F. Kennedy High School, Plainview, NY [*Library symbol Library of Congress*] (LCLS)
NPIMC .... Nassau County Medical Center, Plainview Division, Plainview, NY [*Library symbol Library of Congress*] (LCLS)
NPIMM .... H.B. Mattlin Middle School, Plainview, NY [*Library symbol*] [*Library of Congress*] (LCLS)
NPInRI .... New Plan Realty Trust [*Associated Press*] (SAG)
NPLO .... NATO Production and Logistics Organization (NATG)
NP-L PAC.... National Pro-Life Political Action Committee [*Defunct*] (EA)
NPIPE .... Pasadena Elementary School, Plainview, NY [*Library symbol Library of Congress*] (LCLS)
NPIPwE....... Parkway Elementary School, Plainview, NY [*Library symbol Library of Congress*] (LCLS)
NPLR .... Nyasaland Protectorate Law Reports [*A publication*] (ILCA)
NPLS .... Nonplus (ABBR)
NPLSD .... Nonplused (ABBR)
NPISH......... Plainview-Old Bethpage Senior High School, Plainview, NY [*Library symbol Library of Congress*] (LCLS)
N/PLT.......... Name Plate [*Automotive engineering*]
NPLTC .... National Public Law Training Center (EA)
N PLUR....... Neuter Plural [*Grammar*] (OCD)
NPM........... Counts per Minute (IDOE)
NPM........... Marist College, Poughkeepsie, NY [*Library symbol Library of Congress*] (LCLS)
NPM........... Narrowband Phase Modulation (DEN)
NPM........... National Association of Pastoral Musicians (EA)
NPM........... National Program Manager [*Environmental Protection Agency*] (GFGA)
NPM........... Natural Particulate Matter [*Oceanography*]
NPM........... Naval Provost Martial [*British*]
NPM........... Navy Programming Manual
NPM........... Neonatal-Perinatal Medicine [*Medical specialty*] (DHSM)
Np/m........... Neper per Meter
NPM........... Network Performance Monitor (NITA)
NPM........... New Privateer Mines [*Vancouver Stock Exchange symbol*]
NPM........... Non-Print Media [*Advertising*]
NPM........... North Pahute Mesa [*Nevada*] [*Seismograph station code, US Geological Survey*] (SEIS)
NPM........... Nothing per Mouth [*Medicine*] (DMAA)
NPM........... Nuveen Prem Income Muni 2 [*NYSE symbol*] (TTSB)
NPM........... Nuveen Premium Income Municipal 2 [*NYSE symbol*] (SPSG)
NPMA .... National Piano Manufacturers Association of America [*Later, PMAI*] (EA)
NPMA .... National Podiatric Medical Association (EA)
NPMeP .... National Property Management Association (EA)
NPMA .... Navy Personnel Management Academy (DNAB)
NPMA .... Newspaper Purchasing Management Association (EA)
NPMC .... National Pecan Marketing Council (EA)
NPMCA .... National Paper Marketing Council of Australia
NPMG .... NATO Patriot Management Group (MCD)
NPMH .... Mid-Hudson Libraries, Poughkeepsie, NY [*Library symbol Library of Congress*] (LCLS)
NPMHU....... National Postal Mail Handlers Union (EA)
NPMI .... Nordic Pool for Marine Insurance [*Helsinki, Finland*] (EA)
NPMP .... National Pesticide Monitoring Program [*Later, National Contaminant Biomonitoring Program*] [*US Fish and Wildlife Service*]
NPMR......... National Premium Manufacturers Representatives [*Later, IMRA*] (EA)
NPMTC .... Navy Pacific Missile Test Center (MCD)
NPMTT........ Nuclear Propulsion Mobile Training Team [*Military*] (CAAL)
NPN .... NASA Part Number (MCD)
NPN .... National Particulate Network [*Environmental Protection Agency*] (GFGA)
NPN .... National Party of Nigeria [*Political party*] (PPW)
NPN .... National Performance Network (EA)
NPN .... National Prevention Network (EA)
NPN .... National Prices Network
N-P-N........ Negative-Positive-Negative [*Transistor*] (CET)
NPN .... New Product Network [*Television*]
NPN .... New Pseudonyms and Nicknames [*A publication*]
NPN .... Non-Par Not Approved
NPN .... Nonprotein Nitrogen [*Analytical chemistry*]
NPN .... Normal Propyl Nitrate (MCD)
NPNA .... No Protest Nonacceptance [*Banking*]
NPNCA .... National Parks and Nature Conservation Authority [*Australia*]
NPNP......... Negative-Positive-Negative-Positive [*Transistor*]
NP NS .... Ohio Nisi Prius Reports, New Series [*A publication*] (DLA)
NPO .... Naphthylphenyloxazole [*Biochemical analysis*]

NPO .... NASA Pasadena Office (MCD)
NPO .... National [*or New*] Post Office Building
NPO .... National Project Office
NPO .... Naval Port Officer
NPO .... Navy Post Office
NPO .... Navy Program Objectives (NG)
NPO .... Navy Purchasing Office
NPO .... Negative Positive Zero (IAA)
NPO .... Neighborhood Patrol Office [*or Officer*]
NPO .... New Personnel Orientation (MCD)
NPO .... New Philharmonic Orchestra [*British*]
NPO .... Nil per Os [*Nothing by Mouth*] [*Medicine*]
NPO .... Non Per Os [*Nothing by Mouth*] [*Latin*] (BABM)
NPO .... No Part on Order (MCD)
NPO .... Norpet Resources Ltd. [*Toronto Stock Exchange symbol*]
NPO .... Not Pickled Ordinary [*Metal industry*]
NPO .... Nuclear Plant Operator (NRCH)
NPO .... Nuclear Propulsion Office
NPO .... Strategic Systems Project Office, Washington, DC [*OCLC symbol*] (OCLC)
NPOAA........ National Police Officers Association of America (EA)
NPOC .... National Point of Contact (PDAA)
NPOC .... Navy Polar Oceanographic Center (DNAB)
NPOC .... Nonpurgeable Organic Carbon
NPODS .... Navy Publishing on Demand System (AAGC)
NPOE .... Nitrophenyl Octyl Ether [*Organic chemistry*]
NPOEV .... Nuclear-Powered Ocean Engineering Vehicle [*Minisub*]
NP Ohio ...... Ohio Nisi Prius Reports [*A publication*] (DLA)
NPO/HS....... Nulla per Os Hora Somni [*Nothing by Mouth at Bedtime*] [*Latin Pharmacy*] (MAH)
NPOI .... Navy Prototype Optical Interferometer
NPOI .... Navy Prototype Optical Interferometer
NPOLA .... Navy Purchasing Office, Los Angeles
NPOMHWMGL... National Post Office Mail Handlers, Watchmen, Messengers, and Group Leaders [*Later, NPMHU*] (EA)
NPOPR........ Not Paid on Prior Rolls
NPoq.......... Beekman Community Library Reading Center, Poughquag, NY [*Library symbol Library of Congress*] (LCLS)
NP or D ...... No Place or Date
NPOS .... Nitrite Positive [*Organic chemistry*] (DAVI)
NPOST........ Nonperturbative Open-Shell Theory [*Physics*]
NPot........... Potsdam Public Library, Potsdam, NY [*Library symbol Library of Congress*] (LCLS)
NPotC .... Clarkson College of Technology, Potsdam, NY [*Library symbol Library of Congress*] (LCLS)
NPotU .... State University of New York, College at Potsdam, Potsdam, NY [*Library symbol Library of Congress*] (LCLS)
NPour .... Hiram Halley Memorial Library, Pound Ridge, NY [*Library symbol Library of Congress*] (LCLS)
NPP .... National Patriotic Party [*Liberia*] [*Political party*] (EY)
NPP .... National Peach Partners [*Defunct*] (EA)
NPP .... National People's Party [*Pakistan*] [*Political party*] (FEA)
NPP .... National Periodicals Publications, Inc.
NPP .... National Policy Paper [*Army*] (AABC)
NPP .... National Pretreatment Program [*Metal finishing technology*]
NPP .... National Priority Program [*NHTSA*] (TAG)
NPP .... National Prison Project (EA)
NPP .... National Procurement Point [*Military*] (RDA)
NPP .... National Progressive Party [*Iraq*] [*Political party*] (BJA)
NPP .... National Prohibition Party (EA)
NPP .... Naval Propellant Plant
NPP .... Navy Propellant Plant (DNAB)
NPP .... Negative Picture Phase
NPP .... Nemzeti Paraszt Part [*National Peasant Party*] [*Hungary Political party*] (PPE)
NPP .... Neodymium Pentaphosphate [*Inorganic chemistry*]
NPP .... Net Primary Productivity
NPP .... Network Power Processor [*Acme Electric Corp.*] [*Computer science*] (PCM)
NPP .... Network Protocol Processor
NPP .... New Patriotic Party [*Ghana*] [*Political party*] (ECON)
NPP .... New People's Party [*North Korea Political party*] (FEA)
NPP .... New Physics Project (AIE)
NPP .... New Product Planning (IAA)
NPP .... New Progressive Party [*Puerto Rico*] [*Political party*]
NPP .... Nigerian People's Party [*Political party*] (PPW)
NPP .... Nitrophenyl Phosphate [*Biochemical analysis*]
NPP .... Nitrophenylprolinol [*Organic chemistry*]
NPP .... Nitropropenyl Pivalate [*Organic chemistry*]
NPP .... Non-Penetrating Periscope [*DARPA*]
NPP .... No Passed Proof
NPP .... Normal Pool Plasma [*Clinical chemistry*]
NPP .... North American Power [*Vancouver Stock Exchange symbol*]
NPP .... Nozzleless Performance Program Module (MCD)
NPP .... N-Pentylpalmitamide [*Organic chemistry*]
NPP .... Nuclear Power Plant (IEEE)
NPP .... Nurse Practitioner Project
NPP .... Nuveen Performance Plus Municipal [*NYSE symbol*] (SPSG)
NPP .... Nuveen Perform Plus Muni [*NYSE symbol*] (TTSB)
NPPA .... National Parks and Primitive Areas
NPPA .... National Pickle Packers Association [*Later, PPI*]
NPPA .... National Pizza and Pasta Association (EA)
NPPA .... National Press Photographers Association (EA)
NPPA .... National Probation and Parole Association [*Later, NCCD*]
NPPAC........ National and Provincial Parks Association of Canada

NPPAG........ National Program Production and Aquisition Grant [*Corporation for Public Broadcasting*] [*Radio*] (NTCM)
NPPB .... National Poisons and Pesticides Board [*Sweden*]
NPPB .... National Potato Promotion Board (EA)
NPPB .... Nitro(Phenylpropylamino) Benzoate [*Organic chemistry*]
NPPC .... National Pork Producers Council (EA)
NPPC .... National Power Policy Committee [*World War II*]
NPPC .... Navy Programming Planning Council
NPPC .... Nuclear Power Plant Co. Ltd.
NPPC .... Numeric Parts Preference Code [*Military*] (AFIT)
NPPD .... (Nitrophenyl)pentadienal [*Tracer chemical*] [*Organic chemistry*]
NPPE .... Nitrophenyl Pentyl Ether [*Organic chemistry*]
NPPE .... Nuclear Power Propulsion Evaluation (NG)
NPPF .... National Poultry Producers Federation [*Defunct*] (EA)
NPPI .... Navy Program Progress Item (CAAL)
NPPI .... Norwood Promotional Prd [*NASDAQ symbol*] (TTSB)
NPPI .... Norwood Promotional Products [*NASDAQ symbol*] (SAG)
NPPL .... National Parks and Public Lands [*Victoria, Australia*]
NPPL .... Neuropsychopharmacology Laboratory [*Wayne State University*] [*Research center*]
NPPN .... Nitroxyperoxypropyl Nitrate [*Environmental chemistry*]
NPPN .... NUDO [*Namibia United Democratic Organization*] Progressive Party of Namibia [*Political party*] (PPW)
NPPO .... Navy Program Planning Office
NPPO .... Navy Publications and Printing Office
NP.PP .... Natl Power PLC Interim ADS [*NYSE symbol*] (TTSB)
NPP/QAS..... Naval Propellant Plant Quality Assurance Department [*Indian Head, MD*]
NPPR .... Nationalist Party of Puerto Rico (NADA)
NPPR .... Navy Program Progress Report
NPPR .... Nonproductive Procurement Directive
NPPRE........ Nitrophenyl Propyl Ether [*Organic chemistry*]
NPPS .... Navy Planning and Programming System
NPPS .... Navy Publications and Printing Service
NPPSBO...... Navy Publications and Printing Service Branch Office
NPPSIS........ National Parent to Parent Support & Information Systems, Inc.
NPPSMO..... Navy Publications and Printing Service Management Office
NPPSO .... Navy Publications and Printing Service Office
NPPSSOEASTDIV... Navy Publications and Printing Service, Southeastern Division (DNAB)
NPPSWESTDIV... Navy Publications and Printing Service, Western Division (DNAB)
NPPTA .... National Public Parks Tennis Association (EA)
NPPTS .... Nuclear Power Plant Training Simulator (PDAA)
NPPW .... National Poison Prevention Week
NPQAA .... Natural Products Quality Assurance Alliance
NPR .... Napier [*New Zealand*] [*Seismograph station code, US Geological Survey Closed*] (SEIS)
NPR .... Napper (ABBR)
NPR .... Narodowa Partia Robotnicza [*National Workers Party*] [*Poland Political party*] (PPE)
NPR .... National Aeronautics and Space Administration Procurement Regulation [*A publication*] (AAGC)
NPR .... National Parks and Access to the Countryside Regulations [*Town planning*] [*British*]
NPR .... National Performance Review [*A publication*]
NPR .... National Public Radio [*Washington, DC Telecommunications*] (TSSD)
NPR .... Naval Petroleum Reserves
NPR .... Naval Plant Representative
NPR .... Navy Payroll (DNAB)
NPR .... Navy Preliminary Revision (DNAB)
NPR .... Navy Procurement Regulation
NPR .... Negro Puerto Rican
NPR .... Neoricans in Puerto Rico (EA)
NPR .... Neptune Resources Corp. [*Toronto Stock Exchange symbol*]
NPR .... Net Pool Return
NPR .... Net Protein Ratio [*Nutrition*]
NPR .... New Plan Realty Trust SBI [*NYSE symbol*] (SPSG)
NPR .... New Plan Rlty Tr SBI [*NYSE symbol*] (TTSB)
NPR .... New Production Reactor [*Department of Energy*]
NPR .... Night Press Rate [*of newspapers*]
NPR .... Nisi Prius Reports [*A publication*] (DLA)
NPR .... Noise Power Ratio
NPR .... Noise Prediction and Reduction
NPR .... Noise Preferential Route [*Aviation*] (DA)
NPR .... Nonprocessor Request (IAA)
NPR .... Nonproduction Release (MCD)
NPR .... North Polar Region
NPR .... Notice of Program Reimbursement (MEDA)
NPR .... Notice of Proposed Rule Making [*Federal agencies*] (GFGA)
NPR .... Nozzle Pressure Ratio [*Aviation*]
NPR .... Nuclear Paramagnetic Resonance (MCD)
NPR .... Nuclear Posture Review [*DoD*]
NPR .... Nuclear Power Reactor
NPR .... Nuclear Pulse Rocket [*NASA*]
NPR .... Numerical Position Readout (IAA)
NPr .... Pearl River Public Library, Pearl River, NY [*Library symbol Library of Congress*] (LCLS)
NPrA .... American Cyanamid Co., Lederle Laboratories, Pearl River, NY [*Library symbol Library of Congress*] (LCLS)
NPRA .... National Parks and Recreation Association (NADA)
NPRA .... National Personal Robot Association [*Later, NSRA*] (EA)
NPRA .... National Petroleum Refiners Association (EA)
NPRA .... Naval Personnel Research Activity
NPRA .... Newspaper Personnel Relations Association (EA)
NPR&D .... Navy Property Redistribution and Disposal (AAGC)

NPRC .... National Personnel Records Center [*National Archives and Records Service*]
NPRC .... National Polystyrene Recycling Co.
NPRC .... National Project on Resource Coordination for Justice Statistics and Information [*Canada*]
NPRC .... National Public Relations Council of Health and Welfare Services [*Formerly, NPC*]
NPRC .... National Puerto Rican Coalition (EA)
NPRC .... Newspaper Production and Research Center
NPRC .... Nonproliferation Program Review Committee [*US, multiagency*]
NPRC .... Nuclear Power Range Channel (IEEE)
NPRC (CPR)... National Personnel Records Center (Civilian Personnel Records) [*National Archives and Records Service*] (AFM)
NPRCG........ Nuclear Public Relations Contact Group
NPRC (MPR)... National Personnel Records Center (Military Personnel Records) [*National Archives and Records Service*] (AFM)
NPRD.......... NASA Procurement Regulation Directive
NPRD.......... Nonelectronic Parts Reliability Data (MCD)
NPRD.......... Nuclear Plant Reliability Data
NPRDA......... National Precure Retread Dealers Association [*Defunct*] (EA)
NPRDC........ National Public Resources Defense Council (NUCP)
NPRDC........ Navy Personnel Research and Development Center (GRD)
NPRDL......... Naval Personnel Research and Development Laboratory
NPRDS......... Nuclear Plant Reliability Data System (NRCH)
NPRF.......... National Priority Reserve Fund [*Australia*]
NPRF.......... National Puerto Rican Forum (EA)
NPRF.......... Northrop Pulse Radiation Facility
NPRFT........ Nonprofit (ABBR)
NPRI.......... National Psychiatric Reform Institute
NPRL.......... Navy Prosthetics Research Laboratory
NPRL.......... Nonprocedural Referencing Language
NPRM......... Neopharm Inc. [*NASDAQ symbol*] (TTSB)
NPRM......... Notice of Proposed Rule Making [*Federal agencies*]
NPRMW....... Neopharm Inc. Wrrt [*NASDAQ symbol*] (TTSB)
NPRN......... Neoprene [*Synthetic rubber*]
NPRO......... NaPro Bio Therapeutics [*NASDAQ symbol*] (TTSB)
NPRO......... NaPro BioTherapeutics, Inc. [*NASDAQ symbol*] (SAG)
NPRO......... Naval Petroleum Reserves Office
NPRO......... Navy Plant Representative Office
NPRO......... N-Nitrosoproline [*Organic chemistry*]
NPROA........ Nitrosoprolylalanine [*Organic chemistry*]
NPROG........ Nitrosoprolylglycine [*Organic chemistry*]
NPROW....... Napro Biotheraputics Wrrts [*NASDAQ symbol*] (TTSB)
NPRPA........ Naval Petroleum Reserves Production Act (AAGC)
NPRR.......... National Public Relations Roundtable [*Defunct*]
NPRR.......... Net Pool Return Rule
NPRS.......... NASA Procurement Regulation Supplement
NPRS.......... Negative Poll Response State (IAA)
NPRS.......... Newpark Resources, Inc. [*NASDAQ symbol*] (SAG)
NPRS.......... Nonpersistent (FAAC)
NPRTSN...... Nonpartisan (ABBR)
NPRTSNSP... Nonpartisanship (ABBR)
NPRV.......... Nitrogen Pressure Relief Valve (MCD)
NPRWC........ National Puerto Rican Women's Caucus [*Defunct*] (EA)
NPS .... Counts per Second (IDOE)
NPS .... Honolulu, HI [*Location identifier FAA*] (FAAL)
NPS .... Narcotics Prevention Service (NADA)
NPS .... NASA Planning Studies (KSC)
NPS .... Nationale Partij Suriname [*Surinam National Party*] [*Political party*] (PPW)
NPS .... National Park Service [*Department of the Interior*]
NPS .... National Parole Service [*Canada*]
NPS .... National Periodicals System
NPS .... National Permit Strategy [*Environmental Protection Agency*] (GFGA)
NPS .... National Pesticide Survey [*Environmental Protection Agency*] (GFGA)
NPS .... National Philatelic Society [*Defunct*] (EA)
NPS .... National Phone Services, Inc.
NPS .... National Poetry Secretariat [*British*] [*An association*] (DBA)
NPS .... National Poetry Series
NPS .... National Pony Society [*British*] (DI)
NPS .... National Prisoner Statistics [*An association*]
NPS .... Naval Postgraduate School
NPS .... Navy Personnel Survey
NPS .... Navy Primary Standards (MSA)
NPS .... Neapolis [*Greece*] [*Seismograph station code, US Geological Survey*] (SEIS)
NPS .... Negative Potential Shifts [*Neurophysiology*]
NPS .... Network Processing Supervisor [*Honeywell, Inc.*]
NPS .... Network Processor System (NITA)
NPS .... Neutral Pressure Switch
NPS .... Newspaper Pagination System [*Typography*] (DGA)
NPS .... Night Photographic System
NPS .... Nitrophenyl Sulfenyl [*Organic chemistry*]
Nps .... Nitrophenylthio(nitrophenylsulfonyl) [*Biochemistry*]
NPS .... Noise Power Spectra [*Spectrometry*]
NPS .... Nominal Pipe Size (SAA)
NPS .... Noncumulative Preferred Stock [*Investment term*] (MHDW)
NPS .... Nonperishable Subsistence
NPS .... Non-Pneumatic Spare [*Automotive engineering*]
NPS .... Nonpoint Source Pollution [*Agricultural engineering*]
NPS .... Non-Prior Service
NPS .... No-Par Stock [*Investment term*] (MHDW)
NPS .... No Prior Service [*Military*]
NPS .... Normalized Plateau Slope
NPS .... Normal Pipe Size

NPS .... North Polar Sequence
NPS .... Northwestern Public Service Co. [*NYSE symbol*] (SPSG)
NPS .... Northwestern Pub Svc [*NYSE symbol*] (TTSB)
NPS .... Nuclear and Plasma Sciences (MCD)
NPS .... Nuclear-Powered Ship (NVT)
NPS .... Nuclear Power Source
NPS .... Nuclear Power System
NPS .... Numerical Plotting System (NRCH)
NPS .... NWPS Capital Financing Tr PERCS [*NYSE symbol*] (SAG)
NPSA .... National Passenger Safety Association [*Defunct*] (EA)
NPSA .... National Pecan Shellers Association (EA)
NPSA .... National Pegboard Systems Association (EA)
NPSA .... National Psychic Science Association (EA)
NPSA .... New Program Status Area (IEEE)
NPSA .... Novitiate of Saint Andrew-On-Hudson, Poughkeepsie, NY [*Library symbol Library of Congress*] (LCLS)
NPSAPHA .... New Professionals Section of the American Public Health Association (EA)
NPSAS .... National Postsecondary Student Aid Study [*Department of Education*] (GFGA)
NPSB .... National Prisoner Statistics Bulletin [*Department of Justice*]
NPSB .... News Print Service Bureau
NPSC .... Naval Personnel Separation Center
NPSC .... New Paradigm Sftwr [*NASDAQ symbol*] (TTSB)
NPSC .... New Paradigm Software [*NASDAQ symbol*] (SAG)
NPSC-CL ...... Nursing Policy Studies Centre [*University of Warwick*] [*British*] (CB)
NPS-CL .... Nitrophenyl Sulfenyl Chloride
NPS/CPSU/UW... National Park Service Cooperative Park Studies Unit, University of Washington [*Research center*] (RCD)
NPSCW .... New Paradigm Software Wrrt [*NASDAQ symbol*] (TTSB)
NPSD .... Naval Photographic Services Depot
NPSD .... Neutron Power Spectral Density (OA)
NPSD .... Noise Power Spectre Density
NPSDN .... Nordic Packet Switched Data Network (NITA)
NPSE .... National Premium Sales Executives (EA)
NPSE .... Navy Peridontal Screening Examination (DNAB)
NPSF .... National Pipe Straight Fine [*Mechanical engineering*]
NPSF .... National Straight Pipe Threads for Dry Seal Pressure Tight Joints
NPSFR .... Net Public Sector Financing Requirement [*Business term*]
NPSH .... National Straight Pipe Threads for Hose Couplings and Nipples
NPSH .... Net Positive Suction Head [*Pumps*]
NPSH .... Nonprotein Sulfhydryl [*Biochemistry*]
NPSHA .... Net Positive Suction Head Available [*Pumps*] (PDAA)
NPSHR .... Net Positive Suction Head Required [*Chemical or food processing*]
NPSI .... National Pipe Straight Intermediate [*Mechanical engineering*]
NPSI .... Network Control Program Packet Switching Interface [*Computer science*] (HGAA)
NPSI .... Nursing Performance Simulation Instrument
NPSL .... National Professional Soccer League [*Later, NASL*]
NPSL .... National Straight Pipe Threads for Locknuts and Locknut Pipe Threads
NPSM .... Non-Productive Standard Minute (PDAA)
NPSNL .... South Eastern New York Library Resources Council, Poughkeepsie, NY [*Library symbol*] [*Library of Congress*] (LCLS)
NPSO .... Nonpaired Spatial Orbitals [*Atomic physics*]
NPSP .... National People's Salvation Party [*Zambia*] [*Political party*] (EY)
NPSP .... Net Positive Static Pressure (NASA)
NPSP .... Net Positive Suction Pressure [*Cryogenics*]
NPSP .... N-Phenylselenenylphthalimide [*Organic chemistry*]
NPSP .... NPS Pharmaceutical, Inc. [*NASDAQ symbol*] (SAG)
NPSP .... NPS Pharmaceuticals [*NASDAQ symbol*] (TTSB)
NPsP .... Paul Smiths College, Paul Smiths, NY [*Library symbol Library of Congress*] (LCLS)
NPSPA .... National Pecan Shellers and Processors Association (EA)
NPS Phm ..... NPS Pharmaceutical, Inc. [*Associated Press*] (SAG)
NPSPrA .... NWPS Cap Fin 8.125% Tr Sec 1 [*NYSE symbol*] (TTSB)
NPSR .... No Primary Staff Responsibility [*Army*] (AABC)
NPSRA .... National Professional Squash Racquets Association (EA)
NPSRC .... National Professional Standards Review Council [*Terminated, 1982*] [*HEW*] (EGAO)
NPSRI .... National Public Services Research Institute
NPSS .... IEEE Nuclear and Plasma Sciences Society (EA)
NPSS .... National Police and Security Service [*Republic of Vietnam*]
NPSS .... Noms Propres Sud-Semitiques [*A publication*] (BJA)
NPSS .... Non-Public School Section [*American Association of School Librarians*]
NPSS .... Nuclear and Plasma Science Symposium (MCD)
NPST .... Native Pituitary-Derived Somatotropin [*Endocrinology*]
NPST .... Native Porcine Somatotropin [*Endocrinology*]
NPSTN .... National Public Switched Telecommunications Network (MHDI)
NPSWL .... New Program Status Word Location
NPT .... Nasal Provocation Test [*Immunology*]
NPT .... National Petroleum Corp. Ltd. [*Toronto Stock Exchange symbol*]
NPT .... National Pipe Taper [*Mechanical engineering*]
NPT .... National Taper Pipe [*Thread*]
NPT .... Navy Pointer Tracker (MCD)
NPT .... Neomycin Phosphotransferase [*An enzyme*]
NPT .... Neoprecipitin Test [*Oncology*]
NPT .... Neopyrithiamine Hydrochloride [*Chemistry*] (DAVI)
NPT .... Network Planning Technique [*Computer science*] (IEEE)
NPT .... Neuropsychiatry
NPT .... Neuropsychiatry Technician [*Navy*]
NPT .... New Periodical Titles [*of British Union Catalogue of Periodicals*]
NPT .... Newport [*Rhode Island*] [*Airport symbol*] (OAG)
NPT .... Newport Ebbw Junction [*British depot code*]

NPT .... Nocturnal Penile Tumescence [*Psychiatry*]
NPT .... Non-Packet Mode Terminal (MHDB)
NPT .... Nonpyramidal Tract
NPT .... Normal Pressure and Temperature
NPT .... Nuclear Non-Proliferation Treaty [*United Nations*] (ECON)
NPT .... Nuveen Prem Income Muni 4 [*NYSE symbol*] (TTSB)
NPT .... Nuveen Premium Income Municipal Fund IV [*NYSE symbol*] (SPSG)
NPT .... Portland Terminal R. R. Co. [*Formerly, Northern Pacific Terminal R. R.*] [*AAR code*]
NPTA .... National Paper Trade Association (EA)
NPTA .... National Passenger Traffic Association [*Later, NBTA*] (EA)
NPTA .... National Perishable Transportation Association (EA)
NPTA .... National Piano Travelers Association (EA)
NPTA .... National Postal Transport Association [*Later, APWU*]
NPTA .... New Periodical Title Abbreviations [*A publication*]
NPTA .... Nordstrom Personal Touch America [*E-mail shopping service*]
NPTC .... National Postal and Travelers Censorship [*Army*] (AABC)
NPTC .... National Private Truck Council
NPTC .... National Proficiency Test Council (AIE)
NPtc .... Port Chester Public Library, Port Chester, NY [*Library symbol Library of Congress*] (LCLS)
NPTCO .... National Postal and Travelers Censorship Organization [*Army*] (AABC)
NPtcU .... United Hospital, Port Chester, NY [*Library symbol Library of Congress*] (LCLS)
NPTD .... Nitrogen Phosphorus Thermionic Detector [*Instrumentation*]
NPT/E .... Navy Parachute Team / East Coast (DNAB)
NPte .... Port Ewen Free Library, Port Ewen, NY [*Library symbol Library of Congress*] (LCLS)
NPTF .... National Taper Pipe Threads for Dry Seal Pressure Tight Joints
NPTF .... Nuclear Power Task Force
NPTF .... Nuclear Proof Test Facility [*Proposed, but never built*] (NRCH)
NPTFB .... National Park Trust Fund Board [*Later, NPF*]
NPTG .... Nuclear Power Task Group [*Navy*] (MCD)
NPTH .... NeoPath, Inc. [*NASDAQ symbol*] (SAG)
NPTI .... Nissan Performance Technology, Inc.
NPTjer .... Port Jervis Free Public Library, Port Jervis, NY [*Library symbol Library of Congress*] (LCLS)
NPTL .... National Police Testing Laboratories (EA)
NPTL .... Nuptial (ABBR)
NPTN .... National Pesticide Telecommunication Network (EA)
NPTN .... National Public Telecomputing Network (TNIG)
NPTR .... National Parachute Test Range (MCD)
NPTR .... National Taper Pipe Threads for Railing Fixtures
NPTRL .... Naval Personnel and Training Research Laboratory [*Formerly, Personnel Research Activity*]
NPTS .... Nationwide Personal Transportation Study [*Department of Transportation*] (GFGA)
NPTS .... Nationwide Personal Transportation Survey [*BTS*] [*FHWA*] (TAG)
NPTSM .... Nepotism (ABBR)
NPTST .... Nepotist (ABBR)
NPTU .... Naval Petroleum Training Unit (DNAB)
NPT/W .... Navy Parachute Team / West Coast (DNAB)
NPtw .... Port Washington Public Library, Port Washington, NY [*Library symbol Library of Congress*] (LCLS)
NptwDE .... Daly Elementary School, Port Washington, NY [*Library symbol Library of Congress*] (LCLS)
NPtwGE .... Guggenheim Elementary School, Port Washington, NY [*Library symbol Library of Congress*] (LCLS)
NPtwJSE ...... John Philip Sousa Elementary School, Port Washington, NY [*Library symbol*] [*Library of Congress*] (LCLS)
NptwME .... Manorhaven Elementary School, Port Washington, NY [*Library symbol Library of Congress*] (LCLS)
NPtwMSE .... Main Street Elementary School, Port Washington, NY [*Library symbol Library of Congress*] (LCLS)
NPtwSH .... Paul D. Schreiber High School, Port Washington, NY [*Library symbol*] [*Library of Congress*] (LCLS)
NPtwSSE ...... South Salem Elementary School, Port Washington, NY [*Library symbol Library of Congress*] (LCLS)
NPtwWJ ...... Carrie Palmer Weber Junior High School, Port Washington, NY [*Library symbol*] [*Library of Congress*] (LCLS)
NPTWZI .... North Pacific Trade Winds Zone Investigation (NOAA)
NPTZ .... North Pacific Transition Zone (USDC)
NPTZ .... North Pacific Transition Zone [*Marine science*] (OSRA)
NPU .... National Pharmaceutical Union (PDAA)
NPU .... National Postal Union [*Later, APWU*]
NPU .... Naval Parachute Unit
NPU .... Navigation Processor Unit (MCD)
NPU .... Ne Plus Ultra [*No Further; i.e., the pinnacle of attainment*] [*French*]
NPU .... Net Protein Utilization [*Nutrition*]
NPU .... Network Processing Unit
NPU .... Newspaper Press Union (DGA)
NPU .... Nitrogen Pressure Unit (MCD)
NPU .... Nitrogen Purge Unit (MCD)
NPU .... Nordic Postal Union (EA)
NPU .... Not Passed Urine [*Medicine*]
NPUD .... National Party for Unity and Democracy [*Mauritania*] [*Political party*] (EY)
NPUG .... National Prime User Group (GNE)
NPUP .... National Progressive Unionist Party [*Egypt*] [*Political party*] (PPW)
NPur .... Purchase Free Library, Purchase, NY [*Library symbol Library of Congress*] (LCLS)
NPurMC .... Manhattanville College, Purchase, NY [*Library symbol Library of Congress*] (LCLS)

NPurU .... State University of New York, College at Purchase, Purchase, NY [*Library symbol Library of Congress*] (LCLS)

NPurW .... Westchester Academy of Medicine, Purchase, NY [*Library symbol Library of Congress*] (LCLS)

NPV .... National Present Volume Method [*Management*]

NPV .... Naturpolitische Volkspartei [*People's Party for Nature Policy*] [*Germany Political party*] (PPW)

NPV .... Negative Predictive Value [*Experimentation*]

NPV .... Net Present Value [*Accounting*]

NPV .... New Plymouth Ventures, Inc. [*Vancouver Stock Exchange symbol*]

NPV .... Nitrogen Pressure Valve (KSC)

NPV .... Nonpropulsive Vent (KSC)

NPV .... No Par Value [*Stock exchange term*]

NPV .... Nuclear Polyhedrosis Virus

NPV .... Nuveen VA Prem Inc. Muni Fd [*NYSE symbol*] (TTSB)

NPV .... Nuveen Virginia Premium Income Municipal Fund [*NYSE symbol*] (SPSG)

NPV .... Vassar College, Poughkeepsie, NY [*Library symbol Library of Congress*] (LCLS)

NPVCE .... Net Present Value for Current Expendable Launch Vehicles [*NASA*] (KSC)

NPVH .... Net Present Value at the Horizon (PDAA)

NPVLA .... National Paint, Varnish, and Lacquer Association [*Later, NPCA*] (EA)

NPV-Mu ...... Vassar College, George Sherman Dickerson Music Library, Poughkeepsie, NY [*Library symbol*] [*Library of Congress*] (LCLS)

NPVNE .... Net Present Value for New Expendable Launch Vehicles [*NASA*] (KSC)

NPVS .... No-Par-Value Stock [*Stock exchange term*]

NPVSH .... Net Present Value for Space Shuttle [*NASA*] (KSC)

NPW .... International Union of Allied Novelty and Production Workers

NPW .... National Party of Western Australia [*Political party*]

NPW .... Network for Professional Women [*Hartford, CT*] (EA)

NPW .... Nuveen WA Prem Inc. Muni Fd [*AMEX symbol*] (TTSB)

NPW .... Nuveen Washington Premium Income Municipal Fund [*AMEX symbol*] (SPSG)

NPWA .... National Pure Water Association [*British*]

NPWAC .... National Parks and Wildlife Advisory Council [*Tasmania, Australia*]

NPwADS ...... National Power PLC [*Associated Press*] (SAG)

NPWC .... National Press Women's Club (NTCM)

NPWC .... Navy Public Works Center

NPWD .... Navy Public Works Department

NPWFNSW... National Parks and Wildlife Foundation of New South Wales [*Australia*]

NPWIC .... National Prisoner of War Information Center (DOMA)

NPWOA .... National Piggly Wiggly Operators Association (EA)

NPWRC .... Northern Prairie Wildlife Research Center [*Jamestown, ND*] [*Department of the Interior*] (GRD)

NPWS .... NATO Planning Workshop (NATG)

NPX .... New Pioneer Exploration [*Vancouver Stock Exchange symbol*]

NPX .... Nuveen Ins Prem Inc. Muni 2 [*NYSE symbol*] (TTSB)

NPX .... Nuveen Insured Premium Income Municipal Fund [*NYSE symbol*] (SPSG)

NPY .... Neuropeptide Y [*Biochemistry*]

NPY .... Nuveen PA Prem Inc. Muni 2 [*NYSE symbol*] (TTSB)

NPY .... Nuveen Pennsylvania Premium Income Municipal [*NYSE symbol*] (SPSG)

NPy .... Penn Yan Public Library, Penn Yan, NY [*Library symbol Library of Congress*] (LCLS)

NPYR .... Nitrosopyrrolidine [*Also, NYPYR*] [*Organic chemistry*]

NPYRR .... N-Nitrosopyrrolidine [*Organic chemistry*]

NPZ .... New Plymouth [*New Zealand*] [*Seismograph station code, US Geological Survey Closed*] (SEIS)

NPZ .... North Pyrenean Zone [*Geology*]

NQ .... Cumberland Airlines [*ICAO designator*] (AD)

NQ .... Net Quick Assets

NQ .... Neural Quantum [*Theory*] [*Sensory discrimination*]

nq .... Nicaragua [*MARC country of publication code Library of Congress*] (LCCP)

NQ .... Quoque Library, Quoque, NY [*Library symbol Library of Congress*] (LCLS)

NQA .... Memphis, TN [*Location identifier FAA*] (FAAL)

NQA .... National Quality Award [*LIMRA, NALU*]

NQA .... National Quilting Association (EA)

NQA .... Net Quick Assets

NQA .... North Carolina Agricultural and Technical State University, Greensboro, NC [*OCLC symbol*] (OCLC)

NQAA .... Nuclear Quality Assurance Agency

NQB .... National Quotation Bureau [*Stock market*]

NQB .... No Qualified Bidders [*Investment term*] (DFIT)

NQC .... NASA Quality Control (KSC)

NQC .... National Quotations Committee [*of the National Association of Securities Dealers*]

NQC .... Nuclear Quality Control (DNAB)

NQC .... Nuveen CA Inv Qual Muni [*NYSE symbol*] (TTSB)

NQC .... Nuveen California Investment Quality Municipal Fund [*NYSE symbol*] (SPSG)

NQCC .... Nuclear Quadrupole Coupling Constant [*Physics*]

NQD .... Nonquaded [*Telecommunications*] (TEL)

NQD .... Notice of Quality Discrepancy

NQE .... Nuclear Quality Engineering (DNAB)

NQF .... Nuveen FL Inv Qua Muni [*NYSE symbol*] (TTSB)

NQF .... Nuveen Florida Investment Quality Municipal [*NYSE symbol*] (SPSG)

NQHR .... National Quarter Horse Registry (EA)

NQI .... Kingsville, TX [*Location identifier FAA*] (FAAL)

NQI .... Nuveen Ins Qual Muni [*NYSE symbol*] (TTSB)

NQI .... Nuveen Insured Quality Municipal [*NYSE symbol*] (SPSG)

NQIC .... National Quality Information Centre [*Institute of Quality Assurance*] [*Information service or system*] (IID)

NQJ .... Nuveen New Jersey Investment Quality Municipal [*NYSE symbol*] (SPSG)

NQJ .... Nuveen NJ Inv Qua Muni [*NYSE symbol*] (TTSB)

NQKA .... Northwest Quoin Key Association [*Defunct*] (EA)

NQL .... National Quick Lube Ltd. [*Vancouver Stock Exchange symbol*]

NQL .... North Queensland Libraries: A Directory [*Australia A publication*]

NQL .... Nouveau Quartier Latin [*Paris bookstore*]

NQL .... Nuclear Quadrupole Interaction [*Physics*]

NQLA .... North Queensland Logging Association [*Australia*]

NQM .... Midway/Henderson Naval Station, HI [*Location identifier FAA*] (FAAL)

NQM .... Navy Quality Management

NQM .... Nuveen Investment Quality Municipal [*NYSE symbol*] (SPSG)

NQM .... Nuveen Inv Quality Muni [*NYSE symbol*] (TTSB)

NQMFP .... North Queensland Multifunction Polis [*Australia*]

NQN .... Neuquen [*Argentina*] [*Airport symbol*] (OAG)

NQN .... Nuveen New York Investment Quality Municipal Fund [*NYSE symbol*] (SPSG)

NQN .... Nuveen NY Inv Qual Muni [*NYSE symbol*] (TTSB)

NQN .... Transportes Aereos Neuquen [*Argentina ICAO designator*] (FAAC)

NQO .... Nitroquinoline Oxide [*Organic chemistry*]

NQOS .... Not Quite Our Sort (IIA)

NQP .... Nuveen PA Inv Qua Muni [*NYSE symbol*] (TTSB)

NQP .... Nuveen Pennsylvania Investment Quality Municipal [*NYSE symbol*] (SPSG)

NQPA .... National Quarter Pony Association (EA)

NQPC .... National Quartz Producers Council (EA)

NQPP .... National Quarantine Publicity Program [*Australia*]

NQR .... New Quebec Raglan Mines Ltd. [*Toronto Stock Exchange symbol*]

NQR .... Non-Quadratic Residues (MHDB)

NQR .... Nuclear Quadrupole Resonance [*Frequencies*]

NQRC .... National Quadraphonic Radio Committee

NQRR .... Nuclear Quadrupole Resonance Response

NQS .... Nuveen Select Quality Municipal [*NYSE symbol*] (SPSG)

NQS .... Nuveen Select Qual Muni [*NYSE symbol*] (TTSB)

NQSO .... Nonqualified Stock Options (WYGK)

NQT .... Network Quality Tester (NITA)

NQT .... Newly Qualified to Teach (GFGA)

NQT .... Nonlanguage Qualification Test

NQT .... Nor-Quest Resources Ltd. [*Vancouver Stock Exchange symbol*]

NQTGCA ...... North Queensland Tobacco Growers Cooperative Association [*Australia*]

NQTV .... North Queensland Television [*Australia*]

NQU .... Not Quite Us [*Lower in social status*] [*Slang British*]

NQU .... Nuqui [*Colombia*] [*Airport symbol*] (OAG)

NQU .... Nuveen Qual Income Muni Fd [*NYSE symbol*] (TTSB)

NQU .... Nuveen Quality Income Municipal Fund [*NYSE symbol*] (SPSG)

NQWMI .... Non-Q-Wave Myocardial Infarction [*Cardiology*] (CPH)

NQX .... Key West, FL [*Location identifier FAA*] (FAAL)

NQY .... Newquay [*England*] [*Airport symbol*] (OAG)

NR .... Bosanquet and Puller's New Reports, English Common Pleas [*1804-07*] [*A publication*] (DLA)

NR .... Nachrichtenregiment [*Signal Regiment*] [*German military - World War II*]

NR .... Narrow Resonance [*Nuclear energy*] (NRCH)

NR .... Natal Reports [*South Africa*] [*A publication*] (DLA)

NR .... National Range

NR .... National Recovery Act

NR .... National Recovery Administration [*Voided by Supreme Court, 1935*]

NR .... National Report (OICC)

NR .... National Reporter [*Maritime Law Book Co. Ltd.*] [*Canada Information service or system*] (CRD)

NR .... National Reserve [*British military*] (DMA)

NR .... NATO Restricted (NATG)

NR .... Natural Resources

NR .... Natural Rubber

NR .... Nauru [*ANSI two-letter standard code*] (CNC)

NR .... Naval Rating

NR .... Naval Reactors (GAAI)

NR .... Naval Reserve

NR .... Navigational RADAR

NR .... Navy Regulations

NR .... Near (EY)

nr .... Near (VRA)

NR .... Negative Resistance [*Electronics*]

NR .... Net Register [*Shipping*]

NR .... Neural Retina [*Ophthalmology*]

NR .... Neutral Red [*An indicator*]

NR .... Neutral-Reverse [*Automotive engineering*]

NR .... Newpark Resources [*NYSE symbol*] (TTSB)

NR .... New Range (IAA)

NR .... New Reports [*1862-65*] [*England*] [*A publication*] (DLA)

NR .... Next Renewal

NR .... Next to Reading Matter [*Also, NRM*] [*Advertising*] (NTCM)

NR .... Nicaraguan Resistance [*An association*] (EA)

NR .... Nicolaus Rufulus [*Flourished, 13th century*] [*Authority cited in pre-1607 legal work*] (DSA)

nr .... Nigeria [*MARC country of publication code Library of Congress*] (LCCP)

NR .... Nigeria Regiment [*British military*] (DMA)

NR .... Nitrate Reductase [*An enzyme*]

NR .... Nitrile Rubber [*Organic chemistry*]

NR .... Nodal Rhythm [*Cardiology*] (DAVI)

NR	Noise Rating (NASA)
NR	Noise Ratio
NR	Noise Ration
NR	Noise Reduction (IAA)
NR	[Dolby] Noise Reduction (WDMC)
NR	Nonconformance Report [Nuclear energy] (NRCH)
NR	Nonlinear Resistance (IAA)
NR	Nonrated
NR	Nonreactive [Relay]
NR	Nonrebreathing [Medicine] (AAMN)
NR	Non-Rebreathing
NR	Nonrecoverable (IEEE)
NR	Nonrefundable [Airline fare code]
NR	Nonregistered (AABC)
NR	Non Repetatur [Do Not Repeat] [Pharmacy]
NR	Nonresident [British]
NR	Nonresponder [Strain of mice]
NR	Non-Response (WDMC)
NR	Nonreturnable [Beverage bottles]
NR	Nonreversing (IAA)
NR	Nonspecific Gene Resistance [Genetics]
NR	No Radiation (MAE)
NR	NORAD Region (IAA)
N/R	No Record (AAG)
NR	No Refill [Pharmacy]
NR	No Release (AAG)
NR	No Remittance
NR	No Report [Medicine]
NR	No Requirement
NR	No Residency Requirement [Voter registration]
NR	No Response [Medicine]
NR	Norfolk Rangers [British military] (DMA)
NR	Norgold Russet Potato
NR	No Risk [Business term]
NR	Normal (MAE)
NR	Normal Range
NR	Normal Record [Medicine] (DAVI)
NR	Normal Responder
NR	Normotensive Rat [Medicine] (DMAA)
NR	Northern Range [Navigation]
NR	Northern Rhodesia [Later, Zambia]
NR	North Riding [England] (ROG)
NR	North River [New York, New Jersey]
NR	Northward Aviation Ltd. (MHDW)
NR	Nose Right [Aviation] (MCD)
N/R	Notes Receivable
NR	Notice of Rating Required [Civil Service]
N/R	Notice of Readiness [Shipping]
NR	Not Rated
NR	Not Readable
NR	Not Recorded
N/R	Not Remarkable [Medicine]
NR	Not Reported
NR	Not Required
NR	Not Resolved (MAE)
N/R	Not Responsible For
NR	Nuchal Rigidity [Medicine]
NR	Nuclear Radiation
NR	Nuclear Radiology [Medical specialty] (DHSM)
NR	Nuclear Reactor
NR	Nuclear Research Submarine (MCD)
NR	Nuestra Remesa [Our Remittance] [Spanish Business term]
NR	Nufort Resources, Inc. [Toronto Stock Exchange symbol]
NR	Number (AAG)
NR	Number of Runs
NR	Nurse
NR	Nursing Representative [Red Cross]
NR	Nursing Services (HCT)
NR	Nutritive Ratio
NR	Nystagmus Recorder
NR	Reynold's Number [Viscosity] (MAE)
NR	Rochester Public Library, Rochester, NY [Library symbol Library of Congress] (LCLS)
nr----	Rocky Mountain Region [MARC geographic area code Library of Congress] (LCCP)
NR	Submersible Research Vehicle (Nuclear Propulsion) [Navy ship symbol]
NRA	Coupeville, WA [Location identifier FAA] (FAAL)
NRA	Narrandera [Australia Airport symbol] (OAG)
NRA	NASA Research Announcement
NRA	National Racing Authority (NADA)
NRA	National Reclamation Association [Later, National Water Resources Association] (EA)
NRA	National Recovery Act
NRA	National Recovery Administration [Voided by Supreme Court, 1935]
NRA	National Recreation Area [National Park Service] (GFGA)
NRA	National Recreation Association [Later, NRPA] (EA)
NRA	National Reform Association
NRA	National Register of Archives [Historical Manuscripts Commission] [British]
NRA	National Rehabilitation Association (EA)
NRA	National Remodelers Association [Later, NARI]
NRA	National Renderers Association (EA)
NRA	National Republican Alliance [Australia]
NRA	National Resistance Army [Uganda] (PD)
NRA	National Restaurant Association (EA)
NRA	National Retirement Association [Australia]
NRA	National Rifle Association (NADA)
NRA	National Rifle Association of America (EA)
NRA	National Rivers Authority [British]
NRA	National Roommate Association [Later, ASRS] (EA)
NRA	National Rounders Association [British] (BI)
NRA	NATO Refugees Agency (NATG)
NRA	Naval Radio Activity
NRA	Naval Reserve Association (EA)
NRA	Navy Recruiting Area (DNAB)
NRA	Negative Resistance Amplifier (PDAA)
NRA	Net Rentable Area (ADA)
NRA	Network Resolution Area
NRA	New Era Development Ltd. [Vancouver Stock Exchange symbol]
NRA	New Regional Airliner
NRA	Nitra Air [Slovakia] [FAA designator] (FAAC)
NRA	Non-Recurrrence Action (SAA)
NRA	Nonredundant Array
NRA	Nonregistered Accountable [Military]
NRA	Nonresident Alien
NRA	No Repair Action [Military]
NRA	Normal Retirement Age
NRA	North River [Alaska] [Seismograph station code, US Geological Survey] (SEIS)
NRA	Nothing Recorded Against [Security investigation result] [British]
NRA	Nuclear Radiation Absorber
NRA	Nuclear Reaction Analysis
NRA	Nuclear Regulatory Agency
NRA	Nucleus Raphe Alatus [Neurology]
NRA	Nucleus Retroambigualis [Neurology] (DAVI)
NRA	St. Augustine's College, Raleigh, NC [OCLC symbol] (OCLC)
NRAA	National Railway Appliances Association [Later, REMSA] (EA)
NRAA	National Renal Administrators Association (EA)
NRAA	National Rifle Association of America
NRAB	American Baptist Historical Society, Rochester, NY [Library symbol Library of Congress] (LCLS)
NRAB	National Railroad Adjustment Board
NRAB	National Railroad Adjustment Board Awards [A publication] (DLA)
NRAB	Naval Reserve Aviation Base
NRAB (1st D)	United States National Railroad Adjustment Board Awards, First Division [A publication] (DLA)
NRAB (2d D)	United States National Railroad Adjustment Board Awards, Second Division [A publication] (DLA)
NRAB (3d D)	United States National Railroad Adjustment Board Awards, Third Division [A publication] (DLA)
NRAB (4th D)	United States National Railroad Adjustment Board Awards, Fourth Division [A publication] (DLA)
NRAC	National Resources Analysis Center
NRAC	National Rural Advisory Council (NADA)
NRAC	Natural Resources Audit Council
NRAC	Naval Research Advisory Committee
NRACCO	Navy Regional Air Cargo Central [or Control] Office
NRAD	National Racquetball Association of the Deaf (EA)
NRAD	No Risk After Discharge [Shipping]
NRADUSA	National Racquetball Association of the Deaf of the USA [Later, NRAD] (EA)
NRAF	Naval Reserve Auxiliary Field
NRAF	Navy Recruiting Aids Facility (DNAB)
NRAF	Not Running at Finish [Automobile racing]
NRAG	Naval Research Advisory Group (KSC)
NRAI	National Residential Appraisers Institute (EA)
NRAL	New York State Appellate Division, Law Library, Rochester, NY [Library symbol Library of Congress] (LCLS)
NRAM	Non-Volatile Random Access Memory [Computer science]
NRAMEG	National Restaurant Association Marketing Executives Group [Defunct] (EA)
NRAMRG	National Restaurant Association Market Research Group [Defunct] (EA)
NR & HC	National Rivers and Harbors Congress [Later, WRC]
NRans	Ransomville Free Library, Ransomville, NY [Library symbol Library of Congress] (LCLS)
NRAO	National Radio Astronomy Observatory [Charlottesville, VA] [National Science Foundation] (GRD)
NRAO	Navy Regional Accounts Office
NRAP	Naturally Radioactive Product (NRCH)
NRAS	National Radio Astronomy Observatory [Charlottesville, VA] [National Science Foundation] (GRD)
NRAS	Navy Readiness Analysis System
NRAS	Nuclear Release Authentication System [Seventh Army] (AABC)
NRASF	National Registry of Ambulatory Surgical Facilities (EA)
NRAT	Nonrationed (AABC)
NRB	Mayport, FL [Location identifier FAA] (FAAL)
NRB	National Religious Broadcasters (EA)
NRB	National Research Bureau [Commercial firm] (EA)
NRB	National Resources Board [Terminated, 1935; functions transferred to National Resources Committee]
NRB	National Roads Board (NADA)
NRB	Natural Rubber Bureau [Later, MRB] (EA)
NRB	Naval Reactor Branch (MUGU)
NRB	Naval Repair Base
NRB	Navy Recruiting Bureau
NRB	Navy Reservation Bureau
NRB	New Redundancy Benefit [To reduce unemployment] [British]

NRB	Nonconformance Review Board [*Nuclear Regulatory Commission*] (NRCH)
NRB	Non-Reportable Birth [*Medicine*] (MEDA)
NRB	Nuclear Reactors Branch [*AEC*]
NRB1CL	Nuclear Reactor Operator, First-Class Badge [*Military decoration*] (GFGA)
NRB2CL	Nuclear Reactor Operator, Second-Class Badge [*Military decoration*] (GFGA)
NRBA	National Radio Broadcasters Association [*NAB*] [*Absorbed by*] (EA)
NRBA	National Registered Builders Association [*British*] (DBA)
NRBBAS	Nuclear Reactor Operator, Basic Badge [*Military decoration*] (GFGA)
NRBC	National Rare Blood Club [*Later, NRBC/NYBC*] (EA)
NRBC	Nucleated Red Blood Cell
NRBC/NYBC	National Rare Blood Club/New York Blood Center (EA)
NRBE	Native Races of the British Empire [*A publication*]
NRBF	Number of Rounds between Failures [*Quality control*] (MCD)
NRBL	Bausch & Lomb, Inc., Rochester, NY [*Library symbol Library of Congress*] (LCLS)
NRBL-S	Bausch & Lomb, Inc., SOFLENS Division, Technical Information Center, Rochester, NY [*Library symbol Library of Congress*] (LCLS)
NRBP	Natural Resource-Based Product
NRBP	New Reports of Bosanquet and Puller [*A publication*] (DLA)
NRBQ	New Rhythm and Blues Quartet [*Rock music group*]
NRBQ	Nurses' Registration Board of Queensland [*Australia*]
NRBS	Navy Recruiting Branch Station (DNAB)
NRBS	Nonrebreathing System [*Medicine*] (DAVI)
NRBSUPV	Nuclear Reactor Operator, Shift Supervisor Badge [*Military decoration*] (GFGA)
NRC	Crows Landing, CA [*Location identifier FAA*] (FAAL)
NRC	NAC RE Corp. [*NYSE symbol*] (SAG)
NRC	National Racquetball Club (EA)
NRC	National Radio Club [*Defunct*]
NRC	National Radio Conference [*Broadcast regulations*] (NTCM)
NRC	National Railroad Construction and Maintenance Association, Inc. (EA)
NRC	National Ramah Commission (EA)
NRC	National Reading Conference (EA)
NRC	National Realty Club [*New York, NY*] (EA)
NRC	National Realty Committee [*Washington, DC*] (EA)
NRC	National Reconditioning Order [*National Weather Service*] (USDC)
NRC	National Reconditioning Order [*Marine science*] (OSRA)
NRC	National Records Center
NRC	National Recycling Coalition (EA)
NRC	National Redemption Council [*Ghana*]
NRC	National Referral Center [*Defunct*] (EA)
NRC	National Remodelers Council [*Later, NAHB/RC*] (EA)
NRC	National Reprographic Centre for Documentation [*British*]
NRC	National Republican Club (EA)
NRC	National Republican Convention [*Nigeria*] [*Political party*]
NRCS	National Research Center (NATG)
NRC	National Research Corp.
NRC	National Research Council [*National Academy of Sciences*] [*Washington, DC*]
NRC	National Research Council, Canada [*Research center*] (IRC)
NRC	National Resistance Committee (EA)
NRC	National Resource Center for Paraprofessionals in Special Education and Related Human Services (EA)
NRC	National Resources Committee [*Functions transferred to National Resources Planning Board*]
NRC	National Response Center [*Environmental Protection Agency*]
NRC	National Retreat Centre [*British*] (CB)
NRC	National Riding Committee [*Later, ANRC*] (EA)
NRC	National Rocket Club [*Later, NSC*]
NRC	National Rural Center (EA)
NRC	Natural Resources Center [*University of Alabama*] [*Research center*] (RCD)
NRC	Natural Resources Council of America (EA)
NRC	Natural Rights Center (EA)
NRC	Naval Radio Compass (IAA)
NRC	Naval Radiological Control (DNAB)
NRC	Naval Records Club [*Later, INRO*]
NRC	Naval Recreation Center (DNAB)
NRC	Naval Research Co. - Reserves
NRC	Naval Retraining Command
NRC	Navy Reconnaissance Center (MCD)
NRC	Navy Recruiting Command (DNAB)
NRC	Navy Reserve Centers (NVT)
NRC	Negative Resistance Characteristic [*Electrophysiology*]
NRC	Netherlands Red Cross
NRC	Net Replacement Cost [*Accounting*]
NRC	Networking Routing Center (MHDB)
NRC	Network Reliability Coordinator
NRC	Neutron Radiation Capture
NRC	New Research Centers [*A publication*]
NRC	New Right Coalition (EA)
NRC	Newspaper Research Council (EA)
NRC	Noise-Rating Curve (OA)
NRC	Noise Reduction Coefficient [*of insulation*]
NRC	Nonrecurring Costs [*Accounting*] (KSC)
NRC	Non-Reusable Containers (GNE)
NRC	Norco Resources [*Vancouver Stock Exchange symbol*]
NRC	Normal Retinal Correspondence
NRC	North Carolina State University, Raleigh, NC [*OCLC symbol*] (OCLC)

NRC	Norwegian Refugee Council
NRC	Notch Root Contraction (OA)
NRC	Not Recommended for Children (ADA)
NRC	Not Routine Care [*Medicine*]
NRC	Nuclear Radiation Center [*Washington State University*] [*Research center*] (RCD)
NRC	Nuclear Recycling Consultants (EA)
NRC	Nuclear Regulatory Commission [*Washington, DC*]
NRC	Nuclear Research Council
NRC	Nutrition-Related Complications [*Medicine*]
NRCA	National Reamer Collectors Association (EA)
NRCA	National Rebel Class Association (EA)
NRCA	National Recovery and Collection Association (EA)
NRCA	National Redbone Coonhound Association (EA)
NRCA	National Rehabilitation Counseling Association (EA)
NRCA	National Resources Council of America
NRCA	National Retail Credit Association [*Later, ICA*]
NRCA	National Roofing Contractors Association (EA)
NRC-ACAC	National Research Council Army Countermine Advisory Committee
NRCAR	Nuclear Regulatory Commission Acquisition Regulation (AAGC)
NRCC	National Registry in Clinical Chemistry (EA)
NRCC	National Republican Coalition for Choice (EA)
NRCC	National Republican Congressional Committee (EA)
NRCC	National Research Council of Canada
NRCC	National Resource for Computation in Chemistry [*Lawrence Berkeley Laboratory*] [*Terminated, 1981*]
NRCC	Naval Regional Contracting Center (AAGC)
NRCC	NORAD Region Combat Center [*Military*]
NRCCL	Norwegian Research Centre for Computers and Law (NITA)
NRCCLS	National Resource Center for Consumers of Legal Services (EA)
NRCCS	National Research Council Committee on Salmonella (EA)
NRCD	National Redemption Council Decree [*Ghana*] [*A publication*] (DLA)
NRCd	National Reprographic Centre for Documentation [*Hatfield Polytechnic Institute*] [*Hertfordshire, England Evaluation and information group*] [*Information service or system*]
NRCd	National Reprographic Centre for Documentation Study (NITA)
NRCDA	North Region Cooperative Development Agency [*British*]
NRCDES	National Research Council Division of Earth Sciences (USDC)
NRCDES	National Research Council Division of Earth Sciences [*Marine science*] (OSRA)
NRC/DME	National Research Council of Canada, Division of Mechanical Engineering [*Research center*] (RCD)
NRCHB	Naval Reserve Cargo-Handling Battalion
NRCHMI	National Research Center on Homelessness and Mental Illness (EA)
NRCHTB	Naval Reserve Cargo-Handling Training Battalion
NRCI	National Radio Co., Inc. (IAA)
NRCI	National Rainbow Coalition, Inc. (EA)
NRCI	National Red Cherry Institute (EA)
NRCI	Nuclear Regulatory Commission Issuances [*A publication*] (DLA)
NRCL	National Research Council Library (DIT)
NRCLS	National Resource Center for Consumers of Legal Services (DLA)
NRC-MAC	National Research Council - Mine Advisory Committee
NRC/MAI	National Railroad Construction and Maintenance Association, Inc. (EA)
NRCMC	National Resource Center for Minority Contractors (EA)
NRCMCA	National Radiator Core Manufacturing Credit Association [*Later, NRMCA*] (EA)
NRCMF	NRC Master File (NITA)
NRC-NAS	National Research Council - National Academy of Sciences (AAG)
NRCP	Nonreinforced Concrete Pipe [*Technical drawings*]
NRCPR	Nuclear Regulatory Commission Procurement Regulation (AAGC)
NRCPS	National Research Council on Peace Strategy (EA)
NRCR	Colgate-Rochester Divinity School, Rochester, NY [*Library symbol Library of Congress*] (LCLS)
NRCS	National Roller Canary Society [*British*] (BI)
NRCS	Normalized RADAR Cross Section
NRCS	United States Natural Resources Conservation Service
NRCSA	National Registration Center for Study Abroad (EA)
NRCSA	Neurological Resources Center of South Australia
NRCSL	National Research Center on Student Learning [*University of Pittsburgh*] [*Research center*] (RCD)
NRCSM	Narcissism (ABBR)
NRCST	Narcissist (ABBR)
NRCST	National Referral Center for Science and Technology (MCD)
NRCTK	Narcotic (ABBR)
NRC-TOX	National Research Council - Committee on Toxicology
NRCV	Consolidated Vacuum Corp., Rochester, NY [*Library symbol Library of Congress*] (LCLS)
NRCWA	National Resource Center on Women and AIDS [*Acquired Immune Deficiency Syndrome*] (EA)
NRD	Aeronardi SpA [*Italy ICAO designator*] (FAAC)
NRD	National Range Division [*Air Force*]
NRD	National Range Documentation (MUGU)
NRD	National Registered Designer [*British*]
NRD	Natural Resource Damage [*Environmental science*]
NRD	Natural Resources Division [*An association*] (EAIO)
NRD	Naval Radio Direction Finder (IAA)
NRD	Naval Recruiting Department [*British military*] (DMA)
NRD	Naval Research and Development (KSC)
NRD	Navy Recruiting District (DNAB)
NRD	Negative Resistance Diode
NRD	Nominal Rim Diameter [*Automotive engineering*]
NRD	Nonrenal Death (MAE)
NRD	Nonreplenishable Demand
NRD	Norderney [*Germany Airport symbol*] (OAG)

NRD .... Nordlingen [*Federal Republic of Germany*] [*Seismograph station code, US Geological Survey Closed*] (SEIS)
NRD .... Nord Resources [*NYSE symbol*] (TTSB)
NRD .... Nord Resources Corp. [*NYSE symbol*] (SPSG)
NRD .... No Record of Destination [*Aviation*]
NRD .... Normal Retirement Date
NR/D .... Not Required, but Desired
NRD .... Nuclear Radiation Detector
NRD .... Nucleus Raphe Dorsalis [*Neuroanatomy*]
NRD .... Office of Naval Research and Development
NRDB .... National Residue Database
NRDB .... Nonreversing, Dynamic Braking (IAA)
NRDC .... N-Arginine Dibasic Convertase [*An enzyme*]
NRDC .... Natick Research and Development Center [*Army*] (INF)
NRDC .... National Research & Development Corp. [*Later, BTG*] [*British*]
NRDC .... National Resources Defence Council (ECON)
NRDC .... National Respiratory Disease Conference (DAVI)
NRDC .... National Retail Distribution Certificate [*British*]
NRDC .... National Running Data Center, Inc. [*Defunct*] (EA)
NRDC .... Natural Resources Defense Council (EA)
NRDC .... Navy Relief Society, Washington, DC, Auxiliary
NRDC .... Navy Research and Development Committee
NRDCA .... National Roof Deck Contractors Association (EA)
NRDEC .... Natick Research Development and Engineering Center [*Army*] (INF)
NRDF .... Non-Recursive Digital File (NITA)
NRDF .... Nonrecursive Digital Filter [*Navy*]
NRDFS .... Naval Radio Direction Finder Service
NRDI .... National Rural Development Institute (EA)
NRDL .... Naval Radiological Defense Laboratory
NRDL .... Navy Radiological Defense Laboratory (DNAB)
NRDLS .... National Rural Development Leaders School (OICC)
NRDO .... National Research and Development Organization (WDAA)
NRDO .... Navy Radio (NOAA)
NRDR .... Non-Resetting Data Reconstruction (PDAA)
NRDR-CF ..... Non-Resetting Data Reconstruction with Continuous Feedback (PDAA)
NRDR-DF ..... Non-Resetting Data Reconstruction with Discrete Feedback (PDAA)
NRDS .... Nuclear Rocket Detection System [*NASA*]
NRDS .... Nuclear Rocket Development Station
NRDSCG ...... Naval Research and Development Satellite Communications Group (SAA)
NRDU-V .... Navy Research and Development Unit - Vietnam (MCD)
NRE .... Aviones Are, SA de CV [*Mexico*] [*FAA designator*] (FAAC)
NRE .... Eastman Kodak Co., Rochester, NY [*Library symbol Library of Congress*] (LCLS)
NRE .... National Real Estate Corp. [*NYSE symbol*] (SPSG)
NRE .... National Resource Explorations Ltd. [*Toronto Stock Exchange symbol Vancouver Stock Exchange symbol*]
NRE .... Natl Re Corp. [*NYSE symbol*] (TTSB)
NRE .... Naval Research Establishment
NRE .... Negative Regulatory Element [*Genetics*]
NRE .... Negative Resistance Effect
NRE .... Negative Resistance Element [*Electronics*] (IAA)
NRE .... New and Renewable Energy (PDAA)
NRE .... New York Revised Laws [*A publication*] (DLA)
NRE .... Nonrecurring Engineering Expense
NRE .... Nonrotating Earth (NATG)
NRE .... Not Receiving Additional Irrigation [*Agriculture*]
NRE .... Nuclear Radiation Effect
NRE .... Nuclear Receptor Element [*Biochemistry*]
NRE .... Nuclear Rocket Engine (AAG)
NRe .... [*Reynolds*] Number [*Aerodynamics*] (BARN)
NRE .... Point Mugu, CA [*Location identifier FAA*] (FAAL)
NRE-A .... Eastman Kodak Co., Apparatus Division, Rochester, NY [*Library symbol Library of Congress*] (LCLS)
NREA .... National Rural Education Association (EA)
NREAN .... Northern Rivers Energy Action Network [*Australia*]
NRE-B .... Kodak (Near East) Ltd., Beirut, Lebanon [*Library symbol Library of Congress*] (LCLS)
NREB .... Naval Reserve Evaluation Board (DNAB)
NREC .... National Reconnaissance Executive Committee (LAIN)
NREC .... National Resources Evaluation Center [*of OEP*] [*Nuclear effects*]
NREC .... Natural Resources and Environment Committee [*Victoria, Australia*]
NRECA .... National Rural Electric Cooperative Association (EA)
NREd .... Eastman Dental Center, Basil G. Bibby Library, Rochester, NY [*Library symbol Library of Congress*] (LCLS)
NRed .... Red Hook Public Library, Red Hook, NY [*Library symbol Library of Congress*] (LCLS)
NRedL .... Red Hook Public Library, Red Hook, NY [*Library symbol*] [*Library of Congress*] (LCLS)
NRE-E .... Eastman Kodak Co., Engineering Division, Rochester, NY [*Library symbol Library of Congress*] (LCLS)
NREEC .... Natural Resources and Environmental Education Center [*Oklahoma State University*] [*Research center*] (RCD)
NREF .... North Russia Expeditionary Force [*World War I*] [*Canada*]
NREFA .... National Real Estate Fliers Association [*Later, Real Estate Aviation Chapter*] (EA)
NREH .... Normal Renin Essential Hypertension [*Medicine*] (DMAA)
NREH .... Nuclear Radiation Effects Handbook (SAA)
NRE-L .... Kodak Ltd., Recordak Division, London, Initiated Kingdom [*Library symbol Library of Congress*] (LCLS)
NREL .... National Renewable Energy Laboratory [*Department of Energy*]
NRE-M .... Eastman Kodak Co., Health and Safety Laboratory, Rochester, NY [*Library symbol Library of Congress*] (LCLS)
NREM .... Nonrapid Eye Movement [*Type of sleep*]

NREMS .... Nonrapid Eye Movement Sleep [*Neurology*] (DAVI)
NREMT .... National Registry of Emergency Medical Technicians (EA)
NREMT-P ...... National Registry of Emergency Medical Technicians - Paramedics (DAVI)
NREN .... National Research and Education Network [*Federal government*]
NRenSA .... Saint Anthony-On-Hudson Theological Seminary, Rensselaer, NY [*Library symbol Library of Congress*] (LCLS)
NRenSW ...... Sterling-Winthrop Research Institute, Rensselaer, NY [*Library symbol Library of Congress*] (LCLS)
NRE-P .... Eastman Kodak Co., Photographic Technology Library, Rochester, NY [*Library symbol Library of Congress*] (LCLS)
NREP .... Name Removed from End-Paper [*Antiquarian book trade*]
NREP .... National Registry of Environmental Professionals (EA)
NREP .... National Reliability Evaluation Program [*Nuclear Regulatory Commission*]
NREP .... Neutron Resonance Escape Probability [*Nuclear energy*] (NRCH)
NRE-R .... Eastman Kodak Co., Research Laboratories, Rochester, NY [*Library symbol Library of Congress*] (LCLS)
NRERC .... National Rural Education Research Consortium [*Defunct*] (EA)
NRES .... Natural Resources, Energy, and Environment [*Office of Management and Budget*]
NRES .... Naval Receiving Station
NRES .... Nichols Research [*NASDAQ symbol*] (TTSB)
NRES .... Nichols Research Corp. [*NASDAQ symbol*] (NQ)
NRETN .... Nonreturn
NREVSS .... National Respiratory and Enteric Virus Surveillance System
NRF .... National Republican Foundation (EA)
NRF .... National Research Foundation [*Research center*] (RCD)
NRF .... National Research Foundation [*South Africa*]
NRF .... National Retail Federation (EA)
NRF .... National Roofing Foundation (EA)
NRF .... National Rowing Foundation (EA)
NRF .... National Rural Fellows (EA)
NRF .... Naval Reactor Facility
NRF .... Naval Repair Facility
NRF .... Naval Reserve Fleet [*or Force*]
NRF .... Neurite Retraction Factor [*Biochemistry*]
NRF .... Neurosciences Research Foundation (DAVI)
NRF .... Newport Restoration Foundation (EA)
NRF .... Nitrogen Rejection Facility [*Process engineering*]
NRF .... No Redeeming Features
NRF .... No Reflight
NRF .... No Reinforcement [*Psychology*]
NRF .... Not Running at the Finish [*Automobile racing term*]
NRF .... Nuclear Resonance Fluorescence (IAA)
NRF .... Nutrition Research Foundation [*Australia*]
NRF .... R. T. French Co., Rochester, NY [*Library symbol Library of Congress*] (LCLS)
NRFA .... National Retail Florists Association [*Defunct*]
NRFA .... National Retail Furniture Association [*Later, NHFA*] (EA)
NRFB .... Never Removed from Box [*Doll collecting*]
NRFBS .... National Research Foundation for Business Statistics (EA)
NRFC .... National Railroad Freight Committee (EA)
NRFC .... Navy Regional Finance Center
NRFC-B .... Navy Regional Finance Center, Brooklyn [*New York*] (DNAB)
NRFC-GL ...... Navy Regional Finance Center, Great Lakes (DNAB)
NRFC-N .... Navy Regional Finance Center, Norfolk [*Virginia*] (DNAB)
NRFC-PH ...... Navy Regional Finance Center, Pearl Harbor [*Hawaii*] (DNAB)
NRFC-SD ...... Navy Regional Finance Center, San Diego [*California*] (DNAB)
NRFC-SF ...... Navy Regional Finance Center, San Francisco [*California*] (DNAB)
NRFD .... Not Ready for Data
NRFEA .... National Retail Farm Equipment Association [*Later, NFPEDA*]
NRFF .... National Research Foundation for Fertility [*Inactive*] (EA)
NRFI .... National Rail Freight Initiative [*Australia*]
NRFI .... Nonrecurring Finished Intelligence (MCD)
NRFI .... Not Ready for Issue
NRFL .... National Rugby Football League (NADA)
NRFMAU ...... Naval Reserve Fleet Management Assistance Unit (DNAB)
NRFO .... Navy Regional Finance Office
NRFS .... Naval Reserve Force Study Group (DNAB)
NRFSA .... Navy Radio Frequency Spectrum Activity
NRFSEA .... National Reciprocal and Family Support Enforcement Association [*Later, NCSEA*] (EA)
NRFU .... Nonresponse Follow-Up [*Bureau of the Census*] (GFGA)
NRG .... Energy (ABBR)
NRG .... Nautical Research Guild (EA)
NRG .... Naval Research Group
NRG .... Northern Rhodesia Gazette [*A publication*] (DLA)
NRG .... Ross Aviation, Inc. [*ICAO designator*] (FAAC)
NRG .... Tri-Lite, Inc. [*AMEX symbol*] (SPSG)
NRGA .... National Rice Growers Association [*Defunct*] (EA)
NRGas .... Rochester Gas & Electric Corp., Technical Information Center, Rochester, NY [*Library symbol Library of Congress*] (LCLS)
NRGC .... Nucleus Reticularis Gigantocellularis [*Neuroanatomy*]
NRGD-SC ..... Stromberg-Carlson Corp., Rochester, NY [*Library symbol Library of Congress*] (LCLS)
NRGE .... George Eastman House, Rochester, NY [*Library symbol Library of Congress*] (LCLS)
NRGI .... National Energy Group [*NASDAQ symbol*] (SAG)
NRGN .... Neurogen Corp. [*NASDAQ symbol*] (NQ)
NRGR .... General Railway Signal Co., Rochester, NY [*Library symbol Library of Congress*] (LCLS)
NRGS .... Church of Jesus Christ of Latter-Day Saints, Genealogical Society Library, Rochester Branch, Rochester, NY [*Library symbol Library of Congress*] (LCLS)

NRH.............	Natural Rate Hypothesis [*Economics*]
NRH.............	Nodular Regenerative Hyperplasia [*of liver*] [*Medicine*]
NRH.............	Nonready Hours
NRH.............	No Reply Heard [*ICAO designator*] (FAAC)
NRHA...........	National Radio Heritage Association (EA)
NRHA...........	National Reining Horse Association (EA)
NRHA...........	National Retail Hardware Association (EA)
NRHA...........	National Roller Hockey Association of Great Britain (BI)
NRHA...........	National Rural Health Association (EA)
NRHA...........	Northern Rivers Hydrophonic Association [*Australia*]
NRhbA.........	Astor Home for Children, Rhinebeck, NY [*Library symbol Library of Congress*] (LCLS)
NRHC...........	National Rental Housing Council [*Later, NMHC*] (EA)
NRHC...........	National Rivers and Harbors Congress [*Later, WRC*]
NRHC...........	National Rural Housing Coalition (EA)
NRHCA.........	National Rural Health Care Association [*Formerly, NRPCA*] (EA)
NRhDH.........	Long Island Doctors' Hospital, Roslyn Heights, NY [*Library symbol Library of Congress*] (LCLS)
NRHE...........	Nonregenerative Heat Exchanger [*Nuclear energy*] (NRCH)
NRHGC........	National Republican Heritage Groups (Nationalities) Council (EA)
NRHi...........	Rochester Historical Society, Rochester, NY [*Library symbol Library of Congress*] (LCLS)
NRHP...........	National Register of Historic Places
NRHP...........	National Register of Hypnotherapists and Psychotherapists [*British*] (DBA)
NRHS...........	National Railway Historical Society (EA)
NRHS...........	New Royal Horticultural Society [*British*]
NRHU...........	National Rural Health Unit [*Australia*]
NRHX...........	Nonregenerative Heat Exchanger [*Nuclear energy*] (NRCH)
NRI.............	National Radio Institute
NRI.............	National Research Institute [*Audience research organization*] (NTCM)
NRI.............	National Resource Inventory [*US database on erosion*]
NRI.............	National Rivers Inventory (GNE)
NRI.............	Natural Resources Institute [*University of Greenwich*] [*British*]
NRI.............	Natural Resources International
NRI.............	Net Radio Interface [*Telecommunications*] (TEL)
NRI.............	Neurological and Related Intervention [*Medicine*]
NRI.............	Neutral Regular Insulin
NRI.............	New Records, Inc. [*Record label*]
NRI.............	New Ring Index [*of chemical compounds*] [*A publication*]
NRI.............	Nomura Research Institute (NITA)
NRI.............	Nonrecurring Installation Charge [*Telecommunications*] (TEL)
NRI.............	Nonrecurring Investment (NASA)
NRI.............	Nonrepairable Item (MCD)
NRI.............	Nonresident Instruction (MCD)
NRI.............	Non-Respiratory Infection [*Medicine*] (DMAA)
NRI.............	Noril'sk [*Former USSR Seismograph station code, US Geological Survey*] (SEIS)
NRI.............	Novagold Resources, Inc. [*Toronto Stock Exchange symbol*]
NRI.............	Number of Records Ignored (SAA)
NRIA...........	Narrow Resonance Infinite Absorber (PDAA)
NRIA...........	National Railroad Intermodal Association [*Defunct*] (EA)
NRIAD.........	National Register of Industrial Art Designers [*British*] (DAS)
NRIC...........	National Rehabilitation Information Center [*Catholic University of America*] [*Bibliographic Database*] [*Washington, DC*]
NRIC...........	Negative Return in Cartridge [*Advanced photo system*]
NRIC...........	Non-Reciprocal Impedance Converter (PDAA)
NRIC...........	Nuclear Research Information Center [*American Nuclear Center*] [*Information service or system*] (IID)
NRICH.........	National Resource Institute on Children and Youth with Handicaps [*Defunct*] (EA)
NRID...........	National Registry [*NASDAQ symbol*] (SAG)
NRIIA.........	National Republican Institute for International Affairs (EA)
NRIM...........	Narrow Resonance Infinite Mass [*Nuclear energy*] (NRCH)
NRIM...........	Northrim Bank [*NASDAQ symbol*] (SAG)
NRIMS.........	National Research Institute for Mathematical Sciences [*South Africa*]
NRIP...........	Navy Reserve Intelligence Program (MCD)
NRIP...........	Number of Rejected Initial Pickups
NRIPMVLIC...	Nonresident Interprovince Motor Vehicle Liability Insurance Card [*For travel in Canada*]
NRIS...........	Natural Resource Information System [*Department of the Interior*]
NRIS...........	New Mexico Natural Resources Information System [*New Mexico State Department of Natural Resources*] [*Santa Fe*] (IID)
NRIUW.........	Naval Reserve Inshore Undersea Warfare (DNAB)
NRJ.............	Natural Resources Journal [*A publication*] (BRI)
NRJ.............	Non-Reciprocal Junction (PDAA)
NRK.............	Newark (ABBR)
NRK.............	Normal Rat Kidney
NRK.............	Normotensive Rat Kidney
NRK.............	Norrkoping [*Sweden*] [*Airport symbol*] (OAG)
NRK.............	Norsk Rikskringkasting [*Norwegian Broadcasting Corporation*]
NRK.............	Nurek [*Former USSR Seismograph station code, US Geological Survey Closed*] (SEIS)
NRKF...........	Normal Rat Kidney Fibroblast [*Cytology*]
NRkpJH.......	Rocky Point Junior-Senior High School, Rocky Point, NY [*Library symbol Library of Congress*] (LCLS)
NRL.............	Naneco Resources Ltd. [*Vancouver Stock Exchange symbol*]
NRL.............	National Reference Library [*British*] (NUCP)
NRL.............	National Registry for Librarians (EA)
NRL.............	National Research Laboratory
NRL.............	National Research Library [*Canada*] (DIT)
NRL.............	National Resources Library
NRL.............	Naval Research Laboratory [*Washington, DC Seismograph station code, US Geological Survey Closed*] (SEIS)
NRL.............	Naval Research Laboratory, Washington, DC [*OCLC symbol*] (OCLC)
NRL.............	Network Restructuring Language
NRL.............	New York Revised Laws [*A publication*] (DLA)
NRL.............	Night Ration Locker (MSA)
NRL.............	Normal Rated Load
NRL.............	Normal Response Level
NRL.............	Norrell Corp. [*NYSE symbol*] (SAG)
NRL.............	Norske Reindriftsamers Lansforbund [*Norway*]
NRL.............	North Ronaldsay [*Scotland*] [*Airport symbol*] (OAG)
NRL.............	Nuclear Reactor Laboratory [*Massachusetts Institute of Technology*] [*Research center*] (RCD)
NRLA...........	Network Repair Level Analysis
NRLA...........	Northeastern Retail Lumbermen's Association (EA)
NRLC...........	National Railway Labor Conference (EA)
NRLC...........	National Right to Life Committee (EA)
NRLCA.........	National Rural Letter Carriers' Association (EA)
NRLCHESBAYDET...	Naval Research Laboratory, Chesapeake Bay Detachment (DNAB)
NRLD...........	Norland Medical Systems [*NASDAQ symbol*] (TTSB)
NRLD...........	Norland Medical Systems, Inc. [*NASDAQ symbol*] (SAG)
NRLDA.........	National Retail Lumber Dealers Association [*Later, NLBMDA*]
NRL/EOTPO...	Naval Research Laboratory Electro-Optical Technology Program Office [*Washington, DC*]
NRLETF........	National Right to Life Educational Trust Fund (EA)
NRLF...........	Lincoln First Bank of Rochester, Rochester, NY [*Library symbol Library of Congress*] (LCLS)
NRLFLTSUPPDET...	Naval Research Laboratory, Flight Support Detachment (DNAB)
NRLGY.........	Neurology
NRLN...........	Northern Regional Legal Notice [*1954-61*] [*Nigeria*] [*A publication*] (DLA)
NRLP...........	National Railway Labor Panel [*World War II*]
NRLR...........	Northern Rhodesia Law Reports [*A publication*] (DLA)
NRLREP.......	Naval Research Laboratory Representative (DNAB)
NRLSI.........	National Reference Library of Science and Invention [*of the British Museum*]
NRLSITEDET...	Naval Research Laboratory, Field Site Detachment (DNAB)
NRLSPECPROJDET...	Naval Research Laboratory, Special Projects Detachment (DNAB)
NRL/SVIC...	Naval Research Laboratory Shock and Vibration Information Center [*ONR*]
NRLUWSREFDET...	Naval Research Laboratory, Underwater Sound Reference Detachment (DNAB)
NRM.............	Nara [*Mali*] [*Airport symbol*] (OAG)
NRM.............	National Registry of Microbiologists (DAVI)
NRM.............	National Resistance Movement [*Uganda*] (PD)
NRM.............	National Revolutionary Movement [*France*]
NRM.............	Natural Remanent Magnetism [*or Magnetization*]
NRM.............	Natural Resource Management
NRM.............	Naval Reserve Medal
NRM.............	Next to Reading Matter [*Advertising*] (WDMC)
NRM.............	Nonrecurring Maintenance [*NASA*] (KSC)
NRM.............	Normalize (DEN)
NRM.............	Normal Response Mode
NRM.............	Norm-Referenced Measurement [*Education*]
NRM.............	Northair Mines Ltd. [*Toronto Stock Exchange symbol Vancouver Stock Exchange symbol*]
NRM.............	Northern Rocky Mountains
NRM.............	North Rainier Mesa [*Nevada*] [*Seismograph station code, US Geological Survey*]
NRM.............	Rochester Museum and Science Center, Rochester, NY [*Library symbol Library of Congress*] (LCLS)
NRMA.........	National Reloading Manufacturers Association (EA)
NRMA.........	National Retail Merchants Association [*New York, NY*] (EA)
NRMA.........	Nuclear Records Management Association (EA)
NRMADI......	Non Recedet Malum a Domo Ingrati [*Evil Shall Not Depart from the House of theUngrateful*] [(*After Prov., XVII. 13*) *Motto of Julius, Duke of Braunschweig-Wolfenbuttel (1529-89)*] [*Latin*]
NRMC.........	Monroe Community College, Rochester, NY [*Library symbol Library of Congress*] (LCLS)
NRMC.........	National Records Management Council (EA)
NRMC.........	National Resources Management Corp.
NRMC.........	Naval Records Management Center
NRMC.........	Naval Regional Medical Center (NVT)
NRMC.........	Naval Reserve Manpower Center
NRMC.........	Northeast Rat and Mouse Club (EA)
NRMCA.......	National Radiator Manufacturing Credit Association (EA)
NRMCA.......	National Ready Mixed Concrete Association (EA)
NRMCEN......	Naval Records Management Center
NRME.........	Notched, Returned, and Mitred Ends [*Construction*]
NRMEC........	North American Rockwell Microelectronics Co. [*Obsolete*]
NRMF.........	New Road Map Foundation (EA)
NRMI.........	National Record Mart, Inc. [*NASDAQ symbol*] (SAG)
NRMI.........	National Registry of Myocardial Infarction
NRMI.........	Natl Record Mart [*NASDAQ symbol*] (TTSB)
NRMIUW......	Naval Reserve Mobile Inshore Undersea Warfare (DNAB)
NRML.........	Monroe County Library System, Rochester, NY [*Library symbol Library of Congress*] (LCLS)
NRML.........	Normal (WGA)
NRMLC........	Normalcy (ABBR)
NRMLT........	Normality (ABBR)
NRMLY........	Normally (ABBR)
NRMLZ........	Normalize (ABBR)
NRMLZD......	Normalized (ABBR)
NRMLZG......	Normalizing (ABBR)
NRMLZN......	Normalization (ABBR)

NRMLZR ...... Normalizer (ABBR)
NRMM .... National Register of Microform Masters [*Library of Congress*]
NRMM .... NATO Reference Mobility Model
NRMOMAGU... Naval Reserve Mobile Mine Assembly Group (DNAB)
NRMP .... National Resident Matching Program (EA)
NRMS .... National Registry of Medical Secretaries (EA)
NRMS .... Natural Resource Management System [*Army Corps of Engineers*] [*Database*]
NRMS .... Naval Reserve Midshipmen's School
NRMS .... Neutralization-Reionization Mass Spectrometry
NRMS .... Nominal Root Mean Square (IAA)
NRMS .... Norman Rockwell Memorial Society (EA)
NRMT .... Northern Rocky Mountain Trench [*Geology*]
NRMTC .... Nordoff-Robbins Music Therapy Centre Ltd. [*British*] (CB)
NRMU .... Natural Resources Management [*Organization of Eastern Caribbean States*]
NRMU .... Northern Rhodesia European Mineworkers' Union
NRMV .... Normative (ABBR)
NRMVY .... Normatively (ABBR)
NRMW .... Margaret Woodbury Strong Museum, Rochester, NY [*Library symbol Library of Congress*] (LCLS)
NRN .... Naryn [*Former USSR Seismograph station code, US Geological Survey*] (SEIS)
NRN .... National Resource Network [*Commercial firm*] (EA)
NRN .... Natural Radioactive Nuclides
NRN .... Negative Run Number [*Computer science*] (OA)
NRN .... Northern
NRN .... Royal Netherlands Navy [*ICAO designator*] (FAAC)
nRNA .... Ribonucleic Acid, Nuclear [*Biochemistry, genetics*]
NRNC .... Nazareth College of Rochester, Rochester, NY [*Library symbol Library of Congress*] (LCLS)
NRND .... Norand Corp. [*NASDAQ symbol*] (SAG)
NRNFC .... National Rick Nelson Fan Club (EA)
NRNHD .... Nixon, Hargrave, Devans & Doyle, Rochester, NY [*Library symbol*] [*Library of Congress*] (LCLS)
NRNLR .... Northern Region of Nigeria Law Reports [*A publication*] (DLA)
NRNP .... Nuclear Ribonucleoprotein [*Medicine*] (DMAA)
NRNR .... National Rotorcraft Noise Reduction [*Program to reduce noise of helicopters*]
NRNS .... Nearness (ABBR)
NRO .... National Range Operations (RDA)
NRO .... National Reconnaissance Office [*Air Force/CIA*]
NRO .... National Reconnaissance Organization [*CIA*]
NRO .... Naval Research Objectives
NRO .... Navy Retail Office (AFIT)
NRO .... Negative Resistance Oscillator [*Electronics*]
NRO .... Nobeyama Radio Observatory
NRO .... Nonresident-Owned Funds [*Investment term*]
NRO .... Not RAM [*Reliability, Availability, and Maintainability*] Oriented
NRock .... Rockville Centre Public Library, Rockville Centre, NY [*Library symbol Library of Congress*] (LCLS)
NRockH .... Mercy Hospital, Rockville Centre, NY [*Library symbol Library of Congress*] (LCLS)
NRockHE ..... Hewett Elementary School, Rockville Centre, NY [*Library symbol Library of Congress*] (LCLS)
NRockL .... Lakeview Public Library, Rockville Centre, NY [*Library symbol Library of Congress*] (LCLS)
NRockM .... Molloy College, Rockville Centre, NY [*Library symbol Library of Congress*] (LCLS)
NRockRE ..... Riverside School, Rockville Centre, NY [*Library symbol*] [*Library of Congress*] (LCLS)
NRockSMS ... South Side Middle School, Rockville Centre, NY [*Library symbol*] [*Library of Congress*] (LCLS)
NRockSSH ... South Side Senior High School, Rockville Centre, NY [*Library symbol*] [*Library of Congress*] (LCLS)
NRockWE ..... Wilson Elementary School, Rockville Centre, NY [*Library symbol Library of Congress*] (LCLS)
NRockWR .... Woodfield Road School, Rockville Centre, NY [*Library symbol*] [*Library of Congress*] (LCLS)
NRockWS ..... Floyd B. Watson School, Rockville Centre, NY [*Library symbol*] [*Library of Congress*] (LCLS)
NROE .... Naval Reactor Organic Experiment
nroff .... Nontypesetting Runoff [*Computer science*] (CDE)
NRom .... Jervis Library Association, Rome, NY [*Library symbol Library of Congress*] (LCLS)
NROM .... Noble Roman's, Inc. [*NASDAQ symbol*] (NQ)
NROM .... Noble Romns [*NASDAQ symbol*] (TTSB)
NRomA .... Rome Air Development Center, Rome, NY [*Library symbol Library of Congress*] (LCLS)
NRomAF ...... United States Air Force, Base Library, Griffiss Air Force Base, Rome, NY [*Library symbol Library of Congress*] (LCLS)
NRomAF-R... United States Air Force, Rome Air Development Center, Griffiss, NY [*Library symbol Library of Congress*] (LCLS)
NROO .... Naval Reactors Operations Office
NRoos .... Roosevelt Community Library, Roosevelt, NY [*Library symbol Library of Congress*] (LCLS)
NRoosCE ..... Centennial Elementary School, Roosevelt, NY [*Library symbol*] [*Library of Congress*] (LCLS)
NRoosDP ..... Daniels Primary Center, Roosevelt, NY [*Library symbol*] [*Library of Congress*] (LCLS)
NRoosJH ...... Roosevelt Junior-Senior High School, Roosevelt, NY [*Library symbol*] [*Library of Congress*] (LCLS)
NRoosPK ..... Prekindergarten School, Roosevelt, NY [*Library symbol*] [*Library of Congress*] (LCLS)

NRoosRE ..... Theadore Roosevelt Elementary School, Roosevelt, NY [*Library symbol*] [*Library of Congress*] (LCLS)
NRoosWE .... Washington-Rose Elementary School, Roosevelt, NY [*Library symbol*] [*Library of Congress*] (LCLS)
NROPS .... New Riders of the Purple Sage [*Rock music group*]
NROS .... Naval Reserve Officer School
NRosl .... Bryant Library, Roslyn, NY [*Library symbol Library of Congress*] (LCLS)
NRoslH .... Saint Francis Hospital, Roslyn, NY [*Library symbol Library of Congress*] (LCLS)
NRoslhEI ...... East Hills Intermediate School, Roslyn Heights, NY [*Library symbol*] [*Library of Congress*] (LCLS)
NRoslhHP .... Heights Primary School, Roslyn Heights, NY [*Library symbol*] [*Library of Congress*] (LCLS)
NRoslhHS .... Roslyn High School, Roslyn Heights, NY [*Library symbol*] [*Library of Congress*] (LCLS)
NRoslhJH ..... Roslyn Junior High School, Roslyn Heights, NY [*Library symbol*] [*Library of Congress*] (LCLS)
NRoslHS ...... Roslyn High School, Roslyn, NY [*Library symbol Library of Congress*] (LCLS)
NRoslhWI .... Willets Road Intermediate School, Roslyn Heights, NY [*Library symbol Library of Congress*] (LCLS)
NRoslJH ...... Roslyn Junior High School, Roslyn, NY [*Library symbol Library of Congress*] (LCLS)
NROSS .... Navy Remote Ocean Sensing System [*Proposed*]
NROTC .... Naval Reserve Officers' Training Corps
NROTCBA .... National Reserve Officers' Training Corps Band Association (AEBS)
NROTCU .... Naval Reserve Officers' Training Corps Unit (DNAB)
NROTCUNAVADMINU... Naval Reserve Officers' Training Corps Unit and Administrative Unit (DNAB)
NROVA .... National Record of Vocational Achievement (AIE)
NRP .... National Religious Party [*Hamiflaga Hadatit Leumit*] [*Israel*] [*Political party*] (PPW)
NRP .... National Reporting Program [*National Institute of Mental Health*] [*Department of Health and Human Services*] (GFGA)
NRP .... National Republican Party [*Guyana*] [*Political party*] (EY)
NRP .... National Resistance Party [*Political party*] (BJA)
NRP .... National Review Panel [*Work Incentive Program*] [*Department of Labor*]
NRP .... National Route Program (GAVI)
N/RP .... Neoclassical/Rational Planning
NRP .... Net Rating Point [*Advertising*] (DOAD)
NRP .... Net Rating Points [*Media ratings*] (NTCM)
NRP .... Neurosciences Research Program [*Massachusetts Institute of Technology*]
NRP .... Nevis Reformation Party [*Political party*]
NRP .... New Republic Party [*South Africa*] [*Political party*] (PPW)
NRP .... New Rhodesia Party [*Political party*]
NRP .... Noise Review Program [*Navy*] (DNAB)
NRP .... Nonregistered Publication
NRP .... Nonreportable Property [*Military*]
NRP .... Nonstationary Random Process
NRP .... Non-unit Related Personnel [*Military*] (DOMA)
NRP .... Normal Rated Power
NRP .... Notice of Research Project
NRP .... NRP, Inc. [*Associated Press*] (SAG)
NRP .... Nuclear Reform Project (EA)
NRP .... Nuwe Republiekparty [*New Republic Party*] [*Political party Afrikaans*]
NRP .... People's Republican Party [*Turkey Political party*]
NRP .... Pfaudler Technical Library, Rochester, NY [*Library symbol Library of Congress*] (LCLS)
NRpA .... Ayerst Science Laboratory, Rouses Point, NY [*Library symbol Library of Congress*] (LCLS)
NRPA .... National Recreation and Park Association (EA)
NRPA .... Non-Redundant Pinhole Array (PDAA)
NRPAC .... Naval Reserve Public Affairs Co.
NRPAI .... National Rifle and Pistol Association of Ireland (EAIO)
NRPAIN .... National Register of Prominent Americans and International Notables (EA)
NRPB .... National Radiological Protection Board [*British*]
NRPB .... National Research Planning Board
NRPB .... National Resources Planning Board [*Abolished, 1943*]
NRPB .... Naval Research Planning Board (DNAB)
NRPB .... Naval Research Policy Board (DNAB)
NRPB .... Nickerson RPB Ltd. [*British*] (IRUK)
NRPC .... National Railroad Passenger Corp. [*Government rail transportation*]
NRPC .... National Register Publishing Co. [*Information service or system*] (IID)
NRPC .... Naval Reserve Personnel Center (DNAB)
NRPCA .... National Rural Primary Care Association [*Later, NRHCA*] (EA)
NRPD .... National Radiological Protection Board [*British*]
NRPEO .... Naval Regional Plant Equipment Office [*or Officer*] (DNAB)
NRPF .... National Railroad Pension Forum [*Defunct*] (EA)
NRPF .... National Retinitis Pigmentosa Foundation [*Later, RPFFB*] (EA)
NRPH .... Park Ridge Hospital, Medical Library, Rochester, NY [*Library symbol Library of Congress*] (LCLS)
NRPIO .... Naval Registered Publications Issuing Office
NRPJ .... Nezavisna Radnicka Partija Jugoslavije [*Independent Labor Party of Yugoslavia*] [*Political party*]
NRPlanP ...... Planned Parenthood of Rochester and Monroe County, Rochester, NY [*Library symbol Library of Congress*] (LCLS)
NRPM .... Nonregistered Publications Memoranda
NRPO .... Naval Regional Procurement Office
NRPP .... Pennwalt Corp., Pharmaceutical Division Research Library, Rochester, NY [*Library symbol Library of Congress*] (LCLS)
NRPRA .... Natural Rubber Producers' Research Association [*British*] (BI)

NRPS .... Naval Radiological Protection Service (PDAA)
NRPS .... New Riders of the Purple Sage [Rock music group]
NRPSA .... National Retail Pet Supply Association [Defunct] (EA)
NRPSGA ...... National Retail Pet Store and Groomers Association (EA)
NRPTC .... National Register of Potentially Toxic Chemicals (GNE)
NRR .... Naval Research Reactor
NRR .... Naval Research Requirement
NRR .... Naval Reserve Requirement (MCD)
NRR .... Negative Radial Rake (IAA)
NRR .... Negative Resistance Repeater [Electronics] (IAA)
NRR .... Net Reproductive Rate
NRR .... Net Retail Requirements
NRR .... Noise Reduction Rating [Audio technology] (EG)
NRR .... No Response Required
NRR .... No Resume Required
NRR .... Northern Rhodesia Regiment
NRR .... North Reno [Nevada] [Seismograph station code, US Geological
                 Survey] (SEIS)
NRR .... Note, Record, Report [Medical records and nursing] (DAVI)
NRR .... Nuclear Rocket Reactor
NRR .... Office of Nuclear Reactor Regulation [Nuclear Regulatory
                 Commission]
NRR .... Roosevelt Roads, PR [Location identifier FAA] (FAAL)
NRRA .... National Rail Regulatory Authority [Australia]
NRRA .... National Resource Recovery Association (EA)
NRRA .... National Risk Retention Association (EA)
NRRAD .... Narrated (ABBR)
NRRAG .... Narrating (ABBR)
NRRAN .... Narration (ABBR)
NRR & C ...... Russell and Chesley's Nova Scotia Reports [A publication] (DLA)
NRRAR .... Narrator (ABBR)
NRRAS .... Navy Readiness Reporting and Analysis System (MCD)
NRRAV .... Narrative (ABBR)
NRRB .... National Recovery Review Board [Terminated, 1934]
NRRC .... National Rex Rabbit Club (EA)
NRRC .... Naval Research Reserve Co.
NRRC .... Northern Regional Research Center [Formerly, NRRL] [Peoria, IL]
                 [Department of Agriculture]
NRRC .... Nuclear Risk Reduction Center (DOMA)
NRRD .... Norstan, Inc. [NASDAQ symbol] (NQ)
NRRF .... Naval Radio Receiving Facility (DNAB)
NRRF .... Naval Reserve Readiness Facility (DNAB)
NRRFSS .... National Research and Resource Facility for Submicron Structures
                 [Cornell University] [Research center] (RCD)
NRRI .... National Regulatory Research Institute [Ohio State University]
                 [Research center] (RCD)
NRRI .... Natural Resources Research Institute [Research center] (RCD)
NRRI .... Rochester Institute of Technology, Rochester, NY [Library symbol
                 Library of Congress] (LCLS)
NRRI-C .... Rochester Institute of Technology, Melbert B. Cary, Jr. Graphic Arts
                 Collection, Rochester, NY [Library symbol Library of Congress]
                 (LCLS)
NRRL .... Northern Regional Research Laboratory [Later, NRRC] [Department
                 of Agriculture]
NRRO .... Naval Radio Research Observatory (IAA)
NRRO .... Nuclear Radiation-Resistant Oils (NRCH)
NRRP .... National Reservoir Research Program [Department of the Interior]
                 (GRD)
NRRP .... Sybron Corp., Rochester, NY [Library symbol Library of Congress]
                 (LCLS)
NRRPC .... National Rural and Resources Press Club [Australia]
NRRR .... Rochester Reference Research and Resources Council, Rochester,
                 NY [Library symbol Library of Congress] (LCLS)
NRRS .... Naval Radio Research Station
NRRS .... Nebraska Reading Retrieval System (EDAC)
NRRS .... No Remaining Radiation Service [Unit] [Military]
NRS .... Atlantic Richfield Co. [ICAO designator] (FAAC)
NRS .... Imperial Beach, CA [Location identifier FAA] (FAAL)
NRS .... Name Registration Scheme [Telecommunications] (OSI)
NRS .... National Radio Station (IAA)
NRS .... National Readership Survey [British]
NRS .... National Real Estate Service [Canada]
NRS .... National Reemployment Service
NRS .... National Referral System [British] (DCTA)
NRS .... National Reporter System [Database] [Maritime Law Book Co. Ltd.]
                 [Information service or system] (CRD)
NRS .... National Runaway Switchboard (EA)
NRS .... Nationwide Refrigeration Supplies [British]
NRS .... Naval Radio Station
NRS .... Naval Receiving Station
NRS .... Naval Recruiting Service [British military] (DMA)
NRS .... Naval Recruiting Station
NRS .... Naval Research Section [Library of Congress] (MCD)
NRS .... Naval Rocket Society (IAA)
NRS .... Navy Records Society [British] (DBA)
NRS .... Navy Relief Society (EA)
NRS .... Network Resource Server [J & L Information Systems]
NRS .... Nevada Revised Statutes [A publication]
NRS .... Newborn Rights Society (EA)
NRS .... New Rural Society [HUD project]
NRS .... Night Reconnaissance System
NRS .... Nitrogen Recharge Station
NRS .... Nonconformance Reporting System (NASA)
NRS .... Nonconforming Reporting System
NRSA .... Non-Rising Stem [Valve] (DICI)

NRS .... Normal Rabbit Serum [Culture medium]
NRS .... Normal Rat Serum [Hematology]
NRS .... Normal Reference Serum (MAE)
NRS .... Nuclear Radiation Shield
NRS .... Nuclear Reaction Spectrometry (BARN)
NRS .... Nuclear Rocket Shuttle (KSC)
NRS .... Numerical Rating System [Insurance]
NRS .... Nurse (ABBR)
NRSA .... National Remote Sensing Agency [India]
NRSA .... National Rental Service Association (EA)
NRSA .... National Research Service Awards [Department of Health and
                 Human Services]
NRSA .... National Rose Society of Australia
NRSA .... Natural Rubber Shippers Association (EA)
NRSA .... Northeast Rail Service Act [1981] [Also, NERSA]
NRSB .... Saint Bernard's Seminary and College, Rochester, NY [Library
                 symbol Library of Congress] (LCLS)
NRSC .... National Radio Systems Committee
NRSC .... National Remote Sensing Centre [Royal Aircraft Establishment Space
                 Department] [British] (CB)
NRSC .... National Republican Senatorial Committee (EA)
NRSC .... Naval Reserve Supply Company (DNAB)
NRSC .... Nordic Road Safety Council [See also NTR] [Helsinki, Finland]
                 (EAIO)
NRSCC .... National Reference System in Clinical Chemistry (DAVI)
NRSCC .... National Registry System for Chemical Compounds (DIT)
NRSCO .... Navy Recruiting Station Commanding Officer
NRSD .... Nursed (ABBR)
NRSDNC ...... Nonresidence (ABBR)
NRSDNT ...... Nonresident (ABBR)
NRSE .... Neuron-Restrictive Silencer Element [Neurogenesis]
NRSE .... Nurse (ABBR)
NRSe .... Sear-Brown Associates, PC, Rochester, NY [Library symbol Library
                 of Congress] (LCLS)
NRSED .... Nursed (ABBR)
NRSEG .... Nursing (ABBR)
NRSEMD ...... Nursemaid (ABBR)
NRSEP .... National Roster of Scientific and Engineering Personnel (IAA)
NRSF .... National Rehabilitation and Service Foundation (EA)
NRSF .... National Reye's Syndrome Foundation (EA)
NRSF .... Neuron-Restrictive Silencer Factor [Neurogenesis]
NRSFPS .... National Reporting System for Family Planning Services [National
                 Institutes of Health]
NRSG .... Naval Reserve Security Group (DNAB)
NRSG .... Nursing
NRSH .... Nourish (ABBR)
NRSHD .... Nourished (ABBR)
NRSHG .... Nourishing (ABBR)
NRSHNT ...... Nourishment (ABBR)
NRSI .... National Reading Styles Institute
NRSITD .... Near-Sighted (ABBR)
NRSITNS ..... Near-Sightedness (ABBR)
NRSJ .... Saint John Fisher College, Rochester, NY [Library symbol Library of
                 Congress] (LCLS)
NRSL .... Navy Radio and Sound Laboratory (IAA)
NRSO .... Navy Resale Systems Office
NRSP .... National Remote Sensing Program [Marine science] (OSRA)
NRSP .... National Remote Sensing Programme (USDC)
NRS(R) .... Naval Radio Station (Receiving) (DNAB)
nrsry .... Nursery
NRS(S) .... Naval Radio Station (Sending) (DNAB)
NRSSC .... National Rural and Small Schools Consortium (EA)
NRSSG .... Nuclear Reactor Systems Safety Group [Air Force]
NRSSGP ...... Nuclear Reactor Systems Safety Group [Air Force]
NRSSO .... Navy Resale and Services Support Office (DNAB)
NRSTCTV ..... Nonrestrictive (ABBR)
NRSTK .... Narcisistic (ABBR)
NRSTP .... National Register of Scientific and Technical Personnel (IAA)
NRSV .... Necrotic Ringspot Virus [of prunes]
NRSW .... Nuclear River Service Water (IEEE)
NRSY .... Nordiska Forbundet for Studie- och Yrkesvagledning [Nordic
                 Association for Study and Vocational Guidance - NASVG] (EAIO)
NRSY .... Nursery
NRT .... Burroughs Wellcome & Co., Research Triangle Park, NC [OCLC
                 symbol] (OCLC)
nrt .... Narrator [MARC relator code] [Library of Congress] (LCCP)
NRT .... National Rally Terminology [Automotive competition]
NRT .... National Repertory Theatre Foundation [Defunct] (EA)
NRT .... National Response Team [RSPA] (TAG)
NRT .... National Response Team for Oil and Hazardous Materials Spills
                 [Environmental Protection Agency Washington, DC] (EGAO)
NRT .... Navy Reserve Training
NRT .... Near-Real Time
NR/T .... Near Real-Time
NRT .... Neighbours of the Roundtable (EA)
NRT .... Net Registered Tonnage
NRT .... Net Register Tons [Shipping]
NRT .... Network Readiness Test (KSC)
NRT .... Neuromuscular Re-Education Techniques (DAVI)
NRT .... Nicotine-Replacement Therapy [Medicine]
NRT .... Nonradiating Target
NRT .... Nonreal Time
NRT .... Nonrequestor Terminal (IAA)
NRT .... Normal Rated Thrust (AAG)
NRT .... Norm-Referenced Testing [Education]

NRT .... Nortel Inversora 10%'MEDS' [*NYSE symbol*] (TTSB)
NRT .... Nortel Inversora SA [*NYSE symbol*] (SAG)
NRT .... Northfield [*Vermont*] [*Seismograph station code, US Geological Survey Closed*] (SEIS)
NRT .... Notion Round Table (EA)
NRT .... Nucleus Reticularis Thalami [*Neuroanatomy*]
NRT .... Taylor Instrument Cos., Rochester, NY [*Library symbol Library of Congress*] (LCLS)
NRT .... Tokyo-Narita [*Japan*] [*Airport symbol*] (OAG)
NRTA .... National Retired Teachers Association, Division of AARP (EA)
NRTAC .... National Road Trauma Advisory Council [*Australia*]
NRT & CMA... National Retail Tea and Coffee Merchants Association
NRTB .... Naval Reserve Training Branch
NRTC .... National Retail Trade Centre (EAIO)
NRTC .... Naval Reserve Training Center
NRTC .... Nonreal-Time Conversion Subsystem [*Space Flight Operations Facility, NASA*]
NRTCOMD ... Naval Reserve Training Command
NRTDAS...... Nonreal-Time Data Automation System [*NASA*] (IAA)
NRTEC .... National Rural Teacher Education Consortium [*National Rural Development Institute*] [*Later, NRSSC*] (EA)
NRTF .... Naval Radio Transmitting Facility (DNAB)
NRTH .... North (ABBR)
NrthFce....... North Face, Inc. (The) [*Associated Press*] (SAG)
NRTHSD ...... Northside
NRTHUM...... Northumberland [*County in England*] (ROG)
NRTI .... National Rehabilitation Training Institute [*Defunct*] (EA)
NRTI .... Nooney Realty Trust [*NASDAQ symbol*] (TTSB)
NRTI .... Nooney Realty Trust, Inc. [*NASDAQ symbol*] (NQ)
NRTI .... Nucleoside Revenue Transcript Inhibitor [*Biochemistry*]
NRTIPT .... Naval Reserve Training in Port (NVT)
NRTK .... Nonreceptor Tyrosine Kinase [*An enzyme*]
NRTL .... Non-Random Two-Liquid [*Equation of state*]
NRTO .... National Remotivation Therapy Organization (EA)
NRTOI .... National Range Technical Operating Instructions [*NASA*] (KSC)
NRTP .... Nucleus Reticularis Tegmenti Pontis [*Neuroanatomy*]
NRTR .... Near-Real-Time Reconnaissance (MCD)
NRTR .... Nurture (ABBR)
NRTRD........ Nurtured (ABBR)
NRTRG........ Nurturing (ABBR)
NRTS .... National Reactor Test Station [*INEL*] (NRCH)
NRTS .... Not Repairable This Ship [*Navy*] (AFIT)
NRTS .... Not Reparable This Station
NRTSC .... Naval Reconnaissance and Technical Support Center
NRTSCPAC... Naval Reconnaissance and Technical Support Center, Pacific (DNAB)
NRTWLDEF... National Right to Work Legal Defense and Education Foundation [*Also, NRWLDEF*] (EA)
NRTY .... Norton McNaughton [*NASDAQ symbol*] (TTSB)
NRTY .... Norton McNaughton, Inc. [*NASDAQ symbol*] (SAG)
NRU .... National Reactor Universal
NRU .... National Research Universal [*Nuclear reactor*] [*Canada*]
NRU .... National Rural Utilities Cooperative Finance Corp. [*NYSE symbol*] (SAG)
NRU .... Natural Resource Unit [*Environmental unit*]
NRU .... Nauru [*ANSI three-letter standard code*] (CNC)
NRU .... Network Resource Unit (MHDB)
NRU .... Neuropsychiatric Research Unit [*Navy*]
N Ru .... Nicolaus Rufulus [*Flourished, 13th century*] [*Authority cited in pre-1607 legal work*] (DSA)
NRU .... Nitrogen Rejection Unit [*Process engineering*]
NRU .... Nonreplaceable Unit (IAA)
NRU .... Not Recently Used [*Replacement algorithm*] [*Computer science*] (BYTE)
NRU .... University of Rochester, Rochester, NY [*Library symbol Library of Congress*] (LCLS)
NRU-A .... University of Rochester, Memorial Art Gallery, Rochester, NY [*Library symbol Library of Congress*] (LCLS)
NRUCFC....... National Rural Utilities Cooperative Finance Corp. (EA)
NRU-M........ University of Rochester, School of Medicine and Dentistry, Rochester, NY [*Library symbol Library of Congress*] (LCLS)
NRU-Mus..... University of Rochester, Eastman School of Music, Rochester, NY [*Library symbol Library of Congress*] (LCLS)
NRurU45..... National Rural Utilities Cooperative Finance Corp. [*Associated Press*] (SAG)
NRU-W .... University of Rochester, Women's College, Rochester, NY [*Library symbol Library of Congress*] (LCLS)
NRV .... Navarre Resources [*Vancouver Stock Exchange symbol*]
NRV .... Nerve (ABBR)
NRV .... Net Realizable Value
NRV .... Neubabylonische Rechts- und Verwaltungsurkunden [*A publication*] (BJA)
NRV .... Nonrevenue [*Passengers or cargo*] [*Transportation*]
NRV .... Northamptonshire Rifle Volunteer Corps [*British military*] (DMA)
NRV .... North Carolina State University, School of Veterinary Medicine, Raleigh, NC [*OCLC symbol*] (OCLC)
NRVA .... Net Realizable Value Accounting (ADA)
NRVC .... National Religious Vocation Conference (EA)
NRvCH .... Central Suffolk Hospital, Riverhead, NY [*Library symbol Library of Congress*] (LCLS)
NRVD......... Nerved (ABBR)
NRVG......... Nerving (ABBR)
NRVH......... National RV Holdings, Inc. [*NASDAQ symbol*] (SAG)
NRVH......... Natl R.V.Holding [*NASDAQ symbol*] (TTSB)
NRVI .... Nervy (ABBR)

NRVLS .... Nerveless (ABBR)
NRVMA .... National Roadside Vegetation Management Association (EA)
NRVOC .... National RV [*Recreational Vehicle*] Owners Club (EA)
NRvS .... Suffolk County Historical Society, Riverhead, NY [*Library symbol Library of Congress*] (LCLS)
NRVSBL ...... Nonreversible
NRvSL .... Supreme Court Law Library, Tenth Judicial District, Riverhead, NY [*Library symbol Library of Congress*] (LCLS)
NRVU .... Nervous (ABBR)
NRVUNS ...... Nervousness (ABBR)
NRVUS .... Nervous (ABBR)
NRVUSNS .... Nervousness (ABBR)
NRVUSY...... Nervously (ABBR)
NRVUY....... Nervously (ABBR)
NRVWRKG ... Nerve-Wracking (ABBR)
NRW .... New Right Watch [*An association*] (EA)
NRW .... Nonradioactive Waste [*Nuclear energy*] (NRCH)
NRW .... Norwegian (ABBR)
NRW .... Nuclear RADWASTE (IEEE)
NRW .... Number of Remaining Words
NR/WA .... National Rep/Wholesaler Association (EA)
NRWA .... National Rural Water Association (EA)
NRWC .... National Right to Work Committee (EA)
NRWD .... Narrowed (ABBR)
NRWG .... Narrowing (ABBR)
NRWG .... Neutron Radiography Working Group [*EURATOM*]
NRW-KA ...... National Registry of Willys-Knight Automobiles [*Later, W-O-KR*]
NRWLDEF..... National Right to Work Legal Defense and Education Foundation [*Later, NRWLDF*] (EA)
NRWLDF...... National Right to Work Legal Defense Foundation (EA)
NRWMDD .... Narrow-Minded (ABBR)
NRWMDDNS... Narrow-Mindedness (ABBR)
NRWO .... Nuclear RADWASTE [*Radioactive Waste*] Operator (IAA)
NRWV .... Nonradioactive Waste Vent [*Nuclear energy*] (NRCH)
NRX .... National Research Experiment [*Canadian reactor*]
NRX .... NERVA [*Nuclear Engine for Rocket Vehicle Application*] Reactor Experiment
NRX .... Nuclear Engine Reactor Experiment (NRCH)
NRX .... Nuclear Reactor, Experimental
NRX .... Xerox Corp., Rochester, NY [*Library symbol Library of Congress*] (LCLS)
NRX(C) .... Nonreturn-to-Zero (Change) Recording
NRX-CX....... Nuclear Engine Reactor Critical Assembly (SAA)
NRX-EST ..... NERVA [*Nuclear Engine for Rocket Vehicle Applications*] Reactor Experiment-EngineSystem Test (SAA)
NRY .... Nearly (ABBR)
NRy............ Rye Free Reading Room, Rye, NY [*Library symbol Library of Congress*] (LCLS)
NRyHi .... Rye Historical Society, Rye, NY [*Library symbol Library of Congress*] (LCLS)
NRyS .... Sloan-Kettering Institute for Cancer Research, Rye, NY [*Library symbol Library of Congress*] (LCLS)
NRZ .... Nonreturn to Zero [*Data transmission*]
NRZ .... Null Reception Zone
NRZ1 .... Nonreturn to Zero Change on One (BUR)
NRZC .... Nonreturn to Zero Change
NRZI .... Nonreturn to Zero Inverted [*Recording method*]
NRZI .... NRZ Indicator (NITA)
NRZL .... Nonreturn to Zero Level
NRZL .... Nonreturn to Zero Logic (MCD)
NRZM .... Nonreturn to Zero Mark
NRZ-S .... Non-Return to Zero-Space (MCD)
NS.............. Graduate of the Royal Naval Staff College, Greenwich [*British*]
NS.............. Nachalnik Sektora [*Chief of Sector*] [*Soviet military rank*]
ns .... Nanosecond [*One billionth of a second*] [*Also, nsec*]
NS.............. Naram-Sin (BJA)
NS.............. Narodna Stranka [*People's Party*] [*Montenegro*] [*Political party*] (EY)
NS.............. Narodnye Sotsialisty [*Popular Socialists*] [*Former USSR Political party*] (PPE)
N-S .... Nassi-Schneiderman [*Computer science*]
NS.............. National Savings [*British*]
NS.............. National Scientific [*Vancouver Stock Exchange symbol*]
NS.............. National Seashore (BARN)
NS.............. National Service [*in the armed forces*] [*British*]
NS.............. National Society
NS.............. National Sojourners (EA)
NS.............. National Special [*Thread*]
NS.............. National Standard (IEEE)
NS.............. National Steel [*NYSE symbol*] (SPSG)
NS.............. National Strategy
NS.............. Natjonal Samling [*National Union*] [*Norway*] (PD)
NS.............. Natl Steel 'B' [*NYSE symbol*] (TTSB)
NS.............. NATO Secret (NATG)
NS.............. NATO Surveillance (NATG)
NS.............. Natural Sciences
NS.............. [*The*] Naturist Society (EA)
NS.............. Naval School (MCD)
NS.............. Naval Shipyard
NS.............. Naval Station
NS.............. Naval Stores [*British*]
NS.............. Navigation Subsystem (OA)
NS.............. NAVSHIPS [*Naval Ship Systems Command*] Publication
NS.............. Near Side [*Technical drawings*]
NS.............. Near Space
NS.............. Nederlandse Spoorwegen [*Netherlands Railways*]

NS.............. Neo Sumerian (BJA)
NS.............. Nephrosclerosis [*Medicine*]
NS.............. Nephrotic Syndrome [*Medicine*]
NS.............. Nephrotic Syndrome [*Medicine*] (DAVI)
NS.............. Nerine Society [*Defunct*] (EA)
NS.............. Nervous System
NS.............. Net Sales (MHDW)
NS.............. Net Surplus
NS.............. Network Service [*Computer science*] (TNIG)
NS.............. Neue Sachlichkeit [*New Objectivity*] [*Pre-World War II group of German artists*]
NS.............. Neuroelectric Society [*Defunct*] (EA)
NS.............. Neurologic Signs [*Medicine*] (CPH)
NS.............. Neurologic Survey [*Medicine*] (MAE)
NS.............. Neurosecretory
NS.............. Neurosurgery [*Medicine*]
NS.............. Neuro-Syphilis [*Medicine*]
NS.............. Neurosyphilis [*Medicine*] (DAVI)
NS.............. Neurotic Score [*Psychology*]
N/S.............. Neutrons per Second
NS.............. News [*A radio station format*] (WDMC)
NS.............. New School
NS.............. New Series [*Bibliography*]
NS.............. New Side
NS.............. Newspaper Society [*British*]
n/s.............. Newsstand [*Also N/S*] (WDMC)
NS.............. New Statesman [*A publication*] (BRI)
NS.............. New Style
NS.............. New System [*Computer science*]
NS.............. Next System [*Computer science*]
NS.............. Nickel Silver [*Used in minting coins*]
NS.............. Nickel Steel
Ns.............. Nielsbohrium [*Proposed name and symbol for recently-discovered element*]
NS.............. Nietzsche Society (EA)
NS.............. Nimbostratus [*Cloud*] [*Meteorology*]
NS.............. Nitrogen Supply
NS.............. Nitrogen System
NS.............. Nobelstiftelsen [*Nobel Foundation - NF*] (EAIO)
NS.............. Nockian Society (EA)
NS.............. Nodular Sclerosis [*Medicine*] (AAMN)
NS.............. Noise Sensitivity (IAA)
NS.............. Noise Supressor [*Radio*] (NTCM)
NS.............. Nonscheduled
NS.............. Nonschizophrenic [*Psychology*]
NS.............. Nonsequenced (IAA)
NS.............. Nonserviceable (MSA)
NS.............. Nonshorting (IAA)
NS.............. Nonskew (IAA)
NS.............. Nonslip (ABBR)
NS.............. Nonsmutted [*Plant pathology*]
NS.............. Nonspecified
NS.............. Nonstandard (AABC)
NS.............. Nonstatus Candidates May Apply [*Civil Service*]
NS.............. Nonstimulation
NS.............. Nonstop [*Aviation*]
NS.............. Nonsymptomatic [*Medicine*] (MAE)
NS.............. Nordisk Speditorforbund [*Nordic Forwarding Agents Association - NFAA*] [*Defunct*] (EAIO)
NS.............. Nordisk Svommeforbund [*Nordic Swimming Federations Association - NSFA*] (EAIO)
NS.............. Norfolk Southern Railway Co. [*AAR code*]
NS.............. Normally Shut (NRCH)
NS.............. Normal Saline
NS.............. Normal Segment
NS.............. Normal Serum
NS.............. North Sea - Nonrigid Airship [*Royal Naval Air Service*] [*British*]
N/S.............. North Side [*In outdoor advertising*] (WDMC)
NS.............. North Somerset Imperial Yeomanry [*British military*] (DMA)
NS.............. North-South
NS.............. No Sample (MAE)
NS.............. No Scramble (IAA)
NS.............. Nose [*Horse racing*]
ns.............. No Sequelae [*Aftereffects*] [*Medicine*] (MAE)
NS.............. No Sound [*Script notation*] (NTCM)
NS.............. No Sparring (DS)
NS.............. No Specimen [*Medicine*]
N/S.............. No Stamp [*Deltiology*]
NS.............. No Stimulation [*Neurophysiology*]
NS.............. Nostro Signore [*Our Lord*]
NS.............. No Surgery Performed
NS.............. Notre Seigneur [*Our Lord*] [*French*]
NS.............. Not Seen
NS.............. Not Significant
NS.............. Not Specified
ns.............. Not Specified (WDMC)
NS.............. Not Sprinklered [*Insurance*]
NS.............. Not Stated
NS.............. Not Stocked
NS.............. Not Stung
NS.............. Not Sufficient
n/s.............. Not Sufficient (WDMC)
NS.............. Not Suitable
NS.............. Not Suppressed
NS.............. Not Switchable (MCD)

NS.............. Noun Substantive [*Grammar*] (ROG)
NS.............. Nourishing Stout [*Brewing*] (ROG)
NS.............. Nova Scotia [*Canadian province*] [*Postal code*]
NS.............. Noxious Stimuli
NS.............. Nuclear Science
NS.............. Nuclear Sclerosis [*Ophthalmology*]
NS.............. Nuclear Ship
NS.............. Nuclear Shuttle (NASA)
NS.............. Nuclear Submarine
NS.............. Nuclear Systems
NS.............. Nuernberger [*ICAO designator*] (AD)
N$_s$.............. Number of Secondary Turns (IDOE)
NS.............. Number of Secondary Turns (IAA)
NS.............. Numismatic Society
NS.............. Nursing Services
NS.............. Nursing Sister [*Navy British*]
NS.............. Nutrition Society [*British*] (EAIO)
NS.............. Nylon Suture [*Medicine*]
NS.............. Nzingha Society (EA)
ns.............. Sodium Metasilicate [*CIPW classification*] [*Geology*]
Ns.............. Surface Refractivity (CET)
NSa.............. Bancroft Public Library, Salem, NY [*Library symbol Library of Congress*] (LCLS)
NSA.............. Naphthalene Sulfonic Acid [*Organic chemistry*]
NSA.............. Napoleonic Society of America (EA)
NSA.............. National Safety Association (NADA)
NSA.............. National Sawmilling Association [*British*] (BI)
NSA.............. National Scrabble Association (EA)
NSA.............. National Secretaries Association (International) [*Later, PSI*] (EA)
NSA.............. National Security Act (AAG)
NSA.............. National Security Agency [*Acronym is facetiously translated as No Such Agency or Never Say Anything because of staffers' reluctance to give interviews*] [*DoD*]
NSA.............. National Security Agency, Fort George G. Meade, MD [*OCLC symbol*] (OCLC)
NSA.............. National Security Archive
NSA.............. National Seniors' Association [*Australia*]
NSA.............. National Service Acts [*British*]
NSA.............. National Sheep Association [*British*] (DBA)
NSA.............. National Shellfisheries Association (EA)
NSA.............. National Sheriffs' Association (EA)
NSA.............. National Shipping Authority [*Department of Commerce*]
NSA.............. National Showmen's Association (EA)
NSA.............. National Shuffleboard Association (EA)
NSA.............. National Silo Association [*Later, ISA*] (EA)
NSA.............. National Skating Association of Great Britain
NSA.............. National Ski Association of America [*Later, United States Ski Association*]
NSA.............. National Slag Association (EA)
NSA.............. National Slate Association (EA)
NSA.............. National Smokers Alliance
NSA.............. National Snurfing Association (EA)
NSA.............. National Society of Andersonville (EA)
NSA.............. National Society of Artists (EA)
NSA.............. National Society of Auctioneers [*Later, National Auctioneers Association*]
NSA.............. National Softball Association (EA)
NSA.............. National Sound Archive [*British Library*]
NSA.............. National Speakers Association (EA)
NSA.............. National Spiritual Alliance of the USA (EA)
NSA.............. National Sports Association (EA)
NSA.............. National Sprint Association [*British*] (DBA)
NSA.............. National Sprouting Association (EA)
NSA.............. National Standards Association (NADA)
NSA.............. National Standards Association, Inc. [*Bethesda, MD*]
NSA.............. National Stereoscopic Association (EA)
NSA.............. National Stone Association (EA)
NSA.............. National Stroke Association (EA)
NSA.............. National Student Association [*Later, USSA*]
NSA.............. National Students Association (NADA)
NSA.............. National Sunflower Association (EA)
NSA.............. National System Architecture
NSA.............. Nausea (KSC)
NSA.............. Naval Stock Account
NSA.............. Naval Supply Account
NSA.............. Naval Support Activity [*Vietnam*]
NSA.............. Navy Supply Annex (AFIT)
NSA.............. Neighborhood Strategy Area [*Program*] [*HUD*]
NSA.............. Nepal Studies Association (EA)
NSA.............. Network Software Associates, Inc.
NSA.............. Neurological Society of America (DAVI)
NSA.............. Neurological Society of Australasia
NSA.............. Neurosurgical Society of America (EA)
NSA.............. New Sabina Resources Ltd. [*Vancouver Stock Exchange symbol*]
NSA.............. New Shipborne Aircraft [*Canada*]
NSA.............. New South Africa Fund [*NYSE symbol*] (SAG)
NSA.............. Nichiren Shoshu Soka Gakkai of America [*Buddhist organization*] (EA)
NSA.............. Nile Safaris Aviation [*Sudan*] [*ICAO designator*] (FAAC)
NSA.............. Nitrosylsulfuric Acid [*Inorganic chemistry*]
NSA.............. Node Switching Assembly (SSD)
NSA.............. Noise Suppressor Assembly
NSA.............. Nominal Stress Approach (PDAA)
NSA.............. Nonsequenced Acknowledgment (IAA)
NSA.............. Non-Sterling Area (PDAA)

NSA	Nonylsuccinic Acid [*Organic chemistry*]
NSA	Noosa [*Australia Airport symbol*] (OAG)
NSA	Normal Serum Albumin [*Clinical chemistry*]
NSA	Northeastern Saengerbund of America (EA)
NSA	North Sea Assets [*Investment firm*] [*British*]
NSA	North-South Acceleration
NSA	Norwegian Seamen's Association (EA)
NSA	No Salt Added
NSA	No Serious Abnormality (DAVI)
NSA	No Significant Abnormalities [*Medicine*]
NSA	Not Seasonally Adjusted [*US Census terminology*]
NSA	Nuclear Science Association (NADA)
NSA	Nuclear Stock Association [*British*] (DBA)
NSA	Nuclear Suppliers Association (EA)
NSA	Nuclear Systems Analysis
NSA	Nursery School Association [*British*] (BARN)
NSAA	National Sales Achievement Award [*NALU*]
NSAA	National Ski Areas Association (EA)
NSAA	National Space and Aeronautics Agency (MCD)
NSAA	National Sulphuric Acid Association [*British*] (DBA)
NSAA	National Supply Association of America [*Later, NSDA*] (EA)
NSAA	Norwegian Singers Association of America (EA)
NSAAB	National Security Agency Advisory Board [*Fort George G. Meade, MD*] (EGAO)
NSAAC	Atlantic Co-Operator, Antigonish, Nova Scotia [*Library symbol National Library of Canada*] (NLC)
NSABA	National Spiritual Assembly of Baha'is of Australia
NSABP	National Surgical Adjuvant Breast and Bowel Project (DAVI)
NSABP	National Surgical Adjuvant Breast Project
NSAC	National Society for Autistic Children [*British*]
NSAC	National Society of Accountants for Cooperatives (EA)
NSAC	National Spiritualist Association of Churches (EA)
NSAC	National Sport Aviation Council [*Defunct*] (EA)
NSAC	National Student Action Center (EA)
NSAC	National Student Aid Coalition [*Defunct*] (EA)
NSAC	Nova Scotia Agricultural College
NSAC	NSAC, the National Society for Children and Adults with Autism (EA)
NSAC	Nuclear Safety Advisory Committee (NUCP)
NSAC	Nuclear Safety Analysis Center [*Electric Power Research Institute*] (NRCH)
NSACG	Nuclear Strike Alternate Control Group (NATG)
NSACS	National Society for the Abolition of Cruel Sports [*British*] (BI)
NSACS	Naval Ships Advanced Communications System (SAA)
NSACSS	National Security Agency/Central Security Service (AABC)
NSAD	National Society of Art Directors (EA)
NSAD	Naval Support Activity, Da Nang [*Vietnam*] (VNW)
NSAD	Naval Support Activity Detachment (DNAB)
NSAD	Nuclear Safety Analysis Document (KSC)
NSADN	Daily News, Amherst, Nova Scotia [*Library symbol National Library of Canada*] (NLC)
NSAE	National Society for Art Education [*British*]
NSAE	National Society of Architectural Engineers (EA)
NSAF	National Sanitation Foundation (IAA)
NSAF	Naval Supply Account Fund
NSAFC	National Service Armed Forces Act [*British*]
NSAFF	National Society Against Factory Farming [*British*] (DBA)
NSAG	Negative Channel Self-Aligned Gate (IAA)
NSAGT	New South African Group Test [*Intelligence test*]
NSAH	Heritage Association of Antigonish, Nova Scotia [*Library symbol National Library of Canada*] (NLC)
NSAI	Nashville Songwriters Association, International (EA)
NSAI	National Standards Authority of Ireland [*Irish Science and Technology Agency*] (IRC)
NSAI	Need Satisfaction of Activity Interview
NSAI	Nonsteroidal Anti-Inflammatory [*Pharmacochemistry*]
NSAI	NSA International [*NASDAQ symbol*] (TTSB)
NSAI	NSA International, Inc. [*NASDAQ symbol*] (SAG)
NSAIA	Nonsteroidal Anti-Inflammatory Agent
NSAID	Nonsteroidal Anti-Inflammatory Drug
NSAIN	Indian and Northern Affairs Canada [*Affaires Indiennes et du Nord Canada*],Amherst, Nova Scotia [*Library symbol National Library of Canada*] (BIB)
NSA Int	NSA International, Inc. [*Associated Press*] (SAG)
NSAJ	National Secretariat Australia Jaycees
NSAL	National Society of Arts and Letters (EA)
NSALC	Nonsmoking Attributable Lung Cancer
NSalDH	Salamanca District Hospital, Salamanca, NY [*Library symbol Library of Congress*] (LCLS)
NSALO	National Security Agency Liaison Officer
NSAM	National Security Agency Memorandum
NSAM	Naval School of Aviation Medicine
NSAM	Norwegian Advanced Surface to Air Missile System
NSAMC	Cumberland Regional Library, Amherst, Nova Scotia [*Library symbol National Library of Canada*] (NLC)
NS Am Law Register...	American Law Register (Reprint) [*Ohio*] [*A publication*] (DLA)
NSAMRMS...	Maritime Resource Management Service [*Service d'Amenagement des Ressources des Maritimes*] Amherst, Nova Scotia [*Library symbol National Library of Canada*] (NLC)
NSAN	Nissan Motor Co. Ltd. [*NASDAQ symbol*] (NQ)
NSan	Sanborn-Pekin Free Library, Sanborn, NY [*Library symbol Library of Congress*] (LCLS)
NS & E	New Systems and Enhancements (MCD)
NS & L	NS & L Bancorp, Inc. [*Associated Press*] (SAG)
NS & S	New Statesman & Society [*A publication*] (BRI)

NS & SO	Nervous System and Sense Organs
NS & T	National Status and Trends (GNE)
NS & T	Naval Science and Tactics
NSanF	National Sanitation Foundation
NSANL	Non-Sectarian Anti-NAZI League (EA)
NSanO	Orleans-Niagara Board of Cooperative Educational Services, Associates Special Educational Instruction Materials Center, Sanborn, NY [*Library symbol Library of Congress*] (LCLS)
NSanO-C	Orleans-Niagara Board of Cooperative Educational Services, Educational Communications Center, Sanborn, NY [*Library symbol Library of Congress*] (LCLS)
NSanO-S	Orleans-Niagara Board of Cooperative Educational Services, Sanborn, NY [*Library symbol*] [*Library of Congress*] (LCLS)
NSANY	Nissan Motor Co. ADR [*NASDAQ symbol*] (TTSB)
NSAP	Apia [*Western Samoa*] [*ICAO location identifier*] (ICLI)
NSAP	National Socialist Action Party [*British*]
NSAP	National Society for Animal Protection (EA)
NSAP	Navy Science Assistance Program (CAAL)
NSAP	Network Service Access Point [*Telecommunications*] (OSI)
NSAPAC	National Security Agency Pacific (CINC)
NSAPEA	Nordic Society Against Painful Experiments on Animals (EA)
NSAPI	Netscape Server [*Computer science*] (PCM)
NSAPI	Netscape Server API [*All-Purpose Interface*] [*Computer science*]
NSAR	Annapolis Valley Regional Library, Annapolis Royal, NS [*Library symbol National Library of Canada*] (NLC)
NSAR	Nitrososarcosine [*Organic chemistry*]
NSARC	Navy Systems Acquisition Review Council
NSARF	Fort Anne Museum, Annapolis Royal, Nova Scotia [*Library symbol National Library of Canada*] (NLC)
NSAS	Naval Support Activity, Saigon [*Vietnam*] (VNW)
NSAS	Near Infrared Spectral Analysis Software
NSAS	Nonscheduled Air Services (AAG)
NSAS	Nuclear Sealed Authentication System (AABC)
NSAS	St. Francis Xavier University, Antigonish, Nova Scotia [*Library symbol National Library of Canada*] (NLC)
NSASAB	National Security Agency Scientific Advisory Board [*Ft. George G. Meade, MD*] (EGAO)
NSASC	Chemistry Department, St. Francis Xavier University, Antigonish, Nova Scotia [*Library symbol National Library of Canada*] (NLC)
NSAT	NATO Small Arms Test (MCD)
NSAT	NAVMAT [*Navy Material Command*] Special Assistance Team (DNAB)
NSAT	NII Norsat International, Inc. [*NASDAQ symbol*] (SAG)
NSATE	NII Norsat Intl. [*NASDAQ symbol*] (TTSB)
NSATS	NAVMAT [*Navy Material Command*] Selected Acquisitions Tracking System (DNAB)
NSAU	Asau [*Western Samoa*] [*ICAO location identifier*] (ICLI)
NSau	Saugerties Public Library, Saugerties, NY [*Library symbol Library of Congress*] (LCLS)
NSauF	Ferroxcube Corp., Suagerties, NY [*Library symbol Library of Congress*] (LCLS)
NSA-US	National Spiritual Assembly of the Baha'is of the US (EA)
NSAW	National Society of Asphalt Workers [*A union*] [*British*]
NSay	Sayville Library, Sayville, NY [*Library symbol Library of Congress*] (LCLS)
NSB	Bimini-North [*Bahamas*] [*Airport symbol*] (OAG)
NSB	Nationaal-Socialistische Beweging [*National Socialist Movement*] [*Netherlands Political party*] (PPE)
NSB	National Savings Bank [*British*]
NSB	National Science Board [*National Science Foundation*]
NSB	National Small Business Association [*Later, NSBU*]
NSB	National Socialist Board [*Dutch National Socialist Party of 1931; later, Dutch NAZI Party*] [*Political party*]
NSB	NATO Security Board (NATG)
NSB	Naval Standardization Board
NSB	Naval Studies Board [*National Academy of Sciences*] (DOMA)
NSB	Naval Submarine Base
NSB	Near Surface Burst (MCD)
NSB	Network of Small Businesses [*Lyndhurst, OH*] (EA)
NSB	Newsprint Service Bureau [*Later, API*] (EA)
NSB	Nonspecific Binder
NSB	Non-Statutory Body
NSB	Nonsustained Breakdown (IAA)
NSB	Nordisk Sammanslutning for Barnavard [*Nordic Child and Youth Welfare Alliance - NCYWA*] (EA)
NSB	Nord-Sud [*Benin*] [*ICAO designator*] (FAAC)
NSB	Norges Statsbaner [*Norwegian State Railways*]
NSB	Northern Soviet Boundary
NSB	Not Separately Billed
NSBA	National Saanen Breeders Association (EA)
NSBA	National Safe Boating Association (EA)
NSBA	National School Band Association [*British*] (DBA)
NSBA	National School Boards Association (EA)
NSBA	National Semi-Professional Baseball Association (EA)
NSBA	National Sheep Breeders' Association [*British*] (BI)
NSBA	National Shrimp Breeders Association (EA)
NSBA	National Small Business Association [*Later, NSBU*]
NSBA	National Snaffle Bit Association (EA)
NSBA	National Sugar Brokers Association (EA)
NSBB	National Society for Business Budgeting [*Later, PEI*]
NSBBA	National Small Business Benefits Association (EA)
NSBC	National Safe Boating Council (EA)
NSBC	National Safety Belt Coalition [*NHTSA*] (TAG)
NSBC	National Shoeboard Conference (EA)
NSBC	National Student Book Club

NSBC .... Natural Science Book Club
NS Bcp .... NS Bancorp, Inc. [Associated Press] (SAG)
NSBCSH...... Cape Sable Historical Society, Barrington, Nova Scotia [Library symbol National Library of Canada] (NLC)
NSBD .... Narrow Spectral Band Detection
NSBD .... National Society of Bank Directors [Formerly, NABD] [Later, ASBD] (EA)
NSBDM .... DesBrisay Museum and National Exhibit Centre, Bridgewater, Nova Scotia [Library symbol National Library of Canada] (NLC)
NSBE .... National Society of Black Engineers (EA)
NSBEO .... National Sonic Boom Evaluation Office [Air Force] (MCD)
NSBET .... National Society of Biomedical Equipment Technicians (EA)
NSBF .... National Scientific Balloon Facility [Palestine, TX] [NASA]
NSBGCA...... National Small Business Government Contractors Association [Defunct] (EA)
NSBGW...... National Society of Brushmakers and General Workers [A union] [British] (DCTA)
NSBI .... NS Bancorp, Inc. [NASDAQ symbol] (SAG)
NSbIA .... Institute of Advanced Studies of World Religions, Stony Brook, NY [Library symbol Library of Congress] (LCLS)
NSBISS........ NATO Security Bureau Industrial Security Section (NATG)
NSBJH .... James House, Bridgetown, Nova Scotia [Library symbol National Library of Canada] (NLC)
NSBK .... North Side Savings Bank [NASDAQ symbol] (NQ)
NSBL .... Lighthouse Publishing Ltd., Bridgewater, Nova Scotia [Library symbol National Library of Canada] (NLC)
NSBLE .... Leader, Berwick, Nova Scotia [Library symbol National Library of Canada] (NLC)
NSBM .... Monitor, Bridgetown, Nova Scotia [Library symbol National Library of Canada] (NLC)
NSBMA .... National Small Business Men's Association [Later, NSBU]
NSBNL......... Naval Submarine Base - New London (MCD)
NSBP .... National Society of Black Physicists (EA)
NSBPA .... National Shrimp Breeders and Processors Association (EA)
NSBPH........ National Library Service for the Blind and Physically Handicapped [Library of Congress Washington, DC Library network]
NSBR .... Register, Berwick, Nova Scotia [Library symbol National Library of Canada] (NLC)
NSBRH........ Bear River Historical Society, Nova Scotia [Library symbol National Library of Canada] (NLC)
NSBRO........ National Service Board for Religious Objectors [Later, NISBCO] (EA)
NSBS .... South Shore Regional Library, Bridgewater, Nova Scotia [Library symbol National Library of Canada] (NLC)
NSbSM .... Suffolk Museum at Stony Brook, Stony Brook, NY [Library symbol Library of Congress] (LCLS)
NSBSSA...... National Strict Baptist Sunday School Association [British]
NSBSSN....... South Shore News, Bridgewater, Nova Scotia [Library symbol National Library of Canada] (NLC)
NSbSU .... State University of New York at Stony Brook, Stony Brook, NY [Library symbol Library of Congress] (LCLS)
NSbSU-H ..... State University of New York at Stony Brook, Health Sciences Library, Stony Brook, NY [Library symbol Library of Congress] (LCLS)
NSBT .... National Swiss Battle Tank (MCD)
NSBT .... Not Series by Title (MCD)
NSBU .... National Small Business United [Washington, DC] (EA)
NSBVCA...... Victoria County Archives and Museum, Baddeck, Nova Scotia [Library symbol National Library of Canada] (NLC)
NSBWC........ National Safe Boating Week Committee [Later, NSBC]
NSBWK....... Western King's Memorial Hospital, Berwick, Nova Scotia [Library symbol National Library of Canada] (NLC)
NSC .... Arthur D. Little, Inc. [Research code symbol]
NSC .... Bristol-Myers Co. [Research code symbol]
NSC .... Hoffmann-La Roche, Inc. [Research code symbol]
NSC .... NASCAR [National Association for Stock Car Auto Racing] Street Classics [Later, WW] (EA)
NSC .... National Cancer Institute [Research code symbol]
NSC .... National Safety Corp.
NSC .... National Safety Council (EA)
NSC .... National Safety Council (NADA)
NSC .... National Safflower Council [Defunct] (EA)
NSC .... National Savings Certificates [British] (DAS)
NSC .... National Savings Committee [British]
NSC .... National Science Council [Irish] (MSC)
NSC .... National Security Council
NSC .... National Semiconductor Corp.
NSC .... National Service Center
NSC .... National Shrimp Congress (EA)
NSC .... National Simulation Council (SAA)
NSC .... National Slavic Convention (EA)
NSC .... National Smallgoods Council [Australia]
NSC .... National Snorkellers Club [British] (DBA)
NSC .... National Society of Chauffeurs [A union] [British]
NSC .... National Society of Computer/Genealogists [Defunct] (EA)
NSC .... National Society of Cwens (EA)
NSC .... National Space Club (EA)
NSC .... National Space Council
NSC .... National Spiritualist Church [British]
NSC .... National Staff Committee [Nurses and midwives] [British]
NSC .... National Standards Commission (NADA)
NSC .... National Stinson Club (EA)
NSC .... National Supply Class [Military] (AFIT)
NSC .... National Survey of Children
NSC .... National Synthetics Collection [Smithsonian Institution]

NSC .... NATO [North Atlantic Treaty Organization] Science Committee (EAIO)
NSC .... NATO Steering Committee (NATG)
NSC .... NATO Supply Center (NATG)
NSC .... NATO Supply Classification
NSC .... Naval Coastal Systems Center [Florida]
NSC .... Naval Safety Center (MCD)
NSC .... Naval School Command
NSC .... Naval Sea Cadets
NSC .... Naval Space Command (MCD)
NSC .... Naval Staff College (DOMA)
NSC .... Naval Supply Center
NSC .... Navigation and Sensor Computer
NSC .... Navigation Star Catalogue
NSC .... Navy Service Center
NSC .... Net Sale Certificate (DGA)
NSC .... Network Service Center [Telecommunications]
NSC .... Network Switching Center [Telecommunications] (TEL)
NSC .... Network Systems Corp. [Brooklyn Park, MN] [Telecommunications] (TSSD)
NSC .... Neurosecretory Cells
NSC .... Newscope Resources Ltd. [Toronto Stock Exchange symbol]
NSC .... New Session Cases [Scotland] [A publication] (DLA)
NSC .... Newtex SS [Steamship company] [AAR code]
NSC .... Nicaragua Solidarity Campaign (EAIO)
NSC .... Nippon Steel Corp. [Japan]
NSC .... Nodal Switching Center
NSC .... Noise Suppression Circuit (DEN)
NSC .... Nomenclature Sequence Code [Navy] (AFIT)
NSC .... Nominal Single Dose [Pharmacology] (DAVI)
NSC .... Non-Service-Connected
NSC .... Norfolk Southern [NYSE symbol] (TTSB)
NSC .... Norfolk Southern Railway [NYSE symbol] (SPSG)
NSC .... Northeastern State College [Oklahoma]
NSC .... North Stonington [Connecticut] [Seismograph station code, US Geological Survey] (SEIS)
NSC .... No Significant Change [Medicine]
NSC .... No Significant Cloud [Meteorology] (FAAC)
NSC .... Nothing So Called [Bookselling]
NSC .... Not Service-Connected [Medicine] (MEDA)
nsc.............. Nova Scotia [MARC country of publication code Library of Congress] (LCCP)
NSC .... NSC Corp. [Associated Press] (SAG)
NSC .... Nuclear Science Center [Louisiana State University] [Research center] (RCD)
NSC .... Numerical Sequence Code
NSC .... Nursing Sentence Completions [Nursing school test]
NSC .... Salem College, Winston-Salem, NC [OCLC symbol] (OCLC)
NSCA .... NASCOM [NASA Communications Network] Assembly
NSCA .... National Satellite Cable Association [Defunct] (EA)
NSCA .... National Scrip Collectors Association (EA)
NSCA .... National Senior Citizens Association [Commercial firm] (EA)
NSCA .... National Shrimp Canners Association
NSCA .... National Ski Credit Association (EA)
NSCA .... National Soccer Coaches Association of America (EA)
NSCA .... National Society for Clean Air [British] (DCTA)
NSCA .... National Society of Commercial Agents [Australia]
NSCA .... National Sound and Communications Association (EA)
NSCA .... National Sporting Clays Association
NSCA .... National Strength and Conditioning Association (EA)
NSCA .... Natural Sausage Casings Association [British] (DBA)
NSCA .... Northwest Salmon Canners Association (EA)
NSCA .... Nova Scotia College of Art
NSCA .... Nutrient Starch Cycloheximide Agar [Microbiology]
NSca .... Scarsdale Public Library, Scarsdale, NY [Library symbol Library of Congress] (LCLS)
NSCAA .... National Small College Athletic Association (EA)
NSCAA .... [The] National Society for Children and Adults with Autism 2 [Formerly, NSAC] (EA)
NSCAA .... Nutrient Starch Cycloheximide Antibiotic Agar [Microbiology]
NSCAE .... National Standards Council of American Embroiderers [Later, CAE] (EA)
NSCAEU....... National Service Conference of the American Ethical Union (EA)
NSCAH........ National Student Campaign Against Hunger [Later, NSCAHH] (EA)
NSCAHH ..... National Student Campaign Against Hunger and Homelessness (EA)
NSCAMP...... National Stock Control and Maintenance Point [Army] (AFIT)
NSC & MP ... National Stock Control and Maintenance Point [Army] (AABC)
NSCAR .... National Society of the Children of the American Revolution (EA)
NSCAS .... Archelaus Smith Museum, Centreville (Shelburne Co.), Nova Scotia [Library symbol National Library of Canada] (NLC)
NSCAT .... NASA [or NROSS] Scatterometer [Instrumentation]
N-SCATT...... Navy Scatterometer (MCD)
NSCAV .... National Safety Council of Australia, Victoria Division
NSCB .... NBSC Corp. [NASDAQ symbol] (NQ)
NSCB .... Nordic Society for Cell Biology (EA)
NSCC .... National Securities Clearing Corp.
NSCC .... National Service Coordinating Committee [Ministry of Labour and National Service] [British World War II]
NSCC .... National Siamese Cat Club (EA)
NSCC .... National Social Conditioning Camps [Later, NOC] (EA)
NSCC .... National Society for Crippled Children (DAVI)
NSCC .... Naval Sea Cadet Corps (NVT)
NSCC .... Navy Sea Cargo Coordinator (DNAB)
NSCC .... North Shore Community College [Beverly, MA]
NSCC .... NSC Corp. [NASDAQ symbol] (SAG)

NSCC .... Nuclear Services Closed Cooling (IEEE)
NSCCA .... National Society for Crippled Children and Adults [*Later, NESS*] (EA)
NSCCA .... National Sports Car Club of America
NSCCA .... Nuclear Safety Cross-Check Analysis (DOMA)
NSCCF .... Canadian Forces Base, Cornwallis, Nova Scotia [*Library symbol National Library of Canada*] (NLC)
NSCCFE ...... Ensign, Canadian Forces Base, Cornwallis, Nova Scotia [*Library symbol National Library of Canada*] (NLC)
NSCCLO .... Naval Sea Cadet Corps Liaison Officer (DNAB)
NSCCM .... Cumberland County Museum, Amherst, Nova Scotia [*Library symbol National Library of Canada*] (NLC)
NSCD .... National School Development Council (AEE)
NSCD .... Nonservice-Connected Disability (MAE)
NSCD .... Nuclear Service Control Date (DNAB)
NSCDA .... National Society of Colonial Dames of America (EA)
N Sc Dec ..... Nova Scotia Decisions [*A publication*] (DLA)
NSCDET .... Naval Supply Center Detachment (DNAB)
NSCDP .... Non-Sexist Child Development Project (EA)
NSCDRF .... National Sickle Cell Disease Research Foundation [*Defunct*] (EA)
NSCE .... NetSource Communications, Inc. [*NASDAQ symbol*] (SAG)
NSCEC .... National School Curriculum Center for Educational Computing [*Defunct*] (EA)
NSCEE .... National Schools Committee for Economic Education (EA)
NSCEO .... National Society of Chief Executive Officers [*Defunct*] (EA)
NSCF .... National Skin Cancer Foundation [*Later, SCF*] (EA)
NSCF .... National Student Christian Federation [*Later, UCM*] (EA)
NSCF .... Naval Small Craft Facilities
NSCF .... Northstar Computer Forms [*NASDAQ symbol*] (TTSB)
NSCFA .... Northstar Computer Forms, Inc. [*NASDAQ symbol*] (SAG)
NSCFA .... National Support Center for Families of the Aging [*Defunct*] (EA)
NSCG .... Northeastern Spoon Collectors Guild
NSCH .... Canso Historical Society, Nova Scotia [*Library symbol National Library of Canada*] (NLC)
NSch .... Schenectady County Public Library, Schenectady, NY [*Library symbol Library of Congress*] (LCLS)
NSchC .... Schenectady County Community College, Schenectady, NY [*Library symbol Library of Congress*] (LCLS)
NSchE .... Ellis Hospital, Schenectady, NY [*Library symbol Library of Congress*] (LCLS)
NSCHF .... National Sprint Car Hall of Fame [*Iowa*]
NSchGEKA .... General Atomic Co., Knolls Atomic Laboratory, Technical Library, Schenectady, NY [*Library symbol Library of Congress*] (LCLS)
NSchGEM ..... General Electric Co., Main Library, Schenectady, NY [*Library symbol Library of Congress*] (LCLS)
NSchGER ..... General Electric Co., Research Laboratory, Schenectady, NY [*Library symbol Library of Congress*] (LCLS)
NSchGERB .... General Electric Co., R and D Center, Branch Library, Schenectady, NY [*Library symbol Library of Congress*] (LCLS)
NSchHLC ...... Capital District Library Council, Schenectady, NY [*Library symbol Library of Congress*] (LCLS)
NSchM .... Mohawk Valley Library Association, Schenectady, NY [*Library symbol Library of Congress*] (LCLS)
NSchoCHi .... Schoharie County Historical Society, Schoharie, NY [*Library symbol Library of Congress*] (LCLS)
NSchSC .... Schenectady Chemicals, Inc., Schenectady, NY [*Library symbol Library of Congress*] (LCLS)
N Sch Social Research... [*The*] New School for Social Research (GAGS)
NSchStC ..... Saint Clare's Hospital, Physicians' Library, Schenectady, NY [*Library symbol Library of Congress*] (LCLS)
NSchU .... Union College, Schenectady, NY [*Library symbol Library of Congress*] (LCLS)
NSCI .... NASCOM System Control Interface [*NASA*] (MCD)
NSCI .... National Surgery Centers, Inc. [*NASDAQ symbol*] (SAG)
NSCI .... Natl Surgery Centers [*NASDAQ symbol*] (TTSB)
NSCIA .... National Spinal Cord Injury Association (EA)
NSCIA .... National Supervisory Council for Intruder Alarms [*British*] (DBA)
NSCIC .... National Security Council Intelligence Committee [*Inactive*]
NSCIC .... National Soybean Crop Improvement Council
NSCID .... National Security Council Intelligence Directive [*Pronounced "nee-sid"*] (AFM)
NSCIF .... National Spinal Cord Injury Foundation [*Formerly, NPF*] [*Later, NSCIA*] (EA)
NSCIG .... National Security Council Interdepartmental Group (MCD)
NSCISC .... National Spinal Cord Injury Statistical Center Database [*University of Alabama in Birmingham*] [*Information service or system*] (CRD)
NSCL .... National Superconducting Cyclotron Laboratory [*Michigan State University*] [*National Science Foundation*] [*Research center*] (RCD)
NSCLC .... National Senior Citizens Law Center (EA)
NSCLC .... Non-Small-Cell Lung Cancer [*Oncology*]
NSCLS .... North State Cooperative Library System [*Library network*]
NSCM .... National Society of Cycle Makers [*A union*] [*British*]
NSCM .... NATO Supply Code for Manufacturing (MCD)
NSCM .... Non-Stockpile Chemical Materiel [*Military*] (RDA)
NSCN .... National Socialist Council of Nagaland [*India*] (PD)
NSCNC .... Nascence (ABBR)
NSCNQH .... North Queens Heritage Society, Caledonia, Nova Scotia [*Library symbol National Library of Canada*] (NLC)
NSCNT .... Nascent (ABBR)
NSCO .... National Scientific Committee on Oceanography
NSCO .... Naval Sea Cargo Coordinator (DNAB)
NSCORT .... NASA Specialized Center for Research and Training
NSCP .... National Society of Compliance Professionals (EA)
NSCP .... Naval Stores Conservation Program
NSCP .... Navy Staffing Criteria Program

NSCP .... Netscape Communications [*NASDAQ symbol*] (TTSB)
NSCP .... Netscape Communications Corp. [*NASDAQ symbol*] (SAG)
NSCPA .... National Society of Certified Public Accountants (EA)
NSCPC .... National Student Consumer Protection Council (EA)
NSCPS .... Naval Supply Center, Puget Sound [*Bremerton, WA*] (DNAB)
NSCPT .... National Society for Cardiovascular and Pulmonary Technology (EA)
NSCR .... National Society for Cancer Relief [*British*]
NSCR .... National Sport Custom Registry (EA)
NSCR .... Non-Selective Catalytic Reduction [*Chemistry*]
NSCR .... Nuclear Science Center Reactor
NSCRC .... National Stock Car Racing Commission
NSCRDFO .... National Study Commission on Records and Documents of Federal Officials
NSCS .... National Scouting Collectors Society (EA)
NSCS .... National Sisters Communications Service [*Later, CCM*] (EA)
NSCS .... National Small Craft School [*Red Cross*]
NSCS .... Naval Strategic Communications Simulator (MCD)
NSCS .... Navy Supply Corps School
NSCS .... North Star Computer Society (EA)
NSCS .... Universite Sainte-Anne, Church Point, Nova Scotia [*Library symbol National Library of Canada*] (NLC)
NSCSA .... Centre Acadien, Universite Sainte-Anne, Church Point, Nova Scotia [*Library symbol National Library of Canada*] (BIB)
NSCSC .... National School Calendar Study Committee
NSCSCC .... National Standard for Common System Component Characteristics (MCD)
NSCSWD ..... No Small Craft or Storm Warnings are Being Displayed [*Weather*]
NSCT .... National Students Center for Thailand
NSCT .... Niagara, St. Catharines & Toronto [*AAR code*]
NSCTE .... National Society of College Teachers of Education [*Later, SPE*] (EA)
NSCTI .... National Society for Cardiopulmonary Technology, Inc. (DAVI)
NSCTRN .... Nonsectarian (ABBR)
NSCVPT .... National Society for Cardiovascular and Pulmonary Technology (EA)
NSCVR .... National Student Campaign for Voter Registration (EA)
NSCW .... National Society of Cycle Workers [*A union*] [*British*]
NSD .... Dartmouth Regional Library, Dartmouth, Nova Scotia [*Library symbol National Library of Canada*] (NLC)
NSD .... Ferrosan [*Denmark*] [*Research code symbol*]
NSD .... Geldert and Oxley's Nova Scotia Decisions [*7-9 Nova Scotia Reports*] [*1866-75*] [*Canada*] [*A publication*] (DLA)
NSD .. Nairobi Sheep Disease [*Medicine*] (DMAA)
NSD .... National Silage Demonstration [*British*]
NSD .... National Smooth Dancers (DICI)
NSD .... National-Standard Co. [*NYSE symbol*] (SPSG)
NSD .... National Standard Co. [*NYSE symbol*] (SAG)
NSD .... Naval Stores Department [*British military*] (DMA)
NSD .... Naval Supply Depot
NSD .... Navy Support Date (NG)
NSD .... Network Status Display
NSD .... New Spirit Research [*Vancouver Stock Exchange symbol*]
NSD .... Next Most Significant Digit [*Computer science*]
NSD .... Night Sleep Deprivation [*Medicine*] (DMAA)
NSD .... Noise Suppression Device
NSD .... Nominal Standard Dose [*Medicine*]
NSD .... Non-Self-Destroying
NSD .... Nonsequential Disk [*Computer science*] (IAA)
NSD .... Normal, Spontaneous Delivery [*Obstetrics*]
NSD .... Normal Standard Dose [*Oncology radiation*]
NSD .... Norsk Samfunnsvitenskapelig Datatjeneste [*Norwegian Social Science Data Services*] [*Information service or system*] (IID)
NSD .... Northside Aviation Ltd. [*British ICAO designator*] (FAAC)
NSD .... No Significant Defects [*or Deficiency*] [*Medicine*]
NSD .... No Significant Deviation [*Medicine*]
NSD .... No Significant Difference [*Medicine*]
NSD .... No Significant Disease [*Medicine*]
NSD .... United States Library of Congress, Washington, DC [*OCLC symbol*] (OCLC)
NSDA .... National Soft Drink Association (EA)
NSDA .... National Spasmodic Dysphonia Association (EA)
NSDA .... National Sprayer and Duster Association (EA)
NSDA .... National Supply Distributors Association [*Dayton, OH*] (EA)
NSDA .... National Surplus Dealers Association (EA)
NSDA .... Naval Supply Depot Annex
NSDA .... Nissan Safety Device Advisor [*Driver information system*]
NSDA .... Nonsteroid Dependent Asthmatic [*Medicine*] (DAVI)
NSDAB .... Non-Self-Deployable Aircraft and Boats (MCD)
NSDAP .... Nationalsozialistische Deutsche Arbeiterpartei [*National Socialist German Workers' Party, 1919-45*] [*Political party*]
NSDAP-AO ... NSDAP Auslands- und Aufbauorganisation (EA)
NSDAR .... National Society, Daughters of the American Revolution (EA)
NSDAT .... Naval School of Dental Assisting and Technology (DNAB)
NSDAVNDEPT... Naval Supply Depot Aviation Department (DNAB)
NSDB .... Bedford Institute of Oceanography [*Institut Oceanographique de Bedford*] Dartmouth, Nova Scotia [*Library symbol National Library of Canada*] (NLC)
NSDB .... National Science Development Board
NSDB .... NSD Bancorp [*NASDAQ symbol*] (SAG)
NSD Bc .... NSD Bancorp [*Associated Press*] (SAG)
NSDBE .... National Society, Daughters of the British Empire (EA)
NSDBR .... National Society, Daughters of the Barons of Runnemede (EA)
NSDC .... Courier, Digby, Nova Scotia [*Library symbol National Library of Canada*] (NLC)
NSDC .... National School Development Council (EA)
NSDC .... National Serials Data Centre [*British Library*] (PDAA)
NSDC .... National Square Dance Convention (EA)

NSDC .... National Staff Development Committee [*Australia*]
NSDC .... National Staff Development Council (EA)
NSDC .... Naval Special Devices Center (SAA)
NSDC .... Nonsuppurative Destructive Cholangitis [*Medicine*]
NSDC .... NORAD Sector Direction Center [*Military*]
NSDC .... Northern Shipowners' Defence Club [*See also NORDISK*] (EAIO)
NSDCM .... NORAD Sector Direction Center Manual [*Military*]
NSDD .... National Security Decision Directive
NSDDET .... Naval Supply Depot Detachment (DNAB)
NSDDS .... Dartmouth District School Board, Nova Scotia [*Library symbol National Library of Canada*] (NLC)
NSDE .... Environment Canada [*Environnement Canada*] Dartmouth, Nova Scotia [*Library symbol National Library of Canada*] (NLC)
NSDEA .... National Soda Dispensing Equipment Association (EA)
NS Dec .... Nova Scotia Decisions [*A publication*]
NSDEQ .... National Society, Descendants of Early Quakers (EA)
NSDF .... National Student Drama Festival [*British*]
NSDF .... Navy Standard Distillate Fuel (NVT)
NSDG .... Digby General Hospital, Nova Scotia [*Library symbol National Library of Canada*] (NLC)
NSDGH .... Dartmouth General Hospital, Nova Scotia [*Library symbol National Library of Canada*] (NLC)
NSDH .... Hermes Electronics Ltd., Dartmouth, Novia Scotia [*Library symbol National Library of Canada*] (NLC)
NSDI .... National Sales Development Institute
NSDI .... National Spatial Data Infrastructure [*BTS*] (TAG)
NSDJA .... National Sash and Door Jobbers Association (EA)
NSDL .... National Soil Dynamics Laboratory [*Auburn, AL*] [*Department of Agriculture*] (GRD)
NSDL .... Navy Standard Distribution List (MCD)
NSDLANT/PAC... Naval Supply Depots, Atlantic/Pacific
NSDLMM ..... National Society of Descendants of Lords of the Maryland Manors (EA)
NSDM .... Mirror, Digby, Nova Scotia [*Library symbol National Library of Canada*] (NLC)
NSDM .... National Security Decision Memorandum [*Air Force*]
NSDM .... New School for Democratic Management [*Inactive*] (EA)
NSDM .... Nuclear Sediment Density Meter (PDAA)
NSDMM ...... MacLaren Plansearch Ltd., Dartmouth, Nova Scotia [*Library symbol National Library of Canada*] (NLC)
NSDNHM ...... North Highlands Museum, Dingwall, Nova Scotia [*Library symbol National Library of Canada*] (NLC)
NSDNSH ...... Nova Scotia Hospital, Dartmouth, Nova Scotia [*Library symbol National Library of Canada*] (NLC)
NSDO .... National Seed and Development Organisation [*British*]
NSDP .... NASCOM System Development Plan
NSDP .... National Serials Data Program [*Library of Congress*] (EA)
NSDP .... National Society of Denture Prosthetists [*Later, ADP*]
NSDP .... Norfolk Sample Drug Program
NSDR .... National Ships Destination Room (NATG)
NSDR .... National Silver Dollar Roundtable (EA)
NSDR .... No-son Dependency Ratio [*Demographics*]
NSDRV .... Dartmouth Regional Vocational School, Dartmouth, Nova Scotia [*Library symbol National Library of Canada*] (NLC)
NSDS .... Navy School, Diving and Salvage (NVT)
NSDS .... Neutron Spectrometer Digital System
NSDSA .... Naval Sea Data Support Activity (NVT)
NSDTA .... National Staff Development and Training Association (EA)
NSDU .... Network Service Data Unit [*Telecommunications*] (OSI)
NSDUP .... National Society, Daughters of Utah Pioneers (EA)
NSDV .... Netted Secure Digital Voice (MCD)
NSDWR .... National Secondary Drinking Water Regualtions (GNE)
NSE .... Milton, FL [*Location identifier FAA*] (FAAL)
NSE .... National Sales Executives
NSE .... National Seafood Educators (EA)
NSE .... National Society for Epilepsy [*British*]
NSE .... National Stock Exchange [*Dissolved, 1975*]
NSE .... National Stock Exchange [*India*]
NSE .... National Student Exchange (EA)
NSE .... National Support Elements [*British military*] (DMA)
NSE .... Natural Space Environment
NSE .... Naval Shore Establishment
NSE .... Naval Support Element (DOMA)
NSE .... Navier-Stokes Equation
NSE .... Navigation Support Equipment
NSE .... Network Service Element [*Telecommunications*] (OSI)
NSE .... Network SouthEast [*British Rail*] (ECON)
NSE .... Network Systems Engineer (SSD)
NSE .... Neuron-Specific Enolase [*Formerly, NSP*] [*An enzyme*]
NSE .... Neuropsychological Status Examination [*Psychology*]
NSE .... Nitroguanidine Support Element (MCD)
NSE .... Noise (ABBR)
NSE .... Nonsecurity Exemption [*Military*]
NSE .... Nonspecific Esterase [*An enzyme*]
NSE .... North Steaming Error (SAA)
NSE .... Northwest Sports Enterprises Ltd. [*Vancouver Stock Exchange symbol*]
NSE .... Nuclear Science and Engineering [*A publication*]
NSE .... Nuclear Statistical Equilibrium [*Physics*]
NSE .... Nuclear Support Equipment
NSE .... Nuclear Systems Engineering
NSE .... Number of Simultaneous Engagements [*Military*]
NSE .... Satena Servicios de Aeronavegacion A Territorios Nac [*Colombia*] [*ICAO designator*] (FAAC)
NSEA .... National Standards Educators Association (EA)

NSea .... Seaford Public Library, Seaford, NY [*Library symbol Library of Congress*] (LCLS)
NSeacES ...... Sea Cliff Elementary School, Sea Cliff, NY [*Library symbol*] [*Library of Congress*] (LCLS)
NSEAD .... National Society for Education in Art and Design (EAIO)
NSeaHE .... Seaford Harbor Elementary School, Seaford, NY [*Library symbol*] [*Library of Congress*] (LCLS)
NSeaME .... Seaford Manor Elementary School, Seaford, NY [*Library symbol*] [*Library of Congress*] (LCLS)
NSeaMH ..... Massapequa General Hospital, Seaford, NY [*Library symbol Library of Congress*] (LCLS)
NSeaMS ...... Seaford Middle School, Seaford, NY [*Library symbol*] [*Library of Congress*] (LCLS)
NSeaP .... Plainedge Public Library, Seaford, NY [*Library symbol Library of Congress*] (LCLS)
NSeaSH ...... Seaford Senior High School, Seaford, NY [*Library symbol*] [*Library of Congress*] (LCLS)
NSeaTM ...... Tackapausha Museum, Seaford, NY [*Library symbol Library of Congress*] (LCLS)
nsec .... Nanosecond [*One billionth of a second*] [*Also, ns*]
NSEC .... National Security Group, Inc. [*NASDAQ symbol*] (SAG)
NSEC .... National Service Entertainments Council [*British*]
NSEC .... National Society of Environmental Consultants (EA)
NSEC .... Natl Security Group [*NASDAQ symbol*] (TTSB)
NSEC .... Naval Ship Engineering Center (MCD)
NSecIn .... National Security Group, Inc. [*Associated Press*] (SAG)
NSECINST ...... Naval Ship Engineering Center Instruction
NSEDP .... National Sex Equity Demonstration Project (EDAC)
NSEEC .... Naval Shore Electronics Engineering Center [*Terminated, 1966*] (MCD)
NSEF .... National SANE Education Fund (EA)
NSEF .... National Student Educational Fund (EA)
NSEF .... Navy Security Engineering Facility
NSEF .... New Society Educational Foundation (EA)
NSel .... Middle Country Public Library, Selden Branch, Selden, NY [*Library symbol Library of Congress*] (LCLS)
NSelC .... Suffolk County Community College, Selden, NY [*Library symbol Library of Congress*] (LCLS)
NSelC-E .... Suffolk County Community College, Eastern Campus, Riverhead, NY [*Library symbol Library of Congress*] (LCLS)
NSelC-W ..... Suffolk County Community College, Western Campus, Brentwood, NY [*Library symbol Library of Congress*] (LCLS)
NSELH .... East Lake Ainslie Historical Society, Nova Scotia [*Library symbol National Library of Canada*] (BIB)
NSELS .... Noiseless (ABBR)
NSem .... National Semiconductor Corp. [*Associated Press*] (SAG)
NSEM .... Nederlandsche Standard Electric Maatschappij (NITA)
NSEMA .... National Spray Equipment Manufacturers Association (EA)
NSEN .... Network Simulations Engineer (SSD)
NSENS .... Noisiness (ABBR)
NSEP .... National Security and Emergency Preparedness
NS/EQ .... New Source and Environmental Questionnaire [*Environmental Protection Agency*] (EG)
NSERC .... Natural Sciences and Engineering Research Council of Canada [*Research center*] (IRC)
NSERI .... National Solar Energy Research Institute [*Energy Research and Development Administration*]
NSES .... National Security Electronic Surveillance
NSES .... National Society of Electrotypers and Stereotypers [*British*] (BI)
NSetSP .... Society for the Preservation of Long Island Antiquities, Setauket, NY [*Library symbol Library of Congress*] (LCLS)
NSewCH ...... H.F. Carey High School, Sewanhaka, NY [*Library symbol*] [*Library of Congress*] (LCLS)
NSewEH .... Elmont Memorial High School, Sewanhaka, NY [*Library symbol Library of Congress*] (LCLS)
NSewNH ..... New Hyde Park Memorial High School, Sewanhaka, NY [*Library symbol*] [*Library of Congress*] (LCLS)
NSewSJ ...... Stanforth Junior High School, Sewanhaka, NY [*Library symbol Library of Congress*] (LCLS)
NSF .... Camp Springs, MD [*Location identifier FAA*] (FAAL)
NSF .... National Salvation Front [*Romania*] [*Political party*]
NSF .... National Sanitation Foundation (EA)
NSF .... National Schizophrenia Fellowship [*British*]
NSF .... National Science Foundation (EA)
NSF .... National Science Foundation, Washington, DC [*OCLC symbol*] (OCLC)
NSF .... National Scoliosis Foundation (EA)
NSF .... National Sex Forum [*Later, ET*] (EA)
NSF .... National Sharecroppers Fund (EA)
NSF .... National Ski Federation (BARN)
NSF .... National Soaring Foundation (EA)
NSF .... National Squash Federation [*British*] (DBA)
NSF .... National Stockbrokers Forum [*Later, CFC*] (EA)
NSF .... National Strike Force [*Marine science*] (MSC)
NSF .... Naval Stock Fund
NSF .... Naval Supersonic Facility
NSF .... Naval Supply Force
NSF .... Naval Support Force (MCD)
NSF .... Navy Special Fuel
NSF .... Navy Stock Fund (DOMA)
NSF .... Negotiated Search Facility [*Information retrieval*]
NSF .... NEM [*N-Ethylmaleimide*]-Sensitive Fusion [*Biochemistry*]
NSF .... N-ethylinaleimide Sensitive Fusion
NSF .... N-Ethylmaleimide-Sensitive Fusion (protein) [*Organic chemistry*]
NSF .... Net Square Feet (MCD)

NSF............. Neutron Scattering Facility [*Oak Ridge, TN*] [*Oak Ridge National Laboratory*] [*Department of Energy*] (GRD)
NSF............. Nitrogen Supply Flask
NSF............. Nodular Subepidermal Fibrosis [*Dermatology*]
NSF............. Nodular Subepidermal Fibrosis [*Dermatology*] (DAVI)
NSF............. Noncancerous Skin Fibroblast [*Medicine*]
NSF............. Nonsterile Field Soil [*Agronomy*]
NSF............. Nonstock Fund
NSF............. Nordiska Skattevetenskapliga Forskningradet [*Nordic Council for Tax Research - NCTR*] (EAIO)
NSF............. Not Sufficient Funds [*Banking*]
nsf .... Not Sufficient Funds [*Banking*] (ODBW)
NSF............. Nuclear Safety Facility
NSF............. Nuclear Science Foundation (IAA)
NSF............. Nuclear Structure Facility [*British*]
NSFA .... Faleolo/International [*Western Samoa*] [*ICAO location identifier*] (ICLI)
NSFA .... National Science Foundation Act [*1950*]
NSFA .... Naval Support Force, Antarctica (DNAB)
NSFA .... Nordic Swimming Federations Association (EA)
NSFAC .... National Student Financial Aid Council [*Later, NASFAA*] (EA)
NSFAR .... National Science Foundation Acquisition Regulation [*A publication*] (AAGC)
NSFB .... New School of Family Birthing (EA)
NSFC .... Nancy Sinatra Fan Club (EA)
NSFC .... National Society of Film Critics
NSFC .... Nat Stuckey Fan Club [*Defunct*] (EA)
NSFC .... Natural Science Foudation of China
NSFC .... Natural Science Foundation of China
NSFC .... Northern States Financial Corp. [*NASDAQ symbol*] (SAG)
NSFC .... Northern States Finl [*NASDAQ symbol*] (TTSB)
NSFCCDLR... National Society of Fathers for Child Custody and Divorce Law Reform [*Later, FER*] (EA)
NSFD .... Notice of Structural or Functional Deficiency
NSFFC .... National Save the Family Farm Coalition (EA)
NSFG .... National Survey of Family Growth
NSFH .... North-South Fine, Hundreds
NSFI........... Fagali'I [*Western Samoa*] [*ICAO location identifier*] (ICLI)
NSF-I........... National Science Fair - International
NSF/IDOE..... National Science Foundation Office for the International Decade of Ocean Exploration
NSfK .... Nordiska Samarbetsradet for Kriminologi [*Scandinavian Research Council for Criminology - SRCC*] [*Finland*] (EAIO)
NSFL .... National Sanitation Foundation Laboratory
NSFNET .... National Science Foundation Network
NSFO .... Navy Special [*or Standard*] Fuel Oil
NSFORT....... Non-Standard FORTRAN [*Computer science*] (PDAA)
NSFP .... Non-Sodium Fire Protection [*Nuclear energy*] (NRCH)
NSFPA .... National Suppliers to Food Processors Association (EA)
NSFPR .... National Science Foundation Procurement Regulation [*A publication*] (AAGC)
NSFR .... National Society of Fund Raisers [*Later, NSFRE*] (EA)
NSFR .... Nitroxide Stable Free Radical [*For tissue NMR*]
NSFRC .... National Silver Fox Rabbit Club (EA)
NSFRE .... National Society of Fund Raising Executives (EA)
NSFRE Foundation... National Society of Fund Raising Executives Foundation [*Formerly the National Society of Fund Raisers Institute of Continuing Education and the National Society of Fund Raising Executives*] (NFD)
NSFRE Institute... Former name of the National Society of Fund Rainsing Executives Foundation (NFD)
NSFS .... National Society for Shut-Ins (EA)
NSFS .... Net Section Fracture Strength (PDAA)
NSfSC .... Sullivan County Community College, South Fallsburg, NY [*Library symbol Library of Congress*] (LCLS)
NSF/STAH ..... National Science Foundation Program for Science and Technology Aid to the Handicapped
NSFT........... North-South Fine, Tens
NSFTD .... Normal, Spontaneous, Full Term Delivery [*Obstetrics*]
NSFTL.......... National Sanitation Foundation Testing Laboratory, Inc. (MSA)
NSFU .... Needle Stampers' and Filers' Union [*British*]
NSFU .... North-South Fine, Units
NSG .... Aircompany Liana JSA [*Ukraine*] [*FAA designator*] (FAAC)
NSG .... National Society for Graphology (EA)
NSG .... National Steering Group (AIE)
NSG .... National Supply Group [*Military*] (AFIT)
NSG .... Naval Security Group
NSG .... Network Support Group (NITA)
NSG .... Neurosecretory Granules
NSG .... Newspaper Systems Group (EA)
NSG .... North Seeking Gyro
NSG .... Not So Good
NSG .... Nuclear Suppliers' Group [*Australia*] (ECON)
NSG .... Nursing
NSGA .... National Sand and Gravel Association [*Later, NAA*] (EA)
NSGA .... National Sporting Goods Association (EA)
NSGA .... Naval Security Group Activity
NSGC .... National Self Government Committee (EA)
NSGC .... National Society of Genetic Counselors (EA)
NSGC .... National Swine Growers Council [*Later, NPPC*] (EA)
NSGC .... Naval Security Group Command (DNAB)
NSGCC .... Coastal Courier, Glace Bay, Nova Scotia [*Library symbol National Library of Canada*] (NLC)
NSGCFA....... Aurora, Canadian Forces Base, Greenwood, Nova Scotia [*Library symbol National Library of Canada*] (NLC)

NSGCH......... Naval Security Group Command Headquarters
NSGCT........ Nonsiminomatous Germ Cell Turmors [*Medicine*] (MEDA)
NSGCTT ...... Nonseminomatous Germ Cell Tumors of the Testes
NSGD.......... National Sea Grant Depository [*National Oceanic and Atmospheric Administration Information service or system*] (IID)
NSGD.......... National Support Group for Dermatomyositis (EA)
NS-GFW...... Noise Substest of the Goldman-Fristoe-Woodcock Auditory Skills Test Battery (EDAC)
NSGIB......... NAVSHIPS [*Naval Ship Systems Command*] General Information Book
NSGLS........ Nordisk Sekretariat for Gartneri- Land-, og Skovarbejderforbund [*Nordic Secretariat for Agricultural and Horticultural Workers - NSAHW*] [*Denmark Defunct*] (EAIO)
NSGN.......... Noise Generator (CET)
NSGOC........ Naval Security Group Orientation Course (DNAB)
NSGOC........ Old Court House Museum, Guysborough, Nova Scotia [*Library symbol National Library of Canada*] (NLC)
NS Grp........ NS Group, Inc. [*Associated Press*] (SAG)
Nsg Sta....... Nursing Station (DAVI)
NSGT.......... Non-Self-Governing Territories [*United Nations*]
NSGTMEM ... National Society of General Tool Makers, Engineers, and Machinists [*A union*] [*British*]
NSGTP .... Naval Security Group Training Publication (DNAB)
NSGW......... National Society of Glass Workers [*A union*] [*British*]
NSGW......... Native Sons of the Golden West (EA)
NSH........... Halifax City Regional Library, Nova Scotia [*Library symbol National Library of Canada*] (NLC)
NSh............. John Jermain Memorial Public Library, Sag Harbor, NY [*Library symbol Library of Congress*] (LCLS)
NSH .... Nashua Corp. [*NYSE symbol*] (SPSG)
NSH .... Nashville [*Diocesan abbreviation*] [*Tennessee*] (TOCD)
NSH .... National Society for Histotechnology (EA)
NSH .... National Society of Hypnotherapists (EA)
NSH .... Naval School of Health Sciences, Bethesda, MD [*OCLC symbol*] (OCLC)
NSH .... Nordisk Samarbeidskomite for Husstellundervisning [*Nordic Joint Committee for Domestic Education - NJCDE*] (EAIO)
NSH .... Northern-Southern Hybrid [*Hemoglobin phenotype of Rana pipiens*]
NSH .... Not So Hot [*Slang*]
NSHA .... National Steeplechase and Hunt Association (EA)
NSHA .... National Stock Horse Association (EA)
NSHAC-FP ... National Self-Help Action Center - Food Program (EA)
NSHAG........ Art Gallery of Nova Scotia, Halifax, Nova Scotia [*Library symbol National Library of Canada*] (NLC)
NSHANSS .... Synod Office, Diocese of Nova Scotia, Anglican Church of Canada, Halifax, Nova Scotia [*Library symbol National Library of Canada*] (NLC)
NSHAR......... Algas Resources Ltd., Halifax, Nova Scotia [*Library symbol National Library of Canada*] (NLC)
NSHAVI....... [*The*] Atlantic Provinces Resource Centre for the Visually-Impaired, Halifax, Nova Scotia [*Library symbol National Library of Canada*] (NLC)
NSHBS........ Nova Scotia Barristers Society, Halifax, Nova Scotia [*Library symbol National Library of Canada*] (NLC)
NSHC......... Cambridge Military Library, Halifax, Nova Scotia [*Library symbol National Library of Canada*] (NLC)
NSHC......... National Self-Help Clearinghouse (EA)
NSHC......... National Silver-Haired Congress (EA)
NSHC......... National Syrian Hamster Council [*British*] (DBA)
NSHC......... North Sea Hydrographic Commission [*of the International Hydrographic Organization*] [*Belgium*]
NSHCA........ Nova Scotia College of Art and Design, Halifax, Nova Scotia [*Library symbol National Library of Canada*] (NLC)
NSHCB........ Music and Record Library, Canadian Broadcasting Corp. [*Musicotheque et Discotheque, Societe Radio-Canada*] Halifax, Nova Scotia [*Library symbol National Library of Canada*] (NLC)
NSHCBC....... Canadian British Consultants Ltd., Halifax, Nova Scotia [*Library symbol National Library of Canada*] (NLC)
NSHCBF....... Film Library, CBHT-TV, Halifax, Nova Scotia [*Library symbol National Library of Canada*] (NLC)
NSHCD........ Law Library, Cox, Downie & Co., Halifax, Nova Scotia [*Library symbol National Library of Canada*] (NLC)
NSHCDD....... Nova Scotia Commission on Drug Dependency, Halifax, Nova Scotia [*Library symbol National Library of Canada*] (NLC)
NSHCFM..... Maritime Command Museum, Canadian Forces Base, Halifax, Nova Scotia [*Library symbol National Library of Canada*] (BIB)
NSHCH........ Camp Hill Hospital, Halifax, Nova Scotia [*Library symbol National Library of Canada*] (NLC)
NSHCIC........ National Solar Heating and Cooling Information Center [*Later, CAREIRS*]
NSHCIC........ Nova Scotia Communications and Information Centre, Halifax, Nova Scotia [*Library symbol National Library of Canada*] (NLC)
NSHD.......... Dalhousie University, Halifax, Nova Scotia [*Library symbol National Library of Canada*] (NLC)
NSHD.......... Nodular Sclerosing Hodgkin's Disease [*Medicine*] (DMAA)
NSHDA........ Archives, Dalhousie University, Halifax, Nova Scotia [*Library symbol National Library of Canada*] (BIB)
NSHDAG....... Nova Scotia Department of the Attorney-General, Halifax, Nova Scotia [*Library symbol National Library of Canada*] (NLC)
NSHDCA....... Nova Scotia Department of Consumer Affairs, Halifax, Nova Scotia [*Library symbol National Library of Canada*] (NLC)
NSHDD........ Nova Scotia Department of Industry, Trade, and Technology, Halifax, Nova Scotia [*Library symbol National Library of Canada*] (NLC)
NSHDE........ Nova Scotia Department of the Environment, Halifax, Nova Scotia [*Library symbol National Library of Canada*] (NLC)

NSHDEA...... Resource Centre, Ecology Action Centre, Dalhousie University, Halifax, Nova Scotia [*Library symbol National Library of Canada*] (NLC)

NSHDF.......... Nova Scotia Department of Fisheries, Halifax, Nova Scotia [*Library symbol National Library of Canada*] (NLC)

NSHDH .... Nova Scotia Department of Transportation, Halifax, Nova Scotia [*Library symbol National Library of Canada*] (NLC)

NSHDIP......... Institute of Public Affairs, Dalhousie University, Halifax, Nova Scotia, [*Library symbol National Library of Canada*] (NLC)

NSHDIR .... School of Resources and Environmental Studies, Dalhousie University, Halifax, Nova Scotia [*Library symbol National Library of Canada*] (NLC)

NSHDL......... Law School, Dalhousie University, Halifax, Nova Scotia [*Library symbol National Library of Canada*] (NLC)

NSHDLS......... School of Library Service, Dalhousie University, Halifax, Nova Scotia [*Library symbol National Library of Canada*] (NLC)

NSHDM....... W. K. Kellogg Health Sciences Library, Dalhousie University, Halifax, Nova Scotia [*Library symbol National Library of Canada*] (NLC)

NSHDMA...... Map Library, Dalhousie University, Halifax, Nova Scotia [*Library symbol National Library of Canada*] (NLC)

NSHDOL ...... Nova Scotia Department of Labour and Manpower, Halifax, Nova Scotia [*Library symbol National Library of Canada*] (NLC)

NSHDOM ..... Nova Scotia Department of Mines, Halifax, Nova Scotia [*Library symbol National Library of Canada*] (NLC)

NSHDOS ...... Dalhousie Ocean Studies Programme, Dalhousie University, Halifax, Nova Scotia [*Library symbol National Library of Canada*] (NLC)

NSHDR .... Cultural Affairs Library, Nova Scotia Department of Tourism and Culture, Halifa x, Nova Scotia [*Library symbol National Library of Canada*] (NLC)

NSHDS.......... MacDonald Science Library, Dalhousie University, Halifax, Nova Scotia [*Library symbol National Library of Canada*] (NLC)

NSHE .... [*The*] New Schaff-Herzog Encyclopaedia of Religious Knowledge [*A publication*] (BJA)

NSHEB .... North of Scotland Hydro-Electric Board (ECON)

NShei............ Shelter Island Public Library Society, Shelter Island, NY [*Library symbol Library of Congress*] (LCLS)

NSherb.......... Sherburne Public Library, Sherburne, NY [*Library symbol Library of Congress*] (LCLS)

NSHF .... Fisheries and Oceans Canada [*Peches et Oceans Canada*] Halifax, Nova Scotia [*Library symbol National Library of Canada*] (NLC)

NSHF .... Scotia-Fundy Regional Library, Fisheries and Oceans Canada [*Bibliotheque de la Region Scotia-Fundy, Peches et Oceans Canada*], Halifax, Nova Scotia [*Library symbol National Library of Canada*] (NLC)

NSHFIF .... Federal-Provincial Taxation and Fiscal Relations Library, Nova Scotia Departmentof Finance, Halifax, Nova Scotia [*Library symbol National Library of Canada*] (NLC)

NSHH........... Nova Scotia Department of Health, Halifax, Nova Scotia [*Library symbol National Library of Canada*] (NLC)

NSHHC......... Halifax County Regional Library, Lower Sackville, Nova Scotia [*Library symbol National Library of Canada*] (NLC)

NSHHE.......... Halifax Herald Ltd., Nova Scotia [*Library symbol National Library of Canada*] (NLC)

NSHHI.......... Health Services Library, Halifax Infirmary, Nova Scotia [*Library symbol National Library of Canada*] (NLC)

NSHHR .... Nova Scotia Human Rights Commission, Halifax, Nova Scotia [*Library symbol National Library of Canada*] (NLC)

NSHHS......... Hantsport and Area Historical Society, Nova Scotia [*Library symbol National Library of Canada*] (NLC)

NSHIAP......... Atlantic Regional Library, Parks Canada [*Bibliotheque Regionale de l'Atlantique, Parcs Canada*] Halifax, Nova Scotia [*Library symbol National Library of Canada*] (NLC)

NSHIC........... International Centre for Ocean Development, Halifax, Nova Scotia [*Library symbol National Library of Canada*] (BIB)

NSHJ .... Canada Department of Justice [*Ministere de la Justice*] Halifax, Nova Scotia [*Library symbol National Library of Canada*] (NLC)

NSHK........... University of King's College, Halifax, Nova Scotia [*Library symbol National Library of Canada*] (NLC)

NSHKH.......... Izaak Walton Killam Hospital for Children, Halifax, Nova Scotia [*Library symbol National Library of Canada*] (NLC)

NSHKJ .... School of Journalism, University of King's College, Halifax, Nova Scotia [*Library symbol National Library of Canada*] (NLC)

NSHKMGM... Kitz, Matheson, Green & MacIsaac Law Firm, Halifax, Nova Scotia [*Library symbol National Library of Canada*] (NLC)

NSHL .... Legislative Library, Halifax, Nova Scotia [*Library symbol National Library of Canada*] (NLC)

NSHLA .... Nova Scotia Legal Aid, Halifax, Nova Scotia [*Library symbol National Library of Canada*] (BIB)

NSHLP .... Liberal Party of Nova Scotia, Halifax [*Library symbol National Library of Canada*] (BIB)

NSHM .... Atlantic Regional Laboratory, National Research Council [*Laboratoire Regionalde l'Atlantique, Conseil National de Recherches du Canada*] Halifax, Nova Sco tia [*Library symbol National Library of Canada*] (NLC)

NSHMA........ Nova Scotia Department of Municipal Affairs, Halifax, Nova Scotia [*Library symbol National Library of Canada*] (NLC)

NSHMBA...... National Society of Hispanic MBAs (EA)

NSHMC......... Maritime Conservatory of Music, Halifax, Nova Scotia [*Library symbol National Library of Canada*] (NLC)

NSHMCA...... Archives, Maritime Conference, United Church of Canada Halifax, Nova Scotia [*Library symbol National Conference of Commissioners on Uniform State Laws*] (BIB)

NSHMCR...... Law Library, McInnes, Cooper & Robertson, Halifax, Nova Scotia [*Library symbol National Library of Canada*] (NLC)

NSHML .... Martec Ltd., Halifax, Nova Scotia [*Library symbol National Library of Canada*] (NLC)

NSHMM .... Maritime Museum of the Atlantic, Halifax, Nova Scotia [*Library symbol National Library of Canada*] (NLC)

NSHMO........ Mobil Oil Canada Ltd., Halifax, Nova Scotia [*Library symbol National Library of Canada*] (NLC)

NSHMS......... Nova Scotia Museum, Halifax, Nova Scotia [*Library symbol National Library of Canada*] (NLC)

NSHMT .... Regional Library, Canadian Coast Guard [*Bibliotheque Regionale, Garde CotiereCanadienne*] Dartmouth, Nova Scotia [*Library symbol National Library of Canada*] (NLC)

NSHMTT ...... Information Resource Centre, Maritime Tel & Tel, Halifax, Nova Scotia [*Library symbol National Library of Canada*] (NLC)

NSHN........... Defence Research Establishment Atlantic, Canada Department of National Defence [*Centre de Recherches pour la Defense Atlantique, Ministere de la Defense Nationale*] Dartmouth, Nova Scotia [*Library symbol National Library of Canada*] (NLC)

NSHND .... Reference and Recreational Library (Stadacona), Canada Department of National Defence [*Bibliotheque de Consultation et de Lecture (Stadacona), Ministere de la Defense Nationale*] Halifax, Nova Scotia [*Library symbol National Library of Canada*] (NLC)

NSHNF........ National Film Board [*Office National du Film*], Halifax, Nova Scotia [*Library symbol National Library of Canada*] (NLC)

NSHNI.......... Nova Scotia Nautical Institute, Halifax, Nova Scotia [*Library symbol National Library of Canada*] (NLC)

NSHNP......... Nova Scotia Newspaper Project, Halifax [*Library symbol National Library of Canada*] (BIB)

NSHNS......... Ships Recreational Library, Canadian Forces Base Halifax [*Bibliotheque Recreative, Base des Forces Canadiennes Halifax*], Nova Scotia [*Library symbol National Library of Canada*] (BIB)

NSHO........... Naval Service Headquarters, Ottawa (DNAB)

NShor .... Shoreham-Wading River Public Library, Shoreham, NY [*Library symbol Library of Congress*] (LCLS)

NShorHS...... Shoreham-Wading River High School, Shoreham, NY [*Library symbol Library of Congress*] (LCLS)

NSHP .... Nova Scotia Public Archives, Halifax, Nova Scotia [*Library symbol National Library of Canada*] (NLC)

NSHPC.......... Corporate Research and Information Centre, Nova Scotia Power Corp., Halifax, Nova Scotia [*Library symbol National Library of Canada*] (NLC)

NSHPH........ Atlantic School of Theology, Halifax, Nova Scotia [*Library symbol National Library of Canada*] (NLC)

NSHPI.......... Planning Information Office, City of Halifax, Nova Scotia [*Library symbol National Library of Canada*] (NLC)

NSHPL......... Nova Scotia Union Catalogue, Nova Scotia Provincial Library, Halifax, Nova Scotia [*Library symbol National Library of Canada*] (NLC)

NSHPLX........ Reference Services, Nova Scotia Provinical Library, Halifax, Nova Scotia [*Library symbol National Library of Canada*] (NLC)

NSHPW......... Atlantic Regional Library, Public Works Canada [*Bibliotheque Regionale de l'Atlantique, Travaux Publics Canada*] Halifax, Nova Scotia [*Library symbol National Library of Canada*] (NLC)

NSHQ........... Naval Service Headquarters [*Canada*]

NSHQ........... Naval Staff Headquarters [*British military*] (DMA)

NShr .... John C. Hart Memorial Library, Shrub Oak, NY [*Library symbol Library of Congress*] (LCLS)

NSHR .... National Show Horse Registry (EA)

NSHR .... Nova Scotia Research Foundation, Dartmouth, Nova Scotia [*Library symbol National Library of Canada*] (NLC)

NSHRC.......... National Self-Help Resource Center [*Defunct*] (EA)

NSHRC.......... National Shared Housing Resource Center (EA)

NSHRC.......... Nova Scotia Rehabilitation Centre, Halifax, Nova Scotia [*Library symbol National Library of Canada*] (NLC)

NSHRCA....... Roman Catholic Archdiocesan Archives, Halifax, Nova Scotia [*Library symbol National Library of Canada*] (BIB)

NSHRL......... Nova Scotia Regional Libraries, Halifax, Nova Scotia [*Library symbol National Library of Canada*] (NLC)

NSHRP......... Photogrammetry Division, Nova Scotia Research Foundation, Halifax, Nova Scotia [*Library symbol Obsolete National Library of Canada*] (NLC)

NSHS .... National Slavic Honor Society (EA)

NSHS .... Naval School of Health Sciences [*Bethesda, MD*]

NSHS .... St. Mary's University, Halifax, Nova Scotia [*Library symbol National Library of Canada*] (NLC)

NSHSDET..... Naval School of Health Sciences Detachment (DNAB)

NSHSG.......... Sable Gas Systems Ltd., Halifax, Nova Scotia [*Library symbol National Library of Canada*] (NLC)

NSHSMC....... Stewart, MacKeen & Covert Law Firm, Halifax, Nova Scotia [*Library symbol National Library of Canada*] (NLC)

NSHSP......... Social Development Division Library, Social Planning Department, City of Halifax, Nova Scotia [*Library symbol National Library of Canada*] (NLC)

NSHSPT....... Ferguson Library for Print Handicapped Students, Patrick Power Library, St. Mary's University, Halifax, Nova Scotia [*Library symbol National Library of Canada*] (NLC)

NSHSS......... Nova Scotia Department of Community Services, Halifax, Nova Scotia [*Library symbol National Library of Canada*] (NLC)

NSHSW......... Maritime School of Social Work, Halifax, Nova Scotia [*Library symbol National Library of Canada*] (NLC)

NSHT .... Technical University of Nova Scotia, Halifax, Nova Scotia [*Library symbol National Library of Canada*] (NLC)

NSHTI.......... Nova Scotia Institute of Technology, Halifax, Nova Scotia [*Library symbol National Library of Canada*] (NLC)

NSHTU......... Nova Scotia Teachers Union, Halifax, Nova Scotia [*Library symbol National Library of Canada*] (NLC)

NSHV.......... Mount Saint Vincent University, Halifax, Nova Scotia [*Library symbol National Library of Canada*] (NLC)

NSHVA........ Art Gallery, Mount Saint Vincent University, Halifax, Nova Scotia [*Library symbol National Library of Canada*] (NLC)

NSHVGH ..... Health Sciences Library, Victoria General Hospital, Halifax, Nova Scotia [*Library symbol National Library of Canada*] (NLC)

NSHVH........ Halifax Regional Vocational School, Nova Scotia [*Library symbol National Library of Canada*] (NLC)

NSHVTT .... Nova Scotia Department of Advanced Education and Job Training, Halifax, Nova S cotia [*Library symbol National Library of Canada*] (NLC)

NSHW.......... Atlantic Region, Atmospheric Environment Service, Environment Canada [*Bureau Regional de l'Atlantique, Service de l'Environnement Atmospherique, Environnement Canada*] Halifax, Nova Scotia [*Library symbol National Library of Canada*] (NLC)

NShW .... Sag Harbor Whaling and Historical Museum, Sag Harbor, NY [*Library symbol*] [*Library of Congress*] (LCLS)

NSI............. Handbook of North-Semitic Inscriptions [*A publication*] (BJA)

NSI............. NASA Science Internet

NSI............. NASA [*National Aeronautical and Space Administration*] Standard Indicator

NSI............. NASA Standard Initiator (NASA)

NSI............. National Security Index of the American Security Council [*A publication*] (DLA)

NSI............. National Security Information (NRCH)

NSI............. National Service Industries, Inc. [*NYSE symbol*] (SPSG)

NSI............. National Service [*Life*] Insurance

NSI............. National Shipbuilding Initiative [*MARAD*] (TAG)

NSI............. National Shoe Institute (EA)

NSI............. National Space Institute [*Later, NSS*] (EA)

NSI............. National Supervisory Inspectorate [*British*] (EECA)

NSI............. Natl Service Indus [*NYSE symbol*] (TTSB)

NSI............. Naval Science Instructor (DNAB)

NSI............. Negative Self-Image [*Psychology*]

NSI............. Network Solutions, Inc.

NSI............. Network Solutions Inc.

NSI............. Network Solutions, Inc.

NSI............. Network Strategies, Inc. [*Fairfax, VA*] [*Telecommunications*] (TSSD)

NSI............. Neurosciences Institute (BABM)

NSI............. Neurosciences Institute (DAVI)

NSI............. Next Sequential Instruction

NSI............. Nielsen Station Index [*Nielsen Media Research*] [*Information service or system*]

NSI............. Nitrogen Solubility Index [*Analytical chemistry*]

NSI............. Noise Source Instrumentation

NSI............. Nonsatellite Identification

NSI............. Nonsequenced Information (IAA)

NSI............. Nonspecific Sexually Transmitted Infection [*Medicine*]

NSI............. Nonstandard Item

NSI............. Nonstocked Item

NSI............. Non-Syncytium-Inducing [*Medicine*]

NSI............. Non-Syncytium-Inducing [*Cytology*]

NSI............. Norsk Senter for Informatikk [*Norwegian Center for Informatics*] [*Information service or system*] (IID)

NSI............. North-South Institute [*Canada*] (EAIO)

NSI............. Nuclear Safety Inspection (NVT)

NSI............. Nuclear Safety Institute

NSI............. Nuclear Services International

NSI............. Nuclear Status Indicator (DNAB)

NSI............. Nuclear Surety Inspection

NSI............. San Nicolas Island, CA [*Location identifier FAA*] (FAAL)

NSI-1 .... NASA [*National Aeronautics and Space Administration*] Standard Initiator -Type 1 [*Formerly, SMSI*] (NASA)

NSIA .... National Security and International Affairs [*Office of Management and Budget*]

NSIA .... National Security Industrial Association (EA)

NSIAC .... National Student Involvement Assistance Center [*Boston University*] [*Defunct*]

NSIAD.......... National Security and International Affairs Division (AAGC)

NSIC .... National Spinal Injuries Centre [*Stoke Mandeville Hospital*] [*British*] (CB)

NSIC .... National Storage Industry Consortium

NSIC .... National Strategy Information Center (EA)

NSIC .... Naval Security and Investigative Command

NSIC .... Next Senior in Command [*Navy*]

NSIC .... Noster Salvator Iesus Christus [*Our Savior, Jesus Christ*] [*Latin*]

NSIC .... Nuclear Safety Information Center

NSIC .... Nuclear Strike Information Center

NSiC .... Staten Island Community College, Staten Island, NY [*Library symbol Library of Congress Obsolete*] (LCLS)

NSiCS .... College of Staten Island, St. George Campus, Staten Island, NY [*Library symbol Library of Congress*] (LCLS)

NSID .... National Society of Interior Designers [*Later, ASID*]

NSIDC .... National Snow and Ice Data Center [*National Oceanic and Atmospheric Administration*] (GFGA)

NSIDH.......... National System of Interstate and Defense Highways (AFIT)

NSidHi .... Sidney New York Historical Society, Sidney, NY [*Library symbol*] [*Library of Congress*] (LCLS)

NSidS .... Bendix Corp., Electrical Components Division, Engineering Library, Sidney, NY [*Library symbol Library of Congress*] (LCLS)

NSIDS......... National Shut-In Day Society (EA)

NSIDSC........ National Sudden Infant Death Syndrome Clearinghouse (EA)

NSIDSF........ National Sudden Infant Death Syndrome Foundation (EA)

NSIEE .... National Society for Internships and Experiential Education (EA)

NSIF............ National Swine Improvement Federation (EA)

NSIF............ Near Space Instrumentation Facility [*NASA*] (KSC)

NSIlR .... New York State Department of Mental Hygiene, Institute for Basic Research in Mental Retardation, Staten Island, NY [*Library symbol Library of Congress*] (LCLS)

NSIL .... National Seafood Inspection Laboratory [*Pascagoula, MS*] [*Department of Commerce*] (GRD)

NSIL .... Nonsaturating Inverter Logic (IAA)

NSILA .... Nonsuppressible Insulin-Like Activity [*Cytochemistry*]

NSIIStC .... Saint Columban's Seminary, Silver Creek, NY [*Library symbol Library of Congress Obsolete*] (LCLS)

NSiND .... Notre Dame College of Staten Island, Staten Island, NY [*Library symbol Library of Congress*] (LCLS)

NSIPA .... National Society of Insurance Premium Auditors (EA)

NSIPS .... NRL [*Naval Research Laboratory*] Satellite Image Processing System (USDC)

NSIPS .... NRL [*Naval Research Laboratory*] Satellite Image Processing System [*Marine science*] (OSRA)

NSIR .... Nosier (ABBR)

NSiRC .... Richmond College, Staten Island, NY [*Library symbol Library of Congress Obsolete*] (LCLS)

NSIS .... NASA Software Information System (SSD)

NSIS .... National Shut-In Society (EA)

NSIS .... National Survey of Instructional Staff [*Department of Education*] (GFGA)

NSiSV .... Saint Vincent's Medical Center of Richmond, Staten Island, NY [*Library symbol Library of Congress*] (LCLS)

NSIT .... Insight Enterprises, Inc. [*NASDAQ symbol*] (SAG)

NSIT .... Insiht Enterprises [*NASDAQ symbol*] (TTSB)

NSIT .... Not Safe in Taxis

NSITF .... National Ship Installations Test Facility

NSIX .... Neuromedical Systems [*NASDAQ symbol*] (TTSB)

NSIX .... Neuromedical Systems, Inc. [*NASDAQ symbol*] (SAG)

NSIY .... North Somerset Imperial Yeomanry [*British military*] (DMA)

NSJ............. Nuestro Senor Jesucristo [*Our Lord, Jesus Christ*] [*Spanish*]

NSJC .... National Society of Journeymen Curriers [*A union*] [*British*]

NSJC .... Noster Salvator Jesus Christus [*Our Savior, Jesus Christ*] [*Latin*]

NSJC .... Notre Seigneur Jesus Christ [*Our Lord, Jesus Christ*] [*French*]

NSK .... Nippon Seiko Kabushiki Kaisha [*Japan*]

NSK .... Not Specified by Kind (MHDI)

NSKC .... National Safe Kids Campaign (EA)

NSKER .... Efamol Research Institute, Kentville, Nova Scotia [*Library symbol National Library of Canada*] (NLC)

NSKIP .... Nordiska Samarbetskommitten for Internationell Politik [*Nordic Cooperation Committee for International Politics, Including Conflict and Peace Research*] (EAIO)

NSKKR........ Kings Regional Vocational School, Kentville, Nova Scotia [*Library symbol National Library of Canada*] (NLC)

NSKL .... Wildlife Division, Nova Scotia Department of Lands and Forests, Kentville, Nova Scotia [*Library symbol National Library of Canada*] (NLC)

NSKOK........ Old Kings Courthouse Heritage Museum, Kentville, Nova Scotia [*Library symbol National Library of Canada*] (NLC)

NSKR .... Research Station, Agriculture Canada [*Station de Recherches, Agriculture Canada*] Kentville, Nova Scotia [*Library symbol National Library of Canada*] (NLC)

NSKVH........ Valley Health Services Association, Kentville, Nova Scotia [*Library symbol National Library of Canada*] (NLC)

NSL............. Nasal (ABBR)

NSL............. Nasion-Sella Line [*Brain anatomy*]

NSL............. National Science Laboratories (KSC)

NSL............. National Science Library [*Later, Canada Institute for Scientific and Technical Information*] (DIT)

NSL............. National Service League [*British military*] (DMA)

NSL............. National Soccer League (EA)

NSL............. National Standards Laboratory [*Formerly, IBS, IMR*] [*National Institute of Standards and Technology*]

NSL............. National Story League (EA)

NSL............. Naval Submarine League (EA)

NSL............. Naval Supersonic Laboratory

NSL............. Navigating Sub-Lieutenant [*Navy British*] (ROG)

NSL............. Navy Standards Laboratory

NSL............. Navy Stock List

NSL............. Net Switching Loss [*Telecommunications*] (TEL)

NSL............. New Special Libraries [*A publication*]

NSL............. Nonstandard Label [*Computer science*]

NSL............. Nonstockage List

NSL............. Northrup Space Laboratories (KSC)

NSL............. Norwood & St. Lawrence Railroad Co. [*AAR code*]

NSL............. Not Stock Listed

NSL............. Nuclear Safety Line

NSl............. Saranac Lake Free Library, Saranac Lake, NY [*Library symbol Library of Congress*] (LCLS)

NSLA .... Louisbourg Archives, Nova Scotia [*Library symbol National Library of Canada*] (NLC)

NSLA .... National Society of Literature and the Arts (EA)

NSLA .... National Staff Leasing Association (EA)

NSLAL .... Nova Scotia Land Survey Institute, Lawrencetown, Nova Scotia [*Library symbol National Library of Canada*] (NLC)

NSLB .... NS&L Bancorp [*NASDAQ symbol*] (TTSB)

NSLB .... NS & L Bancorp, Inc. [*NASDAQ symbol*] (SAG)

NSLC .... Nuclear Safety and Licensing Commission

NSLF............ Fortress of Louisbourg, Canada National Historic Park [*Forteresse de Louisbourg, Parc Historique National*] Nova Scotia [*Library symbol National Library of Canada*] (NLC)
NSLF............ National Socialist Liberation Front (NADA)
NSLF............ Nonself
NSLFM........ Fisheries Museum of the Atlantic, Lunenburg, Nova Scotia [*Library symbol National Library of Canada*] (NLC)
NSLFP .... Fort Point Museum, La Have, Nova Scotia [*Library symbol National Library of Canada*] (NLC)
NSIH............ General Hospital of Saranac Lake, Saranac Lake, NY [*Library symbol Library of Congress*] (LCLS)
NSLHS........ Lunenburg Heritage Society, Nova Scotia [*Library symbol National Library of Canada*] (NLC)
NSLI............ National Service Life Insurance
NSLI............ National Service Life Insurance
NSLI............ National Street Law Institute (EA)
NSLIN .... Nonstandard Line Item Number [*Army*] (AABC)
NSLL............ National Save-a-Life League [*Defunct*] (EA)
NSLL............ National Savings and Loan League [*Formerly, NLISA*] (EA)
NSLLS .... Lockeport Little School Museum, Nova Scotia [*Library symbol National Library of Canada*] (NLC)
NSINC......... North Country Community College, Saranac Lake, NY [*Library symbol Library of Congress*] (LCLS)
NSLP .... National School Lunch Program [*Department of Agriculture*]
NSLPE .... Progress-Enterprise, Lunenburg, Nova Scotia [*Library symbol National Library of Canada*] (NLC)
NSLQCM...... Queens County Museum, Liverpool, Nova Scotia [*Library symbol National Library of Canada*] (NLC)
NSLR .... Nova Scotia Law Reports [*A publication*] (DLA)
NSLRB .... National Steel Labor Relations Board [*New Deal*]
NSLRS .... National School Labor Relations Service [*Later, LMRS*] (EA)
NSLS .... National Synchrotron Light Source [*Brookhaven National Laboratory*]
NSLS .... North Suburban Library System, Wheeling, IL [*Library network*]
NSLSA .... National Surf Life Saving Association of America [*Later, USLA*] (EA)
NSLSRA...... National Society of Live Stock Record Associations (EA)
NSIT............ Trudeau Institute, Saranac Lake, NY [*Library symbol Library of Congress*] (LCLS)
N/S-LTI-G/T... National/State Leadership Training Institute on Gifted and Talented (EA)
NSIW .... Will Rogers Memorial Fund, Saranac Lake, NY [*Library symbol Library of Congress*] (LCLS)
NSLY .... Nasally (ABBR)
NSLY .... Noisily (ABBR)
NSM............ National Security Management [*Military*]
NSM............ National Security Medal [*Military decoration*]
NSM............ National Selected Morticians (EA)
NSM............ National Semiconductor Corp. [*NYSE symbol*] (SPSG)
NSM............ National Serviceman [*British military*] (DMA)
NSM............ National Soaring Museum (DICI)
NSM............ National Socialist Movement (EA)
NSM............ Natl Semiconductor [*NYSE symbol*] (TTSB)
NSM............ Naval School of Music
NSM............ Network Security Module
NSM............ Network Space Monitor (SAA)
NSM............ Network Status Monitor [*NASA*] (KSC)
NSM............ Neurosecretory Material (MAE)
NSM............ Neurosecretory Motoneurons
NSM............ New Schools Movement [*Defunct*] (EA)
NSM............ New Smoking Material [*A wood cellulose-based tobacco substitute*]
NSM............ Nice Safe Man [*Slang*]
NSM............ Nitsanim [*Israel*] [*Later, AMT*] [*Geomagnetic observatory code*]
NSM............ Noise Source Meter
NSM............ Nondeterministic Sequential Machine (IAA)
NSM............ Norseman [*Australia Airport symbol*] (OAG)
NSM............ Northern Student Movement [*Defunct*] (EA)
NSM............ North-South Map [*Via orbiter*]
NSM............ Nutrient Sporulation Medium [*Medicine*] (DMAA)
NSm............ Smithtown Public Library, Smithtown, NY [*Library symbol Library of Congress*] (LCLS)
N-S/M² .... Newton Second per Square Meter (WDAA)
NSMA .... Maota [*Western Samoa*] [*ICAO location identifier*] (ICLI)
NSMA .... National Scale Men's Association (EA)
NSMA .... National Seasoning Manufacturers Association (EA)
NSMA .... National Second Mortgage Association [*Center Square, PA*] (EA)
NSMA .... National Shoe Manufacturers Association [*Later, FIA*] (EA)
NSMA .... National Soup Mix Association [*Defunct*] (EA)
NSMAPMAWOL... Not So Much a Programme, More a Way of Life [*British television program*]
NSMATCC..... NATO Small Arms Test Control Commission (MCD)
NSMC .... National Security Management Course [*National Defense University*] (GFGA)
NSMC .... National Student Marketing Corp.
NSMC .... Naval Submarine Medical Center
NSMCA .... National Spirit, Metropolitan Club of America (EA)
NSMCM .... Naval Supplement, Manual for Courts-Martial [*United States*] [*A publication*] (DLA)
NSME........... Eastern Counties Regional Library, Mulgrave, Nova Scotia [*Library symbol National Library of Canada*] (NLC)
NSMEX .... Examiner, Middleton, Nova Scotia [*Library symbol National Library of Canada*] (NLC)
NSMFA .... North Sea Mine Force Association (EA)
NSMG.......... Naval School of Military Government
NSMG & A... Naval School of Military Government and Administration
NSmGH........ Smithtown General Hospital, Smithtown, NY [*Library symbol Library of Congress*] (LCLS)

NSMH .... Nuclear Systems Material Handbook (NRCH)
NSMHC........ National Society for Mentally Handicapped Children [*British*] (BI)
NSmHSE...... Smithtown High School East. Smithtown, NY [*Library symbol*] [*Library of Congress*] (LCLS)
NSmHSW..... Smithtown High School West, Smithtown, NY [*Library symbol*] [*Library of Congress*] (LCLS)
NSML........... Low-Sodium Meal [*Airline notation*] (ADA)
NSMM .... Macdonald Museum, Middleton, Nova Scotia [*Library symbol National Library of Canada*] (NLC)
NSMM .... National Society of Metal Mechanics [*A union*] [*British*] (DCTA)
NSMO .... NASTRAN [*NASA Structural Analysis*] Systems Management Office
NSMP .... National Society of Master Patternmakers [*British*] (BI)
NSMP .... National Society of Mural Painters (EA)
NSMP .... Navy Support and Mobilization Plan (NVT)
NSMPA .... National Screw Machine Products Association (EA)
NSMR .... National Society for Medical Research (EA)
NSMR .... Non-Store Marketing Report [*A publication*]
NSMRL........ Naval Submarine Medical Research Laboratory
NSMRSE ..... National Study of Mathematics Requirements for Scientists and Engineers
NSMRTS ..... Nuclear Submarine Maneuvering Room Training Simulator (PDAA)
NSMS .... National Safety Management Society (EA)
NSMS .... National Sheet Music Society (EA)
NSMS .... Network Server Management System [*Tylink Corp.*]
NSMS .... Soldiers Memorial Hospital, Middleton, Nova Scotia [*Library symbol National Library of Canada*] (NLC)
NSMSES ..... Naval Ship Missile System Engineering Station
NSMSESDETLANT... Naval Ship Missile System Engineering Station Detachment, Atlantic (MUGU)
NSmSJH ..... Saint John's Smithtown Hospital, Smithtown, NY [*Library symbol Library of Congress*] (LCLS)
NSMT.......... National Society of Master Thatchers [*British*] (DBA)
NSMT.......... National Society of Medical Technologists
NSMV .... Valley Mirror, Middleton, Nova Scotia [*Library symbol National Library of Canada*] (NLC)
NSMW .... Naval Schools Mine Warfare
NSN .... Military Sealift Command, Washington, DC [*OCLC symbol*] (OCLC)
NSN .... National Stock Number (MCD)
NSN .... NATO Stock Number (NATG)
NSN .... Nelson [*New Zealand*] [*Airport symbol*] (OAG)
NSN .... Nephrotoxic Serum Nephritis [*Medicine*] (DMAA)
NSN .... Nicotine-Stimulated Neurophysin [*Biochemistry*]
NSN .... North Star Network [*Defunct*] (EA)
NSN .... No Stock Number
Nsn .... Number of Similar Negative Matches
NSN .... Nurses Support Network [*Later, NIT*] (EA)
NSNA .... National Socialist Nederlandse Arbeiders Partij [*Netherlands group favoring integration of the Netherlands into the German reich*] [*World War II*]
NSNA .... National Student Nurses' Association (EA)
NSNA .... Newcomen Society in North America (EA)
NSNC .... Nova Scotia Normal College
NSNCE........ Nuisance (ABBR)
NSNCL .... Nonsensical (ABBR)
NSND .... Nonsymptomatic, Nondisabling (MAE)
NSND .... Normal Saline Nose Drops [*Pharmacology*] (DAVI)
NSNE .... Nappan Experimental Farm, Nova Scotia [*Library symbol National Library of Canada*] (NLC)
NSNEW ...... National Society of New England Women (EA)
NSNF .... Nonstrategic Nuclear Forces (MCD)
NSnfG .... GTE Sylvania, Inc., Electronic Components Group, Seneca Falls, NY [*Library symbol Library of Congress*] (LCLS)
NSNGA........ Aberdeen Hospital, New Glasgow, Nova Scotia [*Library symbol National Library of Canada*] (NLC)
NSNGE........ Evening News, New Glasgow, Nova Scotia [*Library symbol National Library of Canada*] (NLC)
NSNGH .... New Glasgow Senior High School, Nova Scotia [*Library symbol National Library of Canada*] (BIB)
NSNGP........ Pictou-Antigonish Regional Library, New Glasgow, Nova Scotia [*Library symbol National Library of Canada*] (NLC)
NSNHC........ Cabot Archives, Neil's Harbour, Nova Scotia [*Library symbol National Library of Canada*] (NLC)
NSNMDR ..... National Stock Number Master Data Records (MCD)
NSNMK....... Kentville Publishing, New Minas, Nova Scotia [*Library symbol National Library of Canada*] (NLC)
NSNP .... No Space, No Print [*Computer science*] (MHDI)
NSNRP........ Nonstock Numbered Repair Parts
NSNS .... Nonsense (ABBR)
NSNSCLY .... Nonsensically (ABBR)
NSO .... NASA Support Operation (KSC)
NSO .... National Security Office [*or Officer*] (GFGA)
NSO .... National Service Officer [*Ministry of Labour and National Service*] [*British World War II*]
NSO .... National Solar Observatory [*Tucson, AZ*] [*National Science Foundation*] (GRD)
NSO .... National Standardization Office [*US Army Materiel Command*]
NSO .... National Symphony Orchestra
NSO .... Naval Staff Officer
NSO .... Naval Store Officer [*British*]
NSO .... Navy Subsistence Office (DNAB)
NSO .... Neighborhood Service Organization
NSO .... Neosporin Ointment [*Medicine*] (CPH)
NSO .... Network Support Office [*NASA*]
NSO .... Next Standing Order
NSO .... Nitrogen, Sulfur, and Oxygen [*In chemical compounds*]

NSO .... Noise Suppression Oscillator (MCD)
NSO .... Nonferrous Smelter Order [*Environmental Protection Agency*]
nso .... Northern Sotho [*MARC language code Library of Congress*] (LCCP)
NSO .... North State Cooperative Library System, Willows, CA [*OCLC symbol*] (OCLC)
NSO .... No Spares Ordered (AAG)
NSO .... Nuclear Safety Office [*or Officer*] [*Air Force*] (AFM)
NSO .... Numeric Stockage Objective [*Items*] [*DoD*]
NSO .... Scone [*Australia Airport symbol*] (OAG)
NSo .... Somers Library, Somers, NY [*Library symbol Library of Congress*] (LCLS)
NSOA .... National School Orchestra Association (EA)
NSOA .... National Symphony Orchestra Association (EA)
NSOA .... Nuclear Safety Operational Analysis (NRCH)
NSoa .... Rogers Memorial Library, Southampton, NY [*Library symbol Library of Congress*] (LCLS)
NSoaH .... Southampton Hospital, Southampton, NY [*Library symbol Library of Congress*] (LCLS)
NSoaS .... Long Island University, Southampton College, Southampton, NY [*Library symbol Library of Congress*] (LCLS)
NSOB .... New Senate Office Building
NSOC .... National SIGINT [*Signal Intelligence*] Operations Center (MCD)
NSOC .... Navy Satellite Operations Center (NVT)
NSOC .... Norbornene Spiroorthocarbonate [*Organic chemistry*]
NSOD .... Naval School of Ordnance Disposal
NSOEA .... National Stationery and Office Equipment Association [*Later, NOPA*] (EA)
NSOF .... Naval Status of Forces (MCD)
NSOF .... Navy Special Operations Force (AABC)
NSOG .... Navy Special Operations Group [*SEALS that operated in Vietnam*] (VNW)
NSOGA .... National Seniors' Open Golf Association (EA)
NSoHi .... Somers Historical Society, Somers, NY [*Library symbol Library of Congress*] (LCLS)
NSOHSC ...... National Survey of Oral Health in School Children [*Department of Health and Human Services*] (GFGA)
NSOJ .... Journal, Oxford, Nova Scotia [*Library symbol National Library of Canada*] (NLC)
NSOM .... Near Field Scanning Optical Microscopy
NSoo .... Southold Free Library, Southold, NY [*Library symbol Library of Congress*] (LCLS)
NSOP .... National Second Opinion Program (EA)
NSOPCD ...... National Society of Old Plymouth Colony Descendants (EA)
NSOPF .... National Survey of Postsecondary Faculty [*Department of Education*] (GFGA)
NSOR .... No Shop Order Required
NSos .... South Salem Library, South Salem, NY [*Library symbol Library of Congress*] (LCLS)
NSOSG .... North Sea Oceanographical Study Group [*British*]
NSP .... NASA Support Plan (KSC)
NSP .... National Salvation Party [*Milli Selamet Partisi*] [*Turkey Political party*] (PPW)
NSP .... National Sea Products Ltd. [*Toronto Stock Exchange symbol*]
NSP .... National Seoposengwe Party [*Bophuthatswana*] [*Political party*] (PPW)
NSP .... National Ski Patrol System (EA)
NSP .... National Socialist Party [*New Zealand*] [*Political party*] (PD)
NSP .... National Society of Painters [*A union*] [*British*]
NSP .... National Society of Professors [*Later, NEA Higher Education Council*] (EA)
NSP .... National Space Program (AAG)
NSP .... National Stolen Property
NSP .... National Stuttering Project (EA)
NSP .... Native Signal Processing [*Computer science*] (PCM)
NSP .... Navigational Satellite Program [*NASA*] (IAA)
NSP .... Navy Safety Program (DNAB)
NSP .... Navy Space Project
NSP .... Navy Standard Part
NSP .... Navy Support Plan
NSP .... Neighborhood Statistics Program [*Bureau of the Census*] (GFGA)
NSP .... Net Social Profitability
NSP .... Network Service Provider [*Telecommunications*]
NSP .... Network Services Protocol [*Digital Equipment Corp.*] [*Telecommunications*] (TEL)
NSP .... Network Signal Processor (NASA)
NSP .... Network Support Plan [*NASA*] (KSC)
NSP .... Network Support Processor (NITA)
NSP .... Neurological Shellfish Poisoning (USDC)
NSP .... Neuron-Specific Protein [*Later, NSE*] [*Biochemistry*]
NSP .... Neurotoxic Shellfish Poisoning [*Medicine*]
NSP .... New Species
NSP .... Nominal Stagnation Point
NSP .... Non-Self-Propelled
NSP .... Nonseries Parallel (IAA)
NSP .... Nonspecific Prostatitis [*Medicine*] (ADA)
NSP .... Nonstandard Part
NSP .... Nonstorage Protein [*Food technology*]
NSP .... Nordiska Sjoforsakringspoolen [*Nordic Pool for Marine Insurance - NPMI*] (EA)
NSP .... Normal Serum Pool
NSP .... Normal Superphosphate [*Fertilizer*]
NSP .... Northern States Power Co. [*NYSE symbol*] (SPSG)
NSP .... Northern States Pwr [*NYSE symbol*] (TTSB)
NSPA .... No Separate Billing Price (MCD)
NSP .... Nose Shipping Plug

NSP .... Not Separately Priced (NG)
NSP .... Nuclear Strike Plan [*Army*] (AABC)
Nsp .... Number of Similar Positive Matches
NSP .... Numeric Space Character [*Computer science*]
NSP .... Nutritional Support Panel [*Dietetics*] (DAVI)
NSP .... St. Andrews Presbyterian College, Laurinburg, NC [*OCLC symbol*] (OCLC)
NSPA .... Advocate, Pictou, Nova Scotia [*Library symbol National Library of Canada*] (NLC)
NSPA .... National Scholastic Press Association (EA)
NSPA .... National Shrimp Processors Association (EA)
NSPA .... National Socialist Party of America (EA)
NSPA .... National Society of Public Accountants [*Alexandria, VA*] (EA)
NSPA .... National Soybean Processors Association [*Later, NOPA*] (EA)
NSPA .... National Split Pea Association [*Defunct*]
NSPA .... National Standard Parts Association [*Later, ASIA*]
NSPA .... National State Printing Association (EA)
NSPA .... Navy Shore Patrol Administration (WDAA)
NSPA .... Pictou Advocate, Nova Scotia [*Library symbol National Library of Canada*] (NLC)
NSPAC .... National Security Political Action Committee [*Defunct*] (EA)
NSPAR .... Nonstandard Part Approval Request
NSpaT .... Saint Thomas Aquinas College, Sparkill, NY [*Library symbol Library of Congress*] (LCLS)
NSPB .... National Society to Prevent Blindness (EA)
NSPBB .... Burning Bush Museum, Pictou, Nova Scotia [*Library symbol National Library of Canada*] (BIB)
NSPC .... National Security Planning Commission
NSPC .... National Society of Painters in Casein (EA)
NSPC .... National Sound-Program Center [*Telecommunications*] (TEL)
NSPC .... National Standard Plumbing Code Committee (EA)
NSPC .... National Straight Pipe Threads in Pipe Couplings
NSPCA .... National Society for the Prevention of Cruelty to Animals (EA)
NSPCA .... National Society of Painters in Casein and Acrylic (EA)
NSPCB .... National Society for the Preservation of Covered Bridges (EA)
NSPCC .... National Society for the Prevention of Cruelty to Children
NSPCC .... Naval Ships Parts Control Center (MCD)
NSPCM .... National Society for Prevention of Cruelty to Mushrooms (EA)
NSPD .... Naval Shore Patrol Detachment
NSPE .... National Society of Professional Engineers (EA)
NSPE .... Navy Senior Procurement Executive (AAGC)
NSPE .... Specimen Unobtainable [*Laboratory science*] (DAVI)
NSpeB .... Board of Cooperative Educational Services (BOCES), Spencerport, NY [*Library symbol Library of Congress*] (LCLS)
N-SPECS ..... Navy Specifications (AAGC)
NSPF .... National Swimming Pool Foundation (EA)
NSPF .... Not Specifically Provided For
NSPFEA .... National Spray Painting and Finishing Equipment Association [*Later, NSEMA*] (EA)
NSPG .... National Security Planning Group
NSPHM .... Port Hastings Museum and Archives, Nova Scotia [*Library symbol National Library of Canada*] (NLC)
NSPI .... National Society for Performance and Instruction (EA)
NSPI .... National Society for Programmed Instruction (IAA)
NSPI .... National Spa and Pool Institute (EA)
NSPI .... National Spatial Data Infrastructure [*BTS*] (TAG)
NSPI .... Nonstorage Protein Isolate [*Food technology*]
NSPIE .... National Society for the Promotion of Industrial Education [*Later, AVA*]
NSPKU .... National Society for Phenylketonuria and Allied Disorders [*British*] (DBA)
NSPLO .... NATO Sidewinder Production and Logistics Organization [*Missiles*] (NATG)
NSPMH .... McCulloch House, Pictou, Nova Scotia [*Library symbol National Library of Canada*] (NLC)
NSPNC .... North Cumberland Historical Society, Pugwash, Nova Scotia [*Library symbol National Library of Canada*] (NLC)
NSPO .... NATO Sea Sparrow Project Office (MCD)
NSPO .... NATO Sidewinder Production Organization [*Missiles*] (NATG)
NSPO .... NATO Sidewinder Program Office [*Missiles*] (NATG)
NSPO .... Naval Ship Production Overseer [*British*]
NSPO .... Naval Space Projects Office
NSPO .... Navy Special Projects Office
NSPO .... Nuclear Systems Project Office [*Air Research and Development Command*] [*Air Force*] (AAG)
NS-POG .... NAVSHIPS [*Naval Ship Systems Command*] Propulsion Operating Guides
NSPP .... National Serials Pilot Project
NSPP .... Nuclear Safety Pilot Plant [*ORNL*]
NSPPrA .... Non'n St Pwr Minn,$3.60 Pfd [*NYSE symbol*] (TTSB)
NSPPrB .... No'n St Pwr Minn,$4.08 Pfd [*NYSE symbol*] (TTSB)
NSPPrC .... No'n Pwr Minn,$4.10 Pfd [*NYSE symbol*] (TTSB)
NSPPrE .... No's St Pwr Minn,$4.16 Pfd [*NYSE symbol*] (TTSB)
NSPPrG .... No'n St Pwr Minn,$4.56 Pfd [*NYSE symbol*] (TTSB)
NSPPrH .... No'n St Pwr Minn,$6.80 Pfd [*NYSE symbol*] (TTSB)
NSPPrI .... No'n St Pwr Minn,$7.00 Pfd [*NYSE symbol*] (TTSB)
NSPR .... National Society for Park Resources (EA)
NSPR .... National Society of Patient Representatives of the American Hospital Association (EA)
NSPR .... National Society of Pershing Rifles (EA)
NSPR .... Nonstandard Part Approval Request
NSPR .... Record, Parrsboro, Nova Scotia [*Library symbol National Library of Canada*] (NLC)
NSPRA .... National School Public Relations Association (EA)
NSPrD .... No'n St Pwr Minn,$4.11 Pfd [*NYSE symbol*] (TTSB)

NSPRDS	New Systems Personnel Requirements Data System [*Navy*]
NSPRM	National Society of Professional Resident Managers (EA)
NSPRT	Nonsupport (ABBR)
NSPRV	Pictou Regional Vocational School, Nova Scotia [*Library symbol National Library of Canada*] (NLC)
NSprvCH	Bertrand Chaffee Hospital, Springville, NY [*Library symbol Library of Congress*] (LCLS)
NSPS	National Ski Patrol System (EA)
NSPS	National Society of Professional Sanitarians (EA)
NSPS	National Society of Professional Surveyors (EA)
NSPS	National Standards of Performance for Stationary Sources (ACII)
NSPS	National Stockpile Purchase Specification [*for metals*]
NSPS	National Sweet Pea Society [*British*] (BI)
NSPS	New Source Performance Standards [*Environmental Protection Agency*]
NSPS	Nonsynchronous Pulse Suppression (MCD)
NSPS	Nuclear Safety Protection System (NRCH)
NSPS	Nuclear Strike Planning System (MCD)
NSPSE	National Society of Painters, Sculptors, and Engravers [*British*] (DI)
NSPSH	Parrsboro Shore Historical Society, Parrsboro, Nova Scotia [*Library symbol National Library of Canada*] (BIB)
NSPSS	Scotia Sun, Port Hawkesbury, Nova Scotia [*Library symbol National Library of Canada*] (NLC)
NSPST	National Society of Pharmaceutical Sales Trainers (EA)
NSPV	Nandina Stem-Pitting Virus [*Plant pathology*]
NSPV	Number of Scans per Vehicle (OA)
NSPVT	Nonsustained Polymorphic Ventricular Tachycardia [*Cardiology*] (DAVI)
NSPw	Northern States Power Co. [*Associated Press*] (SAG)
NSPWA	National Society Patriotic Women of America
NSQ	Neuroticism Scale Questionnaire [*Psychology*]
NSQ	Not Sufficient Quantity [*Clinical chemistry*]
NSQ	Nurse Satisfaction Questionnaire
NSQC	National Society of Quality Circles [*British*] (DBA)
NSR	Mount Vernon, WA [*Location identifier FAA*] (FAAL)
NSR	Nasoseptal Reconstruction [*Otorhinolaryngology*] (DAVI)
NSR	National Air Charter PT [*Indonesia*] [*ICAO designator*] (FAAC)
NSR	National Scientific Register
NSR	National Security Review (AAGC)
NSR	National Shipping Report [*NATO*]
NSR	National Shipping Representative (NATG)
NSR	National Singles Registry (EA)
NSR	National Slow Rate (NASA)
NSR	National Slow Rate
NSR	NATO Staff Requirements (MCD)
NSR	Naval Supply Requirement (DNAB)
NSR	Net Survival Rate
NSR	Neutron Source Reactor
NSR	New Source Review [*A publication*] (EPA)
NSR	Night Sky Radiation
NSR	Nitrile Silicone Rubber [*Organic chemistry*]
NSR	Noise-to-Signal Ratio (IAA)
NSR	Nominal Slow Rate [*NASA*] (KSC)
NSR	Nonspecific Reaction [*Medicine*] (DMAA)
NSR	Norair Science Report (SAA)
NSR	Nordic Shooting Region (EAIO)
NSR	Nordiska Skidskolans Rad [*Nordic Council of Ski Schools - NCSS*] [*Finland*] (EAIO)
NSR	Nordiska Skogsarbetsstudiernas Rad [*Nordic Research Council on Forest Operations*] [*Sweden*] (EAIO)
NSR	Nordisk Skuespillerrad [*Nordic Actors' Council - NAC*] [*Sweden*] (EAIO)
NSR	Norfolk Southern Railway Co. [*NYSE symbol*] (SAG)
NSR	Normal Sinus Rhythm [*Medicine*] (DMAA)
NSR	Normal Slow Rate Maneuver (NASA)
NSR	Norske Samers Riksforbund [*Norway*]
NSR	Northern Sea Route (NATG)
NSR	North Staffordshire Railway [*British*] (ROG)
NSR	No Staff Responsibility [*Army*] (AABC)
NSR	Not Seen Regularly [*Medicine*] (DAVI)
NSR	Nova Scotia Provincial Library [*UTLAS symbol*]
NSR	Nova Scotia Regiment [*Canada*] (DMA)
NSR	NSR Resources, Inc. [*Toronto Stock Exchange symbol*]
NSR	Nuclear Spin Relaxation [*Physics*]
NSR	Nuclear Structure References [*Brookhaven National Laboratory*] [*Information service or system*]
NSR	Nutrient Supply Rate [*Oceanography*]
NSRA	National Scooter Riders Association [*British*] (DBA)
NSRA	National Service Robot Association (EA)
NSRA	National Shoe Retailers Association (EA)
NSRA	National Shorthand Reporters Association (EA)
NSRA	National Ski Retailers Association (EA)
NSRA	National Smallbore Rifle Association [*British*]
NSRA	National Society for Research into Allergy [*British*]
NSRA	National Street Rod Association (EA)
NSRA	National Swim and Recreation Association (EA)
NSRA	Nuclear Safety Research Association [*See also GAKK*] [*Japan*] (NRCH)
NSRB	National Security Resources Board [*Functions transferred to ODM, 1953*]
NSRB	Nuclear Safety Review Board (NRCH)
NSRBD	National Security Resources Board [*Functions transferred to ODM, 1953*] (GFGA)
NSRC	National Silver Rabbit Club (EA)
NSRC	National Stereophonic Radio Committee

NSRC	NeoSynthesis Research Centre [*Sri Lanka*] (EAIO)
NSRC	North Stratford Railroad Corp. [*AAR code*]
NSR Coch	Cochran's Nova Scotia Reports [*1859*] [*A publication*] (DLA)
NSR Coh	Cohen's Nova Scotia Reports [*A publication*] (DLA)
NSRD	National Security Resources Development
NSRDB	National SIGINT [*Signal Intelligence*] Requirements Database (MCD)
NSRDC	National Standards Reference Data Center
NSRDC	Naval Ship Research and Development Center [*Also, DTNSRDC*]
NSRDC	[*David W. Taylor*] Naval Ship Research and Development Center (AAGC)
NSRDC/A	Naval Ship Research and Development Center, Annapolis [*Maryland*] Division (DNAB)
NSRDC(AD)...	Naval Ship Research and Development Center (Annapolis Division)
NSRDCANNADIV...	Naval Ship Research and Development Center, Annapolis [*Maryland*] Division (DNAB)
NSRDF	Naval Supply Research and Development Facility
NSRDL	Naval Ship Research and Development Laboratory (MCD)
NSRDL/A	Naval Ship Research and Development Laboratory, Annapolis [*Maryland*]
NSRDL/PC ...	Naval Ship Research and Development Laboratory, Panama City [*Florida*] [*Later, NCSC*]
NSRDS	National Standard Reference Data System [*Gaithersburg, MD*] [*National Institute of Standards and Technology*]
NSREC	National Society's Religious Education Centre (AIE)
NSREF	National Society for Real Estate Finance [*Washington, DC*] (EA)
NS Rev Stat...	Nova Scotia Revised Statutes [*Canada*] [*A publication*] (DLA)
NSRF	National Stroke Recovery Foundation (EA)
NSRF	Naval Ship Repair Facility (MCD)
NSRF	Naval Strategic Reserve Fleet
NSRFC	Nova Scotia Research Foundation Corp. [*Crown Corp.*] [*Canada*] (IRC)
NSRG & O ...	Nova Scotia Reports, by Geldert and Oxley [*A publication*] (DLA)
NSRG & R ...	Nova Scotia Reports, by Geldert and Russell [*A publication*] (DLA)
NSRJ	Nova Scotia Reports (James) [*A publication*] (DLA)
NSR (James)...	Nova Scotia Reports (James) [*Canada*] [*A publication*] (DLA)
NSRL	National SIGINT [*Signal Intelligence*] Requirements List (MCD)
NSRL	Nuclear Structure Research Laboratory (NRCH)
NSRM	National Strategy for Rangeland Management [*Australia*]
NSRMCA	National Star Route Mail Contractors Association (EA)
NSRMP	Net Survival Rate for Monocyclic Process
NSRN	National School Resource Network [*Defunct*] (EA)
NSRO	Navy Resale System Office (PDAA)
NSR Old	Oldright's Nova Scotia Reports [*A publication*] (DLA)
NSRP	National Search and Rescue Plan
NSRP	National States Rights Party (EA)
NSRP	Neutral Seat Reference Point (MCD)
NSRP	Nonstandard Part Request
NSRP	Nontechnical Support Real Property
NSRP	Nordic Society for Radiation Protection [*See also NSFS*] [*Helsinki, Finland*] (EAIO)
NSRPr	NorfolkSo'nRy$2.60cmPfd [*NYSE symbol*] (TTSB)
NSR PSU	Non Self-Representing Primary Sampling Unit [*Bureau of the Census*] (GFGA)
NSRQCE	National Symposium on Reliability and Quality Control in Electronics (MCD)
NSRR	Normal Sinus Rate and Rhythm [*Cardiology*] (DAVI)
NSRR	Nuclear Safety Research Reactors (NRCH)
NSRR & C ...	Russell and Chesley's Nova Scotia Reports [*10-12 Nova Scotia Reports*] [*1875-79*] [*A publication*] (DLA)
NSRR & G ...	Russell and Geldert's Nova Scotia Reports [*A publication*] (DLA)
NSRS	National Scholarship Research Service [*Information service or system*] (IID)
NSRS	National Shoreline Refuse Survey [*British*]
NSRS	National Spatial Reference System (USDC)
NSRS	National Spatial Reference System [*Marine science*] (OSRA)
NSRS	National Supply Radio Station (MCD)
NSRS	Naval Supply Radio Station
NSRT	Near-Surface Radiation Thermometer
NSRT	Near Surface Reference Temperature [*Oceanography*]
NSRT	North South Roundtable (EAIO)
NSR Thom...	Thomson's Nova Scotia Reports [*A publication*] (DLA)
NSRU	North Star Universal [*NASDAQ symbol*] (TTSB)
NSRU	North Star Universal, Inc. [*NASDAQ symbol*] (NQ)
NSrU	Ulster County Community College, Stone Ridge, NY [*Library symbol Library of Congress*] (LCLS)
NSRW	Nuclear Service Raw Water (IEEE)
NSR Wall....	Wallace's Nova Scotia Reports [*6 Nova Scotia Reports*] [*1884-1907*] [*A publication*] (DLA)
NSRWP	Nuclear Service Raw Water Pump [*Electronics*] (IAA)
NSRy	Norfolk Southern Railway Co. [*Associated Press*] (SAG)
NSS	National Sample Survey (PDAA)
NSS	National Sculpture Society (EA)
NSS	National Search and Rescue Secretariat [*Canada*] (DA)
NSS	National Secular Society [*British*] (DBA)
NSS	National Seismic Stations
NSS	National Serigraph Society [*Defunct*]
NSS	National Secretariat
NSS	National Slovak Society of the USA
NSS	National Snapdragon Society (EA)
NSS	National Space Society (EA)
NSS	National Space Station [*NASA*] (IAA)
NSS	National Speleological Society (EA)
NSS	National Staff Side [*British*]
NSS	National Stockpile Site
NSS	National Study Service [*Defunct*] (EA)

NSS .... National Supply System (MCD)
NS/S .... Native Seeds/SEARCH [Southwestern Endangered Arid-Land Resource Clearing House] (EA)
NSS .... Naval Sea Systems Command, Washington, DC [OCLC symbol] (OCLC)
NSS .... Naval Security Station (NVT)
NSS .... Naval Simulation System [DoD]
NSS .... Naval Strategic Study
NSS .... Navigation Subsystem Switchboard
NSS .... Navy Secondary Standards (MSA)
NSS .... Navy Shore Station (IAA)
NSS .... Navy Standard Score (DNAB)
NSS .... Navy Strategic Study
NSS .... Navy Supply System
NSS .... Network Supervisor System
NSS .... Network Support System [Computer science]
NSS .... Network Synchronization Subsystem [Telecommunications] (TEL)
NSS .... Neurological Soft Signs [Occupational therapy]
NSS .... Neuropathy Symptom Score
NSS .... Neutral Safety Switch [Automotive engineering]
NSS .... Neutral Speed Stability (PDAA)
NSS .... Neutron Scattering Society
NSS .... Neutron Spectrometer System
NSS .... [The] Newburgh & South Shore Railway Co. [AAR code]
NSS .... New Statesman and Society [A publication]
NSS .... Nitrogen Supply Subsystem
NSS .... Nitrogen Supply System [or Subsystem] (AAG)
NSS .... NMIC [National Military Information Center] Support System (MCD)
NSS .... Nodding Subdish System
NSS .... Noise Suppressor System (MCD)
NSS .... Non-Salt Sensitive
NSS .... Non-Sea Salt
NSS .... Non-Self-Sustaining [Container ship] (MCD)
NSS .... Nonstandard Facilities Setup [Computer science]
NSS .... Nordiska Kommitten for Samordning av Elektriska Sakerhetsfragor [Nordic Committee for Coordination of Electrical Safety Matters] (EAIO)
NSS .... Nordiska Statistiska Sekretariatet [Nordic Statistical Secretariat] (EAIO)
NSS .... Normal Saline Solution
NSS .... Northstar Aviation, Inc. [ICAO designator] (FAAC)
NSS .... Northwest Steam Society (EA)
NSS .... Nortronics System Support
NSSLHA .... Not Statistically Significant (MAE)
NSS .... NS Group [NYSE symbol] (SPSG)
NSS .... Nuclear Science Symposium (PDAA)
NSS .... Nuclear Steam System (NRCH)
NSSA .... National Sanitary Supply Association [Later, ISSA] (EA)
NSSA .... National Scholastic Surfing Association (EA)
NSSA .... National Science Supervisors Association (EA)
NSSA .... National Senior Sports Association (EA)
NSSA .... National Sjogren's Syndrome Association (EA)
NSSA .... National Skeet Shooting Association (EA)
NSSA .... National Sportscasters and Sportswriters Association (EA)
NSSA .... National Suffolk Sheep Association (EA)
NSSA .... National Sunday School Association [Defunct] (EA)
NSSA .... National Swim School Association (EA)
NSSA .... Navy Space Systems Activity [Los Angeles, CA] (MCD)
NSSA .... Nematological Society of Southern Africa (EAIO)
NSSA .... New York Skirt and Sportswear Association (EA)
N-SSA .... North-South Skirmish Association (EA)
NSSA .... Nova Scotia Society of Artists [1922-72] [Canada] (NGC)
NSSAB .... National Selective Service Appeal Board [of SSS] [Inactive since 1975]
NSSAC .... National Society, Sons of the American Colonists [Defunct] (EA)
NSSB .... National Society of Scabbard and Blade (EA)
NSSB .... Norwich Financial [NASDAQ symbol] (TTSB)
NSSB .... Norwich Financial Corp. [NASDAQ symbol] (NQ)
NSSC .... Cape Breton Regional Library, Sydney, Nova Scotia [Library symbol National Library of Canada] (NLC)
NSSC .... Napco Security Sys [NASDAQ symbol] (TTSB)
NSSC .... Napco Security Systems, Inc. [NASDAQ symbol] (NQ)
NSSC .... NASA Safety Standards Committee
NSSC .... National Society for the Study of Communication [Later, ICA] (EA)
NSSC .... National Soil Survey Committee [Canada]
NSSC .... National Space Science Center [British]
NSSC .... Naval Sea [formerly, Ship] Systems Command
NSSC .... Neutral Sulfite Semichemical [Pulp]
NSSCB .... Cape Breton Post, Sydney, Nova Scotia [Library symbol National Library of Canada] (NLC)
NSSCBD ...... Cape Breton Development Corp., Sydney, Nova Scotia [Library symbol National Library of Canada] (NLC)
NSSCBH ...... Cape Breton Hospital, Sydney, Nova Scotia [Library symbol National Library of Canada] (NLC)
NSSCC .... National Space Surveillance Control Center
NSSCDS .... Naval Small Ship Combat Data System (SAA)
NSSCG .... Canadian Coast Guard College [College de la Garde Cotiere Canadienne] Sydney, Nova Scotia [Library symbol National Library of Canada] (NLC)
NSSCM .... Shelburne County Museum, Nova Scotia [Library symbol National Library of Canada] (NLC)
NSSCO .... Coast Guard, Shelburne, Nova Scotia [Library symbol National Library of Canada] (NLC)
NSSD .... National Strategy for Sustainable Development [Australia]
NSSDC .... National Space Science Data Center [Greenbelt, MD] [NASA] (MCD)

NSSDP .... National Society of Sons and Daughters of the Pilgrims (EA)
NSsE .... Empire State College, Saratoga Springs, NY [Library symbol Library of Congress] (LCLS)
NSSE .... National Society for the Study of Education (EA)
NSSE .... National Study of School Evaluation (EA)
NSSEA .... National School Supply and Equipment Association (EA)
NSSEB .... Non-Social Security Equivalent Benefit
NSSET .... National Symposium on Space Electronics and Telemetry [IEEE] (MCD)
NSSF .... National Shooting Sports Foundation (EA)
NSSF .... National Social Science Foundation [Proposed in 1966]
N/SSF .... Novice, Society of St. Francis
NSSFA .... National Single Service Food Association (EA)
NSSFC .... National Severe Storms Forecast Center [National Oceanic and Atmospheric Administration]
NSSFC .... National Society of Student Film Critics [Defunct] (EA)
NSSFFA ...... National Soft Serve and Fast Food Association (EA)
NSSFNS ...... National Scholarship Service and Fund for Negro Students (EA)
NSSG .... National Ski Study Group [Defunct]
NSSHA .... National Spotted Saddle Horse Association (EA)
NSSHA .... National Student Speech and Hearing Association [Later, NSSLHA] (EA)
NSSHCF ...... Canadian Forces Base Barrington, Stone Horse, Nova Scotia [Library symbol National Library of Canada] (NLC)
NSSHDC ...... National Spanish Speaking Housing Development Corp.
NSSHET ...... Newcomen Society for the Study of the History of Engineering and Technology [British] (EAIO)
NSSI .... Nuclear Support Services, Inc. [NASDAQ symbol] (NQ)
NS-SIB .... NAVSHIPS [Naval Ship Systems Command] Ship Information Booklets
NSSIC .... National Student Strike Information Center [Brandeis University]
NSSJD .... Community of the Nursing Sisters of St. John the Divine [Anglican religious community]
NSSK .... National Society of Student Keyboardists (EA)
NSSK .... North-South Station-Keeping (PDAA)
NSSL .... National Seed Storage Laboratory [Department of Agriculture] [Fort Collins, CO] (GRD)
NSSL .... National Service Star Legion (EA)
NSSL .... National Severe Storms Laboratory [National Oceanic and Atmospheric Administration] [Research center]
NSSL .... National Society of State Legislators [Later, NCSL]
NSSL .... National Survey of State Laws [A publication]
NSSLC .... National Social Science and Law Center (EA)
NSSLHA ...... National Student Speech Language Hearing Association (EA)
NSSLP .... National Social Science and Law Project (EA)
NSSM .... National Security Study Memorandum [Obsolete]
NSSM .... Navy Spread Spectrum MODEM (MCD)
NSSMM .... Memorial High School, Sydney Mines, Nova Scotia [Library symbol National Library of Canada] (NLC)
NSSMS .... NATO Sea Sparrow Missile System
NSSN .... National Speed Sport News [A publication]
NSSN .... National Standard Shipping Note (DS)
NSSN .... National Standards Systems Network
NSSNF .... Naval Strategic Systems Navigation Facility
NSSO .... National Society of Student Organists [Later, NSSK] (EA)
NSSO .... National Solar Space Observatory [NASA]
NSSO .... Navy Ships' Store Office [PX]
NSSP .... National Severe Storms Project [National Oceanic and Atmospheric Administration]
NSSP .... National Shellfish Sanitation Program [Food and Drug Administration] (GFGA)
NSSP .... National Syrian Socialist Party [Lebanon] [Political party]
NSSP .... Nava Sama Samaja Party [New Equal Society Party] [Sri Lanka] [Political party] (PPW)
NSSP .... Neutralization Self-Solidification Process (PDAA)
NSSP .... Nonreporting Secondary Stock Point (AFIT)
NSSP .... Normal Size, Shape, and Position [On examination] [Anatomy] (DAVI)
NSSPAVAF... Normal Size, Shape, and Position Anteverted, and Anteflexed [Uterus] [On examination] [Gynecology] (DAVI)
NSSR .... National Spotted Swine Record (EA)
NSSR .... New School for Social Research [New York, NY]
NSSR .... Nordic Society of Space Research
NSSR .... Record, Springhill, Nova Scotia [Library symbol National Library of Canada] (NLC)
NSSRI .... Nervous System Sports-Related Injury [Medicine]
NSSRM .... Soluth Rawdon Museum, Nova Scotia [Library symbol National Library of Canada] (NLC)
NSSS .... National Sewage Sludge Survey [Environmental Protection Agency]
NSSS .... National Space Surveillance System
NSSS .... Nuclear Steam Supply System [Vendor] (NRCH)
NSsS .... Skidmore College, Saratoga Springs, NY [Library symbol Library of Congress] (LCLS)
NSsSA .... Southern Adirondack Library System, Saratoga Springs, NY [Library symbol Library of Congress] (LCLS)
NSsSC .... Supreme Court Library at Saratoga Springs, Saratoga Springs, NY [Library symbol Library of Congress] (LCLS)
NSSSE .... National Study of Secondary School Evaluation [Later, NSSE] (EA)
NSSSRH ...... St. Rita's Hospital, Sydney, Nova Scotia [Library symbol National Library of Canada] (NLC)
NSSSS .... Nuclear Steam Supply Shutoff System (NRCH)
NSST .... Nonspecific ST Segment Changes [On electroencephalogram] [Cardiology] (DAVI)
NSST .... Northwestern Syntax Screening Test [Education]
NSSTA .... National Structured Settlements Trade Association (EA)

NS Stat........ Nova Scotia Statutes [*Canada*] [*A publication*] (DLA)
NSSTC .... National Small Shipments Traffic Conference (EA)
NSSTE .... National Society of Sales Training Executives [*Orlando, FL*] (EA)
NSSTT .... Nonspecific ST and T [*Wave on electrocardiogram*] [*Cardiology*] (DAVI)
NSSU .... National Steam Service Union [*British*]
NSSU .... National Sunday School Union [*British*]
NSSUP........ National Society of the Sons of Utah Pioneers (EA)
NSSX .... National Sanitary Supply Co. [*NASDAQ symbol*] (NQ)
NSSX .... Natl Sanitary Supply [*NASDAQ symbol*] (TTSB)
NSSX .... University College of Cape Breton, Sydney, Nova Scotia [*Library symbol National Library of Canada*] (NLC)
NSSXA .... Archives and General Library, College of Cape Breton, Sydney, Nova Scotia [*Library symbol National Library of Canada*] (NLC)
NSSY .... Norwalk Savings Society [*NASDAQ symbol*] (SAG)
NSSYA .... National Small Sailing Yacht Association (EA)
NST............. Aviacion Ejecutiva del Noroeste SA de CV [*Mexico ICAO designator*] (FAAC)
NST............. Nasty (ABBR)
NST............. National Skills Training
NST............. National Standard Taper (IAA)
NST............. National Symposium on Telemetering (MCD)
NST............. Navy Shipboard Terminal
NST............. Navy Standard Teleprinter (DOMA)
NST............. Nest (ABBR)
NST............. Nesting Module (MCD)
NST............. Network Support Team [*NASA*] (KSC)
NST............. Newfoundland Standard Time [*Aviation*] (AIA)
NST............. New Serial Titles [*A publication of Library of Congress*]
NST............. New Serial Titles, Library of Congress, Washington, DC [*OCLC symbol*] (OCLC)
NST............. Noise Source Tube
NST............. Noise, Spikes, and Transients (PDAA)
NST............. Nonshivering Thermogenesis [*Physiology*]
NST............. Nonslip Tread [*Technical drawings*]
NST............. Nonstress Test [*Gynecology*]
NST............. Normal Sphincter Tone [*Gastroenterology*] (DAVI)
NST............. North Solomon Trench [*Geoscience*]
NST............. Not Sooner Than
NST............. Nuclear and Space Talks (DOMA)
NST............. Numerical Surveying Technique (PDAA)
NST............. Nutritional Support Team [*Dietetics*] (DAVI)
NSTA .... Anesta Corp. [*NASDAQ symbol*] (SAG)
NSTA .... National Safe Transit Association (EA)
NSTA .... National School Transportation Association (EA)
NSTA .... National Science Teachers Association (EA)
NSTA .... National Security Traders Association [*Later, STA*] (EA)
NSTA .... National Shoe Traveler's Association (EA)
NSTA .... National Spasmodic Torticollis Association (EA)
NSTA .... National Squash Tennis Association (EA)
NSTA .... Nova Scotia Agricultural College, Truro, Nova Scotia [*Library symbol National Library of Canada*] (NLC)
NS-TAB .... NAVSHIPS [*Naval Ship Systems Command*] Training Aid Bulletins
NSTAC .... National Security Telecommunications Advisory Committee (NITA)
NSTAF .... National Solar Technical Audience File [*Solar Energy Research Institute*] [*Database*]
NSTAG .... National Science and Technology Advisory Group [*Australia*]
NStand........ National Standard Co. [*Associated Press*] (SAG)
NSTAP .... National Strategic Targeting and Attack Policy (CINC)
NSTARS....... Navy Standard Tracking and Retrieval System (MCD)
NStarU......... North Star Universal, Inc. [*Associated Press*] (SAG)
NSTB .... Biblio-Tech Ltd., Three Fathom Harbor, Nova Scotia [*Library symbol National Library of Canada*] (NLC)
NSTB .... National Science and Technology Board [*Singapore*]
NSTB .... National Science & Technology Board [*Singapore*]
NStBU.......... St. Bonaventure University, St. Bonaventure, NY [*Library symbol Library of Congress*] (LCLS)
NSTC .... Colchester - East Hants Regional Library, Truro, Nova Scotia [*Library symbol National Library of Canada*] (NLC)
NSTC .... National Science and Technology Council [*Formerly, FCCSET*]
NSTC .... National Security Training Commission [*Expired, 1957*]
NSTC .... National Shade Tree Conference [*Later, ISA*]
NSTC .... National Spiritualist Teachers Club (EA)
NSTC .... Nineteenth Century Short Title Catalogue [*Avero Publications Ltd.*] [*Information service or system British*] (CRD)
NSTC .... Nonsmokers' Travel Club [*Defunct*] (EA)
NSTC .... Not Subject to Call (MHDB)
NSTC .... Nova Scotia Teachers College [*Canada*]
NSTC .... Nova Scotia Technical College
NSTCH .... Colchester Historical Society, Truro, Nova Scotia [*Library symbol National Library of Canada*] (BIB)
NST-D .... Navy Standard Transmission [*Dension hydraulics*] (CAAL)
NSTD .... Nested [*Packaging*]
NSTD .... Non-System Training Devices [*USA*]
NSTDB .... National Strategic Target Data Base (CINC)
NSTDH .... National STD [*Sexually Transmitted Disease*] Hotline (EA)
NSTDN .... Daily News, Truro, Nova Scotia [*Library symbol National Library of Canada*] (NLC)
NSTDP .... National Society of Tole and Decorative Painters (EA)
N-STDS....... Navy Standards (AAGC)
NSTE .... National Society of Telephone Employees [*A union*] [*British*]
NSTEP .... National Spit Tobacco Education Program [*An initiative of Oral Health America*]
NSTEP .... Naval Scientist Training and Exchange Program (DNAB)

NSTF.......... Fraser Culture Centre, Tatamagouche, Nova Scotia [*Library symbol National Library of Canada*] (NLC)
NSTF.......... National Scholarship Trust Fund [*An affiliate of the Graphic Arts Technical Foundation*]
NSTF.......... Near Surface Test Facility [*Nuclear energy*] (NUCP)
NSTF.......... Neutron Sensor Testing Facility (IAA)
NSTF.......... Nuclear Science and Technology Facility [*State University of New York at Buffalo*] [*Research center*] (RCD)
NSTFI......... Nuveen Select Tax Free Income Portfolio [*Associated Press*] (SAG)
NSTFI2........ Nuveen Select Tax Free Income Portfolio 2 [*Associated Press*] (SAG)
NSTFI3........ Nuveen Select Tax Free Income Portfolio 3 [*Associated Press*] (SAG)
NSTG .... Nesting (ABBR)
NSTG .... Nuclear Strike Target Graphic (MCD)
NSTI........... NASCOM [*NASA Communications Network*] Simulation Traffic Interface (SSD)
NSTIC .... Naval Science and Technology Information Centre (NITA)
NSTIC .... Naval Scientific and Technical Information Centre [*Later, DRIC*] [*British*] (MCD)
NSTIC .... Navy Scientific and Technical Intelligence Center (IEEE)
NSTICLANT... Naval Scientific and Technical Intelligence Center, Atlantic (DNAB)
NSTICPAC.... Naval Scientific and Technical Intelligence Center, Pacific (DNAB)
NSTIM .... Islands Museum and Tourist Bureau, Tiverton, Nova Scotia [*Library symbol National Library of Canada*] (NLC)
NStj .... Margaret Reaney Memorial Library, St. Johnsville, NY [*Library symbol*] [*Library of Congress*] (LCLS)
NSTK .... Nastech Pharmaceutical [*NASDAQ symbol*] (TTSB)
NSTK .... Nastech Pharmaceuticals [*NASDAQ symbol*] (SAG)
NSTKW .... Nastech Pharmaceutical Wrrt [*NASDAQ symbol*] (TTSB)
NSTL .... National Software-Testing Laboratories [*Computer science*]
NSTL .... National Space Technology Laboratories [*Formerly, MTF*] [*Mississippi*] [*NASA*]
NSTL .... National Strategic Target Line [*or List*] (AFM)
NSTL .... Nestled (ABBR)
NSTL .... Nuclear Services and Training Laboratory [*Ohio State University*] [*Research center*] (RCD)
NSTLG .... Nestling (ABBR)
NSTLG .... Nostalgia (ABBR)
NSTLGC .... Nostalgic (ABBR)
NSTM.......... National School Transportation Management
NSTM.......... Navy Ship Technical Manual (CAAL)
NSTM.......... Navy Standard Test Model (CAAL)
NSTM.......... Nordiska Skeppstekniska Mote [*Joint Committee of Nordic Marine Technology - JCNMT*] (EAIO)
NS-TMI .... NAVSHIPS [*Naval Ship Systems Command*] Technical Manual Index
NSTN .... Nonstandard Telephone Number [*Telecommunications*] (TEL)
NSTN .... [*The*] Nova Scotia Technology Network [*Canada*] [*Computer science*] (TNIG)
NSTNS .... Nastiness (ABBR)
NSTO .... New System Training Office [*Army*]
NSTO .... Non Statutory Training Organisation [*British*]
NSTOA .... National Ski Touring Operators' Association (EA)
NSTP .... National Society of TV Producers (NTCM)
NSTP .... Nuffield Service Teaching Project
NSTPS .... Law Library, Patterson, Smith, Mathews & Grant, Truro, Nova Scotia [*Library symbol National Library of Canada*] (NLC)
NSTR .... Naval Sea Systems Command Technical Representative
NSTR .... Northstar Health Services, Inc. [*NASDAQ symbol*] (SAG)
NSTR .... Record, Truro, Nova Scotia [*Library symbol National Library of Canada*] (NLC)
NSTRE .... Northstar Health Svcs [*NASDAQ symbol*] (TTSB)
NSTS .... National Sea Training Schools [*British*]
NSTS .... National Securities Trading System
NSTS .... National Space Transportation System
NSTS .... National Student Traffic Safety Program [*National Commission on Safety Education*] [*Washington, DC*] (AEBS)
NSTS .... Navy Stockpile to Target Sequence
NSTS .... NCC [*Navy Command Center*] Security Test System
NSTSPO....... National Space Transportation System Program Office (SSD)
NSTT.......... National Sea Training Trusts [*British*] (DS)
NSTT.......... Naval Strategy Think Tank (DOMA)
NSTT.......... Nova Scotia Teachers' College, Truro, Nova Scotia [*Library symbol National Library of Canada*] (NLC)
NSTTF......... National Solar Thermal Test Facility [*Sandia National Laboratories*]
NSTU.......... Pago Pago/International, Tutuila Island [*American Samoa*] [*ICAO location identifier*] (ICLI)
NST-V .... Navy Standard Transmission [*Vickers hydraulics*] (CAAL)
NSTW .... National Science and Technology Week [*An annual outreach program begun in 1985 by the National Science Foundation*]
NSTX .... National Spherical Torus Experiment [*Plasma physics*]
NSTY .... Nastily (ABBR)
NSU .... Naval Scout Unit
NSU .... Neckarsulm [*Location in Wuerttemberg, Germany, of NSU Werke, automobile manufacturer; initialism used as name of its cars*]
NSU .... Neighborhood Stabilization Unit (LAIN)
NSU .... Network Service Unit (NITA)
NSU .... Nitrogen Supply Unit (AAG)
NSU .... Nonspecific Urethritis [*Medicine*]
NSU .... North Stansbury [*Utah*] [*Seismograph station code, US Geological Survey*] (SEIS)
NSU .... Nuova Sinistra Unita [*New United Left*] [*Italy Political party*] (PPE)
NSUA .... Nigerian Students Union in the Americas (EA)
NSuf............ Suffern Free Library, Suffern, NY [*Library symbol Library of Congress*] (LCLS)

NSufA .... Avon Products, Inc., Suffern, NY [*Library symbol Library of Congress*] (LCLS)
NSufR .... Rockland Community College, Suffern, NY [*Library symbol Library of Congress*] (LCLS)
NSUK .... Nichiren Shoshu of the UK [*Buddhist organization*] (DI)
NSUP .... Naval Supply Systems Command Headquarters
NSUPSC ...... Naval Supply Systems Command [*Formerly, Bureau of Supplies and Accounts*] (MCD)
NSURG .... Neurosurgery [*Medicine*]
NSUS .... Newcomen Society of the United States (EA)
NSv .... Finkelstein Memorial Library, Spring Valley, NY [*Library symbol Library of Congress*] (LCLS)
NSV .... National Socialist Vanguard (EA)
NSV .... Negative Supply Voltage
NSV .... Net Sales Value (BUR)
NSV .... Netted Secure Voice [*Military*] (CAAL)
NSV .... Neurosecretory Vesicle [*Neuroanatomy*]
NSV .... Noise, Shock, and Vibration (PDAA)
NSV .... Nonautomatic Self-Verification [*Computer science*] (MDG)
NSV .... Nonspecific Vaginitis [*Medicine*]
NSV .... Nonspinning Vehicle
NSV .... Nova Scotia Savings & Loans Co. [*Toronto Stock Exchange symbol*]
NSV .... Nuclear Service Vessel
NSVA .... Navy Seabee Veterans of America (EA)
NSVA .... New South Wales Vigoro Association [*Australia*]
NSVC .... National Sisters Vocation Conference [*Later, NRVC*] (EA)
NSVD .... Normal Spontaneous Vaginal Delivery [*Obstetrics*] (DMAA)
NSVEA .... Natural-Source Vitamin E Association (EA)
NSVP .... National School Volunteer Program (EA)
NSVP .... National Student Volunteer Program [*Later, NCSL*] (EA)
NSVT .... Nonsustained Ventricular Tachycardia [*Medicine*] (CPH)
NSW .... Ansett Airlines of New South Wales [*Australia ICAO designator*] (FAAC)
NSW .... National Software Works
NSW .... Naval Special Warfare (NVT)
NSW .... NSP Status Word [*NASA*] (GFGA)
NSW .... NSP [*National Aeronautical and Space Administration Support Plan*] Status Word
NSWA .... Acadia University, Wolfville, Nova Scotia [*Library symbol National Library of Canada*] (NLC)
NSWA .... National Social Welfare Assembly [*Later, National Assembly of National Voluntary Health and Social Welfare Organizations*] (EA)
NSWA .... National Soft Wheat Association [*Later, MNF*] (EA)
NSWA .... National Stripper Well Association (EA)
NSWA .... North Shore Writers Alliance (EA)
NSW Adm .... New South Wales Reports, Admiralty [*A publication*] (DLA)
NSWAEM ...... New South Wales Assemblies' Evangelic Mission [*Australia*]
NSWAG .... Department of Geography, Acadia University, Wolfville, Nova Scotia [*Library symbol Obsolete National Library of Canada*] (NLC)
NSWAGTC .... New South Wales Association of Gifted and Talented Children [*Australia*]
NSWAHP ...... New South Wales Association of Health Professions [*Australia*]
NSWALC ...... New South Wales Adult Literacy Council [*Australia*]
NS Wales L .. New South Wales Law [*A publication*] (DLA)
NS Wales LR Eq .. New South Wales Law Reports, Equity [*A publication*] (DLA)
NSWAP .... National Socialist White American Party [*Political party*]
NSWAPA ...... New South Wales Amateur Pistol Association [*Australia*]
NSWAR .... New South Wales Arbitration Reports [*A publication*] (DLA)
NSWAS .... New South Wales Association of Sephardim [*Australia*]
NSWAWL ...... New South Wales Animal Welfare League [*Australia*]
NSWAWPA .... New South Wales Amateur Water Polo Association [*Australia*]
NSWB .... New South Wales Bushmen [*British military*] (DMA)
NSWBA .... New South Wales Bar Association [*Australia*]
NSWBA .... New South Wales Basketball Association [*Australia*]
NSWBA .... New South Wales Bridge Association [*Australia*]
NSWBAC ...... New South Wales Buying Advisory Center [*Australia*]
NSWBACE .... New South Wales Board of Adult and Community Education [*Australia*]
NSWBBA ...... New South Wales Bloodhorse Breeders' Association [*Australia*]
NSWBC .... Black Cultural Centre for Nova Scotia, Westphal [*Library symbol National Library of Canada*] (BIB)
NSWBCS ...... New South Wales Bookmakers' Cooperative Society [*Australia*]
NSWBGA ...... New South Wales Bowling Greenkeepers' Association [*Australia*]
NSWBIC .... New South Wales Banana Industry Committee [*Australia*]
NSWBJE ...... New South Wales Board of Jewish Education [*Australia*]
NSW Bktcy Cas ... New South Wales Reports, Bankruptcy Cases [*A publication*] (DLA)
NSWBL .... New South Wales Basketball League [*Australia*]
NSWBS .... New South Wales Board of Surveyors [*Australia*]
NSWBSA ...... New South Wales Board Sailing Association [*Australia*]
NSWC .... Naval Surface Warfare [*or Weapons*] Center [*Dahlgren, VA*]
NSWCA .... New South Wales Canoe Association [*Australia*]
NSWCA .... New South Wales Coal Association [*Australia*]
NSWCA .... New South Wales Council on the Aging [*Australia*]
NSW CAC Report ... New South Wales Corporate Affairs Commission. Report [*Australia A publication*]
NSWCAF .... Naval Surface Weapons Center Acoustic Facility (GRD)
NSWCC .... New South Wales Canine Council [*Australia*]
NSWCC .... New South Wales Council of Churches [*Australia*]
NSWCCFT .... New South Wales Council for Children's Films and Television [*Australia*]
NSWCCU ...... New South Wales Churches Cricket Union [*Australia*]
NSWC/DL ..... Naval Surface Weapons Center, Dahlgren Laboratory
NSWC Eq ..... New South Wales Law Reports, Equity [*A publication*] (DLA)

NSWCF .... New South Wales Cycling Federation [*Australia*]
NSWCFA ...... New South Wales Canning Fruitgrowers' Association [*Australia*]
NSWCFVI ..... New South Wales Chamber of Fruit and Vegetable Industries [*Australia*]
NSWCGA ...... New South Wales Cane Growers' Association [*Australia*]
NSWCGA ...... New South Wales Cherry Growers' Association [*Australia*]
NSWCGA ...... New South Wales Chicken Growers' Association [*Australia*]
NSWCGC ...... New South Wales Citrus Growers' Council [*Australia*]
NSWCHS ...... New South Wales Cooperative Housing Society [*Australia*]
NSWCMACA ... New South Wales Chinese Martial Arts and Cultural Association [*Australia*]
NSWCMC ...... New South Wales Chicken Meat Council [*Australia*]
NSWCMOA .... New South Wales Coal Mine Owners' Association [*Australia*]
NSWCOA ...... New South Wales Colliery Officials' Association [*Australia*]
NSWCOHO .... New South Wales Council of Heritage Organizations [*Australia*]
NSWCOTA .... New South Wales Council on the Aging [*Australia*]
NSWCPA ...... New South Wales Coal Proprietors' Association [*Australia*]
NSWCPC ...... New South Wales Child Protection Council [*Australia*]
NSWCRL ...... New South Wales Law Reports, Supreme Court [*A publication*] (DLA)
NSWCSA ...... New South Wales Churches Soccer Association [*Australia*]
NSWCSA ...... New South Wales Cold Storage Association [*Australia*]
NSWCTA ...... New South Wales Council of Tourist Associations [*Australia*]
NSWCUA ...... New South Wales Credit Unit Association [*Australia*]
NSWCUA ...... New South Wales Cricket Umpires' Association [*Australia*]
NSWCUEA .... New South Wales Credit Union Employers' Association [*Australia*]
NSWC/WOL ... Naval Surface Weapons Center, White Oak Laboratory
NSWCYMCA ... New South Wales Council of the Young Men's Christian Associations [*Australia*]
NSWDAA ...... New South Wales Domestic Abattoirs Association [*Australia*]
NSWDAA ...... New South Wales Drug and Alcohol Authority [*Australia*]
NSWDAHAC ... National Society Women Descendants of the Ancient and Honorable Artillery Company (EA)
NSWDBA ...... New South Wales Deer Breeders' Association [*Australia*]
NSW Dept Forestry Bull ... New South Wales. Department of Forestry. Bulletin [*Australia A publication*]
NSWDFA ...... New South Wales Dairy Farmers' Association [*Australia*]
NSWDFA ...... New South Wales Deer Farmers' Association [*Australia*]
NSWDFB ...... New South Wales Dried Fruits Board [*Australia*]
NSWDIC .... New South Wales Dairy Industry Conference [*Australia*]
NSWDPA ...... New South Wales Dairy Products Association [*Australia*]
NSWDSC ...... New South Wales Dam Safety Committee [*Australia*]
NSWDU .... New South Wales Debating Union [*Australia*]
NSWEEU ...... New South Wales Education Exports Unit [*Australia*]
NSWEK .... Eastern King's Memorial Hospital, Wolfville, Nova Scotia [*Library symbol National Library of Canada*] (NLC)
NSWEPC ...... New South Wales Egg Producers' Cooperative [*Australia*]
NSWEPOWA .. New South Wales Ex-Prisoners of War Association [*Australia*]
NSW Eq Rep ... New South Wales Law Reports, Equity [*A publication*] (DLA)
NSWETF .... New South Wales Education and Training Foundation [*Australia*]
NSWFA .... New South Wales Farmers' Association [*Australia*]
NSWFB .... New South Wales Fire Brigades [*Australia*]
NSWFBEU .... New South Wales Fire Brigade Employee's Union [*Australia*]
NSWFC .... New South Wales Fitness Council [*Australia*]
NSWFCHA .... New South Wales Farm and Country Holiday Association [*Australia*]
NSWFF .... New South Wales Folk Federation [*Australia*]
NSWFG .... New South Wales Furniture Guild [*Australia*]
NSWFGA ...... New South Wales Flower Growers' Association [*Australia*]
NSWFGHC .... New South Wales Free Growers' Horticultural Council [*Australia*]
NSWFHU ...... New South Wales Friends of the Hebrew University [*Australia*]
NSWFIA .... New South Wales Farmers' Industrial Association [*Australia*]
NSWFIC .... New South Wales Fishing Industry Council [*Australia*]
NSWFITC ..... New South Wales Food Industry Training Council [*Australia*]
NSWFITC ..... New South Wales Furniture Industry Training Council [*Australia*]
NSWFMC ...... New South Wales Flour Millers' Council [*Australia*]
NSWFPA ...... New South Wales Forest Products Association [*Australia*]
NSWFPCA .... New South Wales Federation of Parents and Citizens' Associations [*Australia*]
NSWFS .... New South Wales Fabian Society [*Australia*]
NSWFTO ...... New South Wales Film and Television Office [*Australia*]
NSWG .... Naval Special Warfare Group (NVT)
NSWG .... North Sea Working Group [*Advisory Committee on Pollution of the Sea*]
NSWG .... Nuclear Safety Working Group (CINC)
NSWGA .... New South Wales Golf Association [*Australia*]
NSWGB .... New South Wales Grains Board [*Australia*]
NSWGBOTA ... New South Wales Greyhound Breeders, Owners and Trainers Association [*Australia*]
NSWGC .... New South Wales Gun Club [*Australia*]
NSWGCB ...... New South Wales Guild of Craft Bookbinders [*Australia*]
NSWGCHS ... New South Wales Group of Cooperative Housing Societies [*Australia*]
NSWGCSUA ... New South Wales Glass and Ceramic Silica Users' Association [*Australia*]
NSW Geol Survey Mineral Resour ... New South Wales. Geological Survey. Mineral Resources [*Australia A publication*]
NSWGFL ...... New South Wales Gridiron Football League [*Australia*]
NSWGFM ...... New South Wales Guild of Furniture Manufacturers [*Australia*]
NSWGIS .... New South Wales Government Information Service [*Australia*]
NSWGMA ...... New South Wales Girls' Marching Association [*Australia*]
NSWGMA ...... New South Wales Glass Merchants' Association [*Australia*]
NSWGTC ...... New South Wales Government Travel Center [*Australia*]
NSWH .... Wolfville Historical Museum, Nova Scotia [*Library symbol National Library of Canada*] (NLC)
NSWHA .... New South Wales Hockey Association [*Australia*]
NSWHCA ...... New South Wales Homeless Children's Association [*Australia*]

NSWHEA..... New South Wales Horticultural Exporters' Association [Australia]
NSWHGA .... New South Wales Hospital Group Apprentices Scheme [Australia]
NSWHJ........ Hants Journal, Windsor, Nova Scotia [Library symbol National Library of Canada] (NLC)
NSWHPAC ... New South Wales Hospitals Planning Advisory Center [Australia]
NSWHRA ..... New South Wales Hot Rod Association [Australia]
NSWHS........ New South Wales Humanist Society [Australia]
NSWHTA...... New South Wales Hardcourt Tennis Association [Australia]
NSWI .... National Safe Workplace Institute (EA)
NSWICCA..... New South Wales Indo-China Chinese Association
NSWID........ New South Wales Institute of Dieticians [Australia]
NSWIG........ New South Wales Industrial Gazette [Australia A publication]
NSW Inc Acts... New South Wales Incorporated Acts [A publication] (DLA)
NSW Ind Arbtn... New South Wales Industrial Arbitration Cases [A publication] (DLA)
NSW Ind Arbtn Cas... New South Wales Industrial Arbitration Cases [A publication] (DLA)
NSW Indus Arb R... New South Wales Industrial Arbitration Reports [A publication] (DLA)
NSWIP........ New South Wales Institute of Physiotherapy [Australia]
NSWIP........ New South Wales Institute of Psychotherapy [Australia]
NSWJB .... New South Wales Judgements Bulletin [Australia A publication]
NSWJBD...... New South Wales Jewish Board of Deputies [Australia]
NSWJCU ..... New South Wales Junior Cricket Union [Australia]
NSWJHS ..... New South Wales Jersey Herd Society [Australia]
NSWJT........ Materials Laboratory Library, Nova Scotia Department of Transportation, Windsor Junction, Nova Scotia [Library symbol National Library of Canada] (NLC)
NSWJWM .... New South Wales Jewish War Memorial [Australia]
NSWKE .... King's-Edgehill School, Windsor, Nova Scotia [Library symbol National Library of Canada] (NLC)
NSWL .... New South Wales Lotteries [Australia]
NSW Land App... New South Wales Land Appeal Court Cases [A publication] (DLA)
NSW Land App Cts... New South Wales Land Appeal Courts (DLA)
NSW Law Repts... New South Wales Law Reports [A publication]
NSWLC .... New South Wales Leagues Club [Australia]
NSWLHPB.... New South Wales Ladies Highland Pipe Band [Australia]
NSW Local Gov't R... New South Wales Local Government Reports [A publication] (DLA)
NSWLRC ..... New South Wales Law Reform Commission [Australia] (ILCA)
NSWLSEA ... New South Wales Live Stock Exporters' Association [Australia]
NSWMA...... National Soft Wheat Millers Association [Later, MNF] (EA)
NSWMA...... National Solid Wastes Management Association (EA)
NSWMA...... New South Wales Marching Association [Australia]
NSWMA...... New South Wales Midwives' Association [Australia]
NSWMB...... New South Wales Medical Board [Australia]
NSWMEA .... New South Wales Meat Exporters' Association [Australia]
NSWMEQB... New South Wales Migrant Employment and Qualifications Board [Australia]
NSWMH...... New South Wales Masonic Hospital [Australia]
NSWMIA ..... West Hants Meat Industry Authority [Australia]
NSWNA....... New South Wales Netball Association [Australia]
NSWNCA..... New South Wales National Coursing Association [Australia]
NSWNGA .... New South Wales Nut Growers' Association [Australia]
NSWNPWS... New South Wales National Parks and Wildlife Service [Australia]
NSWNRB ..... New South Wales Nurses' Registration Board [Australia]
NSWO......... Nuclear Surface Warfare Officer [Navy] (DOMA)
NSWODA ..... New South Wales Oyster Distributors' Association [Australia]
NSWOTA ..... New South Wales Occupational Therapy Association [Australia]
NSWOTA ..... New South Wales Operating Theatre Association [Australia]
NSWOTA ..... New South Wales Organic Traders' Association [Australia]
NSWP .... Non-Soviet Warsaw Pact (NATG)
NSWPA........ New South Wales Poker Association [Australia]
NSWPA........ New South Wales Polo Association [Australia]
NSWPACC... New South Wales Police Aero Club Company [Australia]
NSWPBA...... New South Wales Pipe Band Association [Australia]
NSWPC....... New South Wales Parachute Council [Australia]
NSWPC....... New South Wales Parents' Council [Australia]
NSWPC....... New South Wales Prices Commission [Australia]
NSWPEA ..... New South Wales Physical Education Association [Australia]
NSWPGA..... New South Wales Professional Golfers' Association [Australia]
NSWPL....... National New South Wales Police Legacy [Australia]
NSWPMOA... New South Wales Public Medical Officers' Association [Australia]
NSWPOA..... New South Wales Property Owners' Association [Australia]
NSWPP........ National Socialist White People's Party [Formerly, American NAZI Party] (EA)
NSWPP........ New South Wales Parliamentary Papers [A publication]
NSWPR........ Newspaper
NSW Priv Com Papers... New South Wales Privacy Committee. Papers [Australia A publication]
NSWPSPOA... New South Wales Public Service Professional Officers' Association [Australia]
NSW Pub Acts... New South Wales Public Acts [A publication] (DLA)
NSW Pub Stat... New South Wales Public Statutes [A publication] (DLA)
NSWRA........ New South Wales Rifle Association [Australia]
NSWRA........ New South Wales Rowing Association [Australia]
NSWRAA...... New South Wales Rural Assistance Authority [Australia]
NSW Railway & Tramway Mag... New South Wales Railway and Tramway Magazine [Australia A publication]
NSWRCSA ... New South Wales Registered Cereal Seedgrowers' Association [Australia]
NSWRFAC.... New South Wales Recreational Fishing Advisory Council [Australia]
NSWRFL...... New South Wales Rugby Football League [Australia]
NSWRFS...... New South Wales Rod Fishers' Society [Australia]

NSWRITC..... New South Wales Rural Industry Training Committee [Australia]
NSWRLIFA... New South Wales Rugby League Insurance Finance Agency [Australia]
NSWRTA ..... New South Wales Road Transport Association [Australia]
NSWRTEHF... New South Wales Railway and Transport Employees' Hospital Fund [Australia]
NSWRTLA.... New South Wales Right to Life Association [Australia]
NSWRTM ..... New South Wales Rail Transport Museum [Australia]
NSWRTTC .... New South Wales Road Transport Training Council [Australia]
NSWS .... National Surface Water Survey (GNE)
NSWS .... Nuclear Service Water System (NRCH)
NSWSA .... New South Wales Ski Association [Australia]
NSWSA .... New South Wales Softball Association [Australia]
NSWSA .... New South Wales Swimming Association [Australia]
NSWSACW... New South Wales Standing Advisory Committee on Wheat [Australia]
NSWSBA...... New South Wales Sheepbreeders' Association [Australia]
NSWSCC ..... New South Wales Society for Crippled Children [Australia]
NSWSCC ..... New South Wales State Cancer Committee [Australia]
NSWSCR...... New South Wales Supreme Court Reports [A publication] (DLA)
NSW S Ct Cas... New South Wales Supreme Court Cases [A publication] (DLA)
NSW S Ct R... New South Wales Supreme Court Reports [A publication] (DLA)
NSWSDA...... New South Wales Soft Drink Association [Australia]
NSWSES ..... Naval Ship Weapon Systems Engineering Station [Port Hueneme, CA]
NSWSF .... New South Wales Soccer Federation [Australia]
NSWSGA..... New South Wales Seed Growers' Association [Australia]
NSWSHS..... New South Wales School of Hypnotic Sciences [Australia]
NSWSJC ..... New South Wales Show Jumping Council [Australia]
NSWSK....... New South Wales Shorinjiryu Karate-do Association [Australia]
NSWSMBA... New South Wales Stud Merino Breeders' Association [Australia]
NSWSO....... New South Wales Superannuation Office [Australia]
NSWSRCTG... New South Wales Sales Representatives and Commercial Travellers' Guild [Australia]
NSWSS .... New South Wales Supply Service [Australia]
NSWSTC ..... New South Wales Science and Technology Council [Australia]
NSWSTM ..... New South Wales School of Therapeutic Massage [Australia]
NSWTA .... National Senior Women's Tennis Association (EA)
NSWTAFEC... New South Wales Technical and Further Education Commission [Australia]
NSWTC .... New South Wales Taxi Council [Australia]
NSWTC .... New South Wales Tourism Commission [Australia]
NSWTC .... New South Wales Travel Center [Australia]
NSWTEU ..... New South Wales Theatrical Employees' Union [Australia]
NSWTG .... Naval Special Warfare Task Group (CAAL)
NSWTITC ..... New South Wales Timber Industry Training Council [Australia]
NSWTLMB ... New South Wales Tobacco Leaf Marketing Board [Australia]
NSWU .... Naval Special Warfare Unit (DOMA)
NSWVRA...... New South Wales Video Retailers' Association [Australia]
NSWWA ...... New South Wales Wrestling Association [Australia]
NSWWA ...... North Shore Women Writers Alliance [Later, NSWA] (EA)
NSWWAC.... New South Wales Women's Advisory Council [Australia]
NSWWH....... West Hants Historical Society Museum, Windsor, Nova Scotia [Library symbol National Library of Canada] (NLC)
NSWWJA ..... New South Wales Women Justices' Association [Australia]
NSW Worker's Comp R... New South Wales Worker's Compensation Reports [A publication] (DLA)
NSWWP....... New South Wales Water Polo [Australia An association]
NSWWSA..... New South Wales Water Ski Association [Australia]
NSWWSBA... New South Wales Wool Selling Brokers' Association [Australia]
NSXB .... Neutron Star X-Ray Binary [Astrophysics]
NSY .... Naval Shipyard
NSY .... New Scotland Yard
NSY .... Noisy (ABBR)
NSY .... North Salopian Yeomanry [British military] (DMA)
NSY .... North Somerset Yeomanry [British military] (DMA)
NSY .... Nursery (DAVI)
NSy............. Onondaga County Public Library, Syracuse, NY [Library symbol Library of Congress] (LCLS)
NSY .... Western Counties Regional Library, Yarmouth, Nova Scotia [Library symbol National Library of Canada] (NLC)
NSyA........... Allied Corp., Solvay Process Division, Syracuse, NY [Library symbol Library of Congress] (LCLS)
NSYA .... National School Yearbook Association [Later, NSY/NA]
NSyAF.......... United States Air Force, Hancock Air Base Library, Syracuse, NY [Library symbol Library of Congress] (LCLS)
NSyAg.......... Agway, Inc., Syracuse, NY [Library symbol Library of Congress] (LCLS)
NSyBL........... Bristol Laboratories, Syracuse, NY [Library symbol Library of Congress] (LCLS)
NSyC........... Carrier Corp., Syracuse, NY [Library symbol Library of Congress] (LCLS)
NSYC .... Courrier de la Nouvelle-Ecosse, Yarmouth, Nova Scotia [Library symbol National Library of Canada] (NLC)
NSyCA .... United States Court of Appeals, Syracuse, NY [Library symbol Library of Congress] (LCLS)
NSYCDA....... Archives, Diocese of Yarmouth, Catholic Church, Nova Scotia [Library symbol National Library of Canada] (NLC)
NSyCH......... Crouse-Irving Hospital, Syracuse, NY [Library symbol Library of Congress] (LCLS)
NSYD .... Naval Shipyard
NSYDCN ...... Diocese of Central New York, Syracuse, NY [Library symbol Library of Congress] (LCLS)
NSyEd.......... Educational Opportunity Center, Syracuse, NY [Library symbol Library of Congress] (LCLS)
NSYF .... Natural Science for Youth Foundation (EA)

NSYFG .... Fundy Group Publications, Yarmouth, Nova Scotia [*Library symbol National Library of Canada*] (NLC)

NSyGE .... General Electric Co., Syracuse, NY [*Library symbol Library of Congress*] (LCLS)

NSyGH .... Community-General Hospital, Syracuse, NY [*Library symbol Library of Congress*] (LCLS)

NSYHM .... Research Library, Yarmouth County Historical Society, Yarmouth, Nova Scotia [*Library symbol National Library of Canada*] (NLC)

NSyL .... LeMoyne College, Syracuse, NY [*Library symbol Library of Congress*] (LCLS)

NSyLG .... Loretto Geriatric Center, Educational Resource Center, Syracuse, NY [*Library symbol Library of Congress*] (LCLS)

NSyMR .... Maria Regina College, Syracuse, NY [*Library symbol Library of Congress*] (LCLS)

NSyN .... City Normal School, Syracuse, NY [*Library symbol Library of Congress Obsolete*] (LCLS)

NSY/NA .... National School Yearbook/Newspaper Association [*Defunct*] (EA)

NSyo .... Syosset Public Library, Syosset, NY [*Library symbol Library of Congress*] (LCLS)

NSyOB .... Onondaga-Courtland-Madison Board of Cooperative Education Service, Syracuse, NY [*Library symbol*] [*Library of Congress*] (LCLS)

NSyoBaE ..... Baylis Elementary School, Syosset, NY [*Library symbol Library of Congress*] (LCLS)

NSyoBE .... Berry Hill Elementary School, Syosset, NY [*Library symbol Library of Congress*] (LCLS)

NSyOC .... Onondaga Community College, Syracuse, NY [*Library symbol Library of Congress*] (LCLS)

NSyoF .... Fairchild Space and Defense System, Syosset, NY [*Library symbol Library of Congress*] (LCLS)

NSyoG .... United States Geological Survey, Water Resources Division, Syosset, NY [*Library symbol Library of Congress*] (LCLS)

NSyoH .... Syosset Hospital, Syosset, NY [*Library symbol Library of Congress*] (LCLS)

NSyOHi .... Onondaga Historical Association, Syracuse, NY [*Library symbol Library of Congress*] (LCLS)

NSyOL .... Onondaga Library System, Syracuse, NY [*Library symbol Library of Congress*] (LCLS)

NSyoOL .... Our Lady of Mercy Academy, Syosset, NY [*Library symbol*] [*Library of Congress*] (LCLS)

NSyoP .... PRD Electronics, Inc., Information Center Library, Syosset, NY [*Library symbol Library of Congress*] (LCLS)

NSyoRE .... Robbins Elementary School, Syosset, NY [*Library symbol Library of Congress*] (LCLS)

NSyoSGE ..... South Grove Elementary School, Syosset, NY [*Library symbol Library of Congress*] (LCLS)

NSyoSH .... Syosset Senior High School, Syosset, NY [*Library symbol*] [*Library of Congress*] (LCLS)

NSyoSRE .... Split Rock Elementary School, Syosset, NY [*Library symbol Library of Congress*] (LCLS)

NSyoSwJ ..... South Woods Junior High School, Syosset, NY [*Library symbol*] [*Library of Congress*] (LCLS)

NSyoTJ .... Harry B. Thompson Junior High School, Syosset, NY [*Library symbol*] [*Library of Congress*] (LCLS)

NSyoVE .... Village Elementary School, Syosset, NY [*Library symbol Library of Congress*] (LCLS)

NSyoWE ...... Willits Elementary School, Syosset, NY [*Library symbol Library of Congress*] (LCLS)

NSyoWhE .... Whitman Elementary School, Syosset, NY [*Library symbol Library of Congress*] (LCLS)

NSYR .... Medical Library, Yarmouth Regional Hospital, Nova Scotia [*Library symbol National Library of Canada*] (BIB)

NSyR .... Syracuse Research Corp., Syracuse, NY [*Library symbol Library of Congress*] (LCLS)

NSyR .... Syracuse Research Corp., Syracuse, NY [*Library symbol*] [*Library of Congress*] (LCLS)

NSYS .... Nortech Systems [*NASDAQ symbol*] (TTSB)

NSYS .... Nortech Systems, Inc. [*NASDAQ symbol*] (SAG)

NSySC .... New York State Supreme Court Law Library, Syracuse, NY [*Library symbol Library of Congress*] (LCLS)

NSySC .... New York State Supreme Court Law Library, Syracuse, NY [*Library symbol*] [*Library of Congress*] (LCLS)

NSySJ .... Saint Joseph's Hospital, School of Nursing and Medical Library, Syracuse, NY [*Library symbol*] [*Library of Congress*] (LCLS)

NSySJ .... Saint Joseph's Hospital, School of Nursing and Medical Library, Syracuse, NY [*Library symbol Library of Congress*] (LCLS)

NSYSP .... National Summer Youth Sports Program

NSySU-F ..... State University of New York, College of Environmental Sciences and Forestry at Syracuse University, Syracuse, NY [*Library symbol Library of Congress*] (LCLS)

NSySU-M ..... State University of New York, Upstate Medical Center, Syracuse, NY [*Library symbol Library of Congress*] (LCLS)

NSyT .... Technology Club of Syracuse, Syracuse, NY [*Library symbol Library of Congress*] (LCLS)

NSyU .... Syracuse University, Syracuse, NY [*Library symbol Library of Congress*] (LCLS)

NSyU-CE ..... Syracuse University, Library of Continuing Education at Syracuse, NY [*Library symbol Library of Congress*] (LCLS)

NSyU-G .... Syracuse University, Educational Resources Center of the All-University Gerontology Center, Syracuse, NY [*Library symbol Library of Congress*] (LCLS)

NSyVA .... United States Veterans Administration Hospital, Syracuse, NY [*Library symbol Library of Congress*] (LCLS)

NSZP .... Nemzeti Szabadelvu Part [*National Liberal Party*] [*Hungary Political party*] (PPE)

NT .... Iraq-Saudi Arabia Neutral Zone [*ANSI two-letter standard code*] (CNC)

NT .... Lake State Airways [*ICAO designator*] (AD)

N-T .... Nal-Tel [*Race of maize*]

nT .... Nanotesla

NT .... Narrower Term [*Indexing*]

NT .... Naso-Tracheal [*Medicine*]

NT .... National Taranesc [*National Peasant Party*] [*Romania*] [*Political party*] (PPE)

N/T .... National Team

NT .... National Theatre [*Great Britain*]

NT .... National Trust for Historic Preservation

NT .... Natty (ABBR)

NT .... Naturalization Test

NT .... Naval Training

NT .... Navy Type (MSA)

NT .... Neap Tide

NT .... Near Term

NT .... Neat [*Plain*] [*Bookbinding*] (ROG)

NT .... Neonatal Tetanus

NT .... Neotetrazolium

NT .... Nephrostomy Tube [*Nephrology*] (DAVI)

NT .... Nested-Task [*Computer science*] (BYTE)

NT .... Net (WDAA)

NT .... Netilmicin-Ticarcillin [*Antibiotic combination*]

NT .... Nett [*Net*] [*British*] (ROG)

NT .... Net Tax [*IRS*]

N/t .... Net Terms [*Business term*] (DS)

NT .... Net Tons [*Shipping*]

NT .... Network Terminal (MCD)

NT .... Network Termination [*Telecommunications*]

NT .... Neural Tube [*Anatomy*]

NT .... Neurologically Typical [*Psychology*]

NT .... Neurotensin [*Biochemistry*]

NT .... Neurotoxin [*Biochemistry*]

NT .... Neurotrophin [*Neurobiology*]

NT .... Neuter (WGA)

NT .... Neutralization Test [*Chemistry*]

NT .... Neutralizing (MAE)

NT .... Neutron Transmitter [*Nuclear energy*] (NRCH)

NT .... Nevada Territory [*Prior to statehood*]

NT .... News/Talk [*Radio programming format*] (WDMC)

NT .... New Taiwan

NT .... New Technology [*Microsoft operating system*] [*Computer science*] (PCM)

N/T .... New Terms [*Business term*]

NT .... New Territories [*Hong Kong*]

NT .... New Thailand Dollar [*Monetary unit*]

nt .... Newton (NASA)

NT .... Newton

NT .... New Towns [*British*]

NT .... New Translation

Nt. .... Nicotiana tabacum [*Tobacco*]

NT .... Night (ROG)

NT .... Night Telegram

NT .... Night Trunk [*Business term*] (DCTA)

nt .... Nit [*Unit of luminance*]

NT .... Niton (ABBR)

NT .... Node Tracker [*Frye Computer Systems*] [*Telecommunications*] (PCM)

N/T .... None in Town [*Bookselling*]

N/T .... Nonmeasured Time

NT .... Non-T Cell [*Cytology*]

NT .... Nontender (DAVI)

NT .... Nontight (AAG)

NT .... Nontryptophan [*Protein-bound fluorescence*]

NT .... Nontypeable (MAE)

NT .... Nordiska Transportarbetarefederationen [*Nordic Transportworkers' Federation - NTF*] (EAIO)

NT .... Nordisk Traebeskyttelsesrad [*Nordic Wood Preservation Council - NWPC*] (EAIO)

NT .... Normalized and Tempered (MCD)

NT .... Normal Temperature (ADA)

NT .... Normal Tour

NT .... Northern Telecom Ltd. [*NYSE symbol*] (SPSG)

NT .... Northwest Territories [*Postal code*] [*Canada*]

NT .... Nortriptyline [*Antidepressant drug*]

NT .... Note [*Online database field identifier*]

N/T .... No Terms [*Shipping*]

NT .... No Test

NT .... No Tillage [*Agriculture*]

NT .... No Tool (SAA)

NT .... No Trace [*Counterintelligence*]

NT .... No Transmission [*Telecommunications*]

NT .... No Trump [*in game of bridge*]

NT .... Not Tender (DAVI)

NT .... Not Tested

NT .... Not Titled [*Accounting*]

NT .... Not Typical

NT .... Novum Testamentum [*New Testament*] [*of the Bible*]

NT .... Nuclear Transfer

NT .... Nucleotidase [*An enzyme*] (DAVI)

nt .... Nucleotide [*Genetics*] (DOG)

NT .... Nuisance Tax (MHDW)

NT .... Numbering Transmitter

NT................	Nurse Technician
NT................	Thermal Necrosis [*Roentgenology*]
NT................	Troy Public Library, Troy, NY [*Library symbol Library of Congress*] (LCLS)
NT-1............	Network Terminator Type 1 (PCM)
NTA............	Fujisawa Pharmaceutical Co. [*Japan*] [*Research code symbol*]
NTA............	Naphthoyltrifluoroacetone [*Organic chemistry*]
NTA............	Narcotics Treatment Administration [*Washington, DC*]
NTA............	National Tabletop Association (EA)
NTA............	National Tattoo Association (EA)
NTA............	National Tax Association [*Later, NTA-TIA*] (EA)
NTA............	National Taxidermists Association [*Defunct*] (EA)
NTA............	National Taxpayers Alliance (EA)
NTA............	National Teachers Association (AEE)
NTA............	National Technical Association (EA)
NTA............	National Telecommunications Agency
NTA............	National Telefilm Associates, Inc. (NTCM)
NTA............	National Tennis Academy [*Commercial firm*] (EA)
NTA............	National Tennis Association [*Later, IRJA*] (EA)
NTA............	National Threshers Association (EA)
NTA............	National Tour Association (EA)
NTA............	National Tourism Administration [*China*] (EY)
NTA............	National Tourist Association (NADA)
NTA............	National Translator Association (EA)
NTA............	National Trappers Association (EA)
NTA............	National Triton Association (EA)
NTA............	National Trolleybus Association [*British*]
NTA............	National Tuberculosis Association [*Later, American Lung Association*] (EA)
NTA............	National Type Approval (PDAA)
NTA............	Naval Technical Assistants
NTA............	Navy Technical Assessment (MCD)
NTA............	Navy Technician Authorization (NG)
NTA............	Near-Terminal Area [*Airports*]
NTA............	Neher Tetrode Amplifier
NTA............	Net Tangible Assets [*Business term*] (ADA)
NTA............	Net Technical Assessment (MCD)
NTA............	Nevada Test Site Array [*Nevada*] [*Seismograph station code, US Geological Survey*] (SEIS)
NTA............	New Towns Act [*Town planning*] [*British*]
NTA............	Nielsen Television Area (WDAA)
NTA............	Nitrilotriacetic Acid [*Organic chemistry*]
NTA............	Northern Textile Association (EA)
NTA............	Northern Thunderbird Air Ltd. [*Canada ICAO designator*] (FAAC)
NTA............	Northwest Territory Alliance (EA)
NTA............	Norwegian Telecommunications Administration [*or Agency*] [*Oslo*]
NTA............	Nuclear Test Aircraft
NTA............	Nurse Training Act
NTa............	Warner Library, Tarrytown, NY [*Library symbol Library of Congress*] (LCLS)
NTAA............	National Travelers Aid Association (EA)
NTAA............	Tahiti/FAAA [*French Polynesia*] [*ICAO location identifier*] (ICLI)
NTAB............	Nephrotoxic Antibody [*Medicine*] (MAE)
NTAB............	Northern Territory Architects' Board [*Australia*]
NTAB............	Notable (ABBR)
NTAB............	Nuclear Technical Advisory Board [*American National Standards Institute*]
NTABY............	Notably (ABBR)
NTAC............	National Technical Assistance Center on Family Violence [*Defunct*] (EA)
NTAC............	Naval Training Aids Center (DNAB)
NTAC............	New Technology Access Centre (AIE)
NTACF............	Northern Territory Anti-Cancer Foundation
NTACS............	Nationwide Truck Activity Survey [*BTS*] [*FHWA*] (TAG)
NTAF............	Naval Training Aids Facility (DNAB)
NTAG............	Network Technical Architecture Group [*Library of Congress*]
NTaGF............	General Foods Technical Center Library, Tarrytown, NY [*Library symbol Library of Congress*] (LCLS)
NTaHi............	Historical Society of the Tarrytowns, Tarrytown, NY [*Library symbol Library of Congress*] (LCLS)
NTAI............	Nam Tai Electronics, Inc. [*NASDAQ symbol*] (NQ)
NTaI............	Washington Irving Home, Sleepy Hollow Restorations, Tarrytown, NY [*Library symbol Library of Congress Obsolete*] (LCLS)
NTAIDSC............	Northern Territory AIDS [*Acquired Immune Deficiency Syndrome*] Council [*Australia*]
NTAIF............	Nam Tai Electronics [*NASDAQ symbol*] (TTSB)
NTaM............	Marymount College, Tarrytown, NY [*Library symbol Library of Congress*] (LCLS)
NTAM............	New Testament Archaeology Monographs [*A publication*] (BJA)
NTAN............	Nitrilotriacetonitrile [*Organic chemistry*]
NT & SA............	National Trust & Savings Association (MHDB)
NTAP............	National Targeting and Attack Policy (CINC)
NTAP............	National Track Analysis Program [*Aviation*] (FAAC)
NTAP............	Network Appliance [*NASDAQ symbol*] (TTSB)
NTAP............	Network Appliance Corp. [*NASDAQ symbol*] (SAG)
NTAP............	Notices to Airmen Publication [*A publication*] (FAAC)
NTap............	Tappan Free Library, Tappan, NY [*Library symbol Library of Congress*] (LCLS)
NTA Proceedings...	National Tax Association. Proceedings [*A publication*] (DLA)
NTAR............	Nonviolent Techniques Against Rape [*An association*] (EA)
NTAR............	Rurutu [*French Polynesia*] [*ICAO location identifier*] (ICLI)
NTARH............	National Teen Age Republican Headquarters (EA)
NTARS............	National Transportation Analysis Regions [*FHWA*] (TAG)
NTARY............	Notary (ABBR)
NTAS............	Northern Territory Archives Service [*Australia*]
NTaS............	Sleepy Hollow Restorations, Tarrytown, NY [*Library symbol Library of Congress*] (LCLS)
NTAT............	Tubuai/Mataura [*French Polynesia*] [*ICAO location identifier*] (ICLI)
NTATC............	National Transportation Apprenticeship and Training Conference [*Bureau of Apprenticeship and Training*] [*Department of Labor*]
NTA-TIA............	National Tax Association - Tax Institute of America (EA)
NTATN............	Notation (ABBR)
NTATNL............	Notational (ABBR)
NTaUC............	Union Carbide Corp., Tarrytown Technical Center, Tarrytown, NY [*Library symbol Library of Congress*] (LCLS)
NtAust............	National Australia Bank [*Associated Press*] (SAG)
NTAVL............	Not Available (NOAA)
NTB............	National Target Base (MCD)
NTB............	National Test Bed [*Military*] (SDI)
NTB............	Nontariff Barrier [*Kennedy Round*]
NTB............	Nontumor-Bearing
NTB............	Norsk Telegrambyra [*Norwegian News Agency*]
NTB............	Northumbria Tourist Board [*British*] (DCTA)
NTB............	Notable (ABBR)
NTB............	No Talent Bum [*Slang*]
NTB............	Nuclear Test Ban
NTBA............	National Tour Brokers Association (EA)
NTBA............	Northern Territory Bowls Association [*Australia*]
NTBB............	National Temporal Bone Banks Program of the DRF [*Deafness Research Foundation*] (EA)
N/TBC............	Nontuberculous [*Medicine*] (DAVI)
NTBIC............	Northern Territory Buffalo Industry Council [*Australia*]
NTBK............	Notebook (ABBR)
NTBM............	NU-Tech Bio-Med [*NASDAQ symbol*] (TTSB)
NTBM............	Nu-Tech Bio Med, Inc. [*NASDAQ symbol*] (SAG)
NTBPSC............	Nepal, Tibet, and Bhutan Philatelic Study Circle (EA)
NTBR............	Not to Be Resuscitated
NTBRB............	Northern Territory Building Referees' Board [*Australia*]
NTBS............	Northern Territory Board of Studies [*Australia*]
NT BUR STNDS...	National Bureau of Standards [*Department of Commerce*] (WDAA)
NTBY............	Notably (ABBR)
NTC............	Gibson Aviation [*ICAO designator*] (FAAC)
NTC............	National Tasking Center (MCD)
NTC............	National Teachers Corps
NTC............	National Team Championship [*Swimming*] [*British*] (ROG)
NTC............	National Teen Challenge (EA)
NTC............	National Telecommunications Conference [*IEEE*]
NTC............	National Telemedia Council (EA)
NTC............	National Television Center [*Telecommunications*] (TEL)
NTC............	National Territorial Command (MCD)
NTC............	National Test Center (NATG)
NTC............	National Thanksgiving Commission (EA)
NTC............	National Theatre Conference (EA)
NTC............	National Thrift Committee [*Defunct*] (EA)
NTC............	National Timesharing Council (EA)
NTC............	National Traditionalist Caucus (EA)
NTC............	National Trails Council (EA)
NTC............	National Training Center [*Red Cross*] [*Charlottesville, VA*]
NTC............	National Training Center [*Military*] (INF)
NTC............	National Translations Center [*John Crerar Library*] [*Information service or system*]
NTC............	National Transportation Center [*Large city situated at a key junction of rail, air, and highway transportation*] [*Postal Service*]
NTC............	National Travel Club [*Commercial firm*] (EA)
NTC............	National Treatment Consortium for Alcohol and Other Drugs (EA)
NTC............	National Troopers Coalition (EA)
NTC............	Naturally Occurring Top Component [*Virology*]
NTC............	Nautical Training Corps [*British military*] (DMA)
NTC............	Naval Training Center
NTC............	Naval Training Command
NTC............	Navy Test Controller (DNAB)
NTC............	Negative Temperature Coefficient
NTC............	Negative Thermal Coefficient (IAA)
NTC............	Neotetrazolium Chloride [*A dye*]
NTC............	Network Transmission Committee [*Video Transmission Engineering Committee*] (NTCM)
NTC............	Nissan Technical Center [*Automobile manufacturing*]
NTC............	Nordic Temperance Council (EA)
NTC............	Nordic Theater Committee [*Later, NTDC*] (EAIO)
NTaC............	Normal Tour of Duty Completed
ntc............	Northwest Territories [*MARC country of publication code Library of Congress*] (LCCP)
NTC............	Norwich Terrier Club [*Later, NNTC*] (EA)
NTC............	Notice
NTC............	No Traffic Reported [*Air Traffic Control*] (FAAC)
NTC............	Nucleon Transport Code
NTC............	Nu-Trans Cooperative (EA)
NTC............	Nuveen Connecticut Premium Income Municipal Fund [*NYSE symbol*] (SPSG)
NTC............	Nuveen CT Prem Inc. Muni [*NYSE symbol*] (TTSB)
NTCA............	National Telephone Cooperative Association (EA)
NTCA............	National Tile Contractors Association (EA)
NTCA............	National Town Class Association (EA)
NTCA............	National Tribal Chairman's Association [*Defunct*] (EA)
NTCA............	N-Nitrosothioazolidine Carboxylic Acid [*Organic chemistry*]
NTCA............	Northern Territory Cricket Association [*Australia*]
NtCapit............	National Capital Management Corp. [*Associated Press*] (SAG)
NTCAVAL............	Notice of Availability
NTC/AW............	National Training Center / Air Warrior System (DWSG)

NTCB .... (Nitro)thiocyanatobenzoic Acid [*Organic chemistry*]
NTCB .... Northern Territory Convention Bureau [*Australia*]
NTCB .... Noticeable (ABBR)
NTCBY .... Noticeably (ABBR)
NTCC .... Naval Tactical Communications Center (MCD)
NTCC .... Naval Telecommunications Center (DOMA)
NTCC .... Neutron Transport Computer Code
NTCC .... Nimbus Technical Control Center
NTCC .... Northern Territory Conservation Commission [*Australia*]
NTCCDET .... Naval Telecommunications Center Detachment (DNAB)
NTCCS .... Naval Tactical Command and Control System (PDAA)
NTCD .... Nitro(thiocyano)benzoic Acid [*Organic chemistry*]
NTCD .... Noticed (ABBR)
NTCDC .... Northern Territory Counter Disaster Council [*Australia*]
NTCF .... National Telemarketing Fulfillment Center
NTCF .... National Toxic Campaign Fund [*An association*]
NTCFA .... Northern Territory Commercial Fishermen's Association [*Australia*]
NTCFA .... Northern Territory Crab Fishermen's Association [*Australia*]
NTCG .... Noticing (ABBR)
NTCGA .... Northern Territory Community Government Association [*Australia*]
NTCHA .... National Taxi and Car Hire Association [*British*] (BI)
NTCHBA .... National Trust Closely Held Business Association (EA)
NTCI .... National Training Center - Phase I (MCD)
NTCKR .... Nutcracker (ABBR)
NTCL .... Nautical
NTCLP .... Northern Territory Country Liberal Party [*Australia Political party*]
NTCMA .... National Traditional Country Music Association [*Later, NTMA*] (EA)
NtCmcBc .... National Commerce Bancorp [*Associated Press*] (SAG)
NTCMP .... Northern Territory Chamber of Mines and Petroleum [*Australia*]
NtCnv .... National Convenience Stores, Inc. [*Associated Press*] (SAG)
NTCOSS .... Northern Territory Council of Social Service [*Australia*]
NTCOTA .... Northern Territory Council on the Aging [*Australia*]
NTCP .... Near-Term Construction Permit [*Nuclear energy*] (NRCH)
NTCP .... Nightcap (ABBR)
NTCP .... Non-Traditional Casting Project (EA)
NtCptr .... National Computer Systems, Inc. [*Associated Press*] (SAG)
NTCS .... Nonverbal Test of Cognitive Skills [*Intelligence test*]
NTCS-A .... Navy Tactical Command System Afloat (DOMA)
NTCSD .... Naval Training Center, San Diego
NTCSOC .... Naval Telecommunications Command Satellite Operations Center (MCD)
NTCT .... National Tennis Center Trust [*Australia*]
NTCTA .... Northern Territory Clay Target Association [*Australia*]
NTD .... Das Neue Testament Deutsch. Neues Goettinger Bibelwerk [*A publication*] (BJA)
NTD .... NASA Test Director (MCD)
NTD .... National Tap Dance Co. of Canada
NTD .... National Theatre of the Deaf (EA)
NTD .... National Transit Database [*FTA*] (TAG)
NTD .... Naval Training Department [*British military*] (DMA)
NTD .... Neural Tube (Closure) Defect [*Medicine*]
NTD .... Neutron Transmutation Doped [*Silicon for semiconductor use*]
NTD .... New Tyee Resources [*Vancouver Stock Exchange symbol*]
NTD .... Nitroblue Tetrazolium Dye [*Test*] [*Laboratory science*] (DAVI)
NTD .... Nontight Door
NTD .... N-Tone International Ltd. [*Vancouver Stock Exchange symbol*]
NTD .... Nuclear Test Directorate [*Air Force*]
NTD .... Port Hueneme, CA [*Location identifier FAA*] (FAAL)
NTDA .... National Trade Development Association (WDAA)
NTDA .... National Trailer Dealers Association (EA)
NTDA .... National Tyre Distributors Association [*British*] (DBA)
NTDA .... Navy Tactical Doctrine Activity (NVT)
NTDAB .... Northern Territory Drug and Alcohol Board [*Australia*]
NTDB .... National Trade Data Bank (EGAO)
NTDB .... National Trade Database (ACII)
NTDC .... Naval Training Devices Center [*Port Washington, LI*]
NTDC .... Nordic Theatre and Dance Committee (EAIO)
NTDDPA .... Navy Tactical Doctrine Development and Production Activity
NTDE .... North Dakota Tracer Experiment [*Marine science*] (OSRA)
NtDentex .... National Dentex Corp. [*Associated Press*] (SAG)
NTDG .... National Teaching Development Grant [*Australia*]
NTDI .... NATO Target Data Inventory (MCD)
NTDO .... Navy Technical Data Office [*of the Office of Naval Material*]
NTDPMA .... National Tool, Die, and Precision Machining Association [*Later, NTMA*] (EA)
NTDRA .... National Tire Dealers and Retreaders Association (EA)
NTDS .... Naval Technical Data System (IAA)
NTDS .... Navy Tactical Data System
NTDS .... Northern Telecom Data Systems (NITA)
NTDSC .... Nondestructive Testing Data Support Center [*DoD*] (MCD)
NTDS/LBTS .... Naval Tactical Data System / Land-Based Test Site (DNAB)
NTE .... Nantes [*France*] [*Airport symbol*] (OAG)
NTE .... National Teacher Examination
NTE .... National Treasury Employees Union
NTE .... Navy Technical Evaluation (NG)
NTE .... Navy Teletypewriter Exchange [*Later, NTX*]
NTE .... Network Terminating Equipment [*Telecommunications*] (IAA)
NTE .... Network Terminating Equipment (NITA)
NTE .... Neutron Transient Effect
NTE .... Nontactical Equipment
NTE .... Northern Eagle Mines [*Vancouver Stock Exchange symbol*]
NTE .... Not to Exceed [*Aviation*]
NTE .... Nursing the Environment
NTEA .... National Tax Equality Association (EA)
NTEA .... National Telecommunications Electronics Administration
NTEA .... National Time Equipment Association (EA)
NTEA .... National Truck Equipment Association (EA)
NTeam .... National TechTeam, Inc. [*Associated Press*] (SAG)
NTEC .... National Telecommunications Education Committee [*North American Telecommunications Association*] [*Washington, DC Telecommunications service*] (TSSD)
NTEC .... National Traction Engine Club [*British*] (DBA)
NTEC .... Naval Training Equipment Center
NTEC .... Neose Technologies [*NASDAQ symbol*] (TTSB)
NTech .... National Technical Systems, Inc. [*Associated Press*] (SAG)
NTECPE .... Naval Training Equipment Center, Project Engineer
NTEF .... National Tennis Educational Foundation [*Later, NTFHF*] (EA)
NTEG .... Integ Inc. [*NASDAQ symbol*] (SAG)
NTEI .... New Technical Education Initiative (AIE)
NTE/IOTE .... Navy Technical Evaluation/Initial Operational Test and Evaluation (MCD)
NTelpd .... Northwest Teleproductions, Inc. [*Associated Press*] (SAG)
NTEO .... Northern Territory Electoral Office [*Australia*]
NTEP .... National Type Evaluation Program [*Environmental Protection Agency*]
NTER .... Normalized Transmission Energy Requirement
N Terr .... Northern Territory
N Terr Austl Ord .... Northern Territorial Ordinances [*Australia A publication*] (DLA)
NTES .... Northern Territory Emergency Service [*Australia*]
N-TEST .... Nuclear Testing (WDAA)
NTET .... National Traction Engine Trust [*British*] (DBA)
NTEU .... National Treasury Employees Union (EA)
NTeZ .... North Temperate Zone [*Planet Jupiter*]
NTF .... National Tactical Force (NATG)
NTF .... National Tennis Foundation [*Formerly, NTEF*] [*Later, NTFHF*] (EA)
NTF .... National Test Facility [*Military*] (SDI)
NTF .... National Theater File [*Theater Sources, Inc.*] [*Information service or system Defunct*] (IID)
NTF .... National Tidal Facility [*Flinders University*] [*Australia*]
NTF .... National Trainers Federation [*British*] (DBA)
NTF .... National Transonic Facility [*NASA*]
NTF .... National Transport Federation [*Australia*]
NTF .... National Turkey Federation (EA)
NTF .... Naval Task Force
NTF .... Navy Technological Forecast
NTF .... Nigerian Trust Fund [*African Development Bank*]
NTF .... Nordic Transportworkers' Federation [*See also NT*] (EAIO)
NTF .... Nordisk Thoraxkirurgisk Forening [*Scandinavian Association for Thoracic and Cardiovascular Surgery - SATCS*] (EAIO)
NTF .... Normal Throat Flora [*Medicine*] (DMAA)
NTF .... No Trouble Found
NTF .... Nuclear Test Facility
NTFA .... National Teaching-Family Association (EA)
NTFA .... National Track and Field Association [*Superseded by ANG*] (EA)
NTFAO .... National Task Force on Autocratic Options (EA)
NTFC .... National Telemarketing Fulfillment Center
NTFC .... National Television Film Council (EA)
NTFC .... NATO Tactical Fighter Center
NTFC .... Nonlinear Transient Fuel Film Compsensation [*Automotive fuel system*]
NTFDC .... Non Theatrical Film Distributors Council (EA)
NTFEEG .... National Task Force on Education for Economic Growth (EA)
NTFHF .... National Tennis Foundation and Hall of Fame [*Later, ITHOF*] (EA)
NTFIC .... Northern Territory Fishing Industry Council [*Australia*]
NTFITC .... Northern Territory Fishing Industry Training Committee [*Australia*]
NTFL .... National Touch Football Leagues (EA)
NTFNC .... Northern Territory Field Naturalists' Club [*Australia*]
NTFND .... No Trouble Found [*Aviation*] (FAAC)
NTFP .... National Task Force on Prostitution (EA)
NTFS .... Network of Tropical Fisheries Scientists [*Marine science*] (OSRA)
NTFS .... Northern Territory Fire Service [*Australia*]
NTFS .... NT File System [*Computer science*]
NTFTA .... National Toy Fox Terrier Association (EA)
NTFWTC .... NATO Tactical Fighter Weapons Training Center
NTFY .... Notify (AFM)
NTG .... Nitroglycerin [*Also, GTN, NG*] [*Explosive, vasodilator*]
NTG .... Nitrosoguanidine [*Organic chemistry*]
NTG .... Nontactical Generator (RDA)
NTG .... Non-Technical Generator [*Army*]
NTG .... Nontoxic Goiter [*Medicine*]
NTG .... Nontreatment Group [*Medical research*] (DAVI)
NTG .... N-Tolylglycine [*Organic chemistry*]
NTGA .... Anaa [*French Polynesia*] [*ICAO location identifier*] (ICLI)
NTGA .... National Traveler's Gasoline Advisory (DICI)
NTGB .... Fangatau [*French Polynesia*] [*ICAO location identifier*] (ICLI)
NTGC .... Tikehau [*French Polynesia*] [*ICAO location identifier*] (ICLI)
NTGD .... Apataki [*French Polynesia*] [*ICAO location identifier*] (ICLI)
NTGE .... Reao [*French Polynesia*] [*ICAO location identifier*] (ICLI)
NTGF .... Fakarava [*French Polynesia*] [*ICAO location identifier*] (ICLI)
NTGH .... Hikueru [*French Polynesia*] [*ICAO location identifier*] (ICLI)
NTGI .... Manihi [*French Polynesia*] [*ICAO location identifier*] (ICLI)
NTGIS .... National Transit Geographic Information System [*FTA*] (TAG)
NTGJ .... Totegegie [*French Polynesia*] [*ICAO location identifier*] (ICLI)
NTGK .... Kaukura [*French Polynesia*] [*ICAO location identifier*] (ICLI)
NTGk .... New Testament Greek (BARN)
NTGL .... Fakahina [*French Polynesia*] [*ICAO location identifier*] (ICLI)
NTGM .... Makemo [*French Polynesia*] [*ICAO location identifier*] (ICLI)
NTGMA .... Northern Territory Girls' Marching Association [*Australia*]
NTGMB .... Northern Territory Grain Marketing Board [*Australia*]
NTGN .... Napuka [*French Polynesia*] [*ICAO location identifier*] (ICLI)
NTGO .... Nitroglycerine Ointment [*Pharmacy*]

NTGO	Tatakoto [French Polynesia] [ICAO location identifier] (ICLI)
NTGP	Northern Territory Government Publications [Australia]
NTGP	Puka Puka [French Polynesia] [ICAO location identifier] (ICLI)
NTGPE	Northern Territory Government Pipeline Executive [Australia]
NTGPO	Northern Territory Government Printing Office [Australia]
NTGQ	Pukarua [French Polynesia] [ICAO location identifier] (ICLI)
NTGR	Aratica [French Polynesia] [ICAO location identifier] (ICLI)
NTGR	New Testament Greek (BJA)
NTGS	Northwest Territory Genealogical Society (EA)
NTG SL	Nitroglycerin Sublingual [Pharmacology] (DAVI)
NtGsO	National Gas & Oil Corp. [Associated Press] (SAG)
NTGT	Takapoto [French Polynesia] [ICAO location identifier] (ICLI)
NTGU	Arutua [French Polynesia] [ICAO location identifier] (ICLI)
NTGV	Mataiva [French Polynesia] [ICAO location identifier] (ICLI)
NTGW	Nukutavake [French Polynesia] [ICAO location identifier] (ICLI)
NTGY	Tureia [French Polynesia] [ICAO location identifier] (ICLI)
NTH	Hudson Valley Community College, Troy, NY [Library symbol Library of Congress] (LCLS)
NtH	Natural Health Trends Corp. [Associated Press] (SAG)
NTH	New Testament Handbooks [A publication]
NTH	Northern Platinum [Vancouver Stock Exchange symbol]
NTHA	National Temple Hill Association (EA)
NTHA	Northern Territory Hockey Association [Australia]
NTHC	Northern Territory Housing Commission [Australia]
NTHCS	National Toothpick Holder Collector's Society (EA)
NthCsE	North Coast Energy [Associated Press] (SAG)
NthCst	North Coast Energy, Inc. [Associated Press] (SAG)
NthCstE	North Coast Energy [Associated Press] (SAG)
NTHEST	Northeast
NTHESTN	Northeastern
NthfldLb	Northfield Laboratories, Inc. [Associated Press] (SAG)
Nthgat	Northgate Exploration Ltd. [Associated Press] (SAG)
NthHHlt	National Home Health Care Corp. [Associated Press] (SAG)
NTHL	National Treasure Hunters League [Defunct] (EA)
NthLily	North Lilly Mining Co. [Associated Press] (SAG)
NtHlt	National Health Investors [Associated Press] (SAG)
NtHlthE	National Health Enhancement Systems, Inc. [Associated Press] (SAG)
NtHltl	National Health Investors [Associated Press] (SAG)
Nthmb	Northumberland [County in England] (WGA)
NTHN	Northern
NthnTch	Northern Technologies International [Associated Press] (SAG)
NTHP	National Trust for Historic Preservation (EA)
NTHRN	Northern
NthStat	Northern States Financial Corp. [Associated Press] (SAG)
NthstCF	Northstar Computer Forms, Inc. [Associated Press] (SAG)
NthstrHl	Northstar Health Services, Inc. [Associated Press] (SAG)
NTHV	Near-Term Hybrid Vehicle (PDAA)
NTHWST	Northwest
NTHWSTN	Northwestern
NTHZ	N-Nitrosothiazolidine [Organic chemistry]
NTI	Bintuni [Indonesia] [Airport symbol] (OAG)
NTI	Nadic-Terminated Imide [Polymer technology]
NTI	National Tactical Interface (MCD)
NTI	National Technology Initiative [Program introduced by President Bush in February 1992]
NTI	National Theatre Institute (EA)
NTI	National Trade Index
NTI	Naval Travel Instructions
NTI	Nesbitt Thomson, Inc. [Toronto Stock Exchange symbol Vancouver Stock Exchange symbol]
NTI	NeuROM Technology, Inc.
NTI	Neuropsychiatric Interest Checklist
NTI	Nielsen Television Index [Nielsen Media Research] [Information service or system]
NTI	Noise Transmission Impairment [Telecommunications]
NTI	Nonthyroidal Illness [Medicine]
NTI	Nordman [Idaho] [Seismograph station code, US Geological Survey Closed] (SEIS)
NTI	Northern Technology International [AMEX symbol] (SPSG)
NTI	No Travel Involved [Military]
NTIA	National Telecommunications and Information Administration [Department of Commerce] [Washington, DC]
NTIAC	Nondestructive Testing Information Analysis Center [Army Materials and Mechanics Research Center] [Watertown, MA]
NTIB	National Technology and Industrial Base (AAGC)
NTIC	Immaculate Conception Seminary, College of Philosophy, Troy, NY [Library symbol Library of Congress] (LCLS)
NTIC	National Training and Information Center (EA)
NTIC	Naval Technical Intelligence Center [Pronounced N-tech; Formerly, NISC, now NAVMIC] (DOMA)
NTIC	Nondestructive Testing Information Center [Battelle Memorial Institute] [Databank] [Information service or system] (IID)
NTICED	National Training Institute for Community Economic Development (EA)
NTICL	National Technical Information Centre and Library (NITA)
NTID	National Technical Institute for the Deaf [Rochester Institute of Technology] [Research center]
NTIES	National Treatment Improvement Evaluation Study [Department of Health and Human Services]
NTIF	National Taxpayers' Investigative Fund (EA)
NTIH	Normal Terminate Interrupt Handler (MCD)
NTII	Neurobiological Technologies, Inc. [NASDAQ symbol] (SAG)
NTIK	Nontactical Instrumentation Kit [Military] (DWSG)
NTIMS	Negative-Ion Thermal Ionization Mass Spectrometry

NTIOC	No Travel Involved for Officer Concerned [Military]
N-TIP	National Technology Investment Programme [Canada]
NTIP	National Turkey Improvement Plan
NTIPP	Navy Technical Information Presentation Program (MCD)
NTIPS	Navy Technical Information Presentation System (MCD)
NTIR	Nederlands Tijdschrift voor Internationaal Recht [Netherlands A publication] (ILCA)
NTIR	Nontechnical Intelligence Report
NTIRA	National Trucking Industrial Relations Association (EA)
NTIS	National Technical Information Service [Department of Commerce] [Springfield, VA Database producer and database]
NTIS	National Technical Information Service (NADA)
NTIS	NEC [Nippon Electric Company]-Toshiba Information Systems, Inc. [Japan]
NTIS	Nondestructive Testing Information System (SAA)
NTISSC	National Telecommunications and Information System Security Committee (NITA)
NTITC	National Tourism Industry Training Council [Australia]
NTITS	Northern Territory Interpreter and Translator Service [Australia]
NTJ	Nigeria Trade Journal [A publication]
NTK	Need to Know (MCD)
NTK	Newton Tool Kit [Computer science]
NTK	Nontactical Kit [Military] (DWSG)
NTK	Nordisk Teaterkomite [Nordic Theater Committee - NTC] (EAIO)
NTK	Nortek, Inc. [NYSE symbol] (SPSG)
NTK	Nunatak [Alaska] [Seismograph station code, US Geological Survey] (SEIS)
NTK	Tustin, CA [Location identifier FAA] (FAAL)
NTKR	Takaroa [French Polynesia] [ICAO location identifier] (ICLI)
NTL	Jacksonville, NC [Location identifier FAA] (FAAL)
ntL	National (DD)
NTL	National
NTL	National Technology Ltd. (NITA)
NTL	National Temperance League [Later, ACAP] (EA)
NTL	National Tennis League
NTL	National Testing Laboratories [Australia]
NTL	National Training Laboratories [Later, NTLI] (EA)
NTL	Natural Thermo Luminescence (IAA)
NTL	Neon Test Light
NTL	Newcastle [Australia Airport symbol] (OAG)
NTL	Night Telegraph Letter
NTL	Nonthreshold Logic (IAA)
NTL	Nonuniform Transmission Line [Computer science] (IAA)
NTL	Northair Aviation Ltd. [British ICAO designator] (FAAC)
NTL	Northern Technol Intl. [AMEX symbol] (TTSB)
NTL	Northern Telecom Ltd. [Toronto Stock Exchange symbol Vancouver Stock Exchange symbol]
NTL	Northern Territory Library [Australia]
NTL	No Time Lost [Military]
NTL	NovAtel Communications Ltd. [UTLAS symbol]
NTL	Novosti Tehnikskoi Literatury (NITA)
NTL	Nuclear Technology Laboratory [Stanford University] (MCD)
NTL	Nuclear Thermionics Laboratory
NTL	Nuclear Transport Ltd. [British] (IRUK)
NTLA	National Toy Libraries Association [British] (EAIO)
NTLA	Nebraska Test of Learning Aptitude [Education]
NTLAT	Northern Territory Land Acquisition Tribunal [Australia]
NTLB	Northern Territory Land Board [Australia]
NTLC	National Tax-Limitation Committee (EA)
NTLC	National Trades and Labour Congress [Canada]
NTLC	National Traffic Law Center [MHTSA] (TAG)
NtlCity	National City Corp. [Associated Press] (SAG)
NTLDO	Navy Terminal Leave Disbursing Office
NTLEN	Nutlet Length [Botany]
NTLF	National Taxpayers Legal Fund (EA)
NTLF	Northern Troops and Landing Force
NTLGA	Northern Territory Local Government Association [Australia]
NTLGGC	Northern Territory Local Government Grants Commission [Australia]
NTLI	Neurotensin-Like Immunoreactivity
NTLI	NTL Institute (EA)
NtlInco	National Income Realty Trust [Associated Press] (SAG)
NtlIns	National Insurance Group [Associated Press] (SAG)
NtlPict	National Picture & Frame Co. [Associated Press] (SAG)
NtlRlty	National Realty Ltd. [Associated Press] (SAG)
NTLS	National Truck Leasing System (EA)
NTLS	Non-Transposed Loop Sensor (PDAA)
NTLSEA	Northern Territory Live Stock Exporters' Association [Australia]
NtlSecs	National Securities Corp. [Associated Press] (SAG)
NtlWire	National Wireless Holdings, Inc. [Associated Press] (SAG)
NtlWstA	National Westminster Bank Ltd. [Associated Press] (SAG)
NTM	Narrowband Trunk Module [Telecommunications]
NTM	National Technical Means [For monitoring compliance with the provisions of an agreement]
NTM	NAVAIR Test Manual (MCD)
NTM	Nazarene Theological Seminary, Kansas City, MO [OCLC symbol] (OCLC)
NTM	Net Ton Mile [Shipping]
NTM	New Tribes Mission (EA)
NTM	Night Message (MSA)
NTM	Nontariff Measures
NTM	Non-Transition Metal (MCD)
NTM	Normal Transmitting Male [Genetics]
NTM	North American Airlines, Inc. [Canada ICAO designator] (FAAC)
NtM	Norton Micro Images, Inc., Trenton, NJ [Library symbol Library of Congress] (LCLS)

NTM	Notice to Mariners
NTM	Not to My Knowledge
NTMA	National Tank Manufacturers Association [*Defunct*] (EA)
NTMA	National Terrazzo and Mosaic Association (EA)
NTMA	National Tooling and Machining Association (EA)
NTMA	National Traditional Music Association (EA)
NTMB	Nontuberculous Mycobacterium [*A bacterium*] (DAVI)
NTMD	Nuku Hiva [*French Polynesia*] [*ICAO location identifier*] (ICLI)
NTME	Naval Technical Mission in Europe
NtMerc	National Mercantile Bancorp [*Associated Press*] (SAG)
NTMG	Nutmeg Federal Savings & Loan Association [*NASDAQ symbol*] (SAG)
NTMG	Nutmeg Fedl Svgs & Loan [*NASDAQ symbol*] (TTSB)
NTMI	Net Ton of Molten Iron
NTMI	Nontransmural Myocardial Infarction [*Cardiology*] (CPH)
NTMICP	National Topographic Map Inventory Control Point
NTMJ	Naval Technical Mission to Japan
NTML	National Tillage Machinery Laboratory [*Department of Agriculture*] [*Research center*] (GRD)
NTMN	Hiva-Oa/Atuana [*French Polynesia*] [*ICAO location identifier*] (ICLI)
NTMN	National Thrift and Mortgage News [*A publication*]
NTMNG	Nontoxic, Multinodular Goiter [*Medicine*] (DAVI)
NTMP	Nike Target Measurements Program
NTMP	Nitrate Motion Picture (VRA)
NTMP	Ua Pou [*French Polynesia*] [*ICAO location identifier*] (ICLI)
NTMPA	Northern Territory Marine and Ports Authority [*Australia*]
NTMT	Navigation Tender Maintenance Training (DNAB)
NTMU	Ua Huka [*French Polynesia*] [*ICAO location identifier*] (ICLI)
NTMVSA	National Traffic and Motor Vehicle Safety Act
NTMWG	Nuclear Test Monitoring Working Group [*Military*]
NTN	National Airways Corp. (Pty) Ltd. [*South Africa ICAO designator*] (FAAC)
NTN	National TeleAccess Network [*Database of physician opportunities*]
NTN	National Telecommunications Network [*Rockville, MD*] (TSSD)
NTN	National Towing News [*A publication*] (EAAP)
NTN	National Trends Network (EPA)
NTN	Nephrotoxic Nephritis [*Medicine*]
NTN	Network Terminal Number [*Telecommunications*]
NTN	Network Termination Number [*Computer science*] (TNIG)
NTN	Neutral Twisted Nematic [*Computer science*] (PCM)
NTN	Neutron [*A nuclear particle*] (MSA)
NTN	Newton [*Diocesan abbreviation*] [*Melkite United States*] (TOCD)
NTN	Newton College, Newton, MA [*Inactive*] [*OCLC symbol*] (OCLC)
NTN	New Trade Names [*Later, NBTC*] [*A publication*]
NTN	Normanton [*Australia Airport symbol*] (OAG)
NTN	Northern Territory News [*A publication*]
NTN	Norton Co., Coated Abrasive Division, R and D Department, Troy, NY [*Library symbol Library of Congress*] (LCLS)
NTN	NTN Canada, Inc. [*Associated Press*] (SAG)
NTN	NTN Communications [*AMEX symbol*] (TTSB)
NTN	NTN Communications, Inc. [*AMEX symbol*] (SPSG)
NTNA	Northern Territory Nurserymen's Association [*Australia*]
NTNC	NTN Canada, Inc. [*NASDAQ symbol*] (SAG)
NTNC	NTN Cda [*NASDAQ symbol*] (TTSB)
NTN Cda	NTN Canada, Inc. [*Associated Press*] (SAG)
NTNCom	NTN Communications, Inc. [*Associated Press*] (SAG)
NTNCWS	Non-Transient Non-Community Water System [*Environmental Protection Agency*]
NTNF	Norges Teknisk-Naturvitenskapelige Forskningsraad [*Online database*]
NTNG	Nitrate Negative (VRA)
NTNV	Narcissus Tip Necrosis Virus [*Plant pathology*]
NTNYT	Not the New York Times [*A publication*]
NTO	Name To (AAG)
NTO	National Tenants Organization [*Defunct*] (EA)
NTO	National Turnover [*Economics*]
NTO	Natural Transition Orbitals [*Atomic physics*]
NTO	Naval Technology Office [*Arlington, VA*] (GRD)
NTO	Naval Transport Officer
NTO	Network Terminal Operator
NTO	Network Terminal Option [*Computer science*]
NTO	New Technology Opportunities [*Program*] [*US government*]
NTO	Nitrogen Tetroxide [*Inorganic chemistry*]
NTO	Nonorthogonal Timing Error (IAA)
NTO	Nontraditional Occupations
NTO	No Try On [*Purchaser did not have a fitting*] [*Merchandising slang*]
NTO	Not Taken Out [*Insurance*]
NTO	Santo Antao [*Cape Verde Islands*] [*Airport symbol*] (OAG)
NTOC	Naval Telecommunications Operations Center (DNAB)
NTOCDET	Naval Telecommunications Operations Center Detachment (DNAB)
NTOF	National Traumatic Occupational Fatalities [*Surveillance system run by National Institute for Occupational Safety and Health*]
NTOFMS	Neutral Time-of-Flight Mass Spectroscopy [*Aviation*]
NTOL	Near-Term Operating License [*Nuclear energy*] (NRCH)
NTOL	Normal Takeoff and Landing [*Aviation*] (MCD)
NTOMC	National Tung Oil Marketing Cooperative [*Defunct*] (EA)
NTonHi	Historical Society of the Tonawandas, Tonawanda, NY [*Library symbol Library of Congress*] (LCLS)
NTonL	Union Carbide Corp., Linde Division, Tonawanda, NY [*Library asymbol Library of Congress*] (LCLS)
NTonS	Sheridan Park Hospital, Inc., Tonawanda, NY [*Library symbol Library of Congress*] (LCLS)
NTOP	New Technology Opportunities Program [*US government*]
NTORS	Naval Torpedo Station
NTOS	Natural Therapeutic and Osteopathic Society and Register [*British*] (DBA)
NTOTC	National Training and Operational Technology Center [*Environmental Protection Agency*] (IID)
NTP	Nathian [*Pakistan*] [*Seismograph station code, US Geological Survey*] (SEIS)
NTP	National Tasking Plan [*Military*]
NTP	National Toxicology Program [*Department of Health and Human Services*] [*Research Triangle Park, NC*]
NTP	National Transportation Policy
NTP	Naval Tactical Publication (NVT)
NTP	Naval Telecommunications Procedures (NVT)
NTP	Naval Telecommunications Publication (NVT)
NTP	Navy Technological Projections
NTP	Navy Training Plan (NVT)
NTP	Near Time Processing (IAA)
NTP	Network Terminal Protocol
NTP	Network Terminating Point [*Telecommunications*] (TEL)
NTP	Network Termination Processor
NTP	Network Test Panel [*NASA*] (KSC)
NTP	Network Test Panel
NTP	Network Time Protocol
NTP	Neuronal Thread Protein [*Biology*]
NTP	Nistransair [*Republic of Moldova*] [*FAA designator*] (FAAC)
NTP	Nitrol Paste [*Pharmacology*] (DAVI)
NTP	Nitroprusside [*A vasodilator*]
NTP	Nonzero Temperature Plasma
NTP	Normal Temperature and Pressure [*Medicine*]
NTP	Notice to Proceed (KSC)
NTP	No Title Page [*Bibliography*]
NTP	Nuclear Test Plant
NTP	Nuclear Transportation Project (EA)
NTP	Nucleoside Triphosphate [*Biochemistry*]
NTP	Number of Theoretical Plates
NTP	Numerical Tape Punch
NTP	Sodium Nitroprusside [*An antihypertensive and reagent*] [*Pharmacology*] (DAVI)
NTPA	National Tractor Pullers Association (EA)
NTPA	National Trotting Pony Association [*Later, ITPA*]
NTPA	Naval Technical Proficiency Assist (NVT)
NTPA	Northern Territory Planning Authority [*Australia*]
NTPA	Northern Territory Police Association [*Australia*]
NTPAC	Northern Territory Planning Appeals Committee [*Australia*]
NtPatnt	National Patent Development Corp. [*Associated Press*] (SAG)
NTPAW	National Transportation Public Affairs Workshop
NTPC	National Technical Processing Center
NTPC	National Temperance and Prohibition Council (EA)
NTPC	Naval Training Publications Center
NTPC	Navy Training Plan Conference
NTPD	Normal Temperature, Pressure Differential (MCD)
NTPDLB	Northern Territory Plumbers and Drainers Licensing Board [*Australia*]
NTPE	Non-Tactical Peripheral Equipment [*Military*]
NtPenn	National Penn Bancshares, Inc. [*Associated Press*] (SAG)
NTPF	National Tile Promotion Federation [*Defunct*] (EA)
NTPF	Near-Term Prepositioning Forces [*Navy*]
NTPF	Number of Terminals per Failure [*Computer science*]
NTPG	National Textile Processors Guild [*Defunct*] (EA)
NTPH	Nucleosidetriphosphate Pyrophosphatase [*An enzyme*]
NTPHINB	National Trust for Places of Historic Interest or Natural Beauty [*British*] (EAIO)
NTPI	Navy Technical Proficiency Inspection (NG)
NTPI	Nuclear Training Proficiency Inspection [*Navy*] (DOMA)
NTP/IDCSP	Navy Test Plan for Initial Defense Communications Satellite Program (DNAB)
NTPL	Navy Technical Proficiency List
NTPL	Nut Plate (AAG)
NTPNC	Northern Territory Place Names Committee [*Australia*]
NTPO	National Transuranic Waste Program Office [*Department of Energy*] (GAAI)
NTPO	Nitrilotrimethylenephosphonic Acid [*Organic chemistry*]
NTPOC	Navy Technical Point of Contact (DOMA)
NTPP	Normal through Patch Panel (MCD)
NTPR	Nuclear Targeting Policy Review (MCD)
NtPrest	National Presto Industries, Inc. [*Associated Press*] (SAG)
NTPS	Naval Test Pilot School
NTPS	Near-Term Prepositioned Ships
NTPWA	Northern Territory Power and Water Authority [*Australia*]
NtPwADS	National Power PLC [*Associated Press*] (SAG)
NtPwIntr	National Power PLC [*Associated Press*] (SAG)
NTQ	National Trust of Queensland [*Australia*]
NTQ	Nebennieren, Thymus, Quotient [*Test*] [*Medicine*]
NTR	National Tape Repository (EA)
NTR	National Transcontinental Railway [*Canada*]
NTR	Navigational Time Reference (AAG)
NTR	Navy Technical Representative (MCD)
NTR	Negative True Rake (IAA)
NTR	Nernst-Thomson Rule [*Physics*]
NTR	Net-of-Tax Rate (ECON)
NTR	Neutron Test Reactors (KSC)
NTR	New Technology Report
NTR	Next Task Register
NTR	Noise Temperature Ratio (AAG)
NTR	Nontranslated Region [*Genetics*]
NTR	Nordiska Trafiksakerhetsradet [*Nordic Road Safety Council - NRSC*] [*Finland*] (EAIO)

NTR .... Nordisk Tolladministrativt Rad [*Nordic Customs Administrative Council - NCAC*] (EAIO)
NTR .... No Texts Required [*Education*]
NTR .... Nothing to Report
NTR .... No Traffic Reported [*Aviation*]
NTR .... Nuclear Test Reactor [*Also known as GETR*]
NTR .... Nutrition
NTR .... Rensselaer Polytechnic Institute, Troy, NY [*Library symbol Library of Congress*] (LCLS)
NTRA .... National Television Rental Association [*British*]
NTRA .... National Trailer Rental Association (EA)
NTRA .... National Tumor Registrars Association (EA)
NTRA .... National Tyre Recycling Association [*British*] (DBA)
NTRA .... Northern Territory Rifle Association [*Australia*]
N Trans S Dec... National Transportation Safety Board Decisions [*A publication*] (DLA)
NTRC .... National Tourism Review Commission
NTRC .... Natural Toxins Research Center [*Public Health Service*] (GRD)
NTRC .... Northern Territory Rural College [*Australia*]
NTRDA .... National Tuberculosis and Respiratory Diseases Association [*Later, American Lung Association*]
NT Rep .... New Term Reports, English Queen's Bench [*A publication*] (DLA)
NT Repts ..... New Term Reports, English Queen's Bench [*A publication*] (DLA)
NTRG .... New Testament Reading Guide [*Collegeville, MN*] [*A publication*] (BJA)
NTRGLB....... Northern Territory Racing, Gaming and Liquor Board [*Australia*]
NTRL .... NASA Technology Readiness Level (SSD)
NTRL .... Natural
NTRL .... Naval Training Research Laboratory (WDAA)
NtrlH .... Natural Health Trends Corp. [*Associated Press*] (SAG)
NTRLLy........ Naturally
NTRM .... Nitrogen-Tillage-Residue Management (GNE)
NTRMA .... National Tile Roofing Manufacturing Association (EA)
NTRP .... No Traffic Reported [*Aviation*] (FAAC)
NTRS .... National Therapeutic Recreation Society (EA)
NTRS .... Nationwide Trailer Rental System
NTRS .... Northern Trust [*NASDAQ symbol*] (TTSB)
NTRS .... Northern Trust Corp. [*NASDAQ symbol*] (NQ)
NTRS .... Russell Sage College, Troy, NY [*Library symbol Library of Congress*] (LCLS)
NTRU .... Northern Territory Rugby Union [*Australia*]
NTRX .... Netrix Corp. [*NASDAQ symbol*] (SAG)
NTrZ............ North Tropical Zone [*Planet Jupiter*]
NTS............. Cirrus Air, Inc. [*ICAO designator*] (FAAC)
NTS............. Namens Trau- und Sterberegister der Judenschaft [*A publication*] (BJA)
NTS............. Narodno Trudovoi Soyuz [*People's Labor Union*] [*Frankfurt, Federal Republic of Germany*] (PD)
NTS............. NASA Test Support
NTS............. Nasotracheal Suction [*Medical procedure*] (DAVI)
NTS............. National Technical Services
NTS............. National Technical Systems Inc. [*Commercial firm*]
NTS............. National Thespian Society [*Later, ITS*] (EA)
NTS............. National Traffic System [*Amateur radio*]
NTS............. National Transportation Statistics [*or Survey*] [*Department of Transportation*]
NTS............. National Transportation System [*BTS*] (TAG)
NTS............. National Travel Survey [*Census Bureau*]
NTS............. National Trust for Scotland (DI)
NTS............. National Tulip Society [*Defunct*] (EA)
NTS............. Naval Target Subdivision [*G-2, SHAEF*]
NTS............. Naval Telecommunications System (NVT)
NTS............. Naval Torpedo Station
NTS............. Naval Training School
NTS............. Naval Training Station
NTS............. Naval Transportation Service [*Later, MSC*]
NTS............. Navigational Technology Satellite (MCD)
NTS............. Navigation Technology Satellite (PDAA)
NTS............. Navigation Technology System (IAA)
NTS............. Navigator Training Squadron [*Air Force*]
NTS............. Navy Technology Satellite
NTS............. Near Term Schedule (MCD)
NTS............. Negative Torque Signal (MSA)
NTS............. Network/TDRSS [*Tracking and Data Relay Satellite System*] [*NASA*] (MCD)
NTS............. Nevada Test Site [*Department of Energy*]
NTS............. New Tube Shelter [*British*]
NTS............. Nitroglycerin Transdermal System [*Pharmacy*]
NTS............. Nontariff Size
NTS............. Nontemporary Storage [*Personal property*]
NTS............. Non-Traffic Sensitive [*Costs*] [*Telecommunications*]
NTS............. Nontranscribed Spacer [*Genetics*]
NTS............. Nordiske Teleansattes Samarbeidsorgan [*Nordic Telecommunications Association*] (EAIO)
NTS............. Notch Tensile Strength (OA)
NTS............. Notes [*Finance*]
NTS............. Not to Scale [*Drafting*]
NTS............. Nuclear Test Site (MCD)
NTS............. Nuclear Test Stage (AAG)
NTS............. Nucleus Tractus Solitarii [*Brain anatomy*]
NTS............. Number of Theoretical Stages [*Chemical engineering*]
NTS............. Nutrition Today Society [*Defunct*] (EA)
NTS............. Samaritan Hospital, Troy, NY [*Library symbol Library of Congress*] (LCLS)
NTSA .... National Tay-Sachs Association [*Later, NTSAD*] (EA)

NTSA .... National Technical Services Association (EA)
NTSA .... National Traffic Safety Agency [*Federal Highway Administration*]
NTSA .... National Training Systems Association (EA)
NTSA .... National Transportation Safety Association [*Defunct*] (EA)
NTSA .... National T-Shirt Association (EA)
NTSA .... National Tuberous Sclerosis Association (EA)
NTSA .... Naval Telecommunications System Architect (MCD)
NTSA .... Navy Tactical Support Activity (DNAB)
NTSA .... Northern Territory Softball Association [*Australia*]
NTSA .... Norway Technical Science Academy
NTSAD .... National Tay-Sachs and Allied Diseases Association (EA)
NtSanit .... National Sanitary Supply Co. [*Associated Press*] (SAG)
NTSB .... National Traffic Safety Bureau
NTSB .... National Transportation Safety Board [*Independent government agency*] [*Washington, DC*]
NTSB .... Northern Territory Surveyor Board [*Australia*]
NTSC .... National Tax Strike Coalition (EA)
NTSC .... National Technical Systems, Inc. [*NASDAQ symbol*] (NQ)
NTSC .... National Television Standard Code [*Video equipment*] (RDA)
NTSC .... National Television Standards Committee
NTSC .... National Television System Committee [*Formed in 1936*]
NTSC .... Natl Technical Sys [*NQS*] (TTSB)
NTSC .... Naval Training Systems Center [*Orlando, FL*]
NTSC .... Nonextrusion Texturized Soy Concentrate
NTSC .... North Texas State College [*Later, North Texas State University*]
NTSCH .... Naval Training School
NTSDS .... Near-Term Swimmer Defense System
NTSE .... Naval Telecommunications System Engineer (MCD)
NTSE .... Nontactical Support Equipment (MCD)
NTSEA .... National Trade Show Exhibitors Association [*Later, IEA*] (EA)
NTS EIS .... Nevada Test Site Environmental Impact Statement
NtSemi .... National Semiconductor Corp. [*Associated Press*] (SAG)
NTSF .... National Technical Scholarship Foundation (AEBS)
NTSF .... Nonextrusion Texturized Soy Flour
NTSH .... Near-Term Scout Helicopter [*Army*]
NTSI .... National Tire Svcs [*NASDAQ symbol*] (TTSB)
NTSI .... National Tribunal of Second Instance [*Catholic Church*] [*Australia*]
NTSI .... Nonextrusion Texturized Soy Isolate
NTSK .... Nordiska Tele-Satelit Kommitton [*Norway*]
NTSM .... Saint Mary's Hospital, Troy, NY [*Library symbol Library of Congress*] (LCLS)
Ntsmrt .... Netsmart Technologies, Inc. [*Associated Press*] (SAG)
NTSO .... NASA Test Support Office (KSC)
NTSR .... National Tunis Sheep Registry (EA)
NTSR .... NetStar, Inc. [*NASDAQ symbol*] (SAG)
NTSRP .... Nontechnical Services Real Property
NTSRVA ...... Nevada Test Site Radiation Victim Association (EA)
NTSSC .... Northern Territory School Sports Council [*Australia*]
NTST .... Netsmart Technologies, Inc. [*NASDAQ symbol*] (SAG)
NTSTN .... Naval Telecommunications System Test Node (CAAL)
NtSvIn .... National Service Industries, Inc. [*Associated Press*] (SAG)
NTT............. Nasotracheal Tube [*Medicine*] (DAVI)
NTT............. National Training Team [*Operated by the Helen Keller National Center for Deaf-Blind Youths and Adults (HKNC)*] (PAZ)
NTT............. New Technology Telescopes [*Under development*]
NTT............. Nippon Tel & Tel ADS [*NYSE symbol*] (TTSB)
NTT............. Nippon Telegraph & Telephone Co. [*NYSE symbol*] (SAG)
NTT............. Nippon Telegraph & Telephone Corp. [*Telecommunications and videotex company*] [*Japan*]
NTT............. Non-Tactical Tape [*Military*]
NTT............. Nuiatoputapu [*Tonga*] [*Airport symbol*] (OAG)
NTT............. Number Theoretic Transform (MHDI)
NTTA .... National Tobacco Tax Association (EA)
NTTAB .... Northern Territory Totalizator Agency Board [*Australia*]
NTTB .... Bora Bora/Motu-Mute [*French Polynesia*] [*ICAO location identifier*] (ICLI)
NTTBR .... Nineteen Thirty-Two Buick Registry (EA)
NTTC.......... National Tank Truck Carriers [*Alexandria, VA*] (EA)
NTTC.......... National Technology Transfer Center [*NASA*]
NTTC.......... Naval Technical Training Center
NTTC.......... NAVFAC [*Naval Facilities Engineering Command*] Technical Training Center
NTTCIW ...... National Technical Task Committee on Industrial Wastes
NTTE .... Non-Tactical Training Equipment [*Military*]
NTTE .... Tetiaroa [*French Polynesia*] [*ICAO location identifier*] (ICLI)
NTTF.......... Networking and Telecommunications Task Force [*Computer science*] (TNIG)
NTTF.......... Network Test and Training Facility [*Goddard Space Flight Center*]
NTTG .... Rangiroa [*French Polynesia*] [*ICAO location identifier*] (ICLI)
NTTH .... Huahine/Fare [*French Polynesia*] [*ICAO location identifier*] (ICLI)
NTTLC .... Northern Territory Trades and Labor Council [*Australia*]
NTTM .... Moorea/Temae [*French Polynesia*] [*ICAO location identifier*] (ICLI)
NTTO .... Hao [*French Polynesia*] [*ICAO location identifier*] (ICLI)
NTTP .... Maupiti [*French Polynesia*] [*ICAO location identifier*] (ICLI)
NTTPC .... Nippon Telegraph & Telephone Public Corp. [*Telecommunications*] (IAA)
NTTR .... Naval Torpedo Testing Range
NTTR .... Nontactical Telecommunications Requirement [*Army*] (AABC)
NTTR .... Raiatea/Uturoa [*French Polynesia*] [*ICAO location identifier*] (ICLI)
NTTRL .... National Tissue Typing Reference Laboratory (PDAA)
NTTS .... National Technology Transfer Center
NTTT .... Tahiti [*French Polynesia*] [*ICAO location identifier*] (ICLI)
NTTTI......... National Truck Tank and Trailer Tank Institute [*Later, Tank Conference of the Truck Trailer Manufacturers Association*]
NTTX.......... Mururoa [*French Polynesia*] [*ICAO location identifier*] (ICLI)

NTU .... National Taxpayers Union (EA)
NTU .... National Technological University [*Fort Collins, CO*]
NTU .... National Tenants Union [*Defunct*] (EA)
NTU .... Naval Training Unit
NTU .... Navy Toxicology Unit
NTU .... Nephelometric Turbidity Unit [*Analytical chemistry*]
NTU .... Network Terminating [*or Termination*] Unit
NTU .... New Threat Upgrade [*Military*] (CAAL)
NTU .... Nonimmune Transfer Utensil [*i.e., spoon*] [*Slang*]
NTU .... Nordisk Trafikskoleunion [*Nordic Union of Motor Schools Associations - NUMSA*] [*Finland*] (EAIO)
NTU .... Normal Trading Unit
NTU .... Not Taken Up
NTU .... Nuclear Training Unit (MCD)
NTU .... Number of Transfer Units
NTU .... Oceana, VA [*Location identifier FAA*] (FAAL)
NTUC .... National Trades Union Congress (NADA)
NTUC .... National Trade Union Congress [*Singapore*]
NTUC .... National Trade Union Council [*Hungary*]
NTUC .... National Trade Union Council for Human Rights (EA)
NTUC .... Nigerian Trade Union Congress
NTUC .... Nyasaland Trade Union Congress
NTuc .... Tuckahoe Public Library, Tuckahoe, NY [*Library symbol Library of Congress*] (LCLS)
NTucW .... Westchester County Historical Society, Tuckahoe, NY [*Library symbol Library of Congress*] (LCLS)
NTULC .... Negro Trade Union Leadership Council
NTuPSC ...... Sunmount Development Center, Staff Library, Tupper Lake, NY [*Library symbol Library of Congress*] (LCLS)
NTUV .... Vahitahi [*French Polynesia*] [*ICAO location identifier*] (ICLI)
NTuxp .... Tuxedo Park Library, Tuxedo Park, NY [*Library symbol Library of Congress*] (LCLS)
NTuxpl .... International Paper Co., Corporate Research and Development Division, Technical Information Center, Tuxedo Park, NY [*Library symbol Library of Congress*] (LCLS)
NTV .... Nervous Tissue Vaccine (AAMN)
NTV .... Nippon Television Network Corp. [*Japan*]
NTV .... Nontactical Vehicle [*Army*]
NTV .... NTV Oil Services Industries, Inc. [*Vancouver Stock Exchange symbol*]
NTVA .... Nondeterministic Time Variant Automation [*Mathematics*] (IAA)
NTVEI .... New Technical and Vocational Education Initiative (AIE)
NTVLRO ...... National Television Licensing and Records Office [*British*]
NTVS .... Navy Television System
NTVT .... Non-Toxic Vinyl Tubing
NTVU .... National Trust Volunteer Unit [*British*] (EAIO)
NTW .... Navigator Training Wing [*Military*]
NTW .... Non-Pressure Thermit Welding (PDAA)
NTW .... Nose, Tail, Waist [*Aviation*]
NTWA .... National Trust of Western Australia
NTWA .... National Turf Writers Association (EA)
NtwExp .... Network Express, Inc. [*Associated Press*] (SAG)
NTWH .... National Theatre Workshop of the Handicapped (EA)
NTWK .... Network (MSA)
NTWK .... Network Long Distance [*NASDAQ symbol*] (TTSB)
NTWK .... Network Long Distance, Inc. [*NASDAQ symbol*] (SAG)
NtwkC .... Network Connection, Inc. [*Associated Press*] (SAG)
NtwkCn .... Network Connection, Inc. [*Associated Press*] (SAG)
NtwkEq .... Network Equipment Technologies, Inc. [*Associated Press*] (SAG)
NtwkG .... Network General Corp. [*Associated Press*] (SAG)
NtwkLng ..... Network Long Distance, Inc. [*Associated Press*] (SAG)
NtwkPeri ..... Network Peripherals, Inc. [*Associated Press*] (SAG)
NtwkSix ...... Network Six, Inc. [*Associated Press*] (SAG)
NtWnLf .... National Western Life Insurance Co. [*Associated Press*] (SAG)
NTWRK .... Network
NTWRKNG ... Networking
NTWS .... New Threat Warning System [*Military*]
NTWS .... Nontrack while Scan
NtWst .... National Westminster Bank Ltd. [*Associated Press*] (SAG)
NtWstmin ..... National Westminster Bank Ltd. [*Associated Press*] (SAG)
NT WT .... Net Weight
NTX .... National Teletypewriter Exchange (IAA)
NTX .... Naval Teletypewriter Exchange [*Formerly, NTE*]
NTX .... Neonatal Thymectomy [*Medicine*]
NTX .... Networking and Expansion [*Computer science*] (PCM)
NTX .... Northern Air Service, Inc. [*ICAO designator*] (FAAC)
NTX .... Nuveen Texas Quality Income [*NYSE symbol*] (SPSG)
NTX .... Nuveen TX Qual Income Muni [*NYSE symbol*] (TTSB)
NTXQI .... Nuveen Texas Quality Income [*Associated Press*] (SAG)
NTY .... Sun City [*South Africa*] [*Airport symbol*] (OAG)
NTZ .... Indstrie Natuzzi ADS [*NYSE symbol*] (TTSB)
NTZ .... Industrie Natuzzi [*NYSE symbol*] (SPSG)
NTZ .... Iraq-Saudi Arabia Neutral Zone [*ANSI three-letter standard code*] (CNC)
NTZ .... Northern Transgressive Zone [*Geology*]
NTZ .... North Temperate Zone [*Planet Jupiter*]
NU .... Lipnur [*Indonesia*] [*ICAO aircraft manufacturer identifier*] (ICAO)
NU .... Nachalnik Uprovlenia [*Chief of Directorate*] [*Soviet military rank*]
NU .... Name Unknown
nU .... Nanounit [*One billionth of a standard unit*]
NU .... National Union (EA)
NU .... National Unity Party [*British Political party*]
NU .... NATO Unclassified (NATG)
nu .... Nauru [*MARC country of publication code Library of Congress*] (LCCP)

NU .... Nebraska University (MCD)
NU .... Nebraska Unofficial Reports [*A publication*] (DLA)
NU .... Neurology (DAVI)
NU .... New Ulm [*Diocesan abbreviation*] [*Minnesota*] (TOCD)
NU .... New Uses [*Research test*] [*Psychology*]
Nu .... Ngultrum [*Monetary unit*] [*Bhutan*] (BARN)
NU .... Niue [*ANSI two-letter standard code*] (CNC)
NU .... Northeast Utilities [*NYSE symbol*] (SPSG)
NU .... Northern Union [*Rugby*] [*British*] (DAS)
NU .... Northrop Unit [*Of hydrolytic enzyme activity*]
NU .... North Up [*Automotive engineering*]
NU .... Nose Up [*Aviation*]
NU .... Nothing Unsatisfactory (MHDB)
NU .... Not Used
Nu .... Nucleolus [*Cytology*]
nu .... Nude [*Mouse*] [*Medicine*] (DMAA)
NU .... Nu-Gro Corp. [*Toronto Stock Exchange symbol*]
NU .... Nullified Unpostable [*Computer science*]
Nu .... Numbers [*Old Testament book*] (BJA)
NU .... Number Unobtainable [*Telecommunications*]
Nu .... Nusselt Number [*IUPAC*]
NU .... Southwest Airlines [*ICAO designator*] (AD)
NUA .... Nations Unies des Animaux [*United Animal Nations - UAN*] (EA)
NUA .... Net Unrealized Appreciation Tax
NUA .... Network User Address
NUA .... Network Users Association [*Defunct*] (EA)
NUA .... Not Under the Act
NUA .... Nuclear Agency [*Army*]
NUA .... Nuna Air AS [*Denmark ICAO designator*] (FAAC)
NUAAW .... National Union of Agricultural and Allied Workers [*British*]
NUABA .... National United Affiliated Beverage Association (EA)
NUAC .... National Urban Affairs Council (EA)
NUAD .... Nucleus Average Optical Density [*Microscopy*]
NUADC .... National Underwater Accident Data Center
NUAT .... Nordisk Union for Alkoholfri Trafikk [*Scandinavian Union for Non-Alcoholic Traffic - SUNAT*] (EA)
NUATFAC .... Nordiska Unionen for Arbetsledare, Tekniska Funktionarer och andra Chefer [*Nordic Confederation of Supervisors, Technicians and Other Managers*] (EAIO)
NUB .... National Union of Busmen [*British*]
NUB .... Navy Uniform Board (DNAB)
NUB .... Northumberland Mines Ltd. [*Toronto Stock Exchange symbol*]
Nub .... Nubes [*Clouds*] [*of Aristophanes*] [*Classical studies*] (OCD)
nub .... Nubian [*MARC language code Library of Congress*] (LCCP)
NUBA .... National UHF [*Ultrahigh Frequency*] Broadcasters Association (EA)
NUBC .... National Uniform-Billing Committee [*Insurance*] (DAVI)
NUBE .... National Union of Bank Employees [*Later, Banking, Insurance, and Finance Union*] (DCTA)
NUBF .... National Union of British Fishermen
NUBIC .... Nuclear Bunkered Instrumentation Center (MCD)
NUBICWOPS... Nuclear, Biological, and Chemical Warfare Operations [*Military*]
NUBLU .... New Basic Logic Unit [*Computer science*] (MHDI)
NUBOMCWKT... National Union of Blastfurnacemen, Ore Miners, Coke Workers, and Kindred Trades [*British*] (DCTA)
NUBS .... National Unemployment Benefit System [*Department of Health and Social Security*] [*British*]
NUBSO .... National Union of Boot and Shoe Operatives [*British*]
NUBTC .... National Union of Boot Top Cutters [*British*]
NUC .... National Unification Council [*Philippines*] [*Political party*] (FEA)
NUC .... National Union of Carriers [*British*]
NUC .... National University Consortium for Telecommunications in Teaching (EA)
NUC .... National Urban Coalition (EA)
NUC .... Naval Undersea Center [*Later, NOSC*] (MCD)
NUC .... Naval Undersea Research and Development Center (USDC)
NUC .... Naval Undersea Research and Development Center [*Marine science*] (OSRA)
NUC .... Navy Unit Commendation [*Military decoration*]
NUC .... New University Conference
NUC .... Non-Uniformity Correction
NUC .... Nuclear
NUC .... Nuclear (AFM)
NUC .... Nucleated
Nuc .... [*A*] Nucleoside [*Also, N*]
NUC .... Nucleus (WDAA)
NUC .... Nucorr Petroleums Ltd. [*Toronto Stock Exchange symbol*]
NUC .... Nuveen California Quality Income Municipal [*NYSE symbol*] (SPSG)
NUC .... Nuveen CA Qual Income Muni [*NYSE symbol*] (TTSB)
NUC .... San Clemente Island, CA [*Location identifier FAA*] (FAAL)
NUCA .... National Utility Contractors' Association (EA)
NUCAA .... National United Church Association of America (EA)
NUCAL .... National Union Catalog Author List
NUCAP .... Nuclear Cannon Projectile [*Army*]
NUCAP .... Nuclear Capability [*Military*]
NUCAP .... Nuclear Capability Report (CINC)
Nucaps .... National Union of Civil and Public Servants [*British*] (DBA)
NUCAS .... Nuclear Authentication System
NUCAW .... National Union of Clerks and Administrative Workers [*British*]
NUCBO .... National Uniform Certification of Building Operators (EA)
NUCC .... North Up Cursor Centered [*Automotive engineering*]
NUCDEF .... Nuclear Defense (AABC)
NUCDETS ..... Nuclear Detonation Detection and Reporting System (AABC)
Nuc E .... Nuclear Engineer
NUCEA .... National University Continuing Education Association (EA)
NUCEX .... Nuclear Exercise [*Also, NUKEX*] (NVT)

NUCFO......... Nuclear Force Posture
NUCH.......... Nucha [*Nape of the Neck*] [*Latin*] (ROG)
NUCIA......... National Union of Cooperative Insurance Agents [*British*]
NUCINT....... Nuclear Intelligence (MCD)
NUCISE....... National Union of Cooperative Insurance Society Employees [*British*]
NUCL.......... Nuclear
NUCL.......... Nucleus
Nuc L Bull .... Nuclear Law Bulletin [*A publication*] (ILCA)
NUCLE........ Nuclear
Nuclear Reg Rep (CCH)... Nuclear Regulation Reports (Commerce Clearing House)
    [*A publication*] (DLA)
NUCLENOR... Controles Nucleares del Norte, SA [*Spain*]
NUCLEX....... Nuclear Industries Exhibition
NUCLEX....... Nuclear Loadout Exercise [*Military*] (NVT)
NUCM......... North Up Cursor Moving [*Automotive engineering*]
NUCM......... Nuclear Metals [*NASDAQ symbol*] (TTSB)
NUCM......... Nuclear Metals, Inc. [*NASDAQ symbol*] (NQ)
NUCMC....... National Union Catalog of Manuscript Collections [*Library of*
    Congress]
NucMet....... Nuclear Metals, Inc. [*Associated Press*] (SAG)
NUCMUN..... Nuclear Munitions (RDA)
NUCO......... National Union of Certified Officers [*British*]
NUCO......... NuCo2 Inc. [*NASDAQ symbol*] (TTSB)
NUCO......... NuCo2, Inc. [*NASDAQ symbol*] (SAG)
NUCO......... Numerical Code (NATG)
NuCo2......... NuCo2, Inc. [*Associated Press*] (SAG)
NUCOL........ Numerical Control Language [*Computer science*] (PDAA)
NUCOM....... Nuclear Effects on Joint Force Communications (MCD)
NUCOM....... Numerical Contouring Mechanism
Nucor......... Nucor Corp. [*Associated Press*] (SAG)
NUCP......... National Union of Czechoslovak Protestants in America and Canada
    [*Defunct*] (EA)
NUC PHY ..... Nuclear Physics (WDAA)
NUCPS........ National Union of Civil and Public Servants [*British*]
NUCPWR..... Nuclear Powered (NVT)
NucReaOpBasBad... Nuclear Reactor Operator, Basic Badge [*Military decoration*]
    (AABC)
NucReaOpFCBad... Nuclear Reactor Operator, First-Class Badge [*Military*
    decoration] (AABC)
NucReaOpSCBad... Nuclear Reactor Operator, Second-Class Badge [*Military*
    decoration] (AABC)
NucReaOpSftSupvBad... Nuclear Reactor Operator, Shift Supervisor Badge [*Military*
    decoration] (AABC)
NUCREP....... Nuclear Damage Report (AABC)
NUCS.......... National Union of Christian Schools [*Later, CSI*] (EA)
NUCS.......... National Union of Club Stewards [*British*] (DBA)
NUCSAM..... Nuclear Surface-to-Air Missile (NVT)
NUCSE....... National Union of Czechoslovak Students in Exile (EA)
NUCSEQ...... Nucleotide Sequencing Search System [*NIH/EPA Chemical*
    Information System] [*Database*]
NUCSTAT .... Nuclear Operational Status Report (NATG)
NUCUAA ...... National United Church Ushers Association of America (EA)
NUCURES .... Northeastern University Center for Urban and Regional Economic
    Studies [*Research center*] (RCD)
NUCWA....... Nuclear Weapons Accounting (MCD)
NUCWAR..... Nuclear War
NUCWARN... Nuclear Warning Message [*Military*] (ADDR)
NUCWPN ..... Nuclear Weapon (AABC)
NUCWPNSTRACEN... Nuclear Weapons Training Center
NUD.......... Adak, AK [*Location identifier FAA*] (FAAL)
NUD.......... En Nahud [*Sudan*] [*Airport symbol*] (AD)
NUD.......... National Union of the Deaf [*British*]
NUD.......... Naval Unit Disseminator (RDA)
NUD.......... Nebraska University Disease or N. Underdahl Disease [*A disease of*
    swine named both for the place where it was originally identified
    and for the person who isolated the causative agent]
NUD.......... Nonulcer Dyspepsia [*Gastroenterology*] (DAVI)
NUDA & GO... National Union of Domestic Appliances and General Operatives
    [*British*] (DBA)
NUDAC....... Nuclear Data Center (IAA)
NUDAGMW... National Union of Domestic Appliance and General Metal-Workers
    [*British*] (DCTA)
NUDAP....... Nuclear Detonating Data Points (MCD)
NUDAW....... National Union of Shop Distributive and Allied Workers [*British*]
NUDBTW..... National Union of Dyers, Bleachers, and Textile Workers [*British*]
    (DCTA)
NUDET........ Nuclear Detection (MCD)
NUDET........ Nuclear Detonation Evaluation Technique (MCD)
NUDETS...... Nuclear Detection and Reporting System
NUDETS...... Nuclear Detonation Detection and Reporting System
NUDO......... National United Democratic Organization [*Namibia*] [*Political party*]
    (PPW)
NUDORE...... Nuclear Doctrine Organization and Equipment (MCD)
NUDWSS .... National Union of Docks, Wharves, and Shipping Staffs [*British*]
NUE.......... Nitrogen Utilization Efficiency [*Ecology*]
NUE.......... Niue [*Niue Island*] [*Seismograph station code, US Geological*
    Survey] (SEIS)
NUE.......... Nucor Corp. [*NYSE symbol*] (SPSG)
NUE.......... Nuremberg [*Germany Airport symbol*] (OAG)
NUEA......... National University Extension Association [*Later, NUCEA*] (EA)
NUERA........ Nuclear Extended Range Aircraft [*Proposed*] [*Air Force*]
NUESNA...... National Union of Eritrean Students - North America (EA)
NUET .... National Union of Elementary Teachers [*British*]
NuevEn....... Nuevo Energy Co. [*Associated Press*] (SAG)
NUEW......... National Union of Eritrean Women - North America (EA)

NUF .... National Ulcer Foundation (EA)
NUF .... National Unifying Force [*Zimbabwe*] [*Political party*] (PPW)
NUF .... National Union of Firemen [*British*] (DAS)
NUF .... National Unity Front [*Poland Political party*] (PPW)
NUF .... National Urban Fellows (EA)
NUF .... Natural Uranium Fuel
NUF .... Nordisk Urologisk Forening [*Scandinavian Association of Urology -*
    SAU] (EAIO)
NUF .... Nuveen Florida Quality Income Municipal [*NYSE symbol*] (SPSG)
NUF .... Nuveen FL Qual Income Muni [*NYSE symbol*] (TTSB)
NUFAM....... Nuclear Fire Planning and Assessment Model (MCD)
NUFCW....... National Union of Funeral and Cemetery Workers [*British*] (BI)
NUFD......... Naval Unit, Fort Detrick [*Maryland*]
NUFDC....... Northgate Universal Floppy Drive Controller [*Computer science*]
NUFGW....... National Union of Flint Glassworkers [*British*] (DBA)
NUFI .... National Unfinished Furniture Institute [*Defunct*] (EA)
NUFLAT ..... National Union of Footwear, Leather, and Allied Trades [*British*]
    (DCTA)
NUFLV .... National United Front for the Liberation of Vietnam (EA)
NUFON....... Northern UFO Network [*British*]
NUFP .... Not Used for Production (AAG)
NUFP .... Number of Uncorrected Flight Plans (SAA)
NUFRONLIV... National United Front for the Liberation of Vietnam (EA)
NUFS .... National United Front of Somalia [*Political party*] (EY)
NUFS .... National Utility Financial Statement Model [*Department of Energy*]
    (GFGA)
NUFSO .... National Union of Funeral Service Operatives [*British*] (DI)
NUFTIC ...... Nuclear Fuels Technology Information Center (DIT)
NUFTO .... National Union of Furniture Trade Operatives [*British*]
NUFUCO ..... Nuclear Fuel Cost (PDAA)
NUG .... Federation of NCR [*NCR Corp.*] User Groups (EA)
NUG .... National Union of Glovers [*British*]
NUG .... Necrotizing Ulcerative Gingivitis [*Dentistry*]
NUG .... Nonutility Generator
NUGMW...... National Union of General and Municipal Workers [*British*]
NUGS........ Nonutility Generating Source
NUGSAT ..... National Union of Gold, Silver, and Allied Trades [*British*] (DCTA)
NUH .... National Union for the Homeless (EA)
NUHADI ..... Nuclear Helicopter Air Density Indicating [*System*] [*Army*]
NUHC .... Nu Horizons Electronics [*NASDAQ symbol*] (TTSB)
NUHC .... Nu-Horizons Electronics Corp. [*NASDAQ symbol*] (SAG)
NUHELI ...... Nuclear Helicopter Lift Indicator (KSC)
NUHKW....... National Union of Hosiery and Knitwear Workers [*British*] (DCTA)
NuHoriz...... Nu-Horizons Electronics Corp. [*Associated Press*] (SAG)
NUI .... National University of Ireland
NUI .... NetWare Users International
NUI .... Networks Unlimited, Inc. [*Defunct*] (EA)
NUI .... Network User Identifier [*or Identification*] [*Password*]
NUI .... Notebook User Interface [*Penpoint*] [*Computer science*]
NUI .... NUI Corp. [*NYSE symbol*] (SPSG)
NUI .... Nuiqsut [*Alaska*] [*Airport symbol*] (OAG)
NUI .... Patuxent River, MD [*Location identifier FAA*] (FAAL)
NUIA .... National United Italian Associations (EA)
NUIC .... National Urban Indian Council (EA)
NUIR .... National Union for Independence and Revolution [*Chad*] [*Political*
    party]
NUIS .... National Union of Iraqi Students [*British*] (DI)
NUIS .... Navy Unit Identification System (NVT)
NUIU .... New University Industrial Unit [*New University of Ulster*] [*Research*
    center British]
NUIW .... National Union of Insurance Workers [*British*] (DCTA)
NUJ .... National Union of Journalists [*British*]
NUJMB .... Northern Universities Joint Matriculation Board (AIE)
NUK .... Nukutavake [*French Polynesia*] [*Airport symbol*] (OAG)
NUKE......... Nuclear
NUKEX .... Nuclear Exercise [*Also, NUCEX*] (NVT)
NUKO........ Nuko Information Sys [*NASDAQ symbol*] (TTSB)
NUKO........ Nuko Information Systems, Inc. [*NASDAQ symbol*] (SAG)
NukoInfo..... Nuko Information Systems Inc. [*Associated Press*] (SAG)
NuKote....... Nu-Kote Holding, Inc. [*Associated Press*] (SAG)
NUL .... National and University Library [*Israel*] (BJA)
NUL .... National Union for Liberation [*Philippines*] [*Political party*] (PPW)
NUL .... National Urban League (EA)
NUL .... New Universal Library [*A publication*]
NUL .... New Upper Lateral [*Botany*]
NUL .... Nihon University [*UTLAS symbol*]
NUL .... Non-GSE [*Ground Support Equipment*] Utilization List [*NASA*]
    (NASA)
NUL .... No Upper Limit (MHDW)
NUL .... Nu-Lady Gold Mines [*Vancouver Stock Exchange symbol*]
NUL .... Nulato [*Alaska*] [*Airport symbol*] (OAG)
NUL .... Nulato, AK [*Location identifier FAA*] (FAAL)
NUL .... Null (OSI)
NUL .... Null Character [*Keyboard*] [*Computer science*]
NULAC .... Nuclear Liquid Air Cycle Engine
NULACE ..... Nuclear Liquid Air Cycle Engine
NULBA .... National United Licensees Beverage Association [*Later, NUABA*]
    (EA)
NULC .... National Union of Liberal Clubs [*British*] (DBA)
NULCAIS..... Northwestern University Library Computer-Assisted Information
    Service (OLDSS)
NULCW....... National Union of Lift and Crane Workers [*British*]
NULEOA...... National United Law Enforcement Officers Association (EA)
NULF .... National United Liberation Front [*Myanmar*] [*Political party*] (FEA)
nullip .... Nullipara [*obstetrics*] (DAVI)

NULMW .... National Union of Lock and Metal Workers [*British*] (DCTA)
NULO .... NASA Unmanned Launch Operations (MCD)
NULO .... National Union of Labour Organisers [*British*] (DBA)
NULOR .... Neuron Location and Ranging
NULS .... National Underwater Laboratory System [*Marine science*] (MSC)
NULS .... Net Unit-Load Size (MHDB)
NULU .... New Library Utility
NUM .... Error in Use of Numbers [*Used in correcting manuscripts, etc.*]
NUM .... National Union of Mineworkers [*South Africa*]
NUM .... National Unity Movement [*Sierra Leone*] [*Political party*] (EY)
Num .... Numa [*of Plutarch*] [*Classical studies*] (OCD)
NUM .... Numadu [*Japan*] [*Seismograph station code, US Geological Survey Closed*] (SEIS)
NUM .... Number [*or Numerator, or Numeric*]
Num .... Numbers [*Old Testament book*]
NUM .... Numeral [*or Numerical*]
NUM .... Nurse Unit Manager
NUM .... Nuveen Michigan Quality Income Municipal [*NYSE symbol*] (SPSG)
NUM .... Nuveen MI Qual Income Muni [*NYSE symbol*] (TTSB)
NUMA .... National Underwater and Marine Agency (MCD)
NUMA .... Nonuniform - Memory - Access [*Computer science*]
NUMAC .... Northumbrian Universities Multiple Access Computer (NITA)
Numac .... Numac Energy [*Associated Press*]
NUMAR .... Nuclear Magnetic Resonance [*Also, NMR*]
Numar .... Numar Corp. [*Associated Press*] (SAG)
NUMARC .... Nuclear Management and Resources Council (EA)
NUMARCOM... Nuclear Power for Marine Purposes Committee (MCD)
NUMAS .... Numerical Multifactor Assessment System (ADA)
NUMAST ...... National Union of Marine Aviation and Shipping Transport [*British*]
NUMB .... Numbered
Numb .... Numbers [*Old Testament book*]
NUMBR .... Number (DAVI)
NUMC .... Newcastle University Mountaineering Club [*Australia*]
Numd .... Numed Home Health Care, Inc. [*Associated Press*] (SAG)
NUMD .... Numed Home Health Care, Inc. [*NASDAQ symbol*] (SAG)
NUMD .... NuMED Home Hlth Care [*NASDAQ symbol*] (TTSB)
NUMDW .... NuMED Home Health Care Wrrt [*NASDAQ symbol*] (TTSB)
NUMEC .... Nuclear Materials & Equipment Corp.
NUMEC .... Nuclear Uranium Materials and Equipment Corp. (GAAI)
Numed .... Numed Home Health Care, Inc. [*Associated Press*] (SAG)
NumedH .... Numed Home Health Care, Inc. [*Associated Press*] (SAG)
NUMEPS .... Numeric Meta Language Processing System (PDAA)
NUMERALS... Numerical Analysis System (BUR)
Numerex ...... Numerex Corp. [*Associated Press*] (SAG)
Numid .... Numidian
NUMIS .... Navy Uniform Management Information System
NUMIS .... Numismatics
NUMISM .... Numismatics
NUMM .... National Union of Masters and Mates [*British*]
NUMMI .... New United Motor Manufacturing, Inc. [*Joint venture of Toyota Motor Corp . and General Motors Corp.*]
NUMR .... Numar Corp. [*NASDAQ symbol*] (SAG)
NumR .... Numbers Rabbah
NUMS .... Nuclear Materials Security (NRCH)
NUMS .... Numerous (ROG)
NUMSA .... National Union of Metalworkers of South Africa
NUMW .... National Unemployed Workers' Movement [*British*]
NUN .... Network User Name [*Telecommunications*] (OSI)
NUN .... Nunasi-Central Airlines Ltd. [*Canada ICAO designator*] (FAAC)
NUN .... Nuveen New York Quality Income Municipal [*NYSE symbol*] (SPSG)
NUN .... Nuveen NY Qual Income Muni [*NYSE symbol*] (TTSB)
NUN .... Pensacola, FL [*Location identifier FAA*] (FAAL)
NUn .... Uniondale Public Library, Uniondale, NY [*Library symbol Library of Congress*] (LCLS)
NUNA .... Not Used on Next Assembly (AAG)
NUnCCE .... Cornelius Court Elementary School, Uniondale, NY [*Library symbol*] [*Library of Congress*] (LCLS)
NUnCE .... California Elementary School, Uniondale, NY [*Library symbol Library of Congress*] (LCLS)
NUnH .... Uniondale High School, Uniondale, NY [*Library symbol Library of Congress*] (LCLS)
NUnLJ .... Lawrence Junior High School, Uniondale, NY [*Library symbol Library of Congress*] (LCLS)
NUnNE .... Northern Parkway Elementary School, Uniondale, NY [*Library symbol*] [*Library of Congress*] (LCLS)
NUnSE .... Smith Elementary School, Uniondale, NY [*Library symbol Library of Congress*] (LCLS)
NUnStA .... Saint Agnes Cathedral High School, Uniondale, NY [*Library symbol*] [*Library of Congress*] (LCLS)
NUnTHJ .... Turtle Hook Junior High School, Uniondale, NY [*Library symbol Library of Congress*] (LCLS)
NUnWE .... Walnut Elementary School, Uniondale, NY [*Library symbol Library of Congress*] (LCLS)
NUO .... Nugold Enterprises Corp. [*Vancouver Stock Exchange symbol*]
NUO .... Nuveen Ohio Quality Income Municipal [*NYSE symbol*] (SPSG)
NUO .... Nuveen OH Qual Incme Muni [*NYSE symbol*] (TTSB)
NUOL .... Naval Underwater Ordnance Laboratory (NOAA)
NUOM .... Northern Union of Operative Masons [*British*]
NUOS .... Naval Underwater Ordnance Station
NUP .... Nationalist Unionist Party [*Sudan*]
NUP .... National Umma Party [*Sudan*] [*Political party*]
NUP .... National Union of Protestants
NUP .... National United Party [*Vanuatu*] [*Political party*] (EY)
NUP .... National Unity Party [*British Political party*] (EA)
NUP .... Negro Universities Press (AEBS)

NUP .... New Union Party [*Later, IUP*] (EA)
NUP .... Nunapitchuk [*Alaska*] [*Airport symbol*] (OAG)
NUPAD .... Nuclear-Powered Active Detection System
NUpB .... United States Brookhaven National Laboratory, Upton, NY [*Library symbol Library of Congress*] (LCLS)
NUPB & PW... National Union of Printing, Bookbinding, and Paperworkers [*British*] (DGA)
NUpB-MH .... United States Brookhaven National Laboratory, Medical Research Center Hospital, Upton, NY [*Library symbol Library of Congress*] (LCLS)
NUPBP .... National Union of Printing, Bookbinding, and Paperworkers [*British*]
NUPDTU .... National Union of Painters and Decorators Trade Union [*British*]
NUPE .... National Union of Public Employees [*British*]
NUPEC .... Nuclear Power Engineering Test Center (NRCH)
NUPGE .... National Union of Provincial Government Employees [*Canada*]
NUPLEX .... Nuclear Complex
NUPOC .... Nuclear Propulsion Officer Candidate [*Navy*]
NUPOC-S .... Nuclear Propulsion Officer Candidate - Submarine (DNAB)
NUPPS .... Nonuniform Progressive Phase Shift (IAA)
NUPS .... Nordic Union of Private Schools (EA)
NUPT .... National Union of Press Telegraphists [*British*] (DGA)
NUPWR .... Nuclear Power [*or Powered*] (DNAB)
NUPWRU .... Nuclear Power Unit (DNAB)
NUQ .... Mountain View, CA [*Location identifier FAA*] (FAAL)
NUR .... Natchez, Urania & Ruston Railway Co. [*AAR code*]
NUR .... National Union of Railwaymen [*British*]
NUR .... Net Unduplicated Research
Nur .... Nitrosourea [*Biochemistry*]
NUR .... Nonuniformity Ratio
NUR .... Nurmijarvi [*Finland*] [*Seismograph station code, US Geological Survey*] (SEIS)
NUR .... Nurse (AABC)
NUR .... Nurse
NUR .... Nuspar Resources [*Vancouver Stock Exchange symbol*]
NURA .... National Union of Rate-Payers' Associations [*British*] (BI)
NuraTL .... Nur Advanced Technologies Ltd. [*Associated Press*] (SAG)
NURB .... National Uniform Business Rate [*British*]
NURB .... Neville Upper Reservoir Buffer [*Medicine*] (DMAA)
NURBS .... Nonuniform Rational B-Spline [*A type of spline*] [*Computer science*]
NURBS .... Nonuniform Relational B-Spline [*Micro Cadam 3-D*] [*Computer science*]
NURC .... National Undersea Research Center [*Virgin Islands*]
NURC .... National Union of Railway Clerks [*British*]
NURC .... National Union of Retail Confectioners [*British*] (BI)
NURDC .... Naval Undersea Research and Development Center
NURE .... National Uranium Resource Evaluation [*Program*] [*Energy Research and Development Administration*]
NURED .... Nuclear Requirements Determination [*Military*]
NUREG .... Nuclear Regulatory Commission
NUREM .... Nuclear Requirements Methodology [*Military*]
NUREP .... New York University Resonance Escape Probability [*Code*] [*Nuclear energy*] (NRCH)
NUREQ .... Nuclear Requirements [*Military*]
NUREX .... Nuclear Requirements Extrapolation [*Model*] (MCD)
NU/RF .... National Urban/Rural Fellows (EA)
NURF .... National Utility Reference File [*Department of Energy*]
NURF .... Nucleosome Remodeling Factor [*Analytical biochemistry*]
NURIG .... Navy Utility Regulatory Intervention Group (DNAB)
NUROC .... Nuclear Rocket Project (SAA)
NURP .... National Undersea Research Program [*Department of Commerce*] (GRD)
NURP .... Nationwide Urban Runoff Program [*Water pollution*]
NURP .... NOAA [*National Oceanic and Atmospheric Administration*] Undersea Research Program (USDC)
NURP .... NOAA [*National Oceanic and Atmospheric Administration*] Undersea Research Program [*Marine science*] (OSRA)
NURS .... International Nursing Services, Inc. [*NASDAQ symbol*] (SAG)
NURS .... International Nursing Svcs [*NASDAQ symbol*] (TTSB)
NURS .... Nursery
NURS .... Nursing
NURsc .... New Jersey Resources [*Associated Press*] (SAG)
NURSE .... Nurses Underrepresented in Social Equality (BABM)
NURSE .... Nurses Underrepresented in Social Equality (DAVI)
NURSE .... Nursing
NURSEDETS... Nurse Detachments [*Army*]
NURSW .... International Nursing Wrrt [*NASDAQ symbol*] (TTSB)
NURSW .... Nursing System-Wide
NURT .... National Union of Retail Tobacconists [*British*] (BI)
NURTE .... Nur Advanced Technologies Ltd. [*NASDAQ symbol*] (SAG)
NUS .... National Union of Scalemakers [*British*] (DCTA)
NUS .... National Union of Seamen [*British*]
NUS .... National Union of Students [*British*]
NUS .... National University of Singapore
NUS .... National Utility Services [*British*]
NUS .... New Upper Stage [*NASA*] (KSC)
NUS .... Nominal Ultimate Strength (IAA)
NUS .... Nonuniformly Spaced (IAA)
NUS .... Norsup [*Vanuatu*] [*Airport symbol*] (OAG)
NUS .... Nuclear Utility Services
NUS .... NUS Corp. (GAAI)
NUS .... Nu-Start Resource Corp. [*Vancouver Stock Exchange symbol*]
n-us-- .... United States [*MARC geographic area code Library of Congress*] (LCCP)
n-usa- .... Appalachian Area [*MARC geographic area code Library of Congress*] (LCCP)

NUSA .... National Union of Shop Assistants [*British*] (DAS)
N/USA .... National/United Service Agencies
NUSA .... Neighborhoods USA (EA)
NUSA .... Ninth United States Army
NUSAC .... Nuclear Sciences Advisory Committee [*Department of Energy/ National Science Foundation*]
NUSACC .... National United States-Arab Chamber of Commerce (EA)
n-us-ak .... Alaska [*MARC geographic area code Library of Congress*] (LCCP)
n-us-al .... Alabama [*MARC geographic area code Library of Congress*] (LCCP)
n-us-ar .... Arkansas [*MARC geographic area code Library of Congress*] (LCCP)
NUSAR .... Nuclear Sweep and RADAR (IAA)
NUSAS .... National Union of South African Students
NUSAS .... Navy Underwater Swimmer Assault System (SAA)
NUSAT .... Northern Utah Satellite
n-us-az .... Arizona [*MARC geographic area code Library of Congress*] (LCCP)
NUSC .... Naval Underwater Systems Center
NUSC .... Naval Underwater Systems Center/Command (USDC)
n-usc- .... North Central States [*MARC geographic area code Library of Congress*] (LCCP)
n-us-ca .... California [*MARC geographic area code Library of Congress*] (LCCP)
NUSCAT .... New Airborne Scatterometer (MCD)
NUSCDET .... Naval Underwater Systems Center Detachment (DNAB)
NUSC/NL .... Naval Underwater Systems Center, New London [*Connecticut*]
NUSC/NPT .... Naval Underwater Systems Center, Newport [*Rhode Island*]
n-us-co .... Colorado [*MARC geographic area code Library of Congress*] (LCCP)
NUSCOT .... Nuclear Submarine Control Trainer (PDAA)
n-us-ct .... Connecticut [*MARC geographic area code Library of Congress*] (LCCP)
NUSD .... Nucleus Sum Optical Density [*Microscopy*]
n-us-dc .... District of Columbia [*MARC geographic area code Library of Congress*] (LCCP)
n-us-de .... Delaware [*MARC geographic area code Library of Congress*] (LCCP)
n-use- .... Northeast (United States) [*MARC geographic area code Library of Congress*] (LCCP)
NUSEC .... Naval Underwater Systems Engineering Center (MUGU)
NUSFDB .... NUS [*National University of Singapore*] Financial Database [*Information service or system*] (IID)
n-us-fl .... Florida [*MARC geographic area code Library of Congress*] (LCCP)
n-us-ga .... Georgia [*MARC geographic area code Library of Congress*] (LCCP)
NUSGGMW .... National Union of Stove Grate and General Metal Workers [*British*]
NUSGW .... National Union of Stove and Grate Workers [*British*]
NUSH .... Nucleus Shape [*Microscopy*]
n-us-hi .... Hawaii [*MARC geographic area code Library of Congress*] (LCCP)
n-us-ia .... Iowa [*MARC geographic area code Library of Congress*] (LCCP)
n-us-id .... Idaho [*MARC geographic area code Library of Congress*] (LCCP)
n-us-il .... Illinois [*MARC geographic area code Library of Congress*] (LCCP)
n-us-in .... Indiana [*MARC geographic area code Library of Congress*] (LCCP)
n-us-ks .... Kansas [*MARC geographic area code Library of Congress*] (LCCP)
n-us-ky .... Kentucky [*MARC geographic area code Library of Congress*] (LCCP)
n-usl- .... Middle Atlantic States [*MARC geographic area code Library of Congress*] (LCCP)
NUSL .... Naval Underwater Sound Laboratory [*Later, NUSC*]
n-us-la .... Louisiana [*MARC geographic area code Library of Congress*] (LCCP)
n-usm- .... Mississippi River and Basin [*MARC geographic area code Library of Congress*] (LCCP)
n-us-ma .... Massachusetts [*MARC geographic area code Library of Congress*] (LCCP)
n-us-md .... Maryland [*MARC geographic area code Library of Congress*] (LCCP)
n-us-me .... Maine [*MARC geographic area code Library of Congress*] (LCCP)
n-us-mi .... Michigan [*MARC geographic area code Library of Congress*] (LCCP)
n-us-mn .... Minnesota [*MARC geographic area code Library of Congress*] (LCCP)
n-us-mo .... Missouri [*MARC geographic area code Library of Congress*] (LCCP)
n-us-ms .... Mississippi [*MARC geographic area code Library of Congress*] (LCCP)
n-us-mt .... Montana [*MARC geographic area code Library of Congress*] (LCCP)
NUSMWCHDE ... National Union of Sheet Metal Workers, Coppersmiths, Heating and Domestic Engineers [*British*] (DCTA)
n-usn- .... New England [*MARC geographic area code Library of Congress*] (LCCP)
n-us-nb .... Nebraska [*MARC geographic area code Library of Congress*] (LCCP)
n-us-nc .... North Carolina [*MARC geographic area code Library of Congress*] (LCCP)
n-us-nd .... North Dakota [*MARC geographic area code Library of Congress*] (LCCP)
n-us-nh .... New Hampshire [*MARC geographic area code Library of Congress*] (LCCP)
n-us-nj .... New Jersey [*MARC geographic area code Library of Congress*] (LCCP)
n-us-nm .... New Mexico [*MARC geographic area code Library of Congress*] (LCCP)
n-us-nv .... Nevada [*MARC geographic area code Library of Congress*] (LCCP)
n-us-ny .... New York [*MARC geographic area code Library of Congress*] (LCCP)
n-uso- .... Ohio River and Basin [*MARC geographic area code Library of Congress*] (LCCP)
n-us-oh .... Ohio [*MARC geographic area code Library of Congress*] (LCCP)
n-us-ok .... Oklahoma [*MARC geographic area code Library of Congress*] (LCCP)
n-us-or .... Oregon [*MARC geographic area code Library of Congress*] (LCCP)
NUSOS .... Nuclear Underwater Sound Source (NG)
n-usp- .... Pacific and Mountain States [*MARC geographic area code Library of Congress*] (LCCP)
n-us-pa .... Pennsylvania [*MARC geographic area code Library of Congress*] (LCCP)

NUSPRAW ... National Union of Storeworkers, Packers, Rubber and Allied Workers [*Australia*]
n-us-ri .... Rhode Island [*MARC geographic area code Library of Congress*] (LCCP)
NUSRL .... Navy Underwater Sound Reference Laboratory
n-uss- .... Missouri River and Basin [*MARC geographic area code Library of Congress*] (LCCP)
NUSS .... National Union of School Students [*British*] (DI)
NUSS .... Nuclear Safety Standard (PDAA)
n-us-sc .... South Carolina [*MARC geographic area code Library of Congress*] (LCCP)
n-us-sd .... South Dakota [*MARC geographic area code Library of Congress*] (LCCP)
NUSSE .... Nonuniform Simple Surface Evaporated Model (MCD)
n-ust- .... Southwest (United States) [*MARC geographic area code Library of Congress*] (LCCP)
n-us-tn .... Tennessee [*MARC geographic area code Library of Congress*] (LCCP)
n-us-tx .... Texas [*MARC geographic area code Library of Congress*] (LCCP)
NUSU .... Nuclear Superheating (SAA)
n-usu- .... Southern States [*MARC geographic area code Library of Congress*] (LCCP)
NUSU-CX .... Nuclear Superheat Critical Experiment (SAA)
NUSUM .... Nuclear Detonation Summary (NVT)
NUSUM .... Numerical Summary Report [*Military*] (AFM)
n-us-ut .... Utah [*MARC geographic area code Library of Congress*] (LCCP)
n-us-va .... Virginia [*MARC geographic area code Library of Congress*] (LCCP)
n-us-vt .... Vermont [*MARC geographic area code Library of Congress*] (LCCP)
n-usw- .... Northwest (United States) [*MARC geographic area code Library of Congress*] (LCCP)
n-us-wa .... Washington [*MARC geographic area code Library of Congress*] (LCCP)
n-us-wi .... Wisconsin [*MARC geographic area code Library of Congress*] (LCCP)
n-us-wv .... West Virginia [*MARC geographic area code Library of Congress*] (LCCP)
n-us-wy .... Wyoming [*MARC geographic area code Library of Congress*] (LCCP)
NUSZ .... Nucleus Size [*Microscopy*]
NUT .... Mauna Loa Macadamia'A' [*NYSE symbol*] (TTSB)
NUT .... Mauna Loa Macadamia Partners LP [*NYSE symbol*] (SPSG)
NUT .... National Union of Teachers [*British*]
NUT .... Nautilus Resources Ltd. [*Vancouver Stock Exchange symbol*]
N-U-T .... Newcastle-Upon-Tyne [*City in England*]
NUT .... Number Unobtainable Tone [*Telecommunications*] (TEL)
NUt .... Utica Public Library, Utica, NY [*Library symbol Library of Congress*] (LCLS)
NUTA .... National Used Truck Association
NUtC .... Utica College of Syracuse University, Utica, NY [*Library symbol Library of Congress*] (LCLS)
NU-TEC .... Nuclear Detection [*Radiation monitoring device*] (WDAA)
Nu-Tech .... Nu-Tech Bio Med, Inc. [*Associated Press*] (SAG)
NUTEX .... Nuclear Tactical Exercise
NUTG .... National Union of Townswomen's Guilds [*British*]
NUtGE .... General Electric Co., Utica, NY [*Library symbol Library of Congress*] (LCLS)
NUTGW .... National Union of Tailors and Garments Workers [*British*]
NUtHi .... Oneida Historical Society, Utica, NY [*Library symbol Library of Congress*] (LCLS)
NUTI .... NASCOM User Traffic Interface [*NASA*] (MCD)
NUTIS .... Numerical and Textile Information System (PDAA)
NUTL .... Nonuniform Transmission Line (IAA)
NUtM .... Munson-Williams-Proctor Institute, Utica, NY [*Library symbol Library of Congress*] (LCLS)
NUTM .... Nutmeg Industries, Inc. (MHDW)
NutmgFd .... Nutmeg Federal Savings & Loan Association [*Associated Press*] (SAG)
NUtMI .... Utica Mutual Insurance Co., Utica, NY [*Library symbol Library of Congress*] (LCLS)
NUtMM .... Masonic Medical Research Laboratory, Utica, NY [*Library symbol Library of Congress*] (LCLS)
NUtMV .... Mohawk Valley Community College, Utica, NY [*Library symbol Library of Congress*] (LCLS)
NUtMVL .... Mohawk Valley Learning Resource Center, Utica Psychiatric Center, Utica, NY [*Library symbol Library of Congress*] (LCLS)
NUtMY .... Mid-York Library System, Utica, NY [*Library symbol Library of Congress*] (LCLS)
NUTN .... National Union of Trained Nurses [*British*] (DI)
NUTN .... National University Teleconference Network [*Stillwater, OK*] [*Telecommunications*] (TSSD)
NUTP .... National Uranium Tailings Program [*Canada*]
NUtP .... Utica Psychiatric Center, Utica, NY [*Library symbol Library of Congress*] (LCLS)
NUTPW .... National Union of Tin Plate Workers [*British*]
NUTR .... Nutrition (AABC)
NUTRAT .... Nuclear Uses Technology Reaction Analysis Team
NUTRI .... Nutrition
NUTRI .... Nutrition
NUTRL .... Nutritional
NutrLf .... Nutrition For Life International, Inc. [*Associated Press*] (SAG)
NutrLfe .... Nutrition for Life International, Inc. [*Associated Press*] (SAG)
Nutrmax .... NutraMax Products, Inc. [*Associated Press*] (SAG)
NutrMg .... Nutrition Management [*Associated Press*] (SAG)
NutrMgt .... Nutrition Management [*Associated Press*] (SAG)
NUTS .... New Universal Terminology Subjects

NUtSC.......... New York State Supreme Court Law Library, Utica, NY [*Library symbol Library of Congress*] (LCLS)
NUtSU.......... State University of New York, College at Utica-Rome, Utica, NY [*Library symbol Library of Congress*] (LCLS)
NUTT .... National Union of Tobacco Trades [*British*]
NUTTAB ...... Nutrient Data Table
NUTX .... Nucleus Texture [*Microscopy*]
NUU .... New Universal Union (EA)
NUU .... New University of Ulster [*Ireland*] (DI)
NUUSFE....... National Union of United States Forces Employees [*South Korea*]
NUUT .... National Union of Uncertified Teachers [*British*]
NUV .... Near Ultraviolet
NUV .... Norges Unge Venstre [*Norway*]
NUV .... Nuveen Municipal Value Fund, Inc. [*NYSE symbol*] (SPSG)
NUV .... Nuveen Muni Value Fd [*NYSE symbol*] (TTSB)
NuvAZ .... Nuveen Arizona Premium Income [*Associated Press*] (SAG)
NUVB .... National Union of Vehicle Builders [*British*]
NuvCal .... Nuveen California Municipal Value Fund [*Associated Press*] (SAG)
NuvMu .... Nuveen Municipal Value Fund, Inc. [*Associated Press*] (SAG)
NuvPI .... Nuveen Premium Income Municipal Fund, Inc. [*Associated Press*] (SAG)
NuvPI2 .... Nuveen Premium Income Municipal Fund 2 [*Associated Press*] (SAG)
NuvPI4 .... Nuveen Premium Income Municipal Fund 4 [*Associated Press*] (SAG)
NuvPP .... Nuveen Performance Plus Municipal Fund [*Associated Press*] (SAG)
NuvQInc....... Nuveen Quality Income Municipal Fund [*Associated Press*] (SAG)
NuvSel .... Nuveen Select Quality [*Associated Press*] (SAG)
NUVW .... National Union of Vehicular Workers [*British*]
NuvWA......... Nuveen Washington Premium Income Municipal Fund [*Associated Press*] (SAG)
NUW .... National Universities Week [*Canada*]
NUW .... Nu-West Group Ltd. [*Toronto Stock Exchange symbol*]
NUW .... Whidbey Island, WA [*Location identifier FAA*] (FAAL)
NUWA........... National Unemployed Workers Association (NADA)
NUWATI........ Nuclear Work Authorization Technical Instruction (DNAB)
NUWAX........ Nuclear Weapons Accident Exercises
NUWC .... Naval Undersea Warfare Center [*Later, NURDC*]
NUWDAT...... National Union of Wallcoverings, Decorative and Allied Trades [*British*] (DGA)
NUWEDS...... Nuclear Weapons Emergency Destruct System [*Navy*] (ANA)
NUWEP........ Nuclear Weapon Employment Policy (MCD)
NUWEP........ Nuclear Weapons Effect Planning
NUWES .... Naval Undersea Warfare Engineering Station (MCD)
NUWES .... Naval Underwater Weapons Evaluation Station
NUWMF .... Naval Undersea Warfare Museum Foundation (PDAA)
NUWPNSTRACEN... Nuclear Weapons Training Center (MCD)
NUWPNSUPANX... Nuclear Weapons Supply Annex
NUWPNTRACEN... Nuclear Weapons Training Center
NUWPNTRACENLANT... Nuclear Weapons Training Center, Atlantic
NUWPNTRACENPAC... Nuclear Weapons Training Center, Pacific
NUWRES .... Naval Underwater Weapons Research and Engineering Station
NUWS .... Naval Underwater Weapons Station (MCD)
NUWSAMBS... National United Women's Societies of the Adoration of the Most Blessed Sacrament (EA)
NUWSEC ...... Naval Underwater Weapons Systems Engineering Center
NUWT .... National Union of Women Teachers [*British*] (DAS)
NUWT .... National Union of Women Teachers (AIE)
NUWT .... Northeast Utilities [*NASDAQ symbol*] (SAG)
NuWt .... Nu-West Industries, Inc. [*Associated Press*] (SAG)
NUWTW....... Northeast Utils Wrrt [*NASDAQ symbol*] (TTSB)
NUWW .... National Union of Women Workers (MHDB)
NUYC .... Nordic Union of Young Conservatives (EA)
NV................ Naamloze Vennootschap [*Limited Company, Corporation*] [*Netherlands*] (GPO)
NV................ Naked Vision
nV................ Nanovolt [*One billionth of a volt*] (IEEE)
NV................ Near Vertical [*Aerospace*]
NV................ Needle Valve
NV................ Negative Variation [*Medicine*] (MAE)
NV................ Nerve and Vein [*Medicine*] (DAVI)
NV................ Net Value
NV................ Neurovascular [*Anatomy*]
NV................ Neutralization Value (IAA)
NV................ Nevada [*Postal code*]
Nv................ Nevada State Library, Carson City, NV [*Library symbol Library of Congress*] (LCLS)
NV................ New Version [*of the Bible*]
NV................ Next Visit [*Medicine*]
NV................ Night Vision Device [*Optics*]
NV................ Nonvaccinated
NV................ Nonvenereal [*Medicine*]
NV................ Nonveteran
nv................ Non Vidi [*Not Seen*] [*Latin*]
NV................ Nonvintage [*Wine*]
nv................ Nonvirulent [*Pathology*]
NV................ Nonvolatile
NV................ Nonvoting [*Investment term*]
NV................ Nord-Viscount Corp.
NV................ Normal Value [*Clinical chemistry*]
NV................ Norske Veritas [*Norwegian ship classification society*] (DS)
NV................ North Anna [*Virginia*] [*Seismograph station code, US Geological Survey Closed*]
N-V............... Northrop-Ventura (SAA)
NV................ Northwest Territorial Airways [*ICAO designator*] (AD)

NV................ Not Vaccinated [*Medicine*]
N/V............... No Value [*Legal term*] (DLA)
NV................ Nozzle Vanes (AAG)
NV................ Nuisance Value (MHDB)
N/V............... Number of Engine Revolutions per Minute per Vehicle Miles per Hour [*Automotive engineering*]
NVA .... Nationale Volksarmee [*National Peoples' Army*] [*Germany*]
NVA .... National Variety Artists [*Defunct*] (EA)
NVA .... National Velthrow Association (EA)
NVA .... National Veterans Association (EA)
NVA .... National Viatical Association (ECON)
NVA .... National Villa Association [*British*] (BI)
NVA .... National Vista Alliance (EA)
NVA .... National Vulvodynia Association [*Disseminate information about vulvar pain and establish support networks across the country*] [*Medicine*]
NVA .... Native Vegetation Authority [*South Australia*]
NVA .... Near Visual Acuity [*Medicine*]
NVA .... Negative Vorticity Advection [*NWS*] (FAAC)
NVA .... Neiva [*Colombia*] [*Airport symbol*] (OAG)
NVA .... Nile Valley Aviation Co. [*Egypt*] [*ICAO designator*] (FAAC)
NVA .... Non-Violent Alternatives [*An association*] (EA)
NvA.............. Normalized Volt-Ampere
NVA .... North Vietnamese Army
Nva .... Norvaline [*Biochemistry*]
NVA .... NOVA Corp.(Cda) [*NYSE symbol*] (TTSB)
NVA .... Nova Corp. of Alberta [*Later, Nova Corp.*] [*NYSE symbol Toronto Stock Exchange symbol*] (SPSG)
NVA .... No Voltage Amplification [*Electronics*] (IAA)
NVA .... N-Vinylacetamide [*Organic chemistry*]
NVAC .... Natal Voluntary Ambulance Corps [*British military*] (DMA)
NVAC .... National Vaccine Advisory Committee [*Reports to Congress, Health and Human Services*]
NVAC .... North Vietnamese Army Captured
NVAC .... Sunny Von Bulow National Victim Advocacy Center [*Later, NVC*] (EA)
NVACP.......... Neighborhoods, Voluntary Associations and Consumer Protection [*Environmental Protection Agency*] (ERG)
NVAF .... North Vietnamese Air Force
NVAFB .... North Vandenberg Air Force Base (NASA)
NVAL .... National Vision Associates [*NASDAQ symbol*] (SAG)
NVAL .... Natl Vision Associates [*NASDAQ symbol*] (TTSB)
NVAL .... Not Available
NValHi .... Columbia County Historical Library, Valatie, NY [*Library symbol Library of Congress*] (LCLS)
NValhM........ Westchester Medical Center, Valhalla, NY [*Library symbol Library of Congress*] (LCLS)
NValhW........ Westchester Community College, Valhalla, NY [*Library symbol Library of Congress*] (LCLS)
NVAN .... Non-Violent Anarchist Network (EA)
NV & EOL ..... Night Vision and Electro-Optics Laboratory [*Army*] (RDA)
NV & H .... Nuclear Survivability and Hardening
NVAPI .... Nuveen Virginia Premium Income Municipal Fund [*Associated Press*] (SAG)
Nv-Ar .... Nevada State Library, Division of State Archives, Carson City, NV [*Library symbol Library of Congress*] (LCLS)
NVAR .... Normalized Variance (PDAA)
NVAS .... Night Vision Attack System
NVAS .... North Vietnamese Army Suspect
NVASD .... Night Vision Aerial Surveillance Device
NVASS .... Night Vision Airborne Surveillance System
NVATA .... National Vocational Agricultural Teachers' Association (EA)
NVB .... Inco Ltd. [*NYSE symbol*] (SAG)
NVB .... National Volunteer Brigade [*South African equivalent of the British Home Guard*]
NVB .... Navigational Base (KSC)
NVB .... Nederlandse Volksbeweging [*Dutch People's Movement*] [*Political party*] (PPE)
NVB .... Night Vision Binocular
Nvb .... November (CDAI)
NVBA .... National Veteran Boxers Association (EA)
NvBc .... Boulder City Library, Boulder City, NV [*Library symbol Library of Congress*] (LCLS)
NvBcBM ...... United States Bureau of Mines, Boulder City Metallurgy Research Laboratories, Boulder City, NV [*Library symbol Library of Congress*] (LCLS)
NvBcER........ United States Energy Research and Development Administration, Boulder City Metallurgy Research Laboratories, Boulder City, NV [*Library symbol Library of Congress*] (LCLS)
NVBF .... Nordisk Vetenskapliga Bibliotekarie-Forbundet [*Scandinavian Federation of Research Librarians*] (EA)
NvBL .... Lehman Caves National Monument, Baker, NV [*Library symbol Library of Congress*] (LCLS)
NVC .... National Victim Center (EA)
NVC .... National Victims of Crime (EA)
NVC .... National Video Clearinghouse [*Defunct*] (EA)
NVC .... National Video Corp.
NVC .... National Volunteer Center (EA)
NVC .... Nonverbal Communication (ADA)
NVC .... Noverco, Inc. [*Toronto Stock Exchange symbol*]
NVC .... Nuriootpa Viticulture Center [*Australia*]
NVC .... Nuveen California Select Quality Municipal [*NYSE symbol*] (SPSG)
NVC .... Nuveen CA Select Qual Muni [*NYSE symbol*] (TTSB)
NvC .... Ormsby Public Library, Carson City, NV [*Library symbol Library of Congress*] (LCLS)

NVCA .... National Valentine Collectors' Association (EA)
NVCA .... National Van Conversion Association (EA)
NVCA .... National Vehicle Conversion Association
NVCA .... National Venture Capital Association [Arlington, VA] (EA)
NvCAQI .... Nuveen California Quality Income Municipal [Associated Press] (SAG)
NVCC .... Northern Virginia Community College
NVCF .... National Victims of Crime Foundation (EA)
NVCH .... National Volunteer Clearinghouse for the Homeless [Defunct] (EA)
NvCIQ .... Nuveen California Investment Quality Municipal Fund [Associated Press] (SAG)
NV-CJD .... New Variant Creutzfeldt-Jakob Disease [Medicine]
NVCJD .... Newvariant Creutzfeldt-Jakob Disease [Medicine]
NvCMI .... Nuveen California Municipal Income Fund [Associated Press] (SAG)
NVCPP .... Nuveen California Performance Plus Municipal Fund [Associated Press] (SAG)
NVCS .... Nissan Valve Control System [Automotive engineering]
NvCSQ .... Nuveen California Select Quality Municipal Fund [Associated Press] (SAG)
NVCT .... Nonverbal Classification Test
NVCZ .... N-Vinylcarbazole [Organic chemistry]
NVD .... Nausea, Vomiting, Diarrhea [Medicine]
NVD .... Neck Vein Distention [Medicine]
NVD .... Neovascularization of the Disc [Ophthalmology] (DAVI)
NVD .... Nevada, MO [Location identifier FAA] (FAAL)
NVD .... Newcastle Virus Disease [Veterinary medicine] (MAE)
NVD .... Night Vision Device [Optics]
NVD .... Nonvalvular Heart Disease (MAE)
NVD .... North Vancouver District Public Library [UTLAS symbol]
NVD .... No Value Declared [Business term] (DCTA)
NVD .... No Venous Distention [Medicine] (MEDA)
NVDA .... National Vitamin Distributors Association (EA)
NVDM .... Network Virtual Data Manager [Computer science] (IAA)
NVDM .... Novadigm, Inc. [NASDAQ symbol] (SAG)
NVDML .... Network Virtual Data Management Language [Telecommunications] (OSI)
NVE .... Colvin Aviation, Inc. [ICAO designator] (FAAC)
NvE .... Elko County Library, Elko, NV [Library symbol Library of Congress] (LCLS)
NVE .... Native Valve Endocarditis [Medicine]
NVE .... Neovascular Edema [Ophthalmology] (DAVI)
NVE .... Neovascularization Elsewhere [Cardiology] (DAVI)
NVE .... Night Vision Equipment (MCD)
NVE .... Nonvisual Eyepiece
NVe .... Vestal Public Library, Vestal, NY [Library symbol Library of Congress] (LCLS)
NVEBW .... Non-Vacuum Electron Beam Welding (PDAA)
NVEF .... National Vocational Educational Foundation (EA)
NVeGS .... Church of Jesus Christ of Latter-Day Saints, Genealogical Society Library, Ithaca Branch, Vestal, NY [Library symbol Library of Congress] (LCLS)
NvEHi .... Northeastern Nevada Historical Society, Elko, NV [Library symbol Library of Congress] (LCLS)
NVEL .... Navel
NVeL .... Vestal Public Library, Vestal, NY [Library symbol] [Library of Congress] (LCLS)
NvEIGS .... Church of Jesus Christ of Latter-Day Saints, Genealogical Society Library, Ely Branch, Ely, NV [Library symbol Library of Congress] (LCLS)
NVEOC .... Night Vision and Electro-Optics Center [Fort Belvoir, VA] [US Army Communications-Electronics Command] (RDA)
NVEOD .... Night Vision and Electro Optics Directorate [Army] (RDA)
NVEOL .... Night Vision and Electro-Optics Laboratory [Army] (GRD)
NVEPDC ...... National Vocational Educational Professional Development Consortium [Later, NVEPDF] (EA)
NVEPDF ...... National Vocational Educational Professional Development Foundation [Later, NVEF] (EA)
NVESD .... Night Vision and Electronic Sensors Directorate [Army] (RDA)
NVETS .... National Vocational Education and Training System [Australia]
NVF .... National Vitamin Foundation (EA)
NVF .... National Vitiligo Foundation (EA)
NVF .... National Volunteer Force (WDAA)
NVF .... Nordisk Vejteknisk Forbund [Nordic Association of Road and Traffic Engineering] (EAIO)
NVFC .... National Volunteer Fire Council (EA)
NVFEL .... National Vehicle and Fuel Emissions Laboratory
NVFET .... Non-Volatile Field-Effect-Transistor [Electronics]
NvFGS .... Church of Jesus Christ of Latter-Day Saints, Genealogical Society Library, Fallon Branch, Fallon, NV [Library symbol Library of Congress] (LCLS)
NVFI .... National Vitiligo Foundation (PAZ)
NvFL .... Nuveen Florida Investment Quality Municipal Fund [Associated Press] (SAG)
NVFR .... Night Visual Flight Rating
NVG .... National Trust Co. [Toronto Stock Exchange symbol]
NVG .... Neovascular Glaucoma (DAVI)
NVG .... Neoviridogrisein [Antibacterial]
NVG .... Night Vision Goggles
NVG .... Night Vision Group
NVGA .... National Vocational Guidance Association (EA)
NVGGA .... Napa Valley Grape Growers Association (EA)
NVGI .... National Voluntary Groups Institute (EA)
NvGM .... Mormon Station State Park, Genoa, NV [Library symbol Library of Congress] (LCLS)
NVGS .... Night Vision Goggle Sensor (DWSG)

NVGTN .... Navigation
NvH .... Henderson District Public Library, Henderson, NV [Library symbol Library of Congress] (LCLS)
NVH .... Nitrogen Vent Header [Nuclear energy] (NRCH)
NVH .... Noise, Vibration, Harshness [Automotive technology]
NVHA .... National Voluntary Health Agencies (EA)
NvHi .... Nevada State Historical Society, Reno, NV [Library symbol Library of Congress] (LCLS)
NvHV-A .... United States Veterans Administration Hospital, Ambulatory Care Service, Henderson, NV [Library symbol Library of Congress] (LCLS)
NVI .... Night Vision Imaging (DWSG)
NVI .... Non-Value Indicator [Type of postage stamp] (ODBW)
NVI .... Normalized Vegetation Index [Meteorology]
NVIC .... National Vaccine Information Center
NVIC .... Navigational and Vessel Inspection Circular [Coast Guard] (GFGA)
NVIC .... N-Viro International [NASDAQ symbol] (TTSB)
NVIC .... N-Viro International Corp. [NASDAQ symbol] (SAG)
NVICP .... National Vaccine Injury Compensation Program (PAZ)
NVIEW .... NVIEW Corp. [Associated Press] (SAG)
NVII .... Navy Vocational Interest Inventory (NVT)
NvIMO .... Nuveen Insurance Municipal Opportunity Fund [Associated Press] (SAG)
NvInQI .... Nuveen Insured Quality Fund [Associated Press] (SAG)
NvIQI .... Nuveen Investment Quality Municipal Fund [Associated Press] (SAG)
N-ViroInt ..... N-Viro International Corp. [Associated Press] (SAG)
NVIS .... Nearly Vertical Incident Skywave [Propagation model] (MCD)
nVision .... N-Vision, Inc. [Associated Press] (SAG)
NVK .... Milton, FL [Location identifier FAA] (FAAL)
NVK .... Narvik [Norway] [Airport symbol] (OAG)
NVL .... Hunting Aviation Services Ltd. [British ICAO designator] (FAAC)
NvL .... Las Vegas Public Library, Las Vegas, NV [Library symbol Library of Congress] (LCLS)
NVL .... Night Vision Laboratory [Army]
NVL .... Novolazarevskaya [Antarctica] [Seismograph station code, US Geological Survey] (SEIS)
NVLA .... National Vehicle Leasing Association (EA)
NVLA .... National Viewers' and Listeners' Association [British]
NVLAP .... National Voluntary Laboratory Accreditation Program [Gaithersburg, MD] [National Institute of Standards and Technology]
NvLBM .... Basic Magnesium, Inc., Las Vegas, NV [Library symbol Library of Congress Obsolete] (LCLS)
NvLC .... Clark County Library, Las Vegas, NV [Library symbol Library of Congress] (LCLS)
NVLC .... National Veterans Law Center [Defunct] (EA)
NvLGS .... Church of Jesus Christ of Latter-Day Saints, Genealogical Society Library, Las Vegas Branch, Las Vegas, NV [Library symbol Library of Congress] (LCLS)
NvLN .... University of Nevada, Las Vegas, NV [Library symbol Library of Congress] (LCLS)
NVLS .... Novellus Systems [NASDAQ symbol] (TTSB)
NVLS .... Novellus Systems, Inc. [NASDAQ symbol] (CTT)
NVM .... National Voter Mobilization [Defunct] (EA)
NVM .... Nativity of the Virgin Mary
NVM .... Nonvolatile Matter
NVM .... Nonvolatile Memory [Computer science] (HGAA)
NVM .... Non-Volatile Random Access Memory [Computer science]
NVM .... Nova Marketing Ltd. [Vancouver Stock Exchange symbol]
NVMA .... National Veterinary Medical Association (WDAA)
NVMA .... Noise and Vibration Monitor Analyzer [Military] (CAAL)
NvMAd .... Nuveen Municipal Advantage Fund [Associated Press] (SAG)
NvMAP .... Nuveen Massachusetts Premium Income Municipal Fund [Associated Press] (SAG)
NvMcK .... Kinnear Public Library, McGill, NV [Library symbol Library of Congress] (LCLS)
NvMiD .... Douglas County Library, Minden, NV [Library symbol Library of Congress] (LCLS)
NvMIPI .... Nuveen Michigan Premium Income Municipal [Associated Press] (SAG)
NvMO .... Nuveen Municipal Opportunity Fund [Associated Press] (SAG)
NVMS .... Night Visibility Measuring Set
Nvmt .... Novametrics Medical Systems [Associated Press] (SAG)
Nvmt .... Novametrix Medical Systems, Inc. [Associated Press] (SAG)
NvMul .... Nuveen Municipal Income Fund [Associated Press] (SAG)
NvMus .... Nevada State Museum, Capital Complex, Carson City, NV [Library symbol Library of Congress] (LCLS)
NVMV .... Nicotiana Velutina Mosaic Virus [Plant pathology]
NVN .... Nirvana Industries Ltd. [Vancouver Stock Exchange symbol]
NVN .... Non-Von Neumann
NVN .... North Vietnam (VNW)
NVN .... Noun-Verb-Noun [Education of the hearing-impaired]
NVN .... Nuveen New York Select Quality Municipal [NYSE symbol] (SPSG)
NVN .... Nuveen NY Selct Qual Muni [NYSE symbol] (TTSB)
NVNA .... Non-Volatile Nitrosamine [Organic chemistry]
NvNJ .... Nuveen New Jersey Investment Quality Municipal Fund [Associated Press] (SAG)
NvNJPI .... Nuveen New Jersey Premium Income Municipal [Associated Press] (SAG)
NVNN .... North Vietnamese Navy
NvNoIC .... Clark County Community College, North Las Vegas, NV [Library symbol Library of Congress] (LCLS)
NVNTA .... Night Vision Net Technical Assessment (MCD)
NvNYP .... Nuveen New York Performance Plus Municipal Fund [Associated Press] (SAG)
NVNAF .... North Vietnamese Air Force

NvNYQI .... Nuveen New York Quality Income Municipal [*Associated Press*] (SAG)
NVO .... Coalition of National Voluntary Organizations [*Also, National Voluntary Organizations*] (AC)
NVO .... Nevada Operations Office [*Department of Energy*] (MCD)
NVO .... New Vehicle Order
NVO .... Nonverbal Operation
NVO .... Nonvessel Operator [*Shipping*]
NVO .... Nonvolatile Organic [*Residue of thermal processing*]
NVO .... Novo Nordisk A/S ADR [*NYSE symbol*] (SPSG)
NVOAD .... National Voluntary Organizations Active in Disaster (EA)
NVOC .... Nitroveratryloxycarbonyl [*Organic radical*]
NVOC .... Nonvessel-Owning Carrier [*Shipping*] (DS)
NVOCC .... Nonvessel Operating Common Carrier [*Shipping*]
NVOCC .... Non-Vessel Operating Container Carrier
NVOCC .... Nonvessel-Owning Common Carrier [*Shipping*] (DS)
NvoFn .... Nuevo Financing I [*Associated Press*] (SAG)
NVOI .... National Voice of Iran [*Clandestine, Soviet-backed radio station*]
NVOILA .... National Voluntary Organizations for Independent Living for the Aging (EA)
NVOO .... Nevada Operations Office [*Department of Energy*]
NVOP .... National Veteran's Outreach Program (EA)
NVORDCH .... Naval Ordnance Chart
NVP .... National Vaccine Program [*National Institutes of Health*]
NVP .... Nausea and Vomiting in Pregnancy
NVP .... Nevada Power Co. [*NYSE symbol*] (SPSG)
NVP .... Nevirpine [*Organic chemistry*]
NVP .... Nominal Velocity of Propagation [*Electronics*] (PCM)
NVP .... N-Vinylpyrrolidone [*Organic chemistry*]
NVPA .... National Visual Presentation Association (EA)
NvPA .... Nuveen Pennsylvania Investment Quality Municipal Fund [*Associated Press*] (SAG)
NvPAP2 .... Nuveen Pennsylvania Premium Income Municipal Fund [*Associated Press*] (SAG)
NvPIM .... Nuveen Premier Insured Municipal Income Fund [*Associated Press*] (SAG)
NvPMI .... Nuveen Premium Municipal Income Fund [*Associated Press*] (SAG)
NVPO .... Nuclear Vehicle Projects Office [*NASA*]
NVPOWG ..... NASA [*National Aeronautics and Space Administration*]/VAFB Payload Operati ons Working Group [*Vandenberg Air Force Base*] (NASA)
NVPOWG ..... NASA/VAFB [*National Aeronautical and Space Administration/ Vandenburg Air Force Base*] Payload Operations Working Group
NVPP .... National Vehicle Population Profile
NVPS .... Night Vision Pilotage System [*Military*]
NVP-U .... Nationale Volkspartij - Unie [*National United People's Party*] [*Netherlands Antilles*] [*Political party*] (PPW)
NVQ .... National Vocation Qualification [*British*]
NVR .... National Video Resources
NVR .... Naval Vessel Register (MCD)
NVR .... Nonvolatile Residue (NASA)
NVR .... Norfolk Volunteer Regiment [*British military*] (DMA)
NVR .... No Verification Required (NASA)
NVR .... No Voltage Release [*Electronics*]
NVR .... NVA [*North Vietnam Army*] Regulars (VNW)
NVR .... NVR, Inc. [*AMEX symbol*] (SPSG)
NVRAM .... Nonvolatile Random-Access Memory [*Computer science*]
NVRC .... National Retirees Volunteer Coalition [*An association*]
NvREr .... United States Energy Research Development Administration, Reno, NV [*Library symbol Library of Congress*] (LCLS)
NvRFM .... Grand Lodge of the Free and Accepted Masons of the State of Nevada, Reno, NV [*Library symbol Library of Congress*] (LCLS)
NvRGS .... Church of Jesus Christ of Latter-Day Saints, Genealogical Society Library, Reno Branch, Reno, NV [*Library symbol Library of Congress*] (LCLS)
NvRH .... Harrah's Automobile Collection and Pony Express Museum, Reno, NV [*Library symbol Library of Congress*] (LCLS)
NVRIA .... National Vision Research Institute of Australia
NvRNC .... National College of the State Judiciary, Law Library, Reno, NV [*Library symbol Library of Congress*] (LCLS)
NVRS .... National Vegetable Research Station [*Research center British*] (IRC)
NVRS .... Night Vision Reconnaissance System
NVRS .... Numerical Value Rating System [*Navy*]
NvRW .... Washoe County Library, Reno, NV [*Library symbol Library of Congress*] (LCLS)
NvRWL .... Washoe County Law Library, Reno, NV [*Library symbol Library of Congress*] (LCLS)
NVR.WS ...... NVR Inc. Wrrt [*AMEX symbol*] (TTSB)
NVs .... Henry Waldinger Memorial Library, Valley Stream, NY [*Library symbol Library of Congress*] (LCLS)
NVS .... Narrowband Voice Security
NVS .... National Vegetable Society [*British*] (DBA)
NVS .... Neurological Vital Signs [*Medicine*]
NVS .... Neutron Velocity Selector
NVS .... Night Vision Safety [*Automotive rear-view mirrors*]
NVS .... Night Vision System
NVS .... Nonvoting Stock [*Investment term*]
NVS .... Novosibirsk [*Former USSR Seismograph initiation code, US Geological Survey*] (SEIS)
NVS .... Number of Video Samples
NVS .... Southeastern Baptist Theological Seminary, Wake Forest, NC [*OCLC symbol*] (OCLC)
NVSA .... Ablow [*Vanuatu*] [*ICAO location identifier*] (ICLI)

NVSA .... Natuurbestuurvereniging van Suidelike Afrika [*Southern African Wildlife Management Association - SAWMA*] [*Pretoria, South Africa*] (EAIO)
NVSA .... Nematologiese Vereniging van Suidelike Afrika [*Nematological Society of Southern Africa*] (EAIO)
NVsAE .... Alden Terrace Elementary School, Valley Stream, NY [*Library symbol*] [*Library of Congress*] (LCLS)
NVsBAE .... Brooklyn Avenue School, Valley Stream, NY [*Library symbol*] [*Library of Congress*] (LCLS)
NVsBE .... William L. Buck School, Valley Stream, NY [*Library symbol*] [*Library of Congress*] (LCLS)
NVSC .... Sola [*Vanuatu*] [*ICAO location identifier*] (ICLI)
NVsCE .... Robert W. Carbonaro School, Valley Stream, NY [*Library symbol*] [*Library of Congress*] (LCLS)
NVsCSE .... Clear Stream Avenue Elementary School, Valley Stream, NY [*Library symbol*] [*Library of Congress*] (LCLS)
NVsCSH .... Central Senior High School, Valley Stream, NY [*Library symbol Library of Congress*] (LCLS)
NVSD .... Lo-Linua [*Vanuatu*] [*ICAO location identifier*] (ICLI)
NVSD .... National Vital Statistics Division [*National Center for Health Statistics*] [*Obsolete*]
NVSD .... Night Vision System Development [*Military*]
NVsDE .... Devet Elementary School, Valley Stream, NY [*Library symbol Library of Congress*] (LCLS)
NVSDS .... New Vehicle Satisfaction with Dealer Service [*Quality research*]
NVSE .... Emae [*Vanuatu*] [*ICAO location identifier*] (ICLI)
NVSF .... Graig Cove [*Vanuatu*] [*ICAO location identifier*] (ICLI)
NVsFE .... Forest Elementary School, Valley Stream, NY [*Library symbol Library of Congress*] (LCLS)
NVsFH .... Franklin General Hospital, Valley Stream, NY [*Library symbol Library of Congress*] (LCLS)
NVSG .... Longana [*Vanuatu*] [*ICAO location identifier*] (ICLI)
NVSH .... Nonvocal Severely Handicapped
NVSH .... Sara [*Vanuatu*] [*ICAO location identifier*] (ICLI)
NVsHE .... Howell Road School, Valley Stream, NY [*Library symbol*] [*Library of Congress*] (LCLS)
NVSL .... Lamap [*Vanuatu*] [*ICAO location identifier*] (ICLI)
NVSL .... National Veterinary Services Laboratory [*Ames, IA*] [*Department of Agriculture*] (GRD)
NVSM .... Lamen-Bay [*Vanuatu*] [*ICAO location identifier*] (ICLI)
NVSM .... Nonvolatile Semiconductor Memory (MCD)
NVSMD .... Nonvolatile Semiconductor Memory Device (PDAA)
NVsMJH .... Memorial Junior High School, Valley Stream, NY [*Library symbol Library of Congress*] (LCLS)
NvSMM .... Nuveen Select Maturities Municipal Fund [*Associated Press*] (SAG)
NVSN .... Maewo-Naone [*Vanuatu*] [*ICAO location identifier*] (ICLI)
NVSN .... n-Vision Inc. [*NASDAQ symbol*] (TTSB)
NVSN .... N-Vision, Inc. [*NASDAQ symbol*] (SAG)
NVsNSH .... Valley Stream North High School, Valley Stream, NY [*Library symbol*] [*Library of Congress*] (LCLS)
NVSNW .... n-Vision Inc. Wrrt [*NASDAQ symbol*] (TTSB)
NVSO .... Lonorore [*Vanuatu*] [*ICAO location identifier*] (ICLI)
NVsOE .... Ogden Elementary School, Valley Stream, NY [*Library symbol*] [*Library of Congress*] (LCLS)
N-VSOS .... Non-Verbal Scale of Suffering [*Personality development test*] [*Psychology*]
NVSP .... Norsup [*Vanuatu*] [*ICAO location identifier*] (ICLI)
NVSR .... Redcliff [*Vanuatu*] [*ICAO location identifier*] (ICLI)
NVSS .... National Vital Statistics System [*Department of Health and Human Services*] (GFGA)
NVSS .... Nonvolatile Suspended Solids [*Environmental chemistry*]
NVSS .... Normal-Variant Short Stature [*Medicine*]
NVSS .... Santo/Pekoa [*Vanuatu*] [*ICAO location identifier*] (ICLI)
NVsSAE .... Shaw Avenue Elementary School, Valley Stream, NY [*Library symbol*] [*Library of Congress*] (LCLS)
NVsSSH .... South Senior High School, Valley Stream, NY [*Library symbol Library of Congress*] (LCLS)
NVST .... Tongoa [*Vanuatu*] [*ICAO location identifier*] (ICLI)
NVSU .... Ulei [*Vanuatu*] [*ICAO location identifier*] (ICLI)
NVSV .... Valesdir [*Vanuatu*] [*ICAO location identifier*] (ICLI)
NVSW .... Walaha [*Vanuatu*] [*ICAO location identifier*] (ICLI)
NVsWE .... Willow Elementary School, Valley Stream, NY [*Library symbol Library of Congress*] (LCLS)
NVsWhE .... Wheeler Elementary School, Valley Stream, NY [*Library symbol Library of Congress*] (LCLS)
NVSX .... South West Bay [*Vanuatu*] [*ICAO location identifier*] (ICLI)
NVSZ .... North West Santo [*Vanuatu*] [*ICAO location identifier*] (ICLI)
NVT .... Navegantes [*Brazil*] [*Airport symbol*] (OAG)
NVT .... Nelson Vending Technology Ltd. [*Toronto Stock Exchange symbol*]
NVT .... Nerve, Vein, and Tendon (DAVI)
NVT .... Network Virtual Terminal
NVT .... Neuton Velocity Time (IAA)
NVT .... Norton Villiers Triumph [*Automobile manufacturer*] [*British*]
NVT .... Novell Virtual Terminal [*Novell, Inc.*] [*Computer science*] (PCM)
NVT .... Nuisance Valve Tactics
NVTA .... National Visiting Teachers Association (EA)
NVTCS .... Nissan Valve Timing Control System
NVTG .... Norton Villiers Triumph Group [*Automobile manufacturer*] [*British*]
NVTHLSS ..... Nevertheless (ROG)
NV-THS .... National Vocational-Technical Honor Society (EA)
NVTK .... Novatek International, Inc. [*NASDAQ symbol*] (SAG)
NVTOC .... Nonvolatile Total Organic Carbon [*Environmental chemistry*]
NVTS .... National Vocational Training Service
NVTS .... Null Voltage Test Set (MCD)
NVTWUGBI ... National Vehicular Traffic Workers' Union of Great Britain and Ireland

nvu	Nevada [*MARC country of publication code Library of Congress*] (LCCP)
NvU	University of Nevada, Reno, NV [*Library symbol Library of Congress*] (LCLS)
NVUE	NVIEW Corp. [*NASDAQ symbol*] (SAG)
NVVA	Anatom [*Vanuatu*] [*ICAO location identifier*] (ICLI)
NVVA	Napa Valley Vintners Association (EA)
NVVB	Aniwa [*Vanuatu*] [*ICAO location identifier*] (ICLI)
NVVC	National Vietnam Veterans Coalition (EA)
NVVCCG	North Vietnamese and Viet Cong Collecting Group [*Defunct*] (EA)
NVVD	Dillon's Bay [*Vanuatu*] [*ICAO location identifier*] (ICLI)
NVVF	Futuna [*Vanuatu*] [*ICAO location identifier*] (ICLI)
NVVI	Ipota [*Vanuatu*] [*ICAO location identifier*] (ICLI)
NVVJ	Forari [*Vanuatu*] [*ICAO location identifier*] (ICLI)
NVVK	Lenakel [*Vanuatu*] [*ICAO location identifier*] (ICLI)
NVVQ	Quoin Hill [*Vanuatu*] [*ICAO location identifier*] (ICLI)
NVVRS	National Vietnam Veterans Readjustment Study [*Veterans Administration*]
NVVV	Port-Vila/Bauerfield [*Vanuatu*] [*ICAO location identifier*] (ICLI)
NVWA	National Volkswagen Association (EA)
NVWLA	Napa Valley Wine Library Association (EA)
NVWSC	Nonvolatile Whole Smoke Condensate [*Environmental chemistry*] (AAMN)
NVX	North American Vaccine [*AMEX symbol*] (TTSB)
NVX	North American Vaccine, Inc. [*AMEX symbol*] (SAG)
NVY	Royal Navy [*British ICAO designator*] (FAAC)
NW	Naked Weight
NW	Naked Wire (IAA)
nW	Nanowatt [*One billionth of a watt*]
NW	Narrow Widths [*Construction*]
NW	NASA Waiver (KSC)
NW	National Westminster Bancorp, Inc. [*NYSE symbol*] (SPSG)
NW	National Women's Conference Committee [*Formerly, CCNWC*] (EA)
NW	Natl Westminster ADS [*NYSE symbol*] (TTSB)
NW	Nat-War Alliance [*Defunct*] (EA)
NW	Naval Air Systems Command
NW	Net Weight
NW	Network (NASA)
NW	Network Cells [*Botany*]
NW	Net Worth
NW	Neville and Winther's Acid
NW	New
NW	Newsweek [*A publication*] (BRI)
NW	New Wave [*Style of music*]
NW	New World [*Translation of the Holy Scriptures*] [*A publication*] (BJA)
NW	Nominal Width (NATG)
NW	Norfolk & Western Railway Co. [*AAR code*]
NW	Normal Waste [*Nuclear energy*] (NRCH)
NW	North Wales
NW	Northwest
NW	North-Western Provinces, High Court Reports [*India*] [*A publication*] (DLA)
NW	Northwestern Reporter [*A publication*] (DLA)
NW	North Western Reporter [*National Reporter System*] [*A publication*] (DLA)
NW	Northwest Orient Airlines, Inc. [*ICAO designator*]
NW	Nor-Weberine [*Biochemistry*]
NW	Nose Wheel [*Aviation*] (MCD)
NW	Now
NW	No Wait [*Industrial engineering*]
NW	No Wind [*Air*] Position [*Navigation*]
NW	Nuclear Warfare
NW	Nuclear Weapon (NG)
nw----	West Indies [*MARC geographic area code Library of Congress*] (LCCP)
NW2	New River [*California*] [*Seismograph station code, US Geological Survey*] (SEIS)
NW 2d	North Western Reporter, Second Series [*A publication*] (DLA)
NW 2d	North Western Reporter, Second Series [*West*] [*A publication*] (AAGC)
NWA	Moheli [*Comoro Islands*] [*Airport symbol*] (OAG)
NWA	Narrogin [*Australia Seismograph station code, US Geological Survey*] (SEIS)
NWA	National Water Alliance (EA)
NWA	National Waterfowl Alliance, Waterfowl USA [*Later, WUSA*] (EA)
NWA	National Water Well Association, Worthington, OH [*OCLC symbol*] (OCLC)
NWA	National Weather Association (EA)
NWA	National Welders Association [*A union*] [*British*]
NWA	National Wellness Association (EA)
NWA	National Wine Association [*Defunct*] (EA)
NWA	National Wrestling Alliance (DAVI)
NWA	Naval Warfare Analysis (MCD)
NWA	Naval Weapons Annex
NWA	Navy Wifeline Association (EA)
NWA	New Work Authorized (MCD)
NWA	New World Alliance [*Defunct*] (EA)
NWA	Niggers with Attitude [*Rap recording group*]
NWA	Northumbrian Water Authority [*British*] (DCTA)
NWA	Northwest Airlines (MHDB)
NWA	Northwest Airlines, Inc. [*ICAO designator*] (FAAC)
NWA	Northwest Orient Airlines, Inc. (MCD)
NWA	Nothin' Worth Askin' [*Rap recording group*]
NWAA	National Wheelchair Athletic Association (EA)
NWAA	National Women's Automotive Association [*Defunct*] (EA)
NWAAF	Northwest African Air Forces [*World War II*]
NWAB	Necks with Any Boy [*Slang*]
NWAC	National Weather Analysis Center [*Air Force, Navy*]
NWAC	National Wheelchair Athletic Committee
NWAC	National Women's Advisory Council (NADA)
NWAC	Native Women's Association of Canada
NWAC	Northwest Airlines'A' [*NASDAQ symbol*] (TTSB)
NWAC	Northwest Airlines Corp. [*NASDAQ symbol*] (SAG)
NWadd	Hepburn Library, Waddington, NY [*Library symbol Library of Congress*] (LCLS)
NWAFC	Northwest and Alaska Fisheries Center [*National Marine Fisheries Service*] [*Department of Commerce*] [*Research center*] (RCD)
NWAG	Naval Warfare Analysis Group
NWAHACA	National Warm Air Heating and Air Conditioning Association [*Later, ACCA*] (EA)
NWAI	Nuclear Weapons Acceptance Inspection (NG)
NWAIB	Nuclear Weapon Accident Investigation Board (AABC)
NWald	Josephine-Louise Public Library, Walden, NY [*Library symbol Library of Congress*] (LCLS)
NWall	Wallkill Public Library, Wallkill, NY [*Library symbol Library of Congress*] (LCLS)
NWan	Wantagh Public Library, Wantagh, NY [*Library symbol Library of Congress*] (LCLS)
NWanE	Wantagh Elementary School, Wantagh, NY [*Library symbol Library of Congress*] (LCLS)
NWanFLE	Forest Lake Elementary School, Wantagh, NY [*Library symbol Library of Congress*] (LCLS)
NWanJH	Wantagh Junior High School, Wantagh, NY [*Library symbol*] [*Library of Congress*] (LCLS)
NWanJS	Wantagh Junior-Senior High, Wantagh, NY [*Library symbol Library of Congress*] (LCLS)
NWanME	Mandalay Elementary School, Wantagh, NY [*Library symbol Library of Congress*] (LCLS)
NWanSH	Wantagh Senior High School, Wantagh, NY [*Library symbol*] [*Library of Congress*] (LCLS)
NWanSPE	Sunrise Park Elementary School, Wantagh, NY [*Library symbol Library of Congress*] (LCLS)
NWAO	Narrogin [*Australia Seismograph station code, US Geological Survey*] (SEIS)
NWAP	National White American Party (BJA)
NWapA	Mount Alvernia Seminary, Wappingers Falls, NY [*Library symbol*] [*Library of Congress*] (LCLS)
NWAPP	National Woman Abuse Prevention Project (EA)
nwaq--	Antigua [*MARC geographic area code Library of Congress*] (LCCP)
NWas	Moffat Library Association, Washingtonville, NY [*Library symbol Library of Congress*] (LCLS)
NWatfG	General Electric Co., Silicone Products Department, Waterford, NY [*Library symbol Library of Congress*] (LCLS)
NWatt	Roswell P. Flower Memorial Public Library, Watertown, NY [*Library symbol Library of Congress*] (LCLS)
NWattJ	Jefferson Community College, Watertown, NY [*Library symbol Library of Congress*] (LCLS)
NWattJHi	Jefferson County Historical Society, Watertown, NY [*Library symbol Library of Congress*] (LCLS)
NWattKH	Samaritan Keep Nursing Home, Medical Library, Watertown, NY [*Library symbol Library of Congress*] (LCLS)
NWattMH	Mercy Hospital of Watertown, Watertown, NY [*Library symbol Library of Congress*] (LCLS)
NWattN	North Country Library System, Watertown, NY [*Library symbol Library of Congress*] (LCLS)
NWatvlA	Watervliet Arsenal Library, Watervliet, NY [*Library symbol Library of Congress*] (LCLS)
NWAVL	Now Available (NOAA)
NWB	National Wiring Bureau [*Defunct*] (EA)
NWB	Naval Weapons Bulletin
NWB	Nederlandse Waterschapsbank NV [*Waterschaps Bank of the Netherlands*]
NWB	New War Department Building [*Obsolete*]
NWB	Nonweightbearing
NWB	Non-Weight-Bearing [*Orthopedics and physical therapy*] (DAVI)
NWB	Northwestbound [*ICAO designator*] (FAAC)
NWB	North Western Bell (HGAA)
NWB	Northwest Towboat Tariff Bureau, Inc., Seattle WA [*STAC*]
NWB	No Weight-Bearing [*orthopedics*] (DAVI)
NWBA	National Wheelchair Basketball Association (EA)
nwbb--	Barbados [*MARC geographic area code Library of Congress*] (LCCP)
NWBB	Noumea [*New Caledonia*] [*ICAO location identifier*] (ICLI)
NwbBc	Newberry Bancorp, Inc. [*Associated Press*] (SAG)
nwbc--	Barbuda [*MARC geographic area code Library of Congress*] (LCCP)
NWbC	Cardion Electronics, Woodbury, NY [*Library symbol Library of Congress*] (LCLS)
NWBC	National Women's Business Council
NWBC	National Wooden Box Council [*Later, NWPCA*] (EA)
nwbf--	Bahamas [*MARC geographic area code Library of Congress*] (LCCP)
NWBHI	Nuclear Weapon Burst Height Indicator
NWbN	Northwest by North
NWBW	National Women Bowling Writers Association (EA)
NWbW	Northwest by West
NWbW	Waldemar Medical Research Foundation, Woodbury, NY [*Library symbol Library of Congress*] (LCLS)
NWC	National Waco Club (EA)
NWC	National War College [*Later, UND*] [*DoD*]
NWC	National Warning Center [*Civil Defense*]
NWC	National Water Center (EA)
NWC	National Water Commission [*Terminated, 1973*]

NWC .... National Water Council [*British*] (DCTA)
NWC .... National Waterfowl Council (EA)
NWC .... National Watershed Congress (EA)
NWC .... National Waterways Conference (EA)
NWC .... National Wiretap Commission [*Department of Justice*]
NWC .... National Women's Coalition [*Defunct*] (EA)
NWC .... National Woodie Club (EA)
NWC .... National Writers Club (EA)
NWC .... Naval War College
NWC .... Naval Weapons Center
NWC .... Net Working Capital
NWC .... New World Club (EA)
NWC .... New World Coalition (EA)
NWC .... Northwest Cape
NWC .... Northwest College [*Washington*]
NWC .... North West Community College Library [*UTLAS symbol*]
NWC .... Nuclear War Capability (AAG)
NWC .... Nuclear Weapons Control
NWC .... Wingate College, Wingate, NC [*OCLC symbol*] (OCLC)
NWCA .... National Water Carriers Association
NWCA .... National Woodcarvers Association (EA)
NWCA .... National Wrestling Coaches Association (EA)
NWCA .... Navy Wives Clubs of America (EA)
NWCA .... NewCare Health [*NASDAQ symbol*] (TTSB)
NWCA .... New Care Health Corp. [*NASDAQ symbol*] (SAG)
NWCA .... Northwest Cherry Briners Association
NWCAA .... National War College Alumni Association
NWCAEU ..... National Women's Conference of the American Ethical Union (EA)
NWC/ARP .... Naval War College Advanced Research Program [*Newport, RI*]
NWCC .... National Water Co. Conference [*Later, NAWC*]
NWCC .... National Women's Conference Committee (EA)
NWCC .... Neutron Well Coincidence Counter [*Nuclear energy*] (NRCH)
NWCC .... Northwest Christian College [*Oregon*]
NWCC .... Noumea/La Tontouta [*New Caledonia*] [*ICAO location identifier*] (ICLI)
NWCCA .... Naval Weapons Center, Corona Annex [*California*]
NWC/CAR .... Naval War College Center for Advanced Research [*Newport, RI*]
NWCCL .... Naval Weapons Center, Corona Laboratories [*California*]
NWCCS .... Naval Worldwide Command and Control System (MCD)
NWCDC .... North West Cooperative Development Council [*British*]
NWCF .... New Waste Calcining Facility [*Nuclear energy*] (NUCP)
NWCG .... New World Communic Grp'A' [*NASDAQ symbol*] (TTSB)
NWCG .... New World Communictions Corp. [*NASDAQ symbol*] (SAG)
NWCG .... Nuclear Weapons Coordinating Group
NWCI .... New World Coffee [*NASDAQ symbol*] (TTSB)
NWCI .... New World Coffee, Inc. [*NASDAQ symbol*] (SAG)
NWCIEP .... Nation-Wide Committee on Import-Export Policy [*Defunct*] (EA)
nwcj-- .... Cayman Islands [*MARC geographic area code Library of Congress*] (LCCP)
NwCm .... News Communications, Inc. [*Associated Press*] (SAG)
NWCME .... National Winter Convention on Military Electronics [*IEEE*] (MCD)
NWC/NW ...... Naval War College / Naval Warfare Course (DNAB)
nwco-- .... Curacao Group [*MARC geographic area code Library of Congress*] (LCCP)
NWCP .... National Wetlands Conservation Project [*Defunct*] (EA)
NWCP .... Navy Weight-Control Program (DNAB)
NWCR .... Naval War College Review [*A publication*]
NWCR .... Nuclear Weapons Correction Report [*Army*] (AABC)
NWCRB .... Navy War Contracts Relief Board
NWCS .... NATO-Wide Communications System (NATG)
NWCS .... Nuclear Weapons Control System
NWCTU .... National Woman's Christian Temperance Union (WDAA)
nwcu .... Cuba [*MARC geographic area code Library of Congress*] (LCCP)
NWD .... Naval Weapons Directory
NWD .... Network Wide Directory
NWD .... New World Dictionary [*A publication*]
NWD .... Northwest Air Services Ltd. [*Nigeria*] [*ICAO designator*] (FAAC)
NWD .... Northwest Drug Co. Ltd. [*Toronto Stock Exchange symbol*]
NWD .... Number of Words (MSA)
NWDA .... National Wholesale Druggists' Association (EA)
NWDA .... National Wine Distributors' Association (EA)
NwDay .... New Day Beverage, Inc. [*Associated Press*] (SAG)
NWDC .... National Wildlife Defence Council (USDC)
NWDC .... National Wildlife Defense Council [*Marine science*] (OSRA)
NWDC .... Navigation/Weapon Delivery Computer (PDAA)
NWDC .... Northwest Drama Conference (EA)
NWDC/S ...... Navigation/Weapons Delivery Computer/System
NWDEN .... Number of Words per Entry (MSA)
NWDGA .... National Wholesale Dry Goods Association [*Later, NATAD*]
NWdmA .... Woodmere Academy, Woodmere, NY [*Library symbol*] [*Library of Congress*] (LCLS)
NWdmE .... No. 6 Elementary School, Woodmere, NY [*Library symbol*] [*Library of Congress*] (LCLS)
nwdq-- .... Dominica [*MARC geographic area code Library of Congress*] (LCCP)
nwdr-- .... Dominican Republic [*MARC geographic area code Library of Congress*] (LCCP)
NWDS .... National Water Data System [*US Geological Survey*] [*Reston, VA*]
NWDS .... Navigation/Weapons Delivery System
NWDS .... Network Wide Directory System (MHDI)
NWDS .... Noah Worcester Dermatological Society (EA)
NWDS .... Number of Words
NWDSEN ...... Number of Words per Entry
NWE .... Narrow Width Effect (IAA)
NWE .... Newline Resources Ltd. [*Vancouver Stock Exchange symbol*]
NWE .... Nuclear Weapons Effects

NWe .... Westbury Memorial Public Library, Westbury, NY [*Library symbol Library of Congress*] (LCLS)
NWEA .... National Women's Economic Alliance [*Washington, DC*] (EA)
NWEA .... National Wood Energy Association (EA)
NWEB .... Northwestern Electricity Board [*British*]
NWeBE .... Board of Cooperative Educational Services, Nassau Education Resource Center, Westbury, NY [*Library symbol Library of Congress*] (LCLS)
NWeBGE ...... Bowling Green Elementary School, Westbury, NY [*Library symbol*] [*Library of Congress*] (LCLS)
NWebPH ...... Pilgrim Hospital, West Brentwood, NY [*Library symbol Library of Congress*] (LCLS)
NWEC .... Nuclear Weapons Effects Course (MCD)
NWeCJS ...... W. Tresper Clarke Junior-Senior High School, Westbury, NY [*Library symbol*] [*Library of Congress*] (LCLS)
NWED .... Nuclear Weapon Effects Development
NWeDE .... Drexel Elementary School, Westbury, NY [*Library symbol*] [*Library of Congress*] (LCLS)
NWEE .... National Women's Employment and Education [*Defunct*] (EA)
NWEF .... National Women's Education Fund (EA)
NWEF .... Naval Weapons Evaluation Facility [*Kirtland Air Force Base, NM*]
NWEF .... New World Education Fund (EA)
NWEF .... North Western Expeditionary Force [*Norway*] [*World War II*]
NWEF .... Nuclear Weapons Education Fund (EA)
NWef .... Patterson Library, Westfield, NY [*Library symbol*] [*Library of Congress*] (LCLS)
NWefHi .... Chautauqua County Historical Society, Westfield, NY [*Library symbol Library of Congress*] (LCLS)
NWefMH ...... Westfield Memorial Hospital, Inc., Westfield, NY [*Library symbol Library of Congress*] (LCLS)
NWehb .... Westhampton Free Library, Westhampton Beach, NY [*Library symbol Library of Congress*] (LCLS)
NWehbJH ..... Westhampton Beach Junior High School, Westhampton Beach, NY [*Library symbol Library of Congress*] (LCLS)
NWeJH .... Westbury Junior High School, Westbury, NY [*Library symbol*] [*Library of Congress*] (LCLS)
NWel .... David A. Howe Public Library, Wellsville, NY [*Library symbol Library of Congress*] (LCLS)
NWEL .... Nuclear Weapons Effects Laboratory
NWelH .... Jones Memorial Hospital, Wellsville, NY [*Library symbol Library of Congress*] (LCLS)
NWeM .... Metco, Inc., Westbury, NY [*Library symbol Library of Congress*] (LCLS)
NWEO .... Nuclear Weapon Effects Office [*DoD*] (RDA)
NWEO .... Nuclear Weapon Employment Officer (AABC)
NWEP .... Nuclear Weapons Effects Panel
NWePLE ...... Powell's Lane Elementary School, Westbury, NY [*Library symbol*] [*Library of Congress*] (LCLS)
NWePSE ...... Park School Early Childhood Center, Westbury, NY [*Library symbol*] [*Library of Congress*] (LCLS)
NWEQ .... Northwest Equity Corp. [*NASDAQ symbol*] (TTSB)
NWEQ .... Northwest Equity Corp. [*NASDAQ symbol*] (SAG)
NWER .... Nuclear Weapons Effects Research [*Army*]
NWER/T ...... Nuclear Weapons Effects Research and Testing [*Army*] (RDA)
NWES .... Nuclear Weapons Electronic Specialist (AABC)
NWes .... Olive Free Library Association, West Shokan, NY [*Library symbol Library of Congress*] (LCLS)
NWESA .... Naval Weapons Engineering Support Activity (MCD)
NWesbHS .... West Bablyon High School, West Babylon, NY [*Library symbol*] [*Library of Congress*] (LCLS)
NWesbJH .... West Babylon Junior High School, West Babylon, NY [*Library symbol*] [*Library of Congress*] (LCLS)
NWeSH .... Westbury Senior High School, Westbury, NY [*Library symbol*] [*Library of Congress*] (LCLS)
NWesyM ...... Suffolk Marine Museum, West Sayville, NY [*Library symbol Library of Congress*] (LCLS)
NWET .... Nuclear Weapon Effects Test
nweu-- .... Sint Eustatius [*MARC geographic area code Library of Congress*] (LCCP)
NWevNS ...... West Valley Nuclear Services Co., West Valley, NY [*Library symbol Library of Congress*] (LCLS)
NWF .... International Women's Forum [*National Women's Forum*] [*Acronym is based on former name,*] (EA)
NWF .... National War Formulary
NWF .... National War Fund
NWF .... National Welfare Fund (WDAA)
NWF .... National Wildlife Federation (EA)
NWF .... Naval Weapons Factory [*Formerly, NGF*]
NWF .... Naval Working Fund [*Navy, Coast Guard*]
NWF .... New Wilderness Foundation (EA)
NWF .... New World Foundation (EA)
NWF .... Nuclear Waste Fund (NUCP)
NWF .... Numerical Weather Facility
NWFA .... National Wholesale Furniture Association (EA)
NWFA .... National Wood Flooring Association (EA)
NWFA .... Northwest Farm Managers Association (EA)
NWFA .... Northwest Fisheries Association (EA)
NWFAL .... Nation-Wide Fallout (SAA)
NWFC .... Nuclear Weapons Freeze Campaign (EA)
NWFF .... North West Frontier Fellowship (EA)
NWFI .... Non-Woven Fabrics Institute [*Defunct*] (EA)
NWFMA .... Northwest Farm Managers Association
NWFP .... North-West Frontier Province [*Pakistan*] (PD)
NWFP .... Nuclear Weapons Fire Planning (MCD)

NWFP .... Rocky Flats/Nuclear Weapons Facilities Project [*Organization with goal of nuclear disarmament*] (*Defunct*) (EA)
NWF Pak ..... North West Frontier, Pakistan (ILCA)
NWFS .... NWS Capital Financing Trust [*Associated Press*] (SAG)
NWFSPCN... Nahanni National Park, Parks Canada [*Parc National Nahanni, Parcs Canada*] Fort Simpson, Northwest Territories [*Library symbol National Library of Canada*] (NLC)
NWFSPCW.. Wood Buffalo National Park, Parks Canada [*Parc National Wood Buffalo, Parcs Canada*] Fort Smith, Northwest Territories [*Library symbol National Library of Canada*] (NLC)
NWFST .... Thebacha College Library, Fort Smith, Northwest Territories [*Library symbol National Library of Canada*] (NLC)
NWFWA ...... Northwest Forest Workers Association [*Defunct*] (EA)
NWFZ.......... Nuclear Weapons-Free Zone
NWG .... National Wire Gauge
NWG .... New Goliath Minerals Ltd. [*Toronto Stock Exchange symbol Vancouver Stock Exchange symbol*]
nwga-- .... Greater Antilles [*MARC geographic area code Library of Congress*] (LCCP)
NWGA......... National Wool Growers Association [*Later, ASIA*] (EA)
NWGA......... Northwest Guides Association [*Defunct*]
nwgd........... Grenada [*MARC geographic area code Library of Congress*] (LCCP)
NWGDE....... Nordic Working Group on Development Education [*Nordic Council of Ministers*] [*Denmark*] (EAIO)
nwgp-- .... Guadeloupe [*MARC geographic area code Library of Congress*] (LCCP)
NWGP......... Nuclear War Graphics Project [*Defunct*] (EA)
nwgs-- .... Grenadines [*MARC geographic area code Library of Congress*] (LCCP)
NWGS .... Naval Warfare Gaming System
NWGSFW .... National Working Group on Screw Fly Worm [*Australia*]
NWGWU ..... National Warehouse and General Workers' Union [*British*]
NWH .... Nawa Air Transport [*Hungary ICAO designator*] (FAAC)
NWH .... New Hombre Resources [*Vancouver Stock Exchange symbol*]
NWH .... Normal Working Hours
NWh........... West Hempstead Public Library, West Hempstead, NY [*Library symbol Library of Congress*] (LCLS)
NWHA......... National Wholesale Hardware Association (EA)
NWHC......... National Women's Health Coalition [*Later, IWHC*]
NWHC......... Naval Weapons Handling Center
NWhCE .... Cornwell Avenue School, West Hempstead, NY [*Library symbol*] [*Library of Congress*] (LCLS)
NWHF .... National Wildlife Health Foundation (EA)
NWHF .... National Women's Hall of Fame (EA)
NWhh.......... Whitehall Free Library, Whitehall, NY [*Library symbol*] [*Library of Congress*] (LCLS)
NWhHS........ West Hempstead High School, West Hempstead, NY [*Library symbol*] [*Library of Congress*] (LCLS)
nwhi-- .... Hispaniola [*MARC geographic area code Library of Congress*] (LCCP)
NWHI.......... Northwestern Hawaiian Islands
NWHL.......... National Wildlife Health Laboratory [*Department of the Interior*] (GRD)
NWHL.......... Naval Weapons Handling Laboratory
NWhMS .... West Hempstead Middle School, West Hempstead, NY [*Library symbol*] [*Library of Congress*] (LCLS)
NWHN......... National Women's Health Network (EA)
NWHP......... National Women's History Project (EA)
NWhp.......... White Plains Public Library, White Plains, NY [*Library symbol Library of Congress*] (LCLS)
NWhpG .... College of White Plains, White Plains, NY [*Library symbol Library of Congress*] (LCLS)
NWhpI .... IBM Library Processing Center, White Plains, NY [*Library symbol Library of Congress*] (LCLS)
NWhpNC...... Nynex Corp., White Plains, NY [*Library symbol*] [*Library of Congress*] (LCLS)
NWhpNH...... New York Hospital, Westchester Division, White Plains, NY [*Library symbol Library of Congress*] (LCLS)
NWhpSC ...... New York State Supreme Court Law Library, White Plains, NY [*Library symbol Library of Congress*] (LCLS)
NWhpT........ Texaco Inc., Corp. Library, White Plains, NY [*Library symbol*] [*Library of Congress*] (LCLS)
NWhpTI........ Temple Israel Library, White Plains, NY [*Library symbol Library of Congress*] (LCLS)
NWhpW .... Westchester Library System, White Plains, NY [*Library symbol Library of Congress*] (LCLS)
NWHRC....... National Women's Health Resource Center (EA)
NWHRN....... Northwest Territories Public Library Services, Hay River, Northwest Territories [*Library symbol National Library of Canada*] (NLC)
NWHSLC...... Northern Wisconsin Health Science Library Cooperative [*Library network*]
nwht-- .... Haiti [*MARC geographic area code Library of Congress*] (LCCP)
NWhWE .... George Washington School, West Hempstead, NY [*Library symbol*] [*Library of Congress*] (LCLS)
NWI .... National Wetlands Inventory
NWI .... Netherlands West Indies
NWI .... Networking and World Information [*Electronic information and communications exchange service*]
NWI .... Norwich [*England*] [*Airport symbol*] (OAG)
NWI .... Nuclear Weapons Inventory (SSD)
NWI .... Nuinsco Resources Ltd. [*Toronto Stock Exchange symbol*]
NWi .... West Islip Public Library, West Islip, NY [*Library symbol Library of Congress*] (LCLS)
NWIAC........ Arctic College, Iqualuit, Northwest Territories [*Library symbol National Library of Canada*] (BIB)

NWIB .... National Westminster Investment Bank [*British*]
NWIC .... National Water Information Clearinghouse [*Proposed*] [*US Geological Survey*]
NWIC .... National Women's Insurance Center (EA)
NWICO........ New World Information and Communications Order [*UNESCO*]
NWiH .... Good Samaritan Hospital, West Islip, NY [*Library symbol Library of Congress*] (LCLS)
NWII .... Inuvik Scientific Resource Centre, Indian and Northern Affairs Canada [*CentreScientifique de Ressources d'Inuvik, Affaires Indiennes et du Nord Canada*], Northwest Territories [*Library symbol National Library of Canada*] (NLC)
NWIIE .... Eastern Arctic Research Laboratory, Indian and Northern Affairs Canada [*Laboratoire de Recherches Arctique de l'Est, Affaires Indiennes et du Nord Canada*], Igloolik, Northwest Territories [*Library symbol National Library of Canada*] (BIB)
NWiIP .... Willard Psychiatric Center, Willard, NY [*Library symbol Library of Congress*] (LCLS)
NWils........... Wilson Free Library, Wilson, NY [*Library symbol Library of Congress*] (LCLS)
NWilsHi .... Wilson Historical Society, Wilson, NY [*Library symbol Library of Congress*] (LCLS)
NwImag .... New Image Industries, Inc. [*Associated Press*] (SAG)
NWin .... Windham Public Library, Windham, NY [*Library symbol Library of Congress*] (LCLS)
NWIO .... New World Information Order [*Term coined by the Nonaligned Countries at their Fifth Summit Meeting in 1976*]
NWIP .... Naval Warfare Information Publication
NWIP .... Naval Warfare Intercept Procedures (MCD)
NWIP .... North Wales Independent Press
NWIR .... National Wireless Holdings, Inc. [*NASDAQ symbol*] (SAG)
NWIR .... Natl Wireless Hldgs [*NASDAQ symbol*] (TTSB)
NWIRP .... Naval Weapons Industrial Reserve Plant (AFM)
NWIS .... National Water Information System [*Department of the Interior*] (GFGA)
NWIS .... Naval Weaponeering Information Sheet (MCD)
NWISO........ Naval Weapons Industrial Support Office (DNAB)
NWIT .... Nuclear Waste Isolation Technology (NUCP)
NWIYRA...... North West Intercollegiate Yacht Racing Association
NWJA .... National Wholesale Jewelers Association [*Later, AJDA*] (EA)
nwjm .... Jamaica [*MARC geographic area code Library of Congress*] (LCCP)
NWK .... Network Equipment Technologies, Inc. [*NYSE symbol*] (SPSG)
NWK .... Network Equip Tech [*NYSE symbol*] (TTSB)
NWK .... Norwalk Public Library, Norwalk, CT [*Inactive*] [*OCLC symbol*] (OCLC)
NwkCmp ..... Network Computing Devices, Inc. [*Associated Press*] (SAG)
NwkIm .... Network Imaging Corp. [*Associated Press*] (SAG)
NwkImg .... Network Imaging Corp. [*Associated Press*] (SAG)
NWKLS .... Northwest Kansas Library System [*Library network*]
NWL........... National Water Lift Co. (MCD)
NWL........... National Women's League of the United Synagogue of America [*Later, AWL*] (EA)
NWL........... Natural Wavelength
NWL........... Naval Weapons Laboratory [*Later, NSWC*]
NWL........... Newell Co. [*NYSE symbol*] (SPSG)
NWL........... Newline Development [*Vancouver Stock Exchange symbol*]
NWL........... Normal Water Leg [*Nuclear energy*] (NRCH)
NWL........... Normal Water Level (IAA)
nwla-- .... Lesser Antilles [*MARC geographic area code Library of Congress*] (LCCP)
NWLA .... National Women and the Law Association (EA)
NWLA .... Northern Woods Logging Association (EA)
NW Law Rev... Northwestern Law Review [*A publication*] (DLA)
NWLB .... National War Labor Board [*World War II*]
NWLC .... National Women's Law Center (EA)
NWL/D .... Naval Weapons Laboratory / Dahlgren [*Virginia*] (DNAB)
NWldP .... New World Power Corp. (The) [*Associated Press*] (SAG)
NWldPwr ..... [*The*] New World Power Corp. [*Associated Press*] (SAG)
NWLDYA ..... National Wholesale Lumber Distributing Yard Association (EA)
NWLF......... National Watermen and Lightermen's Federation [*A union*] [*British*]
NWLF......... New World Liberation Front
nwli-- .... Leeward Islands [*MARC geographic area code Library of Congress*] (LCCP)
NWLI .... National Western Life Insurance Co. [*NASDAQ symbol*] (NQ)
NWLIA .... Natl Western Life Ins'A' [*NASDAQ symbol*] (TTSB)
NWL Rev ..... North Western Law Review [*Chicago*] [*A publication*] (DLA)
NWLS .... Northwest Wisconsin Library System [*Library network*]
NWM .... Morris County Free Library, Whippany, NJ [*OCLC symbol*] (OCLC)
NWM .... Newfields Minerals Ltd. [*Toronto Stock Exchange symbol*]
NWM .... New Ways Ministry (EA)
NWM .... New World Monkey
NWM .... Northwest Monsoon
NWM .... United States Military Academy, West Point, NY [*Library symbol Library of Congress*] (LCLS)
NWMA .... National Woodwork Manufacturers Association [*Formerly, NDMA*] [*Later, NWWDA*] (EA)
NWMA .... Northwest Mining Association (EA)
NWMAF ...... National Women's Martial Arts Federation (EA)
NWMC .... National Wool Marketing Corp. (EA)
NWMC .... Northwest Michigan College
NWMF .... National Women's Music Festival (EA)
NWMF .... Nuclear Weapons Maintenance Foreman (AABC)
NwMilfd ...... New Milford Bank & Trust Co. [*Associated Press*] (SAG)
nwmj-- .... Montserrat [*MARC geographic area code Library of Congress*] (LCCP)
NWMKT .... Newmarket [*Urban district in England*]

NWML .... National Women's Mailing List (EA)
NWMP .... North-West Mounted Police [*Later, RCMP*] [*Canada*]
nwmq-- .... Martinique [*MARC geographic area code Library of Congress*] (LCCP)
NWMRS .... National Waste Minimization and Recycling Strategy [*Australia*]
NWMS .... Nazarene World Mission Society (EA)
NWMS .... Nuclear Weapons Maintenance Specialist (AABC)
NwmtG .... Newmont Gold Co. [*Associated Press*] (SAG)
NWMTI .... Northwest Medical Team International
NWN .... National Workers Network [*Defunct*] (EA)
NWN .... Newcan Minerals [*Vancouver Stock Exchange symbol*]
NWN .... Nonwhite Noise
NWN .... Northwestern
NWN .... Northwinds Northern Ltd. [*Canada ICAO designator*] (FAAC)
NWN .... Nuclear Waste News [*Business Publishers, Inc.*] [*No longer available online*] [*Information service or system*] (CRD)
nwna-- .... Netherlands Antilles [*MARC geographic area code Library of Congress*] (LCCP)
NWNet .... Northwestern States Network [*Computer science*] (TNIG)
NWNG .... Northwest Natural Gas [*NASDAQ symbol*] (TTSB)
NWNG .... Northwest Natural Gas Co. [*NASDAQ symbol*] (NQ)
NWNSA .... National Women's Neckwear and Scarf Association (EA)
NW-NW .... No Work - No Woo [*Slogan adopted by women war workers in Albina shipyards in Portland, Oregon, who agreed not to date men who were absent from work*] [*World War II*]
NWO .... Directory of National Women's Organizations [*A publication*]
NWO .... NASA Washington Office (KSC)
NWO .... New Work Opportunities [*A publication*]
NWO .... New World Order [*Bush administration*]
NWO .... Nonwoven Oriented
NWO .... Nuclear Weapons Officer
NWOA .... National Woodland Owners Association (EA)
NWOBHM .... New Wave of British Heavy Metal [*Rock music type, 1979-81*]
NWOC .... Naval Weather and Oceanographic Center (DOMA)
NWOFC .... Numerical Weather and Oceanographic Forecasting Center [*Marine science*] (MSC)
NWOO .... NATO Wartime Oil Organization (NATG)
NWOR .... Neworld Bancorp, Inc. [*NASDAQ symbol*] (NQ)
NWP .... National Water Project [*Later, RCAP*] (EA)
NWP .... National Woman's Party (EA)
NWP .... National Writing Project (EA)
NWP .... Nationwide Outdoor Recreation Plan [*Bureau of Outdoor Recreation*]
NWP .... NATO and Warsaw Pact [*Projects*] (NATG)
NWP .... Naval Warfare Procedures (MCD)
NWP .... Naval Warfare Publications
NWP .... Naval Weapons Plant (AAG)
NWP .... Naval Weapons Publications
NWP .... Northwestern Pacific Railroad Co. [*AAR code*]
NWP .... North-Western Provinces, High Court Reports [*India*] [*A publication*] (DLA)
NWP .... Northwest Passage (ROG)
NWP .... Northwest Provinces
NWP .... Nuclear Waste Project [*Defunct*] (EA)
NWP .... Numerical Weather Prediction
NWP .... NWP Resources [*Vancouver Stock Exchange symbol*]
NWp .... Williston Park Public Library, Williston Park, NY [*Library symbol Library of Congress*] (LCLS)
NWPA .... Nuclear Waste Policy Act (NRCH)
NWPA .... Nuclear Waste Policy Act of 1982 (GAAI)
NWPAG .... NATO Wartime Preliminary Analysis Group (NATG)
NwPar .... New Paradigm Software [*Associated Press*] (SAG)
NWPC .... National Women's Political Caucus (EA)
NWPC .... [*The*] New World Power Corp. [*NASDAQ symbol*] (SAG)
NWPC .... Northwest Provinces Code [*India*] [*A publication*] (DLA)
NWPCA .... National Wooden Pallet and Container Association (EA)
NWPCB .... Naval Warfare Planning Chart Bases (MCD)
NWPCE .... New World Power [*NASDAQ symbol*] (TTSB)
NWpCsE .... Center Street Elementary School, Williston Park, NY [*Library symbol*] [*Library of Congress*] (LCLS)
NWPF .... National Water Purification Foundation
NWPF .... Nonwoven Polyester Fabric
NWPHC .... Northwest Provinces, High Court Reports [*India*] [*A publication*] (DLA)
NwpkRs .... Newpark Resources, Inc. [*Associated Press*] (SAG)
NWPL .... Naval Warfare Publications Library (NVT)
NWPMA .... National Wooden Pallet Manufacturers Association [*Later, NWPCA*] (EA)
NWPO .... Northwest Pacific Oceanographers [*An association*] (NOAA)
NWPOG .... Numerical Weather Prediction Operational Grid (SAA)
NWPP .... Nationwide Permit Program [*Army Corps of Engineers*] (GFGA)
NWPPCA ...... Auyuittuq National Park, Parks Canada [*Parc National Auyuittuq, Parcs Canada*] Pangnirtung, Northwest Territories [*Library symbol National Library of Canada*] (NLC)
nwpr-- .... Puerto Rico [*MARC geographic area code Library of Congress*] (LCCP)
NWPrA .... Natl Westminister Pref'A'ADS [*NYSE symbol*] (TTSB)
NWPrB .... Natl Westminister Pref'B'ADS [*NYSE symbol*] (TTSB)
NWPS .... National Wilderness Preservation System
NWPS .... Northwestern Public Service Co. [*Associated Press*] (SAG)
NWPS .... NWPS Capital Financing Tr PERCS [*Associated Press*] (SAG)
NWPSC .... Nationwide Postal-Strike Contingency Plan (DNAB)
NWPU .... Numerical Weather Prediction Unit (DNAB)
NWPW .... Naval Weapons Plant, Washington, DC
NWPX .... Northwest Pipe [*NASDAQ symbol*] (TTSB)
NWPYVO ...... National Working Party of Youth Volunteer Organisers (AIE)

NWQ .... Northwest Digital Ltd. [*Toronto Stock Exchange symbol*]
NWQI .... National Water Quality Inventory [*Environmental Protection Agency*]
NWQL .... National Water Quality Laboratory
NWQSS .... National Water Quality Surveillance System [*Dicontinued, 1981*] [*Environmental Protection Agency*]
NWR .... National Welfare Rights (WDAA)
NWR .... National Wildlife Refuge (WDAA)
NWR .... National Women's Register [*British*] (DBA)
NWR .... Navy Weapons Requirement
NWR .... Next Word Request
NWR .... NOAA [*National Oceanic and Atmospheric Administration*] Weather Radio (NOAA)
NWR .... North Western Railway [*India*]
NWR .... North Western Reporter [*Legal*]
NWR .... Northwestern Reporter [*Commonly cited NW*] [*A publication*] (DLA)
NWR .... Nuclear Weapons Report [*Army*] (AABC)
NWRA .... National Waterbed Retailers Association (EA)
NWRA .... National Water Resources Association (EA)
NWRA .... National Wheel and Rim Association (EA)
NWRA .... National Wildlife Refuge Association (EA)
NWRA .... National Wildlife Rehabilitators Association (EA)
NWRA .... National Women's Rowing Association [*Later, USRA*] (EA)
NWRC .... National Weather Records Center [*Later, National Climatic Center*] [*National Oceanic and Atmospheric Administration*]
NWRC .... National Wildflower Research Center (EA)
NWRC .... Naval Warfare Research Center (MCD)
NWRC .... Nebraska Water Resources Center [*University of Nebraska - Lincoln*] [*Research center*] (RCD)
NWRC .... Northeast Watershed Research Center [*University Park, PA*] [*Department of Agriculture*] (GRD)
NWREL .... Northwest Regional Educational Laboratory [*Portland, OR*] [*Research center*]
NW Rep .... Northwestern Reporter [*Commonly cited NW*] [*A publication*] (DLA)
NW Repr ...... North Western Reporter [*A publication*] (DLA)
NW Rev Ord... Northwest Territories Revised Ordinances [*Canada*] [*A publication*] (DLA)
NWRF .... Naval Weather Research Facility
NWRHB........ North West Regional Health Board [*Tasmania, Australia*]
NWRI .... National Water Research Institute [*Environment Canada*] [*Research center*] (RCD)
NwrldCf....... New World Coffee, Inc. [*Associated Press*] (SAG)
NWRLF........ New World Radical Liberation Front (NADA)
NWRN......... Northwestern (FAAC)
NWRO......... National Women's Rights Organization [*Defunct*]
NWRS......... National Wildlife Refuge System (WDAA)
NWRS......... North-West Recording Society [*Record label*]
NWRS......... Nuclear Weapons Requirements Study (CINC)
NwRSA .... Northwest Region Spinners Association (EA)
NWRT .... National Wildlife Rescue Team (EA)
NWRWA....... North West Regional Water Authority [*Tasmania, Australia*]
NWS .... National Watercolor Society (EA)
NWS .... National Waterways Study [*Marine science*] (MSC)
NWS .... National Weather Service [*Formerly, US Weather Bureau*] [*Silver Spring, MD*] [*National Oceanic and Atmospheric Administration*]
NWS .... National Winter Sports [*Association*] [*Defunct*] (EA)
NWS .... Naval Weapons Station
NWS .... Navy Weather Service
NWS .... [*The*] News Corp. Ltd. [*NYSE symbol*] (SPSG)
NWS .... News Corp. Ltd ADS [*NYSE symbol*] (TTSB)
NWS .... New Workers Scheme (AIE)
NWS .... New World Society (EA)
NWS .... Nimbus Weather Satellite
NWS .... Normal Water Surface (ADA)
NWS .... North Warning System (MCD)
NWS .... North-West Semitic (BJA)
NWS .... Northwest States (ROG)
NWS .... Norway Station [*South Africa*] [*Later, SNA*] [*Geomagnetic observatory code*]
NWS .... Nose Wheel Steering [*Aviation*]
NWS .... Nowsco Well Service Ltd. [*Toronto Stock Exchange symbol*]
NWS .... Nuclear Weapons State
NWS .... Nuclear Weapon State
NWSA .... National Water Slide Association (EA)
NWSA .... National Welding Supply Association (EA)
NWSA .... National Wheelchair Softball Association (EA)
NWSA .... National Winter Sports Association
NWSA .... National Women's Studies Association (EA)
NWSA .... National Women's Suffrage Association (WDAA)
NWSA .... Naval Weapons Support Activity
NWSA .... Naval Weather Service Association (EA)
NWSA .... Nose Wheel Steering Amplifier [*Aviation*] (MCD)
NWSA .... Nuclear Weapons Supply Annex
NWSA Jnl ..... NWSA Journal [*A publication*] (BRI)
NWSAP .... Naval Weapons Station Acceptance Program (MCD)
NWSB .... National Wage Stabilization Board [*Superseded NWLB, 1945; terminated, 1947*]
NWSB .... Northwest Savings Bank [*NASDAQ symbol*] (SAG)
NWSB .... Nuclear Warfare Status Branch (CINC)
nwsb-- .... Saint-Barthelemy [*MARC geographic area code Library of Congress*] (LCCP)
NWSC .... National Water Safety Congress (EA)
NWSC .... National Weather Satellite Center [*Later, National Environmental Satellite Service*]
NWSC .... National Weather Service Center (MCD)
NWSC .... National Women's Student Coalition (EA)

NWSC .... Naval Weapons Support Center (MCD)
NWSC .... Naval Weather Service Command
NWSCA .... National Water and Soil Conservation Agency (BARN)
NWSCC .... Nuclear Weapons System Control Console (MCD)
NWSC/CR .... Naval Weapons Support Center, Crane [Indiana]
Nwscop .... Newscope Resources Ltd. [Associated Press] (SAG)
NWS-CR ..... National Weather Service-Central Region (PDAA)
NWSD .... Naval Weather Service Detachment [or Division]
nwsd-- .... Saba [MARC geographic area code Library of Congress] (LCCP)
NWSED .... Naval Weather Service Environmental Detachment [Navy]
NWSEO .... National Weather Service Employees Organization (EA)
NWS-ER ...... National Weather Service-Eastern Region (PDAA)
NWSF .... Northwest Sea Frontier
NWSF .... Nuclear Weapons Storage Facility [Army] (AABC)
NWSFO .... NWS [National Weather Service] Forecast Office (USDC)
NWSFO .... NWS [National Weather Service] Forecast Office [Marine science] (OSRA)
NWSG .... Nuclear War Study Group (EA)
NWSG .... Nuclear Weapon Systems Surety Group [Army]
NWsH .... Houghton College, Buffalo Campus, West Seneca, NY [Library symbol Library of Congress] (LCLS)
NWSH .... National Weather Service Headquarters
NWsHeaC ... Health Care Plan Medical Center, West Seneca, NY [Library symbol Library of Congress] (LCLS)
NWSI .... New World Services, Inc.
NWSIA .... National Water Supply Improvement Association [Later, IDA] (EA)
NWSLF .... Nowsco WellService [NASDAQ symbol] (TTSB)
NWSLF .... Nowsco Well Services [NASDAQ symbol] (SAG)
NWSM .... Nuclear Weapons Stockpile Memorandum
NWSO .... Naval Weapons Services Office [Also known as NAVWPNSERVO, WEPSO]
NWSO .... Naval Weather Service Office
nwspa .... Newspaper (VRA)
NWSPr .... News Corp. Ltd Pfd ADS [NYSE symbol] (TTSB)
NWSRFS ..... National Weather Service River Forecast System (NOAA)
NWSRS .... National Wild and Scenic Rivers System
NWSS .... National Weather Satellite System (KSC)
NWSS .... National Wool Sorters' Society [A union] [British] (DCTA)
NWSS .... Navy WWMCCS [World-Wide Military Command and Control System] Standardization Software
NWSS .... Network Six, Inc. [NASDAQ symbol] (SAG)
NWSS .... Nuclear Weapons Support Section [Army] (AABC)
NWsS .... West Seneca State School, West Seneca, NY [Library symbol Library of Congress] (LCLS)
NWSSG .... Nuclear Weapons System Safety Group
NWSSG .... Nuclear Weapons System Satellite Group [Military] (IAA)
NWSSGP ..... Nuclear Weapons System Safety Group
NWS-SR ..... National Weather Service-Southern Region (PDAA)
nwst-- .... St. Martin (Sint Maarten) [MARC geographic area code Library of Congress] (LCCP)
NwstAirl ...... Northwest Airlines Corp. [Associated Press] (SAG)
NwstEqty ..... Northwest Equity Corp. [Associated Press] (SAG)
NWSTG .... National Weather Service Telecommunications Gateway
NWSTG .... NWS [National Weather Service] Telecommunications Gateway (USDC)
NWSTG .... NWS [National Weather Service] Telecommunications Gateway [Marine science] (OSRA)
NwStlWr ...... Northwestern Steel & Wire Co. [Associated Press] (SAG)
NwstSBk ..... Northwest Savings Bank [Associated Press] (SAG)
NWSTTC ..... National Weather Service Technical Training Center
nwsv-- .... Swan Islands [MARC geographic area code Library of Congress] (LCCP)
NWSW .... Northwestern Steel & Wire Co. [NASDAQ symbol] (SAG)
NWSW .... Nothwestern Steel & Wire [NASDAQ symbol] (TTSB)
NWS-WR ..... National Weather Service-Western Region (PDAA)
NWSY .... Naval Weapons Station, Yorktown [Virginia]
N WT .... Net Weight
NWT .... New World Translation (of the Holy Scriptures) [A publication] (BJA)
NWT .... Nonwatertight [Packaging] (AAG)
NWT .... Northwestern Terminal R. R. [AAR code]
NWT .... Northwestern Utilities Ltd. [Toronto Stock Exchange symbol]
NWT .... Northwest Territorial Airways [Canada ICAO designator] (FAAC)
NWT .... Northwest Territories [Canada]
NWT .... Nowata [Papua New Guinea] [Airport symbol] (OAG)
NWT .... Nylon Wire Tie
NWTA .... National Waterways Transport Association [British]
NWTA .... National Woman's Trucking Association [Defunct] (EA)
NWTA .... National Wool Trade Association [Defunct] (EA)
NWTA .... North West Territory Alliance (EA)
NWTB .... Northwestern Tariff Bureau
NWTB .... North West Tourist Board [British] (DCTA)
NWTC .... National Wetlands Technical Council (EA)
NWTC .... Naval Weapon Test Center [China Lake, California] [Navy]
NWTC .... Northern Warfare Training Center [Army] (MCD)
NWTC .... Nuclear Weapons Training Center
nwtc-- .... Turks and Caicos Islands [MARC geographic area code Library of Congress] (LCCP)
NWTCL .... Nuclear Weapons Training Center, Atlantic (DNAB)
NWTCP .... Nuclear Weapons Training Center, Pacific (DNAB)
NWTD .... Nonwatertight Door (ADA)
NWTDB .... Naval Warfare Tactical Data Base (DOMA)
NWTEC .... National Wool Textile Export Corp. [British] (BI)
NW Terr ...... Northwest Territories, Supreme Court Reports [A publication] (DLA)
NWTF .... National Wild Turkey Federation (EA)
NWTG .... Nuclear Weapons Training Group (DNAB)

NWTGL .... Nuclear Weapons Training Group, Atlantic (DNAB)
NWTGP .... Nuclear Weapons Training Group, Pacific (DNAB)
NWTH .... Networth, Inc. [NASDAQ symbol] (SAG)
NWTI .... National Wood Tank Institute (EA)
NWTI .... Nuclear Weapons Technical Inspections
NWTK .... North West Token Kai [An association] (EA)
NWTL .... Northwest Teleprod'ns [NASDAQ symbol] (TTSB)
NWTL .... Northwest Teleproductions, Inc. [NASDAQ symbol] (NQ)
NWTLR .... North West Territories Law Reports [A publication] (DLA)
NWTO .... Network for Work Time Options [San Francisco, CA] (EA)
NWT Ord ..... Northwest Territories Ordinances [Canada] [A publication] (DLA)
NWTP .... Naval Warfare Tactical Publication (DNAB)
NWTR .... North West Territories Reports [1885-1907] [Canada] [A publication] (DLA)
nwtr-- .... Trinidad and Tobago [MARC geographic area code Library of Congress] (LCCP)
NWTRB .... Nuclear Waste Technical Review Board [Nuclear energy] (EGAO)
NWTRCC ..... National War Tax Resistance Coordinating Committee (EA)
NWT Rev Ord... Northwest Territories Revised Ordinances [Canada A publication] (DLA)
NWTS .... National Waste Terminal Storage [For radioactive wastes]
NWTS .... National Wilms' Tumor Study [Oncology]
NWTS .... Naval Weapons Test Station
NWT/S .... Nuclear Weapons Technician/Specialist (AAG)
NWTSG .... National Wilms' Tumor Study Group [Oncology]
NWU .... National Workers Union (NADA)
NWU .... National Writers Union (EA)
NWU .... Nebraska Wesleyan University
NWU .... Northwestern University School of Law (DLA)
NWU .... Nose Wheel Up [Aviation]
nwuc-- .... United States Miscellaneous Caribbean Islands [MARC geographic area code Library of Congress] (LCCP)
NWUIS .... Navy Work Unit Information System (DNAB)
NWUS .... Northwestern United States
NWV .... Newcoast Silver Mines [Vancouver Stock Exchange symbol]
NWV .... Norfolk, VA [Location identifier FAA] (FAAL)
nwvb-- .... Virgin Islands, British [MARC geographic area code Library of Congress] (LCCP)
NWvH .... Millard Fillmore Suburban Hospital, Williamsville, NY [Library symbol] [Library of Congress] (LCLS)
nwvi-- .... Virgin Islands of the US [MARC geographic area code Library of Congress] (LCCP)
nwvr .... Virgin Islands [MARC geographic area code Library of Congress] (LCCP)
NWvS .... Sanders Associates, Inc., Williamsville, NY [Library symbol Library of Congress] (LCLS)
NWW .... Newgate Resources [Vancouver Stock Exchange symbol]
NWW .... New Ways to Work (EA)
NWW .... North West Airline [Australia ICAO designator] (FAAC)
NWW .... Nose Wheel Well [Aviation] (MCD)
NWWA .... National Water Well Association [Database producer] (EA)
NWWA .... North-West Water Authority [British] (DCTA)
NWWA .... Tiga, Iles Loyaute [New Caledonia] [ICAO location identifier] (ICLI)
NWWC .... Ile Art/Wala, Iles Belep [New Caledonia] [ICAO location identifier] (ICLI)
NWWC .... National White Wyandotte Club [Defunct] (EA)
NwWCof ...... New World Coffee, Inc. [Associated Press] (SAG)
NWWCSS .... Naval Worldwide Command Support System (MCD)
NWWD .... Kone [New Caledonia] [ICAO location identifier] (ICLI)
NWWDA ...... National Wood Window and Door Association (EA)
NWWE .... Ile Des Pins/Moue [New Caledonia] [ICAO location identifier] (ICLI)
NwWEye ...... New West Eyeworks, Inc. [Associated Press] (SAG)
NWWF .... Voh [New Caledonia] [ICAO location identifier] (ICLI)
NWWH .... Houailou/Nesson [New Caledonia] [ICAO location identifier] (ICLI)
NWWI .... Hienghene/Henri Martinet [New Caledonia] [ICAO location identifier] (ICLI)
nwwi-- .... Windward Islands [MARC geographic area code Library of Congress] (LCCP)
NWWJ .... Poum [New Caledonia] [ICAO location identifier] (ICLI)
NWWK .... Koumac [New Caledonia] [ICAO location identifier] (ICLI)
NWWL .... Lifou/Ouanaham, Iles Loyaute [New Caledonia] [ICAO location identifier] (ICLI)
NWWM .... Noumea/Magenta [New Caledonia] [ICAO location identifier] (ICLI)
NWWN .... Noumea [New Caledonia] [ICAO location identifier] (ICLI)
NWWO .... Ile Ouen/Edmond-Cane [New Caledonia] [ICAO location identifier] (ICLI)
NWWQ .... Mueo/Nickel [New Caledonia] [ICAO location identifier] (ICLI)
NWWR .... Mare/La Roche, Iles Loyaute [New Caledonia] [ICAO location identifier] (ICLI)
NWWS .... NOAA [National Oceanic and Atmospheric Administration] Weather Wire Service (NOAA)
NWWS .... Plaine Des Lacs [New Caledonia] [ICAO location identifier] (ICLI)
NWWU .... Touho [New Caledonia] [ICAO location identifier] (ICLI)
NWWV .... Ouvea/Ouloup, Iles Loyaute [New Caledonia] [ICAO location identifier] (ICLI)
NWWW .... Noumea/La Tontouta [New Caledonia] [ICAO location identifier] (ICLI)
NWWY .... Ouaco/Paquiepe [New Caledonia] [ICAO location identifier] (ICLI)
NWX .... National Westminster Bank PLC [NYSE symbol] (SAG)
NWX .... New Minex Resources Ltd. [Vancouver Stock Exchange symbol]
nwxi-- .... St. Christopher-Nevis-Anguilla [MARC geographic area code Library of Congress] (LCCP)
nwxk-- .... St. Lucia [MARC geographic area code Library of Congress] (LCCP)
nwxm .... St. Vincent [MARC geographic area code Library of Congress] (LCCP)

NWXPrA...... Natl Westminster Bk Ex Cap Sec [*NYSE symbol*] (TTSB)
NWY .... New Penn Energy [*Vancouver Stock Exchange symbol*]
NWy .... Wyoming Free Public Library, Wyoming, NY [*Library symbol Library of Congress*] (LCLS)
NWY .... Yellowknife Public Library, Northwest Territories [*Library symbol National Library of Canada*] (NLC)
NWya.......... Wyandanch Public Library, Wyandanch, NY [*Library symbol Library of Congress*] (LCLS)
NWyaHEC ... LaFrancis Hardiman Early Childhood Center, Wyandanch, NY [*Library symbol*] [*Library of Congress*] (LCLS)
NwyaHS....... Wyandanch Memorial High School, Wyandanch, NY [*Library symbol*] [*Library of Congress*] (LCLS)
NWyaKE....... Martin Luther King Elementary School, Wyandanch, NY [*Library symbol*] [*Library of Congress*] (LCLS)
NWyaOMS ... Milton Olive Middle School, Wyandanch, NY [*Library symbol*] [*Library of Congress*] (LCLS)
NWyaSE....... Straightpath Elementary School, Wyandanch, NY [*Library symbol*] [*Library of Congress*] (LCLS)
NWYC .... Court Library, Department of Justice, Yellowknife, Northwest Territories [*Library symbol National Library of Canada*] (BIB)
NWYCC........ National Write Your Congressman [*Also known as National Write Your Congressman Club*] (EA)
NWYCJ .... Cooper-Johnson, Yellowknife, Northwest Territories [*Library symbol National Library of Canada*] (BIB)
NWYD .... Dene Nation, Yellowknife, Northwest Territories [*Library symbol National Library of Canada*] (BIB)
NWYECW..... Canadian Wildlife Service, Environment Canada [*Service Canadien de la Faune, Environnement Canada*] Yellowknife, Northwest Territories [*Library symbol National Library of Canada*] (NLC)
NWYEEP ...... Assessment and Coordination Branch, Environmental Protection Service, Environment Canada [*Direction de l'Evaluation et de la Coordination, Service de la Protection de l'Environnement, Environnement Canada*] Yellowknife, Northwest Territories [*Library symbol National Library of Canada*] (NLC)
NWYGI........ Government Library, Government of the Northwest Territories, Yellowknife, Northwest Territories [*Library symbol National Library of Canada*] (NLC)
NWYIN........ Indian and Northern Affairs Canada [*Affaires Indiennes et du Nord Canada*] Yellowknife, Northwest Territories [*Library symbol National Library of Canada*] (NLC)
NWYND....... Northern Region Information System (NORIS), Canada Department of National Defence [*Reseau d'Information de la Region du Nord (NORIS), Ministere de la DefenseNationale*] Yellowknife, Northwest Territories [*Library symbol National Library of Canada*] (NLC)
NWYOS........ Dr. Otto Schaefer Health Resource Centre, Yellowknife, Northwest Territories [*Library symbol National Library of Canada*] (NLC)
NWYPC........ Parks Canada [*Parcs Canada*] Yellowknife, Northwest Territories [*Library symbol National Library of Canada*] (NLC)
NWYPW....... Technical Resource Centre, Department of Public Works and Highways, Government of the Northwest Territories, Yellowknife, Northwest Territories [*Library symbol National Library of Canada*] (BIB)
NWYRR........ Renewable Resources Library, Government of the Northwest Territories, Yellowknife, Northwest Territories [*Library symbol National Library of Canada*] (NLC)
NWYWNH .... Prince of Wales Northern Heritage Centre, Government of the Northwest Territories, Yellowknife, Northwest Territories [*Library symbol National Library of Canada*] (NLC)
NX.............. Net Exports
NX............... New Zealand Air Charter [*ICAO designator*] (AD)
nx .... Norfolk Island [*MARC country of publication code Library of Congress*] (LCCP)
NX............... Normal to X-Axis (MCD)
NX............... Nose to X-Axis (MCD)
NX............... Not Exceeding
NX............... Not Expendable (MUGU)
nx .... Nourishment [*Dietetics*] (DAVI)
NX............... Quanex Corp. [*NYSE symbol*] (SPSG)
NXA .... Nodal Exchange Area (MHDB)
NXA .... Nolisair International, Inc. [*Canada ICAO designator*] (FAAC)
NXA .... Norex America [*AMEX symbol*] (TTSB)
NXA .... Norex America, Inc. [*AMEX symbol*] (SPSG)
NXA .... Wake County Public Library, Raleigh, NC [*OCLC symbol*] (OCLC)
NXB .... Neurotoxin B
NXC .... Nuveen Ins CA Sel Tax-Free Inc. [*NYSE symbol*] (TTSB)
NXC .... Nuveen Insured California Select Tax-Free Income [*NYSE symbol*] (SPSG)
NXCI .... National Xeriscape Council, Inc. [*An association*] (EA)
NXCO........... Neurex Corp. [*NASDAQ symbol*] (SAG)
NXDO........... Nike-X Development Office [*Army*] (AABC)
NXGN........... NexGen, Inc. [*NASDAQ symbol*] (SAG)
NXI.............. Oak Harbor, WA [*Location identifier FAA*] (FAAL)
NXL--......... Napoleon Exploration [*Vancouver Stock Exchange symbol*]
n-xl--........... St. Pierre and Miquelon [*MARC geographic area code Library of Congress*] (LCCP)
NXM............ Non-Existent Memory (MHDB)
NXM............ Noramex Minerals [*Vancouver Stock Exchange symbol*]
NXMIS......... Nike-X Management Information System [*Army*]
NXN............ Milton, FL [*Location identifier FAA*] (FAAL)
NXN............ No Christian Name
NXN............ Nuveen Ins NY Sel Tax-Free Inc. [*NYSE symbol*] (TTSB)
NXN............ Nuveen Insured New York Select Tax-Free Income [*NYSE symbol*] (SPSG)
NXP .... Noxe Resources Corp. [*Vancouver Stock Exchange symbol*]

NXP .... Nuveen Select Tax-Free Inc. [*NYSE symbol*] (TTSB)
NXP .... Nuveen Select Tax-Free Income [*NYSE symbol*] (SPSG)
NXP .... Twentynine Palms, CA [*Location identifier FAA*] (FAAL)
NXPM .... Nike-X Project Manager [*Army*] (AABC)
NXPO........... Nike-X Program [*or Project*] Office [*Army*]
NXPRG......... Nike-X Program Review Group [*Army*] (AABC)
NXQ .... Nuveen Selct Tax-Free Inc. 2 [*NYSE symbol*] (TTSB)
NXQ .... Nuveen Select Tax-Free Income 2 [*NYSE symbol*] (SPSG)
NXR .... Noncrossing Rule
NXR .... Nuveen Selct Tax-Free Inc. 3 [*NYSE symbol*] (TTSB)
NXR .... Nuveen Select Tax-Free Income 3 [*NYSE symbol*] (SPSG)
NXS .... Nexus Resources Corp. [*Vancouver Stock Exchange symbol Toronto Stock Exchange symbol*]
NXSM .... Nike-X System Manager [*Army*] (AABC)
NXSMO .... Nike-X System Manager's Office [*Army*]
NXSO .... Nike-X Support Office [*Army*]
NXSPC .... Nexus Telecommunication Systems Ltd. [*NASDAQ symbol*] (SAG)
NXSR .... Non-Extraction Steam Rate (PDAA)
NXT............. Next
NXTR .... NeXstar Pharmaceutical [*NASDAQ symbol*] (SAG)
NXTR .... NeXstar Pharmaceuticals [*NASDAQ symbol*] (TTSB)
NXUL .... Nexus Telecommunication Systems Ltd. [*NASDAQ symbol*] (SAG)
NXULF .... Nexus Telecomm Sys Wrrt [*NASDAQ symbol*] (TTSB)
NXUS .... Nexus Telecommunication Systems Ltd. [*NASDAQ symbol*] (SAG)
NXUSF .... Nexus Telecommns Sys Ltd [*NASDAQ symbol*] (TTSB)
NXUW .... Nexus Telecommunication Systems Ltd. [*NASDAQ symbol*] (SAG)
NXUWF .... Nexus Telecommuns Sys Wrrt'A' [*NASDAQ symbol*] (TTSB)
NXUZ .... Nexus Telecommunication Systems Ltd. [*NASDAQ symbol*] (SAG)
NXUZF .... Nexus Telecommuns Sys Wrrt'B' [*NASDAQ symbol*] (TTSB)
NXW .... University of North Carolina, Wilmington, Wilmington, NC [*OCLC symbol*] (OCLC)
NXWPC .... Nexus Telecommunication Systems Ltd. [*NASDAQ symbol*] (SAG)
NXX .... Willow Grove, PA [*Location identifier FAA*] (FAAL)
NXZPC .... Nexus Telecommunication Systems Ltd. [*NASDAQ symbol*] (SAG)
NY.............. John Dewey [*Final letters of his first and last name used as a pseudonym*] [*American author, 1859-1952*]
NY.............. Navy Yard
NY.............. Nelen Yubu [*A publication*] (APTA)
NY.............. Net Yield
NY.............. New Year
NY.............. New York [*City or state*] [*Postal code*]
NY.............. New York [*Naval Shipyard*]
NY.............. New York Airways, Inc. [*ICAO designator*]
NY.............. New York Court of Appeals Reports [*A publication*] (DLA)
NY.............. New Yorker [*A publication*] (BRI)
NY.............. Noorduyn Aviation Ltd. [*Canada ICAO aircraft manufacturer identifier*] (ICAO)
NY.............. Normal to Y-Axis (MCD)
NY.............. Northamptonshire Yeomanry [*British military*] (DMA)
NY.............. Northumberland Yeomanry [*British military*] (DMA)
NY.............. Nose to Y-Axis (NASA)
NY.............. Nose to Y-Axis
NY.............. No Year [*of publication*] [*Bibliography*]
NY.............. Nuclear Yellow [*A fluorescent dye*]
NY.............. Nuclear Yield
NY.............. Nyasaland (ROG)
NY.............. Yonkers Public Library, Yonkers, NY [*Library symbol Library of Congress*] (LCLS)
NY 2d .... New York Court of Appeals Reports, Second Series [*A publication*] (DLA)
NYA .... National Yogurt Association (EA)
NYA .... National Youth Administration [*Terminated, 1943*]
NYA .... National Youth Alliance (EA)
NYA .... Neighborhood Youth Administration (OICC)
NYA .... New York Airways, Inc. [*Air carrier designation symbol*]
NYA .... Not Yet Answered
nya............. Nyanja [*MARC language code Library of Congress*] (LCCP)
NYAB .... National Youth Advisory Board [*Environmental Protection Agency*]
NYAB .... New York Air Brake Co.
NYABIC........ New York Association for Brain Injured Children
NY Admin Code... Official Compilation of Codes, Rules, and Regulations of the State of New York [*A publication*] (DLA)
NYADS......... New York Air Defense Sector (SAA)
NYAES-C...... New York Agricultural Experiment Station (Cornell University) [*Research center*] (RCD)
NYAIC......... New York Association of Industrial Communicators [*Later, NY/IABC*] (EA)
NYAL .... National Yugoslav Army of Liberation [*World War II*]
NYALR .... New Yorkers for Abortion Law Repeal (EA)
NYAM .... New York Academy of Medicine
NYAM .... New York Academy of Music
NYAMP .... New York Advertising Media Planners [*Defunct*] (EA)
NYANA .... New York Association for New Americans (EA)
NY & E .... New York & Erie Railroad
NY & NE...... New York & New England Railroad [*Nickname: Now You Are Nearing Eternity*]
NY & NH...... New York & New Haven Railroad
NY Ann Ca... New York Annotated Cases [*A publication*] (DLA)
NY Ann Cas... New York Annotated Cases [*A publication*] (DLA)
NY Anno Cas... New York Annotated Cases [*A publication*] (DLA)
NY Anno Dig... New York Annotated Digest [*A publication*] (ILCA)
NY Annot Dig... New York Annotated Digest [*A publication*] (DLA)
NYap............ Middle Island Central Public Library, Yaphank, NY [*Library symbol Library of Congress*] (LCLS)
NYAP .... New York Assembly Program [*Computer science*]

NYAP .... New York Average Price per Share [Stock market]
NY App Dec... New York Court of Appeals Decisions [A publication] (DLA)
NY App Div... New York Supreme Court, Appellate Division Reports [A publication] (DLA)
NYAS .... New York Academy of Sciences (EA)
NYB .... National Youth Bureau [British]
NYB .... New York Bancorp [NYSE symbol] (SAG)
NYB .... New York Bancorp Inc. [AMEX symbol] (SPSG)
NYB .... New York Bight [Oceanography] (MSC)
NYB .... North York Board of Education [UTLAS symbol]
NYBA .... National Young Buddhist Association [Defunct] (EA)
NYBagel ...... New York Bagel Enterprises, Inc. [Associated Press] (SAG)
NYB & M ..... New York, Boston & Montreal Railroad
NY Bank Law... New York Banking Law [A publication] (DLA)
NYBC .... National Yiddish Book Center (EA)
NYBC .... New York Business Communicators [Later, NY/IABC] (EA)
NY Bcp .... New York Bancorp [Associated Press] (SAG)
NY Bcp .... New York Bancorp, Inc. [Associated Press] (SAG)
NYBE .... National Yiddish Book Exchange (EA)
NYBFU .... New York Board of Fire Underwriters (BARN)
NYBG .... New York Botanical Garden
NYBOS......... Navy Yard, Boston, Massachusetts [Obsolete]
NYBPE .... New York Business Press Editors [New York, NY] (EA)
NYBS .... New York Bagel Enterprises, Inc. [NASDAQ symbol] (SAG)
NYBS .... New York Browning Society (EA)
NYBSBC....... New York Bureau of State Building Codes (BARN)
NYBT .... Boyce Thompson Institute for Plant Research, Yonkers, NY [Library symbol Library of Congress] (LCLS)
NYBT .... New York Board of Trade [New York, NY] (EA)
NYC .... Charley [Nevada] [Seismograph station code, US Geological Survey Closed] (SEIS)
NYC .... Neighborhood Youth Corps [Department of Labor] [Terminated]
NYC .... New York Central R. R. [Later, Penn Central] [AAR code]
NYC .... New York Circus (EA)
NYC .... New York City
NYC .... New York, Motor Carrier Conference [STAC]
NYC .... New York [New York]/Newark [New Jersey] [Airport symbol] (OAG)
NYC .... New York, NY [Location identifier FAA] (FAAL)
NYCA .... New York Court of Appeals Reports [A publication] (DLA)
NYC & HR ... New York Central & Hudson River Railroad
NYC & HRR... New York Central & Hudson River Railroad (ROG)
NYC & SL ... New York, Chicago and St. Louis Railroad Co. (IIA)
NYC & STL... New York, Chicago & St. Louis Railroad Co.
NY Cas Err... Caines' New York Cases in Error [A publication] (DLA)
NY Cas in Error... Caines' New York Cases in Error [A publication] (DLA)
NYCB .... New York City Ballet
NYCBA......... New York City Bar Association. Bulletin [A publication] (DLA)
NYCBA Bull... Bulletin. Association of the Bar of the City of New York [A publication] (DLA)
NYCBAN...... New York Center Beacon Alphanumerics [FAA]
NYCC .... New York Candy Club (EA)
NYCCA .... New York Cocoa Clearing Association (EA)
NYCCC......... New York City Community College
NYCCD........ New York Current Court Decisions [A publication] (DLA)
NYCCH........ New York Advance Digest Service (Commerce Clearing House), Cited by Year [A publication] (DLA)
NYCCI .... New York Corset Club (EA)
NYCDC .... New York Curtain and Drapery Club (EA)
NYCE .... New York Cash Exchange [Automated teller machine network]
NYCE .... New York Cocoa Exchange [Later, CSCE]
NYCE .... New York Cotton Exchange (EA)
NYCE .... New York Curb Exchange [Later, AMEX]
NYCER .... New York Conference on Electronic Reliability (MCD)
NYCFMA ...... New York Credit and Financial Management Association [New York, NY] (EA)
NY Ch .... Chancery Sentinel [New York] [A publication] (DLA)
NYCH .... National Youth Coalition on Housing [Australia]
NYCHA .... New York Clearing House Association [New York, NY] (EA)
NYCHARL .... Navy Yard, Charleston, South Carolina
NY Ch Sent... New York Chancery Sentinel [A publication] (DLA)
NYCI .... New York City's First [First beluga whale born at the New York Aquarium, 1981] [Pronounced "Nicky"]
NY City Ct.... New York City Court [A publication] (DLA)
NY City Ct Rep... New York City Court Reports [A publication] (DLA)
NY City Ct Supp... New York City Court Reports, Supplement [A publication] (DLA)
NY City Hall Rec... New York City Hall Recorder [A publication] (ILCA)
NY City H Rec... New York City Hall Recorder [A publication] (DLA)
NY Civ Prac Law & R... New York Civil Practice Law and Rules [A publication] (DLA)
NY Civ Pro... New York Civil Procedure [A publication] (DLA)
NY Civ Proc... New York Civil Procedure [A publication] (ILCA)
NY Civ Proc (NS)... New York Civil Procedure, New Series [A publication] (DLA)
NY Civ Proc R... New York Civil Procedure Reports [A publication] (DLA)
NY Civ Proc Rep... Civil Procedure Reports [New York] [A publication] (DLA)
NY Civ Proc R NS... New York Civil Procedure Reports, New Series [A publication] (DLA)
NY Civ Pro R... New York Civil Procedure Reports [A publication] (ILCA)
NY Civ Pro R NS... New York Civil Procedure Reports, New Series [A publication] (ILCA)
NY Civ Pr Rep... New York Civil Procedure Reports [A publication] (ILCA)
NYCMA .... New York Clothing Manufacturers Association (EA)
NYCMD........ New York Contract Management District (SAA)
NYCME .... New York Clothing Manufacturers Exchange [Later, NYCMA] (EA)
NYCN .... New York Connecting Railroad [AAR code]
NYCO .... New York City Opera

NYCO .... NYCOR, Inc. [NASDAQ symbol] (NQ)
NYCOA .... NYCOR Inc.'A' [NASDAQ symbol] (TTSB)
NY Code R... New York Code Reporter [A publication] (DLA)
NY Code Rep... New York Code Reporter [A publication] (DLA)
NY Code Rep NS... New York Code Reports, New Series [A publication] (DLA)
NY Code Report... New York Code Reporter [A publication] (DLA)
NY Code Report NS... New York Code Reporter, New Series [A publication] (DLA)
NY Code Reports NS... New York Code Reports, New Series [A publication] (DLA)
NY Code Reptr... New York Code Reporter [A publication] (DLA)
NY Code Reptr NS... New York Code Reporter, New Series [A publication] (DLA)
NY Code R NS... New York Code Reports, New Series [A publication] (DLA)
NY Cond ...... New York Condensed Reports [1881-82] [A publication] (DLA)
Nycor .... NYCOR, Inc. [Associated Press] (SAG)
NY Co Rem... New York Code of Remedial Justice [A publication] (DLA)
NYCP .... Civil Procedure Reports [New York] [A publication] (DLA)
NY Cr.......... New York Criminal Reports [A publication] (DLA)
NY Crim ...... New York Criminal Reports [A publication] (DLA)
NY Crim R... New York Criminal Reports [A publication] (DLA)
NY Crim Rep... New York Criminal Reports [A publication] (DLA)
NYCRR......... New York Codes, Rules, and Regulations [A publication] (DLA)
NY Cr R....... New York Criminal Reports [A publication] (DLA)
NY Cr Rep ... New York Criminal Reports [A publication] (DLA)
NYCS .... New York Cipher Society (EA)
NYCSA .... New York Coat and Suit Association (EA)
NYCSA .... New York College Stores Association
NYCSCE....... New York Coffee, Sugar, and Cocoa Exchange
NYCSCE....... New York Coffee, Sugar, and Cocoa Exchange (DFIT)
NYCSE .... New York Coffee and Sugar Exchange [Later, CSCE] (EA)
NYCSG .... New York Constitution Study Group (EA)
NYCSLS....... New York C. S. Lewis Society (EA)
NYCSMA ...... National Young Christian Students' Movement of Australia
NY Ct App.... New York Court of Appeals (DLA)
NYCTC .... New York City Technical College
NYCTCG....... New York Cold Type Composition Group [Later, TANY] (EA)
NYCTNCA..... New York Cotton Exchange, Citrus Associates
NYCTN,CA... New York Cotton Exchange, Citrus Associates (DFIT)
NYCUC .... New York City Urban Corps (EA)
NYD .... Navy Yard
NYD .... New York Datum (NRCH)
NYD .... New York Dock Railway [AAR code]
NYD .... Not Yet Diagnosed [Facetious translation: "Not Yet Dead"] [Medicine]
NYD .... Nycomed ASA ADS [NYSE symbol] (TTSB)
NY Daily L Gaz... New York Daily Law Gazette [A publication] (DLA)
NY Daily L Reg... New York Daily Law Register [A publication] (DLA)
NY Daily Reg... New York Daily Register [A publication] (DLA)
NY Daily Tr... New York Daily Transcript, Old and New Series [A publication] (DLA)
NYDCC .... New York Drama Critics Circle (EA)
NY Dep't R... New York Department Records [A publication] (DLA)
NYDF .... National Youth Development Foundation [Defunct] (EA)
NYDISS........ New York Disposal Surveillance System [U.S. Army Corps of Engineers]
NYDLWC Dec... New York State Department of Labor. Court Decisions of Workmen's Compensation [A publication] (DLA)
NYDO.......... National Youth Development Officer (AIE)
NYDP .... Neighborhood Youth Development Program
NYDR .... New York Department Reports [A publication] (DLA)
Nye .... Nye's Reports [18-21 Utah] [A publication] (DLA)
NYEC .... National Youth Employment Coalition (EA)
NYEG .... New York State Electric & Gas Corp. [Associated Press] (SAG)
NY El Cas.... New York Election Cases [A publication] (DLA)
NY Elec Cas... New York Election Cases [A publication] (DLA)
NY Elect Cas... New York Election Cases [A publication] (DLA)
NYER .... Nyer Med Group [NASDAQ symbol] (TTSB)
NYER .... Nyer Medical Group [NASDAQ symbol] (SAG)
NyerMd....... Nyer Medical Group [Associated Press] (SAG)
NYES .... Elizabeth Seton College, Yonkers, NY [Library symbol Library of Congress] (LCLS)
NYET LC ...... Not Yet in Library of Congress [Suggested name for the Library of Congress computer system]
NYETR .... New York Estate Tax Reports [Prentice-Hall, Inc.] [A publication] (DLA)
NYEWW ...... New York Exchange for Woman's Work [New York, NY] (EA)
NYF............. National Yeomen F [Defunct] (EA)
NYF............. National Youth Foundation [Australia]
NYF............. New York Foundation
NYF............. New York Futures Exchange
NYFBT .... New York Film Board of Trade [Defunct] (EA)
NYFC .... New York Film Critics (EA)
NYFCC .... New York Futures Clearing Corp. [New York Futures Exchange]
NYFD .... New York Fashion Designers [Later, NYFDF]
NYFDF .... New York Fashion Designers and Foundation [Defunct] (EA)
NYFE .... New York Futures Exchange [Pronounced "knife"]
NYFEA .... National Young Farmer Educational Association (EA)
NYFFFBA ..... New York Foreign Freight Forwarders and Brokers Association [New York, NY] (EA)
NYFRF......... New York Fertility Research Foundation [Later, FRF] (EA)
NYFUO......... New York Federation of Urban Organizations
NYFWA........ New York Financial Writers' Association (EA)
NYG .... Geigy Pharmaceuticals, Yonkers, NY [Library symbol Library of Congress] (LCLS)
NYG .... New York State Library, Albany, NY [OCLC symbol] (OCLC)
NYG .... Nyge Aero AB [Sweden ICAO designator] (FAAC)
NYG .... Quantico, VA [Location identifier FAA] (FAAL)
NYGBS........ New York Genealogical and Biographical Society (EA)

NYGC	New York Governor's Conference
NYGJB	New York Guild for Jewish Blind [Later, JGB]
NYH	New York Helicopter Corp. [ICAO designator] (FAAC)
NYHA	National Yacht Harbour Association [British] (BI)
NYHA	New York Heart Association [Classifications I, II, III, and IV] [Cardiology] (DAVI)
NYHA	New York Heart Associaton (MEDA)
NYHC	New York Health Care, Inc. [NASDAQ symbol] (SAG)
NYhI	International Business Machines Corp., Thomas J. Watson Research Center, Yorktown Heights, NY [Library symbol Library of Congress] (LCLS)
NYHlthC	New York Health Care, Inc. [Associated Press] (SAG)
NYhP	Putnam North Westchester S.L.S., Yorktown Heights, NY [Library symbol] [Library of Congress] (LCLS)
NYHSL	New York Health and Safety Laboratory [Energy Research and Development Administration]
NYHT	New York Herald Tribune [Defunct newspaper]
NYI	Sunyani [Ghana] [Airport symbol] (OAG)
NY/IABC	New York/International Association of Business Communicators [New York, NY] (EA)
NYIBC	New York International Ballet Competition
NYIBC	New York Islanders Booster Club (EA)
NYIBS	New York International Bible Society (EA)
NYIC	New York Iroquois Conference (EA)
NYICD	New York Institute for Child Development (EA)
NYIDA	New York Importers and Distillers Association (EA)
NYIE	New York Insurance Exchange
NYIF	New York Index - Finance [Stock market]
NYIF	New York Institute of Finance (ECON)
NYII	New York Index - Industrials [Stock market]
NYIL	Netherlands Yearbook of International Law [A publication] (DLA)
NYIT	New York Index - Transportation [Stock market]
NYIT	New York Institute of Technology
NYIU	New York Index - Utilities [Stock market]
NYJ	Joshua Tree [Nevada] [Seismograph station code, US Geological Survey Closed] (SEIS)
NYJ	National Young Judaea (EA)
NYJO	National Youth Jazz Orchestra [British]
NY Jud Rep	New York Judicial Repository [A publication] (DLA)
NY Jud Repos	New York Judicial Repository [A publication] (DLA)
NY Jur	New York Jurisprudence [A publication] (DLA)
NY Jur	New York Jurist [A publication] (DLA)
NYK	New York [City]
NYK	North York Public Library [UTLAS symbol]
NYKGRP	New York Group [Navy]
NYL	Neodymium YAG [Yttrium Aluminum Garnet] LASER
NYL	Nylon (MSA)
NYL	Yuma, AZ [Location identifier FAA] (FAAL)
NY Law Bul	New York Monthly Law Bulletin [A publication] (DLA)
NY Law Gaz	New York Law Gazette [A publication] (DLA)
NY Law (McKinney)	McKinney's Consolidated Laws of New York [A publication] (DLA)
NY Law Sch	New York Law School (GAGS)
NYLB	[The] New York & Long Branch Railroad Co. [Absorbed into Consolidated Rail Corp.] [AAR code]
NYLC	National Young Life Campaign [British]
NYLC	National Youth Leadership Council (EA)
NYLC Ann	New York Leading Cases, Annotated [A publication] (DLA)
NYL Cas	New York Leading Cases [A publication] (DLA)
NYLE & W	New York, Lake Erie & Western Railroad [Later, EL] [Nickname: Now You Lay Easy and Wait]
NY Leg N	New York Legal News [1880-82] [A publication] (DLA)
NY Leg Obs	New York Legal Observer (Owen) [A publication] (DLA)
NY Leg Reg	New York Legal Register [A publication] (DLA)
NYLEX USA	New York Leather Exposition [American European Trade and Exhibition Center]
NYLG	New York Law Group [Later, BAHRGNY] (EA)
NYL Gaz	New York Law Gazette [A publication] (DLA)
NYLO	New York Legal Observer [A publication] (DLA)
NYLR	Neodymium YAG [Yttrium Aluminum Garnet] LASER Range-Finder
Ny LR	Nyasaland Law Reports [South Africa] [A publication] (DLA)
NYLRB	New York State Labor Relations Board Decisions [A publication] (DLA)
NYLRB Dec	New York State Labor Relations Board Decisions and Orders [A publication] (DLA)
NYL Rec	New York Law Record [A publication] (DLA)
NYLS	New York Law School
NYLS	New York State Longitudinal Study (EDAC)
NYLSMA	New York Lamp and Shade Manufacturers Association (EA)
NYLS Stud L Rev	New York Law School. Student Law Review [A publication] (DLA)
NYLTI	National Youth Leadership Training Institute
NYM	Climax Mine [Nevada] [Seismograph station code, US Geological Survey Closed] (SEIS)
NYM	New York Mercantile Exchange
NYM	New York Movers Tariff Bureau, Inc., New York NY [STAC]
nym	Nyamwezi [MARC language code Library of Congress] (LCCP)
NYM	NYMAGIC, Inc. [Formerly, New York Marine & General Insurance Co.] [NYSE symbol] (SPSG)
NYMA	New York City Metropolitan Area
NYMA	New York Mounters Association [New York, NY] (EA)
NYMAGC	NYMAGIC, Inc. [Formerly, New York Marine & General Insurance Co.] [Associated Press] (SAG)
NYMC	New York Medical College [Valhalla, NY]
NYME	New York Mercantile Exchange (EA)

NY Med C	New York Medicine College (GAGS)
NYMEX	New York Mercantile Exchange (EA)
NYMI	Navy Yard, Mare Island, California
NY Misc	New York Miscellaneous Reports [A publication] (DLA)
NY Misc 2d	New York Miscellaneous Reports. Second Series [A publication] (DLA)
NYMM	New York Merchandise Mart
NYMO	National Youth Ministry Organization (EA)
NY Mo Law Bul	New York Monthly Law Bulletin [A publication] (DLA)
NY Mo L Bul	New York Monthly Law Bulletin [A publication] (DLA)
NY Mo LR	New York Monthly Law Reports [A publication] (DLA)
NY Mo L Rec	New York Monthly Law Record [A publication] (DLA)
NY Month L Bul	New York Monthly Law Bulletin [A publication] (DLA)
NY Month LR	New York Monthly Law Reports [A publication] (DLA)
NY Month L Rep	New York Monthly Law Reports [A publication] (DLA)
NY Monthly Law Bul	New York Monthly Law Bulletin [A publication] (DLA)
NYMPH	Nymphomaniac (DSUE)
nymphm	Nymphaeum (VRA)
NYMPHO	Nymphomaniac (DSUE)
NYMS	New York Microscopical Society (EA)
NY Mun Gaz	New York Municipal Gazette [A publication] (DLA)
NYN	NYNEX Corp. [NYSE symbol] (SPSG)
NYN	Nyngan [Australia Airport symbol]
NYNCY	NYNEX CableCommsGrpADS Unit [NASDAQ symbol] (TTSB)
NYNCY	Nynex Cable Communications Group PLC [NASDAQ symbol] (SAG)
NYNEX	New York New England Exchange [Telecommunications]
Nynex	NYNEX Corp. [Associated Press] (SAG)
NYNH & H	New York, New Haven & Hartford R. R.
NYNJDDA	New York and New Jersey Dry Dock Association [Defunct] (EA)
NYNOR	Navy Yard, Norfolk, Virginia
NYNS	New York Naval Shipyards [Obsolete]
NYNS-ML	New York Naval Shipyard, Material Laboratory (MCD)
NynxCbl	Nynex Cable Communications Group PLC [Associated Press] (SAG)
NYNYD	New York Navy Yard (DNAB)
NYNYK	Navy Yard, New York, New York
NYO	National Youth Orchestra [British] (DI)
NYO	New York Oils Ltd. [Toronto Stock Exchange symbol]
NYO	New York Operations [AEC] (MCD)
NYO	Not Yet Operating (DA)
nyo	Nyoro [MARC language code Library of Congress] (LCCP)
NYo	Youngstown Free Library, Youngstown, NY [Library symbol Library of Congress] (LCLS)
NYO & W	New York, Ontario & Western Railway Co.
NYOD	New York Ordnance District [Military] (MUGU)
NY Off Dept R	New York Official Department Reports [A publication] (DLA)
NYOL	New York On-Line [Information service or system] (IID)
NYoOF	Old Fort Niagara Association, Youngstown, NY [Library symbol Library of Congress] (LCLS)
NY Op Att Gen	Opinions of the Attorneys-General of New York [A publication] (DLA)
NY Ops Atty Gen	Opinions of the Attorney General of New York [A publication] (DLA)
NYOSL	New York Ocean Science Laboratory
NYP	New York-Pennsylvania League [Baseball]
NYP	New York Press (WDMC)
NYP	New York Public Library, Serials, New York, NY [OCLC symbol] (OCLC)
NYP	Not Yet Published
NYPA	New York Port Authority
NYPAA	National Yellow Pages Agency Association [Tucson, AZ] (EA)
NYP & B	New York, Providence & Boston Railroad
NYPC	New York Pigment Club (EA)
NYPD	New York Police Department [Initialism also used as title of TV series]
NYPE	New York Port of Embarkation [Military]
NYPE	New York Produce Exchange [Defunct] (EA)
NYPF	National Young Professionals Forum (EA)
NYPFO	New York Air Force Procurement Field Office
NYPH	Navy Yard, Pearl Harbor, Hawaii
NYPHIL	Navy Yard, Philadelphia, Pennsylvania
NYPIRG	New York Public Interest Research Group
NYPL	New York Public Library [New York, NY]
NYPLC	National Youth Pro-Life Coalition (EA)
NYPLR	New York Prime Loan Rate [Finance] (DS)
NYPM	National Yokefellow Prison Ministry [Later, YPM] (EA)
NYPM	Navy Youth Program Manager (MCD)
NYPMA	New York Paper Merchants Association (EA)
NYPO	New York Publicity Outlet [A publication] (WDMC)
NYPOE	New York Port of Embarkation [Military]
NYPORT	Navy Yard, Portsmouth, New Hampshire
NYPR	New York Practice Reports [A publication] (DLA)
NYPR	N-Nitrosopyrrolidine [Also, NO-PYR] [Biochemistry, organic chemistry]
NYPRPG	New York Publishers Rights and Permissions Group (EA)
NY Pr Rep	New York Practice Reports [A publication] (DLA)
NYPS	National Yellow Pages Service
NYPS	Navy Yard, Puget Sound [Bremerton], Washington
NYPS-SA	National Yellow Pages Service Association (WDMC)
NYPSO	New York Philharmonic Symphony Orchestra
NYPYR	Nitrosopyrrolidine [Also, NPYR] [Organic chemistry]
NYR	National Young Republicans (NADA)
NYR	Neodymium YAG [Yttrium Aluminum Garnet] Range-Finder
NYR	New York Court of Appeals Reports [A publication] (DLA)
NYR	Not Yet Reported [Air Force]
NYR	Not Yet Required (MUGU)

NYR	Not Yet Returned [*Military*]
NYR	Nuclear Yield Requirement (NATG)
NYR	Receiver Site [*Nevada*] [*Seismograph station code, US Geological Survey Closed*] (SEIS)
NYRA	New York Racing Authority [*Cable-television system*]
NYRAPG	New York Rights and Permissions Group (EA)
NYRB	New York Review of Books [*A publication*] (BRI)
NYRC	New York Railroad Commission Reports [*A publication*] (DLA)
NY Rec	New York Record [*A publication*] (DLA)
NY Reg	New York Daily Register [*A publication*] (DLA)
NY Rep	New York Court of Appeals Reports [*A publication*] (DLA)
NY Reps	New York Court of Appeals Reports [*A publication*] (DLA)
NY Reptr	New York Reporter [*A publication*] (ILCA)
NYRFC	New York Rangers Fan Club (EA)
NYRL	New York Revised Laws [*A publication*] (DLA)
NYRMA	New York Raincoat Manufacturers Association (EA)
NYRRC	New York Road Runners Club (EA)
NYRS	New York Revised Statutes [*A publication*] (DLA)
NYRS	New Youth Research Survey [*Religious education test*]
NYS	New York Shavians (EA)
NYS	New York State
NYS	New York State Electric & Gas Corp. [*Associated Press*] (SAG)
NYS	New York State Reporter [*A publication*] (DLA)
NYS	New York State Union List, Albany, NY [*OCLC symbol*] (OCLC)
NYS	New York Supplement [*A publication*] (DLA)
NYS	Not Yet Specified
NYS	Syncline Ridge [*Nevada*] [*Seismograph station code, US Geological Survey Closed*] (SEIS)
NYS	Yonkers School System, Yonkers, NY [*Library symbol Library of Congress*] (LCLS)
NYS 2d	New York Supplement, Second Series [*A publication*] (DLA)
NYSA	New York Shipping Association (EA)
NYSAC	New York State Athletic Commission (BARN)
NYSASS	New York State Association of Service Stations [*Later, NYSASSRS*] (EA)
NYSASSRS...	New York State Association of Service Stations and Repair Shops (EA)
NYSBA Bull...	New York State Bar Association. Bulletin [*A publication*] (DLA)
NY S B BULL...	New York State Bar Bulletin [*A publication*] (LWAP)
NYSC	New York Shipbuilding Corp.
NYSC	Thompson and Cook's New York Supreme Court Reports [*A publication*] (DLA)
NYSCA	National Youth Sports Coaches Association (EA)
NYSCAT	New York State Union Catalog of Film and Video [*Mid-Hudson Library System*] [*Information service or system*] (IID)
NYSCS	New York State Colonization Society [*Defunct*] (EA)
NYS Ct	New York Superior Court Reports [*A publication*] (DLA)
NYSD	New York Society for the Deaf [*Formerly, JSD*] (EA)
NYSDA	New York Security Dealers Association (EA)
NYSDEC	New York State Department of Environmental Conservation
NYSDEC	New York State Department of Environmental Conservation (DOGT)
NYSDR	New York State Department Reports [*A publication*] (DLA)
NYSE	New York Stock Exchange [*New York, NY*] (EA)
NYSE	New York Stock Exchange Guide [*Commerce Clearing House*] [*A publication*] (DLA)
NYSEG	New York State Electric & Gas Corp. [*Associated Press*] (SAG)
NY Sen J	New York Senate Journal [*A publication*] (DLA)
NYSERDA	New York State Energy Research and Development Authority
NYSERNET..	New York State Educational and Research Network
NYSERNet...	New York State Education and Research Network, Inc. [*Telecommunications service*] (TSSD)
NYSF	National Youth Science Foundation
NYSFTCA	New York State Fruit Testing Cooperative Association (EA)
NYSGI	New York Sea Grant Institute [*Albany, NY*] [*Department of Commerce*] (GRD)
NYSIIS	New York State Identification and Intelligence System
NYSILL	New York State Interlibrary Loan [*Network*]
NYSILL	New York State Inter-Library Loans System (NITA)
NYSNY	New York Naval Shipyard (New York)
NYSP	New York School of Printing (DGA)
NYSPCC	New York Society for the Prevention of Cruelty to Children
NY Spec Term R...	Howard's New York Practice Reports [*A publication*] (DLA)
NY Spec Term Rep...	Howard's New York Practice Reports [*A publication*] (DLA)
NYSPI	New York State Psychiatric Institute [*New York State Office of Mental Hygiene*] [*Research center*] (RCD)
NYSR	New York State Reporter [*A publication*] (DLA)
NYSSA	New York Society of Security Analysts [*New York, NY*] (EA)
NYSSDA	New York State Safe Deposit Association [*New York, NY*] (EA)
NYSSTF	New York State Science and Technology Foundation (RDA)
NY St	New York State Reporter [*A publication*] (DLA)
NYST	Nystagmus [*Medicine*]
NY State R...	New York State Reporter [*A publication*] (DLA)
NY State Rep...	New York State Reporter [*A publication*] (DLA)
NY St Ba A...	New York State Bar Association. Bulletin [*A publication*] (DLA)
NY St Bull ...	New York State Bulletin (AAGC)
NY St Dept Rep...	New York State Department Reports [*A publication*] (DLA)
NYStJ..........	Saint Joseph's Seminary, Dunwoodie, Yonkers, NY [*Library symbol Library of Congress*] (LCLS)
NY St R	New York State Reporter [*A publication*] (DLA)
NY St Rep ...	New York State Reporter [*A publication*] (DLA)
NY St Repr...	New York State Reporter [*A publication*] (DLA)
NY Sup Ct...	New York Supreme Court Reports [*A publication*] (DLA)
NY Sup Ct Rep...	Thompson and Cook's New York Supreme Court Reports [*A publication*] (DLA)

NY Sup Ct (T & C)...	Thompson and Cook's New York Supreme Court Reports [*A publication*] (DLA)
NY Super.....	New York Superior Court Reports [*A publication*] (DLA)
NY Super Ct...	New York Superior Court Reports [*Various reporters*]
NY Super Ct R...	New York Superior Court Reports [*A publication*] (DLA)
NY Super Ct Rep...	New York Superior Court Reports [*A publication*] (DLA)
NY Supl	New York Supplement [*A publication*] (DLA)
NY Supp	New York Supplement [*A publication*] (DLA)
NY Supp 2d..	New York Supplement, Second Series [*A publication*] (DLA)
NY Suppl	New York Supplement [*A publication*] (DLA)
NY Supr.......	New York Superior Court Reports [*A publication*] (DLA)
NY Supr Ct...	New York Superior Court Reports [*A publication*] (DLA)
NY Supr Ct R...	New York Superior Court Reports [*A publication*] (DLA)
NY Supr Ct Rep...	New York Superior Court Reports [*A publication*] (DLA)
NY Supr Ct Repts (T & C)...	New York Supreme Court Reports, by Thompson and Cook [*A publication*] (DLA)
NY Suprm Ct...	New York Supreme Court Reports [*A publication*] (DLA)
NYSV	Narcissus Yellow Stripe Virus [*Plant pathology*]
NYSW	New York, Susquehanna & Western Railroad Co. [*AAR code*]
NYSWGGI	New York State Wine Grape Growers, Inc. (EA)
NYT............	National Youth Theatre [*British*]
NYT............	New Yiddish Theater (BJA)
NYT............	New York Testing Laboratories, Inc.
NYT............	[*The*] New York Times Co. [*AMEX symbol*] (SPSG)
NYTA	New York Theatre Annual [*A publication*]
NYTA	New York Times CI'A' [*AMEX symbol*] (TTSB)
NY Tax Cas...	New York Tax Cases [*Commerce Clearing House*] [*A publication*] (DLA)
NYTB	New York Theatre Ballet
NYTB	New York Theatre Ballet
NYTBIO	[*The*] New York Times Biographical File [*The New York Times Co.*] [*Information service or system*] (CRD)
NYTBR	New York Times Book Review [*A publication*] (BRI)
NYTCL	New York Temperance Civic League [*Later, AYE*] (EA)
NYTEI.........	New York Tax Exempt Income Fund [*Associated Press*] (SAG)
Nytest	NYTEST Environmental, Inc. [*Associated Press*] (SAG)
NY Them	New York Themis [*New York City*] [*A publication*] (DLA)
NYT/IB	New York Times Information Bank
NY Tim	[*The*] New York Times Co. [*Associated Press*] (SAG)
NYTIS	New York Times Information Service, Inc. [*Mead Data Central*] [*Database originator and host*] (IID)
NYTLa.........	New York Times (Late Edition) [*A publication*] (BRI)
NYTNS	New York Times News Service
NYTR	New York Term Reports (Caines' Reports) [*A publication*] (DLA)
NY Trans	New York Transcript [*Numbers 1-11*] [*1861 New York City*] [*A publication*] (DLA)
NY Trans App...	New York Transcript Appeals Reports [*A publication*] (DLA)
NY Trans NS...	New York Transcript, New Series [*New York City*] [*A publication*] (DLA)
NY Trans Rep...	New York Transcript Reports [*A publication*] (DLA)
NYT Rep	Caines' Term Reports [*New York*] [*A publication*] (DLA)
NYTS	New York Theological Seminary
NYTS	Nytest Environmental [*NASDAQ symbol*] (TTSB)
NYTS	NYTEST Environmental, Inc. [*NASDAQ symbol*] (NQ)
NYTTS	New York Turtle and Tortoise Society (EA)
nyu............	New York [*MARC country of publication code Library of Congress*] (LCCP)
NYU	New York University
NYU	Nyaung-U [*Myanmar*] [*Airport symbol*] (OAG)
NYU Conf Charitable...	New York University. Conference on Charitable Foundations. Proceedings [*A publication*] (DLA)
NYU Conf Charitable Fdn...	New York University. Conference on Charitable Foundations. Proceedings [*A publication*] (DLA)
NYU Conf on Char Found Proc...	Conference on Charitable Foundations. Proceedings. New York University [*A publication*] (DLA)
NYUL Center Bull...	New York University. Law Center. Bulletin [*A publication*] (DLA)
NYULT	New York University School of Continuing Education, Continuing Education in Law and Taxation [*A publication*] (DLA)
NY Unconsol Laws...	New York Unconsolidated Laws (McKinney) [*A publication*] (DLA)
NYUP	New York University Press (DGA)
NYU Rev Law & Soc...	New York University. Review of Law and Social Change [*A publication*] (DLA)
NYUTI	New York University Tax Institute (DLA)
NYV	Vern [*Nevada*] [*Seismograph station code, US Geological Survey Closed*] (SEIS)
NYWA	National Youth Work Alliance (EA)
NYWASH......	Navy Yard, Washington, DC [*Obsolete*]
NYWC	New York Wine Council (EA)
NYWCC	New York Water Color Club [*1890-1941*] (NGC)
NY Week Dig...	New York Weekly Digest [*A publication*] (DLA)
NY Weekly Dig...	New York Weekly Digest [*A publication*] (DLA)
NYWF	New York World's Fair
NYWGF	New York Wine/Grape Foundation (EA)
NY Wkly Dig...	New York Weekly Digest [*A publication*] (DLA)
NYYP	New York Yellow Pages, Inc.
NYZP	New York Zoological Park
NYZS	New York Zoological Society
NZ.............	Air New Zealand Ltd. (Domestic Division) [*ICAO designator*] (ICDA)
Nz.............	National Library of New Zealand, Wellington, New Zealand [*Library symbol*] [*Library of Congress*] (LCLS)
NZ.............	Neutrality Zone
NZ.............	New Mexico & Arizona Land Co. [*AMEX symbol*] (SPSG)

NZ .... New Mexico/Ariz Land [*AMEX symbol*] (TTSB)
NZ .... New Zealand [*ANSI two-letter standard code*] (CNC)
nz .... New Zealand [*MARC country of publication code Library of Congress*] (LCCP)
NZ .... New Zealand National Airways Corp. [*ICAO designator*]
NZ .... New Zealand Reports [*A publication*] (DLA)
N-Z .... Nike-Zeus [*Missiles*] (AAG)
NZ .... Normal Acceleration
NZ .... Normal to Z-Axis (MCD)
NZ .... Nose to Z-Axis (MCD)
NZ .... Nuclear Zone
NZA .... Niobium Zinc Alloy
NZAA .... Auckland/International [*New Zealand*] [*ICAO location identifier*] (ICLI)
NZAF .... New Zealand Air Force (DAS)
NzAGS .... Church of Jesus Christ of Latter-Day Saints, Genealogical Society Library, Auckland Branch, Auckland, New Zealand [*Library symbol Library of Congress*] (LCLS)
NZAK .... Auckland [*New Zealand*] [*ICAO location identifier*] (ICLI)
NZAP .... New Zealand Associated Press (BARN)
NZAP .... Taupo [*New Zealand*] [*ICAO location identifier*] (ICLI)
NZ App Rep... New Zealand Appeal Reports [*A publication*] (DLA)
NZAPS .... Nike-Zeus Automatic Programming System [*Missiles*]
NZAQ .... Auckland [*New Zealand*] [*ICAO location identifier*] (ICLI)
NZAR .... Ardmore [*New Zealand*] [*ICAO location identifier*] (ICLI)
NzAU .... Auckland University, Auckland, New Zealand [*Library symbol Library of Congress*] (LCLS)
NZ Awards... New Zealand Awards, Recommendations, Agreements, Etc. [*A publication*] (DLA)
NZB .... New Zealand Black [*Mice hybrids*]
NZB .... Nonzero Binary (NASA)
NZB .... Non Zero Binary
NZB .... Royal New Zealand Ballet
NZBC .... New Zealand Broadcasting Corp.
NZBS .... New Zealand Broadcasting Service
NZC .... Jacksonville, FL [*Location identifier FAA*] (FAAL)
NZC .... New Zealand Cross (DAS)
NZCA .... Campbell Island [*New Zealand*] [*ICAO location identifier*] (ICLI)
NzCGS .... Church of Jesus Christ of Latter-Day Saints, Genealogical Society Library, Canterbury Branch, Christchurch, New Zealand [*Library symbol Library of Congress*] (LCLS)
NZCH .... Christchurch/International [*New Zealand*] [*ICAO location identifier*] (ICLI)
NZCI .... Chatham Island/Tuuta [*New Zealand*] [*ICAO location identifier*] (ICLI)
NZCM .... McMurdo Sound, Antarctica [*New Zealand*] [*ICAO location identifier*] (ICLI)
NZCO .... Christchurch [*New Zealand*] [*ICAO location identifier*] (ICLI)
NZ Col LJ ... New Zealand Colonial Law Journal [*A publication*] (DLA)
NzCSI-A .... New Zealand Department of Scientific and Industrial Research, Antarctic Division, Christchurch, New Zealand [*Library symbol*] [*Library of Congress*] (LCLS)
NZ Ct App.... New Zealand Court of Appeals (DLA)
NZ Ct Arb.... New Zealand Court of Arbitration (DLA)
NZD .... Nonzero Digit (ECII)
NZDF .... Christchurch/International [*New Zealand*] [*ICAO location identifier*] (ICLI)
NZDN .... Dunedin [*New Zealand*] [*ICAO location identifier*] (ICLI)
NZE .... Glenview, IL [*Location identifier FAA*] (FAAL)
NZE .... North Zenith East
NZE .... Nzerekore [*Guinea*] [*Airport symbol*] (AD)
N Zea.............. New Zealand (VRA)
NZEF .... New Zealand Employers' Federation (ODBW)
NZF .... Near Zero Field
NZFL .... New Zealand Federation of Labor (ODBW)
NZG .... Near Zero Gravity
NZG .... North Carolina School of the Arts, Winston-Salem, NC [*OCLC symbol*] (OCLC)
NZ Gaz LR... New Zealand Gazette Law Reports [*A publication*] (DLA)
NZGLR .... New Zealand Gazette Law Reports [*A publication*] (DLA)
NZGS .... Gisborne [*New Zealand*] [*ICAO location identifier*] (ICLI)
NZHK .... Hokitika [*New Zealand*] [*ICAO location identifier*] (ICLI)
NZHN .... Hamilton [*New Zealand*] [*ICAO location identifier*] (ICLI)
NZHO .... Wellington [*New Zealand*] [*ICAO location identifier*] (ICLI)
NZIC .... New Zealand Institute of Chemistry
NZIER .... New Zealand Institute of Economic Research
NZ Ind Arb... New Zealand Industrial Arbitration Awards [*A publication*] (DLA)
NZJ .... Naze [*Ryukyu Islands*] [*Seismograph station code, US Geological Survey*] (SEIS)
NZJ .... Santa Ana, CA [*Location identifier FAA*] (FAAL)
NZJP .... New Zealand Justice of the Peace [*1876-77*] [*A publication*] (DLA)
NZ Jur .... New Zealand Jurist [*1873-78*] [*A publication*] (DLA)
NZ Jur Mining Law... Jurist Reports, New Series, Cases in Mining Law [*New Zealand*] [*A publication*] (DLA)
NZ Jur NS.... New Zealand Jurist, New Series [*A publication*] (DLA)
NZKB .... Wellington/Kilbirnie [*New Zealand*] [*ICAO location identifier*] (ICLI)
NZKI .... Kaikoura [*New Zealand*] [*ICAO location identifier*] (ICLI)
NZKL .... Wellington/Kelburn [*New Zealand*] [*ICAO location identifier*] (ICLI)
NZKMB .... New Zealand Kiwifruit Marketing Board
NZKT .... Kaitaia [*New Zealand*] [*ICAO location identifier*] (ICLI)
NZKX .... Kaitaia [*New Zealand*] [*ICAO location identifier*] (ICLI)
NZL .... New Zealand [*ANSI three-letter standard code*] (CNC)
NZ Law Soc N... New Zealand Law Society. Newsletter [*A publication*] (DLA)
NZLGR .... Local Government Reports [*New Zealand*] [*A publication*] (DLA)

NZLJMC .... New Zealand Law Journal, Magistrates' Court Decisions [*A publication*] (DLA)
NZLO .... New Zealand Liaison Officer
NZLP .... New Zealand Labour Party [*Political party*] (PPW)
NZLR .... New Zealand Law Reports [*A publication*] (DLA)
NZLRCA ...... New Zealand Law Reports, Court of Appeal [*A publication*] (DLA)
NZM .... Mount Cook Airlines [*New Zealand*] [*ICAO designator*] (FAAC)
NZMF .... Milford Sound [*New Zealand*] [*ICAO location identifier*] (ICLI)
NZMN .... New Zealand Merchant Navy (DAS)
NZMS .... New Zealand Meteorological Service [*Marine science*] (OSRA)
NZN .... Niedersachsischer Zeitschriftennachweis [*Deutsches Bibliotheksinstitut*] [*Germany Information service or system*] (CRD)
NZNB .... New Zealand Naval Board [*Wellington*]
NZNFC .... Norma Zimmer National Fan Club (EA)
NZNP .... New Plymouth [*New Zealand*] [*ICAO location identifier*] (ICLI)
NZNR .... Napier [*New Zealand*] [*ICAO location identifier*] (ICLI)
NZNS .... Nelson [*New Zealand*] [*ICAO location identifier*] (ICLI)
NZNV .... Invercargill [*New Zealand*] [*ICAO location identifier*] (ICLI)
NZO .... New Zealand Obese [*Mouse*] [*Medicine*] (DMAA)
NZOH .... Ohakea [*New Zealand*] [*ICAO location identifier*] (ICLI)
NZOI .... New Zealand Oceanographic Institute
NZ Ords .... Ordinances of the Legislative Council of New Zealand [*A publication*] (DLA)
NZOU .... Oamaru [*New Zealand*] [*ICAO location identifier*] (ICLI)
NZP .... National Zoological Park [*Smithsonian Institution*]
NZP .... National Zoological Park
NZPA .... New Zealand Press Association
NZPCC .... New Zealand Privy Council Cases [*A publication*] (DLA)
NZPC Cas .... New Zealand Privy Council Cases [*A publication*] (DLA)
NZPM .... Palmerston North [*New Zealand*] [*ICAO location identifier*] (ICLI)
NZPO .... New Zealand Post Office [*Telecommunications*]
NZPP .... Paraparaumu [*New Zealand*] [*ICAO location identifier*] (ICLI)
NZQN .... Queenstown [*New Zealand*] [*ICAO location identifier*] (ICLI)
NZR .... New Zealand Red [*Rabbit*] [*Medicine*] (DMAA)
NZ Rep .... New Zealand Reports, Court of Appeals [*A publication*] (DLA)
NZ Repr Stat... Reprint of the Statutes of New Zealand [*A publication*] (DLA)
NZRN .... Raoul Island [*New Zealand*] [*ICAO location identifier*] (ICLI)
NZRO .... Rotorua [*New Zealand*] [*ICAO location identifier*] (ICLI)
NZRR .... New Zealand Rough Riders [*Military*] (ROG)
NZR Regs & B... Rules, Regulations, and By-Laws under New Zealand Statutes [*A publication*] (DLA)
NZS .... Nonzero Sum [*Genetics*]
NZSC .... New Zealand Supreme Court [*A publication*] (DLA)
NZSEAFRON... New Zealand Sea Frontier
NZSG .... Non-Zero-Sum Game (MHDW)
NZ Stat .... Statutes of New Zealand [*A publication*] (DLA)
NZ Stat Regs... New Zealand Statutory Regulations [*A publication*] (DLA)
NZT .... Nonzero Test (IAA)
NZT .... Nonzero Transfer
NZT .... Telecom Corp. New Zealand [*NYSE symbol*] (SPSG)
NZT .... Telecom Corp. New Zealand ADS [*NYSE symbol*] (TTSB)
NZTBR .... New Zealand Taxation Board of Review Decisions [*A publication*] (DLA)
NZTG .... Tauranga [*New Zealand*] [*ICAO location identifier*] (ICLI)
NZTJWG ..... Nike-Zeus Target Joint Working Group [*Missiles*] (MUGU)
NZTO .... New Zealand Tourism Office (EA)
NZTP .... New Zealand Tourist and Publicity Office [*Later, NZTO*] (EA)
NZTS .... New Zealand Treaty Series [*A publication*] (DLA)
NZTU .... Timaru [*New Zealand*] [*ICAO location identifier*] (ICLI)
NZTV .... Nike-Zeus Target Vehicle [*Missiles*] (IAA)
NzTvGS .... Church of Jesus Christ of Latter-Day Saints, Genealogical Society Library, Temple View Branch, Temple View, New Zealand [*Library symbol Library of Congress*] (LCLS)
NZW .... New Zealand White [*Mice hybrids*]
NZW .... South Weymouth, MA [*Location identifier FAA*] (FAAL)
NZWA .... Chatham Island/Waitangi [*New Zealand*] [*ICAO location identifier*] (ICLI)
NZWB .... Woodbourne [*New Zealand*] [*ICAO location identifier*] (ICLI)
NZWG .... Wigram [*New Zealand*] [*ICAO location identifier*] (ICLI)
NzWGAL ..... General Assembly Library, Wellington, New Zealand, [*Library symbol Library of Congress*] (LCLS)
NzWGS .... Church of Jesus Christ of Latter-Day Saints, Genealogical Society Library, Wellington Stake Branch, Wellington, New Zealand [*Library symbol Library of Congress*] (LCLS)
NZWK .... Whakatane [*New Zealand*] [*ICAO location identifier*] (ICLI)
NzWMW....... New Zealand Ministry of Works and Development, Head Office Library, Wellington, New Zealand [*Library symbol Library of Congress*] (LCLS)
NZWN .... Wellington/International [*New Zealand*] [*ICAO location identifier*] (ICLI)
NzWNA .... National Archives, Wellington, New Zealand [*Library symbol Library of Congress*] (LCLS)
NZWP .... Whenuapai [*New Zealand*] [*ICAO location identifier*] (ICLI)
NZWQ .... Wellington [*New Zealand*] [*ICAO location identifier*] (ICLI)
NZWR .... Whangarei [*New Zealand*] [*ICAO location identifier*] (ICLI)
NZWS .... Westport [*New Zealand*] [*ICAO location identifier*] (ICLI)
NZWU .... Wanganui [*New Zealand*] [*ICAO location identifier*] (ICLI)
NZY .... San Diego, CA [*Location identifier FAA*] (FAAL)
NZYM .... Synthetech, Inc. [*NASDAQ symbol*] (NQ)
NZZA .... Auckland [*New Zealand*] [*ICAO location identifier*] (ICLI)
NZZC .... Christchurch [*New Zealand*] [*ICAO location identifier*] (ICLI)
NZZO .... Auckland [*New Zealand*] [*ICAO location identifier*] (ICLI)
NZZW .... Wellington [*New Zealand*] [*ICAO location identifier*] (ICLI)

O

By Acronym

O .... Absence of Sex Chromosome (DAVI)
O .... An Oige [The Irish Youth Hostels Association] [Founded in 1931]
O .... Deamino [As substituent on nucleoside] [Biochemistry]
O .... Horizontal Opposed [Aircraft engine]
O .... Law Opinions [A publication] (DLA)
O .... New Orleans [Louisiana] [Mint mark, when appearing on US coins] [Obsolete]
O .... New Orleans [Mint mark on U.S. coins] (BARN)
O .... None (DAVI)
O .... Nonmotile [Laboratory science] (DAVI)
O .... Oasis
O .... Oath
O .... Oberst [Colonel] [German military - World War II]
O .... Obiit [He, or She, Died] [Latin]
O .... Object
O .... Objective
O .... Oblast [Governmental subdivision in USSR corresponding to a province or state]
O .... Oboe [Phonetic alphabet] [World War II] (DSUE)
O .... Observation Aircraft [Designation for all US military aircraft]
O .... Observer
O .... Obsolescent (AFIT)
O .... Obstetrics [Medicine] (MAE)
O .... Occasional [Concerning occurrence of species]
O .... Occidental
O .... Occiput [Medicine]
O .... Occlusal [Dentistry]
O .... Occupation (ADA)
O .... Occurrence
O .... Ocean [Maps and charts]
O .... Octal [Number system with a base of eight] [Computer science] (BUR)
O .... Octarius [Pint] [Pharmacy]
O .... Octavo [Book from 20 to 25 centimeters in height] [Bibliography]
O .... October
O .... Octupole [Physics] (OA)
O .... Oculus [Eye] [Latin]
O .... Odericus [Flourished, 1166-1200] [Authority cited in pre-1607 legal work] (DSA)
O .... Off
O .... Offered [Stock exchange term] (SPSG)
O .... Office [or Officer]
O .... Office of Operations [Coast Guard]
O .... Official [Rate] [Value of the English pound]
O .... Ohio
O .... Ohio Reports [A publication] (DLA)
O .... Ohio State Library, Columbus, OH [Library symbol Library of Congress] (LCLS)
O .... Ohm [Electricity]
O .... Ohne [Antigen] [Immunology]
O .... Oil
O .... Oil (VRA)
O .... Oklahoma (DLA)
O .... Old
O .... Olivine Subgroup [Fayalite, forsterite] [CIPW classification Geology]
O .... Omicron [Fifteenth letter of the Greek alphabet] (NASA)
O .... Omicron
O .... Omnipol Foreign Trade Corp. [Former Czechoslovakia] [ICAO aircraft manufacturer identifier] (ICAO)
O .... Omnivore
O .... Oncovin [Leurocristine, Vincristine] [Also, LCR, V, VC, VCR] [Antineoplastic drug]
O .... Ongoing
O .... Only
O .... Ontario (DLA)
O .... Ontario Reports [A publication] (DLA)
O .... Opacity (MCD)
O .... Open [Dancing position]
O .... Open-Air Places [Parks, pools, etc.] [Public-performance tariff class] [British]
O .... Open Circuit
O .... Opening
O .... Operand [Computer science]
O .... Operating Room Attendant [Ranking title] [British Royal Navy]
O .... Operation
O .... Operator

O .... [Telephone] Operator (WDMC)
O .... Operon [Genetics]
O .... Ophthalmology [Medical Officer designation] [British]
O .... Opium [Slang]
O .... Optimus [Best] [Latin]
O .... Optional Dishes [School meals] [British]
O .... Options [Computer science] [Telecommunications]
O .... Oral [Medicine]
O .... Orange [Color] [Medicine] (DMAA)
O .... Orange [Maps and charts]
O .... Orange [Phonetic alphabet] [Royal Navy World War I Pre-World War II] (DSUE)
O .... Orbit [Medicine] (DAVI)
O .... Orchid Flowering [Horticulture]
O .... Ordained
O .... Order
O .... Orderly [Medicine] (DAVI)
O .... Orders Group [British military] (DMA)
O .... Ordinance
O .... Ordinary
O .... Ordinary Level [School graduating grade] [British]
O .... Ordinary Ray [Direction of]
O .... Ordinate [Mathematics] (MSA)
O .... Ordinis [By the Order Of] [Latin]
O .... Ordnance
O .... Ordonnanzoffizier [Special-Missions Staff Officer] [German military - World War II]
O .... Oregon (ROG)
O .... Oregon Reports [A publication] (DLA)
O .... Organ
O .... Organic [Soil]
O .... Organism [Psychology]
O .... Organization
O .... Organized Naval Reserve
O .... Orient [Freemasonry]
O .... Oriental
O .... Origin
O .... Origin (IDOE)
O .... Original
O .... Orotidine [One-letter symbol; see Ord]
O .... Ortho [Chemistry]
O .... Orthodox [Judaism]
O .... Os [Bone] [Latin]
O .... Oscar [Phonetic alphabet] [International] (DSUE)
O .... Oscillation or Fluctuation in Behavior [Psychology]
O .... Oscillators [JETDS nomenclature] [Military] (CET)
O .... Osphradium [An organ in mollusks]
O .... Osten [East] [German]
O .... Ostiole [Biology]
O .... Other
O .... Other Program (NTCM)
O .... Otto's United States Supreme Court Reports [91-107 United States] [A publication] (DLA)
O .... Ouest [West] [French]
O .... Out (NASA)
O .... Out
O .... Outboard (DS)
O .... Outfield [Baseball]
O .... Outlay (GFGA)
O .... Outlet
O .... Output (BUR)
O .... Output (IDOE)
O .... Outside Cylinders [Trains] [British]
O .... Outside Edge [Skating]
O .... Ovary
O .... Ovation (WGA)
O .... Oven
O .... Over
O .... Overall (IAA)
O .... Overall Rating [Broadcasting]
O .... Overcast
O .... Overruled [Ruling in cited case expressly overruled] [Used in Shepard's Citations] [Legal term] (DLA)
O .... Overseer
O .... Ovule [Botany]
O .... Owner

O .... Oxford [*County borough in England*]
O .... Oxygen [*Chemical element*]
O .... Realty Income [*NYSE symbol*] (TTSB)
O .... Realty Income Corp. [*NYSE symbol*] (SAG)
O .... Respirations [*on anesthesia chart*] (DAVI)
O .... Shoulder Season [*Airline fare code*]
O .... Solicitor's Opinion [*A publication*] (DLA)
O .... South African Law Reports, Orange Free State Provincial Division [*1910-46*] [*A publication*] (DLA)
O .... Without Film [*Bacteriology*] (DAVI)
O1 .... Ensign [*Navy*]
O1 .... Organized Naval Reserve Seagoing
O1 .... Second Lieutenant [*Air Force, Army, Marine Corps*]
O^2 .... Both Eyes [*Pharmacy*]
O2 .... First Lieutenant [*Air Force, Army, Marine Corps*]
O2 .... Lieutenant Junior Grade [*Navy*]
O2 .... Organized Naval Reserve Aviation
O$_2$ .... Oxygen (IDOE)
O-2A .... Oligodendrocytes and Type 2 Astrocytes [*Neurology*]
O$_2$ Cap. ...... Oxygen Capacity (MAE)
O$_2$sat .... Oxygen Saturation (MAE)
O$_2$V .... Oxygen Ventilation Equivalent [*Laboratory science*] (DAVI)
O3 .... Captain [*Air Force, Army, Marine Corps*]
O3 .... Lieutenant [*Navy*]
O$_3$ .... Ozone (PS)
O3 .... Ozone
O4 .... Lieutenant Commander [*Navy*]
O4 .... Major [*Air Force, Army, Marine Corps*]
O4O .... October 4th Organization (EA)
O5 .... Commander [*Navy*]
O5 .... Lieutenant Colonel [*Air Force, Army, Marine Corps*]
O6 .... Captain [*Navy*]
O6 .... Colonel [*Air Force, Army, Marine Corps*]
O7 .... Brigadier General [*Air Force, Army, Marine Corps*]
O7 .... Commodore [*Navy*]
O8 .... Major General [*Air Force, Army, Marine Corps*]
O8 .... Rear Admiral [*Navy*]
O9 .... Lieutenant General [*Air Force, Army, Marine Corps*]
O9 .... Vice Admiral [*Navy*]
O10 .... Admiral [*Navy*]
O10 .... General [*Air Force, Army, Marine Corps*]
OA .... Almonte Public Library, Ontario [*Library symbol National Library of Canada*] (NLC)
O-A .... Objective Analytic Batteries [*Personality development test*] [*Psychology*]
OA .... Objective Aperture [*Microscopy*]
OA .... Objective Area [*Military*]
OA .... Oblate Sisters of the Assumption [*Roman Catholic religious order*]
OA .... Obligation Authority [*Army*]
OA .... Obstacle Avoidance (MCD)
OA .... Occipital Artery [*Anatomy*]
OA .... Occiput Anterior [*Medicine*]
OA .... Ocean Acre [*Marine science*] (MSC)
O/A .... Offer Accepted (ADA)
OA .... Office Address (WDAA)
OA .... Office Audit [*IRS*]
OA .... Office Automation
OA .... Office for Accreditation [*American Library Association*]
OA .... Office of Administration [*NASA*]
OA .... Office of Applications [*NASA*]
OA .... Office of Operations Analysis [*Arms Control and Disarmament Agency*] (GRD)
OA .... Office of the Administrator
OA .... Officers Association [*British military*] (DMA)
OA .... Official Assignee (ROG)
OA .... Ohio Appellate Reports [*A publication*] (DLA)
OA .... Oil-Immersed Self-Cooled [*Transformer*] (IEEE)
OA .... Old Account [*Banking*]
OA .... Old Age
OA .... Old Assyrian (BJA)
OA .... Oleic Acid [*Medicine*] (DMAA)
OA .... Olymbiaki Aeroporia [*Olympic Airlines*]
OA .... Olympic Airways [*Greece*] [*ICAO designator*] (OAG)
OA .... Omniantenna
OA .... Omnirange Antenna (IAA)
OA .... On Acceptance [*Business term*]
OA .... On Account [*Business and trade*]
OA .... On Account Of
O/A .... On Application (NITA)
OA .... On Arrival (ADA)
O/A .... On or About (WDAA)
o/a .... On or About (WDMC)
O/A .... Open Access [*Library shelves*] (DGA)
OA .... Open Account
OA .... Open Agility
OA .... Open Annealed [*Metal industry*]
OA .... Open Architecture [*Telecommunications*] (IAA)
OA .... Opera America [*An association*] (EA)
OA .... Operand Address (NITA)
OA .... Operand Address Register [*Computer science*]
OA .... Operating Agency
OA .... Operating Aircraft
OA .... Operating Assemblies [*JETDS nomenclature*] [*Military*] (CET)
OA .... Operating Authorization
OA .... Operational Advice

OA .... Operational Aft (MCD)
OA .... Operational Amplifier [*Telecommunications*] (TEL)
OA .... Operational [*or operations*] Analysis
OA .... Operationally Available (NATG)
OA .... Operation Analysis [*or Analyst*] (WDAA)
OA .... Operation Appreciation (EA)
O/A .... Operations/Administration (SSD)
OA .... Operations Advisor [*NASA*]
OA .... Operations Area
OA .... Operator Access (IAA)
OA .... Opiate Analgesia
OA .... Optical Adjunct
OA .... Optic Atrophy (CPH)
OA .... Optoacoustic [*Cell*]
OA .... Oral Alimentation [*Gastroenterology*] (DAVI)
OA .... Oral Apparatus [*Zoology*]
OA .... Orbital Assembly (MCD)
OA .... Orbit Analysis
OA .... Orbit Analyst (MCD)
OA .... Orbiter Access Arm [*NASA*]
O/A .... Order Authority (MCD)
OA .... Order of AHEPA [*Also known as American Hellenic Educational Progressive Association*] (EA)
OA .... Order of the Alhambra (EA)
OA .... Order of the Arrow (EA)
O/A .... Ordnance Alteration (MCD)
OA .... Ordnance Artificer [*Obsolete Navy British*]
OA .... Organizational Analysis
OA .... Organizational Assessment
O/A .... Original-Abfuellung [*On estate-bottled German wine labels*]
OA .... Originating Agency (SAA)
OA .... Orlando Aerospace [*Martin Marietta*] (RDA)
OA .... Oro Americano [*American Gold*] [*Spanish Business term*]
OA .... Osborne Association (EA)
OA .... Osteoarthritis [*Medicine*]
OA .... Osteogenesis Imperfecta [*Brittle bone disease*]
OA .... Other Appointments
OA .... Other Articles
OA .... Oudh Appeals [*India*] [*A publication*] (DLA)
O/A .... Our Account [*Business term*]
O/A .... Outer Anchorage [*Navigation*]
OA .... Output Amplitude
OA .... Output Axis
OA .... Ovalbumin [*Also, OV, OVA, OVAL*] [*Biochemistry*]
OA .... Overachievers Anonymous (EA)
OA .... Overall [*Technical drawings*]
O/A .... Overall
OA .... Overall
OA .... Overeaters Anonymous (EA)
OA .... Overfire Airport [*Combustion technology*]
OA .... Overtime Authorization (AAG)
OA .... Oxalic Acid [*Organic chemistry*] (AAMN)
OA 2d .... Ohio Appellate Reports, Second Series [*A publication*] (DLA)
OAA .... Hereditary Order of Armigerous Augustans (EA)
OAA .... Nora, AK [*Location identifier FAA*] (FAAL)
OAA .... o-Aminoacetanilide [*Organic chemistry*]
OAA .... Obstetric Anaesthetists Association [*British*] (DBA)
OAA .... Office of Administrative Appeals [*U.S. Department of Labor*] (BARN)
OAA .... Office of Aviation Affairs [*Army*]
OAA .... Old-Age Assistance [*Superseded by SSI*] [*HEW*]
OAA .... Older Americans Act [*1965*]
OAA .... Older Americans Almanac [*A publication*]
OAA .... Ontario Association of Architects [*1890*] [*Canada*] (NGC)
OAA .... Optical Acquisition Aid [*Deep Space Instrumentation Facility, NASA*]
OAA .... Opticians Association of America (EA)
OAA .... Orbiter Access Arm [*NASA*] (NASA)
OAA .... Orbiter Alternate Airfield [*NASA*] (MCD)
OAA .... Order of Australia Association
OAA .... Organic Acidemia Association (EA)
OAA .... Organisation des Nations Unies pour l'Alimentation et l'Agriculture [*Food and Agriculture Organization of the United Nations*]
OAA .... Organization of Athletic Administrators [*Defunct*] (EA)
OAA .... Orient Airlines Association (EA)
OAA .... Other Acronymic Agencies
OAA .... Outdoor Advertising Association (BARN)
OAA .... Oxaloacetic [*or Oxalacetic*] Acid [*Organic chemistry*]
OAA .... Oxley Aviation [*Australia ICAO designator*] (FAAC)
OAAA .... Oceania Amateur Athletic Association (EAIO)
OAAA .... Order of Americans of Armorial Ancestry (EA)
OAAA .... Outdoor Advertising Association of America [*Washington, DC*] (EA)
OAAB .... Objective-Analytic Anxiety Battery [*Psychology*]
OAAC .... Ocean Affairs Advisory Committee [*Department of State*] (MSC)
OAAC .... Older Americans Advocacy Commission [*HEW*]
OAAD .... Amdar [*Afghanistan*] [*ICAO location identifier*] (ICLI)
OAAD .... Ovarian Ascorbic Acid Depletion [*Test*]
OAADM .... Ovarian Ascorbic Acid Depletion Material
OAAIS .... Office of Administrative Analysis, Information, and Statistics [*Red Cross*]
OAAK .... Andkhoi [*Afghanistan*] [*ICAO location identifier*] (ICLI)
OA & C .... Ohio Circuit Court Decisions [*A publication*] (DLA)
OA & M .... Operations, Administration, and Maintenance [*Telecommunications*]
OA & MS .... Office of Administration and Management Services [*Employment and Training Administration*] [*Department of Labor*]
OA & S .... Other Arms and Services [*Military*]
OAAPS .... Organization for Afro-Asian Peoples Solidarity

OAARD............ Office of the Assistant Administrator for Research and Development [*HEW*]

OAAS .... Asmar [*Afghanistan*] [*ICAO location identifier*] (ICLI)

OAA/S .... Observer's Assessment of Alertness / Sedation Scale [*Medicine*]

OAASA .... Office of the Administrative Assistant to the Secretary of the Army

OAASN .... Office of the Administrative Assistant to the Secretary of the Navy

OAAT .... Ortho-Aminoazotoluene [*A dye*] [*Organic chemistry*]

OAAU .... Organization of Afro-American Unity

OAAU .... Orthogonal Array Arithmetic Unit [*Computer science*]

OAAV .... Organization of African-American Veterans (EA)

OAB .... Attawapiskat Band Library, Ontario [*Library symbol National Library of Canada*] (BIB)

OAB .... Moab, UT [*Location identifier FAA*] (FAAL)

OAB .... Oakland [*California*] Army Base (VNW)

OAB .... Ocean Affairs Board [*National Academy of Sciences*] (MSC)

OAB .... Old-Age Benefits

OAB .... Olive Advisory Board [*Defunct*] (EA)

OAB .... Ordnance Assembly Building (MUGU)

OAB .... Organisation Africaine du Bois [*African Timber Organization*] (EAIO)

OAB .... Outer Air Battle [*Navy*] (ANA)

OAB .... Overseas Affairs Branch [*Army*]

OAB .... Overseas Appointments Bureau [*Christian Education Movement*] [*British*] (AEBS)

OAB .... Owners Abroad Aviation Ltd. [*British ICAO designator*] (FAAC)

OAB .... Oxford Annotated Bible [*New York*] [*A publication*] (BJA)

OABA .... Burleigh-Anstruther and Chandos Union Public Library, Apsley, Ontario [*Library symbol National Library of Canada*] (BIB)

OABA .... Outdoor Amusement Business Association (EA)

OABD .... Behsood [*Afghanistan*] [*ICAO location identifier*] (ICLI)

OABETA .... Office Appliance and Business Equipment Trades Association (HGAA)

OABG .... Baghlan [*Afghanistan*] [*ICAO location identifier*] (ICLI)

OABK .... Bandkamalkhan [*Afghanistan*] [*ICAO location identifier*] (ICLI)

OABN .... Bamyan [*Afghanistan*] [*ICAO location identifier*] (ICLI)

OABP .... Organic Anion Binding Protein [*Biochemistry*]

OABR .... Bamar [*Afghanistan*] [*ICAO location identifier*] (ICLI)

OABS .... Sarday [*Afghanistan*] [*ICAO location identifier*] (ICLI)

OABT .... Bost [*Afghanistan*] [*ICAO location identifier*] (ICLI)

OABT .... Ortho-Aminobenzenethiol [*Organic chemistry*]

OAC .... Acton Public Library, Ontario [*Library symbol National Library of Canada*] (NLC)

OAC .... Cleveland Institute of Art, Cleveland, OH [*OCLC symbol*] (OCLC)

OAC .... Oceanic Area Control [*Aviation*] (FAAC)

OAC .... Oceanographic Advisory Committee [*Navy Oceanographer*] (USDC)

OAC .... Oceanographic Advisory Committee [*Marine science*] (OSRA)

OAC .... Office of Academic Computing [*Research center*] (RCD)

OAC .... Officer Advanced Course [*Army*] (INF)

OAC .... Ohio Administrative Code [*A publication*] (AAGC)

OAC .... On Approved Credit

OAC .... Ontario Agricultural College [*Canada*]

OAC .... Ontario Appeal Cases [*Database*] [*Maritime Law Book Co. Ltd.*] [*Information service or system*] (CRD)

OAC .... Ontario Arts Council

OAC .... Open Air Campaigners, US (EA)

OAC .... Operating Agency Code (AFM)

OAC .... Operation Anti-Christ (EA)

OAC .... Operation of Aircraft Costs (DNAB)

OAC .... Operations Analysis Center

OAC .... Operations Analysis Chief [*Air Force*]

OAC .... Optical Acceleration Cancellation [*Vision*]

OAC .... Optical Area Correlator

OAC .... Optimal Automatic Control

OAC .... Optimized Aftercooled [*Truck engineering*]

OAC .... Optimum Approach Course [*Navy*] (NVT)

OAC .... Ordnance Ammunition Command [*Merged with Munitions Command*] [*Army*]

OAC .... Ordo ab Chao [*Order Out of Chaos*] [*Freemasonry*] [*Latin*]

OAC .... Oregon Administrative Code [*A publication*] (AAGC)

OAC .... Oriental Airlines Ltd. [*Nigeria*] [*ICAO designator*] (FAAC)

OAC .... Original Acquisition Cost (AAGC)

OAC .... Original Air Conditioning (IIA)

OAC .... Outer Approach Channel

OAC .... Overseas Automotive Club (EA)

OACB .... Charburjak [*Afghanistan*] [*ICAO location identifier*] (ICLI)

OACC .... Chakhcharan [*Afghanistan*] [*ICAO location identifier*] (ICLI)

OACC .... Oceanic Area Control Centre

OACC .... Older Americans Consumer Cooperative [*Washington, DC*] (EA)

OACD .... Office of Agricultural and Chemical Development [*of TVA*]

OACDT .... Outback Areas Community Developmnent Trust [*Australia*]

OACES .... Ocean-Atmosphere Carbon Exchange Study (USDC)

OACES .... Ocean-Atmosphere Carbon Exchange Study [*Marine science*] (OSRA)

OACG .... Office of the Assistant Comptroller General (AAGC)

OACH .... Acton High School, Ontario [*Library symbol National Library of Canada*] (NLC)

OACI .... Optical Automatic Car Identification

OACI .... Organisation de l'Aviation Civile Internationale [*International Civil Aviation Organization*] [*French United Nations*]

OACI .... Organizacion de Aviacion Civil Internacional [*International Civil Aviation Organization*] [*Spanish United Nations*] (DUND)

OACII .... Operational Approved Configuration Identification Index (SAA)

OACIS .... Ocean-Atmospheric Climatic Interaction Studies

OACIS .... Oregon Advanced Computing Institute [*Research center*] (RCD)

OACO .... Operation and Checkout [*NASA*] (IAA)

OAC of S..... Office of the Assistant Chief of Staff [*Military*]

OACP .... Canada Publishing Corp., Agincourt, Ontario [*Library symbol National Library of Canada*] (BIB)

OACP .... Operational Analysis Code Package (PDAA)

OACR .... Office of the Admiral Commanding Reserves [*Navy British*]

OACS .... Office of the Assistant Chief of Staff [*Military*] (AAG)

OACSA .... Office of the Assistant Chief of Staff for Automation and Communications [*Military*] (MCD)

OACSAC .... Office of the Assistant Chief of Staff for Automation and Communications [*Military*]

OACSC-E...... Office of the Assistant Chief of Staff for Communications-Electronics (AABC)

OACSEA .... Older American Community Service Employment Act [*1975*]

OACSFOR .... Office of the Assistant Chief of Staff for Force Development [*Army*]

OACSI .... Office of the Assistant Chief of Staff for Intelligence [*Army*]

OACSIM .... Office of the Assistant Chief of Staff for Information Management [*Military*]

OACT .... Office of the Actuary [*Department of Health and Human Services*] (GFGA)

OACT .... Officer, Airman, Civilian, and Total (MCD)

OACT .... Organisation Africaine de Cartographie et de Teledetection [*Algeria*] (EAIO)

OACT .... Ormone Adrenocorticotropina [*Italian Medicine*]

OAD .... Adria Laboratories, Inc., Columbus, OH [*OCLC symbol*] (OCLC)

OAD .... Obstructive Airway Disease [*Medicine*]

OAD .... Office of Administration

OAD .... Officers' Accounts Division [*Navy*]

OAD .... Officers' Assignment Division, The Adjutant General's Office [*Army*]

OAD .... Opening of Anterior Digestive [*Gland*]

OAD .... Operational Active Data [*Navy*]

OAD .... Operational Analysis Division [*Air Force*]

OAD .... Operational Availability Data [*Military*]

OAD .... Operational Availability Date [*Nuclear Regulatory Commission*] (GFGA)

OAD .... Optical Activity Detection

OAD .... Orbiter Atmospheric Drag [*NASA*]

OAD .... Ordered, Adjudged, and Decreed (WDAA)

OAD .... Ordered to Active Duty (AABC)

OAD .... Ordering and Distributing (IAA)

OAD .... Organic Anionic Dye [*Medicine*] (DMAA)

OAD .... Organizations and Agencies Directories Series [*A publication*]

OAD .... Original Air Date [*of program's first telecast*]

OAD .... Overall Absolute Deviation [*Mathematics*]

OAD .... Overall Depth (WDAA)

OAD .... Overall Dimensions (IAA)

OAD .... Oxford American Dictionary [*A publication*]

OAD .... Special Audit Division (AAGC)

OADAB .... Office of the Assistant Director of the Army Budget

OADAP .... Office of Alcoholism and Drug Abuse Prevention [*Department of Health and Human Services*]

OADC .... Oleic Acid, Albumin, Dextrose, Catalase

OADD .... Dawlatabad [*Afghanistan*] [*ICAO location identifier*] (ICLI)

OA/DDP........ Office Automation / Distributed Data Processing (MHDI)

OADEMQA.... Office of Acid Deposition, Environmental Monitoring, and Quality Assurance [*Environmental Protection Agency*] (GFGA)

OADF .... Darra-I-Soof [*Afghanistan*] [*ICAO location identifier*] (ICLI)

OA-DG .... Occupational Area Defense Grouping (DNAB)

OADG .... Open Architecture Development Group [*IBM Corp.*] (CDE)

OADH .... One-Arm Dove Hunt Association (EA)

OADH .... Organization of Advanced Disabled Hobbyists (EA)

OADMS .... Office of Automated Data Management Services [*General Services Administration*]

OAdN .... Ohio Northern University, Ada, OH [*Library symbol Library of Congress*] (LCLS)

OADPS .... Office of Automatic Data Processing Services (AAGC)

OADR .... Office of Agricultural Defense Relations [*New Deal*]

OADR .... Originating Agency Determination Required (MCD)

OADS .... Omnidirectional Air Data System

OADV .... Devar [*Afghanistan*] [*ICAO location identifier*] (ICLI)

OADW .... Wazakhwa [*Afghanistan*] [*ICAO location identifier*] (ICLI)

OADZ .... Darwaz [*Afghanistan*] [*ICAO location identifier*] (ICLI)

OAE .... NOAA [*National Oceanic and Atmospheric Administration*]-LISD Seattle Center, Seattle, WA [*OCLC symbol*] (OCLC)

OAE .... Occupational and Adult Education [*Office of Education*] (OICC)

OAE .... Office of Analysis and Evaluation [*Environmental Protection Agency*] (EPA)

OAE .... Officer of Arms Extraordinary [*College of Arms/Heralds' College*] [*British*]

OAE .... Old Antarctic Explorer

OAE .... Optical Alignment Equipment

OAE .... Optima Energy Corp. [*Vancouver Stock Exchange symbol*]

OAE .... Orbiting Astronomical Explorer [*NASA*] (IIA)

OAE .... Orchestra of the Age of Enlightenment [*British*]

OAE .... Organization of Architectural Employees

OAE .... Orzeck Aphasia Evaluation [*Psychology*]

OAE .... Oscillating-Analyzer Ellipsometer (PDAA)

OAEC .... Essa Centennial Library, Angus, Ontario [*Library symbol National Library of Canada*] (BIB)

OAEFT.......... Astorville Branch, East Ferris Township Public Library, Ontario [*Library symbol National Library of Canada*] (NLC)

OAEK .... Keshm [*Afghanistan*] [*ICAO location identifier*] (ICLI)

OAEM .... Eshkashem [*Afghanistan*] [*ICAO location identifier*] (ICLI)

OAEQ .... Islam Qala [*Afghanistan*] [*ICAO location identifier*] (ICLI)

OAET .... Elma Township Public Library, Atwood, Ontario [*Library symbol National Library of Canada*] (NLC)

OAF .... Austrian Air Ambulance [*ICAO designator*] (FAAC)

OAF	Occidentale Afrique Francaise [French West Africa]
OAF	Office of Alcohol Fuels [Department of Energy]
OAF	Officer Assignment Folder [Military] (AFM)
OAF	Ontario Ministry of Agriculture and Food [UTLAS symbol]
OAF	Open Air Factor
OAF	Options for Animals Foundation (EA)
OAF	Orbital Antenna Farm (PDAA)
OAF	Origin Address Field [Computer science] (IBMDP)
OAF	Orthodox and Anglican Fellowship (EA)
OAF	Osteoclast Activating Factor [Endocrinology]
OAF	Oxygen Alternate Fill
OAFB	Offutt Air Force Base [Nebraska] (AAG)
OAFC	Arden Branch, Frontenac County Library, Ontario [Library symbol National Library of Canada] (BIB)
OAFC	Occupational Analysis Field Center
OAFC	Office of Air Force Chaplains
OAFC	Official Aerrage Fan Club [Defunct] (EA)
OAFD	Orbiter Air Flight Deck [NASA] (MCD)
OAFG	Khost-O-Fering [Afghanistan] [ICAO location identifier] (ICLI)
OA/FI	Operational Assurance/Fault Isolation (MCD)
OAFIE	Office of Armed Forces Information and Education
OAFM	On or After Full Moon [Freemasonry] (ROG)
OAFR	Farah [Afghanistan] [ICAO location identifier] (ICLI)
OAFT	Official Air Freight Tariffs
OAFTO	Orbiter Atmospheric Flight Test Office [NASA] (NASA)
OAFZ	Faizabad [Afghanistan] [ICAO location identifier] (ICLI)
OAG	Oblique Anterior Gauche [Left Anterior Oblique Position] [Medicine]
OAG	Office of the Adjutant General [Military] (MCD)
OAG	Office of the Attorney-General
OAG	Official Airline Guide, Inc. [ICAO designator] (FAAC)
OAG	Official Airline Guides, Inc. [Information service or system] (IID)
OAG	Oleoyl(acetyl)glycerol [Organic chemistry]
OAG	Online Airlines Guide [A publication]
OAG	Open Angle Glaucoma [Ophthalmology]
OAG	Opinions of the Attorney General
OAG	Optical Alignment Group
OAG	Orange [Australia Airport symbol] (OAG)
OAGA	Ghaziabad [Afghanistan] [ICAO location identifier] (ICLI)
OAGB	Osteopathic Association of Great Britain
OAGCM	Ocean-Atmosphere General Circulation Model [Oceanography]
OAGD	Gader [Afghanistan] [ICAO location identifier] (ICLI)
OAG-EE	Official Airline Guide-Electronic Edition [Official Airline Guides, Inc.] [Database]
OAGG	Gage Educational Publishing Ltd., Agincourt, Ontario [Library symbol National Library of Canada] (NLC)
OAGL	Gulistan [Afghanistan] [ICAO location identifier] (ICLI)
OAGM	Ghelmeen [Afghanistan] [ICAO location identifier] (ICLI)
OAG Massachusetts	Massachusetts Attorney General Reports [A publication] (DLA)
OAGN	Ghazni [Afghanistan] [ICAO location identifier] (ICLI)
OAGS	Gasar [Afghanistan] [ICAO location identifier] (ICLI)
OAG West Virginia	West Virginia Attorney General Reports [A publication] (DLA)
OAGZ	Gardez [Afghanistan] [ICAO location identifier] (ICLI)
OAH	Ancaster High and Vocational School, Ontario [Library symbol National Library of Canada] (NLC)
OAH	Office of Aboriginal Health [Australia]
OAH	Organization of American Historians (EA)
OAH	Ovarian Androgenic Hyperfunction [Medicine] (DMAA)
OAH	Overall Height [Automotive specifications]
OAH	Overhead Air Hoist
OAHE	Hazrat Eman [Afghanistan] [ICAO location identifier] (ICLI)
OAHJ	Hajigak [Afghanistan] [ICAO location identifier] (ICLI)
OAHN	Khwahan [Afghanistan] [ICAO location identifier] (ICLI)
OAHR	Herat [Afghanistan] [ICAO location identifier] (ICLI)
OAHS	O-Acetylhomoserine (thiol)-lyase [An enzyme]
OAI	Office of Analysis and Inspections [Department of Health and Human Services] (GFGA)
OAI	Office of Audit and Inspection [Energy Research and Development Administration]
OAI	Office of Audit and Investigation [United States Geological Survey]
OAI	Ohio Aerospace Institute
OAI	Open Application Interface
OAI	Optical Associates Inc. (NITA)
OAI	Outside Air Intake (NRCH)
OAIAC	Operational Area Industry Advisory Committee [Civil Defense]
OAIB	Old-Age Insurance Benefit (MHDB)
OAID	Older Americans Information Directory [A publication]
OAIDE	Operational Assistance and Instructive Data Equipment
OAIM	Office of Aviation Information Management [Department of Transportation] [Information service or system] (IID)
OAIP	Ontario Assessment Instrument Pool [Educational test] [Canada]
OAIP	Organic Ablative Insulative Plastic
OAIS	Opinion, Attitude, and Interest Survey [Psychology]
OAIW	International Waxes Ltd., Agincourt, Ontario [Library symbol National Library of Canada] (NLC)
OAJ	Ajax Public Library, Ontario [Library symbol National Library of Canada] (NLC)
OAJ	Jacksonville [North Carolina] [Airport symbol] (OAG)
OAJ	Jacksonville, NC [Location identifier FAA] (FAAL)
OAJ	Opening Altitude Judgement [Parachuting] (DICI)
OAJL	Jalalabad [Afghanistan] [ICAO location identifier] (ICLI)
OAJS	Jabul Saraj [Afghanistan] [ICAO location identifier] (ICLI)
OAJW	Jawand [Afghanistan] [ICAO location identifier] (ICLI)
OAk	Akron Public Library, Akron, OH [Library symbol Library of Congress] (LCLS)

OAK	Oakfield [New York] [Seismograph station code, US Geological Survey Closed] (SEIS)
OAK	Oak Indus [NYSE symbol] (TTSB)
OAK	Oak Industries, Inc. [NYSE symbol] (SPSG)
OAK	Oakland [California] [Airport symbol]
OAK	Oakland Operations Office (DOGT)
OAK	Oakwood College, Huntsville, AL [OCLC symbol] (OCLC)
OAK	Oakwood Petroleums Ltd. [Toronto Stock Exchange symbol]
OAK	Oklahoma-Arkansas-Kansas League [Old baseball league]
OAK	Older Americans Corps [Proposed]
OAK	Optical Alignment Kit (MCD)
OAK	Organization for the Advancement of Knowledge (EA)
OAK	Overhaul Alignment Kit
OAK	San Francisco [California] Oakland [Airport symbol] (OAG)
OAKA	Koban [Afghanistan] [ICAO location identifier] (ICLI)
OAKB	Kabul Ad [Afghanistan] [ICAO location identifier] (ICLI)
OAKC	Oakhurst Capital, Inc. [NASDAQ symbol] (SAG)
OAKC	Oakhurst Co. [NASDAQ symbol] (TTSB)
OAKC	Oakhurst Co., Inc. [NASDAQ symbol] (SAG)
OAkCh	Akron Child Guidance Center, Akron, OH [Library symbol Library of Congress] (LCLS)
OAKD	Kamdesh [Afghanistan] [ICAO location identifier] (ICLI)
OAKE	Organization of American Kodaly Educators (EA)
OAkF	Firestone Tire & Rubber Co., Akron, OH [Library symbol Library of Congress] (LCLS)
OAKF	Oak Hill Financial [NASDAQ symbol] (TTSB)
OAKF	Oak Hill Financial, Inc. [NASDAQ symbol] (SAG)
OAKG	Khojaghar [Afghanistan] [ICAO location identifier] (ICLI)
OAkGr	B. F. Goodrich Co., Akron, OH [Library symbol Library of Congress] (LCLS)
OAkGy	Goodyear Tire & Rubber Co., Akron, OH [Library symbol Library of Congress] (LCLS)
OakHill	Oak Hill Financial, Inc. [Associated Press] (SAG)
OakHill	Oak Hill Sportswear Corp. [Associated Press] (SAG)
OakHillF	Oak Hill Financial, Inc. [Associated Press] (SAG)
Oakhurst	Oakhurst Capital, Inc. [Associated Press] (SAG)
Oakhurst	Oakhurst Co., Inc. [Associated Press] (SAG)
OakInds	Oak Industries, Inc. [Associated Press] (SAG)
OAKJ	Kajaki [Afghanistan] [ICAO location identifier] (ICLI)
OAkk	Old Akkadian (BJA)
OAKL	Konjak-I-Logar [Afghanistan] [ICAO location identifier] (ICLI)
Oakland U	Oakland University (GAGS)
Oakly	Oakly, Inc. [Associated Press] (SAG)
OAKM	Kamar [Afghanistan] [ICAO location identifier] (ICLI)
OAKN	Kandahar [Afghanistan] [ICAO location identifier] (ICLI)
OAKR	Kaldar [Afghanistan] [ICAO location identifier] (ICLI)
OAKS	Khost [Afghanistan] [ICAO location identifier] (ICLI)
OAKS	River Oaks Furniture [NASDAQ symbol] (TTSB)
OAKS	River Oaks Furniture, Inc. [NASDAQ symbol] (SAG)
OAKT	Kalat [Afghanistan] [ICAO location identifier] (ICLI)
OAKT	Oak Technology [NASDAQ symbol] (TTSB)
OAKT	Oak Technology, Inc. [NASDAQ symbol] (SAG)
OakTch	Oak Technology, Inc. [Associated Press] (SAG)
OAkU	University of Akron, Akron, OH [Library symbol Library of Congress] (LCLS)
OAkU-L	University of Akron, School of Law, Akron, Ohio [Library symbol Library of Congress] (LCLS)
Oakwood	Oakwood Homes Corp. [Associated Press] (SAG)
OAKX	Kabul [Afghanistan] [ICAO location identifier] (ICLI)
OAKZ	Karez-I-Mir [Afghanistan] [ICAO location identifier] (ICLI)
OAL	Alliston Memorial Public Library, Ontario [Library symbol National Library of Canada] (BIB)
OAL	Audit Liaison Division (AAGC)
OAL	Coaldale, NV [Location identifier FAA] (FAAL)
OAL	National Oceanic and Atmospheric Administration, Miami Branch, Miami, FL [OCLC symbol] (OCLC)
OAL	Office of Arts and Libraries [British]
OAL	Olympic Airways SA [Greece] [ICAO designator] (FAAC)
OAL	Operational Applications Laboratory [Air Force]
OAL	Operations and Logistics (IAA)
OAL	Order Action List [Military] (DNAB)
OAL	Order of Ancient Lights
OAL	Ordnance Aerophysics Laboratory
OAL	Overall Length [Automotive specifications]
OAL	Overall Level (NASA)
OALAC	Amherstview Branch, Lennox and Addington County Public Library, Ontario [Library symbol National Library of Canada] (NLC)
OALAC	Older Americans' Legal Action Center (DICI)
OAIB	Babcock & Wilcox Co., Alliance, OH [Library symbol Library of Congress] (LCLS)
OALC	Ogden Air Logistics Center (MCD)
OALDCE	Oxford Advanced Learner's Dictionary of Current English
OALF	Organic Acid Labile Fluoride [Chemistry] (AAMN)
OALF	Oromo Abo Liberation Front [Ethiopia] [Political party] (EY)
OALG	Logar [Afghanistan] [ICAO location identifier] (ICLI)
OALJ	Office of Administrative Law Judges [Department of Agriculture] (GFGA)
OALL	Allenford Branch, Bruce County Public Library, Ontario [Library symbol National Library of Canada] (NLC)
OALL	Lal [Afghanistan] [ICAO location identifier] (ICLI)
OAlM	Mount Union College, Alliance, OH [Library symbol Library of Congress] (LCLS)
OALM	Of a Like Mind [An association] (EA)
OALM	Optical Address Light Modulator [Instrumentation]

OALMA	Orthopedic Appliance and Limb Manufacturers Association [*Later, AOPA*]
OALN	Laghman [*Afghanistan*] [*ICAO location identifier*] (ICLI)
OALOS	Office for Ocean Affairs and the Law of the Sea [*United Nations*] (GNE)
OALS	Observer Air Lock System (OA)
OALS	Office of Arid Lands Studies [*University of Arizona*] [*Research center*] (RCD)
OALS	Orbiter Automatic Landing System (MCD)
OALT	Operational Acceptable Level of Traffic [*FAA*] (TAG)
O ALT HOR...	Omnibus Alternis Horis [*Every Other Hour*] [*Pharmacy*] (ROG)
OAM...........	Oamaru [*New Zealand*] [*Airport symbol*] (OAG)
OAM...........	Office of Administration and Management [*Employment and Training Administration*] [*Department of Labor*]
OAM...........	Office of Aerospace Medicine [*NASA*] (MCD)
OAM...........	Office of Alternative Medicine [*National Institutes of Health*]
OAM...........	Office of Automation and Manpower [*Department of Labor*] [*See also OMAT*]
OAM...........	Office of Aviation Medicine [*FAA*]
OAM...........	One Australian Movement [*Political party*]
OAM...........	Onze Alma Mater (BJA)
OAM...........	Open-Air Mission
OAM...........	Operations and Management (MCD)
OAM...........	Optimum Artillery Mix (SAA)
OAM...........	Orbital Assembly Module (MCD)
OAM...........	Order of Ancient Maccabees (BJA)
OAM...........	Organization and Methods [*Military*] (AFIT)
OAM...........	Orthopedic Appliance Mechanic [*Navy*]
OAM...........	Oscillator Activity Monitor [*Telecommunications*] (TEL)
OAMA	Office Automation Management Association (EA)
OAMA	Ogden Air Material Area [*AFLC*]
OAMA	Oil Appliance Manufacturers' Association [*British*] (BI)
OAMAC	Oceanic and Atmospheric Management Advisory Committee [*National Oceanic and Atmospheric Administration*] (EGAO)
OAMCE	Optical Alignment, Monitoring, and Calibration Equipment
OAMDG........	Omnia ad Majorem Dei Gloriam [*All to the Greater Glory of God*] [*Latin*]
OAME.........	Orbital Attitude and Maneuvering Electronics
OAMEX	Ocean-Atmosphere Exchange Processes [*Marine science*] (MSC)
OAMF.........	Fort Malden National Historic Park, Amherstburg, Ontario [*Library symbol National Library of Canada*] (NLC)
OAMHS	Ameliasburgh Historical Society, Ontario [*Library symbol National Library of Canada*] (BIB)
OAMK	Mukur [*Afghanistan*] [*ICAO location identifier*] (ICLI)
OAMN	Maimama [*Afghanistan*] [*ICAO location identifier*] (ICLI)
OAMN	Operations and Maintenance, Navy (AFIT)
OAMP	Optical Analog Matrix Processing
OAMS	Mazar-I-Sharif [*Afghanistan*] [*ICAO location identifier*] (ICLI)
OAMS	Office of Administrative and Management Systems [*Social Security Administration*]
OAMS	Optical Angular Motion Sensor
OAMS	Orbital Altitude and Maneuvering System (IAA)
OAMS	Orbital Attitude and Maneuvering System [*NASA*]
OAMS	Organic and Atmospheric Mass Spectrometer (KSC)
OAMT.........	Munta [*Afghanistan*] [*ICAO location identifier*] (ICLI)
OAN	Curriculum Resources Centre, Niagara South Board of Education, Allanburg, Ontario [*Library symbol National Library of Canada*] (BIB)
OAN	NMFS [*National Marine Fisheries Service*] Southeast Fisheries Center, Beaufort Laboratory, Beaufort, NC [*OCLC symbol*] (OCLC)
OAN	Ocean Aids to Navigation [*Coast Guard*]
OAN	Omega Arts Network (EA)
OANA	Organization of Asia-Pacific News Agencies [*Malaysia*] (EY)
OAND.........	Origin and Destination (NITA)
O & A	Observation and Assessment [*Medicine*]
O & A	October and April [*Denotes semiannual payments of interest or dividends in these months*] [*Business term*]
O & A (Date)...	Oath and Acceptance Date [*Date from which a military officer's commissioned service runs*]
O & B	Opium and Belladonna [*Pharmacy*] (MAE)
O & C	Onset and Course [*of a disease*] [*Medicine*]
o & c	Onset and Course [*Medicine*] (AD)
O & C	Operation and Checkout [*NASA*]
O & C	Oxford and Cambridge Schools Examination Board [*British*] (DCTA)
O & CC	Order and Change Control (AAG)
o & cc	Order and Change Control (AD)
O & CM	Organist and Choir Master (ROG)
O & C/O	Operation and Checkout [*O & C is preferred*] [*NASA*] (KSC)
O & D	Origin and Destination [*Aviation*]
o & d	Origin and Destination (AD)
O & E	Observation and Evaluation [*Medicine*] (DAVI)
O & E	Observation and Examination [*Medicine*]
O & E	Operations and Engineering
o & e	Operations and Engineering (AD)
O & F	Organizations and Functions (MCD)
O & FN	Ordnance and Facilities - Navy
O & FS	Operations and Flight Support [*NASA*] (NASA)
O & G/PF	Oil and Gas/Pipeline Facilities
O & I	Operations and Intelligence [*Section*] [*Army*] (INF)
o & i	Organizational and Intermediate (AD)
O & I	Outline and Installation (MCD)
O & IR	Operation and Inspection Record (KSC)
O & K	Orenstein & Koppel (AD)
O & LS	Ocean and Lake Surveys [*Budget appropriation title*] [*Navy*]
O & M	Ogilvy & Mather [*Advertising agency*]
O & M	Ohio & Morenci Railroad (IIA)
O&M...........	Operating and Maintenance [*USCG*] (TAG)
O & M	Operation and Maintenance (AD)
O & M	Operation and Maintenance (DOMA)
O & M	Operation and Maintenance
O & M	Operations and Management
O & M	Organization and Management
O & M	Organization and Methods (AABC)
O & M	Orientation and Mobility [*for the blind*]
O & MA	Operation and Maintenance Activities (AAG)
O&MA.........	Operation and Maintenance, Army (AAGC)
O & M-DA....	Operation and Maintenance, Defense Agencies [*DoD*]
O & MF	Operation and Maintenance Facilities (MUGU)
O & MFH	Operation and Maintenance, Family Housing [*Army*] (AABC)
O & MMC ...	Operations and Maintenance, Marine Corps
O & MN	Operation and Maintenance, Navy
O & MN	Overhaul and Maintenance, Navy (MCD)
O & MNR....	Operation and Maintenance, Naval Reserve (NVT)
O & N	Oregon & Northwestern Railroad Co. (IIA)
O & O	One and Only (IIA)
O & O	Operational and Organizational (RDA)
O & O	Organization and Operation
O & O	Owned and Operated
O & OP	Organizational and Operational Plan [*Army*]
O & OS	Ordnance and Ordnance Stores [*Navy*]
OANDOS	Ordnance and Ordnance Stores [*Coast Guard*]
O & P	Operations and Procedures (KSC)
O & P	Ova and Parasites [*Medicine*]
O & PC	Owl and the Pussy Cat [*Poem by Edward Lear, 1871*]
O & R	Ocean and Rail [*Shipping*]
OANDR........	Operation and Regulation
OANDR........	Operation and Regulation (FAAC)
O & R	Overhaul and Repair
O & S	Operation and Support Funds [*DoD*] (RDA)
O & S	Operations and Support (MCD)
O & S	Optics and Sensors Program
O & S	Over and Short Account [*Business term*]
O & SCMIS...	Operating and Support Costs Management Information System
O & S HA.....	Operating and Support Hazard Analysis
O & ST	Order and Shipping Time [*Military*] (MCD)
O & T	Operations and Training [*Military*]
O & T	Organization and Training [*Military*]
OANDT........	Organization and Training Division [*Supreme Headquarters Allied Powers Europe*] (NATG)
O & T.........	Oyer and Terminer [*Hear and Determine*] [*Legal term*] (DLA)
O & W	Oldest and Wisest [*Nickname for President Ronald Reagan*]
O & W	Oneida & Western Railroad (IIA)
O & W	Ontario & Western Railroad [*Nickname: Old and Weary*]
O & W Dig....	Oldham and White's Digest of Laws [*Texas*] [*A publication*] (DLA)
O & Y	Olympia & York [*Commercial firm Canada*] (ECON)
OANFE	Operational Aircraft Not Fully Equipped (NG)
OANI	Office of the Administrator of Norfolk Island [*Australia*]
OANM	On or After New Moon [*Freemasonry*] (ROG)
OANR	Nawor [*Afghanistan*] [*ICAO location identifier*] (ICLI)
OANR	Office of Air, Noise, and Radiation [*Environmental Protection Agency*] (ERG)
OANS	Occupied Area News Service [*Military*] (IAA)
OANS	Salang-I-Shamali [*Afghanistan*] [*ICAO location identifier*] (ICLI)
OANT	Normanby Township Community and School Library, Ayton, Ontario [*Library symbol National Library of Canada*] (NLC)
OA/NWOB....	Open Allotments/Navy-Wide Operating Budgets (MCD)
OAO	Arkhangelsk 2 Aviation Division [*Former USSR*] [*FAA designator*] (FAAC)
OAO	National Oceanic and Atmospheric Administration, Miami, Miami, FL [*OCLC symbol*] (OCLC)
OAO	Office of Aircraft Operations [*Miami, FL*] [*National Oceanic and Atmospheric Administration*] (GRD)
OAO	One and Only [*A favorite girl or boy friend*]
OAO	Operational and Organizational (MCD)
OAO	Orbited Assembly Operation
OAO	Orbiting Astronomical Observatory [*NASA*]
OAO	Orthogonalized Atomic Orbital (OA)
OAO	Outdoor Adventure Online [*America Online*]
OAOAF........	Operations Analysis Office, Air Force (MCD)
OAOAFLC....	Operations Analysis Office, Air Force Logistics Command (MCD)
OAOB	Obeh [*Afghanistan*] [*ICAO location identifier*] (ICLI)
OAOG	Urgoon [*Afghanistan*] [*ICAO location identifier*] (ICLI)
OAOI	On and Off Instruments [*Aviation*]
OAOO	Deshoo [*Afghanistan*] [*ICAO location identifier*] (ICLI)
OAOP	Older Adult Offender Project [*of the Alston Wilkes Society*] (EA)
OAOR	Oxygen Adsorption, Out-gassing, and Chemical Reduction (PDAA)
OAP	NMFS [*National Marine Fisheries Service*] Northeast Fisheries Center, WoodsHole, MA [*OCLC symbol*] (OCLC)
OAP	Observation Amphibian Plane [*Coast Guard*]
OAP	Occupational Aptitude Pattern [*US Employment Service*] [*Department of Labor*]
OAP	Oceanic Automation Program [*FAA*] (TAG)
OAP	Office of Adolescent Pregnancy [*Medicine*] (BABM)
OAP	Office of Adolescent Pregnancy (DAVI)
OAP	Office of Aerial Phenomena [*Air Force*]
OAP	Office of Aircraft Production [*World War II*]
OAP	Office of Air Programs [*Obsolete Environmental Protection Agency*]
OAP	Office of Alien Property [*World War II*] (DLA)

OAP	Office of Antarctic Programs [*National Science Foundation*] [*Later, Division of Polar Programs*]
OAP	Office of Atomic Programs [*DoD*]
OAP	Office of the Director of Aerospace Programs [*Air Force*]
OAP	Offset Aiming Point (AFM)
OAP	Oil Analysis Program [*Military*] (AFIT)
OAP	Old-Age Pension [*or Pensioner*]
OAP	On-Axis Pointing (PDAA)
OAP	Oncovin [*Vincristine*], Ara-C, Prednisone [*Antineoplastic drug regimen*]
OAP	Operation Angel Plane (EA)
OAP	Operations and Procedures (IAA)
OAP	Ophthalmic Arterial Pressure [*Medicine*]
OAP	Optical Augmentation Project
OAP	Optically Active Polymer
OAP	Ordinary Alterations Plan [*Navy*] (OAG)
OAP	Organic Ablative Plastic
OAP	Ortho-Aminoacetophenone [*Organic chemistry*]
OAP	Orthogonal Array Processor [*Computer*]
OAP	Osteoarthropathy [*Medicine*] (MAE)
OAP	Outlet Absolute Pressure
OAP	Outline Acquisition Plan [*Army*]
OAP	Overall Average Percentage (DNAB)
OAP	Over Fire Air Port
OAP	Oxygen at Atmospheric Pressure
OAPBC	Office for Advancement of Public Black Colleges [*of the National Association of State Universities and Land Grant Colleges*] (EA)
OAP-BLEO	Oncovin [*Vincristine*] ARA-C [*Cytarabine or cytosine arabinoside*] Prednisone, Bleomycin [*Antineoplastic drug regimen*] (DAVI)
OAPC	Office of Alien Property Custodian [*World War II*]
OAPCA	Organotin Antifouling Paint Control Act of 1988
OAPCB	Old-Age-Pensioner CBer [*Experienced citizens band radio operator*]
OAPEC	Organization of Arab Petroleum Exporting Countries [*See also OPAEP*] [*OPEC Kuwait*] [*Absorbed by*]
OAPEP	Organisation Arabe des Pays Exportateurs de Petrole [*Organization of Arab Petroleum Exporting Countries*]
OAPG	Paghman [*Afghanistan*] [*ICAO location identifier*] (ICLI)
OAPJ	Pan Jao [*Afghanistan*] [*ICAO location identifier*] (ICLI)
OAPM	Optimal Amplitude and Phase Modulation
OAPO	Eastern Pacific Tuna Fishing Organization [*Marine science*] (OSRA)
OAPP	Office of Adolescent Pregnancy Programs [*HEW*]
O App	Ohio Appellate Reports [*A publication*]
O App 2d	Ohio Appellate Reports, Second Series [*A publication*] (DLA)
OAPS	Orbit Adjust Propulsion Subsystem [*NASA*]
OAPU	Overseas Air Preparation Unit [*British military*] (DMA)
OAPWL	Overall Power Watt Level (PDAA)
OAQ	National Climatic Center, Ashville, NC [*OCLC symbol*] (OCLC)
OAQ	Observatorio Astronomico de Quito [*Ecuador*] [*Seismograph station code, US Geological Survey*] (SEIS)
OAQ	Order of Architects of Quebec [*1974, founded 1890 as PQAA*] [*Canada*] (NGC)
OAQD	Qades [*Afghanistan*] [*ICAO location identifier*] (ICLI)
OAQK	Qala-I-Nyazkhan [*Afghanistan*] [*ICAO location identifier*] (ICLI)
OAQM	Kron Monjan [*Afghanistan*] [*ICAO location identifier*] (ICLI)
OAQN	Qala-I-Naw [*Afghanistan*] [*ICAO location identifier*] (ICLI)
OAQPS	Office of Air Quality Planning and Standards [*Environmental Protection Agency*]
OAQQ	Qarqin [*Afghanistan*] [*ICAO location identifier*] (ICLI)
OAQR	Qaisar [*Afghanistan*] [*ICAO location identifier*] (ICLI)
OAQS	Online Associative Query System (NITA)
OAR	Arnprior Public Library, Ontario [*Library symbol National Library of Canada*] (NLC)
OAR	Augustinian Recollect Sisters (TOCD)
OAR	Monterey/Fort Ord, CA [*Location identifier FAA*] (FAAL)
OAR	Offender Aid and Restoration (EA)
OAR	Office of Aerospace Research [*Air Force*]
OAR	Office of AIDS Research [*National Institute of Health*]
OAR	Office of Air and Radiation [*Environmental Protection Agency*] (GFGA)
OAR	Office of Analysis and Review [*Army, Navy*]
OAR	Office of Oceanic and Atmospheric Research [*National Oceanic and Atmospheric Administration*]
OAR	Ohio Appellate Reports [*A publication*] (DLA)
OAR	Ohio Art [*AMEX symbol*] (TTSB)
OAR	[*The*] Ohio Art Co. [*AMEX symbol*] (SPSG)
O-Ar	Ohio State Archives, Columbus, OH [*Library symbol Library of Congress*] (LCLS)
OAR	Ontario Appeal Reports [*A publication*] (DLA)
OAR	Open Architecture Receiver [*Telecommunications*]
OAR	Operand Address Register [*Computer science*] (IAA)
OAR	Operational Address Register [*Computer science*] (IAA)
OAR	Operational Availability and Reliability [*Military*]
OAR	Operations Analysis Report
OAR	Operations and Regulations (IAA)
OAR	Operator Authorization Record [*Computer science*] (IBMDP)
OAR	Optical Angle Readout
OAR	Optical Automatic Ranging
OAR	ORDALT [*Ordnance Alterations*] Accomplishment Requirement (NG)
OAR	Ordering as Required (MHDB)
OAR	Order of the Augustinian Recollects [*Roman Catholic men's religious order*]
oar	Order of the Augustinian Recollects (TOCD)
OAR	Ordnance Allowance Report [*Navy*]
OAR	Ordnance Alteration Reporting
OAR	Ordnance Alteration Requirement (NG)
OAR	Organized Air Reserve
OAR	Original Action Record
OAR	Other Administrative Reasons [*Medicine*] (MAE)
OAR	Over All Rate [*Real estate*] (DICI)
OAR	Overhaul and Repair
OAR	Overtime Authorization Request (MCD)
OAR	Oxford Applied Research [*Software manufacturer*] [*British*]
OARAC	Office of Air Research Automatic Computer
OARB	Azilda Branch, Rayside-Balfour Public Library, Ontario [*Library symbol National Library of Canada*] (NLC)
OARB	Oakland Army Base [*California*] (AABC)
OARBC	Boeing of Canada Ltd., Arnprior, Ontario [*Library symbol National Library of Canada*] (BIB)
OARC	Ordinary Administrative Radio Conference
OARD	Arthur District High School, Arthur, Ontario [*Library symbol National Library of Canada*] (NLC)
OARDC	Ohio Agricultural Research and Development Center [*Ohio State University*] [*Research center*] (RCD)
OARG	Uruzgan [*Afghanistan*] [*ICAO location identifier*] (ICLI)
OARM	Dilaram [*Afghanistan*] [*ICAO location identifier*] (ICLI)
OARM	Middlesex County Public Library, Arva, Ontario [*Library symbol National Library of Canada*] (NLC)
OARM	Office of Administration and Resources Management [*Environmental Protection Agency*] (GFGA)
OARMS	Armstrong Community Library, Ontario [*Library symbol National Library of Canada*] (NLC)
OAR-N	Office of Analysis and Review, Navy (MUGU)
OARnet	[*The*] Ohio Academic Resources Network [*Computer science*] (TNIG)
OARP	Office of Advanced Research Programs [*Later, OART*] [*NASA*]
OARP	Operator Accelerated Retraining Program [*Nuclear energy*] (NRCH)
OARP	Rimpa [*Afghanistan*] [*ICAO location identifier*] (ICLI)
OARS	Ocean Area Reconnaissance Satellite [*Antisubmarine warfare*]
OARS	Ocean Atmosphere Response Studies [*Marine science*] (MSC)
OARS	Ocean Reconnaissance Submarine [*NATO*] (LAIN)
OARS	Office Automation Reporting Service (NITA)
OARS	On-Line Automated Reference Service [*Library science*]
OARS	Opening Automated Report Service [*NYSE*]
OART	Oakland Army Terminal [*California*]
OART	Office of Advanced Research and Technology [*Later, OAST*] [*NASA*]
OAS	O-Acetylserine (thiol)-lyase [*An enzyme*]
OAS	Oasis [*Board on Geographic Names*]
OAS	Oasis Residential [*NYSE symbol*] (SPSG)
OAS	Obstacle Assessment Surface [*Aviation*] (DA)
OAS	Occupational Aspiration Scale [*Education*]
OAS	Occupied Areas Section [*Military government*]
OAS	Offensive Air Support (MCD)
OAS	Offensive Attack System (DOMA)
OAS	Offensive Avionics System
OAS	Office Automation System (NASA)
OAS	Office Automation System
OAS	Office for Advanced Studies (AAG)
OAS	Office of Administrative Systems [*Department of Agriculture*] (GFGA)
OAS	Office of Airline Statistics [*U.S. Department of Transportation*] (BARN)
OAS	Office of Oceanic and Atmospheric Services [*National Oceanic and Atmospheric Administration*] (MSC)
OAS	Office of the Assistant for Study Support [*Air Force*]
OAS	Office of the Assistant Secretary [*Defense*] [*Navy*]
OAS	Ohio Academy of Science (PDAA)
OAS	Old Age and Survivors' Insurance (IAA)
OAS	Old-Age Security
OAS	Olley Air Service Ltd.
OAS	Oman Aviation Services Co. [*ICAO designator*] (FAAC)
OAS	On Active Service
OAS	Open-Hearth Acid Steel
OAS	Operational Announcing System (IAA)
OAS	Optical Alignment Sights [*NASA*]
OAS	Optical Array Spectrometer
OAS	Optical Augmentation System
OAS	Optics and Sensors [*Program*] (MCD)
OAS	Optoacoustic Spectrometry [*Also, PAS*]
OAS	Orbiter Aeroflight Simulator [*NASA*] (NASA)
OAS	Orbiter Atmospheric Simulator [*NASA*] (MCD)
OAS	Orbiter Avionics Simulator [*NASA*] (NASA)
OAS	Orbitor Avionics Simulator [*NASA*]
OAS	Organisation de l'Armee Secrete [*Secret Army Organization*] [*France*] (PD)
OAS	Organizational Accounting Structure (IAA)
OAS	Organization of American States (EA)
OAS	Organization of Arab Students in the USA and Canada (EA)
OAS	Oriental and African Studies
OAS	Origin-of-Assembly Sequence [*Genetics*]
OAS	Orthopedic Appliance Service
OAS	Osmotically Active Substance [*Medicine*] (DMAA)
OAS	Other Active Military Service [*DNAB*]
OAS	Other Approved Studies (ADA)
OAS	Output Amplitude Stability
OAS	Oxygen Activated Sludge (DICI)
OAS²	Officer Accession/Separation System (MCD)
OASAF	Office of Assistant Secretary of Air Force
OASAF	Optical Active Surface Approach Fuze
OASA (FM)	Office of the Assistant Secretary of the Army (Financial Management) (MUGU)
OASA (I & L)	Office of the Assistant Secretary of the Army (Installations and Logistics) (MUGU)

OASAM	Office of the Assistant Secretary for Administration and Management [*Department of Labor*]
OASA(M & RA)	Office of the Assistant Secretary of the Army (Manpower and Reserve Affairs)
OASA (R & D)	Office of the Assistant Secretary of the Army (Research and Development) (MUGU)
OASARDA	Office of the Assistant Secretary of the Army (Research, Development and Aquisition) (RDA)
OASAS	Office of Alcoholism and Substance Abuse Services [*U.S. Department of Health and Human Services*] (BARN)
OASB	Sarobi [*Afghanistan*] [*ICAO location identifier*] (ICLI)
OASBO	Office of Asbestos and Small Business Ombudsman [*Environmental Protection Agency*]
OAsC	Ashland College, Ashland, OH [*Library symbol Library of Congress*] (LCLS)
OASC	Office of Advanced Scientific Computing [*National Science Foundation*]
OASCB	Orbiter Avionics Software Control Board [*NASA*] (NASA)
OASCMIS	Operating and Support Costs Management Information System (MCD)
OASD	Office of the Assistant Secretary of Defense
OASD	Shindand [*Afghanistan*] [*ICAO location identifier*] (ICLI)
OASD(AE)	Office of the Assistant Secretary of Defense (Applications Engineer) (MCD)
OASD-C	Office of the Assistant Secretary of Defense - Comptroller
OASDG	Alexandria Branch, Stormount, Dundas, and Glengarry County Public Library, Ontario [*Library symbol National Library of Canada*] (NLC)
OASD(HA)	Office of the Assisant Secretary of Defense (Health Affairs) (DNAB)
OASDHI	Old-Age, Survivors, Disability, and Health Insurance [*Program*] [*Social Security Administration*]
OASDI	Old-Age, Survivors, and Disability Insurance [*Program*] [*Social Security Administration*]
OASD/IL	Office of the Assistant Secretary of Defense/Installations and Logistics (MCD)
OASD/ISA	Office of the Assistant Secretary of Defense/International Security Affairs (CINC)
OASD/ISP	Office of the Assistant Secretary of Defense for International Security Policy (SDI)
OASD(MRA)	Office of the Assistant Secretary of Defense (Manpower and Reserve Affairs)
OASD (MRA & L)	Office of Assistant Secretary of Defense (Manpower-Reserve Affairs and Logistics) (MCD)
OASD(PA)	Office of the Assistant Secretary of Defense (Public Affairs) (NTCM)
OASD(R & D)	Office of the Assistant Secretary of Defense (Research and Development) (MCD)
OASD(SA)	Office of the Assistant Secretary of Defense (Systems Analysis) (CINC)
OASD(S & L)	Office of the Assistant Secretary of Defense (Supply and Logistics) [*Obsolete*] (MCD)
OASD(T)	Office of the Assistant Secretary of Defense (Telecommunications)
OAS/EOM	Organization of American States Electoral Observation Mission
OASES	Open Access Satellite Education Services (EDAC)
OASES	Organization for American-Soviet Exchanges (EA)
OASET	Office of the Assistant Secretary for Employment and Training [*Department of Labor*]
OASF	Orbiting Astronomical Support Facility (MCD)
OASFP	Old Alliance Society of French Polishers [*A union*] [*British*]
OASG	Office Automation Specialist Group (NITA)
OASG	Sheberghan [*Afghanistan*] [*ICAO location identifier*] (ICLI)
OASH	Obstructive Asymmetrical Septal Hypertrophy [*Medicine*] (CPH)
OASH	Office of the Assistant Secretary for Health [*Department of Health and Human Services*]
OASHA	Operating and Support Hazard Analysis (MCD)
OASHDI	Old Age Survivors Health and Disability Program [*Health insurance*] (GHCT)
OAsht	Ashtabula County District Library, Ashtabula, OH [*Library symbol Library of Congress*] (LCLS)
OAshtK	Kent State University, Ashtabula Regional Campus, Ashtabula, OH [*Library symbol Library of Congress*] (LCLS)
OASI	Office Automation Society International (EA)
OASI	Old-Age and Survivors Insurance [*Program*] [*Social Security Administration*]
OASI	Old America Stores [*NASDAQ symbol*] (TTSB)
OASI	Old Americia Stores, Inc. [*NASDAQ symbol*] (SAG)
OASIA	Office of the Assistant Secretary for International Affairs [*Department of the Treasury*]
OASIS	Occupational Aptitude Survey and Interest Schedule
OASIS	Ocean All-Source Information System
OASIS	Oceanic and Atmospheric Scientific Information System [*National Oceanic and Atmospheric Administration*] (MCD)
OASIS	Office Administration Simulation Study
OASIS	Onboard at Site Invoicing System [*IBM Computer Program*]
OASIS	Online Administrative Information System [*Computer science*] (IAA)
OASIS	Online Automotive Service Information System [*Ford Motor Co.*]
OASIS	Operational Analysis and System Interface System
OASIS	Operational and Supportability Implementation System [*FAA*] (TAG)
OASIS	Operational Applications of Special Intelligence System (MCD)
OASIS	Operational Automatic Scheduling Information System (MUGU)
OASIS	Operation Analysis Strategic Interaction Simulator [*Nuclear war games*]
OASIS	Optimized Air-to-Surface Infrared Seeker
OASIS	Order, Accounting, Stock, Invoicing and Statistics (MHDB)
OASIS	Order and Schedules Input System (MCD)
OASIS	Organization for Applied Science in Society
OASIS	Organized Adoption Search Information Services (EA)
OASIS	Outlook and Situation Information System [*Department of Agriculture*] [*Defunct*] (IID)
OASIS	Outpatient Appointment Scheduling and Information System
OASIS	Over-the-Horizon Airborne Sensor Information System [*Navy*] (DOMA)
OASIS	Ownership Accountability of Selected Secondary Items Stocked
OASIS-AS	Occupational Aptitude Survey and Interest Schedule - Aptitude Survey [*Vocational guidance test*]
OASIS-IS	Occupational Aptitude Survey and Interest Schedule - Interest Schedule [*Vocational guidance test*]
OasisR	Oasis Residential, Inc. [*Associated Press*] (SAG)
OasisRsd	Oasis Residential, Inc. [*Associated Press*] (SAG)
OASK	Serka [*Afghanistan*] [*ICAO location identifier*] (ICLI)
OASL	Salam [*Afghanistan*] [*ICAO location identifier*] (ICLI)
OASM	Office of Aerospace Medicine [*NASA*] (KSC)
OASM	Ohm-Ampere-Second Meter [*System of units*]
OASM	Samangan [*Afghanistan*] [*ICAO location identifier*] (ICLI)
OASMA	Offensive Air Support Mission Analysis
OASMS	Ordnance Ammunition Surveillance and Maintenance School [*Army*]
OASN	Office of the Assistant Secretary of the Navy
OASN	Sheghnan [*Afghanistan*] [*ICAO location identifier*] (ICLI)
OASN(FM)	Office of the Assistant Secretary of the Navy for Financial Management
OASN(I & L)	Office of the Assistant Secretary of the Navy for Installations and Logistics
OASN(M/RA)	Office of the Assistant Secretary of the Navy (Manpower and Reserve Affairs)
OASN(M/RA/L)	Office of the Assistant Secretary of the Navy (Manpower, Reserve Affairs, and Logistics)
OASN(P & RF)	Office of the Assistant Secretary of the Navy for Personnel and Reserve Force
OASN(R & D)	Office of the Assistant Secretary of the Navy for Research and Development
OAS-OGN	Organization of American States-Observer Group in Nicaragua
OASP	Organic Acid Soluble Phosphorus
OASP	Over-All Sound Pressure (PDAA)
OASP	Sare Pul [*Afghanistan*] [*ICAO location identifier*] (ICLI)
OASPL	Overall Sound Pressure Level
OASPrA	Oasis Residential $2.25'A' Pfd [*NYSE symbol*] (TTSB)
OASR	Office of Aeronautical and Space Research [*Later, OART*] [*NASA*]
OASR	Sabar [*Afghanistan*] [*ICAO location identifier*] (ICLI)
OAss	Old Assyrian (BJA)
OASS	Salang-I-Junubi [*Afghanistan*] [*ICAO location identifier*] (ICLI)
OASSO	Operational Applications of Satellite Snowcover Observations [*NASA*]
OAsT	Ashland Theological Seminary, Ashland, OH [*Library symbol Library of Congress*] (LCLS)
OAST	Office of Aeronautical and Space Technology [*Formerly, OART*] [*NASA*]
OAST	Order and Shipping Time [*Military*] (AFIT)
OAST	Overland Air Superiority Training [*Navy*] (DOMA)
OAST	Shur Tepa [*Afghanistan*] [*ICAO location identifier*] (ICLI)
OASTP	Office of the Assistant Secretary for Technology Policy [*U.S. Department of Commerce*] (BARN)
OASU	Oceanographic Air Survey Unit
OASV	Orbital Assembly Support Vehicle
OASW	Office of the Assistant Secretary of War [*World War II*]
OASYS	Obstacle Avoidance System [*Army*] (RDA)
OASYS	Office Automation System
OASYS	Order Allocation System
OAT	Atikokan Public Library, Ontario [*Library symbol National Library of Canada*] (NLC)
OAT	Ocean Acoustic Tomography
OAT	Office for Advanced Technology [*Air Force*]
OAT	On-Air Test [*Telecommunications*] (DOAD)
OAT	One at a Time
OAT	Open-Air Theater
OAT	Operating Ambient Temperature
OAT	Operational Acceptance Test
OAT	Operational Air Traffic (NATG)
OAT	Optical Adaptive Technique
OAT	Optometry Admissions Test (GAGS)
OAT	Ornithineaminotransferase [*An enzyme*]
OAT	Outer Atmospheric Temperature (IAA)
OAT	Outside Air Temperature [*Aviation*]
OAT	Overall Test
OAT	Oxide-Aligned Transistor [*Electronics*] (PDAA)
OAT	Quaker Oats [*NYSE symbol*] (TTSB)
OAT	Quaker Oats Co. [*NYSE symbol Toronto Stock Exchange symbol*] (SPSG)
OAT	Sogervair/Transoceanic Aviation [*France ICAO designator*] (FAAC)
OATA	Optical Acquisition and Tracking Aid Assembly
OATC	Oceanic Air Traffic Center
OATC	Overseas Air Traffic Control
OATD	Toorghondi [*Afghanistan*] [*ICAO location identifier*] (ICLI)
OATG	Tashkurghan [*Afghanistan*] [*ICAO location identifier*] (ICLI)
OATH	Atikokan High School, Ontario [*Library symbol National Library of Canada*] (NLC)
OATHS	One-in-a-Thousand Society (EA)
OATK	Kotal [*Afghanistan*] [*ICAO location identifier*] (ICLI)
OATM	Atikokan Centennial Museum, Ontario [*Library symbol National Library of Canada*] (BIB)
OATM	Orbiter Antenna Test Model [*NASA*]
OATMEAL	Optimum Allocation of Test and Equipment Manpower Against Logistics

OATN	Tereen [*Afghanistan*] [*ICAO location identifier*] (ICLI)
OATP	On-Aircraft Test Procedure (MCD)
OATP	Operational Acceptance Test Procedure (NRCH)
OATQ	Taluqan [*Afghanistan*] [*ICAO location identifier*] (ICLI)
OATS	Office of Air Transportation Security [*FAA*]
OATS	On-Board Acoustic Tracking System [*Navy*] (CAAL)
OATS	Open Architecture Test System (MCD)
OATS	Optical Attitude Transfer System (SSD)
OATS	Optimum Aerial Target Sensor
OATS	Orbit and Attitude Tracking (GAVI)
OATS	Original Article Tear Sheets
OATS	Original Article Tearsheet Service (NITA)
OATS	Original Article Text Service
OATS	Outdoor Advertising Total System (PDAA)
OATS	Overall Test Set
OATS	Over Armor Technology Synthesis (RDA)
OATS	Wild Oats Markets, Inc. [*NASDAQ symbol*] (SAG)
OATUU	Organisation of African Trade Union Unity [*Formerly, AATUF, ATUC*] [*See also OUSA Accra, Ghana*] (EAIO)
OATW	Tewara [*Afghanistan*] [*ICAO location identifier*] (ICLI)
OATZ	Tesak [*Afghanistan*] [*ICAO location identifier*] (ICLI)
OAU	Aurora Public Library, Ontario [*Library symbol National Library of Canada*] (NLC)
OAU	Ohio University, Athens, OH [*Library symbol Library of Congress*] (LCLS)
OAU	Operator Assistance Unit (NITA)
OAU	Optical Alignment Unit
OAU	Organization for African Unity (NADA)
OAU	Organization of African Unity
OAU	Original Sixteen To One Mine [*PC, exchange symbol*] (TTSB)
OAU	Oriol Avia [*Russian Federation*] [*ICAO designator*] (FAAC)
OAUH	Aurora Historical Society, Ontario [*Library symbol National Library of Canada*] (NLC)
OAUHS	PRECIS Project, Aurora High School, Ontario [*Library symbol National Library of Canada*] (NLC)
OAULC	OAU [*Organization of African Unity*] Liberation Committee [*Addis Ababa, Ethiopia*] (EAIO)
OAUM	Aurora Museum, Ontario [*Library symbol National Library of Canada*] (BIB)
OAUS	Sterling Drug Ltd., Aurora, Ontario [*Library symbol National Library of Canada*] (BIB)
OAU/STRC	Organization of African Unity Scientific and Technical Research Commission [*Marine science*] (MSC)
OAUYCE	York County Board of Education, Aurora, Ontario [*Library symbol National Library of Canada*] (NLC)
OAUZ	Kunduz [*Afghanistan*] [*ICAO location identifier*] (ICLI)
O-A-V	Object-Attribute-Value
OAV	Oculoauriculovertebral Dysplasia [*Medicine*] (MAE)
OAV	Omni-Aviacao e Tecnologia Lda. [*Portugal ICAO designator*] (FAAC)
OAV	Operational Aerospace Vehicle
OAVC of SA	Office of the Assistant Vice Chief of Staff, Army [*Later, OAVCSA*] (AABC)
OAVCSA	Office of the Assistant Vice Chief of Staff, Army [*Formerly, OAVC of SA*] (AABC)
OAVD	Oculoauriculovertebral Dysplasia [*Medicine*] (MEDA)
OAVE	Occupational, Adult, and Vocational Education (OICC)
OAvG	B. F. Goodrich Chemical Co. [*of B. F. Goodrich Co.*], Development Center Library, Avon Lake, OH [*Library symbol Library of Congress*] (LCLS)
OAVP	Older Americans Volunteer Program [*ACTION*]
OAVSDG	Avonmore Branch, Stormont, Dundas, and Glengarry County Public Library, Ontario [*Library symbol National Library of Canada*] (BIB)
OAVTME	Office of Adult, Vocational, Technical, and Manpower Education [*Office of Education*]
OAW	Old Abandoned Well (WDAA)
OAW	Overall Width
OAW	Oxyacetylene Welding
OAWCS	Overseas Air Weapons Control System
OAWM	Office of Air and Water Measurement [*National Institute of Standards and Technology*]
OAWOP	Ontario Police College, Aylmer West, Ontario [*Library symbol National Library of Canada*] (NLC)
OAWP	Office of Air and Water Programs (OICC)
OAWP	Operations Analysis Working Paper [*NASA*] (KSC)
OAWR	Office of Agricultural War Relations [*World War II*]
OAWR	Office of Atmospheric Water Resources [*Bureau of Reclamation*]
OAWRMR	Other Acquisition War Reserve Material Requirements (MCD)
OAWU	Wurtach [*Afghanistan*] [*ICAO location identifier*] (ICLI)
OAWZ	Wazirabad [*Afghanistan*] [*ICAO location identifier*] (ICLI)
OAX	Oaxaca [*Mexico*] [*Seismograph station code, US Geological Survey*] (SEIS)
OAX	Oaxaca [*Mexico*] [*Airport symbol*] (OAG)
OAX	Operational Aviation Services - Australia [*ICAO designator*] (FAAC)
OAY	Moses Point, AK [*Location identifier FAA*] (FAAL)
OAY	NOAA [*National Oceanic and Atmospheric Administration*] Geophysical Fluid Dynamics Laboratory, Princeton, NJ [*OCLC symbol*] (OCLC)
OAYM	Aylmer District Museum, Ontario [*Library symbol National Library of Canada*] (BIB)
OAYQ	Yangi Qala [*Afghanistan*] [*ICAO location identifier*] (ICLI)
OAYR	Outstanding Airman of the Year Ribbon [*Military decoration*] (AFM)
OAZB	Zebak [*Afghanistan*] [*ICAO location identifier*] (ICLI)
OAZG	Zaranj [*Afghanistan*] [*ICAO location identifier*] (ICLI)

OB	Brockville Public Library, Ontario [*Library symbol National Library of Canada*] (NLC)
OB	Brought Over (ROG)
Ob	Obadiah [*Old Testament book*]
OB	Oberlerchner [*Joseph Oberlerchner Holzindustrie*] [*Austria ICAO aircraft manufacturer identifier*] (ICAO)
ob	Obese
OB	Obeum [*Nickname for toilets at Cambridge University*] [*Slang British*] (DSUE)
OB	Obidiah [*Old Testament*]
OB	Obiit [*He, or She, Died*] [*Latin*]
ob	Obiter [*Incidentally*] [*Latin*] (GPO)
OB	Obituary Notice (DSUE)
OB	Objection (ROG)
OB	Objective [*Microscopy*]
OB	Objective Benefit (MAE)
OB	Obligation (ROG)
OB	Obligation Bond
OB	Obliteration
OB	Oblong
ob	Oblong [*Bookbinding*] (WDMC)
OB	Oboe
OB	Obolus [*Coin*] [*Latin*] (ADA)
OB	O'Brien Energy & Resources Ltd. [*Toronto Stock Exchange symbol*]
OB	Obscure (KSC)
OB	Observation (WGA)
OB	Observed Bearing [*Navigation*]
OB	Obsolete (AABC)
OB	Obstetrician
OB	Obstetrics [*Medicine*]
OB	Obtuse Bisectrix [*Crystallography*]
OB	Occult Bleeding [*Medicine*]
OB +	Occult Blood Positive [*Medicine*] (DAVI)
OB	Occupational Behavior
OB	Ocean Bottom
OB	Octal-to-Binary [*Computer science*] (BUR)
OB	Octave Band
O-B	Oerlikon-Buehrle [*Switzerland*]
OB	Off-Broadway (WGA)
OB	Offensive Back [*Football*]
OB	Official Board of Ballroom Dancing [*British*] (BI)
OB	Official Bulletin. International Commission for Air Navigation [*A publication*] (DLA)
OB	Oil Bearing (DCTA)
OB	Oil Bomb
OB	Old Babylonian (BJA)
OB	[*The*] Old Bailey [*London court*]
OB	Old Bonded [*Whiskey*] (ROG)
OB	Old Boy [*Communications operators' colloquialism*]
OB	Old Buildings [*British Admiralty*]
OB	Oligoclonal Band [*Analytical biochemistry*]
OB	Ombudsman for Business [*Department of Commerce*]
OB	On Being: the Servant's Servant [*A publication*] (APTA)
OB	On Board
O/B	On Board
OB	On Board
OB	Opal Air [*ICAO designator*] (AD)
OB	Opening of Books
OB	Operating Base [*Navy*]
OB	Operating Budget (AFM)
OB	Operational Base [*Navy*]
O/B	Operational Base
OB	Operation Brotherhood
OB	Optometrists' Board [*Australian Capital Territory*]
OB	Or Better [*Business term*]
OB	Ordered Back
OB	Order of Battle [*Military*]
OB	Order of Burma [*British military*] (DMA)
OB	Order of the Bath
OB	Ordnance Battalion [*Navy*]
OB	Ordnance Board [*Navy*]
OB	Oregon Ballet
OB	Orgelbuechlein [*Little Organ Book*] [*Bach Music*]
OB	Orientalische Bibliographie [*A publication*] (BJA)
OB	Ortsbatterie [*Local Battery*] [*German military - World War II*]
OB	Outboard
OB	Out Board
OB	Outbound (WDAA)
OB	Out-of-Business (OICC)
OB	Output Buffer [*Computer science*]
OB	Output Bus [*Computer science*]
OB	Outside Broadcast (EY)
OB	Outside Bugs [*Nonresident staff at a school*] [*British*] (DSUE)
OB	Outward Bound (EA)
OB	Over Bath [*Classified advertising*] (ADA)
OB	Overboard (AAG)
OB	Overseas Brats [*Commercial firm*] (EA)
OB	Overseas Broadcast [*or Broadcasting*] (IAA)
OB	Owena Bank [*Nigeria*]
OB	Own Brand (MHDB)
OB	Oxford Biographies [*A publication*]
OB	Peru [*International civil aircraft marking*] (ODBW)
OBA	Barrie Public Library, Ontario [*Library symbol National Library of Canada*] (NLC)

OBA .... Oasis Bungera [Antarctica] [Seismograph station code, US Geological Survey Closed] (SEIS)

OBA .... Oberhasli Breeders of America (EA)

OBA .... Object Behavior Analysis [Computer science]

OBA .... Octave Band Analyzer

OBA .... Off Boresight Angle (MCD)

OBA .... Office of Business Administration [Later, Office of Administration] [NASA]

OBA .... Office of Business Affairs [Northern Territory, Australia]

OBA .... Office of Business Analysis [Information service or system] (IID)

OBA .... Open Broadcasting Authority [Noncommercial TV channel] [British]

OBA .... Operating Budget Authority (MCD)

OBA .... Optical Base Assembly (KSC)

OBA .... Optical Brightening Agents

OBA .... Ornithyl-Beta-Alanine [Biochemistry]

OBA .... Outward Bound Australia

OBA .... Over Burner Air

OBA .... Oxygen Breathing Apparatus

OBAALA ...... Organisation for Black Arts Advancement and Learning Activities [British]

Obad .... Obadiah [Old Testament book]

OBAD .... Object Average Optical Density [Microscopy]

OBAD .... Operating Budget Authority Document [Military] (AFIT)

OBADRS ...... Octave Band Automatic Data Reduction System

OBAG .... Georgian Bay Regional Library, Barrie, Ontario [Library symbol National Library of Canada] (NLC)

OBAGC .... Georgian College of Applied Arts and Technology, Barrie, Ontario [Library symbol National Library of Canada] (NLC)

OBAL .... Balmertown Public Library, Ontario [Library symbol National Library of Canada] (NLC)

OBAN .... Bancroft Public Library, Ontario [Library symbol National Library of Canada] (NLC)

OBAN .... Operating Budget Account Number [Air Force]

OB & F .... Ollivier, Bell, and Fitzgerald's Court of Appeal Reports [1878-80] [New Zealand] [A publication] (DLA)

OB & F (CA)... Ollivier, Bell, and Fitzgerald's Court of Appeal Reports [1878-80] [New Zealand] [A publication] (DLA)

OB & FNZ .... Ollivier, Bell, and Fitzgerald's New Zealand Reports [A publication] (DLA)

OB & F (SC)... Ollivier, Bell, and Fitzgerald's Supreme Court Reports [New Zealand] [A publication] (DLA)

OB & PA ...... Office of Budget and Program Analysis [Department of Agriculture] (GFGA)

OBANU .... United Public Library, Carlow, Dungannon, and Mayo Townships, Bancroft, Ontario [Library symbol National Library of Canada] (BIB)

OBAP .... Organization of Black Airline Pilots (EA)

OBAR .... Ohio Bar (NITA)

OBarb .... Barberton Public Library, Barberton, OH [Library symbol Library of Congress] (LCLS)

OBarn .... Barnesville Public Library, Barnesville, OH [Library symbol Library of Congress] (LCLS)

OBAS .... Organ Builders' Amalgamated Society [A union] [British]

OBAS .... Simcoe County Co-Op, Barrie, Ontario [Library symbol National Library of Canada] (NLC)

OBAT .... Augusta Township Public Library, Brockville, Ontario [Library symbol National Library of Canada] (NLC)

OBat............ Clermont County Public Library, Batavia, OH [Library symbol Library of Congress] (LCLS)

OBatC .... Clermont General and Technical College, Batavia, OH [Library symbol Library of Congress] (LCLS)

OBatH .... Clermont Mercy Hospital, Batavia, OH [Library symbol Library of Congress] (LCLS)

OBAWS .... On-Board Aircraft Weighing System (MCD)

OBB .... Barry's Bay Public Library, Ontario [Library symbol National Library of Canada] (NLC)

OBB .... Obbligato [Essential] [Music]

OBB .... Obsidian Butte [California] [Seismograph station code, US Geological Survey] (SEIS)

OBB .... Oesterreichische Bundesbahnen [Austrian Federal Railways]

OBB .... Old Battleship [Navy]

OBB .... Operation Better Block

OBB .... Oxybisbenzene [Organic chemistry]

OBBB .... Bahrain [Bahrain] [ICAO location identifier] (ICLI)

OBBD .... Official Board of Ballroom Dancing [British]

OBBFC .... Official Betty Boop Fan Club (EA)

OBBI .... Bahrain/International [Bahrain] [ICAO location identifier] (ICLI)

Obbl .... Obbligato [Essential] [Music]

OBBM .... Brant County Historical Museum, Brantford, Ontario [Library symbol National Library of Canada] (NLC)

Obbmo......... Obbligatissimo [Your Obedient Servant] [Italian]

OBBMV .... Madawaska Valley District High School, Barry's Bay, Ontario [Library symbol National Library of Canada] (NLC)

OBBO .... Observation Balloon

OBC .... Barwick Community Library, Ontario [Library symbol National Library of Canada] (BIB)

OBC .... Obock [Djibouti] [Airport symbol] (OAG)

OBC .... Oceania Basketball Confederation [Australia] (EA)

OBC .... Off Boresight Correction [Military] (CAAL)

OBC .... Officer Basic Course [Military]

OBC .... Ohio Bell Communications, Inc. [Cleveland] [Telecommunications] (TSSD)

OBC .... Old Boys' Corps [Military British]

OBC .... On-Board Checkout [Aircraft]

OBC .... On-Board Computer (MCD)

OBC .... On-Board Controller [Telecommunications]

OBC .... One Big Computer [Proposed model for automation of the New York and American stock exchanges]

OBC .... Optical Bar Camera [NASA] (LAIN)

OBC .... Order of British Columbia [Canada] (DD)

OBC .... Ouachita Baptist College [Arkadelphia, AR] [Later, OBU]

OBC .... Outboard Boating Club of America [Defunct] (EA)

OBC .... Outside Back Cover [Publishing] (WDMC)

OBC .... Overseas Bankers' Club [British]

OBC .... Overseas Book Centre

OBC .... Oxide-Coated Brush Cathode

OBCA .... Office of Bank Customer Affairs [FDIC]

OBCAB .... Albion-Bolton Branch, Town of Caledon Public Libraries, Bolton, Ontario [Library symbol National Library of Canada] (NLC)

OBCCL .... Canada Cement Lafarge Ltd., Belleville, Ontario [Library symbol National Library of Canada] (NLC)

OBCE .... On-Board Checkout Equipment (MCD)

OBCE .... Operational Baseline Cost Estimate [Army]

OBCGEH...... Housewares and Home Entertainment Department, Canada General Electric Co. Ltd., Barrie, Ontario [Library symbol National Library of Canada] (NLC)

OBCH .... Overseas Booksellers' Clearing House (DGA)

OBCI .... Ocean Bio-Chem [NASDAQ symbol] (TTSB)

OBCI .... Ocean Bio-Chem, Inc. [NASDAQ symbol] (NQ)

OBCI .... On-Board Controller Interface [Telecommunications]

OBCO .... On-Board Checkout [NASA] (KSC)

OB/CP .... Observation/Command Post (DNAB)

OBCP .... Ortho-Benzyl-para-chlorophenol [Disinfectant]

OBCR .... Optical Bar Code Reader (NITA)

OBCS .... Chromatographic Specialties Ltd., Brockville, Ontario [Library symbol National Library of Canada] (NLC)

OBCS .... On-Board Checkout Subsystem [NASA] (NASA)

OBCS .... On-Board Checkout [Instrumentation] System

Obd............. Obadiah [Old Testament book] (BJA)

OBD .... Office of Business Development [Economic Development Administration]

o/bd .... Oil on Board (VRA)

OBD .... Omnibearing Distance

OBD .... On-Board Diagnostics [Chrysler Corp.'s computer system]

OBD .... Open Blade Damper (OA)

OBD .... Operational Base Development (AAG)

OBD .... Operation Buckle Down [NHTSA] (TAG)

OBD .... Optical Beam Deflection

OBD .... Organic Brain Disease

OBD .... Organization for Black Designers

OBDB .... On-Board Data Bank (DNAB)

OBDD .... Ordered Bicontinuous Double Diamond [Phase structure]

OBDE .... Dollman Electronics Canada Ltd., Brampton, Ontario [Library symbol National Library of Canada] (NLC)

OBDII .... On-oard Diagnostics-Second Generation

OB DK......... Observation Deck (WDAA)

OBDO .... Oceanographic, Boarding, and Diving Officer [Navy British]

OBDT .... Obedient

OBDV .... Oat Blue Dwarf Virus [Plant pathology]

OBE............. Belleville Public Library, Ontario [Library symbol National Library of Canada] (NLC)

OBE............. Oberlin College, Oberlin, OH [OCLC symbol] (OCLC)

OBE............. Office of Biological Education (DAVI)

OBE............. Office of Business Economics [Later, Office of Economic Analysis] [Department of Commerce]

OBE............. Officer of the Order of the British Empire (NGC)

OBE............. Okeechobee, FL [Location identifier FAA] (FAAL)

OBE............. On-Board Equipment

OBE............. One-Boson Exchange [Physics] (OA)

OBE............. Operating Basis Earthquake [Nuclear reactor] (NRCH)

OBE............. Operating Basis Event (IEEE)

OBE............. Order of the British Empire [Facetious translations: Old Boiled Egg, Other Buggers' Efforts]

OBE............. Ottawa Board of Education, Library Services Centre [UTLAS symbol]

OBE............. Outcome-Based Education [School reform]

OBE............. Outerback End

OBE............. Out-of-Body Experience [Parapsychology]

OBE............. Overcome [or Overtaken] by Events

OBEA .... Oregon Business Education Association (EDAC)

OBEAB .... Beaverton Branch, Brock Township Public Library, Ontario [Library symbol National Library of Canada] (BIB)

OBEAR .... Beardmore Public Library, Ontario [Library symbol National Library of Canada] (NLC)

OBEATE....... Beaverton-Thorah Eldon Historical Society, Inc., Ontario [Library symbol National Library of Canada] (NLC)

OBECO .... Outboard Engine Cutoff [NASA] (KSC)

OBED .... Beamsville District Secondary School, Ontario [Library symbol National Library of Canada] (NLC)

OBed........... Bedford Public Library, Bedford, OH [Library symbol Library of Congress] (LCLS)

OBedF......... Ferro Corp., Chemical Library, Bedford, OH [Library symbol Library of Congress] (LCLS)

OBEDS .... Deloro Stellite Co., Belleville, Ontario [Library symbol National Library of Canada] (BIB)

OBEE........... Beeton Public Library, Ontario [Library symbol National Library of Canada] (BIB)

OBEGOSC .... Organizational Effectiveness General Officer Steering Committee (MCD)

OBEH .... Hastings County Historical Society, Belleville, Ontario [Library symbol National Library of Canada] (BIB)

OBEHP......... Hastings and Prince Edward County Health Unit, Belleville, Ontario [*Library symbol National Library of Canada*] (BIB)

OBEL........... Loyalist College of Applied Arts and Technology, Belleville, Ontario [*Library symbol National Library of Canada*] (NLC)

OBELF.......... Fleming Branch, Lincoln Public Library, Beamsville, Ontario [*Library symbol National Library of Canada*] (BIB)

OBEM.......... Beachville Ye Olde Museum, Ontario [*Library symbol National Library of Canada*] (BIB)

OBEM.......... One-Boson Exchange Model

OBEM.......... Operational Battery Effectiveness Model (MCD)

OBEMLA ..... Office of Bilingual Education and Minority Language Affairs [*Department of Education*] (GFGA)

O Ben .... Old Benloe's Reports, English Common Pleas [*1486-1580*] [*A publication*] (DLA)

O Benl .... Old Benloe's Reports, English Common Pleas [*1486-1580*] [*A publication*] (DLA)

OBEP .... One-Boson Exchange Potential

OBEr........... OB [*Out-of-the-Body*] Experient [*Parapsychology*]

OBerB .... Baldwin-Wallace College, Berea, OH [*Library symbol Library of Congress*] (LCLS)

OBERS........ Office of Business Economics Research Service (NRCH)

OBERST...... Oberstimme [*Upper Part*] [*Music*]

OBERW....... Oberwerk [*Upper Work*] [*Music*]

OBES .... Office of Basic Energy Services [*Department of Energy*]

OBES .... Orthonormal Basis of an Error Space [*Statistics*]

OBESA .... Stephens-Adamson, Belleville, Ontario [*Library symbol National Library of Canada*] (NLC)

OBESG........ Office of Basic Energy Science/Geosciences [*Department of Energy*]

OBESSU...... Organising Bureau of European School Student Unions (EAIO)

OBEWS .... On-Board Electronic Warfare Simulation [*Air Force*]

OBEX .... Object Exchange [*Computer science*] (PCM)

OBF............ Octave Band Filter

OBF............ One-Bar Function (OA)

OBF............ Operational Base Facility

OBF............ Organ Blood Flow [*Physiology*]

OBF............ Ottawa Board of Education, Library Services Centre (Films) [*UTLAS symbol*]

OBF............ Output Buffer Full [*Computer science*] (IAA)

OBFAR .... Burks Falls, Armour, and Ryerson Union Library, Burks Falls, Ontario [*Library symbol National Library of Canada*] (NLC)

OBFC .... Barriefield Branch, Frontenac County Library, Ontario [*Library symbol National Library of Canada*] (BIB)

OBFC .... O'Leary Brothers Fan Club (EA)

OBFM .... On or Before Full Moon [*Freemasonry*] (ROG)

OBFNO........ Northern Ontario Public School Principals' Association, Burks Falls, Ontario [*Library symbol National Library of Canada*] (NLC)

OBFS .... Octave Band Filter Set

OBFS .... Offshore Bulk Fuel System

OBFS .... Organization of Biological Field Stations (EA)

OBFS .... Overseas Base Facilities Summary [*Navy*]

Ob G .... Obergericht [*Court of Appeal*] [*German*] (DLA)

OBG .... Oberg Industries Ltd. [*Vancouver Stock Exchange symbol*]

OBG .... Obigarm [*Former USSR Seismograph station code, US Geological Survey Closed*] (SEIS)

OBG .... Obstetrics-Gynecology [*Medicine*]

OBG .... Oldie but Goodie [*Music*]

OBgCE .... Conneaut Elementary School, Bowling Green, OH [*Library symbol*] [*Library of Congress*] (LCLS)

OBgCrE .... Crim Elementary School, Bowling Green, OH [*Library symbol*] [*Library of Congress*] (LCLS)

OBgJH .... Bowling Green Junior High School, Bowling Green, OH [*Library symbol*] [*Library of Congress*] (LCLS)

OBgKE .... Kenwood Elementary School, Bowling Green, OH [*Library symbol*] [*Library of Congress*] (LCLS)

OBgRE .... Ridge Elementary School, Bowling Green, OH [*Library symbol*] [*Library of Congress*] (LCLS)

OBGS .... On-Board Gunnery Simulator (PDAA)

OBGS .... Orbital Bombardment Guidance System

OBgSH .... Bowling Green Senior High School, Bowling Green, OH [*Library symbol*] [*Library of Congress*] (LCLS)

OBgSME ...... South Main Elementary School, Bowling Green, OH [*Library symbol*] [*Library of Congress*] (LCLS)

OBGT .... Old Babylonian Grammatical Texts [*A publication*] (BJA)

OBgU .... Bowling Green State University, Bowling Green, OH [*Library symbol Library of Congress*] (LCLS)

OBgU-C....... Bowling Green State University, Center for Archival Collections, Bowling Green, OH [*Library symbol Library of Congress*] (LCLS)

OB-GYN ...... Obstetrician-Gynecologist (PAZ)

OB-GYN ...... Obstetrics-Gynecology [*Medicine*]

OBH .... Office Busy Hour [*Telecommunications*] (TEL)

OBH .... Oil Bath Heater

OBH .... Old Berkeley Hunt [*British*]

OBH .... Old Berkshire Hounds [*British*]

OBH .... Old Highland Blend [*Whisky*] (ROG)

OBH .... Operational Biomedical Harness

OBH .... Wolbach, NE [*Location identifier FAA*] (FAAL)

OBHFC........ Official Bobby Hart Fan Club (EA)

OBHT .... Tecumseh Township Public Library, Bond Head, Ontario [*Library symbol National Library of Canada*] (BIB)

OBI............ Obidos [*Brazil*] [*Airport symbol*] (AD)

OBI............ Obihiro [*Japan*] [*Seismograph station code, US Geological Survey*] (SEIS)

OBI............ Obligated Involuntary Officer [*Military*]

OBI............ Office du Baccalaureat International [*International Baccalaureate Office - IBO*] (EAIO)

OBI............ Office of Basic Instrumentation [*National Bureau of Standards*]

OBI............ Old Babylonian Inscriptions [*A publication*] (BJA)

OBI............ Omnibearing Indicator [*Radio*]

OBI............ Online Book Initiative [*Trademark name*] [*Internet*]

OBI............ Open-Back Inclinable

OBI............ Open-Back Inclinable Press [*Manufacturing term*]

OBI............ Open Buying on the Internet [*Computer science*]

OBI............ Operation Blessing International [*An association*]

OBI............ Order of British India

OBI............ Organisation du Baccalaureat International [*International Baccalaureate Organisation - IBO*] (EAIO)

OBI............ Osaka Bioscience Institute [*Japan*]

O BID.......... Omni Bidus [*Every Two Days*] [*Pharmacy*] (ROG)

OBIE.......... Obie Media Corp. [*NASDAQ symbol*] (SAG)

ObieMed...... Obie Media Corp. [*Associated Press*] (SAG)

OBIFC........ Osmond Boys International Fan Club (EA)

OBIFCO...... On-Board In-Flight Checkout (MCD)

OBIG.......... Oesterreichisches Bundesinstitut fuer Gesundheitswesen [*Austrian National Institute for Public Health*] [*Information service or system*] (IID)

OBIGGS...... On-Board Inert Gas Generator System [*Aviation*] (MCD)

O BIH.......... Omni Bihora [*Every Two Hours*] [*Pharmacy*] (ROG)

OBINXTO..... Obiit in Christo [*Died in Christ*] [*Latin*]

OBIPS......... Optical Band Imager and Photometer System [*Aerospace*]

OBIS.......... Optimum Burn-In Screening

OBIS.......... Outdoor Biology Instructional Strategies [*National Science Foundation project*]

OBIT.......... Obiit [*He, or She, Died*] [*Latin*]

Obit.......... Obiter [*A publication*]

obit.......... Obituary [*Journalism*] [*Also, ob*] (WDMC)

OBIT.......... Obituary Notice (DSUE)

OBIU.......... On-Board Interface Unit (DWSG)

OBIWR........ Whitefish River Band Public Library, Birch Island, Ontario [*Library symbol National Library of Canada*] (NLC)

OBJ............ Intermediate Object Code File [*Computer science*]

OBJ............ Object (AAG)

obj............ Object (VRA)

OBJ............ Objection (WDAA)

OBJ............ Objective

OBJ............ Oklahoma Bar Association. Journal [*A publication*] (DLA)

OBJ............ Operation Buster-Jangle [*Atomic weapons testing*]

OBJ............ Orthodox Black Jews (BJA)

ObjDes........ Object Design, Inc. [*Associated Press*] (SAG)

OBJN.......... Objection

ObjSoft .... ObjectSoft Corp. [*Associated Press*] (SAG)

ObjSys........ Objective Systems Integrators, Inc. [*Associated Press*] (SAG)

OBJV.......... Objective (MSA)

OBK .... Northbrook, IL [*Location identifier FAA*] (FAAL)

OBK .... Organisation pour l'Amenagement et le Developpement du Bassin de la Riviere Kagera [*Organization for the Management and Development of the Kagera River Basin - KBO*] (EAIO)

OBL.......... League of Off-Broadway Theatres and Producers (EA)

OBL.......... Oblast [*Governmental subdivision in USSR corresponding to a province or state*]

OBL.......... Obligation (ADA)

OBL.......... Obligato [*Obbligato*] [*Music*] (ROG)

OBL.......... Oblique (AABC)

OBL.......... Oblong

obl.......... Oblong [*Bookbinding*] (WDMC)

OBL.......... Oceanic Boundary Layer

OBL.......... Office of Business Loans [*Economic Development Administration*]

OBL.......... One Block Look-Ahead [*Computer science*]

OBL.......... Operational Base Launch [*Air Force*]

OBL.......... Order Bill of Lading [*Shipping*]

OBL.......... Outside of the Battery Limits [*Engineering economics*]

OBL.......... Outstanding Balance List [*IRS*]

OBla.......... Blanchester Public Library, Blanchester, OH [*Library symbol Library of Congress*] (LCLS)

OBLAC .... Bath Branch, Lennox and Addington County Public Library, Ontario [*Library symbol National Library of Canada*] (NLC)

OBLACS .... Sandburst Branch, Lennox and Addington County Public Library, Bath, Ontario [*Library symbol National Library of Canada*] (BIB)

OBLAT .... Oblatum [*Cachet*] [*Pharmacy*]

OBLAUTH.... Obligation Authority [*Army*] (AABC)

OBIC .... Bluffton College, Bluffton, OH [*Library symbol Library of Congress*] (LCLS)

OBIC-M .... Bluffton College, Mennonite Historical Library, Bluffton, OH [*Library symbol Library of Congress*] (LCLS)

OBLG .... Obligate (AABC)

OBLH .... Bloomfield-Hallowell Union Library, Bloomfield, Ontario [*Library symbol National Library of Canada*] (BIB)

OBLI.......... Oxford and Bucks Light Infantry [*Military unit*] [*British*]

OBLIGN........ Obligation (ROG)

OBLISERV.... Obligated Services of [*numbers of months indicated*] Required [*Navy*]

OBLISERVNATRA... Obligated to Serve Three and One-Half Years Following Date of Completion of Training within the Naval Air Training Command

OBLISERVONEASIX... Obligated to Serve on Active Duty One Year for Each Six Months Schooling or Fraction Thereof [*Navy*]

OBLISERVTHREETIME... Obligated to Serve on Active Duty a Period Three Times the Length of Period of Education [*Navy*]

OBLISERVTWOYR... Obligated to Serve on Active Duty a Period of Two Years [*Navy*]

OBLN .... Obligation (AFM)

OBLR .... Blind River Public Library, Ontario [*Library symbol National Library of Canada*] (NLC)

OBLu .... Old Babylonian Version of Lu [*A publication*] (BJA)

OBlv .... Bliss Memorial Public Library, Bloomville, OH [*Library symbol Library of Congress*] (LCLS)

OBM .... Aviaobshemash [*Former USSR*] [*FAA designator*] (FAAC)

OBM .... Morobe [*Papua New Guinea*] [*Airport symbol*] (OAG)

OBM .... Oberlin College, Conservatory of Music, Library, Oberlin, OH [*OCLC symbol*] (OCLC)

OBM .... Ocean Biogeochemical Model

OBM .... Optimal Body Mass [*Ecology*]

OBM .... Ordnance Bench Mark (IAA)

OBM .... Oriental Boat Mission [*Later, International Missions*] (EA)

OBM .... Ulan Bator [*Mongolia*] [*Seismograph station code, US Geological Survey Closed*] (SEIS)

OBMA .... Outboard Boat Manufacturers Association [*Later, NMMA*] (EA)

OBMC .... Officers' Basic Military Corps [*Air Force*]

OBMC .... Outbound Midcourse Correction [*NASA*] (KSC)

OBMP .... Bruce Mines and Plummer Additional Union Public Library, Bruce Mines, Ontario [*Library symbol National Library of Canada*] (NLC)

OBMS .... Objectives-Based Management System (ADA)

OBN .... Oban [*Scotland*] [*Airport symbol*] (OAG)

OBN .... Obninsk [*Former USSR Seismograph station code, US Geological Survey*] (SEIS)

OBN .... Occult Blood Negative [*Medicine*] (DAVI)

OBN .... Office Balancing Network [*Telecommunications*] (TEL)

OBN .... Office of Biochemical Nomenclature [*NAS-NRC*]

OBN .... On-Board Navigation

OBN .... Out-of-Band Noise

OBNA .... Only But Not All (NITA)

OBNE .... Department 9911, Northern Telecom Ltd., Belleville, Ontario [*Library symbol National Library of Canada Obsolete*] (NLC)

OBNM .... On or Before New Moon [*Freemasonry*] (ROG)

OBNTC .... Old Boys Network Turtle Club (EA)

OBO .... Obihiro [*Japan*] [*Airport symbol*] (OAG)

OBO .... Obock [*Djibouti*] [*Seismograph station code, US Geological Survey*] (SEIS)

OBO .... Official Business Only (AFM)

OBO .... Oil/Bulk/Ore Carrier [*Multipurpose bulk carrier*] (DS)

OBO .... Or Best Offer [*Classified advertising*]

OBO .... Orbital Bomber (IAA)

OBO .... Order Book Official [*Investment term*]

OBO .... Order by Order

O/B/O .... Ore/Bulk/Oil [*Bulk carrier vessel*]

OBO .... Organization of Bricklin Owners (EA)

OBOA .... Ontario Building Officials Association [*Canada*] (AAGC)

OB/OD .... Open Burning/Open Detonation [*Military*]

OBOE .... Observed Bombing of Enemy

OBOE .... Offensive Burst Operating Environment

OBOE .... Offshore Buoy-Observing Equipment (PDAA)

OBOF .... Old Buffer over Forty [*Elderly recruits*] [*World War I*] [*British*]

OBOG .... On-Board Oxygen-Generation [*For military aviation*]

OBOGS .... On-Board Oxygen Generating System [*Navy*] (CAAL)

OBOLC .... Caledon Public Libraries, Bolton, Ontario [*Library symbol National Library of Canada*] (NLC)

OBOM .... Bowmanville Museum, Ontario [*Library symbol National Library of Canada*] (BIB)

OBON .... Newcastle Public Library Board, Bowmanville, Ontario [*Library symbol National Library of Canada*] (NLC)

OBONF .... Bonfield Public Library, Ontario [*Library symbol National Library of Canada*] (NLC)

OBOS .... Our Bodies Ourselves [*A publication*]

OBP .... Occult Blood Positive [*Medicine*] (DAVI)

OBP .... Occupational Back Pain

OBP .... Odorant-Binding Protein [*Biochemistry*]

OBP .... Oil Breather Pressure

OBP .... On-Base Percentage [*Baseball*]

OBP .... On-Board Processor

OBP .... On-Line Benefits Processing

OBP .... Open Break Position [*Dancing*]

OBP .... Outer (Edge of) Basal Piece

OBP .... Ova, Blood, and Parasites [*Medicine*] (MAE)

obp .... Oxygen at High Pressure (AD)

OBPA .... Outer Banks Protection Act (AAGC)

OBPA .... Oxybisphenoxarsine [*Organic chemistry*]

OB PH .... Oblique Photography (WDAA)

OBPH .... People Helping People, Inc., Brantford, Ontario [*Library symbol National Library of Canada*] (NLC)

OBQ .... Optometrists' Board of Queensland

OBR .... Bradford Public Library, Ontario [*Library symbol National Library of Canada*] (NLC)

OBR .... Office of Budget and Reports

OBR .... One-Button-Recording [*Video technology*]

OBR .... Optical Bar Code

OBR .... Optical Bar Code Reader (MHDB)

OBR .... Optical Bar Recognition [*Commonly known as a bar code*] (WDMC)

OBR .... Outboard Recorder [*Computer science*] (BUR)

OBR .... Owens, B. R., Montebello CA [*STAC*]

OBRA .... Brampton Public Library, Ontario [*Library symbol National Library of Canada*] (NLC)

OBRA .... Office of Business Research and Analysis [*Department of Commerce*]

OBRA .... Omnibus Budget Reconciliation Act [*1987*]

OBRA .... Overseas Broadcasting Representatives Association (IAA)

OBRAC .... Bracebridge Public Library, Ontario [*Library symbol National Library of Canada*] (NLC)

OBRAD .... Oblate Radial (PDAA)

OBRAM .... Chinguacousy Township Public Library, Bramalea, Ontario [*Library symbol National Library of Canada*] (NLC)

OBRAMB .... Bell Northern Research, Bramalea, Ontario [*Library symbol National Library of Canada*] (NLC)

OBRANT .... Northern Telecom, Brampton, Ontario [*Library symbol National Library of Canada*] (NLC)

OBRAPA .... Archives, Region of Peel, Brampton, Ontario [*Library symbol National Library of Canada*] (BIB)

OBRASC .... Brampton Campus, Sheridan College, Brampton, Ontario [*Library symbol National Library of Canada*] (BIB)

OBRC .... Operating Budget Review Committee [*Military*]

OBRER .... Blind River Refinery, Eldorado Resources Ltd., Ontario [*Library symbol National Library of Canada*] (NLC)

OBRET .... Old Breton [*Language, etc.*]

OBrG .... B. F. Goodrich Co., Technical Library, Brecksville, OH [*Library symbol Library of Congress*] (LCLS)

OBRH .... Home Care Program, Brockville, Ontario [*Library symbol National Library of Canada*] (BIB)

OBRI .... Belle River Public Library, Ontario [*Library symbol National Library of Canada*] (NLC)

O Bridg .... Orlando Bridgman's English Common Pleas Reports [*A publication*] (DLA)

O Bridg (Eng)... Orlando Bridgman's English Common Pleas Reports [*A publication*] (DLA)

O Bridgm .... Orlando Bridgman's English Common Pleas Reports [*A publication*] (DLA)

O'Brien .... O'Brien's Upper Canada Reports [*A publication*] (DLA)

OBRIG .... Brighton Public Library, Ontario [*Library symbol National Library of Canada*] (BIB)

O'Bri Lawy... O'Brien's Lawyer's Rule of Holy Life [*A publication*] (DLA)

O'Bri ML .... O'Brien's Military Law [*A publication*] (DLA)

OBRIS .... Smith Township Public Library, Bridgenorth, Ontario [*Library symbol National Library of Canada*] (BIB)

OBRIT .... Britt Area Community Library, Britt, Ontario [*Library symbol National Library of Canada*] (NLC)

OBRIT .... Old British [*Language, etc.*]

OBRM .... W. Ross MacDonald School, Brantford, Ontario [*Library symbol National Library of Canada*] (NLC)

OBRMR .... Mississauga Reserve Library, Blind River, Ontario [*Library symbol National Library of Canada*] (NLC)

OBRNR .... Oil Burner

OBRO .... Oxford-On-Rideau Township Public Library, Burritt's Rapids, Ontario [*Library symbol National Library of Canada*] (BIB)

OBROW .... Ochotnicza Brygada Robotnicza Obrony Warszawy [*A publication*] (BJA)

OBRP .... On-Board Repair Parts [*Navy*]

OBRP .... Pauline Johnson College, Brantford, Ontario [*Library symbol National Library of Canada*] (NLC)

OBRPH .... Library Resources & Information Centre, Brockville Psychiatric Hospital, Ontario [*Library symbol National Library of Canada*] (NLC)

OBRT .... Brantford Public Library, Ontario [*Library symbol National Library of Canada*] (NLC)

OBrV .... United States Veterans Administration Hospital, Brecksville, OH [*Library symbol Library of Congress*] (LCLS)

OBRWI .... [*The*] Woodland Indian Cultural Educational Centre, Brantford, Ontario [*Library symbol National Library of Canada*] (NLC)

OBS .... Aubenas [*France*] [*Airport symbol*] (OAG)

OBS .... Obligations (ROG)

Obs .... Obscene [*Legal term*]

obs .... Obscura (VRA)

OBS .... Obscurant

OBS .... Obscure (ADA)

OBS .... Observation (ROG)

OBS .... Observatory

OBS .... Observe

OBS .... Observe

Obs .... Observer (London) [*A publication*] (BRI)

OBS .... Obsolete (AAG)

OBS .... Obstacle (AABC)

Obs .... Obstacle Light [*Aviation*] (DA)

OBS .... Obstetrical Service [*Medicine*] (MAE)

OBS .... Obstetrics [*Medicine*]

OBS .... Obstruction (WGA)

OBS .... Ocean Bottom Seismometer [*California*] [*Seismograph station code, US Geological Survey Closed*] (SEIS)

OBS .... Ocean Bottom Station

OBS .... Office of Biological Service [*Marine science*] (MSC)

OBS .... Office of Boating Safety [*Coast Guard*]

OBS .... Official Bulletin Station [*Amateur radio*]

OBS .... Old Babylonian Sumerian (BJA)

OBS .... Old Bailey's Sessions Papers [*A publication*] (DLA)

OBS .... Omnibearing Selector [*Radio*]

OBS .... On-Board Spares [*Army*]

OBS .... On-Board System [*Navy*] (CAAL)

OBS .... Online BookStore [*Commercial firm*]

OBS .... On-Line Business Systems, Inc. [*Information service or system*] (IID)

OBS .... Open-Back Stationary Press [*Manufacturing term*]

OBS .... Open-Hearth Basic Steel

OBS .... Opera Ballet School (DICI)

OBS .... Operand Buffering System [*Computer science*] (IAA)

OBS .... Operational Bioinstrumentation System [*NASA*]

OBS .... Operational Biomedical Sensors (NASA)
OBS .... Operational Biomedical Systems (KSC)
OBS .... Optical Beam Scanner
OBS .... Optical Beam Steering
OBS .... Orange Badge Scheme [*Disabled parking permit*] [*British*]
OBS .... Orbital Bombardment System
OBS .... Organic Brain Syndrome [*Psychiatry*]
OBS .... Organization Breakdown Structure [*Computer science*] (PCM)
OBS .... Organized Behavioral System (WDMC)
OBS .... Oriental and Biblical Studies [*A publication*] (BJA)
OBS .... OSIS [*Ocean Surveillance Information System*] Baseline System [*Navy*]
OBS .... Ottawa Board of Education, Library Services Centre (Software) [*UTLAS symbol*]
OBS .... Oxford Bibliographical Society (DGA)
OBS .... Sidney Township Public Library, Batawa, Ontario [*Library symbol National Library of Canada*] (BIB)
OBSC .... Obscure
OBSC .... Obscured Light [*Navigation signal*]
OBSCIS .... Offender Based State Corrections Information System (OICC)
OBSD .... Object Sum Optical Density [*Microscopy*]
OBSD .... Observed
OBSD .... Optical Beam Steering Device
OBSERV .... Observatory
OBSH .... Object Shape [*Microscopy*]
OBSH .... Oxybis(benzenesulfonylhydrazine) [*Organic chemistry*]
OBSHT .... Obstacle Height
OBSL .... St. Lawrence College [*College Saint-Laurent*], Brockville, Ontario [*Library symbol National Library of Canada*] (NLC)
Obs Lt.......... Observer Lieutenant [*British military*] (DMA)
OBSN .... Observation (AAG)
OBSNFL .... Observation Flight (IAA)
OBSOL .... Obsolescent
Obsoles .... Obsolescent
OBSP .... Obiit sine Prole [*Died without Issue*] [*Latin*]
OBSP .... Old Bailey's Sessions Papers [*Legal term British*]
OBSPL .... Octave Band Sound Pressure Level
OBSPM .... Obiit sine Prole Masculus [*He, or She, Died without Male Issue*] [*Latin*]
OBSR .... Observation
OBSRON ...... Observation Squadron
OBSRVTRY.... Observatory
OBSS .... Ocean Bottom Scanning SONAR
Obs Spot...... Observation Spot [*Control point*] [*Nautical charts*]
OBST .... Obstacle (AFM)
OBST .... Obstetric
OBST .... Obstetrics [*Medicine*]
OBST .... Obstruction (AFM)
OBSTET .... Obstetrics [*Medicine*]
obstl .... Obstruction Light (AD)
OBSTN .... Obstruction (MSA)
Obstr.......... Obstruction
obstr.......... Obstruction (AD)
OBSTRN ...... Obstetrician [*Medicine*]
OBSUED....... Oberbefehlshaber Suedost [*Headquarters, Commander-in-Chief, South*] [*Southern Germany and several army groups on the Eastern Front*] [*German military - World War II*]
OBSUM .... Order of Battle Summary [*Military*] (MCD)
OBSV .... Observation (IAA)
obsv.......... Observation (AD)
obsv.......... Observatory (AD)
OBSV .... Observatory (IAA)
OBSV .... Observer
obsv.......... Observer (AD)
OBSVE .... Observe (ROG)
OBSY .... Observatory (AABC)
ob syn .... Organic Brain Syndrome [*Medicine*] (AD)
OBSZ .... Object Size [*Microscopy*]
OBT............. Obedient
obt.............. Obedient (AD)
obt.............. Obiit [*He Died*] [*Latin*] (AD)
OBT............. Obiit [*He, or She, Died*] [*Latin*]
OBT............. Observer Training [*Army*]
OBT............. On-Board Trainer [*Navy*] (CAAL)
OBT............. Oriental Bank & Trust [*NYSE symbol*] (SAG)
OBT............. Oriental Bank & Trust [*NYSE symbol*] (TTSB)
OBT............. Overseas Branch Transfer (AD)
OBT............. Sisters Oblates to the Blessed Trinity (TOCD)
OBTA .... Oak Bark Tanners' Association (AD)
OBTAINDORSETRANS... Obtain Endorsement to Transport (DNAB)
OBTD .... Obtained
obtd .... Obtained (AD)
OBTEX .... Offboard Targeting Experiments (GAVI)
OBTG .... Obtaining (ROG)
OBTN .... Obtain (ROG)
obts .... Offender-Based Transaction Statistics (AD)
OBTS .... Offender Base Transaction Statistical System [*Department of Justice*] [*Database*] [*Information service or system*] (IID)
OBTS .... Organizational Behavior Teaching Society (EA)
OBTVR........ Office for Battlefield Technical Vulnerability Reduction [*Army*] (RDA)
OBTW .... Oh, By the Way [*Computer hacker terminology*] (NHD)
OBTX .... Object Texture [*Microscopy*]
OBU .... Burlington Public Library, Ontario [*Library symbol National Library of Canada*] (NLC)
OBU .... Kobuk [*Alaska*] [*Airport symbol*] (OAG)

OBU .... Kobuk, AK [*Location identifier FAA*] (FAAL)
OBU .... Offshore Banking Unit
OBU .... Oklahoma Baptist University
OBU .... One Big Union [*A reference to Canada*]
OBU .... Operational Base Unit [*British military*] (DMA)
OBU .... Operative Bootmakers Union (AD)
OBU .... Operative Builders' Union [*British*]
OBU .... OSIS [*Ocean Surveillance Information System*] Baseline Upgrade [*Navy*]
OBU .... Ouachita Baptist University [*Arkadelphia, AR*] [*Formerly, OBC*]
OBUC......... Canada Centre for Inland Waters [*Centre Canadien des Eaux Interieures*], Burlington, Ontario [*Library symbol National Library of Canada*] (NLC)
OBUCC........ Canadian Canners Ltd., Burlington, Ontario [*Library symbol National Library of Canada*] (NLC)
OBUFBL ...... Bayfield Laboratory, Ocean Science and Surveys, Fisheries and Oceans Canada [*Laboratoire Bayfield, Science et Leves Oceaniques, Peches et Oceans Canada*] Burlington, Ontario [*Library symbol National Library of Canada*] (NLC)
OBUJB .... Joseph Brant Memorial Hospital, Burlington, Ontario [*Library symbol National Library of Canada*] (BIB)
OBUL .... Lord Elgin High School, Burlington, Ontario [*Library symbol National Library of Canada*] (NLC)
O Bul .... Old Bulgarian (AD)
OBulg.......... Old Bulgarian [*Language*] (BARN)
OBUR .... Burford Public Library, Ontario [*Library symbol National Library of Canada*] (BIB)
OBur .... Burton Public Library, Burton, OH [*Library symbol Library of Congress*] (LCLS)
o/bur.......... Oil on Burlap (VRA)
OBUS .... Obstetric Ultrasound [*Microcomputer system dealing with results of obstetric ultrasound examinations*]
OBUTS .... Organ Builders' United Trade Society [*A union*] [*British*]
OBUV .... Operative Bakers' Union of Victoria [*Australia*]
OBv.......... Bellevue Public Library, Bellevue, OH [*Library symbol Library of Congress*] (LCLS)
OBV .... Bobcaygeon Branch, Victoria County Public Library, Ontario [*Library symbol National Library of Canada*] (BIB)
OBV .... Obligated Volunteer Officer [*Military*]
OBV .... Obstacle Breaching Vehicle [*Military*]
OBV .... Obverse
obv.......... Obverse (AD)
obv.......... Obvious (AD)
obv.......... Ocean Boarding Vessel (AD)
OBV .... Ocean Boarding Vessel
OBV .... Octane Blending Value (PDAA)
obv.......... Octane Blending Value (AD)
OBV .... On-Balance Volume [*Measurement devised by stock market technician Joseph Granville*]
OBV .... Operation Big Vote (EA)
OBV .... Oxidizer Bleed Valve (NASA)
OBVP .... Obiit Vita Patris [*He, or She, Died in the Lifetime of His, or Her, Father*] [*Latin*]
obvy.......... Obviously (AD)
Obw.......... Oberwerk [*Highest Organ Bank*] [*German*] (AD)
OBW .... Oberwerk [*Upper Work*] [*Music*]
OBW .... Observation Window
obw.......... Observation Window (AD)
OBW .... Oxford Bible Warehouse [*British*] (ROG)
OBWC .... Westinghouse Canada, Inc., Burlington, Ontario [*Library symbol National Library of Canada*] (NLC)
OBWO .... O-Type Backward-Wave Oscillator (IDOE)
OBy.......... Old Byblian (BJA)
OBZ .... Outer Border Zone [*Geology*]
OC.......... Air California [*Air carrier designation symbol*] (AD)
OC.......... Cornwall Public Library, Ontario [*Library symbol National Library of Canada*] (NLC)
OC.......... Degrees Celsius
OC.......... Jersey. Ordres du Conseil [*A publication*] (DLA)
OC.......... Oberlin College (AD)
OC.......... Object Class [*Military*]
O/C.......... Object Classification (NG)
OC.......... Objective Capability
OC.......... Oblate College (AD)
OC.......... Observation Car [*British*]
OC.......... Observer-Controller [*Army*] (INF)
OC.......... Observer Corps [*Became ROC, 1941*] [*British*]
OC.......... Obsessive Compulsive (PAZ)
oc.......... Obstetrical Conjugate [*Medicine*] (AD)
OC.......... Obstetric Conjugate [*Pelvic measurement*] [*Gynecology*]
OC.......... Obstruction Chart
OC.......... Occidental
OC.......... Occidental College (AD)
OC.......... Occipital Cortex [*Brain anatomy*]
OC.......... Occlusocervical [*Dentistry*]
OC.......... Occulentum [*Medicine*] (CPH)
Oc.......... Occulting Light [*Navigation signal*]
OC.......... Occupied [*International telex abbreviation*] (WDMC)
OC.......... Occurs (MDG)
OC.......... Ocean
Oc.......... Ocean (AD)
oc.......... Ocean (AD)
OC.......... Oceanographic Devices [*JETDS nomenclature*] [*Military*] (CET)
O/C.......... O'Clock (ROG)

OC.............. Octahedral [*Molecular geometry*]
OC.............. October (ADA)
OC.............. Octyl [*Biochemistry*]
OC.............. Ocular [*Microscopy*]
OC.............. Oculentum [*Eye Ointment*] [*Pharmacy*]
OC.............. Odessa College (AD)
oc.............. Odor Control (AD)
OC.............. Odor Control
OC.............. Oedipus Coloneus [*of Sophocles*] [*Classical studies*] (OCD)
OC.............. Of Course
OC.............. Off-Camera [*Film*] (WDMC)
OC.............. Off Center (WGA)
OC.............. Offensive Center [*Football*]
OC.............. Office Call [*Medicine*]
OC.............. Office Consultation (AD)
OC.............. Office Copy
OC.............. Office of Censorship [*Terminated, 1945*] [*Military*]
OC.............. Office of the Commissioner [*Office of Education*]
OC.............. Office of the Comptroller
O/C.............. Officer Cadet [*British military*] (DMA)
OC.............. Officer Candidate [*Military*]
OC.............. Officer Commanding [*Military*]
O/C.............. Officer-in-Charge [*Army*]
OC.............. Officer in Charge (AD)
OC.............. Officer of the Order of Canada
OC.............. Officer of the Order of Canada (DD)
OC.............. Officers' Cook
OC.............. Official Circular [*Poor Law Board, etc.*] [*A publication*] (DLA)
OC.............. Official Classification
OC.............. Off-Machine Coated [*Paper*] (DGA)
OC.............. Ohio College (AD)
OC.............. Oil Cooler
o/c.............. Oil on Canvas (VRA)
OC.............. Okolona College (AD)
OC.............. Old Carthusian
OC.............. Old Category Code (NITA)
OC.............. Old Catholic
O/C.............. Old Charter [*Business and trade*]
OC.............. Old Cheltonian [*British*] (ROG)
OC.............. Old Code [*Louisiana Code of 1808*] [*A publication*] (DLA)
OC.............. Old Crop
OC.............. Oleoresin Capsicum (BARN)
OC.............. Olivet College (AD)
OC.............. Olympic College (AD)
OC.............. On Call (BUR)
O/C.............. On Camera (WDMC)
OC.............. On Camera (WDMC)
oc.............. On Camera (AD)
OC.............. On Cards
OC.............. On Center [*Technical drawings*]
oc.............. On Center (AD)
OC.............. On-Condition (NASA)
OC.............. On Consignment (MHDB)
OC.............. On Course [*Navigation*]
OC.............. Online Chronicle (NITA)
OC.............. Only Child
OC.............. Ope Consilio [*By Aid and Counsel*] [*Latin Legal term*] (DLA)
OC.............. Open Charter [*Business term*]
oc.............. Open Charter (AD)
OC.............. Open Chock [*Shipfitting*]
OC.............. Open Circuit
o/c.............. Open Circuit (IDOE)
OC.............. Open Circular [*Configuration of DNA*] [*Microbiology*]
O/C.............. Open/Closed [*Mouth*] [*Doll collecting*]
OC.............. Open Collector (IAA)
OC.............. Open College (AIE)
OC.............. Open Contract
O/C.............. Open Cover [*Shipping*]
o/c.............. Open Cover (AD)
oc.............. Open Cup (AD)
OC.............. Open Cup [*Electronics*]
OC.............. Opera-Comique [*Comic Opera*] [*French*] (AD)
OC.............. Opera Company (AD)
OC.............. Operating Characteristic
OC.............. Operating Coil (IAA)
OC.............. Operating Company
OC.............. Operating Curve (NRCH)
OC.............. Operational Capability (AAG)
OC.............. Operational Check (MCD)
OC.............. Operational Computer (IEEE)
OC.............. Operation Code (IAA)
OC.............. Operation CORK [*Joan B. Kroc Foundation*] [*CORK is derived from
　　　　　　the foundation name*] [*Defunct*] (EA)
OC.............. Operation Crossroads [*Atomic weapons testing*]
OC.............. Operations Center [*Military*]
OC.............. Operations Chief [*Deep Space Network, NASA*]
OC.............. Operations Conductor (MUGU)
OC.............. Operations Control
O/C.............. Operations Critical (MCD)
OC.............. Operator Circuit [*Telecommunications*] (IAA)
OC.............. Operator Command (NITA)
OC.............. Opere Citato [*In the Work Cited*] [*Latin*] (WDAA)
oc.............. Opere Citato [*In the Work Cited*] [*Latin*] (AD)
OC.............. Opportunity Cost (MHDB)
OC.............. Optical Cavity [*LASER technology*] (EECA)

OC.............. Optic Chiasm [*Anatomy*]
OC.............. Optometric Corp. (AD)
OC.............. Oral Care [*Denistry*] (DAVI)
oc.............. Oral Contraceptive [*Medicine*] (AD)
OC.............. Oral Contraceptive [*Endocrinology*]
OC.............. Orbital Check (MCD)
OC.............. Order Canceled
OC.............. Order Card
OC.............. Order in Council [*A publication*] (DLA)
OC.............. Orderly Corporal [*British*]
OC.............. Order of Cistercians [*Roman Catholic religious order*]
OC.............. Ordinary Capital Account [*Inter-American Development Bank*]
OC.............. Ordinary Chondrite [*A type of meteorite*]
OC.............. Ordnance Chart (MCD)
OC.............. Ordnance College [*Military British*] (ROG)
OC.............. Ordo Charitatis [*Fathers of the Order of Charity*] [*Roman Catholic
　　　　　　religious order*]
OC.............. Organic Carbon
OC.............. Organizational Chart
o/c.............. Organized Crime (AD)
OC.............. Organochlorine [*Also, OCL*] [*Organic chemistry*]
OC.............. Organo Corale [*Choir Organ*] [*Latin*] (AD)
OC.............. Organ of Consultation
OC.............. Oriel College (AD)
OC.............. Original Claim (MAE)
OC.............. Original Cosmopolitans [*Defunct*] (EA)
OC.............. Original Cover
OC.............. Orion Capital [*NYSE symbol*] (TTSB)
OC.............. Orion Capital Corp. [*NYSE symbol*] (SPSG)
OC.............. Orlando College (AD)
OC.............. Orphans' Court (DLA)
OC.............. Osteocalcin [*Biochemistry*]
OC.............. Otero College (AD)
OC.............. Oudh Cases [*India*] [*A publication*] (DLA)
OC.............. Out Cold [*Slang*]
OC.............. Outflow Channels [*A filamentary mark on Mars*]
OC.............. Outing Club
OC.............. Outlet Contact
O/C.............. Out of Charge [*Customs*]
OC.............. Output Computer
OC.............. Outside Circumference (MSA)
OC.............. Outsiders Club (EAIO)
O/C.............. Overcharge
o/c.............. Overcharge (AD)
OC.............. Over Current
OC.............. Overcurrent
oc.............. Overdraft Charge [*Banking*] (AD)
OC.............. Overseas Chinese (AD)
OC.............. Overseas Commands [*Air Force*]
OC.............. Overseas Country (ODBW)
O/C.............. Over-the-Counter [*Also, OTC*] [*Stock exchange term*]
OC.............. Over-the-Horizon Compressed (MCD)
OC.............. Oxidation Catalyst [*Automotive engineering*]
OC.............. Oxygen Consumed
OC.............. Oxygen Cutting [*Welding*]
OC.............. Public Library of Cincinnati and Hamilton County, Cincinnati, OH
　　　　　　[*Library symbol Library of Congress*] (LCLS)
OC-5.............. Organizing Committee for a Fifth Estate (AD)
OCA .... Aeroservicios Carabobo CA (ASERCA) [*Venzuela*] [*ICAO
　　　　　　designator*] (FAAC)
OCA .... Campbellford Branch, Northumberland County Public Library, Ontario
　　　　　　[*Library symbol National Library of Canada*] (NLC)
OCA .... Carmelite Vietnamese of Our Lady of Mt. Carmel (TOCD)
OCA .... Cincinnati Art Museum, Cincinnati, OH [*Library symbol Library of
　　　　　　Congress*] (LCLS)
OCA .... Creighton University, Alumni Library, Omaha, NE [*OCLC symbol*]
　　　　　　(OCLC)
OCA .... Obsessive-Compulsive Anonymous (EA)
OCA .... Obstacle Clearance Altitude [*Aviation*] (DA)
oca.............. Ocarina (AD)
OCA .... Ocean Control Authority
OCA .... Oceanic Control Area [*ICAO*]
OCA .... Ocean Reef Club [*Florida*] [*Airport symbol*] (OAG)
OCA .... Oceans and Coastal Areas
OCA .... Oculocutaneous Albinism [*Medicine*] (DAVI)
OCA .... Offensive Counterair [*Army*] (ADDR)
OCA .... Office, Comptroller of the Army
OCA .... Office of Competitive Assessment [*Department of Commerce*]
OCA .... Office of Computing Activities [*Later, DCR*] [*National Science
　　　　　　Foundation*]
OCA .... Office of Congressional Affairs [*Energy Research and Development
　　　　　　Administration*]
OCA .... Office of Consumer Advisor [*USDA*]
OCA .... Office of Consumer Affairs [*US Postal Service ombudsman*]
OCA .... Office of the City Attorney (AD)
OCA .... Office of the Community Advocate [*Australian Capital Territory*]
OCA .... Officers' Caterer [*Navy British*]
OCA .... Ohio College Association (AD)
OCA .... Ohio Courts of Appeals Reports [*A publication*] (DLA)
OCA .... Oil Company of Australia (AD)
OCA .... Old Comrades Association [*British military*] (DMA)
OCA .... Oldsmobile Club of America (EA)
OCA .... Olympic Council of Asia [*Hawalli, Kuwait*] (EAIO)
OCA .... Oncovin [*Vincristine*] Cyclophosphamide, Adriamycin [*Doxorubicin*]
　　　　　　[*Antineoplastic drug regimen*] (DAVI)

OCA .... Ontario College of Agriculture
OCA .... Ontario College of Art
OCA .... Opencast Coal Act [Town planning] [British]
OCA .... Open College of Arts [British]
OCA .... Open Communications Architecture (AD)
OCA .... Operational Control Authority [NATO]
OCA .... Operation Crossroads Africa (EA)
OCA .... Oral Contraceptive Agent [Endocrinology]
OCA .... Order of the Crown in America [Later, TOCA] (EA)
OCA .... Oregon Corrections Association (AD)
OCA .... Organisation Combat Anarchiste [Anarchist Combat Organization] [France Political party] (PPW)
OCA .... Organizacion de las Cooperativas de America [Organization of the Cooperatives of America - OCA] (EAIO)
OCA .... Organization of Chinese Americans (EA)
OCA .... [The] Orthodox Church of America
OCA .... Osteopathic Cranial Association [Later, CA]
OCA .... Otterhound Club of America (EA)
OCA .... Outstanding Claims Advance [Insurance] (AIA)
OCA .... Oxychloride Cement Association [Defunct]
OCAA .... Oklahoma City-Ada-Atoka Railway Co. [AAR code]
OCAA .... Organization of Central American Armies (AD)
OCAAF .... Order of the Chief of the Army Air Forces
OCAAR .... Occupational Accidents Analysis and Reporting
OCAB .... Cannington Branch, Brock Township Public Library, Ontario [Library symbol National Library of Canada] (BIB)
OCAC .... Ocean Acre Project [Marine science] (MSC)
OCAC .... Office of the Chief of Air Corps [World War II]
OCAC .... Officer Commanding Administrative Centre [World War I] [British]
OCAC .... Operations, Control, and Analysis Center (DOMA)
OCad .... Cadiz Public Library, Cadiz, OH [Library symbol Library of Congress] (LCLS)
OCAD .... OrCAD Inc. [NASDAQ symbol] (TTSB)
OCAD .... Orcad, Inc. [NASDAQ symbol] (SAG)
OCADA .... Office of the Chief, Air Defense Artillery
OCADS .... Oklahoma City Air Defense Sector (SAA)
OCAE .... United States Army Engineer Division, Ohio River, Technical Library, Cincinnati,OH [Library symbol Library of Congress] (LCLS)
OCAF .... Office, Chief of Aerospace (SAA)
OCAFF .... Office, Chief of Army Field Forces
OCAI .... Orthodontic Centers of Amer [NASDAQ symbol] (TTSB)
OCAI .... Orthodontic Centers of America, Inc. [NASDAQ symbol] (SAG)
OCAJ .... American Jewish Periodical Center, Cincinnati, OH [Library symbol Library of Congress] (LCLS)
OCAJA .... American Jewish Archives, Cincinnati, OH [Library symbol Library of Congress] (LCLS)
OCal .... Caldwell Public Library, Caldwell, OH [Library symbol Library of Congress] (LCLS)
OCAL .... Ocal Inc. [NASDAQ symbol] (TTSB)
OCAL .... Ocal, Inc. [NASDAQ symbol] (SAG)
Ocal .... Ocal, Inc. [Associated Press] (SAG)
Ocal .... Octo Archives, Inc., Laurel, MD [Library symbol] [Library of Congress] (LCLS)
ocal .... On-Line Cryptanalytic Aid Language [Computer science] (AD)
OCAL .... Online Cryptanalytic Aid Language [Computer science]
OCAL .... Organization of Communist Action in Lebanon (PD)
OCAL .... Overseas Containers of Australia, Ltd. (AD)
OCAL .... [The] Oxford Companion to American Literature [A publication]
OCALC .... Oklahoma City Air Logistic Center [Formerly, OCAMA] (MCD)
O'Callaghan New Neth... O'Callaghan's History of New Netherland [A publication] (DLA)
OCAM .... Office, Computing, and Accounting Machinery
OCAM .... Organisation Commune Africaine et Mauricienne [African and Mauritian Common Organization] [Formerly, Organisation Commune Africaine et Malgache]
OCAMA .... Oklahoma City Air Materiel Area [Later, OCALC]
OCAMA-SED... Oklahoma City Air Materiel Area [later, OCALC] Service Engineering Division
OCamd......... Preble County District Library, Camden Branch, Camden, OH [Library symbol Library of Congress] (LCLS)
OCAMM .... Organisation Commune Africaine, Malgache, et Mauricienne [African, Malagasy, and Mauritian Common Organization] [Formerly, Organisation Commune Africaine et Malgache Later, OCAM]
OCan........... Canton Public Library Association, Canton, OH [Library symbol Library of Congress] (LCLS)
OCAN .... Officer Candidate Airman
OC & E .... Oregon, California, and Eastern Railroad (AD)
OC & R .... Operations, Commitments, and Requirements [Military]
OC & S .... Ordnance Center and School [Army] (RDA)
OCanK .... Kent State University, Stark County Regional Campus, Canton, OH [Library symbol Library of Congress] (LCLS)
OCanM........ Malone College, Canton, OH [Library symbol Library of Congress] (LCLS)
OCanS .... Stark County District Library, Canton, OH [Library symbol Library of Congress] (LCLS)
OCanW .... Walsh College, Canton, OH [Library symbol Library of Congress] (LCLS)
OCAO .... Athenaeum of Ohio, Eugene H. Maly Library, Cincinnati, OH [Library symbol] [Library of Congress] (LCLS)
OCAP .... Capreol Public Library, Ontario [Library symbol National Library of Canada] (NLC)
OCAP .... Open Channel Air Preheater [Heat exchanger]
OCAPO......... Office of Compliance Analysis and Program Operations [Environmental Protection Agency] (GFGA)
OCAQ .... Ordre de Comptables Agrees du Quebec [Canada] (DD)

OCAR .... Cargill Branch, Bruce County Public Library, Ontario [Library symbol National Library of Canada] (NLC)
OCAR .... Office of the Chief, Army Reserve (AABC)
OCARD........ Cardinal Public Library, Ontario [Library symbol National Library of Canada] (BIB)
OCareyS ...... Our Lady of Carey Seminary, Carey, OH [Library symbol Library of Congress] (LCLS)
OCarm .... Calced Carmelites (TOCD)
ocarm .... Carmelite Fathers and Brothers (TOCD)
OCarm .... Carmelite Fathers and Brothers (TOCD)
OCarm .... Carmelite Nuns of the Ancient Observance (TOCD)
OCarm .... Carmelite Sisters (Corpus Christi) (TOCD)
OCarm .... Carmelite Sisters for Aged and Infirm (TOCD)
OCarm .... Congregation of Our Lady of Mount Carmel (TOCD)
OCarm .... Institute of the Sisters of Our Lady of Mt. Carmel (TOCD)
OCARM .... Order of Brothers of the Blessed Virgin Mary of Mount Carmel [Rome, Italy] (EAIO)
OCART........ Cartier Public Library, Ontario [Library symbol National Library of Canada] (NLC)
OCart .... Order of Carthusians [Roman Catholic religious order]
ocart .... Order of Carthusians (TOCD)
OCartSC....... Saint Charles Seminary, Carthagena, OH [Library symbol Library of Congress] (LCLS)
OCAS .... Office, Coordinator of Army Studies (AABC)
OCAS .... Office of Carrier Accounts and Statistics [of CAB]
OCAS .... Office of Civil Aviation Security (AD)
OCAS .... Office of the Chief of Air Service [World War II]
OCAS .... Officer-in-Charge of Armament Supply
OCAS .... Ohio Casualty [NASDAQ symbol] (TTSB)
OCAS .... Ohio Casualty Corp. [NASDAQ symbol] (NQ)
OCAS .... Ohio College of Applied Science
OCAS .... Online Cryptanalytic Aid System [Computer science] (IEEE)
OCAS .... Ordnance Configuration Accounting System [Navy]
OCAS .... Organization of Central American States [See also ODECA] [San Salvador, El Salvador] (EAIO)
OCAS .... Out of Controlled Airspace [Aviation] (FAAC)
OCASA .... Overseas Chinese Association of South Australia
O Cat .... Old Catalan (AD)
OCAT .... Optometric College Aptitude Test (WDAA)
OCAT .... Optometry College Admissions Test (WDAA)
OCATOUR .... Office National Centrafricain du Tourisme (EY)
OCAW .... Oil, Chemical, and Atomic Workers (AD)
OCAW .... Oil, Chemical, and Atomic Workers International Union (EA)
OCAW .... Organization of Chinese American Women (EA)
OCB .... Cache Bay Public Library, Ontario [Library symbol National Library of Canada] (NLC)
OCB .... Cincinnati Bible Seminary, Cincinnati, OH [Library symbol Library of Congress] (LCLS)
OCB .... Officer Career Brief [Resume] [Military]
OCB .... Officers' Cadet Battalion [British]
OCB .... Off-Machine Coated Board [Paper] (DGA)
OCB .... Offshore Certification Bureau [British] (CB)
OCB .... Oil [Operated] Circuit Breaker
ocb............. Oil Circuit Breaker (AD)
OCB .... Oil Collection Basin (NRCH)
OCB .... Oil Control Board [British]
OCB .... Operations Coordinating Board [Terminated, 1961] [National Security Council]
OCB .... Outgoing Calls Barred [Telecommunications] (TEL)
OCB .... Output Current Booster
OCB .... Override Control BITS [Binary Digits] [Computer science]
OCB .... Over-the-Counter Batch [Stock exchange term] (MHDW)
OCBA .... Ortho-Chlorobenzoic Acid [Organic chemistry]
OCBC .... Ortho-Chlorobenzyl Chloride [Organic chemistry]
OCBC .... Overseas Chinese Banking Corp. (AD)
OCBH .... Bethesda Base Hospital, Information Resource Center, Cincinnati, OH [Library symbol Library of Congress] (LCLS)
OC/B/L .... Ocean Bill of Lading [Shipping]
oc b/l .... Ocean Bill of Lading (AD)
OCBN .... Ortho-Chlorobenzonitrile [Organic chemistry]
OCBOA .... Other Comprehensive Bases of Accounting (ADA)
OCBR.......... Other than Cost Base Review [DoD]
OCBR.......... Output Channel Buffer Register [Computer science] (IAA)
OCB(S)......... Oil Control Board, Supply [British]
OCC .... CARSTAB Corp., Research Library, Cincinnati, OH [Library symbol] [Library of Congress] (LCLS)
OCC .... Coca [Ecuador] [Airport symbol] (OAG)
OCC .... Object Class Code [Military] (AFM)
OCC .... Occasionally
occ............. Occasionally (AD)
occ............. Occipital [or Occiput] [Anatomy] (MAE)
OCC .... Occluded Corrosion Cell (PDAA)
OCC .... Occlusion
OCC .... Occultation [Astronomy]
Occ .... Occulting (AD)
OCC .... Occulting Light [Navigation signal]
OCC .... Occupation (AFM)
occ............. Occupation (AD)
OCC .... Occupied (IAA)
OCC .... Occupied Command Center [Military]
OCC .... Occurrence
Occ............. Occurs (ILCA)
OCC .... Ocean City College [Maryland]
OCC .... Ocean Coordinating Committee [IEEE] (MSC)
OCC .... Ocean Cruising Club [British] (DI)

OCC .... Oceanic Control Center (OA)
OCC .... OCLC [*Online Computer Library Center*] Library, Columbus, OH [*OCLC symbol*] (OCLC)
OCC .... Octagon Car Club [*Later, MOCC*] (EAIO)
OCC .... Octal Correction Cards [*Computer science*]
OCC .... Ocutech Canada [*Vancouver Stock Exchange symbol*]
OCC .... Office of Cancer Communications [*Department of Health and Human Services*] (GFGA)
OCC .... Office of Contract Compliance [*NASA*] (NASA)
OCC .... Office of the Comptroller of the Currency [*Department of the Treasury*]
OCC .... Office of the Director of Command, Control, and Communications [*Air Force*]
OCC .... Officers' Chief Cook
OCC .... Official Custodian of Charities [*British*]
OCC .... Ohio Circuit Reports [*or Decisions*] [*A publication*] (DLA)
OCC .... Ohio College of Chiropody
OCC .... Ohio Conservation Consortium [*Library network*]
OCC .... Oklahoma Crime Commission (AD)
OCC .... Old Corrugated Container [*Paper recycling*]
OCC .... Olney Communication College (AD)
OCC .... Olympic Committee Congress
OCC .... Omnibus Crime Control and Safe Streets Act [*1968*]
OCC .... Onondaga Community College (AD)
OCC .... Open Channel Cooperative
OCC .... Open Circuit Characteristic (IAA)
OCC .... Operating Characteristics Curve
OCC .... Operational Computer Complex (KSC)
OCC .... Operations Control Center [*or Console*] (AFM)
OCC .... Operator Control Command (BUR)
OCC .... Operator Control Console [*Canadian Navy*]
OCC .... Operator's Computer Console
OCC .... Oppenheimer Capital Ltd. [*NYSE symbol*] (SPSG)
OCC .... Oppenheimer Cap L.P. [*NYSE symbol*] (TTSB)
OCC .... Optical Circuit and Component (NITA)
OCC .... Option Clearing Corp.
OCC .... Oral Contraceptive Council [*Defunct*] (EA)
OCC .... Orange Carpet Crowd [*An association*]
OCC .... Orange Coast College [*Formerly, OCJC*] [*Costa Mesa, CA*]
OCC .... Order of Calced Carmelites [*Roman Catholic religious order*] (DICI)
OCC .... Ordnance Command Converter [*Military*] (IAA)
OCC .... Ordo Carmelitarum Calceatorum [*Carmelites*] [*Roman Catholic religious order*]
OCC .... Organic Carbon Cycle
OCC .... Organic Consultative Committee [*Victoria, Australia*]
OCC .... Organisation Combat Communiste [*Communist Combat Organization*] [*France Political party*] (PPW)
OCC .... Osborne Computer Corporation (NITA)
OCC .... Other Common Carrier [*Telecommunications*]
OCC .... Outer Critics Circle (EA)
OCC .... Output Circuit Check [*Electronics*]
OCCA .... Ocean Cargo Clearance Authority (DOMA)
OCCA .... Office, Chief of Civil Affairs
OCCA .... Officer-in-Charge of Civilian Affairs [*in newly occupied countries*] [*Army World War II*]
OCCA .... Oil and Colour Chemists' Association
OCCA .... Omnibus Crime Control Act of 1970 (OICC)
OCCA .... Organized Crime Control Act of 1970
OCCAS .... Occasional
occas.......... Occasional (AD)
Occas.......... Occasional Light [*Navigation signal*]
OCCASL ...... Occasional
OCCB .... Operational Configuration Control Board (AFM)
OCCB .... Organized Crime Control Bureau (LAIN)
OCC-BL....... Occult Blood [*Medicine*] (DAVI)
OCCBP........ Organization for Collectors of Covered Bridge Postcards (EA)
OCCC .... Oil Control Coordination Committee (AD)
OCCC .... Oocyte-Corona-Cumulus Complex
OCCC .... Open Chest Cardiac Compression [*Cardiology*] (DAVI)
OCCC .... Orange County Community College
OCCC .... Organized Crime-Control Commission [*California*] (AD)
OCCCA .... Office of Congressional, Community, and Consumer Affairs
OCCCE .... Organization for Coordination and Cooperation in the Control of Major Endemic Diseases
Oc C Cm O... Office of the Chief Chemical Officer (AD)
OCCD .... Com Dev Ltd., Cambridge, Ontario [*Library symbol National Library of Canada*] (NLC)
occd........... Occupied (AD)
OCCDC........ Oregon Coastal Conservation and Development Commission (AD)
OCC-E........ Office of the Chief of Communications-Electronics [*Army*] (AABC)
OCCE .... Oklahoma Citizen's Commission on Education (EDAC)
OCCEDCA.... Organization for Co-Ordination in Control of Endemic Diseases in Central Africa (EA)
OCCF .... Oklahoma City Community Foundation (AD)
OCCF .... Operator Communication and Control Facility [*IBM Corp.*]
OCCF .... Optical Cable [*NASDAQ symbol*] (TTSB)
OCCF .... Optical Cable Corp. [*NASDAQ symbol*] (SAG)
OCCGE........ Organisation de Coordination et de Cooperation pour la Lutte Contre les Grandes Endemies [*Organization for Co-Ordination and Co-Operation in the Control of Major Endemic Diseases*] (EAIO)
OCCGERMDL... Army of Occupation of Germany Medal [*Military decoration*]
OCCH .... Children's Hospital Research Foundation, Research Library, Cincinnati, OH [*Library symbol Library of Congress*] (LCLS)
OCCH .... Office, Chief of Chaplains [*Formerly, OC of Ch*] [*Army*] (AABC)
Occ Heal ANZ... Occupational Health Australia and New Zealand [*A publication*]

OCCI .... Optical Coincidence Coordinate Indexing (PDAA)
Occidental C... Occidental College (GAGS)
OCCIM .... Christ Hospital Institute of Medical Research, Research Library, Cincinnati, OH [*Library symbol Library of Congress*] (LCLS)
OCCIN .... Process Technology Department, Inco Ltd., Copper Cliff, Ontario [*Library symbol National Library of Canada*] (BIB)
occip........... Occipital (AD)
OCCIP .... Occiput [*Anatomy*] (WDAA)
OcciPet........ Occidental Petroleum Corp. [*Associated Press*] (SAG)
OcciPt.......... Occidental Petroleum Corp. [*Associated Press*] (SAG)
OCCIS .... Operational Command and Control Intelligence System [*Army*] (AABC)
OCCIS .... Operations Command and Control Information System [*Military*]
occl............. Occlude (AD)
OCCL .... Ontario Community College Librarians [*Canada*] (AD)
OCCM .... Office of Commercial Communications Management (AFM)
OCCM .... Open Chest Cardiac Massage [*Cardiology*] (DAVI)
OCCM .... Optical Counter-Countermeasures
OCCMDL....... Army of Occupation Medal [*Military decoration*]
OCCMED ...... Occupational Medicine (AABC)
OCCMH........ Cambridge Memorial Hospital, Ontario [*Library symbol National Library of Canada*] (BIB)
OCCMLC ...... Office, Chief, Chemical Corps [*Army*]
OCCMLO ...... Office of the Chief Chemical Officer [*Military*]
OCCMS .... Occupational Measurement Squadron [*Air Force*]
OCCN .... Occasion
Occ N.......... Occasional Notes, Canada Law Times [*A publication*] (DLA)
Occ Newsl ... Occasional Newsletter [*American Bar Association, Committee on Environmental Law*] [*A publication*] (ILCA)
OCC NS........ Ohio Circuit Court Reports, New Series [*A publication*] (DLA)
OCCO .... Office Canadien de Commercialisation des Oeufs
OCCO .... Office of the Chief Chemical Officer [*Military*] (AAG)
OCCP .... Octachlorocyclopentene [*Organic chemistry*]
OCCP .... Outside Communications Cable Plant (CET)
Occ Pap Univ NSW... University of New South Wales. Occasional Papers [*A publication*]
OCCPR......... Open-Chest Cardiopulmonary Resuscitation
OCCR .... Cramahe Township Public Library, Castleton, Ontario [*Library symbol National Library of Canada*] (BIB)
OCCR .... Overseas Custody (Child Removal)
OCCS .... Oce Copy Control System (NITA)
OCCS .... Office of Combined Chiefs of Staff [*World War II*]
OCCS .... Office of Computer and Communication Systems (NITA)
OCCS .... Officer Career Counseling System [*Army*] (RDA)
OCCS .... Operational Command and Control System [*Army*] (AABC)
OCCS .... Optical Contrast Contour Seeker
OCCS .... Ordnance and Chemical Center and School [*Army*] (MCD)
OCCSA .... Ohio Correctional and Court Services Association (AD)
OCCSPEC...... Occupational Specialities [*A publication*] (DNAB)
OCCT .... Collingwood Township Public Library, Clarksburg, Ontario [*Library symbol National Library of Canada*] (NLC)
occ th .... Occupational Therapy (AD)
OccTh .... Occupational Therapy [*or Therapist*] (DAVI)
OccuHlt....... Occupational Health & Rehabilitation, Inc. [*Associated Press*] (SAG)
OCCULT ...... Optical Covert Communications Using LASER Transceivers (MCD)
OCCULT ...... Ordered Computer Collation of Unprepared Literary Texts
occup.......... Occupation (AD)
OCCUP .... Occupational
OCCUPON ... Occupation (ROG)
OCCUPTN ... Occupation
OCCUPTNL... Occupational
OccuSys....... OccuSystems, Inc. [*Associated Press*] (SAG)
OCCWC........ Office of Chief of Counsel, War Crimes [*Allied German Occupation Forces*]
OCD .... Carmelitas del Sagrado Corazon (TOCD)
OCD .... Carmelite Sisters of the Most Sacred Heart of Los Angeles (TOCD)
OCD .... Discalced Carmelite Fathers (TOCD)
ocd.............. Discalced Carmelite Friars (TOCD)
OCD .... Discalced Carmelite Nuns (TOCD)
ocd.............. Obsessive Compulsive Disorder [*Medicine*] (AD)
OCD .... Obsessive-Compulsive Disorder [*Psychology*]
OCD .... Occupation Centres for Defectives [*British*]
OCD .... Ocean Chemistry Division [*Atlantic Oceanographic and Meteorological Laboratory*] (USDC)
OCD .... Ocean Chemistry Division [*Marine science*] (OSRA)
OCD .... Office of Child Development [*HEW*]
OCD .... Office of Civil Defense
OCD .... Office of Civilian Defense [*Within Office of Emergency Management*] [*World War II*]
OCD .... Office of Community Development [*HUD*]
OCD .... Offshore and Coastal Dispersion (GNE)
OCD .... Ohio Circuit Court Decisions [*A publication*] (DLA)
OCD .... Online Communications Drive [*or Driver*] [*Computer science*] (WDAA)
ocd.............. On-Line Communications Driver [*Computer science*] (AD)
ocd.............. Operational Capability Date (AD)
OCD .... Operational Capability Date (AAG)
OCD .... Operational Capability Demonstration (AAGC)
OCD .... Operational Capability Development
OCD .... Operational Capability Development (NASA)
OCD .... Operational Concept Document
OCD .... Operations Concept Document
ocd.............. Optical Character Definition [*Computer science*] (AD)
OCD .... Ordnance Classification of Defects [*Navy*]
OCD .... Ordo Carmelitarum Discalceatorum [*Order of Discalced, or Barefoot, Carmelites*] [*Roman Catholic religious order*]

OCD .... Osteochondritis Dissecans [*Medicine*]
OCD .... Other Checkable Deposits [*Federal Reserve system*] (GFGA)
O/C/D .... Out of Collector's District [*Bookselling*] (ROG)
OCD .... Ovarian Cholesterol Depletion [*Test*]
ocd .... Ovarian Cholesterol Depletion [*Medicine*] (AD)
OCD .... Overhaul Consumption Data
o/cdbd .... Oil on Cardboard (VRA)
OCDD .... Octachlorodibenzodioxin [*Organic chemistry*]
OCDE .... Organisation de Cooperation et de Developpement Economiques [*Organization for Economic Cooperation and Development - OECD*] [*France*] (EAIO)
OCDE .... Organizacion de Cooperacion y Desarrollo Economicos [*Organization for Economic Cooperation and Development - OECD*] [*Spain*] (MSC)
OCDETF ...... Organized Crime Drug Enforcement Task Force
OCDF .... Operations Control and Display Facility [*Military*] (RDA)
OCDM .... Office of Civil and Defense Mobilization [*Merged with Office of Emergency Planning*]
OCDMS .... On-Board Checkout and Data Management System (MCD)
OCDN .... Order for Correction of Defect of Nonconformance
OCDQ .... Organizational Climate Description Questionnaire
OCDr .... Drackett Co., Research and Development Library, Cincinnati, OH [*Library symbol Library of Congress*] (LCLS)
OCDR .... Office of Collateral Development Responsibility (AFM)
OCDR .... Officer Control Distribution Report
OCDR .... Orbiter Critical Design Review [*NASA*] (NASA)
OCDRE .... Organic-Cooled Deuterium Reactor Experiment [*Nuclear energy*]
OCDS .... Overseas College of Defence Studies [*British*]
OCDS .... Secular Order of Discalced Carmelites [*Rome, Italy*] (EAIO)
O/CDT .... Officer Cadet [*Military*] (WDAA)
O/Cdt .... Officer-Cadet (AD)
OCDU .... Optics Coupling Data [*or Display*] Unit [*Guidance and navigation*] (KSC)
OCE .... Edgecliff College, Cincinnati, OH [*Library symbol Library of Congress*] (LCLS)
OCE .... Helicocean [*France ICAO designator*] (FAAC)
OCE .... Ocean City [*Maryland*] [*Airport symbol*] (OAG)
OCE .... Ocean Color Experiment [*NASA*]
OCE .... Ocean Covered Earth (OA)
Oce .... Oceanic [*Record label*]
OCE .... Odessa Commodity Exchange [*Ukraine*] (EY)
OCE .... Office, Chief of Engineers [*Army*]
OCE .... Office of Career Education [*Office of Education*]
OCE .... Office of Coastal Environment [*National Oceanic and Atmospheric Administration*]
OCE .... Office of Criminal Enforcement [*Environmental Protection Agency*] (EPA)
OCE .... Office of Cultural Exchange [*Department of State*]
OCE .... Office of the Chief Economist (AAGC)
OCE .... Office of the Director of Civil Engineering [*Air Force*]
OCE .... Officer Commanding Exercises [*Military*]
OCE .... Officer Conducting the Exercise [*Navy, Coast Guard*] [*Military*]
OCE .... Officer Corps Engineers
OCE .... Omega Chi Epsilon [*Honor society*] (EA)
OCE .... OMGUS [*Office of Military Government, United States*] Civilian Employees Association [*Post-World War II, Germany*]
OCE .... Ontario College of Education
OCE .... Open Collaborative Environment [*Apple Computer, Inc.*]
oce .... Operational Control Equipment (AD)
OCE .... Oregon, California & Eastern Railway Co. [*AAR code*]
OCE .... Oregon College of Education
OCE .... Oscillating Current Element
OCE .... Other Controllable Expenses (MEDA)
OCEA .... Outstanding Civil Engineering Achievement [*Award*] [*American Society of Civil Engineers*]
OCEAC .... Organisation de Coordination pour la Lutte Contre les Endemies en Afrique Centrale [*Organization for Co-Ordination in Control of Endemic Diseases in Central Africa - OCCEDCA*] (EAIO)
OCEAN .... Oceanographic Coordination, Evaluation, and Analysis Network
OCEAN .... Organisation de la Communaute Europeenne des Avitailleurs des Navires [*Ship Suppliers' Organization of the European Community - SSOEC*] [*Hague, Netherlands*] (EAIO)
OCEANAV.... Naval Oceanography Command [*Marine science*] (MSC)
OCEANAV.... Oceanographer of the Navy
OCEANAVINST... Naval Oceanographic Office Instruction
OceanB .... Ocean Bio-Chem, Inc. [*Associated Press*] (SAG)
OCEANDEVRON... Oceanographic Development Squadron [*Navy*] (DNAB)
Ocean E .... Ocean Engineer (PGP)
Oceaner .... Oceaneering International, Inc. [*Associated Press*] (SAG)
OceanF .... Ocean Financial Corp. [*Associated Press*] (SAG)
OCEANIC ..... Ocean Network Information Center [*Information service or system*] (IID)
Ocean Inst ... Oceanografiska Institute [*Oceanographic Institute*] [*Goeteborg, Sweden*] (AD)
OCEANLANT... Ocean Subarea (Atlantic) [*NATO*] (NATG)
Ocean Man.. Ocean Management [*A publication*] (ILCA)
oceano .... Oceanologist (AD)
oceanog .... Oceanography (AD)
OCEANOG .... Oceanography
OceanOpt..... Ocean Optique Distributors, Inc. [*Associated Press*] (SAG)
OCEANS .... Omnibus Conference on Experimental Aspects of NMR [*Nuclear Magnetic Resonance*] Spectroscopy (MUGU)
OCEANSYSLANT... Ocean Systems, Atlantic
OCEANSYSPAC... Ocean Systems, Pacific

OCED .... Office of Comprehensive Employment Development [*Department of Labor*]
OCedC .... Cedarville College, Cedarville, OH [*Library symbol Library of Congress*] (LCLS)
OCEFT .... Corbeil Branch, East Ferris Township Public Library, Ontario [*Library symbol National Library of Canada*] (NLC)
OCEI .... Ocean Construction Equipment Inventory (DNAB)
OCel .... Dwyer-Mercer County District Library, Celina, OH [*Library symbol Library of Congress*] (LCLS)
OCEL .... Optical Coating Evaluation Laboratory (AD)
OCEL .... Oxford Companion to English Literature [*A publication*] (AD)
OCELAC .... Camden East Branch, Lennox and Addington County Library, Ontario [*Library symbol National Library of Canada*] (NLC)
OCEleC .... Cincinnati Electronics Corporation, Cincinnati, OH [*Library symbol Library of Congress*] (LCLS)
O Celt .... Old Celtic (AD)
OCEml .... Emery Industries, Inc., Research Library, Cincinnati, OH [*Library symbol Library of Congress*] (LCLS)
OCEN .... Oce-Van der Grinten NV [*Netherlands NASDAQ symbol*]
OCENY .... Oce-van der Grinten ADR [*NASDAQ symbol*] (TTSB)
Oce-NY .... Oce-Van der Grinten NV [*Associated Press*] (SAG)
OCEO .... Office of the Commissioner for Equal Opportunity [*Australia*]
OCEP .... Office of Community Employment Programs [*Department of Labor*]
OCEPA .... United States Environmental Protection Agency, Cincinnati, OH [*Library symbol Library of Congress*] (LCLS)
OCf .... Chagrin Falls Public Library, Chagrin Falls, OH [*Library symbol Library of Congress*] (LCLS)
OCF .... Obsessive Compulsive Foundation (EA)
OCF .... Ocala [*Florida*] [*Airport symbol*] (OAG)
OCF .... Ocala, FL [*Location identifier FAA*] (FAAL)
OCF .... Office of the Chief of Finance [*Military*]
OCF .... Officers' Christian Fellowship of the USA (EA)
OCF .... Officiating Chaplain to the Forces [*Military British*]
OCF .... On-Board Computational Facility [*NASA*] (NASA)
OCF .... Open Channel Flow
OCF .... Open Computing Facility
OCF .... Operational Control Facility (SAA)
OCF .... Operator Console Facility [*Computer science*] (IBMDP)
OCF .... Orbiter Computational Facility [*NASA*] (NASA)
ocf .... Originally Cultured Formulation (AD)
OCF .... Ossining Correctional Facility [*Sing Sing*] (AD)
OCF .... Owens-Corning [*NYSE symbol*] (TTSB)
OCF .... Owens-Corning Fiberglas Corp. [*NYSE symbol*] (SPSG)
OCF .... Ozenji Critical Facility [*Nuclear reactor*] [*Japan*]
OCFA .... Overseas Christian Fellowship Australia
OCF & A ...... Office, Chief of Finance and Accounting [*Army*] (AABC)
OCFC .... Cloyne Branch, Frontenac County Library, Ontario [*Library symbol National Library of Canada*] (BIB)
OCFC .... Ocean Financial Corp. [*NASDAQ symbol*] (SAG)
OCFC .... Overseas Combined Federal Campaign [*Red Cross*]
OCFDA .... United States Food and Drug Administration, Cincinnati, OH [*Library symbol Library of Congress*] (LCLS)
OCFMFP ...... Ontario Centre for Farm Machinery and Food Processing Technology, Chatham, Ontario [*Library symbol National Library of Canada*] (NLC)
OCF-ML .... Organisation Communiste de France - Marxiste-Leniniste [*Communist Organization of France - Marxist-Leninist*] (PPW)
OCFNT .... Occuluded Front [*NWS*] (FAAC)
OCFP .... Office of Commercial and Financial Policy [*Department of Commerce*]
OCFP .... Operator Command Function Processor [*Computer science*] (MHDI)
OCFR .... Oxford Committee for Family Relief [*British*] (AD)
OCFR .... Oxford Committee for Famine Relief [*British*] (DI)
OCFT .... Office of Curriculum Frameworks and Textbooks (AD)
OCG .... Cincinnati General Hospital, Medical Library, Cincinnati, OH [*Library symbol Library of Congress*] (LCLS)
OCG .... Occupational Changes in a Generation [*Socioeconomics*]
OCG .... OCG Technology, Inc. [*Associated Press*] (SAG)
OCG .... Oesterreichische Computer Gesellscahft [*Austrian Computer Society*] [*German*] (AD)
OCG .... Office of Challenge Grants [*National Endowment for the Humanities*] (BARN)
OCG .... Office of the Commanding General [*Army*]
OCG .... Office of the Comptroller General (AAGC)
ocg .... Omnicardiogram [*Medicine*] (AD)
OCG .... Omnicardiogram [*Medicine*] (DMAA)
OCG .... Optimal Code Generation
OCG .... Oral Cholecystography [*or Cholecystogram*] [*Radiology*]
OCG .... Orbital Curve of Growth [*Mathematics*]
OCG .... Osborne & Chappel Goldfields US [*Toronto Stock Exchange symbol*]
OCG .... Oxygen Consumption Gauge
OCGA .... Official Code of Georgia, Annotated [*A publication*] (DLA)
OCGH .... Cornwall General Hospital, Ontario [*Library symbol National Library of Canada*] (NLC)
OCGM .... Office of Cabinet and Government Management [*Australia*]
OCGS .... Church of Jesus Christ of Latter-Day Saints, Genealogical Society Library, Cincinnati Branch, Cincinnati, OH [*Library symbol Library of Congress*] (LCLS)
OCGSH .... Good Samaritan Hospital, Medical Library, Cincinnati, OH [*Library symbol Library of Congress*] (LCLS)
OCGT .... OCG Technology [*NASDAQ symbol*] (TTSB)
OCGT .... OCG Technology, Inc. [*NASDAQ symbol*] (NQ)
OCGT .... Open-Cycle Gas Turbine (PDAA)
OCH .... Chesley Branch, Bruce County Public Library, Ontario [*Library symbol National Library of Canada*] (NLC)

OCh............. Chillicothe and Ross County Public Library, Chillicothe, OH [*Library symbol Library of Congress*] (LCLS)

OCH............. Hebrew Union College - Jewish Institute of Religion, Cincinnati, OH [*Library symbol Library of Congress*] (LCLS)

OCH............. Nacogdoches, TX [*Location identifier FAA*] (FAAL)

OCH............. Obedience Champion [*Dog show term*]

OCH............. Obstacle Clearance Height [*Aviation*] (FAAC)

OCH............. Ochre [*Philately*] (ROG)

och............. Ochre (AD)

OCH............. Office for Communication in the Humanities (NITA)

OCH............. Orbiter Common Hardware [*NASA*] (NASA)

OCH............. Order of the Compassionate Heart (EA)

OCH............. Organ Clearing House (EA)

OCH............. Outpatient Clinic (Hospital) [*Veterans Administration*]

OCHA............. Chatham Public Library, Ontario [*Library symbol National Library of Canada*] (NLC)

OChaG......... Geauga County Public Library, Chardon, OH [*Library symbol Library of Congress*] (LCLS)

OCHAH......... Chatham Public General Hospital, Ontario [*Library symbol National Library of Canada*] (NLC)

OCHAK......... Chatham-Kent Museum, Chatham, Ontario [*Library symbol National Library of Canada*] (NLC)

OCHAKC....... Kent County Public Library, Chatham, Ontario [*Library symbol National Library of Canada*] (NLC)

OCHAMPUS... Office for the Civilian Health and Medical Program of the Uniformed Services (AABC)

OCHAMPUS... Office of Civilian Health and Medical Program of the Uniformed Services (USGC)

OCHAMPUSEUR... Office of the Civilian Health and Medical Program of the Uniformed Services in Europe (DNAB)

OCHAP......... Chapleau Public Library, Ontario [*Library symbol National Library of Canada*] (NLC)

OCharlys...... OCharleys, Inc. [*Associated Press*] (SAG)

OCHAT......... Thames Arts Centre, Chatham, Ontario [*Library symbol National Library of Canada*] (NLC)

OCHC.......... Operator Call Handling Center [*Telecommunications*] (TEL)

OCHCB........ Huron County Board of Education, Clinton, Ontario [*Library symbol National Library of Canada*] (NLC)

OCHDC........ Hilton Davis Chemical Co., Cincinnati, OH [*Library symbol Library of Congress*] (LCLS)

OCHERB...... Chelmsford Branch, Rayside-Balfour Public Library, Chelmsford, Ontario [*Library symbol National Library of Canada*] (NLC)

OCHIN......... Norton Co. Electric, Chippewa, Ontario [*Library symbol National Library of Canada*] (NLC)

OC-HLTHLB... Occupational Health Labels [*Army*]

OCHM......... Haldimand County Museum Board, Cayuga, Ontario [*Library symbol National Library of Canada*] (NLC)

OCHP......... Cincinnati Historical Society, Cincinnati, OH [*Library symbol Library of Congress*] (LCLS)

OCHR......... Oil Catcher

OCHRE........ Optical Character Recognition Engine (PDAA)

OCHS......... Old Colony Historical Society (AD)

OCHSDG...... Chesterville Branch, Stormont, Dundas, and Glengarry County Public Library, Ontario [*Library symbol National Library of Canada*] (BIB)

OChU......... Ohio University, Chillicothe Branch Campus, Chillicothe, OH [*Library symbol Library of Congress*] (LCLS)

OCHWL....... Wollaston and Limerick Public Library, Coe Hill, Ontario [*Library symbol National Library of Canada*] (BIB)

OCI............. Integrated Revolutionary Organizations [*Cuba*] (PPW)

OCI............. Occlude (DA)

OCI............. Ocean Color Imager [*Meteorology*] [*NASA*]

OCI............. OC [*Overseas Crusades*] International (EA)

OCI............. Office of Community Investment [*Federal Home Loan Bank Board*]

OCI............. Office of Computer Information [*Department of Commerce*] [*Originator and database*]

OCI............. Office of Corollary Interest [*DoD*]

OCI............. Office of Criminal Investigation [*Environmental Protection Agency*] (EPA)

OCI............. Office of Current Intelligence (MCD)

OCI............. Office of the Coordinator of Information (AD)

OCI............. Old Canada Investment Corp. Ltd. [*Toronto Stock Exchange symbol*]

OCI............. Olympic Council of Ireland (EAIO)

OCI............. Ontario Cancer Institute [*UTLAS symbol*]

OCI............. Open Circuit Inductance (IAA)

OCI............. Operational Checkout Instruction (AD)

OCI............. Operation Child Identification [*Defunct*] (EA)

OCI............. Operator Control Interface (OA)

OCI............. Optically-Coupled Insulator (IAA)

OCI............. Optically Coupled Isolator

OCI............. Organisation Communiste Internationaliste [*Internationalist Communist Organization*] [*France Political party*] (PPW)

OCI............. Organisation de la Conference Islamique [*Organization of the Islamic Conference - OIC*] [*Jeddah, Saudi Arabia*] (EAIO)

OCI............. Organizational Climate Index [*Test*]

OCI............. Organizational Conflict of Interest (AAGC)

oci............. Organization Conflict of Interest (AD)

OCI............. Organized Crime Intelligence Unit [*Law Enforcement Assistance Administration*]

OCI............. Oryzacystatins I [*Biochemistry*]

OCI............. Outpatient Clinic (Independent) [*Veterans Administration*]

OCI............. Oxide Control and Indication (NRCH)

OCIA............. Organic Crop Improvement Association (EA)

OCIAA......... Office of Coordinator of Inter-American Affairs [*World War II*]

OCIB............. Beausoleil Indian Band Library, Christian Island, Ontario [*Library symbol National Library of Canada*] (BIB)

OCIB............. Organized Crime Intelligence Bureau (AD)

OCIC............. Officer Commanding in Charge [*Facetious acronym*] [*Army British*] (DSUE)

OCIC............. Organisation Catholique Internationale du Cinema et de l'Audiovisuel [*International Catholic Organization for Cinema and Audiovisual*] (EAIO)

OCIE............. Organizational Clothing and Individual Equipment [*Military*]

OCIEP......... Office of the Commissioners of Inquiry for Environment and Planning [*Australia*]

OCIF............. Out Card in File

OCII............. Oryzacystatins II [*Biochemistry*]

OCIL............. Office of Community and Intergovernmental Liaison [*Environmental Protection Agency*] (GFGA)

OCIMF......... Oil Companies International Marine Forum [*British*] (EAIO)

OCINFO........ Office of the Chief of Information [*Military*]

OCIR.......... Operational Capability Inprovement Request Out of Commission, In Reserve [*Vesselstatus*] (DNAB)

OCirP.......... Pickaway County District Public Library, Circleville, OH [*Library symbol Library of Congress*] (LCLS)

OCIS............. Oacis Healthcare Holdings Corp. [*NASDAQ symbol*] (SAG)

OCIS............. Oacis Heathcare Hldgs [*NASDAQ symbol*] (TTSB)

OCIS............. Office for Church in Society (EA)

OCIS............. Office of Computing and Information Services [*University of Georgia*] [*Research center*] (RCD)

OCIS............. Organized Crime Information System [*Federal Bureau of Investigation*] [*Information service or system*] (IID)

OCIS............. OSHA [*Occupational Safety and Health Administration*] Computerized Information System [*Environmental science*]

OCIS............. Oxford Centre for Islamic Studies [*British*]

OcisHlth....... Oacis Healthcare Holdings Corp. [*Associated Press*] (SAG)

ocist............. Cistercian Fathers (TOCD)

OCist............. Cistercian Fathers (TOCD)

OCist............. Cisterdan Nuns (TOCD)

O CIST........ Ordinis Cisterciensis [*Cistercian Order*] (ROG)

OCITA........ Office of the Chemical Industry Trade Advisor

OCIU.......... Optical Cable Interface Unit (MCD)

OCJ............. Ocho Rios [*Jamaica*] [*Airport symbol*] (OAG)

OCJ............. Optional Construction Joint

OCJA............. Oklahoma Criminal Justice Association (AD)

OCJC......... Orange Coast Junior College [*California*] [*Later, OCC*]

OCJCS........ Office of the Chairman, Joint Chiefs of Staff (MCD)

OCJH......... Jewish Hospital, Medical Library, Cincinnati, OH [*Library symbol Library of Congress*] (LCLS)

OCJH-N....... Jewish Hospital, School of Nursing, Cincinnati, OH [*Library symbol Library of Congress*] (LCLS)

OCJP......... Office of Criminal Justice Planning (AD)

OCJP......... Office of Criminal Justice Program (OICC)

OCK............. Chalk River Public Library, Ontario [*Library symbol National Library of Canada*] (BIB)

OCK............. Kent State University, Stark County Regional Campus, Canton, OH [*OCLC symbol*] (OCLC)

OCK............. Operation Control Key [*Computer science*] (IAA)

OCKA.......... Atomic Energy of Canada [*L'Energie Atomique du Canada*] Chalk River, Ontario [*Library symbol National Library of Canada*] (NLC)

OCKE.......... Petawawa National Forestry Institute, Canadian Forestry Service, Environment Canada [*Institut Forestier National Petawawa, Service Canadien des Forets, Environnement Canada*] Chalk River, Ontario [*Library symbol National Library of Canada*] (NLC)

OCl............. Cleveland Public Library, Cleveland, OH [*Library symbol Library of Congress*] (LCLS)

OCL............. Ocean Cargo Line (AD)

OCL............. Ocellus

OCL............. Office of Congressional Liaison [*Environmental Protection Agency*] (GFGA)

OCL............. Offshore Commercial Loan

OCL............. Oil City Lubricants Ltd. [*Vancouver Stock Exchange symbol*]

OCL............. Old Light Cruiser [*Navy symbol*]

OCL............. Operational Check List (MUGU)

OCL............. Operational Control Level

OCL............. Operation Control Language [*Computer programming*]

ocl............. Operator Control Language (AD)

OCL............. Operators Control Language [*Computer science*] (BUR)

ocl............. Optical Communications Linkage (AD)

OCL............. Ordnance Circular Letter

OCL............. Organochlorine [*Also, OC*] [*Organic chemistry*]

OCL............. Orthopedic Casting Laboratory (DAVI)

OCL............. Outgoing Correspondence Log (AAG)

OCL............. Overall Connection Loss [*Telecommunications*] (TEL)

OCL............. Overhaul Cycle Limit

OCL............. Over-Night Cargo Ltd. [*Nigeria*] [*ICAO designator*] (FAAC)

OCL............. Overseas Container Line (AD)

OCL............. Overseas Containers Ltd. (AD)

OCL............. Overseas Currency Loan

OCIA............. Alcan Aluminum Co., Cleveland, OH [*Library symbol Library of Congress*] (LCLS)

OCLA......... Office of Congressional and Legislative Affairs [*U.S. Department of Interior*] (BARN)

OCLA......... Oregon Compiled Laws Annotated [*A publication*]

OCL/ACT...... Overseas Container Lines and Associated Container Transport (AD)

OCLAE........ Organizacion Continental Latinoamericana de Estudiantes [*Latin American Continental Students' Organization*] (EAIO)

OCIAM........ Arthur G. McKee & Co., Cleveland, OH [*Library symbol Library of Congress*] (LCLS)

OCLaw .... Cincinnati Law Library Association, Cincinnati, OH [*Library symbol Library of Congress*] (LCLS)

OCIBE .... Board of Education, Cleveland, OH [*Library symbol Library of Congress*] (LCLS)

OCIBHS .... Benedictine High School, Cleveland, OH [*Library symbol Library of Congress*] (LCLS)

OCI-BPH ...... Ohio Regional Library, Braille and Talking Books Division, Cleveland Public Library, Cleveland, OH [*Library symbol Library of Congress*] (LCLS)

OCIBS .... Blessed Sacrament Seminary, Cleveland, OH [*Library symbol Library of Congress*] (LCLS)

OCIC .... Cleveland Clinic Educational Foundation, Cleveland, OH [*Library symbol Library of Congress*] (LCLS)

OCLC .... Ohio College Library Center (BARN)

OCLC .... Online Computer Library Center (BARN)

OCLC .... Online Computer Library Center [*Formerly, Ohio College Library Center. Initialism used in reference to cataloging system it developed*] [*Information service or system*]

OCICC .... Cuyahoga Community College, Cleveland, OH [*Library symbol Library of Congress*] (LCLS)

OCICh .... Christian Science Reading Room, Cleveland, OH [*Library symbol Library of Congress*] (LCLS)

OCICIM .... Cleveland Institute of Music, Cleveland, OH [*Library symbol Library of Congress*] (LCLS)

OCICo .... Cuyahoga County Public Library, Cleveland, OH [*Library symbol Library of Congress*] (LCLS)

OCID .... Dyke College, Cleveland, OH [*Library symbol Library of Congress*] (LCLS)

OCLD .... Oil-Cooled

OCIDe .... Deaconess Hospital, Medical Library, Cleveland, OH [*Library symbol Library of Congress*] (LCLS)

OCLDP-K ..... Open Court Language Development Program: Kindergarten (EDAC)

OCLE .... Continuing Legal Education, University of Oklahoma Law Center (DLA)

OCIFRB .... Federal Reserve Bank of Cleveland, Cleveland, OH [*Library symbol Library of Congress*] (LCLS)

OCIG .... Glidden Co. Research Library, Cleveland, OH [*Library symbol Library of Congress*] (LCLS)

OCIGC .... Garden Center of Greater Cleveland, Cleveland, OH [*Library symbol Library of Congress*] (LCLS)

OCIGI .... Gould, Incorporated, Gould Information Center, Cleveland, OH [*Library symbol Library of Congress*] (LCLS)

OCIh .... Cleveland Heights-University Heights Public Library, Cleveland Heights, OH [*Library symbol Library of Congress*] (LCLS)

OCLI .... Curve Lake Indian Band Library, Ontario [*Library symbol National Library of Canada*] (BIB)

OCLI .... Optical Coating Lab [*NASDAQ symbol*] (TTSB)

OCLI .... Optical Coating Laboratories, Inc. (PCM)

OCLI .... Optical Coating Laboratory, Inc. [*NASDAQ symbol*] (NQ)

OCLIPS .... Operational Climate Prediction and Services (USDC)

OCLIPS .... Operational Climate Prediction and Services [*Marine science*] (OSRA)

OCIJC .... John Carroll University, Cleveland, OH [*Library symbol Library of Congress*] (LCLS)

OCIL .... General Electric Co., Light Research Laboratory, Cleveland, OH [*Library symbol Library of Congress*] (LCLS)

OCLL .... Office, Chief of Legislative Liaison [*Military*]

OCILH .... Lakeside Hospital, Cleveland, OH [*Library symbol Library of Congress*] (LCLS)

OCLloyd .... Lloyd Library and Museum, Cincinnati, OH [*Library symbol Library of Congress*] (LCLS)

OCIMA .... Cleveland Museum of Art, Cleveland, OH [*Library symbol Library of Congress*] (LCLS)

OCIMGH ...... Cleveland Metropolitan General Hospital, Cleveland, OH [*Library symbol Library of Congress*] (LCLS)

OCIMN .... Cleveland Museum of Natural History, Cleveland, OH [*Library symbol Library of Congress*] (LCLS)

OCIMt .... Mount Sinai Hospital, Cleveland, OH [*Library symbol Library of Congress*] (LCLS)

OCINASA ..... National Aeronautics and Space Administration, Lewis Research Center, Cleveland, OH [*Library symbol Library of Congress*] (LCLS)

OCIND .... Notre Dame College, Cleveland, OH [*Library symbol Library of Congress*] (LCLS)

OCLNR .... Oil Cleaner

OCIP .... Park Synagogue, Cleveland, OH [*Library symbol Library of Congress*] (LCLS)

OCLR .... Oil Cooler

OCIRC .... Rowfant Club, Cleveland, OH [*Library symbol Library of Congress*] (LCLS)

OCISA .... Cleveland Institute of Art, Cleveland, OH [*Library symbol Library of Congress*] (LCLS)

OCISS .... Saint Stanislaus Seminary, Cleveland, OH [*Library symbol Library of Congress*] (LCLS)

OCIStJ .... Saint John College of Cleveland, Cleveland, OH [*Library symbol Library of Congress*] (LCLS)

OCIStM .... Saint Mary's Seminary, Cleveland, OH [*Library symbol Library of Congress*] (LCLS)

OCITem .... Temple Library, Tiffereth Israel Congregation, Cleveland, OH [*Library symbol Library of Congress*] (LCLS)

OCIU .... Cleveland State University, Cleveland, OH [*Library symbol Library of Congress*] (LCLS)

OCLU .... Overseas Container Line Unit (AD)

OCIU-L .... Cleveland-Marshall College of Law, Cleveland State University, Cleveland, OH [*Library symbol Library of Congress*] (LCLS)

OCIUr .... Ursuline College, Pepper Pike, OH [*Library symbol Library of Congress*] (LCLS)

OCLUS .... Outside Continental Limits of United States [*Military*]

OCIV .... United States Veterans Administration Hospital, Cleveland, OH [*Library symbol Library of Congress*] (LCLS)

OCIW .... Case Western Reserve University, Cleveland, OH [*Library symbol Library of Congress*] (LCLS)

OCIW-H .... Case Western Reserve University, Cleveland Health Sciences Library, Cleveland, OH [*Library symbol Library of Congress*] (LCLS)

OCIWHi .... Western Reserve Historical Society, Cleveland, OH [*Library symbol Library of Congress*] (LCLS)

OCIWHi-AM ... Western Reserve Historical Society, Frederick C. Crawford Auto-Aviation Museum, Cleveland, OH [*Library symbol Library of Congress*] (LCLS)

OCIW-L .... Case Western Reserve University, Law Library, Cleveland, OH [*Library symbol*] [*Library of Congress*] (LCLS)

OCIW-LS ..... Case Western Reserve University, School of Library Science, Cleveland, OH [*Library symbol Library of Congress*] (LCLS)

OCIW-S .... Case Western Reserve University, Sears Library, Cleveland, OH [*Library symbol Library of Congress*] (LCLS)

OCIW-SS ..... Case Western Reserve University, School of Applied Social Science, Cleveland, OH [*Library symbol Library of Congress*] (LCLS)

OCM .... Cincinnati Masonic Temple, Cincinnati, OH [*Library symbol Library of Congress*] (LCLS)

OCM .... Creighton University, Health Sciences Library, Omaha, NE [*OCLC symbol*] (OCLC)

OCM .... Matchedash Public Library, Coldwater, Ontario [*Library symbol National Library of Canada*] (BIB)

OCM .... Office of Compliance Monitoring [*Environmental Protection Agency*] (GFGA)

OCM .... Office of Country Marketing [*Department of Commerce*] (IMH)

OCM .... Office of the Commission [*Nuclear energy*] (NRCH)

OCM .... Ohm Centimeter (IAA)

OCM .... Oil Content Monitor [*Navy*] (CAAL)

ocm .... Oil Content Monitor (AD)

OCM .... On-Camera Meteorologist

OCM .... On-Condition Maintenance (AABC)

OCM .... One-Channel Map [*Computer science NASA*]

OCM .... Optical Contour Maximization [*Chemistry*]

OCM .... Optical Countermeasures

OCM .... Ordnance Committee Meeting (AAG)

OCM .... Ordnance Committee Minutes [*Military*]

OCM .... Ordo Constantini Magni [*International Constantinian Order*] (EA)

OCM .... Organic Content Monitor (NASA)

OCM .... Organic Content Monitor

OCM .... Origin of Columellar Muscle

OCM .... Oscillator and Clock Module

OCM .... Outline of Cultural Materials [*Human Relations Area Files*] [*Information retrieval*]

OCM .... Oxford Companion to Music [*A publication*] (AD)

OCM .... Oxidative Coupling of Methane [*Chemistry*]

OCMA .... Oil Companies' Materials Association [*British*] (BI)

OCMCEN ...... Occupational Measurement Center [*Air Force*]

OCMH .... Madonna House Library, Combermere, Ontario [*Library symbol National Library of Canada*] (NLC)

OCMH .... Office of the Chief of Military History [*Army*]

OCMI .... Officer-in-Charge, Marine Inspection Office [*Coast Guard*]

OCMil .... Cincinnati Milacron, Inc., Research Library, Cincinnati, OH [*Library symbol Library of Congress*] (LCLS)

OCMilC .... Cincinnati Milacron, Inc., Corporate Information Center, Cincinnati, OH [*Library symbol*] [*Library of Congress*] (LCLS)

OCMil-T .... Cincinnati Milacron, Inc., Technical Information Center, Cincinnati, OH [*Library symbol Library of Congress*] (LCLS)

OCM-LP .... Organizacao Comunista Marxista-Leninista Portuguesa [*Portuguese Communist Organization, Marxist-Leninist*] [*Political party*] (PPE)

OCMLR .... Organisation Communiste Marxiste-Leniniste de la Reunion [*Reunionese Communist Organization, Marxist-Leninist*] [*Political party*] (PPW)

OCMM .... Office of Civilian Manpower Management [*Later, Office of Civilian Personnel*] [*Navy*]

OCMMINST ... Office of Civilian Manpower Management Instruction [*Navy*]

OCMM-N ..... Office of Civilian Manpower Management - Navy

OCMN .... Merrell-National Laboratories, Cincinnati, OH [*Library symbol Library of Congress*] (LCLS)

OCMODL ..... Operating Cost Model

OCMR .... On-Condition Maintenance Rate (MCD)

OCMR .... Ontario Centre for Materials Research [*Canada Research center*] (RCD)

OCMS .... On-Board Checkout and Monitoring System [*NASA*] (KSC)

OCMS .... Operative Crate Makers' Society [*A union*] [*British*]

OCMS .... Optional Calling Measured Service [*Telecommunications*] (TEL)

OCMS .... Ordnance Command Management System

OCMS .... Ordnance Committee Meeting Standards (AAG)

OCMSq .... Occupational Measurement Squadron [*Air Force*]

OCMU .... Ocmulgee National Monument

OCN .... Canadian Park Service, Environment Canada [*Service Canadien des Parcs, Environnement Canada*], Cornwall, Ontario [*Library symbol National Library of Canada*] (NLC)

OCN .... Ocean

OCN .... Oceanair-Transportes Aereos Regional SA [*Portugal ICAO designator*] (FAAC)

OCN .... Oceanside, CA [*Location identifier FAA*] (FAAL)

OCN .... Oculomotor Nucleus [*Eye anatomy*]

OC-N .... Office of the Comptroller of the Navy

OCN .... Open College Network (AIE)
OCN .... Operation Completion Notice (AAG)
OCN .... Optimal Channel Network [Physics]
OCN .... Optimal Climate Normals [Climatology]
OCN .... Orcana Resources Ltd. [Vancouver Stock Exchange symbol]
OCN .... Order Control Number (NASA)
OCN .... Order Control Number
OCN .... Organization Change Notice
OCN .... Organized Crime Narcotics Program [Department of Justice]
OCN .... Over Castle Rock [New York] [Seismograph station code, US Geological Survey] (SEIS)
OCNAUD ...... Oficina del Coordinador de las Naciones Unidas para la Ayuda en los Desastres [Office of the Coordinator of the United Nations for Help in Disasters] [Spanish] (AD)
OCNAV .... Office of the Oceanographer of the Navy
Ocn Bch ...... Ocean Beach (AD)
OCNC .... Coniston Branch, Nickel Centre Public Library, Ontario [Library symbol National Library of Canada] (NLC)
OCNew .... New Church Library, Cincinnati, OH [Library symbol Library of Congress Obsolete] (LCLS)
OCnf .... Canal Fulton Public Library, Canal Fulton, OH [Library symbol Library of Congress] (LCLS)
OCNGA .... Officer-in-Charge of National Guard Affairs
OCNGH .... Garden Hill Branch, Northumberland County Public Library, Campbellcroft, Ontario [Library symbol National Library of Canada] (BIB)
OCNGS .... Oyster Creek Nuclear Generating Station (NRCH)
OCNHT .... North Himsworth Township Public Library, Callander, Ontario [Library symbol National Library of Canada] (NLC)
OCNIOS .... National Institute for Occupational Safety and Health, Cincinnati, OH [Library symbol Library of Congress] (LCLS)
OCNL .... Occasional
ocnl .... Occasional (AD)
OCNLY .... Occasionally
OCNM .... Oregon Caves National Monument (AD)
OCNMAP ..... Ocean Map [Marine science] (OSRA)
OCNMAP ..... Ocean Map (USDC)
OCNO .... Office of the Chief of Naval Operations
OCNPP .... Oyster Creek Nuclear Power Plant (NRCH)
OCNPR .... Operation and Conservation of Naval Petroleum Reserves [Budget appropriation title]
OCNS .... Oklahoma City NORAD [North American Air Defense] Sector (SAA)
OCNSW .... Outdoor Club of New South Wales [Australia]
OCNWU .... Organizing Committee for a National Writers Union (EA)
OCO .... Cobourg Public Library, Ontario [Library symbol National Library of Canada] (NLC)
OCo .... Columbus Public Library, Columbus, OH [Library symbol Library of Congress] (LCLS)
OCO .... Object Code Only (HGAA)
OCO .... Office, Chief of Ordnance [Army]
OCO .... Office of Central Operations [Bureau of Health Insurance]
OCO .... Office of Civil Operations [Coordinated US civilian pacification efforts in Vietnam] (VNW)
OCO .... Off-Load Control Officer [Navy] (ANA)
OCO .... Old Cornish [Language, etc.]
OCO .... OMS [Orbital Maneuvering Subsystem] Cutoff [NASA] (NASA)
OCO .... OMS [Orbital Maneuvering Subsystem] Cutoff
OCO .... One-Cancels-the-Other Order [Business term]
OCO .... Ontario College of Ophthalmology [Canada] (AD)
oco .... Open-Close-Open (AD)
OCO .... Open-Close-Open [Technical drawings]
OCO .... Operational Capability Objective [Army]
OCO .... Operational Checkout (AAG)
OCO .... Operations Console Operator (MUGU)
OCO .... Optically-Coupled Oscillator [Instrumentation]
OCO .... Ordnance Corps Order (AAG)
OCO .... Public Library of Columbus and Franklin County, Columbus, OH [OCLC symbol] (OCLC)
OCOA .... Art Gallery of Cobourg, Ontario [Library symbol National Library of Canada] (NLC)
OCoa .... Columbiana Public Library, Columbiana, OH [Library symbol Library of Congress] (LCLS)
OCOA .... Organismo Coordinador de Operaciones Antisubversivas [Coordinating Organism of Antisubversive Operations] [Uruguay] (AD)
OCoAC .... American Ceramic Society, Columbus, OH [Library symbol Library of Congress] (LCLS)
OCOAP .... Oscillating-Compensator Oscillating-Analyzer Polarimeter (PDAA)
OCoB .... Battelle-Columbus Laboratories, Columbus, OH [Library symbol Library of Congress] (LCLS)
OCOB .... Cobalt Public Library, Ontario [Library symbol National Library of Canada] (BIB)
OCOBD .... Cobden Public Library, Ontario [Library symbol National Library of Canada] (BIB)
OCoBex .... Bexley Public Library, Columbus, OH [Library symbol Library of Congress] (LCLS)
OCoC .... Capital University, Columbus, OH [Library symbol Library of Congress] (LCLS)
OCOC .... Cochrane Public Library, Ontario [Library symbol National Library of Canada] (NLC)
OCOCC .... Ontario CAD/CAM Centre, Cambridge, Ontario [Library symbol National Library of Canada] (NLC)
OCoC-L .... Capital University, School of Law, Columbus, OH [Library symbol Library of Congress] (LCLS)

OCoCT .... Columbus Technical Institute, Columbus, OH [Library symbol Library of Congress] (LCLS)
OCoCU .... Capital University, Columbus, OH [Library symbol] [Library of Congress] (LCLS)
OCoD .... Ohio Dominican College, Columbus, OH [Library symbol Library of Congress] (LCLS)
OCOD .... Organization for Cooperation in Overseas Development [Canada] (EAIO)
OCoE .... Evangelical Lutheran Theological Seminary, Columbus, OH [Library symbol Library of Congress] (LCLS)
OCOE .... Office of the Chief of Engineers [Army] (RDA)
OCoF .... Franklin University, Columbus, OH [Library symbol Library of Congress] (LCLS)
OC of AC ..... Office of the Chief of Air Corps [World War II]
OC of AS ..... Office of the Chief of Air Staff [World War II]
OC of Ch ..... Office, Chief of Chaplains [Later, OCCH] [Army] (AABC)
OC of F .... Office of the Chief of Finance [Military]
OC of ORD ... Office, Chief of Ordnance [Army]
OC of SA ..... Office, Chief of Staff, Army (AABC)
OC of SptS ... Office of the Chief of Support Services [Army] (AABC)
OC of T .... Office, Chief of Transportation [Army]
OCoG ....: Grandview Heights Library, Columbus, OH [Library symbol Library of Congress] (LCLS)
OCOGF .... General Foods Ltd., Cobourg, Ontario [Library symbol National Library of Canada] (NLC)
OCoGS .... Church of Jesus Christ of Latter-Day Saints, Genealogical Society Library, Columbus Branch, Columbus, OH [Library symbol Library of Congress] (LCLS)
OCOKA .... Observation and Fields of Fire, Cover and Concealment, Obstacles, Key Terrain, Avenues of Approach (MCD)
OCOL .... Collingwood Public Library, Ontario [Library symbol National Library of Canada] (NLC)
OCOLB .... Colborne Public Library, Ontario [Library symbol National Library of Canada] (BIB)
OCoLC .... OCLC Online Computer Library Center, Dublin, OH [Library symbol] [Library of Congress] (LCLS)
OCoLC .... Ohio College Library Center, Columbus, OH [Library symbol Library of Congress] (LCLS)
OCOLD .... Coldwater Memorial Public Library, Ontario [Library symbol National Library of Canada] (BIB)
OCOM .... Oficina Central de Organizacion y Metodos [Central Office of Organization and Methods] [Spain] (AD)
OCOM .... Outlet Communications, Inc. [NASDAQ symbol] (NQ)
OCOMS .... Office of Community Services [Military]
OComS .... Office of Community Services (AD)
OCON .... Northumberland and Newcastle Board of Education, Cobourg, Ontario [Library symbol National Library of Canada] (NLC)
OCON .... Orders for Correction of Nonconformance [Navy] (NG)
OCoNC .... National Center on Educational Media and Materials for the Handicapped, Columbus, OH [Library symbol Library of Congress] (LCLS)
OConCL .... Carnegie Public Library, Conneaut, OH [Library symbol] [Library of Congress] (LCLS)
OCONT .... Oil Control
OConUS ...... Outside Continental Limits of the United States (AD)
OCONUS ..... Outside Continental United States [Military]
OCOO .... Cookstown Public Library, Ontario [Library symbol National Library of Canada] (BIB)
OCoO .... Ohioana Library, Columbus, OH [Library symbol Library of Congress] (LCLS)
OCOO .... Osteopathic College of Ophthalmology and Otorhinolaryngology (EA)
OCoR .... Riverside Methodist Hospital, Columbus, OH [Library symbol Library of Congress] (LCLS)
OCORD .... Office, Chief of Ordnance [Army]
O Corn .... Old Cornish (AD)
OCoSH .... Columbus State Hospital, Columbus, OH [Library symbol Library of Congress] (LCLS)
OCOT .... Office, Chief of Transportation [Army]
OCoV .... Center for Vocational and Technical Education, Ohio State University, Columbus, OH [Library symbol Library of Congress] (LCLS)
OCoY .... Young Men's Christian Association, Columbus, OH [Library symbol Library of Congress] (LCLS)
OCP .... Carleton Place Public Library, Ontario [Library symbol National Library of Canada] (NLC)
OCP .... Obstacle [or Obstruction] Clearance Panel [Aviation] (OA)
OCP .... Occupational Cluster Program (OICC)
OCP .... Ocean Culture Product
OCP .... Octacalcium Phosphate [Inorganic chemistry]
OCP .... Ocular Cicatricial Pemphigoid [Ophthalmology]
OCP .... Office of Civilian Personnel [Military]
OCP .... Office of Commercial Programs [NASA]
OCP .... Office of Consumer Protection (AD)
OCP .... Office of Cultural Presentations (AD)
OCP .... Office of the Chief of Protocol [US Department of State] (AD)
OCP .... Officer Candidate Programme [British military] (DMA)
OCP .... Official Crude Prices [Petroleum Intelligence Weekly] [Information service or system] (CRD)
OCP .... Oficina Central de Personal [Central Personnel Office] [Spain] (AD)
OCP .... Onchocerciasis Chemotherapy Project [WHO]
OCP .... One-Component Plasma
OCP .... Ontario College of Pharmacy
OCP .... Open Circuit Potential (PDAA)
OCP .... Operating [or Operational] Control Procedure (MSA)
OCP .... Operational Capability Plan [Army]
OCP .... Operational Checkout Procedure [NASA] (KSC)

OCP .... Operational Communications Plan (MCD)
OCP .... Operational Control Panel
OCP .... Operations Control Plan (AAG)
OCP .... Optical Character Printing
OCP .... Oral Contraceptive Pill [*Gynecology*] [*Pharmacology*] (DAVI)
OCP .... Orbital Combustion Process (PDAA)
OCP .... Orbital Control Program (SAA)
OCP .... Orbital Correction Program [*NASA*] (KSC)
OCP .... Order Code Processor [*International Computers Ltd.*]
OCP .... Organizational Competitiveness Program [*Motivational program*]
OCP .... Ortho-Chlorophenol [*Organic chemistry*]
OCP .... Ostacalcium Phosphate [*A fertilizer*]
OCP .... Out of Commission for Parts (AFM)
OCP .... Output Control Program
OCP .... Output Control Pulse (NASA)
ocp............. Output Control Pulses (AD)
OCP .... Ova, Cysts, Parasites [*Gastroenterology*] (DAVI)
OCP .... Ova, Cysts, Parasites [*Medicine*] (MEDA)
OCP .... Overland Common Point [*Imported item*] [*Business term*]
ocp............. Overland Common Points (AD)
OCP .... Overload Control Process [*Telecommunications*] (TEL)
OCP .... Overseas Common Point [*Exported item*] [*Business term*]
OCP .... Owners and Contractors Protective [*Insurance*]
OCP .... Oxford Concordance Project (NITA)
OCP .... Public Library of Cincinnati and Hamilton County, Cincinnati, OH [*OCLC symbol*] (OCLC)
OCPA .... Office, Chief of Public Affairs [*Army*]
OCPA .... Office of Congressional and Public Affairs [*FCC*] (TSSD)
OCPA .... Ortho-Chlorophenoxyacetic Acid [*Organic chemistry*]
OCPA .... Ortho-Chlorophenylacetic Acid [*Organic chemistry*]
OCPCA .... Oil and Chemical Plant Constructors' Association [*British*]
OCPCJR ...... Office of Crime Prevention and Criminal Justice Research (AD)
OCPD .... Occult Constrictive Pericardial Disease [*Cardiology*] (CPH)
OCPD .... Officer-in-Charge Police District (AD)
OCPDB .... Organic Chemical Producers Data Base (NITA)
OCPED .... Office de Commercialisation du Poisson d'Eau Douce [*Freshwater Fish Marketing Corp. - FFMC*]
OCPG .... Goodwood Data Systems Ltd., Carleton Place, Ontario [*Library symbol National Library of Canada*] (NLC)
OCPG .... Procter & Gamble Co., Cincinnati, OH [*Library symbol Library of Congress*] (LCLS)
OCPG-H ...... Procter and Gamble Co., Health and Beauty Library, Cincinnati, OH [*Library symbol*] [*Library of Congress*] (LCLS)
OCPG-I........ Procter & Gamble Co., Ivorydale Technical Center, Cincinnati, OH [*Library symbol Library of Congress*] (LCLS)
OCPG-Mv .... Procter & Gamble Co., Miami Valley Laboratories, Cincinnati, OH [*Library symbol Library of Congress*] (LCLS)
OCPG-Sw .... Procter & Gamble Co., Sharon Woods Technical Center, Technical Library, Cincinnati, OH [*Library symbol Library of Congress*] (LCLS)
OCPG-Wh .... Procter & Gamble Co., Winton Hill Technical Center, Cincinnati, OH [*Library symbol Library of Congress*] (LCLS)
OCPH .... Providence Hospital, Medical Library, Cincinnati, OH [*Library symbol Library of Congress*] (LCLS)
OCPINST...... Office of Civilian Personnel Instruction [*Navy*] (MCD)
OCPL .... Leigh Instruments Ltd., Carleton Place, Ontario [*Library symbol National Library of Canada*] (NLC)
OCPL .... Oklahoma City Public Library (AD)
OCPL .... Onondaga Library System [*Library network*]
OCPL .... Orange County Public Library [*Florida*]
OCPLACS .... Ontario Cooperative Program in Latin American and Caribbean Studies [*Research center*] (RCD)
OCPM .... Optically Connected Parallel Machines [*Computer science*]
OCPNA .... Ortho-Chloro-para-nitroaniline [*Organic chemistry*]
OCPO .... Office of Civilian Personnel Operations [*Air Force*]
OCPO .... Office of Computer Processing Operations [*Social Security Administration*]
OCPO .... Operations Cargo Passenger Office (DNAB)
OCPP .... Orbiter Cloud Photopolarimeter [*NASA*]
OCPP .... (Ortho-Chlorophenoxy)propionic Acid [*Organic chemistry*]
OCPR .... Office of Claims and Payments Requirements [*Social Security Administration*]
OCPR .... Office of Collateral Policy Responsibility (AFM)
OCPR .... Operation and Conversion of Naval Petroleum Reserves (DNAB)
OCPS .... I. P. Sharp Associates Ltd., Carleton Place, Ontario [*Library symbol National Library of Canada*] (NLC)
OCPS .... Office Canadien du Poisson Sale [*Canadian Saltfish Corporation*]
OCPS .... Office of Census and Population Studies [*British*]
OCPS .... Officer Candidate Preparatory School (DNAB)
OCPS .... Oxygen Cabin Pressurization Section [*NASA*] (KSC)
OCPSF .... Organic Chemical, Plastic, and Synthetic Fiber
OCPW .... Office of Chief of Psychological Warfare (LAIN)
OCQ .... Membre de l'Ordre des Chimistes du Quebec [*Canada*] (DD)
OCQ .... Oconto, WI [*Location identifier FAA*] (FAAL)
OCQ .... Oneida Ltd. [*NYSE symbol*] (SPSG)
OCQM .... Office of Chief Quartermaster [*Military*]
OCR .... Creemore Public Library, Ontario [*Library symbol National Library of Canada*] (BIB)
OCR .... Norcross, GA [*Location identifier FAA*] (FAAL)
OCR .... Occupational Safety and Health Control Report [*Navy*]
OCR .... O'Connell Ranch [*California*] [*Seismograph station code, US Geological Survey*] (SEIS)
OCR .... Oculocardiac Reflex [*Physiology*]
OCR .... Office for Civil Rights [*Department of Education*]

OCR .... Office of Civilian Requirements [*Division of War Production Board*] [*World War II*]
OCR .... Office of Civil Rights [*Environmental Protection Agency*] (GFGA)
OCR .... Office of Coal Research [*Energy Research and Development Administration*]
OCR .... Office of Collateral Responsibility (AFM)
OCR .... Office of Coordinating Responsibility [*Air Force*]
OCR .... Office of the County Recorder (AD)
OCR .... Oil Circuit Recloser
O Cr .... Oklahoma Criminal Reports [*A publication*] (DLA)
OCR .... Omnicare, Inc. [*NYSE symbol*] (SPSG)
OCR .... Operational Capability Release
OCR .... Operational Change Report [*Military*] (NVT)
OCR .... Operational Control Record [*Nuclear energy*] (NRCH)
OCR .... Operations Capability Reference (SSD)
OCR .... Operations Control Room [*Military*] (CAAL)
OCR .... Optical Character Reader [*Computer science*]
ocr .... Optical Character Reader [*Computer science*] (AD)
ocr .... Optical Character Recognition [*Computer science*] (AD)
OCR .... Optical Character Recognition [*Computer science*]
OCR .... Optical Character Resolution [*Ligature Co.*] (PCM)
OCR .... Optimum Charge Regulator
OCR .... Optional Character Reader [*Computer science*] (DA)
OCR .... Oracle Resources [*Vancouver Stock Exchange symbol*]
OCR .... Order Control Record (SAA)
OCR .... Order of Corporate Reunion [*British*]
OCR .... Order of the Crown of Rumania
OCR .... Ordo Reformatorum Cisterciensium [*Cistercians, Trappists*] [*Roman Catholic men's religious order*]
OCR .... Organic-Cooled Reactor [*Nuclear energy*] (OA)
OCR .... Organisation for the Collaboration of Railways [*See also OSShD*] [*Warsaw, Poland*] (EAIO)
OCR .... Organization Change Request
OCR .... Organized Crime and Racketeering Section [*Department of Justice*] (DLA)
OCR .... Output Control Register
OCR .... Over Consolidated Ratio [*Nuclear energy*] (NUCP)
OCR .... Overcurrent Relay (MSA)
OCR .... Overhaul Component Requirement [*NASA*] (KSC)
OCR .... Overhead Component Requirement (IAA)
OCR .... Oxidizable Carbon Ratio
OCRA .... Optical Character Recognition - ANSI Standard (Font A) [*Computer science*]
OCRA .... Organisation Clandestine de la Revolution Algerienne [*Secret Organization of the Algerian Revolution*] [*France*] (AD)
OCRA .... Overseas Company Registration Agents Ltd. (ECON)
OCRB .... Optical Character Recognition - ANSI Standard (Font B) [*Computer science*]
OCRB .... Optical Character Recognition Bar [*Computer science*] (IAA)
OCRBI......... Organization for Cooperation in the Roller Bearings Industry [*Warsaw, Poland*] (EAIO)
O Cr C .... Oudh Criminal Cases [*India*] [*A publication*] (DLA)
OCRCWA .... Outcare Civil Rehabilitation Council of Western Australia
OCRD.......... Ocean Climate Research Division [*Pacific Marine Environmental Laboratory*] (USDC)
OCRD.......... Ocean Climate Research Division [*Marine science*] (OSRA)
OCRD.......... Office, Chief of Research and Development [*Army*]
OCRE .... Optical Character Recognition Equipment [*Computer science*] (AABC)
ocre .... Optical Character Recognition Equipment [*Computer science*] (AD)
OCRE .... Organizations Concerned about Rural Education (AD)
oCRF........... Ovine Corticotrophin Releasing Factor [*Endocrinology*]
OCRHA........ Overseas Command Records Holding Area [*Army*]
OCRI .... Office Canadien pour un Renouveau Industriel [*Canadian Office for Industrial Revival*]
OCRIT .... Office of Combat Indentification Technology [*Army*]
OCRIT .... Optical Character Recognizing Intelligent Terminal [*Computer science*] (IAA)
ocrit .... Optical Character-Recognizing Intelligent Terminal [*Computer science*] (AD)
OCRM .... Ocean and Coastal Resource Management (GNE)
OCRM .... Office of Coastal Resource Management [*Marine science*] (OSRA)
OCRM .... Office of Coastal Resource Management (USDC)
OCRM .... Officer Commanding Royal Marines [*British military*] (DMA)
OCRM .... Orbiter Crash and Rescue Manuals [*NASA*] (NASA)
OCRM .... Orbiter Crash and Rescue Manuals [*NASA*]
OCRR .... Office of the Coordinator, Regulatory Reform [*Canada*]
OCRS .... Ontario Centre for Remote Sensing [*Canada*]
OCRS .... Optical Character Recognition System (NITA)
OCRS .... Organisation Commune des Regions Sahariennes [*Common Organization of the Saharan Regions*]
OCRS .... Organized Crime and Racketeering Section [*Department of Justice*]
OCRSDG ..... Crysler Branch, Stormont, Dundas, and Glengarry County Library, Ontario [*Library symbol National Library of Canada*] (BIB)
OCRSF .... Organized Crime and Racketeering Strike Force (AD)
OcrstLb .... Ocurest Laboratories, Inc. [*Associated Press*] (SAG)
OCRU .... Office of Communication and Research Utilization (AD)
OCRUA........ Optical Character Recognition Users Association [*Later, RTUA*] (EA)
OCRW .... Raymond Walters General and Technical College, Cincinnati, OH [*Library symbol Library of Congress*] (LCLS)
OCRWM....... Office of Civilian Radioactive Waste Management [*Oak Ridge National Laboratory*]
OCRX .... OncoRx, Inc. [*NASDAQ symbol*] (SAG)
OCS .... Cities Service Co., Technical Center - Energy Resources Group, Research Library,Tulsa, OK [*OCLC symbol*] (OCLC)

OCS .... Obsessive Compulsive Scale [*Psychology*] (EDAC)
OCS .... Obstacle Clearance Surface [*ICAO*] (FAAC)
ocs.............. Obstacle Clearance Surface (AD)
OCS .... Ocean Color Scanner (PDAA)
OCS .... Ocean Culture System
OCS .... Octachlorostyrene [*Organic chemistry*]
OCS .... Octopine Synthase [*An enzyme*]
OCS .... Office, Chief of Staff [*Army*]
OCS .... Office Cleaning Service [*Commercial firm British*]
OCS .... Office Computer System (IAA)
OCS .... Office for Consumer Services [*HEW*]
OCS .... Office of Civilian Supply [*Division of War Production Board*]
OCS .... Office of Commercial Services [*Department of Commerce*]
OCS .... Office of Communication Systems [*Air Force*]
OCS .... Office of Community Services [*Family Support Administration*] [*Department of Health and Human Services*] (GFGA)
OCS .... Office of Community Services [*Bureau of Indian Affairs*]
OCS .... Office of Computing Services [*Georgia Institute of Technology*] [*Research center*] (RCD)
OCS .... Office of Contract Settlement [*Functions transferred to GSA, 1949; now obsolete*]
OCS .... Office of the Chief Scientist
OCS .... Office of the Chief Surgeon [*Military*]
OCS .... Officer Candidate School [*Military*]
OCS .... Officers' Chief Steward [*Navy*]
OCS .... Old Church Slavonic [*Language, etc.*]
OCS .... On-Board Checkout System [*NASA*]
ocs.............. On Company Service (AD)
OCS .... Open Canalicular System [*Hematology*]
OCS .... Open-Circuit-Stable
OCS .... Operational Call Sign (IAA)
OCS .... Operational Characteristics (NATG)
OCS .... Operational Control Segment (SSD)
OCS .... Operations Control System
OCS .... Operator's Connection Set (IAA)
OCS .... Optical Character Scanner [*Computer science*]
OCS .... Optical Communicator System (MCD)
OCS .... Optical Computer System (IAA)
OCS .... Optical Contact Sensor
OCS .... Optical Contrasting Seeker (MCD)
OCS .... Optimum Coordinated Shipboard [*or Shorebased*] Allowance List (DNAB)
OCS .... Orbit Computation System (MCD)
OCS .... Orbit Correction Subsystem (NOAA)
OCS .... Order of the Cross Society (EA)
OCS .... Organe de Controle des Stupefiants [*Narcotic Drug Control Organization*] [*France*] (AD)
OCS .... Oriel Computer Services Ltd. (NITA)
OCS .... Oriental Ceramic Society (EA)
OCS .... Oriental Chair of Solomon [*Freemasonry*]
OCS .... Oriented Cellular Structure
OCS .... Ornithodoros Coriaceus Spirochete [*Entomology*]
OCS .... Outer Continental Shelf
ocs.............. Outler Continental Shelf (AD)
OCS .... Outpatient Clinci Substation [*Medicine*] (DAVI)
OCS .... Outpatient Clinic Substation [*Veterans Administration*]
OCS .... Output Control Subsystem
OCS .... Overload Control Subsystem [*Telecommunications*] (TEL)
OCS .... Overseas Civil Servants (AD)
OCS .... Overseas Courier Service (AD)
OCS .... Overspeed Control System (AAG)
OCS .... Saint Thomas Institute, Cincinnati, OH [*Library symbol Library of Congress*] (LCLS)
OCSA .... Office, Chief of Staff, Army
OCSA .... Orchid Society of South Australia
OCSA .... Outstanding Civilian Service Award
OCSAA .... Official Committee on Service Attaches and Advisers [*British*]
OCSAB .... Office of Contract Settlement Appeal Board [*Abolished, 1952*]
OCSAB .... Outer Continental Shelf Advisory Board [*Marine science*] (MSC)
OCSAN........ Organisation pour la Conservation du Saumon de l'Atlantique Nord [*North Atlantic Salmon Conservation Organization*] [*Scotland*] (EAIO)
OCSC .... Outer Continental Shelf Committee [*Congressional committee*] (MSC)
OCSD .... Obsessive Compulsive Spectrum Disorder [*Psychology*]
OCSDG........ Stormont, Dundas, and Glengarry County Public Library, Cornwall, Ontario [*Library symbol National Library of Canada*] (NLC)
OCSDGL...... Stormont, Dundas, and Glengarry Law Association, Cornwall, Ontario [*Library symbol National Library of Canada*] (BIB)
OCSE .... Office of Child Support Enforcement [*Department of Health and Human Services*]
OCSEA .... Outer Continental Shelf Environmental Assessment [*Marine science*] (MSC)
OCSEAC....... Outer Continental Shelf Environmental Studies Advisory Commission [*Department of the Interior*] (MSC)
OCSEAP....... Outer Continental Shelf Environmental Assessment Program [*Department of Commerce, Department of the Interior*]
OCSEF .... Outer Continental Shelf Events File [*Department of the Interior*] (MSC)
OCSEP .... Outer Continental Shelf Energy Program [*Marine science*] (MSC)
OCSF .... Office Contents Special Form [*Insurance*]
ocsf.............. Office Contents Special Form [*Inventor*] (AD)
OCSIGO....... Office of the Chief Signal Officer
OCSL .... Oriel Computer Services Limited (NITA)
OCSL .... St. Lawrence College [*College Saint-Laurent*], Cornwall, Ontario [*Library symbol National Library of Canada*] (NLC)

OCSLA .... Outer Continental Shelf Lands Act
OCSM .... Organization of Canadian Symphony Musicians [*See also OMOSC*]
OCSM .... Outer Continental Shelf Oil and Gas Supply Model [*Department of Energy*] (GFGA)
ocsn............ Occasion (AD)
ocsnl........... Occasional (AD)
ocsnly......... Occasionally (AD)
ocso............ [*The*] Cistercians Order of the Strict Observance, Trappists (TOCD)
OCSO .... Office of the Chief Signal Officer
OCSO .... Order of Cistercian Nuns of the Strict Observance [*Roman Catholic religious order*]
OCSO .... Order of Cistercians of the Strict Observance [*Trappists*] [*Roman Catholic men's religious order*]
OCSOT........ Overall Combat Systems Operability Test (NVT)
OCSP .... Office of Cued Speech Programs [*Gallaudet College*] [*Research center*] (RCD)
OCSP .... Out of Commission, Special [*Vessel status*] (DNAB)
OCSPC........ Outer Continental Shelf Policy Committee [*California*] (AD)
OCSPWAR .. Office of the Chief of Special Warfare [*Army*]
OCSR .... Optical Cable Signal Repeater (MCD)
OCSR .... Serpent River Band Public Library, Cutler, Ontario [*Library symbol National Library of Canada*] (NLC)
OCSS .... Office of the Chief of Support Services [*Army*]
OCST .... Office of Cable Signal Theft [*National Cable Television Association*] (NTCM)
OCST .... Office of Commercial Space Transportation [*NASA*]
OCST .... Overcast (AABC)
ocst............ Overcast (AD)
OCStFH .... Saint Francis/Saint George Hospital, Cincinnati, OH [*Library symbol Library of Congress*] (LCLS)
OCStG .... Saint Gregory Seminary, Cincinnati, OH [*Library symbol Library of Congress*] (LCLS)
OCSTL .... On-Board Checkout System Test Language [*NASA*] (KSC)
OCSW .... Objective Crew-Served Weapon
OCT .... Cincinnati Technical College, Cincinnati, OH [*Library symbol Library of Congress OCLC symbol*] (LCLS)
OCT .... Octagon (AAG)
oct .... Octagon (AD)
OCT .... Octahedral [*Molecular geometry*] (IAA)
OCT............. Octal [*Number system with a base of eight*] [*Computer science*] (CET)
oct .... Octal (IDOE)
oct .... Octal (AD)
OCT .... Octal
oct .... Octane (AD)
OCT .... Octane (AAG)
OCT .... Octanol [*Organic chemistry*]
Oct .... Octans (AD)
Oct .... Octanus [*Constellation*]
OCT .... Octarius [*Pint*] [*Pharmacy*]
OCT .... Octave (ADA)
oct .... Octave (AD)
OCT .... Octave
Oct .... Octavius (AD)
oct .... Octavo (AD)
OCT .... Octavo [*Book from 20 to 25 centimeters in height*] [*Bibliography*]
oct .... Octet (AD)
Oct .... October (AD)
OCT .... October (EY)
Oct .... October (ODBW)
OCT .... Octuple (MSA)
OCT .... Office, Chief of Transportation [*Army*]
OCT .... Office of Critical Tables [*NAS-NRC*]
OCT .... Officer Candidate Test [*Army*]
OCT .... Officer Classification Test
OCT .... Operational Climatic Testing (MCD)
OCT .... Operational Cycle Time
OCT .... Operations Control Team [*Deep Space Network, NASA*]
OCT .... Optical Coherence Tomography [*Medicine*]
OCT .... Optical Contract Seeker (MCD)
OCT .... Optimal Control Theory
OCT .... Optimal Cutting Temperature [*Material for tissue fixation*]
OCT .... Oral Contraceptive Therapy [*Endocrinology*] (AAMN)
OCT .... Orbital Circularization Technique
OCT .... Organisation Communiste des Travailleurs [*Communist Organization of Workers*] [*France Political party*] (PPW)
OCT .... Ornithine Carbamoyltransferase [*Also, OTC*] [*An enzyme*]
OCT .... Ortho-Chlorotoluene [*Organic chemistry*]
OCT .... Output Clock Trigger (IAA)
OCT .... Overseas Countries and Territories [*Common Market*]
OCT .... Oxford Classical Texts [*A publication*] (OCD)
OCT .... Oxytocin Challenge Test [*Medicine*]
OCTA .... Oceanic Control Area [*Aviation*] (DA)
OCTA .... Octanucleotide [*Biochemistry*]
OCTA .... Octapentadiene [*Toxic chemical*]
OCTA .... On-Line Corporation Tax Assessment [*British*]
OCTA .... Oregon-California Trails Association (EA)
OCTA .... Ortho-Cyclohexanediaminetetraacetic Acid [*Also, DCTA*] [*Organic chemistry*]
OCTA .... Outsized Cargo Tanker Aircraft
OCTAHDR .... Octahedral
OCTANE ...... Operations Control Technique for Actuals Number Extraction (MCD)
OCTAP........ Of Concern to Air Passengers [*Group affiliated with PATCO*] (EA)
OCTB .... Oxford Church Textbooks [*A publication*]
OCTC .... Operator's Control Transfer Channel [*Electronics*] (ECII)

OCTD	Ornithine Carbamoyltransferase Deficiency [*Medicine*]
OCTD	Other Connective Tissue Diseases [*Medicine*]
octe	Optical Component Testing and Evaluation (AD)
Octel	Octel Communications [*Associated Press*] (SAG)
OCTG	Oil Country Tubular Goods [*Metal industry*]
OCTH	Town of Haldimand Public Libraries, Caledonia, Ontario [*Library symbol National Library of Canada*] (NLC)
OCTHB	Office, Chief of Transportation, Historical Branch [*Army*]
OCTI	Office Central des Transports Internationaux par Chemins de Fer [*Central Office for International Railway Transport*] (EAIO)
OCTI	Ordnance Corps Technical Instruction
OCTL	Octel Communications [*NASDAQ symbol*] (TTSB)
OCTL	Octel Communications Corp. [*NASDAQ symbol*] (NQ)
OCTL	Open-Circuited Terminating Line (IAA)
OCTL	Open-Circuited Transmission Line
Octn	Octanus [*Constellation*]
oct pars	Octava Pars [*Eighth Part*] [*Latin*] (AD)
OCTR	Octoraro Railway, Inc. [*AAR code*]
O/CTR	Over Center [*Automotive engineering*]
octr prot	Octrooi Protectie [*Patent Protected*] [*Dutch*] (AD)
OCT/RR	Off Course Target/Remote Reference Display (NG)
OCTS	Open Cooperative Test System [*Trademark of NCR Corp.*]
OCTS	Optical Cable Transmission System (MCD)
Oct Str	Octavo Strange [*Strange's Select Cases on Evidence*] [*A publication*] (DLA)
OCTU	Officer Cadet Training Unit [*Military British*]
octup	Octuplus [*Eightfold*] [*Latin*] (MAE)
octupl	Octuplicate (AD)
octv	Open-Circuit Television (AD)
OCTV	Open-Circuit Television
OCU	Observation Care Unit [*Medicine*] (DAVI)
OCU	Oceanroutes, Inc., Palo Alto, CA [*OCLC symbol*] (OCLC)
OCU	Office Channel Unit (IAA)
OCU	Oklahoma City University
OCU	Operational Control Unit
OCU	Operational Conversion Unit (NATG)
ocu.	Operational Conversion Unit (AD)
OCU	Order of Christian Unity [*British*]
OCU	Orderwire Operator Control Unit (MCD)
OCU	Over-the-Counter Control Unit [*Stock exchange term*] (MHDW)
OCU	University of Cincinnati, Cincinnati, OH [*Library symbol Library of Congress*] (LCLS)
OCUA	Ontario Council on University Affairs [*Canada*] (AD)
OCU-B	University of Cincinnati, Biology Library, Cincinnati, OH [*Library symbol Library of Congress*] (LCLS)
OCUC	Oxford and Cambridge Universities Club [*British*] (DAS)
OCU-DA	University of Cincinnati, Design, Architecture, and Art Library, Cincinnati, OH [*Library symbol Library of Congress*] (LCLS)
OCU-E	University of Cincinnati, Engineering Library, Cincinnati, OH [*Library symbol Library of Congress*] (LCLS)
OCUFA	Ontario Confederation of University Facility Associations [*Canada*] (AD)
OCUG	Union Gas Ltd., Chatham, Ontario [*Library symbol National Library of Canada*] (NLC)
OCUG	Union Graduate School, Cincinnati, OH [*Library symbol Library of Congress*] (LCLS)
OCU-Geo	University of Cincinnati, Geology-Geography Library, Cincinnati, OH [*Library symbol Library of Congress*] (LCLS)
ocul	Oculis [*To the Eyes*] [*Latin*] (AD)
OCUL	Oculo [*To the Eye*] [*Pharmacy*]
OCUL	Ocurest Laboratories, Inc. [*NASDAQ symbol*] (SAG)
OCU-L	University of Cincinnati, Law Library, Cincinnati, OH [*Library symbol Library of Congress*] (LCLS)
OCULENT	Oculentum [*Eye Ointment*] [*Pharmacy*]
oculent	Oculentum [*Eye Ointment*] [*Latin*] (AD)
OCU-M	University of Cincinnati, School of Medicine, Cincinnati, OH [*Library symbol Library of Congress*] (LCLS)
OCU-Math	University of Cincinnati, Mathematics Library, Cincinnati, OH [*Library symbol Library of Congress*] (LCLS)
OCuME	Milton Elementary School, Custar, OH [*Library symbol*] [*Library of Congress*] (LCLS)
OCU-Mu	University of Cincinnati, College Conservatory of Music, Cincinnati, OH [*Library symbol Library of Congress*] (LCLS)
OCU-N	University of Cincinnati, College of Nursing, Cincinnati, OH [*Library symbol Library of Congress*] (LCLS)
OCU-Ph	University of Cincinnati, Physics Library, Cincinnati, OH [*Library symbol Library of Congress*] (LCLS)
OCUS	Oblate Conference of the United States (EA)
OCUSI	United States Industrial Chemicals Co., Research Center Library, Cincinnati, OH [*Library symbol Library of Congress*] (LCLS)
OCV	Bering Sea, AK [*Location identifier FAA*] (FAAL)
OCV	Ocana [*Colombia*] [*Airport symbol*] (OAG)
OCV	Oil Check Valve
OCV	Old Aircraft Carrier [*Navy symbol*]
OCV	Open-Circuit Voltage
ocv	Open-Circuit Voltage (AD)
OCV	Opimian California Vineyards Corp. [*Toronto Stock Exchange symbol*]
OCV	Ordinary Conversational Voice [*Medicine*]
OCV	Ordre des Chevaliers du Verseau [*Knights of Aquarius Order*] (EAIO)
OCV	Overriding Cam Valve
OCV	United States Veterans Administration Hospital, Cincinnati, OH [*Library symbol Library of Congress*] (LCLS)
OCVD	Open-Circuit Voltage Decay [*In silicon devices*]
OCV-L	Oil Control Valve - Low-Speed

OCVRA	Overseas Citizens Voting Rights Act
oc vu	Ocean View (AD)
OCW	Oklahoma College for Women
OCW	Old Cars Weekly [*A publication*]
OCW	Orange Cyan Wideband (IAA)
OCW	Washington, NC [*Location identifier FAA*] (FAAL)
OCW	Waterloo Regional Library, Waterloo, Ontario [*Library symbol National Library of Canada*] (NLC)
OCWCIB	Organizing Committee of the World Congress on Implantology and Bio-Materials [*See also COCMIB*] [*Rouen, France*] (EAIO)
OCWCT	West Carleton Township Public Library, Carp, Ontario [*Library symbol National Library of Canada*] (BIB)
OCWFLU	Operative Coachmakers' and Wheelwrights' Federal Labour Union [*British*]
OCWN	Ocwen Financial Corp. [*NASDAQ symbol*] (SAG)
OcwnFin	Ocwen Financial Corp. [*Associated Press*] (SAG)
OCX	Onex Corp. [*Toronto Stock Exchange symbol*]
OCX	Xavier University, Cincinnati, OH [*Library symbol Library of Congress*] (LCLS)
OCXO	Oven-Controlled Crystal Oscillator
OCY	Young Men's Mercantile Library Association, Cincinnati, OH [*Library symbol Library of Congress*] (LCLS)
OCZ	Lincoln, NE [*Location identifier FAA*] (FAAL)
OCZ	Ocean Container Zebrugge (AD)
OCZ	Operational Control Zone (MCD)
OCZM	Office of Coastal Zone Management [*National Oceanic and Atmospheric Administration*]
OD	Aerovias Condor de Colombia Ltda. (AEROCONDOR) [*Colorado ICAO designator*] (ICDA)
OD	Delaware County District Library, Delaware, OH [*Library symbol Library of Congress*] (LCLS)
OD	Doctor of Ophthalmology (WDAA)
OD	Doctor of Optometry
OD	Doctor of Osteopathy (WDAA)
OD	Drug Overdose [*Emergency Medicine*] (DAVI)
OD	Dundas Public Library, Ontario [*Library symbol National Library of Canada*] (NLC)
OD	Emerald Airlines [*ICAO designator*] (AD)
OD	Obiter Dicta [*Legal term Latin*] (DLA)
OD	Observable Difference
OD	Observed Drift
O-D	Obstacle-Dominance [*Medicine*] (DMAA)
OD	Occupational Disease
OD	Oceanographic Datastation [*Telecommunications*] (TEL)
od	Och Dylika [*And the Like*] [*Swedish*] (AD)
OD	Octal-to-Decimal [*Computer science*] (BUR)
OD	Ocular Density [*Ophthalmology*]
OD	Ocular Dominance [*Opthalmology*]
OD	Oculus Dexter [*Right Eye*] [*Ophthalmology*]
od	Oculus Dexter [*Right Eye*] [*Latin*] (AD)
Od	Odeon [*Record label*] [*Europe, etc.*]
Od	Odericus [*Flourished, 1166-1200*] [*Authority cited in pre-1607 legal work*] (DSA)
Od	Odofredus [*Deceased, 1265*] [*Authority cited in pre-1607 legal work*] (DSA)
od	Odur [*or*] [*German*] (AD)
Od	Odyssey [*of Homer*] [*Classical studies*] (OCD)
OD	Office Decision [*United States Internal Revenue Bureau*] [*A publication*] (DLA)
OD	Office of Disability [*Department of Health and Human Services*] (GFGA)
OD	Office of the Director
OD	Officer of the Day [*or Deck*] [*Also, OOD*] [*Navy*]
OD	Ohio Decisions [*A publication*] (DLA)
OD	Oil Desurger
OD	Oil Distribution (DNAB)
OD	Oil Drainage
OD	Old Dutch [*Language, etc.*]
OD	Olive Drab [*Color often used for military clothing and equipment*]
od	Olive-Drab (AD)
OD	Olive Drab
OD	Omnes Dies [*Every Day*] [*Pharmacy*]
OD	Once a Day [*or Daily*] (DAVI)
O/D	On Deck (KSC)
OD	On Demand [*Business term*]
od	On Demand (AD)
O/D	On Dock (MCD)
OD	On Duty
OD	One Day (SAA)
OD	Onrechtmatige Daad [*Tort or Tortious Act*] [*Netherlands*] (ILCA)
OD	Open Drain (IAA)
OD	Open Drop
OD	Operational Downlink/Downlist (NASA)
OD	Operational DownList
OD	Operation Description
OD	Operations Directive [*or Director*]
OD	Operations Division
OD	Optical Density
od	Optical Density (AD)
OD	Opus Dei (EA)
OD	Orbit Determination
OD	Orbiter (Operational) Downlink [*NASA*]
OD vu	Order Dienst [*Netherlands first organized resistance group, 1940*] [*World War II*]
OD	Order of Daedalians (EA)

OD	Order of DeMolay (EA)
O/D	Order of Deportation
OD	Ordinary Seaman [British] (DMA)
OD	Ordnance Corps [Army] (GFGA)
OD	Ordnance Data [Inspection and test data]
OD	Ordnance Department [or Division]
OD	Ordnance Document [Navy]
OD	Ordnance Drawing
OD	Ordnungsdienst [Military Police Service] [German military - World War II]
od	Organizational Development (AD)
OD	Organization Development
OD	Organization Development [Human resources] (WYGK)
OD	Original Design
od	Original Design (AD)
OD	Original Dirac [Vacuum model] [Physics]
OD	Originally Derived
OD	Origin and Destination [Aviation] (AFM)
O/D	Origin and Destination [OST] (TAG)
OD	Osseous Defect [Medicine]
OD	Other Denomination [British military] (DMA)
OD	Outer Diameter [Mechanical engineering]
OD	Out-of-Date
OD	Output Data (IEEE)
OD	Output Disable
OD	Output Display [Computer science] (IAA)
OD	Outside Diameter
od	Outside Diameter (AD)
od	Outside Dimension (AD)
OD	Outside Dimension
OD	Outstanding Debt [Finance] (MHDB)
od	Oven Dried (AD)
OD	Oven Dry
OD	Overall Depth [Typography] (DGA)
OD	Overburden Drill (PDAA)
O/D	Overdose [of narcotics]
od	Overdose (AD)
OD	Overdraft [or Overdrawn] [Banking]
OD	Overdrive (AAG)
O/D	Overdrive [TII] (TAG)
od	Overdrive (AD)
Od	Overdue
OD	Overload Detection [Telecommunications] (TEL)
OD	Overtly Diabetic [Medicine]
OD	Oxygen Drain (MCD)
OD3	Optical Digital Data Disk
ODa	Dayton and Montgomery County Public Library, Dayton, OH [Library symbol Library of Congress] (LCLS)
ODA	Occipitodextra Anterior [A fetal position] [Medicine] (AAMN)
oda	Occipito-Dextra Anterior (AD)
ODA	Octal Debugging Aid [Computer science]
Oda	Odessa (AD)
ODA	Offa's Dyke Association [British] (DBA)
ODA	Office Document Architecture [Telecommunications] (TSSD)
ODA	Office of Debt [or Depreciation] Analysis [Department of the Treasury]
ODA	Office of Drug Abuse (AD)
ODA	Office of the Defense Attache [Foreign Service]
ODA	Office of the District Administrator (AD)
ODA	Office of the District Attorney (AD)
ODA	Official Development Aid [or Assistance]
ODa	Old Danish (AD)
ODA	Omnidirectional Antenna
ODA	Operational Data Analysis
ODA	Operational Design and Analysis (IEEE)
ODA	Optical Diffraction Analysis [Microscopy]
ODA	Orphan Drug Ace [1983] (BARN)
ODA	Oscillating Doublet Antenna
ODA	Oscillator/Doubler/Amplifier
ODA	Other Design Activity (MSA)
ODA	Ouadda [Central African Republic] [Airport symbol] (AD)
ODA	Overseas Development Administration [British] (EAIO)
ODA	Overseas Development Agency [British]
ODA	Overseas Development Aid
ODA	Overseas Development Assistance (AD)
ODA	Overseas Doctors Association in the United Kingdom [British]
ODA	Oxydianiline [Organic chemistry]
ODAA	Aden/International [People's Democratic Republic of Yemen] [ICAO location identifier] (ICLI)
ODaA	Dayton Art Institute, Dayton, OH [Library symbol Library of Congress] (LCLS)
ODAA	Office of Dependent Area Affairs [Department of State]
ODAB	Beihan [People's Democratic Republic of Yemen] [ICAO location identifier] (ICLI)
ODAC	On Demand Analyzer Computer
ODACA	Original Doll Artists Council of America (EA)
ODaCox	Cox Coronary Heart Institute, Dayton, OH [Library symbol Library of Congress] (LCLS)
ODADC	Omnidirectional Air Data Computer (MCD)
ODaE	Engineers' Club of Dayton, Dayton, OH [Library symbol Library of Congress] (LCLS)
ODAF	Aden [People's Democratic Republic of Yemen] [ICAO location identifier] (ICLI)
ODAG	Al-Gheida [People's Democratic Republic of Yemen] [ICAO location identifier] (ICLI)

ODaGH	Grandview Hospital, Dayton, OH [Library symbol Library of Congress] (LCLS)
ODaGL	Church of Jesus Christ of Latter-Day Saints, Genealogical Society Library, Dayton Ohio Branch, Dayton, OH [Library symbol Library of Congress] (LCLS)
ODaGMI	General Motors Corp., Inland Manufacturing Division, Engineering Library, Dayton, OH [Library symbol Library of Congress] (LCLS)
ODaGS	Good Samaritan Hospital, Dayton, OH [Library symbol Library of Congress] (LCLS)
ODALC	Ogden Air Logistics Center (MCD)
ODALE	Office of Drug Abuse Law Enforcement [Later, Drug Enforcement Administration] [Department of Justice]
ODALS	Omnidirectional Approach Lighting System [Aviation] (FAAC)
ODALS	Omnidirectional Approach Lighting System [FAA] (TAG)
ODAM	Mukeiras [People's Democratic Republic of Yemen] [ICAO location identifier] (ICLI)
ODaMC	Barney Children's Medical Center, Dayton, OH [Library symbol Library of Congress] (LCLS)
ODaMCo	Mead Corp., Dayton, OH [Library symbol Library of Congress] (LCLS)
ODaMNH	Dayton Museum of Natural History, Dayton, OH [Library symbol Library of Congress] (LCLS)
ODaMR	Monsanto Research Corp., Dayton Laboratory, Dayton, OH [Library symbol Library of Congress] (LCLS)
ODAMS	Open Water Disposal Area Management Simulation [US Army Corps of Engineers]
ODaMVH	Miami Valley Hospital, Dayton, OH [Library symbol Library of Congress] (LCLS)
ODAN	Kamaran [People's Democratic Republic of Yemen] [ICAO location identifier] (ICLI)
ODaN	National Cash Register Co., NCR Library, Dayton, OH [Library symbol Library of Congress] (LCLS)
ODAN	Old Danish [Language, etc.]
O'D & Br Eq Dig	O'Donnell and Brady's Irish Equity Digest [A publication] (DLA)
OD and MC	Operational Direction and Management Control (NATG)
OD & RD	Overseas Discharge and Replacement Depot
ODaNR	North Research Stillwater Pioneers, Dayton, OH [Library symbol Library of Congress] (LCLS)
ODaNT	National Cash Register Co., Technical Library, Dayton, OH [Library symbol Library of Congress] (LCLS)
ODA/ODIF	Office Document Architecture/Office Document Interchange Format (DOMA)
O-DAP	Oncovin [Vincristine], Dianhydrogalactitol, Adriamycin, Platinol [Cisplatin] [Antineoplastic drug regimen]
ODAP	Operation Data Analysis Program (IAA)
ODAP	Perim [People's Democratic Republic of Yemen] [ICAO location identifier] (ICLI)
ODAPI	Open Database Applications Program Interface [Microsoft Corp.]
ODAPS	Oceanic Display and Planning System [Air traffic control]
ODAPS	Operational OGE [Operational Ground Equipment] Data Acquisition and Patch Subsystem (GAVI)
ODAQ	Qishn [People's Democratic Republic of Yemen] [ICAO location identifier] (ICLI)
ODAR	Optical Detection and Ranging (DNAB)
ODAR	Riyan [People's Democratic Republic of Yemen] [ICAO location identifier] (ICLI)
ODAS	Ocean Data Acquisition Systems
ODAS	Ocean Data Acquisition Systems, Aids and Devices [Marine science] (OSRA)
ODAS	Ocean Dynamics Advisory Subcommittee [NASA] (MSC)
ODAS	Oral Deaf Adults Section [Later, OHIS] (EA)
ODAS	Socotra [People's Democratic Republic of Yemen] [ICAO location identifier] (ICLI)
ODaSC	Sinclair Community College, Dayton, OH [Library symbol Library of Congress] (LCLS)
ODASD	Office of the Deputy Assistant Secretary of Defense
ODaSR	Standard Register Co., Engineering and Research Library, Dayton, OH [Library symbol Library of Congress] (LCLS)
ODaStE	Saint Elizabeth Hospital, Dayton, OH [Library symbol Library of Congress] (LCLS)
ODaStL	Saint Leonard College, Dayton, OH [Library symbol Library of Congress] (LCLS)
ODAT	Ataq [People's Democratic Republic of Yemen] [ICAO location identifier] (ICLI)
odat	One Day at a Time (AD)
ODaTS	United Theological Seminary, Dayton, OH [Library symbol Library of Congress] (LCLS)
ODaU	University of Dayton, Dayton, OH [Library symbol Library of Congress] (LCLS)
ODaU-L	University of Dayton, Law Library, Dayton, OH [Library symbol Library of Congress] (LCLS)
ODaUM	United Methodist Church, Commission on Archives and History, Dayton, OH [Library symbol Library of Congress] (LCLS)
ODaU-M	University of Dayton, Marian Library, Dayton, OH [Library symbol Library of Congress] (LCLS)
ODaV	United States Veterans Administration Center, Library Services, Dayton, OH [Library symbol Library of Congress] (LCLS)
ODaWU	Wright State University, Dayton, OH [Library symbol Library of Congress] (LCLS)
ODaWU-H	Wright State University, School of Medicine, Fordham Library, Dayton, OH [Library symbol Library of Congress] (LCLS)
ODaWU-W	Wright State University, Western Ohio Branch Campus, Celina, OH [Library symbol Library of Congress] (LCLS)
ODB	Air Service [Mali] [ICAO designator] (FAAC)
ODB	Cordoba [Spain] [Airport symbol] (OAG)

ODB	Ocean Data Buoy [*Marine science*] (MSC)
ODB	Odontoblast
ODB	Office of Dependency Benefits
ODB	Oil-Degrading Bacteria
ODB	Operational Database (SSD)
ODB	Operational Data Book [*NASA*] (KSC)
ODB	Opiate-Directed Behavior
odb	Opiate-Directed Behavior (AD)
ODB	Output Data Buffer
ODB	Output Display Branch [*Computer science*] (IAA)
ODB	Output to Display Buffer [*Computer science*]
odb	Output to Display Buffer [*Computer science*] (AD)
ODB	Oven Dry Basis
ODB	Overseas Development Bank [*Investors' Overseas Services*]
ODB	Oxydibenzil [*Organic chemistry*]
ODBA	Ocean Dumping Ban Act [*1988*]
ODBC	Open Database Connectivity [*Computer science*]
ODBC	Open Database Connectivity
ODBC	Open Database Connectivity
ODBMS	On-Board Database Management System (SSD)
ODC	Oceanographic Data Center (MCD)
ODC	Odometer Data Computer [*Developed by Mileage Validator, Inc.*]
ODC	Office of Defense Cooperation (DOMA)
ODC	Office of Deputy Chief of Staff Programs and Resources [*Air Force*]
ODC	Officer Data Card
ODC	Ohio Dominican College, Columbus, OH [*OCLC symbol*] (OCLC)
ODC	Oil-Dri Corp. of America [*NYSE symbol*] (SPSG)
ODC	Oligodendrocyte [*Also, OLG*] [*Cytology*]
ODC	One-Directional Control [*Engineering*]
ODC	Online Data Capture
ODC	Operational Data Center [*Deep Space Network, NASA*]
ODC	Operational Document Control
ODC	Operation Desert Capture [*DoD*]
ODC	Operation Design Criteria (MCD)
ODC	Optical Disc Controller (NITA)
ODC	Orbital Data Collector
ODC	Order of Discalced Carmelites [*Roman Catholic religious order*]
ODC	Ordinary Decent Criminal [*British prison slang for other than a political prisoner*]
ODC	Organization Development Council [*Defunct*] (EA)
ODC	Original Design Cutoff (AAG)
ODC	Ornithine Decarboxylase [*An enzyme*]
ODC	Oscilloscope Digital Control
ODC	Other Direct Costs [*Accounting*]
odc	Other Direct Costs (AD)
odc	Outer Dead Center (AD)
ODC	Outer Dead Center (DNAB)
ODC	Output Data Control
ODC	Overseas Development Corp. (AD)
ODC	Overseas Development Corporation (NADA)
ODC	Overseas Development Council (EA)
ODC	Overseas Diplomacy Coordinator (DNAB)
ODC	Oxford Decimal Classification
ODC	Oxygen Dissociation Curve [*Medicine*] (DMAA)
ODC	Oxyhaemoglobin Dissociation Curve (PDAA)
ODC	Ozone-Depleting Compound [*Environmental chemistry*]
ODCA	Ocean Dumping Control Act [*Canada*] (MSC)
ODCA	Organizacion Democrata Cristiana de America [*Christian Democratic Organization of America - CDOA*] [*Caracas, Venezuela*]
ODCC	Ohio Decisions, Circuit Court [*Properly cited Ohio Circuit Decisions*] [*A publication*] (DLA)
ODCC	On-Board Digital Computer Control
ODCC	One-Design Class Council (EA)
ODCC	Oxford Dictionary of the Christian Church
ODCC	United States One-Design Class Council (EA)
ODCDR	Orbiter Delta CDR [*NASA*] (GFGA)
ODCM	Office of Defense and Civilian Mobilization [*See also OCDM*] (MUGU)
ODCM	Off-Site Dose Calculation Manual [*Nuclear energy*] (NRCH)
ODC of S	Office of the Deputy Chief of Staff [*World War II*]
ODCP	One-Digit Code Point [*Telecommunications*] (TEL)
ODCPC	Order of Descendants of Colonial Physicians and Chirurgiens [*Defunct*] (EA)
ODCR	Officer Distribution Control Report [*Navy*] (NG)
ODCS	Office of the Deputy Chief of Staff [*World War II*]
ODCS	Online Data Compression System (PDAA)
ODCSCD	Office of the Deputy Chief of Staff, Combat Developments [*Army*]
ODCSI	Office of the Deputy Chief of Staff for Intelligence
ODCSLOG	Office of the Deputy Chief of Staff for Logistics [*Army*] (AABC)
ODCSO	Office of Data Collection and Survey Operations [*Bureau of Labor Statistics*]
ODCSOPS	Office of the Deputy Chief of Staff for Operations and Plans [*Army*]
ODCSPER	Office of the Deputy Chief of Staff for Personnel [*Army*]
ODCSRDA	Office of the Deputy Chief of Staff for Research, Development, and Acquisition [*Army*] (AABC)
ODCTI	Old Dominion College Technical Institute (AD)
ODD	Obsessive-Deductive Disorder [*Facetious term for a malady affecting some taxpayers*]
ODD	Obstacle Detection Device
ODD	Ocean Disposal Database [*US Army Corps of Engineers*]
ODD	Oculodentodigital Dysplasia [*Medicine*] (MAE)
ODD	Offboard Deception Device [*Navy*] (CAAL)
ODD	Old Destroyer [*Navy symbol*]
ODD	Oodnadatta [*Australia Airport symbol*] (OAG)
ODD	Operational Detachment Delta [*Antiterrorist unit*] [*Military*] (LAIN)
ODD	Operator Distance Dialing

odd	Operator Distance Dialing (AD)
ODD	Oppositional Defiant Disorder
ODD	Optical Data Digitizer [*Computer science*]
ODD	Optical Data Disc (NITA)
ODD	Optical Digital Data Disk
ODD	Optical Digital Disc (NITA)
ODD	Organizing District Delegate [*British labor*]
ODD	Ouchterlony Double Diffusion Test [*Immunogel assay*]
ODD	Outside Design and Development
ODD	Overseas Deployment Data [*Military*]
ODDA	Office of Deputy Director for Administration [*Marshall Space Flight Center*] (KSC)
ODDD	Optical Digital Data Disk
ODDDR & R	Office of the Deputy Director of Defense Research and Engineering (RDA)
ODDH	On-Board Digital Data Handling
ODDO	Operation Description Distribution Order
ODDP	Office of the Director of Development Planning [*Air Force*] (MCD)
ODDR & E	Office of the Director of Defense Research and Engineering [*Later, Office of the Under Secretary of Defense for Research and Engineering*] [*Army*]
ODDRD	Office of Deputy Director for Research and Development [*Marshall Space Flight Center*] (KSC)
ODDRE	Office of the Director of Defense Research and Engineering [*Later, Office of the Under Secretary of Defense for Research and Engineering*] [*Army*]
ODDS	Oceanographic Digital Data System [*Navy*]
ODDS	Online Data Entry and Display System [*Job Service*] (OICC)
ODDS	Operational Data Delivery Services (MCD)
ODDS	Optical Disk Data System (NITA)
ODDS	Optional Delivery Dispenser System (MCD)
ODE	Delhi Public Library, Ontario [*Library symbol National Library of Canada*] (NLC)
ODE	Odense [*Denmark*] [*Airport symbol*] (OAG)
ODE	Odessa [*Former USSR Geomagnetic observatory code*]
ODE	Oil Drilling and Exploration (AD)
ODE	Omicron Delta Epsilon [*Fraternity*]
ODE	One Day Event [*Horse-riding*] [*British*] (DI)
ode	One-Day Event (AD)
ODE	One-Dimensional Equilibrium (MCD)
ODE	Online Data Entry (ADA)
ODE	Optical Designation Evaluation (MCD)
ODE	Optimally Designed Experiments
ODE	Orbit Data Editor Assembly [*Space Flight Operations Facility, NASA*]
ODE	Ordinary Differential Equation [*Mathematics*]
ODE	Ortho-Demethylencainide [*Biochemistry*]
ODEAG	Research Station, Agriculture Canada [*Station de Recherches, Agriculture Canada*] Delhi, Ontario [*Library symbol National Library of Canada*] (NLC)
O'Dea Med Exp	O'Dea's Medical Experts [*A publication*] (DLA)
ODEC	Ocean Design Engineering Corp. (AD)
ODECA	Organizacion de los Estados Centroamericanos [*Organization of Central American States - OCAS*] [*San Salvador, El Salvador*] (EAIO)
ODECO	Ocean Drilling and Exploration Co. (AD)
O Dec Rep	Ohio Decisions Reprint [*A publication*] (DLA)
ODEE	[*The*] Oxford Dictionary of English Etymology [*A publication*]
ODef	Defiance Public Library, Defiance, OH [*Library symbol Library of Congress*] (LCLS)
ODefC	Defiance College, Defiance, OH [*Library symbol Library of Congress*] (LCLS)
ODelp	Delphos Public Library, Delphos, OH [*Library symbol Library of Congress*] (LCLS)
odem	Order of Our Lady of Mercy (TOCD)
OdeM	Order of Our Lady of Mercy (TOCD)
OD-ENDOR	Optically Detected Electron Nuclear Double Resonance [*Spectroscopy*]
Odeneal	Odeneal's Reports [*9-11 Oregon*] [*A publication*] (DLA)
ODEPA	Organizacion Deportiva Panamericana [*Pan American Sports Organization - PASO*] [*Mexico City, Mexico*] (EAIO)
ODEPA	Oxapentamethylenediethylenephosphoramide [*Pharmacology*]
ODEPLAN	Oficina de Planificacion Nacional [*Office of National Planning*] [*Spain*] (AD)
O Dep Rep	Ohio Department Reports [*A publication*] (DLA)
Oderi	Odericus [*Flourished, 1166-1200*] [*Authority cited in pre-1607 legal work*] (DSA)
ODES	Deseronto Public Library, Ontario [*Library symbol National Library of Canada*] (NLC)
ODES	Optical Discrimination Evaluation Study [*NASA*] (NASA)
OD-ESR	Optically Detected Electron Spin Resonance [*Spectroscopy*]
OD-ESSA	Ocean Data Environmental Science Services Acquisition [*Buoy*]
ODESSA	Oceanographic Data for the Environmental Science Services Administration (GFGA)
ODESSA	Organisation der Ehemaligen Schutzstaffel Angehoeriggen [*Organization of Former Members of the Elite Guard*] [*Founded after World War II to smuggle war criminals out of Germany and provide them with false identities*]
ODESUR	Organizacion Deportiva Sudamericana [*An association*] (EAIO)
ODESY	Online Data Entry System [*Burroughs Corp.*]
ODET	Odetics, Inc. [*NASDAQ symbol*] (SAG)
ODETA	Odetics, Inc.'A' [*NASDAQ symbol*] (TTSB)
ODETB	Odetics, Inc.'B' [*NASDAQ symbol*] (TTSB)
Odetics	Odetics, Inc. [*Associated Press*] (SAG)
Odf	Odofredus [*Deceased, 1265*] [*Authority cited in pre-1607 legal work*] (DSA)

ODF	Official Development Finance
ODF	Old Dominion Foundation (AD)
ODF	One-Dimension Flow
ODF	Opacity Distribution Function [Spectroscopy]
ODF	Operational Deployment Force (AD)
ODF	Optimal Decision Function
ODF	Orbit Determination Facility (MCD)
ODF	Orientation Distribution Function
ODF	Original Data File (NITA)
ODF	Output Data File
odfc	Outside Diameter of Female Coupling (AD)
ODFFU	Organization for Defense of Four Freedoms for Ukraine (EA)
ODFI	Open Die Forging Institute (EA)
ODFL	Old Dominion Freight Line [NASDAQ symbol] (TTSB)
ODFL	Old Dominion Freight Lines, Inc. [NASDAQ symbol] (SPSG)
ODFR	Oxygen-Derived Free Radicals [Biochemistry]
ODFT	Odd Discrete Fourier Transform (MCD)
ODFW	Oregon Department of Fish and Wildlife Research and Development Section [Oregon State University] [Research center] (RCD)
ODG	Enid, OK [Location identifier FAA] (FAAL)
ODG	Offline Data Generator
ODG	Operational Data Group (MCD)
ODG	Operational Design Group
ODG	Orbit Data Generator [NASA]
Odgers	Odgers on Libel and Slander [A publication] (DLA)
ODGF	Osteosarcoma-Derived Growth Factor [Biochemistry]
Odg Lib	Odgers on Libel and Slander [A publication] (DLA)
Odg Pl	Odgers on Principles of Pleading [20th ed.] [1975] [A publication] (DLA)
ODGSE	Operational Development Ground Support Equipment (AAG)
ODGSO	Office of Domestic Gold and Silver Operations [Department of the Treasury]
ODH	Highland Secondary School, Dundas, Ontario [Library symbol National Library of Canada] (NLC)
ODH	Octanol Dehydrogenase [An enzyme]
ODH	Octopine Dehydrogenase [An enzyme]
ODH	Ontario Department of Health [Canada] (AD)
ODHS	Dundas Historical Society Museum, Ontario [Library symbol National Library of Canada] (BIB)
ODHT	Hagerman Township Public Library, Ontario [Library symbol National Library of Canada] (NLC)
ODHWS	Office of Defense Health and Welfare Services [World War II]
ODI	Nodine, MN [Location identifier FAA] (FAAL)
ODI	Odin Industry Ltd. [Vancouver Stock Exchange symbol]
ODI	Office Document Index
ODI	Office of Director of Intelligence [Military]
ODI	Open Datalink Interface [Computer science]
ODI	Open-Door International [An association] (AD)
ODI	Open Door International for the Economic Emancipation of the Woman Worker [Brussels, Belgium] (EAIO)
ODI	Operational Development Inspection (SAA)
ODI	Optical Digital Imagery
ODI	Optonics Devices Incorporated
ODI	Overseas Development Institute (EA)
ODIC	Outside Diameter of Inner Conductor
ODID	Office of the Director of Industrial Demobilization
ODIF	Office Document Interchange Format (HGAA)
ODIFF	Oil Differential
ODIL	Overseas Development Institute Ltd. (AD)
ODIN	Online Dakota Information Network [Information service or system] (IID)
ODIN	Online Dokumentations und Informationsnetz (NITA)
ODIN	Online Dokumentations- und Informationsverbund [Online Documentation and Information Affiliation]
ODIN	Operational Display Information Network (MCD)
ODIN	Optimal [or Orbital] Design Integration [Computer program]
ODIRP	Office, Director of Personnel [Air Force]
ODIS	Object Design, Inc. [NASDAQ symbol] (SAG)
ODIS	Ocean Dynamics Information System [Marine science] (MSC)
ODIS	Optical Disk Interface System [Computer science]
ODIS	Orbital Design Integration System
ODISTA	Origin Destination Information System [US Postal Service]
ODISTA	Oceanographic Data in Subtrial Areas
ODJ	Ouanda Djalle [Central African Republic] [Airport symbol] (AD)
ODJB	Original Dixieland Jazz Band
ODJS	Office of the Director, Joint Staff (MCD)
ODK	Kodiak, AK [Location identifier FAA] (FAAL)
ODK	Omicron Delta Kappa [Fraternity]
ODK	One-Dimensional Kinetics [Computer program] (MCD)
ODL	Cordillo Downs [South Australia] [Airport symbol] (AD)
ODL	Object Definition Language [Computer science]
ODL	Oceanic Data Link [FAA] (TAG)
ODL	Office Document Language [Telecommunications]
ODL	Office of Defense Lending [Department of the Treasury]
ODL	Office of the Duchy of Lancaster [British]
ODL	Officer Deficiency Letter [Navy] (NVT)
ODL	Open and Distance Learning (AIE)
ODL	Ostwald Dilution Law [Chemistry]
ODL	University of Dayton, Law Library, Dayton, OH [OCLC symbol] (OCLC)
ODLAMP	One-Dimensional LASER and Mixing Program
ODLB	Dwight Branch, Lake Of Bays Township Public Library, Ontario [Library symbol National Library of Canada] (BIB)
ODLB	Optical Dispensers' Licensing Board [New South Wales, Australia]
ODLI	Open Data Link Interface [Computer science]

ODLRO	Off-Diagonal Long-Range Order [Physics]
odlsq	Odalisque (VRA)
ODLY	Orderly (WGA)
ODM	Methodist Theological School in Ohio, Delaware, OH [Library symbol Library of Congress] (LCLS)
ODM	Odiham FTU [British ICAO designator] (FAAC)
ODM	Office of Defense Mobilization [Transferred to Office of Defense and Civilian Mobilization, 1958]
ODM	Oil Debris Monitor
ODM	One Day Mission [NASA] (KSC)
ODM	Operational Data Management (KSC)
ODM	Operational Development Memorandum (AAG)
ODM	Operations Data Message (MCD)
ODM	Ophthalmodynamometry [Ophthalmology] (MAE)
odm	Ophthalmodynamometry [Ophthalmology] (AD)
ODM	Optical Diffractogram
ODM	Optical Disk Memory
ODM	Optical Display Memory [Computer science]
ODM	Optimized Delivery Model [Compaq] [Computer science]
ODM	Optimized Distribution Model [Compaq Computer Corp.] [Computer science]
ODM	Orbital Determination Module
ODM	Order of De Molay (AD)
ODM	Outboard Data Manager [Computer science] (BUR)
ODM	Overseas Development Ministry [British]
ODMA	Office of the Director of Military Assistance [Air Force] (AFM)
ODMA	Open Document Management API [Application Programming Interface] [Computer science]
ODMA	Optical Distributors and Manufacturers Association (AD)
ODMC	Office for Dependents' Medical Care [Army] (AABC)
odmc	Outside Diameter of Male Coupling (AD)
ODMD	Delcan, Don Mills, Ontario [Library symbol National Library of Canada] (NLC)
ODMF	Ortho-Demethylfortimicin [Biochemistry]
ODMG	Object Database Management Group [Computer science] (CDE)
ODMIBM	IBM Canada Ltd., Don Mills, Ontario [Library symbol National Library of Canada] (NLC)
ODMN	National Research Council, Don Mills, Ontario [Library symbol National Library of Canada] (NLC)
ODMO	Office of Defense Management and Organization [Military]
ODMR	Optically Detected Magnetic Resonance [Spectroscopy]
ODMRJ	Rolf Jensen & Associates Ltd., Don Mills, Ontario [Library symbol National Library of Canada] (NLC)
ODMS	Operational Data Management System [FAA] (TAG)
ODMT	Office of the Director of Military Training
ODMWS	Wyda Systems Canada, Inc., Don Mills, Ontario [Library symbol National Library of Canada] (NLC)
ODN	Company of Mary [Roman Catholic women's religious order]
ODN	Dalton-Dalton-Newport, Cleveland, OH [OCLC symbol] (OCLC)
ODN	Long Seridan [Malaysia] [Airport symbol] (OAG)
Odn	Odense (AD)
Odn	Odin (AD)
ODN	Oligodeoxynucleotide [Biochemistry]
ODN	Ophthalmodynamometry [Ophthalmology]
ODN	Organization Development Network (EA)
ODN	Overseas Development Network (EA)
odn	Own Doppler Nullifer (AD)
ODN	Own Doppler Nullifier
ODN	Oxbridge Directory of Newsletters [A publication]
ODNA	Operational Data and Notices to Airmen [FAA]
ODNMR	Optically-Detected Nuclear Magnetic Resonance [Spectroscopy]
ODNP	Ohio Decisions [A publication] (DLA)
ODNR	Oxford Dictionary of Nursery Rhymes [A publication]
ODNRI	Overseas Development Natural Resources Institute [British Information service or system] (IID)
ODNS	Operations Division of Naval Staff [British]
Odo	Odofredus [Deceased, 1265] [Authority cited in pre-1607 legal work] (DSA)
ODO	Odometer [Automotive engineering]
ODO	Office of Disability Operations [Social Security Administration] [Began in 1979] (OICC)
ODO	Opeongo High School, Douglas, Ontario [Library symbol National Library of Canada] (NLC)
ODO	Operations Duty Officer (MUGU)
ODO	Outdoor Officer [Customs] [British]
ODOB	Dobie Public Library, Ontario [Library symbol National Library of Canada] (BIB)
ODOE	Oregon Department of Energy (AD)
OD/OE	Organizational Development/Organizational Effectiveness (MCD)
ODOF	Dowling Branch, Onaping Falls Public Library, Ontario [Library symbol National Library of Canada] (NLC)
Odof	Odofredus [Deceased, 1265] [Authority cited in pre-1607 legal work] (DSA)
Odofr	Odofredus [Deceased, 1265] [Authority cited in pre-1607 legal work] (DSA)
Odofre	Odofredus [Deceased, 1265] [Authority cited in pre-1607 legal work] (DSA)
ODOM	Odometer (AAG)
odom	Odometer (AD)
Odonel Mercandil	Odonellus Mercandilis [Authority cited in pre-1607 legal work] (DSA)
ODONT	Odontology
odont	Odontology (AD)
OdoorS	Outdoor Systems, Inc. [Associated Press] (SAG)
odop	Offset Doppler (AD)

ODOP.......... Offset Doppler
ODOP.......... Orbital Doppler (IAA)
ODOR.......... Dorion Public Library, Ontario [*Library symbol National Library of Canada*] (NLC)
odoram........ Odoramentum [*Perfume*] [*Latin*] (MAE)
odorat......... Odoratus [*Odorous*] [*Latin*] (MAE)
odorl.......... Odorless (AD)
ODOTS........ One-Day One-Trial System (AD)
ODOU......... Douro Public Library, Ontario [*Library symbol National Library of Canada*] (BIB)
ODOW......... Ohio Division of Wildlife
O'Dowd Sh... O'Dowd's Merchant Shipping Act [*A publication*] (DLA)
ODP........... Occipitodextra Posterior [*A fetal position*] [*Medicine*] (AAMN)
odp............ Occipito-Dextra Posterior (AD)
ODP........... Ocean Drilling Program [*Texas A & M University*] [*Research center*] (RCD)
ODP........... Octyl Isodecyl Phthalate [*Organic chemistry*]
ODP........... Oekologisch-Demokratische Partei [*Ecological Democratic Party*] [*Germany Political party*] (PPW)
ODP........... Office Depot [*NYSE symbol*] (TTSB)
ODP........... Office Depot, Inc. [*NYSE symbol*] (SPSG)
ODP........... Office of Defense Planning [*of FRS*]
ODP........... Office of Disability Programs [*Social Security Administration*] (OICC)
ODP........... Office of Disaster Preparedness (AD)
ODP........... Officer Distribution Plan [*Army*]
ODP........... Offshore Drilling Platform
ODP........... Open Data Path (MCD)
ODP........... Open Distributed Processing [*Telecommunications*] (OSI)
ODP........... Open Door Policy
ODP........... Open Dripproof
ODP........... Operational Development Plan [*or Program*]
ODP........... Operational Display Procedure (MCD)
ODP........... Optical Data Processing
ODP........... Orbit Determination Program
odp............ Order-Despatched (AD)
ODP........... Orderly Departure Program [*for Vietnamese refugees*] [*United Nations*]
ODP........... Order of the Sons of Divine Providence
ODP........... Organic Development Problem (SAA)
ODP........... Organized Reservists in Drill Pay Status [*Military*]
ODP........... Original Departure Point
ODP........... Original Document Processing
ODP........... Outline Development Plan [*Army*] (AFIT)
ODP........... Output-to-Display Parity Error [*Computer science*] (SAA)
ODP........... Overall Documentation Plan [*NATO*] (NATG)
ODP........... Overlay Demonstration Program [*Military*]
ODP........... Oviposition-Determining Pheromone
ODP........... Ozone-Depleting [*or Depletion*] Potential [*Environmental science*]
ODP........... Ozone Depletion Potential [*Meteorology*]
OD (PA & E)... Office of the Director (Program Analysis and Evaluation) (MCD)
ODPCS........ Oceanographic Data Processing and Control System (OA)
ODPEX........ Offshore Drilling and Production Exhibition (PDAA)
ODPHP....... Office of Disease Prevention and Health Promotion [*US Public Health Service*] [*Information service or system*] (IID)
ODPI......... Office of Director Public Information [*Military*]
ODP/MT....... Organisation pour la Democratie Populaire/Mouvement du Travail [*Burkina Faso*] [*Political party*] (EY)
ODPP.......... Office of the Director of Public Prosecutions [*Australia*]
ODPP.......... Open Dripproof Protected
O'D Pr & Acc... O'Dedy's Principal and Accessory [*1812*] [*A publication*] (DLA)
ODPS.......... Operational Data Processing Squadron
ODPSK........ Oil Dipstick
ODQ........... Opponens Digiti Quinti [*Muscle*] [*Anatomy*] (DAVI)
ODQ........... [*The*] Oxford Dictionary of Quotations [*A publication*]
ODQM........ Office of the Division Quartermaster
ODR........... Dryden Public Library, Ontario [*Library symbol National Library of Canada*] (NLC)
ODR........... Oculomotor Delayed Response [*Performance test task*]
ODR........... Office of Defense Resources [*Civil Defense*]
ODR........... Office of Dissemination and Resources [*HEW*]
ODR........... Official Discount Rate [*Finance*] (ECON)
ODR........... Omnidirectional Range
ODR........... On Display Racks [*Freight*]
ODR........... Operational Design Resolution (SAA)
ODR........... Operator Data Register [*Telecommunications*] (TEL)
ODR........... Optical Data Recognition [*Computer science*]
ODR........... ORDALT [*Ordnance Alterations*] Deficiency Review (MCD)
odr............ Order (AD)
ODR........... Ordnance Difficulty Report (MCD)
ODR........... Original Data Record
ODR........... Output Data Redundancy (MCD)
ODR........... Output Definition Register
ODR........... Oxygen Diffusion Rate (OA)
ODR........... Roanoke, VA [*Location identifier FAA*] (FAAL)
ODRAN....... Operational Drawing Revision Advance Notice (NASA)
ODRC......... Office of Disaster Relief Coordinator [*United Nations*] (WDAA)
ODRC......... Orbiter Data Reduction Center [*NASA*] (MCD)
OD Re........ Ohio Decisions Reprint [*A publication*] (DLA)
OD Rep...... Ohio Decisions Reprint [*A publication*] (DLA)
ODRI.......... Deep River Public Library, Ontario [*Library symbol National Library of Canada*] (NLC)
ODRI.......... Office of United States Defense Representative, India [*Army*] (AABC)
ODRL......... Delta Branch, Rideau Lakes Union Library, Ontario [*Library symbol National Library of Canada*] (BIB)
ODRM........ Operations Design Reference Mission (MCD)

ODRN........ Orbiting Data Relay Network
ODRP........ Office of Defense Representative, Pakistan [*Army*]
ODRS........ Orbiting Data Relay System (MCD)
ODRS........ Ore Deposits Research Section [*Pennsylvania State University*] [*Research center*] (RCD)
ODRSS....... Orbiting Data Relay Satellite System (MCD)
O/DRV....... Over Drive [*Automotive engineering*]
ODS........... Obstacle Detection System
ODS........... Occupational Demand Schedule (ADA)
ODS........... Ocean Data Station [*Marine science*] (MSC)
ODS........... Octadecylsilane [*Organic chemistry*]
ODS........... Octadeyl(dimethyl)chlorosilane [*Organic chemistry*]
ODS........... Odessa [*Ukraine*] [*Airport symbol*] (OAG)
ODS........... Odessa [*Washington*] [*Seismograph station code, US Geological Survey*] (SEIS)
ODS........... Odessa Explorations Ltd. [*Vancouver Stock Exchange symbol*]
ODS........... Odometer Disclosure Statement
ODS........... Office Dialog System [*Computer science*]
ODS........... Office for Domestic Shipping [*Department of Commerce*]
ODS........... Office of Defender Services (AD)
ODS........... Old Dominion Speedway [*Auto racing*]
ODS........... Open Database Server [*Computer science*]
ODS........... Operating-Differential Subsidy [*Authorized by Merchant Marine Act of 1936*]
ODS........... Operational Data Summary (AAG)
ODS........... Operation Desert Storm [*Military*] (RDA)
ODS........... Operations Directorate Station (SAA)
ODS........... Optical Docking System
ODS........... Optimal Decisions System
ODS........... Orbiter Dynamic Simulator [*NASA*]
ODS........... Ordnance Delivery Schedule [*Navy*] (NG)
ODS........... Orton Dyslexia Society (EA)
ODS........... Osric Dining Society (EA)
ODS........... Output Data Strobe
ODS........... Overall Distance Standard [*for golf balls*] [*Adopted by the United States Golf Association in 1976*]
ODS........... Oxidative-Desulfurization [*Fuel technology*]
ODS........... Oxide Dispersion Strengthened [*Metallurgy*]
ODS........... Oxide Dispersion Strengthened [*Ferrous metallurgy*]
ods........... Oxide Dispersion Strengthened (AD)
ODS........... Oxygen Depletion Sensor
ODS........... Ozone-Depleting Substance (AAGC)
ODSA......... Open Distributed Systems Architecture [*British*]
ODSA......... Operating-Differential Subsidy Agreement [*MARAD*] (TAG)
ODSAS....... Officer Dual Specialty Allocation System
ODSB......... Ocean Data Station Buoy
ODSBA....... Oxford Down Sheep Breeders Association [*British*] (DBA)
ODSD........ Oversea Duty Selection Date [*Air Force*]
odsd.......... Overseas Duty Selection Date (AD)
ODSDG...... Dalkeith Branch, Stormont, Dundas, and Glengarry County Library, Ontario [*Library symbol National Library of Canada*] (BIB)
ODSE......... Open Door Student Exchange (EA)
ODS/FRODS... Observable Differences/Functionally Related Observable Differences (MCD)
ODSI.......... Ocean Data Systems, Inc. [*Information service or system*] (IID)
ODSI.......... Optical Data Systems [*NASDAQ symbol*] (TTSB)
ODSI.......... Optical Data Systems, Inc. [*NASDAQ symbol*] (SAG)
ODSR......... Office of the Director of Scientific Research (AD)
ODSRS....... Orbiting Deep Space Relay Station (MCD)
ODSS......... Ocean Dumping Surveillance System [*Coast Guard*] (MSC)
ODSS......... Order Delivery Schedule Summary (MCD)
ODSY........ Sayun [*People's Democratic Republic of Yemen*] [*ICAO location identifier*] (ICLI)
ODT........... Occipitodextra Transversa [*A fetal position*] [*Medicine*] (AAMN)
odt........... Occipito-Dextra Transverse (AD)
ODT........... Ocean Data Transmitter
ODT........... Octal Debugging Technique [*Computer science*] (IEEE)
odt........... Octal Debugging Technique (AD)
ODT........... Odor Detection Threshold (AD)
ODT........... Odor Detection Threshold (PDAA)
ODT........... Office of Defense Transportation [*Within Office for Emergency Management*] [*World War II*]
ODT........... Oklahoma Department of Transportation
ODT........... Omnidirection Transmission (NVT)
odt........... One-Day Trials (AD)
odt........... On-Line Debugging Technique [*Computer science*] (AD)
ODT........... Online Debugging Technique
ODT........... Operational Demand Time [*Military*] (CAAL)
ODT........... Operational Demonstration Test
ODT........... Operational Development Team (IAA)
ODT........... Optical Data Transmission
ODT........... Order-Disorder Transformation
ODT........... Otago Daily Times [*A publication*] (AD)
ODT........... Outside Diameter Tube (MSA)
ODT........... Overseas Deployment Training [*Army*]
ODTAA....... One Damn Thing After Another [*Title of book by John Masefield*]
ODTACCS.... Office of the Director, Telecommunications, and Command and Control Systems [*DoD*] (PDAA)
ODTC......... Office of Defense Trade Controls (AAGC)
ODTC......... Optic Display Test Chamber
ODTF......... Operational Development Test Facility (AAG)
ODTM........ Orbiter Dynamic Test Model [*NASA*]
ODTS......... Offset Doppler Tracking System (KSC)
ODTS......... Operational Development Test Site (AAG)
ODTS......... Optical Data Transmission System

ODTS	Optical Discrimination and Tracking System [Army]
ODTS	Organic Dust Toxic Syndrome [Medicine]
ODTW	Oppositely-Directed Travelling Wave (PDAA)
ODU	Dunnville Public Library, Ontario [Library symbol National Library of Canada] (NLC)
ODU	Old Dominion University [Virginia]
ODU	Old Dutch [Language, etc.]
ODU	Optical Density Unit
ODU	Optical Display Unit [Computer science] (MCD)
ODU	Output Display Unit [Computer science]
ODUB	Bibliotheque Publique de Dubreuilville, Ontario [Library symbol National Library of Canada] (NLC)
ODUC	Ohio Data Users Center [Columbus] [Information service or system] (IID)
ODUM	Association of American Youth of Ukrainian Descent (EA)
ODUMP	Ocean Dumping Permits [Database] [Environment Canada] [Information service or system] (CRD)
ODUN	Dundalk Public Library, Ontario [Library symbol National Library of Canada] (NLC)
od units	Optical-Density Units (AD)
ODUR	Durham Public Library, Ontario [Library symbol National Library of Canada] (NLC)
ODURF	Old Dominion University Research Foundation [Old Dominion University] [Research center] (RCD)
ODUSD(ES)	Office of the Deputy Under Secretary of Defense (Environmental Security) [DoD] (RDA)
ODUSD (R & AT)	Office of the Deputy Under Secretary of Defense for Research and Advanced Technology [DoD] (RDA)
ODUSM	Office, Deputy Under Secretary for Manpower [Navy]
ODUSN	Office, Deputy Under Secretary of the Navy
ODV	Eau-de-Vie [Taken from the French pronunciation and used to refer to brandy]
ODVA	Open DeviceNet Vendors Association (ACII)
ODVAR	Orbit Determination and Vehicle Attitude Reference
ODVP	Optimal Digital Voice Processor (MCD)
ODW	Oak Harbor [Washington] [Airport symbol] (OAG)
ODW	Office of Drinking Water [Environmental Protection Agency]
ODW	Ohio Wesleyan University, Delaware, OH [Library symbol Library of Congress] (LCLS)
ODW	Omega Dropwindsonde [Meteorology]
ODW	Oregon Draymen & Warehousemen's Association, Portland OR [STAC]
ODW	Organic Dry Weight
ODW	Our Developing World [An association] (EA)
ODW	Output Discrete Word (MCD)
ODW	Oven-Dried Weight
ODW	Workers Health and Safety Centre, Don Mills, Ontario [Library symbol National Library of Canada] (BIB)
ODWA	Odwalla, Inc. [NASDAQ symbol] (SAG)
Odwalla	Odwalla, Inc. [Associated Press] (SAG)
ODWC	West Carleton Secondary School, Dunrobin, Ontario [Library symbol National Library of Canada] (BIB)
ODWIN	Opening Doors Wider in Nursing [Project]
ODWSA	Office of the Directorate of Weapon Systems Analysis [Army] (AABC)
O'Dwyer	Jack O'Dwyer's Newsletter [A publication] [New York, NY] (WDMC)
ODX	Ord, NE [Location identifier FAA] (FAAL)
ODY	Odyssey Industries, Inc. [Toronto Stock Exchange symbol]
ODY	Odyssey International [Canada ICAO designator] (FAAC)
ODZ	Outer Defense Zone
OE	Austria [International civil aircraft marking] (ODBW)
OE	Exeter Public Library, Ontario [Library symbol National Library of Canada] (NLC)
O/E	Observed versus Expected
OE	OE, Inc. [Toronto Stock Exchange symbol]
Oe	Oersted [Unit of magnetizing intensity]
oe	Oersted (AD)
OE	Offensive End [Football]
OE	Office Equipment
OE	Office of Education [HEW]
OE	Office of Energy [Department of Agriculture] (GFGA)
OE	Office of Enforcement [Environmental Protection Agency] (GFGA)
OE	Oil Emulsion [Microbiology]
OE	Oil Equivalent
OE	Old English [Language, etc.] [i.e., before 1150 or 1200]
OE	Old English [Typeface] (WDMC)
OE	Old Etonian [British]
OE	Omission Excepted (IAA)
OE	Omissions Excepted
oe	Omissions Excepted (AD)
o/e	On Examination (AD)
OE	On Examination [Medicine]
OE	Opened Edges [Publishing] (DGA)
OE	Open End (MSA)
oe	Open End (AD)
OE	Operating Engineer (NRCH)
OE	Operating Expense
OE	Operational Evaluation [Army]
OE	Operation Enterprise [Hamilton, NY] (EA)
OE	Operation Enterprise Newsletter [A publication]
OE	Operations Engineering (AAG)
OE	Optical/Electrical Conversion [Telecommunications]
OE	Optical Emission (MCD)
OE	Orbital Engine ADS [NYSE symbol] (SPSG)
O/E	Order/Entry System [Computer science] (DHSM)
OE	Ordnance Electrician [British military] (DMA)

OE	Ordnance Engineer [British military] (DMA)
OE	Oregon Electric Railway Co. [AAR code]
OE	Organizational Effectiveness
oe	Organizational Effectiveness (AD)
OE	Organizational Entity
OE	Organizational Error [Engineering]
OE	Organo Espressivo [Swell Organ] [Music]
oe	Organo Espressivo [Swell Organ] [Italian] (AD)
OE	Orientalium Ecclesiarum [Decree on the Eastern Catholic Churches] [Vatican II document]
OE	Original Entry [Computer science]
OE	Original Equipment [Automobile industry]
OE	Original Error [Navigation]
OE	Orthoenstatite [Mineral]
OE	Other Essays [Literature] (ROG)
OE	Otitis Externa [Medicine]
o/e	Otitis Externa (AD)
oe	Outdoor Education (AD)
OE	Out Island Airways (OAG)
OE	Outlook Express [Computer science] (PCM)
OE	Output Enable [Semiconductor memory] (IEEE)
OE	Over-the-Horizon Expanded (MCD)
OE	Own Exchange [Telecommunications] (TEL)
OE	Samoan [ICAO designator] (AD)
OEA	Archives, City of Etobicoke, Ontario [Library symbol National Library of Canada] (BIB)
OEA	Eastern Oklahoma District Library, Muskogee, OK [OCLC symbol] (OCLC)
OEA	Oahu Education Association [Hawaii] (AD)
OEA	Oblate Education Association [Defunct] (EA)
OEA	OEA, Inc. [NYSE symbol] (SPSG)
OEA	Office Education Association (EA)
OEA	Office Executives Association (AD)
OEA	Office of Economic Adjustment [Air Force] (AFM)
OEA	Office of Economic Analysis [Formerly, Office of Business Economics] [Department of Commerce]
OEA	Office of Environmental Affairs (AD)
OEA	Office of Environmental Analysis [Oak Ridge National Laboratory]
OEA	Office of Ethnic Affairs [Victoria, Australia]
OEA	Office of Export Administration [Formerly, OEC] [Department of Commerce]
OEA	Office of External Affairs [Environmental Protection Agency] (GFGA)
OEA	Ohio Education Association (AD)
OEA	Operational Effectiveness Analysis (MCD)
OEA	Operator Error Analysis
OEA	Ophthalmic Exhibitors' Association [British] (DBA)
OEA	Optometric Editors Association (EA)
OEA	Orchestral Employers' Association [British] (BI)
OEA	Ordnance Electrical Artificer [British military] (DMA)
OEA	Oregon Education Association (AD)
OEA	Organizacion de los Estados Americanos [Organization of American States - OAS] [Spanish]
OEA	Organizational Expense Accounts [Army]
OEA	Outdoor Education Association (EA)
OEA	Overseas Education Association (EA)
OEA	Vincennes, IN [Location identifier FAA] (FAAL)
OEAA	Oil Engineering Apprentices Association (AD)
OEAB	Abha [Saudi Arabia] [ICAO location identifier] (ICLI)
OEac	East Cleveland Public Library, East Cleveland, OH [Library symbol Library of Congress] (LCLS)
OEAH	Al-Ahsa [Saudi Arabia] [ICAO location identifier] (ICLI)
OEal	East Liverpool Carnegie Public Library, East Liverpool, OH [Library symbol Library of Congress] (LCLS)
OEALC	Oficina Regional de Educacion para America Latina y el Caribe [Regional Office for Education in Latin America and the Caribbean-Chile] (IID)
OEalK	Kent State University, East Liverpool Regional Campus, East Liverpool, OH [Library symbol Library of Congress] (LCLS)
OE & TB	Officer Education and Training Branch [BUPERS]
OEAP	Operational Error Analysis Program
OEAQ	Outdoor Educators' Association of Queensland [Australia]
OEAS	Orbital Emergency Arresting System [NASA] (NASA)
OEAS	Organisation Europaischer Aluminium Schmelzhutten [Organization of European Aluminium Foundries] (PDAA)
OEAS	Oxygen Enriched Air System (MCD)
OEB	Officers' Organization for Economic Benefits [Commercial firm] (EA)
OEB	Oregon Educational Broadcasting (AD)
OEB	Organic Electrolyte Battery
OEBA	El-Baha [Saudi Arabia] [ICAO location identifier] (ICLI)
OEBA	Office for Economic and Business Affairs [Department of State]
OEBH	Bisha [Saudi Arabia] [ICAO location identifier] (ICLI)
OEBS	Office of Employee Benefits Security [Department of Labor]
OEBS	Organic Electrolyte Battery System
OEC	Observed Effect Concentration [Environmental science] (ERG)
OEC	Odd-Even Check
Oec	Oeconomica [of Aristotle] [Classical studies] (OCD)
Oec	Oeconomicus [of Xenophon] [Classical studies] (OCD)
OEC	Oesterreichischer Aero-Club [Austrian Aero Club] [German] (AD)
OEC	Office of Emergency Communications [FCC] (NTCM)
OEC	Office of Energy Conservation [Functions transferred to Federal Energy Administration]
OEC	Office of Export Control [Later, OEA] [World War II]
OEC	Office on Educational Credit [Later, OECC] (EA)
OEC	Ohio Edison [NYSE symbol] (TTSB)
OEC	Ohio Edison Co. [NYSE symbol] (SPSG)

OEC.............. Ohio Edison Financing Trust [*NYSE symbol*] (SAG)
OEC.............. Oil Exporting Countries (AD)
OEC.............. Ontario Election Decisions [*A publication*] (DLA)
OEC.............. Open-End Company [*Business term*] (MHDW)
OEC.............. Open-End Credit [*Business term*] (MHDW)
OEC.............. Operational Employment Concept [*Army*] (AABC)
OEC.............. Operational Evaluation Command [*Army*] (DOMA)
OEC.............. Optical Effect Code
OEC.............. Optic-Electronic Corp. (RDA)
OEC.............. Opto-Electronics Center (MCD)
OEC.............. Orbital Electron Capture
OEC.............. Orbiting Experimental Capsule
OEC.............. Ordnance Equipment Chart
OEC.............. Organizational Effectiveness Consultants (INF)
OEC.............. Organizational Entity Code
oec.............. Organizational Entity Code (AD)
OEC.............. Overpaid Entry Certificate (DS)
OECA.............. Oxygen-Evolving Complex [*Photosynthesis*]
OECA.............. Ontario Educational Communications Authority [*Canada*]
OEC & S ..... Organizational Effectiveness Center and School [*Army*]
OECC.............. Office on Educational Credit and Credentials (EA)
OECC.............. Oregon Educational Computing Consortium (EDAC)
OECCNU...... Organizacion para la Educacion la Ciencia, y la Cultura [*Organization for Education, Science, and Culture*] [*United Nations*] (AD)
OECD .... Organization for Economic Cooperation and Development [*Formerly, OEEC*]
OECD/ENC ... Organization for Economic Cooperation and Development/ Environment Committee [*Marine science*] (MSC)
OECD/MEI .... OECD Main Economics Indicators (NITA)
OECD/NIA .... OECD National Income Accounts (NITA)
OECE.............. Organisation Europeenne de Cooperation Economique [*Organization for European Economic Cooperation - OEEC*] [*Later, OECD See also OCDE France*] (MSC)
OECE.............. Organizacion Europea de Cooperacion Economica [*Organization for European Economic Cooperation - OEEC*] [*Later, OECD Spain*]
OECF.............. Overseas Economic Cooperation Fund (AD)
OECIC.............. Open-End Contract Information Circulars (AAGC)
OECM.............. Office of Enforcement and Compliance Monitoring [*Environmental Protection Agency*] (GFGA)
OEC Md ...... OEC Medical [*Associated Press*] (SAG)
OECO .... Outboard Engine Cutoff [*NASA*]
oeco .... Outboard Engine Cutoff (AD)
OECON........ Offshore Engineering Conference (MCD)
OECON........ Offshore Exploration Conference
OECPrA....... Ohio Edison 3.90% Pfd [*NYSE symbol*] (TTSB)
OECPrB....... Ohio Edison, 4.40% Pfd [*NYSE symbol*] (TTSB)
OECPrC....... Ohio Edison 4.44% Pfd [*NYSE symbol*] (TTSB)
OECPrT....... Ohio Edison Fin Tr 9.00% Pfd [*NYSE symbol*] (TTSB)
OECQ.............. Organisation Europeene pour la Controle de la Qualite GG1European Quality-Control OrganizationGG2 [*France*] (AD)
OECQ .... Organisation Europeenne pour la Qualite [*European Organization for Quality -EOQC*] [*Switzerland*]
OECS .... Organisation of Eastern Caribbean States (EAIO)
OECS .... Organization for the Enforcement of Child Support (EA)
OECS .... Organization of East Caribbean States (NADA)
OECSEAS .... Organisation of Eastern Caribbean States, Economic Affairs Secretariat [*St. Johns, Antigua*] (EAIO)
OECT........... European Association of the Textile Wholesale Trade [*EC*] (ECED)
OECT........... Oxford Editions of Cuneiform Texts [*A publication*] (BJA)
oecu........... Outboard Engine Cutoff (AD)
OED .... Ocean Engineering Division [*Coast Guard*]
OED .... Office of Economic Development [*Bureau of Indian Affairs*]
OED .... Operational Engineering Detachment (MCD)
OED .... Operational Engineering Division [*Central Electricity Generating Board*] [*British*] (IRUK)
OED .... Operational Evaluation Demonstration (MCD)
OED .... Operation Effectiveness Demonstration (RDA)
OED .... Orbiting Energy Depot
OED .... Otto Erich Deutsch [*Music cataloger*]
OED .... Oxford English Dictionary [*Information service or system A publication*]
OEDA .... Office of Energy Data and Analysis [*Functions transferred to Federal Energy Administration*]
OEDC .... Office of Engineering Design and Construction [*Tennessee Valley Authority*]
OEDC .... Offshore Energy Development Corp. [*NASDAQ symbol*] (SAG)
OEDIPUS...... Oxford English Dictionary Inputting, Proofing, and Updating Service
OEDIT......... Octal Editor [*Computer science*] (MHDI)
OEDO .... Ordnance Engineering Duty Officer
OEDP .... Office of Employment Development Programs (AD)
OEDP .... Overall Economic Development Program [*Bureau of Indian Affairs*]
OEDR........... Dhahran/International [*Saudi Arabia*] [*ICAO location identifier*] (ICLI)
OEDRC......... Optico-Electronic Device for Registering Coincidences (PDAA)
OEDSF......... On-Board Experimental Data Support Facility
OEE .... Ernst & Whinney, Cleveland, OH [*OCLC symbol*] (OCLC)
OEE .... Essex County Public Library, Essex, Ontario [*Library symbol National Library of Canada*] (NLC)
OEE .... Office of Educational Exchange [*Department of State*]
OEE .... Office of the Assistant Secretary for Export Enforcement [*Department of Commerce*] (GFGA)
OEE .... Ordre de l'Etoile de l'Europe [*Huy, Belgium*] (EAIO)
OEE .... Outer Enamel Epithelium [*Dentistry*]
oee .... Outer Enamel Epithelium (AD)
OEEC........... Organization for European Economic Cooperation [*Later, OECD*]
OEEO .... Office of Equal Educational Opportunities [*Office of Education*]

OEEO .... Office of Equal Employment Opportunity [*Department of Labor*] (OICC)
OEEPE......... Organisation Europeenne d'Etudes Photogrammetriques Experimentales [*European Organisation for Experimental Photogrammetric Research*] [*Research Center Netherlands*] (PDAA)
OEER .... Oceanographic Equipment Evaluation Range (NOAA)
OEES........... Interagency Committee on Ocean Exploration and Environmental Services [*Terminated, 1971*] (EGAO)
OEES........... Organization for Equal Education of the Sexes (EA)
OEET........... Office of Environmental Engineering and Technology [*Environmental Protection Agency*] (EPA)
OEETD .... Office of Environmental Engineering and Technology Demonstration [*Washington, DC Environmental Protection Agency*] (GRD)
OEF.............. Ear Falls Public Library, Ontario [*Library symbol National Library of Canada*] (NLC)
OEF.............. Oceanic Educational Foundation (EA)
OEF.............. Officeholders Expense Funds [*Slush money*]
OEF.............. Oil Emersion Field [*Biochemistry*] (DAVI)
OEF.............. Open-End Funds [*Investment term*]
OEF.............. Optical Evaluation Facility (RDA)
OEF.............. Osteopathic Educational Foundation (AD)
OEF.............. Overseas Education Fund [*Later, OEFI*] (EA)
OEF.............. Oxygen Extraction Fraction [*Medicine*] (DMAA)
OEFD.............. Orbiter Electric Field Detector [*NASA*]
OEFE.............. Flos-Elmvale Public Library, Elmvale, Ontario [*Library symbol National Library of Canada*] (BIB)
OEFI.............. OEF [*Overseas Educational Fund*] International (EA)
OEG .... Eganville Public Library, Ontario [*Library symbol National Library of Canada*] (NLC)
OEG .... Occluded Eye Gunsight [*Military*] (INF)
OEG .... Operational Exposure Guidance [*Military*] (INF)
OEG .... Operations Evaluation Group [*Military*]
OEG .... Organization and Equipment Guide [*Army*] (AABC)
OEG .... Outdoor Ethics Guild (EA)
OEG .... Public Library of Enid and Garfield County, Enid, OK [*OCLC symbol*] (OCLC)
OEGCA......... Old English Game Club of America (EA)
OEGCMJ ..... Officer Exercising General Court-Martial Jurisdiction
OEGN .... Gizan [*Saudi Arabia*] [*ICAO location identifier*] (ICLI)
OEGS .... Gassim [*Saudi Arabia*] [*ICAO location identifier*] (ICLI)
OEGT .... Guriat [*Saudi Arabia*] [*ICAO location identifier*] (ICLI)
oegt .... Observable Evidence of Good Teaching (AD)
OEGT .... Observable Evidences of Good Teaching
OEGT .... Office of Education for the Gifted and Talented [*HEW*]
OEH .... Baltimore, MD [*Location identifier FAA*] (FAAL)
OEHL .... Hail [*Saudi Arabia*] [*ICAO location identifier*] (ICLI)
OEHL .... Hoffman-La Roche Ltd., Etobicoke, Ontario [*Library symbol National Library of Canada*] (NLC)
OEHL .... Occupational and Environmental Health Laboratory [*Brooks Air Force Base, TX*] [*Air Force*]
OEHMO........ Open-Ended Health Maintenance Organization [*Insurance*] (WYGK)
OEI.............. Offshore Ecology Investigation [*Oil study*]
OEI.............. Oficina de Educacion Iberoamericana [*Ibero-American Bureau of Education - IABE*] [*Madrid, Spain*] (EAIO)
OEI.............. One Engine Inoperative [*Aviation*]
OEI.............. Options Exchange Index
OEI.............. Optoelectronic Isolator
OEI.............. Organizacion de Estados Iberoamericanos para la Educacion, la Ciencia, y la Cultura [*Organization of Ibero-American States for Education, Science, and Culture*] (EAIO)
OEI.............. Organizational Entity Identity
oei .... Organizational Entity Identity (AD)
OEI.............. Overall Efficiency Index
OEIAA .... Office Equipment Industry Association of Australia
OEIC........... Ocean Engineering Information Centre [*Memorial University of Newfoundland*] [*Information service or system*] (IID)
OEIC........... Open-End Investment Co. [*Investment term*]
OEIC........... Optoelectronic Integrated Circuit [*Computer science*]
OEIC........... Opto-Electronic Integrated Circuits
OEIC........... Overseas Economic Intelligence Committee [*Military*]
OEID .... Office of Engineering Infrastructure Development [*Washington, DC National Science Foundation*] (GRD)
OEII.............. O'Neill Educational Ideologies Inventory (EDAC)
OEII.............. Operation Everest II [*Army*] (RDA)
OEIO .... Odds and Ends Input/Output (MCD)
OEIPS .... Office of Engineering and Information Processing Standards [*National Bureau of Standards*]
OEIS .... Office of Energy Information Services [*Department of Energy*] (IID)
OEIS .... Orbiter Electrical Interface Simulator [*NASA*]
OEIT .... Open-End Investment Trust [*Investment term*]
OEITFL......... Organisation Europeenne des Industries Transformatrices de Fruits et Legumes [*European Organization of Fruit and Vegetable Processing Industries*] [*Common Market*] [*Belgium*]
OEIU .... Office Employes International Union [*Later, OPEIU*]
OEJB........... Jubail [*Saudi Arabia*] [*ICAO location identifier*] (ICLI)
OEJD........... Jeddah [*Saudi Arabia*] [*ICAO location identifier*] (ICLI)
OEJN........... Jeddah/King Abdul Aziz International [*Saudi Arabia*] [*ICAO location identifier*] (ICLI)
OEKJ........... Al-Kharj [*Saudi Arabia*] [*ICAO location identifier*] (ICLI)
OEKM........... Khamis Mushait [*Saudi Arabia*] [*ICAO location identifier*] (ICLI)
OEL........... Elliot Lake Public Library, Ontario [*Library symbol National Library of Canada*] (NLC)
OEL........... Eugene Public Library, Eugene, OR [*OCLC symbol*] (OCLC)
OEL........... Oakley, KS [*Location identifier FAA*] (FAAL)

OEL............. Occupational Exposure Limit
OEL............. Occupational Exposure Limit
OEL............. Ontario Express Ltd. [*Canada ICAO designator*] (FAAC)
OEL............. Ordnance Engineering Laboratory
OEL............. Ordnance Equipment List [*Navy*] (NG)
OEL............. Organizational Equipment List [*Army*]
OELB......... Oertlicher Landwirtschaftsbetrieb [*Local Agricultural Enterprise*] [*German*]
OELD .... Office of the Executive Legal Director [*Nuclear Regulatory Commission*] (GFGA)
OELF.......... Fort Hope Band Library, Eabamet Lake, Ontario [*Library symbol National Library of Canada*] (BIB)
OELK........... Elk Lake Public Library, Ontario [*Library symbol National Library of Canada*] (BIB)
OELM.......... Elmwood Branch, Bruce County Public Library, Ontario [*Library symbol National Library of Canada*] (NLC)
OELMA........ Ohio Educational Library Media Association (EDAC)
OEL/MA....... Ohio Educational Library/Media Association (AD)
OELMN(A)... Ordnance Electrical Mechanician (Air) [*British military*] (DMA)
OELRR .... Office of Economic Liaison and Regulatory Review [*Western Australia*]
OELS........... Elliot Lake Secondary School, Ontario [*Library symbol National Library of Canada*] (NLC)
OEly........... Elyria Library, Elyria, OH [*Library symbol Library of Congress*] (LCLS)
OElyL.......... Lorain County Community College, Elyria, OH [*Library symbol Library of Congress*] (LCLS)
OEM............ Emo Public Library, Ontario [*Library symbol National Library of Canada*] (NLC)
OEM............ Occupational and Environmental Medicine
OEM............ Office Equipment Maintenance
OEM............ Office for Emergency Management [*World War II*]
OEM............ Office of Electronic Machines [*Commercial firm British*]
OEM............ Office of Environmental Mediation
OEM............ Office of Executive Management
oem .... Oil-Emulsion Mud (AD)
OEM............ On Equipment Materiel [*Army*] (AABC)
OEM............ Open-End Marriage
OEM............ Optical Electronic Microscope (WDAA)
OEM............ Optical Electron Microscope (PDAA)
oem............ Optical Electron Microscope (AD)
OEM....... Ordnance Electrical Mechanic [*British military*] (DMA)
OEM............ Organizational Element Model
OEM............ Original Equipment Manufacturer
OEM............ Original Equipment Manufacturer (AD)
oem .... Original Equipment Manufacturer (AD)
OEM............ Other Equipment Manufacturer (IAA)
OEM............ Other Equipment Manufacturers (CMD)
OEM............ Own Equipment Material
OEMA.......... Madinah [*Saudi Arabia*] [*ICAO location identifier*] (ICLI)
OEMA.......... Office Equipment Manufacturers Association (AD)
OEMA.......... Office Equipment Manufacturers Association (NADA)
OEMA.......... Office of Educational and Manpower Assistance (OICC)
OEMA.......... Office of Export Marketing Assistance [*Department of Commerce*]
OEMCP........ Optical Effects Module Electronic Controller and Processor [*NASA*]
oemcp .... Optical Effects Module Electronic Controller and Processor (AD)
OEMI........... Office Equipment Manufacturers Institute [*Later, CBEMA*]
OEMI........... Office of Energy, Minerals, and Industry [*Environmental Protection Agency*]
OEMI........... Other Equipment Manufacturer's Information (IAA)
OEMN .... Ordnance Electrical Mechanician [*British military*] (DMA)
OEMP.......... Office of Environmental Monitoring and Prediction [*National Oceanic and Atmospheric Research Laboratory*] (USDC)
OEMP........... Office of Environmental Monitoring and Prediction [*Marine science*] (OSRA)
OEN .... Ennismore Township Public Library, Ontario [*Library symbol National Library of Canada*] (BIB)
OEN .... Odd-Even Nuclei
oen .... Oenanthic (AD)
oen .... Oenanthyl (AD)
oen .... oenomancy (AD)
oen .... oenomel (AD)
oen .... oenometer (AD)
oen .... oenophilist (AD)
oen .... oenophobist (AD)
oen .... oenopoetic (AD)
OEN .... Ohio Environmental Protection Agency Library, Columbus, OH [*OCLC symbol*] (OCLC)
OEN .... Organizational Entity Name
OENCO........ Organizational Effectiveness Noncommissioned Officer [*Military*]
OENG .... Englehart Public Library, Ontario [*Library symbol National Library of Canada*] (BIB)
OENG .... Nejran [*Saudi Arabia*] [*ICAO location identifier*] (ICLI)
OENLA .... Enterprise Branch, Lennox and Addington County Library, Ontario [*Library symbol National Library of Canada*] (NLC)
OENR .... Oil-Extended Natural Rubber
OENR .... Organization for European Nuclear Research
OEO .... Office of Economic Opportunity [*Functions transferred to other federal agencies, 1973-75*]
OEO .... Office of Equal Opportunity [*NASA*]
OEO .... Officers' Eyes Only [*Military*] (NVT)
oeo .... Officer's Eyes Only (AD)
OEO .... Ordnance Engineer Overseer (AD)
OEO .... Ordnance Executive Officer [*Military British*]
OEO .... Osceola, WI [*Location identifier FAA*] (FAAL)
OEO .... Oversea Employment Office [*Air Force*] (AFM)

OEOA .... Office for Emergency Operations in Africa [*United Nations*] (EY)
OEOB .... Old Executive Office Building [*Washington, DC*]
OE/OE .... Open Entry/Open Exit (OICC)
OEP .... Occupational Education Project
OEP .... Occupational Exploration Program (OICC)
OEP .... Ocean Education Project (EA)
OEP .... Odd-Even Predominance [*Organic chemistry*]
OEP .... Office of Economic Programs [*of BDSA*]
OEP .... Office of Emergency Planning (AD)
OEP .... Office of Emergency Preparedness [*formerly, Planning*] [*Terminated, 1973*]
OEP .... Office of Energy Planning (NADA)
OEP .... Office of Energy Programs [*NASA*]
OEP .... Office of Environmental Policy [*White House*] (USDC)
OEP .... Office of Environmental Policy [*White House*] [*Marine science*] (OSRA)
OEP .... Office of External Programs [*Environmental Protection Agency*] (GFGA)
OEP .... Oil-Extended Polymer (IAA)
OEP .... Open-Ended Plan [*Human resources*] (WYGK)
OEP .... Operand Execution Pipeline [*Computer science*]
OEP .... Operational Employment Plan [*Army*]
OEP .... Optional Educational Programs (AD)
OEP .... Original Element Processor (MHDB)
OEP .... Outside Engineering Personnel (MCD)
OEP .... Overseas Employment Program [*DoD*]
OEP .... Owen Electric Pictures [*Telecommunications service*] (TSSD)
OEP .... Preble County District Library, Eaton, OH [*Library symbol Library of Congress*] (LCLS)
OEPA .... Hafr Al-Batin Airport [*Saudi Arabia*] [*ICAO location identifier*] (ICLI)
OEPA .... Ohio Environmental Protection Agency
OEPA .... Ohio Environmental Protection Agency (DOGT)
OEPAC .... Office of the Economic Planning Advisory Council [*Australia*]
OEPER .... Office of Environmental Processes and Effects Research [*Environmental Protection Agency Washington, DC*] (GRD)
OEPF .... Optometric Extension Program Foundation (EA)
OEPFC .... Official Elvis Presley Fan Club (EAIO)
OEPP .... Organisation Europeenne et Mediterraneenne pour la Protection des Plantes [*European and Mediterranean Plant Protection Organization - EPPO*] (EAIO)
OEPR .... Office of Environmental Project Review [*Department of the Interior*]
OEPR .... Office of Extramural Program Review [*Department of Health and Human Services*] (GRD)
OEPS .... Office of Educational Programs and Services [*NASA*]
OEPT......... Perry Township Public Library Emsdale, Ontario [*Library symbol National Library of Canada*] (NLC)
OEQ .... Order of Engineers of Quebec [*Canada*] (PDAA)
OEQ .... Organisation Europeenne pour la Qualite [*Switzerland*] (EAIO)
OEQC .... Office of Environmental Quality Control (NADA)
OEQC .... Office of Environmental Quality Control (AD)
OER .... Odd-Even Rule
OER .... Oersted [*Unit of magnetizing intensity*]
OER .... Offensive Efficiency Ratio [*Basketball*]
OER .... Office of Aerospace Research [*Air Force*] (AD)
OER .... Office of Economic Research [*Department of Commerce*]
OER .... Office of Energy Research [*Department of Energy Washington, DC*] (GRD)
OER .... Office of Energy Research [*University of Illinois*] [*Research center*] (RCD)
OER .... Office of Evaluation Research [*University of Illinois at Chicago*] [*Research center*] (RCD)
OER .... Office of Exploratory Research [*Environmental Protection Agency Washington, DC*] (GRD)
OER .... Officer Effectiveness Report [*Air Force*] (AFM)
OER .... Officer Efficiency Report [*Military*]
OER .... Officer Engineering Reserve (AD)
OER .... Officer Evaluation Report [*Military*] (INF)
OER .... Officers' Emergency Reserve [*British*]
OER .... Operational ELINT Requirements (MCD)
OER .... Operational Equipment Requirement (AAG)
OER .... Operations Engineering Report (AAG)
OER .... Organization for European Research (AD)
oer............ Original Equipment Replacement (AD)
OER .... Original Equipment Request (AAG)
OER .... Ornskoldsvik [*Sweden*] [*Airport symbol*] (OAG)
OER .... Osmotic Erythrocyte Resistance
O'ER .... Over (ROG)
OER .... Overhead Expenditure Request
OER .... Oxygen Enhancement Ratio
OER .... Oxygen Evolution Reaction (PDAA)
OERA .... Omnibus Education Reconciliation Act of 1981
OERAHA....... Organisation Europeenne pour des Recherches Astronomiques dans l'Hemisphere Austral [*European Southern Observatory - ESO*] (EAIO)
OERC .... Ontario Educational Research Council [*Canada*] (EDAC)
OERC .... Optimum Earth Reentry Corridor [*Aerospace*]
oerc .... Optimum Earth-Reentry Corridor (AD)
OERCPrD ..... Ohio Edison 4.56% Pfd [*NYSE symbol*] (TTSB)
OERD .... Erin District High School, Erin, Ontario [*Library symbol National Library of Canada*] (NLC)
OERD .... Ocean Environment Research Division [*Formerly, Marine Resources Research Division*] (USDC)
OERD .... Ocean Environment Research Division [*Formerly, MARD, Marine Assessment Research Division and MRRD, Marine Resources Research Division*] [*Marine science*] (OSRA)

OERF .... Orthodontic Education and Research Foundation (EA)
OERF .... Rafha [*Saudi Arabia*] [*ICAO location identifier*] (ICLI)
OERI .... Office of Educational Research and Improvement [*Department of Education Washington, DC*]
OERI .... Office of Energy-Related Inventions [*Gaithersburg, MD*] [*National Institute of Standards and Technology*]
OERK .... Riyadh/King Khalid International [*Saudi Arabia*] [*ICAO location identifier*] (ICLI)
OERL .... Elgin Branch, Rideau Lakes Union Library, Ontario [*Library symbol National Library of Canada*] (NLC)
OERL .... Officer Education Research Laboratory [*Air Force*]
OERL .... Overall Echo Return Loss
OERP .... Overseas Expenditure Reduction Program [*Military*] (AFM)
OERPA .... Office of Exploratory Research and Problem Assessment [*National Science Foundation*] (AD)
OERR .... Arar [*Saudi Arabia*] [*ICAO location identifier*] (ICLI)
OERR .... Office of Emergency and Remedial Response [*Environmental Protection Agency*] (GFGA)
OERS .... Officer Evaluation Reporting System [*Army*]
OERS .... Organisation Europeenne de Recherches Spatiales
OERT .... Succursale d'Embrun, Bibliotheque Publique du Canton de Russell [*Embrun Branch, Russell Township Public Library*] Ontario [*Library symbol National Library of Canada*] (BIB)
OERWM .... Office of Environmental Restoration and Waste Management [*U.S. Department of Energy*] (BARN)
OERY .... Riyadh [*Saudi Arabia*] [*ICAO location identifier*] (ICLI)
OES .... Bureau of Oceans and International Environmental and Scientific Affairs [*Department of State*]
OES .... Espanola Public Library, Ontario [*Library symbol National Library of Canada*] (NLC)
OES .... IEEE Oceanic Engineering Society (EA)
OES .... Occupational Employment Statistics [*Department of Labor*]
OES .... Occupational Exposure Standard [*Environmental chemistry*]
OES .... Office of Economic Stabilization [*World War II*]
OES .... Office of Emergency Service [*Federal disaster planning*]
OES .... Office of Employment Security [*Department of Labor*]
OES .... Office of Endangered Species [*Department of the Interior*]
OES .... Office of Examinations and Supervision [*Federal Home Loan Bank Board*]
OES .... Office of Executive Support [*Environmental Protection Agency*] (GFGA)
OES .... Officer Education System [*Army*] (RDA)
OES .... Official Experimental Station [*Amateur radio*]
OES .... Olympus Endoscopy System [*Gastroenterology*] (DAVI)
OES .... Open-Ended Spinning [*Textile industry*]
OES .... Open-Ended System [*Computer science*]
OES .... Operations and Engineering Squadron
OES .... Operations and Equipment Section (SAA)
OES .... Optical Emission Spectroscopy
OES .... Optical Emission Spectroscopy [*Laboratory science*] (DAVI)
OES .... Orbital-Escape System [*NASA*]
OES .... Orbiter Emergency Site [*NASA*] (NASA)
OES .... Order/Entry System [*Computer science*] (OA)
OES .... Order of the Eastern Star [*Freemasonry*] (EA)
OES .... Organisation Europeenne des Scieries [*European Sawmills Organization*] [*EC*] (ECED)
OES .... Organizacion de Estados Americanos [*Organization of American States*] [*Spain*] (AD)
OES .... Organization of European States (AD)
OES .... Ostrich Eggshell [*Archeological material*]
OES .... Outgoing Echo Suppressor [*Telecommunications*] (TEL)
OES .... Overseas Educational Service [*Defunct*]
OES .... San Antonio Oeste [*Argentina*] [*Airport symbol*] (OAG)
OESA .... Office of Earth Sciences Applications [*Department of the Interior*] (GRD)
OESA .... Office of Employment Service Administration [*US Employment Service*] [*Department of Labor*]
OESBR .... Oil Extended Styrene Butadiene Rubber (PDAA)
oesbr .... Oil-Extended Styrene-Butadiene Rubber (AD)
OESC .... Open-Ended Systems Corp.
OESCA .... Old English Sheepdog Club of America (EA)
OESCAND ... Old East Scandinavian [*Language, etc.*]
OESD .... Ocean Engineering System Development
OESE .... Office of Elementary and Secondary Education [*Department of Education*]
OES/E .... Office of the Environment (US Department of) State/Environment, Health and Natural Resources (GNE)
OES/EGC ..... Office of the Environment (US Department of) State/Office of Global Change (GNE)
OES/EHC ..... Office of the Environment (US Department of) State/Office of Ecology, Health and Conservation (GNE)
OES/ENP ..... Bureau of Oceans and International Environmental and Scientific Affairs/Environmental and Population Affairs [*Department of State*] (MSC)
OES/ENV ..... Office of the Environment (US Department of) State/Office of Environmental Protection (GNE)
OESH .... Shared Library Services, South Huron Hospital, Exeter, Ontario [*Library symbol National Library of Canada*] (BIB)
OESH .... Sharurah [*Saudi Arabia*] [*ICAO location identifier*] (ICLI)
OESK .... Al-Jouf [*Saudi Arabia*] [*ICAO location identifier*] (ICLI)
OESK .... Osteuropeiska Solidaritetskommitten [*East European Solidarity Committee*] (EAIO)
OESL .... Oceanographic and Environmental Service Laboratory [*Raytheon Co.*]
OESL .... Sulayel [*Saudi Arabia*] [*ICAO location identifier*] (ICLI)

OESLA .... Office of Engineering Standards Liaison and Analysis [*National Bureau of Standards*] (IAA)
OES/N .... Office of the Environment (US Department of) State/Nuclear Energy and Energy Technology Affairs (GNE)
OES/NED ..... Office of the Environment (US Department of) State/Office of Export and Import Control (GNE)
OES/NEP ..... Office of the Environment (US Department of) State/Office of Non-Proliferation and Export Policy (GNE)
OES/NTS ..... Office of the Environment (US Department of) State/Office of Nuclear Technology and Safeguards (GNE)
OES/O .... Office of the Environment (US Department of) State/Oceans and Fisheries Affairs (GNE)
OESO .... Organisation Internationale d'Etudes Statistiques pour les Maladies de l'Oesophage [*International Organization for Statistical Studies on Diseases of the Esophagus*] (EAIO)
OESO .... Organizational Effectiveness Staff Officer [*Military*]
OESOC .... Organizational Effectiveness Staff Officer Course [*Army*]
OES/OFA ..... Bureau of Oceans and International Environmental and Scientific Affairs/Ocean and Fishery Affairs [*Department of State*] (MSC)
OES/OFA ..... Office of the Environment (US Department of) State/Office of Fisheries Affairs (GNE)
OES/OLP ..... Office of the Environment (US Department of) State/Office of Ocean Law and Policy (GNE)
oesoph. .... Oesophagus (AD)
OESOPH ...... Oesophagus
OES/OSP ..... Office of the Environment (US Department of) State/Office of Marine Science and Polar Affairs (GNE)
OESP .... O Estado de Sao Paulo [*State of Sao Paulo*] [*Brazil*] [*A publication*] (AD)
OESPCMJ ... Officer Exercising Special Court-Martial Jurisdiction
OESR .... Oil Extended Synthetic Rubber (PDAA)
OESS .... O/ET [*Orbiter/External Tank*] Separation System [*NASA*] (MCD)
OESS .... Office of Engineering Standards Services [*National Bureau of Standards*]
OES/S .... Office of the Environment (US Department of) State/Science and Technology Affairs (GNE)
OESS .... Organizational Effectiveness Survey System [*Army*]
OES/SAT ..... Office of the Environment (US Department of) State/Office of Advanced Technology (GNE)
OES/SCI ...... Bureau of Oceans and International Enviromental and Scientific Affairs/Scientific and Technological Affairs [*Department of State*] (MSC)
OES/SCT ..... Office of Environment (US Department of) State/Office of Cooperative Science and Technology Programs (GNE)
OET .... Objective End Time
OET .... Office of Education and Training (AD)
OET .... Office of Emergency Transportation [*FAA*]
OET .... Office of Engineering and Technology [*Washington, DC FCC*] (GRD)
OET .... Official English Title
OET .... Official Establishments Trust [*Australia*]
OET .... Oldest English Texts
OET .... On Equipment Training (MCD)
O/ET .... Orbiter/External Tank [*NASA*] (NASA)
OET .... Organizacion para Estudios Tropicales [*Organization for Tropical Studies*] (EAIO)
OET .... Overseas Exchange Transactions (AD)
OETA .... Occupied Enemy Territory Administration [*World War II*]
OETA .... Township of Armstrong Public Library [*Bibliotheque Publique Canton Armstrong*], Earlton, Ontario [*Library symbol National Library of Canada*] (BIB)
OET & E ...... Operational Employment Testing and Evaluation (AFM)
OETB .... Ocean Economics and Technology Branch [*United Nations*] (MSC)
OETB .... Offshore Energy Technology Board [*British*]
OETB .... Tabuk [*Saudi Arabia*] [*ICAO location identifier*] (ICLI)
OETC .... Optoelectronics Technology Consortium [*Sponsored by the Department of Defense*]
OETC .... Organizational Effectiveness Training Center [*Army*] (MCD)
OETF .... Taif [*Saudi Arabia*] [*ICAO location identifier*] (ICLI)
OETLC .... Office of Economic Trends and Labor Conditions [*Department of Labor*]
OETP .... Operations Experimental Test Plan (IAA)
OETP .... Orbiter Electron Temperature Probe [*NASA*]
OETR .... Turaif [*Saudi Arabia*] [*ICAO location identifier*] (ICLI)
OEu .... Euclid Public Library, Euclid, OH [*Library symbol Library of Congress*] (LCLS)
OEU .... Operation Eyesight Universal [*Canada*] (EAIO)
OEVE .... Office of Earthquakes, Volcanoes, and Engineering [*US Geological Survey*] (AD)
OEW .... Office of Economic Warfare [*World War II*]
OEW .... Open-End Wrench
OEW .... Operational Empty Weight [*Aviation*]
OEW .... Ordinary Electromagnetic Wave
OEW .... Ordnance and Explosive Waste [*Military*]
OEWG .... Open-Ended Working Group (NATG)
OEWG .... Operation, Evaluation Wartime Group (NATG)
OEWJ .... Wejh [*Saudi Arabia*] [*ICAO location identifier*] (ICLI)
OEX .... Office of Educational Exchange [*Department of State*]
OEX .... Oklahoma City, OK [*Location identifier FAA*] (FAAL)
OEX .... Options Exchange [*Finance*]
OEX .... Orbiter Experiments [*NASA*] (MCD)
OEX .... Standard & Poor's 100 Stock Index (DFIT)
OEXP .... Office of Exploration [*NASA*]
OEYN .... Yenbo [*Saudi Arabia*] [*ICAO location identifier*] (ICLI)
OEZ .... Osteuropaeische Zeit [*East European Time*] [*German*] (AD)
OF .... Degrees Fahrenheit

OF	Fast Airways BV [*Netherlands ICAO designator*] (ICDA)
OF	Fitted for Oil Fuel [*Ships*]
OF	Frankford Public Library, Ontario [*Library symbol National Library of Canada*] (BIB)
OF	Noosa Air [*ICAO designator*] (AD)
OF	Occipitalfrontal [*Diameter of skull*]
OF	Oceanographic Facility
OF	Odd Fellows [*An association*]
Of	Official (DAVI)
OF	Official Files
OF	Offset Printing Program [*Association of Independent Colleges and Schools specialization code*]
OF	Offshore Funds [*Investment term*]
OF	Oil Facility [*International Monetary Fund*]
OF	Oil-Filled (IAA)
OF	Oil Fired (ADA)
OF	Oil Fuel [*British military*] (DMA)
OF	Old Face [*Typography*]
of	Old Face (AD)
OF	Old Field [*Botany*]
OF	Old French [*Language, etc.*]
OF	One of the Firm [*Telecommunications*] (TEL)
OF	Open Forum [*An association*] (EA)
OF	Open Full [*Container*] (DCTA)
OF	Operating Forces [*Navy*]
O/F	Operational Fixed
OF	Operations and Food Analysis
OF	Operations Following (MCD)
OF	Ophthalmological Foundation [*Later, NSPB*]
OF	Optical Fibre (EECA)
OF	Optical Frequency
OF	Optional Feature (IAA)
OF	Optional Form
of	Optional Form (AD)
OF	Orbital Facility (IAA)
O/F	Orbital Flight [*NASA*] (KSC)
OF	Orbitofrontal
OF	Order of the Founder [*Salvation Army*]
OF	Orphan Foundation [*Later, OFA*] (EA)
OF	Orthochromatic Film [*Photography*] (DGA)
OF	Oscillator Frequency [*Telecommunications*] (IAA)
OF	Osfriends (EA)
OF	Osmotic Fragility Test
OF	Osteitis Fibrosa [*Medicine*] (MAE)
OF	Osteopathic Foundation [*Later, NOF*]
OF	Other Medical/Surgical Facility (MEDA)
OF	Outfield [*Baseball*]
O/F	Outfit [*Doll collecting*]
OF	Output Factor [*Computer science*] (IEEE)
OF	Outside Face [*Technical drawings*]
of	Outside Face (AD)
OF	Ovenstone Factor [*Medicine*] (MAE)
Of	Ovenstone Factor (AD)
OF	Overflow
OF	Overfrequency (MSA)
OF	Oxbow Falls (AD)
OF	Oxenstierna Foundation (AD)
OF	Oxford Foundation (AD)
o/f	Oxidation/Fermentation (EA)
O-F	Oxidation-Fermentation [*Growth medium*]
O/F	Oxidizer-to-Fuel [*Ratio*]
o/f	Oxidizer to Fuel Ratio (AD)
of	Oxidizing Flame (AD)
OF	Oxidizing Flame
OF	Oxydizer-to-Fuel [*Ratio*]
OF	Oxygen Fill (NASA)
OFA	Fairfield County District Library, Lancaster, OH [*OCLC symbol*] (OCLC)
OFA	Object Free Area [*FAA*] (TAG)
OFA	Office for the Aging (BARN)
OFA	Office of Family Assistance [*Department of Health and Human Services*] (GFGA)
OFA	Office of Federal Activities [*Environmental Protection Agency*] (GFGA)
OFA	Office of Financial Analysis [*Department of the Treasury*]
OFA	Oficina Alemania [*Chile*] [*Seismograph station code, US Geological Survey*] (SEIS)
OFA	Oil-Immersed Forced-Air-Cooled [*Transformer*] (IEEE)
OFA	Old Folks Association (AD)
OFA	Oncofetal Antigen [*Immunology*]
OFA	Optimized Fuel Assembly [*Nuclear energy*] (NRCH)
OFA	Order for Assignment [*Military*] (CAAL)
OFA	Organic Food Alliance (EA)
OFA	Organized Flying Adjusters (EA)
OFA	Orienteering Federation of Australia
OFA	Oronite Fuel Additive
OFA	Orphan Foundation of America (EA)
OFA	Orthopedic Foundation for Animals (EA)
OFA	Over Fifties Association [*Australia*]
OFA	Over Fire Air [*Combustion technology*]
OFA	Overseas Family Allowance [*British military*] (DMA)
OFA	Oxygenated Fuels Association (EA)
OFAA	Oyster Farmers' Association of Australia
OFAB	Fort Albany Band Library, Ontario [*Library symbol National Library of Canada*] (BIB)

OFACS	Overseas-Foreign Aeronautical Communications Station (MUGU)
OFAD	Ocean Floor Analysis Division [*Later, Sea Floor Division*] [*NORDA*] (EA)
OFAED	Organization Forecast Authorization Equipment Data [*Military*] (AFIT)
OFAF	Metallurgical Research Library, Falconbridge Nickel Mines Ltd., Falconbridge, Ontario [*Library symbol National Library of Canada*] (NLC)
OFAGE	Orthogonal-Field-Alternation Gel Electrophoresis [*Analytical biochemistry*]
OFALF	Omega First Amendment Legal Fund (EA)
OFAM	Office of Financial and Administrative Management [*Department of Labor*]
OFANC	Falconbridge Branch, Nickel Centre Public Library, Ontario [*Library symbol National Library of Canada*] (NLC)
OFANSW	Oyster Farmers' Association of New South Wales [*Australia*]
OFAR	Office of Foreign Agricultural Relations [*Department of Agriculture*]
OFARS	Overseas-Foreign Aeronautical Receiver Station
OFAS	Overseas Flight Assistance Service
OFATS	Overseas-Foreign Aeronautical Transmitter Station
OFavp	Fairview Park Regional Library, Fairview Park, OH [*Library symbol Library of Congress*] (LCLS)
OFB	Oil Forced Blast (IAA)
OFB	Operational Facilities Branch [*NASA*] (MCD)
OFB	Output Feedback (NITA)
OFC	Conference on Optical Fiber Communication [*Optical Society of America*] [*Washington, DC*] (TSSD)
OFC	Foleyet Community Library, Ontario [*Library symbol National Library of Canada*] (NLC)
OFC	High Court Reports, Orange Free State [*A publication*] (DLA)
OFC	Occipitofrontal Circumference [*Anatomy*]
OFC	Oceania Football Confederation
OFC	Oceanography and Fisheries Committee (ASF)
OFC	Office [*or Officer*] (AFM)
ofc	Office (AD)
OFC	Office
OFC	Office of Fishery Coordination [*World War II*]
OFC	Oil Free Compressor
OFC	Oldest Finest Canadian [*Whiskey*] (IIA)
OFC	Old Fired Copper [*Initialism once used as brand name for bourbon*]
OFC	Old French Canadian [*Initialism used in Schenley brand of Canadian whisky*]
OFC	One Flow Cascade Cycle (IAA)
OFC	Open Financial Connectivity [*Microsoft Computer Software*] [*Computer Science*]
OFC	Operational Flight Control [*NASA*]
OFC	Opposing Force Component (MCD)
OFC	Optical File Cabinet [*Computer science*]
OFC	Optical Formatter Controller (NITA)
OFC	Optical Frequency Conversion
OFC	Osteitis Fibrosa Cystica [*Medicine*] (DMAA)
OFC	Outside Front Cover [*Publishing*] (NTCM)
OFC	Overseas Food Corp. (AD)
OFC	Overseas Food Corp. (NADA)
OFC	Oxyfuel-Gas Cutting [*Welding*]
OFCA	Ontario Federation of Construction Associations [*Canada*] (AD)
OFCA	Organisation des Fabricants de Produits Cellulosiques Alimentaires de la CEE [*Organization of Manufacturers of Cellulose Products for Foodstuffs in the European Economic Community*]
OFC-A	Oxyfuel-Gas Cutting - Acetylene [*Welding*]
OFCC	Office of Federal Contract Compliance [*Later, OFCCP*] [*Department of Labor*]
OFCCP	Office of Federal Contract Compliance Programs [*Formerly, OFCC*] [*Department of Labor*]
OFCCP Fed Cont Compl Man	OFCCP Federal Contract Compliance Manual [*A publication*] (AAGC)
OFCE	Office [*or Officer*]
OFC-H	Oxyfuel-Gas Cutting - Hydrogen [*Welding*]
OFCL	Official
ofcl	Official (AD)
OFCL	Official
Of Cl Pac	Officium Clerici Pacis [*A publication*] (DLA)
OFCM	Office of the Federal Coordinator for Meteorological Services and Research
OFC-N	Oxyfuel Cutting - Natural Gas [*Welding*]
OFCO	Offensive Counterintelligence Operations (MCD)
OFCOFASSTSECNAV	Office of the Assistant Secretary of the Navy (DNAB)
OFCOFASSTSECNAV(FINMGMT)	Office of the Assistant Secretary of the Navy (Financial Management) (DNAB)
OFCOFASSTSECNAV(INSTALLOG)	Office of the Assistant Secretary of the Navy (Installations and Logistics) (DNAB)
OFCOFASSTSECNAV(PERSRESFOR)	Office of the Assistant Secretary of the Navy (Personnel and Reserve Force) (DNAB)
OFCOFASSTSECNAV(RSCHDEV)	Office of the Assistant Secretary of the Navy (Research and Development) (DNAB)
OFCOFINFO	Office of Information (DNAB)
OFCP	Ottawa Financial [*NASDAQ symbol*] (TTSB)
OFCP	Ottawa Financial Corp. [*NASDAQ symbol*] (SAG)
OFC-P	Oxyfuel-Gas Cutting - Propane [*Welding*]
OFCR	Officer
OFCS	Office of Foreign Commercial Services [*Abolished 1970, functions transferred to Bureau of International Commerce*]
OFCS	Operational Flight Control System [*NASA*] (KSC)
OFCSAV	Orchardists and Fruit Cool Stores Association of Victoria [*Australia*]
OFD	Object Film Distance [*Optics*]
OFD	Objective Force Designator (MCD)

OFD .... Occipitofrontal Diameter [*of the skull*]
OFD .... Ocean Floor Drilling
OFD .... Ocean Freight Differential [*MARAD*] (TAG)
Ofd.............. Offered [*Stock exchange term*]
OFD .... Ohio Federal Decisions [*A publication*] (DLA)
OFD .... One-Function Diagram
ofd .... One-Function Diagram (AD)
OFD .... Open-Face Dectector [*Instrumentation*]
ofd .... Optical Fire Detector (AD)
OFD .... Optical Gun Fire Director [*Military*] (PDAA)
OFD .... Oral-Facial-Digital [*Genetics*] (DAVI)
OFD .... Oro-Facio-Digital [*Syndrome*] [*Medicine*]
OFD .... Oued Fodda [*Algeria*] [*Seismograph station code, US Geological Survey*] (SEIS)
OFDA .... Office Furniture Distribution Association (EA)
OFDA .... Office of United States Foreign Disaster Assistance [*Agency for International Development*]
OFDAP .... Office of the Field Directorate of Ammunition Plants
OFDC .... Official First Day Cover [*Canada Post Corp.*]
OFDC .... Ontario Film Development Corp. [*Canada*]
OFDG .... Operator Fractionation Decision Guide [*Process control*]
OFDI .... Office of Foreign Direct Investments [*Department of Commerce*]
OFDR .... Off-Frequency Decoupling Resonance [*Physical chemistry*]
OFDS .... Optimal Financial Decision Strategy (MHDI)
OFDS .... Orbiter Flight Dynamics Simulator [*NASA*] (NASA)
OFDS .... Oxygen Fluid Distribution System [*NASA*] (NASA)
OFE .... Odds for Effectiveness [*Navy*]
OFE .... Office of Federal Elections [*Later, FEC*]
OFE .... Office of Fuels and Engergy (AD)
OFE .... Office of Fusion Energy [*Oak Ridge National Laboratory*]
OFE .... Optical Flight Evaluation
OFE .... Order for Engagement [*Military*] (CAAL)
OFE .... Other Further Education
OFE .... Ottawa Fundraising Executives [*Ontario, Canada*]
OFEA .... Office of Foreign Economic Administration [*Lend-Lease*] [*World War II*]
OFEA .... Officer Front End Analysis (MCD)
OFEC .... Office of Federal Employees Compensation [*Department of Labor*]
OFEC .... Office of Foreign Economic Coordination [*World War II*]
OFEC .... Wellington County Museum, Fergus, Ontario [*Library symbol National Library of Canada*] (BIB)
OFEHM .... Fort Erie Historical Museum, Ontario [*Library symbol National Library of Canada*] (BIB)
OFEMA......... Office Francais d'Exportation de Materiel Aeronautique [*French Office for theExportation of Aeronautical Materiel*] (AD)
OFEP .... Fort Erie Public Library, Ontario [*Library symbol National Library of Canada*] (NLC)
OFER .... Fergus Public Library, Ontario [*Library symbol National Library of Canada*] (NLC)
OFERC .... Centre Wellington District High School, Fergus, Ontario [*Library symbol National Library of Canada*] (NLC)
OFERRA....... Office of Foreign Economic Relief and Rehabilitation Administration
OFERW .... Wellington County Public Library, Fergus, Ontario [*Library symbol National Library of Canada*] (NLC)
OFERWM .... Wellington County Museum and Archives, Fergus, Ontario [*Library symbol National Library of Canada*] (BIB)
OFF............. Challenge Air Transport, Inc. [*ICAO designator*] (FAAC)
Off.............. De Officiis [*of Cicero*] [*Classical studies*] (OCD)
OFF............. Fort Frances Public Library, Ontario [*Library symbol National Library of Canada*] (NLC)
OFF............. Offensive
OFF............. Offer
OFF............. Offertory
OFF............. Office [*or Officer*] (AFM)
off............... Office (DD)
OFF............. Office for Families (DICI)
OFF............. Office of Facts and Figures [*Later, Office of War Information*] [*Military*]
Off.............. Officer (AD)
OFF............. Officers' Family Fund
OFF............. Official
OFF............. Offretite [*A zeolite*]
OFF............. Omaha, NE [*Location identifier FAA*] (FAAL)
OFF............. Organization for Femininity
OFFAR .... Office of Fuel and Fuel Additive Registration [*Environmental Protection Agency*]
Off Br......... Officina Brevium [*1679*] [*A publication*] (DLA)
Off Brev...... Officina Brevium [*1679*] [*A publication*] (DLA)
OFF BUS ONLY... Official Business Only (DNAB)
OFFC........... Office
OfcDpt........ Office Depot [*Associated Press*] (SAG)
OFFEE .... Offeree [*Legal shorthand*] (LWAP)
OFFEG .... Offshore Fossil-Fueled Electric Generators
OFFEN .... Offensive [*Ammunition*] (AAG)
offen .... Offensive (AD)
OFFENS ...... Offensive
offeq .... Office Equipment (AD)
offer........... Offertories (AD)
OFFER .... Office of Electricity Regulation [*British*]
Off Ex......... Wentworth's Office of Executors [*A publication*] (DLA)
Off Exec...... Wentworth's Office of Executors [*A publication*] (DLA)
offg............ Offering (AD)
OFFG .... Officiating
Off Gaz Pat Office... Official Gazette. United States Patent and Trademark Office [*A publication*] (DLA)

OFFI............ Official
OFFIC.......... Official
offic........... Official (AD)
OFFIC.......... Officiate
Office Pubns... Office Publications (AD)
Officer........ Officer's Reports [*1-9 Minnesota*] [*A publication*] (DLA)
Official J Ind Comm Prop... Official Journal of Industrial and Commercial Property [*Eire*] [*A publication*] (DLA)
Official Rep III Courts Commission... Official Reports, Illinois Courts Commission [*A publication*] (DLA)
Officmx........ Officemax, Inc. [*Associated Press*] (SAG)
OFFL........... Official (AFM)
OFFM.......... Fort Frances Museum and Cultural Centre, Ontario [*Library symbol National Library of Canada*] (BIB)
OFFMAUTSYS... Officer Master File Automated System (DNAB)
OFFNAVHIST... Office of Naval History [*Also, ONH*]
OFFNAVWEASERV... Office of Naval Weather Service
OFFOR......... Offeror [*Legal shorthand*] (LWAP)
OFFP........... Fenelon Falls Public Library, Ontario [*Library symbol National Library of Canada*] (BIB)
OFFP........... Ovarian Follicular Fluid Peptide [*Endocrinology*]
OFFPROMSYS... Officer Promotion System (DNAB)
OFFR .... Officer
Off Rep .... Official Reports of the High Court of the Transvaal [*A publication*] (DLA)
OffshEnr....... Offshore Energy Development Corp. [*Associated Press*] (SAG)
OFFSHR....... Offshore (NVT)
OffsLog........ Offshore Logistics, Inc. [*Associated Press*] (SAG)
OFF STA ..... Officer Status (DNAB)
off-st pkg ..... Off-Street Parking (AD)
OFFV........... Order of First Families of Virginia, 1607-1624/5 (EA)
OFG .... Opferfuersorgegesetz (BJA)
OFG .... Optical Frequency Generator
OFGAS .... Office of Gas Service [*Government body*] [*British*]
OFGR .... Objective Force Gross Requirement [*Army*] (AABC)
OFGSA .... Organic Farming and Gardening Society of Australia
OFGST .... Organic Farming and Gardening Society of Tasmania [*Australia*]
OFH .... Odd Fellows Hall (ROG)
OFH .... Oil Field Haulers Association Inc., Austin TX [*STAC*]
OFH .... Rutherford B. Hayes Library, Fremont, OH [*Library symbol Library of Congress*] (LCLS)
OFHA.......... Oil Field Haulers Association (EA)
OFHC.......... Oxygen Free Hard Copper (IAA)
ofhc .... Oxygen-Free High-Carbon (AD)
ofhc .... Oxygen-Free High Conductivity (AD)
OFHC.......... Oxygen-Free, High-Conductivity [*Copper*]
OFi .... Findlay-Hancock County District Public Library, Findlay, OH [*Library symbol Library of Congress*] (LCLS)
OFI .... Office of Foreign Investment [*Department of Commerce*]
OFI .... Office of the Federal Inspector (AD)
OFI .... On-Line Free Form Input [*Computer science*] (MHDI)
OFI .... Operational Flight Instrumentation [*NASA*] (NASA)
OFI .... Ornamental Fish International (EAIO)
OFI .... Oxford Forestry Institute [*University of Oxford*] [*British*] (IRUK)
OFIA........... Optical Frame Importers' Association [*British*] (DBA)
OFiC........... Findlay College, Findlay, OH [*Library symbol Library of Congress*] (LCLS)
ofic .... Oficial [*Official*] [*Spanish*] (AD)
OFIC........... Ohio Foundation of Independent Colleges (AD)
OFID........... OPEC [*Organization of Petroleum Exporting Countries*] Fund for International Development (EAIO)
O-FID.......... Oxygen-Flame Ionization Detector
OFIG........... Operational Forces Interface Group [*US Army Natick Research, Development, and Engineering Center*] [*Natick, MA*] (RDA)
OFII............ Otto Fuel II [*Military*] (DNAB)
OFINDMAN... Office of Industrial Management [*Navy*] (DNAB)
OFINTAC...... Offshore Installations Technical Advisory Committee [*British Marine science*] (MSC)
OFIR........... Oceanic Flight Information Region (IAA)
OFIS........... Office Information System (NITA)
OFIS........... Operational Flight Information Service [*ICAO*] (DA)
OFIS........... U.S. Office Products [*NASDAQ symbol*] (TTSB)
OFIS........... US Office Products Co. [*NASDAQ symbol*] (SAG)
OFIX........... Office of the Future Information Exchange (NITA)
OFIX........... Orthofix International [*NASDAQ symbol*] (SAG)
OFIXF......... Orthofix International [*NASDAQ symbol*] (TTSB)
OFJ............. Olafsfjordur [*Iceland*] [*Airport symbol*] (OAG)
OFK............ Norfolk [*Nebraska*] [*Airport symbol*] (OAG)
OFK............ Norfolk, NE [*Location identifier FAA*] (FAAL)
OFK............ Oberfeldkommandantur [*Military government area headquarters*] [*German military - World War II*]
OFK............ Official Flight Kit [*NASA*] (NASA)
OFK............ Official Flight Kit
OFK............ Optical Flight Kit (NASA)
OFL............ Flesherton Public Library, Ontario [*Library symbol National Library of Canada*] (NLC)
OFL............ Official (AABC)
ofl .... Official (AD)
OFL............ Open Fault Locater
OFL............ Optic Fiber Layer
OFL............ Overflow [*Computer science*]
OFL............ Oxidizer Fill Line (AAG)
Oflag.......... Offizierlager [*Officer's Prison Camp*] [*German*] (AD)
OFLAG......... Offizierslager [*Permanent Prison Camp for Captured Officers*] [*German military - World War II*]

OFLC............	Office of Foreign Liquidation Commission
OFLD............	Off-Load (NVT)
OFlem..........	Old Flemish [Language, etc.] (BARN)
OFLIC..........	Office of Foreign Liquidation Commission
OFLINPS......	Open Frame Linear Power Supply [Electronics] (EECA)
OFLT............	Office of Foreign Labor and Trade [Department of Labor]
OFLTR..........	Oil Filter
OFLUSE.......	For Official Use Only [Army]
Ofly.............	Offaly (AD)
ofm.............	Conventual Franciscans, Friars Minor (TOCD)
OFM............	Franciscan Friars (TOCD)
ofm.............	Franciscan Friars, Order of Friars Minor (TOCD)
OFM............	Observation File Maintenance
OFM............	Office of Finance and Management [Department of Agriculture] (GFGA)
OFM............	Office of Financial Management [Bureau of the Budget; later, OMB]
OFM............	Office of Flight Missions [NASA] (MCD)
OFM............	Office of Foreign Missions [Department of State]
OFM............	Optofiber Metric Switch
OFM............	Ordnance Field Manual [Military]
OFM............	Ordo Fratrum Minorum [Order of Friars Minor] [Observant Franciscans] [Roman Catholic religious order] (EA)
OFM............	Organization Field Maintenance
OFM............	Oriental Fruit Moth [Entomology]
OFM............	Orofacial Malformation
OFM............	Our First Men [Slang]
OFM............	Out for Maintenance [Aviation] (FAAC)
OFM............	Oxygen Fill to Missile (AAG)
OFMC..........	Operational Fixed Microwave Council (IAA)
OFMC..........	Order of Friars Minor Conventual [Conventuals] [Roman Catholic religious order]
OFMCap......	[The] Capuchin Friars (TOCD)
ofmcap	[The] Capuchin Friars, Franciscan Fathers (TOCD)
OFM Cap	Order of Friars Minor Capuchin [Capuchins] [Roman Catholic religious order]
OFMConv....	Conventual Franciscans (TOCD)
OFM Conv....	Order of Friars Minor Conventual [Conventuals] [Roman Catholic religious order]
OFMIS	Office of Financial and Management Information Systems (OICC)
OFMP..........	Organization of Facility Managers and Planners [Later, OMERF] (EA)
OFMS..........	Office of Financial and Management Services [Department of Labor]
OFN............	Organization for Flora Neotropica (EA)
OFN	Ottawa Fundraisers Network [Ontario, Canada]
OFN	Overfull Employment [Economics]
OFNCS........	Orange Field Naturalist and Conservation Society [Australia]
OFNPS........	Outstate Facility Network Planning System [Telecommunications] (TEL)
OFNS	Observer Foreign News Service (AD)
OFO	Office of Field Operations [Employment and Training Administration] [Department of Labor]
OFO	Office of Flight Operations [NASA]
OFO	Orbiting Frog Otolith [NASA experimental spacecraft]
Ofo.............	Orfeo [Record label]
OFOC..........	Old Free Order of Chaldeans [Freemasonry] (ROG)
OFOD..........	On-Flight Origin and Destination [International Civil Aviation Organizati on] [Information service or system] (DUND)
OFOFLEGAFFAIRS...	Office of Legal Affairs [Navy] (DNAB)
OFOM	Operational Figure of Merit [Military] (CAAL)
OFOS	Opening Filled Other State [Employment]
OFP.............	Ashland, VA [Location identifier FAA] (FAAL)
OFP.............	Oil Filter Pack
OFP.............	On-the-Fly Printer
OFP.............	Open Fireplace [Classified advertising] (ADA)
OFP.............	Operating Force Plan
OFP.............	Operational Flight Profile [NASA] (NASA)
OFP.............	Operational Flight Profit
OFP.............	Operational Flight Program [NASA] (NASA)
OFP.............	Operational Format Program [NASA] (KSC)
OFP.............	Operative Federal Plasterers [A union] [British]
OFP.............	Orbiter Flight Program [NASA] (NASA)
OFP.............	Order of Friars Preachers [Dominicans] (ADA)
OFP.............	Ordnance Field Park [British]
OFP.............	Organizations, Functions, and Programs [IRS]
OFP.............	Original Flight Plan
OFP.............	Oscilloscope Face Plane
OFP.............	Ozone Forming Potential [Exhaust emissions] [Automotive engineering]
OFPA	Order of the Founders and Patriots of America (EA)
OFPA	Organic Foods Production Act
OFPANA......	Organic Foods Production Association of North America (EA)
OFPCP	Organization of Fitness and Personal Care Professionals [Defunct] (EA)
OFPF	Optical Fiber-Pulling Facility (SSD)
OFPM..........	Office of Fiscal Plans and Management [Bureau of Indian Affairs]
OFP-MIR......	Ozone-Forming Potential-Maximum Incremental Reactivity [Exhaust emissions] [Automotive engineering]
OFPP	Office of Federal Procurement Policy [Executive Office of the President] (MCD)
OFPS	Open Frame Power Supply [Electronics] (EECA)
OFPU	Optical Fiber Production Unit
OFr..............	Franklin Public Library, Franklin, OH [Library symbol Library of Congress] (LCLS)
OFR.............	Ocular Following Reflex [Ophthalmology]
OFR	Off Frequency Rejection [Radio communications]

ofr...............	Off Frequency Rejection (AD)
OFR	Office for Recruitment [American Library Association]
OFR	Office for Research [American Library Association]
OfR	Office for Research (AD)
OFR	Office of the Federal Register
OFR	Officer Fitness Report [Navy] (NVT)
OFR	Official Failure Rate [Military] (AFIT)
OFR	Oil-Filled Resistor
OFR	Old French [Language, etc.]
O Fr	Old French (AD)
OFR	On-Frequency Repeater (IEEE)
OFR	Open Failure Report [NASA] (KSC)
OFR	Open File Report (MCD)
OFR	Operational Failure Report (IAA)
OFR	Operational Fleet Requirements (MCD)
OFR	Ordering Function Register
OFR	Over Frequency Relay
OFR	Overseas Fuel Region (AFIT)
OFR	Oxidation-Fluorination Ratio (MCD)
OFRA	O'Dochartaigh Family Research Association (EA)
OFRAC	On Farm Research Advisory Committee [Australia]
OFR-ALA......	Office of Recruitment-American Library Association (AD)
OFRF	Organic Farming Research Foundation
OFRF	Overland Flow Research Facility [Army]
OFRIS	Old Frisian [Language, etc.]
OFris...........	Old Frisian (AD)
O Frk	Old Frankish (AD)
OFRP	Overseas Family Residence Program [Military] (NVT)
OFRR	Office of Foreign Relief and Rehabilitation [Obsolete]
OFRRO	Office of Foreign Relief and Rehabilitation Operation [Obsolete]
OFrS	Franklin City Schools, Franklin, OH [Library symbol Library of Congress] (LCLS)
OFRW	Oklahoma Federation of Republican Women
OFS	Fauquier-Strickland Public Library, Fauquier, Ontario [Library symbol National Library of Canada] (BIB)
OFS	Octave Filter Set
OFS	Office of Field Service [OSRD] [World War II]
OFS	Office of Field Services [Later, Bureau of Domestic Commerce] [Department of Commerce]
OFS	Office of Oceanographic Facilities and Support [National Science Foundation] (USDC)
OFS	Office of Oceanographic Facilities and Support [Marine science] (OSRA)
OFS	Offset (MSA)
OFS	Oil from Sludge
OFS	One-Function Sketch
ofs	One-Function Sketch (AD)
OFS	Ontario Federation of Students [Canada] (AD)
OFS	Operations Fixed Service [Microwave service] (NTCM)
OFS	Optical Fiber Sensor
OFS	Optical Fuzing System
OFS	Orange Free State [South Africa]
OFS	Orange Free State Reports, High Court [1879-83] [South Africa] [A publication] (DLA)
OFS	Orbital [or Orbiter] Flight System [NASA] (MCD)
OFS	Orbiter Functional Simulator (NASA)
OFS	Orbiter Functional Simulator
OFSA	Ordo Fratrum Sancti Augustini [Order of St. Augustine - OSA] [Rome, Italy] (EAIO)
OFSB	Fort Severn Band Library, Ontario [Library symbol National Library of Canada] (BIB)
OFSB	Ordnance Field Service Bulletin [Military]
OFSC	Ordnance Field Service Circular [Military]
OFSC	Organization and Finance Subcommittee
OFSCC	Orbiter Functional Simulator Control Center (MCD)
OFSD	Operating Flight Strength Diagram
OFSDG	Finch Branch, Stormont, Dundas, and Glengarry County Public Library, Ontario [Library symbol National Library of Canada] (BIB)
OFSE	Operating Forces Support Equipment (DNAB)
OFSM	Operational Flight Safety Monitor (SAA)
OFSMPS	Open Frame Switch Mode Power Supply [Electronics] (EECA)
OFSO	Overfill Shutoff Sensor (KSC)
OFSP	Office of Federal Statistical Policy [Later, OFSPS] [Department of Commerce]
OFSPS	Office of Federal Statistical Policy and Standards [Formerly, OFSP] [Department of Commerce]
OFSSA	Orange Free State, South Africa (ILCA)
OFST...........	Lateral Offset Active Light (GAVI)
OFST...........	Office of the Secretary of the Air Force (AD)
ofst	Offset (VRA)
OFSTED	Office for Standards in Education (AIE)
OFT.............	Field Township Public Library, Ontario [Library symbol National Library of Canada] (NLC)
OFT.............	Observed Fire Trainer [Army] (RDA)
OFT.............	Office of Fair Trading [British]
OFT.............	Often
OFT.............	Ohio Federation of Teachers (AD)
OFT.............	Operational Feasibility Testing (MCD)
OFT.............	Operational Flight Trainer
OFT.............	Optical Fiber Thermometry [Instrumentation]
OFT.............	Optical Fiber Tube
OFT.............	Optical Fibre Technology
OFT.............	Optical Fourier Transform
OFT.............	Optimal Foraging Theory [Animal behavior]

OFT............ Orbital Flight Test [*NASA*] (NASA)
OFT............ Outer Fix Time [*FAA*] (TAG)
OFT............ Outfit (MSA)
OFT............ Outline Feasibility Test [*Army*]
OFTA........... Office for the Aged [*Australia*]
OFTA........... Operational Flight Transfer Airframe
OFTB........... Offshore Technology Board [*British*]
OFTC........... Overseas Finance and Trade Corp. (AD)
OFTD........... Oxygen Furnace Tilt Drive
OFTDA........ Office of Flight Tracking and Data Acquisition [*NASA*]
OFTDS........ Orbital Flight Test Data System [*NASA*] (MCD)
OFTEL......... Office of Telecommunications [*Independent government agency*] [*British*]
OFTF.......... Optical Fibre Transfer Function (EECA)
OFTM.......... On-Orbit Flight Technique Meeting [*NASA*] (MCD)
OFTMS........ Output Format Table Modification Submodule
OFTR.......... Orbital Flight Test Requirement [*NASA*] (NASA)
OFTS.......... Office of Technical Services (AD)
OFTS.......... Office of Transportation Security (AD)
OFTS.......... Officers Training School (AD)
OFTS.......... Operational Flight and Tactics Simulator (MCD)
OFTS.......... Optical Fibre Transmission System (NITA)
OFTS.......... Overseas Fixed Telecommunications System (AD)
OFTT.......... Operational Flight and Tactics Trainer (MCD)
OFTT.......... Organic Failure to Thrive [*Medicine*] (MEDA)
OFU........... Floating Units Division [*Coast Guard*]
OFU........... Franklin University, Columbus, OH [*OCLC symbol*] (OCLC)
OFU........... Ofu Island [*American Samoa*] [*Airport symbol*] (OAG)
OFU........... Ofunato [*Japan*] [*Seismograph station code, US Geological Survey*] (SEIS)
OFV........... Opposing Forces Vehicle [*Military*]
OFV........... Orchid Fleck Virus [*Plant pathology*]
OFW........... Objective Family of Weapons
OFW........... Off Watch [*Aviation*] (FAAC)
OFW........... Operation Fish Watch [*National Oceanic and Atmospheric Administration*] (MSC)
OFW........... Oxyfuel-Gas Welding
OFWAT........ Office of Water Services [*British*]
Ofwat.......... Office of Water Services [*British*] (ODBW)
OFWN.......... Ontario Library Service - Nipigon, Thunder Bay, Ontario [*Library symbol National Library of Canada*] (NLC)
OF/WST....... Operational Flight/Weapons System Trainer (NG)
OFX........... Open Financial Exchange [*Computer science*]
OFX........... Open Financial Exchange [*Computer science*]
OFXT.......... Outer Fix Time [*Aviation*] (FAAC)
OFY........... Opportunities for Youth [*Canada*] (AD)
OFY........... Opportunities for Youth Program [*Canada*]
OFZ........... Fort Sill, OK [*Location identifier FAA*] (FAAL)
OFZ........... Obstacle Free Zone
OG .... Air Guadeloupe [*ICAO designator*] (AD)
OG .... Guelph Public Library, Ontario [*Library symbol National Library of Canada*] (NLC)
OG............ Obergericht [*Court of Appeal*] [*German*] (DLA)
OG............ Oberstes Gericht [*Supreme Court*] [*German*]
OG............ Object Glass (MSA)
OG............ Obscure Glass
OG............ Obstetrics-Gynecology [*Medicine*]
OG............ Occlusogingival [*Dentistry*]
OG............ Octyl Glucoside [*Organic chemistry*]
OG............ Oesterreichische Galerie [*Austrian Gallery*] (AD)
OG............ Offensive Guard [*Football*]
OG............ Off-Gas [*Nuclear energy*] (NRCH)
OG............ Office of Geography [*Functions transferred to Geographic Names Division of Army Topographic Command*] [*Department of the Interior*]
OG .... Officer of the Guard [*Army*]
OG .... Official Gazette [*PTO*] [*A publication*] (AAGC)
OG............ Ogasawara Trench
OG............ Ogden Corp. [*NYSE symbol*] (SPSG)
OG............ Ogdensburg [*Diocesan abbreviation*] [*New York*] (TOCD)
OG............ Ogee [*A molding*] [*Architecture*] (ROG)
OG............ Oh, Gee [*Slang*]
og............ Oh Gee (AD)
OG............ Oil Gauge
og............ Oil Gland (AD)
OG............ Oil Glands [*In propeller shaft*]
OG............ Old Gaelic (AD)
OG............ Old German [*Language, etc.*]
OG............ Old Girl [*A wife*] [*Slang*]
og............ Old Girl (AD)
OG............ Old Greasybeard: Tales from the Cumberland Gap [*A publication*]
OG............ Olive Green [*Army*] (ADDR)
OG............ Olympic Games
OG............ Ongoing (ADA)
OG............ On Grade (DAC)
OG............ On Ground [*Aviation*]
og............ On Ground (AD)
og............ On Guard (AD)
OG............ Operational Group [*World War II*]
OG............ Operation Greenhouse [*Atomic weapons testing*]
OG............ Optic Ganglion
O/G............ Opto/Graphic (AD)
o/g............ Opto-Graphic (AD)
o-g............ Orange-Green (AD)
OG............ Orange Green [*Stain*] [*Medicine*]

OG .... Organic Gardening [*A publication*]
OG .... Organisation Gestosis [*Basel, Switzerland*] (EAIO)
OG .... Or Gate [*Computer science*]
OG .... OR Gate [*Electronics*] (ECII)
OG .... Orientation Group [*Air Force*]
OG .... Original Gravity (BARN)
OG .... Original Gum [*Philately*]
og............ Original Gum (AD)
OG .... Orogastric [*Feeding*] [*Gastroenterology*] (DAVI)
OG .... Outdoor Girl [*Max Factor cosmetic line*]
OG .... Outer Gimbal
O/G .... Outgoing [*Computer science*]
o/g .... Outgoing (AD)
OG .... Output Gate [*Computer science*] (IAA)
OG .... Outside Guard
OG .... Outside Guardian [*Freemasonry*] (ROG)
OG .... Oxygen Gauge (NASA)
OG .... Zero Gravity
OGA .... Obergurgl [*Austria*] [*Seismograph station code, US Geological Survey*] (SEIS)
OGA .... Oesterreichische Gesellschaft fur Akupunktur [*Austrian Society of Acupuncture and Auricular Therapy*] (EAIO)
OGA .... Ogallala, NE [*Location identifier FAA*] (FAAL)
O/GA .... Oil Gauge [*Automotive engineering*]
OGA .... Omega Ltd. [*Ukraine*] [*FAA designator*] (FAAC)
OGA .... Organic Growers Association [*British*] (DBA)
OGA .... Ornamental Growers Association (EA)
OGA .... Orogastric Aspirate [*Medicine*] (AAMN)
OGA .... Outer Gimbal Angle (NASA)
OGA .... Outer Gimbal Assembly (NASA)
OGA .... Outer Gimbal Axis [*NASA*] (IAA)
OGAC .... Galt Collegiate Institute, Cambridge, Ontario [*Library symbol National Library of Canada*] (NLC)
OGAC .... Organizational Governance Advisory Committee [*NERComP*]
O Gael .... Old Gaelic (AD)
OGAL .... Cambridge Public Library, Ontario [*Library symbol National Library of Canada*] (NLC)
OGalG .... Gallia County District Library, Gallipolis, OH [*Library symbol Library of Congress*] (LCLS)
OGALL .... Cavendish Public Library (G. Galloway), Ontario [*Library symbol National Library of Canada*] (BIB)
OGAMA .... Ogden Air Material Area [*AFLC*]
OGAMM .... Optical Glass and Macromolecular Materials [*Imaging*]
OGAN .... Gananoque Public Library, Ontario [*Library symbol National Library of Canada*] (NLC)
OGANSW .... Organic Growers' Association of New South Wales [*Australia*]
OGAR .... OGara Co. (The) [*NASDAQ symbol*] (SAG)
OGaraCo .... OGara Co. (The) [*Associated Press*] (SAG)
OGAWA .... Organic Growers' Association of Western Australia [*Australia*]
OGB .... Beriault Branch, Gloucester Public Library, Ontario [*Library symbol National Library of Canada*] (NLC)
OGB .... Oesterreichischer Gewerkschaftsbund [*Austrian Trade Union Federation*] [*German*] (AD)
OGB .... Orangeburg, SC [*Location identifier FAA*] (FAAL)
OGBD .... Orbiter Gamma Burst Detecter [*NASA*]
OGBG .... Official Gazette Reports, British Guiana [*A publication*] (DLA)
OGBH .... Blackburn Hamlet Branch, Gloucester Public Library, Ontario [*Library symbol National Library of Canada*] (NLC)
OGBKT .... Blessed Kateri Tekakwitha School, Gloucester, Ontario [*Library symbol National Library of Canada*] (NLC)
OGBU .... Gore Bay Union Public Library, Ontario [*Library symbol National Library of Canada*] (NLC)
OGC .... Centennial Collegiate Vocational Institute, Guelph, Ontario [*Library symbol National Library of Canada*] (NLC)
OGc .... Grove City Public Library, Grove City, OH [*Library symbol Library of Congress*] (LCLS)
OGC .... Office of General Counsel
OGC .... Order of the Golden Chain (EA)
OGC .... Oregon Graduate Center for Study and Research [*Research center*] (RCD)
OGCF .... Canadian Farm Management Data System, Agriculture Canada [*Systeme Canadien deDonnees sur la Gestion Agricole, Agriculture Canada*] Guelph, Ontario [*Library symbol National Library of Canada*] (NLC)
OGCH .... College Heights Secondary School, Guelph, Ontario [*Library symbol National Library of Canada*] (NLC)
OGCM .... Ocean General Circulation Model [*Atmospheric science*]
OGCMD .... Ogden Contract Management District (SAA)
OGC-N .... Office of General Counsel - NASA
OGCV .... Guelph Collegiate Vocational Institute, Ontario [*Library symbol National Library of Canada*] (NLC)
OGCW .... Cairine Wilson Secondary School, Gloucester, Ontario [*Library symbol National Library of Canada*] (BIB)
OGCWS .... Office of Government Contract Wage Standards (AAGC)
OGD .... Ogden [*Utah*] [*Airport symbol*]
OGD .... Ogdensburg [*New Jersey*] [*Seismograph station code, US Geological Survey*] (SEIS)
Ogd .... Ogdensburg (AD)
Ogd .... Ogden's Reports [*12-15 Louisiana*] [*A publication*] (DLA)
OGD .... Ogden, UT [*Location identifier FAA*] (FAAL)
OGD .... Old Granulomatus Disease (DAVI)
OGD .... Omega Gamma Delta [*Fraternity*] (EA)
OGD .... Open Government Document (PDAA)
OGDA .... Oyster Growers and Dealers Association (EA)
OGDC .... Oil and Gas Development Corp. (AD)

OGDD.......... Outgoing/Delay Dial [*Telecommunications*] (TEL)

Ogden.......... Ogden Corp. [*Associated Press*] (SAG)

Ogden.......... Ogden's Reports [*12-15 Louisiana*] [*A publication*] (DLA)

OGDH.......... Oxoglutarate Dehydrogenase [*An enzyme*]

Ogdn.......... Ogden Corp. [*Associated Press*] (SAG)

OGDR.......... Uniroyal Research Laboratories, Guelph, Ontario [*Library symbol National Library of Canada*] (NLC)

OGE .... Entomological Society of Ontario, Guelph, Ontario [*Library symbol National Library of Canada*] (NLC)

OGE .... Observer Group Egypt [*UN Truce Supervisor Organization*]

OGE .... Office of Government Ethics

OGE .... OGE Energy Corp. [*NYSE symbol*] (SAG)

OGE .... Oklahoma Gas & Elec [*NYSE symbol*] (TTSB)

OGE .... Oklahoma Gas & Electric Co. [*NYSE symbol*] (SPSG)

OGE .... Omaha Grain Exchange [*Defunct*] (EA)

OGE .... Operating [*or Operational*] Ground Equipment

oge .... Operational Ground Equipment (AD)

OGE .... Optional Ground Equipment (AAGC)

OGE .... Optogalvanic Effect (MCD)

OGE .... Oregon Graduate Center, Beaverton, OR [*OCLC symbol*] (OCLC)

OGE .... Out-of-Ground Effect

OGEC .... Organization of Gas Exporting Countries [*Proposed gas cartel*]

OGEDJ .... E. D. Jones Branch, Gloucester Public Library, Ontario [*Library symbol National Library of Canada*] (NLC)

OGE Engy..... OGE Energy Corp. [*Associated Press*] (SAG)

OGEG .... Georgetown District High School, Ontario [*Library symbol National Library of Canada*] (NLC)

OGEH .... Georgetown Branch, Halton Hills Public Libraries, Ontario [*Library symbol National Library of Canada*] (BIB)

OGELR .... Ecole Secondaire Louis-Riel, Gloucester, Ontario [*Library symbol National Library of Canada*] (BIB)

OGELS .... Observer Group in El Salvador

OGEO .... Georgetown Public Library, Ontario [*Library symbol National Library of Canada*] (NLC)

OGeo .... Mary P. Shelton Library, Georgetown, OH [*Library symbol Library of Congress*] (LCLS)

OGEPrA.......... Okla Gas & Elec,4% Pfd [*NYSE symbol*] (TTSB)

OGER .... Geraldton Public Library, Ontario [*Library symbol National Library of Canada*] (NLC)

OGer .... Germantown Public Library, Germantown, OH [*Library symbol Library of Congress*] (LCLS)

OGE/RPIE..... Operating Ground Equipment/Real Property Installed Equipment (AFM)

OGES .... Operating Ground Equipment Specification [*Italian*] (AD)

OGEV .... Varian Canada, Inc., Georgetown, Ontario [*Library symbol National Library of Canada*] (NLC)

ogf .... Option Growth Fund (AD)

OGF .... Orogastric Feeding [*Gastroenterology*] (DAVI)

OGF .... Ovarian Growth Factor [*Medicine*]

OGFC .... Official Gumby Fan Club (EA)

OGFP .... Obtaining Goods by False Pretense

OGFS .... Oil and Gas Field Study [*Department of the Interior*]

OGG .... GasTOPS Ltd., Gloucester, Ontario [*Library symbol National Library of Canada*] (NLC)

OGG .... Kahului [*Hawaii*] [*Airport symbol*] (OAG)

OGG .... Kahului, HI [*Location identifier FAA*] (FAAL)

ogg .... Oggetto [*Object*] [*Italian*] (AD)

OGG .... Organic Geochemistry Group

OGHC .... Hart Chemicals Ltd., Guelph, Ontario [*Library symbol National Library of Canada*] (NLC)

OGHS .... Gloucester High School, Ontario [*Library symbol National Library of Canada*] (BIB)

OGI .... Gould Information Center, Cleveland, OH [*OCLC symbol*] (OCLC)

OGI .... Oceanic Gamefish Investigations [*National Oceanic and Atmospheric Administration*] (MSC)

OGI .... Oculogyral Illusion [*NASA*]

OGI .... Oesterreichische Gesselschaft fuer Informatik [*Austrian Society for Information Processing*] [*German*] (AD)

OGI .... Off-Gas Isolation [*Nuclear energy*] (NRCH)

OGI .... Ontario Government Information [*Database*] [*Ministry of Culture and Communications*] [*Information service or system*] (CRD)

OGI .... Opera Guilds International (AD)

OGI .... Orientis Graeci Inscriptiones Selectae [*A publication*] (OCD)

OGI .... Outer Grid Injection

OGIB .... Occult Gastrointestinal Bleeding [*Medicine*]

OGID .... Outgoing/Immediate Dial [*Telecommunications*] (TEL)

OGIFC .... Original Gilligan's Island Fan Club (EA)

OGIL .... Open General Import Licence [*British*] (DS)

Ogilvie Dict... Ogilvie's Imperial Dictionary of the English Language [*A publication*] (DLA)

OGIP .... Original Gas in Place [*Natural resources*]

OGIS .... Open Geographic Information System

OGJ .... Oil and Gas Journal [*A publication*] (AD)

OGJ .... Outgoing Junction [*Telecommunications*] (TEL)

OGJFR .... John F. Ross Collegiate Vocational Institute, Guelph, Ontario [*Library symbol National Library of Canada*] (NLC)

OGK .... Kenyon College, Gambier, OH [*Library symbol Library of Congress*] (LCLS)

OGL .... Obscure Glass (AAG)

ogl .... Obscure Glass (AD)

OGL .... Open General License [*Import license*] (DS)

OGL .... Oral Glucose Loading [*Endocrinology*]

OGL .... Outgoing Line

OGLA .... Officer Grade Limitations Act of 1954

Oglbay .... Oglebay Norton Co. [*Associated Press*] (SAG)

OGLE .... Oglebay Norton [*NASDAQ symbol*] (TTSB)

OGLE .... Oglebay Norton Co. [*NASDAQ symbol*] (NQ)

OGLE .... Optical Gravitational Lens Experiment [*Astronomy*]

OGLE .... Organization for Getting Legs Exposed [*Group opposing below-the-knee fashions introduced in 1970*]

Oglethorpe U... Oglethorpe University (GAGS)

OGLPFC .... Official Gary Lewis and the Playboys Fan Club (EA)

OGM .... Office of Grants Management [*Public Health Service*]

OGM .... Office of Guided Missile (IAA)

OGM .... Ontonagon, MI [*Location identifier FAA*] (FAAL)

OGM .... Optimum Gradient Method

OGM .... Ordinary General Meeting

OGM .... Organic Gaseous Mercury [*Environmental chemistry*]

OGM .... Outgoing Message [*Telecommunications*]

OGM .... Outgrowth Medium [*Microbiology*] (DAVI)

OGM .... Outside Gage Marks (SAA)

OGMB .... Mattagami Band Public Library, Gogama, Ontario [*Library symbol National Library of Canada*] (NLC)

OGMC .... Ordnance Guided Missile Center (MCD)

OGMH .... Morrison Hershfield Ltd., Guelph, Ontario [*Library symbol National Library of Canada*] (NLC)

OGMS .... Ordnance Guided Missile School

OGMSD.......... Glen Morris Branch, South Dumfries Township Public Library, Ontario [*Library symbol National Library of Canada*] (BIB)

OGMT .... Orbiter Greenwich Mean Time [*NASA*] (MCD)

OGN .... Obstetric, Gynecologic, and Neonatal

OGN .... Yonagunijima [*Japan*] [*Airport symbol*] (OAG)

OGNB .... Orange National Bancorp [*NASDAQ symbol*] (SAG)

OGNB .... Orange Natl Bancorp [*NASDAQ symbol*] (TTSB)

OGNC .... Garson Branch, Nickel Centre Public Library, Ontario [*Library symbol National Library of Canada*] (NLC)

OGNR .... Oribi Gorge Nature Reserve [*South Africa*] (AD)

OGO .... Abengourou [*Ivory Coast*] [*Airport symbol*] (OAG)

OGO .... City Hall Branch, Gloucester Public Library, Ontario [*Library symbol National Library of Canada*] (NLC)

OGO .... Gould, Inc., Ocean Systems Information Center, Cleveland, OH [*OCLC symbol*] (OCLC)

OGO .... Officer Grade Objectives

OGO .... Oliver Gold Corp. [*Vancouver Stock Exchange symbol*]

OGO .... Orbiting Geophysical Observatory [*NASA*]

OG/OB.......... Office Group/Office Branch [*IRS*]

OGOD .... One Gene One Disorder [*Hypothesis*]

OGOG .... Gogama Community Library, Ontario [*Library symbol National Library of Canada*] (NLC)

OGOH .... Huron County Public Library, Goderich, Ontario [*Library symbol National Library of Canada*] (NLC)

OGOHC .... Huron County Pioneer Museum, Goderich, Ontario [*Library symbol National Library of Canada*] (BIB)

OGOR .... Goulais River Community Library, Ontario [*Library symbol National Library of Canada*] (NLC)

OGOS .... Outward Grade of Service (DNAB)

OGP .... Office of Global Programs [*National Oceanic and Atmospheric Administration*] (USDC)

OGP .... Office of Global Programs [*Marine science*] (OSRA)

OGP .... Original Gross Premium [*Insurance*] (AIA)

OGP .... Outgoing Message Process [*Telecommunications*] (TEL)

OGPA .... Office of Governmental and Public Affairs [*Department of Agriculture*] (GFGA)

OGPA .... Office of the General Purchasing Agent [*Military*]

OGPI .... Optical Glide Path Indicator

OGPr .... Ogden Corp. $1.875 cm Cv Pfd [*NYSE symbol*] (TTSB)

OGPS .... Office of Grants and Program Systems [*Department of Agriculture*]

OGPU .... Obiedinennoye Gosudarstvennoye Politicheskoye Upravlenie [*United State Political Administration*] [*Russian*] (AD)

OGPU .... Otdelenie Gosudarstvenni Politcheskoi Upravi [*Special Government Political Administration*] [*Former Soviet secret service organization, also known as GPU Later, KGB*]

OGR .... B. F. Goodrich Co., Information Center, Brecksville, OH [*OCLC symbol*] (OCLC)

OGr .... Greenville Public Library, Greenville, OH [*Library symbol Library of Congress*] (LCLS)

OGR .... Grimsby Public Library and Art Gallery, Ontario [*Library symbol National Library of Canada*] (NLC)

OGR .... Office of Government Relations [*Environmental Protection Agency*] (GFGA)

OGR .... Office of Government Reports [*New Deal*]

OGR .... Official Guide of the Railways [*A publication*] (AD)

OGR .... Old Garden Rose [*Pre-1870*] [*Horticulture*]

OGR .... Ontario Government Railway [*Canada*] (AD)

OGR .... Operation Grass Roots [*Small communities employment service*]

OGR .... Order of the Golden Rule (EA)

OGR .... Ordnance, Gunnery, and Readiness Division [*Coast Guard*]

OGR .... Original Gross Rate [*Insurance*] (AIA)

OGR .... ORNL [*Oak Ridge National Laboratory*] Graphite Reactor

OGR .... Outgoing Repeater

OGRA .... Gravenhurst Public Library, Ontario [*Library symbol National Library of Canada*] (NLC)

OGraD.......... Denison University, Granville, OH [*Library symbol Library of Congress*] (LCLS)

OGraO.......... Owens-Corning Fiberglas Corp., Granville, OH [*Library symbol Library of Congress*] (LCLS)

OGRC .... Office of Grants and Research Contracts [*NASA*]

OGRE .... Greely Public Library, Ontario [*Library symbol National Library of Canada*] (NLC)

OGRE .... Optical Grating Reflectance Evaluator (PDAA)

OGRE .... Organization of Generally Rotten Enterprises [*Evil organization in television cartoon series "The Drak Pack"*]
OGRL .... Outgoing Rural Line [*Telecommunications*] (IAA)
OGRM .... Grimsby Museum, Ontario [*Library symbol National Library of Canada*] (BIB)
OGRS .... Outgoing Relay Set [*Telecommunications*] (IAA)
OGRS .... Outgoing Rural Selector [*Telecommunications*] (IAA)
OGRV .... Grand Valley Public Library, Ontario [*Library symbol National Library of Canada*] (NLC)
OGS .... Oakland Growth Study [*1932-1964*] [*Sociology*]
OGS .... Obsolete General Supplies [*Military*]
OGS .... Off-Gas System [*Nuclear energy*] (NRCH)
OGS .... Ogdensburg [*New York*] [*Airport symbol*] (OAG)
OGS .... Ogdensburg, NY [*Location identifier FAA*] (FAAL)
OGS .... Ohio Genealogical Society (EA)
OGS .... Ontario Geological Survey [*Ontario Ministry of Northern Development and Mines*] [*Canada*] (IRC)
OGS .... Operative Glovers' Society [*A union*] [*British*]
O-GS .... Operator-to-General Support [*Maintenance*] (MCD)
OGS .... Optical Guidance System
OGS .... Oratory of the Good Shepherd [*British*]
OGS .... Original Ground Surface
OGS .... Outer Glidescope
OGS .... Outer Glide Slope [*Aviation*] (NASA)
OGS .... Outgoing Secondary Switch (IAA)
OGS .... Outgoing Secondary Switches (SAA)
OGS .... Overseas Ground Station (MCD)
OGS .... Oxogenic Steroid (MAE)
OGS .... Oxygen Generation System (NASA)
OGS .... Oxygen Generation System
OGSE .... Operational Ground Support Equipment (AAG)
ogse .... Operational Ground-Support Equipment (AD)
OGSEL .... Operational Ground Support Equipment List (AAG)
OGSESS ...... Operational Ground Support Equipment Systems Specification (SAA)
OGSGS .... Orangeburgh German Swiss Genealogical Society (EA)
OGSI .... Ongard Sys [*NASDAQ symbol*] (TTSB)
OGSI .... On Gard Systems [*NASDAQ symbol*] (SAG)
OGSM .... Office of the General Sales Manager [*Department of Agriculture*]
OGSM .... Stone Shop Museum, Grimsby, Ontario [*Library symbol National Library of Canada*] (NLC)
Ogs Med Jur... Ogston's Medical Jurisprudence [*1878*] [*A publication*] (DLA)
OGSR .... Office of Graduate Studies and Research (AD)
OGST .... Overthread Guide Sleeve Tool [*Nuclear energy*] (NRCH)
o-g stain...... Orange-Green Stain (AD)
OGSTM .... St. Matthew High School, Gloucester, Ontario [*Library symbol National Library of Canada*] (BIB)
OGT .... MIS Division, Turnelle Productions Ltd., Gloucester, Ontario [*Library symbol National Library of Canada*] (BIB)
OGT .... Office for Gifted and Talented [*Education*]
ogt.............. On-Going Thing (AD)
OGT .... Oppenheimer Multi-Government Trust [*NYSE symbol*] (SPSG)
OGT .... Oppenheimer Multi-Gvt Tr [*NYSE symbol*] (TTSB)
OGT .... Outgoing Trunk
OGT .... Outlet Gas Temperature (MSA)
ogt.............. Outlet Gas Temperature (AD)
OGTC .... Outgoing Toll Center [*Telecommunications*] (IAA)
OGTC .... Outgoing Toll Circuit [*Telecommunications*] (IAA)
OGTC .... Tudor and Cashel Public Library, Gilmour, Ontario [*Library symbol National Library of Canada*] (BIB)
OGTM .... Official Gazette. United States Patent and Trademark Office [*A publication*] (DLA)
OGTT .... Oral Glucose Tolerance Test [*Medicine*]
OGU .... Occupational Guidance Unit [*Department of Employment*] [*British*]
OGU .... Ogden Bay [*Utah*] [*Seismograph station code, US Geological Survey*] (SEIS)
OGU .... Outgoing Unit [*Telecommunications*] (IAA)
OGU .... Outgoing Unit [*Military*]
OGU .... University of Guelph, Ontario [*Library symbol National Library of Canada*] (NLC)
OGV .... Outlet Guide Vane
ogv.............. Outlet Guide Vane (AD)
OGV .... Oxygen Gauge Valve (NASA)
OGW .... Overhead Ground Wire
OGW .... Overload Gross Weight (NG)
OGWE .... Education Library, Wellington County Board of Education, Guelph, Ontario [*Library symbol National Library of Canada*] (NLC)
OGWP .... Office of Ground Water Protection [*Environmental Protection Agency*] (GFGA)
OGWS .... Outgoing/Wink Start [*Telecommunications*] (TEL)
OGX .... Ouargla [*Algeria*] [*Airport symbol*] (OAG)
OGY .... O'Gyalla [*Later, HRB*] [*Czechoslovakia*] [*Geomagnetic observatory code*]
OGY .... OGY Petroleum [*Vancouver Stock Exchange symbol*]
OH .... Comair [*ICAO designator*] (AD)
OH .... Finland [*International civil aircraft marking*] (ODBW)
OH .... Hamilton Public Library, Ontario [*Library symbol National Library of Canada*] (NLC)
OH .... Hospitaller Brothers of St. John of God (TOCD)
oh .... Hospitaller Brothers of St. John of God (TOCD)
OH .... Hospitaller Order of St. John of God [*Roman Catholic men's religious order*]
OH .... Hydroxy [*As substituent on nucleoside*] [*Also, HO*] [*Biochemistry*]
OH .... Hydroxycorticosteroid [*Endocrinology*] (DAVI)
OH .... Hydroxyl Radical (AD)
OH .... Oakwood Homes [*NYSE symbol*] (TTSB)

OH .... Oakwood Homes Corp. [*NYSE symbol*] (SPSG)
OH .... Observation Helicopter
OH .... Occipital Horn [*Brain anatomy*]
OH .... Occupational Health
OH .... Occupational History [*Medicine*]
O-H .... Octal-to-Hexadecimal [*Computer science*] (IEEE)
OH .... Ocular Herpes [*Medicine*] (AD)
OH .... Off Hook [*Computer science*]
OH .... Office Hours
oh .... Office Hours (AD)
OH .... Office of the Handicapped
OH .... Official Hostess (BARN)
OH .... Ohio [*Postal code*]
Oh .... Ohio Courts of Appeals Reports [*A publication*] (DLA)
OH .... Ohmic Heating
Oh .... Oholoth (BJA)
OH .... Olduvai Hominid [*Paleoanthropology*]
OH .... Omega House (AD)
oh .... Omni Hora [*Hourly*] [*Latin*] (AD)
OH .... Omni Hora [*Every Hour*] [*Pharmacy*]
OH .... On Hand
oh .... On Hand (AD)
o-H .... On-Hudson (AD)
OH .... Ontario Hydroelectric [*Canada*]
OH .... Open Hearth
oh .... Open Hearth (AD)
OH .... Open Heart Surgery [*Medicine*]
OH .... Opera House (AD)
OH .... Operating Hours (MCD)
OH .... Operational Handbook [*Marine Corps*] (INF)
OH .... Operational Hardware (KSC)
OH .... Operator's Handbook
OH .... Opposite Hand (OA)
OH .... Orah Hayyim Shulhan 'Arukh (BJA)
OH .... Oral Hygiene [*Dentistry*] (DAVI)
OH .... Originating Hospital [*Aeromedical evacuation*]
OH .... Orthostatic Hypotension [*Medicine*]
OH .... Osteopathic Hospital (DAVI)
OH .... Otago Hussars [*British military*] (DMA)
OH .... Out Home [*Men's lacrosse position*]
oh .... Out Home (AD)
OH .... Outlaw HAWK [*Naval Air Development Center*]
OH .... Outpatient Hospital [*Medicine*]
oh .... Oval Head (AD)
OH .... Overall Height [*of the Vehicle*] [*TII*] (TAG)
o/h .... Overhaul (AD)
OH .... Overhaul
OH .... Overhead
oh .... Overhead (AD)
O/H .... Over-the-Horizon Transmission
O/H .... Overzuche Handels Maatschappij [*Foreign Trade Company*] [*Dutch*] (ILCA)
OH .... Ozar Hatorah (EA)
OH .... SFO [*San Francisco and Oakland*] Helicopter Airlines, Inc. [*ICAO designator*] (OAG)
OHA .... Chicago, IL [*Location identifier FAA*] (FAAL)
OHA .... Havelock Public Library, Ontario [*Library symbol National Library of Canada*] (BIB)
OHA .... Hydroxyandrostenedione [*Antineoplastic drug*] (CDI)
OHa .... Lane Public Library, Hamilton, OH [*Library symbol Library of Congress*] (LCLS)
OHA .... Occupational Health Administration (AD)
OHA .... Office of Hearings and Appeals [*In various federal departments*]
OHA .... Officers' Home Advance (ADA)
OHA .... Off-station Housing Allowance (DOMA)
Oha .... Ohaloth (BJA)
OHA .... OH Aviationa [*France ICAO designator*] (FAAC)
Oh A .... Ohio Appellate Reports [*A publication*] (DLA)
OHA .... Operational Hazard Analysis (NASA)
OHA .... Oral History Association (EA)
OHA .... Oral Hypoglycemic Agent [*Medicine*] (CPH)
OHA .... Orbital Height Adjustment Maneuver (MCD)
OHA .... Oriental Herb Association (AD)
OHA .... Oscillator Housing Assembly
OHA .... Outside Helix Angle
oha .... Outside Helix Angle (AD)
OHA .... Overseas Housing Allowance
OHA .... Owner Handler Association of America (EA)
OHA .... Oxygen Hemoglobin Affinity (OA)
Oh A 2d ...... Ohio Appellate Reports, Second Series [*A publication*] (DLA)
OHaBHi........ Butler County Historical Society, Hamilton, OH [*Library symbol Library of Congress*] (LCLS)
OHAD .... Dysart Branch, Haliburton County Public Library, Ontario [*Library symbol National Library of Canada*] (BIB)
OHAG .... Art Gallery of Hamilton, Ontario [*Library symbol National Library of Canada*] (NLC)
OHAI .... Haileybury Public Library, Ontario [*Library symbol National Library of Canada*] (NLC)
OHAINC........ Haileybury School of Mines Campus, Northern College of Applied Arts and Technology, Ontario [*Library symbol National Library of Canada*] (BIB)
OHAL .... Haliburton County Public Library, Ontario [*Library symbol National Library of Canada*] (NLC)
OHALM .... Haliburton Highlands Museum, Haliburton, Ontario [*Library symbol National Library of Canada*] (BIB)

OHaMH .... Mercy Hospital, Health Science Library, Hamilton, OH [*Library symbol Library of Congress*] (LCLS)

OHAN .... Hanover Public Library, Ontario [*Library symbol National Library of Canada*] (NLC)

Oh Ap .... Ohio Appellate Reports [*A publication*] (DLA)

OHAPT .... Orleans-Hanna Algebra Prognosis Test (EDAC)

OHARAG ...... Research Station, Agriculture Canada [*Station de Recherches, Agriculture Canada*] Harrow, Ontario [*Library symbol National Library of Canada*] (NLC)

OhArt .... [*The*] Ohio Art Co. [*Associated Press*] (SAG)

OHAS .... Occupational Health and Safety

OHaU .... Miami University, Hamilton Campus, Hamilton, OH [*Library symbol Library of Congress*] (LCLS)

OHB .... L'Equilibre Biologique [*France*] [*Research code symbol*]

OH-B .... Ocean Hill-Brownsville (AD)

OHBC .... Oregon Highland Bentgrass Commission (EA)

OHBES .... Schools, Hamilton Board of Education, Ontario [*Library symbol National Library of Canada*] (NLC)

OHBHU .... Hilton Union Public Library, Hilton Beach, Ontario [*Library symbol National Library of Canada*] (NLC)

OHBMS ...... On His [*or Her*] Britannic Majesty's Service

OHBP .... Pic Heron Bay Band Public Library, Heron Bay, Ontario [*Library symbol National Library of Canada*] (BIB)

OHC .... Hydroxycholecalciferol [*A form of vitamin D*] (DAVI)

OHC .... Occupational Health Center (KSC)

OHC .... Ocean Heat Convergence

OHC .... Office of Humanities Communication (AD)

OHC .... Office of HUMINT [*Human Intelligence*] Collection [*Military*]

OHC .... O'Higgins [*Antarctica*] [*Seismograph station code, US Geological Survey*] (SEIS)

OHC .... On Board Hard Copier (NASA)

OHC .... Onboard Hard Copier

OHC .... Optics Hand Controller (KSC)

OHC .... Order of the Holy Cross [*Episcopalian religious order*]

OHC .... Oriole Homes Corp. [*AMEX symbol*] (SPSG)

OHC .... Ottumwa Heights College [*Iowa*]

OHC .... Outer Hair Cells [*of cochlea*] [*Anatomy*]

ohc............ Outer Hair Cells (AD)

ohc............ Overhead Cam (AD)

OHC........... Over-Head-Cam [*TII*] (TAG)

OHC........... Overhead Camshaft [*Automotive term*]

OHC........... Overhead Cupboards [*Classified advertising*] (ADA)

OHC........... Overseas Hotel Corp. (AD)

OHC.A......... Oriole HomesCv'A' [*AMEX symbol*] (TTSB)

OHCA......... Otter Hound Club of America [*Later, OCA*] (EA)

OHC.B......... Oriole Homes 'B' [*AMEX symbol*] (TTSB)

OH-Cbl........ Hydroxycobalamin [*Medicine*] (BABM)

OHCC.......... Ordinary High Current Configuration [*Magnetic field*]

Oh Cir Ct ... Ohio Circuit Court Reports [*A publication*] (DLA)

Oh Cir Ct NS... Ohio Circuit Court Reports, New Series [*A publication*] (DLA)

Oh Cir Dec... Ohio Circuit Decisions [*A publication*] (DLA)

OHCS.......... Hydroxycorticosteroid [*Endocrinology*] (AAMN)

OHCS.......... Office of Home Care Services (AD)

OHCU.......... College Universitaire de Hearst, Ontario [*Library symbol National Library of Canada*] (NLC)

OHD........... Office of Human Development [*Later, OHDS*] [*HEW*]

OHD........... Ohrid [*Former Yugoslavia*] [*Airport symbol*] (OAG)

OHD........... Old Hickory Dam [*TVA*]

OHD........... One-Hour Duty (IAA)

OHD........... Optical Heterodyne Detection

OHD........... Ordinary Hydrodynamic

ohd .... Organic Hearing Disease [*Medicine*] (AD)

ohd .... Organic Heart Disease [*Medicine*] (AD)

OHD........... Organic Heart Disease [*Medicine*]

OHD........... Overhead Display

OHD........... Over-the-Horizon Detector [*RADAR*]

OHDA.......... Hydroxydopamine [*Also, HDA, HDM*] [*Biochemistry*]

OHD & W..... Outer Harbor Dock and Wharf (AD)

OHD-B .... Over-the-Horizon Detection RADAR-Backscatter (MCD)

Oh Dec ...... Ohio Decisions [*A publication*] (DLA)

Oh Dec Rep... Ohio Decisions Reprint [*A publication*] (DLA)

OHDET........ Over-the-Horizon Detection [*RADAR*] (SAA)

OHDETS....... Over-the-Horizon Detection System [*RADAR*]

OHDF.......... Dofasco, Inc., Hamilton, Ontario [*Library symbol National Library of Canada*] (NLC)

OHDFR........ Research Information Center, DOFASCO, Inc., Hamilton, Ontario [*Library symbol National Library of Canada*] (NLC)

OHDMS....... Operational Hydromet Data Management System (PDAA)

OH-DOC ..... Hydroxydeoxycorticosterone [*Endocrinology*] (DAVI)

OHDS.......... Office of Human Development Services [*Formerly, OHD*] [*Department of Health and Human Services*]

OHE .... Hearst Public Library, Ontario [*Library symbol National Library of Canada*] (NLC)

OHE .... Office of Health Economics [*British*]

OHE .... Office of the Housing Expediter [*Terminated, 1951*] (GPO)

OHE .... Oxidizer Heat Exchange (MCD)

OHEA.......... Office of Health and Environmental Assessment [*Environmental Protection Agency*] (GFGA)

OHEAT........ Overheat

oheat .... Overheat (AD)

OHEC .... Dr. Harry Paikin Library, Hamilton Board of Education, Ontario [*Library symbol National Library of Canada*] (NLC)

OHEC .... Hamilton Education Centre, Ontario [*Library symbol National Library of Canada*] (NLC)

OhEd .... Ohio Edison Co. [*Associated Press*] (SAG)

OhEd .... Ohio Edison Financing Trust [*Associated Press*] (SAG)

OHEP .... Hepworth Branch, Bruce County Public Library, Ontario [*Library symbol National Library of Canada*] (NLC)

OHER .... Office of Health and Environmental Research [*Department of Energy Washington, DC*]

OHESC .... Ontario Library Service - Escarpment, Hamilton, Ontario [*Library symbol National Library of Canada*] (NLC)

OHET .... Erin Township Public Library, Hillsburgh, Ontario [*Library symbol National Library of Canada*] (NLC)

OHF .... Occupational Health Facility [*NASA*] (KSC)

OHF .... Omsk Hemorrhagic Fever [*Medicine*]

ohf............ Omsk Hemorrhagic Fever (AD)

OHF .... Ordnance Historical Files [*Military*]

ohf............ Overhaul Factor (AD)

OHF .... Overhead Fire (MCD)

OHF .... Overhead Frame (MEDA)

OHF .... Oxalosis and Hyperoxaluria Foundation (EA)

OHFA .... Hydroxy Fatty Acid [*Biochemistry*] (AAMN)

OHFC .... Hartington Branch, Frontenac County Library, Hartington, Ontario [*Library symbol National Library of Canada*] (BIB)

OHFC .... Owen Hart Fan Club (EA)

Oh F Dec .... Ohio Federal Decisions [*A publication*] (DLA)

OH/FH .... Operating Hour/Flight Hour [*Ratio*]

OHG .... Banco OHiggins [*NYSE symbol*] (SAG)

OHG .... Banco O'Higgins ADS [*NYSE symbol*] (TTSB)

OHG .... Offene Handelsgesellschaft [*General Partnership*] [*German*]

OHG .... Old High German [*Language, etc.*]

OHG .... Oral Hypoglycemic [*Endocrinology*] (DAVI)

OHGI .... Over the Hill Gang, International (EA)

OHGS .... Omega Hyperbolic Grid System

OHGVT........ Orbital Horizontal Ground Vibration Test [*NASA*] (NASA)

OHH .... Herrold Hall Learning Resource Center, Zanesville, OH [*OCLC symbol*] (OCLC)

OHH .... Ohio Household Goods Carriers Bureau Inc., Warren OH [*STAC*]

OHH .... Owen Harrison Harding [*of the James W. Ellison novel, "I'm Owen Harrison Harding"*]

OHHA......... Occupational Health Hazard Assessment

OHI .... HUNA International (EA)

OHI .... Occupational Health Institute [*Defunct*] (EA)

OHI .... Ocular Hypertension Indicator

ohi............ Ocular Hypertension Indicator (AD)

OHi .... Ohio Historical Society, Columbus, OH [*Library symbol Library of Congress*] (LCLS)

OHI .... Oil Heat Institute (AD)

OHI .... Oil-Heat Institute of America [*Later, PMAA*]

OHI .... Omega Healthcare Investors [*NYSE symbol*] (SPSG)

OHI .... Open Head Injury [*Medicine*] (PAZ)

OHI .... Ordnance Handling Instructions

OHI .... Organisation Hydrographique Internationale [*International Hydrographic Organization - IHO*] [*Monte Carlo, Monaco*]

OHI .... Other Health Impaired [*Education*]

OHI .... State Library of Ohio, Columbus, OH [*OCLC symbol*] (OCLC)

OHIA .... Oil-Heat Institute of America [*Later, PMAA*] (KSC)

OHIAA......... Hydroxyindolacetic Acid [*Oncology*] (DAVI)

OHIC .... ODPHP Health Information Center (EA)

OHilH .... Highland County District Library, Hillsboro, OH [*Library symbol Library of Congress*] (LCLS)

OHilS .... South Hillsboro City Schools, Hillsboro, OH [*Library symbol Library of Congress*] (LCLS)

Ohio .... Ohio Supreme Court Reports [*1821-51*] [*A publication*] (DLA)

OHIO.......... Over the Hill in October [*Used prior to the bombing of Pearl Harbor to typify a recruit's view of US Army life*]

Ohio Abs..... Ohio Law Abstract [*A publication*] (DLA)

Ohio Abstract... Ohio Law Abstract [*A publication*] (DLA)

Ohio Admin Code... Ohio Administrative Code [*Official compilation published by Banks-Baldwin*] [*A publication*] (DLA)

Ohio App .... Ohio Appellate Reports [*A publication*] (DLA)

Ohio App 2d.. Ohio Appellate Reports, Second Series [*A publication*] (DLA)

Ohio Apps.... Ohio Appellate Reports [*A publication*] (DLA)

Ohio BTA .... Ohio Board of Tax Appeals Reports [*A publication*] (DLA)

OhioCa........ Ohio Casualty Corp. [*Associated Press*] (SAG)

Ohio CA....... Ohio Courts of Appeals Reports [*A publication*] (DLA)

OhioCas....... Ohio Casualty Corp. [*Associated Press*] (SAG)

Ohio CC ...... Ohio Circuit Court Reports [*A publication*] (DLA)

Ohio CC Dec... Ohio Circuit Court Decisions [*A publication*] (DLA)

Ohio CC NS... Ohio Circuit Court Reports, New Series [*A publication*] (DLA)

Ohio CCR.... Ohio Circuit Court Reports [*A publication*] (DLA)

Ohio CCR NS... Ohio Circuit Court Reports, New Series [*A publication*] (DLA)

Ohio CD...... Ohio Circuit Decisions [*A publication*] (DLA)

Ohio C Dec... Ohio Circuit Decisions [*A publication*] (DLA)

Ohio Circ Dec... Ohio Circuit Decisions [*A publication*] (DLA)

Ohio Cir Ct... Ohio Circuit Court Decisions [*A publication*] (DLA)

Ohio Cir Ct (NS)... Ohio Circuit Court Reports, New Series [*A publication*] (DLA)

Ohio Cir Ct R... Ohio Circuit Court Reports [*A publication*] (DLA)

Ohio Cir Ct R NS... Ohio Circuit Court Reports, New Series [*A publication*] (DLA)

Ohio Circuits... Ohio Circuit Court Decisions [*A publication*] (DLA)

Ohio Cir Dec... Ohio Circuit Decisions [*A publication*] (DLA)

Ohio Cond ... Wilcox's Condensed Ohio Reports [*A publication*] (DLA)

Ohio Cond R... Wilcox's Condensed Ohio Reports [*A publication*] (DLA)

Ohio Ct App... Ohio Courts of Appeals Reports [*A publication*] (DLA)

Ohio Dec .... Ohio Decisions [*A publication*] (DLA)

Ohio Dec NP... Ohio Decisions Nisi Prius [*A publication*] (DLA)

Ohio Dec R... Ohio Decisions Reprint [*A publication*] (DLA)

Ohio Dec Re... Ohio Decisions Reprint [*A publication*] (DLA)

Ohio Dec Rep... Ohio Decisions Reprint [*A publication*] (DLA)

Ohio Dec Repr... Ohio Decisions Reprint [*A publication*] (DLA)
Ohio Dep't... Ohio Department Reports [*A publication*] (DLA)
OhioEd......... Ohio Edison Co. [*Associated Press*] (SAG)
Ohio FD...... Ohio Federal Decisions [*A publication*] (DLA)
Ohio F Dec... Ohio Federal Decisions [*A publication*] (DLA)
Ohio Fed Dec... Ohio Federal Decisions [*A publication*] (DLA)
Ohio Gov't... Ohio Government Reports [*A publication*] (DLA)
Ohio Jur ..... Ohio Jurisprudence [*A publication*] (DLA)
Ohio Jur 2d... Ohio Jurisprudence, Second Series [*A publication*] (DLA)
Ohio L Abs... Ohio Law Abstract [*A publication*] (DLA)
Ohio Law Abs... Ohio Law Abstract [*A publication*] (DLA)
Ohio Law Abst... Ohio Law Abstract [*A publication*] (DLA)
Ohio Law Bull... Weekly Law Bulletin [*Ohio*] [*A publication*] (DLA)
Ohio Law J... Ohio Law Journal [*A publication*] (DLA)
Ohio Law R... Ohio Law Reporter [*A publication*] (DLA)
Ohio Law Rep... Ohio Law Reporter [*A publication*] (DLA)
Ohio Law Repr... Ohio Law Reporter [*A publication*] (DLA)
Ohio Laws ... State of Ohio: Legislative Acts Passed and Joint Resolutions Adopted [*A publication*] (DLA)
Ohio LB ...... Weekly Law Bulletin [*Ohio*] [*A publication*] (DLA)
Ohio L Bull... Ohio Law Bulletin [*A publication*] (DLA)
Ohio Legal N... Ohio Legal News [*A publication*] (DLA)
Ohio Legis Bull... Ohio Legislative Bulletin (Anderson) [*A publication*] (DLA)
Ohio Legis Serv... Ohio Legislative Service [*A publication*] (DLA)
Ohio Leg N... Ohio Legal News [*A publication*] (DLA)
Ohio Leg News... Ohio Legal News [*A publication*] (DLA)
Ohio LJ........ Ohio Law Journal [*A publication*] (DLA)
Ohio Low Dec... Ohio Lower Court Decisions [*A publication*] (DLA)
Ohio Lower Dec... Ohio Lower Court Decisions [*A publication*] (DLA)
Ohio LR........ Ohio Law Reporter [*A publication*] (DLA)
Ohio LR & Wk Bul... Ohio Law Reporter and Weekly Bulletin [*A publication*] (DLA)
Ohio L Rep... Ohio Law Reporter [*A publication*] (DLA)
OHIO M........ Ohio Magazine [*A publication*] (ROG)
Ohio Misc... Ohio Miscellaneous Reports [*A publication*] (DLA)
Ohio Misc 2d... Ohio Miscellaneous Reports, Second Series [*A publication*] (DLA)
Ohio Misc 3d... Ohio Miscellaneous Reports, Third Series [*A publication*] (DLA)
Ohio Misc Dec... Ohio Miscellaneous Decisions [*A publication*] (DLA)
Ohio Monthly Rec... Ohio Monthly Record [*A publication*] (DLA)
OHIONET...... Ohio Network (NITA)
Ohio (New Series)... Ohio State Reports, New Series [*A publication*] (DLA)
Ohio Nisi Prius... Ohio Nisi Prius Reports [*A publication*] (DLA)
Ohio Nisi Prius (NS)... Ohio Nisi Prius Reports, New Series [*A publication*] (DLA)
Ohio No U ... Ohio Northern University (GAGS)
Ohio NP...... Ohio Nisi Prius Reports [*A publication*] (DLA)
Ohio NP NS... Ohio Nisi Prius Reports, New Series [*A publication*] (DLA)
Ohio NS....... Ohio State Reports, New Series [*A publication*] (DLA)
Ohio O .... Ohio Opinions [*A publication*] (DLA)
Ohio O .... Ohio Opinions, Annotated [*A publication*] (DLA)
Ohio O 2d ... Ohio Opinions, Second Series [*A publication*] (DLA)
Ohio Op...... Ohio Opinions [*A publication*] (DLA)
Ohio Op 2d... Ohio Opinions, Second Series [*A publication*] (DLA)
Ohio Op 3d... Ohio Opinions, Third Series [*A publication*] (DLA)
Ohio Ops ..... Ohio Opinions [*A publication*] (DLA)
Ohio Prob.... Ohio Probate Reports, by Goebel [*A publication*] (DLA)
Ohio Prob Ct... Goebel's Probate Reports [*Ohio*] [*A publication*] (DLA)
Ohio R........ Ohio Report [*A publication*] (DLA)
Ohio R Cond... Ohio Reports Condensed [*A publication*] (DLA)
Ohio Rev Code Ann... Ohio Revised Code, Annotated [*A publication*] (DLA)
Ohio Rev Code Ann (Anderson)... Ohio Revised Code, Annotated (Anderson) [*A publication*] (DLA)
Ohio Rev Code Ann (Baldwin)... Ohio Revised Code, Annotated (Baldwin) [*A publication*] (DLA)
Ohio Rev Code Ann (Page)... Ohio Revised Code, Annotated (Page) [*A publication*] (DLA)
Ohio S .... Ohio State Reports [*A publication*] (DLA)
Ohio S & CP... Ohio Superior and Common Pleas Decisions [*A publication*] (DLA)
Ohio S & CP Dec... Ohio Superior and Common Pleas Decisions [*A publication*] (DLA)
Ohio SBA Bull... Ohio State Bar Association. Bulletin [*A publication*] (DLA)
Ohio SR....... Ohio State Reports [*A publication*] (DLA)
Ohio S Rep ... Ohio State Reports [*A publication*] (DLA)
Ohio St .... Ohio State Reports [*A publication*] (DLA)
Ohio St 2d ... Ohio State Reports, Second Series [*A publication*] (DLA)
Ohio St 3d ... Ohio State Reports, Third Series [*A publication*] (DLA)
Ohio State ... Ohio State Reports [*A publication*] (DLA)
Ohio State Rep... Ohio State Reports [*A publication*] (DLA)
Ohio State R (NS)... Ohio State Reports, New Series [*A publication*] (DLA)
Ohio St R... Ohio State Reports [*A publication*] (DLA)
Ohio St Rep... Ohio State Reports [*A publication*] (DLA)
Ohio St Report... Ohio State Reports [*A publication*] (DLA)
Ohio St R (NS)... Ohio State Reports, New Series [*A publication*] (DLA)
Ohio St U..... [*The*] Ohio State University (GAGS)
Ohio SU....... Ohio Supreme Court Decisions, Unreported Cases [*A publication*] (DLA)
Ohio Sup & CP Dec... Ohio Superior and Common Pleas Decisions [*A publication*] (DLA)
Ohio Supp ... Ohio Supplement [*A publication*] (DLA)
Ohio Turn .... Ohio Turnpike (AD)
Ohio U .... Ohio University (GAGS)
Ohio Unrep... Ohio Supreme Court Decisions, Unreported Cases [*A publication*] (DLA)
Ohio Unrep Jud Dec... Pollack's Ohio Unreported Judicial Decisions Prior to 1823 [*A publication*] (DLA)
Ohio Unrept Cas... Ohio Supreme Court Decisions, Unreported Cases [*A publication*] (DLA)

Ohio U Pr ... Ohio University Press (AD)
OhioVal...... Ohio Valley Banc Corp. [*Associated Press*] (SAG)
OHIP........... Ontario Hospital Insurance Plan [*Canada*] (AD)
OHIR.......... Operating House of Ill Repute
OHirC.......... Hiram College, Hiram, OH [*Library symbol Library of Congress*] (LCLS)
OHirP.......... Portage County District Library, Hiram, OH [*Library symbol Library of Congress*] (LCLS)
OHIS .... Oral Hearing-Impaired Section [*of the Alexander Graham Bell Association for the Deaf*] (EA)
OHI-S......... Oral Hygiene Index-Simplified
OHJ........... Old-House Journal [*A publication*]
OHJD .... John Deere Ltd., Hamilton, Ontario [*Library symbol National Library of Canada*] (NLC)
Oh Jur .... Ohio Jurisprudence [*A publication*] (DLA)
OHK .... Hawkesbury Public Library, Ontario [*Library symbol National Library of Canada*] (NLC)
OHKAC........ Resource Centre, Algonquin College of Applied Arts and Technology [*Centre de Documentation, College Algonquin des Arts Appliques et de la Technologie*], Hawkesbury, Ontario [*Library symbol National Library of Canada*] (BIB)
OHKC .... CIP Research Ltd., Hawkesbury, Ontario [*Library symbol National Library of Canada*] (NLC)
OHKGH .... Hawkesbury General Hospital, Ontario [*Library symbol National Library of Canada*] (BIB)
OHL .... Oberste Herresleitung [*Supreme Headquarters*] [*German*] (AD)
OHL .... Ontario Hydro Library [*UTLAS symbol*]
OHL .... Oral Hairy Leukoplakia [*Medicine*]
OHL .... Overhaul
OHL .... Oxford Higher Local Examination [*British*] (ROG)
OHLA .... Anthony Pape Memorial Law Library, Hamilton Law Association, Ontario [*Library symbol National Library of Canada*] (BIB)
Oh L Bul...... Ohio Law Bulletin [*A publication*] (DLA)
Oh L Ct D .... Ohio Lower Court Decisions [*A publication*] (DLA)
OHLEG .... East Gwillimbury Public Libraries, Holland Landing, Ontario [*Library symbol National Library of Canada*] (NLC)
Oh Leg N ..... Ohio Legal News [*A publication*] (DLA)
OHLH .... Overhead Heavy Load Handling [*Nuclear energy*] (NRCH)
Ohlinger Fed Practice... Ohlinger's Federal Practice [*A publication*] (DLA)
Oh LJ.......... Ohio Law Journal [*A publication*] (DLA)
Oh L Rep ..... Ohio Law Reporter [*A publication*] (DLA)
OHM .... McMaster University, Hamilton, Ontario [*Library symbol National Library of Canada*] (NLC)
OHM .... Miami University, Hamilton Campus, Hamilton, OH [*OCLC symbol*] (OCLC)
OHM .... Office of Hazardous Materials [*Department of Transportation*]
OHM .... OHM Corp. [*NYSE symbol*] (SPSG)
OHM .... Ohmmeter [*Engineering*] (AAG)
ohm .... Ohmmeter (AD)
OHM .... Oil and Hazardous Materials Incidence
OHMA .... Archives and Special Collections Division, McMaster University, Hamilton, Ontario [*Library symbol National Library of Canada*] (NLC)
OHMA .... Office of Health and Medical Affairs (GHCT)
OHMAH........ Department of Art and Art History, McMaster University, Hamilton, Ontario [*Library symbol National Library of Canada*] (NLC)
OHMAR .... Oral History in the Mid-Atlantic Region [*An association*]
OHMB .... Health Sciences Library, McMaster University, Hamilton, Ontario [*Library symbol National Library of Canada*] (NLC)
OHMC .... Mohawk College of Applied Arts and Technology, Hamilton, Ontario [*Library symbol National Library of Canada*] (NLC)
OHMcGF ...... Odyssey House McGrath Foundation [*Australia*]
OHMCL .... Library Technician Program, Mohawk College of Applied Arts & Technology, Hamilton, Ontario [*Library symbol National Library of Canada*] (NLC)
OHM-CM ...... Ohm-Centimeter (AAG)
ohm-cm ...... Ohm-Centimeter (AD)
OHM Cp ...... OHM Corp. [*Associated Press*] (SAG)
OHMDBA...... Canadian Baptist Archives, McMaster Divinity College, McMaster University, Hamilton, Ontario [*Library symbol National Library of Canada*] (NLC)
OHMEA .... Office of Hazardous Materials Exemptions and Approvals [*RSPA*] (TAG)
OHMES .... Occupational Health Monitoring and Evaluation System (PDAA)
OHMIS .... Occupational Health Management Information System [*Military*] (GFGA)
Oh Misc ...... Ohio Miscellaneous Reports [*A publication*] (DLA)
OHMM .... Map Library, McMaster University, Hamilton, Ontario [*Library symbol National Library of Canada*] (NLC)
OHMM .... Ohmmeter [*Engineering*]
OHMM .... Ohmmeter
ohm/m .... Resistence per Meter
OHMO.......... Office of Hazardous Materials Operations [*Department of Transportation*] (DLA)
OHMO.......... Office of Health Maintenance Organization [*Insurance*] (DHSM)
OHMP .... Oral Health Maintenance Program [*Army*] (AABC)
OHMR .... Office of Hazardous Materials Regulation [*Department of Transportation*] (OICC)
OHMS .... Office of Hazardous Materials Standards [*RSPA*] (TAG)
OHMS .... Onboard Health Monitoring System (AD)
OHMS .... On His [*or Her*] Majesty's Service
OHMS .... Our Helpless Millions Saved [*Title of early film*]
OHMS .... Overhead Machine Screw [*Technical drawings*]
OHMSB........ Oil and Hazardous Materials Spills Branch [*Environmental Protection Agency*] (GRD)

OHMSETT .... Oil and Hazardous Materials Simulated Environmental Test Tank [Leonardo, NJ] [Environmental Protection Agency]
OHMT .... Office of Hazardous Materials Transportation [Department of Transportation] (GFGA)
OHM-TADS... Oil and Hazardous Materials Technical Assistance Data System [Databank] [Environmental Protection Agency] (IID)
OHN .... Hastings Branch, Northumberland County Public Library, Ontario [Library symbol National Library of Canada] (BIB)
OHN .... Memphis, TN [Location identifier FAA] (FAAL)
OHN .... Occupational Health Nurse [Government classification]
OHN .... OHIONET, Columbus, OH [OCLC symbol] (OCLC)
OHNC .... Occupational Health Nursing Certificate [British]
OHNN .... Otorhinolaryngology and Head/Neck Nurses (EA)
OHNO .... Occupational Health Nursing Officer (AD)
Oh NP .... Ohio Nisi Prius Reports [A publication] (DLA)
Oh NP (NS).. Ohio Nisi Prius Reports, New Series [A publication] (DLA)
OHNS .... Occupational Health Nursing Sister (AD)
Oh NU Intra LR... Ohio Northern University. Intramural Law Review [A publication] (DLA)
OHO .... Ohio Resources Corp. [Vancouver Stock Exchange symbol]
Oho .... Oholoth (BJA)
OHO .... Order Holding Office
OHO .... Ordnance Handling Officer [Navy] (DOMA)
oho .... Out-of-House Operation (AD)
OHOHS .... Canadian Centre for Occupational Health and Safety [Centre Canadien d'Hygieneet de Securite au Travail] Hamilton, Ontario [Library symbol National Library of Canada] (NLC)
Ohol .... Oholoth (BJA)
OHP .... Hydroxypyroline [Biochemistry] (AAMN)
OHP .... Oban-Heliport [Scotland] [Airport symbol] (OAG)
OHP .... Operational Hydrology Program [World Meteorological Organization] (GFGA)
OHP .... Order of the Holy Paraclete [Anglican religious community]
OHP .... Outer Helmholtz Plane [Physics]
ohp .... Overhead Projection (AD)
OHP .... Overhead Projector (ADA)
OHP .... Oxygen at High Pressure [Also, HBO, HPO] (MCD)
OHP .... Oxygen under Hyperbaric Pressure [For hyperbaric oxygen therapy] [Medicine] (DAVI)
OhP25.......... Ohio Power Co. [Associated Press] (SAG)
OH PED....... Ohne Pedal [Without Pedal] [Music]
oh Ped......... Ohne Pedale [Without Pedals] [German] (AD)
OHPO .... Organization Health Program Officer (AFM)
OHPR .... Outstanding Hardware Problem Report (MCD)
Oh Prob ..... Ohio Probate [A publication] (DLA)
OHPS .... Oil Hydraulic Power Switch
OHQ .... Overseas Headquarters [British military] (DMA)
OHR .... Office of Health Research [Environmental Protection Agency Washington, DC] (GRD)
OHR .... Of Human Rights (EA)
OHR .... O'Hara Resources Ltd. [Vancouver Stock Exchange symbol]
OHR .... Ohrid [Yugoslavia] [Seismograph station code, US Geological Survey] (SEIS)
OHR .... Operational Hazard Report [Air Force] (AFM)
OHR .... Over-the-Horizon RADAR
OHRB .... Royal Botanical Gardens, Hamilton, Ontario [Library symbol National Library of Canada] (NLC)
OHRC .... Redeemer College, Ancaster, Ontario [Library symbol National Library of Canada] (NLC)
ohrf .... Overhaul Replacement Factor (AD)
OHRG .... Official Hotel and Resort Guide [A publication] (AD)
OHRI .... Occupational Health & Rehabilitation, Inc. [NASDAQ symbol] (SAG)
OHRI .... Oral Health Research Institute [Indiana University] [Research center] (RCD)
OHRI .... Overhaul Recurrent Item (CINC)
OHRI .... Overhaul Removal Interval [Military] (AFIT)
OHRI .... Overhaul Removal Item (CINC)
OHRIM......... Office of Human Resource Information Management [Department of Health and Human Services] (GFGA)
OHRM .... Office of Human Resources Management [Environmental Protection Agency] (GFGA)
OHRR........... Open Heart Recovery Room [Cardiology] (DAVI)
OHRS........... Overflow Heat Removal System [Nuclear energy] (NRCH)
OHS .... Hamilton Spectator, Ontario [Library symbol National Library of Canada] (NLC)
OHS .... Obesity Hypoventilation Syndrome
OHS .... Occupational Health and Safety
OHS .... Occupational Health Services, Inc. [Secaucus, NJ] [Medical databank originator] [Information service or system]
OHS .... Occupational Hearing Service
OHS .... Off-Hook Service [Telecommunications] (TEL)
OHS .... Office of Highway Safety [of BPR]
OHS .... Ontario Humane Society [Canada] (AD)
ohs............. Open-Hearth Steel (AD)
OHS .... Open-Hearth Steel
OHS .... Open Heart Surgery [Medicine]
OHS .... Optometric Historical Society (EA)
OHS .... Oral Hygiene Service (AD)
OHS .... Oral Hygiene Society (NADA)
OHS .... Organ Historical Society (EA)
OHS .... Organization Health Survey [Test]
OHSETT .... Organization of Historical Studies (EA)
OHS .... Organization of Historical Studies (AD)
OHS .... Oval-Headed Screw (DAC)
OHS .... Ovarian Hyperstimulation Syndrome [Medicine] (DMAA)

OHS .... University of Oregon, Health Sciences Library, Portland, OR [OCLC symbol] (OCLC)
OHSA .... Occupational Health and Safety Authority [Victoria, Australia]
Oh S & CP... Ohio Superior and Common Pleas Decisions [A publication] (DLA)
OHSC .... Oak Hill Sportswear [NASDAQ symbol] (TTSB)
OHSC .... Oak Hill Sportswear Corp. [NASDAQ symbol] (NQ)
OHSCC .... Steel Company of Canada, Hamilton, Ontario [Library symbol National Library of Canada] (NLC)
Oh SCD ...... Ohio Supreme Court Decisions, Unreported Cases [A publication] (DLA)
OHSCSA....... Occupational Health and Safety Commission of South Australia
OHSGT .... Office of High-Speed Ground Transportation [Department of Transportation]
OHSI .... Omega Health Systems [NASDAQ symbol] (TTSB)
OHSI .... Omega Health Systems, Inc. [NASDAQ symbol] (SAG)
OHSI .... Oral Health Status Index [Dentistry]
OHSIP .... Ontario Health-Services Insurances Plan [Canada] (AD)
OHSL .... OHSL Financial Corp. [NASDAQ symbol] (SAG)
OHSL Fn ...... OHSL Financial Corp. [Associated Press] (SAG)
OHS MSDS... Occupational Health Services Material Safety Data Sheets [Database]
OHSPAC....... Occupational Health-Safety-Programs Accreditation Commission (AD)
OHSRC .... Occupational Health Safety and Rehabilitation Council [New South Wales, Australia]
OHSS .... Occupational Health and Safety Staff [Environmental Protection Agency] (GFGA)
OHST .... Occupational Health and Safety Technologist
Oh St .... Ohio State Reports [A publication] (DLA)
OHST .... Overhead Storage Tank [Nuclear energy] (NRCH)
OHSU .... Oregon Health Sciences University (IID)
OHT .... Hornepayne Township Public Library, Ontario [Library symbol National Library of Canada] (NLC)
OHT .... Ocean Heat Transport
OHT .... Ocular Hypertensive [Ophthalmology]
OHT .... Office of Housing Technology [National Bureau of Standards]
OHT .... Ohio Historical Society, Columbus, OH [OCLC symbol] (OCLC)
OHT .... Ohio Tank Truck Carriers Bureau, Worthington OH [STAC]
OHT .... Overheating Temperature (PDAA)
oht .... Overheating Temperature (AD)
OHT .... Oxygen at High Temperature (OA)
OHTA .... Office of Health Technology Assessment [HHS]
OHTA .... Organ Historical Trust of Australia
OHTCS .... Outer Head Temperature Control System [Nuclear energy] (NRCH)
OHTE .... Ohmic Heating Toroidal Experiment [Nuclear fusion device]
OHTEX .... Ocean Heat Transport Experiment [Japan] [Marine science] (OSRA)
OHTR .... Theological College of the Canadian Reformed Churches, Hamilton, Ontario [Library symbol National Library of Canada] (NLC)
OHTS .... Oil-Hardened Tool Steel
OHu .... Hubbard Public Library, Hubbard, OH [Library symbol Library of Congress] (LCLS)
OHU .... Huntsville Public Library, Ontario [Library symbol National Library of Canada] (NLC)
ohu .... Ohio [MARC country of publication code Library of Congress] (LCCP)
OHU .... Overseas Homeported Units [Navy] (NVT)
OHUM .... Muskoka Pioneer Village, Huntsville, Ontario [Library symbol National Library of Canada] (BIB)
OHur .... Huron Public Library, Huron, OH [Library symbol Library of Congress] (LCLS)
OHV .... Off-Highway Vehicle
OHV .... Overhead Valve
ohv .... Overhead Valve (AD)
OHV .... Overhead Vent (WDAA)
OHVE .... Hanmer Branch, Valley East Public Library [Succursale Hanmer, Bibliotheque Publique de Valley-East], Ontario [Library symbol National Library of Canada] (NLC)
OHW .... Electronic Systems Library, Westinghouse Canada Ltd., Burlington, Ontario [Library symbol National Library of Canada] (NLC)
OHW .... Oak Harbor [Washington] [Seismograph station code, US Geological Survey] (SEIS)
OHW .... Oxyhydrogen Welding
OHWL .... Wentworth Public Library, Hamilton, Ontario [Library symbol National Library of Canada] (NLC)
OHWM.......... Open Heart World Mission (EA)
OHWS.......... Overhead Wood Screw [Technical drawings]
OHY .... Onur Hava Tasimacilik AWMS [Turkey] [ICAO designator] (FAAC)
OI............... Ingersoll Public Library, Ontario [Library symbol National Library of Canada] (NLC)
OI............... Odyssey Institute [Later, OIC] (EA)
OI............... Office Instruction (AFM)
OI............... Office of Information (AFM)
OI............... Office of Investigations [Environmental Protection Agency] (GFGA)
OI............... Ohashi Institute (EA)
OI............... Oil-Immersed
oi............... Oil-Immersed (AD)
OI............... Oil-Insulated
OI............... Old Icelandic [Language] (BARN)
OI............... ONE, Inc. (EA)
OI............... On Instruments [Aviation]
OI............... Opener Inhibitor
OI............... Opening of Intestine
OI............... Operating Income [Accounting]
OI............... Operating Instructions
OI............... Operational Instrumentation (NASA)
OI............... Operational Intelligence

OI .... Operational Issue [Military]
OI .... Operation Identity (EA)
OI .... Operations Interface (MCD)
OI .... Operator Input
OI .... Operator Interface (ACII)
OI .... Opportunistic Infection [Medicine]
OI .... Opsconic Index [Laboratory science] (DAVI)
OI .... Opsonic Index [Medicine]
o/i .... Opsonic Index (AD)
OI .... Optical Isolator [Nuclear energy] (NRCH)
OI .... Optimist International (EA)
OI .... Optimum Interpolation [Marine science] (OSRA)
OI .... Orbiter Instrumentation [NASA] (NASA)
OI .... Orbit [or Orbital] Insertion
OI .... Ordinary Interest [Banking]
OI .... Organizational/Intermediate (MCD)
OI .... Organization Integration [Military]
OI .... Orgasmic Impairment [Medicine]
o-i .... Orgasmic Impairment (AD)
OI .... Oriental Institute (AD)
OI .... Orientation Inventory [Psychology]
OI .... Orthopedically Impaired
OI .... Osteogenesis Imperfecta [Medicine]
OI .... Ote Iwapo [All That Is Must Be Considered] [of OI Committee International, a third-world lobby opposing systematic birth control Swahili]
OI .... Ours, Inc. (EA)
OI .... Output Impedance
O/I .... Overseas Investment [Economics]
OI .... Owens-Illinois [NYSE symbol] (TTSB)
OI .... Owens Illinois [NYSE symbol] (SAG)
OI .... Owens-Illinois, Inc. [NYSE symbol] (SPSG)
OI .... Oxygen Income [or Intake] [Medicine]
OI .... Oxygen Index [Medicine] (DAVI)
OI .... Oxygen Intact [Medicine] (DAVI)
OIA .... Municipal Income Opportunity Trust [Formerly, Allstate Municipal Income Opportunities Trust] [NYSE symbol] (SPSG)
OIA .... Municipal Income Opp Tr [NYSE symbol] (TTSB)
OIA .... Ocean Industries Association (AD)
OIA .... Office of Impact Analysis [Environmental Protection Agency] (BARN)
OIA .... Office of Industrial Associates (AD)
OIA .... Office of Inspector and Auditor [Nuclear Regulatory Commission] (NRCH)
OIA .... Office of International Activities [American Chemical Society]
OIA .... Office of International Administration [Department of State]
OIA .... Office of International Affairs [NASA, HUD]
OIA .... Oil Import Administration [Later, Office of Oil and Gas] [Department of the Interior]
OIA .... Oil Insurance Association [Later, Industrial Risk Insurance] (EA)
OIA .... Oishiyama A [Japan] [Seismograph station code, US Geological Survey] (SEIS)
OIA .... Operative Ironmoulders' Association [A union] [British]
OIA .... Optical Immunoassay [Clinical chemistry]
OIA .... Optics Inertial Analyzer (SAA)
OIA .... Orbiter Interface Adapter [NASA] (NASA)
OIA .... Organizacion Internacional del Azucar [International Sugar Organization - ISO] (EAIO)
OIA .... Outboard Industry Association [Later, NMMA] (EA)
OIAA .... Abadan/International [Iran] [ICAO location identifier] (ICLI)
OIAA .... Office of Inter-American Affairs [Later, BIAA]
OIAA .... Office of International Aviation Affairs [FAA]
OIA & TU .... Office of Industry Affairs and Technology Utilization [NASA]
OIAB .... Boostan [Iran] [ICAO location identifier] (ICLI)
OIAB .... Oil Import Appeals Board (AD)
OIAC .... Organizacion Internacional de la Aviacion Civil [International Civil Aviation Organization] [Spanish] (AD)
OIAD .... Dezful [Iran] [ICAO location identifier] (ICLI)
OIAF .... Office of Information for the Armed Forces (DNAB)
OIAG .... Aghajari [Iran] [ICAO location identifier] (ICLI)
OIAH .... Gachsaran [Iran] [ICAO location identifier] (ICLI)
OIAI .... Masjed Soleiman [Iran] [ICAO location identifier] (ICLI)
OIAJ .... Office for Improvements in the Administration of Justice (AD)
OIAJ .... Omidyeh [Iran] [ICAO location identifier] (ICLI)
OIAK .... Haft-Gel [Iran] [ICAO location identifier] (ICLI)
OIAL .... Lali [Iran] [ICAO location identifier] (ICLI)
OIAM .... Bandar Mahshahr [Iran] [ICAO location identifier] (ICLI)
OIAN .... Andimeshk [Iran] [ICAO location identifier] (ICLI)
OI & C .... Office of Investigation and Compliance [Employment and Training Administration] [Department of Labor]
OI & I .... Office of Invention and Innovation [Disbanded] [National Institute of Standards and Technology]
OIAS .... Observer Impression Assessment Scale
OIAS .... Occupational Information Access System (WDAA)
OIAT .... Abadan [Iran] [ICAO location identifier] (ICLI)
OIATU .... Office of Industry Affairs and Technology Utilization [NASA]
OIAW .... Ahwaz [Iran] [ICAO location identifier] (ICLI)
OIB .... Briggs-Lawrence County Public Library, Ironton, OH [Library symbol Library of Congress] (LCLS)
OIB .... Iron Bridge Public Library, Ontario [Library symbol National Library of Canada] (NLC)
OIB .... Municipal Income Opportunity Trust [Formerly, Allstate Municipal Income Opportunities Trust] [NYSE symbol] (SPSG)
OIB .... Municipal Income Op Tr II [NYSE symbol] (TTSB)
OIB .... Oceanic Island Basalt [Geology]
OIB .... Official Information Base

OIB .... Ohio Inspection Bureau (AD)
OIB .... Oishiyama B [Japan] [Seismograph station code, US Geological Survey] (SEIS)
OIB .... Oklahoma Inspection Bureau (AD)
OIB .... Oligoclonal Immunoglobulin Bands [Clinical chemistry]
OIB .... Olympic Installations Board
OIB .... Operating Impedance Bridge (IAA)
OIB .... Operation Instruction Block (NITA)
OIB .... Operations Integration Branch [NASA] (KSC)
OIB .... Orbiter Interface Box [NASA] (NASA)
OIB .... Orbiter Interface Box
OIB .... Ortho-Iodobenzoic (Acid) [Biochemistry]
OIBA .... Abumusa Island [Iran] [ICAO location identifier] (ICLI)
OIBA .... Office of Industrial Base Assessment (DOMA)
OIBB .... Bushehr/Bushehr [Iran] [ICAO location identifier] (ICLI)
OIBD .... Bandar Deylam [Iran] [ICAO location identifier] (ICLI)
OIBF .... Forouz Island [Iran] [ICAO location identifier] (ICLI)
OIBG .... Ganaveh [Iran] [ICAO location identifier] (ICLI)
OIBH .... Bastak [Iran] [ICAO location identifier] (ICLI)
OIBI .... Golbandi [Iran] [ICAO location identifier] (ICLI)
OIBK .... Kish Island [Iran] [ICAO location identifier] (ICLI)
OIBL .... Bandar Lengeh [Iran] [ICAO location identifier] (ICLI)
OIBN .... Borazjan [Iran] [ICAO location identifier] (ICLI)
OIBQ .... Khark Island [Iran] [ICAO location identifier] (ICLI)
OIBS .... Siri Island [Iran] [ICAO location identifier] (ICLI)
OIBT .... Bushehr [Iran] [ICAO location identifier] (ICLI)
OIBV .... Lavan Island [Iran] [ICAO location identifier] (ICLI)
OIBX .... Tonb Island [Iran] [ICAO location identifier] (ICLI)
OIC .... Municipal Income Opportunity Trust [Formerly, Allstate Municipal Income Opportunities Trust] [NYSE symbol] (SPSG)
OIC .... Municipal Income Opp Tr III [NYSE symbol] (TTSB)
OIC .... Norwich, NY [Location identifier FAA] (FAAL)
OIC .... Objective Individual Combat Weapon
OIC .... Oceanographic Instrumentation Center [Navy]
OIC .... Oceans Institute of Canada (IRC)
OIC .... Octyl Isocyanate [Organic chemistry]
OIC .... Odyssey Institute Corp. (EA)
OIC .... Offer in Compromise [IRS]
OIC .... Office of Independent Counsel [U.S. Department of Justice] (BARN)
OIC .... Office of Industrial Cooperation [AEC]
OIC .... Office of International Conferences [Department of State]
OIC .... Office of International Cooperation [in CAA]
OIC .... Office of the Insurance Commissioner (AD)
O-i-C .... Officer-in-Charge (AD)
OIC .... Officer-in-Charge
OIC .... Ohio Improved Chesters [Initialism itself now used as name of breed of swine]
OIC .... Oh, I See [Computer science] (DOM)
OIC .... Oil Industry Commission (AD)
OIC .... Oishiyama C [Japan] [Seismograph station code, US Geological Survey] (SEIS)
OIC .... Okinawa Interboard Committee [Absorbed by Interboard Committee for Christian Work in Japan] (EA)
OIC .... Online Instrument and Control Program [Computer science] (NRCH)
OIC .... Operational Intelligence Centre [British military] (DMA)
OIC .... Operations Instrumentation Coordinator [NASA] (KSC)
OIC .... Operator's Instruction Chart
OIC .... Opportunities Industrialization Center (OICC)
OIC .... Optical Integrated Circuit (IEEE)
OIC .... Optimized Image Compression (PCM)
OIC .... Orbiter Integrated Checkout [NASA] (NASA)
O-I-C .... Order-in-Council [Canada]
oic .... Order of the Imitation of Christ (TOCD)
OIC .... Order of the Imitation of Christ (TOCD)
O-I-C .... Organisation Interafricaine du Cafe [Inter-African Coffee Organization] [French] (AD)
OIC .... Organisation Internationale Catholique
OIC .... Organisation Internationale du Commerce [International Organization for Commerce] [France]
OIC .... Organization for International Cooperation (EA)
OIC .... Organization of Islamic Countries [Intergovernmental group]
OIC .... Organization of the Islamic Conference [See also OCI] [Jeddah, Saudi Arabia] (EAIO)
OIC .... Overseas Investment Commission (AD)
OICA .... Azna [Iran] [ICAO location identifier] (ICLI)
OICA .... Ontario Institute of Chartered Accountants [Canada] (DD)
OIC/A .... Opportunities Industrialization Centers of America (EA)
OICA .... Organisation Internationale des Constructeurs d'Automobiles (EAIO)
OICB .... Baneh [Iran] [ICAO location identifier] (ICLI)
OICC .... Bakhtaran [Iran] [ICAO location identifier] (ICLI)
OICC .... Officer-in-Charge of Construction [Navy]
OICC .... Operational Intelligence Crisis Center [Defense Intelligence Adgency] (DOMA)
OICC .... Operations Interface Control Chart (KSC)
OICC .... Organization of Islamic Capitals and Cities (EA)
OICCFE .... Officer-in-Charge of Construction, Far East [Navy]
OICCSOWESPAC... Officer-in-Charge of Construction, South Western Pacific (DNAB)
OICD .... Abdanan [Iran] [ICAO location identifier] (ICLI)
OICD .... Office of International Cooperation and Development [Department of Agriculture]
OICD .... On-Board Information Compression Device [Aerospace]
OICE .... Bijar [Iran] [ICAO location identifier] (ICLI)
O ICE .... Old Icelandic [Language, etc.] (ROG)
OIcel .... Old Icelandic [Language] (BARN)

OICF	Naft-E-Shah [Iran] [ICAO location identifier] (ICLI)
OICF	Oklahoma Independent College Foundation (AD)
OICF	Oregon Independent College Foundation (AD)
OICG	Ghasre-Shirin [Iran] [ICAO location identifier] (ICLI)
OICH	Islam Abad [Iran] [ICAO location identifier] (ICLI)
OICI	Ilam [Iran] [ICAO location identifier] (ICLI)
OICI	Oficina Internacional Catolica de la Infancia [International Catholic Child Bureau]
OICI	Organizacion Ibero-Americana de Cooperacion Intermunicipal [Ibero-American Municipal Organization] (EAIO)
OICI	Organizacion Interamericana de Cooperacion [Inter-American Cooperation Organ ization] [Spanish] (AD)
OICI	Organizacion Interamericana de Cooperacion Intermunicipal [Interamerican Municipal Organization]
OICJ	Boroujerd [Iran] [ICAO location identifier] (ICLI)
OICJ	Office of International Criminal Justice (AD)
OICK	Khorram Abad [Iran] [ICAO location identifier] (ICLI)
OICL	Sare Pole Zahab [Iran] [ICAO location identifier] (ICLI)
OICM	Mehran [Iran] [ICAO location identifier] (ICLI)
OICM	Organisation Internationale pour la Cooperation Medicale [International Organization for Medical Cooperation]
OICMA	Organisation Internationale Contre le Criquet Migrateur Africain [International African Migratory Locust Organization] (EAIO)
OICMATU	Officer-in-Charge, Marine Air Traffic Control Unit (DNAB)
OICMILDEPT	Officer-in-Charge, Military Department (DNAB)
OICNA	Overseas Indian Congress of North America [Defunct] (EA)
OICO	Office of Integration and Checkout
OICO	OI Corp. [NASDAQ symbol] (NQ)
OICO	Songhor [Iran] [ICAO location identifier] (ICLI)
OI Corp	OI Corp. [Associated Press] (SAG)
OICP	Office of International Communications Policy (NITA)
OICP	Paveh [Iran] [ICAO location identifier] (ICLI)
OICQ	Takab [Iran] [ICAO location identifier] (ICLI)
OICR	Dehloran [Iran] [ICAO location identifier] (ICLI)
OICR	Office of International Commercial Relations [Department of State]
OICS	Office of Interoceanic Canal Studies [National Oceanic and Atmospheric Administration] (NOAA)
OICS	Operational Intelligence Collection System
OICS	Organe International de Controle des Stupefiants [International Narcotics Control Board] (EAIO)
OICS	Sanandaj [Iran] [ICAO location identifier] (ICLI)
OICT	Bakhtaran [Iran] [ICAO location identifier] (ICLI)
OICTP	Outline Individual and Collective Training Plan [Army]
OICW	Objective Individual Combat Weapon [Army] (INF)
OICW	Objective Individual Combat Weapon [USA]
OICY	Malavi [Iran] [ICAO location identifier] (ICLI)
OICZ	Aligoodarz [Iran] [ICAO location identifier] (ICLI)
OID	Object Identifier [Computer science]
OID	Octal Identifier [Computer science] (KSC)
OID	Ofensiva de Izquierda Democratica [Offensive of the Democratic Left] [Bolivia] (PPW)
OID	Optoelectronic Imaging Device
OID	Order Initiated Distribution
OID	Organism Identification Number [Medicine] (BABM)
OID	Organism Identification Number [Microbiology] (DAVI)
OID	Original Issue Discount [Business term]
oid	Original Issue Discount (AD)
OID	Original Issue Discount Obligations (TDOB)
OID	Outline and Installation Drawing
OIDA	Ordnance Industrial Data Agency
OIDC	Oil Importing and Developing Country
OIDI	Optically Isolated Digital Input
OI DIV	Operations/Combat Information Center Division (DNAB)
OIDL	Object Interface Definition Language [Computer science]
OIDMM	Office Internationale de Documentation de Medecine Militaire [International Office of Documentation on Military Medicine - IODMM] (EAIO)
OIDP	Oversea Internal Defense Policy [Army] (AABC)
OIDPS	Oversea Intelligence Data Processing System
OIE	Central Library, Albright & Wilson Americas, Islington, Ontario [Library symbol National Library of Canada] (NLC)
OIE	Office International des Epizooties [International Office of Epizootics] [Research center France] (IRC)
OIE	Office of Indian Education [Department of Education] (GFGA)
OIE	Office of Inspection and Enforcement [Nuclear Regulatory Commission]
OIE	Office of International Epizootics (AD)
O/I/E	Offsites/Infrastructure/Establishment [Engineering]
OIE	Operational Independent Evaluator
OIE	Optical Incremental Encoder
OIE	Optical Infrared Equipment
OIE	Organisation Internationale des Employeurs [International Organization of Employers]
OIEA	Organismo Internacional de Energia Atomica [International Atomic Energy Agency] [Spanish United Nations] (DUND)
OIEC	Office International de l'Enseignement Catholique [Catholic International Education Office - CIEO] (EAIO)
OIEO	Ocean Instrumentation Engineering Office [National Oceanic and Atmospheric Administration] (MSC)
OIER	Office of International Acronomics Research (AD)
OIER	Official Intermodal Equipment Register [Intermodal Publishing Co.] [Information service or system] (IID)
OIES	Oxford Institute for Energy Studies [British]
OIESA	Office of International Economic and Social Affairs [Department of State]

OIF	American Opportunity Income [NYSE symbol] (SPSG)
OIF	Amer Opportunity Income [NYSE symbol] (TTSB)
OIF	Iroquois Falls Public Library, Ontario [Library symbol National Library of Canada] (NLC)
OIF	Observed Intrinsic Frequency [Medicine] (DMAA)
OIF	Office for Intellectual Freedom [American Library Association]
OIF	Office Interconnect Facility [Computer science] (BTTJ)
OIF	Office of International Finance [Department of the Treasury]
OIF	Oil Immersion Field (MAE)
OIF	Osteogenesis Imperfecta Foundation (EA)
OIF	Osteoinductive Factor [Biochemistry]
OIF	Other Intelligence File (MCD)
OIFB	Boroujen [Iran] [ICAO location identifier] (ICLI)
OIFC	Ghamsar [Iran] [ICAO location identifier] (ICLI)
OIFC	Oil-Insulated, Fan-Cooled
OIFD	Ardestan [Iran] [ICAO location identifier] (ICLI)
OIFF	Soffeh [Iran] [ICAO location identifier] (ICLI)
OIFG	Golpaygan [Iran] [ICAO location identifier] (ICLI)
OIFH	Esfahan [Iran] [ICAO location identifier] (ICLI)
OIFI	Semirom [Iran] [ICAO location identifier] (ICLI)
OIFIG	Official Irish FORTH [Programming language] Interest Group (EAIO)
OIFJ	Najaf Abad [Iran] [ICAO location identifier] (ICLI)
OIFK	Kashan [Iran] [ICAO location identifier] (ICLI)
OIFL	Felavarjan [Iran] [ICAO location identifier] (ICLI)
OIFM	Esfahan [Iran] [ICAO location identifier] (ICLI)
OIFN	Naein [Iran] [ICAO location identifier] (ICLI)
OIFO	Khomeini Shahr [Iran] [ICAO location identifier] (ICLI)
OIFR	Ghomsheh [Iran] [ICAO location identifier] (ICLI)
OIFS	Shahrekord [Iran] [ICAO location identifier] (ICLI)
OIFT	Esfahan [Iran] [ICAO location identifier] (ICLI)
OIFU	Fereidan [Iran] [ICAO location identifier] (ICLI)
OIFW	Khomein [Iran] [ICAO location identifier] (ICLI)
OIFY	Meymeh [Iran] [ICAO location identifier] (ICLI)
OIFZ	Natanz [Iran] [ICAO location identifier] (ICLI)
OIG	Ignace Public Library, Ontario [Library symbol National Library of Canada] (NLC)
OIG	Office of the Inspector General [Army]
OIG	Optically Isolated Gate (IEEE)
OIG	Organisation Intergouvernementale [Inter-Governmental Organization] [French] (AD)
OIGA	Astara [Iran] [ICAO location identifier] (ICLI)
OIGF	Fouman [Iran] [ICAO location identifier] (ICLI)
OIGG	Rasht [Iran] [ICAO location identifier] (ICLI)
OIGH	Hashtpar [Iran] [ICAO location identifier] (ICLI)
OIGIS	Office of the Inspector-General of Intelligence and Security [Australia]
OIGK	Khailkhal [Iran] [ICAO location identifier] (ICLI)
OIGL	Langerood [Iran] [ICAO location identifier] (ICLI)
OIGM	Manjil [Iran] [ICAO location identifier] (ICLI)
OIGN	Lahijan [Iran] [ICAO location identifier] (ICLI)
OIGP	Bandar Anzali [Iran] [ICAO location identifier] (ICLI)
OIGR	Office of Industrial Growth and Research [of BDSA]
OIGR	Office of Intergovernmental Relations [US Congress] [Washington, DC] (GRD)
OIGR	Roodsar [Iran] [ICAO location identifier] (ICLI)
OIGT	Rasht [Iran] [ICAO location identifier] (ICLI)
OIGU	Roodbar [Iran] [ICAO location identifier] (ICLI)
OIH	Oceanic Institute of Hawaii
OIH	Office of International Health [Department of Health and Human Services]
OIH	Ortho-Iodohippurate [Clinical chemistry] (AAMN)
OIH	Ovulation-Inducing Hormone [Endocrinology]
OIH	Ovulation-Producing Hormone [Medicine] (AD)
OIHA	Orthoiodohippuric Acid [Clinical chemistry] (DAVI)
OIHA	Takestan [Iran] [ICAO location identifier] (ICLI)
OIHB	Asad Abad [Iran] [ICAO location identifier] (ICLI)
OIHD	Shahzand [Iran] [ICAO location identifier] (ICLI)
OIHF	Tafresh [Iran] [ICAO location identifier] (ICLI)
OIHG	Kharaghan [Iran] [ICAO location identifier] (ICLI)
OIHH	Hamadan [Iran] [ICAO location identifier] (ICLI)
OIHJ	Avaj [Iran] [ICAO location identifier] (ICLI)
OIHM	Malayer [Iran] [ICAO location identifier] (ICLI)
OIHN	Nahavand [Iran] [ICAO location identifier] (ICLI)
OIHP	Office International d'Hygiene Publique [United Nations]
OIHQ	Kangavar [Iran] [ICAO location identifier] (ICLI)
OIHR	Arak [Iran] [ICAO location identifier] (ICLI)
OIHS	Hamadan [Iran] [ICAO location identifier] (ICLI)
OIHT	Hamadan [Iran] [ICAO location identifier] (ICLI)
OIHU	Tooyserkan [Iran] [ICAO location identifier] (ICLI)
OII	Oceaneering International, Inc. [NYSE symbol] (SPSG)
OII	Oceaneering Intl. [NYSE symbol] (TTSB)
OII	Office of International Investment [Department of Commerce]
OII	Office of Invention and Innovation (AD)
OII	Oil Investment Institute [Washington, DC] (EA)
OII	Operations Integration Instruction [NASA] (NASA)
OII	Ourobourus Institute (EA)
OIIA	Abe-Ali [Iran] [ICAO location identifier] (ICLI)
OIIC	Kushke Nosrat [Iran] [ICAO location identifier] (ICLI)
OIIC	Oil Industry Industrial Committee [Australia]
OIID	Tehran/Doshan Tappeh [Iran] [ICAO location identifier] (ICLI)
OIIE	Abyek [Iran] [ICAO location identifier] (ICLI)
OIIF	Firouzkouh [Iran] [ICAO location identifier] (ICLI)
OIIFDRES	Oficina Internacional de Informacion del Frente Democratico Revolucionario de ElSalvador [International Information Office of the Democratic Revolutionary Front of El Salvador - IIODRFES] [San Jose, Costa Rica] (EAIO)

OIIG .... Tehran/Ghaleh Morghi [Iran] [ICAO location identifier] (ICLI)
OIIH .... Mahallat [Iran] [ICAO location identifier] (ICLI)
OIII............. Tehran/Mehrabad International [Iran] [ICAO location identifier] (ICLI)
OIIJ .... Karaj [Iran] [ICAO location identifier] (ICLI)
OIIK .... Ghazvin [Iran] [ICAO location identifier] (ICLI)
OIIM .... Khoram Dareh [Iran] [ICAO location identifier] (ICLI)
OIIM .... Overseas Issues Identification Meeting (DNAB)
OIIN .... Delijan [Iran] [ICAO location identifier] (ICLI)
OIIQ .... Ghom [Iran] [ICAO location identifier] (ICLI)
OIIR .... Garmsar [Iran] [ICAO location identifier] (ICLI)
OIIS .... Semnan [Iran] [ICAO location identifier] (ICLI)
OIIT .... Tehran [Iran] [ICAO location identifier] (ICLI)
OIIU .... Damghan [Iran] [ICAO location identifier] (ICLI)
OIIV .... Seveh [Iran] [ICAO location identifier] (ICLI)
OIIW .... Varamin [Iran] [ICAO location identifier] (ICLI)
OIIX .... Tehran [Iran] [ICAO location identifier] (ICLI)
OIJ .... Octarius Duos [Two Pints] [Pharmacy] (ROG)
OIJ .... Organisation Internationale des Journalistes [International
                   Organization of Journalists - IOJ] (EAIO)
OIJSS........... Octarios Duobus cum Semisse [Two and a Half Pints] [Pharmacy]
                   (ROG)
OIK............. Ocean City, MD [Location identifier FAA] (FAAL)
OIKA .... Shahre Babak [Iran] [ICAO location identifier] (ICLI)
OIKB .... Bandar Abbas [Iran] [ICAO location identifier] (ICLI)
OIKD .... Darband/Ravar [Iran] [ICAO location identifier] (ICLI)
OIKE............ Anar [Iran] [ICAO location identifier] (ICLI)
OIKF .... Baft [Iran] [ICAO location identifier] (ICLI)
OIKI .... Bandar Khamir [Iran] [ICAO location identifier] (ICLI)
OIKJ .... Jiroft [Iran] [ICAO location identifier] (ICLI)
OIKK .... Kerman [Iran] [ICAO location identifier] (ICLI)
OIKM .... Bam [Iran] [ICAO location identifier] (ICLI)
OIKN .... Narmashir [Iran] [ICAO location identifier] (ICLI)
OIKO .... Minab [Iran] [ICAO location identifier] (ICLI)
OIKQ .... Gheshm Island [Iran] [ICAO location identifier] (ICLI)
OIKR .... Rafsanjan [Iran] [ICAO location identifier] (ICLI)
OIKS .... Shahdad [Iran] [ICAO location identifier] (ICLI)
OIKT .... Kerman [Iran] [ICAO location identifier] (ICLI)
OIKU .... Hengam Island [Iran] [ICAO location identifier] (ICLI)
OIKW .... Kahnooj [Iran] [ICAO location identifier] (ICLI)
OIKX .... Hormoz Island [Iran] [ICAO location identifier] (ICLI)
OIKY .... Sirjan [Iran] [ICAO location identifier] (ICLI)
OIKZ .... Zarand [Iran] [ICAO location identifier] (ICLI)
OIL............. Ocelot Industries Ltd. [Toronto Stock Exchange symbol]
OIL............. Office of Intergovernmental Liaison [Environmental Protection
                   Agency] (GFGA)
OIL............. Oil City, PA [Location identifier FAA] (FAAL)
OIL............. Oklahoma Information Lines [Oklahoma State Department of
                   Libraries] [Oklahoma City] [Information service or system] (IID)
OIL............. Only Input Line (MHDI)
OIL............. Operation Inspection Log (AAG)
OIL............. Orange Indicating Light (MSA)
OIL............. Orbital International Laboratory
OIL............. Ordnance Investigation Laboratory
OIL............. Triton Energy [NYSE symbol] (TTSB)
OIL............. Triton Energy Corp. [NYSE symbol] (SPSG)
OILA .... Office of International Labor Affairs [Department of Labor]
Oil & Gas .... Oil and Gas Reporter [A publication] (DLA)
Oil & Gas LR... Oil and Gas Law Review [A publication] (DLA)
Oil & Gas Reptr... Oil and Gas Reporter [A publication] (DLA)
Oil & Gas Rptr... Oil and Gas Reporter [A publication] (DLA)
OILB............ Organisation Internationale de Lutte Biologique Contre les Animaux
                   et les Plantes Nuisibles [International Organization for Biological
                   Control of Noxious Animals and Plants - IOBC] (EAIO)
OILD .... Occupationally Induced Lung Disease
OilDri.......... Oil-Dri Corp. of America [Associated Press] (SAG)
Oilgear .... [The] Oilgear Co. [Associated Press] (SAG)
oiloff.......... Oil Ripoff (AD)
OILSR.......... Office of Interstate Land Sales Registration (AD)
OIM............ Office of Industrial Managers [Navy]
OIM............ Office of Industrial Mobilization [of BDSA]
OIM............ Office of Intergovernmental Management (OICC)
OIM............ Offshore-Installation Manager [Oil well drilling]
OIM............ On Its Merits [British] (ROG)
OIM............ Orbit Insertion Maneuver
OIM............ Organic Insulating Material
OIM............ Organizational Intermediate Maintenance [Military] (AFIT)
OIM............ Oriental Institute Museum [University of Chicago] (AD)
OIM............ Oshima Island [Japan] [Airport symbol] (OAG)
OIMA .... Torbat-E-Jam [Iran] [ICAO location identifier] (ICLI)
OIMB .... Birjand [Iran] [ICAO location identifier] (ICLI)
OIMC .... Office of Information Services (AAGC)
OIMC .... Sarakhs [Iran] [ICAO location identifier] (ICLI)
OIMD .... Goonabad [Iran] [ICAO location identifier] (ICLI)
OIME .... Esfarayen [Iran] [ICAO location identifier] (ICLI)
OIMF .... Ferdous [Iran] [ICAO location identifier] (ICLI)
OIMG .... Ghaen [Iran] [ICAO location identifier] (ICLI)
OIMH .... Torbat-E-Heidarieh [Iran] [ICAO location identifier] (ICLI)
OIMJ .... Emam Shahr [Iran] [ICAO location identifier] (ICLI)
OIMK .... Nehbandan [Iran] [ICAO location identifier] (ICLI)
OIML .... Janat Abad [Iran] [ICAO location identifier] (ICLI)
OIML .... Organisation Internationale de Metrologie Legale [International
                   Organization of Legal Metrology] (EAIO)
OIMM .... Mashhad [Iran] [ICAO location identifier] (ICLI)
OIMN .... Bojnord [Iran] [ICAO location identifier] (ICLI)
OIMO .... Ghoochan [Iran] [ICAO location identifier] (ICLI)

OIMP .... Taybad [Iran] [ICAO location identifier] (ICLI)
OIMQ .... Kashmar [Iran] [ICAO location identifier] (ICLI)
OIMR .... Fariman [Iran] [ICAO location identifier] (ICLI)
OIMS .... Orbiter Ion Mass Spectrometer [NASA]
OIMS .... Oscillator Instability Measurement System
OIMS .... Sabzevar [Iran] [ICAO location identifier] (ICLI)
OIMSJ .... Micropower/St. Joseph's High School, Islington, Ontario [Library
                   symbol National Library of Canada] (NLC)
OIMT .... Tabas [Iran] [ICAO location identifier] (ICLI)
OIMV .... Mashhad [Iran] [ICAO location identifier] (ICLI)
OIMW .... Shirvan [Iran] [ICAO location identifier] (ICLI)
OIMX .... Shahr Abad [Iran] [ICAO location identifier] (ICLI)
OIMY .... Neishaboor [Iran] [ICAO location identifier] (ICLI)
OIMYFC .... Official International Michael York Fan Club (EA)
OIN............. Oberlin, KS [Location identifier FAA] (FAAL)
OI-N............ Office of Information, Navy
OIN............. Organisation Internationale de Normalisation [International
                   Organization for Standardization]
OIN............. Organization of International Numismatists
OIN............. Osrodek Informacji Naukowej [Scientific Information Center] [Polish
                   Academy of Sciences Warsaw] [Information service or system]
                   (IID)
OINA .... Amol [Iran] [ICAO location identifier] (ICLI)
OINA .... Oyster Institute of North America [Later, SINA] (EA)
OINB .... Babolsar [Iran] [ICAO location identifier] (ICLI)
OINC .... Chalous [Iran] [ICAO location identifier] (ICLI)
OINC .... Officer-in-Charge [Navy]
O in C .... Officer-in-Charge
OINCABCCTC... Officer-in-Charge, Advanced Base Combat Communication Training
                   Center [Pearl Harbor] [Navy]
OIND .... Minoo Dasht [Iran] [ICAO location identifier] (ICLI)
OINE .... Kalaleh [Iran] [ICAO location identifier] (ICLI)
OInF .... Ferro Corp., Independence, OH [Library symbol Library of
                   Congress] (LCLS)
OING .... Gorgan [Iran] [ICAO location identifier] (ICLI)
OING .... Organisation Internationale Non-Gouvernementale
                   [Non-Governmental International Organization] [French] (AD)
OINH .... Behshahr [Iran] [ICAO location identifier] (ICLI)
OINI .... Ghaem Shahr [Iran] [ICAO location identifier] (ICLI)
OINK .... Gonbad Ghabous [Iran] [ICAO location identifier] (ICLI)
Oink .... One Income, No Kids [Lifestyle classification]
OINL .... Alamdeh [Iran] [ICAO location identifier] (ICLI)
OINM .... Mahmood Abad [Iran] [ICAO location identifier] (ICLI)
OINN .... Noshahr [Iran] [ICAO location identifier] (ICLI)
OINO .... Noor [Iran] [ICAO location identifier] (ICLI)
OINP .... Azad Shahr [Iran] [ICAO location identifier] (ICLI)
OINQ .... Kelardasht [Iran] [ICAO location identifier] (ICLI)
OINR .... Ramsar [Iran] [ICAO location identifier] (ICLI)
OINS .... Sari [Iran] [ICAO location identifier] (ICLI)
OINT .... Ointment
oint .... Ointment (AD)
OINV .... Tonkabon [Iran] [ICAO location identifier] (ICLI)
OINY .... Bandar Torkaman [Iran] [ICAO location identifier] (ICLI)
OINZ .... Dasht-E-Naz [Iran] [ICAO location identifier] (ICLI)
OIO .... Obligated Involuntary Officers [Used in movie "Spies Like Us"]
OIO .... Office of International Operations [of IRS]
OIO .... Oklahomans for Indian Opportunity (AD)
OIO .... Operations Integration Officer [NASA] (MCD)
OIOPSWL.... Old Input/Output Program Status Word Location [Computer
                   science] (MHDB)
OIP............. Eastland, TX [Location identifier FAA] (FAAL)
OIP............. Office of Import Programs [Functions transferred to Domestic and
                   International Business Administration] [Department of
                   Commerce]
OIP............. Office of Industrial Programs [Department of Energy]
OIP............. Office of International Programs [National Science Foundation]
OIP............. Oil-in-Place
oip .... Oil in Place (AD)
OIP............. Ontario Institute of Painters, Toronto [1958] [Canada] (NGC)
OIP............. Operating Internal Pressure [Nuclear energy] (NRCH)
OIP............. Operational Improvement Plan [or Program] [Navy]
OIP............. Operational Instruction Pamphlet
OIP............. Optical Image Processor
OIP............. Optical Improvement Program [Army]
OIP............. Orbital Improvement Program
OIP............. Ordnance Installation Plan (MCD)
OIP............. Organic Insulative Plastic
OIP............. Organisation Internationale de la Paleobotanique [International
                   Organization of Paleobotany]
OIP............. Organisation Internationale de Psychophysiologie [International
                   Organization of Psychophysiology - IOP] (EAIO)
OIP............. Organisation Internationale pour le Progres [Austria] (EAIO)
OIP............. Organizacion Iberoamericana de Pilotos [Ibero-American
                   Organization of Pilots - IOP] [Mexico City, Mexico] (EAIO)
OIP............. Organizing Interstitial Pneumonia [Medicine]
oip .... Oxford India Paper (AD)
OIPA .... Ortho-Isopropylaniline [Organic chemistry]
OIPAAR........ Office of Industrial Personnel Access Authorization Review [Army]
                   (AABC)
OIPC .... Organisation Internationale de Police Criminelle [International
                   Criminal Police Organization] [French] (AD)
OIPC .... Organisation Internationale de Protection Civile [International Civil
                   Defense Organization - ICDO] (EAIO)
OIPCFC .... Official International Peter Coyote Fan Club (EA)

OIPEEC .... Organisation Internationale pour l'Etude de l'Endurance des Cables [*International Organization for the Study of the Endurance of Wire Ropes - IOSEWR*] (EAIO)

OIPH .... Office of International Public Health (AD)

Oipi .... One Income plus Inheritance [*Lifestyle classification*]

OIPMT .... Optimum Insect Pest Management Trial [*Department of Agriculture*]

OIPO .... Optimum Installation Position Only (MCD)

OIPR .... Office of Information, Publications, and Reports [*Department of Labor*]

OIPR .... Office of Intelligence Policy and Review [*U.S. Department of Justice*] (BARN)

OIPS .... Optical Image Processing System

OIPT .... Overarching Integrated Product Team [*Army*]

OIQ .... Ordre des Ingenieurs du Quebec [*Canada*] (DD)

OIQ .... Sioux City, IA [*Location identifier FAA*] (FAAL)

OIR .... Iroquois Public Library, Ontario [*Library symbol National Library of Canada*] (BIB)

OIR .... Office of Indian Rights [*Department of Justice*]

OIR .... Office of Industrial Relations [*Superseded, 1966, by Office of Civilian Manpower*] [*Navy*]

OIR .... Office of Industrial Research [*University of Manitoba*] [*Canada Research center*] (RCD)

OIR .... Office of Institutional Relations [*Energy Research and Development Administration*]

OIR .... Office of Inter-American Radio (AD)

OIR .... Office of International Research [*National Institutes of Health*]

OIR .... Office of International Resources [*Department of State*]

OIR .... Okushiri [*Japan*] [*Airport symbol*] (OAG)

OIR .... Old Irish [*Language, etc.*]

OIr .... Old Irish (AD)

OIR .... Online Information Retrieval Ltd. [*Information service or system Defunct*] (IID)

OIR .... Open Item Review (KSC)

OIR .... Operations Integration Review (NASA)

OIR .... Orbiter Infrared Radiometer [*NASA*]

OIR .... Organisation Internationale de Radiodiffusion [*International Radio Organization*] [*Later, OIRT*]

OIR .... Other Intelligence Requirements [*Army*] (MCD)

OIR .... Slov-Air [*Slovakia*] [*ICAO designator*] (FAAC)

OIRA .... Office of Industrial Resource Administration (AAGC)

OIRA .... Office of Information and Regulatory Affairs [*Office of Management and Budget*]

OIRA .... Officials of the Irish Republican Army [*Northern Ireland*]

OIRB .... Oregon Insurance Rating Bureau (AD)

OIRD .... Object-to-Image Receptor Distance [*Radiology*] (DAVI)

OIRE .... Optical Infrared Equipment

OIRM .... Office and Industrial Records Management (AD)

OIRM .... Office of Information Resources Management [*General Services Administration*]

OIR-N .... Office of Industrial Relations, Navy [*Superseded, 1966, by Office of Civilian Manpower*]

OIRS .... Occupational Interest Rating Scale [*Vocational guidance test*]

OIRS .... Operation and Inspection Route Sheet (DNAB)

OIRSA .... Organismo Internacional Regional de Sanidad Agropecuaria [*Regional International Organization of Plant Protection and Animal Health*] [*El Salvador*]

OIRT .... Organisation Internationale de Radiodiffusion et Television [*International Radio and Television Organization*] [*Formerly, OIR*] (EAIO)

OIS .... Obstacle Identification Surface [*Aviation*] (DA)

OIS .... Occupational Information System [*Department of Labor*]

OIS .... Occupational Interest Survey [*Aptitude test*]

OIS .... Office of Industrial Security [*DoD*]

OIS .... Office of Information Services [*Council of State Governments*] [*Lexington, KY*]

OIS .... Office of Information Systems [*Social and Rehabilitation Service, HEW*]

OIS .... Office of International Services [*Red Cross*]

OIS .... Oishiyama [*Japan*] [*Seismograph station code, US Geological Survey*] (SEIS)

OIS .... OIS Optical Imaging Systems, Inc. [*Associated Press*] (SAG)

OIS .... Oncology Information Service [*University of Leeds*] [*England*] [*Information service or system*] (IID)

OIS .... Operating Information System [*Army*]

OIS .... Operational Insertion System

OIS .... Operational Instrumentation System

OIS .... Operational Intercommunication System [*NASA*] (KSC)

OIS .... Optical Image Sensor

OIS .... Optical Imaging Systems (RDA)

OIS .... Optical Information System [*Computer science*]

OIS .... Orbiter Instrumentation Systems [*NASA*] (MCD)

OIS .... Ounce-Inches per Second (IAA)

OIS .... Overseas Investors Services (AD)

OISA .... Abadeh [*Iran*] [*ICAO location identifier*] (ICLI)

OISA .... Office of International Science Activities [*National Science Foundation*]

OISA .... Office of International Scientific Affairs (AD)

OIS & T .... Office of Information Systems and Telecommunications [*Veterans Administration*] (TSSD)

OISB .... Bavanat [*Iran*] [*ICAO location identifier*] (ICLI)

OISC .... Ardakan-E-Fars [*Iran*] [*ICAO location identifier*] (ICLI)

OISC .... Oil-Insulated, Self-Cooling

OISCA .... Organization for Industrial, Spiritual, and Cultural Advancement International [*Tokyo, Japan*] (EAIO)

OISD .... Darab [*Iran*] [*ICAO location identifier*] (ICLI)

OISDG .... Ingleside Branch, Stormont, Dundas, and Glengarry County Library, Ontario [*Library symbol National Library of Canada*] (BIB)

OISE .... Estahbanat [*Iran*] [*ICAO location identifier*] (ICLI)

OISE .... Office of Industrial Security, Europe [*DoD*]

OISE .... Ontario Institute for Studies in Education [*University of Toronto*] [*Research center*] (RCD)

OISF .... Fasa [*Iran*] [*ICAO location identifier*] (ICLI)

OISH .... Farashband [*Iran*] [*ICAO location identifier*] (ICLI)

OISI .... Dehbid [*Iran*] [*ICAO location identifier*] (ICLI)

OISI .... Office of Industrial Security, International [*DoD*] (MCD)

OISI .... Ophthalmic Imaging Sys [*NASDAQ symbol*] (TTSB)

OISI .... Ophthalmic Imaging Systems, Inc. [*NASDAQ symbol*] (SAG)

OISJ .... Jahrom [*Iran*] [*ICAO location identifier*] (ICLI)

OISK .... Kazeroun [*Iran*] [*ICAO location identifier*] (ICLI)

OISL .... Lar [*Iran*] [*ICAO location identifier*] (ICLI)

OISLGR .... Office of Industry and State and Local Government Relations [*Energy Research and Development Administration*]

OISM .... Mamassani [*Iran*] [*ICAO location identifier*] (ICLI)

OISN .... Neiriz [*Iran*] [*ICAO location identifier*] (ICLI)

OISP .... Overseas Internal Security Program [*Army*]

OISP .... Persepolis/Marvdasht [*Iran*] [*ICAO location identifier*] (ICLI)

OISQ .... Ghir/Karzin [*Iran*] [*ICAO location identifier*] (ICLI)

OISR .... Lamerd [*Iran*] [*ICAO location identifier*] (ICLI)

OISR .... Office of Interstate Sales Registration [*HUD*]

OISR .... Open Item Status Report (NASA)

OISRU .... Office of Intergovernmental Science and Research Utilization [*National Science Foundation*]

OISS .... Office of Information Systems and Services (AAGC)

OISS .... Online Information Search Service [*Computer science*] (AD)

OISS .... Operational Intelligence Support System (MCD)

OISS .... Organizacion Iberoamericana de Seguridad Social [*Ibero-American Social Security Organization*]

OISS .... Shiraz/International [*Iran*] [*ICAO location identifier*] (ICLI)

OISSP .... Office of Interim Space Station Program [*NASA*] (NASA)

OISSP .... Office of Interim Space Station Program [*NASA*]

OIST .... Operator Integration Shakedown Test

OIST .... Shiraz [*Iran*] [*ICAO location identifier*] (ICLI)

OISTV .... Organisation Internationale pour la Science et la Technique du Vide [*International Organization for Vacuum Science and Technology*] [*French*] (AD)

OISU .... Abarghou [*Iran*] [*ICAO location identifier*] (ICLI)

OISW .... Kohkiloyeh [*Iran*] [*ICAO location identifier*] (ICLI)

OISX .... Khonj [*Iran*] [*ICAO location identifier*] (ICLI)

OISY .... Yasouj [*Iran*] [*ICAO location identifier*] (ICLI)

OISZ .... Firouzabad [*Iran*] [*ICAO location identifier*] (ICLI)

OIT .... Object Identification Test

OIT .... Oblique-Incidence Transmission

OIT .... Office of International Trade [*Department of Commerce*]

O i T .... Officer in Training (AD)

OIT .... Oil Interceptor Trap

OIT .... Oita [*Japan*] [*Seismograph station code, US Geological Survey*] (SEIS)

OIT .... Oita [*Japan*] [*Airport symbol*] (OAG)

O IT .... Old Italian [*Language, etc.*] (ROG)

O It .... Old Italian (AD)

OIT .... Ontario Ministry of Industry, Trade, and Technology [*UTLAS symbol*]

OIT .... Operator Interface Terminal (MCD)

OIT .... Optimum Insulation Thickness (DICI)

OIT .... Orbiter Integrated Test [*NASA*] (NASA)

OIT .... Oregon Institute of Technology, Klamath Falls, OR [*OCLC symbol*] (OCLC)

OIT .... Organic Integrity Test [*Psychology*]

OIT .... Organisation Internationale du Travail [*International Labor Organization*] [*French United Nations*] (EAIO)

OIT .... Organizacion Internacional del Trabajo [*International Labor Organization*] [*Spanish United Nations*] (DUND)

OIT .... Organization Iberoamericaine de Television (NTCM)

OITA .... Office of International Tax Affairs [*Department of the Treasury*]

OITA .... Sarab [*Iran*] [*ICAO location identifier*] (ICLI)

OITAF-NACS... Organizzazione Internazionale dei Trasporti a Fune [*International Organization for Transportation by Rope*] - North American Continental Section (EA)

OITB .... Mahabad [*Iran*] [*ICAO location identifier*] (ICLI)

OITC .... Sardasht [*Iran*] [*ICAO location identifier*] (ICLI)

OITD .... Marand [*Iran*] [*ICAO location identifier*] (ICLI)

OITDA .... Optoelectronic Industry and Technology Development Association [*Japan*]

OITDS .... Operations and Intelligence Tactical Data Systems (MCD)

OITF .... Office of International Trade and Finance [*Department of State*]

OITF .... Office of International Trade Fairs [*Department of Commerce*]

OITF .... Organisation Intergouvernementale pour les Transports Internationaux Ferroviaires [*Intergovernmental Organization for International Carriage by Rail*] (EAIO)

OITG .... Naghadeh [*Iran*] [*ICAO location identifier*] (ICLI)

OITH .... Khaneh/Piranshahr [*Iran*] [*ICAO location identifier*] (ICLI)

OITI .... Mianeh [*Iran*] [*ICAO location identifier*] (ICLI)

OITJ .... Julfa [*Iran*] [*ICAO location identifier*] (ICLI)

OITK .... Khoy [*Iran*] [*ICAO location identifier*] (ICLI)

OITM .... Maragheh [*Iran*] [*ICAO location identifier*] (ICLI)

OITN .... Meshgin Shahr [*Iran*] [*ICAO location identifier*] (ICLI)

OITO .... Mian Do Ab [*Iran*] [*ICAO location identifier*] (ICLI)

OITP .... Office for Information Technology Policy [*American Library Association*]

OITP .... Office of International Trade Promotion [*Department of State*]

OITP .... Parsabad/Moghan [*Iran*] [*ICAO location identifier*] (ICLI)

OITQ .... Ahar [Iran] [ICAO location identifier] (ICLI)
OITR .... Uromiyeh [Iran] [ICAO location identifier] (ICLI)
OITS .... Saghez [Iran] [ICAO location identifier] (ICLI)
OITT .... Outpulser, Identifier, Trunk Test
OITT .... Tabriz [Iran] [ICAO location identifier] (ICLI)
OITU .... Makou [Iran] [ICAO location identifier] (ICLI)
OITV .... Tabriz [Iran] [ICAO location identifier] (ICLI)
OITW .... Azar Shahr [Iran] [ICAO location identifier] (ICLI)
OITX .... Sareskand [Iran] [ICAO location identifier] (ICLI)
OITY .... Marivan [Iran] [ICAO location identifier] (ICLI)
OITZ .... Zanjan [Iran] [ICAO location identifier] (ICLI)
OIU .... Operator Interface Unit [Computer science]
OIV .... Octarios Quatior [Four Pints] [Pharmacy] (ROG)
OIV .... Office International de la Vigne et du Vin [International Vine and
                  Wine Office] (EAIO)
OIV .... Overhead Inlet Valve [Automotive engineering]
OIV .... Oxidizer Isolation Valve (MCD)
OIVS .... Orbiter Interface Verification Set [NASA] (NASA)
OIVS .... Orbiter Interface Verification Set
OIVV .... Office Internationale de la Vigne et du Vin [International Office of
                  Vines and Wines] [French] (AD)
OIW .... Oceanographic Institute of Washington [Marine science] (MSC)
OIW .... Oceanographic Institute Wellington New Zealand (AD)
OIW .... Office of Indigenous Women [Australia]
OIW .... Oiwake [Japan] [Seismograph station code, US Geological Survey
                  Closed] (SEIS)
OIW .... Order of the Indian Wars (EA)
OIWC .... Oil-Insulated, Water-Cooled
OIWP .... Oil Industry Working Party (AD)
OIWR .... Office of Indian Water Rights [Bureau of Indian Affairs]
OIX .... Ottawa, IL [Location identifier FAA] (FAAL)
OIYA .... Ardakan-E-Yazd [Iran] [ICAO location identifier] (ICLI)
OIYB .... Bafgh [Iran] [ICAO location identifier] (ICLI)
OIYD .... Dehshir [Iran] [ICAO location identifier] (ICLI)
OIYF .... Taft [Iran] [ICAO location identifier] (ICLI)
OIYK .... Khor/Jandagh [Iran] [ICAO location identifier] (ICLI)
OIYM .... Mehriz [Iran] [ICAO location identifier] (ICLI)
OIYN .... Khore Beyabanak [Iran] [ICAO location identifier] (ICLI)
OIYQ .... Khezr Abad [Iran] [ICAO location identifier] (ICLI)
OIYT .... Yazd [Iran] [ICAO location identifier] (ICLI)
OIYY .... Yazd [Iran] [ICAO location identifier] (ICLI)
OIYZ .... Ashkezar [Iran] [ICAO location identifier] (ICLI)
OIZA .... Jalagh [Iran] [ICAO location identifier] (ICLI)
OIZB .... Zabol [Iran] [ICAO location identifier] (ICLI)
OIZC .... Chah Bahar/Konarak [Iran] [ICAO location identifier] (ICLI)
OIZD .... Dashtyari [Iran] [ICAO location identifier] (ICLI)
OIZG .... Ghasre Ghand [Iran] [ICAO location identifier] (ICLI)
OIZH .... Zahedan [Iran] [ICAO location identifier] (ICLI)
OIZI .... Iran Shahr [Iran] [ICAO location identifier] (ICLI)
OIZJ .... Jask [Iran] [ICAO location identifier] (ICLI)
OIZK .... Khash [Iran] [ICAO location identifier] (ICLI)
OIZL .... Zabolee [Iran] [ICAO location identifier] (ICLI)
OIZM .... Mirjaveh [Iran] [ICAO location identifier] (ICLI)
OIZN .... Bazman [Iran] [ICAO location identifier] (ICLI)
OIZO .... Sarbaz [Iran] [ICAO location identifier] (ICLI)
OIZP .... Bampoor [Iran] [ICAO location identifier] (ICLI)
OIZR .... Bask [Iran] [ICAO location identifier] (ICLI)
OIZS .... Saravan [Iran] [ICAO location identifier] (ICLI)
OIZT .... Zahedan [Iran] [ICAO location identifier] (ICLI)
OIZY .... Nik-Shahr [Iran] [ICAO location identifier] (ICLI)
OJ .... Air Texana [ICAO designator] (AD)
OJ .... Jackson Public Library, Jackson, OH [Library symbol Library of
                  Congress] (LCLS)
OJ .... Ohne Jahr [Without Date of Publication] [Bibliography] [German]
oJ .... Ohne Jahr [Without Year] [German] (AD)
oj .... Open-Joint (AD)
OJ .... Open-Joisted [Technical drawings]
OJ .... Open Web Joist [Technical drawings]
OJ .... Operation Joshua (EA)
OJ .... Opium Joint [Slang]
OJ .... Orange Co. [NYSE symbol] (SPSG)
OJ .... Orange-Co. [NYSE symbol] (TTSB)
OJ .... Orange Juice
oj .... Orange Juice (AD)
OJ .... Order of Jamaica
OJ .... Orenthal James [Given names of football player O. J. Simpson]
OJ .... Orenthal James Simpson [Sports personality] (ECON)
OJ .... Originating Junctor [Telecommunications] (TEL)
OJ .... Orthomode Junction [Electronics]
OJ .... Orthoplast Jacket [Orthopedics] (DAVI)
OJ .... Outer Jacket
OJA .... Onklos-Jonathan Aramaic (BJA)
OJA .... Oriental Pearl Airways Ltd. [British ICAO designator] (FAAC)
OJA .... Weatherford, OK [Location identifier FAA] (FAAL)
OJAC .... Amman [Jordan] [ICAO location identifier] (ICLI)
OJ Act .... Ontario Judicature Act [A publication] (DLA)
OJAF .... Amman [Jordan] [ICAO location identifier] (ICLI)
OJA-G .... Office of the Judge Advocate General [British]
OJAI .... Amman/Queen Alia [Jordan] [ICAO location identifier] (ICLI)
OJAJ .... October, January, April, and July [Denotes quarterly payments of
                  interest or dividends in these months] [Business term]
OJAM .... Amman/Marka [Jordan] [ICAO location identifier] (ICLI)
OJapan ...... Order of Japan (DD)
OJAQ .... Aqaba [Jordan] [ICAO location identifier] (ICLI)

OJARS .... Office of Justice Assistance, Research, and Statistics [Department of
                  Justice]
OJBD .... Irbid [Jordan] [ICAO location identifier] (ICLI)
OJC .... North Central Regional Library, Ojibway Cree Project [UTLAS
                  symbol]
OJC .... Occupied Japan Club (EA)
OJC .... Office of Job Corps [Department of Labor]
OJC .... Olathe, KS [Location identifier FAA] (FAAL)
OJC .... Order of Jacques-Cartier [Canada] (BARN)
OJC .... Organisation Juive de Combat [Jewish Combat Organization]
                  [French] (AD)
OJC .... Orlando Junior College [Florida]
OJC .... Otero Junior College [La Junta, CO]
OJC .... Overseas Jazz Club (EA)
OJCE .... Orchestre des Jeunes de la Communaute Europeenne [European
                  Community Youth Orchestra - ECYO] (EAIO)
OJCN .... Jarvis Branch, City of Nanticoke Public Library, Ontario [Library
                  symbol National Library of Canada] (BIB)
OJCS .... Office of the Joint Chiefs of Staff (AFM)
OJCS .... Organization of the Joint Chiefs of Staff
OJD .... Order of Job's Daughters
OJDYD .... Office of Juvenile Delinquency and Youth Development [Later, Youth
                  Development Bureau] [HEW]
OJE .... Okumenischer Jugendrat in Europa [Ecumenical Youth Council in
                  Europe - EYCE] (EAIO)
OJE .... On-the-Job Education
OJE .... On-the-Job Evaluation (OICC)
OJE .... On-the-Job Experience
OJE .... Orthodox Job Enrichment (PDAA)
OJEC .... Official Journal of the European Communities [A publication] (AD)
OJG .... Ordnance Job Guide
OJHF .... Hotel Five [Jordan] [ICAO location identifier] (ICLI)
OJHR .... Hotel Four [Jordan] [ICAO location identifier] (ICLI)
oji .... Ojibwa [MARC language code Library of Congress] (LCCP)
OJI .... On-the-Job Injuries
OJI .... On-the-Job Injuries (AD)
oji .... On-the-Job Injuries (AD)
OJJ .... Office of Juvenile Justice (AD)
OJJDP .... Office of Juvenile Justice and Delinquency Prevention [Department of
                  Just ice] [Washington, DC]
OJJO .... Jericho [Jordan] [ICAO location identifier] (ICLI)
OJJR .... Jerusalem [Jordan] [ICAO location identifier] (ICLI)
OJL .... Josephine County Library System, Grants Pass, OR [OCLC
                  symbol] (OCLC)
OJMF .... Mafraq [Jordan] [ICAO location identifier] (ICLI)
OJNRF .... O. J. Noer Research Foundation (EA)
OJOP .... Olympic Job Opportunities Program
OJP .... Office of Justice Programs [Department of Justice]
OJP .... Ontong Java Plateau [Geology]
OJP .... Orlando, FL [Location identifier FAA] (FAAL)
OJPR .... Office for Jewish Population Research [Defunct] (EA)
OJQ .... Objective Judgment Quotient
OJR .... Old Jamaica Rum (ROG)
oJr .... Old Jamaica Rum (AD)
OJRL .... Optoelectronics Joint Research Laboratory [Japan]
OJS .... Las Oblatas de Jesus Sacerdote [Oblates of Jesus the Priest]
                  [Roman Catholic women's religious order]
OJS .... Optical Jammer Source
OJSA .... Orthomode Junction and Switching Assembly [Electronics]
OJT .... On-the-Job Training
ojt .... On-the-Job Training (AD)
OJT .... Over-Water Jet Transport (MCD)
OJTA .... Officer Job/Task Analysis [Military]
O Jur .... Ohio Jurisprudence [A publication] (DLA)
OJW .... Otjiwarongo [South-West Africa] [Airport symbol] (AD)
OJY .... Florida Air, Inc. [ICAO designator] (FAAC)
OJZ .... White Plains, NY [Location identifier FAA] (FAAL)
OJZZ .... Amman [Jordan] [ICAO location identifier] (ICLI)
OK .... All Right [From Oll Korrect; or from Old Kinderhook, a political club
                  that supported the 1840 presidential campaign of Martin Van
                  Buren]
OK .... Czechoslovak Airlines [ICAO designator] (AD)
OK .... Kingston Public Library, Ontario [Library symbol National Library of
                  Canada] (NLC)
O-K .... Object-Kowal [Object in the solar system]
OK .... Odorless Kerosene
OK .... Ohne Kosten [Without Cost] [German]
ok .... Ohne Kosten [Without Cost] [German] (AD)
OK .... Okay [International telex abbreviation] (WDMC)
OK .... Okinawa [Japan]
OK .... Oklahoma [Postal code]
Ok .... Oklahoma Department of Libraries, Oklahoma City, OK [Library
                  symbol Library of Congress] (LCLS)
OK .... Okonite (IAA)
OK .... Oktal (IAA)
OK .... Ola Kala [All Is Well] [Greek]
ok .... Ola Kala [All is Fine] [Greek] (AD)
OK .... Old Kinderhook (IIA)
OK .... Old Kingdom [Egyptology] (ROG)
OK .... Optical Klystron (PDAA)
ok .... Optical Klystron (AD)
OK .... Order of Knights (ADA)
OK .... Oskar Kokoschka [Austrian painter] [1886-1980]
OK .... Outer Keel
ok .... Outer Keel (AD)
OKA .... Bethany Nazarene College, Bethany, OK [OCLC symbol] (OCLC)

OKA .... Kingston Laboratories, Alcan International Ltd., Ontario [*Library symbol National Library of Canada*] (NLC)

OKA .... Okayama [*Japan*] [*Seismograph station code, US Geological Survey*] (SEIS)

OKA .... Okinawa [*Japan*] [*Airport symbol*] (OAG)

OKA .... Otherwise Known As

oka............. Otherwise Known As (AD)

OKA .... Out-of-Kilter Algorithm [*Mathematics*]

OKAA .... Kuwait Directorate General of Civil Aviation [*Kuwait*] [*ICAO location identifier*] (ICLI)

OKAAN........ Optokinetic After-After-Nystagmus [*Ophthalmology*]

OKAB .... Beaverbrook Branch, Kanata Public Library, Ontario [*Library symbol National Library of Canada*] (NLC)

OKAC .... Kuwait [*Kuwait*] [*ICAO location identifier*] (ICLI)

OkAd........... Ada Public Library, Ada, OK [*Library symbol Library of Congress*] (LCLS)

OkAdE .... East Central State College [*Later, East Central Oklahoma State University*], Ada, OK [*Library symbol Library of Congress*] (LCLS)

OKAER .... Radiochemical Co., Atomic Energy of Canada Ltd., [*Societe Radiochimique, L'Energie Atomique du Canada Ltee.*], Kanata, Ontario [*Library symbol National Library of Canada*] (NLC)

OKAF .... Kuwait Air Force [*Kuwait*] [*ICAO location identifier*] (ICLI)

OKAH .... Hazeldean Branch, Kanata Public Library, Ontario [*Library symbol National Library of Canada*] (NLC)

OKAI .... Research & Technology Centre, AMCA International Ltd., Kanata, Ontario [*Library symbol National Library of Canada*] (NLC)

OKAKS .... Synod Office, Diocese of Keewatin, Anglican Church of Canada, Kenora, Ontario [*Library symbol National Library of Canada*] (NLC)

OkAl............ Altus Library, Altus, OK [*Library symbol Library of Congress*] (LCLS)

OKAL .... Aluminum Co. of Canada Ltd., Kingston, Ontario [*Library symbol National Library of Canada*] (NLC)

OkAlS.......... Southern Prairie Library System, Altus, OK [*Library symbol Library of Congress*] (LCLS)

OkAlvN........ Northwestern State College, Alva, OK [*Library symbol Library of Congress*] (LCLS)

OKAN .... Kanata Public Library, Ontario [*Library symbol National Library of Canada*] (BIB)

OKAN .... Optokinetic After-Nystagmus [*Ophthalmology*]

OKANA........ Arctec Canada Ltd., Kanata, Ontario [*Library symbol National Library of Canada*] (NLC)

OKAOS........ Synod Office, Diocese of Ontario, Anglican Church of Canada, Kingston, Ontario [*Library symbol National Library of Canada*] (NLC)

OKAP .... Kapuskasing Public Library, Ontario [*Library symbol National Library of Canada*] (NLC)

OkArC .... Chickasaw Library System, Ardmore, OK [*Library symbol Library of Congress*] (LCLS)

OKASG........ St. George's Cathedral, Anglican Church of Canada, Kingston, Ontario [*Library symbol National Library of Canada*] (NLC)

OKAYJ .... A. Y. Jackson High School, Kanata, Ontario [*Library symbol National Library of Canada*] (BIB)

OkB .... Bartlesville Public Library, Bartlesville, OK [*Library symbol Library of Congress*] (LCLS)

OKB .... Kashechewan Band Library, Ontario [*Library symbol National Library of Canada*] (BIB)

OKB .... Oklahoma Baptist University, Shawnee, OK [*OCLC symbol*] (OCLC)

OKB .... Orchid Beach [*Australia Airport symbol*]

OkBERDA.... United States Energy Research Development Administration, Energy Research Center, Bartlesville, OK [*Library symbol Library of Congress*] (LCLS)

OkBetC........ Bethany Nazarene College, Bethany, OK [*Library symbol Library of Congress*] (LCLS)

OKBK .... Kuwait/International [*Kuwait*] [*ICAO location identifier*] (ICLI)

OkBP........... Phillips Petroleum Co., Research and Development Department, Bartlesville, OK [*Library symbol Library of Congress*] (LCLS)

OkBP-NR...... Philips Petroleum Co., Exploration and Production Library, Bartlesville, OK [*Library symbol*] [*Library of Congress*] (LCLS)

OkBr............ Bristow Public Library, Bristow, OK [*Library symbol Library of Congress*] (LCLS)

OKBT .... Billings Township Public Library, Kagawong, Ontario [*Library symbol National Library of Canada*] (NLC)

OkBUSM ...... United States Bureau of Mines, Petroleum Research Center, Bartlesville, OK [*Library symbol Library of Congress Obsolete*] (LCLS)

OKC .... Cameron University, Lawton, OK [*OCLC symbol*] (OCLC)

OKC .... Canadian Forces School of Communications and Electronics, Kingston, Ontario [*Library symbol National Library of Canada*] (BIB)

OKC .... Okanagan College Learning Resources Centre [*UTLAS symbol*]

OKC .... Oklahoma City [*Oklahoma*] [*Airport symbol*] (OAG)

OKC .... Will Rogers World Airport [*FAA*] (TAG)

OKCAA .... Archives, Archdiocese of Kingston, Catholic Church, Ontario [*Library symbol National Library of Canada*] (NLC)

OkChicW...... Oklahoma College of Liberal Arts, Chickasha, OK [*Library symbol Library of Congress*] (LCLS)

OKCKT .... King Township Public Library, King City, Ontario [*Library symbol National Library of Canada*] (NLC)

OkCl............ Clinton Public Library, Clinton, OK [*Library symbol Library of Congress*] (LCLS)

OkClaW........ Will Rogers Library, Claremore, OH [*Library symbol Library of Congress*] (LCLS)

OkClW .... Western Plains Library System, Clinton, OK [*Library symbol Library of Congress*] (LCLS)

OKCM .... Canadian Marconi Co., Kanata, Ontario [*Library symbol National Library of Canada*] (NLC)

OKD .... Oklahoma Department of Libraries, Oklahoma City, OK [*OCLC symbol*] (OCLC)

OKD .... Research Centre Library, Du Pont Canada, Inc., Kingston, Ontario [*Library symbol National Library of Canada*] (NLC)

OKD .... Sapporo/Okadama [*Japan*] [*Airport symbol*] (OAG)

OKDBMS...... Operations Knowledge Data Base Management System [*NASA*]

OKDC .... Du Pont Canada, Inc., Kingston, Ontario [*Library symbol National Library of Canada*] (NLC)

OkDurS .... Southeastern State College, Durant, OK [*Library symbol Library of Congress*] (LCLS)

OKE .... Kenora Public Library, Ontario [*Library symbol National Library of Canada*] (NLC)

OKE .... Metropolitan Library System, Capitol Hill Branch, Oklahoma City, OK [*OCLC symbol*] (OCLC)

OKE .... Okino Erabu [*Japan*] [*Airport symbol*] (OAG)

OKE .... ONEOK, Inc. [*NYSE symbol*] (SPSG)

OKE .... Optical Kerr Effect [*Birefringence induced in an electrical field*]

OkE .... Public Library of Enid and Garfield County, Enid, OK [*Library symbol Library of Congress*] (LCLS)

OKEA .... Kearney and Area Public Library, Kearney, Ontario [*Library symbol National Library of Canada*] (NLC)

OkEdT .... Central State University, Edmond, OK [*Library symbol Library of Congress*] (LCLS)

OKEE .... Keewatin Public Library, Ontario [*Library symbol National Library of Canada*] (NLC)

O'Keefe Ord.. O'Keefe's Order in Chancery [*Ireland*] [*A publication*] (DLA)

Oke Fish L... Oke. Fisher Laws [*4th ed.*] [*1924*] [*A publication*] (DLA)

OkEG.......... Phillips University, Graduate Seminary, Enid, OK [*Library symbol Library of Congress*] (LCLS)

Oke Game L... Oke. Game Laws [*5th ed.*] [*1912*] [*A publication*] (DLA)

OKEH .... Okehampton [*England*]

OKEM.......... Kemptville Public Library, Ontario [*Library symbol National Library of Canada*] (NLC)

OKEMAF ...... Ontario Ministry of Agriculture and Food, Kemptville, Ontario [*Library symbol National Library of Canada*] (NLC)

Oke Mag Form... Oke. Magisterial Formulist [*19th ed.*] [*1978*] [*A publication*] (DLA)

Oke Mag Syn... Oke. Magisterial Synopsis [*14th ed.*] [*1893*] [*A publication*] (DLA)

OKEMC .... Kemptville College of Agricultural Technology, Ontario [*Library symbol National Library of Canada*] (BIB)

OKEMS .... Earl of March Secondary School, Kanata, Ontario [*Library symbol National Library of Canada*] (NLC)

OKEN .... Old Kent Financial Corp. [*NASDAQ symbol*] (NQ)

OKEN .... Old Kent Finl [*NASDAQ symbol*] (TTSB)

OKentU .... Kent State University, Kent, OH [*Library symbol Library of Congress*] (LCLS)

OkEP........... Phillips University, Enid, OK [*Library symbol Library of Congress*] (LCLS)

OkErC.......... El Reno Junior College Learning Resource Center, El Reno, OK [*Library symbol*] [*Library of Congress*] (LCLS)

OKES .... Georgina Township Public Library, Keswick, Ontario [*Library symbol National Library of Canada*] (NLC)

OKET........... Euphrasia Township Public Library, Kimberley, Ontario [*Library symbol National Library of Canada*] (NLC)

OKetBD .... BDM International, Information Service Center, Kettering, OH [*Library symbol*] [*Library of Congress*] (LCLS)

OKetH .... Kettering Memorial Hospital, Kettering, OH [*Library symbol Library of Congress*] (LCLS)

OKetK .... Charles F. Kettering Foundation, Kettering, OH [*Library symbol Library of Congress*] (LCLS)

Oke Turn...... Oke. Turnpike Laws [*2nd ed.*] [*1861*] [*A publication*] (DLA)

OKF............. Fort Frontenac Library, Canada Department of National Defence [*Bibliotheque Fort Frontenac, Ministere de la Defense Nationale*] Kingston, Ontario [*Library symbol National Library of Canada*] (NLC)

OKFC .... Frontenac County Library, Kingston, Ontario [*Library symbol National Library of Canada*] (NLC)

OKFCSM ...... Frontenac County Schools Museum Association, Kingston, Ontario [*Library symbol National Library of Canada*] (BIB)

OKFI............ Siltronics Ltd., Kanata, Ontario [*Library symbol National Library of Canada*] (NLC)

OkFsAGM..... United States Army, Artillery and Guided Missile School, Fort Sill, OK [*Library symbol Library of Congress*] (LCLS)

OKG .... Oak Grove [*Tennessee*] [*Seismograph station code, US Geological Survey*] (SEIS)

OKG .... Okoyo [*Congo*] [*Airport symbol*] (OAG)

OKG .... Phillips University, Graduate Seminary Library, Enid, OK [*OCLC symbol*] (OCLC)

OKGH .... Kingston General Hospital, Ontario [*Library symbol National Library of Canada*] (NLC)

OkGoP .... Panhandle State College, Goodwell, OK [*Library symbol Library of Congress*] (LCLS)

OkGuC .... Catholic College of Oklahoma for Women, Guthrie, OK [*Library symbol Library of Congress Obsolete*] (LCLS)

OkGuy......... Guymon City Library, Guymon, OK [*Library symbol Library of Congress*] (LCLS)

OKH .... Oberkommando des Heeres [*Army High Command*] [*German military - World War II*]

OKH .... Okha [*Former USSR Seismograph station code, US Geological Survey*] (SEIS)

OKH .... University of Oklahoma, Health Science Center Library, Oklahoma City, OK [*OCLC symbol*] (OCLC)

OKHD .... Hotel-Dieu Hospital, Kingston, Ontario [*Library symbol National Library of Canada*] (NLC)

OkHenn........ Hennessey Public Library, Hennessey, OK [*Library symbol Library of Congress*] (LCLS)

OkHi............ Oklahoma Historical Society, Oklahoma City, OK [*Library symbol Library of Congress*] (LCLS)

OKI.............. Choctaw Nation Multi-County Library, McAlester, OK [*OCLC symbol*] (OCLC)

OKI.............. Kincardine Branch, Bruce County Public Library, Ontario [*Library symbol National Library of Canada*] (NLC)

OKI.............. Ohio-Kentucky-Indiana Regional Planning Authority

OKI.............. Oki Island [*Japan*] [*Airport symbol*] (OAG)

OKI.............. Okijuku [*Japan*] [*Seismograph station code, US Geological Survey Closed*] (SEIS)

OKIESMO..... Oklahoma Machismo [*Term coined by author Mark Singer*]

OKIL............. Killaloe Public Library, Ontario [*Library symbol National Library of Canada*] (NLC)

OkIM............ McUrtain County High Education Program, Idabel, OK [*Library symbol*] [*Library of Congress*] (LCLS)

Okin............. Okinawa (AD)

OKIT............ Kitchener Public Library, Ontario [*Library symbol National Library of Canada*] (NLC)

OKITC .... Learning Resource Centre, Conestoga College of Applied Arts and Technology, Kitchener, Ontario [*Library symbol National Library of Canada*] (NLC)

OKITD .... Doon Pioneer Village, Kitchener, Ontario [*Library symbol National Library of Canada*] (BIB)

OKITM .... Ontario Library Service - Saugeen, Kitchener, Ontario [*Library symbol National Library of Canada*] (NLC)

OKITW .... Kitchener-Waterloo Record, Kitchener, Ontario [*Library symbol National Library of Canada*] (NLC)

OKITWC .... Waterloo County Board of Education, Kitchener, Ontario [*Library symbol National Library of Canada*] (NLC)

OKJ.............. Okada Airlines Ltd. [*Nigeria*] [*ICAO designator*] (FAAC)

OKJ.............. Okayama [*Japan*] [*Airport symbol*] (OAG)

OKJ.............. Oklahoma City Community College, Oklahoma City, OK [*OCLC symbol*] (OCLC)

OKK .... Charles F. Kettering Foundation, Dayton, OH [*OCLC symbol*] (OCLC)

OKK .... Kokomo [*Indiana*] [*Airport symbol*] (OAG)

OKK .... Kokomo, IN [*Location identifier FAA*] (FAAL)

OKKBWP...... One Kind Kiss Before We Part [*Slang*]

OKL............. Lake Ontario Regional Library System, Kingston, Ontario [*Library symbol Obsolete National Library of Canada*] (NLC)

OkL............. Lawton Public Library, Lawton, OK [*Library symbol Library of Congress*] (LCLS)

OKL............. Oberkommando der Luftwaffe [*Air Force High Command*] [*German military - World War II*]

Okl.............. Oklahoma (DLA)

OKL............. Oklahoma City [*Diocesan abbreviation*] [*Oklahoma*] (TOCD)

Okl.............. Oklahoma Reports [*A publication*] (DLA)

OKL............. University of Oklahoma, Law Library, Norman, OK [*OCLC symbol*] (OCLC)

OKLA .... Oklahoma (AFM)

Okla .... Oklahoma (AD)

Okla............. Oklahoma (ODBW)

Okla............. Oklahoma Criminal Reports [*A publication*] (DLA)

Okla............. Oklahoma Supreme Court Reports [*A publication*] (DLA)

Okla Ap Ct Rep... Oklahoma Appellate Court Reporter [*A publication*] (DLA)

OklaC........... Oklahoma City (AD)

Okla City U... Oklahoma City University (GAGS)

Okla Cr .... Oklahoma Criminal Reports [*A publication*] (DLA)

Okla Crim .... Oklahoma Criminal Reports [*A publication*] (DLA)

Okla CULR... Oklahoma City University. Law Review [*A publication*] (DLA)

OklaG........... Oklahoma Gas & Electric Co. [*Associated Press*] (SAG)

Okla Gaz...... Oklahoma Gazette [*A publication*] (DLA)

OklaGE......... Oklahoma Gas & Electric Co. [*Associated Press*] (SAG)

Oklahoma..... Oklahoma Reports [*A publication*] (DLA)

Okla ICR...... Oklahoma Industrial Commission Reports [*A publication*] (DLA)

Okla Lawy ... Oklahoma Lawyer [*A publication*] (DLA)

Okla LJ .... Oklahoma Law Journal [*A publication*] (DLA)

Okl App....... Oklahoma Court of Appeals (DLA)

Okla SBJ..... Oklahoma State Bar Journal [*A publication*] (DLA)

Okla Sess Laws... Oklahoma Session Laws [*A publication*] (DLA)

Okla Sess Law Serv... Oklahoma Session Law Service (West) [*A publication*] (DLA)

Okla Stat .... Oklahoma Statutes [*A publication*] (DLA)

Okla Stat Ann (West)... Oklahoma Statutes, Annotated (West) [*A publication*] (DLA)

Okla St U.... Oklahoma State University (GAGS)

OkLaU.......... Langston University, Langston, OK [*Library symbol Library of Congress*] (LCLS)

OkLC........... Cameron University, Lawton, OK [*Library symbol Library of Congress*] (LCLS)

Okl City UL Rev... Oklahoma City University. Law Review [*A publication*] (DLA)

OkLC-M........ Cameron College, Medical Library Resource Center, Lawton, OK [*Library symbol Library of Congress*] (LCLS)

Okl Cr .... Oklahoma Criminal Reports [*A publication*] (DLA)

Okl Cr R ...... Oklahoma Criminal Reports [*A publication*] (DLA)

OKLEM......... McMichael Canadian Collection, Kleinburg, Ontario [*Library symbol National Library of Canada*] (NLC)

OKLFC .... Official Kate Linder Fan Club (EA)

OKLN .... Northeastern Regional Library, Kirkland Lake, Ontario [*Library symbol National Library of Canada*] (NLC)

OKLN .... Ontario Library Service - James Bay, Kirkland Lake, Ontario [*Library symbol National Library of Canada*] (NLC)

OKLNC........ Kirkland Lake Campus, Northern College, Ontario [*Library symbol National Library of Canada*] (NLC)

Okl St Ann ... Oklahoma Statutes, Annotated [*A publication*] (DLA)

OKLT............ Teck Centennial Public Library, Kirkland Lake, Ontario [*Library symbol National Library of Canada*] (NLC)

OKLU .... Lumonics, Inc., Kanata, Ontario [*Library symbol National Library of Canada*] (NLC)

OKM............ Mitel Corp., Kanata, Ontario [*Library symbol National Library of Canada*] (NLC)

OKM............ Oberkommando der Kriegsmarine [*Navy High Command*] [*German military - World War II*]

OKM............ Oberkommando der Marine [*Naval High Command*] [*Germany*] (AD)

OKM............ Okmulgee, OK [*Location identifier FAA*] (FAAL)

OKM............ Pioneer Multi-County Library, Norman, OK [*OCLC symbol*] (OCLC)

OKMC .... Miller Communications Systems Ltd., Kanata, Ontario [*Library symbol National Library of Canada*] (NLC)

OkMcC .... Choctaw Nation Multi-County Library, McAlester, OK [*Library symbol Library of Congress*] (LCLS)

OkMcO .... Oscar Rose Junior College, Midwest City, OK [*Library symbol Library of Congress*] (LCLS)

OKMD .... Digital Equipment of Canada Ltd., Kanata, Ontario [*Library symbol National Library of Canada*] (NLC)

OKME .... Metro Canada Ltd., Kingston, Ontario [*Library symbol National Library of Canada*] (NLC)

OKMM .... Marine Museum of the Great Lakes at Kingston, Ontario [*Library symbol National Library of Canada*] (NLC)

OkMu .... Muskogee Public Library, Muskogee, OK [*Library symbol Library of Congress*] (LCLS)

OkMuE .... Eastern Oklahoma District Library, Muskogee, OK [*Library symbol Library of Congress*] (LCLS)

OkMuV .... United States Veterans Administration Hospital, Muskogee, OK [*Library symbol Library of Congress*] (LCLS)

OKMV .... Okra Mosaic Virus [*Plant pathology*]

OKN............ Northeastern Oklahoma State University, Tahlequah, OK [*OCLC symbol*] (OCLC)

OKN............ Okmulgee Northern Railway Co. [*AAR code*]

OKN............ Okondja [*Gabon*] [*Airport symbol*] (OAG)

OKN............ Optokinetic Nystagmus [*Ophthalmology*]

OkN............ Pioneer Multi-County Library, Norman, OK [*Library symbol Library of Congress*] (LCLS)

OKNC .... Newbridge Communication Network Corp., Kanata, Ontario [*Library symbol National Library of Canada*] (BIB)

OkNNS .... National Severe Storms Laboratory, Norman, OK [*Library symbol Library of Congress*] (LCLS)

OKNO .... Kuwait International NOTAM Office [*Kuwait*] [*ICAO location identifier*] (ICLI)

OKO............ Oral Roberts University, Tulsa, OK [*OCLC symbol*] (OCLC)

OKOH........... Penrose Division, Ongwanada Hospital, Kingston, Ontario [*Library symbol National Library of Canada*] (NLC)

OkOk........... Oklahoma County Libraries, Oklahoma City, OK [*Library symbol Library of Congress*] (LCLS)

OkOkB .... Oklahoma Library for the Blind and Physically Handicapped, Oklahoma City, OK [*Library symbol Library of Congress*] (LCLS)

OkOkC .... Oklahoma Christian College, Oklahoma City, OK [*Library symbol*] [*Library of Congress*] (LCLS)

OkOkCGS .... Oklahoma City Geological Survey, Inc., Oklahoma City, OK [*Library symbol*] [*Library of Congress*] (LCLS)

OkOkD .... Deaconess Hospital, Oklahoma City, OK [*Library symbol Library of Congress*] (LCLS)

OkOke .... Okemah Public Library, Okemah, OK [*Library symbol*] [*Library of Congress*] (LCLS)

OkOkFA........ United States Federal Aviation Administration, Civil Aeromedical Institute, Oklahoma City, OK [*Library symbol Library of Congress*] (LCLS)

OkOkGS .... Church of Jesus Christ of Latter-Day Saints, Genealogical Society Library, Oklahoma City Branch, Oklahoma City, OK [*Library symbol Library of Congress*] (LCLS)

OkOkK .... Kerr-McGee Corp., Oklahoma City, OK [*Library symbol Library of Congress*] (LCLS)

OkOkM .... Mid-America Bible College, Oklahoma City, OK [*Library symbol*] [*Library of Congress*] (LCLS)

OkOkSO .... Oklahoma City Community College, Learning Resources Center, Oklahoma City, OK [*Library symbol Library of Congress*] (LCLS)

OkOkU .... Oklahoma City University, Oklahoma City, OK [*Library symbol Library of Congress*] (LCLS)

OkOkU-L ...... Oklahoma City University, Law Library, Oklahoma City, OK [*Library symbol Library of Congress*] (LCLS)

OkOkV .... United States Veterans Administration Hospital, Oklahoma City, OK [*Library symbol Library of Congress*] (LCLS)

OKOT .... Otonabee Township Library, Keen, Ontario [*Library symbol National Library of Canada*] (NLC)

OKP............ Citizens' Parliamentary Club [*Poland*] [*Political party*]

OKP............ Oksapmin [*Papua New Guinea*] [*Airport symbol*] (OAG)

OKP............ O'okiep Copper ADR [*AMEX symbol*] (TTSB)

OKP............ O'Okiep Copper Co. Ltd. [*AMEX symbol*] (SPSG)

OKP............ Optimized Kill Probability

OKP............ Southern Prairie Library System, Altus, OK [*OCLC symbol*] (OCLC)

OkPo........... Ponca City Public Library, Ponca City, OK [*Library symbol Library of Congress*] (LCLS)

OkPoC......... Continental Oil Co., R and D Technical Information Service, Ponca City, OK [*Library symbol Library of Congress*] (LCLS)

OkPot.......... Buckley Public Library, Poteau, OK [*Library symbol Library of Congress*] (LCLS)

OKQ............ Okaba [*Indonesia*] [*Airport symbol*] (OAG)

OKQ............ Queen's University, Kingston, Ontario [*Library symbol National Library of Canada*] (NLC)

OKQA .... Agnes Etherington Art Centre, Queen's University, Kingston, Ontario [*Library symbol National Library of Canada*] (NLC)

OKQAR .... Archives, Queen's University, Kingston, Ontario [*Library symbol National Library of Canada*] (NLC)

OKQCI .... Canadian Institute of Guided Ground Transport, Queen's University, Kingston, Ontario [*Library symbol National Library of Canada*] (NLC)

OKQG .... Department of Geography, Queen's University, Kingston, Ontario [*Library symbol National Library of Canada*] (NLC)

OKQGS .... Department of Geological Sciences, Queen's University, Kingston, Ontario [*Library symbol National Library of Canada*] (NLC)

OKQH .... Bracken Library, Queen's University, Kingston, Ontario [*Library symbol National Library of Canada*] (NLC)

OKQL .... Law Library, Queen's University, Kingston, Ontario [*Library symbol National Library of Canada*] (NLC)

OKQM .... McArthur College of Education, Queen's University, Kingston, Ontario [*Library symbol National Library of Canada*] (NLC)

OKQMA .... Map Collection, Douglas Library, Queen's University, Kingston, Ontario [*Library symbol National Library of Canada*] (NLC)

OKR .... Optical Key Reader [*Automotive engineering*]

OKR .... Royal Military College of Canada, Kingston, Ontario [*Library symbol National Library of Canada*] (NLC)

OKRC .... Regiopolis - Notre Dame High School, Kingston, Ontario [*Library symbol National Library of Canada*] (NLC)

Ok Reg .... Oklahoma Register [*A publication*] (AAGC)

OKRGI .... Rutherford and George Island Township Public Library, Killarney, Ontario [*Library symbol National Library of Canada*] (NLC)

OKRS .... Science Engineering Library, Royal Military College of Canada, Kingston, Ontario [*Library symbol National Library of Canada*] (BIB)

OKS .... Ohio Kache Systems Corp.

OKS .... Okanagan Skeena Group Ltd. [*Vancouver Stock Exchange symbol Toronto Stock Exchange symbol*]

OkS .... Oklahoma State University, Stillwater, OK [*Library symbol Library of Congress*] (LCLS)

OKS .... Old King's Scholars Association [*Canterbury, England*]

OKS .... Oshkosh, NE [*Location identifier FAA*] (FAAL)

OKSB .... Southwest Bancorp [*NASDAQ symbol*] (SAG)

OKSBP .... Southwest Bcp 9.2% cm 'A'Pfd [*NASDAQ symbol*] (TTSB)

OkShB .... Oklahoma Baptist University, Shawnee, OK [*Library symbol Library of Congress*] (LCLS)

OKSL .... St. Lawrence College of Applied Arts and Technology, Kingston, Ontario [*Library symbol National Library of Canada*] (NLC)

OKSMG .... Gibson Medical Library, St. Mary's of the Lake Hospital, Kingston, Ontario [*Library symbol National Library of Canada*] (NLC)

OkS-T .... Oklahoma State University Technical Institute Library, Oklahoma City, OK [*Library symbol Library of Congress*] (LCLS)

OkSt .... Stillwater Public Library, Stillwater, OK [*Library symbol Library of Congress*] (LCLS)

OkS-TBO ...... Oklahoma State University Technical Branch, Okmulgee, OK [*Library symbol*] [*Library of Congress*] (LCLS)

OKT .... [*The*] Oakland Terminal Railway [*Later, OTR*] [*AAR code*]

okt .... Oktober [*October*] [*GRM*] (AD)

okt .... Oktyab [*October*] [*Russian*] (AD)

OKT .... Oslo Kommune Tunnelbanekontoret [*Oslo Subway System*] (AD)

OkT .... Tulsa City-County Library System, Tulsa, OK [*Library symbol Library of Congress*] (LCLS)

OKT .... University of Tulsa, Tulsa, OK [*OCLC symbol*] (OCLC)

OKT .... Yoakum, TX [*Location identifier FAA*] (FAAL)

OkTA .... American Association of Petroleum Geologists, Energy Resources Library, Tulsa, OK [*Library symbol*] [*Library of Congress*] (LCLS)

OkTahN .... Northeastern State College, Tahlequah, OK [*Library symbol Library of Congress*] (LCLS)

OkTAm .... AMOCO Production Co., Research Center Geology Library, Tulsa, OK [*Library symbol Library of Congress*] (LCLS)

OkTC .... Ceja Corp., Tulsa, OK [*Library symbol Library of Congress*] (LCLS)

OkTCS .... Cities Service Co., Energy Resources Group, E & P Library, Tulsa, OK [*Library symbol Library of Congress*] (LCLS)

OkTG .... Thomas Gilcrease Institute of American History and Art, Tulsa, OK [*Library symbol Library of Congress*] (LCLS)

OkTGS .... Church of Jesus Christ of Latter-Day Saints, Genealogical Society Library, TulsaBranch, Tulsa, OK [*Library symbol Library of Congress*] (LCLS)

OkTo .... Tonkawa Public Library, Tonkawa, OK [*Library symbol Library of Congress*] (LCLS)

OkTOR .... Oral Roberts University, Learning Resources Center, Tulsa, OK [*Library symbol Library of Congress*] (LCLS)

OkTPA .... Pan American Oil Corp., Research Library, Tulsa, OK [*Library symbol Library of Congress*] (LCLS)

OkTPh .... Philbrook Art Center, Tulsa, OK [*Library symbol*] [*Library of Congress*] (LCLS)

Oktronics ..... Oklahoma Electronics (AD)

OkTU .... University of Tulsa, Tulsa, OK [*Library symbol Library of Congress*] (LCLS)

OkTU-L .... University of Tulsa, College of Law, Tulsa, OK [*Library symbol Library of Congress*] (LCLS)

oku .... Oklahoma [*MARC country of publication code Library of Congress*] (LCCP)

OKU .... Omicron Kappa Upsilon [*Fraternity*]

OkU .... University of Oklahoma, Norman, OK [*Library symbol Library of Congress*] (LCLS)

OkU-C .... University of Oklahoma, Communication Department, Political Communications Center, Political Commercial Archives, Norman, OK [*Library symbol*] [*Library of Congress*] (LCLS)

OkU-L .... University of Oklahoma, Law School, Norman, OK [*Library symbol Library of Congress*] (LCLS)

OkU-M .... University of Oklahoma, Health Sciences Center, Oklahoma City, OK [*Library symbol Library of Congress*] (LCLS)

OkU-P .... University of Oklahoma, College of Pharmacy, Norman, OK [*Library symbol Library of Congress*] (LCLS)

OKUTD .... Urban Transportation Development Corp., Kingston, Ontario [*Library symbol National Library of Canada*] (NLC)

OkU-TM .... University of Oklahoma, Tulsa Medical College, Tulsa, OK [*Library symbol Library of Congress*] (LCLS)

OkU-W .... University of Oklahoma, Western History Collections, Norman, OK [*Library symbol*] [*Library of Congress*] (LCLS)

OKV .... University of Oklahoma, Library School, Norman, OK [*OCLC symbol*] (OCLC)

OKW .... Brookwood, AL [*Location identifier FAA*] (FAAL)

OKW .... Oberkommando der Wehrmacht [*Armed Forces High Command*] [*German military - World War II*]

OKW .... University of Tulsa, College of Law, Tulsa, OK [*OCLC symbol*] (OCLC)

OK W/C .... Okay Except for [*with*] the Corrections [*Proofreading*] (WDMC)

OkWeaT .... Southwestern State College, Weatherford, OK [*Library symbol Library of Congress*] (LCLS)

OkWo .... Woodward Carnegie Library, Woodward, OK [*Library symbol Library of Congress*] (LCLS)

OKX .... Central State University, Edmond, OK [*OCLC symbol*] (OCLC)

OKXS .... Xenotech Systems, Inc., Kitchener, Ontario [*Library symbol National Library of Canada*] (NLC)

OKY .... Oakey [*Queensland*] [*Airport symbol*] (AD)

OKY .... Oklahoma City University, Law Library, Oklahoma City, OK [*OCLC symbol*] (OCLC)

OKZ .... Phillips University, Zollars Memorial Library, Enid, OK [*OCLC symbol*] (OCLC)

OKZ .... Sandersville, GA [*Location identifier FAA*] (FAAL)

OL .... London Public Library, Ontario [*Library symbol National Library of Canada*] (NLC)

O/L .... Observation/Losing [*Army*] (ADDR)

OL .... Occupational Level

OL .... Ocean Letter

OL .... October League

ol .... Oculus Laevus [*Left Eye*] [*Latin*] (AD)

OL .... Oculus Laevus [*Left Eye*] [*Ophthalmology*]

OL .... Odd Lot [*Stock exchange term*]

OL .... Office Lady [*Japan*] (ECON)

OL .... Officer of the Order of Leopold

OL .... Official Liquidator [*British*] (ROG)

OL .... Ohio Laws [*A publication*] (DLA)

ol .... Oil [*Pharmacy*] (CPH)

OL .... Oil Level (AAG)

ol .... Oil Level (AD)

OL .... Oil Lighter [*Shipping*] [*British*]

OL .... Oiseau-Lyre [*Record label*] [*France*]

OL .... Oldham [*Postcode*] (ODBW)

OL .... Old Latin [*Language, etc.*]

Ol .... Oldradus da Ponte de Laude [*Deceased, 1335*] [*Authority cited in pre-1607 legal work*] (DSA)

OL .... Oleum [*Oil*] [*Pharmacy*]

ol .... Oleum [*Oil*] [*Latin*] (AD)

OL .... Oligoblastic Leukemia [*Oncology*]

OL .... Olivary [*Neurology*]

ol .... Olive [*Philately*]

ol .... Olive [*Political party*] (AD)

ol .... Olivine [*CIPW classification*] [*Geology*]

OL .... Olsen Line (AD)

OL .... Olympian [*of Pindar*] [*Classical studies*] (OCD)

OL .... Olympic

OL .... Olympic Lift [*Sports*]

OL .... Online

OL .... Only Loadable [*Computer science*] (IAA)

OL .... Open Learning (AIE)

OL .... Open Loop

OL .... Operating Level (IEEE)

OL .... Operating License

ol .... Operating License (AD)

OL .... Operating Location [*Army*]

OL .... Operating Log

OL .... Operating Loss

OL .... Operational Left

OL .... Operation Liftoff (EA)

O/L .... Operations/Logistics

o/l .... Operations/Logistics (AD)

OL .... Orbital Launch

OL .... Order of Lafayette (EA)

OL .... Ordinary Leave [*Military*] (AFM)

OL .... Ordnance Lieutenant [*Navy British*]

OL .... Organization List (MCD)

OL .... Original Learning [*Psychometrics*]

OL .... Or Less

ol .... Or Less (AD)

OL .... Oscillating Limiter (IAA)

OL .... Ostfriesische Lufttransport GmbH [*Germany ICAO designator*] (ICDA)

OL .... Other Line [*Telecommunications*] (TEL)

OL .... Outgoing Letter

o/l .... Outlook (AD)

OL .... Output Latch

OL .... Outside Left [*Soccer position*]

OL.............. Overflow Level
OL.............. Overhead Line
OL.............. Overlap
OL.............. Overlay (NASA)
OL.............. Overload
O/L............. Overload
OL.............. Overload
OLA............ Lakefield Public Library, Ontario [*Library symbol National Library of Canada*] (NLC)
OLA............ National Oceanic and Atmospheric Administration, Rockville, MD [*OCLC symbol*] (OCLC)
OLA............ Occipitolaeva Anterior [*A fetal position*] [*Medicine*] (AAMN)
ola............. Occipito-Laeva Anterior (AD)
OLA............ Occupiers' Liability Act [*1957*] [*British*] (DCTA)
OLA............ Office of Legislative Affairs
OLA............ Office of Legislative Analysis [*Environmental Protection Agency*] (GFGA)
OLA............ Official Languages Act [*Canada*]
OLA............ Ohio Law Abstract [*A publication*] (DLA)
OLA............ Ohio Library Association (AD)
OLA............ Oklahoma Library Association (AD)
OLA............ Oligonucleotide Ligation Assay [*Analytical biochemistry*]
OLA............ Ontario Library Association [*Canada*] (AD)
OLA............ Optical Laboratories Association (EA)
OLA............ Optical Link in the Atmosphere (PDAA)
OLA............ Optimally Localized Averages [*Mathematics*]
OLA............ Orbital Lock Assembly
OLA............ Orland [*Norway*] [*Airport symbol*] (OAG)
OLA............ Osteopathic Libraries Association [*Defunct*] (EA)
OLA............ Overview Latin America (EA)
OLAA.......... Office of Legal Aid Administration
OL Abs........ Ohio Law Abstract [*A publication*] (DLA)
OLAC.......... Offline Adaptive Computer [*Computer science*]
OLAC.......... Online Audiovisual Catalogers [*An association*] (EA)
OLADE........ Organizacion Latin-Americana de Energia [*Latin American Energy Organization*] [*Spanish*] (AD)
OLAFL......... Front of Leeds and Lansdowne Public Library, Lansdowne, Ontario [*Library symbol National Library of Canada*] (NLC)
OLAFS........ Office of Legal Aid and Family Services
OLAFS........ Orbiting and Launch Approach Flight Simulator
OLAG......... London Research Center, Agriculture Canada [*Centre de Recherches de London, Agriculture Canada*] London, Ontario [*Library symbol National Library of Canada*] (NLC)
OLAG......... Oesterreichische Luftverkehrs Aktiengesellschaft [*Austrian Airlines*]
OLak.......... Lakewood Public Library, Lakewood, OH [*Library symbol Library of Congress*] (LCLS)
OLakB........ Lakewood Board of Education, Lakewood, OH [*Library symbol Library of Congress*] (LCLS)
OLAL.......... Bibliotheque Publique du Canton d'Alfred [*Alfred Township Public Library*],Lefaivre, Ontario [*Library symbol National Library of Canada*] (BIB)
OLAMINE.... Ethanolamine [*Also, EA, Etn*] [*USAN*] [*Organic chemistry*]
OLAN......... Landsdowne Public Library, Ontario [*Library symbol National Library of Canada*] (BIB)
OLA-N........ Office of Legislative Affairs, Navy (MUGU)
OLAN......... On-Board Local Area Network [*Aviation*]
O/LAND....... Overland
O/LANDED ... Overlanded
OL & T........ Owners, Landlords, and Tenants [*Liability insurance*]
ol & t......... Owners, Landlords, and Tenants (AD)
OLanF........ Fairfield County District Library, Lancaster, OH [*Library symbol Library of Congress*] (LCLS)
OLanU .... Ohio University, Lancaster Branch Campus, Lancaster, OH [*Library symbol Library of Congress*] (LCLS)
OLAP......... Online Analytical Processing [*Computer science*] (CDE)
OLAPEC ...... Organization of Latin American Petroleum Exporting Countries (AD)
OLAR.......... On-Line Analytical Processing [*Computer science*]
OLAS.......... Office of Arid Land Studies [*University of Arizona*] (AD)
OLAS.......... On-Line Acquisitions Systems [*Brodart, Inc.*] [*Book acquisition system*] [*Information service or system*] (IID)
OLAS.......... Organizacion Latino-Americana de Solidaridad [*Latin American Solidarity Organization*] [*Spanish*] (AD)
OLAS.......... Organization of Latin American Students (AD)
OLATN........ Township of Norfolk Public Library, Langton, Ontario [*Library symbol National Library of Canada*] (NLC)
OLAU .... Lanark Union Public Library, Lanark, Ontario [*Library symbol National Library of Canada*] (BIB)
Olav Tryg..... Olav Trygvason (AD)
OLB........... London Board of Education, Ontario [*Library symbol National Library of Canada*] (NLC)
OLB........... Odd-Lot Broker [*Finance*] (MHDW)
OLB........... Oertlicher Landwirtschaftsbetrieb [*Local Agricultural Enterprise*] [*German*]
OLB........... Official Log Book [*Ship's diary*] (DS)
OLB........... Ohio Law Bulletin [*A publication*] (DLA)
OLB........... Olbia [*Italy*] [*Airport symbol*] (OAG)
OLB........... Omaha, Lincoln & Beatrice Railway Co. [*AAR code*]
OLB........... Online Batch (NITA)
OLB........... Open Liver Biopsy [*Medicine*] (DMAA)
OLB........... Open-Loop Bandwidth [*Also, OLBW*]
OLB........... Open Lung Biopsy
OLB........... Outer Lead Bond [*Integrated circuit technology*]
OLB........... Outside Linebacker [*Football*]
OLBA.......... Beirut/International [*Lebanon*] [*ICAO location identifier*] (ICLI)
OLBGFC ...... Official Lane Brody Global Fan Club (EA)

OLBIEN .... Olsen's Biomass Energy [*G. V. Olsen Associates*] [*Information service or system*] (CRD)
olbm.......... Orbital Launched Balistic Missile (AD)
OLBM......... Orbital Launched Ballistic Missile [*Military*] (WDAA)
OLBM......... Overlay Battle Manager
OLBR .... Brescia College, London, Ontario [*Library symbol National Library of Canada*] (NLC)
OlBr .... Olive Brown (AD)
OLBR .... Operational LASER Beam Recorder
OLBS .... OnLine Bookstore
OLBV .... Beirut [*Lebanon*] [*ICAO location identifier*] (ICLI)
OLBW .... Open-Loop Bandwidth [*Also, OLB*]
olc............ Brothers of Our Lady of Providence (TOCD)
OLC........... Catholic Central High School, London, Ontario [*Library symbol National Library of Canada*] (NLC)
OLC........... Linfield College, McMinnville, OR [*OCLC symbol*] (OCLC)
OLC........... Oak Leaf Cluster [*Military decoration*]
OLC........... Office of Legal Counsel [*Department of Justice*]
Olc............ Olcott's United States District Court Reports, Admiralty [*A publication*] (DLA)
OLC........... Olema [*California*] [*Seismograph station code, US Geological Survey*] (SEIS)
OLC........... Oneida, TN [*Location identifier FAA*] (FAAL)
OLC........... Online Computer [*System*] [*Computer science*]
olc............ On-Line Computer (AD)
OLC........... Ontario Ladies College
OLC........... Ontario Library Co-Operative [*UTLAS symbol*]
OLC........... Operation Load Code (MCD)
OLC........... Operator-Level Chart (AFIT)
OLC........... Order Location and Control (MCD)
OLC........... Oubain-Like Compound [*Biochemistry*]
OLC........... Outgoing Line Circuit
OLC........... Overseas Liaison Committee [*of the American Council on Education*] [*Later, Division of International Educational Relations of the American Council on Education*] (EA)
OLC........... Sisters of Our Lady of Charity (TOCD)
OLCA .... Online Circuit Analysis [*System*] [*Computer science*]
Olc Adm ...... Olcott's United States District Court Reports, Admiralty [*A publication*] (DLA)
OLCAO .... Orthogonalized Linear Combination of Atomic Orbitals [*Optics*]
OLCC .... Ontario Cancer Clinic, London, Ontario [*Library symbol National Library of Canada*] (NLC)
OLCC .... Optimum Life Cycle Costing (PDAA)
olcc.......... Optimum Life-Cycle Costing (AD)
OLCC .... Ordinary Low Current Configuration [*Magnetic field*]
OLCC .... Our Lady of Cincinnati College [*Ohio*]
OLCC .... Overseas Labour Consultative Committee [*British*] (DCTA)
OLCD .... Overseas Liaison and Consultancy Department (NITA)
OLCG .... Clarkson Gordon, London, Ontario [*Library symbol National Library of Canada*] (BIB)
OLCM......... Olicom AS [*NASDAQ symbol*] (SAG)
OLCMF....... Olicom A/S [*NASDAQ symbol*] (TTSB)
Ol Conv....... Oliver's Conveyancing [*A publication*] (DLA)
Olcott........ Olcott's United States District Court Reports, Admiralty [*A publication*] (DLA)
Olcott Adm (F)... Olcott's United States District Court Reports, Admiralty [*A publication*] (DLA)
Olcott's Adm... Olcott's United States District Court Reports, Admiralty [*A publication*] (DLA)
OLCP......... Online Complex Processing [*Computer science*] (CDE)
OLCPR........ Canadian Peace Research Institute, London, Ontario [*Library symbol National Library of Canada*] (NLC)
OLCR .... Clark Road Secondary School, London, Ontario [*Library symbol National Library of Canada*] (NLC)
O L Cr......... Ordinance Lieutenent-Commander (AD)
OLCR .... Ordnance Lieutenant-Commander [*Navy British*]
OLCR .... Sisters of Our Lady of Charity of Refuge [*Roman Catholic religious order*]
OLCS .... On-Line Computer System (AD)
OLCSSCP.... Children's Psychiatric Research Institute, Ontario Ministry of Community and Social Services, London, Ontario [*Library symbol National Library of Canada*] (NLC)
OLCT.......... Tax Services, Canada Trust Co., London, Ontario [*Library symbol National Library of Canada*] (BIB)
OLCV .... Century Village, Lang, Ontario [*Library symbol National Library of Canada*] (BIB)
OLD .... Odd Lot Dealer
OLD .... Office of Legislative Development [*Bureau of Indian Affairs*]
OLD .... Ohio Lower Court Decisions [*A publication*] (DLA)
Old............ Oldradus da Ponte de Laude [*Deceased, 1335*] [*Authority cited in pre-1607 legal work*] (DSA)
Old............ Oldright's Nova Scotia Reports [*A publication*] (DLA)
OLD .... Old Town, ME [*Location identifier FAA*] (FAAL)
OLD .... Online Debug [*Computer science*] (IAA)
OLD .... Open-Loop Damping
OLD .... Operating Level Days
OLD .... Operations and Liquidations Division [*Federal Savings and Loans Insurance Corporation*]
OLD .... Our Lady of Deliverance Syriac, Union City [*Diocesan abbreviation*] [*New Jersey*] (TOCD)
OLD .... Oxford Latin Dictionary [*A publication*]
OldAmer...... Old America Stores, Inc. [*Associated Press*] (SAG)
OLDAP........ Online Data Processor (PDAA)
OLDB .... Old National Bancorp [*NASDAQ symbol*] (NQ)
OLDB .... Old Natl Bancorp(Ind) [*NASDAQ symbol*] (TTSB)

OLDB .... Online Database [or Data Bank]

Old Bailey ... London's Central Criminal Court [England] (AD)

Old Bailey Chr... Old Bailey Chronicle [A publication] (DLA)

Old Ben .... Benloe in Benloe and Dalison's English Common Pleas Reports [A publication] (DLA)

Old Benloe... Benloe in Benloe and Dalison's English Common Pleas Reports [A publication] (DLA)

OLDC .... Online Data Collection [Computer science] (MCD)

OLDD .... Beirut [Lebanon] [ICAO location identifier] (ICLI)

OldDom .... Old Dominion Freight Lines, Inc. [Associated Press] (SAG)

Old Dom U... Old Dominion University (GAGS)

OLD ECC..... Ordinary Linear Differential Equations with Constant Coefficients [Mathematics]

Old Ent .... Rastell's Old Entries [A publication] (DLA)

OLDERT ...... On-Line Executive for Real-Time [Computer science] (MHDB)

old-fash ...... Old Fashioned (AD)

Oldfos .... Old Established Forces (AD)

OLDFOS ...... Old Established Forces [Military] (CINC)

OLDHM .... Oldham [City in England]

OLDI .... Online Data Interchange (DA)

OLDIV .... Operations/Lookout and Recognition Division (DNAB)

OldKent....... Old Kent Financial Corp. [Associated Press] (SAG)

Old Maid's ... Old Maid's Day [June 4] (AD)

Old Nat Brev... Old Natura Brevium [A publication] (DLA)

OldNB .... Old National Bancorp Industries [Associated Press] (SAG)

Oldn Pr........ Oldnall's Sessions Practice [A publication] (DLA)

Oldr .... Oldradus da Ponte de Laude [Deceased, 1335] [Authority cited in pre-1607 legal work] (DSA)

Oldr .... Oldright's Nova Scotia Reports [A publication] (DLA)

Oldra .... Oldradus da Ponte de Laude [Deceased, 1335] [Authority cited in pre-1607 legal work] (DSA)

Oldra de Lau... Oldradus da Ponte de Laude [Deceased, 1335] [Authority cited in pre-1607 legal work] (DSA)

old rep........ Old Repertory (AD)

OldRep .... Old Republic International Corp. [Associated Press] (SAG)

Oldr NS....... Oldright's Nova Scotia Reports [A publication] (DLA)

OldRp .... Old Republic International Corp. [Associated Press] (SAG)

OLDS .... Off-Axis LASER Detection System (MCD)

OLDS .... Offshore Lease Data System [Department of the Interior] [Information service or system] (IID)

OLDS .... Oldsmobile [Automotive engineering]

Olds .... Oldsmobile (AD)

OLDS .... On-Line Detection System [Nuclear energy]

OLDS SC ..... Online Display System [Computer science]

Old SC .... Old Select Cases [Oudh, India] [A publication] (DLA)

OldSecBc .... Old Second Bancorp, Inc. [Associated Press] (SAG)

OLDSS .... Online Database Search Services Directory [A publication]

Old Test...... Old Testament (AD)

OLE .... Lane Community College, Eugene, OR [OCLC symbol] (OCLC)

OLE .... Leamington Public Library, Ontario [Library symbol National Library of Canada] (NLC)

OLe .... Lebanon Public Library, Lebanon, OH [Library symbol Library of Congress] (LCLS)

OLE .... Object Linking and Embedding [Windows] [Computer science]

OLE .... Office for Library Education [American Library Association]

OLE .... Olean [New York] [Airport symbol] (AD)

OLE .... Olean, NY [Location identifier FAA] (FAAL)

OLE .... On-Line Encyclopedia [Hypergraphics Corp.]

OLE .... Online Enquiry [System]

OLE .... Ontario Land Economist [Canada] (DD)

OLE .... Oral Language Evaluation [English and Spanish test]

OLE .... Organizational Leadership for Executives [Military] (RDA)

OLE .... Oriole Communication [Vancouver Stock Exchange symbol]

OLE .... Outside Location Engineer (MCD)

OLEA .... Office of Law Enforcement Assistance (AD)

OLeC.......... Lebanon Correctional Institution Library, Lebanon, OH [Library symbol Library of Congress] (LCLS)

Oleck Corporations... Oleck's Modern Corporation Law [A publication] (DLA)

OLED .... Organic Light-Emitting Device [Photonics]

OLED .... Organic Light Emitting Diode [Electronics]

OLE DB .... OLE Database [Computer science]

O Legal News... Ohio Legal News [A publication] (DLA)

OLEI............ Point Pelee National Park, Parks Canada [Parc National de la Pointe-Pelee, Parcs Canada] Leamington, Ontario [Library symbol National Library of Canada] (NLC)

OLELB......... Lyn Branch, Elizabethtown Township Public Library, Ontario [Library symbol National Library of Canada] (BIB)

OLEM.......... Other Loans Especially Mentioned (TDOB)

oleo .... Oleomargarine [Dietetics] (DAVI)

oleo .... Oleoresins (AD)

OLEP.......... Office of Law Enforcement and Planning (AD)

OLEP.......... Office of Law Enforcement and Planning (NADA)

OLEP.......... Office of Law Enforcement Programs [Federal government]

OLEP.......... Office of Legal Enforcement Policy [Environmental Protection Agency] (EPA)

OLEP.......... Organization for the Lifelong Establishment of Paternity (EA)

OLER .... Olericulture

olericult....... Olericulture (AD)

OLERT .... Online Executive for Real Time [Computer science] (IEEE)

OLES.......... Online Editorial System [Computer science] (DGA)

OLESS .... Open Learning Electronic Support Services [Australia]

O level........ Ordinary Level [ODBW]

O-levels...... Ordinary Levels [of educational tests] (AD)

OLeWHi...... Warren County Historical Society, Lebanon, OH [Library symbol Library of Congress] (LCLS)

OLF............ Ohio Library Foundation (AD)

OLF............ Old Low Franconian [Language, etc.]

olf............... Olfactory [Medicine] (DAVI)

OLF............ Online Filing [Computer science] (PDAA)

olf............... On-Line Filing (AD)

OLF............ Only Living Father [of Newfoundland's confederation with Canada in 1949] [Epithet for Joseph R. Smallwood]

OLF............ Open Learning Federation [British] (DI)

OLF............ Orbital Launch Facility

OLF............ Orbiter Landing Facility [NASA] (NASA)

OLF............ Organ Literature Foundation (EA)

OLF............ Oromo Liberation Front [Ethiopia] [Political party] (PD)

OLF............ Outline Font [Computer science] (PCM)

OLF............ Outlying Field [Army]

OLF............ Wolf Point [Montana] [Airport symbol] (OAG)

OLF............ Wolf Point, MT [Location identifier FAA] (FAAL)

OLFC.......... Fanshawe College of Applied Arts and Technology, London, Ontario [Library symbol National Library of Canada] (NLC)

OLFDEMO... Outline Font Demonstration [Computer science]

OLFO.......... Open-Loop Feedback Optimal (PDAA)

OLG............ Nordmaling [Sweden] [Airport symbol] (AD)

OLG............ Oberlandesgericht [District Court of Appeal] [German] (DLA)

OLG............ Ohio Legislative Service Commission, Columbus, OH [OCLC symbol] (OCLC)

OLG............ Old Low German [Language, etc.]

OLG............ Oligodendrocyte [Also, ODC] [Cytology]

OIG............ Olive Green (AD)

OLG............ Open-Loop Gain

OLG............ Sisters of Guadalupe [Roman Catholic religious order]

OLG............ Sisters of Our Lady of the Garden [Roman Catholic religious order]

OLGA.......... On-line Guitar Archive [Internet site]

OLGC.......... Orthologic Corp. [NASDAQ symbol] (SAG)

OLGR.......... [The] Oilgear Co. [NASDAQ symbol] (NQ)

OLH............ Huron College, London, Ontario [Library symbol National Library of Canada] (NLC)

OLH............ Old Harbor [Alaska] [Airport symbol] (OAG)

OLH............ Old Harbor, AK [Location identifier FAA] (FAAL)

OLH............ Orpen's Light Horse [British military] (DMA)

OLH............ Ovine Lactogenic Hormone [Endocrinology] (MAE)

OLH............ Ovine Luteinizing Hormone [Endocrinology]

OLH............ Oxfordshire Light Horse [British military] (DMA)

OLHC.......... Old Lyme Holding Corp. [NASDAQ symbol] (SAG)

OLHM .... London Historical Museums, Ontario [Library symbol National Library of Canada] (BIB)

OLHMIS .... On-Line Hospital Management Information System [Computer science]

Ol Horse ...... Oliphant's Law of Horses [6th ed.] [1908] [A publication] (DLA)

OLI............. Lindsay Public Library, Ontario [Library symbol National Library of Canada] (NLC)

OLI............. Ocean Living Institute [Defunct] (EA)

OLI............. Olafsvik [Iceland] [Airport symbol] (OAG)

OLI............. Oliktok, AK [Location identifier FAA] (FAAL)

Oli.............. Oliver (AD)

OLI............. Online Information

OLI............. Open Learning Institute [UTLAS symbol]

OLI............. Open Link Interface (TNIG)

OLI............. Out-of-Line Igniter [Military] (CAAL)

OLI............. Out-of-Line Interrupter (MCD)

OLI............. Overlay Interceptor

OLI............. Oxfordshire Light Infantry [Military unit] [British]

OLiC............ Columbiana County Court House, Lisbon, OH [Library symbol Library of Congress] (LCLS)

OLIC........... Online Information Centre (NITA)

OL-IC.......... Operating Location-Iceland (DNAB)

O-license .... Operator's License (AD)

Olicom........ Olicom AS [Associated Press] (SAG)

OLICU......... Little Current Public Library, Ontario [Library symbol National Library of Canada] (NLC)

OLICUS .... Sucker Creek Indian Band Public Library, Little Current, Ontario [Library symbol National Library of Canada] (NLC)

OLIDS......... Open Loop Insulin Delivery System [Medicine] (DMAA)

OLIF........... Orbiter Landing Instrumentation Facilities [NASA] (NASA)

OLIFLM....... Online Image Forming Light Modulator

Olig............ Oligocene (AD)

OLIH........... Lion's Head Branch, Bruce County Public Library, Ontario [Library symbol National Library of Canada] (NLC)

OLIM........... Olimpiadas [Ministerio de Cultura] [Spain Information service or system] (CRD)

OLima......... Lima Public Library, Lima, OH [Library symbol Library of Congress] (LCLS)

OLimaAL..... Allen County Law Library, Lima, OH [Library symbol Library of Congress] (LCLS)

OLIMCH ...... Open Learning Information and Materials Clearing House [Australia]

Olin............ Olin Corp. [Associated Press] (SAG)

OLIP........... Online Instrument Package [Computer science] (NRCH)

Oliph Hor .... Oliphant's Law of Horses [6th ed.] [1908] [A publication] (DLA)

OLIS........... Listowel Public Library, Ontario [Library symbol National Library of Canada] (NLC)

OLIS........... Online Information Services [Mercer County Community College Library] (OLDSS)

OLIS........... Oregon Legislative Information System [Information service or system]

OLIS........... Oxford Library Information System (TNIG)

OLIS........... Oxide Layer Isolation Structure

OLISF........... Frost Campus Library, Sir Sandford Fleming College, Lindsay, Ontario [Library symbol National Library of Canada] (NLC)

OLIT............. OPEN LOOK Intrinsic Toolkit

OLitW.......... Wagnalls Memorial Library, Lithopolis, OH [Library symbol Library of Congress] (LCLS)

OLIV............ Oleum Olivae [Olive Oil] [Pharmacy] (ROG)

OLIV............ Victoria County Public Library, Lindsay, Ontario [Library symbol National Library of Canada] (NLC)

Oliv B & L... Oliver, Beavan, and Lefroy's English Railway and Canal Cases [A publication] (DLA)

Oliv Conv..... Oliver's Conveyancing [A publication] (DLA)

Olive............ Olivera (AD)

OLIVER........ Online Instrumentation via Energetic Radioisotopes [Computer science] (PDAA)

OLIVER........ Online Interactive Variable Editing Reporter [Computer science] (IAA)

Olivet Naz U... Olivet Nazarene University (GAGS)

Oliv Prec .... Oliver's Precedents [A publication] (DLA)

OLIVW .... Walden Public Library, Lively, Ontario [Library symbol National Library of Canada] (BIB)

OLJ............. Ohio Law Journal [A publication] (DLA)

OLJ............. Order of St. Lazarus of Jerusalem [British]

OLJ............. Oudh Law Journal [India] [A publication] (DLA)

OLJ............. Spokane, WA [Location identifier FAA] (FAAL)

OL Jour....... Ohio Law Journal [A publication] (DLA)

OL Jour....... Oudh Law Journal [India] [A publication] (DLA)

OLK............. King's College, London, Ontario [Library symbol National Library of Canada] (NLC)

OLK............. Salomon, Inc. [AMEX symbol] (SPSG)

OLK............. Salomon Inc, 7.25% ORCL'ELKS' [AMEX symbol] (TTSB)

OLK............. Wolf Lake, IN [Location identifier FAA] (FAAL)

OLKK .... Tripoli [Lebanon] [ICAO location identifier] (ICLI)

OLKV .... Tripoli [Lebanon] [ICAO location identifier] (ICLI)

OLL............. Larder Lake Public Library, Ontario [Library symbol National Library of Canada] (BIB)

OLL............. Office of Legislative Liaison (AD)

OLL............. Ollague [Chile] [Seismograph station code, US Geological Survey Closed] (SEIS)

OLL............. Organic Liquid LASER

OLL............. Our Lady of Lebanon of Los Angeles [Diocesan abbreviation] [California] (TOCD)

OLL............. Output Logic Level

OLLA........... Office of Lend-Lease Administration [World War II]

OLLA........... Oil Lands Leasing Act

Oll B & F... Ollivier, Bell, and Fitzgerald's New Zealand Reports [A publication] (DLA)

OLLC........... Office of the Liquor Licensing Commissioner [South Australia]

OLLC........... Our Lady of the Lake College [Texas]

OLLCR .... Labatt's Central Research Library, London, Ontario [Library symbol National Library of Canada] (NLC)

OLLE........... Lake Erie Regional Library System, London, Ontario [Library symbol National Library of Canada] (NLC)

OLLE........... Ontario Library Service - Thames, London, Ontario [Library symbol National Library of Canada] (NLC)

OLLI............ Online Library Index [Western Michigan University]

OLLIE.......... Operation Last Laugh Independence Expenditure [Political Action Committee opposed to Oliver North's candidacy for United States Senator of Virginia]

OL LINI SI ... Oleum Lini sine Igne [Cold-Drawn Linseed Oil] [Pharmacy] (ROG)

Olliv B & F... Ollivier, Bell, and Fitzgerald's New Zealand Reports [A publication] (DLA)

OLLL........... Beirut [Lebanon] [ICAO location identifier] (ICLI)

OLLS........... Online Logical Simulation System [Computer science] (KSC)

OLLT........... Office of Libraries and Learning Technologies (NITA)

OLLU .... Our Lady of the Lake University [Texas]

OLM............ Lloyd Library and Museum, Cincinnati, OH [OCLC symbol] (OCLC)

OLM............ Office for Laboratory Management [DoD] (MCD)

OLM............ Olympia [Washington] [Airport symbol] (AD)

OLM............ Olympia, WA [Location identifier FAA] (FAAL)

OLM............ Olympic Financial Ltd [NYSE symbol] (TTSB)

OLM............ Online Monitor [Computer science]

OLM............ Organic Leach Model [Landfill technology]

OLM............ Sisters of Charity of Our Lady of Mercy [Roman Catholic religious order]

OLMAT........ Otis Lennon Mental Ability Test (EDAC)

OLMC.......... Output Logic Macrocell [Computer science]

OLMR.......... Office of Labor Management Relations (AD)

OLMR.......... Organic Liquid Moderated Reactor

olmr............ Organic Liquid-Moderator Reactor (AD)

Olms........... Decisions of the Judicial Committee of the Privy Council re the British North American Act, 1867, and the Canadian Constitution [A publication] (DLA)

OLMS.......... Office of Labor-Management Standards [Department of Labor]

OLMS.......... Osborn Laboratories of Marine Sciences [New York Zoological Society] [Research center] (RCD)

Olmsted...... Olmsted's Privy Council Decisions [1867-1954] [A publication] (DLA)

OLMT.......... Organizational Level Maintenance Timer

OLMUG........ Online Librarian's Microcomputer User Group [Teleconferencing system]

OLMWPR.... Office of Labor-Management and Welfare-Pension Reports [Department of Labor]

OLN .... Colonia Sarmiento [Argentina] [Airport symbol] (AD)

OLN .... Lane Public Library, Hamilton, OH [OCLC symbol] (OCLC)

OLN .... Ohio Legal News [A publication] (DLA)

OLN .... Old Man, AK [Location identifier FAA] (FAAL)

OLN .... Olin Corp. [NYSE symbol] (TTSB)

OLN .... Online News (NITA)

OLO .... Longlac Public Library, Ontario [Library symbol National Library of Canada] (NLC)

OLO .... Olomouc [Czechoslovakia] [Airport symbol] (AD)

OLO .... Olotillo [Race of maize]

OLO .... Online Operation [Computer science]

OLO .... Oologah [Oklahoma] [Seismograph station code, US Geological Survey Closed] (SEIS)

OLO .... Operations Launch Order (MUGU)

OLO .... Orbital Launch Operation

OLOC........... Old Lesbians Organizing for Change [An association] (EA)

OLOE........... Online Order Entry

OLOF........... Levack Branch, Onaping Falls Public Library, Ontario [Library symbol National Library of Canada] (NLC)

Olofson........ Olofsson Corp. [Associated Press] (SAG)

OLOFV......... Olofsson Corp. [NASDAQ symbol] (SAG)

OLOG........... Offshore Logistics [NASDAQ symbol] (TTSB)

OLOG........... Offshore Logistics, Inc. [NASDAQ symbol] (NQ)

OLogC.......... Logan-Hocking County District Library, Logan, OH [Library symbol Library of Congress] (LCLS)

OLOGP......... Offshore Logistics, Inc. (MHDW)

OLOGS......... Open-Loop Oxygen-Generating System [Air Force]

ol ol............. Olive Oil (AD)

ol oliv........... Oleum Olivae [Olive Oil] [Pharmacy] (AD)

OLOM.......... Orbiter Lift-Off Mass [NASA] (KSC)

OLor............ Lorain Public Library, Lorain, OH [Library symbol Library of Congress] (LCLS)

OLOS .... Oakridge Secondary School, London, Ontario [Library symbol National Library of Canada] (NLC)

OLOS .... Office for Library Outreach Service [American Library Association]

OLOS .... Out of Line of Sight (NATG)

olos .... Out of Line of Sight (AD)

OLou............ Loudonville Public Library, Loudonville, OH [Library symbol Library of Congress] (LCLS)

OLOW .... Orbiter Lift-Off Weight [NASA]

olow............ Orbiter Liftoff Weight (AD)

O Lower D ... Ohio Lower Court Decisions [A publication] (DLA)

OLP............. Brothers of Our Lady of Providence (TOCD)

OLP............. Lewis and Clark College, Portland, OR [OCLC symbol] (OCLC)

OLP............. Missionaries of the Third Order of St. Francis of Our Lady of the Prairies [Roman Catholic women's religious order]

OLP............. Observation Landplane [Coast Guard]

OLP............. Occipitolaeva Posterior [A fetal position] [Medicine] (AAMN)

olp............. Occipito-Laeva Posterior (AD)

OLP............. Office of Labor Production [WPB] [World War II]

OLP............. Off-Line Program [Computer science]

OLP............. Olympic Dam [Australia Airport symbol] (OAG)

OLP............. One Liberty Properties [AMEX symbol] (TTSB)

OLP............. One Liberty Properties, Inc. [AMEX symbol] (SPSG)

OLP............. Online Processor (TEL)

OLP............. Online Programming

OLP............. Open Learning Programme (AIE)

OLP............. Optical Line Pair

OLP............. Oral Lichen Plannus [Medicine]

OLP............. Organizacion para la Liberacion Palestina [Palestinian Liberation Organization] [Spanish] [Political party] (AD)

olp............. Original List Price (AD)

OLP............. Outside Left Position [Dancing]

OLP............. Oxygen at Low Pressure (KSC)

OLP............. Oxygen Lance Powder (IAA)

OLP............. Oxygen Lime Powder [Steelmaking process]

OLP............. Sisters of Our Lady of Providence [Roman Catholic religious order]

olpar........... Other Large Phased-Array RADAR (AD)

OLPARS...... Online Pattern Analysis and Recognition System [Computer science] (MCD)

OL/PBAR..... Online Patient Billing and Accounts Receivable System [Computer science] (PDAA)

OLPH .... London Psychiatric Hospital, Ontario [Library symbol National Library of Canada] (NLC)

OLPHS......... Parkwood Hospital Services, London, Ontario [Library symbol National Library of Canada] (BIB)

OLPP .... One Liberty Prop $1.60 Cv Pfd [AMEX symbol] (TTSB)

OLPR .... Office of Library Personnel Resources [American Library Association]

Ol Prec .... Oliver's Precedents [A publication] (DLA)

OLPS .... Online Programming System [Computer science]

OLPT........... Oxford Library of Practical Theology [A publication]

OLPT........... Pinchas Troester Library, Congregation B'Nai Israel, London, Ontario [Library symbol National Library of Canada] (NLC)

OLQ .... Biloxi, MS [Location identifier FAA] (FAAL)

OLQ .... Officer-Like Qualities [British military] (DMA)

olq .... Officer-Like Qualities (AD)

OLQ .... Olsobip [Papua New Guinea] [Airport symbol] (OAG)

OLR .... Oak-Leaf Roller [Moth] [Entomology]

OLR .... Objective Loudness Rating [of telephone connections] (IEEE)

OLR .... Office Loop Repeater (MHDB)

OLR .... Office of Labor Racketeering [Department of Labor]

OLR .... Office of Legislative Reference [Bureau of the Budget; later, OMB]

OLR .... Offline Reader [Bulletin board]

OLR .... Offline Recovery [Telecommunications] (TEL)

OLR .... Off Load Route [Aviation] (DA)

OLR .... Ohio Law Reporter [A publication] (DLA)

O-LR .... Ohio Legislative Reference Bureau, Columbus, OH [Library symbol Library of Congress] (LCLS)

OLR .... On-Line Research, Inc. [Information service or system] (IID)

OLR .... On Location Repair (MCD)

OLR .... Ontario Law Reporter [*A publication*] (DLA)
OLR .... Ontario Law Reports [*A publication*] (DLA)
OLR .... Open-Loop Receiver [*or Response*]
OLR .... Operator's Local Representative (AIA)
OLR .... Organisation pour la Liberation du Rwanda [*Organization for the Liberation of Rwanda*]
OLR .... Oudh Law Reports [*India*] [*A publication*] (DLA)
OLR .... Outgoing Long-Wave Radiation [*Satellite sensed*]
OLR .... Overload Relay
olr .... Overload Relay (AD)
OLR .... Robarts School Library, London, Ontario [*Library symbol National Library of Canada*] (BIB)
OLRAG .... London Regional Art Gallery, Ontario [*Library symbol National Library of Canada*] (NLC)
OLRB .... Ontario Labor Relations Board [*Canada*] (AD)
OLRB .... Ontario Labour Relations Board Monthly Report [*A publication*] (DLA)
O/L-RC .... Overload-Reverse Current [*NASA*]
OL Rep .... Ohio Law Reporter [*A publication*] (DLA)
OI Res .... Oleoresin [*Also, OR*] [*Pharmacy*]
ol res .... Oleoresin (AD)
OLRI .... Office & Factory, Rochevert Industrie, Inc., Lindsay, Ontario [*Library symbol National Library of Canada*] (NLC)
OL RIC .... Oleum Ricini [*Castor Oil*] [*Pharmacy*] (ROG)
OLRL .... Lyndhurst Branch, Rideau Lakes Union Library, Ontario [*Library symbol National Library of Canada*] (BIB)
OLRM .... Medical Library, Ross Memorial Hospital, Lindsay, Ontario [*Library symbol National Library of Canada*] (BIB)
OLRS .... Optical LASER Ranging System
OLRT .... Online Real Time [*Computer science*]
olrt .... On-Line Real Time [*Computer science*] (AD)
OLRV .... Olive Latent Ringspot Virus [*Plant pathology*]
OLS .... Nogales, AZ [*Location identifier FAA*] (FAAL)
OLS .... Office of Legal Services [*of Office of Economic Opportunity*]
OLS .... Office of Library Services (AAGC)
OLS .... OLS Asia Holdings Ltd. [*Associated Press*] (SAG)
OLS .... Olsten Corp. [*NYSE symbol*] (SAG)
OLS .... Online Scan [*Computer science*] (CAAL)
OLS .... Online Search (NITA)
OLS .... Online System [*Computer science*]
OLS .... Ontario Land Surveyor [*Canada*] (DD)
OLS .... Open-Loop System [*Chemical engineering*]
OLS .... Operational Launch Station (AAG)
OLS .... Operational Linescan System [*Navy*] (ANA)
OLS .... Operational Lines of Succession [*Defense readiness*]
OLS .... Operation...Life Support [*Online lobbying for the television show "My So-Called Life"*]
OLS .... Optical Landing System
OLS .... Orbiting Lunar Station [*NASA*]
OLS .... Ordinary Least Squares [*Statistics*]
OLS .... Original Line of Sight
OLS .... Overlap Shear
OLS .... Sisters of Our Lady of Sorrows [*Roman Catholic religious order*]
OLS .... Spartan of Canada Ltd., London, Ontario [*Library symbol National Library of Canada*] (NLC)
OLSA .... Off-Line Selectric Analyser [*Computer science*] (IAA)
OLSA .... OLS Asia Holdings Ltd. [*NASDAQ symbol*] (SAG)
OLSA .... Orbiter Logistics Support Plan [*NASA*]
OLSA .... Orbiter/LPS [*Launch Processing System*] Signal Adapter [*NASA*] (NASA)
OLS AH .... OLS Asia Holdings Ltd. [*Associated Press*] (SAG)
OL'SAM ...... Online Database Search Assistance Machine [*Franklin Institute*] [*Information service or system Defunct*] (IID)
OL'SAM ...... Online Search Assistance Machine (NITA)
OLSASS ...... Online System Availability and Service Simulation [*Computer science*] (PDAA)
OLSAT .... Otis-Lennon School Ability Test [*Education*]
OLSAY .... OLS Asia Hlds ADS [*NASDAQ symbol*] (TTSB)
OLSC .... Online Scientific Computer [*Computer science*]
olsc .... On-Line Scientific Computer (AD)
OLSCA .... Orientation Linkage for a Solar Cell Array
OLSCG .... Latchford Senior Citizens Group, Ontario [*Library symbol National Library of Canada*] (BIB)
OLSD .... Office for Library Service to the Disadvantaged [*American Library Association*]
OLSDG .... Lancaster Branch, Stormont, Dundas, and Glengarry County Library, Ontario [*Library symbol National Library of Canada*] (BIB)
OLSE .... Ordinary Least-Squares Estimators [*Statistics*]
OLSF .... Online Subsystem Facility [*Computer science*] (MCD)
OLSH .... Our Lady of the Sacred Heart (ADA)
OLSIDI-F ..... Oral Language Sentence Imitation Diagnostic Inventory - Format Revised [*Educational test*]
OLSILC .... On the Lighter Side, International Lighter Collectors (EA)
OLSIST-F .... Oral Language Sentence Imitation Screening Test - Format Revised [*Educational test*]
OLSJ .... St. Joseph's Hospital, London, Ontario [*Library symbol National Library of Canada*] (NLC)
OLSOR .... Object Location and Small Object Recovery [*Military*] (DNAB)
OLSP .... Office of Life Science Programs [*Obsolete NASA*]
OLSP .... Operational Logistic Support Plan
OLSP .... Orbiter Logistics Support Plan [*NASA*] (NASA)
OLSP .... Orbiter Logistics Support Plan
OLSP .... St. Peter's Seminary, London, Ontario [*Library symbol National Library of Canada*] (NLC)
OLSS .... Online Software System [*Computer science*] (IEEE)
OLSS .... Operational Logistic Support Summary [*Military*] (CAAL)

OLSS .... Overseas Limited Storage Site [*Army*]
OLSSDG ...... Long Sault Branch, Stormont, Dundas, and Glengarry County Public Library, Ontario [*Library symbol National Library of Canada*] (BIB)
Olsten .... Olsten Corp. [*Associated Press*] (SAG)
OLSUS .... Online System Use Statistics (NITA)
OLSWF .... OLS Asia HLDS ADS Wrrt [*NASDAQ symbol*] (TTSB)
OLT .... Occipitolaeva Transversa [*A fetal position*] [*Medicine*] (AAMN)
olt .... Occipito-Laeva Transverse (AD)
OLT .... Oddity-Learning Task [*Psychology*]
OLT .... Official Latin Title
Olt .... Old Italian (AD)
OLT .... Online Test [*Computer science*]
OLT .... Orange Light
OLT .... Orthotopic Liver Transplantation [*Medicine*]
OLT .... Ostfriesische Lufttransport GmbH [*Germany ICAO designator*] (FAAC)
OLT .... Oxford Library of Translations [*A publication*]
OLT .... United Lodge of Theosophists, London, Ontario [*Library symbol National Library of Canada*] (NLC)
OLTE .... Online Test (NITA)
OLTE .... Online Test Executive Program [*Computer science*] (PDAA)
OLTE .... Organizational Level Test Equipment (MCD)
OLTEP .... On-Line Test Executive Program [*IBM Corp.*] [*Computer science*]
OLTL .... One Life to Live [*Television program*]
OLTMC .... Technical Information Centre, 3M Canada, Inc., London, Ontario [*Library symbol National Library of Canada*] (NLC)
OLTP .... On-Line Transaction Processing [*Tandem Computers*]
OLTS .... On-Line Mainframe Testing System [*Computer science*] (IAA)
OLTS .... Online Test Section (NITA)
OLTS .... Online Test System [*Computer science*] (BUR)
OLTS .... Online Time Share [*Computer science*]
OLTS .... Online Transaction System [*Computer science*] (IAA)
OLTT .... Online Teller Terminal
oltt .... On-Line Teller Terminal [*Computer science*] (AD)
OLTT .... Online Terminal Test [*Computer science*] (IBMDP)
OLU .... Columbus [*Nebraska*] [*Airport symbol*] (OAG)
OLU .... Outdoing Line Unit (IAA)
OLU .... University of Western Ontario, London, Ontario [*Library symbol National Library of Canada*] (NLC)
OLUC .... Lucknow Branch, Bruce County Public Library, Ontario [*Library symbol National Library of Canada*] (NLC)
OLUC .... Office of Land Use Coordination [*Abolished, 1944*] [*Department of Agriculture*]
OLUC .... Online Union Catalog [*Online Computer Library Center, Inc.*] [*Information service or system*] (CRD)
OLuCF .... Southern Ohio Correctional Facility, Lucasville, OH [*Library symbol Library of Congress*] (LCLS)
OLUD .... Online Update (TEL)
OLUE .... Engineering Library, University of Western Ontario, London, Ontario [*Library symbol National Library of Canada*] (BIB)
OLUG .... Department of Geography, University of Western Ontario, London, Ontario [*Library symbol National Library of Canada*] (NLC)
OLUG .... Office Landscape Users Group [*Later, OPUG*] (EA)
OLUH .... University Hospital, London, Ontario [*Library symbol National Library of Canada*] (NLC)
OLUL .... Law Library, University of Western Ontario, London, Ontario [*Library symbol National Library of Canada*] (NLC)
OLUM .... Online Update Control Module (TEL)
OLUM .... Sciences Library, Natural Sciences Centre, University of Western Ontario, London, Ontario [*Library symbol National Library of Canada*] (NLC)
OLUMG .... MacIntosh Gallery, University of Western Ontario, London, Ontario [*Library symbol National Library of Canada*] (NLC)
OLUNO .... Northern Outreach Library Service, University of Western Ontario, London, Ontario [*Library symbol National Library of Canada*] (BIB)
OLURC .... London Urban Resource Centre, Ontario [*Library symbol National Library of Canada*] (NLC)
OLUS .... Online Update System (RDA)
OLUS .... School of Library and Information Science, University of Western Ontario, London, Ontario [*Library symbol National Library of Canada*] (NLC)
OLuS .... Scioto Technical College, Lucasville, OH [*Library symbol Library of Congress Obsolete*] (LCLS)
OLUVA .... Visual Arts Department, University of Western Ontario, London, Ontario [*Library symbol National Library of Canada*] (NLC)
OLUWP .... Office of Land Use and Water Planning [*Abolished, 1976*] [*Department of the Interior*]
olv .... Olivaceous (AD)
olv .... Olive (AD)
OLV .... Olive Branch, MS [*Location identifier FAA*] (FAAL)
OLV .... Oliver Resources [*Vancouver Stock Exchange symbol*]
OLV .... One-Lung Ventilation [*Medicine*]
olv .... On-Line Validation [*Computer science*] (AD)
OLV .... Onze Lieve Vrouw [*Our Lady*] [*Dutch*] (AD)
OLV .... Open-Frame Low Voltage (IEEE)
OLV .... Orbital Launch Vehicle
OLVG .... Open-Loop Voltage Gain
OLVH .... Medical Library, South Street Campus, Victoria Hospital Corp., London, Ontario [*Library symbol National Library of Canada*] (NLC)
OLVL .... Oil Level
O-LVL .... Organizational Level (MCD)

OLVM............ Our Lady of Victory Missionary Sisters [*Roman Catholic religious order*]
olvn .... Olivine [*Philately*]
OLVP .... Office of Launch Vehicle Programs [*Obsolete NASA*]
Olwine's LJ (PA)... Olwine's Law Journal [*Pennsylvania*] [*A publication*] (DLA)
OLX............... Linn-Benton Community College, Albany, OR [*OCLC symbol*] (OCLC)
OLX............... Off-Line Express [*Mustang Software, Inc.*] (PCM)
OLX............... On-Line Executive [*Computer science*] (MHDB)
OLY............... Olney-Noble, IL [*Location identifier FAA*] (FAAL)
Oly............... Olympia (AD)
Oly............... Olympic (AD)
OLY............... Olympic Aviation SA [*Greece*] [*ICAO designator*] (FAAC)
Olym............ Olympia (AD)
OLYM............ Olympiad
OLYM............ Olympic Financial Ltd. [*NASDAQ symbol*] (NQ)
OLYM............ Olympic National Park
OlymF.......... Olympic Financial Ltd. [*Associated Press*] (SAG)
OlymFn........ Olympic Financial Ltd. [*Associated Press*] (SAG)
OLYMP........ Olympic Finl Cv Exch Pfd [*NASDAQ symbol*] (TTSB)
Olympic ...... Olympic National Park, Washington (AD)
OlympStl...... Olympic Steel, Inc. [*Associated Press*] (SAG)
OLZ............... Oelwein, IA [*Location identifier FAA*] (FAAL)
OM............... Air Mongol [*ICAO designator*] (AD)
Om............... Book of Omni (AD)
OM............... Member of the Order of Merit [*Canada*] (DD)
OM............... Minim Fathers (TOCD)
om............... Minim Fathers (TOCD)
OM............... Mississauga Public Library, Ontario [*Library symbol National Library of Canada*] (NLC)
OM............... Obermanual [*Upper Manual*] [*Music*]
OM............... Observer's Mate [*British military*] (DMA)
OM............... Obtuse Marginal [*Medicine*] (MAE)
OM............... Occipitomental [*Diameter of skull*]
OM............... Occupational Medal [*as used with special reference to Germany or Japan*] [*Military decoration*]
OM............... Occupational Medicine
OM............... Oceanography and Meteorology
OM............... Ochsner-Mahorner [*Echocardiogram*] (DAVI)
OM............... Oduma Magazine [*A publication*]
OM............... Odyssey of the Mind
OM............... Oesterreichische Monatsschrift fuer den Orient (BJA)
OM............... Office Manager
OM............... Office Messenger [*Military*]
OM............... Officine Meccaniche [*Italian auto manufacturer*]
OM............... Old Man [*Communications operators' colloquialism*]
om............... Old Man (AD)
om............... Old Measurement (AD)
OM............... Old Measurement
OM............... Olympus Mons [*A filamentary mark on Mars*]
Om............... Omaha (AD)
OM............... Omaha [*Diocesan abbreviation*] [*Nebraska*] (TOCD)
Om............... Oman (AD)
OM............... Oman [*IYRU nationality code*] [*ANSI two-letter standard code*] (CNC)
om............... Omit
OM............... Omni Mane [*Every Morning*] [*Pharmacy*]
om............... Omni Mane [*Every Morning*] [*Latin*] (AD)
OM............... On Margin [*Investment term*]
OM............... Opaque Media [*X-ray microscopy*]
OM............... Open Market
OM............... Open Matching [*Parapsychology*]
OM............... Open Mouth [*Doll collecting*]
OM............... Opera di Maria [*Work of Mary*] [*An association*] (EAIO)
OM............... Opera Mundi [*Book-packaging firm based in Paris*]
OM............... Operating Memorandum
OM............... Operating Memory (KSC)
OM............... Operational Management [*Computer science*] (IAA)
OM............... Operational Monitor (IAA)
om............... Operational Monitor (AD)
OM............... Operation Mainstream (OICC)
OM............... Operation Mobilisation [*Religious movement*] [*British*]
OM............... Operation Monkees (EA)
OM............... Operations Maintenance
OM............... Operations Manager
OM............... Operations Manager [*The assistant manager at some radio stations*] (WDMC)
OM............... Operations Manual (NITA)
OM............... Operations Memorandum [*Department of Agriculture*] (GFGA)
OM............... Operator's Manual
OM............... Opticalman [*Navy rating*]
OM............... Opticalman [*Navy*] (DAVI)
OM............... Optical Master (KSC)
OM............... Optical Media [*Computer graphics*]
OM............... Optical Microscope (ECII)
OM............... Optical Microscopy
OM............... Optimus Maximus [*Greatest and Best*] [*Latin*]
OM............... Options for Men [*A publication*]
OM............... Options Market [*Finance*]
OM............... Orbit Modification (IAA)
OM............... Order of Merit
Om............... Ordinance Map (AD)
OM............... Ordnance Mission (AAG)
OM............... Ordo [*Fratrum*] Minimorum [*Minims of St. Francis of Paul*] [*Roman Catholic men's religious order*]
OM............... Organic Matter
om............... Organic Matter (AD)

OM............... Organizational Maintenance (MCD)
OM............... Orthogonal Memory (MHDB)
OM............... Osborne Mendel Rat [*Medicine*] (DMAA)
OM............... Osmiophilic Layer [*Botany*]
OM............... Osteomalacia [*Medicine*] (MAE)
OM............... Osteomyelitis [*Medicine*]
OM............... Ostmark [*Monetary unit*] [*Germany*]
OM............... Otitis Media [*Medicine*]
OM............... Otolitic Membrane [*Otology*]
om............... Our Memo (AD)
OM............... Our Message
OM............... Outboard Marine [*NYSE symbol*] (TTSB)
OM............... Outer Marker [*Part of an instrument landing system*] [*Aviation*]
om............... Outer Marker (AD)
OM............... Outer Membrane [*Biochemistry*]
OM............... Output Module
OM............... Outside Manufacturing
O/M............. Outside of Metal (MSA)
OM............... Overall Modernity [*Sociological scale*]
OM............... Overhaul Manual (MCD)
OM............... Overland Monthly [*A publication*] (ROG)
OM............... Overseas Mail [*British*]
OM............... Overseas Minister [*World War I*] [*Canada*]
OM............... Overt Meditation
OM............... Overturning Moment
OM............... Ovulation Method [*Birth control*]
OM............... Owners Manual
O/M............. Oxygen-to-Metal [*Ratio*] (NRCH)
OM1............. Opticalman, First Class [*Navy rating*]
OM2............. Opticalman, Second Class [*Navy rating*]
OM3............. Opticalman, Third Class [*Navy rating*]
OMA............ Eppley Airfield [*FAA*] (TAG)
OMA............ Markham Public Library, Ontario [*Library symbol National Library of Canada*] (NLC)
OMA............ Object Management Architecture [*Computer science*] (CDE)
OMA............ Ocean Mining Administration (NADA)
OMA............ Ocean Mining Administration (AD)
OMA............ Oceanography and Marine Assessment (USDC)
OMA............ Oceanography and Marine Assessment [*Marine science*] (OSRA)
OMA............ Office of Management and Administration [*Social Security Administration*] (OICC)
OMA............ Office of Maritime Administration [*Navy*]
OMA............ Office of Maritime Affairs (AD)
OMA............ Office of Military Affairs
OMA............ Office of Military Applications [*Department of Energy*]
OMA............ Office of Military Assistance
OMA............ Office of Minority Affairs [*Department of Agriculture*] (GFGA)
OMA............ Oilskin Manufacturers' Association of Great Britain Ltd. (BI)
OMA............ Oklahoma Military Academy
OMA............ Omaezaki [*Japan*] [*Seismograph station code, US Geological Survey*] (SEIS)
OMA............ Omaha [*Nebraska*] [*Airport symbol*]
Oma............ Omaha, Nebraska (AD)
OMA............ Ontario Medical Association [*Canada*] (AD)
OMA............ Operational Maintenance Activity (NVT)
OMA............ Operation Medicare Alert
OMA............ Operations and Maintenance Appopriation [*Army*]
OMA............ Operations and Maintenance, Army
OMA............ Operations Maintenance Area (NASA)
OMA............ Operations Management Application (SSD)
OMA............ Operations Monitor Alarm
OMA............ Optical Manufacturers Association (EA)
OMA............ Optical-Mechanical Assembly [*Apollo*] [*NASA*]
OMA............ Optical Multichannel Analyzer [*Spectrometry*]
OMA............ Orbiter Maintenance Area [*NASA*] (MCD)
OMA............ Orderly Marketing Agreement
oma............ Orderly Marketing Arrangement (AD)
OMA............ Organizational Maintenance Activity
OMA............ Oriental Merchants Association [*Defunct*] (EA)
OMA............ Outstanding Merchandising Achievement Award
OMA............ Overall Manufacturers' Association (AD)
OMA............ Overall Manufacturers' Association of Great Britain (BI)
OMAA.......... Abu Dhabi/International [*United Arab Emirates*] [*ICAO location identifier*] (ICLI)
OMAA .... Occupational Medical Administrators' Association (EA)
OMAA .... Office of Management Analysis and Audit [*Civil Service Commission*]
OMAAEEC .... Organisation Mondiale des Anciens et Anciennes Eleves de l'Enseignement Catholique [*World Organization of Former Pupils of Catholic Schools*] (EAIO)
OMAB.......... Buhasa [*United Arab Emirates*] [*ICAO location identifier*] (ICLI)
OMABP........ Abitibi-Price, Inc., Mississauga, Ontario [*Library symbol National Library of Canada*] (NLC)
OMAC.......... Alkaril Chemicals Ltd., Mississauga, Ontario [*Library symbol National Library of Canada*] (NLC)
OMAC.......... Asab [*United Arab Emirates*] [*ICAO location identifier*] (ICLI)
OMAC.......... Online Manufacturing, Accounting, and Control System
OMAC.......... Online Manufacturing Control (NITA)
OMAC.......... Open Modular Architecture Controller (ACII)
OMAC.......... Operator Measures and Criteria (MCD)
OMACON...... Optimized Magnetohydrodynamic Conversion
OMACS........ Online Manufacturing and Control System [*Computer science*] (PDAA)
OMAD.......... Abu Dhabi/Bateen [*United Arab Emirates*] [*ICAO location identifier*] (ICLI)

OMAD .... Madoc Public Library, Ontario [*Library symbol National Library of Canada*] (BIB)

OMAD .... Oncovin [*Vincristine*], Methotrexate, Adriamycin, Dactinomycin [*Actinomycin D*] [*Antineoplastic drug regimen*]

OMAD .... Optical Mark and Automatic Dialing [*Facsimile transmission*] (DGA)

OMADA ...... Airway Centre, AES Data Ltd., Mississauga, Ontario [*Library symbol National Library of Canada*] (NLC)

OMAE .... Emirates Flight Information Region [*United Arab Emirates*] [*ICAO location identifier*] (ICLI)

OMAECL ...... AECL International, Mississauga, Ontario [*Library symbol National Library of Canada*] (NLC)

OMAF .... Operations and Maintenance, Air Force

OMAG .... Geac Computers International, Markham, Ontario [*Library symbol National Library of Canada*] (NLC)

OMAG .... Orbiter Magnetometer [*NASA*]

OMAH .... Al Hamra [*United Arab Emirates*] [*ICAO location identifier*] (ICLI)

OMAH .... Markham High School, Ontario [*Library symbol National Library of Canada*]

OMAHM ...... Markham District Historical Museum, Ontario [*Library symbol National Library of Canada*] (BIB)

OMAI .... Allelix, Inc., Mississauga, Ontario [*Library symbol National Library of Canada*] (NLC)

OMAI .... Organisation Mondiale Agudath Israel [*Agudas Israel World Organization - AIWO*] (EAIO)

OMAJ .... Jebel Dhana [*United Arab Emirates*] [*ICAO location identifier*] (ICLI)

OMAL .... Al Ain [*United Arab Emirates*] [*ICAO location identifier*] (ICLI)

O'Mal & H... O'Malley and Hardcastle's Election Cases [*England*] [*A publication*] (DLA)

OMAM .... Abu Dhabi/Al Dhafra [*United Arab Emirates*] [*ICAO location identifier*] (ICLI)

OMAN .... Manitouwadge Public Library, Ontario [*Library symbol National Library of Canada*] (NLC)

O-MAN ...... Overhead Manipulator [*For handling loads in a nuclear environment*]

OMancAH .... Alfred Holbrook College, Manchester, OH [*Library symbol Library of Congress Obsolete*] (LCLS)

OMancO ...... Ohio Valley Local District Free Public Library, Manchester, OH [*Library symbol Library of Congress*] (LCLS)

O'M & H ...... O'Malley and Hardcastle's Election Cases [*England*] [*A publication*] (DLA)

O'M & H El Cas... O'Malley and Hardcastle's Election Cases [*England*] [*A publication*] (DLA)

OM & MG .... Organizational Manual and Management Guide

OM & S .... Osteopathic Medicine and Surgery

OMANO .... Manotick Public Library, Ontario [*Library symbol National Library of Canada*] (NLC)

OMans .... Mansfield Public Library, Mansfield, OH [*Library symbol Library of Congress*] (LCLS)

OMansK ...... Kingwood Center Library, Mansfield, OH [*Library symbol Library of Congress*] (LCLS)

OMansU ...... Ohio State University, Mansfield Regional Campus, Mansfield, OH [*Library symbol Library of Congress*] (LCLS)

OMAP .... Object Module Assembly Program

OMAP .... Operations and Maintenance Application Part [*Telecommunications*]

OMAP .... Vaughan Public Library, Maple, Ontario [*Library symbol National Library of Canada*] (NLC)

OMAPC .... Astra Pharmaceuticals Canada Ltd., Mississauga, Ontario [*Library symbol National Library of Canada*] (NLC)

OMAPFW .... Ontario Ministry of Natural Resources, Maple, Ontario [*Library symbol National Library of Canada*] (NLC)

OMAQ .... Quarmain [*United Arab Emirates*] [*ICAO location identifier*] (ICLI)

OMAR .... Arzana [*United Arab Emirates*] [*ICAO location identifier*] (ICLI)

omar .... Congregation of Maronite Monks (TOCD)

OMar .... Congregation of Maronite Monks (TOCD)

OMAR .... Marathon Public Library, Ontario [*Library symbol National Library of Canada*] (NLC)

OMAR .... Office of Medical Applications of Research [*Bethesda, MD*] [*Department of Health and Human Services National Institutes of Health*]

OMAR .... Operations and Maintenance, Army Reserve (AABC)

OMAR .... Optical Mark Reader [*Computer science*]

omarb .... Omarbetad [*Revised*] [*Swedish*] (AD)

OMarion ...... Marion Carnegie Public Library, Marion, OH [*Library symbol Library of Congress*] (LCLS)

OMarionU .... Ohio State University, Marion Campus, Marion, OH [*Library symbol Library of Congress*] (LCLS)

OMARK .... Markdale Public Library, Ontario [*Library symbol National Library of Canada*] (NLC)

OMARNG ..... Operation and Maintenance, Army National Guard (AABC)

OMARS .... Outstanding Media Advertising by Restaurants (AD)

OMAS .... Assiginack Public Library, Manitowaning, Ontario [*Library symbol National Library of Canada*] (NLC)

OMAS .... Das Island [*United Arab Emirates*] [*ICAO location identifier*] (ICLI)

OMas .... Massillon Public Library, Massillon, OH [*Library symbol Library of Congress*] (LCLS)

OMAS .... Off-Magic-Angle-Spinning [*Spectroscopy*]

OMAS .... One-Man Atmospheric Submersible (PDAA)

OMAS .... Operational Miscellaneous Audio Subsystem

OMAST .... Massey and Township Public Library, Ontario [*Library symbol Library network*] (NLC)

OMAT .... Matheson Public Library, Ontario [*Library symbol National Library of Canada*] (NLC)

OMAT .... Ocean Measurement and Array Technology [*Navy*] (CAAL)

OMAT .... Office of Manpower, Automation, and Training [*See also OAM*] [*Department of Labor*]

OMATT .... Mattawa Public Library, Ontario [*Library symbol National Library of Canada*] (NLC)

OMAU .... Magnetawan Area Union Public Library, Magnetawan, Ontario [*Library symbol National Library of Canada*] (NLC)

OMAZ .... Zirku [*United Arab Emirates*] [*ICAO location identifier*] (ICLI)

OMB .... Midhurst Branch Library, Ontario [*Library symbol National Library of Canada*] (NLC)

OMB .... Object Management Architecture [*Computer science*]

OMB .... Office of Management and Budget [*Executive Office of the President*] [*Formerly, Bureau of the Budget Washington, DC*]

OMB .... Omboue [*Gabon*] [*Airport symbol*] (OAG)

Omb .... Ombudsman (AD)

OMB .... Operational Maintenance Battalion [*Army*] (DOMA)

OMB .... Ordnance Maintenance Bulletin

OMB .... Outboard Motorboat

OMB .... Outer Marker Beacon [*Part of an instrument landing system*] [*Aviation*]

OMB .... Out-of-Home Measurement Bureau [*Later, TABMM*] (EA)

OMBAC .... Old Mission Beach Athletic Club (AD)

OMBC .... Beak Consultants, Mississauga, Ontario [*Library symbol National Library of Canada*] (NLC)

OMB Circular... Office of Management and Budget Circular (AAGC)

OMBE .... Office of Minority Business Enterprise [*Later, MBDA*] [*Department of Commerce*]

OMBE .... Oxford Mission Brotherhood of the Epiphany [*Anglican religious community*]

OMB/FPPO... Office of Management and Budget/Federal Procurement Policy Office (OICC)

OMBI .... Observation-Measurement-Balancing and Installation [*Production analysis*]

OMBI .... Overcoming Mobility Barriers International (EA)

om bid .... Omnibus Bidendis [*Every Two Days*] [*Latin*] (AD)

OMBR .... Ontario Municipal Board Reports [*A publication*] (DLA)

OMBUU .... Orbiter Midbody Umbilical Unit [*NASA*] (NASA)

OMBVT .... Minesing Branch, Vespra Township Public Library, Ontario [*Library symbol National Library of Canada*] (BIB)

OMBW .... Bangor, Wicklow, McClure, and Monteagle Union Public Library, Maynooth, Ontario [*Library symbol National Library of Canada*] (BIB)

OMBW .... OMB [*Office of Management and Budget*] Watch (EA)

OMC .... Chief Opticalman [*Navy rating*]

OMc .... Herbert Wescoat Memorial Library, McArthur, OH [*Library symbol Library of Congress*] (LCLS)

OMC .... Marietta College, Marietta, OH [*Library symbol Library of Congress*] (LCLS)

OMC .... Mayo Clinic Library, Rochester, MN [*OCLC symbol*] (OCLC)

OMC .... Office of Military Cooperation [*Foreign Service*]

OMC .... Office of Motor Carriers [*FHWA*] [*NHSTA*] [*RSPA*] (TAG)

OMC .... Office of Munitions Control [*Department of State*]

OMC .... Official Mail Center [*Air Force*] (AFM)

OMC .... Off-Machine Coated [*Paper*] (DGA)

OMC .... Omnicom Group [*NYSE symbol*] (TTSB)

OMC .... Omnicom Group, Inc. [*NYSE symbol*] (SPSG)

OMC .... One-Man Control (DNAB)

OMC .... Opel Motorsport Club AG (EA)

OMC .... Open Market Committee [*Also, FOMC*] [*Federal Reserve System*]

OMC .... Operating and Maintenance Costs

OMC .... Operations Monitoring Computer

OMC .... Opticalman, Chief [*Navy rating*] (DNAB)

OMC .... Orbiter Maintenance and Checkout [*NASA*] (NASA)

OMC .... Orbiter Maintenance and Checkout

OMC .... Ordnance Missile Command [*Later, Missile Command*]

OMC .... Ordo Minorum Cappucinorum [*Capuchins*] [*Roman Catholic men's religious order*]

OMC .... Ordo Minorum Conventualium [*Conventual Franciscans*] [*Roman Catholic men's religious order*]

OMC .... Organic Molecular Crystal

OMC .... Orion Molecular Cloud [*Astronomy*]

OMC .... Outboard Marine Corp.

OMC .... Oxford Military College (ROG)

OMC .... Oxford Mission to Calcutta [*British*] (ROG)

OMC1 .... Orion Molecular Cloud 1 [*Astronomy*]

OMCA .... Ontario Motor Coach Association

OMCA .... Organic-Moderated Critical Assembly [*Nuclear energy*] (NRCH)

OMCA .... Otitis Media, Catarrhal, Acute [*Medicine*] (MAE)

OMCB .... Off-Machine Coated Board [*Paper*] (DGA)

OMCC .... Open Minded Comics Club [*Defunct*] (EA)

OMCF .... Operations and Maintenance Control File [*NASA*] (NASA)

OMCF .... Orbiter Maintenance and Checkout Facility [*NASA*] (NASA)

OMCG .... Ciba/Geigy Canada Ltd., Mississauga, Ontario [*Library symbol National Library of Canada*] (NLC)

OMCHE .... Organic Material Hydrocarbon Equivalent [*Materials science*]

OMCI .... Organisation Maritime Consultatif Intergouvernementale [*Intergovernmental Maritime Consultative Organization*]

OMCILCR..... Chemical Research Laboratory, CIL, Inc., Mississauga, Ontario [*Library symbol National Library of Canada*] (NLC)

OMcL .... Herbert Wescoat Memorial Library, McArthur, OH [*Library symbol Library of Congress*] (LCLS)

OMCM .... Master Chief Opticalman [*Navy rating*]

OMCM .... Omnicom Group, Inc. (MHDW)

OMCO .... Official Mail Control Officer (MCD)

OMCR .... Chippewa Resource Centre, Muncey, Ontario [*Library symbol National Library of Canada*] (NLC)

OMCR .... Organic-Moderated Cooled Reactor

OMCR .... Organized Marine Corps Reserve

OMCS .... Office of Motor Carrier Standards [*Federal Highway Administration*]
OMCS .... Senior Chief Opticalman [*Navy rating*]
OMCS .... Sheridan Park Research Community, Cominco Ltd., Mississauga, Ontario [*Library symbol National Library of Canada*] (NLC)
OMCSDG...... Moose Creek Branch, Stormount, Dundas, and Glengarry County Public Library, Ontario [*Library symbol National Library of Canada*] (NLC)
OMCSG .... Canada Systems Group, Mississauga, Ontario [*Library symbol National Library of Canada*] (NLC)
OMCT.......... Carnarvon Township Public Library, Mindemoya, Ontario [*Library symbol National Library of Canada*] (NLC)
OMCT.......... Office of Motor Carrier Transportation [*Federal Highway Administration*]
OMCT.......... Organisation Mondiale Contre la Torture [*World Organization Against Torture*] [*Switzerland*] (EAIO)
OMCTS .... Octamethylcyclotetrasiloxane [*Organic chemistry*]
OMCT/SOST... Organisation Mondiale la Torture/SOS-Torture [*World Organization Against Torture/SOS-Torture*] [*Geneva, Switzerland*] (EAIO)
OM-CVD....... Organometallic Chemical Vapor Deposition [*Also, OM-VPE, MO-CVD, MO-VPE*] [*Semiconductor technology*]
OMCVH....... Credit Valley Hospital, Mississauga, Ontario [*Library symbol National Library of Canada*] (NLC)
OMD .... Doctor of Oriental Medicine
OMD .... Du Pont Canada, Inc., Maitland, Ontario [*Library symbol National Library of Canada*] (NLC)
OMD .... Ocean Margin Drilling [*Program*] [*National Science Foundation*]
OMD .... Ocean Movement Designator
OMD .... Ocular Muscle Dystrophy [*Ophthalmology*] (MAE)
OMD .... Office of Management Development [*Later, OMPR*] [*NASA*]
omd .... Off-Market Date (AD)
OMD .... Oldsmobile Motor Division [*General Motors Corp.*]
OMD .... O-Methyldopa [*Biochemistry*]
OMD .... Open Macrodefinition
OMD .... Operations and Maintainer Decision
OMD .... Operations and Maintenance Documentation [*NASA*] (NASA)
OMD .... Orbiter Mating Device [*NASA*] (NASA)
OMD .... Orbiter Mating Device [*NASA*]
OMD .... Orchestral Manoeuvres in the Dark [*Pop music group*]
OMD .... Ordnance Medical Department [*British military*] (DMA)
OMD .... Organic Mental Disorder [*Neurology*] (CPH)
OMD .... Oriental Medicine Doctor [*Medicine*]
OMDB .... Dubai [*United Arab Emirates*] [*ICAO location identifier*] (ICLI)
OMDB .... Over My Dead Body
OMDC .... Du Pont Canada, Inc., Mississauga, Ontario [*Library symbol National Library of Canada*] (NLC)
OMDCPL ..... Patent & Legal Library, DuPont Canada, Inc., Mississauga, Ontario [*Library symbol National Library of Canada*] (NLC)
OMDEAC ..... Dearborn Chemical Co. Ltd., Mississauga, Ontario [*Library symbol National Library of Canada*] (NLC)
OMDG .... Dominion Glass Co. Ltd., Mississauga, Ontario [*Library symbol National Library of Canada*] (NLC)
OMDIR......... Research Library, Duracell, Inc., Mississauga, Ontario [*Library symbol Obsolete National Library of Canada*] (NLC)
OMDL .... Marmora, Deloro, and Lake Union Public Library, Marmora, Ontario [*Library symbol National Library of Canada*] (BIB)
OMDM .... Optomechanical Display Module
OMDO .... Corporate Library, Domglas, Inc., Mississauga, Ontario [*Library symbol National Library of Canada*] (NLC)
OMDP .... Ocean Margin Drilling Program [*National Science Foundation*]
OMDR .... Dunlop Research Centre, Sheridan Park, Mississauga, Ontario [*Library symbol National Library of Canada*] (NLC)
omdr............ Off-Market Date Received (AD)
OMDR .... Operation and Maintainability Data Record
OMDR .... Operations and Maintenance Data Record [*NASA*] (KSC)
OMDR .... Optical Memory Disc Recorder (DOM)
OMDR .... Optic Memory Disk Recorder
OMDS .... Delphax Systems, Mississauga, Ontario [*Library symbol National Library of Canada*] (NLC)
OMDS .... Online Diver Monitoring System
OMDW .... Diversey Wyandotte, Inc., Mississauga, Ontario, [*Library symbol National Library of Canada*] (NLC)
OME .... Erindale College, University of Toronto, Mississauga, Ontario [*Library symbol National Library of Canada*] (NLC)
OME .... Nome [*Alaska*] [*Airport symbol*] (OAG)
OME .... Object Management Extension
OME .... Office of Management Engineer
OME .... Office of Manpower Economics [*Department of Employment*] [*British*]
OME .... Office of Minerals Exploration [*Functions transferred to Geological Survey*] [*Department of the Interior*]
OME .... Office of the Medical Examiner (DAVI)
Ome .... Omega [*Record label*] [*Belgium, etc.*]
OME .... Ometepe [*Nicaragua*] [*Seismograph station code, US Geological Survey*] (SEIS)
OME .... Open Messaging Environment [*Computer science*] (CDE)
OME .... Operational Mission Environment (MCD)
OME .... Orbital [*or Orbiter*] Main Engine [*NASA*] (NASA)
OME .... Orbital Maneuvering Engine [*NASA*] (KSC)
OME .... Ordnance Mechanical Engineer [*British military*] (DMA)
OME .... Organisation Mondiale de l'Emballage [*World Packaging Organization - WPO*] (EAIO)
OME .... Ormont Explorations Ltd. [*Vancouver Stock Exchange symbol*]
OME .... Otitis Media with Effusion [*Medicine*]
OMEA......... Meaford Public Library, Ontario [*Library symbol National Library of Canada*] (NLC)

OMEA......... Office of Multicultural and Ethnic Affairs [*Australia*]
OMEC......... Optimized Microminiature Electronic Circuit
OMEC......... Organization of Mineral Exporting Countries [*Proposed*]
OMED .... Oxboro Medical International, Inc. [*NASDAQ symbol*] (SAG)
OMED .... Oxboro Med Intl. [*NASDAQ symbol*] (TTSB)
OMEF......... Office Machines and Equipment Federation [*British*] (DIT)
OMEF......... Omega Financial [*NASDAQ symbol*] (TTSB)
OMEF......... Omega Financial Corp. [*NASDAQ symbol*] (SAG)
OMEG .... Omega Environmental [*NASDAQ symbol*] (SPSG)
OMEGA .... Off-Road Mobility Evaluation and Generalized Analysis [*Army*]
OMEGA .... Operation Model Evaluation Group, Air Force (MCD)
OMEGA .... Optimal Missile Engagement Guidance Algorithm (AD)
OmegaEn..... Omega Environmental, Inc. [*Associated Press*] (SAG)
OmegFn..... Omega Financial Corp. [*Associated Press*] (SAG)
OmegHlt..... Omega Healthcare Investors [*Associated Press*] (SAG)
OMeH .... Holden Arboretum, Mento, OH [*Library symbol*] [*Library of Congress*] (LCLS)
OM/EH .... Occupational Medicine/Environmental Health Evaluation Center [*Emory University*]
OMEI .... Office of Minority Economic Impact [*Department of Energy*]
OMEI .... Other Major End Item [*Military*] (AFIT)
OMEL .... Orient Mid-East Lines (AD)
OMEN .... Ohio Medical Education Network [*Ohio State University*] [*Columbus*] (TSSD)
OMEN .... Orthogonal Mini-Embedment (MHDI)
OMEP......... Office of Marine and Estuarine Protection [*Environmental Protection Agency*] (EPA)
OMEP......... Organisation Mondiale pour l'Education Prescolaire [*World Organization for Early Childhood Education*] (EAIO)
OMER .... Merrickville Public Library, Ontario [*Library symbol National Library of Canada*] (NLC)
OMER .... Operations Management Education and Research Foundation (EA)
OMERAD...... Office of Medical Education Research and Development [*Michigan State University*] [*Research center*] (RCD)
OMerc......... Order of Mercedarians [*Also, MMB*] [*Roman Catholic women's religious order*]
OMERF .... Operations Management Education and Research Foundation [*Formerly, OFMP*] (EA)
O-Mess........ Officer's Mess [*Military*] (AD)
OMET......... Orbiter Mission Elapsed Time [*NASA*] (MCD)
OMET......... Ordnance Middle East Tasks [*Military*]
OMET......... Organization Manning Equipment Table (MCD)
OMETA........ Ordnance Management Engineering Training Agency [*Army*]
OMEW .... Office of Missile Electronic Warfare [*Army*] (RDA)
OMEWG .... Orbiter Maintenance Engineering Working Group [*NASA*] (NASA)
OMF.......... Moose Factory Library, Ontario [*Library symbol National Library of Canada*] (BIB)
OMF.......... Object Management Facility [*Computer science*]
OMF.......... Object Module File [*Computer science*] (IAA)
OMF.......... Object Module Format
OMF.......... Office of Management and Finance (AD)
OMF.......... Office of Management and Finance (NADA)
OMF.......... Officer Master File [*Army*] (INF)
OMF.......... Old Master File
OMF.......... Omniflys SA de CV [*Mexico ICAO designator*] (FAAC)
OMF.......... Open Media Framework (DOM)
OMF.......... Operational Mission Failure (MCD)
OMF.......... Operation and Maintenance of Facilities [*Army*]
OMF.......... Optical Matched Filter
OMF.......... Order Materials For
OMF.......... Organizational Master File [*Army*]
OMF.......... Oscillatory Magnetic Field
OMF.......... Overseas Missionary Fellowship, USA Headquarters (EA)
OMFBAA ..... Operation and Maintenance of Facilities Budget Activity Account [*Army*] (AABC)
OMFBR........ Organic-Moderated Fluidized Bed Reactor
OMFC......... Overseas Military Forces of Canada [*World War I*]
OMFCA .... Operation and Maintenance of Facilities Cost Account [*Army*] (AABC)
OMFCU .... Outboard Message Format Conversion Unit (MCD)
OMFD .... Mount Forest District High School, Mount Forest, Ontario [*Library symbol National Library of Canada*] (NLC)
OMFE......... Front of Escott Public Library, Mallorytown, Ontario [*Library symbol National Library of Canada*] (NLC)
OMFJ .... Fujeirah/International [*United Arab Emirates*] [*ICAO location identifier*] (ICLI)
OMFP......... Obtaining Money by False Pretense
omfp.......... Obtaining Money by False Pretenses (AD)
OMFP......... Ortho-Methylfluorescein Phosphate [*Biochemistry*]
OMFS......... Office Master Frequency Supply [*Telecommunications*] (TEL)
OMFS......... Optimum Metric Fastener System
OMFSCA ..... Operation and Maintenance of Facilities Summary Cost Account [*Army*] (AABC)
OMFT......... Optical Matched Filter Technique
OMFTS........ Operational Maneuver from the Sea [*Marine Corps*] (DOMA)
OMFUG .... Other Music for Urban Gormandizers [*Acronym used as subtitle to the New York City nightclub name, CBGB*]
OMFY......... Front of Yonge Township Public Library, Mallorytown, Ontario [*Library symbol National Library of Canada*] (BIB)
OMG .... Aeromega Ltd. [*British ICAO designator*] (FAAC)
OMG .... Object Management Group [*Computer science*]
OMG .... Object Management Group
OMG .... Office Machines Group [*Business Equipment Manufacturers Association*]
OMG .... Office of Marine Geology [*United States Geological Survey*]
OMG .... Office of Military Government

OMG .... Older Metamorphic Group [*Geology*]
OMG .... Omega [*Namibia*] [*Airport symbol*] (OAG)
OMG .... Omni MultiMedia Group [*AMEX symbol*] (TTSB)
OMG .... Omni Multimedia Group, Inc. [*AMEX symbol*] (SAG)
OMG .... Operational-Maneuver Group [*Military*]
OMG .... Opthalmology Medical Group (AD)
OMG .... Outlaw Motorcycle Gang
OMGA .... Golder Associates, Mississauga, Ontario [*Library symbol National Library of Canada*] (NLC)
OMGA .... Operations Management Ground Application (SSD)
OmgaHI ...... Omega Health Systems, Inc. [*Associated Press*] (SAG)
OMGB .... Georgian Bay Township Public Library, Mactier, Ontario [*Library symbol National Library of Canada*] (BIB)
OMGB .... Office of Military Government for Bavaria [*US Military Government, Germany*]
OMGBS .... Office of Military Government for Berlin Sector [*US Military Government, Germany*]
OMGCR .... Research & Development, Gulf Canada Ltd., Mississauga, Ontario [*Library symbol National Library of Canada*] (NLC)
OMGCR .... Technical Library, Petro-Canada Products, Mississauga, Ontario [*Library symbol National Library of Canada*] (NLC)
OMGE .... Organisation Mondiale de Gastroenterologie [*World Organization of Gastroenterology - WOG*] [*Edinburgh, Scotland*] (EAIO)
OMGH .... Office of Military Government for Hesse [*US Military Government, Germany*]
OMGI .... OM Group [*NASDAQ symbol*] (TTSB)
OMGI .... OM Group, Inc. [*NASDAQ symbol*] (SAG)
OMGL .... Gartner Lee Associates Ltd., Markham, Ontario [*Library symbol National Library of Canada*] (NLC)
OMGR .... Omni Insurance Group [*NASDAQ symbol*] (TTSB)
OMGR .... Omni Insurance Group, Inc. [*NASDAQ symbol*] (SAG)
OM Grp .... OM Group, Inc. [*Associated Press*] (SAG)
OMGT .... Overall Missile Guidance Tests (MCD)
OMGUS .... Office of Military Government, United States
OMGWB .... Office of Military Government for Wuerttemberg-Baden [*US Military Government, Germany*]
OMH .... Health Sciences Library, Mississauga Hospital, Ontario [*Library symbol National Library of Canada*] (BIB)
OMH .... Office of Mental Health (AD)
OMH .... Omega Hydrocarbons Ltd. [*Toronto Stock Exchange symbol*]
OMH .... Orumieh [*Iran*] [*Airport symbol Obsolete*] (OAG)
OMHCE .... Organic Material Hydrocarbon Equivalent [*Automotive emissions control*]
OMHL .... Occupational Medicine and Hygiene Laboratory [*British*] (IRUK)
OMH-RC ...... Office of Minority Health Resource Center
OMHT .... Hagar Township Public Library, Markstay, Ontario [*Library symbol National Library of Canada*] (NLC)
OMI .... Middletown Public Library, Middletown, OH [*OCLC symbol*] (OCLC)
OMI .... Midland Public Library, Ontario [*Library symbol National Library of Canada*] (NLC)
OMI .... Oblates of Mary Immaculate (TOCD)
omi .... Oblates of Mary Immaculate (TOCD)
OMI .... Oblats de Marie Immaculee [*Oblates of Mary Immaculate*] [*Rome, Italy*] (EAIO)
OMI .... Office of Management Improvement [*Department of Agriculture*]
OMI .... Office of Management Information [*Military*] (AFIT)
OMI .... Office of Multicultural Interests [*Western Australia*]
OMI .... Ohio Mechanics Institute
OMI .... Old Myocardial Infarction [*Medicine*]
OMI .... Olympic Media Information (AD)
OMI .... OMI Corp. [*Associated Press*] (SAG)
OMI .... Omnibus Computer Graphics, Inc. [*Toronto Stock Exchange symbol*]
OMI .... Oocyte Maturation Inhibitor [*Endocrinology*]
OMI .... Open Messaging Interface [*Lotus Development Corp.*] (PCM)
OMI .... Operating Memorandum - Information
OMI .... Operational Maintenance Instruction (AAG)
OMI .... Operation Move-In [*New York City*]
OMI .... Opinions about Mental Illness [*A questionnaire*]
OMI .... Optical Measurement Instrument (SAA)
OMI .... Ordnance Modifications Instructions
OMI .... Organisation Maritime Internationale [*International Maritime Organization - IMO*] (EAIO)
OMI .... Organisation Meteorologique Internationale
OMI .... Organizacion Maritima Internacional [*International Maritime Organization*] [*Spanish United Nations*] (DUND)
OMI .... Organizacion Maritima Internacional [*International Maritime Organization*] [*Spanish*] (AD)
OMI .... Organization for Microinformation
OMI .... Organizations Master Index [*A publication*]
OMI .... Other Manufacturing Industries [*Department of Employment*] [*British*]
OMI .... Our Main Interest (LAIN)
OMI .... Owens & Minor [*NYSE symbol*] (TTSB)
OMI .... Owens & Minor, Inc. [*NYSE symbol*] (SPSG)
OMIA .... Operating, Maintenance, Interest, and Adaptability
OMiabM .... Monsanto Research Corp., Mound Laboratory, Miamisburg, OH [*Library symbol Library of Congress*] (LCLS)
OMiabMI ...... Mead Imaging, Miamisburg, OH [*Library symbol*] [*Library of Congress*] (LCLS)
OMiabMM ... Monarch Marking Systems, Pitney Bowes, Chemical Research and Development Library, Miamisburg, OH [*Library symbol Library of Congress*] (LCLS)
OMIBAC ...... Ordinal Memory Inspecting Binary Automatic Computer (IEEE)
OMIBM .... IBM Canada Ltd., Markham, Ontario [*Library symbol National Library of Canada*] (NLC)
OMICA .... Organized Migrants in Community Action [*Florida*] [*Defunct*]

OMid .... Middletown Public Library, Middletown, OH [*Library symbol Library of Congress*] (LCLS)
OMidAR ...... Armco, Inc., Research Center, Technical Library, Middletown, OH [*Library symbol Library of Congress*] (LCLS)
OMidH .... Middletown Hospital Association, Ada Leonard Memorial Library, Middletown, OH [*Library symbol*] [*Library of Congress*] (LCLS)
OMidU .... Miami University, Middletown Campus, Middletown, OH [*Library symbol Library of Congress*] (LCLS)
OMIH .... Huronia Historical Park, Midland, Ontario [*Library symbol National Library of Canada*] (NLC)
OMIHM .... Halton Region Museum, Milton, Ontario [*Library symbol National Library of Canada*] (BIB)
OMIHS .... Institute for Hydrogen Systems, Mississauga, Ontario [*Library symbol National Library of Canada*] (NLC)
OMII .... Oxy Metal Industries International (AD)
OMIKK .... Orszagos Muszaki Informacios Kozpont es Konyvtar [*National Technical Information Center and Library*] [*Information service or system*] (IID)
OMIL .... Milton Public Library, Ontario [*Library symbol National Library of Canada*] (NLC)
OMILD .... Mildmay Branch, Bruce County Public Library, Ontario [*Library symbol National Library of Canada*] (NLC)
OMiII .... Holmes County Public Library, Millersburg, OH [*Library symbol Library of Congress*] (LCLS)
OMILL .... Millbrook Public Library, Ontario [*Library symbol National Library of Canada*] (BIB)
OMILV .... Milverton Public Library, Ontario [*Library symbol National Library of Canada*] (NLC)
OMiM .... Megis Local School District Public Library, Middleport Branch, Middleport, OH [*Library symbol Library of Congress*] (LCLS)
OMiM .... Online Mendelian Inheritance in Man [*Genetics*]
OMiM .... Outer Mitochondrial Membrane [*Also, OMM*] [*Cytology*]
OMIN .... Inco Ltd., Mississauga, Ontario [*Library symbol National Library of Canada*] (NLC)
OMIOM .... Original Meaning Is the Only Meaning [*Writing term*]
omiom .... Original Meaning Is the Only Meaning (AD)
OMIP .... Office of Minority Institutions Program [*U.S. Department of the Interior*] (BARN)
OMIS .... Office of Management and Information Systems (USGC)
OMIS .... Office of Management Information Systems [*Office of Administration and Management*] [*Department of Labor*]
OMIS .... Omission (AAG)
OMIS .... Operational Management Information System [*Computer science*]
O Misc .... Ohio Miscellaneous Reports [*A publication*] (DLA)
OMISS .... Operation and Maintenance Instruction Summary Sheet [*NASA*] (MCD)
OMIT .... Mitchell Public Library, Ontario [*Library symbol National Library of Canada*] (NLC)
omit .... Orinthine-Decarboxylase, Motility, Indole, Trytophandeaminase (AD)
OMITT .... Omittatur [*Let It Be Omitted*] [*Pharmacy*] (ROG)
OMJ .... Ohmine [*Japan*] [*Seismograph station code, US Geological Survey*] (SEIS)
OMJ .... Orthomode Junction [*Electronics*]
OMJAT .... J. A. Turner Professional Library, H. J. A. Brown Education Centre, Mississauga, Ontario [*Library symbol National Library of Canada*] (NLC)
OMK .... Omak, WA [*Location identifier FAA*] (FAAL)
OMK .... Owl Monkey Kidney [*Cell line*]
omkr .... Omdring [*About*] [*Norwegian*] (AD)
OMKR .... Outer Marker [*Part of an instrument landing system*] [*Aviation*]
OMKT .... Open Market [*NASDAQ symbol*] (TTSB)
OMKT .... Open Market, Inc. [*NASDAQ symbol*] (SAG)
OML .... One-Man-LAN [*Linked Access Network*] [*PC Interconnect, Inc.*] [*Telecommunications*] (PCM)
OML .... Ontario Ministry of Labour Library [*UTLAS symbol*]
OML .... Ontario Motor League [*Canada*] (AD)
OML .... Operations Manual Letter [*National Weather Service*] (NOAA)
OML .... Orbiter Mold Line [*NASA*]
OML .... Orbiting Military Laboratory (AAG)
OML .... Order of Merit List [*Army*] (AABC)
OML .... Ordnance Material Letter (SAA)
OML .... Ordnance Missile Laboratories (KSC)
OML .... Ordnance Muzzle Loading [*British military*] (DMA)
OML .... Organic Materials Laboratory [*Watertown, MA*] [*Army*] (GRD)
OML .... Organizational Maintenance Level (NVT)
OML .... Outer Mold Line (NASA)
OML .... Outgoing Matching Loss [*Telecommunications*] (TEL)
OML .... Outside Mold Line [*Technical drawings*]
oml .... Outside Mold Line (AD)
OML .... University of Cincinnati, Marx Law Library, Cincinnati, OH [*OCLC symbol*] (OCLC)
OMLA .... Organizational Maintenance Level Activity (MCD)
OMLAC .... Oxfordshire Modern Languages Achievement Certificate [*British*] (AIE)
OMLCSA ...... Old Mine Lamp Collectors Society of America (EA)
OMLE .... Organization of Spanish Marxist-Leninists (PD)
OMLIT .... One-Man Live Interception Test (SAA)
OMLJ .... Officer of Merit, Order of St. Lazarus of Jerusalem (DD)
OMLP .... Ohio Midland Light & Power [*AAR code*]
OMLT .... [*The*] Learning Tree, Mississauga, Ontario [*Library symbol National Library of Canada*] (NLC)
OMLTA .... Ohio Modern Language Teachers Association (EDAC)
OMM .... Miami University, Middletown Campus, Middletown, OH [*OCLC symbol*] (OCLC)
OMM .... Office of Marine Minerals

OMM............ Office of Minerals Mobilization [*Later, OMSF*] [*Department of the Interior*]
OMM............ Officer Message Mail [*Military*]
OMM............ Officer of the Order of Military Merit
OMM............ Officer of the Order of Military Merit [*Canada*] (DD)
OMM............ Oil Market Module [*Department of Energy*] (GFGA)
OMM............ OMI Corp. [*NYSE symbol*] (SAG)
OMM............ OMI Corp. [*NYSE symbol*] (TTSB)
OMM............ Ommatidium [*Arthropod eye anatomy*]
OMM............ Operation and Maintenance Manual
OMM............ Orbital Maintenance Mission [*NASA*] (SSD)
OMM............ Organisation Meteorologique Mondiale [*World Meteorological Organization - WMO*] (EAIO)
OMM............ Organizacion Meteorologica Mundial [*World Meteorological Organization - WMO*] [*Spanish*]
OMM............ Organometallic Material
OMM............ Outer Mitochondrial Membrane [*Also, OMiM*] [*Cytology*]
OMM............ Oxford Medical Manuals [*A publication*]
OMMA .... Outboard Motor Manufacturers Association [*Later, MEMA*] (EA)
OMMB ...... Information Centre, Molson Breweries of Canada Ltd., Mississauga, Ontario [*Library symbol National Library of Canada*] (NLC)
OMMC ...... Officer Message Mail Center [*Military*]
OMMCS ...... Ordnance Missile and Munitions Center and School [*Army*]
Om Mer Sh... Omond's Merchant Shipping Acts [*1877*] [*A publication*] (DLA)
OMMH .... Orbiter Maintenance Man-Hours [*NASA*] (NASA)
OMMI............ Magna International, Inc., Markham, Ontario [*Library symbol National Library of Canada*] (BIB)
OMMI.......... Oblate Missionaries of Mary Immaculate (TOCD)
OMMIC ...... Ordnance Maintenance Management Information Center [*Navy*]
OMMLT........ Murchison Lyell Township Community Library, Madawaska, Ontario [*Library symbol National Library of Canada*] (NLC)
OMMM........ Moore Museum, Mooretown, Ontario [*Library symbol National Library of Canada*] (BIB)
OMMMSA..... Oil Mill Machinery Manufacturers and Supply Association (EA)
OMMS .... Office of Merchant Marine Safety [*Coast Guard*]
OMMS .... Organizational Missile Maintenance Squadron [*Air Force*]
OMM(S)C..... Officer Messenger Mail (Sub) Center [*Navy*]
OMMSQA..... Office of Modeling, Monitoring Systems, and Quality Assurance [*Environmental Protection Agency*]
OMN .... Mansfield-Richland County Public Library, Mansfield, OH [*OCLC symbol*] (OCLC)
OMN .... Octamethylnaphthalene [*Organic chemistry*]
OMN .... Oman [*ANSI three-letter standard code*] (CNC)
OMN .... Omnivorous
OMN .... Ormond Beach, FL [*Location identifier FAA*] (FAAL)
OMN .... Orthomin
omn 2 hor ... Omni Secunda Hora [*Every Two Hours*] [*Latin*] [*Pharmacy*] (DAVI)
OMN BID .... Omni Bidus [*Every Two Days*] [*Pharmacy*] (ROG)
OMN BIH .... Omni Bihora [*Every Two Hours*] [*Pharmacy*]
omn bih...... Omni Bihora [*Every Two Hours*] [*Latin*] (AD)
Omncre...... Omnicare, Inc. [*Associated Press*] (SAG)
OMNCS ...... Office of the Manager National Communications System [*GSA*]
OMNET ...... Organizational Maintenance New Equipment Training [*Army*] (INF)
OMNG .... Operations and Maintenance, National Guard [*Army*]
OMN H........ Omni Hora [*Every Hour*] [*Pharmacy*]
OMN HOR ... Omni Hora [*Every Hour*] [*Pharmacy*]
OMNI .... Omnidirectional
omni............ Omnidirectional [*Microphone*] (WDMC)
Omni............ Omni Multimedia Group, Inc. [*Associated Press*] (SAG)
omni............ Omnirange (AD)
omni............ Omnivisual (AD)
omni............ Omnidirectional (AD)
OMNI .... On-Site Multiple Network Installation [*Thomas & Betts Corp.*]
Omnicm...... Omnicom Group, Inc. [*Associated Press*] (SAG)
Omnilns...... Omni Insurance Group, Inc. [*Associated Press*] (SAG)
OmniMult .... Omni Multimedia Group, Inc. [*Associated Press*] (SAG)
Omnipt........ Omnipoint Corp. [*Associated Press*] (SAG)
OMNIRANGE... Omnidirectional Radio Range (MSA)
OMNITAB...... Omnibus Program with Tabular Numerical Functions [*Programming language*] [*1965*] (CSR)
OMNITENNA... Omnirange Antenna
OmniUSA...... Omni USA, Inc. [*Associated Press*] (SAG)
OMN MAN ... Omni Mane [*Every Morning*] [*Pharmacy*]
omn man...... Omni Mane [*Every Morning*] [*Latin*] (AD)
OMNMPS..... Operative Machine Needle Makers' Protection Society [*A union*] [*British*]
OMN NOCT... Omni Nocte [*Every Night*] [*Pharmacy*]
omn noct.... Omni Nocte [*Every Night*] [*Latin*] (AD)
omn quad hor... Omni Quadrante Hora [*Every quarter of An Hour*] [*Latin*] [*Pharmacy*] (DAVI)
OMN QUADR HOR... Omni Quadrante Horae [*Every Quarter of an Hour*] [*Pharmacy*] (ROG)
OMNT .... Northern Telecom, Mississauga, Ontario [*Library symbol National Library of Canada*] (NLC)
OMO .... Moonbeam Public Library, Ontario [*Library symbol National Library of Canada*] (BIB)
OMO .... Mostar [*Yugoslavia*] [*Airport symbol*] (AD)
OMO .... Oblates of the Mother of Orphans (TOCD)
OMO .... Office of Marine Operations [*Marine science*] (OSRA)
OMO .... Office of Marine Operations (USDC)
OMO .... Office of the Director of Manpower and Organization [*Air Force*]
OMO .... Old Man's Out [*Facetious translation of Omo, a brand of detergent*] [*British*]
OMO .... Omoco Holdings [*Vancouver Stock Exchange symbol*]
OMO .... One-Man-Operated Bus [*London, England*]

OMO .... One Man Operation [*Railroad*] [*British*]
OMO .... Open Market Operations [*Economics*]
OMO .... Ordinary Money Order
OMO .... Singly-Occupied Molecular Orbital [*Physical chemistry*]
OMOAM .... Ontario Agricultural Museum, Milton, Ontario [*Library symbol National Library of Canada*] (NLC)
OMOB .... Offensive Missile Order of Battle (MCD)
OMODE .... Ordinary Mode (MCD)
OMOL .... Oliver Township Public Library, Murillo, Ontario [*Library symbol National Library of Canada*] (BIB)
OMOO .... Moosonee Public Library, Ontario [*Library symbol National Library of Canada*] (BIB)
omor............ One Man, One Responsibility (AD)
OMorS .... Salem Township Public Library, Morrow, OH [*Library symbol Library of Congress*] (LCLS)
OMORSDG ... Morewood Branch, Stormont, Dundas, and Glengarry County Public Library, Ontario [*Library symbol National Library of Canada*] (BIB)
OMOSC .... Organisation des Musiciens d'Orchestres Symphoniques du Canada [*Organization of Canadian Symphony Musicans - OCSM*]
OMOSDG ..... Morrisburg Branch, Stormont, Dundas, and Glengarry County Public Library, Ontario [*Library symbol National Library of Canada*] (NLC)
OMOT .... Metcalfe Branch, Osgoode Township Library, Ontario [*Library symbol National Library of Canada*] (BIB)
OMOTH .... Osgoode Township High School Library, Metcalfe, Ontario [*Library symbol National Library of Canada*] (BIB)
OMOV .... One Member, One Vote [*System to select parliamentary candidates*] [*British*]
OMP .... Espe [*Germany*] [*Research code symbol*]
OMP .... Marion Public Library, Marion, OH [*OCLC symbol*] (OCLC)
OMP .... Ocean Microwave Package (SSD)
OMP .... Office of Metric Programs [*Department of Commerce*]
OMP .... Olfactory Marker Protein [*Biochemistry*]
OMP .... Oligo-N-methylmorpholinopropylene Oxide [*Pharmacology*]
OMP .... OM Group, Inc. [*NYSE symbol*] (SAG)
OMP .... Operating Maintenance Panel (IAA)
OMP .... Operating Maintenance Procedure (IAA)
OMP .... Operating Memorandum - Policy
OMP .... Operations and Maintenance Plan [*NASA*] (NASA)
OMP .... Optical Mark Printer (NITA)
omp .... Organo-Metallic Polymer (AD)
OMP .... Organometallic Polymer (CAAL)
OMP .... Ormetoprim [*Potentiator for antibacterials*] [*Veterinary medicine*]
OMP .... Orotidine Monophosphate [*Organic chemistry*]
OMP .... Outer Membrane Protein [*Biochemistry*]
OMP .... Output Makeup
OMP .... Overseas Manpower [*British*]
OMP .... Oxford Medical Publications [*A publication*]
OMpA .... American Society for Metals Library, Metals Park, OH [*Library symbol*] [*Library of Congress*] (LCLS)
OMPA .... Octamethylpyrophosphoramide [*Insecticide*]
OMPA .... Office of Marine Pollution Assessment [*National Oceanic and Atmospheric Administration*] (ASF)
OMPA .... One-Man Pension Arrangement [*Management*]
ompa .... One-Man Pension Arrangement (AD)
OMPA .... Operating Memorandum - Personnel Assignment
OMPA .... Otitis Media, Purulent, Acute [*Medicine*]
OMPA .... Outer Membrane Protein A [*Biochemistry*]
OMPC .... Office of Municipal Pollution Control [*Environmental Protection Agency*] (GFGA)
OMPC .... Overseas Military Personnel Charter (MCD)
OMPD .... Office of Mineral Policy Development [*Department of the Interior*]
OMPE .... Office of Management Planning and Evaluation [*Environmental Protection Agency*] (EPA)
OMPE & R... Office of Manpower Policy, Evaluation, and Research [*Department of Labor*]
OMPEC .... Offshore Mechanics and Polar Engineering Council
OMPER .... Office of Manpower Policy, Evaluation, and Research [*Department of Labor*]
OMPF .... Official Military Personnel File [*Army*] (AABC)
ompf .... Omphaloskepsis (AD)
OMPI .... Ordnance Master Publication Index (MCD)
OMPI .... Organisation Mondiale de la Propriete Intellectuelle [*World Intellectual Property Organization - WIPO*] [*Information service or system*] (IID)
OMPI .... Organizacion Mundial de la Propiedad Intelectual [*World Intellectual Property Organization*] [*Spanish United Nations*] (DUND)
OMPI .... Oxo(mercaptoethyl)(phenyl)imidazolidine [*Biochemistry*]
OMPO .... Oahu Metropolitan Planning Organization [*Hawaii*] (AD)
OMPR .... Office of Management Planning and Review [*Formerly, OMD*] [*NASA*]
OMPR .... Operational Maintainability Problem Reporting (NASA)
OMPR .... Optical Mark Page Reader [*Computer science*] (AABC)
ompr .... Optical Mark Page Reader (AD)
OMPRA .... Office of Minerals Policy and Research Analysis (AD)
OMPRA .... One-Man Propulsion Research Apparatus [*NASA*]
OMPS .... Orbit Maneuvering Propulsion System [*NASA*] (KSC)
OMPSA .... Organisation Mondiale pour le Promotion Sociale des Aveugles [*World Council for the Welfare of the Blind - WCWB*] (EAIO)
OMPT.......... Observed Man [*or Mass*] Point Trajectory [*NASA*] (KSC)
OMPT.......... Omnipoint Corp. [*NASDAQ symbol*] (TTSB)
OMPT.......... Omnipoint Corp. [*NASDAQ symbol*] (SAG)
OMPU .... Oficina Municipale de Planeamiento Urbano [*Municipal Office of Urban Planning*] [*Spain*] (AD)

OMPUS....... Official Munitions Production United States
OMPW......... Pratt & Whitney Aircraft Ltd., Mississauga, Ontario [*Library symbol National Library of Canada*] (NLC)
OMPX.......... OCLC Microcomputer Program Exchange (NITA)
OM QUAR HOR... Omni Quarta Hora [*Every Quarter of An Hour*] [*Latin*] [*Pharmacy*] (DAVI)
OMR .... Midland-Ross Corp., Library, Cleveland, OH [*OCLC symbol*] (OCLC)
OMR .... Office Methods Research
omr.............. Office Methods Research (AD)
OMR .... Office of Marine Resources [*Department of the Interior*] (NOAA)
OMR .... Officer Master Record [*Air Force*] (AFM)
OMR .... Online Medical Record (HCT)
OMR .... Operational Modification Report (IAA)
OMR .... Operation Management Room [*NASA*] (KSC)
OMR .... Operations and Maintenance Requirements (NASA)
OMR .... Operations Management Room [*NASA*]
OMR .... Operations Manager's Report
OMR .... Operative Morality Rate [*Statistics*] [*Medicine*] (DAVI)
OMR .... Optical Mark Reader [*Computer science*]
omr.............. Optical Mark Reader (AD)
omr.............. Optical Mark Recognition (AD)
OMR .... Optical Mark Recognition [*Computer science*] (MCD)
OMR .... Optical Meter Relay
OMR .... Orad [*Romania*] [*Airport symbol*] (OAG)
OMR .... Orbiter Management Review [*NASA*] (NASA)
OMR .... Organic Magnetic Resonance
OMR .... Organic-Moderated Reactor [*Nuclear energy*]
OMR .... Our Material Returned (AAG)
OMR .... Overhaul, Maintenance, and Repair (MCD)
OMR .... Overhead Materials Requirement [*Manufacturing*]
OMRB .... Operating Material Review Board [*NASA*] (NASA)
OMRC .... Operational Maintenance Requirements Catalog [*NASA*] (MCD)
OMRC .... Optical Mark Reader Card [*Computer science*] (MHDI)
OMRCA .... Organic-Moderated Reactor Critical Assembly [*Nuclear energy*]
OMRD .... Office of Manpower Research and Development [*National Academy of Sciences*]
OMRD .... Overseas Mineral Resource Development (AD)
OMRE .... Organic-Moderated Reactor Experiment [*Nuclear energy*]
OMRF .... Oklahoma Medical Research Foundation [*University of Oklahoma*] [*Research center*]
OMRI .... Oklahoma Medical Research Institute
OMRI .... Open Media Research Institute [*Non-profit news and analysis organization covering Eastern Europe and the former Soviet Union*] (ECON)
OMRI .... Open Media Research Institute
OMRK .... Ras Al Khaimah/International [*United Arab Emirates*] [*ICAO location identifier*] (ICLI)
OMRM .... Manitou Library (Ojibway of Manitou Rapids Indian Band), Manitou Rapids, Ontario [*Library symbol National Library of Canada*] (BIB)
OMRO .... Ordnance Materials Research Office [*Later, AMMRC*] [*Army*] (MCD)
OMR/P .... Operations and Maintenance Requirements/Plan [*NASA*] (NASA)
OMRR .... Ordnance Material Research Reactor [*Nuclear energy*]
OMRS .... Operations and Maintenance Requirements Specifications (NASA)
OMRS .... Optical Mark Reader Sheet [*Computer science*] (MHDI)
OMRS .... Orders and Medals Research Society (EA)
OMRSD........ Operational Maintainability Reporting Systems Document [*NASA*] (NASA)
OMRSD........ Operational Maintenance Requirements and Specifications Document [*NASA*] (NASA)
OMRSD........ Operations and Maintenance Requirements and Specification Documentation (NASA)
OMRSD........ Operations and Maintenance Requirements and Specifications Documentation
OMRV .... Operational Maneuvering Reentry Vehicle (MCD)
OMRW .... Optical MASER [*Microwave Amplification by Stimulated Emission of Radiation*] Radiation Weapon (AAG)
OMS............. Ocean Minesweeper
OMS............. Octahedral Molecular Sieve [*Inorganic chemistry*]
OMS............. Office Management System [*Computer science*] (IAA)
OMS............. Office of Management Services [*Department of Agriculture*]
OMS............. Office of Management Studies (EA)
OMS............. Office of Management Support [*Environmental Protection Agency*] (EPA)
OMS............. Office of Marketing Services [*of BDSA*]
OMS............. Office of Mobile Sources [*Environmental Protection Agency*] (GFGA)
OMS............. Oil Market Simulation Model [*Department of Energy*] (GFGA)
OMS............. Omsk [*Former USSR Airport symbol*] (OAG)
OMS............. On-Board Maintenance System [*Aviation*]
OMS............. One-Minute Superstar [*Actor whose bit part in a television series results in instant stardom*]
OMS............. Opcode MIDI [*Musical Instrument Digital Interface*] System
OMS............. Open Mail System [*Raindrop Software Co.*] (PCM)
OMS............. Open Management System [*Vitalink Communicatons Corp.*]
OMS............. Open Measurement Solution
OMS............. Operational Maintenance System
OMS............. Operational Meteorological Satellite [*NASA*]
OMS............. Operational Mission Summary [*Army*]
OMS............. Operational Mode Summary
OMS............. Operational Monitoring System (MCD)
OMS............. Operations Management System (SSD)
OMS............. Oppenheimer Multi-Sector [*NYSE symbol*] (TTSB)
OMS............. Oppenheimer Multi-Sector Income Trust [*NYSE symbol*] (SPSG)
OMS............. Optical MASER [*Microwave Amplification by Stimulated Emission of Radiation*] System

OMS............. Optical Modulation System
OMS............. Optimum Mode Selector (CAAL)
OMS............. Oral and Maxillofacial Surgery
OMS............. Orbital Maneuvering System [*or Subsystem*] [*NASA*]
OMS............. Orbital Multifunction Satellite
OMS............. Ordnance Machine Shop
OMS............. Organic Mass Spectroscopy
OMS............. Organic Mental Syndrome [*Medicine*] (DMAA)
OMS............. Organisation Mondiale de la Sante [*World Health Organization - WHO*] [*Switzerland*]
OMS............. Organizacion Mundial de la Salud [*World Health Organization*] [*Spanish United Nations*] (DUND)
OMS............. Organizational Maintenance Shop [*Army*]
OMS............. Organizational Maintenance Squadron [*Air Force*] (MCD)
OMS............. Organizational Maintenance Support
OMS............. Oriental Missionary Society [*Later, OMS International*] (EA)
OMS............. Outdoor Microphone System
OMS............. Output Multiplex Synchronizer
oms.............. Output per Man Shift
oms.............. Output per Man Shift (AD)
OMS............. Overnight Message Service [*Diversified Data Processing and Consulting, Inc.*] [*Oak Park, MI*] [*Telecommunications*] (TSSD)
OMS............. Overseas Mission Society [*Defunct*] (EA)
OMS............. Ovonic Memory Switch (PDAA)
OMS............. Spectravac Power Conversion Systems, Inc., Mississauga, Ontario [*Library symbol National Library of Canada*] (NLC)
OMSA .... Offshore Marine Service Association [*New Orleans, LA*] (EA)
OMSA .... Orders and Medals Society of America (EA)
OMSA .... Ordnance Missile Support Agency (SAA)
OMSA .... Otitis Media, Suppurative, Acute [*Medicine*]
OMSA .... Seaman Apprentice, Opticalman, Striker [*Navy rating*]
OMSA .... Simcoe County Archives, Minesing, Ontario [*Library symbol National Library of Canada*] (NLC)
OMSAPC ..... Office of Mobile Source Air Pollution Control [*Environmental Protection Agency*]
OMSB .... Outcomes Management System Information Board
OMSC .... Organisation Mondiale pour la Systemique et la Cybernetique [*World Organization of Systems and Cybernetics*] (EAIO)
OMSC .... Otitis Media, Secretory, Chronic [*Medicine*] (DAVI)
OMSC .... Otitis Media, Suppurative, Chronic [*Medicine*]
OMSDG........ Maxville Branch, Stormount, Dundas, and Glengarry County Public Library, Ontario [*Library symbol National Library of Canada*] (NLC)
OMSE .... Office of Management Systems and Evaluation [*Environmental Protection Agency*] (GFGA)
Om Sea ...... Omond's Law of the Sea [*1916*] [*A publication*] (DLA)
OMSF .... Office of Manned Space Flight [*NASA*]
OMSF .... Office of Minerals and Solid Fuels [*Formerly, OMM*] [*Abolished, 1971 Department of the Interior*]
OMSG .... Official Mail Study Group [*Defunct*] (EA)
OMSG .... Our Message [*Aviation*] (FAAC)
OMSI .... Oregon Museum of Science and Industry
OMSIP .... Ontario Medical Surgical Insurance Plan [*Canada*] (AD)
OMSITE ...... Oral and Maxillofacial Surgery In-Training Examination
OMSJ.......... Sharjah/International [*United Arab Emirates*] [*ICAO location identifier*] (ICLI)
OMSJB .... St. Jean Bosco Library, Matachewan, Ontario [*Library symbol National Library of Canada*] (BIB)
OMSK .... Smith, Kline & French Canada Ltd., Mississauga, Ontario [*Library symbol National Library of Canada*] (NLC)
OMSLMSq ... Organizational Missile Maintenance Squadron [*Air Force*]
OMSM .... Medical Library, Syntex, Inc., Mississauga, Ontario [*Library symbol National Library of Canada*] (NLC)
OMS/MP ...... Operational Mode Summary/Mission Profiles (MCD)
OMSMT....... South Marysburgh Township Public Library, Milford, Ontario [*Library symbol National Library of Canada*] (BIB)
OMsn .... Mason Public Library, Mason, OH [*Library symbol Library of Congress*] (LCLS)
OMSN .... Seaman, Opticalman, Striker [*Navy rating*]
OMSP .... Operational Maintenance Support Plan [*NASA*] (MCD)
OMSq.......... Organizational Maintenance Squadron [*Air Force*] (AFM)
OMSQA .... Office of Monitoring Systems and Quality Assurance [*Environmental Protection Agency*] (EPA)
OMSRADS ... Optimum Mix of Short Range Air Defense Systems
OMST.......... Object Manipulation Speed Test
OMSWG ...... Operations and Maintenance Security Working Group (SSD)
OMT............. McKellar Township Public Library, Ontario [*Library symbol National Library of Canada*] (NLC)
OMT............. Metropolitan Toronto Library, Multilanguage Service [*UTLAS symbol*]
OMT............. Object Modeling Technology [*Ungermann-Bass, Inc.*]
OMT............. Ocean Marine Technology [*Vancouver Stock Exchange symbol*]
OMT............. Oceanography and Marine Technology [*Defunct*] (USDC)
OMT............. Office of Manufacturing Technology [*DARCOM*] [*Army*] (RDA)
OMT............. Officiating Minister to the Troops [*British*]
OMT............. Old Merchant Taylors [*School*] [*British*] (ROG)
OMT............. Oleoyl Methyl Taurate [*Organic chemistry*]
OMT............. O-Methylthreonine [*Biochemistry*]
OMT............. Ophthalmic Medical Assistant (DAVI)
OMT............. Ophthalmic Medical Technician [*or Technologist*] (HCT)
OMT............. Oral Mucosal Transudate [*Clinical chemistry*]
OMT............. Ordnance Maintenance Truck [*British*]
OMT............. Organizational Maintenance Technician [*Army*] (AABC)
OMT............. Organizational Maintenance Trainer (MCD)
OMT............. Orthogonal Mode Transducer (IAA)
OMT............. Orthomode Transducer [*Electronics*]

omt............ Orthomode Transducer (AD)
OMT............ Ortho-Mycaminosyltylonolide [*Antibacterial compound*]
OMT............ Orthotropic Multicell Tank
OMT............ Osteopathic Manipulative Therapy (CPH)
OMT............ Other Military Target
OMTA.......... Office of Management and Technical Assessment [*Environmental Protection Agency*] (GFGA)
OMTA.......... Ovulation Method Teachers Association (EA)
OMTBP........ Octamethyltetrabenzporphyrin [*Organic chemistry*]
OMTC.......... Ontario Ministry of Transportation and Communications [*Downsview, ON*] [*Telecommunications*] (TSSD)
OMTD.......... Operator/Maintenance Task Description (DNAB)
OMTN.......... Other Military Teletypewriter Network (CET)
OMTNS......... Over Mountains [*NWS*] (FAAC)
OMTR.......... Officer Master Tape Record [*Army*] (AABC)
OMTS.......... Organizational Maintenance Test Station [*Army*]
OMtsjC.......... College of Mount St. Joseph-On-The-Ohio, Mount St. Joseph, OH [*Library symbol Library of Congress*] (LCLS)
OMTSS......... Ordnance Multiple-Purpose Tactical Satellite System
OMtv.......... Mount Vernon Public Library, Mount Vernon, OH [*Library symbol Library of Congress*] (LCLS)
OMtvN.......... Mount Vernon Nazarene College, Mount Vernon, OH [*Library symbol Library of Congress*] (LCLS)
OMU.......... Operational Mock-Up
OMU.......... Operative Mechanics' Union [*British*]
OMU.......... Optical Measuring Unit (KSC)
OMUC.......... Upper Canada Village, Morrisburg, Ontario [*Library symbol National Library of Canada*] (NLC)
OMUP.......... Organization and Management User Parts [*Telecommunications*] (OSI)
OMV.......... Oat Mosaic Virus [*Plant pathology*]
omv............ Oblates of the Virgin Mary (TOCD)
OMV.......... Oblates of the Virgin Mary (TOCD)
OMV.......... Orbital Maneuvering Vehicle [*NASA*]
OMV.......... Overseas Media Visitor
OMV.......... Oxygen Manual Valve (NASA)
OMVC.......... Mattice-Val Cote Public Library, Mattice, Ontario [*Library symbol National Library of Canada*] (BIB)
OMVC.......... Open Mitral Valve Commissurotomy [*Medicine*]
OMVCC........ Orbital Maneuvering Vehicle Control Center [*NASA*] (SSD)
OMVG.......... Organisation pour la Mise en Valeur du Fleuve Gambie [*Gambia River Basin Organisation*] (EAIO)
OMVI.......... Operating a Motor Vehicle Intoxicated (MEDA)
OM-VPE....... Organometallic Vapor Phase Epitaxy [*Also, OM-CVD, MO-CVD, MO-VPE*] [*Semiconductor technology*]
OMVTO........ Office Motor Vehicle Transportation Officer [*Army*] (AABC)
OMVUIL....... Operating Motor Vehicle under the Influence of Liquor [*Traffic offense charge*]
OMVWI....... Operating Motor Vehicle while Intoxicated [*Traffic offense charge*]
OMW.......... Office of the Mining Warden [*Victoria, Australia*]
OMW.......... Omak [*Washington*] [*Seismograph station code, US Geological Survey*] (SEIS)
OMWG.......... Object Model Working Group
OMWM......... Open Marsh Water Managed [*Ecology*]
OMX.......... Officemax, Inc. [*NYSE symbol*] (SAG)
OMX.......... Xerox Research Centre of Canada, Mississauga, Ontario [*Library symbol National Library of Canada*] (NLC)
OMZ.......... Oamaru [*New Zealand*] [*Seismograph station code, US Geological Survey*] (SEIS)
OMZ.......... Oxygen-Minimum Zone [*Oceanography*]
OMZ.......... Oxymorphonazine [*An analgesic*]
ON.......... Air Nauru [*ICAO designator*] (AD)
ON.......... Central Branch, Nepean Public Library, Ontario [*Library symbol National Library of Canada*] (NLC)
ON.......... McKinley Memorial Library, Niles, OH [*Library symbol Library of Congress*] (LCLS)
ON.......... New Order [*Revolutionary group*] [*Italy*]
ON.......... Octane Number [*Fuel terminology*]
on............ Octane Number (AD)
ON.......... Oculonasal [*Anatomy*]
ON.......... Office Nurse
ON.......... Officer's Name (NITA)
ON.......... Official Number (DS)
ON.......... Off Normal
ON.......... Ogden Nash
ON.......... Oil-Immersed Natural-Colled Transformer (IAA)
ON.......... Old Norse [*Language, etc.*]
ON.......... Olfactory Nerve [*Neuroanatomy*]
ON.......... Oligonucleotide [*Chemistry*]
ON.......... Omega Navigation (PDAA)
ON.......... Omega Neuron [*Neuroanatomy*]
ON.......... Omni Nocte [*Every Night*] [*Pharmacy*]
on............ Omni Nocte [*Every Night*] [*Latin*] (AD)
ON.......... Oncology [*Medical specialty*] (DHSM)
ON.......... Onions (ROG)
on............ Onomastikon [*Lexicon*] [*Greek*] (AD)
On.......... Onorevole [*Honorable*] [*Italian*] (AD)
ON.......... Onorevole [*Honorable*] (EY)
On.......... Onsdag [*Wednesday*] [*Danish*] (AD)
on............ Onstage [*Theater*] (WDMC)
ON.......... Ontario [*Canadian province*] [*Postal code*]
ON.......... Ontario Northland Railway [*Canada*] (AD)
ON.......... Opera News [*A publication*] (BRI)
ON.......... Operation Notice (AAG)
ON.......... Optic Nerve [*Anatomy*]

O/N.......... Order Notify [*Bill of lading*] [*Shipping*]
ON.......... Order Number (NITA)
ON.......... Oregon [*Obsolete*] (ROG)
ON.......... Original Negative (MCD)
ON.......... Ortho-Novum [*A contraceptive*] [*Ortho Pharmaceutical Corp.*] (DAVI)
ON.......... Orthopedic Nurse
ON.......... Our Neighbours [*A publication*]
O/N.......... Own Name
o/n............ Own Name (AD)
ON.......... Oxidation Number (IAA)
ONA.......... Nakina Public Library, Ontario [*Library symbol National Library of Canada*] (BIB)
ONA.......... Office of National Assessments [*Australia*]
ONA.......... Onahama [*Japan*] [*Seismograph station code, US Geological Survey*] (SEIS)
ONA.......... Oneita Industries [*NYSE symbol*] (SAG)
ONA.......... Open Network Architecture [*Computer science*]
ONA.......... Optical Navigation Attachment (WDAA)
ONA.......... Orthonitroaniline (DICI)
ONA.......... Overseas National Airways [*Belgium ICAO designator*] (FAAC)
ONA.......... Overseas National Airways, Inc.
ONA.......... Overseas News Agency
ONA.......... Winona [*Minnesota*] [*Airport symbol*] (AD)
ONA.......... Winona, MN [*Location identifier FAA*] (FAAL)
ONAC.......... Office of Noise Abatement and Control [*Environmental Protection Agency*]
ONAC.......... Operating Network Advisory Committee [*NERComP*]
ONAIS......... Organization of North American Indian Students [*Defunct*] (EA)
ONAL.......... Off-Net Access Line [*Telecommunications*] (TEL)
ONAP.......... Orbit Navigation Analysis Program
ONAP.......... Organisation Nationale d'Anti-Pauvrete [*Canada*]
ONAS.......... Outpatient Nonavailability Statement [*DoD*]
OnAssign.... On Assignment, Inc. [*Associated Press*] (SAG)
O-NAV......... On-Board Navigation (MCD)
ONAX.......... Overseas National Airways, Inc. [*Air carrier designation symbol*]
ONB.......... Monkey Bay [*Malawi*] [*Airport symbol*] (AD)
ONb.......... New Breman Public Library, New Breman, OH [*Library symbol Library of Congress*] (LCLS)
ONB.......... North Bay Public Library, Ontario [*Library symbol National Library of Canada*] (NLC)
ONB.......... Octane Number Barrel [*Fuel terminology*]
ONB.......... Old Natura Brevium [*A publication*] (DLA)
ONB.......... Ortho-Nitrobiphenyl [*Organic chemistry*]
ONBA.......... Centre de Ressources, Ecole Secondaire Algonquin, North Bay, Ontario [*Library symbol National Library of Canada*] (NLC)
ONBCC......... Canadore College, North Bay, Ontario [*Library symbol National Library of Canada*] (NLC)
Onbcp.......... ONBANcorp, Inc. [*Associated Press*] (SAG)
ONBD.......... On Board (NASA)
ONBD.......... On Board
ONBK.......... Onbancorp, Inc. [*NASDAQ symbol*] (NQ)
ONBKP.......... ONBANCorp 6.75% Cv 'B' Pfd [*NASDAQ symbol*] (TTSB)
ONBM.......... Belmont and Methuen Township Public Library, Nephton, Ontario [*Library symbol National Library of Canada*] (BIB)
ONBNU........ Nipissing University College, North Bay, Ontario [*Library symbol National Library of Canada*] (NLC)
ONBOSUB.... On Board a Submarine [*Navy*]
ONBOWCOM... Duty on Board that Vessel when Placed in Commission [*Navy*]
ONBOWSERV... Duty on Board that Vessel when Placed in Service [*Navy*]
ONBP.......... Staff Library, North Bay Psychiatric Hospital, Ontario [*Library symbol National Library of Canada*] (NLC)
ONBT.......... Orbiter Neutral Buoyancy Trainer [*NASA*] (MCD)
ONBT.......... Regroupement des Organisations Nationales Benevoles [*Also, National Voluntary Organizations*] (AC)
ONBWF........ West Ferris Secondary School, North Bay, Ontario [*Library symbol National Library of Canada*] (NLC)
ONC.......... Confederation High School, Nepean, Ontario [*Library symbol National Library of Canada*] (NLC)
ONC.......... Office of Narcotics Coordinator [*Later, NARCOG*] [*CIA*]
ONC.......... Office of New Careers [*HEW*]
ONC.......... Olivet Nazarene College [*Kankakee, IL*]
ONC.......... Oncology (DAVI)
ONC.......... Oncor, Inc. [*AMEX symbol*] (SAG)
ONC.......... On-Site Container (DOMA)
onc............ Ontario [*MARC country of publication code Library of Congress*] (LCCP)
ONC.......... Open Network Computing [*Computer science*] (PCM)
ONC+.......... Open Network Computing Plus [*Computer science*] (PCM)
ONC.......... Operational Navigation Charts [*Air Force*]
ONC.......... Optimists National Corps [*British military*] (DMA)
ONC.......... Ordinary National Certificate [*British*]
ONC.......... Oregon-Nevada-California [*Truck line*] (IIA)
ONC.......... Orthopedic Nursing Certificate
ONC.......... Overall NATO Command (NATG)
ONCB.......... Centennial Branch, Nepean Public Library, Ontario [*Library symbol National Library of Canada*] (NLC)
ONC/D.......... Ordinary National Certificate/Diploma (ACII)
ONCE.......... Office of National Cost Estimates [*Department of Health and Human Services*] (GFGA)
ONCF.......... Office National des Chemins de Fer [*Moroccan Railways*]
ONCFM.......... Office National des Chemins de Fer du Maroc [*Moroccan Railways*] (DCTA)
ONCG-A.......... Oncogenic Virus Battery - Acute [*Oncology*] (DAVI)
ONcM.......... Muskingum College, New Concord, OH [*Library symbol Library of Congress*] (LCLS)

ONCMM .... Cosby, Mason, and Martland Public Library, Noelville, Ontario [*Library symbol National Library of Canada*] (NLC)

ONCN .... [*An*] O'Neill Concordance [*A publication*]

ONCO .... Office of NOAA [*National Oceanic and Atmospheric Administration*] Corps Operations (USDC)

ONCO .... Office of NOAA [*National Oceanic and Atmospheric Administration*] Corps Operations [*Marine science*] (OSRA)

OnCo .... On Command Corp. [*Associated Press*] (SAG)

ONCO .... On Command Corp. [*NASDAQ symbol*] (SAG)

Onco .... OncoRx, Inc. [*Associated Press*] (SAG)

Oncogn .... Oncogene Science, Inc. [*Associated Press*] (SAG)

ONCOL .... Oncologist

OnCom .... On Command Corp. [*Associated Press*] (SAG)

OnComm ...... On Command Corp. [*Associated Press*] (SAG)

Oncor .... Oncor, Inc. [*Associated Press*] (SAG)

ONCORE ...... On-Command Restartable (MCD)

Oncormd ...... OncorMed, Inc. [*Associated Press*] (SAG)

OncoRx .... OncoRx, Inc. [*Associated Press*] (SAG)

ONCRC .... Central Resource Centre, Carleton Roman Catholic School Board, Nepean, Ontario [*Library symbol National Library of Canada*] (NLC)

ONCS .... Oncogene Science [*NASDAQ symbol*] (TTSB)

ONCS .... Oncogene Science, Inc. [*NASDAQ symbol*] (NQ)

ONCU .... Cumberland Township Library, Navan, Ontario [*Library symbol National Library of Canada*] (BIB)

OND .... Office for Network Development [*Ottawa, ON*] [*National Library of Canada Telecommunications service*] (TSSD)

OND .... Office of Neighborhood Development (OICC)

OND .... Office of the Nominal Defendant [*Australia*]

OND .... Ondangua [*Namibia*] [*Airport symbol*] (OAG)

OND .... Operator Need Date (NASA)

OND .... Ophthalmic Nursing Diploma

OND .... Ordinary National Diploma [*British*]

OND .... Orthopaedic Nursing Diploma [*British*]

OND .... Other Neurological Disorders

OND .... Own Number Dialing [*Telecommunications*] (OA)

ONDA .... Norwich and District Archives, Norwich, Ontario [*Library symbol National Library of Canada*] (BIB)

ONDCP .... Office of National Drug Control Policy [*Executive Office of the President*]

ONDE .... Office of Naval Disability Evaluation (NVT)

ONDI .... Ontrack Data International, Inc. [*NASDAQ symbol*] (SAG)

ONDS .... Dipix Systems Ltd., Nepean, Ontario [*Library symbol National Library of Canada*] (NLC)

ONDS .... Optic Nerve Decompression Surgery

ONDS .... Oriental Nocturnal Death Syndrome [*Neurology*] (DAVI)

ONE .... Banc One Corp. [*NYSE symbol*] (SPSG)

ONE .... Current Tech [*Vancouver Stock Exchange symbol*]

ONE .... Current Technology [*VS, exchange symbol*] (TTSB)

ONe .... Nelsonville Public Library, Nelsonville, OH [*Library symbol Library of Congress*] (LCLS)

ONE .... Newmarket Public Library, Ontario [*Library symbol National Library of Canada*] (NLC)

ONE .... Northeastern Ohio University, College of Medicine, Rootstown, OH [*OCLC symbol*] (OCLC)

ONE .... Office National de l'Energie [*National Energy Board - NEB*] [*Canada*]

ONE .... Office Network Exchange [*Honeywell, Inc.*]

ONE .... Onepusu [*Solomon Islands*] [*Airport symbol Obsolete*] (OAG)

ONE .... Onerahi [*Whangarei*] [*New Zealand*] [*Seismograph station code, US Geological Survey*] (SEIS)

ONE .... Open Network Environment [*Netscape network*] [*Computer science*]

ONE .... Optimum Nutritional Effectiveness [*Brand name of dog food*] [*Ralston Purina Co.*]

O'Neal Neg L... O'Neal's Negro Law of South Carolina [*A publication*] (DLA)

ONEC .... OneComm Corp. [*NASDAQ symbol*] (SAG)

OneCm .... OneComm Corp. [*Associated Press*] (SAG)

ONEG .... O Negative [*Blood type*] [*Hematology and laboratory*] (DAVI)

ONeH .... Hocking Technical College, Nelsonville, OH [*Library symbol Library of Congress*] (LCLS)

Oneida .... Oneida Ltd. [*Associated Press*] (SAG)

Oneita .... Oneita Industries [*Associated Press*] (SAG)

ONELAC ...... Newburgh Branch, Lennox and Addington County, Ontario [*Library symbol National Library of Canada*] (BIB)

OneLb .... One Liberty Properties, Inc. [*Associated Press*] (SAG)

Onelibt .... One Liberty Properties, Inc. [*Associated Press*] (SAG)

ONEMRCM... BCC Library, CANMET, Energy, Mines, and Resources Canada [*Bibliotheque du CBC, CANMET, Energie, Mines, et Ressources Canada*], Nepean, Ontario [*Library symbol National Library of Canada*] (NLC)

ONEO .... Office of Navajo Economic Opportunity

ONEOK .... ONEOK, Inc. [*Associated Press*] (SAG)

ONEP .... Office National d'Edition et de Presse [*News agency*] [*Niger*] (EY)

ONEP .... Pickering College, Newmarket, Ontario [*Library symbol National Library of Canada*] (NLC)

ONEPI .... Office National d'Edition, de Presse, et d'Imprimerie [*Publisher*] [*Benin*] (EY)

OnePrice...... One Price Clothing Stores, Inc. [*Associated Press*] (SAG)

ONER .... Oceanic Navigational Error Report [*Aviation*] (FAAC)

Onet .... Ontario Regional Network [*Canada*] [*Computer science*] (TNIG)

ONEU .... Neustadt Village Public Library, Ontario [*Library symbol National Library of Canada*] (NLC)

OneVall....... One Valley Bancorp of West Virginia, Inc. [*Associated Press*] (SAG)

ONew .... Newark Public Library, Newark, OH [*Library symbol Library of Congress*] (LCLS)

ONewU .... Ohio State University, Newark Campus, Newark, OH [*Library symbol Library of Congress*] (LCLS)

OneWve...... OneWave, Inc. [*Associated Press*] (SAG)

ONF .... Niagara Falls Public Library, Ontario [*Library symbol National Library of Canada*] (NLC)

ONF .... Office National du Film du Canada [*National Film Board of Canada - NFB*]

ONF .... Old Norman French [*Language, etc.*]

ONF .... Old Northern French [*Language, etc.*]

ONF .... Optic Nerve Fiber [*Anatomy*]

ONFA .... Acres Consulting Services Ltd., Niagara Falls, Ontario [*Library symbol National Library of Canada*] (NLC)

ONFCY .... Cyanamid, Niagara Falls, Ontario [*Library symbol National Library of Canada*] (NLC)

ONFJC .... John Coutts Library Services Ltd., Niagara Falls, Ontario [*Library symbol National Library of Canada*] (NLC)

ONFLC .... Lanmer Consultants Ltd., Niagara Falls, Ontario [*Library symbol National Library of Canada*] (NLC)

ONFM .... On or Nearest Full Moon [*Freemasonry*] (ROG)

ONFR .... Old Northern French [*Language, etc.*]

ONFWM .... Willoughby Historical Museum, Niagara Falls, Ontario [*Library symbol National Library of Canada*] (BIB)

ONFWPL...... W. P. London & Associates, Niagara Falls, Ontario [*Library symbol National Library of Canada*] (NLC)

ONG .... Donalsonville, GA [*Location identifier FAA*] (FAAL)

ONG .... Mornington Island [*Australia Airport symbol*] (OAG)

ONG .... Ongar [*England*]

ONG .... Ongoro [*Peru*] [*Seismograph station code, US Geological Survey Closed*] (SEIS)

ONG .... Osteopathic and Naturopathic Guild [*British*] (DBA)

ONGA .... Overseas Number Group Analysis [*Telecommunications*] (TEL)

ONGC .... Office des Normes Generales du Canada

OnGrd .... On Gard Systems [*Associated Press*] (SAG)

OnGrdSy ..... On Gard Systems [*Associated Press*] (SAG)

ONGRT .... North Gower Branch, Rideau Township Library, Ontario [*Library symbol National Library of Canada*] (BIB)

ONGS .... Office of National Geodetic Survey [*National Ocean Survey*]

ONH .... Office of Naval History [*Also, OFFNAVHIST*]

ONH .... Oneonta [*New York*] [*Airport symbol*] (OAG)

ON/H .... On the Hatch Cover [*Stowage*] (DNAB)

ONHI .... Niagara Historical Society, Niagara-On-The-Lake, Ontario [*Library symbol National Library of Canada*] (NLC)

ONHIC .... ODPHP [*Office of Disease Prevention and Health Promotion*] National Health Information Center (IID)

ONI .... Moanamani [*Indonesia*] [*Airport symbol*] (OAG)

ONI .... Nipigon Public Library, Ontario [*Library symbol National Library of Canada*] (NLC)

ONI .... Office of Naval Intelligence

ONI .... Oficina Nacional de Informacion [*National Information Office*] [*Press agency Peru*]

ONI .... Oni [*Former USSR Seismograph station code, US Geological Survey*] (SEIS)

ONI .... Operator Number Identification [*Bell System*]

ONIO .... Office of Naval Inspectors of Ordnance

ONIP .... Office of National Industry Promotion [*Bureau of Apprenticeship and Training*] [*Department of Labor*]

OnIssues...... On the Issues [*A publication*] (BRI)

ONJ .... Olivia Newton-John [*Singer*]

ONJSW .... J. S. Woodsworth Secondary School, Nepean, Ontario [*Library symbol National Library of Canada*] (NLC)

Onk .... Targum Onkelos (BJA)

ONL .... New Liskeard Public Library, Ontario [*Library symbol National Library of Canada*] (NLC)

ONL .... Office of Naval Liaison [*NASA*] (KSC)

ONL .... Ohio Northern University, Law Library, Ada, OH [*OCLC symbol*] (OCLC)

ONL .... O'Neill, NE [*Location identifier FAA*] (FAAL)

ONL .... Outer Nuclear Layer [*Anatomy*]

ONL .... Overnight Loan (ADA)

ONLAC .... Lennox and Addington Counties Public Library, Napanee, Ontario [*Library symbol National Library of Canada*] (NLC)

ONLAH......... Lennox and Addington Historical Society, Napanee, Ontario [*Library symbol National Library of Canada*] (BIB)

ONLAM........ Lennox and Addington Museum, Napanee, Ontario [*Library symbol National Library of Canada*] (NLC)

ONLAS .... Optical Night Landing Approach System [*Aviation*] (PDAA)

ONLICATS.... Online Shared Cataloging System [*Computer science*]

ONLP .... On-Line Program Development [*Computer science*] (MHDB)

ONIP .... Perry County District Library, New Lexington, OH [*Library symbol Library of Congress*] (LCLS)

ONLS .... Sunnidale Township Public Library, New Lowell, Ontario [*Library symbol National Library of Canada*] (BIB)

ONLY .... Online Yield [*Computer science*]

ONM .... Condamine [*Queensland*] [*Airport symbol*] (AD)

ONM .... Office of Naval Material [*Later, NMCOM*]

ONM .... OncorMed, Inc. [*AMEX symbol*] (SAG)

ONM .... Socorro, NM [*Location identifier FAA*] (FAAL)

ONMB .... Merivale Road Branch, Nepean Public Library, Ontario [*Library symbol National Library of Canada*] (BIB)

ONMINST..... Office of Naval Material Publication Type Instruction

ONMM .... On-Board Microwave MODEM [*Telecommunications*] (LAIN)

ONMPC .... Office of Naval Material - Permanent Cadre

ONMS .... Orbiter Neutral Mass Spectrometer [*NASA*]

ONMSS .... Office of Nuclear Materials Safety and Safeguards [*Nuclear Regulatory Commission*]

ONN .... Fort Meade, MD [*Location identifier FAA*] (FAAL)
ONN .... O'Nyong-Nyong Virus
ONNI .... Office of National Narcotics Intelligence [*Later, Drug Enforcement Administration*] [*Department of Justice*]
ONNM .... On or Nearest New Moon [*Freemasonry*] (ROG)
ONO .... Norwood Public Library, Ontario [*Library symbol National Library of Canada*] (BIB)
ONO .... Office of Naval Operations
ONO .... Ontario [*Oregon*] [*Airport symbol*] (AD)
ONO .... Ontario, OR [*Location identifier FAA*] (FAAL)
ONO .... Organization of News Ombudsmen (EA)
ONO .... Or Nearest [*or Near*] Offer [*Business term*] (ADA)
ONOC .... Oceania National Olympic Committee [*Australia*]
ONocHE ...... Hoover Co., Engineering Division, North Canton, OH [*Library symbol Library of Congress*] (LCLS)
ON-OFF....... Oscillatory, Nonoscillatory Flip-Flop [*Computer science*]
ONOL .... Niagara-On-The-Lake Public Library, Ontario [*Library symbol National Library of Canada*] (BIB)
Onom .... Onomasticon [*of Eusebius*] (BJA)
ONOMAT..... Onomatopoeia (ROG)
ONOO.......... Outline NATO Operational Objective (MCD)
ONOP .... Office of Naval Officer Procurement
ONOP .... Officer-in-Charge, Branch Office of Naval Officer Procurement (DNAB)
ONowdM...... Athenaeum of Ohio, Norwood, OH [*Library symbol Library of Congress*] (LCLS)
ONOZ .... Oil Nozzle
ONP .... Newport [*Oregon*] [*Airport symbol Obsolete*] (OAG)
ONP .... Office of National Programs [*Employment and Training Administration*] [*Department of Labor*]
ONP .... Ohio Nisi Prius Reports [*A publication*] (DLA)
ONP .... Old Newspaper [*Recycling*]
ONP .... Onex Packaging, Inc. [*Toronto Stock Exchange symbol*]
ONP .... Open Network Provision
ONP .... Operating Nursing Procedure
ONP .... Original Net Premium [*Insurance*] (AIA)
ONP .... Ortho-Nitrophenol [*Organic chemistry*]
ONPA .... Office of National Projects Administration [*Department of Labor*]
ONPG .... O-Nitrophenyl-beta-D-galactopyranoside [*Test*] [*Microbiology*]
ONPG .... O-Nitrophenyl Galactoside (DOG)
ONPG .... Operational Nuclear Planning Group [*Military*]
ONP-GAL ..... Ortho-Nitrophenyl-B-Galactosidase [*Organic chemistry*] (MAE)
ONpK .... Kent State University, Tuscarawas County Regional Campus, New Philadelphia, OH [*Library symbol Library of Congress*] (LCLS)
ONPNS........ Ohio Nisi Prius Reports, New Series [*1903-13*] [*A publication*] (DLA)
OnPointT..... On-Point Technology Systems, Inc. [*Associated Press*] (SAG)
ONPOSR ...... Office of Naval Petroleum and Oil Shale Reserves
ONPR.......... Office of New Production Reactors [*U.S. Department of Energy*] (BARN)
ONPR.......... One Price Clothing Stores, Inc. [*NASDAQ symbol*] (NQ)
ONPR.......... One Price Clothing Strs [*NASDAQ symbol*] (TTSB)
ONPT .... On-Point Technology Systems, Inc. [*NASDAQ symbol*] (SAG)
ONR .... Monkira [*Queensland*] [*Airport symbol*] (AD)
ONR .... Oboz Narodowo-Radykalny [*Radical Nationalist Camp*] [*Poland Political party*] (PPE)
ONR .... Octane Number Requirement [*Automotive engineering*]
ONR .... Office of Naval Research [*Arlington, VA*]
ONR .... Official Naval Reporter [*British*]
ONR .... Ontario Northland Railway
ONR .... Operational NonRADAR Directed Flights (NATG)
ONR .... Original Net Rate [*Insurance*] (AIA)
ONR .... Phillips Petroleum Co., Exploration and Product Library, Bartlesville, OK [*OCLC symbol*] (OCLC)
ONRARO ...... Office of Naval Research, Area Research Office (DNAB)
ONR BR ...... Branch Office, Office of Naval Research
ONRBRO...... Office of Naval Research Branch Research Office
ONRC .... Office of Naval Research, Chicago
ONRDB .... Ruth E. Dickinson Branch, Nepean Public Library, Ontario [*Library symbol National Library of Canada*] (BIB)
ONRDET...... Office of Naval Research Detachment (DNAB)
ONREAST.... Office of Naval Research, East Coast Regional Office (DNAB)
ONRFE .... Office of Naval Research, Far East Regional Office (DNAB)
ONRI .... Octane Number Requirement Increase [*Automotive engineering*]
ONRL .... Office of Naval Research, London
ONRO.......... ODA Natural Resources Office
ONRRR .... Office of Naval Research Resident Representative
ONRS.......... Oceanic Navigation Research Society (EA)
ONRS.......... Office of National Range Support (SAA)
ONRT.......... Office of Naval Research, Tokyo
ONRT.......... Online Real Time [*Computer science*] (ADA)
ONRWEST.... Office of Naval Research, West Coast Regional Office (DNAB)
ONRY.......... Ogdensburg Bridge & Port Authority [*AAR code*]
ONS .... Northwestern School of Law, Lewis and Clark College, Portland, OR [*OCLC symbol*] (OCLC)
ONS .... Oconee Nuclear Station (NRCH)
ONS .... Office for National Statistics [*British*]
ONS .... Office of Nuclear Systems (SAA)
ONS .... Off-Normal Switch
ONS .... Omega Navigation System
ONS .... Oncology Nursing Society (EA)
ONS .... Onslow [*Australia Airport symbol Obsolete*] (OAG)
ONS .... Open Network Server [*Tylink Corp.*]
ONS .... Operational Needs Statement [*Army*]
ONS .... Oriental Numismatic Society [*Reading, Berkshire, England*] (EAIO)

ONSDG .... Newington Branch, Stormont, Dundas, and Glengarry County Library, Ontario [*Library symbol National Library of Canada*] (BIB)
On Serv ...... On Service [*A publication*]
ONSHR .... On Shore [*NWS*] (FAAC)
ONSI .... Orion Network Systems [*NASDAQ symbol*] (TTSB)
ONSI .... Orion Network Systems, Inc. [*NASDAQ symbol*] (SAG)
ONSIDIV ...... On-Sight Surveys Division
OnSiteS ...... On-Site Sourcing, Inc. [*Associated Press*] (SAG)
Onsl NP ...... Onslow's Nisi Prius [*A publication*] (DLA)
ONSOD .... Omega Navigation System Operations Detail
ONSR .... Sir Robert Borden High School, Nepean, Ontario [*Library symbol National Library of Canada*] (BIB)
ONSS .... On-Site Sourcing, Inc. [*NASDAQ symbol*] (SAG)
ONST .... Outline NATO Staff Target
ONT .... Air Ontario Ltd. [*Canada ICAO designator*] (FAAC)
ONT .... Office Nationale du Tourisme [*Algeria*] (EY)
ONT .... Office of Naval Technology (MCD)
ONT .... Ombudsman of the Northern Territory [*Australia*]
ONT .... Ontario [*California*] [*Airport symbol*]
ONT .... Ontario [*Canadian province*]
Ont............. Ontario [*Canada*] (DD)
Ont............. Ontario (ODBW)
ONT .... Ontario City Library, Ontario, CA [*OCLC symbol*] (OCLC)
ONT .... Ontario Northland Railway [*AAR code*]
Ont............. Ontario Reports [*A publication*] (DLA)
ONT .... Ordinary Neap Tide (WDAA)
ONT .... Our New Thread [*Clark thread designation*]
Ont 2d .... Ontario Reports, Second Series [*Canada*] [*A publication*] (DLA)
Ont A .... Ontario Appeals [*A publication*] (DLA)
ONTAP......... Online Training and Practice (NITA)
ONTAP......... On-Line Training and Practice File [*Lockheed*] [*Computer science*]
Ont App ...... Ontario Appeal Reports [*A publication*] (DLA)
Ontario Cons Reg... Ontario Consolidated Regulations [*Canada*] [*A publication*] (DLA)
ONTC .... ON Technology [*NASDAQ symbol*] (TTSB)
ONTC .... ON Technology Corp. [*NASDAQ symbol*] (SAG)
ONTC .... On Technology Corp. [*NASDAQ symbol*] (SAG)
ON Tch .... ON Technology Corp. [*Associated Press*] (SAG)
ON Tch .... ON Technology Corp. [*Associated Press*] (SAG)
Ont Dig....... Digest of Ontario Case Law [*A publication*] (DLA)
Ont El Cas ... Ontario Election Cases [*1884-1900*] [*Canada A publication*] (DLA)
Ont Elec...... Ontario Election Cases [*1884-1900*] [*Canada A publication*] (DLA)
Ont Elec C ... Ontario Election Cases [*1884-1900*] [*Canada A publication*] (DLA)
Ont Elect..... Ontario Election Cases [*1884-1900*] [*Canada A publication*] (DLA)
ONTERIS...... Ontario Education Resources Information System [*Ontario Ministry of Education*] [*Toronto*] [*Information service or system*] (IID)
ONTG .... Oral Nitroglycerine [*Medicine*]
ONTK .... OnTrak Systems [*NASDAQ symbol*] (TTSB)
ONTK .... On Trak Systems, Inc. [*NASDAQ symbol*] (SAG)
Ont L .... Ontario Law Reports [*A publication*] (DLA)
Ont LJ......... Ontario Law Journal [*A publication*] (DLA)
Ont LJ (NS)... Ontario Law Journal, New Series [*A publication*] (DLA)
Ont LR .... Ontario Reports [*A publication*] (DLA)
Ont L Rep ... Ontario Law Reports [*A publication*] (DLA)
ONTOLT....... Onion, Tomato, or Lettuce [*Notation on restaurant checks*]
Ont Pr........ Ontario Practice [*A publication*] (DLA)
Ont PR .... Ontario Practice Reports [*A publication*] (DLA)
Ont Pr Rep... Ontario Practice Reports [*A publication*] (DLA)
Ont R .... Ontario Reports [*A publication*] (DLA)
ONTR .... Orders Not to Resuscitate [*Medicine*]
OnTrak........ OnTrak Systems, Inc. [*Associated Press*] (SAG)
Ont R & WN... Ontario Reports and Ontario Weekly Notes [*Canada*] [*A publication*] (DLA)
OntrDta....... Ontrack Data International, Inc. [*Associated Press*] (SAG)
Ont Reg ...... Ontario Regulations [*Canada*] [*A publication*] (DLA)
Ont Regs .... Ontario Regulations [*Canada A publication*] (DLA)
Ont Rev Regs... Ontario Revised Regulations [*Canada A publication*] (DLA)
Ont Rev Stat... Ontario Revised Statutes [*Canada*] [*A publication*] (DLA)
Ont Rgt....... Ontario Regiment [*Canada*] (DMA)
Ont Stat ...... Ontario Statutes [*Canada*] [*A publication*] (DLA)
Ont Tax Rep (CCH)... Ontario Tax Reporter (Commerce Clearing House) [*A publication*] (DLA)
Ont Week N... Ontario Weekly Notes [*A publication*] (DLA)
Ont Week R... Ontario Weekly Reporter [*A publication*] (DLA)
Ont Wkly N... Ontario Weekly Notes [*A publication*] (DLA)
Ont Wkly Rep... Ontario Weekly Reporter [*A publication*] (DLA)
Ont WN .... Ontario Weekly Notes [*A publication*] (DLA)
Ont WR....... Ontario Weekly Reporter [*A publication*] (DLA)
Ont WR Op... Ontario Weekly Reporter. Opinions of United States Attorneys General [*A publication*] (DLA)
ONU .... Kongoussi [*Upper Volta*] [*Airport symbol*] (AD)
ONU .... Ohio Northern University [*Ada, OH*]
ONU .... Ohio Northern University, Ada, OH [*OCLC symbol*] (OCLC)
ONU .... Ono-I-Lau [*Fiji*] [*Airport symbol Obsolete*] (OAG)
ONU .... Optical Network Unit [*Telecommunications*]
ONU .... Organisation des Nations Unies [*United Nations French*]
ONU .... Organizacion de las Naciones Unidas [*United Nations*] [*Spanish*] (DUND)
ONU .... Organizzazione Nazioni Unite [*United Nations*] [*Italian*]
ONUC.......... Organisation des Nations Unies au Congo [*United Nations Organization in the Congo*]
ONUDI .... Organisation des Nations Unies pour le Developpement Industriel [*United Nations Industrial Development Organization*]

ONUDI .... Organizacion de las Naciones Unidas para el Desarrollo Industrial [*United Nations Industrial Development Organization*] [*Spanish*] (DUND)

ONU Intra LR... Ohio Northern University. Intramural Law Review [*A publication*] (DLA)

ONULP .... Ontario New Universities Library Project

Onuphr De Interp Voc Eccles... Onuphrius. De Interpretatione Vocum Ecclesiae [*A publication*] (DLA)

ONV .... Organisations Nationales Volontaires [*Canada*]

ONVL .... Over-the-Nose Vision Line (PDAA)

ONW .... Office of Naval Weapons

ONW .... On Watch

ONW .... Oregon & Northwestern Railroad Co. [*AAR code*]

ONWI .... Office of Nuclear Waste Isolation (MCD)

ONWL .... Whitefish Lake Band Public Library, Naughton, Ontario [*Library symbol National Library of Canada*] (NLC)

ONWS .... Office of Naval Weather Service

ONX .... Colon [*Panama*] [*Airport symbol*] (OAG)

ONX .... Mount Olive, NC [*Location identifier FAA*] (FAAL)

onx .... Onyx (VRA)

ONX .... Onyx Petroleum Exploration Co. Ltd. [*Toronto Stock Exchange symbol*]

ONXX .... ONYX Pharmaceuticals [*NASDAQ symbol*] (TTSB)

ONXX .... Onyx Pharmaceuticals, Inc. [*NASDAQ symbol*] (SAG)

ONY .... Olney, TX [*Location identifier FAA*] (FAAL)

ONYX .... Onyx Acceptance [*NASDAQ symbol*] (TTSB)

ONYX .... Onyx Acceptance Corp. [*NASDAQ symbol*] (SAG)

OnyxAcc ...... Onyx Acceptance Corp. [*Associated Press*] (SAG)

OnyxPh .... Onyx Pharmaceuticals, Inc. [*Associated Press*] (SAG)

OO .... Belgium [*International civil aircraft marking*] (ODBW)

OO .... Naval Oceanographic Office [*Also known as NOO; formerly, HO, NHO, USNHO*]

OO .... Oakly, Inc. [*NYSE symbol*] (SAG)

OO .... Oberlin College, Oberlin, OH [*Library symbol Library of Congress*] (LCLS)

OO .... Object-Oriented (BYTE)

OO .... Observation Officer [*Military*]

OO .... Oceanographic Office

OO .... Ocean Outlook (EA)

OO .... Office of Operations [*Department of Agriculture*] (GFGA)

O/O .... Office of Origin (AFM)

O/O .... Off Ocean (SAA)

OO .... Ohio Opinions [*A publication*] (DLA)

OO .... Ohne Ort [*Without Place of Publication*] [*Bibliography*] [*German*]

O/O .... Oil/Ore [*Ship*] (DS)

OO .... Old Orkney [*Whisky*] (ROG)

OO .... Once Over [*To examine cursorily*] [*Slang*]

o-o .... Once-Over [*Theater*] [*Slang*] (WDMC)

O/O .... Only to Order (DGA)

O/O .... On Orbit (MCD)

OO .... On Order

OO .... Oophorectomized [*Gynecology*]

OO .... Open Order

OO .... Operation Order [*Military*]

OO .... Operations Office [*Environmental Protection Agency*] (GFGA)

OO .... Operations Officer [*Navy British*]

OO .... Orderly Officer [*British*]

O/O .... Order Of [*Business term*]

OO .... Ordnance Office [*or Officer*]

OO .... Orthopaedics Overseas (EA)

OO .... Osobyi Otdel [*Counterintelligence surveillance unit in military formation until 1943*] [*Former USSR*]

O/O .... Owner/Operator

OO .... Own Occupation [*Banking*]

OO .... Sunaire Lines [*ICAO designator*] (AD)

OO 2d .... Ohio Opinions, Second Series [*A publication*] (DLA)

OOA .... Object of Affections [*Slang*]

OOA .... Object-Oriented Analysis [*Computer science*]

OOA .... Office of Ocean Affairs [*Navy*]

OOA .... Office of the Americas [*An association*] (EA)

OOA .... Olive Oil Association (EA)

OOA .... On or About (WDAA)

OOA .... Open Ocean Area (SAA)

OOA .... Optimum Orbital Altitude (AAG)

OOA .... Oskaloosa, IA [*Location identifier FAA*] (FAAL)

OOA .... Out of Action (MCD)

OOA .... Out of Area (NVT)

OOA .... Owner Operators of America [*Boston, NY*] (EA)

OOA .... Public Archives [*Archives Publiques*] Ottawa, Ontario [*Library symbol National Library of Canada*] (NLC)

OOAA .... Olive Oil Association of America [*Later, OOA*] (EA)

OOAC .... Algonquin College of Applied Arts and Technology, Ottawa, Ontario [*Library symbol National Library of Canada*] (NLC)

OOACC .... Colonel By Campus, Algonquin College of Applied Arts and Technology, Ottawa, On tario [*Library symbol National Library of Canada*] (NLC)

OOACF .... Alta Vista Branch, Ontario Cancer Foundation, Ottawa, Ontario [*Library symbol National Library of Canada*] (NLC)

OOACH .... Heron Park Campus, Algonquin College of Applied Arts and Technology, Ottawa, Ontario [*Library symbol National Library of Canada*] (BIB)

OOACL .... Library Technician Program, Algonquin College of Applied Arts & Technology, Ottawa, Ontario [*Library symbol National Library of Canada*] (NLC)

OOACR .... Rideau Campus, Algonquin College of Applied Arts and Technology, Ottawa, On tario, [*Library symbol National Library of Canada*] (NLC)

OOAD .... Object-Oriented Analysis & Design [*Computer science*] (CDE)

OOADE .... Archives Deschatelets (Oblats de Marie-Immaculee), Ottawa, Ontario [*Library symbol National Library of Canada*] (NLC)

OOAEA .... Ethnic Archives of Canada, Public Archives [*Archives Ethniques du Canada, Archives Publiques*] Ottawa, Ontario [*Library symbol National Library of Canada*] (NLC)

OOAECB ...... Atomic Energy Control Board [*Commission de Controle de l'Energie Atomique*]Ottawa, Ontario [*Library symbol National Library of Canada*] (NLC)

OOAER .... Research Co., Atomic Energy of Canada Ltd. [*Societe de Recherches, L'Energie Atomique du Canada Ltee*] Ottawa, Ontario [*Library symbol National Library of Canada*] (NLC)

OOAF .... Bibliotheque de l'Ambassade de France, Ottawa, Ontario [*Library symbol National Library of Canada*] (BIB)

OOAFN .... Assembly of First Nations, Ottawa, Ontario [*Library symbol National Library of Canada*] (NLC)

OOAG .... Libraries Division, Agriculture Canada [*Division des Bibliotheques, Agriculture Canada*] Ottawa, Ontario [*Library symbol National Library of Canada*] (NLC)

OOAGA .... Animal Diseases Research Institute, Agriculture Canada [*Institut de Recherches Veterinaires, Agriculture Canada*] Ottawa, Ontario [*Library symbol National Library of Canada*] (NLC)

OOAGAR ..... Animal Research Institute, Agriculture Canada [*Institut de Recherches Zootechniques, Agriculture Canada*] Ottawa, Ontario [*Library symbol National Library of Canada*] (NLC)

OOAGB .... Plant Research Library, Biosystematics Research Institute, Agriculture Canada [*Bibliotheque de Recherches sur les Vegetaux, Institut de Recherches Biosystematiques, Agriculture Canada*] Ottawa, Ontario [*Library symbol National Library of Canada*] (NLC)

OOAGCH ...... Neatby Library, Agriculture Canada [*Bibliotheque Neatby, Agriculture Canada*] Ottawa, Ontario [*Library symbol National Library of Canada*] (NLC)

OOAGE .... Entomology Research Library, Biosystematics Research Institute, Agriculture Canada [*Bibliotheque de Recherches Entomologiques, Institut de Recherches Biosystematiques, Agriculture Canada*] Ottawa, Ontario [*Library symbol National Library of Canada*] (NLC)

OOAGER ...... Engineering and Statistical Research Centre, Agriculture Canada [*Centre de Recherche Technique et de Statistique, Agriculture Canada*] Ottawa, Ontario [*Library symbol National Library of Canada*] (NLC)

OOAGFP .... Laboratory Services Section, Food Production and Marketing Branch, Agriculture Canada [*Section des Services d'Analyse, Direction de la Production et de la Commercialisation des Aliments, Agriculture Canada*] Ottawa, Ontario [*Library symbol National Library of Canada*] (NLC)

OOAGFR ...... Food Research Centre, Agriculture Canada [*Centre de Recherches sur les Aliments,Agriculture Canada*], Ottawa, Ontario [*Library symbol National Library of Canada*] (BIB)

OOAGO .... Research Station, Agriculture Canada [*Station de Recherches, Agriculture Canada*] Ottawa, Ontario [*Library symbol National Library of Canada*] (NLC)

OOAGSR ...... Soil Research Institute, Agriculture Canada [*Institut de Recherches sur les Sols, Agriculture Canada*] Ottawa, Ontario [*Library symbol National Library of Canada*] (NLC)

OOAI .... AMCA International Ltd., Ottawa, Ontario [*Library symbol National Library of Canada*] (NLC)

OOAK .... Oakville Public Library, Ontario [*Library symbol National Library of Canada*] (NLC)

OOAKA .... Appleby College, Oakville, Ontario [*Library symbol National Library of Canada*] (NLC)

OOAKG .... G. D. Searle Co. of Canada Ltd., Oakville, Ontario [*Library symbol National Library of Canada*] (BIB)

OOAKM .... Oakville Museums, Ontario [*Library symbol National Library of Canada*] (BIB)

OOAKS .... Shell Research Centre, Oakville, Ontario [*Library symbol National Library of Canada*] (NLC)

OOAKSC .... Sheridan College, Oakville, Ontario [*Library symbol National Library of Canada*] (NLC)

OOAKSCL ..... Library Techniques, Sheridan College, Oakville, Ontario [*Library symbol National Library of Canada*] (NLC)

OOAMA .... National Map Collection, Public Archives [*Collection Nationale des Cartes et Plans, Archives Publiques*] Ottawa, Ontario [*Library symbol National Library of Canada*] (NLC)

OOAMA .... Office, Ogden Air Material Area [*AFLC*]

OOAM & S... On-Orbit Assembly, Maintenance, and Service [*NASA*] (SSD)

OOAMS .... Manuscript Division, Public Archives [*Division des Manuscrits, Archives Publiques*] Ottawa, Ontario [*Library symbol National Library of Canada*] (NLC)

OOANF .... National Film Archives, Public Archives [*Archives Nationales du Film, Archives Publiques*] Ottawa, Ontario [*Library symbol National Library of Canada*] (NLC)

OOAOA .... Archives, Diocese of Ottawa, Anglican Church of Canada, Ontario [*Library symbol National Library of Canada*] (NLC)

OOAR .... Canadian Broadcasting Corp. [*Societe Radio-Canada*] Ottawa, Ontario [*Library symbol National Library of Canada*] (NLC)

OOASH .... Ashbury College, Ottawa, Ontario [*Library symbol National Library of Canada*] (NLC)

OOB .... Bank of Canada [*Banque du Canada*] Ottawa, Ontario [*Library symbol National Library of Canada*] (NLC)

OOB .... Off-Off Broadway [*Theater*]

OOB	Off Our Backs [*A publication*] (BRI)
OOB	Opening of Business (MCD)
OOB	Operations Operating Budget [*Military*] (AFIT)
OOB	Order of Battle [*Military*] (NVT)
OOB	Ordnance Office Bulletin [*Military*]
OOB	Out of Band [*Telecommunications*] (TEL)
OOB	Out of Bed [*Medicine*]
OOB	Out of Body [*Parapsychology*]
OOB	Out of Bounds (IIA)
OOBA	Brewers Association of Canada, [*Association des Brasseurs du Canada*], Ott awa, Ontario [*Library symbol National Library of Canada*] (NLC)
OOBA	Off Off Broadway Alliance [*Later, ART/NY*]
OOBBRP	Out of Bed with Bathroom Privileges [*Medicine*] (DAVI)
OOBC	Bowmar Canada Ltd., Ottawa, Ontario [*Library symbol National Library of Canada*] (NLC)
OOBE	Ottawa Board of Education, Ontario [*Library symbol National Library of Canada*] (NLC)
OOBE	Out-of-Body Experience [*Parapsychology*]
OOBE	Out-Of-Box Experience [*Computer hacker's terminology*] (PCM)
OOBH	Information Library, British High Commission, Ottawa, Ontario [*Library symbol National Library of Canada*] (BIB)
OOBLA	Onset of Blood Lactose Accumulation [*Metabolism*]
OOBM	Bartonian Metaphysical Society, Ottawa, Ontario [*Library symbol National Library of Canada*] (NLC)
OOBMC	Bureau of Management Consulting, Department of Supply and Services [*Bureau des Conseillers en Gestion, Ministere des Approvisionnements et Services*] Ottawa, Ontario [*Library symbol National Library of Canada*] (NLC)
OOBMI	Bell Canada Market Information Centre, Ottawa, Ontario [*Library symbol National Library of Canada*] (NLC)
OOBMM	Medical Library, Bristol-Myers Pharmaceutical Group, Ottawa, Ontario [*Library symbol National Library of Canada*] (NLC)
OOBR	Buraimi [*Oman*] [*ICAO location identifier*] (ICLI)
OOC	Junior Optimist Octagon International [*Formerly, Optimist Octagon Clubs*] (EA)
OOC	Oberlin College, Conservatory of Music, Oberlin, OH [*Library symbol Library of Congress*] (LCLS)
OOC	Office of Censorship [*Terminated, 1945*] [*Military*]
OOC	Office of Corrections [*Victoria, Australia*]
OOC	Office of Olympic Coordination [*New South Wales, Australia*]
OOC	Off-On Control
OOC	Operating Vehicle without Owner's Consent [*Traffic offense charge*]
OOC	Operational Oceanography Center (USDC)
OOC	Operation Oceanography Center [*Marine science*] (OSRA)
OOC	Organized Occupational Curricula
OOC	Ottawa Public Library [*Bibliotheque Publique d'Ottawa*] Ontario [*Library symbol National Library of Canada*] (NLC)
OOC	Out of Commission (NVT)
OOC	Out of Control
OOC	Over-Ocean Communications
OOC	Overseas Operating Committee [*World War II*]
OOCAA	Canadian Astronautics, Ottawa, Ontario [*Library symbol National Library of Canada*] (NLC)
OOCAAS	Canadian Automobile Association, Ottawa, Ontario [*Library symbol National Library of Canada*] (BIB)
OOCAB	Canadian Association of Broadcasters [*Association Canadienne des Radiodiffuseurs*] Ottawa, Ontario [*Library symbol National Library of Canada*] (NLC)
OOCAC	Canada Council [*Conseil des Arts du Canada*] Ottawa, Ontario [*Library symbol National Library of Canada*] (NLC)
OOCACR	Research and Evaluation Section, Canada Council [*Service de Recherche et d'Evaluation, Conseil des Arts du Canada*], Ottawa, Ontario [*Library symbol National Library of Canada*] (BIB)
OOCACSW	Documentation Centre, Canadian Advisory Council on the Status of Women [*Centre de Documentation, Conseil Consultatif Canadien de la Situation de la Femme*] Ottawa, Ontario [*Library symbol National Library of Canada*] (NLC)
OOCAM	Canadian Association of Medical Radiation Technologists, Ottawa, Ontario [*Library symbol National Library of Canada*] (BIB)
OOCANM	Canadian Museum Association [*Association des Musees Canadiens*], Ottawa, Ontario [*Library symbol National Library of Canada*] (NLC)
OOCAR	Canadian Arctic Resources Committee, Ottawa, Ontario [*Library symbol National Library of Canada*] (NLC)
OOCARE	Care Canada, Ottawa, Ontario [*Library symbol National Library of Canada*] (BIB)
OOCAS	Children's Aid Society of Ottawa-Carleton, Ottawa, Ontario [*Library symbol National Library of Canada*] (NLC)
OOCB	Colonel By Secondary School, Ottawa, Ontario [*Library symbol National Library of Canada*] (NLC)
OOCBC	Conference Board of Canada, Ottawa, Ontario [*Library symbol National Library of Canada*] (NLC)
OOCBE	Carleton Board of Education, Ottawa, Ontario [*Library symbol National Library of Canada*] (NLC)
OOCBH	Human Resources Department, Canadian Broadcasting Corp. [*Departement des Ressources Humaines, Societe Radio-Canada*], Ottawa, Ontario [*Library symbol National Library of Canada*] (BIB)
OOCC	Carleton University, Ottawa, Ontario [*Library symbol National Library of Canada*] (NLC)
OOCCAH	Department of Art History, Carleton University, Ottawa, Ontario [*Library symbol Obsolete National Library of Canada*] (NLC)
OOCCFA	Canadian Centre for Films on Art [*Centre Canadien du Film sur l'Art*] Ottawa, Ontario [*Library symbol National Library of Canada*] (NLC)
OOCCG	Geography Department, Carleton University, Ottawa, Ontario [*Library symbol Obsolete National Library of Canada*] (NLC)
OOCCJ	Church Council on Justice and Correction [*Conseil des Eglises pour la Justiceet la Criminologie*], Ottawa, Ontario [*Library symbol National Library of Canada*] (BIB)
OOCCL	County of Carleton Law Library, Ottawa, Ontario [*Library symbol National Library of Canada*] (NLC)
OOCCR	Canada Centre for Remote Sensing, Energy, Mines and Resources Canada [*Centre Canadien de Teledetection, Energie, Mines et Ressources Canada*] Ottawa, Ontario [*Library symbol National Library of Canada*] (NLC)
OOCCU	Canadian Commission for UNESCO, Ottawa, Ontario [*Library symbol National Library of Canada*] (BIB)
OOCD	Canadian International Development Agency [*Agence Canadienne de DeveloppementInternational*] Ottawa, Ontario [*Library symbol National Library of Canada*] (NLC)
OOCDA	Canadian Dental Association, Ottawa, Ontario [*Library symbol National Library of Canada*] (NLC)
OOCDC	Computing Devices of Canada, Ottawa, Ontario [*Library symbol National Library of Canada*] (NLC)
OOCDP	College Dominicain de Philosophie et de Theologie, Ottawa, Ontario [*Library symbol National Library of Canada*] (NLC)
OOCEEC	Delegation of the Commission of the European Communities [*Delegation de la C ommission des Communautes Europeennes*], Ottawa, Ontario [*Library symbol National Library of Canada*] (BIB)
OOCES	Combustion Engineering Superheater Ltd., Ottawa, Ontario [*Library symbol National Library of Canada*] (NLC)
OOCESC	Centre d'Animation Pedagogique, Conseil des Ecoles Separees Catholiques d'Ottawa, Ontario [*Library symbol National Library of Canada*] (BIB)
OOCF	Canadian Film Institute [*Institut Canadien du Film*] Ottawa, Ontario [*Library symbol National Library of Canada*] (NLC)
OOCFB	Canadian Forces Base, Ottawa, Ontario [*Library symbol National Library of Canada*] (BIB)
OOCHA	Canadian Hospital Association [*Association des Hopitaux du Canada*] Ottawa,Ontario [*Library symbol National Library of Canada*] (NLC)
OOCHAC	Catholic Health Association of Canada [*Association Catholique Canadienne de la Sante*], Ottawa, Ontario [*Library symbol National Library of Canada*] (NLC)
OOCHC	Canadian Horticultural Council [*Conseil Canadien de l'Horticulture*], Ottawa, Ontario [*Library symbol National Library of Canada*] (BIB)
OOCHEO	Children's Hospital of Eastern Ontario [*Hopital pour Enfants de l'Est de l'Ontario*] Ottawa, Ontario [*Library symbol National Library of Canada*] (NLC)
OOCHI	Chreod International, Ottawa, Ontario [*Library symbol National Library of Canada*] (NLC)
OOCHP	Common Heritage Programme, Ottawa, Ontario [*Library symbol National Library of Canada*] (BIB)
OOCHR	Canadian Human Rights Commission [*Commission Canadienne des Droits de la Personne*] Ottawa, Ontario [*Library symbol National Library of Canada*] (NLC)
OOCI	Department of Consumer and Corporate Affairs [*Ministere de la Consommation etdes Corporations*] Ottawa, Ontario [*Library symbol National Library of Canada*] (NLC)
OOCIC	Documentation Centre, Canadian Intergovernmental Conference Secretariat [*Centre de Documentation, Secretariat des Conferences Intergouvernementales Canadiennes*], Ottawa, Ontario [*Library symbol National Library of Canada*] (NLC)
OOCIFE	Field Exploration Library, Inco Ltd., Copper Cliff, Ontario [*Library symbol National Library of Canada*] (NLC)
OOCIHM	Canadian Institute for Historical Microreproductions [*Institut Canadien de Microreproductions Historiques*] Ottawa, Ontario [*Library symbol National Library of Canada*] (NLC)
OOCIIPS	Canadian Institute for International Peace and Security [*Institut Canadien pour la Paix et la Securite Mondiales*] Ottawa, Ontario [*Library symbol National Library of Canada*] (NLC)
OOCIRS	Canadian Institute for Radiation Safety, Ottawa, Ontario [*Library symbol National Library of Canada*] (NLC)
OOCITT	Canadian International Trade Tribunal [*Tribunal Canadien du Commerce Exterieur*], Ontario [*Library symbol National Library of Canada*] (BIB)
OOCL	Capital Library Wholesale, Ottawa, Ontario [*Library symbol National Library of Canada*] (NLC)
OOCLA	Canadian Library Association, Ottawa, Ontario [*Library symbol National Library of Canada*] (BIB)
OOCLC	Canadian Labour Congress [*Congres du Travail du Canada*] Ottawa, Ontario [*Library symbol National Library of Canada*] (NLC)
OOCLCG	Coopers & Lybrand Consulting Group, Ottawa, Ontario [*Library symbol National Library of Canada*] (BIB)
OOCLM	Canadian Labour Market and Productivity Centre [*Centre Canadien du Marche du Travail et de la Productivite*], Ottawa, Ontario [*Library symbol National Library of Canada*] (NLC)
OOCM	Canadian Housing Information Centre, Canada Mortgage and Housing Corp. [*Centre Canadien de Documentation sur l'Habitation, Societe Canadienne d'Hypotheques et de Logement*] Ottawa, Ontario [*Library symbol National Library of Canada*] (NLC)
OOCMA	Canadian Medical Association, Ottawa, Ontario [*Library symbol National Library of Canada*] (NLC)

OOCMC .... Children's Environments Advisory Service, Canada Mortgage and Housing Corp. [*Service Consultatif sur l'Environnement de l'Enfant, Societe Canadienne d'Hypotheques et de Logement*] Ottawa, Ontario [*Library symbol National Library of Canada*] (NLC)

OOCMF .... Office of the Commissioner for Federal Judicial Affairs [*Bureau du Commissaire a la Magistrature Federale*], Ottawa, Ontario [*Library symbol National Library of Canada*] (BIB)

OOCN .... Canadian Nurses' Association [*Association Canadienne des Infirmieres*] Ottawa, Ontario [*Library symbol National Library of Canada*] (NLC)

OOCNET ...... Office of Corrections Network

OOCNP .... CNP Resource Centre, Energy, Mines, and Resources Canada [*Centre d'Information EESP, Energie, Mines, et Ressources Canada*] Ottawa, Ontario [*Library symbol National Library of Canada*] (NLC)

OOCO .... Department of Communications [*Ministere des Communications*] Ottawa, Ontario [*Library symbol National Library of Canada*] (NLC)

OOCOAC ...... Consumer's Association of Canada, Ottawa, Ontario [*Library symbol National Library of Canada*] (BIB)

OOCOG .... COGLA [*Canada Oil and Gas Lands Administration*] Ocean Mining Resource Centre , Ottawa, Ontario [*Centre de Ressources sur l'Extraction de Minerais Oceaniques, Administration du Petrole et du Gaz des Terres du Canada*] [*Library symbol National Library of Canada*] (NLC)

OOCOI .... Cognos, Inc., Ottawa, Ontario [*Library symbol National Library of Canada*] (BIB)

OOCOL .... Commissioner of Official Languages [*Commissaire aux Langues Officielles*] Ottawa, Ontario [*Library symbol National Library of Canada*] (NLC)

OOCOT .... Competition Tribunal [*Tribunal de la Concurrence*], Ottawa, Ontario [*Library symbol National Library of Canada*] (BIB)

OOCOW .... Cowater International, Inc., Ottawa, Ontario [*Library symbol National Library of Canada*] (BIB)

OOCP .... Community Planning Association of Canada [*Association Canadienne d'Urbanisme*] Ottawa, Ontario [*Library symbol National Library of Canada*] (NLC)

OOCPA .... Canadian Payments Association, Ottawa, Ontario [*Library symbol National Library of Canada*] (BIB)

OOCPB .... Planning and Development Library, City of Ottawa, Ontario [*Library symbol National Library of Canada*] (BIB)

OOCPR .... Canadian Public Relations Society [*Societe Canadienne des Relations Publiques*], Ottawa, Ontario [*Library symbol National Library of Canada*] (BIB)

OOCRC .... Canadian Red Cross Society [*Societe Canadienne de la Croix-Rouge*] Ottawa, Ontario [*Library symbol National Library of Canada*] (NLC)

OOCRI .... Canadian Research Institute for the Avancement of Women [*Institut Canadien deRecherches sur les Femmes*] Ottawa, Ontario [*Library symbol National Library of Canada*] (NLC)

OOCRLF ...... Canadian Rights and Liberties Federation, Ottawa, Ontario [*Library symbol National Library of Canada*] (NLC)

OOCRM .... Canadian Royal Mint [*Monnaie Royale Canadienne*] Ottawa, Ontario [*Library symbol National Library of Canada*] (NLC)

OOCS .... Public Service Commission [*Commission de la Fonction Publique*] Ottawa, Ontario [*Library symbol National Library of Canada*] (NLC)

OOCSC .... Canada Safety Council [*Conseil Canadien de la Securite*] Ottawa, Ontario [*Library symbol National Library of Canada*] (NLC)

OOCT .... Canadian Teachers Federation, Ottawa, Ontario [*Library symbol National Library of Canada*] (NLC)

OOCTI .... Canadian Textiles Institute [*Institut Canadien des Textiles*], Ottawa, Ontario [*Library symbol National Library of Canada*] (BIB)

OOCU .... Association of Universities and Colleges of Canada [*Association des Universites et Colleges du Canada*], Ottawa, Ontario [*Library symbol National Library of Canada*] (NLC)

OOCUI .... Canadian Unity Information Office [*Centre d'Information sur l'Unite Canadienne*] Ottawa, Ontario [*Library symbol National Library of Canada*] (NLC)

OOCUS .... CUSO [*Canadian University Service Overseas*], Ottawa, Ontario [*Library symbol National Library of Canada*] (NLC)

OOCVB .... Central Volunteer Bureau of Ottawa-Carleton [*Bureau Central des Benevoles d'Ottawa-Carleton*] Ottawa, Ontario [*Library symbol National Library of Canada*] (BIB)

OOCW .... Canadian Council on Social Development [*Conseil Canadien de Developpement Social*] Ottawa, Ontario [*Library symbol National Library of Canada*] (NLC)

OOCWC .... Canadian Wood Council [*Conseil Canadien du Bois*] Ottawa, Ontario [*Library symbol National Library of Canada*] (NLC)

OOCZ .... Ottawa Citizen, Ontario [*Library symbol National Library of Canada*] (NLC)

OOD .... Object-Oriented Design [*Computer science*]
OOD .... Office of Disability [*Australia*]
OOD .... Office Operations Department
OOD .... Officer of the Day [*or Deck*] [*Also, OD*] [*Navy*]
OOD .... Operations Orientation Director [*NASA*]
OOD .... Orbiter on Dock [*NASA*] (KSC)
OOD .... Woodstown, NJ [*Location identifier FAA*] (FAAL)
OODB .... Dominion Bridge Co. Ltd., Ottawa, Ontario [*Library symbol National Library of Canada*] (NLC)
OODB .... Object-Oriented Database [*Computer science*] (CDE)
OODBMS ...... Object-Oriented Database Management System [*Objectivity, Inc.*] [*Computer science*]

OODBS .... DOBIS (Dortmunder Bibliothekssystem), Ottawa, Ontario [*Library symbol National Library of Canada*] (NLC)

OODCH .... DCH Consultants, Inc., Ottawa, Ontario [*Library symbol National Library of Canada*] (NLC)

OODE .... Office of Overseas Dependent Education [*Military*]
OODEP .... Owner, Officer, Director, or Executive Personnel (MCD)
OODF .... Officer-of-the-Deck (Fleet Task Force Operations) [*Navy*] (DNAB)
OODI .... Officer-of-the-Deck (Independent) [*Navy*] (DNAB)
OODL .... Object-Oriented Dynamic Language [*Computer science*] (PCM)
OODLAC .... Odessa Branch, Lennox and Addington County Library, Ontario [*Library symbol National Library of Canada*] (NLC)

OODLC .... Library Education Services, Data Logic Canada, Ottawa, Ontario [*Library symbol National Library of Canada*] (NLC)

OODM .... Dali Management [*Gestion Dali*], Ottawa, Ontario [*Library symbol National Library of Canada*] (BIB)

OODMR .... DMR Group, Inc., Ottawa, Ontario [*Library symbol National Library of Canada*] (BIB)

OODP .... Department of Supply and Services [*Ministere des Approvisionnements et Services*] Ottawa, Ontario [*Library symbol National Library of Canada*] (NLC)

OODP .... Out-of-Detent Pitch [*Aviation*] (MCD)
OODPS .... Superannuation Division, Compensation Services Branch, Department of Supply and Services [*Division des Pensions de Retraite, Direction des Services de Renumeration, Ministere des Approvisionnements et Services*] Ottawa, Ontario [*Library symbol National Library of Canada*] (NLC)

OODQ .... Oliver Organization Description Questionnaire [*Test*]
OODR .... Out-of-Detent Roll [*Aviation*] (MCD)
OODRC .... Defence Research Establishment Ottawa, Department of National Defence [*Centrede Recherches pour la Defense Ottawa, Ministere de la Defense Nationale*] Ont ario [*Library symbol National Library of Canada*] (NLC)

OODR-MPI ... Optical-Optical Double Resonance Multiphonton Ionization [*Spectrocopy*]

OODSIS .... Directorate of Scientific Information Services, Department of National Defence [*Services d'Information Scientifique, Ministere de la Defense Nationale*] Ottawa, Ontario [*Library symbol National Library of Canada*] (NLC)

OODV .... Orbit-on-Demand Vehicle
OOE .... Department of External Affairs [*Ministere des Affaires Exerieures*] Ottawa,Ontario [*Library symbol National Library of Canada*] (NLC)

OOE .... Office of Employment [*Victoria, Australia*]
OOE .... Office of Energy [*New South Wales, Australia*]
OOE .... Office of Ocean Engineering [*National Oceanic and Atmospheric Administration*] (MSC)

OOE .... Opening of Oesophagus
OOE .... Out-of-Ecliptic Mission [*NASA*] (EGAO)
OOEA .... Embassy of Argentina, Ottawa, Ontario [*Library symbol National Library of Canada*] (BIB)

OOEAB .... Archaeological Research, Environment Canada [*Recherches Archeologiques, Environnement Canada*] Ottawa, Ontario [*Library symbol National Library of Canada*] (NLC)

OOEAPT .... River Road Environmental Technology Centre, Environment Canada [*Centre de Techologie Environnementale de River Road, Environnement Canada*] Ottawa, Ontario [*Library symbol National Library of Canada*] (NLC)

OOEB .... Elisabeth Bruyere Health Center [*Centre de Sante Elisabeth Bruyere*] Ottawa, Ontario [*Library symbol National Library of Canada*] (NLC)

OOEC .... Economic Council of Canada [*Conseil Economique du Canada*] Ottawa, Ontario [*Library symbol National Library of Canada*] (NLC)

OOEC .... Oxford Orthopaedic Engineering Centre [*British*] (IRUK)
OOECS .... ECS [*Energy Conversion Systems*] Power Systems, Inc., Ottawa, Ontario [*Library symbol National Library of Canada*] (NLC)

OOECW .... Canadian Wildlife Service, Environment Canada [*Service Canadien de la Faune, Environnement Canada*] Ottawa, Ontario [*Library symbol National Library of Canada*] (NLC)

OOECWN ...... National Wildlife Research Centre, Canadian Wildlife Service, Environment Canada[*Centre National de Recherche sur la Faune, Service Canadien de la Faune, En vironnement Canada*] Ottawa, Ontario [*Library symbol National Library of Canada*] (NLC)

OOEDC .... Export Development Corp. [*Societe pour l'Expansion des Exportations*] Ottawa, Ontario [*Library symbol National Library of Canada*] (NLC)

OOEE .... Engineering and Economic Research Technologies, Inc., Ottawa, Ontario [*Library symbol National Library of Canada*] (BIB)

OOEIB .... Interpretation Division, Environment Canada - Parks [*Direction de l'Interpretation, Environnement Canada - Parcs*], Ottawa, Ontario [*Library symbol National Library of Canada*] (NLC)

OOEK .... Embassy of Korea, Ottawa, Ontario [*Library symbol National Library of Canada*] (BIB)

OOELB .... Legal Branch, Department of External Affairs [*Direction des Operations Juridiques, Ministere des Affaires Exterieures*] Ottawa, Ontario [*Library symbol National Library of Canada*] (NLC)

OOELC .... Elections Canada, Ottawa, Ontario [*Library symbol National Library of Canada*] (NLC)

OOELS .... Legal Services, Environment Canada [*Services Juridiques, Environnement Canada*] Ottawa, Ontario [*Library symbol National Library of Canada*] (NLC)

OOEMB .... Embassy of Brazil, Ottawa, Ontario [*Library symbol National Library of Canada*] (BIB)

OOEN .... Cameco Research Center, Ottawa, Ontario [*Library symbol National Library of Canada*] (NLC)

OOEO .... Eastern Ontario Regional Library, Ottawa, Ontario [*Library symbol National Library of Canada*] (NLC)

OOEO .... Ontario Library Service - Rideau, Ottawa, Ontario [*Library symbol National Library of Canada*] (NLC)

OOEOB .... Conservation Division, Environment Canada [*Division de la Conservation, Environnement Canada*] Ottawa, Ontario [*Library symbol National Library of Canada*] (NLC)

OOEPC .... Emergency Planning Canada [*Planification d'Urgence Canada*] Ottawa, Ontario [*Library symbol National Library of Canada*] (NLC)

OOEPSE ...... Socio-Economic Research Division, Parks Canada Program, Environment Canada [*Division de la Recherche Socio-Economique, Programme Parcs Canada, Environnement Canada*] Ottawa, Ontario [*Library symbol National Library of Canada*] (NLC)

OOESC .... Ecole Secondaire Champlain, Ottawa, Ontario [*Library symbol National Library of Canada*] (NLC)

OOEU .... Euroline, Ottawa, Ontario [*Library symbol National Library of Canada*] (BIB)

OOEY .... Eyretechnics Ltd., Ottawa, Ontario [*Library symbol National Library of Canada*] (NLC)

OOF .... Department of Finance [*Ministere des Finances*] Ottawa, Ontario [*Library symbol National Library of Canada*] (NLC)

OOF .... Offense Only Fighter (MCD)

OOF .... Office of Fisheries [*National Oceanic and Atmospheric Administration*] (GFGA)

OOF .... Office of the Family [*Western Australia*]

OOF .... Office of the Future (IAA)

OOFA .... Documentation Centre, Family Action [*Centre de Documentation, Action Famille*], Ottawa, Ontario [*Library symbol National Library of Canada*] (NLC)

O of A .... Order of Amaranth (EA)

OOFC .... Federal Court of Canada [*Cour Federale du Canada*] Ottawa, Ontario [*Library symbol National Library of Canada*] (NLC)

OOFCC .... Farm Credit Corp., Ottawa, Ontario [*Library symbol Obsolete National Library of Canada*] (NLC)

OOFD .... Fahud [*Oman*] [*ICAO location identifier*] (ICLI)

OOFE .... Federal Environmental Assessment Review Office [*Bureau Federal d'Examen des Evaluations Environnementales*], Ottawa, Ontario [*Library symbol National Library of Canada*] (BIB)

OOFF .... Departmental Library, Environment Canada [*Bibliotheque du Ministere, Environnemet Canada*] Ottawa, Ontario [*Library symbol National Library of Canada*] (NLC)

OOFI .... Fisheries and Oceans Canada [*Peches et Oceans Canada*] Ottawa, Ontario [*Library symbol National Library of Canada*] (NLC)

OOFL .... Federal Liberal Agency of Canada, Ottawa, Ontario [*Library symbol National Library of Canada*] (NLC)

OOFM .... Mining Library, Falconbridge Ltd., Onaping, Ontario [*Library symbol National Library of Canada*] (NLC)

OOFP .... Forintek Canada Corp., Ottawa, Ontario [*Library symbol National Library of Canada*] (NLC)

OOFQ .... Firq [*Oman*] [*ICAO location identifier*] (ICLI)

OOFS .... Sport Information Resource Centre [*Centre de Documentation de Reference pour le Sport*] Ottawa, Ontario [*Library symbol National Library of Canada*] (NLC)

OOG .... Geological Survey of Canada [*Commission Geologique du Canada*] Ottawa, Ontario [*Library symbol National Library of Canada*] (NLC)

OOG .... Office of Gambling [*Victoria, Australia*]

OOG .... Office of Oil and Gas [*Functions transferred to Energy Research and Development Administration*] [*Department of the Interior*]

OOG .... Officer of the Guard [*Navy British*]

OOG .... Olive Oil Group [*Later, OOA*] (EA)

OOG .... Oscillating Output Geneva

OOG .... Out of Gauge [*Shipping*] (DCTA)

OOGB .... Ghaba Central [*Oman*] [*ICAO location identifier*] (ICLI)

OOGDC .... Gandalf Data Ltd., Ottawa, Ontario [*Library symbol National Library of Canada*] (NLC)

OOGE .... Canadian Government Expositions Centre, Department of Supply and Services [*Centre des Expositions du Gouvernement Canadien, Ministere des Approvisionnements et Services*] Ottawa, Ontario [*Library symbol National Library of Canada*] (NLC)

OOGG .... Documentation Centre, Goss, Gilroy & Associates, Ottawa, Ontario [*Library symbol National Library of Canada*] (BIB)

OOGGH .... Grace General Hospital, Ottawa, Ontario [*Library symbol National Library of Canada*] (NLC)

OOGH .... Reference Library, Government House [*Salle de Reference, Residence du Gouverneur-General*] Ottawa, Ontario [*Library symbol National Library of Canada*] (NLC)

OOGKS .... Gottlieb Kaylor & Stocks, Ottawa, Ontario [*Library symbol National Library of Canada*] (BIB)

OOGOH .... Gowling & Henderson, Ottawa, Ontario [*Library symbol National Library of Canada*] (NLC)

OOGUI .... Object-Oriented Graphical User Interface [*Computer science*]

OOH .... Heraldry Society of Canada [*Societe Heraldique du Canada*], Ottawa, Ontario [*Library symbol National Library of Canada*] (BIB)

OOH .... Occupational Outlook Handbook [*A publication*] (OICC)

OOHA .... Haima [*Oman*] [*ICAO location identifier*] (ICLI)

OOHC .... Heritage Canada Foundation [*Fondation Canadienne pour la Protection du Patrimoine*] Ottawa, Ontario [*Library symbol National Library of Canada*] (NLC)

OOHG .... Ottawa General Hospital [*Hopital General d'Ottawa*] Ontario [*Library symbol National Library of Canada*] (NLC)

OOHI .... Historical Society of Ottawa Library and the Bytown Historical Museum, Ontario [*Library symbol National Library of Canada*] (NLC)

OOH-OOH ...... On the One Hand, On the Other Hand

OOHUR .... Huronia Regional Centre, Orillia, Ontario [*Library symbol National Library of Canada*] (NLC)

OOI .... Informetrica Ltd., Ottawa, Ontario [*Library symbol National Library of Canada*] (NLC)

OOI .... Memphis, TN [*Location identifier FAA*] (FAAL)

OOI .... Oxygen/Ozone Indicator

OOIA .... Ibra [*Oman*] [*ICAO location identifier*] (ICLI)

OOIB .... Imperial Ballet of Canada, Ottawa, Ontario [*Library symbol National Library of Canada*] (NLC)

OOIC .... Information Centre, Investment Canada [*Centre d'Information, Investissement Canada*] Ottawa, Ontario [*Library symbol National Library of Canada*] (NLC)

OOICC .... Indian Claims Commission [*Commission d'Etude des Revendications des Indiens*] Ottawa, Ontario [*Library symbol National Library of Canada*] (NLC)

OOICCS .... International Council for Canadian Studies [*Conseil International d'Etudes Canadiennes*], Ottawa, Ontario [*Library symbol National Library of Canada*] (BIB)

OOICP .... Phototheque, National Film Board [*Phototheque, Office National du Film*] Ottawa, Ontario [*Library symbol National Library of Canada*] (NLC)

OOID .... International Development Research Centre [*Centre de Recherches pour le Developpement International*] Ottawa, Ontario [*Library symbol National Library of Canada*] (NLC)

OOIDA .... Owner-Operator Independent Drivers Association

OOIHC .... India High Commission, Ottawa, Ontario [*Library symbol National Library of Canada*] (BIB)

OOII .... Ibri [*Oman*] [*ICAO location identifier*] (ICLI)

OOIJC .... International Joint Commission [*Commission Mixte Internationale*], Ottawa, Ontario [*Library symbol National Library of Canada*] (NLC)

OOIN .... Office of the Superintendent of Financial Institutions Canada [*Bureau du Surintendant des Institutions Financieres Canada*] Ottawa, Ontario [*Library symbol National Library of Canada*] (NLC)

OOIP .... Original Oil in Place [*Petroleum*]

OOIPC .... Offices of the Information and Privacy Commissioners of Canada [*Bureaux des Commissaires a l'Information et a la Protection de la Vie Privee du Canada*] Ottawa, Ontario [*Library symbol National Library of Canada*] (NLC)

OOIRB .... Immigration and Refugee Board [*Commission d'Immigration et du Status de Refugie*], Ottawa, Ontario [*Library symbol National Library of Canada*] (BIB)

OOIRP .... Institute for Research on Public Policy [*Institut de Recherches Politiques*], Ottawa, Ontario [*Library symbol National Library of Canada*] (NLC)

OOIRS .... Irving R. Silver Associates Library [*IRSA*], Ottawa, Ontario [*Library symbol National Library of Canada*] (NLC)

OOIT .... Inuit Tapirisat of Canada, Ottawa, Ontario [*Library symbol National Library of Canada*] (NLC)

OOIZ .... Izki [*Oman*] [*ICAO location identifier*] (ICLI)

OOJ .... Department of Justice [*Ministere de la Justice*] Ottawa, Ontario [*Library symbol National Library of Canada*] (NLC)

OOJ .... Obstruction of Justice

OOJN .... Jarf North [*Oman*] [*ICAO location identifier*] (ICLI)

OOK .... On-Off Keying [*Computer science*] (IEEE)

OOK .... Toksook [*Alaska*] [*Airport symbol*] (OAG)

OOKB .... Khasab [*Oman*] [*ICAO location identifier*] (ICLI)

OOkiep .... O'Okiep Copper Co. Ltd. [*Associated Press*] (SAG)

OOL .... Coolangatta [*Queensland*] [*Airport symbol*] (AD)

OOL .... Gold Coast [*Australia Airport symbol*] (OAG)

OOL .... Labour Canada [*Travail Canada*] Ottawa, Ontario [*Library symbol National Library of Canada*] (NLC)

OOL .... Oberlin Public Library, Oberlin, OH [*Library symbol Library of Congress*] (LCLS)

OOL .... Object-Oriented Language [*Computer science*] (BYTE)

OOL .... Office of Oceanography and Limnology [*Smithsonian Institution*] (MCD)

OOL .... Operator-Oriented Language [*Computer science*]

OOL .... Optimized Optical Link

OOL .... Out of Orbit Launch [*NASA*] (LAIN)

OOLAP .... Occupational Safety and Health Branch, Labour Canada [*Direction de la Securite et de l'Hygiene, Travail Canada*] Ottawa, Ontario [*Library symbol National Library of Canada*] (NLC)

OOLC .... Labour College of Canada, Ottawa, Ontario [*Library symbol National Library of Canada*] (NLC)

OOLHMD ...... Optimized Optical Link Helmet-Mounted Display

OOLK .... Lekhwair [*Oman*] [*ICAO location identifier*] (ICLI)

OOLM .... Computing Department, Loeb's MIS, Ottawa, Ontario [*Library symbol National Library of Canada*] (BIB)

OOLML .... Lang, Michener, Lash & Johnston, Ottawa, Ontario [*Library symbol National Library of Canada*] (BIB)

OOLR .... Law Reform Commission [*Commission de Reforme du Droit*] Ottawa, Ontario [*Library symbol National Library of Canada*] (NLC)

OOLR .... Ophthalmology, Otology, Laryngology, Rhinology

OOLR .... Overall Objective Loudness Rating [*of telephone connections*] (IEEE)

OOLRB .... Canada Labour Relations Board [*Conseil Canadien des Relations de Travail*] Ottawa, Ontario [*Library symbol National Library of Canada*] (NLC)

OOLRS .... Research Library, LRS Trimark Ltd., Ottawa, Ontario [*Library symbol National Library of Canada*] (BIB)

OOLUG .... Oklahoma On Line Users Group (NITA)

OOLWB .... Women's Bureau, Labour Canada [*Bureau de la Main-d'Oeuvre Feminine, Travail Canada*] Ottawa, Ontario [*Library symbol National Library of Canada*] (NLC)

OOM .... CANMET [*Canada Centre for Mineral and Energy Technology*] Library, Energy, Mines, and Resources Canada , Ottawa, Ontario [*Bibliotheque CANMET, Energie, Mines, et Ressources Canada*] [*Library symbol National Library of Canada*] (NLC)

OOM .... Cooma [*Australia Airport symbol*] (OAG)

OOM .... Office of Ocean Management [*Marine science*] (MSC)

OOM .... Office of Organization and Management [*NASA*]

OOM .... Officers' Open Mess [*Military*] (AFM)

OOM .... Oomiya [*Japan*] [*Seismograph station code, US Geological Survey Closed*] (SEIS)

OOM .... Open Ocean Mining

OOM .... Open Order Master (MCD)

OOM .... Organized Organic Monolayer [*Organic chemistry*]

OOM .... Original Online Module [*Computer science*] (PDAA)

OOMA .... Masirah [*Oman*] [*ICAO location identifier*] (ICLI)

OOMAD .... Michael A. Dagg Associates [*Michael A. Dagg Associes*], Ottawa, Ontario [*Library symbol National Library of Canada*] (NLC)

OOMFC .... Ompah Branch, Frontenac County Library, Ontario [*Library symbol National Library of Canada*] (BIB)

OOMHC .... Malaysia High Commission, Ottawa, Ontario [*Library symbol National Library of Canada*] (NLC)

OOMHS .... Merivale High School, Ottawa, Ontario [*Library symbol National Library of Canada*] (NLC)

OOMI .... Employment and Immigration Canada [*Emploi et Immigration Canada*] Ottawa, Ontario [*Library symbol National Library of Canada*] (NLC)

OOMIL .... MIL Systems Engineering, Inc., Ottawa, Ontario [*Library symbol National Library of Canada*] (BIB)

OOMJ.......... Macera & Jarzyna, Ottawa, Ontario [*Library symbol National Library of Canada*] (BIB)

OOML .... Metropolitan Life Insurance Co., Ottawa, Ontario [*Library symbol National Library of Canada*] (NLC)

OOMM .... Muscat [*Oman*] [*ICAO location identifier*] (ICLI)

OOMM .... Organizational Operations and Maintenance Manual (NASA)

OOMNA .... National Air Photo Library, Energy, Mines, and Resources Canada [*BibliothequePhotographie Aerienne Nationale, Energie, Mines, et Ressources Canada*], Otta wa, Ontario [*Library symbol National Library of Canada*] (BIB)

OOMO .... Oxford Mills Branch, Oxford-On-Rideau Township Public Library [*Library symbol National Library of Canada*] (BIB)

OOMP .... Physical Metallurgy Division, Energy, Mines and Resources Canada [*Division dela Metallurgie Physique, Energie, Mines et Ressources Canada*] Ottawa, Ontari o [*Library symbol National Library of Canada*] (NLC)

OOMPR .... Microtel Pacific Research Ltd., Ottawa, Ontario [*Library symbol National Library of Canada*] (NLC)

OOMR .... Headquarters Library, Energy, Mines and Resources Canada [*Bibliotheque Centrale, Energie, Mines et Ressources Canada*] Ottawa, Ontario [*Library symbol National Library of Canada*] (NLC)

OOMS .... Muscat/Seeb International [*Oman*] [*ICAO location identifier*] (ICLI)

OOMSD........ Ministry of State for Social Development [*Ministere d'Etat au Developpement Social*] Ottawa, Ontario [*Library symbol National Library of Canada*] (NLC)

OOMSS .... Ministry of State for Science and Technology [*Ministere d'Etat pour les Sciences et la Technologie*], Ottawa, Ontario [*Library symbol National Library of Canada*] (NLC)

OON .... Canada Institute for Scientific and Technical Information, National Research Council (CISTI) [*Institut Canadien de l'Information Scientifique et Technique, Conseil National de Recherches (ICIST)*] Ottawa, Ontario [*Library symbol National Library of Canada*] (NLC)

OON .... Odd-Odd Nuclei

OON .... Officer of the Order of Niger

OONAB........ Administration Building Library, Canada Institute for Scientific and Technical Information [*Bibliotheque de l'Edifice de l'Administration, Institut Canadien de l'Information Scientifique et Technique*] Ottawa, Ontario [*Library symbol National Library of Canada*] (NLC)

OONAM........ Aeronautical and Mechanical Engineering Branch, Canada Institute for Scientific and Technical Information [*Division du Genie Aeronautique et Mecanique, Institut Canadien de l'Information Scientifique et Technique*] Ottawa, Ontario [*Library symbol National Library of Canada*] (NLC)

OONAMC...... NABU Manufacturing Corp., Ottawa, Ontario [*Library symbol National Library of Canada*] (NLC)

OONBR .... IRC [*Institute for Research in Construction*] Library, National Research Council Canada Ottawa, Ontario [*Bibliotheque IRC (Institut de Recherche en Construction), Conseil National de Recherches Canada*] [*Library symbol National Library of Canada*] (NLC)

OONC .... Chemistry Library, Canada Institute for Scientific and Technical Information [*Division de Chimie, Institut Canadien de l'Information Scientifique et Technique*] Ottawa, Ontario [*Library symbol National Library of Canada*] (NLC)

OONCC......... National Capital Commission [*Commission de la Capitale Nationale*] Ottawa, Ontario [*Library symbol National Library of Canada*] (NLC)

OOND .... Department of National Defence [*Ministere de la Defense Nationale*] Ottawa,Ontario [*Library symbol National Library of Canada*] (NLC)

OONDAT ...... Air Technical Library, Department of National Defence [*Bibliotheque Techniquede l'Aviation, Ministere de la Defense Nationale*] Ottawa, Ontario [*Library symbol National Library of Canada*] (NLC)

OONDC .... Communications and Electronics Engineering Library, Department of National Defence [*Bibliotheque du Genie Electronique et des Communications, Ministere de laDefense National*] Ottawa, Ontario [*Library symbol National Library of Canada*] (NLC)

OONDCP ...... Chief, Construction and Properties, Library, Department of National Defence [*Bibliotheque, Chef - Construction et Immeubles, Ministere de le Defense Nationale*] Ottawa, Ontario [*Library symbol National Library of Canada*] (NLC)

OONDCS ...... Communications Security Establishment, Department of National Defence [*Centrede la Securite des Telecommunications, Ministere de la Defense Nationale*] Ot tawa, Ontario [*Library symbol National Library of Canada*] (NLC)

OONDH .... Directorate of History, Department of National Defence [*Bureau du Service Historique, Ministere de la Defense Nationale*] Ottawa, Ontario [*Library symbol National Library of Canada*] (NLC)

OONDIS .... Directorate of Information Services, Department of National Defence [*Servicesd'Information, Ministere de la Defense Nationale*] Ottawa, Ontario [*Library symbol National Library of Canada*] (NLC)

OONDJ......... Judge Advocate General, Department of National Defence [*Jugeavocat General, Ministere de la Defense Nationale*] Ottawa, Ontario [*Library symbol National Library of Canada*] (NLC)

OONDLT....... Land Technical Library, Department of National Defence [*Bibliotheque Technique (Terre), Ministere de la Defense Nationale*] Ottawa, Ontario [*Library symbol National Library of Canada*] (NLC)

OONDM........ National Defence Medical Centre, Department of National Defence [*Centre Medical de la Nationale, Ministere de la Defense Nationale*] Ottawa, Ontario [*Library symbol National Library of Canada*] (NLC)

OONDMC ..... Mapping and Charting Establishment, Department of National Defence [*Service de la Cartographie, Ministere de la Defense Nationale*] Ottawa, Ontario [*Library symbol National Library of Canada*] (NLC)

OONDMT...... Maritime Technical Library, Department of National Defence [*Bibliotheque Technique (Mer), Ministere de la Defense Nationale*] Ottawa, Ontario [*Library symbol National Library of Canada*] (NLC)

OONDORAE... Operational Research and Analysis Establishment, Department of National Defence [*Centre d'Analyse et de Recherche Operationnelle, Ministere de la Defense Nationale*] Ottawa, Ontario [*Library symbol National Library of Canada*] (NLC)

OONDT......... Secretary of State Library at National Defence [*Bibliotheque du Secretariat d'Etat a la Defense Nationale*], Ottawa, Ontario [*Library symbol National Library of Canada*] (NLC)

OONE .... National Energy Board [*Office National de l'Energie*] Ottawa, Ontario [*Library symbol National Library of Canada*] (NLC)

OONFP......... National Farm Products Marketing Council [*Conseil National de Commercialisation des Produits Agricoles*], Ottawa, Ontario [*Library symbol National Library of Canada*] (BIB)

OONG.......... National Gallery of Canada [*Galerie Nationale du Canada*] Ottawa, Ontario [*Library symbol National Library of Canada*] (NLC)

OONH .... Department of National Health and Welfare [*Ministere de la Sante Nationale etdu Bien-Etre Social*] Ottawa, Ontario [*Library symbol Obsolete National Library of Canada*] (NLC)

OONHAC ...... Federal Centre for AIDS [*Acquired Immune Deficiency Syndrome*], Health Protection Branch, Health and Welfare Canada , Ottawa, Ontario [*Centre Federal du SIDA, Direction Generale de la Protection de la Sante, Sante et Bien-Etre Social Canada*] [*Library symbol National Library of Canada*] (BIB)

OONHBR ...... Banting Research Centre Library, Department of National Health and Welfare [*Bibliotheque du Centre de Recherches Banting, Ministere de la Sante Nationale et du Bien-Etre Social*] Ottawa, Ontario [*Library symbol National Library of Canada*] (NLC)

OONHFV ...... National Clearinghouse on Family Violence, Health and Welfare Canada [*Centre National d'Information sur la Violence dans la Famille, Sante et Bien-Etre Social Canada*], Ottawa, Ontario [*Library symbol National Library of Canada*] (BIB)

OONHH .... Environmental Health Directorate, Health Protection Branch, Department of National Health and Welfare [*Direction de l'Hygiene du Milieu, Direction Generale de la Protection de la Sante, Ministere de la Sante Nationale et du Bien-Etre Social*] Ottawa, Ontario [*Library symbol National Library of Canada*] (NLC)

OONHHP ...... Library Services Division, Health Protection Branch, Health and Welfare Canada [*Service de Bibliotheque, Direction Generale de la Protection de la Sante, Sante et Bien-Etre Social Canada*] Ottawa, Ontario [*Library symbol National Library of Canada*] (NLC)

OONHHS ...... Health Services and Promotion Branch, Department of National Health and Welfare [*Direction Generale des Services et de la Promotion de la Sante, Ministere dela Sante Nationale et du Bien-Etre Social*] Ottawa, Ontario [*Library symbol National Library of Canada*] (NLC)

OONHL........ Laboratory Centre for Disease Control, Health Protection Branch, Department of National Health and Welfare [*Laboratoire de Lutte Contre la Maladie, DirectionGenerale de la Protection de la Sante, Ministere de la Sante Nationale et du Bi en-Etre Social*] Ottawa, Ontario [*Library symbol National Library of Canada*] (NLC)

OONHP .... Vanier Reading Room, Place Vanier, Health Protection Branch, Health and Welfare Canada [*Salle de Lecture de Vanier, Place Vanier, Direction Generale de la Protection de la Sante, Sante et Bien-Etre Social Canada*], Ottawa, Ontario [*Library symbol National Library of Canada*] (NLC)

OONHPP ...... Library Services, Policy, Communications, and Information Branch, Health and Welfare Canada [*Services de Bibliotheque, Direction Generale de la Politique, des Communications, et de l'Information, Sante et Bien-Etre Social Canada*] Ottawa, Ontario [*Library symbol National Library of Canada*] (NLC)

OONIN .... National Institute of Nutrition [*Institut National de la Nutrition*], Ottawa, Ontario [*Library symbol National Library of Canada*] (BIB)

OONL .... National Library of Canada [*Bibliotheque Nationale du Canada*] Ottawa, Ontario [*Library symbol National Library of Canada*] (NLC)

OONLB .... Union Catalogue of Books, National Library of Canada [*Catalogue Collectif desLivres, Bibliotheque Nationale du Canada*] Ottawa, Ontario [*Library symbol National Library of Canada*] (NLC)

OONLC .... Canadiana Acquisitions, National Library of Canada [*Acquisitions pour Canadiana, Bibliotheque Nationale du Canada*] Ottawa, Ontario [*Library symbol National Library of Canada*] (NLC)

OONLD .... Information Technology Services, National Library of Canada [*Services de Technologie de l'Information, Bibliotheque Nationale de Canada*], Ottawa, Ontario [*Library symbol National Library of Canada*] (NLC)

OONLD .... Library Systems Centre, National Library of Canada [*Centre des Systemes de Bibliotheque, Bibliotheque Nationale du Canada*] Ottawa, Ontario [*Library symbol National Library of Canada*] (NLC)

OONLG .... Official Publications, National Library of Canada [*Publications Officielles, Bibliotheque Nationale du Canada*] Ottawa, Ontario [*Library symbol National Library of Canada*] (NLC)

OONLI .... ISDS Canada, National Library of Canada [*ISDS Canada, Bibliotheque Nationale du Canada*], Ottawa, Ontario [*Library symbol National Library of Canada*] (BIB)

OONLMBS .... Multilingual Biblioservice, National Library of Canada [*Biblioservice Multilingue, Bibliotheque Nationale du Canada*] Ottawa, Ontario [*Library symbol National Library of Canada*] (NLC)

OONLN .... Newspaper Division, National Library of Canada [*Division des Journaux Bibliotheque Nationale du Canada*] Ottawa, Ontario [*Library symbol National Library of Canada*] (NLC)

OONLP .... Serials Record, National Library of Canada [*Enregistrement des Publications en Serie, Bibliotheque Nationale du Canada*] Ottawa, Ontario [*Library symbol National Library of Canada*] (NLC)

OONLR .... Retrospective Bibliography, National Library of Canada [*Bibliographie Retrospective, Bibliotheque Nationale du Canada*] Ottawa, Ontario [*Library symbol National Library of Canada*] (NLC)

OONLS .... Union Catalogue of Serials, National Library of Canada [*Catalogue Collectif des Periodiques, Bibliotheque Nationale du Canada*] Ottawa, Ontario [*Library symbol National Library of Canada*] (NLC)

OONM .... National Museums of Canada [*Musees Nationaux du Canada*] Ottawa, Ontario [*Library symbol National Library of Canada*] (NLC)

OONMA .... National Aviation Museum [*Musee National de l'Aviation*], Ottawa, Ontario [*Library symbol National Library of Canada*] (NLC)

OONMC .... Canadian War Museum [*Musee de Guerre du Canada*] Ottawa, Ontario [*Library symbol National Library of Canada*] (NLC)

OONMCC ..... Canadian Conservation Institute, National Museums of Canada [*Institut Canadien de Conservation, Musees Nationaux du Canada*] Ottawa, Ontario [*Library symbol National Library of Canada*] (NLC)

OONMM ...... Canadian Museum of Civilization, National Museums of Canada [*Musee Canadien des Civilisations, Musees Nationaux du Canada*] Ottawa, Ontario [*Library symbol National Library of Canada*] (NLC)

OONMNS ..... National Museum of Natural Sciences [*Musee National des Sciences Naturelles*], Ottawa, Ontario [*Library symbol National Library of Canada*] (NLC)

OONMS .... National Museum of Science and Technology [*Musee National des Sciences et de la Technologie*] Ottawa, Ontario [*Library symbol National Library of Canada*] (NLC)

OONORE ...... Bell Northern Research, Ottawa, Ontario [*Library symbol National Library of Canada*] (NLC)

OONP .... Division of Physics, Canada Institute for Scientific and Technical Information [*Division de Physique, Institute Canadien de l'Information Scientifique et Technique*] Ottawa, Ontario [*Library symbol National Library of Canada*] (NLC)

OONR .... Customs and Excise Division, Department of National Revenue [*Division des Douanes et de l'Accise, Ministere du Revenu National*] Ottawa, Ontario [*Library symbol National Library of Canada*] (NLC)

OONR .... Marmul/Nasir [*Oman*] [*ICAO location identifier*] (ICLI)

OONRE .... Electrical Engineering Division, Canada Institute for Scientific and Technical Information [*Division de Genie Electrique, Institut Canadien de l'Information Scientifique et Technique*] Ottawa, Ontario [*Library symbol National Library of Canada*] (NLC)

OONRT .... Taxation Division, Department of National Revenue [*Division de l'Impot, Ministere du Revenu National*] Ottawa, Ontario [*Library symbol National Library of Canada*] (NLC)

OONRTC ...... Centre for Career Development, Revenue Canada - Taxation [*Centre de Developpement Professionnel, Revenu Canada - Impot*] Ottawa, Ontario [*Library symbol National Library of Canada*] (NLC)

OONS .... Sussex Library, Canada Institute for Scientific and Technical Information [*Bibliotheque Sussex, Institut Canadien de l'Information Scientifique et Technique*] Ottawa, Ontario [*Library symbol National Library of Canada*] (NLC)

OONSE .... Natural Sciences and Engineering Research Council of Canada [*Conseil de Recherches en Sciences Naturelles et en Genie du Canada*], Ottawa, Ontario [*Library symbol National Library of Canada*] (NLC)

OONSF .... National Science Film Library [*Cinematheque Nationale Scientifique*] Ottawa, Ontario [*Library symbol National Library of Canada*] (NLC)

OONSI .... North-South Institute [*L'Institut Nord-Sud*], Ottawa, Ontario [*Library symbol National Library of Canada*] (NLC)

OOnt .... Order of Ontario [*Canada*] (DD)

OONU .... Uplands Library, Canada Institute for Scientific and Technical Information [*Bibliotheque d'Uplands, Institut Canadien de l'Information Scientifique et Technique*] Ottawa, Ontario [*Library symbol National Library of Canada*] (NLC)

OONUL .... Union List of Scientific Serials in Canadian Libraries [*Catalogue Collectif des Publications Scientifiques dans les Bibliotheques Canadiennes*] Ottawa, Ontario [*Library symbol National Library of Canada*] (NLC)

OONVRC ..... National Victims Resource Centre [*Centre National de la Documentation sur lesVictimes*] Ottawa, Ontario [*Library symbol National Library of Canada*] (NLC)

OONZ .... Nizwa [*Oman*] [*ICAO location identifier*] (ICLI)

OOO .... Earth Physics Branch, Energy, Mines and Resources Canada [*Direction de la Physique du Globe, Energie, Mines et Resources Canada*] Ottawa, Ontario [*Library symbol National Library of Canada*] (NLC)

OOO .... Geophysics Collection, Geological Survey of Canada [*Collection de la Geophysique, Commission Geologique du Canada*], Ottawa, Ontario [*Library symbol National Library of Canada*] (NLC)

OOO .... Grants Pass, OR [*Location identifier FAA*] (FAAL)

OOO .... Office of the Ombudsman

OOO .... Oleum Olivae Optimum [*Best Olive Oil*] [*Pharmacy*] (ROG)

OOO .... Order of Owls (EA)

OOO .... O Sapientia, O Radix, O Adonai [*Three anthems sung in Roman Catholic churches before Christmas*] (ROG)

OOO .... Out of Order [*Telecommunications*] (TEL)

OOOA .... City of Ottawa Archives, Ontario [*Library symbol National Library of Canada*] (NLC)

OOOAG .... Office of the Auditor General [*Bureau du Verificateur General*] Ottawa, Ontario [*Library symbol National Library of Canada*] (NLC)

OOOCF .... Ottawa Clinic, Ontario Cancer Foundation, Ontario [*Library symbol National Library of Canada*] (NLC)

OOOCH .... Ottawa Civic Hospital, Ontario [*Library symbol National Library of Canada*] (NLC)

OOOCM .... Information Services, Ontario Centre for Microelectronics, Nepean, Ontario [*Library symbol National Library of Canada*] (NLC)

OOOF .... Onaping Branch, Onaping Falls Public Library, Ontario [*Library symbol National Library of Canada*] (NLC)

OOOI .... Out-Off-On-In [*Telecommunications*]

OOOL .... Optotek Ltd., Ottawa, Ontario [*Library symbol National Library of Canada*] (NLC)

OOOS .... Object-Oriented Operating System [*Computer science*] (CDE)

OOOTQFUE... Omnipotent Overseer of the Quest for Unsurpassable Excellence [*Rank in the Junior Woodchucks organization mentioned in Donald Duck comic by Carl Barks*]

OOP .... Library of Parliament [*Bibliotheque du Parlement*] Ottawa, Ontario [*Library symbol National Library of Canada*] (NLC)

OOP .... Object-Oriented Programming [*Computer science*]

OOP .... Oceanographic Observations of the Pacific

OOP .... Office of Organization Planning

OOP .... Offline Orthophoto Printer [*Computer science*] (PDAA)

OOP .... Optimum Optical Pump

OOP .... Ounce of Prevention [*A publication*]

OOP .... Out of Pelvis [*Obstetrics*] (DAVI)

OOP .... Out-of-Phase [*Gynecology*]

OOP .... Out of Plane

OOP .... Out of Plant

OOP .... Out of Plaster [*Orthopedics*] (DAVI)

OOP .... Out-of-Pocket [*Costs/expenses*]

OOP .... Out-of-Pocket (MHDW)

OOP .... Out of Position (MCD)

OOP .... Out of Print [*Also, OP*] [*Publishing*]

OOP .... Out on Pass [*Medicine*]

OOPA .... National Arts Centre [*Centre National des Arts*] Ottawa, Ontario [*Library symbol National Library of Canada*] (NLC)

OOPA .... One and Only Parents Association (EA)

OOPAC .... Chaudiere Branch, Departmental Library, Environment Canada [*Succursale Chaudiere, Bibliotheque du Ministere, Environnement Canada*] Ottawa, Ontario [*Library symbol National Library of Canada*] (NLC)

OOPART .... Out of Place Artifact [*Archeology*]

OOPC .... Management Information Centre, Privy Council Office [*Regie Interne de l'Information, Bureau du Conseil Prive*] Ottawa, Ontario [*Library symbol National Library of Canada*] (NLC)

OOPC .... Office of Operational Planning and Control [*Social Security Administration*]

OOPC .... Owners & Officers of Private Companies [*A publication*]

OOPCF .... Parliamentary Centre for Foreign Affairs and Foreign Trade [*Centre Parlementaire pour les Affaires Etrangeres et le Commerce Exterieur*], Ottawa, Ontario [*Library symbol National Library of Canada*] (NLC)

OOPEC .... Office for Official Publications of the European Communities (ECED)

OOPEC .... Petro-Canada, Ottawa, Ontario [*Library symbol National Library of Canada*] (NLC)

OOPED .... Pylon Electronic Development Co. Ltd., Ottawa, Ontario [*Library symbol National Library of Canada*] (NLC)

OOPF .... Resource Centre, Ottawa Police Force, Ontario [*Library symbol National Library of Canada*] (BIB)

OOPH .... Perley Hospital, Ottawa, Ontario [*Library symbol National Library of Canada*] (NLC)

OOPI .... Petroleum Incentives Program, Energy, Mines and Resources Canada [*Programmes d'Encouragement Petrolier, Energie, Mines et Ressources Canada*] Ottawa, Ontario [*Library symbol National Library of Canada*] (NLC)

OOPIP .... Professional Institute of the Public Service of Canada [*Institut Professionnel de la Fonction Publique du Canada*], Ottawa, Ontario [*Library symbol National Library of Canada*] (BIB)

OOPL .... Object-Oriented Programming Language [*Computer science*] (PCM)

OOPLFC & A ... Only Official Peggy Lee Fan Club and Archives (EA)

OOPM .... National Postal Museum [*Musee National des Postes*] Ottawa, Ontario [*Library symbol National Library of Canada*] (NLC)

OOPMF .... Marten Falls Band Library, Ogoki Post, Ontario [*Library symbol National Library of Canada*] (BIB)

OOPMP ...... Peat, Marwick & Partners, Ottawa, Ontario [*Library symbol National Library of Canada*] (NLC)

OOPO .... Canada Post [*Postes Canada*] Ottawa, Ontario [*Library symbol National Library of Canada*] (NLC)

OOPOM .... Meriline Branch, Canada Post [*Postes Canada*], Ottawa, Ontario [*Library symbol National Library of Canada*] (BIB)

OOPOR .... Ports Canada, Ottawa, Ontario [*Library symbol National Library of Canada*] (NLC)

OOPS .... Object-Oriented Pieces of Something [*Computer science*]

OOPS .... Object-Oriented Programming (BYTE)

OOPS .... O'Brien's Oil Pollution Service of New Orleans [*Oil spill cleanup service*]

OOPS .... Office for Operations in Political Systems

OOPS .... Off-Line Operating Simulator [*Computer science*]

OOPS .... Online Object Patching System [*Computer science*] (PDAA)

OOPS .... Originals on Permanent Sale

OOPS .... Public Service Staff Relations Board [*Commission des Relations de Travail dans la Fonction Publique*] Ottawa, Ontario [*Library symbol National Library of Canada*] (NLC)

OOPSAC .... Public Service Alliance of Canada [*Alliance de la Fonction Publique du Canada*] Ottawa, Ontario [*Library symbol National Library of Canada*] (NLC)

OOPSLA .... Object-Oriented Programming Systems, Languages, and Applications [*Computer conference*]

OOPW .... Public Works Canada [*Travaux Publics Canada*] Ottawa, Ontario [*Library symbol National Library of Canada*] (NLC)

OOPWC .... Capital Region Library, Public Works Canada [*Bibliotheque de la Region de la Capitale, Travaux Publics Canada*] Ottawa, Ontario [*Library symbol National Library of Canada*] (NLC)

OOPWR .... Research and Development Laboratories, Public Works Canada [*Laboratoires de Recherche et de Developpement, Travaux Publics Canada*] Ottawa, Ontario [*Library symbol Obsolete National Library of Canada*] (NLC)

OOQ .... Officer of the Quarters

OOQA .... Director-General, Quality Assurance Library, Department of National Defence [*Bibliotheque du Directeur General-Assurance de la Qualite, Ministere de la Defense Nationale*], Ottawa, Ontario [*Library symbol National Library of Canada*] (NLC)

OOQC .... Queensway-Carleton Hospital, Ottawa, Ontario [*Library symbol National Library of Canada*] (NLC)

OOQM .... Queen Mary Street School, Ottawa, Ontario [*Library symbol National Library of Canada*] (BIB)

OOR .... Mooraberrie [*Queensland*] [*Airport symbol*] (AD)

OOR .... Office for Ordnance Research [*Later, Army Research Office*]

OOR .... Open Ocean Release

OOR .... Operator Override [*Telecommunications*] (TEL)

OOR .... Out of Room (DAVI)

OOR .... Out-of-Roundness [*Manufacturing term*]

OOR .... Oxygen/Ozone Recorder

OOR .... RCMP Headquarters [*Direction Generale de la GRC*] Ottawa, Ontario [*Library symbol National Library of Canada*] (NLC)

OOR .... RCMP [*Royal Canadian Mounted Police*] Law Enforcement Reference Centre, Ottawa, Ontario [*Centre de Documentation Policiere, Gendarmerie Royale du Canada*] [*Library symbol National Library of Canada*] (NLC)

OORA .... Orangeville Public Library, Ontario [*Library symbol National Library of Canada*] (NLC)

OORCS .... Ottawa Roman Catholic Separate School Board, Ontario [*Library symbol National Library of Canada*] (NLC)

OORD .... Indian and Northern Affairs Canada [*Affaires Indiennes et du Nord Canada*] Ottawa, Ontario [*Library symbol National Library of Canada*] (NLC)

OORH .... Riverside Hospital, Ottawa, Ontario [*Library symbol National Library of Canada*] (NLC)

OORI .... Orillia Public Library, Ontario [*Library symbol National Library of Canada*] (NLC)

OORIA .... J. L. Richard & Associates Ltd., Ottawa, Ontario [*Library symbol National Library of Canada*] (NLC)

OORIGC .... Learning Resources Centre, Georgian College of Applied Arts and Technology, Orillia, Ontario [*Library symbol National Library of Canada*] (NLC)

OORIMT .... Mara Township Public Library, Orillia, Ontario [*Library symbol National Library of Canada*] (BIB)

OORISMH ... OSMH Health Sciences Library, Orillia Soldiers' Memorial Hospital, Ontario [*Library symbol National Library of Canada*] (NLC)

OORM .... Planning Department Library, Regional Municipality of Ottawa-Carleton, Ottawa, Ontario [*Library symbol National Library of Canada*] (NLC)

OORM .... Rima [*Oman*] [*ICAO location identifier*] (ICLI)

OORMT .... Transportation-Works Department, Regional Municipality of Ottawa-Carleton, Ottawa, Ontario [*Library symbol National Library of Canada*] (NLC)

OORO .... Royal Ottawa Hospital, Ontario [*Library symbol National Library of Canada*] (NLC)

OORORR ...... Royal Ottawa Regional Rehabilitation Centre, Royal Ottawa Hospital, Ontario [*Library symbol National Library of Canada*] (NLC)

OORP .... Rockliffe Park Public Library, Ottawa, Ontario [*Library symbol National Library of Canada*] (BIB)

OORPL .... Communications Research Centre, Department of Communications [*Centre de Recherches sur les Communications, Ministere des Communications*] Ottawa, Ontario [*Library symbol National Library of Canada*] (NLC)

OORQ .... Rostaq [*Oman*] [*ICAO location identifier*] (ICLI)

OORR .... Regional Realty Ltd., Ottawa, Ontario [*Library symbol National Library of Canada*] (BIB)

OOrrW .... Wayne General and Technical College, Orrville, OH [*Library symbol Library of Congress*] (LCLS)

OORS .... RCMP Scientific Information Centre [*Centre d'Information Scientifique de la GRC*] Ottawa, Ontario [*Library symbol National Library of Canada*] (NLC)

OORSFC ...... Only Official Rolling Stones Fan Club (EAIO)

OORSS .... CSIS [*Canadian Security Intelligence Service*] Open Information Centre Ontario [*Bibliotheque du SCRS (Service Canadien du Renseignement de Securite), Ottawa*] [*Library symbol National Library of Canada*] (NLC)

OORT .... Canadian Radio-Television and Telecommunications Commission [*Conseil de la Radiodiffusion et des Telecommunications Canadiennes*] Ottawa, Ontario [*Library symbol National Library of Canada*] (NLC)

OORTA .... Roads and Transportation Association of Canada [*Association des Routes et Transports du Canada*] Ottawa, Ontario [*Library symbol National Library of Canada*] (NLC)

OOS .... Occupational Overuse Syndrome

OOS .... Ocean Observing System [*Marine science*] (OSRA)

OOS .... Office of Operations Support [*Law Enforcement Assistance Administration*]

OOS .... On-Orbit Station [*NASA*] (NASA)

OOS .... On-Orbit Support

OOS .... Operational Operating System [*Telecommunications*] (TEL)

OOS .... Orbit-to-Orbit Shuttle [*NASA*]

OOS .... Orbit-to-Orbit Stage [*NASA*] (NASA)

OOS .... Out of School (OICC)

OOS .... Out of Sequence (NRCH)

OOS .... Out of Service (NRCH)

OOS .... Out-of-Shot [*Photography*] (ADA)

OOS .... Out of Stock

OOS .... Statistics Canada [*Statistique Canada*] Ottawa Ontario [*Library symbol National Library of Canada*] (NLC)

OOSA .... National Social Services Consultant and Government Relations Officer, Salvation Army Library, Ottawa, Ontario [*Library symbol National Library of Canada*] (BIB)

OOSA .... Salalah [*Oman*] [*ICAO location identifier*] (ICLI)

OOSAR .... Government Relations Office, Spar Aerospace Ltd., Ottawa, Ontario [*Library symbol National Library of Canada*] (BIB)

OOSB .... Smart & Biggar, Ottawa, Ontario [*Library symbol National Library of Canada*] (BIB)

OOSC .... Out-of-Sight Control (MUGU)

OOSC .... Supreme Court of Canada [*Cour Supreme du Canada*] Ottawa, Ontario [*Library symbol National Library of Canada*] (NLC)

OOSCA .... Archives des Soeurs de la Charite d'Ottawa, Ontario [*Library symbol National Library of Canada*] (NLC)

OOSCAC ...... Scanada Consultants Ltd., Ottawa, Ontario [*Library symbol National Library of Canada*] (NLC)

OOSCC .... Out-of-Site Control Center (SAA)

OOSCC .... Science Council of Canada [*Conseil des Sciences du Canada*] Ottawa, Ontario [*Library symbol National Library of Canada*] (NLC)

OOSCL .... Census Library, Statistics Canada [*Bibliotheque du Recensement, Statistique Canada*] Ottawa, Ontario [*Library symbol National Library of Canada*] (NLC)

OOSCM .... Census Map Library, Statistics Canada [*Cartotheque du Recensement, Statistique Canada*] Ottawa, Ontario [*Library symbol National Library of Canada*] (NLC)

OOSD .... Object Oriented Structured Design [*Computer science*]

OOSDP .... On-Orbit Station Distribution Panel [*NASA*] (MCD)

OOSG .... Ministry of the Solicitor General [*Ministere du Solliciteur General*] Ottawa, Ontario [*Library symbol National Library of Canada*] (NLC)

OOSGO .... Osgoode Public Library, Ontario [*Library symbol National Library of Canada*] (BIB)

OOSH .... Oshawa Public Library, Ontario [*Library symbol National Library of Canada*] (NLC)

OOSH .... Out of School Hours

OOSH.......... Sohar [*Oman*] [*ICAO location identifier*] (ICLI)

OOSHD .... Durham College of Applied Arts and Technology, Oshawa, Ontario [*Library symbol National Library of Canada*] (NLC)

OOSHH .... Education Resource Centre, Oshawa General Hospital, Ontario [*Library symbol National Library of Canada*] (BIB)

OOSHR .... Robert McLaughlin Gallery, Oshawa, Ontario [*Library symbol National Library of Canada*] (NLC)

OOSHT .... Technical Library, Systemhouse Ltd., Ottawa, Ontario [*Library symbol National Library of Canada*] (NLC)

OOSJ .... La Bibliotheque Deschatelets Peres Oblats [*Closed to the public*] Ottawa, Ontario [*Library symbol National Library of Canada*] (NLC)

OOSLM .... Montfort Hospital [*Hopital Montfort*] Ottawa, Ontario [*Library symbol National Library of Canada*] (NLC)

OOSLR .... S. L. Ross Environmental Research, Ottawa, Ontario [*Library symbol National Library of Canada*] (BIB)

OOSM .... Sahma [*Oman*] [*ICAO location identifier*] (ICLI)

OOSM .... Surveying and Mapping Library, Cartographic Information and Distribution Centre,Energy, Mines, and Resources Canada [*Bibliotheque des Leves et de Cartograph ies, Centre d'Information et de Distribution Cartographiques, Energie, Mines, et Ressources Canada*] Ottawa, Ontario [*Library symbol National Library of Canada*] (NLC)

OOSMM .... Map Library, Energy, Mines and Resources Canada [*Cartotheque, Energie, Mines et Ressources Canada*] Ottawa, Ontario [*Library symbol National Library of Canada*] (NLC)

OOSN .... Six Nations Public Library, Ohsweken, Ontario [*Library symbol National Library of Canada*] (BIB)

OOSP .... Patent and Copyright Office, Department of Consumer and Corporate Affairs [*Bureau des Brevets et du Droit d'Auteur, Ministere de la Consommation et des Corporations*] Ottawa, Ontario [*Library symbol National Library of Canada*] (NLC)

OOSPD .... Ocean Observing System Development Panel [*Marine science*] (OSRA)

OOSPX .... St.-Pius X High School, Ottawa, Ontario [*Library symbol National Library of Canada*] (BIB)

OOSQ .... Saiq [*Oman*] [*ICAO location identifier*] (ICLI)

OOSR .... Sur [*Oman*] [*ICAO location identifier*] (ICLI)

OOSS .... Department of the Secretary of State [*Secretariat d'Etat*] Ottawa, Ontario [*Library symbol National Library of Canada*] (NLC)

OOSS .... Outpatient Ophthalmic Surgery Society (EA)

OOSS .... Overseas Operational Storage Site [*Army*]

OOSSHRC .... Social Sciences and Humanities Research Council of Canada [*Conseil de Recherches en Sciences Humaines du Canada*] Ottawa, Ontario [*Library symbol National Library of Canada*] (NLC)

OOSSTE .... Terminology and Documentation Branch, Translation Bureau, Department of the Secretary of State [*Direction generale de la Terminologie et de la Documentation,Bureau des Traductions, Secretariat d'Etat*] Ottawa, Ontario [*Library symbol National Library of Canada*] (NLC)

OOSSTE .... Terminology Library, Information Resource Services Directorate, Secretary of State [*Bibliotheque de la Terminologie, Direction Info-Ressources, Secretariat d'Etat*], Ottawa, Ontario [*Library symbol National Library of Canada*] (NLC)

OOSSTM ...... Multilingual Services Directorate, Translation Bureau, Department of the Secretary of State [*Direction des Services Multilingues, Bureau des Traductions, Secretariat d'Etat*] Ottawa, Ontario [*Library symbol National Library of Canada*] (NLC)

OOSSTR .... Translation Services Branch, Translation Bureau, Department of the Secretary of State [*Direction Generale des Services de Traduction, Bureau des Traductions,Secretariat d'Etat*] Ottawa, Ontario [*Library symbol National Library of Canada*] (NLC)

OOST .... Standards Council of Canada, Ottawa, Ontario [*Library symbol National Library of Canada*] (BIB)

OOSTI .... Scientific and Technical Information Centre, Laboratory and Scientific Services Division, Revenue Canada Customs and Excise [*Centre d'Information Scientifique et Technique, Division du Laboratoire et des Services Scientifiques, Revenu Canada Douanes et Accise*] Ottawa, Ontario [*Library symbol National Library of Canada*] (NLC)

OOSTM .... Careerware Reference Centre, STM Systems Corp., Ottawa, Ontario [*Library symbol National Library of Canada*] (BIB)

OOSU .... St. Paul University [*Universite St-Paul*] Ottawa, Ontario [*Library symbol National Library of Canada*] (NLC)

OOSUA .... Archives, St. Paul University [*Archives, Universite St-Paul*] Ottawa, Ontario [*Library symbol National Library of Canada*] (NLC)

OOSV .... St. Vincent Hospital [*Hopital St-Vincent*] Ottawa, Ontario [*Library symbol National Library of Canada*] (NLC)

OOSW .... Status of Women Canada [*Condition Feminine Canada*] Ottawa, Ontario [*Library symbol National Library of Canada*] (NLC)

OOSWH .... Soloway, Wright & Houston Law Firm, Ottawa, Ontario [*Library symbol National Library of Canada*] (BIB)

OOT .... Object-Oriented Technology [*Computer science*] (CDE)

OOT .... Oil Out Temperature

OOT .... Onotoa [*Kiribati*] [*Airport symbol*] (OAG)

OOT .... Ootomari [*Former USSR Seismograph station code, US Geological Survey Closed*] (SEIS)

OOT .... Out of Oxygen Tent

OOT .... Out of Tolerance (FAAC)

OOT .... Out-of-Town [*Word processing*]

OOT .... Transport Canada [*Transports Canada*] Ottawa, Ontario [*Library symbol National Library of Canada*] (NLC)

OOTA .... Airworthiness Library, Transport Canada [*Bibliotheque de la Navigabilite Aerienne, Transports Canada*], Ottawa, Ontario [*Library symbol National Library of Canada*] (NLC)

OOTAC .... Airports and Construction Services, Transport Canada [*Service des Aeroports et de la Construction, Transports Canada*] Ottawa, Ontario [*Library symbol National Library of Canada*] (NLC)

OOTAS .... Canadian Aviation Safety Board [*Bureau Canadien de la Securite Aerienne*] Ottawa, Ontario [*Library symbol National Library of Canada*] (NLC)

OOTB .... Tourism Reference and Documentation, Regional Industrial Expansion [*Centre deReference et de Documentation Touristique, Expansion Industrielle Regionale*] , Ottawa, Ontario [*Library symbol National Library of Canada*] (NLC)

OOTC .... Department of Regional Industrial Expansion [*Ministere de l'Expansion Industrielle Regionale*] Ottawa, Ontario [*Library symbol National Library of Canada*] (NLC)

OOTC .... Oceania Olympic Training Center [*Australia*]

OOTC .... Old Old Timers Club (EA)

OOTCI .... Documentation Centre, Communications and Informatics, Transport Canada [*Centre de Documentation, Communications et Informatique, Transports Canada*], Ottawa, Ontario [*Library symbol National Library of Canada*] (BIB)

OOTCO .... Telecommunications Library, Transport Canada [*Bibliotheque de Telecommunications, Transports Canada*], Ottawa, Ontario [*Library symbol National Library of Canada*] (NLC)

OOTCT .... TransCanada Telephone System, Ottawa, Ontario [*Library symbol National Library of Canada*] (NLC)

OOTE .... Out-of-Town Executive

OOTEL .... Telesat Canada, Ottawa, Ontario [*Library symbol National Library of Canada*] (NLC)

OOTFS .... Technical Library AAFBAA, Flight Services Directorate, Transport Canada [*Bibliotheque Technique AAFBAA, Direction Generale du Service des Vols, Transports Canada*], Ottawa, Ontario [*Library symbol National Library of Canada*] (NLC)

OOTH .... Thumrait [*Oman*] [*ICAO location identifier*] (ICLI)

OOTI .... Technical Information Centre, Transport Canada Training Institute [*Centre d'Information Technique, Institut de Formation Transports Canada*], Cornwall, Ontario [*Library symbol National Library of Canada*] (NLC)

OOTIR .... Traffic Injury Research Foundation of Canada [*Fondation de Recherches sur lesBlessures de la Route au Canada*] Ottawa, Ontario [*Library symbol National Library of Canada*] (NLC)

OOTN .... Trade Negotiations Office, External Affairs Canada [*Affaires Exterieures Canada*] Ottawa, Ontario [*Library symbol National Library of Canada*] (NLC)

OOTR .... Tax Court of Canada [*Cour Canadienne de l'Impot*] Ottawa, Ontario [*Library symbol National Library of Canada*] (NLC)

OOTRAT .... Les Traductions Tessier SCC (Division de Multiscript International), Ottawa, Ontario [*Library symbol National Library of Canada*] (BIB)

OOTRS .... Road Safety and Motor Vehicle Regulation Branch, Transport Canada [*Direction de la Securite Routiere et de la Reglementation Automobile, Transports Canada*], Ottawa, Ontario [*Library symbol National Library of Canada*] (NLC)

OOTRT .... Railway Transportation Directorate, Transport Canada [*Direction du Transport Ferroviaire, Transports Canada*] Ottawa, Ontario [*Library symbol National Library of Canada*] (NLC)

OOTSSA .... St. Lawrence Seaway Authority, Transport Canada [*Administration de la Voie Maritime du Saint-Laurent, Transports Canada*] Ottawa, Ontario [*Library symbol National Library of Canada*] (NLC)

OOTT .... National Transportation Agency of Canada [*Office National des Transports du Canada*], Ottawa, Ontario [*Library symbol National Library of Canada*] (NLC)

OOTTD .... Technical Data Resource Centre, Transport Canada [*Centre de la Documentation Technique, Transports Canada*], Ottawa, Ontario [*Library symbol National Library of Canada*] (NLC)

OOTTE .... Telecommunications and Electronics Directorate, Transport Canada [*Direction des Telecommunications et de l'Electronique, Transports Canada*] Ottawa, Ontario [*Library symbol Obsolete National Library of Canada*] (NLC)

OOTW .... Operations Other Than War [*Army*] (INF)

OOU .... Out of Use (IAA)

OOU .... University of Ottawa [*Universite d'Ottawa*] Ontario [*Library symbol National Library of Canada*] (NLC)

OOUA .... Archives, Universite d'Ottawa [*Archives, University of Ottawa*], Ontario [*Library symbol National Library of Canada*] (BIB)

OOUC .... Department of Criminology, University of Ottawa [*Departement de Criminologie,Universite d'Ottawa*] Ontario [*Library symbol National Library of Canada*] (NLC)

OOUD .... Faculty of Civil Law, University of Ottawa [*Faculte de Droit Civil, Universite d'Ottawa*] Ontario [*Library symbol National Library of Canada*] (NLC)

OOUG .... Oregon Online User Group (NITA)

OOUH .... Health Sciences Library, University of Ottawa [*Bibliotheque des Sciences de la Sante, Universite d'Ottawa*] Ontario [*Library symbol National Library of Canada*] (NLC)

OOUI .... Object-Oriented User Interface [*Computer science*]

OOUIC .... Institute of International Cooperation, University of Ottawa [*Institut de Cooperation Internationale, Universite d'Ottawa*] Ontario [*Library symbol National Library of Canada*] (NLC)

OOUM .... Vanier Library, University of Ottawa [*Bibliotheque Vanier, Universite d'Ottawa*] Ontario [*Library symbol National Library of Canada*] (NLC)

OOUMA .... Map Library, University of Ottawa [*Cartotheque, Universite d'Ottawa*] Ontario [*Library symbol National Library of Canada*] (NLC)

OOURC	Centre de Recherche en Civilisation Canadienne-Francaise, Universite d'Ottawa [*Centre for Research on French Canadian Culture, University of Ottawa*], Ontario [*Library symbol National Library of Canada*] (BIB)
OOUSA	United States Information Service, Ottawa, Ontario [*Library symbol National Library of Canada*] (NLC)
OOUSC	Unitarian Service Committee of Canada, Ottawa, Ontario [*Library symbol National Library of Canada*] (BIB)
OOV	Objects of Verification [*Arms control*] (DOMA)
OOV	Orbit-to-Orbit Vehicle (MCD)
OOV	Out of View
OOV	Out of Vision [*Films, television, etc.*]
OOVIF	Vanier Institute of the Family [*Institut Vanier de la Famille*] Ottawa, Ontario [*Library symbol National Library of Canada*] (NLC)
OOVV	Versatile Vickers Systems, Inc., Ottawa, Ontario [*Library symbol National Library of Canada*] (NLC)
OOW	Officer of the Watch [*Navigation*]
OOW	Owen Sound Public Library, Ontario [*Library symbol National Library of Canada*] (NLC)
OOWC	Wordcount, Creative Writing Services, Inc., Ottawa, Ontario [*Library symbol National Library of Canada*] (NLC)
OOWD	Western Diversification [*Diversification de l'Ouest*], Ottawa, Ontario [*Library symbol National Library of Canada*] (BIB)
OOWGC	Georgian College Resource Centre, Owen Sound, Ontario [*Library symbol National Library of Canada*] (NLC)
OOWGM	Health Sciences Library, General & Marine Hospital, Owen Sound, Ontario [*Library symbol National Library of Canada*] (NLC)
OOWGM	Health Sciences Library, Grey Bruce Regional Health Centre, Owen Sound, Ontario [*Library symbol National Library of Canada*] (NLC)
OOWIC	West Island College of Ontario, Ottawa [*Library symbol National Library of Canada*] (BIB)
OOWLS	Sir Wilfrid Laurier High School Library, Carleton Board of Education, Ottawa, Ontario [*Library symbol National Library of Canada*] (BIB)
OOWM	Owen Sound Museum, County of Grey, Ontario [*Library symbol National Library of Canada*] (BIB)
OOWT	Tom Thomson Memorial Gallery, Owen Sound, Ontario [*Library symbol National Library of Canada*] (NLC)
OOWU	Briefing Centre, World University Services of Canada [*Centre de Ressources, Entraide Universitaire Mondiale du Canada*], Ottawa, Ontario [*Library symbol National Library of Canada*] (NLC)
OOX	XIOS Research Corp., Ottawa, Ontario [*Library symbol National Library of Canada*] (BIB)
OOxM	Miami University, Oxford, OH [*Library symbol Library of Congress*] (LCLS)
OOxM-S	Miami University, Scripps Foundation for Research in Population Problems, Oxford, OH [*Library symbol Library of Congress*] (LCLS)
OOYB	Yibal [*Oman*] [*ICAO location identifier*] (ICLI)
OOZ	Open Ocean Zone [*Oceanography*]
OOZE	Object-Oriented Z Environment [*Computer science*]
OP	Air Panama Internacional [*ICAO designator*] (AD)
Op	De Opficio Mundi [*Philo*] (BJA)
OP	Dominican Contemplative Nuns (Cloistered) (TOCD)
OP	Dominican Contemplative Sisters (TOCD)
OP	Dominican Contemplative Sisters (Cloistered) (TOCD)
OP	Dominican Rural Missionaries (TOCD)
OP	Dominican Sisters (Adrian, MI) (TOCD)
OP	Dominican Sisters (Akron, OH) (TOCD)
OP	Dominican Sisters (Amityville, NY) (TOCD)
OP	Dominican Sisters (Blauvelt, NY) (TOCD)
OP	Dominican Sisters (Caldwell, PA) (TOCD)
OP	Dominican Sisters (Colombia) (TOCD)
OP	Dominican Sisters (Columbus, OH) (TOCD)
OP	Dominican Sisters (Ecuador) (TOCD)
OP	Dominican Sisters (Edmonds, WA) (TOCD)
OP	Dominican Sisters (Fall River, MA) (TOCD)
OP	Dominican Sisters (Grand Rapid, MI) (TOCD)
OP	Dominican Sisters (Great Bend, KS) (TOCD)
OP	Dominican Sisters (Hawthorne, NY) (TOCD)
OP	Dominican Sisters (Houston, TX) (TOCD)
OP	Dominican Sisters (Justice, IL) (TOCD)
OP	Dominican Sisters (Kenosha, WI) (TOCD)
OP	Dominican Sisters (Media, PA) (TOCD)
OP	Dominican Sisters (Nashville, TN) (TOCD)
OP	Dominican Sisters (Newburgh, NY) (TOCD)
OP	Dominican Sisters (New Orleans, LA) (TOCD)
OP	Dominican Sisters of Carondelet (TOCD)
OP	Dominican Sisters of Charity of the Presentation of the Blessed Virgin (TOCD)
OP	Dominican Sisters of Mt. Thabor (TOCD)
OP	Dominican Sisters of Our Lady of the Most Holy Rosary (TOCD)
OP	Dominican Sisters of Our Lady of the Rosary and of Saint Catherine of Siena, Cabra (TOCD)
OP	Dominican Sisters of the Roman Congregation (TOCD)
OP	Dominican Sisters (Ossining, NY) (TOCD)
OP	Dominican Sisters (Oxford, MI) (TOCD)
OP	Dominican Sisters (Oxford, South Africa) (TOCD)
OP	Dominican Sisters (Racine, WI) (TOCD)
OP	Dominican Sisters (San Jose, CA) (TOCD)
OP	Dominican Sisters (San Rafael, CA) (TOCD)
OP	Dominican Sisters (Sinsinawa, WI) (TOCD)
OP	Dominican Sisters (Sparkill, NY) (TOCD)

OP	Dominican Sisters (Spokane, WA) (TOCD)
OP	Dominican Sisters (Springfield, IL) (TOCD)
OP	Dominican Sisters (St. Catherine, KY) (TOCD)
OP	Dominican Sisters (Tacoma, WA) (TOCD)
OP	Dominican Sisters (Vietnam) (TOCD)
OP	Eucharistic Missionaries of St. Dominic (TOCD)
OP	Hermanas Dominicanas de la Doctrine Cristiana (TOCD)
OP	Marian Society of Dominican Catechists (TOCD)
OP	Object Program (IAA)
OP	Obligated Position [*Civil Service*]
OP	Observation Plane
OP	Observation Point [*or Post*]
OP	Observation Post [*Military*]
OP	Observed Position [*Navigation*]
OP	Occasional Paper
OP	Occipitoparietal [*Medicine*] (AAMN)
OP	Occiput Posterior [*Medicine*]
OP	Occupational Psychologist
OP	Oceanus Procellarum [*Lunar area*]
OP	Octapeptide [*Biochemistry*]
OP	Offering Price
OP	Office of Personnel [*Department of Agriculture*] (GFGA)
OP	Office of Pesticides [*Public Health Service*]
OP	Office of Policy [*NASA*]
OP	Office of Preparedness (DNAB)
OP	Office Pass (AAG)
OP	Office Product (IAA)
OP	Officer Program [*Military*] (DNAB)
OP	Official Publication (ADA)
O/P	Off Peak (WDAA)
O-P	Off-Price [*A retail outlet selling discounted merchandise*]
o/p	Oil on Panel (VRA)
OP	Oil Pressure
OP	Oilproof
OP	Oil Pump
OP	Old Particular [*Marsala*]
OP	Old [*Previously seen*] Patient
OP	Old Pattern [*British military*] (DMA)
OP	Old Persian [*Language, etc.*]
OP	Old Price [*Riots*] [*Occurred for 67 nights, beginning December 30, 1808, opening night of rebuilt Covent Garden Theatre, London, because of new and higher prices*]
OP	Olfactory Peduncle [*Medicine*] (DMAA)
OP	Omega Project (EA)
O/P	On Proof [*Publishing*] (DGA)
OP	Opaque [*Envelopes*]
OP	Open [*Stock exchange term*]
OP	Open
OP	Opening Pressure [*Medicine*]
OP	Opening Price [*Stock exchange term*]
OP	Opening Purchase [*Stock exchange term*]
OP	Open Policy
OP	Open Position [*Dancing*]
op	Opera [*Works*] [*Italian*]
OP	Opera
Op	Opera et Dies [*of Hesiod*] [*Classical studies*] (OCD)
OP	Operand [*Computer science*]
op	Operate (IDOE)
OP	Operate
OP	Operating Plan [*Management term*] (MCD)
OP	Operating Point (IAA)
OP	Operating Policy [*Military*]
OP	Operating Procedure [*Management term*] (KSC)
OP	Operating Profit [*DoD*]
OP	Operation (AFM)
OP	Operational (CAAL)
op	Operational (IDOE)
OP	Operational Priority
OP	Operational Procedure (MCD)
OP	Operational Project [*Army*] (AABC)
OP	Operation Overlord Preparations [*World War II*]
OP	Operation Plans
OP	Operations (KSC)
OP	Operations Order (MCD)
OP	Operations Plan (IAA)
OP	Operative Procedure
OP	Operator [*Computer science*]
op	Operator (IDOE)
OP	Ophthalmology
OP	Opinion (ADA)
O-P	Oppenheimer-Phillips [*Process*]
OP	Opposed (NVT)
OP	Opposite
op	Opposite (WDMC)
OP	Opposite Prompt [*i.e., the left side*] [*A stage direction*]
OP	Optical Probe (AAG)
OP	Optical Technician Program [*Association of Independent Colleges and Schools specialization code*]
OP	Optime [*Best*] [*Latin*] (ROG)
OP	Optional
OP	Optional Flag [*Navy British*]
OP	Opus [*Work*] [*Latin*]
op	Opus (WDMC)
OP	Orange Pekoe [*Tea*]
OP	Orbital Period (AAG)

OP..............	Orbital Probe [*NASA*]
op...............	Order of Preachers, Dominican Fathers (TOCD)
OP...............	Order of Preachers (Dominicans) (TOCD)
OP...............	Order of Preceptors
OP...............	Order Policy [*Insurance*]
OP...............	Ordinis Praedicatorum [*Of the Order of Preachers, or Dominicans*] [*Latin*]
OP...............	Ordnance Pamphlets
OP...............	Ordnance Personnel
OP...............	Ordnance Publications [*Navy*] (MCD)
OP...............	Ordo Praedicatorum [*Order of Preachers*] [*Dominicans*] [*Roman Catholic religious order*]
OP...............	Organic Phosphates (GNE)
OP...............	Organophosphorus [*Organic chemistry*]
OP...............	Orient Press [*Press agency*] [*South Korea*]
OP...............	Original Policy (ADA)
OP...............	Original Premium [*Insurance*]
OP...............	Orthogonal Polynomial (OA)
OP...............	Orthomat Plot (MCD)
OP...............	Osmotic Pressure
OP...............	Osteopoetin [*Biochemistry*]
OP...............	Osteoporosis [*Orthopedics*] (DAVI)
OP...............	Osterogenic Protein
OP...............	Other Papers (ROG)
OP...............	Other People's [*Borrowed money, cigarettes, etc.*] [*Slang*]
OP...............	Other Procurement
OP...............	Other than Psychotic
OP...............	Outer Panel (AAG)
OP...............	Out-of-Press [*Recordings*]
OP...............	Out of Print [*Also, OOP*] [*Publishing*]
op...............	Out of Print [*Publishing*] (WDMC)
op...............	Outpatient [*Medicine*]
OP...............	Outpost
OP...............	Output (AAG)
OP...............	Output Primary [*Electronics*]
OP...............	Outside Production
OP...............	Overall Position [*Tertiary entrance*]
OP...............	Over Pressure (AAG)
O/P.............	Overpriced (WDAA)
OP...............	Overprint
op...............	Overprint [*Journalism*] (WDMC)
OP...............	Overproof [*Distilling*]
OP...............	Overseas Post (ADA)
OP...............	Overtime Pay (MHDB)
OP...............	Ovine Prolactin [*Endocrinology*]
O/P.............	Ownership Purpose Code [*Army*] (AABC)
OP...............	Oxazolinylphenoxy [*Organic radical*]
OP...............	Oxygen Pressure Process [*Ore leach process*]
OP...............	Oxygen Purge [*NASA*] (NASA)
OP...............	Paulding County Carnegie Public Library, Paulding, OH [*Library symbol Library of Congress*] (LCLS)
OP...............	Perth Public Library, Ontario [*Library symbol National Library of Canada*] (NLC)
OP...............	Religious Missionaries of St. Dominic (Spanish Prov.) (TOCD)
OPA.............	Kopasker [*Iceland*] [*Airport symbol*] (OAG)
OPa.............	Morley Library, Painesville, OH [*Library symbol Library of Congress*] (LCLS)
OPA.............	Obscene Publications Act [*British*]
OPA.............	Office of Petroleum Allocation [*Federal Energy Administration*]
OPA.............	Office of Policy Analysis [*Environmental Protection Agency*] (GFGA)
OPA.............	Office of Population Affairs [*HEW*]
OPA.............	Office of Price Administration [*World War II*]
OPA.............	Office of Producer Affairs [*Federal Telecommunications Commission*]
OPA.............	Office of Program Analysis [*Department of Energy Washington, DC*]
OPA.............	Office of Program Appraisal [*Navy*]
OPA.............	Office of Public Affairs [*in various government agencies*]
OPA.............	Office of the Pardon Attorney [*Department of Justice*]
OPA.............	Officer Personnel Act
o/pa...........	Oil on Paper (VRA)
OPA.............	Oil Pollution Act of 1990 [*MARAD*] (TAG)
OPA.............	Onafhankelijke Partij [*Independent Party*] [*Netherlands Political party*] (PPW)
OPA.............	Opal Air Pty Ltd. [*Australia ICAO designator*] (FAAC)
OPA.............	Opal Air Pty Ltd. [*Australia FAA designator*] (FAAC)
OPA.............	Opana [*Hawaii*] [*Seismograph station code, US Geological Survey*] (SEIS)
OPA.............	Opaque [*Type of ice formation*]
Opa.............	Opera of the Month Club [*Record label*]
OPA.............	Operations Planning Analysis [*NASA*] (MCD)
OPA.............	Operator Priority Access (NITA)
OPA.............	O-Phthalaldehyde
OPA.............	Optical Plotting Attachment (WDAA)
OPA.............	Optical Publishing Association (EA)
OPA.............	Optoelectronic Pulse Amplifier
OPA.............	Orbiter Plasma Analyzer [*NASA*]
OPA.............	Organophosphorous Acid [*Organic chemistry*]
OPA.............	Organ Procurement Agency [*Department of Health and Human Services*] (GFGA)
OPA.............	Ortho-Phthaldehyde [*Organic chemistry*]
OPA.............	Ortho-Propylaniline
OPA.............	Other Procurement, Army (AABC)
OPA.............	Output Plate Assembly (MCD)
OPA.............	Ovarian Papillary Adenocarcinoma [*Oncology*]
OPA.............	Overall Probability of Attack (DNAB)
OPA.............	Overhead Precautionary Approach

OPAA.........	Organophosphorous Acid Anhydrase [*An enzyme*]
OPAAW.......	Organization of Pan Asian-American Women (EA)
OPAB.........	Abbottabad [*Pakistan*] [*ICAO location identifier*] (ICLI)
OPAC.........	Online Public Access Catalog [*Silicon Valley Information Center - SVIC*] [*San Jose, CA*] [*Information service or system*] (IID)
OPAC.........	Overall Performance Appraisal Certification [*Environmental Protection Agency*] (GFGA)
OPAC.........	Resource Centre, School of Lanark County, Algonquin College of Applied Arts & Technology, Perth, Ontario [*Library symbol National Library of Canada*] (NLC)
OPACK.......	Operation Acknowledge [*Computer science*] (MHDI)
OPACS.......	Office of Price Administration and Civilian Supply [*Name changed to Office of Price Administration*] [*World War II*]
OPACS.......	Order Planning and Control System (MCD)
OPACT.......	Organization of Professional Acting Coaches and Teachers (EA)
OPaD.........	Diamond Shamrock Corp., Research Library, Painesville, OH [*Library symbol Library of Congress*] (LCLS)
OPADEC.....	Optical Partial Decoy (IAA)
OPADEC.....	Optical Particle Decoy
OPADR.......	Operand Address [*Computer science*] (IAA)
OPAE.........	Office of Program Analysis and Evaluation [*DoD*]
OPAEP.......	Organisation des Pays Arabes Exportateurs de Petrole [*Organization of Arab Petroleum Exporting Countries*] (EAIO)
Op AG........	Opinions of the Attorney General [*A publication*] (DLA)
OPAGREE....	Operational Agreement (DNAB)
OPAGY.......	Operating Agency [*Military*]
OPAH.........	Oil Pump Assembly Housing (MCD)
OPAI..........	Paisley Branch, Bruce County Public Library, Ontario [*Library symbol National Library of Canada*] (NLC)
OPaL.........	Lake Erie College, Painesville, OH [*Library symbol Library of Congress*] (LCLS)
OPAL.........	Lakehead University, Thunder Bay, Ontario [*Library symbol National Library of Canada*] (NLC)
OPAL.........	Ocean Process Analysis Laboratory [*University of New Hampshire*] [*Research center*] (RCD)
OPAL.........	Older People with Active Lifestyles [*Lifestyle classification*]
OPAL.........	Oncovin [*Vincristine*], Prednisolone, Adriamycin, L-Asparaginase [*Antineoplastic drug regimen*]
OPAL.........	Opal, Inc. [*NASDAQ symbol*] (SAG)
OPAL.........	Operation Alert [*Designed to test ability to recover from an enemy attack*]
OPAL.........	Operational Performance Analysis Language [*Computer science*]
OPAL.........	Operation Plan Analysis Logic [*Search technology*]
OPAL.........	Optical Platform Alignment Linkage
OPAL.........	Orientation Program in American Law [*of AALS*]
OPALE........	Faculty of Education, Lakehead University, Thunder Bay, Ontario [*Library symbol National Library of Canada*] (NLC)
OPALG.......	Department of Geography, Lakehead University, Thunder Bay, Ontario [*Library symbol National Library of Canada*] (NLC)
OPALs........	Older People with Active Lifestyles [*Lifestyle classification*]
Opals.........	Older People with an Active Lifestyle [*Lifestyle classification*]
OP AMP.....	Operational Amplifier [*Computer science*]
op amp......	Operational Amplifier (IDOE)
OPANAL......	Operations Analysis [*Navy*] (NG)
OPANAL......	Organismo para la Proscripcion de las Armas Nucleares en la America Latina [*Agency for the Prohibition of Nuclear Weapons in Latin America*] (EAIO)
OP & I........	Office of Patents and Inventions
OP & I........	Office of Publications and Information [*Department of Commerce*]
OP & PB.....	Oceanographic Plans and Policy Board (SAA)
OP & R.......	Offset Printing and Reprographics [*A publication*] (DGA)
OPAPE.......	Organisation Pan-Africaine de la Profession Enseignante [*All Africa Teachers' Organization*] (EAIO)
OPAQ........	Offer Parent-Adolescent Questionnaire [*Personality development test*] [*Psychology*]
OPAQUE.....	Optical Atmospheric Quality in Europe (MCD)
OPAR.........	Office of Policy Analysis and Review [*Environmental Protection Agency*] (GFGA)
OPAR.........	Paris Public Library, Ontario [*Library symbol National Library of Canada*] (NLC)
Op Arch......	Opuscula Archaeologica [*A publication*] (OCD)
OPAREA......	Operating Area (CAAL)
op art........	Optical Art (WDMC)
op art........	Optical Art (ODBW)
OPAS.........	Operational Assignment (DA)
OPAS.........	Operational Assistance [*United Nations Development Program*]
OPAS.........	Operational Public Address System
OPAS.........	Overpass
OPAS.........	Overpass [*Postal Service standard*] (OPSA)
OPASTCO.....	Organization for the Protection and Advancement of Small Telephone Companies (EA)
OPat..........	Pataskala Public Library, Pataskala, OH [*Library symbol Library of Congress*] (LCLS)
Op Att Gen...	Opinions of the Attorneys-General [*United States*] [*A publication*] (DLA)
OPATTI.......	Office de Promotion et d'Animation Touristique de Tahiti et ses Iles (EY)
Op Att'y Gen..	Opinions of the Attorney General [*A publication*] (DLA)
Op Attys Gen..	Opinions of the Attorneys-General [*United States*] [*A publication*] (DLA)
OPB..........	Occupational Pensions Board [*British*] (DCTA)
OPB..........	Office of the Publication Board [*Department of Commerce*]
OPB..........	Open Bay [*Papua New Guinea*] [*Airport symbol*] (OAG)
OPB..........	Other People's Butts [*Cigarette butts garnered from ash trays*] [*Slang*]

OPB .... Outpatient Basis [Medicine]
OPB .... Oxidizer Preburner (KSC)
OPB .... Pikangikum Band Library, Ontario [Library symbol National Library of Canada] (BIB)
OPBAT .... Operation Bahamas, Antilles, and Turks [Air Force]
OPBCT .... Providence Bay Branch, Carnarvon Township Public Library, Ontario [Library symbol National Library of Canada] (NLC)
OPBDR......... Office of Program and Budget Development and Review [Bureau of Apprenticeship and Training] [Department of Labor]
OPBE .... Office of Planning, Budgeting, and Evaluation [National Institute of Education]
OPBG .... Bhagtanwala [Pakistan] [ICAO location identifier] (ICLI)
OPBL .... Bela [Pakistan] [ICAO location identifier] (ICLI)
OPBMA .... Ocean Pearl Button Manufacturers Association [Defunct]
OPBN .... Bannu [Pakistan] [ICAO location identifier] (ICLI)
OPBOV .... Oxidizer Preburner Oxidizer Valve (NASA)
OPBR .... Bahawalnagar [Pakistan] [ICAO location identifier] (ICLI)
OPBU .... Operating Budget
OPBW .... Bahawalpur [Pakistan] [ICAO location identifier] (ICLI)
OPC .... Occult Papillary Carcinoma [Oncology]
OPC .... Ocean Policy Committee [Marine science] (MSC)
OPC .... Ocean Products Center (USDC)
OPC .... Ocean Products Center [Marine science] (OSRA)
OPC .... Office de la Protection du Consommateur [Quebec, PQ]
OPC .... Office of Policy Coordination (LAIN)
OPC .... Office of Price Control [World War II]
OPC .... Office of Primary Concern [DoD]
OPC .... Office of Private Cooperation [Department of State]
OPC .... Office of Procurement and Contracts [Department of Housing and Urban Development] (GFGA)
OPC .... Office of the Protective Commissioner [Australia]
OPC .... Ogren, Paul C., South Bend IN [STAC]
OPC .... Oil Policy Committee [Office of Emergency Preparedness] [Obsolete]
OPC .... Oldsmobile Performance Chapter (EA)
OPC .... OLE [Object Linking and Embedding] for Process Control (ACII)
OPC .... Oligonucleotide Purification Cartridge [Chromatography]
OPC .... Olivetti Personal Computers
OPC .... One Pound Charge (MCD)
OPC .... Online Plotter Controller [California Computer Products, Inc.]
OPC .... Open Printed Circuit (IAA)
OPC .... Open Promoter Complex [Genetics]
OPC .... Operated Preference Controls
OPC .... Operation Code
OPC .... Operations Code [Army] (IAA)
OPC .... Operations Control (IAA)
OPC .... Operator Position Controller [Telecommunications]
OPC .... Optical Particle Counter (PDAA)
OPC .... Optical Phase Conjugator [LASER-aiming device]
OPC .... Optical Photoconductor (PCM)
OPC .... Optical Photo Coupler
OPC .... Optional Calling Plans [Telecommunications] (TEL)
OPC .... Orange Pigment Cell
OPC .... Ordinary Portland Cement
OPC .... Ordnance Procurement Center [Army]
OPC .... Organic Photoconductor
OPC .... Outer Passenger Cabin
OPC .... Outer Proliferative Center [Brain anatomy]
opc.............. Out of Print and Cancelled [Publishing] (WDMC)
OPC .... Out of Print, Canceled [Publishing]
OPC .... Outpatient Clinic [Medicine]
OPC .... Outpatient Psychiatric Care [Health insurance] (GHCT)
OPC .... Overall Performance Category
OPC .... Overseas Press Club of America (EA)
OPC .... Ownership Purpose and Condition Code [Navy] (DNAB)
OPC .... Oxford Pocket Classics [A publication] (ROG)
OPC .... Oxypneumocardiogram [Cardiology] (DAVI)
OPC .... Perth Courier, Ontario [Library symbol National Library of Canada] (NLC)
OPC .... QC Optics [AMEX symbol] (SAG)
OPCA .... Occupational Program Consultants Association (EA)
OPCA .... Olivopontocerebellar Atrophy [Neurology]
OPCA .... Opium Poppy Control Act of 1942
OPCA .... Overseas Press Club of America (WDAA)
OP-CAL .... Operation California (EA)
Op Cal Att'y Gen... Opinions of the Attorney General of California [A publication] (DLA)
OPCC .... Office of Preschool and Child Care [Victoria, Australia]
OPCC .... Offutt Air Force Base Processing and Correlation Center (MCD)
OPCC .... Optical Product Code Council (EA)
OPCC .... Outpatient Psychiatric Care Coverage
Op CCCG...... Opinion, Chief Counsel, United States Coast Guard [A publication] (DLA)
OPCE .... Operator Control Element [Computer science] (IBMDP)
OPCEN .... Operations Center [INTELSAT]
OPCG .... Original Print Collectors Group (EA)
OPCGE .... Organic/Polymer Crystal Growth Experiment (SSD)
OPCGF .... Organic/Polymer Crystal Growth Facility (SSD)
OPCH .... Chitral [Pakistan] [ICAO location identifier] (ICLI)
OP CIT .... Opere Citato [In the Work Cited] [Latin]
op cit........... Opere Citato [In the work cited] [Latin] (WDMC)
OPCIT .... Opus Citatum (IAA)
OPCL .... Chilas [Pakistan] [ICAO location identifier] (ICLI)
OPCM .... Operative Plasterers and Cement Masons International Association of the US and Canada

OPCMIA .... Operative Plasterers and Cement Masons International Association of US and Canada (EA)
OPCML .... Township of Muskoka Lakes Public Library Board, Port Carling, Ontario [Library symbol National Library of Canada] (BIB)
OPCO .... Operating Plan Change Orders [Coast Guard publication]
OPCO .... Outside Production Consignment Order
OP-COD .... Operating Code [Computer science]
op code .... Operation Code (IDOE)
OPCODE....... Operations Code [Army] (AABC)
OP-COM .... Opera-Comique [Comic Opera] [Music]
OPCOM........ Operational Command [Military] (MCD)
OP-COM .... Operations-Communications
OPCOMCTR.. Operational Command Center [Navy] (NVT)
OPCON......... Operational Control [Army] (NVT)
OPCON......... Operation Control [Military] (VNW)
OPCON......... Operations and Control System (IAA)
OPCON......... Operator's Console
OPCON......... Optimizing Control [Military]
OPCONCEN... Operational Control Center [Navy]
OPCONCTR... Operational Control Center [Navy] (NVT)
OPCOSAL...... Optimum Coordinated Shipboard [or Shorebased] Allowance List
OPCPL .... Port Colborne Public Library, Ontario [Library symbol National Library of Canada] (NLC)
OPCR .... Chachro [Pakistan] [ICAO location identifier] (ICLI)
OPCR .... One-Pass Cold-Rolled [Steel sheets]
OPCS .... Office of Population Census and Surveys [British] (ECON)
OPCS .... Office of Population Censuses and Surveys [Department of Employment] [British]
OPCS .... Operational Planning and Control System [Department of Labor] (OICC)
OPCT .... Chirat [Pakistan] [ICAO location identifier] (ICLI)
OPCTR .... Operation Counter (IAA)
OPCTR .... Operations Center [Military]
OPCV .... Office of Planning, Control, and Validation [Social Security Administration]
OPCW .... Office of Petroleum Coordination for War [New Deal]
OPCW .... Organization for the Prohibition of Chemical Weapons [Proposed, 1992]
OPD .... Audit Programs Division (AAGC)
OPD .... Delayed Opening
OPD .... Observed Position Data
OPD .... Office of Policy Development [Executive Office of the President]
OPD .... Office of Program Development [Environmental Protection Agency] (GFGA)
OPD .... Office of Program Development [NASA]
OPD .... Officer Personnel Directorate [Army]
OPD .... Officer Professional Development [Military] (INF)
OPD .... Ohio College of Podiatric Medicine, Cleveland, OH [OCLC symbol] (OCLC)
OPD .... One Per Desk (NITA)
OPD .... Opened [Stock exchange term] (SPSG)
OPD .... Opening Posterior Digestive [Gland]
OPD .... Operand [Computer science]
OPD .... Operational Programming Department [Telecommunications] (TEL)
OPD .... Operations Division [War Department General Staff] [World War II]
OPD .... Operations Planning Division [Manned Spacecraft Center]
OPD .... Optical Particle Detector [for evaluating film quality]
OPD .... Optical Path Difference (MCD)
OPD .... Optical Phase Distortion (PDAA)
OPD .... Optical Proximity Detector
OPD .... Oral and Pharyngeal Development [Section] [National Institute of Dental Research]
OPD .... Orbiting Propellant Depot [NASA]
OPD .... Original Pack Dispensing [For drugs] [Packaging]
OPD .... Ortho-Phenylenediamine [Organic chemistry]
OPD .... 'Osef Piskei Din shel ha-Rabanut ha-Rashit le-'Erets Yisrael (BJA)
OPD .... Oto-Palato-Digital [Syndrome]
OPD .... Outpatient Department [or Dispensary] [Medicine]
OPD .... Overall Program Design (OICC)
O/PD .... Overpaid (ROG)
OPD .... Overseas Policy Defence Committee [British]
OPD .... Oxford Paperback Dictionary [A publication]
OPD .... Port Dover Centennial Public Library, Ontario [Library symbol National Library of Canada] (NLC)
OPDAC.......... Optical Data Converter (NOAA)
OPDAG........ Original Paper Doll Artists Guild (EA)
OPDAR........ Optical Detection and Ranging
OPDARS ...... Optical Detection and Ranging System (IAA)
OPDATS....... Operational Performance Data System
OPDB .... Dalbandin [Pakistan] [ICAO location identifier] (ICLI)
OPDC .... Overseas Policy Defence Committee [British] (DI)
OPDD .... Dadu [Pakistan] [ICAO location identifier] (ICLI)
OPDD .... Operational Plan Data Document [Military] (AFM)
O,p-DDD ...... Ortho, Para-Dichloro-Diphenyldichlorethane [Mitotane] [Antineoplastic drug regimen] (DAVI)
OPDEC......... Operational Deception [Navy] (NVT)
OpDent .... Operative Dentistry (BABM)
Opdent......... Operative Dentistry (DAVI)
OPDET .... Operational Detachment (MCD)
OPDEVFOR... Operational Development Forces
OPDG .... Dera Ghazi Khan [Pakistan] [ICAO location identifier] (ICLI)
OPDI .... Dera Ismail Khan [Pakistan] [ICAO location identifier] (ICLI)
OPDI .... Operator Please Deliver Immediately
OP DIAP ...... Open Diapason [Organ stop] [Music]
OPDIF.......... Operational Planning Identification File [Military]

OPDIN.......... Ocean Pollution Data and Information Network [*Washington, DC Department of Commerce*] (GRD)
OPDIN.......... Ocean Pollution Data Center (USDC)
OPDIN.......... Ocean Pollution Data Center [*Marine science*] (OSRA)
OP DIV.......... Operations/Air Intelligence Photography Division (DNAB)
OPDK.......... Daharki [*Pakistan*] [*ICAO location identifier*] (ICLI)
OPDL.......... Office of Production and Defense Lending [*Department of the Treasury*]
OPDO.......... Oromo People's Democratic Organization [*Ethiopia*] [*Political party*] (EY)
OPDOC.......... Operational Documentation [*Military*]
OPDP.......... Officer Professional Development Program [*Pronounced "opey-dopey"*] [*Canadian Navy*]
OPDPE.......... Office of Policy Development Planning and Evaluation [*Pronounced "opey dopey"*] [*NIMH*]
OPDR.......... Office of Primary Development Responsibility (AFM)
OPDS.......... Office Professional Development System (MCD)
OPDS.......... Offshore Petroleum Distribution System
OPDU.......... Operation Protocol Data Unit [*Telecommunications*] (OSI)
OPDU.......... Powassan and District Union Public Library, Powassan, Ontario [*Library symbol National Library of Canada*] (NLC)
OPDUA.......... Operative Painters amd Decorators' Union of Australia
OPD WDGS... Operations Division, War Department General Staff [*World War II*]
OPE.......... Eldorado Nuclear Ltd., Port Hope, Ontario [*Library symbol National Library of Canada*] (NLC)
OPE.......... Office of Planning and Evaluation [*Office of Personnel Management*] (GRD)
OPE.......... Office of Policy Evaluation [*Nuclear energy*] (NRCH)
OPE.......... Office of Postsecondary Education [*Department of Education*] (GFGA)
OPE.......... Office of Program Eligibility (AAGC)
OPE.......... Office of Program Evaluation [*Office of Policy, Evaluation, and Research*] [*Department of Labor*]
OPE.......... One-Pion Exchange [*Nuclear energy*]
OPE.......... Open Point Expanding [*Bullet*] (DICI)
OPE.......... Operational Planning Estimate
OPE.......... Operations Project Engineer [*NASA*] (KSC)
OPE.......... Optical Pointing Error
OPE.......... Optical-Probe Experiment [*Giotto probe of Halley's comet*] [*European Space Agency*]
OPE.......... Optimized Processing Element
OPE.......... Orbiting Primate Experiment (MCD)
OPE.......... Oregon, Pacific & Eastern Railway Co. [*AAR code*]
OPE.......... Other Plant Equipment [*DoD*]
OPE.......... Other Project Element (NASA)
OPE.......... Other Project Element
OPE.......... Outer Planets Explorer [*NASA*]
OPE.......... Societe 3S Aviation (Aerope) [*France ICAO designator*] (FAAC)
OPE.......... Topeka, KS [*Location identifier FAA*] (FAAL)
OPEAA.......... Outdoor Power Equipment Aftermarket Association (EA)
OPEB.......... Bruce County Public Library, Port Elgin, Ontario [*Library symbol National Library of Canada*] (NLC)
OPEC.......... Oil Producers' Economic Cartel (NADA)
OPEC.......... Organization of Petroleum Exporting Countries (NADA)
OPEC.......... Organization of Petroleum Exporting Countries [*Also, OAPEC*] [*Vienna, Austria*]
OPECNA.......... OPEC [*Organization of Petroleum Exporting Countries*] News Agency [*See also APOPEC*] [*Vienna, Austria*] (EAIO)
OPECO.......... Operations Coordinator [*Marine science*] (MSC)
OP-ED.......... Opposite Editorial Page [*in a newspaper*] [*Usually consists of opinion columns by various guest writers or syndicated columnists*]
op ed.......... Opposite - the Editorial Page [*Newspapers*] (WDMC)
OPED.......... Other Pay Entry Date [*Army*] (AABC)
OPED.......... Point Edward Public Library, Ontario [*Library symbol National Library of Canada*] (NLC)
OPEDA.......... Organization of Professional Employees of the United States Department of Agriculture (EA)
OPEDA.......... Outdoor Power Equipment Distributors Association (EA)
OPEDC.......... Overseas Private Enterprise Development Corp. [*Proposed successor to Agency for International Development*]
OPeeO.......... Ohio Valley Local District Free Public Library, Peebles Branch, Peebles, OH [*Library symbol Library of Congress*] (LCLS)
OPEF.......... Overall Plume Enhancement Factor [*Space Shuttle*] [*NASA*]
OPEI.......... Office of Public Education and Information [*NASA*]
OPEI.......... Outdoor Power Equipment Institute (EA)
OPEIU.......... Office and Professional Employees International Union (EA)
OPEM.......... One-Pion Exchange Model [*Nuclear energy*]
OPEM.......... Pembroke Public Library, Ontario [*Library symbol National Library of Canada*] (NLC)
OPEMA.......... Oilfield Production Equipment Manufacturers Association [*Defunct*] (EA)
OPEMAC.......... Upper Ottawa Valley Campus Resource Centre, Algonquin College, Pembroke, Ontario [*Library symbol National Library of Canada*] (NLC)
OPEMO.......... Ottawa Valley Historical Society, Pembroke, Ontario [*Library symbol National Library of Canada*] (BIB)
OPEN.......... Fund for an Open Society (EA)
OPEN.......... Oncovin, Prednisone, Etopside, Mitoxantrone [*Antineoplastic drug*] (CDI)
OPEN.......... Online Public Education Network
OPEN.......... Open Environment [*NASDAQ symbol*] (TTSB)
OPEN.......... Open Environment Corp. [*NASDAQ symbol*] (SAG)
OPEN.......... Open Protocol Enhanced Network [*Northern Telecom communications network*] [*Canada*]

OPEN.......... Organisation des Producteurs d'Energie Nucleaire [*Paris, France*] (EAIO)
OPEN.......... Origins of Plasma in the Earth's Neighborhood [*Ad Hoc Advisory Committee terminated, 1981*]
OPEN.......... Penetanguishene Public Library, Ontario [*Library symbol National Library of Canada*] (BIB)
OPENAH.......... Operational Evaluation of Armed Helicopters (MCD)
OPENE.......... Ecole Secondaire le Caron, Penetanguishene, Ontario [*Library symbol National Library of Canada*] (BIB)
OPENM.......... Mental Health Centre, Penetanguishene, Ontario [*Library symbol National Library of Canada*] (NLC)
OpenMkt.......... Open Market, Inc. [*Associated Press*] (SAG)
OpenPln.......... Open Plan Systems, Inc. [*Associated Press*] (SAG)
OpenTxt.......... Open Text Corp. [*Associated Press*] (SAG)
OpenVis.......... OpenVision Technologies, Inc. [*Associated Press*] (SAG)
OPEO.......... Oakland-Pontiac Enthusiast Organization (EA)
OPEO.......... Octylphenol Polyethoxylate [*Organic chemistry*]
OPEOS.......... Outside Plant Planning, Engineering, and Construction Operations System (MCD)
OPEP.......... Orbital-Plane Experiment Package [*NASA*]
OPEPB.......... Eastern Pentecostal Bible College, Peterborough, Ontario [*Library symbol National Library of Canada*] (NLC)
OPER.......... Office of Policy and Economic Research [*Federal Home Loan Bank Board*] [*Washington, DC*] (GRD)
OPER.......... Office of Policy, Evaluation, and Research [*Employment and Training Administration*] [*Department of Labor*]
OPer.......... Old Persian [*Language*] (BARN)
OPER.......... Operating [*Automotive engineering*]
OPER.......... Operation [*or Operational*] (KSC)
oper.......... Operation (DD)
OPER.......... Operator (IAA)
OPER.......... Operator
OPERA.......... Operational Analysis (IAA)
OPERA.......... Ordnance Pulses Experimental Research Assembly [*Nuclear reactor*]
OPERA.......... Out-of-Pile Expulsion and Reentry Apparatus [*Nuclear energy*]
OPERATORS... Optimization Program for Economical Remote Trunk Arrangement and TSPS [*Traffic Service Positions System*] Operator Arrangements [*Telecommunications*] (TEL)
OPERG.......... Operating (MDG)
O-PERS.......... Officer Personnel Office (DNAB)
OPers.......... Old Persian [*Language*] (BARN)
OPERSCRS... Officer Personnel Course [*Air Force*]
OPersLex.......... Old Persian Grammar Texts Lexicon [*A publication*] (BJA)
OPERUN.......... Operation Planning and Execution System for Railway Unified Network (PDAA)
OPES.......... Centre de Documentation, Ecole Secondaire de Plantagenet [*Documentation Centre, Plantagenet Secondary School*], Ontario [*Library symbol National Library of Canada*] (BIB)
OPET.......... Organization, Personnel Equipment and Training [*Group*]
OPET.......... Oriented Polyethylene Terephthalate [*Organic chemistry*]
OPET.......... Trent University, Peterborough, Ontario [*Library symbol National Library of Canada*] (NLC)
OPETA.......... Trent University Archives, Peterborough, Ontario [*Library symbol National Library of Canada*] (NLC)
OPETAL.......... Trent Audio Library Services, Trent University, Peterborough, Ontario [*Library symbol National Library of Canada*] (NLC)
OPETC.......... Trent Canal Office, Peterborough, Ontario [*Library symbol National Library of Canada*] (BIB)
OPETCG.......... Canadian General Electric Co. Ltd., Peterborough, Ontario [*Library symbol National Library of Canada*] (NLC)
OPETCM.......... Peterborough Centennial Museum and Archives, Ontario [*Library symbol National Library of Canada*] (BIB)
OPETHS.......... Hutchison House Museum, Peterborough Historical Society, Ontario [*Library symbol National Library of Canada*] (BIB)
OPETM.......... Map Library, Trent University, Peterborough, Ontario [*Library symbol National Library of Canada*] (NLC)
OPETP.......... Peterborough Public Library, Ontario [*Library symbol National Library of Canada*] (NLC)
OPETSF.......... Brealy Library, Sir Sandford Fleming College, Peterborough, Ontario [*Library symbol National Library of Canada*] (NLC)
OPETSFD.......... Daniel Library, Sir Sandford Fleming College, Peterborough, Ontario [*Library symbol National Library of Canada*] (BIB)
OPEV.......... Petawawa Village and Township Union Public Library, Ontario [*Library symbol National Library of Canada*] (NLC)
OPEVAL.......... Operational Evaluation [*Navy*] (NG)
OPEX.......... Operational, Executive, and Administrative Personnel Program [*United Nations*]
OPEX.......... Operational Extension
OPF.......... Miami, FL [*Location identifier FAA*] (FAAL)
OPF.......... Official Personnel File (MCD)
OPF.......... Official Personnel Folder [*Military*]
OPF.......... One-Piece Folder [*Publishing*] (WDMC)
OPF.......... Open-Pore Foam [*Plastic*]
OPF.......... Operations Flight [*Military*]
OPF.......... Optical Propagation Facility
OPF.......... Orbiter Processing Facility [*NASA*] (NASA)
OPF.......... Overseas Project Fund [*British Overseas Trade Board*] (DS)
OPFA.......... Faisalabad [*Pakistan*] [*ICAO location identifier*] (ICLI)
OPFAC.......... Operating Facilities [*Coast Guard publication*]
OPFAC.......... Operational Facility (RDA)
OPFAD.......... Outer-Perimeter Fleet Air Defense
OPFC.......... Hinchinbrooke Public Library, Frontenac County Library, Parkham, Ontario [*Library symbol National Library of Canada*] (BIB)
OPFC.......... Orbiter Preflight Checklist [*NASA*] (MCD)

OPFCA .... Ornamental Pool and Fountain Constructors Association [*British*] (DBA)

OPFCO .... Operational Program Functional Checkout (MCD)

OPFI .... Office of Program and Fiscal Integrity (USGC)

OPFM .... Outlet Plenum Feature Model [*Nuclear energy*] (NRCH)

OPFOR .... Opportunity to Confront the Best Opposing Force [*Army*] (INF)

OPFOR .... Opposing Force [*Military*] (INF)

OPFRC .... Clarendon-Miller Branch, Frontenac County Library, Plevna, Ontario [*Library symbol National Library of Canada*] (NLC)

OPFT .... Other than Permanent Full-Time (GFGA)

OPFTE .... Other than Permanent Full-Time Equivalent (GFGA)

OPG .... Oculoplethysmograph [*Instrumentation*]

OPG .... Office Of Global Programs [*Marine science*] (OSRA)

OPG .... Office of the Postmaster General [*Obsolete*]

OPG .... Opening

OPG .... Operating

OPG .... Operational Performance Goals

OPG .... Operational Planning Grant (OICC)

OPG .... Operations Planning Group [*Military*]

OPG .... Original Proof Gallon

OPG .... Outside Production Group

OPG .... Overseas Products Group [*Department of Trade*] [*British*]

OPG .... Oxypolygelatin [*Plasma extender*]

Op GA Att'y Gen... Opinions of the Attorney General of Georgia [*A publication*] (DLA)

OPG/CPA ..... Oculoplethysmography/Carotid Phonoangiography [*Medicine*] (DAVI)

Op GCT .... Opinion, General Counsel, United States Treasury Department [*A publication*] (DLA)

OPGD .... Gwadar [*Pakistan*] [*ICAO location identifier*] (ICLI)

OPGE .... OEEC [*Organization for European Economic Cooperation*] Petroleum Industry Emergency Group (NATG)

OP/GSA .... Office of Preparedness, General Services Administration [*Later, Federal Preparedness Agency*]

OPGT .... Gilgit [*Pakistan*] [*ICAO location identifier*] (ICLI)

OPGT .... Outer Planets Grand Tour [*NASA*]

OPGUID .... Optimum Guidance [*Technique*] (NASA)

OPGW .... Optical Groundwire [*Telecommunications*] (TSSD)

OPH .... Obliterative Pulmonary Hypertension [*Medicine*]

OPH .... Old Parliamentary Hand [*Political*] [*British*]

OPh .... Old Phoenician (BJA)

OPH .... Operational Propellant Handling [*NASA*] (AAG)

OPH .... Ophicleide [*Musical instrument*]

Oph .... Ophiuchus [*Constellation*]

OPH .... Ophthalmodynamometry [*Ophthalmology*]

OPH .... Ophthalmolgist

OPH .... Ophthalmology [*or Ophthalmoscopy*]

OPH .... [*The*] Ophthalmoscope [*London*] [*A publication*] (ROG)

Oph .... Ophthalmoscopic [*or Ophthalmoscope*] [*Ophthalmology*] (DAVI)

OPH .... Opposite Hand [*Technical drawings*]

OPH .... Organophosphorus Hydrolase [*An enzyme*]

OPH .... Public Library, Port Hope, Ontario [*Library symbol National Library of Canada*] (NLC)

OPHC .... Office of Prepaid Health Care [*Department of Health and Human Services*] (GFGA)

Oph D .... Doctor of Ophthalmology

OPHF .... Orbital Polarized Hartree-Fock [*Atomic physics*]

Ophi .... Ophiuchus [*Constellation*]

OPHIR .... Organic Power and Heat Industrial Reactor

Ophn .... Orpheon [*Record label*] [*Poland*]

OPHQ .... Karachi [*Pakistan*] [*ICAO location identifier*] (ICLI)

OPHR .... Olympic Project for Human Rights

Op Hrs .... Operation Hours (DA)

OPHS .... Operational Propellant Handling System [*NASA*] (AAG)

OPHT .... Ophthalmic

OPHTH .... Ophthalmology (AABC)

OPHTHAL ..... Ophthalmology

OphtImg .... Ophthalmic Imaging Systems [*Associated Press*] (SAG)

OPHTS .... Operational Propellant Handling Test Site [*NASA*] (AAG)

OPHWA .... Nuclear Products Department, Westinghouse Canada, Inc., Port Hope, Ontario [*Library symbol National Library of Canada*] (NLC)

OPi .... Flesh Public Library, Piqua, OH [*Library symbol Library of Congress*] (LCLS)

OPI .... Oculoparalytic Illusion [*Ophthalmology*]

OPI .... Office of Primary Interest

OPI .... Office of Programs Integration [*Energy Research and Development Administration*]

OPI .... Office of Public Information [*UNESCO*]

OPI .... Office of Public Information [*NASA*]

OPI .... Off-Site Production Inspection (AAG)

OPI .... Oil Patch Group, Inc. [*Toronto Stock Exchange symbol*]

OPI .... Oil Pressure Indicator

OPI .... Omnibus Personality Inventory [*Psychology*]

OPI .... One Person's Impact [*An association*] (EA)

OPI .... Open for Public Inspection [*Patent applications*]

OPI .... Open Prepress Interface [*Computer science*] (PCM)

OPI .... Open Protocol Interface [*Telecommunications*]

OPI .... Optical Publishing, Inc. [*Information service or system*] (IID)

OPI .... Orbital Position Indicator

OPI .... Orbiter Payload Interrogator [*NASA*] (MCD)

OPI .... Ordnance Procedure Instrumentations (AAG)

OPI .... Ordnance Procurement Instructions [*Army*]

OPI .... Organophosphate Insecticide

OPI .... Output Productivity Index

OPI .... Outside Procurement [*or Purchase*] Inspection (AAG)

OPI .... Overall Performance Index [*Finance*]

OPI .... Picton Public Library, Ontario [*Library symbol National Library of Canada*] (NLC)

OPIAT .... Opiates [*Chemical dependency*] [*Pharmacology*] (DAVI)

OPIC .... Oficina Permanente Internacional de la Carne [*Permanent International Meat Office*] (EAIO)

OPIC .... Overseas Private Investment Corp. [*US International Development Cooperatio n Agency*] [*Washington, DC*]

OPIC .... Overseas Private Investment Corp.

OPIC .... Pickering Public Library, Ontario [*Library symbol National Library of Canada*] (NLC)

OPID .... Operational Procedures Interface Document (MCD)

OPIDF .... Operational Planning Identification File (MCD)

OPIDF .... Operational Planning Identification File

OPIDN .... Organophosphate Induced Delayed Neural Toxicity

OPiE .... Edison State Community College, Piqua, OH [*Library symbol Library of Congress*] (LCLS)

OPIE .... Ohio Program of Intensive English (EDAC)

OPIET .... Eco-Tec Ltd., Pickering, Ontario [*Library symbol National Library of Canada*] (NLC)

OPIG .... Picton Gazette, Ontario [*Library symbol National Library of Canada*] (NLC)

OPIL .... Opalescent Indicating Light

Op III Att'y Gen... Illinois Attorney General's Opinion [*A publication*] (DLA)

OPIM .... Order Processing and Inventory Monitoring [*Computer science*]

Opin .... Opinions of the Attorneys-General [*United States*] [*A publication*] (DLA)

Opinc .... Options Income (BARN)

OPINE .... Operations in a Nuclear Environment [*DoD*]

Opine .... Option Income [*Business term*]

OPINM .... North Marysburgh Museum, Picton, Ontario [*Library symbol National Library of Canada*] (BIB)

OpinRsh .... Opinion Research Corp. [*Associated Press*] (SAG)

OPINT .... Optical Intelligence

OPINTEL ...... Operational Intelligence

OPIRL .... Operator Interface Rolling Loop

OPIS .... Operational Priority Indicating System (NATG)

OPIS .... Orbiter Prime Item Specification [*NASA*] (NASA)

OPIS .... Pelee Island Public Library, Ontario [*Library symbol National Library of Canada*] (NLC)

OP(IT) .... Operation Overlord Preparations, Inland Transport [*World War II*]

OPIT .... Operator Interface Table (MCD)

OPiWU .... Wright State University, Piqua Branch Campus, Piqua, OH [*Library symbol Library of Congress*] (LCLS)

OPJ .... Ohio Power 8.16% Jr Sub Debs [*NYSE symbol*] (TTSB)

OPJA .... Jacobabad [*Pakistan*] [*ICAO location identifier*] (ICLI)

Op JAGAF .... Opinion, Judge Advocate General, United States Air Force [*A publication*] (DLA)

Op JAGN ...... Opinion, Judge Advocate General, United States Navy [*A publication*] (DLA)

OPJC .... Jacobabad [*Pakistan*] [*ICAO location identifier*] (ICLI)

OPJI .... Jiwani [*Pakistan*] [*ICAO location identifier*] (ICLI)

Op Judge Adv Gen... Opinion of the Judge Advocate General (AAGC)

OPK .... Operative Personenkontrolle [*Operational Person Control*] [*German*]

OPK .... Optokinetic

OPK .... Ovulation Predictor Kit

OPKA .... Cape Monze [*Pakistan*] [*ICAO location identifier*] (ICLI)

Op Kan Att'y Gen... Opinions of the Attorney General of Kansas [*A publication*] (DLA)

OPKC .... Karachi/International [*Pakistan*] [*ICAO location identifier*] (ICLI)

OPKD .... Hyderabad [*Pakistan*] [*ICAO location identifier*] (ICLI)

OPKE .... Chore [*Pakistan*] [*ICAO location identifier*] (ICLI)

OPKE .... Knudsen Engineering Ltd., Perth, Ontario [*Library symbol National Library of Canada*] (BIB)

OPKF .... Gharo [*Pakistan*] [*ICAO location identifier*] (ICLI)

OPKH .... Khuzdhar [*Pakistan*] [*ICAO location identifier*] (ICLI)

OPKK .... Karachi/Korangi Creek [*Pakistan*] [*ICAO location identifier*] (ICLI)

OPKL .... Kalat [*Pakistan*] [*ICAO location identifier*] (ICLI)

OPKN .... Kharan [*Pakistan*] [*ICAO location identifier*] (ICLI)

OPKO .... Kohat [*Pakistan*] [*ICAO location identifier*] (ICLI)

OPKR .... Karachi [*Pakistan*] [*ICAO location identifier*] (ICLI)

OPKT .... Kohat [*Pakistan*] [*ICAO location identifier*] (ICLI)

Op KY Att'y Gen... Opinion of Attorney General, State of Kentucky [*A publication*] (DLA)

OPL .... Air Cote d'Opale [*France ICAO designator*] (FAAC)

OPL .... Oberlin Public Library, Oberlin, OH [*OCLC symbol*] (OCLC)

OPL .... Ocean Pressure Laboratory

OPL .... Office of Presidential Libraries [*National Archives*] (BARN)

OPL .... Official Publications Library [*The British Library*]

OPL .... Old Product Line (IAA)

OPL .... One-Person Library

OPL .... Opelousas, LA [*Location identifier FAA*] (FAAL)

OPL .... Open Problem List (NASA)

OPL .... Open Problem List

OPL .... Operational (AFM)

OPL .... Operations Plan (KSC)

OPL .... Optical Path Length

OPL .... Organizer Programming Language [*Computer science*]

OPL .... Orient-Pacific Line [*Shipping*] (ROG)

OPL .... Ottawa Public Library [*UTLAS symbol*]

OPL .... Outer Plexiform Layer [*Retina*]

OPL .... Out-of-Phase Loading

OPL .... Outpost Line

OPL .... Overpaid Last Account

OPL .... Ovine Placental Lactogen [*Medicine*] (DMAA)

OPLA .... Lahore [*Pakistan*] [*ICAO location identifier*] (ICLI)

Op LA Att'y Gen... Opinions of the Attorney General of Louisiana [*A publication*] (DLA)
OPLAC .... Argyle Community Library, Port Loring, Ontario [*Library symbol National Library of Canada*] (NLC)
OPLAN .... Operation Plan [*Army*]
OPLAN SEA... Operation Plan, Southeast Asia [*Military*]
OPLC .... Organizacion para la Liberacion de Cuba [*Organization for the Liberation of Cuba*] (PD)
OPLC .... Overpressure Layer Chromatography
OPLE .... Omega Position Location Experiment [*NASA*]
Op Let .... Opinion Letter [*A publication*] (DLA)
OPLF .... Orbiter Processing and Landing Facility [*NASA*] (MCD)
OPLG .... Oil Plug
OPLH .... Lahore/Walton [*Pakistan*] [*ICAO location identifier*] (ICLI)
OPLL .... Loralai [*Pakistan*] [*ICAO location identifier*] (ICLI)
OPLL .... Ossification of Posterior Longitudinal Ligament [*Orthopedics*] (DAVI)
OPLP .... Pickle Pat Public Library, Pickle Lake, Ontario [*Library symbol National Library of Canada*] (NLC)
OPLR .... Lahore [*Pakistan*] [*ICAO location identifier*] (ICLI)
OPLR .... Outpost Line of Resistance
OPLSS .... Optimized Portable Life-Support System [*NASA*]
OPM .... Occult Primary Malignancy [*Oncology*]
OPM .... Office of Personnel Management [*Supersedes Civil Service Commission*]
OPM .... Office of Planning and Management [*DoD*]
OPM .... Office of Policy and Management [*Environmental Protection Agency*] (GFGA)
OPM .... Office of Procurement and Materiel [*Army*]
OPM .... Office of Production Management [*Superseded by WPB, 1942*]
OPM .... Office of Program Management [*Unemployment Insurance Service*] [*Department of Labor*]
OPM .... Office of Program Management [*Environmental Protection Agency*] (GFGA)
OPM .... Office, Personnel Manager [*Army*] (MUGU)
OPM .... Operating Plane Months [*Navy*] (NG)
OPM .... Operating Procedure for Ministers
OPM .... Operations Message (SSD)
OPM .... Operations per Minute [*Performance measure*]
OPM .... Operator Programming Method [*Computer science*]
OPM .... Ophthalmodynamometry [*Ophthalmology*]
OPM .... Optically Projected Map
OPM .... Optical Power Meter
OPM .... Options Pricing Model
OPM .... Ordnance Proof Manual (SAA)
OPM .... Organisasi Papua Merdeka [*Papua Independent Organization*] [*Indonesia*] (PD)
OPM .... Organizacion Politico-Militar [*Politico-Military Organization*] [*Paraguay*] (PD)
OPM .... Oscillating Pressure Method
OPM .... Other People's Money
OPM .... Outer Planet Mission
OPM .... Output per Man (ODBW)
OPM .... Output Position Map [*Computer science*] (OA)
OPM .... Output Processor Module (MCD)
OPM .... Owner President Management Program (DD)
OPM .... Oxford Policy Management [*British*]
OPM .... Perth Museum, Ontario [*Library symbol National Library of Canada*] (NLC)
OPMA .... Mangla [*Pakistan*] [*ICAO location identifier*] (ICLI)
OPMA .... Office Products Manufacturers Association (EA)
OPMA .... Open Pit Mining Association (EA)
OPMA .... Ophthalmic Prescription Manufacturers Association [*British*] (DBA)
OPMA .... Overseas Press and Media Association [*British*] (EAIO)
OPMAC .... Operations for Military Assistance to the Community (PDAA)
OPMACC ..... Operation Military Aid to the Civil Community [*British military*] (DMA)
OPMARV ..... Operational Maneuvering Reentry Vehicle (MCD)
OPMC .... One Player Median Competitive (PDAA)
OPMCS .... Otto Pre-Marital Counseling Schedules [*Psychology*]
OPMD .... Officer Personnel Management Directorate [*Military*]
OPME .... Office of Personnel Management Evaluation (DNAB)
OPME .... Office of Program Management and Evaluation [*Environmental Protection Agency*] (GFGA)
OPMET .... Operational Meteorological Information [*ICAO*] (FAAC)
OPMF .... Muzaffarabad [*Pakistan*] [*ICAO location identifier*] (ICLI)
OPMG .... Office of the Provost Marshal General [*Army*]
OpMG .... Oppenheimer Multi-Government Trust [*Associated Press*] (SAG)
OPMH .... Occupations for Patients in Mental Hospitals [*British*]
OPMI .... Mianwali [*Pakistan*] [*ICAO location identifier*] (ICLI)
OPMI .... Open Perfusion Micro-Incubator
OPMI .... Operation Microscope [*Surgery*]
Op Minn Att'y Gen... Opinions of the Attorney General of Minnesota [*A publication*] (DLA)
OPMIS .... Optical Propulsion Management Interface System
OPMJ .... Moenjodaro [*Pakistan*] [*ICAO location identifier*] (ICLI)
OPMK .... Mir Pur Khas [*Pakistan*] [*ICAO location identifier*] (ICLI)
OPMN .... Miranshah [*Pakistan*] [*ICAO location identifier*] (ICLI)
OPMN .... Port McNicoll Public Library, Ontario [*Library symbol National Library of Canada*] (NLC)
OPMO .... Office of Program Management Operations [*Environmental Protection Agency*] (GFGA)
OPMOPLAN... Operation Missouri Plan [*Program for five-day state funeral planned several years in advance for ex-President Harry Truman*] [*Army*]
OPMPR .... Office of Personnel Management Procurement Regulations [*A publication*] (AAGC)
OPMR .... Karachi/Masroor [*Pakistan*] [*ICAO location identifier*] (ICLI)

OPMR .... Optimal Robotics Corp. [*NASDAQ symbol*] (SAG)
OPMS .... Miranshah [*Pakistan*] [*ICAO location identifier*] (ICLI)
OPMS .... Office of Physical Measurement Services [*Gaithersburg, MD*] [*National Institute of Standards and Technology*] (GRD)
OPMS .... Office of Program Management and Support [*Environmental Protection Agency*] (GFGA)
OPMS .... Officer Personnel Management System [*Army*]
OPMS .... Outplant Procurement Manufacturing Specification (SAA)
OPMSO .... Outside Production Material Sales Order
OPMT .... Multan [*Pakistan*] [*ICAO location identifier*] (ICLI)
OPMW .... Mianwali [*Pakistan*] [*ICAO location identifier*] (ICLI)
OPMX .... Optimax Industries, Inc. [*NASDAQ symbol*] (SAG)
OPMX .... Otimax Industries [*NASDAQ symbol*] (TTSB)
OPMXZ .... Optimax Inds Wrrt'BB' [*NQS*] (TTSB)
OPN .... Norwell District Secondary School, Palmerston, Ontario [*Library symbol National Library of Canada*] (NLC)
OPN .... Office of the Chief of Naval Operations
OPN .... Office Productivity Network [*Computer science*]
OPN .... Oil Pan
OPN .... Open (AAG)
OPN .... Operation
OPN .... Opercular Nerve
OPN .... Ophthalmic Nurse (DAVI)
OPN .... Opinion (ROG)
OPN .... Option (ADA)
OPN .... Ora pro Nobis [*Pray for Us*] [*Latin*]
OPN .... Other Procurement, Navy
OPNAV .... Chief of Naval Operations (AAGC)
OPNAV .... Office of the Chief of Naval Operations
OPNAVCOMMO... Office of the Chief of Naval Operations, Communications Office (DNAB)
OPNAVINST... Office of the Chief of Naval Operations Instruction
OPNAVO ...... Office of the Chief of Naval Operations
OPNAVSUPPACT... Office of the Chief of Naval Operations, Support Activity (DNAB)
OPNAVSUPPACTDET... Office of the Chief of Naval Operations, Support Activity Detachment (DNAB)
OPNAVSUPPACT FIG... Office of the Chief of Naval Operations, Support Activity Flight Information Group (DNAB)
OPNAVSUPPACT TCC... Office of the Chief of Naval Operations, Support Activity Telecommunications Center (DNAB)
OPNAVSUPPACT WWMCCS DP... Office of the Chief of Naval Operations, Support Activity, Worldwide Military Command Control System, Data Processing (DNAB)
OPNAVSUPPACT WWMCCS EMPSKED... Office of the Chief of Naval Operations, Support Activity, Worldwide Military Command Control System, Employment Schedule (DNAB)
OPNAVSUPPACT WWMCCS FORSTAT... Office of the Chief of Naval Operations, Support Activity, Worldwide Military Command Control System, Force Status (DNAB)
OPNAVSUPPACT WWMCCS MOVREP... Office of the Chief of Naval Operations, Support Activity, Worldwide Military Command Control System, Movement Reports (DNAB)
OPNAVTCC... Ofice of the Chief of Naval Operations, Telecommunications Center (DNAB)
OPND .... Operand (ECII)
Op ND Att'y Gen... Opinions of the Attorney General of North Dakota [*A publication*] (DLA)
OpnEnv .... Open Environment Corp. [*Associated Press*] (SAG)
OPNET .... Operator's Training New Equipment Training [*Army*] (INF)
Op Nev Att'y Gen... Official Opinions of the Attorney General of Nevada [*A publication*] (DLA)
OPNG .... Opening (AAG)
OPNH .... Nawabshah [*Pakistan*] [*ICAO location identifier*] (ICLI)
OpnhCa .... Oppenheimer Capital Ltd. [*Associated Press*] (SAG)
OPNJC .... Ora pro Nobis Jesu Christe [*Pray for Us, Jesus Christ*] [*Motto of Ernst, Duke of Bavaria (1554-1612)*] [*Latin*]
OPNK .... Naushki [*Pakistan*] [*ICAO location identifier*] (ICLI)
OPNL .... Operational
OPNML .... Operations Normal (FAAC)
OPNMR .... Optically Pumped Nuclear Magnetic Resonance [*Physics*]
OPNOTE .... Operational Note (MCD)
OPNS .... Operations (NASA)
OPNSEVAL & TNGSq... Operational Evaluation and Training Squadron [*Air Force*]
Op NY Atty Gen... Opinions of the Attorneys-General of New York [*A publication*] (DLA)
OPo .... Megis Local School District Public Library, Pomeroy, OH [*Library symbol Library of Congress*] (LCLS)
OPO .... Office of Personnel Operations [*Army*]
OPO .... Officer of the Post Office [*British*]
OPO .... Oil Pressure Out
OPO .... One-Person Operation [*Slang Business term*] (DCTA)
OPO .... One Price Only (WDAA)
OPO .... Oporto [*Portugal*] [*Airport symbol*] (OAG)
OPO .... Optical Parametric Oscillator [*Tunable LASER device*]
OPO .... Orbiter Project Office [*NASA*] (MCD)
OPO .... Orbiting Planetary Observatory
OPO .... Ordnance Personnel Office [*Army*]
OPO .... Organ Procurement Organization [*Generic term*] [*Medicine*]
OPO .... Organ Procurement Organizations (USGC)
OPO .... Other Programmed Operations (IAA)
OPO .... Outside Production Order (SAA)
OPO .... Outside Purchase Order (SAA)
OPO .... Overseas Press Club (NADA)
OPOC .... On-Board Pilot-Observer Camera (SAA)

OPOEB......... Port Elgin Branch, Bruce County Public Library, Ontario [*Library symbol National Library of Canada*] (NLC)

Op Off Legal Counsel... Opinions of the Office of Legal Counsel [*A publication*] (DLA)

Op Ohio Att'y Gen... Opinions of the Attorney General of Ohio [*A publication*] (DLA)

OPOK........... Okara [*Pakistan*] [*ICAO location identifier*] (ICLI)

Op Okla Att'y Gen... Opinions of the Attorney General of Oklahoma [*A publication*] (DLA)

OPOL.......... Offshore Pollution Liability Association Ltd. (EA)

OPOL.......... Optimization-Oriented Language

OPOMP........ Overall Planning and Optimization and Machining Process (MHDI)

OPON.......... Opinion (ROG)

OPOR........... Ormara [*Pakistan*] [*ICAO location identifier*] (ICLI)

Op Or Att'y Gen... Opinions of the Attorney General of Oregon [*A publication*] (DLA)

OPORC........ Port Carling Public Library, Ontario [*Library symbol National Library of Canada*] (BIB)

OPORD .... Operations Order [*Army*]

OPORPL........ Oppose Replenishment [*Navy*] (NVT)

OPOS.......... Optical Property of Orbiting Satellite [*NASA*] (PDAA)

OPOS.......... Outside Production Operation Sheet (MCD)

O-POS.......... Oxygen-Dope Polysilicon (PDAA)

OPOSENT...... Oppose Entry [*Navy*] (NVT)

OPosm......... Portsmouth Public Library, Portsmouth, OH [*Library symbol Library of Congress*] (LCLS)

OPosmG....... Goodyear Atomic Corp., Portsmouth, OH [*Library symbol Library of Congress*] (LCLS)

OPosmS....... Shawnee State College, Portsmouth, OH [*Library symbol Library of Congress*] (LCLS)

OPosmU ...... Ohio University, Portsmouth Branch Campus, Portsmouth, OH [*Library symbol Library of Congress Obsolete*] (LCLS)

OPOSORT .... Oppose Sortie [*Navy*] (NVT)

OPOSS......... Office of Personnel Operations Standards and Systems Office [*Army*]

OPOSSMS...... Options to Purchase or Sell Specific Mortgage-Backed Securities [*Merrill Lynch & Co.*] [*Finance*]

OPOSTOR .... Oppose Sortie [*Navy*] (ANA)

OPOV.......... Oxidizer Preburner Oxidizer Valve (MCD)

OPowS......... Scioto Village High School, Powell, OH [*Library symbol Library of Congress*] (LCLS)

OPP .... Occiput Posterior Position (DAVI)

OPP .... Octal Print Punch [*Computer science*]

OPP .... Office of Pesticide Programs [*Environmental Protection Agency*]

OPP .... Office of Plans and Policy (LAIN)

OPP .... Office of Polar Programs [*Later, Division of Polar Programs*] [*National Science Foundation*]

OPP .... Office of Policy and Planning [*Office of Policy, Evaluation, and Research*] [*Department of Labor*]

OPP .... Office of Productivity Programs [*Office of Personnel Management*] (GRD)

OPP .... Office of Program Planning (AAGC)

OPP .... Office of Public Programs [*National Archives*] (BARN)

OPP .... Office of Public Prosecutions [*Northern Territory, Australia*]

OPP .... Off-Load Preparation Party [*Navy*] (ANA)

OPP .... Oncovin [*Vincristine*], Procarbazine, Prednisone [*Antineoplastic drug regimen*]

OPP .... Ontario Provincial Police [*UTLAS symbol*]

OPP .... Open-Pore Polyurethan [*Plastic*]

OPP .... Operator Preparation Program (IAA)

OPP .... Opponent

OPP .... Opportunity (ADA)

OPP .... Opportunity

opp .... Opposed (DAVI)

OPP .... Opposed To

OPP .... Opposite (AAG)

opp .... Opposite (WDMC)

OPP .... Opposite

OPP .... Oppure [*Otherwise*] [*Music*]

OPP .... Organizational Project Plan [*Civil Defense*]

OPP .... Organization and Personnel Plan [*Army*]

OPP .... [*The*] Organization of Plastics Processors

OPP .... Oriented Polypropylene [*Plastics technology*]

OPP .... Ortho-Phenylphenol [*Disinfectant*]

OPP .... Other Physical Principles [*Defense system*]

OPP .... Outer Planet Project

OPP .... Out of Print at Present [*Publishing*]

OPP .... Out of Print at Present [*Publishing*] (WDMC)

opp .... Out of Print at Present [*Publishing*] (WDMC)

OPP .... Oxidative Pentose Phosphate (PDAA)

OPP .... Oxygen Partial Pressure

OPPA .... Octylpyrophosphoric Acid [*Organic chemistry*]

OPPA .... Office of Publications and Public Affairs [*National Endowment for the Humanities*] (BARN)

OPPA .... Operation Plan Package Appraisal (AFM)

Op PA Att'y Gen... Opinions of the Attorney General of Pennsylvania [*A publication*] (DLA)

OPPAR........ Orbiter Project Parts Authorization Request [*NASA*] (NASA)

OPPC .... Optima Petroleum Corp. [*NASDAQ symbol*] (SAG)

OPPC .... Outpatient Professional Psychiatric Clinic [*Health insurance*] (GHCT)

OPPC .... Parachinar [*Pakistan*] [*ICAO location identifier*] (ICLI)

OPPCE .... Opposite Commutator End (IEEE)

OPPCF .... Optima Petroleum [*NASDAQ symbol*] (TTSB)

OPPD .... Omaha Public Power District

OPPE .... Office of Plans and Program Evaluation (SAA)

OPPE .... Office of Policy, Planning, and Evaluation [*Environmental Protection Agency*] (GFGA)

OPPE .... Office of Program Planning and Evaluation [*National Institutes of Health*]

OPPE .... Operational Propulsion Plant Examination [*Navy*] (NVT)

OPPE .... Operations Planning Project Engineer [*Deep Space Instrumentation Facility, NASA*]

OPPG .... Oculopneumoplethysmography (DAVI)

OPPG .... Office of Propulsion and Power Generation (SAA)

OPPG .... Panjgur [*Pakistan*] [*ICAO location identifier*] (ICLI)

OPP HND.... Opposite Hand (MSA)

OPPI .... Office of Policy, Planning, and Information [*Environmental Protection Agency*] (GFGA)

OPPI .... Pasni [*Pakistan*] [*ICAO location identifier*] (ICLI)

Opp Int L .... Oppenheim's International Law [*A publication*] (DLA)

OPPL .... Orbiter Project Parts List [*NASA*] (NASA)

OPPLAN...... Operations Plan (KSC)

OPPM .... Office of Policy and Program Management [*Environmental Protection Agency*] (GFGA)

OppMS........ Oppenheimer Multi-Sector Income Trust [*Associated Press*] (SAG)

OPPN .... Pishin [*Pakistan*] [*ICAO location identifier*] (ICLI)

OPPOR........ Opportunity (AABC)

OPPORT...... Opportunity (ADA)

OPPOSIT...... Optimization of a Production Process by an Ordered Simulation and Iteration Technique (IEEE)

OPPP .... Office of Program Policy and Planning [*Social Security Administration*] (OICC)

OPPP .... Port Perry High School, Ontario [*Library symbol National Library of Canada*] (NLC)

OPPR .... Offset Printing Press

OPPR .... Operating Program

OPPS .... Office of Planning and Program Services [*Office of Field Operations*] [*Department of Labor*]

OPPS .... Overpressurization Protection Switch (IEEE)

OPPS .... Overpressurization Protection System (IEEE)

OPPS .... Oxygen Partial Pressure Sensor

OPPS .... Peshawar [*Pakistan*] [*ICAO location identifier*] (ICLI)

OPPSL .... Office of Private and Public Sector Liaison [*Environmental Protection Agency*] (GFGA)

OPPWFA...... Operative Plasteres amd Plaster Workers' Federation of Australia

OPPY .... Opportunity (ROG)

OPQ .... Occupational Personality Questionnaires [*Employment test*]

OPQ .... Occupying Public Quarters [*Military*]

OPQS .... Qasim [*Pakistan*] [*ICAO location identifier*] (ICLI)

OPQT .... Quetta/Samungli [*Pakistan*] [*ICAO location identifier*] (ICLI)

OPR .... Lifts Operating [*Skiing*]

OPR .... Office of Planning and Research [*International Trade Administration*] (GRD)

OPR .... Office of Pre-Claims Requirements [*Social Security Administration*]

OPR .... Office of Primary Responsibility [*Air Force*]

OPR .... Office of Private Resources [*Department of State*]

OPR .... Office of Professional Responsibility [*Department of Justice*]

OPR .... Office of Public Relations [*Later, PUBINFO*] [*Navy*]

OPR .... Offsite Procurement Request (IEEE)

OPR .... Off-Site Procurement Request (NRCH)

OPR .... Old Prussian [*Language, etc.*]

OPR .... Ontario Practice Reports [*A publication*] (DLA)

OPR .... Opener (MSA)

OPR .... Open Pool Reactor [*Nuclear energy*] (NRCH)

OPR .... Operand [*Computer science*]

OPR .... Operate [*or Operator*] (AAG)

OPR .... Operational Preference (DA)

OPR .... Operational Project Requirements (AABC)

OPR .... Operations Planning Review (NASA)

OPR .... Operations Procedure (MUGU)

OPR .... Operator

OPR .... Operator

OPR .... OP Resources Ltd. [*Vancouver Stock Exchange symbol*]

OPR .... Optical Page Reader [*Computer science*]

OPR .... Optical Pattern Recognition

OPR .... Optimized Palette Reduction [*Algorithm*] [*Computer Presentations, Inc.*] (PCM)

OPR .... Optional Parts Request (SAA)

OPR .... Orbit/Payload Recorder [*NASA*] (MCD)

OPR .... Order Point Recognition (ADA)

OPR .... Outpatient Rate [*Medicine*] (AFM)

OPR .... Outstanding Performance Rating [*Military*] (RDA)

OPR .... Overall Pressure Ratio

OPR .... Oxygen Pressure Regulator (MCD)

OPR .... Oxygen Production Rate [*Biochemistry*]

OPR .... Port Rowan Public Library, Ontario [*Library symbol National Library of Canada*] (NLC)

OPR .... Santander Overseas Bank [*NYSE symbol*] (SPSG)

OPRA .... Observation Post Royal Artillery [*British military*] (DMA)

OPRA .... Office Products Reps Association (EA)

OPRA .... Ohio Penal Racing Association (EA)

OPRA .... Options Price Reporting Authority [*Information service or system*] (IID)

OPRAD........ Operations Research and Development Management (PDAA)

OPraem .... Canons Regular of Premontre (TOCD)

opraem........ Canons Regular of Premontre, Premonstratensians, Norbetines (TOCD)

OPraem .... Ordo Canonicorum Regularium Praemonstatenstium [*Order of the Canons Regular of Premontre*] [*Norbetines*] [*Roman Catholic men's religious order*]

OPRAF........ Office of Passenger Rail Franchising [*British*] (ECON)

OPRD .... Office of Production Research and Development

OPRD.......... Organic Process Research & Development [*A publication*]
OPRDY....... Operationally Ready [*Army*] (AABC)
OPRE.......... Prescott Public Library, Ontario [*Library symbol National Library of Canada*] (NLC)
OPRED........ Operations Reduction [*Government term*]
OPREDS...... Operational Performance Recording and Evaluation Data System [*Military*] (CAAL)
OPREG........ Operation Register (IAA)
OPrem........ Ordre de Premontre [*Order of the Canons Regular of Premontre*] [*Rome, Italy*] (EAIO)
OPREP........ Operational Reporting [*Army*]
OPREPS....... Operational Reporting System [*Military*]
OPREQ........ Operation Request [*Computer science*] (MHDI)
OPREX........ Operational Exercise [*NATO*] (NATG)
OPRFLT....... Operator Fault (AAG)
OPRG.......... Oxygenated Fuels Program Reformulated Gasoline
OPRI........... Office de la Propriete Industrielle [*Department of Industrial Property*] [*Ministry of Economic Affairs*] (IID)
OPRI........... Office de Protection contre les Rayonnements Ionisants [*France*]
OPRIC......... Operator in Charge (IAA)
OPRIS......... Ohio Project for Research in Information Service (NITA)
OPRK......... Rahimyarkhan [*Pakistan*] [*ICAO location identifier*] (ICLI)
OPRL.......... Ovine Prolactin [*Endocrinology*]
OPRL.......... Portland Branch, Rideau Lakes Union Library, Ontario [*Library symbol National Library of Canada*] (BIB)
OPRLFT ...... Operator Fault [*Computer science*] (MHDI)
OPRN......... Islamabad/Chaklala [*Pakistan*] [*ICAO location identifier*] (ICLI)
OPRN......... Operation
OPRNL........ Operational (AAG)
OPRNTL..... Operational
OpRobt....... Optimal Robotics Corp. [*Associated Press*] (SAG)
OPROM....... Optical Programmable Read-Only Memory [*Disk*] (BYTE)
OProv......... Old Provencal [*Language*] (BARN)
OPRPrC...... Santander Overseas Bk'C'Pfd [*NYSE symbol*] (TTSB)
OPRPrD...... Santander Overseas Bk 'D'Pfd [*NYSE symbol*] (TTSB)
OPRQ......... Shorekote/Rafiqui [*Pakistan*] [*ICAO location identifier*] (ICLI)
OPRR.......... Office for Protection from Research Risks [*Bethesda, MD*] [*National Institutes of Health*] (GRD)
OPRR.......... Outside Production Requirement Record (SAA)
OPRRB........ Officer Personnel Record Review Board [*Air Force*] (AFM)
OPRRE........ Office of Public Roads and Rural Engineering [*Later, Bureau of Public Roads*]
OPRS.......... Office of Professional Research Services [*American Occupational Therapy Association*]
OPRS.......... Oil Pressure
OPRS.......... Operational Planning and Review Systems [*Employment and Training Administration*] [*Department of Labor*]
OPRS.......... Risalpur [*Pakistan*] [*ICAO location identifier*] (ICLI)
OPRT.......... Operator Table
OPRT.......... Rawalakot [*Pakistan*] [*ICAO location identifier*] (ICLI)
OPRTNTY..... Opportunity
OPRU......... Oil Pollution Research Unit [*British*] (ARC)
OPruss........ Old Prussian [*Language*] (BARN)
OPRV......... Oxygen Pressure Relief Valve (MCD)
OPS .... Oblique Photo Sketcher
OPS .... Obscene Publications Squad [*British*] (DI)
OPS .... Obstacle Planner Software (RDA)
OPS .... Occupational Preparation Scheme (AIE)
OPS .... Ocean Platform Station [*National Data Buoy Office*] (NOAA)
OPS .... Office of Pipeline Safety [*Department of Transportation*]
OPS .... Office of Population Surveys [*British*]
OPS .... Office of Price Stabilization [*Terminated, 1953*]
OPS .... Office of Products Safety [*FDA*]
OPS .... Office of Product Standards [*Department of Commerce*] (WDAA)
OPS .... Office of Programmatic Systems [*Social Security Administration*]
OPS .... Office of Program Services [*US Employment Service*] [*Department of Labor*]
OPS .... Office of Publishing Services (AAGC)
OPS .... Official Phone Station [*Amateur radio*]
OPS .... Official Production System [*Production-system language*]
OPS .... Official Public Service Reports [*New York*] [*A publication*] (DLA)
OPS .... Off-Premise Station [*Telecommunications*] (TEL)
OPS .... Offshore Power Systems (NRCH)
OPS .... Oil Pressure Switch
OPS .... Oil Production Stock
OPS .... Omnidirectional Point Source (PDAA)
OPS .... On-Line Process Synthesis [*Computer science*]
OPS .... On-Site Inspection Agency [*DoD ICAO designator*] (FAAC)
OPS .... Open Pan Sulphitation [*Sugar production*]
OPS .... Open Profiling Standard [*Firefly Network*] [*Computer science*]
OPS .... Open Profiling Standard [*Computer science*]
OPS .... Operational Paging System [*NASA*] (KSC)
OPSIM........ Operational Performance Standard [*Aviation*] (DA)
OPS .... Operational Power Supply
OPS .... Operational Protection System [*Nuclear energy*] (NRCH)
OPS .... Operational Station (SAA)
OPS .... Operational Support (MCD)
OPS .... Operation and Support (MCD)
OPS .... Operations (MCD)
OPS .... Operations Division [*NATO*] (NATG)
OPS .... Operations per Second (IAA)
OPS .... Operations Sequence [*NASA*] (MCD)
OPS .... Operations Squadron
OPS .... Operations Staff [*Military British*]
OPS .... Operator's Subsystem [*Telecommunications*] (TEL)

OPS .... Operator System Program [*Manufacturing engineering*] [*Computer science*]
OPS .... Ophthalmic Photographers' Society (EA)
Ops .... Opinions [*Legal term*] (DLA)
OPS .... Opposite Prompters' Side [*i.e., the left side*] [*Stage direction*] (ROG)
OPS .... Opposite Surface [*Technical drawings*]
OPS .... OPSEC [*Operations Security*] Professional Society (EA)
OPS .... Optical Power Spectrum (PDAA)
OPS .... Optical Processing System
OPS .... Oracle Parallel Server [*Computer science*]
OPS .... Orbiter Project Schedules [*NASA*] (NASA)
OPS .... Orbiting Primate Spacecraft (MCD)
OPS .... Organisation Panamericaine de la Sante [*Pan American Health Organization*] (MSC)
OPS .... Oriented Polystyrene [*Plastics technology*]
OPS .... Ortho-Phosphoserine [*Biochemistry*]
OPS .... Other Personal Services
ops............ Out of Print and Searching [*Publishing*] (WDMC)
OPS .... Out of Print, Searching [*Publishing*]
OPS .... Out of Production Spares (MCD)
OPS .... Outpatient Section (DAVI)
OPS .... Outpatient Service [*Medicine*]
OPS .... Outpatient Surgery [*Health insurance*] (GHCT)
OPS .... Outside Production Service (SAA)
OPS .... Overhead Positioning System [*AEC*]
OPS .... Overpressure [*or Overpressurization*] Protection System [*Nuclear energy*] (NRCH)
OPS .... Oxidized Porous Silicon [*Materials science*]
OPS .... Oxidizer Particle Size
OPS .... Oxygen Purge System [*or Subsystem*] [*NASA*]
OPS .... Parry Sound Public Library, Ontario [*Library symbol National Library of Canada*] (NLC)
OPS .... Phillips Petroleum Co., Research and Development Department, Bartlesville, OK [*OCLC symbol*] (OCLC)
OpS............ Specialist in Optical Science (GAGS)
OPSA .... Algonquin Regional Library, Parry Sound, Ontario [*Library symbol Obsolete National Library of Canada*] (NLC)
OPSA .... Optimal Pneumatic Systems Analysis (PDAA)
Ops AAG POD... United States Post Office Department. Official Opinions of the Solicitor [*A publication*] (DLA)
Ops AG .... Opinions of the Attorney General [*A publication*] (DLA)
OPSAM .... Optical Storage Access Method [*Computer science*] (PDAA)
OP(S)ARMYJAG... Opinion(s) of the Army Judge Advocate General
OPSAS .... Office of Program Support and Advanced Systems (SAA)
OPSATCOM.... Optical Satellite Communications (MCD)
Ops Atty Gen... Opinions of the Attorney General [*A publication*] (DLA)
Ops Atty Gen Wisc... Wisconsin Attorney General Reports [*A publication*] (DLA)
OPSB .... Orbiter Processing Support Building [*NASA*] (NASA)
OPSB .... Orbiter Processing Support Building
OPSB .... Sibi [*Pakistan*] [*ICAO location identifier*] (ICLI)
OPSC .... Office of Planning Standards and Coordination [*HUD*]
OPSC .... Office of the Public Service Commissioner [*Australia*]
OPSC .... Optical Security Group [*NASDAQ symbol*] (TTSB)
OPSC .... Optical Security Group, Inc. [*NASDAQ symbol*] (SAG)
OPSCAN...... Optical Scanning [*Computer science*] (WDAA)
OPSCOMM.... Operations Communications (MCD)
OPSCON...... Operations Control [*NASA*] (KSC)
OPSCOP...... Operations Control [*Monitor*] Program
OPSCT........ Christie Township Public Library, Parry Sound, Ontario [*Library symbol National Library of Canada*] (NLC)
OPSD .... Office of Placement Support and Development [*US Employment Service*] [*Department of Labor*]
OPSD .... Openside
OPSD .... Skardu [*Pakistan*] [*ICAO location identifier*] (ICLI)
OPSDEP .... Operations Deputy [*In JCS system*] [*Military*]
OPSEC .... Operational Security
OPSEC .... Operations per Second (IAA)
OPSEC .... Operations Security Program (AAGC)
OPSEC .... OPSEC Professionals Society [*Later, OPS*] (EA)
OPSET .... Optimal Set [*of Parameters*] [*Hydrology*]
OPSF .... Karachi/Shara-E-Faisal [*Pakistan*] [*ICAO location identifier*] (ICLI)
OP SF .... Office of Preparedness, General Services Administration [*later, Federal Preparedness Agency*], Special Facility
OPSF .... Orbital Propellant Storage Facility (MCD)
OPSG .... Operation Plans Steering Group (DOMA)
OPSHT........ Humphrey Township Public Library, Parry Sound, Ontario [*Library symbol National Library of Canada*] (NLC)
OPSI .... Optical Sensors [*NASDAQ symbol*] (TTSB)
OPSI .... Optical Sensors, Inc. [*NASDAQ symbol*] (SAG)
OPSI .... Ordnance Publications for Supply Index [*Military*]
OPSI .... Overwhelming Post-Splenectomy Infection [*Medicine*]
OPSIM........ Operational Simulator [*Coast Guard*]
OPSIMS...... Operational Simulation Subsystem (MCD)
Ops JAG ...... Opinions of the Judge Advocate General, United States Army [*A publication*] (DLA)
OPSK .... Sukkur [*Pakistan*] [*ICAO location identifier*] (ICLI)
OPSKS .... Optimum Phase Shift Keyed Signals [*Telecommunications*]
OPSM .... Office of Public Sector Management [*Australian Capital Territory*]
OPSMB .... Organization of Progressive Socialists of the Mediterranean Basin
OPSO .... Office of Pipeline Safety Operations [*Department of Transportation*] (DLA)
OPS O.......... Operations Officer [*Navy*] (DOMA)
Op Sol Dept... Opinions of the Solicitor for the Department of Labor [*United States*] [*A publication*] (DLA)

Op Sol Dept Labor... Opinions of the Solicitor for the Department of Labor Dealing with Workmen's Compensation [*A publication*] (DLA)
Op Solic PO Dep't.. Official Opinions of the Solicitor for the Post Office Department [*A publication*] (DLA)
Op Sol POD... Opinions of the Solicitor for the Post Office Department [*United States*] [*A publication*] (DLA)
OPSP .... Office of Product Standards Policy [*Gaithersburg, MD*] [*Department of Commerce*] (GRD)
OPSP .... Operations Panel [*ICAO*] (DA)
OPSP .... Shekhupura [*Pakistan*] [*ICAO location identifier*] (ICLI)
OPSR .... Office of Pipeline Safety Regulation [*Department of Transportation*] (OICC)
OPSR .... Office of Professional Standards Review [*Medicare and Medicaid*] [*HEW*]
OPSR .... Operations Supervisor [*NASA*] (MCD)
OPSR .... Sargodha [*Pakistan*] [*ICAO location identifier*] (ICLI)
OPSRDY ...... Operations Readiness (MCD)
OPSREP....... Operations Report [*NATO*] (NATG)
OPSRO......... Office of Professional Standards Review [*Medicare and Medicaid*] Organization [*HEW*]
OPSS .... Orbital Propellant Storage Subsystem (MCD)
OPSS .... Saidu Sharif [*Pakistan*] [*ICAO location identifier*] (ICLI)
OP(ST)......... Operation Overlord Preparations, Service Leave and Travel [*World War II*]
OPST .... Out-of-Pile Systems Test [*Nuclear energy*] (NRCH)
OPSTACOM.. Optical Satellite Communications
OPSTAT .... Operational Status [*Navy*] (NVT)
OPSTATUSREP... Operations Status Report (NATG)
OPSTR......... Operating Strength [*Army*] (AABC)
OPSU.......... Sui [*Pakistan*] [*ICAO location identifier*] (ICLI)
OPSUB......... Operational SUBPAY (DNAB)
OPSUM........ Operational Summary [*Navy*] (NVT)
OPSUPPFAC... Operational Support Facility (MCD)
OPSW.......... Sahiwal [*Pakistan*] [*ICAO location identifier*] (ICLI)
OPSWL .... Old Program Status Word Location
OPS-X.......... Operational Teletype Message
OPSYS......... Operating System [*Computer science*]
OPT.............. International Finance Corp. [*NYSE symbol*] (SAG)
OPT.............. Office of the Public Trustee [*Australian Capital Territory*]
OPT.............. Oil Point [*Alaska*] [*Seismograph station code, US Geological Survey*] (SEIS)
OPT.............. Oil Pressure Transmitter
OPT.............. Operability Testing [*Military*] (CAAL)
OPT.............. Operate (WGA)
OPT.............. Operational Pressure Transducer (MCD)
OPT.............. Operation Prime Time [*Television*]
OPT.............. Operations and Telling (SAA)
OPT.............. Operations Planning Team [*Air Force*] (DOMA)
OPT.............. Opportunities for Professional Transition [*An association*] (EA)
OPT.............. Optative [*Grammar*]
OPT.............. Optic (IAA)
OPT.............. Optical (AAG)
OPT.............. Optical Point Transfer
OPT.............. Optician
OPT.............. Optics
OPT.............. Optics
OPT.............. Optimization Study [*Nuclear energy*] (NRCH)
OPT.............. Optimized Production Technology
OPT.............. Optimum (AAG)
OPT.............. Optimum
OPT.............. Optimus [*Best*] [*Latin*]
OPT.............. Option [*Shares*]
OPT.............. Option
OPT.............. Optional (AAG)
opt.............. Optional (IDOE)
OPT.............. Other People's Tobacco [*Slang*]
OPT.............. Outpatient [*Medicine*] (AAMN)
OPT.............. Outpatient Physical Therapy [*Health insurance*] (GHCT)
OPT.............. Outpatient Therapy (DAVI)
OPT.............. Outpatient Treatment [*Medicine*]
OPT.............. Output Transformer (IAA)
OPT.............. Overhead Projection Transparency (MCD)
OPT.............. Pakenham Township Public Library, Ontario [*Library symbol National Library of Canada*] (BIB)
OPT.............. Payne Theological Seminary, Wilberforce, OH [*OCLC symbol*] (OCLC)
Opta............ Opta Food Ingredients, Inc. [*Associated Press*] (SAG)
OPTA .... Optimal Performance Theoretically Attainable (IEEE)
OPTA .... Organ and Piano Teachers Association [*Defunct*] (EA)
OPTA .... Terbela [*Pakistan*] [*ICAO location identifier*] (ICLI)
OPTACON.... Optical-to-Tactile Converter [*Electronic reader for the blind*]
OPTADS....... Operations Tactical Data Systems [*Army*] (RDA)
OPTAG........ Optical Aimpoint Guidance System [*Weaponry*]
OPTAG........ Optical Pickoff Two-Axis Gyroscope (SAA)
OPTAN........ Operations Target Analysis [*of strike missions in North Vietnam*]
OPTAR........ Operating Target
OPTAR........ Optical Automatic Ranging
OPTARE....... Office of Planning, Technical Assistance, Research, and Evaluation [*Washington, DC Department of Commerce*] (GRD)
OPTASK....... Operational Tasking (DOMA)
OPTB .... Operational Program Time Base [*NASA*] (MCD)
OPTC .... Optelecom, Inc. [*NASDAQ symbol*] (NQ)
OptCble........ Optical Cable Corp. [*Associated Press*] (SAG)
OptclData .... Optical Data Systems [*Associated Press*] (SAG)
OptclDt .... Optical Data Systems, Inc. [*Associated Press*] (SAG)

Opt Clm ...... Optional Claiming Race (WGA)
OPTCN......... Optician
Opt County Gov't... Optional County Government [*A publication*] (DLA)
Opt D .... Doctor of Optometry
OPT'D .... Optioned [*Automotive advertising*]
OPTE............ Operational Proficiency Training Equipment [*Roland International Corp.*] (MCD)
OPTEC......... Operational Test and Evaluation Command [*Army*] (RDA)
OPTEC .... Optical Properties Technical Evaluation Center
OPTEMPO.... Tempo of Operations (MCD)
Op Tenn Att'y Gen... Opinions of the Attorney General of Tennessee [*A publication*] (DLA)
OPTEV .... Operational Test and Evaluation [*Military*]
OPTEVFOR... Operational Test and Evaluation Force [*Norfolk, VA*] [*Navy*]
OPTEVFORDET.. Operational Test and Evaluation Force Detachment (DNAB)
OptEx .... Optional Exchange [*Dietetics*]
Op Tex Att'y Gen... Opinions of the Attorney General of Texas [*A publication*] (DLA)
OPTH .... Ophthalmic (ROG)
OPTH .... Talhar [*Pakistan*] [*ICAO location identifier*] (ICLI)
OPTI............ Office of Productivity, Technology, and Innovation [*Department of Commerce*]
OPTI............ OPTI, Inc. [*NASDAQ symbol*] (SAG)
OPTIC.......... Ophthalmological Products Trade and Industry Conference [*British*] (DBA)
OPTIC.......... Optical
OPTIC.......... Optical Procedural Task Instruction Compiler
OPTIC.......... Oryx Pecos Test Inquiry and Control System (NITA)
Opticam....... Optics Automation and Management (RDA)
OpticC......... Optical Coating Laboratory, Inc. [*Associated Press*] (SAG)
OPTIM......... Occupational Projections and Training Information for Michigan [*Information service or system*] (IID)
OPTIM......... Order Point Technique for Inventory Management (BUR)
Optima......... Optima Petroleum Corp. [*Associated Press*] (SAG)
OPTIMA....... Organization for the Phyto-Taxonomic Investigation of the Mediterranean Area [*Berlin, Federal Republic of Germany*] (EAIO)
OptImag....... Optika Imaging Systems, Inc. [*Associated Press*] (SAG)
Optimax....... Optimax Industries, Inc. [*Associated Press*] (SAG)
OPTIMUM ... Obtain Increased Productivity through Improved Modernization of Facilities and Updating Maintenance Tools, Equipment, and Methods [*Military*]
OPTIMUS..... Office of Public Trustee Information Management User System [*Canada*]
OPTINT .... Optical Intelligence (MCD)
OPTIS .... Oxfordshire Project for the Training of Instructors and Supervisors [*British*] (AIE)
OptiSG .... Optical Security Group, Inc. [*Associated Press*] (SAG)
OPTK .... Optika Imaging Systems, Inc. [*NASDAQ symbol*] (SAG)
OPTL........... Optional (MSA)
OPTLC .... Overpressurized Thin-Layer Chromatography
OptIcm .... Optelecom, Inc. [*Associated Press*] (SAG)
OPTM.......... Optometry
OPTMTRC.... Optometric
Optmx......... Optimax Industries, Inc. [*Associated Press*] (SAG)
OPTN .... [*The*] National Organ Procurement and Transplantation Network [*Information service or system*] (IID)
OPTN .... Option [*Legal shorthand*] (LWAP)
OPTN .... OPTION CARE [*NASDAQ symbol*] (TTSB)
OPTN .... Option Care, Inc. [*NASDAQ symbol*] (SAG)
OptnCr .... Option Care, Inc. [*Associated Press*] (SAG)
OPTNET ...... Optimum Private Trunk Network Embodying Tandems (PDAA)
OPT-NSC..... Outpatient Treatment/Nonservice-Connected [*Veterans Administration*] (DAVI)
OPTOL .... Optimized Test-Oriented Language [*Computer science*] (PDAA)
OPTOM .... Optometrist
Optom.......... Optometry
OPTOMA...... Ocean Prediction through Observation, Modeling, and Analysis [*Experimental program*]
OPT/OSP...... Outpatient Physical Therapy/Outpatient Speech Pathology Services [*Department of Health and Human Services*] (GFGA)
OPTQ .... Ocean Optique Distributors, Inc. [*NASDAQ symbol*] (SAG)
OPTQ .... Ocean Optique Dstr [*NASDAQ symbol*] (TTSB)
OPTRA......... Operational Training (DNAB)
OPTRAK...... Optical Tracking and Ranging Kit (PDAA)
OPTRAN...... Operational Transit (GAAI)
OPTRARON... Operational Training Squadron (DNAB)
OPTS .... Office of Pesticides and Toxic Substances [*Environmental Protection Agency*]
OPTS .... Office of Program and Technical Services [*Employment and Training Administration*] [*Department of Labor*]
OPTS .... Online Peripheral Test System
OPTS .... Online Program Testing System [*Computer science*] (IAA)
OPTS .... Opta Food Ingredients [*NASDAQ symbol*] (TTSB)
OPTS .... Opta Food Ingredients, Inc. [*NASDAQ symbol*] (SAG)
OPT-SC........ Outpatient Treatment/Service Connected [*Veterans Administration*] (DAVI)
OptSens....... Optical Sensors, Inc. [*Associated Press*] (SAG)
OPTT........... Optek Technology [*NASDAQ symbol*] (TTSB)
OPTT........... Taftan [*Pakistan*] [*ICAO location identifier*] (ICLI)
OPTU .... Turbat [*Pakistan*] [*ICAO location identifier*] (ICLI)
OPTUL .... Optical Pulse Transmitter Using LASER
OPTV .... Operative
OPTX .... Optex Biomedical [*NASDAQ symbol*] (TTSB)
OPTYP .... Opalotype (VRA)

OPTZU .... Optical-Pan-Tilt-Zoom Unit (SAA)
OPU .... Balimo [*Papua New Guinea*] [*Airport symbol*] (OAG)
OPU .... Operational Performance Unit (ADA)
OPU .... Operations Priority Unit
OPU .... Overseas Plexiglas Unit
OPU .... Pacific University, Forest Grove, OR [*OCLC symbol*] (OCLC)
OPU .... Unemployed Peoples Union (NADA)
OPUR .... Object Program Utility Routine
OPUS .... Octal Program Updating System [*Computer science*]
OPUS .... Offshore Persistent Upwelling Structure
OPUS .... Optical Prism Uniformity System
OPUS .... Organisation of Professional Users of Statistics
OPUSC .... Opuscula [*Minor Works*] [*Latin*] (ROG)
OPV .... Bedarfsflugunternehmen Dr. L. Polsterer [*Austria ICAO designator*] (FAAC)
OPV .... Offshore Patrol Vessel (DOMA)
OPV .... Ohms per Volt
OPV .... Optical Path-Length Variation (PDAA)
OPV .... Oral Polio Vaccine [*Also, Sabin vaccine*] (PAZ)
OPV .... Oral Poliovirus [*Infectious diseases*] (DAVI)
OPV .... Oral Polio Virus Vaccine
Op VA Att'y Gen... Opinions of the Attorney General and Report to the Governor of Virginia [*A publication*] (DLA)
OPVN .... OpenVision Technologies, Inc. [*NASDAQ symbol*] (SAG)
OPVN .... Open Vision Technology [*NASDAQ symbol*] (TTSB)
OPW .... Objective Personal Weapon
OPW .... Oboz Polski Walczacej [*A publication*] (BJA)
OPW .... Office of Public Works (WDAA)
OPW .... Opawica Explorations, Inc. [*Toronto Stock Exchange symbol*]
OPW .... Open Pilot Warranty [*Insurance*] (AIA)
OPW .... Operating Weight [*Air Force*]
OPW .... Optical Window
OPW .... Opuwa [*Namibia*] [*Airport symbol*] (OAG)
OPW .... Orthogonalized Plane Wave
OPW .... Porter Public Library, Westlake, OH [*OCLC symbol*] (OCLC)
OPW .... Whitney Public Library, Porcupine, Ontario [*Library symbol National Library of Canada*] (NLC)
Op Wash Att'y Gen... Office of the Attorney General (State of Washington) Opinions [*A publication*] (DLA)
Op Wis Att'y Gen... Opinions of the Attorney General of Wisconsin [*A publication*] (DLA)
OpWldBd ..... Oppenheimer World Bond Fund [*Associated Press*] (SAG)
OPWN .... Wana [*Pakistan*] [*ICAO location identifier*] (ICLI)
OPWS .... Orbiter Payload Work Station (MCD)
Op Wyo Att'y Gen... Opinions of the Attorney General of Wyoming [*A publication*] (DLA)
OPX .... Off-Premise Extension [*Nuclear energy*] (NRCH)
OPX .... Orthopyroxene [*A silicate mineral*]
OPY .... Salomon, Inc. [*AMEX symbol*] (SAG)
OPZ .... Opsonized Zymosan [*Biochemistry*]
OPZB .... Zhob [*Pakistan*] [*ICAO location identifier*] (ICLI)
OQ .... Officers' Quarters [*Military*]
OQ .... Oil Quench (IAA)
OQ .... Operational Qualification (ACII)
OQ .... Optical Quality
OQ .... Order Quantity (DNAB)
OQ .... Ordre du Quebec [*Order of Quebec*] [*Canada*] (DD)
OQ .... Royale Airlines [*ICAO designator*] (AD)
OQA .... Operations Quality Assurance [*Nuclear energy*] (NRCH)
OQA .... Optical Quantum Amplifier (PDAA)
OQA .... Reidsville, NC [*Location identifier FAA*] (FAAL)
OQAP .... Oil Quality Assessment Program [*Society of Automotive Engineers, Inc.*]
O-QAR .... Optical Quick Access Recorder (GAVI)
OQC .... Office of Quality Control [*Social and Rehabilitation Service, HEW*]
OQC .... Operator Quality Control [*RADAR*]
OQC .... Outside Quality Control (KSC)
OQD .... Optical Quantum Detector
OQE .... Objective Quality Evidence (MCD)
OQG .... Optical Quantum Generator
OQI .... Oil Quantity Indicator
OQL .... Observed Quality Level
OQL .... Online Query Language
OQL .... Outgoing Quality Level
OQL .... Outgoing Quality Limit
OQM .... Office of the Quartermaster [*Military*]
OQMG .... Office of the Quartermaster General [*Military*]
OQP .... Optimum Qualification Procedure
O-QPSK ...... Offset QPSK (NITA)
OQQ .... Officer Qualification Questionnaire [*Navy*] (DOMA)
OQR .... Officer's Qualification Record [*Army*]
OQSMAT ...... Otis Quick Scoring Mental Abilities Tests [*Psychology*] (DAVI)
OQT .... Officer Qualification Test
OQTD .... Operational Qualifications Test Deficiency [*Air Force*]
OQU .... North Kingstown, RI [*Location identifier FAA*] (FAAL)
OQW .... Maquoketa, IA [*Location identifier FAA*] (FAAL)
OQZ .... Union City, TN [*Location identifier FAA*] (FAAL)
OR .... Air Comores [*ICAO designator*] (AD)
Or .... Indian Law Reports, Orissa Series [*A publication*] (DLA)
OR .... Oak Ridge Complex [*Department of Energy*] [*Oak Ridge National Laboratory*] (GAAI)
OR .... Oak Ridge Operations Office (DOGT)
OR .... Objective Reliability (MCD)
OR .... Observed Ratio (MCD)
OR .... Octane Rating [*Automotive engineering*]

OR .... Octane Requirement [*Mechanical engineering*]
OR .... Odds Ratio [*Statistics*]
O/R .... Office of Record (AFM)
OR .... Officer Records [*Military*] (AFM)
OR .... Official Receiver
OR .... Official Records
OR .... Official Referee
OR .... Official Reports, South Africa [*A publication*] (DLA)
OR .... Off-Radial (RDA)
OR .... Oil Rehabilitation Committee [*British*]
OR .... Oil Retention [*Enema*] [*Medicine*]
OR .... Oil Ring (MSA)
OR .... Old Roman (ADA)
OR .... Oleoresin [*Also, Ol Res*] [*Pharmacy*]
OR .... Olfactory Receptor [*Biochemistry*]
OR .... Oligomer Restriction [*Genetics*]
OR .... Omnidirectional Radio Range (MCD)
O/R .... On Request
OR .... On Return
OR .... Ontario Reports [*A publication*] (DLA)
OR .... Open Reduction [*Orthopedics*] (DAVI)
OR .... Open Registry [*Flag of convenience*] [*Shipping*] (DS)
OR .... Operating Reactor [*Nuclear energy*] (NRCH)
OR .... Operating Resources (AFM)
OR .... Operating Room [*Medicine*]
OR .... Operational Equipment Requirement (IAA)
OR .... Operationally Ready (MCD)
OR .... Operational Readiness [*Army*]
OR .... Operational Reliability [*Army*] (AABC)
OR .... Operational Report (AAG)
OR .... Operational Requirement
OR .... Operational Research
OR .... Operational Right
OR .... Operation Reach-Out [*Department of Labor*]
OR .... Operation Record
OR .... Operation Rescue (EA)
OR .... Operations Request [*Military*]
OR .... Operations Requirements
OR .... Operations Research [*Computer science*]
OR .... Operations Review [*NASA*] (MCD)
OR .... Operations Room
OR .... Operator (IAA)
OR .... Operculum Ridge
OR .... Ophthalmic Rete [*Bird anatomy*]
OR .... Opponents' Runs [*Baseball*]
OR .... Optical Reader [*Computer science*] (BUR)
O+R .... Optiram, St. Helier, Jersey, Channel Islands, United Kingdom [*Library symbol*] [*Library of Congress*] (LCLS)
OR .... Orange
Or .... Oratio [*A publication*] (OCD)
Or .... Orationes [*of Julian*] [*Classical studies*] (OCD)
Or .... Orationes [*of Dio Chrysostomus*] [*Classical studies*] (OCD)
OR .... Oratorians
OR .... Ordered Recorded
OR .... Ordering Register (IAA)
OR .... Orderly Room
OR .... Order of the Road [*British*] (DBA)
OR .... Order Pennant [*Navy British*]
OR .... Order [*or Ordering*] Register (SAA)
OR .... Ordnance Report
OR .... Ordnance Requirement
OR .... Oregon [*Postal code*]
Or .... Oregon State Library, Salem, OR [*Library symbol Library of Congress*] (LCLS)
Or .... Oregon Supreme Court Reports [*A publication*] (DLA)
Or .... Orestes [*of Euripides*] [*Classical studies*] (OCD)
OR .... Organized Reserves [*Military*]
OR .... Organ Recovery (EA)
OR .... Orient
OR .... Oriental (ROG)
OR .... Orienting Response [*Psychology*]
Or .... Origen [*Deceased circa 254*] [*Authority cited in pre-1607 legal work*] (DSA)
OR .... Original (ADA)
O/R .... Originator or Recipient [*Telecommunications*] (OSI)
OR .... O-Ring [*Automotive engineering*]
'Or .... 'Orlah (BJA)
OR .... Orosomucoid [*Biochemistry*]
or .... Orthoclase [*CIPW classification*] [*Geology*]
OR .... Orthopedic
OR .... Orthopedic Research [*Medicine*]
OR .... Oswestry Rangers [*British military*] (DMA)
OR .... Other (ROG)
OR .... Other Ranks [*Ranks other than officers*] [*Military*]
OR .... Outer Roll [*Aviation*] (MCD)
OR .... Out of Range
OR .... Output Register (MSA)
OR .... Outside Radius [*Technical drawings*]
OR .... Outside Right [*Soccer position*]
OR .... Overall Report
OR .... Overall Resistance (IAA)
OR .... Overhaul and Repair
OR .... Overload Relay (KSC)
O/R .... Overrange [*System or element*] (IEEE)
O/R .... Override (KSC)

OR .... Over Run (MHDW)
OR .... Overseas Replacement [Military]
OR .... Owasco River [AAR code]
OR .... Owner's Risk [Shipping]
OR .... Own Recognizance [Legal term]
O-R .... Oxidation-Reduction
OR .... Oxygen Enchancement Ratio (IAA)
OR .... Oxygen Relief (NASA)
O/R .... Oxygen Relief
OR .... Renfrew Public Library, Ontario [Library symbol National Library of
                  Canada] (NLC)
ORA .... Montauk Caribbean Airways, Inc. [ICAO designator] (FAAC)
ORA .... Office of Records Administration [National Archives] (BARN)
ORA .... Office of Redress Administration [Department of Justice]
ORA .... Office of Regulatory Analysis [Federal Energy Regulatory
                  Commission]
ORA .... Office of Research Administration [University of Pennsylvania]
                  [Research center] (RCD)
ORA .... Office of Research Administration [North Carolina A & T State
                  University] [Research center] (RCD)
ORA .... Office of Research Administration [St. Louis University] [Research
                  center] (RCD)
ORA .... Office of Research Administration [University of Hawaii] [Research
                  center] (RCD)
ORA .... Office of Research Analysis [Air Force]
ORA .... Office of Rural Affairs [Victoria, Australia]
ORA .... Oil Refiners Association (NADA)
ORA .... Operating Room Attendant [British military] (DMA)
ORA .... Operational RADAR Directed Flights (NATG)
ORA .... Operational Readiness Assessment
ORA .... Operation Response Area (MCD)
ORA .... Operations Research Analyst [Army] (AABC)
ORA .... Opportunity Resources for the Arts (EA)
ORA .... Optical Reference Axis
ORA .... Oran [Argentina] [Airport symbol] (AD)
ORA .... Order for Reinforced Alert (NATG)
Or A .... Oregon Court of Appeals Reports [A publication] (DLA)
ORA .... Organisation de Resistance de l'Armee [France]
ORA .... Organisation Revolutionnaire Anarchiste [Revolutionary Anarchist
                  Organization] [France Political party] (PPE)
ORA .... Organizacao Revolucionaria Armada [Terrorist group] [Portugal] (EY)
ORA .... Organizational Role Analysis (PDAA)
ORA .... Orifice Rod Assembly [Nuclear energy] (NRCH)
ORA .... Output Reference Axis (IAA)
ORA .... Output Register Address
ORA .... Ramore Library, Ontario [Library symbol National Library of
                  Canada] (BIB)
ORA .... Ross Laboratory Library, Columbus, OH [OCLC symbol] (OCLC)
ORAAP .... Outstanding Reserve Airman Appointment Program
ORAC .... Oxygen Radical Absorbance Capacity [Analytical Chemistry]
ORACLE .... Oak Ridge Automatic Computer and Logical Engine
ORACLE .... Observation Research and Classroom Learning Evaluation (AIE)
ORACLE .... On-Line Retrieval and Computational Language for Economists
                  [Computer science]
ORACLE .... Optical Reception of Announcements by Coded Line Electronics
ORACLE .... Optimized Reliability and Component Life Estimate
ORACLE .... Optimum Record Automation for Court and Law Enforcement
ORACLE .... Optional Reception of Announcements by Coded Line Electronics
                  [Independent Television "newspaper"] [British] (DI)
ORACLE .... Optional Recovery of Announcements by Coded Line Electronics
                  (NITA)
Oracle .... Oracle Systems Corp. [Associated Press] (SAG)
ORACLE .... Ordnance Rapid Area Clearance [Military] (CAAL)
ORACLE .... Organic Rankine Cycle
ORACLE .... Oversight of Resources and Capability for Logistics Effectiveness
                  (PDAA)
ORACT .... Operational Readiness and Confidence Test
OrAd .... Adams Public Library, Adams, OR [Library symbol] [Library of
                  Congress] (LCLS)
ORAD .... Office of Rural Areas Development [Later, Rural Community
                  Development Service] [Department of Agriculture]
ORAD .... Orbiter RADAR [NASA]
Or Admin R... Oregon Administrative Rules [A publication] (DLA)
Or Admin R Bull... Oregon Administrative Rules Bulletin [A publication] (DLA)
ORADS .... Optical Ranging and Detection System
Or Ad Sh...... Supreme Court of the State of Oregon Advance Sheets
                  [A publication] (DLA)
ORAE .... Office de Repartition des Approvisionnements d'Energie [Canada]
ORAE .... Operational Research and Analysis Establishment (MCD)
OrAg .... Agness Community Library, Agness, OR [Library symbol Library of
                  Congress] (LCLS)
ORaH .... Robinson Memorial Hospital, Ravenna, OH [Library symbol] [Library
                  of Congress] (LCLS)
OrAh .... Washington County Cooperative Library Services, Aloha, OR [Library
                  symbol] [Library of Congress] (LCLS)
OrAl .... Albany Public Library, Albany, OR [Library symbol Library of
                  Congress] (LCLS)
ORAL .... Oral Access to Library
OrAlBM .... United States Bureau of Mines, Education and Training Center,
                  Albany, OR [Library symbol Library of Congress] (LCLS)
OrAIC .... Linn-Benton Community College, Albany, OR [Library symbol Library
                  of Congress] (LCLS)
OrAlH .... Albany General Hospital, Albany, OR [Library symbol Library of
                  Congress] (LCLS)
Oral Roberts U... Oral Roberts University (GAGS)

OrAIT .... Teledyne-Wah Chang Albany, Albany, OR (LCLS)
OrAm .... Amity Public Library, Amity, OR [Library symbol Library of
                  Congress] (LCLS)
ORAN .... Orange [Laboratory science] (DAVI)
ORAN .... Orbital Analysis
ORAN .... Organisation Regionale Africaine de Normalisation [African Regional
                  Organization for Standardization - AROS] (EAIO)
OR&F.......... Operations, Research and Facilities (USDC)
OR&F.......... Operations, Research and Facilities [Marine science] (OSRA)
OR & N .... Oregon Railroad & Navigation Co.
OR & SP ...... Office of Research and Sponsored Programs [Research center]
                  (RCD)
Orange........ Orange PLC [Associated Press] (SAG)
OrangN .... Orange National Bancorp [Associated Press] (SAG)
OranRk .... Orange & Rockland Utilities, Inc. [Associated Press] (SAG)
ORANS .... Oak Ridge Analytical Systems
Or App .... Oregon Reports, Court of Appeal [A publication] (DLA)
OrAr .... Arlington Public Library, Arlington, OR [Library symbol Library of
                  Congress] (LCLS)
Or-Ar........... Oregon State Archives, Salem, OR [Library symbol Library of
                  Congress] (LCLS)
ORAR .... Rainy River Public Library, Ontario [Library symbol National Library of
                  Canada] (NLC)
ORAS .... Oil Recovery and Separation Technology [Jastram Werke]
ORASA .... Operational Research and Systems Analysis (PDAA)
OrAshS .... Southern Oregon College, Ashland, OR [Library symbol Library of
                  Congress] (LCLS)
OrAst .... Astor Library, Astoria, OR [Library symbol Library of Congress]
                  (LCLS)
OrAstC .... Clatsop Community College, Astoria, OR [Library symbol Library of
                  Congress] (LCLS)
OrAstM .... Columbia River Maritime Museum, Astoria, OR [Library symbol
                  Library of Congress] (LCLS)
Orat .... Oration [or Orator or Oratorio]
Orat .... Orator ad M. Brutum [of Cicero] [Classical studies] (OCD)
ORAT .... Oratorical
ORATE .... Ordered Random Access Talking Equipment
ORATMS...... Off-Route Antitank Mine System (MCD)
ORATS .... Operational Readiness Assessment and Training System (MCD)
ORAU .... Oak Ridge Associated Universities (EA)
OraVax .... OraVax, Inc. [Associated Press] (SAG)
ORAW.......... Oil Remaining after Waterflooding [Petroleum technology]
OrB .... Beaverton City Library, Beaverton, OR [Library symbol Library of
                  Congress] (LCLS)
ORB .... Object Request Broker [Computer science]
ORB .... Oceanic Ridge Basalts
ORB .... Oceanographic Research Buoy
ORB .... Ocean Research Buoy (IAA)
ORB .... Offenders' Review Board [New South Wales, Australia]
ORB .... Officer Record Brief [Army] (AABC)
ORB .... Offsets Review Board [New South Wales, Australia]
ORB .... Omnidirectional Radio Beacon
ORB .... Operational Research Branch [Canada]
ORB .... Operations Record Book [Air Ministry] [British World War II]
ORB .... Optometrists' Registration Board [Victoria, Australia]
ORB .... Orbe [Switzerland] [Seismograph station code, US Geological Survey
                  Closed] (SEIS)
Orb............. Orbis [Record label] [Germany, etc.]
ORB .... Orbit
ORB .... Orbital (KSC)
ORB .... Orbiter [NASA] (NASA)
ORB .... Orbiter
ORB .... Orbit Oil & Gas Ltd. [Toronto Stock Exchange symbol]
ORB .... Order
ORB .... Orebro [Sweden] [Airport symbol] (OAG)
ORB .... Organizational Records Branch [Army]
ORB .... Orr, MN [Location identifier FAA] (FAAL)
ORB .... Outer Radiation Belt
ORB .... Outside Reactor Building [Nuclear energy] (NRCH)
ORB .... Owner's Risk of Breaking [Shipping]
ORB 1-G ...... Orbiter One-G Trainer [NASA] (NASA)
OrBa .... Banks Community Library, Banks, OR [Library symbol Library of
                  Congress] (LCLS)
ORBA .... Erbil [Iraq] [ICAO location identifier] (ICLI)
ORBACT....... Optometrists' Registration Board of the Australian Capital Territory
OrBak.......... Baker County Public Library, Baker, OR [Library symbol Library of
                  Congress] (LCLS)
OrBakSE ...... Saint Elizabeth Hospital, Baker, OR [Library symbol Library of
                  Congress] (LCLS)
OrBan .... Bandon Public Library, Bandon, OR [Library symbol Library of
                  Congress] (LCLS)
Or Bar Bull... Oregon Bar Bulletin [A publication] (DLA)
ORBAT........ Order of Battle Report [Military] (NATG)
ORBB .... Sirsenk/Bamarni [Iraq] [ICAO location identifier] (ICLI)
ORBC .... Baghdad/Soica Headquarters [Iraq] [ICAO location identifier] (ICLI)
ORBC .... Ox Red Blood Cell [Medicine] (DMAA)
OrBe .... Deschutes County Library, Bend, OR [Library symbol Library of
                  Congress] (LCLS)
ORBE .... Open Reciprocating Brayton Engine (PDAA)
OrBeBR....... Bend Research, Inc., Bend, OR [Library symbol] [Library of
                  Congress] (LCLS)
OrBeC .... Central Oregon Community College, Bend, OR [Library symbol
                  Library of Congress] (LCLS)
OrBeCJ .... Cascade Junior High School, Bend, OR [Library symbol] [Library of
                  Congress] (LCLS)

OrBeHS........ Bend Senior High School, Bend, OR [*Library symbol*] [*Library of Congress*] (LCLS)

OrBeMC........ Saint Charles Medical Center, Medical Library, Bend, OR [*Library symbol Library of Congress*] (LCLS)

OrBeMH........ Mountain View High School, Bend, OR [*Library symbol*] [*Library of Congress*] (LCLS)

OrbEng........ Orbital Engine Corp. Ltd. [*Associated Press*] (SAG)

OrBeOHM .... Oregon High Desert Museum, Bend, OR [*Library symbol*] [*Library of Congress*] (LCLS)

OrBePJ........ Pilot Butte Junior High School, Bend, OR [*Library symbol*] [*Library of Congress*] (LCLS)

OrBFP.......... Floating Point Systems, Inc., Beaverton, OR [*Library symbol Library of Congress*] (LCLS)

OrBG.......... Oregon Graduate Center, Beaverton, OR [*Library symbol Library of Congress*] (LCLS)

OrBGS.......... Church of Jesus Christ of Latter-Day Saints, Genealogical Society Library, Beaverton Branch, Beaverton, OR [*Library symbol Library of Congress*] (LCLS)

ORBI.......... Orbital Sciences Corp. [*NASDAQ symbol*] (SAG)

ORBI.......... Rocky Band No. 1 Indian Band Library, Ontario [*Library symbol National Library of Canada*] (BIB)

ORBIFC........ Oak Ridge Boys International Fan Club (EA)

ORBIS.......... Orbiting Radio Beacon Ionospheric Satellite [*NASA*]

ORBIS.......... Ordering and Billing System

ORBIS.......... Oregon Business Information System [*Oregon State Economic Development Department*] [*Information service or system Defunct*] (IID)

ORBIS CAL.. Orbiting Radio Beacon Ionosphere Satellite for Calibration [*NASA*] (PDAA)

ORBIT........ Oak Ridge Binary Internal-Translator

ORBIT........ Office Research into Buildings and IT (NITA)

ORBIT........ On-Line, Real-Time, Branch Information Transmission [*IBM Corp.*] [*Computer science*]

ORBIT........ On-Line Reduced Bandwidth Information Transfer [*Computer science*]

ORBIT........ On-Line Retrieval of Bibliographic Text [*Search system*] [*Computer science*]

ORBIT........ ORACLE Binary Internal Translator [*Algebraic programming system*]

ORBIT........ Orbit, Ballistic Impact, and Trajectory [*Computer*] (MUGU)

Orbit.......... Orbit International Corp. [*Associated Press*] (SAG)

ORBIT........ Order Billing Inventory Technique (PDAA)

ORBK.......... Orbotech Ltd. [*Formerly, Optrotech Ltd.*] [*NASDAQ symbol*] (SPSG)

ORBKF........ Orbotech Ltd Ord [*NASDAQ symbol*] (TTSB)

ORBM.......... Mosul [*Iraq*] [*ICAO location identifier*] (ICLI)

OrBo.......... Boardman Public Library, Boardman, OR [*Library symbol Library of Congress*] (LCLS)

Orbotch........ Orbotech [*Associated Press*] (SAG)

OrBP.......... Oregon Regional Primate Research Center, Beaverton, OR [*Library symbol Library of Congress*] (LCLS)

Or-BPH........ Oregon State Library, Services for the Blind and Physically Handicapped, Salem, OR [*Library symbol Library of Congress*] (LCLS)

ORBR.......... Baghdad/Rasheed [*Iraq*] [*ICAO location identifier*] (ICLI)

OrBroo........ Chetco Community Public Library, Brookings, OR [*Library symbol Library of Congress*] (LCLS)

ORBS.......... Baghdad/Saddam International [*Iraq*] [*ICAO location identifier*] (ICLI)

ORBS.......... Off Reservation Boarding School (EDAC)

ORBS.......... Orbital Rendezvous Base System

OrbSci........ Orbital Sciences Corp. [*Associated Press*] (SAG)

ORBT.......... Orbit International [*NASDAQ symbol*] (TTSB)

ORBT.......... Orbit International Corp. [*NASDAQ symbol*] (NQ)

OrBT.......... Tektronix, Inc., Beaverton, OR [*Library symbol Library of Congress*] (LCLS)

OrbtSemi ..... Orbit Semiconductor Co. [*Associated Press*] (SAG)

Or Bull........ Oregon Bulletin [*A publication*] (AAGC)

ORBV.......... Optometrists' Registration Board of Victoria [*Australia*]

ORBW.......... Baghdad/Muthenna [*Iraq*] [*ICAO location identifier*] (ICLI)

ORBWA........ Optometrists' Registration Board of Western Australia

ORBZ.......... Ain Zalah [*Iraq*] [*ICAO location identifier*] (ICLI)

OrC.......... Corvallis Public Library, Corvallis, OR [*Library symbol Library of Congress*] (LCLS)

ORC.......... Occupational Research Centre [*Hatfield Polytechnic*] [*British*] (CB)

ORC.......... Office of Regional Counsel [*Environmental Protection Agency*] (GFGA)

ORC.......... Office of Reserve Components [*Army*]

ORC.......... Office of the Regional Commissioner [*Social Security Administration*] (OICC)

ORC.......... Officers' Reserve Corps [*Later, Army Reserve*]

ORC.......... Offshore Racing Council

ORC.......... Oilseeds Research Council [*Australia*]

ORC.......... On-Line Reactivity Computer [*Nuclear energy*] (NRCH)

ORC.......... On-Road Costs [*Motor vehicles*]

orc.......... Operarios del Reina de Cristo (TOCD)

ORC.......... Operarios del Reina de Cristo (TOCD)

ORC.......... Operational Readiness Check

ORC.......... Operational Reports Control [*Military*] (AFM)

ORC.......... Operational Requirements Committee [*Ministry of Defence*] [*British*]

ORC.......... Operations Research Center [*Massachusetts Institute of Technology*] [*Research center*] (KSC)

ORC.......... Opinion Research Center

ORC.......... Optical Radiation Corp.

ORC.......... Optical Recording Corp.

ORC.......... Orange City, IA [*Location identifier FAA*] (FAAL)

ORC.......... Orange River Colony [*Later, Orange Free State*] [*South Africa*]

ORC.......... Orbital Research Centrifuge [*NASA*] (KSC)

ORC.......... Orcadas Del Sur [*Argentina*] [*Geomagnetic observatory code*]

ORC.......... Orcatech, Inc. [*Toronto Stock Exchange symbol*]

ORC.......... Orderly Room Corporal [*British*]

ORC.......... Order of the Red Cross

ORC.......... Ordnance Rocket Center (KSC)

ORC.......... Organic Rankine Cycle [*for power generation*] (PDAA)

ORC.......... Organization Requirements Clerk [*Defense Supply Agency*]

ORC.......... Organization Resources Counselors (MCD)

ORC.......... Organized Reserve Corps [*Later, Army Reserve*]

ORC.......... Origin Recognition Complex [*Genetics*]

ORC.......... Orthogonal Row Computer

ORC.......... Outbound RADAR Control

ORC.......... Overrun Clutch

ORC.......... Overseas Reconstruction Committee [*British World War II*]

ORC.......... Overseas Research Center [*Wake Forest University*] [*Research center*] (RCD)

ORC.......... Owner's Risk of Chafing [*Shipping*]

ORC.......... Oxidation-Resistant Coating

ORC.......... Oxidized Regenerated Cellulose [*Hemostatic*] [*Organic chemistry*]

ORC.......... Ozarks Regional Commission [*Department of Commerce*]

ORC.......... Reed College, Portland, OR [*OCLC symbol*] (OCLC)

ORC.......... Reports of the High Court of the Orange River Colony [*South Africa*] [*A publication*] (DLA)

ORCA.......... Ocean Resource Coordination and Assessment [*National Oceanic and Atmospheric Administration*]

ORCA.......... Ocean Resources Conservation Association [*British*]

ORCA.......... Oldtime Radio-Show Collector's Association (EA)

ORCA.......... Online Resource Control Aid [*Computer science*] (HGAA)

ORCA.......... Oregon Caves National Monument

ORCA.......... Organisme Europeen de Recherche sur la Carie [*European Organization for Caries Research*] (EAIO)

ORCA.......... Organized Resistance to Capture in Alaska [*Defunct*] (EA)

Orcad.......... Orcad, Inc. [*Associated Press*] (SAG)

ORCALMIS... Ordnance Calibration Management Information System [*Navy*] (DNAB)

OrCan.......... Canby Public Library, Canby, OR [*Library symbol Library of Congress*] (LCLS)

OrCanHS...... Canby Union High School, Canby, OR [*Library symbol Library of Congress*] (LCLS)

ORCATS........ Oldtime Radio Collectors and Traders Society (EA)

OrCb.......... Coos Bay Public Library, Coos Bay, OR [*Library symbol Library of Congress*] (LCLS)

ORCB.......... Order of Railway Conductors and Brakemen [*Later, United Transportation Union*] (EA)

OrCbS.......... Southwestern Oregon Community College, Coos Bay, OR [*Library symbol Library of Congress*] (LCLS)

OrCC.......... Corvallis Clinic, Corvallis, OR [*Library symbol Library of Congress*] (LCLS)

ORCC.......... Online Resources Communications Co.

ORCC.......... Outward-Rectifying Chloride Channel [*Biochemistry*]

ORCCA.......... Open Road Camper Clubs of America [*Later, ORSAC*] (EA)

ORCEN.......... Overseas Records Center [*Military*]

OrCEPA........ United States Environmental Protection Agency, Corvallis Environmental Research Laboratory, Corvallis, OR [*Library symbol Library of Congress*] (LCLS)

OrCg.......... W. A. Woodward Memorial Library, Cottage Grove, OR [*Library symbol Library of Congress*] (LCLS)

OrCGS.......... Church of Jesus Christ of Latter-Day Saints, Genealogical Society Library, Corvallis Branch, Corvallis, OR [*Library symbol Library of Congress*] (LCLS)

OrCGSH........ Good Samaritan Hospital, Corvallis, OR [*Library symbol Library of Congress*] (LCLS)

ORCH.......... Orchard

ORCH.......... Orchard

orch.......... Orchestra (ODBW)

ORCH.......... Orchestra

ORCHARD.... Orchard [*Commonly used*] (OPSA)

ORCHD.... Orchestrated (By) [*Music*]

ORCHIS........ Oak Ridge Computerized Hierarchical Information System [*AEC*] (IID)

ORCHL.......... Orchestral [*Music*]

ORCHRD...... Orchard [*Commonly used*] (OPSA)

OrchSHw...... Orchard Supply Hardware Stores Corp. [*Associated Press*] (SAG)

ORCI.......... Opinion Research [*NASDAQ symbol*] (TTSB)

ORCI.......... Opinion Research Crop. [*NASDAQ symbol*] (SAG)

ORCID.......... Optical Readout Cherenkov Imaging Detector [*Computer science*] (PDAA)

OrckitCo...... Orckit Communications Ltd. [*Associated Press*] (SAG)

ORCL.......... Oracle Corp. [*NASDAQ symbol*] (TTSB)

ORCL.......... Oracle Systems Corp. [*NASDAQ symbol*] (NQ)

OrCIS.......... Sunnyside Medical Library, Clackamas, OR [*Library symbol Library of Congress*] (LCLS)

ORCMD........ Orlando Contract Management District (SAA)

OrCMG........ Mid-Valley Genealogical Society, Corvallis, OR [*Library symbol Library of Congress*] (LCLS)

ORCO.......... Central Ontario Regional Library, Richmond Hill, Ontario [*Library symbol National Library of Canada*] (NLC)

OrCo.......... Coquille Public Library, Coquille, OR [*Library symbol Library of Congress*] (LCLS)

ORCO.......... Ontario Library Service - Trent, Richmond Hill, Ontario [*Library symbol National Library of Canada*] (NLC)

OrColHS........ Colton High School, Colton, OR [*Library symbol Library of Congress*] (LCLS)

OrCon.......... Condon Public Library, Condon, OR [*Library symbol Library of Congress*] (LCLS)

ORCON	Observation Report Conversion [*Program*]
ORCON	Organic Control
ORCON	Originator Controlled [*Information dissemination*]
ORCON	Originator Controlled [*CIA terminology*]
ORCON	Originator-Controlled Information (MCD)
OrCor	Cornelius Public Library, Cornelius, OR [*Library symbol Library of Congress*] (LCLS)
OrCS	Oregon State University, Corvallis, OR [*Library symbol Library of Congress*] (LCLS)
ORCS	Organic Rankine Cycle System [*For power generation*]
ORCS	Organic Reactions Catalysis Society (EA)
ORCSA	Orange River Colony, South Africa (ILCA)
OrCS-Ar	Oregon State University Archives, Corvallis, OR [*Library symbol Library of Congress*] (LCLS)
OrCS-MB...	Oregon State University, Institute of Marine Biology, Coos Bay, OR [*Library symbol Library of Congress*] (LCLS)
OrCS-MSC ...	Oregon State University, Hatfield Marine Science Center, Newport, OR [*Library symbol*] [*Library of Congress*] (LCLS)
ORCT	Orckit Communications Ltd. [*NASDAQ symbol*] (SAG)
OrCuHS.......	Culver Senior High School, Culver, OR [*Library symbol*] [*Library of Congress*] (LCLS)
ORCUS	Operational Research Co., Universal Systems
ORCV	Outdoor Recreation Center Victoria [*Australia*]
ORCV	Overriding Cam Valve
ORC youth ...	Opinion Research Corporation Youth (NITA)
ORD	CAP PA Gutierrez [*Hernando R.*] Ordonez [*Mexico ICAO designator*] (FAAC)
ORD	Chicago [*Illinois*] O'Hare Airport [*Derived from former name: Orchard Field*] [*Airport symbol*]
ORD	Office for Research and Development [*American Library Association*] (AEBS)
ORD	Office of Regional Development [*Organization of American States*]
ORD	Office of Research and Development [*Washington, DC Environmental Protection Agency*] (GRD)
ORD	Office of Research and Development [*National Oceanic and Atmospheric Administration*] (GFGA)
ORD	Office of Research Development [*Office of Policy, Evaluation, and Research*] [*Department of Labor*]
ORD	Office of Rubber Director [*WPB*] [*World War II*]
ORD	Off-Range Distance (MCD)
ORD	Ohio River Division [*Army Corps of Engineers*]
ORD	Once-Run Distillate (PDAA)
ORD	Operational Readiness Date
ORD	Operational Readiness Demonstration [*FAA*] (TAG)
ORD	Operational Ready [*or Readiness*] Data [*NASA*] (GFGA)
ORD	Operational Ready Data
ORD	Operational Research Division [*Department of National Defence*] [*Canada*]
ORD	Operations [*or Operational*] Requirement Document
ORD	Optical Reference Device
ORD	Optical Rotary Dispersion
ORD	Orbital Requirements Document
ORD	Ordained
ORD	Order
ORD	Orderly
ORD	Ordinal
ORD	Ordinance
ORD	Ordinance
ORD	Ordinary (MSA)
ORD	Ordinary Seaman [*British*]
ORD	Ordnance (AAG)
ORD	Ordovician [*Period, era, or system*] [*Geology*]
Ord.............	Orotidine [*Also, O*] [*A nucleoside*]
ORD	Overseas Replacement Depot [*Military*]
ORD	Owner's Risk of Damage [*Shipping*]
ORDA	Ober Ramstadt Depot Activity [*Germany*] [*Army*]
ORDA	Office of Recombinant DNA Activities [*Bethesda, MD*] [*National Institute of Allergy and Infectious Diseases*]
ORDAC........	Overrange Detection and Correction [*Analytical chemistry*]
OrDal	Dallas Public Library, Dallas, OR [*Library symbol Library of Congress*] (LCLS)
ORDALT.......	Ordnance Alterations
Ord Amst	Ordinance of Amsterdam [*A publication*] (DLA)
Ord Antw	Ordinance of Antwerp [*A publication*] (DLA)
ORD BD	Ordnance Board [*Military*] (WDAA)
Ord Bilb.......	Ordinance of Bilboa [*A publication*] (DLA)
ORDBN	Ordnance Battalion
OrdBrd	Ordnance Board [*British*]
ORDC..........	Orbiter Data Reduction Center [*NASA*]
ORDC..........	Ordnance Corps [*Army*]
ORDC..........	Ordnance Research and Development Center [*Aberdeen Proving Ground, Maryland*] [*Navy*]
ORDCAL	Ordnance Calibration [*Navy*] (NVT)
ORDCAN	Orders Canceled [*Air Force*]
ORDCIT........	Ordnance Department and California Institute of Technology [*Army*] (RDA)
ORDCONCAN...	Orders Considered Canceled [*Air Force*]
ORDCONTECH...	Ordnance Control Technician (DNAB)
Ord Copen ...	Ordinance of Copenhagen [*A publication*] (DLA)
ORDCOR	Orders Corrected [*Air Force*]
ORDCORPS...	Ordnance Corps [*Army*]
ORDCU	Occupational Research and Development Coordinating Unit
ORDD..........	Office of Research, Development, and Demonstrations [*Federal Railroad Administration*]
ORDD..........	Ordered (ROG)

ORD DEPT ...	Ordnance Department [*Military*] (WDAA)
ORDDIS	Ordinary Discharge [*Military*]
ORDEAL.......	Oak Ridge Data Evaluation and Analysis Language [*Department of Energy*] (PDAA)
ORDEAL.......	Orbital Rate Drive Electronics for Apollo and LM [*NASA*]
ORDEAL.......	Orbit Rate Display - Earth and Lunar [*NASA*]
ORDENG	Ordnance Engineering
ORDER........	On-Line Order Entry System [*Computer science*] (MHDB)
ORDER........	Outstanding Requisitions Defeat Endurance Readiness (DNAB)
ORDET	Orbit Determination Group
ORDet	Owner's Risk of Deterioration [*Shipping*]
ORDFAC.......	Ordnance Facility
Ord Flor......	Ordinance of Florence [*A publication*] (DLA)
Ord Gen......	Ordinance of Genoa [*A publication*] (DLA)
ORDHAC	Ordnance Systems Command Hydroballistics Advisory Committee [*Obsolete Navy*]
Ord Hamb....	Ordinance of Hamburg [*A publication*] (DLA)
ORDINST......	Ordnance Instruction
ORDIP	Ordnance Alteration Installation Plan [*Navy*]
ORDIR	Omnirange Digital RADAR
ORDIS	Optical Reading Direct Input System (IAA)
ORDIS	Ordnance Discharge (DNAB)
Ord Konigs...	Ordinance of Konigsberg [*A publication*] (DLA)
ORDL	Ohio River Division Laboratory [*Army Corps of Engineers*] (KSC)
ORDL-EC......	Ohio River Division Laboratory, Engineer Corps [*Army*] (MCD)
Ord Leg.......	Ordinance of Leghorn [*A publication*] (DLA)
ORDLIS........	Ordnance Logistics Information System [*Navy*]
ORDM..........	Ordnance Corps Manual (AAG)
ORDMAINTCO....	Ordnance Maintenance Company [*Navy*] (DNAB)
Ord Med Jur...	Ordronaux's Medical Jurisprudence [*A publication*] (DLA)
ORDMOD	Orders Modified [*Navy*]
ORDN..........	Ordnance (KSC)
ORDNA	Organismes de Radiodiffusion des Pays NonAlignes [*Broadcasting Organizations of Non-Aligned Countries - BONAC*] (EAIO)
ORDNG	Ordering
ORDNTR	Ordinator
ORDO..........	Ordinario [*Ordinarily*] [*Music*] (ROG)
Ordo Nob Urb...	Ordo Nobilium Urbium [*of Ausonius*] [*Classical studies*] (OCD)
ORDP..........	Office of Rural Development Policy [*Department of Agriculture*]
ORDP..........	Ordnance Corps Pamphlet [*Army*] (MCD)
ORDPDS	Offender Rehabilitation Division of the Public Defender Service (EA)
Ord Port......	Ordinance of Portugal [*A publication*] (DLA)
Ord Prus......	Ordinance of Prussia [*A publication*] (DLA)
ORDR..........	Order
ORDRAT	Ordnance Dial Reader and Translator
ORDREV	Ordnance Procedures Review [*Military*] (NVT)
Ordr Jud Ins...	Ordronaux on Judicial Aspects of Insanity [*A publication*] (DLA)
Ordr Med Jur...	Ordronaux's Medical Jurisprudence [*A publication*] (DLA)
Ord Rott......	Ordinance of Rotterdam [*A publication*] (DLA)
ORDRPT.......	Ordnance Report
ORDS..........	Observation Requirements Data Sheet (IAA)
ORDS..........	Office of Research, Demonstrations, and Statistics [*Health Care Financing Administration*]
ORDS..........	Ordinary Shares (WDAA)
ORDSER	Ordnance Support Element Review (NVT)
Ord Sgt.......	Ordnance Sergeant [*Military*] (DMA)
Ords NZ	Ordinances of the Legislative Council of New Zealand [*A publication*] (DLA)
ORDSTA......	Ordnance Station
Ord Swe	Ordinance of Sweden [*A publication*] (DLA)
ORDSYSCOM...	Ordnance Systems Command [*Formerly, Bureau of Naval Weapons; later, Naval Sea Systems Command*]
ORDT..........	Office of Research, Demonstrations, and Training [*Social and Rehabilitation Service, HEW*]
Ord Us........	Ord on Usury [*A publication*] (DLA)
ORDVAC.......	Ordnance Variable Automatic Computer
ORDY..........	Ordinary (AABC)
OrE..............	Eugene Public Library, Eugene, OR [*Library symbol Library of Congress*] (LCLS)
ORE	Greendale Aviation Co. [*Nigeria*] [*FAA designator*] (FAAC)
ORE	Greenfield [*Massachusetts*] [*Airport symbol*] (AD)
ORE	Obtained Radiation Emittance
ORE	Occupational Radiation Exposure (NRCH)
ORE	Oceanographic Research Equipment
ORE	Office of Regional Economics [*Department of Commerce*]
ORE	Office of Research and Evaluation [*Bureau of Labor Statistics*] (GRD)
ORE	Officer Responsible for the Exercise [*Navy*] (NVT)
ORE	On-Orbit Repair Experiment [*NASA*] (NASA)
ORE	On-Orbit Repairs Experiment
ORE	Operational Readiness [*Navy*] (NG)
ORE	Operational Readiness Evaluation [*Army*]
ORE	Operational Readiness Exercise (MCD)
ORE	Optimum Resource Extraction (PDAA)
ORE	Orange, MA [*Location identifier FAA*] (FAAL)
ORE	Oregon (AAG)
Ore...........	Oregon (ODBW)
ORE	Oregon Resources Corp. [*Vancouver Stock Exchange symbol*]
ORE	Oregon State University, Corvallis, Corvallis, OR [*OCLC symbol*] (OCLC)
ORE	Ornitologia Rondo Esperantlingva [*Esperantist Ornithologists' Association*] (EAIO)
ORE DEPT ...	Orthophoto Resolution Enhancer [*Army*]
ORE	Output Register Empty (MHDB)
ORE	Overall Reference Equivalent (NITA)
ORE	Overhaul, Rebuild, and Exchange (MCD)

ORE .... Overtraining Reversal Effect

OREALC .... Regional Office for Education in Latin America and the Caribbean [*UNESCO*] [*Acronym is based on foreign phrase*]

Ore App .... Oregon Court of Appeals Reports [*A publication*] (DLA)

OrEc .... Echo Public Library, Echo, OR [*Library symbol*] [*Library of Congress*] (LCLS)

OREC .... Eramosa Community Library, Rockwood, Ontario [*Library symbol National Library of Canada*] (NLC)

OREC .... Optimises Rectangles [*AERE Harwell*] [*Software package*] (NCC)

ORECHL .... Centre Hospitalier Le Gardeur, Repentigny, Quebec [*Library symbol National Library of Canada*] (NLC)

OrECoAr .... Lane County Archives, Eugene, OR [*Library symbol Library of Congress*] (LCLS)

OrECoL .... Lane County Law Library, Eugene, OR [*Library symbol Library of Congress*] (LCLS)

ORE/ERO ...... Organisation Regionale de la Federation Internationale Dentaire pour l'Europe [*European Regional Organization of the International Dental Federation*] (EAIO)

OREF .... Orthopedic Research and Education Foundation [*Medicine*] (DMAA)

OREG .... Operation Register (IAA)

OREG .... Ordinary Multiple Regression [*Statistics*]

OREG .... Oregon (AFM)

Oreg. .... Oregon (ODBW)

OregMt .... Oregon Metallurgical Corp. [*Associated Press*] (SAG)

Oregon........ Oregon Reports [*A publication*] (DLA)

Oreg Rev Stat... Oregon Revised Statutes [*A publication*] (DLA)

OrEGS .... Church of Jesus Christ of Latter-Day Saints, Genealogical Society Library, Eugene Branch, Eugene, OR [*Library symbol Library of Congress*] (LCLS)

Oreg SB Bull... Oregon State Bar Bulletin [*A publication*] (DLA)

Ore Health Sci U... Oregon Health Sciences University (GAGS)

OReilyAu ...... O'Reilly Automotive [*Associated Press*] (SAG)

OrEL .... Lane Community College, Eugene, OR [*Library symbol Library of Congress*] (LCLS)

OREL .... Ocean Research and Engineering Laboratory (SAA)

ORELA .... Oak Ridge Electron Linear Accelerator [*Oak Ridge, TN*] [*Department of Energy*]

OREM .... Objective Reference Equivalent Measurement (IAA)

OREM .... Office of Research and Evaluation Methods [*National Institute of Justice*] (GRD)

OREM .... Oregon Metallurgical [*NASDAQ symbol*] (TTSB)

OREM .... Oregon Metallurgical Corp. [*NASDAQ symbol*] (NQ)

OREN .... Orthorhombic Enstatite [*Geology*]

OrENC .... Northwest Christian College, Eugene, OR [*Library symbol Library of Congress*] (LCLS)

OrEnW .... Wallowa County Library, Enterprise, OR [*Library symbol Library of Congress*] (LCLS)

OrEnWM ...... Wallowa Memorial Hospital, Burton Carlock Memorial Library, Enterprise, OR [*Library symbol Library of Congress*] (LCLS)

OREO .... Orbiting Radio Emission Observatory [*Satellite*]

OREO .... Other Real Estate Owned (TDOB)

O Rep .... Ohio Reports [*A publication*] (DLA)

OrEPM .... Lane County Museum [*Formerly, Lane County Pioneer Museum*], Eugene, OR [*Library symbol Library of Congress*] (LCLS)

OREPS .... Operational Research in Electrical Power Systems (PDAA)

ORER .... Official Railway Equipment Register [*National Railway Publication Co.*] [*Information service or system*] (IID)

Ore Rev Stat... Oregon Revised Statutes [*A publication*] (DLA)

ORERP .... Off-Site Radiation Exposure Review Project [*Department of Energy*]

OrEs .... Estacada Public Library, Estacada, OR [*Library symbol Library of Congress*] (LCLS)

OrESH .... Sacred Heart General Hospital, Eugene, OR [*Library symbol Library of Congress*] (LCLS)

OrEsHS .... Estacada High School, Estacada, OR [*Library symbol Library of Congress*] (LCLS)

Ore St B Bull... Oregon State Bar Bulletin [*A publication*] (DLA)

OreStl .... Oregon Steel Mills [*Associated Press*] (SAG)

Ore St U ...... Oregon State University (GAGS)

Ore Tax Ct ... Oregon Tax Court Reports [*A publication*] (DLA)

OREX .... Isolyser Co. [*NASDAQ symbol*] (TTSB)

OREX .... Isolyser Company, Inc. [*NASDAQ symbol*] (SAG)

ORF .... Norfolk/Virginia Beach [*Virginia*] [*Airport symbol*] (OAG)

ORF .... Obesity Research Foundation [*British*] (DI)

ORF .... Oceanic Research Foundation [*Australia*]

ORF .... Oesterreichischer Rundfunk [*Radio and television network*] [*Austria*]

ORF .... Officers' Recreation Facility

ORF .... Olfactory Research Fund

ORF .... Oman Royal Flight [*ICAO designator*] (FAAC)

ORF .... Ontario Research Foundation [*Canada Research center*] (RCD)

ORF .... Open Reading Frame [*Genetics*]

ORF .... Operational Readiness Float (AABC)

ORF .... Oral Rehydration Fluid

ORF .... Oratorum Romanorum Fragmenta [*A publication*] (OCD)

Orf .... Orfeo [*Record label*]

ORF .... Orifice (NASA)

ORF .... Orifice

ORF .... Ortho Pharmaceutical Corp. [*Research code symbol*]

ORF .... Overhaul Replacement Factor (MCD)

ORF .... Owner's Risk of Fire [*Shipping*]

ORF .... Owner's Risk of Freezing [*Shipping*]

OrF............. Rogers City Public Library, Forest Grove, OR [*Library symbol Library of Congress*] (LCLS)

OrFc........... Falls City Public Library, Falls City, OR [*Library symbol Library of Congress*] (LCLS)

ORFC .... Orifice (AAG)

ORFEUS....... Orbiting Far and Extreme Ultraviolet Spectrometer [*Telescope*]

OrFFM .... Oregon Masonic Grand Lodge, Forest Grove, OR [*Library symbol Library of Congress*] (LCLS)

OrFl .... Florence Public Library, Florence, OR [*Library symbol Library of Congress*] (LCLS)

ORFLS .... Oak Ridge Full Matrix Least Squares

ORFM .... Outlet Region Feature Model [*Nuclear energy*] (NRCH)

Orf ML .... Orfila's Medecine Legale [*A publication*] (DLA)

OrFP .... Pacific University, Forest Grove, OR [*Library symbol Library of Congress*] (LCLS)

OrFS .... Orange Free State (DAS)

ORFS .... Origin Rail Freight [*MARAD*] (TAG)

ORG .... Glen Robertson Branch, Stormont, Dundas, and Glengarry County Public Library, Ontario [*Library symbol National Library of Canada*] (BIB)

ORG .... Office of Racing and Gaming [*Western Australia*]

ORG .... [*The*] Official Recreation Guide [*Applied Information Services, Inc.*] [*Whitefish, MT*] [*Information service or system*] (IID)

ORG .... Olympics Research Group [*University of Calgary*] [*Canada Research center*] (RCD)

ORG .... Operations Research Group

org .... Orange [*Philately*]

ORG .... Orange [*Diocesan abbreviation*] [*California*] (TOCD)

ORG .... Orange, TX [*Location identifier FAA*] (FAAL)

ORG .... Organ

ORG .... Organic

ORG .... Organism (ADA)

ORG .... Organization [*or Organizational*] (AAG)

Org............ Organization (AAGC)

ORG .... Organogenesis, Inc. [*AMEX symbol*] (SPSG)

ORG .... Organon [*Netherlands*] [*Research code symbol*]

ORG .... Oriental Airlines (Gambia) Ltd. [*ICAO designator*] (FAAC)

ORG .... Origin (MDG)

ORG .... Original New York Seltzer of Canada Ltd. [*Vancouver Stock Exchange symbol*]

org .... Originator [*MARC relator code*] [*Library of Congress*] (LCCP)

ORG .... Paramaribo [*Surinam*] Zorg En Hoop Airport [*Airport symbol*] (OAG)

ORGA .... Organizacion Regional Gallega Autonoma [*Regional Galician Autonomy Organization*] [*Spain Political party*] (PPE)

ORGALIME... Organisme de Liaison des Industries Metalliques Europeennes [*Liaison Group for the European Engineering Industries*] [*Brussels, Belgium*] (EAIO)

ORGAN .... Organisation Regionale Africaine de Normalisation [*African Regional Organization for Standardization - AROS*] (EA)

ORGAN .... Organization

Organik........ Organik Technologies, Inc. [*Associated Press*] (SAG)

organiz .... Organization [*or Organizational*] (DAVI)

OrGb .... Curry Public Library, Gold Beach, OR [*Library symbol Library of Congress*] (LCLS)

OrgBehav..... Organizational Behaviour (DD)

ORgC .... Rio Grande College, Rio Grande, OH [*Library symbol Library of Congress*] (LCLS)

ORGD.......... Organized

ORGDP......... Oak Ridge Gaseous Diffusion Plant [*Department of Energy*]

ORGEL .... Organique et Eau Lourde [*Organic liquid and heavy water nuclear reactor*]

Org Exp........ Organo Espressivo [*Swell Organ*] [*Music*]

OrGH.......... Josephine Memorial Hospital, Grants Pass, OR [*Library symbol*] [*Library of Congress*] (LCLS)

ORGK.......... Organik Technologies [*NASDAQ symbol*] (TTSB)

ORGK.......... Organik Technologies, Inc. [*NASDAQ symbol*] (SAG)

ORGKL......... Organik Tech Wrrt [*NASDAQ symbol*] (TTSB)

ORGKW....... Organik Technologies Wrrt'A' [*NASDAQ symbol*] (TTSB)

ORGKZ......... Organik Technologies Wrrt'B' [*NASDAQ symbol*] (TTSB)

OrGl............ Gladstone Public Library, Gladstone, OR [*Library symbol Library of Congress*] (LCLS)

ORGL.......... Organizational (AFM)

ORGL.......... Overall Reading Grade Level (MCD)

OrGIHS........ Gladstone High School, Gladstone, OR [*Library symbol Library of Congress*] (LCLS)

ORGM.......... Outdoor Recreation Grants-in-Aid Manual

ORGN.......... Organization (AFM)

ORGN.......... Organization

Orgngn........ Organogenesis, Inc. [*Associated Press*] (SAG)

Orgnik........ Organik Technologies, Inc. [*Associated Press*] (SAG)

ORGNL......... Organizational

ORGNL......... Organizational

ORGO.......... Organo [*Organ*] [*Music*] (ROG)

OrGR.......... Rogue Community College, Grants Pass, OR [*Library symbol Library of Congress*] (LCLS)

OrGrC.......... Mount Hood Community College, Gresham, OR [*Library symbol Library of Congress*] (LCLS)

OrGrGS........ Church of Jesus Christ of Latter-Day Saints, Genealogical Society Library, Gresham Branch, Gresham, OR [*Library symbol Library of Congress*] (LCLS)

ORGSBS....... Oak Ridge Graduate School of Biomedical Sciences [*Tennessee*]

ORGSC......... Oregon Ryegrass Growers Seed Commission (EA)

ORGT.......... Organist

ORGY.......... Organization for the Rational Guidance of Youth [*Fictitious organization in film, "The Man from ORGY"*]

ORH .... Occupational Role History [*Psychology*]

ORH .... Office of Rural Health (MEDA)

ORH .... Operational Requirements Handbook

ORH .... Orchard Supply Hardware Strs [*NYSE symbol*] (TTSB)

o-rh............ Orthorhombic [*Crystallography*]

ORH.............. Richmond Hill Public Library, Ontario [*Library symbol National Library of Canada*] (NLC)

ORH.............. Worcester [*Massachusetts*] [*Airport symbol*] (OAG)

OrHe.............. Hermiston Public Library, Hermiston, OR [*Library symbol Library of Congress*] (LCLS)

OrHeGS....... Good Shepherd Hospital, Hermiston, OR [*Library symbol Library of Congress*] (LCLS)

OrHep.......... Heppner Public Library, Heppner, OR [*Library symbol Library of Congress*] (LCLS)

OrHepPM..... Pioneer Memorial Hospital, Heppner, OR [*Library symbol Library of Congress*] (LCLS)

ORHFC......... Official Rocky Horror Fan Club (EA)

OrHi.............. Oregon Historical Society, Portland, OR [*Library symbol Library of Congress*] (LCLS)

OrHil............ Hillsboro Public Library, Hillsboro, OR [*Library symbol Library of Congress*] (LCLS)

OrHilHI........ Tuality Health Information Resource Center, Hillsboro, OR [*Library symbol*] [*Library of Congress*] (LCLS)

OrHilT.......... Tuality Community Hospital, Hillsboro, OR [*Library symbol Library of Congress*] (LCLS)

OrHilW........ Washington County Law Library, Hillsboro, OR [*Library symbol Library of Congress*] (LCLS)

OrHr............. Hood River County Library, Hood River, OR [*Library symbol Library of Congress*] (LCLS)

OrHx............ Helix Pubic Library, Helix, OR [*Library symbol*] [*Library of Congress*] (LCLS)

Orl............... Independence Public Library, Independence, OR [*Library symbol Library of Congress*] (LCLS)

ORI................ Ocean Research Institute (WDAA)

ORI................ Ocean Resources Institute (NADA)

ORI................ Octane Requirement Increase [*Mechanical engineering*]

ORI................ Ocurrence of Reinforcing Information (PDAA)

ORI................ Office of Research and Inventions

ORI................ Office of Research Integrity [*Department of Health and Human Services*]

ORI................ Office of Road Inquiry [*Later, Bureau of Public Roads*]

ORI................ Office Research Institute (NADA)

ORI................ Old Republic International Corp. [*NYSE symbol*] (SPSG)

ORI................ Old Republic Intl. [*NYSE symbol*] (TTSB)

ORI................ Omni Resources, Inc. [*Vancouver Stock Exchange symbol*]

ORI................ Operating and Repair Instruction

ORI................ Operational Readiness Inspection [*Army*]

ORI................ Operational Readiness Instruction [*Military*]

ORI................ Operations Research, Inc. [*Information service or system*]

ORI................ Ophthalmic Research Institute (EA)

ORI................ Oregon Research Institute

ORI................ Orient Air Ltd. [*British ICAO designator*] (FAAC)

ORI................ Orientation Inventory [*Vocational guidance test*]

Ori................. Oriole [*Record label*] [*Great Britain*]

Ori................. Orion [*Constellation*]

ori................. Oriya [*MARC language code Library of Congress*] (LCCP)

ORI................ Outdoor Recreation Institute (EA)

ORI................ Overhaul and Repair Instruction

ORI................ Port Lions [*Alaska*] [*Airport symbol*] (OAG)

ORIA............ Oriental Rug Importers Association of America (EA)

ORIADOC... Orientation and Access to Information and Documentation Sources in France [*Commission de Coordination de la Documentation Administrative*] [*Database*]

ORIC............ Oak Ridge Isochronous Cyclotron [*Department of Energy*]

ORIC............ Operational Readiness Inspection Committee [*NASA*]

ORICAT....... Original Cataloguing System (NITA)

ORIDE......... Override (KSC)

ORIE............ Operational Radiation Instrumentation Equipment (SAA)

ORIEN......... Orientation (AABC)

ORIENT...... Orientation

OrientB....... Oriental Bank & Trust [*Associated Press*] (SAG)

ORIF........... Open Reduction with Internal Fixation [*Medicine*]

Orig............. Origen [*Deceased circa 254*] [*Authority cited in pre-1607 legal work*] (DSA)

ORIG........... Origin [*or Original*] (AAG)

orig............. Origin (VRA)

ORIG........... Originator (MSA)

ORIGAN....... Origanum [*Marjoram*] [*Pharmacology*] (ROG)

ORIG BDS.... Original Boards [*Graphic arts*] (DGA)

ORIGEN2..... Oak Ridge Isotope Generation and Depletion Code [*Department of Energy*] (GAAI)

ORIGINATG... Originating (ROG)

ORIGINS..... Oklahoma Resources Integrated General Information Network System

ORIGL......... Original (ROG)

ORINS......... Oak Ridge Institute of Nuclear Studies [*Later, ORAU*] (EA)

Orio............. Orion [*Constellation*]

OriolH......... Oriole Homes Corp. [*Associated Press*] (SAG)

ORION......... Online Retrieval of Information over a Network

ORION......... Operational Radio Interferometry Observing Network (MCD)

OrionCap..... Orion Capital Corp. [*Associated Press*] (SAG)

OrionNS...... Orion Network Systems, Inc. [*Associated Press*] (SAG)

ORIP........... Ripley Branch, Bruce County Public Library, Ontario [*Library symbol National Library of Canada*] (NLC)

ORIPrH........ Old Republic Int 8.75% Pfd'H' [*NYSE symbol*] (TTSB)

Oris.............. All India Reporter, Orissa [*A publication*] (DLA)

ORIS............ Office of Regulatory Information Systems [*Energy Regulatory Commission*] (IID)

ORIS............ Officeworker Reader Information Services [*British*]

ORIS............ South Carleton High School, Richmond, Ontario [*Library symbol National Library of Canada*] (NLC)

ORISE......... Oak Ridge Institute for Science and Education [*Oak Ridge Associated Universities*] [*Research center*] (RCD)

Orissa.......... All India Reporter, Orissa [*A publication*] (DLA)

ORIT............ Operational Readiness Inspection Team [*Air Force*]

ORIT............ Operational Readiness Inspection Test [*Air Force*]

ORIT............ Organization Regional Interamericana de Trabdjadores [*Inter-American Labor Organization*] [*Spanish*] (BARN)

ORJ.............. Corry, PA [*Location identifier FAA*] (FAAL)

ORJ.............. Ohio Power Co. [*NYSE symbol*] (SAG)

ORJ.............. Oneida Resources, Inc. [*Vancouver Stock Exchange symbol*]

OrJ.............. Orange Juice

ORJ.............. Orinduik [*Guyana*] [*Airport symbol*] (OAG)

OrJc............ Junction City Public Library, Junction City, OR [*Library symbol Library of Congress*] (LCLS)

OrJe............ Jefferson Public Library, Jefferson, OR [*Library symbol Library of Congress*] (LCLS)

ORJETS........ On-Line Remote Job Entry Terminal System [*Computer science*]

OrJM........... Jacksonville Museum, Jacksonville, OR [*Library symbol Library of Congress*] (LCLS)

OrJvHS .... Jordan Valley High School, Jordan Valley, OR [*Library symbol Library of Congress*] (LCLS)

ORK .... Air Orkney [*British ICAO designator*] (FAAC)

ORK .... Cork [*Ireland*] [*Airport symbol*] (OAG)

OrK .... Klamath County Library, Klamath Falls, OR [*Library symbol Library of Congress*] (LCLS)

ORK .... Orkney [*County in Scotland*] (ROG)

OrKM .... Merle West Medical Center Library, Klamath Falls, OR [*Library symbol*] [*Library of Congress*] (LCLS)

OrKT .... Oregon Technical Institute, Klamath Falls, OR [*Library symbol Library of Congress*] (LCLS)

ORL .... Observed Range Limit

ORL .... Olivetti Research Laboratory Ltd. [*British*] (IRUK)

ORL .... On Air Ltd. [*Canada ICAO designator*] (FAAC)

ORL .... Optimum Repair Level Analysis

ORL .... Orbital Research Laboratory [*NASA*]

ORL .... Ordnance Research Laboratory [*Later, Applied Research Laboratory*] [*Pennsylvania State University*] (MCD)

ORL .... Orion Resources Ltd. [*Vancouver Stock Exchange symbol*]

'Orl .... 'Orlah (BJA)

ORL .... Orlando [*Florida*] [*Airport symbol*] (OAG)

ORL .... Orlando Public Library, Orlando, FL [*OCLC symbol*] (OCLC)

ORL .... Otorhinolaryngology [*Medicine*]

ORL .... Owner's Risk of Leakage [*Shipping*]

ORL .... Red Lake Public Library, Ontario [*Library symbol National Library of Canada*] (NLC)

ORLA .... Optimum Repair Level Analysis [*Air Force*]

ORLA .... Optimum Repair Level Authorization (MCD)

ORLA .... Optimum Report Level Analysis [*Military*]

OrLak.......... Lake County Library, Lakeview, OR [*Library symbol*] [*Library of Congress*] (LCLS)

OrLan.......... Langlois Public Library, Langlois, OR [*Library symbol Library of Congress*] (LCLS)

Or Laws...... Oregon Laws and Resolutions [*A publication*] (DLA)

Or Laws Adv Sh... Oregon Laws Advance Sheets [*A publication*] (DLA)

Or Laws Spec Sess... Oregon Laws and Resolutions [*A publication*] (DLA)

Orl Bridg...... Orlando Bridgman's English Common Pleas Reports [*A publication*] (DLA)

Orl Bridgman... Orlando Bridgman's English Common Pleas Reports [*A publication*] (DLA)

Orleans App... Orleans Court of Appeals [*Louisiana*] (DLA)

Orleans TR... Orleans Term Reports [*1, 2 Martin*] [*Louisiana*] [*A publication*] (DLA)

OrLeH.......... Lebanon Community Hospital, Lebanon, OR [*Library symbol*] [*Library of Congress*] (LCLS)

OrLg........... La Grande Public Library, La Grande, OR [*Library symbol Library of Congress*] (LCLS)

OrLgE......... Eastern Oregon College, La Grande, OR [*Library symbol Library of Congress*] (LCLS)

OrLgFS....... United States Forest Service, Range and Wildlife Habitat Laboratory, La Grande, OR [*Library symbol Library of Congress*] (LCLS)

OrLgGRH..... Grande Ronde Hospital, LaGrande, OR [*Library symbol Library of Congress*] (LCLS)

OrLgGS....... Church of Jesus Christ of Latter-Day Saints, Genealogical Society Library, La Grande Branch, La Grande, OR [*Library symbol Library of Congress*] (LCLS)

ORLIS.......... Orts-, Regional-, und Landesplanung Literaturinformationssystem [*Literature Information System for Town and Regional Planning*] [*1974-1978 Database*]

ORLL........... Operational Reports - Lessons Learned [*Army*] (AABC)

OrLo............ Lake Oswego Public Library, Lake Oswego, OR [*Library symbol Library of Congress*] (LCLS)

OrLoHS....... Lake Oswego High School, Lake Oswego, OR [*Library symbol Library of Congress*] (LCLS)

OrLoJS........ Lake Oswego Junior High School, Lake Oswego, OR [*Library symbol Library of Congress*] (LCLS)

OrLoLHS..... Lakeridge High School, Lake Oswego, OR [*Library symbol Library of Congress*] (LCLS)

OrLpHS....... La Pine Senior High School, La Pine, OR [*Library symbol*] [*Library of Congress*] (LCLS)

OrlPID........ Industrial Design Corp., Portland, OR [*Library symbol*] [*Library of Congress*] (LCLS)

ORLPP........ Office of Research, Legislation, and Program Policies [*Unemployment Insurance Service*] [*Department of Labor*]

ORLS .... Selco Mining Corp., Red Lake, Ontario [*Library symbol National Library of Canada*] (NLC)

Or LSJ .... Oregon Law School Journal [*1902-03*] [*A publication*] (DLA)

ORLSTJ........ St. Joseph Township Public Library, Richards Landing, Ontario [*Library symbol National Library of Canada*] (NLC)

Orl TR.......... Orleans Term Reports [*1, 2 Martin*] [*Louisiana*] [*A publication*] (DLA)

ORLY .... O'Reilly Automotive [*NASDAQ symbol*] (SAG)

ORLY .... Overload Relay (IEEE)

ORM .... Northampton [*England*] [*Airport symbol*] (AD)

ORM .... Office of Recycled Materials [*National Bureau of Standards*]

ORM .... Office of Regional Management [*Employment and Training Administration*]

ORM .... Office of Regulated Material [*Environmental Protection Agency*] (GFGA)

ORM .... Off-Road Mobility

ORM .... Off-Route Mine

ORM .... Operators Reference Manual (IAA)

ORM .... Optical Reference Manual

ORM .... Opytnyi Reaktivnyi Motor [*Experimental Reaction Motor*] [*Former USSR*]

orm.............. Ormolu (VRA)

ORM .... Other Regulated Material

ORM .... Overhaul and Repair Manual

ORM .... Overlapping Resolution Mapping [*Computer science*]

ORMA .... Office of Refugee and Migration Affairs [*Department of State*]

OrMaC .... Marylhurst College, Marylhurst, OR [*Library symbol Library of Congress*] (LCLS)

OrMad .... Jefferson County Library, Madras, OR [*Library symbol Library of Congress*] (LCLS)

OrMadHS..... Madras High School, Madras, OR [*Library symbol*] [*Library of Congress*] (LCLS)

OrMadJH ..... Madras Junior High School, Madras, OR [*Library symbol*] [*Library of Congress*] (LCLS)

ORMAK........ Oak Ridge TOKAMAK [*Energy Research and Development Administration*]

ORMAS........ Operational Resource Management Assessment System [*Military*]

OrMc........... McMinnville Public Library, McMinnville, OR [*Library symbol Library of Congress*] (LCLS)

ORMC .... Off-Route [*Smart*] Mine Clearance [*Military*]

OR/MC .... Operational Requirements/Military Characteristics (NG)

OrMcL.......... Linfield College, McMinnville, OR [*Library symbol Library of Congress*] (LCLS)

OrMeGS....... Church of Jesus Christ of Latter-Day Saints, Genealogical Society Library, Medford Branch, Medford, OR [*Library symbol Library of Congress*] (LCLS)

OrMeJ.......... Jackson County Library System, Medford, OR [*Library symbol Library of Congress*] (LCLS)

OrMePH ...... Providence Hospital, Medford, OR [*Library symbol*] [*Library of Congress*] (LCLS)

OrMeRM ...... Rogue Valley Medical Center, Medford, OR [*Library symbol*] [*Library of Congress*] (LCLS)

OrMf .... Milton-Freewater Public Library, Milton-Freewater, OR [*Library symbol Library of Congress*] (LCLS)

OrMi .... Milwaukie Public Library, Milwaukie, OR [*Library symbol Library of Congress*] (LCLS)

ORMI .... Oak Ridge Military Institute

OrMiCHS...... Clackamas High School, Media Center, Milwaukie, OR [*Library symbol Library of Congress*] (LCLS)

OrMiD .... Dwyer Community Hospital, Medical Library, Milwaukie, OR [*Library symbol Library of Congress*] (LCLS)

OrMiHS........ Milwaukie High School, Milwaukie, OR [*Library symbol Library of Congress*] (LCLS)

OrMiLHS...... La Salle High School, Milwaukie, OR [*Library symbol Library of Congress*] (LCLS)

OrMiPHS...... Rex Putnam High School, Milwaukie, OR [*Library symbol Library of Congress*] (LCLS)

ORMM .... Basrah/Magal [*Iraq*] [*ICAO location identifier*] (ICLI)

ORMOA........ Office for Relations with Military and Occupation Authorities

OrMol .... Molalla Public Library, Molalla, OR [*Library symbol Library of Congress*] (LCLS)

OrMolHS ..... Molalla Senior High School, Molalla, OR [*Library symbol Library of Congress*] (LCLS)

OrMolMS .... Molalla Mid-High School, Molalla, OR [*Library symbol*] [*Library of Congress*] (LCLS)

OrMon .... Monmouth Library, Monmouth, OR [*Library symbol Library of Congress*] (LCLS)

Ormond........ Ormond's Reports [*19-107 Alabama*] [*A publication*] (DLA)

OrMonO .... Oregon College of Education, Monmouth, OR [*Library symbol Library of Congress*] (LCLS)

ORMONS ..... Operational Readiness Monitoring System (MCD)

OrMonW ..... Western Oregon State College, Monmouth, OR [*Library symbol*] [*Library of Congress*] (LCLS)

OrMp .... Myrtle Point Public Library (Flora M. Laird Library), Myrtle Point, OR [*Library symbol Library of Congress*] (LCLS)

ORMS .... Basrah/Shaibah [*Iraq*] [*ICAO location identifier*] (ICLI)

ORMS .... Operational Readiness Management System

OR/MS .... Operations Research or Management Science

ORMS .... Operative Roller Makers' Society [*A union*] [*British*]

ORMS .... Other Regulated Materials (GNE)

OrMta .... Mount Angel Public Library, Mount Angel, OR [*Library symbol Library of Congress*] (LCLS)

OrMtaC .... Mount Angel College [*Later, Cesar Chavez College*], Mount Angel, OR [*Library symbol Library of Congress*] (LCLS)

ORMU.......... Orbital Remote Maneuvering Unit

OrN .... Newberg Library Association, Newberg, OR [*Library symbol Library of Congress*] (LCLS)

ORN .... Oak Ridge National Laboratory, Oak Ridge, TN [*OCLC symbol*] (OCLC)

ORN .... Olfactory Receptor Neuron [*Biochemistry*]

ORN .... Operating Room Nurse [*Medicine*]

ORN .... Oran [*Algeria*] [*Airport symbol*] (OAG)

ORN .... Orange (AAG)

ORN .... Organization of Revolutionaries of the North [*Lebanon*] (PD)

ORN .... Orient Airways [*Pakistan*] [*ICAO designator*] (FAAC)

ORN .... Ornament (MSA)

ORN .... OrNda Healthcorp [*NYSE symbol*] (TTSB)

Orn.............. Ornithine [*Same as DAV*] [*An amino acid*]

ORN .... Ornithology

ORN .... Orthopedic Nurse

ornam.......... Ornament (VRA)

ORNAM........ Ornamental

OrNb .... North Bend Public Library, North Bend, OR [*Library symbol Library of Congress*] (LCLS)

OrNbGS........ Church of Jesus Christ of Latter-Day Saints, Genealogical Society Library, Coos Bay Stake Branch, North Bend, OR [*Library symbol Library of Congress*] (LCLS)

ORND .... Ornda Healthcorp [*Formerly, Republic Health Corp.*] [*NASDAQ symbol*] (SPSG)

Ornda.......... Ornda Healthcorp [*Associated Press*] (SAG)

OrNep .... Newport Public Library, Newport, OR [*Library symbol Library of Congress*] (LCLS)

OrNepH........ Pacific Communities Hospital Library, Newport, OR [*Library symbol*] [*Library of Congress*] (LCLS)

ORNG.......... Orange

ORNG.......... Orange PLC [*NASDAQ symbol*] (SAG)

OrngCo........ Orange-Co., Inc. [*Associated Press*] (SAG)

OrNGF......... George Fox College, Newberg, OR [*Library symbol Library of Congress*] (LCLS)

ORNGY .... Orange PLC ADR [*NASDAQ symbol*] (TTSB)

ORNITH........ Ornithology

ORNITHOL ... Ornithology

ORNL .... Oak Ridge National Laboratory [*Oak Ridge, TN*] [*Department of Energy*]

ORNL-PCA ... Oak Ridge National Laboratory Pool Critical Assembly (SAA)

ORNLY-NDP.. Oak Ridge National Laboratory Nuclear Data Project [*Database producer*]

ORNMT .... Ornament

ORNTL .... Ornamental

OrNyGS........ Church of Jesus Christ of Latter-Day Saints, Genealogical Society Library, Nyssa Branch, Nyssa, OR [*Library symbol Library of Congress*] (LCLS)

OrNyMH....... Malheur Memorial Hospital, J. J. Sarazin Memorial Library, Nyssa, OR [*Library symbol Library of Congress*] (LCLS)

ORO .... Oak Ridge Operations Office (MCD)

ORO .... Office of Regional Operations [*Office of Field Operations*] [*Department of Labor*]

ORO .... Office of Regional Operations [*Environmental Protection Agency*] (GFGA)

ORO .... Official Receiver's Office [*Australia*]

ORO .... Oil Red O [*A stain*]

ORO .... Operations Research Office

ORO .... Orapouche [*An arbovirus*] [*Medicine*] (BABM)

ORO .... Orapouche [*An arbovirus*] [*Laboratory science*] (DAVI)

OrO .... Oregon City Public Library, Oregon City, OR [*Library symbol Library of Congress*] (LCLS)

ORO .... Orofino Resources Ltd. [*Toronto Stock Exchange symbol Vancouver Stock Exchange symbol*]

ORO .... Oropa [*Italy*] [*Seismograph station code, US Geological Survey Closed*] (SEIS)

ORO .... Oropouche [*An arbovirus*]

Oro.............. Orotate [*Biochemistry*]

Oro.............. Orotic Acid [*Biochemistry*]

ORO .... Orthicon Read-Out

ORO .... Porto Seguro [*Brazil*] [*Airport symbol*] (AD)

ORO .... Rockland Public Library, Ontario [*Library symbol National Library of Canada*] (NLC)

OrOa .... Oakridge Public Library, Oakridge, OR [*Library symbol Library of Congress*] (LCLS)

OROA........... Oroamerica, Inc. [*NASDAQ symbol*] (SAG)

Oroamer....... Oroamerica, Inc. [*Associated Press*] (SAG)

OROAP........ Organizacion Regional del Oriente para la Administracion Publica [*Eastern Regional Organization for Public Administration*] (EAIO)

OrOC........... Clackamas County Public Library, Oregon City, OR [*Library symbol Library of Congress*] (LCLS)

OrOCC......... Clackamas Community College, Oregon City, OR [*Library symbol Library of Congress*] (LCLS)

OROCS......... Optical Recognition of Chemical Structures Program [*IBM Almaden Research Center*] [*San Jose, CA*]

OrOgCL........ Cooperative Library Network of Clackamas County, Oak Grove, OR [*Library symbol*] [*Library of Congress*] (LCLS)

OrOHS .... Oregon City Senior High School, Oregon City, OR [*Library symbol Library of Congress*] (LCLS)

OROM .... Optical Read-Only Memory [*Computer science*]

OrOn .... Malheur County Library, Ontario, OR [*Library symbol Library of Congress*] (LCLS)

OrOnHR........ Holy Rosary Hospital, Weise-Biggs Memorial Medical Library, Ontario, OR [*Library symbol Library of Congress*] (LCLS)

OrOnT .... Treasure Valley Community College, Ontario, OR [*Library symbol Library of Congress*] (LCLS)

ORootN .... Northeastern Ohio Universities, College of Medicine, Basic Medical Sciences Library, Rootstown, OH [*Library symbol Library of Congress*] (LCLS)

OROS .... Optical Read-Only Storage [*Computer science*]

OROS .... Oral Osmotic [*System for delivering drugs into the bloodstream*] [*Alza Corp. trademark*]

OROS .... Rosseau Public Library, Ontario [*Library symbol National Library of Canada*] (NLC)

OROSS .... Operational Readiness-Oriented Supply System [*Army*] (PDAA)

OrOWH .... Willamette Falls Community Hospital, Oregon City, OR [*Library symbol Library of Congress*] (LCLS)

OrP .... Library Association of Portland [*Public Library for Portland and Multnomah County*], Portland, OR [*Library symbol Library of Congress*] (LCLS)

ORP .... Objective Rally [*or Rallying*] Point [*Military*]

ORP .... Objective Release Point [*Army*] (INF)

ORP .... Office of Radiation Programs [*Environmental Protection Agency*]

ORP .... Office of Regulatory Programs [*Federal Energy Administration*] [*Obsolete*]

ORP .... Officer Requirements Plan (DNAB)

ORP .... OFS [*Orbital Flight System*] Retransmission Processor [*NASA*] (GFGA)

ORP .... OFS [*Orbiter Functional Simulator*] Retransmission Processor [*NASA*]

ORP .... Operational Readiness Panel

ORP .... Operational Readiness Platform [*Aviation*] (DA)

ORP .... Optical Rotary Power

ORP .... Orapa [*Botswana*] [*Airport symbol Obsolete*] (OAG)

ORP .... Orbital Rendezvous Procedure (AAG)

ORP .... Ordinary, Reasonable, and Prudent [*Legal term*] (BARN)

ORP .... Organ Recovery Program (EA)

ORP .... Ormara [*Pakistan*] [*Airport symbol*] (AD)

ORP .... Outside Right Position [*Dancing*]

ORP .... Oxidation-Reduction Potential

ORP .... Oxygen-Regulated Protein [*Biochemistry*]

ORP .... Phelps Community Library, Redbridge, Ontario [*Library symbol National Library of Canada*] (NLC)

ORPA .... Orbiter Retarding Potential Analyzer [*NASA*]

ORPA .... Organizacion Revolucionaria del Pueblo en Armas [*Revolutionary Organization of the People in Arms*] [*Guatemala*] [*Political party*] (PD)

OrP-A .... Portland City Archives, Portland, OR [*Library symbol Library of Congress*] (LCLS)

OrPAA .... Arthur Anderson & Co., Portland, OR [*Library symbol Library of Congress*] (LCLS)

OrPAB .... Academic Book Center, Portland, OR [*Library symbol*] [*Library of Congress*] (LCLS)

OrPB .... Bonneville Power Administration, Portland, OR [*Library symbol Library of Congress*] (LCLS)

OrPBC .... Blue Cross/Blue Shield of Oregon, Portland, OR [*Library symbol*] [*Library of Congress*] (LCLS)

OrPBK .... Bess Kaiser Foundation Hospital, Medical Library, Portland, OR [*Library symbol Library of Congress*] (LCLS)

OrPC .... Cascade College, Portland, OR [*Library symbol Library of Congress*] (LCLS)

ORPC .... Office of Rail Public Counsel [*Terminated, 1979*] [*Affiliated with Interstate Commerce Commission*]

ORPC .... Old Radio Program Collectors Club (EA)

OrPCA .... Roman Catholic Archdiocese of Portland in Oregon, Chancery Office, Portland, OR [*Library symbol Library of Congress*] (LCLS)

OrPCC .... Concordia College, Portland, OR [*Library symbol Library of Congress*] (LCLS)

OrPCM .... Cedar Mill Community Library, Portland, OR [*Library symbol Library of Congress*] (LCLS)

OrPCNM .... National College of Naturopathic Medicine, Portland, OR [*Library symbol Library of Congress*] (LCLS)

OrPCol .... Columbia Christian College, Portland, OR [*Library symbol Library of Congress*] (LCLS)

OrPD .... Protestant Episcopal Church, Diocesan Library, Portland, OR [*Library symbol Library of Congress*] (LCLS)

OrPeB .... Blue Mountain Community College, Pendleton, OR [*Library symbol Library of Congress*] (LCLS)

OrPeCH .... Pendleton Community Hospital, Pendleton, OR [*Library symbol Library of Congress*] (LCLS)

OrPEH .... Emanuel Hospital, Portland, OR [*Library symbol Library of Congress*] (LCLS)

OrPeSA .... Saint Anthony Hospital, Pendleton, OR [*Library symbol Library of Congress*] (LCLS)

OrPeU .... Umatilla County Library, Pendleton, OR [*Library symbol Library of Congress*] (LCLS)

OrPFW .... United States Fish and Wildlife Service, Portland, OR [*Library symbol Library of Congress*] (LCLS)

OrPGE .... Portland General Electric Co., Portland, OR [*Library symbol Library of Congress*] (LCLS)

OrPGF .... Genealogical Forum of Portland, Portland, OR [*Library symbol Library of Congress*] (LCLS)

OrPGH .... Good Samaritan Hospital and Medical Center, Portland, OR [*Library symbol Library of Congress*] (LCLS)

OrPGS .... Church of Jesus Christ of Latter-Day Saints, Genealogical Society Library, Portland Branch, Portland, OR [*Library symbol Library of Congress*] (LCLS)

OrPGSE .... Church of Jesus Christ of Latter-Day Saints, Genealogical Society Library, Portland East Branch, Portland, OR [*Library symbol Library of Congress*] (LCLS)

ORPH .... Orphan [*or Orphanage*]

ORPH .... Orphan Medical, Inc. [*NASDAQ symbol*] (SAG)

ORPH .... Orphan Med Inc. [*NASDAQ symbol*] (TTSB)

OrphanM .... Orphan Medical, Inc. [*Associated Press*] (SAG)

Orph Frag ... Orphica Fragmenta [*A publication*] (OCD)

ORPHIC .... Organized Projected Hypotheses for Innovations in Curriculum [*Educational planning*]

OrPHP .... Holladay Park Hospital, Medical Library, Portland, OR [*Library symbol Library of Congress*] (LCLS)

OrPHS-D ...... Oregon Health Sciences University, Dental Library, Portland, OR [*Library symbol Library of Congress*] (LCLS)

ORPI .... Organ Pipe Cactus National Monument

ORPICS .... Orbital Rendezvous Positioning, Indexing, and Coupling System

OrPK .... Bess Kaiser Foundation Hospital, Medical Library, Portland, OR [*Library symbol Library of Congress*] (LCLS)

OrPKF .... Kaiser Foundation Hospitals, Health Services Research Center, Portland, OR [*Library symbol Library of Congress*] (LCLS)

OrPL .... Lewis and Clark College, Portland, OR [*Library symbol Library of Congress*] (LCLS)

ORPL .... Office de Protection contre les Rayonnements Ionisants [*Office for Protecti on Against Ionizing Radiation*] [*France*]

ORPL .... Overseas Replacement [*Military*]

OrPL-L .... Northwestern School of Law, Lewis and Clark College, Portland, OR [*Library symbol Library of Congress*] (LCLS)

OrPM .... Office of Research Program Management [*Environmental Protection Agency*] (GFGA)

OrPMB .... Multnomah School of the Bible, Portland, OR [*Library symbol Library of Congress*] (LCLS)

OrPML .... Multnomah County Law Library, Portland, OR [*Library symbol Library of Congress*] (LCLS)

OrPNA .... Northwest Association of Private Colleges and Universities, Microform Center, Portland, OR [*Library symbol Library of Congress*] (LCLS)

OrPNR .... Northwest Regional Educational Laboratory, Information Center Library, Portland,OR [*Library symbol Library of Congress*] (LCLS)

OrPO .... Oregonian Publishing Co. Library, Portland, OR [*Library symbol Library of Congress*] (LCLS)

OrPOF .... Oregon Odd Fellows Grand Lodge, Portland, OR [*Library symbol Library of Congress*] (LCLS)

OrPOj .... Oregon Daily Journal, Portland, OR [*Library symbol*] [*Library of Congress*] (LCLS)

OrPoL .... Hazel M. Lewis Library (Powers Public Library), Powers, OR [*Library symbol*] [*Library of Congress*] (LCLS)

ORPOS .... Office of Regulatory Policy, Oversight, and Supervision [*Federal Home Loan Bank Board*]

OrPP .... Port of Portland Library, Portland, OR [*Library symbol Library of Congress*] (LCLS)

OrPPC .... Portland Community College, Portland, OR [*Library symbol Library of Congress*] (LCLS)

OrPPCP .... Precision Cast Parts, Portland, OR [*Library symbol*] [*Library of Congress*] (LCLS)

OrPPL .... Pacific Power & Light Co., Portland, OR [*Library symbol Library of Congress*] (LCLS)

OrPPM .... Providence Medical Center, Portland, OR [*Library symbol Library of Congress*] (LCLS)

OrPPS .... Portland Public School District, Portland, OR [*Library symbol Library of Congress*] (LCLS)

OrPr .... Crook County Library, Prineville, OR [*Library symbol Library of Congress*] (LCLS)

OrPR .... Reed College, Portland, OR [*Library symbol Library of Congress*] (LCLS)

OrPRAM .... Oregon Royal Arch Masons Grand Chapter Archives, Portland, OR [*Library symbol Library of Congress*] (LCLS)

OrPrC .... Crook County Library, Prineville, OR [*Library symbol*] [*Library of Congress*] (LCLS)

OrPrH .... Pioneer Memorial Hospital Library, Prineville, OR [*Library symbol*] [*Library of Congress*] (LCLS)

OrPrK .... Pilot Rock Public Library, Pilot Rock, OR [*Library symbol*] [*Library of Congress*] (LCLS)

OrPRP .... Riverside Psychiatric Hospital, Portland, OR [*Library symbol Library of Congress*] (LCLS)

ORPS .... Overseas Return Placement System [*Military*]

OrPS .... Portland State University, Portland, OR [*Library symbol Library of Congress*] (LCLS)

OrPSMA .... Saint Mary's Academy, Portland, OR [*Library symbol Library of Congress*] (LCLS)

OrPS-MI .... Metropolitan Instructional Support Laboratory, Portland State University, Portland, OR [*Library symbol*] [*Library of Congress*] (LCLS)

OrPStV .... Saint Vincent Hospital and Medical Center, Portland, OR [*Library symbol Library of Congress*] (LCLS)

ORPSU .... Organized Reserve Port Security Unit [*Military*]

OrPT .... Temple Beth Israel, Portland, OR [*Library symbol Library of Congress*] (LCLS)

OrPTC .... Town Center Library at Tanasbourne, Portland, OR [*Library symbol Library of Congress*] (LCLS)

OrPto .... Port Orford Public Library, Port Orford, OR [*Library symbol Library of Congress*] (LCLS)

OrPU .... University of Portland, Portland, OR [*Library symbol Library of Congress*] (LCLS)

OrPUCA .... United States Court of Appeals, Portland, OR [*Library symbol*] [*Library of Congress*] (LCLS)

Or PUC Ops... Oregon Office of the Public Utilities Commissioner. Opinions and Decisions [*A publication*] (DLA)

OrPUDC .... United States District Court, Central Library, Portland, OR [*Library symbol*] [*Library of Congress*] (LCLS)

OrPV .... United States Veterans Administration Hospital, Portland, OR [*Library symbol Library of Congress*] (LCLS)

OrPW .... Western Evangelical Seminary, Portland, OR [*Library symbol Library of Congress*] (LCLS)

OrPWB .... Western Conservative Baptist Theological Seminary, Portland, OR [*Library symbol Library of Congress*] (LCLS)

OrPWP .... Warner Pacific College, Portland, OR [*Library symbol Library of Congress*] (LCLS)

OrPWS .... Western States Chiropractic College, Portland, OR [*Library symbol Library of Congress*] (LCLS)

OrPWsC ...... West Slope Community Library, Portland, OR [*Library symbol Library of Congress*] (LCLS)

ORQ .... Norwalk, CT [*Location identifier FAA*] (FAAL)

ORQ .... Outstanding Performance Rating with Quality Step Increase [*Military*] (DNAB)

ORQMC .... Orderly Room Quartermaster-Corporal [*British military*] (DMA)

ORQMS .... Orderly Room Quartermaster-Sergeant [*British military*] (DMA)

ORR .... Oak Ridge Research Reactor [*ORNL*] (NRCH)

ORR .... Oak Ridge Reservation

ORR .... Oak Ridge Reservation

ORR .... Oak Ridge Reservation (DOGT)

ORR .... Office of Ready Reserve [*Army*]

ORR .... Office of Refugee Relief [*Department of Health and Human Services*]

ORR .... Office of Refugee Resettlement (USGC)

ORR .... Omnidirectional RADAR Range (IAA)

ORR .... Omnidirectional Radio Range (IAA)

ORR .... Onsager Reciprocal Relations [*Thermodynamics*]

ORR .... Operational Readiness Reporting

ORR .... Operational Readiness Review (NASA)

ORR .... Operational Ready Rate (MCD)

ORR .... Operations Requirements Review (NASA)

ORR .... Optical Ratio Reflector

ORR .... Orbital Rendezvous RADAR (AAG)

ORR .... Orroval Valley, Australia, Tracking Station [*NASA*] (NASA)

ORR .... Orthographic RADAR Restitutor

ORR .... Oudh and Rohilkand Railway Rifles [*British military*] (DMA)

ORR .... Overhaul Replacement Rate

ORR .... Owner's Risk Rates [*Shipping*]

ORR .... Red Rock Public Library, Ontario [*Library symbol National Library of Canada*] (NLC)

ORR .... Rogue Community College Library, Grants Pass, OR [*OCLC symbol*] (OCLC)

ORRA .... Orbit Semiconductor [*NASDAQ symbol*] (SAG)

ORRA .... Oriental Rug Retailers of America (EA)

ORRAS .... Optical Research Radiometrical Analysis System (IEEE)

ORRCAT ...... Ridgetown College of Agricultural Technology, Ontario [*Library symbol National Library of Canada*] (NLC)

OrRed .... Redmond Public Library, Redmond, OR [*Library symbol Library of Congress*] (LCLS)

OrRedDH ..... Central Oregon District Hospital, Medical Library, Redmond, OR [*Library symbol Library of Congress*] (LCLS)

OrRedHS ..... Redmond Senior High School, Redmond, OR [*Library symbol*] [*Library of Congress*] (LCLS)

OrRedOJ ..... Obsidian Junior High School, Redmond, OR [*Library symbol*] [*Library of Congress*] (LCLS)

OrRedTE ..... John Tuck Elementary School, Redmond, OR [*Library symbol*] [*Library of Congress*] (LCLS)

Or Rep .... Oregon Reports [*A publication*] (DLA)

Or Rev Stat ... Oregon Revised Statutes [*A publication*] (DLA)

ORRMIS .... Oak Ridge Regional Modeling Information System

OrRoD .... Douglas County Library, Roseburg, OR [*Library symbol Library of Congress*] (LCLS)

OrRoM .... Douglas County Museum, Roseburg, OR [*Library symbol Library of Congress*] (LCLS)

OrRoMM ...... Mercy Medical Center, Roseburg, OR [*Library symbol Library of Congress*] (LCLS)

OrRoU .... Umpqua Community College, Roseburg, OR [*Library symbol Library of Congress*] (LCLS)

OrRoV .... United States Veterans Administration Hospital, Roseburg, OR [*Library symbol Library of Congress*] (LCLS)

ORRR .... Oak Ridge Research Reactor [*Department of Energy*] (NRCH)

ORRRC .... Outdoor Recreation Resources Review Commission [*Terminated, 1962*] [*Department of the Interior*]

ORRT .... Operational Readiness and Reliability Test

ORRTA .... Office of the Registrar of Restrictive Trading Agreements (PDAA)

ORRV .... Off-Road Recreation Vehicle

ORS .... Obligated Reserve Section [*Air Force*] (AFM)

ORS .... Oceanographic Research Ship

ORS .... Octahedral Research Satellite [*NASA*]

ORS .... Office for Research & Statistics [*American Library Association*]

ORS .... Office of Radiation Standards [*AEC*]

ORS .... Office of Regulatory Support [*Environmental Protection Agency*] (GFGA)

ORS .... Office of Rent Stabilization [*Functions transferred to Office of Defense Mobilization, 1953*]

ORS .... Office of Research and Statistics [*Social Security Administration*]

ORS .... Office of Revenue Sharing [*Department of the Treasury*]

ORS .... Official Relay Station [*Amateur radio*]

ORS .... Off-Site Repair and Support (MCD)

ORS .... Oil Recovery System

ORS .... Old Red Sandstone

ORS .... Olfactory Reference Syndrome [*Medicine*] (DMAA)

ORS .... Online Reference Service [*Thunder Bay Public Library*] [*Canada*] (OLDSS)

ORS .... Online Research Systems [*Information service or system*] (IID)

ORS .... Operational Reactor Safeguards (DNAB)

ORS .... Operational Research Society [*British*]

ORS .... Operational Research Station [*Air Ministry*] [*British World War II*]

ORS .... Optimal Real Storage (CMD)

ORS .... Oral Electrolyte Solution [*Nutrition*]

ORS .... Oral Rehydration Salts [*or Solution*]

ORS .... Oral Surgeon

ORS .... Orbital Refueling System [*NASA*] (NASA)

ORS .... Orbiter Refueling System [*NASA*]

ORS .... Orbiter Relay Simulator [*NASA*]

ORS .... Orbiting Research Satellite [*NASA*]

ORS .... Orderly Room Sergeant [*British*]

ORS .... Oregon Revised Statutes [*A publication*] (AAGC)

ORS .... Organization Rating Scale

ORS .... Originating Register Sender

ORS .... Orpheus Island [*Australia Airport symbol*]

ORS .... Orsett [*England*]

ORS .... Orsina Resources [*Vancouver Stock Exchange symbol*]

ORS .... Orthopedic Research Society (EA)

ORS .... Orthopedic Surgeon

ORS .... Oscillographic Recording System

ORS .... Others

ORS .... Outboard Rotating Shield

ORS .... Outstanding Requisition System (DNAB)

ORS .... Oval Ring Seal

ORS .... Overlay Reproducer System

ORS .... Ownership Reporting System [*Securities and Exchange Commission*] (GFGA)

ORS .... Owner's Risk of Shifting [*Shipping*]

ORS .... Oxfordshire Record Society [*British*] (DBA)

ORS .... Research and Development Library, Shaw Industries, Rexdale, Ontario [*Library symbol National Library of Canada*] (BIB)

ORSA .... Operations Research Society of America (EA)

OR/SA .... Operations Research/Systems Analysis [*Army*]

ORSA .... Order of Recollects of St. Augustine

ORSA .... Oregon Revised Statutes Annotated [*A publication*]

OrSa .... Salem Public Library, Salem, OR [*Library symbol Library of Congress*] (LCLS)

OrSaC .... Chemeketa Community College, Salem, OR [*Library symbol Library of Congress*] (LCLS)

ORSAC .... Oak Ridge Systems Analysis Code

ORSAC .... Open Road "See America" Club [*Defunct*] (EA)

OR/SAEC ...... Operations Research/Systems Analysis Executive Course [*Army*]

OrSaGS .... Church of Jesus Christ of Latter-Day Saints, Genealogical Society Library, SalemBranch, Salem, OR [*Library symbol Library of Congress*] (LCLS)

OrSaH .... Salem Hospital, Salem, OR [*Library symbol Library of Congress*] (LCLS)

OrSaMHi ...... Marion County Historical Society, Salem, OR [*Library symbol*] [*Library of Congress*] (LCLS)

OrSan .... Sandy Public Library, Sandy, OR [*Library symbol Library of Congress*] (LCLS)

ORSANCO .... Ohio River Valley Water Sanitation Commission

OrSanHS ...... Sandy Union High School, Sandy, OR [*Library symbol Library of Congress*] (LCLS)

ORSAR .... Official Reports, South African Republic [*A publication*] (DLA)

OrSaSH .... Oregon State Hospital, Medical Library, Salem, OR [*Library symbol*] [*Library of Congress*] (LCLS)

OrSaT .... Oregon Department of Transportation, Salem, OR [*Library symbol*] [*Library of Congress*] (LCLS)

OrSaW .... Willamette University, Salem, OR [*Library symbol Library of Congress*] (LCLS)

OrSaWB .... Western Baptist Bible College, Salem, OR [*Library symbol Library of Congress*] (LCLS)

OrSaW-L ...... Willamette University, Law Library, Salem, OR [*Library symbol Library of Congress*] (LCLS)

Or SB Bull ... Oregon State Bar. Bulletin [*A publication*] (ILCA)

ORS(BC) ...... Operational Research Section (Bomber Command) [*British World War II*]

Or-SC .... Oregon Supreme Court, Salem, OR [*Library symbol Library of Congress*] (LCLS)

ORSDI .... Oak Ridge Selective Dissemination of Information [*Department of Energy*] (NASA)

ORSE .... Operational Reactor Safeguard Examination (NVT)

ORSE .... Otherwise

ORSEP .... Operational Reentry Systems Evaluation Program (SAA)

ORSER .... Office for Remote Sensing of Earth Resources [*Pennsylvania State University*] [*Research center*]

OrSh .... Sherwood Public Library, Sherwood, OR [*Library symbol Library of Congress*] (LCLS)

OrShe .... Sheridan Public Library, Sheridan, OR [*Library symbol Library of Congress*] (LCLS)

OrSi .... Sisters Public Library, Sisters, OR [*Library symbol Library of Congress*] (LCLS)

OrSibyll .... Sibylline Oracles (Pseudepigrapha) (BJA)

OrSil .... Silverton Public Library, Silverton, OR [*Library symbol Library of Congress*] (LCLS)

ORSIP .... Office of Research, Statistics, and International Policy [*Later, ORS*] [*Social Security Administration*] (IID)

ORSL .... Order of the Republic of Sierra Leone

ORSociety ..... Operational Research Society [*British*] (DBA)

ORSociety ..... Operational Research Society (ACII)

ORSON .... Orient, Spell Out, Nail Down [*Method for organizing and communicating information, proposed by Barry Tarshis in his book "How to Write without Pain"*]

ORSORT	Oak Ridge School of Reactor Technology [*Department of Energy*]
OrSp	Springfield Public Library, Springfield, OR [*Library symbol Library of Congress*] (LCLS)
ORS(S)	Operational Research Section (Singapore) [*Military*]
OrSt	Stayton Public Library, Stayton, OR [*Library symbol Library of Congress*] (LCLS)
OR St B	Operation Rescue Saint Bernard [*Test given to Junior Woodchucks in Donald Duck comic by Carl Barks*]
Or St B Bull	Oregon State Bar Bulletin [*A publication*] (DLA)
OrStbM	Mount Angel College, Mount Angel Abbey, St. Benedict, OR [*Library symbol Library of Congress*] (LCLS)
OrStf	Stanfield Public Library, Stanfield, OR [*Library symbol*] [*Library of Congress*] (LCLS)
OrSthDH	Columbia District Hospital, Medical Library, St. Helens, OR [*Library symbol Library of Congress*] (LCLS)
ORSTOM	Office de la Recherche Scientifique et Technique Outre-Mer (USDC)
ORSV	Odontoglossum Ringspot Virus [*Plant pathology*]
ORT	Northway, AK [*Location identifier FAA*] (FAAL)
ORT	Oak Ridge [*Tennessee*] [*Seismograph station code, US Geological Survey*] (SEIS)
ORT	Object Relations Technique [*Psychology*]
ORT	Ooty Radio Telescope [*India*]
ORT	Operating Room Technician [*Medicine*]
ORT	Operationally Ready Time
ORT	Operational Readiness Test
ORT	Operational Readiness Training [*Army*]
ORT	Optical Relay Tube (MCD)
ORT	Optical Rotary Table
ORT	Optimum Resolution Technique
ORT	Oral Rehydration Therapy
ORT	Orbital Rendezvous Technique (AAG)
ORT	Orbit Readiness Test [*NASA*] (NASA)
ORT	Order of Railroad Telegraphers [*Later, Transportation-Communication Employees Union*] (EA)
ORT	Ordnance Repair Truck [*British*]
ORT	Organization for Rehabilitation through Training [*Acronym is used in names of several Jewish social welfare organizations*]
ORT	Orient-Avia [*Former USSR*] [*FAA designator*] (FAAC)
ORT	Original Running Time [*Movies*] (CDAI)
Ort	Ortho Diagnostics
ORT	Overhaul RADAR Technology
ORT	Overland RADAR Technology (MCD)
ORTA	Office of Research and Technology Applications [*Gaithersburg, MD*] [*National Institute of Standards and Technology*] (GRD)
ORTA	Office of Research and Technology Applications [*Berkeley, CA*] [*Lawrence Berkeley Laboratory*] [*Department of Energy*] (GRD)
ORTA	Office of Research and Technology Applications [*Army*] (RDA)
ORTA	Optical Relay Tube Assembly (MCD)
ORTAG	Operations Research Technical Assistance Group [*Army*] (PDAA)
ORTAI	Orbit-to-Air Intercept (IAA)
ORTC	Organized Reserve Training Center [*Military*]
ORTC	Ortec International, Inc. [*NASDAQ symbol*] (SAG)
ORTC	Ortec Intl. [*NASDAQ symbol*] (TTSB)
ORTC	Ortec Intl. Wrrt'B' [*NASDAQ symbol*] (TTSB)
ORT/CTL	Operational Readiness Training - Combat Training Launch [*Military*] (SAA)
ORTCW	Ortec Intl. Wrrt'A' [*NASDAQ symbol*] (TTSB)
ORTE	Operational Readiness Training Equipment [*Military*] (SAA)
ORTEC	Oak Ridge Technical Enterprises Corp.
OR tech	Operating Room Technician (DAVI)
OrtecInt	Ortec International, Inc. [*Associated Press*] (SAG)
Ortel	Ortel Corp. [*Associated Press*] (SAG)
ORTF	Office de la Radio et de la Television Francaise [*State-owned radio and television network*] [*France*]
ORTF	Office de Radiodiffusion-Television Francaise [*National Broadcasting Organization*] [*France*] (NTCM)
ORTF	Organization Radio Television France (IAA)
ORTH	Orthodox
ORTH	Orthography
ORTH	Orthopedic
ORTH	Orthopedic Technology, Inc. [*NASDAQ symbol*] (SAG)
Orthfx	Orthofix International [*Associated Press*] (SAG)
orthg	Orthogonals (VRA)
Ort Hist	Ortolan's History of the Roman Law [*A publication*] (DLA)
Orthlog	Orghologic Corp. [*Associated Press*] (SAG)
ORTHO	American Orthopsychiatric Association (EA)
ORTHO	Orthochromatic [*Photography*] (ROG)
ORTHO	Orthopedic
ORTHO	Orthopedic
Orthodon	Orthodontic Centers of America, Inc. [*Associated Press*] (SAG)
ORTHOG	Orthagonal
ORTHOG	Orthogonal (NASA)
Ortho-K	Orthokeratology [*Medicine*]
orthop	Orthopnea [*Medicine*] (DAVI)
orthopod	Orthopedist [*Orthopedic Physician*] (DAVI)
OrthopT	Orthopedic Technology, Inc. [*Associated Press*] (SAG)
OrTig	Tigard Public Library, Tigard, OR [*Library symbol Library of Congress*] (LCLS)
Ort Inst	Ortolan's Justinian's Institutes [*A publication*] (DLA)
OrtInt	Ortec International, Inc. [*Associated Press*] (SAG)
ORTL	Ortel Corp. [*NASDAQ symbol*] (SAG)
ORTN	Officie Radiodiffusion Television du Niger [*Radio and television network*] [*Niger*]
ORTO	Olympics Radio and Television Organization [*Organisme de Radio-Television des Olympiques*] [*Canada*]
ORTP	Operational Readiness Training Program [*Military*] (AABC)
Or TR	Oregon Tax Reporter [*A publication*] (DLA)
Or T Rep	Oregon Tax Reporter [*A publication*] (ILCA)
Or T Rep	Orleans Term Reports [*1, 2 Martin*] [*Louisiana*] [*A publication*] (DLA)
Ort Rom Law	Ortolan's History of the Roman Law [*A publication*] (DLA)
ORTS	Operational Readiness Test System [*Military*] (CAAL)
ORTS	Optional Residential Telephone Service [*Telecommunications*] (TEL)
ORTT	Operational Readiness Training Test [*Army*] (AABC)
ORTT	Overreaching Transfer Trip (IAA)
ORTU	Organized Reserve Training Unit [*Military*]
OrTua	Tualatin Public Library, Tualatin, OR [*Library symbol Library of Congress*] (LCLS)
ORTUAG	Organized Reserve Training Unit, Vessel Augmentation [*Military*]
OrTuaM	Meridian Park Hospital, Medical Library, Tualatin, OR [*Library symbol Library of Congress*] (LCLS)
ORTUAM	Organized Reserve Training Unit, Administration of Mobilization [*Military*]
ORTUAV	Organized Reserve Training Unit, Aviation Support [*Military*]
ORTUEL	Organized Reserve Training Unit, Electronics [*Military*]
ORTUF	Organized Reserve Training Unit, Coastal Force [*Military*]
ORTUPS	Organized Reserve Training Unit, Port Security [*Military*]
ORTUPS(0)	Organized Reserve Training Unit, Port Security (Operational) [*Military*]
ORTUR	Organized Reserve Training Unit, Rescue Coordination Center [*Military*]
OrTW	Wasco County Library, The Dalles, OR [*Library symbol Library of Congress*] (LCLS)
ORTX	Ortner Air Service [*Air carrier designation symbol*]
ORU	On-Line Replacement Unit [*Computer science*] (MCD)
ORU	Operational Readiness Unit
ORU	Optical Reference Unit
ORU	Optimal Replaceable Unit (IAA)
ORU	Oral Roberts University [*Oklahoma*]
ORU	Orange & Rockland Utilities, Inc. [*NYSE symbol*] (SPSG)
ORU	Orange/Rockland Util [*NYSE symbol*] (TTSB)
ORU	Orbital Replaceable Unit (SSD)
ORU	Orbital Replacement Unit (MCD)
oru	Oregon [*MARC country of publication code Library of Congress*] (LCCP)
ORU	Organization for Rebirth of Ukraine (EA)
ORU	Oruro [*Bolivia*] [*Airport symbol*] (AD)
ORU	Other than Ship or Squadron Reinforcement Unit [*Naval Reserve*] (DNAB)
ORU	Russell Branch, Russell Township Public Library, Ontario [*Library symbol National Library of Canada*] (BIB)
OrU	University of Oregon, Eugene, OR [*Library symbol Library of Congress*] (LCLS)
ORU	University of Oregon Library, Eugene, OR [*OCLC symbol*] (OCLC)
OrU-C	University of Oregon, Computing Center, Eugene, OR [*Library symbol Library of Congress*] (LCLS)
OrU-D	University of Oregon, Dental School, Portland, OR [*Library symbol Library of Congress*] (LCLS)
ORUEF	Oral Roberts University Educational Fellowship (EA)
ORUFE	Operational Research Unit, Far East
OrUk	Ukiah Public Library, Ukiah, OR [*Library symbol*] [*Library of Congress*] (LCLS)
OrU-L	University of Oregon, Law Library, Portland, OR [*Library symbol Library of Congress*] (LCLS)
OrU-M	University of Oregon, Medical School, Portland, OR [*Library symbol Library of Congress*] (LCLS)
OrUma	Umatilla Public Library, Umatilla, OR [*Library symbol*] [*Library of Congress*] (LCLS)
OrUmaH	Umatilla Hospital, Umatilla, OR [*Library symbol*] [*Library of Congress*] (LCLS)
OrUmH	Umatilla Hospital, Umatilla, OR [*Library symbol Library of Congress*] (LCLS)
OrUn	Carnegie Public Library, Union, OR [*Library symbol Library of Congress*] (LCLS)
O/RUNN	Overrunning [*Automotive engineering*]
OrU-O	University of Oregon, Ocean and Coastal Law Center, Eugene, OR [*Library symbol*] [*Library of Congress*] (LCLS)
OrU-Or	University of Oregon, Oriental Museum, Portland, OR [*Library symbol Library of Congress*] (LCLS)
ORUP	Ocean Resource Utilization Program (ASF)
ORUS	Official Register of the United States
OrU-S	University of Oregon, Science Division Library, Eugene, OR [*Library symbol Library of Congress*] (LCLS)
ORuss	Old Russian [*Language*] (BARN)
OrV	Fern Ridge Community Library, Veneta, OR [*Library symbol Library of Congress*] (LCLS)
ORV	Noorvik [*Alaska*] [*Airport symbol*] (OAG)
ORV	Oceanographic Research Vessel
ORV	Ocean Range Vessel [*Air Force*]
ORV	Off-Road Vehicle
ORV	Orbital Reentry Vehicle [*NASA*] (IAA)
ORV	Orbital Rescue Vehicle [*NASA*] (KSC)
ORV	Orbital Return Vehicle [*NASA*]
ORV	Oroville [*California*] [*Seismograph station code, US Geological Survey*] (SEIS)
ORVAT	Organizational Vehicle Automatic Tester
ORVC	River Valley Community Library, Ontario [*Library symbol National Library of Canada*] (NLC)
ORVID	Online X-ray Evaluation over Video-Display Including Documentation (PDAA)
ORVR	On-Board Refueling Vapor Recovery [*Automotive engineering*]

ORVR............ On-Board Refueling Vapor Recovery
ORVX........... OraVax, Inc. [NASDAQ symbol] (SAG)
ORW............ Norwich, CT [Location identifier FAA] (FAAL)
ORW............ Orange Walk [British Honduras] [Airport symbol] (AD)
ORW............ Orwell Resources Ltd. [Vancouver Stock Exchange symbol]
ORW............ Orwex [Poland ICAO designator] (FAAC)
ORW............ Outstanding Resource Waters [Water quality standards] [Environmental Protection Agency]
ORW............ Owner's Risk of Becoming Wet [Shipping]
ORW............ Raymond Walters General and Technical College, Blue Ash, OH [OCLC symbol] (OCLC)
OrWe .... Weston Public Library, Weston, OR [Library symbol] [Library of Congress] (LCLS)
OrWel .... West Linn Public Library, West Linn, OR [Library symbol Library of Congress] (LCLS)
OrWelH......... West Linn High School, West Linn, OR [Library symbol Library of Congress] (LCLS)
ORWG........... Operational Requirements Working Group (DOMA)
OrWi .... Willamina Public Library, Willamina, OR [Library symbol Library of Congress] (LCLS)
ORWISE....... Otherwise (ROG)
OrWo .... Woodburn Public Library, Woodburn, OR [Library symbol Library of Congress] (LCLS)
ORWP.......... Optical Radiation Weapon Program (AAG)
ORX............. Oriximina [Brazil] [Airport symbol] (AD)
ORX............. Oryx Aviation [South Africa ICAO designator] (FAAC)
ORX............. Oryx Energy Co. [NYSE symbol] (SPSG)
ORY .... Paris [France] Orly Airport [Airport symbol] (OAG)
Oryx............ Oryx Energy Co. [Associated Press] (SAG)
ORYX........... Oryx Technology [NASDAQ symbol] (TTSB)
ORYX........... Oryx Technology Corp. [NASDAQ symbol] (SAG)
OryxTc......... Oryx Technology Corp. [Associated Press] (SAG)
ORYXW........ Oryx Technology Wrrt [NASDAQ symbol] (TTSB)
ORZ............. Omnirange Zero (IAA)
ORZ............. Omnirange Zone
ORZ............. Orange Walk [Belize] [Airport symbol Obsolete] (OAG)
ORZ............. Outer Radiation Zone
OS............... Austrian Airlines [ICAO designator] (AD)
OS............... By Mouth [Pharmacy] (DAVI)
OS............... Obese Strain [White leghorn]
OS............... Object-Subject [Education of the hearing-impaired]
OS............... Oblique Sounding [Telecommunications] (OA)
OS............... Observation-Scouting Plane [When first two letters in Navy designation]
OS............... Observing Station [Marine science] (MSC)
OS............... Occupational Safety (DAVI)
OS............... Oceanic Society (EA)
OS............... Ocean Station [Maps and charts]
OS............... Octavian Society (EA)
OS............... Oculus Sinister [Left Eye] [Ophthalmology]
OS............... Odd Symmetric
OS............... Office of Systems [NASA] (KSC)
OS............... Office of the Secretary
OS............... Officers' Steward [Ranking title] [British Women's Royal Naval Service]
OS............... Office System
OS............... Official Station
OS............... Off Scale (IAA)
OS............... Off Screen [or Stage]
OS............... Offset
OS............... Ohio State Reports [A publication] (DLA)
OS............... Oil Solenoid
OS............... Oil Switch
OS............... Old Saxon [Language, etc.]
OS............... Old School
OS............... Old Series
OS............... Old Side
OS............... Old Standard [Currency] (ROG)
OS............... Old Style [Printing] (NTCM)
OS............... Old Style [Calendar, previous to 1752]
OS............... Omega Society [Defunct] (EA)
OS............... Omnibus Society [British]
OS............... One Shot
OS............... One Side
OS............... One-Stop [Aviation]
OS............... Only Son
OS............... On-Orbit Station [NASA] (MCD)
OS............... On Sale
OS............... On Sample
OS............... On Schedule
O/S.............. On Sea [In place names] [British] (ROG)
OS............... On Sheet (WGA)
OS............... On Side
OS............... On-Site
OS............... On Spot (ROG)
OS............... On Station [Military]
OS............... On Switch
OS............... Opening Snaps [Cardiology]
OS............... Operating Schedule [Field stations] (MCD)
OS............... Operating Software (MCD)
OS............... Operating System [Computer science] (BUR)
O/S.............. Operational Assist Project/Shipborne Application
OS............... Operational Sequence (KSC)
OS............... Operational Sheets
OS............... Operational Specialist [Navy]

OS............... Operational Suitability
OS............... Operational Supplements [Air Force] (MCD)
OS............... Operation Sandstone [Atomic weapons testing]
OS............... Operation Smile (EA)
OS............... Operation Snapper [Atomic weapons testing]
OS............... Operations Specialist [Navy] (DNAB)
OS............... Operation Suburbia [Defunct] (EA)
OS............... Operator's Set
OS............... Optical Scanning [Computer science]
OS............... Optical Society (NADA)
OS............... Optics Subsystem
OS............... Optics Subsystem (NASA)
OS............... Option Spreading [Investment term]
OS............... Oral Surgery
OS............... Oral Suspension [Pharmacy]
OS............... Orbiter CEI [Contract End Item] Specification [NASA] (NASA)
OS............... Order of Servites
OS............... Order Sheet
OS............... Ordinary Seaman [British]
OS............... Ordnance School [Army] (MCD)
OS............... Ordnance Services [Military British]
OS............... Ordnance Specifications [Navy]
OS............... Ordnance Survey
OS............... Oregon Steel Mills [NYSE symbol] (SPSG)
OS............... Organizational Source [Online database field identifier] [Computer science]
OS............... Organizations System (IAA)
OS............... Original Series
OS............... Ornamental Stitching (DNAB)
OS............... Oro Sellado [Standard Gold] [Business term Spanish]
O/S.............. Orthopaedic Surgery [Medical Officer designation] [British]
OS............... Orthopedics (DAVI)
OS............... Orthopedic Surgery (DAVI)
OS............... Orton Society [Later, ODS] (EA)
OS............... Osgood-Schlatter's Disease [Medicine]
Os................ Osmium [Chemical element]
OS............... Osmotic Shock
OS............... Osteogenic Sarcoma [Medicine]
OS............... Osteosarcoma [Oncology]
OS............... Osteosclerosis [Medicine] (DAVI)
OS............... Other Side [A publication] (BRI)
OS............... Other Sources
OS............... Otherwise Specified (MSA)
OS............... Outer Sheath [Botany]
OS............... Outlaw Shark [RADAR surveillance] [Naval Electronic Systems Command]
OS............... Outline Square Condition [Vision]
O/S.............. Out of Service (AFM)
O/S.............. Out-of-Shot [Photography]
OS............... Out of Stock (NTCM)
OS............... Output Secondary [Electronics]
OS............... Outside
OS............... Outside Sentinel
OS............... Outsize [Of clothes]
O/S.............. Outstanding
OS............... Outstation (MCD)
OS............... Out Stealing [Baseball]
OS............... Overlong Sentence [Used in correcting manuscripts, etc.]
OS............... Overscene [Films, television, etc.]
OS............... Oversea [Military]
O/S.............. Overshipped (MCD)
OS............... Oversize (AAG)
OS............... Overspecificity [Psychometrics]
OS............... Over-the-Horizon Targeting System (MCD)
OS............... Over-the-Shoulder Cinematography (NTCM)
OS............... Over the State [Regarding distribution]
OS............... Own Ship [Navy] (CAAL)
OS............... Oxygen Sensor [Automotive engineering]
OS............... Oxygen Service (DNAB)
OS............... Sarnia Public Library, Ontario [Library symbol National Library of Canada] (NLC)
OS............... Shell Development Co. [Research code symbol]
OS............... Test Oscilloscope [JETDS nomenclature] [Military] (CET)
OS............... Warder Public Library of Springfield and Clark County, Springfield, OH [Library symbol Library of Congress] (LCLS)
OS/2............ Operating System 2 [Computer science]
OS 2d .... Ohio State Reports, Second Series [A publication] (DLA)
OSA .... Aero Astra [Mexico ICAO designator] (FAAC)
OSA .... Augustinian Nuns of Contemplative Life (TOCD)
OSA .... [The] Augustinians (TOCD)
osa .... [The] Augustinians (TOCD)
OSA .... Augustinian Sisters of Our Lady of Consolation (TOCD)
OSA .... Congregation of Augustinian Sisters Servants of Jesus and Mary (TOCD)
OSA .... Obstructive Sleep Apnea [Medicine]
OSA .... Occupational Safety Aid
OSA .... Office of Savings Associations [Formerly, FHLIC]
OSA .... Office of Services to the Aging (DAVI)
OSA .... Office of Special Activities (CINC)
OSA .... Office of State Administration [Australia]
OSA .... Office of the Secretary of the Army
OSA .... Office of the Special Assistant to the Ambassador
OSA .... Official Secrets Act [British]
OSA .... Offshore Acquisition [Army] (AABC)
OSA .... Oklahoma Statutes Annotated [A publication] (DLA)

OSA .... Old South Arabic (BJA)
OSA .... Old Style Antique [*British*]
OSA .... Omnibus Society of America (EA)
OSA .... Ontario Society of Artists [*Canada*] (BARN)
OSA .... Open Systems Architecture [*Computer science*]
OSA .... Operational Support Aircraft [*or Airlift*]
OSA .... Operational Support Airlift [*Air Force*] (DOMA)
OSA .... Operational Support Area (NASA)
OSA .... Operational Support Area
OSA .... Operation Sciences Appliquees [*Quebec*]
OSA .... Optical Society of America (EA)
OSA .... Optimization by Simulated Annealing [*Mathematics*]
OSA .... Order for Simple Alert (NATG)
OSA .... Order of St. Anne [*Anglican religious community*]
OSA .... Order of St. Augustine [*See also OFSA*] [*Rome, Italy*] (EAIO)
OSA .... Order-Sorting Aperture [*Instrumentation*]
OSA .... Ormec Serro Analyst (NITA)
osa .... Osage [*MARC language code Library of Congress*] (LCCP)
OSA .... Osaka [*Japan*] [*Seismograph station code, US Geological Survey*] (SEIS)
OSA .... Osaka [*Japan*] [*Airport symbol*] (OAG)
OSA .... Ossa Resources, Inc. [*Vancouver Stock Exchange symbol*]
OSA .... Outfit Supply Activity (MCD)
OSA .... Overseas Supply Agency [*Military*]
OSA .... Overspenders Anonymous (EA)
OSa .... Sabina Public Library, Sabina, OH [*Library symbol Library of Congress*] (LCLS)
OSA .... Sisters of St. Augustine (TOCD)
OSA .... Sisters of St. Rita (TOCD)
OSAA .... Operational Satellite Active Archive [*Marine science*] (OSRA)
OSAA .... Operational Satellite Active Archive (USDC)
OSA (ABCMR)... Office, Secretary of the Army (Army Board for Correction of Military Records)
OSAC .... Orifice Spark Advance Control [*Valve*] [*Automotive technology*]
OSAC .... Overseas Schools Advisory Council [*Department of State*] [*Washington, DC*] (EGAO)
OSAC .... Overseas Security Advisory Council [*Department of State*] [*Washington, DC*] (EGAO)
OSACI .... Ecumenical Study and Action Centre on Investment [*Netherlands*]
OSAD A & L... Office of the Secretary of the Army for Development / Acquisition and Logistics
OSADBU ...... Office of Small and Disadvantaged Business Utilization (AAGC)
OS/AEL .... Operating Space/Allowance Equipage List
OSAF .... Office of the Secretary of the Air Force
OSAFO .... Office of the Special Assistant for Field Operations [*Formerly, CORDS*] (VNW)
OSAH .... Health Sciences Library, Sudbury Algoma Hospital, Sudbury, Ontario [*Library symbol National Library of Canada*] (NLC)
OSAHRC ...... Occupational Safety and Health Review Commission [*Department of Labor*]
OSAI .... Office of Systems Analysis and Information [*Department of Transportation*]
OSAIS .... Oil Spillage Analytical and Identification Service [*Laboratory of the Government Chemist*] (PDAA)
OSAIS .... Oil Spillage Analytical Information Service (NITA)
OSAK .... OSI [*Open Systems Interconnection*] Applications Kernel [*Computer science*] (TNIG)
Osaka Pref Bull... Osaka Prefecture. University. Bulletin [*A publication*] (DLA)
Osaka ULR... Osaka University. Law Review [*A publication*] (DLA)
Osaka UL Rev... Osaka University. Law Review [*A publication*] (DLA)
Osaka Univ L Rev... Osaka University. Law Review [*Osaka, Japan*] [*A publication*] (DLA)
OSAL .... Opening of Salivary [*Gland*]
OSal .... Salem Public Library, Salem, OH [*Library symbol Library of Congress*] (LCLS)
OSALC .... Savant Lake Community Library, Ontario [*Library symbol National Library of Canada*] (NLC)
OSalK .... Kent State University, Columbiana Regional Campus, Salem, OH [*Library symbol Library of Congress*] (LCLS)
OSALSAA .... Office, Special Assistant for Logistical Support of Army Aircraft (AABC)
OSALSTC ..... Office, Special Assistant for Logistical Support of Tactical Communications (AABC)
OSAM .... Overflow Sequential Access Method [*Computer science*]
OSAMM .... Optimum Supply and Maintenance Model [*Army*] (RDA)
OSAMS .... Synod Office, Diocese of Moosonee, Anglican Church of Canada, Schumacher, Ontario [*Library symbol National Library of Canada*] (NLC)
OSand .... Sandusky Library Association, Sandusky, OH [*Library symbol Library of Congress*] (LCLS)
OS & CP Dec... Ohio Superior and Common Pleas Decisions [*A publication*] (DLA)
OS & D .... Over, Short, and Damaged [*Report*] [*Shipping*] (MSA)
OS & DR ..... Over, Short, and Damaged Report [*Shipping*]
OS & FM ..... Office of Systems and Financial Management [*DoD*]
OS & RP ..... On-Board Spares and Repair Parts [*Navy*] (DNAB)
OS & TD ...... Ocean Science and Technology Division [*Office of Naval Research*] (DNAB)
OS & W ...... Oak, Sunk, and Weathered [*Construction*]
OS & Y .... Outside Screw and Yoke
OSAP .... Aleppo/Neirab [*Syria*] [*ICAO location identifier*] (ICLI)
OSAP .... Ocean Surveillance Air Patrol (CINC)
OSAP .... Ocean Survey Advisory Panel [*Marine science*] (MSC)
OSAP .... Office of Substance Abuse Prevention [*Department of Agriculture*] (EGAO)
OSAP .... Office Space Allocation Plan (MCD)

OSAPI .... Operating System/Application Program Interface [*Computer science*]
OSAR .... Operations Suitability Assessment Report (SSD)
OSAR .... Optical Storage and Retrieval [*Computer science*]
OSAR .... Overhead Systems Apprearance Research (IAA)
OSarS .... Southern State Community College, Sardinia, OH [*Library symbol Library of Congress*] (LCLS)
OSART .... Operational Safety Review Team [*International Atomic Energy Agency*]
OSAS .... Obstructive Sleep Apnea Syndrome [*Medicine*] (DMAA)
OSAS .... Ohio Social Acceptance Scale (EDAC)
OSAS .... Open Systems Accounting Software [*Computer science*]
OSAS .... Overseas Service Aid Scheme
OSASF .... Overseas Supply Agency, San Francisco [*Military*] (CINC)
OSASN .... Office of Special Assistant, Secretary of the Navy
OSAT .... Office for the Study of Automotive Transportation [*Department of Transportation*]
OSAT .... Office of the Special Assistant for Training [*Army*] (RDA)
OSAT .... Optical Sensor and Tracker
OSATA .... Order of Saint Andrew the Apostle (EA)
OSAY .... Outside Screw and Yoke (IAA)
OSB .... Benedictine Congregation of Our Lady of Monte (TOCD)
OSB .... Benedictine Monks (TOCD)
osb .... Benedictine Monks, Olivetan Benedictines, Sylvestrine Benedictines (TOCD)
OSB .... Benedictine Nuns (TOCD)
OSB .... Benedictine Nuns of the Congregation of Solesmes (TOCD)
OSB .... Benedictine Nuns of the Primitive Observance (TOCD)
OSB .... Benedictine Sisters (TOCD)
OSB .... Benedictine Sisters of Liberty (TOCD)
OSB .... Benedictine Sisters of Pontifical Jurisdiction (TOCD)
OSB .... Benedictine Sisters of Sacred Heart (TOCD)
OSB .... Congregation of Jesus Crucified (TOCD)
OSB .... Congregation of the Benedictine Sisters of Perpetual Adoration of Pontifical Jurisdiction (TOCD)
OSB .... Congregation of the Benedictine Sisters of the Sacred Heart (TOCD)
OSB .... Contemplative Sisters of St. Benedict (TOCD)
OSB .... Missionary Benedictine Sisters (TOCD)
OSB .... Ocean Sciences Board [*NASA*] (MSC)
OSB .... Office of Savings Bonds [*Navy*]
OSB .... Officer Selection Battery [*Military*]
OSB .... Officer Selection Board
OSB .... Olivetan Benedictine Sisters (TOCD)
OSB .... One-Statement Banking (MHDB)
OSB .... Operational Status BIT [*Binary Digit*]
OSB .... Operations Stations Book [*Navy*]
OSB .... Operations Support Building [*NASA*] (KSC)
OSB .... Operative Society of Bricklayers [*A union*] [*British*]
OSB .... Orangeburg [*South Carolina*] [*Seismograph station code, US Geological Survey*] (SEIS)
OSB .... Orbital Solar Observation (IAA)
OSB .... Order of Shepherds of Bethlehem (EA)
OSB .... Order of the Stars and Bars [*Later, MOSB*] (EA)
OSB .... Ordinis Sancti Bernardi [*Order of St. Bernard*] [*Latin*] (ROG)
OSB .... Ordnance Supply Bulletin
OSB .... Ordo Sancti Benedicti [*Order of St. Benedict*] [*Roman Catholic religious order*]
OSB .... Oriented-Strand Board [*A plywood panel composition*]
OSB .... Osage Beach [*Missouri*] [*Airport symbol Obsolete*] (OAG)
OSB .... Sauble Beach Branch, Bruce County Public Library, Ontario [*Library symbol National Library of Canada*] (NLC)
OSBA .... Outlet and Switch Box Association [*Defunct*] (EA)
OSBA Bull... Ohio State Bar Association. Bulletin [*A publication*] (DLA)
OSBC .... Old Second Bancorp [*NASDAQ symbol*] (TTSB)
OSBC .... Old Second Bancorp, Inc. [*NASDAQ symbol*] (SAG)
OSBCam ...... Camaldolese Benedictine Sisters (TOCD)
osbcam .... Camaldolese Hermits (TOCD)
OSBCam ...... Camaldolese Hermits (TOCD)
OSBF .... Damascus [*Syria*] [*ICAO location identifier*] (ICLI)
OSBF .... OSB Financial [*NASDAQ symbol*] (SAG)
OSBF .... OSB Finl Corp. [*NASDAQ symbol*] (TTSB)
OSB Fn .... OSB Financial [*Associated Press*] (SAG)
OSBL .... Outside Battery Limits [*Chemical engineering*]
OSBM .... Morrison Library Outpost, Severn Bridge, Ontario [*Library symbol National Library of Canada*] (NLC)
OSBM .... Office of Space Biology and Medicine [*Proposed for NASA*]
osbm .... Order of St. Basil the Great (TOCD)
OSBM .... Ordo Sancti Basil Magni [*Order of St. Basil the Great*] [*Roman Catholic religious order*]
OSBM .... Sisters of the Order of St. Basil the Great (TOCD)
OSBN .... Osborn Communications [*NASDAQ symbol*] (TTSB)
OSBN .... Osborn Communications Corp. [*NASDAQ symbol*] (NQ)
Osborn .... Osborn Communications [*Associated Press*] (SAG)
Osborn .... Osborne Communications Corp. [*Associated Press*] (SAG)
OSBR .... Seeley's Bay Branch, Rideau Lakes Union Library, Ontario [*Library symbol National Library of Canada*] (BIB)
OSBRD .... Office of Small Business Research and Development [*National Science Foundation*] (GRD)
OSBS .... Oblate Sisters of the Blessed Sacrament [*Roman Catholic religious order*]
OSBT .... Officer Selection Battery Test [*Military*]
OSC .... Canonici Regulares Ordinis Sanctae Crucis [*Canons Regular of the Order of the Holy Cross*] [*Crosier Fathers*] [*Roman Catholic religious order*]
osc .... Canons Regular of the Order of the Holy Cross, Crosier Fathers (TOCD)

OSC .... Clan Grant No. 17, Order of Scottish Clans (EA)
OSC .... Clark County Technical Institute, Springfield, OH [Library symbol Library of Congress] (LCLS)
OSC .... Complete Operational Software [Telecommunications] (TEL)
OSC .... Oak Satellite Corp. (NITA)
OSC .... Obedience Stewards Club (EA)
OSC .... Objective Supply Capability [Army] (RDA)
OSC .... Oblate Spherical Coordinates
OSC .... Oblati Sancti Caroli [Oblate Fathers of St. Charles] [Roman Catholic religious order]
OSC .... Occupational Standards Council (AIE)
OSC .... Ocean Science Committee [National Academy of Sciences/Ocean Affairs Board] (NOAA)
OSC .... Ocean Sciences Center [Memorial University of Newfoundland] [Canada]
OSC .... Office of Space Communications [NASA] (BARN)
OSC .... Office of Special Counsel [Federal agency]
OSC .... Office of the Security Council
OSC .... Officer Specialty Code [Army] (INF)
OSC .... Offshore Survival Centre [Robert Gordon's Institute of Technology] [British] (CB)
OSC .... Ogden [Utah] Service Center [IRS]
O-SC .... Ohio Supreme Court, Columbus, OH [Library symbol Library of Congress] (LCLS)
OSC .... One Shoe Crew [An association] (EA)
OSC .... On-Scene Commander [Navy] (NVT)
OSC .... On-Scene Coordinator [Environmental Protection Agency] (FFDE)
OSC .... On-Site Safety Committee (IAA)
OSC .... Ontario Securities Commission (HGAA)
OSC .... Operational Simulator Console
OSC .... Operational Summary Console
OSC .... Operational Support Center (NRCH)
OSC .... Operational Support Chart [Nuclear energy] (NUCP)
OSC .... Operational Switching Cabinet
OSC .... Operations Sequence Chart (MCD)
OSC .... Operator Services Complex [Telecommunications] (TEL)
OSC .... Optical Sciences Center [University of Arizona] [Research center] (RCD)
OSC .... Optical Signature Code
OSC .... Optical String Switch Controller (NITA)
OSC .... Orangeburg [South Carolina] [Seismograph station code, US Geological Survey Closed] (SEIS)
OSC .... Orbital Sciences Corp.
OSC .... Orbit Shift Coil
OSC .... Order of St. Clare [Roman Catholic women's religious order]
OSC .... Order to Show Cause
OSC .... Ordnance Store Corps [British military] (DMA)
OSC .... Ordnance Systems Command [Formerly, Bureau of Naval Weapons; later, Naval Sea Systems Command]
OSC .... Oregon State College [Later, OSU]
OSC .... Organic Sulfur Compound [Organic chemistry]
OSC .... Organizational Structure Code [Air Force] (AFIT)
OSC .... Organizational Supply Code [Army] (AABC)
OSC .... Oscillate [or Oscillation, Oscillator, Oscillograph, Oscilloscope] (KSC)
osc .... Oscillator (IDOE)
OSC .... Oscoda, MI [Location identifier FAA] (FAAL)
OSC .... Osmotically Sensitive Cell
OSC .... Outer Space Contact
OSC .... Out of Stock, Canceled [Business term]
OSC .... Output State Check [Electronics]
OSCN .... Out, See Copy [Proofreader's note]
OSC .... Overlapping Spreading Centers [Geology]
OSC .... Overlap Slotted Container [Packaging]
OSC .... Overseas Settlement Committee [World War I] [British]
OSC .... Overseas Staff College [British]
OSC .... Overseas Supply Committee [World War II]
OSC .... Own Ship's Course [Navy]
OSC .... Oxidatively Solubilized Coal [Fuel technology]
OSC .... Oxygenated Sterol Compound [Biochemistry]
OSC .... Royal Clan, Order of Scottish Clans [Later, Independent Order of Foresters] (EA)
OSC .... Scugog Public Library, Ontario [Library symbol National Library of Canada] (NLC)
OSC .... Sisters of St. Clare (TOCD)
OSC .... Southern State Community College, Wilmington, OH [OCLC symbol] (OCLC)
OSCA .... Office of Saver and Consumer Affairs [Federal Reserve Board]
OSCA .... Office of Senior Citizens Affairs (NADA)
OSCA .... Office of State Corporate Affairs [Western Australia]
OSCA .... Optical Sensors Collaborative Association [British] (DBA)
OSCAA .... Oil Spill Control Association of America [Later, SCAA] (EA)
oscam .... Camillian Fathers and Brothers (TOCD)
OS Cam .... Order of St. Camillus [Camillians] [Roman Catholic religious order]
OSCAND .... Old Scandinavian [Language, etc.]
OSCAP .... Operating System Communication Application Program [Computer science]
OSCAR .... Observation Schedule and Records
OSCAR .... Online Serials Control at Ratcliffe (NITA)
OSCAR .... On-Site Computer Assisted Research [Oscar, Inc.] [Information service or system] (IID)
OSCAR .... Operating Sequence Control Array [NASA]
OSCAR .... Operational System Characteristics
OSCAR .... Operations, Scheduling, Control, and Reporting (MCD)
OSCAR .... Optically Scanned Character Automatic Reader [Computer science] (DIT)

OSCAR .... Optical Submarine Communications by Aerospace Relay
OSCAR .... Optimum Survival Containment and Recovery (AAG)
OSCAR .... Optimum System for the Control of Aircraft Retardation
OSCAR .... Optimum Systems Covariance Analysis Results (IEEE)
OSCAR .... Orbiting Satellite Carrying Amateur Radio [Telecommunications] (TEL)
OSCAR .... Order Status Control and Reporting [Telecommunications] (TEL)
OSCAR .... Oregon State Conversational Aid to Research [Computer science] (CSR)
OSCAR .... Organisation for Sickle Cell Anemia Research [British]
OSCAR .... Organization for Scientific Coordination in AIDS [Acquired Immune Deficiency Syndrome] Research, Inc. [New York, NY]
OSCAR .... Oscillogram Scan and Recorder System (PDAA)
OSCAR .... Overnight Statewide Customer Accounting Reporting (IAA)
OSCAR II .... Outside Cable Rehabilitation II [Army] (RDA)
OSCARS .... Order Status Control and Reporting System [Telecommunications]
OSCB .... College Bibliocentre, Scarborough, Ontario [Library symbol National Library of Canada] (BIB)
OSCCap .... Capuchin Poor Clares (TOCD)
OSCCB .... On-Site Change Control Board [Military] (CAAL)
OSCCJA .... Casimir, Jennings, and Appleby Public Library, St. Charles, Ontario [Library symbol National Library of Canada] (NLC)
OSCD .... Ohio Supreme Court Decisions, Unreported Cases [A publication] (DLA)
OSCD .... Ontario Securities Commission Decisions [QL Systems Ltd.] [Information service or system Canada] (CRD)
OSCE .... Office of Child Support Enforcement (USGC)
OSCE .... Office Statistique des Communautes Europeennes [Statistical Office of the European Communities - EUROSTAT] [Commission of the European Communities]
OSCE .... Organisation for Security and Co-Operation in Europe (ECON)
OSCER .... Offshore Survival Craft Emergency Radiotelephone [Telecommunications] (PDAA)
OSCF .... Operations Support Computing Facility (MCD)
OSCG .... Information Resource Centre, Consumers Gas, Scarborough, Ontario [Library symbol National Library of Canada] (NLC)
OSCG .... Oscillating
OSCG .... Oscillograph, String
OSCGRM .... Oscillogram [Engineering]
OSCH .... Schreiber Public Library, Ontario [Library symbol National Library of Canada] (NLC)
OSCILAB .... Ocean Science Laboratory [Oceanography]
OSCILLOSC .. Oscilloscope (IAA)
OSCL .... Operating System Control Language (NITA)
OSCL .... Own Ship's Centerline [Navy]
OSCMF .... Oxygen Scavenging Cell Membrane Fragment [Biochemistry]
OSCMIS .... Operating and Support Costs Management Information System (MCD)
OSC-MULT ... Oscillator-Multiplier [Telecommunications] (TEL)
OSCO .... Organizational Source Code (NITA)
OSCOM .... Oslo Commission (EAIO)
OSCOT .... Overall Systems Combat Operability Test [Navy] (ANA)
OSCP .... Ocean Sediment Coring Program [National Science Foundation]
OSCP .... Oscilloscope (AAG)
OSCP .... Oscilloscope Panel
OSCPS .... Oxygen Supply and Cabin Pressurization Section [Apollo] [NASA]
OSCR .... Ocean Surface Current RADAR
OSCR .... Operating and Support Cost Reduction [Army]
OSCR .... Operations and Sustainment Cost Reduction Strategy (RDA)
OSCRL .... Operating System Command and Response Language
OSCRN .... Oil Screen
OSCUT .... Oil Spill Clean-Up Technology (ASF)
OSD .... Dow Chemical Co., Sarnia, Ontario [Library symbol National Library of Canada] (NLC)
OSD .... Office of Standards Development [Abolished] [Nuclear Regulatory Commission]
OSD .... Office of Student Detachment [Navy]
OSD .... Office of Systems Development [Social Security Administration]
OSD .... Office of the Secretary of Defense
OSD .... Officer Service Date [Air Force] (AFM)
OSD .... Officers Service Dress [British military] (DMA)
OSD .... Online System Drivers [NCR Corp.]
OSD .... Open Shelter Deck [Shipping] (DS)
OSD .... Open Software Description [Computer science]
OSD .... Operational Sea Vehicle Diagram (MCD)
OSD .... Operational Sequence Diagram (IEEE)
OSD .... Operational Support Directive [Military] (AFM)
OSD .... Operational Systems Development (MCD)
OSD .... Operations Subdirective
OSD .... Optical Scanning Device [Computer science]
OSD .... Ordinis Sancti Dominici [Order of St. Dominic] [Latin] (ROG)
OSD .... Ordnance Safing Device
OSD .... Ordnance Store Department [British] (ROG)
OSD .... Ordnance Supply Depot
OSD .... Osgood Semantic Differential [Occupational therapy]
OSD .... Ostersund [Sweden] [Airport symbol] (OAG)
OSD .... Out of Stock for the Duration [Business term] (DGA)
OSD .... Overseas Duty
OSD .... Overseas Settlement Department [World War I] [British]
OSD .... Overseas Standards Digest [A publication] (ADA)
OSD .... Overseas Supply Division [Military]
OSD .... Over, Short, and Damaged [Report] [Shipping] (MCD)
OSD .... Overside Drainage [Medicine] (DAVI)
OSD .... Own Ship's Distance [Navy] (MCD)
OSD .... Oxygen Selective Detector [Chromatography]

OSDA.......... Oceanic System Development and Support [*FAA*] (TAG)
OSDBMC...... Office of the Secretary of Defense, Ballistic Missile Committee
OSDBU........ Office of Small and Disadvantaged Business Utilization [*See also SDBU/CR*] [*Agency for International Development*]
OSD/CSD ..... Open Shelter Deck/Closed Shelter Deck [*Shipping*] (DS)
OSD/DSAA ... Office of the Secretary of Defense, Defense Security Assistance Agency (MCD)
OSDH......... Orbiter System Definition Handbook [*NASA*] (NASA)
OSDI.......... Damascus/International [*Syria*] [*ICAO location identifier*] (ICLI)
OSDIDBAD... Office of the Secretary of Defense Identification Badge [*Military decoration*] (GFGA)
OSDIdentBad... Office of the Secretary of Defense Identification Badge (AABC)
OSD/ISA...... Office of the Secretary of Defense for International Security Affairs
OSDIT........ Office of Software Development and Information Technology [*General Services Administration*]
OSDIU........ Over-the-Horizon Targeting System Digital Interface Unit
OSDM......... Optical Space-Division Multiplexing (EECA)
OSDMT .... Organization for the Support of Democratic Movement of Taiwan (EA)
OSDOC........ Offshore Discharge of Container-Ships (RDA)
OSDOC........ Over-the-Shore Discharge of Cargo [*Navy*] (CAAL)
OS/DOS....... Operating System/Disk Operating System [*Software*]
OSDP .... On-Site Data Processing [*or Processor*] [*NASA*]
OSDP .... Operational System Development Program
OSDP .... Operations System Development Program [*Marine science*] (OSRA)
OSD(PA & E)... Office of the Secretary of Defense for Program Analysis and Evaluation (MCD)
OSDPT........ Optimization of Systems for Data Processing and Transmission (PDAA)
OSDR......... Oil Slick Detection RADAR
OSD-SA....... Office of the Secretary of Defense - Systems Analysis
OSDSAC...... Office of the Secretary of Defense, Scientific Advisory Committee
OSDT .... Damascus [*Syria*] [*ICAO location identifier*] (ICLI)
OSDU .... Output Signal Distribution Unit (MCD)
OSDV .... Oat Sterile Dwarf Virus [*Plant pathology*]
OSDZ .... Deir Ez Zor [*Syria*] [*ICAO location identifier*] (ICLI)
OSE........... Bethel, AK [*Location identifier FAA*] (FAAL)
OSE........... Edwardsburg Township Public Library, Spencerville, Ontario [*Library symbol National Library of Canada*] (BIB)
OSE........... Occupational Supplies and Equipment [*Red Cross*]
OSE........... Ocean and Science Engineering Inc.
OSE........... Oceanic Society Expeditions (EA)
OSE........... Office of Systems Engineering [*Social Security Administration*]
OSE........... Officer Scheduling the Exercise [*Navy*] (NVT)
OSE........... Olefin Strain Energy [*Organic chemistry*]
OSE........... Omniforce Spatial Environment (AAG)
OS/E.......... Operating System/Environment [*Computer science*] (BYTE)
OSE........... Operational Security Evaluation (MCD)
OSE........... Operational Support Equipment
OSE........... Operation Status Equipment
OSE........... Orbital Sequence of Events [*NASA*] (IAA)
OSE........... Orbiter Support Equipment [*NASA*] (NASA)
OSE........... Order of the Star in the East [*A theosophical organization*]
OSE........... Organizational Support Equipment [*Army*]
OSE........... Osaka Stock Exchange [*Japan*]
OSE........... Osec Petroleum [*Vancouver Stock Exchange symbol*]
OSE........... Overall System Effectiveness (IAA)
OSE........... Overseas Security Eligibility [*DoD*]
OSE........... Salem Public Library, Salem, OR [*OCLC symbol*] (OCLC)
OSE........... Union Mondiale pour la Protection de la Sante des Populations Juives et Oeuvres de Secours aux Enfants
OSEAP .... Oil Shale Environmental Advisory Panel [*Department of the Interior*]
OSEAS........ Ocean Sampling and Environmental Analysis System (PDAA)
O/SEAS .... Overseas
OSEC......... Office of the Secretary
OSEC......... Office Systems Education and Counseling (HGAA)
OSECCA...... Old Sleepy Eye Collectors' Club of America (EA)
OSECY .... Office of the Secretary to the Staff [*NATO*] (NATG)
OSEDS........ Operational Support Equipment Design Specification
OSEE......... Optically Stimulated Electron Emission [*Also, PEE*] [*Physics*]
O/SEER .... Overseer
OSEH......... Order of St. Elizabeth of Hungary [*Anglican religious community*]
OSEM......... Office of Systems Engineering Management [*Department of Transportation*]
OSEOS........ Operational Synchronous Earth Observatory Satellite [*Telecommunications*] (TEL)
OSEP .... Office of Scientific and Engineering Personnel [*National Academy of Sciences*] [*Information service or system*] (IID)
OSEP .... Office of Special Education Programs [*Also, SEP*] [*Department of Education*]
OSERS........ Office of Special Education and Rehabilitative Services [*Department of Education*]
OSES .... Operations Systems Engineering Support (MCD)
OSESG........ Oil Sands Environmental Study Group [*Canada*]
OSF........... Bernardine Sisters of the Third Order of St. Francis (TOCD)
OSF........... Congregation of the Religious Brothers of the Third Order Regular of St. Francis (TOCD)
OSF........... Congregation of the Sisters of the Third Order of St. Francis Oldenburg, IN (TOCD)
OSF........... Congregation of the Third Order of St. Francis of Mary Immaculate, Joliet IL (TOCD)
OSF........... Franciscan Brothers of Christ the King (TOCD)
osf........... Franciscan Brothers of Christ the King (TOCD)
osf........... Franciscan Brothers of the Third Order Regular (TOCD)
OSF........... Franciscan Missionaries of Our Lady (TOCD)

osf .... Franciscan Missionary Brothers of the Sacred Heart of Jesus (TOCD)
OSF........... Franciscan Missionary Brothers of the Sacred Heart of Jesus (TOCD)
OSF........... Franciscan Missionary Sisters for Africa (TOCD)
OSF........... Franciscan Missionary Sisters of Our Lady of Sorrows (TOCD)
OSF........... Franciscan Missionary Sisters of the Immaculate Conception (TOCD)
OSF........... Franciscan Sister, Daughters of the Sacred Hearts of Jesus and Mary (TOCD)
OSF........... Franciscan Sisters of Allegany, New York (TOCD)
OSF........... [*The*] Franciscan Sisters of Baltimore (TOCD)
OSF........... Franciscan Sisters of Chicago (TOCD)
OSF........... Franciscan Sisters of Christian Charity (TOCD)
OSF........... Franciscan Sisters of Christ the Divine Teacher (TOCD)
OSF........... Franciscan Sisters of Little Falls, Minnesota (TOCD)
OSF........... Franciscan Sisters of Our Lady of Perpetual Help (TOCD)
OSF........... Franciscan Sisters of St. Paul (TOCD)
OSF........... Franciscan Sisters of the Immaculate Conception (TOCD)
OSF........... Franciscan Sisters of the Immaculate Conception and St. Joseph for the Dying (TOCD)
OSF........... Franciscan Sisters of the Sacred Heart (TOCD)
OSF........... Fransciscan Brothers of the Third Order Regular (TOCD)
OSF........... Hospital Sisters of the Third Order of St. Francis (TOCD)
OSF........... Missionary Franciscan Sisters of the Immaculate Conception (TOCD)
OSF........... Obtain Service From [*Navy*] (NVT)
OSF........... Ocean Simulation Facility [*Naval Coastal Systems Laboratory*] (DNAB)
OSF........... Odd Side Flat
OSF........... Office of Space Flight [*NASA Washington, DC*] (NASA)
OSF........... Office of Space Flight [*NASA*]
OSF........... Office Systems Family (HGAA)
OSF........... Open Software Foundation
OSF........... Open Systems Foundation
OSF........... Operational Service Fee (WDAA)
OSF........... Operation Support Facility [*National Weather Service*] (USDC)
OSF........... Operation Support Facility [*Marine science*] (OSRA)
OSF........... Optically-Shaped Film
OSF........... Order of St. Francis [*Franciscans*] [*Roman Catholic religious order*]
OSF........... Ordinary Shareholders Fund (WDAA)
OSF........... Ordnance Storage Facility (KSC)
OSF........... Organ System Failure [*Medicine*]
OSF........... Osaka Stock Futures [*Japan*] (ECON)
OSF........... Outer Spiral Fibers [*Ear anatomy*]
OSF........... Out of Stock, To Follow [*Business term*]
OSF........... Overgrowth Stimulating Factor [*Cancer cause*]
OSF........... Oxidation-Induced Stacking Fault (PDAA)
osf........... Religious Brothers of the Third Order Regular of St. Francis (TOCD)
OSF........... School Sisters of St. Francis (TOCD)
OSF........... School Sisters of the Third Order of St. Francis (Bethlehem, PA) (TOCD)
OSF........... School Sisters of the Third Order of St. Francis (Panhandle, TX) (TOCD)
OSF........... School Sisters of the Third Order of St. Francis (Pittsburgh, PA) (TOCD)
OSF........... Servants of the Holy Infancy of Jesus (TOCD)
OSF........... Sisters of Saint Francis, Clinton, Iowa (TOCD)
OSF........... Sisters of Saint Francis of Milvale, Pennsylvania (TOCD)
OSF........... Sisters of Saint Francis of the Providence of God (TOCD)
OSF........... Sisters of St. Francis (TOCD)
OSF........... Sisters of St. Francis of Christ the King (TOCD)
OSF........... Sisters of St. Francis of Penance and Christian Charity (TOCD)
OSF........... Sisters of St. Francis of Perpetual Adoration (TOCD)
OSF........... Sisters of St. Francis of Savannah, MO (TOCD)
OSF........... Sisters of St. Francis of the Congregation of Our Lady of Lourdes, Sylvania, Ohio (TOCD)
OSF........... Sisters of St. Francis of the Holy Cross (TOCD)
OSF........... Sisters of St. Francis of the Holy Eucharist (TOCD)
OSF........... Sisters of St. Francis of the Holy Family (TOCD)
OSF........... Sisters of St. Francis of the Immaculate Conception (TOCD)
OSF........... Sisters of St. Francis of the Immaculate Heart of Mary (Hankinson, North Dakota) (TOCD)
OSF........... Sisters of St. Francis of the Martyr St. George (TOCD)
OSF........... Sisters of St. Francis of the Third Order Regular (Williamsville, New York) (TOCD)
OSF........... Sisters of the Third Franciscan Order (TOCD)
OSF........... Sisters of the Third Order of St. Francis of Penance and Charity (TOCD)
OSF........... Sisters of the Third Order of St. Francis (Peoria, IL) (TOCD)
OSF........... Sisters of the Third Order Regular of St. Francis of the Congregation of Our Lady of Lourdes (TOCD)
OSF........... St. Francis Mission Community (TOCD)
OSF........... The Sisters of St. Francis of Assisi (TOCD)
OSF........... The Sisters of St. Francis of Philadelphia (TOCD)
OSFA......... Office of Student Financial Assistance [*Department of Education*] (GFGA)
OSFA......... Offshore Shrimp Fisheries Act of 1973
OSFAR........ Sturgeon Falls Branch of the Algonquin Regional Library System, Ontario [*Library symbol National Library of Canada*] (NLC)
OSFC .... Fiberglas Canada, Inc., Sarnia, Ontario [*Library symbol National Library of Canada*] (NLC)
OSFC .... Ordinis Sancti Francisci Capuccini [*Franciscan Capuchins*] [*Roman Catholic men's religious order*]
OSFCO........ Office of Solid Fuels Coordinator [*Military*] (DNAB)
OSFCSR....... Rideau Regional Centre, Ministry of Community and Social Services, Smiths Falls, Ontario [*Library symbol National Library of Canada*] (NLC)
OSFCW .... Office of Solid Fuels Coordinator for War [*World War II*]

OSFD .... Office of Space Flight Development [*Obsolete NASA*]
OSFI .... Office of the Superintendent of Financial Institutions [*Department of Insurance*] [*Ottawa, ON*] [*Information service or system*] (IID)
OSFI .... Open Steel Flooring Institute [*Defunct*]
OSFM .... Office of Spacecraft and Flight Missions [*NASA*]
OSFP .... Office of Space Flight Programs [*Obsolete NASA*]
osfs .... Oblates of St. Francis de Sales (TOCD)
OSFS .... Oblates of St. Francis de Sales (TOCD)
OSFS .... Oblati Sancti Francisci Salesii [*Oblate Fathers or Sisters of St. Francis of Sales*] [*Roman Catholic religious orders*]
OSFT .... ObjectSoft Corp. [*NASDAQ symbol*] (SAG)
OSG .... Occupations Study Group [*British*]
OSG .... Office of Sea Grant [*National Oceanic and Atmospheric Administration*]
OSG .... Office of the Secretary General [*United Nations*]
OSG .... Office of the Solicitor General [*Department of Justice*]
OSG .... Office of the Surgeon General [*of Public Health Service; later, absorbed by office of Assistant Secretary for Health and Scientific Affairs*]
OSG .... Operand Select Gate [*Computer science*]
OSG .... Operations Support Group [*Nuclear energy*] (NRCH)
OSG .... Organization and Staffing Guide [*Department of Labor*] (OICC)
OSG .... Osphradial Ganglion [*In mollusks*]
OSG .... Otosclerosis Study Group (EA)
OSG .... Overseas Shiphldg [*NYSE symbol*] (TTSB)
OSG .... Overseas Shipholding Group, Inc. [*NYSE symbol*] (SPSG)
OSG .... South Gillies Library, Ontario [*Library symbol National Library of Canada*] (BIB)
OSGB .... Orchid Society of Great Britain (EAIO)
OSGD .... Office of Sea Grant Development [*National Oceanic and Atmospheric Administration*] (MSC)
OSGLI .... Office of Servicemen's Group Life Insurance
OSGP .... Office of Sea Grant Programs [*National Oceanic and Atmospheric Administration*]
OSGR .... Oscillator Single Gain Region (PDAA)
OSGS .... Office of the Secretary of the General Staff
OSGS .... Stittsville Branch, Goulbourn Township Public Library, Ontario [*Library symbol National Library of Canada*] (NLC)
OSH .... Community Hospital of Springfield, Springfield, OH [*Library symbol Library of Congress*] (LCLS)
OSH .... National Institute for Occupational Safety and Health, Cincinnati, OH [*OCLC symbol*] (OCLC)
OSH .... Occupational Safety and Health [*Department of Labor*]
OSH .... Office on Smoking and Health Database [*Centers for Disease Control*] [*Information service or system*] (CRD)
OSH .... Omni Singula Hora [*Every Hour*] [*Pharmacy*]
OSH .... Ordo Sancti Hieronymi [*Hieronymites*]
OSH .... Oshawa Group Ltd. [*Toronto Stock Exchange symbol*]
OSH .... Oshima [*Japan*] [*Seismograph station code, US Geological Survey*] (SEIS)
OSH .... Oshkosh [*Wisconsin*] [*Airport symbol*] (OAG)
OSH .... Oshman's Sporting Gds [*AMEX symbol*] (TTSB)
OSH .... Oshman's Sporting Goods, Inc. [*AMEX symbol*] (SAG)
OSH .... Own Ship's Heading [*Navy*]
OSh .... Shaker Heights Public Library, Shaker Heights, OH [*Library symbol Library of Congress*] (LCLS)
OSH .... Shelburne Public Library, Ontario [*Library symbol National Library of Canada*] (NLC)
OSHA .... Occupational Safety and Health Act [*1970*]
OSHA .... Occupational Safety and Health Administration [*Department of Labor*] [*Washington, DC*]
OSHA .... Office of Special Housing Assistance [*HUD*]
Oshap .... OSHAP Technologies Ltd. [*Associated Press*] (SAG)
OSHB .... One-Sided Height Balanced [*Telecommunications*]
OshB .... Oshkosh B'Gosh, Inc. [*Associated Press*] (SAG)
OSHB .... Sheshegwaning Band Public Library, Ontario [*Library symbol National Library of Canada*] (NLC)
OSHC .... Orchard Supply Hardware Stores Corp. [*NASDAQ symbol*] (SAG)
OSHC .... Outside School Hours Care
OSHC .... Overseas Student Health Coverage
OSH Cas ...... Occupational Safety and Health Cases [*A publication*] (DLA)
OSHD .... Occupational Safety and Health Decisions [*A publication*] (DLA)
OSH Dec ...... Occupational Safety and Health Decisions [*A publication*] (DLA)
OShelS .... Sacred Heart Seminary, Shelby, OH [*Library symbol Library of Congress*] (LCLS)
OSHI .... Occupational, Safety, and Health Institute [*University of Houston*] [*Research center*] (RCD)
OSHJ .... Oblate Sisters of the Sacred Heart of Jesus [*Roman Catholic religious order*]
OshkT .... Oshkosh Truck Corp. [*Associated Press*] (SAG)
OShL .... Shaker Heights Public Library, Shaker Heights, OH [*Library symbol*] [*Library of Congress*] (LCLS)
Oshmn .... Oshman's Sporting Goods, Inc. [*Associated Press*] (SAG)
OSHRC .... Occupational Safety and Health Review Commission [*Department of Labor*]
OSHS .... Occupational Safety and Health Statistics [*Bureau of Labor Statistics*] (GFGA)
OSHS .... OSHAP Technologies Ltd. [*NASDAQ symbol*] (NQ)
OShS .... Shaker Heights City School District, Shaker Heights, OH [*Library symbol Library of Congress*] (LCLS)
OSHSF .... Oshap Technologies Ltd. [*NASDAQ symbol*] (TTSB)
OSHT .... Grand Lodge Order of the Sons of Hermann in Texas [*San Antonio, TX*] (EA)
OSHT .... Sharon Temple, Sharon, Ontario [*Library symbol National Library of Canada*] (NLC)

OSI .... Aerosi SA de CV [*Mexico ICAO designator*] (FAAC)
OSI .... National Institute for Occupational Safety and Health, Rockville, MD [*OCLC symbol*] (OCLC)
OSI .... Office of Samoa Information [*Press agency*]
OSI .... Office of Scientific Information [*National Science Foundation*] (MCD)
OSI .... Office of Scientific Integrity [*National Institutes of Health*]
OSI .... Office of Scientific Intelligence [*Fictitious government agency on TV series "The Six Million Dollar Man"*]
OSI .... Office of Seniors' Interests [*Australia*]
OSI .... Office of Special Investigation [*Air Force*]
OSI .... Office of Strategic Information [*DoD*]
OSI .... Office of Strategic Intelligence [*Air Force*] (INF)
OSI .... Office of Systems Integration [*Social Security Administration*]
OSI .... Office Systems Interconnection [*Telecommunications*] (TSSD)
OSI .... Offshore Islands (CINC)
OSI .... On-Site Inspection
OSI .... Open Space Institute (EA)
OSI .... Open Standards Interconnection [*International Standards Organisation*]
OSI .... Open System Interconnections [*Networking technique*]
OSI .... Open Systems Interconnect
OSI .... Operating Space Item [*Military*] (CAAL)
OSI .... Operating System Interface
OSI .... Operating Systems, Inc. (MCD)
OSI .... Operational Status Indicator (MUGU)
OSI .... ORDALT [*Ordnance Alterations*]/SHIPALT Inspector [*Ship Alteration*] (MCD)
OSI .... Organic Sign Index [*Psychology*]
OSI .... Oriental Shorthairs International (EA)
OSI .... Osijek [*Former Yugoslavia*] [*Airport symbol*] (OAG)
OSI .... Other Support Items
OSI .... Out of Stock, Indefinite [*Business term*]
OSI .... Overhead Supply Inventory (MCD)
OSI .... Oyster Shell Institute (EA)
OSI .... Ozark Society (EA)
OSI .... Research Technical Information Centre, ESSO Petroleum Canada, Sarnia, Ontario [*Library symbol National Library of Canada*] (NLC)
OSI .... Woodside, CA [*Location identifier FAA*] (FAAL)
OSIA .... Office, Services and Information Agency [*Military*] (AABC)
OSIA .... On-Site Inspection Agency [*DoD*]
OSIA .... Order Sons of Italy in America (EA)
OSIA .... Outdoor Systems [*NASDAQ symbol*] (TTSB)
OSIA .... Outdoor Systems, Inc. [*NASDAQ symbol*] (SAG)
OSIASL .... Order Sons of Italy in America Supreme Lodge [*Later, OSIA*] (EA)
OSIC .... Ocean Science Information Center [*University of Hawaii*] (NOAA)
OSIC .... Oil Spill Information Center [*Santa Barbara, CA*]
OSIC .... Optimization of Subcarrier Information Capacity
OSICOM .... Open Systems Interconnections Division [*Now Open Systems Interconnection Division*] (ACII)
Osicom .... Osicom Technologies, Inc. [*Associated Press*] (SAG)
OSICS .... Commission Scolaire de Sept-Iles, Quebec [*Library symbol National Library of Canada*] (NLC)
OSID .... Open Systems Interconnection Division (ACII)
OSID .... Operational System Interface Document (MCD)
OSIDM .... Eva Brook Donly Museum, Simcoe, Ontario [*Library symbol National Library of Canada*] (NLC)
OSIE .... Office of Software Improvement and Engineering [*Social Security Administration*]
OSIE .... Open Systems Interconnection Environment [*Telecommunications*] (OSI)
OSIE .... Operational Support Integration Engineering
OS/IES .... On-Site Integrated Energy System
OSIGA .... Ohio State Inventory of Guidance Awareness
OSIGO .... Office of the Chief Signal Officer
OSII .... Objective Sys Integrators [*NASDAQ symbol*] (TTSB)
OSII .... Objective Systems Integrators, Inc. [*NASDAQ symbol*] (SAG)
OSIL .... Lynwood Arts Centre, Simcoe, Ontario [*Library symbol National Library of Canada*] (NLC)
OSIL .... Operating System Implementation Language
OSINH .... Norfolk Historical Society, Simcoe, Ontario [*Library symbol National Library of Canada*] (NLC)
OSI/NMF ...... Open Systems Interconnect Network Management Forum [*Computer science*] (BTTJ)
OSIP .... Operational and Safety Improvement Program (NVT)
OSIP .... Operational Suitability Improvement Program [*Aviation*]
OSIP .... Simcoe Public Library, Ontario [*Library symbol National Library of Canada*] (NLC)
OS/IPC .... Operating System/Inter-Process Communications (DOMA)
OSIQ .... Offer Self-Image Questionnaire
OSIQA .... Offer Self-Image Questionnaire for Adolescents (EDAC)
OSIR .... Office of Scientific Integrity Review [*US Secretary of Health*]
OSIR .... Oil Spill Intelligence Report
Os-Ir .... Osmiridium (IDOE)
OSIR .... Out of Service in Reserve [*Military*] (CINC)
OSIRIS .... Online Search Information Retrieval Information Storage [*Computer science*] (PDAA)
OSIS .... Ocean Surveillance Information System [*Navy*] (MCD)
OSIS .... Office of Science Information Service [*National Science Foundation*]
OSITOP .... Open Systems Interconnection Technical and Office Protocols [*Telecommunications*] (OSI)
OSJ .... Oblates of St. Joseph [*Roman Catholic religious order*]
osj .... Oblates of St. Joseph (TOCD)
OSJ .... Office of Supervisory Jurisdiction [*Investment term*]
OSJ .... Sovereign Order of Saint John of Jerusalem (EA)

OSJD	Ordinis Sancti Joannis de Deo [Order of St. John of God]
OSK	Osaka [Takayasuyama] [Japan] [Seismograph station code, US Geological Survey] (SEIS)
OSK	Oskarshamn [Sweden] [Airport symbol] (OAG)
OSKAR	Outstanding Superior Kitchen All-Rounder [Trademark of Sunbeam Corp.]
OSKL	Kamishly [Syria] [ICAO location identifier] (ICLI)
OSKL	Swastika Branch, Kirkland Lake Public Library, Ontario [Library symbol National Library of Canada] (BIB)
OSKNC	Skead Branch, Nickel Centre Public Library, Ontario [Library symbol National Library of Canada] (NLC)
OSKY	Mahaska Investment [NASDAQ symbol] (TTSB)
OSKY	Mahaska Investment Co. [NASDAQ symbol] (SAG)
OSL	International Order of Saint Luke the Physician (EA)
OSL	Oil Seal
OSL	Old [Church] Slavonic [Language, etc.]
OSL	Old Style Latin (ADA)
OSL	Open/Short Locator
OSL	Operating System Language
OSL	Operator Set Loop [Electronics] (ECII)
OSL	Optically Stimulated Luminescence [Analytical Chemistry]
OSL	Optical Storage Ltd.
OSL	Orbiting Space Laboratory
OSL	Order of St. Luke the Physician of America (EA)
OSL	Ordnance Sub-Lieutenant [British military] (DMA)
OSL	Oregon Short Line Railroad [of Union Pacific Railroad Co.]
OSL	Osler Resources, Inc. [Vancouver Stock Exchange symbol]
OSL	Oslo [Norway] [Airport symbol] (OAG)
OSL	O'Sullivan Corp. [AMEX symbol] (SPSG)
OSL	Outstanding Leg [NASA] (KSC)
OSL	Sioux Lookout Public Library, Ontario [Library symbol National Library of Canada] (NLC)
OSL	University of Oregon, School of Librarianship, Eugene, OR [OCLC symbol] (OCLC)
OSLA	Stella Branch, Lennox and Addington County Library, Ontario [Library symbol National Library of Canada] (NLC)
O Slav	Old [Church] Slavic [Language] (BARN)
OSLB	Operational Search Lower Bound [RADAR]
OSLC	Lambton College of Applied Arts and Technology, Sarnia, Ontario [Library symbol National Library of Canada] (NLC)
OSLEAS	Association Sectorielle de Fabrication d'Equipement de Transport et de Machines,St.-Leonard, Quebec [Library symbol National Library of Canada] (NLC)
OSLFC	Sharbot Lake Branch, Frontenac County Library, Ontario [Library symbol National Library of Canada] (BIB)
OSLI	Office of Servicemen's Life Insurance (OICC)
OSLJ	Law Journal. Student Bar Association. Ohio State University [A publication] (DLA)
OSLK	Latakia/Latakia [Syria] [ICAO location identifier] (ICLI)
OSLM	Operations Shop/Laboratory Manager [NASA] (MCD)
OSLM	Operations Shop/Laboratory Manager
OSLR	Intergovernmental Committee for Ocean Science and Living Resources [Marine science] (OSRA)
OSLT	On-Site Logistics Team (MCD)
OSM	Mantellate Sisters, Servants of Mary of Blue Island (TOCD)
OSM	Mental Health Services for Clark County, Springfield, OH [Library symbol] [Library of Congress] (LCLS)
OSM	Mosul [Iraq] [Airport symbol] (AD)
OSM	Oblates of St. Martha (TOCD)
OSM	Office of Spectrum Management [US National Telecommunications and Information Administration] (TSSD)
OSM	Office of Surface Mining [Department of the Interior] (AAGC)
OSM	Office of Surface Mining Reclamation and Enforcement [Department of the Interior]
OSM	Off-Screen Model [Computer science]
OSM	Omnispectra Miniature
OSM	Oncostatin [Antibiotic]
OSM	On-Screen Manager [Computer science]
OSM	On-Screen Manager [Computer science]
OSM	On-Site Maintenance
OSM	On Station Mode
OSM	Operating Service Month
OSM	Operating System Manual (MCD)
OSM	Operating System Monitor
OSM	Operator's Service Manual
OSM	Opisu Struktur Mikroprogramowynch [Programming language] (CSR)
OSM	Optical Section Microscope
OSM	Option Select Mode [Computer science] (OA)
OSM	Orbital Service Module [NASA] (MCD)
OSM	Ordnance Safety Manual [Military]
OSM	Ordo Servorum Mariae [Order of Servants of Mary] [Servites] [Roman Catholic religious order]
OSM	Oscillating Secondary Mirror [Telescope]
osM	Osmolar [Chemistry] (DAVI)
Osm	Osmole [Physical chemistry]
OSM	Osmonics, Inc. [NYSE symbol] (SPSG)
OSM	Osmotic
OSM	Output Switch Module [Automotive engineering]
OSM	Outside Mail (AFM)
OSM	Outside of Metal
OSM	Ovine Submaxillary Mucin [Medicine] (DMAA)
OSM	Oxygen Saturation Meter (MAE)
OSM	Oxygen Steel Making
OSM	Schumacher Memorial Library, Ontario [Library symbol National Library of Canada] (BIB)
OSM	Servants of Mary (TOCD)
osm	Servite Fathers (TOCD)
OSM	Servites (TOCD)
OSMA	Occidental Society of Metempiric Analysis (EA)
OSMA	Office of Small Manufacturers Assistance [FDA]
OSMA	Optical Spectrometric Multichannel Analyzer [Instrumentation]
OSMA	Orthopedic Surgical Manufacturers Association (EA)
OSMA	Overseas Sales and Marketing Association of America [Lake Bluff, IL] (EA)
OSME	Oral Speech Mechanism Screening Examination [Educational test]
OSME	Ornithological Society of the Middle East (EAIO)
OSMED	Otospondylomegaepiphyseal Dystrophy [Medicine] (DAVI)
OSMF	Smith Falls Public Library, Ontario [Library symbol National Library of Canada] (NLC)
OS/MFT	Operating System/Multiprogramming Fixed Task (NITA)
OS/MFT	Operating System/Multiprogramming with a Fixed Number of Tasks [IBM Corp.] [Computer science]
OSML	McNeil Laboratories (Canada) Ltd., Stouffville, Ontario [Library symbol National Library of Canada] (NLC)
OSMM	Mercy Medical Center, Springfield, OH [Library symbol Library of Congress] (LCLS)
OSMM	Office of Safeguards and Materials Management [AEC]
OSMM	Optimum Supply and Maintenance Model
osmo	Osmolality [Chemistry]
osmol	Osmole [Measurement] (DAVI)
Osmonic	Osmonics, Inc. [Associated Press] (SAG)
OSMOS	Own Ship's Motion Simulator [Navy]
OSMOS	Own Ship's Motion System [Navy]
OSMP	Operational Support Maintenance Plan [NASA] (MCD)
OSMR	Office of Systems Modernization Requirements [Social Security Administration]
OSMRE	Office of Surface Mining Reclamation and Enforcement [Also, OSM] [Department of the Interior]
OSMS	Organizational Supply Management System [Army] (INF)
OSM S	Osmolarity Serum [Biochemistry] (DAVI)
OSMU	Oesterreichische Schuhmusterschau [Austrian Footwear Exhibition] [Wiener Messen und Kongress GmbH] (TSPED)
OSM U	Osmolarity Urine [Biochemistry] (DAVI)
OSMV	Oat Striate Mosaic Virus [Plant pathology]
OSMV	One Shot Multivibrator (MSA)
OS/MVS	Operating System/Multiprogramming with Virtual Storage [Computer science]
OS/MVT	Operating System/Multiprogramming with a Variable Number of Tasks [Computer science]
OSN	Ocean Science News (USDC)
OSN	Ocean Science News [Marine science] (OSRA)
OSN	Office of the Secretary of the Navy
OSN	Off Service Note [Medicine] (DAVI)
OSN	Osphradial Nerve [In mollusks]
OSN	Output Sequence Number
OSN	Sioux Narrows Public Library, Ontario [Library symbol National Library of Canada] (NLC)
OSNAP	Object Snap [Auto CAD] [Computer science]
OSNC	Sarnia Northern Collegiate, Ontario [Library symbol National Library of Canada] (NLC)
OSNLR	Ocean Science in Relation to Non-Living Resources [Marine science] (OSRA)
OSNS	Shedden Public Library, Spanish, Ontario [Library symbol National Library of Canada] (NLC)
OSNSW	Office of the Sheriff of New South Wales [Australia]
OSO	Ocean Systems Operation [NASA]
OSO	Office of Systems Operations [Social Security Administration]
OSO	Officer Selection Office (DNAB)
OSO	Offshore Suppliers Office [British]
OSO	Onsala Space Observatory [Sweden]
OSO	Operations Scheduling Office (SSD)
OSO	Orbiting Satellite Observer (IEEE)
OSO	Orbiting Scientific Observatory (IAA)
OSO	Orbiting Solar Observatory [A satellite]
OSO	Ordnance Supply Office
OSO	Oregon State Library, Salem, OR [OCLC symbol] (OCLC)
O/S/O	Ore/Slurry/Oil [Supertanker]
OSO	Origination Screening Office [Telecommunications] (TEL)
OSO	Southampton Branch, Bruce County Public Library, Ontario [Library symbol National Library of Canada] (NLC)
OSOB	Old Senate Office Building [Also, RSOB] [Washington, DC] (DLA)
OSOC	Off-Site Originated Change (AAG)
OSODS	Office of Strategic Offensive and Defensive Systems [Navy]
OSOG	Office Systems Owners Group (HGAA)
OSOIPB	Ordnance Supply Office Illustrated Parts Breakdown [Navy]
OSol	Odes of Solomon (BJA)
OSOL	Office of the Solicitor [Department of Labor]
OS/OLM	On-Site/On-Line Maintenance
OSOM	Bruce County Museum, Southampton, Ontario [Library symbol National Library of Canada] (BIB)
OSOP	Off-Site Operations Plan (SSD)
OSOP	Orbiter Systems Operating Procedures [NASA] (NASA)
OSOR	Operational Standoff Range (NVT)
OSoSJ	Saint Joseph's Priory, Somerset, OH [Library symbol Library of Congress] (LCLS)
OSOT	Oakland Township Public Library, Scotland, Ontario [Library symbol National Library of Canada] (BIB)
OSOTM	Sombra Township Museum, Ontario [Library symbol National Library of Canada] (BIB)
OSP	Obiit sine Prole [Died without Issue] [Latin]

OSP .... Oblate Sisters of Providence [*Roman Catholic religious order*]
OSP .... Ocean Surveillance Product (DOMA)
OSP .... Ocean Survey Plan [*or Program*] [*Navy*]
OSP .... Office of Science Policy [*National Science Foundation*]
OSP .... Office of Scientific Personnel [*NAS-NRC*]
OSP .... Office of Special Technology [*Formerly, Office of Special Projects*] [*Washington, DC Department of Energy*] (GRD)
OSP .... Office of Staffing Policy [*Office of Personnel Management*] [*Washington, DC*] (GRD)
OSP .... Office of Surplus Property [*Superseded by War Assets Corporation*] [*World War II*]
OSP .... Office of the Special Prosecutor [*Queensland, Australia*]
OSP .... Offshore Procurement [*Army*]
O-SP .... Off-Street Parking
OSP .... Oficina Sanitaria Panamericana [*Pan-American Sanitary Bureau - PASB*] [*Washington, DC*]
OSP .... Oil Suction Pump (MSA)
OSP .... On Station Position (MUGU)
OSP .... Operating Steam Pressure (MSA)
OSP .... Operating System Plan (SAA)
OSP .... Operational Surveillance Program [*Nuclear Regulatory Commission*] (NRCH)
OSP .... Operational Survival Plan [*Civil Defense*]
OSP .... Operations Support Plan [*Navy*] (NG)
OSP .... Optical Signature Program [*Military*] (CAAL)
OSP .... Optimum Sustainable Population [*Marine science*] (MSC)
OSP .... Optoelectronic Systems Programme [*British*]
OSP .... Orbital Support Plan (MCD)
OSP .... Order of St. Paul [*Anglican religious community*]
OSP .... Order of St. Paul the First Hermit [*Pauline Fathers*] [*Roman Catholic religious order*]
OSP .... Original Set Pattern [*Ice dancing*]
OSP .... Outer Surface Protein [*Cytology*]
OSP .... Outfitting Stock Point
OSP .... Outside Plant [*Telecommunications*] (TEL)
OSP .... Outside Procured Stores (AAG)
OSP .... Outside Purchase (WDAA)
OSP .... Own Ship's Position [*Navy*] (MCD)
OSP .... Polysar Ltd., Sarnia, Ontario [*Library symbol National Library of Canada*] (NLC)
OSP .... Slupsk [*Poland*] [*Airport symbol*] (OAG)
OSPA .... Open Signal Coprocessing Architecture [*Computer science*]
OSPAAAL ..... Organization of Solidarity of the Peoples of Africa, Asia, and Latin America
OSPCS .... Charles M. Shields Centennial Library, South Porcupine, Ontario [*Library symbol National Library of Canada*] (BIB)
OSPD .... Office of Sponsored Program Development [*State University of New York at Binghamton*] [*Research center*] (RCD)
OSPE .... Organizational Spare Parts and Equipment [*Army*]
OSPES .... Outer Shell Photoelectron Spectroscopy
OSPF .... Open Shortest Path First [*Communications routing protocol*]
OSPG .... Original Society of Painters and Glaziers [*A union*] [*British*]
OS-PIF .... Office of the Secretary of Defense Productivity Investment Funding
OSPIRG .... Oregon State Public Interest Research Group [*Research center*] (RCD)
OSPJ .... Offshore Procurement, Japan
OSpM .... Mental Health Services for Clark County, Springfield, OH [*Library symbol Library of Congress*] (LCLS)
OSPNC .... Porcupine Campus, Northern College of Applied Arts and Technology, South Porcupine, Ontario [*Library symbol National Library of Canada*] (NLC)
OSPPE .... Pauline Fathers (TOCD)
osppe .... Pauline Fathers (TOCD)
OSPR .... Office of Oil Spill Prevention and Response
OSPR .... Palmyra [*Syria*] [*ICAO location identifier*] (ICLI)
OSPRDS ...... Oblate Spheroid (PDAA)
OSPREY .... Ocean Swell Powered Renewable Energy [*United Kingdom*]
OSPRO .... Ocean Shipping Procedures
OSPTM .... Timmins Museum, South Porcupine, Ontario [*Library symbol National Library of Canada*] (BIB)
OSQ .... Officer Separation Questionnaire (DNAB)
OSQ .... Officer Student Quarters (DNAB)
OSQ .... San Antonio, TX [*Location identifier FAA*] (FAAL)
OSR .... Occupational Survey Report
OSR .... Office of Scientific Research [*AFSC*]
OSR .... Office of Security Review [*Obsolete DoD*]
OSR .... Office of Sport and Recreation [*Australian Capital Territory*]
OSR .... Office of Standards and Regulations [*Environmental Protection Agency*] (GFGA)
OSR .... Office of Systems Requirements [*Social Security Administration*]
OSR .... Ohio State Reports [*A publication*] (DLA)
OSR .... Old Style Roman (ADA)
OSR .... Onsite Review [*Military*]
OSR .... Operand Storage Register [*Computer science*]
OSR .... Operational Scanning Recognition
OSR .... Operational Status Release [*Navy*] (NG)
OSR .... Operational Support Readiness
OSR .... Operational Support Requirement [*Military*]
OSR .... Operations Support Room [*NASA*] (KSC)
OSR .... Operations Support Room [*NASA*]
OSR .... Optical Scanning Recognition [*Computer science*]
OSR .... Optical Solar Reflector
OSR .... Optical Sound Recorder
OSR .... Optical Still Recorder [*LASER-disc technology*]
OSR .... Optimum Ship Routing [*Obsolete*]

OSR .... Ordnance Status Report (NG)
OSR .... Originators Status Report [*Army*]
OSR .... Oscar Resources Ltd. [*Vancouver Stock Exchange symbol*]
OSR .... Ostrava [*Former Czechoslovakia*] [*Airport symbol*] (OAG)
OSR .... Output Shift Register
OSR .... Output Signal Range
OSR .... Output Status Register
OSR .... Oversea Returnee [*Military*]
OSR .... Overseas Service Ribbon [*Military decoration*]
OSR .... Over-the-Shoulder Rating
OSR .... Own Ship's Roll [*Navy*]
OSR .... Oxide-Stable Resin
OSRA .... Office Systems Research Association [*Cleveland, OH*] (EA)
OSRAC .... Ocean Shipping Requirements and Capabilities
OSRC .... Oil Sands Research Centre [*Alberta*]
OSRD .... Office of Scientific Research and Development [*World War II*]
OSRD .... Office of Standard Reference Data [*Gaithersburg, MD*] [*National Institute of Standards and Technology*]
OSRDB .... Office of Standard Reference Data Bibliography [*National Institute of Standards and Technology*]
OS Rep .... Ohio State Reports [*A publication*] (DLA)
OSREPL .... Oversea Replacement [*Army*]
OSRET .... Oversea Returnee [*Army*]
OSRF .... Smooth Rock Falls Public Library, Ontario [*Library symbol National Library of Canada*] (NLC)
OSRI .... Originating Station Routing Identifier
OSRL .... Organizations and Systems Research Laboratory [*Army*] (RDA)
OSRM .... Office of Standard Reference Materials [*Gaithersburg, MD*] [*National Institute of Standards and Technology*] (GRD)
OSRM .... South River-Machar Union Public Library, South River, Ontario [*Library symbol National Library of Canada*] (NLC)
OSRO .... Office for the Sahelian Relief Operation [*UN Food and Agriculture Organization*]
OSRO .... Operations Support Requirements Office [*NASA*] (KSC)
OSRP .... Occupant Safety Research Partnership
OSRP .... Oil Spill Response Plan [*Pollution prevention*]
OSRPA .... Offices, Shops, and Railway Premises Act [*1963*] [*British*]
OSRR .... Spanish River Reserve Band Public Library, Ontario [*Library symbol National Library of Canada*] (NLC)
OSRS .... Operational Status Recording Subsystem
OSRTN .... Office of the Special Representative for Trade Negotiations [*Later, Office of the United States Trade Representative*] [*Executive Office of the President*]
OSRU .... Optical Sensors Research Unit (NITA)
OSRV .... Outside Rear View [*Mirrors*] [*Automotive features*]
OSS .... Los Angeles, CA [*Location identifier FAA*] (FAAL)
OSS .... Objective Supply System [*Army*]
OSS .... Object Sorting Scales [*Psychology*]
OSS .... Observing Simulation System (USDC)
OSS .... Observing Stimulation System [*Marine science*] (OSRA)
OSS .... Occupational Superannuation Standard
OSS .... Oceanic Scanning Spectrophotometer
OSS .... Oceanic Space Subcommittee [*Congressional committee*] (MSC)
OSS .... Ocean Surveillance Satellite (MCD)
OSS .... Ocean Surveillance System [*Navy*] (SAA)
OSS .... Ocean Survey Ship (NOAA)
OSS .... OEX [*Orbiter Experiments*] Support System [*NASA*] (NASA)
OSS .... OEX [*Orbiter Experiments*] Support System [*NASA*]
OSS .... Office of Safeguards and Security [*Department of Energy Washington, DC*] (GRD)
OSS .... Office of Senate Security [*Congress*]
OSS .... Office of Space Science [*NASA*]
OSS .... Office of Space Systems [*Air Force*]
OSS .... Office of Statistical Standards [*Bureau of the Budget; later, OMB*]
OSS .... Office of Strategic Services [*Facetiously translated as "Oh So Social" because some of its staff were socially prominent*] [*World War II*]
OSS .... Office of Support Services [*Army*]
OSS .... Office of Systems Operations [*National Weather Service*] (USDC)
OSS .... Offshore Surveillance System
OSS .... Old Submarine [*Navy symbol*]
OSS .... One Stop Shop [*Small business advice*] [*British*] (ECON)
OSS .... Ontario Secondary School Teachers' Federation [*UTLAS symbol*]
OSS .... Operating System Software [*Personal computers*]
OSS .... Operating System Supervisor
OSS .... Operating System Support (NITA)
OSS .... Operational Storage Site [*Army*]
OSS .... Operational Support System [*Computer science*]
OSS .... Operations Support System (DOMA)
OSS .... Optical Sensor Subsystem [*Military*] (CAAL)
OSS .... Optical Sight System
OSS .... Optical Subsystem (KSC)
OSS .... Optical Surveillance System (AAG)
OSS .... Optimized Systems Software [*San Jose, CA*]
OSS .... Orbital Space Station Study [*NASA*] (IAA)
OSS .... Orbital Stabilization System (MCD)
OSS .... Orbiting Space Station [*NASA*]
OSS .... Orbiting Space Station [*NASA*]
OSS .... Ordnance Safety Switch [*Military*] (IAA)
OSS .... Organised Science Series [*A publication*]
OSS .... Organization for Cooperation of Socialist Countries in the Domain of Posts and Telecommunications [*Defunct*] (EAIO)
OSS .... Osisko Lake Mines Ltd. [*Toronto Stock Exchange symbol*]
oss .... Ossetic [*MARC language code Library of Congress*] (LCCP)
OSS .... Ossory [*Ireland*] (ROG)
OSS .... Outer Solar System

OSS	Overhead Speaker System [Automotive engineering]
OSS	Overseas Switch [Military]
OSS	Over-the-Shoulder Shot [Photography] (WDMC)
OSS	Own Ship's Speed [Navy]
OSS	Oxygen Sleep Starvation
OSS	Religious of the Order of the Blessed Sacrament and Our Lady [Sacramentine Nuns] [Roman Catholic religious order]
OSS	Sacramentine Nuns (TOCD)
OSS	Shawnee State Community College, Portsmouth, OH [OCLC symbol] (OCLC)
OSSA	Office of Space Science and Applications [Washington, DC NASA]
OSSA	Order Scheduled Shipment Analysis (MCD)
OSSA	Order Secular of St. Augustine [See also ASAS] [Rome, Italy] (EAIO)
OSSC	Oblati Sacratissimi Cordis [Oblate Fathers of the Sacred Heart] [Roman Catholic religious order]
OSSC	Ordnance Storage and Shipment Chart [Army] (MCD)
OSSD	Office of Space Systems Development [NASA]
OSSD	Off-Site Surveillance Data [Military]
OSSE	Object/Surface/Special Effect
OSSE	Observing Systems Simulation Experiments [National Center for Atmospheric Research]
OSSE	Oriented Scintillation Spectrometer Experiment [Instrumentation in Gamma Ray Observatory] [NASA]
OSSF	Operating System Support Facility (MHDI)
OSSF	Overseas Services Storage Facility
OSShD	Organisation fur die Zusammenarbeit der Eisenbahnen [Organisation for the Collaboration of Railways - OCR] (EAIO)
OSSI	Outback Steakhouse [NASDAQ symbol] (TTSB)
OSSI	Outback Steakhouse, Inc. [NASDAQ symbol] (SPSG)
OSSJ	St. Joseph's Hospital, Sarnia, Ontario [Library symbol National Library of Canada] (BIB)
OSSKC	Operative Society of Spring Knife Cutlers [A union] [British]
OSSL	Operating System Simulation Language [1971] [Computer science] (CSR)
OSSM	Oil Spill Simulation Model
OSSMJ	Order of the Societies of Mary and Joseph (ROG)
OSSN	Operational Specialist Supervisor, Night [Navy]
OSSN	Other Specialty Serial Numbers [Air Force]
OSSNSS	Ordnance Supply Segment of the Navy Supply System
OSSO	Office of State Systems Operations [Social and Rehabilitation Service, HEW]
OSSP	Operational Supply Support Plan (MCD)
OSSP	Outer Solar System Probe
OS-SPT	Osmolality Urin-Spot [Test] [Biochemistry] (DAVI)
OSSR	Oblates of the Most Holy Redeemer (TOCD)
OSSR	Oblates [or Order] of the Most Holy Redeemer [Roman Catholic women's religious order]
OSSR	Order of the Most Holy Redeemer (TOCD)
OSSR	Own Ship's Speed Repeater [Navy]
OSSRH	Orbiter Subsystem Requirements Handbook [NASA] (NASA)
OSSRS	Optimum Step Size Random Search [Computer science] (IAA)
osss	Brigittine Monks (TOCD)
OSsS	Brigittine Monks (TOCD)
OSSS	Damascus [Syria] [ICAO location identifier] (ICLI)
OSSS	Optical Space Surveillance Subsystem (AAG)
OSSS	Optical Space Surveillance System [or Subsystem] (IAA)
OSSS	Orbital Space Station Study
OSSS	Orbital Space Station System [of NASA]
OSSS	Order of the Most Holy Savior [Bridgettine Sisters] [Roman Catholic religious order]
OSSS	The Brigittine Sisters (TOCD)
OSST	Ocean Ship Surveillance Training
OSST	Official Summary of Security Transactions and Holdings
OSST	Offshore Storage Tank
OSST	Order of the Holy Trinity (TOCD)
osst	Order of the Most Holy Trinity, Trinitarian Fathers (TOCD)
OSsT	Ordo Sanctissimae Trinitatis Redemptionis Captivorum [Order of the Most Holy Trinity] [Trinitarians] [Roman Catholic religious order]
OSST	Sisters of the Most Holy Trinity (TOCD)
OSSU	Operator Services Switching Unit [Telecommunications] (TEL)
OSSU	Sundridge & Strong Union Public Library, Sundridge, Ontario [Library symbol National Library of Canada] (NLC)
OS Supp	Oklahoma Statutes, Supplement [A publication] (DLA)
OST	Austria Fund [NYSE symbol] (SPSG)
OST	Objectives, Strategy, and Tactics [Management system]
OST	Objective Start Time
OST	Object Sorting Test [Psychology]
OST	Observation Skills Test
OST	Ocean Surface Temperature [Marine science] (OSRA)
OST	Office of Science and Technology [Terminated 1973, functions transferred to National Science Foundation] [Later, CSTD]
OST	Office of Systems Operations [Marine science] (OSRA)
OST	Office of the Secretary of Transportation [Department of Transportation]
O St	Ohio State Reports [A publication] (DLA)
OST	One-Station Training
OST	On Same Terms (WDAA)
OST	On-Shift Test (IEEE)
OST	On-Site Test (IAA)
OST	Operational Suitability Test [Aviation]
OST	Operational System Test (KSC)
OST	Operations Support Team [NASA] (MCD)
OST	Optical Sensing Trigger
OST	Optical Star Tracker
OST	Optic Support Table

OST	Orbiter Support Trolley [NASA] (NASA)
OST	Orbit Stay Time
OST	Order Ship Time [DoD]
OST	Ordinary Spring Tides
OST	Ordnance Shock Test [Military]
OST	Ordnance Special Training (AAG)
OST	Ordnance Suitability Test
OST	Organisation Socialiste des Travailleurs [Socialist Workers' Organization] [Senegal] [Political party] (PPW)
OST	Organizacion Socialista de los Trabajadores [Socialist Workers' Organization] [Costa Rica] [Political party] (PPW)
OST	Organizacion Socialista de los Trabajadores [Socialist Workers' Organization] [Bolivia] [Political party] (PPW)
OST	Originating Station Treatment [Telecommunications] (TEL)
OST	Ostend [Belgium] [Airport symbol] (OAG)
OST	Osteopathic (WGA)
Ost	Osteotomy [Orthopedics] (DAVI)
OST	Osterhout Free Library, Wilkes-Barre, PA [OCLC symbol] (OCLC)
OST	Out of Stock, Temporary [Business term]
OST	Overseas Students Trust [British] (AEBS)
OST	Over Stress Testing
OST	Oxford Superconductive Technology [Manufacturing company] [British]
OST	Stratford Public Library, Ontario [Library symbol National Library of Canada] (NLC)
OSTA	Office of Space and Terrestrial Applications [NASA] (GRD)
OSTA	Optical Storage Technology Association (CDE)
OSTA	Stayner Public Library, Ontario [Library symbol National Library of Canada] (NLC)
OSTAC	Bibliotheque Publique Cambridge-St.-Albert, St.-Albert, Ontario [Library symbol National Library of Canada] (NLC)
OSTAC	Ocean Science Technology Advisory Committee [Terminated, 1976] [National Security Industrial Association] (MSC)
OSTAG	Gallery Stratford, Ontario [Library symbol National Library of Canada] (NLC)
OSTAR	Observer Single-Handed Transatlantic Race [Sailing]
OSTARE	Old Scientific Technical Aerospace Reports Extended
OSTARS	Orbiting Surveillance and Target Acquisition Relay [Army] (RDA)
OSTASDG	St. Andrews Branch, Stormount, Dundas, and Glengarry County Library, Ontario [Library symbol National Library of Canada] (BIB)
O State	Ohio State Reports [A publication] (DLA)
OSTB	Office of the State Training Board [Australia]
OSTC	St. Catharines Public Library, Ontario [Library symbol National Library of Canada] (NLC)
OStcB	Belmont Technical Institute, St. Clairsville, OH [Library symbol Library of Congress] (LCLS)
OSTCB	Brock University, St. Catharines, Ontario [Library symbol National Library of Canada] (NLC)
OSTCBG	Department of Geography, Brock University, St. Catharines, Ontario [Library symbol National Library of Canada] (NLC)
OSTCG	Grantham High School, St. Catharines, Ontario [Library symbol National Library of Canada] (NLC)
OSTCGL	Genaire Ltd., St. Catharines, Ontario [Library symbol National Library of Canada] (NLC)
OSTCH	Hotel-Dieu Hospital, St. Catharines, Ontario [Library symbol National Library of Canada] (BIB)
OSTCM	St. Catharines Historical Museum, Ontario [Library symbol National Library of Canada] (BIB)
OSTCMEC	Monenco Consultants Ltd., St. Catharines, Ontario [Library symbol National Library of Canada] (NLC)
OSTCOOP	Office of the Secretary of Transportation Continuity of Operations Plan
OSTCT	St. Catharines Teachers' College, Ontario [Library symbol National Library of Canada] (NLC)
OSTCTR	St. Catharines Teachers' Reference Library, Ontario [Library symbol National Library of Canada] (NLC)
OStcU	Ohio University, Belmont County Branch Campus, St. Clairsville, OH [Library symbol Library of Congress] (LCLS)
OSTD	Office of Supersonic Transport Development [Department of Transportation] [Obsolete]
OSTD	Off-Site Technical Director (MHDI)
OSTD	Ontario Society for Training and Development [Canada] (EDAC)
OSTD	Ordnance Standards
OSTD	Ordnance Standard Technical Directives [Obsolete]
OSTDS	Office of Space Tracking and Data Systems [NASA] (NASA)
OSTE	Osteotech, Inc. [NASDAQ symbol] (SAG)
OSte	Public Library of Steubenville and Jefferson County, Steubenville, OH [Library symbol Library of Congress] (LCLS)
OSteC	College of Steubenville, Steubenville, OH [Library symbol Library of Congress] (LCLS)
osteo	Osteoarthritis [Medicine]
OSTEO	Osteomyelitis [Medicine]
Osteo	Osteomyelitis [Orthopedics] (DAVI)
OSTEO	Osteopathic
OSTEOPTH	Osteopath
Osteotch	Osteotech, Inc. [Associated Press] (SAG)
OSTEST	Operating System Test [Telecommunications] (TEL)
Ostex	Ostex International, Inc. [Associated Press] (SAG)
OSTF	Operational Silo Test Facility
OSTF	Operational Suitability Test Facility [Aviation]
OSTF	Operational System Test Facility [Air Force]
OSTFC	Storrington Branch, Frontenac County Library, Ontario [Library symbol National Library of Canada] (BIB)
OSTG	Ocean Science and Technology Group [Navy] (MCD)

OSTG .... St. Georges Branch, South Dumfries Public Library, Ontario [*Library symbol National Library of Canada*] (BIB)

OSTI............ Bibliotheque Publique de St.-Isidore, Ontario [*Library symbol National Library of Canada*] (NLC)

OSTI............ Office of Scientific and Technical Information [*Later, BLR & DD*] [*British Library*]

OSTI............ Office of Scientific and Technical Information [*Department of Energy*] [*Information service or system*] (IID)

OSTI............ Organization for Social and Technical Innovation

OSTIR .... Stirling Public Library, Ontario [*Library symbol National Library of Canada*] (BIB)

OSTIV .... Organisation Scientifique et Technique Internationale du Vol a Voile [*International Technical and Scientific Organization for Soaring Flight*]

OStJ .... Officer of the Order of St. John of Jerusalem [*British*]

ostk............ Oilstick (VRA)

OSTL .... Operating System Table Loader [*Telecommunications*] (TEL)

OSTL .... Ovary Style Length [*Botany*]

OSTM .... Sault Ste. Marie Public Library, Ontario [*Library symbol National Library of Canada*] (NLC)

OSTMA .... Algoma College, Sault Ste. Marie, Ontario [*Library symbol National Library of Canada*] (NLC)

OSTMAAS .... Synod Office, Diocese of Algoma, Anglican Church of Canada, Sault Ste. Marie, Ontario [*Library symbol National Library of Canada*] (NLC)

OStmaC .... Chatfield College, St. Martin, OH [*Library symbol Library of Congress*] (LCLS)

OSTMAS ...... Research Library, Algoma Steel Corp. Ltd., Sault Ste. Marie, Ontario [*Library symbol National Library of Canada*] (NLC)

OSTMB .... Batchewana Indian Band, Sault Ste. Marie, Ontario [*Library symbol National Library of Canada*] (NLC)

OSTMEF .... Sea Lamprey Control Centre, Fisheries and Oceans Canada [*Centre de Controle des Lamproies de Mer, Peches et Oceans Canada*] Sault Ste. Marie, Ontario [*Library symbol National Library of Canada*] (NLC)

OSTMF......... Great Lakes Forest Research Centre, Canadian Forestry Service [*Centre de Recherches Forestieres des Grands Lacs, Service Canadien des Forets*] Sault Ste. Marie, Ontario [*Library symbol National Library of Canada*] (NLC)

OSTMFF....... Forest Pest Management Institute, Canadian Forestry Service [*Institut pour laRepression des Ravageurs Forestiers, Service Canadien des Forets*], Sault-Ste.-Marie, Ontario [*Library symbol National Library of Canada*] (NLC)

OSTMGH...... General Hospital, Sault Ste. Marie, Ontario [*Library symbol National Library of Canada*] (NLC)

OSTMH .... Sault Ste. Marie and 49th (SSM) Field Regiment RCA Historical Society, Ontario [*Library symbol National Library of Canada*] (NLC)

OSTMM........ Strathroy Middlesex Museum, Strathroy, Ontario [*Library symbol National Library of Canada*] (BIB)

OSTMNA ...... Aviation and Fire Management Centre, Ontario Ministry of Natural Resources, Sault Ste. Marie [*Library symbol National Library of Canada*] (BIB)

OSTMPH...... Plummer Public Hospital, Sault Ste. Marie, Ontario [*Library symbol National Library of Canada*] (NLC)

OSTMSC ...... Sault College of Applied Arts and Technology, Sault Ste. Marie, Ontario [*Library symbol National Library of Canada*] (NLC)

OSTMY .... St. Mary's Public Library, Ontario [*Library symbol National Library of Canada*] (NLC)

OSTMYM ..... St. Mary's District Museum, St. Mary's, Ontario [*Library symbol National Library of Canada*] (BIB)

OSTO .... Office of Space Transportation Operations [*NASA*] (NASA)

OST-ONA ..... Office of the Secretary of Transportation Office of Noise Abatement

OSTP .... Office of Science and Technology Policy [*Executive Office of the Presiden t*] [*Washington, DC*]

OSTP .... On-Site Test Procedure

OSTP .... Orbiting System Test Plan [*NASA*] (NASA)

OSTP .... Strathroy Public Library, Ontario [*Library symbol National Library of Canada*] (NLC)

OSTPA .... Stratford-Perth Archives Board, Ontario [*Library symbol National Library of Canada*] (BIB)

O St R .... Ohio State Reports [*A publication*] (DLA)

OSTR .... Streetsville Public Library, Ontario [*Library symbol National Library of Canada*] (NLC)

O St Rep..... Ohio State Reports [*A publication*] (DLA)

OSTRO......... Stroud Branch, Township of Innisfil Public Library, Ontario [*Library symbol National Library of Canada*] (NLC)

OSTS .... Office of Space Transportation System [*NASA*]

OSTS .... Office of Space Transportation Systems [*NASA*] (GRD)

OSTS .... Office of State Technical Services [*Also, STS*] [*Abolished, 1970 Department of Commerce*]

OSTS .... Official Seed Testing Station (WDAA)

OSTS .... Operational Suitability Test Site [*Aviation*] (AAG)

OSTT........... Damascus [*Syria*] [*ICAO location identifier*] (ICLI)

OSTT........... Open Systems Technology Transfer Programme [*British*]

OSTT........... St. Thomas Public Library, Ontario [*Library symbol National Library of Canada*] (NLC)

OSTTE......... Elgin County Public Library, St. Thomas, Ontario [*Library symbol National Library of Canada*] (NLC)

OSTTP .... St. Thomas Psychiatric Hospital, Ontario [*Library symbol National Library of Canada*] (NLC)

OSTV .... Operational Support Television [*Military*] (AFM)

OSTX .... Ostex International, Inc. [*NASDAQ symbol*] (SAG)

OSTX .... Ostex Intl. [*NASDAQ symbol*] (TTSB)

OSU .... Columbus, OH [*Location identifier FAA*] (FAAL)

OSU .... Irish Ursuline Union (TOCD)

OSU .... Ohio State University [*Columbus*]

OSu .... Ohio State University, Columbus, OH [*OCLC symbol*] (OCLC)

O Su .... Ohio Supplement [*A publication*] (DLA)

OSU .... Ohio Supreme Court Decisions, Unreported Cases [*A publication*] (DLA)

OSU .... Oklahoma State University

OSU .... Older-Worker Service Unit [*US Employment Service*] [*Department of Labor*]

OSU .... Open Systems Unit [*British*]

OSU .... Operational Switching Unit

OSU .... Operation Sisters United (EA)

OSU .... Optical Scanning Unit (DNAB)

OSU .... Optical Service Unit [*Telecommunications*]

OSU .... Order of St. Ursula [*Roman Catholic women's religious order*]

OSU .... Oregon State University [*Formerly, OSC*]

OSU .... O'Sullivan Industries Hldg [*NYSE symbol*] (TTSB)

OSU .... O'Sullivan Industries Holding [*NYSE symbol*] (SPSG)

OSU .... Own Ship's Use [*Navy*] (DNAB)

OSU .... Sudbury Public Library, Ontario [*Library symbol National Library of Canada*] (NLC)

OSU .... Ursuline Nuns of the Congregation of Paris (Cincinnati, OH) (TOCD)

OSU .... Ursuline Nuns of the Congregation of Paris (Cleveland, OH) (TOCD)

OSU .... Ursuline Nuns of the Congregation of Paris (Kansas City, KS) (TOCD)

OSU .... Ursuline Nuns of the Congregation of Paris (Louisville, KY) (TOCD)

OSU .... Ursuline Nuns of the Congregation of Paris (Owensboro, KY) (TOCD)

OSU .... Ursuline Nuns of the Congregation of Paris (St. Martin, OH) (TOCD)

OSU .... Ursuline Nuns of the Congregation of Paris (Toledo, OH) (TOCD)

OSU .... Ursuline Nuns of the Congregation of Paris (Youngstown, OH) (TOCD)

OSU .... Ursuline Sisters of Belleville (TOCD)

OSU .... Ursuline Sisters of the Congregation of Tildonk, Belgium (TOCD)

OSUBE .... Educational Media Centre, Sudbury Board of Education, Ontario [*Library symbol National Library of Canada*] (NLC)

OSUC .... Cambrian College, Sudbury, Ontario [*Library symbol National Library of Canada*] (NLC)

OSUCS........ Civic Square, Information and Reference, Sudbury Public Library, Ontario [*Library symbol National Library of Canada*] (NLC)

OSUE .... On-Site User Evaluation (MCD)

OSUGH .... Sudbury General Hospital, Ontario [*Library symbol National Library of Canada*] (NLC)

OSUK .... Ophthalmological Society of the United Kingdom

OSUL .... Laurentian University [*Universite Laurentienne*] Sudbury, Ontario [*Library symbol National Library of Canada*] (NLC)

OSUL .... Ohio State University Libraries (NITA)

OSULH .... Medical Library, Laurentian Hospital, Sudbury, Ontario [*Library symbol National Library of Canada*] (BIB)

OSullvnC..... O'Sullivan Corp. [*Associated Press*] (SAG)

OSulvInd..... O'Sullivan Industries Holdings [*Associated Press*] (SAG)

OSUM .... Ohio State University Museum of Zoology [*Research center*] (RCD)

OSUME .... Ontario Ministry of Education, Sudbury, Ontario [*Library symbol National Library of Canada*] (BIB)

OSUN.......... North Central Regional Library, Sudbury, Ontario [*Library symbol National Library of Canada*] (NLC)

OSUN.......... Ontario Library Service - Voyageur, Sudbury, Ontario [*Library symbol National Library of Canada*] (NLC)

OSUNB........ Brock Township Public Library, Sunderland, Ontario [*Library symbol National Library of Canada*] (NLC)

OSUOP........ Northeastern Ontario Oncology Program [*Programme d'Oncologie du Nord-Est de l'Ontario*], Sudbury, Ontario [*Library symbol National Library of Canada*] (NLC)

OSUP .... Ohio State University Press (DGA)

OSUPE .... Ohio State University Psychological Exam (EDAC)

O Supp .... Ohio Supplement [*A publication*] (DLA)

OSUR .... Ohio State University Reactor

OSUREP....... Overseas Unit Replacement System [*Military*] (AFIT)

OSURF .... Ohio State University Research Foundation

OSURO .... Ohio State University Radio Observatory

OSUT .... One-Station-Unit Training [*Army*]

OSUT .... On-Site User Test

OSUT .... On-Site User Training

OSUT .... Ordinary Seamen Under Training [*Canadian Navy*]

OSUT-COFT... One-Station-Unit Training - Conduct of Fire Trainer [*Army*] (MCD)

OSUU .... University of Subury [*Universite de Sudbury*] Ontario [*Library symbol National Library of Canada*] (NLC)

OSV .... Ocean Station Vessel

OSV .... Office of Space Vehicles

OSV .... Offscreen Voice [*Films, television, etc.*]

OSV .... Offshore Supply Vessel [*Coast Guard*] (GFGA)

OSV .... On Station Vehicle (MCD)

OSV .... Orbital Support Vehicle

OSV .... Order of St. Vincent (EA)

OSV .... Oriented Space Vehicle

OSV .... Output Serving Voltage

OSV .... Over-Sand Vehicle

OSVA .... Off-Site Vital Area (MCD)

OS/VS .... Operating Schedule/Virtual System

OS/VS .... Operating System/Virtual Storage [*Computer science*] (MDG)

OSW .... Oblique Shock Wave

OSW .... Office of Saline Water [*Later, OWRT*] [*Department of the Interior*]

OSW .... Office of Secretary of War [*Obsolete*]

OSW .... Office of Solid Waste [*Environmental Protection Agency*] (EPA)

OSW .... Old Swedish [*Language, etc.*]

OSW .... Operational Switching Unit

OSW	Operations Support Wing [NASA]
OSW	Order of the Sacred Word [Affiliate of the magical society, Aurum Solis]
OSW	Oswego, KS [Location identifier FAA] (FAAL)
OSW	Oswestry [British depot code]
OSW	Wittenberg University, Springfield, OH [Library symbol Library of Congress] (LCLS)
OSWA	Off-Shift Work Authorization (AAG)
OSWA	Orchid Society of Western Australia
OSWA	Organ Society of Western Australia
OSWAC	Ordnance Special Weapons Ammunition Command [Later, Weapons Command]
OSWC	Ordnance Special Weapons Command [Merged with Missile Command] [Army]
OSWD	Office of Special Weapons Development [Army]
OSWER	Office of Solid Waste and Emergency Response [Environmental Protection Agency Washington, DC]
OSWG	Optical Systems Working Group (MUGU)
OSWI	Old Spaghetti Warehouse, Inc. (MHDW)
OSWMP	Office of Solid Waste Management Programs [Environmental Protection Agency]
OSWS	Operating System Workstation [Computer science]
OSWS	Whitchurch-Stouffville Public Library, Stouffville, Ontario [Library symbol National Library of Canada] (NLC)
OSWV	Osteryoung Square Wave Voltammogram [Electrochemistry]
OSX	Kosciusko, MS [Location identifier FAA] (FAAL)
OSY	Namsos [Norway] [Airport symbol] (OAG)
OSY	National Institute for Occupational Safety and Health, Morgantown, WV [OCLC symbol] (OCLC)
OSY	Odyssey Resources Ltd. [Vancouver Stock Exchange symbol]
OSYC	Officer Supervising Yardcraft [Canadian Navy]
OSYFC	Sydenham Branch, Frontenac County Library, Ontario [Library symbol National Library of Canada] (BIB)
OSYS	OccuSystems, Inc. [NASDAQ symbol] (SAG)
OSyS	Sylvania Schools, Sylvania, OH [Library symbol] [Library of Congress] (LCLS)
OSZ	Koszalin [Poland] [Airport symbol] (OAG)
OSZ	Offshore Surf Zone
OSZ	Washington, DC [Location identifier FAA] (FAAL)
OSzK	Orszagos Szechenyi Konyvtar [National Szechenyi Library] [Information service or system] (IID)
OT	Evergreen Helicopters of Alaska [ICAO designator] (AD)
OT	Objective Test [Psychology]
OT	Object Technology [Computer science] (CDE)
OT	Observer Target [Army]
OT	Occipitotransverse [Obstetrics]
OT	Occlusion Time (MAE)
OT	Occupational Therapist [or Therapy] [Medicine]
OT	Occupational Therapy Technician [Navy]
OT	Occupational Training (AIE)
OT	Occupied Territories (BJA)
OT	Ocean Systems Technician [Navy] (DNAB)
OT	Ocean Transportation [Military]
OT	Ocular Tension [Medicine]
OT	Oedipus Tyrannus [of Sophocles] [Classical studies] (OCD)
OT	Offensive Tackle [Football]
OT	Office of Telecommunications [Department of Commerce]
OT	Office of Territories [Department of the Interior]
OT	Office of Transportation [Department of Agriculture]
OT	Off Time (WDAA)
OT	Oil Temperature [Automotive engineering]
OT	Oil-Tempered (IAA)
OT	Oil-Tight
OT	Old Term
OT	Old Terminology
OT	Old Testament [of the Bible]
OT	Old Timer [Communications operators' colloquialism]
OT	Old Tom [British slang term for gin] (ROG)
OT	Old Top [Communications operators' colloquialism]
OT	Old [or Original] Tuberculin [Also, TO] [Medicine]
OT	Olfactory Threshold
OT	Olfactory Tubercle [Neuroanatomy]
OT	On a Track [Rail] [Shipping] (DCTA)
OT	Once-Through [Nuclear reactor technology]
OT	One Time
OT	On Target [Military] (CAAL)
O/T	On Thames [In place names] [British] (ROG)
OT	On Time
O/T	On Trent [In place names] [British] (ROG)
OT	On Truck [Shipping]
OT	Open Topped [Container] [Packaging] (DCTA)
OT	Open Transport [Computer science]
OT	Operating Temperature [Nuclear energy]
OT	Operating Theater
OT	Operating Time
OT	Operational Technology [Nuclear energy] (NRCH)
OT	Operational Test (AFM)
OT	Operational TIROS [NASA]
OT	Operational Training (MCD)
OT	Operational Trajectory [Aerospace] (KSC)
OT	Operations Team (MCD)
OT	Optatam Totius [Decree on Priestly Formation] [Vatican II document]
OT	Optical Tool
OT	Optical Tracking [NASA] (KSC)
OT	Optical-Transient [Astronomy]

OT	Optic Tectum [Anatomy]
O/T	Oral Temperature (DAVI)
OT	Oral Testimony (BJA)
OT	Oral Thrush [Medicine] (MEDA)
OT	Oregon Territory [Prior to statehood]
OT	Oregon Trunk Railway [AAR code]
OT	Organizational Table
OT	Organization Table
OT	Orienteering Tasmania [Australia An association]
OT	Orifice Tube [Automobile air conditioning system]
OT	Original Tuberculin [Medicine] (DMAA)
OT	Orotracheal [Medicine]
O-T	Orthohombic-Tetragonal [Temperature transition]
OT	Ortho Tolidine (PDAA)
OT	Oscillation Transformer [Radio]
OT	Osmium Tetroxide [Inorganic chemistry]
OT	Other Than
OT	Other Time
OT	Otis Test [Psychiatry] (DAVI)
OT	Otolaryngology [Medicine]
OT	Otology [Medicine]
OT	O'Toole's Group, Inc. [Toronto Stock Exchange symbol]
Ot	Otto Papiensis [Flourished, 12th century] [Authority cited in pre-1607 legal work] (DSA)
Ot	Otto's United States Supreme Court Reports [91-107 United States] [A publication] (DLA)
OT	Ought (ROG)
OT	Outer Table (MCD)
OT	Outer Tube
OT	Outfit
OT	Out of Tolerance
OT	Output [Computer science] (IAA)
OT	Output Terminal
OT	Out Temperature (MCD)
OT	Overall Test (KSC)
OT	Overhead Transparencies
OT	Overlap Technician
OT	Overlap Telling (MCD)
OT	Overseas Territories (MCD)
OT	Overseas Trade
OT	Overseas Trading [A publication]
O/T	Overtemperature (KSC)
OT	Over There (ADA)
OT	Overtime
OT	Overtone
OT	Ovotransferrin [Biochemistry]
OT	Oxytocin [Endocrinology]
OT	Stations Open Exclusively to Operational Traffic of the Services Concerned [ITU designation] (CET)
OT	Tara Branch, Bruce County Public Library, Ontario [Library symbol National Library of Canada] (NLC)
OT	Toledo-Lucas County Public Library, Toledo, OH [Library symbol Library of Congress] (LCLS)
OTA	Academy of Medicine, Toronto, Ontario [Library symbol National Library of Canada] (NLC)
OTA	Mota [Ethiopia] [Airport symbol] (AD)
OTA	Occupational Therapists Association (NADA)
OTA	Occupied Territory Administration [World War II]
OTA	Office of Tax Analysis [Department of the Treasury]
OTA	Office of Technical Assistance (USGC)
OTA	Office of Technology Assessment [Congressional study group] [Washington, DC]
OTA	Office of Technology Assistance [General Services Administration]
OTA	Office of Telecommunications Applications [US National Telecommunications and Information Administration] (TSSD)
OTA	Officer Training Allowance [Naval Reserve]
OTA	Off-the-Air Record Club [Record label]
OTA	Oil Trades Association of New York (EA)
OTA	Old Testament Abstracts [A publication] (BJA)
OTA	Omnidirectional Transmitter Antenna
OTA	Open Test Assembly [Nuclear energy] (NRCH)
OTA	Operational Test Agency (DOMA)
OTA	Operational Transconductance Amplifier (IEEE)
OTA	Operation Town Affiliations [An association] (EA)
OTA	Operation-Triggered Architecture [Computer science]
OTA	Optical Telescope Assembly [NASA]
OTA	Optical Tracking Aid [Deep Space Instrumentation Facility, NASA]
OTA	Organic Trade Association
OTA	Organisation Mondiale du Tourisme et de l'Automobile [World Touring and Automobile Organization]
OTA	Orthodontic Technicians Association [British] (DBA)
OTA	Ortho-Tolidine Arsenite [Organic chemistry]
OTA	Other Talk Address (IAA)
OTA	Other than Air (CINC)
ota	Ottoman Turkish [MARC language code Library of Congress] (LCCP)
OTA	Outer Transport Area
OTA	Output Transformerless Amplifier (DICI)
OTA	Outside-Wheel Turning Angle [Automotive engineering]
OTAA	AASTRA Aerospace, Inc., Downsview, Ontario [Library symbol National Library of Canada] (BIB)
OTAA	Office of Trade Adjustment Assistance [Department of Labor]
OTAC	Acres Consulting Services Ltd., Toronto, Ontario [Library symbol National Library of Canada] (NLC)
OTAC	Oceanic Trade Alliance Council International

OTAC .... Ordnance Tank-Automotive Command [*Merged with Weapons and Mobility Command*] [*Army*]

OTACS .... Old Timer Assay Commissioners Society [*Defunct*] (EA)

OTAD .... Addiction Research Foundation, Toronto, Ontario [*Library symbol National Library of Canada*] (NLC)

OTAD .... Office of Tributary Area Development [*Tennessee Valley Authority*]

OTAD .... Oversea Terminal Arrival Date [*Army*] (AABC)

OTADA .... Office of Tracking and Data Acquisition [*NASA*]

OTADL .... Outer Target Azimuth Datum Line

OTAE .... Atomic Energy of Canada [*L'Energie Atomique du Canada*] Toronto, Ontario [*Library symbol National Library of Canada*] (NLC)

OTAE .... [*The*] Old Testament in the Light of the Ancient East [*A publication*] (BJA)

OTAF .... Office of Technology Assessment and Forecast [*Patent and Trademark Office*] [*Washington, DC*]

OTAF .... Ontario Ministry of Agriculture and Food, Toronto, Ontario [*Library symbol National Library of Canada*] (NLC)

OTAF .... Operating Time at Failure (MCD)

OTAF Data Base... Office of Technology Assessment and Forecasts Data Base (NITA)

OTAG .... Art Gallery of Ontario, Toronto, Ontario [*Library symbol National Library of Canada*] (NLC)

OTAG .... Office of the Adjutant General [*Military*]

OTAGAV ...... Audiovisual Library, Art Gallery of Ontario, Toronto, Ontario [*Library symbol National Library of Canada*] (NLC)

Otago Pol Gaz... Otago Police Gazette [*1861-64*] [*New Zealand*] [*A publication*] (DLA)

OTAL .... Arts and Letters Club, Toronto, Ontario [*Library symbol National Library of Canada*] (NLC)

OTAN .... Organisation du Traite de l'Atlantique Nord [*North Atlantic Treaty Organization - NATO*] [*Brussels, Belgium*]

OTAN .... Organizacao do Tratado do Atlantico Norte [*North Atlantic Treaty Organization*] [*Portuguese*]

OT & E .... Operational Test and Evaluation [*Military*] (AFM)

OT&E .... Operational Testing and Evaluation (USDC)

OTANY .... Oil Trades Association of New York (EA)

OTAP .... Alternative Press Centre, Toronto, Ontario [*Library symbol National Library of Canada*] (NLC)

OTAQ .... Offer Therapist-Adolescent Questionnaire [*Personality development test*] [*Psychology*]

OTAR .... Archives of Ontario, Toronto, Ontario [*Library symbol National Library of Canada*] (NLC)

OTAR .... Overseas Tariffs and Regulations (DS)

OTARC .... Centennial College of Applied Arts and Technology, Scarborough, Ontario [*Library symbol National Library of Canada*] (NLC)

OTAS .... Observer Target Acquisition Subsystem (MCD)

OTAS .... On Top and Smooth [*NWS*] (FAAC)

OTASO .... Organizacao do Tratado da Asia Sul-Oriental [*South-East Asia Treaty Organization*] [*Portuguese*]

O T AUTIC ... Other than Automatic [*Freight*]

OTAWA .... Occupational Therapy Association of Western Australia

Otb .... October (CDAI)

OTB .... Off the Board [*Investment term*]

OTB .... Off-Track Betting

OTB .... Old Tired Broads

OTB .... On the Bow [*Nautical*]

OTB .... Open to Buy

OTB .... Orbiting Tanker Base [*NASA*] (NASA)

OTB .... Ordnance and Terminal Ballistics

OTB .... Ortho-Toluidine Boric Acid [*Organic chemistry*]

OTB .... Overseas Trust Bank [*Hong Kong*]

OTB .... Waverly Resource Library, Thunder Bay Public Library, Ontario [*Library symbol National Library of Canada*] (NLC)

OTBA .... Ocean Thermal Boundary Analysis Charts [*Marine science*] (MSC)

OTBA .... Owners, Traders, Breeders Association (NADA)

OTBA .... Terrace Bay Public Library, Ontario [*Library symbol National Library of Canada*] (NLC)

OTBBR .... Brodie Resource Library, Thunder Bay, Ontario [*Library symbol National Library of Canada*] (NLC)

OTBC .... Canadian Broadcasting Corp. [*Societe Radio-Canada*] Toronto, Ontario [*Library symbol National Library of Canada*] (NLC)

OTBCC .... Confederation College, Thunder Bay, Ontario [*Library symbol National Library of Canada*] (NLC)

OTBCG .... Blake, Cassels & Graydon, Toronto, Ontario [*Library symbol National Library of Canada*] (NLC)

OTBCGC ...... Staff Library, Baycrest Centre for Geriatric Care, Toronto, Ontario [*Library symbol National Library of Canada*] (BIB)

OTBCIR .... Bell Canada Information Resource Centre, Toronto, Ontario [*Library symbol National Library of Canada*] (NLC)

OTBCO .... Technical Information Facility, Canadien Imperial Bank of Commerce, Toronto, Ontario [*Library symbol National Library of Canada*] (NLC)

OTBCP .... Program Archives, Canadian Broadcasting Corp. [*Archives des Emissions, Societe Radio-Canada*] Toronto, Ontario [*Library symbol National Library of Canada*] (NLC)

OTBD .... Doha/International [*Qatar*] [*ICAO location identifier*] (ICLI)

OTBD .... Outboard (ADA)

OTBD .... Outboard

OTBDHC ...... Thunder Bay District Health Council, Thunder Bay, Ontario [*Library symbol National Library of Canada*] (NLC)

OTBE .... Ontario Ministry of Education, Thunder Bay, Ontario [*Library symbol National Library of Canada*] (NLC)

OTBE .... Out of the Body Experiences [*Parapsychology*] (ECON)

OTBE .... Overtaken by Events [*Military*]

OTBGH .... General Hospital of Port Arthur, Thunder Bay, Ontario [*Library symbol National Library of Canada*] (NLC)

OTBH .... Thunder Bay Historical Museum Society, Ontario [*Library symbol National Library of Canada*] (NLC)

OTBHS .... Hammarskjold High School, Thunder Bay, Ontario [*Library symbol National Library of Canada*] (NLC)

OTBLA .... Audio Library Services of Northwestern Ontario, Lakehead University, Thunder Bay, Ontario [*Library symbol National Library of Canada*] (NLC)

OTBLL .... School of Library Technology, Lakehead University, Thunder Bay, Ontario [*Library symbol National Library of Canada*] (NLC)

OTBLP .... Staff Library, Lakehead Psychiatric Hospital, Thunder Bay, Ontario [*Library symbol National Library of Canada*] (NLC)

OTBM .... Technical Information Centre, Bank of Montreal, Willowdale, Ontario [*Library symbol National Library of Canada*] (NLC)

OTBMB .... Mary J. L. Black Library, Thunder Bay, Ontario [*Library symbol National Library of Canada*] (NLC)

OTBMBI .... Business Information Centre, Bank of Montreal, Toronto, Ontario [*Library symbol National Library of Canada*] (NLC)

OTBMC .... Medical Library, McKellar General Hospital, Thunder Bay, Ontario [*Library symbol National Library of Canada*] (NLC)

OTBML .... Music Library, Canadian National Institute for the Blind, Toronto, Ontario [*Library symbol National Library of Canada*] (BIB)

OTBNL .... National Library Division, Canadian National Institute for the Blind, Toronto, Ontario [*Library symbol National Library of Canada*] (NLC)

OTBNR .... Learning Resource Centre, BNR Ltd., Toronto, Ontario [*Library symbol National Library of Canada*] (NLC)

OTBNS .... Bell Northern Software Research, Toronto, Ontario [*Library symbol National Library of Canada*] (NLC)

OTBOC .... Ontario Cancer Treatment and Research Foundation, Thunder Bay, Ontario [*Library symbol National Library of Canada*] (NLC)

OTBP .... Blaney, Pasternak, Smela, Eagleson & Watson, Toronto, Ontario [*Library symbol National Library of Canada*] (NLC)

OTBQ .... Occupational Therapists' Board of Queensland [*Australia*]

OTBR .... Barringer Research Ltd., Rexdale, Ontario [*Library symbol National Library of Canada*] (NLC)

OTBS .... On-the-Bottom Sonobuoy (MCD)

OTBSL .... Bassel, Sullivan & Leake, Toronto, Ontario [*Library symbol National Library of Canada*] (NLC)

OTBSSC ...... Over Thirty but Still Swinging Club

OTBV .... Oxidizer Turbine Bypass Valve (KSC)

OTBV .... Victoriaville Branch, Thunder Bay Public Library, Ontario [*Library symbol National Library of Canada*] (BIB)

OTC .... Bol [*Chad*] [*Airport symbol*] (AD)

OTC .... Faculty of Education, University of Toronto, Ontario [*Library symbol National Library of Canada*] (NLC)

OTC .... Objective, Time, and Cost

OTC .... Office of Technical Cooperation [*United Nations*]

OTC .... Office of Temporary Controls

OTC .... Officer in Tactical Command [*Air Force*]

OTC .... Officers' Training Camp [*World War I*]

OTC .... Officers' Training Corps

OTC .... Officers Transit Camp [*British military*] (DMA)

OTC .... Officer Training Center [*Navy*]

OTC .... Offshore Technology Conference

OTC .... Ohio Motor Freight Tariff Committee Inc., Columbus OH [*STAC*]

OTC .... Old Testament Commentary [*A publication*] (BJA)

OTC .... Old Timers' Club (EA)

OTC .... Once-Through Cooling [*Nuclear energy*] (NRCH)

OTC .... One-Stop Tour Charter [*Airline fare*]

OTC .... One-Time Carbon [*Paper*] (PDAA)

OTC .... Open Tubular Column [*For gas chromatography*]

OTC .... Operado de Terminal de Contenedores [*Container Terminal Operator*] [*Shipping*] [*Spanish*]

OTC .... Operador de Transporte Combinado [*Combined Transport Operator*] [*Spanish Business term*]

OTC .... Operating Telephone Co. [*Bell System*] (TEL)

OTC .... Operational Techniques Conference

OTC .... Operational Test Center [*NASA*] (KSC)

OTC .... Operational Test Coordinator [*Military*] (CAAL)

OTC .... Operational Training Capability [*Air Force*] (AFM)

OTC .... Operational Training Command (MCD)

OTC .... Operatore di Trasporto Combinato [*Combined Transport Operator*] [*Italian Business term*]

OTC .... Orbiter Test Conductor [*NASA*] (NASA)

OTC .... Orbiting Trajectory Computations

OTC .... Order of Three Crusades (EA)

OTC .... Ordnance Technical Committee [*Military*] (MUGU)

OTC .... Ordnance Training Command [*Army*]

OTC .... Organization for Trade Cooperation [*GATT*]

OTC .... Organize Training Center (EA)

OTC .... Organotin Compound [*Organic chemistry*]

OTC .... Original Trenton Cracker Co. [*Maker of Chowder & Oyster Crackers, claimed by some to be the oldest continuously manufactured American food product*]

OTC .... Originating Toll Center [*Telecommunications*] (TEL)

OTC .... Originating Toll Circuit [*Telecommunications*] (IAA)

OTC .... Originating Trunk Center [*Telecommunications*] (IAA)

OTC .... Ornithine Transcarbamoylase [*Also, OCT*] [*An enzyme*]

OTC .... Ornithine Transcarbamylase [*An enzyme*] (DAVI)

OTC .... Oshkosh Truck Corp.

OTC .... Otterbein College, Westerville, OH [*OCLC symbol*] (OCLC)

OTC .... Outer Tube Centerline

OTC .... Overseas Telecommunications Commission (NITA)

OTC............. Overseas Telecommunications Commission of Australia (BARN)
OTC............. Over-the-Calf [Women's fashions] (IIA)
OTC............. Over-the-Capacitor [Sockets]
OTC............. Over-the-Counter [Pharmacy]
OTC............. Over-the-Counter [Also, O/C] [Stock exchange term]
OTC............. Oxygen Transfer Compressor
OTC............. Oxytetracycline [Antibiotic]
OTC............. Ozone Transport Commission [State environmental agencies]
OTCA .... Olson 30 Class Association (EA)
OTCA .... Ontario College of Art, Toronto, Ontario [Library symbol National Library of Canada] (NLC)
OTCA .... Oxothiazolidinecarboxylic Acid [Biochemistry]
OTCAG .... Canada Arctic Gas Study Ltd., Toronto, Ontario [Library symbol National Library of Canada] (NLC)
OTCAS .... Canadian Association in Support of the Native Peoples, Toronto, Ontario [Library symbol National Library of Canada] (NLC)
OTCBS .... Central Baptist Seminary and Bible College, Toronto, Ontario [Library symbol National Library of Canada] (NLC)
OTCC .... Operator Test Control Console (MCD)
OTCC .... Organic Thermal Control Coating
OTCC .... United Church of Canada Archives, Toronto, Ontario [Library symbol National Library of Canada] (NLC)
OTCCC .... Cross Cultural Communication Centre, Toronto, Ontario [Library symbol National Library of Canada] (NLC)
OTCCC .... Open Type Control Circuit Contacts (MSA)
OTCCL .... Currie, Coopers & Lybrand Ltd., Toronto, Ontario [Library symbol National Library of Canada] (NLC)
OTCCP .... Canadian Centre for Philanthropy, Toronto, Ontario [Library symbol National Library of Canada] (NLC)
OTCCRT .... Technical Standards Division, Ontario Ministry of Consumer and Commercial Relations, Toronto, Ontario [Library symbol National Library of Canada] (NLC)
OTCD .... Over-the-Counter-Drug [MEDA]
OTCE .... Central Library, North York, Ontario [Library symbol National Library of Canada] (NLC)
OTCEA .... [The] Canadian Education Association [L'Association Canadienne d'Education] Toronto, Ontario [Library symbol National Library of Canada] (NLC)
OTCF........... H. Ward Smith Library, Centre of Forensic Sciences, Toronto, Ontario [Library symbol National Library of Canada] (NLC)
OTCFA .... Occupational Therapy Comprehensive Functional Assessment
OTCGL .... Campbell, Godfrey & Lewtas, Toronto, Ontario [Library symbol National Library of Canada] (NLC)
OTCGR .... Canadian Gas Research Institute, Don Mills, Ontario [Library symbol National Library of Canada] (NLC)
OTCGW .... Clarkson, Gordon, Woods, Gordon, Toronto, Ontario [Library symbol National Library of Canada] (NLC)
OTCH .... Anglican Church House, Toronto, Ontario [Library symbol National Library of Canada] (NLC)
OTCH .... Obedience Trial Champion [Dog training]
OTCh........... Obedience Trial Champion [Prefix]
OTCHA......... Canadian Hospital Association [Association des Hopitaux du Canada] Toronto, Ontario [Library symbol National Library of Canada] (NLC)
OTCHAR...... Anglican Church of Canada Archives, Toronto, Ontario [Library symbol National Library of Canada] (NLC)
OTCI............ OTC [Overseas Telecommunications Commission] International Ltd. [Australia Telecommunications service] (TSSD)
OTCIA .... Canadian Institute of International Affairs [Institut Canadien des Affaires Internationales] Toronto, Ontario [Library symbol National Library of Canada] (NLC)
OTCIB .... Canadian Imperial Bank of Commerce, Toronto, Ontario [Library symbol National Library of Canada] (NLC)
OTCIL......... Central Library, C-I-L, Inc., North York, Ontario [Library symbol National Library of Canada] (NLC)
OTCILL........ Law Library, C-I-L, Inc., North York, Ontario [Library symbol National Library of Canada] (NLC)
OTCIXS .... Officer in Tactical Command Information Exchange Subsystem [Navy] (ANA)
OTCJC.......... Genealogical Society Library, Church of Jesus Christ of Latter-Day Saints, Etobicoke, Ontario [Library symbol National Library of Canada] (NLC)
OTCL........... Connaught Laboratories Ltd., Willowdale, Ontario [Library symbol National Library of Canada] (NLC)
OTCLA .... Confederation Life Association, Toronto, Ontario [Library symbol National Library of Canada] (NLC)
OTCLANT ..... Fleet Operational Training Command, Atlantic [Usually, COTCLANT]
OTCLH .... Research and Information Library, Canadian Life and Health Insurance Association, Toronto, Ontario [Library symbol National Library of Canada] (BIB)
OTCM .... Canadian School of Missions and Ecumenical Institute, Toronto, Ontario [Library symbol National Library of Canada] (NLC)
OTCM .... Ocean Systems Technician, Master Chief [Navy rating] (DNAB)
OTCM........... Orbiter Thermal Control Model [NASA]
OTCM......... Ordnance Technical Committee Minutes [Military]
OTCM......... Royce Micro-Cap Tr [NASDAQ symbol] (TTSB)
OTCM......... Royce OTC [Over the Counter] Micro Capital Fund [NASDAQ symbol] (SAG)
OTCMC .... Canadian Memorial Chiropractic College, Toronto, Ontario [Library symbol National Library of Canada] (NLC)
OTCMCC ...... Old Time Country Music Club of Canada (EA)
OTCMH .... Saul A. Silverman Library, C. M. Hincks Treatment Centre, Toronto, Ontario [Library symbol National Library of Canada] (BIB)
OTCMHA...... Canadian Mental Health Association, Toronto, Ontario [Library symbol National Library of Canada] (BIB)

OTCMLA ...... Canadian Music Library Association [Association Canadienne des Bibliotheques Musicales] Toronto, Ontario [Library symbol National Library of Canada]
OTCMS .... Operations Training Certification Management System [NASA]
OTCOM .... Cominco Ltd., Toronto, Ontario [Library symbol National Library of Canada] (NLC)
OTCOP .... Olympic Training Center Outreach Program
OTCOS .... Concord Scientific Corp., Downsview, Ontario [Library symbol National Library of Canada] (NLC)
OTCOU........ Council of Ontario Universities, Toronto, Ontario [Library symbol National Library of Canada] (NLC)
OTCP .... Canada Packers Ltd., Toronto, Ontario [Library symbol National Library of Canada] (NLC)
OTCPAC ...... Fleet Operational Training Command, Pacific [Usually, COTCPAC]
OTCPB .... Toronto City Planning Board Library, Ontario, [Library symbol National Library of Canada] (NLC)
OTCQM .... Office of the Theater Chief Quartermaster [World War II]
OTCR .... Office of Technical Cooperation and Research [Department of State]
OTCR .... Ontario Ministry of Culture and Communications, Toronto, Ontario [Library symbol National Library of Canada] (NLC)
OTCRC .... National Office Library, Canadian Red Cross Society [Bibliotheque du Siege Social, Societe Canadienne de la Croix-Rouge] Toronto, Ontario [Library symbol National Library of Canada] (NLC)
OTCRx .... Over-the-Counter Drug (MEDA)
OTCS .... Ocean Systems Technician, Senior Chief [Navy rating] (DNAB)
OTCS .... Ontario Ministry of Correctional Services, Toronto, Ontario [Library symbol National Library of Canada] (NLC)
OTCS .... Operational Teletype Communications Subsystem
OTCS .... Optical Transient Current Spectroscopy
OTCSA .... Canadian Standards Association, Rexdale, Ontario [Library symbol National Library of Canada] (NLC)
OTCSAO...... Construction Safety Association of Ontario, Toronto, Ontario [Library symbol National Library of Canada] (NLC)
OTCSC .... Civil Service Commission of Ontario, Toronto, Ontario [Library symbol National Library of Canada] (NLC)
OTCSE .... Canadian Selection, Toronto, Ontario [Library symbol National Library of Canada] (NLC)
OTCSS .... CANEBSCO Subscription Service Ltd., Toronto, Ontario [Library symbol National Library of Canada] (NLC)
OTCT........... Canadian Tax Foundation [Association Canadienne d'Etudes Fiscales] Toronto, Ontario [Library symbol National Library of Canada] (NLC)
OTCTA .... Canadian Telebook Agency, Toronto, Ontario [Library symbol National Library of Canada] (NLC)
OTCTAR ...... Division of Records and Archives, City of Toronto (NLC)
OTCTH .... Town Hall, Collins Canada, Toronto, Ontario [Library symbol National Library of Canada] (NLC)
OTCTVN ...... CTV News Research Library, CTV Television Network, Toronto, Ontario [Library symbol National Library of Canada] (NLC)
OTCW .... Canada Wire & Cable Co. Ltd., Toronto, Ontario [Library symbol National Library of Canada] (NLC)
OTCWB .... Welding Institute of Canada, Oakville, Ontario [Library symbol National Library of Canada] (NLC)
OTCWT .... Canadian Waste Technology, Inc., Toronto, Ontario [Library symbol National Library of Canada] (NLC)
OTD .... Contadora [Panama] [Airport symbol] (OAG)
OTD .... Doctor of Occupational Therapy (PGP)
OTD .... Ocean Travel Development (DS)
OTD .... Official Table of Distances (AFM)
OTD .... Offset, Tilted Dipole [Model of Uranus' magnetic field]
OTD .... Oil Turbine Drive
OTD .... On the Deck
OTD .... Operational Technical Documentation [NASA] (NASA)
OTD .... Operational Test Director [Navy]
OTD .... Operations and Technical Data [Engineering]
OTD .... Optical Time Domain (EECA)
OTD .... Optical Tracking Device
OTD .... Optical Transient Detector
OTD .... Optimal Terminal Descent (PDAA)
OTD .... Oral Temperature Device (MCD)
OTD .... Orbiter Test Director [NASA] (NASA)
OTD .... Orbit Test Direction [or Directive] (IAA)
OTD .... Organ Tolerance Dose
OTD .... Original Transmission Density (OA)
OTD .... Ortho-Toluenediamine [Organic chemistry]
OTD .... Out the Door (DAVI)
OTD .... Overseas-Trained Doctors
OTDA .... DSMA Acton Ltd., Toronto, Ontario [Library symbol National Library of Canada] (NLC)
OTDA .... Office of Tracking and Data Acquisition [NASA]
OTDAR........ Alexander Raxlen Memorial Library, Doctors Hospital, Toronto, Ontario [Library symbol National Library of Canada] (NLC)
OTDC .... Dominion Colour Ltd., Toronto, Ontario [Library symbol National Library of Canada] (NLC)
OTDC .... Observational Test and Development Center [National Weather Service] (NOAA)
OTDC .... Optical Target Designation Computer
OTDCB .... Dictionary of Canadian Biography, Toronto, Ontario [Library symbol National Library of Canada] (BIB)
OTDD .... Optical Target Detecting Device
OTDE .... Ontario Ministry of Education, Toronto, Ontario [Library symbol National Library of Canada] (NLC)
OTDH .... Ontario Ministry of Health, Toronto, Ontario [Library symbol National Library of Canada] (NLC)

OTDHA......... De Havilland Aircraft of Canada Ltd., Downsview, Ontario [*Library symbol National Library of Canada*] (NLC)

OTDHC......... Oceanographic Technical Data Handling Committee

OTDHL......... Laboratory Services, Ontario Ministry of Health, Toronto, Ontario [*Library symbol National Library of Canada*] (NLC)

OTDL........... Ontario Ministry of Labour, Toronto, Ontario [*Library symbol National Library of Canada*] (NLC)

OTDM.......... Mines Library, Ontario Ministry of Natural Resources, Toronto, Ontario [*Library symbol National Library of Canada*] (NLC)

OTDO........... Donwood Institute, Toronto, Ontario [*Library symbol National Library of Canada*] (BIB)

OTDR........... Optical Fiber Time-Domain Reflectometer [*Computer science*]

OTDR........... Optical Time Domain Reflectometer (NITA)

OTDR........... Outdoor

OTDR........... Scientific Information Centre, Defence and Civil Institute of Environmental Medicine, Canada Department of National Defence [*Centre d'Information Scientifique, Institut Militaire et Civil de Medecine de l'Environnement, Ministere de la Defense Nationale*] Downsview, Ontario [*Library symbol National Library of Canada*] (NLC)

OTDRE......... Ontario Ministry of Treasury and Economics, Toronto, Ontario [*Library symbol National Library of Canada*] (NLC)

OTDT........... Ontario Ministry of Transportation and Communications, Toronto, Ontario [*Library symbol National Library of Canada*] (NLC)

OTDT........... Operational Test, Development Test

OTDT........... Operations Training Development Team [*Air Force*]

OTDU........... Ontario Ministry of Colleges and Universities, Toronto, Ontario [*Library symbol National Library of Canada*] (NLC)

OTDW.......... Day-Wilson-Campbell, Toronto, Ontario [*Library symbol National Library of Canada*] (BIB)

OTE............. Emmanuel College, Victoria University, Toronto, Ontario [*Library symbol National Library of Canada*] (NLC)

OTE............. On-Target Earnings [*Sales industry*] (ODBW)

OTE............. Ontario Ministry of Treasury and Economics Library [*UTLAS symbol*]

OTE............. Operational Test and Evaluation [*Army*] (AABC)

OTE............. Operational Test Equipment [*NASA*] (KSC)

OTE............. Optically Transparent Electrode

OTE............. Optical Tracking Electronics

OTE............. Organismos Tilepikoinonion Ellados [*Hellenic Telecommunications Organization*] [*Greek*]

OTE............. Other Technical Effort

OTE............. Outer Tube Equipment

OTE............. Overtaken by Events [*US Congress*]

OTE............. Oxalyl Thiolester [*Biochemistry*]

OTEA........... Operational Test and Evaluation Agency [*Army*]

OTEA........... Oval Track Equipment Association (EA)

OTEAOW...... Atmospheric Environment Service (ODIT Ontario Weather Centre), Environment Canada [*Service de l'Environnement Atmospherique (Centre Meteorologique de l'Ontario), Environnement Canada*] Toronto, Ontario [*Library symbol National Library of Canada*] (NLC)

OTEBE......... Resource Library, Board of Education for the City of Etobicoke, Ontario [*Library symbol National Library of Canada*] (NLC)

OTEC........... Education Centre, Toronto Board of Education, Ontario [*Library symbol National Library of Canada*] (NLC)

OTEC........... Ocean Thermal Energy Conversion

OTEC........... Operational Test and Evaluation Command [*Army*] (AAGC)

OTEC........... Osage Tribal Education Committee [*Department of the Interior*] [*Muskogee, OK*] (EGAO)

OTECA......... Ocean Thermal Energy Conversion Act of 1980

OTECS......... Ocean Thermal Energy Conversion Systems [*Department of Energy*]

OTECU......... Colleges and Universitites, Ontario Ministry of Education, Toronto, Ontario [*Library symbol National Library of Canada*] (NLC)

OTEE........... Teeswater Branch, Bruce County Public Library, Ontario [*Library symbol National Library of Canada*] (NLC)

OTEF........... Operational Training and Evaluation Facility

OTEM........... ESSO [*Standard Oil*] Minerals of Canada, Toronto, Ontario [*Library symbol National Library of Canada*] (NLC)

OTEMAC...... Temagami Community Library, Ontario [*Library symbol National Library of Canada*] (NLC)

OTEMAS...... Osaka International Textile Machinery Show

OTEMC......... Elizabeth McRae Associates, Toronto, Ontario [*Library symbol Obsolete National Library of Canada*] (NLC)

OTEMP......... Overtemperature (NASA)

OTEMP......... Overtemperature

OTEMPO...... Operating Temporaries

OTEMR........ Conservation and Renewable Energy Office, Energy, Mines, and Resources Canada [*Bureau de la Conservation de l'Energie et de l'Energie Renouvelable, Energie, Mines, et Ressources Canada*] Toronto, Ontario [*Library symbol National Library of Canada*] (NLC)

OTEP........... Office of Transportation Energy Policy [*Department of Transportation*]

OTEP........... Operational Test and Evaluation Plan [*Military*] (AFM)

OTEPL......... Etobicoke Public Library, Ontario [*Library symbol National Library of Canada*] (NLC)

OTEPS......... Environmental Protection Service, Environment Canada [*Service de la Protection de l'Environnement, Environnement Canada*] Toronto, Ontario [*Library symbol National Library of Canada*] (NLC)

OTEPSE....... Environmental Emergency Library, Environmental Protection Service, Environment Canada [*Bibliotheque des Incidences Environnementales, Service de la Protection de l'Environnement, Environnement Canada*] Toronto, Ontario [*Library symbol National Library of Canada*] (NLC)

OTER........... Ontario Institute for Studies in Education, Toronto, Ontario [*Library symbol National Library of Canada*] (NLC)

OTES........... Operational Test and Evaluation Squadron [*Military*]

OTES........... Optical Technology Experiment System

OTES........... Orbiter Thermal Effects Simulator [*NASA*]

OTET........... Ontario Educational Communications Authority, Toronto, Ontario [*Library symbol National Library of Canada*] (NLC)

OTET........... TVOntario, Toronto, Ontario [*Library symbol National Library of Canada*] (NLC)

OTEU........... Office and Technical Employees (International) Union

O TEUT........ Old Teutonic [*Language, etc.*] (ROG)

OTEX........... Open Text Corp. [*NASDAQ symbol*] (SAG)

OTEXA......... Office of Textiles and Apparel [*Department of Commerce*] (GFGA)

OTEXF......... Open Text [*NASDAQ symbol*] (TTSB)

OTEY........... East York Public Library, Toronto, Ontario [*Library symbol National Library of Canada*] (NLC)

OTEYBE....... Professional Library, Board of Education for the Borough of East York, Toronto, Ontario [*Library symbol National Library of Canada*] (NLC)

OTF............. Institute of Environment Studies, University of Toronto, Ontario [*Library symbol National Library of Canada*] (NLC)

OTF............. Octamer Transcription Factor [*Genetics*]

OTF............. Off-the-Film [*Photography*] (WDMC)

OTF............. Off-the-Film Metering [*Olympus cameras*]

OTF............. Ontario Teachers Federation (AEBS)

OTF............. On the Floor [*Computer language*] [*Computer science*]

OTF............. On-the-Fly [*Computer compression program*] (PCM)

OTF............. Open Token Foundation (BTTJ)

OTF............. Optical Transfer Function

OTF............. Optimum Traffic Condition [*Radio*] (IAA)

OTF............. Optimum Traffic Frequency [*Radio*]

OTF............. Oral Transfer Factor [*Virology*]

OTF............. Orbital Test Flight (MCD)

OTF............. Other than Flat [*Freight*]

OTFC........... Official 3 Stooges Fan Club [*Defunct*] (EA)

OTFC........... Ontario Ministry of Consumer and Commercial Relations, Toronto, Ontario [*Library symbol National Library of Canada*] (NLC)

OTFC........... Overflight Traffic [*Aviation*] (FAAC)

OTFCS......... On-Target Fire Control System (MCD)

OTFE........... Optical Terminal Flight Evaluation

OTFEC......... Fenco Consultants Ltd., Toronto, Ontario [*Library symbol National Library of Canada*] (NLC)

OTFH........... Forest Hill Public Library, Toronto, Ontario [*Library symbol National Library of Canada*] (NLC)

OTFM........... Fire Marshal of Ontario, Toronto, Ontario [*Library symbol National Library of Canada*] (NLC)

OTFN........... Information Centre, Falconbridge Nickel Mines Ltd., Toronto, Ontario [*Library symbol National Library of Canada*] (NLC)

OT/FOT........ Operational Test/Follow-On Operational Test

OTFP........... Fisons Corp. Ltd., Markham, Ontario [*Library symbol National Library of Canada*] (NLC)

OTFP........... Octylthio(trifluoro)propanone [*Biochemistry*]

OTFP........... Operational Traffic Flow Planning (GAVI)

OTFP........... Other than Full Paid [*IRS*]

OTFR........... Overall Transfer Function Response

OTFT........... Financial Times, Don Mills, Ontario [*Library symbol National Library of Canada*] (NLC)

OT/FT.......... Operational Test/Follow-On Test [*Missiles*] (DOMA)

OTFTS......... Outfits

OTG............. Information Centre, Glaxo Canada, Inc., Toronto, Ontario [*Library symbol National Library of Canada*] (BIB)

OTG............. Oil Temperature Gauge (MSA)

OTG............. OPTEVFOR [*Operational Test and Evaluation Force*] Tactics Guide [*Navy*] (CAAL)

OTG............. Option Table Generator

OTG............. Otolith Test Goggles [*NASA*] (KSC)

OTG............. Worthington [*Minnesota*] [*Airport symbol*] (OAG)

OTGA........... Information Centre, Giffels Associates Ltd., Rexdale, Ontario [*Library symbol National Library of Canada*] (NLC)

OTGAR......... Engineering Library, Garrett Canada, Rexdale, Ontario [*Library symbol National Library of Canada*] (BIB)

OTGB........... Library and Audio-Visual Services, George Brown College of Applied Arts and Technology, Toronto, Ontario [*Library symbol National Library of Canada*] (BIB)

OTGFM......... Management Science Department, General Foods, Inc., Don Mills, Ontario [*Library symbol National Library of Canada*] (NLC)

OTGG........... Goodman & Goodman, Toronto, Ontario [*Library symbol National Library of Canada*] (BIB)

OTGH........... Fudger Medical Library, Toronto General Hospital, Ontario [*Library symbol National Library of Canada*] (NLC)

OTGHPP....... Ocean Thermal Gradient Hydraulic Power Plant

OTGM........... Globe and Mail, Toronto, Ontario [*Library symbol National Library of Canada*] (NLC)

OTGMC........ Gulf Minerals Canada Ltd., Toronto, Ontario [*Library symbol National Library of Canada*] (NLC)

OTGOH........ Gowling & Henderson, Toronto, Ontario [*Library symbol National Library of Canada*] (NLC)

OTGS........... Gore & Storrie Ltd., Toronto, Ontario [*Library symbol National Library of Canada*] (NLC)

OTGS........... Ocean Thermal Gradient System [*National Science Foundation*]

OTGSB......... Bibliographic Centre, Ontario Ministry of Government Services, Toronto, Ontario [*Library symbol National Library of Canada*] (NLC)

OTGSI .... CTS Information Resource Centre, Ontario Ministry of Government Services, Toronto [*Library symbol National Library of Canada*] (BIB)

OTH .... Independent Institute, NAD, Dublin, OH [*OCLC symbol*] (OCLC)

OTH .... North Bend [*Oregon*] [*Airport symbol*] (OAG)

OTH .... Oil-Tight Hatch [*Shipfitting*]

OTH .... Ontario Hydro, Toronto, Ontario [*Library symbol National Library of Canada*] (NLC)

OTH .... Optical Time History (MCD)

Oth .... Othello [*Shakespearean work*]

OTH .... Othello [*Washington*] [*Seismograph station code, US Geological Survey*] (SEIS)

oth .... Other (VRA)

OTH .... Other (DAVI)

OTH .... Other than Hand [*Freight*]

OTH .... Other than Honorable Conditions [*Military*] (AABC)

OTH .... Over-the-Horizon [*RADAR*]

OTHA .... Hatch Associates Ltd., Toronto, Ontario [*Library symbol National Library of Canada*] (NLC)

OTHB .... Over-the-Horizon Back-Scatter [*RADAR*]

OTHB .... Toronto Historical Society, Ontario [*Library symbol National Library of Canada*] (BIB)

OTHC .... Humber College of Applied Arts and Technology, Rexdale, Ontario [*Library symbol National Library of Canada*] (NLC)

OTH/DA .... Over-the-Horizon/Damage Assessment [*Navy*] (CAAL)

OTHDC & T... Over-the-Horizon Detection, Classification, and Targeting (NVT)

OTH-E .... Over-the-Horizon - Expanded

OTHE .... Thessalon Union Public Library, Ontario [*Library symbol National Library of Canada*] (NLC)

OTHER .... Open Tubular Heterogeneous Enzyme Reactor [*Biochemical engineering*]

OTH-F .... Over-the-Horizon - Forward Scatter

OTHL .... Advanced Technology Centre, Honeywell Ltd., Willowdale, Ontario [*Library symbol National Library of Canada*] (NLC)

OTHMC .... Information Resources, Hay Management Consultants, Toronto, Ontario [*Library symbol National Library of Canada*] (NLC)

OTHMH .... Humber Memorial Hospital, Weston, Ontario [*Library symbol National Library of Canada*] (NLC)

OTHO .... Thornbury Public Library, Ontario [*Library symbol National Library of Canada*] (NLC)

OTHOP .... Quebec & Ontario Paper Co. Ltd., Thorold, Ontario [*Library symbol National Library of Canada*] (NLC)

OTHOR .... Thornhill Public Library, Ontario [*Library symbol National Library of Canada*] (NLC)

OTHORF ...... Metallurgical Laboratory, Falconbridge Nickel Mines Ltd., Thornhill, Ontario [*Library symbol National Library of Canada*] (NLC)

OTHORO ...... Thorold Public Library, Ontario [*Library symbol National Library of Canada*] (BIB)

OTHR .... Ontario Hydro Research, Toronto, Ontario [*Library symbol National Library of Canada*] (NLC)

OTHR .... Over-the-Horizon RADAR (MCD)

OTHSA .... Orphan Train Heritage Society of America (EA)

OTHSC .... Hospital for Sick Children, Toronto, Ontario [*Library symbol National Library of Canada*] (NLC)

OTHSSM ...... Over-the-Horizon Ship-to-Ship Missile

OTHT .... Over-the-Horizon Targeting (NVT)

OTHU .... Huntec Ltd., Toronto, Ontario [*Library symbol National Library of Canada*] (NLC)

OTI .... Morotai Island [*Indonesia*] [*Airport symbol*] (OAG)

OTI .... Newport, RI [*Location identifier FAA*] (FAAL)

OTI .... Office of Technical Information (MUGU)

OTI .... Office of Trade and Investment [*Victoria, Australia*]

OTI .... Office of Treatment Improvement [*U.S. Public Health Service*] (BARN)

OTI .... Official Test Insecticide

OTI .... Optimum Time Invariant (IAA)

OTI .... Ordnance Technical Instructions [*Navy*]

OTI .... Oregon Technical Institute

OTI .... Original Title [*Online database field identifier*]

OTI .... Otiai [*Former USSR Seismograph station code, US Geological Survey Closed*] (SEIS)

OTI .... OT Industries, Inc. [*Vancouver Stock Exchange symbol*]

OTI .... Ovomucoid Trypsin Inhibitor [*Medicine*] (DMAA)

OTI .... Oxide Throat Insert

OTI .... Timmins Public Library, Ontario [*Library symbol National Library of Canada*] (NLC)

OTIA .... Office of Technical Information Agency [*Army*] (MCD)

OTIA .... Ordnance Technical Intelligence Agency (AAG)

OTIAP .... IAPA [*Industrial Accident Prevention Association*] Library, Toronto, Ontario [*Library symbol National Library of Canada*] (NLC)

OTIBI .... IBI Group, Toronto, Ontario [*Library symbol National Library of Canada*] (BIB)

OTIC .... Idea Corp., Toronto, Ontario [*Library symbol National Library of Canada*] (NLC)

OTIC .... Innovation Ontario Corp., Toronto, Ontario [*Library symbol National Library of Canada*] (NLC)

OTICA .... Institute of Chartered Accountants of Ontario, Toronto, Ontario [*Library symbol National Library of Canada*] (NLC)

OTID .... Industrial Disease Standards Panel, Toronto, Ontario [*Library symbol National Library of Canada*] (BIB)

OTID .... Office of Talented Identification and Development [*Johns Hopkins University*] (EDAC)

OTID .... Office of Talented Indentification and Development [*Johns Hopkins Institute*] (WDAA)

OTIEP .... Office of Technical Information and Educational Programs [*Terminated NASA*]

OTIF .... Organisation Intergouvernementale pour les Transports Internationaux Ferrovaires [*Intergovernmental Organization for International Carriage by Rail*] (EAIO)

OTif .... Tiffin Seneca Public Library, Tiffin, OH [*Library symbol Library of Congress*] (LCLS)

OTifH .... Heidelberg College, Tiffin, OH [*Library symbol Library of Congress*] (LCLS)

OTIG .... Office of the Inspector General [*Army*] (AABC)

OTIHM .... Tillsonburg and District Historical Museum Society, Tillsonburg, Ontario [*Library symbol National Library of Canada*] (NLC)

OTII .... Our Torah Institutions of Israel (EA)

OTIL .... Tilbury Public Library, Ontario [*Library symbol National Library of Canada*] (NLC)

OTIM .... Pontifical Institute of Mediaeval Studies, University of Toronto, Ontario [*Library symbol National Library of Canada*] (NLC)

OTIN .... International Nickel Co. of Canada Ltd., Toronto, Ontario [*Library symbol National Library of Canada*] (NLC)

OTINF .... Infomart, Toronto, Ontario [*Library symbol National Library of Canada*] (NLC)

OTINP .... Information Plus Library, Toronto, Ontario [*Library symbol National Library of Canada*] (BIB)

OTIO .... United Kingdom Information Office, Toronto, Ontario [*Library symbol National Library of Canada*] (NLC)

OTIOL .... Imperial Oil Ltd., Toronto, Ontario [*Library symbol National Library of Canada*] (NLC)

OTIP .... Occupational Therapist in Independent Practice

OTIP .... Tillsonburg Public Library, Ontario [*Library symbol National Library of Canada*] (NLC)

OTIR .... Operational Test Incident Report (MCD)

OTIS .... Observer's Thermal Imaging System (PDAA)

OTIS .... Occupational Training Information System

OTIS .... Offset Target Indicator System (MCD)

OTIS .... Oklahoma Teletype Interlibrary System [*Library network*]

OTIS .... Once-Through Integral System [*Nuclear energy*] (NRCH)

OTIS .... One Term In-Service Course (AIE)

OTIS .... Online Telecommunications Information Service [*Connections Telecommunications, Inc.*] [*West Bridgewater, MA*] [*Telecommunications service*] (TSSD)

OTIS .... Operational Test Instrumentation Ship [*Navy*]

OTIS .... Operation, Transport, Inspection, Storage (MHDB)

OTIS .... Ordnance Telemetry Instrumentation Station [*Army*] (AABC)

OTIS .... Oregon Total Information System [*Eugene*] [*Information service or system*] (IID)

OTIS .... Other than Iron or Steel [*Freight*]

OTIS .... Overstayer Tracing and Intelligence System [*British*]

Otis Art Inst... Otis Art Institute of Parsons School of Design (GAGS)

OT/ITS .... Office of Telecommunications Institute for Telecommunication Sciences [*Boulder, CO*] [*Department of Commerce*]

OTIU .... Overseas Technical Information Unit [*Department of Trade*] [*British*]

OTIV .... Tiverton Branch, Bruce County Public Library, Ontario [*Library symbol National Library of Canada*] (NLC)

OTJ .... Off-the-Job

OTJ .... On the Job

OTJ .... Toronto Regional Office, Department of Justice Canada [*Bureau Regional de Toronto, Ministere de la Justice du Canada*] Toronto, Ontario [*Library symbol National Library of Canada*] (NLC)

OTJAE .... John Arpin Enterprises, Inc., Toronto, Ontario [*Library symbol National Library of Canada*] (NLC)

OTJAG .... Office of the Judge Advocate General [*Army*] (AABC)

OTJFM .... James F. MacLaren Ltd., Willowdale, Ontario [*Library symbol National Library of Canada*] (NLC)

OTJL .... Judges Library, Ontario Ministry of the Attorney General, Toronto, Ontario [*Library symbol National Library of Canada*] (NLC)

OTJPS .... Sands Pharmaceutical Division, Jerram Pharmaceuticals Ltd., Toronto, Ontario [*Library symbol National Library of Canada*] (NLC)

OTJT .... On the Job Training

OTJWT .... Information Centre, J. Walter Thompson Co. Ltd., Toronto, Ontario [*Library symbol National Library of Canada*] (NLC)

OTK .... Knox College, University of Toronto, Ontario [*Library symbol National Library of Canada*] (NLC)

OTK .... Oil Tank

OTK .... Oxidizer Tank (MCD)

OTKC .... Kidd Creek Mines Ltd., Toronto, Ontario [*Library symbol National Library of Canada*] (NLC)

OTKDF .... Other than Knocked Down Flat [*Freight*]

OTKE .... Kilborn Engineering Ltd., Toronto, Ontario [*Library symbol National Library of Canada*] (NLC)

OTL .... Boutilimit [*Mauritania*] [*Airport symbol*] (AD)

OTL .... Legislative Library of Ontario, Toronto, Ontario [*Library symbol National Library of Canada*] (NLC)

OTL .... Libbey-Owens-Ford Glass Co., Technical Library, Toledo, OH [*Library symbol Library of Congress*] (LCLS)

OTL .... Observer Target Line (NVT)

OTL .... Office Technology Ltd. (NITA)

OTL .... Ogden Technology Laboratories [*NASA*] (KSC)

OTL .... Ohio Theological Librarians [*Library network*]

OTL .... Oil-Tight Light

OTL .... [*The*] Old Testament Library [*A publication*] (BJA)

OTL .... Online Task Loader

OTL .... Operating Temperature Limit

OTL .... Operating Time Log (AAG)

OTL .... Oracle Teletext Ltd. (NITA)
OTL .... Order Trunk Line [*Telecommunications*] (OA)
OTL .... Ordnance Test Laboratory (NASA)
OTL .... Outer Tube Limit [*Chemical engineering*]
OTL .... Outland Resources [*Vancouver Stock Exchange symbol*]
OTL .... Output-Transformerless (SAA)
OTL .... Out to Lunch
OTL .... Over the Line (WDAA)
OTL .... Ovine Testicular Lymph [*Endocrinology*]
OTL .... Oxidizer Topping Line (AAG)
OTLAC .... Tamworth Branch, Lennox and Addington County Library, Ontario [*Library symbol National Library of Canada*] (BIB)
OTLC .... Information Section, Ontario Ministry of Natural Resources, Toronto, Ontario [*Library symbol National Library of Canada*] (NLC)
OTLC .... Open Tubular Liquid Chromatography
OTLC .... Orbiter Timeline Constraints [*NASA*] (NASA)
OTLCC .... Lummus Co. Canada Ltd., Willowdale, Ontario [*Library symbol National Library of Canada*] (NLC)
OTLF .... Natural Resources Library, Ontario Ministry of Natural Resources, Toronto, Ontario [*Library symbol National Library of Canada*] (NLC)
OTLH .... Laventhol & Horwath, Toronto, Ontario, [*Library symbol National Library of Canada*] (BIB)
OTLK .... Outlook [*NWS*] (FAAC)
OTLMO .... Orde des Technologistes de Laboratoire Medical de l'Ontario (AC)
OTLO .... Libbey-Owens-Ford Glass Co., Corporate Library, Toledo, OH [*Library symbol Library of Congress*] (LCLS)
OTLP .... Ledbury Park Junior High School, Toronto, Ontario [*Library symbol National Library of Canada*] (NLC)
OTLR .... Research Branch, Ontario Ministry of Natural Resources, Toronto, Ontario [*Library symbol National Library of Canada*] (NLC)
OTLS .... Law Society of Upper Canada, Toronto, Ontario [*Library symbol National Library of Canada*] (NLC)
OTLSC .... Litton Systems Canada Ltd., Rexdale, Ontario [*Library symbol National Library of Canada*] (NLC)
OTM .... Atmospheric Environment Service, Environment Canada [*Service de l'Environnement Atmospherique, Environnement Canada*] Downsview, Ontario [*Library symbol National Library of Canada*] (NLC)
OTM .... Odd Transversal Magnetic (IAA)
OTM .... Office of Telecommunications Management [*Later, OTP*] [*FCC*]
OTM .... Once-through-Methanol [*Fuel technology*]
OTM .... On the Mark - Mark Hamill Fan Club (EA)
OTM .... On-Time Marker [*Computer science*]
OTM .... Optical Tool Master (MCD)
OTM .... Organo-Transition-Metal (PDAA)
OTM .... Original Turkey Mill [*Paper*] (DGA)
OTM .... Ortho-Tolidine Manganese Sulphate
OTM .... Other than Mexican [*Term applied by US Border Patrol to certain illegal immigrants*]
OTM .... Ottumwa [*Iowa*] [*Airport symbol*] (OAG)
OTM .... Timken Co., Research Library, Canton, OH [*OCLC symbol*] (OCLC)
OTM .... Toledo Museum of Art, Toledo, OH [*Library symbol Library of Congress*] (LCLS)
OTMA .... Office Technology Management Association [*Defunct*] (EA)
OTMA .... Oilfield Tank Manufacturers Association (EA)
OTMAG .... Ontario Ministry of the Attorney General [*Ministere du Procureur-General*],Toronto [*Library symbol National Library of Canada*] (BIB)
OTMB .... McMillan, Binch, Toronto, Ontario [*Library symbol National Library of Canada*] (NLC)
OTMC .... Massey College, Toronto, Ontario [*Library symbol National Library of Canada*] (NLC)
OTMC .... Medical College of Ohio at Toledo, Toledo, OH [*Library symbol Library of Congress*] (LCLS)
OTMCL .... Metropolitan Toronto Library, Ontario [*Library symbol National Library of Canada*] (NLC)
OTME .... Ontario Ministry of Energy, Toronto, Ontario [*Library symbol National Library of Canada*] (NLC)
OTMEN .... Ontario Ministry of the Environment, Toronto, Ontario [*Library symbol National Library of Canada*] (NLC)
OTMENL ...... Laboratory, Ontario Ministry of the Environment, Rexdale, Ontario [*Library symbol National Library of Canada*] (NLC)
OTMF .... McIntyre-Falconbridge Library, Toronto, Ontario [*Library symbol National Library of Canada*] (NLC)
OTMH .... Financial Post, Toronto, Ontario [*Library symbol National Library of Canada*] (NLC)
OTMI .... Royal Canadian Military Institute, Toronto, Ontario [*Library symbol National Library of Canada*] (NLC)
OTMIO .... Employment and Immigration Canada [*Emploi et Immigration Canada*] Toronto, Ontario [*Library symbol National Library of Canada*] (NLC)
OTMIO .... Ontario Region Library, Employment and Immigration Canada [*Bibliotheque de laRegion de l'Ontario, Emploi et Immigration Canada*], North York, Ontario [*Library symbol National Library of Canada*] (NLC)
OTMIP .... One-Time Mortgage Insurance Premium (GFGA)
OTMIS .... Medical Information Services, Toronto, Ontario [*Library symbol National Library of Canada*] (BIB)
OTMJ .... Outgoing Trunk Message Junction [*Telecommunications*] (OA)
OTML .... Law Library, Manufacturers Life Insurance Co., Toronto, Ontario [*Library symbol National Library of Canada*] (BIB)
OTML .... Oatmeal [*Freight*]
OTMM .... Mary Manse College, Toledo, OH [*Library symbol Library of Congress*] (LCLS)

OTMM .... McCarthy & McCarthy, Barristers & Solicitors, Toronto, Ontario [*Library symbol National Library of Canada*] (NLC)
OTMMB .... Ontario Milks Marketing Board, Toronto, Ontario [*Library symbol National Library of Canada*] (NLC)
OTMML .... Micromedia Ltd., Toronto, Ontario [*Library symbol National Library of Canada*] (NLC)
OTMMM .... Marshall-Macklin-Monaghan Library, Don Mills, Ontario [*Library symbol National Library of Canada*] (NLC)
OTMN .... Oxotremorine [*Cholinergic agent*]
OTMO .... Monopros Ltd., Toronto, Ontario [*Library symbol National Library of Canada*] (BIB)
OTMOF .... MacDonald Ophthalmic Foundation, Toronto, Ontario [*Library symbol National Library of Canada*] (NLC)
OTMS .... Mount Sinai Hospital, Toronto, Ontario [*Library symbol National Library of Canada*] (NLC)
OTMS .... [*The*] Old Testament and Modern Study [*A publication*] (BJA)
OTMS .... Operational Technical Managerial System (NVT)
OTMSM .... Management Services Department Library, Municipality of Metropolitan Toronto, Ontario [*Library symbol National Library of Canada*] (BIB)
OTMSS .... Professional Library, Metropolitan Separate School Board, Willowdale, Ontario [*Library symbol National Library of Canada*] (NLC)
OTMT .... Monetary Times, Toronto, Ontario [*Library symbol National Library of Canada*] (NLC)
OTMTC .... Economic Development Division, Metro Toronto Chairman's Office, Toronto, Ontario [*Library symbol National Library of Canada*] (BIB)
OTMTS .... Metropolitan Toronto School Board, Ontario [*Library symbol National Library of Canada*] (NLC)
OTMTSS ...... Secondary Schools, Metropolitan Toronto School Board, Ontario [*Library symbol National Library of Canada*] (NLC)
OTMW .... Department of Works, Municipality of Metropolitan Toronto, Ontario [*Library symbol National Library of Canada*] (BIB)
OTN .... Lastp-Linhas Aereas de Sao Tome e Principe [*ICAO designator*] (FAAC)
OTN .... Newtonbrook Secondary School, Willowdale, Ontario [*Library symbol National Library of Canada*] (NLC)
OTN .... Oaktown, IN [*Location identifier FAA*] (FAAL)
OTN .... Octal Track Number [*Computer science*]
OTN .... Operational Teletype Network
OTN .... Operational Test, Non-Major Systems (MCD)
OTN .... Over the Nose [*Aviation*]
OTN .... Own-the-Night [*Technology*] [*Army*] (INF)
OTNA .... Ontario Ministry of Northern Development and Mines, Toronto, Ontario [*Library symbol National Library of Canada*] (NLC)
OTNC .... International Council for Adult Education, Toronto, Ontario [*Library symbol National Library of Canada*] (BIB)
OTNG .... Observer Training [*Army*] (AABC)
OTNGH .... Health Sciences Library, Northwestern General Hospital, Toronto, Ontario [*Library symbol National Library of Canada*] (BIB)
OTNH .... National Heritage Ltd., Toronto, Ontario [*Library symbol National Library of Canada*] (NLC)
OTNHH .... Health Protection Branch, Canada Department of National Health and Welfare [*Direction Generale de la Protection de la Sante, Ministere de la Sante Nationale et du Bien-Etre Social*] Toronto, Ontario [*Library symbol National Library of Canada*] (NLC)
OTNI .... Industrial Development Office, National Research Council Canada [*Bureau du Developpement Industriel, Conseil National de Recherches Canada*], Scarborough, Ontario [*Library symbol National Library of Canada*] (NLC)
OTNIMR .... G. Allan Roeher Institute, Downsview, Ontario [*Library symbol National Library of Canada*] (NLC)
OTNIMR .... National Institute on Mental Retardation [*Institut National pour la Deficience Mentale*] Toronto, Ontario [*Library symbol National Library of Canada*] (NLC)
OTNM .... Northern Mines, Toronto, Ontario [*Library symbol National Library of Canada*] (NLC)
OTNM .... Over-Thirty-Never-Married [*Lifestyle classification*]
OTNP .... Other than New Procurement [*Navy*] (DNAB)
OTNR .... Survey Records Branch, Ontario Ministry of Natural Resources, Toronto, Ontario [*Library symbol National Library of Canada*] (BIB)
OTNS .... Bank of Nova Scotia [*Banque de Nouvelle-Ecosse*], Toronto, Ontario [*Library symbol National Library of Canada*] (NLC)
OTNY .... North York Public Library, Willowdale, Ontario [*Library symbol National Library of Canada*] (NLC)
OTNYE .... F. W. Minkler Library, North York Board of Education, Willowdale, Ontario [*Library symbol National Library of Canada*] (NLC)
OTO .... Oil Temperature Out
OTO .... One-Time-Only
OTO .... Operator-to-Operator [*Military*] (CAAL)
OTO .... Optical Tracker Operator (MUGU)
OTO .... Ordo Templi Orientis [*Order of the Oriental Templars*] [*A mystical lodge*] [*Latin*] (ADA)
Oto .... Otolaryngology [*Medicine*]
OTO .... Otology [*Medicine*]
OTO .... Otology
oto .... Otomian [*MARC language code Library of Congress*] (LCCP)
OTO .... Otorhinolaryngology [*Medicine*] (DHSM)
OTO .... Otto, NM [*Location identifier FAA*] (FAAL)
OTO .... Out-to-Out (AAG)
OTO .... Owens-Illinois, Inc., Technical Information Service-NTC, Toledo, OH [*Library symbol Library of Congress*] (LCLS)

OTO .... Tottenham Public Library, Ontario [*Library symbol National Library of Canada*] (NLC)

OTOB .... Tobermory Branch, Bruce County Public Library, Ontario [*Library symbol National Library of Canada*] (NLC)

OTOC .... Ontario Cancer Institute, Toronto, Ontario [*Library symbol National Library of Canada*] (NLC)

OTOCTA ...... Optimum Technical Operational Concept to Accomplish

OTOD .... Organization of Teachers of Oral Diagnosis (EA)

OTOE .... Omnispace Environments Ltd., Toronto, Ontario [*Library symbol National Library of Canada*] (NLC)

OTOEB .... Ontario Energy Board, Toronto, Ontario [*Library symbol National Library of Canada*] (NLC)

OTOGR......... Canadian Geriatrics Research Society, Toronto, Ontario [*Library symbol National Library of Canada*] (NLC)

OTOH .... Ontario Ministry of Municipal Affairs and Housing, Toronto, Ontario [*Library symbol National Library of Canada*] (NLC)

OTOH .... On the Other Hand [*Internet language*] [*Computer science*]

OTOHCR ...... Central Records, Ontario Hydro, Toronto, Ontario [*Library symbol National Library of Canada*] (NLC)

OTOL .... Ontario Lottery Corporation, Toronto, Ontario [*Library symbol National Library of Canada*] (BIB)

OTOL .... Otology [*Medicine*]

Otolar .... Otolaryngology [*Medicine*] (DAVI)

OTOLR .... Ontario Labour Relations Board [*Commission des Relations de Travail de l'Ontario*], Toronto, Ontario [*Library symbol National Library of Canada*] (NLC)

OTOLRC .... Ontario Law Reform Commission, Toronto, Ontario [*Library symbol National Library of Canada*] (BIB)

OTOMA .... Ontario Medical Association, Toronto, Ontario [*Library symbol National Library of Canada*] (NLC)

OTOME .... Information Resource Centre, Ontario Municipal Employees Retirement Board, Toronto [*Library symbol National Library of Canada*] (BIB)

OTOMR........ Ontario Ministry of Revenue, Toronto, Ontario [*Library symbol National Library of Canada*] (NLC)

OTONA........ Ontario Nurses Association, Toronto, Ontario [*Library symbol National Library of Canada*] (NLC)

OTO NAVSUPPACT... Overseas Transportation Office, Naval Support Activity (DNAB)

O to O .... Out to Out [*Technical drawings*]

OTOPC .... Ortho Pharmaceutical Canada Ltd., Don Mills, Ontario [*Library symbol National Library of Canada*] (NLC)

OTOPCT .... Planning and Research Library, Technical Services Branch, Ontario Police Commission, Toronto, Ontario [*Library symbol National Library of Canada*] (NLC)

OTOS .... Orbit-to-Orbit Stage [*NASA*] (MCD)

OTOSC .... Ontario Securities Commission, Toronto, Ontario [*Library symbol National Library of Canada*] (NLC)

OTOSS .... Ontario Secondary School Teachers Federation, Toronto, Ontario [*Library symbol National Library of Canada*] (NLC)

OTOW .... Resource Centre, Ontario Women's Directorate [*Library symbol National Library of Canada*] (BIB)

OTP .... Ocean Test Platform [*Marine science*] (MSC)

OTP .... Office of Telecommunications Policy [*Terminated, 1978*] [*Executive Office of the President*]

OTP .... Office of Trade Promotion [*Department of Commerce*]

OTP............. Office Technology Plus [*General Services Administration*]

OTP............. Of This Parish

OTP............. Of True Position (MSA)

OTP............. One-Time Pad [*Navy British*]

OTP............. One-Time Programmable [*Computer science*]

OTP............. On Top [*Aviation*]

OTP............. Open Top [*Freight*]

OTP............. Operational Test Plan

OTP............. Operational Test Procedure (KSC)

OTP............. Operations Turnaround Plan (NASA)

OTP............. Oscillation Test Point [*British military*] (DMA)

OTP............. Otepa [*Tuamotu Archipelago*] [*Seismograph station code, US Geological Survey*] (SEIS)

OTP............. Other than Portable [*Freight*]

Ot P .... Otto Papiensis [*Flourished, 12th century*] [*Authority cited in pre-1607 legal work*] (DSA)

OTP............. Outline Test Plan [*Army*]

OTP............. Overhead Trickle Purification (PDAA)

OTP............. Overtime Premium (MCD)

OTP............. Ovine Trophoblast Protein [*Biochemistry*]

OTP............. Oxidizer Tanking Panel (AAG)

OTP............. Ozone Trends Panel [*NASA*]

OTP............. Toronto Public Libraries, Ontario [*Library symbol National Library of Canada*] (NLC)

OTPA .... Institute of Public Administration of Canada [*Institut d'Administration Publique du Canada*] Toronto, Ontario [*Library symbol National Library of Canada*] (NLC)

OTPAL .... PAL Reading Service, Toronto, Ontario [*Library symbol National Library of Canada*] (NLC)

OTPEC .... Officer Training Program Examining Center [*Air Force*]

OTPFA .... Fine Arts Library, Northern District, Toronto Public Libraries, Ontario [*Library symbol National Library of Canada*] (NLC)

OTPG .... Polar Gas Library, Toronto, Ontario [*Library symbol National Library of Canada*] (NLC)

OTPH .... History Section, Metropolitan Toronto Library, Ontario [*Library symbol National Library of Canada*] (NLC)

OTPHC .... Prentice Hall Canada, Inc., Scarborough, Ontario [*Library symbol National Library of Canada*] (NLC)

OTPHR .... Resource Centre, Department of Public Health, City of Toronto, Ontario [*Library symbol National Library of Canada*] (BIB)

OTPI............ On Top Position Indicator [*Navy*] (NG)

OTPI............ Operational Test Program Instruction (MCD)

OTPM.......... Peat, Marwick & Partners, Toronto, Ontario [*Library symbol National Library of Canada*] (NLC)

OTPMG .... Office of the Provost Marshal General [*Army*]

OTPNL .... Outer Pane [*Aerospace*] (IAA)

OTPP .... Ocean Thermal Power Plant

OTPP .... Office of Transport, Policy and Planning [*South Australia*]

OTPP .... Ontario Provincial Police, Toronto, Ontario [*Library symbol National Library of Canada*] (NLC)

Ot Pp .... Otto Papiensis [*Flourished, 12th century*] [*Authority cited in pre-1607 legal work*] (DSA)

OTPPC .... Ontario Provincial Police College, Toronto, Ontario [*Library symbol National Library of Canada*] (NLC)

OTPR .... Proctor & Redfern Group, Don Mills, Ontario [*Library symbol National Library of Canada*] (NLC)

OTPROM ...... One-Time Programmable Read Only Memory [*Computer science*]

OTP/RS .... Outline Test Plan/Resume Sheet (MCD)

OTPRW .... National Office Library, Price Waterhouse & Co., Toronto, Ontario [*Library symbol National Library of Canada*] (BIB)

OTPS .... Oceanic Traffic Planning System [*FAA*] (TAG)

OTPS .... Operational Test Program Set (MCD)

OTPT .... Operational Test Program Tape (MCD)

OTPT........... Output (KSC)

OTPW .... Ontario Ministry of Community and Social Services, Toronto, Ontario [*Library symbol National Library of Canada*] (NLC)

OTPWC .... Ontario Regional Library, Public Works Canada [*Bibliotheque Regionale de l'Ontario, Travaux Publics Canada*] Toronto, Ontario [*Library symbol National Library of Canada*] (NLC)

OTQ .... On the Quarter

OTQE .... Queen Elizabeth Hospital, Toronto, Ontario [*Library symbol National Library of Canada*] (NLC)

OTQL .... Quaere Legal Resources Ltd., Toronto, Ontario [*Library symbol National Library of Canada*] (NLC)

OTQRM........ [*The*] Queen's Own Rifles of Canada Regimental Museum, Toronto, Ontario [*Library symbol National Library of Canada*] (NLC)

OTQSM .... Queen Street Mental Health Centre, Toronto, Ontario [*Library symbol National Library of Canada*] (NLC)

OTR .... Coto 47 [*Costa Rica*] [*Airport symbol*] (OAG)

OTR .... [*The*] Oakland Terminal Railway [*Formerly, OKT*] [*AAR code*]

OTR .... Observed Temperature Rise

OTR .... Occupational Therapist, Registered

OTR .... Oceanic Transition Route [*FAA*] (TAG)

OTR .... Office of Technical Resources

OTR .... Off-the-Road

OTR .... Old Time Radio

OTR .... One Touch Recording

OTR .... Open-Tubular Reactor

OTR .... Operating Temperature Range

OTR .... Operational Time Record (AAG)

OTR .... Optical Tracking [*NASA*] (KSC)

OTR .... Optical Transition Radiation [*Physics*]

OTR .... Oregon Tax Reports [*A publication*] (DLA)

OTR .... Organic Test Reactor [*Nuclear energy*]

OTR .... Orotek Resources Corp. [*Vancouver Stock Exchange symbol*]

OTR .... Outer (MSA)

OTR .... Outer

OTR .... Ovarian Tumor Registry [*Medicine*]

OTR .... Over-the-Road [*Automotive engineering*]

OTR .... Oxygen Transfer Rate [*Chemical engineering*]

OTR .... Ryerson Polytechnical Institute, Toronto, Ontario [*Library symbol National Library of Canada*] (NLC)

OTr.............. Troy-Miami County Public Library, Troy, OH [*Library symbol Library of Congress*] (LCLS)

OTRA .... Other than Regular Army (AABC)

OTRA .... Oversea Theater Requisitioning Authority [*Military*]

OTRA .... Royal Astronomical Society [*Societe Royale d'Astronomie*] Toronto, Ontario [*Library symbol National Library of Canada*] (NLC)

OTRAC .... Oscillogram Trace Reader [*Non-Linear Systems, Inc.*] [*Computer science*]

OTRAG........ Orbital Transport- und Raketen-Aktiengesellschaft [*Rocket company*] [*Germany*]

OTRAL .... Rio Algom Ltd., Toronto, Ontario [*Library symbol National Library of Canada*] (NLC)

OTRAN .... Ocean Testing Ranges and Instrumentation Conference

OTRAR .... Other than Regular Army

OTRBI .... Information Resources, Royal Bank of Canada, Toronto, Ontario [*Library symbol National Library of Canada*] (NLC)

OTRBSA .... Occupational Therapists' Registration Board of South Australia

OTRC .... Canadian Forces College, Toronto, Ontario [*Library symbol National Library of Canada*] (NLC)

OTRCF .... Royal Commission on the Future of the Toronto Waterfront, Toronto, Ontario [*Library symbol National Library of Canada*] (BIB)

OTRCL .... Reichhold Chemicals Ltd., Weston, Ontario [*Library symbol National Library of Canada*] (NLC)

OTRCR .... Trout Creek Community Library, Ontario [*Library symbol National Library of Canada*] (NLC)

OTRCS .... Canadian Forces Staff School, Canada Department of National Defence [*College d'Etat-Major des Forces Canadiennes, Ministere de la Defense Nationale*] Toronto, Ontario [*Library symbol National Library of Canada*] (NLC)

OTRE .... Trenton Public Library, Ontario [*Library symbol National Library of Canada*] (NLC)

OTREC .... Regis College, Toronto, Ontario [*Library symbol National Library of Canada*] (NLC)

OTReg .... Occupational Therapist Registered [*Canada*] (BABM)

OTReg .... Occupational Therapist Registered [*Canada*] (DAVI)

OTREN .... Northumberland County Public Library, Warkworth, Ontario [*Library symbol National Library of Canada*] (NLC)

OTREX .... Canada Department of Regional Industrial Expansion [*Ministere de l'Expansion Industrielle Regionale*] Toronto, Ontario [*Library symbol National Library of Canada*] (NLC)

OTR Ex .... OTR Express, Inc. [*Associated Press*] (SAG)

OTRF .... Ontario Research Foundation, Sheridan Park, Mississauga, Ontario [*Library symbol National Library of Canada*] (NLC)

OTRG .... Office Technology Research Group [*Defunct*] (EA)

OTRG .... Old Testament Reading Guide [*Collegeville, MN*] [*A publication*] (BJA)

OTRHNLRGYNGY... Otorhinolaryngology

OTRIC .... Collins Canada Division, Rockwell International, Toronto, Ontario [*Library symbol National Library of Canada*] (NLC)

OTRK .... Oshkosh Truck Corp. [*Oshkosh, WI*] [*NASDAQ symbol*] (NQ)

OTRKB .... Oshkosh Truck'B' [*NASDAQ symbol*] (TTSB)

OTRL .... Reed Ltd., Toronto, Ontario [*Library symbol National Library of Canada*] (NLC)

OTrL .... Troy-Miami County Public Library, Troy, OH [*Library symbol*] [*Library of Congress*] (LCLS)

OTRM .... Royal Ontario Museum, Toronto, Ontario [*Library symbol National Library of Canada*] (NLC)

OTRMC .... Canadiana Department, Royal Ontario Museum, Toronto, Ontario [*Library symbol National Library of Canada*] (NLC)

OTRMF .... Far Eastern Department, Royal Ontario Museum, Toronto, Ontario [*Library symbol National Library of Canada*] (NLC)

OTRO .... Overhaul Test Requirement Outline

OTROT .... Corporate Information Centre, Royal Trust, Toronto, Ontario [*Library symbol National Library of Canada*] (BIB)

OTRPM .... Rothmans of Pall Mall Ltd., Don Mills, Ontario [*Library symbol National Library of Canada*] (NLC)

OTRR .... Operation Test Readiness Review [*Army*]

OTRS .... Operational Test Readiness Statement

OTRT .... Operating Time Record Tag (AAG)

OTRT .... Rose Technology Group Ltd., Toronto, Ontario [*Library symbol National Library of Canada*] (NLC)

OTRX .... OTR Express [*NASDAQ symbol*] (TTSB)

OTRX .... OTR Express, Inc. [*NASDAQ symbol*] (SAG)

OTS .... Object Time System (MHDB)

OTS .... Occipital Temporal Sulcus [*Medicine*] (DMAA)

OTS .... Octadecyltrichlorosilane [*Organic chemistry*]

OTS .... Office of Technical Services [*Later, CFSTI, NTIS*] [*National Institute of Standards and Technology*]

OTS .... Office of Technical Support [*US Employment Service*] [*Department of Labor*]

OTS .... Office of Thrift Supervision [*Department of the Treasury*] [*Superseded Federal Home Loan Bank Board, 1989*]

OTS .... Office of Toxic Substances [*Environmental Protection Agency*]

OTS .... Office of Transportation Security [*Department of Transportation*]

OTS .... Officers' Tactical School [*Navy*] (NVT)

OTS .... Officers' Training School

OTS .... Off the Shelf

OTS .... Ohio Carriers Tariff Service Inc., Cleveland OH [*STAC*]

OTS .... One-Time Source (MCD)

OTS .... On-Line Terminal System [*Computer science*] (MHDB)

OTS .... Open Two Seater [*Style of automobile*]

OTS .... Operational Test Site (AAG)

OTS .... Operational Time Sync

OTS .... Operational Training Squadron (MCD)

OTS .... Operational Training System [*HAWK*]

OTS .... Opportunities to See [*Business term*]

OTS .... Optical Technology Satellite

OTS .... Optical Tracking Satellite [*NASA*] (IAA)

OTS .... Optical Transport Systems (IEEE)

OTS .... Orbital Test Satellite [*Communications satellite*] [*European Space Agency*]

OTS .... Orbital Transport Systems (MCD)

OTS .... Organization for Tropical Studies (EA)

OTS .... Organized Track System [*Aviation*]

OTS .... Orotracheal Suction [*Medicine*] (DAVI)

OTS .... Ortho-Toluenesulfonamide [*Used in manufacture of saccharin*]

OTS .... Outside Temperature Sensor [*Automotive engineering*]

OTS .... Overlap Technician Supervisor (SAA)

OTS .... Overlap Telling and Surveillance (SAA)

OTS .... Overseas Telephone Services (DAS)

OTS .... Over-the-Shoulder [*Cinematography*]

OTS .... Over-the-Side [*Navy*] (CAAL)

OTS .... Ovonic Threshold Switch

OTS .... Own Time Switch [*Connection or call*] [*Telecommunications*] (TEL)

OTS .... Oxford Text System (NITA)

OTS .... Oxygen Test Stand (KSC)

OTS .... Statistics Canada [*Statistique Canada*] Toronto, Ontario [*Library symbol National Library of Canada*] (NLC)

OTSA .... Ocean Systems Technician, Seaman Apprentice [*Navy rating*] (DNAB)

OTSA .... Orthodox Theological Society in America (EA)

OTSA .... Salvation Army, Toronto, Ontario [*Library symbol National Library of Canada*] (NLC)

OTSAA .... Officer Training School Alumni Association (EA)

OTSAC .... Sanco Consultants Ltd., Toronto, Ontario [*Library symbol National Library of Canada*] (NLC)

OTS-AES ...... Optical Technology Satellite - Apollo Extension System (DNAB)

OTSAP .... Spar Aerospace Products, Toronto, Ontario [*Library symbol National Library of Canada*] (NLC)

O/TSC .... Other than Special Consultants [*Military*]

OTSC .... Seneca College, Willowdale, Ontario [*Library symbol National Library of Canada*] (NLC)

OTSCC .... Scarborough College, Ontario [*Library symbol National Library of Canada*] (NLC)

OTSCI .... Sulzer Canada, Inc., Toronto, Ontario [*Library symbol National Library of Canada*] (NLC)

OTSCL .... Shell Canada Ltd., Toronto, Ontario [*Library symbol National Library of Canada*] (NLC)

OTSCLT .... Library Techniques, Seneca College of Applied Arts and Technology, Willowdale, Ontario [*Library symbol National Library of Canada*] (NLC)

OTSD .... Operational Test Supportability Demonstration

OTSE .... Toronto Stock Exchange Library, Ontario [*Library symbol National Library of Canada*] (BIB)

OTSED .... Scarborough Borough Board of Education, Toronto, Ontario [*Library symbol National Library of Canada*] (NLC)

OTSG .... Office of the Surgeon General [*Public Health Service*]

OTSG .... Once-Through Steam Generator [*Nuclear energy*]

OTSGS .... Once-Through Steam Generating System [*Nuclear energy*] (IEEE)

OTSLI .... Sun Life of Canada, Toronto, Ontario [*Library symbol National Library of Canada*] (NLC)

OTSM .... St. Michael's Hospital, Toronto, Ontario [*Library symbol National Library of Canada*] (NLC)

OTSMC .... Sunnybrook Medical Centre, Toronto, Ontario [*Library symbol National Library of Canada*] (NLC)

OTSMG .... St. Mary's General Hospital, Timmins, Ontario [*Library symbol National Library of Canada*] (NLC)

OTSML .... Selco Mining Corp., Toronto, Ontario [*Library symbol National Library of Canada*] (NLC)

OTSN .... Ocean Systems Technician, Seaman [*Navy rating*] (DNAB)

OTSO .... Office of Telecommunications Systems Operations [*Social Security Administration*]

OTSOA .... Overseas Telegraph Superintending Officers' Association [*A union*] [*British*]

OTSOG .... On the Shoulders of Giants [*Literature*]

OTSP .... Office of Technology Support Programs [*Washington, DC Department of Energy*] (GRD)

OTSP .... Office of Transportation Systems and Planning [*Battelle Memorial Institut e*] [*Department of Energy Also, an information service or system*] (IID)

OTSP .... Scarborough Public Library, Ontario [*Library symbol National Library of Canada*] (NLC)

OTSPA .... Albert Campbell Branch, Scarborough Public Library, Ontario [*Library symbol National Library of Canada*] (NLC)

OTSPC .... Cedarbrae Branch, Scarborough Public Library, Ontario [*Library symbol National Library of Canada*] (NLC)

OTS-PST ...... Orbiting Transition State-Phase Space Theory [*Physical chemistry*]

OTSQ .... Offer Teacher-Student Questionnaire [*Personality development test*] [*Psychology*]

OTSR .... Once-Through Superheat Reactor [*Nuclear energy*]

OTSR .... Optimum Track Ship Routing [*Navy*] (NVT)

OTSS .... Office of Technical and Special Services [*Office of Field Operations*] [*Department of Labor*]

OTSS .... Off-the-Shelf System [*Bell System*]

OTSS .... Ontario Regional Library, Secretary of State Canada [*Bibliotheque Regionale de l'Ontario, Secretariat d'Etat*], Toronto, Ontario [*Library symbol National Library of Canada*] (NLC)

OTSS .... Open Transport and Session Support (NITA)

OTSS .... Operational Test Support System

OTSS .... Optical Tracking Servo

OTS SB .... Office of Technical Service, Selective Bibliographies [*US government*]

OTST .... Ontario Science Centre, Toronto, Ontario [*Library symbol National Library of Canada*] (NLC)

OTSTA .... St. Augustine's Seminary, Toronto, Ontario [*Library symbol National Library of Canada*] (NLC)

OTSTB .... St. Basil's Seminary [*Collection transferred to OTSTM*] Ontario [*Library symbol National Library of Canada*] (NLC)

OTSTF .... Ontario Film Institute, Ontario Science Centre Library, Don Mills, Ontario [*Library symbol National Library of Canada*] (NLC)

OTSTG .... St. George's College, Toronto, Ontario [*Library symbol National Library of Canada*] (NLC)

OTSTJ .... George Pennal Library, St. Joseph's Health Centre, Toronto, Ontario [*Library symbol National Library of Canada*] (BIB)

OTSTM .... University of Saint Michael's College, Toronto, Ontario [*Library symbol National Library of Canada*] (NLC)

OTSZH .... Other than Steel or Zinc Heads [*Freight*]

OTT .... Nottingham, MD [*Location identifier FAA*] (FAAL)

OTT .... Ocean Transport and Trading [*British*]

OTT .... Office of Technology Transfer [*University of Illinois*]

OTT .... One-Time Tape

OTT .... Operational Training Test (NVT)

OTT .... Operator Tactics Trainer [*Patriot air defense system*] (MCD)

OTT .... Optional Team Targeting (MCD)

OTT .... Oral Trade Tests [*Department of Labor*]

OTT .... Orotracheal Tube [*Medicine*] (DAVI)

OTT .... Ottava [*Octave*] [*Music*]

OTT .... Ottawa [*Ontario*] [*Seismograph station code, US Geological Survey*] (SEIS)

OTT .... Ottery Saint Mary [*Urban district in England*]

Ott .... Otto's United States Supreme Court Reports [*91-107 United States*] [*A publication*] (DLA)
OTT .... Outgoing Teletype
OTT .... Outgoing Trunk Terminal [*Telecommunications*] (IAA)
OTT .... Outside Trim Template (MSA)
OTT .... Over-the-Top [*Marshall-MacIntosh knee operation*]
OTT .... Over the Top [*British Slang*]
OTT .... Oxygen Tolerance Test
OTT .... Teledyne CAE Engineering Library, Toledo, OH [*Library symbol Library of Congress*] (LCLS)
OTT .... Toronto Transit Commission, Ontario [*Library symbol National Library of Canada*] (NLC)
OTT .... University of Ottawa Library [*UTLAS symbol*]
OttawFn ...... Ottawa Financial Corp. [*Associated Press*] (SAG)
OTTB .... Optically-Thin Thermal Bremsstrahlung [*Astrophysics*]
OTTC .... University of Trinity College, Toronto, Ontario [*Library symbol National Library of Canada*] (NLC)
OTTCA .... University of Trinity College Archives, Toronto, Ontario [*Library symbol National Library of Canada*] (NLC)
OTTDB .... Toronto-Dominion Bank, Toronto, Ontario [*Library symbol National Library of Canada*] (NLC)
OTTE .... Operational Testing, Training, and Evaluation
OTTEC .... Toronto Teachers' College, Ontario [*Library symbol National Library of Canada*] (NLC)
OTTER .... Operational Training, Test, and Evaluation RADAR
OTTEX .... Texaco Canada, Inc., Don Mills, Ontario [*Library symbol National Library of Canada*] (NLC)
OTTFC .... Official Tim Topper Fan Club [*Defunct*] (EA)
OTTI .... Ontario Ministry of Industry and Trade, Toronto, Ontario [*Library symbol National Library of Canada*] (NLC)
OTTLE .... Optically Transparent Thin-Layer Electrode
OTTO .... Olympic Technology Trailer Operations
OTTO .... Once Through, Then Out [*Fuel management system*]
OTTO .... Optical-to-Optical (IAA)
Otto .... Otto's United States Supreme Court Reports [*91-107 United States*] [*A publication*] (DLA)
OTTOA .... Ontario Region, Canadian Air Transportation Administration, Transport Canada [*Region de l'Ontario, Administration Canadienne des Transports Aeriens, Transports Canada*] Toronto, Ontario [*Library symbol National Library of Canada*] (NLC)
OTTR .... Otter Tail Power [*NASDAQ symbol*] (TTSB)
OTTR .... Otter Tail Power Co. [*NASDAQ symbol*] (NQ)
OTTR .... Thomson, Rogers, Barristers & Solicitors, Toronto, Ontario [*Library symbol National Library of Canada*] (NLC)
OTTRAC ...... Travelers Canada, Toronto, Ontario [*Library symbol National Library of Canada*] (BIB)
OTTRC .... Thistletown Regional Centre for Children and Adolescents, Rexdale, Ontario [*Library symbol National Library of Canada*] (NLC)
OTTRC .... Touche Ross & Co., Toronto, Ontario [*Library symbol National Library of Canada*] (NLC)
OttrTP .... Otter Tail Power Co. [*Associated Press*] (SAG)
OTTS .... Operations Training and Technical Services [*Nuclear Regulatory Commission*] (NRCH)
OTTS .... Organisation of Teachers of Transport Studies [*British*]
OTTS .... Outgoing Trunk Testing System [*Telecommunications*] (TEL)
OTTST .... Toronto School of Theology, Toronto, Ontario [*Library symbol National Library of Canada*] (NLC)
OTTSU .... Open Tech Training Support Unit (AIE)
Ott's US Sup Ct R ... Otto's United States Supreme Court Reports [*91-107 United States*] [*A publication*] (DLA)
OTTT .... Tory, Tory, DesLauriers & Binnington, Toronto, Ontario [*Library symbol National Library of Canada*] (BIB)
OTTW .... Optical Telescope Technology Workshop [*NASA*] (PDAA)
OTTWH .... Health Sciences Library, Toronto Western Hospital, Ontario [*Library symbol National Library of Canada*] (NLC)
OTU .... Office of Technology Utilization [*NASA*]
OTU .... Officers' Training Unit [*Air Force British*]
OTU .... Ogden Test Unit (SAA)
OTU .... One-Time Use
OTU .... Operating Time Update
OTU .... Operational Taxonomic Unit [*Numerical taxonomy*]
OTU .... Operational Test Unit (KSC)
OTU .... Operational Training Unit [*Military*]
OTU .... Opetus-ja Tutkimusalan Unioni [*Teaching and Research Employees Union*] [*Finalnd*] (EY)
OTU .... Orthopedic Transcription Unit
OTU .... Otu [*Colombia*] [*Airport symbol*] (OAG)
OTU .... Output Terminal Unit (SSD)
OTU .... University of Toledo, Toledo, OH [*Library symbol Library of Congress*] (LCLS)
OTU .... University of Toronto, Ontario [*Library symbol National Library of Canada*] (NLC)
OTUA .... Institute for Aerospace Studies, University of Toronto, Ontario [*Library symbol National Library of Canada*] (NLC)
OTUAN .... Department of Anatomy, University of Toronto, Ontario [*Library symbol National Library of Canada*] (NLC)
OTUAP .... Department of Applied Physics, University of Toronto, Ontario [*Library symbol National Library of Canada*] (NLC)
OTUAR .... University of Toronto Archives, Ontario [*Library symbol National Library of Canada*] (NLC)
OTUAV .... Audio-Visual Library, University of Toronto, Ontario [*Library symbol National Library of Canada*] (NLC)
OTUB .... Department of Biochemistry, University of Toronto, Ontario [*Library symbol National Library of Canada*] (NLC)

OTUBP .... Banting-Best Physiology Library, University of Toronto, Ontario [*Library symbol National Library of Canada*] (NLC)
OTUC .... Department of Chemistry, University of Toronto, Ontario [*Library symbol National Library of Canada*] (NLC)
OTUCC .... Institute of Computer Science, University of Toronto, Ontario [*Library symbol National Library of Canada*] (NLC)
OTUCE .... Department of Chemical Engineering and Applied Chemistry, University of Toronto,Ontario [*Library symbol National Library of Canada*] (NLC)
OTUCI .... Department of Civil Engineering, University of Toronto, Ontario [*Library symbol National Library of Canada*] (NLC)
OTUCR .... Centre of Criminology, University of Toronto, Ontario [*Library symbol National Library of Canada*] (NLC)
OTUCS .... Institute of Child Study, University of Toronto, Ontario [*Library symbol National Library of Canada*] (NLC)
OTUD .... David Dunlap Observatory, University of Toronto, Ontario [*Library symbol National Library of Canada*] (NLC)
OTUDB .... Department of Botany, University of Toronto, Ontario [*Library symbol National Library of Canada*] (NLC)
OTUDM .... Department of Mathematics, University of Toronto, Ontario [*Library symbol National Library of Canada*] (NLC)
OTUDP .... Clarke Institute of Psychiatry, University of Toronto, Ontario [*Library symbol National Library of Canada*] (NLC)
OTUE .... Engineering Library, University of Toronto, Ontario [*Library symbol National Library of Canada*] (NLC)
OTUEE .... Department of Electrical Engineering, University of Toronto, Ontario [*Library symbol National Library of Canada*] (NLC)
OTUFA .... Department of Fine Art, University of Toronto, Ontario [*Library symbol National Library of Canada*] (NLC)
OTUFD .... Faculty of Dentistry, University of Toronto, Ontario [*Library symbol National Library of Canada*] (NLC)
OTUFM .... Faculty of Music, University of Toronto, Ontario [*Library symbol National Library of Canada*] (NLC)
OTUFP .... Faculty of Pharmacy, University of Toronto, Ontario [*Library symbol National Library of Canada*] (NLC)
OTUG .... Department of Geological Sciences, University of Toronto, Ontario [*Library symbol National Library of Canada*] (NLC)
OTUGL .... Geophysics Laboratory, University of Toronto, Ontario [*Library symbol National Library of Canada*] (NLC)
OTUH .... Science and Medicine Library, University of Toronto, Ontario [*Library symbol National Library of Canada*] (NLC)
OTUHO .... Occupational & Environment Health Unit, Science and Medicine Library, Universityof Toronto, Ontario [*Library symbol National Library of Canada*] (NLC)
OTUINC .... Innis College, University of Toronto, Ontario [*Library symbol National Library of Canada*] (NLC)
OTUIRN .... [*The*] Jean and Dorothy Newman Industrial Relations Library, Center for Industrial Relations, University of Toronto, Ontario [*Library symbol National Library of Canada*] (NLC)
OTUL .... Faculty of Law, University of Toronto, Ontario [*Library symbol National Library of Canada*] (NLC)
OTU-L .... University of Toledo, Law Library, Toledo, OH [*Library symbol Library of Congress*] (LCLS)
OTULAS ...... UTLAS [*University of Toronto Library Automation System*] International Canada, Toronto, Ontario [*Library symbol National Library of Canada*] (NLC)
OTULS .... Faculty of Library Science, University of Toronto, Ontario [*Library symbol National Library of Canada*] (NLC)
OTUM .... Department of Mechanical Engineering, University of Toronto, Ontario [*Library symbol National Library of Canada*] (NLC)
OTUMA .... Map Library, University of Toronto, Ontario [*Library symbol National Library of Canada*] (NLC)
OTUME .... Department of Metallurgical Engineering, University of Toronto, Ontario [*Library symbol National Library of Canada*] (NLC)
OTUMI .... Department of Mining Engineering, University of Toronto, Ontario [*Library symbol National Library of Canada*] (NLC)
OTUMS .... Faculty of Management Studies, University of Toronto, Ontario [*Library symbol National Library of Canada*] (NLC)
OTUN .... Faculty of Nursing, University of Toronto, Ontario [*Library symbol National Library of Canada*] (NLC)
OTUNC .... Union Carbide Canada Ltd., Toronto, Ontario [*Library symbol National Library of Canada*] (NLC)
OTUNWC ..... New College, University of Toronto, Ontario [*Library symbol National Library of Canada*] (NLC)
OTUP .... Department of Physics, University of Toronto, Ontario [*Library symbol National Library of Canada*] (NLC)
OTUPA .... Department of Pathology, Banting-Best Institute, University of Toronto, Ontario [*Library symbol National Library of Canada*] (NLC)
OTUPG .... Information Centre, Programme in Gerontology, University of Toronto, Ontario [*Library symbol National Library of Canada*] (NLC)
OTUS .... Office of the Treasurer of the United States
OTUSA .... School of Architecture, University of Toronto, Ontario [*Library symbol National Library of Canada*] (NLC)
OTUSP .... School of Physical and Health Education (Women), University of Toronto, Ontario [*Library symbol National Library of Canada*] (NLC)
OTUSW .... School of Social Work, University of Toronto, Ontario [*Library symbol National Library of Canada*] (NLC)
OTUTD .... Urban Transportation Development Corp., Toronto, Ontario [*Library symbol National Library of Canada*] (NLC)
OTUTF .... Thomas Fisher Rare Book Library, University of Toronto, Ontario [*Library symbol National Library of Canada*] (NLC)
OTUTP .... University of Toronto Press, Ontario [*Library symbol National Library of Canada*] (NLC)

OTUUC........ University College, University of Toronto, Ontario [*Library symbol National Library of Canada*] (NLC)

OTUZ .... Department of Zoology, University of Toronto, Ontario [*Library symbol National Library of Canada*] (NLC)

OTV............. Operational Television (KSC)

OTV............. Operational Test Vehicle (IAA)

OTV............. Optimum Time Varying (IAA)

OTV............. Orbiter Transfer Vehicle [*NASA*]

OTV............. Otavi [*South-West Africa*] [*Airport symbol*] (AD)

OTV............. Victoria University, Toronto, Ontario [*Library symbol National Library of Canada*] (NLC)

OTVC .... Open Top Vapor Cleaner [*Engineering*]

OTVCT .... Outer Tube Vertical Centerline Target

OTVL........... V & L Enterprises, Downsview, Ontario [*Library symbol National Library of Canada*] (NLC)

OTW............ Off the Wall [*Slang*]

OTW............ Over the Wing [*Aircraft*]

OTW............ Owner's Tank Wagons [*Shipping*]

OTW............ Owning the Weather [*Army*] (RDA)

OTW............ Wycliffe College, Toronto, Ontario [*Library symbol National Library of Canada*] (NLC)

OTWC .... Ontario Workmen's Compensation Board, Toronto, Ontario [*Library symbol National Library of Canada*] (NLC)

OTWCA .... Ontario Workers' Compensation Appeals Tribunal, Toronto, Ontario [*Library symbol National Library of Canada*] (NLC)

OTWCH .... Medical Library, Women's College Hospital, Toronto, Ontario [*Library symbol National Library of Canada*] (NLC)

OTWE........... Tweed Public Library, Ontario [*Library symbol National Library of Canada*] (BIB)

OTWEN .... Ontario Ministry of Northern Development and Mines, Tweed [*Library symbol National Library of Canada*] (BIB)

OTWFC .... Old Time Western Film Club (EA)

OTWH .... Wellesley Hospital, Toronto, Ontario [*Library symbol National Library of Canada*] (NLC)

OTWL........... William Lyon Mackenzie Collegiate Institute, Downsview, Ontario [*Library symbol National Library of Canada*] (NLC)

OTWLC .... Warner-Lambert Canada Ltd., Scarborough, Ontario [*Library symbol National Library of Canada*] (NLC)

OTWM .... William M. Mercer Ltd., Toronto, Ontario [*Library symbol National Library of Canada*] (NLC)

OTWR......... Oblique Tape Wound Refrasil

OTWRC........ Weston Research Centre, Toronto, Ontario [*Library symbol National Library of Canada*] (NLC)

OTWY .... Medical Library, Wyeth Ltd., Downsview, Ontario [*Library symbol National Library of Canada*] (BIB)

OTX............. Oiltex International Ltd. [*Toronto Stock Exchange symbol*]

OTXRA........ X-Ray Assay Laboratories Ltd., Don Mills, Ontario [*Library symbol National Library of Canada*] (NLC)

OTY............. Oria [*Papua New Guinea*] [*Airport symbol Obsolete*] (OAG)

OTY............. York University, Toronto, Ontario [*Library symbol National Library of Canada*] (NLC)

OTYA .... York University Archives, Toronto, Ontario [*Library symbol National Library of Canada*] (NLC)

OTYBE .... Professional Library, Board of Education for the City of York, Toronto, Ontario [*Library symbol National Library of Canada*] (NLC)

OTYBE .... York Borough Board of Education, Toronto, Ontario [*Library symbol National Library of Canada*] (NLC)

OTYBES ...... Schools, Board of Education for the City of York, Toronto, Ontario [*Library symbol National Library of Canada*] (NLC)

OTYF........... Hospital Library, York-Finch General Hospital, Downsview, Ontario [*Library symbol National Library of Canada*] (BIB)

OTYL........... Law Library, York University, Toronto, Ontario [*Library symbol National Library of Canada*] (NLC)

OTYLR .... Listening Room, York University, Toronto, Ontario [*Library symbol National Library of Canada*] (NLC)

OTYP .... City of York Public Library, Toronto, Ontario [*Library symbol National Library of Canada*] (NLC)

OTZ............. Kotzebue [*Alaska*] [*Airport symbol*] (OAG)

OTZ............. Ortiz [*New Mexico*] [*Seismograph station code, US Geological Survey*] (SEIS)

OTZ............. Oxothiazolidine [*Biochemistry*]

OU .... City Express [*ICAO designator*] (AD)

OU .... Object Unit (NITA)

OU .... Observation Unit

OU .... Oculi Unitas [*Both Eyes Together*] [*Ophthalmology*]

OU .... Oculus Uterque [*Each Eye*] [*Ophthalmology*]

OU .... Odor Unit [*Air pollution*]

OU .... Official Use (WDAA)

OU .... Ohio State University, Columbus, OH [*Library symbol Library of Congress*] (LCLS)

OU .... Ohio University [*Athens*]

OU .... Oklahoma University

OU .... Open University [*British*]

OU .... Operation Unit

OU .... Opposition Unie [*United Opposition*] [*The Comoros*] [*Political party*] (EY)

OU .... Otonabee Airways [*ICAO designator*] (AD)

ou .... Ounce [*Unit of weight*] (CDAI)

OU .... Output Unit [*Computer science*] (IAA)

OU .... Oxford University [*England*]

OU .... University of Oklahoma, Norman (USDC)

OU .... University of Oklahoma, Norman [*USA*] [*Marine science*] (OSRA)

OUA .... Office of University Affairs [*NASA*]

OUA .... Order of United Americans (NADA)

OUA .... Organisation de l'Unite Africaine [*Organization of African Unity - OAU*] (EAIO)

OUA .... Ouagadougou [*Burkina Faso*] [*Airport symbol*] (OAG)

OUA .... Ouanaham [*Loyalty Islands*] [*Seismograph station code, US Geological Survey*] (SEIS)

OUa .... Upper Arlington Public Library, Upper Arlington, OH [*Library symbol Library of Congress*] (LCLS)

OUAM .... Order of United American Mechanics

OUAS .... Oxford University Air Squadron [*British*] (DI)

OUAT .... Once upon a Time (The Prisoner Fan Club) (EA)

OUBD .... Outbound [*ICAO designator*] (FAAC)

OU-BP......... Ohio State University, Byrd Polar Research Center, Goldthwait Polar Library, Columbus, OH [*Library symbol*] [*Library of Congress*] (LCLS)

OUBS .... Open University Business School [*British*]

OUC .... Ocracoke, NC [*Location identifier FAA*] (FAAL)

OUC .... Ohio University, Chillicothe Branch Campus, Chillicothe, OH [*OCLC symbol*] (OCLC)

OUCA .... Chemical Abstracts, Ohio State University, Columbus, OH [*Library symbol Library of Congress*] (LCLS)

OUCC .... Ohio University Cartographic Center [*Research center*] (RCD)

OUCH .... Off-Line Universal Command History [*Computer science*] (KSC)

OUCTA .... Order of United Commercial Travelers of America (EA)

OUD .... AMOCO Production Co., Library, Tulsa, OK [*OCLC symbol*] (OCLC)

OUD .... Operational Use Data

OUD .... Oujda [*Morocco*] [*Airport symbol*] (OAG)

Oud C .... Oudh Code [*India*] [*A publication*] (DLA)

Oudh C .... Oudh Code [*India*] [*A publication*] (DLA)

Oudh LJ ...... Oudh Law Journal [*India*] [*A publication*] (DLA)

Oudh LR ...... Oudh Law Reports [*India*] [*A publication*] (DLA)

Oudh Rev Sel Cas... Revised Collection of Selected Cases Issued by Chief Commissioner and Financial Commissioner of Oudh [*A publication*] (DLA)

Oudh Wkly N... Oudh Weekly Notes [*India*] [*A publication*] (DLA)

Oudh WN .... Oudh Weekly Notes [*India*] [*A publication*] (DLA)

OUDP.......... Officer Undergraduate Degree Program [*Army*] (AABC)

OUDS.......... Oxford University Dramatic Society [*British*] (AIE)

OUE .... National Oceanic and Atmospheric Administration, National Severe Storms Laboratories, Norman, OK [*OCLC symbol*] (OCLC)

OUE .... Operational Utility Evaluation

OUE .... Orbital Uncertainty Estimate

OUE .... Ouesso [*Congo*] [*Airport symbol*] (OAG)

OUE .... Ouvriers Unis de l'Electricite, de la Radio, et de la Machinerie d'Amerique [*United Electrical, Radio, and Machine Workers of America - UE*]

OUF .... Northwestern Oklahoma State University, Library, Alva, OK [*OCLC symbol*] (OCLC)

OUF .... Optimum Usual Frequency Radio (IAA)

OUF .... Order of Use File (MCD)

OUF .... Oxygen Utilization Factor

OUG .... Oklahoma Children's Memorial Hospital, Library, Oklahoma City, OK [*OCLC symbol*] (OCLC)

OUG .... Organisation de l'Unite Guineenne [*Organization of Guinean Unity*] (PD)

OUG .... Ouahigouya [*Upper Volta*] [*Airport symbol*] (AD)

Ought .... Oughton's Ordo Judiciorum [*Order of Judgments*] [*A publication*] (DLA)

OUG/I.......... Online Users' Group/Ireland (EAIO)

OU-H........... Ohio State University, Health Sciences Library, Columbus, OH [*Library symbol Library of Congress*] (LCLS)

OUH .... Oklahoma College of Osteopathic Medicine and Surgery, Library, Tulsa, OK [*OCLC symbol*] (OCLC)

OUH .... Oudtshoorn [*South Africa*] [*Airport symbol*] (OAG)

OUHSC........ Oklahoma University Health Sciences Center

OUI .... Ban Houei Sai [*Laos*] [*Airport symbol*] (AD)

OUI .... Office of Unemployment Insurance [*Employment and Training Administration*] [*Department of Labor*]

OUI .... Oklahoma Osteopathic Hospital, Library, Tulsa, OK [*OCLC symbol*] (OCLC)

OUI .... Organisation Universitaire Interamericaine [*Inter-American Organization for Higher Education*] (EAIO)

OUI .... Outdoors Unlimited (EA)

OUI .... Outer Integument [*Botany*]

OUIL .... Operating a Vehicle while under the Influence of Liquor [*Traffic offense charge*]

OUJ............. Oklahoma State University, Technical Institute Library, Oklahoma City, OK [*OCLC symbol*] (OCLC)

OUK .... Operation Upshot-Knothole [*Atomic weapons testing*]

OUK .... Oscar Rose Junior College Library, Midwest City, OK [*OCLC symbol*] (OCLC)

OUL .... Air Atonabee Ltd. [*Canada ICAO designator*] (FAAC)

OU-L........... Ohio State University, College of Law, Columbus, OH [*Library symbol Library of Congress*] (LCLS)

OUL .... Ohio University, Lancaster Branch Campus, Lancaster, OH [*OCLC symbol*] (OCLC)

OUL .... Orbital Utility Light

OUL .... Oulu [*Finland*] [*Airport symbol*] (OAG)

OUL .... Oulu [*Finland*] [*Seismograph station code, US Geological Survey*] (SEIS)

OULCS .... Ontario University Libraries Cooperative System (NITA)

Oult Ind ...... Oulton's Index to Irish Statutes [*A publication*] (DLA)

Oult Laws Ir... Oulton's Laws of Ireland [*A publication*] (DLA)

OUM .... Philbrook Art Center Library, Tulsa, OK [*OCLC symbol*] (OCLC)

OUMC.......... Otago University Medical Corps [*British military*] (DMA)

OUN............. Norman, OK [*Location identifier FAA*] (FAAL)

OUN	Ohio University, Athens, OH [*OCLC symbol*]　(OCLC)
OUNPSA	Office of United Nations Political and Security Affairs [*Department of State*]
OUNS	Office of Urban Neighborhood Services [*HUD*]
OUNSAF	Office of the Under Secretary of the Air Force
OUO	Official Use Only
OUO	United States Army, Morris Swett Library, Fort Sill, OK [*OCLC symbol*]　(OCLC)
OUP	Official Unionist Party [*Northern Ireland*]　(PPW)
OUP	OFS [*Orbital Flight System*] Uplink Processor [*NASA*]　(GFGA)
OUP	OFS [*Orbiter Functional Simulator*] Uplink Processor [*NASA*]
OU-P	Ohio State University, Pharmacy and Bacteriology Library, Columbus, OH [*Library symbol Library of Congress*]　(LCLS)
OUP	Operative United Painters [*A union*] [*British*]
OUP	Operative United Plumbers [*A union*] [*British*]
OUP	Oxford University Press　(NADA)
OUP	Oxford University Press, Inc. [*New York, NY*]
OUP	University of Portland, Portland, OR [*OCLC symbol*]　(OCLC)
OUPT	Output　(AAG)
OUQ	United States Army, Nye Library, Fort Sill, OK [*OCLC symbol*]　(OCLC)
OUR	Batouri [*Cameroon*] [*Airport symbol*]　(OAG)
OUR	Organizacion de Unidad Revolucionaria [*Organization of Revolutionary Unity*] [*Bolivia*] [*Political party*]　(PPW)
OUR	Oxygen Uptake Rate [*Biochemistry*]
OUR	Oxygen Utilization Rate [*Photosynthesis*]
OUR	United States Federal Aviation Administration, Aeronautical Center Library, Oklahoma City, OK [*OCLC symbol*]　(OCLC)
OUrC	Urbana College, Urbana, OH [*Library symbol Library of Congress*]　(LCLS)
OURD	[*The*] Ogden Union Railway & Depot Co. [*AAR code*]
OURI	Oklahoma University Research Institute
Our Lady Lake U ...	Our Lady of the Lake University　(GAGS)
OURQ	Outer Upper Right Quadrant [*Anatomy*]
OURS	Orangutan Recovery Service [*Later, IUCN*]
OURS	Organization for United Response [*Later, AFA (Adoptive Families of America)*]　(PAZ)
OURTEL	Our Telegram　(NATG)
OUS	Oklahoma Union List of Serials Project, Stillwater, OK [*OCLC symbol*]　(OCLC)
OUS	Ourinhos [*Brazil*] [*Airport symbol*]　(OAG)
OUS	Outdoor Unit Substation
OUSA	Office of the Under Secretary of the Army
OUSA	OMNI U.S.A. [*NASDAQ symbol*]　(TTSB)
OUSA	Omni USA, Inc. [*NASDAQ symbol*]　(SAG)
OUSA	Open University Students' Association [*British*]
OUSA	Operation USA [*An association*]　(EA)
OUSA	Organisation de l'Unite Syndicale Africaine [*Organisation of African Trade Union Unity - OATUU*] [*Accra, Ghana*]　(EAIO)
OUSAF	Office of the Under Secretary of the Air Force
OUSAIRA	Office of the United States Air Attache　(CINC)
OUSARMA ...	Office of the United States Army Attache
OUSCS	Office of Urban Studies and Clearinghouse Services [*HUD*]
OUSD	Office of the Under Secretary of Defense　(MCD)
OUSDA	Office of the Under Secretary of Defense for Acquisition
OUSD(A & T) ...	Office of the Under Secretary of Defense (Acquisition and Technology)　(RDA)
OUSD(P)	Office of the Under Secretary of Defense (Policy)　(MCD)
OUSDRE	Office of the Under Secretary of Defense for Research and Engineering
OUSH	Uxbridge-Scott Historical Society, Uxbridge, Ontario [*Library symbol National Library of Canada*]　(BIB)
OUSN	Office of the Under Secretary of the Navy
OUSOFA	Office of the Under Secretary of the Army
OUST	Office of Underground Storage Tanks [*Environmental Protection Agency*]
OUSW	Office of the Under Secretary of War [*Obsolete*]
OUT	Bousso [*Chad*] [*Airport symbol*]　(AD)
OUT	Orbiter Utilities Tray [*NASA*]　(NASA)
OUT	Organizacao Unida de Trabalhadores [*United Organization of Workers*] [*Portugal Political party*]　(PPE)
OUT	Organization for Unemployed Teachers
OUT	Organization for Use of the Telephone　(EA)
Out	Outerbridge's State Reports [*97, 98 Pennsylvania*] [*A publication*]　(DLA)
OUT	Outgoing
OUT	Outing　(ROG)
OUT	Outlet [*Hawaii*] [*Seismograph station code, US Geological Survey*]　(SEIS)
OUT	Output　(NASA)
OUT	United States Federal Aviation Administration, CAMI Library, Oklahoma City, OK [*OCLC symbol*]　(OCLC)
OUT	Uxbridge Township Public Library, Uxbridge, Ontario [*Library symbol National Library of Canada*]　(NLC)
OUTA	Ouvriers Unis des Textiles d'Amerique [*United Textile Workers of America - UTWA*]
OUTBD	Outboard　(AAG)
OUTBD	Outboard
OUTBD	Outbound
OUTbdM	Outboard Marine Corp. [*Associated Press*]　(SAG)
OUTBGS	Outbuildings　(ROG)
OutbkStk	Outback Steakhouse, Inc. [*Associated Press*]　(SAG)
OUTC	Ordnance Unit Training Center [*Military*]
OUTCONUS ...	Outside Continental Limits of the United States [*Military*]　(DNAB)
OUTG	Outage　(KSC)

OUTHO	Outhouse　(ROG)
OUTL	Outlet
outl	Outline　(VRA)
OUTL	Outlook Group [*NASDAQ symbol*]　(TTSB)
OUTL	Outlook Group Corp [*NASDAQ symbol*]　(SPSG)
Outlet	Outlet Communications, Inc. [*Associated Press*]　(SAG)
OUTLIM	Output Limiting Facility [*Computer science*]　(MDG)
OutlkGrp	Outlook Group Corp. [*Associated Press*]　(SAG)
OUTLT	Outlet
OUTPUTM	Output Measures for Public Libraries [*Clarion University of Pennsylvania*] [*Information service or system*]　(IID)
OUTRAN	Outlet
OUTRAN	Output
OUTRAN	Output Translator [*IBM Corp.*]
OUTREG	Output Register　(IAA)
OUTS	Operational Unit Transportable System　(MCD)
OUTSTDG	Outstanding [*Business term*]
outstg	Outstanding [*Business term*]　(MHDW)
OUTUS	Outside the United States
OUTWATS	Outgoing Wide-Area Telephone Service [*Telecommunications*]　(TEL)
OUTWD	Outward　(ROG)
OUTXLTR	Output Translator [*IBM Corp.*]　(MSA)
OUU	University of Oklahoma, Tulsa Medical College Library, Tulsa, OK [*OCLC symbol*]　(OCLC)
OUUI	Decisions Given by the Office of the Umpire (Unemployment Insurance) Respecting Claims to Out-of-Work Donation [*England*]　(DLA)
OUUIBD	Benefit Decisions of the British Umpire [*A publication*]　(DLA)
OUUID	Umpire Decisions, Benefit Claims [*England*] [*A publication*]　(DLA)
OUUISD	Benefit and Donation Claims, Selected Decisions of Umpire [*England*] [*A publication*]　(DLA)
OUV	University of Science and Arts of Oklahoma Libraries, Chickasha, OK [*OCLC symbol*]　(OCLC)
OUVB	Oxford University Volunteer Battalion [*British military*]　(DMA)
OUVS	Orbiter Ultraviolet Spectrometer [*NASA*]
OUW	Elkins, WV [*Location identifier FAA*]　(FAAL)
OUW	Western Oklahoma State College, Library, Altus, OK [*OCLC symbol*]　(OCLC)
OUZ	Zouerate [*Mauritania*] [*Airport symbol*]　(OAG)
OV	Observed Vehicle　(WDAA)
OV	Obvious　(AAMN)
OV	Offense Variable [*Criminal sentencing*]
OV	Office of Volunteers [*Red Cross*]
OV	Office Visit [*Medicine*]
OV	Ohio Valley
OV	Oil of Vitriol
OV	One Village [*An association*]　(EAIO)
OV	One Voice: a Magazine about Church Music [*A publication*]　(APTA)
OV	Open Ventilated　(MSA)
OV	Operation Venus　(EA)
OV	Orbital [*or Orbiter*] Vehicle [*NASA*]
OV	Orphan Voyage　(EA)
OV	Output Voltage
OV	Oval
OV	Ovalbumin [*Also, OA, OVA, OVAL*] [*Biochemistry*]
OV	Ovarian Volume [*Gynecology*]
OV	Ovary　(ADA)
OV	Oven [*Refers to the open space below the stage in a theater*] [*Slang*]　(DSUE)
OV	Over　(AAG)
ov	Over　(VRA)
OV	Overflow
OV	Overruled [*Legal shorthand*]　(LWAP)
OV	Overseas National Airways　(GAVI)
OV	Overture　(ROG)
OV	Overventilation [*Medicine*]
OV	Overvoltage
O/V	Over Voltage
OV	Ovid [*Roman poet, 43BC-17AD*] [*Classical studies*]　(ROG)
OV	Ovulate [*Gynecology*]　(DAVI)
OV	Ovum [*Egg*] [*Latin*]
OV	Owner's Vans [*Shipping*]
OV	Oxygen Vent [*NASA*]
OVA	Bekily [*Madagascar*] [*Airport symbol*]　(OAG)
OVA	Office of Veterans' Affairs
OVA	Offshore Valve Association　(EA)
OVA	Organic Vapor Analyzer [*Chromatography*]
OVA	Ottava [*Octave*] [*Music*]
OVA	Ovalbumin [*Also, OA, OV, OVAL*] [*Biochemistry*]
OVA	Overhead Value Analysis　(ADA)
OVAB	Orbiting Vehicle Assembly Building [*Later, OVSB*]
OVAC	Organisation Value Analysis Chart　(PDAA)
OVAC	Overseas Visual Aids Centre [*British*]
OVAE	Office of Vocational and Adult Education [*Department of Education*]　(OICC)
OVAG	Horticultural Research Institute of Ontario Ministry of Agriculture and Food, Vineland Station, Ontario [*Library symbol National Library of Canada*]　(NLC)
OVAGR	Research Station, Agriculture Canada [*Station de Recherches, Agriculture Canada*] Vineland Station, Ontario [*Library symbol National Library of Canada*]　(NLC)
OVAL	Oval [*Postal Service standard*]　(OPSA)
OVAL	Ovalbumin [*Also, OA, OV, OVA*]
OVAL	Ovalocytes [*Laboratory science*]　(DAVI)
OVAL	Overalls [*Freight*]

OVALO .... Ovalocytosis [*Laboratory science*] (DAVI)

OVAM .... Orbital Vehicle Assembly Mode [*NASA*]

OVAMS .... Office of Vulnerability Assessment and Management Services [*Department of Commerce*]

OVAN .... Vanier Public Library, Ontario [*Library symbol National Library of Canada*] (NLC)

OVAS .... Offshore Vessels Availability System [*Alpha Asia Systems Pte. Ltd.*] [*Defunct Information service or system*] (CRD)

OVATE .... Okumenische Vereinigung der Akademien und Tagungzentren in Europa [*Ecumenical Association of Laity Centres and Academies in Europe - EALCAE*] [*Bad Boll, Federal Republic of Germany*] (EAIO)

OVAX .... Ovariectomized [*Gynecology*]

OVB .... Novosibirsk [*Former USSR Airport symbol*] (OAG)

OVB .... Overseas Visitors Bureau [*Department of Trade*] [*British*]

OVBC .... Ohio Valley Banc Corp. [*NASDAQ symbol*] (TTSB)

OVBC .... Ohio Valley Banc Corp. [*NASDAQ symbol*] (SAG)

OVBD .... Overboard (AAG)

OVC .... Office for Victims of Crime [*Department of Justice*]

OVC .... Ohio Valley Conference [*Collegiate sports*]

OVC .... Ontario Veterinary College

OVC .... Optimized Valence Configuration [*Air Force*]

ovc .... Other Valuable Considerations [*Commerce*] (BARN)

OVC .... Overcast

OVC .... Oxidizer Vent Control

OVC .... Valley East Public Library, Val Caron, Ontario [*Library symbol National Library of Canada*] (NLC)

OVCA .... Ovarian Carcinoma [*Oncology*]

OVCO .... Operational Voice Communication Office [*NASA*] (MCD)

OVCP .... Orbiting Vehicle Checkout Procedure

OVCS .... Operational Voice Communication Subsystem

OVCST .... Overcast (AFM)

OVCT .... Caldwell Township Public Library, Verner, Ontario [*Library symbol National Library of Canada*] (NLC)

OVD .... Occlusal Vertical Dimension [*Dentistry*]

OV/D .... Operational Verification/Demonstration

OVD .... Optically Variable Device

OVD .... Optical Video Disk

OVD .... Outer Vapor Phase Deposition [*Coating technology*]

OVD .... Outside Vapor Deposition [*Coating technology*]

OVD .... Oviedo [*Spain*] [*Airport symbol*] (OAG)

OVDED .... Overdeduction

OVDF .... Official Visitors to Departmental Facilities [*New South Wales, Australia*]

OVDR .... Observed Vertical Detection Range

OVE .... Ohio Valley Electric Railroad

OVE .... On Vehicle Equipment

OVE .... Optimum Value Engineered (Home)

OVE .... Orator Verbis Electric (IAA)

OVE .... Oroville, CA [*Location identifier FAA*] (FAAL)

OVE .... Overton [*Nevada*] [*Seismograph station code, US Geological Survey Closed*] (SEIS)

OVE .... Owen Vapor Engine

OVEATP ...... Ohio Vocational Education Achievement Test Program (EDAC)

OVEN .... Italian Oven [*NASDAQ symbol*] (TTSB)

OVEN .... [*The*] Italian Oven, Inc. [*NASDAQ symbol*] (SAG)

OVER .... Optimum Vehicle for Effective Reconnaissance [*Air Force*] (PDAA)

Over .... Overtone [*Record label*]

Over .... Overton's Tennessee Supreme Court Reports [*1791-1816*] [*A publication*] (DLA)

Overl .... Overland [*A publication*]

OVERPASS... Overpass [*Commonly used*] (OPSA)

Overr .... Overruled In [*or Overruling*] [*Legal term*] (DLA)

OVERS .... Orbital Vehicle Reentry Simulator [*NASA*]

OVERS .... Overplus (DGA)

Overt .... Overton's Tennessee Supreme Court Reports [*1791-1816*] [*A publication*] (DLA)

Overt Pr ...... Overton's Iowa and Wisconsin Practice [*A publication*] (DLA)

OVF .... Overfill (NASA)

OVF .... Overfill

OVF .... Overflow [*Computer science*]

OVF .... Overvoltage Factor (IAA)

OVF .... Over-Voltage Factor (PDAA)

OVF .... Oxygen Vent Fill

OVFL .... Overflow (AAG)

ovflo .... Overflow (HGAA)

OVG .... Oberverwaltungsgericht [*Provincial Administrative Court of Appeal*] [*German*] (DLA)

OVG .... Office of the Valuer-General [*Northern Territory, Australia*]

OVH .... Vankleek Hill Public Library, Ontario [*Library symbol National Library of Canada*] (NLC)

OVHD .... Oval Head

OVHD .... Overhead (AAG)

OVHDLD ...... Overhandled [*Freight*]

OVHD PWR CAB... Overhead Power Cable [*Nautical charts*]

OVHG .... Overhanging

OVHL .... Overhaul (AAG)

OVHT .... Overheat (NASA)

OVHT .... Overheat

OVHT .... Tay-Victoria Harbour Union Library, Victoria Harbour, Ontario [*Library symbol National Library of Canada*] (BIB)

OVI .... Office of Volunteerism Initiatives (BARN)

OVI .... Operational Validation Inspection (MCD)

OVIC .... Orbiting Vehicle Integrating Contractor

OVID .... Ovid Technologies [*NASDAQ symbol*] (SAG)

OvidTec ...... Ovid Technoloiges [*Associated Press*] (SAG)

OVIR .... Office of Visas and Registrations [*Former USSR*]

OVIS .... Ohio Vocational Interest Survey [*Vocational guidance test*]

OVL .... Office of Volunteer Liaison [*ACTION*]

OVL .... Optically Void Liquid

OVL .... Oval [*Commonly used*] (OPSA)

OVL .... Overlap (IAA)

OVL .... Overlay (IAA)

OVL .... Overlay File [*Computer science*]

OVLAY .... Overlay

OVLBI .... Orbital Very-Long Baseline Interferometer [*Communications satellite*] [*Telecommunications*] (IEEE)

OVLD .... Overload (AAG)

OVLD .... Overload

OVLMA .... Orbiting Vehicle Limited Maintenance Area

OVLP .... Overvoltage Load Protection

OVLT .... Organum Vasculosum of the Lamina Terminalis [*Medicine*]

OVM .... Congregation of the Oblates of the Virgin Mary [*Rome, Italy*] (EAIO)

OVM .... McGarry Public Library, Virginiatown, Ontario [*Library symbol National Library of Canada*] (BIB)

OVM .... On Vehicle Materiel [*Military*]

OVM .... Orbiting Velocity Meter

OVNGT .... Overnight (FAAC)

OVO .... North Vernon, IN [*Location identifier FAA*] (FAAL)

OVON .... OIS Optical Imaging Sys [*NASDAQ symbol*] (TTSB)

OVON .... OIS Optical Imaging Systems, Inc. [*NASDAQ symbol*] (SAG)

OVONIC ...... Ovshinsky and Electronic [*Excitation processing term formed by combining name of Stanford Ovshinsky, energy researcher, and "electronic"*]

OVOT .... Vernon Branch, Osgoode Township Library, Ontario [*Library symbol National Library of Canada*] (NLC)

OVP .... Oesterreichische Volkspartei [*Austrian People's Party*] [*Political party*] (PPW)

OVP .... Office of the Vice-President

OVP .... Oil-Vapor Pump

OVP .... Outside Vendor Personnel

OVP .... Oval Paint

OVP .... Ovarian Vein Plasma [*Endocrinology*]

OVP .... Overseas Private Investment Corp., Washington, DC [*OCLC symbol*] (OCLC)

OVP .... Overvoltage Protection

OVPC .... Ovary Pubescence - Curly [*Botany*]

OVPD .... Overpaid (AFM)

OVPG .... Ovary Pubescence, Glandular [*Botany*]

OVPO .... Outside Vapor Phase Oxidation [*Glass technology*]

OVPR .... Over-Voltage Protection Relay [*Electrical engineering*]

OVPRESS..... Overpressurized

OVPU .... Over-Voltage Protection Unit [*Computer science*] (EECA)

OVPUS .... Office of the Vice President of the United States (BARN)

OVPWR .... Overpower

OVR .... Office of Vocational Rehabilitation [*Later, Vocational Rehabilitation Administration*] [*HEW*]

OVR .... Orbiting Vehicle Requirements

OVR .... Oudtshoorn Volunteer Rifles [*British military*] (DMA)

OVR .... Overlay File [*Computer science*]

OVR .... Overvoltage Relay

OVRD .... Override (AAG)

OVRD .... Override

OVRH .... Val Rita-Harty Public Library, Val Rita, Ontario [*Library symbol National Library of Canada*] (BIB)

OVRHD .... Overhead

OVRN .... Overrun (AFM)

OVRN .... Overrun Standard Approach Lighting System [*Aviation*] (DA)

OVRNG .... Overrunning (DA)

OVRO .... Owens Valley Radio Observatory [*California Institute of Technology*] [*Research center*] (RCD)

OVRP .... Organizacion de Voluntarios para la Revolucion Puertorriquena [*Organization of Volunteers for the Puerto Rican Revolution*] (PD)

OVRR .... Office of Veterans Reemployment Rights [*Department of Labor*]

OVRS .... Operational Voice Recording Subsystem

OVRSGHT ... Oversight

OVS .... Official Visitors' Scheme

OVS .... Online Version Storage [*Computer science*] (PDAA)

OVS .... Operational Voice System (MCD)

OVS .... Optical Viewing System

OVS .... Orbiting Vehicle System

OVS .... Ovarian Vein Serum [*Endocrinology*]

OVS .... Overhaul Specification (NG)

OVS .... Oversize

OVSB .... Overvoltage Sensing (MCD)

OVSB .... Orbiting Vehicle Support Building [*Formerly, OVAB*]

OVSEA .... Overseas [*Aviation*] (FAAC)

OvShip .... Overseas Shipholding Group, Inc. [*Associated Press*] (SAG)

OVSP .... Overspeed (AAG)

OVSR .... Office of Vehicle Systems Research [*Later, Safety System Laboratory*] [*National Institute of Standards and Technology*]

OVSTFD ...... Overstuffed [*Freight*]

OVT .... Occupational-Vocational-Technical Training

OVT .... Operational Verification Test

OVT .... Optical Van Trailer

OVTK .... Overtake (FAAC)

OVTR .... Operational Video Tape Recorder [*Air Force*] (MCD)

OVTR .... Overtravel

OVUIL .... Operating Vehicle under Influence of Liquor or Narcotic Drugs [*FBI standardized term*]

OVUREP ...... Overseas Unit Replacement [*System*] [*Army*]

O/V-U/V ...... Over Voltage - Under Voltage (MCD)

OVV .... Optically Violently Variable [*QUASAR*]

OVV .... Overvoltage

OVV .... Ovvero [*Otherwise*] [*Music*]

OVWA .... On-Line Voltammetric Wastewater Analyzer [*Biochemistry*]

OVWD .... Operating Vehicle while Drunk [*Traffic offense charge*]

OVWV .... One Valley Bancorp [*NASDAQ symbol*] (TTSB)

OVWV .... One Valley Bancorp of West Virginia, Inc. [*NASDAQ symbol*] (NQ)

OVX .... Ovariectomized [*Gynecology*]

OVX .... Ovariectomized [*Gynecology*] (DAVI)

OW .... Obere Winkelgruppe [*Angles above 45*] [*German military - World War II*]

OW .... Observation Ward [*British*]

OW .... Ocellus Width

OW .... Offer Wanted

OW .... Office of Water [*Environmental Protection Agency*] (GFGA)

OW .... Officer's Writer [*British military*] (DMA)

OW .... Ohne Wert [*Without Value*] [*German*]

O/W .... Oil-dispersed-in-Water [*Emulsion*]

OW .... Oil-Immersed Water-Cooled [*Transformer*] (IEEE)

O/W .... Oil in Water

O/W .... Oil-Water [*Ratio*] [*Laboratory science*] (DAVI)

OW .... Older Worker

OW .... Old Wellingtonian [*Wellington College*] [*British*]

OW .... Old Welsh [*Language, etc.*]

OW .... Old Woman [*A wife*] [*Slang*]

OW .... One Way [*Fare*]

OW .... Open Wedge [*Osteotomy*] [*Orthopedics*] (DAVI)

OW .... Open Wheel [*A publication*]

OW .... Open Wire (NATG)

OW .... Optical Window (NASA)

O/W .... Optional With [*Automotive engineering*]

OW .... Options for Women [*Later, Options*] (EA)

OW .... Order Wire [*Military*] (AABC)

OW .... Order Writing (IAA)

OW .... Ordinary Warfare

O-W .... Ordinary Wave (MCD)

OW .... Ordinary Welfare (BABM)

OW .... Ordinary Welfare (DAVI)

OW .... Outer Wing

OW .... Out of Wedlock

OW .... Over-Achieving Women

OW .... Overall Width [*of the Vehicle*] [*TII*] (TAG)

OW .... Overseas Writers (EA)

OW .... Over Water (WDAA)

Ow .... Owen's English Common Pleas Reports [*A publication*] (DLA)

Ow .... Owen's English King's Bench Reports [*1556-1615*] [*A publication*] (DLA)

OW .... Owner's Wagons [*Shipping*]

OW .... Trans Mountain Airlines [*ICAO designator*] (AD)

OW .... Warren Public Library, Warren, OH [*Library symbol Library of Congress*] (LCLS)

OW .... Windsor Public Library, Ontario [*Library symbol National Library of Canada*] (NLC)

OWA .... Optical Wholesalers Association [*Later, OLA*] (EA)

OWA .... Organics-in-Water Analyzer [*Instrumentation*]

OWA .... Owase [*Japan*] [*Seismograph station code, US Geological Survey*] (SEIS)

OWA .... Owatonna, MN [*Location identifier FAA*] (FAAL)

OWA .... University of Windsor, Ontario [*Library symbol National Library of Canada*] (NLC)

OWAA .... Anderson Associates Ltd., Willowdale, Ontario [*Library symbol National Library of Canada*] (NLC)

OWAA .... Outdoor Writers Association of America (EA)

OWAAD .... Organisation of Women of Asian and African Descent [*British*] (DI)

OWAB .... Wasaga Beach Public Library, Ontario [*Library symbol National Library of Canada*] (BIB)

OWAEC .... Organization for West African Economic Co-operation

OWAG .... Art Gallery of Windsor, Ontario [*Library symbol National Library of Canada*] (NLC)

OWAIT .... Airy Township Public Library, Whitney, Ontario [*Library symbol National Library of Canada*] (NLC)

OWAL .... Law Library, University of Windsor, Ontario [*Library symbol National Library of Canada*] (NLC)

OWALK .... Walkerton Branch, Bruce County Public Library, Ontario [*Library symbol National Library of Canada*] (NLC)

OWALL .... Wallaceburg Public Library, Ontario [*Library symbol National Library of Canada*] (NLC)

OWAP .... Overhead Warning Annunciator Panel (MCD)

OWaP .... Pike County Free Public Library, Waverly, OH [*Library symbol Library of Congress*] (LCLS)

OWAP .... Waterford Public Library, Ontario [*Library symbol National Library of Canada*] (NLC)

OWAR .... Warkworth Public Library, Ontario [*Library symbol National Library of Canada*] (NLC)

OWARNP ..... Percy Township Branch, Northumberland County Public Library, Warkworth, Ontario [*Library symbol National Library of Canada*] (BIB)

OWas .... Carnegie Public Library, Washington Court House, OH [*Library symbol Library of Congress*] (LCLS)

OWASU .... Old World Archaeological Study Unit (EA)

OWAT .... Wainfleet Township Library, Ontario [*Library symbol National Library of Canada*] (NLC)

OWAV .... OneWave, Inc. [*NASDAQ symbol*] (SAG)

OWAVE .... Ordinary Wave (MSA)

OWay .... Mary L. Cook Public Library, Waynesville, OH [*Library symbol Library of Congress*] (LCLS)

OWB .... Oppenheimer World Bond Fund [*NYSE symbol*] (SAG)

OWB .... Owensboro [*Kentucky*] [*Airport symbol*] (AD)

OWB .... Owensboro [*Kentucky*] [*Airport symbol*] (OAG)

OWB .... West Bay Public Library, Ontario [*Library symbol National Library of Canada*] (NLC)

OWBC .... Health Sciences Library, Bloorview Children's Hospital, Willowdale, Ontario [*Library symbol National Library of Canada*] (BIB)

OWBE .... Office of Women's Business Enterprise [*Federal government*]

OWBE .... Windsor Board of Education, Ontario [*Library symbol National Library of Canada*] (NLC)

OWBL .... Beaver Lake Branch, Walden Public Library, Ontario [*Library symbol National Library of Canada*] (NLC)

OWBL .... Office of Work-Based Learning [*U.S. Department of Labor*] (BARN)

OWBMS ...... Manitoulin Secondary School Library, West Bay, Ontario [*Library symbol National Library of Canada*] (BIB)

OWBO .... Office of Women's Business Ownership [*Small Business Administration*]

OWBPA .... Older Workers Benefit Protection Act of 1990 (WYGK)

OWBR .... Bartlet & Richardes, Windsor, Ontario [*Library symbol National Library of Canada*] (BIB)

OWC .... Centennial Secondary School, Windsor, Ontario [*Library symbol National Library of Canada*] (NLC)

OWC .... Officers' Wives Club [*Military*]

OwC .... Omniwest Corporation, Salt Lake City, UT [*Library symbol Library of Congress*] (LCLS)

OWC .... Ontario Workers' Compensation Appeals Tribunal [*UTLAS symbol*]

OWC .... Order of Woodcraft Chivalry [*British*] (DBA)

OWC .... Ordinary Wave Component

OWC .... Ordnance Weapons Command [*Later, Weapons Command*]

OWC .... Outline of World Cultures [*Human Relations Area Files*] [*Information retrieval*]

OWC .... Owner Will Carry [*Banking*]

OWC .... Owning Work Center [*Military*] (AFIT)

OWC .... Wood County District Public Library, Bowling Green, OH [*OCLC symbol*] (OCLC)

OWCA .... Canadian Automobile Workers Union, Willowdale, Ontario [*Library symbol National Library of Canada*] (BIB)

OWCC .... Cape Croker Public Library, Wiarton, Ontario [*Library symbol National Library of Canada*] (NLC)

OWCF .... Canadian Federation of Independent Business, Willowdale, Ontario [*Library symbol National Library of Canada*] (BIB)

OWCL .... Octane Weekly Cost Ledger (MCD)

OWCP .... Office of Workers' [*formerly, Workmen's*] Compensation Programs [*Formerly, Bureau of Employees' Compensation*] [*Department of Labor*]

OWCS .... Outer Wing Canted Station (MCD)

OWCSC ...... Old Water Colour Society's Club (EA)

OWD .... Norwood, MA [*Location identifier FAA*] (FAAL)

OWD .... Oil-in-Water Dispersion [*Pollution*]

OWD .... One-Way Doppler

OWD .... On-Line Wholesale Distribution System [*Computer science*] (BUR)

OWDC .... Office of Water Data Coordination [*US Geological Survey*] [*Reston, VA*]

OWDE .... One-Way Doppler Extraction

OWE .... Eagle, CO [*Location identifier FAA*] (FAAL)

OWE .... Office of Water Enforcement [*Environmental Protection Agency*] (ERG)

OWE .... Operating Weight Empty [*of space shuttle*] [*NASA*]

OWE .... Optimum Working Efficiency

OWE .... Outer Window Envelope [*Business stationery*]

OWE .... Welland Public Library, Ontario [*Library symbol National Library of Canada*] (NLC)

OWE .... Western Plains Library System, Clinton, OK [*OCLC symbol*] (OCLC)

OWe .... Westerville Public Library, Westerville, OH [*Library symbol Library of Congress*] (LCLS)

OWEB .... Webbwood Public Library, Ontario [*Library symbol National Library of Canada*] (NLC)

OWEC .... Centennial Secondary School, Welland, Ontario [*Library symbol National Library of Canada*] (NLC)

OWel .... Sylvester Memorial Wellston Public Library, Wellston, OH [*Library symbol Library of Congress*] (LCLS)

OWEL .... Wellington Public Library, Ontario [*Library symbol National Library of Canada*] (BIB)

OWEN .... Niagara College of Applied Arts and Technology, Welland, Ontario [*Library symbol National Library of Canada*] (NLC)

OWEN .... Owen Healthcare, Inc. [*NASDAQ symbol*] (SAG)

Owen .... Owen's English King's Bench Reports [*1556-1615*] [*A publication*] (DLA)

Owen Bankr... Owen on Bankruptcy [*A publication*] (DLA)

OwenC .... Owens-Corning Fiberglas Corp. [*Associated Press*] (SAG)

OWENC .... Westport-North Crosby Public Library, Westport, Ontario [*Library symbol National Library of Canada*] (NLC)

OwenHlt ...... Owen Healthcare, Inc. [*Associated Press*] (SAG)

OWENL .... Library Technician Program, Niagara College of Applied Arts & Technology, Welland, Ontario [*Library symbol National Library of Canada*] (NLC)

OwensIll ...... Owens Illinois [*Associated Press*] (SAG)

OwensM ...... Owens & Minor Inc. Holding Co. [*Associated Press*] (SAG)

OWeO .... Otterbein College, Westerville, OH [*Library symbol Library of Congress*] (LCLS)

OWEP .... Office of Water Enforcement and Permits [*Environmental Protection Agency*] (GFGA)

OWESBC ...... Borden Chemical, Westhill, Ontario [*Library symbol National Library of Canada*] (NLC)

OWEST .... Asphodel Township Public Library, Westwood, Ontario [*Library symbol National Library of Canada*] (BIB)

OWF .... Oceania Weightlifting Federation [*Australia*] (EA)

OWF .... On Weight of Fiber

OWF .... Optimum Working Facility (NITA)

OWF .... Optimum Working Frequency [*Telecommunications*]

OWF .... Orbital, Weightless Flight (IAA)

OWG .... Oil, Water, Gas

OWG .... Washington, DC [*Location identifier FAA*] (FAAL)

OWGL .... Obscure Wire Glass

OWH .... Herman Collegiate Institute, Windsor, Ontario [*Library symbol National Library of Canada*] (NLC)

OWH .... Warren General Hospital, Warren, OH [*Library symbol*] [*Library of Congress*] (LCLS)

OWHA .... Oliver Wendell Holmes Association

OWHD .... Medical Library, Hotel-Dieu of St. Joseph Hospital, Windsor, Ontario [*Library symbol National Library of Canada*] (NLC)

OWHM .... Hiram Walker Historical Museum, Windsor, Ontario [*Library symbol National Library of Canada*] (BIB)

OWHM .... Office of Water and Hazardous Materials (OICC)

OWHP .... Whitby Public Library, Ontario [*Library symbol National Library of Canada*] (NLC)

OWI .... Ocellus Width Index

OWI .... Office of War Information [*World War II*]

OWI .... Office of Waste Isolation [*Department of Energy*]

OWI .... OneWorld Internet [*Global Village Communication*] [*Internet gateway service*]

OWI .... Open Work Items (KSC)

OWI .... Operating Vehicle while Intoxicated [*Traffic offense charge*]

OWI .... Ottawa, KS [*Location identifier FAA*] (FAAL)

OWI .... Owens-Illinois, Inc., Technical and Business Information Services, Toledo, OH [*OCLC symbol*] (OCLC)

OWI .... Wiarton Branch, Bruce County Public Library, Ontario [*Library symbol National Library of Canada*] (NLC)

OWIB .... Wikwemikong Band Public Library, Ontario [*Library symbol National Library of Canada*] (NLC)

OWibfC .... Central State University, Wilberforce, OH [*Library symbol Library of Congress*] (LCLS)

OWibfP .... Payne Theological Seminary, Wilberforce, OH [*Library symbol Library of Congress*] (LCLS)

OWibfU .... Wilberforce University, Wilberforce, OH [*Library symbol Library of Congress*] (LCLS)

OWicB .... Borromeo Seminary of Ohio, Wickliffe, OH [*Library symbol Library of Congress*] (LCLS)

OWIFC .... Wolfe Island Branch, Frontenac County Public Library, Ontario [*Library symbol National Library of Canada*] (NLC)

OWIJC .... International Joint Commission [*Commission Mixte Internationale*] Windsor, Ontario [*Library symbol National Library of Canada*] (NLC)

OWil .... Willard Memorial Library, Willard, OH [*Library symbol Library of Congress*] (LCLS)

OWillo .... Willoughby-Eastlake Public Library, Willowick, OH [*Library symbol Library of Congress*] (LCLS)

OWilm .... Wilmington Public Library, Wilmington, OH [*Library symbol Library of Congress*] (LCLS)

OWilmC ...... Wilmington College, Wilmington, OH [*Library symbol Library of Congress*] (LCLS)

OWilmH ...... Clinton Memorial Hospital, Health Resource Center, Wilmington, OH [*Library symbol Library of Congress*] (LCLS)

OWilm-O ..... Southwestern Ohio Rural Library, Wilmington, OH [*Library symbol Library of Congress*] (LCLS)

OWilmS ...... Southern State Community College, Wilmington, OH [*Library symbol Library of Congress*] (LCLS)

OWin .... Adams-Brown County Bookmobile, Winchester, OH [*Library symbol Library of Congress*] (LCLS)

OWIN .... Office of Work Incentive Program [*Office of Comprehensive Employment Development*] [*Department of Labor*]

OWINF .... F. E. Madill Secondary School, Wingham, Ontario [*Library symbol National Library of Canada*] (NLC)

OWISDG ...... Williamstown Branch, Stormount, Dundas, and Glengarry County Library, Ontario [*Library symbol National Library of Canada*] (NLC)

OWIU .... Oil Workers International Union [*Later, OCAW*]

OWK .... Kent State University, Trumbull Regional Campus, Warren, OH [*Library symbol Library of Congress OCLC symbol*] (LCLS)

OWK .... Norridgewock, ME [*Location identifier FAA*] (FAAL)

OWL .... Lowe Technical School, Windsor, Ontario [*Library symbol National Library of Canada*] (NLC)

OWL .... Maui Airlines, Inc. [*ICAO designator*] (FAAC)

OWL .... National Order of Women Legislators (EA)

OWL .... Object Windows Library [*Borland International*] [*Computer science*] (PCM)

OWL .... Office Workstations Ltd. (NITA)

OWL .... Older Women's League (EA)

OWL .... Older Women's Liberation [*Feminist group*] [*Defunct*]

OWL .... Olympic-Wallowa Lineament [*Geology*]

OWL .... Online without Limits

OWL .... Online Writing Lab [*Purdue University*] [*Computer science*]

OWL .... Other Woman Limited [*An association*]

OWL .... Westerville Public Library, Westerville, OH [*OCLC symbol*] (OCLC)

OWLA .... Organization of Women for Legal Awareness (EA)

OWLaw .... Trumbull County Law Library, Warren, OH [*Library symbol Library of Congress*] (LCLS)

OWLB .... Wunnummin Lake Band Library, Ontario [*Library symbol National Library of Canada*] (BIB)

OWL/D .... Optical Warning Locator/Detector (MCD)

OWLEF .... Older Women's League Educational Fund (EA)

OWIGS .... Church Jesus Christ of Latter-Day Saints, Genealogical Society Library, Cleveland Branch, Westlake, OH [*Library symbol*] [*Library of Congress*] (LCLS)

OWIGS .... Church of Jesus Christ of Latter-Day Saints, Genealogical Society Library, Cleveland Branch, Westlake, OH [*Library symbol Library of Congress*] (LCLS)

OWLI .... Lively Branch, Walden Public Library, Ontario [*Library symbol National Library of Canada*] (NLC)

OWLS .... Office Workers Link Shift [*After-hours production workers*] [*World War II*]

OWLS .... Operation Work Load Scheduling (MCD)

OWLS .... Outagamie-Waupaca Counties Federated Library System [*Library network*]

OWLS .... Overseas Weapons, Logistically Supported (MCD)

OWLS .... Oxford Word and Language Service [*A service of the Oxford English Dictionary group*]

OWLS .... Oxford Word and Language Service [*British*] (DAVI)

OWM .... Office of War Mobilization [*Succeeded by OWMR, 1944*]

OWM .... Office of Weights and Measures [*National Institute of Standards and Technology*]

OWMMD ...... M. M. Dillon Ltd., Willowdale, Ontario [*Library symbol National Library of Canada*] (NLC)

OWMR .... Office of War Mobilization and Reconversion [*Succeeded OWM, 1944; became part of Office of Temporary Controls, 1946*]

OWMR .... Other War Materiel Requirements [*Army*]

OWMT .... Michipicoten Township Public Library, Wawa, Ontario [*Library symbol National Library of Canada*] (NLC)

OWN .... Naughton Branch, Walden Public Library, Ontario [*Library symbol National Library of Canada*] (NLC)

OWN .... Ontario Weekly Notes [*A publication*] (DLA)

OWN .... Oudh Weekly Notes [*India*] [*A publication*] (DLA)

OWN .... Overwintered Nest [*Ornithology*]

OWN .... Owen Healthcare [*NYSE symbol*] (TTSB)

OWN .... Owensboro [*Diocesan abbreviation*] [*Kentucky*] (TOCD)

OWN .... Owens Group Ltd. [*New Zealand*] [*ICAO designator*] (FAAC)

OWN .... Owen Ventures Ltd. [*Vancouver Stock Exchange symbol*]

OWN .... Owner (MCD)

OWN .... Wise, VA [*Location identifier FAA*] (FAAL)

OWNR .... Owner

OWO .... On Work Order [*Military*] (AFIT)

OWo .... Wayne County Public Library, Wooster, OH [*Library symbol Library of Congress*] (LCLS)

OWO .... Woodstock Public Library, Ontario [*Library symbol National Library of Canada*] (NLC)

OWoA .... Ohio Agricultural Research and Development Center, Wooster, OH [*Library symbol Library of Congress*] (LCLS)

OWOBC .... J. William Horsey Library, Ontario Bible College, Ontario Theological College, Willowdale, Ontario [*Library symbol National Library of Canada*] (NLC)

OWoC .... College of Wooster, Wooster, OH [*Library symbol Library of Congress*] (LCLS)

OWOH .... Huron Park Secondary School, Woodstock, Ontario [*Library symbol National Library of Canada*] (NLC)

OWoH .... Wooster Community Hospital, Wooster, OH [*Library symbol*] [*Library of Congress*] (LCLS)

OWOL .... Ontario Library Co-Operative, Wyoming, Ontario [*Library symbol National Library of Canada*] (NLC)

OWOM .... Woodstock Museum, Ontario [*Library symbol National Library of Canada*] (BIB)

OWOO .... Oxford County Public Library, Woodstock, Ontario [*Library symbol National Library of Canada*] (NLC)

OWor .... Worthington Public Library, Worthington, OH [*Library symbol*] [*Library of Congress*] (LCLS)

OWorNW .... National Water Wall Association, Ground Water Library/Information Center, Worthington, OH [*Library symbol*] [*Library of Congress*] (LCLS)

OWorP .... Pontifical College Josephinum, Worthington, OH [*Library symbol Library of Congress*] (LCLS)

OWOS .... Owosso Corp. [*NASDAQ symbol*] (SAG)

Owosso .... Owosso Corp. [*Associated Press*] (SAG)

OWoWCL .... Wayne County Law Library, Wooster, OH [*Library symbol Library of Congress*] (LCLS)

OWP .... Oboz Wielkiej Polski [*Camp of Great Poland*] (PPE)

OWP .... Office of Water Policy [*Department of the Interior*]

OWP .... Office of Water Programs [*Abolished*] [*Environmental Protection Agency*]

OWP .... One-Way Polar [*Telegraph*]

OWP .... One-Write Plus [*Computer software*]

OWP .... Operations Work Procedure [*Nuclear energy*] (NRCH)

OWP .... Orange Washed Pulp [*Citrus processing*]

OWP .... Organization of Wildlife Planners (EA)

OWP .... Outer Wing Panel

OWP .... Warner Pacific College, Portland, OR [*OCLC symbol*] (OCLC)

OWpAR .... United States Air Force, Aerospace Research Laboratories, Wright-Patterson Air Force Base, OH [*Library symbol Library of Congress*] (LCLS)

OWpDI......... United States Air Force, Defense Institute of Security Administration Management, Wright-Patterson Air Force Base, OH [*Library symbol Library of Congress*] (LCLS)

OWPE.......... Office of Waste Programs Enforcement [*Environmental Protection Agency*] (EPA)

OWPH.......... Whitby Psychiatric Hospital, Ontario [*Library symbol National Library of Canada*] (NLC)

OWpIT......... United States Air Force Institute of Technology, Wright-Patterson Air Force Base, OH [*Library symbol Library of Congress*] (LCLS)

OWpL.......... United States Air Force, Air Force Logistics Command, Wright-Patterson Air ForceBase, OH [*Library symbol Library of Congress*] (LCLS)

OWpM.......... United States Air Force, Medical Center Library, SGEL, Wright Patterson AFB, OH [*Library symbol Library of Congress*] (LCLS)

OWPO.......... Office of Water Program Operations [*Environmental Protection Agency*] (EPA)

OWPP.......... Office of Welfare and Pension Plans [*Department of Labor*]

OWPR.......... Ocean Wave Profile Recorder (IEEE)

OWPS.......... Offshore Windpower System [*Proposed system to generate electricity by wind turbines mounted on offshore platforms*]

OWpT.......... United States Air Force, Wright-Patterson Technical Library, Wright-Patterson Air Force Base, OH [*Library symbol Library of Congress*] (LCLS)

OWR .... Obligated War Reserves [*Army*] (AABC)

OWR .... Office of Worship Resources [*Later, WRO*] (EA)

OWR .... Omega West Reactor [*Los Alamos, NM*] [*Department of Energy*]

OWR .... Ontario Weekly Reporter [*A publication*] (DLA)

OWR .... Order of the White Rose of Finland (DD)

OWR .... Riverside Secondary School, Windsor, Ontario [*Library symbol National Library of Canada*] (NLC)

OWR .... Worthington Public Library, Worthington, OH [*OCLC symbol*] (OCLC)

OWRAP........ Office of Worker Retraining and Adjustment Programs [*U.S. Department of Labor*] (BARN)

OWRB.......... RC Reid-Bicknell Eng. Ltd., Woodbridge, Ontario [*Library symbol National Library of Canada*] (NLC)

OWRC.......... Old West Regional Commission [*Department of Commerce*]

OWRC.......... White River Community Library, Ontario [*Library symbol National Library of Canada*] (NLC)

OWRD.......... Ratter and Dunnet Public Library, Warren, Ontario [*Library symbol National Library of Canada*] (NLC)

OWRHS........ Ontario and Western Railroad Historical Society (EA)

OWRL.......... One-Way Radio Link [*Telecommunications*] (LAIN)

OWRM......... Office of Weather Research and Modification [*National Oceanic and Atmospheric Administration*] (GRD)

OWRM........ Other War Reserve Materiel

OWRMR....... Other War Reserve Materiel Requirement (AFIT)

OWRMS....... Other War Reserve Materiel Stocks [*Army*] (AABC)

OWRR.......... Office of Water Resources Research [*Later, OWRT*] [*Department of the Interior*]

OWRRI........ Oklahoma Water Resources Research Institute [*Stillwater, OK*] [*Department of the Interior*] (GRD)

OWRS.......... Office of Water Regulations and Standards [*Environmental Protection Agency*] (GFGA)

OWRT.......... Office of Water Research and Technology [*Formerly, OSW, OWRR*] [*Abolished, 1982 Department of the Interior*]

OWS .... Cargosur [*Spain ICAO designator*] (FAAC)

OWS .... Occupational Wage Survey

OWS .... Ocean Weather Ship

OWS .... Ocean Weather Station (MCD)

OWS .... Oil Water Separator [*Navy*] (CAAL)

OWS .... Old West Saxon [*Language, etc.*] (ROG)

OWS .... Oliphant Washington Service [*Information service or system*] (IID)

OWS .... Operational Weather Support

OWS .... Orbital Weapon System (AAG)

OWS .... Orbital Workshop [*NASA*]

OWS .... Ordnance Weapon Systems [*Army*]

OWS .... Outer Wing Station (MCD)

OWS .... Overload Warning System (MCD)

OWS .... Overwear Syndrome [*Of contact lens*]

OWS .... Southwestern Regional Library, Windsor, Ontario [*Library symbol Obsolete National Library of Canada*] (NLC)

OWS .... Willamette University, Salem, OR [*OCLC symbol*] (OCLC)

OWSA.......... Spar Aerospace Ltd., Weston, Ontario [*Library symbol National Library of Canada*] (NLC)

OWSAH........ Salvation Army Grace Hospital, Windsor, Ontario [*Library symbol National Library of Canada*] (BIB)

OWSC.......... Old West Scandinavian [*Language, etc.*]

OWSC.......... St. Clair College, Windsor, Ontario [*Library symbol National Library of Canada*] (NLC)

OWSCC........ Simon-Carves of Canada Ltd., Willowdale, Ontario [*Library symbol National Library of Canada*] (NLC)

OWSCL........ Senes Consultants Ltd., Willowdale, Ontario [*Library symbol National Library of Canada*] (NLC)

OWSDG........ Winchester Branch, Stormount, Dundas, and Glengarry County Public Library, Ontario [*Library symbol National Library of Canada*] (NLC)

OWSE.......... Otherwise

OWSG.......... Older Worker Specialists Group

OWSJ.......... Off the Wall Street Journal [*Parody of the Wall Street Journal*]

OWSM......... Seagram Museum, Waterloo, Ontario [*Library symbol National Library of Canada*] (BIB)

OWT .... Organic Weather Team

OWT.......... Waterloo Public Library, Ontario [*Library symbol National Library of Canada*] (NLC)

OWT.......... Willamette University, Law Library, Salem, OR [*OCLC symbol*] (OCLC)

OWTA .... Kitchener-Waterloo Academy of Medicine, Kitchener, Ontario [*Library symbol National Library of Canada*] (NLC)

OWTAI........ Airworthiness Library, Ontario Region, Transport Canada [*Bibliotheque de la Navigabilite Aerienne, Region de l'Ontario, Transports Canada*], Willowdale, Ontario [*Library symbol National Library of Canada*] (NLC)

OWTG .... Kitchener-Waterloo Hospital, Kitchener, Ontario [*Library symbol National Library of Canada*] (NLC)

OWTL.......... Wilfrid Laurier University [*Formerly, Waterloo Lutheran University*] Waterloo, Ontario [*Library symbol National Library of Canada*] (NLC)

OWTM .... Legal Reference Centre, Manufacturers' Life Insurance Co., Waterloo, Ontario [*Library symbol National Library of Canada*] (BIB)

OWTML........ Corporate Library, Mutual Life of Canada, Waterloo, Ontario [*Library symbol National Library of Canada*] (BIB)

OWTO .... Ontario Library Services Center, Waterloo, Ontario [*Library symbol National Library of Canada*] (NLC)

OWTS .... St. Mary's General Hospital, Kitchener, Ontario [*Library symbol National Library of Canada*] (NLC)

OWTU .... University of Waterloo, Ontario [*Library symbol National Library of Canada*] (NLC)

OWTUE .... Environmental Studies Library, University of Waterloo, Ontario [*Library symbol National Library of Canada*] (NLC)

OWU .... Office of War Utilities [*War Production Board*]

OWU .... Ohio Wesleyan University [*Delaware, OH*]

OWU .... Ohio Wesleyan University, Delaware, OH [*OCLC symbol*] (OCLC)

OWU .... Open-Window Unit (MSA)

OWU .... Overload Warning Unit (MCD)

OWU .... Woodward, OK [*Location identifier FAA*] (FAAL)

OW-USS ...... Our World-Underwater Scholarship Society (EA)

OWV .... Ocean Weather Vessel [*Shipping*] (AIA)

OWVM .... Vincent Massey Secondary School, Windsor, Ontario [*Library symbol National Library of Canada*] (NLC)

OWW .... Walkerville Collegiate Institute, Windsor, Ontario [*Library symbol National Library of Canada*] (NLC)

OWWA .... Waters Branch, Walden Public Library, Ontario [*Library symbol National Library of Canada*] (NLC)

OWWH .... Whitefish Branch, Walden Public Library, Ontario [*Library symbol National Library of Canada*] (NLC)

OWWM .... Office of Water and Waste Management (ERG)

OWX .... Office of the Assistant for Weather [*Air Force*]

OWX .... Ottawa, OH [*Location identifier FAA*] (FAAL)

OWY .... Owyhee, NV [*Location identifier FAA*] (FAAL)

OWYL......... Lambton County Public Library, Wyoming, Ontario [*Library symbol National Library of Canada*] (NLC)

OW/YM .... Older Woman / Younger Man (WDAA)

OX.............. Air Atlantic Airlines [*ICAO designator*] (AD)

OX.............. Oxacillin [*Antibacterial compound*]

OX.............. Oxford [*England*]

Ox.............. Oxford [*Record label*]

OX.............. Oxidant [*Photochemical*] (ERG)

OX.............. Oxide [*or Oxidizer*] (AAG)

ox.............. Oxides (VRA)

OX.............. Oxygen [*Chemical element*] (IAA)

ox.............. Oxygen (IDOE)

OX.............. Oxymel [*Syrup of vinegar and honey*] [*Pharmacy*]

OXA.......... Oxalic Acid [*Organic chemistry*]

OXB.......... Baldwin-Wallace College, Berea, OH [*OCLC symbol*] (OCLC)

OxboroM...... Oxboro Medical International, Inc. [*Associated Press*] (SAG)

OXBRIDGE ... Oxford/Cambridge [*England*]

OXC.......... Oxford, CT [*Location identifier FAA*] (FAAL)

OXC.......... Oxidizing Catalyst [*Automotive engineering*]

OXC.......... Waterbury [*Connecticut*] [*Airport symbol*] (AD)

OXCI.......... Oxford Consolidated, Inc. [*NASDAQ symbol*] (NQ)

OXD............ Oxford [*England*] [*Seismograph station code, US Geological Survey Closed*] (SEIS)

OXD............ Oxford, OH [*Location identifier FAA*] (FAAL)

OXD............ Oxidized (MSA)

OXDZR........ Oxidizer (NASA)

OXDZR........ Oxidizer

OXe.......... Greene County District Library, Xenia, OH [*Library symbol Library of Congress*] (LCLS)

OXE.......... OEC Medical Sys [*NYSE symbol*] (TTSB)

OXE.......... OEC Medical Systems [*Formerly, Diasonics, Inc.*] [*NYSE symbol*] (SPSG)

OXE.......... Oxaero [*British*] [*FAA designator*] (FAAC)

OXeGH....... Greene Memorial Hospital, Health Resource Library, Xenia, OH [*Library symbol Library of Congress*] (LCLS)

OXERA .... Oxford Economic Research Associates Ltd

OXF.......... Oxford [*England*]

OXF.......... Oxford [*British depot code*]

OXF.......... Oxford [*Mississippi*] [*Seismograph station code, US Geological Survey Closed*] (SEIS)

OXF.......... Oxford [*England*] [*Airport symbol*] (AD)

OXF.......... Oxford Properties Canada Ltd. [*Toronto Stock Exchange symbol*]

OXFAM .... Oxford Committee for Famine Relief [*Acronym is now organization's official name British*] (EA)

OXFD .... Oxford Resources CI'A' [*NASDAQ symbol*] (TTSB)

OXFD .... Oxford Resources Corp. [*NASDAQ symbol*] (SAG)

OxfdHlt .... Oxford Health Plans, Inc. [*Associated Press*] (SAG)

OxfdRsc .... Oxford Resources Corp. [*Associated Press*] (SAG)

Oxf Lawy ..... Oxford Lawyer [*1958-61*] [*A publication*] (DLA)

Oxford	Oxford Industries, Inc. [*Associated Press*] (SAG)
Oxford Law	Oxford Lawyer [*1958-61*] [*A publication*] (DLA)
OxfrdC	Oxford Consolidated, Inc. [*Associated Press*] (SAG)
OXGN	Oxigene, Inc. [*NASDAQ symbol*] (SAG)
OXGNW	OXIGENE Inc. Wrrt [*NASDAQ symbol*] (TTSB)
OXH	Oxygen Heat Exchanger (KSC)
OXHP	Oxford Health Plans [*NASDAQ symbol*] (SPSG)
OXI	Knox, IN [*Location identifier FAA*] (FAAL)
OXI	Orbex Industries, Inc. [*Vancouver Stock Exchange symbol*]
OXID	Oxidizer (AAG)
OXIDN	Oxidation
Oxigene	Oxigene, Inc. [*Associated Press*] (SAG)
Oxign	Oxigene, Inc. [*Associated Press*] (SAG)
OXIM	Oxide-Isolated Monolith
OXINE	Oxyquinoline [*Organic chemistry*]
OXIS	Oxide Isolated (NITA)
OXIS	Oxide Isolation (IAA)
OXIS	OXIS International [*NASDAQ symbol*] (TTSB)
OXIS	Oxis International, Inc. [*NASDAQ symbol*] (SAG)
OXK	Belleville, IL [*Location identifier FAA*] (FAAL)
OXLAT	Oxalate [*Laboratory science*] (DAVI)
Oxley	Oxley's Railway Cases [*1897-1903*] [*A publication*] (DLA)
Oxley	Young's Nova Scotia Vice-Admiralty Decisions, Edited by Oxley [*A publication*] (DLA)
OXM	Oxford Indus [*NYSE symbol*] (TTSB)
OXM	Oxford Industries, Inc. [*NYSE symbol*] (SPSG)
OXM	Oxtotitlan [*Mexico*] [*Seismograph station code, US Geological Survey*] (SEIS)
OXN	Oxin Industries Ltd. [*Vancouver Stock Exchange symbol*]
OXO	Million Air, Inc. [*ICAO designator*] (FAAC)
OXO	Orbiting X-Ray Observatory [*NASA*]
OXO	Orientos [*Queensland*] [*Airport symbol*] (AD)
OXON	Oxfordshire [*County in England*]
OXON	Oxonia [*Oxford University*] [*Latin*]
OXON	Oxoniensis [*Of Oxford University*] [*Latin*]
OXP	Oxford Poets [*A publication*]
OXP	Oxprenolol [*Vasodilator*]
OXPHOS	Oxidative Phosphorylation [*Medicine*]
OXR	Oxnard [*California*] [*Airport symbol*] (OAG)
OXRB	Oxygen Replacement Bottles
OXV	Knoxville, IA [*Location identifier FAA*] (FAAL)
OXY	Occidental Petroleum Corp. [*NYSE symbol Toronto Stock Exchange symbol*] (SPSG)
OXY	Occidental Petrol'm [*NYSE symbol*] (TTSB)
OXY	Oxley [*British depot code*]
OXY	Oxygen [*Chemical element*] [*Symbol is O*] (AAG)
OXY	Oxygen
OXY	Oxytocin [*Endocrinology*]
OXYG	Oxygen [*Chemical element*] [*Symbol is O*]
OXYM	Oxymel [*Syrup of vinegar and honey*] [*Pharmacy*] (ROG)
OXYPrA	Occidental Petr $3 Cv Pfd [*NYSE symbol*] (TTSB)
OY	Denmark [*International civil aircraft marking*] (ODBW)
OY	New Jersey Airways [*ICAO designator*] (AD)
OY	Optimum Yield
OY	Orange Yellow
Oy	Osakeyhtioe [*Limited Company*] [*Finland*]
OY	Public Library of Youngstown and Mahoning County, Youngstown, OH [*Library symbol Library of Congress*] (LCLS)
OYA	Goya [*Argentina*] [*Airport symbol*] (OAG)
OYA	Orthodox Youth of America [*Later, SOYO*]
OYAP	Outstanding Young American Pianist
OYAS	Abbs [*Yemen*] [*ICAO location identifier*] (ICLI)
OYBI	Al-Beida [*Yemen*] [*ICAO location identifier*] (ICLI)
OYBO	Al-Bough [*Yemen*] [*ICAO location identifier*] (ICLI)
OYBT	Barat [*Yemen*] [*ICAO location identifier*] (ICLI)
OYC	Conair AS [*Denmark ICAO designator*] (FAAC)
OYC	Corpus Christi, TX [*Location identifier FAA*] (FAAL)
OYC	Out Year Costs (MCD)
OYCV	Optimum Yaw Control Vertical (SAA)
OYD	Rome, GA [*Location identifier FAA*] (FAAL)
OYDV	Onion Yellow Dwarf Virus [*Plant pathology*]
OYE	Old Yellow Enzyme [*Biochemistry*]
OYE	Oyem [*Gabon*] [*Airport symbol*] (OAG)
OYesA	Antioch College, Yellow Springs, OH [*Library symbol Library of Congress*] (LCLS)
OYesF	Fels Research Institute, Yellow Springs, OH [*Library symbol Library of Congress*] (LCLS)
OYesK	Charles F. Kettering Foundation, Research Laboratory Library, Yellow Springs, OH [*Library symbol Library of Congress*] (LCLS)

OYG	Operating Year Guidance (GFGA)
OYHD	Hodeidah [*Yemen*] [*ICAO location identifier*] (ICLI)
OYK	Oiapoque [*Brazil*] [*Airport symbol*] (AD)
OYKM	Kamaran [*Yemen*] [*ICAO location identifier*] (ICLI)
OYM	Outstanding Young Man (DICI)
OYM	Oyama [*Japan*] [*Seismograph station code, US Geological Survey*] (SEIS)
OYM	St. Mary's, PA [*Location identifier FAA*] (FAAL)
OYMB	Marib [*Yemen*] [*ICAO location identifier*] (ICLI)
OYMC	Mokha [*Yemen*] [*ICAO location identifier*] (ICLI)
OYMHi	Mahoning Valley Historical Society, Arms Museum, Youngstown, OH [*Library symbol Library of Congress*] (LCLS)
OYMV	Ononis Yellow Mosaic Virus [*Plant pathology*]
OYO	Tres Arroyos [*Argentina*] [*Airport symbol*] (OAG)
OYOG	OYO Geospace Corp. [*NASDAQ symbol*] (SAG)
OYOGeo	OYO Geospace Corp. [*Associated Press*] (SAG)
OYP	Office of Youth Programs [*Department of Labor*]
OYP	Opportunities for Youth Program [*Canada*]
OYS	Otsar Yehude Sefarad (BJA)
Oys	Oysters [*Quality of the bottom*] [*Nautical charts*]
OYS	Yosemite National Park [*California*] [*Airport symbol Obsolete*] (OAG)
OYSH	Saada [*Yemen*] [*ICAO location identifier*] (ICLI)
OYSN	Sanaa/International [*Yemen*] [*ICAO location identifier*] (ICLI)
OYSREA	Office of Youth, Sport, Recreation and Ethnic Affairs [*Northern Territory, Australia*]
OYTZ	Taiz/Ganad [*Yemen*] [*ICAO location identifier*] (ICLI)
OYU	Youngstown State University, Youngstown, OH [*Library symbol Library of Congress*] (LCLS)
OYY	Columbus, OH [*Location identifier FAA*] (FAAL)
OYZM	Al-Hazm [*Yemen*] [*ICAO location identifier*] (ICLI)
Oz	Ooze [*Quality of the bottom*] [*Nautical charts*]
OZ	Ounce [*Unit of weight*] (AAG)
oz	Ounce (IDOE)
OZ	Ozark Airlines, Inc. [*ICAO designator*] (OAG)
OZ	Ozone
oz	Ozone (IDOE)
OZA	Ozark (MCD)
OZA	Ozark Airlines (MHDB)
OZA	Ozona, TX [*Location identifier FAA*] (FAAL)
OZ AP	Apothecaries' Ounce (WDAA)
oz apoth	Apothecaries Ounce (BARN)
OZAR	Ozark National Scenic Riverways [*National Park Service designation*]
OZARC	Ozone ARCAS [*All-Purpose Rocket for Collecting Atmospheric Soundings*] [*Navy*]
OZav	John McIntire Public Library, Zanesville, OH [*Library symbol Library of Congress*] (LCLS)
OZavU	Ohio University, Zanesville Branch Campus, Zanesville, OH [*Library symbol Library of Congress*] (LCLS)
OZC	Cleveland Heights-University Heights Public Library, Cleveland Heights, OH [*OCLC symbol*] (OCLC)
OZC	Ozamis City [*Philippines*] [*Airport symbol*] (OAG)
OZD	Observed Zenith Distance [*Navigation*]
OZE	Outer Zone Electron
OZEM	OzMail Ltd. [*NASDAQ symbol*] (SAG)
OzEmail	OZEmail Ltd. [*Associated Press*] (SAG)
OZEMY	OzEmail Ltd ADR [*NASDAQ symbol*] (TTSB)
OZEP	Outer Zone Electron Precipitation
OZ-FT^2	Ounce Foot (AAG)
OZ/FT^2	Ounces per Square Foot
OZ/GAL	Ounces per Gallon
OZH	Zaporozh'ye [*Former USSR Airport symbol Obsolete*] (OAG)
OZ-IN	Ounce Inch (AAG)
oz-in	Ounce-Inch (IDOE)
oz-in	Ounce-Inches (IDOE)
OZ/IN^2	Ounces per Square Inch
OZ/IN^3	Ounces per Cubic Inch
OZIPP	Ozone Isopleth Plotting Package (GFGA)
OZIPPM	Ozone Isopleth Plotting Package, Modified (GFGA)
OZN	St. George, UT [*Location identifier FAA*] (FAAL)
OZO	Orbiting Zoological Observatory to Track Animals
OZON	Cyclc3PSS Corp. [*NASDAQ symbol*] (SAG)
OZON	Cyclopss Corp. [*NASDAQ symbol*] (TTSB)
OZ/PT	Ounces per Pint
OZR	Ozark, Fort Rucker, AL [*Location identifier FAA*] (FAAL)
OZRF	Opposed Zone Reheating Furnace (PDAA)
OZT	Ounces Troy [*Unit of weight*]
OZX	Oneonta, NY [*Location identifier FAA*] (FAAL)
OZ/YD^2	Ounces per Square Yard
OZZ	Ouarzazate [*Morocco*] [*Airport symbol*] (OAG)
OZZ	Ozark, AR [*Location identifier FAA*] (FAAL)